QFINANCE

THE ULTIMATE RESOURCE

QFINANCE

THE ULTIMATE RESOURCE

BLOOMSBURY

First published in 2009 by
Bloomsbury Information Ltd
36 Soho Square
London
W1D 3QY
United Kingdom

The information contained in this book is for general information purposes only. It does not constitute investment, financial, legal, or other advice, and should not be relied upon as such. No representation or warranty, express or implied, is made as to the accuracy or completeness of the contents. The publisher and the authors disclaim any warranty or liability for actions taken (or not taken) on the basis of information contained herein.

The views and opinions of the publisher may not necessarily coincide with some of the views and opinions expressed in this book, which are entirely those of the authors. No endorsement of them by the publisher should be inferred.

Every reasonable effort has been made to trace copyright holders of material reproduced in this book, but if any have been inadvertently overlooked then the publisher would be glad to hear from them. For legal purposes the credits on pages 2159–2160 constitute extensions of the copyright page.

A CIP record for this book is available from the British Library.

Standard edition
ISBN-10: 1-84930-000-3
ISBN-13: 978-1-84930-000-1

Special edition
ISBN-10: 1-84930-001-1
ISBN-13: 978-1-84930-001-8

Middle East edition
ISBN-10: 1-84930-002-X
ISBN-13: 978-1-84930-002-5

Mixed Sources
Product group from well-managed forests and recycled wood or fiber
www.fsc.org Cert no. TT-COC-002231
© 1996 Forest Stewardship Council
FSC

Cover design by Sean Gladwell
Page design by Fiona Pike, Pike Design, Winchester, UK
Typeset by RefineCatch Limited, Bungay, Suffolk, UK
Printed in the UK by CPI William Clowes, Beccles, NR34 7TL

     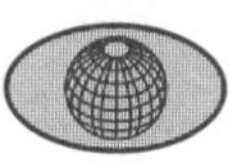   

Contents

 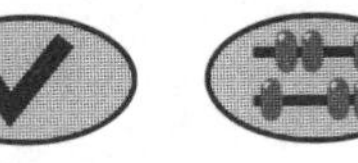   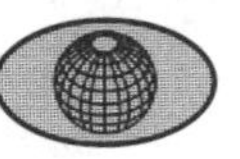   

  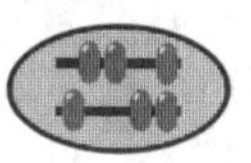   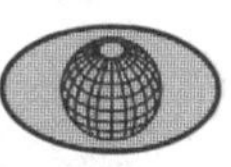   

Contents

     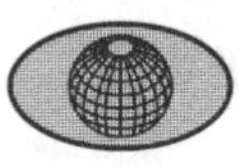   

Contents

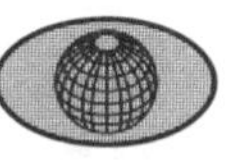

     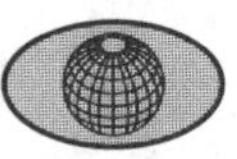   

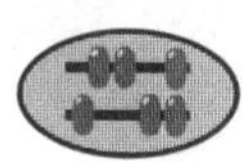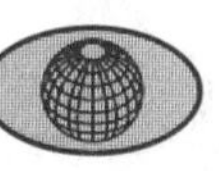

     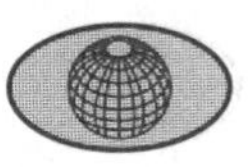   
a–z

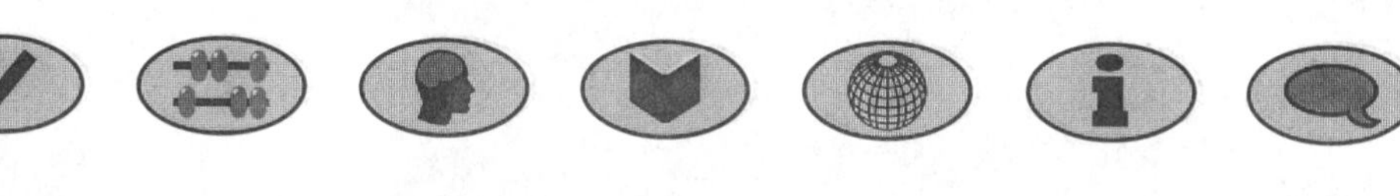

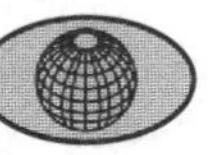

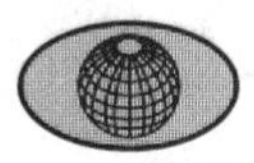

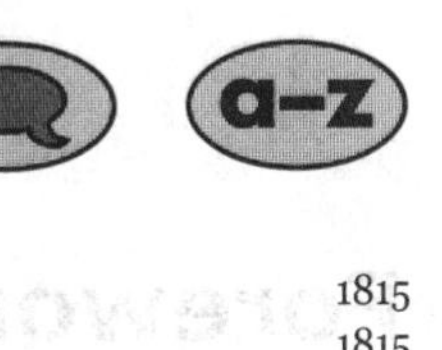

     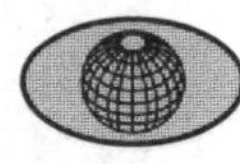   

Foreword
by HE Yousef Hussain Kamal, Minister of Economy and Finance of the State of Qatar and Chairman of the Qatar Financial Centre Authority

The world of finance is changing dramatically, but despite its current challenges finance remains the bedrock of global development. Never in this generation's lifetime has best financial practice needed to be reinforced so clearly.

Qatar Finance: The Ultimate Resource (*QFINANCE*) is a project of immense dimensions and scope. It combines the vast experience and knowledge of some 300 experts in the world of finance and provides a wealth of examples of best practice, an understanding of basic and applied principles of finance, and a financial reference point on which users can depend.

The State of Qatar, through the Qatar Financial Centre Authority, is proud to partner Bloomsbury Publishing in the creation of *QFINANCE*. This project reflects everything that Qatar is striving for as a nation. It is progressive in that it gives to the world of finance a platform of knowledge that does not exist in one place anywhere else. It is reliable in that those who have supported *QFINANCE* and contributed to it as it has come into being are all recognized as experts in their respective fields. And it is educational, to ensure that this and future generations have the best sources of learning at their disposal.

As a young but dynamic country, Qatar represents the future. We are investing in our financial sector to help us develop Qatar into an economy that is fully diversified and which can sustain itself for generations to come. The contribution that we believe *QFINANCE* will make to the world's financial practitioners, students, and commentators is a gift which we believe goes well beyond the investment we have made in it.

     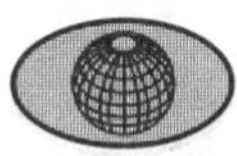   

Advisory Panel

HE Sheikh Hamad bin Jabor bin Jassim Al-Thani was appointed director-general of the General Secretariat for Development Planning (GSDP) and acting chairman of the Qatar Statistics Authority in 2007. At GSDP, Sheikh Hamad is in charge of day-to-day management and, with the secretary-general, provides leadership on strategic direction. Sheikh Hamad also takes a keen interest in GSDP's project work and has played an instrumental role in projects such as the KBE and SMEs projects. Sheikh Hamad serves as a member of the board of directors of Hamad Medical Corporation, Qatar Chemical Company, Qatar Electricity and Water Company, Qatar National Bank, Ansbacher, and ictQatar. He is also a member of the board of trustees of Qatar University, chairman of the Permanent Population Committee, a member of the governing board for the UNESCO Institute for Statistics, and a deputy chairman of the AIDS Control Committee. Previously, Sheikh Hamad was the secretary-general of the Planning Council for four years, which had the responsibility for planning Qatar's social and economic policies. Sheikh Hamad earned his managerial skills from working at Qatar Petroleum for fifteen years, including a position as a Manager of Human Resources and Director of Administration.

Zvi Bodie is professor of finance and economics at Boston University School of Management. He holds a PhD from the Massachusetts Institute of Technology, has served on the finance faculty at the Harvard Business School and MIT's Sloan School of Management, and is a member of the Pension Research Council of the Wharton School, University of Pennsylvania. Professor Bodie has published widely on pension finance and investment strategy in leading professional journals. His books include *The Foundations of Pension Finance*, *Pensions in the US Economy*, *Issues in Pension Economics*, and *Financial Aspects of the US Pension System*. His textbook *Investments* is the market leader and is used in the certification programs of the Financial Planning Association and the Society of Actuaries. His textbook *Finance* is coauthored by Nobel Prize-winning economist Robert C. Merton. His latest book is *Worry-Free Investing: A Safe Approach to Achieving Your Lifetime Financial Goals*.

Ian Cormack is a senior non-executive director at the Pearl Group and a non-executive director at the Qatar Financial Centre Authority (QFCA). He was a senior partner in Cormack Tansey Partners, a strategic consulting firm for financial institutions, from 2003 to 2005. He was chief executive officer of AIG, Inc's insurance financial services and asset management in Europe from 1997 to 2000, chairman of Citibank International plc, and co-head of the Global Financial Institutions Client Group at Citigroup. He was also country head of Citicorp in the UK from 1992 to 1996. He now holds a number of non-executive positions with various companies (public and private) and charities in the UK and abroad.

Florence Eid, PhD, is managing director for MENA at Passport Capital, having previously been vice president and senior economist for MENA at JP Morgan and professor of finance and economics at the American University of Beirut. She has worked for the World Bank, the Ford Foundation, and with Save the Children.

Hatem El-Karanshawy is the founding dean of the Qatar Faculty of Islamic Studies (QFIS). His efforts have been instrumental in building the faculty from the ground up. He came to QFIS after a long and distinguished career both in academia and policy. Before joining QFIS, Dr El-Karanshawy was professor of finance and director of the Public Administration Program at the American University in Cairo. He was also dean at the Faculty of Commerce in Al Azhar University. Dr El-Karanshawy was also a member of the board of directors of the Central Bank of Egypt. He has and continues to advise extensively on Islamic finance and economic development. In addition to advising the Prime Minister of Egypt and other senior cabinet members, he has contributed to negotiations with the World Bank, the African Development Bank, the International Monetary Fund, and the US State Department.

Robert Gray is chairman of Debt Finance & Advisory at HSBC Bank. He joined HSBC in 1994 as chairman of HSBC Markets Ltd, with particular responsibility for developing HSBC's capital markets capabilities globally. In 1999, he was appointed vice chairman of Client Development at HSBC Investment Bank, and to his current position in March 2001. Prior to joining HSBC, Gray was head of JP Morgan's capital markets (Europe). Previously he was president and Tokyo branch manager of JP Morgan Securities Asia Ltd. He also headed JP Morgan's worldwide loan syndication group and was responsible for their Eurobond underwriting activities.

Hasung Jang is a professor of finance and a director of the Asian Institute of Corporate Governance at Korea University. Since 1996, Professor Jang has been the leader of a minority shareholder activist's civil group (PSPD) in Korea and has been at the forefront of improving the corporate governance in Korea. In recognition of his contributions, he, with two other distinguished figures, Sir Adrian Cadbury and Ira Millstein, was given the first Annual Award from the International Corporate Governance Network (ICGN) in July 2001. The *Financial Times* selected him as one of five "prominent figures in the world of corporate governance" in December 2004, and *Business Week* recognized him by placing him among the Asian Star 50 in 1998 and 1999. He and his group were given the Economic Justice Citizen's Award in 1998.

Robert C. Merton is currently the John and Natty McArthur University Professor at the Harvard Business School. After receiving a PhD in Economics from the Massachusetts Institute of Technology (MIT) in 1970, he served on the finance faculty of MIT's Sloan School of Management until 1988 when he moved to Harvard. Professor Merton is past President of the American Finance Association, a member of the National Academy of Sciences, and a Fellow of the American Academy of Arts and Sciences. He received the Alfred Nobel Memorial Prize in the Economic Sciences in 1997.

Jim O'Neill is head of Global Economic Research for Goldman Sachs, and has been in this position since September 2001. In this role, he oversees the firm's economic research globally. He joined Goldman Sachs in 1995 as a partner, co-head of Global Economics and Chief Currency Economist. Prior to this, he was head of research at Swiss Bank Corporation (SBC), which he joined in 1988 to set up the fixed income research group in

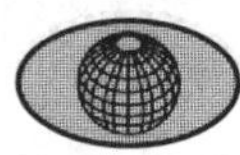

London. O'Neill moved to Goldman Sachs from International Treasury Management, a division of Marine Midland Bank and worked for a brief spell at Bank of America in 1983. O'Neill received his PhD in 1982 from the University of Surrey after graduating in economics from Sheffield University in 1978.

Michael K. Ong is the director of the finance program at Illinois Institute of Technology. He was executive vice president and chief risk officer for Credit Agricole Indosuez in New York, where he held enterprise-wide responsibility for all risk management functions for corporate banking, merchant banking, asset management, capital markets activities, and the Carr Futures Group. He was a member of the executive committee and chaired the Risk Management Committee, Credit Committee, Market Risk Committee, Equity Investment Committee, and the Operational Risk Committee. Dr Ong was also head of Enterprise Risk Management for ABN-AMRO Bank. He was responsible for management information and decision support function for the Executive Committee regarding enterprise-wide market, credit, operational, and liquidity risk, as well as RAROC, ROE, and related optimization models. Previously, Dr Ong was head of the Corporate Research Unit for First Chicago NBD Corporation (now Bank One).

Sir John Stuttard has spent his career with accountants PricewaterhouseCoopers, of which he is now a vice-chairman. He has focused on auditing, acquisitions, stock exchange listings, and privatizations for UK, US, and Scandinavian companies. He was made a Knight, and then a Commander, of the Order of the Lion of Finland and has been chairman of the Finnish-British Chamber of Commerce. He served in the Cabinet Office for two years and spent five years in China as PwC executive chairman. He has also been a director of the China Britain Business Council. He is currently pro-chancellor of City University London, a trustee of Charities Aid Foundation and of Morden College, a governor of King Edward's School Witley and on the board of other charities. He served as Sheriff of London in 2005–2006 and Lord Mayor in 2006–2007.

Jackson Tai was made a member of the supervisory board at ING in 2008. He is former vice chairman and CEO of DBS Group Holdings and former managing director in the Investment Banking Division of JP Morgan, where he held senior management positions in New York, Tokyo and San Francisco. He also holds a number of non-directorships including MasterCard Incorporated, CapitaLand, and non-executive chairman of Brookstone, Inc. He is a member of the Bloomberg Asia-Pacific Advisory Board, Harvard Business School Asia-Pacific Advisory Board and a trustee of Rensselaer Polytechnic Institute.

Laura Tyson is the S. K. and Angela Chan professor of global management at the Haas Business and Public Policy Group at UCLA. Professor Tyson was dean of the London Business School from January 2002 to 2006, and was previously dean of the Walter A. Haas School of Business at the University of California, Berkeley, where she had been professor of economics and business administration. Professor Tyson served in the Clinton administration from 1993 to 1996. Between February 1995 and December 1996 she served as the President's National Economic Adviser and was the highest-ranking woman in the Clinton White House. A key architect of President Clinton's domestic and international policy agenda during his first term in office, she also served as a member of the President's National Security Council and Domestic Policy Council. Prior to this appointment Laura Tyson was the sixteenth chairman of the White House Council of Economic Advisers, the first woman to hold that post.

     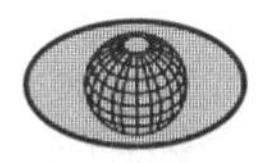   

Publishing, Editorial, and Production Staff

Chief Executive
Nigel Newton

Publisher
Kathy Rooney

Project Director
Conrad Gardner

Production Director
Oscar Heini

Project Manager
Ben Hickling

Database Managers
Martin Dowling
Katy McAdam

Consultant Editor
Amarendra Swarup

Commissioning Editors
Ian Fraser
Conrad Gardner
Anthony Harrington
Wendy Morris
Tim Penn
Stuart Rutherford
Dave Stauffer
Amarendra Swarup

Marketing Manager
Paula Soutinho

Project Editor
Lizzy Kingston

Project Assistant
Sarah Latham

Cross-References
Tom Horncastle

Copy Editors
Romilly Hambling
Corinne Orde
Claire Annals
Louise Bolotin
Adèle Linderholm
Val Rice
Deborah Smith
Frances Worlock

Proofreaders
Sheila Cameron
Laurie Donaldson
Ann Ridgway
Daniel Sefton

Inputter
Bernadette Crowley

Other Contributors and Advisers

Checklists
Anthony Beachey
Michael Beachey
Louise Bolotin
David Thomson
Anca Toma-Thomson

Calculations and Ratios
Sally Whittle

Finance Thinkers and Leaders
Laurie Donaldson
Stuart Rutherford
Lauren Mills

Finance Library
Laurie Donaldson
Stuart Rutherford
Lauren Mills

Country and Sector Profiles
Anthony Beachey
Anthony Harrington
Ian Fraser
Radhika Dogra Swarup

Finance Information Sources
Laurie Donaldson
Danielle Pellikaan
Neha Bhargava
Chartered Management Institute

Quotations
Market House Books

Dictionary
Susan Jellis
Lesley Brown
John Butler
Faye Carney
John Y. Fishman
Stephen Handorf
Marcus Johnson
Julie Plier
David Pritchard
Howard Sargeant

Referees
Habib Ahmed
Manzurul Alam
Seth Armitage
Buddy Baker
Ruth Bender
Paul Beretz
Janusz Brzeszczyński
Terry Carroll
Andrew Cox
Shane Edwards
John Ferry
Jonathan Fletcher
Norman Goldstein
Ashish Gupta
Andrew Higson
Vijyata Kirpalani
Vinod Lall
Tanja Maffei
Roger Mattar
Tom McKaig
Nigel Morgan
John Mosher
Kristian Niemietz
Martin O'Donovan
Justin Oliver
Emilia Onyema
Jeremy Phillips
David Sadtler
Olgun Fuat Sahin
Shireen Smith
Gabriel Stein
Pearl Tan Hock Neo
Siri Terjesen
Steve Wallace
Véronique Weets
Juergen Weiss
Lawrence White
Suzanne White
Priscilla Wisner

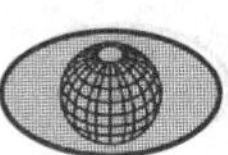

Contributors

Mark Abkowitz is professor of civil and environmental engineering at Vanderbilt University and specializes in managing the risks associated with accidents, intentional acts, and natural disasters. He has a specific interest in the safety and security of hazardous materials and in risk mitigation using advanced information technologies. Dr Abkowitz has appeared on National Public Radio, Fox National News, and CNBC, discussing various risk management topics. Since June 2002, he has been a member of the US Nuclear Waste Technical Review Board.

Viral V. Acharya is professor of finance at the London Business School and New York University's Stern School of Business, academic director of the Coller Institute of Private Equity, and a research affiliate of the Centre for Economic Policy Research (CEPR). He gained a PhD in finance from Stern and a bachelor's degree in computer science and engineering from the Indian Institute of Technology. Dr Acharya has received numerous awards and recognition for his research. He was appointed as a senior Houblon-Norman research fellow at the Bank of England in summer 2008 to conduct research on the efficiency of the interbank lending markets.

Reena Aggarwal is the Stallkamp fellow and professor of finance at Georgetown University in Washington, DC. She specializes in international stock markets, demutualization of stock exchanges, initial public offerings, international investments by mutual funds, and international corporate governance and market valuation. She has been named among "outstanding faculty" in the *Business Week Guide to the Best Business Schools*. She is also a faculty associate of the Capital Markets Research Center. Dr Aggarwal is a frequent guest on local and international radio and television stations. Her research and comments have been cited in the *Wall Street Journal*, *Washington Post*, and the *Financial Times* among other publications.

Amjid Ali, senior manager at HSBC Amanah Global is recognized as one of the most influential Muslims in the United Kingdom by the Muslim Power 100 awards, and has 22 years of branch banking experience with Midland Bank and HSBC in the United Kingdom. He joined HSBC Amanah UK in 2003 as senior business development manager, and took over as UK head in January 2005 with responsibility for strategy, distribution, and sales. He was appointed as senior manager, HSBC Amanah Global, in August 2008, where he works as part of the HSBC Amanah central team headquartered in Dubai.

Noël Amenc is professor of finance and director of research and development at EDHEC Business School, where he heads the Risk and Asset Management Research Centre. He has a masters in economics and a PhD in finance and has conducted active research in the fields of quantitative equity management, portfolio performance analysis, and active asset allocation, resulting in numerous academic and practitioner articles and books. He is an associate editor of the *Journal of Alternative Investments* and a member of the scientific advisory council of the AMF (the French financial regulatory authority).

Seth Armitage is director of the MSc in finance and investment at the University of Edinburgh Business School. His research is mainly in the area of corporate finance and includes projects on rights issues and open offers, the cost of capital, the role of banks in funding companies, and mutual financial institutions. He is author of *The Cost of Capital: Intermediate Theory* (Cambridge University Press, 2005). He was on the faculty of the University of Edinburgh from 1989 to 2002, and before rejoining in 2007 he was head of the Department of Accounting and Finance at Heriot-Watt University.

Jacques Attali was recently appointed by President Sarkozy to head the commission to promote growth in the French economy. Formerly he was a special adviser to President Mitterand, then founder and first president of the European Bank for Reconstruction and Development. He is founder and currently president of PlaNet Finance, and chairman of an investment bank and private equity vehicle specializing in the development of European IT start-ups. Attali has degrees from the French "grandes écoles," and he has taught economics at several leading French universities. He is the author of over 50 books on topics ranging from mathematical economy to music, as well as novels, songs, short stories and theatre plays. His main work in economics and sociology has been on trends in history and their use to forecast the future. He forecast the global economic crisis back in 2006. In 1989 he launched an international action program against massive floods in Bangladesh.

Buddy Baker has over 30 years of experience in international trade finance. In May 2009 he joined Fifth Third Bank, where he manages the Trade Services Sales team. Prior to Fifth Third Bank, Buddy worked for Atradius Trade Credit Insurance, ABN AMRO Bank, Bank of America, Wachovia Bank, and The First National Bank of Chicago. Buddy is a recognized expert in trade finance, a long-time member of the National Letter of Credit Committee of the International Financial Services Association, and is actively involved in establishing national and worldwide standard practices for L/Cs. He also serves on the board of directors of the FCIB, a multinational association of export credit managers. Buddy received his undergraduate degree from Yale University and his MBA from Northwestern.

Angela Baron is a chartered member of the Chartered Institute of Personnel and Development (CIPD), for which she is currently an adviser on organization and resourcing. She has been responsible for numerous research programs including corporate culture, psychological testing, counseling in the workplace, performance management, HR strategy and recruitment practice. Her current research covers investigating the underlying links between people management, productivity, and profitability. She is also steering work on human capital, developing measures and reporting systems for practitioners. Baron has coauthored a number of books in the field, including *The Job Evaluation Handbook* and *Strategic HRM*.

Paul Barrett is assistant director, financial regulation, and taxation, at the Association of British Insurers (ABI). His team leads on a number of strategic risk and regulatory issues, including Solvency II, developing proposals to support the UK and European industry agenda in partnership with the CEA (the European insurance and reinsurance federation), and other stakeholders. Barrett coordinates the ABI's regulation priority work and was responsible for producing the industry guide to the individual capital assessment (ICA) process and the ABI's unit-linked guide of good practice. Previously he worked at the Financial Services Authority.

     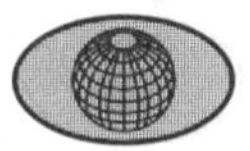   

Wim Bartels has been global head of KPMG's sustainability services network since October 2007. He studied business economics and accountancy at Amsterdam's Vrije Universiteit before qualifying as a chartered accountant in 1993. In 2001 he became a KPMG partner with overall responsibility for the group's sustainability services, including the provision of sustainability assurance services to multinational businesses such as BASF, DSM, Heineken, KLM, Philips, and Rabobank. Bartels is closely involved with the UN's Global Reporting Initiative, and he sits on the council of AccountAbility. In his spare time he sings and plays trumpet in a band that performs cover versions of 1970s and 1980s hits and which performs for good causes.

Ilias G. Basioudis is senior lecturer in financial accounting and auditing at Aston Business School. He is also chairman of the Auditing Special Interest Group of the British Accounting Association, a fellow of the UK Academy of Higher Education, and an adjunct senior lecturer at the University of South Australia. Dr Basioudis has published widely in academic and professional journals and has recently been commissioned by Pearson to write a textbook on financial accounting. His research interests lie primarily in the area of empirical auditing, corporate governance, and accounting education. He is a member of various international accounting associations and is on the editorial board of the *International Journal of Auditing*.

Paul Belok, principal and actuary at Aon Consulting, has been involved in providing actuarial and benefits consulting advice to trustees and corporate clients for over 20 years. As head of settlement solutions for Aon Consulting, including responsibility for bulk annuity issues, Belok is a regular commentator in the press and at conferences on pension issues.

Ruth Bender is a senior lecturer at Cranfield School of Management. She joined the faculty in 1994, having completed her MBA there. Prior to this she was a partner in Grant Thornton, where latterly she specialized in corporate finance, including a time on secondment as a private equity investment manager in the City of London. She is a chartered accountant, and was a committee member of the Institute of Chartered Accountants in England and Wales' Faculty of Finance and Management. Other outside roles have included non-executive directorships of a health authority and an NHS trust. Bender's main teaching areas include financial strategy, working capital management, and corporate governance. Her doctorate is in corporate governance.

Samy Ben Naceur is a professor of finance at ESSEC Tunis. He has worked as a consultant with the Economic Research Forum, the European Union, and the World Bank. He was previously associate professor of finance at IHEC Carthage and Université Libre de Tunis (ULT). Professor Ben Naceur's areas of academic research cover accounting, financial structure, corporate valuation, and economics, with particular emphasis on Middle Eastern and North African financial markets.

Paul Beretz, CICE (Certified International Credit Executive), is managing director of Pacific Business Solutions, Clayton, CA, a company he created in 1999. In addition, he is a partner of Q2C (Quote to Cash) Solutions. He brings over 30 years of global management experience in telecommunications, semiconductors, forest products, and chemicals. His faculty postings include St Mary's College, California (MA in leadership), University of California, Berkeley, Michigan State University, and Dartmouth College. He has designed and facilitates online courses in international credit and general business. He currently serves on the advisory committee of the Export–Import Bank of the United States.

Jagdish Bhagwati is university professor, economics and law, at Columbia University and senior fellow in international economics at the Council of Foreign Relations. One of the world's leading economists today, he writes frequently in leading newspapers and magazines.

Harold Bierman, Jr is Nicholas H. Noyes professor of business administration at the Johnson Graduate School of Management, Cornell University, New York. Professor Bierman's interests are in investment and corporate financial policy decisions. He has consulted for many public organizations and industrial firms and is the author of more than 150 books and articles in the fields of accounting, finance, investment, taxation, and quantitative analysis. In 1985 he was named winner of the prestigious Dow Jones Award of the American Assembly of Collegiate Schools of Business for his outstanding contributions to collegiate management education.

Keith Black is an associate of Ennis Knupp + Associates. He is a member of the opportunistic strategies group, which advises foundations, endowments, and pension funds on their asset allocation and manager selection strategies in the alternative investment space. His prior professional experience includes commodities derivatives trading at First Chicago Capital Markets, stock options research and trading for Hull Trading Company, building stock selection models for Chicago Investment Analytics, and teaching finance at the Illinois Institute of Technology. He has earned the Chartered Financial Analyst (CFA) and the Chartered Alternative Investment Analyst (CAIA) designations. Black is the author of the book *Managing a Hedge Fund*.

Anthony Bolton managed one of the United Kingdom's most successful and largest mutual funds, Fidelity Special Situations, from 1979 to 2007. Over that period the fund generated an annualized return of 20% (against some 8% for the FTSE All-Share Index). He graduated from Cambridge University with a degree in engineering before entering the City as an investment analyst at investment bank Keyser Ullman. In 1979 he was hired by Fidelity, the Boston-based investment group, as one of its first London-based investors, and he subsequently pursued a contrarian and bottom-up approach to investing, with immense success. In surveys of professional investors he is regularly named the fund manager most respected by his peers. Since stepping down from day-to-day fund management in December 2007, Bolton has focused on mentoring Fidelity's younger fund managers and analysts and overseeing its investment process.

Lena Booth is associate professor of finance at the Thunderbird School of Global Management and served as the first executive director of the Thunderbird Private Equity Center (TPEC). Dr Booth has been a member of the Thunderbird faculty since 1995 and has taught and presented research in many countries around the world. Her research interests lie mainly in capital raising and security issuance by firms, with the primary focus on initial public offerings. She has received several teaching and research awards during her tenure at Thunderbird. Born and raised in Malaysia, Dr Booth holds a BBA from the National University of Singapore, MBA from Northern Arizona University, and PhD (finance) from Arizona State University.

     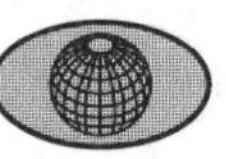   

Roger Bootle is one of the City of London's most respected economists and now runs his own consultancy, Capital Economics. He is also economic adviser to Deloitte & Touche, a specialist adviser to the House of Commons Treasury Committee, and a visiting professor at Manchester Business School. He was formerly group chief economist of the HSBC Group and, before the change of government, a member of the former Chancellor's panel of independent economic advisers, the so-called "wise men." Bootle studied at Oxford University before becoming a lecturer in economics at St Anne's College, Oxford. He has written many articles and is a regular columnist on the *Sunday Telegraph*. He also frequently appears on national television and radio.

R. Brayton Bowen is author of *Recognizing and Rewarding Employees* (McGraw-Hill) and leads the Howland Group, a strategy consulting and change management firm committed to "building better worlds of work." His documentary series *Anger in the Workplace*, distributed to public radio nationally in the United States, continues to be regarded as a benchmark study on the subject of workplace issues and change. A *Best Practice* editor and contributing author to the hallmark work *Business: The Ultimate Resource* (Bloomsbury Publishing and Perseus Books), he has written for *MWorld*, the online magazine of the American Management Association. He currently serves as executive adviser for the Center for Business Excellence at McKendree University.

Stavros Brekoulakis, LLB (Athens), LLM (London), and PhD (London) is a lecturer in international dispute resolution. Dr Brekoulakis lectures at Queen Mary, University of London, on the Master of Laws (LLM) courses on international comparative and commercial arbitration, international commercial construction, international commercial litigation, and conflict of laws. He is also academic director of the diploma course (taught by distance learning) on international arbitration. His academic research focuses on international commercial arbitration, conflict of laws, multiparty and complex dispute resolution, issues on jurisdiction of tribunals and national courts, and enforcement of awards and national judgments. He is a member of the Athens Bar, having practiced shipping law and dispute resolution.

Ian Bremmer's career spans academic, investment, and policymaking communities. His research focuses on states in transition, global political risk, and US foreign policy. Dr Bremmer founded the research and consulting firm Eurasia Group, which today is the preeminent global political risk consultancy. In 2001, he authored Wall Street's first global political risk index, now the Global Political Risk Index (GPRI). Throughout his career, Dr Bremmer has spent much of his time advising world leaders on US foreign policy, including US presidential candidates from both Democratic and Republican parties, Russian Prime Minister Sergei Kiriyenko, and Japanese Prime Minister Shinzo Abe.

Lawrence Brotzge's business background includes 11 years with Ernst & Young, 10 years as corporate controller and CFO for two major divisions of Providian Corp (a Fortune 500 financial services company), and five years as a founder of a corporate venturing project, which resulted in Providian establishing an entirely new business. Since 1994, Brotzge has been an independent consultant and an angel investor. He has an ownership position in several small/start-up businesses and consults with a number of other companies.

Tom Brown served as a *Best Practice* editor and wrote the keynote essay for *Business: The Ultimate Resource*, which is the largest handbook/database ever assembled on modern managerial leadership. He has contributed to the Drucker Foundation's *Leader to Leader*, *Harvard Management Update*, London's *Financial Times*, and the *Wall Street Journal*. He also edits the quarterly journal of the London Business School, *Business Strategy Review*. Brown's writings are based on his extensive work in leadership development going back to 1977, when he helped to create the Honeywell Aerospace Management Development Center. Today, as publisher of BrownHerron Publishing, he has become the e-publisher for over 50 authors and is seen as a pioneer in 21st century publishing.

Janusz Brzeszczyński is a senior lecturer in the Department of Accountancy, Economics and Finance at Heriot-Watt University, Edinburgh, and specializes in international finance, financial markets, and financial econometrics. Before joining Heriot-Watt, he held a Fulbright scholarship in the United States and worked as a visiting professor in the Department of Economics, Arizona State University. He was also a visiting scholar at the Swiss Institute of Banking and Finance, University of St Gallen, Switzerland, and assistant/associate professor at the Chair of Econometric Models and Forecasts, University of Lodz, Poland. Besides the Fulbright scholarship, he was also awarded an ESKAS post-doctoral scholarship at the Swiss Institute of Banking and Finance and a DAAD doctoral scholarship at Kiel University, Germany. Dr Brzeszczyński has published in a number of finance journals.

Todd Buchholz is a former director of economic policy at the White House, a managing director of the US$15 billion Tiger hedge fund, and an economics teacher at Harvard. He advised President Bush Snr and is a frequent commentator on ABC News, PBS, and CBS. He recently hosted his own show on CNBC. He is also co-founder and managing director of Two Oceans Management, LLC. He has written numerous books, including *Market Shock: 9 Economic and Social Upheavals that Will Shake Your Financial Future*, *New Ideas from Dead Economists* and *From Here to Economy*. His latest works, *New Ideas from Dead CEOs* and *The Castro Gene*, were published in 2007. Buchholz is a contributing editor at *Worth* magazine, where he writes the "Global markets" column. His editorials in the *Wall Street Journal* correctly forecast the 2001 slowdown in the US. He won the Allyn Young teaching prize at Harvard and holds advanced degrees in economics and law from Cambridge and Harvard.

Patrick Buchmann is a principal at the Hamburg office of the Boston Consulting Group. He joined the company in 2001 and is a core group member of the industrial goods, operations, and corporate development practice areas. He is an expert on net working capital optimization. Over the past years he has led and supported a number of international projects, with a focus on the optimization of processes and inventories as well as creditor and debtor management. Buchmann holds a master's degree from the Technical University of Berlin in industrial engineering with emphasis on production technology and logistics, and he studied business administration at the Cass Business School in London.

Kevin Burrows is a senior investment analyst and portfolio adviser for the Nedgroup range of funds of funds, which totals approximately US$600,000,000. His areas of primary responsibility include fixed-income, event-driven, distressed debt, and global macro-strategies, where he performs extensive and in-depth manager

     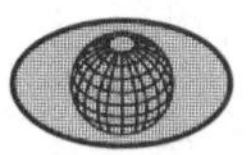   

search and due diligence for initial investment and on an ongoing basis. He is involved in all aspects of the Nedgroup fund products through his participation on the investment committee. Burrows graduated with a BA in economics from Yale University and holds an MPhil in finance from Cambridge University.

Sir Adrian Cadbury studied economics at Cambridge before joining the Cadbury business in 1952. He became chairman of Cadbury Ltd in 1965 and retired as chairman of Cadbury Schweppes in 1989. He was chairman of the UK Committee on the Financial Aspects of Corporate Governance, which published its *Report* and *Code of Best Practice* in December 1992. Sir Adrian received the International Corporate Governance Network Award in 2001. His book, *Corporate Governance and Chairmanship—A Personal View*, was published by Oxford University Press in 2002 and has been translated into Japanese, Chinese, and Italian. In 2005 he was awarded the Laureate Medal for Corporate Governance.

Mark Camp is director of institutional liquidity funds for Henderson Global Investors, where he is responsible for marketing a comprehensive range of such funds. He was formerly a business development manager for AIM Global money market funds, part of the Amvescap Group. Camp joined the Amvescap Group soon after its inception and made a significant contribution to getting money market funds accepted for regulatory purposes for the insurance and public sectors. Before that, he worked for over 10 years in the UK insurance market with banking and investment responsibilities.

Terry Carroll heads up corporate finance and advisory services for Broadhead Peel Rhodes, following a highly successful career as finance director and CEO of a range of businesses. He was also for some years a business and financial consultant, working especially with SMEs and growing businesses. A qualified banker, corporate treasurer, and chartered accountant who trained with KPMG, Carroll has experience of many different corporate finance projects, including banking, financing, business restructuring, mergers and acquisitions, MBO/MBI, and venture and private capital. With five books and scores of published articles, he is also an established business author.

Susan Cartwright is professor of organisational psychology and head of the subject area group at Manchester Business School. She worked in industry for 12 years before joining the Manchester School of Management (now MBS) in 1987, where she completed a master's degree in 1988 and a PhD in 1990, which was supported by an ESRC competitive scholarship. Professor Cartwright is a fellow of the British Academy of Management, of which she is currently president. She has been an associate editor of the *British Journal of Management* for more than seven years, is a past editor of the *Leadership & Organization Development Journal*, and is the recipient of the first Meritous Reviewer Award presented by Human Relations.

Richard E. Cascarino is CEO of Richard Cascarino & Associates, based in Colorado, with over 26 years' experience in audit training and consultancy. Well known in international auditing circles as one of the most knowledgeable practitioners in the field, he is a regular speaker at national and international conferences and has presented courses throughout Africa, Europe, the Middle East, and the United States. He is a past president of the Institute of Internal Auditors (IIA) in South Africa, was the founding regional director of the Southern African Region of the IIA, and is a member of ISACA and the American Institute of Certified Fraud Examiners. He is also a visiting lecturer at the University of the Witwatersrand.

Peter Casson is a senior lecturer in accounting at the School of Management of the University of Southampton. He graduated with BTech and PhD degrees in psychology from Brunel University and an MSc in occupational psychology from Birkbeck College, University of London. He is a fellow of the Institute of Chartered Accountants in England and Wales. After holding a number of research posts in psychology, he trained as a chartered accountant before starting an academic career in accounting. His research interests are mainly in accounting for financial instruments, stock option compensation, corporate governance, and company taxation.

Andrew Chambers works for Management Audit LLP advising on corporate governance and internal auditing, and is also a professor at London South Bank University. Described in an editorial in *The Times* (September 15, 2006) as "a worldwide authority on corporate governance," he chairs the Corporate Governance and Risk Management Committee of the Association of Chartered Certified Accountants and is a member of the Financial Reporting Council's Auditing Practices Board. Professor Chambers has been dean of what is now the Cass Business School, London. He is also a member of the Institute of Internal Auditors' international Internal Audit Standards Board.

Moorad Choudhry is head of treasury at Europe Arab Bank plc in London. He was previously head of treasury at KBC Financial Products, and before that he worked at JP Morgan Chase, ABN Amro Hoare Govett Ltd and Hambros Bank Ltd. Dr Choudhry is visiting professor at the Department of Economics, London Metropolitan University, visiting research fellow at the ICMA Centre, University of Reading, and a fellow of the Securities and Investment Institute. He is on the editorial board of the *Journal of Structured Finance*.

Subir Chowdhury is chairman and CEO of ASI Consulting Group, LLC. A respected quality strategist, Chowdhury's clients include global Fortune 100 companies as well as small organizations in both the public and private sectors. He is the author of 12 books and has received numerous international awards for leadership in quality management and major contributions to various industries worldwide. He has a graduate degree in aerospace engineering from the Indian Institute of Technology, Kharagpur, a postgraduate degree in industrial management from Central Michigan University, and an honorary doctorate in engineering from Michigan Technological University. Chowdhury is frequently cited in national and international media.

Diana Choyleva joined the World Service at Lombard Street Research (LSR) in 2000 after graduating with a master's degree in economics from the University of Warwick. She was promoted to the position of director and head of the UK Service in 2005. Choyleva's work covers global issues, with a particular focus on the United Kingdom and Chinese economies. In 2006 she published her first book, *The Bill from the China Shop*, coauthored with Charles Dumas. She has also specialized in research on monetary and financial flows, and her work on estimating potential output and output gaps is the basis for producing LSR's proprietary global leading indicators. Choyleva's research has been extensively quoted in the international press and she gives regular TV and radio interviews.

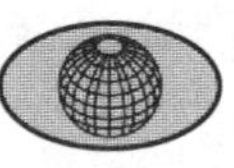

Andrew Cox has been a senior executive in the governance, risk management, and internal audit field with Centrelink in Canberra and the Northern Territory government in Darwin, and has managed eight internal audit activities over his career. Apart from internal audit, his previous experience has covered a number of areas including business continuity, security, strategic planning, IT planning, and industrial relations. Until recently he was a member of the Institute of Internal Auditors' International Committee on Quality in internal auditing. Cox has given presentations on internal auditing in forums both in Australia and internationally, and he has taught internal auditing in Australia and other countries.

Tom Coyne has been a chief investment strategist at the Index Investor since 2000. He received a BS in economics from Georgetown University and MBA from Harvard University. He began his career at Chase Manhattan Bank in South America, and for many years specialized in turnaround and growth consulting at the MAC Group in London and Bristol Partners in San Francisco. He has also been both the CFO and CEO of a publicly traded environmental technology company in Canada.

Henrik Cronqvist is assistant professor of financial economics at the Robert Day School of Economics and Finance at Claremont McKenna College. He received his PhD in finance from the Graduate School of Business at the University of Chicago. His main areas of research cover corporate finance and behavioral finance. He is also a research affiliate at the Swedish Institute for Financial Research. He has published papers in a number of academic journals including the *Journal of Finance*, *Journal of Financial Economics*, and the *Review of Financial Studies*. He regularly gives seminars to executives and policy-makers, and his research has been featured in *The Economist*, the *Financial Times*, and the *Wall Street Journal*.

Aswath Damodaran is a professor of finance at the Stern School of Business at New York University, where he teaches corporate finance and equity valuation. He also teaches on the TRIUM Global Executive MBA program, an alliance of NYU Stern, the London School of Economics, and HEC School of Management. Professor Damodaran is best known as author of several widely used academic and practitioner texts on valuation, corporate finance, and investment management. He is also widely published in leading journals of finance, including the *Journal of Financial and Quantitative Analysis*, *Journal of Finance*, *Journal of Financial Economics*, and the *Review of Financial Studies*.

Simon D'Arcy is currently head of internal audit for a joint venture between two global banks. He began his career in internal auditing in 1986 with the UK Department of the Environment. Later he joined Abbey National, where he spent 14 years fulfilling a variety of roles. In 2003 he left Abbey National to become associate director, audit services, for the Portman Building Society, where he remained until its merger with Nationwide. D'Arcy has been a volunteer member of the Institute of Internal Auditors UK and Ireland (IIA) since 1996, and he was president of the IIA in 2007/08. He regularly speaks on a range of governance, risk management, and internal audit subjects and contributes on the same topics to professional publications and periodicals.

Andy Davies joined Terra Nova in 1994 as group financial controller of Terra Nova Bermuda Holdings. In 2000 he became finance director at Markel International, with responsibility for reporting into Markel Corporation and overseeing the operations of the finance and RAO departments.

Sir Howard Davies is director of the London School of Economics and Political Science. Prior to his current appointment, he was chairman of the Financial Services Authority, served for two years as deputy governor of the Bank of England, and spent three years as director general of the Confederation of British Industry. From 1987 to 1992 he was controller of the Audit Commission. From 1982 to 1987 he worked for McKinsey & Company in London, and in 1985–1986 was seconded to the Treasury as special adviser to the Chancellor of the Exchequer.

Paul Davies is managing director of Onshore Offshore Ltd. He has been responsible for a wide range of business transformation projects, whether establishing companies offshore, providing consultancy for entering offshore markets, creating the most appropriate offshoring approaches and environments, recruiting the appropriate staff and management, managing the procurement of offshore services, providing interim management, transferring contracts under employment legislation, or creating new business strategies. With a management background in the United Kingdom and India and sales and marketing experience across Europe, Dr Davies has formed a team of professionals who can address a wide range of business issues and provide solutions in management, finance, business efficiency, and global talent management.

Graham Dawson studied philosophy, politics and economics at University College, Oxford, and holds a PhD in philosophy from the University of Keele. He is the author of *Inflation and Unemployment: Causes, Consequences and Cures* and of articles in journals including *Philosophy and Economics*, *Risk, Decision and Policy*, *Philosophy*, and *Economic Affairs*. He recently retired from the post of senior lecturer in economics at the Open University and is currently visiting fellow at the Max Beloff Centre for the Study of Liberty at the University of Buckingham.

Augusto de la Torre is the chief economist for Latin America and the Caribbean at the World Bank. Since joining the Bank in 1997, he has held the positions of senior adviser in the Financial Systems Department and senior financial sector adviser for the Latin American and Caribbean regions. From 1993 to 1997 he was the head of the Central Bank of Ecuador, and in November 1996 *Euromoney* nominated him as the year's "Best Latin American Central Banker." From 1986 to 1992 he worked at the International Monetary Fund, where, among other positions, he was the IMF's resident representative in Venezuela (1991–1992). de la Torre has published on a broad range of macroeconomic and financial development topics. He is a member of the Carnegie Economic Reform Network.

Elisabeth de Nadal is a partner at Cuatrecasas, Gonçalves Pereira, and heads the arbitration practice at the Barcelona office. She has extensive experience in general commercial litigation, both in judicial proceedings and through alternative dispute resolutions. de Nadal specializes in corporate lawsuits, disputes arising over acquisitions (M&A), and disputes in the areas of competition law, commercial distribution agreements, entertainment, and sport. She is the author and coauthor of several legal publications such as *International Civil Procedure* (Kluwer Law International), the new Spanish Arbitration Act 60/2003 (Mealey Publications), *Dispute Resolution*

     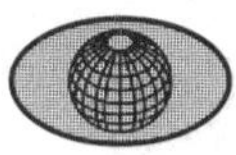   

Handbook 2005 (Spanish chapter), and *International Comparative Guide to International Arbitration* 2005, 2006, and 2007 (Global Legal Group). She is a lecturer on arbitration in the LLM degree in dispute resolution at the Universidad Pompeu Fabra School of Law, Barcelona.

Bert De Reyck is a professor of management science and innovation at University College London and adjunct professor at the London Business School. Previously, he held positions at the Kellogg School of Management, Northwestern University, and the Rotterdam School of Management. He is an authority on decision-making, risk management, project management, and project portfolio management. Professor De Reyck's award-winning research has been published in numerous scientific and professional journals, and applications of his work can be found in industries such as pharmaceuticals, energy, and aerospace. He is also a multiple award-winning educator. He is a member of the Institute for Management Science and Operations Research (INFORMS), the Institute of Industrial Engineers (IIE), and the Project Management Institute (PMI).

Todd DeZoort is professor of accounting and accounting advisory board fellow at the University of Alabama. He joined the university's accounting faculty in 2001 and has published 40 articles with many in top academic journals such as *Accounting, Organizations and Society*, *Contemporary Accounting Research*, *Auditing: A Journal of Practice & Theory*, *Journal of Accounting Literature*, and *Behavioral Research in Accounting*. He also has received several research grants from the American Institute of Certified Public Accountants, KPMG's Audit Committee Institute, and the Institute of Internal Auditors. Dr DeZoort is currently a member of the AICPA's reliability task force and an advisory council member at the Academy for Ethics in Financial Reporting.

Eric R. Dinallo has been superintendent of insurance for New York State since January 2007. During his tenure the New York State Insurance Department has been given the 2008 Esprit de Corps award by the National Association of Insurance Commissioners (NAIC) for outstanding service to state insurance regulation. He has worked with the United States Treasury Department, the Federal Reserve Bank of New York, and others in the rescue of financial services giant AIG. He is chair of the 50-state task force of the NAIC charged with safeguarding AIG insurance interests during the federal government's stewardship of the company. He has served as chair of the NAIC's Life and Annuities Committee since January 2008.

Rajiv Dogra is a diplomat by profession, an engineer by training, a writer by choice, and an artist by inclination. Currently he is based in New Delhi and is a well-known commentator and columnist. He became a member of the Indian Diplomatic Service in 1974. During the course of a wide-ranging professional career he was India's ambassador to Italy, Romania, Moldova, Albania, and San Marino. He was also India's permanent representative to United Nations agencies in Rome (FAO, WFP, and IFAD) and India's last full-time consul general in Karachi. He is the author of two novels, *Footprints in Foreign Sands* and *Almost an Ambassador*. Among the honors he has received is an honorary doctorate.

David A. Doney is vice-president of internal audit for SIRVA, Inc., a global moving and relocation services company, where he oversees the audit team and is the coordinator for the company's Sarbanes–Oxley (SOX) compliance efforts. Prior to SIRVA, Doney led the SOX assessment efforts for Bally Total Fitness from 2004 to 2007. He has also worked for Sears, Roebuck & Company in the internal audit and financial planning areas, and for Ingersoll-Rand Company as a financial management trainee. He is a frequent speaker at the MIS Training Institute on internal audit and SOX and gave presentations at the Institute of Internal Auditors' international conferences in 2002 and 2008. Doney is a registered Certified Public Accountant (CPA) and a Certified Internal Auditor (CIA).

Emma Du Haney is senior fixed-income product specialist on the fixed-income team at Insight Investment. Previously she worked at Henderson Global Investors as investment director. Her focus now is Insight's developing client base outside the United Kingdom, especially in Europe. Emma has over 20 years of fixed-income experience in both fund management and product specialist roles. Before Henderson she spent most of her career at Credit Suisse Asset Management.

Leif Edvinsson is the world's leading expert on intellectual capital (IC). He has been vice president and the world's first corporate director of IC at Skandia of Stockholm, Sweden, and has held the world's first professorship in IC at Lund Universtiy, Sweden, since 2000. In 1996 he received awards from the American Productivity and Quality Center and from Business Intelligence in the United Kingdom for his pioneering work on IC. In light of his work in both training and IC, Professor Edvinsson has been a special adviser on service trade to the Swedish Ministry of Foreign Affairs. He is also special adviser to the United Nations International Trade Centre and is a cofounder of the Swedish Coalition of Service Industries.

Shane Edwards is managing director and global head of equity structuring at the Royal Bank of Scotland. His team has won numerous "best in country" and innovation awards and is responsible for structured products across the entire client spectrum from retail investors to large institutions and major hedge funds. Edward's research on derivatives markets has been published in industry and academic journals, and he is frequently a speaker at derivatives conferences and interviewed by journalists. Prior to the Royal Bank of Scotland, he worked in a similar capacity and as an algorithmic trader at Deutsche Bank, Macquarie Bank, and a private hedge fund. He is one of the youngest ever winners of the Dow Jones' *Financial News* Top 100 Rising Stars in Europe Award.

Rainer Ender is managing director of Adveq. Before joining Adveq in 2001, he was an underwriter for alternative risk transfer at Zurich Reinsurance Company. From 1997 to 2000 he was a manager in the financial risk management practice at Arthur Andersen. He also served for several years on the board of DTS, a regulated derivatives trader in Switzerland. Dr Ender holds an MSc in physics and a PhD in natural sciences from the Swiss Federal Institute of Technology (ETH), and he is a CFA charter holder.

Marc J. Epstein is distinguished research professor of management at Jones Graduate School of Management at Rice University, Houston, Texas. He was also recently visiting professor and Wyss visiting scholar at Harvard Business School. Prior to joining Rice, Dr Epstein was a professor at Stanford Business School, Harvard Business School, and INSEAD (European Institute of Business Administration). He has completed extensive academic research and has extensive practical experience in the implementation of corporate strategies and the development of performance

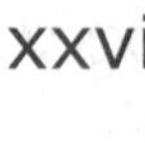

metrics for use in these implementations. Dr Epstein has extensive industry experience and has been a senior consultant to leading corporations and governments for over 25 years.

Javier Estrada, professor of financial management at Barcelona-based IESE Business School, set the cat among the pigeons with his ground-breaking research, *Black Swans and Market Timing: How Not to Generate Alpha*. Published in 2008, this revealed that investors who seek to time the market are unlikely to reap rewards. His research focuses on risk, portfolio management, investment strategies, emerging markets, and insider trading. The founding editor of the *Emerging Markets Review*, he also has several visiting professorships in Scandinavia and Latin America. His first degree, a BA in economics, was from the National University of La Plata in Buenos Aires, and he has an MSc and PhD from the University of Illinois at Urbana—Champaign.

Frank J. Fabozzi is professor in the practice of finance at Yale School of Management and specializes in investment management and structured finance. He is editor of the *Journal of Portfolio Management* and has authored and edited many acclaimed books, three of which were coauthored with the late Franco Modigliani and one coedited with Harry Markowitz. Professor Fabozzi is a consultant to several financial institutions, is on the board of directors of the BlackRock complex of closed-end funds, and is on the advisory council for the Department of Operations Research and Financial Engineering at Princeton University. He was inducted into the Fixed Income Analysts Society Hall of Fame in November 2002 and is the 2007 recipient of the C. Stewart Sheppard Award given by the CFA Institute.

Alain Fayolle is professor and director of the entrepreneurship research center at EM Lyon Business School, France. He is also visiting professor at Solvay Brussels School of Economics and Management, Belgium, and HEC Montréal, Canada. His current research work focuses on the dynamics of entrepreneurial processes, the influence of cultural factors on organizations' entrepreneurial orientation, and the evaluation of entrepreneurship education. Professor Fayolle's most recent books are *Entrepreneurship and New Value Creation: The Dynamic of the Entrepreneurial Process* (Cambridge University Press, 2007) and *The Dynamics between Entrepreneurship, Environment and Education* (Edward Elgar, 2008).

Frank Feather is a business futurist, with a remarkably accurate 30-year forecasting track record that often defies conventional explanation. He is ranked as one of the "Top 100 Futurists of All Time" by Margaret MacMillan's *Encyclopedia of the Future*. A best-selling author and dynamic keynote speaker, Feather was born in the United Kingdom but is now based in Toronto, Canada. He has consulted for companies including Ericsson, IBM, Ford, Nokia, and Shell. He has been special adviser to China on economic modernization and market reforms continuously since 1984, and has seen many of his ideas implemented there. Previously, he worked for Barclays Bank, Toronto-Dominion Bank, and the Canadian Imperial Bank of Commerce (CIBC).

Björn Flismark is a senior vice president, product management and development, within global transaction services at Skandinaviska Enskilda Banken (SEB). Formerly he was responsible for infrastructure projects on payments, securities, and foreign exchange, and he is now involved in SEB's preparations for the Single European Payments Area (SEPA) and the Payment Service Directive (PSD). Flismark is deputy chairman of the Euro Banking Association (EBA) and chairs the SEPA and PSD compliance working group, which produced "Banks preparing for SEPA" and "Banks preparing for PSD." He is also a member of the European Payments Council and the Coordination Committee and is chairman of the Information Security Support Group (ISSG).

Julian Franks is professor of finance and academic director at London Business School's Centre for Corporate Governance. His research focuses on bankruptcy and financial distress and corporate ownership and control, a field in which he has won two international prizes. He served as a member of a UK government working party reviewing the insolvency code and advised (with London Business School professor Richard A. Brealey) the Office of Constitutional Affairs on the issue of outside equity for law firms. He is also an adviser to the regulator, Ofcom, and BAA. His qualifications include a BA (Sheffield), an MBA (Columbia), and PhD (London).

Ian Fraser is professor of accounting at the University of Stirling, Scotland, and he has previously held academic posts at the University of Strathclyde and Glasgow Caledonian University. He trained for membership of the Institute of Chartered Accountants of Scotland (ICAS) with Thomson Mclintock & Co. (one of the predecessor firms of KPMG). Professor Fraser has wide-ranging research interests in the fields of auditing, financial reporting, and corporate governance, and he has published on these areas in many academic journals. He has a particular interest in the interfaces between auditing, risk, and risk management. He is currently carrying out a major funded research project on the audit of narrative corporate reporting.

Martin S. Fridson is a former managing director of Merrill Lynch & Co. Inc. and was a member of *Institutional Investor*'s All-America Fixed-Income Research Team. He is the author of *It Was a Very Good Year*, *Investment Illusions*, and *Financial Statement Analysis*. He serves on the board of the Association for Investment Management and Research. According to the *New York Times*, Fridson is "one of Wall Street's most thoughtful and perceptive analysts." The Financial Management Association International named him its financial executive of the year in 2002. In 2000 Fridson became the youngest person ever inducted into the Fixed Income Analysts Society Hall of Fame.

Hung-Gay Fung is a professor of Chinese studies at the College of Business Administration of the University of Missouri, St Louis. He holds a BBA (1978) from the Chinese University of Hong Kong and a PhD (1984) from Georgia State University, in both cases majoring in finance with a minor in economics. His teaching areas are investments, risk management, corporate finance, and international investments. His research focuses on international finance, banking, derivative markets, and small business finance. In 1999 he won a best paper award (with G. Lai, R. MacMinn and Bob Witt) given by the Committee on Online Services (COOS) of the Casualty Actuarial Society.

James Gifford is executive director of Principles for Responsible Investment (PRI) and has been guiding the initiative since its inception in November 2003. He was also a member of the Global Reporting Initiative working group that developed the environmental sector supplement for the finance sector. As well as leading the PRI, he has recently completed a PhD at the Faculty of Economics and Business,

     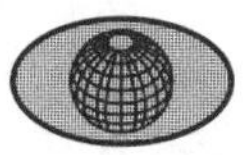   

University of Sydney, on the effectiveness of shareholder engagement in improving corporate environmental, social, and corporate governance performance. He has degrees in commerce and law from the University of Queensland, and a master's in environment management from the University of New South Wales.

John Gilligan is a corporate finance partner in PKF (UK) LLP and has worked in the private equity and venture capital industry for 21 years. He started his career in 1988 at 3i Group plc as a financial analyst. He joined what is now Deloitte in 1993 and was a partner from 1998 to 2003. He is a special lecturer at Nottingham University Business School and has also taught at Cranfield University Business School. He has a degree in economics from Southampton University and an MBA in financial studies from Nottingham University. He is the coauthor with Mike Wright of *Private Equity Demystified.*

Martin Gold is a senior lecturer at the Sydney Business School, University of Wollongong, having joined academia after a successful career in the investment industry. He is an experienced funds manager and investment analyst who has held senior analytical and managerial positions in financial institutions and investment research firms. Dr Gold coauthored *Corporate Governance and Investment Fiduciaries* (Thomson Lawbook Co., 2003), and he has also published a number of articles on innovative investment products and the related fiduciary obligations of fund managers and pension fund trustees.

Beverly Goldberg is senior fellow and editor-at-large at the Century Foundation. She is the author of *Age Works: What Corporate America Must Do to Survive the Graying of the Workforce* (Free Press, 2000) and *Overcoming High-tech Anxiety: Thriving in a Wired World* (Jossey-Bass, 1999) and coauthor of *Corporation on a Tightrope: Balancing Leadership, Governance, and Technology in an Age of Complexity* (Oxford, 1996) and *Dynamic Planning: The Art of Managing Beyond Tomorrow* (Oxford, 1994). Goldberg was the former vice president and director of publications at the Century Foundation.

Vidhan Goyal is a professor of finance at the Hong Kong University of Science and Technology. His research interests are in empirical corporate finance, with an emphasis on capital structure and corporate governance. His research papers have been published in the *Journal of Finance, Journal of Financial Economics, Journal of Business, Journal of Financial Intermediation, Finance Research Letters, Journal of Corporate Finance*, and the *Pacific Basin Finance Journal.* Professor Goyal is a member of the American Finance Association, the Western Finance Association, and Beta Gamma Sigma.

John C. Groth is professor of finance in the Department of Finance, Mays Business School, at Texas A&M University. He has received many teaching awards, authored numerous publications, and been cited as a major contributor to the finance literature. Dr Groth received his PhD from the Krannert School, Purdue University. He also holds degrees in physics and in industrial administration. He serves as a consultant in the areas of corporate finance and management education and conducts executive development programs. In addition to his work in finance, he researches and speaks on human capital and creativity and is a keynote speaker. In 2006 he was designated a Mays Faculty Fellow in Teaching Innovation.

Raj Gupta is research director of the Center for International Securities and Derivatives Markets (CISDM) at the University of Massachusetts, Amherst. He is also a visiting faculty at Clark University and has taught finance at the University of Massachusetts, Amherst. Gupta is assistant editor for the *Journal of Alternative Investments* and has published articles in the *Journal of Portfolio Management, Journal of Alternative Investments, Journal of Investment Consulting, Journal of Trading, Alternative Investment Quarterly, IMCA Monitor*, and the *Journal of Performance Measurement.* He is a frequent speaker at industry conferences on topics such as performance measurement, asset allocation, and risk management. He holds a PhD in finance from the University of Massachusetts, Amherst.

Stephen Haddrill took up his post as director general of the Association of British Insurers in 2005, focusing on maintaining and developing its influential relationship with government and regulators. Previously he was a civil servant, joining UK government service in 1978 and ultimately rising to the position of director general, Fair Markets Group, at the Department of Trade and Industry (DTI). Between 1990 and 1994 he worked for the Hong Kong government as a member of the Governor's central policy unit. Haddrill was recently appointed chief executive of the Financial Reporting Council, and will begin this new role in November 2009.

Ray Halagera is founder/partner of the Profit Ability Group, Inc., a consulting and training company specializing in finance and strategy. Over the past 20 years he has held leadership positions in other global training companies serving Fortune 500 clients. Before his career in the learning industry, Halagera was vice president of planning and management information systems for Chromalloy American Corporation, a Fortune 100 conglomerate, and a senior associate at A.T. Kearney, an international broad-line management consulting firm and subsidiary of EDS.

Bill Hambrecht has been in the securities business since 1958. He cofounded the San Francisco-based investment bank Hambrecht & Quist in 1968. Noted for its focus on the technology sector, H&Q was the pioneer of Silicon Valley's venture capital industry. Hambrecht resigned from H&Q in December 1997 to form WR Hambrecht + Co, which has introduced a new "Dutch auction" technique that has increased the amount that companies can raise through flotations. He is currently a director of Motorola Inc. and is on the advisory council to the J. David Gladstone Institutes. He graduated from Princeton University in 1957 and was inducted to the American Academy of Arts and Sciences in October 2006.

Stewart Hamilton is professor of accounting and finance at IMD business school in Lausanne. He has held that post since 1981 and has been dean of finance and administration since 2008. His areas of interest are corporate failure, governance, risk management, and investor protection. Formerly a senior partner of a UK national accounting firm, Hamilton has served on professional committees and working parties on company law reform, the conduct of serious fraud trials, and financial services legislation. He is the author of numerous case studies on corporate failure, including the Barings collapse and the Enron collapse. Professor Hamilton is a graduate of the University of Edinburgh and a member of the Institutes of Chartered Accountants of Scotland, of Alberta, and of Ontario.

Gail Harden is internal audit manager with Specialized Technology Resources, Inc. (STR). She created the internal audit function at both STR and her previous

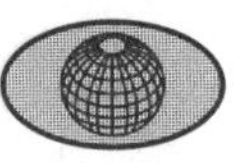

employer, United Natural Foods, Inc. Harden has been the sole internal auditor at each company, utilizing creative and insightful ways to meet the demands and standards of the internal audit profession with limited resources. At United Natural Foods she was responsible for implementing the Sarbanes–Oxley compliance process. Gail has seven years experience in internal audit and 13 years experience in accounting. She holds a bachelor's degree in accounting and MS in business administration and is a certified internal auditor (CIA).

Robert P. Hartwig is president of the Insurance Information Institute, where for the last 11 years he has focused on improving the understanding of key insurance issues across all industry stakeholders. He previously served as director of economic research and senior economist with the National Council on Compensation Insurance (NCCI). He has also worked as senior economist for the Swiss Reinsurance Group and as senior statistician for the US Consumer Product Safety Commission. Dr Hartwig is a published author and is frequently quoted in leading publications such as the *Wall Street Journal* and *The Economist*. He has a PhD and MSc in economics from the University of Illinois and a BA in economics cum laude from the University of Massachusetts.

Rita Herron Brown has been a business educator and editor for more than 25 years. She is editor-in-chief at BrownHerron Publishing and an editor of *Business Strategy Review*, the quarterly journal of the London Business School. Previously she developed the curriculum for marketing programs at Honeywell's Aerospace Management Development Center in Minneapolis. She also served as associate director of the executive program at Indiana University's Kelley School of Business, where she was involved in both curriculum development and marketing. She gained her BA and MBA degrees from Indiana University.

Andrew Higson is a lecturer in accounting and financial management at the Business School, Loughborough University. After qualifying as a chartered accountant, he studied for a PhD. Dr Higson's research has covered a wide range of topics, including accounting theory, the conceptual framework of financial reporting, the expectations gap in financial statements, external auditing, and fraud. He is on the editorial board of the *Icfai University Journal of Audit Practice*, which is based in Hyderabad, India.

Andrew Hiles was founding director and is a fellow of the Business Continuity Institute. He was chairman of the European Information Market (EURIM) group, which supports the UK Parliament's all-party EURIM group in handling European legislation that impacts IT. He is a director of Kingswell International, an international consultancy specializing in managing business risk. Hiles is a published writer and international speaker on business continuity and risk management. He has presented at numerous conferences in Europe, the United States, Africa, the Middle East, the Pacific Rim, Australia, and New Zealand and has broadcast on IT topics on radio and television. He is a member of the British Computer Society.

Tim Hindle is a freelance writer and editor. Educated at Worcester College, Oxford, and Heriot-Watt University, Edinburgh, he was a research analyst in the City of London before joining *The Banker* magazine as deputy editor. He subsequently wrote for *The Economist* for many years, acting as finance editor in the 1980s before taking on the new role of management editor. He launched *EuroBusiness* magazine in the early 1990s and then relaunched the Institute of Directors' magazine, *Director*, later that decade. He has written a number of books. *The Essential Manager's Manual*, published by Dorling Kindersley, was a worldwide bestseller. His latest book, *Guide to Management Ideas and Gurus*, was published in 2008 to widespread acclaim.

Christopher Holt founded AllAboutAlpha in 2006 and was formerly the head of institutional sales for JC Clark, a $400 million Canadian hedge fund manager. Prior to JC Clark, Holt spent a decade in the management consulting industry with various firms, including Ernst & Young. During this time he worked as both a consultant and a research director, providing counsel to major clients in the financial services and telecom sectors. For 10 years he acted as a consultant to the annual meeting of the World Economic Forum in Davos, Switzerland. Holt has an MBA from from Duke University and holds the Chartered Alternative Invesment Analysis (CAIA) designation.

Zahirul Hoque is associate dean (research) and professor of accounting in the Faculty of Law and Management of La Trobe University in Australia, where he is also deputy director of the Public Sector Governance and Accountability Research Centre. Prior to that he held a number of faculty posts at universities in Australia, New Zealand, Bangladesh and Saudi Arabia. His research interests include accounting and organizational change, management accounting, performance management, public sector accounting, and a general interest in the interdisciplinary research in organizational designs. Professor Hoque has published a number of articles, book chapters, two edited volumes, and two books, namely *Handbook of Cost and Management Accounting* and *Strategic Management Accounting*. He is founding editor of the *Journal of Accounting & Organizational Change*.

Arne-G. Hostrup has been a managing director at netzwerk|nordbayern since January 2003. His main remits are fiscal planning and private equity finance of high-growth companies by business angels and venture capital. He has gained professional experience in several positions: as commercial leader of a German medium-sized company, in the franchise operations of an international fast-food company, as project leader of the Northern Bavarian Business Plan Competition, and as finance director and involved in building a start-up in the media area. As a member of the board of the European Business Angel Network (EBAN) and leader of the Best Practice Committee of the German Business Angel Network, he has committed himself to the establishment of the business angel culture in Northern Bavaria, Germany.

Peter Howson is a director of AMR International, a London-based strategic consultancy that specializes in commercial due diligence. His particluar focus is on manufacturing, building, and construction. He has over 20 years of M&A experience, gained both in industry and as an adviser. Previously he worked in corporate finance at Barings, where he focused on domestic and cross-border deals in manufacturing industries. He has also worked for TI Group plc, transforming the company from a UK supplier of mainly commodity engineering products into a global specialist engineering company through a series of acquisitions and disposals. He has also held senior finance and M&A roles with British Steel and T&N.

Frank Hoy is the Paul Beswick professor of entrepreneurship and director of the Collaborative for Entrepreneurship and Innovation at Worcester Polytechnic

  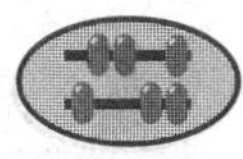 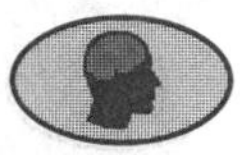  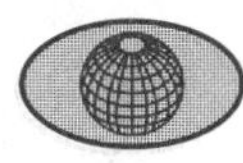   

Institute. Dr Hoy earned his PhD at Texas A&M University, where he developed a small business outreach program for the Texas Agricultural Extension Service. Subsequently, he became director of the Small Business Development Center for the State of Georgia. He moved from the University of Georgia to Georgia State University in 1988 as the Carl R. Zwerner professor of family-owned businesses. From 1991 to 2001 Dr Hoy was dean of the College of Business and subsequently director of the entrepreneurship program at the University of Texas at El Paso.

Fred Hu is chairman of Greater China at Goldman Sachs. He has advised the Chinese government on financial reform, pension reform, and macroeconomic policies, and has worked closely with China's leading companies on business strategy, capital raising, and cross-border mergers and acquisitions. He is a member of the strategic development committee for the Government of Hong Kong Special Administrative Region and the advisory committee for the Hong Kong Securities and Futures Commission. Co-director and professor at the National Center for Economic Research (NCER) at Tsinghua University in Beijing, he teaches a graduate course in international finance and macroeconomics. Dr Hu has published widely on economics and financial markets.

Bridget Hutter is chair of risk regulation at the London School of Economics and Political Science and director of the ESRC Centre for Analysis of Risk and Regulation (CARR), a multidisciplinary research center which focuses on the organizational and institutional settings of risk management and regulation. She has held research and teaching appointments at the universities of Oxford and London and is former editor of the *British Journal of Sociology*. Professor Hutter is author of numerous publications on the subject of risk regulation and has an international reputation for her work on compliance, regulatory enforcement, and business risk management. She is regularly involved with policy-making and business discussions, particularly with international bodies such as the World Economic Forum and with business organizations and regulatory agencies.

Boulis Ibrahim is a lecturer in finance at the School of Management and Languages at Heriot-Watt University (HWSML). Dr Ibrahim joined the Department of Accountancy and Finance as a lecturer in 1996 and teaches on both the undergraduate and postgraduate courses. His academic research covers portfolio theory, asset allocation, asset pricing theory, volatility modeling, asset–liability modeling, market microstructure, and trading mechanisms. He currently coordinates the undergraduate second year and teaches the finance, structure, and regulation of capital markets and derivatives at the HWSML. He also teaches petroleum economics at the Institute of Petroleum Economics and consults on the same subject through the Energy Academy at Heriot-Watt.

Hao Jiang is assistant professor of finance at Rotterdam School of Management, Erasmus University. Dr Jiang's main research areas include asset pricing, investments, the behavior of institutional and individual investors, and international finance. At Erasmus he teaches portfolio management, investments, advanced asset pricing, and behavioral finance. His work will appear in the *Journal of Financial Economics* and he has conducted industry and academic presentations across Europe, the United States, and Asia.

Irena Jindrichovska is a senior lecturer in finance and accounting at the University of Buckingham, where she is a program director of the MSc in accounting and finance. She has a broad experience in the financial sector and in consulting and executive training. Previously she worked at several British and European universities. She acts as a lead researcher in British and international projects. She is an author of academic articles in the field of market-based accounting and a coauthor of books on corporate finance, financial derivatives, and financial statement analysis. Her current academic interests include corporate financing decisions and corporate governance in transitional countries.

Scott S. Johnson is the CEO of SJ Partners, LLC, a middle-market leveraged buyout group. He is on the boards of portfolio companies European Soaps LLC and Audio Messaging Solutions LLC. He previously worked in equity research at Salomon Smith Barney and Merrill Lynch. Johnson earned his BA, MIA (Master of International Affairs), and MBA from Columbia University.

Tim Johnson is a director at Regester Larkin, a specialist reputation strategy and management consultancy. He advises some of the world's leading public and private organizations on reputation management, helping them to develop their approach to sensitive, long-term issues and respond to acute, short-term reputational risks. He works extensively with senior executives, coaching them on their presentation and media handling skills.

Udo Jung is a senior partner and managing director in the Frankfurt office of the Boston Consulting Group. He joined BCG in 1990 and leads the operations practice in Europe. His work focuses on performance improvement, value lever management, and cash-flow optimization (including net working capital management) for industrial goods companies, with a focus on the chemical and logistics industries. He supports companies mainly in Europe, the Middle East, and Asia. Dr Jung holds a PhD in business administration and studied at Philipps-University of Marburg in Germany and the University of Illinois, USA.

Jonathan M. Karpoff has a particular interest in what drives executives to commit corporate crimes and misdemeanors, believing that a breakdown of trust can have long-term repercussions for individual corporations and that it contributed to the wider financial collapse of 2007–08. A professor of finance at the University of Washington's Michael G. Foster School of Business, Karpoff is also associate editor of a number of academic journals including the *Journal of Finance*. He won the best paper award in the CRSP Forum at the University of Chicago in 2006 and 2008 for his research into corporate and financial scandals. He was founding director of the University of Washington's environmental management program and was director of its CFO Forum in 2004–07.

Paul Kasriel joined the economic research unit of the Northern Trust Company in 1986 as vice president and economist, and was made senior vice president and director of economic research in 2000. In 2006 he received the prestigious Lawrence R. Klein Award for making the most accurate economic forecast among the Blue Chip survey participants for the years 2002 through 2005. The accuracy of Kasriel's 2008 economic forecast was ranked in the top five of the *Wall Street Journal* survey panel of economists. In January 2009, the *Wall Street Journal* and *Forbes* cited him as one of the few who identified early on the formation of the housing bubble and foresaw the economic and financial market havoc that would ensue after the bubble burst. Kasriel began his career as a research economist at the Federal Reserve Bank of Chicago. He is coauthor of a book entitled *Seven Indicators that Move Markets*, and he serves on the Economic Advisory Committee of the American Bankers Association.

Giles Keating is a managing director of Credit Suisse in the Private Banking Division. He is head of private banking research and also responsible for the research groups of asset management. He is also chair of the Global Economics and Strategy Group of Credit Suisse. Before joining Credit Suisse First Boston in 1986, Keating was a research fellow at the London Business School Centre for Economic Forecasting, where he built an econometric model of the UK financial system. He spent six years at the Confederation of British Industry, finishing as head of the Economic Forecasting Department. He has published widely in academic and general media on macroeconomics, financial markets, and public policy.

Alison Kemper is completing her PhD in strategic management under the supervision of Roger Martin. She is studying the impact of social ratings on the behavior of firms. For many years she was a leader and activist in the nonprofit sector. She completed her BA in religious studies at Yale College, her MDiv and MTh at Trinity College, Toronto, and her MBA at the Rotman School of Management, University of Toronto.

Shân Kennedy is an independent consultant who advises on IFRS and valuation issues. Her background includes more than 20 years with Ernst & Young and Deloitte. She has also spent four years working at the UK Accounting Standards Board developing UK GAAP guidance on accounting for goodwill and intangible assets; this included developing the impairment test. Kennedy has presented at many IFRS conferences in London and Europe. She has recently acted as technical consultant to the International Valuation Standards Council to develop its guidance on the valuation of intangible assets, both generally and for IFRS purposes.

Peter Killing is professor of strategy at IMD, Lausanne, Switzerland. His major interest is the interface between strategy and leadership. His teaching, research, and consulting activities focus on leaders who are working with their teams to create the right strategy and at the same time set the ground for effective implementation. In the area of mergers, acquisitions, and alliances, Professor Killing has written and edited four books and several articles, including one in the *Harvard Business Review*. He also runs in-company programs for a variety of clients including BMW, Allianz, Sika, and Vestas, the Danish wind turbine company.

Kelvin King's early career was spent with the UK government division responsible for private company, business, intellectual property, and intangible asset valuation. He established a valuation unit for an accountancy practice. Before the founding of Valuation Consulting, a BNP Paribas company, he was managing director of a specialist valuation company within an international Swiss bank. Since 1996 he has been a separately listed UK expert witness in intellectual property, intangible asset, and unquoted company valuation. King is a founder of the Society of Share and Business Valuers, founding expert of Lord Woolf's Expert Witness Institute, associate member of the Licensing Executive Society, Chartered Institute of Patent Agents, fellow of the Royal Institution of Chartered Surveyors, and a member of the International Association of Consultants, Valuers and Analysts.

Joachim Klement is a CFA charter holder and a CFP certificant. Currently he is head of the UBS Wealth Management Research strategic research team. His focus is on asset allocation topics (including nontraditional asset classes), portfolio construction, and financial planning. To support these efforts, he develops quantitative investment models and works with advisers and clients on topics such as financial planning, behavioral finance, and strategic asset allocation. Since joining UBS in 2003 as an investment consultant for Swiss institutional clients, Klement has gained expertise in institutional asset management and quantitative analysis and as head of equity strategy within Wealth Management Research.

Ruud Kleynen is professor of asset–liability management in the Faculty of Economics and Business Administration at the University of Maastricht. His main areas of research cover the risk management and asset–liability management for pension funds and insurance companies. He also runs his own consultancy bureau, Kleynen Consultants, which aims to apply knowledge in the field of asset–liability management to offer state of the art solutions to large clients.

Angela Knight, CBE, is chief executive of the British Bankers' Association. She is also a non-executive director on the boards of International Financial Services, London (IFSL), Brewin Dolphin plc, and the Financial Services Skills Council. From 1987 to 1992 she was councillor and chief whip on Sheffield City Council. She entered the British Parliament in 1992 as MP for Erewash and was economic secretary to the Treasury between 1995 and 1997, when she lost her seat at the general election. She was chief executive of the Association of Private Client Investment Managers and Stockbrokers from 1997 to 2006. Knight has an honors degree in chemistry from Bristol University.

Theo Kocken, founder and CEO of the Cardano Group, graduated in business administration (Eindhoven) and econometrics (Tilburg) and gained his PhD at Vrije Universiteit (VU), Amsterdam. From 1990 on he headed the market risk departments at ING and Rabobank International. In 2000 he started Cardano, a specialized organization that supports end users such as pension funds and insurance companies around Europe with strategic derivatives solutions and portfolio optimization. Cardano, now with over 60 employees, has offices in Rotterdam and London. Kocken is coauthor of various books and articles in the area of risk management. In 2006 he wrote *Curious Contracts: Pension Fund Redesign for the Future*, in which he applied embedded option theories as a basis for pension fund risk management and redesign.

Leslie L. Kossoff is an internationally renowned executive adviser specializing in strategy and corporate turnaround. For over 20 years she has assisted clients ranging from Fortune 50 to small and mid-sized firms in a broad range of industries and sectors in the United States, Japan, and Europe. Her clients include Fidelity Investments, Sony, TRW, Kraft Foods, Baxter Healthcare, the UK National Health Service, Seiko/Epson, 3M, Infonet and GM/Hughes. A former C-level executive in the aerospace/defense, pharmaceutical, and entertainment industries, Kossoff enjoys an outstanding reputation as an invited speaker. She is the author of two books and more than 100 articles in journals and newspapers, including the *Financial Times* and *CEO Magazine*.

Peter Koveos is professor and chair of the Finance Department at the Whitman School of Management, Syracuse University. He is also the Kiebach chair in

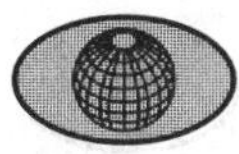

international business, director of the Kiebach Center, and executive director of the Africa Business Program at the Whitman School. As director of ExportNY, an institute for international business executives, and the International Business Forum he works closely with New York companies to develop their international business strategies. He is also president of the Central New York International Business Alliance and has worked extensively in Asia. Professor Koveos is editor of the *Journal of Developmental Entrepreneurship* and his work has appeared in numerous professional journals.

Klaus Kremers is a partner at Roland Berger Strategy Consultants in London. He is also a member of Berger's Restructuring & Corporate Finance Competence Center. Kremers has more than 10 years' experience in strategic, operational, and financial restructuring in turnaround situations. He advises international sponsors/financiers and European corporate clients across a range of industries. Prior to joining Roland Berger in 2000, he worked for KPMG Transaction and Corporate Recovery Services in Frankfurt. He has studied in Germany, the United States, the Netherlands, and the United Kingdom. He holds a degree in international business administration and a master's in business administration with special focus on finance.

Satya Kumar is an associate at Ennis Knupp and manages consulting assignments for several retainer and project clients. Prior to joining Ennis Knupp in 2004, he served as a research associate involved in risk management and quantitative strategy development with a proprietary options trading firm. Kumar holds a BComm degree from the University of Madras and earned a MS degree in finance from the Illinois Institute of Technology. He is a CFA charterholder and a member of CFA Institute and the CFA Society of Chicago. He is also an associate member of the Institute of Chartered Accountants of India.

Chiraz Labidi is assistant professor of finance at the College of Business and Economics, United Arab Emirates University in Al Ain. She was previously assistant professor of finance at IHEC Carthage. Her areas of academic research cover international financial markets, emerging markets, and dependence structures.

Gene C. Lai is Safeco distinguished professor of insurance and chairperson of the Department of Finance, Insurance, and Real Estate at Washington State University. His publications have appeared in many journals, including the *Journal of Risk and Insurance*. Professor Lai has won numerous best paper awards, including one from the Casualty Actuarial Society. He serves as a coeditor for the *Journal of Insurance Issues* and as associate editor for many other journals, including the *Journal of Risk and Insurance*. He is vice president of the American Risk and Insurance Association (ARIA).

Vinod Lall is adjunct professor at the Graduate School of Management and Technology at the University of Maryland University College, which he joined in 2007. He is also an associate professor of operations management at Minnesota State University Moorhead, where he teaches courses in operations management, management science, project management, and supply chain management. He is an APICS Certified Supply Chain Professional (CSCP), and he runs training courses for APICS. He has taught an EMBA course in operations management for the American University in Bulgaria for the last couple of years.

Meziane Lasfer is professor of finance at Cass Business School, London, which he joined in 1990. He has written extensively on corporate finance, capital markets, and corporate governance issues. His research is widely reported in the financial press and is published in top academic journals such as the *Journal of Finance*, *Journal of Finance and Quantitative Analysis*, *Journal of Banking and Finance*, *Journal of Corporate Finance*, *Journal of Business Finance and Accounting*, *Financial Management*, *National Tax Journal*, and *European Financial Management*. He is a visiting professor at University Paris-Dauphine. He teaches extensively masters, PhDs, and executives at Cass and abroad.

Graeme Leach is chief economist and director of policy at the Institute of Directors, London. He is also visiting professor of economics at the University of Lincoln. Prior to joining the IoD he was an economics director at the Henley Centre, analyzing future economic and social change.

Ernst Ligteringen is chief executive of the United Nations' Global Reporting Initiative, which he has run since it was established as an independent organization in 2002. He has overall responsibility for secretariat operations and the coordination of a global network of stakeholders. A Dutch national, Ligteringen previously worked for a number of international organizations including the International Federation of Red Cross and Red Crescent Societies, Oxfam, and Terres des Hommes in Africa, the Caribbean, Latin America, Asia, the Middle East, and Europe.

Justin Yifu Lin has been the World Bank's chief economist since June 2008, and is the first person from an emerging market to hold this role since the World Bank was founded over 60 years ago. He was previously professor and founding director of the China Center for Economic Research at Peking University. Lin, who received his PhD in economics from the University of Chicago in 1986, has written 16 books, including *The China Miracle: Development Strategy and Economic Reform*, published in seven languages, and *State-owned Enterprise Reform in China*. Among his public roles in China, Lin has served as a deputy in the National People's Congress and as vice chairman of the All-China Federation of Industry and Commerce. He has also served on international task forces and groups including the United Nations Millennium Task Force on Hunger, the National Committee on United States–China Relations, the working group on the future of the OECD, and the Reinventing Bretton Woods Committee. He gave the 2007–2008 Marshall Lectures at Cambridge University.

Joseph LiPuma is an affiliate professor in strategic management at EMLYON Business School. He has a BS in mathematics and an MBA from SUNY Buffalo, and received his doctorate in business strategy and policy from Boston University. LiPuma has nearly 20 years of professional experience, including senior management, operating committee and board-level roles. He has established new businesses (information technology consultancies) in both US domestic and international environments. His research focuses on international entrepreneurship, specifically new venture internationalization and its relationship to the manner in which ventures are capitalized. He teaches masters-level courses in strategy, international business, and entrepreneurship.

Roger Lister is a chartered accountant and a professor of finance at Salford University. After reading modern languages as a major open scholar at Oriel

 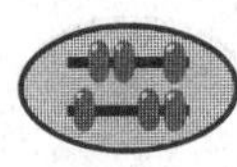  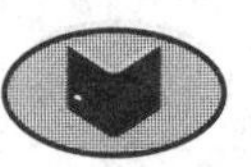 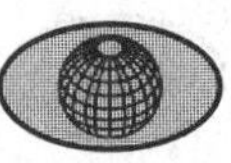   

College, Oxford, he worked for international accounting firms KPMG and PwC, specializing latterly in corporate taxation with particular interest in the taxation of groups. In his academic posts at Liverpool and Salford universities, Lister has taught accounting, corporate finance, and corporate tax and given specialized courses on capital structure. His research and publications have focused on corporate finance. Recent work has included an interdisciplinary perspective in which he examines alternative cultural models and advocates a role for the arts in business education.

Augusto Lopez-Claros is an international consultant based in Geneva, Switzerland, specializing in economic, financial, and development issues. Until 2006 he was chief economist and director of the Global Competitiveness Program at the World Economic Forum in Geneva. Before joining the Forum he held senior positions at Lehman Brothers International and the International Monetary Fund in Washington. Dr Lopez-Claros has written and lectured extensively on a wide range of topics in his field and is a sought-after speaker. He has a degree in mathematical statistics from Cambridge University and a PhD in economics from Duke University.

Montague Lord is a leading economist in trade, macroeconomics, international finance, and private sector development. Following his work as a principal research economist at the Inter-American Development Bank, he founded Montague Lord International LLC and is currently undertaking research and consulting assignments throughout the world. He has directed projects for business organizations, universities, governments and international development partners such as the World Bank, IMF, OECD, ADB, IDB, USAID, JICA, and WTO. Articles by Lord have been published in numerous academic journals, and he has written books on international trade and applied macroeconomics. He divides his time between his offices in the United States, Spain, and Thailand

Jay W. Lorsch is Louis Kirstein professor of human relations at Harvard Business School and chairman of the School's global corporate governance initiative. As a consultant, his clients have included Citicorp, Deloitte & Touche, DLA Piper Rudnick, Goldman Sachs, Tyco International, and Shire Pharmaceuticals. He is currently a director of Computer Associates. Lorsch graduated from Antioch College in 1955 and has an MSc in business from Columbia University and a doctorate in business administration from HBS. He is a fellow of the American Academy of Arts and Sciences.

Steven Lowe is a director at Pension Corporation. Previously he was a senior credit portfolio manager with Legal and General Investment Management (LGIM), where he focused on structured solutions, derivatives, and investment-grade credit for pension fund clients. Before working at LGIM, he worked at Barclays Global Investors, State Street Global Advisors and Baring Asset Management. Lowe has 15 years of investment experience and was awarded the Chartered Financial Analyst designation in 1997.

David Magee is an award-winning columnist for newspapers that include the *Wall Street Journal*, *New York Times*, and *Boston Globe*, and he is the nonfiction author of eight books, including the just-released *The South is Round* and the upcoming *How Toyota Became #1*. He is the co-owner of Chattanooga's largest independent bookstore, Rock Point Books, and the founder of Jefferson Press, a niche publisher distributed nationally by the Independent Publishers Group. A former newspaper editor, columnist, freelance writer, business owner, and small-town politician, Magee was named one of Mississippi's top business leaders under the age of 40 in 1998. Since 1999 he has been writing full time.

Thierry Malleret is a managing partner at Rainbow Insight, an advisory boutique that provides tailor-made intelligence to high-net-worth individuals and investors. Until April 2007 he headed the Global Risk Network at the World Economic Forum. Dr Malleret has organized the Davos annual forum and has spoken at global, industry, and regional events for several consecutive years. Prior to that, he worked in investment banking, think tanks and academia, and in government. He has written several business and academic books. Malleret was educated at the Sorbonne and École des Hautes Études en Sciences Sociales (EHESS) in Paris and St Antony's College, Oxford. He holds a PhD in economics.

Robin Mann is head of the Centre for Organisational Excellence Research, New Zealand, chairman of the Global Benchmarking Network, advisory board member of the Hamdan bin Mohammed e-University, and cofounder of BPIR.com Ltd. Dr Mann's experience includes managing the UK's Food and Drinks Industry Benchmarking and Self-assessment Initiative (1995–1998), the New Zealand Benchmarking Club (2000–2004), the Sheikh Saqr Government Excellence Program, UAE (2005–2007), and leading TRADE benchmarking projects in Singapore (from 2007 on). He worked in Edinburgh (1992–1995) for Burton's Biscuits as a process improvement manager and obtained his PhD in total quality management at Liverpool University in 1992.

Víctor Manuel Sánchez is associate attorney at Cuatrecasas, Gonçalves Pereira. He has experience in international and domestic arbitration and in judicial proceedings. He has participated in institutional arbitrations before the International Chamber of Commerce, the London Court of International Arbitration, and the Tribunal Arbitral de Barcelona in the defense of clients in collaboration with international law firms in multijurisdictional arbitrations. He holds bachelor degrees in law and in business administration from Universidad Pompeu Fabra in Barcelona and a master of laws (LLM) from the University of Manchester. He is an associate lecturer at the Universidad Pompeu Fabra School of Law, Barcelona.

Aldo Mareuse has been chief financial officer of Orascom Telecom Holding since 2002. He is also CFO of Weather Investments SpA, a private company that owns a majority stake in Orascom Telecom. Prior to joining Orascom Telecom, Mareuse worked in various positions for the investment bank Credit Suisse First Boston. He holds an engineering degree from Ecole Centrale de Lyon. When he is not traveling between Islamabad, Cairo, Rome, or New York, in the winter he enjoys back-country skiing in the Alps or the Rockies and in the summer he likes to cruise on the Mediterranean on his boat. He is married and has three children.

John L. Mariotti is the president/CEO and founder of the Enterprise Group, a coalition of time-shared executive advisers. Mariotti currently serves as a director on several corporate boards, including World Kitchen, Henkel Consumer Adhesives, Petmate, DF Co. LLC, Levick Strategic Communications, and HomeCare Industries. Prior to this he was president of Rubbermaid Office Products Group (1992–1994), a multinational group of nine divisions spanning North America, Europe, Asia, and

     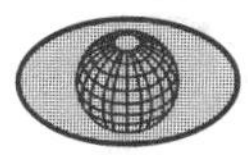   

Australia. Before joining Rubbermaid, Mariotti led Huffy Bicycles (1982–1992) as its president to the preeminent position of industry leader and the world's largest bicycle company at the time. He is also a former management consultant and contributing editor for *IndustryWeek* magazine.

Neil Marriott, BSc, MBA, PhD, DipM, CPFA, FHEA, is dean of the Winchester Business School and in 2008 and 2009 was chair of the British Accounting Association (BAA). Professor Marriott has also been the chair of the BAA's Special Interest Group in Accounting Education for 10 years. His publications include five textbooks and tutor manuals covering financial and management accounting, as well as a specialized work for NHS financial managers. His research interests include small business financial management and auditing, public sector accounting, and accounting education. Marriott is editor of the *International Journal of Management Education*, published by the Higher Education Academy.

Duncan Martin is a partner and managing director in the risk management practice at the Boston Consulting Group (BCG), based in London. Prior to joining BCG, he was the head of Wholesale Credit Risk Analytics at the Royal Bank of Scotland in London, the director of Strategic Risk Management at Dresdner Kleinwort, and a senior manager at Oliver Wyman & Company. Martin was educated at Cambridge University and the Wharton School of the University of Pennsylvania. He is the author of *Managing Risk in Extreme Environments* (Kogan Page, 2008).

Roger Martin has served as dean of the Rotman School of Management since 1998. He also serves as an adviser on strategy to the CEOs of several major global corporations. He has published two books: *The Opposable Mind* (2007) and *The Responsibility Virus* (2002). His third book, *The Design of Business: Why Design Thinking is the Next Competitive Advantage*, will be published in November 2009 (Harvard Business School Press). In 2007, *Business Week* named him one of the 10 most influential business professors in the world. He received his AB from Harvard College, with a concentration in economics, in 1979, and his MBA from the Harvard Business School in 1981.

María Soledad Martínez Pería is a senior economist in the finance team of the Development Economics Research Group of the World Bank. Her published research has focused on currency and banking crises, depositor market discipline, and foreign bank participation in developing countries. Currently she is conducting research on financial sector outreach and on the impact of remittances on financial development. Prior to joining the World Bank, she worked at the Brookings Institution, the Central Bank of Argentina, the Federal Reserve Board, and the International Monetary Fund. She holds a PhD in economics from the University of California, Berkeley, and a BA from Stanford University.

Andrew Mayo is associate professor of human capital management at Middlesex Business School, where he teaches human resource strategy, and his main research interest is in people-related measures. He is also a fellow and program director for in-company programs at the Centre for Management Development at the London Business School, where he has worked since 1996. He runs his own consultancy company, MLI Ltd (Mayo Learning International), specializing in organizational strategies for growing human capital and translating the rhetoric of "people are our most important asset" into reality. Mayo is president of the HR Society in the United Kingdom and is a frequent speaker at conferences around the world.

Thomas McKaig is a Canadian author, professor, and keynote international business speaker. He is the founder of international development advisers Thomas McKaig International. He is an adjunct professor in the Department of Marketing and Consumer Studies at the University of Guelph and has been executive in residence at the University of Tennessee. He has advised a Canadian crown corporation on Central American regulatory and housing finance issues and has been a private and public sector adviser in several industries. McKaig has worked in international equities and served as adviser to the US Mint's Gold Eagle bullion coin program and as European sales manager for the Royal Canadian Mint.

Hamish McRae is a London-based economic journalist. He is the principal economic commentator of *The Independent* and *The Independent on Sunday*. His most recent awards are the David Watt Prize for outstanding political journalism in 2005, Business and Finance Journalist of the Year in the 2006 British Press Awards, and Communicator of the Year in the 2007 Business Journalist Awards. He was educated at Fettes College, Edinburgh, and has an MA in economics and political science from Trinity College, Dublin. He was deputy editor of *The Banker* and editor of *Euromoney* before becoming financial editor of *The Guardian* in 1975. In 1989 he moved to *The Independent*, where he is now associate editor.

Wondimu Mekonnen is a program director of accounting and finance and a lecturer in management accounting at the University of Buckingham. Before joining the University of Buckingham, he lectured at Addis Ababa University for many years and briefly at Grafton College. He also worked for seven and a half years for JSA Services Ltd, a firm of chartered accountants based in Watford, England, in the capacity of accountant and corporate tax accountant, where he gained extensive experience of dealing with small investors and private entrepreneurs.

Damian Merciar is managing director of Merciar Business Consulting, a niche business economics consultancy founded in 1998. He is experienced in the transition environments of nationalized to private sector state utilities and the senior practice of commercial management, advisorial consultancy, and implementation. He has carried out policy advisory work for government ministries and been an adviser to institutional bodies proposing changes to government. He holds an MBA from the University of Kent at Canterbury (1993), went to the Hebrew University of Jerusalem, International Relations and Language (1992), for which he won a competitive international scholarship, and has a BA (Hons) in economic history and political economy from the University of Portsmouth (1991).

Andrew Milligan joined Standard Life Investments in 2000 as global investment strategist before being appointed head of global strategy in 2001. Prior to joining Standard Life Investments, he was employed by HM Treasury, followed by Lloyds Bank, where he was an economic adviser, and Smith New Court as an international economist. In 1994 he was appointed chief economist at New Japan Securities Europe. He then moved to Morley Fund Management in 1996 as director of economic research and business risk. He is a governing board member of the Technology Strategy Board, an executive nondepartmental public body established by the government to stimulate innovation in the United Kingdom.

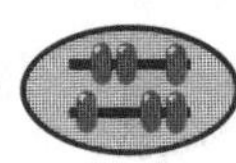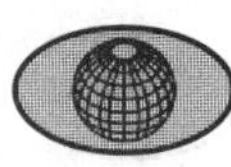

Lauren Mills is a senior financial journalist with 17 years' experience working for business publications and national newspapers. She was retail correspondent for the *Sunday Telegraph* for more than five years and went on to become enterprise editor at the *Sunday Express*, before joining the *Mail on Sunday*'s financial desk covering a range of sectors that now includes banking, insurance, private equity, mining, pharmaceuticals, and manufacturing. She has also contributed business articles to the *Sunday Times*, *Daily Telegraph*, *Daily Mail*, *Financial Times* and *Independent on Sunday*.

John Milton-Smith is a graduate of Sydney, Monash, and Cambridge universities. He worked in international trade, marketing, and consulting while completing his earlier studies on a part-time basis. Between 1990 and 2007 he held appointments at Curtin University, Western Australia, as deputy vice-chancellor, Curtin Business School (1990–1997) and Curtin International (1998–2002) and as professor of management (2002–2007). The author of nine books and more than 60 refereed articles, Curtin University appointed him emeritus professor in 2007. Professor Milton-Smith is currently a senior management consultant specializing in corporate coaching and leadership development with the Catalyst Group, Perth.

Bruce Misamore was chief financial officer and deputy chairman of Yukos, Russia's largest oil company, from 2001 until 2005. While there, he introduced world-class standards of corporate governance, financial transparency, and accounting. However, his reforms were unwound after the company had its domestic assets seized by the Russian government after 2004 and the arrest of its chief executive, Mikhail Khodorkovsky. Misamore resigned in December 2005 and has since been instrumental in a global legal campaign to ensure that Yukos's thousands of legitimate stakeholders receive compensation from the Russian government. Before joining Yukos, Misamore worked in senior-level finance roles with US oil companies PennzEnergy, PennzOil Co., and Marathon Oil. Misamore taught finance at Bowling Green State University in Ohio in the 1970s and says that the winters there are even colder than they are in Moscow.

Maureen J. Miskovic has been executive vice-president and chief risk officer at Boston-based State Street Corporation since April 2008. In this capacity she oversees a global team of more than 250 multidisciplinary enterprise risk professionals. She was previously senior adviser at Eurasia Group, a global political risk advisory and consulting firm based in New York. She has also worked at Lehman Brothers in New York, and at Morgan Stanley, S.G. Warburg, and Morgan Grenfell in London. Miskovic has published a book titled *Futures and Options—A Handbook for Institutional*. She holds a BA in Russian and German from King's College, London University.

Mark Mobius joined Templeton in 1987 as president of Templeton Emerging Markets Fund, Inc. He has spent more than 30 years working in emerging markets and currently directs analysts based in Templeton's emerging markets offices and manages the emerging markets portfolios. He was appointed joint chairman of the World Bank and OECD's global corporate governance forum investor responsibility taskforce. Dr Mobius has received many awards, including Emerging Markets Equity Manager of the Year 2001 from *International Money Marketing* and nomination as one of the Ten Top Money Managers of the 20th Century by the Carson Group in 1999. He earned bachelor's and master's degrees from Boston University and a PhD in economics and political science from MIT. He is the author of the books *Trading with China*, *The Investor's Guide to Emerging Markets*, *Mobius on Emerging Markets*, and *Passport to Profits*.

Scott Moeller is the director of the M&A Research Centre at Cass Business School, London, and a former senior executive at Deutsche Bank and Morgan Stanley. While at Deutsche Bank, Professor Moeller held roles as global head of the corporate venture capital unit, managing director of the Global eBusiness division, and managing director responsible for worldwide strategy and new business acquisitions. Prior to his career in investment banking he was a management consultant with Booz, Allen & Hamilton (now Booz & Co). He is a non-executive director of several nonprofit and financial services companies in the United States, the United Kingdom, and Continental Europe.

James Montier, an expert in behavioral finance, argues that investors would have a greater chance of spotting the formation of bubbles if they could only brush up on their history and have a greater awareness of human psychology. Co-head of global strategy at Société Générale, he has been described as an "enfant terrible" by *Frankfurter Allgemeine Zeitung*, an "iconoclast" by the *Financial Times*, a "maverick" by the *Sunday Times*, and "a prophet" by *Fast Company*. Montier has been a top-rated strategist in the annual Thomson Reuters Extel survey for the last five years. When not reading, writing, or speaking, Montier can usually be found swimming with sharks and blowing bubbles at fishes.

Mike Moore is special adviser to the UN Global Compact for Business and Development. He was prime minister of New Zealand in 1990 and director general of the World Trade Organization from 1999 to 2002. He has had a distinguished career in politics and was the driving force behind important changes in the WTO. His term at the WTO coincided with momentous changes in the global economy and multilateral trading system, and he is widely credited with restoring confidence in the system following the setback of the Third Ministerial Conference in Seattle in 1999. Moore was the youngest member elected to the New Zealand parliament in 1972 and became an active participant in international discussions on trade liberalization. When minister of overseas trade and marketing, he played a leading role in launching the Uruguay round of GATT negotiations. He is the recipient of many global honors.

Rod Morris is vice president in charge of the political risk insurance program for the Overseas Private Investment Corporation. He first came to OPIC in 2000 after serving as a senior vice president at CNA Insurance Company, where he was in charge of a number of products and divisions as well as the branch offices in Omaha and Phoenix. He has also served as the chief regulator for the captive insurance program in Arizona and has authored a number of articles and training texts on underwriting and captives. Morris has been a member of the United Nation's Expert Group on Public-Private Risk Sharing.

Jon Moulton is managing partner of the United Kingdom-based private equity firm Alchemy Partners, which has invested £2 billion of equity and specializes in dealing with troubled companies. Alchemy also has a £300 million European special opportunities fund that invests in distressed debt. Moulton previously worked with Citicorp Venture Capital (now

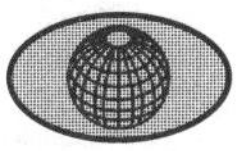

CVC Capital Partners), Permira and Apax. He is currently a director of the United States-based Irvin-GQ parachute business, the Cedar IT business, and Sylvan (timber) among others. An active angel investor, he has a degree in chemistry from Lancaster University and started his career as a chartered accountant with Coopers & Lybrand.

Arun Muralidhar is cofounder and chairman of AlphaEngine Global Investment Solutions (AEGIS) and its parent company, Mcube Investment Technologies. Muralidhar earned an undergraduate degree in economics in 1988 from Wabash College in Indiana. After gaining a PhD in managerial economics at the Sloan School of Management he joined the World Bank, where he rose to become head of investment research for the bank's pension fund. He has also worked as managing director and head of currency research at J.P. Morgan Investment Management and FX Concepts.

Sanjay Muralidhar, cofounder and CEO of AlphaEngine Global Investment Solutions (AEGIS) and its parent company, Mcube Investment Technologies, is devoted to helping clients to make better investment decisions and improve returns. Muralidhar earned an undergraduate degree in accounting in 1984 from Bombay University and an MBA from the University of Pennsylvania. He has worked in senior finance positions at Bristol-Myers Squibb, Reader's Digest, and iVillage.

Ravi Nedungadi is president and group CFO of Bangalore-based United Breweries (UB) Group. From the start of his career in 1990, he has held various positions from corporate treasurer to finance director of the group's international businesses. Appointed president and group CFO in 1998, he has led the way to sharpening the group's focus on areas of core competence and global reach. Under his leadership the market capitalization of the three principal group companies has grown to US$7.7 billion, up from $145 million three years earlier. Nedungadi's achievements have been recognized by many awards, including the Udyog Ratan Award and the IMA Award for CFO of the Year (2007). He lives in Bangalore with his wife and two children.

Sue Newell is Cammarata professor of management at Bentley University in Waltham, Massachusetts, and a part-time professor of information management at Warwick University in the United Kingdom. She gained her BSc and PhD from Cardiff University and is currently PhD director at Bentley University. Professor Newell's research focuses on understanding the relationships between innovation, knowledge, and organizational networking (IKON)—primarily from an organizational theory perspective. She was one of the founding members of IKON, a research center based at Warwick University. Newell has published more than 80 journal articles on organizational studies and management and information systems, as well as numerous books and book chapters.

Hansjörg Nymphius is director of market infrastructures at Deutsche Bank's Global Transaction Bank, and global product manager for financial supply chain management. He previously held the position of global head of methodologies and performance management. Over the course of his career he has actively participated in various domestic and international industry bodies, both at working group level and in policy-making. Currently he is chairman of the board of the Euro Banking Association (EBA), Paris. Nymphius has been a key driver behind the integration of EU payments markets over the past decade. As a senior manager he has made significant contributions to the successful deployment of euro market infrastructures, business rules, and standards.

Martin O'Donovan is assistant director, policy and technical, at the Association of Corporate Treasurers (ACT). The ACT is the international body for finance professionals working in treasury, risk, and corporate finance. With 3,600 members in over 60 countries, the ACT defines and promotes best practice in treasury and is the world's leading examining body for treasury. O'Donovan qualified as a chartered accountant and has spent his career working in treasury at Redland, Hertz, BTR, and, most recently, as group treasurer of National Grid Group. He is a fellow of the Association of Corporate Treasurers.

Kevin Ow Yong is an assistant professor of accounting at Singapore Management University. He graduated with a bachelor of accountancy (first class honors) from Nanyang Technological University and a PhD from Duke University. He is a Certified Public Accountant (CPA) and a Chartered Financial Analyst (CFA) holder. His research has been cited in two of Singapore's highest-circulation newspapers, the *Straits Times* and the *Business Times*, as well as in *Pulses* (previously, the *Singapore Stock Exchange Journal*), *Smart Investor*, and *CFO Asia*, a publication of The Economist Group.

Nenad Pacek is a leading authority on Central and Eastern Europe, the Middle East and Africa (CEEMEA), advising companies on building successful strategies for these and other emerging markets. He works for the Economist Group as a director of the Economist Intelligence Unit, directing the corporate network programs in CEEMEA. He also heads Economist Conferences' global government roundtables business. He chairs senior business-to-government dialogues with some 20 heads of state every year across Europe, Eastern Europe, Africa, and the Middle East. Pacek has cowritten two books and lectures on emerging markets at the University of Vienna and on the MBA program at ESSEC Business School, Paris. He graduated in economics and business from the University of Vienna.

Michael J. Panzner is a 25-year veteran of the global stock, bond, and currency markets who has worked for such leading companies as HSBC, Soros Funds, ABN Amro, Dresdner Bank, and JP Morgan Chase. He has authored books including *When Giants Fall: An Economic Roadmap for the End of the American Era* (Wiley, 2009), and *Financial Armageddon: Protecting Your Future from Four Impending Catastrophes* (Kaplan, 2007). He has also been a columnist for TheStreet.com's RealMoney paid subscription service and a contributor to AOL's BloggingStocks.com. In addition, Panzner is a New York Institute of Finance faculty member specializing in equities, trading, global capital markets, and technical analysis. He is a graduate of Columbia University.

Michael Parkinson, CIA, CISA, is an internal auditor of more than 20 years' experience. While working as a government employee he was the chief audit executive of three different government agencies. He is currently a director in the government services practice of KPMG Canberra. Parkinson joined the board of the Institute of Internal Auditors Australia (IIA-Australia) in 1996, was elected vice-president in 1998, and became national president in 1999, serving until 2001. He is a respected educator and author in internal auditing. He currently serves on the Standards Australia OB-007 Risk Management Committee.

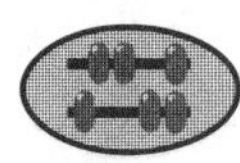

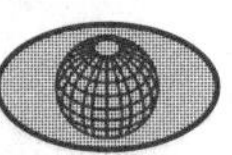

Graham Partington is currently an associate professor at the University of Sydney. He has extensive experience in research and teaching at universities around the world and has designed several very successful degrees in finance. He is coauthor of four textbooks and many research papers, including prize-winning work. His particular research interests lie in dividends, valuation, and the cost of capital, and he provides consulting advice in these areas. From 2002 to 2008 he was education director of the Capital Markets Cooperative Research Centre, where he ran one of the world's largest and most successful PhD programs in capital markets research.

Zaril Patel is the first female finance director of the BBC, a position she has held since 2004. As a member of the BBC's executive board, Patel is responsible for financial strategy, planning, control, and corporate reporting activities. Before joining the BBC in 1998, she had previously spent 15 years with one of the "big four" accountants, KMPG. She graduated in economics at the London School of Economics in 1982. Named as one of the most powerful people in the British media by *The Guardian*, Patel recently graduated from Harvard Business School. She is also a governor for the University of the Arts, London.

Jeremy Phillips is an intellectual property consultant, author, lecturer and commentator on patents, trademarks, copyrights, and most contemporary issues involving intellectual property rights. He is an intellectual property consultant at Olswang solicitors, director of research at the Intellectual Property Institute, and visiting professorial fellow, Queen Mary Intellectual Property Research Institute, Queen Mary, University of London. Cofounder and blogmeister of the IPKat weblog, Phillips is currently involved in the development of weblog-based intellectual property communities.

Lawrence Phillips, visiting professor of decision science at the London School of Economics and a director of Facilitations Ltd, is a leading expert on ways in which organizations can improve their decision-making. He has long been fascinated by the challenges associated with deciding how best to deploy limited resources across a range of projects and getting people to buy into the outcome—the quintessential budgeting and, indeed, management problem. Dr Phillips teaches decision science to graduates and undergraduates at the LSE and conducts training courses on decision science and facilitation skills to external organizations. In 2005 he was awarded the Frank P. Ramsey medal for distinguished contributions to decision analysis by the Decision Analysis Society of INFORMS.

Ramesh Pillai is CEO and group managing director of Friday Concepts (Asia). He is also the risk management adviser to AmanahRaya/KWB and a nominee director for Bank Negara Malaysia (Central Bank of Malaysia). Previously he was the risk management adviser to Tabung Haji. He holds a bachelor of economics with accountancy (honours) degree from Loughborough University. A member of the Institute of Chartered Accountants in England and Wales and the Malaysian Institute of Accountants, as well as a Certified Risk Professional, Pillai was also a regional director for the Global Association of Risk Professionals and is one of the founding members of the Malaysian chapter of the Professional Risk Managers International Association.

David Pitt-Watson is senior adviser to Hermes Fund Managers. He is cofounder and former chief executive of Hermes' shareholder activist activities. Following an early career at 3i and McKinsey & Co, Pitt-Watson was cofounder and ultimately managing director of Braxton Associates Ltd, which became the strategic consulting arm of Deloitte & Touche. In that role he had 17 years' experience of boardroom decision-taking and corporate transformation. A graduate of Oxford and Stanford universities, Pitt-Watson was visiting professor of strategic management at Cranfield School of Management from 1990 to 1995.

Neuman F. Pollack teaches entrepreneurship at Florida Atlantic University and has been director of the Stuart-James Research Center, the Adams Center for Entrepreneurship, and the Office of Executive Relations at the Kaye College of Business. As founding dean of the Huizenga School of Business and Entrepreneurship at Nova Southeastern University, Dr Pollack developed business partnerships in the United States, Caribbean, Southeast Asia, and Western Europe. As president of the Building Owners and Managers Institute (BOMI) he promoted research and development in the property management industry. He is a director of Emotional Endurance Institute, a nonprofit entrepreneurial support organization, FreshPeek, an entrepreneurial development company, and Parking and Security Systems, a technology-based security enterprise.

Yves Poullet holds a bachelor's degree in electronic engineering from the Katholieke Universiteit Leuven and a degree in business administration from the Université Catholique de Louvain. Starting his career in 1991 at Euroclear, Poullet held a variety of senior management positions in the finance, risk management, corporate strategy, and product management divisions. Before taking up his current role as CEO of Euroclear Bank, he has held positions as the head of Euroclear Bank's operations, and deputy general manager of Euroclear France. Outside of work, he spends most of his time with his family (four children), enjoying amongst other activities the family sport, tennis. He is also an avid reader.

Price Pritchett is founder and CEO of Pritchett LP, a Dallas-based consulting firm recognized internationally for its expertise in mergers, culture, and organizational change. Dr Pritchett's book, *After the Merger: Managing the Shockwaves*, named one of the 10 best business books of the year, was the first ever written on merger integration strategy. He is also author of the all-time best seller on mergers, *The Employee Guide to Mergers and Acquisitions*, plus various other titles. More than 20 million copies of his books are in print worldwide, with translations into many foreign languages. Almost all of the Fortune 500 have used some combination of Pritchett LP's consulting, training, and handbooks.

Marc Quintyn has been division chief, Africa, at the IMF Institute since 2006, where he teaches macroeconomics and more specialized topics. He has been with the IMF since 1989 and worked most of his career on monetary and financial sector issues in surveillance and program missions, financial sector assessment programs (FSAPs), and technical assistance work. He received his PhD from the University of Ghent, Belgium. Before joining the IMF, he held various positions at the University of Ghent (1979–83), the Research Department, National Bank of Belgium (1984–89), and the University of Limburg, Belgium (1986–89). Dr Quintyn is a published author of numerous books, papers, and articles.

Bilal Rasul is the registrar of modaraba companies and of the Modarabas, Securities and Exchange Commission of

     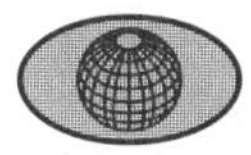   

Pakistan (SECP). A British Council (Chevening) scholar, Rasul gained his master's degrees in public administration and in economics and finance in the United Kingdom. He has 15 years of varied experience in capital market regulation, including the securities market and nonbanking and finance companies, as well as the nonfinancial sector. As registrar, he is responsible for heading the Islamic finance initiative for the capital market in Pakistan. He is also the focal person of the Islamic Financial Services Board (IFSB) at SECP, responsible for the implementation and adoption of IFSB standards and principles.

Philip Ratcliffe left Oxford University to start his life-long career in internal audit with Unilever, where he qualified as a chartered management accountant. He later became head of internal audit at a number of large multinational companies involved in manufacturing, distribution, and natural resources. He is currently chief audit executive at a publicly quoted UK paper and packaging company. A long-term member and fellow of the Institute of Internal Auditors (in the United Kingdom, Brazil, and Belgium), Ratcliffe joined the council of the IIA, UK and Ireland, in 2006, becoming its president for 2008/09.

Jenny Rayner is director and principal consultant at Abbey Consulting, which she established in 1999 to provide consultancy and training on the positive management of risk to improve business performance and protect and enhance reputation. Prior to this, her wide-ranging career spanned more than 20 years with ICI and Zeneca in a variety of sales, marketing, purchasing, logistics, supply chain, and general business management roles, and latterly she was a chief internal auditor with ICI. Rayner also writes and lectures on risk management, corporate governance, corporate social responsibility, and reputation.

Brian Reading is a director of Lombard Street Research. He has a first-class honors degree in philosophy, politics, and economics from Wadham College, Oxford. After earning his degree he was appointed adviser to the Governor of the Bank of England, worked in the government's Department of Economic Affairs, and from 1966 to 1972 was an adviser to Edward Heath. Since then he has been economics editor of *The Economist*, consultant to Dillon Reed and with US Advisory Associates, and adviser to Nomura Asset Management. In 1991 he founded the Lombard Street Research International Service and is also founder of Ernst & Young's Item Club.

Riccardo Rebonato is global head of market risk and global head of the Quantitative Research Team at the Royal Bank of Scotland (RBS). He also sits on the Investment Committee of RBS Asset Management. Dr Rebonato is a visiting lecturer at Oxford University and adjunct professor at Imperial College's Tanaka Business School. He sits on the board of directors of ISDA (International Swaps and Derivatives Association) and the board of trustees for GARP (Global Association of Risk Professionals). He is an editor for several financial journals, and has written several books. He holds a doctorate in nuclear engineering and a PhD in condensed matter physics/science of materials from Stony Brook University, NY.

Luc Renneboog is a lecturer at Tilburg University, the Netherlands. Before joining Tilburg, he taught at the Catholic University of Leuven and at Oxford University. Dr Renneboog graduated with a BSc/MSc in management engineering from the University of Leuven, followed by an MBA from the University of Chicago, a BA in philosophy from Leuven, and a PhD in financial economics from the London Business School. He has also been a visiting researcher at the London Business School, HEC Paris, and Venice University. He is a widely published author, with research interests are corporate finance, corporate governance, mergers and acquisitions, and the economics of art.

Jeffrey Ridley is currently visiting professor of auditing at the London South Bank University and Birmingham City University. He teaches and researches internal auditing, corporate governance, corporate social responsibility, and quality management. He has been a member of the International IIA Board of Regents, a member of that institute's Committee on Quality, and a member of the IIA Research Foundation Board of Research Advisors. He is currently an editorial assistant for the IIA's *Internal Auditor* journal. Ridley has researched other internal auditing practices and written many articles and presented papers on the results. He coauthored *Leading Edge Internal Auditing* in 1998 and authored *Cutting Edge Internal Auditing* in 2008.

Steve Robinson was director of open executive programs at Henley Business School until the end of 2007. Previously he was with Ashridge Business School for 14 years, latterly as director of executive MBA programs. Robinson has designed and taught on a variety of management development and qualification programs in the United States, Europe, Asia, and Australia. He is the author of the *Financial Times Handbook of Financial Management* and is an external examiner at the Cass Business School, City University, London. He is now an independent educator, writer, and consultant working closely with Duke Corporate Education and with the Henley, Warwick, and Kingston Business Schools.

Jim Rogers was educated at Yale and Balliol College, Oxford. After he cofounded the Quantum Fund with George Soros in 1970, the fund surged by 4,200% over the next decade, while the Standard & Poor's index rose by 47%. Rogers has worked as a professor of finance at Columbia University, columnist, author, and a contrarian investor. In the early 1990s he traveled 65,000 miles through six continents on a BMW motorcycle and ended up with a portfolio of investments in some of the world's most unexpected markets. In 1998 he became bullish about commodities, predicting an enduring commodities rally, and later launched the Rogers International Commodities Index.

Gerasimos G. Rompotis is a senior auditor at KPMG Greece and also a researcher at the Faculty of Economics of the National and Kapodistrian University of Athens. His main areas of research cover the evaluation of mutual fund managers' selection and market timing skills, the performance of exchange-traded funds, calendar effects on the performance and volatility of equity investments, and intervaling effects on the systematic risk of ETFs. His work has been published in a number of industry journals such as the *Guide to Exchange Traded Funds and Indexing Innovations* issued by Institutional Investor Journals and the *International Research Journal of Finance and Economics*, including the European conferences.

Alan Rugman holds the L. Leslie Waters Chair of International Business at the Kelley School of Business, Indiana University, where he is professor of international business and professor of business economics and public policy. He has also been Thames Water Fellow in strategic management at Templeton College, University of Oxford. Dr Rugman has published widely and has served as a consultant to major private sector

 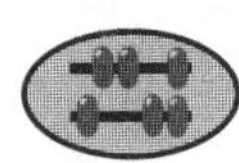   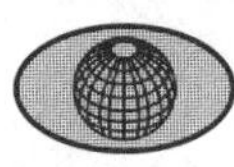   

companies, research institutes, and government agencies, and as an outside adviser on free trade, foreign investment, and international competitiveness to two Canadian prime ministers. Dr Rugman was president of the Academy of International Business from 2004 to 2006.

Tarun Sabarwal is assistant professor of economics and Oswald Scholar at the University of Kansas. He received his doctorate from the University of California at Berkeley. His research interests include microeconomic theory and financial economics. Sabarwal's work has been published in a number of academic journals, most recently in *Economic Theory*, in *Regional Science and Urban Economics* and in *Annals of Finance*, among others. He has presented his work at conferences around the world.

David Sadtler is an associate of the Ashridge Strategic Management Centre. His research, teaching, consulting, and writing activities are concentrated on questions of corporate-level strategy. A graduate of Brown University (mathematics and economics) and of Harvard Business School, his career has been divided between consulting and industry. Sadtler was the corporate development director and a main board director of London International Group plc, a diversified healthcare company, for eight years and is a two-time alumnus of McKinsey & Company, having served a broad range of clients on questions of strategy in the New York, Amsterdam, and London offices.

James S. Sagner is an internationally recognized expert in financial management and economic analysis. He teaches undergraduate and MBA management, finance, and international business and is currently a lecturer in the Executive Education Finance Program at the University of North Carolina. He has written business finance books, papers and articles as well as being a former editor of *Treasury Views*. He is a graduate of Washington and Lee University, has an MBA from the Wharton School of the University of Pennsylvania, and holds a PhD in business and economics from the American University in Washington, DC.

John Schaetzl has a breadth of experience in the healthcare sector. Most recently, he was a portfolio manager at GE Asset Management, prior to which he held marketing and planning roles at Bayer's Miles Laboratories. He was a consultant to the pharmaceutical industry at Healthcare Forecasting Inc. and Scott Levin Associates. Schaetzl has taught and held administrative positions at several universities and is a non-executive director of SustainAbility and Columbus House. He is the coauthor of *Practical Politics and American Government* (Macmillan, 1976) and *Project 18: Effectively Influencing Political Decisions* (Edinburgh, 1973). He has an MA from the University of Pennsylvania and a BA from Harvard College.

Hans-Dieter Scheuermann has extensive experience at SAP, the business software developer, in the areas of financials and insurance solutions. Since 2003 he has headed the SAP Business Solution Architects Group, deploying his 30 years of experience directly in strategic customer relationships. Before assuming his current post, he had global responsibility for the General Business Unit (GBU) Financials. In 1998–2000 he was director of the Industry Business Unit (IBU) Insurance. Prior to that, from 1991 he was head of development for the financials and accounting application. He started his career at SAP in 1978 as a developer for financial accounting solutions. Scheuermann studied mathematics at the University of Heidelberg.

Sergio Schmukler is lead economist with the Development Research Group of the World Bank. He has also worked continuously for the Office of the Chief Economist for Latin America and for the East Asia and South Asia regions. Besides his work for the World Bank, he has been treasurer of LACEA (Latin American and Caribbean Economic Association) since 2004, was associate editor of the *Journal of Development Economics* (2001–2004), taught in the Department of Economics, University of Maryland (1999–2003), and worked in the International Monetary Fund Research Department (2004–2005). He gained his PhD at the University of California at Berkeley.

Louise Scholes is a research fellow at Nottingham University Business School. Her main research interests include entrepreneurial activity, family firms, private equity and venture capital (particularly management buyouts), and science and business. Dr Scholes has published articles in a number of journals, including *Entrepreneurship Theory and Practice*, *Small Business Economics*, *International Small Business Journal*, and *Journal of Applied Corporate Finance*. She is a member of the Royal Society of Chemistry and the British Academy of Management.

James E. Schrager is clinical professor of entrepreneurship and strategy at the University of Chicago and has numerous awards for his teaching. He is an active strategy adviser to companies small and large. His articles have appeared in the *Wall Street Journal* and *Chicago Tribune* among others, and he is frequently quoted in the press. He is founding and current editor of the *Journal of Private Equity*, published by Institutional Investors. Dr Schrager's education includes a bachelor's degree in economics, an MBA in accounting, a CPA certificate, and a juris doctor of laws, and he graduated with a PhD in organizational behavior and policy from the University of Chicago.

Neil Seitz is professor of finance and prior dean at the John Cook School of Business, Saint Louis University. He holds a PhD in finance from Ohio State University (1973) and an MBA from the University of Hawaii (1969). He worked on consulting and executive development programs for AT&T, Barclays, Caterpillar Inc., Citicorp, Household International, and Standard Chartered Bank. He has also done acquisition planning for Telecheck International (1969) and inventory planning and long-range forecasting for the Cooper Tire and Rubber Company (1966–1968). He has published six books, including two on capital budgeting.

Samuel Sender founded MC2 Finance, an independent consulting firm for life and mutual insurance companies, before joining FINALYSE, a consultancy specializing in risk and performance measurement, as a senior insurance consultant and asset–liability management specialist. Formerly with the economics, strategy, and quantitative research unit at HSBC Asset Management Europe, and then head of asset–liability management at Erisa, the French life insurance subsidiary of HSBC, he graduated in statistics and economics from ENSAE (école Nationale de la Statistique et de l'Administration Economique) in Paris.

Bill Sharon has been conducting seminars, workshops, and consulting assignments in the area of risk management for the past 12 years. He has 30 years' experience in the financial services and marketing/communications industry in a variety of C-level positions and consultancies. He has been featured in numerous industry

  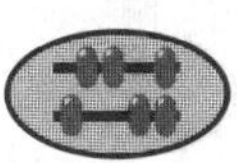   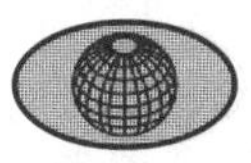   

magazines (*CIO Magazine*, *Business Finance*, *Business Credit Magazine*) and has authored numerous articles as well as a blog (www.sorms.blogspot.com) that is read in more than 80 countries. Sharon holds a clinical degree, and for the first 10 years of his professional life he worked with adolescents—an experience that taught him the very difficult skill of how to listen.

David Shimko holds a PhD in finance from Northwestern University. He has taught finance at the Kellogg Graduate School of Management at Northwestern University, the Marshall School of Business at the University of Southern California, the Harvard Business School, and the Courant Institute at New York University. His professional career included positions at J.P. Morgan, Bankers Trust, and Risk Capital, an independent risk advisory firm that was sold to Towers Perrin in 2006. Currently, Shimko sits on the board of trustees of the Global Association of Risk Professionals (GARP). He acts as an independent financial consultant and continues to teach part-time at the Kellogg School.

Gary Silha has more than 25 years of treasury management experience and is currently assistant treasurer at Tenneco Inc., where he has responsibility for worldwide treasury operations. Prior to joining Tenneco in 2000, he was the director of worldwide treasury operations at the American National Can Company, the largest beverage can manufacturer in the world. Silha holds bachelor's and master's degrees in business from Illinois State University, is a Certified Treasury Professional, and is a former president of the Treasury Management Association of Chicago.

William Sjostrom is a professor of law at the James E. Rogers College of Law at the University of Arizona. He graduated magna cum laude from Notre Dame Law School in 1996, where he was an editor of the *Law Review* and a Dean's Scholar. Prior to law school, Professor Sjostrom worked as an options trader at the Chicago Board Options Exchange. He received his undergraduate degree in finance with high honors from the University of Illinois in 1991. Before entering academia, Sjostrom worked for four years at the Minneapolis law firm of Fredrikson & Byron, where he focused on public and private securities offerings, venture capital financing, and mergers and acquisitions.

Leigh Skene is an independent economic consultant specializing in financial markets. Previously, he was head of fixed-income trading at investment bank Burns, Fry and Company (now BMO Nesbitt Burns), later becoming chief economist. In 1980 he left Burns, Fry and established himself as an independent economic consultant specializing in financial markets. He has been a director of Lombard Street Associates since 2004. In 2007 Skene wrote three key reports: "The ABC of 21st century risk," "The sub-prime mortgage fiasco—The start of something big," and "Credit and credibility," which pointed out the dangers of the new financial system, warned of the impending credit crunch, and forecast the ensuing financial turmoil.

Chris Skinner is well known as an authority on the future of banking. He chairs the Financial Services Club, a European networking group, works with the media, and presents extensively at conferences globally, speaking about the future of banking. He has written several books on the subject and keeps a daily blog at www.thefinanser.co.uk. Previously, he was vice president of marketing and strategy for Unisys Global Financial Services and strategy director with NCR Financial Services. Skinner is also a cofounder of the website for strategists www.shapingtomorrow.com.

Shireen Smith founded Azrights Solicitors in 2005. The firm is a niche intellectual property and technology law practice based in London. It focuses on online branding, encompassing trade mark, domain name, and copyright registration, along with litigious matters, e-commerce and internet law, and the filing of patents. She is particularly interested in social media and, through a separate business, Ferreter, has developed a close understanding of internet business, websites, search engine optimization, pay-per-click advertising, and reputation monitoring. Smith brings this knowledge to bear in her law practice, advising businesses that engage with social media and internet service providers. She has an LLM in intellectual property law and is a frequent speaker on this area.

Bernhard Speyer has been the head of the banking, financial markets, and regulation department of Deutsche Bank Research, the in-house think tank of Deutsche Bank Group, since 2001. In this role, he is responsible for briefing the senior management of the bank on regulatory issues as well as on structural issues in the financial industry. He was previously senior economist at Deutsche Bank Research. Before joining Deutsche Bank Research, he was a lecturer in the economics department of Freie Universität Berlin, where he taught international monetary policy and trade policy. A trained banker, Speyer studied economics at the University of Leicester and the Freie Universität Berlin, from which he graduated.

Will Spinney joined the treasury department at Johnson Matthey plc after a brief career in the Royal Navy, and took the first ever Association of Corporate Treasurers (ACT) corporate treasury exams in 1985. He has been a practicing treasurer now for 25 years, working for several companies that have included most recently Eaton Corporation and Invensys plc, where his experience ranged from risk management, cash management, and extensive refinancings to pension investment strategies. He has been a speaker at several ACT conferences and has been involved in education and training programmes with the ACT for several years, both writing resources and as a member of the MCT examination board.

Roger Steare is a corporate philosopher and visiting professor of organizational ethics at Cass Business School, City University. He studied philosophy at Royal Holloway College, London University. He worked for Midland Bank (now HSBC) in the City in 1979–1981 before becoming chief executive of City recruiters Jonathan Wren. He left to found Roger Steare Consulting in 1998 and has specialized in ethics since 2002. His "ethicability" framework has been used or endorsed by organizations including HSBC, Tomorrow's Company, and the Institute of Business Ethics. Steare is a director of the Centre for Applied and Professional Ethics and a fellow of the Royal Society for the Arts.

Gabriel Stein graduated from the Stockholm School of Economics with an MSc in 1980. In 1981 he worked for the International Relations Department of the Israeli Ministry of Finance. From 1982 to 1991 he ran his own economics and public affairs consultancy, Stein Brothers, first in Stockholm and then from 1990 in London. He joined Lombard Street Research in 1991 and, together with Brian Reading, set up the World Service. He became a director in 1995. On behalf of the Adam Smith Institute he calculates Tax Freedom Day for the United Kingdom. His research follows all global trends.

Achim Steiner has been executive director of the United Nations Environment

     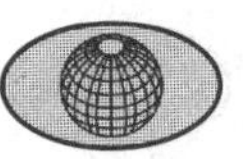   

Program (UNEP) since June 2006. He was director-general of the World Conservation Union from 2001 to 2006. In 1998–2001 he was secretary-general of the World Commission on Dams, based in South Africa, where he managed a multistakeholder program to develop a global policy process on dams and development. Steiner has a BA from the University of Oxford and MA in international development and environment policy from the University of London. He has also studied at the German Development Institute in Berlin and the Harvard Business School. He serves on a number of international advisory boards, including the China Council for International Cooperation on Environment and Development (CCICED).

Erik Stern, president international of Stern Stewart & Co., has advised numerous organizations on their implementation of EVA. He coauthored the EVAluation report on cascading EVA to shop-floor employees, "The capitalist manifesto," and has written for many publications, including the *Financial Times*. A global value ranking based on his pioneering metric, the Wealth Added Index (WAI), was highlighted in *The Economist* (December 1, 2001). His book *The Value Mindset* was published in 2004. Stern has an MBA from the University of Chicago and a BA (Hons) from Brown University.

Thomas A. Stewart is chief marketing and knowledge officer of Booz & Company. Before that he was for six years editor of the *Harvard Business Review*, and he was editorial director of *Business 2.0* magazine and a member of the board of editors of *Fortune*. He is author of the books *Intellectual Capital: The New Wealth of Organizations* and *The Wealth of Knowledge: Intellectual Capital and the 21st Century Organization*. Stewart has won numerous awards and honors, including an honorary degree from City University, London, and has been named one of the 50 most influential management thinkers by the *Financial Times*. He has a degree in English literature from Harvard College.

Sir John Stuttard has spent his career with accountants PricewaterhouseCoopers, of which he is now a vice-chairman. He has focused on auditing, acquisitions, stock exchange listings, and privatizations for UK, US, and Scandinavian companies. He was made a Knight, and then a Commander, of the Order of the Lion of Finland, and has been chairman of the Finnish–British Chamber of Commerce. He served in the Cabinet Office for two years and spent five years in China as PwC executive chairman. He has also been a director of the China–Britain Business Council. He is currently a trustee of the Charities Aid Foundation. Sir John served as sheriff of London in 2005–2006 and lord mayor in 2006–2007.

Pavan Sukhdev leads two programs for UNEP: the Economics of Ecosystems and Biodiversity program and the Green Economy Initiative. He also holds two board-level positions with Deutsche Bank subsidiaries, including chairman of its Mumbai-based Global Markets Centre, a captive offshoring facility that he helped to establish in 2006. After joining Deutsche Bank in 1994, Sukhdev held capital markets, trading, and sales management roles in Singapore, London, and India. In the mid-1990s he played a major role in the development of India's currency and interest rate derivatives markets. His involvement with the environmental movement in India has included roles with the Green Indian States Trust and Conservation Action Trust.

John Surdyk is director of the Initiative for Studies in Transformational Entrepreneurship at the Wisconsin School of Business in Madison, Wisconsin. He has advised companies bringing emerging technologies to market for international consultancies for 10 years. Surdyk spent more than a decade consulting with high-technology start-ups, Fortune 500 firms, and nonprofit organizations at SRI International in Menlo Park and, later, Navigant Consulting in Chicago. He has also evaluated policy initiatives at the National Center for Environmental Economics at the US Environmental Protection Agency. He now teaches on social entrepreneurship at the University of Wisconsin, Madison.

Amarendra Swarup is a partner at Pension Corporation, a United Kingdom-based pension buyout firm. He advises on allocations to alternative assets and strategies, asset–liability and risk management, and portfolio construction. Swarup was previously at Altedge Capital, an AAA-rated hedge fund of funds based in London, and has a PhD in cosmology from Imperial College, London. He is a CAIA (Chartered Alternative Investment Analyst) charter-holder and a member of the CAIA examinations council. He has written extensively for a range of media and academic publications. He is currently working with the London School of Economics on Pensions Tomorrow, a research initiative looking into the economic, sociopolitical, and financial aspects of pensions and longevity.

Simon Taylor is lecturer in finance at Cambridge University's Judge Business School. His main areas of research include how capital markets monitor and influence company decision-making and methods of valuation used by equity research analysts. Taylor spent nine years as an equity analyst at a number of investment banks, including BZW, J.P. Morgan, and Citigroup, where he was involved in several major equity transactions and takeovers. In 2001 he became deputy head of European equity research at J.P. Morgan, where he was responsible for the technical and quantitative research teams and for the technology, media, and telecoms sectors. He has been a consulting editor for *HedgeQuest* magazine and a consultant to a number of hedge funds.

Aziz Tayyebi works as financial reporting officer of the Association of Chartered Certified Accountants (ACCA). Tayyebi is the key technical contributor to ACCA's thought leadership in the field of Islamic finance, contributing articles and discussion papers on the subject and responding to external consultations in this area. He represents the ACCA on the Federation of European Accountants (FEE) task force on XBRL and on the UKTI accounting subgroup on Islamic finance. Previously, he worked as a manager with Ernst & Young, managing a portfolio of audit clients ranging from large privately owned companies to listed companies.

Siri Terjesen holds a PhD from Cranfield School of Management (2006), a master's in international business from the Norwegian School of Economics and Business Administration (Norges Handelshùyskole), where she was a Fulbright scholar (2002), and a BS in business administration from the University of Richmond, Virginia (1997). She is an assistant professor in the Kelley School of Business at Indiana University and a visiting research fellow in the entrepreneurship, growth, and public policy group at the Max Planck Institute of Economics in Jena, Germany. She has been widely published in leading journals and is a coauthor of *Strategic Management: Logic & Action* (Wiley, 2008).

Jean-Claude Trichet is an Inspecteur général des Finances and Ingénieur civil

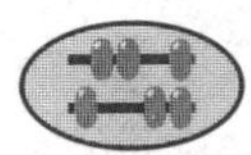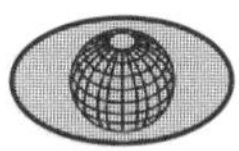

des Mines (ICM). Between 1978 and 1998 he held numerous positions, from head of international affairs and director of the Treasury, to governor of the Banque de France and alternate governor of the International Monetary Fund and the World Bank. He was elected chairman of the Group of Ten (G10) governors in June 2003, and was appointed president of the European Central Bank in October of the same year. Trichet was named "Person of the Year" by the *Financial Times* (2007), "Central Banker of the Year" by *The Banker* (2008), "European Banker of the Year 2007" by the Group of 20 + 1 (2008), and "Central Bank Governor of the Year 2008" by *Euromoney*.

Edmund Truell is group CEO and founder of Pension Corporation. Initially trained at Bankers Trust, he moved to Hambros Bank in 1986 and then cofounded the buyout group Hambro European Ventures (HEV). He led the 1998 buyout and formation of Duke Street Capital, having been chief executive of HEV since 1994. During his tenure as group chief executive officer, Duke Street Capital's private equity funds under management grew to more than €2 billion. In 2000 Truell was responsible for creating and building Duke Street Capital Debt management, one of Europe's largest and most successful leveraged loan managers, which was sold to Babson Capital in 2004.

Jon Tucker is professor of finance at the Bristol Business School of the University of the West of England and is director of the Centre for Global Finance there. He holds a PhD in European corporate finance (1995) and a BSc in applied economics (1991), both from the University of Plymouth. He has published frequently in leading finance journals and is associate editor of the *Journal of Finance* and *Management in Public Services*. He is chief examiner in investment analysis for the Securities and Investment Institute and visiting professor at Universitatea Babes-Bolyai, in Romania.

Bruce Turner has been chief internal auditor at the Australian Taxation Office since February 2007. As chief audit executive at one of Australia's largest and most prestigious public sector agencies, he provides strategic leadership for the Tax Office's internal audit activities and works closely with the audit committee. He has extensive experience in leading and managing internal audit areas, having previously held chief audit executive roles in the energy and transport sectors in Australia. In 2008 the Institute of Internal Auditors Australia presented him with the Bob McDonald Award in recognition of his contribution to internal audit services and the profession.

Shaun Tyson is emeritus professor of human resource management at Cranfield University. He holds a PhD from the London School of Economics and is a fellow of the Chartered Institute of Personnel and Development, a fellow of the Royal Society of Arts, and a member of the British Psychological Society. He has written 19 books on human resource management and has published extensively on human resource strategy and policies. He has carried out consultancy assignments and research with a wide range of public and private sector organizations in the United Kingdom and overseas. He chaired the remuneration committee of the Law Society for four years.

Roger Urwin is global head of investment content at Watson Wyatt after having been global head of the investment practice from 1995 to 2008. He joined Watson Wyatt in 1989 to start the firm's investment consulting practice. His prior career involved investment consulting for Hewitt, heading the investment practice at Mercer, and leading the business development and quantitative investment functions at Gartmore Investment Management. He is author of a number of papers on asset allocation policy, manager selection, and governance. Urwin is on the boards of the Chartered Financial Analyst Institute and the Institute for Quantitative Investment Research (INQUIRE), and also on the editorial board of MSCI.

Sheryl Vacca is the senior vice president/chief compliance and audit officer at the University of California (UC). Previous to UC, she served as the West Coast practice leader and national lead for internal audit, life sciences and healthcare. She was also the vice president of internal audit and corporate compliance officer for a large healthcare system in northern California. Vacca has published and presented nationally in the fields of healthcare compliance and internal audit to professional organizations such as the Institute of Internal Auditors, Health Care Compliance Association, Healthcare Financial Management Association, and the Practising Law Institute.

Jos van Bommel is a lecturer in finance at Oxford University's Said Business School and conducts empirical and theoretical research in various areas of corporate finance. He has completed several studies on IPOs, but is also interested in private equity, venture capital, and international finance. He also studies the market's microstructure and investigates the strategic behavior of informed and less informed traders to better understand how information is incorporated into market prices. Dr van Bommel holds a university degree in engineering from the University of Eindhoven, an MBA from the IESE Business School, and a PhD in finance from INSEAD. In between his studies he worked in international sales and marketing.

Vishal Vedi is a partner in Deloitte's financial services advisory practice in London. His key responsibilities include Basel II advisory services, financial risk advisory services, capital management, and banking regulation. He is Deloitte's EMEA lead for risk and capital management. He has conducted a variety of engagements for major financial institutions globally and has extensive experience of dealing with complex risk and regulatory issues. Vedi has spent over two years on secondment to the United Kingdom's Financial Services Authority in its banking policy unit and is a frequent presenter on risk and capital issues.

Daud Vicary Abdullah is the managing director of DVA Consulting. Since 2002 he has focused exclusively on Islamic finance. He is a distinguished fellow of the Islamic Banking and Finance Institute Malaysia (IBFIM), a Chartered Islamic Finance Professional (CIFP), and a former board member of the Accounting and Auditing Organization for Islamic Financial Institutions (AAOIFI). He was the first managing director of Hong Leong Islamic Bank, after which he became chief operating officer and ultimately acting CEO at the Asian Finance Bank. He is now engaged by Deloitte to assist in the setting up of their global Islamic finance practice. Abdullah is a frequent speaker and commentator on matters relating to Islamic finance.

Nigel Walder is the CEO of Business Control Solutions (BCS). He founded the Buttonwood Tree Group in 2001, which merged with B2B Systems in 2005 to form BCS. Walder has more than 17 years' experience in the financial technology industry and is recognized as one of the sector's leading professionals. Before founding Buttonwood Tree Group, he worked as managing director for Europe at Moneyline. Before that, he worked for

  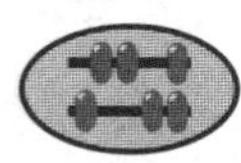   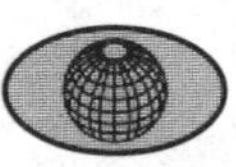   

nearly five years at NatWest Global Financial Markets, where he held the position of global head of technology and was recognized as one of NatWest's most up and coming managers. Walder has a BCS honors degree in civil engineering from the University of Nottingham.

Steve Wallace joined the Chartered Alternative Investment Analyst (CAIA) Association as associate director of industry relations in June 2008 and is based in England. Prior to joining the CAIA Association he managed client relations for several UK firms—most recently with an emerging market equity hedge fund as well as ING Wholesale Banking and Société Générale Corporate & Investment Banking. In addition, he spent seven years working in the private wealth management sector in Australia, primarily in investment strategy for high net worth individuals at firms, including the private bank division of National Australia Bank and AXA Australia.

Norbert Walter is chief economist of Deutsche Bank. He was previously director at the renowned Kiel Institute for World Economics and was a John J. McCloy distinguished research fellow at the American Institute for Contemporary German Studies at the Johns Hopkins University in Washington, DC. At Deutsche Bank he is responsible for a globally integrated approach to economic research and is a member of the management of the Deutsche Bank think tank. He is a member of the Committee of Wise Men on the Regulation of European Securities Markets (the Lamfalussy group) and was also a valued adviser to Gerhard Schrðder's government.

Wang Jiwei is a professor of accounting at Singapore Management University. He graduated with honors from Xi'an Jiaotong University with a bachelor's degree in economics and obtained his PhD in accounting from Hong Kong University of Science and Technology. He has many years of industry and academia experience in auditing, corporate reporting, financial statements analysis, and equity valuation. Dr Wang has been doing practical research on Chinese accounting standards and securities regulation. He has published research papers in prestigious international journals and serves on the editorial board of the *Singapore Accountant*. His research has also been profiled in the *Financial Times* and the *Straits Times*.

Véronique Weets is founder and managing partner of Cethys. She is a professor of international accounting and a faculty member of the Vrije Universiteit Brussel (VUB) and the University of Antwerp. She has several years of practical experience in one of the big four firms, where she was involved in client work on matters such as the transition to IFRS and the subsequent application of IFRS by listed companies. Weets also facilitates IFRS-related training programs for organizations such as IASeminars, Euromoney, and Quorum Training, and is a widely published author. She holds an IFRS certificate from the Association of Chartered Certified Accountants.

Juergen Weiss worked for almost 11 years at SAP AG in the SAP ERP (enterprise resource planning) financials area. In his last position he was consulting director for financial supply chain management and corporate performance management. He also worked as director of application solution management ERP and held global responsibility for financial supply chain management, particularly for SAP solutions in the areas of electronic bill presentment and payment, dispute management, credit management, in-house cash, and customer and vendor accounting. Prior to joining SAP in 1997 he worked for Westdeutsche Landesbank in Dösseldorf, Germany. He has degrees in economics and business.

Richard Werner is director of international development and founding director of the Centre for Banking, Finance and Sustainable Development at the University of Southampton. He holds a BSc in international and development economics from the London School of Economics and an MSc in economics from Oxford University. In 1990 he joined the Graduate School at the University of Tokyo and became a researcher at the Nomura Research Institute. He was chief economist at Jardine Fleming Securities (Asia) Ltd, after which he joined the faculty of Sophia University, Tokyo. In 1998 he set up a consulting firm, Profit Research, which conducts macroeconomic research and market forecasting on 37 countries.

Lawrence J. White is Arthur E. Imperatore professor of economics at New York University's Stern School of Business and deputy chair of the Economics Department at Stern. He was a board member on the Federal Home Loan Bank Board and director of the Economic Policy Office, Antitrust Division, in the US Department of Justice. Professor White received his BA from Harvard University (1964), MSc from the London School of Economics (1965), and PhD from Harvard University (1969). He has written many books and articles and is editor or coeditor of 11 academic volumes. He also served on the senior staff of the President's Council of Economic Advisers in 1978–1979.

Suzanne White, FCII, is chief executive officer of JWZ Solutions. Before founding JWZ Solutions, Dr White's most recent position was at a banking and finance institute in the Gulf, where, in addition to leading the insurance and accounting teaching teams, she was involved in other projects for the Chartered Insurance Institute as a member of the senior management team. A major responsibility and achievement was to establish the CII Academy at the Bahrain Institute of Banking and Finance (BIBF). Dr White has over 15 years of consultancy and training experience with educational and corporate entities, and she holds a PhD in educational research.

William C. White IV is a senior financial executive with CFO, treasury, corporate development, accounting, and auditing experience in Fortune 500/FTSE 100 companies such as Brown-Forman, Humana, and British American Tobacco. He has extensive knowledge and practice in mergers and acquisitions, venture capital investment, production finance, and multinational audit functions. White earned a BS degree in accounting from the University of Kentucky and a master's in management from Northwestern University's Kellogg School of Management. He has written in-depth essays on finance and accounting and appeared in *Business: The Ultimate Resource* (Bloomsbury, 2002). He is a member of the American Institute of Certified Public Accountants.

Paul Wilmott is a financial consultant specializing in derivatives, risk management, and quantitative finance. He has worked with many leading US and European financial institutions. He studied mathematics at St Catherine's College, Oxford, where he also received his DPhil. He founded the Diploma in Mathematical Finance at Oxford University and the journal *Applied Mathematical Finance*. He was a founding partner of the volatility arbitrage hedge fund Caissa Capital, which managed $170 million. Dr Wilmott is the proprietor of www.wilmott.com, the popular quantitative finance community website, and the quant magazine *Wilmott*, and he is

     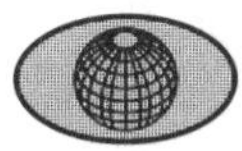   

course director for the world's largest quant education program, the Certificate in Quantitative Finance (CQF).

Rodney Wilson is director of postgraduate studies at Durham University. Formerly visiting professor at the Universities of Kuwait and Paris X, the International University of Japan, and the Qatar Foundation's Qatar Faculty of Islamic Studies, he is a world expert on Islamic economics and finance, Middle Eastern political economy, and the political economy of oil and gas. He currently chairs the academic committee of the Institute of Islamic Banking and Insurance in London and is acting as consultant to the Islamic Financial Services Board with respect to its *shariah* governance guidelines.

Priscilla Wisner is an associate professor of accounting at Montana State University. She formerly taught at the Thunderbird School of Global Management, and her research has been widely published in journals and books, including *Management International Review* and the *Harvard Business School Balanced Scorecard Report*. She also has more than 15 years' experience of consultancy with corporations. Dr Wisner earned her PhD at the University of Tennessee, an MBA degree from Cornell University, and a BA in international economics from the George Washington University.

Marlene Wittman is group managing director of Aquitaine Investment Advisors Ltd and oversees the group's pan-Asian investment management services and strategies. She has approximately 20 years' experience in the Asian region in the investment in and research of Asian companies and capital markets. Prior to founding Aquitaine, she was a director of Nikko Securities (Hong Kong) and Nikko Europe Plc (London). Her experience of investment management stems from her experience with a Boston-based investment advisory and with a Hong Kong-based private equity group. Wittman is a registered investment adviser with the Securities and Futures Commission (SFC) of Hong Kong.

Mike Wright is professor of financial studies and director of the Centre for Management Buy-out Research at Nottingham University Business School, which he founded in 1986. His research interests include international dimensions of entrepreneurial management buyouts and venture capital, technology transfer, and corporate governance in emerging markets. Professor Wright is the author of over 300 papers in international journals. He is also author or editor of some 50 books, the most recent of which are *Private Equity Demystified* (with John Gilligan, 2008) and *Private Equity and Management Buyouts* (with Hans Bruining, 2008). He is a member of the British Venture Capital Association Advisory Board.

David Wyss is chief economist at Standard & Poor's. He is responsible for S&P's economic forecasts and publications. Wyss joined Data Resources, Inc., in 1979 as an economist in the European Economic Service in London, which was acquired by McGraw-Hill. He returned to the United States in 1983 as chief financial economist for DRI/McGraw-Hill, became chief economist for Standard & Poor's DRI in 1992, and chief economist for Standard & Poor's in 1999. Wyss holds a BS from the Massachusetts Institute of Technology and a PhD in economics from Harvard University. He is on the board of the National Association for Business Economics.

George Yip is dean of Rotterdam School of Management, Erasmus University. Professor Yip holds BA and MA degrees in economics from Cambridge University and an MBA and doctorate from Harvard Business School. A native of Asia, he is a dual citizen of the United Kingdom and the United States. Before joining the Rotterdam School of Management, Yip was vice president and director of research and innovation at Capgemini Consulting. He has been a professor at Cambridge University, the London Business School, and UCLA. He is one of the world's leading authorities on global strategy and marketing, managing global customers, and internationalization.

S. David Young is a professor at INSEAD (France and Singapore), holds a PhD from the University of Virginia, and is both a certified public accountant (United States) and a chartered financial analyst. His main research interests are value-based management, executive compensation, and corporate financial reporting. Most of his efforts focus on how businesses can align key management systems with the value creation imperative. His research has appeared in a wide range of academic and professional journals, including the *Harvard Business Review*. He is also a consultant, having advised many firms in Europe, North America, and Asia.

Pierre Yourougou is associate professor of finance at the Whitman School of Management, Syracuse University. He is also managing director of the Africa Business Program at the Whitman School. His research and teaching interests are in the areas of corporate finance, financial institutions and markets, and emerging markets. Prior to joining Syracuse University in 2006, Professor Yourougou worked for the World Bank, where he held various senior level positions in the corporate finance, financial products development, and public debt management departments. He received his PhD in banking and finance from New York University's Stern School of Business

Abdel-Rahman Yousri Ahmad, PhD in economics (1968) from St Andrews University, Scotland, is professor and ex-chair of the Department of Economics at Alexandria University. He is a former director general of the International Institute of Islamic Economics at the International Islamic University, Islamabad, Pakistan. He is a member of the Economic Research Council and the Academy of Scientific Research and Technology, Ministry of Higher Education and Scientific Research, Egypt, and is a deputy and visiting professor to many universities and institutes in the Middle East, Asia, and Europe. Professor Yousri Ahmad is the author of nine textbooks and of 30 articles, most on Islamic economics and Islamic finance.

Linda Yueh is an economist and commentator on global economic and business issues. She is a fellow in economics at the University of Oxford, a visiting professor at the London Business School, and an associate of the Centre for Economic Performance at the London School of Economics and Political Science. Previously, she worked internationally as a corporate lawyer, based in New York, Hong Kong, and Beijing. She has authored and co-authored numerous books and is editor of the series of books on economic development and growth published by World Scientific Publishing. Dr Yueh is an adviser to the World Economic Forum in Davos, Switzerland, and the UK government.

Muhammad Yunus is the founder and managing director of Grameen Bank, which provides microcredit to millions of poor people in Bangladesh. In 2006 he was awarded the Nobel Peace Prize. Professor Yunus' vision is the total eradication of poverty from the world. The World Bank

  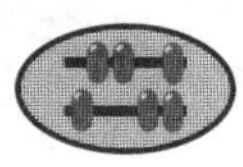   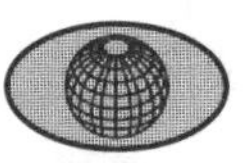   

recently acknowledged that "this business approach to the alleviation of poverty has allowed millions of individuals to work their way out of poverty with dignity." Professor Yunus serves on the boards of many national and international organizations. Besides Grameen Bank, he has created a number of companies in Bangladesh to address diverse issues of poverty and development.

Chendi Zhang is assistant professor of finance at Warwick Business School. His main areas of research include corporate finance, behavioral finance, ethical/social investments, and emerging economies. He is junior extramural fellow of the CentER for Economic Research, Tilburg, the Netherlands, and was previously lecturer in finance at the University of Sheffield. He has also held positions as consultant/ researcher at the World Bank and the International Finance Corporation (IFC), Washington, DC. Dr Zhang has published in academic journals such as the *Journal of Corporate Finance* and *Journal of Banking and Finance*. He holds a PhD in financial economics from Tilburg University, the Netherlands.

Guofu Zhou is professor of finance at Olin Business School, Washington University. His teaching and research interests include asset pricing tests, asset allocation, portfolio optimization, Bayesian learning and model evaluation, econometric methods in finance, futures, options, and derivatives, the term structure of interest rates, and the real option valuation of corporate projects. Before joining Olin Business School in 1990, Zhou studied at Duke University for his PhD in economics and MA in mathematics, at Academia Sinica for an MS in numerical analysis, and at Chengdu College of Geology for a BS.

Peter Zollinger is senior vice-president at the environmental and social governance consultancy SustainAbility, where his clients include Aracruz (Brazil), Credit Suisse, MasterCard, Rabobank, Standard Chartered Bank, and UBS. Before joining SustainAbility he was a founder of the Business Council for Sustainable Development (now WBCSD) and of AVINA, which invests in sustainability and social entrepreneurs in Latin America. Zollinger was educated at the University of St Gallen, Switzerland, and speaks five languages.

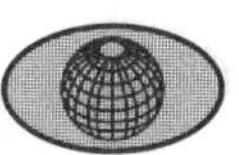

QFINANCE User Guide

QFINANCE is a one-stop guide for finance professionals, compiled by 300+ expert advisers and contributors, covering topics such as Corporate Balance Sheets and Cash Flow, Governance and Business Ethics, Insurance and Financial Markets, Making and Managing Investments, Mergers and Acquisitions, Operations Management, Raising Finance, Regulation and Compliance, and Strategy and Performance.

QFINANCE includes:

- 250+ original best practice essays written by leading international finance experts and market movers
- 300+ step-by-step guides to solving everyday problems and making calculations
- analysis of 102 countries and 26 industry sectors
- definitions for 9,000+ financial terms
- 125 influential finance books summarized
- 2,000+ insightful quotations
- coverage of subject areas ranging from accounting to wealth management
- concise biographies of the world's key thinkers behind modern finance

The material is split into nine distinct sections to ensure ease of navigation. Each section is extensively cross-referenced across and within topics.

BEST PRACTICE

Putting the expertise of the world's leading finance writers, educators, and practitioners to work for you

The **Best Practice** section presents a powerful array of practical advice and fresh thinking reflecting the full spectrum of issues that define finance today.

Internationally renowned finance leaders, experts, and educators distil the most important aspects of finance best practice. Contributors include Riccardo Rebonato, Paul Wilmott, Ian Bremmer, James Montier, Scott Moeller, Muhammad Yunus, Sir John Stuttard, Howard Davies, Michael Panzner, Todd Buchholz, and Diana Choyleva.

Essays

Each essay begins with an **Executive Summary** for quick reference, outlining the main points in the article. The **Making It Happen** feature illustrates practical applications of the principles and concepts, and where relevant authors have provided illustrative case studies and definitions of technical terms. In addition the **More Info** section includes recommendations of related books, articles, reports, and websites, and is linked to detailed hands-on advice in the **Checklists, Calculations and Ratios**.

Viewpoints

Viewpoints have been contributed by some of the world's most prominent financial minds. The articles and interviews are forward-looking and agenda-setting explorations of personal perspectives on the future of finance in an environment of constant challenge and change.

CHECKLISTS

Finding practical solutions to everyday finance problems

The **Checklists** section provides a comprehensive handbook of practical answers to the daily challenges of modern finance. Each checklist is a step-by-step guide to achieving the best results in areas including hedging interest rate risk, governance practices, project appraisal, estimating enterprise value, and managing credit ratings. Each checklist reflects current thinking and best practice, and includes a list of "dos" and "don'ts" as well as critical reflection on the topic at hand.

CALCULATIONS AND RATIOS

The **Calculations and Ratios** section presents the essential mathematical tools the finance professional needs for finding solutions to daily numerical problems. This section includes how to calculate return on investment, return on shareholders' equity, working capital productivity, EVA, risk-adjusted rate of return, CAPM, and many more.

FINANCE THINKERS AND LEADERS

Profiling the top finance thinkers and leaders

This section provides over 50 profiles of the most influential or controversial finance writers, thinkers, and entrepreneurs; those who shaped modern finance through their contributions to both theory and practice. These profiles offer insights into the background, defining moments, and legacies of each of the key characters including Joseph de la Vega, Franco Modigliani, Louis Bachelier, Franco Modigliani, Paul Samuelson, and Myron Scholes.

FINANCE LIBRARY

Summarizing the most influential finance books

The canon of finance literature is vast, with hundreds more publications emerging every year. This section distills the main lessons from most influential finance books both past and present, from the cornerstones to the most popular reads, from *Against the Gods* to *Portfolio Theory and Capital Markets* and *The Great Crash*.

Each summary includes a concise overview and analysis of the book's most distinctive contributions to finance thinking and practice, along with bibliographic information for the featured title and related works by the author.

COUNRY AND SECTOR PROFILES

Country and Sector Profiles provide an in-depth analysis of 102 countries comprising EU, OECD, and OPEC members, and composites of MSCI, emerging markets, and MENA indexes, plus coverage of 26 industry sectors from automobiles to water.

     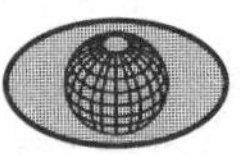   

FINANCE INFORMATION SOURCES

Providing the quickest and easiest route to the best financial information available

Finance Information Sources brings together the best financial information sources from around the world. Organized into over 60 subject areas, this carefully selected list includes authoritative books, magazines, journals, and websites, as well as key organizations.

QUOTATIONS

This section includes more than 2,000 quotations on finance, management, leadership, money, and business.

DICTIONARY

The most up-to-date global finance dictionary

Over 9,000 terms providing a comprehensive global dictionary of finance and banking vocabulary.

factoring FINANCE **1.** transferring of foreign debts the practice of transferring title to foreign accounts receivable to a third-party factor that assumes responsibility for collections, administrative services, and any other services requested. Major exporters use factoring as a way of reducing exchange rate risk. The fee for this service is a percentage of the value of the receivables, anywhere from 5% to 10% or higher, depending on the currencies involved. Companies often include this percentage in selling prices to recoup the cost. **2.** selling firm's debts at discount the sale of accounts receivable to a third party (the factor) at a discount, in return for cash. A factoring service may be "with recourse," in which case the supplier takes the risk of the debt not being paid, or "without recourse," when the factor takes the risk. *See also* ***invoice discounting*** **3.** buying of debts the practice of buying up a business's accounts receivable, providing it with working capital

QFINANCE ONLINE

To complement your print copy of *QFINANCE*, a fully searchable electronic version can be found at **qfinance.com.** The online edition of the book will be regularly updated to incorporate the very the latest developments in this fast-moving area.

FEEDBACK

We welcome any comments you may have about how ***QFINANCE*** might be improved. Let us know, too, if you disagree with any of the points made, or have any corrections, we welcome your views. Write to us at qfinance@bloomsbury.com.

BEST PRACTICE

     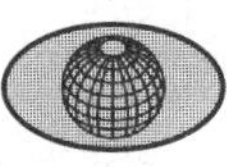   

Best Practice

Putting the expertise of the world's best business thinkers to work for you

The purpose of the Best Practice section is to provide you with incisive information covering key problems and finance-related issues you are likely to face during your working life.

With over 250 contributors, this section presents a powerful array of practical advice and thinking from some of the world's leading finance authors, educators, and practitioners.

However, don't expect easy answers to every problem. These essays are not designed to be the last word on the subject, but an easy-to-read and practical introduction. There are extensive links to detailed hands-on advice on "how to do it" in later sections.

We have tried to organize these essays so you can browse them quickly. The section is therefore divided into nine broad themes: Corporate Balance Sheets and Cash Flow, Governance and Business Ethics, Insurance and Financial Markets, Making and Managing Investments, Mergers and Acquisitions, Operations Management, Raising Finance, Regulation and Compliance, and Strategy and Performance.

At the beginning of each essay is an **Executive Summary** for quick reference, outlining the key areas in the article

The **Making It Happen** section shows you how you can apply what has been discussed in practice. Where relevant, authors have provided examples to show how theories have been implemented.

Most essays provide you with a short directory entitled **More Info**, as well as quick links to other sections in *QFINANCE*.

We have also provided a number of distinguished **Viewpoints**, which provide you with perspectives on a number of finance-related themes including the rise of China, the future of asset management, and financial regulation. These are based on a number of exclusive interviews and essays contributed by some of the world's leading finance thinkers such as Anthony Bolton, Mark Mobius, James Montier, Sir John Stuttard, Michael Panzner, Michael Moore, and Augusto Lopez-Claros. Our aim here is to stimulate, to provoke, and to inspire.

     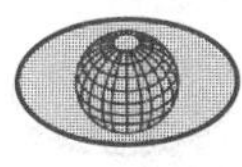   

Contents

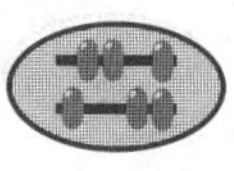
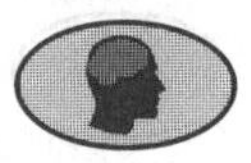

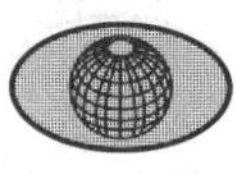

Making and Managing Investments

   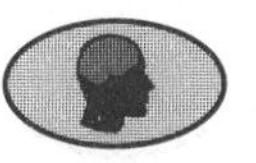  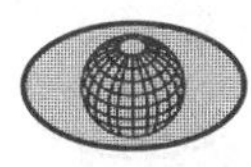   

  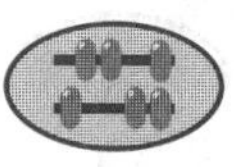   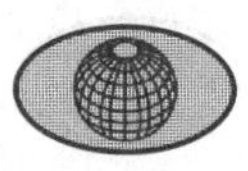   

Regulation and Compliance

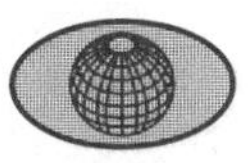

Strategy and Performance

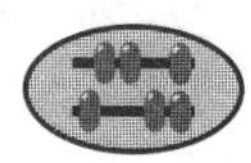

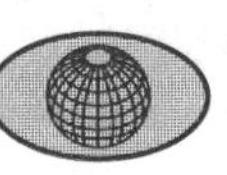

Advantages of Finance Best Practice Networks

by Hans-Dieter Scheuermann

EXECUTIVE SUMMARY

The article describes the needs of complex finance transformations projects and how finance best practice networks can help an organization find the best practices that fit its specific requirements.

- Most business transformation projects require that the finance function is prepared to enable and accompany change.
- Governance and stewardship is one role. Finance excellence in operations and business partnering is the second one.
- Finance best practice networks are the platform to exchange experiences: Examples from Roche, BHP Billiton, Nestlé, BP, and Philips illustrate such projects.

INTRODUCTION

The Best Practice Network for Finance and HR is a network for senior executives and best practice leaders at the senior executive level—spanning nations and industries. The goal is to facilitate networking, and allow the business leaders of large customers to exchange experiences and their use of best practices. The Best Practice Network for Finance and HR injects ideas and concepts into a cross-company network of professionals to identify best practices, disseminate information members can learn from, test new ideas, and develop practical solutions that work in specific company environments.

By tapping into the vast amount of experiences out there, and a new willingness to share and connect, companies stand to gain. Why not learn from an insurance company how best to prepare for risk, and why not talk to an oil company to learn how to handle the current trend to be green?

FINANCE TRANSFORMATION PROJECTS

Many companies currently undergo big projects such as a finance transformation, responding to the needs of corporate governance, and, at the same time, optimizing the organization of their finance functions. Finance transformation projects typically follow four main areas for improvement: Processes, organization, information systems, and people. From the viewpoint of an IT (information technology) company, it is of utmost importance that the goal, the process, and the organizational structure are clearly laid out, agreed on, and planned, before they are set in stone by the implementation of an IT system. What is required is a multi-step process towards management of information management—according to Peter Drucker "focusing on the 'I' in 'IT,' not on technology first." First, it is important to understand the critical business and chief financial officer (CFO) issues, and their mission. The second step is to design or redesign the finance and/or business architecture, and its processes. The final step, only after completion of the first two, is to design or re-engineer the IS architecture and solutions. Only by integrating all three views, can IT/IS (information system) create maximum value, enabling the possibility for optimal trade-off decisions.

The structure and goals of finance transformation projects reflect what the production and supply-chain side of companies have already addressed under the umbrella of "lean manufacturing"–the acceleration, automation, and simplification of processes; the reduction of working capital; the implementation of centers of expertise; the saving on labor costs; etc. It is possible to create more value with less work, by dispensing with wasteful activities, and applying best practices. On the financial side, companies look at shared services, simplify the charts of accounts, optimize their financial supply chain, put their management reporting on a diet, and implement employee and manager self-services. Reporting does happen in a "pull mode" by the business user instead of being "pushed" on a periodic schedule.

As financial transformation most often leads to automation and efficiency gains as well, financial capacity is freed to support the business in a different way from before. Where better analytics and real-time business insight become available in an ever-more complex world, the finance function can and must develop from a bean-counting report provider into a trusted, well-equipped, knowledgeable, and respected business partner. "If we are honest, most finance professionals are still at the backend of the pipeline, still analyzing what others have done. The challenge in the future will be to help to develop the pipeline rather than reporting on the pipeline and on the ideas of others," says Paul Koppelman, CFO of BHP Billiton Marketing, in his presentation at the European CFO Roundtable on July 9–10, 2007, in Hamburg, Germany.

FINANCE AS THE BUSINESS PARTNER

Dominic Moorhead, head of finance and accounting at F. Hoffmann-La Roche Pharma, and his team put the following quote rather nicely into their finance credo, which he presented at the European CFO Roundtable in Hamburg, Germany: "Our winning finance team will navigate the path to new heights of business performance, leading with our partners in crafting and executing value enhancing decisions, while ensuring financial peace."

At the basic level, finance transformation requires a secure foundation of

Figure 1. General Electric (Jeff Immelt's view). (*Source*: Björn Bergabo, CFO of GE Commercial Finance, SAP Finance Best Practice Workshop, September 22, 2005, Barcelona)

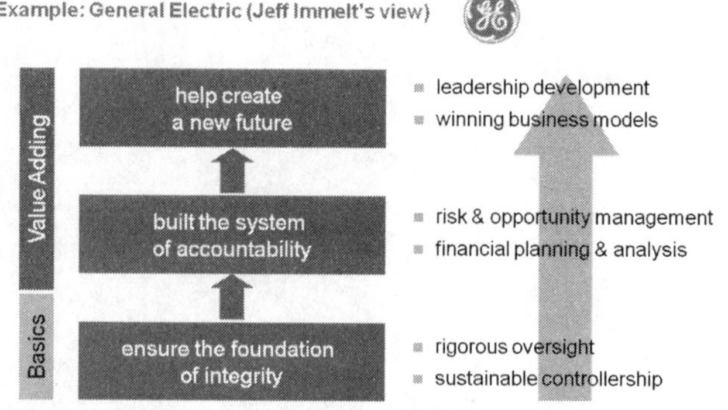

"For top executives to award themselves these kinds of compensation packages in the midst of this economic crisis is not only bad taste, it's bad strategy—and I will not tolerate it as president." Barack Obama

     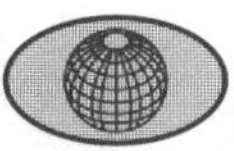   

rigorous oversight and sustained controllership to ensure integrity of the function. It adds value as soon as a system of accountability is built, by introducing risk and opportunity management, and financial planning and analysis. However, the greatest step towards the creation of a new future is being done by leadership-development and winning-business models, where finance comes in as the business partner, according to Jeff Immelt, chief executive officer (CEO) of General Electric.

The result can be a "house of finance," as described, for example, by the former CFO of Nestlé, Paul Polman. Polman established four pillars that support profitable growth: Co-pilots/business partners (grouped along countries, product lines, etc.); specialist services (for example, for tax); business services (for example, for accounting), and decision-support services (for example, costing).

In the networked business environment of today, many have come to the conclusion that you can no longer be excellent on your own. A. G. Lafley, CEO of P&G, said: "In 2000, a little more than 10% of our innovation was partnered. . .last year, a bit more than 40% of what we commercialized had at least one external partner." So, apart from optimal processes, a stable infrastructure, and an effective leadership development program, intelligent business networks could be an important element of what a high-performing organization requires.

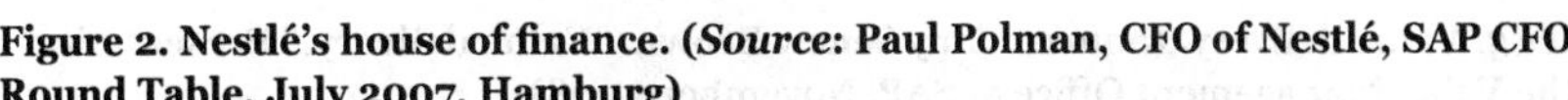

Figure 2. Nestlé's house of finance. (*Source*: Paul Polman, CFO of Nestlé, SAP CFO Round Table, July 2007, Hamburg)

Figure 3. The different roles of finance. (*Source*: Daum, J. H. *ZfCM—Zeitschrift für Controlling & Management* 52 (June 2008))

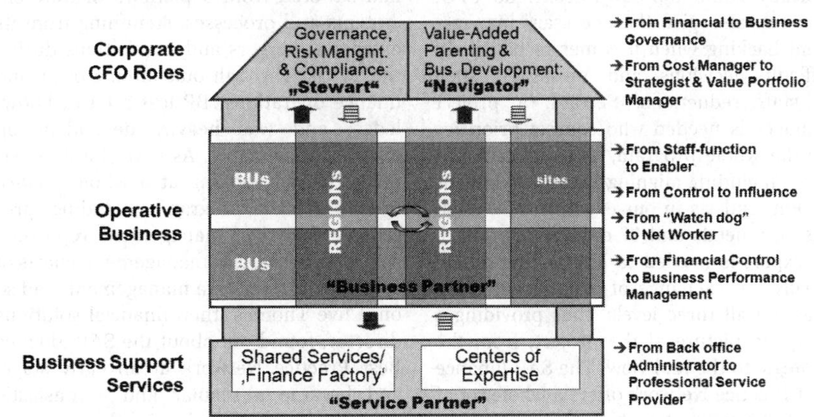

Figure 4. The multi-level finance best practice network. (*Source*: H. D. Scheuermann, SAP CFO Round Table, July 2007, Hamburg)

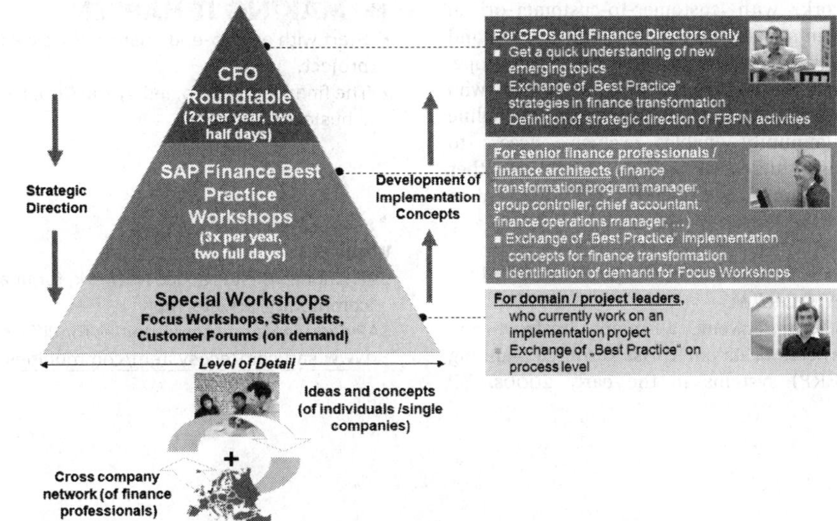

FINANCE BEST PRACTICE NETWORKS

There are a number of business networks out there that may support an organization's striving for learning and exchange, and help it to cope with the challenges ahead.

The Conference Board, for example, runs regular meetings that focus on IT, shared services, and other topics with attendees from multinational organizations.

The Corporate Executive Board reports on case studies and presents the results at conferences.

Hackett and other benchmark providers run surveys and share the resulting studies in annual conferences.

And also the major consulting companies offer a variety of events to enable networking among peers.

THE SAP FINANCE BEST PRACTICE NETWORK

The SAP Finance Best Practice Network offers peer-to-peer exchange of experiences and learning, with a special focus on three dimensions of the aforementioned complex projects. First, the green light and budget

"The bonus system has proved to be wrong. Substantial cash bonuses do not reward the right kind of behaviour." Andy Hornby

Figure 5. Value delivery. (*Source*: Amy Senew Brown. "Value delivery." Presentation for the Value Management Office at SAP, November 2008)

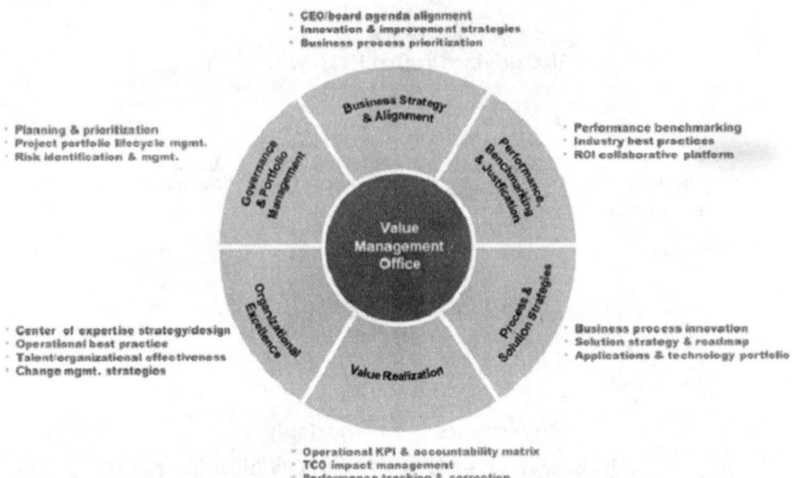

typically come top-down from the CFO, who can also give the necessary management backing when it comes to politically difficult decisions and measures, such as staff reductions. Second, a project manager is needed who can set priorities for the whole program, align its different parts, including aligning it with the organization, and, as in our example, also align business needs and IT capabilities. Third, an expert is needed to look at the detail. Ideally, an exchange of experiences takes place on all three levels, thus providing a complete picture of the project, from the strategic to the tool view. The SAP Finance Best Practice Network offers a whole set of events targeted at each management level participating in a finance transformation program, as described earlier.

It is a business-specific customer network, with customer-to-customer-driven events that has developed into a strong and vibrant community of executives in Europe, North and Latin America, and Asia who share best practices globally. Its online community enables exclusive access to case studies, as well as contacting other community members and holding online discussions.

BP'S FINANCE TRANSFORMATION PROGRAM

BP underwent a major restructuring process of its enterprise resource planning (ERP) systems in the early 2000s. BP had suffered from a plethora of different systems and processes, stemming from its extensive mergers and acquisitions during the 1990s. Through outsourcing of IT and finance operations, BP lost a lot of knowledge, and was heavily dependent on external consultants. As part of a five-year plan, BP was looking at a whole finance transformation program, including processes, analytics, management reporting, shared services, risk management, charts of accounts, master data management, and so on. Clive Thomas, then financial solutions director, found out about the SAP Finance Best Practice Network at an early stage, and became a regular and enthusiastic attendee, as the topics in the meetings fitted his needs perfectly. Away from consulting spin and sales pitches, he was able to learn and research how organizations from his own and other industries had conquered the same unknown lands. "Many great companies have done many great things—we needed to filter these and see which areas were appropriate for BP," Thomas says. Among the case studies Thomas looked at, in the exclusive circle of companies gathered in the network around him, were how Siemens had solved the puzzle of complex organizational models, how Philips in the Netherlands had harmonized its multitude of charts of accounts, and how BHP Billiton had got to grips with risk management. BP, in return, shared its Sarbanes–Oxley activities with Shell, helped Nestlé to consolidate its African banking and treasury operations, and helped Barclays set up operations where currencies run into too many digits. After the first two meetings, Thomas even arranged his travel to Singapore, London, and Houston to match the schedule of the sessions. He wanted to: "listen to real-life customer experiences, and look and see what went well and what didn't."

Networking helped BP to compare itself to other customers, and find out about innovations and opportunities within its own organization, while benchmarks gave reliable figures that helped to create a sense of urgency to change. BP was able to access a collaborative platform online with all past case studies, and even find out about relevant solutions and roadmaps from an IT perspective, by using the SAP network. All that knowledge helped BP to prioritize and plan the project, knowledge which was also an important cornerstone in the sense of being effective risk management for the endeavor.

▸▸ MAKING IT HAPPEN

- Start with end-to-end finance processes and a bridge to IT before starting an IT project.
- The finance function, led by the CFO, has a strong role in business change projects as a business partner.

▸▸ MORE INFO

Websites:

SAP Finance Best Practice Network, for finance professionals: www.sap.com/community/private/fbpn

SAP overview of its communities for different information needs and target groups: www.sap.com/ecosystem/communities

"You can blame it on me and close the book, but it doesn't come close to explaining what happened."
Sir Fred Goodwin

  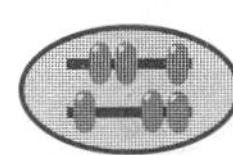   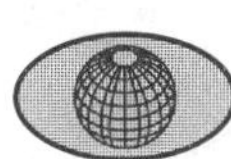   

Allocating Corporate Capital Fairly by John L. Mariotti

EXECUTIVE SUMMARY

- The principal job of management is the allocation of scarce resources—people, time, and money—to opportunities that yield the greatest returns.
- There is always a shortage of capital and an excess of worthy projects. There are many methods of capital allocation, but most do not fund the best opportunities.
- The key task is to allocate capital to support the greatest opportunities, those that match strategic objectives.

INTRODUCTION

The appetite of organizations for capital is insatiable. Understanding the nature of capital and its effective allocation is essential to organizational success. Classical economics defines land, labor, and capital as the determinants of wealth, each being exclusive to its owner. Now there is a fourth determinant of wealth—information—and it is nonexclusive. The more information is shared, the more valuable it becomes. Business is a competition in which the score is kept in money, and thus allocation of capital, in all its forms, is a critical success factor.

The challenge is to decide which division, project, or acquisition gets the scarce capital. The challenge varies with the source of capital. Venture capitalists' and hedge funds' tolerance for risk is offset by their high return expectations. The low risk of municipal bonds and banks is matched by low returns. Hedge funds make increasingly larger "bets," while equity investors carefully consider exit strategies in capital allocation decisions. Privately owned companies strive to enhance shareholder value, matching investment choices to their investors' expectations. Public companies are servants of the public stock markets and investment analysts. Each master has different expectations, and thus capital allocation must vary accordingly.

ALLOCATING CAPITAL

If capital is allocated foolishly, or to poorly defined projects, it is wasted. The game is a simple one: invest the least possible amount, borrow the rest, and put it in projects with the greatest potential return (or occasionally the lowest risk). Deciding which ventures to invest in has always occupied management attention. There are many quantitative methods for allocating capital. Most of these remain valid, but they share one problem: they all depend on a forecast of future events, which is uncertain. The challenge is to allocate capital to the best opportunities, given the risk-reward profile of the investors, and to choose projects that have the best chance of earning good returns.

The Typical Plan: Allocation for Strategic Purposes and Objectives

Capital allocation must be aligned with the strategic purposes and objectives of the investor. The implication is that these are well defined and clearly understood. However, this is frequently not the case. Often the strategies and goals are unclear or poorly understood.

The Typical Practice: An Artifact—The Capital Budget

Organizations develop capital expenditure budget needs for annual review by boards and lenders. A common breakdown of a capital budget is by category or type of expenditure—for example, new products, new facilities, maintenance of existing products or facilities, and infrastructure needs. This is a theoretically sound method since each category has a different strategic purpose: for example, sustaining current activities or revenue streams, creating new revenue streams, or providing infrastructure to support current or new business needs. These category splits are intended to allow senior management and boards to allocate capital fairly according to the company's strategic needs. The problem is that there is an enormous gap developing those artifacts of bygone eras—capital budgets—and the actual intent of the investments. This traditional route is a sure path to sustained mediocrity or steady decline.

MAKING IT HAPPEN

The Capital Appropriation Process

When management has determined what it believes is an effective use of capital, it must find a means to communicate that need and its worthiness relative to other needs. Larger organizations use a formal capital appropriation process. This process involves documentation of the intended use, description of the assets to be acquired, time frames for the investments, and benefits to be gained. A financial analysis is a required part of the capital appropriation request

The methods used to compare and evaluate capital investments are based on projections of future revenue streams and a calculation of some combination of:

- internal rate of return (IRR)
- net present value (NPV)
- breakeven
- economic value added (EVA)
- economic profit created (EP)
- risk-adjusted return on capital (RAROC)

This approach rewards the best analysts, politicians, and sycophants, but not the best projects. The most innovative, high-potential projects are seldom easy to analyze and quantify. Yet these are the very ideas that turn out to be outstanding—but only in retrospect—and only if they ever get funded. In traditional allocation, the capital tends to be spent either protecting the past or perfecting the present, with precious little left for funding the future. For reasons of personal or organizational pride, differing goals, or political power, appropriation requests often do not match corporate goals. Competing executives or organizations will scuffle for scarce capital, and even if their intentions are good (which they usually aren't) the resulting conflicts can be ugly. Who is to resolve these conflicts

Approvals and the Capital Appropriation Committee

In some companies the authority level for heads of business units is high—assuming funds have been budgeted—in the category needed. This means there is a chance that good, innovative ideas might receive financing. In central-control-oriented companies spending approval levels are kept low, forcing corporate reviews of most investments.

Appropriation requests go up the ladder to be approved by successively higher levels of management, and the higher one goes, the less informed the management tends to be. The originator's chain of command includes gatekeepers from finance and accounting. Other functions affected often have sign-off rights, too. This creates a time-consuming, bureaucratic, and often contentious process that wrings the creativity out of any proposal, replacing it with conservatism, caution, and capital "constipation."

"Capital as such is not evil; it is its wrong use that is evil. Capital in some form or other will always be needed."
Mahatma Gandhi

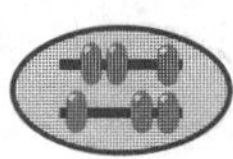

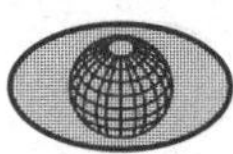

After running the divisional bureaucratic gauntlet, the appropriation goes to the corporate capital appropriation committee, where it is subjected to more scrutiny by even less informed people. This review is supposedly based on alignment with corporate strategies, return versus competing capital needs, and the requesting unit's budget. The larger the organization the more levels there may be, but the process varies surprisingly little from company to company.

When small companies grow rapidly, capital allocation is efficient and effective—and involves only a few well-informed people. As the company gets larger or is acquired by a larger entity, it implements a more formal capital approval process. This process now includes approval at higher authority levels. While this is considered necessary, it is noticeably slower and less efficient. The successive layers of capital appropriation processes and committees can slow down or even kill most creative projects and divert capital to safer, less rewarding uses.

Historically, depreciation was designed to fund the replacement of assets by expensing non-cash charges, thereby reserving the cash (capital) for new expenditures. Thus the norm was for capital allocation to equal depreciation. To spend more is equivalent to putting in new money, and to spend less is in effect using up the business. Many lending agreements also contain restrictive covenants that limit capital spending to formulae—the right spending level is a function of what happened in the past adjusted by management's or investors' wishes. The obvious corollary is that, if the company is struggling, it is often starved of the necessary capital to rebuild itself.

Other Challenges in Capital Allocation

Cash-rich companies also have a problem. A low return on conservatively invested cash reduces overall returns. Companies are expected to earn higher returns than banks. A common alternative is to repurchase stock, a less than exciting capital allocation. In other cases, company treasurers are tempted to use high-risk investments like derivatives to elevate returns on excess cash. Multinational companies encounter another issue: currency exchange rate fluctuations, which can negate the best analyses. Hedging currency by buying futures can protect the downside, but, like all insurance, this too comes at a cost. Then there are fiascos in which capital allocation is based on equity markets and stock prices. The dot-com deals involving stock swaps quickly revealed the flaws here: huge profits disappeared overnight, replaced by unexpected write-offs. Misadventures like Enron illustrate how easily a bogus capital structure can tumble like a house of cards.

Furthermore, what happens to budgeted but unspent money? The government model—use it or lose it—is often used. The rush to spend unused budgeted capital results in waste, misallocation, or both. Alternatively, a passive indecision deprives the enterprise of funding for its growth or rejuvenation.

Nonmoney "Capital"

Finally, there are critical non-capital resources to be allocated—people, knowledge, or time. The people part is often called "human capital," an appropriate name. If this human capital is in short supply, all the monetary capital in the world will not help. Capital must be spent wisely or allocating it well is useless. People spend the capital, and thus the most important question to ask is not what it will be spent on, but who will be spending it and what is their track record? Choosing the right people to bet on is the critical decision.

An Alternative to Allocation?

In the bubble era of 2000–2001 capital flowed freely to those perceived to deserve it; those perceived as undeserving were starved. Many decisions were bad, but consider the concept. Instead of allocating capital, think of "earning it and/or deserving it." Innovative ideas seldom survive bureaucratic battles, particularly if they threaten to cannibalize existing businesses. Harvard's Clayton Christensen has written at length about "disruptive technologies" and their impact on markets. In the real world, an idea should either be able to attract capital or not. No corporate committee says yea or nay. The idea must prove that it deserved the capital by being successful. That is capital allocation's model for the 21st century.

CONCLUSION

Companies usually allocate capital on the basis of one of three mindsets:

- The first is *protecting the past*, in which case they will always be following the competition and reacting to a leader's moves, simply trying to hang on to past glories.
- The second mindset is the attractive trap of *perfecting the present*. Such moves are always easier to analyze, and make short-term goals, except when new, disruptive technology or a competitor enters the fray, upsetting the applecart.
- The third mindset is the critical one—to allocate capital by investing in *funding the future*. This is harder and riskier, but it is the only true path to success. The capital need must attract the needed capital based on its potential success.

Few traditional appropriation processes accommodate this approach, which is why so few companies succeed over the longer term. Companies trying to fund the future are often led by "escapees" from the other kind of companies—people seeking outlets for creative brilliance and thwarted by bureaucratic, inwardly focused capital appropriation processes, policies, and committees. The best rule for capital allocation is to allocate very little to protecting the past and just enough to perfecting the present, leaving plenty to spend on funding the future. That is where real wealth and excitement lies—if only management and boards will finance it.

▸▸ MORE INFO

Books:

Drucker, Peter F. *Management Challenges for the 21st Century*. New York: HarperBusiness, 1999.

Hamel, Gary. *Leading the Revolution*. Cambridge, MA: Harvard Business School Press, 2000.

Hamel, Gary, and C. K. Prahalad. *Competing for the Future*. Boston, MA: McGraw-Hill, 1996.

Selden, Larry, and Geoffrey Colvin. *Angel Customers & Demon Customers*. New York: Portfolio, 2003.

Websites:

The Enterprise Group: www.mariotti.net

Telling It Like It Is, John L. Mariotti's blog: mariotti.blogs.com/my_weblog

See Also:

★ Managing Capital Budgets for Small and Medium-Sized Companies (pp. 72–74)
✔ The Objectives of Corporate Planning and Budgeting (p. 877)
Adam Smith (p. 1196)
Mastering Financial Management: Demystify Finance and Transform Your Financial Skills of Management (p. 1296)

"Investing is an act of faith. We entrust our capital to corporate stewards in the faith—at least with the hope—that their efforts will generate high rates of return on our investments." John Clifton Bogle

  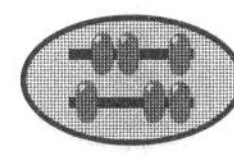   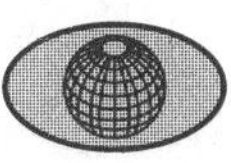   

Asset Liability Management for Pension Funds by R. H. M. A. Kleynen

EXECUTIVE SUMMARY

- Asset liability management (ALM) is an overall risk management technique for pension funds.
- ALM requires the board to formulate guidelines for its strategy on contribution and indexing levels, and its attitude to risk.
- ALM is based on stochastic simulation and is used as a basis for decisions on the distribution of future contributions, funding, and indexing levels.
- Practicing ALM requires an assets and liabilities committee (ALCO). An ALCO consists of senior pension fund management, with the chief risk officer as chairman. The committee converts the guidelines into formal proposals on the investment strategy and the contributions and indexing policies.
- ALM does not predict the future, but it gives insight into the possible risks a pension fund is exposed to and how to handle them.
- An ALM model should be as parsimonious and uncomplicated as possible. The purpose of such models is to act as a tool to help management understand what is really going on, and how to reach responsible and internally consistent decisions.

INTRODUCTION

The management of a pension fund has to make decisions about its strategic asset allocation, its contributions policy, and its indexing policy in a context of acceptable financial risk. It has to meet the return requirements necessary to improve benefit payments on the one hand, and to stay in line with the solvency requirements of the regulator on the other. But what is an acceptable contributions and indexing policy, and how is an acceptable risk attitude defined? ALM forces the board to think about these aspects, and to quantify them. That is not an easy job. But only by giving clear guidelines does risk management have practical and measurable value. Putting ALM into practice is not a solo achievement but requires a multidisciplinary team of specialists who are willing to work together. Formalization normally results in the so-called assets and liabilities committee, or ALCO, with the chief risk officer as chairman.

THE AIM OF ALM

A crucial stage in the exploration of an ALM strategy is the development of the funding level. The funding level is the ratio of the market value of the assets and the market value of the liabilities. Funding levels below 100% are disliked because the assets do not cover the total value of the liabilities. So management of the funding level in general, and the possibility of underfunding in particular, is of primary importance. Generating high funding levels is easy to accomplish. Just increasing the contributions and investing them in low-risk assets will generate attractive funding levels. However, neither employers nor employees will be too enthusiastic about this solution because they are faced with high pension contributions.

Another important concern is the indexing policy. Pension funds aim to index their benefit payments based on the price inflation of the previous year to protect pensioners from loss of purchasing power. Such indexing clauses are conditional, as full indexing can only be implemented if the funding level is high enough. The closer the funding level falls to the 100% mark, the less the benefits will be increased. If benefit payments are to be made inflation-resistant, adequate indexing levels are very important.

ALM, therefore, is the search for a balanced perspective. By practicing ALM we want to find a balance between future contributions on the one hand and future funding and indexing levels on the other. To accomplish this, the choice of strategic asset allocation plays an important role, as Figure 1 shows.

WHY IS ALM IMPORTANT?

Within a pension fund, investment managers, risk managers, accountants, actuaries, CEOs, and CFOs have to communicate, and communication is not that easy. How nice it would be if we all spoke the same language. ALM helps us. ALM is a technique that pension funds employ in coordinating the management of assets and liabilities. An ALM approach forces all parties to quantify the relevant factors and bundles them into an overall framework. The effects of separate decisions are analyzed in an overall context. Isolated decision-making is no longer possible. ALM is therefore a financial risk assessment and asset planning tool used by pension funds to help them choose the strategic policy under uncertainty, and in a coherent and consistent balance sheet approach.

ALM MODELING

In the complex environment in which pension funds have to operate, ALM requires an instrument to identify and manage risks. Such an instrument is a stochastic simulation model, which mimics the behavior of a pension fund by incorporating randomness to obtain a statistical sample of possible outcomes. ALM modeling is thus a key method in strategic risk management. It involves developing mathematical scenarios of the future evolution of assets and liabilities,

Figure 1. The impact of asset allocation on returns. © Kleynen Consultants bv

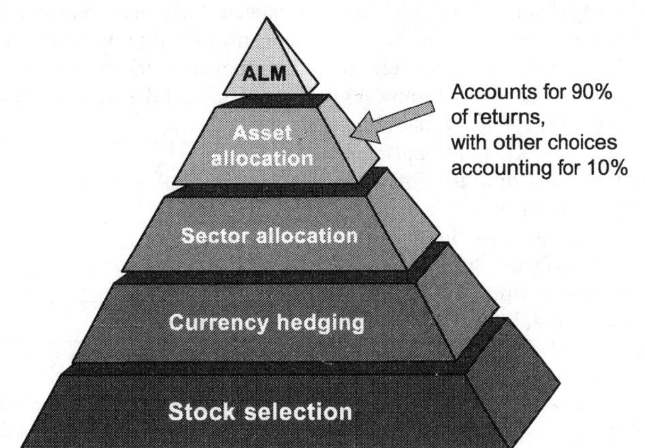

"Companies that have been around for 50 years are another world to me. I entered the technology arena the same year that Microsoft was started. And the arena has always felt like a meritocracy, though there were never many women." Ann Winblad

  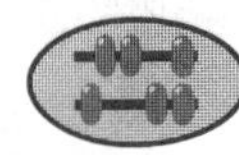 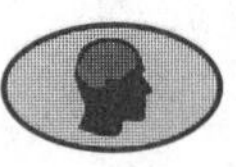  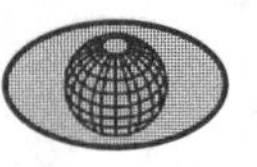   

Figure 2. Examples of pension fund cash flow and term structure. © Kleynen Consultants bv

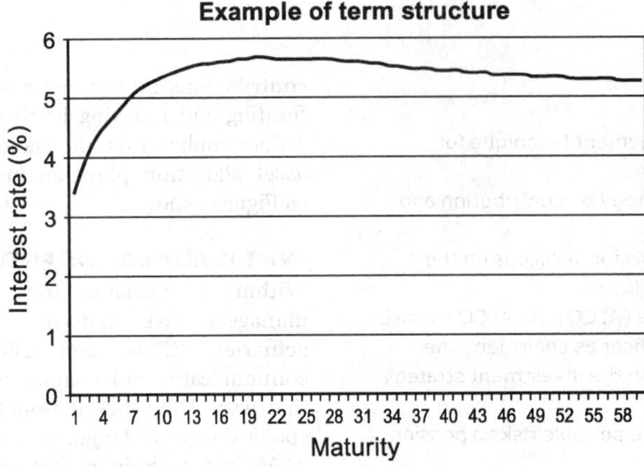

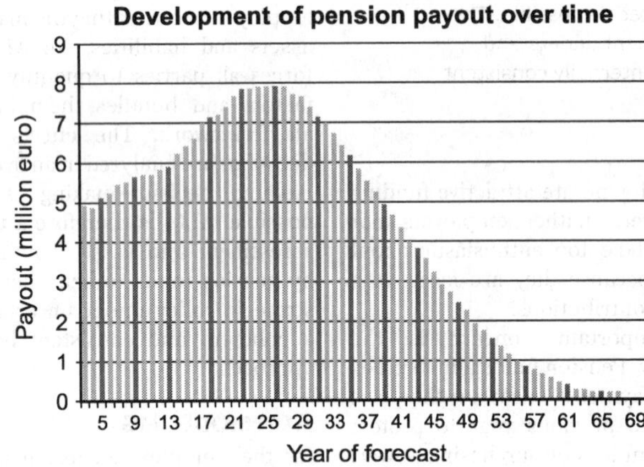

given certain assumptions about the statistical properties of the variables that affect the evolution of assets and liabilities. Though dynamic models have proven a better fit for real world scenarios, they do have their drawbacks, as due to their complexity they may be harder to understand and interpret.

There are many ways to generate these scenarios. The traditional method was to create a central scenario, and to carry out some stress testing around it. With time the models have become more sophisticated, involving stochastic simulation of assets and liabilities. Modern ALM studies rely on stochastic models that generate thousands of scenarios, with different probabilities attached to each. While the traditional ALM studies focused on asset optimization with a deterministic view of liabilities, today ALM is increasingly used to simulate the consequences of policies for different stakeholders while complying with the requirements of the regulatory authorities. In this sense, ALM systems are used as integrated planning systems to simultaneously determine investment, funding, and—if applicable—indexation policies, thereby balancing the goals of the different stakeholders. Each ALM system has its own unique characteristics, principally governed by the underlying stochastic processes and distribution functions.[1] The main financial uncertainty comes from changing asset prices and interest rates, and from transition probabilities. But how do they behave? Questions such as "Are there differences between short-term and long-term behavior?"[2] have to be asked, and if the answer is yes, they should be modeled. Furthermore, modeling normally concentrates only on stocks and bonds, so the question arises whether investment products should also be included.[3]

CASE STUDY

ALM is a widely accepted risk management tool in the Netherlands. The new regulatory framework introduced in January 2007 requires the use of ALM studies, with stochastic analysis prescribed as of 2010. Although these stochastic analyses are voluntary until 2010, most pension funds have already integrated this kind of analysis into their daily practice. But how is this done? The example below gives an idea of how an ALM study is structured and the results presented.

Pension Fund XYZ: Some Characteristics

The ALM study for pension fund XYZ starts with assumptions about investments, participants, financial construction, contribution policy, and indexing.

Investments: The total value of the investment portfolio at year-end is 150,000 million euros. The structure of the portfolio is assumed to be the same as that of the strategic investment portfolio. This implies a portfolio based on a constant mix of 65% fixed income, 25% equity, and 10% real estate.

Charges: The charge for solvency, set by the rules formulated by the pension regulator De Nederlandsche Bank, is equal to 23% of the net reserve. The charge is based on the portfolio structure, the cash flow scheme of payouts, and the term structure.

Contributions: Contributions are assumed to be equal to 35% of the contribution base. The contribution base equals the salary minus an offset of 15,000 euros.

Indexing: Indexing is based on price inflation in the previous year. Indexing policy is as follows:

- if the funding level is less than 110%, there is no indexing
- between 110% and 130% indexing is increased linearly
- between 130% and 135% there is full indexing
- above 135% any lost indexing is restored
- if funding levels remain below 105% for more than a year, pension rights are cut until they reach 105% again

Category	Return (%)	Standard deviation (%)
Stocks	7.5	18.5
Bonds	4.5	8.5
Real estate	6.0	14
Wage inflation	3.0	2.0
Price inflation	2.0	2.0

Test statistic: The resulting risk/return profile is accepted if the probability of underfunding (meaning when the funding level is below 100%) at year 10 is less than 2.5%.

"It was the kind of blind, gulping, insensate greed that you associate with some milk-eyed creature in a volcanic fissure at the bottom of the Marianas Trench—an organism with no understanding of the existence, let alone the feelings, of other members of the ecosystem." Boris Johnson

Economy: In order to make forecasts, assumptions with respect to the future risk/return profiles of economic variables have to be made. The regulator has given guidelines on the mean values of these variables. With regard to these basic risk characteristics, the pension fund has made its own assumptions, as set out in the table below.

A SURVEY OF PENSION FUND XYZ

A prime concern for pension funds is the cash flow scheme of the benefit payments, as the development of this scheme over time, in combination with the term structure, determines the required reserve. An example of such a cash flow and term structure is given in Figure 2.

Based on this information, profiles of contribution levels, probabilities of underfunding, and indexing levels can be derived. The probability of underfunding is now considered in more detail; it has the characteristics shown in Figure 3.

We see that after 10 years the probability of underfunding exceeds the limit of 5%. Therefore one has to conclude that the policy of this pension fund will have to be changed if it is to meet its requirements.

CONCLUSION

ALM is not just an analytical tool that generates suitable strategies for pension fund management—it also forces departments to cooperate and to reach joint conclusions. It makes decision-making very transparent, and it helps pension funds to maneuver in a consistent way in uncertain and sometimes difficult times. ALM is all about understanding what is really going on and how to make responsible decisions. It is not some technical *tour de force*, but rather a practical tool that assists management in making systematically sound strategic decisions under conditions of uncertainty.

Figure 3. Main characteristics of the probability of underfunding. © Kleynen Consultants bv

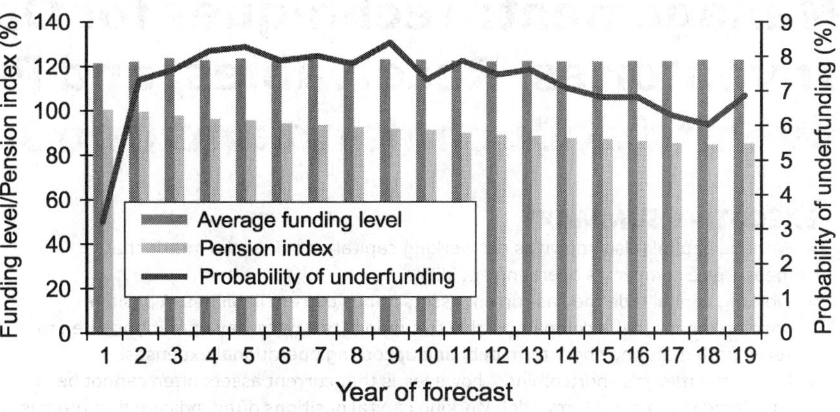

⏩ MAKING IT HAPPEN

- Implementation of ALM is a top-down process.
- The board formulates the required contribution and indexing levels.
- The ALCO transforms these requirements into a practical proposal that outlines the pros and cons of the possible ALM strategies.
- The board formulates an investment strategy and sets contribution levels and any increase in pension payouts.
- Investment strategy is implemented in daily practice—contributions are collected and pensions are indexed.
- The control cycle starts. The ALCO monitors the environment to see if expectations and reality still meet. If not, alternatives are presented and the board reconsiders its earlier decisions.

⏩ MORE INFO

Articles:

Campbell, J. Y., and L. M. Viceira. "The term structure of the risk–return trade-off." *Financial Analysts Journal* 61:1 (2005): 34–44.

Gerstner, T., *et al.* "A general asset-liability management model for the efficient simulation of portfolios of life insurance policies." *Insurance: Mathematics and Economics* 42 (2008): 704–716.

Gibbs, S., and E. McNamara. "Practical issues in ALM and stochastic modelling for actuaries." Paper presented to the Institute of Actuaries of Australia Biennial Convention, September 23–26, 2007.

See Also:

✔ Understanding Asset–Liability Management (Full Balance Sheet Approach) (p. 889)
Peter Bernstein (p. 1154)
Against the Gods: The Remarkable Story of Risk (p. 1215)

NOTES

1 See Gibbs and McNamara (2007).

2 See e.g. Campbell, J. Y., and L. M. Viceira. *Strategic Asset Allocation: Portfolio Choice for Long-Term Investors*. Clarendon Lectures in Economics. Oxford: Oxford University Press, 2002.

3 Hoevenaars, R. P. M. M., *et al.*. "Strategic asset allocation with liabilities: Beyond stocks and bonds." Working paper, Maastricht University, 2007.

  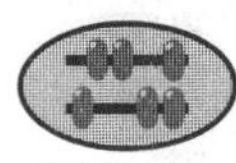  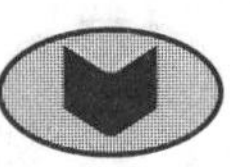 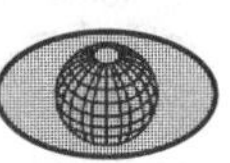   

Best-Practice Working Capital Management: Techniques for Optimizing Inventories, Receivables, and Payables

by Patrick Buchmann and Udo Jung

EXECUTIVE SUMMARY

- Working capital (also known as net working capital) is a financial metric that measures a company's operating liquidity.
- Working capital is defined as current assets minus current liabilities. A positive position means that a company is able to support its day-to-day operations—i.e., to serve both maturing short-term debt and upcoming operational expenses.
- One of the metric's shortcomings, however, is that current assets often cannot be liquidated in the short term. High working capital positions often indicate that there is too much money tied up in accounts receivable and inventory, rather than short-term liquidity.
- All companies should therefore focus on the tight management of working capital. Inventory, accounts receivable, and accounts payable are of specific importance since they can be influenced most directly by operational management.
- Companies that improve their working capital management are able to free up cash and thus can, for example, reduce their dependence on outside funding, or finance additional growth projects.
- If done right, working capital management generates cash for growth together with streamlined processes along the value chain and lower costs.

INTRODUCTION

Many companies still underestimate the importance of working capital management as a lever for freeing up cash from inventory, accounts receivable, and accounts payable. By effectively managing these components, companies can sharply reduce their dependence on outside funding and can use the released cash for further investments or acquisitions. This will not only lead to more financial flexibility, but also create value and have a strong impact on a company's enterprise value by reducing capital employed and thus increasing asset productivity.

High working capital ratios often mean that too much money is tied up in receivables and inventories. Typically, the knee-jerk reaction to this problem is to apply the "big squeeze" by aggressively collecting receivables, ruthlessly delaying payments to suppliers and cutting inventories across the board. But that only attacks the symptoms of working capital issues, not the root causes. A more effective approach is to fundamentally rethink and streamline key processes across the value chain. This will not only free up cash but lead to significant cost reductions at the same time.

NWC: DEFINITION AND MEASUREMENT

Working capital, also referred to as net working capital (NWC), is an absolute measure of a company's current operative capital employed and is defined as:

(Net) working capital = Current assets – Current liabilities

Current assets are assets which are expected to be sold or otherwise used within one fiscal year. Typically, current assets include cash, cash equivalents, accounts receivable, inventory, prepaid accounts which will be used within a year, and short-term investments.

Current liabilities are considered as liabilities of the business that are to be settled in cash within the fiscal year. Current liabilities include accounts payable for goods, services or supplies, short-term loans, long-term loans with maturity within one year, dividends and interest payable, or accrued liabilities such as accrued taxes.

Working capital, on the one hand, can be seen as a metric for evaluating a company's operating liquidity. A positive working capital position indicates that a company can meet its short-term obligations. On the other hand, a company's working capital position signals its operating efficiency. Comparably high working capital levels may indicate that too much money is tied up in the business.

The most important positions for effective working capital management are inventory, accounts receivable, and accounts payable. Depending on the industry and business, prepayments received from customers and prepayments paid to suppliers may also play an important role in the company's cash flow. Excess cash and nonoperational items may be excluded from the calculation for better comparison.

As a measure for effective working capital management, therefore, another more operational metric definition applies:

(Operative) net working capital = Inventories + Receivables – Payables – Advances received + Advances made

where:

- inventory is raw materials plus work in progress (WIP) plus finished goods;
- receivables are trade receivables;
- payables are non-interest-bearing trade payables;
- advances received are prepayments received from customers;
- advances made are prepayments paid to suppliers.

When measuring the effectiveness of working capital management, relative metrics (for example, coverage) are generally applied. They have the advantage of higher resistance to growth, seasonality, and deviations in (cost of) sales. In addition to better comparison over time, they also allow better benchmarking of operating efficiency with internal or external peers.

A frequently used measure for the effectiveness of working capital management is the so-called cash conversion cycle, or cash-to-cash cycle (CCC). It reflects the time (in days) it takes a company to get back one monetary unit spent in operations. The operative NWC positions are translated into "days outstanding"—the number of days during which cash is bound in inventory and receivables or financed by the suppliers in accounts payable. It is defined as follows:

CCC[1] = DIO + DSO – DPO

where:

- days inventories outstanding (DIO) = (average inventories ÷ cumulative cost of sales) × 365 = average number of days that inventory is held;
- days sales outstanding (DSO) = (average receivables ÷ cumulative sales) × 365 = average number of days until a company is paid by its customers;
- days payables outstanding (DPO) =

"**Cash is king.**" Proverb

  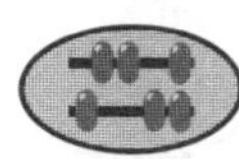   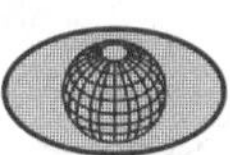   

Figure 1. Holistic approach to working capital management

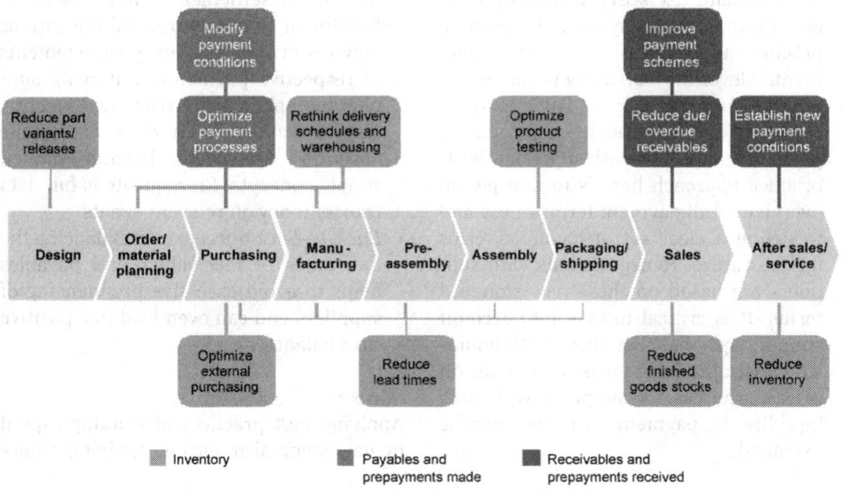

Note: Value chain and relevance of levers may vary with industry and business model
Source: BCG

(average payables ÷ cumulative purchasing volume) × 365 = average number of days until a company pays its suppliers.

Optimizing the three components of operative NWC simultaneously not only accelerates the CCC, but also goes hand in hand with further improvements. Figure 1 illustrates how an NWC optimization impacts the value added and free cash flow of a company. However, applying the right measures will not only increase value added by lowering capital employed. Improved processes will also lead to reduced costs and higher earnings before income and taxes (EBIT).

HOLISTIC APPROACH TO WORKING CAPITAL MANAGEMENT

By streamlining end-to-end processes, companies can, for example, reduce stock, decrease replenishment times from internal and external suppliers, and optimize cash-collection and payment cycles. The key is to uncover the underlying causes of excess operative working capital. In order to address the often hidden interdependencies among the different components and achieve maximum savings from a working capital program, companies must analyze the entire value chain, from product design to manufacturing, sales and after-sales support. They must also look for ways to simplify and streamline processes and eliminate waste, always keeping potential tradeoffs in mind. For instance, cutting inventories of spare parts or reducing product customization could lead to a major reduction in inventory. But how would these measures affect service quality, market positioning, or other aspects of the business?

MANAGING THE THREE OPERATIONAL COMPONENTS OF NWC

So, what are the relevant levers of working capital management, and how are they applied? In effect, receivables and payables are just different ways of financing inventories. Companies need to manage all three components simultaneously across the value chain so as to drive fundamental reductions in asset levels. Given the wide range of possible actions, focus is critical. A realistic plan with clear priorities is the best approach. An overly ambitious agenda can overstrain internal capabilities and deliver suboptimal results. Instead, companies should concentrate on the most promising actions that will not impair flexibility and performance. These actions will vary depending on industry and competitive situation, and have to be adapted to country specifics and regulations. In the following paragraphs some typical (but just exemplary) levers are described.

Reduce Inventories

Excess inventory is one of the most overlooked sources of cash, typically accounting for almost half of the savings from working capital optimization projects. By streamlining processes within the company—as well as processes involving suppliers and customers—companies can minimize inventory throughout the value chain.

- *Enhanced forecast accuracy and demand planning:* Improved forecast accuracy and regular updates of customer demand lead to a much more reliable planning process and help companies not only to reduce their inventory but also to improve the ability to deliver.
- *Advanced delivery and logistics concepts:* In order to keep inventories at lower levels, top-performing companies establish advanced and demand-driven logistics concepts with their suppliers, such as vendor-managed inventory, just in time (JIT) or just in sequence (JIS), and collaborate with their suppliers in terms of a holistic supply chain management with mutual benefits.
- *Optimized production processes:* An important lever to reduce work-in-progress inventory is the redesign of production processes. The main objectives here are to reduce non-value-adding time ("white-space reduction") and excessive inventory between production steps. Promising measures are removing bottlenecks and migrating from push concepts to demand-driven pull systems.
- *Service level adjustments:* An increased service level for products which are critical to the customer (and thus allow higher prices) and a decreased service level for products which are uncritical to the customer will not only lead to optimized stocks. A more sophisticated approach to calculating security stocks based on target availability and deviations in production and demand will also reduce out-of-stock situations for critical parts.
- *Variance management:* Reducing product complexity and carefully tracking demand of product variants in order to identify low-turning products is one way to reorganize and tighten the assortment and concentrate on the most important products. Moreover, where applicable, components should be standardized. Customization of products should take place as late in the process as possible.

SPEED UP RECEIVABLES COLLECTION

Many companies are early payers and late collectors—a formula for squandering working capital. Other companies—particularly project-based businesses and manufacturers of large, costly products with lengthy production cycles—have cash flow problems caused by a mismatch in timing between costs incurred and customer payments. Therefore, efficient management of receivables and prepayments received is crucial. An optimization can yield significant potential.

- *Invoicing cycle:* The main target in this respect is to get invoices to the customers as quickly as possible. Processes and systems should be aligned to allow invoicing promptly after dispatch or

     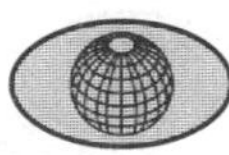   

service provision. All disruptions of the process by unnecessary interfaces should be eliminated. Furthermore, companies should reduce invoicing lead times by multiplying their invoicing runs.

- *Early reminders/dunning cycles:* Experience shows that a number of customers seem to postpone their payments to the receipt of the first payment reminder. Early reminders and short dunning cycles thus have a direct impact on late payments. Best-in-class companies reduce grace periods to a minimum or remind their customers of upcoming payments even before the due date. Establishing direct debiting with main customers is the most effective means to avoid overdue payments.
- *Payment terms:* Renegotiated payment terms will lead to reduced DSO. The first step is often a harmonization and reduction of available conditions to decrease discretionary application. When preparing negotiations, companies should analyze their customers' bargaining power and specific preferences in order to identify improvement potential in the terms and conditions for payments.
- *Payment schedule:* Companies operating in project business should introduce more advantageous payment schemes that cover costs incurred. Percentage of completion (POC) accounting helps to define relevant payments along milestones. But also for companies with small series productions, the introduction of prepayments and advances can significantly improve liquidity.

Rethink Payment Terms with Suppliers

If fast-paying companies are at one end of the spectrum, then companies that "lean on the trade" and use unpaid payables as a source of financing are at the other. Between these two extremes there is a more effective, integrated approach to payment renegotiation that takes into account all aspects of the customer–supplier relationship, from price and payment terms to delivery time frames, product acceptance conditions, and international trade definitions.

- *Payment cycle:* Payment runs for payables should be limited to the required frequency. Here, of course, country- and industry-specific business conventions apply. Moderate adjustments of payment runs just require some changes in the accounting systems, and tend to be a "quick hit."
- *Avoidance of early payments:* Payments before the due date should be strictly avoided. Payments should be accomplished with the next payment run after the due date (*ex post*). Switching from *ex ante* to *ex post* payments is common practice and entails an easily implemented lever for increasing payables.
- *Payment conditions:* A DPO increase can often be achieved by renegotiating payment conditions with suppliers. Best-practice approach here is to first get an overview of all payment terms in use and to define a clear set of payment terms for the future. Renegotiations with suppliers are based on these new standard terms. It is critical to take into account supplier specifics. For those with liquidity constraints the focus should lie on prices, whereas for suppliers with high liquidity the payment term can often be extended.
- *Product acceptance conditions:* Connecting the settlement of payables to the fulfillment of all contractual obligations may result in significant postponements of respective payments. Enforcing supplier compliance to stipulated quality, quantity, and delivery dates is also the basis for optimized, demand-oriented supply concepts. Prerequisite is full data transparency on relevant events.
- *Back-to-back agreements*: Balancing the due dates of receivables and payables helps to avoid excessive prefinancing of suppliers and can even lead to a positive cash balance.

Mind the Tradeoffs

Applying best practices of working capital management also means applying value-

Figure 2. Value creation and free cash flow are overarching targets

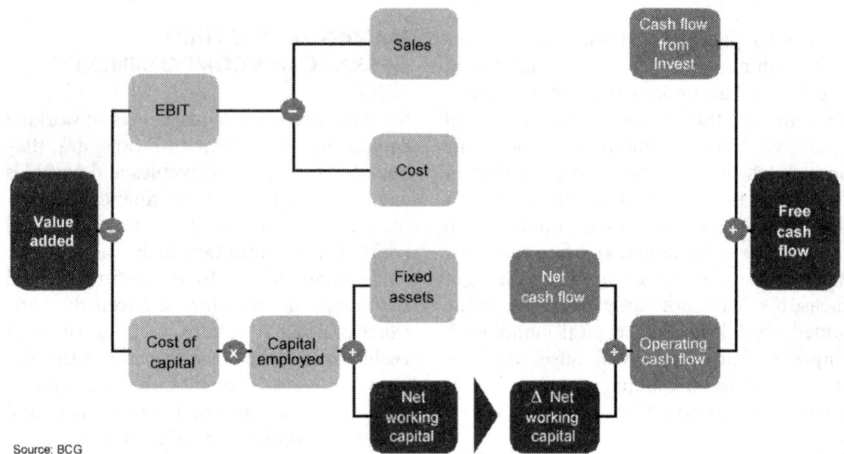

Source: BCG

CASE STUDY

A leading industrial conglomerate with worldwide sales presence in all of its divisions recently conducted a comprehensive, group-wide working capital program with a strong commitment of top management levels. Critical success factors were a holistic approach to the entire value chain and the definition of clear and practicable measures, together with employees responsible for implementation on the operational level.

Improvement measures ranged from more easily implemented quick wins, such as optimizing payment processes, to complete restructuring of production processes. Quick wins not only paid off the initiative after a few months, but also served as a beacon for the initiative and proof of concept. The overall NWC reduction added up to more than 40%. Roughly half of the improvement potential was already realized within one year from start of the implementation.

In order to anchor working capital management in the organization, a pragmatic controlling tool was set up and regular reporting cycles were established. Working capital goals were integrated into budgets and incentive programs to further foster sustainability.

Before the program brought the change, a number of initiatives had fallen short of expectations. The main reasons had been an undifferentiated top-down approach, and the lack of a comprehensive perspective on working capital. Thus, the symptoms rather than the root causes of excess accounts receivable and inventory or low positions in payables had been approached and no sustainable results had been achieved.

"Normally, we do not so much look at things as overlook them. " Zen quote by Alan Watts

  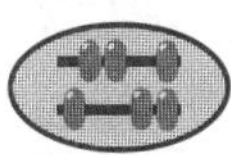   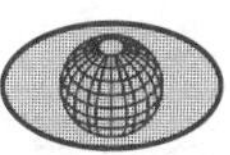 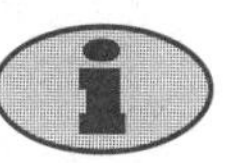  

oriented management of tradeoffs between NWC and fixed assets, and between NWC and costs. The isolated treatment of individual levers has its boundaries and, therefore, all elements of tied-up capital across the balance sheet (fixed assets, inventories, receivables, payables, and cash) have to be considered as a whole. For example, it may be advantageous to acquire a new and more flexible machine (fixed asset) in order to reduce inventories. As another example, negotiations in purchasing cannot only focus on payment targets. The company also has to consider the resulting prices and discount conditions. Therefore, a best-practice NWC optimization is not just a pure reduction of NWC; it is rather a holistic optimization with value creation as the overarching target.

CONCLUSION

Best-in-class companies understand the company- and industry-specific drivers behind each component of operative working capital, and focus on optimizing the most promising ones. During this process, they consider the entire value chain to reveal the root causes of tied-up cash and take into account all interdependencies between the respective components. They apply a holistic approach in which they do not randomly reduce costs but consider all tradeoffs with costs and capital employed to optimize the company value. By applying the appropriate levers for each component, obstacles that slow cash flow can be removed and overall company processes can be improved.

▸▸ MAKING IT HAPPEN

Since working capital optimization affects many areas of a company, detailed planning and a holistic approach are crucial for the success of a project. The following points provide some success factors of implementation:

- *How should we approach a working capital optimization project?* A benchmarking for the company and for all segments/business units should be conducted in order to identify the most promising areas for improvement and respective units. Following this, the project should start with a few selected pilots. Once these pilots have been executed, knowledge gains can be transferred to other business units, and further projects can be rolled out to the entire company.
- *How do we ensure that a working capital initiative is sustainable?* There are four main aspects to successfully anchoring an NWC project into an organization and making it sustainable: 1. Commitment and resources (sponsorship by top management, clear responsibilities, dedicated teams, internal experts as multipliers). 2. Communication and enabling (conveying motivation and necessity, fostering know-how exchange and best-practice sharing, providing training on NWC principles). 3. Incentives (inclusion in budget planning, linking variable salary to target achievements, recognizing jobs well done). 4. Controlling (integration into existing reporting formats, tracking target achievement and implementation progress).
- *How long does it take to optimize NWC?* In order to keep a momentum for change and to get a proof of concept, the right mix of quick wins and deep-dive improvements should be aimed for. Quick wins are usually realized within less than a year. They can make up roughly 30% of the overall potential. The overall sustainable optimization takes about three years, depending on company size and industry. According to project experience, the next 40% of the overall potential can be realized in the second year and the rest (about 30%) in the third year.

▸▸ MORE INFO

Articles:

Karaian, Jason. "Dash for cash." *CFO Europe Magazine* (July/August 2008). Online at: www.cfo.com/article.cfm/11661328

Websites:

Atradius has further survey data on agreed payment terms and delays: global.atradius.com

CFO Magazine and *CFO Europe Magazine* have articles on working capital management: www.cfo.com

Dun and Bradstreet has information on payment terms and late payment: www.dnb.com

Intrum Justitia compiles in its European Payment Index Report data on average agreed payment terms and delays in a European country comparison: www.europeanpayment.com

NOTES

1 For some businesses (i.e., project business) prepayments should be included as well. Prepayments received should be related to cumulative sales (as receivables). Prepayments paid should be related to the purchasing volume (as payables).

     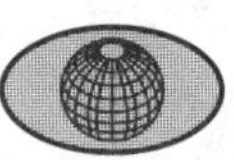   

Business Implications of the Single Euro Payments Area (SEPA) by Juergen Bernd Weiss

EXECUTIVE SUMMARY

- The Single Euro Payments Area (SEPA) affects all companies doing business with European partners and sending or collecting payments in euros.
- SEPA introduces two new pan-European payment instruments, replaces local payment formats, and requires the utilization of new master data for payments.
- Companies can simply try to comply with the new SEPA framework or pursue a strategic approach involving the redesign of their business processes.
- The German Würth Group implemented a strategic change program that included corporate connectivity with SWIFT and further cash management centralization.

A BRIEF HISTORY OF SEPA

SEPA is one of the largest projects in the history of pan-European monetary transactions. It is another major step toward a common financial market following the introduction of the euro in 1999. SEPA, which became effective in January 2008, affects all companies doing business with European partners and sending or collecting payments in euros. SEPA not only erases the boundaries between payment service systems in the European Union (EU), but also forces corporations to comply with new payment standards, change master data, and reconsider their business processes in financial accounting, cash, and corporate treasury management.

SEPA is the result of actions taken by the banking industry in 2002, when the industry created the European Payments Council (EPC) to define the standards, frameworks, and rules for euro payments. SEPA enables individuals, companies, and other stakeholders to make and receive payments in euros within Europe, whether across or within national boundaries, under the same basic conditions, rights, and obligations, regardless of their location. The political driver behind SEPA is the European Commission along with the European Central Bank.

BACKGROUND

SEPA applies to all national and cross-border euro payments within and between the 27 member states of the European Union, the three European Economic Area ountries, and Switzerland. All of these 31 countries must gradually harmonize their payment systems and procedures. This means establishing European standards for processing payments, reducing barriers to market entry, increasing efficiency, and lowering transfer costs. Setting such standards will lead to payment format and master data changes—not only for companies in Europe, but also in the United States and other countries that have subsidiaries in Europe. So-called one-leg-out payments—where either the payment service provider of the payer or the beneficiary is not located within the SEPA—are not subject to SEPA payment regulations.

The official SEPA roadmap allows for a transitional period in which both the old and the new payment formats coexist. This is similar to the roadmap for the euro. After a critical mass of payment transactions using the new SEPA payment formats has been reached, the old formats will be abolished by the European banking industry. Although there is currently no fixed end date defined for this event (the initial plan envisioned 2010, which is rather unrealistic), such a date will undoubtedly be set and all enterprises doing business in Europe will have to become SEPA-compliant eventually.

NEW PAYMENTS INSTRUMENTS

SEPA introduces two new payment instruments to be provided by banks for their customers: SEPA credit transfers (launched in 2008) and SEPA direct debits (scheduled to be introduced by November 2009). These new payment instruments are identical across SEPA. They provide significant payment efficiencies for the daily business of corporations.

The two new payment instruments are fundamentally different from each other. While SEPA credit transfers are used by debtors to initiate payments, SEPA direct debits are initiated by creditors to collect outstanding receivables. The processing of SEPA credit transfers is relatively straightforward, but SEPA direct debits are more complex because they require a mandate that has to be sent by the creditor to the debtor and signed by the debtor. From a legal perspective, a mandate encompasses two different functions. First, it is an authorization by the debtor to debit his or her account, and second, it is a payment order to the debtor's bank to initiate a payment to the creditor. Although SEPA direct debits and credit transfers can both

CASE STUDY

The German Würth Group decided to seize the opportunity of the advent of SEPA and implement a strategic approach. Würth's core business is worldwide trade in fixing and assembly materials, including screws, screw accessories, dowels and plugs, chemical products, furniture and construction fittings, tools, and stock keeping and picking systems. The group's 420 companies are located in 86 countries (half of them in Europe), with almost 63,000 employees. Würth's 2007 turnover totaled almost 8.8 billion euros.

The main business issue for the group was its nontransparent financial supply chain, since the group's many companies maintained their own banking interfaces for their payment transactions. Additional obstacles were high processing costs as a result of manual business processes, use of numerous access channels, and a lack of straight-through-processing (STP). The group was already managing 18 banks in a shared-service center and processing up to 2.5 million incoming payment transactions annually. Not only was the existing electronic banking component non-SEPA compatible, it had reached its capacity limits both from internationalization and compliance perspectives. In addition, Würth wanted to increase the current level of automation to achieve greater process savings.

Würth decided to implement a vendor's commercial bank communication solution and use the SWIFTNet infrastructure to route its SEPA payments to the group's banking partners. Würth is modifying all of its payment transactions, replacing domestic payment formats, and setting up a new payment approval process. The group also plans to bring additional banks and affiliates into the new SWIFT infrastructure. A key objective is to improve the processing of account statements further and increase the automatic reconciliation quota of open items within its enterprise resource planning (ERP) system.

"A handful of men have become very rich by paying attention to details that most others ignored." Henry Ford

     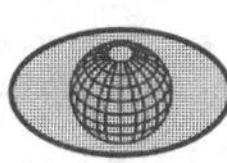   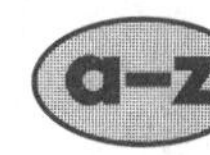

be used for business-to-business as well as business-to-consumer transactions, it is very likely that SEPA direct debits will become more common for smaller, potentially recurring business-to-consumer transactions such as utility or telecommunications bills. A huge benefit of the two new payment instruments is their universal usage across the SEPA area; this differentiates them from domestic payment solutions that don't work across borders and are today much more expensive.

The two payment instruments provide a number of additional advantages. For example, exporters no longer require expensive, difficult to manage, incoming payment accounts at foreign correspondents' banks. Companies can set up payment factories and shared service centers for financial operations, enabling them to centralize their financial accounting, cash, and corporate treasury management functions. SEPA affects card payments as well. Holders of Euro Cheque (EC) cards and credit cards can use them within SEPA to make payments at their usual national rates.

Both SEPA credit transfer and SEPA direct debit payments are based on International Organization for Standardization (ISO) 20022 payment processing standards and are defined as XML (eXtensible Markup Language) formats. Both the SEPA credit transfer and the SEPA direct debit are defined by ISO as PAIN (Payment Initiation) messages. There are also CAMT (Cash Management) messages, which define XML-based account statements for corporate-to-bank communication.

One of the key benefits of ISO 20022 messages—which are sometimes also referred to as UNIFI (Universal Financial Industry Message Scheme)—is the standardization and simplification of today's heterogeneous and flat-file-based payment messages. In the medium term, it is also foreseen that the UNIFI standard will replace the common message types which are used today in the SWIFT (Society for Worldwide Interbank Financial Telecommunication) environment such as SWIFT MT940.

The SEPA credit transfer does not differ significantly from the existing standard credit transfer within the EU, but it eliminates the current 50,000 euro value limit. The SEPA direct debit is a more complex payment instrument, requiring the creditor to receive a mandate from the creditor's debtors. The mandate is the authorization and expression of consent given by the debtor to the creditor, allowing the collection of outstanding receivables from a specified debtor account. Creditors must store mandate information in their systems as proof of legitimate collections, as well as to transfer mandate-related data to their financial institutions.

Both the SEPA credit transfer and the SEPA direct debit payment instruments require the use of an international bank account number (IBAN) and bank identifier code (BIC). The IBAN is a standard which was jointly developed by ISO and the European Committee for Banking Standards (ECBS).

Because only 45 countries have defined IBAN structures so far, this standard is not sufficient for routing payments, which means the BIC is needed as well. BIC (often also called SWIFT) codes are assigned by SWIFT. Companies have to update their IT systems to support both IBAN and BIC.

SEPA credit transfers are already in use and SEPA direct debits will be gradually introduced to the market by the banking industry. In the medium term, both payment instruments will replace the current domestic payment formats such as DTAUS (Datentraegeraustauschverfahren) in Germany and BACS (Bankers' Automated Clearing Services) in the United Kingdom.

One of the prerequisites for the introduction of SEPA direct debits is the Payment Services Directive, which establishes important intervals and other rules for payments. The European Parliament and the European Council (which consists of all the ministers of finance and economic affairs within the EU) approved this directive in 2007 and requested the member states to implement it before November 2009 in national law.

▸▸ MAKING IT HAPPEN

Strategic Options for SEPA

Enterprises can respond to the SEPA challenge with two basic strategies:

- **They can invest only the bare minimum to become SEPA-compliant.** This would imply the adoption of IBAN and BIC master data, as well as the implementation of the new payment instruments and formats. From an IT perspective, this strategy would require companies to evaluate the SEPA compatibility of their existing human resources, financial accounting, payment, and cash management system—including relevant master data.
- **They can view the changes as a strategic opportunity to benefit from lower market barriers and adapt their business processes.** On the business side, this could include the centralization of cash management activities, the implementation of payment factories, and the use of international payment service providers such as SWIFT. From the IT side, this could include consolidation of various IT systems in shared-service centers that would cover different European markets. Such operations should lead to improved economies of scale, better capacity utilization, and reduced total cost of ownership (TCO).

The right strategy depends on various factors, such as the geographical extent of a company's sourcing and sales, the savings potential in SEPA compliance, the number of customers in various markets, the level of competition in these markets, and the potential for consolidation of IT systems.

▸▸ MORE INFO

Books:

Skinner, C. (ed). *The Future of Finance After SEPA*. Hoboken, NJ: Wiley, 2008.

Reports:

Capgemini, ABN AMRO, and EFMA. "World Payments Report 2007." Online at: www.capgemini.com/resources/thought_leadership/world_payments_report_2007

Capgemini. "SEPA: Potential benefits at stake: Researching the benefits of SEPA on the payments market and its stakeholders." 2008. Online at: ec.europa.eu/internal_market/payments/docs/sepa/sepa-capgemini_study-final_report_en.pdf

European Commission. "Directive on payment services." Online at: ec.europa.eu/internal_market/payments/framework/index_en.htm

Logica CMG. "SEPA—The forgotten customer." White paper, 2005. Online at: www.logicacmg.com/pSecured/admin/countries/_app/assets/forgotten_customer_sept05-10252005.pdf

Viner, N., A. Creyghton, C. Rutstein, and N. Storz. "Navigating to win." Boston Consulting Group White paper, 2006. Online at: www.bcg.com/impact_expertise/publications/files/Global_Payments06_excerpt.pdf

"In epochs when the cash payment has become the sole nexus of man to man." Thomas Carlyle

     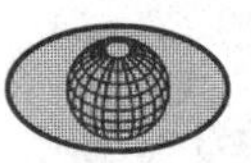   

Websites:

Euro Banking Association: www.abe-eba.eu
European Central Bank: www.ecb.europa.eu
European Committee for Banking Standards: www.ecbsnet.org
European Payments Council: www.europeanpaymentscouncil.eu
International Organization for Standardization. ISO20022 Standards: www.iso20022.org
SWIFT (Society for Worldwide Interbank Financial Telecommunication): www.swift.com

  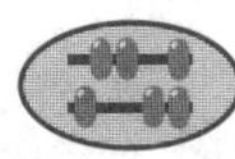   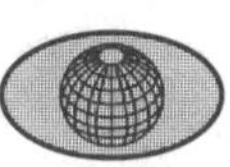   

Capital Budgeting: The Dominance of Net Present Value by Harold Bierman, Jr

EXECUTIVE SUMMARY

- The time value of money is highly relevant.
- Net present value (NPV) is a very reliable method of analysis.
- Use incremental cash flows.
- NPV profile is an excellent summary.

INTRODUCTION

A capital budgeting decision is characterized by costs and benefits that are spread out over several time periods. This leads to a requirement that the time value of money be considered in order to evaluate the alternatives correctly. Although to make decisions we must consider risks as well as time value, I restrict the discussion to situations in which the costs and benefits are known with certainty. There are sufficient difficulties in just taking the time value of money into consideration. Moreover, when the cash flows are allowed to be uncertain, I would suggest the use of procedures that are based on the initial recommendations made with the certainty assumption, so nothing is lost by making the assumption of certainty.

A financial executive made the following interesting observation (Bierman, 1986):

"The real challenge is creativity and invention, not analysis. Timely execution of projects by entrepreneurial managers is also more critical than sophistication of analytical budgeting techniques."

RATE OF DISCOUNT

We shall use the term time value of money to describe the discount rate. One possibility is to use the rate of interest associated with default-free securities. This rate does not include an adjustment for the risk of default; thus risk, if present, would be handled separately from the time discounting. In some situations, it is convenient to use the firm's borrowing rate (the marginal cost of borrowing funds). The objective of the discounting process is to take the time value of money into consideration. We want to find the present equivalent of future sums, neglecting risk considerations.

Although the average cost of capital is an important concept that should be understood by all managers and is useful in deciding on the financing mix, I do not advocate its general use in evaluating all investments. Different investments have different risks.

DEPENDENT AND INDEPENDENT INVESTMENTS

In evaluating the investment proposals presented to management, it is important to be aware of the possible interrelationships between pairs of investment proposals. An investment proposal will be said to be economically independent of a second investment if the cash flows (or equivalently the costs and benefits) expected from the first investment would be the same regardless of whether the second investment were accepted or rejected. If the cash flows associated with the first investment are affected by the decision to accept or reject the second investment, the first investment is said to be economically dependent on the second.

In order for investment A to be economically independent of investment B, two conditions must be satisfied. First, it must be technically possible to undertake investment A whether or not investment B is accepted. Second, the net benefits to be expected from the first investment must not be affected by the acceptance or rejection of the second. The dependency relationship can be classified further. In the extreme case where the potential benefits to be derived from the first investment will completely disappear if the second investment is accepted, or where it is technically impossible to undertake the first when the second has been accepted, the two investments are said to be mutually exclusive.

STATISTICAL DEPENDENCE

It is possible for two or more investments to be economically independent but statistically dependent. Statistical dependence is said to be present if the cash flows from two or more investments would be affected by some external event or happening whose occurrence is uncertain. For example, a firm could produce high-priced yachts and expensive cars. The investment decisions affecting these two product lines are economically independent. However, the fortunes of both activities are closely associated with high business activity and a large amount of discretionary income for the "rich" people. This statistical dependence may affect the risk of investments in these product lines because the swings of profitability of a firm with these two product lines will be wider than those of a firm with two product lines having less statistical dependence.

INCREMENTAL CASH FLOWS

Investments should be analyzed using after-tax incremental cash flows. Although we shall assume zero taxes so that we can concentrate on the technique of analysis, it should be remembered that the only relevant cash flows of a period are after all tax effects have been taken into account.

The definition of incremental cash flows is relatively straightforward: If the item changes the bank account or cash balance, it is a cash flow. This definition includes opportunity costs (the value of alternative uses). For example, if a warehouse is used for a new product and the alternative is to rent the space, the lost rentals should be counted as an opportunity cost in computing the incremental cash flows of using the space.

The computations in this article make several assumptions that are convenient and that simplify the analysis:

- Capital can be borrowed and lent at the same rate.
- The cash inflows and outflows occur at the beginning or end of each period, rather than continuously during the periods.
- The cash flows are certain, and no risk adjustment is necessary.

In addition, in choosing the methods of analysis and implementation, it is assumed that the objective is to maximize the well-being of stockholders, and more wealth is better than less.

TWO DISCOUNTED CASH FLOW METHODS

The two primary discounted cash flow investment evaluation procedures are net present value (NPV) and internal rate of return (IRR). We shall conclude that the net present value method is better than the other possible methods of analyzing investments.

Net Present Value

The two most important measures of investment worth are called the discounted cash flow (DCF), measures. It is desirable to

"Large firms rely heavily on present value techniques and the capital asset pricing model, while small firms are relatively likely to use the payback criterion." John R. Graham and Campbell R. Harvey

explain the concept of the present value of a future sum because in one way or another this concept is utilized in both these measures.

The present value of $100 payable in two years can be defined as that quantity of money necessary to invest today at compound interest in order to have $100 in two years. The rate of interest at which the money will grow and the frequency at which it will be compounded will determine the present value. I shall assume that funds are compounded annually. Assume that we are given a 0.10 annual rate of interest. Let us examine how the present value of a future sum can be computed by using that rate of interest.

Suppose that an investment promises to return a total of $100 at the end of two years. Because $1.00 invested today at 10% compounded annually would grow to $1.21 in two years, we can find the present value at 10% of $100 in two years by dividing $100 by 1.21 or by multiplying by the present value factor, 0.8264. This gives $82.64. Therefore, a sum of $82.64 that earns 10% interest compounded annually will be worth $100 at the end of two years. By repeated applications of this method, we can convert any series of current or future cash payments (or outlays) into an equivalent present value. Because tables, hand calculators, and computers are available that give the appropriate conversion factors for various rates of interest, the calculations involved are relatively simple.

The net present value method is a direct application of the present value concept. Its computation requires the following steps:

1 Choose an appropriate rate of discount.
2 Compute the present value of the cash proceeds expected from the investment.
3 Compute the present value of the cash outlays required by the investment.
4 Add all the present value equivalents to obtain the net present value.

The sum of the present values of the proceeds minus the present value of the outlays is the net present value of the investment. The recommended "accept or reject" criterion is to accept all independent investments whose net present value is greater than or equal to zero and to reject all investments whose net present value is less than zero.

With zero taxes, the net present value of an investment may be described as the maximum amount a firm could pay for the opportunity of making the investment without being financially worse off. If no such payment must be made, the expected net present value is an unrealized capital gain from the investment, over and above the cost of the investment used in the calculation. The capital gain will be realized if the expected cash proceeds materialize.

The following example illustrates the basic computations for discounting cash flows—that is, adjusting future cash flows for the time value of money, using the net present value method.

Assume that there is an investment opportunity with the cash flows given in Table 1.

Table 1. An investment's cash flows

	Period		
	0	*1*	*2*
Cash flow	–$12,337	$10,000	$5,000

We want first to compute the net present value of this investment using 0.10 as the discount rate. The present value of $1 due zero periods from now discounted at any interest rate is 1.000. The present value of $1 due one period from now discounted at 0.10 is 0.9091 or $(1.10)^{-1}$. The present value of $1 due two periods from now discounted at 0.10 is 0.8264 or $(1.10)^{-2}$.

The net present value of the investment is the algebraic sum of the three present values of the cash flows (Table 2).

The net present value is positive, indicating that the investment is acceptable. Any investment with a net present value equal to or greater than zero is acceptable using this single criterion. Since the net present value is $886, the firm could pay an amount of $886 in excess of the cost of $12,337 and still break even economically by undertaking the investment. The net present value calculation is a reliable method for evaluating investments.

Internal Rate of Return

Many different terms are used to describe the internal rate of return concept. Among these terms are: yield, interest rate of return, rate of return, return on investment, present value return on investment, discounted cash flow, investor's method, time-adjusted rate of return, and marginal efficiency of capital. IRR and internal rate of return may be used interchangeably.

The internal rate of return method utilizes present value concepts. The procedure is to find a rate of discount that will make the present value of the cash proceeds expected from an investment equal to the present value of the cash outlays required by the investment. Such a rate of discount may be found by trial and error. For example, with a conventional investment, if we know the cash proceeds and the cash outlays in each future year, we can start with any rate of discount and find for that rate the present value of the cash proceeds and the present value of the outlays. If the net present value of the cash flows is positive, then using some higher rate of discount would make them equal. By a process of trial and error, an approximately correct rate of discount can be determined. This rate of discount is referred to as the internal rate of return of the investment, or its IRR.

The IRR method is commonly used in security markets in evaluating bonds and other debt instruments. The yield to maturity of a bond is the rate of discount that makes the present value of the payments promised to the bondholder equal to the market price of the bond. The yield to maturity on a $1,000 bond having a coupon rate of 10% will be equal to 10% only if the current market value of the bond is $1,000. If the current market value is greater than $1,000, the IRR to maturity will be something less than the coupon rate; if the current market value is less than $1,000, the IRR will be greater than the coupon rate.

The internal rate of return may also be described as the rate of growth of an investment. This is more easily seen for an investment with one present outlay and one future benefit. For example, assume that an investment with an outlay of $1,000 today will return $1,331 three years from now.

Table 3 shows a 0.10 internal rate of return, and it is also a 0.10 growth rate per year.

The internal rate of return of a conventional investment represents the highest rate of interest an investor could afford to pay, without losing money, if all

Table 2. Present value calculations

	Period		
	(1)	*(2)*	*(3)*
	Cash flow	Present value factor	Present value
Period			(col. 1 × col. 2)
0	–$12,337	1.0000	–$12,337
1	10,000	0.9091	9,091
2	5,000	0.8264	4,132
	Net present value =		**$886**

"**John W. Kluge is the only 90-year old I know that invests with a 30-year time horizon.**" Kenneth D. Moeks

  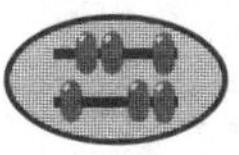 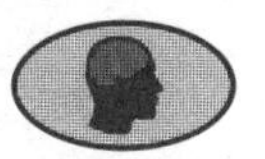  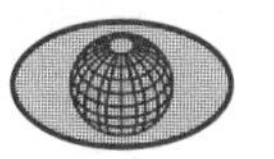   

the funds to finance the investment were borrowed and the loan (principal and accrued interest) was repaid by application of the cash proceeds from the investment as they were earned.

We shall illustrate the internal rate of return calculation using the example of the previous section where the investment had a net present value of $886 using 0.10 as the discount rate.

We want to find the rate of discount that causes the sum of the present values of the cash flows to be equal to zero. Assume that our first choice (an arbitrary guess) is 0.10. In the preceding situation, we found that the net present value using 0.10 is a positive $886. We want to change the discount rate so that the present value is zero. Since the cash flows are conventional (negative followed by positive), to decrease the present value of the future cash flows we should increase the rate of discount (thus causing the present value of the future cash flows that are positive to be smaller).

Table 3. Cash flow

Beginning-of-Time period	Growth of cash investment	Growth	Growth divided by beginning-of-period flow investment
0	$1,000	$100	$100/$1,000 = 0.10
1	1,100	110	$110/$1,100 = 0.10
2	1,210	121	$121/$1,210 = 0.10
3	1,331	—	

Table 4. NPV using 0.20

		Present value	
Period	Cash flow	Factor	Present value
0	–$12,337	1.0000	–$12,337
1	10,000	0.8333	8,333
2	5,000	0.6944	3,472
	Net present value =		$532

Table 5. NVP using 0.16

		Present value	
Period	Cash flow	Factor	Present value
0	–$12,337	1.0000	–$12,337
1	10,000	0.8621	8,621
2	5,000	0.7432	3,716
	Net present value =		**0**

Figure 1. Net present value profile

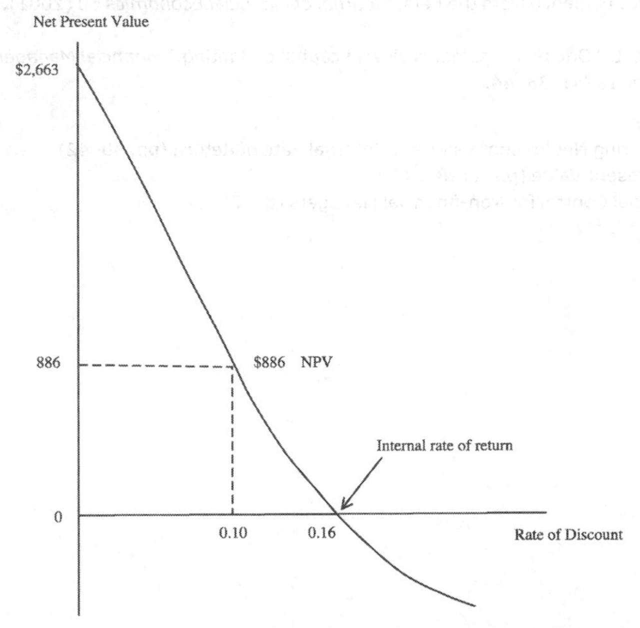

In Table 4 we try 0.20 as the rate of discount.

The net present value is negative, indicating that the 0.20 rate of discount is too large. We shall try a value between 0.10 and 0.20 for our next estimate. Assume that we try 0.16 (Table 5).

The net present value is zero using 0.16 as the rate of discount, which by definition means that 0.16 is the internal rate of return of the investment.

Although tables give only present value factors for select interest rates, calculators and computers can be used for any interest rate.

NET PRESENT VALUE PROFILE

The net present value profile is one of the more useful devices for summarizing the profitability characteristics of an investment. On the horizontal axis we measure different discount rates; on the vertical axis we measure the net present value of the investment. The net present value of the investment is plotted for all discount rates from zero to some reasonably large rate. The plot of net present values will cross the horizontal axis (have zero net present value) at the rate of discount that is called the internal rate of return of the investment.

Figure 1 shows the net present value profile for the investment discussed in the previous two sections. If we add the cash flows, assuming a zero rate of discount, we obtain

–$12,337 + $10,000 + $5,000 = $2,663

The $2,663 is the intersection of the graph with the Y axis. We know that the graph has a height of $886 at a 0.10 rate of discount and crosses the X axis at 0.16, since 0.16 is the internal rate of return of the investment. For interest rates greater than 0.16, the investment's net present value is negative.

Note that for a conventional investment (negative cash flows followed by positive cash flows), the net present value profile slopes downward to the right.

THE ROLLBACK METHOD

On a simple hand calculator that lacks a present value button, it is sometimes convenient to use a rollback method of calculation to compute the net present value of an investment. One advantage of this procedure is that the present values at different moments in time are obtained. Consider the investment in Table 6.
Assume that the discount rate is 0.10.

The first step is to place the cash flow of period 3 ($1,100) in the calculator and divide by 1.10 to obtain $1,000, the value at

"If you dislike change, you're going to dislike irrelevance even more." General Eric Shineski

Table 6. The rollback example

Time	Cash flow
1	–$7,000
1	5,000
2	2,300
3	1,100

time 2. Add $2,300 and divide the sum by 1.10 to obtain $3,000, the value at time 1. Add $5,000 and divide by 1.10 to obtain $7,273, the value of time 0. Subtract $7,000 to obtain the net present value of $273.

CONCLUSION

There are many different ways of evaluating investments. In some situations, several of the methods will lead to identical decisions. We shall consistently recommend the net present value method as the primary means of evaluating investments.

The net present value method ensures that future cash flows are brought back to a common moment in time called time 0. For each future cash flow, a present value equivalent is found. These present value equivalents are summed to obtain a net present value. If the net present value is positive, the investment is acceptable.

The transformation of future flows back to the present is accomplished using the mathematical relationship $(1 + r)^{-n}$, which we shall call the present value factor for r rate of interest and n time periods.

In cases of uncertainty, additional complexities must be considered, but the basic framework of analysis will remain a discounted present value method.

A Stanford Research Institute publication (1966) stated the situation well (p. 3): "The growth in corporate long range planning has intensified interest in corporate objectives, and has created a critical need to evaluate the financial impact of alternative courses of action."

Table 7. Financial Analysis for the chemical company

	NPV (0.15)	*IRR*
Most probable outcome	$80,000,0000	0.38
A 20% decrease in expected volume	50,000,0000	0.30
A 10% decrease in gross margin	70,000,0000	0.35
A 20% decrease in volume and10% decrease in gross margin	44,000,0000	0.20

CASE STUDY

A chemical company had sales of $14 billion and net earnings of $380 million in 20X1. Sales grew at 8% in the period 2001–20X1 and earnings at 10%.

Management was concerned that the firm's growth rates would fall as its product lines were maturing and the firm was finding it difficult to develop desirable investments. Management wanted the firm to grow at least 10% per year.

The firm used a 15% (after tax) hurdle rate as the required return.

The European plant was designed to manufacture a new proprietary polyethylene terephthalate (PET) that could be used, if successful, to package bottled water. A test tube quantity had been prepared but the new product had never been manufactured.

Demand for water bottles was expected to double in the next six years. The materials currently being used were neither environmentally sound nor safe. The new bottle would also have a better appearance. The average European drinks three times as much bottled water as the average resident in the United States.

The economic analysis presented for this plant was as given in Table 7.

Question: Should the plant being considered be accepted?

Answer: The plant has risk (the product has never been manufactured), but the likely profits look good. Accept. For all the listed events, the outcomes are acceptable.

▸▸ MORE INFO

Books:

Bierman, Harold. *Implementation of Capital Budgeting Techniques*. Financial Management Survey & Synthesis Series, FMA, Tampa, FL, 1986.

Bierman, Harold, Jr, and Seymour Smidt. *The Capital Budgeting Decision*. 9th ed. New York: Routledge, 2007.

Bierman, Harold, Jr, and Seymour Smidt. *Advanced Capital Budgeting*. New York: Routledge, 2007.

Stanford Research Institute. *Financial Management in Transition*. Menlo Park, CA, 1966.

Articles:

Graham, John R., and Campbell R. Harvey. "The theory and practice of corporate finance: Evidence from the field." *Journal of Financial Economics* 60 (2001): 187–243.

Hastie, K. L. "One businessman's view of capital budgeting." *Financial Management* 3 (Winter 1974): 36–44.

See Also:

★ Comparing Net Present Value and Internal Rate of Return (pp. 40–42)

Net Present Value (pp. 1118–1119)

Financial Control for Non-financial Managers (p. 1257)

"Don't say yes until I finish talking." Darryl Zanuck

  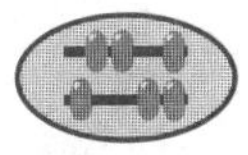 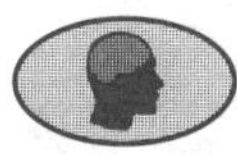  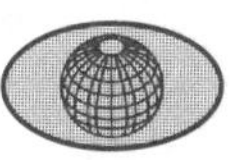   

Capital Structure: Implications by John C. Groth

EXECUTIVE SUMMARY

- Reducing the weighted cost of capital increases the net economic returns, and adds to company value.
- Place the company in a position that it can choose what it wants to do, rather than have circumstances force it to take a course of action.
- The use of too little debt (L) results in a lower stock price, and too much debt (M) also lowers the stock price.
- The more uncertain an environment, the greater the importance of the choice of and the strategy for managing capital structure.
- If a company's business risk is very sensitive to economic cycles, a company should manage its debt/equity (D/E) ratio across the cycle.
- Knowledge of capital structure theory and practice is important in stock repurchase programs, mergers and acquisitions, divestitures, leveraged buyouts, and strategies aimed at defeating takeover.

INTRODUCTION

A tax environment that allows for the deduction of interest charges, but not the deduction of dividends, results in an optimal capital structure for a company. The optimal structure results in a lower weighted cost of capital (WCOC) for reasons examined in the article, Capital Structure: Perspectives on pages (pp. 31–34). This article examines the implications of capital structure, and some of the key factors that influence capital structure.

KEY IMPLICATION: WCOC AND VALUE

Recognizing the behavior of the WCOC when there are changes in the D/E ratio, we now review how the correct capital structure ultimately adds benefits in terms of economic margins and resultant value.

Figure 1 illustrates the origin of value, and the significance of lowering the WCOC that results from selecting the optimal D/E ratio for a company. Recall that value arises from earning a net economic return that exceeds the cost of capital. For example, the net present value of a project represents the dollar value of having earned economic returns in excess of the cost of capital while the capital is in a project.

In Figure 1, with no debt the economic returns are labeled NER @ D/E = 0. Moving down the WCOC curve in the diagram increases the net economic returns, with attendant increases in value. The WCOC is for projects that do not alter the business risk of the firm.

Figure 2 graphically illustrates the impact of capital structure on stock price, keeping in mind that as we go from no debt to an increasing D/E we are reducing the number of shares. The use of too little debt (L) results in a lower stock price, and too much debt (M) also lowers the stock price.

Moving from L to the optimal level is quite easy. Borrow money and buy back some shares. Moving from M back to the optimal level is, in theory, equally easy, but in practice may face challenges depending on market conditions. Capital structure strategy is discussed in the article, Capital Structure: A Strategy that Makes Sense (pp. 526–530)

Figure 1. WCOC and net economic returns as D/E ratio varies

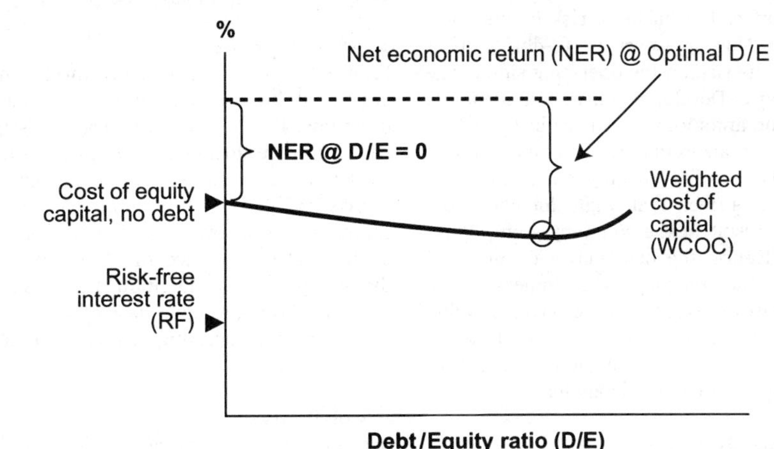

Figure 2. Capital structure and stock price

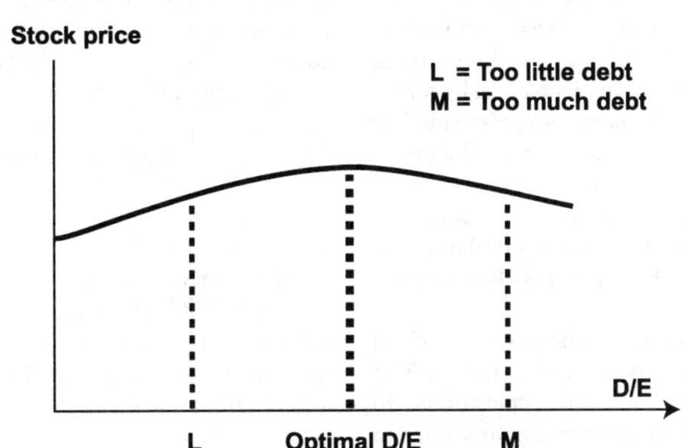

The Core Implication

Reducing the weighted cost of capital increases the net economic returns, and adds to company value. Remember that the relationship between WCOC and value is non-linear, making the choice and management of D/E particularly important.[1]

OTHER IMPLICATIONS

Capital structure has numerous additional implications, including the following.

Business Risk Change and Capital Structure

- Recall that business risk is the risk associated with the asset side and operations of the company. The greater the business risk of the company, the higher the cost of equity, and the lower the optimal debt/equity ratio. Changes in business risk stem from one or more of the following:
- Changes in market conditions: For example, an increase in competition, trends in consumer preferences, greater

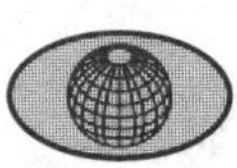

uncertainty about the costs of inputs, political risk, and other forces over which a company normally has no or little control;

- Changes in how things are done: for example, management of the operating cycle, decisions on working capital, cost control, efficiency of operations, effectiveness of product design, marketing.
- Changes in what is done: for example, the markets pursued, and the investments made to support those choices.

Investments and Optimal Structure

The interrelationships between capital structure, assets, and a dynamic environment have implications in terms of risk, value, choice, strategy, and actions. For example, if a company changes the nature or structure of its assets by investing in projects of greater risk than its current risk, and/or if external changes and trends in markets alter the business risk of the company, then the optimal capital structure changes.[2]

Effects of Financial Risk on Business Risk

In imperfect markets, excess financial risk resulting from the financing of the firm may affect the business risk of the company.[3] This crossover or feedback effect alters the risk on the operating side of the company. Developments in the economy, and the automotive industry in the fall of 2008 are an examples. A company offers a 100,000-mile warranty on its cars, but customers feel that high financial risk might result in the company going bankrupt. Hence, the high perceived financial risk of the company by customers affects purchase decisions, and the perceived value of the warranty in their purchase decision. In reality, the asset side and finance side of a company are not independent.

Cyclical Business

The choice of capital structure has an impact on alternatives, decisions, and strategy—especially across economic cycles. In a cyclical business, the patterns and magnitudes of expected cash generation from the business, or "asset side," of the company are subject to the influence of the economy, an influence over which a company has no control. In this scenario, the business risk of the company changes as it lives through the ebbs and flows in the economy.

The sensitivity of companies to a cyclical economy varies. A company may adjust its asset structure and operations in anticipation of, or in response to swings in the economy. However, other than adding liquidity in anticipation of a deteriorating economy, major changes in other assets are often costly, or not practical.[4] Some companies may also try to insulate the adverse effects of the cycle on the business risk of company with other strategies, such as in-house finance companies to support credit sales.[5]

A change in the business risk (BR) alters the optimal capital structure of the company. An increase (decrease) in BR decreases (increases) the optimal D/E. A significant sensitivity to the business cycle has important implications.[6] A company will survive (or perish), or have opportunities (or miss opportunities), according to its strategy and financial position at a point in time.

Place the company in a position that it can choose what it wants to do—rather than have circumstances force it to take a course of action.[7]

The implication is that a company that generates cash flow in a cyclical pattern should reduce its debt during periods of high cash generation, moving its D/E to the lower D/E limit of the target capital structure, consistent with the discussion in the article, Capital Structure: A Strategy that Makes Sense (pp. 526–530).

Stock Repurchase

Knowledge of capital structure theory and practice is important in stock repurchase programs. If the company does not issue new common stock—for example, issuing stock for an acquisition, or as a result of the exercise of options—the repurchase of a company's own stock is a reduction in equity that will reduce the D/E ratio of the company. To maintain the desired target D/E ratio, a repurchase of stock will require a corresponding reduction in the company's debt.

Acquisitions

A company making an acquisition should consider the implications in terms of optimal capital structure. To the extent the business risk of the target and acquiring companies differ, the optimal D/E ratios for the target and acquiring companies differ. One may adjust to the desired post-acquisition target D/E, coincident with the acquisition and attendant financing arrangements. Additional issues are important, including the following.

Independent of any operational or "synergistic effects" that may result from a merger, a pure financial merger benefit may exist. Lewellen (1971) offered astute arguments addressing this issue. Essentially, one can demonstrate that the mere combination of firms may offer financial benefit. The combined cash flows of the two companies may result in lower risks to creditors, with this reduction stemming from a co-insurance effect.

Capital structure opportunities may also exist if the target company does not have an optimal capital structure. These particular benefits differ from the pure financial rationale, and their realization is not dependent on the acquisition. If the current management of the target company has ignored the prescriptions of capital structure theory, the acquiring company may benefit by adjusting the capital structure concurrently with the acquisition. In a merger, "good" or "bad" debt capacity in the target or acquiring firms has practical implications.[8] Returning to Figure 2, we can consider two scenarios:

- Assume the target company has too little debt, shown by the D/E of L. The target company has unused good-debt capacity, and also a share price that is lower than the optimal level. The acquiring company can use this unused good-debt capacity to help finance the acquisition, and, at the same time, realize the increment in share price represented by the change from the D/E of L to the optimal D/E.
- Assume the target company has too much debt, shown by the D/E of M. Unused good-debt capacity does not exist in the target company. However, if the acquiring company "refinances" the acquisition and, in effect, moves the acquired company to the optimal D/E, the acquiring company realizes the value represented by the share-price gain that would result from the company moving from M D/E back to the optimal D/E.

Again, the gains for these scenarios have nothing to do with acquisition itself, but result from correcting the mistakes made by management in the capital structure of the target company.

Divestments

Capital structure in the divesting of a portion of the company is important. Separate from the appropriateness of the divestment, casting off the new company with the optimal D/E ratio will maximize the value realized.

Tax Issues

Assuming interest is tax-deductible, uncertainty about future tax rates and other changes in taxes do influence capital structure decisions. If one knew the effective dates of new tax rates, or thought

"I believe that banking institutions are more dangerous to our liberties than standing armies." Thomas Jefferson

  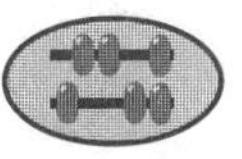 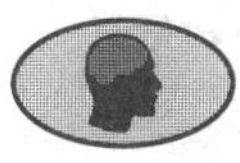  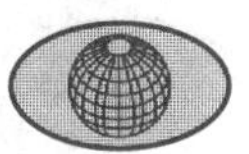  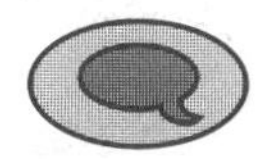 

tax rates would increase (decrease) in the future, one would consider altering the target D/E ratio. Recall that the higher the tax rate, the lower the after-tax cost of debt—if the company has sufficient pretax income to allow the interest deduction.

Implications for capital structure would exist if dividends also became deductible. If the tax-rate effect was the same for dividends or interest deductions, under some circumstances an optimal D/E would no longer exist, as debt offers no advantage over equity. If interest and dividend payments were both deductible, but the tax rate applicable to these deductions varied, an optimal D/E would remain.[9]

In many tax environments, a company may carry back or forward certain tax variables, and realize tax effects in previous or future periods. This results in timing the realization of tax benefits, and thus affects the present value of the tax treatment. In addition, tax issues can be very important in an acquisition, especially if certain tax options will expire at a point in time. In some tax environments and circumstances, an acquisition with attendant changes in capital structure might allow realization of a tax benefit, or at least preserve it for a future period.

Other Implications

Strategies aimed at defeating a potential takeover have, some assert, included exceeding the optimal amount of debt to make the company an unattractive target. Following this practice is inappropriate, and generally not aligned with shareholder interests. However, the observation reflects that a management might understand and employ capital structure theory to promote management's rather than shareholder interests.

In a leveraged buyout (LBO), equity participants often intentionally ignore the guidelines of capital structure in an attempt to maximize personal wealth. For example, in an LBO those with an equity position attempt to maximize personal return on equity. Consequently, over the shorter term, they allow the company to greatly exceed the optimal D/E ratio, as they seek to maximize the future value of equity interest, rather than a current share price. With this approach, the plan is that, over time, the company can pay down debt, and attain an optimal D/E ratio. Then those with the equity interest take the company public with a stock issue, and the pricing of the equity issue reflects the now-optimal D/E ratio.

CONCLUSION

The fact that interest is tax-deductible in many economies is an argument for the use of some debt in financing a company. The right combination of debt and equity results in a capital structure that reduces the weighted cost of capital. The lower weighted cost of capital results in a higher net economic margin—the difference between the economic return on a project and the weighted cost of capital.

The expected benefit of the tax deduction flows to shareholders, who bear the added financial risk associated with the debt. As long as shareholders view the expected value of the tax benefits as attractive compared to the added financial risk, then they welcome the use of debt.

A dynamic environment complicates decisions. Understanding core issues allows one to make/manage prudent actions in a dynamic environment. In particular, we should recognize that although a company should have a target capital structure, its management must remain sensitive to internal changes as well as changes in the markets and economies, and pursue a strategy that "makes sense." For example, if a company alters its business risk, it should adjust its debt/equity ratio. Similarly, if management perceives greater/less risk in the external environment, it should decrease/increase the debt/equity ratio.

In the end, we see the need for a keen awareness of circumstance and future possibility, coupled with an understanding of fundamental concepts better equip us to make judgments—and then take actions that add value.

➧➧ MAKING IT HAPPEN

The implications of capital structure theory are many. We have shared some of the most important. In summary:

- Recognize that changes in what you do, and how you do it (markets pursued, capital investments) influence the capital structure decision, and the management of capital structure.
- Changing the business risk of a company changes its optimal capital structure.
- Changing the capital structure of a company will change its risk, and its value.
- Reducing unnecessary business risk (see "Risk: Perspectives and Common Sense Rules for Survival") allows one to derive greater benefits from capital structure since one will enjoy a higher optimal debt/equity ratio.
- The interrelationships between capital structure, assets, and a dynamic environment have implications in terms of risk, value, choice, strategy, and actions.
- The nature of liabilities in terms of maturity, variable versus fixed interest rate, principal repayment schedules, restrictive covenant of debt, etc., influence the optimal capital structure.
- Reduce uncertainty in investors' minds by adopting and disclosing an optimal target D/E ratio. Provide a simple explanation of the logic for the company's target D/E ratio, and the strategy the company will follow. The article, "Capital Structure: A Strategy That Makes Sense," focuses on issues in capital structure, and strategy.
- If a company's business risk is very sensitive to economic cycles, a company should manage and adjust its D/E across the cycle. Reducing the D/E ratio during periods of robust economic activity and high cash generation restores debt capacity to sustain and support the pursuit of opportunities during downturns in the economy.

➧➧ MORE INFO

Articles:

Israel, Ronen. "Capital structure and the market for corporate control: The defensive role of debt financing." *Journal of Finance* 46 (1991): 1391–1409.

Lewellen, W. G. "A pure financial rationale for the conglomerate merger." *Journal of Finance* 26 (1971): 521–37.

Prezas, Alexandros P. "Effects of debt on the degrees of operating and financial leverage." *Financial Management* 16:2 (1987): 39–44.

Prezas, Alexandros P. "Interactions of the firm's real and financial decisions." *Applied Economics* 20 (1988): 551–560.

Website:

Basic Modigliani–Miller theorem: en.wikipedia.org/wiki/Modigliani-Miller_theorem

"Wealth consists not in having great possessions, but in having few wants."
Epicurus, 341–270 BC, ancient Greek philosopher

  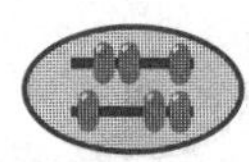   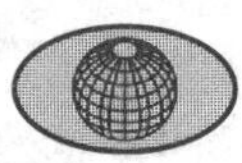   

See Also:

NOTES

1 As addressed in the article, Risk—Perspectives and Common Sense Rules for Survival (pp. 811–814).

2 If investing in projects with a risk different from the company's normal investment, one must be careful to adjust the cost of capital used in project evaluation.

3 For example, perfect capital markets assume no cost to bankruptcy—clearly not the case for shareholders, creditors, customers, the economy, and society.

4 A company might also seek to mitigate or hedge certain risks that influence the asset side of the company.

5 Some companies sales and operations are quite sensitive to interest rates, and the availability of credit to their customers. Some suggest one strategy (we do not): have an in-house finance company to finance sales to customers; engage in actions to offset the interest-rate risk in the finance company; and then attempt to reduce the impact on sales of economic and consumer credit conditions by offering customers cut-rate financing. Remember that an in-house finance company does not make the risk go away, but rather parks the risk in a different place. This doesn't sound like a good idea. For example, if in the business of making and selling appliances, focusing on making and selling appliances sounds like the correct strategy. If one wants to be in consumer credit or speculate on interest rates, then do that elsewhere.

6 Theorists might argue that capital markets anticipate potential changes in the economy, and recognize that some companies are more sensitive to economy-wide swings than are other companies. Consequently, some argue these "variances in business risk" across time are recognized, and already captured in the market-derived estimates of an optimal D/E and attendant WCOC.

7 See the article, Risk—Perspectives and Common Sense Rules for Survival (pp. 811–814)

8 A discussion of good and bad capacity appears in the article, Capital Structure: A Strategy that Makes Sense (pp. 526–530).

9 The issues and arguments concerning these issues are beyond the scope of this article. For example, whether a company would or would not pay a cash dividend would influence the decisions. Issues to do with control might also be an argument for debt rather than equity. For example, if a company issues equity, those with control dilute their ownership unless they invest at least proportionately in the new equity issue.

"I just made a smart deal for myself. This is America. This isn't the Soviet Union. It's the supply-and-demand of the marketplace." Michael Ovitz

  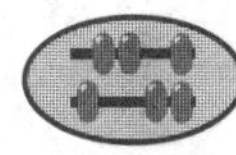 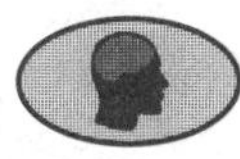  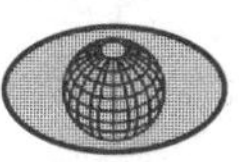   

Capital Structure: Perspectives by John C. Groth

EXECUTIVE SUMMARY

- Capital structure reflects the financing strategy and potentially influences the value of a company.
- The potential value to shareholders of capital structure depends on the tax environment.
- Understanding the logic of capital structure and the origin of potential value is of import to leaders, strategists, and managers.
- The greater the business risk, the lower the optimal debt/equity (D/E) ratio.
- Tax strategy and management should consider capital structure. The higher the expected tax rate, the more important are capital structure decisions and management.

INTRODUCTION

Capital has three forms: human, tangible, and financial. In this article, we focus on how financing choices influence the cost of financial capital and company value. Capital structure focuses on the sources of financial capital. The choice of structure affects firm value in some economies.[1]

The seminal works of Nobel laureate Franco Modigliani conceived important relationships and issues in capital structure. Subsequently, researchers have nourished the development of capital structure theory and the related literature, and they have influenced practice. Many companies follow the prescriptions of capital structure theory, and create value for stockholders and society.[2]

We do not have the "perfect" capital markets described by economists, and key factors influence the choice of capital structure. For example, investors are concerned with the potential for, and cost of, bankruptcy. If a company disappoints investors by using too little or too much debt, its stock price will suffer. Understanding exactly how the use of some debt may add to company value is essential to understanding capital structure.

First, we will clarify the meaning of capital structure. Then we will address other issues.

CAPITAL STRUCTURE

The decision on capital structure is the choice of how to finance a company. Capital structure represents the proportion of each source of financing relative to total financing. Types of financing fall into broad categories: equity, representing ownership; debt; and preferred financing. Interestingly, in some economies the concept of equity or ownership was unfamiliar until recently, as historically individuals did not enjoy the privilege of ownership.

Capital structure is about dividing up expected economic returns (not accounting returns) and risk, in exchange for providing capital. Those divisions are specific. For example, a pecking order exists amongst the different creditors. The "covenants" of debt arrangements, as well as precedent in practice and legal arrangements, address these relationships. For example, in practice "normal" trade credit is often not formalized, and the company routinely pays trade creditors.[3]

In the context of capital structure and an "ongoing enterprise," equity ownership is last in line with a claim on what others have not claimed of the returns. Equity holders also bear the risks which the creditors and preferred shareholders (if present) have not accepted. In the event of financial distress or bankruptcy, in most economies very specific rules apply to dividing up the carcass.[4]

In Figure 1, the balance sheet depicts the "assets" and the source of financing, and, consequently, the claim on the assets. For simplicity, we will focus on financing with a combination of debt and equity, ignoring preferred shares as a source of capital. In fact, many firms do not have preferred shares.

The choice of assets, how well we manage the assets, and the nature and success of our providing product/services to markets, taxes, and other factors determine the business risk of the company. The business risk influences the cost of equity capital. For a firm without debt, or an "unlevered" firm, the cost of equity equals the risk-free rate of interest plus a premium for business risk. Collectively, the business risk factors will determine the expected level and risk of cash flows that originate in the asset side of the company. These expected cash flows that come from the asset side of the company must service any debt. After debt service and the payment of taxes, the net remaining cash flows provide the expected returns to equity holders.

The higher the business risk of a company—and hence, the greater the uncertainty in cash flows from the asset side of the business—the less financial risk a company should have, and the lower the optimal D/E ratio.

Consequently, the more uncertain the environment, and the greater the sensitivity of the business side of the company to the economic environment, the more important it is that one select a capital structure with care. Companies with high sensitivity to the cyclical effects of the economy should consider a more conservative capital structure, and have a strategy to manage the structure across economic cycles.

For the purposes of discussion, Figure 1 shows four alternative financing arrangements. In financing alternative A, only equity holders provide capital. In finance

Figure 1. Alternative capital structures

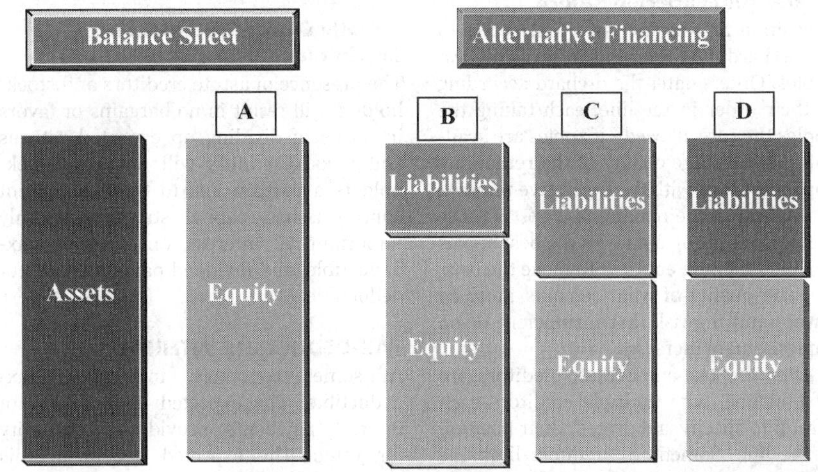

  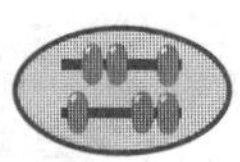   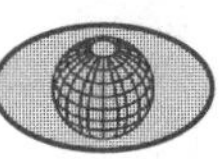   

jargon, situation A represents an unlevered firm. Each equity holder has a claim on the after-tax benefits of owning and operating the assets, as well as on the assets themselves. The proportion of total shares owned determines the claims of each. In some instances, different classes of equity exist, with the rights of each class defined accordingly.

Alternatives B and C represent different ways of financing the same assets, with C having a higher debt/equity ratio than B. Assuming that the nature of liabilities (discussed shortly) for B and C are the same, C, which has the higher debt/equity ratio, has greater financial risk. We will explain alternative D later in the chapter.

Relative Position and Risk

Capital structure does not involve sharing, but dividing and ordering. Deciding to use debt and/or preferred ownership entails dividing expected returns and risk, and ordering claims—both for "normal" times, as well as in the event of bankruptcy. Think of a line of people, an uncertain future, and expected benefits that may stem from the operation or sale of a company's assets, or benefits that might arise from the financing of the company.

A metaphor helps in understanding the issues and relationships. Imagine an apple orchard. Uncertainty exists about future crops in terms of the size, and quality, of the apples. Variance in quality means not all apples in a crop have equal value. Let's see how the ordered line works.

Governments are first in line, taking the most certain and best apples for taxes. Some taxes are ardent claims, which are due independent of the sufficiency of the crop. Equity holders bear this tax responsibility. However, tax circumstances also affect creditors and other providers of capital.

Fundamental Principle: The Division of Risk and Expected Return

A position first in line gives first access to the orchard, and the right to take the best apples. Others enter the orchard according to their order in the line, each taking the apples they are allowed—if apples are available. The average quality of the remaining apples declines with the successive removal of the best of the remaining crop, as those in line are careful and claim the best apples to which they are entitled. Remove the best, and the quality of what remains must be lower—and the risk that insufficient or no apples remain increases.

After the tax authorities, creditors are next in line, with multiple creditors each careful to specify and protect their position in the line. Sometimes creditors limit the number and/or magnitude of other credit claims in line. Preferred stockholders (if the company has any) have a position in line ahead of common stockholders, but behind creditors. A company may have different classes of stockholders, with the classes also ordered.

Equity holders are last in line, expecting to get the lower-quality (higher-risk) apples that are left, and having a claim on all that are left. Equity holders, last in line, have the most risk, but also the possibility of unlimited returns. Equity holders bear the risk that others have not accepted, and they get what is left over. Different classes of equity holders may exist, with these classes differentiated and "labeled," for example, class A. The classification scheme specifies the positions, potential rights, and claims of each class.

With distress or bankruptcy, the provisions of the various sources of financing specify the relative position and claims of each party, but with one usual modification: tax liabilities, attorneys, and related costs often take first from the carcass. After that, an ordered picking over the corpse follows.

Motivation for Using Debt

A logical question surfaces: why would equity holders allow others to go ahead of them in the line? There are two main reasons for this: garnering incremental value; and/or issues of control.

Increased Value

Potential increases in value stem from "leveraging effects" (stockholders) and tax effects (total firm value). Capital structure theory generally focuses on the value that may originate in tax effects that result from the use of debt. This article focuses on capital structure, but we will first briefly comment on the classic financial leverage reasons for using debt.

Equally Clever Creditors and Stockholders Have Implications

The presence of astute creditors and stockholders will result in no bargains or favors in terms of dividing up expected returns and risks. Creditors will not give stockholders a bargain just to be nice. Absent control issues, capital structure is only important if interest on debt is tax-deductible, and dividend payments are not deductible.

TAX-DEDUCTIBLE INTEREST

In some economies, interest is tax-deductible. The expected deductibility of interest payments provides opportunity for value. The expected benefit of this deduction flows to stockholders, which is best illustrated with an example.

Example

A company borrows money at a fixed rate of 10%. The tax rate is 30%. The company expects to have sufficient pretax income to allow the deduction of the interest before calculating taxes. The net effects are:

- Lenders expect payment of 10%, whether the company has taxable income or not.
- If the company realizes the tax deduction, the after-tax cost = 10% (1 – 0.3) = 7%.
- The expected benefit of the tax deduction goes to stockholders.
- The stockholders have increased financial risk that stems from the borrowing—and letting creditors precede them in line.
- Stockholders are astute. Increased risk increases the cost of equity capital.
- However, if the expected value of the tax savings is attractive to stockholders relative to the added risk of borrowing, stockholders are happy, and the share price increases.
- The right choice of capital structure will result in a reduction of the weighted cost of capital—even though the cost of both equity and debt capital increase with debt, as Table 1 illustrates, and we discuss below.

Importantly, the tax deduction and its benefit is an expected benefit, as the uncertain pretax income (EBIT or NOI in several economies) must be large enough to allow the interest deduction.

Tax Rate and Implications

Notice that the higher the tax rate, the greater the potential impact of the deductibility of interest on the after-tax cost of debt. For example, with the same 10% borrowing rate but a 40% tax rate, the after-tax cost is 10% (1 – 0.4) = 6%.

We take care not to confuse issues. We don't benefit from higher tax rates. However, the higher the tax rate we endure, the more important becomes the choice of capital structure.

To reiterate, the tax benefits of using debt do not alter the promised cash flows in the form of interest or principle to creditors. Any tax benefits therefore precipitate to stockholders, and that is core to understanding how capital structure can create value.[5]

Asymmetry of Effects

The use of some debt in place of some equity will lever up (down) the expected returns to stockholders. If interest is tax-deductible, the potential good or bad

"**What we obtain too cheap, we esteem too lightly; it is dearness only that gives everything its value.**"
Thomas Paine

     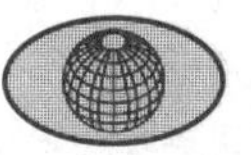   

leveraging effects are asymmetric. If the company has returns on its assets that exceed the cost of debt, a positive leveraging effect accrues to stockholders. If stockholders view these returns as attractive, given the financial risk of the added debt, the stock value increases.

If the EBIT for tax accounting is insufficient to allow the deduction of interest, stockholders must now bear the full cost of debt rather than benefit from a lower after-tax cost.[6] This shift in tax impact results in a greater and adverse leveraging effect on returns to stockholders, as equity investors must now cover the full cost of debt, rather than the after-tax cost of debt. Using the original example above, the cost of debt rises from the after-tax 7% to the full 10%. The inability to realize the interest deduction results in an asymmetric effect on expected returns to stockholders.

BEHAVIOR OF WEIGHTED COST OF CAPITAL

An example showing the behavior of the component costs of capital and the weighted cost of capital (WCOC) appears in Table 1. For simplification, we consider only equity and debt sources of capital. One might employ one or more models, or different forms of models, as well as alternative econometric procedures to estimate the costs of the components of capital for different levels of leverage.[7]

Entries reflect the raising of money from debt and equity in different proportions. The more debt that is used as a proportion of the total, the less equity (and fewer shares). Costs are after-tax costs to the company. The cost of debt represents the weighted cost of debt, reflecting the fact that first-in-line creditors have lower risk, and the borrowing cost is lower. Creditors that follow in line have greater risk, and demand a higher rate.

For all entries in this table, the company is getting the same amount of money. The values show the effects of getting this money in different proportions from debt and equity, which is the capital structure decision.

Choices of capital structure seek to increase the value of the firm. Hence, in Table 1 and all discussion in this article and the article, "Capital Structure: A Strategy That Makes Sense" (pp. 526–530), debt and equity refer to the market values of debt and equity. Hence, the D/E ratio we calculate uses the market values of the debt and equity.

Note in Table 1 that the weighted cost of capital (WCOC) at first decreases, reaching a minimum when about 30% of capital comes from debt and 70% from equity. Observe also that this decrease occurs even though the weighted cost of debt increases with the use of an increased proportion of debt capital. Recognize that successive increments of debt cost more, as successive creditors in the line of claimants demand higher expected returns to compensate for their higher risk.

With an increase in the use of debt, the cost of equity increases as well. Equity holders recognize the greater financial risk attendant with a higher D/E ratio, and demand increased expected returns.

Seemingly, the WCOC could not decline if the cost of components increased. The reason for the decline stems entirely from the expected tax-deductibility of debt, and equity holders think the value of the tax benefit is attractive compared to the added risk. As the D/E ratio increases, the amount of equity decreases because we are raising the same amount of capital everywhere in Table 1. If we raise more from debt, less comes from equity. The use of some debt rather than all equity amplifies the effect on a per-share basis, as the company needs fewer shares for the same amount of capital. The result is that with an increasing D/E the expected tax benefits increase, and these are spread over fewer shares.

In the example in Table 1, note that obtaining more than 30% of capital from debt results in an increase in the WCOC. Above 30% debt, stockholders do not think that the incremental tax benefits of more debt are attractive enough to compensate them for the incremental financial risk, and the uncertainty of realizing the tax benefits. Hence, the demanded rate of increase in the cost of equity and debt overpowers the effects on value of the expected incremental tax benefits of employing more debt.

Table 1. Calculation of weighted cost of capital (WCOC)

Source of capital	*Relative proportion*	*Cost of component*	*Weighted cost of component*	*Weighted cost of captial*
Debt	0%	5.40%	0.00%	
Equity	100%	13.00%	13.00%	
				13.00%
Debt	10%	5.40%	0.54%	
Equity	90%	13.40%	12.10%	
				12.64%
Debt	20%	6.10%	1.22%	
Equity	80%	13.90%	11.12%	
				12.34%
Debt	**30%**	6.60%	1.98%	
Equity	**70%**	14.50%	10.15%	
				12.13%
Debt	40%	7.60%	3.04%	
Equity	60%	15.50%	9.30%	
				12.34%
Debt	50%	9.00%	4.50%	
Equity	50%	17.20%	8.60%	
				13.10%

Summary

Given a particular business risk of a company, determined by the asset side of the business and how well the company employs its assets, an optimal capital structure exists—optimal, as it lowers the WCOC of the company. For example, in Table 1, using about 30% from debt and 70% from equity will result in the lowest weighted cost of capital.[8] Note in the table that the cost of components increases in a nonlinear manner as the use of debt increases. This behavior is related to several factors, including: the risk of realizing the expected tax benefit of debt; potential distress caused by excess debt, and its effects on operations as well as opportunities and investments; and possible bankruptcy with attendant loss.

OTHER ISSUES

The Nature of Liabilities and Optimal D/E

The nature of the liabilities influences the choice of capital structure. Let alternative D in Figure 1 represent the same capital structure as in alternative C. Suppose that certain characteristics of the liabilities for C and D differ. To illustrate, assume that the weighted maturity of liabilities in D is less than that in C, and/or that C represents borrowing at a fixed rate while some debt in D has a variable rate of interest.

Despite the same D/E ratio, the financial risk of D is greater than that of C because D is bearing interest-rate risk if the debt has a variable rate of interest, and D has more risk as it faces refunding of debt sooner. Less flexibility in the timing of refunding the debt is a potentially important issue, as capital market conditions vary over time. The developments and difficulty for firms of obtaining "replacement" credit in the 2008 crisis illustrate this refunding risk.

Logically, the nature of the liabilities therefore affects the optimal D/E ratio. For A, B, C, and D, the business risk is still the same. The use of liabilities with greater risk (in this scenario, maturity and interest rate risk) results in a lower optimal D/E, despite the same business risk on the asset side of the company. Thus, if the structure shown for C is optimal, the structure shown for D is incorrect. D should have a lower optimal D/E ratio than C, as the nature and structure of liabilities for D results in higher risk on the financing side of the company.

CONCLUSION

The tax deductibility of interest provides the opportunity to add to company value by employing the correct amount of debt relative to equity. The underlying relationships that cause this potential increment in value rest on the logical behavior of informed investors who agree to divide risks and expected returns. The deductibility of interest has expected economic benefits that flow to equity holders. Consequently, the use of debt is logical if interest is tax deductible and we expect to realize the benefit of that deduction. The higher the corporate tax rate we must endure, the greater the value of issuing debt.

The choice of how to finance the company, and its resulting debt/equity ratio, is the capital structure decision. Issues relating to the strategy and management of capital structure are discussed in the article, "Capital Structure: A Strategy that Makes Sense" (pp. 526–530)

▸▸ MAKING IT HAPPEN

- Remember that the expected tax deductibility of interest is the origin of any value that arises from the choice of capital structure.
- In capital structure decisions, the examination focuses on the market value of debt and equity.
- Changes in the tax rate will influence the optimal capital structure.
- The greater the business risk, the lower the optimal D/E ratio.
- The choice of capital structure will influence the cost of the individual sources of capital, and, in turn, the weighted cost of capital.
- "Real world" considerations argue for a target capital structure, and a strategy to pursue that structure. The chapter, "Capital Structure: A Strategy that Makes Sense," examines these issues and offers guidance on a strategy.

▸▸ MORE INFO

Articles:

Groth, John C., and Ronald C. Anderson. "Capital structure: Perspectives for managers." *Management Decision* 35:7 (1997): 552–561.

Miller, Merton H. "The Modigliani–Miller propositions after thirty years." *Journal of Applied Corporate Finance* 2:1 (1989): 6–18.

Website:

Weighted average cost of capital: en.wikipedia.org/wiki/Weighted_average_cost_of_capital

NOTES

1 Issues of control can influence choice of capital structure, for example, with current managers not willing to issue equity as the issuance would dilute management's "personal" control percentage, or alter the distribution of shares in float.

2 Actions that lower the cost of capital result in benefits to individuals in economies and societies. In contrast, in 2008 we have witnessed the adverse and spreading effects that result from interruptions in the availability and/or cost of capital in economies.

3 If suppliers perceive unnecessary risk or the likelihood of financial distress, suppliers may demand trade notes payable. Trade notes payable formalize trade credit, and seek to clearly identify the obligation. Hence, requiring formalization of obligation with trade notes payable clarifies as well as "perfects" the supplier's interest, and relative claimant position. This formalization can alter the risks to the suppliers of receipt of payment, both during ongoing operations as well as in the case of bankruptcy. Normally, the existence of trade notes payable on a balance sheet signals concerns by trade creditors of the financial viability of the company.

4 Multiple classes of equity may exist, with specified relative claimant positions during normal operations as well as in bankruptcy.

5 In imperfect markets with multiple periods, and with certain tax rules, the risk of promised cash flows to creditors may be reduced by the tax-deductibility of interest in previous periods or by carry-back tax effects. These issues are beyond the scope of this article.

6 In some environments, differences exist in accounting for taxes, and accounting for financial reporting.

7 The most common approaches include several different model forms based on the capital asset pricing model, multi-factor models, discounted cash flow models, risk-premium models, and other pricing models.

8 This is an approximation. Estimating the WCOC curve and finding the minimum point is not a precise science.

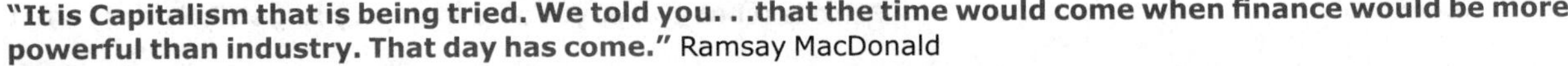

"It is Capitalism that is being tried. We told you. . .that the time would come when finance would be more powerful than industry. That day has come." Ramsay MacDonald

     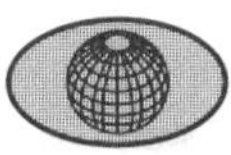   

Viewpoint: Sir Howard Davies

Mend the Balance Sheet

INTRODUCTION

Sir Howard Davies is director of the London School of Economics and Political Science. Prior to his current appointment, he was chairman of the Financial Services Authority.

He served for two years as deputy governor of the Bank of England. Prior to that, he spent three years as director general of the Confederation of British Industry. From 1987 to 1992 he was controller of the Audit Commission. From 1982 to 1987 he worked for McKinsey & Company in London, and during 1985–1986 was seconded to the Treasury as special adviser to the Chancellor of the Exchequer. He has also worked at the Treasury and the Foreign and Commonwealth Office, including two years as private secretary to the British ambassador in Paris.

THE NEW RULES OF THE GAME

This is a remarkably challenging time to be a chief financial officer (CFO). All the comfortable assumptions of the last decade or more have been overturned in a very short time; the credit crunch is rapidly rewriting the rules of the game.

For years, banks have been almost embarrassingly keen to lend. That has been particularly true in the case of lending to individuals. We have all received credit card cheques through the mail, and regular encouragements to take out larger and larger loans. As a result household debt in the United Kingdom is even higher than in the United States, as a percentage of GDP. It has been reasonably easy to secure credit for companies too, even those without a great story to tell. In a booming economy, the rising tide lifted all boats. Now all that has changed. Banks are not at all keen to lend, and the terms on which they do so have been deteriorating rapidly.

Why is that the case? Well, the simplest answer is that they need to repair their balance sheets to cope with the effects of the lending binge and the associated hangover. The losses on mortgage and other lending are massive. In its Financial Stability Report of October 2008, the Bank of England assessed the write-offs for British banks at around £130 billion. That is reflected in banks share prices, and their need to rebuild their reserves. Until that process is complete, and it may well take some time, their appetite for new exposures will be extremely limited.

While many of us may understand, intellectually, why banks are behaving in this way it does not make the consequences for companies any easier to manage. Now good credits are finding it hard to raise finance. Suddenly, cash is king, in a way it has not been in some time.

Of course, the simple point is that we are entering a recession. That is a novel experience for many. We have not experienced a downturn in the United Kingdom since the spring of 1992. The British economy enjoyed 64 consecutive quarters of growth. In fact, the economy began to pick up at exactly the same time I was appointed director general of the Confederation of British Industry. Not even I would claim a direct connection, but my point is that the last downturn was so long ago that most of those in senior management positions in British companies have little memory of how recessions affect corporate life.

Companies were slow to react. Indeed, I think this is one of the reasons why the recession took some time to hit us, but it hit us with some force in the second half of 2008. In the 1970s and 1980s, when downturns were more frequent, companies knew how to react. At the first sign of trouble a hiring freeze would be put into place, followed by a memo from the CFO saying that every order for a pencil should be signed by him personally. This time, there was a delayed action response, as people tried to pretend for a while that it wasn't really happening. Now they know that it is for real, and it is likely to be painful.

But this recession may be unlike those we used to know. There is a famous sentence at the beginning of Tolstoy's *Anna Karenina* to the effect that all happy families are happy in the same way, while all unhappy families have their own particular sadness. I suspect that this is true of the economy as well, and that each recession has its own particular characteristics. This time, the most marked feature is availability of credit. We know that, for households, the borrowing boom of the last decade is over, and that our saving rates will need to rise. Something similar will be true for companies also. For the moment, I imagine that many investment projects have been put on hold. That will not last forever, of course. But when it is time to invest again, there will be a premium on the use of retained earnings as far as possible. Just as banks will be looking for larger deposits from borrowers in the mortgage markets, and lower income multiples, so they will also be looking for companies to fund more of their investment projects themselves. This mechanism will, of course, reduce the speed of the upturn when it comes, but I fear that is an inevitable consequence of the type of recession we will see this time. Regulation will have an impact on borrowing costs too. I hope we avoid overreaction, but it is inevitable that capital requirements on banks will be tightened, which will increase the cost of borrowing. If banks are required to hold larger reserves, their ability to lend is constrained.

We can also expect some of the more imaginative and complex funding schemes, which banks and investment banks have been promoting in recent years, to be less in evidence for a while at least. The credit default swap market will certainly decline, and other derivatives markets will suffer as well. Financial regulators will be keeping a much closer eye on this kind of financial engineering than they have done in the past. It is clear that credit expanded more rapidly than the authorities foresaw, through the use of derivatives and off-balance-sheet vehicles. Regulators will try to prevent that happening in future.

SLOW ROAD TO RECOVERY

All this sounds rather pessimistic, and I fear that does reflect my state of mind at present. The latest economic data in the

"The problem with the bank managers was not that they were malevolent but that they were mediocre."
Christopher Caldwell

     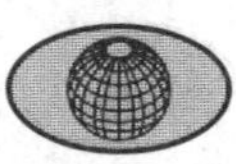   

United Kingdom is very bad, worse than the market expected. The recession is likely to be deeper than those we experienced a couple of decades ago. The recovery process may be slower too, as banks engage in defensive behavior. When you have been through a near-death experience, survival is the top priority, ahead of expanding into new business opportunities.

But there will be some upsides. I suspect that we may experience quite a lengthy period of low interest rates. Inflationary pressures are likely to be weak, which will give the Bank of England's monetary policy committee more flexibility with interest rates than it has had for some time. The commodity and oil price spike, which was boosting UK inflation, appears to be behind us. I also expect that the exchange rate will be quite weak, especially against the dollar. This will be part of the rebalancing of the British economy which we need to see. Our balance of payments has been in structural deficit for some time. While it is possible to run a trade deficit for a long period if the rest of the world is prepared to invest in your country, as has been the case in the United Kingdom for a while, it not possible to run a deficit indefinitely, without having some impact on the real exchange rate. There are already some signs that overseas investors are less ready to buy British government debt. That is depressing the pound.

The period from 1997 to 2008 when sterling was relatively high has altered the shape of the British economy, with a smaller exporting sector. My hunch, and it is no more than that, is that it will become somewhat easier to export goods and services from the United Kingdom than it has been in the recent past. So there will be an upside for some businesses. The impact on manufacturing is often discussed, but manufacturers will not be the only people to benefit. I write as the chief executive of a university with a lot of overseas students, which is in effect a service export business at the center of London. 70% of students at the LSE come from other countries. In the recent past, with the pound at two dollars and housing costs in London extravagantly high, we have been an expensive option for students from Asia and North America. At the beginning of 2009 we are already looking significantly more competitive, which is a positive development for us, and for other British universities, training companies, and the like.

Overall, though, there is no hiding the fact that these will be testing times for CFOs. In many cases, funding for 2008 was already in place, with undrawn facilities. 2009 will be tougher, and companies will need to explore alternative sources of funding wherever they can find them. Conserving resources, especially cash, will be at the top of the agenda in many companies for some time. CFOs may become rather unpopular with their colleagues in the process. But if their company survives, while others fail, that unpopularity will have been worth it.

▸▸ MORE INFO

Report:

Bank of England. "Bank of England Financial Stability Report." October 2008. Online at www.bankofengland.co.uk

"The business of banking ought to be simple. If it is hard it is wrong. The only securities which a banker, using money that he may be asked at short notice to repay, ought to touch, are those which are easily saleable and easily intelligible." Walter Bagehot

  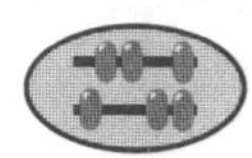   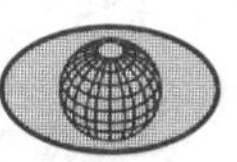   

Cash Flow Best Practice for Small and Medium-Sized Enterprises by Rita Herron Brown

EXECUTIVE SUMMARY

- Cash is the oxygen of a business: it must have cash in order to operate.
- Cash flow management entails measuring cash coming in (receivables) and cash going out (payables).
- It's not uncommon for smaller businesses to need a line of credit to bridge the gap between receivables and payables—but this facility comes at a cost.
- Many cash flow issues are due more to inattention or sloppy management than to problems with customers. Nonetheless, it's important for managers to know who they are doing business with, and customers need to know the terms of any sales transactions.

INTRODUCTION

In late summer 2008, a Californian company that helped businesses to cut their power consumption costs, BluePoint Energy, found itself in very hot water. BluePoint's CEO, Guy Archbold, had stated a year earlier that the company would soon lock down contracts to bring in more than US$50 million in revenue. However, this didn't happen. And when newspapers reported that Archbold had been suspended, they also reported that the company had lost US$14.3 million on sales of only US$1.3 million. The story ended unhappily for all involved, and there are many management lessons that could be learned from it—with the importance of cash flow management at the top of the list. A 2008 survey by Discover Financial Services showed that some 44% of small-business owners said they had experienced cash flow problems.[1] In a tough economy, that number is assuredly higher. What can a manager do?

MASTER DAY-TO-DAY FINANCIAL METRICS

Every business needs a budget that allocates income and outgoings in well-defined categories. The best budget system is based on the history of the business, i.e. a detailed listing of where money was earned and spent in the past; but, essentially, what a manager is trying to do is pin down (on at least a quarterly basis) his yearly receivables, and from whom and where, and his yearly expenditures. Then, against that budget, the manager should track business operations to see whether budget projections are turning out to be reality. It's important for a manager to account for every dollar that comes into the business and every dollar that goes out. And, in a pinch, he needs to know where the business is, against budget, *right now.*

TRACK AND FORECAST RECEIVABLES

The part of any budget that is most critical, of course, is the cash coming in—not the cash that might possibly come in (projected or booked business), but the cash for which a business has performed work, or for which it has a contract with a firm payment schedule. Yet here too, the tieback to a budget is quite important: Every manager needs to know (based on past experience as well as future plans) *when* he can reasonably expect those dollars to be in the mailbox or, better, electronically transferred to a business bank account. Thus, managers need to know on a weekly (some say daily) basis whether the to-date income projected is actually in hand. If it is, a manager can then start to disburse payments (salaries, supplier invoices, and so forth); if the business is running short of income, a manager needs to take other forms of action (as will be discussed later).

KNOW THE CUSTOMERS AND SET TERMS

It's not hard to find stories of businesses that did work for a new customer only to have the order canceled just as the product is about to be shipped. Worse still is the customer who takes delivery and pays with a check without having enough cash in the bank to cover it. On any substantial customer order, it's not improper to ask for references (which must be checked!)—and, on any order, it's not unusual to state before beginning the work how the business expects to be paid and when. Does a customer pay on completion of work? If the customer takes 30 days or more to pay, are there any penalties? What if a customer pays immediately or within a week: Is there a discount? Is the amount due the same if the bill is paid with cash rather than a credit card, or in installments? Knowing the customer—and making sure that each customer knows the terms of any business transaction—is key to cash flow management.

BILL PROMPTLY AND OFFER DISCOUNTS

Many businesses, of course, do the work and bill later. Amazingly, many businesses are lax when it comes to cutting the invoice, and often this is because it's viewed as too much work to take time to raise invoices when there's "real" work to be done. Nonsense. The quicker a business bills for completed work (no matter what the terms of payment are), the quicker that business can expect cash to show on the balance sheet. That's why many businesses offer incentives to customers to pay earlier. Incentives can be as high as 3%, although a manager needs to decide the discount rate by judging how much it's worth to receive payment sooner rather than later.

DON'T LET CASH SIT AROUND

It's easy to allow the work in process to dominate one's attention, yet there's no excuse for allowing checks received for past work to lie in an inbox, unattended for days. But a manager doesn't have to have checks sitting on a desk to be guilty of cash flow dereliction. Even if all receivables arrive on time and are deposited in the bank promptly, many businesses allow their cash to sit in business checking accounts that often pay *zero* interest. This, too, is letting cash sit around. Depending on when a business will need the cash to pay its own bills, there are ways to put that money to work, via short-term certificates of deposit or other financial instruments that bankers can quickly explain.

TRACK AND FORECAST PAYABLES

Each time a manager pays anything, it should be logged properly via a chart of accounts that lists the category of the expense and ties it to a specific business check or direct-from-bank payment. There are many software programs that can help a small business to manage these details. Yet the most important thing is that a business has a precise plan in place for any expense that a manager can project. When a manager is surprised that "payroll ran so high this month," or complains that "energy prices are way out of line," such comments reveal that his attention to cash flow detail is lacking. If, in fact, the business is large enough that such details can't be managed by the senior

     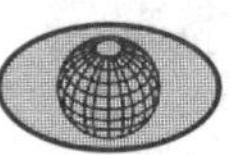   

manager, they should be delegated to someone who can report on income and outgoings—in precise detail—at a moment's notice. The list of payables should be divided into those that must be paid (required spending) and those which can be deferred or delayed (discretionary spending). Payroll and rent are required payments; new carpeting for the manager's office is discretionary.

WHEN CASH FLOW DIPS

In 1997, Francine Glick started a company, Hands2Go, that sells hand-sanitizing products. Glick says that, from day one, she was on top of the financials of her successful business. But has her company always had more cash on hand or coming in than it needed to operate? As with the vast majority of businesses, she'd be the first to say hers did not. For those times when she might need cash in a downturn, or when receivables were running late, Glick set up credit lines *before* she needed to draw on such resources. "As long as you only use it for emergencies and don't become dependent on it, a line of credit is a useful tool," she says.

The key, of course, is to use a line of credit (a company credit card is, in essence, the same thing) only when a manager can, with certainty, pinpoint when the business will receive income that can be used to pay down that credit line. Otherwise, one is borrowing blindly or on faith; either way, that's not good business. One more point: Many a small business has borrowed liberally when facing a cash flow dip, received income in due course, and then failed to pay down its debt. Cash that comes from a line of credit should be considered as receivables that have already been spent. Keeping credit line balances close to zero will mean that a business has full access to dollars it may critically need during even tougher times to come.

CASE STUDY

Omni Graphics Printing & Copying

Jim Hahn runs Omni Graphics Printing & Copying in Kentucky, a small firm that handles all kinds of printing jobs—from business cards to publishing booklets such as annual reports for sports teams. In business since the mid-1980s, Hahn's operation increased its year-on-year revenues by 3–5% without the need to market extensively. His five-man business serves both walk-in customers and large business-to-business clientele. Word of mouth sustained his business growth; and, as his business grew, he added printing equipment and employees to boost his productivity and profits.

Yet, by the end of 2008, Hahn could sense that something was wrong. As the American economy started to tank, Hahn could feel that his revenue was sliding and that his bills and payroll were starting to exceed income. But he didn't know exactly what was happening. That's because Hahn did not really use a budget or cash flow tracking. "For years, I didn't need to worry about such things," he says. "Revenues always handily exceeded expenses."

The economic downturn has actually helped to make Hahn an even better businessman. "Now, I have a budget that pins down all my expenses; I've even listed how much my advertisement in the local phone book costs me. More than that, I have identified where 80% of my income has been coming from, so I know who my best customers have been, their industries, and thus, the probable source for potential future income."

Hahn's cash flow management is now a daily activity. First, Hahn has quadrupled the amount of time he is spending on marketing; he now personally checks on his top customers and is attending group business luncheons and making dozens of cold calls to attract customers with a profile that matches those of his best customers in the past. Second, on payables, Hahn has been reducing expenses by tracking every dollar that flows out of his business. He has found that employees have been flexible in temporarily reducing work hours and salaries, that he doesn't need to stock as much paper and other supplies, that his expensive advertisement in the local phone book doesn't have the return on investment that he thought, that every large equipment purchase planned for the next year can be deferred, and that numerous other expenses—once deemed essential, such as four telephone lines—can be cut back. Third, Hahn is documenting his case to establish a business line of credit at his bank, so as to be ready to handle downturns in the future.

Hahn admits that this new attention to cash flow management has not been easy. Nevertheless, although these practices were implemented during harsh business times and have boosted his chances of sustaining his business for another 20 years, the exercise in cash flow management has taught him an enormous lesson: "If I can find ways to eke out a profit using these techniques in tough times, imagine how much more profitable my business can be if I manage exactly the same way when the good times return."

▶▶ MAKING IT HAPPEN

- Create systems for budgeting, receivables, and payables to establish how healthy the business is in a financial sense. Create a cash flow statement.
- Don't perform work for customers that can't be relied on to pay promptly. Share with all customers the terms of payment, including any incentives and penalties.
- Keep a close eye on both payments the business will be required to make and payments that could be delayed or deferred because they are not essential to current business operations.
- When the business is cash negative, don't panic. As long as the business has predictable, reliable income from customers in the near future, a manager can access lines of credit—if he has been wise enough to establish those before they become a critical need. And when income arrives, such short-term debt should be paid down immediately.

"One of the symptoms of an approaching nervous breakdown is the belief that one's work is terribly important." Bertrand Russell

     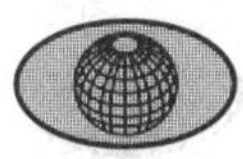   

►► MORE INFO

Books:

Forsyth, Patrick, and Frances Kay. *Tough Tactics for Tough Times: How to Maintain Business Success in Difficult Economic Conditions.* Philadelphia, PA: Kogan Page, 2009.

Jordan, Caroline Grimm. *Stop the Cash Flow Roller Coaster, I Want to Get Off! What Every Small Business Owner Should Know About Cash Flow. . .But Most Don't.* Lincoln, NE: iUniverse, 2007.

Articles:

Bernabucci, Bob. "Improving your cash flow problems." *Entrepreneur.com* (August 2, 2005). Online at: www.entrepreneur.com/money/moneymanagement/financialanalysis/article79084.html

Campbell, Philip. "The 10 rules of cash flow 101." *About.com Small Business Information*. Online at: sbinformation.about.com/cs/accounting/a/uccashflow.htm

Glick, Francine. "Get your hands around cash flow." *Open Forum* (September 18, 2007). Online at: www.openforum.com:80/management/article_getyourhands.html

ScotiaBank. "A blueprint for cash-flow success." *Get Growing for Business*. Online at: www.getgrowingforbusiness.com/mylibrary-business/featured-articles-details.asp?article_id=161

Websites:

About.com Small Business Resource Center: smallbusiness.specials.about.com

Business Owner's Toolkit, "Managing your cash flow": www.toolkit.com/small_business_guide/sbg.aspx?nid=P06_4001

Inc., the daily resource for entrepreneurs, "Cash management basics": www.inc.com/guides/start_biz/20675.html

See Also:

★ Best-Practice Working Capital Management: Techniques for Optimizing Inventories, Receivables, and Payables (pp. 16–19)

★ How to Better Manage Your Financial Supply Chain (pp. 57–59)

★ Navigating a Liquidity Crisis Effectively (pp. 86–88)

✔ Building an Electronic Invoicing System (p. 973)

✔ Identifying Weak Points in Your Liquidity (p. 868)

✔ Invoicing and Credit Control for Small and Medium-Sized Enterprises (p. 993)

✔ Managing Working Capital 872

✔ Understanding and Using the Cash Conversion Cycle (p. 888)

Cashflow Reengineering: How to Optimize the Cashflow Timeline and Improve Financial Efficiency (p. 1234)

NOTES

1 "Small business economic confidence continues to slide. 2 in 3 small business owners rate economy as poor; 3 in 4 see it getting worse." Discover Financial Services Small Business Watch, November 2008: www.discovercard.com/business/watch/2008/november.html

"I have enough money to last me the rest of my life, unless I buy something." Jackie Mason

     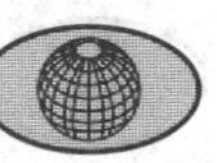   

Comparing Net Present Value and Internal Rate of Return by Harold Bierman, Jr

EXECUTIVE SUMMARY

- Net present value (NPV) and internal rate of return (IRR) are two very practical discounted cash flow (DCF) calculations used for making capital budgeting decisions.
- NPV and IRR lead to the same decisions with investments that are independent.
- With mutually exclusive investments, the NPV method is easier to use and more reliable.

INTRODUCTION

To this point neither of the two discounted cash flow procedures for evaluating an investment is obviously incorrect. In many situations, the internal rate of return (IRR) procedure will lead to the same decision as the net present value (NPV) procedure, but there are also times when the IRR may lead to different decisions from those obtained by using the net present value procedure. When the two methods lead to different decisions, the net present value method tends to give better decisions.

It is sometimes possible to use the IRR method in such a way that it gives the same results as the NPV method. For this to occur, it is necessary that the rate of discount at which it is appropriate to discount future cash proceeds be the same for all future years. If the appropriate rate of interest varies from year to year, then the two procedures may not give identical answers.

It is easy to use the NPV method correctly. It is much more difficult to use the IRR method correctly.

ACCEPT OR REJECT DECISIONS

Frequently, the investment decision to be made is whether to accept or reject a project where the cash flows of the project do not affect the cash flows of other projects. We speak of this type of investment as being an independent investment. With the IRR procedure, the recommendation with conventional cash flows is to accept an independent investment if its IRR is greater than some minimum acceptable rate of discount. If the cash flow corresponding to the investment consists of one or more periods of cash outlays followed only by periods of cash proceeds, this method will give the same accept or reject decisions as the NPV method, using the same discount rate. Because most independent investments have cash flow patterns that meet the specifications described, it is fair to say that in practice, the IRR and NPV methods tend to give the same accept or reject recommendations for independent investments.

MUTUALLY EXCLUSIVE INVESTMENT

If undertaking any one of a set of investments will change the profitability of the other investments, the investments are substitutes. An extreme case of substitution exists if undertaking one of the investments completely eliminates the expected proceeds of the other investments. Such investments are said to be mutually exclusive.

Frequently, a company will have two or more investments, any one of which would be acceptable, but because the investments are mutually exclusive, only one can be accepted. Mutually exclusive investment alternatives are common in industry. The situation frequently occurs in connection with the engineering design of a new installation. In the process of designing such an installation, the engineers are typically faced at a great many points with alternatives that are mutually exclusive. Thus, a measure of investment worth that does not lead to correct mutually exclusive choices will be seriously deficient.

INCREMENTAL BENEFITS: THE SCALE PROBLEM

The IRR method's recommendations for mutually exclusive investments are less reliable than are those that result from the application of the NPV method because the former fail to consider the size of the investment. Let us assume that we must choose one of the following investments for a company whose discount rate is 10%: Investment A requires an outlay of $10,000 this year and has cash proceeds of $12,000 next year; investment B requires an outlay of $15,000 this year and has cash proceeds of $17,700 next year. The IRR of A is 20%, and that of B is 18%.

A quick answer would be that A is more desirable, based on the hypothesis that the higher the IRR, the better the investment. When only the IRR of the investment is considered, something significant is left out, and that is the size of the investment. The important difference between investments B and A is that B requires an additional outlay of $5,000 and provides additional cash proceeds of $5,700. Table 1 shows that the IRR of the incremental investment is 14%, which is clearly worthwhile for a company that can obtain additional funds at 10%. The $5,000 saved by investing in A can earn $5,500 (a 10% return). This is inferior to the $5,700 earned by investing an additional $5,000 in B.

Figure 1 shows both investments. It can be seen that investment B is more desirable

Table 1. Two mutually exclusive investments, A and B

	Cash flows		
Investment	0	1	IRR (%)
A	–$10,000	$12,000	20
B	–15,000	17,700	18
Incremental (B–A)	–$5,000	+$5,700	14

Figure 1. Two mutually exclusive investments, A and B

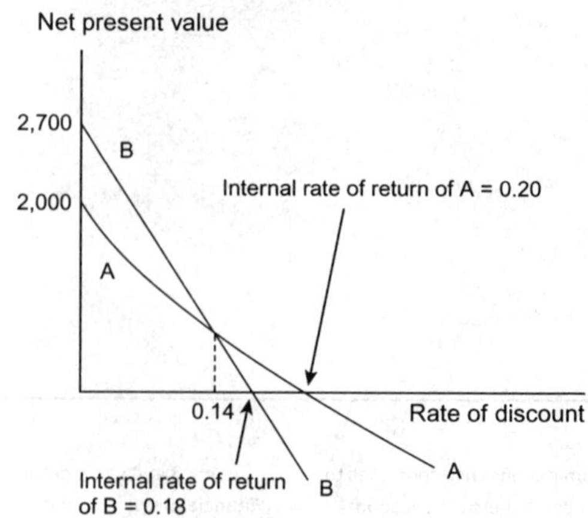

(has a higher present value) as long as the discount rate is less than 14%.

We can identify the difficulty just described as the scale or size problem that arises when the IRR method is used to evaluate mutually exclusive investments. Because the IRR is a percentage, the process of computation eliminates size; yet, size of the investment is important.

TIMING

Assume that there are two mutually exclusive investments both requiring the same initial outlay. This case seems to be different from the one we have just discussed because there is no incremental investment. Actually, the difference is superficial. Consider investments Y and Z, described in Table 2. Suppose that Y and Z are mutually exclusive investments for a company whose cost of money is 5%. The IRR of Y is 20%, whereas that of Z is 25%. If we take the present value of each investment at 5%, however, we find that the ranking is in the opposite order. The present value of Z is less than the present value of Y.

Table 2. Cash flows for two investments, Y and Z

Cash flows for period				*IRR (%)*	*NPV at 5%*
Investment	*0*	*1*	*2*		
Y	–$100.00	$20.00	$120.00	20	$27.89
Z	–100.00	100.00	31.25	25	23.58

Suppose that we attempt to make an incremental comparison, as shown in Table 3. We see that the cash flow of Y is $80.00 less in year 1 and $88.75 more than Z in year 2. As before, we can compute the IRR on the incremental cash flow. An outlay of $80.00 that returns $88.75 one year later has an IRR of 10.9%. An investment such as this would be desirable for a company whose cost of money is less than 10.9%. Again, we are really dealing with a problem of the scale of the investment, but in this case, the opportunity for the additional investment occurs one year later.

Table 3. Incremental comparison of cash flows for investments Y and Z

Period 0	0.00	Cash flows identical
Period 1	–$80.00	Cash flow of Y is less than that of Z
Period 2	$88.75	Cash flow of Y exceeds that of Z

The same result can be reached by a somewhat different route if we ask how much cash the company would have on hand at the end of the second year if it accepted investment Y or if it accepted investment Z. Both investments give some cash proceeds at the end of the first year. The value of the investment at the end of the second year will depend on what is done with cash proceeds of the first year. Assume that the cash proceeds of the first year could be reinvested to yield 5%. Then investment Y would result in a total cash accumulation by the end of the year of $141 (105% of $20 plus $120). Investment Z would result in a cash accumulation of only $136.25 (105% of $100 plus $31.25).

Figure 2 shows that investment Y is to be preferred as long as the appropriate discount rate is less than 10.9%. If the rate is in excess of 10.9, then Z is to be preferred.

One disadvantage associated with the use of the IRR method is the necessity of computing the IRR on the incremental cash proceeds in order to determine which of a pair of mutually exclusive investments is preferable. If there are more than two mutually exclusive investments, we shall have to conduct an elimination tournament among the mutually exclusive investments. Taking any pair, we compute the IRR on the incremental cash flow and attempt to decide which of the two investments is preferable. The winner of this round would then be compared in the same manner with one of the remaining investments until the grand champion investment is discovered. If there are 151 investments being considered, there will have to be 150 computations, because 150 investments would have to be eliminated.

Figure 2. Two mutually exclusive investments, Y and Z

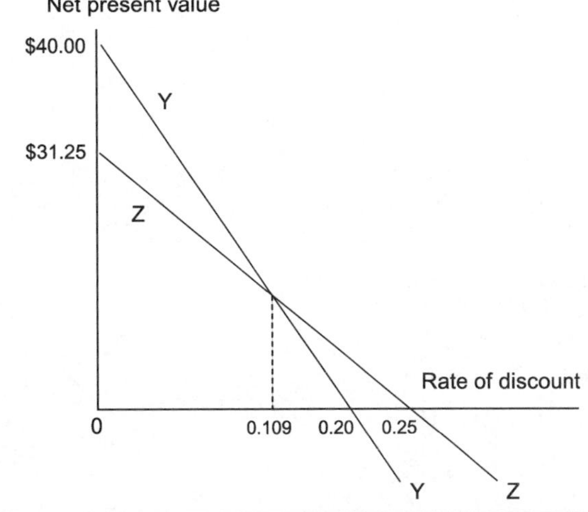

WHY IRR IS POPULAR

Managers like the IRR method, since they consider it important to know the differential between the proposed investment's IRR and the required return. This is a measure of safety that allows an evaluation of the investment's return compared to its risk. If an investment has an IRR of 0.30 when the required return is 0.12, this is a large margin that allows for error. An NPV measure does not give the same type of information to management.

CONCLUSION

An effective understanding of present value concepts is of great assistance in the understanding of a wide range of areas of business decision making. The concepts are especially important in managerial decision making, since many decisions made today affect the firm's cash flows over future time periods.

It should be stressed that I have only discussed how to take the timing of the cash flows into consideration. Risk and tax considerations must still be explained before the real-world decision maker has a tool that can be effectively applied. In addition, there may be qualitative factors that management wants to consider before accepting or rejecting an investment.

It is sometimes stated that refinements in capital budgeting techniques are a waste of effort because the basic information being used is so unreliable. It is claimed that the estimates of cash proceeds are only guesses and that to use anything except the simplest capital budget procedures is as futile as using complicated formulas or observations of past market levels to determine which way the stock market is going to move next. For example, in 1974 K. Larry Hastie published his classic

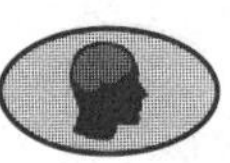

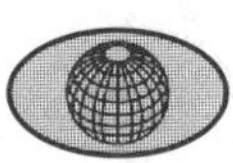

paper, "One Businessman's View of Capital Budgeting." His position is that firms should avoid excessively complex measurement techniques. He states: "Investment decision making could be improved significantly if the emphasis were placed on asking the appropriate strategic questions and providing better assumptions rather than on increasing the sophistication of measurement techniques" (1974, p. 36).

It is true that in many situations reliable estimates of cash proceeds are difficult to make. Fortunately, there are a large number of investment decisions in which cash proceeds can be predicted with a fair degree of certainty. But even with an accurate, reliable estimate of cash proceeds, the wrong decision is frequently made because incorrect methods are used in evaluating this information.

While it is not possible to make a single estimate of cash proceeds that is certain to occur, it does not follow that incorrect methods of analysis are justified. When all the calculations are completed, judgmental insights may be included in the analysis to decide whether to accept or reject a project.

CASE STUDY

A Decision in Mexico

A major Mexican steel corporation had a major decision. It could stand relatively pat (a marginal investment of $50,000,000) with its present steel making facilities and earn indefinitely (after maintenance capital expenditures) $8,000,000 per year. This is an IRR of 0.16. The pesos have been translated to dollars.

The alternative is to invest $10,000,000,000 and earn $1,500,000,000 per year indefinitely, an IRR of 0.15.

What should the corporation do if it has a cost of capital of 0.10 for steel making facilities?

The solution is:

$$\text{NPV (stand pat)} = \frac{8{,}000{,}000}{0.10} - 50{,}000{,}000$$
$$= 80{,}000{,}000 - 50{,}000{,}000$$
$$= \$30{,}000{,}000$$

$$\text{NPV (major investment)} = \frac{1{,}500{,}000{,}000}{0.10} - 10{,}000{,}000{,}000$$
$$= 15{,}000{,}000{,}000 - 10{,}000{,}000{,}000$$
$$= \$5{,}000{,}000{,}000$$

IRR says stand pat (0.16 is larger than 0.15). NPV says rebuild ($5 billion is larger than $30 million).

▸▸ MORE INFO

Books:

Bierman, Harold, Jr. *Implementation of Capital Budgeting Techniques*. Financial Management Survey & Synthesis Series, FMA, Tampa, FL, 1986.

Bierman, Harold, Jr, and Seymour Smidt. *Advanced Capital Budgeting*. New York and London: Routledge, 2007.

Bierman, Harold, Jr, and Seymour Smidt. *The Capital Budgeting Decision*. 9th ed. New York and London: Routledge, 2007.

Article:

Hastie, K. L. "One businessman's view of capital budgeting." *Financial Management* 3 (Winter 1974): 36–44.

"Harvey & Thompson, the UK's largest listed pawnbrokers, yesterday announced good trading and a record number of store openings." Anonymous

  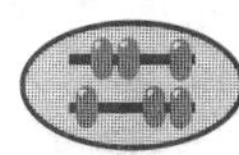   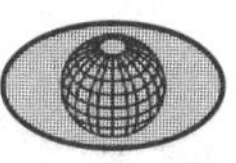   

Corporate Finance for SMEs by Terry Carroll

EXECUTIVE SUMMARY

- Corporate finance has evolved over many years to become a sophisticated specialism, for which the fees may be substantial.
- The principles are the same for SMEs (small and medium enterprises) as for any larger company.
- Often transaction-led, it is recommended that a wider full balance sheet approach be adopted because of the strategic financial significance.
- SMEs often originate as owner/proprietor businesses, and this structure can often trigger transactions such as change of ownership or disposal for tax purposes.
- By applying the same basic principles, there is no reason why similar sophistication should not be available to SMEs at affordable rates.
- Working capital is a fundamental need in a recession. In order to survive, SMEs should strategically review and simplify the business, exploring all available sources of capital.

INTRODUCTION

The term "corporate finance" is widely, and sometimes loosely, used in business. In accounting firms it typically relates to a department or function that primarily deals with:

- mergers, acquisitions, and disposals (M&A);
- raising finance (early stage through to mature businesses);
- flotations;
- management buyouts and buy-ins;
- business valuations;
- due diligence;
- succession planning and exit strategies.

These might represent the practical application of corporate finance. In theory, however, its primary role is to maximize the value of the business while minimizing the financial risks. The essence of the present article is that the practice of corporate finance has become over-simplified—potentially to the detriment of the business.

Furthermore, while corporate finance is usually a specialized department in larger accounting firms and in some smaller ones, its application in SMEs can often be quite different. Here, accessing and managing sources of working capital becomes a fundamental need, especially in a recession.

We shall propose a wider approach to corporate finance, based on asset/liability management principles and the *full balance sheet approach*, that is just as applicable to SMEs as it is to larger, more sophisticated companies.

A FULL BALANCE SHEET APPROACH

A full balance sheet approach is recommended as the underlying principle of applying corporate finance. This involves looking at each and every asset in the context of the liabilities that actually or notionally finance them. Two key measures are:

- The amount by which the profit would increase or decrease as the overall result of a 1% change in interest rates.
- The difference between the average *duration* (i.e. asset life weighted by value) of the assets and the average duration of the liabilities that fund them. The importance of this is that, if the duration of the liabilities is shorter than that of the assets and, for example, interest rates rise, there will be an additional cost to the profit and loss account that cannot be recovered by the assets.

A MORE SOPHISTICATED APPROACH TO CORPORATE FINANCE FOR SMEs

SMEs are often started and/or owned by owner/entrepreneurs. Corporate finance transactions may be precipitated by owners, their bankers, accountants, or lawyers, or by approaches from elsewhere. For example, two sets of circumstances have recently led to a flurry of transactions:

1. The British Government changed the capital gains tax (CGT) arrangements for businesses from April 6, 2008, ending taper relief. One result was that, leading up to this date, accounting and law firms were deluged by a spate of entrepreneurs seeking advice on financial restructuring or sale of their businesses to children, managers, and other interested parties so as to minimize CGT.
2. A growing number of owner/entrepreneurs are approaching retirement age and want to pass their businesses on to their children or managers.

Both of these typical situations create the need for advice and support on corporate finance, funding, and tax and legal advice.

The transactions referred to in points 1 and 2 are circumstantial. Other typical examples are refinancing the business, management buyouts and buy-ins, and M&A. These are routine corporate finance transactions, but if we return to the theory and apply it there are many more sophisticated possibilities which can be more appropriately driven by business or financial strategy, rather than circumstance. One of the less obvious times to consider these is during a recession or economic slowdown.

BUSINESS IN THREE BOXES

Entrepreneurs who have started their own business often end up trying to juggle all of what are known as the "three boxes," though such a simplified approach is entirely appropriate in a recession. The three boxes are:

- business development, which includes both sales and marketing and the development of the business itself, whether organically or by acquisition;
- operations, including delivery;
- finance and administration.

It has been possible to outsource the last of these for at least 20 years. Not every business can afford or justify the appointment of a full-time finance director, but even that function can be contracted out these days at an economic cost—creating the "virtual F.D.". By doing so, the entrepreneur is able to focus on those aspects where his or her skills and experience are usually best applied—in the first two boxes. These should go hand in glove, as together they represent the "end to end" customer-focused processes.

RECESSION, REVIEW, AND THE APPLICATION OF CORPORATE FINANCE

A recession or similar downturn is absolutely the time to do a root and branch review, "lift the drains," and spring-clean the business. Why? Two reasons: First, because you have more time to do it during a recession; and second, because having done so, you will emerge lean and mean when the economic cycle turns favorable once more.

So often, corporate finance is transaction-led. Most accountants routinely offer the corporate finance services listed at the top of this article, but (and not just in the application of theory) there are many more opportunities, both holistically and in detail, to add measurable and lasting value to the business—and better understand it—if a corporate finance transaction starts with strategy and a thorough business review.

BUSINESS AND FINANCIAL REVIEWS

Any accountancy firm worth its salt can do a financial review of sorts. This would probably focus on the profit and loss account, or tax, and how you can thereby save money. But the central focus of corporate finance is much more on the balance sheet. For example, an acquisition needs financing, either by debt or equity, or by both. Both need to be seen in the context of and integrated into the existing financial structure of the balance sheet.

A thorough financial review should ideally begin with a thorough *business* review. Every financial transaction is the consequence of a business decision. The business review starts with a review of strategy—especially the marketing strategy. It can go all the way through to the business processes and the systems that support them.

It's rather too simplistic to think that corporate finance transactions result solely from a need such as raising more working capital, financing capital expenditure, saving tax, selling or passing the business on, etc. Even if these are the circumstances that trigger a corporate finance transaction, each transaction should still be preceded by a thorough business and balance sheet review to see how it fits into the whole and ensure that the overall goal of *maximizing the return on the balance sheet at a managed level of risk* can be achieved.

CORPORATE FINANCE IN A CREDIT CRUNCH

Credit shortages and squeezes are not unusual; they typically follow a credit "bubble," where credit has grown so fast that it necessitates an economic readjustment. More importantly, the recent credit crunch has actually been a liquidity shortage. Funds have been scarce and the cost of borrowing has gone higher because the banks could not raise sufficient, or even any, longer-term funds to lend to business.

The smaller the enterprise, the harder it is to raise sufficient funds and the higher the likely cost. It's hard enough that the economic slowdown has squeezed financial performance. Being unable to find additional funds readily when they are most needed can all too often lead to business failure. It's not lack of capital but lack of cash that busts businesses. So creativity in corporate finance becomes even more important.

SO WHAT CAN SMEs DO?

Few SMEs have the opportunity to float via either an Alternative Investment Market (AIM) or full listing on the London Stock Exchange. Furthermore, the new issues market is unlikely to return to anywhere near normal before 2010. Most corporate finance transactions for SMEs involve rather less finance than might be raised through an IPO (initial public offering, or flotation).

One factor that unites all SMEs is the need to find and manage working capital. Many are wedded to the idea of unsecured debt—usually an overdraft. Some will even resort to moving banks just to get a bigger unsecured overdraft facility.

This may not be the most efficient or, especially, the cheapest means, however. The credit crunch produced some fundamental changes in the commercial and corporate banking markets (many UK bankers refer to finance for companies with turnovers of up to $1.5 million as "commercial" and above that level as "corporate"; there is no real difference in principle). First, it accelerated the transition from overdraft finance to invoice discounting. One of the key reasons for this was because in most cases banks wanted security for the debt.

This security can take many forms. The most common is assets—property, machinery, other capital assets, cash, stock, receivables, etc. The practice of taking unsecured personal guarantees has decreased, but banks may routinely ask for a statement of personal assets and liabilities. Ideally, they prefer to take a charge on personal assets, such as the owner's or director's house.

Parallel with these changes has been the move away from base rate related finance. At the worst of the credit crunch, Libor (the London Interbank Offered Rate, i.e. the rate at which banks lend each other money) diverged by up to 1.6% from base rate (usually equal to the Bank of England Base Rate as reviewed and set by the FOMC monthly), so banks preferred to use Libor as the basis for their lending rates. It also allowed them to blur the edges from one bank to another, as opposed to the common metric of the base rate.

So unsecured overdrafts became relatively dearer (up to 5% or more above base rate) and invoice discounting relatively cheaper (as low as 1.2% over base rate, although it rose as high as 2% above as Libor diverged).

THE CHEAPEST FORM OF WORKING CAPITAL

The cheapest form is that generated by the business itself, i.e. from sales. It is amazing how many SMEs approach their advisers or bankers seeking to borrow more money for working capital purposes when they could devote more time to selling and less to administration. This is the principle of working *in* the business rather than *on* the business. Sir Alan Sugar, the British entrepreneur and businessman, is not alone in referring to the concept of the "busy fool"—someone who works long hours and makes little or no profit.

OTHER FORMS OF FUNDING

Beyond sales and shorter-term borrowing, banks offer several other forms of financing, at various cost levels:

Asset-backed

- property finance;
- asset finance, including leasing, HP, etc.;
- stock finance.

Quasi-secured

- payroll finance;
- invoice discounting (not the same as factoring, but similar).

Unfortunately, as the credit crunch deepened, the availability of finance fell and the price increased. In particular, property finance became scarcer, with much lower loan-to-value (LTV) rates, as banks found they were yet again overcommitted to commercial property finance less than 20 years after the last property crash.

In summary, therefore, funding has always been available for well-run, profitable companies of any size generating regular cash flows and with assets to act as collateral. With little interbank lending taking place, resulting in shrinking wholesale funding and a liquidity squeeze, it has been no surprise that banks in general became more cautious about the scale and security of their lending.

TRANSACTION-BASED CORPORATE FINANCE

As in the wider markets, M&A activity has slowed dramatically, due both to a shortage of funds and to the greater overall perceived risk of corporates in a slowdown. In the case of both M&As and management buyouts/buy-ins, the transaction is primarily based on the track record of sales and profit generation and the capability of the business being acquired.

The more doubtful the recent and projected profit record, the more likely it is that the majority, if not all, of the funding will need to be based on assets and/or quasi-assets.

TAX, LEGAL, AND PROFESSIONAL ADVICE

Some may think that corporate finance is an industry invented by professionals to

"We face prolonged tough times." Paul Williams

generate fat fees. However, there are many pitfalls in trying to do it yourself. The finance director or owner is generally unlikely to get the best terms possible, even if they run a competitive auction.

Professional advisers, such as the accountancy firms, will usually have better and more banking and financing contacts. They should also be able to exert more leverage on the banks, as they have their whole clientele as the lever, rather than the business and assets of a single company or business.

Many people also resent paying what they regard as high or exorbitant fees, especially to lawyers. While there may be the odd less scrupulous professional adviser, in the main you will be paying for massive accumulated experience of the best and most efficient ways to source, transact, and document the finance, as well as avoiding myriad pitfalls.

While sale and purchase agreements and shareholder agreements may have a standard form at their core, each company and set of directors is different. Finally, there will be tax implications for every corporate finance transaction, whether for the organization or the individuals concerned. If you have the right advisers, there is no harm in taking a degree of responsibility on yourselves, but your advisers can save you money and help you avoid penal costs and consequences.

CONCLUSION

Corporate finance can mean different things to different people; even the banks divide it into at least three categories: commercial finance, corporate finance, and structured finance. In truth, however, it is about just one thing—how the business is financed. The key is the *whole balance sheet approach*, looking not only at the optimum mix of short- and longer-term finance, but also at the overall picture: which liability funds which asset, at an optimum balance of cost and risk.

At its best in practice, corporate finance can be a sophisticated science. This does not make it any less applicable to SMEs. While the scale and nature of transactions may often be smaller or simpler, there is no reason why similar principles and practices shouldn't be applied. Equally, for firms that have the necessary breadth of skills, the fees do not need to be exorbitant either.

▸▸ MORE INFO

See Also:

Joseph Schumpeter (p. 1192)
Financial Management for the Small Business (p. 1260)

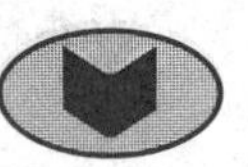
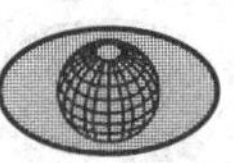

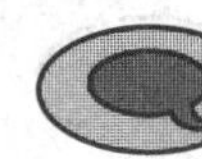

Dangers of Corporate Derivative Transactions by David C. Shimko

EXECUTIVE SUMMARY

- Derivatives can be extremely effective risk management tools when used correctly.
- Used incorrectly, derivatives can cost firms hundreds of millions of dollars and damage the hard-won reputations of firms and managers.
- Most derivative debacles could have been avoided had appropriate checklists been followed and corrective action taken.
- Successful derivative transactions require significant analysis, senior management understanding and judgment, and due skepticism regarding advice from conflicted counterparties.

OVERLOOKED RISKS

It's easy for managers to overlook risks. Financial risk managers may ignore non-financial risks. Business managers responsible for a particular line item (such as costs) may downplay risks unrelated to their particular line item. Firms often manage their risks compartmentally—for example: the treasury department for foreign exchange and interest rates; the procurement department for commodity purchases; and the insurance department for catastrophic risks.

By its nature, any derivatives transaction introduces an enterprise-wide risk, even if it has a narrow purpose. Therefore, derivative transactions must be analyzed and managed systematically to ensure consistency with corporate objectives, suitability of the transaction, and avoidance of unintended consequences of the process.

Many soft risks can be avoided by following the steps on this derivatives transaction checklist:

- Verify consistency with risk policy and corporate objectives. Has the risk policy been updated to reflect current business strategy?
- Consider the impact of potentially offsetting risks on the balance sheet.
- Examine legal and regulatory requirements to assure compliance.
- Anticipate possible future legal and regulatory changes.
- Simulate possible outcomes of the derivative transaction under many scenarios.
- Establish the correct accounting treatment.
- Ensure the accounting treatment has the desired result in all scenarios.
- Understand when the desired accounting treatment cannot be attained.
- Make sure the firm has the personnel and systems to trade, monitor, and report derivatives activity.
- Communicate objectives to all stakeholders.
- Plan communication strategies for alternative future outcomes.
- Anticipate reputational risk due to possible adverse outcomes.
- Predetermine performance measurement criteria.
- Undertake review by audit committee (some firms will have a risk management committee).
- In the absence of sufficient internal expertise, seek outside evaluation.
- Determine in advance how ongoing valuations and risk assessments will be performed.
- Provide updated performance reports referencing communicated objectives.
- Study exit strategies in the event that conditions change materially.
- Consider personal political risk to managers under different outcome scenarios.

FAILURE TO REDUCE RISK

Although a derivative usually meets its narrow goal of reducing a particular risk, it is often the case that the derivatives transaction fails to reduce corporate risk materially. Indeed, some may actually increase the overall net risk profile.

For example, many firms hedge their foreign exchange risk carefully, perhaps not realizing that foreign exchange risk may be a very small part of the overall corporate risk profile.[1] In many cases, tacit speculation occurs under the guise of hedging, particularly if the trading activity gets hedge accounting treatment.

More generally, derivative transactions supported by a particular department will likely reduce departmental risk but may not reduce the overall risk of the firm. For example, a large software firm may want to hedge its interest rate risk, without realizing that the interest rate risk pales in comparison to the business risks of software development and sales.

The only remedy for this problem is to build a firm-wide risk model, even if it is approximate in many ways, to understand the impact of a particular derivatives strategy on the firm. The firm-wide risk model should include market, credit, operational, and event risks in order to be as complete as possible. With this kind of model in place, the benefits of risk management can be more precisely measured in order to compare the benefits to the costs. The following steps may be added to the checklist above:

- Build a model of the firm that simulates all material risks.
- Overlay the proposed derivative on the firm model.
- Test cash margin requirements, credit exposures, and accounting outcomes from the model.
- Document courses of action for select scenarios.

CREATION OF NEW RISKS WITH DERIVATIVES

There is a kind of law of conservation of risk in the universe. Risk is neither created nor destroyed, merely transformed into different risks.[2] Hedging market risk creates margin risk if hedging is done on exchanges, and it creates counterparty risk if it is done over-the-counter. Hedging also creates operational risks if the hedger is ill-prepared to manage the unanticipated consequences of hedging. In this section we will describe the three major risks created by derivative transactions.

Market risk. Hedging creates incremental market risk in many different scenarios. For example, most hedgers cannot hedge their risk perfectly—a corn farmer in Vermont may hedge with Illinois corn futures, exposing the farmer to fluctuations in corn value between Vermont and Illinois. Market risk is also created when the hedger overhedges, such as when an oil producer hedges planned production from a well to find out that the well does not end up producing oil. Finally, market risk is created when the underlying risk profile of the company changes and its derivative contract does not. For example, the size of an exposure to counterparty default will generally vary with changes in market prices. If the company hedges counterparty risk but the exposure doubles, it is no longer hedged.

"Many. . .corporations use derivatives conservatively, to offset risks from fluctuating currency and interest rates. But over the years, companies. . .have run into serious financial trouble using derivatives in a more dangerous fashion—to speculate." Knowledge@Wharton

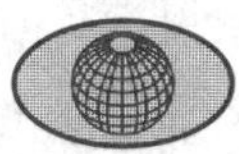

Credit risk. Hedging creates credit risk whenever a specific counterparty is involved. This may be a bank party to an OTC derivatives trade, or it may be an insurance company. A company's own credit may be impaired by hedging if hedging creates future cash margin requirements that compromise the company (see SemGroup example below).

Operational risk. The large number of soft risks may be inferred from the list above. Here we emphasize that even a firm that hedges may find it does not have the valuation, validation, monitoring, reporting, and execution skills to maintain derivative strategies. In some cases, strategies were designed poorly because of the unfamiliarity of the analysts with the risks they were modeling.[3] Particularly when a company chooses to reverse a particular strategy, it is prone to losing significant sums due to trading with sophisticated counterparties.

Several of the world's largest and most successful companies have suffered derivative disasters of one form or another. One such listing is the "Wheel of Misfortune" on a website provided by Sungard (see Table 1 and More Info section).

These debacles are documented on Sungard's website. The most important thing for the CFO is to be aware of the dangers in order to manage them. Derivatives comprise a specialized subfield of financial management requiring specialized skills. A CFO with analytic support from people experienced in derivative transactions and risk management stands a better chance of executing derivative strategies successfully than one who does not have this support.

Table 1. Disasters cited in Sungard's "Wheel of Misfortune"

	Credit risk	*Market risk*	*Operational risk*
Allied Irish Banks		•	•
Bank of Credit and Commerce International			•
Bankers Trust		•	•
Bankgesellschaft Berlin	•		
Barings		•	•
Bausch and Lomb			•
California power crisis 2000–2001	•	•	
Cendant			•
Confederation Life	•		•
Continental Illinois	•		•
Credit Lyonnais			•
Daiwa			•
First National Bank of Keystone	•		•
HIH Insurance			•
Lloyd's	•		•
Long-Term Capital Management	•	•	•
Metallgesellschaft (MG)		•	•
Morgan Grenfell		•	•
NatWest Markets			•
Orange County		•	•
Power Company of America (PCA)	•	•	
US savings and loan crisis	•	•	

FITCH RELEASE ON SEMGROUP ENERGY PARTNERS LP

Corporate CFOs often enter derivative transactions with the best of intentions, but leave them as unintended consequences develop. As an example, in 2008, SemGroup suffered significant financial distress as a result of its hedging activities.

"The downgrades and Watch Negative status reflect liquidity pressures related to the sustained elevated level of crude oil prices and SemGroup's ability to continue its marketing and storage businesses in the current price environment. Spot prices for WTI crude at Cushing, OK have increased by as much as 43% since April 1, 2008. SemGroup hedges a large percentage of its inventories and would be required to post additional margin to increase the collateral support for its hedging program. Specifically, Fitch is concerned that the company may not have sufficient available capacity from its bank facilities to meet requests for additional margin. SemGroup is a privately held midstream energy partnership focused primarily on providing gathering, transportation, processing, and marketing services for crude oil and refined products in the US Midcontinent region and Canada." (July 17, 2008)

REGRETS EXPRESSED BY CFOS WHO HAVE HEDGED WITH DERIVATIVES

To understand the dangers of corporate derivatives transactions, it is useful to share the personal experiences of CFOs who have hedged using derivatives. While there are many success stories, here are some paraphrased quotes from CFOs that have not been as successful:

"When we make money on the hedge, we are told we are doing our jobs. When we lose money on the hedge, we are responsible. Management should realize the purpose of the hedge is to reduce risk, not make money."

"Are we really hedging, or are we speculating under the guise of hedge accounting treatment?"

CASE STUDY

We consider the case of a US-based petroleum refinery seeking to reduce its net income variations with a strategy using either exchange-traded or OTC derivatives. What are the problems the refinery may have?

- It may not consider all risks in its derivatives strategy. For example, the risk of plant failure due to operational failures may end up not being factored into the analysis, causing the refinery to over-hedge.
- A transaction designed to reduce the risk surrounding crude oil purchases may actually end up increasing risk for the refinery. This happens because the margin between crude and crude products becomes more variable if costs are hedged but revenues are not.
- New risks may be introduced by hedging. If the refinery hedges on a futures exchange, it is subject to cash margin calls it may not have anticipated. If the refinery transacts on the OTC market, it can expect to take additional risk due to potential counterparty failure.
- As the refiner's risk profile changes, the derivative strategy may be discovered to be inappropriate. For example, if refinery margins shrink and become negative, it may make more sense for the refinery to stop producing rather than continuing to produce at a loss for the purpose of honoring a delivery contract, especially if the delivery requirement can be arranged elsewhere more cheaply. Clearly, the refinery must consider its entire risk profile if it seeks to manage one of its risks.

     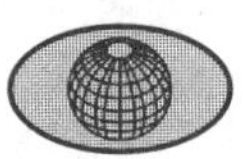   

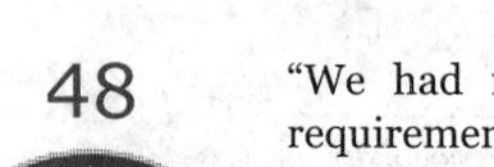

"We had no idea how bad the margin requirements could get. This trade may bankrupt us."

"Is this risk really material to our business? We spend 80% of our time hedging 20% of our risk, exactly the wrong way around."

CONCLUSION

Unfortunately, many CFOs have nowhere to turn but to their counterparties for advice. This is like asking the wolf to guard the sheep. The counterparty has a position of conflict and, even if qualified, should not advise a corporation on derivatives strategy.

Another problem CFOs have is that senior management expect them to have the skills necessary to evaluate and execute derivative transactions, even though this is a highly specialized subfield of financial management. Yet, the best source of advice is an independent adviser who is familiar with the company's risk policies and profile, and familiar with the markets and instruments under consideration for the hedge.

It is tempting to think that a financial executive need only read a textbook on derivatives to be effective, but this could not be further from the truth. In fact, unscrupulous counterparties can take advantage of executives whose knowledge is textbook-oriented.

Nothing beats practical experience. Nevertheless, there are some excellent textbooks where the financial executive should begin. These are listed in the More Info section.

▸▸ MAKING IT HAPPEN

The checklist items given earlier would surely need to be completed in an exhaustive derivatives analysis. The most important steps for minimizing derivative dangers are summarized below:

- *Risk Policy*. Risk policy must be consistent with shareholder and board preferences, and with corporate strategy generally. Risk governance must be clear; risk control must be independent; and standards for derivatives performance need to be articulated precisely in advance of the transaction.
- *Risk Measurement*. Risk must be measured in the context of the entire firm and reported in terms familiar to managers.
- *Scenario analysis*. The derivative outcomes should be analyzed under many different scenarios to ensure the firm has created a contingency plan for management of the transaction under these scenarios.
- *Suitability*. It should be determined that the type of transaction and its terms are suitable for the company, given its level of experience and expertise.
- *Performance*. Performance must be consistent with policy goals, rather than just the profit or loss of the hedge program in isolation.

▸▸ MORE INFO

Books:

Brown, Gregory W., and Donald H. Chew (eds). *Corporate Risk: Strategies and Management*. London: Risk Books, 1999.

Hull, John C. *Options, Futures and Other Derivatives*. 7th ed. Harlow, UK: Prentice Hall, 2008.

Kolb, Robert W., and James A. Overdahl. *Understanding Futures Markets*. 6th ed. Malden, MA: Blackwell, 2006.

McDonald, Robert L. *Derivatives Markets*. 2nd ed. Boston, MA: Addison-Wesley, 2005.

Smithson, Charles W. *Managing Financial Risk: A Guide to Derivative Products, Financial Engineering, and Value Maximization*. 3rd ed. New York: McGraw-Hill, 1998.

NOTES

1 Copeland, Thomas E., and Yash Joshi. "Why derivatives don't reduce foreign exchange risk." *McKinsey Quarterly* (February 1996): 66–79.

2 Shimko, David. "As if by magic." *Risk Magazine* 11:10 (1998): 45.

3 Edwards, Franklin R., and Michael S. Canter. "The collapse of Metallgesellschaft: Unhedgeable risks, poor hedging strategy, or just bad luck?" *Journal of Futures Markets* 15:3 (1995): 211–264.

"Derivatives are financial weapons of mass destruction." Warren Buffett

  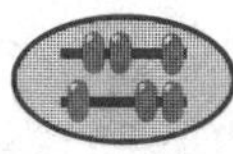   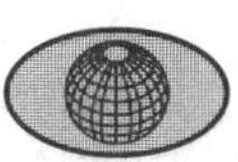   

Factoring and Invoice Discounting: Working Capital Management Options

by Irena Jindrichovska

EXECUTIVE SUMMARY

- Factoring is often understood by businesses to be invoice discounting. However, it is, in fact, the sale of receivables, whereas invoice discounting is borrowing, where receivables are used as collateral.
- In recent years, factoring has experienced substantial growth, as it has become an important source of financing for both small and medium-size enterprises (SMEs), as well as for export corporations.
- Both factoring and invoice discounting are methods that help to speed up the collection of receivables, and thus increase asset turnover and profit generation for corporate shareholders.
- Both factoring and invoice discounting directly affect the performance of corporations as they impact on working capital, and affect the performance of asset turnover and profit generation.

FACTORING

Factoring is provided by financial institutions, for example banks and individual factoring brokers. It is a form of asset-based financing, where the factor provides funding based upon the values of a borrower's accounts receivable, i.e. corporate debtors. The receivables are purchased by the factor rather than used as collateral for a loan. This means that the ownership of receivables shifts from the seller to the factor. Factoring generally includes more than just financing, and it also includes funding and collection (Booth and Cleary, 2007).

Factoring and invoice discounting in the UK is being used by more than 47,000 companies, with a total volume of €170,000 billion in 2003 (Bakker *et al.*, 2004). It is a popular method of working capital management in many countries, and is especially helpful for start-up companies, as well as small and medium-size corporations, to use their working capital more effectively.

Factoring offers some advantages for the factor over lending, and is likely to become more important in transitional and developing countries. The funding provided to the customer is explicitly linked to the value of their underlying assets (working capital), and not to the borrower's overall creditworthiness. This portfolio of assets (receivables) is being continuously managed, to ensure that the value of the underlying assets always exceeds the amount of credit.

FEATURES AND PARAMETERS OF FACTORING

Factoring can be done on both a recourse and non-recourse basis. In developed financial markets, factoring is done on a non-recourse basis. The factor does not have a claim against its client (the borrower) if the accounts default. In less-mature financial markets, recourse factoring is used, where the factor has a claim against its borrower for deficiencies of purchased receivables. Therefore, the factor would suffer a loss only if the underlying accounts are not paid, while, at the same time, the borrower cannot cover the deficiency. In recourse factoring, all the debts are at the client's risk in the event of customer failure. The factoring company is taking little risk. In these cases, one might expect that the factor would not be restrictive as to whom the company is selling the product. However, factors impose credit risks and concentration limits that restrict the funding of their clients. This is also an important aspect of risk management on the part of factors.

Factoring can be also be done on a notification and a non-notification basis. Under notification, the debtors are notified that their payables have been sold to a factor. In general, factoring with recourse does not include notification, but factoring without recourse does. (In many countries, factoring has a negative connotation, so some clients prefer factors that do not notify their debtors.)

In reality, a factor provides three linked services: financing, assuming credit risk, and a collection service. The collection service involves collecting current accounts, and the collecting of non-performing accounts. This helps to minimize losses associated with bad debts to the client.

Factors typically pay less than 100% of the face value of receivables, even though they take ownership of the whole amount. The difference between those amounts creates a reserve held by the factor. This reserve will be used to cover deficiencies in the payment of invoices.

In world trade, factorable products often flow from developing countries to developed countries. This creates opportunities for export factoring. Export factoring is the principal type of factoring in most developing and transitional countries because it is, in many cases, easier and safer to factor export receivables than domestic receivables. Obviously, in these cases, all parties to the transaction will face an exchange-rate risk, which needs to be mitigated with the help of financial institutions.

FACTORING EXAMPLE AND THE COST OF FACTORING

Factoring represents a sale of accounts receivable to a financial institution, which acts as a factor. This may be a bank, or an independent factoring broker. There are three parties to this transaction: a client company (a producer that has provided services or produced goods, and issued invoices to its debtors, who need to pay invoices to the company under certain conditions); a debtor (the company that ought to pay the invoice to the producer in due time); and a factor that facilitates the transaction through buying the invoice from the client, and finances the amount over an agreed period.

Simple Illustration

The factor purchases £100 from its client under a factoring contract. The client company (borrower) receives, from the factor, 70% of the value of the invoice minus interest and service fees, and minus a factoring commission of, say, 2%. The client receives the remaining 30% upon receiving the payment from its customer. The amount of £30 serves as a reserve amount, and is kept by the factor until the invoice is paid.

At the beginning of the transaction, the factor advances £68 and acquires ownership of the whole receivable. When the invoice is paid in 31 days, the factor sends £30 to the client on day 31. The size of the reserve depends on the perceived risk of the

"What does a Great Depression for the relatively wealthy look like? If you spend lots of your budget on 'luxuries'—especially durables—it is easy to postpone their consumption. This might cause GDP to fall more rapidly than if people were poorer." Tyler Cowen

  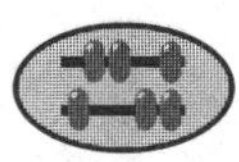   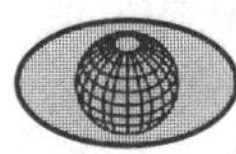   

client. There will be an additional cost, which will be the interest on the outstanding balance of receivables. The interest can be deducted at the beginning, at the same time as factoring the commission.

The client company pays a commission fee for the factoring service to the factor, as well as interest for the period of financing. The factor bears the risk of non-paying customers. The factor buys the receivable at a discount, which ranges from 0.35% to 4%. The interest for factoring is usually 1.5 to 3 percentage points above the base rate, reflecting the overall risk of the transaction, as well as current market conditions. The rates are roughly equivalent to bank overdraft rates, and can occasionally be better.

CASE STUDY

The Cost of Factoring: A Short Summary

Background: The turnover of a client company is £750,000 per year, and debtors are taking an average of 50 days to pay on commencement of the factoring agreement.

The factoring company provides the following conditions:

Factoring commission:	1.25%
Factoring interest:	7.0% pa
Average credit period:	50 days
Convention 360 days in a year	
Factoring commission cost:	
1.25% x £750,000	£9,375
Factoring interest cost:	
(£750,000 – £9,375) × 7% × 50 ÷ 360	£7,200
Total factoring costs:	£16,575

The total cost of funding over the period of 50 days is £16,575. This needs to be compared with other funding options (e.g. bank loan) for optimization. (Adapted from Factoring solutions: www.factoringsolutions.co.uk, accessed December 10, 2008.)

REGULATION OF THE INDUSTRY

Company cash flow, and its financial health, are very much affected by performance of its short-term assets. In this regard, the way factoring is arranged and managed is extremely important, as it directly affects the cash flow and financial health of a client company. Companies, therefore, need to pay close attention to choosing a good quality factor, because selecting the wrong factor can have a damaging effect on the company.

"Unfortunately, there isn't any regulation of factoring companies, and equally unfortunately, as any knowledgeable factoring insider will tell you, the industry is badly in need of regulation, as currently the factoring companies exercise far too much power, and on the occasions when they abuse that power, the poor client has no one to complain to." (*Source*: www.factoring-broker.org.uk, accessed December 10, 2008.)

Factoring is a complex, long-term agreement that could have major effects on the management and development of the client company. It is, therefore, advisable to take legal advice on the legal and financial implications of factoring.

INVOICE DISCOUNTING

Invoice discounting is another policy used by firms to speed up collection of receivables. Invoice discounting is an alternative way of drawing money against a company's receivables, i.e., issued invoices. In this case, the business retains control over the administration of receivables. It provides a cost-effective way for profitable businesses to improve their cash flow.

There are two parties to this transaction: the client company and the invoice discounter.

This service is provided by banks and financial institutions to businesses that sell products or services on credit to other businesses. It is normally available to businesses with a proven track record, and annual turnover of at least £500,000, and is usually a long-term relationship between the business and the invoice discounter.

The Mechanics of Invoice Discounting

The invoice discounter first checks the client company, its accounting, and production systems. It reviews the client's accounting system, its customers, and its overall creditworthiness, and will then agree to pay a certain percentage of its total outstanding receivables.

The client company pays a monthly fee and interest on the net amount advanced. Typical fees range from 0.2% to 0.5% of discounted receivables. These fees are less than factoring fees, because only the financing service is provided.

"For example, if the invoice discounter agrees to advance 80% of the total owing, and the total of outstanding invoices is steadily changing, then so will the amount you receive. If the outstanding debt drops month on month, you must repay 80% of the fall in debt. If the debt rises month on month, you will receive 80% of the increase." (*Source*: Adapted from Business Link, www.businesslink.gov.uk, accessed December 10, 2008.)

SHORT-TERM FINANCE AND WORKING CAPITAL MANAGEMENT

Short-term finance consists of the management of short-term assets and liabilities. Both methods—factoring and invoice discounting—reduce the cash cycle in the business, and the need to finance short-term assets of the company. The shortcomings of these methods are that if the factor is not a good-quality organization, the corporate client will suffer and have problems with cash flow. Lack of regulation in the industry may also be a problem in using factoring. Invoice discounting is less complex as the discounter provides only financing, while the company retains total control over its sales ledger.

There are also many other services provided by the financial sector that can improve the use of cash in a company, including debt factoring, invoice factoring, and asset-based lending. The topic remains the same: turn the company's unpaid

▸▸ MAKING IT HAPPEN

Factoring services in particular are provided by many companies and therefore it pays to look around for the best deal. Financial companies usually provide both factoring and invoice discounting services. Factors are usually linked with bigger banks to provide secure funding. Some examples of providers of commercial finance and asset financing are provided in the next section.

"Private equity has absolutely no reason to exist. The private equity holder has all the upside and the banks all the downside." Nassim Nicholas Taleb

     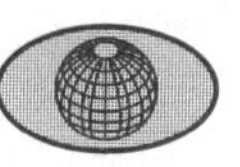 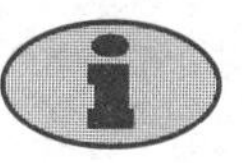  

invoices into cash that can be put to work immediately. An invoice-discounting facility grows with the volume of issued invoices. Therefore, there is no need to renegotiate funding or increase the overdraft facility to free business capacity in order to enable a quick reaction to market opportunities.

▸▸ MORE INFO

Books:

Bakker, M., L. Klapper, and G. Udell. *Financing Small and Medium-size Enterprises with Factoring: Global Growth and Its Potential in Eastern Europe*. Washington, DC: World Bank, 2004.

Booth, L., and W. S. Cleary. *Introduction to Corporate Finance*. Toronto, ON: Wiley, 2007.

Klapper, L. *The Role of Factoring for Financing Small and Medium Enterprises*. Washington, DC: World Bank, 2005.

Meckin, D. *Naked Finance: Business and Finance Pure and Simple*. London: Nicolas Brealey Publishing, 2007.

Article:

Soufani, K. "Factoring as a financing option: Evidence from the UK." Working paper, Concordia University, 2003.

Websites:

Factoring Solutions, independent factoring firm: www.factoringsolutions.co.uk

HSBC, information on factoring: www.hsbc.co.uk/1/2/business/finance-borrowing/invoice-finance

Independent Factoring Brokers Association: www.factoring-broker.org.uk

Lloyds TSB, information on factoring: www.ltsbcf.co.uk/factoring

Royal Bank of Scotland, information on factoring: www.decision-finance.co.uk/royal_bank_of_scotland_factoring.html

UK government-sponsored advice agency, Business Link: www.businesslink.gov.uk

"I want them poor and they deserve to be poor. You can't have capitalism without punishment."
Nassim Nicholas Taleb

     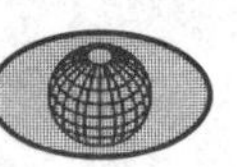 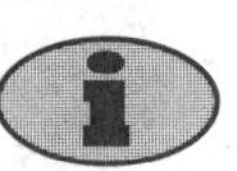  

A Holistic Approach to Business Risk Management by Terry Carroll

EXECUTIVE SUMMARY

- The events of 2008 make it unsurprising that we are preoccupied with financial risk.
- Financial risk is part of overall business risk—business risks have financial consequences.
- As well as being viewed individually, risks should be viewed holistically.
- A holistic approach to risk means looking at each risk in the context of others.
- Managing business risk can be positive and offer opportunities.
- The credit crunch is an example for all companies, not just banks.
- There is a simple, clearly defined process for managing business risks.
- Risk pervades every element of the overall business process.
- The whole organization should be engaged in the risk management process.

INTRODUCTION

After arguably the greatest credit crisis in history, it is unsurprising that lenders, borrowers, and investors alike have become preoccupied with financial risk. Its magnitude seems to have dwarfed all other business risk considerations. It can be hard to take a pragmatic view when the strictures in the financial markets may have put the corporation at risk, but the correct perspective is for all risk to be captured in a holistic framework.

Apart from the consequences of events in the financial markets, some recent risk considerations have been imposed rather than occurring naturally. Among those that were more prevalent prior to the credit crunch were the issue of corporate manslaughter and the need to comply with burgeoning health and safety regulation.

What seems sometimes to have been overlooked is that all financial risks are business risks (i.e. a risk to the business), and all business risk has financial consequences. There are those, especially in the public sector, who seem preoccupied with budgets and spending, rather than planning. The advent of business process reengineering (BPR) in the 1980s seemed to coincide with downsizing or rightsizing, as companies trimmed or even slashed their budgets.

What BPR and business planning have in common is the need to put the horse in front of the cart. Financial transactions are the consequence of business decisions. Budgets are the consequence of business planning. Cost efficiencies should only arise from BPR where the exercise is to design or redesign the organization to deliver the current strategy in the current markets and circumstances.

In summary, all risks have potential consequences for financial and business continuity. A holistic approach means looking at each risk in the context of others, and of the business and financial risk as a whole.

RISK IS A NATURAL CONSEQUENCE OF BUSINESS

Financial risk is a subset of business risk, which is a consequence of business decisions. You cannot be in business without taking risks. Whether you accept these risks or not is a function of whether your business thinking is proactive or reactive.

No one can eliminate all business or financial risk. Either you don't have a business, or the premiums you would need to pay to eliminate risk would transcend any prospect of profit.

It could be argued that in the public sector, and with the latter's growing influence in commerce (for example through public/private partnerships), risk has become an industry in itself. The public sector does not have a profit imperative. If it is decreed that risk shall be actively managed or insured against, the cost is picked up by the taxpayer. The growth of the health and safety industry in the United Kingdom has undoubtedly saddled the taxpayer with burgeoning costs. It has impacted industry in much the same way, but with less chance to pass this on to the customer.

WHAT IS BUSINESS RISK?

"Risk is a threat that a company will not achieve its corporate objectives."[1] A typical dictionary definition would be: "Risk is the possibility of suffering harm or loss." Such a definition characteristically has implicit negative connotations. Here we are talking about a more objective approach, where risk is recognized as part and parcel of enterprise.

The management of risk is fundamentally about ownership and accountability for the management and business processes, and their possible opportunities and consequences.

The process can be characterized by four simple components:

- evaluation;
- control;
- transfer;
- constructive damage limitation (insurance or hedging).

Managing risk is a continuous process, as opposed to something that you do just once. Starting from strategy, and considered throughout the organizational processes, risk is present and has potential impacts at every step of the way. The trick is in being able to see it in a positive and opportunistic way rather than in a negative light. Ideally, the whole organization should be constructively engaged and empowered in the recognition and management of risk.

LESSONS FOR COMPANIES

In the infamous 1980s Barings case, the board either was not aware of the scale of risk being created, and/or it did not have sufficient or satisfactory controls, including the separation of functions. Nor does it appear to have had a sufficient, or a holistic, view that would have considered the burgeoning risk in the context of the whole of Barings' business, which the materialization of this risk ultimately brought down.

We don't have enough information to be sure whether the boards of the US institutions had sufficient oversight over the nature and scale of the risks being created. We do, however, know that the financial authorities, and especially the Bank of England, had become increasingly concerned about the lack of control or regulation of what have been labeled "toxic assets" long before the problems became critical to the markets.

This is a clear lesson for the boards and executives of companies. Not just in relation to financial risk, but to business risk in general. We do not propose a new industry of risk management, but we do strongly recommend that risk management should be a core business function. It does not sit apart from business planning and decision-making, but it is a close cousin of audit, and may ideally be viewed as internal consultancy, informing and improving the quality of management decisions.

Similarly, in the public sector, risk management in its many guises has come

"There are not only trade unions in England, but also alliances between workers and capitalists in a particular industry for the purpose of raising prices and robbing everybody else." Vladimir Ilich Lenin

to resemble a core function that is sometimes "the tail that wags the dog." The risk management function should be woven into mainstream decision-making; it should start with, and encompass, the whole of business risk; and it should enrich and inform management rather than constrain and curtail, otherwise it misses the point.

A SIMPLE FORMULATION

Holistic business risk management starts with strategy formulation and goes right through to business and financial planning, and ultimately implementation. At every stage, the simple question is "What are the consequences of this decision?"

For some, risk management or risk review seems to be more of an afterthought. For example, prospectuses and project plans seem always to finish with a summary and evaluation of the risks. This is done with an eye to investors or stockholders, to satisfy them that management has thought of all the significant consequences of a plan or proposal. Often it amounts to little more than a rhetorical flourish: "See, we've done the risk evaluation."

It would be better if management wove risk evaluation into every stage of planning and decision-making. It should be at the heart of all high-quality management thinking, and should be seen to enrich the quality and rigor of decisions, rather than holding them back or, worse still, being a mechanical afterthought, and only when demanded or requested.

There is a simple pattern to the consideration of risks as part of business decision-making:

- determine the risk;
- analyze it;
- evaluate it;
- manage it;
- ignore it;
- insure against it;
- control it;
- improve the management and business processes that are the basis of the risk.

A WHOLE ORGANIZATION ENTERPRISE

It has been characteristic for management to be directive rather than consultative. Managing risk in a holistic way can be time-consuming, but, like success, it touches the whole enterprise. Singular decisions were taken for US institutions to drive into subprime assets. Would it have been different if the whole organization had been engaged in the decision? It is important to see managing risk as a central business need, woven throughout the fabric of the organization.

CASE STUDY

The Credit Crunch and the Irresponsible Creation of Financial Risk

The credit crunch has been a highly illustrative case study in dysfunctional risk management. What brought the financial markets to their knees was the irresponsible and inadequately controlled creation of excessive risk, with little or no consideration of the consequences.

In a climate where interest rates were historically low from 2001, and with bonus-fueled incentives to grow the balance sheet, US financial institutions identified a new group of customers. These were people at the bottom of the economic food chain, living in rented property, who were persuaded that with interest rates so low it was cheaper to buy their homes than to rent them.

As interest rates rose and fixed-rate deals matured, a growing proportion of this new army of borrowers found they could not meet the repayments. Unsophisticated, many of them simply defaulted on the payments, and some even walked away. The result was what became known as subprime assets.

The problem was compounded in at least two further ways, however. The new assets had been securitized into packages that could be sold on to fund new lending, and some had even been disaggregated into their component parts, to be sold on to other investors such as hedge funds and other investment funds. So long as the returns were good nobody complained, but as the markets unraveled investors became increasingly concerned about where their money was invested.

Many of these assets were off balance sheet, and even offshore. Often they weren't regulated. When, in August 2007, BNP Paribas found that it couldn't value three of its funds because there was no longer a sound market for these esoteric assets, the whole global financial system began to crumble.

Ultimately, the management of risk is the responsibility of the board. As the governance medium of the organization, the board approves and oversees strategy and policy. At the strategic level, some other questions and issues that arise are:

- What is risk in the context of our business organization?
- What does managing risk imply for us and our management processes?
- Where does responsibility for the management of risk lie?
- Why should we manage risk?
- What are the benefits of managing risk?
- Are we complying with legislation, good practice, standards, regulation, and sound governance?

Managing risk will always be a balance between evaluating and optimizing opportunity on the one hand, and identifying and dealing with the potential related risks on the other.

Do you need a specific department to manage risk? Might one actually create confusion within other departments? If you were establishing your organization from scratch today, would you set up a specific function called risk management? Ideally, it should be woven as an integral part into the management and business processes. The mature organization instinctively scans for, and is aware of, risk in everything it does.

SO HOW DO WE DO THIS?

World class organizations have world class management practices and processes. By all means set up a risk management function, but it should be a servant to, not a constraint on, the organization. It should be participative, engaging, and integrated with the internal audit process, in the nature of an internal consultancy.

It should be engaged end to end in the entire management processes—from strategy formulation to implementation and delivery. It should especially facilitate management, and indeed the whole enterprise, to make the consideration of risk fundamental to every business decision in a positive, objective, and contributory way, rather than as a constraint on enterprise.

Where such risk evaluation results in a decision to insure against risk, rather than manage it, this should also be the consequence of objective evaluation rather than defensiveness. Excess insurance is a brake on enterprise, and has financial consequences for the bottom line. Where it comes in the form of derivatives or hedges, it can sometimes create more rather than less risk if there is not a "total balance sheet" approach.

CONCLUSION

Risk management was born out of the insurance industry. It has become endemic in the public sector, with consequent burgeoning costs. It has had negative rather than positive results. All great entrepreneurs are risk-takers. The best either have a sound, intuitive awareness of risk

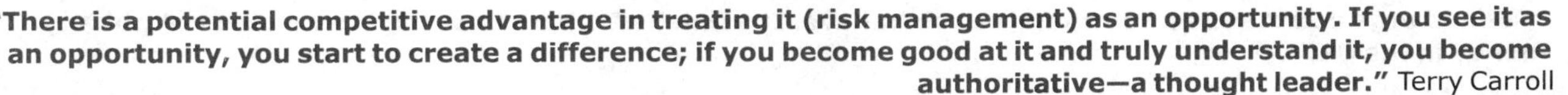

"There is a potential competitive advantage in treating it (risk management) as an opportunity. If you see it as an opportunity, you start to create a difference; if you become good at it and truly understand it, you become authoritative—a thought leader." Terry Carroll

and its balance with enterprise, or are secure enough to lead the evaluation of possible consequences, so as to enrich rather than inhibit business decisions.

Now is the time to see the management of risk as a holistic business process that is inherent in every decision. As opposed to being seen to hold back enterprise, the consideration and evaluation of risk should be seen as enriching the quality of business decisions. It is, however, sensible to capture the risk evaluation alongside the decision. You make the decision *including* the risk consequences, rather than despite them.

As well as being woven into the management and business processes, holistic risk management should embrace as much of the organization as is practicable. What-ifs, constructive challenge, and objective review should be celebrated rather than shunned. Financial transactions are the consequence of business decisions. Negative risk outcomes and their financial costs should not be a surprise, except where they arise from chance.

Insurance, whether through premiums or derivatives, should not merely be a safety net. It should be the result of mature identification, consideration, and evaluation of risk scenarios and consequent management decisions. That way, the net financial outcomes can be predicted with reasonable accuracy and consistency.

Those organizations that take a holistic, constructive, and proactive view of risk are less likely to be caught out, are more likely to succeed in the long run, and produce more predictable and manageable results. Where they engage as many of the staff as possible in the process, the by-products could well be better reputation and trust with investors, customers, and staff, and better long-term market value.

Above all, this objective, positive, holistic approach to business risk management empowers organizations, management, and individuals to grow through openness and mature evaluation, rather than feel constrained by a process that seems to sit apart from the core enterprise.

›› MORE INFO

Book:

Carroll, Terry, and Mark Webb. *The Risk Factor: How to Make Risk Management Work for You in Strategic Planning and Enterprise*. Harrogate, UK: Take That Books, 2001.

Article:

Carroll, Terry. "A risky business." *Exec* online magazine (August 2007): www.execdigital.co.uk

Website:

Association of Corporate Treasurers (ACT) risk management main page: www.treasurers.org/Risk+Management

See Also:

Peter Bernstein (p. 1154)
Mastering Risk Volume 1: Concepts (p. 1297)

NOTES

1 Harris-Jones, J., and L. Bergin. "The management of corporate risk—A framework for directors." London: Association of Corporate Treasurers, 1998.

"I would urge you to sell any sterling you might have. It's finished. I hate to say it, but I would not put any money in the UK." Jim Rogers

  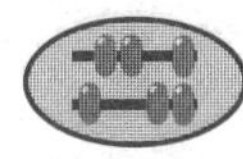 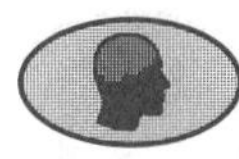  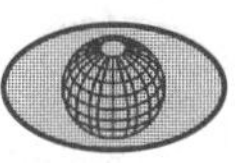   

How Taxation Impacts on Liquidity Management by Martin O'Donovan

EXECUTIVE SUMMARY

- Efficient cash and liquidity management will involve centralizing cash within a single entity, on a country, regional, or even global basis.
- The movement of cash between entities and between countries will create complex tax considerations, so that all loans and rates of interest applied must be at arm's-length pricing.
- The cash centralization is normally arranged with the group's bankers who can offer a notional pooling or a physical movement of cash.
- Interest payable on the balances arising from the cash centralization or from the overall funding structure of the group can be subject to withholding tax (WHT), which may be reduced to zero by tax treaties or may be reclaimable through a variety of mechanisms.

THE BASIS FOR TAXATION

Taxation is highly dependent on the specifics of the companies concerned and the tax jurisdictions to which they are subject. Nonetheless, there are sufficient structural similarities between countries so that background generalizations can be made, although the specific rules and tax rates vary over time and will need to be verified with local tax experts.

Tax is initially assessed on the basis of each legal entity in isolation, but various allowances exist that enable operations to be examined from a group or subgroup perspective.

The legal grouping of companies, the managerial grouping, the accounting grouping and taxation group may each be on a different basis.

Taxable profit is not calculated in the same way as accounting profit. The latter may be generated using IFRS (International Financial Reporting Standards) or local GAAP (Generally Accepted Accounting Principles) using cash accounting or some taxation specific rules.

Efficient liquidity management for an international group involves making best use of the cash resources existing or being required or generated across the group.

In order to manage the daily flows of cash across the group there are normally efficiencies to be gained by centralizing cash flows within a central entity for each country or region, or, if practical, globally. The consequent movement of cash around the group, whether buying and selling goods between companies, or lending cash backward and forward, have significant tax consequences, made complicated by the interaction of different national and international rules.

Tax is therefore a major issue in the selection of a treasury center location. Areas set up specifically to attract treasury may be located in tax environments where local taxes are low and where there is special treatment of foreign earnings. They will be located in countries with extensive tax treaties, and there will be no WHT on interest earned or paid, or on income from dividends. These locations should also enable the repatriation of profits without tax deductions. Note, however, that in common with many business decisions, tax is not the only factor. Issues over staff availability and retention, proximity to management and major investors (for example, in London) are equally important factors.

TRANSACTING WITH CONNECTED PARTIES

Transfer Pricing

Most developed tax systems contain provisions that allow the tax authorities to increase the taxable profit, or reduce the allowable loss, of an entity which has entered into transactions with affiliates on non-arm's-length terms. In some jurisdictions, including the United Kingdom, this now includes domestic transactions as well as cross-border items. The concern for tax authorities is that profits are artificially moved between countries and, in particular, from a high tax area to a lower tax area.

Transfer pricing rules concern the provision of services as well as goods, and so they affect not only intragroup funding and hedging arrangements but also the provision of centralized treasury services. From a practical perspective, this means that apart from keeping contemporaneous documentary evidence of group transactions:

- all intercompany loans should carry a market rate of interest or other finance charge;
- commercial foreign exchange rates should be used when transacting between group companies;
- central treasury services should be recharged among those group members that benefit from them.

In-house re-invoicing and factoring centers usually receive particular scrutiny from the tax authorities of all the countries where participating group members are based.

Thin Capitalization

A company is said to be "thinly capitalized" where it is particularly highly geared. The tax authorities are concerned to ensure that companies do not receive debt funding from affiliates at levels that mean their profits are largely sheltered by interest expense. Many jurisdictions have now passed rules that set out what they consider to be an acceptable level of gearing for tax purposes. In some cases, for example in the United States, Germany, or Australia, the rules prescribe a maximum debt/equity ratio or required interest cover, and in others, such as the United Kingdom, the rules restrict finance charges by reference to the company's capacity to borrow from a third party on a stand-alone basis. Where the acceptable level of debt is based on subjective tests, it is frequently possible to secure advance clearance from the fiscal authorities on the proposed level of gearing.

For companies, the downside is that if transfer pricing or thin cap rules are breached a tax deduction for interest expense may be denied, while at the other end of the transaction the lending company is still taxed on the interest income.

WITHHOLDING TAXES

WHT is a tax that is deducted at source on earnings, which include employment income, dividends, and interest payments, and can also include intangible services. It is a charge on the recipient. It is not tax that is charged on the remitter and has no effect on tax payable by the latter. This tax is withheld by the remitter and is paid over to the domestic tax authority in which the income arose. A tax treaty may lower the withholding rate between certain countries—sometimes to zero. Double tax relief may also be available to offset WHT against a domestic tax liability. It may be necessary to apply in advance in order to obtain the reduced rate. As there are considerable differences in WHT rules between countries,

  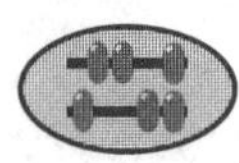   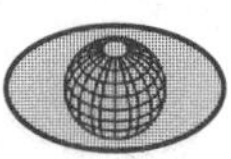   

companies need to carry out due diligence at the country level first and then look at the tax treaties that are available in order to obtain a full appreciation of the impact of WHT on their activities.

From a liquidity perspective, the major areas where withholding taxes can be an issue are:

- Dividends and royalties.
- Bank interest applied at source: The company may, or may not, be able to reclaim or deduct the WHT from income when the corporate tax return is filed, but there is inevitably a cash flow delay.
- Deemed bank interest applied by the corporate treasury, for example when reallocating interest on deemed bank interest arising from a notional pool. In some countries, such as the United Kingdom and the Netherlands, banks pay corporate interest gross, i.e. without deduction of WHT. This is one of the reasons why these countries are popular as cash pool centers.
- Interest on intercompany loans applied by the corporate treasury or created by cash concentration sweeping.
- Payments considered "in lieu of interest," such as guarantee and arrangement fees. The tax is due irrespective of whether or not an actual payment was received or a charge made for the service.

The WHT tax paid may become a final tax burden for the lender if it cannot be refunded or claimed as a tax credit or deduction. In some countries the WHT can be offset against corporate taxes due.

TAX TREATIES/DOUBLE TAX RELIEF

Tax treaties (also known as double taxation treaties) are a set of bilateral agreements between two countries that set out the taxation rights of each country in respect of tax charged in the other.

When a company receives income from overseas that has been taxed at the local level there are three options in dealing with the potential for double taxation. In order of most advantageous to the company:

- If the tax treaty calls for participation exemption (which prevents the same income from being taxed twice), the income may not be taxed again at the shareholder level.
- The overseas tax is used to offset and reduce any domestic tax liability, i.e. the amount of the tax already paid reduces the amount of the tax due at home by an equal amount.
- The overseas tax may simply be allowed as a tax deduction against domestic tax liability, i.e. the tax paid overseas is used as a deduction against income, thereby reducing taxable income.

TAX IMPLICATIONS OF NOTIONAL POOLING

Notional pooling means that credit and debit balances of various companies are notionally aggregated and netted by the group's bank, without actual transfer of ownership of the funds taking place. The following issues are associated with notional pooling:

- Notional pooling is usually considered to be a form of bank lending and treated as if interest is paid to the bank, although in fact the interest may actually be paid through intercompany transactions.
- Transfer pricing regulations require that any interest paid as an intercompany transaction is reallocated to the subsidiaries on an arm's-length basis.
- Transfer pricing will also look into the issues of pricing for the value of cross-guarantees that would normally be paid to a third party.
- There may be withholding tax (WHT) on the interest paid through intercompany transactions.
- A debit balance in a notional pool may also be used to calculate thin capitalization ratios.
- Notional pooling requires cross-guarantees and a legal right of offset to secure the position of creditors. Strictly, both these should be charged for.
- Legal constraints, such as not allowing cross-border legal right of offset, prohibiting the co-mingling of resident and non-resident accounts or requiring central bank reporting and reserves to be maintained on a gross basis, render pooling unviable or difficult in some countries.

TAX IMPLICATIONS OF CASH CONCENTRATION

With cash concentration, the funds move physically into the concentration account, with a resulting change of ownership. These are the major issues that arise from cash concentration:

- It creates intercompany loans and is taxed accordingly.
- No cross-guarantees or legal right of offset are required.
- Transfer pricing regulations require that any interest paid as an intercompany transaction is reallocated to the subsidiaries on an arm's-length basis.
- There may be WHT on the interest paid through intercompany transactions.
- Thin capitalization is likely to be an issue.
- It may attract deemed dividends.
- In some countries there may be additional stamp duties on cross-border intercompany loans (for example Austria, Italy, Portugal).
- Regulations prohibiting cross-border transfers will restrict participation in an overseas concentration scheme.
- Reference accounts are a way to pool cash without transfer of ownership.

▸▸ MAKING IT HAPPEN

- Taxation considerations should be built in at an early stage in the planning of liquidity management structures and processes.
- The best location for a cash management center will often be within a country with an extensive network of tax treaties and with no WHT on interest or dividends.
- Intra-group financial transactions should be priced at market prices (including margin where appropriate), and there should be contemporaneous independent documentation in place to support the prices used (for example, Reuters, Bloomberg, or the *Wall Street Journal*). Justification of margin can be more subjective. Possible comparators might be alternative facilities offered by banks locally or perhaps bond spreads, or credit default spreads (from Markit for instance).
- Where there is a central treasury operation or an in-house bank, borrowing rates and other terms and conditions should be formalized in the same manner as they would be with an external commercial bank.
- The same applies where a parent company is obliged to guarantee a subsidiary as a means of securing the subsidiary a lower borrowing rate. The parent should charge a guarantee fee.
- Structures such as "shared service centers," where a centralized group resource provides services to affiliates, also attract particular attention from tax authorities. Pricing and service levels should be similar to those that might be offered by a third-party provider.

▸▸ MORE INFO

Websites:

Deloitte International Tax and Business Guides: www.deloitte.com

"How to Manage Your Global Liquidity—A six part guide": www.gtnews.com/feature/85.cfm

"Everyone wants a more simple tax system. But if this means that certain tax breaks have to be cut, people are no longer so enthusiastic." Angela Merkel

  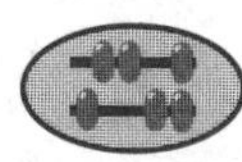   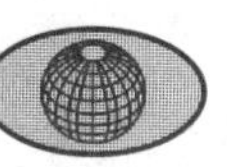   

How to Better Manage Your Financial Supply Chain by Juergen Bernd Weiss

EXECUTIVE SUMMARY

- Financial supply chain management (FSCM) addresses a number of initiatives that can help to make finance organizations more efficient and improve the working capital position of an enterprise.
- There are a number of indicators for an inefficient financial supply chain including low straight through processing rates and a high amount of uncollectible receivables on the balance sheet.
- Key performance indicators such as days sales outstanding or days in receivables can be used by companies to benchmark themselves with their peers.
- Microsoft decided to improve its financial supply chain to better utilize working capital, to reduce bank fees, to process payments more effectively and to gain better control of cash flows.

INTRODUCTION

Benchmarks of business performance indicate that enterprise resource planning (ERP) systems and other enterprise technologies have transformed customer and supply chain processes but that the performance of the finance function has hardly changed. Although some companies have managed to improve the performance of their financial processes profoundly, financial functions are still neglected in many businesses, and days sales outstanding (DSO) and working capital needs are very high in several industries. The working capital scorecard for 2008 from *CFO Magazine* demonstrates that there are significant differences between high and low performers within an industry. In the automotive industry, for example, the best score in DSO was 44, while the worst score was 241—five times more than the sector median of 47. Research from the Hackett Group indicates that finance department costs continue to consume more than 1% of revenues in many companies, and CFOs struggle with poor transparency of their daily cash flows.

In times when unprecedented economic uncertainty and soaring stockholder expectations are putting every function under closer scrutiny than ever before, the finance function should be driving business, not holding it back. Financial supply chain management (FSCM) can help companies to remove some of the inefficiencies in operational processes in order to become more effective.

DEFINITIONS OF FINANCIAL SUPPLY CHAIN MANAGEMENT

There are different definitions of the term *financial supply chain*, which appeared for the first time in 2000 and 2001. According to the research company Killen & Associates (2001), the financial supply chain "parallels the physical or materials supply chain and represents all transaction activities related to the flow of cash from the customer's initial order through reconciliation and payment to the seller." The Aberdeen Group, another research company, calls the financial supply chain "a range of B-to-B trade-related intra- and inter-company financial transaction-based functions and processes [which] begin before buyers and suppliers establish contact and proceed beyond the settlement process." The two definitions emphasize different topics. Killen's focuses on the parallelism between the physical and the financial supply chain, and it stresses a section of the cash flow cycle that I'll discuss in more detail below. The Aberdeen Group's definition focuses on the collaborative nature of financial supply chain management and reveals that the financial value chain isn't limited to the inner walls of a company but includes communication and cooperation with business partners.

Both definitions focus on a process-oriented view of the financial supply chain that is basically correct; however, in many respects the explanations do not go far enough:

- They focus very much on the collaboration between companies—specifically, suppliers and customers—and they do not consider other important business partners within the financial supply chain, such as banks.
- They describe primarily the status quo, and do not stress the various dimensions for the optimization of business processes within the financial supply chain.
- The motivation, as well as the key performance indicators, for an efficient financial supply chain are not obvious.

Another definition that includes these three aspects is the following: Financial supply chain management (FSCM) is the holistic and comprehensive planning and controlling of all financial processes which are relevant within a company and for communication with other enterprises. The goal of FSCM is to increase the transparency and the level of automation of business processes along the financial value chain. The purpose is to save processing costs and reduce the working capital of the company. This definition doesn't consider where the financial supply chain actually begins and ends, because there are also analytical processes that are not directly related to a business process but which belong nonetheless to the financial supply chain. Let's now have a closer look at the indicators of an *inefficient* financial supply chain.

INDICATORS OF AN INEFFICIENT FINANCIAL SUPPLY CHAIN

As we have seen, the financial supply chain is different from the physical supply chain because it deals with the flow of cash instead of goods. Just as in the physical supply chain, though, every day that's lost in the cash-to-cash cycle equals lost revenue. But how do you know that your financial value chain isn't working properly? Besides a number of rather operational problems, there are also several concrete key performance indicators and metrics that you can use to analyze your financial supply chain. You are most likely aware of the fact that the financial supply chain stretches across many different business processes. These are, in a broader sense, the two processes *order-to-cash* and *purchase-to-pay*, which consist of various sub-processes that are relevant to the financial aspects of the value chain.

The order-to-cash process includes, from the perspective of a supplier (or creditor), the following business process steps:

1 Creditworthiness check.
2 Invoice creation.
3 Cash forecast.
4 Financing of working capital.
5 Processing of dispute cases.
6 Cash collection.
7 Settlement and payment.
8 Account reconciliation.

From the perspective of a customer (or debtor), the purchase-to-pay process consists of the following business processes:

1 Procurement.

"I don't think there is a sound UK bank now, at least, if there is one I don't know about it. The City of London is finished, the financial centre of the world is moving east. All the money is in Asia. Why would it go back to the West? You don't need London." Jim Rogers

     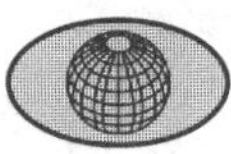   

2 Cash forecast.
3 Financing of working capital.
4 Receipt of invoices.
5 Resolution of discrepancies or exceptions.
6 Invoice approval.
7 Settlement and payment.
8 Account reconciliation.

There are a number of operational factors within the order-to-cash and purchase-to-pay processes that can serve as indicators of a suboptimal financial supply chain. Some examples are:

- The number of paper-based business processes is very high and there are several changes in medium (for example, the creation of invoices).
- The straight-through processing rate is low, which means that there are multiple manual interventions and process steps.
- Companies struggle with a large number of dispute cases during the creation of invoices, and it takes them a lot of time to process these.
- There is a large amount of uncollectable receivables on the balance sheet, and many employees in receivables or collections management are involved in the resolution process.
- Enterprises haven't implemented a consistent credit management policy, which results in a number of bad debt losses.
- Management has difficulties in predicting cash flows.
- There is no centralized cash management to control payment streams, and the company maintains too many bank connections.

KEY PERFORMANCE INDICATORS

There are various key performance indicators that are relevant for measurement in financial supply chain management. One key metric is the cash flow cycle, which defines the period from delivery by suppliers until the cash collection of receivables from customers (Figure 1). It is the time period required for the company to receive the invested funds back in the form of cash. The cash flow cycle can be divided into the *operating cycle*—which is the time period between delivery by suppliers and the actual cash collection of receivables, and the *cash flow cycle*—which is the time period between the cash payment for inventory and the cash collection of receivables. The longer the cash flow cycle, the greater is the working capital requirement of a company, which means that a reduction of the cash flow cycle will immediately free up liquidity.

Within the cash flow cycle we can differentiate the following parameters, which are delimited in Figure 1 with curly brackets:

Figure 1. The cash flow cycle

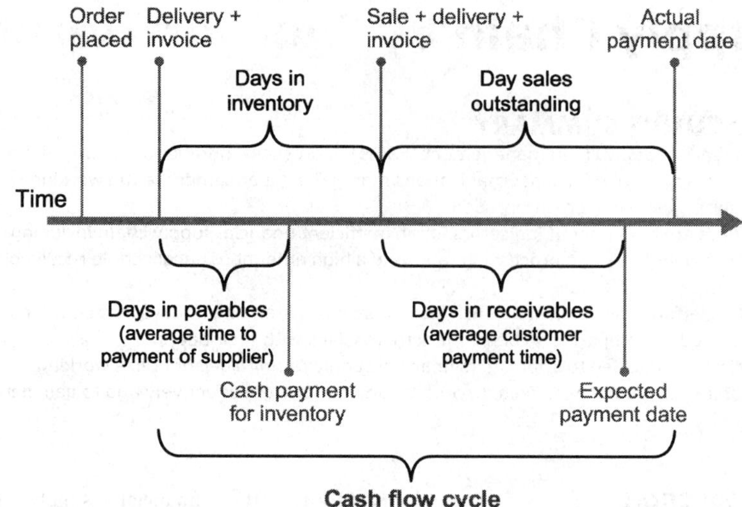

- *Days in inventory*: This is the length of time between the delivery of the goods and the invoice from the supplier, and the sale of the goods and the invoice to the customer. It describes the average number of days the goods of a company remain in inventory before being sold. This metric is the focus for all activities around classical supply chain management.
- *Days in payables:* This is the length of time between delivery of the goods and the invoice from the supplier, and the actual payment for the inventory. This figure describes the average time it takes to pay a supplier. The parameter considers the outstanding receivables of a company, and is an important metric for debtors concentrating on their efforts to optimize the purchase-to-pay cycle.
- *Days sales outstanding:* This is the length of time between the sale of the

CASE STUDY

Microsoft

US company Microsoft decided to improve its financial supply chain by replacing third-party and in-house developed legacy software systems that were very costly to maintain. Microsoft, which is headquartered in Redmond, Washington, provides information technology, operating systems, middleware solutions, small/mid-size business applications, professional services, and other software solutions. The company reported annual sales in 2008 of more than US$60 billion and had more than 90,000 employees worldwide.

The main business drivers for the company were:

- Better data integration between applications.
- Elimination of manual intercompany processes and month-end bank account reconciliation.
- More transparent accessibility to real-time data such as bank account balances, financial transactions, and accounts receivable and payable.
- More efficient usage of excess funds and better working capital management.
- Increased straight-through processing of foreign exchange trading.
- Reduction of bank fees and more cost-effective processing of payments.
- Risk reduction and better control of cash flows.
- Better utilization of human resources.

Microsoft decided to implement a vendor's financial supply chain management solution to complement its existing enterprise resource planning (ERP) landscape. The company realized a number of benefits from the project and was, for example, able to automate the confirmation process in the foreign exchange settlement fully. Exception rates are now smaller than 5%, the settlement process went from four hours to less than 15 minutes, and the percentage of settlement errors is approaching 0%.

"We were on our own for years and we went too far, too fast, in too little time. . .We're just like kids whose parents went away for the weekend and we trashed the whole house." Hallgrimur Helgason

     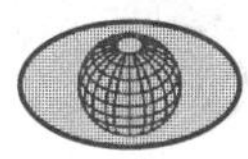   

goods and the invoice to the customer, and the actual payment date of the customer. This metric measures the average number of days companies need to collect revenue after a sale has been made. A high DSO number means that an enterprise is selling to its customers on credit and taking longer to collect money. The figure is an important figure for creditors, to optimize the order-to-cash cycle.

- *Days in receivables:* This is the length of time between the sale of the goods and the invoice to the customer, and the expected payment date. This key performance indicator is similar to DSO, and indicates the average time, in days, that receivables are outstanding. Days in receivables can also be called best possible DSO, since the company would collect all receivables before the due date.

Within the cash flow cycle there is potential to reduce both days in inventory and days sales outstanding. Days in payables can be reduced but should be monitored carefully to avoid putting supplies at risk. Days in receivables can be reduced by optimizing cash collection. Another important indicator for an efficient financial supply chain management is working capital, which is a balance sheet metric and part of the liquid assets. Working capital is calculated as current assets less current liabilities, and is a measure of the liquid reserve and short-term solvency of an enterprise, available to satisfy contingencies and uncertainties. One of the key objectives of financial supply chain management is to optimize the working capital by reducing, for instance, outstanding receivables.

MORE INFO

Books:

Bhalla, V. K. *Working Capital Management: Text and Cases*. New Delhi: Anmol Publications, 2006.

Horcher, Karen A. *Essentials of Managing Treasury*. Hoboken, NJ: Wiley, 2006.

Salek, John G. *Accounts Receivable Management Best Practices*. Hoboken, NJ: Wiley, 2005.

Schaeffer, Mary S. *Essentials of Credit, Collections, and Accounts Receivable*. Hoboken, NJ: Wiley, 2002.

Scheuermann, Hans-Dieter, the Mysap Financials Team, and Cedric Read. *The CFO as Business Integrator*. Hoboken, NJ: Wiley, 2003.

Articles:

Hartley-Urquhart, Roland. "Managing the financial supply chain." *Supply Chain Management Review* (2006). Online at: www.scmr.com/article/CA6376439.html

Karaian, Jason. "Working capital scorecard 2008." *CFO Europe Magazine* (July 7, 2008). Online at: www.cfo.com/article.cfm/11661239?f=search

Websites:

CFO—News and insight for financial executives: www.cfo.com

gtnews—Library for finance and treasury professionals: www.gtnews.com

The Hackett Group: www.thehackettgroup.com

See Also:

✔ Assessing Cash Flow and Bank Lending Requirements (p. 854)

✔ Creating a Cash Flow Statement (p. 1092)

✔ Preparing a Cash Flow Forecast (p. 880)

Cashflow Reengineering: How to Optimize the Cashflow Timeline and Improve Financial Efficiency (p. 1234)

  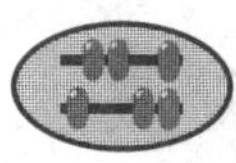   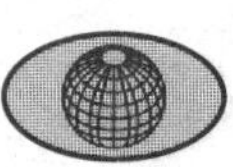   

Viewpoint: Lawrence Phillips
Moving Away from Traditional Budgeting

INTRODUCTION

Dr Lawrence Phillips, Visiting Professor of Decision Science at the London School of Economics and a director of Facilitations Ltd, is a leading expert on ways in which organizations can improve their decision-making. He has long been fascinated by the challenges associated with deciding how best to deploy limited resources across a range of possible projects and getting people to buy into the outcome—the quintessential budgeting and indeed management problem. He teaches decision science to graduates and undergraduates at the LSE and conducts training courses on decision science and facilitation skills to external organizations. His expertize is in applying a wide variety of approaches, particularly decision and risk analysis, to issues of strategic and operational management, option evaluation, prioritization, resource allocation, and crisis management. In November 2005, Dr Phillips was awarded the Frank P. Ramsey Medal for distinguished contributions to decision analysis by the Decision Analysis Society of INFORMS.

Every organization has finite resources and must, therefore, assign priorities to a range of possible options when allocating its budget. However, in my experience, very few organizations do this particularly well.

The traditional approach to budgeting invariably leads to "silo decisions," in which resources are allocated on a project-by-project basis. The individual judgments that are being made preclude any coherent analysis of the wider options available, often resulting in missed opportunity for the organization concerned. However, by applying the principles of decision analysis, it becomes possible to create a portfolio of options that really do make the best use of the available resources.

Budgeting is generally an exercise in balancing costs, benefits, and risks. It involves persuading a wide constituency of stakeholders to sign up to these decisions. In the process, multiple stakeholders with different agendas will compete for limited resources. A classic example is the UK government spending round, in which different spending departments slug it out for a slice of the Treasury's pie.

Resource allocations that are optimal to the individual organizational units are rarely collectively optimal, and those who are dissatisfied with the outcome can become jaundiced and resistant to implementation. In this article, I explain three current approaches to resource allocation, taken from the worlds of corporate finance, operational research, and decision analysis; the latter is one of my expertizes. I draw heavily on an earlier paper coauthored with Carlos A. Bana e Costa in 2007, entitled "Transparent prioritisation, budgeting and resource allocation with multi-criteria decision analysis and decision conferencing."

What I want to sketch out is a technical process, multi-criteria portfolio analysis, which makes it possible to balance the conflicting elements, and a social process, decision conferencing, which ensures that all relevant players are engaged in the modeling process, ensuring their ownership of the model and their satisfaction when it comes to implementation.

The essence of much decision-making, including budgeting, is that, when presented with a large number of opportunities, decision-makers have insufficient knowledge of each option to be able to make informed choices. Another problem is that the benefits associated with these opportunities are typically characterized by multiple objectives, which themselves often conflict.

A DELICATE BALANCE

What is needed is an approach that enables decision-makers to balance costs, risks, and multiple benefits; to construct portfolios of investments across different areas to ensure that collective best use is made of the limited total resource; to consult the right people in a structured, coherent way, so that their multiple perspectives can be brought to bear; and to engage with key players to ensure they are aligned with the way forward, while preserving their individual differences of approach.

That may sound a tall order. But it can be accomplished by blending a technical solution that captures the differing perspectives with a social process that engages with the people concerned. The technical solution I am suggesting is multi-criteria decision analysis (MCDA), blended with decision conferencing.

We need to distinguish between resource allocation, which is done by a manager bearing the responsibility for this allocation (ultimately the responsibility is borne by the board in a public company) and resource prioritization, which can involve input from multiple line-management functions. It is also useful to distinguish between two prioritization tasks: the appraisal of options, and the construction of portfolios.

The former orders options within an area, the latter refers to the appraisal of options across multiple areas (a portfolio of options), with the aim of finding the best combination of options for a given level of resource.

The three main perspectives on portfolio resource allocation decisions are derived from the worlds of corporate finance, operations research optimization, and decision analysis. Each places a different emphasis on how benefits, costs, and risks can best be handled.

In the corporate finance perspective, it is assumed that benefits are expressed in monetary terms and that the appraisal of a project's worth is determined by calculating its net present value (NPV). One of the commonest budgeting techniques is to select from a universe of options by ranking them in terms of highest to lowest NPV, and assigning the budget to options until the resource reaches zero.

It seems logical and it is widely deployed in the finance departments of major corporations. But this approach conceals a schoolboy howler. The essence of the

"The SEC now is 3500 chickens, and we need to get some foxes in there." Harry Markopolos

   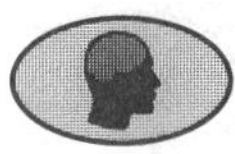  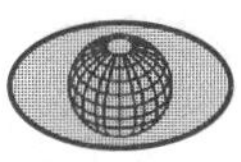   

howler is that the method uses a simple "screen" that masks out the possibility that other budget combinations, based on a ratio of NPV over cost, will deliver far better returns.

There is no substitute, in short, for carrying out a scoring and weighting analysis of all the options. In all cases with finite budgets, which effectively means in all budgets, the appropriate criterion is not just a positive NPV (or highest ranking NPV), but rather the ratio of NPV to the investment cost. This is a profitability index that represents value for money.

THE BINARY KNAPSACK

Unlike the corporate finance perspective, the optimization perspective of operations research takes the "binary knapsack" approach. This casts the problem as one of maximizing the sum of the benefits of all investments subject to the constraints of the budget. Each chosen project is put into the "knapsack" and when this is full, it's full. The challenge is to fill it with the most valuable projects. The hidden "risk" in this approach is that in the real world, it is more realistic to think of the options as varying degrees of funding the projects, not as "go, no-go" alternatives for each project. In this way, allocating more resources to the more promising projects can be accomplished by spending less on the projects that are characterized by lesser opportunities.

The third perspective, decision analysis, comes in two flavors. In the first flavor, each project's risks can be modeled using "decision trees," as can the possible future decisions. Typically, NPV is used to provide a "score" with the discount rate set as "risk-free."

Why? The answer is simple and straightforward. All the uncertainties about future events are intended to be fully modeled as probabilities in the decision tree (what else is it?). This point is missed again and again, even by academics who really ought to know better.

I have lost count of the number of times that I have found people building risk into NPV discount rates in decision trees. Uncertainty about the future is better modeled by probabilities of later events, followed by downstream decisions, a true options analysis that provides expected (weighted average) monetary values as the basis for valuing the options, and, when divided by costs, providing indices for constructing portfolios.

The second flavor relies on multi-criteria decision analysis for placing values on the consequences of the options. In this way, monetary and nonmonetary values can be incorporated in the model, with common units of added-value across all the criteria. Thus, it is not necessary to use money as the common unit, easing the process of valuation. Risks here often become criteria, which many people find congenial because they think of risks as negative values rather than as probabilities.

All three approaches, financial modeling, operations research, and decision analysis, conform to the principle that the correct basis for prioritization in budgeting, the one that ensures that the best value is obtained for the available resource, is risk-adjusted benefit divided by cost.

Weakness Remains Widespread

However, in practice, I and the coauthor of the original paper, who have amassed some 35 years of experience working with organizations between us, have not once come across an organization that really makes this principle work in practice.

What they actually do amounts to a variant of the following five steps:

1 List the projects they wish to support;
2 Determine the benefit that each project is expected to create;
3 Rank the projects from most to least benefit;
4 Associate a forward cost to each project;
5 Go down the list, choosing projects until the budget is exceeded.

In short, projects are prioritized on the basis of benefits only. It is easy to show that this does not make the best use of the budget and that choosing on the basis of the benefit-to-cost ratio is always a better way of maximizing the total benefit.

One further important point needs to be made. Insofar as future benefits are uncertain, then the benefits should be risk-adjusted. In decision theory, this is accomplished by multiplying the benefits by the probability of realizing them, a necessary step to ensure consistency of preference between projects with different benefits and probabilities of success.

To be useful to decision-makers, models need to be able to accommodate all of the following: financial and nonfinancial benefit criteria, risk and uncertainty, data, and judgment. They should also be transparent (in a way that real-option analysis, for example, most certainly is not), and should provide an audit trail which enables a review, after the fact, of how particular decisions were reached and what the underlying assumptions were. Decision analysis does all this exceptionally well.

Allow me to provide a perhaps grossly oversimplified example of decision analysis.

A tossed coin has a 50–50 probability of landing heads or tails up. If I offer you a ticket that entitles you to one toss of the coin to win £10,000, you will judge yourself to have a one in two chance of winning. A risk-adjusted view of the benefit conferred on your ticket would value it at £5,000. If we say that the ticket is transferable, it immediately has a value, probably some value less than £5,000, unless the buyer happens to be a Muggins.

How much would you sell that ticket for, trading off a potential win which you only have a 50–50 chance of securing, in return for real cash in your pocket now? The answer you give places a cash weighting on the decision, and indeed the difference between your minimum selling (or reserve) price and £5,000 gives a measure of your risk aversion. If we imagine a collection of people with a stake in the ticket, then their collective answer provides a group view of the value, which would probably be different from most of the individual views, and this gives us the basis for a decision conference. Note that the whole process builds in the possibility that the coin toss will not be favorable and so the consequence of the coin toss will turn out to be valueless in reality when that moment of truth arrives.

BUILDING CONSENSUS

Today decision conferences, where all the key players in a decision process come together to work on an issue of concern to their organization, are becoming best practice in many organizations. They create a model of their decisions, which always involves assigning values to the consequences of the options and taking account of uncertainty that the consequences may or may not occur.

It is a highly effective way of ensuring that everyone buys into the final decisions that inform a budget. Assisted by a decision conference facilitator, who is a specialist in decision analysis, and whose job it is to help people in how to think about the issues, and not what to think, the process aims to get the whole group thinking more clearly about the issues involved.

The model represents the collective view of the group at any point during its generation and modification, and serves as a way of examining the impact of differences in perspective or vagueness in the data. Everyone should understand the formation of the model as it is constructed, so that they can see and understand the impact of their own participation in it. In practice, we have discovered that decision conferences are a tremendous way of getting organizations to think creatively and to move away from merely pumping resources into maintaining or slightly adjusting the status quo.

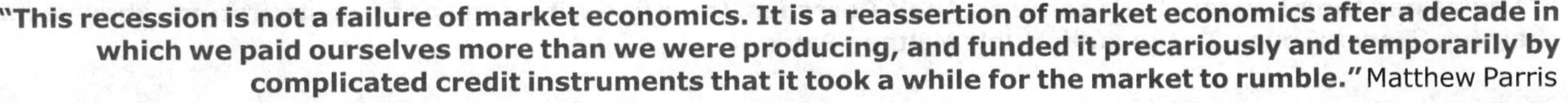
"This recession is not a failure of market economics. It is a reassertion of market economics after a decade in which we paid ourselves more than we were producing, and funded it precariously and temporarily by complicated credit instruments that it took a while for the market to rumble." Matthew Parris

  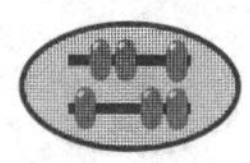   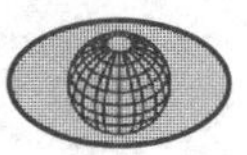   

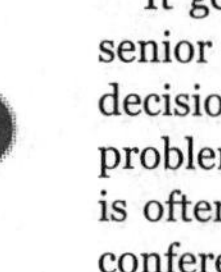

It generally takes around two weeks for senior staff to digest the results of the decision conference fully. For larger problems, a sustained workshop approach is often required, utilizing several decision conferences along with workshops, interviews, and individual meetings. But one outcome is certain—better decisions, and decisions in which the participants really believe, will be achieved.

MORE INFO

Books:

Clemen, Robert T., and Terence Reilly. *Making Hard Decisions with DecisionTools*. 2nd ed. Pacific Grove, CA: Duxbury Thomson Learning, 2004.

Goodwin, Paul, and George Wright. *Decision Analysis for Management Judgment*. 3rd ed. Chichester, UK: Wiley, 2003.

Hammond, John S., Ralph L. Keeney, and Howard Raiffa. *Smart Choices: A Practical Guide to Making Better Decisions*. Boston, MA: Harvard University Press, 1999.

Keeney, Ralph L. *Value-Focused Thinking: A Path to Creative Decisionmaking*. Cambridge, MA: Harvard University Press, 1992.

Article:

Phillips, Lawrence D., and Carlos A. Bana e Costa. "Transparent prioritisation, budgeting and resource allocation with multi-criteria decision analysis and decision conferencing." *Annals of Operations Research* 154:1 (2007): 51–68.

"They've had their heyday, their bonuses, their Porsches, their fine wines and oafish ostentation—they've had their fun. Now for ours. To the guillotine!" Matthew Parris

     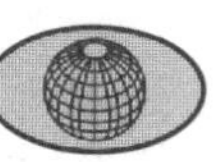   

How to Manage Pension Costs by Edmund Truell

EXECUTIVE SUMMARY

- The financial implications of rising longevity, in particular with regard to pensions, pose significant challenges to society. The re-allocation of the financial burden among governments, businesses, and individuals will significantly affect pension systems.
- The upward trend in life expectancy and the consequent aging population has led to large unanticipated retirement costs for businesses and governments, particularly in developed countries.
- Governments have increased the long-term sustainability of the public finances by reducing the future generosity of state pension entitlements and encouraging greater private sector involvement.
- In response to government initiatives, corporate sponsors have closed their defined benefit pension schemes, and moved employees into defined contribution schemes—thus shifting investment and longevity risk onto individuals.
- To deal with the legacy of previous commitments, managers have created a range of new solutions for the financial markets, from hedging liabilities to passing all or part of the risk and responsibility to specialist third-party providers.

INTRODUCTION

A huge increase in life expectancy is one of the great achievements of the human race over the past two centuries. Increased longevity has transformed both individuals' lives and their societies, with the most marked changes taking place in the developed world. Actual increases in life expectancy have been far more substantial than previously projected, with the result that governments, businesses, financial markets, and individuals must radically readjust their plans.

Moreover, the current trend shows no sign of leveling off. For example, between 1981 and 2000 the life expectancy for 65-year-old males in the United Kingdom increased by approximately three months for every year, and future life expectancy is widely expected to continue to increase. Therefore, it is increasingly important that governments, businesses, and individuals consider the economic, societal, and financial implications of an aging society in diverse but important policy areas such as pensions, health care, and long-term care provision. For example, pension liabilities increase by 3% or more for every added year of life expectancy.

CHANGES TO THE PENSIONS LANDSCAPE

Pension reform has been high on the political agenda in most Organizations for Economic Co-operation and Development (OECD) countries during the past decade. In most instances the key objective of reform has been to increase the long-term sustainability of public finances in the light of an aging population. Governments have frequently reduced the future generosity of state pension entitlements through several means, such as indexing future pension increases to inflation rather than earnings growth, increasing the official pension age to compensate for expected longevity increases, and, in some cases, developing new measures to automatically reallocate the financial burden of unexpected future increases in longevity between the state and the individual.

To compensate for planned reductions, most reform packages also include measures aimed at encouraging greater private sector involvement. This shift has led to a reallocation of risk, including longevity risk, away from the state and onto businesses and individuals. However, shifting the responsibility of future pension provision to businesses or individuals does not solve all the problems.

Countries such as the United States, the United Kingdom, and the Netherlands, with traditionally larger private sector involvement in pension provision, face unique challenges due to the defined benefit (DB) nature of their pension schemes. In these countries, DB pensions are linked to the salary earned by the individual, and are often index-linked and passed on to dependents in the event of death. Although DB schemes are attractive and arguably help to foster employee loyalty, they have become increasingly onerous for companies to maintain. The United Kingdom, the United States, and the Netherlands have all witnessed an accelerated closure of DB schemes, as businesses respond to new accounting standards and recognize more clearly the substantial longevity risk borne with DB schemes.

Some firms have opted for defined contribution (DC) schemes, in which a contribution of salary is paid regularly into the scheme by the individual and typically is matched by an employer contribution. The contributions are then invested, with the assumption that the compounded return on these investments over time will be sufficient to provide a pension in retirement. The shift from DB to DC schemes places more risk on individuals. Taken together with less generous state pensions, this move raises the question: Will future pensioner incomes be sufficient to meet the expectations of future pensioners? There is an additional danger for companies in some countries, where planned compulsory pensions for all employees are likely to lead to large costs because of the significant increase in employer contributions.

LEGACY ISSUES

There is also another issue. Although closing DB pension schemes to new entrants means that no new liabilities will be added to the existing stock, dealing with the legacy issues still remains a formidable challenge for companies and pension fund trustees. Today's corporate pension managers face the problem of maintaining a set of financial commitments made in another era, when assumptions and expectations were vastly different. These commitments are difficult to measure, let alone anticipate, and are tied to the health and well-being of the corporate sponsor of the fund, which is required to underwrite any deficit.

Similarly, pension fund trustees are attempting to steer a secure course through a sea of investment strategies, taking account of increasing longevity exposure, while also keeping an eye on the financial robustness of their corporate sponsor. The issue is further complicated by the fact that the time horizon within which most companies operate will generally be much shorter than that covered by pension funds, with the result that corporate sponsors are also charged with maintaining open-ended commitments for a very long period ahead. These obligations frequently stretch beyond the tenure of current managers or stockholders.

Corporate sponsors that initiated DB pension funds in the past now find their pension-inflated balance sheets at the mercy of volatile markets. These inflated balance sheets can dramatically affect share price, ability to maneuver, and, ironically,

     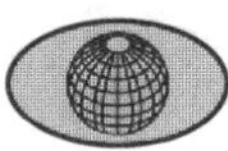   

the very security of the pension commitments they are obliged to maintain.

SOLUTIONS AND CASE STUDIES

There are a number of different approaches to dealing with pension cost issues in the private sector. The overriding prerequisite is for assets and liabilities to be run as a combined analysis. This is because the true benchmark for any pension scheme is the liabilities that have to be paid out over time. Managers should also be cognizant of the risks associated with these liabilities, particularly the effect of interest rates and inflation, in addition to the better understood market risks present within the assets.

Over the last few years, the financial markets have innovated and provided a range of tools and solutions. For example, the liabilities can be hedged against the effect of interest rate changes and inflation through traditional instruments such as government securities and corporate bonds, or through interest rate and inflation swaps. Interest rate and inflation swaps are often preferable and more efficient from an asset–liability management standpoint, as they free up assets for investment in a diversified pool of return-seeking assets: This can then help schemes potentially turn around a deficit over time.

Large companies may choose to embrace the risks and potential returns offered by the pension fund, establishing asset and liability teams to understand, coordinate, and manage asset–liability and balance sheet risk.

CONCLUSION

The exponential increase in life expectancy over the last century is a staggering achievement. However, the experiences of economies with strong private sector involvement in pensions show that a mixed system poses its own complex challenges. For example, in the United Kingdom many firms have concluded that they are not well placed to deal with these challenges and have closed their defined benefit schemes as a result. Although such a move deals with the accrual of future liabilities, it does not address legacy issues. Businesses have turned to the financial markets to offer innovative solutions, though here cost will be a critical factor in dealing with future pension provision. Nevertheless, these new approaches have expanded the choice set available to policymakers, businesses, and individuals, and as, such, are likely to play an important role in designing a sustainable pension environment for the future.

CASE STUDY 1

British Telecom, Dutch Pension Schemes and Insurance Options

One of the most interesting examples of a large company choosing to establish an asset and liability team is British Telecom (BT) in the United Kingdom. BT's pension obligations and assets were initially managed by an in-house investment team. The team was so successful that demand for its services increased and BT created a separate fund management entity, Hermes Asset Management, predominantly owned by the BT Pension Scheme. However, the risks taken by this team were larger than originally identified, and the team is now being dismantled. In some countries, such as the Netherlands, interest in managing assets and liabilities as a holistic entity has also led to the advent of third-party fiduciary managers, who take on the responsibility of hedging the liabilities and managing the assets to help trustees and companies meet their funding targets.

A permanent solution that is gaining increased attention in Anglo-Saxon economies, notably the United Kingdom, is to pass the risk and responsibility to a specialist third-party pension solutions provider. A third-party insurer can provide members with improved security through a bespoke insurance solution, securing member benefits for the long term. Furthermore, the sponsor company removes all future pension uncertainties from its balance sheet. This route also has the advantage that the liabilities are covered for all risks, including longevity risk. The most common mechanism is a pension insurance buyout—a bulk annuity policy secured with an insurer, which ensures that all benefits are met in exchange for an upfront premium. Historically, this route was used as part of insolvency procedures or in the case of a winding-up. However, increasing scrutiny of the health of corporate sponsors by financial markets and the practical difficulties associated with DB schemes for companies have meant that, in recent years, many companies have sought to transfer the liabilities to specialists. This usually increases the security for scheme members. Traditionally, operating businesses have been perceived to provide security for the promise of future contributions. In contrast, insurance companies have no such operating assets and, under FSA rules, need to hold assets and regulatory capital in excess of the accounting liabilities. Moreover, pension insurance buyout costs are typically higher than pension liabilities on an accounting basis, due to the more conservative assumptions used for the assessment of liabilities and projected asset returns. As a result, there has also been rapid recent growth in more cost-effective alternatives such as partial buyouts, where only part of the liabilities is insured, and buyins, where an insurance policy is purchased as an asset to precisely match some proportion of the liabilities.

CASE STUDY 2

Thorn Pension Scheme

An alternative approach was followed by UK-based Thorn Ltd. Thorn's active business was sold off and gradually reduced over time, to end up with a large £1.2 billion pension fund supported by a very small corporate covenant. In this situation, the trustee decided that the safest way to secure the 24,000 pensioners' obligations was to buy out their current and future obligations with a registered insurance company, using all the assets in the pension fund.

But not all firms are necessarily interested in fully shedding their pension liabilities, particularly in the case of pension schemes where there are strong reasons not to sever links with the sponsoring employer. Although many firms have managed everything themselves along the approaches discussed earlier, these firms are still faced with the key outstanding risk of increased future longevity. Though nascent, the insurance industry that is now developing aims to decouple longevity risk and investment risk. Some financial services companies, such as J.P. Morgan, have sought to construct longevity indices that can be used as the basis for hedging longevity, while others have sought solutions tailored to the specific longevity profile of a particular scheme. Either way, the common mechanism is a longevity swap, which allows the scheme to lock into an agreed level of future longevity. The cost of any future pension payments that arises from pensioners living longer than expected is swapped by the pension fund for fixed annual premiums set at the inception of the swap. This can also be structured as an insurance contract, removing the counterparty issues and the limited time frame enshrined in most derivative contracts.

"Surely I'm not the only person to ask the obvious question: How different, really, is Mr. Madoff's tale from the story of the investment industry as a whole?" Paul R. Krugman

   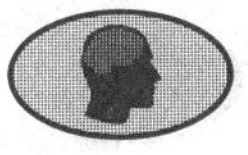  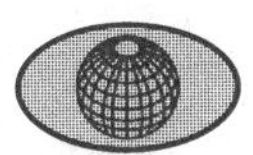   

Figure 1. The global liquidity management structure review process

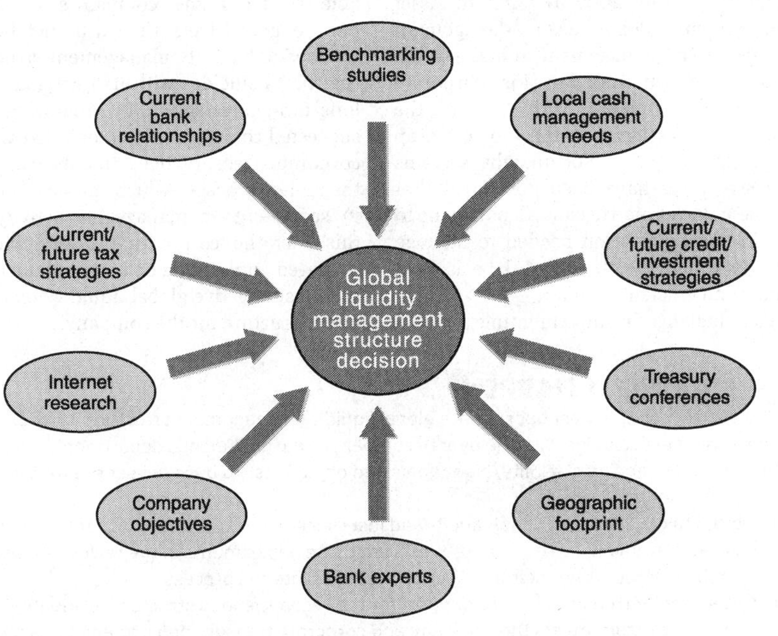

easily attained via an internet search. These will provide the company with a foundation for discussing these structures in greater depth with potential service providers.

Utilize the Money Center Banks that Provide Global Liquidity Management Services

As of this writing there are only a handful of banks that can provide a true global liquidity management solution. These banks have staffs of experts who live, breathe, and sleep these structures. These bankers are more than willing to assist companies in developing a global liquidity management structure that best fits a company's needs and objectives.

The more experienced banks will have implemented similar structures for other companies and are therefore able to provide firsthand knowledge of the twists and turns of implementation in each country in which the company operates. Although for liability reasons most banks will defer to the company's own tax, legal, insurance, audit, and accounting departments on specific issues, the more experienced banks will be able to demonstrate how other companies faced with exactly the same issues were able to resolve them.

Benchmark Companies that Have Implemented Successful Global Liquidity Management Solutions

Experience usually does not come cheap, although it is attainable by finding companies that are willing to benchmark their successes. The global liquidity management providers which a company considers for its business should be able to set up several benchmark meetings with companies that have similar footprints, needs, and objectives.

Through these meetings a company will be able to attain an understanding of, among other things, why these companies ended up with the service provider they selected, how they went about managing their implementation, the issues that caught them by surprise, the specific successes and failures they experienced in their implementation, and the ease of managing their structure on an ongoing basis.

Utilize the Availability of Corporate Treasury Conferences

There are several large corporate treasury management conferences where, for a nominal fee, an attendee will gain access to presentations of case studies of companies that have implemented successful global liquidity management structures. These conferences also offer one-stop shopping in their exhibit halls with banks that offer global liquidity management solutions. Although the amount of information an attendee will receive at these conferences can be overwhelming, the greatest benefit of attending one is the ability to introduce the company to the banks and to establish follow-up meetings with potential service providers. Having access to these banks within a day, or over a couple of days, will greatly accelerate the attendee's global liquidity management review process.

Do the Work Yourself

Shortcuts taken in managing the review process will inevitably return to haunt a company in the end. Though there are consultants that will manage the review process, the client will end up either implementing or managing on an ongoing basis the global solution that is developed. A thorough understanding of why specific aspects of the structure were adopted or excluded is necessary to ensure the successful implementation and management of the structure. There is no substitute for hands-on learning. Outsourcing the review process to a consultant will leave the company at a disadvantage when issues arise down the road.

SERVICE PROVIDER REVIEW

The process of understanding the various forms of liquidity management structures and identifying the company's global liquidity management needs and objectives can take several months to complete. Once the company's needs and objectives are finalized, the company is in a position to entertain presentations by potential service providers. Detailed below are three tips related to comparing the various bank-provided solutions:

Spend Most of the Review Period Evaluating the Reporting Systems Provided by the Global Service Providers

When reviewing the various reports provided by the global service providers, drill down on each individual field within each report. Although this can make for a very tedious meeting, it is the only way to determine whether the timeliness of the information being reported meets the company's needs.

Inquire where each field of information in each report comes from, how often these systems are updated, and how often these systems feed each other. Inquire about each system's downtime and recovery time, when the last upgrade to the system was implemented, the changes that were made in the last upgrade, and how long it has been since the previous upgrade. Finally, inquire about whether the reporting system can accommodate value-dated transactions without human intervention, whether the system has ad-hoc reporting capabilities, and whether the system can provide interest accrual reports during the company's accounting close.

Without a timely, robust reporting system to support the global liquidity

"Before anything else, preparation is the key to success." Alexander Graham Bell

     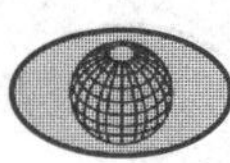   

management structure, a company will end up with a great number of bank accounts, with a great volume of transactions flowing through them, with no visibility to the transactions and resulting balances. This is a corporate treasurer's nightmare. Asking about the specifics of the bank's reporting system will reveal those banks that have truly invested in their global liquidity management reporting systems—in other words, who are the true players and who are the posers.

Evaluate the Bank's Commitment to Their Global Liquidity Management Structure

Global liquidity management solutions require the support of enhanced electronic reporting systems. The investment to develop and maintain these systems is substantial. These products therefore need to be core to the bank's overall global cash management strategy. The last thing you want to do is align the company with a service provider that is not going to keep pace with the market on a product that can take the company up to a year to implement.

Get to Know the People on the Company's Account

Depending on the number of entities in the pool the worldwide implimentation of the structure could take up to a year to complete. The bank's implementation team, in coordination with the company's in-house project manager, will have the greatest impact on the success of the implementation.

An experienced bank implementation manager will have already implemented several similar structures for companies with a similar geographic footprint, thereby ensuring knowledge of the specific local customs and hurdles which will need to be addressed. Just as important, this individual must have a thorough understanding of the internal processes needed to open bank accounts and set up the services required from the global structure.

Ask about the background of the implementation manager who will be assigned to the company. Meet specifically with this individual to discuss the implementation plan that will be developed. Ask for references from clients for which this manager has previously worked. The bank's implementation manager will be working with the company on a daily basis. Making sure the company is comfortable with this individual's abilities is imperative to the ultimate success of the company's implementation.

CONCLUSION

According to the 2007 JP Morgan Asset Management Global Cash Management Survey, cash management remained the most important function for corporate treasury departments, with 53% of the respondents assigning it the top score, up from 45% in 2006. Fortunately, systems and structures have been developed that enable a corporate treasury department to obtain the information needed to manage this daily activity on a global basis in a timely and efficient manner.

The challenge in implementing a global liquidity management structure is in being able to focus the company's attention on the key drivers that will dictate the worldwide liquidity management structure that best coincides with its own goals and long-term strategies. By following the suggested courses of action detailed above, corporate treasury departments can turn the review process—which can be daunting in scope—into a manageable activity. In this way the corporate treasury will be prepared for deciding on and implementing the most effective global liquidity management structure for the company.

▸▸ MAKING IT HAPPEN

The decision on the most appropriate global liquidity management structure for your company must coincide with the overall company, treasury/finance department, business unit, and local facility/plant goals and objectives. To build consensus for the recommended structure:

- Obtain tax, accounting, legal, audit, and insurance department support for the structure by involving representatives from these departments in the review process, thereby incorporating their needs and objectives into the process.
- Obtain senior treasury/finance support for the recommended structure by identifying how the structure meets the company and corporate treasury department goals and strategies.
- Obtain senior business unit support by identifying how the recommended structure will improve operations at the business unit level.
- Obtain facility/plant support for the recommended structure by considering its local cash management needs and identifying how the structure will improve its local operations.

▸▸ MORE INFO

Book:

van der Wielen, Lex, Willem van Alphen, Joost Bergen, and Phillip Lindow. *International Cash Management: A Practical Guide to Managing Cash Flows, Liquidity, Working Capital and Short-term Financial Risks*. 2nd ed. Treasury and Management Finance Series. Driebergen, Netherlands: Riskmatrix, 2006.

Articles:

Diamond, Nick, and Michael Golden. "Achieving new heights through a truly global liquidity structure." Online at: www.ibm.com/us (search on "Diamond Golden").

gtnews.com with ABN AMRO. "How to manage your global liquidity—Part 2: Cross-currency pooling." September 28, 2005. Online at: www.gtnews.com/feature/85_2.cfm

gtnews.com with ABN AMRO. "How to manage your global liquidity—Part 4: The next wave of enhancements." January 24, 2006. Online at: www.gtnews.com/feature/85_4.cfm

Hawser, Anita. "Bringing it all together." *Global Finance* (December 2005). Online at: www.gfmag.com/2005/Dec/c_ci/fe_art03.php

Potter, St John. "Global provider: Do all banks live up to the label?" *JP Morgan Treasury Services*. Online at: www.jpmorgan.com (search on "Potter global provider").

Seifert, Erik, and Robert Pehrson. "Corporate cash management trends—Part 4: Liquidity management." gtnews.com, March 4, 2008. Online at: www.gtnews.com/feature/225_4.cfm

Skerritt, Susan. "European treasury structures: Compare and contrast." *Treasury Management International* (February 2003): 14–18. Online at: www.treasurystrat.com/resources/articles/EuropeanTreasuryStructures.pdf

Website:

Association for Financial Professionals (AFP), Bethesda, MD: www.afponline.org

"**Nothing happens quite by chance. It's a question of accretion of information and experience.**" Jonas Salk

  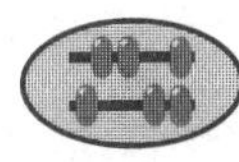   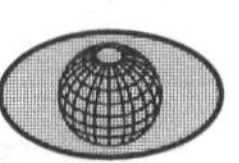   

Integrated Corporate Financial Risk Policy by David C. Shimko

EXECUTIVE SUMMARY

- Corporate risk is any threat to financial objectives, measured in financial terms.
- Risk is defined not necessarily as absolute risk, but relative to a benchmark.
- If risk is free, corporate departments will squander it. By putting a price on risk, it is managed when it should be.
- Corporate treasuries tend to minimize risk, probably not consistently with corporate objectives.
- Procurement risk problems often come from fixed budget levels.
- Marketing risk problems often come from giveaways in customer contracts.
- An integrated corporate risk policy defines how risk should be measured, priced, and rewarded in the corporation, leading to better corporate decisions in all departments.

DEFINING RISK—HARDER THAN IT SEEMS

Risk can be described as the threat of an adverse outcome. Many firms take the benchmark strategy of doing nothing (i.e., investing in Treasury Bills), and measure their risk in absolute terms relative to the strategy of doing nothing. Others measure their risk-taking behavior relative to what might be considered risky benchmarks. Mutual funds, for example, do not focus on the absolute risk of their portfolios; rather, they determine how far away they are from a market benchmark, such as being long the S&P 500. Corporations should explicitly determine their proper benchmarks.

For example, when a gold company hedges its exposure to gold prices, it is arguably reducing risk. However, shareholders may see this as an increase in risk, since it moves the company away from its natural gold exposure. Similarly, shareholders own all sorts of assets and diversify their risks; if a company moves away from its natural risk profile it is making the shareholder portfolio less diversified.

Most financial institutions should measure their risks relative to holding Treasury Bills, since that is an appropriate benchmark strategy for its shareholders. Furthermore, because financial institutions' risk capital levels are regulated, risk is a scarce resource that must be consumed wisely.

In all cases, shareholder preferences should be considered in establishing the risk benchmark, risk measure, and risk appetite. This is the first critical step in establishing a best practice integrated risk policy.

RISK INTEGRATION

Many treatments of risk deal with risk silos: treasury risk, insurance risk, budget risk, procurement risk, sales price risk, and marketing risk. While specialized knowledge in each of these areas informs risk management and execution, it does not address questions like the following:

- How important is one risk *vis-à-vis* the corporation's entire risk profile?
- Is it better to manage a risk operationally or through financial means?
- Are there natural risk offsets to consider before targeting a particular risk for elimination?
- What are the interactions among risks and the natural diversification benefit companies generally have?

The following sections consider selected risks that are shared by many corporations, within the framework that good risk management in each area must be consistent with the overall corporate standard. The overall corporate standard should include a cost for risk to prevent it from being squandered, measures of risk that are consistent with corporate objectives, consistent policies for treasury and insurance risk, best practices in procurement and marketing risk, corporate hedging policy to hedge integrated risk (not in each silo), and risk-based performance measurement to reward those who manage risk prudently.

THE COST OF RISK

Financial institutions often place an explicit cost on risk to ensure it is being taken prudently. For example, a bank may require that a transaction that risks $100 million in bank capital must earn at least $25 million in present value. This cutoff percentage (25%) can be called a risk-adjusted return on capital, or RAROC.

Bank capital is affected by market risk (changes in market prices), credit risk (default risk and counterparty performance risk), and operational risk (people, processes, and systems). Any activity that increases risk should not be voluntarily undertaken without earning a commensurate return. The logic is as simple as net present value: if money were free, people would squander it more. When risk is free, it is also squandered. Nonbanks also need measures of the cost of risk, although the measures may be different.

The risk-based performance measurement process is designed to ensure that managers take risk prudently, by reflecting the cost of risk in assessments of their performance, and thereby affecting their compensation.

MEASURING AND REPORTING RISK

If risk is the threat of an adverse outcome, that threat should be measured against the corporation's business objective. If the business objective is to "maximize shareholder value," then the logical risk measure is the potential reduction in share price. If the business objective is to "maximize earnings while keeping an investment grade rating," then the appropriate risk measures are "earnings at risk," a probabilistic statement of how bad earnings can get, and the probability of a ratings downgrade.

Many corporations report their risks in terms of value-at-risk or, worse, Greek letters such as sigma (standard deviation) and delta (sensitivity to a pricing benchmark). Best practice firms report their risks not only in financial terms that senior managers can understand easily, but also in terms that map directly into financial goals.

TREASURY

A company's treasury usually has the best opportunity to manage risk, since it deals mostly with issues related to interest rates and foreign exchange. A treasury risk policy that requires 100% hedging may be at odds with corporate objectives. For example, a large corporation with little debt probably does not need to worry about whether its debt is financed on a fixed or floating basis. Since floating debt is usually cheaper, it may be better not to hedge. The same thing is true of foreign exchange. If the risks are small relative to the company, the question should be asked if hedging is necessary.[1] If the risks are large, hedging may be justified.

Other treasuries trade quite a lot within their hedging boundaries, creating a pocket of speculative activity within the firm.

"Ultimately we will enhance transparency by providing investors and issuers with our views of a management team's ability to understand, articulate and successfully manage risk." Standard & Poors

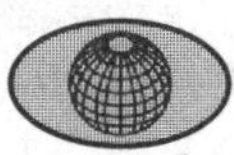

Unless the firm can demonstrate a core competence in trading foreign exchange, this does not usually contribute positively to corporate objectives.

PROCUREMENT AND BUDGETING

Fixed price budgets are the classic example of a procurement risk management policy that may be inconsistent with corporate risk policy. Budgets create the artificial incentive to hedge regardless of the cost of doing so, as long as the realized price is within budget. Other procurement policies have to do with portfolio price risk management of the company's factors of production. This subportfolio of the company must also be managed in a way that is consistent with overall corporate objectives.

The other major procurement risks include supplier performance, often modeled as a credit risk, and supply chain management, usually modeled as an operational risk. By establishing a cost of risk at the corporate level, a procurement division can make intelligent choices about which risks to take, which risks to manage, and how to manage them most efficiently.

Risk problems in procurement and budgeting can be best demonstrated in the accompanying case study.

CASE STUDY

A large multinational corporation operates a distribution facility in Puerto Rico. The facility maintains automobiles and light trucks, requiring the use of significant amounts of diesel over the year. The price of diesel is determined by a local index that fluctuates roughly along the lines of US gas prices. The company's procurement officer has a budget to meet for the year, and will not meet his target if diesel prices increase over the year. He has two alternatives: to try to fix a price with a small distributor, or to try to hedge the price using market derivatives. What should he do?

Answer: First, since this is a large corporation, it is likely that it does not need to manage this risk. In other words, the costs of managing risk are probably greater than the benefits. The only driver for hedging is the policy that affects the procurement officer's compensation. Therefore, the procurement officer should seek a solution whereby his budget is adjusted in line with the changes in diesel prices; if diesel prices go up $0.50, his budget should go up as well. His budget should drop if diesel prices fall, so he is not rewarded for a windfall outside his control.

Regarding the hedging methods, both are problematic. By fixing the price with a small distributor, he may be using his market clout to put the distributor in jeopardy, since the distributor may have to take the deal and will not be able to hedge. Since there are not many diesel distributors in Puerto Rico, this may not be wise, since the distributor could go bankrupt. By hedging the price with derivatives, the procurement officer will see increased trading costs, including risk of rogue trading (see the Ford debacle on platinum), margining, and counterparty credit risk (see the article in this volume on Dangers of Corporate Derivative Transactions: pp. 46–48).

MARKETING AND SALES

While most companies are well aware of the credit risk in their receivables, they are usually less aware of the risks in their sales contracts. For example, a product warranty creates a potentially costly obligation for the company that needs to be considered in product pricing. That calculation should include not only the expected warranty service costs, but also consideration for the risk that warranty claims may be much higher than expected.

Other sales contracts may be inadvertently giving away valuable options:

- renewal options (at the same price);
- cancellation options;
- options to increase or decrease purchase quantities;
- options to match price (for example, a most-favored nation clause);
- requirements to post collateral (financial products);
- options for additional free services.

In many environments, salespeople are rewarded on the basis of revenue. Hence, they are loath to cut price. An alternative for many of them is to continue to "throw in options" until the deal gets done, hoping they will never be valuable, but running that risk for the company. They are hoping those risks will never be quantified or attributed to the sales group.

Best practice risk management in marketing prices the various contract features considering both expected losses and risks, and charges the sales department for the costs of the options it gives away.

RISK-BASED PERFORMANCE MEASUREMENT

The common theme in all the corporation's departments is that if risk has no cost, departments should not be penalized for taking it (as with the case study). If risk has a cost, it should be quantified and charged to the department to make sure they take risk only when it is appropriate (as with the marketing example). Policies that require minimizing risk are usually inappropriate (such as the treasury example), since that is not the corporate objective.

The risk-based performance measure for a company that measures risks relative to earnings would be:

Department's contribution to earnings over benchmark
– (Earnings-at-risk department contribution
× Cost of earnings risk)

For example, if a procurement is expected to cost 25 cents per share in earnings, has the risk of going up to 30 cents per share, but ends up costing 24 cents per share, its earnings contribution is 1 cent, its earnings-at-risk contribution is 5 cents, and its performance measure (assuming cost of risk of 25%) is –0.25 cents per share. If the department can cut its risk in half at no cost, its contribution is +0.38 cents per share. This performance measure gives explicit guidance on procurement risk management, and rewards procurement for finding a way to reduce risk.

Finally, risk-based performance measurement systems, like any performance measurement systems, invite abuse from those whose compensation depends on those systems. Care must be taken in the design of these systems to reduce or eliminate the risk of "gaming the system."

OVERALL HEDGING POLICY

Many firms prefer to manage their risks in silos, with separate departments for insurance risk, treasury risk, procurement risk, and pensions. This has the benefit of putting decision authority where the expertise lies, and can improve execution of policy. However, the cost is that the departments may have different objectives and may manage risk in inconsistent ways.

Some firms establish a single central hedging authority that takes ownership of all the departmental risks and decides how to hedge those risks at the portfolio level for the benefit of the company. This process tends to ensure that small risks are not managed, but large risks that cross department lines are actively measured and managed.

CONCLUSION

Risk management policy is more than a risk control policy. It sets out defined threats to corporate objectives, measures threats relative to the financial indicators that define success, and ensures consistent

"There are risks and costs to a program of action. But they are far less than the long-range risks and costs of comfortable inaction." John F. Kennedy

interpretation and pricing of risk throughout the company. A widely used measure at financial institutions is RAROC or something similar. A corporation's choice of risk measure and cost will depend on its own particular circumstances.

MAKING IT HAPPEN

- Determine if risk is a scarce resource for your company.
- If it is, seek to identify risks in all parts of the firm.
- Risks are often hidden in contracts, procurement, budgeting, marketing, sales, and even risk mitigation.
- Put a cost on risk to facilitate a culture of smart risk-taking.

MORE INFO

Many good books specialize in enterprise risk management for financial institutions, but there are few titles available on enterprise risk for corporations generally.

Books:

Chew, Donald H. (ed). *Corporate Risk Management*. New York: Columbia University Press, 2008.

Damodaran, Aswath. *Strategic Risk Taking: A Framework for Risk Management*. Upper Saddle River, NJ: Wharton School Publishing, 2008.

Smithson, Charles W. *Managing Financial Risk: A Guide to Derivative Products, Financial Engineering, and Value Maximization*. 3rd ed. New York: McGraw-Hill, 1998.

See Also:

★ Dangers of Corporate Derivative Transactions (pp. 46–48)
★ Managing Counterparty Credit Risk (pp. 75–77)
★ Quantifying Corporate Financial Risk (pp. 97–99)
★ Real Options: Opportunity from Risk (pp. 808–810)
Mastering Risk Volume 1: Concepts (p. 1297)

NOTES

1 Copeland, Thomas E., and Yash Joshi. "Why derivatives don't reduce foreign exchange risk." *McKinsey Quarterly* (February 1996): 66–79.

"By definition, risk-takers often fail. So do morons. In practice it's difficult to sort them out." Scott Adams

     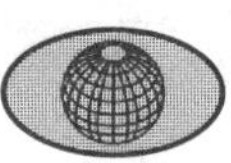   

Managing Capital Budgets for Small and Medium-Sized Companies by Neil Seitz

EXECUTIVE SUMMARY

- Small and medium-sized enterprises have distinct capital budgeting best practices, distinct because they result from top management's intimate knowledge of the business.
- The search for investment opportunities depends on effective communication of strategy.
- Best practice in capital investment analysis starts with strategic importance, followed by profitability and risk assessment.
- Funding decisions must consider cost, control, flexibility, and risk.
- Monitoring capital investments is the essential, but frequently neglected, final phase.

INTRODUCTION

Capital budgeting irrevocably shapes the direction of a business, and our collective capital budgeting decisions "determine the kind of society that we and our children will live in—not just this year but many years from now as well."[1] Investment of revenue from their oil industry by Gulf countries is "profoundly reshaping global capitalism."[2] Decisions of such magnitude must be made correctly.

All corporate finance books, including books by the present author, offer the same advice: Choose investments with positive net present values. The NPV rule is important, but it is only one element of best practice. This article highlights best practices in four phases of managing capital budgets for small and medium-sized businesses (SMEs):

- Create proposals;
- Select investments;
- Fund investments;
- Monitor results.

THE NPV RULE

Net present value (NPV) is the present value of cash inflows minus the present value of cash outflows. A capital investment is desirable if the NPV is positive, and the greater the NPV, the more desirable is the investment. Let us say that a proposed project generates a cash inflow of $1,100 in one year. Suppose that the *hurdle rate*, the rate investors could earn elsewhere with similar risk, is 10%. The present value—the amount you would have to invest elsewhere at 10% to get $1,100 in one year—is $1,000. The proposed project happens to cost only $950, which is $50 less than the present value; the NPV of the project is $50. The internal rate of return (IRR) is the rate of return actually earned on the investment. For this example, the IRR is 15.8%: $950 invested at 15.8% would grow to $1,100 in one year. If the NPV is positive, the IRR is greater than the hurdle rate, and vice versa.

CREATE PROPOSALS

The results of capital budgeting cannot exceed the set of capital investment proposals. Some large bureaucracies announce a process for submitting proposals—and then wait passively. The shape and direction of a company are determined by capital budgeting decisions, so a passive approach gives the CEO little role in shaping the future of the business.

An *active capital budgeting approach* is best practice, and it starts with strategy. Strategy creates competitive advantage, and therefore adds value. Without competitive advantage there are no projects with positive NPV. Managers in a position to identify capital investment opportunities must understand the company's strategy, and how capital investments are a major part of strategy implementation.

A second aspect of the active approach is that many people have vested interests in the status quo. A new strategic direction requires aggressive top management involvement to identify investment opportunities.

An advantage of a SME is that the CEO is generally close to the action. The CEO is well positioned to communicate strategy, spot opportunities, and evaluate investments. A potential weakness of a SME is failure of the CEO to maintain a disciplined, strategic approach, and failure to communicate strategy to other managers. Best practice responsibility in generating proposals in a SME falls heavily on top management. Strategy, communication, and discipline are key elements.

SELECT INVESTMENTS

General rules for capital investment decisions are the same at global conglomerates and SMEs. Application of the rules is different at a SME, because the CEO is usually not far removed from the person proposing an investment. The CEO is often the originator of a large project, particularly one of strategic importance.

Strategy is the best place to start. Clever wordsmiths can explain why anything and everything is consistent with the company's strategy. It is the job of top management to make a critical, independent judgment of the strategic importance of the project. To aid in that judgment, Carroll and Mui (2008) stress that "Reviewers should ask for a detailed written description of the strategy—not spreadsheets and slides."[3]

The second step in the capital budgeting process is NPV analysis. Project proponents will compute an NPV if asked, and will generally predict positive NPV. Herein lies a subtle danger. If a pet project has a negative NPV, there is a temptation to adjust the sales forecast enough to make it positive. Studies have shown that, on average, proposals overestimate NPV.[4]

What are best practices for avoiding excess optimism? First, know the people in your company well enough to know who is likely to be overly optimistic. The SME has an advantage in this regard because of its size. Second, seek independent input on critical assumptions for major investments. Third, and this is essential, establish an effective monitoring system, so that managers expect to be accountable for their forecasts.

One reason for starting with strategy rather than NPV is that there are strategic decisions for which accurate NPV estimates are virtually impossible. One example is the Scott Seed Company, which invests in research to maintain its enviable brand recognition for the best lawn grass seed. It would be difficult for Scott to measure the NPV of a particular research project. The project approval process must allow for the funding of critical activities of this type, even though they would lose out if the first hurdle was *proven* NPV.

Decision speed is another best practice. Many organizations still use an annual budget cycle, in which all proposals for the year are considered together. This might be consistent with the speed of business in another century, but not today. The process must be open to respond to rapidly changing challenges and opportunities. SMEs have a capital investment decision speed advantage, because fewer layers of management are involved.

"One of the most important responsibilities of corporate managers is to evaluate and choose among major investment projects." Laughton *et al.* (2008)

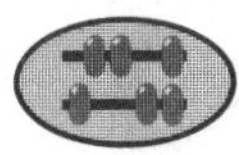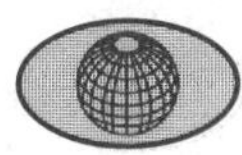

Risk analysis is different for SMEs compared to large, publicly traded companies, which are typically owned by diversified investors who are concerned about risk to their portfolio. For large companies, sensitivity to overall market conditions is the relevant risk, and risks unique to one company will average out across their portfolio. Owners of SMEs may have most of their wealth in one company, so the welfare of the company is of importance to them. For SMEs, the relevant risk of a particular capital investment is its impact on the overall health of the company.

Stress testing is a best practice for risk assessment. Identify possible problems, such as a recession or loss of a major customer. Prepare pro forma financial statements for the company in these unfortunate scenarios, with and without the proposed capital investment. Although income is important, the critical variable is cash: Will the proposed capital investment push the company into a vulnerable cash position in difficult times?

FUND INVESTMENTS

Funding is an essential part of the decision for a large capital investment. The major considerations in funding are cost, control, flexibility, and risk. Debt is often seen as less expensive than equity, partly because the cost of debt is tax-deductible. Sale of new equity is often seen as undesirable, because it dilutes ownership and weakens management control. The trade-offs are in flexibility and risk. Heavy debt levels reduce financing alternatives and may force the company to abandon its strategy in difficult financial markets. An often ignored best practice is always to maintain some unused borrowing ability so you can respond to changing circumstances.

The risk associated with debt is determined primarily by the cash flow needed to service the debt, not the amount of debt. Risk analysis using pro forma financial statements highlights the combined impacts of the proposed investment and its funding on the risk of running out of cash. A project funded with intermediate-term debt may raise the risk of a cash crisis to an unacceptable level, though the same project funded with long-term debt or equity would not be excessively risky.

MONITOR RESULTS

The most common deviation from best practice is a failure to monitor capital investments after the decision is made. First, the expectation of monitoring helps control excess optimism about costs and benefits. Second, deviations are more likely to be correctable if detected early. Third, monitoring is a learning tool for improving the capital budgeting process.

The first stage of monitoring occurs as the capital investment is being acquired and made operational. Are costs and timing consistent with the proposal? If there are deviations, can they be corrected? The second stage is monitoring the investment once it is operational. Are results what we expected, can we make improvements, and what can we learn from the experience?

CONCLUSION

Capital budgeting is the implementation of strategy, and it commits the firm to directions that are not easily changed. Best practice requires that strategy determines capital investments, not the other way round. Best practice requires a disciplined process, with the involvement of the CEO and CFO, and clear communication from proposal development through capital budgeting, funding, and monitoring.

CASE STUDY

Bass Family Electric

Bass Family Electric (the name has been changed for confidentiality) was an electronic contractor with a 20-year history of success in small commercial building projects. The founder made a strategic decision to leapfrog into much larger projects, increasing debt to fund the needed capital investment. Small projects typically lasted a few weeks, but big projects stretched over a couple of years. The sad result of expansion was a series of losses and looming bankruptcy.

The problem was failure to fully implement the strategic decision. The company continued to prepare bids as it had done for small projects, ignoring the fact that long-term projects were capital investments. One capital investment that was not made was a monitoring system for long-term projects. A brief study of past projects made clear which types of projects and conditions were leading to losses.

The prescription was to avoid the types of projects that created losses temporarily, modify the bid process to recognize large projects as capital investments, and institute monitoring that allowed a rapid response to deviations. Bass was then positioned to expand its range of business, including the types of projects that had previously contributed to losses.

▸▸ MAKING IT HAPPEN

- Determine who will be responsible for managing the capital budgeting process (typically the CFO). In addition to managing the process, the CFO will recommend financing.
- Communicate business strategy clearly to everyone involved.
- Establish and publish hurdle rates.
- Create standards with regard to what must be in capital investment proposals, including general description, strategic impact, NPV, and risk analysis.
- Establish responsibility for capital investment decisions. Managers at various levels may be given authority to decide on smaller investments, while large, strategic investments are decided by top management. A capital investment committee is frequently used, with membership including the CEO, CFO, and other senior managers.
- Establish a time schedule and process for monitoring. The monitoring process may be done as often as once a week during implementation, and may be part of the annual review thereafter.

▸▸ MORE INFO

Books:

Martin, John, and Sheridan Titman. *Valuation: The Art and Science of Corporate Investment Decisions*. Harlow, UK: Addison-Wesley, 2008.

Seitz, Neil, and Mitch Ellison. *Capital Budgeting and Long-term Financing Decisions*. Cincinnati, OH: Cengage, 2005.

Articles:

Laughton, D., R. Guerrero, and D. R. Lessard. "Real asset valuation: A back-to-basics approach." *Journal of Applied Corporate Finance* 20:2 (2008): 46–65.

Statman, M., and T. Tyebjee. "Optimistic capital budgeting forecasts: An experiment." *Financial Management* 14:3 (1985), 27–33.

"In most instances, the avoidable fiascos resulted from flawed strategies—not inept execution."
Carroll and Mui (2008)

  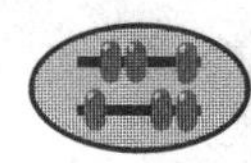   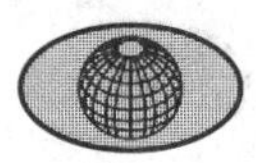   

Website:
AllBusiness resources and advice: www.allbusiness.com

NOTES

1 *Report of the President's Commission to Study Capital Budgeting*. Washington, DC. February 1999. Online at: clinton3.nara.gov/pcscb/report_pcscb.html

2 Abdelal, Rawi, Ayesha Khan, and Tarun Khanna. "Where the oil-rich nations are placing their bets." *Harvard Business Review* (September 2008): 119.

3 Carroll, Paul B., and Chunka Mui. "7 ways to fail big." *Harvard Business Review* (September 2008): 82–91.

4 Malmendier, Ulrike, and G. Tate. "CEO overconfidence and corporate investment." *Journal of Finance* 60 (2005): 2661–2700; Statman, Meir, and Tyzoon Tyebjee. "Optimistic capital budgeting forecasts: An experiment." *Financial Management* 14:3 (1985): 27–33.

"Post-audits generally reveal that actual project costs exceed their forecasts, and actual project revenues fall short of their forecasts." Statman and Tyebjee (1985)

     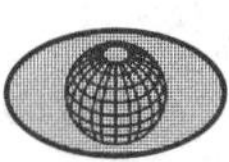   

Managing Counterparty Credit Risk by David C. Shimko

EXECUTIVE SUMMARY

- Counterparty risk exposure is the financial measure of performance risk in any contract.
- Many contract exposures are managed through operational or legal means; this article focuses on financial risk management.
- Counterparty credit exposure equals *current exposure* (accounts receivable minus collateral) plus an adjustment for *potential future exposure* based on possible increases in future net receivables.
- A comprehensive credit risk management policy addresses counterparty initiation and monitoring, contracting standards, credit authorities and limits, the transaction approval process, credit risk reporting, and reserving and capital policy.
- Credit risk mitigation is best handled through collateral, but there are legal and financial means to mitigate credit risk as well.
- Credit insurance can fit the exposure perfectly, but may be costly.
- Credit default swaps are linked to credit events and payments that may not correspond exactly to counterparty exposures, but may be cheaper than credit insurance.

DEFINING COUNTERPARTY RISK

Counterparty risk is the risk to each party of a contract that the counterparty will not live up to its contractual obligations; it is otherwise known as default risk.

Counterparty risk relates closely to performance risk. It arises whenever one entity depends on another to honor the terms of a contract. If a parts supplier fails to provide steering wheels to General Motors, GM will be damaged because of its inability to deliver complete cars. The resulting profit reduction is defined as the *exposure* that GM runs to its supplier. Similarly, GM runs a credit exposure to its customers who have not yet paid for their cars. This would include dealers and end customers who are financed by GMAC, GM's financing subsidiary.

Normally, performance risk is managed operationally—i.e., GM would use alternative suppliers, reserve supplies of steering wheels, and contractual nonperformance remedies to manage its performance risk. Also, to manage risk to its dealers, it may retain title to vehicles, verify insurance coverage, obtain some advance payment, and use legal means to minimize their collections risk. In addition to these counterparty risk situations, GM will experience counterparty risk from its derivative contracts.

Suppose GM wanted to purchase steering wheels on an ongoing basis from a European supplier, and protect itself from devaluation of the US dollar. It would likely enter a foreign exchange swap transaction with a bank. After entering the contract, rates would continue to change, bringing the contract in-the-money to either GM or the bank. If the dollar were to devalue, the contract would move in-the-money to GM, which would expose GM to the possible failure of the bank to honor its contract. Conversely, if the dollar were to strengthen, the bank would have an in-the-money contract with GM, and subsequently become concerned about GM's possible default risk.

MEASURING COUNTERPARTY RISK

Counterparty risk exposure can be divided into accounts receivable exposure and potential future exposure. If collateral is held as a bond for performance risk, the amount of the collateral is deducted from the gross exposure calculation. If the collateral itself is risky, such as a deposit of traded securities rather than cash, the collateral may not get full credit. Therefore, total credit exposure can be defined as follows:

Current exposure = Maximum of {Accounts receivable (A/R) – discounted collateral value} and 0

Potential future exposure = Current credit exposure plus maximum likely increase in future credit exposure

The maximum likely increase in future credit exposure is defined relative to a timeframe and relative to a statistical confidence interval, typically 95%. To demonstrate this concept simply, assume a potential foreign exchange transaction as an expected value of zero with an annual standard deviation of σ, a duration of τ, and a normally distributed risk. This is illustrated in Figure 1.

Figure 1. Exposure distribution for GM

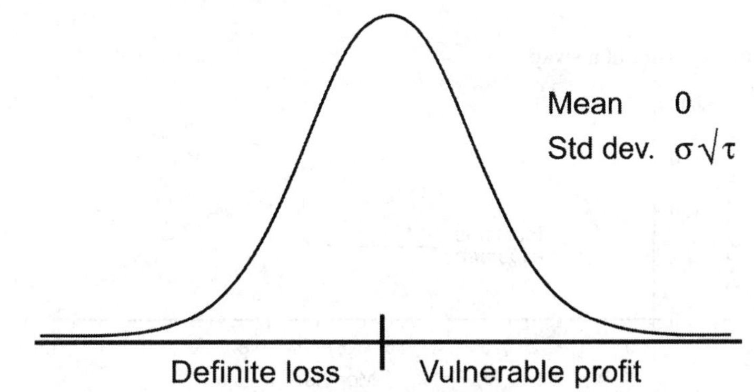

The *definite loss* shows in which cases GM will owe money to the bank, while *vulnerable profit* shows cases where the bank may owe money to GM. It is called vulnerable on account of the default risk of the bank. Although the current exposure is zero, the vulnerable profit could be as great as 1.65 standard deviations using a 95% confidence interval. This is also known as the *peak exposure*. The probability-weighted average of all the exposure figures, both zero and positive, is known as the *expected exposure*. For the normal distribution case, the expected exposure is 0.40 times the standard deviation.

To determine the expected loss conditional on default, we need to have two more pieces of information. One is the probability of default, which we will call π. The other is the *loss given default*, i.e., the percentage of the exposure that we never recover, even after settlement or bankruptcy. We call this estimate λ. Given these assumptions, we may summarize:

"The struggle itself toward the heights is enough to fill a human heart." Albert Camus

Peak exposure = $1.65\sigma\sqrt{T}$

Expected exposure = $0.40\sigma\sqrt{T}$

Expected loss = $0.40\pi\lambda\sigma\sqrt{T}$

For example, if GM determines the Euro volatility to be 15% per year, the contract to be three months in duration (0.25 years), its bank to have a default likelihood of 10%, and the loss given default to be 50%, its expected loss is $(0.40 \times 0.10 \times 0.50 \times 0.15 \times \sqrt{0.25}) = 0.0015$ times the size of the transaction—i.e., $1500 per million dollars hedged.

In the case of a swap rather than a single forward transaction, the amortization of the swap payments reduces exposure over time, so that it does not necessarily rise with the square root of time. In this case, the peak and expected exposure can be determined as in Figure 2.

The peak exposure can be used to understand how much risk is being taken with respect to the counterparty, whereas the expected exposure is an indicator of expected losses.

CREDIT RISK MANAGEMENT POLICY

Best practice credit risk management policy includes the following items:

- counterparty initiation and monitoring;
- contracting standards;
- credit authorities and limits;
- transaction approval process;
- credit risk reporting;
- a reserving and capital policy.

Counterparty initiation refers to the first time a company wishes to enter a transaction with a proposed counterparty. The credit department typically reviews available public information, credit agency reports, and counterparty financials before agreeing to trade with the counterparty. The financial status of the counterparty should be continually monitored to proactively detect situations where counterparty credit quality might deteriorate. It is also important to segregate counterparties according to legal entities; trading with a subsidiary of a triple-A company may provide little to no financial protection in the event of a default. Furthermore, one should assume in general that a benefit of trading with one legal entity *cannot* be netted against a loss to another legal entity of the same firm. For example, if a company is owed $1 million by subsidiary X, and owes $1 million to subsidiary Y of the same counterparty, and X defaults, it will still have an obligation to Y.

Contracting standards refer to the types of contracts that may be entered with an appropriately initiated counterparty. For example, in most derivative contracts, a standard contract such as the International Swaps and Derivatives Association (ISDA) contract is used. Even standard contracts require customization, however. The Credit Support Annex (CSA) of the ISDA details the unilateral or bilateral collateral posting requirements of the counterparties. It also typically contains provisions for Material Adverse Changes (MAC) in the credit quality of the counterparties, perhaps calling for more collateral when credit ratings downgrade. Finally, the CSA details rules for termination of contracts—for example, upon failure to supply collateral. ISDA Master Agreements should be established to guarantee netting across different legal entities of the same counterparty.

Credit limits refer to the amount of credit risk that may be taken to approved counterparties with approved contract forms. In most firms, credit limits are set on an aggregate basis by counterparty or credit rating—for instance, the firm is unwilling to take more than $100 million in credit risk to any one bank with a AA rating.

Credit authorities refer to the ability of any individual trader or trading desk to enter into new transactions with a counterparty, considering the possible impact on current or future credit exposure. Best practice firms use some measure of *potential future exposure* in setting their credit limits, although many focus only on *current exposure*. Some firms will also set portfolio concentration limits, for example, restricting the company's credit exposure to a particular industry. In all cases, firms must establish exception policies to deal with situations where credit limits are inadvertently or deliberately breached.

Transaction approval is a verification process to ensure that, before an individual transaction is executed, all of its requirements have been met: Counterparty initiation, contracts, collateral provisions, collateral collection if applicable, and compliance with authorities and with limits. Some firms allow slack in the process, such as transactions under a given materiality threshold with an uninitiated counterparty. These are a practical consequence of business dealings, but credit risk departments should strive to minimize these occurrences.

Credit risk reporting should address credit risk across the firm, whether risk is run in treasury, procurement, or sales. Aggregate receivables, potential future exposure, and aggregate collateral should be brought together in a comprehensive report by a non-netted legal entity. Best practice reporting includes portfolio risk measures, such as aggregate credit exposure, concentrations, and sensitivity of exposure to key economic drivers.

A reserving policy for expected credit losses, to be taken as a charge against earnings and reversed if losses never materialize, should be established by the office of the chief financial officer. This practice ensures that business units are held responsible for credit risk in their contracting processes. Some firms also charge business units for credit risk usage, but practices vary considerably. As a general statement, if a firm puts a price on credit risk, then business units must ensure that the profitability of their projects includes a cost factor for the credit risk being used. In general, the formula to adjust project NPV (net present value) for credit is as follows:

Project NPV = Starting NPV − Expected PV of credit losses − Cost of credit risk × PV of credit risk consumed for unexpected credit losses

In the marketing department, credit risk calculations are sometimes used as a determinant in product pricing. For example, credit card companies will factor expected collection costs and losses into its fee structure for retail clients.

CREDIT RISK MITIGATION

The most important credit risk mitigation tool is the collection of collateral and ongoing diligence with respect to enforcing collateral requirements. This may include the threat of forced terminations for failure

Figure 2. Exposure of a swap

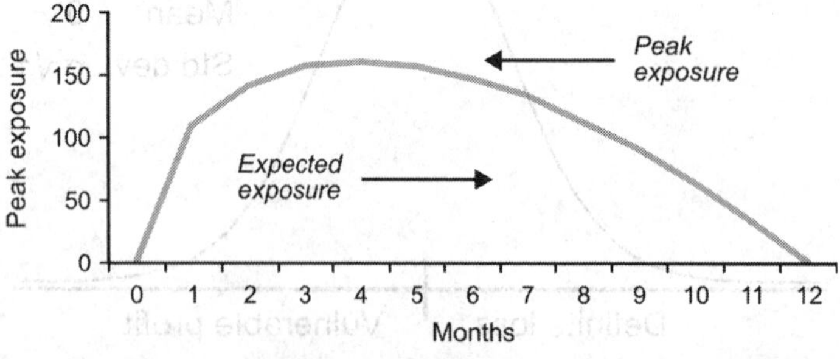

"Receivables and payables by the billions become concentrated in the hands of a few large dealers who are apt to be highly leveraged in other ways as well . . . It's not just whom *you* sleep with, but also whom *they* are sleeping with." Warren Buffett.

  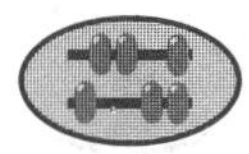   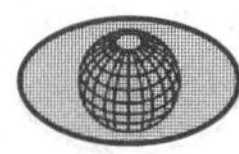   

to provide collateral. If collateral is not an option, due to contract limitations, then there are other options.

When a company determines that it has too much exposure to a single counterparty, and it is unable to collect collateral, it may undertake several actions. First, attempts may be made to close out some trading positions with the counterparty, or initiate new trading positions that have the effect of reducing the risk. Second, the company may attempt to novate a contract—i.e., reassign the contract to a different counterparty for some consideration. Third, a firm may try to "book out" a trade, if it finds it has identical and offsetting trades to two different counterparties. All of these options require counterparty agreement.

Barring these operational strategies, there are two financial strategies for mitigating credit risk. One is to obtain credit insurance for the actual realized loss to a defaulting counterparty. The other is to enter a credit default swap (CDS), which is essentially a contingent payment triggered by a counterparty credit event and made by a third-party derivatives trading counterparty.

Insurance can be tailored to provide specific coverage of the actual realized loss, but because of its specificity, the insurance company margin can be seen as being excessive by some corporations. Credit default swaps can be cheaper, since they trade in broader over-the-counter (OTC) markets.

Using CDSs to manage credit risk creates three problems. First, in most trading situations, the actual exposure is variable, making it difficult to target 100% protection. Second, in CDS markets, the payment triggering event may not correspond exactly to a counterparty's default event. For example, when Fannie Mae and Freddie Mac were put into receivership by the US government in 2008, this was classified as a default event in CDSs and synthetic collateralized debt obligations (CDOs), which were built from those CDSs—even though there was no default. Third, as we learned in 2008, CDS spreads can become extremely high and can be subject to their own performance risk, as Lehman Brothers' counterparties discovered.

OTHER CONSIDERATIONS

Contagion. Most models of credit focus on bilateral credit arrangements, without recognizing that credit relationships are multilateral. For example, GM's supplier mentioned above may depend on other suppliers for parts. While the supplier itself may be creditworthy, its own suppliers may not be creditworthy. GM may not know how vulnerable it is to its counterparty's counterparty.

Consequences. While counterparty risk is often measured in terms of the counterparty's failure, it may be the case that default by a counterparty leads to much greater damage for a company. Many financial institutions were compromised in 2008 when the credit crisis caused a domino-like effect of systemic corporate collapse. Counterparty credit risk assessment, therefore, must include all the costs of counterparty failure, including the cost of lost reputation, lower credit rating, and, in the most extreme cases, bankruptcy.

CONCLUSION

Although a relatively young discipline, credit risk management has matured rapidly. Improved risk measurement and reporting techniques paired with comprehensive credit risk policies can provide extremely effective protection against credit risk losses. The best risk management techniques are operational and legal, with collateral providing the best financial risk mitigation. Credit insurance and credit default swaps offer financial protection against default, but each at its own cost—which must be compared to the benefits of reducing the specific risk it is intended to mitigate.

▸▸ MAKING IT HAPPEN

- Set a corporate policy for credit risk management that recognizes the links to financial strategy.
- Identify corporate contracts and relationships with credit or performance risk.
- Model and quantify the organization's exposure to credit losses.

▸▸ MORE INFO

Books:

Saunders, Anthony, and Linda Allen. *Credit Risk Measurement: New Approaches to Value at Risk and Other Paradigms*. 2nd ed. New York: Wiley, 2002.

Servigny, Arnaud de, and Olivier Renault. *Measuring and Managing Credit Risk*. New York: McGraw-Hill, 2004.

"Never cheat, but do not be soft. It is a hard world. Be harder. But, and this is the test, at the same time, obviously, a good fellow." Gerald Sparrow

     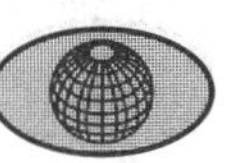   

Managing Interest Rate Risk by Will Spinney

EXECUTIVE SUMMARY

- Interest rate risk can manifest itself in several different ways.
- It is best managed within the context of the firm and a risk framework.
- Proper evaluation or measurement is key.
- Selection of a good key performance indicator is essential.
- A typical response to interest rate risk is a transfer of risk to another party.
- Many risk transfer tools are available, of which interest rate swaps are the most popular.
- The risk is usually transformed rather than eliminated.

INTRODUCTION

Almost all firms are exposed to interest rate risk, but it can manifest itself in different ways. A proper response to this risk can only come following a full understanding of the context of the firm and its strategy, along with a full evaluation of the risk. Firms should generate a well thought out key performance indicator (KPI) and then apply one or more of the many tools available in the market to transfer interest rate risk.

MAJOR WAYS THAT A FIRM CAN BE AFFECTED

Interest rate risk is the exposure of the firm to changing interest rates. It has four main dimensions:

Changing Cost of Interest Expense or Income

Companies with debt charged at variable rates (for example, based on Libor, and also called floating rates) will be exposed to increases in interest rates, whereas companies whose borrowing costs are totally or partly fixed will be exposed to falls in interest rates. The reverse is obviously true for companies with cash term deposits. This is usually the key risk that firms consider.

Impact on Business Performance by a Changing Business Environment

Changes in interest rates also affect businesses indirectly, through their effect on the overall business environment. In normal times, for example, construction firms enjoy a rise in business activity when interest rates fall, as investors build more when the cost of projects is lower. Conversely, some firms may benefit from high levels of activity that prompt a high interest rate response by central banks. So some firms may have a form of natural hedge against the other forms of interest rate risk, although for any one firm the effect may lead or lag actual changes in rates.

Impact on Pension Schemes Sponsored by the Firm

Pension schemes that carry liability and investment risk for the sponsor have interest rate risk in that liabilities act in a similar way to bonds, rising in value as interest rates fall and vice versa.

Changing Market Values of Any Debt Outstanding

Although a nonfinancial firm will usually report its bonds on issue in financial statements, at substantially their face value, early redemptions must be done at the market value. This may be significantly different, as interest rates will change the value of fixed-rate debt. This risk is not commonly considered by most nonfinancial firms.

INTEREST RATE RISK IN THE CONTEXT OF THE FIRM

Investors do expect firms to take risks, especially with regard to their core business competencies. It may be that investors expect the firm to take interest rate risk. On the other hand, investors would probably not expect a firm to breach a financial covenant because of rising interest rates.

RISK MANAGEMENT FRAMEWORK

A risk management framework includes the following key stages:

- Identification and assessment of risks;
- Detailed evaluation of the highest risks;
- Creation of a response to each risk;
- Reporting and feedback on risks.

Evaluation is crucial to the management of interest rate risk and will discover exactly how a firm might be affected, thus guiding the response to the risk. Evaluation techniques include: sensitivity analysis, modeling changes in a variable against its effect; and value at risk (VaR) analysis, based on volatilities to calculate the chances of certain outcomes.

Let us look at a simple firm with earnings before interest and tax (EBIT) of 100, borrowings of 400 (all on a floating rate), an interest rate of 6% (as a base case), and a tax rate of 30%, and apply some of these techniques.

Evaluation 1: Sensitivity Analysis

A 1% move in interest rates has an effect of 4 (1% of 400) on the annual interest charge. This is not very helpful because there is no context for the effect.

Evaluation 2: Sensitivity Analysis

A table can be constructed to show the effect on earnings and interest cover (Table 1). In the table items in bold represent the base case, whereas other columns represent the sensitivities to this base case. Earnings are earnings after interest and tax.

This is much more helpful, showing the effect on both earnings and interest cover. If the firm has an interest cover covenant of, say, 3.75, then the table shows a high risk of a breach, depending on how likely a rise in rates might be.

Evaluation 3: Sensitivity Analysis

Suppose now that EBIT displays volatility. We can construct a further table (Table 2) showing interest cover under variations in EBIT and the interest rate. Italic numerals indicate a covenant breach, and the number in bold is the base case described in Table 1.

A drop of 5 in EBIT and a rise of 0.5% in interest rates will cause a breach, a clear risk factor for the firm. If a relationship between EBIT and interest rates can be established, then further conclusions could be drawn.

Sensitivity analysis does not show the probability of these changes, but if they are available—for example from a study of

Table 1. The effect of interest rate changes on earnings and interest cover

	Interest rate						
	4.5%	5.0%	5.5%	**6.0%**	6.5%	7.0%	7.5%
EBIT	100.0	100.0	100.0	**100.0**	100.0	100.0	100.0
Interest	(18.0)	(20.0)	(22.0)	**(24.0)**	(26.0)	(28.0)	(30.0)
Tax	(24.6)	(24.0)	(23.4)	**(22.8)**	(22.2)	(21.6)	(21.0)
Earnings	57.4	56.0	54.6	**53.2**	51.8	50.4	49.0
Interest cover	5.56	5.00	4.55	**4.17**	3.85	3.57	3.33

"This firm has a policy of fixing rates on 80% of their borrowing, but no-one could tell me why that was."
Anonymous

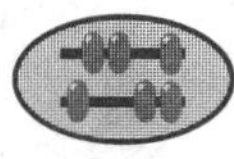

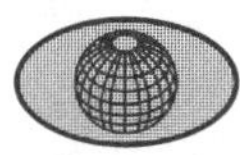

Table 2. Interest cover under variations in EBIT and interest rate

	Interest rate						
	4.5%	5.0%	5.5%	6.0%	6.5%	7.0%	7.5%
EBIT							
80	4.44	4.00	3.64	3.33	3.08	2.86	2.67
85	4.72	4.25	3.86	3.54	3.27	3.04	2.83
90	5.00	4.50	4.09	3.75	3.46	3.21	3.00
95	5.28	4.75	4.32	3.96	3.65	3.39	3.17
100	5.56	5.00	4.55	**4.17**	3.85	3.57	3.33
105	5.83	5.25	4.77	4.38	4.04	3.75	3.50
110	6.11	5.50	5.00	4.58	4.23	3.93	3.67
115	6.39	5.75	5.23	4.79	4.42	4.11	3.83
120	6.67	6.00	5.45	5.00	4.62	4.29	4.00

market volatility—a probability distribution for a covenant breach can easily be obtained.

Evaluation 4: VaR

Suppose that investigation of the assets and liabilities in the firm's pension scheme shows that the scheme has a deficit of 50. As an illustration, VaR might tell us that, based on the volatility of the long-term interest rates used to calculate liabilities, and taking into account that the scheme has some bond investments (in which value moves are opposite to liabilities), there is a 1 in 20 chance that the deficit will increase in the next year, because of interest rate changes alone, by 15 or more.

Interest rate risk inside a pension scheme (or other scheme for future employee benefits) often dwarfs interest rate risk inside the firm.

Evaluation should reveal where a firm is sensitive to interest rates. It could be:

- Earnings, perhaps where earnings per share (EPS) is an important issue.
- Cash flow.
- Interest cover ratios, perhaps because of financial covenants.
- Other ratios, such as those used by credit rating agencies.

ESTABLISHING A KPI AND RESPONSE TO THE RISK

Evaluation should lead the firm to establish a key performance indicator (KPI) for interest rate risk. A good example of a KPI would be: *Interest cover to be greater than 3.75, on a 99% confidence basis, over an 18-month period.* This is better than using a simple interest cover ratio or a fixed/floating ratio as a KPI, because it speaks specifically about the risk to the firm.

The KPI should guide the response to the risk. Possible responses include:

- *Avoid*: It is hard to avoid interest rate risk.
- *Accept*: Simply accept the risk and take no further action. This may be suitable if there are no significant issues such as proximate financial covenants.
- *Accept and reduce*: It may be possible to reduce the risk through internal actions, such as reducing cash balances as far as possible to repay debt.
- *Accept and transfer*: Many market products are available that enable a firm to change the character of interest payments. This process is called hedging.

ESTABLISHING A POLICY

The factors we have seen should be formalized in a policy, as should approaches to all risks. The policy should set out:

- The overall direction of the policy.
- How the risk is to be measured.
- Who has responsibility for the risk management.
- What procedures should be in place to control the risk.
- A framework for decision-making.
- The key performance indicator.
- A reporting mechanism to view the performance of the policy.

TOOLS AVAILABLE TO TRANSFER INTEREST RATE RISK

There are a large number of tools available for the transfer of interest rate risk (Table 3).

Interest Rate Swap

This key instrument deserves a little more explanation. It is an instrument that, in its usual form, transforms one kind of interest stream to another, such as floating to fixed or fixed to floating. Each swap has two counterparties, and therefore in each swap one party pays fixed and receives floating, while the other party receives fixed and pays floating.

There are two classic uses of swaps by nonfinancial firms:

Table 3. Tools that can be used to transfer interest rate risk

Tool	*Description*	*Comment*
Forward rate agreement (FRA)	An FRA is a tool for fixing future interest rates (or unfixing them) over shorter periods, up to say 1-2 years.	A 3v6 FRA allows a firm to fix the three-month Libor (or other reference) rate in three months time. It is dealt over the counter (with banks).
Future	Futures have the same function as FRAs.	Futures are traded on an exchange, and thus have less flexibility.
Cap	A cap is an option instrument. The buyer of a cap pays a maximum interest rate over the life of the cap but enjoys lower rates as they come down. Caps have a premium.	Caps are usually dealt over the counter by firms, and the classic use is for a borrower to buy a cap that is higher than current interest rates, thus providing insurance for the borrower.
Floor	A floor is an option instrument. The buyer of a floor receives a minimum interest rate over the life of the floor but enjoys higher rates as they increase. Floors have a premium.	Floors are usually dealt over the counter by firms, and the classic use is for a depositor to buy a floor that is lower than current interest rates, thus providing insurance for the depositor.
Collar	A collar is a combination of a cap and a floor, thus providing a firm with a corridor of possible interest rates between a maximum and a minimum.	A borrower would buy a cap and sell a floor, usually over the counter, thus creating a "collar," or corridor, of rates.
Interest rate swap	An interest rate swap is probably the most widely used and popular risk transfer instrument in the field of interest rate risk. It changes the nature of a stream of interest payments from floating to fixed or vice versa.	Swaps (as they are usually called) are dealt over the counter and the market is large and (usually) deep. Terms of 5 to 7 years are common with nonfinancial firms, although terms of 30 or more years are often used by pension schemes, reflecting their different maturity horizon.
Swaption	A swaption is an instrument where the buyer of a swaption has the right to enter into an interest rate swap at a particular rate, thus protecting the buyer against adverse movements in long-term rates, while allowing him or her to benefit from favorable moves.	Swaptions are not very popular with nonfinancial firms but might be used near the time of bond issues, for example.

"A quick look at the pension scheme showed that it was carrying way more risk to interest rates than our trading operations." Unnamed bank to author

Figure 1. Floating-rate borrower uses swap to convert to a fixed rate

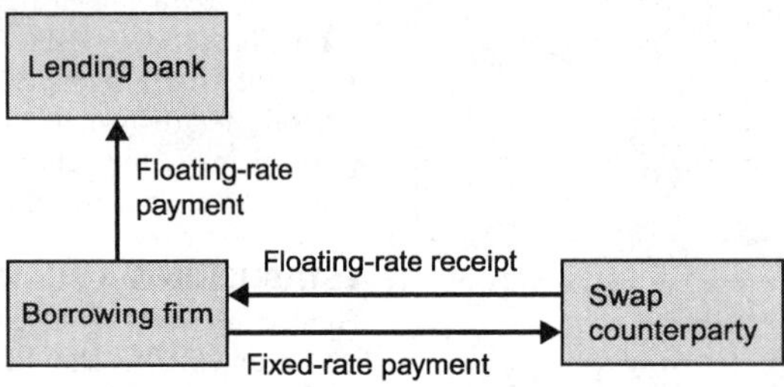

Figure 2. Fixed-rate borrower uses swap to convert to a floating rate

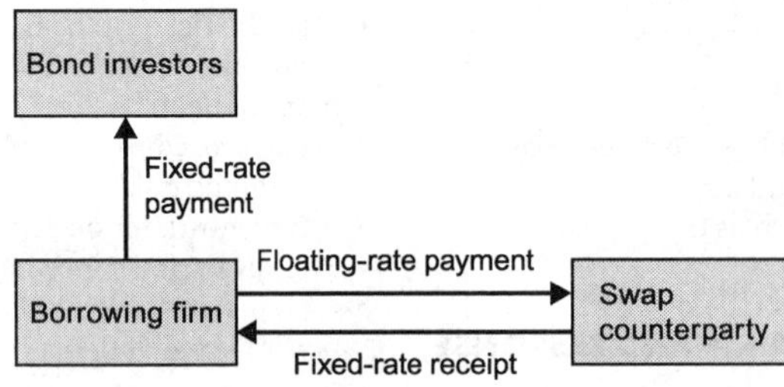

Table 4. Interest cover under variations in EBIT and interest rate for firm that pays fixed swap (see text for details)

	Interest rate						
	4.5%	5.0%	5.5%	6.0%	6.5%	7.0%	7.5%
EBIT							
80	*3.56*	*3.48*	*3.40*	*3.33*	*3.27*	*3.20*	*3.14*
85	3.78	*3.70*	*3.62*	*3.54*	*3.47*	*3.40*	*3.33*
90	4.00	3.91	3.83	3.75	*3.67*	*3.60*	*3.53*
95	4.22	4.13	4.04	3.96	3.88	3.80	3.73
100	4.44	4.35	4.26	4.17	4.08	4.00	3.92
105	4.67	4.57	4.47	4.38	4.29	4.20	4.12
110	4.89	4.78	4.68	4.58	4.49	4.40	4.31
115	5.11	5.00	4.89	4.79	4.69	4.60	4.51
120	5.33	5.22	5.11	5.00	4.90	4.80	4.71

- *A floating-rate borrower converts to a fixed rate.* In this case a borrower has floating-rate bank debt and carries out a pay-fixed swap, converting the debt to a fixed rate. This is shown diagrammatically in Figure 1. The two floating-rate streams cancel each other out for the borrower, leaving it to pay only a fixed-rate stream.
- *A fixed-rate borrower converts to a floating rate.* In this case a borrower has fixed-rate bond debt and undertakes a receive-fixed swap, converting the debt to a floating rate (Figure 2). The two fixed-rate streams cancel each other out for the borrower, leaving it to pay only a floating-rate stream.

Let's suppose that our firm from above has responded to the risk of covenant breach by deciding to enter into a pay-fixed swap for 75% of its borrowing. It will pay 6% on the fixed-rate leg of the swap. The interest cover table we considered in Table 2 is now as shown in Table 4.

The italicized cells (covenant breach) now cover the width of the table but are less deep. Our firm has a lower risk of a breach from interest rates alone but has increased the risk from a falling EBIT. As interest rates are believed to be more volatile than EBIT, the overall risk to our firm has been reduced through the transfer of risk.

FIXING PRODUCTS VERSUS OPTIONS

There is a key difference between interest-rate-fixing products (such as swaps) and options. A fixing instrument binds its user to the rate that is set when it is transacted. An option allows the buyer to walk away. So a firm taking out a pay-fixed swap, following which rates decline, is left paying the higher rates. The risk is thus transformed, rather than transferred. Exposure to rising rates has become an exposure to falling rates. Firms must be clear about this when establishing their response to risk.

Accordingly, option products may seem to be an ideal product to deal with interest rate risk, and for those prepared to pay, they can be. However, costs rise with two main factors:

- *Time*: The longer an option has until expiry, the higher the premium.
- *Volatility*: The higher the volatility in the underlying risk being hedged, the higher the premium.

Both these factors tend to deter firms from using options, and for the longer-term risk transfer-response interest rate swaps are usually the instrument of choice.

CONCLUSION

The effects of changes in interest rates on a firm can be complex, but techniques are available to evaluate and respond to any risks this presents. A clear reference back to business and financial strategy will put interest rate risk in its context, allow a suitable response, and help the firm to achieve its goals.

▸▸ MAKING IT HAPPEN

- Assess how the firm is affected by changes in interest rates.
- Evaluate the risk according to the firm's strategy, using tools such as sensitivity analysis or VaR.
- Establish a key performance indicator for the risk.
- Choose whether to avoid or to accept the risk.
- If the choice is to accept, either:
  - accept and reduce; or
  - accept and transfer, such as with interest rate swaps or options.
- Make frequent reports to give feedback on the risk.

▸▸ MORE INFO

Books:

Buckley, Adrian. *Multinational Finance*. 5th ed. Harlow, UK: Pearson Education, 2004.

Chapman, Robert J. *Simple Tools and Techniques for Enterprise Risk Management*. Chichester, UK: Wiley, 2006.

Websites:

Association for Finance Professional (AFP): www.afponline.org

Association of Corporate Treasurers (ACT): www.treasurers.org

National Association of Corporate Treasurers (NACT): www.nact.org

"I prefer to keep interest rates floating so that if our sales fall in a recession, we don't suffer too much because the Bank of England will simply cut rates to help the economy." Treasurer of a retail firm

  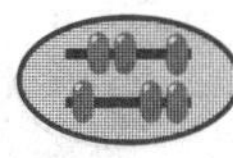   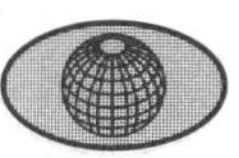   

Managing Liquidity in China—Challenging Times

by Marlene R. Wittman

EXECUTIVE SUMMARY

- Companies operating in China should monitor carefully the People's Republic of China's financial and foreign exchange (forex) regulatory landscape.
- The treasury operations and their traditional liquidity management tools usually employed in other regimes, such as intercompany loans, have not been permissible under Chinese law.
- China's regulatory framework is a fragmented system that is based on a bifurcation between foreign and local currency movements, with greatest importance given to control of the renminbi (the local currency), foreign currency flows, and the maintenance of the exchange rate.
- Since 2005, China's financial and forex regulators have increased their liberalization momentum, following a path that is meant to entice multinationals; this deregulation has been rolled out in a series of pilot programs.
- In volatile market conditions it is unclear how a global liquidity crunch will affect China's momentum towards policy relaxation.
- The best advice for treasurers coping with cash and liquidity management in China: Keep close track of the large foreign and local banks since they are in the best position to monitor regulatory intentions.
- A company's paramount asset in challenging liquidity times is its treasury talent—a treasurer should be able to anticipate and interpret the effect of the regulatory changes on the mechanics of cash management.

INTRODUCTION

Efficient cash and liquidity management in China is a multifaceted challenge—a treasurer has to scrutinize China's regulatory environment constantly. In the past regulation has been "lyrical" at best and arbitrary at worst. Up to recent market events, it had been tending towards liberalization. The treasurer has to match various limited and unique "China-derived" treasury solutions with the capital structures of his China entities. He has to anticipate the next direction of the regulators on both the financial and the forex fronts. In turbulent global credit conditions, the mandate becomes challenging but will create, we believe, a more robust set of treasury solutions for the China market.

UNDERSTANDING CHINA'S REGULATORY ENVIRONMENT

A China treasurer has to understand the fragmented yet punitive nature of the regulatory framework in which financial transactions and forex are regulated. A good rule of thumb is that the capital structure of an entity in China will determine what liquidity and repatriation tools are possible. If the company entered China operations fairly soon after China's market opening, the relevant capital structures –such as equity joint ventures, cooperative joint ventures, wholly owned foreign enterprises (WOFEs), and representative offices—have varying levels of restrictive regimes for the movement of local and foreign currencies. Structures sanctioned later by the government have more favorable regulatory treatment regarding the types of liquidity tools that can be employed. For example, from July 2006, the holding company and the regional headquarter (RHQ) structure was approved in order to encourage multinational companies (MNCs) to establish their regional operations in Shanghai. Since the move was to promote MNCs, the measure might not be useful to smaller companies operating in China.

China's regulatory backdrop for cash management is best viewed as a dual system that is designed to maintain the nonconvertible nature of the renminbi, ensuring that the renminbi forex level is maintained within a band of a basket of currencies. There are regulatory nuances to an entity's holding, movement, and account opening of foreign currency and renminbi, as well as cash repatriation. Foreign currency accounts within China, which require the State Administration of Foreign Exchange (SAFE) approval, are designated for certain capital injection exercises and for loan proceeds. Local currency is controlled in a number of ways, including physical flow of notes, control of local currency interest rates, and mechanisms for moving funds from corporate to individual accounts.

Renminbi currency accounts have more flexibility, and are used for daily operational needs, such as payroll, payables and receivables, and trade-related activities. The capital structure of the China entity determines the types of account the treasurer may open: For example, a representative office can only open one type of renminbi account, the basic account, which covers physical cash withdrawals and payroll.

Forex control and the maintenance of the renminbi-forex rate within a designated band is controlled by SAFE. SAFE, at the time of writing, has 34 branches and 807 sub-branches, a vast improvement over the previous centralized bureaucracy. SAFE oversees foreign currency-related matters in three main areas: (1) direct investment, in which case the nature of the investment must be examined for Department of Commerce approval (is the foreign direct investment "promoted," "restricted," or "prohibited"?); (2) SAFE also checks that transactions involving the use of foreign currency are "genuine"—the company must submit invoices, sales contracts, receipts and/or tax certificates to the appropriate SAFE subbranch for verification; and (3) SAFE oversees the limit on an entity's foreign debt, including foreign guarantees—for example foreign debt cannot exceed "total investment" ("registered capital" as defined by the Chinese). SAFE also provides the approval mechanism for foreign currency short-term debt levels, while a sister agency (the National Development and Reform Commission) oversees mid-term debt.

Relaxation of regulations in 2005–07 included the following: encouragement of MNCs to set up in China via the RHQ provisions; support for large Chinese corporations to set up outside China, thereby allowing renminbi flows to "temporarily" exit China; and implementation of deregulatory efforts via pilot programs. These "Nine Measures," promulgated in December 2005, were released to allow more flexibility for both foreign and Chinese qualified MNCs to manage their liabilities, including foreign currency cash pooling for domestic group entities, establishment of offshore accounts for overseas liquidity management, lending of foreign investors' surplus renminbi to overseas investors, execution of renminbi–foreign currency forward and renminbi–foreign currency swap transactions, and simplification of non-trade-related (or services-related) payment processes. In April 2006 the "Pudong Nine," as they became known, allowed certain companies to open multiple foreign currency accounts and liberalized foreign currency movements. In July 2006 a portion of the "menu" of forex reform measures for holding companies with RHQ status and SAFE approval was at the very beginning of its rollout phase—just as the liquidity crisis started to become apparent on a global basis.

CASH AND LIQUIDITY MANAGEMENT—THE OPTIONS IN CHINA

One way of looking at the myriad of overly restrictive regulations is as follows: The Chinese government, since its inception in 1949, has had as one of its dominant political mindsets the physical control or protection of the renminbi, its "people's money." This explains the limited options for onshore renminbi cash management and the fact that offshore entities are not allowed to hold renminbi accounts.

Renminbi Cash Management

Conventional cash and liquidity management solutions available to a treasurer in China are limited by what Chinese law permits. Direct intercompany lending is prohibited unless it is a trade-related transaction, or a payment of service, or a royalty fee. In the early days of China's opening, trading companies established onshore utilized transfer pricing methodologies to balance the levels of renminbi working capital within China, while monies were remitted out of the country under a documented trade transaction. The documentation required for this sort of transaction has expanded over the years as the Chinese tax authorities have become involved: They check that the transfer price is on an arm's length basis in order to assess the relevant taxes.

Second, if the Chinese company is part of a larger global trade structure of several entities, leading and lagging techniques can be used to facilitate a trade-backed transfer of funds. This technique obviously only applies to corporates with global operations that have subentities with varying levels of, and requirements for, working capital (balancing "cash-poor" entities versus "cash-rich" entities on a global basis).

The third method for circumventing the prohibition of intercompany loans is the entrustment loan structure (Figure 1). This is one of those uniquely "China-derived" structures that manages to solve the liquidity problem while satisfying the law proscribing intercompany lending. The structure basically replicates an intercompany loan; it started out as an ideal arrangement for single-source stable medium-term liquidity needs. It has since become a very elaborate structure, meeting more and more of the specific liquidity needs of onshore entities.

Figure 1. Mechanics and money flows involved in the entrustment loan system

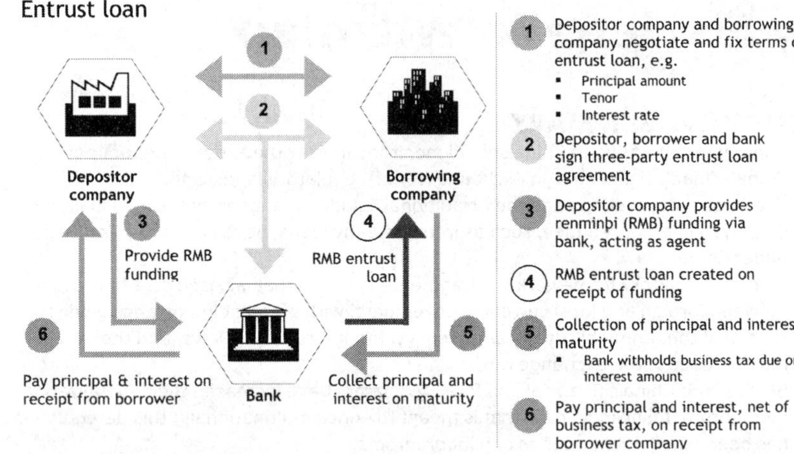

Source: Citibank China (Shanghai), Cash Management Division (2008).

Under a trilateral entrustment renminbi loan structure, the designated bank is "entrusted" by a depositor to lend on funds provided solely by the depositor to a designated borrower. The bank essentially acts as an intermediary between the parties to meet the regulatory prohibition on intercompany lending. The bank receives a commission and takes no credit risk in the transactions. In this way, companies with a shortfall on internally generated cash flow can make use of the surplus that cash-rich companies have generated via a third (fee-receiving) party.

The entity placing the deposit specifies the terms of the loan to the borrower: use of loan proceeds or purpose of loan, loan amount, tenor, and interest rate. The rate must be seen to be set using arm's length principles. Again, the Chinese tax authorities are on the scene: There is a business tax on the gross interest income earned on the loan, plus stamp duty.

Foreign banks operating in China have managed to refine the entrustment structure so that it is more efficient for group companies. For example, multiple entities within China can use the same legal structure for several transactions with simplified documentation. The advances in clearing infrastructures in China and the intensified competition among international banks entering this market have ensured that the entrustment framework is no longer a cumbersome transaction-by-transaction process.

Bank competition in China has resulted in further product development for renminbi cash management. Renminbi physical cash pooling—zero balancing (ZBA) and target balancing (TBA)—is essentially an automated daily entrustment loan structure. Physical cash pooling is a physical movement of funds between accounts of separate but legal entities with the object of achieving a "target balance" in each account at the end of the day. (If the target balance of the subaccount is set to zero, then that is the origin of the ZBA action.) Depending on the bank infrastructure, balances are physically "swept" to a header account (i.e. an active operating account). Conceptually, the renminbi cash pooling replicates intercompany cash pooling—ideal for multisource, variable-tenor liquidity needs. Also, depending on the bank, an overdraft facility may be provided, enabling the header and child accounts to deal with any overnight cash deficit position or intraday exposure. Therefore, renminbi cash pooling can cover the following treasury situations: shortage of funds on header account, surplus of funds on some of the accounts, funding of exact temporary shortages, and arrangement of sublimits for child accounts.

The China treasurer should take into account the facilities that the designated bank uses for this pooling arrangement. If dealing with a foreign bank, the treasurer should note that some cities in China are not yet fully "open" to foreign banking operations. If the entity requires cash pooling services on a pan-China basis, the treasurer needs to check that the foreign bank has arrangements in place with local banks to provide renminbi daily cash concentration services in these particular cities.

"There is a serious tendency towards capitalism among the well-to-do peasants." Mao Zedong

  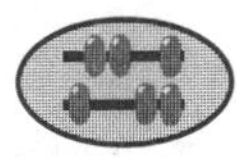   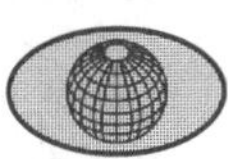   

Since the cash pooling is a variation on the entrustment loan structure, again there are tax implications, namely stamp and business tax, in addition to the usual bank fees for the facility.

Renminbi Short-Term Investment or Yield Enhancement

Similarly, there are limited options open to a treasurer wishing to put surplus renminbi to use. (In conditions of squeezed liquidity worldwide this is an important consideration.) The size of the entity will determine which instruments are cost-effective given the amount of surplus renminbi to invest. For example, MNCs invest surplus renminbi balances in call and time deposits. Since they are onshore renminbi instruments, they have regulated rates. Additionally, renminbi money market and bond funds are available to the MNC treasurer.

Depending on the bank, some treasurers are able to use the entrustment loan structure to maximize renminbi yield. The surplus renminbi is lent out to an unrelated party, and the bank provides a bank guarantee. The entrustment structure limits risk to the lender to bank risk rather than corporate risk. Since the interest rate can be higher than the regulated interest for onshore bank balances, the loan structure allows for enhanced yield.

Foreign Currency Cash Management

In general, the foreign currency management options available to a China treasurer are limited by the capital structure of the entity operating in China. In general, the larger the China-based operation, the more options are available to the treasurer, both onshore and offshore. This is entirely in keeping with the long-standing Chinese regulatory trend toward favoring large companies over small ones during times of policy liberalization.

Select MNCs operating in China—those with a Chinese holding company or a RHQ in China—may be permitted, with SAFE approval, to set up a foreign currency cash pooling structure. This allows companies to lend excess foreign currency funds temporarily to related group entities domestically within China or overseas prior to formal declaration and payment of dividends (within a set, predetermined time frame). For domestic borrowing and lending of foreign currency, the arrangement is again facilitated through an entrustment loan agreement with a regulated party as an agent. As in the renminbi cash pooling scheme (above), using the entrustment loan arrangement in this manner means that the foreign currency accounts—capital accounts and settlement accounts—are transformed into a collection and payment cash flow and, depending on the bank used, automatically "swept" to a daily ZBA.

Obviously, the MNC will have to choose a bank capable of offering all the services involved in the above structure and, if required, on a pan-China basis.

Cross-border borrowing and lending of foreign currency is only open to MNCs that are designated as holding companies and have RHQ status; these transactions are structured with SAFE approval and within an entrustment arrangement. This flexibility is, at the time of writing, still in a pilot program phase.

Foreign Currency Short-Term Investment/Yield Enhancement

Foreign currency surpluses may be placed in time deposits, where the interest rate is higher than in one of the regular foreign currency accounts. It is unlikely that companies operating in China will want to keep substantial foreign currency onshore because regulations stipulate the time frame in which foreign currency, if sitting onshore, must be converted into renminbi balances.

There are a number of bank-designed treasury solutions that may be applied on a "menu basis," depending upon how the bank offers the services. For example, for

CASE STUDY

Capricho Douro was founded in 1999 as a luxury wine distributor, with an initial business plan that concentrated on the import and sale of select Douro ports and wines from the port-making region of Portugal to first- and second-tier cities in China. The Douro in Portugal is the oldest demarcated wine-growing region in the world, and was designated a World Heritage Site in 2001 by UNESCO. The company's name, Capricho Douro ("golden Douro") captures the richness of the region, not only in terms of exclusivity and rareness of brand, but also in terms of historical significance.

The initial business plan included the importation of some of the rarer port wines to Shanghai and Beijing, with the main customers being luxury hotels, corporate clients, clubs, and restaurants. In each of the major cities the product launch was in the form of a month-long series of promotional food plus beverage events in the main five and six star hotels, featuring a Portuguese chef and Portuguese menus, and exclusive port wine tastings priced for corporate clients. In addition, the port wine producers hosted tastings and competitions in these venues. Once the distribution and sales became a substantial flow, Capricho Douro expanded the operations to other cities, hotels, and venues.

In third-tier cities in China, the rollout plan for port wine distribution focused more on the less expensive table wines (*vinho de mesa*) and the sweeter ports, targeting affluent women as the main client base. The last stage of the product rollout included the importation and distribution of Portuguese specialty food items: sausages, olives, olive oil, etc., from the Douro region to restaurants and hotels in select first-tier cities.

Capricho Douro is a growing, Shanghai-based company with registered capital of approximately US$15 million. It is not part of a global trading company, it does not qualify as a MNC or holding company, and it is not of a size to be considered a RHQ any time soon. Therefore, its cash and liquidity solutions are limited to those available to smaller companies operating in China. The Capricho Douro treasurer wished to be aware of all the possible treasury solutions available to a company of this size. So he held a "beauty contest" with a number of foreign and local banks capable of providing facilities not only in Shanghai but also in some of the second- and third-tier cities where Capricho Douro does business.

The treasurer considered manual control of flows as an option since the bank charges for automatic pooling, etc., were seen as high. The manual option would be manageable for the treasurer, but the company operates on a pan-China level, albeit modestly. Therefore, the treasurer chose a bank that arranged for single party ZBA for all renminbi accounts, and auto sweeping to a higher-yield deposit. He arranged for the bank to shorten day sales outstanding via accounts receivable financing. He also signed on to the bank's electronic platform for Capricho Douro's renminbi payments, such as payroll and other short-term liabilities. Essentially, the treasurer chose a bank with pan-China connections and sufficient infrastructure to deal with the company's fairly modest renminbi flows. The treasurer will monitor the situation onshore to see what will be possible on the repatriation front should Capricho Douro decide to capitalize on its earnings in the China market. From a strategic point of view, repatriation in current conditions would be difficult, so the treasurer is in a market intelligence mode. This suits the company's business strategy since the sales revenues for the port wines and the table wines have remained robust in the first-tier cities despite the market conditions globally.

   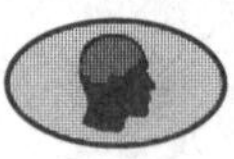  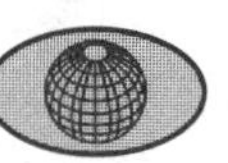   

accounts receivable management, banks may offer bank acceptance draft (BAD), an early form of trade financing in China, and corporate acceptance draft (CAD) financing; accounts receivable selling (without or limited recourse), financing, and purchase; and trade financing. For accounts payable management, most banks offer a CAD program, and some offer supplier financing of varying terms and conditions. On the cash/short-term investments and short-term liabilities side of the working capital matrix, the larger banks will offer the cash pooling, auto sweeping, and overdraft facilities, as described above. Whether these services are funneled through a shared service center, or whether they are provided on a fully automated infrastructure on a pan-China basis, is likewise dependent on the bank's operations in China.

Repatriation

Maintaining an effective cash management program and liquidity position is unfortunately only one, albeit huge, piece of the China treasury puzzle. Getting a company's hard earned capital out of China is yet another treasury nightmare. After all the effort on the liquidity front, the treasurer is then confronted with the problem of facilitating the cash flow from China to the parent company. Not surprisingly, the Chinese regulators have not deregulated this side of the liquidity equation in favor of the foreign company operating in China, so many of the conventional (and awkward) methods for repatriation still stand.

The traditional method is repatriation via dividend payments, where the main drawback is the tax treatment, timing, and potential SAFE approval. Payment of management fees, service fees, or royalty fees is another method, although the service and fee level is subject to regulatory scrutiny, as is the case with trade-related payments (i.e. justification of transfer pricing methods). Cross-border entrusted loans can also be utilized, but the destination and timing of the surplus funds is limited. Moreover, this solution is really only applicable to holding companies and RHQs.

While many companies have looked into a preference share scheme for this purpose, it is currently still not feasible. Treasurers, therefore, have to persuade their banks to create an instrument that manages to repatriate cash, perhaps in a synthetic format. The more products that are demanded, the more likely it is that the bank's onsite product development teams will find a way of designing the solution. In China, the treasurers provide the momentum for banks' product development, and competition in the banking industry means that the treasurers are not ignored.

MANAGING IN DIFFICULT MARKET CONDITIONS—ISSUES

Use of Treasury Products—Cost versus Benefit

The entry of foreign banks into China means that renminbi and foreign currency treasury products have been developed for companies operating in China and wishing to optimize their liquidity. The astute treasurer, however, will know that an automated, pan-China treasury product is not cheap. The cost of the treasury solution—fully automated "platforms" for auto sweeping etc.—may not be justified for small companies. As an alternative, treasurers may want to retain manual control of flows.

Your Bank in China—Domestic versus International

The choice of bank will be based on the relative size and capital structure of the entity in China. For example, a one-office requirement compared to the multinational with hundreds of operations and requirements for auto sweeping, shared service centers, and a myriad of trade and distributor-related financing. The treasurer then has the extra burden of ascertaining the stability and creditworthiness of the chosen bank(s). The global credit picture has been turned upside down by recent events, so the China treasurer cannot take credit ratings as the final word on the stability of their service providers.

Finding Funding for a China Operation—The Global Liquidity Squeeze

The China treasurer is currently faced with two squeezes: funding restrictions and/or timing issues from the parent/group, and frozen facilities from local banks. While the Chinese government has committed to inject liquidity into the macro-system, it is unlikely that this will filter down to the entity level in the short term. The treasurer is faced with having to examine supplier arrangements, trade terms, and ruthless extension/shortening of the accounts receivable/accounts payable cycle—the traditional methods in these conditions.

►► MAKING IT HAPPEN

Managing Expectations on the Regulatory Front

The legal and regulatory framework in which cash and liquidity solutions are deployed by companies in China is rapidly evolving. Prior to the global credit crisis, a China treasurer could assume that the dynamic nature of this regulatory landscape meant that the direction was definitely towards deregulation. Credit crisis market conditions invalidate that assumption. The treasurer therefore has to be *extra vigilant* in monitoring the following:

- changes in the regulations affecting methods of cash repatriation;
- the areas of liquidity management—accounts receivable/accounts payable, trade finance, leasing, entrustment structures—that are likely to be liberalized or tightened;
- developments in regulations that will affect banks, both foreign and local, operating in China.

On-Site Market Intelligence

China watchers assume that the regulators are most likely to enact measures that will protect the nation's currency and give support to policies that assist troubled domestic firms and workers. The best market intelligence for the treasurer is the banking community, and he or she should monitor the regulators as closely as possible. Moreover, the banks may have input into the regulators' next policy moves, to anticipate the following:

- What is the next likely step for the regulators in respect of relieving the liquidity squeeze?
- What is the banks' take on future directions of financial and forex regulations?
- What types of products, platforms, and structures are in the development pipeline that would alleviate the liquidity squeeze for companies operating in China?

The Value of Human Capital

From the parent company standpoint, the starting point for successful liquidity management in China is the human asset: Sourcing and retaining sharp treasury talent in China is critical. Infrastructure can go only so far in revealing your cash position;

"Daring ideas are like chessmen moved forward. They may be beaten, but they may start a winning game."
Johann Wolfgang von Goethe

a good treasurer has the ability to anticipate changes and flag problems from a bank and regulatory standpoint. As treasury is a relatively new discipline in China, it is crucial that the parent is proactive in recruiting local expertise, and then motivating the new recruits to go forward. China treasury expertise that is savvy and creative is a rarity, so once found it should be nurtured.

More Information

China is a relative newcomer to the world of working capital management, having spent its formative years in the "planned production" socialist style of operations. Moreover, the landscape in which liquidity is managed is evolving, especially on the regulatory side. Therefore, the bulk of relevant case studies and papers on the subject, where they do exist, are in the Chinese language. However, there is an industry source that does provide a global source of treasury information, where the majority of the case studies are in English. This is Eurofinance, a subsidiary of The Economist Group. Eurofinance produces many conferences in emerging areas of the world in which issues related to treasury and cash management issues are confronted and discussed. Among these conferences and industry groupings, the reader may find case studies from China treasurers that illustrate the latest approaches to liquidity problems in China. findings are also available on the EuroFinance website.

▸▸ MORE INFO

Report:

Economist Intelligence Unit (EIU). "Country Finance China." August 2008. Available on-line by subscription: store.eiu.com/country/CN.html?ref=country_list

Website:

EuroFinance cash, treasury, and risk management: www.eurofinance.com

"An army of experts assured us on a daily basis that this boom couldn't possibly crash like previous booms because this boom was still going on whereas all previous booms had ended." Mark Steel

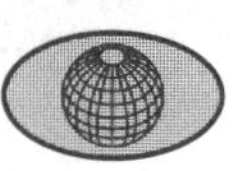

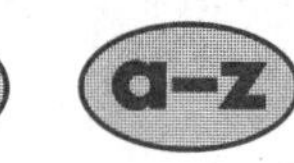

Navigating a Liquidity Crisis Effectively by Klaus Kremers

EXECUTIVE SUMMARY

- Liquidity crises are usually the symptoms of underlying strategic and operational crises that must be tackled to avoid repeated cash crises.
- The levers to address liquidity crises are not just operational and financial but also behavioral.
- CFOs must recognise the liquidity crisis and communicate openly to crucial stakeholders as a first step; they need to build trust with current and new financing stakeholders by producing a predictable rolling liquidity forecast.
- Cash constraints can be addressed by collecting and controlling existing cash, reducing net working capital, and restructuring the balance sheet.
- The control of cash requires very conservative cash authorizations and aggressive control from the financial team on all operations.
- Reducing net working capital is a well-known source of cash, but requires care to avoid deteriorating relationships with clients or suppliers.
- Restructuring the balance sheet is a medium/long-term solution. It mainly involves selling assets and raising/refinancing debt and/or equity.

INTRODUCTION

Until 2007, debt had become very cheap and accessible. Most companies sharply increased their leverage. In Germany, for example, the net-debt-to-EBITDA ratio extremes moved from around 3 in 2002 to around 7 in early 2008. However, a downturn in company performance or an external financial crisis—where lending becomes scarce and borrowing expensive—can make this approach risky.

WHAT IS A LIQUIDITY CRISIS?

A company's liquidity is its ability to quickly pay off its short-term debts as they fall due, and still have enough cash to keep operating. Liquidity crises can be broadly split into company-specific crises, and those driven by external factors—by market or general economic changes. In both cases, the company experiences a loss of investor confidence, making it difficult to raise further cash. If the company has insufficient cash reserves, it can very quickly run into serious difficulty. A familiar vicious circle takes hold, where a company cannot pay its debts because it has no funds, but cannot raise funds as its financial difficulties result in the downgrading of its debt.

HOW TO RESPOND TO A LIQUIDITY CRISIS

Once a company finds itself struggling to meet its short-term obligations, it needs to urgently access sources of cash, both internal and external. The following five-step approach covers the key elements of any response:

1. Tackle the Root of the Crisis

Normally, a liquidity crisis is only the last symptom of pre-existing root issues such as strategic or profitability crises (for example, losing one key customer contract, misalignment of product portfolio and market, a company overstretching itself by entering too many markets). A liquidity crisis needs to be addressed right away, but ignoring the crisis' root causes will merely postpone the next liquidity crisis. In these times of urgency, the support of external advisers can bring highly needed extra resources, experience of crisis management, and an independent perspective.

2. Be Honest

It is essential that a company is honest about its current situation, and creates a climate of transparency. It must comply with any regulatory requirements to inform the market, which can be applicable to listed companies. A CFO only has one chance to put things right with the banks:

- Give an honest assessment of the situation;
- Communicate appropriate information to all stakeholders; banks, shareholders, employees, suppliers, credit insurers, etc. so as not to mislead, or make fraudulent misrepresentations. Be sure to present an accurate picture of the current situation; account for all received bills (from experience, purchase ledgers do not include all received invoices, with many invoices hidden in staff drawers).

3. Gain or regain trust

Regaining the trust of banks, shareholders, and other stakeholders is a prerequisite to maintaining, or raising external funding. This requires communicating robust and realistic plans, delivering on these plans and building relationships.

- The main tool for trust building is a bullet-proof rolling liquidity forecast on which you will deliver (see Rolling Liquidity Forecast).
- In a liquidity crisis, a company's usual banking relationship can be replaced by a workout banker with different expectations and greater experience of liquidity crises.

4. Harvest Cash

There are three main ways to improve cash position:

1. Collect and control existing cash
2. Reduce working capital
3. Restructure the balance sheet

4.1. Collect and control existing cash

Companies usually have large amounts of cash spread across business entities and regions:

- Know where the cash is and who is responsible for it;
- Establish cash pooling: minimise cash held by operational entities (no cash constraint on operational entities means no tough cash discipline);
- Make managers ask for cash if they want to spend;
- If the company has one main bank lender, try to keep all the company's cash within this bank, to increase transparency.

4.2. Reduce net working capital

Working capital reduction obviously uses three levers: receivables, inventories, and payables. Keep some key points in mind while reducing working capital:

- Fix a deadline for finalizing collection and deciding on write-offs for receivables;
- Promptly claim refunds of taxation, if due;
- Reduce inventories by both reducing replenishment of production inventories, and by selling low-rotation inventories to generate cash;
- Be careful when extending payment conditions for suppliers, and keep in touch with the credit insurer—if they pull the cover, the company would have to prepay its suppliers, with disastrous consequences for its liquidity.

The potential for reduction in working

"CFOs live and die by liquidity. While CEOs may be able to talk themselves out of their strategic miscalculations, CFOs do not survive the loss of a company's liquidity." Klaus Kremers

     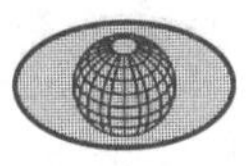   

capital is also very much industry-specific, depending on the make-up of the industry's working capital requirements. For example:

- The construction industry has far greater potential for cash realization (up to 20% of working capital employed) than the oil and gas industry (far less than 10% of working capital employed).
- This difference is from the type of long-term contracts normally used in the construction industry, creating significant work in progress and inventory balances.

4.3. Restructure balance sheet

Restructuring the balance sheet is a medium/long-term option, and usually involves third parties. Three main approaches exist:

1 *Reduce investments*: short-term solution of freezing or cancelling investments:
   - Before freezing expenditures, critically analyze impacts on future earnings;
   - Investments should be modular as far as possible, so that if a project is curtailed or postponed, the investment already made is itself still viable;
   - The cash return on investment should be a maximum of three years for generic industries (longer for asset intensive industries).
2 *Sell fixed assets*: medium/long-term solution. A liquidity crisis gives the opportunity to redefine the core businesses and sell non-core activities:
   - Selling assets always takes much longer than planned—consider it an upside rather than part of the main solution;
   - Within the core business, consider the sale and leaseback of assets.
3 *Raise debt and/or equity*: medium to long-term solution. This approach may seem the easiest solution, but at the end of 2008, banks reduced credit lines, and stock markets closed to capital increases.

Following the aforementioned steps will better enable the company to raise finance in the future. Remember, too, that keeping the supplier insurers on side and informed indirectly generates a source of credit through creditor balances.

CASE STUDY

Roland Berger

- A mid-sized mechanical engineering company with assets of €500m was in a liquidity crisis following two years of losses. External funding sources had dried up due to poor performance. Our project focused on generating cash from internal sources. A team of four consultants released €51m cash in around six months. The methods used for extracting cash included:
- In the first two months:
  - Putting a cash control and liquidity plan put in place
  - Selling raw materials back to suppliers (€6m)
  - Postponement of non-essential projects (€4m)
  - Review of accounts receivable (€16m) and accounts payable (€2m)
- Over the course of the next four months:
  - Cash pooling across sites
  - Giving site managers targets for raising cash – further cut in inventories (€12m)
  - Operational and strategic restructuring defined and implementation started, for example loss making activities identified and plans put in place for site and product rationalization

In the first 12 months, an additional €11m of liquidity was generated through asset disposal, as well as sale and leaseback of fixed assets. Short-term measures allowed the company some breathing space to enable it to find an investor; longer-term measures provided the negotiation basis for the entry of an additional investor. The company is now trading profitably and has a new investor, brought in on reasonable terms.

MAKING IT HAPPEN

A few dos and don'ts that management should bear in mind during a liquidity crisis:

Do

- Announce problems early and honestly to all relevant stakeholders.
- Build and monitor a reliable rolling liquidity forecast.
- Develop an action plan early on to demonstrate control of the situation.
- Empower managers to look for potential to extract cash in their areas from the bottom up.
- Maintain regular and open contact with external stakeholders.
- Be honest with employees and involve them in the process.
- Perform financial restructuring in conjunction with operational restructuring.
- Always prepare for the worst: in a crisis situation the worst case is always the real case.

Don't

- Ignore the situation hoping that things will turn themselves around.
- Look for profit instead of liquidity: avoid paying early for cash discounts, and collect value adjusted receivables rather than keep your write-offs down.
- Throw good money after bad: accept sunk cost rather than continuously burn new cash.
- Forget to include an additional buffer for peaks in cash requirements in your liquidity forecast: there will always be unexpected events, and most will hit you.
- Stop spending and investing completely: do not risk a complete breakdown of operations.
- Look for perfect solutions: take a practical approach, and react quickly to avoid rumours spreading and a domino effect.

5. Manage Cash Sustainability

Finally, a company needs to ensure a sustainable liquidity position. As mentioned above, strategic and operational root causes for the last crisis must be understood and tackled to avoid reoccurrences of liquidity crises; then companies can implement the following techniques to keep control of liquidity:

- Implementation of *KPI-based management* that includes liquidity and capital tied-up indicators.
- *Active risk management* of the business, including operations, legal contracts, financing decisions and structure, investments, and image/reputation. For example, a European pharmaceutical company lacking cash flows decided to finance a €80m factory with short-term loans. Due to poor performance, banks decreased the credit facility, causing a liquidity crisis which forced the company to restructure.
- *Change of the company culture:*
  - Encourage staff to take care of the company's cash as if it were their own;
  - Encourage realistic forecasts and

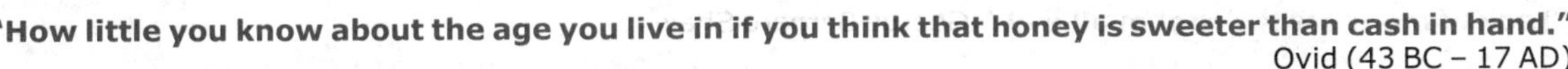
"How little you know about the age you live in if you think that honey is sweeter than cash in hand."
Ovid (43 BC – 17 AD)

   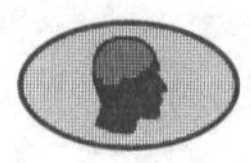  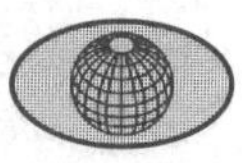   

planning: use scenario modelling techniques to limit future surprises;
  - Change employees' incentivization (long-term focus).
- *Ongoing communication* with internal and external stakeholders to further build trust and confidence.
- Continuous implementation of a "*tool box*" of operational measures to optimize cash management, working capital, and information accuracy.
- Further operational, financial and strategic *flexibility* to enable the company to react early and quickly once issues become apparent.

ROLLING LIQUIDITY FORECAST

- This is not "just another financial report": it shows where your company liquidity is—and will be—when negotiating with external and internal parties.
- All departments communicate their cash impacts (purchasing, sales, operation/investment, etc) and are responsible for impacts and timing.
- Obviously, take into account business seasonality and a reasonable buffer. Avoid surprises, as one cannot ask twice for an extension of credit lines: the CFO's credibility would not survive.
- The frequency with which the forecast is updated depends on the liquidity stretch: daily rolling liquidity plans are usual during periods of high crisis.
- Carrying out these simple steps properly will put the company in favourable light with banks: a Roland Berger study showed that only 30% of companies with a liquidity crisis have implemented a rolling liquidity forecast.

CONCLUSION

The outlined approach to a liquidity crisis describes the worst-case scenario. In less severe cases, not all levers need to be utilized. Even in good times, however, the best companies are already using most of these tools.

▸▸ MORE INFO

Books:

Blatz, Michael, Karl-J. Kraus, and Sascha Haghani. *Corporate Restructuring: Finance in Times of Crisis.* New York: Springer, 2006.

Graham, Alistair. *Cash Flow Forecasting and Liquidity*. Chicago, IL: AMACOM, 2001.

Websites:

Association of Corporate Treasurers, contingency planning: www.treasurers.org/contingencyplanning

Roland Berger, restructuring: www.rolandberger.com/expertise/functional_issues/restructuring

Turnaround Management Association: www.turnaround.org

See Also:

Cashflow Reengineering: How to Optimize the Cashflow Timeline and Improve Financial Efficiency (p. 1234)

Viewpoint: Zarin Patel
How the BBC Reshaped Its Finance Function

INTRODUCTION

In the past four years Zarin Patel has focused on repositioning the BBC's finance department, boosting its efficiency and finding new and innovative ways of reducing costs. Her key focus is now on delivering more with the same amount of money and resources. She became the broadcasting corporation's first female finance director in 2004. A member of the BBC's executive board, Patel is responsible for financial strategy, planning, control, and corporate reporting activities. She joined the BBC in 1998, having previously spent 15 years with KPMG, one of the "Big Four" accountancy firms. She qualified as a chartered accountant after graduating in economics at the London School of Economics in 1982. Named as one of the most powerful people in the British media by *The Guardian*, Patel recently graduated from Harvard Business School, where she spent two months before returning to her role at the BBC in November 2008. She is also Governor of the University of the Arts, London.

When a business has to adapt to an economic downturn, finance's instinctive role might be to keep the creative drive in check, to communicate tough messages and to shepherd the business through an uncertain period.

In such an environment, you might expect the focus on financial stability to influence the core skills that are sought in finance managers. At the BBC, where finance's role is so much about demonstrating value in our decision-making and how we spend the licence fee, this expectation might be even more pronounced.

The current economic downturn has given rise to unprecedented levels of uncertainty across all business sectors. People have had to contend with new jargon, and with language, previously reserved for the trading floor, being used in news reports and staff communications. In addition, every area of the business is being challenged to find new and innovative ways to reduce its cost base, to create headroom against already pressured budgets, and to actively manage financial risk.

The BBC has been facing similar challenges and financial pressures; however, operating in a fixed revenue business, with clear accountability not only to the BBC Trust, the group of independent trustees, but also to the licence fee payers themselves, adds an extra dynamic to our approach to risk. Our reputation, both editorial and financial, has to be a constant consideration in decision-making.

One of the biggest and most reported casualties of the recent downturn has been the property market; and there seems to be limited respite predicted from the current conditions in the coming financial year. Following the licence fee settlement back in 2006, the BBC embarked on a review of its property strategy to raise additional income to invest in program making.

The strategy which emerged, to streamline our property portfolio and exit 30% of our buildings over the coming five years, has inevitably been affected by such a sharp decrease in commercial property activity. Empty offices across the UK give us a very clear indication that we need to review our timetable. Even though the longer-term strategy remains intact, we have had to revisit both the assumptions we made in valuation of assets, and the timing of any receipts.

Property is, of course, only one of several areas where we have been streamlining our activities and making bold decisions to reduce our cost base and generate additional income.

FINANCE REDESIGN

BBC Finance embarked on an ambitious redesign of the entire function in 2005, with the target of reducing the cost of finance to below 1% of annual income and, as part of this, reducing finance headcount by approximately 50%. By simplifying processes and our operating model, we aimed to drive out cost and create efficiencies across all areas of the business. The new finance structure, including a shared service center based in Cardiff, has now been operating successfully for two years.

Our ambition for finance did not stop at simply reviewing and restructuring internal processes. The complementary, and equally important aspect of the remodeling exercise, was the re-tender of the Finance and Accounting Services contract, which moved to a lower cost model with a new partner, Steria (a leading European IT service provider), at the start of 2007. The contract re-tender alone delivered £20 million per annum of savings back to the BBC.

The contract with Steria is just one of a number of strategic contracts that have been placed with supply partners over the past five years for services such as human resources and technology, to ensure that the BBC's resources are focused on its core remit, which is producing quality output.

The new contract with Steria involved the off-shoring of elements of both core and noncore finance services. At the time, this was an entirely new approach to contract delivery for the BBC, and a decision which inevitably attracted debate. However, once the decision had been taken, the benefits have given us confidence to consider other ways of delivering value to the license fee payer through our outsourced contracts. The move has also served to further highlight the need for strong governance and clear and consistent communication between our own finance community and our supply partner.

Now that we are two years into this 10-year contract, we have the opportunity to move into the next stage of the relationship, with a much clearer understanding of the services provided and the governance required to develop the relationship.

For me as CFO, a clear indicator of success for this contract will be its ability to keep moving and adjusting its model in line with developments in corporate governance and technology. Innovation has always been a huge part of our ambition for the contract, and we aim to lead the way, in terms of contract management, to develop new ways of solving old problems.

The first stage of the finance redesign, as described above, was very much about delivering efficiency and reducing costs. We needed core finance and change management skills in the business to implement new processes, roll out new reporting processes, and embed new models.

We anticipated that the BBC and its needs were likely to develop and evolve, as indeed they have.

STRATEGY AND INNOVATION

The increasingly rapid pace of change in the broadcasting and technology arenas requires us to serve both the linear and nonlinear agenda.

The BBC's strategy has been to respond to audience demands and to our own desire to be the leading protagonist in developing the way in which broadcasters deliver content to their audiences. A prime example of this was iPlayer. Launched at the end of 2007, iPlayer was ahead of the field in making BBC linear content available on-demand, allowing the audience to personalize its content and make it more relevant and responsive to its needs. The continued success of the iPlayer relies on its continual adaptability and development, through either further technical enhancements or through partnership with other broadcasters, such as the recent agreement to make the iPlayer available via SkyPlayer.

More recently, BBC One and BBC Two have been made available online. This means that all BBC channels are now simulcast and available to watch on computers or portable devices. Such a move is hugely important in our continuous efforts to make the BBC's content accessible to the widest population possible, and to give the audience the freedom to consume this output as and when they choose.

The continual dynamic between changes in technology, broadcasting and governance is driving the BBC's Finance agenda.

It has to go beyond being efficient and finding new and innovative ways of reducing costs. Effectiveness and delivering more with the same money and resources, is now even more at the heart of our agenda. A good example of this is the current efficiency program, which is targeted to deliver 3% cumulative efficiencies by 2012. The success of this program will be judged on whether cash savings are achieved without a detrimental impact on the performance of our output.

We must be flexible and continue to evolve to support our business. Most importantly, we must make ourselves part of the decision-making process to enable us to add value in every intervention we make.

For our finance managers, it is still about the timeliness and accuracy of the numbers. However, it is also now about how you use the available information to inform and shape the business you support.

The current economic environment presents both a challenge and a huge opportunity for finance—the adaptability and flexibility needed when a business is short on cash represent an opportunity to add real value to decision-makers and change the shape of finance for future years.

If a business is required to identify and prioritize scarce resources, finance can be a source of reliable information and advice. It can also provide both tactical and strategic solutions to business issues.

FACING THE TRUTH

The economic downturn has meant that we have had to carry out the most honest and far-reaching assessment of our financial risk in recent years. Although this exercise has been led mainly by finance, it has required the full commitment and engagement of all areas of the business, including editorial, production and professional services.

Sharing responsibility for this challenge has helped us move away from the perception of the finance manager as a function of business decisions towards being an active stakeholder in those decisions.

Bold decisions need to be taken to mitigate financial risk. Current constraints simply enhance the need for the BBC to invest in finance managers who not only display an innate curiosity but can also demonstrate strong business and advisery skills, matched with a more traditional accounting skill-set.

Delivering an effective finance function was always the next stage of our development and we feel that we are making good progress. The realities of an economic downturn have only served to bring this more sharply into focus.

▸▸ MORE INFO

Books:

Collins, Jim. *Good to Great: Why Some Companies Make the Leap. . . and Others Don't*. New York: Collins Business, 2001.

PricewaterhouseCoopers Finance and Cost Management team. *CFO: Architect of the Corporation's Future*. Chichester, UK: Wiley, 1997.

Taleb, Nassim Nicholas. *The Black Swan: The Impact of the Highly Improbable*. London: Allen Lane, 2007.

Periodicals:

Harvard Business Review

McKinsey Quarterly

See Also:

★ Viewpoint: Howard Davies (pp. 35–36)

Cost and Effect: Using Integrated Cost Systems to Drive Profitability and Performance (p. 1244)

Media (pp. 1523–1525)

"Blaming the hedge funds for the crisis is like blaming the passengers in a bus crash." Paul Marshall

  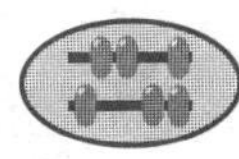 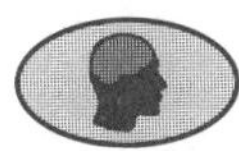  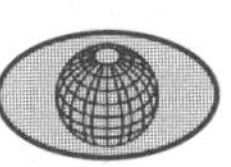   

Payment Factories: How to Streamline Financial Flows by Chris Skinner

EXECUTIVE SUMMARY

- The world's largest businesses and their banks have been bringing their major global payments structures together into a rationalized, single platform known as a "payment factory."
- This platform is not a single system, but a single payments application that runs across multiple centers around the world.
- These payment factories replace the previously disparate, fragmented, and nonintegrated payments applications that businesses ran historically, whereby every country had its own system and operation.
- The aim is to gain the efficiencies and cost savings that such global integration can deliver through economies of scale, alongside fault-tolerant, mission-critical operations because each technical center now provides a real-time backup to the others.
- The single payments platform also allows all payment transactions and currencies put through it to be managed globally in real time, which helps greatly with managing a firm's cash position, liquidity, and risk.

INTRODUCTION

During the past few years, banks and their clients have been consolidating their payments infrastructures into single, global platforms. Payment consolidation helps to overcome the issues of fragmentation between systems that have been set up over the years. For large international banks and businesses in particular, having duplicate systems in different geographies just does not make sense. As a result, international banks and companies have been transforming their back-office operations with streamlined services based on refreshed processes and the latest technologies.

THE CHALLENGE

When you consider any large bank or global corporation, you think of multiple operations in multiple countries. Now think of a business and how it began, and you will probably think of one office in one town. There lies the challenge for any business: How can it grow operations effectively?

Growth may require new offices in new locations with new staff, and throughout the 20th century it often meant implementing more robust systems to handle payroll, general ledgers, and general office support. The problem is that, as the business expands, managers are forced to implement hundreds of systems to handle payments. The systems are often incompatible because they have been implemented at different times, to handle different currencies, and in different countries with differing tax regimes over a long period of time.

In the payments world, there are also many payment instruments and processes, covering cash, checks, and electronic payments, as well as accounts payable and receivable, with all of these differing domestically and internationally. This is why historically the payments world has been such a mess for multinational businesses—a mess of payments practices, processes, and systems, across the world.

THE SOLUTION

Over the past decade, many firms have decided to rationalize their payment infrastructures and to consolidate all of their payment applications, systems, and services into a single, global platform. This has been prompted by a range of factors, including the increasing costs and risks of regulatory exposures created by Sarbanes–Oxley.

A single, global platform does not mean a single computer, as that would create too much risk exposure should such a system fail. It means bringing together all the payments for a function or instrument, such as all cash management, into a single application. This application will often operate on three or more physical computer sites globally, with each site copying the others to replicate all data and applications. The result is that one has a single view of the data on a single application, working in real time, with fault tolerance and backup across systems in case any of the physical operations fail.

Banks and financial departments call this a payments factory. The phrase is a loose term that covers the rationalization and consolidation of a payment service into these global hubs. The aim is to have a single track of payments for invoices, purchase orders, payroll, cash management, and more, that can be easily managed, tracked, and changed regardless of where these are happening.

WHAT IS IMPLEMENTED?

There are many suppliers of payments factory services in the technology industry. The usual method of implementing such a capability is to analyze what a firm has in place today, and then put into play a rationalization plan. This plan would normally be based on putting in place a new payments platform as the first global hub near the firm's home office. The reason is that this makes the first project highly controllable, with the firm's main resources and expertise available.

The reason for it being near the home office, rather than within head office, is due to the risks of changing all the key payments applications: invoicing, purchase orders, receivables, payroll, and so on. These are all applications that are fundamental to an organization's financial health, and therefore nothing should be changed too fast. A typical project runs for 18 to 24 months.

Once this is achieved, however, the rationalization can be started much more rapidly because the risks are now known and controllable. Change can therefore be implemented reasonably rapidly thereafter.

Within this context, it should be borne in mind that not all implementations are the same. In some instances, firms will replace their local system with an approved corporate package, which is integrated across the network into the head office, to ensure that a single view of payments data is available. In other instances, some businesses will take out the local payments system and use networking services to allow local business users to access the payments hub in their nearest regional hub center.

In all implementations in a business context, one of the primary drivers for making the changes from local payment systems to a global payment factory is to control payment inflows and outflows more effectively so as to reduce costs. Another driver is to gain efficiencies through removing fragmented and incompatible systems, ensuring that there is a single and consistent approach worldwide that is compliant with regulations.

In the context of removing costs, one of the biggest cost-reducing factors is the

"In terms of IT investments, it won't be the IT manager who writes the investment proposal for the payments processing engine. He's going to work with the payments factory owner, where the payments factory owner will develop the investment proposal and business plan." Ching Wei Hong, Head of Operations and IT, OCBC Bank

ability to work closely with a bank. As mentioned, many corporations have local currency systems with differing tax implications. The result is that most businesses have a different bank in every country of operation. In part, this has also been due to the lack of availability of global banking services, but today, with HSBC, Deutsche Bank, Citibank, JPMorgan, and others offering globalized account services, this is possible.

Therefore, as another key part of the change process, corporations will work closely with a global bank partner in their implementation of a payments factory, as illustrated by P&O and others. The reorganization undertaken by Philips is described in the case study that follows. The importance of a strong banking partner in this context cannot be underestimated. For example, just as a technology firm understands the technological requirements of change, a bank understands payment processes, practices, and instruments. With the right bank partner working with the corporation, moving all payment instructions from a smaller, local bank to a global facility becomes routine. The bank will take over most of the responsibilities of making the transition.

The result is that a company can reduce its bank accounts throughout the world from hundreds down to just a few, although it is worth noting that most corporations will rarely consolidate all global payments to a single bank partner as they do not want to be exposed to a single dominant bank for fees and charges purposes. In other words, they like to maintain some form of competitive relationship with banks.

WHAT NEXT?

After the implementation of a payments factory, which focuses on consolidation, costs savings, and a centralized platform, most firms develop more sophisticated functions of risk management. This means that new processes and functions are integrated into the core system, for example real-time cash management reporting. This requires even more focus on technology, as the integration required across many different systems, formats, and services—both internal and external, including the banks—is considerable.

Therefore, most firms would partner with technology organizations, and possibly their number one global bank partner, to implement this range of services. Following this, the more information services and reporting a corporate can provide to its treasury, finance, and end-user population the better.

CASE STUDY

Philips

gtnews reported Philips' major reorganization of disparate systems into a single payments factory between 1998 and 2004.[1] In 1999 the first replacement system was implemented near Philips' main office at Eindhoven in the Netherlands. In the second year 40 sites were replaced, and in the third year a further 100. In each instance, replacing the local facilities did not necessarily entail removal of their payment systems. Six years after the project's commencement, 630 sites around the world had migrated to the new global payments factory platform, which was processing 70,000 payments per month.

A range of benefits was gained from consolidating payments into a payments factory. For example, it is believed that a typical company with annual revenues of around $1 billion would save over 1% of its costs per year (i.e. $10 million per annum through such consolidation. Certainly, the Philips case study bears this out, with savings of around 50 staff, bank fees and netting fees down by almost €7 million per annum, and systems maintenance savings of around €1 million per annum.

Other benefits include:

- Real-time management of all cash and netting positions.
- An accurate picture of risk and liquidity.
- Improved bank relationships and transaction management.
- More effective negotiation of cross-border positions and currency transactions.

▸▸ MAKING IT HAPPEN

Any organization considering the implementation of a payments factory should take the proven path of consolidation by following these steps:

1 Consider the costs of processing payments based upon the range of systems and processes involved and discuss with senior management the rationale for maintaining such a range;

2 Agree to move towards a payments factory approach and invite key providers of such services to discuss what would be involved;

3 Based upon the firms you invite to discuss this with your firm, identify up to six organizations that may be appropriate to deliver a payments factory solution;

4 Ask each firm to outline the approach they would take and then invite two or three to prepare a formal proposal;

5 Review each proposal and ensure that:

  a they clearly articulate how they will identify the global structure of payments processes across the corporation;

  b they explicitly identify how they will audit the systems, software and platforms involved including their age, resilience and compatibilities, or incompatibilities;

  c the benefits and issues of consolidation are clear;

  d you are comfortable they can do the job and have strong references to prove they have worked with similar organizations to your own.

As long as all of the above are clear and proven, select an organization to work with and make it happen.

▸▸ MORE INFO

Book:

Skinner, Chris. *The Future of Finance after SEPA*. Chichester, UK: Wiley, 2008.

Websites:

Financial Services Club (UK): www.fsclub.co.uk

Financial Services Club blog: www.thefinanser.com

gtnews.com—treasury and finance network: www.gtnews.com

PaymentsNews.com: www.paymentsnews.com

NOTES

1 Capachin, Jeanne. "Implementing a payments factory at Philips." gtnews (November 15, 2004). Online at: www.gtnews.com/article/5678.cfm

"One of the objectives was to achieve one way of working across the product divisions, simplifying accounts payable processes." Simon Braaksma, European Cash Manager at Royal Philips Electronics

  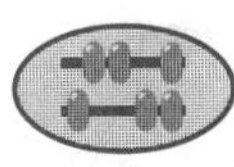   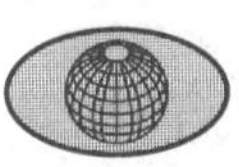   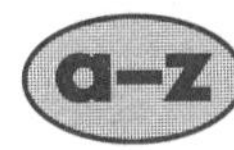

Pension Schemes: A Unique and Unintended Basket of Risks on the Balance Sheet by Amarendra Swarup

EXECUTIVE SUMMARY

- Pension schemes are often the most overlooked part of a company's balance sheet, despite the large hidden and complex risks they can pose. Some of the unique risks within pension schemes are exposure to interest rates, inflation, market risk, and longevity.
- The problem is particularly acute for defined-benefit pension schemes—common in many developed countries—where the benefits are predetermined, are often index-linked, and can be passed on to dependents. The present cost of bearing these risks has risen sharply in recent decades, and many companies have closed their pension schemes to new members.
- In the short term, changing economic, financial, and demographic perceptions can materially alter the valuation of a pension scheme's assets and liabilities from one day to the next, potentially leaving many finance directors with an uncontrolled liability on otherwise well-managed balance sheets.
- The waters can be muddied further by another fundamental problem: for most schemes, liabilities are calculated infrequently using ad hoc or out-of-date assumptions, which can often present a less than prudent valuation of the true costs.
- Options to manage and even reduce these uncertainties are now appearing. The key is to have a proactive and realistic approach to the risks that are being carried on the balance sheet.

INTRODUCTION

The only function of economic forecasting, the late American economist J. K. Galbraith once noted, was to make astrology look respectable. And, knowingly or not, it's a belief that's endemic in the corporate world.

The overriding concern is to find the hidden value in companies—whether in their balance sheet or in their intellectual property—and extract it in the most efficient way possible. Every financial and operational risk is carefully studied and, where possible, mitigated. Lines of credit are negotiated at known terms to suit the company's horizon. Capital structures are continually redrawn to maximize efficiency. Balance sheets are scrutinized line by line and operations are streamlined.

There is no obsession with predicting GDP, or agonizing over the evolution of the labor market over the next decade, for example. No, these are all nebulous questions for economic forecasters to ponder. For the seasoned financial director, the wider economy only matters insofar as it affects that all important cash flow.

Yet, hidden in that otherwise well-managed balance sheet might be a host of unconstrained liabilities that threaten to undo the most meticulous business plan and expose companies to a whole host of unknown risks—all housed within an often overlooked pension plan.

The problem is particularly acute for defined benefit schemes—occupational schemes where the pension benefits are fixed in advance and are often calculated as a proportion of an employee's final salary. Many include provision for dependents such as widows, and can even be indexed to inflation. These proved to be enormously popular in the aftermath of the Second World War, when many companies saw them as an effective way to defer compensation for workers to future years. However, these schemes placed a host of unintended and poorly understood risks with the sponsoring employer, such as exposure to longevity, to future interest rates, and to the capricious whims of financial markets.

In recent decades, as companies found themselves confronted with declining employment and a growing retiree problem, the present cost of bearing these risks has escalated sharply, and many have closed their pension schemes to new members. Furthermore, pension schemes and, in some jurisdictions, their associated healthcare liabilities, are increasingly a growing factor in corporate finance transactions.

A potentially attractive merger or acquisition may become unstuck because of the pension fund, or, worse still, an existing company may hit difficulties as the full cost of the pension obligation becomes known. The abortive takeover of Sainsbury's in the United Kingdom and the well-publicized troubles at General Motors in the United States are but the most visible tip of the proverbial iceberg, and are indicative of a problem that can consign businesses to a slow decline.

But more than just eroding stockholder value in the present, defined benefit schemes are also a danger to a company's long-term survival in an increasingly competitive global economy. Many management teams now face the problem of maintaining a set of financial commitments made in another era, when assumptions and expectations were vastly different. These commitments are difficult to measure—let alone anticipate—and they are tied to the health of the corporate sponsor of the pension fund, which is legally required to underwrite any deficit. If the company does go under, the responsibility of meeting at least part of these liabilities may then be transferred to governments and taxpayers. This may create additional problems, as pension scheme members will likely receive reduced benefits, and the addition of significant numbers of liabilities to the government balance sheet is eventually likely to become politically unpalatable.

A GROWING PROBLEM

Anyone who doubts the potential scale of the problem only has to look at the case of the American Civil War veterans' pension fund—one of the earliest defined benefit schemes. Originally set up during the war to pay pensions to disabled veterans, the scheme was gradually extended to include all veterans and their dependants, making its final payment only in 2004—nearly 140 years after the war ended. By then, the scheme had cost the US government hundreds of billions in today's dollars, and at its peak in the early 1890s, it had even constituted over 40% of the annual federal budget.

It's a stark warning for many pension schemes and their corporate sponsors today.

Any views on interest rates over the next decade? Your debt financing may have excellent terms, and it may seem a moot

"It sounds extraordinary, but it's a fact that balance sheets can make fascinating reading." Mary Archer

     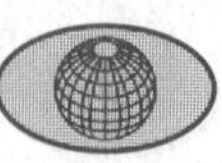   

point, but the pension fund's liabilities and their associated accounting costs will swing violently over the next few decades with movements in the prevailing interest rates. By some estimates, the drop in long-term interest rates from 1999 to 2002 increased the value of pension liabilities by 30–40%.

How about inflation—any thoughts on how it might evolve over the next half century? Many scheme members, particularly in the United Kingdom, have index-linked pensions, and the burden of payments can quickly become onerous. Figures from Britain's Office for National Statistics show that from 1970 to 2007, annual employer contributions to pension schemes went up a factor of 53, and they have trebled over the last seven years alone (Figure 1). Wage inflation too can rapidly push up costs.

And what about people living longer? For individuals and society, increased longevity is desirable, but living longer can often also create large unanticipated costs. Ever since German Chancellor Otto von Bismarck thought he'd pulled off a politically brilliant move back in 1889, by promising pensions at 70 when the average German lived to less than 50 years of age, the continual improvements in life expectancies have rapidly unraveled the best-laid pension plans. Even more troubling, the current upward trend shows little sign of leveling off, and it is increasingly clear that this is the most significant risk to the finances of pension schemes and their sponsors. The rising life expectancies for males and females in the United Kingdom are shown in Figure 2.

In a field typified by extremes, the case of Jeanne Calment is a situation that's humorlessly reminiscent of reality for many pension schemes. When Madame Calment's lawyer agreed in 1965 to pay her an annual income worth one-tenth of the value of her flat on the understanding that he would inherit the property on her death, it seemed like a shrewd bargain. Madame Calment was then 90 years old, and it seemed unlikely that she had much longer to go on this particular journey. Unfortunately, bearing testament to perhaps one of the most misjudged investment decisions ever, Jeanne went on to live to the ripe old age of 122. Along the way, she also became the oldest rap artist ever, releasing an album at 121, but that is unlikely to have provided much consolation to her poor aforementioned lawyer. By then, he was long dead and his widow was still making the payments.

THE DANGERS OF VOLATILE MARKETS

It's a complex basket of risks and, in the short term, changing economic and demographic perceptions can materially alter the valuation of a pension scheme's liabilities from one day to the next. Even the assets are not immune, as many pension schemes have more than half their assets in equities—a consequence of their long-term perspective, adherents argue. In the short term, however, volatility in the markets can materially alter the valuation of a pension scheme from one day to the next. It's a headache for many finance directors, who are left with an uncontrolled liability on otherwise well-managed balance sheets.

It becomes extremely difficult under these circumstances to determine the ability of a defined benefit pension scheme to pay its annuities 40 years down the track. Throw in the increasingly common belief that the economic environment in the coming years is likely to be far less favorable than in recent years, and increased volatility seems inevitable.

In 2008 alone, Aon Consulting estimated that sharp falls in the FTSE caused UK pension schemes to lose $60 billion in just a single week, wiping out all the gains made in 2007. More worryingly for companies, equity markets—excluding the buoyant energy and mining sectors—have declined significantly since mid-2007, and are now close to the depths reached at the bottom of the last recession in 2003. Given that these companies are often older, and therefore have a much greater role as pension sponsors than the percentage of market capitalization that they represent, sponsor risk is also an increasingly major concern across the board.

It's a growing headache for many firms, for whom such risks often lie far from familiar territory and who are charged with looking after a broad church of stakeholders, not just pensioners. Though the increased pension fund liabilities are often longer term than most corporate horizons, they must be carried on the company's balance sheet, reducing net asset value and increasing financial leverage. As the corporate sponsor, they generally also have an obligation to fund at least part of these unexpected costs, giving them an uncertain command over their own cash flow and reducing future distributions to investors. The impact can go far beyond the immediate cash flow hit—filtering through to the P & L, lowering profits, hurting competitiveness, and, ultimately, even impacting the share price.

In the case of General Motors, for example, net obligations are estimated to be about $170 billion across all of GM's US operations, dwarfing its current market cap of $3 billion. To meet its soaring obligations, the company contributed an astonishing $30 billion to its US pension plans in 2003 and 2004, but the accounts are still tens of billions of dollars in deficit. Now, pension and healthcare costs make up more of the average GM vehicle's price tag than the steel used to build it. Consequently, the company is inexorably losing ground to a wave of foreign competitors with lower cost bases and less debt on their balance sheets—resulting in a catastrophic decline in stock price for investors, from $55 in January 2004 to under $10 today.

MUDDY WATERS

The waters are muddied further by another fundamental problem. For most schemes, liabilities are calculated infrequently, using out-of-date longevity assumptions and ad hoc discount rates, and often presenting a less than prudent valuation of the true costs of delivering pensioners full financial security. As people live longer—15 minutes more for every passing hour by some estimates—and accounting standards move more toward valuing balance sheets on a mark-to-market basis, the immediately calculable costs can rise

Figure 1. Annual contributions to UK pension schemes by employers and employees 1970–2007. (*Source*: Office for National Statistics)

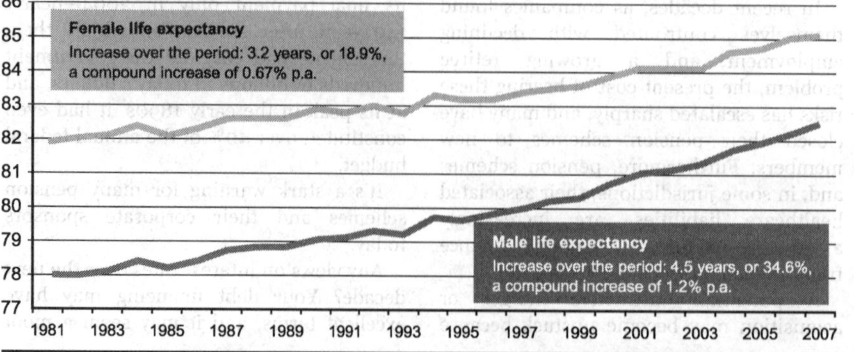

"Most businesses tie up a tremendous amount of assets anticipating things that may not happen. If they had a system that was customer demand driven, they would be much more efficient." Michael Del

Figure 2. Increasing life expectancy in the United Kingdom for 65-year-olds. (*Source*: Office for National Statistics)

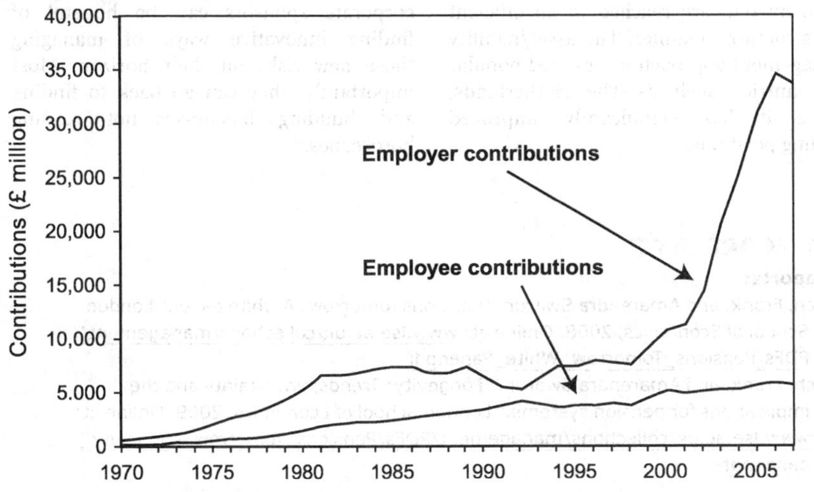

dramatically as outdated assumptions are revised.

Many pension schemes value their liabilities by using a discount rate that is implicitly linked to the assumed return on their assets. The problem is that they are effectively banking on an uncertain set of future gains to pay off their obligations to millions of current and future pensioners. Even worse, the discount rates vary from scheme to scheme. Some may choose a point in time and a single discount rate for all their liabilities, while others may choose to be more sophisticated and look at evolving discount rates over time. Regardless, most discount rates are ultimately linked to AA-rated corporate bond yields—the result of an implicit belief that returns of this order can be harvested without difficulty.

This is not to say that corporate bonds are not good investments. They are an investment staple with good reason and can provide low-risk returns. However, they are not risk-free, and any prudent investor needs to be cognizant of the default, credit, and liquidity risks that go with the asset class. In recent months, the problem has been highlighted by the credit crunch, which has seen prices of AA corporate bonds collapse and their yields soar. No wonder many schemes were feeling pleasantly flush and in surplus over the last couple of years—their liabilities dramatically lessened over the same time period!

It's a false optimism. The downturn in prices reflects the increasing fear that some of these corporate bonds might default. Even if one claimed that investing everything in AA corporate bonds today could still provide these returns at low risk, there simply aren't enough around. Taking the United Kingdom as an example, the total value of AA corporate bonds floating around the British financial markets at last count was just over $142 billion—a fraction of the some $1,200 billion of liabilities they are supposed to underpin.

It's a troubling mismatch problem. Although there is a tradition of pension schemes and insurers "booking" some potential asset gains in advance, it is important for companies not to bank on future gains to work out their liabilities. An unembellished picture of the liabilities, stripped of any assumed risk premiums, can often be a good guide when setting investment targets and managing the risk on your balance sheet.

The area is also coming under increased regulatory scrutiny, with more stringent accounting standards being imposed. For example, the pensions regulator in the United Kingdom is now pushing schemes to adopt more realistic mortality assumptions that reflect the latest scientific evidence—a change that could equate to an additional cost of $40 billion for the UK defined benefit industry with every added year of life expectancy. This also presents additional shorter-term risks for sponsors, as they may have to divert extra cash into the scheme to meet these future liabilities via a contribution notice.

SOLUTIONS ON THE HORIZON

Company finance directors must feel victimized. Constrained by ever-growing liabilities on the balance sheet and a volatile pension asset portfolio, they often find themselves on the wrong side of the window when it comes to securing their retirees' benefits. Changing interest rates, rising inflation, and ever-increasing allowances for longevity mean that the liabilities are often a fast-moving target. Throw in a worsening economic environment, and keeping apace is complicated by potentially thorny negotiations with trustees and retirees for additional injections.

So how are trustees and sponsors to manage these new, troubling risks? It's hard enough to judge market returns over the next few years, without crystal ball gazing to estimate the lifespan of all the scheme members under your responsibility—past, present, and future.

The answer today is that it is largely a dark art. The current trend is unlikely to be your friend here; longevity improvements have repeatedly defied the hopeful shackles of successive actuarial models, despite the most Orwellian filtering of data by job, medical history, and even postcode. The latest models—even if true—give scant comfort. For example, by 2050 a 65-year-old UK male might live to be between 86 and 97 years old, up from 83 today.

However, there are options. Like any other risk, these uncertainties can be managed, and even reduced, once understood. The key is to have a proactive and realistic approach to the risks that are being carried on the balance sheet. Sponsors need to engage actively with trustees and walk a fine line between investors' expectations and the funding needs for the pension scheme.

Unique solutions are now appearing in the market. A whole industry has now sprung up in the United Kingdom offering full insurance buyouts, where the pension liabilities are transferred away to dedicated specialists. This can often improve the situation for pension scheme members, as these specialist insurers are tightly regulated, operate within strict investment and asset/liability guidelines, and have to hold capital against any extreme losses.

It also helps troubled sponsors: Securing pension liabilities away from balance sheets improves their ability to raise finance, and removes the situation where, in a falling equity market with a commensurate fall in the valuation of a scheme's assets, a sponsor looking to invest in the business might also find trustees coming cap in hand. Above all, it enables management to get on with running the business, free from the peripheral distractions of administering a pension scheme.

However, insurance buyout valuations use more cautious longevity assumptions and paint a truer picture of the hidden arrears, increasing the liabilities and the premiums required significantly. Like customers outside a Ferrari showroom peering in through the window, it is simply

"Inflation is as violent as a mugger, as frightening as an armed robber, and as deadly as a hit man."
Ronald Reagan

   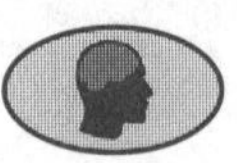  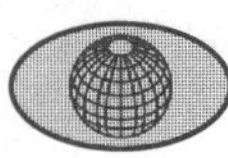   

unaffordable for many companies and not available in many countries.

But there are alternatives to help transfer risk. Schemes can execute partial buyouts for some of their liabilities, such as current pensioners. If that overshoots the budget and the deficit is still too large, or the options are not available in your jurisdiction, there are now innovative corporate solutions to help transfer risk, ranging from taking on the entire scheme and its myriad liabilities, to specific solutions for specific risks.

For example, trustees and sponsors can implement bond or swap-based hedging strategies to nullify the impact of interest rates and inflation on their liabilities, and thereby on the balance sheet. There is even a growing market in longevity swaps, allowing people also to hedge this idiosyncratic risk. Although they introduce new risks in lieu, such as the health of the counterparties on the other side of the swap, these steps are cost-effective and can ensure that the larger part of a scheme's risk—its volatile liabilities—is better constrained, while precious assets are freed up to invest in assets with higher returns.

Another alternative is to delegate the holistic management of all the scheme's assets and liabilities to a third-party fiduciary manager, who will manage them on a real-time basis within tight guidelines agreed with the trustees. These specialists will typically hedge all the liabilities where possible and diversify the assets among a range of best of breed providers. This ensures that the funding position is improved, and its ultimate targets, such as a full buyout, are reached in an efficient and structured manner. The asset/liability management approach has proved popular in countries such as The Netherlands, where it has significantly improved funding positions.

It's a rapidly evolving environment, and, with new solutions appearing fast, corporate sponsors can be hopeful of finding innovative ways of managing these new risks on their horizon. Most importantly, they can go back to finding and building businesses—not reading horoscopes.

▸▸ MORE INFO

Reports:

Eich, Frank, and Amarendra Swarup. "Pensions tomorrow: A white paper." London School of Economics, 2008. Online at: www.lse.ac.uk/collections/management/PDFs/Pensions_Tomorrow_White_Paper.pdf

Eich, Frank, and Amarendra Swarup. "Longevity: Trends, uncertainty and the implications for pension systems." London School of Economics, 2009. Online at: www.lse.ac.uk/collections/management/PDFs/Pensions_Tomorrow_Longevity_paper.pdf

Website:

London School of Economics—Pensions Tomorrow, an initiative launched by the LSE to stimulate debate on how to take pension systems forward: www.lse.ac.uk/collections/management/pensionsTomorrow

See Also:

★ Asset Liability Management for Pension Funds (pp. 13–15)
★ Mixflation (pp. 353–356)
★ The Role of Institutional Investors in Corporate Financing (pp. 572–575)
★ Valuing Pension Fund Liabilities on the Balance Sheet (pp. 113–115)
✔ Investing in Employee Pension Plans: Understanding the Risks and Returns (p. 940)
✔ Preparing Financial Statements: Balance Sheets (p. 1043)
✔ Understanding Asset-Liability Management (Full Balance Sheet Approach) (p. 889)
✔ Understanding the Balance Sheet (p. 894)
✔ Understanding the Relationship between the Discount Rate and Risk (p. 896)
Gary Brinson (p. 1156)

"In business a reputation for keeping absolutely to the letter and spirit of an agreement, even when it is unfavorable, is the most precious of assets, although it is not entered in the balance sheet."
Oliver Lyttelton Chandos

     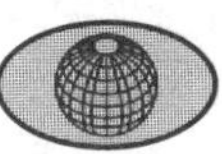  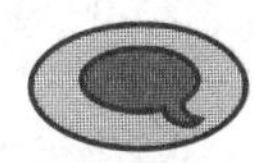 

Quantifying Corporate Financial Risk by David C. Shimko

EXECUTIVE SUMMARY

- Standard pro forma cash flow analysis considers risk in a crude way, usually with a subjectively determined upside and downside to cash flows.
- Stochastic analysis generates a large number of scenarios to better understand risk interactions, business linkages, optionality, and contracts designed to mitigate risk.
- Simple models can be built in spreadsheets, but one must take care to model financial assets, commodity prices, interest rates, and exchange rates appropriately.
- Stochastic pro-formas can lead to better capital budgeting, valuation, and risk management decisions, particularly when risk is important to decision-making.
- Even the most sophisticated models are still subject to model risk; and they do not likely capture all the risks affecting an enterprise.

EXAMPLE OF A STOCHASTIC PRO FORMA

Consider the case of a company that has experienced six months of cash flows this year and wants to forecast the next six months. The usual way to do this is to predict a cash flow growth rate—expected, high, and low—and to base the analysis on these choices. A sample cash flow projection might be illustrated graphically in Figure 1.

In reality, of course, several different cash flow patterns might emerge for the last six months of the year. Using the same risk model, we could run a large number of simulations and see what the outcomes might be. Eight possible outcomes are plotted in Figure 2.

Clearly the stochastic analysis, albeit more realistic, is not as simple and not as attractive at first blush as deterministic analysis. And there are many situations where stochastic analysis is not needed. Yet there are certain results that one can get from stochastic analysis that cannot be gained from deterministic analysis. Table 1 gives some examples.

Stochastic analysis is needed in situations where risk assessment is required, where the future company decisions depend on an unknown variable, where options are present, and when the company wants to study risk mitigation strategies.

Stochastic modeling of the income statement can be done at the aggregate level as it has been demonstrated here, or the components can be broken down into smaller components, such as the prices of products, inputs, interest rates, foreign exchange rates, and the like. The benefit of breaking down the income statement into its market-driven components is that we can find much more information on market-quoted prices and rates. This historical information is usually used as a starting point in determining how to best model these prices and rates.

MODELING MARKET RISK

Risk analysts need to spend significant time and effort to correctly model the risk of the inputs to their stochastic models. Incorrect specifications for market prices will lead to incorrect results. There are several models available to model market price risk. The choice of the best model generally is made by looking at the market's historical performance and making judgments about market price behavior.[1]

For example, if our risk model depends on fluctuations in the stock market index, a popular approach is to represent the index as following a random walk in percentage terms. Thus, any given day's return is normally distributed with a constant mean and standard deviation, and statistically independent from the previous day's return. This approach was popularized in the Black–Scholes (1973) and Merton (1973) papers on option pricing. The random walk works reasonably well, except that with specialized knowledge one could argue that the average return should not be constant, the volatility should not be constant, and there are sometimes events

Figure 1. Deterministic cash flow forecast for last six months

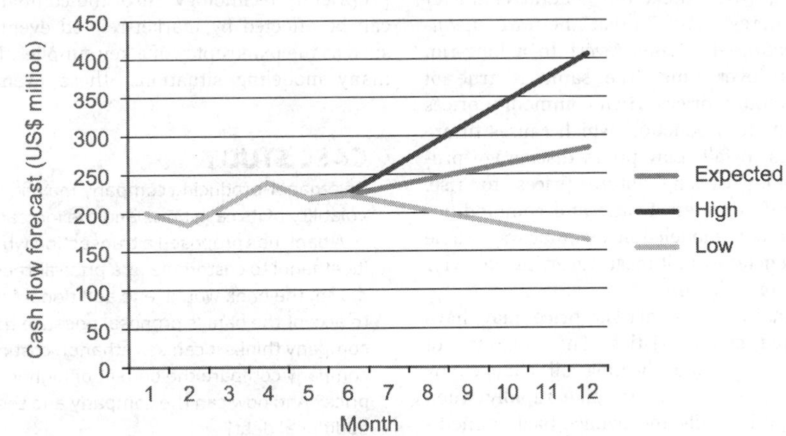

Figure 2. Stochastic cash flow projection for last six months

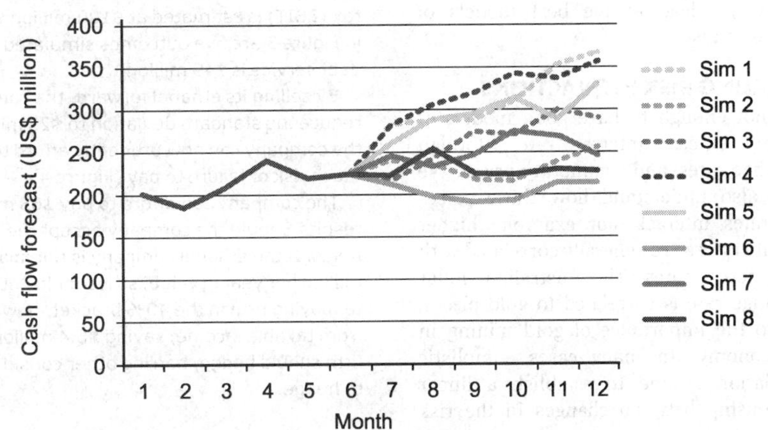

"They are like looters after a hurricane." Andrew Cuomo

     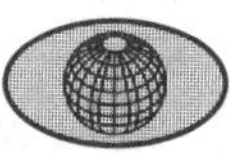   

Table 1. Incremental analyses produced by stochastic pro formas

Analysis	*Sample question*
Probabilities of outcomes	What is the likelihood we will need to borrow?
Risk of outcomes	What is the most likely range for annual cash flows at year-end?
Interactions	If we invest more in capital expenditures only when cash flows are up, how do we reflect that in the analysis, and what impact does it have?
Options	Our loan contracts have floating rates, but the rates are capped. How does this affect the probabilities of different cash flow levels?
Worst case	We probably won't have the worst case revenues and the worst case costs in the same year; how does that reflect on our expectation of the worst case?
Events	There's a 10% chance we get a major contract that will increase our cash flows significantly. How do we incorporate this in the model?
Risk mitigation	The treasurer wants to lock in foreign exchange rates for our foreign buyers. How will this affect cash flow volatility?
Capital structure	What is our capacity to make interest payments on debt with 99% certainty?

which cause stock prices not to be normally distributed. For this reason, the S&P 500 index may reasonably follow a random walk, but the stock of a small pharmaceutical company will not, since it is prone to occasional major events such as FDA drug approval or discovery of legal liability.

Other market prices, such as interest rates, do not follow random walks. Overly high and overly low interest rates tend to correct over time to equilibrium levels. Although that equilibrium level may change over time, the general character of interest rates is that they are *mean-reverting*—i.e., they revert to a long-run mean over time. The same is true of commodity prices. High commodity prices stimulate production, which causes future prices to fall. Low prices discourage production, causing future prices to rise. Therefore, interest rates and commodities need to be modeled in a similar way. Some currencies exhibit mean-reverting behavior and some do not.

Finally, every market price may have unique characteristics. The volatility of natural gas and heating oil changes by season. Power prices spike rapidly when generation fails and bounce back immediately as generation comes back on line. Careful modeling of critical market price inputs will lead to the best models of stochastic results.

MODELING RISK INTERACTIONS

It is not enough to have good models of security prices, interest rates, foreign exchange rates, and commodity prices. We must also understand how those prices and rates interact. For example, higher security prices are generally correlated with low interest rates. The Australian dollar exchange rate is correlated to gold prices, due to the importance of gold mining in its economy. In many cases, simplistic correlation is fine to establish a linear relationship between changes in the risk variables. However, in other cases, the correlations may not be linear, requiring a more subtle approach. For some firms, that subtlety will be important enough to build a precise model of the interaction between two risks of importance to the company.

MODELING EVENT RISK

Every corporation is subject to risks from significant events, such as losing a major lawsuit, or obtaining a patent on its proprietary technology. Also, the company can be affected by market-related events, such as the bankruptcy of a key supplier. In many modeling situations, these events play an important role in determining the probability distributions of future cash flows.

It is tempting to think of event risks as being random outcomes, independent of everything else in the model. This is the biggest mistake a modeler can make. The credit crisis of 2008, for example, showed vividly how default risks across investment banks were correlated, owing to the similarity of their risk-taking activities.

AGGREGATING CASH FLOW RISKS TO THE INCOME STATEMENT

Once all the drivers of the income statement have been modeled, they are compiled to the income statement in the same way that a pro-forma income statement would normally be generated. For example, suppose a refinery in Brazil buys crude oil in dollars, sells products in reais, shuts down production when it is not profitable to produce, and runs the risk of operational failures according to some statistical model. In this case, the modeler could build stochastic formulas for the price of crude, the price of products, the dollar foreign exchange rate, the shutdown policy of the firm, and the unplanned outage rates due to operational risk. The result is a determination of net income for each particular simulated environment. These net income numbers can be simulated as

CASE STUDY

An ethanol-producing company may be reluctant to issue more debt because of the high volatility of its cash flows and the increased risk of being put into bankruptcy.

A bank has proposed a transaction where the company would reduce its risk by selling its ethanol to customers at a price agreed today—i.e., entering forward contracts. If it did so, the bank would lend additional funds at the same rate. The company is reluctant to accept the bank's proposal because the sales price falls below the level at which the company thinks it can sell ethanol, costing the company $2 million per year. How can the company compare the benefit of higher debt with the cost of selling at a distressed price? And how can the company and the bank determine an appropriate level of additional debt?

A stochastic pro forma analysis could be done for the company before and after the proposed transaction. Before the transaction, the average earnings before interest and tax (EBIT) is estimated at $100 million with a standard deviation of $50 million. Shown in Figure 3 are five outcomes simulated over an eight-year period. The current annual debt service is $49 million.

By selling its ethanol forward, the company expects to lose $2 million per year, but reduce the standard deviation to $25 million. The resulting stochastics demonstrate that the company can now prudently afford to make higher interest payments without having much risk of failure to pay (Figure 4).

The company can afford to pay $65 million in interest safely, after hedging its results.Should the company accept the hedging program? The answer depends on taxes. If the ethanol company is not in a tax-paying situation, it has lost an expected $2 million per year in value, so it should not hedge unless there are other reasons to do so. A taxpaying firm in the 40% bracket, however, will be able to deduct the interest expense from taxable income, saving $6.4 million per year (40% of 65 minus 49). The taxpaying firm should hedge, barring other considerations that might cause the firm not to want to hedge.

"I didn't understand how they were turning all this garbage into gold."

  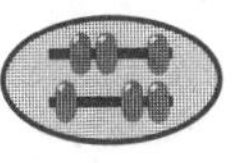   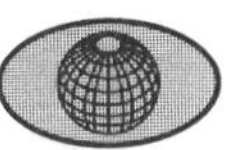   

Figure 3. Current EBIT stochastics

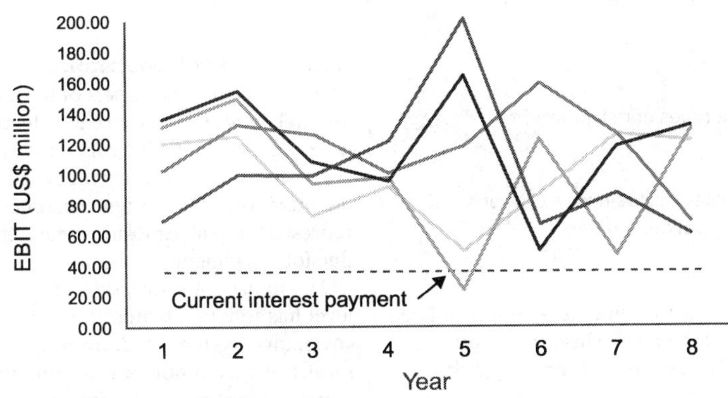

Figure 4. EBIT stochastics post-hedging

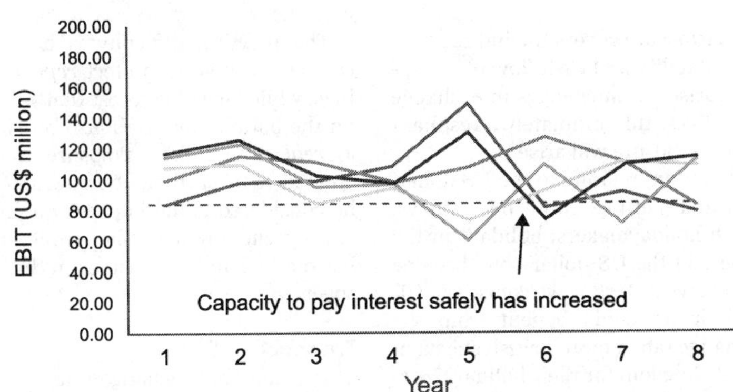

many times as required to determine the volatility of cash flows, the value of the shutdown option, and the answer to any of the questions posed above.

MODELING RISKS OTHER THAN CASH FLOW

Some risks may not affect cash flows but could affect earnings, such as a mark-to-market liability. In these cases, similar risk models can be built to model earnings risk, or to model the likelihood of a credit downgrade. Stochastic models can be simple or extremely complex, but they all are built fundamentally to make deterministic models more realistic and able to answer questions related to risk, risk management, optionality, capital structure, and much, much more.

CONCLUSION

Stochastic pro forma analysis answers many financial questions that cannot be addressed with usual deterministic pro-forma analysis. The case study demonstrates how hedging and capital structure may be evaluated using stochastic pro formas. Other applications include evaluation of real options,[2] the study of credit ratings, and the development of probability statements around cash flow or earnings.

Like any other type of analysis, poor assumptions lead to poor conclusions. Good simulation models take a great deal of care in specifying the correct models for all the risk drivers and the interactions between them. Finally, more realistic risk-based models lead to better corporate financial decisions.

In the final analysis, however, even a very sophisticated model is still a model, and is therefore subject to model risk. Thus, the model may not fully identify or quantify all risks that affect an enterprise, and can thereby lead to a false sense of security. Accordingly, decision-makers should consider model risk as one of the components of any financial decision based on stochastic pro forma analysis.

▸▸ MAKING IT HAPPEN

- Begin with a project or corporate pro forma.
- Consider every assumption and ask if it is vulnerable to risk.
- Produce a risk model to simulate all the assumptions consistently and simultaneously.
- Use this model (stochastic pro forma) to design best and worst cases.
- Simulate outcomes of all key financial variables and communicate the risks.

▸▸ MORE INFO

Most of the literature in "stochastic processes" is extremely technical and not suitable for the average business reader. Even "stochastic processes in finance" tends to lead to models of security prices and interest rates for building value-at-risk models and option pricing models.

The topic "financial statement simulation" in an internet search engine leads to simulation software providers, such as Palisade, Finance 3.0, and @Risk. These providers offer written materials to supplement their software services. In addition, the reader is invited to request additional materials from the author.

Articles:

Black, Fischer, and Myron Scholes. "The pricing of options and corporate liabilities" *Journal of Political Economy* 81:3 (1973): 637–654.

Merton, Robert C. "Theory of regional option pricing" *Bell Journal of Economics and Management Science* 4:1 (1973): 141–183.

NOTES

1 Analysts should never expect that historical price behavior will represent future price behavior—only to realize that there is usually no better source of information for modeling purposes.

2 See the article on real options in this volume (pp. 808–810).

"That Wall Street has gone down because of this is justice. . .They built a castle to rip people off. Not once in all these years have I come across a person inside a big Wall Street firm who was having a crisis of conscience."
Steve Eisman

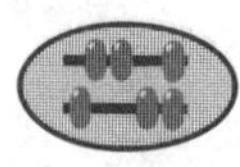

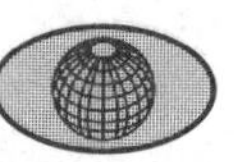

To Hedge or Not to Hedge by Steve Robinson

EXECUTIVE SUMMARY

- How currency risks are created and managed and the types of risk inherent in international trading.
- The techniques for managing currency risks.
- A framework for selecting appropriate techniques in specific business situations.
- An outline and illustration of the use, of the main financial derivatives.

INTRODUCTION

Business has become increasingly international, and companies cannot ignore the impact of currency changes on cash flows, profitability, and their asset and liability position. No company is wholly immune—the cash received from exporting is affected by the relationship between the currency used by the customer to pay and the currency in which the cost of providing the product or service is denominated.

Many commodity prices have been volatile, rising and falling dramatically in recent years—driven by exploding or plummeting demand from fast-developing countries. Copper, tin, wheat, platinum, and of course oil, have risen dramatically, and this has had a significant impact on costs for many industries. Declines can be equally sudden, although falling costs often take more time to work through to market prices.

A spectacular result was the sudden collapse of several airline businesses in late 2007 and early 2008. Among them was EOS, a business-class only carrier operating mainly between London and New York, which started only in 2005. Also, Oasis Hong Kong Airlines, an innovative long-haul discount operator between Hong Kong, London, and Vancouver, MAXjet Airways, and some smaller low-cost US carriers, have all ceased trading very suddenly. Although other factors, such as reduced business travel and turbulent financial markets, have had an impact, the price of aviation fuel is the main cost driver, closely followed by the impact of currency changes—airlines pay all their costs in US dollars.

The risks extend beyond the trading sphere. Many banks have had to write down the value of their assets—largely complex "trading" securities. Finance is a global industry, and companies borrow and invest in many currencies. It is not sufficient that only financial people know how currency risks are created and managed.

WHAT ARE THE RISKS?

Currency risk is the net potential effect of exchange rate movements on the cash flow, profit, and balance sheet of a business. There are three types of currency risk:

Economic, Strategic, or Competitive Risk

Economic exposure covers the indirect risk to the profitability and cash flow of a company that arises from changes in exchange rates. It is likely that ultimately a resultant transaction exposure will arise.

An illustration, relating to the US dollar, the euro, and sterling, could be holidays. For British holidaymakers, holidays in the euro zone and the US dollar zone become more expensive if sterling weakens. The UK holiday industry could benefit from the euro exchange rate if more British stayed in the United Kingdom for their holidays.

Translation Risk

Translation risk arises when amounts denominated in foreign currency are converted to domestic equivalents for financial reporting purposes. There is no immediate cash impact. Translation can affect both the profit and loss account and the balance sheet. Increasingly, converging accounting standards under International Financial Reporting Standards (IFRS, which do not apply to unquoted companies) are removing some previous distortions. The most common accounting policy is to convert trading profit and loss numbers at an average exchange rate during the accounting period, and to convert assets and liabilities at the year-end rate.

Profit and Loss Statement Translation

The profit and loss translation is only a paper figure initially, but it may become a real transaction exposure if cash interest or dividends need to be paid. A company with a large proportion of its income, or of its cash, in other currencies, will have a translation issue, but this can be helped by effective communication to investors, persuading them that short-term currency fluctuations will not necessarily lead to reduced long-term stockholder value creation.

Balance Sheet Translation

The foreign currency assets of the company are not exposed to currency fluctuations unless they are to be sold and the cash converted to another currency. Liabilities denominated in foreign currencies will represent a real exposure when they are due for repayment.

The impact of translation on the gearing level has to be evaluated to ensure that no covenants are breached, even if only technically. A very simple way around this is to match investment in foreign currency assets with loans dominated in equivalent currencies.

The practical difficulty is how far the company can go to protect *reported* earnings, while incurring a cost that will impact on the bottom line. It is also possible that a *real* transaction exposure could be created by a currency borrowing. Also to be considered is the impact of a fair value adjustment, on both the profit and loss bottom line and on reserves in the balance sheet.

Transaction Risk

This risk is that exchange rate movements affect the value of foreign currency cash flows. It is the only risk that has a direct and immediate impact on cash, and arises when a transaction is entered into to actually convert from one currency to another.

The most common trading situation creating this exposure is the sale or purchase of goods or services on extended payment terms in foreign currencies. Another common situation arises when dividend or interest payments are paid or received.

This type of risk is usually predictable and quantified, making the protection or hedging process straightforward. Really successful management of currency exposures needs to cope with transactions that have not yet been identified but are likely to occur.

SPECIFIC SITUATIONS

Price List Exposure

Scenario: An exporting company publishes a price list in a local currency. It is commercially impractical to change prices in less than six months.

Risk: A potential exposure is created for up to six months, plus any extended payment term. Actual exposure arises when an invoice is issued.

Possible solutions:

- Small print "right to impose surcharges" clauses. This is legally possible, but

"**In the middle of difficulty lies opportunity.**" Albert Einstein

commercially highly damaging. Airlines have had to resort to this, but it is easier for them given the high profile of oil price movements and the fact that almost all of the competitors are doing it!

- Hedging a proportion of projected sales, from the date of publication of the price list, is advisable. What proportion is a risk management decision, dependent on the corporate attitude to risk, the corporate memory of past situations, and the degree of volatility between currencies.

Capital expenditure: This investment is usually planned and committed over a long period. There may be no actual transaction exposure until purchase contracts are awarded, so the exposure can be identified, quantified, and handled by a hedging technique.

Tender to Control Exposure

Scenario and risk exposure: Companies that regularly submit tenders for the supply of goods and services are exposed from the date of submitting the tender to the date(s) cash is received. Until an order has been received, this is potential exposure; after that event there is real exposure, and from the invoice date transaction exposure exists.

Possible solutions:

- Using historic data for guidance, assess the success rate from tender to contract. Apply that rate—with a value weighting—to all tenders issued, hedging the proportion that's likely to be successful. Additionally, where good market intelligence exists, add in those contracts likely to be won.
- Treat the exposure after winning the contract as a transaction, and hedge using an appropriate technique.
- Try to offset as many costs as possible by buying in the currency of the payer.

MANAGING CURRENCY RISKS

A range of techniques exists that enable companies to limit their exposure to the effect of fluctuating exchange rates. The decision to protect or hedge is made after an assessment of the significance of the risk to the business of exchange rate movements. The selection of hedging technique is made for each specific situation, following a risk assessment of the impact on the business. Factors considered in the risk assessment are:

- The percentage of the company's turnover that is exposed to currency risk. The greater the proportion of sales paid in international currencies versus the home currency, the greater the risk to the business.
- The individual size of a single exposure. Depending on the volatility of the currency, this could be a very high risk, even threatening the continuity of the business.
- The market position of the company. Its financial strength and consequent ability to react to competitive pressures.
- The portfolio of currencies in which the company trades, and whether there are potential off-setting transactions.
- The relationship of cost to sales within trading blocs, particularly currencies that move in lockstep with the US dollar—those of Canada, Hong Kong, Malaysia, Singapore, and Saudi Arabia.
- The ability to match the currency of sales with the currency of costs.
- The previous experience of the company in relation to currency losses, and its forecasting experience.
- The level of currency management expertise within the company.

HEDGING TECHNIQUES

Internal

Sometimes known as commercial or natural, these techniques are within the internal management control of the company.

Pricing:

- In the currency in which the majority of the costs are incurred.
- In the domestic currency of the main competitors, so that comparative prices are less affected by exchange rate variations.
- Inserting an exchange rate variation clause (always difficult commercially) to protect margins.

Matching:

- Setting up an equal and opposite commercial transaction when the original exposure is created—for example, using the currency receivable to buy a commodity used by the business.
- Borrow in the same currency as that needed to complete the asset purchase.

Netting:

- A partial alternative to matching—a net amount is still left exposed, but the overall risk is reduced.

Leading and lagging:

- Simply, either delaying payment, or settling early, in anticipation of falling or rising exchange rates. Safe, and simple to manage, but there is a reliance on the accuracy of a forecast.

Intercompany payment discipline:

- Intercompany payables and receivables are real exposure and should be ranked equally for settlement with external liabilities.
- There is no canceling gain or loss situation within a group. When the transaction interacts with the market there will be a gain or a loss—and it will be real.

External

When the use of internal techniques has been exhausted, external ones should be used. There are four main instruments:

- Forward contracts;
- Lending and borrowing;
- Options;
- Swaps.

Forward Contracts

A forward contract is an agreement to exchange a fixed amount of one currency for a fixed amount of another currency at an agreed date in the future. The effective exchange rate is derived from the comparative interest rates of the two currencies being exchanged. Its suitability depends on being able to forecast the currency flows confidently. If the forecast proves not to be accurate, the business has in reality created an exposure rather than protected an existing one, because the forward contract is a binding agreement to deliver a quantity of one currency and receive a quantity of another. The key features of a forward contract are:

- Certainty and simplicity—enabling good cash management;
- Off balance sheet—it does not count as borrowings that affect gearing;
- Normally sourced from a bank.

Lending and Borrowing

As an alternative to a forward contract, the currency could be exchanged immediately in the spot market, i.e. where the transaction is agreed on the "spot" and takes place immediately. The exchange rate is known as fixed, the transaction immediate (two days delivery normally), and the administration and monitoring of forward contracts are avoided. The currency is normally deposited in an interest-bearing currency account until needed.

Illustration: A forward transaction to buy yen for a capital equipment purchase has been made. Delivery will be late. A way around this problem would be to take delivery of the yen as agreed and put the amount on deposit until needed. As yen interest rates are lower than for sterling, there will be an effective interest cost. If delivery was available earlier and agreed to by the company, yen could be borrowed short term and repaid when the forward contract matured.

Options

An option is the right, but not the obligation, to exchange a fixed amount of one

     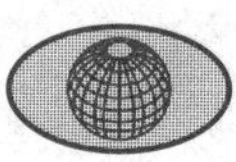   

currency for a fixed amount of another within, or at the end of, a predetermined period. In effect, it is a forward contract that can be walked away from, where you lose only the cost of the option, which could be 3–5% of the contract value. It therefore has the advantage of limiting the downside, as the maximum cost is known at the beginning, while leaving unlimited profit potential. These options are ideally suited to translations, where the size or existence of the exposure is uncertain, for example tender-to-contract or price list exposures.

Illustration: A quantity of a commodity (or currency to pay for it) is needed in three months' time. A dealer is willing to accept US$100 per ton to supply a predetermined quantity at US$2,000 per ton. If the price of this commodity in three months' time is US$1,700 per ton, then the option would be thrown away, the product bought in the spot market, and the cost to the company would be US$1,800 per ton. The tender-to-contract or price list item would have been safeguarded, and the price could even be reduced by US$200 per ton if competitive conditions demanded. If the price of the commodity rose, the cost to the company would be contained. The option could be sold at a profit if the product was not needed, or the loss would in any event be limited to US$100 per ton.

There are two types of option:

- **Calls**—giving the right to buy a currency;
- **Puts**—giving the right to sell a currency.

Currency Options

The exchange rate (known as the strike price) and the expiry date of the option are chosen by the customer at the outset. The cost (known as the premium) of the option is calculated based on these decisions and the volatility of the currency involved. Options can be exchange-traded where they exist in standardized form, or bought over the counter, where they are written to fit a customer's particular circumstances.

There are two styles of option:

- **American option**. The buyer can exercise the option (make the exchange of currencies) at any time up to the expiry date.
- **European option**. This can be exercised on the expiry date only, and is slightly cheaper because of its lack of flexibility.

Options may have a resale value, determined by the same criteria as the original cost. When the exercise price of an option is better than the current spot exchange rate, it is called "in the money"; when it is the other way round, it is "out of the money."

Swaps

Swaps are like long-dated forward contracts. They involve the exchange of a liability now, with the exchange back at a predetermined future time, and the compensation of the other party for costs in the intervening period. Swaps are used primarily to protect an investment or portfolio of borrowings. They involve a back-to-back loan between companies with a matching but opposite need. What is "swapped" is essentially a series of cash flows.

Illustration: A UK company wishes to raise cash to invest in developing its business in the United States. It is quoted in the United Kingdom only, which means it does not have access to US capital markets and it does not have a rating, so it would be extremely difficult to borrow in the United States.

What sources of funds are available?

- Raise equity via a UK rights issue;
- Borrow sterling from a UK bank;
- Borrow in US dollars.

The first two of these options will appear on a balance sheet as sterling liabilities, but the asset will appear as a dollar asset, creating a translation exposure. The returns from the investment will be in dollars, which will create a translation exposure when they are converted to sterling income in the profit statement, and a transaction exposure when they need to be converted to pay interest or dividends in sterling.

A solution is to swap the currency flows for the duration of a loan, paying or receiving a sum of money from the other party, leaving both sides in an equivalent cash flow position but having avoided specific payments in another currency. The loan would revert to the borrowing currency on maturity.

CONCLUSION

Managing currency and related transactions is a core part of corporate risk management within the Treasury Function. Its importance will continue to demand boardroom time and the highest standard of corporate governance. Massive and unpredictable fluctuations in currency markets have made forecasting more difficult and the need to safeguard the value of assets, liabilities and transactions is paramount.

▶▶ MORE INFO

Books:

Arnold, Glen. *Corporate Financial Management*. 4th ed. Harlow, UK: FT Prentice Hall, 2008.

Boakes, Kevin. *Reading and Understanding the Financial Times*. Harlow, UK: FT Prentice Hall, 2008.

Matza, Peter (ed). *The International Treasurer's Handbook 2009*. 19th ed. London: Association of Corporate Treasurers, 2008.

Shomah, Shani Beverley. *A Foreign Exchange Primer*. 2nd ed. Chichester, UK: Wiley, 2009.

Slatyer, Will. *The Debt Delusion: Evolution and Management of Financial Risk*. Boca Raton, FL: Universal Publishers, 2008.

Websites:

DailyFX: www.dailyfx.com

Reuters Business and Finance: www.reuters.com/finance

TMI Online: www.treasury-management.com

"To a bystander like me, those who made 190 million pounds deliberately underselling the shares of HBOS, in spite of its very strong capital base, and drove it into the bosom of Lloyds TSB Bank, are clearly bank robbers and asset strippers." Dr John Sentamu

  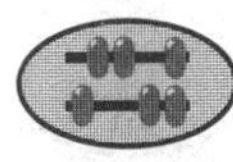   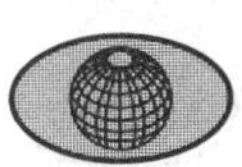   

A Total Balance Sheet Approach to Financial Risk by Terry Carroll

EXECUTIVE SUMMARY

- Because the oil price rose rapidly and the wider commodities market followed suit, inflation rose to its highest level for many years. Following a protracted boom, property prices have been savaged. Only interest rates have remained comparatively benign.
- Protecting or insulating yourself or your company against financial risks is known as "hedging." Most businesses use a transaction-driven approach. The generic name often used by bankers for these hedging instruments is "treasury products."
- Bankers can provide a derivative-based hedge to reduce or neutralize an interest rate, inflation, or commodity price risk. A derivative is a financial instrument whose value changes in relation to an underlying variable such as interest rates, commodity prices, or house prices.
- Price increases and currency fluctuations, as well as interest rate movements, can be hedged. The most common source of long-term capital, fixed by nature, is retained profits. A mismatch between, say, fixed-rate assets and variable-rate liabilities may cause you to want to hedge or renegotiate more fixed-rate liabilities to produce a better match and more overall certainty, with, by definition, lower overall risk.

INTRODUCTION

We are living in some of the most volatile times in the history of the global financial markets. One of the reasons is exactly because they have become truly global. As banks seek to restore profitability, they may increase their offering of "treasury products" to customers. This article argues that these should be considered only in the context of a total balance sheet approach rather than transaction by transaction.

MANAGING INCREASED FINANCIAL RISK

We have seen a period in which the oil price rose to $147 a barrel and then fell back dramatically. The wider commodities market followed suit. Inflation rose to its highest level for many years before easing back. Property prices have been savaged, following a protracted boom. Only interest rates have remained relatively benign compared to the extremes of the past.

Volatility has been traded as a market index for many years, but in 2008 alone it hit several spikes. It has become a fact of life. Markets are now driven mainly by fear—fear of being caught out when prices fall or fear of not being in the market as prices rise. Add to that the power of short sellers and you have a scary scenario for borrowers and investors, whether individuals or corporate.

Protecting or insulating yourself or your company against financial risks is known as "hedging." The principle of hedging is easily understood—it's like an insurance premium. In practice, the instruments generally used are known as "derivatives." These are poorly understood and, given the recent financial mess, probably viewed with fear or trepidation.

This article attempts two things: first, to put forward a more objective approach for companies wishing to improve their financial efficiency at a managed level of risk; and second, to demystify financial risk, making it a more approachable topic for the average manager or director.

WHAT IS A DERIVATIVE?

A derivative is a financial instrument whose value changes in relation to an underlying variable, for example: interest rates, the rate of inflation, commodity prices, share or bond prices, house prices, etc. Its most general use is for the purpose of "hedging" a given risk, i.e. neutralizing or taking the opposite position to a given risk, such as commodity prices, exchange or interest rates.

The problem with derivatives is that although they were created for the primary purpose of insuring against financial risks, the proportion of derivatives trading done for speculative purposes now dramatically outweighs that for ordinary trade purposes.

MOST HEDGING IS TRANSACTION-BASED

In this article we shall be proposing a "full balance sheet approach" to the management of financial risk. Most businesses currently use a transaction-driven approach. This could result in overall risk being increased rather than decreased.

By a transaction-driven approach, we mean that each transaction or set of similar transactions is individually hedged. This is the most common situation, whether the use of derivatives is recommended by a bank or requested by the customer. The generic title often used by bankers for these hedging instruments is "treasury products."

Trading and managing the use of derivatives is a highly skilled and often complex process. They are usually created and dealt with by the treasury or special products division of a bank. In the United Kingdom, these "rocket scientists," as they are sometimes known, are usually based in the City of London, embedded within the financial markets.

If you wish to hedge a risk, your bank will usually put you in touch with such a treasury specialist. Alternatively, the bank may make the first move. Not surprisingly, banks have increasingly been offering these products in the climate of increasing volatility for all the commodities and financial facilities that companies use.

A TRANSACTION-BASED APPROACH CAN ACTUALLY INCREASE OVERALL RISK

There is an important difference between the profit and loss account approach and the balance sheet approach to improving financial efficiency. Any accountant or banker worth their salt can look at the profit and loss account and come up with suggestions on how to improve profitability or reduce risk. If you fear interest rate, inflation, or commodity price risks, your banker can provide you with a derivative-based hedge to reduce or neutralize that risk. Accountants like certainty, so that they can sleep easy at night.

The danger of this approach is that it can actually increase the risk of loss for the company. Take a simple example:

Suppose you have a commercial property—the business premises for example—that you own and plan to keep for the long term. It is by nature, therefore, a fixed asset. It has a fixed notional return, i.e. its long-term value to the business. You wouldn't think of financing it out of short-term overdraft. You want a long-term debt, ideally, to finance it. This may well be at an interest rate linked to bank base rate.

Your bank draws your attention to the possibility that interest rates may increase. Wouldn't you like to hedge that risk? Their treasury products division can sell you an

     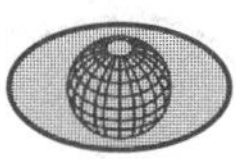   

interest rate hedge that swaps the variable-rate risk into a fixed-rate risk, thereby insulating you against the cost of rising interest rates.

Now consider two worrying circumstances. The first is that interest rates actually fall. In those circumstances you have not only lost the value of the "premium" you paid, i.e. the cost of the derivative contract, but you've also lost the opportunity to gain from the interest rate falls, because you're now effectively stuck with a stream of fixed-rate payments.

So the first and most important consideration is not to use hedging on a transaction by transaction basis, because you may actually be increasing the overall risk profile of the company.

Take another example: sterling is falling against the dollar and, because commodities are usually priced in dollars, the effective cost you are paying for your raw materials is increasing. So you decide to hedge against the risk of a rising dollar. But suppose you also sell much of your finished product overseas. Whether or not you are invoicing in dollars—but especially if you are—the currency you receive will be exchanging into more and more pounds. This could be counterbalancing your raw material price increases.

Of course, you could decide to hedge the raw material currency risk alone and profit from the widening margins in sterling. But again, if the currency rates swing round the other way, your sales income in sterling will be falling and you won't benefit from the fact that raw material prices are also falling. This again illustrates the importance of looking at both sides of the trading account or balance sheet.

A HOLISTIC OR FULL BALANCE SHEET APPROACH

So, the first point we are making is that when you are looking at your trading, before entering into a hedge on one side of the transaction, i.e. the buying or selling side, you should also consider what is happening on the other side. You can hedge price increases and currency fluctuations, as well as interest rate movements.

There is also a range of products that can make the holistic hedging approach even more effective. As well as swapping variable interest rate payments for fixed, you can also buy what is called a "cap" or a "collar." A cap protects you from interest rate increases above a certain level but enables you still to benefit if rates fall; and a collar gives you protection from interest rate fluctuations both up and down, outside of a given band of rates, and may be cheaper.

Having considered trading transactions on both sides of the equation (such as the inflation of selling prices matching out the inflation of raw material costs), the most significant and generally underexploited area is the balance sheet.

Many of you will have come across fixed-rate mortgages for home purchase. Although 25-year fixed-rate mortgages have been available in recent years, few have been taken out to date. Normally fixes are for up to five years. The problem is that, on a 25-year mortgage term, after five years you are exposed to the risk of rising rates again. In other words, you don't have a perfect hedge.

And so with balance sheets. It would seem to be folly to fund long-term fixed assets from overdrafts, but that is exactly what some businesses effectively do. By taking the whole balance sheet perspective, you can not only ensure that you reduce overall financial risk, but you can also increase profitability without increasing risk.

EFFECTING THE FULL BALANCE SHEET APPROACH

You may still wish to seek the help of a treasury specialist, but here you want them to look at the whole balance sheet.

To take the earlier example: you may have funded the purchase of a commercial property that you intend to use and keep indefinitely, by borrowing on a five-year term at a margin over bank base rate. There is certainly logic in swapping this into a fixed rate if you think interest rates may rise, but this can also be a gamble because if they fall, you are not gaining the benefit.

Furthermore, the most common source of long-term capital, fixed by nature, is retained profits. So, suppose that your retained profits are at least as great in value as the cost of the property. Given that both are retained for the long term, they could be said to match each other. This leaves the cash that you have borrowed on a variable rate free to fluctuate. If you also generate spare cash on the other side of the balance sheet, then, in order not to increase the overall financial risk in the balance sheet, either this should be invested at a variable rate, or, if it is at a fixed rate, then the cost of the debt should be swapped to variable.

When you put all those assets and liabilities together in the balance sheet, you have not only reduced the financial risk in the balance sheet, but you have also significantly improved the certainty of the net cost or profit arising from those matched transactions.

THE CONCEPT OF DURATION RISK

The final piece of the jigsaw is known as "duration." In simple terms, duration is the length of the life of the particular asset or liability. The importance of this is as follows.

Most people understand the likely folly of borrowing short to lend long. You wouldn't borrow money for six months to buy your house. You might borrow money for 25 years with a fixed rate for the first five to give you relative certainty, but because of the constant risk of rising interest costs it is no surprise when people are looking to refix the rate for another two, three, or five years—for example, when the first fixed rate runs out. It may cost more, but that is the price of certainty.

So, the final piece is duration, and we bring this together with the whole balance sheet approach. First, you analyze your whole balance sheet by looking at each of the assets and determining which liabilities are funding which assets. If you have a mismatch between, say, fixed-rate assets and variable-rate liabilities, you may want to hedge or renegotiate more fixed-rate liabilities to produce a better match and more overall certainty, with, by definition, lower overall risk.

The next stage is to look at the average duration (or maturity/life) of the assets and the same for the liabilities. If there is a mismatch, either you will have greater overall certainty and lower risk because the average duration of the liabilities is longer than that of the assets, or you may have greater overall risk and less certainty if the balance is the other way. In the latter case, you may wish to increase the average duration of the liabilities, perhaps by refinancing.

> "Hedging through the use of the increasingly sophisticated range of derivative-based products can both reduce risk and increase either or both the overall return and the certainty of costs or return."

CONCLUSION

We have introduced some complex concepts here, but this is for at least two important reasons: first, if you have, or know of, a risk that you face and choose to do nothing about it, that decision alone increases the risk to the corporation. Hedging through the use of the increasingly sophisticated range of derivative-based

  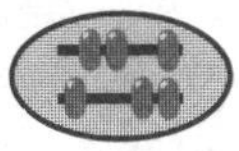   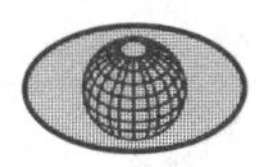   

products can both reduce risk and increase either or both the overall return and the certainty of costs or return.

This can only be guaranteed if you use the full balance sheet approach or look at both sides of the transaction. If you allow yourself to be persuaded to hedge individual transactions, you may by definition actually be speculating and, worse still, increasing the overall risk profile of the business.

Any worthwhile treasury products specialist at your bank should understand all the principles and concepts introduced in this article and would find it hard to disagree with the overall premise. Business finance should be about improving returns and the certainty of returns and reducing or neutralizing risk. Never has this been truer than in these increasingly volatile times.

▸▸ MORE INFO

Books:

Choudhry, Moorad. *Bank Asset and Liability Management: Strategy, Trading, Analysis.* Singapore: Wiley, 2007.

Van Deventer, Donald R., Kenji Imai, and Mark Mesler. *Advanced Financial Risk Management: Tools and Techniques for Integrated Credit Risk and Interest Rate Risk Management.* Singapore: Wiley, 2005.

Article:

Roy, Sayonton. "Asset liability management in risk framework." Online at: www.coolavenues.com/know/fin/sayonton_1.php3

Website:

RiskGlossary.com—see entry for "asset-liability management": www.riskglossary.com

See Also:

★ Dangers of Corporate Derivative Transactions (pp. 46–48)
★ Risk Management: Beyond Compliance (pp. 510–513)
Peter Bernstein (p. 1154)

"The Robert Mugabe school of economics provides a salutary warning about uncontrolled monetary expansion in generating hyper-inflation. The road to Harare is not as long as we might hope." Vince Cable

  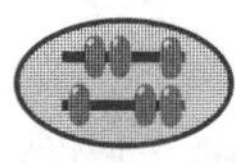   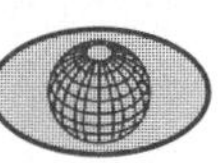   

Using Structured Products to Manage Liabilities by Shane Edwards

EXECUTIVE SUMMARY

- Structured products (SPs) are derivative contracts that are tailored for a specific purpose, such as hedging the value of an uncertain future liability.
- The value of a SP is derived from one or many underlying reference asset values, which causes uncertainty in the value of the liability to be hedged.
- SPs are typically transacted between a client and an investment bank, and can take various legal forms.
- The fact that SPs are flexible and can be tailored to client needs distinguishes them from standard derivatives, which have generic fixed terms.
- However, SPs tend to be regarded as more complex financial instruments, and they are more difficult to value than vanilla derivatives.

INTRODUCTION

Only a decade ago, the use of structured products (SPs) was largely confined to sophisticated institutions that used them for risk management purposes. Now SPs are embraced across the client spectrum and are owned by millions—from retail individuals investing in capital-protected equity products, to global corporations that tailor SPs to meet their often complex and highly specific liability management needs.

In the liability management arena, SPs have an important role to play due to their highly customizable nature. They are used by corporate treasurers as a way of actively managing borrowing costs and hedging foreign exchange liabilities. Many companies have also embraced SPs, outside of treasury, to manage expected future liabilities (for example, airlines hedging the price of jet fuel or importers/exporters hedging the foreign exchange rate). SPs are also used by many pension funds as a strategic initiative to manage the asset–liability mismatch and tailor the pension deficit risk profile.

The increased appetite for SPs is a result of improved client education and the rapid pace of innovation at investment banks, where SPs have become a major source of business. The growth in SP volumes is expected to continue its rapid pace in the years ahead.

ANATOMY OF A STRUCTURED PRODUCT

A derivative is a financial instrument that derives its value from one or more underlying reference asset values. Derivatives can range in complexity from very simple with standardized terms (vanilla derivatives), to very complex with highly customized features (exotic derivatives). Broadly, there are three levels of complexity in derivatives, listed here in order of complexity:

Linear derivatives (for example, futures, forwards, zero strike calls), which reflect the performance of an underlying asset on an almost one-to-one basis but without legal ownership of the underlying asset. These derivatives can be simply priced through arbitrage (cost of carry) arguments.

Nonlinear derivatives (for example, call options), where at expiry the price of the derivative will vary linearly with the underlying asset price if the underlying is above a predefined strike level. If this is not the case, the option price will be worth zero. Well-understood models are available that rely heavily on the volatility of the underlying asset to determine the derivative price.

Exotic derivatives, which have path-dependent payouts, restriking features, or hybrid (multiasset class) characteristics. They require sophisticated mathematical models to price and are highly sensitive to calibrations of the underlying probability distribution and correlation assumptions (in the case of multiasset underlyings).

Any of the three derivative types may be regarded as structured products due to the amount of customization that is contained in the contract terms. Common customizations include:

- *Underlying assets (underlyings)*: These may include anything that is transparent and tradable, such as equities, interest rates, foreign exchange rates, commodities, and inflation. Hybrid SPs can be created where multiple asset classes are used.
- *Tenor*: Clients are able to tailor the maturity of a SP to any extent where the counterparty providing the hedge allows it, which in turn is dictated by the liquidity of the underlying asset. SPs can include features that allow early maturity, such as: puttability (where the client may choose to early-terminate the structure with preagreed payout), callability (where the hedge counterparty can terminate at its discretion), or automatic termination (where maturity will occur once a predefined event has occured).
- *Path dependency*: The payouts of many SPs are determined with reference to how the underlyings have performed through the life of the product, and not simply as a function of the final underlying asset level. Examples are Asian options (where the average level of an underlying is calculated) and lookback or barrier options (where the highest or lowest observed levels of an underlying determine the payout).
- *Payouts*: SPs can have interim payouts (coupons) and/or a final payout at maturity as specified.
- *Currency*: SP payouts are often requested in currencies other than the currency of the underlying asset; such products are known as quanto or composite options.

LEGAL FORM

A structured product is a legally binding financial contract between a client and an investment bank, stating the specific terms that have been agreed. The legal form of the transaction is referred to as a wrapper, and the most common wrappers are:

Over-the-counter (OTC). This typically means that a client makes an upfront payment equal to the offer price of the SP. In return, the bank (as per the terms of the SP) may pay the client coupons and/or a payment at maturity, all of which are typically dependent on the performance of the underlying reference assets.

Structured note. The client pays the principal amount to the bank at inception. In return, the bank sells the client a note, which is typically a senior unsecured debt obligation of the bank. The note will reflect the terms of the transaction and specify payments, normally including the return of the principal amount at maturity (for principal protected notes), or possibly some principal loss (in the case of nonprincipal protected notes), depending on the performance of the underlying.

Swap. In a swap there is no exchange of principal. Typically, the client will pay

"The government increasingly resembles somebody who is trying to give the kiss of life to a corpse." Vince Cable

  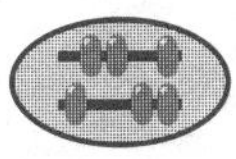   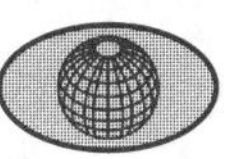   

floating Libor (minus a spread) and the investment bank will pay periodic amounts contingent on the performance of the underlying.

Other forms. There are myriad wrappers that find preference with certain clients or in certain jurisdictions, depending on the tax consequences, counterparty risk exposure, and local regulation. Other wrappers include structured deposits and UCITS III funds,[1] for example.

CLIENT TYPES AND COMMON USES OF STRUCTURED PRODUCTS IN LIABILITY MANAGEMENT

Due to their flexibility, SPs are chosen in a variety of liability management situations and by an array of users. They are implemented as both a proactive (value enhancing) and a reactive (risk hedging) tool. Some examples are given below for corporate treasurers who manage interest rate exposure, borrowing requirements, and currency exposure, and for pension managers who employ SPs in the asset–liability management framework.

Managing interest rate exposure (reactive example). A corporation has existing floating-rate debt and is concerned that interest rates will increase. It may buy a cap with the same remaining debt maturity, which means it will pay a premium upfront and will receive periodic payments if the floating reference rate is above the agreed cap rate. Thus the company can ensure that its net floating payments will not exceed a capped rate.

Managing interest rate exposure (proactive example). A corporation is aware that its business revenue varies inversely with the level of prevailing interest rates. Working with an investment bank, the treasurer decides to restructure its borrowing and issue an inverse floater, which means that its interest payments will decline as the floating reference rate rises (and its business revenues contract), and its interest payments will rise if floating reference rates fall (and business revenues expand), providing profit stabilization through the economic cycle.

Using SPs for new borrowing requirements (hybrid example). A Japanese company could borrow in US dollars to establish a US-based distribution center for products it manufactures in Japan for a fixed cost in Japanese yen. A major threat to profit is the selling price, which is fixed in US dollars. Again, looking to stabilize profit, the company could buy a SP where it will receive coupons if the dollar depreciates or if the US interest rate rises.

Hedging input prices. Steel is a vital input for automobile manufacturers. In forecasting the budget, auto makers will estimate the number of cars they need to complete over the following period and the associated revenues and costs. Clearly, fluctuating input prices could threaten the bottom line. A variety of SPs can hedge this risk, including a forward purchase agreement that guarantees a fixed price or an option to buy steel at a fixed price in the future, for which the company could pay an upfront premium.

Pension asset–liability management. Pension managers receive plan contributions and must grow the asset base so that it exceeds the expected liabilities that arise from funding the future retirement benefits of fund members. The desire to invest in higher-growth assets (for example, equities) is tempered by the knowledge that they are also higher risk. The fund could invest in low-risk assets (for example, government bonds) and gain exposure to the outperformance of an equity index over a bond index, floored at zero, through a tailored hybrid SP. This would allow it to substantially outperform fixed-income investments during good times, though it would slightly underperform during bad times since the SP premium paid would detract from a bond-only portfolio.

PRACTICAL CONSIDERATIONS

The attributes that make SPs so desirable—namely their flexibility and highly customizable nature—may also be their biggest disadvantage. Some predominant practical considerations are:

- *Pricing*: This can be complicated and requires mathematical models and computing power. Most structured products are priced in a Monte Carlo framework, which is a statistical technique involving the simulation of many paths for each underlying to assess the expected payout of the SP.
- *Mark-to-market valuation*: Although many SPs have a clearly defined payout at maturity (intended to match a specific liability, for example), the fluctuations in mark-to-market valuations also depend on other variables. Such variables include changes in the underlying's volatility, correlation, or interest rates. Mark-to-market fluctuations can cause balance sheet volatility, depending on how hedge accounting is implemented.
- *Secondary market*: A client wishing to terminate an SP before its maturity date may be granted an unwind price from the bank it originally traded with, or enter into a directly opposite trade with another investment bank. This may leave residual credit risk.
- *Asset mismatch*: Sometimes the precise underlying that constitutes the source of a future liability cannot be used as the underlying for the SP because it is not readily tradable. This is a particular concern with commodity SPs, which are often linked to commodity futures rather than physical commodities.
- *Counterparty risk*: Many of the typical SP wrappers, such as OTC, note, and swap, contain credit risk—that is, the investment bank may not be able to fulfill its obligations when they fall due. This can be mitigated by requiring the bank to post high-quality collateral against mark-to-market valuations.

CONCLUSION

Structured products represent a powerful instrument for the active management of specific liabilities, a liability portfolio, or asset–liability dilemmas. They can be linked to a wide variety of underlying assets and are fully flexible with regard to maturity date and conditions observed

MAKING IT HAPPEN

Most SP experts are found at the major investment banks. As a potential client, a useful starting point is to have clarity on a specific liability or liability portfolio, and an objective that the company would like to achieve—for example, hedging of price uncertainties, smoothed performance over business cycles, or achieving a higher return with less risk on surplus funds. Clients can approach this in a number of ways:

- Advanced clients will often propose the details of an SP to investment banks and ask for pricing and trade terms to see whether they are favorable.
- Less-experienced clients will request a meeting with a bank at which SP experts will propose a range of potentially appropriate products and indicative terms.
- Always conduct a scenario analysis of how the liability portfolio behaves before and after the inclusion of an SP that is being considered, and consider mark-to-market and accounting effects.
- Many courses are available that teach elementary SP pricing. This knowledge will help you to understand how different variables may affect a valuation.

"We ultimately witnessed the demise of an ideology that says the only rule for government is always to get out of the way." Douglas Alexander

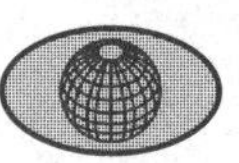

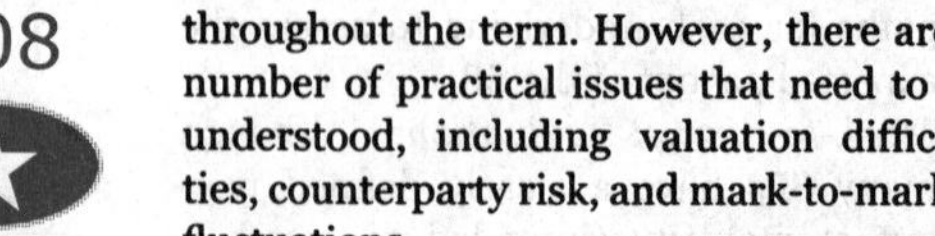

throughout the term. However, there are a number of practical issues that need to be understood, including valuation difficulties, counterparty risk, and mark-to-market fluctuations.

MORE INFO

Books:

Adam, Alexandre. *Handbook of Asset and Liability Management: From Models to Optimal Return Strategies*. Chichester, UK: Wiley, 2007.

Hull, John C. *Options, Futures, and Other Derivatives*. 7th ed. Upper Saddle River, NJ: Prentice Hall, 2008.

Rebonato, Riccardo. *Volatility and Correlation: The Perfect Hedger and the Fox*. 2nd ed. Chichester, UK: Wiley, 2004.

Wilmott, Paul. *Paul Wilmott on Quantitative Finance*. 2nd ed. Chichester, UK: Wiley, 2006.

Articles:

Black, Fischer, and Myron Scholes. "The pricing of options and corporate liabilities." *Journal of Political Economy* 81:3 (1973): 637–654.

Dupire, B. "Pricing with a smile." *Risk* 7:1 (1994): 18–20.

Heston, Steven. L. "A closed-form solution for options with stochastic volatility with applications to bond and currency options." *Review of Financial Studies* 6:2 (1993): 327–343.

Magazines:

Risk, Structured Products, Euromoney, Derivatives Week.

See Also:

- John Cox (p. 1160)
- Stephen Ross (p. 1186)

NOTES

1 Undertakings for Collective Investments in Transferable Securities (UCITS) are a set of European Union directives that allow compliant collective investment schemes to operate freely throughout the European Union. These funds are a versatile legal structure that often includes embedded structured products.

"Currently the prime minister is the equivalent of a doctor who is asked to save the same person's life several times. Originally the relatives are grateful but then start to wonder why his services are required so often."
Steve Richards

  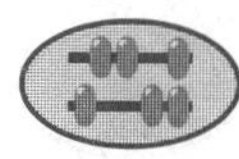 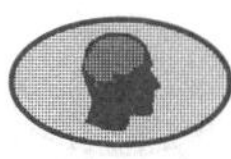  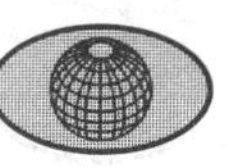   

The Value and Management of Intellectual Property, Intangible Assets, and Goodwill by Kelvin King

EXECUTIVE SUMMARY

- Intellectual capital is recognized as the most important asset of many of the world's largest and most powerful companies.
- It is the foundation for the market dominance and continuing profitability of leading corporations.
- It is often the key objective in mergers and acquisitions, and knowledgeable companies are increasingly using licensing routes to transfer these assets to low-tax jurisdictions.
- Accounting standards have traditionally not been helpful in representing the worth of intellectual property rights (IPR) and intangible assets in company accounts.
- Future winners will be those who own and effectively manage intellectual capital, which asset—such as a brand, patent portfolio, etc.—has become possibly the most critical success factor. No sector has been untouched by IPR.

INTRODUCTION

The role of IPR in business is insufficiently understood. It is probably undervalued, undermanaged or underexploited, and there is little coordination between the different professionals dealing with an organization's IPR. You probably need to have a better understanding about intellectual capital and its ownership, acquisition, and use. You probably need a practical source of knowledge and guidance about intellectual property and other intellectual capital in a commercial context. You might be a chief executive of an intellectual capital company, or a brand-based business, or both. You might be a manager of such a business, or a research director, or academic. Maybe you are a student on a management program, or an accountant, a corporate finance professional, an investor, or a venture capitalist. In your studies intellectual capital will not have been a core subject. Whatever the reason, you need to understand intellectual capital, especially IPRs, to do your job better or to be more successful in your career. IPRs are both important and complex. Therefore the questions to be addressed are often:

- What are the IPRs used in the business?
- What are their value (and hence level of risk)?
- Who owns it (could I sue or could someone sue me)?
- How may it be better exploited (e.g. licensing in or out of technology)?
- At what level do I need to insure the IPR risk?

THE BENEFITS OF IPR MANAGEMENT

You cannot "manage" without having some understanding of value, and the benefits of good IPR management include:

- Increased returns on capital invested in the business, particularly capital tied up in intellectual property.
- Increased shareholder value.
- A thorough understanding of the alignment of intellectual property development or acquisitions and business strategic objectives.
- The ability to make informed decisions about intellectual property development or acquisition.
- The creation of new and diverse revenue streams from intellectual capital, and especially from underused intellectual capital.
- The ability to distinguish between valuable intellectual capital (perhaps within a large portfolio) and so protect it fully, and intellectual capital of no significant value, which might be sold or abandoned.
- Achieving lower overall costs associated with intellectual capital development or acquisition, protection, and utilization.
- Creating internal awareness of the importance of intellectual capital to success.

CURRENT BIG ISSUES FOR IPR VALUATION

- Accounting standards.
- Corporate governance.
- Litigation (defence and attack).
- Fairness opinions.
- In-process R&D.

IFRS 3 Business Combination Valuation Allocations, IAS 38 Recognition of IPR in Accounts, and IAS 36 Valuation Impairment Tests

Purchase accounting must be applied to all acquisitions (business combinations are also treated as acquisitions, and there is no more merger accounting). Many intangible assets that would previously have been subsumed within goodwill must be separately identified and valued. Explicit guidance is provided for the recognition of such intangible assets, and IFRS 3 includes a list of assets that are expected to be recognized separately from goodwill.

The valuation of such assets is a complex process and nearly always requires specialist intellectual property (IP) valuation skills, and frequently an IP lawyer to undertake the categorization which the valuer requires. Examples of intangible assets to be separately recognized and categorized within the purchase cost are set out in the regulations and include those which are: marketing-related (trademarks, brands, domain names, newspaper mastheads), customer-related (customer lists and contracts), artistic-related (television programs, photographs, films, publications), contract-based (e.g. licensing and royalty agreements, contracts for numerous situations such as advertising, construction and supply), and technology-based (patents, computer software, databases, trade secrets, etc.).

IFRS 3 is mandatory for all new transactions from March 31, 2004.

Additionally, under IAS 36 valuations need to be independently tested for impairment by the valuer on a regular basis. Obviously one of the valuer's first questions will be (with advice from the IP lawyer, or patent or trademark attorney): Has there been any diminution of the legal nature of the originally categorized IP?

Corporate Governance

Statute and case law is being developed which will compel boards of directors to accept that they must undertake and lead IP decisions rather than leave them to management.

- Sarbanes–Oxley: The provision of valuation services for audit clients is prohibited.
- Caremark International 1996 imposed

"Our data shows that capital markets will reward companies that focus on the intangible assets of innovation and intellectual property." J.M. Torres and N. Kossovsky

on directors the duty to ensure adequate reporting.

- A Walt Disney case in 2003 and Research in Motion (the Blackberry case) establish the potential liability of directors in respect of IP.
- Find case references at www.valuation-consulting.co.uk/services/oxley_act.html

IPR AND THE VALUATION EXPERT

For the valuer, this process of understanding is not usually a problem when these rights have been formally protected through trademarks, patents, or copyright. This is not the case with intangibles such as know-how (which can include the talents, skill, and knowledge of the workforce), training systems and methods, designs, technical processes, customer lists, distribution networks, etc. These assets are equally valuable but more difficult to identify in terms of the earnings and profits they generate. With many intangibles a very careful initial due diligence process needs to be undertaken together with IP lawyers and in-house accountants.

Overall risk affects valuation analysis; corporate valuation must reflect risk, and, most importantly, risk assessment should reflect IPR value.

One of the key factors affecting a company's success or failure is the degree to which it effectively exploits intellectual capital and values risk. Management obviously need to know the value of the IPR and those risks for the same reason that they need to know the underlying value of their tangible assets; this is because business managers need to know, or should know, the value of all assets and liabilities under their stewardship and control, to make sure that values are maintained. Markets (restricted or otherwise), institutions, and shareholders need to be educated. Exploitation can take many forms, ranging from outright sale of an asset, to a joint venture or a licensing agreement. Inevitably, exploitation increases the risk assessment.

The valuation procedure is, essentially, a bringing together of the economic concept of value and the legal concept of property. The presence of an asset is a function of its ability to generate a return and the discount rate applied to that return. The cardinal rule of commercial valuation is: the value of something cannot be stated in the abstract; all that can be stated is the value of a thing in a particular place, at a particular time, in particular circumstances. The questions "to whom?" and "for what purpose?" must always be asked before a valuation can be carried out. This rule is particularly significant as far as the valuation of intellectual property rights is concerned. More often than not, there will be only one or two interested parties, and the value to each of them will depend on their circumstances. Failure to take these circumstances, and those of the owner, into account will result in a meaningless valuation.

There are four main value concepts, namely, owner value, market value, tax value, and fair value. *Owner value* often determines the price in negotiated deals and is often led by a proprietor's view of the value if he or she were deprived of the property. The basis of *market value* is the assumption that if comparable property has fetched a certain price, then the subject property will realize a similar price. The *fair value* concept is essentially the desire to be equitable to both parties. It recognizes that the transaction is not in the open market and that vendor and purchaser have been brought together in a legally binding manner. *Tax valuation* has been the subject of case law worldwide since the turn of the century and is an esoteric practice. There are also quasi-concepts of value which impinge on each of these main areas, namely, investment value, liquidation value, and going-concern value.

METHODS FOR THE VALUATION OF IPR

Acceptable methods for the valuation of identifiable intangible assets and intellectual property fall into three broad categories. They are either *market-based*, *cost-based*, or *based on estimates of future economic benefit*. In an ideal situation an independent expert will always prefer to determine a market value by reference to comparable market transactions. This is difficult enough when valuing assets such as bricks and mortar because it is never possible to find a transaction that is exactly comparable. In valuing an item of intellectual property, the search for a comparable market transaction becomes almost futile. This is not only due to lack of comparability, but also because intellectual property is generally not developed to be sold, and many sales are usually only a small part of a larger transaction and details are kept extremely confidential. There are other impediments that limit the usefulness of this method, namely, special purchasers, different negotiating skills, and the distorting effects of the peaks and troughs of economic cycles. In a nutshell, this summarizes my objection to such statements as "this is a rule of thumb in the sector."

Cost-based methodologies, such as the cost to create or the cost to replace, assume that there is some relationship between cost and value, and the approach has very little to commend itself other than ease of use. The method ignores changes in the time value of money, and maintenance.

The *method of valuation flowing from an estimate of past and future economic benefits* can be broken down into four limbs: (1) capitalization of historic profits, (2) gross profit differential methods, (3) excess profits methods, and (4) the relief from royalty method.

Discounted cash flow (DCF) analysis sits across the last three methodologies. DCF mathematical modeling allows for the fact that one euro in your pocket today is worth more than one euro next year or one euro the year after. The time value of money is taken into account by adjusting expected future returns to today's monetary values using a discount rate. The discount rate is used to calculate economic value and includes compensation for risk and for expected rates of inflation.

The *capitalization of historic profits* arrives at the value of IPRs by multiplying the maintainable historic profitability of the asset by a multiple that is assessed after scoring the relative strength of the IPR. For example, a multiple is arrived at after assessing a brand in the light of factors such as leadership, stability, market share, internationality, trend of profitability, marketing, and advertizing support and protection. While this capitalization process recognizes some of the factors which should be considered, it has major shortcomings, mostly associated with historic earning capability. The method pays little regard to the future.

Gross profit differential methods are often associated with trademark and brand valuation. These methods adopt the differences in sale prices, adjusted for differences in marketing costs. That is, the difference between the margin of the branded and/or patented product and an unbranded or generic product. This formula is used to drive out cash flows and calculate value. Finding generic equivalents for a patent and identifiable price differences is far more difficult than for a retail brand.

The *excess profits method* looks at the current value of the net tangible assets employed as the benchmark for an estimated rate of return to calculate the profits that are required in order to induce investors to invest into those net tangible assets. Any return over and above those profits required to induce investment is considered to be the excess return attribut-

"Intangible assets are valuable and quantifiable financial assets. That value needs to be managed, risks to that value need to be mitigated, and the resulting enhancement and conservation of that value needs to be communicated to shareholders in quantitative terms." J. M. Torres and N. Kossovsky

able to the IPRs. Although theoretically relying on future economic benefits from the use of the asset, the method has difficulty in adjusting to alternative uses of the asset.

Relief from royalty considers what the purchaser could afford, or would be willing to pay, for the licence. The royalty stream is then capitalized, reflecting the risk and return relationship of investing in the asset.

Discounted Cash Flow Analysis

Discounted cash flow analysis is probably the most comprehensive of appraisal techniques. Potential profits and cash flows need to be assessed carefully and then restated to present value through use of a discount rate, or rates. With the asset you are considering, the valuer will need to consider the operating environment of the asset to determine the potential for market revenue growth. The projection of market revenues will be a critical step in the valuation. The potential will need to be assessed by reference to the enduring nature of the asset and its marketability, and this must subsume consideration of expenses together with an estimate of residual value or terminal value, if any. This method recognizes market conditions, likely performance and potential, and the time value of money. It is illustrative, demonstrating the cash flow potential of the property, and is highly regarded and widely accepted in the financial community.

The discount rate to be applied to the cash flows can be derived from a number of different models, including common sense, the build-up method, dividend growth models, or the capital asset pricing model (CAPM), utilizing a weighted average cost of capital. This appraisal technique will probably be the preferred option.

These processes lead one nowhere unless due diligence and the valuation process quantify remaining useful life and decay rates. This will quantify lives such as the following, and which is the shortest: physical, functional, technological, economic, and legal. This process is necessary because, just like any other asset, IPR has a varying ability to generate economic returns that depend on these main lives. For example, in the discounted cash flow model it would not be correct to drive out cash flows for the entire legal length of copyright protection—which may be 100 plus years—when a valuation concerns computer software with only a short economic life span of one to two years. However, patent legal protection of 20 years can prevent infringement situations which may be important, as is often illustrated in the pharmaceutical sector where generic competitors enter the marketplace at a speed that dilutes a monopoly position when protection ceases.

The message is that, when undertaking DCF modeling, never project longer than is realistic by testing against these major lives.

CASE STUDY

IP financings can unlock value that markets and capital providers have overlooked. Tax-effective strategies concerning the management of IP, and the attendant ability for structures to provide attractive securitization prospects, have become more widely known. As reported by *Business Week* in 2007, the largest ever IP-backed securitization, US$1.8 billion for Sears' Kenmore Craftsman and DieHard brands, may be a harbinger of things to come for IP as an asset class.

Sears has disclosed that it created a "separate, wholly owned, bankruptcy-remote subsidiary"—essentially a company within a company. Called KCD IP (for Kenmore, Craftsman, DieHard, intellectual property), the entity issued US$1.8 billion worth of bonds backed by the intellectual property of Sears' three biggest brands, according to filings with the Patent & Trademark Office.

Sears, in essence, created licensing income. First it transferred ownership of the brand names into KCD, which charges Sears royalty fees to license bonds to the insurance subsidiary, where, like any other security on an insurer's books, it serves as protection against future loss. The insurer, meanwhile, protects Sears from financial trouble—and, because it is a subsidiary, it does so at a lower cost than Sears could get from an outside party.

The payments net out to zero because Sears owns every piece. But that would change if Sears were to sell the bonds to outsiders. Sears would be holding up to US$1.8 billion in case, and investors would be holding the bonds.

The KCD bonds have a higher credit rating than Sears' regular bonds. Moody's Investors Service gave KCD an investment-grade rating of Baa2, four rungs better than Sears' junk rating of Ba1. How so? If Sears were to go bankrupt, bondholders wouldn't be able to get their hands on Kenmore, Craftsman and DieHard trademarks, the company's crown jewels.

Following this, Eric Hedman, a director in S&P's Structural Finance Group, said "interest [in intellectual property deals] is exploding."

►► MAKING IT HAPPEN

In the book I coauthored with John Sykes, an IP lawyer (Sykes and King, 2003), we established a number of general principles concerning the management and valuation of intellectual property:

- Make intellectual capital a part of the business's strategic thinking and planning. For example, risk control, maximizing value, being aware of emerging technologies, seeking appropriate legal protection, etc.
- Understand the role of intellectual capital. This involves assessing the importance of intellectual capital now and in the future to the market position and future success of your business. Part of this is the challenge of identifying the intellectual property of others and avoiding infringement of the associated legal rights.
- Be aware of competing intellectual capital.
- Know your own intellectual capital. Use rigorous processes to identify and evaluate the existing intellectual capital in the business, creating a comprehensive record of results, and developing a process for identifying future IPR. Carry out positive due diligence. Success or not is dependent on a management process to do the aforementioned.
- Identify required intellectual capital, which is a process of forecasting future needs.
- Acquire any required intellectual capital.
- Think tax and balance sheet.
- Be ready to protect your rights.
- Measure improvements as an essential part of good intellectual capital management, to develop measures of success for the management and evaluation of IPR.
- Spread the message, because just as important as measuring improvements is communicating a strategy and a process, not least via financial PR, etc.
- Know the cost and value of your intellectual capital.

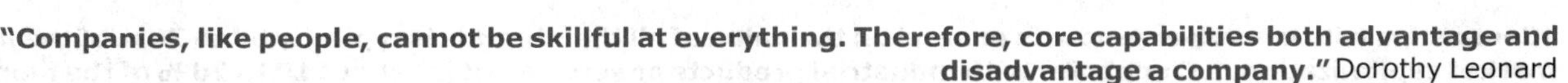

"Companies, like people, cannot be skillful at everything. Therefore, core capabilities both advantage and disadvantage a company." Dorothy Leonard

It must also be acknowledged that, in many situations, after these lives have been examined carefully to produce cash flow forecasts it is often not credible to forecast beyond, say, four to five years. The mathematical modeling allows for this by using, at the end of the period when forecasting becomes futile but clearly the cash flows will not "fall of a cliff," a terminal value that is calculated using a modest growth rate (say inflation) at the steady state year but also discounting this forecast to the valuation date.

Valuation is more an art than a science and is an interdisciplinary study drawing on law, economics, finance, accounting, and investment. It is rash to attempt any valuation adopting so-called industry/sector norms in ignorance of the fundamental theoretical framework of valuation.

▸▸ MORE INFO

Books:

King, Kelvin. *The Valuation and Exploitation of Intangible Assets*. Welwyn Garden City, UK: EMIS Professional Publishing, 2003.

Sykes, John, and Kelvin King. *Valuation and Exploitation of Intellectual Property and Intangible Assets*. Welwyn Garden City, UK: EMIS Professional Publishing, 2003.

Articles:

Sexton, Donald E. "Valuing brand equity." *The Advertiser* (March 2000).

Torres, J. M., and N. Kossovsky. "Intangible assets and shareholder value." *Intellectual Asset Management* 32 (October/November 2008): 18–22.

Websites:

American Society of Appraisers (ASA): www.appraisers.org

International Asset Management magazine: www.iam-magazine.com

International Valuation Standards Committee (IVSC): www.ivsc.org

Society of Share and Business Valuers (SSBV): www.ssbv.org

Valuation Consulting, the website of the author's company: www.valuation-consulting.co.uk

"Companies with consumer products or service; the value of all their brands is typically 50 to 70% of the firm's market capitalization. . .Companies with industrial products or services [it is] about 10 to 20% of the market capitalization." Donald Sexton

   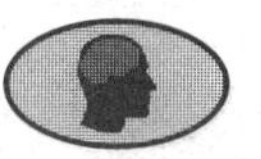  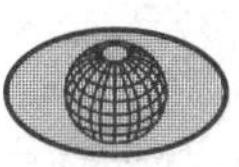 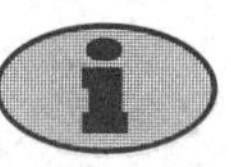  

Valuing Pension Fund Liabilities on the Balance Sheet by Steven Lowe

EXECUTIVE SUMMARY

- Accounting standards affect how pension liabilities are reported in company accounts. FAS 158 requires that the net of pension fund assets and liabilities are reported in the main accounts. Traditional accountancy measures allow a more subjective measurement, and relegate pension information to the accounting notes.
- The real issue is how a company calculates and values the projected liability—which depends on the discount rate selected, the actuarial assumptions relating to future inflation, wage increases, and, most importantly, the expected longevity of employees.
- Different pension stakeholders will favor different liability measures, resulting in differing investment risk tolerances and strategies, which in turn can impact the corporate balance sheet.
- Accounting measures and buyout measures of pension liabilities differ. Finance directors need to be aware of both types of measure, their assumptions, and the interaction between them, as they can impact pension strategies and, consequently, financial reporting.

INTRODUCTION

With a pension plan, companies agree to provide certain benefits to their employees, by specifying either a defined contribution (where a fixed contribution is made to the plan each year by the employer, with no promises as to the future benefits that will be delivered by the plan) or a defined benefit (where the employer undertakes to pay a certain benefit to the employee at some point in the future). Under the latter, the employer has to put sufficient money into the plan each period such that the amounts, with reinvestment, are sufficient to meet the defined benefits due as plan members retire.

With a defined contribution plan, the firm meets its obligation once it has made the prespecified contribution to the plan, and its valuation on the balance sheet is reasonably straightforward. With a defined benefit plan, the firm's obligations are much more difficult to estimate, since they will be determined by a number of variables, including the benefits that employees are entitled to (which will change as their salary and employment status change), the prior contributions made by the employer (and the returns they have earned), the expected retirement date of employees, and the rate of return that the employer expects to make on current contributions.

As these variables change, the value of the pension fund assets can be greater than, less than, or equal to the pension fund liabilities (which include the present value of promised benefits). Recent changes to accounting regulations have increased the transparency of pension funding, and this has sparked an increased debate about the goals of defined benefit pension funds. The stakeholders of a pension fund (sponsor, trustees, and the various classes of pensioner) often have different goals, and therefore require the asset and liability information to be presented using different assumptions. These assumptions can materially affect both profit and loss (P&L) and balance sheet statements.

A pension fund whose assets exceed liabilities is an overfunded plan, whereas one in which assets are less than liabilities is underfunded, and disclosures to that effect have to be included in financial statements. When a pension fund is overfunded the firm has several options: It can withdraw the excess assets from the fund, it can discontinue contributions to the plan, or it can continue to make contributions on the assumption that the overfunding is a transitory phenomenon that could well disappear by the next period. When a fund is underfunded, the firm has a liability that must be recognized on the balance sheet.

ACCOUNTING STANDARDS

In late 2006, the Financial Accounting Standards Board issued its final Statement of Financial Accounting Standards No. 158 (FAS 158), which deals with the rules for reporting the obligations and expenses of pension plans, retiree health plans, nonqualified deferred compensation plans, and other post retirement benefits. Among many changes, FAS 158 moved information about the funded status of pension plans and other postretirement employee benefit plans from the footnotes of the financial statements to the balance sheet itself. The idea behind FAS 158 was to create more transparency and to make information about pension plans and other postretirement employee benefit plans available to investors. It requires companies to include on the balance sheet the full net value of pension assets and obligations. These are to be measured as the difference between the fund assets and the projected benefit obligations. A company does not have to show the full value of assets and the full value of liabilities—just the net of the two. If the fund assets are higher than the pension obligation, it will show as an asset; if not, it will be a liability.

Before FAS 158, the effects of certain events, such as plan amendments or actuarial gains and losses, could be given delayed recognition in the balance sheet. Alternatively, market returns could be smoothed over several years rather than recognized at once. As a result, a plan's funded status (plan assets less obligations) rarely reflected the true position and so was not reported on the balance sheet. FAS 158 requires companies to report their plan's funded status, which is likely to cause reported pension liabilities to rise significantly. The traditional actuarial approach is incorporated to a degree in International Accounting Standard 19 (IAS 19), which means that the balance sheet generated on an IAS 19 basis does not necessarily reflect the full net asset or liability position of the pension plan. Whichever accountancy basis is adopted, the real issue is how to identify the projected benefit obligation.

Typically, the assets held by the sponsor's pension fund are liquid, have publicly accessible pricing data, and are subject to market value fluctuations. The liabilities, however, are rarely traded, are particular to the individual pension scheme, and, depending on the valuation method adopted, can be considerably less volatile. Assets are measured at market value, whereas the discount rate for valuing liabilities is based on the actuaries' assessment of long-run returns on the assets in the pension fund.

CALCULATING ACCOUNTING LIABILITIES

The projected benefit obligation is the actuarial present value of the benefit obligations made by the pension plan. This liability, according to most accounting standards (FRS 17, FAS 87, IAS 19), is

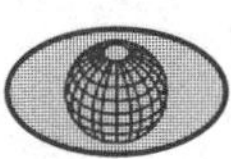

calculated by reference to the yield on AA corporate bonds. These in turn are affected by movements in interest rates, and also variations in the cost of credit.

This accounting measure of liabilities makes no allowance for the actual investment policy pursued by the pension scheme. It does, however, include actuarial forecasts of inflation, expected future salary increases, and current longevity assumptions. These assumptions are taken as being best-guess estimations, and often cause keen debate between a corporate sponsor's actuaries and those advising the trustees during the triennial funding discussion. The rate of inflation and forecast salary increases are usually fairly straightforward and based on recent experience, but forecasts of longevity lead to more discussion. Longevity has been increasing exponentially since the Second World War, and actuaries have consistently underestimated life expectancy. Any increase in assumed life expectancy will increase the liability of the pension fund and thus increase the annual contributions required by the sponsor, as well as increasing the total liability on the balance sheet. It is estimated that an increase of one year of life expectancy will add approximately 7% to pension liability. Given that life expectancy for a 65-year-old male is improving at the rate of one year's increase in life expectancy in every five years, this has the potential to have a huge impact on corporate investment plans.

The assumptions made about inflation, salary increases, and longevity are a key subject of discussion when trustees and sponsor debate proposed future funding strategies for the pension plan. The other key topic for discussion should be the expected investment returns from the asset strategy undertaken by the trustees. Both the actuarial assumptions and the investment risk assumed by the pension fund are likely to greatly influence the size and scale of future sponsor contributions.

The funding strategy is normally assessed on a going concern principle, resting on the assumption that the sponsor will be around for many years and is able and willing to provide the support necessary to the pension scheme if the investment strategy produces returns below those expected, or if life expectancy or any of the other actuarial assumptions exceeds the forecast. There are a number of factors that should be considered by both sponsor and trustees in determining how much risk there is to the ability of the pension fund to meet its future liabilities:

- *Covenant or sponsor business risk*: The stronger the covenant (the lower the business risk), the more risk can be taken with the pension fund investment and the less conservative the actuarial assumptions need to be.
- *Maturity of pension scheme*: The longer the funding period (i.e., the younger the potential beneficiaries or pension scheme membership), the more investment risk can be taken without compromising the security of the final benefit payments. Conversely, the higher the longevity risk which a younger scheme incorporates, the greater is the risk that even minor improvements in life expectancy will cause a large movement in the value of future pension promises and, hence, liability on the balance sheet.
- *Surplus*: The larger the accounting surplus, the more investment risk can be taken. Conversely, with a large deficit there will also be pressure to take increased investment risk.

The minimal risk approach argues that assets should be valued at market prices and that liabilities should be valued consistently using the market returns on appropriate assets and conservative longevity assumptions. The optimal asset allocation would then be determined using horizon matching. This uses bonds, with their reliable cash flows, to meet current and near-maturing pension obligations (using a strategy called cash flow matching), and equity and property, with their growth potential, to match long-maturing liabilities that grow in line with earnings (using a strategy called surplus management). This second strategy is justified because of the long-run constancy of factor shares in national income (which makes capital and land ideal long-term matching assets for a liability that is linked to the return on labor), and because of the positive long-run equity risk premium and mean-reversion in equity returns (which implies that long-run equity returns are more stable than short-run returns). Such an asset allocation should mean that changes in pension liabilities caused by moves in interest rates, inflation, or longevity are matched by a mixture of bond and equity returns, thus immunizing the balance sheet from any unexpected changes in value of either asset or liability metric. With a stable balance sheet, planning future pension contributions can be done with more certainty, thus limiting the impact of volatile contributions on the P&L.

BUYOUT LIABILITY

Another, different, way of calculating the pension position is based on the assets required to buy out the pension liabilities at a specific point in time. This can be thought of as the market price of passing all the liabilities of a pension fund to a specialist insurer. Five years ago, this only happened in the case of insolvency, but increasingly niche insurers are starting to specialize in pooling longevity risk and offering prices to remove all pension assets and liabilities from a sponsor's balance sheet. The buyout deficit shows the additional funds needed if the accrued liabilities were to be settled by purchasing matching annuities from these insurers. Under UK legislation, this is also the contingent debt that could be served on the sponsor by the trustees of the pension scheme, should the sponsor decide to discontinue the scheme.

The volatility of this measure is dictated by the terms on which insurance companies are prepared to deal. Annuities are usually priced at yields well below the prevailing

▸▸ MAKING IT HAPPEN

- A defined benefit pension scheme is one where the employer promises to pay a certain benefit to the employee on retirement. It is funded by contributions to a pension plan and the investment return on those contributions while the employee is working, which, over time, the employer hopes will match the benefits promised.
- Both the assets and liabilities are accounted for on the corporate balance sheet, introducing a complicated variable into financial reporting that usually has little to do with the main business of the employer.
- Assets are valued using market rates, but future liabilities are valued by selecting a discount rate and making assumptions about future inflation, wage increases, and longevity.
- Each of these factors (inflation, wages, and longevity) can have a large influence not only on the financial information reported, but also on the strategy and risk tolerance of the pension fund and its stakeholders.
- Because of this, it is vital that the employer understands a variety of different measures for the pension liabilities, such as the accounting/funding basis and the buyout liability, as these can impact how the pension fund assets and liabilities are ultimately reported on the balance sheet each year.

"The superior man is distressed by his want of ability." Confucius

  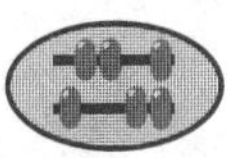   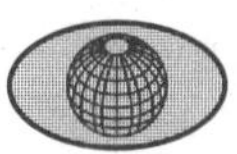   

yields on government bonds and with a cautious view of future longevity trends. Therefore, the liabilities assessed on this measure are significantly higher than those assessed on the accounting and funding measures.

ACCOUNTING IMPACT

The current accounting methodology has three main impacts. First, balance sheets have become more volatile due to the inclusion of net pension assets or liabilities, which are dependent on publicly traded debt prices. This volatility may trigger loan covenants or borrowing limits, or otherwise affect corporate behavior. Second, the P&L retains some volatility due to pension impacts, since changes in the balance sheet funding position affect the level of sponsor contributions and, hence, flow through to the P&L. Finally, financial statements have increased in complexity as noncash pension items are now included. Some items, such as the current service cost and amortization of past service costs within operating cost, the unwinding of the pension liability discount, and the expected return on assets within financing costs, are highly complex in themselves.

CONCLUSION

There is no doubt that the accounting measure has been, and continues to be, hugely influential in corporate decision-making and short-term risk management. It provides the basis for funding discussions with the trustees and is therefore important for cash flow management, particularly in companies where the corporate covenant is not strong. The buyout measure of pension liabilities is becoming more important, since the discharge of all pension obligations by the sponsor is growing in desirability as the full risks of longevity increases are increasingly recognized. Additionally, trustees often find that a buyout, with the security provided by a regulated insurer rather than a corporate sponsor, is a goal for pension funding in itself. Buyout pricing also establishes a target for a closed defined benefit scheme (over a suitable time horizon).

Therefore it is vital that finance directors monitor the development of assets and liabilities using both accounting and buyout measures, as well as understanding the assumptions that each employs and interactions between them.

▸▸ MORE INFO

Book:

Fridson, Martin, and Fernando Alvarez. *Financial Statement Analysis: A Practitioner's Guide*. 3rd ed. New York: Wiley, 2002.

Articles:

Financial Education. "Balance sheet recognition of pension liabilities under International Accounting Standards (IAS)." Online at: tinyurl.com/anupfb

JP Morgan. "Implementing FAS 158 for year-end financial reporting." January 18, 2007. Online at: tinyurl.com/dj7mrq

Juliens, Dennis. "The impact of pension accounting on financial statements and disclosures." CFA Institute Publications. Online at: www.cfapubs.org/doi/abs/10.2469/cp.v2005.n3.3484

Riley, Leigh C., and Katherine L. Aizawa. "Pension fund issues in the boardroom: Is your pension plan becoming too expensive?" Chicago, IL: Foley & Lardner, 2007. Online at: www.foley.com/files/tbl_s31Publications/FileUpload137/4091/PensionFund.pdf

Zion, David. "Beginning to overhaul the pension accounting rules." *CFA Institute Conference Proceedings Quarterly* 24:2 (2007): 38–44.

  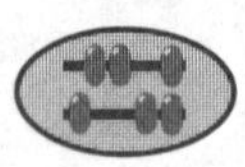   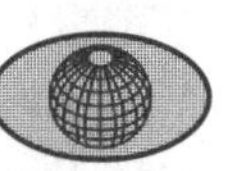   

Balancing Senior Management Compensation Arrangements with Shareholders' Interests by Henrik Cronqvist

EXECUTIVE SUMMARY

- Appropriately designed executive compensation schemes can add substantial value for the firm's shareholders.
- Base salaries should be competitive with those awarded by similar-sized firms in the industry in order to attract and retain superior top-executive talent.
- Most perquisite-type compensation is now outdated, fails to align manager–shareholder interests in any obvious way, and should be avoided.
- Annual cash bonuses should be based on measures that can't be easily manipulated through accounting practices adopted by management.
- Long-term, equity-based compensation in the form of stock options or grants is the most effective way to harmonize the interests of senior management and shareholders.
- It is important to anticipate increased disclosure and scrutiny of executive compensation structures by the media when a particular compensation structure is being designed.

INTRODUCTION

The board of directors, and specifically the compensation committee (or remuneration committee), has the challenging task of designing a compensation structure for the chief executive officer (CEO) and other senior managers that balances their interests with those of the shareholders. The general idea is to make an executive's pay sensitive to the value created for the firm's shareholders. In this way, everyone shares the common goal of maximizing shareholder value.

Corporate executives can in principle be compensated in three different ways:

- base salary and perquisites, or "perks";
- annual cash bonus;
- shares.

No one form will perfectly align the interests of senior management and shareholders. The task of designing a value-adding compensation structure is therefore about identifying the mix between these different forms of compensation that best incentivizes senior management to create value for the shareholders.

DESIGNING A VALUE-ADDING COMPENSATION STRUCTURE

The base salary is the starting point for the compensation package and is commonly set through benchmarking based on a survey of similar-sized firms in the company's industry. Because of risk aversion, most executives will not accept a purely performance-based pay package. Though not sensitive to company performance, the base salary can still play a key role in attracting and retaining superior managerial talent.

Perks such as country club membership and private use of a corporate aircraft used to be common. There is, however, a trend towards the use of fewer perks, mainly because of increased disclosure and scrutiny by media and "watch-dog" groups.[1] For example, in an article with the headline "Only the little people pay for lawn care," columnist Gretchen Morgenson of the *New York Times* wrote that Donald J. Tyson, the former CEO of Tyson Foods, received $84,000 in compensation for "lawn maintenance costs" during 1997–2001.[2] Though the perk was an insignificant portion of his pay during this period, the public's perception of its size can be much more significant than its monetary value. Perks perceived as excessive can cause customer resentment and, as a result, adversely affect both brand and shareholder value.

In contrast to base salary and perks, annual cash bonuses are conditional on short-term financial or nonfinancial goals being met by the firm or individual senior managers. Executives' bonuses, other than for the CEO should be based on their particular business unit's performance, though a part may be based on overall firm performance or cooperation among executives managing different business units.[3] Nonfinancial targets can include successfully launching a new product line, meeting a certain customer satisfaction level, or appointing a new chief financial officer (CFO). These objectives should be specific, attainable, and measurable in the short run. Examples of financial performance targets are earnings per share (EPS), earnings before interest, taxes, depreciation, and amortization (EBITDA), and economic value added (EVA). Regardless of which measure is chosen, a particular threshold has to be attained before a minimum bonus is paid. If the performance is above that threshold, the bonus should increase in increments up to a prespecified maximum. One advantage of annual cash bonuses is that they are one-time compensation for past, realized performance—unlike base salary raises, which are permanent.

Using accounting-based performance targets, such as EBITDA, carries two potential risks. First, short-term performance measures can result in myopic behavior by management: For example, managers trading off short-term earnings growth at the expense of creating shareholder value through valuable R&D projects. Second, accounting-based measures can lead to earnings management, and in the extreme case even manipulation, in order to boost current earnings.

Equity-based compensation, in the form of options or stock, can be used to circumvent some of the problems with short-term, accounting-based cash bonuses. Stock options are the most common form of long-term incentive pay. These allow the executive to purchase a certain number of shares at a prespecified exercise price, commonly the stock price on the day of the option grant, and with a specific period length, often 10 years.

To see how stock options can consolidate manager and shareholder interests, suppose that the stock price at the time of a grant of 250,000 options to a CEO is $50. If the stock price doubles over a couple of years, the CEO will make a profit of $12.5 million (250,000 shares × ($100 − $50)). In contrast, suppose that the stock price declines to $25. Then the options are said to be "underwater" and worth nothing, but the CEO does not lose any money. If the CEO creates value for the shareholder by taking actions that result in the stock price going up, he or she will be rewarded with a slice of that value added. Granted stock options commonly vest (reach a point where they cannot be taken away) over time according to a schedule, or after the firm meets certain performance targets. Executives cannot exercise options before they have vested.

"Management is doing things right; leadership is doing the right things." Peter Drucker

  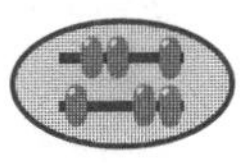 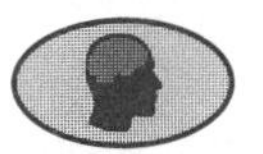  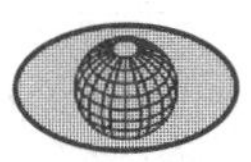   

One problem with stock options is that they reward executives even if the reason for the firm's stock price increase is completely beyond their control. Suppose that the world market price of oil increases significantly; the stock prices of oil companies increase too, but for reasons that have no relation to anything an oil executive may have done. One potential solution is to benchmark the exercise price of executive stock options to the overall stock market or to a portfolio of firms in the firm's industry—i.e. oil companies in this example. In practice, however, such indexed executive stock options are extremely rare.

Another form of equity-based compensation is stock grants. One argument in favor of stock grants is that options provide executives with an asymmetric incentive because their value goes to zero if the stock price falls below the exercise price; the value of a stock grant does not go to zero. Restricted stock is a form of stock grant that involves common stock of the firm, but with the condition that a certain period of time, for example 10 years, has to pass or a target has to be met before the executive can sell the shares. Performance shares are another form of stock grant. These consist of common stock granted to an executive provided that specific firm performance targets, for example EPS, are met. The performance shares become more valuable if the stock price goes up after the grant is made.

In addition to the three forms of compensation discussed above, severance pay packages, also referred to as "golden parachutes," are also common. There are several reasons why appropriately designed severance pay for a firm's CEO can be in the interests of value-maximizing shareholders. First, shareholders want to avoid a situation in which a CEO is resisting a value-enhancing takeover of the firm because the executive's job will then be eliminated. A golden parachute can provide an incentive for a CEO to step down rather than trying to fight a takeover threat. Second, the severance pay can compensate the CEO for signing a restrictive and lengthy noncompete contract with the firm. Such a contract can be in the interest of value-maximizing shareholders, especially in R&D-intensive industries, because it prevents the individual who knows the most about the corporation's business practices from sharing them with the competition.

CONCLUSION

The design of an executive compensation structure is crucial when providing managerial incentives to create shareholder value, but in practice it is a very challenging task. Management compensation should be sensitive to a firm's performance, should reward superior current performance, and should provide incentives for similar strong results in the future. At the same time, it should prevent the firm from paying a premium for poor performance. Because compensation of senior management in public firms is subject to increased disclosure requirements and scrutiny by media and various interest groups, public perception of what constitutes "reasonable" pay is another important factor to consider.

▸▸ MAKING IT HAPPEN

A review of the compensation structure for senior management should focus on the following:

- How can the interests of senior management and shareholders be harmonized? Annual cash bonuses make executives focus on year-to-year performance targets. Grants of options and restricted stock provide long-term incentives to create shareholder value.
- What are the advantages of stock grants over options? Because options, unlike restricted stock grants, reward superior performance but do not penalize poor performance, they can result in excessive risk-taking.
- What can be done to avoid a debate about excessive CEO pay? Perks that do not align manager and shareholder interests should not be provided. The board also has to consider the likelihood of mega-payoffs from the proposed compensation scheme.

CASE STUDY

Equity-Based Compensation at Disney

Based on his 1989 employment agreement with the Walt Disney Company, CEO Michael Eisner was granted millions of stock options as part of his compensation package. If shareholder value could be created through Eisner's actions, then he would be rewarded with a slice of that value added. Billions of dollars of shareholder value was indeed created: The stock price doubled between 1992 and 1998. Eisner's base salary was $750,000 in 1998, and his cash bonus was $5 million, based on an EPS growth target. He also exercised previously granted and vested stock options and realized a total profit of about $570 million. Since Eisner was a central to the creation of over $10 billion of shareholder value, it makes sense that he should have been rewarded appropriately.

But this compensation structure can be questioned. Was more than half a billion dollars in rewards really necessary to create a strong incentive for Eisner? Was such compensation "reasonable" from the perspective of the public, in particular the ordinary working person who is also a Disney customer?

The problem is that Disney's stock performed much less impressively from the late 1990s until Eisner resigned in 2005, to the extent that, from 1998 to 2001, more than half of the shareholder value created before 1998 was lost. In 2001 Eisner received $1 million in base salary but no cash bonus because he did not meet the short-term accounting performance targets. Nor did he exercise any stock options.

Stock option grants may incentivize a CEO to create shareholder value, but this case also emphasizes potential problems associated with them of which boards have to be aware. In particular, option grants can result in mega-payoffs that can be next to impossible to explain to the public. Also, there is nothing shareholders can do once stock options are granted, even if most or all of the previously created value is subsequently destroyed during the tenure of the very same CEO.

NOTES

1 An example is CIO-AFL's Executive PayWatch, www.aflcio.org/corporatewatch/paywatch

2 "Only the little people pay for lawn care." *New York Times* (May 1, 2005).

3 For example, Citigroup recently announced that a part of senior managers' bonuses will be determined by how well they interact with other executives during meetings of a division's management committee. See the *Financial Times* (October 14, 2008).

"When you hire people that are smarter than you are, you prove you are smarter than they are." R. H. Grant

     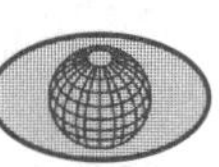   

Viewpoint: Wim Bartels

The Growth of Sustainability Reporting

INTRODUCTION

Wim Bartels has been global head of KPMG's Sustainability Services Network since October 2007. He studied business economics and accountancy at Amsterdam's Vrije Universiteit before qualifying as a chartered accountant in 1993. He has worked as an auditor and forensic accountant. In 2001 he became a KPMG partner, taking overall responsibility for the group's sustainability services, including the provision of sustainability assurance services to multinational businesses such as BASF, DSM, Heineken, KLM, Philips and Rabobank. Wim is closely involved with initiatives including the UN's Global Reporting Initiative and AccountAbility. In his spare time Wim sings and plays trumpet in a band that performs cover versions of 1970s and 1980s hits, for charitable causes. He is also involved in a foundation that supports children in Tanzania.

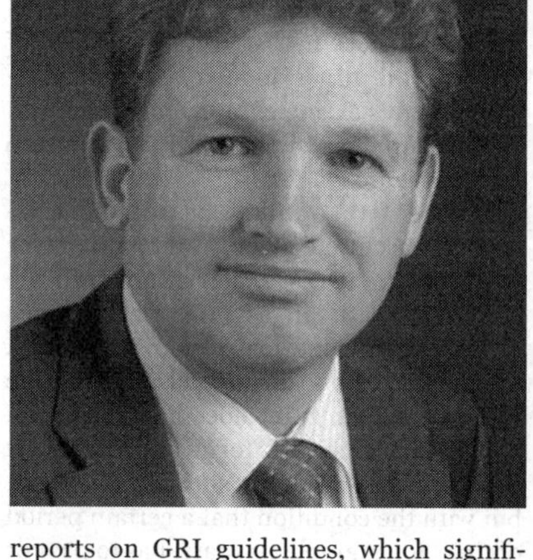

Social and environmental reporting has come a long way in the past decade. However it still has a long way to go.

Back in the 1990s, when sustainability reporting was still in its infancy, it was often seen to be used by corporates as a form of window-dressing or "greenwash."

Responsibility for corporate social responsibility reporting was often handed to the communications department. In many cases, corporates were perceived to embark on the journey for largely cosmetic reasons—whereas their intentions may already have been different. In the wake of reputational disasters like the Brent Spar, the production of glossy corporate social responsibility (CSR) reports was seen as the perfect antidote to interfering non-government organizations (NGOs) and socio-environmental campaigners.

Today, all that has changed. Companies have now widely recognized that, in order to give themselves a long-term future, they are going to have to become more serious, accountable and transparent where sustainability is concerned.

This implies first of all a different way of structuring it and a proper approach to embedding it within the corporate management systems. Businesses are also recognizing that they will need a properly thought-out strategy to address pressing global issues such as global warming, resource depletion and demographic change—and find ways to accurately reflect such a strategy in their reporting.

For their part, investors are demanding greater access to transparent, accountable, robust, reliable, and comparable data from companies about their "nonfinancial" performance. And this is not just out of altruism or personal ethical curiosity; it is because asset managers increasingly believe that having such knowledge will enable them to make better investment decisions and achieve superior returns for their own clients. This means that the non-financial information has effectively become as important as financial information.

MOVING UP THE CORPORATE AGENDA

Recent research by KPMG Global Sustainability Services confirmed that sustainability reporting is moving up the corporate agenda and is now mainstream.

The report, which assessed the sustainability reports of 2,200 companies across 22 countries worldwide, found that far from being put together for appearances' sake, these are now regarded as an internal management tool that enables companies to prioritize issues likely to contribute to their long-term success.

For a growing band of larger, quoted companies worldwide, sustainability reporting has become a core part of their strategy development processes and business reporting cycles. The KPMG International Survey of Corporate Responsibility Reporting, published in October 2008, found that that 80% of Global Fortune 250 (G250) companies now disclose their sustainability performance in "sustainability" or "corporate responsibility" reports, a jump from 50% in 2005.

Reporting also increased on a national level, and a further rise is expected. Among the hundred largest companies by revenue in 22 countries worldwide (N100 companies), only 45% are reporting their own sustainability performance, albeit with marked variations between countries. Mexico was lowest at 18%, while Japan and the UK ranked highest, both scoring over 85%.

NO ROOM FOR COMPLACENCY

Encouragingly, the 2008 survey also revealed that growing numbers of companies worldwide base their sustainability reports on GRI guidelines, which significantly boosts the value of what they are doing, since it contributes significantly to the professionalism and comparability of corporate responsibility reporting.

However, the report also revealed that there is little room for complacency. A surprisingly large proportion of the world's largest companies (25%) still think they can manage perfectly well without any sustainability strategy. And the report also identified some surprising weaknesses where reporting on sustainability practices within the supply chain are concerned. This was especially true among the N100 companies. Also only few companies surveyed were making an explicit link between risk management and CSR within their reports. An insufficient number alluded to the business risk of climate change in their sustainability reports, while a disappointing proportion provided data on the size of their carbon footprints.

However, the main findings of the tri-annual survey were positive. Sustainability is moving up the corporate agenda, and responsibility for it is moving away from the corporate communications department—where it was often considered more in presentational than in material terms—and closer to the chief executive. Nowadays, it is often the responsibility of a CSR officer or sustainability manager who, though unlikely to be a member of the main board, tend to report directly to an executive board member.

Also, more than half of the G250 have disclosed business opportunities and/or the financial value of corporate responsibility.

"You must make use of people according to their abilities and realizerealise that absolutely no one is perfect."
Françoise d'Aubigné Maintenon

     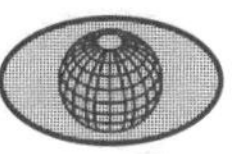   

This value could be in terms of bottom line savings due to efficiency or risk aversion, or top line growth due to new innovations in products and services as a direct response to social or environmental challenges.

Corporate structures clearly play a big role in how CSR issues are handled within an organization. One of the dangers of having responsibility for CSR set too low down within an organization, or apart from normal business line reporting and management, is that it falls between two stools and therefore gets ignored.

This was recently highlighted by Michael Dell, founder, chairman, and chief executive of the Dell, Inc, who admitted on a visit to London that his company was having difficulties persuading its corporate customers to pay a tiny margin for energy-efficient personal computers, servers, and other hardware. Chief technology officers, said Dell, are reluctant to pay the premium for these pieces of kit, largely because energy does not come under their budget. As a result, they don't personally believe that they have anything to gain from paying a premium for equipment that would reduce corporate energy use. Instead, they think they have something to lose.

FINANCIAL IMPACT OF NONFINANCIAL ISSUES

To avoid this sort of situation arising, I believe the ultimate responsibility for sustainability reporting ought, in future, to rest with the chief financial officer (CFO). The so-called "nonfinancial issues" often have a financial impact, and since CFOs have profound experience of managing risk and installing good internal controls, they are well-placed to take this under their belts too. If CSR reporting and control were to become their responsibility, I think that it could play a major part in changing corporate behavior.

Overnight, the CFO would become less obsessed with financial performance and more open to the significance of other types of performance. They are already used to gathering and assembling accurate performance data from all levels within their companies. They are also used to questioning and auditing this data to ensure its veracity.

CFOs also produce timely and accurate performance information, according to a strict reporting cycle. Given this experience, why shouldn't they take responsibility for ensuring their companies produce accurate and timely nonfinancial data too?

There are, of course, psychological and practical barriers. For a start, finance directors do not yet necessarily know how to integrate nonfinancial indicators into their model. This can be overcome if they think about sustainability reporting as a means of reporting on risk factors that drive the company's full performance (for example, the level of carbon emissions, safety at work or diversity).

The perfect situation for me would be for nonfinancial standards to be seamlessly integrated into both internal and external assessments of a company's performance.

At a practical level, the CFO would need to get connected with those who have access to nonfinancial information, such as HSE professionals and HR staff and persuade them to become part of the company's financial planning and control cycle.

Some CFOs remain prejudiced against, or even dismissive of, nonfinancial indicators. However, they are increasingly aware that corporate social responsibility can have a major impact on a company's finance, such as its stock market valuation. In the end, I believe they will accept the need to measure corporate performance in a holistic way, not just through a narrow financial angle.

This process has, to an extent, already started, through projects like the Enhanced Analytics Initiative. Established by a group of prominent European institutional investors in 2004, this project aims to persuade sell-side analysts that they should take greater cognizance of a company's nonfinancial performance when assessing its overall performance.

The credit crunch is a turning point here. The positive side of what occurred between August 2007 and October 2008 is that lessons will be learned. The unprecedented downfall of so many once-revered banks and other financial institutions across Europe and the United States, in the autumn of 2008, provided an illustration that an extremely single-minded focus on financial indicators—short-term profits growth; earnings before interest, taxes, depreciation and amortization; earnings per share, and return on investment—can be a recipe for disaster.

If a bank is managed using only such measurements, it makes it near impossible for it to be managed responsibly. During 2002–2008, banks' and investors' obsession with financial performance prompted many banks to take extraordinary risks, that can be seen as socially irresponsible, without considering whether their actions could risk their own futures or even the destruction of the entire financial system.

While greater commitment to CSR would not necessarily have prevented the banks from collapsing in the way that they did, it might at least have reduced the carnage and the costs that have had to be borne by taxpayers.

The experience of mutually owned banks such as Rabobank (based in the Netherlands) and the Cooperative Bank (based in Manchester, UK) demonstrates that when a bank's top management thinks beyond narrow financial parameters, and considers other measures to be of equal importance, it is more likely to survive and prosper in the long term. It is perhaps telling that, whereas it might have been mocked at the height of the credit bubble, Rabobank is today seen as one of the strongest and well-managed banks around. Admittedly, being a mutual is a different position to being a listed bank, since its management is under no pressure to maximize profits every quarter.

With the credit crunch behind us, CSR is likely to become even more critical to how companies are perceived and rated by investors. A growing numbers of organizations, even listed ones, will start to think along similar lines to banks like Rabobank.

Once shareholders become convinced that it makes more sense to invest in organizations that want to secure themselves a long-term future, rather than in the ones that are designed to maximize short-term profits but are at risk of going bust at any time, then this battle will have been won.

MORE INFO

Article:

Becchetti, Leonardo, and Rocco Ciciretti. "Corporate responsibility and stock market performance." Centre for International Studies on Economic Growth Research Paper Series. Working paper no. 79. March 2006.

Reports:

KPMG and SustainAbility. "Count me in—the readers' take on sustainability reporting." 2008.

United Nations Environment Programme Finance Initiative Asset Management Working Group and Mercer. "Demystifying responsible investment performance: A review of key academic and broker research on ESG factors." October 2007.

Website:

A sustainability report of a bank currently seen as well-managed and strong: www.sustainabilityreport2007rabobank.com

     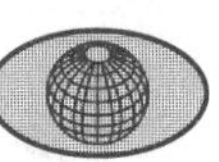   

Best Practice in Investment Governance for Pension Funds by Roger Urwin

EXECUTIVE SUMMARY

- This article demonstrates the influence of governance by institutional fund asset owners on their performance.
- Using examples from across the whole spectrum of institutional funds by type and geography, we illustrate the principles and practice of good governance.
- A number of lessons can be learned from our examples, and we boil these down to a set of 12 findings about global best practice.
- We suggest best-practice models for funds that employ significant investment staff and a separate model for those funds whose decision-taking is done by boards and investment committees.
- We conclude that funds tend to perform better when they correctly assess their governance and determine their investment strategy commensurate with their capabilities. Although there are ways to adapt the governance budget over time, with implications for likely investment performance and pay-offs, there is currently an unpreparedness in the industry to consider in-house resources as anything other than highly visible "costs," whereas external spending on managers and transactions costs tend to be seen as "performance benefits." This has always seemed like a case of tortured logic and a false economy.
- It is only at the high end of this spectrum that we see funds succeeding with the challenges of running complex multi-asset and multi-manager program.

INTRODUCTION

There is increasing evidence to support a link between superior investment performance and an institutional investor's strong governance. Recent research conducted jointly by the author and Gordon Clark of Oxford University, entitled *Best-practice investment management: lessons for asset owners*, further clarified this link and identified 12 best-practice factors as being indicative of future success in meeting institutional goals.

The research focused on 10 of the top institutional funds around the world. All had made the move up from being seen as 'good' in their field to something close to 'great' by committing passion and excellence to their mission through their governance structure. If there is one marker of this excellence, it seems to lie in having a strong investment leader or CIO on the staff, but sadly most funds don't take this step.

Many pension funds are beginning to realize that their governance arrangement should be a top priority, not only through responsibility to literally billions of individuals, but also because it creates an opportunity for wealth creation. At the same time, it is important to point out that while strong governance (with "governance" defined quite broadly as *all the resources applied to investment decision-making*) is hugely important in institutional investment, it is a very difficult area to get right, with only the most conscientious and gifted succeeding in all areas. Among this number are some prominent institutional investment funds that made the right sort of strides with their governance arrangements and have successfully shown the world that very good performance can come from those strides.

For a long time governance has been seen simply as a constraint. Funds have learned to simply get by without being adequately resourced. However, the investment world has now changed irrevocably, and the last 10 years have added more complexity than any period in history. Greater regulation, product proliferation, and much competition for effective investment strategies and products have complicated the sorts of decisions that funds have to face. Among the critical issues to be faced are: how much risk, what types of risk, what types of return (absolute or relative); what types of strategy (mainstream or alternatives), beta or alpha. But, stepping back, the managers of institutional funds must first deal with a higher-level question: how much time and resource should be committed to governance, and how should this effort be organized?

According to our research, only a minority of pension funds worldwide have investment strategies and governance arrangements that are aligned. The research shows that the more common misalignment is to be overambitious in their investment structures, introducing too much complexity for their governance to cope with.

THREE TYPES OF GOVERNANCE

As a simple step, we consider three types of governance arrangements (grouped by the size of their governance budget) and then suggest investment arrangements that are aligned and can be implemented with confidence and good outcomes. Governance budget is defined as a combination of time, expertise, and organizational effectiveness of the decision-makers.

Limited governance budget: The *cost minimizer*—compatible with the lowest governance resources—is a set of arrangements that manage down all costs and focus on easily available investment returns. Being the least sophisticated investment strategy, it would have only bonds and equities and use mainly passive managers.

Mid-range governance budget: The *diversity seeker*—with greater governance available, the fund can pursue more value creation opportunities. The focus would be mainly on improving market exposure diversity outside equities and bonds. Generally these arrangements would again not contain large exposures to active management, simply because alpha is the hardest part of the investment spectrum to create value from.

Advanced governance budget: The *diversity and skill exploiter*—with very strong governance, the arrangements would major on diversification, but also include a significant amount of risk in active manager structures. There is greater emphasis on identifying manager skill opportunities, including ones where the market return and the active manager return are difficult to separate, as is the case with many absolute return products.

We acknowledge that in practice funds may not find it easy to position themselves this way. Most have taken their different investment strategy routes by reference to a peer group mentality that has established one institutional norm, rather than by reference to governance budgets. This needs to change, and indeed there are some positive signs that this is occurring.

Research Findings on the Relation between Governance and Fund Performance

One of these is the growing body of research showing a clear link between

"**Great ability develops and reveals itself increasingly with every new assignment.**" Baltasar Gracián

     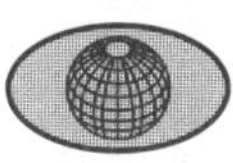   

superior performance and strong governance, particularly among larger funds. It is perhaps not surprising that the best-governed funds tend to perform better than averagely governed funds. While quantitative data on the precise size of the "bad–good governance gap" is relatively scarce, in *The Ambachtsheer Letter* of June 2006, Keith Ambachtsheer uses estimates from his database research that the gap has been worth 1–2% of additional return per annum.[1]

We have also recently undertaken our own research (in combination with Oxford University) into actual practice at top funds around the world. The research, entitled "Best-practice investment management: lessons for asset owners,"[2] involved case studies on 10 funds across the world that were cherry-picked for their exceptional reputation and strong sustained performance. The 10 comprise six pension funds, two endowments, and two sovereign funds, located in North America (five funds), Europe (three funds) and Asia–Pacific (two funds), and they are all large in terms of assets, ranging from around US$5 billion to well over US$50 billion.

The study identified five main areas of critical significance to institutional funds where these funds excel, namely: risk management; time–horizon focus on the long term; innovative capabilities; clarity of mission; and effective management of external fund managers and other agents. However, even these funds with exceptionally strong governance capabilities find it difficult to overcome certain constraints. The research shows that the most common constraints are inherited regulations and systems of control, and the competing claims of multiple stakeholders. In addition, it shows that there is an unpreparedness in the industry to consider in-house resources as anything other than highly visible "costs," whereas external spending on managers and transactions costs tend to be seen as "performance benefits." This has always seemed like an extreme case of tortured logic.

The central finding of the research was in isolating 12 best-practice factors as being indicative of future success in meeting institutional goals. Six of these are assessed as being within the reach of most institutional funds, and are called "core attributes;" they are: mission clarity; effective focusing of time; investment committee leadership; strong beliefs; risk budgeting framework; and a fit-for-purpose manager line-up.

Six further global best-practice factors were isolated in the research and described as requiring significant resources, including an executive team, usually with a CIO. The research suggests that these "exceptional attributes" are not easy for most funds to achieve. They are: a highly competent investment executive; high-level board competencies; supportive compensation; real-time decision-making; the ability to exploit competitive advantage; and learning organization.

In terms of structure, leading funds tend to split the key functions between a board, which governs, and an executive, which implements and manages. The board also appoints and supervises the CIO. In terms

▸▸ MAKING IT HAPPEN

The 12 governance factors associated with organizational effectiveness are:

Core Attributes

- mission clarity
- effective focusing of time
- investment committee leadership
- strong beliefs
- a risk budgeting framework
- fit-for-purpose manager line-up

Exceptional Attributes

- highly competent investment executive
- high-level board competencies
- supportive compensation
- real-time decision-making
- ability to exploit competitive advantage
- a learning organization

The six exceptional best-practice attributes differentiate what one might call the "great" funds from the rest.

- **Investment executive**: The merits of separating governance into a governing function, which sets the framework, monitors, and controls, and an executive function, which makes the decisions within the given framework and implements them cannot be understated. Not only does this improve efficiency and accountability, but it also allows for the concentration of investment expertise within the executive function. Best-practice funds adopt a clear separation of governing and executive functions, with a strong culture of accountability. Furthermore, the executive function has a high level of investment competency, enabling the funds to implement and monitor complex investment arrangements.
- **Board selection and competence**: Sound investment competencies are also observed at the board level of best-practice funds. Board members ideally have strong numeric skills and the ability to think logically within a probability-based domain, such skills enabling the board to function effectively in its long-horizon mission.
- **Supportive compensation**: Leading funds address this at both the board and executive level, with some success at using compensation to attract appropriate skills and align actions to the goals of the fund. Current practice among funds in general appears to result in significantly more being paid to external agents. There is scope to address this imbalance through greater use of internal resources—an approach that is becoming more widely adopted.
- **Competitive advantage**: Investment is a highly competitive activity, and, for funds to succeed, they need to be aware of their competitive advantages and disadvantages and adapt their decision-making accordingly. Much of their competitive advantage will be built on a sound belief structure, but will also maximize their own particular areas of competence. It is equally important that funds should be aware of areas where they have no expertise, and seek to limit their strategy accordingly.
- **Real-time decisions**: Most funds are geared toward making decisions around a calendar-based series of meetings. Best-practice funds, however, tend to have processes in place that enable decisions to be taken as and when necessary, based on investment market conditions. Making such a change from calendar to real-time focus involves more delegation and a clear definition of responsibilities.
- **Learning organization**: Best-practice funds tend to be innovative. To be successful they need to operate in a culture that learns from experience. They also need to be willing to challenge conventional wisdom and deal enthusiastically with change.

"Those who believe in our ability do more than stimulate us. They create for us an atmosphere in which it becomes easier to succeed." John Lancaster Spalding

  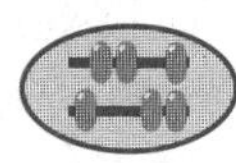   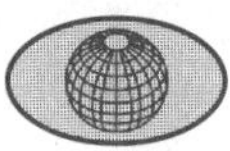   

of people, the CIO will tend to have a very high degree of investment expertise and be supported by strong researchers. Processwise, leading funds are extremely skilled at maximizing any sustainable comparative advantage they have over competing funds, and tend to have impressively efficient decision-making structures.

Aside from societal responsibility, the potential return advantage should be a strong motivator among pension funds to improve governance and then align it with investment strategy. However, it is clear that for many funds the "governance gap"—insufficient governance for the complexity of the investment strategy pursued—is widening because a lack of focus on these core attributes coincides with the greater complexity of prime investment opportunities. Some investors will see merit in improving their governance arrangements by increasing the time they spend on investment issues, adding expertise, and rethinking their organizational structures. However, it is unrealistic to suppose that all pension funds can improve their arrangements to such an extent that they become high-governance funds.

As such, governance is likely to become one of the bigger polarizing factors among pension funds, which would indeed be a welcome development.

To conclude, I find strong evidence that investment success and value creation are driven by the quality of the decision-making involved. It follows that there should be a much stronger link between governance and investment strategy. The potential to destroy value through unsuitable investment strategies can be significantly reduced if pension fund trustees are honest with themselves about their governance capabilities in the first instance. And if funds can start to treat governance as a variable and not a constraint, and make some moves in the direction of best practice, things could look altogether brighter for their considerable numbers of stakeholders. We are living in a period of extreme investment conditions. Such times reinforce the idea that we should give more attention to the governance factor.

▸▸ MORE INFO

Articles:

Ambachtsheer, Keith. "How much is good governance worth?" *The Ambachtsheer Letter* 245 (June 2006). Online at: www.kpa-advisery.com/ambachtsheer.htm

Ambachtsheer, Keith, Ronald Capelle, and Tom Scheibelhut. "Improving pension fund performance." *Financial Analysts Journal* (November/December 1998): 15–21.

Reports:

Clark, Gordon L., and Roger Urwin. "Best-practice investment management: Lessons for asset owners from the Oxford–Watson Wyatt project on governance." White paper, October 2007. Online at: www.watsonwyatt.com/europe/research/resrender.asp?id=BPIM-2007-A&page=1

Watson Wyatt and Oxford University. "Best-practice investment governance: 'Good to great' opportunities. Case study research by Watson Wyatt and Oxford University on governance and investment capabilities." An online slide-show presentation: www.watsonwyatt.com/europe/research/resrender.asp?id=BPIM-2007-B&page=1.

See Also:

★ Best Practices in Risk-Based Internal Auditing (pp. 611–613)
★ Boardroom Roles (pp. 130–131)
★ Internal Audit and Partnering with Senior Management (pp. 668–671)
★ Internal Auditors and Enterprise Risk Management (pp. 680–682)
✔ Corporate Governance and Its Interpretations (p. 902)
✔ Directors' Duties: A Primer (p. 909)
✔ Requirements of the UK Combined Code on Corporate Governance (p. 913)
Gary Brinson (p. 1156)

NOTES

1 See "How much is good governance worth?" *The Ambachtsheer Letter*, June 2006. For additional evidence in this area, see Ambachtsheer, Capelle, and Scheibelhut (1998).

2 Clark and Urwin (2007).

"Balance sheets are meaningless. Our accounting system is still based on the assumption that 80 per cent of costs are manual laborlabour." Peter F. Drucker

  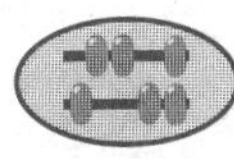 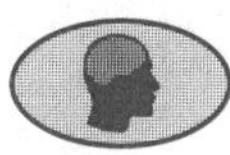  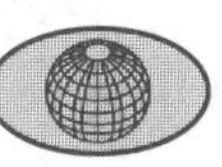   

Best Practices in Corporate Social Responsibility

by Alison Kemper and Roger Martin

EXECUTIVE SUMMARY

- Business leaders throughout the world are under increasing pressure to make socially responsible decisions even as they comply with legal requirements and generate sufficient profits.
- Corporate social responsibility (CSR) decisions demand new skills: managers must understand not only the responsibilities demanded of all firms, but also the opportunities they introduce.
- While the marketplace does not reward all good deeds, thoughtful strategies can increase the likelihood that firms increase their value while creating positive outcomes for society.
- In this essay, we review the complexity of the issue, the opportunities CSR presents, and one approach to identifying CSR opportunities.

MANAGING IN COMPLEXITY—CIVIL VS STRATEGIC

As business has become increasingly global, the values and principles that guide managers are no longer local. Raw materials from Canada and Indonesia are transformed by manufacturers in India and Brazil under contract to firms in the United States and Germany. Social activists, investors, accountants, workers, politicians, environmentalists, regulators, and customers in each and every location work to influence management's decisions. Normal business practices in one location can be objectionable to customers and investors in other areas, while labor and environmental principles in one region appear to be protectionist to businesses in other regions.[1] Companies would like to do the right thing but seldom have reliable means to choose a direction or level of investment.

For most companies, CSR presents complex problems and great opportunities. CSR allows companies to engage in sophisticated nonmarket strategies that can influence customers, regulators, and employees. It also can reveal firm weaknesses. There are no global laws. There is no single right way. Firms must distinguish the legitimate demands of multiple governments, assess the claims of diverse groups, and identify the significant problems they can best resolve.

WHAT WORKS?

Many researchers have looked for the elusive factor that will turn a firm's good deeds into profits, searching in vain for missing magic. The right answer to the question "Does doing result in doing well?" is "It depends." Firms that select a specific type of social or environmental opportunity consistent with their identity and strategy will reap rewards. Firms which make choices based on the most recent request for help or on a particular manager's enthusiasm will likely not.

The most critical factors in the success of any firm's CSR strategy are not about CSR. A successful CSR strategy builds on basics. First, a firm must be viable in order to create an effective, valuable approach to society and the environment. It is unlikely that a good CSR strategy will reverse bad business decisions. Second, firms must meet their legal and regulatory commitments. Compliance is essential. Enron's ethics policies were widely admired, but the company was nevertheless in violation of the law. Third, firms must meet basic expectations of their industry and the communities in which they operate. A company known for spilling toxic effluent is unlikely to make gains from sponsoring a children's sports team. This sequence of responsibility is illustrated in the CSR value curve IBM has described (Figure 1).

IBM recommends that firms ask their employees, suppliers, and customers what kind of CSR strategy would be optimal. Engagement with these groups helps managers identify their best strategies in many settings. The IBM report suggests that consulting these groups will also help identify good CSR strategies. This is consistent with recent economic theory that makes the case for strategic approaches not only to financial gains, but also to social output.[2]

Meeting the demands of disparate social agents disperses the energy and creativity of the firm. Deliberate, strategic choices maximize social effectiveness and firm opportunities.

THE ROLE OF FINANCIAL FIRMS

Financial institutions can choose to play another, powerful role: increasingly often, they determine whether new initiatives carry more social and environmental risks than potential economic benefits.[3] Good analysts will be able to see the ways in which future growth prospects are enhanced or reduced by the social and environmental characteristics of the firms and projects they finance.

Financial analysts and investors now recognize that a firm's ability to work with indigenous people and their property rights is critical to the success of new mineral extraction projects. Corporate finance professionals in companies like Procter & Gamble know that their sustainability principles must be factored into their investment decisions and growth forecasts.[4]

Figure 1. CSR value curve. (*Source*: IBM Institute for Business Value)

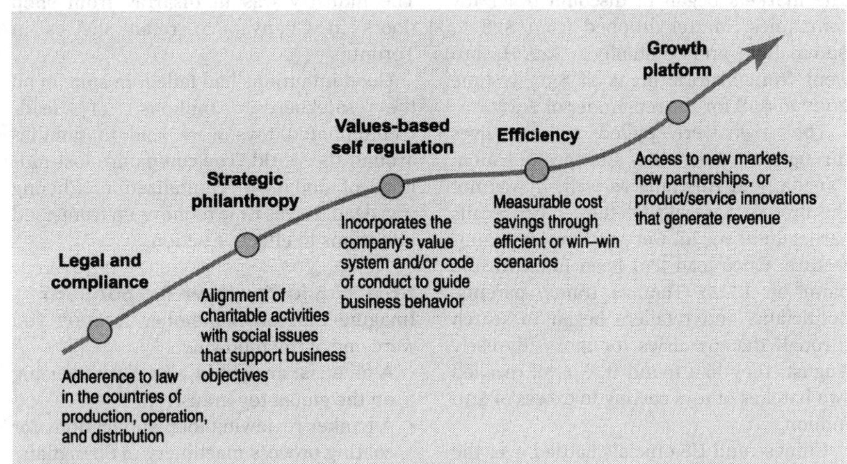

"I used to play football. . .you always know the score. Now, we are ice-skating,. . . [with] a bunch of judges shouting out scores." Robert Nardelli

  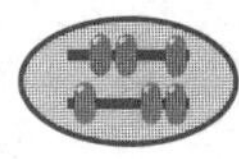   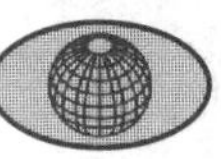   

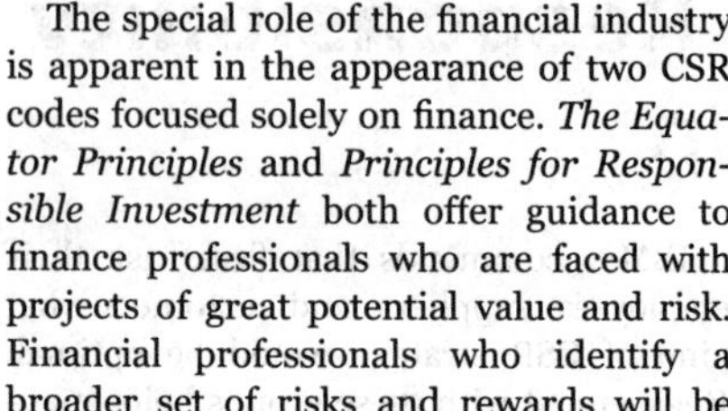

The special role of the financial industry is apparent in the appearance of two CSR codes focused solely on finance. *The Equator Principles* and *Principles for Responsible Investment* both offer guidance to finance professionals who are faced with projects of great potential value and risk. Financial professionals who identify a broader set of risks and rewards will be more effective.

CASE STUDY

Thomas the Tank Engine Runs Off the Rails

The spring of 2007 was promising for the global toy industry. In early June 2007, RC2 (RCRC), the manufacturer of Thomas & Friends Wooden Railway Toys, was trading at over $45 per share, the highest level it had ever reached. Mattel's stock also reached historic highs in spring 2007. In May, a trade journal announced that "China's coatings industry is benefiting from the country's thriving consumer goods market, to which it supplies almost 4.5 M tonnes/y of paint. . . In the electronic and computerized toys segment, coatings suppliers will be hoping to tap the country's 290 M children."[5] Painted toys were a key segment of China's manufacturing sector, and the global demand for colorful, inexpensive toys seemed insatiable.

In 2007, China's manufacturers accounted for approximately 80% of the world market for toys and employed more than 4 million workers.[6] Their business depended on the tight ties in the value chain: the links between consumers, the brands, and their personalities, the toy company giants, the Hong Kong brokers, and the Chinese manufacturers were close and profitable.

Everything changed in mid-June, when RC2 recalled 1.5 million Thomas toys that had been sprayed with lead paint.[8] RC2's share price dipped below $40 on the news. The markets began to discount other toy companies: Mattel dropped from $28 to $26 in June, and eventually to $22. Hasbro went from historic highs of $32 in June 2007 to $28 for the remainder of 2007.

The toys were pulled from shelves throughout Asia, the European Union, Canada, and Australia as well. It was not the first such recall: Of the 24 US recalls earlier in 2007, all were of Chinese manufacture. Once lead had been found in the paint on RC2's Thomas trains, parents, politicians, and retailers began to search through the toy aisles for more. By early August, they had found it. Mattel recalled two batches of toys costing in excess of $30 million.

Chinese and US officials battled over the issue: were there enough safeguards on Chinese exports? Which government was at fault?

The Hong Kong industrialists were devastated. Companies were banned from exporting goods. One toy manufacturer, Cheung Shue Hung, committed suicide.[9] The industry was in disarray from shop floors in Guanyao to retail shelves in Toronto.

Good intentions had failed. In spite of all the safeguards, millions of lead-contaminated toys were sold to families around the world. Toy companies lost millions of dollars of capitalization. Cheung was dead. It was time to move up from good intentions to effective action.

Figure 2. The virtue matrix

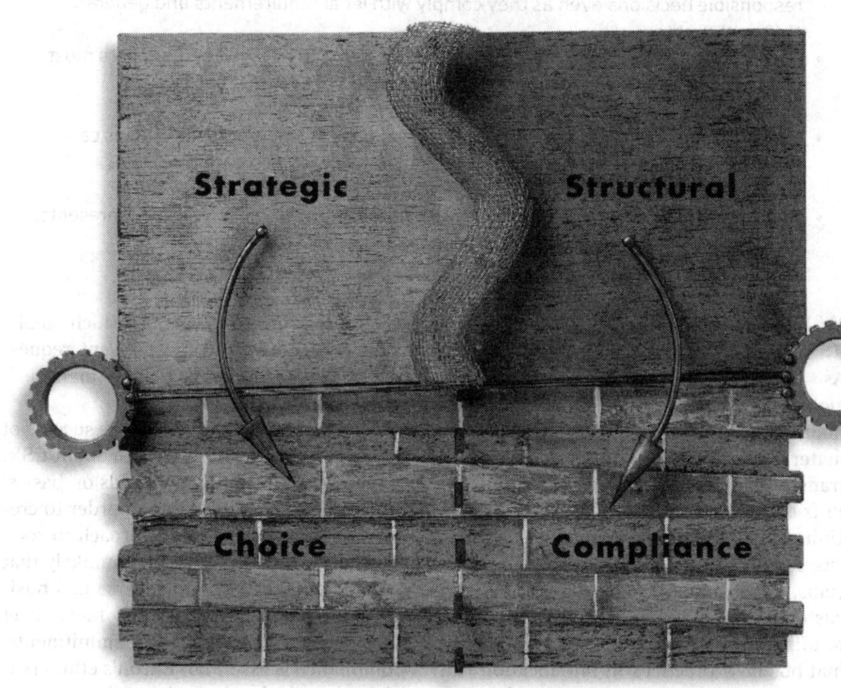

How Would *You* Have Responded?

Imagine that on September 1, 2007 you were one of the following:

- A financial analyst in New York focusing on the global toy industry;
- A banker reviewing loan applications for coating process machinery in Shanghai;
- Plant manager of a coating factory in Guan
- Chief of manufacturing export regulations in Beijing;
- Regional manager of Toys"R"Us retail operations in California;
- Global brand manager of Thomas & Friends Wooden Railway Toys;
- Research director at Al Tawfeek, a leading provider of *shariah*-compliant investment funds.

From the perspective of the person whose position is most similar to yours, first list the strategic opportunities and risks you see in the situation you face. Then consider these issues:

1. What do governments require? Do you need to ensure that these requirements are being met?
2. What do consumers and other groups expect of businesses in this situation? Does your work meet their expectations?
3. Where are the opportunities for a single firm or brand to gain advantage over its competitors? Can you identify and harness them?

"It is to the advantage of the firm to act in a strategic manner. . .a strategic focus increases the firm's social output." Husted Corregan and Salazar

4 Where is there no likelihood of profit but a great likelihood of harm? Is this impossible to resolve by firms that must make profits? Can your organization contribute to a resolution?

5 From your professional standpoint, do you support a market solution based on competitive dynamics? Do you think that voluntary industry codes will work? Would you support increased regulation?

What are the issues here? Why did the Chinese toy debacle happen? Why did the incentives allow this to happen repeatedly? What can prevent its recurrence?

▸▸ MAKING IT HAPPEN

The Virtue Matrix[10] as an Action Framework

By distinguishing four types of "virtue," companies can approach CSR effectively. When a firm recognizes the specific type of social activity demanded, it can respond optimally. Roger Martin's "virtue matrix" maps out these four kinds of virtue, each of which demands a different decision-making logic.

To identify and enact CSR strategies, a broad-based working group of managers can ask:

- *Compliance:* What are the firm's legal and regulatory requirements?
- *Choice:* Which codes of conduct and other expectations govern the choices of business in this context?
- *Strategic:* What problems can be tackled that will enhance the value, brand, or profits of a specific firm?
- *Structural:* What are the problems that no business can solve alone?

The best business opportunities lie in the area where a firm's unique resources and skills match social and environmental gaps or needs. Competitive advantage does not emerge from compliance with the law, from tackling systemic issues single-handedly, or from meeting the demands of civil society. Each of those must be addressed as distinct ways of doing good.

This need not be a mysterious process. Mapping the demands and opportunities requires environment scanning and research, capacities that businesses use daily. IBM suggests asking employees and suppliers to make recommendations. For most firms, there are likely to be many more opportunities to do good than there is capacity

Having gathered a planning team and a list of options, a firm might then match each idea to a quadrant in the virtue matrix and assign a priority

- Compliance issues are the most straightforward: Noncompliance is too risky for most businesses.
- Choice issues are more complex. What are the social norms? Are there any rankings or indices that give firms information about their competitive position with regard to the issues? What kind of identity does the firm wish to project? What can it afford?
- Structural issues demand the alignment of firms, governments, industries, and/or civil groupings. Each structural problem identified demands the formation of a working group or coalition. A firm can then ask if the potential benefit to a resolution warrants participation in such a group.
- Finally, strategic opportunities can be evaluated for their potential benefit to the reputation, position, or profits of a firm. Their implementation can be assessed through the same processes as are used for other business strategies.

By categorizing each type of CSR, a firm can make better decisions.

▸▸ MORE INFO

Books:

Crane, Andrew, Abagail McWilliams, Dirk Matten, Jeremy Moon, and Donald S. Siegel (eds). *The Oxford Handbook of Corporate Social Responsibility*. Oxford: Oxford University Press, 2008.

Kline, John M. *Ethics for International Business: Decision Making in a Global Political Economy*. London: Routledge, 2005.

Prahalad, C. K., Michael E. Porter, and Charles Handy (eds). *Harvard Business Review on Corporate Responsibility*. Boston, MA: Harvard Business School Press, 2003.

Vogel, David. *The Market for Virtue: The Potential and Limits of Corporate Social Responsibility*. Washington, DC: Brookings Institution, 2005.

Websites:

Global organizations

International Finance Corporation: www.ifc.org and www.ifc.org/sustainability

Organisation for Economic Co-operation and Development (OECD): www.oecd.org

United Nations. See especially the United Nations Global Compact, starting here: www.un.org/partners

United Nations Conference on Trade and Development (UNCTAD); search on "ISAR" to find the webpages of the Intergovernmental Working Group of Experts on International Standards of Accounting and Reporting: www.unctad.org

"It is to the advantage of the firm to act in a strategic manner. . .a strategic focus increases the firm's social output." Husted Corregan and Salazar

     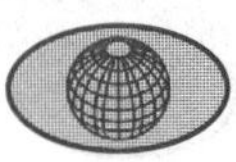   

World Bank. The bank's website has many useful resources, including CSR links and information on the Inclusive and Sustainable Business Program and Business Fighting Corruption. Search from the home page: www.worldbank.org

Accounting and reporting standards

AA1000: www.accountability21.net
Global Reporting Initiative: www.globalreporting.org
ISO 14000: www.iso.org/iso/iso_catalogue/management_standards/iso_9000_iso_14000/iso_14000_essentials.htm
Social Accountability 8000 (SA8000): www.sa8000.org

Other sources

Business for Social Responsibility: www.bsr.org
Equator Principles, a benchmark for the financial industry to manage social and environmental issues in project financing: www.equator-principles.com
Ethical Corporation: www.ethicalcorp.com
Global Reporting Initiative: www.globalreporting.org
Industry Canada: www.ic.gc.ca
Principles for Responsible Investment, a UN-based initiative which provides a framework to integrate responsible investment into mainstream decision-making: www.unpri.org
Social Investment Forum: www.socialinvest.org
Wikipedia: en.wikipedia.org/wiki/Corporate_social_responsibility
World Business Council on Sustainable Development: www.wbcsd.org

See Also:

★ CSR: More than PR, Pursuing Competitive Advantage in the Long Run (pp. 147–149)
Muhammed Yunus (p. 1205)
The Caring Economy: Business Principles for the New Digital Age (p. 1233)

NOTES

1 Kline, 2005.
2 Husted, B. W., and Jose De Jesus Salazar, "Taking Friedman seriously: Maximizing profits and social performance." *Journal of Management Studies* 43:1 (2006): 75–91.
3 See the Equator Principles: www.equator-principles.com
4 Procter & Gamble. "P&G 2007 Global Sustainability Report." Online at: www.pg.com/company/our_commitment/pdfs/gsr07_execsum.pdf
5 "China has enormous potential in paint and coatings for cars, electronics and computerized toys." *ICIS Chemical Business* (May 21, 2007). Online at: www.icis.com/Articles/2007/05/18/4502632/China-has-enormous-potential-in-paint-and-coatings-for-cars-electronics-and-computerised.html
6 Chen, Shu-Ching Jean. "Trapped in the Chinese toy closet." Forbes.com (August 21, 2007). Online at: www.forbes.com/2007/08/21/china-toy-industry-markets-equity-cx_jc_0821markets1.html
7 Dee, Jonathan. "A toy maker's conscience." *New York Times* (December 23, 2007): magazine section. Online at: www.nytimes.com/2007/12/23/magazine/23Mattel-t.html
8 Chen, Shu-Ching Jean. "Subcontractor at heart of Fisher-Price toy recall is apparent suicide." Forbes.com (August 13, 2007). Online at: www.forbes.com/2007/08/13/mattel-subcontractor-suicide-face-cx_jc_0813autofacescan02.html
9 *Ibid.* 2007.
10 Martin, Roger L. "The virtue matrix: Calculating the return on corporate responsibility." *Harvard Business Review* 80:3 (2002): 68–75.

"It is to the advantage of the firm to act in a strategic manner. . .a strategic focus increases the firm's social output." Husted Corregan and Salazar

  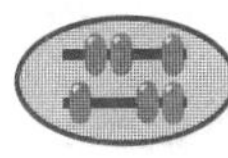   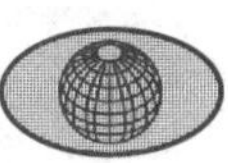   

Viewpoint: Stewart Hamilton

Regulation, Corporate Governance, and Boardroom Performance Must Be Shaken Up If We Are to Avoid Another Financial Crisis

INTRODUCTION

Stewart Hamilton, professor of accounting and finance at business school IMD, argues that corporate governance failures, and particularly a lack of expertise among nonexecutive directors, were largely to blame for the financial crisis. Here he proposes a number of solutions, including that shareholders should take more of an interest in the qualifications of company directors, and that the "Big Four" accountancy firms should be broken up. He has been professor of accounting and finance at IMD since 1981, and dean of finance and administration since 2008. His areas of interest are corporate failure, governance, risk management, and investor protection. Formerly a senior partner of a UK national accounting firm, Hamilton has served on professional committees and working parties on company law reform, conduct of serious fraud trials, and financial services legislation. He is the author of numerous cases on corporate failure, including *The Barings Collapse* and *The Enron Collapse*. Hamilton is a graduate of the University of Edinburgh, and a member of the Institutes of Chartered Accountants of Scotland, of Alberta, and of Ontario.

Did the regulators do enough to rein in irresponsible behavior in the banking sector in the 1990s and 2000s?

Two years before the collapse of Barings Bank in 1994–1995, I met a board director of the Swiss National Bank (the central bank of Switzerland). He told me that his greatest worry—one which he said was at that time widely shared by central bankers across Europe—was that the directors of the institutions they were supposed to be monitoring had very little understanding of the risks they were taking. He said this was particularly true where the rapidly growing derivatives market was concerned. Not nearly enough was done to address that.

Given that the wholesale funding markets briefly froze up after 9/11, why do you think the boards of banks dependent on these markets were oblivious to the risk that this might happen again?

It comes down to flawed assumptions. It is worth taking a look at Long-Term Capital Management. That was a highly sophisticated, computer-based options pricing model on a massive scale. The problem was that the models it used were based on a number of unreasonable assumptions—including that there is perfect liquidity. Long-Term Capital Management collapsed because the liquidity in the market in which it operated totally dried up.

Isn't it bizarre that people who are supposedly very bright are capable of making such flawed assumptions?

The Black–Scholes model for derivatives pricing, the Chicago School of Economics, and the perfect market hypothesis have heavily influenced financial thinking. My concern is that the use of these models, with their flawed assumptions, has replaced judgment. The models were primarily designed by people with a limited understanding of banking—they were mainly mathematicians and physicists—and they were being used by people who didn't even understand the models. The lack of resources among bank regulators meant they took far too much on trust where these models are concerned. This is reflected in the Basel II liquidity proposals, where the concerns of individual central banks have been brushed aside.

Would one solution be to pay the regulators more, as already happens in Singapore?

The Singapore regulators are very smart, knowledgeable, and well-resourced. They are also streets ahead of the bankers in their ability to identify risk. They picked up on the lessons from the Barings collapse, in marked contrast to the Bank of England, which was much more complacent.

If regulators in the United Kingdom and United States had responded better to earlier crises, would the credit bubble of 2000–2007 have reached such devastating proportions?

It would probably have been punctured at an earlier stage. If the regulators had extended their analysis of what was going on to the business models themselves, then I'm sure there would have been mutterings about capital adequacy at a much earlier stage.

Do you believe that there were particular inadequacies in the boards of banks and other financial institutions in the run up to the crisis?

One problem was that the people who became nonexecutive directors of banks had very little knowledge, experience, or understanding of banking. Most probably had checkbooks and some might also have had a mortgage, but they lacked any profound understanding of banking. This meant they were incapable of doing a proper risk assessment.

"The problem with the bank managers was not that they were malevolent but that they were mediocre." Christopher Caldwell

     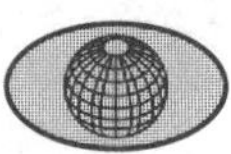   

Were the boards of directors—and particularly the nonexecutives—at most banks pretty useless?

There was this assumption that just because somebody is good at managing one business, they would automatically be good at managing or overseeing another. I call it the arrogance of the Harvard MBA. The reality is that the most successful managers are people who have a deep understanding of the business that they're running—like Jack Welch at GE or Ian Wood at Wood Group.

Many of the executive directors at banks were afflicted by the "master-of-the-universe" bug. Derivatives are only part of the story. Another was their reckless lending on property. That is nothing new. It happened in the United States during the savings and loans crisis. There was the same easing of regulation, the same lowering of lending standards, the same lack of controls, and the same encouragement of debt—and there was also politicians' general view that home ownership is a right. Margaret Thatcher and Ronald Reagan have a lot to answer for.

Can you identify specific or general failures within audit committees—and can you propose ways of ensuring that audit committees become more effective?

In the case of Nick Leeson at Barings, John Rusnak at Allied Irish Banks, and Jerome Kerviel at Société Générale, the underlying factors were more or less identical; there was a failure to have adequate internal controls, very poor risk management, and a weak internal audit function. These are precisely the roles that the audit committee is supposed to oversee.

At both the Royal Bank of Scotland and at HBOS there was prima facie evidence that the audit committees failed to properly assess or understand the risks that the institutions were taking. Having some retired partners from "Big Four" accountancy firms is not good enough. Just because they have worked for a "Big Four" firm, it does not mean they understand banking or even that they are particularly bright. You also have to question where the audit committee of Fortis were during this time. The audit committees of banks like Citigroup and Lehman Brothers also clearly failed.

Can you summarize the role of an audit committee?

The audit committee is there to monitor the risks, not just the financial risks. In 2003, Sir Robert Smith (currently chairman of Scottish & Southern Energy and Weir Group) produced some recommendations on audit committees, and these were integrated into the Combined Code of Corporate Governance. Smith clearly laid down what audit committees should be doing and what the standards should be. Two of the key recommendations were that, over and above ensuring the integrity of a company's financial statements, they should be reviewing the company's internal financial controls and risk management systems. Smith also said that audit committee members need to be "tough, knowledgeable and independent-minded." However, despite this becoming part of the combined code, quite a few institutions seem only to have paid lip-service to it.

What else could be done to ensure the abuses that occurred ahead of the credit crisis do not happen again?

I would strengthen the capability of people sitting on the boards of public listed companies. They need to be people who are capable of exercising independent judgment. They should also have a proper understanding of business in general, and a sufficient number of them must be reasonably experienced in the industry in which the company is involved.

There should also be a limit in the number of directorships that an individual can hold; in Saudi Arabia the limit is either four or five, which ensures that you don't get serial directors. To properly perform the role of nonexecutive director, people need to be able to devote an adequate amount of time to it. Remuneration should also be fixed by the shareholders. I would eliminate the entire compensation consulting industry, which I believe is as conflicted as the rating agencies.

Do you think the main role of remuneration consultants is, in fact, to drive executive pay up?

Yes. A lot of these pay awards are self-serving. In his book *Annals of the Abiding Liberal*, economist John Kenneth Galbraith wrote that: "The salary of the chief executive of the large corporation is not a market award for achievement. It is frequently in the nature of a warm personal gesture by the individual to himself."

Another thing that should happen is that regulators should be beefed up, adequately remunerated, and their scope should be extended to making judgments about the quality of the boards of the financial institutions—and the appropriateness of the individuals serving on them.

I can imagine the response that Adam Smith free-marketeer types would have to that suggestion.

The problem is that those free-marketeer types you describe haven't actually read Adam Smith. If you look at Adam Smith and the invisible hand—that was tempered by recognition that there was such a thing as society, that governments did have some responsibility to curtail excesses and, in particular, the point he made about whenever businessmen get together for a chat, it invariably ends up as a conspiracy against the public. So, having a free market implies some sense of responsibility. In the recent past, that sense of responsibility has been conspicuously absent.

Do you think it would help if the wider investment community had more say in director appointments?

In the United States there's some momentum behind the idea that shareholders should have a greater say in the appointment of directors. I also hope that analysts will wake up and start asking questions about the qualifications and knowledge of board members, particularly directors on audit committees.

Do you have any other proposals?

You have to ask where were the auditors were in this. I think the time has come to break up the "Big Four" accounting firms. There is inadequate choice in the market. It is clear that in doing their risk assessment, which they are supposed to do as part of their audit, they have not either considered the risks adequately, or given sufficient warning. The lack of choice in the audit market has bred an inherent complacency. I think the auditors need to be sorted out, as do the ratings agencies. The ratings agencies were hugely culpable in all of this. They should go back to the way in which they were financed in the past. Then, if you wanted the rating of a company, you paid for it. Now, it is the rated companies that pay the ratings agencies. There is a huge conflict inherent in that.

Are there any other specific reforms that you would call for?

In the United Kingdom, I think the government should have another good look at the Companies Act—specifically the clauses on the duties and responsibilities of directors. The whole debate about the capping of auditors' liability also needs to be looked at again.

"Think of the way almost everyone important missed the warning signs of an impending crisis. How was that possible? ... The answer, I believe, is that there's an innate tendency on the part of even the elite to idolize men who are making a lot of money, and assume that they know what they're doing." Paul R. Krugman

     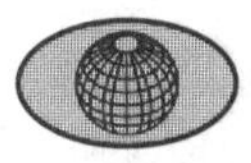   

▸▸ MORE INFO

Books:

Bernstein, Peter L. *Against the Gods: The Remarkable Story of Risk*. New York: Wiley, 1996.

Galbraith, John Kenneth. *The Great Crash: 1929*. Penguin, 1992.

Hamilton, Stewart, and Alicia Micklethwait. *Greed and Corporate Failure: The Lessons from Recent Disasters*. London: Palgrave, 2006.

Kindleberger, Charles P. *Manias, Panics, and Crashes: A History of Financial Crises.* New York: Basic Books, 1989.

Lowenstein, Roger. *When Genius Failed: The Rise and Fall of Long-Term Capital Management*. London: Fourth Estate, 2001.

Morris, Charles R. *Money, Greed & Risk*. Chichester, UK: Wiley, 1999.

Partnoy, Frank. *Infectious Greed: How Deceit and Risk Corrupted the Financial Markets.* London: Profile Books, 2003.

Shiller, Robert J. *Irrational Exuberance*. Princeton, NJ: Princeton University Press, 2000.

Steinherr, Alfred. *Derivatives: The Wild Beast of Finance*. Chichester, UK: Wiley, 1998.

"History records no case where the bubble gracefully deflated, accompanied by a slight hiss of escaping optimism. The speculative episode always ends with a loud explosion." Andreas Whittam Smith

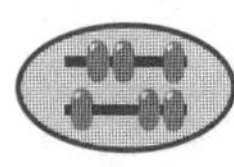

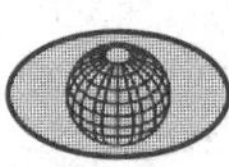

Boardroom Roles by Sir Adrian Cadbury

EXECUTIVE SUMMARY

- The role of the board is to direct, not to manage.
- Balance of board membership and choice of individuals are key.
- Chairmen are responsible for the effectiveness of their boards.
- Nonexecutive directors have a particular contribution to make to the work of a board.
- Board committees are important structurally and for the tasks they undertake.
- Executive directors should be appointed solely for the value they can add to the board.
- Board members have different roles; what matters is how they combine to form the board team.

THE ROLE OF THE BOARD

The crispest definition of a board's role is Sir John Harvey-Jones's: *"to create tomorrow's company out of today's."* Boards are in place to direct and control, not to manage. Boards have the task of defining the purpose of their enterprises and of agreeing the strategy for achieving that purpose. They are responsible for appointing chief executives to turn strategic plans into action, for supporting and counseling them in so doing, and if necessary for replacing them. Above all, boards are there to provide leadership, and it is in that context that the roles of board members need to be considered.

BOARD COMPOSITION

A single board at the head of a company is the commonest form of board structure. Unitary boards of this nature are made up of executive and nonexecutive or outside directors. Two-tier boards separate these two kinds of director, and their structure is covered briefly in the next section. Given that both executive and outside directors sit on unitary boards, the first issue is the balance between them. In the United States the chief executive is often the only executive on the board, and is usually its chairman as well. Fifteen years ago the ratio on UK boards was around two-thirds executive directors and one-third outside directors. This has now moved through parity to the position where outside directors are in the majority.

The Combined Code on Corporate Governance,[1] in provision A.3.2, states: *"Except for smaller companies, at least half the board, excluding the chairman, should comprise non-executive directors determined by the board to be independent. A smaller company should have at least two independent non-executive directors."* The issue of independence is dealt with under the heading of the Role of Non-Executive Directors.

In addition to the question of balance, there is the question of size. There is a clear move to smaller boards, both in Britain and the United States. Martin Lipton and Jay W. Lorsch, in their "Modest proposal for improved corporate governance" (*Business Lawyer* vol. 48, no. 1, Nov. 1992), recommend a maximum board size of ten and favor eight or nine. The argument for smaller boards is that they enable all the directors to get to know each other and to contribute effectively in board discussions, thus arriving at a true consensus. The crucial point is that boards are teams and provide collective leadership. So the balance of membership and choice of individuals are key to forming the team.

TWO-TIER BOARDS

These boards are constituted of a supervisory board whose members are all nonexecutive and a management board made up of executive directors. The management board is responsible for strategy as well as for running the business. The supervisory board appoints and can dismiss the management board, and no one can be on both boards. The legal responsibilities of the two boards and of their directors are different, whereas with a unitary board all directors have the same legal duties however the board is structured.

Since supervisory boards may have employee members, this raises the question of their role on boards.[2] My own view is that employees can most effectively participate at levels below the board, where the decisions are taken that affect them most directly and to which they can contribute knowledgeably.

THE CHAIRMAN'S ROLE

Chairmen are responsible for the effectiveness of their boards. This responsibility rests with chairmen whatever their other duties. It leads on to the point that all companies are different and the issues they face are constantly changing. Individual boards have to follow accepted board principles, but in ways which meet their particular circumstances. It is chairmen who have the responsibility of ensuring that the make-up of their boards is appropriate for the challenges ahead. Similarly, it is chairmen who have the task of welding their directors into an effective team. Effective boards are not brought into being simply by sitting competent individuals around a board table. Creating effective boards requires effort by their members, but above all coaching and leadership by their chairmen. This is an argument for chairmen not also being chief executives.

Chairmen are responsible for the running of their boards. Their responsibilities include the agenda, the provision of adequate and timely information to all directors, and the actual conduct of board meetings. They are also, provided they are not chief executives, responsible for putting in place a means by which their boards can evaluate their own performance.

Where chairmen are also chief executives, their duties in relation to their boards remain the same, but the senior independent nonexecutive director would be responsible for the appraisal of the chief executive and for the review of the board's performance.

ROLE OF NONEXECUTIVE DIRECTORS

All directors are equal in that they all carry the same legal responsibilities. Outside or nonexecutive directors are in that sense no different from their executive colleagues. They do, however, have particular contributions to make to their boards by virtue of standing further back from the business. One is in reviewing the performance of the chief executive and of the executive team; clearly the outside directors are the only board members in a position to do this objectively.

Another is in relation to potential conflicts of interest, such as those between the interests of the executives and those of the shareholders. Examples are directors' pay, dividends versus re-investment, and whether top appointments should be made from within or from outside the company. Decisions on these matters are ultimately decisions of the whole board, but the outside directors are well-placed to give a lead over where the best interests of the company—to which all directors owe their duty—lie.

Outside directors bring with them their experience in fields which are different from those of the executive directors, and this external experience is of particular value in the formulation of strategy. The potential advantage which the unitary

     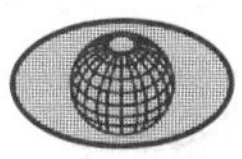   

board has over the two-tier board is that it provides the opportunity to combine, in the same body, the depth of knowledge of the business of the executives with the breadth of knowledge of the outside directors. Once again, it is up to chairmen to make the most of these different viewpoints by the way they structure board debates.

The role of outside directors in helping to resolve conflicts of interest does not imply that they have higher ethical standards than their executive colleagues. The difference is simply that they can judge these matters more objectively because their interests are less directly involved. Not all nonexecutive directors are considered independent. The Combined Code, provision A.3.1, states: "*The board should identify in the annual report each nonexecutive director it considers to be independent. The board should determine whether the director is independent in character and judgement and whether there are relationships or circumstances which are likely to affect, or could appear to affect, the director's judgement.*" Nonexecutive directors who do not meet these tests may be valued board members in their own right, but they cannot be classed as independent.

Another provision of the Combined Code, A.3.3, requires that boards "*Should appoint one of the independent nonexecutive directors to be the senior independent director. The senior independent director should be available to shareholders if they have concerns which contact through the normal channels of chairman, chief executive or finance director has failed to resolve or for which such contact is inappropriate.*"

ROLE OF BOARD COMMITTEES

As the responsibilities of directors have become more demanding, boards have increasingly formed committees to deal with some of their more detailed work. The Combined Code requires all quoted companies to establish audit and remuneration committees and, unless they have a small board, nomination committees. These committees strengthen the position of the nonexecutive directors, of whom they are made up, and are important for the work they do. The essential point is that they are committees of the board. It is the board which appoints them, sets their terms of reference, and turns their recommendations into decisions.

ROLE OF EXECUTIVE DIRECTORS

The duties of executive directors are the same as those of the nonexecutive directors. They are as responsible for the monitoring task of the board as the nonexecutive directors, who in turn are as responsible for the strategy and leadership of the company as the executives. This means that executive directors have to take their executive hats off on entering the boardroom and put on their directorial ones. They should only be appointed for the contribution they can make to the board, and they are there to further the company's interests, not those of their function or department. It is not an easy transition to make, and executive directors can be helped to adopt their new governance role through appropriate training or through a nonexecutive directorship elsewhere.

ROLE OF THE COMPANY SECRETARY

Chairmen and board members should be able to look to the company secretary for impartial and professional guidance on their responsibilities, and all directors should have access to the advice and services of a company secretary, who is responsible for ensuring that board procedures are followed.

CONCLUSION

Although board members have different roles, what counts is the way those roles are combined in the board team. This is why board selection is so fundamental. Directors should only be appointed for the value they can add to their boards. All directors should have terms of office to enable renewal to take place, although I am personally against rigid rules tying retirement to age or length of board service, preferring to rely on the judgement of boards and their shareholders.

The search for nonexecutive directors should be purposeful, with the aim of filling gaps in the experience and backgrounds of the existing directors, and their selection should involve the board as a whole. Chairmen, however, have a particular responsibility for the choice of board members since it is they who have to turn them into an effective team.

▸▸ MORE INFO

Books:

Carver, John. *John Carver on Board Leadership*. San Francisco, CA: Jossey-Bass, 2002.

Charkham, Jonathan. *Keeping Better Company: Corporate Governance Ten Years On*. 2nd ed. Oxford: Oxford University Press, 2005.

Harvey-Jones, John. *Making It Happen: Reflections on Leadership*. London: Profile Books, 2003.

NOTES

1 The Combined Code on Corporate Governance was published by the London Stock Exchange in July 2003; it includes Guidance on Internal Control and on Audit Committees and Suggestions for Good Practice from the Higgs Report. Companies listed on the London Stock Exchange are required to disclose how far they comply with the Code as a condition of listing. The latest version was published in June 2008 by the Financial Reporting Council, which is now responsible for the Combined Code, but it does not include the Turnbull and Smith guidance.

2 Although the supervisory boards of German companies above a certain size include employee members, Dutch supervisory boards, for example, do not.

"I get many invitations but I only join the boards of companies where I admire the management and believe in the company." Jill Ker Conway

   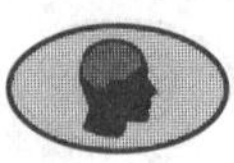  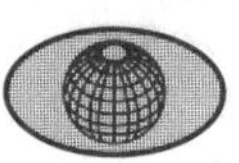   

Viewpoint: Tim Hindle
Ladies in Waiting

INTRODUCTION

Tim Hindle is a freelance writer and editor. Educated at Worcester College, Oxford, and Heriot-Watt University, Edinburgh, he was a research analyst in the City of London before joining *The Banker* magazine as deputy editor. He subsequently wrote for *The Economist* for many years, acting as finance editor in the 1980s before taking on the new role of management editor.

He launched *EuroBusiness* magazine in the early 1990s, and then re-launched the Institute of Directors' magazine, *Director*, later that decade. He has written a number of books. *The Essential Manager's Manual*, published by Dorling Kindersley, was a worldwide bestseller. His latest book, *Guide to Management Ideas and Gurus*, was published in 2008 to widespread acclaim. Hindle has also written extensively about Turkey. His wife is Turkish and he has visited the country over 100 times in the past 35 years. During that time he has seen the country grow from an underdeveloped agricultural economy into a thriving European neighbor, a vital geopolitical bridge between Christian and Muslim nations.

There are too few women in key jobs in the financial sector. Promoting them is not just a matter of fairness; it's a matter of prudent regulation.

Remember *Liar's Poker*, Michael Lewis's best-selling tale of his life as a Salomon Brothers' bond trader in the 1980s? It is a story of how macho traders on Wall Street fleeced innocents on the high street, including front-line mortgage lenders like the Savings & Loan Associations. The book's most memorable line—"If he could make millions of dollars come out of those phones, he became that most revered of all species: A Big Swinging Dick"—epitomized the financiers' *modus operandi* at the time.

Twenty years on, little has changed. The ethos of Wall Street-type firms is still male, rude, and ruthless. If anything, it has become worse. In the 1980s the commanding positions in these firms were taken mostly by graduate investment bankers. But in recent years the biggest profit-makers have been the traders of both old- and new-fangled securities. Traders tend to be rough and ready, and to have a limited interest in the world outside their dealing rooms. Their rewards and their status have risen to reflect their growing contribution to their employers' profits.

Traders, however, have shown that, uncontrolled, they can be lethal. At very short notice, they can throw banks into deep trouble. Nick Leeson, who brought down Barings in the 1990s, was a trader. His story was published as a book (and made into a film) under the title *Rogue Trader*. Jerome Kerviel, a Frenchman whose wildly spiraling deals at the beginning of 2008 lost US$7 billion for a much bigger bank, Société Générale, was also a trader.

These two rogues had other things in common. In the first place, both were young (in their twenties at the time) and male. And both came from humble backgrounds: Leeson's father was a plasterer; Kerviel's mother was a hairdresser. They had had little money of their own before billions of dollars of other people's was thrust into their care.

NO PLACE FOR WOMEN

As yet, few women have made their mark in this particular world. While they have made great strides in entering the lower echelons of financial services firms, women in the industry have largely been excluded from its trading rooms and its corridors of power. Where women have reached high levels it has usually been in "softer" areas, including fund management, public affairs, or as a general counsel. At the time of writing, Goldman Sachs has only three women on its management committee of 29. Credit Suisse has none.

What's more, the few women who really make breakthroughs seem to fall (or be felled) at the final hurdle. In 2007 Zoe Cruz, who started her banking career as a trader with Morgan Stanley, was fired just as she was about to take over as boss of the whole organization. The following year, Sally Krawcheck was eased out of Citigroup after being effectively demoted from the job of CFO.

Meanwhile, the bank that made the most creditable attempts to promote women, Lehman Brothers, is no more. Its much vaunted scheme to persuade female alumni to return after some years of absence evaporated when the bank went bust. At the same time, the Lehman Brothers Centre for Women in Business at the London Business School has, perhaps unsurprisingly, dropped the bank's name from its title.

I believe promoting more women on Wall Street and in the City of London is part of the solution to the world's financial ills, helping to ensure that banks and other institutions resist the urge to pursue suicidal strategies.

What the financial services industry needs is not just re-regulation in the place of deregulation, but more women in the place of men. It is not merely a matter of fairness. There is growing evidence that women are better suited to the work.

Writing in the *Financial Times* in April 2008, John Coates, a research fellow at Cambridge University who also once worked as a trader in New York, claimed that "as levels of testosterone rise, effective risk-taking gradually turns into dangerous behavior. . . testosterone is likely to rise in a bull market, increase risk and exaggerate the rally." On average, men produce 40-60 times more testosterone than women. And young men, who are a majority in most trading rooms, produce much more than older men.

Coates then pointed to another hormone, cortisol—the so-called "stress hormone" —as having a similar effect, but in the opposite direction. "Chronic cortisol exposure," he wrote, "promotes feelings of anxiety. . .and a tendency to find danger

"The secret isn't counting the beans, it's growing more beans." Roberto Goizueta

where none exists. Cortisol is likely to rise in a crash, make traders dramatically and perhaps irrationally risk-averse, and exaggerate the sell-off."

And guess what? Cortisol production is dampened under stress by yet another hormone, oxytocin, which is produced in far larger quantities in women than it is in men. Which explains the very different reactions of the two sexes to stress. Men tend towards the "fight or flight" option, both of them choices which leave them fending for themselves.

Women, on the other hand, tend towards each other. They seek the comfort and strength that comes from being part of a group. Hence, so the argument goes, if trading floors were run by women rather than men, market booms and busts would be far less extreme.

MALE PREJUDICE AND FEMALE RESIGNATION

Why then are there so few women in high places in the industry? Based on the endocrinal evidence, the market's invisible hand should be firmly pushing them forward.

The answer is a mix of male prejudice and female resignation. Women naturally opt out of an arena where the ultimate accolade is to become a "big swinging dick." They say that exclusion from the industry's male-dominated informal networks is one of the main reasons why so few of them reach the top rungs of the corporate ladder. Jock talk and late-night boozing oil the wheels of progress in many corporations, not just those in finance. A trip round the City of London's bars after 7pm any weekday provides ample evidence. The general increase in heavy female drinking in recent years may, in part, be a sad reflection of women's attempts to climb these particular corporate ladders on men's terms.

Katherine Bucknell, an author and the wife of a one-time top investment banker, recently wrote: "The size of a banker's pile of money is like the size of anything else in a macho environment: you need the biggest one to show that you are good at what you do. The pile does not necessarily reflect personal greed, it reflects the need to be the best banker." Women tend to find reward in things that lie beyond size—be it of paychecks, bonuses, air-miles, or just the working day.

At the same time, the male tribe which lucratively occupies the financial services high ground has successfully excluded them. The people who make the decisions as to who does what jobs within large organizations—essentially old, white men—are (unconsciously and unavoidably) biased in favor of their own kind (as are all such small groups in power). The ability of unconscious bias to distort management decisions in this way is now undeniable.

Women (who, of course, have their own biases) believe that organizations are biased against them. A survey undertaken by the publication *Financial News* in September 2008, found that 60% of a sample of 1,350 women in financial services firms in the City of London (one-third of them in investment banks) believed that their gender made it harder for them to succeed.

Women complain that they are in a Catch-22 situation. While several studies show that those who actively promote their own interests are seen as aggressive, uncooperative, and selfish (Zoe Cruz was known as the "Cruz missile"), a similar number of studies show that when women don't promote their own interests they don't get anywhere.

A recent report by management consultants McKinsey quotes Julie Daum, a headhunter who specializes in recruiting company board directors. She said that senior women on boards still lose out by not speaking up: "They hang back if they think that they have nothing new to say or that their ideas fall short of profound." Men don't worry so much about profundity. And they see people who do as weak and indecisive—i.e., not fit to run large financial institutions.

There are areas of life where male dominance makes sense. Women are unlikely ever to play rugby for the New Zealand All-Blacks or American football for the New York Giants. We need take no action to rectify these imbalances.

But with financial services it is different. The continuing absence of women at the top of the industry really does matter. The links between the rational and emotional parts of the brain are greater in women than they are in men. When emotions are high, as when markets are dramatically rising or dramatically falling, women are able to keep in closer touch with their intelligence. Testosterone and cortisol are less likely to get in the way.

BREAKING THE BARRIER

The only country that has managed to break the barrier that is preventing women from rising to levels where they can influence key decisions is Norway. And it achieved that by legislation. In 2003 it passed a law decreeing that by 2008 40% of the directors of all quoted companies should be women.

From all accounts, the Norwegian experiment has been a great success despite widespread initial skepticism. It may be a coincidence, but Norwegian banks have been less scathed by the global financial crisis than banks in many other countries.

Now countries like Spain and the Netherlands are considering taking similar steps, and others should quickly follow suit. For promoting women is now not just about sexual equality, it is about prudent regulation. We need many more women in high places in the financial services industry well before the next time hormonal madness hits the markets.

▸▸ MORE INFO

Books:

Bazerman, Max B., and Don A. Moore. *Judgment in Managerial Decision Making.* Hoboken, NJ: Wiley, 2009.

Lewis, Michael. *Liar's Poker.* London: Hodder Paperbacks, 2006.

Thomson, Peninah, and Jacey Graham. *A Woman's Place is in the Boardroom.* Basingstoke, UK: Palgrave Macmillan, 2005.

Articles:

Barsh, Joanna, Susie Cranston, and Rebecca Craske. "Centered leadership: How talented women thrive." *McKinsey Quarterly* (September 2008). Online at: www.mckinseyquarterly.com/Organization/Talent/Centered_leadership_How_talented_women_thrive_2193

Coates, John. "Traders should track their hormones." *Financial Times* (April 14, 2008). Online at: www.ft.com/cms/s/0/9973fb0a-0a1d-11dd-b5b1-0000779fd2ac.html

Economist. "Helping women get to the top." July 23, 2005. Online at: www.economist.com/opinion/displaystory.cfm?story_id=E1_QTJRPGP

Fabrikant, Geraldine. "When Citi lost Sallie". *New York Times* (November 15, 2008). Online at: www.nytimes.com/2008/11/16/business/16sallie.html

Report:

Catalyst. "The connection between women board directors and women corporate officers." July 2008.

"My father would look at my books and pull his hair, I just never got involved with the whole cash-flow thing. My attitude was, creativity will see me through." Adrienne Landau

  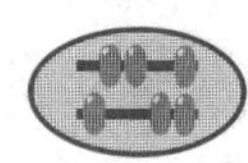 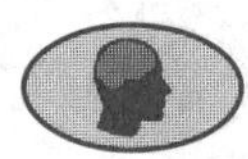  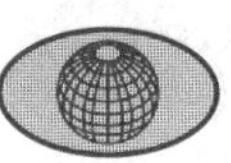   

Business Ethics by Sue Newell

EXECUTIVE SUMMARY

- Business ethics focuses on identifying the moral standards of right and wrong as they apply to behavior within and across business institutions and other related organizations.
- Corporations sometimes behave unethically, having a harmful effect on people or the environment.
- Unethical behavior is typically not caused by a single "bad apple," but is a result of complex interactions between individuals, groups, and organizational cultures.
- Ethical behavior can be defined either as behavior that maximizes happiness and minimizes harm or as behavior that is motivated by principles of duty.
- While behaving unethically may have some short-term benefit for a company, in the long term it will harm stakeholder support.
- Long-term sustainability comes from concentrating on the *triple bottom line*: that is, social, environmental, and financial performance (Elkington, 1998).

INTRODUCTION

Look in the newspaper on virtually any day of the week and you will find at least one business scandal in which a corporation appears to have violated the rules or standards of behavior generally accepted by society. Company finances have been manipulated in order to show a better balance sheet than actually exists, toxic waste has been allowed to flow into a river, bribes have been paid to secure a business deal, child labor has been used to assemble a product, discriminatory practices have prevented the employment or promotion of members of a particular group. When businesses behave unethically, they act in ways that have a harmful effect on others and in ways that are morally unacceptable to the larger community. This is very serious because corporate power and impact are increasing as corporations become larger (indeed, global) and as profit-making concerns take over functions that were once publicly controlled, such as the railroads, water utilities, and healthcare. Increasingly, it is the private sector that determines the quality of the air we breathe, the water we drink, our standard of living, and even where we live and how easily we can move around.

COMMON ETHICAL PROBLEMS WITHIN CORPORATIONS

Given the increasing social impact of business, business ethics has emerged as a discrete subject over the last 20 years. Business ethics is concerned with exploring the moral principles by which we can evaluate business organizations in relation to their impact on people and the environment. Trevino and Nelson (2004) categorize four types of ethical problems that are commonly found in business organizations.

First are the *human resource problems*: These relate to the equitable and just treatment of current and potential employees. Unethical behavior here involves treating people unfairly because of their gender, sexuality, skin color, religion, ethnic background, and so on.

Second are ethical problems arising from *conflicts of interest*, when particular individuals or organizations are given special treatment because of some personal relationship with the individual or group making a decision. A company might get a lucrative contract, for example, because a bribe was paid to the management team of the contracting organization, not because of the quality of its proposal.

Third are ethical problems that involve *customer confidence*. Corporations sometimes behave in ways that show a lack of respect for customers or a lack of concern with public safety. Examples here include advertisements that lie (or at least conceal the truth) about particular goods or services, and the sale of products, such as drugs, where a company conceals or obfuscates negative data about safety and/or efficacy.

Finally, there are ethical problems surrounding the *use of corporate resources* by employees who make private phone calls at work, submit false expense claims, take company stationery home, etc.

The financial scandals that have rocked the corporate world in recent years (Enron, WorldCom, Parmalat, Lehman Brothers, for example) have involved a number of these different ethical issues. In these cases, senior managers have engaged in improper bookkeeping, making companies look more financially profitable than they actually are. As a consequence the stockholder value of the company increases, and anyone with stock profits directly. Among those profiting will be those making the decisions to manipulate the accounts—and so there is a conflict of interest. However, the fallout from the downfall of these companies affects stockholders, employees, and society at large negatively, with innocent people losing their retirement reserves and/or savings, and employees losing their jobs.

Another category can be added to this list—ethical problems surrounding the *use of the world's environmental resources*. Many organizations have externalized the costs associated with their negative impact on the environment, whether in relation to their own operations to produce goods and services, or in terms of the use and later the disposal of the goods that they have sold. Externalizing means that organizations do not themselves pay for the environmental costs that they create. For example, carbon dioxide emissions, a by-product of energy use for all kinds of organizations, are now recognized as contributing to global warming; computer equipment contains toxic waste that pollutes the land where it is dumped; and packaging of all kinds, including plastic bags that are handed out by supermarkets, are creating mounting problems as local authorities run out of landfill sites. Increasingly, ethical business is seen to require that a business takes into account and offsets its "environmental footprint" so that it engages in sustainable activity. Sustainability broadly means that a business meets the needs of the present without compromising the ability of future generations to meet their needs.

ACCOUNTING FOR ETHICAL AND UNETHICAL BEHAVIOR

While it may be very easy to identify and blame an individual or small group of individuals, to see these individuals as the perpetrators of an unethical act—the "bad apple"—and hold them responsible for the harm caused, is an oversimplification. Most accounts of unethical behavior that are restricted to the level of the individual are inadequate. Despite popular belief, decisions harmful to others or the environment that are made within organizations are not typically the result of an isolated, immoral individual seeking to gain personally. Although an individual's level of moral maturity or the locus of control (for example, the degree to which they perceive they control their behaviors and actions) are factors, we also need to explore the decision-making context—the group dynamics and the organizational practices

"To see what is right and not to do it is want of courage." Confucius

     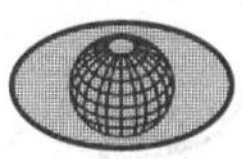   

and procedures—to understand why an unethical decision was made.

Group dynamics influence the decision-making process. A particularly important group-level influence is *groupthink*, a phenomenon identified by Irving Janis (1982) in his research on US foreign policy groups. The research demonstrates the presence of strong pressures towards conformity in these groups: individual members suspend their own critical judgment and right to question, with the result that they make bad and/or immoral decisions. Janis defines groupthink as "the psychological drive for consensus at any cost that suppresses dissent and appraisal of alternatives in cohesive decision-making groups."

The degree to which decisions are ethical is also influenced by organizational culture or climate. Organizational ethical climates can differ; some are more egoistic, others are more benevolent, still others are highly principled, and these contexts can shape a manager's ethical decision-making. Smith and Johnson (1996) identify three general approaches that organizations take to corporate responsibility:

- **Social obligation**: The corporation does only what is legally required.
- **Social responsiveness**: The corporation responds to pressure from different stakeholder groups.
- **Social responsibility**: The corporation has an agenda of proactively trying to improve society.

In a company in which the dominant approach to business ethics is social obligation, it is likely to be difficult to justify a decision based on ethical criteria; morally irresponsible behavior may be condoned as long as it does not break the law. Legal loopholes, for example, may be exploited in such a company if these can benefit the company in the short term, even if they might have a negative influence on others in society.

ETHICAL DILEMMAS

Sometimes it is clear that a business has behaved unethically—for example, where a drug is sold illegally, the company accounts have been falsely presented, or where client funds have been embezzled. Of more interest, and much more common, are situations that pose an ethical dilemma—situations that present a conflict between right and wrong or between values and obligations—so that a choice is necessary. For example, a corporation may want to build a new factory on a previously undeveloped and popular tourist site in a location where there is large-scale unemployment among the local population. Here we have a conflict between the benefits of wealth and job creation in a location in which these are crucial and the cost of spoiling some naturally beautiful countryside. Philosophers have attempted to develop prescriptive theories providing universal laws that enable us to differentiate between right and wrong, and good and bad, in these situations.

PRESCRIPTIVE ETHICAL THEORIES

Essentially there are two schools of thought. The consequentialists argue that behavior is ethical if it maximizes the common good (happiness) and minimizes harm. The opposing nonconsequentialists argue that behavior is ethical if it is motivated by a sense of duty or a set of moral principles about human conduct—regardless of the consequences of the action.

Consequentialist Accounts of Ethical Behavior

Philosophers who adopt the consequentialist approach (sometimes also referred to as utilitarianism) consider that behavior can be judged ethical if it has been enacted in order to maximize human happiness and minimize harm. Jeremy Bentham (1748–1832) and John Stuart Mill (1806–73) are two of the best-known early proponents of this view. Importantly it is the common good, not personal happiness, that is the arbiter of right and wrong. Indeed, we are required to sacrifice our personal happiness if doing so enhances the total sum of happiness. For someone faced with a decision choice, the ethical action is the one that achieves the greatest good for the greatest number of people after weighing the impact on those involved. Common criticisms of this approach are that it is impossible to measure happiness adequately and that it essentially condones injustice if this is to the benefit of the majority.

Nonconsequentialist Accounts of Ethical Behavior

Philosophers who adopt a nonconsequentialist approach (also referred to as deontological theory) argue that behavior can be judged as ethical if it is based on a sense of duty and carried out in accordance with defined principles. Immanuel Kant (1724–1804), for example, articulated the principle of *respect for persons*, which states that people should never be treated as a means to an end, but always as an end in themselves; leading to the easy to remember maxim – do as you would be done by. The idea here is that we can establish moral judgments that are true because they can be based on the unique human ability to reason. One common criticism of this approach is that it is impossible to agree on the basic ethical principles of duty or their relative weighting in order to direct choices when multiple ethical principles are called into question at the same time, or when decisions cut across cultures with different ethical principles.

WHY BEHAVING ETHICALLY IS IMPORTANT FOR BUSINESS

Choosing to be ethical can involve short-term disadvantages for a corporation. Yet in the long term it is clear that behaving ethically is the key to sustainable development. When you're faced with an ethical dilemma in which the immoral choice looks appealing, ask yourself three questions:

1 **What will happen when (not if) the action is discovered?** Increasingly, the behavior of corporations is under scrutiny from their various stakeholders—customers, suppliers, stock-

▸▸ MAKING IT HAPPEN

While the two approaches to evaluating behavior described above are clearly different, they can be integrated to create a checklist that will help an individual or group make sound ethical decisions.

- Gather the facts: What is the problem, and what are the potential solutions?
- Define the ethical issues. This is a step that is often neglected, so that the ethical dilemmas raised by a particular decision are never even considered.
- Identify the various stakeholders involved.
- Think through the consequences of each solution: What happiness or harm will be caused?
- Identify the obligations and rights of those potentially affected: What is my duty here? Can I uphold my duty to avoid doing harm and make reasonable efforts toward that end?
- Check your gut feeling.

The last step is crucial. Those involved need to ask themselves what they would feel like if friends or family found out they had been involved in making a particular corporate decision, whether personally or collectively.

  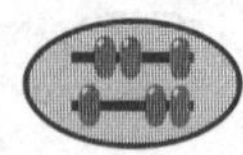   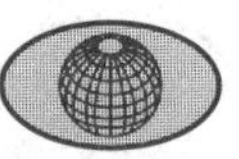   

holders, employees, competitors, regulators, environmental groups, and the general public. People are less willing to keep quiet when they feel an injustice has been done, and the internet and other media give them the means to make their concerns very public, reaching a global audience. Corporations that behave unethically are unlikely to get away with it, and the impact when they are discovered can be catastrophic. This leads to the second question.

2 **Is the decision really in the long-term interests of the corporation?** Many financial services companies in the United Kingdom generated short-term profits in the 1990s by miss selling personal pensions to people who would have been better off staying in their company's pension plan. However, in the long term these companies have suffered by having to repay this money and pay penalties. Most significantly, the practice has eroded public confidence. The same is true of many banks and mortgage brokers in the first part of the 21st century when they sold mortgages to individuals who could not afford to repay their debts. The eventual result was that large numbers defaulted, causing a meltdown in the global financial system beginning in 2008.

3 **Will organizations that behave unethically attract the employees they need?** Corporations that harm society or the environment are actually harming their own employees, including those who are making the decisions. For example, corporations that pour toxins into the air are polluting the air their employees' families breathe. Ultimately, a business relies on its human resources. If a company cannot attract high-quality people because it has a poor public image based on previous unethical behavior, it will certainly flounder.

Behaving ethically is clearly key to the long-term sustainability of any business. Focusing on the triple bottom line—the social and environmental as well as the economic impact of a company—provides the basis for sound stakeholder relationships that can sustain a business into the future.

▸▸ MORE INFO

Books:

Elkington, John. *Cannibals with Forks: The Triple Bottom Line of 21st Century Business*. Gabriola Island, BC: New Society Publishers, 1998.

Janis, Irving L. *Groupthink: Psychological Studies of Policy Decisions and Fiascoes*. 2nd ed. Boston, MA: Houghton Mifflin College, 1982.

Smith, Ken G., and Phil Johnson. *Business Ethics and Business Behaviour*. Boston, MA: International Thomson Business Press, 1996.

Trevino, Linda K., and Katherine A. Nelson. *Managing Business Ethics: Straight Talk About How to Do It Right*. New York: Wiley, 2004.

Velasquez, M. *Business Ethics: Concepts and Cases*. 6th ed. Upper Saddle River, NJ: Prentice Hall, 2006.

Websites:

Aspen Institute: www.aspeninstitute.org

Bentley University Center for Business Ethics: www.bentley.edu/cbe/about

Business in Society Gateway: www.businessinsociety.eu

Institute of Business Ethics: www.ibe.org.uk

International Business Ethics Institute: www.business-ethics.org

See Also:

★ Best Practices in Corporate Social Responsibility (pp. 123–126)
★ CSR: More than PR, Pursuing Competitive Advantage in the Long Run (pp. 147–149)
★ Ethical Funds and Socially Responsible Investment: An Overview (pp. 306–308)
★ The Impact of Climate Change on Business (pp. 775–777)
✔ Business Ethics in Islamic Finance (p. 900)
✔ The Triple Bottom Line (p. 917)

"Management is doing things right; leadership is doing the right things." Peter Drucker

  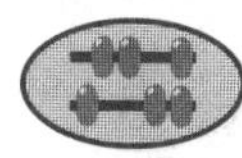 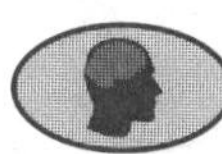  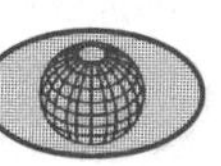   

Corporate Board Structures by Vidhan Goyal

EXECUTIVE SUMMARY

- Firms choose their board structures based on a value-maximizing process.
- Large and outsider-dominated boards are optimal for complex firms (such as large firms, firms with multiple business segments, and complex operational and financial structures). Conversely, small and insider-dominated boards are optimal for small, young, and high-growth firms.
- CEOs who also hold the title of chairman appear to have greater influence on the board. In firms with combined titles, boards do not dismiss poorly performing CEOs at the same rate as they do in firms with CEO and chairman titles vested in different individuals.
- Politically connected directors add substantial value to the firms. They matter more in firms in which politics plays an important role, such as firms where sales to government, exports, and lobbying are greater.
- Women in the boardroom have a positive impact on how firms are governed. Women have fewer attendance problems, and they improve the attendance behavior of male directors.

INTRODUCTION

The job of the board is to control the managerial succession process (involving hiring, assessing, promoting, and if required, dismissing the CEO), and to provide high-level counsel to top management.

There is a widespread skepticism of the effectiveness of boards. Recent accounting scandals at firms such as Enron, WorldCom, and Parmalat have resulted in intense scrutiny of the function of boards. Critics point out that corporate boards have failed primarily because of poor board structures. Top management and board members are tied together though a web of personal and business connections, compromising a board's ability to monitor firms. Michael Jensen puts it more bluntly by stating that, in large US corporations, "even the outside directors basically see themselves as employees of the CEO. . . And this means that, in American companies, the CEO effectively has no boss."[1]

Many scholars, regulators, legislators, and investors are, therefore, calling for a reform of corporate boards. The codes of conduct for good corporate governance frequently recommend that boards should be small, and comprised largely of independent directors.[2] TIAA-CREF, one of the largest pension funds, will only invest in firms that have boards consisting of a majority of outside directors. CalPERS, another large pension fund, recommends that the CEO should be the only inside director on the board. The Sarbanes-Oxley Act of 2002 mandates that audit committees of boards should consist entirely of outside directors. The stock exchanges, such as the NYSE and the NASDAQ, require listed firms to use a majority of outside directors. These intense institutional, regulatory, and legislative pressures are indeed working. YiLin Wu (2004), for example, shows that after firms are publicly named for poor governance by CalPERS, the number of inside board members declines, and board sizes shrink.[3] Governance activists have also been calling for boards to elect their directors annually, to separate the CEO and chairman positions, and for greater diversity on boards.

This article reviews the literature that inquires into whether differences in board structures affects the way in which boards conduct themselves, and whether boards affect firm performance. Board sizes and board compositions differ across firms. Many firms continue to operate with large boards and boards with high insider representation. Boards are often elected on staggered terms, and it is common in large corporations to have the CEO and chairman positions vested in the same individual. If these board structures are suboptimal, as the critics of existing board structures claim, then why do they persist? Should we compel all firms to conform to a single model of board structure?

The emerging academic evidence suggests that the conventional wisdom on board structures is misguided. Recent work suggests that boards are organized according to a value-maximizing calculus. This work carefully highlights the trade-offs associated with different board structures, and shows that the observable variation in board structures reflects careful attention to these trade-offs. Firms choose the board structures that suit their circumstances.

CAUSES AND CONSEQUENCES OF BOARD STRUCTURES

Board Size

It is often asserted that small boards are more effective than large boards. For example, Martin Lipton and Jay Lorsch (1992) argue that, "[W]hen a board has more than 10 members it becomes more difficult for them all to express their ideas and opinions."[4] Michael Jensen (1993) takes up this theme, and conjectures that "keeping boards small can help improve their performance. When boards get beyond seven or eight people they are less likely to function effectively and are easier for the CEO to control."[5] These conjectures are supported by David Yermack (1996), who finds that smaller boards are associated with higher firm value.[6]

However, a careful examination of the forces affecting board structures reveals that firms face a tradeoff in determining board sizes. As boards become larger, the directors collectively possess more information that is important for both monitoring and advisery functions. Each prospective director brings additional information to the board. Consequently, larger boards have more aggregate information about product markets, technology, regulation, financing choices, and mergers and acquisition opportunities.

However, the costs of decision-making increase as boards become large, because of higher coordination costs and the free-rider problems associated with larger boards. With an increase in board size, each member considers its influence on board decisions to be of lesser significance. This reduces the directors' incentives to incur the private costs of acquiring information and actively monitoring top management. In other words, the decision to add a new member to the board is determined by a trade-off between the additional information that a prospective director brings to the board against the increased coordination costs and free-rider problems.

Large firms with more diverse operations find the additional information that a prospective director brings more valuable. Large firms and those with more complex operations have a higher volume of activity and larger information requirements. These firms frequently engage in mergers and acquisitions, and more often use sophisticated financing techniques. Thus, large firms benefit from the specialized information that new board members bring to the firm.

"Many major corporations still play things straight, but a significant and growing number. . .have come to the view that it's okay to manipulate earnings to satisfy what they believe are Wall Street's desires. . .many CEOs think this kind of manipulation is not only okay, but actually their duty." Warren Buffett

     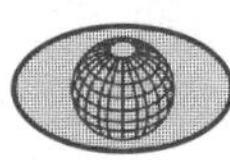   

On the other hand, young, fast-growing firms with lots of intangible assets should optimally keep their boards small. A primary reason is that large information differences exist among managers and outside directors in young and high-growth firms. These information differences increase monitoring costs. By keeping their boards small, firms ensure that board members will have sufficient private interest to bear the high costs of monitoring. In addition, young and high-growth firms will find the slow and deliberate decision-making associated with large boards more costly. Young and high-growth firms, particularly those operating in more volatile environments, face rapid technological changes and unstable market shares. Smaller boards are likely to be more nimble, providing these firms with the flexibility to react quickly.

The empirical evidence is consistent with these predictions. Kenneth Lehn, Sukesh Patro, and Mengxin Zhao (2009) examined a sample of 81 firms that survived over the period 1935–2000, and show that "two variables, firm size and growth opportunities, explain a large amount of cross-sectional and inter-temporal variation in the size and composition of boards."[7] Audra Boone, Laura Field, Jonathan Karpoff, and Charu Raheja (2007) studied the development of corporate boards during the first 10 years after a firm's initial public offering.[8] They found that as firms become larger, older, and start to add more segments, boards become larger. Conversely, boards become smaller as a firm's environment becomes noisier, as R&D expenditures increase, and as growth opportunities become more abundant.

Recent work by Jeffrey Coles, Naveen Daniel and Lalitha Naveen (2008) showed that firm value is increasing in board size in firms with greater advising needs (such as large firms, diversified firms, and high debt firms).[9] Their evidence suggests that certain classes of firms actually benefit from larger boards, contrary to the calls from governance activists requiring all boards to reduce their sizes.

Board Composition

Typically, boards of directors can be divided into two groups—inside directors (management), or outside directors (non-management). Inside directors are full-time employees of the firm, while outside directors are not employed by the firm. Often, outside directors are taken to be independent, but sometimes they are not because of business or personal relationships with the firm or the CEO. On average, outside directors make up about 55–60% of the total directors of large US firms. This proportion has increased in the last decade, particularly for listed firms, since the enactment of the Sarbanes-Oxley Act of 2002, which led to an increase in the number of outside directors on US firms.

Conventional wisdom suggests that outsider-dominated boards are more effective boards. Following up on this conventional wisdom, there is a general push from institutional investors, regulators, and legislators towards more independent boards. Martin Lipton and Jay Lorsch (1992) suggested that there be at least two independent directors for every affiliated director. Michael Jensen (1993) goes even further and writes that, "it is almost impossible for those who report directly to the CEO to participate openly and critically in effective evaluation and monitoring of the CEO. . ., the only inside board member should be the CEO." A large number of codes of conduct for good governance put forth by various countries recommend firms to have a majority of independent directors on their boards.

Similar to our discussion of board sizes, a serious consideration of trade-offs reveals that firms choose the board composition that is optimal for their circumstances. Independent-outsider-dominated boards serve important advisery and monitoring functions. CEOs of large firms, firms with diverse operations, and firms with complex operating and financing structures have greater need for advice. These firms benefit more from the specialized expertise outside directors bring to the firm. At the same time, small, young, high-growth firms will find it optimal to have fewer outside directors. The reason is that information problems are relatively more severe in small and high-growth firms. Outside board members find it relatively costly to obtain information that is relevant for monitoring and advisery functions. These information differences also slow down decision-making associated with outsider-dominated boards in small, young, high-growth firms.

The available evidence suggests that, indeed, outside directors are effective monitors. Michael Weisbach (1988) finds that in firms with outsider-dominated boards, poorly performing CEOs are removed at a relatively higher frequency compared to that in firms with insider-dominated boards.[10] However, the size of these effects remains controversial.

The research cited earlier also finds systematic cross-sectional variation in board independence. Large firms, firms with diversified operations, and high-debt firms have more independent boards. Small, young, and high-growth firms have boards that consist largely of insiders.[11]

Classified Boards

Boards also differ in the terms they offer to their directors. A majority of US firms have classified boards, which stagger the annual election of director slates. With classified boards, directors are grouped into distinct classes (typically three), with a single class of directors standing for re-election each year. Thus, in classified boards, directors serve for three-year terms. In firms with a single class of directors, directors are elected for one-year terms. Almost 60% of major US firms have classified boards.

Many scholars criticize classified board structures for their anti-takeover properties. Paul Gompers, Joy Ishii, and Andrew Metrick (2003) suggest that board classification is "one of the few provisions that clearly retains some deterrent value in modern takeover battles."[12] Similarly, Lucian Bebchuk and Alma Cohen (2005) criticize board classification by arguing that it raises the expected costs of bidders contemplating a hostile change-in-control bid.[13] They argue that by insulating management from takeovers, classified boards entrench management, and, consequently, reduce shareholder wealth.

On the other side of the debate, several commentators point out the advantages of classified boards. By providing multi-year terms, classified boards increase board stability and board independence. If directors are elected to multi-year terms, they will have greater incentives to invest in the information required to monitor managers actively, and to provide advice and guidance to top managers. John Wilcox (2002) argued that classified boards increase board stability, and enhance director independence by insulating directors from outside pressures.[14] Thomas Bates, David Becher, and Michael Lemmon (2008) argued that in takeover situations, board classification can facilitate bargaining for a greater share of transaction surplus.[15]

The costs and benefits of classified boards are likely to vary across firms. Seoungpil Ahn, Vidhan Goyal, and Keshab Shrestha (2009) argued that staggered terms are likely to be most useful when firms have greater advising needs, and outside directors can more effectively monitor managers.[16] Advising needs are often greater in firms with a greater scope and complexity of operations. These firms are more likely to benefit from classified boards. Classified boards tend to be less

"The attitude of disrespect that many executives have today for accurate reporting is a business disgrace. And auditors. . .have done little on the positive side. Though auditors should regard the investing public as their client, they tend to kowtow instead to the managers who choose them and dole out their pay." Warren Buffett

  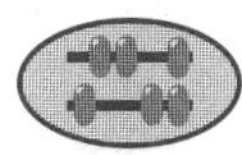   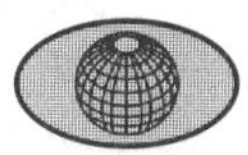   

useful, even value-destroying, in firms where monitoring managers by outside directors is particularly difficult. Outsider-controlled boards are generally less effective in monitoring firms that are relatively opaque (firms with high R&D intensity or with lots of intangible assets). Staggering the terms of these insider-controlled boards would further entrench management, and it is optimal for these firms to have a single class of directors.

The evidence continues to be controversial. It is unclear whether classified boards actually reduce the likelihood of a firm becoming a takeover target, as recent research by Thomas Bates, David Becher, and Michael Lemmon (2008) showed that takeover targets with a classified board are acquired at an equivalent rate to targets with a single class of directors. Moreover, target firms with classified boards do obtain a larger proportional share of the total value gains in merger and acquisition transactions.

Research by Seoungpil Ahn, Vidhan Goyal, and Keshab Shrestha (2009) showed that certain classes of firms actually benefit from board classification, as their market value is higher when they adopt classified boards. In particular, firms with greater advising needs (large and more complex operations) and low monitoring costs (low R&D intensity) have higher market value when they adopt classified boards.

OTHER BOARD ATTRIBUTES

CEO-Chairman Duality

In a large fraction of major US firms, CEOs also hold the title of chairman of the board. Many commentators have called for a prohibition of the CEO serving as chairman, based on the argument that this structure gives CEOs greater control at the expense of other board members. Michael Jensen (1993) argued that "the function of the chairman is to run board meetings and oversee the process of hiring, firing, evaluating, and compensating the CEO. Clearly, the CEO cannot perform this function apart from his or her personal interest. . .for the board to be effective, it is important to separate the CEO and chairman positions."

Indeed, CEOs who also hold the chairman title have greater power. For example, Vidhan Goyal and Chul Park (2002) found that in firms with combined titles, boards do not dismiss poorly performing CEOs at the same rate compared to firms where the CEO and chairman titles are vested in different individuals.[17] Overall, the evidence in the literature confirms that combined titles provide CEOs with greater influence in the firm. There is little evidence, however, that combining or separating CEO and chairman titles leads to any appreciable differences in corporate performance.[18]

Politically Connected Boards

Boards can also add value through the connections they provide with politicians. Anup Agarwal and Charles Knoeber (2001) showed that firms in which politics matter more tend to have a larger number of political directors.[19] These politically experienced directors are more common in firms where sales to government, exports, and lobbying are greater. Similarly, firms that are exposed to costly environmental regulation appoint more directors with backgrounds in law. Firms also respond to changes in regulation by adjusting board composition. In the 1990s, as retail competition in electricity became an increasingly political issue, outside directors with political backgrounds increased in number and importance on the boards of US electric utilities.

The stock prices of firms nominating politically connected directors to their boards increase on the announcement dates of such nominations. Research by Eitan Goldman, Jörg Rocholl, and Jongil So (2009) showed that in the 2000 presidential election in the United States, companies with political connections to the Republican Party increased in value upon the Republican win, while companies with connections to the Democratic Party suffered a drop in value.[20] If politically connected boards add value in countries with strong legal systems, as has been shown in the existing research, the added value of politically connected directors would be even larger in other countries with relatively weak legal systems.

Women in the Boardroom

Boards worldwide are under increasing pressure to choose female directors. Renée Adams and Daniel Ferreira (2008) confronted the issue of whether women directors affect the functioning of boards.[21] The evidence suggests that women have fewer attendance problems than men. In fact, having women directors on boards improves the attendance behavior of male directors. Boards with greater gender diversity meet more often, and offer more performance-based pay to board members. Overall, women have a positive impact on how boards are governed.

CONCLUSION

In the last 10 years, boards have become more independent and diligent. Contributing to this change is the increased pressure from institutional investors, greater regulation, litigation threats from shareholders, and new exchange requirements regarding the composition of boards. Data show that the proportion of outside directors on boards is now larger than in previous decades. Importantly, outside directors nominated to boards since 2000 are relatively more independent, more of them have financial acumen, and more of them are women. The increasing independence of boards has changed the way boards operate. A direct impact of this can be seen in the shortening of CEO tenure in the last decade, compared to earlier periods.

Overall, the academic evidence suggests that a "one size fits all" approach to board structures is misguided. A large part of variation in board structures can be explained by underlying firm characteristics suggesting that there is an underlying economic logic at work in determining these structures. Greater regulation on board structures may force firms towards an inefficient board structure, imposing heavy deadweight costs on firm and their shareholders.

▸▸ MAKING IT HAPPEN

- Large, multidivisional firms should optimally choose bigger and more independent boards. Small, young, fast-growing firms should optimally choose smaller boards.
- Large and multidivisional firms, where boards have a greater number of outside directors, should consider staggering the election of directors. By contrast, small, young, fast-growing firms should consider electing their directors every year.
- The titles of CEO and chairman should be vested in different individuals.
- Politically experienced directors add substantial value in firms that sell to the government, or those which are exposed to costly regulation. Women on boards positively affect the governance of firms. Boards with more women meet more often and offer more performance-based pay to board members.

"A buck in the hand is worth two on the books." David J. Farber

  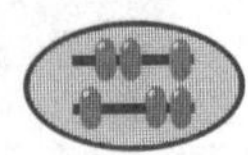   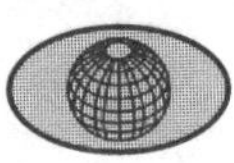   

▸▸ MORE INFO

Books:

Harvard Business Review on Corporate Governance. Boston, MA: Harvard Business School Press, 2000.

Macey, Jonathan R. *Corporate Governance: Promises Kept, Promises Broken*. Princeton, NJ: Princeton University Press, 2008.

Monks, Robert A. G., and Nell Minow. *Corporate Governance*. Chichester, UK: Wiley, 2008.

Articles:

Ahn, S., V. K. Goyal, and K. Shrestha. "The differential effects of classified boards on firm value." Working paper, National University of Singapore, HKUST, and Nanyang Technological University, 2009.

Boone, A. L., L. C. Field, J. M. Karpoff, and C. G. Raheja. "The determinants of corporate board size and composition: An empirical analysis." *Journal of Financial Economics*. 85 (2007): 66–101.

Coles, J. L., N. D. Daniel, and L. Naveen. "Boards: Does one size fit all?" *Journal of Financial Economics* 87 (2008): 329–356.

Goyal, V. K., and C. W. Park. "Board leadership structure and CEO turnover." *Journal of Corporate Finance* 8 (2002): 49–66.

Jensen, M. C. "The modern industrial revolution, exit and the failure of internal control systems." *Journal of Finance* 48 (1993): 831–880.

Lehn, K., S. Patro, and M. Zhao. "Determinants of the size and structure of corporate boards: 1935–2000." *Financial Management* (2009 forthcoming).

Website:

European Corporate Governance Initiative: www.ecgi.com

NOTES

1 "US corporate governance: Accomplishments and failings: A discussion with Michael Jensen and Robert Monks." *Journal of Applied Corporate Finance*. (Spring/Summer 2008): 28–46.

2 The codes of conduct for good governance can be accessed from the homepage of the European Corporate Governance Initiative (www.ecgi.org).

3 Wu, YiLin. "The impact of public opinion on board structure changes, director career progression, and CEO turnover: Evidence from CalPERS' corporate governance program." *Journal of Corporate Finance* 10 (2004): 199–227.

4 Lipton, M., and J. W. Lorsch. "A modest proposal for improved corporate governance." *Business Lawyer* 48 (1992): 59–77.

5 Jensen, M. C. (1993).

6 Yermack, D. "Higher market valuation of companies with a small board of directors." *Journal of Financial Economics* 40 (1996): 185–212.

7 Lehn, K., S. Patro, and M. Zhao (2009, forthcoming).

8 Boone, A. *et al.* (2007): 66–101.

9 Coles, J. L., N. D. Daniel, and L. Naveen (2008): 329–356.

10 Weisbach, M. S. "Outside directors and CEO turnover." *Journal of Financial Economics* 20 (1988): 431–460.

11 See Boone *et al.* (2007), Coles *et al.* (2008), and Lehn *et al.* (2009).

12 Gompers, P., J. Ishii, and A. Metrick. "Corporate governance and equity prices." *Quarterly Journal of Economics*. 118 (2003): 107–155.

13 Bebchuk, L. A., and A. Cohen. "The costs of entrenched boards." *Journal of Financial Economics* 78 (2005), 409–433.

14 Wilcox, J. C. "Two cheers for staggered boards." *Corporate Governance Adviser* 10 (2002): 1–5.

15 Bates, T. W., D. A. Becher, and M. L. Lemmon. "Board classification and managerial entrenchment: Evidence from the market for corporate control." *Journal of Financial Economics* 87 (2008): 656–677.

16 Ahn, S., V. K. Goyal, and K. Shrestha (2009).

17 Goyal, V. K., and C. W. Park (2002).

18 See Brickley, J. A., J. L. Coles, and G. Jarrell. "Leadership structure: Separating the CEO and chairman of the board." *Journal of Corporate Finance* 3 (1997): 189–220.

19 Agarwal, A., and C. R. Knoeber. "Do some outside directors play a political role?" *Journal of Law and Economics* 44 (2001): 179–198.

20 Goldman, E., and J. Rocholl. So, J. "Do politically connected boards affect firm value?" *Review of Financial Studies* (2009, forthcoming).

21 Adams, R. B., and D. Ferreira. "Women in the boardroom and their impact on governance and performance." Working paper, University of Queensland, London School of Economics, CEPR, and ECGI (2008).

"Insanity is often the logic of an accurate mind overtasked." Oliver Wendell Holmes

  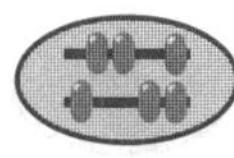   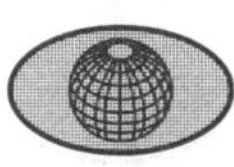   

Viewpoint: Jonathan M. Karpoff

The Importance of Trust—In Everything

INTRODUCTION

Jonathan M. Karpoff has particular interest in what drives executives to commit corporate crimes and misdemeanors. Here, he explains how a breakdown of trust can have long-term repercussions for individual corporations and how it led to the wider financial collapse of 2008–2009.

A professor of finance at the University of Washington's Michael G. Foster School of Business, Karpoff is also associate editor of a number of academic journals including the *Journal of Finance*. Karpoff won the best paper award in the CRSP Forum at the University of Chicago in both 2006 and 2008 for his research into corporate and financial scandals. Karpoff was the founding director of the University of Washington's environmental management program and was director of its CFO Forum from 2004–2007.

Karpoff's extra-curricular activities include rock climbing, mountaineering, and adventure skate skiing in the Cascade Mountains. He received his BA (1978) from the University of Alaska/Anchorage, and his MA (1980) and PhD (1982) degrees from UCLA.

Most investors had a terrible 2008. But stockholders in Xerox Corporation have had a bad *decade*. Xerox's story contains an important lesson because, in addition to a decreasing demand for copiers, its struggles have been compounded by a lack of trust in its financial reporting.

Xerox's share price was flying high until October 8, 1999, when the firm announced that its quarterly earnings would fall short of expectations. As investors soon discovered, the company's prior strong financial performance had been a mirage.

Since early 1997, managers had manipulated the books by recognizing as current revenue its customers' promises to pay on long-term equipment lease contracts. The manipulation worked for a couple of years, and the share price peaked at US$59.01 on May 3, 1999. But revenue-acceleration schemes like that at Xerox have a way of catching up with the perpetrators. Eventually, Xerox had to restate its earnings to reflect the lower revenues that it had actually received.

Xerox's financial reporting misconduct proved costly. Controlling for market movements, Xerox's market capitalization fell by a cumulated amount of US$5 billion on the days that news of its misconduct was first reported to investors. My colleagues Scott Lee, Jerry Martin, and I have determined that US$1.14 billion of this loss represents the adjustment back to Xerox's pre-inflated level—the market cap that Xerox would have attained had its books never been cooked in the first place. Another US$523 million of the loss is due to penalties imposed by the SEC and a class action lawsuit by angry investors.

But most of Xerox shareholders' loss—US$3.34 billion or 67% of the total—represents something more powerful than even the disciplinary arm of the SEC. It is the direct financial cost from the breakdown in investors' trust in the company and the transparency of its financial reports.

We all know the value of a good reputation. Indeed, as parents one of our greatest tasks is to instill in our children an appreciation for honesty and integrity. But recent research has shed new light on the role of trust and reputation in business. In many cases—as with Xerox—researchers can even put a dollar value on the loss in reputation that comes when a firm behaves badly and loses the trust of its customers, suppliers, and investors.

As I use them here, "trust" and "reputation" are not fuzzy, feel-good terms. By reputation I mean the present value of the income that accrues from repeat business on profitable terms. And repeat business comes from trust. Firms that act opportunistically undermine that trust, and face tougher terms of trade with counterparties, who learn to be wary of such opportunism.

By tougher terms of trade, I mean such things as higher borrowing costs and lower sales. In recent research, John Graham, Si Li, and Jaiping Qiu show that firms that restate earnings subsequently face greater borrowing restrictions, including higher loan rates, when seeking loans from banks. Deborah Murphy, Ronald Shrieves, and Samuel Tibbs show that firms caught in various types of misconduct, including misreporting, suffer a double whammy: they experience a higher cost of capital and they lose sales.

Xerox's experience is by no means unusual. In January, Satyam Computer Services' share price fell more than 88% in the two days after its founder and chairman, B. Ramalinga Raju, disclosed that the Hyderabad-based firm's assets had been inflated by more than US$1 billion. Parmalat, the Italian dairy company was declared bankrupt in December 2003, in the wake of revelations of financial misconduct involving its top officers. Shares in Ahold, the Dutch grocery chain, dropped two-thirds of their value upon revelation that a subsidiary's profits were overstated by US$500 million. And in 2007, Royal Dutch Shell settled investor lawsuits for US$352.6m (£178.3m) for previously inflating its oil and gas reserves by 20%.

Each of these firms reflects the pattern documented in a recent study that I conducted with Scott Lee and Jerry Martin. Using data from all firms disciplined by the US SEC for financial misrepresentation, we found that shareholders lose a tremendous amount of value when their firms are caught cooking the books.

The average firm loses 38% of its market capitalization. Even more importantly, two-thirds of this loss is from lost reputation. The lost reputation is the decrease in present value as these firms face a higher cost of capital and less attractive terms when trading with their (now) more skeptical customers and suppliers.

Stated differently, managers are putting a lot at risk when they cook the books. Financial manipulation can inflate prices over the short term. But when the manipulation is discovered, the firm loses much more than the short-term price inflation.

"Our trust in those who made the financial system work has been decimated-no less than we would lose faith in the water company if the taps started dripping cyanide." Peggy Drexler

For every dollar the stock price was artificially inflated, the firm loses this dollar plus US$3 more. Of this additional loss, most is from lost reputation (the rest is from legal pelaties.). This is the real impact of financial misrepresentation on the firm's long-term operations. By cheating investors, the firm faces a higher cost of financial capital until it can reestablish trust and a new reputation for financial transparency—and that can take a very long time.

The reputational effects for managers and directors also are severe. In a related study, Lee, Martin, and I found that over 92% of executives involved in financial misrepresentations lose their jobs. Most are fired. Fully 42% are barred from serving as officers or directors, and 28% are indicted on criminal charges. Directors also have a lot of reputation at stake. Anil Shivdasani and Eliezer Fich found that directors of firms that are sued for financial misconduct become tainted. As a result, they lose 50% of their seats on other boards, on average.

TRUST MATTERS

A firm's trust and reputation are important not only for its investors. They affect the firm's relationships with all counterparties. Culinary gourmets might sneer at McDonalds's hamburgers, but those burgers sell by the millions because customers know what they will get when they walk through the golden arches. That trust from customers—and the profit stream that accrues because of it—is McDonalds's reputational capital. It is every bit as valuable as the firm's proprietary method of deep-frying French fries.

Different firms invest in, and accumulate, different levels of reputation. Johnson & Johnson, the maker of Tylenol, has a huge reputational investment in Tylenol, which it protects through elaborate quality control measures. Generic producers of acetaminophen, in contrast, have little reputational capital. Customers know this, and infer that Johnson & Johnson has much greater incentives to control the quality of its product. That is, Johnson & Johnson has more reputational capital at stake. As we see in sales figures, some people are willing to pay for the extra assurance of quality provided by the Tylenol™ brand name.

A good reputation encourages customers to buy from the firm and investors to buy the stock. But reputation is a double-edged sword, because any hint that the firm has failed to provide the expected quality imposes a large penalty. This is especially true for firms that defraud or cheat their customers or investors. Businesses that cheat their customers lose future sales. Those that cheat suppliers or employees find it difficult to keep their inventory stocked and workforce productive. And, as we have seen, those that cheat their investors by misreporting financial statements find it difficult to raise new capital.

ABSENCE OF TRUST

The importance of trust illuminates the issues at the core of the current financial crisis. Fraudsters like Bernie Madoff exploit other people's trust. What is remarkable about the Madoff experience is not only the size and devastation of his pyramid scheme, but the fact that he had acquired —and sacrificed—a huge amount of reputational capital.

Madoff's scam could be so large only because—as a highly respected member of the financial community and former chairman of NASDAQ—he had such a good reputation. Had he acted honestly, Madoff could have enjoyed a lifetime of wealth and social prestige about which most people can only dream. By perpetrating a fraud, in contrast, Madoff enjoyed years of the appearance of phenomenal success, but at a cost of all his reputational capital.

Beyond the Madoff scandal, trust—or its lack—lies at the heart of the broader financial crisis. The crisis has many causes, including overleveraged financial institutions, bad loans, a housing bubble, and interlocking credit default swaps. But what shocked central bankers around the world into pumping billions of dollars into the financial system was the specter of a massive credit crunch. And the credit crunch is, in essence, a breakdown of trust. The reason anyone lends money is the trust that they will be repaid. When such trust evaporates, so does the willingness to lend.

Trust is central to the financial crisis. The fear of a deep worldwide recession is exacerbated by the prospect of a credit freeze, which in turn results from the breakdown in trust between lenders and borrowers. Many firms were highly leveraged—indeed, the average asset-to-equity ratio of US securities broker-dealers in the middle of last year was approximately 32, an historically high ratio. European banks' leverage ratios were even higher, approaching 40. With a decrease in asset values, many financial institutions sought at once to deleverage by dumping assets and hoarding cash.

Many of these same firms' assets were of uncertain quality. Firms such as Lehman Brothers and Washington Mutual sought short-term financing to weather the storm, but potential counterparties could not determine the value of these firms' collateral, or the likelihood that they were solvent.

Both effects—high leverage and poor asset quality—eroded trust in many firms' abilities to pay off new loans. This breakdown of trust has increased the cost of private borrowing for both financial and industrial firms, increasing operational costs and dramatically slowing economic investment and growth. Trust, or its absence, continues to be at the centre of the financial crisis.

REPUTATION IS ALL

Business gurus frequently advise us to do well by treating our customers, suppliers, and investors well. This is sound advice, but its impact is limited by the absence of hard data to back it up. The paucity of data may

Figure 1. Xerox's cumulated market-adjusted returns from January 1997 through December 2008

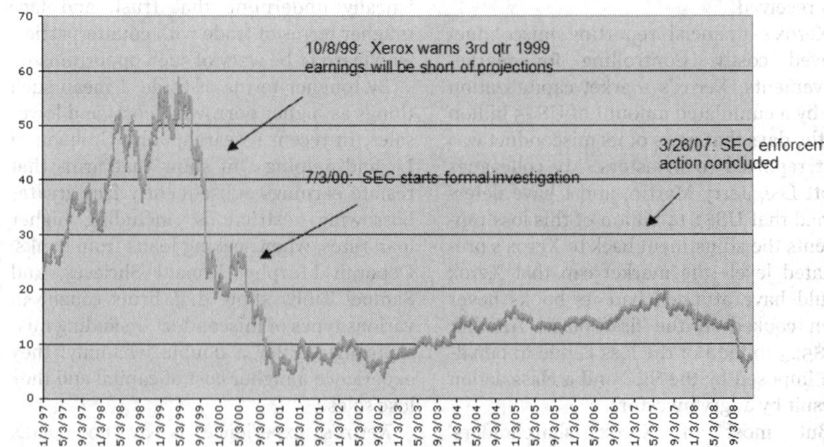

"The argument that rigorous oversight will somehow stifle Wall Street's "creativity" is no longer convincing. Any system that permits a scam artist like Madoff to deceive, not just widows and orphans, but also sophisticated investors . . . isn't a market at all; it's a shooting gallery." Charles Handy

  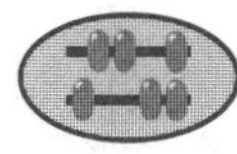   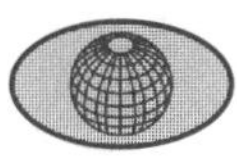   

be one reason executives frequently underestimate the importance of trust and the cost of squandering their firm's reputation with investors or customers.

There is a story, perhaps apocryphal, that years ago Ford Motor Company calculated the financial costs and benefits of reengineering the gas tank in its Pinto automobile. On paper, the costs appeared be greater than the benefits, so no change was made. Several Pintos subsequently were involved in horrific accidents that resulted in large punitive damage awards. Ford had anticipated such costs in its calculations.

What the car company had not considered, however, was the reputational cost from having a potentially lethal car in its fleet. In researching the impact of punitive damage-seeking lawsuits, John Lott and I discovered that the direct cost of a damage award is only a small portion of the total cost to the paying company. The mere publicity of the lawsuit and the punitive award scares away customers and investors, decreasing the firm's future sales, and increasing its cost of capital.

To the extent that this story is true, Ford's Pinto experience highlights a managerial experience that is all too common: underestimating the importance of trust and the value of reputation. Events or actions that undermine trust in their firms—from accounting irregularities, to charges of fraud, to lawsuits seeking punitive awards—scare away customers, suppliers, and investors. Such events have repercussions that extend far beyond the immediate crisis because they affect counterparties' future willingness to do business with the firm.

Managing a firm's reputation—that is, building a track record that attracts customers and investors—is not simply a feel-good concept from the latest trendy management book. Rather, it is a core competency that has real and measurable impact on firm operations and value.

▸▸ MORE INFO

Articles:

Alexander, Cindy. "On the nature of the reputational penalty for corporate crime: Evidence." *Journal of Law and Economics* 42 (1999): 489–526.

Fich, Eliezer M., and Anil Shivdasani. "Financial fraud, director reputation, and shareholder wealth." *Journal of Financial Economics* 86:2 (2007): 306–336.

Graham, John R., Si Li, and Jaiping Qiu. "Corporate misreporting and bank loan contracting, *Journal of Financial Economics*, 89:1 (2008): 44–61.

Karpoff, Jonathan, D. Scott Lee, and Gerald S. Martin. "The consequences to managers for financial misrepresentation." *Journal of Financial Economics* 88:2 (2008): 193–215.

Karpoff, Jonathan, D. Scott Lee, and Gerald S. Martin. "The cost to firms of cooking the books." *Journal of Financial and Quantitative Analysis* 43:3 (2008): 581–612.

Karpoff, Jonathan M., and John R. Lott, Jr. "The reputational penalty firms bear from committing criminal fraud." *Journal of Law and Economics* 36 (October 1993): 757–802.

Karpoff, Jonathan M., and John R. Lott, Jr. "On the determinants and importance of punitive damage awards." *Journal of Law and Economics* 62:1 (1999): 527–573.

Murphy, Deborah L., Ronald E. Shrieves, and Samuel L. Tibbs. "Understanding the penalties associated with corporate misconduct: An empirical examination of earnings and risk." *Journal of Financial Quantitative Analysis* 44:1 (2009): 55–83. Online at: ssrn.com/abstract=993479

See Also:

★ Effective Financial Reporting and Auditing: Importance and Limitations (pp. 623–625)
★ The Rationale of International Financial Reporting Standards and their Acceptance by Major Countries (pp. 709–711)
★ What Are the Leading Causes of Financial Restatements? (pp. 729–731)
✔ IFRS: The Basics (p. 1036)
✔ Key Accounting Standards and Organizations (p. 1038)
✔ The Ten Accounting Principles (p. 1050)

"Brands are all about trust. You buy the brand because you consider it a friend." Michael Perry

  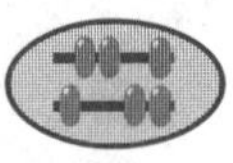   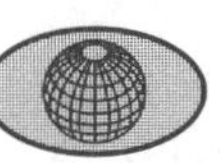   

Corporate Responsibility in a Global World: Marrying Investment in Human Capital with Focus on Costs by Angela Baron

EXECUTIVE SUMMARY

- A human capital approach to the management of people shifts the emphasis of people management from minimization of cost to maximization of return on investment.
- Human capital is an important element of intellectual capital, and hence the market value of an organization.
- The importance of human capital has increased as the shift to knowledge-based work and a knowledge-based economy has accelerated.
- Human capital management combines information on the value and contribution of people with management processes, to direct their efforts and behavior.
- Human capital information can be collected on a number of levels, all of which have value to the organization.
- At its highest level, human capital information can produce meaningful insights to enhance business decision-making, or assist the achievement of strategic objectives.

INTRODUCTION

Love it or loathe it, the term human capital has entered the HR vocabulary for keeps. The term is much criticized for implying that people can be subjected to the same rules as more traditional forms of capital, regardless of personal aspirations and objectives. Yet the same grounds for criticism are also the impetus for a fundamental shift in organizational thinking in terms of the people employed. Organizations that adopt a human capital approach to the management of their workforce immediately shift that workforce from the cost to the asset side of the balance sheet. People become assets to be invested in, and from which a return that can be maximized is expected, as opposed to a set of costs to be kept to a minimum.

Immediately the focus of people is asset-based, the organization needs to rethink a whole set of assumptions and people-management actions. When organizations treat people as costs, they assume:

- that people need to be incentivized to work harder;
- that people should be bought in with the highest possible value for the lowest possible cost;
- that it is only worth investing in training if there is an immediate need;
- that the removal of people from the organization is primarily a cost decision.

When people are assets, organizations assume:

- people will work better when they have interesting and challenging work to do;
- people work harder when they are motivated and committed to their work, experiencing high levels of satisfaction;
- people should be brought into the organization on the basis of their potential to develop and grow;
- investment in training and skills is worthwhile, if there is likely to be a return on that investment in the medium to long term;
- when people leave the organization, there are knowledge retention and capacity issues to be considered and managed.

This, therefore, has given rise to a whole new set of rules about how we recruit, develop, and finally exit people from the organization.

A DEFINITION OF HUMAN CAPITAL

There have been many definitions of human capital over the years. However, there now seems to be general agreement that human capital is the knowledge, skills, abilities, and capacity to develop and innovate possessed by people in an organization. It is an aspect of intellectual capital—the stocks and flows of knowledge available to an organization—and is associated with the concepts of social capital—the knowledge derived from relationships within and outside the organization—and

CASE STUDY

Nationwide Building Society

Nationwide has been investigating the links between employee commitment, customer commitment, and business performance for some years. Its objectives were to:

- establish the key drivers of customer commitment;
- measure the impact of improved employee commitment on customer commitment, and business performance;
- identify activities that can be undertaken, at corporate and local levels, to leverage this knowledge, and bring about business improvements.

It collected data from four main sources:

- HR data: from PeopleSoft;
- employee opinion data: from the "Viewpoint" survey;
- customer satisfaction and commitment data: from the "Member Perception" questionnaire;
- business performance data: from the Operational Sales database.

Analysis revealed that employee commitment and length of service were the most critical factors driving customer commitment and sales. Further modeling demonstrated that areas generating the best performance were also those with the highest average length of service.

It was then possible to investigate further the drivers of employee commitment, and means of increasing employee tenure. Five key drivers were found to have the most effect on employee retention, which in turn affect positively customer satisfaction and business performance, as follows:

- employees' perceptions of pay levels;
- average age of employees;
- levels of resource during peak times;
- understanding and promoting the values of Nationwide;
- management behaviors emphasized in Nationwide's organizational development program, PRIDE.

(*Note*: The full version of this case study is available in the CIPD guide, "Human capital reporting: An internal perspective," which can be downloaded from www.cipd.co.uk/humancapital.)

  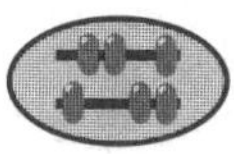   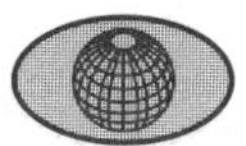   

Figure 1. Human capital as an intangible asset

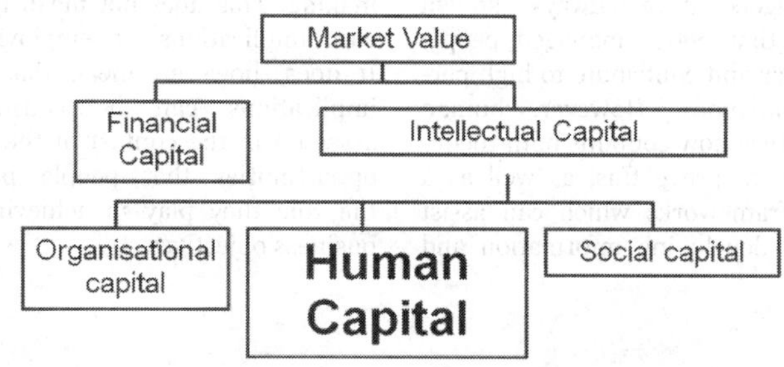

organizational capital, the institutionalized knowledge possessed by an organization which is stored in databases, manuals, etc. It hence contributes to the market value of an organization through its contribution to intellectual value, which also accounts for the value of brand and reputation. Our research at the Chartered Institute & Personnel (and Development) (CIPD) has resulted in the following definition of human capital (Figure 1), viewed as an element of intangible value, and it is this definition that has shaped our work to date.

Human capital management is important because it enables organizations to make more productive use of people through measurements, analysis, and evaluation rather than guesswork. It provides guidance on the development of HR and business strategies which enable improvements in levels of business performance, and higher levels of engagement to be achieved by such means as better selection, training, and leadership. It encourages the initiation of processes for the assessment and satisfaction of future people requirements. It provides the basis for developing policies and practices which enhance the inherent capacities of people—their contributions, potential, and employability—by providing learning, and continuous development opportunities. It also shapes the way in which people share and apply their knowledge. Therefore, if human capital management processes are aligned with business processes, it can ensure that the effort and behavior of people are focused on the things that are important for the business, and the achievement of strategic objectives.

The impact human capital can have on markets is huge. In advanced economies, the only distinctive asset which cannot be imitated easily is the skills, talent, and know-how of people. The 1999 Competitiveness White Paper, "Building the Knowledge-Driven Economy," published by Peter Mandelson while UK Secretary of State for Trade and Industry, argued that "...we will only compete successfully in the future if we create an economy that is genuinely knowledge-driven." It is no accident, therefore, that interest in human capital, how to measure it, and how to manage it has increased as the knowledge-intensive sector of the economy has expanded.

WHAT INFORMATION SHOULD BE COLLECTED TO INFORM HUMAN CAPITAL MANAGEMENT?

Effective human capital management relies on credible and appropriate data, which informs managers of the drivers of individual performance, and enables informed business decision-making on the people capacity available to implement strategy, and achieve strategic objectives. There are several levels at which data can be collected, which are described in Table 1 below.

Table 1. Levels of human capital data collection and analysis

	Level		
	Basic	*Intermediate*	*Higher*
Action	Collect basic input data, e.g., absence, employee turnover Identify useful data already available, such as data from pay reviews, performance management, job evaluation, training, the recruitment process Use this data to communicate essential information to managers about absence, turnover, or accident levels, compared by department look for trends or patterns in the data, and investigate their causes	Design data collection for specific human capital needs. For example, conduct an employee attitude survey to measure satisfaction, or follow up on training activity to monitor implementation and use Use this data to inform the design and implementation of people-management policies and processes Look for correlations between data, for example, whether high levels of job satisfaction occur when certain HR practices are in place, such as performance management, career management, or flexible working Communicate the value of processes to line managers, and identify specific actions to improve people management	Identify key performance indicators relating to the business strategy, and design and implement data collection processes to measure against them Feed both quantitative and qualitative information into an analysis model, such as a balanced scorecard Provide managers with indicators on a range of measures designed to inform them on performance and progress in their department Accompany this with specific actions to be taken, informed by the resulting human capital data Interpret and communicate data in ways that will be meaningful to a range of audiences
Outcome	Measures of efficiency and effectiveness Basic information for managers on headcount, make-up of the workforce, and so on Identification of any action that might be needed as a result of these measures, for example to reduce accident rates, to improve the diversity profile of the workforce, or to reduce absence	Measures of process Information to help design the HR model that is most likely to contribute to performance Communication to managers, not just how to implement processes but with accompanying information on why they are important, and what they can achieve	Identification of the drivers of business performance Information that will enable better-informed decision-making, both internally on the management of people, and externally on the progress with regard to strategy

"Knowledge is power." Sir Francis Bacon

The collection, development, and analysis of human capital data is still a relatively new process for the majority of organizations. Most of those making systematic efforts to collect information to describe the contribution of people are using existing data, often collected for another purpose. So, for example, most organizations collect data on absence, retention, training provision, pay, health, and safety (i.e., the number of accidents). This is the basic level of data, and can be very useful in terms of identifying patterns, or trends, and informing management action. It can also be important for informing external stakeholders about their commitment and understanding of factors which might impact on future performance, such as retention of key staff, and management of risk.

However, higher levels of data are more likely to be of use to the investment community, particularly data likely to provide insight into the drivers of business performance. It is these factors which can enable informed decision-making, both assessing the impact of cost, and the return on investment in people. Although many organizations are making huge progress in this area, it represents a significant investment in terms of time and effort.

CONCLUSION

Good managers have always known instinctively that better managed people perform better and contribute to high performance outcomes. However, human capital literature now contains both theory and evidence to prove this, as well as a number of frameworks which can assist managers in developing information and insight to inform their business decision-making. This does not mean ignoring the cost implications of employing people. It does, however, mean that these cost implications can be considered and assessed in the context of the investment opportunities that people present and the role they play in achieving strategic business objectives.

▸▸ MORE INFO

Books:

Baron, Angela, and Michael Armstrong. *Human Capital Management: Achieving Added Value through People*. London: Kogan Page, 2007.

Kinnie, Nicholas, Juani Swart, Mark Lund, Shad Morris, Scott A. Snell, and Sung-Choon Kang. *Managing People and Knowledge in Professional Service Firms*. London: CIPD, 2006.

Article:

Kinnie, Nicholas, and Juani Swart. "The alchemists." *People Management* 12:7 (April 6, 2006): 42–45.

Websites:

Chartered Institute of Personnel and Development, section on human capital: www.cipd.co.uk/humancapital

Human Capital Management magazine: www.humancapitalmanagement.org

Institute for Employment Studies: www.employment-studies.co.uk

PricewaterhouseCoopers: www.pwc.com

Society for Human Resource Management: www.shrm.org

  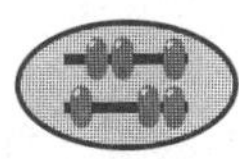   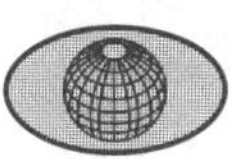   

CSR: More than PR, Pursuing Competitive Advantage in the Long Run by John Surdyk

EXECUTIVE SUMMARY

- Consumers increasingly expect companies to act in "responsible" ways.
- Because of their scale and reach, companies have unusual opportunities to address social concerns in innovative and productive ways.
- Evidence suggests that corporate social responsibility (CSR) practices produce long-term benefits with financial performance gains.
- Advancing CSR is made easier with modern risk management tools, reporting guidelines, and committed leadership and employees.

THE EMERGENCE OF CORPORATE SOCIAL RESPONSIBILITY

Global greenhouse gas emissions continue to rise. Diseases wreak havoc across entire continents. An entire host of seemingly intractable issues confront governments throughout the world, which are sometimes unable to effect positive changes. With the emergence of companies as some of the most powerful institutions for innovation and social change, more shareholders, regulators, customers, and corporate partners are increasingly interested in understanding the impact of these organizations' regular activities upon the community and its natural resources. With the world's largest 800 nonfinancial companies accounting for as much economic output as the world's poorest 144 countries, the importance of these organizations in addressing trade imbalances, income inequality, resource degradation, and other issues is clear. While companies are not tasked with the responsibilities of governments, their scale and their ability to influence these issues necessitate their involvement and create opportunities for forward-looking organizations to exercise great leadership.

In public opinion surveys, consumers admit that they prefer to buy products and services from companies they feel are socially responsible (72%) and that they sell shares of those companies they feel don't pass muster (27%). Challenging Nobel laureate Milton Friedman's notion that companies' only responsibility is to make profit, executives are increasingly seeking ways to combine economic gain with social well-being in ways that will produce more customer loyalty, better relationships with regulators, and a host of other advantages. CSR practices may, in fact, prove pivotal to the success of a company.

Sometimes described simply as "doing well by doing good," corporate social responsibility initiatives gained traction in the 1990s as consumer interest in management practices erupted in the wake of several substantial incidences of executive malfeasance and of escalating environmental challenges. While originally focused on environmental factors, CSR reports increasingly include social measures. Likewise, company leaders today express interest in business models that weave together explicit goals for profit, environmental performance, and social factors, at the same time recognizing that these efforts will likely yield no short-term financial benefits but rather long-term performance improvements.

A CLOUDY CONCEPT BEGINS TO CRYSTALLIZE

The phrase "corporate social responsibility" (CSR) describes both:

- A social movement;
- A collection of specific management practices and initiatives.

Business leaders, government professionals, and others use these principles and tools to assess and report on organizations' impact on society.

Globally, CSR is an evolving concept without a clear definition, yet it describes a set of corporate obligations and practices somewhere on the spectrum between traditional charitable giving on the one hand and merely strict compliance with laws on the other.

While operating definitions remain elusive, the term "CSR" generally refers to a company's efforts to include social and environmental concerns explicitly in its decision-making along with a commitment to increasing the organization's positive impact on society. Beneath these efforts is a realization that improved CSR reporting and better risk-management systems generally promote the transparency and accountability essential to good company governance and improved financial performance. These systems, in effect, enable a company to anticipate and respond to opportunities when it senses that society's expectations aren't being met by its performance.

BENEFITS FROM CSR

The benefits of corporate social performance reporting spread over an entire organization. Areas of greatest gain for a company's

Table 1. Benefits of CSR

Business Area	*Reduce Costs*	*Create Value*
License to Operate	More favorable government relations; reduced shareholder activism; reduced risk of lawsuits	Increased community support for the company's operations ("a bank account of goodwill")
Reputational Capital	Reduced negative consumer activism/boycotts; positive media coverage/"free advertising"; positive "word-of-mouth" advertising	Increased customer attraction; increased customer retention
Human Resources	Increased employee retention and morale	Enhanced recruitment; increased productivity
Finance		Social screens and investment funds are attracted to companies perceived as good social performers

CASE STUDY

Beginning with $1,000 in a garage in 1990, Greg Erickson founded a new energy bar company, Clif Bars, Inc., in Berkeley, California. Committed to exercising environmental stewardship, Greg made expensive investments in organic ingredients and renewable energy while pursuing progressive employment practices such as six-month sabbaticals for employees. Refusing acquisition overtures from other companies, Clif Bars' commitments to corporate responsibility laid a strong, long-term foundation for the growing $100+ million company and its meteoric rise against titans like Kellogg and Quaker Oats.

"Society never advances. It recedes as fast on one side as it gains on the other. Society acquires new arts, and loses old instincts." Ralph Waldo Emerson

   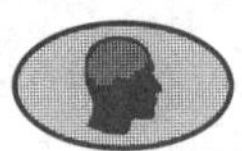  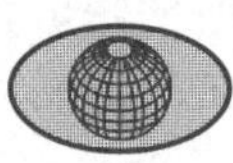   

market value, operational efficiency, access to capital, and brand value typically come from:

- Establishing ethics, values, and principles for the organization;
- Improving environmental processes or reducing environmental impact;
- Improving workplace conditions.

Other efforts, such as better governance measures, also tend to yield positive benefits for companies.

MAKING CSR REAL

Traditional rhetoric about "private versus public" responsibilities is diminishing while companies operate more and more with an understanding of an acknowledged (if tacit) role to play in society. In the United States many people feel companies should be doing more to improve society through changing their business practices.

Although implementing CSR initiatives in modern companies is a daunting prospect because of their increasingly complex and global operations, many CSR management frameworks have moved onto the international stage. Approximately 400 companies—including many of the world's largest—use all or some of the Global Reporting Initiative (GRI), and combined environmental and social reports are increasingly common alongside companies' regular sustainability reports. Launched in 1997 by the Coalition of Environmentally Responsible Economies, the GRI report contains 50 core environmental, social, and economic indicators for a broad range of companies. It also offers additional modules with distinct metrics for companies, depending on their industry sector and operations. The price range for producing a report spans from $100,000 for a basic GRI to more than $3 million for complex organizations like Shell.

Other major initiatives and reporting standards provide helpful guidance and principles; among them are:

- The United Nations Global Compact;
- Global Environmental Management Initiative;
- International Standards Organization guidelines (for example, ISO14000).

The continued growth of the socially responsible investment movement, especially in the United States and Europe, is stimulating companies' adoption of GRI and other instruments. In the United States alone, capital available to socially responsible companies reached $2.29 trillion in 2005.

CHALLENGES TO CSR

The majority of corporations in the world do not produce any reports on their CSR practices. Executives often cite several concerns, including:

- Fear that they may undertake a CSR program while competitors do not, meaning they incur expenses and refocus management talent that may put them at a competitive disadvantage.
- No feeling of urgency to act on many societal issues.
- No accepted standard of what type of information should be reported or at what depth.
- Concern that if they only achieve goals they largely establish for themselves, they may appear only half-heartedly committed—or they may even open themselves to lawsuits.
- Trouble identifying stakeholders, meaning the audience for their reports may be ambiguous, which may, in turn, undermine the quality of the reporting generally.
- Belief that traditional philanthropy fulfils an organization's commitment to society.
- Reporting on the entire scope of a company's impact on society and the environment is increasingly complex.

Recognizing "that one size does not fit all," more companies are exercising greater discretion in reporting initiatives to highlight key information for their sector or the parts of the world in which they operate.

HOW TO GET STARTED

These principles must be grounded in an organization for CSR management frameworks to yield their maximum benefit.

▸▸ MAKING IT HAPPEN

There is no consensus among government bodies, companies, or consumers about what precisely constitutes a definition—or even a consistent set of management topics—under the umbrella of corporate social responsibility. Several intergovernmental bodies, company federations, and nonprofits have advanced competing definitions. Among the most influential are:

- *World Bank*. "Corporate Social Responsibility, or CSR, is the commitment of business to contribute to sustainable economic development, working with employees, their families, the local community, and society at large to improve their quality of life, in ways that are both good for business and good for development."
- *World Economic Forum*. "Corporate Citizenship can be defined as the contribution a company makes to society through its core business activities, its social investment and philanthropy programs, and its engagement in public policy. The manner in which a company manages its economic, social, and environmental relationships, as well as those with different stakeholders, in particular shareholders, employees, customers, business partners, governments, and communities, determine its impact."
- *Business for Social Responsibility*. "CSR is operating a business in a manner that meets or exceeds the ethical, legal, commercial, and public expectations that society has of business. CSR is seen by leadership companies as more than a collection of discrete practices and occasional gestures, or initiatives motivated by marketing, public relations, or other business benefits. Rather, it is viewed as a comprehensive set of policies, practices, and programs that are integrated throughout business operations, and decision-making processes that are supported and rewarded by top management."
- *Center for Corporate Citizenship at Boston College*. "Corporate Citizenship refers to the way a company integrates basic social values with everyday business practices, operations, and policies. A corporate citizenship company understands that its own success is intertwined with societal health and well-being. Therefore, it takes into account its impact on all stakeholders, including employees, customers, communities, suppliers, and the natural environment."
- *International Business Leaders Forum*. "Corporate Social Responsibility means open and transparent business practices that are based on ethical values and respect for employees, communities, and the environment. It is designed to deliver sustainable value to society at large as well as to shareholders."
- *United Nations*. While not advocating a particular definition of corporate social responsibility, the United Nations uses the term "global corporate citizenship" to describe international companies' obligations to respect human rights, improve labor conditions, and protect the environment. The UN Research Institute for Sustainable Development, which follows academic work in this area, typically concentrates on ethical issues and principles guiding how a company's management engages stakeholders.

"Corporate courage is usually no greater than personal courage." Edward Teller

     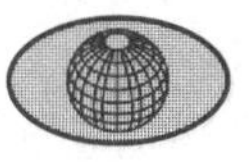   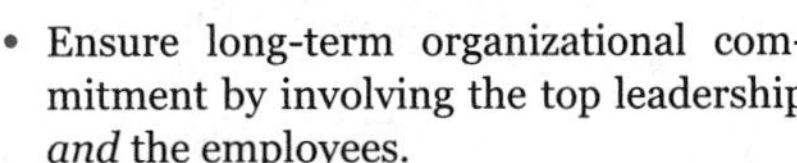

- Ensure long-term organizational commitment by involving the top leadership *and* the employees.
- Don't adopt every reporting system: select one that makes the most sense for your industry and scale.
- Carefully identify stakeholders to help develop feedback loops so you can adjust your course.
- Consider benchmarking against peer companies.
- Communicate your results widely.
- Don't be afraid to revise standards or develop new metrics of your own.

CONCLUSION

Evidence is mounting that CSR provides tangible benefits and lasting competitive advantage to organizations. While difficult to implement, corporate social responsibility practices and frameworks provide companies with a chance to influence the rules of competition positively while playing a crucial—and increasingly expected—role in the world.

FUN FACTS

The Institute of Business Ethics published a study of FTSE 250 companies, providing evidence that those with an ethical code in place for over five years generated greater economic value and market value than their peers over the period 1997–2000.

For 79% of fund managers and analysts surveyed in 2003, the management of social and environmental risks has a positive impact on a company's market value in the long term.

▸▸ MORE INFO

Book:

United Nations Conference on Trade and Development. *Disclosure of the Impact of Corporations on Society: Current Trends and Issues*. New York: United Nations, 2004. Online at: www.unctad.org/en/docs/iteteb20037_en.pdf

Websites:

Business for Social Responsibility: www.bsr.org
CSR Network: www.csrnetwork.com
Ethical Corp: www.ethicalcorp.com
SustainAbility: www.sustainability.com
World Business Council for Sustainable Development: www.wbcsd.org

See Also:

★ Best Practices in Corporate Social Responsibility (pp. 123–126)
★ Business Ethics (pp. 134–136)
★ Corporate Responsibility in a Global World: Marrying Investment in Human Capital with Focus on Costs (pp. 144–146)
★ Ethical Funds and Socially Responsible Investment: An Overview (pp. 306–308)
★ Understanding Reputation Risk and Its Importance (pp. 514–516)
★ Value Creation—Perspectives and Implications (pp. 834–838)
✔ Business Ethics in Islamic Finance (p. 900)
✔ Creating a Sustainable Development Policy (p. 905)
Muhammed Yunus (p. 1205)
The Caring Economy: Business Principles for the New Digital Age (p. 1233)

NOTES

1 Source: Simon Webley & Elise More, "Does Business Ethics Pay?" April 2003.

2 Source: CSR Europe, Deloitte & Euronext (2003) *Investing in Responsible Business: The 2003 Survey of European Fund Managers, Financial Analysts and Investor Relations Officers*, CSR Europe & Deloitte.

"Business doesn't have to choose ... between economic success and ethical responsibility, between satisfying the customer and meeting the demands of other stakeholders ... we don't have to make a choice between profits and principles." Jeroen Van der Vee

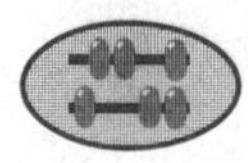

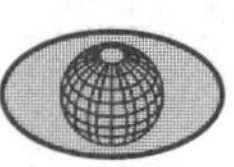

Viewpoint: Jay W. Lorsch

Lessons from the Credit Crisis: Governing Financial Institutions

INTRODUCTION

Jay W. Lorsch is an internationally recognized expert in boards and corporate governance. Here he argues that the lack of experienced bankers on bank boards was a major contributor to the 2008 financial crisis. He believes that the "independence" criteria played a big part in banks' preference for nonbankers as nonexecutives, and must now be reconsidered. Lorsch also argues that US companies should keep the roles of chairman and CEO separate as is the case in the United Kingdom.

Lorsch is Louis Kirstein Professor of Human Relations at Harvard Business School and Chairman of the school's global corporate governance initiative. He has taught in all of HBS's educational programs. As a consultant, Lorsch's clients have included Citicorp, Deloitte & Touche, DLA Piper Rudnick, Goldman Sachs, Tyco International, and Shire Pharmaceuticals.

Lorsch graduated from Antioch College in 1955. He has an MSc in business from Columbia University and a doctorate in business administration from HBS. From 1956–1959, he served as a lieutenant in the US Army Finance Corp. He is also a Fellow of the American Academy of Arts & Sciences.

In the many commentaries about the credit crisis, blame has been placed squarely on the management of the failed financial institutions. While these leaders certainly bear some responsibility, the boards of directors to whom they report should not be let off the hook so easily. After all, boards are ultimately responsible for the performance of their companies.

In this essay I explore the lessons we should draw from these failures about the role of boards in overseeing complex financial institutions. I do so with two caveats. First, boards are not the only governance body that has failed. Government regulators, credit rating agencies, and accounting firms, among others, must also bear some of the responsibility. Second, knowing how boards of directors failed must largely be a matter of informed speculation on my part, since in the current legal environment the board members directly involved are not willing to talk about what went wrong. I say "informed speculation" because I have had the opportunity to consult for boards of such firms in more halcyon times.

BOARDROOM REALITIES

While boards on both sides of the Atlantic are the ultimate legal authority in corporations, their ability actually to carry out this duty is constrained by several realities. The central factor among these is what directors know and understand about their companies' plans, activities, and results.

To an extent, such knowledge can be affected by the number of times the directors meet. The less time directors spend in discussions together and with management, the less informed they may be.

However, a cursory examination of proxy statements reveals that, in 2007, the boards of the large Wall Street institutions did meet much more often than the average American company's board—on average 10 times a year for the Wall Street firms, and six times for the typical company. Even more impressively, the audit committees of these financial institutions met an average of 11 times during 2007. All of this I believe is evidence that these directors were spending time trying to understand the complexity of their companies.

However, what directors understand about these institutions is obviously the result of more than just how much time they spend together. Another significant factor can be the depth of knowledge directors bring to the boardroom about financial markets, products, and institutions from prior career experience. Unfortunately, current rules and best practices make such transfer of knowledge unlikely. The emphasis in selecting board members in the United States is on finding individuals who are "independent."

This generally means selecting directors who have no current or recent experience working for the company, its competitors or clients. The underlying idea is to create boards whose members have no conflicts of interest. While this is an understandable and worthy goal, a significant result is that most boards of financial institutions in the United States have few nonmanagement directors with prior experience in that industry.

Again, looking at the boards of the 12 largest Wall Street firms, each has at most two independent directors with prior financial experience. The other independent directors, experienced and accomplished as they may be in other industries and professions, start with a sizeable handicap.

Whether independent or not, and whether they have a prior experience of financial organizations, board members must rely on their management as the most important source of information about future plans and current company activities, risks, and results. There is no other way for directors to understand what is happening in their companies.

Trying to understand the debacles in these financial firms from outside the boardroom, it is not clear whether management understood the problems that their companies faced and chose to withhold this knowledge from the board, or else whether the top management itself did not understand the situation. However, it really doesn't matter, because either way the directors, even those few who might have had deep knowledge of financial issues, were unaware of the storm that was about to break upon them.

The fact that these boards were unaware of the catastrophe that struck their companies until after it had occurred points to the fact that boards need knowledge for two reasons.

"Accuracy is to a newspaper what virtue is to a lady, but a newspaper can always print a retraction."
Adlai E. Stevenson

   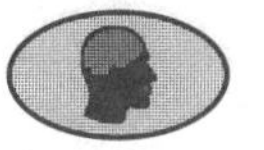  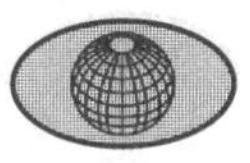   

One is to understand and make judgments about how well their company has been performing, to look in the rear view mirror. Their failure in this regard is what many observers are most likely to criticize.

However, I believe that their more serious sin occurred many years earlier, as they approved (or should have approved) the strategic plans for their company. It was at this stage that they allowed their managements to set off in new directions, which eventually did so much damage to the companies and the wider economy. My hunch is that the reception for these innovative new "products," if they were presented to the board by management, was as enthusiastic among the directors as it was among the managers proposing them.

With so little financial knowledge among the board members, my hunch is that they were reluctant or unable to raise any doubts about management's "exciting" new ideas. At least this is too often the case in boards with which I am familiar. Further, it is unlikely that the directors understood the necessity to create monitoring systems, which would keep them aware of any new risks associated with the newfangled innovations.

It may be unfair or even unreasonable to expect directors to have been able to predict or anticipate the failures in the financial system, when top executives, regulators, and academic experts with much greater knowledge were unable to do so.

Yet, I cannot ignore the fact that the boards of these institutions have a legal and moral obligation for the health of their company, including its equity value for shareholders, and the safety of investor assets entrusted to the company. While it is unhelpful to cast blame on these boards, I do want to consider what they can do going forward to prevent future calamities.

LOOKING TO THE FUTURE

Over the past two decades there have been plenty of ideas about boardroom best practices, including that they should have a preponderance of independent directors, the requisite committees, discussions among independent directors without management present, and board approval of strategic plans. While these innovations have been helpful to many boards, they did not go far enough to prevent the crisis that hit and, in some cases, nearly destroyed their companies.

Even assiduously adopting all these practices does not go far enough to prevent a recurrence of such problems, unless the independent directors have the information and knowledge to assess plans and results intelligently. Thus, I believe that attention needs to be focused primarily on solving this part of the problem.

I would start by requiring the boards of financial companies to have more independent directors who have deep knowledge and experience of the world of financial markets and institutions. I have in mind a principle similar to that used in the Sarbanes–Oxley Act's definition of the competence required for members of audit committees.

Based on my own experience, I believe it is possible to find directors who meet both the test of independence and have deep financial understanding. Finding such individuals requires dropping the assumption that the best directors for these financial firms are prestigious CEOs or other comparable high-status individuals. It will also require corporate governance committees and any consultants they choose to use to search more carefully for candidates who meet both criteria.

Second, these boards should adopt an idea first proposed in 1972 by the late Justice Arthur Goldberg, who was on the board of Trans World Airlines. He asked that the board create a small staff to support it with analysis and interpretation of data. This proposal was rejected at the time, but I believe it is an idea whose time has come for complex financial institutions.

There is simply too much complicated data about performance and risks for independent directors to understand, even if boards do meet monthly and consist of more members with deep financial expertise. I envision a relatively small "staff" of young professionals with the relevant expertize.

Third, I believe that these boards should recognize that their company's complexity requires them to have a chair who is not the CEO. While this idea is widely accepted in the United Kingdom and the rest of Europe, there is resistance to it in the United States.

However, it seems clear that boards which are meeting almost monthly, and which face such complicated issues, need a leader who has no other obligations within the company.

Some may see this proposal as a reheating of an old campaign from corporate governance reformers. However, I would remind the reader that I was one of the originators of the concept of a lead director, as an alternative to a separate chair for US boards. I am proposing the idea of a separate chair because I truly believe it is relevant for the boards of these complex financial institutions.

In doing so, I recognize that one requirement for its successful implementation is a very clear and explicit definition of the chair's job. It should be to lead the board in its oversight duties. This includes assuring that the board has appropriate membership and committees, the right agendas, sufficient information, and overseeing the board's staff proposed above, as well as presiding at board meetings. What the chair's job must not entail is being a personal "boss" of the CEO, or usurping the board's duties in this regard.

While I do not believe that these changes alone will prevent a repetition of the failures of so many financial institutions, I do believe that, along with improved regulatory oversight, they should vastly improve the odds that boards can be the guardians of their companies that society has the right to expect.

▸▸ MORE INFO

Books:

Carter, Colin B., and Jay W. Lorsch. *Back to the Drawing Board: Designing Corporate Boards for a Complex World*. Cambridge, MA: Harvard Business School Press, 2003.

Lawrence, Paul R., and Jay W. Lorsch. *Organization and Environment: Managing Differentiation and Integration*. Cambridge, MA: Harvard Business School Press, 1967.

Lorsch, Jay W., and Elizabeth McIver. *Pawns or Potentates: The Reality of America's Corporate Boards*. Cambridge, MA: Harvard Business School Press, 1989.

Lorsch, Jay W., and Thomas J. Tierney. *Aligning the Stars: How to Succeed when Professionals Drive Results.* Cambridge, MA: Harvard Business School Press, 2002.

See Also:

★ Boardroom Roles (pp. 130–131)

★ Identifying the Right Nonexecutive Director Terry Carroll (pp. 165–167)

Irrational Exuberance (p. 1286)

  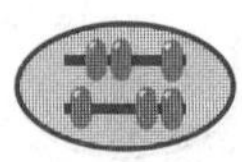   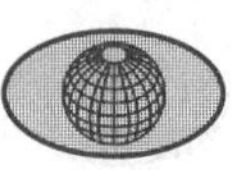 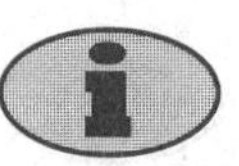  

Dividend Policy: Maximizing Shareholder Value by Harold Bierman, Jr

EXECUTIVE SUMMARY

- Dividend policy (or distribution policy) distributes some amount of cash (possibly zero) to its investors.
- Retained earnings is a very tax efficient (zero dividend) policy.
- If cash is to be distributed, with most tax systems and taxed investors, share repurchase is the preferred method.
- The choice of method is important on several different dimensions.

INTRODUCTION

The amount of dividends can affect stock prices. Barsky and De Long (1993) stated:

"... changes in current and expected future dividends can account for the bulk of long-run stock price fluctuations, although much less so for short-term price movements."[1]

The title of this paper could be "Distribution Policy," since dividends are not the only way of implementing a policy aimed at financially rewarding a firm's stockholders. The various methods of distributing cash (or not distributing cash), listed in order of preference order from an economic–finance perspective of maximizing shareholder wealth, are:

- retained earnings;
- share repurchase;
- sale of firm (or part of a firm);
- LBOs (buyouts);
- cash dividends with a dividend reinvestment plans (DRIP);
- cash dividends.

RETENTION: TAX DEFERRAL

It has been proven that, with enough assumptions, dividend policy is not relevant to the valuation of the common stock equity of a firm. However, the proof assumes zero investor taxes; thus it does not apply to a real-world situation in which such taxes exist. With income taxes, an investor benefits from being able to defer the payment of taxes as well as from the fact that some types of income (capital gains) for individuals may be taxed at lower rates than other types of income (dividends).

If a company retains \$100, earns 0.10 in one period, and then pays a dividend of \$110, the investor taxed at a rate of 0.40 will net: \$110 × (1 – 0.4) = \$66.

If the same company had paid a dividend of \$100 and if the investor also could earn 0.10 before tax and 0.06 after tax on the \$60 after tax proceeds, the investor receiving the \$100 dividend (\$60 after tax) would have after one period: 60 × 1.06 = \$63.60.

The investor is better off by \$2.40 with the one-period delay in cash distribution. The investor "defers" \$40 of taxes that earn 0.10, or \$4. The \$4 is taxed (\$1.60) and the investor is better off by \$2.40.

If desired, one could compute the return necessary for the firm to justify retention. It would be equal to the after-tax return (0.06) available in the market to the investor. Thus, if the corporation could earn 0.06 and then pay a dividend, the investor would net: \$100 × 1.06 × (1 – 0.4) = \$63.60. This is the same as the investor would net with an immediate cash dividend.

If the planning horizon is n periods instead of one period, then 0.06 still measures the return that the firm must earn to justify retention. If the earning opportunities available to the corporation are greater than 0.06, retention is more desirable than an immediate dividend.

If the planning horizon is n periods, the dollar advantage of tax deferral increases. For example, if the firm can earn 0.10 and the time horizon is 20 years with retention and then a tax rate of 0.40, the investor has:

$$\$100 \times 1.10^{20} \times (1 - 0.4) = \$100 \times 6.73 \times 0.6 = \$404$$

With an immediate \$100 cash dividend and the investment of \$60 by the stockholder to earn 0.06 after tax for 20 years, the investor would have:

$$\$60 \times 1.06^{20} = \$60 \times 3.207 = \$192$$

With a planning horizon of 20 years, the advantage of tax deferral is \$212 for the retention of the \$100 earnings. There will be 19 other years between now and the end of the 20 years that will generate comparable tax deferral savings (although of decreasing amounts).

CAPITAL GAINS

To this point, we have assumed that all income is taxed at one rate. Now we assume that a capital gains tax rate of 0.20 applies to capital gains income. This assumes that retention of earnings leads to stock price increases and that these increases can be realized by investors as capital gains.

Returning to the 20-year horizon, with retention and then capital gains taxation of 0.20, the investor would have:

$$\$100 \times 1.10^{20} \times (1 - 0.20) = \$100 \times 6.73 \times 0.80 = \$538$$

The cash dividend and an after-tax earning rate of 0.06 again leads to a value of \$192 after 20 years.

The net advantage of retention is \$538 – \$192 = \$346. Capital gains taxation increases the value of retention from the \$212 obtained above to \$346.

Again, if we considered the tax consequences of the dividend decision for all subsequent years, the value of the difference would be even larger. Tax deferral and capital gains are two powerful factors that must be considered in deciding a distribution policy.

SHARE REPURCHASE

A number of explanations of the motivation behind share repurchase (where a company buys its own stock) have been suggested. It has been argued, for example, that firms buy back their own shares to have them available to acquire other companies or to fulfill the obligations of stock option plans. Unquestionably, some repurchasing has been done for these reasons. Income tax considerations may make it possible for firms to acquire other companies more cheaply for stock than for cash, and the use of stock options and restricted stock as forms of executive compensation have been widespread. However, the growth of share repurchasing cannot be explained by merger and stock option plans. There is no essential reason why firms should use repurchased shares for these purposes, rather than newly issued shares.

Corporations also repurchase shares with the intention of retiring them, or at least holding them indefinitely in the treasury. It has been suggested that firms with excessive liquid assets have one or more of the following motives to repurchase shares:

- repurchasing shares is the best investment that can be made with these assets;
- repurchasing shares has beneficial leverage effects;
- repurchasing shares, rather than paying dividends, has a significant tax advantage for stockholders.

"The word revolution is entirely appropriate for describing the changes in financial institutions and instruments that have occurred in the past twenty years." Merton H. Miller

   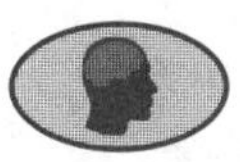  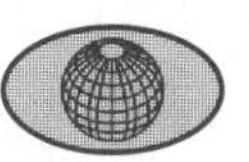 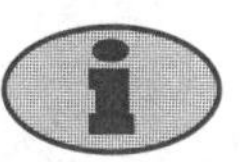  

Is a firm's purchase of its own common stock an investment? There are authors who think so: "The repurchase of its own stock by a company is an investment decision—plain and simple."[2]

Share Repurchasing as an Investment

Share repurchasing does not possess the same general characteristics as other acts of investment by a firm—for instance, purchasing plant and equipment. Normal investments increase the size of the firm and do not decrease the stockholders' equity balance. A firm's repurchase of its own common stock, on the other hand, reduces the size of the enterprise. Specifically, the cash balance is decreased and the stockholders' equity balance is reduced. In short, repurchasing shares has few characteristics which identify it as a normal investment.

While share repurchasing is clearly not an investment by the firm, there is a change in the relative proportions of ownership if some stockholders sell their shares and some do not sell. The investors who do not sell are implicitly making an investment compared with the investors who do sell. Also, investors not selling make an investment in the firm compared with what would have happened if they had received a cash dividend.

Even though share repurchasing is not an investment, it may be the best use of corporate cash from the point of view of the present investors. This may be the case if the present stock price is below the intrinsic value of the shares.

Taxes and Share Repurchasing

The tax laws can provide powerful incentives for firms with excess liquid assets to repurchase shares rather than pay dividends. The tax code may lead individuals to prefer capital gains to ordinary income, assuming that the top marginal rate of taxation on ordinary income is higher than the rate on capital gains.

Consider now a corporation with excess cash that it desires to pay out to stockholders in the form that will be most attractive from its shareholders' point of view. If it distributes the assets as dividends, they will represent ordinary income to shareholders, and will be taxed accordingly. If, on the other hand, the corporation buys back shares, the tax basis of the stock will be regarded as a return to the shareholders' capital and will not be taxed at all, while that portion of the return which is taxed—i.e., the capital gain—will be subject to a lower rate than ordinary income. In addition, the investor who merely wants to reinvest and does not sell is not taxed at all.

Abby Cohen (1994) captures the essence of this thought:[3] "First, shareholders are not thrilled by the prospect of double taxation on cash dividends. Many prefer that corporations 'pay out' the cash indirectly to shareholders in the form of share repurchases, rather than in the form of cash dividends."

Given these incentives for returning cash to stockholders by repurchasing shares, a relevant question would seem to be: Why, if the tax law is as described, do firms pay dividends? One important answer is that many stockholders do not pay tax on the dividends they receive (for example, Cornell University and low-income retirees). A second reason (related to the first) is that the receipt of cash dividends to low-tax investors reduces the transaction costs for those investors who need cash. But even if one were to accept the above explanations, the basic question still remains. Why do firms pay dividends to investors who are taxed at high ordinary income tax rates?

Example

A firm has 100,000 shares outstanding and $100,000 available for distribution. Should it pay a dividend or repurchase shares? Assume that the personal tax rate is 0.36 and the capital gains tax rate is 0.20. The initial stock price is $20. Assume that the tax basis is also $20. There is an investor who owns 1,000 shares. With a $1,000 cash dividend for this investor we have:

Dividend	
Cash received	$1,000
Tax (0.36)	$360
Net	$640

If the company acquires 100,000/20 = 5,000 shares and the investor tenders 0.05 of the 1,000 shares held, we have:

Stock repurchase	
Cash received (50 × $20)	$1,000
Tax	$0
Net	$1,000

There is a $360 cash flow advantage for share repurchase compared to a cash dividend.

With a zero tax basis and a 0.20 tax rate, we have for the share repurchase:

Stock repurchase	
Cash received	$1,000
Tax (0.20)	$200
Net	$800

Not selling, the investor's percentage ownership goes up from 0.01 to 0.0105 (that is, 1,000/95,000). The investor has a choice of receiving cash (selling some stock) or increasing the relative investment in the firm.

When capital gains and ordinary income have different tax treatment, the value of the firm's stock is influenced by the form of its cash distribution. In addition, with share repurchase and a positive-tax basis, part of the cash distribution is not taxed. There are three factors at work that cause the buying back of shares to be more profitable than dividend payments (from the stockholders' point of view) under any reasonable set of assumptions that includes taxation of income. For one thing, part of the distribution under the share-repurchasing arrangement is considered a return of capital and is not taxed. Secondly, that part of the distribution subject to tax (i.e., the capital gain) is generally taxed at a lower rate than ordinary income. Finally, the investor can avoid all taxes by not selling.

Stock Option Plans

Share repurchase programs by corporations enhance the value of stock options compared to cash dividends by forcing the stock price up relative to a cash dividend of equal dollar amount (the number of shares outstanding is reduced). The stock price effect is not a real advantage to the investor, but it is an advantage to the holders of stock options.

For example, suppose a firm has one million shares outstanding selling at $40 per share. The value of the stock equity is $40 million. If it pays a $4 million cash dividend, the value of the stock equity will be $36 million. Then, as a result of the cash dividend:

Stock price per share	$36
Cash received	$4
Total value to investor per share	$40

The investor is indifferent to the share repurchase and dividends (with zero taxes), but the holder of the stock options prefers the share repurchase.

The firm could buy 100,000 shares with the $4 million. The value of the firm after purchase will be $36 million, and the stock price per share will be $40 (that is, $36,000,000/900,000 = $40). The investor is indifferent to share repurchase and cash dividend (with no taxes), but the holder of a stock option prefers the $40 market price with share repurchase to the $36 price with cash dividends.

The stock price after one year is interesting. Assume that the stock equity is again $40 million (the firm made earnings of $4 million during the year).

"Special or Extra Dividends have been used by some firms to distribute excess cash." Merton H. Miller

  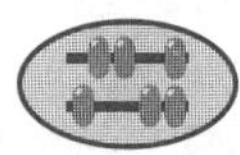   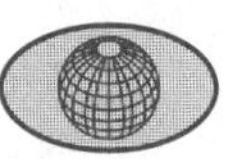   

Having paid a $4 million dividend last year, the stock value per share would be $40. If the firm had repurchased 100,000 shares instead of a dividend, the stock value per share would be $40,000,000/900,000 = $44.44.

A share repurchase program, all things equal, will result in an increasing stock price through time compared to the price with dividends being paid. With a stock option contract (not adjusted for share repurchases) the increase in stock price resulting from a share repurchase strategy rather than a cash dividend is valuable for the holder of the stock option.

Of course, the owner of an exercisable option can convert it to stock and receive any dividend that is paid. This will require a cash outlay equal to the option's exercise price. Also, the cash dividend is taxed. With the stock repurchase by the firm and the owner not exercising the option, the tax on the cash dividend is avoided and the cash outlay of the option's exercise price is delayed.

A Flexible Dividend

One tax advantage of stock repurchase in lieu of cash dividends is that investors who do not want to convert their investments into cash do not sell their stock back to the corporation. By not selling, they avoid realization of the capital gain and do not have any taxation on the increment to the value of their wealth (they also avoid transaction costs).

The investors who want to receive cash sell a portion of their holdings, and even though they pay tax on the gain, it is apt to be less than if the cash distribution were taxed as ordinary income. By using stock repurchase as the means of the cash distribution, the company tends to direct the cash to those investors who want the cash and bypass the investors who do not need cash at the present time. Also, the tax consequences are favorable for investors.

THE SIGNALING EFFECT OF REPURCHASE

Would management be more likely to launch a share repurchase program if the firm's stock is overvalued or undervalued? While many companies implement share repurchase programs irrespective of whether the stock price is too low or too high, there is evidence that firms are more likely to buy stock that is undervalued by the market. Thus, some investors will consider the start of a stock buyback program as a signal that management thinks the stock is undervalued. Two studies that find evidence supporting this signaling effect are Dann (1981) and Vermaelen (1981).

Investors Like Dividends

The attitude of investors is an important factor to be considered. Consistently increasing dividends are generally welcomed by investors as indicators of profitability and safety. Uncertainty is increased by lack of dividends or dividends that fluctuate widely. Grigoli (1986) agrees with this conclusion: "Because investors value stable dividends, it may not be in a corporation's best interests to raise dividends to unsustainable levels."[4]

Dividends are thought to have an information content; that is, an increase in dividends means that the board of directors expects the firm to do well in the future. This "signaling effect" might favorably affect the firm's common stock price. On the other hand, if income expectations do not justify the optimism, the indication of a more positive future than is justified by the facts is not likely to lead to a favorable outcome.

Since trust officers can only invest in securities with a consistent dividend history, firms like to establish a history of dividends so that they can make the "trust legal list." This consideration sometimes leads to the payment of cash dividends before the firm would otherwise start paying a dividend.

Another important reason for the payment of dividends is that a wide range of investors need the dividends for consumption purposes. Although such investors could sell a portion of their holdings, this latter transaction has relatively high processing costs compared with cashing a dividend check. The presence of investors desiring cash for consumption makes it difficult to change the current dividend policy. One group of investors may benefit from a change in dividend policy, but another group may be harmed. Although we see that income taxes paid by investors tend to make a retention policy more desirable than cash dividends, the presence in the real world of zero tax and low tax investors needing cash dictates that we consider each situation individually and be flexible in arriving at a dividend policy.

There are stockholders who desire cash. A dividend supplies cash without the investor incurring brokerage expense. If cash is retained by the corporation, the stockholders wanting liquidity will have to sell a fraction of their holdings to obtain cash, and this process will result in brokerage fees. Retired individuals living off their dividends and tax-free universities are apt to prefer dividend-paying corporations to corporations retaining income. While a 100% earnings payout cash dividend has the advantage of giving cash to those investors who desire cash, the policy also results in cash being given to those investors who do not desire cash, and who must incur brokerage fees to reinvest the dividends, and who pay taxes.

Dividend Changes and Signaling

A study by Liu, Szewczyk, and Zantout (2008) shows that "there is no compelling evidence of a post-dividend-reduction or post-dividend-omission price drift" (p. 987).

Assume that a firm's stock is fairly priced. Let us assume that this firm's management thinks that if dividends are increased, the market will conclude that this is a favorable signal and the stock price will increase significantly. If the stock was fairly priced to begin with, the stock price after the dividend increase will be too high. This means that with no other changes, the new stockholders will earn less than the firm's required return on stock. Thus, if a stock is fairly priced initially, an increase in dividends that leads to an unjustifiable stock price is not desirable since it leads to investor returns that are less than those required by the new stockholders.

CONCLUSION

If investors in a high tax bracket expect the price of a stock to increase because of improved earnings (and a higher level of future dividends), they will be willing to pay more for a stock knowing that if their expectations are realized the stock can be sold and be taxed at the relatively lower capital gains tax rate. Whereas the lower capital gains tax rate tends to increase the

CASE STUDY

Microsoft (2003–2004)

In 2003, the US tax rates on dividends and capital gains were reduced to a maximum rate of 0.15. Microsoft had over $40 billion in cash.

In January of 2003, Microsoft issued its first cash dividend of $0.02 per quarter. Some investors thought the dividend too low. Others thought the company should have repurchased more shares rather than pay a cash dividend. In July of 2004, the company announced a special $3 cash dividend. With almost 11 billion shares outstanding, this dividend would require a cash outlay of $33 billion.

"A corporation may want to choose its dividend policy under the assumption that changes in dividend policy will have no permanent effect on its stock price." Fisher Black and Myron Scholes

  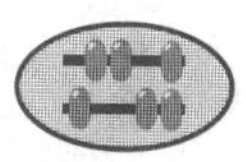 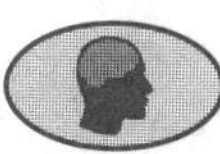  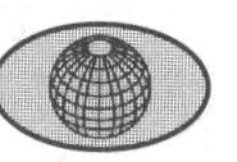   

value of a share of stock, we have shown that another powerful factor arises from the ability of the stockholder to defer paying taxes if the corporation retains income rather than paying dividends. Tax deferral is an extremely important advantage associated with the retention of earnings by a corporation.

The present tax law allows deferral of tax payment (or complete avoidance) on capital gains, and recognized gains may be taxed at a lower rate than ordinary income. Dividend policies of firms have relevance for public policy in the areas of taxation of both corporations and individuals. As corporate managers adjust their decision-making to include the tax law considerations, the makers of public policy must decide whether the results are beneficial to society.

It is not being argued that all firms should discontinue dividend payments. There is a place for a variety of payout policies, but there is a high cost to investors for all firms attempting to cater to the dividend and reinvestment preferences of an average investor. However, it is entirely appropriate that not all corporations appeal to all investors and that corporations design their common stock (and other securities) in the same way they design their consumer products. A corporation should have a financial personality resulting from its various financial policies (especially capital structure and dividend policies) that is attractive to a given group of investors, and is inappropriate for other groups. Corporate securities should have clienteles.

Define the price (and value) of a share of common stock as being equal to the present value of the next dividend (assumed to be declared and paid one period from now) and the price of the share at the time the dividend is paid. If we keep repeating the substitution process, we find that the value of the firm is equal to the present value of all future dividends, where the word "dividend" is used to include all cash distributions made from the firm to its investors. We replace the price at each future moment in time by the dividends that causes the stock to have value.

A board of directors acting in the interests of the stockholders of a corporation sets the dividend policy of a firm. The ability of an investor to defer income taxes as a result of the company retaining earnings is an important consideration. In addition, the distinction between ordinary income and capital gains for purposes of income taxation by the federal government accentuates the importance of investors knowing the dividend policy of the firm whose stock they are considering purchasing or have already purchased. In turn, this means that the corporation (and its board) has a responsibility to announce its dividend policy and to attempt to be consistent in its policy, changing only when its economic situation changes significantly. In the particular situation in which a firm is expanding its investments rapidly and is financing this expansion by issuing securities to its stockholders, the payment of cash dividends is especially vulnerable to criticism.

▸▸ MORE INFO

Book:

Bierman, Harold, Jr. *Increasing Shareholder Value: Distribution Policy, A Corporate Finance Challenge*. Norwell, MA: Kluwer Academic Publishers, 2001.

Articles:

Barsky, Robert B., and J. Bradford De Long. "Why does the stock market fluctuate?" *The Quarterly Journal of Economics* 108:2 (May 1993): 291–311.

Black, Fisher. "The dividend puzzle." *Journal of Portfolio Management* (Winter 1976): 5–8.

Dann, Larry Y. "Common stock repurchases: An analysis of returns to bondholders and stockholders." *Journal of Financial Economics* 9:2 (June 1981): 113–38.

Liu, Y., H. Szewczyk, and Z. Zantout. "Under-reaction to dividend reductions and omissions." *Journal of Finance* 63:2 (April 2008): 987–1020.

Miller, Merton H., and Franco Modigliani. "Dividend policy, growth, and the valuation of shares." *Journal of Business* 34:4 (Jan 1961): 411–433.

Rundell, C. A. "From the thoughtful businessman." *Harvard Business Review* 43:6 (November–December, 1965): 39.

Vermaelen, Theo. "Common stock repurchase and market signaling." *Journal of Financial Economics* 9:2 (June 1981): 139–83.

Reports:

Cohen, Abby Joseph. "No problem with dividend growths." Goldman Sachs Portfolio Strategy, August 12, 1994, p. 1.

Grigoli, Carmine J. "The great corporate de-financing." Merrill Lynch, March 1986, p. 5.

See Also:

★ Attracting Small Investors (pp. 523–525)
★ How Stockholders Can Effectively Engage With Companies (pp. 319–320)
★ Reinvesting in the Company versus Rewarding Investors with Distributions (pp. 172–173)
✔ Calculating Total Shareholder Return (p. 936)
✔ An Overview of Stockholders' Agreements (p. 1019)
✔ Setting Up a Dividend Policy (p. 881)
✔ Using Shareholder Value Analysis (p. 953)
Jack Welch (p. 1204)

NOTES

1 Barsky and De Long (1993).
2 Rundell (1965), p. 39.
3 Cohen (1994), p. 1.
4 Grigoli (1986), p. 5.

"They seldom pretend to understand anything of the business of the company...but receive contentedly such half yearly or yearly dividends, as the directors think proper to make them." Adam Smith

  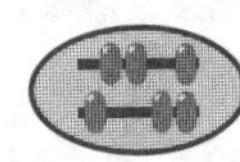 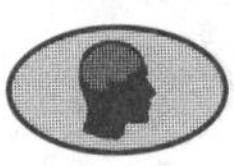  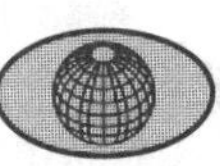   

Executive Rewards: Ensuring That Financial Rewards Match Performance by Shaun Tyson

EXECUTIVE SUMMARY

- Executive pay is used to attract and retain executives, and to drive performance.
- Business strategy objectives are cascaded down the organization and used as performance targets for the variable element in the reward package, in order to provide a clear line of sight.
- Reward packages for executive pay include base pay, short-term incentives, benefits, long-term incentives, and perks. Base pay is determined by the market rate in similar organizations.
- Variable pay incentives usually take the form of an annual bonus scheme, or, in the case of long-term incentives, deferred bonus and/or stock option plans.
- Reward packages are decided by remuneration committees as an important aspect of good corporate governance; the decisions are made by nonexecutive directors, with transparent reporting in annual reports. In the United Kingdom stockholders vote on the report.

INTRODUCTION

Effective management of executive rewards resides at the heart of a network of pressures and issues of central relevance to the management of organizational performance. These pressures can be represented diagrammatically to show how stockholder interests and corporate governance issues impact on business performance, objective setting, the motivation of executives, and the position of the organization as an employer in specific labor markets; and how all of these are affected by corporate values/culture and vision (Figure 1).

However, the economic events of 2008 have reminded us all that these issues are conditioned by the broader economic climate in which corporations operate, where survival is more risky and uncertain irrespective of size, sector, or ownership structure. The rapid disappearance of banks such as Lehman Brothers, the exposure of massive manufacturers such as General Motors, Chrysler, and Ford to recessionary problems, the collapse of house prices, of normal financial processes, and of currencies means that organizations are facing a strategic inflection point, which is affecting all aspects of reward. The topic of executive rewards must be seen as a dynamic field, and this caveat informs all that follows. Nevertheless, there are systematic and enduring influences in the linkages between reward and performance.

We will examine rewards to show the major impact of reward policies and practices on organizational performance. This article takes rewards from the organizational perspective, and the starting point is an examination of the significance of corporate values, vision, and the culture of rewards.

CORPORATE VALUES/CULTURE/VISION

Corporate values and vision statements are an explicit expression of the formal values and vision of the organization, including the sometimes implicitly preferred behaviors and attitudes of managers in their leadership roles. These values may be published but, if not explicitly stated, will still emerge in the actions of senior managers and the founders. The objectives of a reward policy can be summarized as:

- Building stockholder value (or sustaining value for the citizen in the public sector).
- Being competitive in the recruitment of executives.
- Motivating and retaining executives.
- Being cost-effective.
- Being seen as fair by employees.
- Providing a degree of security for employees.

How these objectives are interpreted in any organization is contingent on that organization's values and the nature of its objectives—for example, profit maximization, market share, and service provision.

A number of authors have suggested that there are specific best practices to drive a philosophy of rewards that will support the corporate vision. For example *The New Pay*, by Schuster and Zingheim (1996), was a reward ideology that emphasized the strategic role of rewards and the supremacy of the marketplace. Key features of *The New Pay* were:

- Emphasis on external market-sensitive pay rather than annual increases.
- Risk-sharing partnership with employees rather than entitlements.
- Variable, performance-based pay.
- Flexibility in pay systems.
- Lateral promotions rather than career paths.
- Employability, not job security.

Later, the same authors argued that there are general reward principles that include aligning rewards with business goals; extending the "line of sight" of all employees to see the relationship between individual performance, corporate performance, and their rewards; and recognizing the market value of the individual with base pay, while rewarding results with variable pay (Zingheim and Schuster, 2000).

These ideas have gained currency over the last 20 years. Even though the economic storm now raging across the globe challenges some of this received wisdom, the ideas remain consistent with the prevailing concepts of market capitalism.

Figure 1. Reward at the centre of internal and external pressures

"The top 20% must be loved, nurtured and rewarded in the soul and wallet because they are the ones who make magic happen." General Electric

     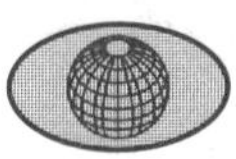   

RELATING BUSINESS PERFORMANCE TO REWARDS

According to economic logic, there is a clear and consequential relationship, or line of sight, between the economic climate, the organization's performance, and the rewards provided (Figure 2).

Certain linkages, such as that between strategies and accountabilities, are critical. The diagram demonstrates the importance of line of sight. There is also the question of how quickly strategies, accountabilities, and rewards can adapt in response to changes in the economic climate.

Objective Setting and Targets

Objectives are normally "cascaded" down from the business strategy—each business unit or department having agreed short-term (next year) and longer-term (three to five year) plans. Objectives are usually both financial and qualitative. Financial objectives are typically total stockholder returns (TSR) and return on capital employed (ROCE). Budget targets are also often used, as well as share price. In remuneration planning, the performance objectives should be measured, and they should be designed to drive the business forward: "Paying for value creation is the most reliable way of generating it" (Credit Suisse First Boston). Targets are usually discussed and agreed at the annual performance review.

The Reward Package

Reward packages are pay policies aimed at achieving behaviors and actions by senior managers that accomplish business objectives. A package consists of base pay, short-term incentives, benefits, long-term incentives, and perks (perquisites). Base pay is decided by reference to pay rates in comparable organizations (see below), and usually according to internal relativities decided by the job evaluation scheme in use.

The decision of where to be in the market is a matter for corporate policy (for example, at the market median, or the upper quartile rate), reflecting labor market pressures and attraction and retention strategies. Short-term incentives are usually annual bonus schemes. Long-term incentive plans (LTIPs) use stock options and/or bonuses, merit pay, company-wide share plans, and the like.

Benefits include pensions to which the employer makes a contribution, private health plans, life insurance, and similar personal benefits. Perks are fringe benefits such as status cars, concierge services, use of company accommodation, etc. In most countries such perks are taxable as benefits in kind, although the package as a whole should be constructed to be as tax-effective as possible. Benefits may be flexible, so that individuals can choose a mix of benefits and perks within the agreed total value package. In some organizations there will also be the opportunity to sacrifice a proportion of salary for benefits.

Reward specialists structure executive reward packages taking into account the proportion of the base pay to variable pay available in the bonus opportunities, and typically they seek to balance the various elements in the package to drive the performance (both short and long term) required to achieve corporate objectives. The trend is toward variable pay based on performance being a high proportion of the total reward package, especially as managers become more senior. In this way senior managers take a larger risk with their rewards, since variable rewards are related more directly to the performance of the business in market conditions, which may vary for any number of reasons. Irrespective of these market conditions, directors and senior managers are accountable for profit, cost, and market share objectives.

LTIPs are normally constructed using bonus and stock option plans. Stock options give the right to purchase a defined quantity of stock at a stipulated price over a given period, according to predetermined eligibility requirements. There may be stock appreciation rights—the share award is triggered by increases in the share price, at a time chosen by the executive in the time period allowed.

Stock options have been popular as a way to retain key executives, to provide them with a stake in the company, and, at a time when share prices were rising, the opportunity to acquire real wealth. The change from a bull to a bear market has diminished enthusiasm for stock option schemes because the schemes depend on rising share prices so that executives can gain in wealth either by owning an appreciating asset, or by selling the shares and realizing the difference between the stipulated price (the strike price) and the enhanced market price.

Various performance conditions may be attached to the granting of a stock option or bonus. These include improvements in TSR, ROCE, EPS, and EBITDA (earnings before interest, taxation, depreciation, and amortization), usually in the corporate figures produced for the annual accounts. Table 1 is example from BP in 2007 to show how the package works.

There is an annual bonus scheme. Performance measures and targets were set at the beginning of the year. Bonus opportunities were: on target (120%), and maximum (150%), of salary. The remuneration committee can, in exceptional circumstances, increase these payments, or reduce them to zero if appropriate. Targets for 2007 and 2008 were: half of the bonus is based on financial measures (EBITDA, ROCE, and cash flow), the other half on nonfinancial measures and individual performance. Nonfinancial targets were safety and people (including values and culture); individual performance targets were results and leadership.

The LTIP had three elements: shares, stock options, and cash; up to 5.5 times salary could be awarded in performance shares. Performance measured in TSR was compared to other oil companies. Although in this particular case shares were not vested (i.e. not passed into the ownership of the executives for 2007, due to operational problems that affected performance compared to other oil companies), high performance in previous years had resulted in substantial numbers of shares being vested. This demonstrates how the package reflects performance.

Figure 2. Linkages between objectives and rewards

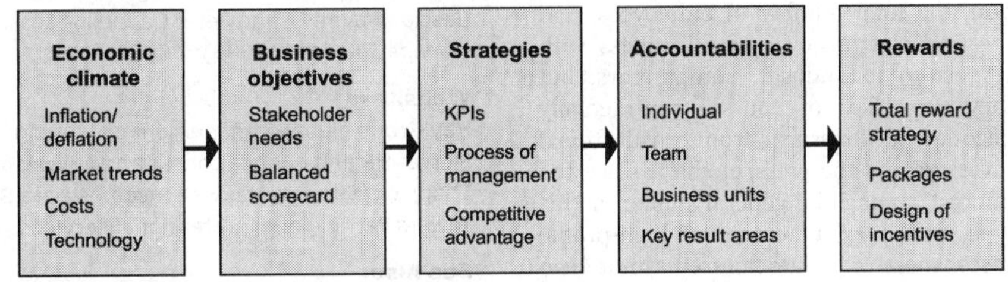

Table 1. Example of a reward package: BP executive directors as at December 2007. (*Source:* IDS *Executive Compensation Review* April 2008, ECR 326, p. 12)

Chief executive	£877,000	£1,262,000	£14,000	Zero vested	£2,153,000
Chief finance officer	£591,755	£781,117	£5,036	Zero vested	£1,377,908

  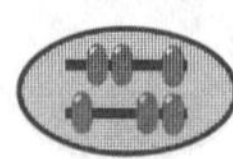   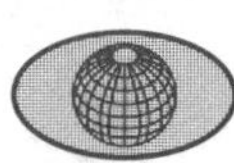   

CORPORATE GOVERNANCE ISSUES

Reward for Failure

Much attention has been paid to excessive pay increases and bonuses for senior executives, especially where these appear to be awarded regardless of the corporate performance achieved.

Criticism of directors for receiving massive bonus and termination payments typically happens when there seems to be an element of reward for failure. UK directors in the FTSE 100 companies are paid more than in the rest of the FTSE companies, but they do not receive the massive sums seen in Fortune 500 companies in the United States. There is a tradition of higher rewards in financial services. A big bonus culture existed in financial services among those dealing in the markets, as well as in the boardroom. Whether this was a cause of the recession is not yet clear, but it may have increased the propensity of managers and traders to take higher risks.

For most directors in the United Kingdom, pay and bonus awards were marginally reduced in the period from 2003. There are a number of possible reasons. Some companies have reduced notice periods for chief executives to around 12 months, which has encouraged more reasonable termination payments. Stockholder activism among both institutional stockholders, such as the Association of British Insurers, and small stockholder groups means that stockholders are likely to be consulted before new schemes are introduced. The court of public opinion is assisted by a vigilant press and the transparency rules. Accounting rules are now generally applied that require the cost of stock options and LTIPs to be fully expensed in the accounts. Increased volatility in share prices and the massive fall from the last quarter of 2008 onward have made stock options much less attractive, so there is less likelihood of big payouts at a later time when the executive cashes in the shares.

Base pay and total rewards are typically decided according to the market capitalization, the total number of employees, and the financial turnover of a business with respect to its industry comparators, but they are also, of course, contractually negotiated. Pressure from institutional investors and the press/media has created interest among the general public in this area, fueled by a number of high-profile cases where corporate failure has not been reflected in reductions in bonus or reward. As a consequence, director-level rewards are now very highly regulated and scrutinized compared to other employee groups.

Remuneration Committees

There is a convergence in corporate governance arrangements, based on the principles of transparency, the need to justify pay awards, the independent judgments of a remuneration committee, an accent on the process rather than on the content of rewards, and compliance with the rules as a condition of being listed on the appropriate stock exchange. Some of these principles were found in the original voluntary rules of the stock exchanges (for example in the Combined Code of the London Stock Exchange). Statutory provision has reinforced these rules—Directors' Remuneration Report Regulations 2002 (UK), Sarbanes–Oxley 2002 (US), SEC rules (US), NRE Act 2001 (France), and in Germany, the Cromme Code (2002). The UK regulations of 2002 require listed companies to have a remuneration committee of independent (nonexecutive) directors, which must produce and publish a report as part of the annual company report. This must include a statement of reward policy, the role of the remuneration committee, proposals for directors' pay going forward, and must include a graph showing comparisons in terms of TSR with a named broad equity index over the previous five years, stating the reasons for selecting the index. Stockholders must be given the opportunity to vote on the remuneration committee report at the AGM. The stockholders' vote is not binding, but it would be unusual for a company and CEO to implement a pay award to the directors if this was voted down.

▸▸ MAKING IT HAPPEN

- Effective reward policies for senior managers and directors can only be created if there is a clear line of sight between their performance goals and the business objectives. This requires:
  - strategic planning and accurate budgeting;
  - clear accountabilities, cascaded down the business;
  - realistic, measurable, demanding performance targets for the short and long term.
- Job evaluation techniques such as the Hay system can help to review accountabilities systematically.
- Base pay should be decided from market data on rates, with comparator organizations in the same industry sector that have similar market capitalization and employee numbers.
- Variable pay is used to recognize and drive performance. Short-term performance will need bonus schemes to be designed with annual performance targets, and there are design decisions to be made about whether there should be a threshold performance level, any weighting on particular targets, etc. Bonus is normally a percentage of base pay (typically 20%–40%). Long-term incentives might include a deferred bonus paid out after two or three years, with further performance conditions attached, and/or stock option schemes.
- Decisions on rewards are made by remuneration committees for director-level pay in quoted companies, with annual public reporting and stockholder involvement.

▸▸ MORE INFO

Articles:

Balkin, D. B., and L. Gomez-Mejia, "Matching compensation and organizational strategies." *Strategic Management Journal* 11:1 (1990): 153–169.

Cascio, Wayne F., and Peter Cappelli. "Lessons from the financial services crisis." *HR Magazine* 54:1 (2009): 46–50.

Websites:

Hay Group global management consulting: www.haygroup.co.uk

Mercer HR and finance consultancy: www.mercer.com

Thomson/Sweet & Maxwell Incomes Data Services (IDS): www.incomesdata.co.uk

Towers Perrin global professional services: www.towersperrin.com

See Also:

★ Balancing Senior Management Compensation Arrangements with Shareholders' Interests (pp. 116–117)

✔ The Board's Role in Executive Compensation (p. 899)

✔ Creating Executive Compensation (p. 906)

"Numerous examples exist of reward systems that are fouled up in that the types of behavior rewarded are those that the rewarder is trying to discourage, while the behavior desired is not being rewarded at all."

Steven Kerr

  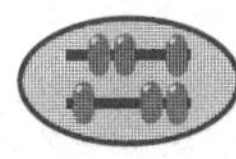   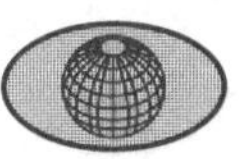   

Viewpoint: Bruce Misamore
Lessons from Russia

INTRODUCTION

Bruce Misamore was Chief Financial Officer and Deputy Chairman of Yukos, Russia's largest oil company, from 2001 until 2005. While there, he introduced world-class standards in corporate governance, financial transparency and accounting. However, Misamore's reforms were unwound when the company had its domestic assets seized by the Russian government after 2004 and Russia arrested its chief executive Mikhail Khodorkovsky. Misamore resigned in December 2005 and has since been instrumental in a global legal campaign to ensure that Yukos's thousands of legitimate stakeholders receive compensation from the Russian government. Before joining Yukos, Misamore held senior-level finance roles with US oil companies PennzEnergy, Pennzoil Co and Marathon Oil. Misamore taught finance at Bowling Green State University in Ohio in the 1970s and says that the winters there are even colder than in Moscow.

Why did you choose to move to Russia and become Yukos's CFO?

During my initial conversations with the CEO of Yukos, Mikhail Khodorkovsky, he made it clear that he wanted Yukos to become a transparent stakeholder-focused company. His aspiration was, in fact, to set the agenda for other Russian companies and oil companies globally, making Yukos a world leader for operational excellence, corporate governance, financial reporting, and investor relations. It seemed like a place where I would be able to make a major positive contribution, not just to the company itself, but also to the wider Russian economy.

What processes did you introduce to improve transparency and the quality of reporting and what did you find most questionable about Russian accounting practice?

Russian accounting had not really evolved since the Soviet era. It was primarily cash accounting, and they had no such thing as consolidation accounting. This meant that each individual legal entity was treated as a separate accounting entity and had to report to the government as such. This made it impossible to create a consolidated financial statement, which in turn caused a lack of sensible financial reporting and other practical problems. Michel Soublin, Yukos' former CFO, and Khodorkovsky had already recognized that Russian accounting standards were inappropriate for a company like Yukos and had made a choice between International Financial Reporting Standards or US GAAP. Before I arrived, they had chosen the latter, in view of their plan to seek a listing for Yukos on a US stock exchange.

Were there any tensions between the use of US GAAP and statutory requirements Yukos had to also report using Russian accounting?

Yes. Despite the move to US GAAP, Yukos was still required to maintain Russian books for domestic tax and financial reporting purposes. As Russian accounts could not be consolidated, the eliminations you would normally make in consolidated statements needed to be tossed out the window, and accruals to reflect the true state of the business were nonexistent. Because of the lack of intercompany eliminations, no reader of the Russian financials could have been properly informed of the true situation of the group as a whole.

What about the tensions over the reporting of oil and gas reserves? Does that remain a criminal offence in Russia?

In the Soviet Union the reporting of reserves was illegal, and technically that remains the case in Russia today. In the late 1990s and early 2000s, companies like Yukos, Lukoil, and TNK-BP elected to begin reporting in either International Financial Reporting Standards or US GAAP, which compelled them to report reserves. In the early Putin years, the government turned a blind eye to the existing Soviet-era law and didn't bother to harass companies over this. The government seemed to recognize that, if Russian oil companies were going to raise capital in the international financial markets, they were going to have to comply with Western rules. However, after the Kremlin decided to renationalize a large portion of the country's oil reserves, Yukos and other companies started to be harassed by the Ministry of Natural Resources over their reporting of reserves. While we certainly did not ignore these calls, we were committed to reporting our reserves, and did not believe that we would be subject to criminal sanctions.

Was Yukos one of the first Russian companies to adopt US GAAP?

Yes. We were the first Russian oil company to publish full US GAAP financial statements, including quarterly US GAAP financials. From 2002 onwards, there emerged a movement called "Yukosization," in which other Russian companies sought to emulate what we had achieved in financial reporting and corporate governance. There were even seminars on it. The focus on transparent financial reporting and good corporate governance meant that Yukos had become recognized as a leader in financial reporting, corporate governance, and investor relations not just in Russia, but across the emerging markets. This was why I had gone to Russia—not only to improve Yukos but to drive forward standards across Russia's industrial base.

However, when Yukos was attacked by the Russian government, most of the other companies backed off, especially on the corporate governance aspects. A key issue was over the identity of major shareholders. No other company in Russia had done that before we did. Companies that had been considering following us down that road scrapped their plans. Once the real Putin stepped forward, there was a significant regression in terms of corporate governance in Russia.

"Facts, when combined with ideas, constitute the greatest force in the world. They are greater than armaments, greater than finance, greater than science, business, and law because they are the common denominator of them all." Carl William Ackerman

  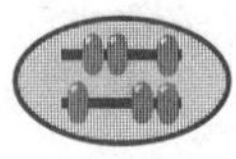   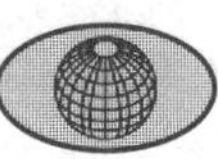   

Why do you think the Russian government singled out Yukos?

There were several factors. In April 2003, we announced a merger with Sibneft, another leading Russian oil company, with Yukos as the dominant partner. That would have created by far the dominant Russian oil company and one of the biggest oil companies in the world. While Mr Putin originally supported the deal, he may later have seen this as a threat.

He also had a growing, though not at that stage explicit, desire to renationalize the commanding heights of the Russian economy—and particularly to exert more control over the country's resources. He also may have resented the fact that Yukos had a number of Americans in senior roles and that its principal shareholder group was having talks with major Western oil companies about possible share interests and cross-shareholdings.

Another factor was that Mr Khodorkovsky was supporting reform candidates in the 2003 Duma elections. Mikhail was doing that, among other things, out of concern that Mr Putin was poised to reverse many of the reforms put in place by Boris Yeltsin during the 1990s.

Did relations between Yukos and the Russian government deteriorate thenceforth?

In December 2003, the Russian government singled out Yukos for retroactive reinterpretation of Russian tax law, and the group started to be hit with massive tax bills. Initially, there was a bill of over US$3bn, but ultimately this rose to over US$30bn. The Kremlin got court judgments against us, freezing all assets, which made it impossible for us to pay the taxes by selling assets, and started removing all cash from the company.

We continued the legal battle with the government, but by late 2004 it had become clear that they would prevail, at least with respect to Yukos' Russian assets. The most significant blow came when the Russian government auctioned off Yukos's biggest subsidiary, Yuganskneftegaz, to pay some off the alleged back taxes. The Russian government ultimately expropriated all of Yukos's Russian assets through a legally questionable bankruptcy process, and the assets ended up with the state-owned companies Rosneft and Gazprom.

Were you able to do anything about this?

In early December 2004, we appointed the Houston-based law firm Fulbright & Jaworski, who represented us in the US Federal bankruptcy court. The court issued an injunction against the Yuganskneftegaz auction. However, the Russian government totally ignored this injunction. We had intended to use the US bankruptcy as a means of protecting the assets of the entire company for the sake of its stakeholders—including employees, legitimate creditors, and the 50,000 plus shareholders who have to date received zero compensation from the Russian government.

But in March 2005 the US Bankruptcy Court determined that, since the Russian government was the largest creditor and the Russian government was not co-operating in the bankruptcy process, it would be impossible for the bankruptcy to conclude successfully. This meant the case was discontinued and we lost the protection of the US bankruptcy courts. We then started looking around for alternative ways of protecting the remaining assets, believing that while Yukos's international assets could probably be protected, its Russian domestic assets probably could not.

When and why did you leave Russia?

In late November 2004 I was at a meeting in London and received a phone call telling me that I should not go back to Russia because I risked being arrested upon my return. I never went back and, indeed, around that time virtually every member of the management committee of Yukos had left Russia never to go back. I arrived in Houston December 4 and we began the bankruptcy process in the United States.

Under the circumstances, was it hard to focus on your original mission of improving standards of corporate governance etc at Yukos?

The focus had to change. We had a major battle on our hands trying to save the company and to convince the Russian government that we were good corporate citizens. We tried all kinds of tax settlement negotiations throughout 2004, including bringing in some very high profile international political figures. These included the former prime minister of Canada, Jean Chrétien, who employed the assistance of some other prominent world leaders to try to reach a settlement. They all had conversations with Mr Putin, who made promises, which he failed to deliver.

What happened to Mr Mikhail Khodorkovsky?

In October 2003 Mikhail was arrested and charged on a personal basis for alleged crimes, primarily related to a fertilizer company that his group had acquired in the mid-1990s. Since his arrest, Mikhail has not been out of jail for a single minute. He was, of course, found guilty of all charges and was sentenced to prison in Eastern Siberia. He is now on trial again in Moscow on phony charges, primarily limited to stealing all of Yuko's oil production from 1998–2003. That trial is a political show trial and will take several months.

What are your chances of securing compensation for Yukos shareholders from the Russian government?

During 2004 and 2005 we scoured the world during for legal structures to protect Yukos's international assets and we found a structure in the Netherlands called a Stichting, a Dutch "foundation" structure. We now have formed two stichtings in which we have put all of Yukos's international assets. The Stichtings have served us extremely well.

We are still battling off attacks from Rosneft and other entities and fronts of the Russian government, which keep trying to seize those assets.

However, we have won virtually every meaningful court case outside Russia, including a key victory in October 2007, which said that the Russian bankruptcy would not be recognized in the Netherlands. There is a strong chance that sizeable verdicts will be levied against the Russian government. In January 2009, the main Yuko case was admitted to the European Court of Human Rights.

However, it is going to be years before any money is collected for the parties that have been harmed. If the cases that are currently being heard under the European Energy Charter Treaty and in the European Court of Human Rights were to rule against Russia, it would hopefully serve as a wake up call for the country.

This is the main reason I continue to be involved. The Russian public and political community need to understand that expropriation is not the way to improve the economy.

What is the outlook for the transparency of financial reporting in Russia?

Through its intimidation campaign, the Russian government has compromised the move to more transparency in Russian entities, including the disclosure of major shareholders. This has led to questionable disclosure by a lot of Russian companies. However, whenever Russian companies are seeking to raise money in international capital markets, they will have to provide reasonable financial statements. I think that even Mr Putin understands that.

  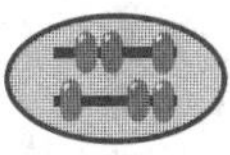 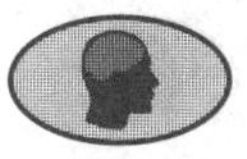  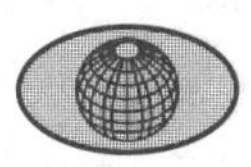   

What is the outlook for the Russian economy?

Russia has become an autocracy and this is bad news for the economy. It means that Russian companies will never get a consistently strong inflow of Western capital. This is very different from other economies in Eastern Europe. Few other former Soviet or Warsaw Pact republics, other than Belarus, have regressed as far as Russia has. As a result, the Western banking crisis has had a far bigger impact on Russia. There's been a massive flight of capital out of Russia and a more pronounced stock market crash there, a crash in the rouble and a significant decrease in purchasing power.

What is your advice to someone from a developed country who is considering taking on a CFO role in a Russian company right now?

I would not want to share my talents with Russia today because the situation there is far, far different from what it was like when I went there in 2001. Until the Russian government explicitly supports transparency in its businesses and gets a handle on government corruption, I don't think anyone should waste their time in Russia. There's currently no sign of that happening.

Are there lessons for transparency in other emerging markets?

The only way for emerging market companies to achieve the kind of results they want is through financial transparency and good corporate governance. This also needs to be understood by the politicians and others within those countries. In India, because of its British background, there is more transparency. However, I believe that China will achieve less economically in comparison with what it could otherwise achieve because of the country's apparent failure to encourage transparency.

▸▸ MORE INFO

Books:

Baker, Peter, and Susan Glasser. *Kremlin Rising: Vladimir Putin's Russia and the End of Revolution*. New York: Lisa Drew/Scribner, 2005.

Economides, Michael J., and Donna Marie D'Aleo. *From Soviet to Putin and Back: the Dominance of Energy in Today's Russia*. Houston, TX: Energy Tribune Publishing, 2008.

Jack, Andrew. *Inside Putin's Russia*. London: Granta Books, 2004.

Norman, James R. *The Oil Card: Global Economic Warfare in the 21st Century*. Walterville, OR: Trine Day, 2008.

See Also:

★ Geopolitical Risk: Countering the Impact on Your Business (pp. 465–467)
✔ Defining Corporate Governance: Its Aims, Goals, and Responsibilities (p. 907)
✔ IFRS: The Basics (p. 1036)
✔ Key Accounting Standards and Organizations (p. 1038)
✔ The Ten Accounting Principles (p. 1050)
✔ Understanding the Key Components of GAAP: The Continuing Concern Concept (p. 1054)
🌐 Russia (pp. 1461–1463)

"In all pointed sentences, some degree of accuracy must be sacrificed to conciseness." Samuel Johnson

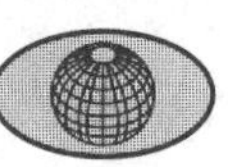

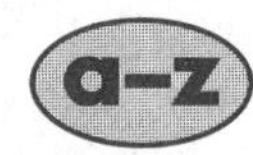

Financial Reporting: Conveying the Message Down the Line by Leslie L. Kossoff

EXECUTIVE SUMMARY

- Finance department participation must be cross-organizational to ensure the financial health and welfare of the enterprise.
- Financial data should be better shared, and finance personnel become more involved, at all levels of the organization.
- Middle management presents the greatest barrier to finance messaging. To overcome this, finance must present data sharing as a verifiable win to them.
- Integrating into ad-hoc or lean-team initiatives provides finance personnel with the opportunity to become friendly advisers to the organization as a whole.

INTRODUCTION

Of all the functions in an enterprise that cannot, indeed *must not*, be the province of the function itself is finance. In fact, the more finance is separated from the rest of the organization's thinking and operations, the greater the risk for the enterprise and its stakeholders.

Finance people not only know the numbers behind what's going on, they also know why those numbers exist. From greasing the wheels to get things done, to putting the brake on projects that carry too high a financial risk, finance knows the answers—and acts on them.

The problem is that when you ask those in other parts of the organization what finance does, what you'll hear will likely be either resounding silence from a lack of knowledge, a description of some of its most basic tasks, or a stream of complaints about the problems and obstacles that finance causes.

Yet, in best of breed organizations, finance is there as much to help the body of the organization as it is to ensure the strategic and tactical financial health and welfare of the enterprise. The beauty of the function is that it can be as overarching and as specific as necessary—simultaneously and serially. The data are there to be used to help, not hurt, or obstruct. So are the people.

Until that word gets out, however, finance will be at best a boring function left to others or, at worst, seen as an enemy within the enterprise.

That's why finance has to change its image across all divisions, directorates, departments, and levels. Finance has to become an organizational player.

REDEFINING THE ROLE OF FINANCE

The problem with becoming a player is that, first, you have to want to play. That is very often the prime difficulty for the people who work in finance. Starting at the highest level and systematically working down through the enterprise, finance people must become some of the most familiar—and welcome—faces in the organization.

And so, as with every other successful organizational initiative, it starts at the top. The CEO and CFO have to agree that more financial information will be shared throughout the enterprise. They have to discuss with the senior executive team which information should be shared, when, and with whom. That means safety checks and limits on what information is given to whom—because the given is that someone, somehow, is going to give the game away outside the enterprise. As a result, damage control measures must be put in place before information is shared.

The chances are that these measures and limits are already in place. The chances are even higher that comparatively few executives or managers have accessed the information available to them. Even if they have, it probably hasn't been adequately communicated (if it was communicated at all), or they didn't know what to do with it once it was in their hands.

That is where finance's role changes from a service that is perceived to be "outside" and auditing in nature (for which read obstructive), to the organization's most involved, friendly adviser.

The goal, of course, is to turn every employee into a mini-CFO in their own job within their own department. From senior manager to frontline employee, everyone needs to understand where the organization stands financially, why, and, most importantly, how their particular job or functional area is contributing to that state of affairs. Good or bad.

BUILDING SUPPORT AMONG MIDDLE MANAGEMENT

The biggest challenge is to involve middle management positively in the process—and it's a big challenge.

Executives understand the need for financial data. The senior team will be onside as you look at how you are going to inculcate financial thinking into the larger organization.

Middle management, on the other hand, will either see the offer of financial advice and guidance as a potential threat, or as a weapon they can use at some later date against some other part of the organization. Even though they never touch a banknote, the more they see in their spreadsheet coffers, the more they believe they can manipulate the rest of the organization into doing things the way they want. Budgeting, to middle management, is empire building. It's fiefdoms. It's silos.

Enter finance. With all the good intentions in the world, your people will be facing an audience who, at least in part, are frightened that seeing your faces means the end of the world as they've known it. Fear will be the prevailing—if hidden—emotion.

It gets worse. As you bring financial knowledge to the lower levels of the enterprise, middle management will become even more frightened at the prospect of their power base being dissolved.

This means that finance has to develop a strategy to make not just knowing, but also sharing, financial information a benefit to the middle management group as well as to their employees. The good news is that, because they believe information is power, if you position what you're offering as something that will enable them to improve their position in the organization, you will achieve at least a first-level sell. They'll be open to what you have to offer.

From there, use what you're providing to make them shine. To help them succeed. To make them open to your next step—bringing finance to the front line in every department.

Because the real goal—the thing that will make the biggest change, both in the way that finance is seen and in the extent to which smart financial thinking becomes standard operating procedure in the organization—is when you start working with the lower levels. Then, just watch what happens. Even the middle managers will join in and see the win at that point.

"Even if your idea is worth stealing, the hard part is implementing the idea, not coming up with it."
Guy Kawasaki

  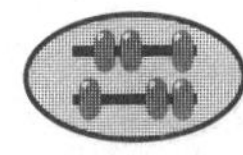   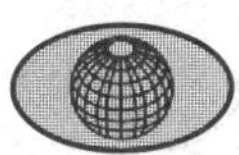   

CASE STUDY

Sony Electronics

When one of Sony Electronics' technology divisions decided it was time to look at cost reductions, senior management at one of the US plants decided it was make-or-break time. They had to show headquarters in Japan what they could do.

Adopting and adapting the Sony Six Sigma management system for a Western audience, they immediately brought finance in as a centerpiece of the initiative. The process and results were:

- Management at all levels, from manufacturing floor supervisors to external sales managers to R&D directors, were briefed and briefed again on how the financials fit into the initiative—and, by extension, into every decision they were to make.
- Dedicated finance representatives worked with management and teams to ensure that the decisions being made were financially sound, simultaneously dovetailing with and enhancing decisions made across the enterprise.
- Finance team members became operations specialists and, for the first time, fully understood the organization they were supporting.
- External contracts were both expanded and discarded, based on verifiable financial data.
- Within four months, overall productivity increased in the double digits, with a corresponding reduction in operating costs.
- For the first time in the plant's history, management returned budget to headquarters at the end of the fiscal year.

CREATING THE WIN

At the middle and lower levels of the organization, employees know that there are financial underpinnings to what they are doing, but they have little to no idea what those underpinnings are. What they do know is that they are, all too often, told that the company can't afford what would, from the employees' perspective, make all the difference in the world.

By bringing financial knowledge to all levels of the enterprise, finance breaks the existing mold. Suddenly the mystery behind the decisions is gone. The veil has been lifted and everyone knows and understands things in the same way.

Employees gain a new respect for how the finances of the company act as a driver for overall success. They begin to understand that there are financial implications in every action they make and decision they take. There is, suddenly, a direct, causal correlation between what they are doing and how it is impacting the organization, positively or negatively.

That is your chance. The more you position finance as a friendly adviser to departments and workgroups at all levels, the faster the decisions will improve across the organization. Employees at every level will know exactly what's in it for them to participate positively.

Moreover, if there are teams of any kind—from ad-hoc groups to an ongoing lean initiative—the more both they and finance will shine.

Teams are formed to generate options, recommendations, and, in some cases, decisions to move the organization from where it is to where senior executives want it to go. Unfortunately, those teams rarely have a full understanding of the financial foundations or consequences of the recommendations they make.

Too often, that results in finance having to come in after the fact and, like the villain of the piece, tell the teams they can't go forward with their ideas because they are not financially viable. Finance becomes, once again, the bad guy.

Instead, by insinuating finance into every existing and forming team in the enterprise, senior management is assured—from the get-go—that they won't have to be concerned about what the recommendations are going to cost. Instead, they'll be presented with recommendations that have annual costs, with detail on the associated savings, avoidances, and return on investment, that each recommendation brings.

Sweet.

Even better, as the organization gets smarter at using financial data at all levels, the enterprise can start moving toward stretch goals—those infamous goals so typical of best of breed organizations. That's when, even though management knows what its budget is for any fiscal year, their greater goal is not to meet budget, but to meet and exceed productivity and output targets, while returning anywhere from 10 to 15% of the annual budget back to the organization.

Really sweet.

But that can only happen if finance has developed a system for working with the rest of the enterprise. And that means taking it back to basics.

BUILDING THE FRIENDLY ADVISOR

Every employee in the finance function needs to practice relationship building with the rest of the enterprise. Finance personnel must become the first choice go-to guys as everyone, from senior executives to middle managers to line level employees, looks at what's next.

The challenge for you and your personnel will be learning a new language to explain what, to you, is self-evident.

People in the body of the organization don't know how elegant the finance function is. They don't understand that the data are there to provide answers which are simultaneously overarching and exquisitely specific, strategic, and tactical.

They don't know what you do. That puts the onus on you not only to determine what information is shared, but also how best to share it. This is a learning process for everyone—both those within the finance function and those they will be assisting.

Be clear on what you want to achieve as you take employees at all levels through the learning process. Be prepared to explain things that you don't think need explanation. They do. Moreover, those to whom you're providing guidance probably won't ask for the explanations they need, if only because they're concerned that they might not look as clever as they would like. Take it

▸▸ MAKING IT HAPPEN

- The CEO and CFO, with executive management, put together a plan for sharing financial data across the organization.
- Data protection and damage control plans are put into place, in case any financial data are released without permission.
- Finance personnel are trained to become participants in educating and supporting the organization to use financial data to make better decisions.
- Middle management is co-opted to incorporate financial data and finance department support in all planning and decision-making.
- Teams (ad-hoc, lean, departmental, etc.) are assigned dedicated finance representatives to assist in using financial data for sound decision-making.

   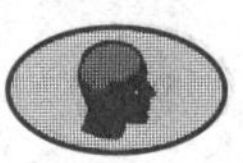  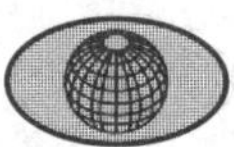   

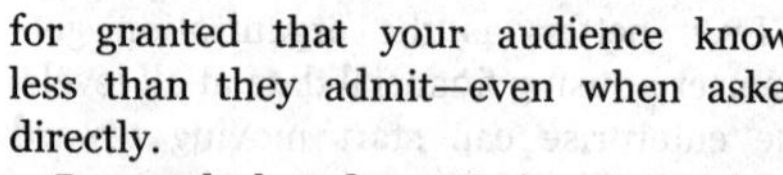

for granted that your audience knows less than they admit—even when asked directly.

Be gentle but firm. You're giving them the ability to succeed in ways that transcend anything they've achieved before. Not only will they have answers, they will also have financially sound solutions, which can lead to quantum leaps in everything from productivity to profits.

They will finally know what you yourself know about the job you do—that it's one of the most exciting and satisfying functions out there. Especially when everyone is involved.

▸▸ MORE INFO

Books:

Creelman, James. *Creating a World-Class Finance Function: Five Core Capabilities That Generate Added Business Value*. London: Business Intelligence, 2005.

Donegan, Michael C. *Growth and Profitability: Optimizing the Finance Function for Small and Emerging Businesses*. Hoboken, NJ: Wiley, 2002.

Articles:

Desai, Mihir A. "The finance function in a global corporation." *Harvard Business Review* 86:7/8 (2008).

Pohl, Herbert. "Building a competitive finance function: An executive roundtable." *McKinsey Quarterly* (December, 2007). Online at: www.nemrod-partners.com/Building.pdf

Report:

IBM Global Business Services. "Balancing risk and performance with an integrated finance organization: The global CFO study 2008." 2008. Online at: www-935.ibm.com/services/us/gbs/bus/html/2008cfostudy.html

Website:

CFO.com news and insight for financial executives: www.cfo.com

"**I don't look to jump over seven-foot bars; I look around for one-foot bars that I can step over.**" Warren Buffet

  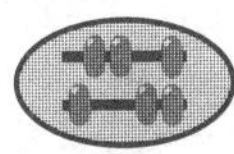   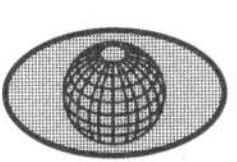   

Identifying the Right Nonexecutive Director by Terry Carroll

EXECUTIVE SUMMARY

- In the past, some have seen NED posts as a sinecure.
- Risk, diligence, and compliance factors may have changed this.
- Companies and prospective NEDs need the role to be seen as more professional.
- Remuneration for the right NED should reflect the increased "risk premium."
- NEDs should protect all stakeholders and apply sound corporate governance.
- Independence is paramount.
- Governance regulations and best practice continue to evolve.
- Successive Companies Acts have growing impact and change demands.
- The "right" NED needs wider skills and relevant business and sector experience.
- A range of sources exists, but thorough evaluation and selection are required.
- The quantity of candidates may reduce but the quality should increase.

INTRODUCTION

The "Credit Crunch" has thrown up many challenges and controversies. The extraordinary losses at Société Générale were reminiscent of the Barings debacle. The unaccountable losses suffered by many banks, especially in America, also beg serious questions about nonexecutive directors (NEDs). Never have times been tougher, or the challenges greater—and not just for banks but for all companies. Never has there been a clearer need for the right NEDs.

This article examines the challenges for all companies from a British perspective and suggests some key characteristics that are needed in the "right" NED. It also looks at wider aspects of the role, and where and how suitable candidates may be found.

GOVERNANCE AND MORE GOVERNANCE

On March 22, 2007, Naguib Kheraj resigned as finance director of Barclays, quoted by *Accountancy Age* as being "sick of compliance." As an executive director he was required to understand the same governance and regulatory matters as a NED.

In the past, some saw the role of NED as a sinecure. Now they may be rethinking that jaundiced view, as the toll of legislation, regulation, compliance, and the globalized economy increase the risk for those who occupy the role. There may still be some who approach the task altruistically, but, in general, to attract the best this increased risk should be reflected in higher remuneration.

Whether or not reward and recognition have been motivators in the past, the growing risk, diligence, and compliance factors may now be more important considerations in the mind of a prospective NED.

THE ROLE OF THE NED

In its simplest terms, the NED is there to protect the interests of the owners of the business. But now, major considerations such as health and safety, derivatives, new legislation concerning companies and employment, and risk management have added immeasurably to the potential legal and practical consequences for a NED—and, correspondingly, to the risks. These are in addition to the economic and commercial challenges that may have been the greatest for years.

To the layperson, the remuneration a NED receives may seem generous. Often it is the FTSE100 companies that hit the headlines in this respect. Not far below this level, NED packages are much more modest, and, although the scale and complexity may not be as vast as for big companies, the weight of regulation and compliance is similar.

The 2003 Higgs Review[1] drew on many of the strands of corporate governance that had been developing since the Cadbury Report in 1992.[2] It created a wholesome debate about the composition and responsibilities of the board. NEDs are now expected to play a more active role in the corporation, while being required to maintain their independence.

Two days a month is a reasonable expectation for a NED, whose day rate may be equal to that of a management consultant. But how can any diligent person be expected to perform their board and committee duties, spend time in the company, *and* keep up to date with information that, if ignored or overlooked, may land them in court, in two days per month?

COMBINED CODE OF CORPORATE GOVERNANCE

Every company needs NEDs, but not all can afford them. The law is pretty much the same for most companies; governance and guidance vary little except for small companies and quoted companies. It would do no harm for more companies to embrace the standards of the Combined Code,[3] whether or not they are required to. It would improve any company and is a useful starting point to guide any prospective NED.

RISK AND REWARD

> "For some, the burden of being a NED in a public company is too onerous in terms of time and the potential financial or reputational risk. A point of inflexion is reached when good candidates say "no thanks". In this increasingly litigious world, NEDs should be adequately rewarded for their effort in proportion to the risks they run."
>
> Virginia Bottomley, Head of Practice at Odgers Ray & Berndtson

As the demands and the potential exposure grow, so there is a commensurate increase in the risk factor. Ignorance or incompetence is no excuse; insurance and indemnity only go so far. Remuneration should increase to recognize the risk factor and reward the professional.

While NEDs are not responsible for, or engaged in, the day-to-day management, they are nevertheless subject to legal duties and responsibilities similar to those of the executives and are similarly liable for dismissal. Furthermore, it is also recommended that their remuneration should *not* be a significant proportion of their overall income.

So, will we see the emergence of the "professional" NED? A growing number are striking a balance between number of appointments and diligence. Enlightened companies encourage executive directors to accept NED appointments elsewhere to widen their perspective and personal development.

EVOLUTION OF THE ROLE

According to the Higgs Review, NEDs should:

- contribute to and constructively challenge the development of company strategy;
- scrutinize management performance;

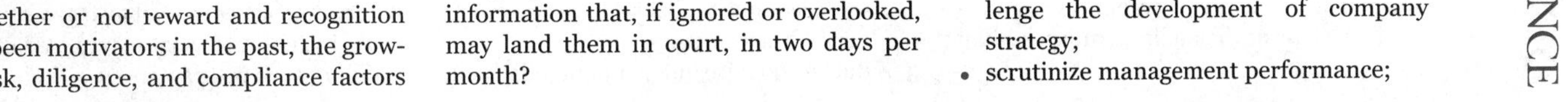
"The First Duty of a newspaper is to be Accurate. If it is Accurate, it follows that it is Fair." Herbert Bayard Swope

   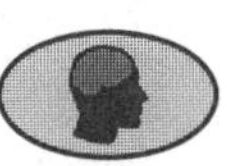  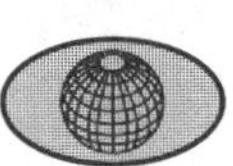 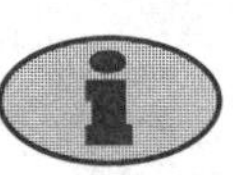  

- satisfy themselves that financial information is accurate and ensure that robust risk management is in place;
- meet at least once a year without the chairman or executive directors;
- be prepared to attend AGMs and discuss issues relating to their roles;
- have a greater exposure to major shareholders.

If only it was that simple. And according to Higgs, 60% of NEDs are still recruited with no formal process.

NEDs are, however, increasingly being sourced through search and selection. Since Higgs, diversity has been a more significant factor. Many would-be NEDs may prefer to go into private companies, where there are fewer governance requirements and financial rewards can still be attractive. Also, government and public bodies have opened themselves to advertised selection, but the fees they offer are much lower or even zero.

Executive secondment and private companies are a good proving ground. There is still, however, an apparent shortage of suitably qualified NED candidates. Organizations such as Directorbank (www.directorbank.com) have attempted to address this challenge.

The best boards should provide the newly recruited NED with a formal induction and an ongoing training program, whatever the degree of experience. Key aspects would include strategy, governance and regulation, and, of course, an introduction to the company itself, and its key people, products, and services.

This still leaves the onus on the individual to keep up to date and prepare diligently. Some take the view that this would require up to 30 days a year.

KEY ISSUES

According to Ernst & Young's annual survey in 2006, ("Concerns that keep Non-Executives awake at night"; *E&Y Newsletter*, June 2006) NEDs now spend up to 40% of their time on governance. The matters that most preoccupy them are:

- understanding a new sector;
- audit and finance;
- overseas knowledge;
- technology and security;
- remuneration policy in the company as a whole;
- the company's reputational risk.

Furthermore, a MORI poll cited in the same survey suggested that people were less likely to accept a NED appointment, and much less likely to accept an appointment as chair of the audit committee, than a year before.

INDEPENDENCE

Best practice and regulation dictate the need for independence. It's not just about individual thinking, because teamwork between the NEDs and with the executive is highly desirable. Share options as incentives for NEDs are, however, actively discouraged for quoted companies, and performance-related rewards should be geared to the share price rather than profits or sales.

The NED is required to judge and act in the best interests of the shareholders, yet, ironically, this begins with having the company's best interests at heart. Those who seek personal reward or recognition as a result of their directorship may not instinctively make impartial judgments where the company's interests should prevail.

Above all, integrity, teamwork, and trust across the board are paramount. Consensus is ideal, with a vote hardly ever needed. Consequently, these qualities matter most of all in the selection of the chairman of the board or audit committee.

THE EFFECTS OF THE 2006 COMPANIES ACT

The Companies Act 2006 came into effect in the United Kingdom in October 2008. While it codified the guidance and requirements from many sources, ultimately it made the duties even more significant and onerous. Alongside this, you have the extension of the crime of "corporate manslaughter" to the company itself, thereby effectively doubling the directors' liability.

The Act clearly sets out the seven general duties of directors:

1 A duty to act in accordance with the company's constitution, and to use powers only for the purposes for which they were conferred.
2 A duty to promote the success of the company for the benefit of its members. In doing this the directors are required to take account of:
   - the likely long-term consequences of their decisions;
   - the interests of the company's employees;
   - the need to foster the company's business relationships with suppliers, customers, and others;
   - the impact of the company's operations on the community and the environment;
   - the desirability of maintaining a reputation for high standards of business conduct;
   - the need to act fairly as between members of the company.
3 A duty to exercise independent judgment.
4 A duty to exercise reasonable care, skill, and diligence.
5 A duty to avoid conflicts of interest.
6 A duty not to accept benefits from third parties.
7 A duty to declare to the company's other directors any interest a director has in a proposed transaction or arrangement with the company.

It is likely that the new provisions will cause the greatest difficulty for directors who sit on more than one board. The Act introduces a new statutory right of shareholders to sue directors, in the company's name, to recover on the company's behalf loss it has suffered as a result of the directors' negligence, default, breach of duty, or breach of trust.

The new statutory right, or "derivative action," will undoubtedly make it easier for shareholders to take directors to court. Considerable concern has been expressed that this, taken together with the statutory statement of duties—particularly the detailed list of factors to which directors are to have regard—will lead to significant risks for directors.

Even if directors are able to obtain indemnity or insurance, the above requirements not only codify the requirements of best practice or regulation from a number of different sources, they also increase individual risks and exposure significantly.

One might wonder why anyone would want to be a nonexecutive director. The risks, responsibilities, and liabilities have increased considerably, as has the amount of knowledge and understanding now required of them.

Nevertheless, there will always be a supply of would-be NEDs, and not just for the money. We shall inevitably see the growth of the profession of director, which the United Kingdom's Institute of Directors has done much to foster, through collectivization and training. There will always be some people who either wish to carry their executive experience into semi-retirement or have the personal and professional qualities to perform the role. In addition, there is a ready supply from the executive ranks of other companies.

SO HOW DO YOU FIND AND IDENTIFY THE RIGHT NEDS?

First, all companies of a certain size should encourage their executive directors to seek a NED appointment elsewhere as part of their personal development. This opportunity not only helps them grow as individuals and executives, it also gives them an acute insight into what is required of those fulfilling such roles.

     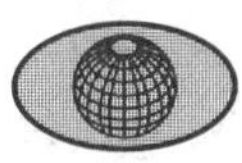   

While it is not beyond the whit of a chairman to seek out people with directly relevant sectoral experience and/or skills, there is no reason why this process should be any different from that of selecting executives. Search consultants have been playing an increasing role in identifying and selecting suitable candidates, but ultimately it is for the board to apply an appropriate and objective recruitment and selection process for the right candidate.

It has been too often said in the past that there aren't enough good and suitable candidates. Certainly, not only the diligent governance requirements, but also the personal qualities needed, justify significant expense and a rigorous process of selection.

Ultimately, the fundamental role of NEDs is to protect the interests of the owners of the business. They need to be dispassionate, courageous, and of the highest integrity. The remuneration may not always have compensated for the potential corporate and personal risks, but maybe this is because they weren't always recognized either. Now the British Government and others are ensuring that these considerations are paramount.

ESSENTIAL CHARACTERISTICS

Ideally, a prospective NED should have experience relevant to the business or to the sector in which it operates. However, alongside this goes a set of professional skills. If you can identify the core executive roles, it would be ideal to have an equivalent "shadow" on the board. This is most evident in the case of the finance director. A senior professional from another company, or maybe a retired executive director, can be a coach, mentor, and sounding board.

Above all, the board needs to be capable of acting as a team—NEDs and executives together, comprehensive and all-embracing; neither shy of their collective responsibility to the shareholders, nor of their commitment to the long-term success of the enterprise.

Executive directors may be rigorously reviewed and vetted for their relevant skills; but those required of the NED go one step beyond. If the post ever was a sinecure, it should be no longer. Not only the future of the company, but that of a country's economy and wider reputation lie in the hands of this new generation. The chairman and his colleagues may realize that they are protecting interests beyond their own and those of the owners in having a thorough, objective, and professional identification and selection process for their new NED colleagues.

STILL INTERESTED?

The growth of regulation and the duties of governance may drive some prospective NEDs away. If Naguib Kheraj found life too onerous as an executive director, what might many who contemplate putting themselves forward as candidates for a nonexecutive directorship think? Others, increasingly professional, may be drawn by the challenge, complexity, and variety, together with the intellectual and increasingly appropriate financial reward for a job diligently and well done.

▸▸ MORE INFO

Website:

Directorbank, for executive and non-executive recruitment: www.directorbank.com

NOTES

1 Derek Higgs. *Review of the Role and Effectiveness of Non-executive Directors.* London: The Stationery Office, 2003.

2 *Report of the Committee on the Financial Aspects of Corporate Governance.* "The Cadbury Report." London: Gee, 1992.

3 Financial Reporting Council (FRC). *The Combined Code on Corporate Governance.* London: FRC, 2008.

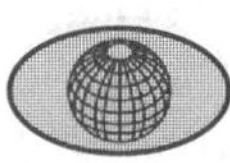

Viewpoint: Roger Steare

The Morals of Money—How to Build a Sustainable Economy and Financial Sector

INTRODUCTION

Roger Steare is a corporate philosopher and visiting professor of organizational ethics at Cass Business School, City University, London. Roger studied philosophy at Royal Holloway College, London University, where he was tutored by Lord Conrad Russell, son of philosopher Bertrand Russell. He worked for Midland Bank (now HSBC) in the City between 1979 and 1981, and then had stints as a social worker and executive coach before becoming chief executive of the City recruiters Jonathan Wren, a subsidiary of Adecco, the world's largest recruitment firm, in 1994. He left to found Roger Steare Consulting in 1998, and has specialized in ethics since 2002. His ethicability® framework has been used or endorsed by organizations including HSBC, Tomorrow's Company, and the Institute of Business Ethics. He is the co-founder of the Soul Gym at Worth Abbey, a Benedictine monastery in West Sussex, a director of the Centre for Applied and Professional Ethics, and a Fellow of the Royal Society for the Arts. Roger is interested in astronomy and lives in Sevenoaks, Kent.

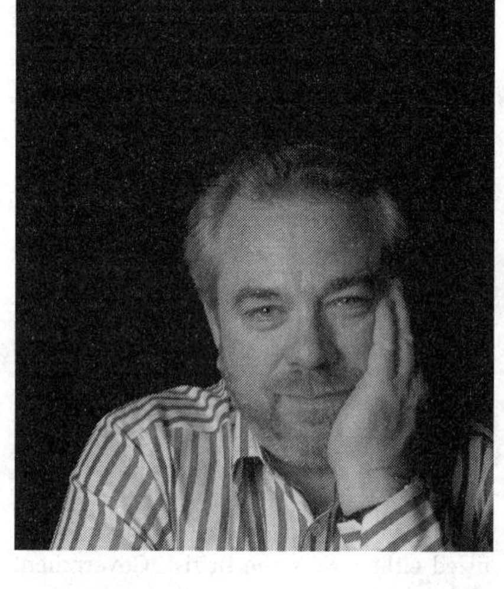

The credit crisis of 2007–2008 and the subsequent economic recession were the direct consequence of serious ethical failures. Banks lent money that they didn't have to borrowers who wanted goods and services they couldn't afford or didn't actually need. Human greed and fear were the fundamental drivers of the crisis. Unfortunately, however, the crisis is certain to be repeated, unless or until human beings learn to exercise greater restraint, courage, humanity, and judgment.

The ethical failures that lay behind the crisis go to the heart of modern economic theory. If we want economic growth, we must also accept economic decline. We inhabit a closed planetary ecosystem with finite resources. While solar radiation, wind energy, and gravity offer virtually unlimited energy resources, fossil fuels, fresh water, fertile soil, a benign climate, and biodiversity are either limited or fragile.

In 1950, there were two billion human beings on the planet. In 2008, the world's human population had risen to nearly seven billion, and the United Nations estimates it will have risen to nine billion by 2050. Many more people want better material lifestyles.

But if we accept that our planet has a limited and fragile ecosystem, how can it support this constant and infinite economic growth? I know it is not a particularly popular view, but perhaps the philosophy of perpetual economic growth has more in common with the cancer cell—a terminal disease—than it does with sustainable organisms. Only a minority of economists, such as Herman Daly, Juan Martinez-Alier, and Robert Constanza, acknowledge that the economics of infinite growth is essentially suicidal. Amongst politicians, only the Green movement accepts the alternative that Daly describes as "steady state" economics.

Current accounting standards are another part of the problem. These are only capable of accurately describing 20% to 25% of the full economic value of any enterprise. The alternative of "triple bottom line" accounting standards is beginning to address this issue, but we are still left with a massive void—our failure to measure the value of human relationships, with all stakeholders, that are the core fundamentals of all human activity.

RESTORING TRUST

So what does all this mean for financial services firms and for financial services centers? Quite simply, it depends on whether or not these arguments are persuasive or not. But, given that "trust" is the greatest asset a financial services firm or center can possess, I recommend that prudence, restraint, fairness, and other moral values should once again become the foundation stone for those who look after other people's money.

How is trust restored? Well, firstly it is going to take time. Patience here, as with most things in life, is a virtue. But having worked closely with a number of enlightened financial services firms, professional bodies, and regulators since 2003, I would like to share with you this is not just wishful thinking, but the evidence of my experiences and insights. I have worked with over 6,000 senior executives from over 100 different private, public sector, and not-for-profit organizations. Together, we have explored:

- why we do right and wrong;
- what we mean by doing the right thing;
- how we decide what's right;
- how we build a culture of integrity.

This journey of exploration offers insights into over 2,500 years of moral philosophy; about 50 years of behavioral and social psychology; some brain physiology; the concept of moral leadership; and last, but not least, a decision-making framework which is road-tested with relevant and realistic business dilemmas.

The experience is both meaningful and memorable for participants because it gives them the opportunity and the permission to think and speak constructively about issues that go to the core of who they are as human beings, and how they behave within their organizations or communities. This often comes as a relief to those who feel that we have created a world today where other people have taken it upon themselves to tell us what's right, instead of trusting us as moral adults to work it out for ourselves. In the media, these people include politicians, journalists, and commentators. At work, there are regulators, lawyers, compliance officers, HR executives, and, of course, bosses.

I would contend that regulation alone is no substitute for moral character and moral leadership.

"There is no royal flower-strewn path to success. And if there is, I have not found it for if I have accomplished anything in life it is because I have been willing to work hard." C. J. Walker

MORAL DNA

In 2008, we constructed and published the ethicability® Moral DNA Test to understand how people prefer to make moral decisions. Between July and August 2008 over 20,000 people from 162 countries completed the test, which was supported by Cass Business School, Pricewaterhouse-Coopers, and *The Times* in London.

Those who work in financial services scored lower than average, indicating greed, fear, or moral immaturity. But the test measures not just our overall ethics score compared with others, it also describes how we make moral choices based on three moral dimensions: Rule compliance, social conscience, and principled conscience.

Rule compliance means obedience and is the first conscience we develop as young children. Don't think—just do as you're told—or else. Social conscience means altruism and is based on the idea that doing the right thing is doing what's best for others. This part of our conscience appears to be almost fully developed by the time we are in our teens. Finally, principled conscience means character or virtue. Doing the right thing is about making decisions based on how we apply principles such as courage, fairness, and honesty to the choices we make. This appears not to develop fully until we are in our late 50s.

When things go wrong, the response of governments and regulators is to treat us like children and try to change behaviors by devising even more rules and regulations. But the test results clearly demonstrated that this only serves to increase the risk of more wrong-doing, as it means people take less personal responsibility for their actions. Instead of bothering with this, they will simply check if it's okay with compliance or HR.

Then, if things do go wrong, they don't blame themselves, but blame the system or the market. The response of government and regulators to wrong-doing has been to add ever-increasing volumes of rules and regulations that tell us what's right and how to behave. We can no longer be trusted to know what is right or, indeed, to do it. We have to be told.

If we do the right thing, we are rewarded. But if we do the wrong thing—and get caught—then we are punished. And, if the transgression is newsworthy enough to get the attention of politicians, we will get even more rules, structures, and processes to tell us what's right.

It is my experience that in order to do the right thing in any organization, people have to have the following:

- a clear and moral purpose
- a clear set of moral values that guide behavior
- leaders who set a personal example consistent with these values
- a living community of employees, customers, suppliers, shareholders, and others, in which people will able to resolve together the inevitable challenges and conflicts which are faced in every endeavor

They will be guided by the values of the organization, the personal example of their leaders, and a shared approach and framework to ethical decisions. This approach should permeate every human aspect of business from recruitment, through training, appraisals and rewards.

The challenges that we face today in business are not economic, social, or political—they are ethical challenges that demand a more mature response. Moral grown-ups in business don't need others to tell them what's right, they ought to be trusted to discuss it and work it out for themselves. A great customer proposition is not delivered in the form of complex rules and procedures; it is delivered by mature adults who really do care about other people and the quality of goods and services they buy.

But the greatest challenge of all will be to confront the brutal truth that our current assumptions about economics are fundamentally flawed. This planet that we all share is a closed ecosystem with finite resources. Yet the other assumptions we make are that human beings have unlimited wants; that growth is good; that we can all strive for what we want rather than what we need.

This economic philosophy of growth for its own sake is as bankrupt as the philosophy of the cancer cell. "Homo economicus" is riddled with malignant growths. We need to re-discover the philosophy of "homo sapiens." We need to find the wisdom to confront this awful truth; and then deploy our intelligence to find a new and sustainable model of moral capitalism, founded on a moral financial sector where trust is the ultimate reserve currency.

▸▸ MORE INFO

Books:

Bakan, J. *The Corporation: The Pathological Pursuit of Profit and Power*. Toronto, ON: Penguin Books, 2004.

Bellini, J., and K. St Clair. *The Bullshit Factor: The Truth about Corporate Disguises, Lies and Denial*. London: Artesian Publishing, 2006.

Collins, J. *Good to Great*. New York: HarperCollins, 2001.

Common, M., and S. Stagl. *Ecological Economics: An Introduction*. New York: Cambridge University Press, 2005.

Website:

www.ethicability.org Take the free ethicability® Moral DNA Test

  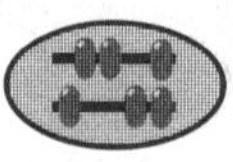   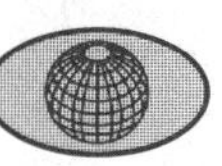   

Improving Corporate Profitability Through Accountability by Marc J. Epstein and Priscilla S. Wisner

EXECUTIVE SUMMARY

- Traditional measures of performance are of limited use to modern businesses, being rooted in evaluating past performance. They are a poor guide to true value, often missing the key factors that promote long-term worth.
- It is essential to include the leading financial and nonfinancial indicators of performance that drive long-term value. This provides broader and more sophisticated information that highlights future trends.
- Effectively managing and communicating a broader set of performance measures reduces uncertainty, ensures better relationships with stockholders and analysts, and enables improved financial performance.
- Full accountability and disclosure, combined with improved measures and new systems to drive the process throughout the organization, create greater value for stakeholders, promoting future success.

INTRODUCTION

Improved governance requires the right employees, the right culture and values, and the right systems, information, and decision-making. Unfortunately, most organizations are attempting to steer their information-age businesses using industrial-age measurements. Managers have struggled for decades with accounting systems that fail to measure many of the variables that drive long-term value. The historical lagging indicators of performance that are commonly used by accountants are of limited value in determining the value of businesses for external stakeholders, and are of little use in guiding the business internally. Financial data on profitability and return on investment are valuable measures of corporate performance, but they are lagging indicators that measure past performance. A broader set of financial measures is necessary (for example, measurement of intangible assets such as intellectual capital and research-and-development value), in addition to an expanded set relating to customers, internal processes, and organizational measures.

The metrics must include the *leading* financial and nonfinancial indicators of performance that are the drivers and predictors of future financial performance. For example, fines and penalties may be a leading indicator of corporate reputation, employee turnover is a leading measure of future recruitment and training costs, and product quality is a leading measure of customer satisfaction, which in turn is a leading measure of market share. Each of these factors (reputation, employee-related costs, customer satisfaction, and market share) impacts financial performance.

IMPROVED INTERNAL AND EXTERNAL REPORTING

Just as companies expand their performance measurement parameters, they must also expand their performance reporting models. Employees, stockholders, financial analysts, activists, customers, suppliers, government regulators, and others increasingly demand detailed information about corporate activities, and the internet has made the dissemination of that information easier and faster. No longer can managers claim they don't have the information. The data are easy to collect, and it's essential to have broader and more forward-looking information to effectively manage the diverse issues that managers now confront daily. Managers should collect this broader array of information on activities and impacts both inside and outside the company, and select a set of data to provide adequate disclosure to their various stakeholders. External stakeholders need a broader set of information to effectively evaluate corporate performance, and voluntary disclosure of this information is critical for corporate accountability. This accountability, both inside and outside the company, through an effective corporate communications strategy, is an essential element of effective and responsible corporate governance.

Proactively managing external disclosures should be a fundamental part of corporate communications strategy. By externally disclosing a more comprehensive set of measures, company executives are seizing the initiative to describe the company's strategy, set expectations, increase transparency, and ensure goal alignment between the company and a broad set of stakeholders. Disclosing performance measures allows investors and other stakeholders to view the

CASE STUDY

The Campbell Soup Company has continually improved corporate governance.

Changes undertaken in the early 1990s required a majority of directors to come from outside the organization. All directors must stand for election every year and must own at least 6,000 shares of stock within three years of election. Among other provisions, interlocking directorships are not allowed and insiders are banned from certain key committees. In 1995, the board began a rotating yearly performance evaluation of directors, board committees, and the board as a whole. In 2000, the board approved a new director compensation program to closely link director compensation to the creation of stockholder value; only 20% is paid in cash (tied to attendance at meetings). The full set of Campbell Soup's governance standards and current performance review are disclosed in the annual proxy statement to stockholders.

The Cooperative Bank, based in the United Kingdom and with 4,000 employees, has won numerous awards for the high degree of transparency and accountability the company has exhibited. The bank has identified six partners in its quest for corporate value: stockholders, customers, staff and their families, suppliers, national and international societies, and past and future generations of cooperators. The company surveys all stakeholder groups to determine the critical elements in creating value for each, and performance targets are set on the basis of this information. In 2003, 70 targets were established in three principal areas: delivering value, social responsibility, and ecological sustainability. The Cooperative Bank 2004 Sustainability Report states that 33 targets were fully achieved, acceptable progress was made on 22, and 15 were not achieved. The bank reports progress on each target, providing data and management commentary, and establishes targets for the coming year.

"Good men prefer to be accountable." Michael Owen Edwardes

     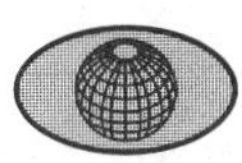   

company through the eyes of management. A clear, comprehensive communications strategy is highly valued by stockholders and analysts alike.

CONCLUSION

Once a company has decided to improve corporate governance, measure a broader set of indicators of past and future success, and report internally and externally, managers must develop systems to drive these decisions through the organization. Leading companies are developing integrated, closed-loop planning, budgeting, and feedback systems to help align strategy implementation with corporate performance. While leadership at the top is critical, buy-in at the shop floor level is essential for the success of any system implementation. Metrics must be linked to strategy and must be consistent throughout the organization. Companies are increasingly stating desires to become more customer focused or more socially responsible, yet many are still basing employee rewards on meeting revenue and profit goals. If companies expect employees to be more customer focused or more socially or environmentally responsible, part of overall performance evaluations and rewards should be on the basis of customer focus or social responsibility.

Accountable managers encourage not only continuous judgment, but continuous improvement. They insist that everyone in the organization participate in decision-making. They implement a culture of constant learning and insist on building learning organizations. Accountable managers communicate constantly, setting a tone of forthright feedback and transparency.

Full accountability comes only when a company combines a strong governance structure, improved and broad measurement of relevant performance impacts, timely and full internal and external reporting, and comprehensive management systems to drive the accountability model throughout the organization. By combining these elements companies are creating value for the stakeholders whose support they need in order to prosper—customers, investors, employees, suppliers, communities, the public, regulators, and other government officials.

▸▸ MAKING IT HAPPEN

The rewards from building the accountable organization are much like those from building the quality organization—the more committed the managers and workers and the better integrated the concept with company line operations, the greater the benefit. As a first step, managers must build accountable systems and practices within the company. Then they can build bridges to the outside. As they move toward full accountability—well-governed, measured, managed, and publicly responsive—they will position themselves to reap many benefits:

- Executing strategy: the accountable organization articulates each strategy and tactic with specific measures that align direction in ways that broader objectives cannot. The hard measures then give managers objective feedback on what the strategy execution is achieving.
- Improving decision-making: the accountable organization generates a wealth of information on performance, which in turn informs decision-making through facts, not intuition. People inside and outside the company can make more effective decisions to further company strategy and goals.
- Empowering people: the accountable organization thins the ranks of middle managers that distil and convey information and empowers decision-making authority to the front lines. As management articulates what it wants with concrete quantitative measures, workers have clear guidance of goals and objectives and how they relate to strategy.
- Accelerating learning: the accountable organization installs feedback systems that yield rapid-fire learning from people both across and outside the company. The company with the most feedback loops—internal and external—is the most successful.
- Communicating the story: the accountable organization delivers its story of value with credible financial and nonfinancial numbers. As senior managers report more numbers externally, exposing performance transparently, stockholders and analysts have less reason to undervalue their stock.
- Inspiring loyalty: the accountable organization markets its value on a basis of reliable performance measures. The no-smoke-and-mirrors approach spurs cooperation and inspires the loyalty of investors, customers, suppliers, employees, business partners, and communities.

▸▸ MORE INFO

Books:

Epstein, Marc J., and Bill Birchard. *Counting What Counts: Turning Corporate Accountability to Competitive Advantage*. Cambridge, MA: Perseus, 2000.

Epstein, Marc J., and K. O. Hanson (eds). *The Accountable Corporation*. Westport, CT: Praeger Publications, 2006.

Monks, Robert A. G. *The Emperor's Nightingale: Restoring the Integrity of the Corporation in the Age of Shareholder Activism*. Cambridge, MA: Perseus, 1999.

Ward, Ralph D. *Improving Corporate Boards: The Boardroom Insider Guidebook*. New York: Wiley, 2000.

Articles:

Botosan, Christine. "Disclosure level and the cost of equity capital." *Accounting Review* 72:3 (July 1997): 323–349.

Epstein, Marc J., and Krishna Palepu. "What financial analysts want." *Strategic Finance* (April 1999): 48–52.

Healy, Paul, Amy Hutton, and Krishna Palepu. "Stock performance and intermediation changes surrounding sustained increases in disclosure." *Contemporary Accounting Research* 16:3 (Fall 1999): 485–520.

Hutton, Amy. "Beyond financial reporting—An integrated approach to corporate disclosure." *Journal of Applied Corporate Finance* 16:4 (Fall 2004): 8–16.

Sengupta, Partha. "Corporate disclosure quality and the cost of debt." *Accounting Review* 73:4 (October 1998): 459–474.

Report:

Engen, Travis, and Samuel DiPiazza. "Beyond reporting: Creating business value and accountability." World Business Council on Sustainable Development, June 2005. Online at: www.wbcsd.org/plugins/DocSearch/details.asp?ObjectId=MTU5MDk

"We are responsible for actions performed in response to circumstances for which we are not responsible."
Allan Massie

     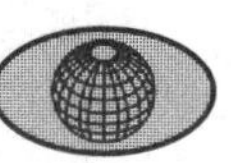   

Reinvesting in the Company versus Rewarding Investors with Distributions by Ruth Bender

EXECUTIVE SUMMARY

- Dividend payouts will always depend on having sufficient retained profits and cash.
- Companies should invest in growth if doing so will generate a return above the cost of capital, as this will increase stockholder value. If there are no value-enhancing investments, surplus cash should be returned to stockholders.
- Stockholder expectations will drive dividend policy, and changes to that policy should be signaled clearly to investors.

INTRODUCTION

Stockholders gain value from their investments in two ways—either by receiving dividends or by realizing a capital gain. Dividend policy is determined directly by a company's board, which has to decide whether to make a payout or to reinvest.

Although many factors underlie the dividend decision, there is one basic rule: If there are investment opportunities where the expected return exceeds the company's cost of capital, value will be created by making the investment and it should be done. If there are insufficient value-creating opportunities, the surplus cash should be distributed to stockholders.

Therefore, the question to ask when considering reinvestment versus distribution to investors should be: Will this create stockholder value?

DIVIDEND POLICY

Companies that pay dividends try to increase the absolute level of dividend each year in order to meet investor expectations.

Two numbers are relevant to understanding dividend policy: The level of the annual dividend (which may in practice be paid in quarterly or semi-annual installments), and the dividend payout ratio (the dividend for the year as a percentage of after-tax income). Stockholders are concerned with the absolute level of dividend they receive, but will also have an eye on the dividend payout ratio.

If the payout ratio is kept constant, then, as profits grow, the absolute level of dividend will become progressively larger. However, volatility in profits would mean volatility in payouts, and this is unsatisfactory to investors. Accordingly, most companies have a more flexible attitude to the payout ratio, aiming to smooth the distribution, increasing dividends annually but not exactly in line with the change in profits.[1] This is particularly relevant in cyclical industries, where a progressive dividend implies a changing payout ratio over the cycle.

DRIVERS OF DIVIDEND POLICY

Two fundamentals underlie a company's ability to pay dividends to its stockholders—is there enough cash, and are there enough profits?

The issue of cash is a universal one: If a company does not have sufficient liquidity to manage its operations in the way it needs to, it would be foolish to deplete cash resources by making payouts. As to whether there are sufficient profits, this is often a legal issue, and so specific to a particular jurisdiction. However, a general rule is that dividends should only be paid out of realized retained profits.

Moving beyond these fundamentals, a key issue for management to consider is the business of the company. Companies in different industries, or at different stages of their life cycle, have different cash needs and investment opportunities, and these will drive dividend policy.

Investors in an early-stage business have different expectations from those investing in a mature business. The early-stage business has low (if any) profits but high growth potential, and the investor will be seeking a capital gain. That gain will come from growing the business, which is likely to involve considerable investment along the way. So for these types of business, paying a dividend would reduce the growth potential; investors would not, therefore, expect a high payout.

In a mature company there are fewer investment opportunities and so less growth is expected. To obtain the required returns, stockholders will expect a large dividend. Indeed, if a company with no clear investment opportunities were to retain profits rather than paying them out as dividends, stockholders could rightly query the executives' motives in doing so as this is not a value-creating strategy.

In determining their dividend policy, boards also need to ensure that the capital structure of the business is sound. Because debt is a cheaper form of finance than equity, companies generally want a proportion of their finance to be debt. However, too much debt will drive a business to bankruptcy. Accordingly, the dividend decision has to be consistent with the financing policy—a riskier business will have more equity in its capital structure, and it is unlikely that a company that is equity-financed would pay out a large dividend. Table 1 illustrates this.

For an early-stage operation there is no point in paying a dividend, as this would deplete the company's much needed cash resources, and the only source of replacement funds would be the same stockholders that are receiving the dividend. However, as the business gains the traction to use more debt-based instruments, a higher payout to stockholders can be made. For declining business there will be few, if any, value-enhancing investment opportunities, so the dividend payout should be as great as cash flow allows, probably paying out previously retained profits.

A further consideration in deciding dividend policy is the tax situation of the company and its investors. In many jurisdictions, investors are taxed more highly on dividends than on capital gains, which means that they might prefer to receive value by selling their shares in the market at a time of their choosing (or selling them to the company in a buyback) rather than taking this highly taxed income. Also, in some jurisdictions, companies can face a tax penalty for paying dividends.

Table 1. Financing and dividend policy over the business life cycle. (*Source*: Bender and Ward, 2009)

	Stage of life cycle			
	Launch	*Growth*	*Maturity*	*Decline*
Capital required to support value-enhancing growth	Very high	High	Medium	Negative
Main source of finance for the business	Equity (venture capital)	Equity	Equity and debt	Debt
Dividend policy	Nil	Nil or low	Substantial	100% payout

"The worst crime against working people is a company which fails to operate at a profit." Samuel Gompers

  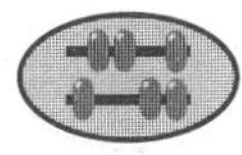   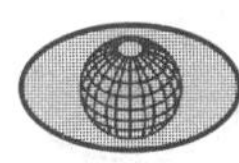   

THE IMPACT OF CHANGING DIVIDEND POLICY

A strong influence on how much dividend a company pays out is the level of dividends in previous years. Stockholders prefer a predictable and sustainable dividend strategy, and companies have particular clienteles of investors with different requirements for distributions. Investors who want their value creation to come from capital gains tend not to invest too much in high-yielding shares. Similarly, those who need a stream of income from dividends seek out companies that will provide this.

Given that the dividend decision is made by balancing the company's cash needs and its investment needs, significant changes in a company's level of dividend could be seen as good or bad by the investment community; it depends on the story that the company is telling, and whether the markets believe it. Table 2 illustrates this.

If the dividend on a high-yielding stock was cut without this being properly signaled, the income-seeking stockholders will be obliged to sell shares in order to make good the shortfall in the inflows they were expecting. And if a growth stock suddenly starts paying a dividend, this might be unwelcome (for example, for tax reasons) to its particular stockholder constituency, who again might become sellers. So an unexpected change in dividend policy can lead, in the short term, to the share price falling because there are too many sellers.

BUYBACKS AS AN ALTERNATIVE TO CASH DIVIDENDS

Companies that do not want to commit to a regular dividend, or those making one-off large distributions to stockholders (for example, the proceeds of a major disposal), may do so by way of a share buyback rather than a dividend. For tax purposes, the proceeds of a buyback are often treated as capital rather than income, which favors some investors. Another advantage to investors is that, depending on how the transaction is structured, they can choose whether or not to sell their shares to the company, giving them more flexibility in managing their investment. And, from the company's point of view, the buyback does not create expectations in the same way that a regularly increasing dividend does.

However, buybacks are not permitted in all jurisdictions. Also, these programs are more expensive for companies to administer than are dividends.

CONCLUSION

Ultimately, all the profits a business creates will be paid out to its stockholders; dividends are just a payment on account to those that currently own its stock. The board has a practical decision to make: Whether to make that payment now, or to retain the money and put it to use by reinvesting in the business.

In addition to the availability of cash and profits to support the dividend, other factors to influence the board's decision should include the company's investment opportunities and stockholder expectations.

Investors value stability in dividend policy, and an increasing payout.

Table 2. What might a change in dividend signal?

	Increase dividend	*Reduce dividend*
Interpreted as good news	Company is prospering and throwing off cash	A change of strategy means that the directors see more profitable investment opportunities and future profitable growth
Interpreted as bad news	Directors have run out of investment ideas for profitable growth	Falls in profits and cash flow have led to the need to preserve cash

CASE STUDY

Microsoft[2]

Microsoft, one of the largest and most profitable companies in the world, has a somewhat unusual track record on distributions. Although enormously cash-generative, until 2003 the company had never paid out a dividend to its stockholders, though it had returned money to them through buybacks. (In 2003 the tax treatment of US dividends was eased, although the company stated that this was a coincidence.) A quarterly dividend is now paid, which has grown steadily each year.

In 2004 Microsoft announced its quarterly dividend (US$0.08), and also a special one-off dividend of US$3 per share, plus plans for a buyback program of up to US$30 billion.

At the time, Steve Ballmer, the CEO, explained the distributions as follows: "We are confident in our long-term ability to grow revenue, profits and shareholder value. . .We will continue to make major investments across all our businesses, and maintain our position as a leading innovator in the industry, but we can now also provide up to $75 billion in total value to shareholders over the next four years."

In this way the payout was clearly signaled as a growth story, with excess cash rather than a lack of managerial ideas for the future.

Bringing the story up to date, in September 2008, following its abortive bid for Yahoo!, Microsoft announced a US$0.02 increase in its quarterly dividend (to US$0.13), and a new US$40 billion share repurchase program, to expire in 2013. (And this at a time when most companies were preserving cash because of the credit crunch.) The company stated that it had returned more than US$115 billion to stockholders via dividends and buybacks in the last five years and that the new buyback program reflected its confidence in Microsoft's long-term growth. This return of equity to stockholders may be funded by bringing debt into the capital structure.

▸▸ MAKING IT HAPPEN

In setting dividend policy, the board should consider several key factors. For example:

- What are the current investment opportunities (organic and by acquisition) available to the business, and are they likely to change in the next few years?
- What is the current cash position? Do we have sufficient cash for our needs in the foreseeable future? Are we holding too much cash? How accurately can we forecast this?
- Legally, are there any restraints on paying out a dividend this year?
- If we change our dividend policy, how will the markets react?

NOTES

1 Lintner, J. "Distribution of incomes of corporations among dividends, retained earnings, and taxes." *American Economic Review* 46 (1956): 97–113.

2 *Source*: www.microsoft.com.

"If a business does well, the stock eventually follows." Warren Buffett

     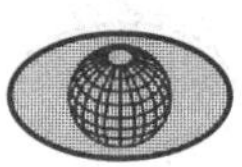   

Viewpoint: Amjid Ali
Shariah Law—Bringing a New Ethical Dimension to Banking

INTRODUCTION

Amjid Ali, senior manager, HSBC Amanah Global, believes that *shariah* finance is broadening its appeal and reach—both among Muslims and non-Muslims—as a result of the banking and financial crisis. Recognized as one of the most influential Muslims in the UK by the Muslim Power 100 Awards, Ali has 22 years of branch banking experience with Midland Bank and HSBC in the UK. In September 2003 he joined HSBC Amanah UK as senior business development manager, with responsibility for raising the profile of Amanah Home Finance in the UK. He took over as UK head in January 2005, with responsibility for strategy, distribution, and sales, and was appointed senior manager, HSBC Amanah Global, in August 2008. In this role Ali is working as part of the HSBC Amanah central team headquartered in Dubai.

What are the underlying principles of *shariah* law from a financial perspective? In other words, what defines the kind of model to which a financial institution that seeks to offer *shariah*-compliant services to its Muslim customers will have to adhere?

Shariah is the body of Islamic faith and has two main sources. The first is the Qur'an, the sacred book that records the word of God as revealed to the prophet Muhammad, Peace Be Upon Him (PBUH). To quote directly from the Qur'an: "God has permitted trade and forbidden interest," Qur'an, Chapter 2, Verse 275. The fundamental underlying principle is that interest is prohibited.

The second source is the Hadith, the body of documents that records the *sunnah* (the practice, or "life example") of the Prophet Muhammad (PBUH).

From these two sources there are five main prohibitions that must be observed in the creation of a *shariah*-compliant financial services model. They overlap somewhat and are mutually supportive.

1 *Riba*: the prohibition of interest.
2 *Gharar* (translated as "uncertainty" or opacity): there must be a full and fair disclosure (e.g., certainty as to the price of a contract before it is concluded.)
3 *Maysair*: the prohibition of speculation or gambling ("obtaining something easily or becoming rich without effort".)
4 Profit: the Islamic financier should only generate benefit from the project in which they invest and must take some risk, since risk equates to effort and potential loss.
5 Unethical investment: Islam prohibits investing or dealing in certain products such as alcohol, armaments, and pork, and in activities such as gambling, entertainment, and hotels. (Exactly how this last prohibition is interpreted varies widely depending on where in the Muslim world one is.)

Is this list sufficient to define *shariah*-compliant financial services?

No, there are other factors to keep in mind when constructing product offerings. Very importantly, one has to keep in mind the Islamic view of money. In Islam money is not a commodity; it has no intrinsic use and it can only be exchanged for the same par value. Also, Islam allows the use of securities to support a transaction, which guards against the wilful wrongdoing or carelessness of partners.

HSBC, Lloyds, and other banks now offer *shariah*-compliant mortgages for house purchase. How can this be reconciled with the principles you have outlined?

If we are supporting a customer in the buying of a property, it is done under a contract known as diminishing *musharakah*. This translates as co-ownership. In this transaction, the bank and the customer buy the home jointly, in joint names. As time progresses the customer buys more and more of the property from the bank and the bank's share in the home diminishes, until the bank no longer has any stake in the home. It is proper for the bank to take a reward for bearing the initial risk, but this reward is not interest on a loan but a rental charge for the portion the asset owned by the bank. This method follows the underlying principle that "you cannot make money on money," but it is permissible to "make money on the use or the exchange of an asset."

Can you provide a sense of the growing scale and importance of *shariah* finance around the world?

Islamic banking is already large and it is growing very substantially. The target market is the world's 1.6 billion Muslims, who represent 25 per cent of the world's population, and are largely concentrated in emerging economies. The industry's total funds under management are estimated to be worth around US$450 billion to US$500 billion, excluding Iran. The annual growth rate for Islamic finance is currently running at 30%, which suggests that the market will reach US$1 trillion in funds under management by 2010. These figures were provided in a recent issue of *The Banker*.

While the Muslim community in general views *shariah* banking as the only acceptable method of banking we have to accept that, when viewed globally, *shariah* banking is an alternative to, rather than a replacement for, the conventional, traditional model of Western banking. The latter has been in existence for centuries and has developed into a very sophisticated global industry. By contrast, Islamic finance is still very much an emerging, developing form of banking, which continues to evolve almost on a daily basis. At this moment, no *shariah* bank has a complete set of products that would mirror the portfolio of products on offer in a traditional bank.

     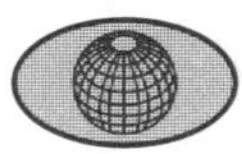   

Following the financial crisis, there have been calls for a more ethical financial infrastructure in the West. Does *shariah* banking have anything to offer to non-Muslims on this front?

If you look at the ethical platform of *shariah* banking, it will undoubtedly appeal not only to the Muslim community, but to the wider community as well. The transparency of products and the sharing of risk, together with the emphasis on like-for-like benefits are very appealing universally. What is also very clear is that, with any *shariah* bank, the principle of treating customers fairly must be at the heart of the bank's practice or it cannot be *shariah*-compliant. There are lessons for all from the credit crisis and subsequent global recession. However, I personally do not believe that Islamic financing can be considered a replacement for traditional banking. However, as it stands today, it is a credible alternative for non-Muslims. And for Muslims, it is really the only way for a Muslim to do business and sleep peacefully at night.

The prohibition against interest is not just an incidental or minor detail. It is the only prohibition in the Qur'an which is actually specified that to be in breach of this principle is to "make war on God and on his messenger," the Prophet Muhammad PBUH. This is a fundamental dividing point between traditional banking practice and *shariah* banking and it is not something that a Muslim can "fudge" and be happy.

I should point out that both the Christian and the Jewish traditions have a long history of being against usury, or the payment and receipt of interest. So the three traditions are not very far apart on this point.

You have provided an example of mortgage finance *shariah*-style. What other products are available?

One that comes to mind is *ijarah*, a lease-backed contract, which "mirrors" asset-based finance in traditional banking. In *ijarah*, the bank buys the asset in its entirety and then leases it back to the client and charges a rental. With *ijarah*, the return going to the bank from the customer is rent not interest, and Islam is comfortable with the concept of rent. Here the bank is making money on the use of an asset.

Another product area is pensions. The restrictions of *riba* mean that pensions cannot be invested in government securities, as these are pure interest-bearing investments. However, certain equities are perfectly acceptable because the investor is a partner in the company so he or she shares its risks and losses. Therefore, our pension product is very heavily based on equities, although property is also allowed as an asset class if the transaction is structured correctly.

The whole pensions area is much undeveloped in the Muslim community. Because of *riba*, Muslims naturally look to rental income and property ownership as the most natural way of funding their retirement. There is a real culture clash in the area of pensions, and it is something that we have been in longstanding discussions with the HM Revenue and Customs about. In the UK, the law mandates that at the age of 75 you have no other option but to buy an annuity with your pension. And annuities, being interest-based, are not ideal for Muslims. We have made this point through the Islamic Finance Experts Group that the Government has set up, of which I participate. But it is not an issue that can be resolved overnight.

Then there are wholesale products, such as support for major corporates that are Muslim-owned. Again this is very much a developing area in Islamic banking.

It seems that Islamic banks and traditional banks do coexist in some areas, perhaps because they are serving different markets. In others, Islamic financial institutions are predominant. And there are also areas where Western banks are developing Islamic finance arms, such as HSBC's Amanah proposition. Is this how you see things progressing?

Today there are over 500 institutions around the world offering *shariah*-compliant products in 47 countries across the globe. I expect this to continue to expand, particularly in the Middle East, Indonesia, and Malaysia. The market is big enough to accommodate both wholly Islamic financial institutions as well as those who have "window" operations which offer Islamic products through existing branch networks.

At HSBC we have adopted a three-pronged approach:

- Window Model—this offers Islamic products through existing branch networks, and is used in UAE, Bahrain, UK, and Indonesia.
- Partnership Model—a joint venture between HSBC and Saudi British Bank. This unique partnership has given us access to one of the biggest markets in the Muslim world.
- Islamic Subsidiary—HSBC's Malaysian subsidiary was the first international bank offered this license in Malaysia. This is a unique proposition available for HSBC with the option of opening branches outside Malaysia (Brunei and Bangladesh).

It is all about understanding the local market and deciding which model works best.

The window model, offering *shariah*-compliant products through an existing branch network, works extremely well for us in markets where the idea of *shariah* banking remains unfamiliar. In the UK, for example, there is not a particularly developed understanding of what makes a product *shariah*-compliant, even among British Muslims. There is also a lack of understanding of how a *shariah*-compliant financial product might benefit a Muslim customer. There are invariably many questions and one needs the interaction with a customer and trained branch staff who can make clear how a *shariah* product differs from a conventional one.

Is it necessary for a bank wishing to have a *shariah* banking service to have a body of Islamic scholars overseeing its *shariah* products and its operations?

It is absolutely fundamental. It is the key to gaining credibility and integrity in the eyes of the market. Right from the outset, in 1998, when HSBC first set up HSBC Amanah as the Islamic financial services division of the group, we established an independent board of leading Muslim scholars to be our *shariah* advisers. These are very eminent and respected scholars from across the Muslim world. Success in this market depends on a *shariah* bank's ability to deliver in a way that continually demonstrates a respect and understanding of cultural differences, and of the importance of Islam in the daily life of a Muslim.

▸▸ MORE INFO

Books:

El-Gamal, Mahmoud A. *Islamic Finance: Law, Economics, and Practice*. Cambridge, UK: Cambridge University Press, 2008.

Usmani, Muhammad Taqi. *The Authority of Sunnah*. New Delhi: Kitab Bhavan, 1998.

Usmani, Muhammad Taqi. *An Introduction to Islamic Finance*. New Delhi: Idara Isha'at-e-Diniyat, 1999.

Zarabozo, Jamal Al-Din. *The Authority of and Importance of the Sunnah*. Denver, CO: Al-Basheer Publications, 2000.

  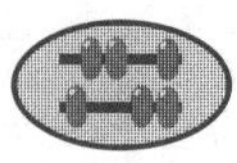  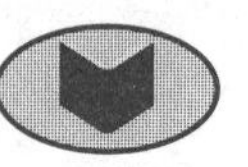 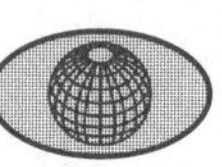 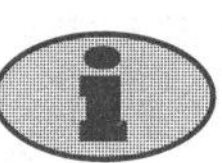  

Banks and Small and Medium-Sized Enterprises: Recent Business Developments

by Sergio Schmukler, Augusto de la Torre, and María Soledad Martínez Pería

EXECUTIVE SUMMARY

- Banks consider SMEs to be core strategic businesses with a high profit potential.
- To serve SMEs, banks are now establishing separate dedicated units, standardized processes, and risk-management systems.
- The relationship manager's role is crucial for attracting new customers, and selling products to existing SME customers.
- Banks are increasingly serving SMEs through different transactional technologies. which emphasize cross-selling.
- Large, multiple-service banks are the main players in the SME market.

INTRODUCTION

A common perception is that small and medium-sized enterprises (SMEs) cannot access appropriate financing. This perception is often supported by academic and policy circles' "conventional wisdom" that banks are generally not interested in dealing with SMEs, mainly due to SMEs' perceived opaqueness[1] and higher informality.[2] As capital markets do not compensate for these deficiencies in the banking sector, the need to receive special assistance, such as government programs to increase lending, has been suggested.[3] In recent years, SME financing initiatives included government-subsidized lines of credit and public guarantee funds.[4]

In the academic literature, there is evidence that banks (especially small and niche players) engage with SMEs through relationship lending. Relationship lending can overcome opaqueness due to the primary reliance on "soft" information gathered by the loan officer through continuous, personalized, direct contacts with SMEs.[5] However, in a series of studies recently conducted by the World Bank, new stylized facts point to a gap between the conventional view and the way banks are actually interacting with SMEs.[6]

First, new evidence suggests that most banks, including large and foreign banks, indeed serve SMEs, finding this segment very profitable.[7] Second, different transactional technologies that facilitate arms-length lending (such as credit scoring and significantly standardized risk-rating tools and processes, as well as special products such as asset-based lending, factoring, fixed-asset lending, and leasing) are increasingly applied to SME financing.[8] Third, banks try to serve SMEs in a holistic way through a wide range of products and services, with fee-based products rising in importance, placing cross-selling at the heart of their business strategy.

Under this new model of bank engagement with SMEs, larger, multiple-service banks exhibit, through the use of new technologies, business models, and risk-management systems, a comparative advantage in offering a wide range of products and services on a large scale, becoming leaders in this business segment.

NEW BUSINESS MODEL

Banks' high level of interest towards SMEs has, consequently, brought major changes to business models. First, as SMEs have become a strategic sector, banks are changing their organizational set-up to approach and serve this segment efficiently. Two main structures can be broadly categorized. The first combines the work of a commercial and credit risk team established at headquarters, with relationship managers distributed throughout the branches. The second consists of business centers or regional centers that operate as mediators between headquarters and branches, with a team leader or regional manager who controls and trains the relationship managers of the corresponding branches. In addition, banks are establishing separate, dedicated units with new strategies to cater adequately for the specific needs of SMEs. These dedicated business units approach SMEs in an integrated way, offering them a wide variety of products and services, including both deposits and loan products. In this set-up, relationship managers (RMs) are instrumental in attracting new customers, and selling products to existing ones. RMs look for new clients and prepare the information of each SME that is presented at the regional centers or at headquarters. They develop a relationship with the client, and, in some cases, RMs are allowed to express their opinion, make recommendations, or even present the case to the credit committee.

Second, the new model serves SMEs at all branches, and with standardized processes, facilitating the reduction of the high transaction costs that dealing with each SME entails. In most cases, branches and headquarters complement each other and undertake different functions. The initial stages of granting loans to SMEs are decentralized in most banks, while later stages, such as risk analysis or loan recovery, are usually centralized. In addition, banks exploit the synergies of working with different types of clients. Using information from existing firm databases, such as credit bureaus, relying on existing deposit clients, and attracting clients with bank credit are also common approaches that banks use to identify prospective SMEs.

Third, regarding credit-risk management, banks are reorganizing their systems, with a greater degree of sophistication among international banks and the leading, large domestic banks. Typically, risk management is a process that is organizationally separated from sales, and primarily done independently at headquarters. In most large banks, credit-risk management is not automated. Furthermore, in most cases, credit-risk management involves a credit-risk analyst, who is in charge of conducting both qualitative and quantitative risk assessments on the SME. The quality rating of SME management and SWOT (strengths, weaknesses, opportunities, and threats) analysis are the main components of qualitative assessments, while the financial analysis and projections of the SME firm and the SME owner are the main quantitative assessments. Qualitative assessments usually include an analysis of the SMEs' products, their demand and market structure, the quality of the owners and managers (including the degree of separation between management and owners),

"Enthusiasm and hard work are indispensable ingredients of achievement. So is stick-to-it-iveness."
Clarence Birdseye

the degree of informality, the years of activity in the sector, and the vulnerability to foreign-exchange-rate fluctuations. Quantitative assessments entail an analysis of profitability, cash-flow generation capacity, solvency, quality of assets, structure of balance sheets, and global guarantees. Moreover, scoring models are still being developed, and primarily applied to small loans.

Monitoring of the credit-risk outlook is standardized at the majority of banks. Some monitoring mechanisms used frequently are preventive triggers and alerts automatically generated to signal the deterioration of the SMEs' payment capacity. However, credit-risk monitoring still depends on the diligence of the relationship manager or the credit-risk analyst. Some banks use a system that allows different individuals to provide input on each enterprise (such as auditors, back-office staff, sales personnel, and risk analysts).

The business and risk-management models described above can be better pursued by large universal banks, especially foreign ones, which can be more aggressive in reaching out to SME clients, and are better suited to conduct lending based on automated scoring models for small loans (as they have the know-how and models to do so) and template-type rating systems for larger loans (based on streamlined, standardized versions of corporate rating).

SME EVIDENCE

SMEs interact with banks using a variety of products, mostly checking and savings accounts, as well as term loans.[9] Furthermore, SMEs do not exclusively obtain financing via "relationship loans." SMEs access financing products that do not depend on the bank processing soft information on the firm.[10] An interesting finding is that the provision of loans through public programs or guarantees is low. The highest usage of public programs observed is in Chile, with 8% of SMEs reporting using them; other countries are reporting percentages of around 3%.[11]

Nonetheless, while SMEs increasingly interact with banks to purchase a range of products and services, SMEs still appear unable to obtain access to crucial products such as loans secured by certain forms of collateral (for example, accounts receivable, inventories, equipment, cattle, and intangible assets), or long-term, fixed-interest rate loans in domestic currency. However, it is still unclear how much SMEs in developing countries would be able to rely on banks to obtain those products. As the US literature indicates (Carey et al., 1993; and Berger and Udell, 1996), SMEs might have to rely on private placements and non-bank institutions. Bank financing for certain SMEs, such as start-ups (in particular, those in high-tech or research-based industries), is also likely to remain limited, as has proven to be the case in developed markets such as the United States.

CONCLUSION

In summary, the new evidence shows that the whole spectrum of private banks (large and small, domestic and foreign) has started to perceive SMEs as a strategic sector. Banks are aggressively expanding, or planning to expand, their operations in the SME segment. As a consequence, the

CASE STUDY

Government Interventions in Colombia[12]

While direct government funding programs have been described as relatively unsuccessful, policy innovations could still prove important for SME financing. For example, in Colombia, several policy measures targeted towards the micro and SME segments have been introduced since 2004. On the one hand, non-financial instruments have been implemented, including training programs to increase competitiveness, and promote technological development and exports. On the other hand, financial instruments have been introduced, including the further expansion of existing government programs, and promoting the development of alternative financing instruments (investment funds, factoring/supplier financing, fiduciary structures, etc).

Colombian government programs include long-term development funds and partial credit guarantees. Longer-term development funding is mainly provided in the form of rediscounting lines at below-market rates by the state-owned, second-tier credit institutions, Bancóldex,[13] Finagro,[14] and Findeter.[15] Partial credit guarantees—typically around 50% loan-loss coverage—are provided by FNG,[16] as well as by FAG[17] for the agricultural sector. The role of these institutions—particularly Bancóldex and FNG—has been cited as instrumental in promoting access to credit for SMEs.

The authorities have recently embarked on an initiative to improve financial access, including for SMEs. The low level of financial penetration in Colombia, both in response to pre-crisis levels and in comparison to regional peers, has prompted the authorities to take measures to expand access to credit and other financial services. Both demand- and supply-side barriers have been identified, and will be tackled via regulatory reforms and the *Banca de las Oportunidades* initiative. Recent policy measures include the introduction of correspondent banking arrangements, changes in the definition of the interest-rate ceiling, the passage of legislation on credit reporting, and the strengthening of creditor rights via a new bankruptcy law. Additional proposed reforms include changes to the civil code on enforcement procedures and to the financial system structure, as well as plans for the introduction of a special savings account for low-income households. In addition, the *Banca de las Oportunidades* initiative aims to design and propose measures to stimulate financial access, particularly for low-income households.

▸▸ MORE INFO

Articles:

Berger, A., and G. Udell. "Universal banking and the future of small business lending." In A. Saunders, I. Walter (eds). *Financial System Design: The Case for Universal Banking*. Burr Ridge, IL: Irwin, 1996: 559–627.

Carey, M., S. Prowse, J. Rea, and G. Udell. "The economics of the private placements: A new look." *Journal of Financial Markets, Institutions and Instruments* 2 (1993): 1–66.

Carter, D., J. McNulty, and J. Verbrugge. "Do small banks have an advantage in lending? An examination of risk-adjusted yields on business loans at large and small banks." *Journal of Financial Services Research* 25 (2004): 233–252.

De la Torre, A., M. S. Martinez Peria, M. Politi, S. Schmukler, V. Vanasco. "How do banks serve SMEs? Business and risk management models." In Benoît Leleux, Ximena Escobar de Nogales, and Albert Diversé (eds). *Small and Medium Enterprise Finance in Emerging and Frontier Markets*. IMD and IFC, 2008c forthcoming.

DeYoung, R. "Mergers and the changing landscape of commercial banking (part II)". *Federal Reserve Bank of Chicago, Chicago Fed Letter* 150, 2000.

DeYoung, R., and W. Hunter. "Deregulation, the internet, and the competitive viability of large and community banks." In B. Gup. (ed). *The Future of Banking*. Westport, CT: Quorom Books, 2003: 173–202.

SME market is becoming increasingly competitive, although far from saturated. The evidence suggests that banks are learning how to deal with SMEs, and, at the same time, making the investments to develop the structure to deal with a growing market in the years to come. As banks have recently discovered a key, untapped segment, it is likely that the models to work with SMEs will evolve significantly as the involvement with the SME segment increases.

However, there are issues that remain for future work. Although banks appear to have become more involved with SMEs, banks may not be able to measure comprehensibly their exposure to the segment in terms of income, costs, or risk. Furthermore, banks are not adequately tracking their loan-loss experiences. We might be witnessing a process in which banks are only now developing the structure to deal with SMEs, and, through their interactions with the segment, they will be able to reduce the involved costs and risks.

DeYoung, R., W. Hunter, and G. Udell. "The past, present, and probable future for community banks." *Journal of Financial Services Research* 25 (2004): 85–133.

Reports:

Beck, T., A. Demirgüç-Kunt, and M. S. Martínez Pería. "Bank financing for SMEs around the world. Drivers, obstacles, business models, and lending practices." World Bank Policy Research Working Paper 4785, 2008.

De la Torre, A., J. C. Gozzi, and S. Schmukler. "Innovative experiences in access to finance: Market friendly roles for the visible hand?" Washington, DC: World Bank, 2009.

De la Torre, A., M. S. Martinez Peria, and S. Schmukler. "Bank involvement with SMEs: Beyond relationship lending." World Bank Policy Research Working Paper 4649, 2008b.

Independent Evaluation Group. "Financing micro, small, and medium enterprises through financial intermediaries." Washinton, DC: International Finance Corporation, World Bank, 2008.

OECD. "The SME financing gap: Theory and evidence". OECD Publishing, 2006.

Stephanou, C. and C. Rodriguez. "Bank financing to small- and medium-sized enterprises (SMEs) in Colombia." World Bank Policy Research Working Paper 4481, 2008.

WEC. "Securing a place in an uncertain economic landscape." World Economic Forum on Latin America, Cancún, Mexico, April 15–16, 2008.

World Bank. "Bank financing to small and medium enterprises: Survey results from Argentina and Chile." 2007a.

World Bank. "Bank lending to small and medium enterprises: The Republic of Serbia." 2007b.

NOTES

1 Opaqueness means that it is difficult to ascertain if firms have the capacity to pay (for example, viable projects) and/or the willingness to pay (due to moral hazard). For example, lack of audited financial statements prevents banks from engaging in what is known as financial-statement lending, by which the loan contract terms are set on the basis of the company's expected future cash flow and current financial condition, as reflected in audited statements (see Berger and Udell, 2006).

2 If firms do not reliably report their full financial activity on their financial statements, banks do not count, for example, with complete information on warranties for lending. See OECD (2006) for more on the factors that drive SMEs to operate in the informal economy, especially in emerging economies.

3 The need to provide support to SMEs through critical government investments was stated at the World Economic Forum on Latin America Summit in 2008. In addition, re-examination of tax regimes, regulatory reforms, and provision of capital through public-private partnerships were mentioned. See WEC (2008).

4 Chile's *Fondo de Garantía para Pequeños Empresarios* (FOGAPE) is a fund created to encourage bank lending to SMEs through partial credit guarantees. The Colombian *Fondo Nacional de Garantías* (National Guarantee Fund) provides similar partial credit guarantees. Structured finance transactions arranged by FIRA, a Mexican development financial institution focused on the agricultural sector, are another example of a government effort to provide financing to rural SMEs. Furthermore, the Mexican development bank, NAFIN, has initiated a reverse factoring program to provide working capital financing to SMEs through a process of online sale of receivables from large buyers. See de la Torre *et al.* (2008a).

5 See DeYoung (2000), DeYoung, and Hunter (2003), Carter *et al.* (2004), and DeYoung *et al.* (2004) for a discussion of the comparative advantages that small community banks have in lending to small firms through relationship lending.

6 See de la Torre *et al.* (2008b, 2008c) for a comprehensive analysis. Case studies are also available for Argentina, Chile, Colombia, and Serbia, describing the institutional and macroeconomic contexts, their banking industries and trends, and the data in detail. See World Bank (2007a and 2007b) and Stephanou and Rodriguez (2008).

7 Using data from 91 banks in 45 countries, Beck *et al.* (2008) found that all banks in the sample have SME customers, over 80% perceive the market to be big and prospects to be good, and more than 60% have a separate department managing their relations with SMEs. On average, the share of bank loans to small (medium) enterprises averages 11% (13%), compared to 32% in the case of large firms. The share of non-performing loans for small (medium) enterprises is 7.4% (5.7%), compared to 4% in the case of large firms.

8 See Berger and Udell (2006).

9 Banks have developed a wide range of fee-based, non-lending products and financial services for SMEs. Loans are not all always the main product offered to SMEs. Moreover, loans are often offered as a way to cross-sell other lucrative fee-based products and services. See de la Torre *et al.* (2008b, 2008c).

10 De la Torre *et al.* (2008b) argue that banks are developing new technologies and business models to serve the SME segment, reducing their dependence on "relationship lending" and the gathering of "soft" information, which is costly and time-consuming.

11 See World Bank (2007a).

12 This case study can be found in Stephanou and Rodriguez (2008).

13 Bancóldex's main aim is to provide low-interest lines of credit via first-tier credit institutions for exporters and SMEs.

14 Finagro's main aim is to provide low-interest financing for agriculture, livestock, forestry, and related rural projects.

15 Findeter was set up in order to lend (via first-tier banks) to subnational entities for infrastructure and other development projects.

16 FNG is a guarantee fund that "backs" credits to all economic sectors (except agriculture) with the primary objective of facilitating access to credit for micro enterprises and SMEs.

17 FAG is a guarantee fund that "backs" working capital and investment loans for the agricultural sector that are financed either with Finagro discounting, or with a credit institution's own funds.

"If offended, take the initiative to clear it up." Stephen Covey

  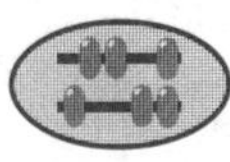   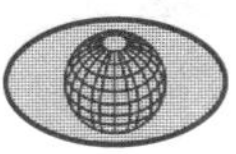   

Viewpoint: Jacques Attali
Microfinancing

INTRODUCTION

Jacques Attali is an economic theorist, with degrees from the renowned French "grandes écoles." In 2007 he was appointed head of the commission to promote growth in the French economy by President Nicolas Sarkozy. He is chairman of A&A, an international consulting firm based in Paris, and Founder and President of PlaNet Finance, an international nonprofit organization focusing on structuring the microfinance sector. Attali founded PlaNet Finance in 1998, and is also Chairman of an investment bank and private equity vehicle specializing in the development of European IT startups, from software to genomics.

In his book *Millennium*, published in 1990, Attali created the concept of "nomad society" to characterize the nature of future civilization. This theory of "nomadism" was an inspiration for the creation of the Java programming language by Bill Joy and John Gage at Sun Microsystems, and for the titanium-clad Guggenheim museum in Bilbao, Spain, designed by architect Frank Gehry.

Attali is a former special adviser to François Mitterand (1981–1990), and was the first President of the European Bank for Reconstruction and Development (1991–1993). In 1984 he created *Eureka*, the main European program on new technologies, and in 1989 he launched an international action program.

The existence and aim of microfinance are justified by one goal—the fight against poverty, humanity's key concern today. Out of the 6.7 billion inhabitants on the planet, three billion people live on less than US$2 per day, and 80% of the world's population has no access to financial services.

Microfinance has existed in different forms for centuries, but has only really started to be structured in the last 30 years. It can be defined as the provision of financial services (especially savings, credit, and insurance) to poor people, excluded from the financial sector, in particular the working poor, the microentrepreneurs, who have no access to banks and traditional financial institutions. Microfinance aims to find adapted solutions for people who live in developing countries, allowing them to start and develop a business project. It is an efficient and ethical way of giving them means to escape poverty in dignity. Today, more than 150 million people worldwide, served by more than 10,000 microfinance institutions (savings and credit cooperative, NGOs, microfinance banks, and commercial banks), benefit directly or indirectly from microfinance activities. But it is estimated that over 500 million entrepreneurs remain excluded from financial services.

Microfinancing is based on two principles which are linked to each other. First, that everyone who has an income-generating project should have the ability to become a microentrepreneur and to implement ideas and develop successful enterprises. In this way, microfinance gives an opportunity for the self-financing income generating ideas rather than providing a costless help. Secondly, we believe that the credit relationship can be based on trust. Since microfinance relies on this value, microfinance can avoid a biased relationship between credit providers and their clients, as it has been seen, for example, in the subprime crisis.

Microfinance is based on two lending models: joint (or grouped) microloans and individual contracts. Individual contracts are more similar to traditional loans—a person receives a certain amount of money and must repay it, with interest, within a relatively short period of time (a few weeks or months). The loan amount is generally higher than in joint loans. Joint microloans are granted to a group of people who are jointly responsible for repaying the loan. Individual defaults are avoided and group pressure serves as a strong incentive in ensuring responsible behavior.

Although microfinancing includes interest payment, as the loans are small and must be paid back quickly, the sums to be repaid are affordable for clients, especially considering the output of their income-generating activities. Interest rates in microfinance institutions are high, since MFIs grant many more small loans than traditional banks do, using a methodology that implies higher operating and processing costs. The interest rates cover the cost of the loan, the risk associated with nonreimbursement and expenses relating to the microcredit administrative and processing tasks. Although microcredit costs are substantially higher than those of "traditional loans," MFIs' loan officers appear to be far more productive. In viable MFIs, a loan officer manages an average of 359 microborrowers (Microfinance Information eXchange).

Interest rates are determined by local rules and regulations—concerning the ceiling fixed on interest rates: often, the local financial administration or central bank determines a fixed interest rate for the MFIs operating in the country. Interest rates can also be established according to the expenses related to microfinance activities, the type of institution (not-for-profit or profit-oriented MFIs), as well as by technologies or innovations that allow the MFI to enhance productivity and reduce operating costs. More has to be achieved, as far as regulations and best practices are concerned. For example, the Consultative Group to Assist the Poor (CGAP) has been working for years on the development of sound legal and regulatory frameworks for financial service providers that serve the billions of poor people who lack access to the global financial system.

Microfinance is facing new challenges today. First, more has to be done in order to reach more people. Over 500 million microentrepreneurs remain excluded from financial services and poverty is spreading in both rural and urban areas, as has been cruelly demonstrated by the ongoing agricultural and food crisis.

Reinforcing and supporting microfinance institutions enables a greater number of low income entrepreneurs to develop

". . . there should be some kind of safety net, we should not tolerate, in an affluent society, extreme levels of poverty or deprivation." Camille Paglia

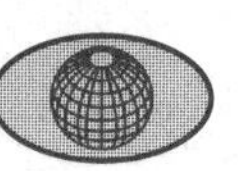
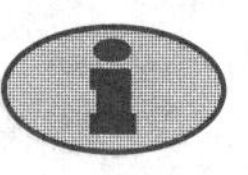

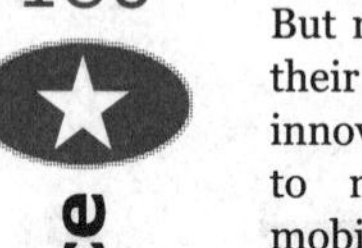

microenterprises and increase their income. But microfinance players need to diversify their products as well as come up with innovative ways to give more people access to microfinance. The development of mobile banking initiatives (including mobile banking credit, savings, and insurance on the use of existing mobile phone infrastructures to reduce MFI transactional costs and broaden their reach to rural and remote areas) can be an efficient and innovative way of giving access to a considerable number of people to financial services.

Microfinance can also play an important role in areas such as healthcare, education, and the environment. The development of microfinance programs associated with health and education initiatives is very positive. It allows the clients of microfinance institutions to be informed about issues that are as diverse as HIV/AIDS or malaria, or biodiversity and best practices in education.

The current financial crisis will have serious consequences for microfinancing. Microfinance represents €30 billion that could be impacted by the financial crisis. Furthermore, the coming recession will have very damaging consequences for the poorest people on the planet. Rich countries may transfer less money to developing countries, which would be negative for the development of microfinance, and local activities could be affected because of the global economic slowdown.

One could think that microfinance will be a victim of the current crisis. But I think that, if properly managed, microfinance can be one of the possible solutions to the financial crisis. This would work in two ways. Firstly, microfinance is an ethical answer to traditional finance. Therefore, it creates the conditions to help people develop the real economy. More than any other area of finance, microfinance aims to reach the 80% of the planet's population who have no access to financial services in order to include them in the real economy.

Secondly, microfinance has a very important role to play in the resolution of the crisis because the current crisis will only be solved if the global economy is able to find new ways to grow. This growth can only be achieved if millions of people become new consumers and are included in an economy based on consumption, production, and exchanges. Only microfinance can do that. Microfinance can reach people who are excluded from our global economy and allow them to produce exchange and consume in the long term, and hence boost the global economy.

But the challenges remain. The crisis will impact microfinance, which is as threatened as the traditional financial services sector.

The erratic development, in some places, of credit for consumption is very different from the key principle of microfinance, which is to help the development of activities that generate income.

Allowing individuals to obtain credit for their daily consumption can be a real danger. Microfinance providers have to keep an eye on their clients to prevent them obtaining multiple lines of credit, even if these are for the development of income-generating activities.

The crisis should make us learn from the failures of the subprimes. Microfinance's main aim is to help people to develop income generating activities and we must not forget that. Delinquent financial products and excessive debt are the roots of today's global financial crisis and are now threatening microfinance as well. Microfinance providers have to be cautious to avoid repeating the same mistakes.

Finally, one must not forget that microfinancing is not, and will never be, the only solution to help the population of developing countries escape poverty. Microfinance is an essential tool in the fight against poverty worldwide but it is no panacea for the world's poverty. Microfinance can only work alongside developments in new information technologies and democracy, which are basic conditions for poverty to be eradicated in any country.

▸▸ MORE INFO

See Also:

★ Best Practices in Corporate Social Responsibility (pp. 123–126)
★ Ethical Funds and Socially Responsible Investment: An Overview (pp. 306–308)
★ The Impact of Climate Change on Business (pp. 775–777)
★ Viewpoint: Muhammad Yunus (pp. 274–276)
★ Viewpoint: Roger Steare (pp. 168–169)
✔ Creating a Sustainable Development Policy (p. 905)
✔ The Triple Bottom Line (p. 917)
Muhammed Yunus (p. 1205)
Banker to the Poor: The Story of the Grameen Bank (p. 1222)

"Today's corporations have global responsibilities because their decisions affect world problems concerning economics, poverty, security and the environment." Anita Roddick

     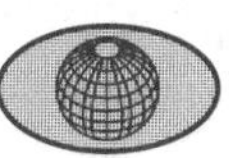   

Viewpoint: Jagdish Bhagwati
Lessons from the Current Crisis

INTRODUCTION

Jagdish Bhagwati is University Professor, Economics and Law, at Columbia University and Senior Fellow in International Economics at the Council of Foreign Relations. One of the world's leading economists today, he writes frequently in the leading newspapers and magazines.

The current crisis—or perhaps two crises, one financial or Wall Street, the other macroeconomic or Main Street, both are intertwined—has caused not only panic, but also much anguished thought about its implications for capitalism and globalization. Clear thinking is necessary to prevent both of these principles being undermined in the populist reaction that seems to have emerged.

MARKET FUNDAMENTALISM

The financier George Soros and the economist Joseph Stiglitz, in particular, have gone around saying that the crisis has put an end to "market fundamentalism," and that it represents for capitalism and globalization what the collapse of the Berlin Wall did for communism. Both arguments must be rejected.

The post-war shift to more reliance on markets, greater integration of national economies into the world economy (which we call globalization), and the shift away from knee-jerk expansion of public-sector enterprises into activities beyond utilities that are "natural monopolies" was a shift from "anti-market fundamentalism" towards a more pragmatic center. It was not, as these critics claim, a shift from pragmatism to "market fundamentalism."

Besides, the analogy with the collapse of the Berlin Wall is laughable. The Wall's collapse signified the epitaph of a failed communism, which had landed its supporters in authoritarianism and economic wilderness. The current crisis follows instead decades of post-war prosperity, ushered in by the shift to the pragmatic center and away from anti-market fundamentalism. It also follows a steady shift of more of the world's nations to democracy, with economic and political liberalization often reinforcing each other.

GLOBALIZATION AND FINANCIAL INNOVATION

Again, we must avoid the fallacy of aggregation. Globalization, in the shape of freer trade and multinational investments, has been generally a force for good and economic prosperity. But it has also advanced, rather than harmed, social agendas such as gender equality and reduction of child labor, as demonstrated in my 2004 book, *In Defense of Globalization*. But, as every sophisticated economist knows, the financial sector offers asymmetries *vis-à-vis* international trade and, while it provides credit, which is the lifeblood of capitalist (or indeed any) systems, it can also lead to huge downsides and requires monitoring and informed regulation.

In relation to freeing capital flows and capital account convertibility that led to the East Asian financial crisis in the 1980s, I illustrate this asymmetry by using a couple of analogies.

Regarding trade, if I exchanged some of my toothbrushes for some of your toothpaste, and we both remembered to brush our teeth, we would both have white teeth and the probability of our teeth being knocked out in the process would be pretty slim.

However, the analogy for free capital flows is different. It is like fire, which enables me to turn veal into delicious "wiener schnitzel," but it can also burn down my house. The downside is huge, as we discovered at the time of the East Asian crisis.

This insight applies to financial innovation, which underlies recent crises, including the one we are in right now, perfectly. The long-term capital management crisis was precipitated by the financial innovation of derivatives which few understood. The innovation, and its downside when things got rough, had gone beyond comprehension by most, including the regulators. Currently, we have had similarly dangerous financial innovations like the credit default swaps and securitized mortgages. I am afraid few people realized the downside potential of these instruments. Yes, there were some warning voices. But they did not belong to what I have called the Wall Street–Treasury Complex: players who go back and forth, like Treasury Secretary Robert Rubin, between the Treasury and Wall Street (in his case, he went from Goldman Sachs to the Treasury and back to Citigroup). This Complex shared the euphoria about the financial innovations. So, they took us right into what turned into the bonfire.

The point we need to learn is that nonfinancial and financial innovations have important differences. Nonfinancial innovations (such as the innovation of the personal computer) raise the issue of what Schumpeter called "creative destruction" (i.e. smoothing into obsolescence the typewriter). With financial innovations, the problem is that there is a potential downside which can turn it into a "destructive creation." Therefore, we need a high-level "Standing Committee of Experts" whose job would be to look hard at the potential downside of whatever is the latest innovation being created by Wall Street.

Again, an analogy helps. The United States, under the Cheney–Rumsfeld leadership, went to war against Iraq based on the assumption that the war would last six weeks. They did not have a scenario where it would last six years, which it has! They had not worked out the downside scenarios, and the cost of that omission, as with the current financial crisis, has turned out to be enormous. We may not be able to figure out the downside with prescience; after all, Keynes once said, with characteristically brilliant exaggeration: "The inevitable never happens. It is always the unexpected." The task of the "Standing Committee of Experts" which I have proposed would be to reduce the unexpected whenever possible.

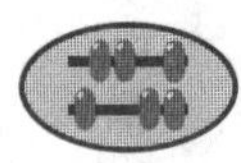

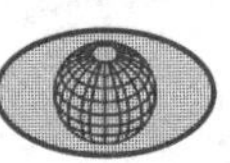

FINANCIAL REGULATION

We therefore need to fix the financial sector and the problems that affect it. In this vein, let me also say that the US Congress was remiss in encouraging home ownership through its quasi-governmental agencies Freddie Mac and Fannie Mae, in effect regardless of adequate collateral, with many mortgages being given to people who could not possibly have qualified under normal commercial criteria. These agencies also "bribed" congressmen from both political parties with political contributions into effectively providing lax oversight. And again the big investment banks, such as Goldman Sachs, pressured the Securities and Exchange Commission into exempting them from the prudential reserve requirements, leading to gross over-leveraging. In turn, politicians like Senator Schumer of New York supported such irresponsible actions by arguing that, if New York imposed prudential requirements on the investment banks, the business would go to London, suggesting that the new financial architecture must seek some basic coordination of regulations so we do not get a dangerous "race to the bottom."

FREE TRADE, NOT PROTECTIONISM

The current crisis has also made the critics of free trade more confident. But trade did not cause the crisis, and protectionism will not cure it. The East Asians were smart enough to know that premature capital account convertibility (i.e. freeing of capital flows which is the "financial sector") caused the crash from their remarkable growth for nearly three decades, which was attributable to outward orientation in trade. So, after the crisis, they refused to throw the trade baby out with the financial bath water. Surely, we are not going to be less smart than they were. So, the G20 has been right to urge that protectionism must be kept at bay.

On the other hand, the United States has failed to provide the lead in holding the line on protectionism, with the Congress working with the Buy America provisions in its Stimulus Bill. President Sarkozy, in keeping with the French skepticism over free trade, has even gone so far as to suggest that French firms should return to France from Eastern Europe. Apart from that, many leaders face demands to fire legal and illegal workers first, and to hire them last. So, the protectionism and anti-foreigner discrimination is showing incipient signs of breaking out, in trade, in foreign investment, in immigration, and labor markets. Only determined leadership will hold the line; and only time will tell whether it will be forthcoming in the way it should.

MORALITY IN THE FINANCIAL SECTOR

One final word is necessary. Many populists have concluded that the current crisis shows that markets are incompatible with morality. This is, of course, an old debate, ever since Adam Smith's time. Let me make just two observations.

First, markets affect our morality less than morality affects how we behave when we work in these markets. Our morality comes from our family, school, church, and even from literature, such as the great Russian novels which explore the ethical dilemmas of its characters. In turn, this affects how we conduct ourselves in the marketplace. Thus, we observe different types of capitalism: the Scandinavian version reflects egalitarianism, for example. In the same industry, again, we find some practicing corporate social responsibility, whereas others do not. It is therefore nothing short of vulgar quasi-Marxism to claim that where and how we work affects our morals.

Second, the corruption that we have seen in the financial sector should be put down not to greed (which suggests compulsive pursuit of self-interest to the exclusion of other virtues and vices) but often to the mere fact that the financial sector offers such enormous returns to skullduggery that, given the same propensity to cheat, the actual cheating is far greater than it would be without such returns. The greater the temptation, the greater the likelihood that you will succumb to it. So, you observe that, in agriculture, the display of "greed" is less than in the manufacturing sector, and it is the worst in the financial sector.

➤➤ MORE INFO

Book:

Bhagwati, Jagdish. *In Defense of Globalization*. Revised paperback ed. New York: Oxford University Press, 2008.

"Since business is a get things done institution, creativity without action-oriented follow-through is a barren form of behavior." Theodore Levitt

     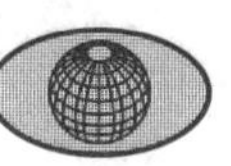   

Climate Change and Insurance

by Stephen Haddrill

EXECUTIVE SUMMARY

- A discussion of the likely impact of climate change
- The scenario 50 years on
- Present responses to extreme weather
- Insurance sector agreements with government
- The limits to insurance

INTRODUCTION

Starting from the fact that climate change is a reality that is happening now, and that we can see its impact across the world, what role does the insurance sector have in covering this? There is no doubt that climate change is of enormous importance to the insurance industry. The costs of flooding, wind damage, and abnormal heat are all huge, and climate change threatens to increase all those costs.

Work done so far on climate change shows the threat has arrived. The carbon produced in the last century is already causing extreme weather. The scientific consensus is that flooding has increased in severity due to sea level rises and more rain. Wind-storms are fiercer. Heat waves are more intense. Again, the scientific consensus is that reducing carbon emissions will not reverse this trend for decades. More extreme views, such as that by the founder of Gaia theory, James Lovelock, argue that we have probably already gone past the point of no return, but this pessimistic approach is not mainstream thinking. What is clear is that both the insurance sector and the world at large have to adapt and look to protect themselves.

Failure to adapt will generate extreme economic costs. Even relatively low percentage increases in weather phenomena, such as the footprint of a flood area, lead to massively increased costs. For example, a 5% increase in the footprint of a flood can lead to a 75% increase in the consequent bill for damages.

EXTREME WEATHER CONDITIONS

Over the next 50 years, we expect to see:

- Windstorm losses increase by two-thirds to US$27bn per year worldwide.
- Additional flooding costs of €100–120 billion a year in Europe.
- A 15-fold increase in UK flood costs, to £22 billion.
- Subsidence costs increasing by 50% in average clay-soil areas.

At the same time, heat stress on people, animals, machinery, and property will also increase. It is quite possible that by the 2040s, the summer of 2003 will be regarded as normal. If this becomes reality, then a quarter of working hours will be hotter than "comfort levels" in London offices, increasing the demand for air conditioning, and creating heat islands.

Last year's floods in the United Kingdom present a good example of our concerns. While it is difficult to point to one isolated storm or flood and say conclusively, "there we have proof of climate change", the floods of 2007 nevertheless give us a picture of the effects we are facing. Torrential rain did not just lead to rivers bursting their banks. Crucially, the drains failed also, as flash flooding overwhelmed them. In all, some 180,000 people made claims, or four times the annual average of flood claimants. Another way of putting this is that the industry experienced four years' worth of claims in just two months.

At the same time, the floods put a significant percentage of the United Kingdom's infrastructure at great risk. Reservoir banks threatened to fail. The electricity supply to 600,000 homes was almost lost, and the water supply to those homes was in fact lost for a while—this despite the fact that the insurance industry has issued repeated warnings to government about the vulnerability of critical infrastructure.

THE RESPONSE OF INSURANCE COMPANIES

To date, the insurance industry has coped with extreme weather events extremely well. In the 2007 floods in the United Kingdom, most insurers had loss adjusters on the ground within 24 hours, often calling in staff from overseas. People were put in temporary housing within days, and almost all are now back in their homes. Two hundred families were still displaced at the end of September, but virtually all because they required special building work.

There are, however, some lessons to learn. People talk to each other in a crisis. If a loss adjuster representing one insurer gives information to one household, while another gives different information to a neighbor, people get confused. The sector therefore came together to standardize the process of communicating with citizens in an afflicted area after an extreme weather event.

People in hard-hit areas worry greatly whether they will be able to obtain insurance again. The industry has been tremendously resourceful in continuing to provide insurance cover in "at-risk" areas, and it has done so at very reasonable premium prices. However, there is a need for governments around the world to be alert to the dangers of allowing building on flood plains and low-lying coastal areas in an era of rising sea levels.

Insurance covers risk. It is not there to cover loss that is absolutely certain to be incurred—you cannot insure your house once it is on fire! It is a fact that, in both America and the United Kingdom, and in many European countries, some of the most valuable properties, infrastructure assets, and concentrations of people live in areas that are going to be more at risk from tidal surges, flooding, and rising sea levels in the years and decades ahead.

The 2007 floods were the result of extreme rainfall. Water also threatens us from the seas, particularly as sea levels are expected to increase by at least a meter this century. If nothing is done, the risk of the 1953 flood being repeated will increase from 1 in 1000 in 2000, to 1 in 100 by 2100 (figures from the UK Environmental Agency).

The financial cost of a major storm on the UK east coast, for example, could reach £15–20 billion, as quoted in an Association of British Insurers report, "Coastal Flood Risk—Thinking for Tomorrow, Acting Today," published in November 2006. This is not a fantastical, or a remote possibility. In 2008, the United Kingdom was just hours away from a combination of a tidal surge, strong east winds, and high water levels in the Thames causing flooding in London, according to the London Meteorological Office. The ABI report used insurance catastrophe models to examine the effects of a rise in sea levels on flood risk.

Handling such an event would be extremely difficult. A high proportion of our emergency facilities are on the coastal flood plain. It is worth bearing in mind that the number of people over the age of 75 (the least-mobile members of our community) living on the UK coast is expected to double in the next 30 years, according to ABI research.

Taking all this together, the adaptation of homes, business, and the infrastructure

"All across the world . . . increasingly dangerous weather patterns . . . are abruptly putting an end to the long-running debate over whether or not climate change is real. Not only is it real, it's here, and its effects are giving rise to a frighteningly new global phenomenon: the man-made natural disaster." Barack Obama

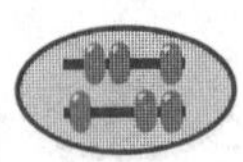
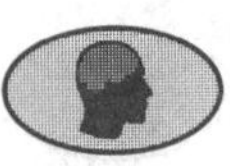
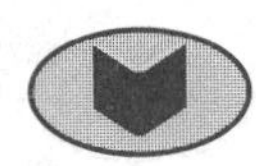
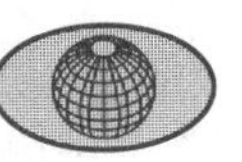

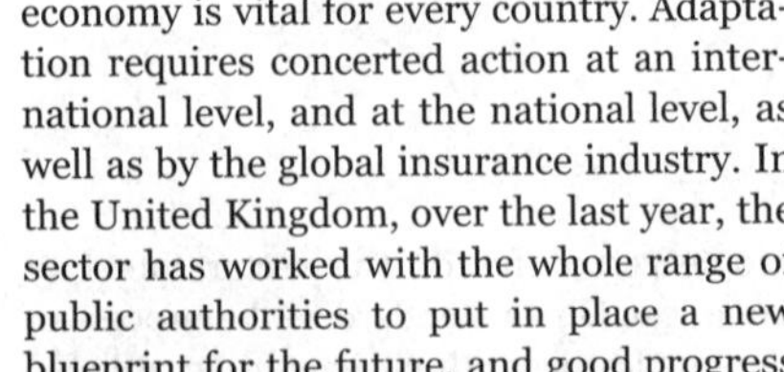

economy is vital for every country. Adaptation requires concerted action at an international level, and at the national level, as well as by the global insurance industry. In the United Kingdom, over the last year, the sector has worked with the whole range of public authorities to put in place a new blueprint for the future, and good progress has been made on all sides.

INTERNATIONAL AND BRITISH STRATEGIES

First, the international dimension: There is already international action on carbon reduction. That international cooperation needs to be repeated for adaptation. Globally agreed principles need to feed into EU strategic plans. Storms do not respect borders, nor do rivers in flood. Across the EU, we need a better understanding of risk, and we need agreement on the standard of protection required across Europe.

Such international strategies must, however, promote and encourage national and local action. Successful adaptation requires a framework that allows regional and local authorities to develop their individual action plans, responding to the specific threats affecting each locality.

The UK government has proposed new legislation to start creating this framework. We need to see two fundamental measures. First, there needs to be a commitment to a properly coordinated flood-management system in the United Kingdom, with clarity about who will be responsible for drainage. The government is talking here about a new strategic role for the Environment Agency, but the details will be critical.

Secondly, the United Kingdom and Europe need a commitment to a new, long-term, flood-management strategy, with a commitment to invest consistently over the long term. The industry needs to ensure that flood insurance remains as affordable and widely available as possible, so that consumers and small businesses can continue to be able to protect themselves from the financial cost of flooding.

Since 2000, this has been achieved in the United Kingdom through the "Statement of Principles on Flood Insurance," which commit insurers to provide flood insurance to homes that are already covered, provided the risk is not worse than 1:75, or if flood protection works are planned within five years. Under this arrangement, half a million homes at high risk of flooding have been protected. In fact, the sector is probably protecting an additional 400,000 homes that are not strictly covered by the agreement.

The statement has been a good deal for consumers in many respects, but it has not been entirely good for the market. The cost has fallen on existing insurers alone. New entrants to the market have no obligation to existing customers, and so are not affected. Specialist insurance for higher-risk customers has not developed, and because insurers have insured more people than they need to, inappropriate new property developments have secured insurance cover.

In its latest agreement with the UK government, the UK insurance industry has addressed these points. The new agreement sets out a series of government actions that are necessary to enable flood insurance to continue to be as widely available as possible in the future.

These include:

- Agreement by government to move away from a short-term, three-year approach to flood-risk management. Instead, the Environment Agency will publish next year a paper setting out a range of options for protecting the country over the next 25 years. This will facilitate a full debate about the best way forward. The government will then publish its response by the next spending review, setting out long-term aims and the associated funding.
- Risk data will be improved by the Environment Agency, and these will be made more readily available.
- Planning policy will be evaluated by early 2009, to ensure the new planning rules are delivering at both strategic and practical levels (it must be said that the early evidence is positive).
- Properties built from 2009 onwards are now explicitly excluded from the statement so that the onus clearly lies on developers to ensure their development is insurable.

Another important feature of this agreement is that it sets an end-date for the insurer commitments of June 30, 2013, after which what is, after all, a market distortion, will be removed. This instance shows how national governments can cooperate with the insurance industry to provide insurance, even under difficult circumstances.

However, the ABI and the industry are very keen to ensure that it is made obvious whether a new development is a good flood risk or not. We are working with the Royal Institute of Chartered Surveyors to develop a kitemark that can be applied to new homes. This will assure prospective owners whether their new home will be insurable or not. In this way, the market can be made to work for adaptation. Second, both the ABI and the industry will do more to promote better understanding of climate risk among the general population.

To this end, we will be publishing research on the economic costs of climate impacts. We will disseminate new climate data within the industry by hosting discussions among insurers and scientists about new climate science scenarios. We will also be working with government to educate the general public, by offering advice and tools for individuals to understand climate risks.

Home owners can also be encouraged to make their homes more resilient to flooding, and the ABI will produce new guidance for property developers about making new developments more climate-resilient. It will also research the cost of resilient repairs, and will continue to work with the industry and government on options for increasing the take-up of cost-effective resilience measures.

ClimateWise

Finally, the ABI is a strong supporter of the ClimateWise initiative. ClimateWise is a set of principles that commits insurers and the wider insurance industry to build climate change into their business operations. ClimateWise was developed by the UK industry, with the support of the Prince of Wales, to strengthen efforts to tackle climate change, including carrying out further research into climate change, and to promote the findings.

The insurance industry reaches into millions of homes and businesses, and has a key role to play in enabling customers to prepare for changing weather, as well as encouraging them to reduce their own emissions.

CONCLUSION

The UK sector has had warning of the scale of the threat. The floods of 2007 showed that new effort is needed. It did not tell us exactly what to do, nor where or how to do it. Since then the industry, and those outside the industry, have come up with many good ideas for a safer future. These ideas now need to be acted on.

▸▸ MORE INFO

Reports:

Association of British Insurers. "Climate adaption—Guidance on insurance issues for new developments". Online at: www.abi.org.uk/BookShop/ResearchReports/Climate%20Adaptation%20Guide%20Final.pdf

Haddrill, Stephen. "Preparing the UK for climate change." Speech, January 27, 2009. Online at: www.abi.org.uk/Document_Vault/ABI_adaptation_event_SH_Speech_27th_Jan.pdf

"Climate change should be seen as the greatest challenge to face man and treated as a much bigger priority in the United Kingdom." Prince Charles

Viewpoint: Roger Bootle
How to Rescue the World Economy from Disaster

INTRODUCTION

One of the City of London's most respected economists, Roger Bootle now runs his own consultancy, Capital Economics, which specializes in macroeconomics and the economics of the property market. He is also Economic Adviser to Deloitte & Touche, and a Specialist Adviser to the House of Commons Treasury Committee. He was formerly Group Chief Economist of the HSBC Group and, before the change of government, he was a member of the former Chancellor's panel of Independent Economic Advisers, the so-called "Wise Men."

Roger Bootle studied at Oxford University and then became a Lecturer in Economics at St Anne's College, Oxford. Most of his subsequent career has been spent in the City of London.

He has written many articles and books on monetary economics. *The Death of Inflation*, was published in 1996 and became a best-seller, translated into nine languages. Initially dismissed as extreme, this book is now widely recognized as prophetic. His next book, *Money for Nothing*, was widely acclaimed. It anticipated much of the current crisis. His latest book, *The Trouble with Markets*, is due out later this year.

A regular columnist on *The Daily Telegraph*, Roger also appears frequently on national television and radio.

At the start of 2009 the world economy was at a crossroads. There is a real danger that the current recession will evolve into a downturn similar in depth and length to that of the Great Depression of the 1930s. To avoid such an outcome, there are six things which policymakers should do—and one thing that they should avoid at all costs.

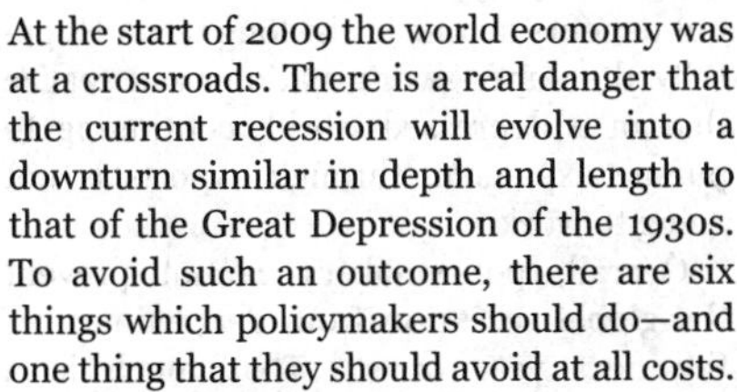

First, policymakers need to maintain very low interest rates and they should take further steps to reduce longer-term rates of interest, principally the yield on government bonds, first by keeping official interest rates low for a very long time and second by buying government bonds, and, if need be, private securities.

Once short-term interest rates have reached zero, conventional monetary policy has reached the end of the road, but that does not mean that monetary policy has shot its bolt. In particular, central bank purchases of assets, so-called quantitative easing can continue without limit. To get the desired result, central banks need to declare to the markets that they are prepared, if necessary, to continue with the policy without limit. The more this message is believed, the less they will have to do.

Second, some governments need to invoke the ghost of Keynes and implement large expansionary fiscal policies. Again, global policymakers have already put in place fiscal packages.

But these measures are not large enough. To be really effective, policymakers must give the impression that they will do whatever it takes to lift aggregate demand. If they succeed, then they will have to do comparatively little. Small measures, which do not bring about this result, could be next to useless. Indeed, a succession of footling measures, which leave the private sector with the impression that, after trying this succession, the state had given all it has got, could actually make matters worse. The problem is that public debt is now so high in some countries – the UK, for instance – that they do not have much scope to do a lot more. But two key countries – China and Germany – have lots of scope. They need to act.

SUSTAINABLE BORROWING

Of course, such action would place a large hole in government finances. And, at some point, measures will need to be put in place to bring government borrowing back to more sustainable levels. But now is not the time for such a move. If a temporary, albeit large, increase in government borrowing helps to avoid a depression, then the cost is well worth bearing.

People are undoubtedly wary of such a policy. I often hear people ask why, if excessive borrowing got us into this mess, even more borrowing can get us out of it. Although excessive borrowing did get us to this position, it was excessive borrowing by the private sector. And, because of the excesses, the danger now is that the private sector will be borrowing too little. It is that which could bring on depression. The solution can hardly be to borrow and spend still less. So, given that the private sector will find it difficult to borrow in present circumstances, it is up to the public sector to fill the gap. As far as the public finances are concerned, there is a time for prudence—but this isn't it.

Third, policymakers need to take more action to recapitalize the banks. The US$700bn (5% of GDP) granted under the US Emergency Economic Stabilization Act, the £50bn (3.3% of GDP) injected into UK banks and the €160bn (1.8% of GDP) injected into Euro-zone banks have prevented a full-blown collapse of the global financial system. But, ultimately, that may only be enough to cover the losses banks have made on new-fangled products such as mortgage-backed securities. It will not be enough to cover the old-fangled defaults on plain vanilla mortgages, commercial property mortgages, credit cards and business loans, which will result from the global recession. Governments need to be more proactive and should be ready to inject much more cash into the banking system.

Fourth, policymakers need to take more action to induce banks to lend. It is all very well pumping money into the banks, but it is not going to make a blind bit of difference unless they lend it out. Over the past 18 months, the banks have had their fingers badly burned and they are reluctant to engage in new lending. This much is obvious in the available data on lending. Once you strip out the distortions caused by the logjam in the wholesale lending markets, it is very clear that banks are content to sit on their cash. In the UK, the annual growth rate of lending by banks and building societies to companies has fallen from 18% a

"The scarce people are the ones who have the know-how, energy, daring, and staying power to implement ideas. . .Since business is a get-things-done institution, creativity without action-oriented follow-through is a barren form of behavior. In a sense it is irresponsible." Theodore Levitt

  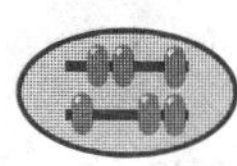 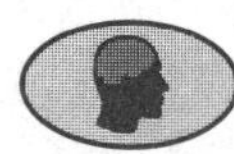  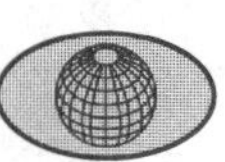   

year ago to 8% now and that to households has dropped from 10% to 6%. What's more, in the last few months, the total stock of loans has been just about stationary.

LENDING MEASURES

Accordingly, policymakers need to do more to force the banks to lend. This may involve banks signing commitments to keep lending at certain levels or other such codes of conduct. But such agreements are notoriously hard to measure and even harder to enforce. In the end, policymakers may have to consider going the whole hog and nationalizing the banks. Admittedly, for policymakers who have imbibed free-market doctrine at their mother's knee, this will be philosophically painful—as well as practically troublesome. The consequence would be that government debt would shoot up through the stratosphere. But this may be the only way to force lenders to lend.

Admittedly, simply increasing the supply of lending is not a miraculous solution to all the world's woes. After all, in an environment where asset prices are falling and unemployment is rising, demand for lending may be subdued, regardless of the supply. Nonetheless, there is no point in trying to increase demand for credit by lowering interest rates and expanding fiscal policy, unless you ensure that there is going to be enough supply.

Fifth, in selected cases, countries should allow their exchange rates to depreciate to provide a further boost to activity over and above that stemming from low interest rates and expansionary fiscal policy. Of course, not every country in the world can enjoy a boost from a weak currency. But the exchange rates of those that need the boost the most should nonetheless fall.

Indeed, history shows that lower exchange rates are often a prerequisite to a sustained economic recovery. It was largely down to the ability of the UK to pursue a lower exchange rate after it left the Gold Standard in 1931 that it started to recover from the Great Depression. And, although the Great Depression in the US lasted for a number of years after it left the Gold Standard in 1933, it is likely that it would have been even longer and deeper if the dollar was not allowed to fall. The same is true during more recent downturns. The UK only really emerged from its deep recession in the early 1990s once the pound fell sharply after it was ejected from the European Exchange Rate Mechanism in September 1992.

Some policymakers may be concerned about the inflationary consequences of much lower exchange rates. But in current conditions inflation is a red herring. In an environment where businesses and consumers are reluctant to spend, any boost to inflation from a lower exchange rate would be trivial. And, if deflationary conditions would otherwise prevail, a bit of inflation may not go amiss.

SPEND, SPEND, SPEND

Sixth, the super-saving nations of Asia must break the habit of a lifetime—and spend. The willingness of these nations to run large current account surpluses and thereby suck demand out of the rest of the world contributed to the credit crisis by forcing policymakers in the West to keep interest rates low, which ultimately created the housing bubbles that are now bursting. These super-saving nations need to play a more significant role in contributing to global aggregate demand. They need to use interest rates and fiscal policy to boost aggregate demand in their own economies, thus stimulating the demand for the exports of the rest of the world. And these are the countries that exchange rates have to rise to accommodate exchange rate depreciation by the dollar and the pound, and quite possibly the Euro. The currencies of the whole Asian bloc need to rise. China holds the key.

Unfortunately, this result will be very tricky to achieve. Governments are fond of their export sectors and tend to be keen to protect them. So keen, indeed, that protection may readily go beyond exchange rate policy to encompass trade barriers. The one thing that policymakers need to resist at all costs is the lure of protectionism. This is dangerously appealing in the short term, but benefits no one in the long term. Hopefully the super-saving nations will realize that in a depressed world, continuing to pursue expansion through exports is not going to work.

Overall, policymakers cannot prevent the global recession from deepening over the next year or so. That much is a given and we are all going to have to deal with it. But there is a way to prevent the recession from evolving into a full-blown depression. They should take it—before it is too late.

"When I saw something that needed doing, I did it." Nellie Cashman

  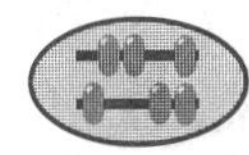   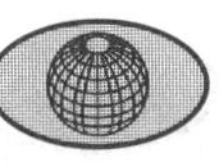   

The Crash and the Banking Sector—The Road to Recovery by Angela Knight

EXECUTIVE SUMMARY

The British Bankers' Association (BBA) has been heavily involved in many of the UK's landmark discussions on the financial crisis. This article explains the BBA's perspective on how the crisis came about, the response of the markets, how the financial regulation of the future might look, and sounds a warning that, for all its benefits, globalization comes at a price. The article looks at:

- The availability of cheap credit, and its impact on fueling the bubble;
- Globalization and its impact on contagion;
- The disappearance of non banks and non-UK lenders from the market;
- The shape of regulation to come.

INTRODUCTION

With the empowering gift of hindsight, there were some telling signs leading to the financial crisis, which has now become a global recession. Global imbalances had been growing for a decade. The United Kingdom and other Western economies imported raw materials, manufactured goods, gas, and oil from the East, exported their inflation, and, in the case of the United Kingdom, sought to fill the balance of payments deficit in tangible goods through financial services. These activities increased the current account deficits in countries such as the United Kingdom, United States, Spain, and other European countries, and increased the surpluses in Japan, China, and other Asian economies. The imbalance laid the foundations for the credit crunch.

Interest rates were low and investors wanted a better return. Credit was freely available, which fueled the property price boom. Innovation in financial services took place to feed the demand for credit, on the one hand, and a better return for investors on the other. Securitization became complex securitizations; leverage resulted in apparently better returns. Markets did what they always do, becoming overoptimistic on the up and overpessimistic on the down. Bubbles developed most noticeably in raw materials, energy, and housing.

A HARSH LESSON ON GLOBALIZATION

For years, we have also lived with a number of unchallenged assumptions: that globalization is only a force for good; that liberalization of credit brings broad and sustainable benefits to companies and individuals; and that the only real monetary policy tool needed is the control of an inflation target.

It was assumed that if a bubble forms, authorities know what to do about it and can mop it up quickly if it bursts. Many assumed that new regulatory arrangements plus more sophistication generally would provide protection. And, of course, many assumed that economies had come to the end of boom and bust. The experiences of a global recession show that these assumptions are flawed. As we all know, hindsight is a great teacher.

THE MARKET RESPONSE—THE STATISTICS TELL THE STORY

In responding to the situation, the industry and authorities have to deal with many issues. One issue gaining immediate attention is lending. The statistics here tell an interesting story.

Eighteen months ago, there were more than 100 mortgage lenders operating in the United Kingdom. Now there are just the five main High Street banks, plus two or three building societies. On average, throughout 2008, major High Street banks each month wrote some 50,000 remortgages, plus 26,000 new mortgages.

Then, in December 2008, demand for mortgages fell substantially. Figures show that the demand by individuals for all types of credit has fallen, and savings have started to rise. At the same time, lending to small firms by the major banks remains either constant or is increasing. Deposits by these companies have also remained constant.

The problem is that many non-UK banks and non-bank lenders have, like mortgage providers, disappeared from the market, taking with them a sizeable chunk of small business lending capacity. Treasury says the gap could be more than £100 billion, which major banks are now being asked to pick up.

Bank of England statistics also show that UK savings rates fell steeply from 2005, leaving a gap between demand for credit and supply of something like £300 billion, which was largely filled by the wholesale market. The whole dynamics of credit supply and demand have changed, and reaching a solution will not be easy.

It will also take time and a great deal of effort to rebuild confidence. As the voice of the industry, we acknowledge that not all banks have been appropriately vigilant in managing risk. What has happened should not have happened. The industry expresses its regret and has apologized. It looks forward to the apologies of other contributors, including from rating agencies, governments, regulators, institutional investors, central banks, economists, and commentators. They, too, are part of all this.

As the world responds to the turmoil, all sectors and parties need to work together; global challenges demand global responses. We have seen major economies working together to restore stability to markets. Policy makers must now avoid piecemeal regional or national responses in regulation and policy, which could distort international trade and undercut its benefits.

THE SHAPE OF REGULATION TO COME

As governments, regulators, and the financial services sectors around the world look to address regulatory weaknesses, it is important to recognize the benefits of financial innovation also. What is needed is not more regulation, but better regulation. The impact of new regulation should be balanced against the risks to economic recovery, which would follow from requiring banks to overcapitalize and deleverage. An international industry must operate in an international framework where regulators and policy makers cooperate.

There are specific UK initiatives in the Banking Act, which effectively codifies the intervention that has already taken place, and clarifies how the UK authorities work together. The European Commission has, meanwhile, set up an expert group, led by French banker, Jacques de Larosière, to recommend reforms to the shape of EU financial supervision.

The BBA has been a longstanding contributor to the development of the EU supervisory architecture, and keenly supports what is known as the Lamfalussy Process, which devolved to a series of committees the responsibility of working on cross-border rules and requirements. In drawing up a blueprint for the future, de

"Action without a name, without a who attached to it, is meaningless." Hannah Arendt

  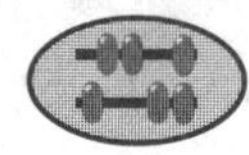   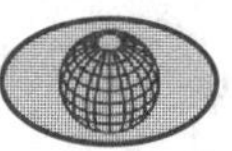   

Larosière needs to bear in mind that the underlying principles must:

- be consistent with global initiatives;
- embrace the whole EU, and not subgroups such as the Eurozone;
- build on a broad consensus of member states, financial institutions, and end-users;
- focus on desired regulatory outcomes, rather than on processes;
- build on existing initiatives such as supervisory cooperation; and
- focus on developing existing EU bodies, where possible, rather than creating new ones.

The BBA has itself proposed major enhancements to the EU regulatory architecture.

The first is to develop a formalized European Financial Stability Forum (EFSF) out of the existing roles of Europe's Economic and Financial Committee and Financial Services Committee. The EFSF should include finance ministers, central banks, and supervisors, and report to member states with actions it considers should be taken. It should work towards better monitoring of macro issues that either arise inside the EU, or have an impact on the EU, and it needs to link to the global Financial Stability Forum (FSF).

Secondly, the BBA proposes bolstering the role of the Committee of European Banking Supervisors (CEBS) in coordinating regulation. Its responsibilities should include a greater role in establishing colleges of regulators for cross-border banks; maintaining the focus of the colleges on relevant issues, including capital and liquidity; and increasing the quality of regulators across Europe.

Thirdly, while some debate the need for a single European regulator, the BBA remains convinced of the value of colleges of supervisors, albeit that their role and operation must be reviewed to meet future requirements. All cross-border banks should have a college of supervisors, with an inner core grouping consisting of the home-state supervisor and supervisors from other countries, where either the bank has a significant operation, or it is deemed to be systemic by a jurisdiction. Colleges should apply rules to give equivalent outcomes across all EU countries in which a bank operates.

In the view of the BBA, and of many regulators around the world, experience has shown that where colleges have been put in place properly, they have worked. Failed US bank, Lehman Brothers, on the other hand, did not have a properly working college.

While the BBA believes that the EU has an important role in responding to the financial turmoil in the ways outlined, it must not act in isolation. A regional EU solution will be counterproductive unless there is global coordination and a global framework.

The BBA shares the UK government's vision of a global financial system based on global standards, developed by specialist standard-setters and enforced nationally. This should be achieved through the development of existing structures. Global institutions should be made to work better, rather than creating new institutions.

The BBA supports the work of the G20 and FSF in coordinating the global approach, and believes these are the appropriate bodies for charting the way forward.

Any debate on the future of global regulation must involve as wide a group of nations as possible, including new and emerging financial powers such as China and India, to achieve global consistency and cooperation. We urge the UK government to continue to champion an open and inclusive debate, and to press for a fundamental review of the membership of organizations, including the Basel Committee for Banking Supervision, IOSCO, the International Monetary Fund, the World Bank and FSF. Among other issues the G20 and FSF should address are Basel II and the Capital Requirements Directive, which has required banks to increase their capital at just the wrong time. In simplistic terms, as the market has turned down so the risk-weighting of the assets banks hold has increased, along with the amount of capital they have to hold just to stand still.

This was exacerbated by statements in the United Kingdom and elsewhere by governments and other authorities last October. The effect has been to reduce banks' ability to provide new lending, or to use capital to absorb losses as we enter recession.

Other issues for G20 attention include credit-rating agencies, in part responsible for the credit crunch, and hedge funds, whose activities have, at the very least, added to volatility, and, at worst, destroyed value and jeopardized the system. International accounting standards, stress testing, remuneration structures, and corporate governance also need to be addressed.

CONCLUSION

There is much work to be done and the challenges may appear daunting. But by working together to take up the lessons presented by the recent turmoil, we will pave the way for continued growth and prosperity in the decades to come.

▸▸ MORE INFO

Report:

Financial Services Authority. "The Turner review: A regulatory response to the global banking crisis." March 2009. Online at: www.fsa.gov.uk/pubs/other/turner_review.pdf

Website:

Financial Services Authority, contains a number of relevant documents: www.fsa.gov.uk

"An activist—the guy who clears the river, not the guy who concludes it's dirty." H. Ross Perot

   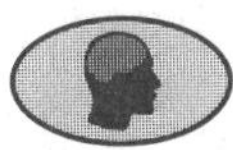  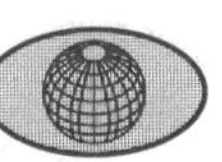   

Viewpoint: Todd Buchholz
Trust, Fear, and a Dead Economist

INTRODUCTION

Todd Buchholz is a former Director of Economic Policy at the White House, a managing director of the US$15 billion Tiger hedge fund, and an economics teacher at Harvard.

Buchholz advised President Bush Snr and is a frequent commentator on ABC News, PBS, and CBS. He recently hosted his own show on CNBC. He is also Co-Founder and Managing Director of Two Oceans Management, LLC. He delivered a lecture at the White House entitled "Clarity, Honesty and Modesty in Economics," and has been a keynote speaker for corporations such as Microsoft, Citibank, and IBM.

He has written numerous books, including *Market Shock: 9 Economic and Social Upheavals that Will Shake Our Financial Future*, *New Ideas from Dead Economists*, and *From Here to Economy*. His latest works, *New Ideas from Dead CEOs* and *The Castro Gene*, were published in 2007.

Buchholz is a contributing editor at *Worth* magazine, where he writes the "Global Markets" column. He has written articles for the *New York Times*, *Wall Street Journal*, *Forbes*, and *Reader's Digest*. His editorials in the *Wall Street Journal* correctly forecasted the 2001 slowdown in the US.

He won the Allyn Young Teaching Prize at Harvard and holds advanced degrees in economics and law from Cambridge and Harvard.

Trust is dead. President Teddy Roosevelt proclaimed himself a proud "trust-buster." But that was about cartels. Wall Street fraudsters like Bernie Madoff and the crooked Illinois Governor Blagojevich are busting the trust that people had in markets and in government.

Therefore, the collapse of the world economy is not like the Great Depression. It's more like the fall of South Vietnam. Or the Fall of Rome, with barbarians figuring out how to pick the locks of the gates.

The stock market crash of 1929 tumbled into the Great Depression when central banks hoarded cash, and the Federal Reserve Board watched as the money supply evaporated like yesterday's rain puddle. Meanwhile, the protectionist Ross Perots of 1930 blamed scurrilous foreigners and then jacked up barriers to trade, led by the US Smoot–Hawley tariff. Politicians compounded the error by strangling American workers with higher tax rates, raising them more than four-fold for lower income earners and three-fold for high-income earners.

Today's government economic policy is not nearly so reckless and stupid. Central banks have slashed interest rates and, so far, only small protectionist hand grenades have been lobbed.

So where does the Vietnam analogy come in? Early in my career, I wrote an academic paper called "Revolution, reputation effects and time horizons," arguing that when an invader conquers a country, the economy will collapse, tracking a catastrophic mathematical function.[1] What drives the collapse? Not guns. Not nooses. The catastrophe comes when time horizons shrink. Why? Because merchants must believe that their counterparties will be around next year, or next month. The Latin root for "credit" means trust. Would you lend to fly-by-night traveling salesmen? The current crisis has turned nearly every company into a fly-by-nighter, grabbing onto the last chopper out of Saigon.

BORROWING BY THE HOUR

Today, only a starry-eyed gambler will lend to the Sands Casino company for more than an hour. On the Las Vegas strip you could always find talent who rented by the hour. Now its CFOs must borrow by the hour.

Even if the Fed Funds and UK base rates scrape along near 0%, commercial credit suffers. While I am concerned about people paying back current debts, I am just as worried about a refusal to loan to businesses for new endeavors. A world-class company like AT&T should not have to pay 9% to borrow when government debt earns just 3%.

I heard US House Ways and Means Chairman Charles Rangel joke that at his age (78), he doesn't buy green bananas. Rangel is fast becoming a symbol of the entire world economy, and not just because he doesn't understand his tax returns.

What can we do, when time horizons shrink? How can President Obama, Prime Minister Gordon Brown, the Federal Reserve, and the Bank of England (BoE) stretch them? It is damn tricky. They have two avenues. The populist route has the government simply guaranteeing private debts, paying for people's mortgages and car loans, and even paying for unions to make cars that nobody wants to buy. While this will save some hides, it will not stir the "animal spirits" and arouse *new* activity.

PIGOU'S LAST CHANCE

The second avenue brings us to Arthur Cecil Pigou. Pigou has been dead 50 years, and this is his last chance.

During the Great Depression, this Cambridge professor was kicked about by his former pupil, John Maynard Keynes. To Keynes, Pigou was just another fuddy-duddy who would not revise his economic models even though Britain was being ripped apart in the economic equivalent of Gallipoli. This was trench warfare, and Pigou looked too genteel for the job.

Poor Pigou just could not rebut the dazzling intellect of Keynes, and turned into a kind of straight man for Keynes's *bon mots*. Scroll ahead 75 years, and now the world is tackling a new economic monster, grown from Wall Street banks and homebuyers drunk on leverage and equipped with all the logic and foresight of a palm reader at a circus tent.

Today our headlines blare with stories about falling oil and food prices, after a blistering run-up in 2007 and the first half of 2008. Many economists warn that this could bring on a Greater Depression. After all, the world suffered slumping commodity prices then.

Pigou had another take. He argued that falling prices can make us feel wealthier. And that if, when we go shopping, we feel as

"We do not need, and indeed never will have, all the answers before we act. . .It is often through taking action that we can discover some of them." Charlotte Bunch

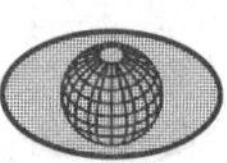

if we have more buying power, consumers can lead the country out of recession. Today, you might feel a little better when you swerve into your local gasoline station and see a price starting with a US$2 instead of a US$4, for example.

Unfortunately, this "Pigou Effect" flopped in the early 1930s. Keynes declared the free market is dead, and Pigou's theory slumped into a corner of our dusty textbooks.

But why did the Pigou Effect fail? Because central bankers yanked the electrical cord out of their printing presses and sat on their hands. The Pigou Effect basically takes the money supply and divides it by the price level. But during the 1930s, both the money supply *and* the price level dove into a sinkhole. In the US, the money supply sank by 30%, as 40% of banks bolted their doors shut.

Now, A.C. Pigou and Ben Bernanke have a second chance. If the Federal Reserve Board can stomp on the money supply accelerator, the Pigou fraction can climb, and the economy can find some hope. The latest readings show the US M2 money supply rising at a 13.8% pace (up from 7.7% this summer). But even more must be done, because the vicious de-leveraging among banks and hedge funds has ignited a destructive bonfire of capital.

Still, collapsing gasoline and home heating oil prices should pump over US$300 billion into the pockets of Americans, roughly US$300 per month for a typical family. In the UK, a tank of petrol costs almost £20 less than in the summer of 2008. Cheaper turkeys and chickens are flocking their way to the supermarket, too. Amazon.com keeps emailing me about "free shipping" (and all I wanted for Christmas was to clear my office of the stuff they sent free last year). Last week, I saw a burly guy outside Costco apparently trying to fold a huge bargain-priced flat-screen TV into the back of his Toyota Prius.

ECONOMIC BATTLE

We are witnessing a furious battle in the economy. On one side is the frightened consumer. She has more buying power via the Pigou Effect. But she is fighting the fear of new job losses. Even in a very serious recession, about 90% of households will likely keep their jobs. Here's the question, though: Will those 90% have the confidence to deploy their new spending power when the threat of layoffs glares from across the playing field?

The Pigou route is powerful but does not fit on bumper stickers. The government must force down longer-term real interest rates. High long-term interest rates tell us: "Give up on the future. Today's dollar won't be worth much in the future." The Federal Reserve Board, European Central Bank (ECB) and BoE must inject liquidity into every part of the yield curve. Traditionally, the Fed has preferred to create a steeper yield curve in recessions to widen bank spreads on lending, but we are now facing a corporate lending crunch that requires a flattening structure between 10-year commercial paper and the Fed Funds rate. Then Congress should cut the Social Security payroll tax, and for Pete's sake, don't jack up taxes on capital, as the Obama campaign promised last year.

Won't this ignite inflation? Nope. Inflation is a yellowed newspaper headline ready for the shredder. The Fed may be running the printing presses overtime, but that is merely offsetting the destruction of money as banks, insurance companies, and hedge funds dump and de-lever.

The inflation scare last spring looked like the Y2K hoax. Yes, commodities skyrocketed, but they were bubbles. As the bubble was popping, I was asking Ben Bernanke to shout *En guard*!, slap ECB chief Jean-Claude Trichet across the face with a white glove, and challenge him to a duel on the future path of inflation. Trichet was constipated. In November, when the BoE had pushed rates down to the lowest since 1955, Trichet and the ECB still had not pushed rates even below their 2006 level. Today's economy is starting to looks less like 2006 and more like 6 A.D.

We must also have a legal strategy to reduce the incentive to bet against the future. That's where US$65 trillion in credit default swaps come in. My proposal will test President Obama's Harvard law school education. President Obama should march the Attorney General into the Supreme Court to declare CDSs void, unless the buyer has a stake in the underlying company. There is precedent. For example, I cannot take out a life insurance on you, because I would then have a strong incentive to nudge you onto the subway tracks. For a hundred years courts have nullified impersonal life insurance contracts as "void as against the public interest." Because CDSs are called "swaps," they have escaped this insurance rule. 90% of CDSs have been bought, not to hedge, but to profit on the death of companies. When you combine these with short-sellers, there's simply too much incentive to light a match to the entire world economy.

No path looks attractive, of course. A hedge fund friend told me that John McCain should've bragged more about Sarah Palin's hunting skills. At the rate we're going, the only industry left will be hunting and gathering. It's not that bad. But it is that urgent.

Earlier in my career I worked at the White House with Treasury Secretary designate Tim Geithner, and taught with Larry Summers at Harvard. Summers and Bernanke are masters of Pigou and Keynes. Now, they must use the collective wisdom of the last hundred years, not to settle a decrepit academic dispute, but to save our standard of living.

It's not just Pigou's last chance.

NOTES

1 Buchholz, Todd G. "Revolution, Reputation Effects and Time Horizons." *Cato Journal* 8:1 (1988): 185–197.

"Don't study the idea to death with experts and committees. Get on with it and see if it works." Kenneth Iverson

  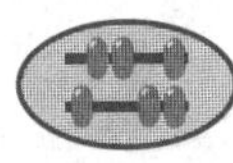 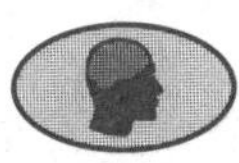  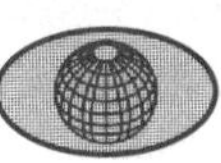   

Viewpoint: Bill Hambrecht
Bringing Trust Back to Wall Street

INTRODUCTION

Bill Hambrecht believes that Obama should steer clear of knee-jerk regulatory responses and instead restore transparency, fairness, and trust into the capital markets through solutions including forcing all derivatives trading onto regulated exchanges. Hambrecht, 73, has been in the securities business since 1958. He co-founded the San Francisco-based investment bank Hambrecht & Quist in 1968. Noted for its focus on the technology sector, H&Q was one of the pioneers of Silicon Valley's venture capital industry. Hambrecht resigned from H&Q in December 1997 to form WR Hambrecht + Co., which has introduced a new "Dutch auction" technique that has increased the amount that companies can raise through flotations. Hambrecht is currently a director of Motorola, Inc., and on the advisery council to The J. David Gladstone Institutes. He is also in the wine business, owning several hundred acres of vineyards in Sonoma County and a winery in Healsburg, California. Hambrecht graduated from Princeton University in 1957. He was inducted to the American Academy of Arts and Sciences in October 2006.

PRINCIPLES, NOT RULES, WILL SORT OUT THIS MESS

Warren Buffett once famously described derivatives as "financial weapons of mass destruction" that were in danger of exploding at any time, taking with them the institutions that traded in them and perhaps also the entire economic system. Made in the 2002 Berkshire Hathaway annual report, it has proved a remarkably accurate prediction.

So what lay behind the great disruption of September and October 2008, when a number of leading banks nearly followed Lehman Brothers into oblivion and the world came perilously close to systemic financial meltdown—and what can be done to ensure it doesn't happen again?

The view that finance was most likely to flourish in a regulatory vacuum, held by the administration of George W. Bush throughout its period in office, certainly played a major part. In the absence of regulation, questionable practices came to be seen as the norm.

In a regulatory vacuum, the investment banks were able to shift their emphasis away from being agency-based, service-oriented businesses towards being proprietary traders, and in the process they were able to leverage up their balance sheets to a previously unimaginable extent.

WHEN PROFIT IS KING

In pursuit of ever-greater profits and higher compensation for their executives, most investment banks transformed themselves into highly leveraged hedge funds. Meanwhile, the commercial banks, whose focus had traditionally been on direct lending, transformed themselves into packagers and sellers of loans, and started to encroach on the investment banks' territory.

The banks found they were able to give themselves unprecedented amounts of leverage through the use and abuse of customer deposits. While the commercial banks relied on their "time and demand" deposits, the investment banks used deposits in brokerage accounts and the huge cash balances created through short sales.

As the two groups of banks converged, they found that the most interesting opportunities lay in quant-based, leveraged trading in unregulated markets, with a particular focus on lightly regulated debt instruments that traded from dealer to dealer.

Highly complex debt instruments based on the exploding market of prime and nonprime mortgage loans soon became their vehicles of choice, and banks bought and sold packages of these loans even though they were so complex they were barely understood, even by the ratings agencies that were supposed to assess their creditworthiness.

Because no independent or transparent pricing information was available, the issuers and underwriters of these opaque instruments had a huge amount of latitude when it came to establishing their value. It didn't take long for the link between prices and fundamentals to get broken.

As the underwriters of the mortgage-related instruments were paid according to the volume of deals they completed, they had a vested interest in marking valuations as high as possible as well as in continuing to find buyers for these securities. When new buyers became thin on the ground, the investment banks became significant buyers themselves, leaving their balance sheets bloated with illiquid securities.

Essentially, it was the absence of any continuous or transparent market in these securities that made all this possible. And it was only when the US housing price bubble burst that holders of this paper were forced to come clean and admit there were was a huge gulf between their model valuations and real market values.

Ultimately, this is what lay behind the breakdown in trust which provoked the crisis of September and October 2008, something that few involved in the world of finance would like to see repeated any time soon, and which is now taking such a heavy toll on the wider global economy.

REGULATION WILL PUT THE MARKET BACK ON TRACK

Clearly President Barack Obama does not share his predecessor's view that, where financial matters are concerned, no regulation is good regulation. Already, in January 2009, the new administration made some positive early steps which will go some way towards ensuring that this sort of thing does not happen again.

Overall, however, Obama's administration is going to have to resist the siren calls for stringent new regulations or knee-jerk responses. Many of the people who work on Wall Street are very smart, and would soon find ways around such new rules.

Instead, the new administration should be focusing its energies on reintroducing soundness and transparency into the system. One way of achieving this would be to force all derivatives trading onto a properly regulated exchange (or exchanges)—and preferably ones that deploy an open auction process.

If all trades in derivatives and related instruments were forced onto such exchanges—something that would, of course, have to done gradually given the huge quantities of these instruments which are out there in the marketplace—I believe it would have a remarkably positive effect.

This would have the positive effect of forcing the creators and underwriters of the instruments to make them more transparent and more standardized; it would also rebuild the link between prices and fundamentals, bringing trust back into what had become a dysfunctional market. Market participants would find it much easier to establish the true worth of each contract, fair market pricing would be restored, and other important exchange-based protections would come in too.

Shifting derivatives trading onto an exchange would also boost the demand for independent research, creating immediate opportunities for independent research houses, as well as for the existing brokerages, to get into the analysis of the formerly opaque products.

I believe that the Federal Reserve could kick-start the process of driving derivatives trading onto regulated exchanges. At the height of the crisis in October 2008, the Fed lent huge sums to the banks in order to avert a catastrophe, and the collateral for these loans was opaque paper and a lot of other hard-to-value instruments. Were the Fed to insist that, within say a six month time frame, every new issue has to be exchange traded, or else it would be ineligible as collateral, everything would rapidly migrate onto an exchange.

If the banks were to have been bailed out without any changes to the rules, it would of course have been a recipe for disaster. To quote the Spanish philosopher George Santayana: "Those who cannot remember the past are condemned to repeat it." However, if the rules are changed and if, in future, the Fed refuses to lend against securities unless they are exchange traded, I believe it would change the system for the better.

At its heart, a functioning exchange has a number of advantages to the opaque dealer-to-dealer market, including:

1 Transparency of trades: All orders concentrate at one point, trades are disclosed to everyone.
2 Continuous trading market to determine value, as opposed to model-based pricing. Markets look ahead and predict future assumptions, while models look backward.
3 Control of leverage: Margin requirements have contained bubbles in the equity markets without the threat of contagion and should be equally reviewed and adjusted in the debt market.
4 Independent research for both new issues and in the aftermarket.
5 A functioning clearing house.
6 Counterparty risk assumed by the exchange. If there are counterparty losses, they are shared by all members of an exchange. The participants always recognize undue risk before the regulators, and this usually assures strong self-regulation.

THE END OF "FREE" MONEY

It is also imperative that, in future, the investment banks are prevented from abusing their customers' deposits in order to build up their leverage for proprietary trading.

Rather than re-enact the Glass–Steagall Act—which separated underwriting from lending in the wake of the crash of 1929—the Obama administration should bring in legislation that separates agency and money-management business from proprietary trading business.

If people want to run a hedge fund, that's all very well. But if they do, they must be obliged to borrow the money themselves. If they are obliged to go out and borrow on the open market, whoever lends to them is going to ensure that the collateral is priced correctly and that there is adequate margin. It was crazy that investment banks were able to borrow 97 cents on the dollar on order to buy paper that nobody really understood. It had become far too tempting for traders to use such "free" money to trade on their own accounts.

Allowing the investment banks to convert into bank holding companies and merge with commercial banks—which is what happened in October 2008—might at first glance seem like a dangerous thing to do. It gave them access to deposits, which they could conceivably abuse in similar ways to what they did before. However, the saving grace is that the FDIC (the Federal Deposit Insurance Corporation) controls commercial banks' leverage limits.

The ratings agency model is also going to have to be reformed. The only way you get decent ratings is for the buyers of the securities and other instruments—the marketplace—to pay for the ratings, not the underwriters and issuers. One way of doing that would be to put a tax on trading.

Transparency and fairness are going to be at the heart of any solution to this crisis. The enemy of a successful approach is going to be a lack of transparency, whether it is in the prices that are ultimately paid for these assets, or the perceived interests of the buyers and sellers in any transaction that is ultimately culminated.

Only when the inherent benefits of a truly transparent and functioning marketplace are applied to this portion of the financial system is the public going to feel that their interests are truly protected, and will much-needed confidence flow back into Wall Street.

▸▸ MORE INFO

Books:

Christensen, Clayton M. *The Innovator's Dilemma: When New Technologies Cause Great Firms to Fail*. Watertown, MA: Harvard Business School Press, 1997.

Christensen, Clayton M., Curtis W. Johnson, and Michael B. Horn. *Disrupting Class: How Disruptive Innovation Will Change the Way the World Learns*. New York: McGraw-Hill, 2008.

Ellis, Charles D. *The Partnership: The Making of Goldman Sachs*. London: Penguin Press, 2008.

Grossman, Jerome H., and Jason Hwang. *The Innovator's Prescription: A Disruptive Solution for Health Care*. New York: McGraw-Hill, 2008.

Schroeder, Alice. *The Snowball: Warren Buffett and the Business of Life*. London: Bloomsbury, 2008.

Surowiecki, James. *The Wisdom of Crowds: Why the Many Are Smarter Than the Few and How Collective Wisdom Shapes Business, Economies, Societies and Nations*. London: Little Brown, 2004.

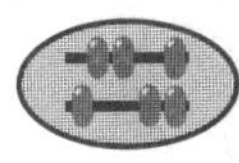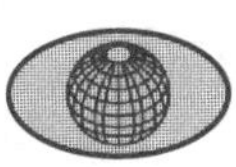

Credit Derivatives—The Origins of the Problem[1] by Eric Dinallo

EXECUTIVE SUMMARY

The nature of credit swaps explained:

- The difference between insurance and speculation in CDSs.
- "Anti-bucket shop" legislation as a precursor to the CDS debate.
- The origins of the exemption for CDSs.
- The role of the New York Insurance Department.
- Steps to bring CDSs under control.

INTRODUCTION

There is no doubt that credit default swaps (CDSs) have played a major role in the financial problems the world now faces. As the insurance regulator for New York, the New York Insurance Department had a role to play in the development of CDSs. As they developed, there was a question about whether or not they were insurance. As they initially were used by owners of bonds to seek protection or insurance in the case of a default by the issuer of the bonds, this was a reasonable question. In 2000, under a prior administration, the New York Insurance Department was asked to determine if swaps were insurance, and said no. That is a decision the department has since revisited and reversed as incomplete. We are now unambiguously in favor of the regulation of CDSs.

Since 2007, when the author took office, the impact of CDSs has been one of the major issues the department has had to confront. In the first instance, the department tackled the problems of financial guarantee companies, known as bond insurers. CDSs were a major factor in their difficulties. More recently, the department was involved in the rescue of AIG. Again, credit default swaps were the biggest source of that company's problems.

WHAT IS A CREDIT DEFAULT SWAP AND HOW MANY VARIETIES ARE THERE?

A CDS is a contract in which the seller, for a fee, agrees to make a payment to the protection buyer in the event that the referenced security, usually some kind of bond, experiences any number of various "credit events," such as bankruptcy, default, or reorganization. If something goes wrong with the referenced entity, the protection buyer can put the bond to the protection seller and be made whole. Or a net payment can be made by the seller to the buyer. Originally, credit default swaps were used to transfer, and thus reduce risk, for the owners of bonds. If you owned a bond in company X and were concerned that the company might default, you bought the swap to protect yourself. The swaps could also be used by banks who loaned money to a company. This type of swap is still used for hedging purposes.

Over time, however, swaps came to be used not to reduce risk, but to assume it. Institutions that did not own the obligation bought and sold credit default swaps to place what Wall Street calls a directional bet on a company's creditworthiness. Swaps bought by speculators are sometimes known as "naked credit default swaps" because the swap purchasers do not own the underlying obligation. The protection becomes more valuable as the company becomes less creditworthy. This is similar to naked shorting of stocks.

I have argued that these naked credit default swaps should not be called swaps, because there is no transfer or swap of risk. Instead, risk is created by the transaction. For example, you have no risk on the outcome of the third race until you place a bet on horse number five to win.

WHEN IS A SWAP INSURANCE AND WHEN IS IT PURE SPECULATION?

We believe that the first type of swap—let's call it the covered swap—is insurance. The essence of an insurance contract is that the buyer has to have a material interest in the asset or obligation that is the subject of the contract. That means the buyer owns property or a security and can suffer a loss from damage to, or the loss of value of that property.

With insurance, the buyer only has a claim after actually suffering a loss. With the covered swaps, if the issuer of a bond defaults, then the owner of the bond has suffered a loss and the swap provides some recovery for that loss. The second type of swap contains none of these features.

Because the credit default swap market is not regulated, there is no valid data on the number of swaps outstanding, and how many are naked. Estimates of the market were as high as US$62 trillion. By comparison, there is only about US$6 trillion in corporate debt outstanding, US$7.5 trillion in mortgage-backed debt and US$2.5 trillion in asset-backed debt. That's a total of about US$16 trillion in private-sector debt.

BUCKET SHOPS AND ANTI-BUCKET SHOP LEGISLATION IN THE US—AN IMPORTANT PIECE OF HISTORY IN THE CDS DEBACLE

Some history here would be useful. Betting or speculating on movements in securities or commodities prices without actually owning the referenced security or commodity is nothing new. As early as 1829, "stock jobbing," an early version of short selling, was outlawed in New York. The Stock Jobbing Act was ultimately repealed in 1858 because it was overly broad and captured legitimate forms of speculation. However, the issue of whether to allow bets on security and commodity prices outside of organized exchanges continued to be an issue.

"Bucket shops" arose in the late 19th Century. Customers "bought" securities or commodities on these unauthorized exchanges, but, in reality, the bucket shop was simply booking the customer's order without executing on an exchange. In fact, they were simply throwing the trade ticket in the bucket, which is where the name comes from, and tearing it up when an opposite trade came in. The bucket shop would agree to take the other side of the customer's "bet" on the performance of the security or commodity.

Bucket shops sometimes survived for a time by balancing their books, but were wiped out by extreme bull or bear markets. When their books failed, the bucketeers simply closed up shop and left town, leaving the "investors" holding worthless tickets. The Bank Panic of 1907 is famous for J. P. Morgan, the leading banker of the time, calling all the other bankers to a meeting and keeping them there until they agreed to form a consortium of bankers to create an emergency backstop for the banking system.

At the time there was no Federal Reserve. However, a more lasting result was the passage of New York's anti-bucket shop law in 1909. The law, General Business Law Section 351, made it a felony to operate or be connected with a bucket shop or "fake exchange." Because of the specificity and severity of the much-anticipated legislation, virtually all bucket

  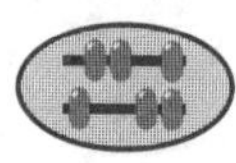   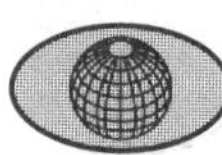   

shops shut down before the law came into effect, and little enforcement was necessary. Other states passed similar laws.

Section 351 prohibits the making or offering of a purchase or sale of a security, commodity, debt, property, options, bonds, etc., without intending a *bona fide* purchase or sale of the security, commodity, debt, property, options, bonds, etc. If you think that sounds exactly like a naked credit default swap, you are right. What this tells us is that back in 1909, 100 years ago, people understood the risks and potential instability that comes from betting on securities prices, and outlawed it.

HOW CDSS CAME TO BE EXEMPT FROM ANTI-BUCKET-SHOP LEGISLATION

With the growth of various kinds of derivatives in the late 20th Century, there was legal uncertainty as to whether certain derivatives, including credit default swaps, violated state bucket-shop and gambling laws. The Commodity Futures Modernization Act of 2000 (CFMA), signed by President Clinton on December 21, 2000, created a "safe harbor" by (1) pre-empting state and local gaming and bucket-shop laws, except for general antifraud provisions; and (2) exempting certain derivative transaction on commodities and swap agreements, including credit default swaps, from CFTC regulation.

CFMA also amended the Securities and Exchange Acts of 1933 and 1934 to make it clear that the definition of "security" does not include certain swap agreements, including credit default swaps, and that the SEC is prohibited from regulating those swap agreements, except for its anti-fraud enforcement authority.

So, by ruling that credit default swaps were not subject to state laws or SEC regulation, the way was cleared for the growth of the market. But there was one other issue. If the swaps were considered insurance, then they would be regulated by state insurance departments. If this were the case, then the capital and underwriting limits in insurance regulation would have curtailed the rapid growth in the market for these derivatives.

THE ROLE OF THE NEW YORK INSURANCE DEPARTMENT

So, at the same time, in 2000, the New York Insurance Department was asked a very carefully crafted question. "Does a credit default swap transaction, wherein the seller will make payment to the buyer upon the happening of a negative credit event, and such payment is not dependent upon the buyer having suffered a loss, constitute a contract of insurance under the insurance law?"

Clearly, the question was framed to ask only about naked credit default swaps. Under the facts we were given, the swap was not insurance, because the buyer had no material interest and the filing of claim does not require a loss. However, the entities involved were careful not to ask about covered credit default swaps. Nonetheless, the market took the Department's opinion on a subset of credit default swaps as a ruling on all swaps.

In sum, in 2000, as a society we chose not to regulate credit default swaps. Why did that matter? As we have seen, the financial system has been placed in peril because there was no comprehensive management of counterparty risk. Deals were made privately between two parties. These bilateral arrangements mean that there are no standards for the solvency of counterparties. The buyer does not know how much risk the seller is taking on. And there are no requirements for the seller to hold reserves or capital against the risks it is taking on by selling swaps.

None of this was a problem as long as the value of everything was going up, and defaults were rare. But the problem with this sort of unregulated protection scheme is that when everyone needs to be paid at once, the market is not strong enough to provide the protection everyone suddenly needs.

CDSs AND MARKING TO MARKET

Unlike insurance, credit default swaps are marked to market. That means the value of the swap reflects the current market value, which can swing sharply and suddenly. Value changes require the sellers to post collateral. Sudden and sharp changes in the credit rating of the issuer of the bonds, or of the bonds themselves, can produce large swings in the value of the swaps, and thus the need to post large and increasing amounts of collateral. That capital strain can produce sudden liquidity problems for sellers. The seller may own enough assets to provide collateral, but the assets may not be liquid, and thus not immediately accessible.

When many sellers are forced to sell assets, the price of those assets falls and sellers are faced with taking large losses just to meet collateral requirements. As the prices of the assets are driven down by forced sales, mark-to-market losses increase, and the collateral posting cycle continues. Meanwhile, the underlying assets may continue to perform, paying interest and principal in full.

STEPS TO BRING CDSS UNDER CONTROL

On September 22, we announced that New York State would, beginning in January 2009, regulate the insurance part of the credit default swap market, which has, to date, been unregulated—the part which the Insurance Department has jurisdiction to regulate.

That announcement played an important role in spurring national discussion about a comprehensive regulatory structure for the CDS market. The result has been exactly what was envisioned—a broad debate and discussion about the best way to bring controls and oversight to this huge and important market, and concrete progress toward a centralized risk management, trading, and clearing system.

After our announcement, SEC Chairman Cox asked for the power to regulate the credit default swap market. The New York Federal Reserve began a series of meetings with the dealer community to discuss how to proceed. We believe that there are appropriate uses for credit default swaps.

CONCLUSION

We acknowledge that some amount of speculation can provide useful information and market liquidity. We also recognize that the best route to a healthy market in credit default swaps is not to divide it up among regulators. It would not be effective or efficient for New York to regulate some transactions under the insurance law, while other transactions are either not regulated or regulated under some other law. The best outcome is a holistic solution for the entire credit default swap market.

▸▸ MORE INFO

Article:

Dinallo, Eric. "We modernized ourselves into this ice age." *Financial Times* (March 30, 2009).

Other:

Testimony by Eric Dinallo to the US House of Representatives: Hearing to review the role of credit derivatives in the US economy. Online at: www.ins.state.ny.us/speeches/pdf/sp0811201.pdf

NOTES

[1] Drawn from Dinallo's testimony to the US Congress on November 20, 2008, at a hearing to review the role of credit derivatives in the US economy.

"Action to be effective must be directed to clearly conceived ends." Jawaharlal Nehru

  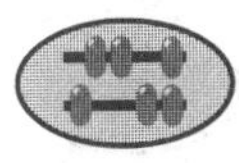   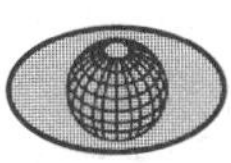   

Viewpoint: Fred Hu

China's Financial System: Challenges and Opportunities

INTRODUCTION

Dr Fred Hu is Chairman of Greater China at Goldman Sachs. He has advised the Chinese government on financial reform, pension reform andmacroeconomic policies, and has worked closely with China's leading companies onbusiness strategy, capital raising, and cross-border mergers and acquisitions.

He is a member of the Strategic Development Committee for the Government of Hong Kong Special Administrative Region and the Advisery Committee for the Hong Kong Securities and Futures Commission.

Co-director and professor at the National Center for Economic Research (NCER) at Tsinghua University in Beijing, he teaches a graduate course in international finance and macroeconomics. He has published widely on economics and financial markets. He earned an MS in Engineering Science from Tsinghua University and an MA and PhD in Economics from Harvard University.

The global financial crisis triggered by the US subprime fiasco has sent shock waves throughout the world economy and taken a devastating toll on the global financial system. China's economy has also been negatively impacted owing to the country's heavy reliance on exports. Nevertheless China's financial sector, once considered the weakest link of the country's otherwise dynamic economy, has escaped the current global crisis largely unscathed and demonstrated remarkable stability. Indeed, a stable and healthy financial sector at the moment has set China apart from United States, Europe, and other leading emerging markets such as Russia.

> "China is well poised to build a well-functioning, liquid, and deep financial system that can allocate capital efficiently to sustain its rapid economic growth."

In contrast to many Western financial institutions battered by toxic assets, liquidity crunch, and capital shortfalls, Chinese banks, insurance companies, and securities firms generally boast strong balance sheets, with adequate capital, good asset quality, and impressive earnings performance. With average loan to deposit ratio at 60%, there is plenty of liquidity and funding in the Chinese banking system. Out of the world's top 10 largest banks by market capitalization, at least three are now Chinese—ICBC, China Construction Bank, and Bank of China. China Life and Ping An are among the world's largest insurance companies. ICBC, with net earnings at 110 billion renminbi (US$16.2 billion) for 2008, is easily the world's most profitable financial institution.

These achievements reflect successful financial reforms undertaken over the past decade, which put China's ailing banking sector on a much healthier footing. However, there is little cause for China to rest on its laurels. The financial stability China currently enjoys could quickly come under threat if China's economy should experience a much sharper and more prolonged slowdown. Continuous and steep interest rate cuts by the People's Bank of China (PBOC), the Chinese central bank, may compress lending margins and cloud outlook for bank earnings. Nonperforming loans, presently at very low levels, may start to rise as numerous export-oriented manufacturing firms experience financial distress in the face of plunging overseas orders and, importantly, China's once red-hot real estate sector remains sluggish. Chinese insurance companies, securities firms, and fund management companies, once buoyed by a bullish and fast-rising stock market, may be bracing for a tough period ahead if the country's stock market remains weak and depressed.

CHINA'S INEFFICIENT FINANCIAL SYSTEM

Short-term problems aside, China faces a multitude of medium- to long-term challenges. Despite significant progress in recent years, China's financial system remains under developed and inefficient. Chinese banks continue to rely mainly on interest income, with little diversification in business lines, assets, and revenues. With few exceptions, large financial institutions (banks, insurance companies, and securities firms) remain under state control. Though the global financial crisis has triggered a tidal wave of nationalization of Western financial institutions, China's longstanding experience with state controlled financial sector shows that state ownership can be, at best, a mixed blessing. The government, as the majority and controlling shareholder of banks and as regulator, often sets policy objectives at odds with prudent and profit-maximizing banking practices. With the state in firm control of the boards, standards of corporate governance are severely compromised. Senior executives at the largest financial institutions continue to be appointed by the government and the ruling party based primarily on political patronage instead of professional qualifications, and the compensation system for bank managers, undifferentiated from the one designed for public service, does poorly in attracting, motivating and retaining the best talent. As a result, China's state-controlled financial sector faces an acute shortage of human capital, especially at the senior level. IT infrastructure for China's finance industry, while fast improving, remains a key bottleneck. There continue to be significant gaps in risk management, internal control, and balance sheet optimization. With regulatory functions and responsibilities divided by four agencies—the PBOC (the central bank), China Banking Regulatory Commission (CBRC), China Securities Regulatory

  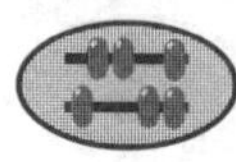   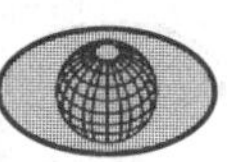   

Commission (CSRC), and China Insurance Regulatory Commission (CIRC), China faces its own regulatory fragmentation and coordination problems. While lax regulation and excessive innovation in the West may have been a contributing factor for the current global financial meltdown, most observers would agree that in the case of China, the country clearly suffers too much, not too little, regulation, and that there is too little, not too much, financial innovation.

With commercial banks dominating China's financial landscape, capital markets play only a secondary role in capital formation and economic growth. China's domestic stock market capitalization, currently at US$2.2 trillion, accounts for 55% of GDP. The total value of domestic bonds outstanding amounts to US$2.6 trillion, or 68% of GDP. By contrast, China's outstanding bank assets amount to more than US$8.7 trillion, or 228% of GDP. In 2008, total new corporate equity and bond issuance amounted to US$112 billion (of which, equity financing US$48 billion), which is less than one fifth of the bank credit extended for the year. Even allowing for exceptionally difficult capital market conditions in 2008, bank credit is far more important as a source of financing than equities and bonds in China.

SME FINANCING HURDLES

Ironically and most worrisome, China's small and medium-sized enterprises (SMEs), long the most dynamic part of the Chinese economy, and the leading source of job creation, continue to face significant hurdles in accessing capital. China's rural population of 600 million is also appallingly underserved by the country's financial system, contributing to widening urban/rural income inequality, a cause of grave concern for a country that puts such a premium on social and political stability. Consumer finance is woefully underdeveloped, which explains the fact that retail banking represents less than one fifth of revenues for the average Chinese bank. Apart from mortgages, which experienced rapid growth over the past decade, Chinese households, even in urban areas, have little access to consumer credit, contributing to China's persistently sub-par consumption growth. Clearly, it is difficult to revamp China's investment-led and export-led growth model and rebalance its economy without a major overhaul of the country's lopsided financial sector.

BANKING ON GROWTH

Yet China has a golden opportunity to develop and modernize its financial system. With the world's highest domestic savings rate, the world's largest foreign exchange reserves at US$2 trillion, and a host of favorable macroeconomic fundamentals, China is well poised to build a well-functioning, liquid, and deep financial system that can allocate capital efficiently to sustain its rapid economic growth.

China's banking sector, already one of the world's largest, can build on the progress it has made over the past decade, by fine-tuning business model, optimizing balance sheet, improving operating efficiencies, investing in advanced IT and risk management systems, thereby achieve sustainable high return on assets and on equity. While building on its traditional strength of corporate banking, Chinese banks should prudently seek diversification, especially in expanding retail banking businesses to serve Chinese consumers. In light of its size and dominance, a sound and vibrant banking sector holds the key to systemic financial stability in China for years to come.

DEVELOPING THE BOND AND EQUITY MARKETS

While continuing to strengthen its banking industry, China should assign a top priority to the development of domestic bond market as well as equity market. Existing listing rules are overly cumbersome and should be streamlined to facilitate more initial public offerings (IPOs) for promising Chinese companies especially fast-growing small and medium-sized enterprises. Chinese regulators should make vigorous efforts to improve liquidity, transparency, and corporate governance to engender investor confidence. Despite the global financial turmoil, China should not unduly delay the planned introduction of new products, such as stock index futures and short selling into the Chinese markets. China's existing commodities exchanges have failed to keep pace with the demand arising from China's rapid industrialization and urbanization, and must develop a far greater number and variety of futures contracts, including products designed to promote climate and emission trading, as well as those on traditional agricultural products, crude oil, nonferrous and precious metals.

In light of the massive pool of savings and rapid wealth accumulation in China, investment management is another increasingly important growth segment of China's financial sector. China's mutual fund industry has expanded rapidly in recent years, but there is much further to go to achieve world class scale and size in terms of assets under management, as well as in quality and performance. Other institutions, such as sovereign wealth funds including China Investment Corp (CIC), pension funds, insurance, and trust companies are also expected to play a more proactive and significant role in China's nascent investment management industry. To promote and support entrepreneurial activity, China has now paid growing attention to the development of a domestic private equity/ venture capital (PE/VC) industry that sources yuan-denominated capital primarily from domestic sources, as opposed to sourcing capital mainly from overseas for most existing China-focused PE/VC funds.

RISING TO THE CHALLENGE

Over the medium term, China will also have to respond to the challenges and opportunities arising from a more open capital account and greater integration with the international financial markets. At the present time, China's currency, the yuan, is still inconvertible under capital account transactions, which in part explains why the Chinese financial sector has been largely shielded from the US subprime debacle. Understandably, the Chinese authorities have become more cautious towards the financial market opening up in general, and capital account liberalization in particular, in the aftermath of the worst global financial crisis since the Great Depression. But as the world's third largest economy and a leading trading nation, China is rather unique to continue to maintain extensive and draconian capital control. The exceptional degree of openness of the Chinese economy to international trade, the significant inflows of international capital, the accumulation of massive foreign exchange reserves, the undervalued currency, the build-up in macro imbalances in the economy, and the growing desire of Chinese companies and households to deploy assets abroad and invest in global markets, will exert intensifying pressure on China to open up its capital account. China can have the option to initiate and manage this process in a gradual, orderly and prudent way, not in a rushed, potentially disruptive and destabilizing big bang. But it may not have the luxury to postpone the necessary reform indefinitely.

The ongoing global financial crisis may have created a major opportunity for China. While largely immune to the worst carnage, China can carefully study the current crisis and learn valuable lessons from it. It was after the Asian financial crisis a decade ago that China embarked on a comprehensive banking reform program that has clearly

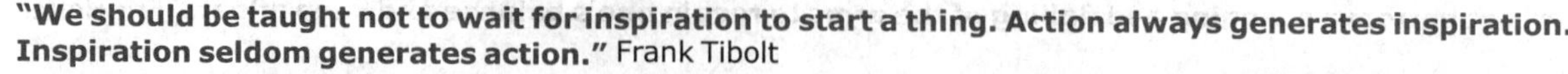

born fruit. The current crisis may well serve as yet another catalyst for China to deepen financial reforms, strengthen risk management, improve regulations and supervisions, and safeguard systemic stability in China's financial sector.

The next five years will likely be a crucial period for China's financial development. It will be apparent whether China stands a real chance to emerge as a global financial powerhouse in the same way it has become a global manufacturing juggernaut. If China can harness the numerous opportunities and at the same time effectively overcome the many challenges, China will likely succeed in building a globally competitive, sophisticated and stable financial system that may one day become the envy of the world.

MORE INFO

See Also:

★ Managing Liquidity in China—Challenging Times (pp. 81–84)
★ Viewpoint: Frank Feather (pp. 763–764)
★ Viewpoint: Linda Yueh (pp. 270–271)
✓ China (pp. 1374–1375)

    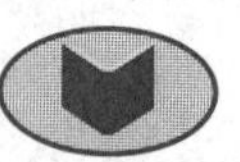 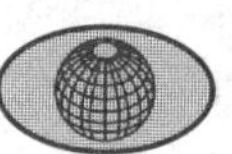   

ERM, Best's Ratings, and the Financial Crisis by Gene C. Lai

EXECUTIVE SUMMARY

- The objective of ERM should be to maximize the wealth of all stakeholders, including stockholders, policy-holders, creditors, and employees.
- To have a successful ERM process, a company needs to have an effective risk culture, and have the support of the CEO and other executive officers, such as the CRO or CFO.
- The ERM process should include capital modeling tools, and hold high quality and sufficient capital.
- An effective ERM will have a positive impact, not only on the BCAR but also on Best's overall ratings.
- In addition to the traditional ERM, and recent improvements such as dynamic hedging models, an effective ERM needs to consider the systemic risks that made some insurance companies insolvent in the recent financial crisis.

INTRODUCTION

The recent financial crisis has raised some questions, such as why enterprise risk management (ERM) was not able to prevent some large insurance companies from either insolvency (for example, AIG) or suffering large losses of their market value (for example, Lincoln National), and whether rating agencies properly perform their jobs.[1] It is critical that insurance companies have effective ERM programs, and that rating agencies provide adequate ratings to prevent insurance companies from bankruptcy. Initially, many insurance companies adopt ERM because rating agencies consider ERM as part of their rating. Adopting ERM for the sole purpose of fulfilling the requirements of a rating agency may not be the best practice. A recent survey conducted by Towers Perrin showed that 32% of companies names identifying and quantifying risk as the main purpose. We believe these companies are moving in the right direction, but more improvements to the current ERM process are needed.

EFFECTIVE ERM

To have an effective ERM, a company needs to have an effective risk culture. To achieve an effective risk culture, a company needs to start from the chief executive officer (CEO) and other senior executive officers (including the chief financial officer (CFO) and/or the chief risk officer (CRO)).

ERM usually involves a process that identifies and assess risks, determines a response strategy and techniques, and implements and monitors the risk-management program for the enterprise. The objective of an ERM program is to maximize the wealth of the stakeholders, including stockholders, policy-holders, creditors, and employees sustainably over the long term. It should be noted that wealth maximization is not equivalent to risk minimization. Risk and return are trade-offs. Insurance companies need first to establish their risk tolerance level and minimize unnecessary risk.

Some major categories of risk are credit risk, market risk, underwriting risk, operational risk, and strategic risk. Detailed items for each category of risk can be found in one of Best's articles.[2] In terms of credit risk, insurance companies should pay special attention to counterparty risk if they hold credit default swaps (CDSs). The recent collapse of AIG provides a good lesson for insurance companies not knowing the counterparty risk.

As a result of recent events such as September 11, 2001, the financial crisis which started in 2008, and major hurricanes in 2004 and 2005 (including Katrina, Rita, and Wilma), longevity issues have increased the risk profile of insurance companies. Insurance companies have to take action to deal with the increased uncertainty and volatility that they face. In addition, the regulatory changes regarding EU Solvency II and principles-based requirements have also resulted in improvements to the traditional risk management programs. Recent developments in ERM include catastrophe modeling, dynamic hedging modeling, and an enterprise-wide view of risk for insurance companies. Catastrophe modeling aims to deal with the rapid escalation in natural disasters caused by global warming, because it has been more difficult to predict catastrophic events. While the retirement of the baby-boomer generation presents opportunities for insurance companies to manage retirement savings, it also creates capital market-based risk. Insurance companies have developed some products that guarantee certain returns on the invested assets. The guarantees create additional risks related to capital market performance. To reduce the risk of the guarantees, insurance companies have developed and implemented sophisticated hedging models to protect both the policy holders and the companies against adverse movements in the capital markets. The recent financial crisis has shown that the hedging programs are far from perfect. Many insurance companies have suffered from rating downgrades and potential bankruptcy. The new emphasis on ERM today is a heuristic approach, rather than a silo approach. Not only the risk of individual unit, but also the correlations among the units, are critical to the success of ERM. More importantly, ERM today should pay more attention to systemic risk, which can be defined as the risk of collapse of an entire financial system or capital market. One reason for the recent failure of the financial systems is that ERM does not consider the systemic risk.

ERM, BCAR, AND A. M. BEST RATINGS

There are different rating agencies that rate insurance companies. Among them, A. M. Best is deemed as one of the most important. This chapter therefore focuses on the relationship between ERM and A. M. Best

CASE STUDY

ERM and the Ratings of USAA and its Subsidiaries

In December 2008, A. M. Best confirmed it had given USAA and its subsidiaries (hereafter USAA) the financial strength rating (FSR) of A++ (superior) rating, issuer credit rating (ICR) of "aaa," and the debt rating of "aaa." The ratings reflect "USAA's superior capitalization and strong operating results through focused business and financial strategy." Diversified sources of earnings, capital accumulation, and strong ERM are also key factors for superior ratings. In addition, good catastrophe management, a sound reinsurance program to preserve the finance capital, and a conservative investment strategy were mentioned. The USAA case demonstrates that Best's ratings reflect the effectiveness of USAA's ERM.

"You may not realize it when it happens, but a kick in the teeth may be the best thing in the world for you."
Walt Disney

     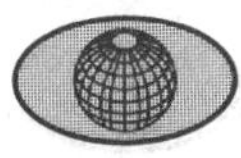   

ratings. A. M. Best expects each insurance company to customize its ERM process to their integrated risk profile and risk management needs in order to maintain acceptable ratings. The ERM process should include capital modeling tools (such as dynamic financial analysis) to maintain appropriate capital. The process also needs to include a discussion of the impact of the company's ERM on its rating in its annual meetings.

The objective of A. M. Best's rating system is to "provide an opinion of an insurer's financial strength, and ability to meet ongoing obligations to policyholders." One of the most important factors of Best's rating is balance sheet strength. Best uses the best capital adequacy ratio (BCAR) to proxy balance sheet strength. BCAR is defined as the ratio of adjusted surplus to net required capital (NRC). The main components of adjusted surplus are reported surplus, equity adjustments, debt adjustments, and other adjustments. NRC includes fixed-income securities, equity securities, interest rate, credit risk, loss and loss-adjustment-expense reserves, net written premium, and off-balance-sheet. The BCAR formula also contains an adjustment for covariance, reflecting the correlation between individual components. BCAR is similar to the calculation of the National Association of Insurance Commissioners' (NAIC's) risk-based capital, but BCAR includes some important risk factors that are not considered by the NAIC's risk-based capital. BCAR can make adjustments to respond to various market issues such as rate changes, the stage of underwriting cycles, and reinsurance. It should be noted that more than two-thirds of an insurance company's gross capital requirements of BCAR comes from the company's loss reserve and net premiums written. Less than one-third of the gross capital requirements comes from investment risk, interest risk, and credit risk. After Best calculates a company's initial BCAR, it performs various sensitivity tests including the catastrophe, terrorism stress test.

While BCAR is a critical quantitative model to measure financial strength and serve as a consistent baseline for Best ratings, it is not the sole basis for determining the final ratings. A corporate culture of risk awareness and accountability in daily operations, operating performance, business profile, and the quality of capital are also very important considerations for Best's ratings. ERM has an impact on a company's financial strength, operating performance (such as relative earnings and loss-ratio volatility), business profile (for example, catastrophe and terrorism risk exposures), and the quality of capital. Thus, an effective ERM has an important impact on the Best rating. An insurance company with a strong ERM can be allowed to lower its BCAR, compared with another company with a relatively weak ERM. It is even possible that an insurance company can keep its BCAR lower than the guideline level, on a case-by-case basis, and vice versa.

ERM AND THE FINANCIAL CRISIS

This section does not intend to examine the causes of the recent financial crisis, but to discuss whether an effective ERM can mitigate the negative impact of the financial crisis on insurance companies. In the insurance industry, AIG is now 80% owned by the US government. MetLife and Prudential, among other insurance companies, may seek the aid from the government. Why did ERM fail to prevent these companies from near collapse? Here are some possible answers. First, even though the concept of ERM has been popular for more than 10 years, insurance companies had not very seriously implemented ERM until recently. The current process is not perfect; while it considers the correlations among individual risks, it fails to consider the systemic risk facing the whole financial system, and the counterparty risk of derivative securities. To prevent future failures, the ERM approach needs to recognize that the solvency approach may not be appropriate in a financial crisis environment. Insurance companies need to have more capital than BCAR requires, because additional capital is difficult to obtain during a financial crisis. Second, CROs need to resist the temptation of selling complex products without really understanding the consequence of selling those products. The CDSs of AIG is an example. Finally, insurance companies should focus on their core business, underwriting business, rather than investing in exotic derivatives.

CONCLUSION

ERM has been becoming more and more important in recent years. The recent financial crisis makes ERM even more critical for the success and survival of an enterprise. To have a successful ERM process, a company needs to have support from the CEO and other executive officers such as the CRO or CFO. The ERM process should include capital modeling tools, and hold sufficient high-quality capital. An effective ERM will have a positive impact not only on the BCAR but also on Best's overall ratings. In addition to traditional ERM, and recent improvements such as dynamic hedging models, an effective ERM needs to consider the systemic risks that made many insurance companies insolvent in the recent financial crisis.

▸▸ MORE INFO

Books:

Moeller, Robert. *COSO Enterprise Risk Management: Understanding the New Integrated ERM Framework*. Hoboken, NJ: Wiley, 2007.

Articles:

Best, A. M. "Risk management and the rating process for insurance companies." *Methodology Report* (January 25, 2008).

Kenealy, Bill. "Sifting through the ashes to assess ERM's value—In a collection of essays, actuaries ponder the role of risk management in the financial crisis." *Insurance Networking News* (March 2009).

Mueller, Hubert, Eric Simpson, and Edward Easop. "The best of ERM—A. M. Best's enterprise risk management (ERM) criteria further confirm ERM as a central tool for insurers to manage their risk, capital and strategic decisions more effectively." *Emphasis* (March 2008).

Mosher, Matthew C., FCAS, MAAA. "Special report: A. M. Best comments on enterprise risk management and capital models." A. M. Best, February 2006.

A collection of essays: *Risk Management: The Current Financial Crisis, Lessons Learned and Future Implications*. Society of Actuaries, Casualty Actuarial Society, and the Canadian Institute of Actuaries, 2008. Online at: www.soa.org/library/essays/rm-essay-2008-toc.aspx

NOTES

1 In addition, Prudential Financial Inc. and Hartford Financial Services Group Inc. reported losses of more than $1 billion in the second half of 2008.

2 See "Risk management and the rating process for insurance companies." *Best's Methodology* (January 25, 2008).

  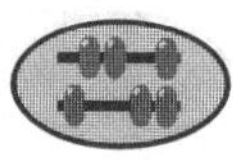   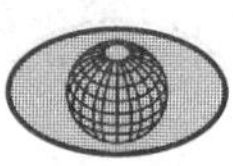   

Viewpoint: Justin Yifu Lin

Coping with the Crisis: Risks, Options, and Priorities for Developing Countries

INTRODUCTION

Justin Yifu Lin has been the World Bank's chief economist since June 2008. He is the first person from an emerging market to hold this role since the World Bank was founded over 60 years ago.

He was previously professor and founding director of the China Centre for Economic Research at Peking University. Lin, who received his PhD in economics from the University of Chicago in 1986, has written 16 books including *The China Miracle: Development Strategy and Economic Reform*, published in seven languages, and *State-owned Enterprise Reform in China*, which is available in Chinese, Japanese, and English. Among his public roles in China, Lin has served as a deputy of China's People's Congress and Vice Chairman of the All-China Federation of Industry and Commerce. He has also served on international task forces and groups including the United Nations Millennium Task Force on Hunger, the National Committee on United States–China Relations; the Working Group on the future of the OECD (Organization for Economic Co-operation and Development) and the Reinventing Bretton Woods Committee. He gave the 2007–2008 Marshall Lectures at Cambridge University.

As the world economy is buffeted by the worst financial crisis for many decades—a crisis that entails grave implications for developing countries and threatens to undo the hard-won gains in growth and development of the past years—the world needs international economic cooperation more than ever.

Until the summer of 2008, there was a view that the "decoupling" theory of global economics would prevail, ensuring that developing economies would remain mainly immune to the financial crisis and economic downturn that was sweeping through the developed world. Now, that looks like wishful thinking.

Developing countries, which like the developed nations had thrived on the back of the 2002–2007 global economic boom, have faced the triple jeopardy of food, fuel and financial crises. Many are entering a danger zone. The international community is going to have work together to overcome this crisis and prevent it from triggering a development and humanitarian crisis.

Developing economies are feeling the fall-out in a number of ways, with countries with high balance of payments and fiscal deficits being the most vulnerable. Many nations are facing a rapid decline in exports, as the runaway trade expansion of 2002–2007 has sharply slowed. Commodity exporters were among those hit hard, since the reversal in GDP growth was accompanied by a drop in prices for food, fuel, and metals.

The crisis also dealt a major blow to investment in emerging markets. Portfolio investment fell, as investors removed their capital or chose to keep it closer to home. Foreign direct investment, though historically more resilient to economic and financial shocks, will also decline.

In addition, developing countries which still had access to capital started having to pay higher interest rates for the privilege, owing to the flight to safety and greater risk-aversion among lenders. Also, as labor markets slacken, foreign workers have suffered a disproportionate impact on their earnings, with remittances falling as a share of GDP.

Second-round effects of the crisis are likely to deepen the slowdown. Because of the investment surge of the past five years, many investment projects are underway in emerging economies. As investment financing dries up, two outcomes are possible. In some cases projects may be mothballed, making them unproductive and saddling banks' balance sheets with nonperforming loans. In other cases, once the projects are completed, they will add to excess production capacity, increasing the risk of deflation.

As a result of all these factors, developing countries' collective GDP growth is expected to slow to 2.1% in 2009, compared with an average of more than 7% in 2004–2007. Meanwhile, high income countries are in deep recession this year, with OECD economies likely to contract 3% and other high income countries 2%.

This highly synchronous growth collapse cannot be solely explained by trade linkages, but illustrates also that developing countries have been directly hit in their domestic economies by the financial crisis. The reversal of capital flows, collapse in stock markets, and in general the deterioration in financing conditions have brought investment growth in the developing countries to a halt, and in many developing countries investment is sharply declining.

DEVELOPING COUNTRIES HAVE GREATER RESILIENCE NOW

Nevertheless, developing countries entered this crisis with advantages that they lacked during the shocks of the 1980s or 1990s. These included stronger macroeconomic policies and better-managed sovereign debt. Also, the move to flexible exchange rate arrangements has enhanced their ability to absorb shocks through exchange-rate adjustments.

The number of people worldwide living in extreme poverty has fallen by more than 300 million since the 1998 Asian crisis. The onset of the current crisis has also diminished inflationary pressures and reduced commodity prices, which has been a benefit for some developing countries.

Policymakers in the developing world will need to tap into all these advantages if they are to limit the fall-out from this crisis. Their first priority has been to prevent financial contagion from crippling their domestic banking sectors. Stock markets have declined sharply, some currencies have depreciated, and sovereign interest-rate spreads have risen with the "flight to safety" in world markets.

"Multinational organisations and those governments truly concerned about Africa should be directing all their efforts to creating and supporting a...policy of real diplomatic sticks and large economic carrots untainted by protectionism." Nicky Oppenheimer

In the case of countries that entered the crisis with large balance of payments and fiscal deficits, many vulnerabilities are looming. Their larger financing and adjustment needs have strained the balance sheets of domestic firms and banks, raising the risks of a cascade of bankruptcies and bank failures. If fiscal resources are strained, they may find it difficult to mount domestically financed rescues of their financial sectors.

In the case of a prolonged credit crisis, the global economy could enter a period of deflation, similar to that experienced by Japan in the 1990s. In this scenario, the emerging economies would have greater scope for credit-financed industrial upgrading than their more developed counterparts.

The chances that monetary easing would ease the effects of the crisis are of course greater in countries that can afford such measures. However this tool is not available to all emerging economies. Some will, in fact, be forced to tighten their monetary policy and raise interest rates in a bid to avoid currency depreciations or capital outflows.

On the fiscal side, developing country governments have a number of tools at their disposal. Governments that still have the fiscal headroom can inject some fiscal stimulus into their economies, for example by boosting much-needed infrastructure investment, in order to stimulate domestic demand and offset the fall in foreign demand.

A second area of fiscal stimulus entails investing in social protection and human development to ensure that a temporary shock does not prompt permanent declines in the welfare of poorer households. There are many programs that have proved effective in this regard; governments should prioritize those that most effectively buffer the impact of crises on the poorest households.

In sum, policymakers in the developing countries face some difficult dilemmas. Solving them successfully will depend on how they behaved during the boom. Their ability to respond depends on whether they have freedom of maneuver to act in a prudent counter-cyclical way by boosting domestic demand without sacrificing the fundamentals. Some developing countries are going to find this much easier than others.

IFIs TO THE RESCUE?

Armed with the lessons of past crises, the International Monetary Fund (IMF) is well-placed to help emerging markets make balance of payments adjustments to what should be temporary reversals in capital flows.

The World Bank Group is in a position to substantially boost its financial support to developing countries, focusing on the structural and social areas that are its mandate. The US$41.6 billion replenishment of its low-income-country window gives the Bank sufficient resources to help many countries invest in the infrastructure and social sectors.

In the case of middle-income countries, the International Bank for Reconstruction and Development (IBRD), the arm of the Bank that lends to emerging market countries, is in a position to make new commitments of up to US$100 billion over the next three years.

The International Finance Corporation (IFC), the Bank's private sector arm, is launching four new facilities for bank recapitalization, infrastructure financing, trade facilitation, and refocused advisery services. Combined with financing mobilized from others, these new facilities could provide more than US$30 billion over the next three years.

In summary, the World Bank Group can help countries mitigate the risk of the financial crisis turning into a humanitarian crisis. It can also shore up banking systems and support the adoption of other financial reforms.

THE ROAD TO RECOVERY

In an increasingly integrated world, where crises are able to spread rapidly across the globe, the response needs to be global, coordinated, and fast. Policy challenges need to be addressed at the country level, but it is critical that the international community acts in a coordinated and supportive way to make each country's task easier.

It is also critical that aid flows to developing countries be maintained, and that past commitments are honored and indeed supplemented. At some US$100 billion per annum, official development assistance volumes are modest in comparison to the trillions of dollars being spent on addressing the financial crisis in developed countries.

In the face of a prospective decline in private capital flows to developing countries, we must also intensify our efforts to catalyze and leverage private capital in support of development, including through innovative public–private partnerships. On current projections, net private capital flows to developing countries could drop from about US$1 trillion in 2007 to roughly half that level in 2009.

Governments need to coordinate approaches to avoid a return to "beggar-thy-neighbor" policies. I welcome the G20's reaffirmation at the April 2009 summit of its commitment not to raise new barriers to investment or to trade in goods and services and commend leaders' willingness to stick to the goal of concluding the Doha Development Round. With world trade volume in goods and services set to decline by 6.1% in 2009, pressing ahead with trade openness is crucial to global recovery.

The current global financial crisis poses significant challenges, but it also creates opportunities. A vigorous response to the crisis could set the stage for a new multilateralism that supports sustainable and inclusive globalization.

SPECIFIC RECOMMENDATIONS

- We need to lay the foundation for a new economic multilateralism that is more responsive to today's realities and challenges.
- The IFIs must become more flexible and inclusive to accommodate rising economic powers such as the BRIC countries (Brazil, Russia, India, and China) and representatives of poorer countries. They must also embrace issues beyond trade and finance to include development, climate change and fragile states.
- We need concerted responses to reignite demand globally.
- Financial supervision needs to become more global.
- Financial supervision needs to keep pace with financial innovation.
- National governments must consider whether to add the control of asset price bubbles to the mandate of their monetary policy authorities.

›› MORE INFO

Books:

Claessens, S., D. Klingebiel, and L. Laeven. "Crisis resolution, policies and institutions: Empirical evidence." In P. Honohan and L. Laeven (ed). *Systemic Financial Crises: Containment and Resolution*. New York: Cambridge University Press, 2005.

Easterly, W., and L. Serven. *The Limits of Stabilization: Infrastructure, Public Deficits and Growth in Latin America*. Palo Alto, CA: Stanford University Press, 2003.

"The trade of the East has always been the richest jewel in the diadem of commerce. All nations, in all ages, have sought it; and those which obtained it, or even a share of it, attained the highest degree of opulence, refinement, and power." Thomas Hart Benton

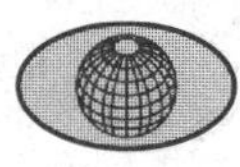

Article:

Didier, T., P. Mauro, and S. Schmukler. "Vanishing financial contagion?" *Journal of Policy Modeling* 30:5 (September–October 2008): 775–791.

Report:

Caprio, G., A. Demirguc-Kunt, and E. Kane. "The 2007 meltdown in structured securitization: Searching for lessons not scapegoats." Policy research working paper 4756, World Bank, 2008.

"The trade of the East has always been the richest jewel in the diadem of commerce. All nations, in all ages, have sought it; and those which obtained it, or even a share of it, attained the highest degree of opulence, refinement, and power." Thomas Hart Benton

   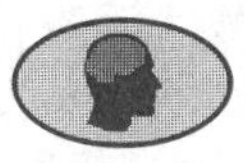  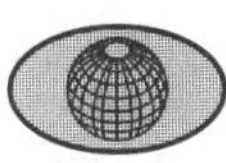   

Viewpoint: Augusto Lopez-Claros

What Would a New Bretton Woods Mean for the IMF?

INTRODUCTION

Augusto Lopez-Claros was the Chief Economist and Director of the Global Competitiveness Program at the World Economic Forum in Geneva until 2006.

He has been the editor of the Forum's Global Competitiveness Report and, in late 2006, he established himself as an international consultant based in Geneva, Switzerland, specializing in economic, financial and development issues.

He has a degree in mathematical statistics from Cambridge University, England, and a PhD in economics from Duke University in the United States. Before joining the Forum in 2003 he was Executive Director and Senior International Economist with Lehman Brothers International, in London. Before Lehman he worked as an economist with the International Monetary Fund in Washington, which he joined in the mid-1980s. During his time in the Fund, he worked in the main policy making department and was the IMF's Resident Representative in the Russian Federation during 1992–1995. Prior to the IMF, he was Professor of Economics at the University of Chile, Santiago, where, in addition to his teaching duties, he also headed a research team, financed by the Ministry of Health, which examined the economic aspects of alcohol abuse in Chile.

The 2008 global economic crisis and earlier episodes of market volatility during the past decade raise fundamental questions about the resilience of the international financial system and its ability to cope with shocks. It has become clear that we do not have the appropriate institutions and institutional mechanisms in place to deal with this new type of crisis, which originates in the inner workings of the financial system itself. This, in turn, has highlighted the huge costs associated with our present approach to crisis management, which involves a considerable degree of improvisation and ad-hockery. The recent calls by Messrs. Brown, Sarkozy, and others for a new Bretton Woods conference reflect the growing realization that, with tightly integrated financial markets and evermore complex linkages among them, a global economy may need some form of global economic governance, a task for which the International Monetary Fund (IMF) is woefully unprepared. In this article we explore some of the ways in which the IMF could be strengthened to enhance its role as a global crisis manager.

A BUDDING LENDER OF LAST RESORT

During much of the past decade the IMF has found itself in the middle of virtually all major emerging market crises, and questions about its effectiveness have been raised; indeed some have argued that the organization is no longer needed in an environment of largely floating exchange rates. It is clear, however, that in a world of fully globalized financial markets and in which policy missteps in one country have costly spillover effects on others, an institution that will have sufficient resources to deal with episodes of financial instability and that will help cushion or prevent the effects of future crises is indispensable.

As presently structured, the IMF falls far short of the role played by central banks in national economies. Like a central bank, it can create international liquidity through its lending operations and the occasional allocations to its members of SDRs, its composite currency. The IMF is already, in a limited sense, a small international bank of issue. As seen during much of the past decade and a half, the Fund can also play the role of lender of last resort for an economy experiencing debt-servicing difficulties. But the amount of support it can provide has traditionally been limited by the size of the country's membership quota and there is obviously an upper limit on *total* available resources; as of early 2009 this amounted to US$250 billion, a sum which includes about US$53 billion of resources potentially available under special arrangements negotiated with a few rich countries.

In addition to the relative paucity of resources, which do not allow the Fund to respond to more than a handful of crises in a few medium-sized countries, there are other serious flaws in its lender of last resort functions. To begin with, its regulatory functions are extremely rudimentary. Its members are sovereign nations that are bound, in theory, by the Fund's Articles of Agreement, but the institution has no real enforcing authority, other than some limited functions through the "conditionality" it applies to those countries using its resources. In particular, the Fund has no authority to enforce changes in policies when countries are engaged in misguided or unsustainable policy paths but are otherwise not borrowing from the Fund—this was the case with the Asian countries in 1997 and it certainly is the case with the current crisis, which originated in the United States with the bursting of the housing bubble. What little enforcement authority the IMF does have is sometimes eroded when the country in question has a powerful patron, who may try to persuade the Fund and its managers to exercise leniency or turn a blind eye if policies appear to be going awry.

There are a number of ways to deal with these shortcomings. One proposal some years back was to create an International Financial Stability Fund to supplement IMF resources. This would be a facility that could be financed by an annual fee on the stock of cross-border investment. This would also partially delink its lender of last resort functions from the periodic allocations of national currencies that currently form the basis of IMF liquidity growth. An alternative and more promising proposal would give the Fund the authority to create SDRs as needed, as a national central bank can in theory, to meet calls on it by would-be borrowers.

When this idea was first put forward, in

  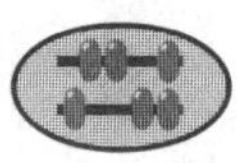   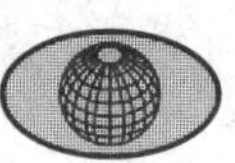   

the early 1980s, concerns were raised about the possibly inflationary implications of such liquidity injections, but international inflation was a serious problem then in ways that, in the midst of a global recession, it is clearly not one today and measures could be introduced to safeguard against this. This, of course, would involve giving the Fund considerably more leverage vis-à-vis the policies of those countries willing to have much larger potential access to its resources. Nobody questions the right of central banks to have a major say over the prudential and regulatory environment underlying the activities of the commercial banks under their jurisdiction; it is seen as a legitimate counterpart of its lender of last resort functions. A much richer Fund would, likewise, have to have much stronger leverage and independence.

MODERNIZING LENDING MECHANISMS

One criticism often directed at the Fund has been that it does not provide resources in a way that efficiently restores confidence. From the moment when it becomes clear that a country will need additional funding because it is facing a liquidity crisis until the time the money is available, several months may have passed. This is valuable time during which the underlying causes of the crisis may have deteriorated, further undermining investor sentiment. These delays are largely dictated by the demands of IMF conditionality, the tedious and lengthy process of negotiating loan conditions "while the house is effectively on fire." This feature of IMF operations is well-known. In a nut shell, the IMF does not lend freely in the midst of a crisis to a country that may be illiquid but otherwise solvent. Rather, it disburses funds in tranches as the country meets a variety of "performance criteria." Since these conditions may be quite onerous and take many months to implement, it will typically not be clear to the market whether the resources committed will actually be disbursed. This undermines confidence and makes the country vulnerable to speculative attacks. In contrast, a well-developed central bank facing a liquidity crisis in the financial system can typically respond in a manner of hours, as it understands that it must shape and manage expectations. Partly in response to this criticism the IMF created a special quick disbursing facility called the Emergency Financing Procedure, but it has been used only twice this decade, by Turkey in 2001 and Georgia in 2008. In any case, it is clear that giving the Fund potential access to a much larger volume of resources (as agreed by the G20 at their April 2009 London Summit) would have to be accompanied by significant internal reforms, both in terms of the content of the policies it advocates, as well as its internal management.

BETTER POLICY PRESCRIPTIONS

The above says nothing about the kinds of policies which the IMF advocates and whether these are generally welfare enhancing or not. IMF involvement in past crises has generated heated debates as to whether the IMF is part of the problem, part of the solution, or a bit of both.

If the Fund is to be given more of the functions of a lender of last resort, then it needs to modernize its philosophy, bringing into the center of its conditionality the kinds of concerns and policies which, so far, it has only tended to espouse in theory. In their speeches the Fund's managers speak of transparency, social protection, good governance, and "high quality growth," but they have not yet managed to incorporate these laudable aims into IMF program design. Indeed, most IMF programs yield distressingly disappointing results. Not surprisingly, the Fund finds itself often blamed for the failure of its policy prescriptions. This, in turn, undermines its credibility and prevents those who recognize the importance of the organization in today's globalized financial markets from endorsing proposals aimed at enhancing its influence.

The above would need to be accompanied by a structural reorganization, whereby the Fund's shareholders assigned it a greater measure of intellectual independence, making it at the same time more accountable for the consequences of its decisions. It would seem desirable to separate the Fund's surveillance activities from its decisions in respect of lending, so that glaring conflicts of interest might be avoided. The emphasis in recent years on the implementation of code standards for fiscal, monetary, and other policies to diminish the likelihood of future crises is certainly a step in the right direction. Surely the focus should overwhelmingly shift to crisis prevention rather than crisis resolution.

GOVERNANCE

But even an updated set of policy prescriptions is unlikely to suffice without corresponding reforms in the internal workings of the organization. There are several dimensions to this issue. First, the voting power of its member countries needs to be updated and made to reflect the major changes which have taken place in the structure of the global economy during the past quarter century. It is simply absurd that the voting power of the EU should stand at 32.4%, whereas the combined voting power of the United States, China, India, Brazil and Russia comes to 26.9%, though, collectively, these countries account for a much larger share of global GDP. This distribution of power leads to such anomalies as Belgium having a larger quota than India and China having a quota only marginally higher than Italy's and well below that of France. Not surprisingly, Asian countries do not see they have a stake in empowering the IMF, regarding it increasingly as embodying power relationships which no longer reflect contemporary realities. (To add insult to injury, against the background of the current global credit crunch, surplus countries like China are being asked to recycle some of their ample reserves through the IMF to other emerging markets in crisis, clearly a third-best approach to boosting the institution's liquidity and counter to its multilateral character.) An IMF without credibility is of no use to the international community, particularly at a time of world-engulfing crises.

Second, the international community might finally break with the convention adhered to ever since the IMF's creation, which establishes that its managing director must be an EU citizen. (A similar recommendation applies to the World Bank, whose president has traditionally been a US citizen.) The organization is too important and its mistakes too socially costly for the nationality of the candidate for managing director to be the determining factor in assessing suitability for the job. The unseemly negotiating process, that is entered into every few years as efforts are once more set in train to locate the most suitable candidate from a specific country, is inherently offensive to the peoples of those countries who have to endure the rigors of IMF austerity, not to mention that it exemplifies that very inefficiency which IMF officials are quick to condemn in dealings with the Fund's member countries. In this respect a further desirable reform would be to accord the managing director a nonrenewable fixed term of service, thereby freeing him from the conflict that may otherwise result between the interests of those who hold his appointment in their hands, and the countries which it is his mission to serve. In this way, he may never feel himself under pressure to forgo his principles by reconciling these divergent stances.

The present organizational structure has implications too for the Fund staff,

"In adversity a man is saved by hope." Menander

  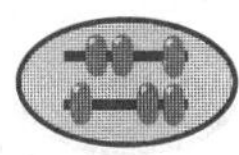   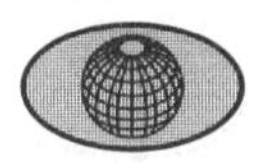   

who cannot under the present regime be held accountable for policy miscalculations. Deprived of full freedom to make intellectually independent assessments, inasmuch as the controlling influence rests with the large shareholders, they are constrained to represent themselves merely as executors—not a role calculated to enhance their standing with their counterparts in the Fund's member countries.

A NEW BRETTON WOODS

Emerging from the 1944 Bretton Woods conference at which both the IMF and the World Bank were created, John Maynard Keynes expressed the view: "As an experiment in international cooperation, the conference has been an outstanding success." The world has changed beyond recognition in the meantime, and, with the emergence of a global economy, the case for an institution that will help further the cause of international cooperation has only become stronger. Conditions seem now indeed propitious for the convocation of a global conference to consult upon the policy and institutional requirements for a more stable world financial system, one that will turn the International Monetary Fund into a more flexible and effective instrument for the promotion of global welfare.

The Globalization of Inflation by Diana Choyleva

EXECUTIVE SUMMARY

- The past ten years saw the clash between China's semi-command saver economy and the market economies of the West. Interaction between supply and demand for goods, services, factors of production, and assets has been polarized on a global scale. Inflation or deflation in the modern world has to be analyzed in the framework of the balance between global demand and supply.
- The low-inflation decade that preceded the overheating of 2007 and early 2008 gave central bankers God-like status. But they fell seriously behind the curve by failing to grasp the profound global changes at play and their implications for economic, financial, and price developments. The central bankers' mistakes could cost the world a dangerous lurch into deflation.

INTRODUCTION

The surge in global consumer price inflation in 2007 and most of 2008 caught many by surprise. The low-inflation decade that preceded this overheating had given central bankers God-like status. But improved monetary policy had at best a supporting role in the global Goldilocks story. The protagonist was the Eurasian savings glut. The setting was the process of globalization. Central bankers across the world fell seriously behind the curve by failing to grasp the profound global changes at play and their implications for economic, financial, and price developments. Their mistakes could cost the world a dangerous lurch into deflation.

The past ten years saw the global clash between China's semi-command saver economy and the market economies of the West. China's supersonic expansion turned it into the manufacturing hub of the world. But final demand for manufacturing goods came from the developed borrower countries. China provided the world with an endless supply of low-cost labor and mispriced, cheap capital. Developed countries provided most of the supply of real and financial assets. Interaction between supply and demand for goods, services, factors of production, and assets has been polarized on a global scale. Globalization did not alter the nature of inflation. But inflation in the context of the modern world has to be analyzed in the framework of the balance between global demand and supply.

THE IMPACT OF CHINA'S ECONOMIC EXPANSION

China's reawakening has transformed the global economy. For many centuries it was the world's greatest. Chinese steel production in 1066, using blast furnaces, exceeded Britain's in 1866. But China ignored the 18th and 19th century Industrial Revolution. It then failed to tackle its 20th century weakness, culminating in the 30-year economic catastrophe of Mao's leadership. Since 1978, China has gone down the export-led, catch-up path pioneered by Japan and Korea, with a similar annual growth rate of almost 10%. Growth of GDP per capita at purchasing power parity averaged a huge 12%, meaning the standard of living doubled every six and a bit years. In 2007 China was the second largest manufacturer, after the United States. Much of China's manufacturing is low value-added assembly, where China now dominates both global output and capacity.

While China was fast becoming the world's manufacturing powerhouse, the emergence of the Chinese consumer remained a chimera. Final demand for manufacturing goods came from the developed, especially the borrower, economies. The reason is that China saves excessively out of its income, more than a half. This negates the possibility of a mass consumer market. Savings are high for structural reasons. These reasons include the lack of universal social security, pension provision, and poor health care; the one-child policy, which has destroyed family security; migration into cities, which has broken up families; and limited financial products to channel savings between the old and the young, or into the private corporate side of the economy.

Instead, China provided the world not only with what seemed like an endless supply of low-cost labor, but also with mispriced, cheap capital. China's high savings cannot be invested profitably in the domestic economy. In a command economy they have no need to be. Profitability and return on capital are irrelevant. Instead, command economies are incredibly good at wasting savings through misallocating investment. China can waste its excess savings either domestically or abroad.

In the first half of this decade its excess savings went into a massive domestic investment boom. There was a huge buildup of excess capacity. The mainly state-owned banking system played an instrumental role in this. It has the bulk of the domestic savings, and the bulk of its lending goes to state firms and local governments. It is not done according to market principles and proper credit risk assessment. State banks are unwilling or unable to provide much finance to private firms or households. Access to cheap money gave state firms an unfair competitive advantage over private firms. But for private firms, China's incorporation into the global economy, especially since its entry in the World Trade Organization (WTO) in 2001, was a boon, providing both the markets and a source of funds. Moreover, Beijing kept its exchange rate fixed to the dollar and the capital account closed.

Unsurprisingly, overinvestment and a pegged currency led to falling global manufacturing goods prices. Meanwhile, energy and commodity prices surged on the world market as China's production was extremely energy-inefficient. But this was not reflected in the price of manufacturing goods because Beijing does not allow domestic energy prices to be set by the market. Ultimately, China could not escape the business cycle. By mid-2004 it had run into severe energy and transport shortages, which curbed its investment frenzy. Over the next two years domestic demand growth slowed significantly. China was still saving excessively, but now it had to find another channel to waste the savings—this time exporting them to the Americans. The yuan–dollar peg had also forced the Tigers and Japan, which had excess savings for their own reasons, to do the same.

China's current account surplus surged. Beijing was investing its huge savings in low-risk, low-yield dollar assets, and so did most of the other Asians. Globally this led to a collapse in real yields. But while China was providing the world with the excess savings, developed countries provided most of the supply of real and financial assets. In simplistic terms, when the huge population of China was bolted onto the global economy, the demand for assets shot up. Naturally, the supply of assets shot up in response. The booms in real estate and in mergers and acquisitions in the borrower economies were an expression of that. They were also the source of yet another

"Adversity is wont to reveal genius, prosperity to hide it." Horace

  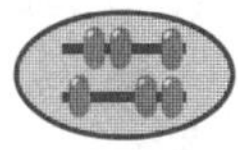   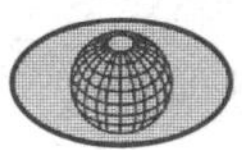   

boom—that of a purely financial type of asset: the asset-backed security and its derivatives.

BANKERS FAILED TO CURB AN OVERHEATING MARKET

Unfortunately, central bankers across the world fell seriously behind the curve by failing to grasp the profound global changes at play. In the developed countries they believed that globalization meant a change in relative prices. Eventually, they started to talk about China "exporting deflation" and then "exporting inflation." But in terms of their remit, their focus remained firmly at home. They failed to realize how manufacturing prices were set globally; where the "low bond yield conundrum" came from; and why the surge in energy prices did not translate into higher domestic wage inflation. Importantly, they did not pay attention to money and asset price developments.

But the harbingers of the global overheating that began in 2006 came in the form of above-trend broad money growth and asset price inflation. Central banks in the developed economies ignored their message and kept policy rates too low for too long, spawning asset price bubbles and the buildup of excessive debt. The Chinese authorities also made a mistake. They allowed some appreciation of the yuan versus the dollar, but in effective exchange rate terms the yuan was up by a lot less as Beijing was taking advantage of the stronger euro and stronger growth in euroland. Beijing thought the yuan–dollar peg was serving China well. The economy industrialized at breakneck speed, and international influences were kept at bay. The authorities failed to realize that China could no longer be immune to global developments. If Beijing did not allow the exchange rate to appreciate, inflation had to accelerate.

By 2006 most developed and developing economies were overheating. At the start of 2008 the global economy was still operating above its capacity, but the developed and the developing economies had distinctly different cyclical positions. The borrower economies' ability to take up debt was exhausted. The trigger was the emergence of the US subprime mortgage problems in early 2007. This caused global risk-aversion to surge, leading to a global liquidity crunch, followed by a fundamental failure of the banks' funding model, and severe de-leveraging. By the middle of 2008 most developed economies were already operating below capacity—the United States, the United Kingdom, and Japan—or close to their capacity in the case of euroland.

However, most developing economies, led by China and India, were still operating above capacity. Their overheating and the oil and commodity bubbles, which were stoked by investment demand and the Fed's misguided early slashing of policy rates, exacerbated the hit from the credit crunch. Developed economies saw cost-push inflation cutting into real incomes. But spare capacity in their economies suggested that a wage-inflation spiral like the 1970s was unlikely to ensue. For the borrower economies this meant they could not rely on inflating away their excessive household debt. The workout had to involve rising defaults, domestic demand deflation, currency depreciation and falling asset prices. The borrower economies, with the most conspicuous big ones being the United States, the United Kingdom, and Spain are in for a prolonged period of significantly below-trend growth.

"If Beijing goes for a state-directed investment binge that boosts manufacturing capacity and production when global consumer demand is flagging, there is even the possibility that price deflation—a sustained fall in the price level—could rear its ugly head."

About 60% of Western Europe and Japan does not suffer from excess household debt. But these countries have been primarily export-led and are also in for a sharpe cyclical growth correction. Both the developing and the developed countries are likely to see headline inflation start to ease sharply in 2009 as the oil and commodity bubbles burst. While lower headline inflation will not help revive the battered consumer in the excess debt countries, where any increase in real income is likely to be saved rather than spent, it could help kick-start a domestic demand recovery in the countries where excess debt is not a problem. Lower interest rates should also lend support. But in both of the borrower and saver economies, willingness to boost public spending substantially will be needed to pull them out of the doldrums in 2010.

In terms of the overall global story, China is crucial. It seems that slumping external demand has finally pulled the rug from under China's expansion. The crucial question is how drastic the externally driven slowdown is set to be. Ever since China joined the WTO, external demand has provided the main genuine source of final demand. The share of exports in output was 36% in 2007. But the share of exports tells you about the composition of output, not about the cause of growth. To determine the cause of growth one has to look at the change in the shares of output of the various expenditure components.

Exports were indeed a key growth driver in the early stages of China's boom. Over the past two years consumer spending has taken over. But the increase in the propensity to consume came on the back of strong export income growth and accelerating wage inflation in the context of overheating. Going forward, with incomes hit and unemployment on the rise, it is difficult to see the Chinese consumer becoming an independent source of final demand. Moreover, the change in investment is determined by the change in the growth of demand, making investment the most volatile component of output. In China the share of investment in output remains ridiculously high at 40%. Consequently, slumping external demand should present a serious hit to China's economy.

CONCLUSION

By the middle of 2009 the global economy is likely to be operating significantly below its potential, pointing to severe disinflation—in other words minimal rises in core prices. For the medium term, China's policy choices will be crucial for the world. China is currently at a major crossroads. The positive path is turning into a fully fledged market economy that allocates its savings efficiently, whether domestically or abroad, and invests its wealth and savings in search of high returns. This involves reforming the banking sector, allowing the yuan to move freely, opening up the capital account, and supporting consumer spending.

The negative path is a return to the bad old ways—state resources thrown into wasteful domestic investment to counteract the global downswing. Public infrastructure spending is the least bad option, but you cannot turn the state spending tap on fast. The worst option will be to force banks to lend support to the struggling manufacturing sector. If Beijing goes for a state-directed investment binge that boosts manufacturing capacity and production when global consumer demand is flagging, there is even the possibility that price deflation—a sustained fall in the price level—could rear its ugly head.

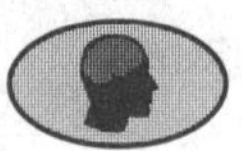

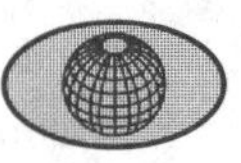

MORE INFO

Books:

Congdan, T. *Keynes, the Keynesians and Monetarism*. Cheltenham, UK: Edward Elgar Publishing, 2007.

Dumas, C. *China and America: A Time of Reckoning*. London: Profile Books, 2008.

Dumas, C., and D. Choyleva. *The Bill from the China Shop: How Asia's Savings Glut Threatens the World Economy*. London: Profile Books, 2006.

Pepper, G., and M. Oliver. *The Liquidity Theory of Asset Prices.* Chichester, UK: Wiley, 2006.

Report:

Beyer, A., and L. Reichlin (eds). "The role of money—Money and monetary policy in the twenty-first century." Fourth ECB Central Banking Conference, November 2006. Frankfurt am Main, Germany: European Central Bank, 2008. Online at: www.ecb.int/press/pr/date/2008/html/pr080225.en.html

Articles:

Ball, L. M. "Has globalization changed inflation?" NBER working paper 12687, 2006. Online at: ideas.repec.org/p/nbr/nberwo/12687.html

Borio, C. E. V., and A. Filardo. "Globalization and inflation: New cross-country evidence on the global determinants of domestic inflation." Bank for International Settlements working paper 227, 2007. Online at: ideas.repec.org/p/bis/biswps/227.html

Choyleva, D. "US liquidity crunch—The slow motion crisis." *Lombard Street Research Monthly Review* 219 (August 2007).

Choyleva, D. "The globalisation of inflation." *Lombard Street Research Monthly Review* 234 (October 2008).

Congdon, T. "Money and asset prices in boom and bust." Institute of Economic Affairs, 2005. Online at: accessible.iea.org.uk/record.jsp?type=book&ID=291

Guilloux, S., and E. Kharroubi. "Some preliminary evidence on the globalization-inflation nexus." Federal Reserve Bank of Dallas, Globalization and Monetary Policy Institute working paper 18, 2008. Online at: www.dallasfed.org/institute/wpapers/2008/0018.pdf

International Monetary Fund. "How has globalization changed inflation?" IMF World Economic Outlook, Chapter III, April 2006: 97–134. Online at: imf.org/external/pubs/ft/weo/2006/01/pdf/c3.pdf

Loungani, P., and A. Razin. "Globalization and disinflation: The efficiency channel." CEPR discussion paper 4895, 2005. Online at: ideas.repec.org/p/cpr/ceprdp/4895.html

Pain, N., I. Koske, and M. Sollie. "Globalization and inflation in the OECD economies." OECD Economics Department working paper 524, November 2006. Online at: ideas.repec.org/p/oec/ecoaaa/524-en.html

Rogoff, K. "Globalization and global disinflation." Paper presented at Federal Reserve Bank of Kansas City conference on "Monetary policy and uncertainty: Adapting to a changing economy." August 2003. Online at: www.kc.frb.org/publicat/sympos/2003/pdf/Rogoff.0910.2003.pdf

Wynne, M. A., and G. R. Solomon. "Obstacles to measuring global output gaps." *Federal Reserve Bank of Dallas Economic Letter* 2:3 (March 2007). Online at: www.dallasfed.org/research/eclett/2007/el0703.html

See Also:

★ Globalization and Regional Business Strategy (pp. 769–771)
★ Interdependence of National and International Markets: The Foreign Information Transmission (FIT) Model (pp. 330–333)
★ Mixflation (pp. 353–356)
★ Viewpoint: Linda Yueh (pp. 270–271)
✔ Methods for Dealing With Inflation Risk (p. 876)
✔ Understanding and Using Inflation Swaps (p. 886)
Joseph Stiglitz (p. 1198)
Globalization and Its Discontents (p. 1270)

"**Without humanity a man cannot long endure adversity, nor can he long enjoy prosperity.**" Confucius

  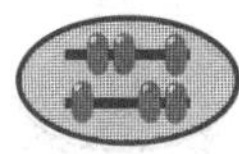   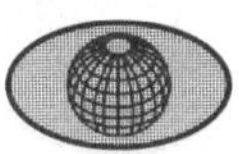   

Viewpoint: Maureen J. Miskovic
Risk Management at a Crossroads

INTRODUCTION

Maureen J. Miskovic believes that in the post-crash period risk managers of banks and financial institutions are going to step out of the back office and into front-line roles. Miskovic has been Executive Vice-President and Chief Risk Officer at Boston-based State Street since April 2008. In this capacity, she oversees a global team of more than 250 multidisciplinary enterprise risk professionals.

Miskovic, born in the United Kingdom, is also a member of State Street's operating group. She was previously Senior Adviser at Eurasia Group, a global political risk advisery and consulting firm based in New York. She has also worked at Lehman Brothers in New York, and Morgan Stanley, SG Warburg, and Morgan Grenfell in London.

Miskovic has published a book titled *Futures and Options—A Handbook for Institutional Investors* and serves as an honorary member of the leadership council of the Betty Ford Foundation. She holds a Bachelor of Arts degree in Russian and German from King's College, London University.

The crisis that is gripping the global economy has given rise to many thousands of words and many hours of discussions over perceived failures in risk management. It is tempting to point an accusatory finger at the use and misuse of risk models, but the truth is more complex and lies more appropriately in the failure of an entire risk culture.

The sub-prime crisis, which was and still may be at the heart of the crisis, was the child of two greedy parents: investors seeking higher yields and loan originators who led a race to sign up ever-less-creditworthy borrowers and then pass on the loans, thereby retaining no interest in those loans. But this explanation is too simplistic.

The behavior of these greedy parents was facilitated by many, including politicians who advocated a policy of home ownership; credit rating agencies which were in many cases conflicted and which failed to adjust their rating models even in the light of default experience; banks which were incented to make loans appear as profitable as those issued by their rivals; boards of directors who should have asked more searching questions about the risk of the portfolios; banking analysts and a central bank that kept the funds flowing cheaply; and lastly, regulators who certainly had access to all of the relevant information and could have had a consolidated view of systemic risk. All of these constituencies bear some part of the blame for the worst recession since the 1930s.

The year 2008 is likely to be regarded by history as marking a revolution in the financial services industry. By the end of last year we had seen unprecedented intervention and assistance to banks and other financial institutions particularly in Europe and the United States.

In 2009, further remedies have already been required. As the pace of recession quickens, unemployment rises and consumer defaults increase, it is quite possible there will be further pressure on certain mortgage- and other asset-backed securities. This pressure may increase further if measures currently being discussed with regard to loan modification are successful. Furthermore, as this recession charts its course, many believe that we will see significantly higher rates of default on corporate debt. These factors will almost certainly lead to further reorganization in the financial services industry.

Indeed, just as the Lehman Brothers bankruptcy was the watershed event of 2008, the breakup of Citigroup may be the watershed event of 2009. Here we see the rather counter-intuitive phenomenon of "too big to fail, yet too big to succeed."

GETTING TO GRIPS WITH COMPETITIVE ADVANTAGE

As the "originate to distribute model" is mostly broken and derivatives are passed through clearing houses—thus eliminating counterparty risk but also requiring standardization—banks' balance sheets are going to be looking more vanilla than at any time over the past few years. Banks will therefore need to consider where their strategic and competitive advantages lie.

Some will choose to excel in providing agency trading services to their clients, others may choose to offer specialized services to high-net-worth individuals, a small group may decide that their advantage lies in proprietary trading and some regional banks will have the strategic advantage of being preeminent in a local market. Each will seek to differentiate themselves by gravitating toward unique areas of excellence.

Overall, however, the trend may be toward further consolidation among financial services firms. This in turn will lead to a concentration of available counterparties to transactions and as a result there will be a greater focus on collateral provisions and documentation.

It also seems certain that the industry will come under greater regulatory scrutiny than at any time since the Great Depression. Indeed with the administration of Barack Obama in office in the United States, there has been much speculation regarding the consolidation of regulatory bodies and the most appropriate form of oversight. Regulation going forward will demand greater transparency and will also be more intrusive.

Furthermore, since the market meltdown has been global, there are going to be far greater levels of international regulatory cooperation than ever before. Regulators completely understand that business will flow to more lightly regulated jurisdictions and thus they will strive to agree on common principles for oversight. Given the press coverage of the losses associated with funds run by Bernard Madoff, hedge funds and fund of funds will not escape increased regulatory scrutiny. As 2009 progresses, attention will begin to turn from the immediate need to support the banking system and kick-start lending to reviewing all aspects of risk management, encompassing both the qualitative and quantitative.

"Whenever our neighbour's house is on fire, it cannot be amiss for the engine to play a little on our own."
Edmund Burke

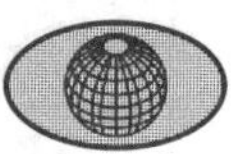

In the years leading up to the credit crunch, while banks were making unprecedented profits—in many cases based on unprecedented levels of leverage—risk management took a back seat. This will certainly change.

Boards of directors will undoubtedly spend more time seeking insight into the risks that the institutions undertake and therefore develop closer links to risk management organizations. There is already a vigorous debate on the need for dedicated board risk committees.

Current practice suggests it has become more usual for financial institutions to have such a committee, but it is by no means the norm. Many boards incorporate risk oversight into their audit committees' responsibilities. As a result of the conditions associated with government infusions of capital into US banks, executive compensation committees are also being asked to consider risk management, since senior risk officers must now attest that the chief executive and other senior staff have not subjected the institution to excessive risk-taking.

RISK MANAGEMENT HIGHER ON THE AGENDA

For the next few years at least, risk management is going to enjoy a much higher profile. Establishing a strong and independent risk management department is going to be a priority. In many institutions, the role of the chief risk officer will be elevated to a position that reports directly to the chief executive officer rather than one that reports lower in the structure. This in turn will ensure that the chief risk officer—who in this paradigm will need to have broad business experience—has a seat at the table and will be able to offer a risk perspective on strategic initiatives as well as ensure that senior colleagues are apprised of the risk profile of the organization.

This is important because few chief risk officers can set the tone for risk-taking in financial services organization by themselves. Ideally, chief risk officers help to establish a risk appetite for the company and then facilitate risk-taking within that risk appetite.

This facilitation requires that the risk management organization work side by side with business units to ensure that the company receives a proper return for the appropriate level of risk.

Risk takers must come to trust and rely on risk managers for advice and counsel. Risk managers will need to maintain independence and not hold back from raising a red flag when they have agreed to disagree with business units on the type or amount of risk that businesses wish to take. It has been suggested that risk managers are there "for the obedience of fools and guidance of wise men."

The founding principles of risk management—identification, measuring, monitoring and reporting of risk—will continue to be of fundamental importance. These basic disciplines require skilled staff and technology support. Collecting and consolidating data about market, credit, counterparty, and operational risks are onerous, but they are only a starting point.

REVOLUTION AND VOLATILITY

The value-added part of risk management comes from analysis. It is now very clear that many of the analysis tools are insufficient to provide a proper view of risk, particularly in extreme and illiquid markets. Going forward, quantitative models will still be important but they will be increasingly augmented by more qualitative techniques where assumptions are tested using future forecasts rather than historical data.

This suggests that, while financial engineers will continue to have a role in risk management organizations, they will either need to have direct business unit experience, or risk management departments will need to recruit those with experience to work alongside quantitative analysts.

All revolutions are marked by extreme volatility and the financial revolution that we're currently living through is no exception. As with any revolution there will be many false dawns. We should remember that though the headline stock market crash preceding the Great Depression was in 1929, the stock market did not bottom out until 1932. It is, therefore, impossible to predict how the next year will play out and, since our world has changed so much since the early 1930s, history will not give us a detailed roadmap of future outcomes.

Past failures in risk management notwithstanding, we can be sure that the discipline is going to be of renewed and critical importance going forward. By pushing risk management deep into the culture of the organization and hiring broad strategic thinkers into the risk management function who can be aligned to, though independent from, the risk takers, firms have an opportunity to build strategic advantage by aligning return expectations with risk tolerance. Now is the time for risk managers to step out of the back office and become part of the senior strategy team.

▸▸ MORE INFO

Books:

Bernstein, Peter. *Against the Gods: The Remarkable Story of Risk*. Chichester, UK: Wiley. 1998.

Cerulo, Karen. *Never Saw it Coming: Cultural Challenges to Envisioning the Worst*. Chicago, IL: Chicago University Press, 2006.

Kahneman, Daniel, Paul Slovic, and Amos Tversky (eds). *Judgment under Uncertainty: Heuristics and Biases*. Cambridge, UK: Cambridge University Press, 1982.

Lowenstein, Roger. *When Genius Failed: The Rise and Fall of Long-term Capital Management*. London: Fourth Estate, 2002.

MacKay, Charles. *Extraordinary Delusions and the Madness of Crowds*. Ware, UK: Wordsworth Reference, 1995.

McLean, Bethany, and Peter Elkind. *The Smartest Guys in the Room: The Amazing Rise and Scandalous Fall of Enron*. London:Penguin, 2004.

Plous, Scott. *The Psychology of Judgment and Decision Making*. New York: McGraw-Hill, 1993.

Taleb, Nassim Nicholas. *Fooled by Randomness: The Hidden Role of Chance in Life and in the Markets*. New York: Texere Publishing, 2004.

Taleb, Nassim Nicholas. *The Black Swan: The Impact of the Highly Improbable*. London: Penguin, 2008.

"When business conditions got tough in recent years, we did not take meat cleavers to our product."
Colin Marshall

  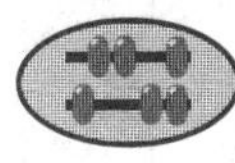 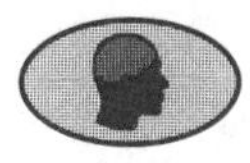  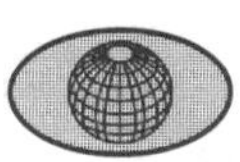   

How the Settlement Infrastructure Is Surviving the Financial Meltdown by Yves Poullet

EXECUTIVE SUMMARY

Few people outside the banking sector are aware of the national and cross-border settlement systems that enable counterparties across the financial services industry to settle their transactions securely. This article examines how these systems were stressed by the global banking crisis. It explains the post-trade infrastructure, the procedures that dealt with the failure of Lehman Brothers, the use of collateral to minimise counterparty risk, the varieties of collateral, the necessity for stress-testing infrastructure, the crucial role of collateral valuation, the growing interoperability between settlement infrastructure providers, and the road ahead.

INTRODUCTION

While the headlines are dominated by the plight of the banking sector, and the wider economic implications of the financial crisis, it is our job to make sure that the securities settlement infrastructure on which you have come to rely continues to function well. As if that was not challenging enough these days, we are committed to delivering an infrastructure that offers even greater efficiency, with reduced risk, and at the lowest possible prices.

Securities settlement systems, however, have not been immune from the recent market turmoil. They have had to deal with record transaction flows, and the liquidation or partial nationalization of a number of market participants. Procedures relating to the liquidation of collateral that, for many, had only ever been tested in theory, have now been put into practice.

The good news is that the clearing and settlement infrastructure across the globe has stood up well to immense strains—processing record peaks in volumes and values. Recent market developments have spotlighted, in the most extreme fashion, the ramifications of international capital market co-dependencies. For example, interbank lending has become more and more difficult, with the erosion of trust between counterparties. Fully collateralized transactions are now more the rule than the exception, in order to protect a counterparty against another's possible default during the middle of a transaction.

SETTLEMENT UNCOVERED

Euroclear is a user-owned, user-governed Brussels-based organization that specializes in the settlement of securities transactions. It was founded in the 1960s as part of JP Morgan and Co. to settle international securities, so-called "Eurobonds."

Today, as the world's largest international central securities depository (ICSD), Euroclear Bank provides settlement and custody services, as well as value-added services such as collateral management, to clients from all corners of the globe. In 2008, Euroclear Bank processed securities transactions worth €280 trillion, which is equivalent to more than 3,000 times Qatar's GDP of 2008. A brief explanation might be in order here about how this segment of the market works.

When trades are conducted on a regulated exchange, they are cleared and settled by post-trade infrastructure providers. Central counterparties (CCPs), also known as clearing houses, often reduce risk by acting as the sole buyer to the seller and the sole seller to the buyer, as well as netting trades between the same counterparties to make the settlement process more efficient and less expensive. The various national and international CSDs take responsibility for simultaneously exchanging cash for securities, which is called settlement, once the transactions are cleared and netted. This is actually the point where there is an irrevocable transfer of ownership of the asset.

Take a situation where two institutions are conducting thousands of trades between themselves, on or off an exchange. The clearing house may be able to net the aggregated trading activity down to a single netted trade by acting as the central counterparty for both institutions. Counterparty risk is minimized in this process, and is further reduced because CSDs and international CSDs operate an irreversible mechanism to conclude settlement, known as "delivery versus payment," where securities are only ever transferred against actual payment received—simultaneously.

In the current climate, it has been tremendously important for market participants that the (I)CSDs continue to provide safe settlement. Euroclear Bank, as a single purpose settlement bank which is owned and governed by its clients, is a systemically important piece of market infrastructure that must have very robust risk-management practices. Indeed, as a multi-currency, multi-market ICSD, Euroclear Bank also grants credit and securities loans to its 1,500 clients, to facilitate settlement and maximize settlement efficiency.

Euroclear Bank's business practices ensure that around 99% of the credit Euroclear Bank grants to its clients is fully collateralized. This gives Euroclear Bank the resilience required to continue to help liquidity flow between financial firms, and to contribute an element of safety during the settlement process.

RIDING OUT THE STORM

To operate efficiently, particularly during adverse market conditions, it is good practice to stress test, on a regular basis, systems and procedures under very extreme scenarios. No institution in the capital markets can afford to drop the ball.

When Lehman Brothers was placed into administration, this was considered by Euroclear Bank as an extreme situation that had to be managed quickly and efficiently. As a result of the Lehman situation, panic and shock pervaded the

Figure 1. Differing roles in the international capital markets

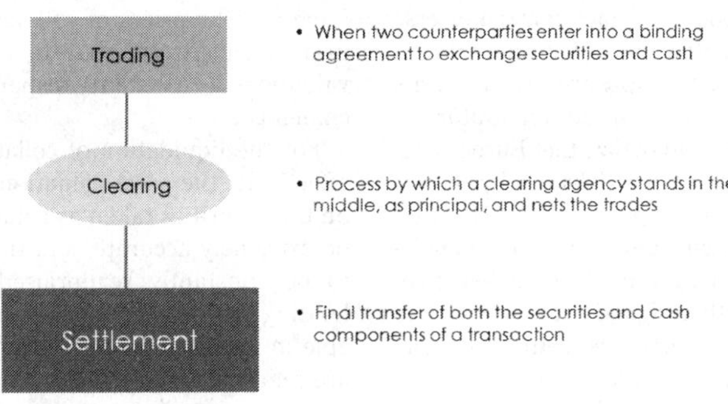
Trading
• When two counterparties enter into a binding agreement to exchange securities and cash
Clearing
• Process by which a clearing agency stands in the middle, as principal, and nets the trades
Settlement
• Final transfer of both the securities and cash components of a transaction

"After calamities, more caution." Desiderius Erasmus

     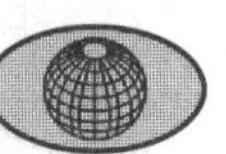 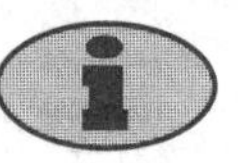  

capital markets, spiraling into fear that other trading counterparties could also be experiencing severe financial and/or liquidity difficulties. This was a major challenge for Euroclear Bank, as it needed to continue the processing of transactions to support client activity, without reducing credit facilities more than was absolutely necessary. Had Euroclear managed the situation differently, this would have reduced the ability of key market participants to shift liquidity around at a time when they most needed to do so.

Euroclear managed this market shock by carefully monitoring events, and staying in very close contact with regulators and central banks, as well as with clients, in order to then take the best possible measures and actions, while managing and mitigating the risks to which it was exposed.

In fact, the collapse of a firm of Lehman's stature was a scenario that Euroclear Bank had prepared for during previous business contingency rehearsals and drills. Just weeks prior to the Lehman crisis, a stress-test scenario was presented to various Euroclear teams where a major financial firm "failed." Therefore, well-rehearsed crisis management procedures and protocols were put into practice during this "live" Lehman event, enabling management to take informed decisions quickly and effectively.

One of the outcomes of the crisis exercise was an understanding of the emphasis to be placed on the various responsibilities that Euroclear Bank bears as the world's largest ICSD, processing trillions of euros in transactions everyday. As well, as an intraday provider of credit, Euroclear Bank has an equally vital role to keep liquidity circulating smoothly. Thus, it also has the duty of protecting itself.

Running disaster simulations helped the ICSD to realize how rapidly systemic risk could spread, and what measures would be required to contain risks. Consequently, when Lehman Brothers was put into administration, Euroclear was comfortable about its decision to take rapid action by selling off the securities it had received from Lehman's as collateral to cover its credit risk exposure. In fact, this risk-averse model saw sufficient collateral sold to cover the initial exposure, with excess collateral returned to the administrators.

It is important to realize that Euroclear is not responsible for the risks run by clients. The delivery versus payment (DvP) settlement mechanism and collateral management operated by Euroclear on behalf of clients, are both designed to allow clients to manage counterparty risk, settlement risk, and credit risk more effectively.

DEFINITIONS OF RISK

- Counterparty risk is the risk of a monetary loss that a firm may be exposed to if the counterparty to a transaction with it encounters difficulties meeting its obligations under the terms of the agreement.
- Settlement risk is the risk that a counterparty does not deliver a security or its value in cash, as per agreement, when the security was traded after the other counterparty or counterparties have already delivered security or cash value, as per the trade agreement.
- Credit risk/default risk is the risk of loss due to a debtor's nonpayment of a loan or other line of credit (either the principal or interest (coupon) or both).

NOT ALL COLLATERAL IS EQUAL

Of course, not all collateral is equal, and the more the markets become nervous about counterparty risk, the higher the benchmark tends to go as far as what constitutes acceptable collateral. Typically, government and supranational bonds remain sought after as high-quality collateral, while other types of collateral, such as corporate bonds, structured products and equities are either in low demand, or substantially discounted.

The recent, difficult market conditions have tested collateral valuation tools and processing methods, and have taught firms a great deal about these domains, particularly their strengths and weaknesses during times of crisis.

Institutions acting as triparty collateral management agents, such as Euroclear Bank, offer a service which ensures a complete match between the cash lender's collateral requirements, and the basket of collateral offered by the cash borrower.

Offering such a service necessitates the daily mark-to-market of the value of collateral used to cover exposures on behalf of the counterparties, but this is not a trivial task. It requires that the collateral agent has access to the portfolio of securities held by the cash borrower, and fully understands the collateral criteria specified by the cash lender. Indeed, as the markets fluctuate, the prices of collateral can move dramatically from hour to hour, making valuation a constant responsibility and challenge.

For the liquidation of collateral to work effectively, the asset valuation calculations on the securities taken as collateral have to be extremely accurate, and they then have to be constantly reappraised during the holding period, or losses will be unavoidable in a falling market. Often, limitations are set and agreed by both parties as to the type and grading of the securities to be included in the collateral mix, among other criteria. For example, the collateral taker can automatically exclude in the mix any security issued by the collateral giver. The triparty agent, therefore, will take responsibility to ensure that, for example, Lehman's own stock was never posted as collateral to any of its counterparties that expressly excluded Lehman stock in their collateral eligibility criteria.

At the same time, the valuation of securities taken as collateral are subject to "haircuts" (when securities of higher risk are valued lower than their market value), which reflect the rating, volatility, and liquidity of the paper.

One has to remember that what is poisoning interbank lending today is the lack of trust between the counterparties, due to the subprime losses suffered. However, lenders are able to take sound collateral from the borrower as a form of protection, which should ease the nervousness of actively engaging in this business again. That is where efficient and risk-averse settlement systems can facilitate the smooth transfer of collateral between borrowers and lenders, which can have a hugely positive effect on the overall liquidity of the markets.

INTEROPERABILITY, IF NOT CONSOLIDATION

What has undoubtedly helped ease tensions during the current liquidity crisis is the interoperability that already exists between various securities settlement providers, such as between Euroclear Bank and Clearstream in Luxembourg. Euroclear Bank has worked with Clearstream over the years to further improve what has become the model of ICSD interoperability, so that securities and liquidity can move easily across borders, and between institutions.

While interoperability is important, it does not compare with the efficiencies and cost savings that infrastructure consolidation can deliver. Euroclear recently completed the launch of ESES (Euroclear Settlement of Euronext-zone Securities), a single platform for the processing of all fixed-income securities in Belgium, France, and the Netherlands, as well as equity transactions traded on the Amsterdam, Brussels, and Paris Euronext exchanges. This common settlement solution is in full support of Euronext's Single Order Book, and is one of the cornerstones of Euroclear's multi-market platform consolidation process, founded on harmonized market rules and practices.

By 2011, Euroclear will have a multi-currency single platform for real-time

"Prosperity doth best discover vice; but adversity doth best discover virtue." Francis Bacon

settlement, custody, and other services. It will cover the three ESES markets, British and Irish securities, as well as all transactions processed for Euroclear Bank clients. Following immediately thereafter, the final two markets in the Euroclear group—Finland and Sweden—will also join the single platform.

The ability to create a single order book for Euronext securities, and a common ESES settlement solution across three important markets (France, Belgium, and the Netherlands), means that all the complexities and difficulties of cross-border trading and settlement vanish. In essence, what has been created is the foundation for a pan-European domestic market for trading and settlement. Once Euroclear completes its single platform, it expects to deliver more than €300 million per year in savings to the market.

Without this kind of platform integration among CSDs, a cross-border deal between a French investor buying a Belgian share from a Dutch investor could cost somewhere between €5 and €15 in post-trade transaction costs, depending on the number of intermediaries involved in the chain to settle the bargain. With a single platform for these three countries now available, the cost of such a trade has fallen to under €1 in post-trade costs. This will certainly serve to encourage even more cross-border flows of securities and liquidity.

THE ROAD AHEAD

Right now, it is clear that the market is highly risk- and cost-conscious. In the short term, it is likely that firms will be prudent on approving new IT and integration projects generally. However, it is also very clear that the financial markets are now essentially global markets, with a compelling need to move towards tighter integration of the settlement infrastructure. Asia is still in the early stages of developing a sophisticated, interoperable CSD infrastructure, and a globally integrated, post-trade infrastructure is probably still many, many years away.

Looking forward, one has to be optimistic that over the course of the next five to 10 years, Europe will bring about a fully integrated, smoothly operating settlement infrastructure. This will enable liquidity and investments to flow seamlessly across national boundaries. Furthermore, a Europe where market practices are fully harmonized will alleviate unnecessary costs for intermediaries and investors alike. This is an ambitious, but realistic dream: a domestic market for Europe.

▸▸ MORE INFO

Books:

Attali, Jacques. *Gandhi*. Paris: Fayard, 2007.

Attali, Jacques. *A Brief History of the Future: A Brave and Controversial Look At the Twenty-First Century*. New York: Arcade Publishing, 2009.

Drew, John, Blair McCallum, and Stefan Roggenhofer. *Journey to Lean: Making Operational Change Stick*. New York: Palgrave Macmillan, 2004.

Larsson, Stieg. Millennium Series. Arles, France: Actes Sud, 2006.

Tolle, Eckhart. *Power of Now*. Novato, CA: New World Library, 2004.

See Also:

Banking and Financial Services (pp. 1500–1502)

"Prosperity is not without many fears and distastes; and Adversity is not without comfort and hope."
Francis Bacon

  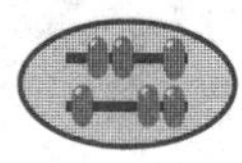   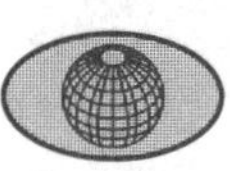   

Viewpoint: Jon Moulton
A Not So Cheerful Future for LBOs

INTRODUCTION

Jon Moulton is Managing Partner of UK-based private equity firm Alchemy Partners, which has invested £2 billion of equity and specializes in dealing with troubled companies. Alchemy also has a £300 million European special opportunities fund investing in distressed debt. Moulton previously worked with Citicorp Venture Capital (now called CVC Capital Partners) in New York and London, Permira, and Apax. He has been a director of five public companies, numerous private companies and is currently a director of the US-based Irvin parachute business, the Cedar IT business, and Sylvan (timber), amongst others.

An active angel investor, he has a chemistry degree from Lancaster University and started his career as a chartered accountant with Coopers & Lybrand. He has publicly criticized private equity firms that flatter their own income by using a loophole to avoid paying tax on management fees.

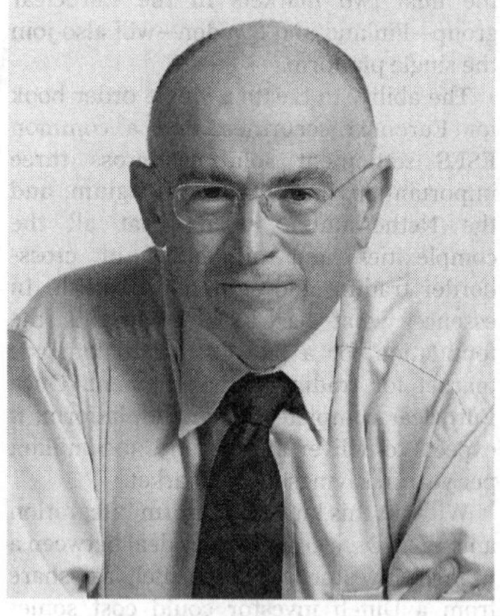

The large buy-outs which took place in the bubble years of 2005 to mid 2007 now look like horrible aberrations. In fact, they were horrible aberrations. Many of these deals were priced at such levels that real profits now need to grow by 50% or more for equities to achieve the same value buyers paid when the deal was closed. This is a big ask in normal conditions, and is much, much harder in a recession which is moving towards a depression.

Then, of course, there are the balance sheets of most of these deals, where debt levels are high by any historic measure. Debt at eight to 10 times EBITDA (earnings before interest, taxation, depreciation, and amortization) is far from unusual—and much of this debt is now trading below 65p to the £1. Refinancing at current levels seems impossible in the tortured debt markets now prevalent, where even three times EBITDA is often impossible to fund.

Debt terms and structures vary, but very many of these large deals will run into financing problems over the next few years, indeed some are already doing so.

Deals were done with long "bullet" amortization and with few, or even no, traditional covenants. Leverage was so high that a recessionary breeze was sufficient to make cash become a real problem. We now face a recessionary gale.

Given that the original equity investment in these deals is really now an expensive and massively out-of-the-money option, investors in the large leverage buy-out (LBO) funds are going to be unenthusiastic about the refinancing of the companies owned by those funds. The notion of investing simply for the benefit of debt-holders to maintain the possibility of a company recovering is likely to be heartily disliked. The only reason to keep the companies afloat is so that the LBO firm can cynically maintain the appearance of infallibility.

A lot of time is going to be spent trying to repair the balance sheets of large LBOs in 2009 and later. Already whole industries focused on restructuring distressed debt markets have sprung up. These industries are growing fast and are likely to be sorely needed.

Given the changed world, investors will rightly be worried about the situation of funds where perhaps half of the fund has, sadly, been propelled into worthless-looking wreckage from the bubble period. Carried interest from aggregate gains is unlikely ever to emerge in such a fund, yet generous management fees will continue to be taken out by the LBO firm—in part to cover the "management" of corporate corpses.

The situation of a firm with a part invested, largely lost, fund is going to be at best uncomfortable. The firm's ability to refinance itself will be a concern, so the firm can have a future that is precisely measurable in a few years.

So what are the options for such a private equity firm? It will probably seek to maximize its profitability by minimizing staff and costs. If there is no likely prospect of carried interest, then there is no incentive to sell portfolio companies, since their continued presence in the portfolio generates an opportunity for continued income. As regards new investments, the motivation might be to "put it all on number 36" and take a wild risk/reward bet to try to get carried interest. Individual motivation in a firm in this state is likely to be pretty low. Activity will be modest and likely to decline, promotion opportunities will be nonexistent and morale horrible.

In order to avoid some of these issues, it may well be in the interests of general partners and limited partners mutually to consider a new (lower) target for carried interest in exchange for lower fees and/or reduced commitments. It will be interesting to see if many firms promote such ideas.

UNCOMFORTABLE TRUTH

The LBO debt market is going to remain pretty terrible throughout 2009. Given the backdrop of bank capital shortages, increased regulatory involvement, and government direction of banks, it is unlikely that scarce lending funds are going to be steered into LBO lending. Indeed, lenders are more likely to be seeking repayment actively. Low interest levels will generally be helpful to the LBO world (except those who fixed their interest rates) and are one of the clear positives in an otherwise bleak background.

One uncomfortable truth that is being recognized, at a pace reflecting the pain of this recognition, is that buying a company with 40% equity and 60% debt in mid-2007 meant that by the end of 2008, even if profits remained stable, the equity had no real value. Mark-to-market, a phenomenon relatively new to the world of private equity investing (especially in the United States), means terrible reported returns for the many funds that invested into the bubble. Investors are unlikely to be encouraged.

So what else is there to be cheerful about? Well, first there is a lot of liquidity in many of the large funds—around about the same amount that was exuberantly projected into bubble investments remains to

"Inflation is as violent as a mugger, as frightening as an armed robber, and as deadly as a hit man."
Ronald Reagan

be invested more sensibly now. Investments will be made, albeit at low leverage, but at much lower prices. Some very good deals will be done in this environment; some funds will use these opportunities to recover their performance.

As a general rule, LBO firms are going to have to become more skilful if they are to make money—businesses will have to be managed more smartly rather than being simply seen as targets for advanced financings. Traditional business management skills, including having good teams, strategy, and operations, will distinguish the good LBO firm from the bad one. In the long term, this is likely to be a very good thing for the industry and its image.

The substantial closure of the IPO, debt, and equity markets means that private equity has much less competition in 2009. Again, this means private equity firms can and should be able to buy well. Conversely, good exits will be very difficult in 2009.

And, quite likely, after a brief decline in inflation caused by the recession, the printing of money by many governments will generate inflation at levels that used to be great for LBOs. Debt vanishes nicely in inflationary times, and I fear that is going to happen after 2009.

INVESTMENT SLOWDOWN

The mid-market (and smaller) LBO firms are going to have their problems too. Typically, they will have been unable to obtain the extravagant levels of leverage that the mega-firms got from their well-rewarded friends in the investment banking world (a.k.a. The Last Chance Saloon). This means the smaller private equity firms will have one less headache to contend with. However, the drop in equity markets will have hit the value of their portfolios and the recessionary tide will hit their companies too. Failures will occur. As a result, whilst their performances are likely to be better than the performance of the mega-funds, they will still be weak, given that they will have to invest with even modest leverage into weak financial and economic markets.

Venture capital of the traditional variety had a very hard time in 2008—the absence of IPOs has greatly suppressed returns and the arrival of recession hurts companies relying on the take-up of innovative new ideas. In any case, in Europe, venture capital remains a relatively small and underdeveloped section of the market, following a long period of weak overall performance, which has discouraged money from being dedicated to this area. This part of private equity will probably shrink a little more in 2009.

Investors, squeezed by losses in the rest of their portfolios and in private equity, will inevitably be slow to invest in new private equity funds in 2009. A bizarre game is being played; because private equity has been slow to write-down its values, it has risen beyond target percentages of the assets in investors' portfolios. This switches off investment into the asset class, so it would actually be better for the industry if valuations were written down quickly. That is somewhat counter-intuitive. Alchemy Partners has been quick off the mark in pointing out to competitors the need to honor their duties to the private equity community by writing things down quickly and robustly.

Public vehicles in private equity have had a horrible year with big share price declines and shares trading at massive discounts to stated values. Valuations were simply not believed. Many investors will simply not invest in new funds given all these issues.

Indeed, in some cases, investors such as fund-of-funds (some public, some not) had rashly over-committed to private equity funds, betting that distributions would forever exceed calls. The year 2008 showed this strategy to be optimistic, particularly where the capability of investors to meet calls is concerned. This has led to efforts to reduce fund sizes (TPG and Permira have both recently announced fund reductions). It may yet lead to investors being unable to meet calls and certainly will lead to forced sales of existing fund holdings to the benefit of secondary investors.

So in the future we are going to see a smaller private equity industry, where there will be fewer mega-deals and a great need to show outstanding managerial skills to justify the private equity industry's continuation into better days.

▸▸ MORE INFO

Books:

Brickhill, Paul. *The Great Escape*. New York: WW Norton & Co, 2004.

The Book of Ecclesiastes. Edinburgh, UK: Canongate Books, 1998.

Vogel, Arthur Israel, B. S. Furnis, A. J. Hannaford, and P. W. G. Smith. *Textbook of Practical Organic Chemistry*. 5th ed. Harlow, UK: Pearson, 1989.

See Also:

★ Leveraged Buyouts and Recession (pp. 405–408)
★ Leveraged Buyouts: What, Why, When, and How (pp. 409–411)
Barbarians at the Gate: The Fall of RJR Nabisco (p. 1223)

"Private capital markets are the fundamental building block of the capitalist system of resource allocation across activities and over time. Such markets can function properly only if investors bear the costs of their bad decisions and bad luck and reap the benefits of their good decisions and good luck." Alan Greenspan

  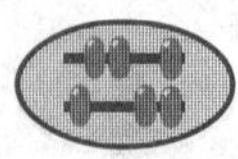  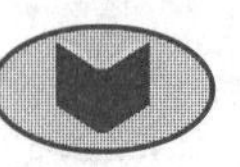 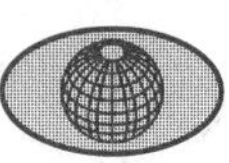 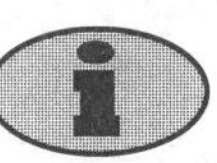  

Viewpoint: Michael J. Panzner

Forecasting the Credit Crunch and Future Market Prospects

INTRODUCTION

Michael J. Panzner is a 25-year veteran of the global stock, bond, and currency markets who has worked in New York and London for such leading companies as HSBC, Soros Funds, ABN Amro, Dresdner Bank, and J.P. Morgan Chase. He is the author of When Giants Fall: An Economic Roadmap for the End of the American Era (Wiley, 2009), Financial Armageddon: Protecting Your Future from Four Impending Catastrophes (Kaplan, 2007), and The New Laws of the Stock Market Jungle: An Insider's Guide to Successful Investing in a Changing World (FT Prentice Hall, 2004). He has also been a columnist at TheStreet.com's RealMoney paid-subscription service and a contributor to AOL's BloggingStocks.com. In addition, Mr. Panzner is a New York Institute of Finance faculty member specializing in Equities, Trading, Global Capital Markets, and Technical Analysis, and is a graduate of Columbia University.

What brought about the worst financial crisis since the Great Depression?

There are many reasons why we reached this point, but one, in particular, stands out: hubris. By the spring of 2007, for instance, the conventional wisdom on Wall Street was that the financial world had been totally transformed and the business cycle had been repealed. People were confident that reams of research and the lessons of history would prevent policymakers from repeating the mistakes of the past. Powerful technology and rapid innovation would ensure that risk was fully monitored and efficiently managed. Industry consolidation and the globalization of finance would allow any excessive or unwanted exposure to be offset. In sum, the "masters of the universe" thought they had it all figured out—which, of course, they didn't.

Was it just those who worked in the financial industry who felt this way?

Not really. Insiders and outsiders alike—including central bankers, regulators, and the political establishment—came to believe that markets and economies were virtually bullet-proof, no longer exposed as they once were to the fallout from exogenous shocks and endogenous eruptions. In a sense, the prevailing view was that with all the rules, strategies, and mechanisms that were in place, neither Wall Street nor Main Street would again find themselves taken by surprise, as they were during the Asian financial crisis of 1997–1998, the 1998 meltdown of hedge fund Long Term Capital Management, and on many other occasions before that.

How about the man on the street?

To be sure, confidence about existing conditions and the notion that the good times could carry on indefinitely was widespread. Although there were clear signs that something was amiss, many people drank the bullish Kool-Aid and warmed to the fantasy of a Goldilocks economy. They believed that society no longer had to be a slave to market and other natural forces. In today's sophisticated and globalized world, people were the masters of their own destiny, economic or otherwise. Not surprisingly, these perspectives spawned widespread complacency. Unhealthy imbalances were permitted to grow and fester. Prudence was seen as highly overrated. Planning for hard times took a back seat to riding the crest of the wave. In the end, of course, those notions proved dangerously misguided.

Are you suggesting that the failure to prepare for the worst ensured that it would happen?

To some extent, yes. In fact, throughout society, many of the mechanisms and backstops that people were counting on for protection in the event that things somehow went awry had unintended negative consequences. Instead of enhancing the resiliency of the system, the latticework of safety measures engendered a false sense of security, leading homeowners, investors, policymakers, business executives, and others to act naively or recklessly. Economists call this the moral hazard effect. Under these circumstances, everyone has an incentive to be on their worst behavior. In hindsight, it's clear that a lot of people took that message to heart.

So far, at least, the financial system seems to have suffered the most.

That's not too surprising, given that those who worked on Wall Street and in other financial centers made some of biggest miscalculations, at least in terms of the amounts they were playing around with. Among other things, many supposedly savvy operators failed to grasp that just because risks were being sliced, diced, repackaged, and shifted elsewhere, they weren't being eliminated. On the contrary, the new financial alchemy meant that all sorts of dangerously unfamiliar combinations were being created and that no one really had a solid handle on overall exposure. Moreover, with risk being shoved into every nook and cranny of the global financial system, it meant that few places on earth would be spared following a major shock to the system, like, for example, a bursting credit bubble.

Presumably, people are looking at things differently now?

There's no doubt that the events of the past few years are forcing a major rethink in certain quarters. Formerly free-spending Americans, for example, are beginning to cut back on purchases, slash borrowing, and boost the amount of money they have in savings. Yet not everyone grasps what is clearly a sea change. The fact that so many "strategists"—I use that term loosely—failed to see what was coming and were utterly surprised by the breadth and depth of the collapse hasn't stopped them from offering wrong-footed theories about what may happen next. Many are simply delud-

"I believe that crisis really tends to help develop the character of an organization." John Sculley

ing themselves with short memories and wishful thinking. Indeed, ever since the "Great Unraveling" began, there has been no shortage of prognosticators claiming to see a light at the end of the tunnel.

Could it be that they were merely early and the storm will soon blow over?

Sure, but the odds are against it. With the world enmeshed in what is acknowledged to be the worst financial crisis since the Great Depression and, by all accounts, with most developed countries now entering the first synchronized slowdown since World War II, it's clear that what we've been experiencing is not a garden-variety cyclical event. Given that, a quick read of history, the kind that extends beyond the past decade or even the post-war era, suggests the outlook for the immediate years ahead is for more hardship and pain than we've seen already. Ironically, given how many ivory-tower theories have been discredited by events of the past few years, recent academic research would appear to confirm that outlook.

What are the details?

According to a December 2008 paper by Carmen M. Reinhart and Kenneth S. Rogoff, entitled *The Aftermath of Financial Crises*, episodes like the one that began in 2007 have traditionally been a bad omen.

"Broadly speaking, financial crises are protracted affairs. More often than not, the aftermath of severe financial crises share three characteristics. First, asset market collapses are deep and prolonged. Real housing price declines average 35% stretched out over six years, while equity price collapses average 55% over a downturn of about three and a half years. Second, the aftermath of banking crises is associated with profound declines in output and employment. The unemployment rate rises an average of 7 percentage points over the down phase of the cycle, which lasts on average over four years. Output falls (from peak to trough) an average of over 9%, although the duration of the downturn, averaging roughly two years, is considerably shorter than for unemployment. Third, the real value of government debt tends to explode, rising an average of 86% in the major post-World War II episodes."

That's worrying, to be sure, but some would say that the past is not destiny. Are there other reasons to be pessimistic?

Sure, plenty. First, there are myriad imbalances that still need to be resolved in one way or another. In the United States, for example, even though a bursting housing bubble has brought prices in some areas back into line with incomes and rents, overall values are still high relative to secular trends, based on data derived from studies by Yale University professor Robert J. Shiller, author of *Irrational Exuberance*. As of the second quarter of 2008, for example, the benchmark S&P Case-Shiller Real Home Price Index was still more than 40% above its long-term median. As prices continue their inevitable reversion to the mean—and, more likely, given the pattern of past boom–bust cycles, overshoot—the fallout from the negative wealth effect alone will cast a powerful and persistent pall over the economy for quite a while.

What else?

Let's start with debt. Even though the upheavals of the past few years have forced banks and other intermediaries to cut back on lending, the amount of obligations outstanding is still staggering. At the end of 2008, for instance, total US credit market debt was more than three-and-a-half times as large as gross domestic product (GDP), or 15% higher than the prior record set during the Great Depression. One way or another, whether because of widespread defaults or frantic efforts to reduce leverage, those borrowings represent a substantial drag on future growth prospects. In addition, there are untenable cross-border imbalances that can only be rectified through economic pain, or bone-jarring upheaval. One example includes the United States' long-running current account deficit, which, at nearly 5% of GDP, reflects a propensity towards over-consuming and over-borrowing that cannot be sustained.

These are serious concerns, but won't America bear the brunt of the damage?

The United States accounts for a quarter of global GDP, so America's problem is, by definition, everybody's problem. More recent developments regarding global trade and capital flows, for example, have proved that. The once popular notion that the rest of the world could somehow "decouple" from the United States was laughable, given how dependent other nations were on the spending power of the American consumer. No doubt that formula will change as developing nations like China eventually shift their focus away from export markets towards domestic consumption. However, this adjustment will take time. Otherwise, in terms of the imbalances that exist outside the United States, you only have to look at how property prices are deflating throughout Europe, Asia, and South America to realize that others had their share of excesses and bad behavior.

What else makes you think that the risks are to the downside as far as markets and economies are concerned?

Two factors, in particular. First, the global system for intermediating credit has become seriously impaired. Not only is the securitization model, which has been a key driver of growth-enhancing liquidity, on its last legs—as evidenced by the dramatic collapse in issuance of and trading volumes in asset-backed and other derivative securities—but banks around the world have clearly demonstrated that they are neither willing nor able to do what they supposedly know best: make loans. The vast majority of financial institutions are capital constrained, and in many cases, literally or effectively insolvent. Despite all the bailouts and rescue efforts, including government-sponsored lines of credit, taxpayer-funded equity injections, and the loosening of regulatory and accounting constraints, there are few signs that the money is benefiting the real economy.

But isn't it just a matter of time before that happens?

I wouldn't want to rule that out, but as of now, the facts suggest it will be a long time before we go back to anything resembling "normal." Among other things, some of the efforts being made now to fix things are actually causing more damage. Again, we are seeing the unintended consequences of government actions. For example, by stepping in as the intermediaries of last resort, the Federal Reserve and other central banks have effectively discouraged financial institutions from working together to repair the damage caused to the interbank lending market as a result of worries over counterparty risk. In addition, many banks seem unduly focused on getting their fair share of the bailout pie, instead of reworking anachronistic business models and making the painful adjustments they need to survive beyond the current crisis.

You noted that there was another factor that makes you pessimistic?

As I see it, there has clearly been a secular shift in attitudes towards risk and risk-taking. Anecdotal and other evidence suggest that individuals and businesses are not only increasingly concerned with digging themselves out from under the obligations they took on during the go-go days, but they are also rethinking how they want to travel the road ahead. Instead of pie-in-the-sky forecasts, companies are insisting on realistic assessments. Cushions and allowances that once seemed adequate are being expanded to take account of heightened economic uncertainty, counterparty risk,

  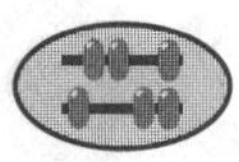   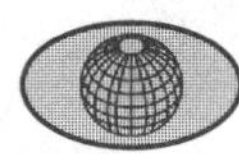   

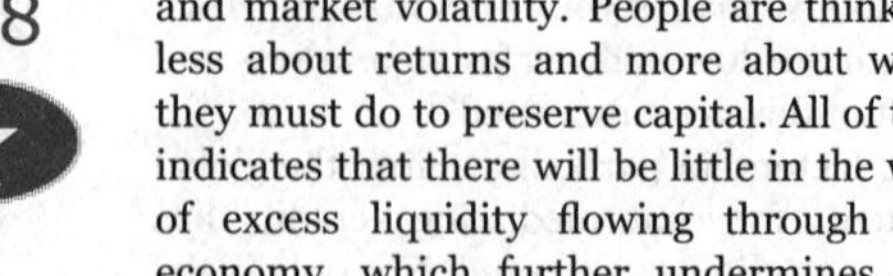

and market volatility. People are thinking less about returns and more about what they must do to preserve capital. All of this indicates that there will be little in the way of excess liquidity flowing through the economy, which further undermines the prospects for recovery.

Is there anything else?

Although I can think of many other problems looming on the horizon, one that is probably not on too many radar screens stems from a nascent but ultimately seismic shift in the global order. Up until now, the world has benefited tremendously from the United States' role as the consumer and policeman of last resort. With the fallout from the credit crunch and subsequent economic unraveling calling the first role into question, and the quagmires in the Middle East, among other things, casting doubt on the second, it may be no time at all before other countries and regions lose faith in US and Western sponsored systems, mechanisms, and institutions. With that, we can expect to see serious disruptions of capital and trade flows. These schisms will inhibit and, increasingly, reverse efforts to expand economic and financial integration, which will have a negative effect on credit, liquidity, and growth.

▸▸ MORE INFO

Books:

Cohan, William D. House of Cards: *A Tale of Hubris and Wretched Excess on Wall Street*. Doubleday, 2009.

Morris, Charles R. *The Trillion Dollar Meltdown: Easy Money, High Rollers, and the Great Credit Crash*. PublicAffairs, 2008.

Phillips. Kevin. *Bad Money: Reckless Finance, Failed Politics, and the Global Crisis of American Capitalism*. Penguin, 2009.

Ritholtz, Barry. *Bailout Nation: How Greed and Easy Money Corrupted Wall Street and Shook the World Economy*. Wiley, 2009

Woods, Thomas E., Jr. *Meltdown: A Free-Market Look at Why the Stock Market Collapsed, the Economy Tanked, and Government Bailouts Will Make Things Worse*. Regnery, 2009.

Websites:

Naked Capitalism: www.nakedcapitalism.com
Calculated Risk: www.calculatedriskblog.com
Mish's Global Economic Trend Analysis: globaleconomicanalysis.blogspot.com
The Big Picture: www.ritholtz.com
FT Alphaville: ftalphaville.ft.com
Financial Armageddon: www.financialarmageddon.com
When Giants Fall: www.economicroadmap.com
Paul Kedrosky's Infectious Greed: paul.kedrosky.com
Credit Writedowns: www.creditwritedowns.com
Zero Hedge: zerohedge.blogspot.com

See Also:

Irrational Exuberance (p. 1286)

"Whom prosperity maketh our friend, adversity will make our enemy." Boethius

  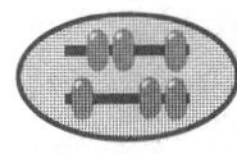   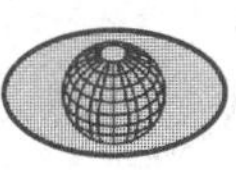   

Insurance—Bruised, Not Crushed

by Robert P. Hartwig

EXECUTIVE SUMMARY

- Compared with the banking sector, the insurance industry has been able to continue business as usual through the crash thanks to some crucial differences between the two sectors.
- The sector faces some specific challenges posed by "long-tailed" business in the downturn as it seeks to match assets against liabilities.
- Low returns in an era of near zero interest rates will push up premium prices.
- The sector has a number of anxieties concerning potential regulatory responses to the crash.
- Risk appraisal is a key differences between banks and insurance companies.

INTRODUCTION

There is no doubt that, compared with the banks and the investment banks, the insurance sector has come through the crash in relatively good order. The sector has not escaped entirely. AIG, the world's biggest insurer, needed a US$85 billion bailout from the Federal Reserve to help the company unwind its credit default swap (CDS) positions "in an orderly manner," without precipitating one of the biggest insolvencies ever in US insurance history. However, it is important to realize that AIG was a very unusual insurance company, and a leader in the CDS market, which went sour when the liquidity crunch set in. AIG's business model and profile of operations have no real parallel in the rest of the sector.

The vast majority of what the United States calls property and casualty insurers, and Europe terms general insurers, are working through the current deep recession with the fundamental business of insurance operating normally, with the transfer of risk from client to insurer and from insurer to re-insurer continuing as normal, and with no shortage of capacity.

None of this is true of the banking market, and this is where the fundamental difference between these two components of the financial services sector manifests itself most strikingly. In the banking sector, of course, loan activity has been greatly reduced, and, by early 2009, there was really very little that could be termed "normal" about many of the world's major banks.

Of course, the insurance sector as a whole is not immune to a general economic downturn, and particularly not to a full-blown, deep, global recession. The sector is less sensitive to fluctuations in the economy than most industries, as in many instances insurance is not an option but a necessity. However, to the extent that economies are not growing, the sector cannot advance.

A RISK-AVERSE MARKET

We have a more general challenge, however, in the sector, and this has to do with the fact that many insurance risks are "long-tailed;" they run for many years into the future. In an ideal world, you would look to match your liabilities with your assets. Today, however, there is very little yield available on long-term instruments, and we even had the bizarre situation on December 4, 2008, when long-dated Treasury bills slipped into nominal negative returns. This kind of position shows a tremendous level of risk aversion in the market, with short-term fear outweighing long-term needs. It created a bubble in the price of Treasuries that leads to unsustainable programs.

What all this means is that insurers are not going to tie up their investment money in a 20-year yield at these very low rates, as, if the rates went up in a few years' time, these instruments would sustain a significant loss. This, in turn, means that investment income will decline in the medium term for insurers, as short-term investments are likely to provide very meagre rates of return.

A "SOFT MARKET"

For the insurance sector, there are only two possible sources of income. These are investment income premiums on business written, and low investment returns have a very direct impact on premium prices, which will almost certainly rise. There is very little option about this for the industry. The sector's anticipated losses are not going to be any the less because investment yields are down. Natural catastrophes happen every year, and they cost a great deal, whatever the investment climate.

This, then, creates a fear that insurance prices will become too high for the market to bear. We are currently in a period of declining prices for insurance premiums; what the industry calls a "soft market." Prices have been declining for four straight years, and the price of many types of insurance in the United States today are below where they were in 2004. This is one of the features of the sector. Insurance is nothing if not cyclical, and every player in the sector knows this very well.

However, even if rising prices cause the insurance sector to "flip flop" from a declining price market to a rising price market, the cost of premiums, despite the current difficult economic circumstances, is highly unlikely to become an onerous burden on an individual's or a company's budget. The last "hard market," when the industry was able to charge high prices because the market in general was pricing high, was in the period 2000–2003, and we could be seeing a return to that period.

To understand how pricing affects the industry, it is worth pointing out, perhaps, that the hard pricing of 2000–2003 brought the industry through the 9/11 period with its massive payouts, and, when insurers experienced record catastrophe losses in 2004 and 2005, the industry had to build up sufficient capital to come through in good shape. At the same time, 2006 and 2007 were low loss years as far as natural disasters were concerned. That all turned around in 2008, where we had poor investment returns and high catastrophe payouts.

It is probably too soon, at the time of writing in February 2009, to say that insurance markets are definitely heading back to a hard market, with a rapid and sustained price rise ahead. The industry globally needs to take a very severe hit before that happens, and we are possibly not there yet.

Despite the adverse features of 2008 for the industry, the underwriting performance was not that bad, and was consistent with four years of a soft pricing market. The problem the sector has is that, with the economic downturn, asset categories that were thought of as safe have lost significant amounts of value, and the sector has to invest its premium income to generate returns.

To sum up then, the industry went into the financial crisis extremely well capitalized. However, much of that surplus capital has been eroded through the underwriting and investment losses 2008. So now,

     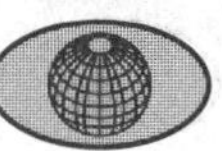   

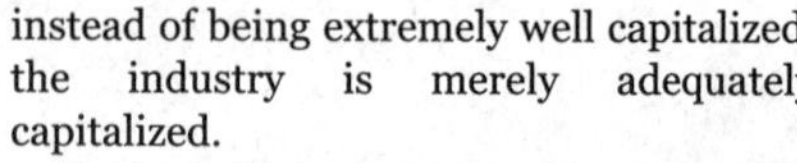

instead of being extremely well capitalized, the industry is merely adequately capitalized.

One of the common misconceptions about the challenges facing the industry is that global warming, and the more energetic and extreme weather events that are predicted to follow from this, will be too much for the sector to handle. In actual fact, extreme weather conditions are nothing new for the sector. It has been dealing with the consequences of extreme weather events for centuries. The key here, as elsewhere, is to be able to price the business appropriately. The increased risk has to be priced into the cost of insurance.

The insurance sector has been extremely strong in Europe and, more recently, in the United States, in voicing its concerns about global warming and the need for concerted action. However, it is undoubtedly true that the current crisis has somewhat overwhelmed environmental concerns.

REGULATORY RESPONSE

A great source of anxiety, going forward, is how the regulators will respond. There is no doubt at all that there will be a change in the regulatory environment faced by the industry. In the United States, regulation has traditionally been carried out on a state-by-state basis, and there is now speculation that we could be seeing the end of a 135-year tradition of state-based regulation in favor of centralized federal regulation. Smaller insurers, particularly, would much rather continue to be faced with local regulators, than some central regulator in far-away Washington DC.

Another unknown is whether any new federal regulatory structure would regulate for solvency, or for rates and forms. Many larger multinational insurers would prefer that solvency regulation be moved to the federal level and that there be no regulatory hand on the price of insurance. The remaining months of 2009 will see a good deal of debate on these themes.

On top of all this, we have new regulations, such as Solvency II and the international accounting standards. It seems clear from the current financial crisis that accounting systems were clearly not up to the task. There were also undoubted problems, both in the United States and in Europe, in the regulation of financial services, and there will need to be a good deal of discussion here before some kind of a global regulatory system can be imposed. The regulatory and oversight regimes in both the United States and Europe have been shown to be faulty, so no one, at this point in time, has a template without its shortcomings.

CONTROLLING SYSTEMATIC RISK

As far as the United States is concerned, it is already clear that the focus will be on controlling systemic risk, and on identifying points across the financial services sector that have the potential to bring down the system, as was the case with poorly priced credit derivatives products. The insurance sector invested in some of these instruments, but, by and large, with the exception of AIG, it was not deeply involved. It seems a reasonable guess, therefore, that the general insurance sector will emerge from this crisis with its risk management model more intact than any other sector of the financial service industry.

A key reason for this is that, unlike banks, which spun off risks away from themselves by wrapping the risk up in securitized products and selling it on, the insurance sector retains in whole or in part the risks associated with the business it writes. Therefore, it does not have the "out of touch," "out of control" motivation to keep on creating very risky products to maximize volume, fees and profitability, *á la* the banks. The endpoint of all this for the banks was a total collapse of risk management, and catastrophic losses.

With hindsight, now that we know both how reliant many banks were on liquidity in the credit markets to sustain their business models, and how subprime mortgages were used in asset-backed securities on a grand scale (securities that were taken up, also on a grand scale, by the banks themselves), the collapse does not appear that surprising. What was surprising was the fact that this out-of-control model in the banking world could continue for so long, and that it was able to blow the bubble up to such a proportion without check.

Not only do insurance companies retain a stake in every contract they write, the operating model in the sector is not based on debt. We now see that the model for some of the best-known investment banks was to have one dollar of capital for US$30 of debt, and then to invest most of it in highly risky assets. The equivalent behavior in the insurance world would be for an insurer to leverage up their capital by a factor of 30, and then to use the money to write insurance policies on every home on the coast of Florida.

Again, the key difference with the banks is that, in insurance, there is an alignment of interests between the insurer and the consumer—the insurer bears the risk if the contract does not perform. In a securitization deal, the bank that originates the deal has sold the risk on to the investor, and the risk becomes the investor's risk. The bank is "free" from the risk. Whether selling "toxic" products was an appropriate way to treat one's investors seems not to have been considered. Of course, not all sellers of structured credit products knew they were toxic before the collapse of the asset-backed market, but with hindsight one has to question the due diligence model being used.

Another point to stress is that insurers are accustomed to applying a great deal of care, discipline, and accuracy to the treatment and pricing of risk. Underwriting is a real discipline, and no organization survives the challenges involved in being an underwriter if there is anything loose or sloppy in its approach and methodology. You have to be focused on managing your potential loss exposure, or it will destroy you. The model adopted by the banks emphasized leverage, volume, and short-term rewards, and was blind to any risk that was not immediate, or that did not have an impact on the banks' regulatory capital requirements.

CONCLUSION

Off-balance-sheet special purpose vehicles (SPVs) had no impact on bank capital adequacy requirements, and the potential impact on bank solvency of the business written by such entities was not considered. The insurance sector is more stringently regulated than the banking sector, and the focus is much more on transparency. In 2008, there were 25 bank failures in the United States, including the largest bank failure in history, Washington Mutual, with US$307 billion in assets. No insurer has, so far, failed in the current credit crunch and downturn.

▸▸ MORE INFO

Presentation:

Hartwig, Robert. "Financial crisis, economic stimulus and the future of the P/C insurance industry: Trends, challenges and opportunities." Online at: www.iii.org/media/presentations/westchester

Website:

Insurance Information Institute: www.iii.org

See Also:

Insurance (pp. 1520–1521)

"In business, when things aren't working it's time to mix it up." Donald J. Trump

  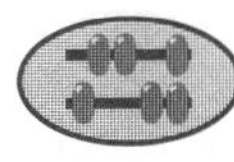   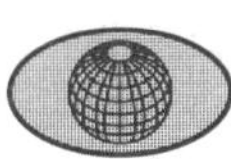   

Viewpoint: Brian Reading

New Dollar Area: The Makings of the Mess

INTRODUCTION

Brian Reading 73, Director Lombard Street Research. First class honours, PPE, Wadham college, Oxford 1958. George Webb Medley Senior Prize. Nuffield College 1958–60. Lecturer, Christchurch, Oxford 1960–62. Adviser to the Governor, Bank of England 1962–64. Department of Economic Affairs 1964–66. Adviser to Edward Heath as Leader of the Opposition and then as Prime Minister, 1966-72. Economics Editor, The Economist 1972–77. Consultant to Dillon Reed, 1975–1981. Consultant with US Adivory Associates, 1981–91. Adviser to Nomura Assel Management 1985–, founder, LOmbard Street Research International Service 1991–, Founder, the Item Club. Sometime adviser to the Commons Treasury Commitee and visiting Professor Strathclyde University. Author of numerous articles in the Investors Chronicle, the Sunday Times, the Financial Times and other newspapers. Author 'Japan the Coming Collapse' 1991.

They called it "Bretton Woods 2." A better name would have been the "new dollar area" (NDA), especially when the November 2008 G20 summit to fix the global financial architecture was labeled by the media as Bretton Woods 2. It is an informal, fixed, or semi-fixed exchange rate regime centered on the dollar. Whatever it is called, it did much to cause the world financial crisis. While the two are intimately linked, they are rarely discussed together.

NDA members comprise countries that peg their currencies to the dollar, or dirty float against it. China, Hong Kong, and developing Asia are at the core. The periphery is fuzzy. Membership is best defined by the accumulation of excessive foreign currency reserves (mostly dollars, although the currency content of international reserves is not available by individual country holdings).[1] Broadly speaking, members also include Asian newly industrialized countries (NICs), Japan (off and on, because it does not always intervene to manage the yen/dollar rate), and Russia. Most Gulf oil producers peg to the dollar, but as long-standing members rather than new. The NDA, including the United States, accounts for half the world's GDP.

FEARS FOR A DOLLAR FREEFALL UNFOUNDED

Martin Wolf, writing in the *Financial Times*, has credited economists at Deutsche Bank with coining the name Bretton Woods 2.[2] Prominent among many discussing the issue were Michael Dooley, David Folkerts-Landau, and Peter Gaber working together.[3] Dooley *et al* set the ball rolling in 2003, by suggesting the new system could sustain large US current account deficits for years to come. Their thesis was that when import-substituting developing countries and ex-command economies opened up to the world, they discovered that their capital stock was obsolete. They needed to rebuild their economies, as did war-devastated Europe and Japan after 1945. The "revived" Bretton Woods model was similar to Europe and Japan's post-war relationship with the United States until those nations were strong enough to stand on their own feet. China and Asia's undervalued exchange rates against the dollar (the United States is the world's largest manufactured goods market) and secured export/investment-led growth. In this way, they could build up large and high-quality physical capital stocks, at the expense of acquiring large and low-quality financial capital.

The United States was the other side of a symbiotic relationship. Fiscal policy could be eased aggressively in 2001–2002 to counter the recession caused by the burst dotcom bubble, without driving up interest rates.[4] The consequent current-account deterioration was accommodated without the dollar crashing.[5] On the contrary, the Federal Reserve was able progressively to cut its Fed funds target rate from 6.5% in December 2000 to 1.0% in June 2003, and hold it there until June 2004. The trade-weighted dollar appreciated strongly until early 2002 before sliding, and then only against the euro and other floaters.[6] It took new dollar area currencies down with it.

This analysis spawned a debate in 2004–05 concerning the durability of the regime. A widely held view was that the ever-increasing US current account deficit was unsustainable. Like Bretton Woods, the system was expected to collapse because of a run on the dollar, causing it to go into freefall. US interest rates would soar and the economy crash. The argument was not whether this would happen, but when. Dooley's suggestion of "several more years" was challenged. The US economists Nouriel Roubini and Brad Setser, and many others, feared the dollar's collapse was imminent.[7] There was much discussion of the extent to which it must fall to reduce the US current account deficit to a manageable 3% of GDP. A trade-weighted decline of 30% from its 2002 peak was widely regarded as necessary to shift demand and output from nontraded goods and services to traded goods (as a rule of thumb, a 10% fall equals a 1% shift). Martin Wolf, reporting work by Morris Obstfeld and Kenneth Rogoff, made clear that, in the absence of dollar depreciation, US GDP would need to fall by 7% in order to produce a 3% GDP points improvement in the current account deficit.[8] He did not explain why, if the United States could finance its deficit without the dollar depreciating, it would

Figure 1. The trade-weighted dollar and euro. (*Source*: Federal Reserve Bank of St Louis, FRED database)

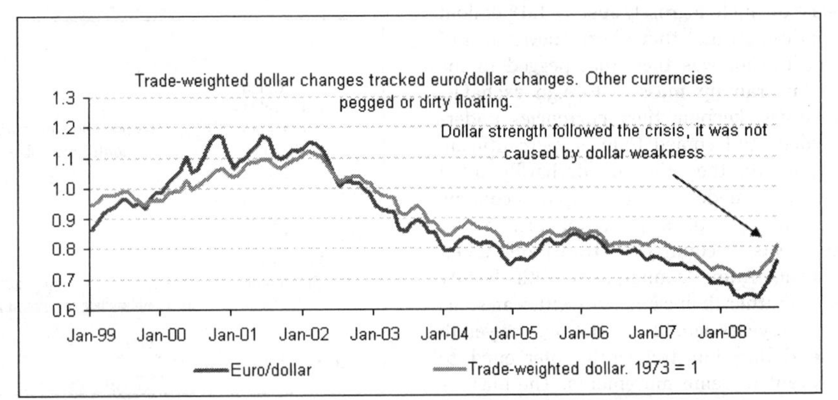

     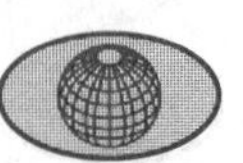   

need to reduce the deficit. The trade-weighted dollar did depreciate by more than 30%, but not withstanding China's managed crawl and a suspension of yen intervention, this was almost exclusively against the euro. (At time of writing in March 2009, the United States was in recession, and, according to cycle-dating, has been in one since January 2008.[9] It is likely the peak-to-trough fall will not be as much as 7%, but 3–4% is possible.)

HOW SOME FORECASTS ERRED

This analysis erred in three major respects. It provided an *ex-post* rationalization of the system, not an explanation of its actual genesis. It foresaw a debt trap where there was none. It ignored the possibility that the United States would bring it down, meaning it was blind to the danger that the financial bubble it spawned would burst. Many commentators then made a fourth error—they assumed the developing world could decouple from the United States. Chris P. Dialynas and Marshall Auerback exposed the first error.[10] China was responsible for the genesis of the system. It adopted a pegged and deeply undervalued yuan exchange rate in 1995, deliberately to promote export-led growth so as to absorb a massive surplus of cheap rural labor. China's move was the logical consequence of the transition from a closed command economy to an open-market one. Command economies are extremely efficient at wasting savings in value-subtracting investment. Transition to a market economy exposed a Chinese savings glut. The pegged and undervalued yuan allowed China to waste its excess savings by lending to the United States, so that Americans could buy its excess products. It thereby avoided, if perhaps only for a time, an economic and political catastrophe.

The undervalued yuan undermined south-east Asian competitiveness, helping to precipitate the 1997–98 Asian crisis. The consequences were so traumatic (GDP collapsing and unemployment soaring, not least owing to a grossly austere IMF bailout conditions) that they swore "never again." The upshot was they, too, pegged to the dollar, ran up massive foreign exchange reserves, keeping their currencies undervalued, and copied China's mercantilism. Japan, on the other hand, hardly fitted Dooley's model of a developing economy upgrading its physical capital stock. Yet it, too, was a country in transition, albeit glacial, from "communism with beauty spots rather than capitalism with warts," as I put it years ago.[11] It did not peg the yen to the dollar, but frequently intervened to prevent extreme movements. The bias, as witnessed by the accumulation of nearly $1 trillion of foreign exchange reserves (20% of Japan's GDP), was to maintain yen competitiveness, and foster export-led growth.

The NDA has created a tripolar world. Asian and other member countries, the first pole, managed capital flows by official intervention. Their central banks financed the United States' twin current account and budget deficits by purchasing US Treasury and agency paper, regardless of risk or return. The second pole, the United States, is the center of the area, operating no controls over international trade or capital flows. However, it enjoyed the freedom to live beyond its means. The third pole is the floaters. Their private capital flows underwrite current account balances on commercial terms, causing exchange and interest rates to adjust as and when necessary to clear markets. The other great divide is between the savings gluttons and the profligate. The gluttons run large current account surpluses; they are the world's savers and lenders. The profligate run large current account deficits; they are the world's borrowers and spenders. The gluttons include most NDA member countries, particularly China and Japan. But some NDA members, such as India,[12] are not gluttons. Equally, some gluttons, such as Germany and its northern European neighbors, are not NDA members.[13] Until the crisis and recession, the United States was by far the greatest profligate, absorbing 50% of global surplus savings. It was joined by the United Kingdom and the southern hemisphere trio of Australia, South Africa, and New Zealand (plus southern Europeans such as Spain, Greece, and Ireland, but see note 12).

PARADOXICALLY THE SAVINGS GLUT SPAWNED A WORLD BOOM

The savings gluttons should have stagnated unless and until they boosted domestic demand. The profligate should have been prevented from generating grotesque and unsustainable domestic sector financial imbalances. The global economy would have foregone an unprecedented boom—four years of 5% GDP growth—largely concentrated in vibrant Asia, but, equally, it would have escaped the present recession. My colleague, Charles Dumas, was first to draw attention to the consequences of the Eurasian savings glut, subsequently popularized by Ben Bernanke.[14] Incredibly, the Eurasian savings glut spawned a global boom. Eurasian parsimony caused US profligacy, and not the other way round. If US spending had crowded out Asian spending, interest rates would have been historically high and global inflation rapid. Instead, Asian saving crowded out US savings by making credit abnormally plentiful and cheap. Without a glut, there could have been no spree; but without a spree, there could have been no glut. And, without NDA pegs and dirty floating, leading to Asian central banks financing the US twin deficits regardless of risk or return, there could have been neither. Private investors would never have lent on so massive a scale, faced with the risk of a dollar freefall. Yuan and yen appreciation would have stifled export-led growth.

US consumers went on a spending spree. Personal savings evaporated. The household sector's financial balance (the difference between income and all spending, consumption plus capital investment, especially in real estate) moved into an unprecedented deficit. Debt levels consequently rose to unprecedented and unsustainable levels. The other factor of the utmost importance was the explosion in financial innovation. It would take a book to explain the mechanics of the US credit bubble. It was not simply caused by the Eurasian savings glut lowering interest

Figure 2. Current account balances, $bn, 2007. (*Source*: IMF World Economic Outlook Database)

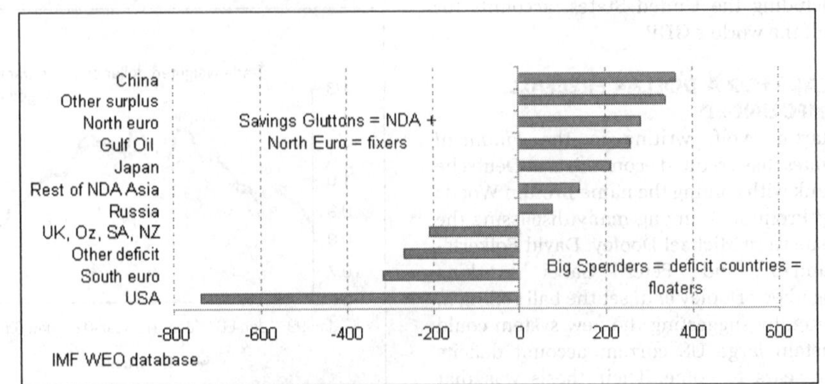

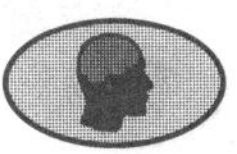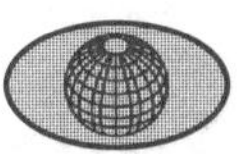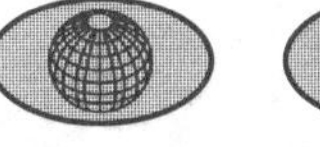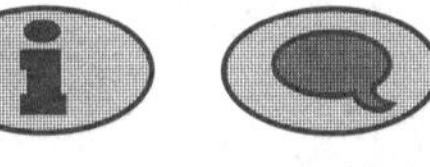

rates. The witches' brew included: Structured finance; the need and greed for high returns; obscene bonuses; regulatory and information black holes; interest-conflicted rating agencies given power without responsibility; flawed Basel rules; central banking bubble bingers; mark-to-model or make-believe; and so on. However, the point is that the crunch did not come from an inability to finance the US external deficit, but from unsustainable domestic imbalances and the inevitability of burst credit bubbles. The credit crash came because Ponzi finance required asset prices to rise for ever. As the gap between asset prices and output prices (i.e., incomes) widened, so the ability to service and repay debt diminished. New loans were increasingly required to refinance old.

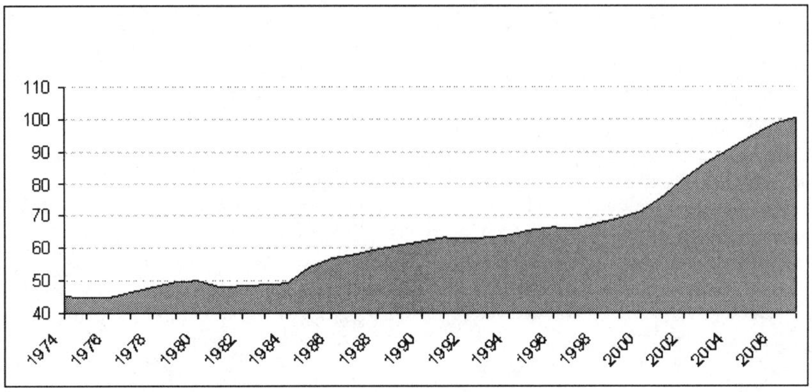

The belief that the NDA collapse would come because member countries would no longer be willing to finance US profligacy was wholly mistaken.[15] The dollar has not gone into freefall, nor have Treasury rates soared. The reverse has happened. The NDA remains alive and kicking. Indeed, it was obvious that this would be so. The Eurasian savings glut has not evaporated. The gluttons' desire to save and lend has, in no way, been satiated. There is no limit to the extent to which creditors can accumulate assets, regardless of risk and return, when the alternative is a domestic economic slump, driven by falling exports and investment. China's prime minister, Wen Jiabo, has made this "crystal clear."[16] The limit has been the US ability to borrow and spend, as it was certain to be. It was thought that the US current account deficit would have to be reduced because it could no longer be financed. It was expected that policy tightening would be needed to cause the economy to contract, because the dollar's freefall and foreigners' flight from Treasuries would threaten inflation. The public sector deficit would have to be reduced in order that its twin, the current account deficit, could be brought down. Monetary policy would have to be tightened to stop consumers living beyond their means. This view was widely held even as the crisis began to unfold.

Figure 3. US Household Debt, % GDP. (*Source:* IMF World Economic Outlook Database)

CONCLUSION

It has not worked out that way at all. Instead, the economy's contraction is causing the US current account deficit to diminish. The public sector deficit is increasing as the current account deficit falls. This simply means that both the public sector's and foreigners' financial balances are deteriorating, as consumers have stopped borrowing, started saving, and are reducing their debts. The improvement in the household sector's financial balance is the driver, not the driven. Hence the strength of the dollar and continued cheap, but unobtainable, credit (except by the government). Indeed, the banking crisis has led to government bailouts and risk aversion, and has reduced the availability of credit, while the collapse in asset values has simultaneously reduced consumers' ability and desire to borrow. It follows that if household debts are reduced, so must be lending to households.

The Asian decoupling notion was ever absurd. What would make frugal Eurasian savers and lenders become profligate borrowers and spenders, as long as they enjoyed a free ride on export-led growth? The November 2008 summit advocated fiscal synchro-stimuli. The April 2009 summit faced this issue with a proposal, favored by the United States, Japan, and (half-heartedly) the United Kingdom, that all G20 countries should increase public spending and cut taxes to the tune of 2% of GDP. The French and Germans were against this proposal. The aim of synchronized fiscal stimulation was to prevent free-riding on exports to those that did expand domestic demand. It was the right policy for big savers, but only a temporary expedient for the former profligates. When households no longer borrow and spend, for their governments to do so instead merely slows down the correction in financial imbalances by trashing public sector balance sheets. The savings gluttons cannot indefinitely be rescued from the Keynesian consequences of their own thrift by deficit countries' spending—now public instead of private. Consequently, they are suffering a more severe recession than the United States. After all, as American consumers are stopping living beyond their means, they have stopped buying Asia's surplus products. Asian exports crashed in early 2009 by up to 50%. The opposite of export-led growth is import-fed sloth. As Asia is denied the former, the United States can escape the latter. The Asian investment-accelerator-driven recession is sharper, but at least for China it will probably be shorter than the US consumer-retrenchment-driven one. Technically, the United States should escape from recession in late 2009, but growth is expected to remain feeble.

One final word. Deficit countries have few sanctions with which to persuade surplus ones to revalue and/or reflate. One is to threaten trade protection. If synchro-stimuli trash deficit countries' public sector balance sheets before big savers start to spend, protection will become a serious prospect.

MORE INFO

See Also:

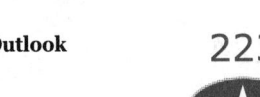

Nouriel Roubini (p. 1187)

United States (pp. 1493–1495)

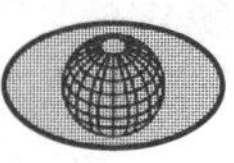
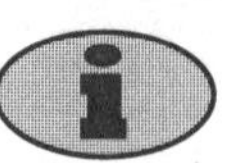

NOTES

1 See the IMF's COFER quarterly database. IMF members' foreign currency reserves totalled $7 trillion at end-June 2008. Only some $4.3 trillion was allocated among currencies, and identified US dollar holdings were $2.7 trillion, or 62%.

2 May 9, 2006.

3 "An Essay on the Revived Bretton Woods System," NBER Working Paper 9971, September 2003.

4 Between 2000 and 2003, the US general government balance went from 1.6% of GDP surplus to a 4.8% deficit, an adverse swing of 6.4% points. The cyclical deterioration was a mere one percentage point. OECD, *Economic Outlook*, 83, Appendix tables 27 and 28.

5 The current account deficit climbed from 3.3% of GDP in 1999 to 4.8% in 2003, on its way to a 6.2% peak in 2006, or a record $800 billion. OECD, *op. cit.,* Table 50.

6 The Fed's trade-weighted dollar exchange rate against major currencies climbed 16% between December 1999 and February 2002, and did not drop back below its 1999 level until May 2003. St Louis Federal Reserve database, FRED II.

7 "Will the Bretton Woods 2 regime unravel soon? The risk of a hard landing in 2005-06", paper written for the Federal Reserve Bank of San Francisco and UC Berkley conference on *The Revived Bretton Woods System*, February 2005.

8 "Let the dollar fall or risk global disorder," *Financial Times*, May 10, 2006; Obstfeld and Rogoff, "The Unsustainable US Current Account Position Revisited," NBER working paper 10869, 30 November 30, 2005.

9 NBER recession data is available on www.nber.org/cycles.

10 "Renegade economics: The Bretton Woods II fiction", PIMCO. September 2007.

11 Reading, Brian. *Japan: The Coming Collapse*. London:George Weidenfeld and Nicholson Ltd, 1992.

12 According to the IMF's WEO database, India ran a current account deficit of around 1% of GDP during the three-year period 2005–07. A current account balance equals the surplus or deficit in national savings over domestic investment.

13 However, they are members of a different "fixed exchange rate regime," the European common currency, the euro. The Eurozone, like the NDA, has its savers and lenders (northern Europe), and borrowers and spenders (southern Europe). This is for the same reason. Exchange rate changes are not allowed to clear markets, so payments imbalances can persist.

14 Charles Dumas, and Diana Choyleva. *The Bill from the China Shop–How Asia's Savings Glut Threatens the World Economy,* Lombard Street Research January 2006. Martin Wolf wrote: "In 2005, incoming Fed Chairman Ben Bernanke argued that a global savings glut is causing the huge US current account deficits. Charles Dumas recognized this truth long before him." *Financial Times* 28 March 2006.

15 Brad Setser has admitted as much in his blog, *Follow the Money*. See "The end of Bretton Woods 2," blog entry, October 21, 2008.

16 "We must be crystal clear that without a certain pace of economic growth, there will be difficulties with employment, fiscal revenues, and social developments. . . and factors damaging social stability will grow." Speech by Wen Jiabo, reported by the *Financial Times*, November 2, 2008.

"Advertising is what you do when you can't go see somebody. That's all it is." Fairfax Cone

  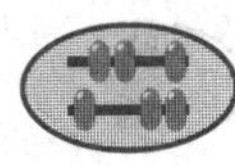   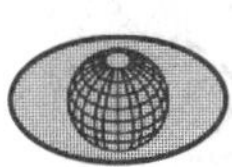   

The Insurance Sector: Plenty of Silver Lining to Be Found by Andrew Milligan

EXECUTIVE SUMMARY

- Why the insurance sector came out of the downturn better than the banks.
- The important effect the yield curve has on insurance liquidity and the real economy.
- The need for Governments to act on a number of fronts.
- The shift in wealth from savers to spenders.
- The importance of not rushing to judgement on regulatory matters.

INTRODUCTION

If one looks at the devastation wrought on the global finance community, there is no doubt that the insurance sector has come out of this in very much better shape than the banks. There have been casualties—AIG in the United States, for example. However, AIG was a special case, being much more of a financial conglomerate than a "pure" insurance company.

The reasons why the insurance sector has been less affected by the financial services "meltdown" are complex. An important factor is that there was no parallel to the way the banks—and the shadow banking system that sprang up in recent years—leveraged themselves. Relying on a constant supply of new funding to keep their business models running meant the eventual liquidity crunch left certain banks high and dry.

This does not mean that the insurance sector does not have issues to face in the future. It will have to deal with the aftershocks of the economic downturn, with weakness and volatility in the stock, bond, and property markets, or with movements in annuity rates, all of which will pose serious challenges.

THE SHAPE OF THE YIELD CURVE IS IMPORTANT

It is already clear that the shape of the yield curve is going to be of considerable importance in the months ahead. So far, governments have tended to implement monetary policy by urging central banks to reduce short-term interest rates. The next step in this program has been quantitative easing (QE), namely governments going out and buying certain private and public-sector assets in significant amounts, to the tune of hundreds of billions of pounds. At present, government and then corporate bonds are to be top of the shopping list.

Such QE policies could eventually flatten parts of the interest-rate structure. This may possibly have an impact on annuity rates, driving them down. Historically, the level of long-term interest rates is more correlated with the weakness of the economy than with the supply of new government bonds. Conversely, it is possible that the very sizeable public-sector debt issuance expected in the coming months and years could be skewed towards the longer end of the yield curve, as a means of keeping long-dated yields higher. We could end up with some very peculiar yield curve shapes in the years ahead. Either way, coordination between the Bank of England and the Debt Management Office in the United Kingdom, and counterparts in other countries, will be vital in the coming months.

The shape of the curve also has strong implications for the real economy. In normal circumstances, changes in interest rates have an impact fairly quickly on economic activity. However, the precise interest rate does matter. The United Kingdom may have very low base rates, but, in fact, the mortgage market is very heavily based on the level of two- to five-year interest rates. In the United States, it is the 30-year bond yield which matters more for mortgages. European companies are generally financed by a mix of medium-term bank lending and corporate bonds.

There is a major impact, of course, on savings rates. Savers are being affected by very low base rates. This produces a strong incentive for people to spend, or to invest in something other than cash. For example, it is already clear that there is a growing demand for corporate bonds. Although there are concerns about the number of companies that could fail during the recession, the high yield on good quality corporate bonds means investors buying a diversified portfolio should normally be rewarded for the risk in buying such an asset. It is the case, though, that an investor who classically needs a 5% return on his or her money, for example, to finance his or her retirement, does not have many options right now, apart from buying some corporate bonds, some equity or even some commercial property. However, an investor should note that as and when the economic recovery begins, and government bonds are likely to be sold off, corporate bonds will then also suffer, though by less than public-sector debt.

The shape of the yield curve also gives signals about investor sentiment. A singularly odd shape in the curve occurred in the United States in early December 2008. For a few days, the interest on three-month Treasury bills actually went negative, which means that buying those bills and holding them to maturity would return less than the capital sum, even before the impact of inflation is factored in. The only way to explain such negative interest rates is complete and utter risk aversion dominating the market. When people fear there is no safe haven for cash, they will take a slightly negative rate as the best way of conserving whatever possible value. As investor sentiment has recovered in recent weeks, so by the end of April, three-month US Treasury bills were paying positive, albeit at only 0.2% interest, just above US inflation running at –0.1% a year.

GOVERNMENT POLICIES

As insurance companies hold large equity, bond, and property portfolios, the outlook for government policies to kickstart the world economy is important. Alongside QE, another issue to consider is the "bad bank" plan, where the government sets up a special purpose vehicle to remove some of the toxic assets from bank books, freeing them to lend more. This may work alongside programs which act to stabilize asset prices, perhaps with some direct government intervention in the housing market to slow or stop the downward spiral of asset values in the sector. It is clear that no one step will be sufficient, and governments will need to act on a number of fronts. What cannot be ignored is that in order to help finance the next phase of the business cycle, a range of fiscal, monetary, regulatory, and quantitative-easing measures looks likely to be required.

The scale of the actions being taken by governments, with many hundreds of billions of pounds being spent, has led to a widening in the credit default swap (CDS) spreads on sovereign debt (a financial instrument akin to an insurance policy, which pays out should a government default on its debt). There has, indeed, been talk in the media about the increased risk of

"Advertising is the business of telling someone something that should be important to him. It is a substitute for talking to him." Fairfax Cone

     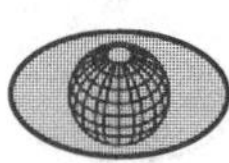   

one or another government defaulting on its debt. However, the word "default" has to be thought about rather carefully when it is applied to a government, rather than to an individual or a company. True, we have relatively recent historical instances of sovereign default, with Russia and Ecuador declaring that they are not going to meet payments on some foreign-currency debt. However, there is very little chance of a major Western government, particularly the UK or the US, going down this route. Governments have a range of options when they are in difficulties, not least because they can "print money". Generating inflation lowers the real value of the debt. This may also depress the domestic currency versus the creditor's currency, and, again, makes the debt easier to pay.

In other words, modern states do not default on the nominal amount of the debt, but the true cost to an overseas lender of some actions open to government can be severe. Instead of talking about the risk of government defaults, a more accurate way of interpreting widening CDS spreads for Europe and the United States may be to think of some investors as becoming more concerned about the potential for inflation and adverse currency movements in those countries.

If we take the examples of Italy and Japan, both of which are OECD economies with very high public-sector debt-to-GDP ratios, we see that one impact of debt on this scale is to constrain growth in those economies. Japan has a very flat interest-rate structure, partly to ensure that the burden of servicing such debt does not become too onerous. The economy still functions well, but the high debt-to-GDP ratio rules out certain avenues of action, such as repeating the wave of public-sector infrastructure investment which took place in the 1990s—one of the options being examined in the United States and the United Kingdom. High tax burdens are often seen as a drag on economic growth.

All in all, there is a difficult balancing act ahead for governments across Europe, as they try to encourage consumers to start spending again, yet the levels of indebtedness at all levels of society mean that paying down of debt is also a priority. These two cannot be achieved simultaneously, but the effect of the two can be created by generating inflation, which would drive down the real value of the stock of debt. Whether governments can generate that inflation at will is questionable, but the easy monetary policy, weak currencies, and massive liquidity stimulus may have an effect in the end.

INSURANCE COMPANIES

Insurance companies are, of course, in constant dialogue with wealth managers and financial advisers, all of whom are concerned to find viable solutions for their clients. There is considerable anxiety among such advisers concerning the ability of the stock market to deliver reasonable dividend growth in the next few years. At the same time, such managers want help in trying to determine the outlook for deflation in the short term, and inflation in the longer term. These are all issues that are being avidly discussed across the industry.

The insurance sector has to concern itself with savings decisions, and people's attitude to mid-to-long-term savings. Right now, there is a generational shift in wealth from older people, who tend to have built up significant savings, to younger people, who do not have much of a savings profile and who are buying on credit. Younger people are net gainers, as interest on credit has come down significantly, while older people are seeing the income from their savings plummet, and negative real deposit rates starting to erode the value of their savings pot, i.e. after adjusting for inflation. This equates to a transfer of wealth from the older generation to the younger generation.

Markets and investors try to look ahead beyond the immediate factors that are playing out in the economy today. As the financial markets take the longer-term view, the realization that the United States will begin issuing US$2 trillion of debt per year over the next few years—up from US$500 billion of debt, which was the average a few years ago—is a matter of considerable concern. It is one factor behind the higher US bond yields seen through late 2008 and early 2009. The willingness of overseas governments to continue to buy a very large part of the US debt is going to be very material for the US dollar and US long-term interest rates, and will also determine whether the US Federal Reserve is required to accept some extreme forms of quantitative easing.

In the United Kingdom, we have already seen what happens when a large number of overseas investors decide that they are becoming uncomfortable about UK policy and direction. They started to dispose of some of their UK assets, and the result was a precipitous drop in the value of sterling. In fact, sterling lost some 25% of its value in 2008, a truly stunning amount. That was the fall against a basket of currencies that consist of all the United Kingdom's major trading partners, with the dollar and the euro being the major constituents. To put this fall in context, it is larger than the roughly 20% fall sterling experienced when the United Kingdom fell out of the Exchange Rate Mechanism. Of course, this time round, the fall has been spread over 18 months, rather than over the course of a few days, but that should not blind us to the scale of the fall.

> "Markets and investors try to look ahead beyond the immediate factors that are playing out in the economy today."

However, currency movements should be seen as neutral by investors. They have both positive and negative impacts. The export of goods and services is much easier for a devalued currency. As a service sector, the insurance sector in the United Kingdom is well placed to profit from the fact that pricing has moved in its favor as it seeks to sell its services in Asia, Europe, and the Americas. Similarly, we are already seeing more of an appetite on the part of overseas investors for good value in the United Kingdom, for example, distressed UK property, which is now looking very cheap to them. At the same time, as the prices of import goods are higher as a result of the drop in the value of sterling, this helps to move the economy out of deflation and to trigger some inflation again. In addition, overseas investors can, and, according to the latest statistics, are buying more UK debt, particularly gilts, because sterling has fallen, and they can buy more bonds for their, for example, euros than they used to. This is a good example of the positive and negative impacts of currency movements. All this is positive in helping the economy to rebalance.

The insurance sector will hope that as governments seek to formulate and impose new regulatory regimes on the banks, and possibly on hedge funds, they do not rush into judgment on the insurance sector. It seems clear that the sector has done a good job under very difficult circumstances. They are still doing the basics: taking in premiums, investing them, and providing payoffs, be it in, for example, pensions or protection products, at a future date. The business model for all insurance companies is tougher, as can be expected in the face of the worst financial crisis in 60 years, but the industry is generally sound.

It is clear that the top 20 or 40 banks in the world are going to be subjected to much more searching regulation in future. The likely outcome is that we will see a

"There have been many disputes by advertisers and their agencies about articles published . . . and scheduled advertising has been canceled. But I can see no difference between this and the action of an irate individual who cancels his subscription because of an article or story that he doesn't like." Fairfax Cone

  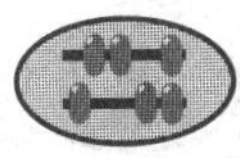   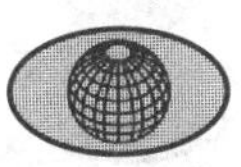   

lot of effort to produce specific tools for regulating different sectors—interest rates alone are simply not enough of a lever for directing the economy. The insurance sector needs to be closely involved in this debate, not least because we own shares in a large part of the economy, particularly the financial sector.

CONCLUSION

Looking ahead, we already have new financial conglomerates emerging, with the likes of Bank of America now including Merrill Lynch, and regulators will have to work to see that one part of such new conglomerates does not bring the rest down with it. This was an issue with the rise of the credit derivative markets, but another form of risk is now appearing in the conglomerates that rapid market consolidation is generating.

This will require regulation, not just by government regulators but also by independent regulators, in other words, by non-executive directors and major shareholders of these new conglomerates. They will have to see that the organizations in which they have invested create value in a prudent manner, rather than taking irrational risks with their clients' money.

▸▸ MORE INFO

Report:

International Association of Insurance Supervisors (IAIS). "Roadmap for a common structure and common standards for the assessment of insurer solvency." IAIS, February 16, 2006. Online at: www.iaisweb.org/__temp/Roadmap_for_a_common_structure_and_common_standards.pdf

Websites:

International Association of Insurance Supervisors: www.iaisweb.org

The Geneva Association: The International Association for the Study of Insurance Economics: www.genevaassociation.org

See Also:

Insurance (pp. 1520–1521)

  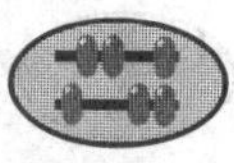   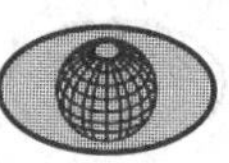   

Viewpoint: Ricardo Rebonato
What Models Do We Need for Risk Management?

INTRODUCTION

Dr Riccardo Rebonato is Global Head of Market Risk and Global Head of Quantitative Analytics at RBS. He is a Visiting Lecturer at Oxford University (Mathematical Finance) and Adjunct Professor at Imperial College (Tanaka Business School). He sits on the Board of Directors of ISDA and on the Board of Trustees for GARP. He is an Editor for the International Journal of Theoretical and Applied Finance, for Applied Mathematical Finance, for the Journal of Risk and for the Journal of Risk Management in Financial Institutions. He is the author of the books Plight of the Fortune Tellers – Why We Need To Manage Financial risk Differently (2007), Volatility and Correlation in Option Pricing (2004, 1999), Modern Pricing of Interest-Rate Derivatives (2002), Interest-Rate Option Models' (1998, 1996).

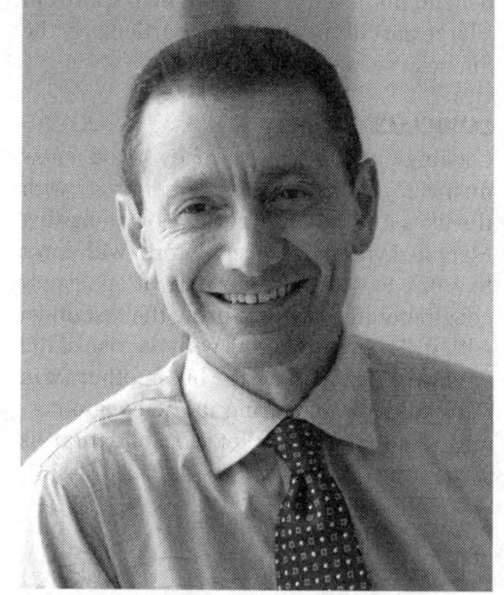

"All models are wrong, but some models are useful." Anon

Quantitative models have come under intense scrutiny in the wake of the recent, and still unfolding, financial crisis. And justly so, as the way models have been used in these turbulent times has left a lot to be desired. Much of the criticism, however, has been misplaced, and, often, not even reasonably well-informed. The conspiracy theorists, for instance, who see in the blind acceptance by the "establishment" of the Normal distribution as the root of all evil, have, quite simply, missed the point. Those critics who have complained about "imperfect model assumptions" do not seem to appreciate that, if a model did not have some imperfect assumptions, it would not be a model at all, and that some very successful models in the hardest science of all (physics) often make outrageously unrealistic assumptions, yet can be just as outrageously successful. As I have been involved with models throughout all of my professional life, both as practitioner and academic, I intend to touch on the topic of models from an insider's perspective. However, generalizing about "models in finance" would cause whatever conclusions or suggestions I might reach to be rather bland and generic. I therefore intend to focus on one particular set of applications: i.e., on the use of models for financial risk management.

ONE MODEL OR MANY MODELS?

I intend to argue that there exist a plurality of interpretative models of financial reality, and that each can be adopted or abandoned by market participants in an unpredictable fashion. If this view is correct, the search for the "true" model, for the unique "correct" mapping from information to prices, may be futile and some of the modeling risk-management efforts to date have been misguided. This has important consequences: the existence of competition among models and the resulting "fluctuations" between them can give rise to coordination among agents and feed back mechanisms into prices. This complex dynamic is beginning to be well-understood in some areas of finance and economics, but has not received sufficient attention in financial risk management. This, I believe, is dangerous, and has been one of the contributing factors to the current financial turmoil.

REDUCED-FORM AND MICROSTRUCTURAL MODELS

I referred above to a plurality of interpretative models. What does this mean? Models come in all forms and stripes. The most ambitious are microstructural models that attempt to explain and predict aggregate observables (for example, price movements), starting from the specification of the behavior of individual agents. Traditional micromodels in economics are fully prespecified, i.e. they make strong assumptions about how agents make their choices given inputs (for example, utility functions, etc). They assume the inputs to these models are fixed, and that we know them; there is a "communism of models," the assumption is made that "all agents inside the model, econometricians and God all share the same model."[1] These models can, of course, be stochastic, but, even when they are, they still assume that the nature of the uncertainty (for example, the parameters of the chosen distribution) is perfectly known to all the agents, to the econometrician (and, hopefully, to God).[2]

Reduced-form models are less ambitious. They dispense with the description of the underlying micromechanisms, and simply account for the statistical properties of a phenomenon at an aggregate level. Intensity models of credit default, for instance, where the frequency of default becomes an exogenous quantity, belong to this class. In the risk management domain, all analyses of risk that simply look at price movements, without asking what mechanisms brought about the observed changes, firmly fall in to the reduced-form camp.

Reduced-form models look less assumption-laden (and therefore presumably safer) than the microstructural ones. However, they give no indication as to when their conditions of validity may fail to apply—just because they do not look under the bonnet. Their strength is, in this respect, also their weakness. These reduced-form models are therefore adequate for day-to-day, "nothing-much-has-changed" type of applications. They can also work in the tails of a return distribution if we have enough data and the underlying phenomenon is stationary. But reduced-form models are intrinsically unable to deal with the unexpected, the new—with the real tail event.

Those who preach power laws, more-or-less-truncated Levy flights, Cauchy distributions, or other exotica, without offering a mechanism capable of explaining how and *when* these distributional features occur are therefore still solidly in the reduced-form camp—despite their claims, they are still fundamentally ill-equipped to deal with the unexpected. Unless coupled with model(s) of reality, these distributional suggestions ultimately give us no real handle on black swans.

The microstructural models loved by economists have in principle far more

"The cosmetics industry should be promoting health and well-being; instead it hypes an outdated notion of glamour and sells false hopes and fantasies." Anita Roddick

  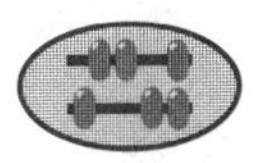   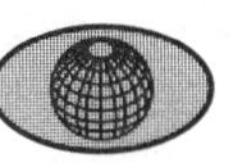  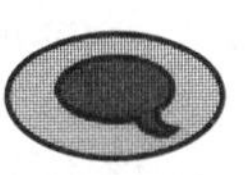 

power, because they specify the mechanisms that bring about certain outcomes, and we can therefore ask ourselves whether these mechanisms still apply. They are not without problems, though, and it is to these problems that I now turn.

A DIFFERENT PICTURE OF THE DATA/MODEL INTERACTION

From the discussion above, a strong case can be made that for day-to-day risk management reduced-form models can do a good (and "cheap") job; but if we want to capture truly exceptional risk, microstructural models that link aggregate outputs to the behavior of agents via a simplified mechanism of financial reality, seem to be needed.

For the purpose of financial risk management, the aggregate variables of interest are asset prices. Asset prices are, in turn, determined by the actions of traders. In order to understand how prices evolve, it is therefore essential to understand how traders react to information.

One paradigm (Efficient Market Hypothesis, Rational Expectation Hypothesis) is that of the perfectly efficient Bayesian agent, who (almost) instantaneously updates his prior beliefs in the light of new information. Depending on the application, this picture may or may not be useful as a model that links microbehavior (utility maximization and Bayesian updating) and market institutional set-ups to aggregate outcomes (prices of assets). It certainly leaves behind important features of real price dynamics:

1 overreaction to news cannot happen;
2 traders can adjust their beliefs almost instantaneously;
3 traders are principals, not agents, or, if agents, the principal/agent set-up perfectly aligns the actions of the agent with the interests of the principal;
4 there are no limits to (pseudo-)arbitrage.

For the reasons alluded to above, it is futile and unproductive to say that "these assumptions are not met in practice." The relevant question is whether these simplifications of reality are so strong as to make the predictions uninteresting or useless for the purposes of the management of financial risk. Unfortunately, there is abundant evidence that suggests that important features are left out of the stylized description above, especially in situation of market distress.

A more realistic model of how traders react to information and, by so doing, affect prices, may go along the following lines.

- Traders are agents—with all the problems of incentivization and principal-agent alignment that this entails.
- Traders are smart—they understand that, in order to make sense of the minute-by-minute flow of information, they need "stories" that can help them organize this enormous amount of data. These stories are often very "micro" in nature, in the sense that they assume complex mechanisms to link economic data to aggregate outputs—we have all heard the "stories" (or "rationalizations") that run along the lines of: "pension funds are buying index-linkers to cover their liabilities," "exotic traders are rehedging their negative gamma," "sellers of variance swaps are dumping stock in the last twenty minutes of opening," etc.
- Traders are fickle—each of the above models seems *prima facie* like a mini microstructural model. However, unlike economists, traders are unashamedly ready to dump their perfect fully prespecified micromodel for the new flavor-of-the-month/week/day fully prespecified micromodel—how quickly did we go from the "oil-at-$300 story" to "oil-at-US$20 story?" From a world with out-of-control inflation to a deflationary world? From a decoupling story to full synchronicity of the world economies?
- Traders are selective in their choice of data—they never let inconvenient data get in the way of today's good story, at least until tomorrow when the new story is all the rage.

The interaction of several competing models into a dynamic, not-fully-prespecified picture of reality has been picked up in the academic economics domain by the Imperfect Knowledge Economics (IKE) school—the approach offers very interesting applications to FX dynamics, and an explanation of how FX rates can stray from "fundamentals" for so long. I suggest that a similar way of looking at financial risk may be very profitable.

From this perspective, for risk management purposes the important observation from the above is that it is advantageous for market participants to coordinate their actions. In many situations, this can give rise to feedback mechanisms that can produce wild moves of prices away from fundamentals and that can ultimately leave a signature in the tail behavior of price returns.

The existence of this competing heuristic to make sense of data cannot, of course, be proven by anecdotes, but a conversation I had with the head of a commodity trading desk in the late summer of 2008, when oil prices were testing US$140, and there were fears that Israel may attempt a preemptive strike on Iran's nuclear facilities, is very telling. I wanted to confirm with the trader my intuition that the feared bombing would send oil prices even higher. "A strike by Israel will have two effects," the trader confidently said: "either the oil price will go up a lot. Or it will go down a lot." His reasoning was that the military action may cause a restriction of supply, or that the action would have such a negative effect on global sentiment, as to tip toward recession a world already shaken by the unfolding financial crisis. The merits of either argument are not the point here. What *is* the point is the readiness of the trader to embrace two such discordant models of reality, and his need to coordinate his action with the perceived interpretation of the other traders. What springs to mind, of course, is Keynes's beauty contest, where the judges have to choose not the most attractive contestant, but the contestant that the other judges will choose as the most attractive.

The view of trading that I propose is therefore consistent with a coordination game played by the market participants; as information arrives, traders have to analyze it and process it in a very short time. It is plausible that they use relatively simple heuristics in doing so. They have to categorize this information in one of the "market modes" they recognize—the inflationary story, the commodity-demand-from-emerging-markets story, the decoupling story. Then they have to coordinate their categorization with what the other market participants are doing, because the worst situation for an individual trader is not to be wrong, but to give the "wrong" (i.e. dissonant) categorization in comparison to the rest of the market. And, in periods of turmoil or great uncertainty, the swings from one temporary paradigm to another can be wild (both in amplitude and in rapidity): ". . .investors have an incentive to coordinate, *which may generate self-fulfilling beliefs and multiple equilibria.* Using insights from global games, [one can] pin down investors' beliefs, analyze equilibrium prices, and show that *strong feedback leads to higher excess volatility...*"[3] (my emphasis).

In order to anticipate, at least at a qualitative level, how prices might behave tomorrow, an understanding of these imperfect models and heuristics and how they can be temporarily adopted or dropped is therefore indispensable. Blind adherence to any one model, even to the intellectually most satisfactory or the empirically least wrong one, will therefore leave us unprepared to cope with what reality will throw at us tomorrow.

  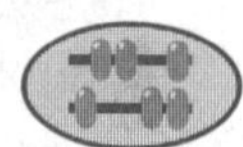   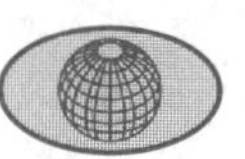   

THE CURRENT QUANTITATIVE APPROACH TO FINANCIAL RISK MANAGEMENT

How do these views square with current thinking about quantitative financial risk management? Even a cursory analysis of what is presented as best practice immediately shows that the prevailing paradigm is one where reduced-form models reign supreme. The obsessive interest in the study of the return distribution is, of course, the ultimate reduced-form-model approach, with all the limitations highlighted above. The frequently heard statement, "All the statistical information of interest is contained in the multivariate joint distribution of returns—pity that it is so difficult to obtain, and, if we had it, more difficult to interpret" must be strongly qualified. All the statistical information of relevance is indeed in the return distribution, but only for time-stationary phenomena and *over the same time horizon over which the returns have been calculated.*[4] This means that, if I have vectors of daily returns, I can hope to have all the statistical information I need about 1-day changes. But if I am interested in 2-day, 10-day, or 1-year changes there is no sure-proof, model-independent, assumption-free way of aggregating these data for the longer time frames of interest.

Of course, if perfect independence of returns applied and one were dealing with a time-stationary phenomenon, one could in principle obtain the distribution of one-year changes from the distribution of one-minute changes: the way to do it is by convolution. But there is overwhelming evidence that shows that the "synthetic" long-horizon distributions calculated by repeated convolutions starting from the short-horizon distribution are very different from the empirical long-horizon distribution.[5] Why not using the long-horizon distribution to start with? Because the longer the horizon, the fewer the independent observation points, the less we can say about the tails of the distribution, the less confident we can be of the relevance of very "ancient" data to the current market conditions. I have expanded at length on this aspect in Rebonato (2006), and I will therefore not pursue this line here.

Ultimately, the joint distribution of n-day returns does give full information about what n-day returns have been in the past (over the time horizon equal to the frequency of data collection). The link between this information and future n-day returns, however, is not in the data, but in our model(s) of reality. When it comes to financial risk management, are we interested in understanding the past or predicting the future?

DESIGNING A MORE REALISTIC MODELING APPROACH

If these insights are correct, the (self-organizing) switching between modes of understanding reality referred to above should leave a signature in the distribution of returns. To see how this can happen, suppose that one of the prevalent market reactions to very bad economic news is the expectation of a pronounced steepening of the yield curve. Then one would expect to be able to identify a subset of data associated with large downward moves at the short end, high maturity-adjusted volatility, high correlation among short-dated yields, and lower correlation between short and long-dated yields. Or suppose that a mode of reaction to unexpected inflationary evidence is a flattening of the yield curve, with short rates moving up much more than long rates and high maturity-adjusted volatility at the short end. One should be able to identify in a subset of the data the signature of these market responses as well.

As long as there is not an infinity of modes of reaction to economic news (and this is likely to be the case as a result of the traders' need to organize information in digestible soundbites), these modes of deformation should be recognizable in the full time series of returns (but not at all in the cumulative distribution).

As pieces of information do not come with ready-made labels, if different market participants chose their heuristic models independently, there would be little chance for the result of a single mode of organization of reality to become apparent. However, for the reasons explained above, market participants must develop the ability to "lock into" a coordinated market response. The market creates a small number of filters through which information is passed. The filters are changed occasionally (with a frequency ranging from a few days to a few months).

The good news is that the signature onto the prices of the different modes of reaction to economic news *is* detectable. There now exist powerful analytical methods to identify (i) how many modes of deformation exist; and (ii) what happens (to volatilities, correlations, etc.) in each of these modes.[6] It is also often possible to give a narrative interpretation—for example, a flight-to-liquidity mode, for some (or most) of the modes so identified. And, *looking at each mode in isolation*, it is not unreasonable to expect that quantities such as correlations or volatilities might be constant (conditional homoskedasticity).

So, despite recent events, models are not dead. Models don't kill financial systems—people who don't understand how to use models sometimes do. But we must realize that, without an interpretative model of reality, data analysis, however sophisticated, is mute. We will be better served by a plurality of imperfect, but richer, microstructurally inspired models than by a supposedly all-encompassing, reduced-form supermodel. And most of all, we need people—analysts, traders and, yes, also senior managers—who can use models more effectively.

▸▸ MORE INFO

There are similarities between the views I presented and the much wider reflexivity model proposed by Soros (2003) and Soros (2008). About the shortcomings of fully prespecified microstructural models, and an application to FX rates, see Frydman and Goldberg (2007). About the effect on asset prices of heterogeneous beliefs, see, for example, Shefrin (2008) and Buraschi (2006). The effects of coordination in general are nicely presented in Chamley (2004). The techniques presented in this text do not deal, however, with the case when the actions of the coordinating agents affect the prices. To explore this angle, see Cipriani and Guarino (2008).

Books:

Chamley, Christophe P. *Rational Herds: Economic Models of Social Learning*. Cambridge, UK: Cambridge University Press, 2004.

Frydman, Roman, and Michael D. Goldberg *Imperfect Knowledge Economics: Exchange Rates and Risk*. Princeton, NJ: Princeton University Press, 2007.

Rebonato R. *The Plight of the Fortune Tellers*—Why We Need to Manage Financial Risk Differently, Princeton, NJ: Princeton University Press, 2007.

Shefrin Hersh. *A Behavioral Approach to Asset* Pricing. 2nd ed. Oxford: Academic Press, 2008.

Soros, George. *The Alchemy of Finance*. 3rd ed. Hoboken, NJ: Wiley, 2003.

Soros, George. *The New Paradigm for Financial Markets: The Credit Crisis of 2008 and What It Means.* New York: Public Affairs, 2008.

"Imagine if advertisers used their creative skills to make watching learning-oriented shows a first choice for kids." Geraldine Laybourne

     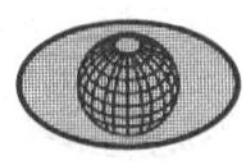   

Articles:

Buraschi, A. "Model uncertainty and option markets with heterogeneous beliefs." *Journal of Finance* 61:6 (December 2006): 2841–2898.

Cipriani, M., and A. Guarino. "Herd behaviour and contagion in financial markets." *Berkley Electronic Journal of Theoretical Economics* 8:1 (2008): article 28. Online at: www.bepress.com/bejte/vol8/iss1/art24

NOTES

1 Interview with Thomas Sargent in Frydman (2006), Imperfect Knowledge Economics, PUP.

2 I note in passing that behavioural finance, often offered as a cure to all of our neoclassical woes, is in this respect no exception—it is still a fully pre-specified model that happens to make different assumptions about human "rationality" (for example, it questions the actual prevalence of Bayesian updating of beliefs).

3 Ozdenoren E, Yuan K. "Feedback effects and asset prices," Journal of Finance, LXIII, 4, August 2008, 1939-1975.

4 If we are interested in properties such as drawdowns—and, as risk managers, we certainly should—we must also add the assumption of independence of draws for the return distribution to be all-informative.

5 See, for example, Malevergne, Y., and D. Sornette. *Extreme Financial Risks: From Dependence to Risk Management*. Springer Verlag, 2005.

6 See, for example, Doust, Chen, and Rebonato. "Identification of the modes of deformation of the US$ yield curve." RBS Working Paper, 2008.

  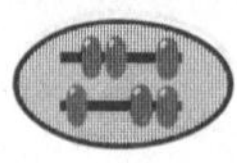   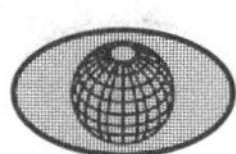   

Viewpoint: Jim Rogers

Asia: Future Perspectives

INTRODUCTION

Jim Rogers grew up in Alabama and started out in business, aged six, selling peanuts and soft drinks at baseball games. He was educated at Yale and Balliol College, Oxford. After he co-founded the Quantum fund in 1970, the fund surged by 4,200% over the next decade, while the Standard & Poor's index rose by 47%. Having earned enough money to "retire" at the age of 37, Rogers has since worked as a professor of finance at Columbia University, columnist, author, and a contrarian investor. In the early 1990s he traveled 100,000 miles through six continents on a BMW motorcycle and ended up with a portfolio of investments in some of the world's most unexpected markets. In 1998 Rogers became bullish about commodities, predicting an enduring commodities rally and later launched the Rogers International Commodities Index. Believing that the future belongs to Asia, he sold his mansion house in New York's Riverside Avenue in 2007 and now lives in Singapore, partly so that his two young daughters can learn Mandarin.

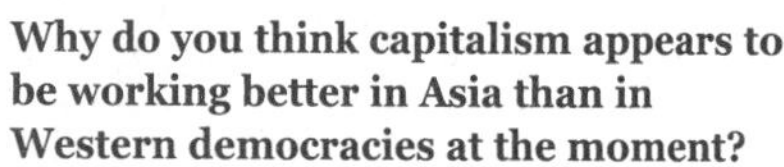

Why do you think capitalism appears to be working better in Asia than in Western democracies at the moment?
It is because in Asia they're fresher at it and they haven't yet had the chance to get corrupted and corroded. In China, they still call themselves Communists. They didn't have a stock market 20 years ago, nor did Vietnam. Thirty years ago Mao Tse-tung was still running China; Indira Gandhi and Nehru were ruining India; East and West Pakistan had just had a big split; Vietnam had been destroyed by war. So, 30 years ago Asia was not in the game.

Is the current financial crisis a tipping point, with developed nations losing their status as financial centers and Asian centers taking over?
Yes, definitely. This is a period that we will look back on and say, "Oh, yes, that's when it all really changed." The money now is in Asia. The largest creditor nations in the world are China, Japan, South Korea, Taiwan, Singapore, and Saudi Arabia. Forty years ago none were in Asia. Experience tells us that; money is not dumb. It goes where the money already is; everybody follows the money. That's why New York became the world's financial center: because America had the money, the balance of trade, the reserves, and the economy. But America doesn't have the money any more and nor does the United Kingdom.

If Asia is poised to take over as the world's next financial center, which city do you think is going to be dominant?
No single financial center has emerged in Asia yet. Singapore and Hong Kong are working at it, and they both have a lot going for them. Hong Kong has a negative, which could turn out to be a positive, in that its neighbor is China. China has a blocked currency, so it cannot emerge yet. Seoul is saying that they want to become one, but they still have a host of unbelievable regulations, and even the Koreans themselves aren't on top of these regulations. You can't have a financial center without a free flow of capital. There's no free flow of capital in South Korea right now.

Do you believe Singapore or Hong Kong more likely to emerge as Asia's leading financial center?
I think it'll be Singapore, at least in the medium term, because no one really knows what's going to happen with Hong Kong and China. Dubai says it wants to, but Dubai is essentially a short-sell now. There's also Tokyo. Over the last 40 years, Tokyo should have been emerging as a financial center. On paper it looks like it ought to be the world's financial center. The trouble is that, for whatever reason, the Japanese just don't want to open up to the outside world and keep doing ludicrous things, like having their interest rates at almost zero.

Why do believe that Dubai was a short-sell?
Dubai's "model" has been to develop the country and the economy based on real estate speculation. They don't have any oil; they ran out of oil. So they've come up with all these fabulous plans on paper to become a media center, to become a high-tech center, an entertainment center, etc. It's all based on massive amounts of real estate speculation with borrowed money. Now, maybe their cousins in Abu Dhabi will continue to bail them out, but it's going to be a big, big, big bite to bail out.

What lessons do you think the developed economies can learn from the banking crisis? How should they be reforming their financial systems to ensure they can recover?
The lesson that they should learn is to let the market work. During the past 15 years, in the United States especially, they refused to allow the market do its work. Alan Greenspan swore every day that he believed in market forces, but every time there was a problem he over-rode the market. If he had allowed "Long-term Capital Management" to go broke, we would not have had these problems now. That allowed people at Bear Stearns and Lehman's, who were incompetent before, to carry on. Instead of licking their wounds and learning how to drive cabs, they went off looking for the next fish to fry. At the time everybody thought Greenspan knew what he was doing. But if you look back at some of the things he said, we now know he was a fool. Through his policies, he goosed up a consumption and a housing bubble. He said, "The derivatives markets are great. They're a fabulous thing to help the financial system." He came out and said all these things out loud, officially, under oath.

Do you think derivatives will have to be more tightly regulated?
There's no need. The markets have taken care of that. Do you think anybody is out there writing derivatives now? There are

   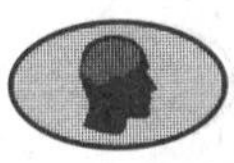  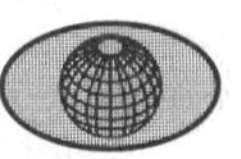   

simply no buyers out there. The regulators still don't understand derivatives.

What is the commercial bank of the future going to look like do you think?
They are going to take deposits and make loans to people they know, and they're going to make a living. Securitization will come back someday but, if and when it does, it will be on an entirely different basis. It will be pretty straightforward and transparent. One thing that was lacking in the market before was transparency. Nobody could see what they were buying or selling. Some of these derivative instruments had offering circulars of over 1,000 pages, which I doubt anybody read, including the people who wrote them. Nobody knew what was in this stuff.

Were the people who bought those things greedy or naive, or both?
Well, I guess they were certainly naïve. I hope they were naïve, maybe they were just crooks. Greedy? Well, everybody was out there trying to make as much money as they could. The first securitizations were fine.

What is the investment bank of the future going to look like?
Well, it's going to look like the investment bank of 20 years ago. There was nothing wrong with the model back in 1929; it's just that everybody went out and did some strange things with the model. And it had a revival, but some of the practices are yet to have a revival.

Does this mean the United States is effectively bankrupt?
There's no doubt about it. Greenspan and Ben Bernanke have ensured the demise of the Federal Reserve. America has had three central banks. The first two disappeared and these two clowns have ensured the current one will also disappear. Bernanke tripled the balance sheet of the Federal Reserve in something like four months and filled it with garbage. The Federal Reserve used to have almost 100% government bonds; now it's got who knows what percent of garbage. I wrote this in a book five years ago, expecting the Fed to disappear some time after 2010. I think it could happen much sooner now.

A year ago, the US government had debt of about US$5 trillion, which had been built up over the 200 years of the republic. Then, over a single weekend in September, Hank Paulson doubled that. He did this by assuming the debt for Fanny Mae and Freddie Mac, which had US$6 trillion of debt. Some of that debt perhaps has good assets behind it, but Fanny Mae and Freddie Mac also had untold trillions of off-balance-sheet derivatives. The government assumed those as well. In taking over AIG, the government assumed untold trillions of AIG's off-balance-sheet derivatives obligations. The government tripled or quadrupled its debt in a few months.

What are the key challenges facing President Barack Obama?
Obama ran on a platform of taxing capital and protectionism, and won, at a time when the world knows that those two platforms are crazy. But he did it. Throughout history we know that the taxation of capital has been a disaster. It leaves a country with less capital and, if that's done during a crisis, it makes capital flee. As for protectionism, that has never worked. Nobody has ever won a trade war in history. In 1930 America passed the Smoot–Hawley tariff, which promptly led to the Great Depression. Politicians have done dumb things throughout history. So far, Obama has shown a distinct lack of understanding of what is happening and certainly has continued his anti-capital approach.

Given Obama's economic policies, are you worried about the future of America?
The hope is that he didn't mean it, that it was just in the heat of campaigning. Or, even if he meant it, that somebody will pull him aside and say, "Look, Mr Obama, this would be a disaster." And that he would listen. But who knows? Of course I'm worried. This is one of the reasons that markets kept falling in the build-up to November's presidential election. Everybody knew Obama was going to win and everybody knew what his policies were.

What does the future hold for the City of London?
The game is up for the City of London. A lot of business, including a lot of derivatives business, some initial public offerings, and some underwriting, migrated there because of Sarbanes–Oxley and other things. But most of that business is now in chaos and has been devastated. The City of London has been particularly error-prone in the derivatives market. I cannot see the City of London making a quick revival.

What role did regulation or the lack of it play in that?
As usual, the people in the business (the entrepreneurs) are way ahead of the regulators. The regulators are usually people who cannot get jobs elsewhere and are basically bureaucrats, and they're older. In Singapore, they have a better approach to that. They pay their cabinet ministers US$1 million a year, which gives them no incentive to be corrupt and ensures that high-quality people are attracted to the job. Everybody, including the regulators, is well paid, which means they're not easily corruptible.

Could London reinvent itself by pursuing a different strand of business?
Sterling is in serious trouble—what does the United Kingdom have to sell now? The United Kingdom went from being a net exporter of oil to a net importer, that is a gigantic swing in the balance of trade. Thirty or 40 years ago, the United Kingdom went bankrupt and sterling went to parity with the dollar, almost one-to-one. But then North Sea oil started flowing and both sterling and the economy had a big revival. Margaret Thatcher took the credit for that. However, basically, any country that opens up the largest oil field in the world is going to have a good time. That's what rescued the United Kingdom. But now that the country's oil production is declining, the United Kingdom is soon going to be importing oil again, which will create a gigantic hole in the balance of trade.

What does the future hold for the UK economy?
Over the past 30 years, North Sea oil and the City of London have been pretty much

▸▸ MORE INFO

Books:

Rogers, Jim. *Investment Biker: Around the World with Jim Rogers*. Chichester, UK: Wiley, 1994.

Rogers, Jim. *Adventure Capitalist: The Ultimate Investors' Road Trip*. Chichester, UK: Wiley, 2003.

Rogers, Jim. *Hot Commodities: How Anyone Can Invest Profitably in the World's Best Market*. Chichester, UK: Wiley, 2004.

Rogers, Jim. *A Bull in China: Investing Profitably in the World's Greatest Market*. Chichester, UK: Wiley, 2007.

Rogers, Jim. *A Gift to my Children: A Father's Lessons for Life and Investing*. Chichester, UK: Wiley, 2009.

"It is a bloodless extrapolation of a satisfying life. You dine off the advertiser's sizzle and not the meat of the steak." J. B. Priestley

all the extra, new items the United Kingdom has had to sell to the rest of the world. But both have entered a period of rapid decline. It's a self-reinforcing process. If sterling goes down, it makes people less inclined to do their financial business in London and, as the financial business lessens, there's less to support sterling, so the whole thing spirals downwards.

See Also:

- China (pp. 1374–1375)
- Hong Kong (pp. 1400–1401)
- Singapore (pp. 1466–1467)

"In a stable world, knowledge of standard situations and the routine ways of dealing with them is sufficient. Not so in a changing world. . .judgments from the past may be inadequate, misleading, and dangerous."
Edward de Bono

  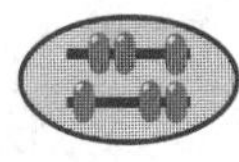 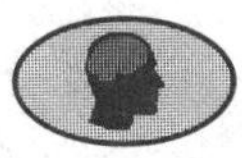  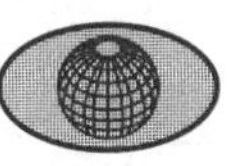   

Islamic Capital Markets: The Role of *Sukuk* by Rodney Wilson

EXECUTIVE SUMMARY

- Conventional bills, bonds, and notes which pay interest are unacceptable from an Islamic perspective.
- Tradable financial instruments using Islamic structures were introduced in Pakistan in 1980 and Malaysia in 1990.
- The defining characteristic of *sukuk* is their asset backing.
- There remains much controversy over *sukuk* structures, especially amongst *shariah* scholars.
- There is growing worldwide interest in *sukuk*, including from the Treasury in the United Kingdom.

INCOMPATIBILITY OF CONVENTIONAL FINANCIAL MARKET INSTRUMENTS WITH *SHARIAH* LAW

Islamic capital markets are made up of two components, stock markets and bond markets. This contribution is primarily concerned with the latter rather than *shariah*-compliant stock determination. In particular it is *sukuk* that have become the accepted Islamic alternative to conventional bills, bonds, and notes, and hence are the major focus here.

Conventional capital market instruments such as treasury bills, bonds, and notes are unacceptable from a *shariah* Islamic legal perspective as they involve interest payments and receipts. Interest is equated with *riba*, an unjust addition to the principal of a debt, and is seen as potentially exploitative. Islamic economists prefer equity to debt financing because of the risk-sharing characteristics of the former, which is viewed as fairer to all parties. They are also concerned about the injustices that often arise with excessive indebtedness, as in the case of developing country debt, or simply the higher interest charges often faced by those with no collateral to offer and the poor more generally.

Nevertheless, government and corporate borrowing is unavoidable, and can indeed be beneficial if the finance is used productively for investment that can contribute to employment and prosperity. Bank lending, however, commits assets on a long-term basis and reduces liquidity. The advantage of using capital market instruments to raise finance is that investors can exit at any time rather than wait for assets to mature. Furthermore, the investment banks that arrange the issuances earn fees and do not have to commit their own resources, unless the bill, bond, or note issue is not taken up, in which case, as underwriters, they will have to purchase the issuance.

THE INTRODUCTION OF ISLAMIC CAPITAL MARKET INSTRUMENTS

There are no *shariah* objections to financial markets, only to the interest-based instruments which are traded in the markets. Therefore, the first attempt to develop *shariah*-compliant debt instruments involved securitizing traditional Islamic financing instruments, as with the *mudaraba* certificates issued in Pakistan from 1980 onward after a law was passed giving legal recognition to the certificates. *Mudaraba* involves the establishment of partnership companies with investors, and the company managers share in the profits, but the financiers alone bear any losses. In 2008 the original law was amended to bring the *mudaraba* companies under the regulatory supervision of the Securities and Exchange Commission of Pakistan, the aim being to ensure better investor protection.

In Malaysia, where Islamic banking started in 1983, a natural innovation was to securitize the debt instruments used, mainly *murabaha* financing, where a bank would purchase a commodity on behalf of a client and resell it to the client for a markup, with settlement through deferred payments. The first instrument was issued by the Shell oil company's Sarawak subsidiary in 1990, with Bank Islam Malaysia as the arranger. By attracting third-party investors interested in benefiting from these deferred payments the bank could use its capital for further financing rather than having it committed on a long-term basis. This debt trading, known as *bai al-dayn,* is permitted by the Malaysian interpretation of the Shafii School of Islamic jurisprudence which prevails in Malaysia and Indonesia, but is not permitted in Saudi Arabia or the Gulf. Scholars of Islamic jurisprudence in the Gulf believe that debtors should know who they are indebted to, rather than having their debt obligations traded in an impersonal market.

ASSET-BACKED *SUKUK*

Given the concerns with *bai al-dayn*, it became clear that an alternative approach was needed to the securitization of debt instruments, and it was this that resulted in the emergence of *sukuk*. The defining characteristic of *sukuk* is that they are asset backed, which implies that when they are traded the investors are buying and selling the rights to an underlying real asset, usually a piece of real estate or a movable asset such as equipment or vehicles. It is this that makes the transaction legitimate, as under *sura* 2.275 in the Qur'an, it states that "God hath permitted trade but forbidden *riba*."

The Accounting and Auditing Organization for Islamic Financial Institutions (AAOIFI) has stated that for "*sukuk*, to be tradable, (they) must be owned by *sukuk* holders, with all the rights and obligations of ownership in real assets."[1]

Again, it was Malaysia that took the lead in *sukuk* issuance, the first being for Malaysian Newsprint Industries in 2000, with an eight-year maturity. It was, however, the Malaysian government's global *sukuk* in June 2002 that brought international attention, this being the first ever sovereign *sukuk*, with maturity after five years, the sum raised being $US 600 million. State-owned land provided the asset backing, and an *ijara* structure was used, with the government selling the land to a special purpose vehicle (SPV) and leasing it back, and the investors in the SPV receiving a rental income as indirect owners rather than interest payments. The returns were, however, benchmarked to the London Inter-Bank Offer Rate (LIBOR), the return being LIBOR + 0.95%, which meant the *sukuk* had similar financial characteristics to a floating rate note. HSBC Amanah the Islamic finance affiliate of HSBC acted as arranger.

Since 2002 *sukuk* issuance has risen remarkably, with *sukuk* issuance peaking at $US 46.6 billion in 2007, representing 205 issuances. The subprime crisis in asset-backed securities had a negative impact on *sukuk* issuance from August 2007 onward, demonstrating that Islamic finance was not immune from global financial developments. However, it mainly affected dollar-denominated issuance, as issuers who were asked to pay much more for their

"Tradable *sukuk* must represent ownership for the *sukuk* holders in real assets that may be possessed and disposed of legally and in accordance with *shariah*." Accounting and Auditing Organisation for Islamic Financial Institutions, (AAOIFI), Clarification on *Sukuk*, Bahrain, 2008, p. 1

financing decided to postpone or abandon planned *sukuk*. Hence, US dollar-denominated issuance fell to just over $US 1 billion over the September 2007 to September 2008 period. *Sukuk* issuance in other currencies was less affected, however, with the equivalent of $US 15.4 billion issued in Malaysian ringgit over the same period, and $US 6.6 billion in UAE dirham, even though the latter currency is pegged to the dollar. The need for funds for project finance continues to propel *sukuk* issuance in the Gulf, with the Saudi Arabian Basic Industries Corporation, the region's leading petrochemical producer, issuing *sukuk* worth $US 1.3 billion in May 2008, with the *sukuk* being riyal-denominated and paying SAIBOR (Saudi Arabia Inter-Bank Offer Rate) plus 48 basis points over a 20-year period.

AAOIFI has identified 14 types of *sukuk* with different risk and return characteristics. *Salam sukuk,* for example, are a short-term substitute for conventional bills, as they yield a fixed return, usually over a 90-day period, and are regarded as very low-risk instruments, not least because the issuers are usually sovereign governments rather than corporate clients. The major limitation of *salam sukuk,* however, is that they cannot be traded, unlike treasury bills, as the investors are paying in advance for the delivery of an asset in 90 days. Under *shariah* investors can only trade assets they own, and not those that they hope to own at a future date.

With the *ijara sukuk* cited above there is a return risk, as payments are usually linked to LIBOR which varies, and typically the issuance is for three to five years, which increases the possibility of default risk. *Ijara sukuk* can, however, be traded as the investors have a title to the underlying assets. This also applies in the case of *mudaraba sukuk*, which in some respects are less risky than their *ijara* equivalents as they pay a fixed return.

UNRESOLVED *SHARIAH* CONCERNS WITH *SUKUK*

Despite the success of *sukuk* there remain fundamental questions about their legitimacy from a *shariah* perspective, as the current structures have been devised by lawyers and investment bankers and are not *shariah*-based, as the contracts in traditional Islamic jurisprudence, *fiqh*, are significantly different. The *sukuk* are *shariah*-compliant in the sense that they have been approved by the *shariah* boards of the institutions undertaking their arrangement, but the *shariah* scholars serving on the boards have not been involved in the structuring of the financial instruments.

The first concern is over pricing, as although with *mudaraba sukuk* the returns are profit shares and with *ijara sukuk* they are rents, the benchmarks used, whether LIBOR or SAIBOR, are interest rate proxies. These are used so that the returns to *sukuk* investors are competitive with those on comparable conventional bonds and bills, but this is driven by market considerations and not by *shariah*. The second concern is that the returns to Islamic investors are supposed to be justified by risk-sharing, the notion of taking on each other's burden. With *sukuk,* however, the main risk for the investors is of default, and in such circumstances the investors can be expected to instigate legal proceedings against the issuer to try to reclaim as much of their investment as possible. Most *sukuk* are rated, and the rating reflects the probability of default risk, which in turn is reflected in the pricing. For sovereign *sukuk,* for example, Pakistan has to pay a higher return than Qatar or Malaysia, reflecting country risk perceptions, yet it is the government of Pakistan that can least afford the debt servicing.

Sheikh Taqi Usmani, a leading *shariah* scholar who specializes in Islamic finance, alleged in a speech in November 2007 that most *sukuk* were not *shariah*-compliant, as the investors expected to get the nominal value of their capital returned on maturity, avoiding exposure to market risk. In the case of *mudaraba* and *musharaka sukuk,* he believed that the amount the investor gets returned on maturity should reflect the terminal market value of the asset backing the *sukuk* and not simply its initial nominal value. The asset used as backing for the *sukuk* should have real financial significance and not simply be used as a legal proxy to justify *sukuk* trading.

Unlike equity investors, however, *sukuk* investors do not want market exposure. There may be justifiable reasons for this. Firstly, investors may want a balanced portfolio and may be willing to risk a proportion of their capital for a potentially higher return, but they may not be willing to take excessive risk. Furthermore, Islamic *takaful* insurance operators hold significant amounts of *sukuk* in their asset portfolios in the same way as conventional insurance companies hold bonds and notes. If their capital diminished, they would be unable to meet the claims of their members. If asset values are at risk this may also distort the type of *sukuk* which can be offered. The first Saudi Arabian *sukuk* was by HANCO, a car rental company, with the vehicles used as the underlying asset. If the original vehicles had been revalued on maturity after three years, they would have been worth less, and the investors would have lost some of their capital. Where real estate is used investors may gain, but those wanting exposure to the real estate market will invest directly, rather than through *sukuk*.

THE GLOBALIZATION OF *SUKUK*

Despite controversies over the structuring and characteristics of *sukuk*, they have become an established asset class of interest to conventional as well as Islamic financial institutions. In the United Kingdom, HM Treasury published a consultation document on *sukuk* in November 2007 declaring that such an issuance could "deliver greater opportunities to British Muslims—and also entrench London as a leading centre for Islamic finance".[2] Following responses to the consultation, another document was published in June 2008 indicating that the Treasury was planning a series of *sukuk* bills issues, probably starting in 2009, which would provide a benchmark against which sterling corporate *sukuk* could be priced.

There have been *sukuk* issues already in other Western countries, with the German state of Saxony–Anhalt issuing a Euro-denominated *ijara sukuk* in July 2004 and the East Cameron Gas Company issuing a *sukuk* in the United States in June 2006. The major potential is in the Islamic world however, and it is notable that in the most populous Muslim country, Indonesia, interest in *sukuk* is increasing, with Metrodata Electronics issuing an *ijara sukuk* in April 2008 to fund its expansion in telecommunications. Qatar has been particularly active in *sukuk* issuances, with major sovereign *sukuk* issued in September 2003 and January 2008, and twelve corporate *sukuk*, including by leading Doha-based real estate and transportation companies. In the years ahead the Qatar Financial Centre may well become a major center for *sukuk* trading, contributing to the country's diversification into financial services.

The temporary pause in dollar-denominated *sukuk* issuance provides an opportunity for reviewing *sukuk* structures, and in this context the debate that followed Sheikh Taqi Usmani's remarks is timely. There can be no doubt that once the market in conventional asset-backed securities revives internationally, dollar-denominated *sukuk* issuance will revive. The weakness over the 2000–07 period, however, was that although there was much new *sukuk* issuance, trading was limited, apart from in Kuala Lumpur in ringgit-denominated

"An analysis of commercial terms and legal structures shows that *sukuk* performance may not be governed by asset performance alone." HM Treasury, Consultation on the Legislative Framework for the Regulation of Alternative Finance Investment Bonds (*Sukuk*), London, 2008, p. 10

sukuk. The investment banks and regulators of financial centers in the Gulf, and indeed London, will have to consider how more active trading can be facilitated, as until this occurs *sukuk* will not fulfill their potential in providing long-term financing while maintaining investor liquidity.

►► MORE INFO

Books:

Nathif, Adam, and Thomas Abdulkader. *Islamic Bonds: Your Guide to Issuing, Structuring and Investing in* Sukuk. London: Euromoney Books, 2004.

Obaidullah, Mohammed. "Securitization in Islam." In *Handbook of Islamic Banking*, M. Kabir Hassan and Mervyn K. Lewis (eds). Cheltenham, UK: Edward Elgar, 2007, pp. 191–199.

Articles:

Cox, Stella. "The role of *sukuk* in managing liquidity issues." *New Horizon: Global Perspective on Islamic Banking and Insurance* 163 (January–March 2007): 38–39. Online at: www.newhorizon-islamicbanking.com/index.cfm?action=view&id=10430§ion=features

Jabeen, Zohra. "*Sukuk* as an asset securitisation instrument and its relevance for banks." *Review of Islamic Economics* 12:1 (2008): 57–72.

Samsudin, Anna Maria. "*Sukuk* strikes the right chord." *Islamic Finance Asia* (August/September 2008): 16–24. Online at: www.islamicfinanceasia.com (click on Archives).

Wilson, Rodney. "Innovation in the structuring of Islamic *sukuk* securities." *Humanomics: The International Journal of Systems and Ethics* 24:3 (2008): 170–181.

Report:

Islamic Financial Services Board. "Exposure draft on capital adequacy requirements for *sukuk* securitisations and real estate." Online at: www.ifsb.org/docs/ed_sukuk_english.pdf

Website:

Accounting and Auditing Organization for Islamic Financial Institutions: www.aaoifi.com

NOTES

1 Accounting and Auditing Organization for Islamic Financial Institutions. *Shariah Board Statement*. Bahrain (February 13 and 14, 2008), p. 1. www.aaoifi.com/sharia-board.html

2 HM Treasury. *Government Sterling Sukuk Issuance: A Consultation*. London, November 2007, p. 3. Online at: www.hm-treasury.gov.uk/5703.htm

"Although the current level of *sukuk* issuance remains a fraction of the global issuance of conventional bonds and ABS, the market for *sukuk* has been growing rapidly despite the global financial crisis." IMF Policy Discussion Paper, Number 3, Washington, 2008, p. 4

     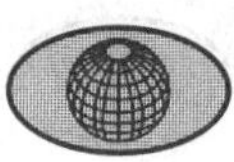   

Viewpoint: Leigh Skene

A One-in-Fifty-Year Event

INTRODUCTION

Leigh Skene is a Canadian who has been involved in financial markets ever since he first purchased equities when he was a teenager. He became involved in debt analysis and trading at the Sun Life Assurance Company of Canada. He moved to the sell side and became Head of Fixed Income Trading at inves tm ent bank Burns, Fry and Company (now BMO Nesbitt Burns), then became Chief Economist. In 1980, he left Burns Fry and established himself as an independent economic consultant specializing in financial markets and wrote articles for several publications. He has been a director of Lombard Street Associates since 2004, and wrote three key reports in 2007; The ABC of 21st Century Risk; The Sub-prime Mortgage Fiasco—The Start of Something Big; and Credit and Credibility which pointed out the dangers of the new financial system, warned of the impending credit crunch and forecast the ensuing financial turmoil. He has published four books on money and credit and his fifth, a treatise on the long term outlook, is scheduled for publication this autumn.

People are comparing today's problems to the 1930s, but they're considerably smaller. The Great Depression was the biggest economic event in US history. Ameritrust has calculated the deviation from trend for the American economy since 1790. The Great Depression held the economy below trend for 10¾ consecutive years with a maximum deviation of 51% from trend. There is no danger of experiencing anything like the Great Depression in the United States or in Europe in the foreseeable future because the monetary system is different.

The modern fiat money system, with flexible exchange rates, guarantees the destruction of debt and money that occurred in the 1930s will not occur in the next few years, so the economic repercussions of the credit difficulties will be far less than in the 1930s. Nevertheless, an extended period of weakness will occur—largely because economies are structurally weak. For example, US GDP growth has averaged 3.4% growth a year since 1947, but only 2.3% so far this century because recoveries became weaker. The fastest rate of growth in the recovery now ending was barely above average, even though a falling savings rate greatly enhanced growth (see Figure 1).

The reasons for slower growth were:

1 The aging population is slowing the growth rate of the labor force and increasing the burden of taxes, especially for pensions.
2 Capital productivity has fallen sharply due to a gross misallocation of capital (see Figure 2).

These two factors plus the long overdue rise of savings rates to more normal levels will hinder growth for a long time.

THE THREE STAGES OF THE CREDIT CYCLE

Debt is the main counterpart to money. Debt and money grew at about the same rate until the early 1980s, when the biggest disintermediation of lending in history started (see Figure 3). Efficient capital allocation would have returned debt to its historical relationship to money after the bank correction had been completed, and debt would be about 35% to 50% lower than it is today. Disintermediation misallocated capital into a huge credit bubble because fiat money has bestowed unlimited ability to create credit. However, creditworthiness falls if debt outstanding rises faster than nominal GDP. In the 1970s, the American economist Hyman Minsky described the credit cycle created by debt rising faster than GDP.

In the first stage of the credit cycle,

Figure 1. Year-on-year US GDP growth

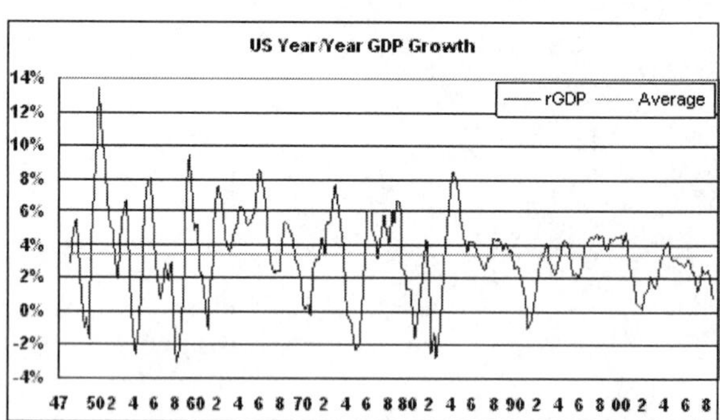

Figure 2. US capital productivity

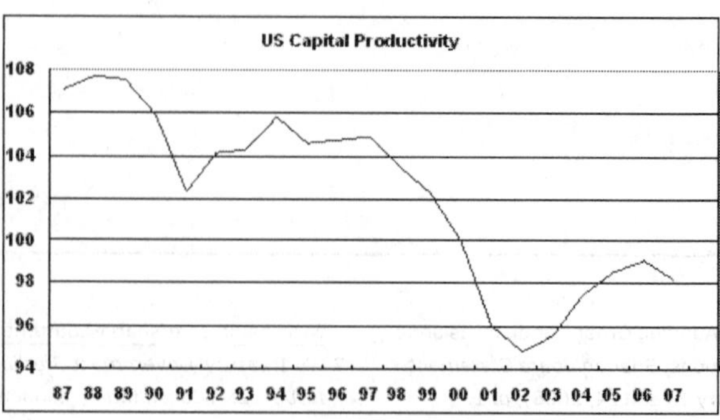

"The way a lot of advertising works is negative, in an if you have this you'll be younger, better, perfect sort of way. That's not my message." Jeanine Lobell

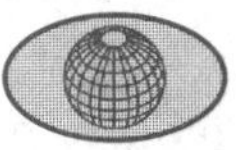

Figure 3. US debt and broad money vs GDP

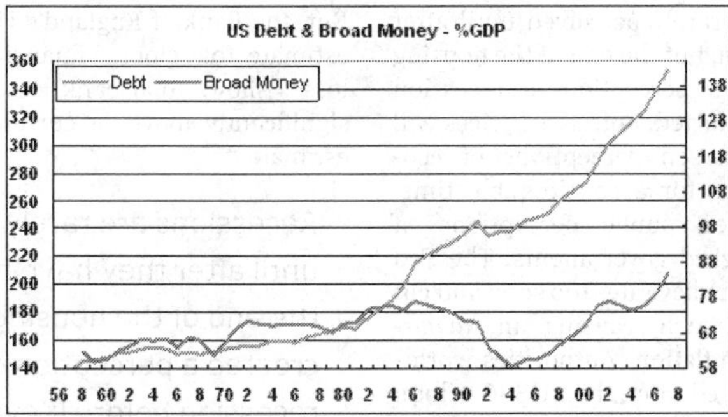

most borrowers can meet both interest and principal repayments from cash flow. Borrowers intend to repay their debts in full, so moral hazard and the default rate are inconsequential. The first stage of the current credit cycle lasted from the end of the depression until over borrowing began in the 1960s, which ultimately caused the credit crunch in the early 1980s. The second stage began in the aftermath of that credit crunch.

In the second stage of the credit cycle, most borrowers can service only interest payments from cash flow. They assume liquid capital markets will let them refinance the principal amount of their debts. Assuming debt will never be reduced turns debt into cheap equity, so borrowers worry only about how much more they can borrow, never about their ability to repay existing debts. Thus, a drop in liquidity causes an explosion of defaults, as occurred in 2001–2002. Defaults panic officialdom into excessive ease and bailouts, which creates moral hazard. Lenders learn they can make ever more risky loans that pay handsomely when investments turn out well, and get bailed out of the losses if they turn out badly. Moral hazard caused the third stage.

In the third stage of the credit cycle, many borrowers can service neither interest nor principal payments from cash flows. The prices of the assets they invested in must rise to enable them to keep refinancing their debts. Negative amortization mortgages and covenant-light private equity buyouts are textbook examples. The need for rising asset prices to service debts is a pyramid scheme, making the third stage a bubble that must deflate. Rising house prices supported the pyramid debt in the third stage. The subprime mortgage fiasco began soon after house prices began to fall, exposing the thorough trashing of household balance sheets. Also, private equity had over levered a meaningful part of corporate net worth.

THE END OF THE CREDIT CYCLE MEANS TODAY'S CREDIT PROBLEMS ARE STRUCTURAL—NOT CYCLICAL

Household net worth is 70% of the total and so is the foundation of the credit structure. It began falling in the second quarter of 2007, which immediately initiated big problems in financial markets. The spread between the three-month Eurodollar rate and the three-month Treasury bill rate is the most reliable single indicator of the health of credit markets. This spread soared to a record high in October, in spite of US$6 trillion of government bailouts, indicating the current credit problems are the most serious since the 1930s (see Figure 4).

Also, bank finances are deteriorating rapidly. The Texas ratio successfully identified banks likely to fail in the oil bust in Texas in the 1980s by comparing the ratio of bad loans to their ability to absorb bad loans. Banks are likely to fail if the ratio exceeds 100%. In the second quarter of 2008, the Texas ratio for US commercial banks was 26%, more than double the figure two years previously (see Figure 5).

The irresponsibility of lending and borrowing in the third stage of the credit cycle ended an expansion in leverage that had lasted for over 60 years. Lender liquidity went from lavish to almost nonexistent, lending from cautious to irresponsible, and leverage from almost nonexistent to grotesquely excessive. The losses from the irresponsible lending and excessive leverage, plus low growth, will ultimately return us to the first stage of the next credit cycle. The current credit crunch is a 1-in-50-year event because credit cycles tend to last at least 50 years.

The big disintermediation weakened the credit structure by:

1 Dubious to fraudulent lending practices;

Figure 4. Three-month Eurodollars minus three-month US Treasury bills

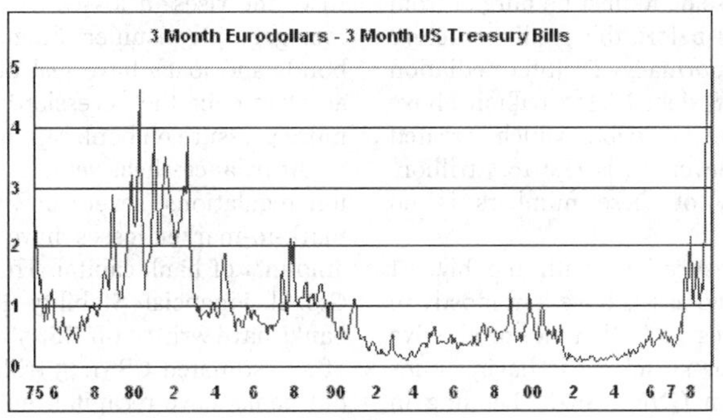

Figure 5. Texas ratio for US commercial banks

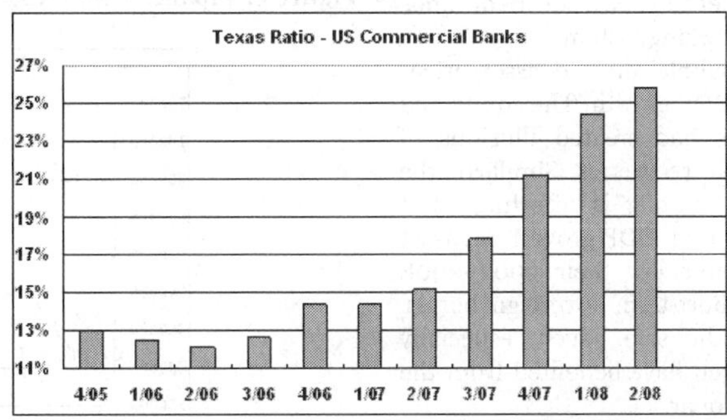

"Those who prefer their English sloppy have only themselves to thank if the advertisement writer uses his mastery of vocabulary and syntax to mislead their weak minds." Dorothy L. Sayers

     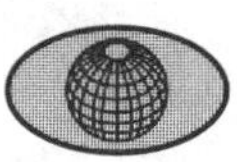   

2 Creating opaque securities of unknown value;

3 Grossly excessive leverage.

Lending standards are being tightened, but that's the only abuse that is being addressed so far. Opaque securities of unknown value abound and their embedded losses must be identified and excised before credit conditions can return to normal. Governments and Wall Street don't want to know, so this process hasn't started yet. Also, statements about massive deleveraging are somewhat misleading.

The acceleration of gearing up from 2000 to the second quarter of 2007 created the illusion of unlimited liquidity. The deceleration of gearing up thereafter reduced the excess liquidity in a financial system accustomed to excess liquidity always rising. This created the illusion that liquidity had suddenly vanished. It hasn't. Short-term sovereign yields have been far below policy rates for some time, showing excess liquidity, not lack of liquidity. Also, banks are still lending to creditworthy borrowers. The trouble is creditworthy borrowers are hard to find.

Leverage dropped to zero in the second quarter of 2008. The painful process of gearing down probably started in the third quarter, even though the authorities are doing everything they can to prevent it. Gearing down is not a problem; it is the solution. Excess debt must be purged from balance sheets before the credit structure can function normally. Disintermediation has created US debt US$17 trillion above optimal. Financial debt, which created the excessive leverage, is US$16.5 trillion. The similarity of these numbers is no coincidence.

Financial institutions with the biggest portfolios of bad assets have lent mostly to fund derivatives and other nonproductive purposes. Their shrinkage is having minimal impact on GDP growth. Lending in the interbank market is having an equally minimal impact. An individual bank can obtain funding in this market, but the interbank market can't be a source of funds for the whole banking system.

The credit bubble affected asset prices far more than GDP growth. The equity and housing booms had created illusions of strength in weak recoveries. Similarly, the credit bubble bursting is affecting asset prices far more than GDP growth. All asset classes are well below their 2007–2008 highs except short-term sovereign bonds. They've been the safe haven, especially Treasuries, which have benefited from the rise in the US dollar.

THE PROBLEM IS SOLVENCY, NOT LIQUIDITY

Recessions are rarely perceived until after they have begun, but the end of the housing boom created a perception of recession before it even started. Soft asset prices will continue to worsen perceptions of economic weakness for a considerable time. The exaggerated public perceptions of weakness panicked governments. The Fed began slashing policy rates too soon and cut them far too much, causing an unwarranted rise in inflation. Authorities worldwide have pledged more than US$6 trillion to combat the credit crunch—most of it to increase liquidity. However, there's no liquidity problem, so most of the increase was used to acquire the sovereign bonds that funded the liquidity. This merry-go-round drove sovereign yields far too low, but did little to free up other financial markets.

The problem is solvency. Defaults and credit spreads usually peak a year or two after the recession ends. However, balance sheets have been weakened so badly that most credit spreads have risen to the widest levels since the Great Depression before the recession. The wide spreads probably herald record high default rates. The Alt A, jumbo, and prime mortgage problems are just starting. They constitute the vast majority of residential mortgages and their total losses will exceed subprime losses. Also, the rises in losses from commercial mortgages, consumer finance, and junk bonds and loans have just begun and will accelerate in the recession, putting even more pressure on bank capital.

Off-balance-sheet vehicles to avoid capital regulations, severe downgrading, and mark-to-market losses have drained vast amounts of bank capital. The World Bank Global Financial Stability Report shows banks have written off US$585 billion, 40% of an estimated US$1.45 trillion total loss, but banks have recapitalized only US$439 billion of the write offs. More than US$1 trillion of bank losses must be recapitalized—even if total losses don't rise further. But, the Bank of England's US$2.8 trillion estimate of global financial institution losses shows total bank losses should rise significantly above the current World Bank estimate.

> "Recessions are rarely perceived until after they have begun, but the end of the housing boom created a perception of recession before it even started."

Governments have finally begun to address the need for bank recapitalization more than a year after it became obvious solvency was a major factor in the credit crunch. Bank capital could become a financial black hole and the recapitalizations will decimate the equity of current shareholders in weak banks.

The end of the credit cycle is deflationary in spite of more than US$6 trillion in government bailouts. Global equity market losses have been estimated at US$16 trillion, housing losses at about half that, and untold more trillions have been lost in structured finance and derivatives. Japan has shown a rising money supply doesn't prevent deflation (see Figure 6). A mild deflation, as occurred in Japan, is likely in the US and Europe.

The bailing out of financial institutions and deposit guarantees are multiplying the direct and contingent liabilities of many nations. Government debt to GDP ratios are likely to double and some smaller nations lack the resources required to honor the liabilities they've assumed. Iceland has already reneged on its guarantees, and others may follow. Many sovereign credits will be downgraded and rising interest costs will transfer wealth out of taxpayer pockets, impeding growth in GDP and living standards for many years.

Figure 6. Japanese money supply: M2

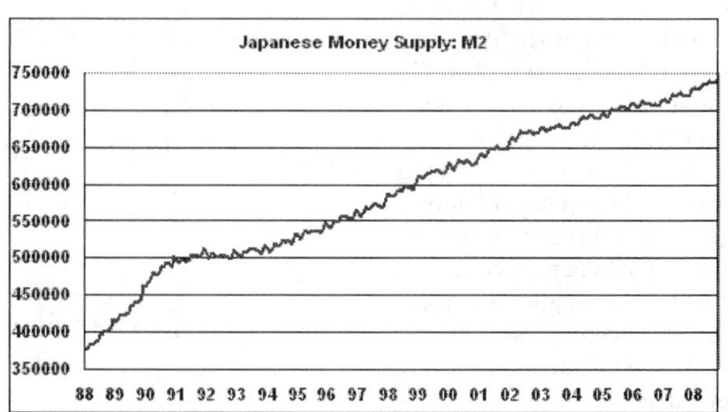

"The reality remains that the power to persuade has to be demonstrated in old-fashioned conventional terms."
Michael Perry

  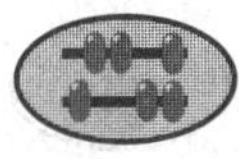   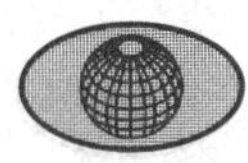   

INVESTMENT AND ECONOMIC CONSEQUENCES

Most credit spreads have increased to the widest levels since the Great Depression even though creditworthy borrowers have been able to borrow throughout and the rest shouldn't borrow. Bargains abound in investment-grade corporate bonds. Junk bonds and loans are a different kettle of fish. The Finra junk bond average yields about 20%. This high cost has closed financial markets to below-investment-grade companies as few would buy equity in a company with a 20% cost of borrowing. Distressed debt gives a better rate of return than equity in all but the most advantageous circumstances. Slow growth and the threat of deflation don't create the most advantageous circumstances for distressed debt, or equities.

Shareholder returns come from reported earnings, not the higher operating earnings numbers analysts like to use, and executive stock options often further reduce shareholder returns. Reported earnings for the S&P 500 for the last four quarters total US$50.52 for a current price–earnings ratio of 20 times, well above the long-term average. Earnings will fall for several quarters, so price–earnings ratios will rise unless prices fall further. It will take some time for earnings to return to current levels, so equities are expensive. At first glance the S&P 500 appears expensive relative to European indexes, but adjusting for differing accounting methods, industry compositions and earnings outlooks would make price–earnings ratios similar.

Housing is also expensive. Professor Robert Shiller calculated an index of real prices for existing housing from 1890 to 2006. A house costing 100 in 1890 reached a 25% premium only twice up to 2000, in 1894 and 1989. However, the premium was 99% in 2006, double "fair value." Real house prices must fall by 50% from that peak to return to "fair value." They have fallen 27% so far, so the correction may be about half over, but overshoot is likely. Housing in the United Kingdom, Ireland, and Spain is similarly expensive.

This isn't a cyclical adjustment; it's a period of structural change. Credit conditions won't return to normal until the following five truths have been learned.

1 **Deleverage and falling asset prices are two sides of the same coin and so offset each other,** making balance sheet repair difficult. Only increased saving and debt write-offs can repair balance sheets without inflation. Weak economies make saving difficult, so write-offs will do the heavy lifting and credit problems will last a long time.
2 **The banking system is not fit for purpose**. IBM has found a big difference between what banks think their customers want and what the customers actually want. Bank regulation is high on the agenda, but most regulations are counter-productive. Canada has strong banks because it regulates bank leverage, something few other nations have even considered. Hopefully, others will follow Canada's lead.
3 **Aging populations exposed the pyramid-scheme nature of the welfare state.** The welfare state needs labor forces to expand fast enough to be able to produce the output needed to satisfy their needs, plus those of the growing number of beneficiaries. Recent labor-force growth hasn't been fast enough to do this, so taxes are rising and benefits falling. As a result, the rise in living standards has reversed for some people.
4 **Bailouts are aggravating the fall in living standards.** The transfer of wealth from taxpayers due to the big rises in government interest costs from the bailouts and guarantees will reverse the rise in living standards for most people. The days of big government are numbered.
5 **Last and most important,** the attitudes of the borrow-and-spend nations must be converted to save-and-invest. Only saving and investment can create growth. America and Europe are condemned to stagnation until the majority put saving and investment at the top of their list of priorities.

➧ MORE INFO

Articles:

Broda, Christian, and David Weinstein. "How bad is deflation in Japan?" *Vox* (October 22, 2007). Online at: www.voxeu.org/index.php?q=node/624

Klingebiel, Daniela, and Luc Laeven. "Managing the real and fiscal costs of banking crises." World Bank Discussion Paper #428, 2002.

Minsky, Hyman P. "The financial instability thesis." Jerome Levy Institute Working Paper #74, May 1992.

Rothbard, Murray N. "Deflation, free or compulsory." The Free Market, Ludwig von Mises Institute, April 1991.

Greene, Richard J. "Fiat money systems." *Gold Eagle* (March 21, 2004). Online at: www.gold-eagle.com/editorials_04/greene032104.html

See Also:

★ Booms, Busts, and How to Navigate Troubled Waters (pp. 286–288)

The Black Swan: The Impact of the Highly Improbable (p. 1227)

"If you pretest your product with consumers and pretest your advertising, you will do well in the marketplace."
David Ogilvy

     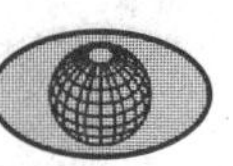   

Islamic Insurance Markets and the Structure of *Takaful* by Suzanne White

EXECUTIVE SUMMARY

- Islamic scholars object to the concept of conventional insurance due to three key elements: *riba* (usury), *gharar* (uncertainty), and *maysir* (gambling).
- Islamic insurance or *takaful* operators have therefore redesigned their management and accounting practices to comply with *shariah* law.
- *Takaful*, and conventional or traditional insurance policy wordings, both operate in a similar way, with the protection that is provided to the client being exactly the same.
- The differences between Islamic and conventional insurance lie in the ownership and financing of the company, in the management and accounting systems, and in the entities in which the premiums are invested.
- Islamic insurance is a very close concept to that of "mutual insurers" in the West and, in particular, to those we call "ethical" insurers.

INTRODUCTION

Insurance plays a vital role in supporting both national and international economic development and growth. Islamic countries are no exception. The main issue for insurers in the Islamic world is that many Islamic scholars view conventional insurance as prohibited by Islam.

Muslim scholars are not against the concept of risk mitigation, risk sharing, or risk management, including risk financing, *per se*. In fact, they support the compensation of victims of misfortune. However, many scholars consider some aspects of conventional insurance contracts as being prohibited from a *shariah* (Islamic law) point of view. *Shariah* covers all aspects of a Muslim's life, not just worship.

PROHIBITED FACTORS OF INSURANCE

Several *fatawa* (the plural of *fatwa*, meaning an answer to a question related to an issue of *shariah*) have been issued by eminent Muslim scholars on the subject of insurance. The objections tend to relate to the insurance contract itself or to insurance market practice in general.

Objections relating to the insurance contract itself are those of *riba* (usury), *gharar* (uncertainty), and *maysir* (gambling). The other objections relating to market practice are usually concerned with two issues: The first is that insurance companies' investment policies are generally interest-bearing (which is not acceptable in Islam), and the second issue is the fact that life assurance is considered to breach Islamic inheritance rules by distributing the sum assured among beneficiaries. These objections relating to market practice can be easily overcome by the insurer making changes to their company policy, as they do not affect the insurance contract itself.

The objections related to the contract itself, however, require the restructuring of insurance contracts to be in line with *shariah*.

Riba (Usury)

Under a conventional insurance contract, the insured pays the insurance company a premium (either as a lump sum in general insurance or as installments in life insurance), in exchange for financial compensation at the time of a claim, subject to the happening of an insured occurrence or event. Claims are generally larger amounts than the premium paid. Islamic law objects to this payment on the grounds that a small amount of money (premium) is being exchanged for a larger amount of money (claim). Scholars consider this an unjustified increase of money, and therefore *riba*. Islamic insurers therefore have to structure their operations and investments to avoid *riba*.

Gharar (Uncertainty)

Gharar can be defined as uncertainty or ambiguity. Islamic law seeks to avoid ambiguity in contracts, in order to prevent disputes and conflict between parties. This is a general Islamic principle that must be applied to all contracts, including insurance.

In the case of conventional insurance, neither the insurer nor the insured knows the outcome of the contract (i.e., whether a loss will occur or not). The insurer is entitled to get the premium in all cases, whereas the insured may not receive a claim because the payment of claims depends on the probability of loss occurrence (which is a random variable). Other uncertain elements are as to when the claim may be paid and how much the insured may receive.

In life assurance contracts, *gharar* can be seen to exist even in the premium, as the insured party does not know how much he will pay to the insurance company each year, or for how many years. The insured may know the monthly or yearly premium, but he does not know how much he will pay to the insurer before he dies. In general insurance (nonlife insurance), the premium is pre-agreed, but there is *gharar* in the claim amount. Therefore *gharar* exists in all insurance contracts, either in premiums or in claims. In Islamic insurance, scholars agree that engaging in *takaful* transactions, with a donation element as part of their contribution, offsets *gharar*.

Maysir (Gambling)

Some arguments against conventional insurance are based on the grounds that insurance contracts are basically gambling contracts. Islam rejects any contract where financial gain comes from chance or speculation. Insurance, however, needs to comply with the principle of insurable interest. This principle requires a financial and legal relationship between the insured and the subject matter of insurance. The insured is only entitled to get a claim if he proves his insurable interest, and this feature therefore nullifies the notion that insurance is a gamble.

The other difference between gambling and insurance is that the first is a speculative risk (which is uninsurable), while the latter consists of pure risk only (i.e., the insured should not make a gain but should be put back into the same financial position as before the loss occurred).

THE CONCEPT OF ISLAMIC INSURANCE

The first Islamic insurance company was set up in Sudan in 1979. Today there are many Islamic insurance operators in Muslim as well as non-Muslim countries. The main concept of Islamic insurance is that it is an alternative to conventional insurance, with characteristics and features that comply with *shariah* requirements. This is done by eliminating the objections against conventional insurance. "The term *takaful* is an infinitive noun which is derived from the Arabic root verb *kafal*' or *kafala*, meaning to guarantee or bear responsibility for." (Kassar, 2008, p. 26).

The main features of Islamic insurance are:

"Good copy can't be written with tongue in cheek, written just for a living. You've got to believe in the product."
David Ogilvy

  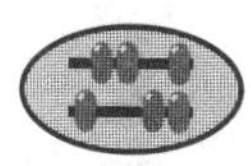   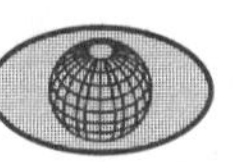   

- cooperative risk sharing by using charitable donations to eliminate *gharar* and *riba*;
- clear financial segregation between the participant (insured) and the operator (insurance company);
- *shariah*-compliant underwriting policies and investment strategies.

Cooperative Risk Sharing

The characteristics of a cooperative include self-responsibility, democracy, equality, equity, solidarity, honesty, openness, social responsibility, and caring for others. While mutuality or cooperative risk sharing is at the core of Islamic insurance, it cannot alone create an Islamic insurance operation. Islamic insurance is based on more than one contractual relationship: The first relationship is a mutual insurance contract between policyholders (contributors) and each other. This is similar to a pure mutual insurance relationship, taking into consideration the concept of donation *(tabarru)* instead of premiums and an ethical framework of Islamic transactions. The main features behind cooperative insurance are:

- Policyholders pay premiums to a cooperative fund with the intention of it being a donation to those who will suffer losses (*tabarru*).
- Policyholders are entitled to receive any surplus resulting from the operation of the cooperative insurance fund.
- Policyholders are liable to make up for any deficits that result from the operation of the cooperative insurance fund.
- The amount of contribution (premium) differs from one participant to another, based on the degree of risk in general insurances and actuarial principles in life assurance.
- There is no unified system to operate the treatment of surplus and deficit. There is therefore more than one model accepted by *shariah* scholars being used in practice.

Clear Segregation Between Participant and Operator

In conventional insurance, the insurance company is a profit-making organization that aims to maximize profit by accepting the financial burden of others' losses. The insurance company is owned by shareholders who are entitled to receive any profit and are responsible for financing any deficit. Under Islamic insurance, the system is that the insurance company's role is restricted to managing the portfolio and investing the insurance contributions for and on behalf of the participants. The relationship between the participants and the insurance company (as an operator, not as an insurer) is different. There are four different models in operation: The *mudarabh* model, the *wakalah* model, the hybrid *mudarabh–wakalah* model, and the pure cooperative model (non-profit). "The overarching goal of Takaful is brotherhood, solidarity, protection and mutual cooperation between members" (Kassar, 2008, p. 66).

Shariah-Compliant Policies and Strategies

Ethical insurers invest money in a responsible way in industries that are ethically sound and do not harm the environment or people. Islamic insurance is similar, except that the ethical considerations are extended to those which do not contravene the religion of Islam and are monitored by a *shariah* board, which is part of the company structure. In particular, the investment and underwriting policies need to be free of any involvement with the prohibited activities of gambling, alcohol, pork, armaments, tobacco, and interest-bearing activities, loans, and securities.

CONCLUSION

Islamic insurance has grown out of the need of many stakeholders in the Islamic world to have protection for assets and liabilities. This protection was required in a similar fashion to that provided by conventional insurance, which, for a variety of reasons, was often viewed as prohibited in Islam. *Takaful* or Islamic insurers have been structured in such a way that Islamic scholars are satisfied that the main objections to insurance, which are *riba*, *gharar*, and *maysir*, have been addressed.

CASE STUDY

American Insurance Group (AIG)

The potential for *takaful* business is evidenced by the fact that almost all new insurance license applications in the Middle Eastern region are for *takaful* companies. Even many Western insurers, such as American Insurance Group (AIG), have realized the potential of *takaful* and have set up their own *takaful* operations. AIG *Takaful*, known as *Enaya*, which means "care," was established in 2006 in Bahrain with a $15 million paid-up capital and licensed by the Central Bank of Bahrain (CBB). *Enaya's* plan was to start business in the Gulf region and then expand into the Far East and Europe.

►► MAKING IT HAPPEN

Islamic insurance is the fastest-growing area of insurance throughout the world, including in Western countries. In order to call a company Islamic, there are features that need to be built into the structure:

- cooperative risk sharing, by using charitable donations to eliminate *ghara*r and *riba;*
- clear financial segregation between the participant (insured) and the operator (insurance company);
- *shariah*-compliant underwriting policies and investment strategies.

►► MORE INFO

Books:

El-Gamal, M. *A Basic Guide to Contemporary Islamic Banking and Finance*. Houston, TX: Rice University, 2000.

Jaffer, S. (ed). *Islamic Insurance: Trends, Opportunities and the Future of Takaful.* London: Euromoney Books, 2007.

Kassar, Khaled, Omar Clark Fisher, *et al. What's Takaful—A Guide to Islamic Insurance.* Beirut: BISC Group, 2008.

Ma'sum Billah, M. *Islamic Insurance (Takaful)*. Kuala Lumpur: Ilmiah Publishers, 2003.

Websites:

Institute of Islamic Banking and Finance: www.islamic-banking.com
Islamic Banking and Finance: www.islamicbankingandfinance.com
Middle East Insurance Review: www.meinsurancereview.com

See Also:

Insurance (pp. 1520–1521)

"Every advertisement should be thought of as a contribution to the complex symbol which is the brand image."
David Ogilvy

     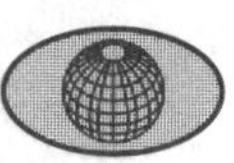   

Viewpoint: Bernhard Speyer and Norbert Walter

Fragment or Unite—But Decide! The Future of EU Financial Supervision

INTRODUCTION

Since mid-2001, Mr Speyer has been the head of the "Banking, Financial Markets and Regulation" depar tm ent of Deutsche Bank Research, the in-house think-tank of Deutsche Bank Group. In this role, he is responsible for briefing the senior management of Deutsche Bank on regulatory issues as well as on structural issues in the financial industry. In addition, he represents Deutsche Bank on these issues in discussions with clients, authorities, parliaments and the general public.

Mr Speyer had joined Deutsche Bank Research in January 1998 as a Senior Economist responsible for the coverage of issues relating to international monetary and trade policy, structural developments in banking and financial markets as well as regulation and supervision. Current areas of special interest include the structure of financial supervision in the European Union, EU financial market integration, and the governance of the international financial system.

Before joining Deutsche Bank Research, Speyer was a lecturer at the Economics Department of Freie Universität Berlin, where he taught international monetary policy and trade policy from 1993–1997. A trained banker, he studied economics at the University of Leicester, U.K. and the Freie Universität Berlin, where he graduated. Mr Speyer holds a doctorate in economics from the Freie Universität. He is an alumnus of the British-German Forum (2001), the Young Leaders' Programmes of the American Council on Germany (2005) and of the Chicago Council on Foreign Relations / Dräger Foundation (2000).

Norbert Walter is chief economist of Deutsche Bank. He was previously director at the renowned Kiel Institute for World Economics and was a John J. McCloy Distinguished Research Fellow at the American Institute for Contemporary German Studies at the Johns Hopkins University, in Washington, DC.

At Deutsche Bank, he is responsible for a globally integrated approach in economic research and is a member of the management of the Deutsche Bank think-tank, which covers a wide spectrum of issues, ranging from economic forecasting to country rating and sector analysis.

He is a member of the Committee of Wise Men on the Regulation of European Securities Markets ("Lamfalussy group"), and was also a valued adviser to Gerhard Schroder's government.

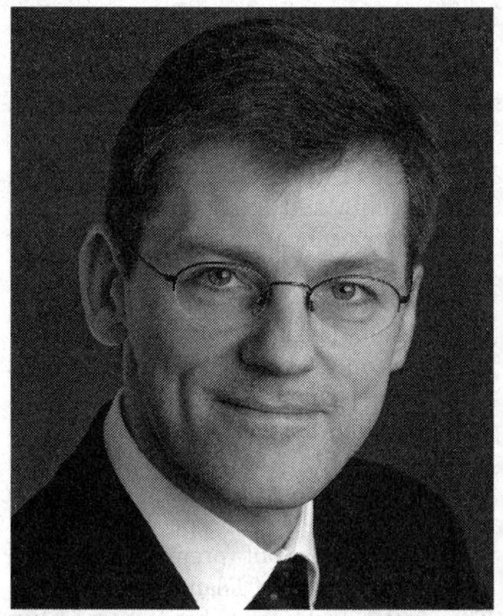

THE GEOPOLITICS OF THE FINANCIAL MARKETS

The grave financial crisis, which has engulfed the global economy since 2008, has raised many questions. Many of these are directed at the economic and financial aspects of the crisis, and clearly these must be at the foreground at this stage. But many commentators have also wondered what the financial crisis—which was originated in what traditionally was regarded as the most sophisticated financial market in the world—will ultimately mean for the geopolitics of financial markets and financial regulation in the future.

A KEY ROLE FOR THE EUROPEAN UNION?

Some protagonists—not least in France—have already boldly proclaimed that the European Union will emerge as a winner from this crisis. It is asserted that the "Anglo-Saxon model of capitalism" has failed and that the European Union will assume the lead in reshaping the global financial architecture.

This may yet happen. But, for now, reality speaks a different language. It is indeed correct that the agreement of, initially, eurozone members and, subsequently, all EU members on common principles and elements for the rescue packages for the banking industry represented a major breakthrough—an urgently needed one, one hastens to add.

But honesty also warrants observing the following:

- EU members only managed to present a common front after prior isolated action by individual member states had only aggravated the crisis; the Irish government's guarantee for deposits held at Irish banks (only!) was the most blatant example of this.
- While EU member states have agreed on common principles for their rescue packages, conditions differ markedly when it comes to detail. It is already obvious that this will lead to competitive distortions.
- More fundamentally, the failure of several cross-border financial groups has clearly demonstrated that current structures of financial supervision in Europe are neither conducive to effective supervision nor useful for effective crisis management—and they are not at all suitable for preserving the single market for financial services.

PAN-EUROPEAN STRUCTURE OR FRAGMENTED NATIONAL MARKETS?

Against this background, it is clear that the European Union is at the crossroads. Either the financial crisis will give an impetus for member states finally to build a pan-European structure for financial supervision, that is commensurate with the objective and the realities of a single market for financial services, or the achievements made towards building that single market will unravel and the European Union will relapse into a collection of fragmented national markets.

For many years, academics, international organizations, such as the IMF, and large parts of Europe's financial industry have pointed out the deficiencies of the current supervisory structure. To its credit, the European Parliament has been increasingly

  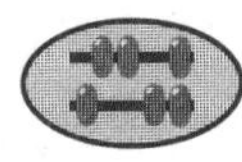   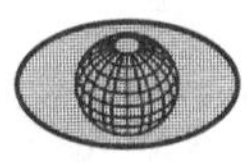   

responsive to these calls. In contrast, the European Commission (fearing political defeat at the hands of member states) and, a fortiori, national governments have turned a blind eye and a deaf ear to the obvious challenges. The progress made—whatever its form—has been haphazard and piecemeal.

True, with the establishment of the Lamfalussy process, a greater coherence of national supervisory processes has explicitly been formulated as a European policy objective. It is also true that, with the establishment of the so-called level 3 committees (CEBS, CESR and CEIOPS), supervisory cooperation has got fora, albeit ones that are firmly rooted in intergovernmental structures. However, the improvements that these new structures have brought are minimal and, as the financial crisis has demonstrated, utterly insufficient.

In response to the crisis, the EU Commission and member states have indicated that they will use the upcoming revision of the Capital Requirements Directive (CRD) to make some amendments to the supervisory structure. Essentially, the proposals aim at establishing supervisory colleges for all cross-border groups and strengthening the role of the consolidated supervisor. Specifically, the CRD revision would extend the existing rules of Art 129 concerning model approval to Pillar 2 issues and reporting duties.

Unfortunately, even those minor improvements appear to be too much for the majority of member states to digest. If the fate of the similarly designed Solvency II proposal, which just got stuck in the Council because of fervent opposition by many member states to a strengthening of the rights of the consolidate supervisor, is any guide, the analogous provisions in the CRD will probably never see the light of day.

BUILDING A SUPERVISORY ARCHITECTURE

This cannot continue. Europe must make up its mind. If it wants to stick to the political objective of an integrated market, it must be ready to build a supervisory architecture that is commensurate with it. This will require a two-step approach.

In a first and interim step, the revision of the CRD must be used to strengthen the role of the consolidated supervisors. This will require action on three fronts:

- First, supervisory colleges must become more than mere talking shops, which, today, they often are. They must produce a full operational integration of supervisory operations leading to greater financial stability, greater efficiency, better quality, and lower cost of financial supervision for firms. We need a single group-wide supervisory process based upon close cooperation and ideally joint work in colleges that function as teams cutting across the supervisory agencies involved.
- Second, this in turn requires strong process leadership and binding decision-making by the consolidated supervisor. The consolidating supervisor has to have the final say and must have the power to act. His or her decision must have legal effect for all EEA-based operations—which may require a review of the law and, if necessary, the creation a European administrative act, without which integrated supervision cannot be achieved.
- Third, the establishment of colleges and the strengthening of the respective roles of the consolidated supervisor may only aggravate the problem of inconsistent supervisory practices, as they exists today. Hence, in addition to stronger colleges and a leading role for the consolidated supervisor, we need centralized governance based on a stronger role for the Level 3 committees, which will ensure competitive neutrality and identical quality in the work of colleges. An effective annual review mechanism should be established; financial groups concerned should be allowed to give their input into these reviews.

In the second step, we need to build a truly pan-European system of financial supervision.

- A European System of Financial Supervision (ESFS), modeled on the ESCB, would comprise a new EU-level institution (a European FSA, or EFSA), which would supervise the systemically relevant financial institutions that operate on a pan-European basis and would be the final authority on interpretation and implementation of EU financial market rules in cases of conflicts between national regulators.
- Small and domestically oriented institutions would continue to be supervised by national authorities, acting on the basis of common rules and subject to the final say of EFSA.
- EFSA would collaborate closely with the ECB, which has an important role in the area of macroprudential supervision.

Only such a comprehensive, supranational approach is able to overcome the present deficiencies; only such a system is competitively neutral and institutionally stable. It should also be noted that, from a political point of view, an ESFS system, while difficult to agree upon in the first place, would have one significant advantage over the lead supervisor regime: smaller countries that would essentially lose direct supervisory authority under a consolidated supervisor regime would regain an influence via a pan-European structure. In a way, the ESFS would thus bear some noticeable resemblance to monetary policy, with small countries that had passively followed German monetary policy prior to EMU regaining a voice in setting monetary policy by means of pooling sovereignty.

THE INTERNATIONAL DIMENSION OF EU CHOICES

A final thought—finding an appropriate institutional structure for financial supervision in the European Union is not only about Europe. Europe's governments, not only, but especially those with grander ambitions, would also be well advised to recall that political procrastination on the issue damages the European Union in its international role too. The European Union's obvious inability to deal effectively with the failure of large cross-border financial institutions and the fall-out of a systemic crisis has already damaged the reputation of EU financial markets.

More generally, it seems that many decision-makers are still not sufficiently aware of the international dimension of our choices. The European Union, as the second largest financial market in the world, has a responsibility to make sure that its financial markets are stable and secure. Furthermore, in competition and in cooperation with third countries—be it the United States or upcoming new financial centers—the European Union must be able to argue convincingly that it has world-class regulation and supervision across the entire European Union. Otherwise, we will seriously undermine our negotiating position and trustworthiness as a partner in global affairs.

In building its new supervisory structure, Europe needs pragmatism and vision. Vision without pragmatism will not get us going, but pragmatism without vision lacks direction and will lead us to undesirable results. Hopefully, the High Level Group, appointed by President Barroso and chaired by Jacques de Larosière, will deliver the necessary blueprints for this. Even if it does, it is the European Union's legislators that must act, and the time to do so is now. Failure is not an option—we cannot afford even larger losses for our economies and societies.

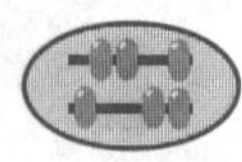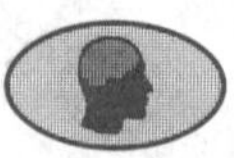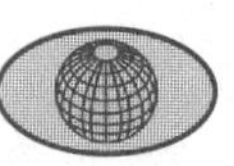

Viewpoint: Achim Steiner and Pavan Sukhdev

Why the World Needs a Green New Deal

INTRODUCTION

Achim Steiner has been executive director of the United Nations Environment Program (UNEP) since June 2006. He was director-general of the World Conservation Union from 2001 to 2006. From 1998 to 2001, he was secretary-general of the World Commission on Dams, based in South Africa, where he managed a multi-stakeholder program to develop a global policy process on dams and development. Steiner has a BA from the University of Oxford and an MA in international development and environment policy from the University of London. He has also studied at the German Development Institute in Berlin and the Harvard Business School. He serves on a number of international advisery boards, including the China Council for International Cooperation on Environment and Development.

Pavan Sukhdev is leading two programs for UNEP: The Economics of Ecosystems and Biodiversity program and the Green Economy Initiative. He also holds two board-level positions with Deutsche Bank subsidiaries, including chairman of its Mumbai-based Global Markets Centre, a captive offshoring facility that he helped establish in 2006. After joining Deutsche Bank in 1994, Sukhdev held capital markets, trading, and sales management roles in Singapore, London, and India. In the mid-1990s he played a major role in the development of India's currency and interest rate derivatives markets. His involvement with the environmental movement in India has included roles with the Green Indian States Trust and Conservation Action Trust.

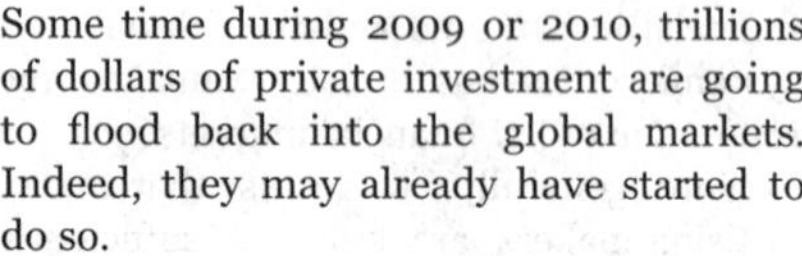

Some time during 2009 or 2010, trillions of dollars of private investment are going to flood back into the global markets. Indeed, they may already have started to do so.

The question is whether these investments are going to go into the old, brown economy of the 19th and 20th centuries or into the new, green one that will pave the way for the resource-efficient, innovative, and employment-orientated economy that the world so urgently needs in the 21st century.

The food, fuel, and financial crises of 2008 were, in large part, based on speculation. But they also provided a glimpse into a not-too-distant future of mounting instability, intensifying natural hazards, and natural resource scarcity. Unless the international community forges a more sustainable path, there's a risk that these sorts of crises will become commonplace.

The science is clear. According to the UN Environment Programme's (UNEP) latest Global Environment Outlook, over 60% of the earth's ecosystems—economically important assets from forests and grasslands to coral reefs and wetlands—are degraded or else being used unsustainably. Commercial fish stocks may run out in just a few decades, and fertile agricultural land is heading in the same direction.

Economists estimate that over US$2.5 trillion of goods and services are being lost annually as a result of deforestation. We are living off the Earth's capital; we need to learn to live off the interest.

Climate change, perhaps the biggest market failure of them all, will cost the world economy five to 20% of global GDP over the coming years if left unchecked.

Meanwhile 1.3 billion people around the world are either unemployed or underemployed, with 500 million young people estimated to join the workforce over the coming decade.

Is the solution to find all these people old-style manufacturing jobs, just so that everyone can own several motor cars or have a laptop computer in every room, which is the logical endgame of the current economic model? Or is there another way?

It is our contention that the industrial and services-led "growth at any cost" credo may have hit the buffers—both in terms of job creation and in terms of its ecological footprint on the world's increasingly scarce nature-based assets. GDP, as a measure of real wealth and as a bellwether of economic success or failure, may too have had its day in its current, narrow configuration.

OVERTURNING MYTHS

These are among the drivers for the Global Green New Deal and the inspiration for the new UNEP Green Economy Initiative, both of which aim to challenge the status quo and overturn some of the myths that so often stand in the way of real innovation and transformational change.

Take solar power, for example. Governments and experts still contend that this renewable energy will only be competitive with traditional energy sources in 20 or more years.

However, at the last UN climate convention meeting in Poznan, Poland, the heads of three key solar energy companies (First Solar of the United States, SunTech of China, and SolarCentury of the United Kingdom) declared they believe they can be fully competitive with traditional sources of energy within three to five years.

Steering the global economy onto a sustainable path and delivering a Global Green New Deal is not about sentiment. It's about hard economics, real choices, and a new compass for delivering genuine and lasting wealth creation.

It is not about cutting growth but about

finding a path to more intelligent and sustainable growth that captures the true value of human and nature-based capital, as opposed to focusing narrowly on financial and industrial capital.

It is also about rebalancing, refocusing, and redirecting investments and markets in ways that deal with multiple challenges and deliver multiple benefits in the both the northern and the southern hemispheres, while emphasizing "real" value rather than the speculation that all too often benefits the few over the many.

The pillars of new green deal initiative are:

- clean energy and clean technologies, including recycling
- rural energy, including renewables and sustainable biomass
- sustainable agriculture, including organic agriculture
- ecosystem infrastructure
- reduced emissions from deforestation and forest degradation (REDD)
- sustainable cities including planning, transportation, and green building.

We are not starting from ground zero here. In 2007, US$148 billion was invested in the renewable energy market, 60% more than the year before.

Much of this has been spurred by creative market mechanisms such as the feed-in tariffs which, in a few short years, have transformed Germany into one of the world's leading renewable economies. The country's renewable energy sector employ an estimated half a million people and have an annual turnover of €24 billion.

QUIET REVOLUTION

And it is not just in developed economies. In Bangladesh, Grameen Shakti, founded in 1996 by the microfinance pioneer and Nobel Peace Prize winner Professor Muhammad Yunus, has been leading a quiet renewables revolution. It has done this by selling and financing solar photovoltaic panels and greening the energy supply of over 8,000 Bangladeshi homes every month. Women who buy its panels become village electricity distributors, selling their solar electricity to neighboring homes at no more than the monthly cost of kerosene, their normal fuel.

Grameen Shakti's chief executive officer (CEO), Dipal Barua, has a vision of greening energy use, bringing the women of Bangladesh out of poverty and ill-health, and converting a million homes from health-damaging kerosene stoves to solar electricity by next year.

Meanwhile the current global market for environmental goods and services is worth over US$1.3 trillion, and this could easily double by 2020. Venture capital investments in the United States alone in energy efficiency and clean energy reached close to US$2.5 trillion in 2007. Investments in improved energy efficiency in buildings could generate between two and 3.5 million additional green jobs in Europe and the United States, and the potential is even higher in developing countries. India could create 900,000 jobs by 2025 in biomass gasification. Recycling and waste management employs an estimated 10 million in China and 500,000 in Brazil today, reflecting both the business opportunities and the rollercoaster costs of commodities. Several countries, including Costa Rica, Iceland, New Zealand, and Norway, have joined with cities and companies to pledge a zero emission future. They are part of UNEP's Climate Neutral Network, which is aimed at showcasing inspiring policies and actions, and creating "a common space" in which these ideas can be exchanged, tested, and mainstreamed elsewhere.

Under the carbon markets initiative, an estimated 4,200 projects, covering areas such as wind and solar power, are currently in the pipeline, with projects covering tidal and geothermal power in places like Indonesia and Korea now emerging. Mexico, for example, has registered or has in the pipeline close to 190 projects, including clean energy ones; it exported US$2.3 billion worth of solar panels last year.

By some estimates, boosting the fuel efficiency of the US car fleet to 35 mpg could generate savings for consumers of close to US$40 billion, which could be spent in the wider economy.

These transformations are happening as a result of "soft" market signals and, in many cases, with only minimal government intervention. Imagine if the incentives were to become harder and more imaginative?

Take forests, the world's great water storage, carbon-absorbing, soil conserving public "utilities." Just US$45 billion a year invested in the world's 100,000 National Parks and protected areas could not only secure services worth some US$5.2 trillion, but also boost employment and livelihoods for literally millions of indigenous and rural people. This could come from the public purse or via reduced emissions from deforestation and degradation funds or an expanded carbon market.

REAPING THE BENEFITS

Since launching the Green Economy Initiative in October 2008, we have been heartened by the response from so many economies and world leaders. Many of the multi-billion dollar stimulus packages currently being deployed around the world have elements of the Global Green New Deal built into them.

In Australia, efforts are being made to allocate AUS$4.7 billion out of the Canberra government's AUS$10.4 billion stimulus package for investment in green homes over four years. It is estimated that such improvements could reduce greenhouse emissions by 3.8 million tons a year, and that over 160,000 people will be employed in the auditing and installation services.

In the United States, it is estimated that US$100 billion will be spent over two years on improving the energy efficiency of buildings and cities, and that this will generate two million new jobs.

The financial mechanisms proposed in the US green stimulus package include:

1. US$50 billion tax credits to finance commercial and residential building retrofits and renewable energy systems;
2. US$46 billion direct government spending to support public building retrofits, the expansion of mass transit, freight rail, smart electrical grid systems, and new investments in renewable energy;
3. US$4 billion Federal loan guarantees to underwrite private credit extended to finance building retrofits and investments in renewable energy.

Over US$140 billion of China's US$570 billion stimulus package is for investments in renewable energy and energy efficiency, including switching the transportation of freight and passengers off the roads and onto the railways.

We are determined to bring forward throughout 2009 and deliver by 2010 a full, but not final package of smart market mechanisms and inspirational case studies that will act as a green economy toolkit for nations in both North and South.

The UN climate change convention meeting, to be held in Denmark from November 30 to December 11, 2009, is going to be a crucial moment and perhaps the litmus test as to whether governments have truly embarked on a new sustainability path for the 21st century.

If a deep and decisive deal can be reached, this could prove to be the biggest stimulus package yet, and one that should accelerate the transition to a low carbon society and give the global green economy real legs.

Faced with a full-scale economic and employment emergency over 70 years ago, Franklin D. Roosevelt did what presidents and prime ministers are elected to do: He

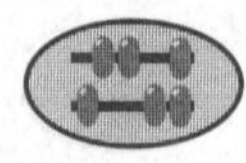

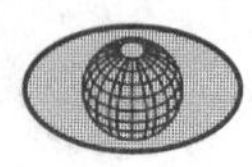

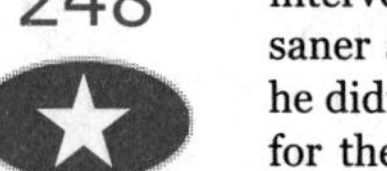

intervened to steer the markets onto a saner and more sensible path. In doing so he didn't kill the economy. He set the stage for the biggest growth the world has ever seen.

The transition to a green economy is not about some unreachable and whimsical Nirvana, but a way of powering the world out of its current malaise. A Global Green New Deal echoes the even greater challenges of today—it could also set the stage for unprecedented green growth for six billion rising to nine billion people without short-changing either them or the planet.

  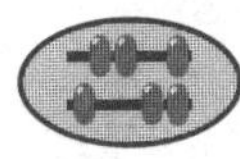   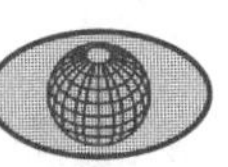   

Longevity, Reserves, and Annuities—A Difficult Circle to Square by Paul Belok

EXECUTIVE SUMMARY

Increasing longevity increases funding costs and adds risk to the business of providing annuities. This article looks at a range of pressures that determine annuity pricing and the impact of pricing on the annuities market. Topics covered are:

- The difficulty of estimating longevity accurately.
- The impact of longevity on annuities, and why falling annuity rates represent a major risk to those about to retire.
- The role of corporate bond pricing on annuities.
- Quantitative easing and annuities, and the way inflation affects bond prices.
- Stresses and strains in the annuities market.

INTRODUCTION

According to best estimates from the actuarial profession, longevity is currently increasing at the rate of 12 minutes an hour. This may be good news for most of us, but it is not particularly good news for the sponsors and trustees of pension schemes, since it increases the cost of funding pensions very substantially. Moreover, the most unsettling thing about longevity creep is that no one knows how far the gains in the average length of the human life span will go, or whether the rate of gain will speed up or slow down. What we can say with certainty is that the current rate of increase is beyond what the originators of annuity policies considered 20, or even 10, years ago.

That said, life insurers—and annuity providers by and large are life insurers—have a huge amount of data to draw on when forming their view about probable mortality figures. The UK entity called the Continuous Mortality Investigation Bureau analyzes data tracked by life insurance companies, and publishes standard mortality tables for use by the actuarial profession. These give the profession a very good handle on the mortality implications of particular lifestyles and employment. This information is then matched with data from consumer databases on what people resident in a particular postcode area tend to earn and eat, how much they exercise, gym membership, and so on.

However, what these figures track is how the past has affected things up to this point in time. What is much more difficult to track is what the impact on longevity will be of changes in diet and general health, as well as medical breakthroughs yet to happen. The life insurance companies pay a great deal of attention to research that looks at trends in the underlying causes of death, with the big killers being heart attacks, strokes, and cancers. They take input from the medical and pharmaceutical industries about leading-edge developments and their likely impact, to see if anything is known that could cause a step change in our mortality assumptions.

From the standpoint of an employer with a final salary scheme, the risks associated with longevity, which only ever seem to make such schemes more expensive, are one of many factors that are pushing companies to abandon them. The government, too, would love to be able to move away from guaranteeing a set level of benefit but, so far, moving the public sector away from final salary schemes to a more affordable money purchase style of arrangement has proved impossible for politicians to achieve.

THE IMPACT ON ANNUITIES

We have seen some interesting developments recently, with annuity providers cutting the return on index-linked annuities from around 6% to 4%, a cut of 33%. This is an enormous amount for potential pensioners to lose from their pension, and one needs to understand why insurers have made this move.

Much of this has to do not so much with longevity as with the much more temporary position of corporate bonds in the current economic climate (March 2009). Many insurers look to corporate bonds to back their annuity book. They seek exposure to the corporate bond market because of the additional return this can generate for them over and above investments in risk-free government gilt debt. Historically the extra yield, which is the spread on corporate bonds over risk-free investments such as government gilts, has been somewhere between 0.5% and 1.0%.

However, over the last several months, because the market has become much more risk-averse, the interest on corporate bonds has had to move up to reflect the increased likelihood that the company could fail and so not be in a position to repay the debt on maturity. The spread has now moved up to more than 2%, or at least four times what it was.

Part of this increase is compensation for liquidity risk, which is to say that as corporate bonds get more risky, fewer people want to buy them, so the market in those bonds becomes more illiquid. The other key factor, of course, is that if the company does default, the value the bondholder can expect to get will be considerably less than the face value of the bond—typically, companies going into administration or insolvency pay around 40% to bondholders, though the amounts vary widely from case to case.

The Financial Services Authority (FSA) in the United Kingdom, and other regulators elsewhere, realize this, so the FSA issued a bulletin in September 2008 advising that life insurers need to think about the risk of default when they are pricing annuity business. The FSA has so far not been prescriptive about its expectations as to what would constitute realistic pricing, but its comments put the matter on the radar.

The end of March is the end of the annual reporting period for life insurance companies, and the big focus this year is on the amount they are factoring in for corporate bond defaults. To take one example, Legal & General's share price suffered because the market became concerned that it might not be making sufficient allowance for default in relation to its bond portfolio.

After the market reacted, Legal & General announced that it was increasing its default allowance. That had two effects. First, increasing the allowance reduces surplus assets, so although a life insurer might believe that it has a sufficient cushion to meet any adverse future circumstances, that cushion is diminished. Second, this feeds through into the market perception of the financial strength of insurers. Lowering the annuity rates is a natural consequence, as it lessens the company's future liabilities in writing annuity business and improves its overall position.

Another impact on annuity rates comes from the UK government's quantitative easing program. This is being implemented by the Bank of England buying back bonds, which drives up bond prices and reduces the yield on bonds. Again, this means that

"Retirement at sixty-five is ridiculous. When I was sixty-five I still had pimples." George Burns

  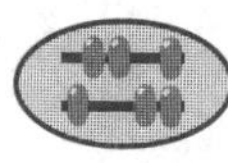   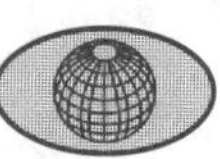   

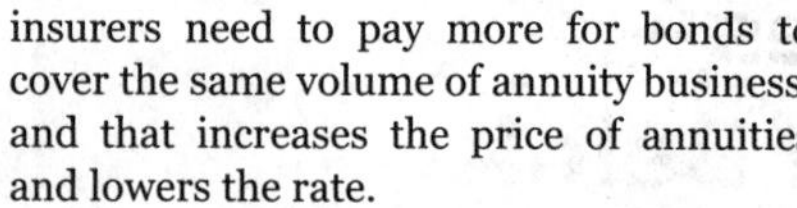

insurers need to pay more for bonds to cover the same volume of annuity business, and that increases the price of annuities and lowers the rate.

So the net result of all of this for someone buying an annuity when they are about to retire is a double whammy: their pension pot, which probably had a chunk of equities or corporate bond investments, is reduced in value at the same time as the cost of buying an annuity goes up—you get less money annually in retirement for each £100,000 you spend on buying an annuity.

There is an interesting conundrum in all of this for government as it thinks about the relationship between pensions and taxation, and ponders ways of getting individuals to take greater responsibility for their own pensions rather than relying on the state. Simply put, if the life insurance industry were to play too safe and lower the rates on annuities too far, people would simply lose interest in annuities. At 4%, the return is probably already perilously close to a level that many people would not feel attracted by. With the UK government already committed to introducing personal pension accounts, it is difficult to see how these could be marketed successfully in an era of really low annuity rates. If one follows this line of thinking, it becomes clear that the insistence of the UK Treasury on forcing people to buy an annuity with their pension pot as a fair exchange for getting tax relief on their pension contributions will be difficult to maintain. Already we have seen some tweaking of the rules on annuities, and the point at which the individual now has to buy an annuity has moved from the moment of retirement to age 75. Up to that point they can choose to opt for drawdown under the drawdown rules set by the Government Actuary's Department.

THE TECHNICAL BACKGROUND TO THE ANNUITIES MARKET

There are some technical reasons for some of the stresses and distortions that we are starting to see coming through the annuities market. One of the big problems is that, in an ideal world, insurers would like to match their long-term liabilities—that is, the amounts they expect to pay out in pensions—against long-dated fixed-interest stock. If they could get an exact match, then one whole area of risk would vanish.

However, there is not enough long-dated fixed interest stock available to achieve such a match. So insurers constantly have to juggle the value of the assets they hold, some of which are much shorter term in nature than their liabilities and whose value can be quite volatile, against these long-term liabilities. Their job is made more difficult by regulators who, after the current banking sector turmoil, can be expected to take a very conservative view of asset values. The result will be that insurers will have to hold much higher capital reserves—and this, again, will raise the price of annuities. From the government's perspective there is a danger here, as we have said, of annuities reaching a price point where they no longer make sense to the public. However, that is not the regulator's concern. Their remit is to make annuity products secure from the consumer's point of view, so that if they are bought the products will do what they say they will do. If that means that the price rises to such a level that demand disappears, that is not the regulator's problem. This clearly creates some issues and concerns about just how joined up government policy is on pensions, and how this downward drift in annuity values and upward drift in annuity pricing squares with the desire of government to lighten the state's burden as far as the provision of pensions is concerned.

"Insurers constantly have to juggle the value of the assets they hold, some of which are much shorter term in nature than their liabilities and whose value can be quite volatile, against these long-term liabilities."

Solvency II, the equivalent in the life insurance sector of Basel II in the banking world, is still being worked through and there are question marks over how it will be implemented. However, there is a possibility that a more extreme implementation of Solvency II, which has been mooted in Europe, would require insurers to hold risk-free assets against their annuity book. Since the returns on risk-free assets are very low, this again would drive up the price of annuities substantially.

One idea that has informed pension advice and pension planning over recent years is that of matching, where people invest increasingly in corporate bonds and gilts in the run up to retirement. The thinking here is that if the yields on bonds go down, and so annuities get more pricy, it means that there is plenty of demand for bonds, so the pension fund's assets will go up in value as well (demand, of course, generates rising prices for bonds). In that way, although you get less income per $100,000 of annuity, you have more of a pension pot to buy the annuity with, and the thinking was that these two trends would balance each other. However, if you get a step change, such as the 2% reduction in annuity rates, which equates to a 33% drop in pension benefit, then matching doesn't work and the model is broken. This kind of step change can be caused by two different factors, as we have seen. Either longevity increases can make annuities suddenly very expensive, or a sudden step change in the reserves that insurers need to hold can have the same effect. Either way, individuals have no mechanism that will allow them to hedge against this risk.

It is worth pointing out that this puts a question mark over the whole approach of lifestyling pension investments, since by definition it means moving out of potentially high-yielding equity assets and into lower-yielding assets. If the rationale for this is that the individual is hedging annuity price risk by such a move, that strategy is now broken since, as we have shown, there are other factors that they do not have the power to cover off. In this instance, one could make an argument that the only salvation lies in high returns. Being risk-averse will not do the job, so the argument goes, individuals need to stay invested in assets that might be able to deliver a reasonable pension despite the annuity price risk. There is no doubt that this will be an uncomfortable philosophy for many who are approaching retirement, because no one likes to gamble with their retirement income.

▸▸ MAKING IT HAPPEN

- Longevity issues now require very careful consideration by employers as scheme sponsors, by annuity providers, and by scheme actuaries.
- Annuity "risk," or the possibility that annuity rates will be substantially lower when they retire, is a factor that those approaching retirement need to give serious consideration.
- Lifestyle matching now needs to be examined in context to see that it delivers the expected benefits, to compensate for potential loss of returns.

"Retirement kills more people than hard work ever did." Malcolm S. Forbes

CONCLUSION

As far as investors looking to secure a pension pot are concerned, playing safe will not get the job done in an era of very low annuity rates. There are challenges here for government, for the pensions industry, for the individual, and for society that everyone involved in the sector is only just beginning to square up to.

▶▶ MORE INFO

Articles:

Aon Consulting. "Flexibility key to managing pension burden as pensions deficits soar again." News release, March 2, 2009. Online at: aon.mediaroom.com/index.php?s=43&item=1476

Aon Consulting. "Market slump prompts record pensions losses." News release, March 5, 2009. Online at: aon.mediaroom.com/index.php?s=43&item=1497

Testimony of Cameron Findlay, Executive Vice President and General Counsel, Aon Corporation, on behalf of the Council of Insurance Agents and Brokers before the Committee on Financial Services, London, November 18, 2008. (A short document that is of interest in that it is about the difficulty of pricing risk in markets where there is insufficient transparency, a state of affairs that typifies the present pensions market.) Online at: aon.mediaroom.com/file.php/348/Testimony+Nov+18+2008.pdf

     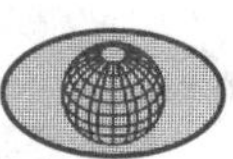   

Viewpoint: Jean-Claude Trichet
Solutions to the Current Crisis

INTRODUCTION

Jean-Claude Trichet is an Inspecteur géné des Finances and IngÝnieur civil des Mines. Between 1978 and 1998 he held numerous positions from Head of International Affairs and Director of the Treasury, to Governor of the Banque de France and Alternate Governor of the International Monetary Fund and the World Bank. He was also Chairman of the Monetary Policy Council of the Banque de France, a member of the Council of the European Monetary Institute, and a member of the Governing Council of the European Central Bank.

Jean-Claude Trichet was elected Chairman of the Group of Ten (G10) Governors in June 2003, and was appointed President of the European Central Bank in October 2003. He was named "Person of the Year" by the Financial Times (2007), "Central Banker of the Year" by The Banker (2008), "European Banker of the Year 2007" by The Group od 20 + 1 (2008), and "Central Bank Governor of the Year 2000" by Euromonet.

The following article is compiled from a recent speech by the president of the European Central Bank, delivered at the roundtable at the international colloquium, "Nouveau Monde, Nouveau Capitalisme," held in Paris on January 9, 2009.

The current crisis stands out because it affects the heart of the global financial system. Its root cause was a widespread undervaluation of risk in the global financial system, especially in the most advanced economies. This included an underestimation of the quantity of risk that financial institutions took upon themselves and an underpricing of the unit of risk. Risk was underpriced because, among other things, financial market participants largely extrapolated ongoing trends and the very low levels of volatility in financial markets and in the real economies going forward.

A number of policymakers indicated at the time that these trends and continuing low volatility could not be taken for granted. At the Global Economy Meetings of central bank governors in Basel, this was the sentiment reported by the meeting. The central bankers also said publicly, long before the difficult time we are going through today, that the private sector had to prepare for a market correction, because such a correction was inevitable.

The aim of this urging was to try to ensure that the correction itself would be as orderly as possible. Yet, one of the main reasons for the lack of preparation had its basis in the widely held view that regulation should not stifle financial innovation, and that markets knew best and could—for the most part—regulate themselves adequately.

The turmoil has shown how complacent and misleading this attitude was. When the turmoil set in, many financial institutions realised that their risk management systems were not as reliable and robust as they had believed them to be and, indeed, should have been. Most importantly at the time, market liquidity, that is the ability of financial markets to express appropriate prices at all times, which had wrongly been taken for granted, evaporated in large segments of the financial markets.

Investment-banking business models typically featured high-leverage, marking-to-market accounting, large maturity mismatches and relatively limited liquidity and capital reserves. This model was efficient as long as markets kept booming and functioned properly, but it left those banks with little or no shock-absorption capacity. We have seen the result: investment banking, as we knew it, has disappeared before our eyes, and all banking institutions have come under severe pressure.

The financial authorities—both in Europe and in other parts of the world—reacted promptly. Central banks, including prominently—and from the very start of the turmoil—the ECB, provided short-term liquidity support to prevent contagion. A number of the central banks' actions were coordinated internationally. Regulators gave priority to comprehensive policy responses, addressing the more fundamental weaknesses. Coordinated guidelines were put forward at the European and international level by the Financial Stability Forum, the Eurogroup and the European Council, in particular, and were reflected in the declaration of the G20 summit. This bears witness to the importance of measures to be applied consistently in all countries. A global financial system requires a globally coordinated response, and the official sector has been providing just such a response.

Looking ahead, we should correct the substantial flaws in the financial system that have now become evident. Of course, we should not throw the baby out with the bath water by discarding the market economy setup that underlies the system. It is the only setup that has proved able, over time and globally, to deliver sustained prosperity, and it has no equal in overall efficiency. But our basic aim should be to improve very significantly the resilience of the financial system: the fragility that has become apparent since August 2007 and more acute since mid-September last year is not acceptable. We have to draw lessons from the present situation without any complacency.

To be specific in terms of avenues for reform, there are three areas where change is particularly needed: 1) short-termism, 2) pro-cyclicality, and 3) transparency. I believe that shortcomings in these areas were instrumental in creating the conditions for this crisis and for amplifying its severity.

First, among financial market participants (traders, managers, risk committees, and boards of directors alike) for a long time there has been an excessive focus on short-term profits to the detriment of longer-term business performance. This has resulted in excessive risk-taking and, particularly, an underestimation of low probability risks stemming from excessive leverage and concentration. We now need to create more balanced and forward-looking incentive frameworks for management compensation and more

"If it doesn't sell, it isn't creative." David Ogilvy

  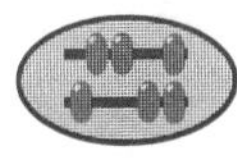   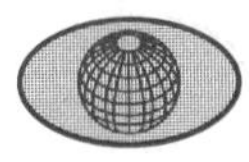   

effective internal risk measurement and control systems that take into account not only near-term profitability, but also sustainability and durable financial strength. This is an area where improvement will depend crucially on private decisions, in addition to public action.

Second, we need to reexamine all aspects of the current regulatory framework to ensure it does not contribute to the intrinsic cyclicality of banking. A number of potential sources of pro-cyclicality need to be investigated, including fair value accounting and leverage, capital requirements, and provisioning regimes. Looking forward, new mechanisms should be devised to ensure that banks accumulate resources in good times to cushion the shock when the cycle turns. Measures could include requiring banks to hold additional capital and liquidity buffers, and introducing dynamic provisioning systems that require banks to build up a general reserve that can be drawn on in downturns. Market economies inevitably entail cyclical swings; it is up to regulatory and supervisory bodies to ensure that their regulations and actions do not amplify those swings.

Third, in recent decades transparency has not matched the increasing level of sophistication and complexity of financial instruments, creating significant gaps in investor information and financial education. These need to be filled with enhanced risk disclosure at all levels, particularly in institutions and markets that are currently unregulated but can—as recent experience has shown—exert a relevant systemic impact. Financial regulation should be reviewed to reflect the role of highly leveraged institutions better in particular—namely private equity, hedge funds, and special purpose vehicles—and of derivatives markets in general, including, but not exclusively, credit derivatives. Particularly welcome here is the initiative to improve the infrastructure of over-the-counter markets by establishing central counterparty clearing for the CDS market.

In the current, very demanding situation, the swiftness and the magnitude of the decisions taken by central banks as regards the supply of liquidity, and the decisive actions taken by governments and parliaments as regards recapitalisation in the financial sector, and the provision of guarantees have proved effective in avoiding a meltdown of global finance. But it would be a mistake to underestimate the structural fragility of the present state of global finance and, consequently, of the global economy.

This is the heart of the matter: we need a paradigm change in the global economy. The previous paradigm was based on the concept of relatively short-term financial market equilibrium. What we need is a new paradigm. It should be a paradigm based upon the following three fundamental notions. First, the notion of medium and long-term sustainability, which will require us to be much more resolute in distinguishing between the stable equilibria on the one hand and the unstable equilibria on the other hand, which should not be accepted.

Second, the notion of resilience to shocks, taking into account the fact that whatever the level of sustainability of a particular financial situation, we can never eliminate the occurrence of unpredictable shocks. These shocks can come not only from the economic and financial sphere—the present stress test is a very powerful example—but also from the geopolitical sphere, or they can be triggered by natural catastrophes. Resilience is therefore essential; it is a necessary complement to sustainability.

The third notion is holism. The present global financial system depends on the appropriate handling of a very large number of factors: prudential practices, accounting rules, audit quality, liquidity management, risk management, and credit assessment, to mention but a few. This holistic approach must also comprehend a fundamental factor, namely the long-term sustainability and resilience of public macro policies—whether, in particular, fiscal or structural—and the associated progressive, but resolute elimination of those large domestic and external imbalances that are one of the major causes of global economic and financial instability.

Such a paradigm change, including the three notions of medium and long-term sustainability, resilience, and a holistic approach of the global financial system, is now absolutely essential to correct the fragility of the market economy which we are presently experiencing.

  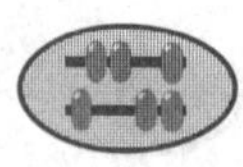   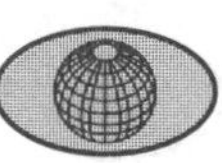   

Middle East and North Africa Region: Financial Sector and Integration

by Samy Ben Naceur and Chiraz Labidi

EXECUTIVE SUMMARY

- With a population of 345.5 million and a GDP of about $1,593 billion in 2007, the Middle East and North Africa (MENA) region has great potential, but faces major challenges.
- By reforming their economies, most of the MENA countries have achieved macroeconomic stability, and increased their growth.
- A more developed and well-functioning financial sector is essential to boosting sustainable economic growth in the region.
- Given the existing complementarities between MENA countries, there are numerous possibilities for intra-regional integration. Financial integration within the region will also help deepen financial markets, and increase their efficiency.

INTRODUCTION

The Middle East and North Africa region, as defined by the World Bank in the MENA 2008 Economic Developments and Prospects (EDP) report,[1] comprises Algeria, Bahrain, Djibouti, Egypt, Iran, Iraq, Jordan, Kuwait, Lebanon, Libya, Morocco, Oman, the Palestinian Territories (West Bank and Gaza), Qatar, Saudi Arabia, Syria, Tunisia, the United Arab Emirates, and Yemen.

The World Bank classifies these countries within three groups: Resource-poor, labor-abundant economies (Djibouti, Egypt, Jordan, Lebanon, Morocco, Tunisia, and the West Bank and Gaza); resource-rich, labor-abundant economies (Algeria, Iran, Iraq, Syria, and Yemen); and resource-rich, labor-importing economies (Bahrain, Kuwait, Libya, Oman, Qatar, Saudi Arabia, and the United Arab Emirates).

In 2007, these 19 countries and territories represented about 5% (345.5 million) of the world's population. The region's GDP was approximately $1,593 billion (at current exchange rates), or about 3% of world GDP.

The Gulf Cooperation Council (GCC) countries—Bahrain, Kuwait, Oman, Qatar, Saudi Arabia, and the United Arab Emirates—account for less than 11% of the population of MENA countries, but for some 49% of the region's GDP and around 80% of the area's stock-market capitalization.[2] The GCC region's wealth is, in large part, a product of its petroleum resources.

In 2007, the MENA region experienced GDP growth of 5.7% (see Table 1), and five years of growth at a rate higher than 5%. This performance occurred in the context of a continued rise in the oil price in recent years having important spillover effects on the financial and real-estate sectors, as well as on job creation. It has also brought more interest in intra-regional integration as a means of sharing prosperity within the region, and as a catalyst for global integration and competitiveness.

However, the increased interests of MENA banks and investors in the volatile equity and real-estate markets have made some economies more vulnerable to contagion effects. During 2008, the recession in developed economies and the slowdown in emerging markets affected some MENA countries. More precisely, the region and, especially, GCC countries experienced reduced financial liquidity and a sharp drop in shares values.

FINANCIAL SECTOR

A well-developed and dynamic financial sector is essential to achieve sustainable economic growth. Many attempts have been made in the last decade to improve the performances and efficiency of the MENA financial sector. However, there still exists a wide gap if compared to other developed and emerging regions. Although MENA countries present different levels of the financial sector's development, some broad generalizations can be made. Overall, the banking sector dominates MENA's financial system, and stock and bond markets remain a minor alternative option for raising funds.

Table 1. Real GDP growth. (*Source*: World Bank)

	2000–04	2005	2006	2007
MENA region	4.6	5.8	5.8	5.7
Resource-poor, labor-abundant*	4.2	3.7	6.3	5.4
Resource-rich, labor-abundant†	5.1	6.5	5.7	5.8
Resource-rich, labor-importing‡	5.1	7.3	6.2	5.8

* Djibouti, Egypt, Jordan, Lebanon, Morocco, and Tunisia (West Bank and Gaza are excluded because of data limitations).

† Algeria, Iran, Iraq, Syria, and Yemen.

‡ Bahrain, Kuwait, Libya, Oman, Qatar, Saudi Arabia, and the United Arab Emirates.

Banking Sector

Banks dominate MENA's financial systems and, over the past years, the exceptional increases in liquidity stemming from oil revenues have fed a rapid rise in bank deposits, and a growing demand for credit from the real economy. The credit growth has supported real-estate loans and mortgage lending. This has been complemented by housing finance reform efforts throughout the region. Particularly in the Gulf economies, the banking sector has increased credit and relaxed financing terms to the real-estate sector.

The MENA financial sector is also experiencing prodigious growth in the Islamic banking sector (15–20% over the past decade), which is based on the principles of Islamic law (also known as Sharia law). Two basic principles behind Islamic banking are the prohibition of the collection and payment of interest (known as *riba*), and the prohibition of profit-sharing or leasing without underlying tangible assets. These principles contribute to make lending more prudent and linked to real economic activity, and explain the resiliency of the sector to the credit crunch crisis.

However, according to the MENA 2008 EDP report, "These positive developments are overshadowed by a number of factors. The financial sector in MENA is still dominated by commercial banks that are vulnerable to shocks from the equity and the real markets. A disconnect between the financial sector and the real economy is still observed, public sector ownership is high, and access to banking services is low." Indeed, the heavy public-sector ownership, as well as the limited openness in some countries, had had a significant impact on the direction of credit in MENA, as well as the operating efficiency and the ability of the banking sector to conduct robust risk analysis.

Capital Markets

The MENA capital markets are generally

  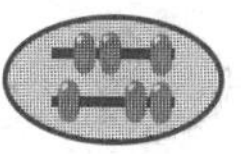   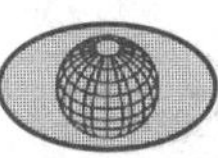   

Table 2. Stock market indicators. (*Source*: World Bank and AMF)

Indicator	*2003*	*2004*	*2005*	*2006*	*2007*	*2008*
Market capitalization (US$ millions)	361,078	620,364	1,287,696	883,497	1,333,620	765,784
Value traded (US$ millions)	230,417	568,158	1,434,908	1,684,029	1,107,177	997,331
Number of listed firms	1,723	1,549	1,616	1,571	1,498	1,503

perceived as less developed than other emerging markets.

The privatization process launched during the 1990s has been slow, and has not reached its promise with regard to capital markets development. There are many reasons for the markedly slow privatization in the region, and its consequences in terms of capital markets underdevelopment. In some cases, there is evidence of a lack of political will, and some pressure by interest groups. More generally, the considerable involvement of governments in economic activities and related overstaffing, as well as the slow pace of job creation in the private sector, represent barriers to a rapid privatization process.

However, following continuous liberalization efforts and improvements to the underlying legal framework, some MENA stock markets have been successfully revitalized during the last few years. As shown in Table 2, market development indicators such as market capitalization, value traded, and number of listed firms have significantly increased. GCC capital markets can be considered as the most developed, and they account for about 73% of the region's stock market capitalization (see Figure 1), but for only 40% of the total number of listed companies. There are also bond markets in almost all MENA countries, but they haven't yet reached a sufficient level of development due to low governmental and institutional investors' participation, and to the relative scarcity of large private corporations able to issue debt.

Overall, a key challenge for capital markets in the MENA countries is to channel available liquidity into the real economy, boosting sustainable and efficient growth. However, academic research shows that stock market informational efficiency (in the sense defined by Eugene Fama) is essential to achieve this goal. Lagoarde-Segot and Lucey (2008)[3] investigated informational efficiency in a set of seven MENA stock markets, excluding GCC countries, while other studies focused on the GCC stock markets. See, for example, Abraham et al., (2002),[4] Al Loughani (2003),[5] and Al Saad and Moosa (2005).[6] Most of these studies found evidence of a significant departure from the efficient market hypothesis. After constructing an efficiency index, Lagoarde-Segot and

Figure 1. Relative market capitalization (2008). (*Source*: AMF)

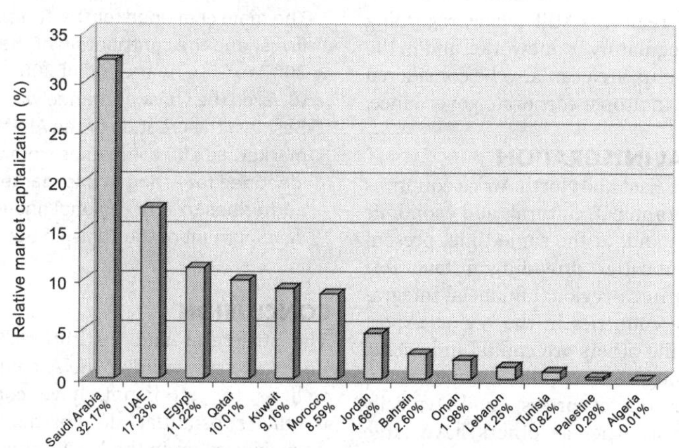

Lucey highlighted heterogeneous levels of efficiency in the MENA stock markets. Their results indicate that informational efficiency in the MENA markets is primarily affected by market depth, and corporate governance factors.

Indeed, in most MENA countries, stock markets are characterized by the concentration of ownership and the limited role of market forces. These aspects, among others, have a negative impact on transparency and disclosure standards, in particular, and on corporate governance practices in general. Recent surveys[7] show evidence of a corporate governance gap in the MENA region, if the benchmark of the

CASE STUDY

Tunisia's Stock Exchange

Overview

Tunisia's Stock Exchange (TSE) is composed of an equity market and a bond market, while there are no derivative instruments traded. The equity market consists of an Official Market, which contains 51 listed firms, and an Alternative Market, which was set up in 2007 and has one listed firm. There is also an unlisted market comprising four companies. Two-thirds of the stocks, representing 63% of the market capitalization by the end of 2007, are continuously priced.

Institutions

The TSE is managed by the Bourse des Valeurs Mobilières de Tunis (BVMT), which is owned by the 24 financial intermediaries, supervised by the Conseil du Marché Financier (CMF), and for which stock and bonds transactions are deposited and cleared by the Société Tunisienne Interprofessionnelle de Compensation et de Dépôt des Valeurs Mobilières (STICODEVAM).

Markets

The TSE is dominated by retail investors, and foreign participation stood at 28% of the whole market by the end of 2007. Any foreign participation above 50% of a firm's capital needs authorization. There are two market indices. The unweighted BVMT index, created in September 1990, includes the most liquid stocks on the market with at least six months' listing. The other index is TUNINDEX, which has been published since 1998 and weighted by market capitalization. It also covers listed firms that have at least six months' of quotations. The TSE implemented in December 2007 a new electronic trading platform, which uses the same trading system as NYSE. New trading rules have been introduced, such as the increase in the minimum daily trading margin from 4.50% to 6.09% on the equity market.

"There is one category of advertising which is totally uncontrolled and flagrantly dishonest: the television commercials for candidates in Presidential elections." David Ogilvy

OECD's corporate governance principles and practice in developed countries are considered. Despite the fact that the corporate governance framework is already in place, there is still room for improvement with respect to transparency, disclosure, protection of noncontrolling shareholders, directors' independence, qualifications, and compensation. The challenges the region is still facing regarding legal and regulatory frameworks, and in the property rights area can also be considered as barriers to proper corporate governance.

FINANCIAL INTEGRATION

The Middle East and North Africa countries share geographical, cultural, and economic similarities and, at the same time, present complementarities providing a favorable context for intra-regional financial integration. Some countries in the region export capital, while others are capital importers. Some countries have small populations, are major oil exporters, and typically import labor, whereas others have large populations and face unemployment issues.

Moreover, the wealthiest countries had traditionally invested their surpluses in the major international financial centers, and are now seeking to diversify their investments by placing an increased share of their funds in the region. As a consequence, intra-regional foreign direct investments (FDI) and portfolio investments have risen in many MENA countries. In particular, between 2002 and 2006, about US$60 billion, or 11% of total GCC capital outflows, went to other MENA countries.[8]

Direct foreign investment flows have been boosted by the improved business climate in some MENA countries, and many GCC investors, operating in several sectors (telecommunications, real estate, tourism, banking), are targeting countries such as Egypt, Lebanon, Syria, and Tunisia.

As for capital market integration, the amount of funds that actually flows intra-regionally depends on regulatory aspects related to stock markets and foreign investments. Investors from the GCC are showing interest in stocks of non-GCC countries. However, most countries impose barriers and restrictions on foreign investments in domestic equities, preventing deeper capital market integration (for example, Amman Stock Exchange imposes a ceiling of 50% foreign ownership for companies operating in some specific sectors, foreign investors are allowed to own a maximum of 49% of UAE corporations, and foreign ownership in Omani companies is generally limited to 70%).

The debt market is small compared to the equity market, as it represents less than 10% of market transactions in the period 2003–2007. Bond issues reached US$1.2 billion in 2007, with the state representing 83.4% of bond issues by value in 2007. The corporate bond market is monopolized by financial institutions. Banks tend to use it to finance mortgages, and leasing companies to balance their books. New legislation allowing foreign investors to own up to 20% of government bonds from January 2007 will certainly stimulate trading in the debt market.

Challenges

The main challenge for the Tunisian Stock Exchange is to increase the number of listed firms, and the contribution of the capital market to finance the economy[9] from 8% in 2007 to 20% by the end of 2009. The recent reallocation of the privatization program towards the stock exchange will certainly have a strong impact on developing the TSE. Besides, the creation of the Alternative Market in 2007 is expected to boost the capital market, as 100 companies from the Tunisian Modernization Program have been identified for listing in this market. Finally, the willingness of the Maghreb countries' authorities to spur regional financial integration will also be another contributor to the development of the Tunisian Stock Exchange.

CONCLUSION

The structural and institutional reforms undertaken by many MENA countries, as well as the oil boom, have contributed to the substantial development of the financial system in the MENA region in the last decade. Despite this progress, much remains to be done, and the region is still facing a number of issues with regard to its banking sector and capital markets. Good corporate governance practices are also essential in ensuring efficient access to financing, in attracting foreign investors, and, more generally, in promoting sustainable development. In addition, more pronounced intra-regional integration should enable investors throughout the region to achieve more portfolio diversification, and improve resources allocation. Hence, deeper regional cooperation should be encouraged if MENA is to keep up in an increasingly competitive global environment.

▸▸ MAKING IT HAPPEN

- A healthy and dynamic financial sector entails achieving sustainable and efficient economic growth in the MENA region.
- Good corporate governance is crucial for the region to achieve its challenge of becoming a global player.
- The efficiency of the banking system is one of the key aspects that the MENA countries need to face the challenges of globalization, and support economic growth. A more developed capital markets infrastructure should make it easier for borrowers and investors to operate.
- Economic and financial integration within the region could represent stepping stones towards the ultimate goal of development and global competitiveness.

▸▸ MORE INFO

Books:

Molyneux, Philip, and Iqbal Munawar. *Banking and Financial Systems in the Arab World*. New York: Palgrave Macmillan, 2005.

Noland, Marcus, and Howard Pack. *The Arab Economies in a Changing World*. Washington, DC: Peterson Institute for International Economics, 2007.

Websites:

Arab Monetary Fund: www.amf.org.ae
International Monetary Fund: www.imf.org
OECD information on MENA: www.oecd.org/mena
The World Bank's Middle East and North Africa site: www.go.worldbank.org/DT45JDVOKO

See Also:

✔ Middle East: Regulatory Structure and Powers (p. 1041)
Prince Al-Walid bin Talal (p. 1150)

"It was something you only spoke of in hushed tones. Advertising is a bit of an anathema." Michael Bungey

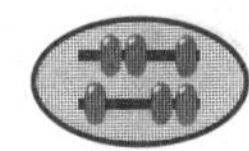

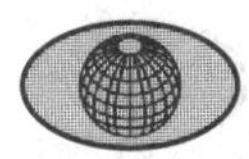

NOTES

1 Middle East and North Africa Region, 2008, Economic Developments and Prospects: Regional Integration for Global competitiveness, World Bank, 2008.

2 Excluding Tehran's stock exchange capitalization.

3 Lagoarde-Segot, T., and B. M. Lucey. "Efficiency in emerging markets: Evidence from the MENA region." *International Financial Markets, Institutions and Money* 18 (2008): 94–105.

4 Abraham, A., F. J. Seyyed, and S. A. Alsakran. "Testing the random walk behavior and efficiency of Gulf stock markets." *The Financial Review* 37 (2002): 469–480.

5 Al Loughani, N. E. "The seasonal characteristics of stock returns in the Kuwaiti stock market." *Journal of Gulf and Arabian Peninsula Studies* 29 (2003): 15–40.

6 Al Saad, K., and A. I. Moosa. "Seasonality in stock returns: Evidence from an emerging market." *Applied Financial Economics* 15 (2005): 63–71.

7 See, for example, "Advancing the corporate governance agenda in the Middle East and North Africa: A survey of legal and institutional frameworks." MENA-OECD Investment Program.

8 Source: World Bank.

9 Three possible sources of financing are considered: bank credits, bonds, and equity.

"Advertising is our printed salesman. It may not be pretty, but it has to be true." William Wrigley

     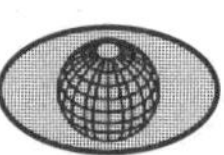   

Viewpoint: Richard A. Werner

Understanding and Forecasting the Credit Cycle—Why the Mainstream Paradigm in Economics and Finance Collapsed

INTRODUCTION

Professor Richard A. Werner, D.Phil. (Oxon), B.Sc. (Economics, LSE), began his academic career as Marie Curie Fellow of the European Commission at the University of Oxford. From 1997 to 2004 he was Assistant Professor at Sophia University, Tokyo. Since 2004 he has been at the University of Southampton, School of Management, where he is Chair in International Banking and founding director of the Centre for Banking, Finance and Sustainable Development.

Professor Werner has two decades of experience in the financial sector, including as chief economist at Jardine Fleming Securities (Asia) Ltd., Senior Managing Director at Bear Stearns Asset Management, and as senior consultant or visiting researcher at the Asian Development Bank, the Japanese Ministry of Finance, the Bank of Japan, the Japan Development Bank and the Nomura Research Institute. Richard served as member of the asset allocation board of a US$6.5bn Japanese corporate pension fund, and has been working as global macro fund manager and provider of forecasting services and economic policy advice to investors and governments.

His book 'Princes of the Yen' was a No. 1 bestseller in Japan in 2001. In his 2005 book New Paradigm in Macroeconomics, he warned about the dangers of "recurring banking crises," including the pending financial collapse in the UK, and detailed the required policy responses. Richard has been voted one of the top economists by investor surveys and is sought as a commentator by the media. The World Economic Forum, Davos, selected him as "Global Leader for Tomorrow" in 2003.

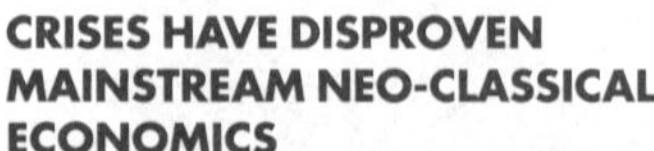

CRISES HAVE DISPROVEN MAINSTREAM NEO-CLASSICAL ECONOMICS

The global financial crisis has led many observers to question the success of an array of government policies adopted in the past decade or so in many countries. Most have been directly or indirectly based on the thinking that markets should be the ultimate arbiter, and hence deregulation, liberalization, and privatization was the policy mantra.

The doubters are now in good company. For about two decades, Alan Greenspan, chairman of the Board of Governors of the Federal Reserve System from August 1987 to January 2006, has been considered the oracle on any issue involving banking, monetary, fiscal, and economic policy. The "Maestro" has been a staunch champion of the deregulation mantra and the belief that markets, if left unregulated and to their own devices, would produce the best possible outcome for society. Likewise, he also believed that bankers should not be further regulated as their self-interest would ensure an optimal result. This thinking is commonly known as "mainstream" or "neo-classical" economics. From about 1980 onwards, it was initially adopted by international organizations such as the IMF and the World Bank in their policies imposed on dozens of developing countries, but since the mid-1980s it has became the guideline of other Washington-based decision-making bodies, such as the US government (hence it is often called the "Washington Consensus" on economic policy). It has since also become the basis of government policies worldwide, such as in Thatcherite and New Labour Britain, or more recently in Japan, Korea, or Germany. Even nonmarket economies such as China have begun to adopt a growing set of recommendations derived from this free market economics.

Dr Greenspan, an academically trained economist and key promoter of this creed, has, however, now changed his mind. On October 23, 2008, he admitted—reluctantly, under cross-examination by irate Congressmen—that this entire approach to economics is flawed and that his faith in the free markets had been wrong. Greenspan had been summoned to give formal testimony to the House Committee on Oversight and Government Reform of the US House of Representatives about his role and involvement in the events that led to the financial crisis. His testimony must be considered a watershed in the debate about different economic theories and policy recommendations.

Representative Henry Waxman of California, chairman of the committee, asked him: "You had the authority to prevent irresponsible lending practices that led to the subprime mortgage crisis. You were advised to do so by many others. Do you feel that your ideology pushed you to make decisions that you wish you had not made?"

Greenspan: "...Yes. I've found a flaw. I don't know how significant or permanent it is. But I've been very distressed by that fact." The exchange goes on:

Waxman: "You found a flaw in the reality." Greenspan: "...[A] flaw in the model that I perceived as the critical functioning structure that defines how the world works, so to speak."

Waxman: "In other words, you found that your view of the world, your ideology was not right. It was not working." Greenspan: "Precisely. That's precisely the reason I was shocked..."

There was a second admission, concerning the methods used to calculate and manage risk in the entire financial sector: "This modern risk-management paradigm held sway for decades. The whole intellectual edifice, however, collapsed in the summer of last year," Greenspan testified.

     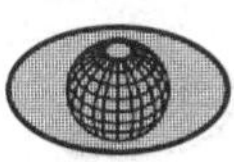   

The crisis has with one stroke not only discredited the particular decisions by those responsible for the crisis—central bankers, financial regulators, and bankers—but it has disproved the entire mainstream "neo-classical" paradigm of thinking about economics and economic policy. The Washington Consensus, the basis for recent government and central bank policies all over the world, has been proven wrong.

But the current crisis is not the only piece of evidence that there has been something seriously amiss with the mainstream economic theories and the policies based on them. Other evidence includes the increasingly visible environmental destruction, or the many previous financial and economic crises the world has seen. Indeed, banking and financial crises have recurred with such frequency over the past centuries that their occurrence must be considered one of the few constants in economic life. Each time, much surprise is exhibited by the experts. Over the past three decades, the number of banking and financial crises has increased (to over 100 countries) and the swings of the business cycle have become more pronounced. (It is noteworthy that this happened, as central bank independence and power over economic policy has increased significantly during this time period).

Thus the experience in many countries has contradicted key aspects of mainstream theories. There is one country, however, where the number of "anomalies" or contradictions of the mainstream approaches has been the largest: this is Japan, the second largest economy in the world. First, Japan's meteoric postwar rise, which was based on nonmarket policies, cartels, and "guidance" of industries and credit, could not be explained. Then, in the 1980s, Japan experienced a surge in asset prices and capital outflows that economists had not expected (and could not explain). Just when observers were predicting that Japan was about to take over the world, in the early 1990s, asset prices fell sharply and economic growth decelerated for over a decade (soon we will have clocked up two decades). These almost twenty years of recession, deflation, and economic depression have occurred despite all the textbook recommendations having been implemented. During the 1990s, record fiscal spending delivered record government debts, but there was no recovery. Lowering interest rates to zero failed to accelerate growth. Structural changes increased deflation and bankruptcies, but did not boost demand.

WHAT'S WRONG WITH MAINSTREAM ECONOMICS?

Just why is it that, while science is constantly making visible progress, economics seems to be stuck in a time warp, without making any visible advances? Here we are in the 21st century, with man having been on the moon, and with the most advanced telecommunications technology spreading knowledge faster than ever before. Yet, the financial markets are allowed to generate the same kind of boom–bust cycle as in earlier centuries.

Could it be that mainstream economics suffers from adhering to some fundamental errors that must compromise all its results? The most familiar diagram in economics is that of a downward-sloping demand and an upward-sloping supply curve. Most observers, but also most economists believe that economics has shown that prices move to equalize demand and supply so that, thanks to the working of the markets, we experience "equilibrium" or market clearing. But, actually, economics has done no such thing. Quite to the contrary, it has shown that such market clearing would only be possible if and only if we lived in a world of perfect information, complete markets, and where many other unrealistic assumptions held—all of which are necessary to achieve this textbook outcome. Since it is evident to everyone that these assumptions do not hold on the planet we live on, it should be clear that economics really has proven that in our world we cannot expect any market ever to clear. But instead of learning from this finding that equilibrium cannot exist, and hence any economics based on equilibrium needs to be discarded, the unrealistic fictional equilibrium models have become the mainstream. Economists are obliged to pretend that the emperor is not naked, that markets clear, that there is equilibrium, and, even more preposterous, that markets deliver the best possible outcome for society.

For Dr Greenspan it took over 40 years to have his eyes opened. Let's hope that others will be quicker. But how is it possible that theories that have no bearing on reality could become the foundation of an entire approach that in turn becomes the dominant ideology globally, influencing government policy and even the thinking of ordinary people?

The theoretical sleight of hand is that economics, as virtually the only discipline, has got away with arguing that its theories do not need to be based on the fundamentals of economic reality (a methodology called "inductive"), but can exclusively be based on "axioms" and assumptions (the deductive methodology) that have been assembled as it suited best to obtain a predetermined ideological goal—the goal to present market outcomes as supreme. No surprise, then, that the performance of such economics has been dismal.

So what would nonfiction economics look like? Markets cannot clear, because information, time, and money are rationed. So what happens in the world we live in, where markets do not clear? Demand does not equal supply. And such rationed markets are determined by quantities, not prices. Their outcome follows the "short-side principle:" whichever is smaller, demand or supply, that quantity will be transacted. And that short side can extract additional, nonmarket benefits.

This has far-reaching political implications. While the rhetoric is of a globalized world, dominated by anonymous market forces, which decide the flow of goods, services, and capital across the globe, the reality is that the majority of trade flows are decided by planners—bureaucrats or bureaucrat-like managers at large-scale corporations, who make discrete allocation decisions. The reality of "market capitalism" is therefore that the market plays a much smaller role than is widely claimed. Recognizing pervasive rationing and lack of market clearing implies that instead of the dream-world of efficient (and hence politically neutral) markets, we live in a reality of powerful allocators who make decisions that suit them, but which are in no way linked to what is best for the overall economy or society. This sharply lowers the hurdle for government intervention to be beneficial to society.

Mainstream economics purports to have shown that government intervention is almost always inefficient and creates distortions. However, this finding only comes about, because government intervention has to beat the super efficient markets of the illusory theoretical dream world – and by definition it cannot do that. But if we leave the dream world oftheoretical mainstream economics, we find that on our planet markets are not just often failing, they are virtually never in equilibrium. This sharply lowers the hurdle for government intervention to become beneficial to society. And it explains the otherwise puzzling finding that many countries, such as 20th century East Asian economies and 19th century Germany, succeeded so spectacularly in developing their economies quickly on the basis of strategic though pervasive government intervention.

"The things we have to sell won't take the place of the Ten Commandments. . .Copy can be casually optimistic, but no more." Bernice Fitz-Gibbon

   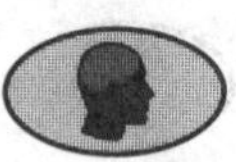  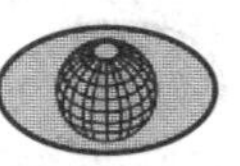   

THE REALITY OF CREDIT CREATION: THERE IS NO SUCH THING AS A BANK LOAN

What are the implications for finance and banking? For small firms, the price of money (the interest rate) is usually less important than the question of whether a loan can be obtained at all. Banks prefer to ration and allocate credit—even in the best of times—because due to the high demand for this useful thing called money, the theoretical market-clearing interest rate would be so high as to leave them with only risky projects, while sensible projects could not service the loans. This explains why interest rates are far less important in the economy than is generally claimed. Instead, the quantity of credit is the most important variable determining growth, asset prices, and exchange rates.

The most important institutional reality that has been neglected by theoretical equilibrium economics is the key function banks perform: they create between 95% and 98% of the money supply. The first and most important form of privatization that has swept the world has been the privatization of the creation and allocation of money, which is implemented by privately-owned commercial banks.

This means that there is no such thing as a "bank loan." Banks do not lend money. "Lending" refers to transferring control of the lent object to the borrower. If I lend you my car, I can't drive it at the same time. That's not what banks do when they issue a "bank loan." Instead, they are allowed by the current regulatory framework to create new money out of nothing—which is called "credit creation." The collective decisions of commercial bank staff thus determine how much money is created, who gets the newly created money and to what use it is put.

Mainstream economics assumes that the best possible outcome will be achieved if banks are left alone in making their decisions about how much money should be created, to whom it should be handed over, and for what purpose. But the current crisis has demonstrated that we can't expect banks' credit decisions to be in any way beneficial to the overall economy, social welfare, or even the bankers themselves—as Alan Greenspan has now admitted. The incentive structure at banks is such that they tend to create too much credit, when not needed, and for unproductive use. This is followed by banks creating too little money, when more would be needed.

There are some simple rules for sound banking and sound economics that need to be followed. Whenever credit is created and used to increase the amount of goods and services provided, it will result in noninflationary growth; more money comes about, but also more goods and services. Whenever credit is created and used for unproductive purposes, inflation comes about; more money chases limited goods or assets. The unproductive credit creation can take two forms. When credit is extended for consumption, it will result in consumer price inflation. When credit is extended for non-GDP transactions (which means mainly financial and real estate transactions), there will be asset inflation. Both cases are unsustainable and, if sufficiently large, result in banking and economic crises.

In the research experience of this author, this framework (first proposed in a 1992 paper, published as Werner, 1997) delivers the most reliable models for forecasting nominal GDP growth, equity markets, bond markets, and even currencies. Credit used for GDP transactions is the most reliable forecaster of nominal GDP growth. Credit used for non-GDP transactions ends up driving up real estate and asset prices, and ultimately turns into bad debts. It is thus a key variable to watch by policy makers, if one wants to prevent asset bubbles and banking crises, as I have suggested many times in the past two decades. Empirical evidence and further details can be found in the book, *New Paradigm in Macroeconomics*.

> "What should be done to end the current crisis and avoid large-scale unemployment?"

To prevent banking crises, it must be ensured that the bulk of credit creation is used for productive purposes. Specifically, aggregate bank credit for transactions that are not part of GDP (something that can be easily verified by loan officers) needs to be monitored, and suppressed when it rises in excess of overall bank credit growth (see Werner, 1997, 1999). This simple measure would have prevented the credit bubbles in the United States, the United Kingdom, Ireland, Spain, and many emerging markets, which have now burst and caused the current crisis. It would also have prevented the Japanese depression since 1990 or the US Depression of the 1930s, among others. Central banks used to monitor precisely this but, following the deregulation advice of mainstream economics, they chose to abolish their "credit guidance" policies and instead let rip the unproductive bank credit expansions. Ironically, now the UK, French, and German governments want to monitor the allocation of new bank lending (to small firms) policy advice of the kind I have given consistently and repeatedly since 1991, but which was rejected as 'inefficient interference' in 'free markets'. This amounts to closing stable doors when the horse has already bolted.

Thus one also needs to ask why those institutions that could have prevented the bubbles have singularly failed to do so, although they had been given unusually strong powers with little accountability to democratic institutions—the central banks. They cannot feign ignorance: apart from employing the largest number of economists of any institution and spending vast resources on 'research' (none of it on the taboo topic of credit creation), I have also contacted many central banks and finance ministries and have in the past twenty years published many articles based on my credit model, warning of pending crises (such as today's UK banking collapse) and indicating that bubbles and subsequent collapses could easily be prevented by monitoring and restricting speculative (non-GDP) credit creation. Central banks – and governments for that matter – were not interested. This suggests that the very independence and lack of accountability of central banks has been a factor in allowing the creation of credit bubbles and the propagation of the current crisis. Central banks should be made to monitor credit flows and be more directly accountable to democratically elected assemblies for the macroeconomic results.

HOW TO FIX THE BANKING SYSTEM AND ENSURE EMPLOYMENT

What should be done to end the current crisis and avoid large-scale unemployment? Just like the Japanese government in the early 1990s, governments have responded by increasing fiscal expenditure, funded by borrowing, and central banks have responded by lowering interest rates. Neither will help. The privately owned creators of the bulk of the money supply are battening down the hatches; in their increased risk aversion they will reduce credit creation. Just as their excessive credit creation affects us all, so does their reduction of credit. For economic growth, as traditionally measured, credit creation is necessary. This is why the current policies will not help. Fiscal policy on its own does not create credit. By borrowing more, national debt is increased, but the money for the fiscal stimulation is the same money that is removed from the economy through bond issuance. Thus fiscal policy, if not backed by credit creation, will crowd out private demand dollar by dollar. And lower interest rates will not help—even if they drop to zero—if the quantity of credit does not

"A good ad should be like a good sermon: It must not only comfort the afflicted—it must afflict the comfortable!" Bernice Fitz-Gibbon

increase. This is why Japan will soon be in the twentieth year of recession after its own credit bubble burst in 1990. (My predictions and recommendations to this effect over the past twenty years have been met with stony silence or outright rejection by policy makers.)

The solution is simple: fiscal stimulation, in the form of purchases of nonperforming assets from banks, and public purchases of bank equity, should be funded either by the issuance of government money (such as Kennedy's 1963 "United States Notes," to give a graphic example), or, failing that, undertaken directly by the central banks, for their own account. In both cases, national debt and interest liabilities will not increase, but credit creation will. Growth will not collapse. This also makes sense from a moral hazard perspective. The tax payer is not responsible for the current mess, the central banks are—so let them pay.

In countries, where central banks are not cooperative with governments, credit creation can still be jump-started by stopping the issuance of government bonds and instead funding the public sector borrowing requirement through direct borrowing from the commercial banks (a policy I first proposed in 1996). All of the above proposals I termed 'quantitative easing' in my publications, such as articles for the Nikkei in 1995 and 1996. When the Bank of Japan adopted my terminology (which has now conquered the world), it unfortunately chose to use my label, but not the actual policies: it focused on expanding banks' reserves, which I had already explained would not help.

▸▸ MORE INFO

Book:

Richard A. Werner. *New Paradigm in Macroeconomics*. Basingstoke, UK: Palgrave Macmillan, 2005.

Articles:

Werner, Richard A. "Towards a new monetary paradigm: A quantity theorem of disaggregated credit, with evidence from Japan." *Kredit und Kapital* (1997): 276–239.

Werner, Richard A. "Soundness of Financial Systems: Bank restructuring and its impact on the economy, paper presented at the International Conference on Central Banking Policies," 14–15 May 1999, Macao, published as Werner, Richard A., Post-crisis banking sector restructuring and its impact on economic growth. *The Japanese Economy*, 6 (2002): 3–37.

See Also:

★ Viewpoint: Roger Bootle (pp. 185–186)
Friedrich Hayek (p. 1170)

"Any seeming deception in a statement is costly, not only in the expense of the advertising but in the detrimental effect produced upon the customer, who believes she has been misled." John Wanamaker

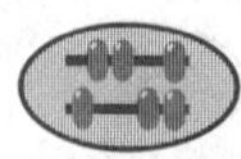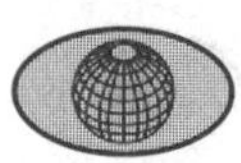

The Payment Services Directive: A Crucial Step Toward Payment Harmonization Across the EU by Björn Flismark

EXECUTIVE SUMMARY

This article looks at the impact and implications of the Payment Services Directive (PSD), which EU member countries will be enacting into law by November 2009 at the latest. The PSD is another step on the road to an integrated Europe-wide payments market. The article considers:

- The objectives of the PSD;
- Its scope and impact;
- The differences between SEPA (Single Euro Payments Area) and the PSD;
- The benefits of the PSD for customers;
- The impact of the PSD on banks.

INTRODUCTION

The Payment Services Directive (PSD) provides a legal framework for payment services in the internal market of the EU and the European Economic Area (EEA). It was adopted by European legislators on November 13, 2007, and must be transposed into national law by the 27 EU member states by November 1, 2009, at the latest. The three non-EU EEA countries—Iceland, Liechtenstein, and Norway—are also committed to transposing the PSD into their national law. The EU and EEA countries plus Switzerland together form the Single Euro Payments Area (SEPA) for euro payments.

The PSD is one additional step in the efforts of the European legislators to achieve an integrated payments market. This process started with the introduction of the euro in 1999 (as an electronic currency) and 2002 (bank notes and coins), the implementation of new payments-related legislation at EU level, such as Regulation EC2560/2001, and the launch in 2008 of the first Single Euro Payments Area (SEPA) instrument for handling credit transfers as well as of the SEPA Cards Framework. In November 2009, SEPA Direct Debit Schemes (Core and B2B) will be launched, and at the same time an updated version of Regulation EC2560/2001 is expected to come into force that will cover direct debit transactions as well.

In November 2012, the EU Commission will publish a report reviewing the functioning of the PSD and measuring the progress toward establishing a single European payments market. This review will also focus on whether the scope of the PSD should be expanded with regard to non-EU/EEA currencies and to transactions where only one of the payment service providers involved is located in the EU/EEA. Thus, the PSD should be seen as a further step, rather than as the final step, in Europe's drive for harmonization.

OBJECTIVES OF THE PSD

The PSD has five main objectives:

- To establish a single payments market in the EU;
- To provide the regulatory framework for a single payments market;
- To create a level playing field and to enhance competition;
- To ensure that there is consistent consumer protection and improved transparency;
- To create the potential for greater efficiency in EU payments systems.

By removing legal barriers to the provision of payment services across Europe and fulfilling these objectives, the PSD will enable citizens and businesses to make all kinds of intra-EU/EEA payments—at both national and cross-border level—easily, safely, efficiently, cost-effectively, and in a timely manner. The new legal framework supports the SEPA payment instruments, particularly the SEPA Direct Debit Scheme, and removes barriers to entry into new markets within the EU/EEA.

The PSD also creates a clear set of rules for payment institutions (PIs), a new category of payment service providers. Once authorized to provide and execute payment services in one member state, a PI can operate throughout the EU/EEA. PIs have to meet specific capital requirements and fulfill a number of other requirements, such as specific obligations related to record keeping.

THE SCOPE AND IMPACT OF THE PSD

As the PSD applies to payment services between payment service providers (PSPs) and payment service users (PSUs) within the EU/EEA, it affects everyone carrying out payment transactions, from private banking customers to businesses and corporates, as well as financial institutions, governments, local authorities, merchants, credit card providers, and so on.

The PSD will have a particularly far-reaching impact on the way banks process payments. It affects not only euro payments, but also payments carried out in non-euro currencies of all EU/EEA countries. SEPA instruments, as well as existing national payment instruments, fall under the provisions of the PSD. The PSD covers credit transfers, direct debits, card payments, and some cash transactions such as cash deposits. Excluded are a number of paper-based instruments, as well as some transactions that do not fall directly under the PSP–customer relationship.

DIFFERENCES BETWEEN SEPA AND THE PSD

The building of the Single Euro Payments Area (SEPA) is an initiative to establish a truly integrated European payments landscape, where euro payments are subject to a uniform set of standards, rules, and conditions and can be executed as easily, quickly, securely, and efficiently as in national markets. SEPA was launched in January 2008 with the SEPA Credit Transfer and the SEPA Cards Framework.

Although both the PSD and the SEPA initiatives are aimed at enabling and facilitating the integration of the European payments market, their scope and areas of impact are not identical, in spite of some overlap. The PSD is a European directive that will be transposed into national law across the EU/EEA, whereas SEPA is a self-regulatory initiative of the European Payments Council. While SEPA focuses only on the euro, the PSD embraces all currencies within the EU/EEA. SEPA coverage is slightly wider than the PSD in that it includes Switzerland. Most importantly, the main focus of the PSD is the payment service users (the customers) and their relationship to the PSP, whereas the main focus of SEPA is to establish binding standards and business practices for the bank-to-bank relationship. The PSD also covers a wider range of transaction types, including cash deposits and withdrawals.

"If you want to know what God thinks of money, just look at the people he gave it to." Dorothy Parker

  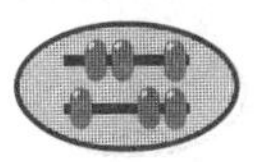   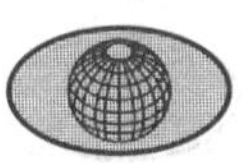   

BENEFITS OF THE PSD FOR CUSTOMERS

The PSD provides significant benefits to customers as it contains a number of protective measures that will need to be applied uniformly across the EU/EEA to payment services offered to private consumers and, to some extent, corporate customers. The directive spells out in detail the obligations of payment service providers (PSPs) with respect to customers. Among others, it stipulates maximum execution times for the banks' payment processes and imposes strict rules on value dating.

In general, customers can expect a more harmonious and transparent service under the PSD, since the directive mandates full transparency of conditions and requires the PSP to provide a high standard of information to the customer. Key provisions include:

- PSPs have to provide a great deal of free payment-related information to the customer.
- PSPs may be required by the different EU/EEA member states to provide paper information updates to customers once a month free of charge.
- PSPs need to be given a unique identifier by the customer for a payment to be properly executed.
- PSPs must provide full transparency to customers before and after a payment is executed, i.e., inform customers of the maximum execution time and of all charges payable, provide a breakdown of charges, and confirm any exchange rate that may apply.

BENEFITS AND CHALLENGES FOR BANKS

The Payment Services Directive will have a major impact on the banks' payments business, as it requires changes to many payment-related processes that are in place today. All banks operating in the EU/EEA today will have to undergo the costly exercise of adjusting their existing internal systems and platforms, as well as their services and underlying terms and conditions, to the PSD requirements.

Beside the cost of compliance, the PSD will also impose an additional burden on banks. The directive will negatively impact some of the revenue streams of the banks because there are provisions, such as the requirement to provide some information services free of charge, that will reduce the banks' ability to charge for certain services. Bank revenue might also be impacted by increased obligations vis-à-vis customers, such as the responsibility to inform customers of the PSD, and by the maximum execution times and value dating rules stipulated by the PSD.

The articles on maximum execution times and on obligations with regard to value dating will be among those that banks need to study particularly closely. Among others, they detail that:

- The payer's PSP may set a cutoff time toward the end of its business day, after which a payment order can be treated as if it had been received on the following business day.
- Payments within the EU/EEA should generally be subject to a D + 1 execution time, with up to D + 3 being a possible exception until January 1, 2012, if agreed between PSP and payer.
- Longer execution times of up to D + 4 may be applied to a number of transaction scenarios involving currency conversions—but only if they have been agreed on between PSP and PSU.
- The debit value date of a payment is no earlier than the point in time at which the payment is debited to a payer's account.
- The credit value date of a payment is no later than the business day on which the PSP's own account has been credited with the amount of the payment and the PSP has to put the amount at the PSU's disposal immediately after the PSU has received it in its own account.

The PSD also represents an opportunity for banks, as they can use the PSD to explore new business opportunities. For example, the fact that the PSD implements the same legislation concerning payment services across the EU/EEA makes it easier for banks to develop new products and services that can be offered at a pan-European level. This opens up the possibility of expanding into new markets without having to establish a physical presence in those new markets. Standardized service offerings also provide the opportunity to simplify both account documentation and terms and conditions for customers across Europe. What is more, necessary investments in the adjustment of payment processes provide the opportunity to modernize and streamline these processes.

THE PSD'S IMPACT ON BANKS: A HIGH-LEVEL OVERVIEW

On a practical level, the PSD will impact the following areas and functions within a bank:

- Payment products and cash management businesses will be affected, and there will be a need to implement changes in product offerings to ensure PSD compliance.
- IT systems will require modification to ensure that shortened execution time requirements can be met.
- Information channels, including electronic banking systems, will have to be adjusted.
- Additional operational procedures, including enhanced risk management, may have to be put in place. For example, if a payment service provider refuses to execute a payment, the reason for this and the procedure for correcting the problem will need to be notified to the customer within the time frame specified in the PSD (normally D + 1).
- Banking documentation (account opening documentation, framework contracts, etc.) will have to be adjusted.
- Customer communication will have to reflect the impact of the PSD.

Figure 1. Value dating and availability of funds when both payer's and payee's banks are located in the EU/EEA. (*Source*: Euro Banking Association, "Banks preparing for PSD," 2008)

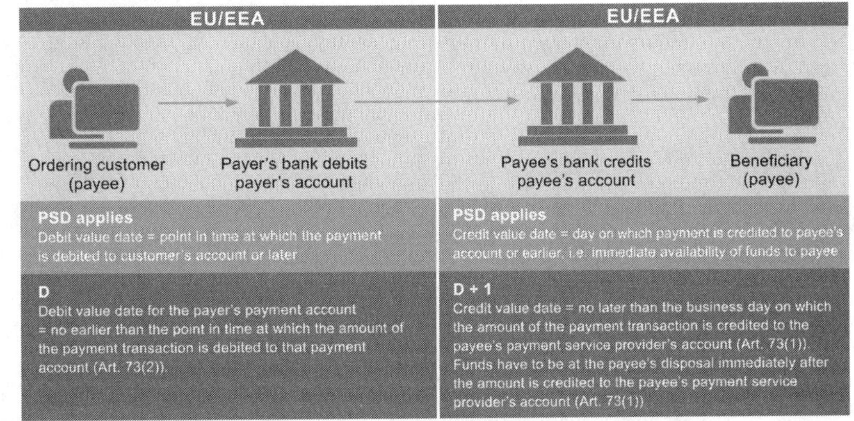

Note: D + 3 is possible until January 1, 2012, if there is an agreement between ordering customer (payer) and payer's bank (+1 possible in case of paper-initiated transactions).

"My problem lies in reconciling my gross habits with my net income." Erroll Flynn

- Staff education and training will be needed to ensure that customer service staff, as well as product, sales, operational, and IT staff, are able to communicate with customers and make the necessary internal bank changes.
- Third-party agreements (existing agreements with technical providers, intermediaries, clearing houses, correspondents, etc.) will have to be reviewed and/or renegotiated.
- Financial planning (revenue and cost budgets will be impacted because of reduction of float, full amount to be paid, investments in system changes, etc.).

On a strategic level, the PSD will need to be considered in terms of:

- The opportunity it offers to agree that certain articles should not apply when the customer is not a consumer; this opportunity, which is called the corporate opt-out, is detailed in Article 51 and should be evaluated by each bank.
- The competitive environment in which a bank operates.
- The impact of new market entrants (for example, the PIs) and their product offering on a bank's current client base.
- Potential changes in strategy regarding products and services, expansion into new markets, and targeting of customer segments.

Overall, the implementation of the PSD will require a major effort involving many different functions and areas. It will undoubtedly generate an increased demand for skilled resources, funding of systems enhancements, and legal and compliance expertize, plus it will take up a significant amount of senior managements' attention and focus. As a result of changes in execution times, banks will have to review their operational risk management procedures and will potentially need to set up new processes and ensure that there are sufficient resources available. The rules governing refunds are also impacted.

CONCLUSION

There is no doubt that PSD requires banks to do work and to make investments to conform to the requirements of the directive. However, it also brings opportunities, particularly for national players to move into pan-European and EEA markets, even without having to establish a physical presence in those markets. As such, the directive can be seen as an opportunity rather than as a burden. As banks across Europe are running their internal PSD projects involving their legal, compliance, and operations teams, they also need to participate in and closely follow the work of their national PSD working groups and liaison groups in order to keep track of national transposition processes and their outcome. The PSD will transform the European payments industry, resulting in greater standardization and more consistent and harmonized market practices, which should benefit both the providers and the users of payment services.

➤➤ MORE INFO

Articles:

Euro Banking Association (ABE/EBA). "Banks preparing for PSD: A guide for bankers on the Payment Services Directive." Paris: ABE/EBA, November 2008. Online at: tinyurl.com/dy2x54

Euro Banking Association (ABE/EBA). "Banks preparing for SEPA: Issues to be addressed to achieve SEPA compliance." Paris: ABE/EBA, May 25, 2008. Online at: tinyurl.com/dy2x54

Website:

Euro Banking Association (ABE/EBA): www.abe-eba.eu

See Also:

★ Business Implications of the Single Euro Payments Area (SEPA) (pp. 20–21)
★ How to Successfully Assess a Company's Global Treasury Needs and Objectives (pp. 66–68)
★ Payment Factories: How to Streamline Financial Flows (pp. 91–92)
★ What the Rise of Global Banks Means for Your Company (pp. 596–597)

"**Finance is the art of passing money from hand to hand until it finally disappears.**" Robert W. Sarnoff

  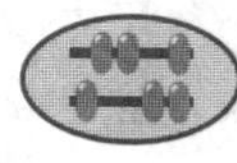   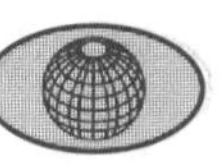   

Viewpoint: Paul Wilmott

The Problem with Derivatives, Quants, and Risk Management Today

INTRODUCTION

Paul Wilmott is a financial consultant, specializing in derivatives, risk management and quantitative finance. He has worked with many leading US and European financial institutions. Paul studied mathematics at St Catherine's College, Oxford, where he also received his DPhil. He founded the Diploma in Mathematical Finance at Oxford University and the journal Applied Mathematical Finance. He is the author of *Paul Wilmott Introduces Quantitative Finance* (Wiley 2007), *Paul Wilmott On Quantitative Finance* (Wiley 2006), *Frequently Asked Questions in Quantitative Finance* (Wiley 2006), and other financial textbooks. He has written over 100 research articles on finance and mathematics. Paul Wilmott was a founding partner of the volatility arbitrage hedge fund Caissa Capital which managed $170million. His responsibilities included forecasting, derivatives pricing, and risk management. Dr Wilmott is the proprietor of www.wilmott.com, the popular quantitative finance community website, the quant magazine *Wilmott* and is the Course Director for the world's largest quant education programme the Certificate in Quantitative Finance (www.cqf.com).

The press has recently vilified derivatives and Warren Buffett famously called them "weapons of financial mass destruction." What's your feeling?

A decade ago, I wrote about how the derivatives market now exceeded the size of the underlying market. Small quantities of derivatives are fine, but if you look at the derivatives trading on the back of IBM or HBOS shares, the sheer quantity of trading that goes on is both worrying and lethal to the health of the underlying companies as well as the broader economy.

If you can make some money on a small number of derivatives, then people will naturally lever up to make greater returns —and that's when things get dangerous. Banks have being selling these instruments for years now without worrying about the repercussions. I'm surprised that just because Warren Buffett started talking a few years ago about the danger of derivatives, people started wondering for the first time, "Hang on, can that be right?" It's staggering how little people think for themselves.

What's the solution, then, as derivatives seem here to stay, be it for hedging and portfolio efficiency, or for unique different trading strategies? Is the answer greater transparency as some people have called for?

I'm not sure greater transparency would help. Ratings agencies and regulators go into banks all the time to examine their instruments and models.

The problem is that they are all using similar—and poor—risk models, and everyone is doing the same trades in large numbers and sizes. A ratings agency, for example, will walk into one bank and see what trades they're doing. It will then go into the neighboring bank and see the exact same trades. Realistically, anybody should have immediately seen how dangerously correlated the whole system is.

There is plenty of transparency at the moment where regulators and ratings agencies are seeing this. The problem is that they all still sign off and give the Triple A ratings. For me, there is a distinct moral hazard in the way ratings agencies are compensated: banks and companies pay them millions of dollars to get ratings, which creates a system that is inherently conflicted. When the lawsuits start in a few months' time, I hope that ratings agencies will suffer the largest damages.

As well as transparency, you need someone to do something about what they see—and that simply isn't happening today.

What about the regulators, then? Increasingly, there have been calls for greater regulation to solve the problems within the system, such as the nature of compensation.

As far as regulations are concerned, there are two sorts that should come into force.

The first is diversification. You have to diversify and spread your risk amongst a range of instruments that are as uncorrelated as possible—that reduces risk. However, this will be very hard to implement, and an alternative might be to instead target limits on the large quantities that banks can otherwise trade in a small pool of derivatives.

The other issue is compensation—and that can be regulated. We have got to stop compensating people for taking ridiculous risks with other people's money, and this could be implemented in a day if politicians really wanted to.

There are lots of ways to do this. Link the compensation to the maturity of the instrument. If a banker is responsible for putting together a five-year CDO (collateralized debt obligation), trickle out their bonus over five years. Then, you have a system similar to the royalties that musicians receive long after they have recorded a song. This also encourages people to trade shorter-term instruments that have greater transparency.

Pay their bonuses in company shares, for example, so that they bear the risk of loss. If you stick with the current status quo, where bankers get paid on the upside annually without any downside risk, then you're still encouraging them to bet as much of other people's money as possible, with obvious and now well-known consequences. The compensation needs to be smaller as well. Bankers can't be paid the vast amounts they're receiving now for risking other people's money—it's just not morally right.

Let's talk about the instrument that's been most in the press, credit default swaps (CDS), where the size of the

  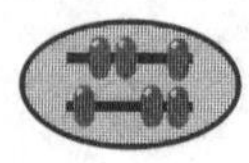 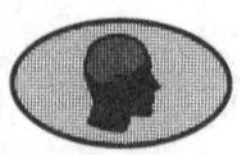  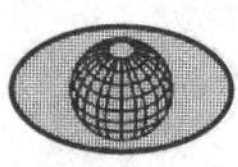   

market has become ridiculously large compared to the companies whose defaults they're underwriting. What do you see as their future?

Nassim Taleb and I have talked out for years now about the size of these markets and how, in some cases, you're even buying protection on a company from itself, which seems crazy. These risks have always been clear but no one has ever admitted it, as they've all been busy making too much money.

To deal with the problem, you can set up an exchange and have standardized contracts. With simple CDS, this can give greater transparency as people can see how many there actually are. But more complicated structures are harder to standardize. While there's nothing inherently wrong with these, it is essential to see how many are being used for hedging and how many for speculation, as you cannot have more speculation than there are underlying assets. Most should really be used for hedging, such as companies looking to hedge the risk of their suppliers going bust.

Otherwise, you increase the risk of contagion and systemic failure, as no one knows who the ultimate counterparty is. Their sheer size also matters, as it wouldn't matter if these contracts were traded in small quantities. But the quantities are so large, and everything is continually repackaged and moved from one bank to another, that no one knows anymore how much there actually is out there and, more importantly, how much is still outstanding. You need to see who has what, and who they're trading with.

One thing that seems certain is that leverage is not going to be the same going forward. What's the bank of the future going to look like?

In some ways, it won't be all that different. Banks will always hire expensive quants, accountants, and lawyers to work their way around these obstacles. Leverage had been crazy and there might well be some regulation, but there will doubtless also be people to get around this.

Also, people forget. Once a disaster is over, people very rapidly forget how bad it was. So I don't know if banks will really change—it just depends on if regulators will bring in new laws before people get bored and move onto the next disaster.

Hedge funds have been particularly blamed for their role in the credit crunch. Were they culpable or just one of the culprits, along with banks and those investors who drove the demand for securitization?

Hedge funds do have a role, though not as big as the banks. Hedge funds are largely all the same, i.e., they follow fashions in strategy. This makes them dangerous as they all end up in the same trades, but people are largely wary of them. Also, the investors in hedge funds are people with lots of money and expertise, while many of those in banks are normal people—your man on the street who can't afford to lose his money.

Banks are supposed to take excess money from people with too much and lend to those with too little money, to do useful things such as buying a house or starting a business. Banks should not be lending to people to buy trivial items that should be saved up for, such as Christmas presents and shoes. Banks are ultimately responsible for the credit crunch as they extended such easy credit to people to live far beyond their means.

The problem has now moved on from the financial sphere into the real economy. How do you wean people off this easy credit?

That's an important consideration. Can it be done gradually or should it be undertaken with a short, sharp shock? There is a generation of people today around the age of thirty, who have only ever lived off credit. How will they survive without credit?

If you tell them they can't have the latest iPhone, it's going to be a shock to them. It's symptomatic of the society we live in, where we believe the economy has to keep growing, otherwise all hell breaks loose.

Running is the new standing still, so to speak.

Quants have also had a rough ride recently thanks to CDOs and the like. What are your thoughts and what is the future for them?

Once banks have been exposed to quantitative methods and approaches, it's hard to go back to the old world. So, they are here to stay despite their large role in the credit crunch. Without quants, you wouldn't have such methods as value at risk (VaR) to quantify the risks we are running.

Ironically, the problem is that once you start quantifying risks, you can also manipulate them. VaR is a perfect example where, thanks to your underlying assumptions and models, you can believe there is no risk. In reality, you're likely running lots of risk but, by reporting such a small amount, it's possible to trade bigger and bigger amounts. So, in some cases, the consequences of measuring risk better is that you end up with more!

There are also different types of quants. I train more quants than anyone else on this planet, and there are two types—sensible and stupid. Unfortunately, the stupid—the purist, abstract mathematics-loving quants—are in the majority.

Let me explain. Many quant books contain vast volumes of unrealistic mathematics. Some people get carried away with the beauty of this mathematics with no corresponding understanding of finance and, more importantly, of human nature. These people are dangerous, as you cannot talk to them about the real world. If you tell them their models do not work, they'll talk of all sorts of abstract notions, proving themselves right in their heads. Unfortunately, all this is without any reference to the real world. And in finance—which is as much about people as mathematics—if you can't grasp that, then that is dangerous.

I have always advocated the mathematics "sweet spot," that fine balance between a sufficiently advanced knowledge of mathematics to do the job in the real world, while not being so abstract as to lose your head in the clouds. You must not dumb down quantitative math, else you cannot understand more complicated derivative products. But, equally, you do not want to stray into the even more dangerous area of really high-level math, where people get carried away by the subject's beauty. There are some 5,000–10,000 Masters in Financial Engineering graduates churned out each year, and I would not employ a single one of them myself, as they are so hopelessly out of touch.

I hope that everyone—people, banks, risk managers, hedge funds, governments, and regulators—all realize that while a certain level of mathematics is important, transparency and robustness in the models are the key, not valuing derivatives to 10 decimal places.

People often don't realize that any theory is only as good as its axioms. So what can be done about this?

They just love the mathematics, which is fantastic—I love mathematics too. But if that's what you want, then get a job in a university or do it in your free time. Don't do it in the bank's time.

I'm a great believer in quantifying everything, but are we actually dealing with a science? Finance is a very "soft" science—it's a science because you have all this data that you can analyze, but it's also soft because, despite all these theorems, human beings have an annoying habit of not obeying the rules.

So while there is always going to be a

"What does a Great Depression for the relatively wealthy look like? If you spend lots of your budget on 'luxuries'—especially durables—it is easy to postpone their consumption. This might cause GDP to fall more rapidly than if people were poorer." Tyler Cowen

need for mathematics, we need people to ask difficult questions. When these quants with their PhDs are talking math, intelligent people have got to have the confidence to ask them the difficult and embarrassing questions, such as "When do your models break down?"

Similarly, risk managers need to act as devil's advocates. They need to ask, "We've lost a billion. How did that happen?" At the moment, it's the other way round as people look only at scenarios. The problem is that everybody misses one, such as Long-Term Capital Management (LTCM) overlooking the scenario where all their uncorrelated risks suddenly all became correlated. However, there is an implicit moral hazard too, as managers know that if there is a bad enough scenario with high enough risk, the bank wouldn't be allowed to trade, so they may choose not to acknowledge some risks at all, such as rising defaults.

One of my favorite examples of the need to think outside the box is the magician's card trick, where he hands an ordinary pack of cards to a random member of the audience, and asks another random person to pick a card. The person says "ace of hearts," and the magician now turns back to the first member, feel around inside the deck and pulls out a card. What is the probability of that card being the Ace of Hearts?

Most people would say one in 52. But you have to think of where all this is happening. You're in a magic show, so you expect something impressive. The other obvious answer is that the probability is one.

This is such an important question because most quants will say one in 52, a few will then stop to consider, and fewer still will take the magic element into account. But you do need to consider these possibilities. If you have $1bn riding on it not being the ace of hearts, and every time the magician picks a card it is the ace of hearts, you've just lost $1bn.

Risk managers have to be able to think laterally, though even realizing just these two scenarios is not good enough. Picking the ace of hearts may just be boring. Maybe it's a different trick, where he picks the wrong card and the ace of hearts is actually in the second person's pocket. Perhaps the card instead contains the winning lottery numbers for that night, which will be chosen in 15 minutes' time. One in 52—the quant answer—doesn't even begin to scratch at the possibilities.

Let's end with the question that resonates most in the minds of financial leaders these days. What lessons, if any, can we take from the credit crunch?

I don't actually think there are any lessons to learn, as we cannot expect people to stop having a herd mentality. As far back as 2000, I warned about a mathematician-led market meltdown, thanks to the dangers of all these credit instruments and what quants were doing. It was all there for everyone to see—bad models, self-serving regulations, the moral hazard with the compensation schemes within ratings agencies, and so on.

But people in general are like sheep. So, the lesson for me is the same old lesson that people will always make the same mistakes. There will doubtless be new regulations, but there will also be people who will be paid tremendous sums of money to work their way around these regulations. Fundamentally, it comes back to my earlier point that what has to change is the way people are compensated. With the way the bonus structure is currently set within banks, people take as much risk as they can—they wouldn't care if they blow up the entire banking system as long as they got their tens of millions of dollars.

▸▸ MORE INFO

Books:

Wilmott, Paul. *Frequently Asked Questions in Quantitative Finance*. Chichester, UK: Wiley, 2006.

Wilmott, Paul. *Paul Wilmott on Quantitative Finance*. 2nd ed. Chichester, UK: Wiley, 2006.

Wilmott, Paul. *Paul Wilmott Introduces Quantitative Finance*. 2nd ed. Chichester, UK: Wiley, 2007.

See Also:

★ Dangers of Corporate Derivative Transactions (pp. 46–48)
★ Viewpoint: Maureen J. Miskovic (pp. 209–210)
★ Viewpoint: Ricardo Rebonato (pp. 228–231)
✔ Derivatives Markets: Their Structure and Function (p. 924)
✔ Establishing a Framework for Assessing Risk (p. 1034)

"The bonus system has proved to be wrong. Substantial cash bonuses do not reward the right kind of behavior." Andy Hornby

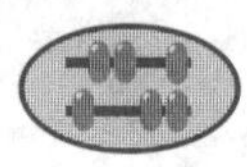
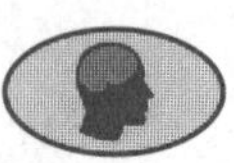

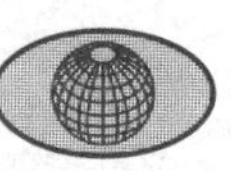

The Perfect Storm—Why Did No One See It Coming? The Missing Piece in Risk Management by Nigel Walder

EXECUTIVE SUMMARY

With hindsight, the author suggests a practical process for re-inputting the people element to create an "early warning system" to prevent another perfect storm.

- In a near-global systemic meltdown, a contributing factor was inadequate transparency through the levels of the organization.
- As financial regulation revisions bite, there is an opportunity to re-input the "people" element in offering an early warning.
- By encouraging contributions at all levels through a systematic approach, CEOs, CFOs, risk, and top management can be more aware earlier of potential problems.
- Encouraging a climate of more openness would help, but this does not work in all cultures.
- The real challenge remains to extend that transparency as far as the regulator.

INTRODUCTION

It's been an unforgettable 12 months, with multi-billion write-offs every week, well-established firms collapsing, fire sales, runs on banks, and as near to a totally global systemic meltdown as any of us will ever want to get. And we're not out of it yet.

How can such well-established firms get it so wrong? Why did the risk departments and regulators fail so dramatically? Hindsight is a wonderful thing, but I firmly believe that one of the major contributing factors is the lack of transparency within financial service organizations; not only to the shareholders, but to senior management as well. When you combine this with record trading volumes, the complexity and opacity of derivatives, and the apparent acceptance of a greed culture, we clearly were hit hard by the perfect storm.

As an organization specializing in putting people and their input back into automated operations in the financial services arena, we have been very cynical for the last six or seven years about the traditional operational risk department's focus. In a nutshell, it was clear to us that you cannot risk to manage trading and operational activities from the center of an organization, unless you have very strong personal input from the coalface, and total change in the culture.

Coming from the coalface, it has been clear to us that senior risk managers have very little visibility as to what is going on across the length and breadth of their organization, particularly where whole swathes of processes have been or are being outsourced, or sent offshore. In fact, I'd broaden that statement to say that most senior management struggle to have transparency over their own operation, let alone a risk manager.

My own background is in applications development. As a former chief information officer (CIO) at NatWest Global Financial Markets, I think of myself as someone who focuses on business problems and tries to generate sensible solutions to those problems. That is not quite the way things have been played in the regulatory field in financial services. Instead of a sensible approach to a business problem, we have a situation where the regulator sets the boundaries and the various players then push the envelope as hard and as creatively as they can.

So, when I watched the implementation of regulatory regimes such as Sarbanes-Oxley and Basel II, and saw the industry trying to "game" the regulations as they emerged, it seemed inevitable that these well-intentioned regulations were unlikely to serve their intended purpose. This is despite the fact that there is very little in the regulations that best practice or sensible management wouldn't cover. Indeed, the firms thought they were being smart, whereas in reality most got a very poor return on investment from implementing solutions to such regulations.

THE ROLE OF OUTSOURCING AND OFFSHORING IN COMPLICATING CONTROL

Of course, the financial industry—both the banks and the life companies—have been under tremendous competitive pressure over the last decade. This has driven them to look for efficiencies wherever possible, and has pushed the move to outsourcing and offshoring faster than is reasonable.

I know some senior operations heads in large banks who resigned because they were being asked to offshore processes so aggressively that they knew they could not do this in the time frame being set for them, while still retaining control.

USING SYSTEMS TO RECONNECT SENIOR MANAGEMENT WITH THE COALFACE

In an earlier era, management in banks could go round and talk to their people. Issues would emerge, and management would get a real feel for what was going on. Today, senior management has become detached from what is going on in the trenches. To combat this, what is needed are systems that directly address the necessity for gathering the views of people at every level of the organization, from the most junior sign-off levels upwards.

At a simplistic level, this can be achieved through a narrative workflow approach that forces sign-off at every level for specific processes, and collects subjective views at the same time from the person responsible for the sign-off. An example of the latter would be asking the person concerned to rate whether the item they were signing off was "issue-free," on a scale of one to seven, say, where one was issue-free, and seven was critical. At the same time, the system should capture a narrative explanation of the individual's input.

A manager at the next level up might judge that something that his junior rated as serious was in fact not an issue at all, because they had a better and deeper view of the matter. So they in turn could rate the issue. However, their view would not eradicate the junior's view, which would stay on the system.

When this system of sign-off and issue rating is translated into a dashboard approach, it means that a senior manager or CEO looking at a bunch of green indicators, which seem to show that all is well, could drill down through the various levels until they can see the warning lights that were implemented right down at the coalface, as they started to appear. They would also see a written account of why a particular junior person felt that there was an issue. This would put people back into automated processes, and give management a measure of control that would otherwise be sadly lacking.

CULTURAL PROBLEMS IN REPORTING ISSUES TO SENIOR MANAGEMENT

This approach works particularly well in

"**In writing advertising it must always be kept in mind that the customer often knows more about the goods than the advertising writers because they have had experience in buying them.**" John Wanamaker

  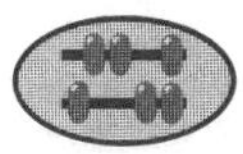   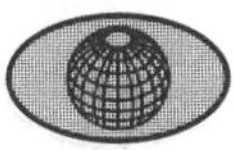   

enabling top-level executives, such as the CEO and chief financial officer (CFO) of an international bank, for example, to "hear" opinions and views that very junior subordinates would be extremely loath to present to them face to face. One senior client, for example, with this kind of a system in place, says that he has noticed a definite trend for those reporting directly to him to log more concerns and issues onto the system than they are willing to raise with him in his weekly meetings with them.

"They should feel comfortable raising any issue with me, but it seems that even relatively senior people are a lot more comfortable about raising a critique in the more anonymous realm of a work-flow document or e-mail, than they are face to face," was his comment.

In some Asian cultures, there is a real problem with reporting issues. It is seen as a weakness to admit that there is a problem with any process. As a result, some of the large Asian banks, and some Western banks with large processing centers in Asia, have a huge challenge in getting to grips with how good their control of their processes actually is, as no one wants to report weaknesses.

However, when private logging of views is enabled through a system, it is somehow seen as a more neutral and less threatening way of logging a concern. It is "just a technical exercise." So, junior staff feel easier about adding their views as they sign off on the processes that involve them, and that enables information about potential problem areas to start flowing up the chain to senior management in a way that it has not been able to do before.

THE IMPACT ON SECURITY AND FRAUD PREVENTION OF RE-INSERTING PEOPLE AND PERSONAL RESPONSIBILITY INTO AUTOMATED PROCESSES

While I would not make the claim that frauds such as the multi-billion loss experienced by Société Générale at the hands of its Paris-based trader, Jerome Kerviel, would automatically be prevented by this kind of system, it tends to be the case that in retrospect, when the fraud is analyzed in detail, one finds many little problems that were noticed by staff around the fraud that, if they were viewed holistically, would have rung some alarm bells.

A system that gathers up this sense of unease, and is available all the way to the board, can be of great assistance in bringing things to light far sooner than might otherwise be the case. Balance-sheet substantiation across a large organization is an ideal application zone for this kind of system. It makes it much more feasible for a CFO, for example, to ensure that every single account or line item is "owned" by someone specific who has the responsibility for signing off on that specific item.

That way, no one can walk away and say, "I didn't think that that was my problem, I thought it was in Bloggs' neck of the woods." There are often a number of dubious or "grey" ownership areas between finance and operations in many organizations, for example, and forcing through signing responsibility down to the level of each item or account clarifies these kinds of muddles wonderfully.

For example, if a particular account has a profit and loss (P&L) break of greater than x, and it is a derivatives account, you can force the immediate flagging-up of a problem all the way to a level where effective probing or remedial action can be taken.

DISTINGUISHING BETWEEN DATA AND INFORMATION

One of the biggest problems that management in large, complex, international financial institutions faces is that they receive far too much data, and far too little real information. The management information packs that hit their desks at regular intervals are generally out of date before they are printed, they take so long to gather. So, bringing transparency and immediacy back into the frame is a hugely positive thing.

However, implementing this kind of system can have its political challenges. It is not unusual to find resistance from middle managers, who begin to worry that a system like this could make their part of things all too visible to those above them. So, implementing this kind of narrative gathering system requires strong top-down direction and commitment if it is going to happen effectively. It needs board-level championing.

People have said that implementing this kind of system is as much a cultural change as it is a process change. The process change part is simple. Crudely put, it is about interrupting automated processes by forcing personal sign-off at optimal designated points, and capturing narrative at the same time. The cultural change is about getting people to accept that, while they might well get fired for saying there is no problem when there is a problem, they will get nothing but praise for flagging up real issues or things that concern them about a process.

It is a bit like the way some financial institutions deal with their relationship with the regulator. They put a buffer zone in the way, between them and the regulator, then they game what the regulator needs to see. Imagine the transformation in the industry if the regulators could see the same reports that management sees. However, that is likely to be a tough nut to crack, although the regulators clearly have more clout than ever before.

From the CFO's perspective, what is important about a sign-off process across a large, balance sheet substantiation process that could involve in excess of a million accounts, is that the system will let them see at a glance, at any point in time, just what percentage of accounts have been signed off as problem-free, what percentage is still pending, and which have been flagged as problematic.

CONCLUSION

This, plus the ability to drill down to the most junior levels, and look at real annotations by the people actually doing the jobs, is a powerful way of putting management back in control. And, as we have all seen from the recent turmoil across the financial sector, there are not that many management boards in the sector that, by the start of 2009, could put their hands on their hearts and say that they were fully in control of all aspects of their operation!

➡ MORE INFO

Websites:

Business Control Solutions (BCS) Operational Control Architecture: www.bcsplc.com/pg.asp?p=ocaHowitWorks

Securities and Exchange Commission (US), Sarbanes-Oxley Act 2002: www.sec.gov/about/laws/soa2002.pdf

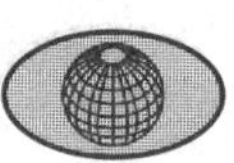
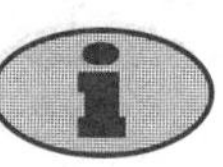

Viewpoint: Linda Yueh

China and the Global Financial Crisis

INTRODUCTION

Dr Linda Yueh is an economist and commentator on global economic and business issues. She is a fellow in economics at the University of Oxford, a visiting professor at the London Business School, and an associate of the Centre for Economic Performance at the London School of Economics and Political Science. Previously, she worked as a corporate lawyer internationally, based in New York, Hong Kong and Beijing. Recent books include *Macroeconomics* (co-authored with Graeme Chamberlin) and *Globalisation and Economic Growth in China* (co-edited with Yang Yao). Forthcoming books include *The Law and Economics of Globalisation: New Challenges for a World in Flux* (editor) and *The Future of Asian Trade and Growth: Economic Development with the Emergence of China* (editor). Dr Yueh is editor of the Economic Development and Growth book series published by World Scientific Publishing, and serves as an adviser to the World Economic Forum in Davos, Switzerland, and the UK government. She is a frequent commentator for the media, including the BBC, CNBC, CNN and *The Guardian*.

Although it is certainly true that excessive risk-taking by financiers and inadequate regulatory supervision are to blame for the global financial crisis, international macroeconomic forces should not be overlooked as a contributing factor. This is particularly the case as any lasting resolution must address the causes of the most significant global economic crisis in recent memory.

The economic crisis of 2008 has its roots in the last recession. Ever since the US central bank used loose monetary policy to stave off a technical recession in 2001, after the dot-com bubble burst, low interest rates in developed economies became the norm as economic growth continued to be strong. Cutting interest rates to stimulate the economy during a downturn is the usual use of monetary policy, but the extent of globalization in a fundamentally changed global economy of the 2000s altered its effects.

The mispriced risk, which was at the heart of the US subprime mortgage crisis, is a result of low interest rates and excess liquidity. Credit was cheap and plentiful, which is peculiar in a country with a low rate of saving as well as a high level of consumer debt and highly leveraged firms. Normally, with a savings deficit, borrowing would be more expensive given the low supply of funds.

The liquidity did not cause inflation. This is due to globalization and the global appetite for US debt, which kept down prices and the cost of borrowing. The US Federal Reserve then missed the signal that money was too cheap and lenders continued to seek borrowers, even if they were subprime ones.

This strong demand for US treasuries stemmed from the trade surpluses in the Middle East (due to oil exports) and China and elsewhere in Asia (due to cheap manufactured goods). When combined with a high savings rate, particularly in Asia, large foreign exchange reserve holdings accumulated in their coffers. As a result of the fixed exchange rates operated by these countries, purchases of US treasuries were necessary even if the American interest rate, and therefore returns, were low.

CHINESE STRATEGY

This fixed exchange rate regime also forestalled a quick re-balancing of the global economy. For instance, when China, recorded trade a surplus reaching some 14% of GDP in 2007, the currency should have experienced irresistible pressure to appreciate. By so doing, goods purchased from China would have been more expensive for American consumers who would then buy less, thereby reducing the US trade deficit and concurrently causing the Chinese trade surplus to fall.

This, however, did not happen, as the Chinese intervened to manage their currency and used measures to raise reserve requirements in the banking sector to manage the large increase in liquidity in the economy. This was not entirely successful, as inflows continued to come in and China experienced the prospect of an overheating economy when investment, particularly in fixed assets and construction, grew rapidly and led to the prospect of an asset bubble.

Exchange rates are not the only reason for such economic movements. Demand for the US dollar, which has the status of being a reserve currency, does not depend purely on supply and demand caused by trade balance and capital movements. If that were the case, then the US 'twin deficits' (budget and trade) would have become unsustainable long before the crisis. Indeed, the US external deficit, which reflects consumption based on borrowing from abroad, was a phenomenon in the 1980s, well before China's significant opening to the world economy after 1992.

It is not unusual for China or other developing countries to want a stable and competitive currency as their economy grows. Nevertheless, the so-called global imbalances seen in 2008 saw the West, which had low savings, importing savings from the (Far and Middle) East. Also the appetite for US dollars kept liquidity high and cheap (as well as interest rates low) in the United States.

THE DEVELOPMENT OF A GLOBAL CRISIS

The financial crisis followed, as financiers created ever more sophisticated instruments and sold them around the world. To resolve the situation, there will need to be a rebalance in the global economy. This should be done gradually; liquidity from China and emerging economies is needed to help the West to deal with the credit crunch. This liquidity would alleviate some of the necessary belt-tightening experienced by Western consumers and help deflate the asset bubbles that have been building up in emerging economies. It would also help stabilize the rich countries, home to most of the world's consumers upon whom most emerging economies depend for export growth.

"Advertising as a marketing and communications tool will never command the respect it deserves until the correlation between share of voice and profitable growth is firmly established." DeWitt Frederick Helm, Jr

  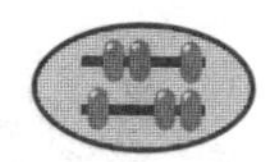   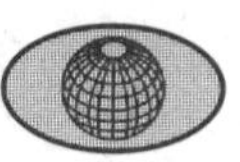   

Some sovereign wealth funds have already helped to re-capitalize Wall Street and European banks, for example Singapore's investments in Citigroup and UBS. And, imagine what would have happened if China's sovereign wealth fund had bought Lehman Brothers. Buying well-priced but illiquid companies is not new, as was seen in the rise of merger and acquisition activity in the aftermath of the Asian financial crisis.

However, the political reaction to sovereign wealth funds strongly suggests that private and commercial firms investing in the West would be more feasible. But China only allowed commercial outward foreign direct investment in the past five years and, even then, it was tightly controlled.

From the perspective of developed countries, it is a small economic step to take direct capital investments from emerging economies through sovereign wealth funds, but a large one politically. Alternatively, commercial capital outflows from Asia would allow a re-balancing without much of the political backlash. However, doing so would also erode capital controls in countries such as China, which will make a fixed exchange rate harder to maintain. This is not a position that China is ready to take nor, it appears, is the Middle East.

However, it should be in the interest of emerging economies to allow greater flexibility in their exchange rates to protect themselves against a currency-led financial crisis, especially considering that a floating currency appreciates/depreciates to absorb external shocks while a fixed exchange rate can be attacked by speculators.

Also, countries such as India and Vietnam had experienced double digit inflation as a result of their low exchange rates, making imports more expensive and investment cheap, factors that can lead to economic overheating and an eventual crash. Moreover, with China and India leading global economic growth, as the developed economies fall into recession, those looking for capital returns are likely to contribute to potential future market bubbles (particularly housing) in these countries, which could cause the next financial crisis.

Also, Western governments will have to borrow to fund the rescue packages and fiscal stimulus measures to fight the recession. These government bonds are likely to be bought by governments from emerging economies, with high levels of savings, such as China. Therefore, rather counter-intuitively, although global imbalances led to this crisis, these imbalances (whereby liquidity flows from East to West) should be maintained for some time longer so that Asian savings can help fuel Western recovery and gradually achieving a rebalanced global economy.

Reducing liquidity at a time when the West is drawing upon it to fund rescue efforts will likely lead to a long and painful period of austerity. The recovery of the Western economies and their markets is in the global interest, particularly China's as the world's second largest trader.

China has played a notable, albeit an indirect role, in the global financial crisis. Its actions, along with other major emerging economies, can also help to resolve it. Doing so is not just geared at aiding a US-led crisis, but to restore a global economic and financial stability that has brought real prosperity to China and much of the developing world over the past decade.

▸▸ MORE INFO

Books:

Dollar, David. "Asian century or multi-polar century?" In Natalia Dinello and Wang Shaoguang (eds). *China, India and Beyond: Drivers and Limitations of Development*. Cheltenham, UK: Edward Elgar, 2009.

Wolf, Martin. *Fixing Global Finance*. New Haven, CT: Yale University Press, 2008.

Yueh, Linda. "Perspectives on China's economic growth: Prospects and wider impact." In Natalia Dinello and Wang Shaoguang (eds). *China, India and Beyond: Drivers and Limitations of Development*. Cheltenham, UK: Edward Elgar, 2009.

Article:

Bean, Charles. "Some lessons for monetary policy from the recent financial turmoil." Speech at Conference on Globalisation, Inflation and Monetary Policy, Istanbul, Turkey, November 22, 2008.

     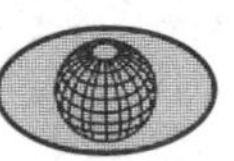   

Why Printing Money Sometimes Works for Central Banks by Paul Kasriel

EXECUTIVE SUMMARY

- There is a logical and defensible rationale for running the printing presses in the current economic climate.
- The banks and two-year Treasury notes, how the banks are recapitalized.
- Options that do not involve monetizing the debt–their disadvantages improve the argument for the monetizing approach.
- Why TALF is essentially a Structured Investment Vehicle.
- The possibility of a second recession in 2012.

INTRODUCTION

At the start of March 2009, even after the signing of the US$787 billion fiscal stimulus package from President Obama, doom and gloom was the order of the day from most commentators. The markets were extremely volatile, anticipating the imminent nationalization of one or more major US banks. The US commerce department released its fourth-quarter GDP data for 2008, which showed that the economy had contracted at an annualized rate of 6.2%, the sharpest contraction since the first quarter of 1982, when the economy fell back by 6.4%. In the light of this and the deepening global recession, very few economists were predicting growth restarting in Q4 2009.

RUNNING THE PRESSES AT HIGH SPEED

Yet there is a very clear route and rationale for growth to come about in this sort of time frame. It all depends on how the Obama fiscal stimulus package is put into effect. In explaining this, we will, simultaneously, be demonstrating how it is that for a central bank, with an economy in this kind of difficulty, running the printing presses at high speed can be a highly responsible course of action.

Of course, if printing money were always a good thing, the Zimbabwean economy in 2009 would be a thing of wonder for the world, instead of the unmitigated disaster it certainly is. Printing money ultimately leads to price inflation, and from there, down the slippery slope to hyperinflation. Before things reach this pass, however, in the early stages, good things can be achieved, as we will demonstrate.

The basis for predicting growth in the fourth quarter of 2009 is an anticipation—at the time of writing, this was not yet a certainty—that the effects of increased federal government spending and tax rebates from the fiscal stimulus will come from the stimulus being largely financed by the banking system and/or the Federal Reserve. When the Federal Reserve and the banking system team up to buy debt, in combination they are, in effect, printing money.

GETTING 65 BASIS POINTS FOR FREE—NICE WORK IF YOU CAN GET IT

How does this work? At today's overnight Fed funds market rate, banks can fund themselves at a cost of about 0.25%. At the same time, two-year Treasury securities are yielding approximately 0.9%. So, if the banks load themselves up with two-year Treasury securities, all funded at 0.25%, they generate a healthy 65 basis-point profit for absolutely no risk. By loading up on Treasuries, banks are, in effect, replenishing their depleted capital. It is a "trick" that worked extremely well for the banks in the 1990s, when they needed to repair depleted capital structures, and it will work again this time round.

It is important here to realize that, because of the Federal Government's ability to tax, there is no credit risk involved in the purchase of Treasury securities. So, there is no risk-based capital charge incurred when banks purchase them. The only meaningful constraint on bank purchases of Treasury securities is their respective overall leverage ratios—total assets in relation to their capital.

There is some slight interest-rate risk, in that if the Federal Reserve began to raise the overnight rate, the profitability of the two-year bills to the banks would diminish, and possibly even turn into a loss. But that is the only risk, and it is likely to be well into 2010 before the Federal Reserve will need to worry about inflation, which might cause it to want to push rates up.

There seems little likelihood or risk of stagflation for the US economy. Stagflation usually occurs when there is some supply constraint on the economy; for example, where the economy has run out of labor and cannot grow any faster because it does not have the labor to produce the goods and services, or where there is a sharp reduction in energy supplies, which constrains industry. The United States is a net debtor nation, and falling prices of goods, services, and income make a very hostile environment for debtors. The nominal value of the debt contracted for does not fall, but the revenue of the debtor nation falls, making the debt much harder to pay back. So, the United States has an interest in generating a modest amount of inflation as it restarts the economy. It also has plenty of excess capacity in the economy, with unemployment likely to go above 9% in the months ahead, and underutilized capacity rising in US factories. The real factor holding back GDP growth in the United States right now is the lack of aggregate demand for goods from households and businesses, as well as from state and local government.

How does the monetization of debt (with the Fed printing money to pay the banks and the banks buying Treasury debt) affect the banks' ability to lend? The process of borrowing cheaply and buying debt for a net 65 basis-points profit allows the banks' capital to increase, and that, in turn, allows the banks to start to extend more credit to the private sector. This is exactly what happened during the early 1990s, and although the situation is more severe now, the yield curve is steeper. In the early 1990s, by the second half of 1993, this process of gaining capital through buying Treasuries had recapitalized the banks sufficiently for them to resume near-normal lending.

However, there are two other options where the debt is not monetized, via the banks buying Treasury bills and the Fed printing money. Option one is where the Federal Government acquires funding via increasing the taxes it collects—which does not look to be on the agenda now, despite President Obama's pre-election promise to increase taxes on incomes in excess of US$250,000. Option two is where the Fed increases its bond sales to the non-bank public—a method much used by Argentina after it defaulted on its sovereign debt. Neither of these options, increasing taxes and selling to the non-bank public, lead to any new spending in the economy. In the first option, the private sector cuts back on spending to pay for the new taxes. In the second, it cuts back on spending to pay for the new bonds (in other words it saves, rather than spends, and increased

"**A hard sell advertisement, like a diesel motor, must be judged on whether it performs what it was designed to do.**" Rosser Reeves

saving at the cost of spending deepens the recession).

However, where the Fed prints money to fund increased spending, the private sector is not supplied with a new motive for cutting back on spending, so the new spending by the government is a real net additional spend in the economy. That is the first part of the monetization process. The second part is the improvement in bank-retained earnings.

Of course, in addition to taking these measures, the federal government is also doing other things to encourage the economy to move forward. Both TARP (the Troubled Assets Relief Program) and the Federal Reserve's Term Asset-backed securities Lending Facility (TALF) are crucial here. The goal of TALF is to begin a thawing process in the frozen, asset-backed securities (ABS) market. These asset-backed securities involve many types of private-sector credit, such as credit cards, auto loans, student loans, residential real-estate mortgages, and commercial real-estate mortgage debt. The idea is that, through TALF, the Federal Reserve will provide non-recourse financing to entities that purchase newly issued securitized debt with a credit rating of AAA. The term of these loans would be three years. The borrowers could opt for a floating-rate loan, priced at 100 basis points over one-month Libor, or a fixed-rate loan priced at 100 basis points over three-year Libor. The Fed would not lend 100% of the face value of these securities, but would lend an amount something less than face value in order to protect the taxpayer against some future loss in the value of these securities. However, due to the non-recourse nature of the loan, if the value of the securities were to fall below this discounted value, then the Fed would have to accept the credit loss.

When TALF was first proposed, back in November 2008, its funding allocation was US$200 billion. Under the Treasury's new Financial Stability Package (FSP), TALF's funding amount has been increased five-fold, to US$1 trillion.

Interestingly, the TALF program is essentially a structured investment vehicle (SIV), much like the banks' off-balance-sheet SIVs that got us all into this mess in the first place. The one really important distinction, however, is that the Fed, which has the largest capacity in the world to absorb losses, is providing the financing. So, unlike the case with the original SIVs, there are no parties in a position to make margin calls in the TALF version. (It was the margin calls that were triggered as the collateral in the SIVs deteriorated that first opened up the debt abyss for the banks.)

With previous facilities, the Fed had already begun creating credit for the non-bank private sector in the United States. For example, the Fed has been purchasing commercial paper, short-term uncollateralized loans, from corporate issuers (borrowers). TALF expands the capacity for the Fed, in effect, to create credit for the private sector. It is, therefore, very likely that TALF will be the most important element of the federal government's Financial Stability Package, as far as increasing the flow of credit to the private sector over the coming 12 months is concerned.

Another part of the FSP is, as far as can be seen at this stage, a kind of "purge and merge" program, whereby the Fed's "stress test" is supposed to show which banks have a decent chance of surviving the recession, and which do not. The "terminally ill" will be purged of their poisonous assets and merged into those with a better chance of survival. In the process, it is likely that stockholder equity in the terminally ill banks will be wiped out. Taxpayers will bear the costs of any unrecoverable losses of purged assets.

CONCLUSION

There is a reasonable case to be made, as of the beginning of March 2009, that the combination of the US$1 trillion TALF program and the US$787 billion fiscal stimulus program, assuming it is financed by the banking system and the Fed, will have a salutary effect on aggregate real activity in the US economy, with a reasonable chance of inducing an economic recovery by the fourth quarter of 2009.

However, because a key part of this upturn will rely on the Fed running the printing presses as hard as it can, there is also a reasonable likelihood that rising inflation will return as we go through 2010. This, in turn, will prompt the Fed to tighten credit again, which could have a second recessionary impact by 2012. So, one possible shape for the future of the United States, and possibly of the global economy, is not a "V" but a "W". However, that would still, in all probability, be a better outcome than a multi-year recession.

▸▸ MORE INFO

Websites:

Northern Trust Bank: www.ntrs.com

Paul Kasriel's The EContrarian: www.northerntrust.com/pws/jsp/display2.jsp?XML=pages/nt/0601/1138283681241_6.xml&TYPE=interior

"Advertising began as an art. . .and too many advertising people want it to remain that way—a never-never land where they can say this is right because we feel it is right." Rosser Reeves

  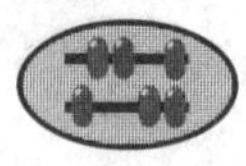 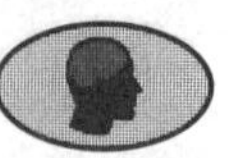  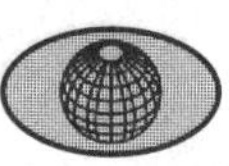   

Viewpoint: Muhammad Yunus
The Financial Crisis and the World's Poor

INTRODUCTION

Professor Muhammad Yunus is the founder and Managing Director of Grameen Bank which provides micro-credit to millions of poor people in Bangladesh. In 2006 he was awarded the Nobel Peace Prize.

Yunus pioneered microcredit, the innovative banking program that provides the poor—mainly women—with small loans they use to launch businesses and lift their families out of poverty. Yunus's vision is the total eradication of poverty from the world. This work is a fundamental rethink on the economic relationship between the rich and the poor, their rights and their obligations. The World Bank recently acknowledged that "this business approach to the alleviation of poverty has allowed millions of individuals to work their way out of poverty with dignity." Credit is the last hope left to those faced with absolute poverty. That is why Yunus believes that the right to credit should be recognized as a fundamental human right.

Yunus serves on the boards of many national and international organisations. Besides Grameen Bank he has created a number of companies in Bangladesh to address diverse issues of poverty and development.

The recession of 2008–2009 has well and truly shaken the foundations of global finance. Financial pundits and central banks are now analyzing how they got here and how to prevent things from crashing through the floor. The stimulus packages announced in the richest economies of the world are being widely judged as being insufficient. Quarter on quarter output changes published in *The Economist* for the G7 countries are painting a ghastly picture. There is much concern that the developed world is not spending enough on stimulus packages (despite Obama's fiscal stimulus package of US$787 billion—the largest in US history, and China, which is spending 6.9% of its GDP), which will, in turn, hurt the developing countries that sell goods and services to them.

The developing countries are not expected to enter into stimulus spending on this large scale, mainly because they do not have the liquidity to borrow in the first place. Financial pundits in Bangladesh, for example, are in fact trying to explain the "time lag" between the global recessionary economy and Bangladesh's own economy, which is partially shielded from feeling the aftershocks. They are, however, advising the government to take advantage of the time lag by designing stimulus packages for the banking system and government spending with the goals of creating new jobs and improving the long-term competitiveness of the economy. They are creating financial packages so that they can lend more to retail and business customers.

All of this, no doubt, makes sound financial sense, but I would like to ask a few questions: What is the future of global capitalism when there is no financial package for the protection of the world's poorest? What is the goal of financial planning at a time of recession if no one talks about those who are too poor to even have a bank account? What kind of changes should we be looking for that protect the interests of people who have no access to food and nutrition even when the markets are bullish?

CAPITALISM AND POVERTY

Poverty is not created by the poor. Rather, it is created by the economic and social system that we have designed for the world. It is created by the institutions that we have built, the concepts we have developed, by the policies borne out of our reasoning and theoretical framework. In order to overcome poverty, we have to go back to the drawing board and redesign our concepts and institutions of capitalism. There is something fundamentally wrong with an institution that leaves out more than half the population of the world, because they are not considered creditworthy. This is what my work with Grameen Bank has been about: to design a banking method that can deliver the financial service to the people left out, particularly for the women who are the most difficult to reach.

In the context of the global banking crisis of 2008–2009, it is paramount that we redesign the way finance is handled globally, which has been described in the media as casino capitalism or irresponsible capitalism. Credit markets were originally created to serve human needs, to provide business people with capital to start or expand companies, and to enable families to buy homes. In return for these services, bankers and other lenders earned a reasonable profit. Everyone benefited. In recent years, however, the credit markets have been distorted by a relative handful of individuals and companies with a different goal in mind, to earn unrealistically high rates of return through clever feats of financial engineering. They repackaged mortgages and other loans into sophisticated instruments whose risk level and other characteristics were hidden or disguised. Then they sold and resold these instruments, earning a slice of profit on every transaction. All the while, investors eagerly bid up the prices, scrambling for unsustainable growth, and gambling that the underlying weakness of the system would never come to light. The poor, as usual, will feel the worst effects. As economies falter, as government budgets collapse, and as contributions to charities and NGOs dwindle, efforts to help the poor will diminish. With the slowing down of economies everywhere, the poor will lose their jobs and income from self-employment.

Even if we can overcome the problem of the financial crisis, we will still be left with some fundamental questions about the effectiveness of capitalism in tackling many other unresolved problems. In my view, the theoretical framework of capitalism that is in practice today is a half-done structure. The theory of capitalism holds that the marketplace is only for those who are interested in making money, for the people who are interested in profit only. This interpretation of human beings in the theory

"**Advertising is merely a substitute for a personal sales force – an extension, if you will, of the merchant who cried about his wares."** Rosser Reeves

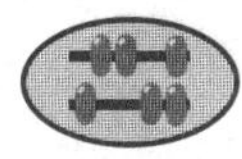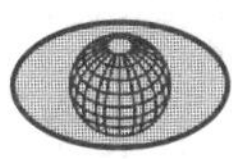

treats people as one-dimensional beings. But people are multi-dimensional. While they have their selfish dimensions, at the same time they also have their selfless dimensions. Capitalism, and the marketplace that has grown up around the theory, makes no room for people's selfless dimensions. If some of the self-sacrificing drives and motivations that exist in people could be brought into the business arena to tackle problems that face the world, there would be very few problems that we could not solve.

The present structure of the economic theory does not allow these dimensions of people to play out in the marketplace. I argue that, given the opportunity, people will come into the marketplace to express their selfless urges by running special types of businesses, let us call them social businesses, to make a change in the world. In the absence of such opportunity in the marketplace, people express their selflessness through charities. Charitable efforts have been with us always, and they are noble and needed. But we have seen that business is able to innovate, expand, and reach more and more people through the power of the free market. Imagine what we could achieve if talented entrepreneurs and business executives around the world devoted themselves to ending, say, malnutrition, without any intention of making money for themselves or investors?

THE BANKS VS THE GRAMEEN MODEL

Banks explain that poor people are not creditworthy. The Grameen Bank model challenges that, and continues to do that during the worst recession in recent memory. At Grameen Bank, there are no legal instruments between lender and borrower, no guarantees, no collateral. You cannot get riskier than that, and yet our money comes back while the prestigious banks all over the world are going down with all their intelligent paperwork, all their collateral, all the lawyers and legal systems to back up their lending.

When people ask me, "How did you figure out all the rules and procedures that are now known as the Grameen system?" my answer is: "That was very simple and easy. Whenever I needed a rule or a procedure in our work, I just looked at the conventional banks to see what they do in a similar situation. Once I learned what they did, I just did the opposite." That's how I got our rules. Conventional banks go to the rich, we go to the poor; their rule is: "The more you have, the more you get." So our rule became: "The less you have, the more attention you get. If you have nothing, you are top priority." They ask for collateral, we abandoned it, as if we had never heard of it. They need lawyers in their business. We do not. No lawyer is involved in any of our loan transactions. The rich own them; ours is owned by the poorest, the poorest women. I can go on adding more to this list to show how Grameen does things quite the opposite way. Was it really a systematic policy to do it the opposite way? No, it was not. But that is how it turned out ultimately, because our objective was different. I had not even noticed it until a senior banker admonished me by saying: "Dr Yunus, you are trying to put the banking system upside down." I quickly agreed with him. I said: "Yes, because the banking system is standing on its head."

SOCIAL BUSINESS FROM THE GRAMEEN BANK

Corporate social responsibility (CSR) is considered to be a part of company policy nowadays in many developed and developing countries. CSR usually means let us make money, and then use part of that wealth to help society. This is an important development in the business world. But this still does not let business people express their selfless urges within the framework of the market. Just as an individual person who makes money in business then gives away a part of his income to charity, similarly now a company, a legal person, does the same, it makes money and gives part of it to charity.

I am proposing a different structure for the market itself. I am proposing a second type of business to operate in the same market alongside the existing profit-maximizing businesses. I am not opposed to the existing type of business (although I call for many improvements, as many others do). I am proposing a new business in addition to the existing one. This new type of business I call "social business," because it is for the collective benefit of others.

This is a business the purpose of which is to address and solve the social problems faced by the poorest people, not to make money for its investors. It is a nonloss, nondividend company. Investors can recoup their investment capital, but beyond that, there are no profits to be taken out as dividends. The profits remain with the company and are used to expand its reach, improve the quality of the product or service it provides, and design methods to bring down the cost of the product or service. If the efficiency, the competitiveness, and the dynamism of business could be harnessed to deal with specific social problems, the world would be a much better place.

BIRTH OF SOCIAL BUSINESS

The concept of a social business crystallized in my mind through my experience with Grameen companies. Over the years, Grameen created a series of companies to address different problems faced by the poor in Bangladesh. Whether it is a company to provide renewable energy or a company to provide healthcare or yet another company to provide information technology to the poor, we were always motivated by the need to address social needs. We always designed them as profitable companies, but only to ensure their sustainability so that the product or service could reach more and more of the poor on an ongoing basis. In all these cases, the social need was the only focus; making personal money was no consideration at all. That is how I realized that businesses could be built that way, from the ground up, around a specific social need, without motive for personal gain.

SOCIAL BUSINESS IN MOTION

The idea of social business took wings when we launched a joint venture with Danone (known as Dannon in the United States). Together we have formed Grameen Danone Foods Ltd and we produce nutritious fortified yogurt for the undernourished children of rural Bangladesh. The yogurt, called Shakti Doi, is made with full-cream milk that contains protein, vitamins, iron, calcium, zinc, and other micronutrients which poor people might not get in their regular diet. Each pot is sold at 5 taka (about 5 UK pence) in Bangladeshi villages, so it is easily affordable. Grameen Danone Foods is a prime example of social business because it sources raw materials locally and employs local people. But more importantly, neither we nor Danone will make money from this venture beyond recuperating our initial investment. Bottom line for the company is to see how many children overcome their nutritional deficiencies each year. We currently have one plant operating in Bangladesh, and we hope to grow to have 50 such plants throughout the country.

In 2006 we set up the Grameen Health Care Services Ltd, with the idea of contributing to the healthcare sector in Bangladesh. Under that initiative in 2007, we started an eye care hospital in Bogra, Bangladesh, targeting about 3.5 million poor Bangladeshis. Grameen eye hospital is charging patients based on their ability to pay: wealthier patients are charged at a normal rate while poor patients pay a subsidized rate. The fee for an eye exam is 50 taka (about 50 UK pence). A second eye hospital is being built, and two more are in the pipeline.

     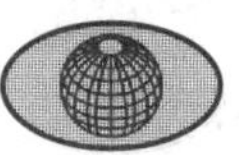   

We have created a joint venture with Veolia of France to deliver safe drinking water to the villages of Bangladesh. Under the company, we are building a small water treatment plant in a rural part of Bangladesh to bring clean water to 100,000 villagers in an area where the existing supply of water is highly contaminated with arsenic. We will sell the water at a very affordable price to the villagers to make the company sustainable, but no financial gain will come to Grameen or Veolia. This social business water company will be a prototype for supplying safe drinking water in a sustainable and affordable way to people who are faced with water crises. Once it is perfected, it can be replicated in other villages, within and outside Bangladesh.

Our next initiative came from Credit Agricole of France. We created the Grameen Credit Agricole Microfinance Foundation to provide financial support to microfinance organizations and social businesses. We have signed a joint venture agreement with Intel Corporation to create a social business company called Grameen-Intel, which will bring information technology-based services to the poor in healthcare, marketing, education, and remittances. We also signed a social business joint venture agreement with Saudi-German Hospital Group to set up a series of hospitals in Bangladesh. In March 2009, BASF SE and Grameen Healthcare Trust have announced the establishment of a joint social business venture to supply at reasonable cost, dietary supplement sachets containing vitamins and trace elements, and impregnated mosquito nets that offer protection against insect-borne diseases. BASF Grameen Ltd is not a charity. It combines business sense with social needs.

Many more companies from around the world are showing interest in such social business joint ventures. A leading shoe company wants to create a social business to make sure that nobody goes without shoes. One leading pharmaceutical company wishes to set up a joint venture social business company to produce nutritional supplements appropriate for Bangladeshi pregnant mothers and young women at the cheapest possible price.

Some people are skeptical. Who will create these businesses? Who will run these businesses? I always say that, to begin with, there is no dearth of philanthropists in the world. People give away billions of dollars. Imagine if those billions could be used in a social business way to help people. These billions will be recycled again and again, and the social impact could be that much more powerful. Companies' CSR money could easily go into social businesses. Each company can create its own range of social businesses.

Once the concept of social business is included in the economic theory, millions of people will come forward to invest because they all have those social dreams in their hearts. We will need to create social stock markets to channel these funds to appropriate social businesses.

SOCIAL STOCK MARKET

To connect investors with social businesses, we need to create a social stock market where only the shares of social businesses will be traded. An investor will come to this stock exchange with a clear intention of finding a social business that has a mission of his or her liking. Anyone who wants to make money will go to the existing stock market. To enable a social stock exchange to perform properly, we will need to create rating agencies, standardization of terminology, definitions, impact measurement tools, reporting formats, and new financial publications, such as "The Social Wall Street Journal." Business schools will offer courses and business management degrees on social businesses to train young managers in how to manage social business enterprises in the most efficient manner, and, most of all, to inspire them to become social business entrepreneurs themselves.

Once social business is recognized in law, many existing companies will come forward to create social businesses in addition to their foundation activities. Many activists from the nonprofit sector will also find this an attractive option. Unlike the nonprofit sector, where one needs to collect donations to keep activities going, a social business will be self-sustaining and create surplus for expansion since it is a nonloss enterprise. Social business will go into a new type of capital market of its own to raise capital.

HOW TO BEGIN CHANGE

I have talked a lot about how the current financial crisis brings new risks to the world's poor. It is time to change. The thought that always energizes me is that poverty is not created by the poor people. Poverty is an artificial imposition on people. Poor people are endowed with the same unlimited potential of creativity and energy as any other human being of any walk of life, anywhere in the world. It is a question of removing the barriers to unleash poor people's creativity to solve their own problems. They can change their lives, but only if we give them the same opportunity that we get. Creatively designed social businesses in all sectors can make this happen in the fastest way. To make a start, all each one of you has to do is to design a business plan for a social business. Each prototype of a social business can be a cute little business. If it works out, the whole world can be changed by replicating it in thousands of locations.

Three basic interventions will make a big difference in the existing system:

1. Broadening the concept of business by including "social business" in the framework of the marketplace;
2. Creating inclusive financial and healthcare services which can reach out to every person on the planet;
3. Designing appropriate information technology devices and services for the most deprived people and making these easily available to them.

CONCLUSION

I always insist that poverty does not belong in civilized society. Poverty belongs only in museums, where our children and grandchildren can go to see what inhumane conditions people had to suffer, and where they will ask themselves how their ancestors allowed it to persist for so long. We overcame slavery; we overcame apartheid. Together, if we face the recession of 2008–2009 through changing capitalism and its institutions, we can change the way people think. Social businesses can be an important part of that vision.

▸▸ MORE INFO

See Also:

✔ Bangladesh (pp. 1355–1356)
Muhammad Yunus (p. 1205)
Banker to the Poor: The Story of the Grameen Bank (p. 1222)

"Each day of our lives, twelve billion display ads, two and a half million radio commercials, and over three hundred thousand television commercials are dumped into the collective conscience." Ronald Collins

     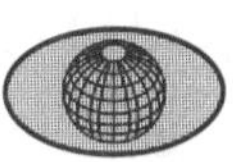   

The Ability of Ratings to Predict the Performance of Exchange-Traded Funds
by Gerasimos G. Rompotis

EXECUTIVE SUMMARY

- Rating of the past performance of securities is considered crucial by investors when they make investment decisions.
- Several rating methods are used in the financial literature and by the investing community to rate the performance of securities.
- Performance is considered to be in some way predictable, and prediction is based on past performance.
- This article empirically assesses the rating of exchange-traded funds (ETFs) and prediction of their performance.
- The methods examined are the Morningstar rating process, the excess return, the Sharpe ratio, and the Treynor ratio.
- The empirical results reveal a high consistency among the rating methods and a sufficient level of predictability of ETF performance.
- ETF performance is persistent over the short term.

INTRODUCTION

Exchange-traded funds, or ETFs, are a relatively new investment product, but they are very important for both institutional and retail investors. ETFs are hybrids of ordinary corporate stocks and open-ended mutual funds which invest in baskets of shares that closely replicate the performance and risk levels of specific broad sector and international indexes. As such, ETFs offer investors a considerable level of risk diversification with just a single transaction. The risk of investing in ETFs can be moderated by choosing non-equity investments such as corporate bonds or treasury bonds, both of which are less risky choices than the most common equity-linked ETFs. Also, fixed-income ETFs, which usually carry low risk, are available for investors along with commodity and real estate ETFs.

ETFs are cheap investment tools because their administrative costs are low. This is reflected in low expense ratios due to their passive investment character, which requires managers simply to follow the tracking indexes and not to develop complicated and high-cost investment strategies. Nevertheless, it should be borne in mind that extremely frequent trading can offset the benefits of low expense ratios. The level of ETF expense ratios varies. In particular, ETFs that track broadly diversified indexes have the lowest expenses, followed by those that track sector indexes and others which invest in international indexes. Beyond managerial costs, ETFs pay commission to brokerage companies.

ETFs provide significant trading flexibility since they offer continuous pricing and the ability to trade throughout the day, unlike most mutual funds, which are traded at the end of the day. Furthermore, ETFs offer opportunities for the implementation of both passive and active trading strategies. The most common investment strategy in ETFs is the passive buy-and-hold strategy, the return of which depends exclusively on market performance. Also, ETFs allow active intraday trading and enable investors to buy and sell, in essence, all of the securities that make up an entire market with a single trade. They therefore provide the flexibility to get into or out of a position at any time throughout the day.

Another significant element of ETFs is the potential for high tax efficiency that they offer, since they tend to generate fewer capital gains than traditional mutual funds. The tax efficiency of ETFs arises from their discrete "in kind" creation/redemption process. ETFs are created in block-sized units of 25,000, 50,000, or 100,000 shares by large investors and institutions. The creator of an ETF purchases and deposits with a trustee a portfolio of stocks that approximates the composition of a specific index. In return for this deposit, the creator receives a fixed number of ETF shares, all of which are then usually traded on a secondary exchange market. The redemption of ETFs follows the reverse direction. Buying and selling of ETF shares usually takes place among shareholders and, as a result, there is no need for the ETF to sell its assets to meet redemptions. This advantageous feature of ETFs restricts the realization of taxable capital gains.

The trading price of ETFs usually deviates from their corresponding net asset value, providing arbitrage opportunities for big investors. If the value of the underlying portfolio of stocks is greater than the ETF price, the institutional investor will redeem the low-priced units of ETF by receiving the high-priced securities. In contrast, if the value of the underlying stocks is lower than the ETF price, the investor will exchange the low-priced securities for a newly created unit of the ETF.

Finally, ETFs are characterized by large liquidity, which contributes to easy and rapid trading near their fair market value and to the narrowness of bid/ask spreads and volatility. The liquidity of an ETF is not related to its daily trading volume but rather to the liquidity of the stocks contained in the index. The high liquidity of ETFs is achieved due to the ability of market-makers, which are usually large brokerage houses, to create and redeem shares of ETFs perpetually in response to market demand.

Because of their success, ETFs have begun to attract significant interest in the finance literature. An issue that so far has not been thoroughly examined is the rating of ETF performance and the ability of ratings to predict future performance. Nevertheless, several companies provide ranking services. The most popular is Morningstar, Inc., which rates ETFs on a scale of one to five stars according to past performance. Here we provide an introduction to ETF performance rating by investigating whether ratings are indicative of future returns. We do so using a sample of 50 Barclays iShares.

PERFORMANCE RATING

Morningstar

We first rate the performance of ETFs by using the Morningstar star rating. We calculate the "Morningstar" return, which is adjusted for expenses such as management fees, 12b-1 fees (annual marketing or distribution fees charged by some mutual funds), custodian fees, and other costs that are deducted from the assets of ETFs. Then we divide average excess return by either the average excess return or the average risk-free rate. The risk-free rate is used

"The need to trade an entire portfolio in a single transaction was the generator of ETFs." Gary Gastineau

Table 1. Consistency in performance rating

Estimated model	alpha	t-test	beta	t-test	R^2	F-stat
Morningstar return = $\alpha_0 + \beta$ (Excess return) + υ	0.270	1.360	0.910*	15.206	0.828	231.23*
Morningstar return = $\alpha_0 + \beta$ (Sharpe ratio) + υ	0.210	1.193	0.930*	17.530	0.865	307.29*
Morningstar return = $\alpha_0 + \beta$ (Treynor ratio) + υ	0.240	1.279	0.920*	16.263	0.846	264.50*
Excess return = $\alpha_0 + \beta$ (Sharpe ratio) + υ	0.090	0.773	0.970*	27.644	0.941	764.18*
Excess return = $\alpha_0 + \beta$ (Treynor ratio) + υ	0.030	0.444	0.990*	48.621	0.980	2364.06*
Sharpe ratio = $\alpha_0 + \beta$ (Treynor ratio) + υ	0.120	0.895	0.960*	23.753	0.922	564.24*

* Statistically significant at the 1% level.

Table 2. Correlation coefficients among performance ratings

	Morningstar	Excess	Sharpe	Treynor
Morningstar	1.000	0.910	0.930	0.920
Excess	0.910	1.000	0.970	0.990
Sharpe	0.930	0.970	1.000	0.960
Treynor	0.920	0.990	0.960	1.000

Excess Return, Sharpe Ratio, and Treynor Ratio

The second performance measure we consider is the average daily excess return of ETFs, which is simply calculated by subtracting a fund's risk-free performance from its return. The third performance measure is the Sharpe ratio. Sharpe ratio is calculated by dividing the average daily excess return of ETFs by the standard deviation of daily excess returns. The last performance measure is the Treynor ratio. This is computed by dividing the average daily excess return of ETFs by their systematic risk. Systematic risk is estimated by the single index market model, where the daily excess return of each ETF is regressed on the excess return of its benchmark.

Table 3. Regression results in predicting performance

Variables	δ_0	δ_4 (4-star)	δ_3 (3-star)	δ_2 (2-star)	δ_1 (1-star)	R^2	F-stat
Morningstar return	0.525	−0.147	−0.846	−0.913	−0.438	0.200	1.510
Excess return	0.060	−0.016	−0.032	−0.036	−0.028	0.196	2.874
Sharpe ratio	0.044	−0.006	−0.011	−0.022	−0.011	0.142	2.041
Treynor ratio	0.061	−0.018	−0.033	−0.038	−0.029	0.201	2.957

when the average excess return is negative or lower than the average risk-free rate. Morningstar return is expressed by the following formula:

$$\text{Morningstar return} = \frac{(\text{Expense- and load-adjusted return of ETF} - \text{Treasury bill})}{\{\max[(\text{Average sample return} - \text{Treasury bill}),\ \text{Treasury bill}]\}}$$

The risk-free return is used in the dominator of the equation in cases where the average excess return of ETFs is negative or very low.

We then calculate "Morningstar" risk by summing up all the negative average daily excess returns of each ETF and dividing by the number of days in the assessing time period. Morningstar risk is represented by the following equation:

$$\text{Morningstar risk} = \frac{(\text{Average underperformance of ETF})}{(\text{Average underperformance of sample})}$$

Finally, the ETF's star rating is calculated by subtracting its Morningstar risk from its Morningstar return. Afterwards, we classify ETFs in five classes, each of which includes 10 ETFs.

Morningstar, Inc., adjusts the returns of funds for expenses such as management fees, 12b-1 fees, custodian fees, and other costs that are deducted from the assets of funds. Return is also adjusted for front-end and deferred loads. However, here we do not need to adjust for expenses and loads because we start out by calculating returns with expense-free net asset values, meaning that we can then treat ETFs as no-load funds and removing the need to adjust for loads.

Table 4. Regression results in performance persistence

Period	alpha	t-test	beta	t-test	R^2	F-stat
Dependent variable: Morningstar return						
2001–02	−9.305*	−7.359	0.744*	3.447	0.198	11.883*
2002–03	0.009	0.056	0.001	0.060	0.000	0.011
2003–04	0.000	0.000	0.853**	2.141	0.217	13.318*
2004–05	−0.044	−0.115	0.065	0.207	0.226	6.699*
2005–06	−0.009	−0.051	−0.145**	−2.447	0.176	3.127**
2006–07	−0.487	−0.723	0.077	0.107	0.154	4.187**
Dependent variable: Excess return						
2001–02	−0.058*	−3.288	0.296*	3.302	0.185	10.904*
2002–03	0.103*	7.968	−0.247***	−1.956	0.168	4.636**
2003–04	−0.004	−0.257	0.538*	4.748	0.320	22.542*
2004–05	−0.009	−1.048	0.530*	2.927	0.242	15.319*
2005–06	0.059*	4.616	−0.044	−0.190	0.291	6.006*
2006–07	−0.017	−1.221	0.588*	2.940	0.153	8.645*
Dependent variable: Sharpe ratio						
2001–02	−0.034*	−6.139	0.266*	2.936	0.078	4.596**
2002–03	0.124*	13.624	0.377**	2.022	0.168	4.089**
2003–04	0.007	0.299	0.547**	2.392	0.248	15.851*
2004–05	0.005	0.524	0.280***	2.010	0.077	4.039***
2005–06	0.068*	3.317	−0.557*	−4.344	0.367	6.095*
2006–07	−0.006	−0.501	0.298***	1.867	0.068	3.486***
Dependent variable: Treynor ratio						
2001–02	−0.059*	−8.282	0.302*	3.367	0.191	11.334*
2002–03	0.108*	4.990	−0.197	−0.698	0.141	3.783**
2003–04	−0.007	−0.520	0.565*	5.222	0.362	27.274*
2004–05	−0.009	−1.045	0.529*	2.929	0.243	15.406*
2005–06	0.060*	4.526	−0.031	−0.136	0.300	6.275*
2006–07	−0.017	−1.229	0.584*	2.972	0.155	8.831*

*Statistically significant at the 1% level. **Statistically significant at the 5% level. ***Statistically significant at the 10% level.

"The first thing is character. . .before money or anything else. Money cannot buy it. . .because a man I do not trust could not get money from me on all the bonds in Christendom." J. P. Morgan

  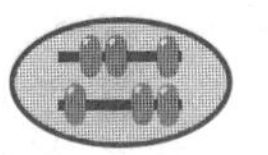   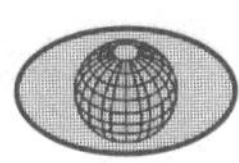   

PERFORMANCE PREDICTION

We examine predictability following regression analysis, represented by the next equation:

$$P_i = \delta_0 + \delta_4 D4_i + \delta_3 D3_i + \delta_2 D2_i + \delta_1 D1_i + u$$

where P_i is the out-of-sample performance of ETFs. Performance is, successively, the Morningstar return, the excess return, the Sharpe ratio, and the Treynor ratio. The control factors of the model are four variables symbolized as D4, D3, D2, and D1, representing the ETFs that receive four, three, two, and one stars, respectively. The class of top-performing ETFs that are assigned five stars is represented by the δ_0 coefficient. This class is the reference group, and hence deltas account for the difference between the top-performing ETFs and other classes.

To estimate the model represented by this equation, we first compute all the performance measures of ETFs in a specific year between 2001 and 2006 and rank them in five classes in descending order. Then, we calculate each of the four types of performance for the subsequent period (2002–07, 2003–07, 2004–07, 2005–07, 2006–07, and 2007). The predictive ability of the model is confirmed when, first, δ estimates are negative and statistically significant and, second, when deltas become more negative as we move from δ_4 to δ_1.

It has been shown in the literature that there is a positive correlation between fund flows and persistence of performance (e.g. Wermers, 2003). Given that investors tend to put more money in mutual funds or ETFs that receive high grades from Morningstar or other agencies, we assume that this new money pushes up prices and returns and therefore that there should be a meaningful relationship between ratings and future performance.

PERFORMANCE PERSISTENCE

We examine persistence by applying simple regression analysis—specifically, cross-sectional regression of ETFs' performance in a given year on their performance in the previous year. The beta coefficient of the model is the indicator of persistence. Positive and significant betas imply persistence, and evidence of persistence strengthens as beta approaches unity. Significant negative beta values reflect inversions of ETF performance, while insignificant betas imply unsystematic variation of performance.

This study is presented in the next section.

CASE STUDY

Barclays iShares

Here we will empirically examine the rating and predictability of ETF performance using a sample of 50 Barclays Global Investors iShares during the period 2001–07. Of this sample, 27 ETFs track domestic broad market or sector indexes (20 and 7 ETFs, respectively), while the other 23 ETFs track the country indexes of Morgan Stanley or other international indexes (21 and 2 ETFs, respectively).

The average estimates of the four performance measures are as follows. The average Morningstar performance is negative and equal to –0.496. The average excess return and Sharpe and Treynor ratios are 0.017, 0.013, and 0.017, respectively.

We evaluate the consistency among the ratings by applying a simple cross-sectional model. Specifically, we regress the rating of ETFs according to method *i* to the rating of ETFs according to method *j*. More specifically, we regress the rankings of ETFs (i.e. rankings 1, 2, 3, 4, and 5) and not the actual estimates derived by the Morningstar rating method on the rankings derived by excess return. We repeat the regression for all the pairs of methods used to evaluate the performance of ETFs. The measure of consistency is the beta of the model. Positive beta estimates indicate consistency among ratings. Negative or statistically insignificant betas indicate inconsistency among the ratings. Alternatively, we assess consistency by calculating the correlation coefficients among the rankings obtained using the four methods.

The results, presented in Table 1, reveal high consistency among the performance measures. All betas are positive and significant and approach unity, ranging from 0.910 for the regression between Morningstar and excess return ratings to 0.990 for the pairing of excess return and Treynor ratio. This means that the best performing ETFs receive five stars almost consistently regardless of the rating method. This is also the case for ETFs in the other four classes. Table 2 presents the correlation coefficients among the rankings given by the four methods. Correlation coefficients are all greater than 0.900 and approximate unity, confirming the high consistency among the ranking results. Overall, the results reveal that there is no best method for the rating of ETF performance, and therefore investors (could) consult various alternative methods to make their investment choices based on the available information.

The regression results for performance prediction are reported in Table 3. To begin with, the average δ_0 estimates are positive for each performance measure. Second, the average δ_4, δ_3, δ_2, and δ_1 estimates are all negative. Informationally, the majority of individual δ_0 in the individual regressions performed for each year of the period are positive and statistically significant, while the majority of δ_4 to δ_1 estimates are negative. Considering the significance of the δ_4 to δ_1 estimates, the results of individual regressions indicate that there is no significant difference between the ETFs included in classes 5 and 4, while there is a definite difference between the top-performing ETFs and medium- and low-performing ETFs.

The results are interpreted as follows: First, the positive δ_0 estimates indicate that the top-rated ETFs display a constant behavior through time. In other words, an ETF that performs well now is likely to perform well in the future. Second, there is no significant difference in the performance of the top-rated and second-rank ETFs. Third, there is evidence that the performance of the medium- and low-rated ETFs is sufficiently predictable, the performance of both these groups being inferior to that of the highly rated ETFs.

The sufficient predictability of ETF returns on the basis of rating in a specific year or period revealed by the results indicates that institutional and retail investors should take into consideration the published ratings of ETFs when they assess their investment choices. However, investors should always bear in mind that returns are not guaranteed and markets can move both up and down. Therefore, ratings are useful but should not be the only criterion in choosing among the bulk of ETFs. Other features, such as risk and expenses, should also be taken into consideration by investors.

Regression results for performance persistence are presented in Table 4. Regarding Morningstar, beta estimates provide evidence for short-term persistence in ETF performance during the periods 2001–02 and 2003–04 but a reversal for the period 2005–06. Beta estimates for the first two periods are positive and significant, while the beta for the third mentioned period is significantly negative. Considering excess return and Treynor ratio, the results indicate short-term persistence in the periods 2001–02, 2003–04, 2004–05, and 2006–07. The excess return results indicate a reversal of

     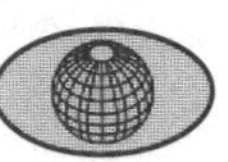   

CONCLUSION

We have investigated the ability of ETF performance ratings to predict the future performance of these funds. We ranked ETFs using the overall Morningstar star rating methodology along with three alternative performance measures: the excess return, the Sharpe ratio, and the Treynor ratio.

First, the results reveal a high level of consistency among the four types of performance measure. In other words, all assign similar ratings to ETFs without significant deviations among them. Going further, regression analysis showed that the performance of ETFs is sufficiently predictable. More specifically, the results show that the highly graded ETFs perform well through time, while low-rated ETFs deliver consistently poor performance. In addition, it was found that there is no significant difference between ETFs assigned five and four stars, respectively.

Considering the predictive ability of each performance measure, the results show that the Treynor ratio produces the most significant results—specifically, it has better predictive ability than the other performance measures. The Morningstar rating has less predictive ability than Treynor ratio and excess return while it is essentially equivalent to Sharpe ratio. Finally, the results provide strong evidence for persistence in the performance of ETFs, at least in the short term.

performance during the period 2002–03. With respect to Sharpe ratio, the results reveal performance persistence for all the sub-periods except 2005–06, when performance reversed.

Overall, the beta estimates provide sound evidence for persistence patterns in ETF performance at the short-term level. These findings boost the results obtained for the predictability of ETF performance. In other words, persistence may be explained by the performance of either the top- or the bottom-rated ETFs. Combining the predictability and persistence of performance, investors may find profitable opportunities by investing in ETFs.

MAKING IT HAPPEN

- ETFs provide investors with a large range of investment choices covering a variety of domestic, regional, international, and global markets. In addition, ETFs are invested in stocks, bonds, commodities, currencies, and fixed-income products.
- The assets of ETFs have shown continuous worldwide growth after their introduction on Amex in 1993.
- ETFs are preferable for both retail and institutional investors due to their trading convenience, low cost, tax efficiency, risk diversification, and portfolio transparency.
- Information on ETF profiles, management, trading processes, return, risk, holdings, and characteristics can be found from a range of sources.
- Investors should consider both the rating of an ETF's past performance and the past performance itself. However, they should bear in mind that past performance does not guarantee future returns.
- Investors should select an ETF after assessing their own investment profile and evaluating both returns and risks.

MORE INFO

Articles:

Blake, C. R., and M. R. Morey. "Morningstar ratings and mutual fund performance." *Journal of Financial and Quantitative Analysis* 35:3 (2000): 451–483.

Blume, Marshall E. "An anatomy of Morningstar ratings." *Financial Analysts Journal* 54:2 (1998): 19–27.

Khorana, A., and E. Neilling. "The determinants and predictive ability of mutual fund ratings." *Journal of Investing* (Fall 1998): 61–66.

Sharpe, William F. "Morningstar's risk-adjusted ratings." Working paper, Stanford University, 1998. Online at: www.stanford.edu/~wfsharpe/art/msrar/msrar.htm

Wermers, Russ. "Is money really 'smart'? New evidence on the relation between mutual fund flows, manager behavior, and performance persistence." Working paper, Robert H. Smith School of Business, University of Maryland, November 2003.

Websites:

Morningstar: www.morningstar.com

NASDAQ: www.nasdaq.com

Seeking Alpha's ETF sector page: www.etfinvestor.com

"My initial plan was to conquer the world, but in reality, the world is not an easy place to conquer. I learned through the years that I had to build step by step, solidly." Lise Watier

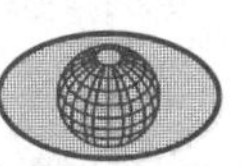

Asset Allocation Methodologies by Tom Coyne

EXECUTIVE SUMMARY

- Asset allocation is both a process and a collection of methodologies that are intended to help a decision-maker to achieve a set of investment objectives by dividing scarce resources between different alternatives.
- Theory assumes that asset allocations are made in the face of risk, where the full range of possible future outcomes and their associated probabilities are known. In the real world this is rarely the case, and decisions must be made in the face of uncertainty.
- The appropriate asset allocation methodology to use, in part, depends on an investor's belief in the efficacy of forecasting. Assuming you believe that forecasting accuracy beyond luck is possible, there remains an inescapable trade-off between a forecasting model's fidelity to historical data and its robustness to uncertainty. Confidence in prediction also increases when models based on different methodologies reach similar conclusions. In fact, averaging the results of these models has been shown to raise forecast accuracy.
- The traditional methodology for asset allocation problems is mean–variance optimization (MVO), which is an application of linear programming that seeks to maximize the return for any given level of risk. However, MVO has many limitations, including high sensitivity to input estimation error and difficulty in handling realistic multiyear, multiobjective problems.
- Alternative techniques include equal weighting, risk budgeting, scenario-based approaches, and stochastic optimization. The choice of which to use fundamentally depends on your belief in the predictability of future levels of risk and return.
- Although they are improving, all quantitative approaches to asset allocation still suffer from various limitations. For that reason, relatively passive risk management approaches such as diversification and automatic rebalancing occasionally need to be complemented by active hedging measures, such as going to cash or buying options.

INTRODUCTION

Everyone has financial goals they want to achieve, whether it is accumulating a target amount of money before retirement, ensuring that a pension fund can provide promised incomes to retirees, or, in a different context, achieving an increase in corporate cash flow. Inevitably, we do not have unlimited resources available to achieve these goals. We often face not only financial constraints, but also shortages of information, time, and cognitive capacity. In many cases, we also face additional constraints on how we can employ available resources to achieve our goals (for example, limits to the maximum amount of funds that can be invested in one area, or the maximum acceptable probability of a result below some threshold).

Broadly, these are all asset allocation problems. We solve them every day using a variety of methodologies. Many of these are nonquantitative, such as dividing resources equally between options, using a rule of thumb that has worked in the past, or copying what others are doing. However, in cases where the stakes are high, the allocation problem is complicated, and/or our choice has to be justified to others, we often employ quantitative methodologies to help us identify, understand, and explain the potential consequences of different decision options. This article considers a typical asset allocation problem: how to allocate one's financial assets across a range of investment options in order to achieve a long-term goal, subject to a set of constraints.

THE CORE CHALLENGE: DECISION MAKING UNDER UNCERTAINTY

All investment asset allocation methodologies start with two core assumptions. First, that a range of different scenarios could occur in the future. Second, that investment alternatives are available whose performance will vary depending on the scenario that eventually develops. A critical issue is the extent to which a decision-maker believes it is possible to predict future outcomes accurately. Traditional finance theory, which is widely used in the investment management industry, assumes that both the full range of possible outcomes and their associated probabilities are known to the decision maker. This is the classic problem of making decisions in the face of risk.

However, when you dig a bit deeper, you find that this approach is based on some questionable assumptions. The obvious question is: how can a decision maker know the full range of possible future outcomes and their associated probabilities? One explanation is that they understand the workings of the process that produces future outcomes. In physical systems, and even in simple social systems, this may be true. But this is likely not to be the case when it comes to investment outcomes. Financial markets are complex adaptive systems, filled with positive feedback loops and nonlinear effects caused by the interaction of competing strategies (for example, value, momentum, and passive approaches), and underlying decisions made by people with imperfect information and limited cognitive capacities who are often pressed for time, affected by emotions, and subject to the influence of other people. An investor can never fully understand the way this system produces outcomes.

Even without such causal understanding, an investor could still believe that the range of possible future outcomes can be described mathematically, based on an analysis of past outcomes. For example, you could use historical data to construct a statistical distribution to describe the range of possible future outcomes, or devise a formula for projecting a time series into the future. The validity of both these approaches rests on two further assumptions. The first is that the historical data used to construct the distribution or time-series algorithm contain sufficient information to capture the full range of possible future outcomes. The second is that the unknown underlying process that generates the historical data will remain constant, or only change slowly over time. Over the past decade, we have seen repeated evidence that in financial markets these two assumptions are not true, for example in the meltdown of the Long Term Capital Management hedge fund in 1998, the crash of the technology stock bubble in 2001, and the worldwide financial market panic in 2008. In these cases, models based on historical data failed to identify the full range of possible outcomes, or to assess the probability of the possible outcomes they identified

  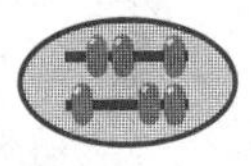 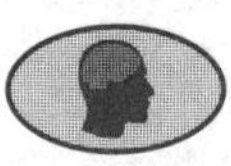  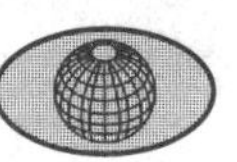 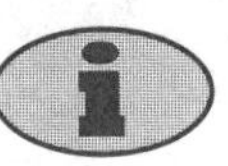  

accurately. People will live with the consequences of these failures for years.

This is not to say that skilled forecasters do not exist, however. They certainly do. Unfortunately, it is usually easier to identify them with the benefit of hindsight (which also helps to distinguish between skill and luck) than it is to pick them in advance.

This discussion leads to an important conclusion. In the real world, asset allocators must make decisions not in the face of *risk*, but rather under conditions of true *uncertainty*, in which neither the full range of possible future outcomes nor their associated probabilities are fully known in advance. This has two critical implications. First, there is an inescapable trade-off between any forecasting model's fidelity to historical data and its robustness to uncertainty. The more carefully a model is backtested and tightly calibrated to reproduce *past* outcomes accurately, the less likely it is to predict the future behavior of a complex adaptive system accurately. Second, confidence in a forecast increases only when models based on differing methodologies (for example, causal, statistical, time-series, and judgmental forecasts) reach similar conclusions, and/or when their individual forecasts are combined to reduce the impact of their individual errors. In short, decision-making under uncertainty is much harder than decision-making under risk.

Asset Allocation: A Simple Example

Let us now move on to a more concrete, yet still simple, example to illustrate some key issues that underlie the most common asset allocation methodology in use today. Our quantitative data and results are summarized in the following table:

	Asset A	*Asset B*
Year 1 return	1%	3%
Year 2 return	5%	7%
Year 3 return	9%	20%
Year 4 return	5%	−5%
Year 5 return	1%	8%
Sample arithmetic mean	4.2%	6.6%
Standard error of the mean	1.5%	4.1%
Sample geometric mean	4.1%	6.3%
Sample standard deviation	3.3%	9.1%
Covariance of A and B	0.12%	
Correlation of A and B	0.41	
Asset weight	40%	60%
Expected arithmetic annual portfolio return	5.6%	
Expected portfolio standard deviation	6.1%	
Expected geometric annual portfolio return	4.9%	

Our portfolio comprises two assets, for which we have five years of historical data. In line with industry norms, we will treat each data point as an independent sample (i.e. we will assume that no momentum or mean-reversion processes are at work in our data series) drawn from a distribution which includes the full range of results that could be produced by the unknown return-generating process. As you can see, the sample mean (i.e. arithmetic average) annual return is 4.2% for Asset A and 6.6% for Asset B. So it is clear that Asset B should produce higher returns, right? Wrong. The next line of the table shows the standard error for our estimate of the mean. The standard error is equal to the sample standard deviation (which we'll discuss below) divided by the square root of the number of data points used in the estimate (in our case, there are five). Assuming that the data come from a normal distribution (that is, one in the shape of the bell curve), there is a 67% chance that the true mean will lie within plus or minus one standard error of our sample mean, and a 95% chance that it will lie within two standard errors. In our example, the short data history, along with the relatively high standard deviation of Asset B's returns, means that the standard errors are high relative to the sample means, and we really can't be completely sure that Asset A has a higher expected return than Asset B. In fact, we'd need a lot more data to increase our confidence about this conclusion. Assuming no change in the size of the standard deviations, the size of the standard error of the mean declines very slowly as the length of the historical data sample is increased—the square root of 5 is about 2.2; of 10, about 3.2; and of 20, about 4.5. Cutting the standard error in half—that is, doubling the accuracy of your estimate of the true mean—requires about a fourfold increase in the length of the data series. Considering that 20 years is about the limit of the available data series for many asset classes, you can see how this can create problems when it comes to generating asset allocation results in which you can have a high degree of confidence.

The next line in the table, the sample geometric mean, highlights another issue: As long as there is any variability in returns, the average return in a given year is not the same as the actual compound return that would be earned by an investor who held an asset for the full five years. In fact, the realized return—that is, the geometric mean—will be lower, and can quickly be approximated by subtracting twice the standard deviation squared from the arithmetic mean. In summary, the higher the variability of returns, the larger the gap will be between the arithmetic and the geometric mean.

The following line in the table shows the sample standard deviation of returns for Assets A and B. This measures the extent to which they are dispersed around the sample mean. In many asset allocation analyses, the standard deviation (also known as volatility) is used as a proxy for risk. Common sense tells you that the correspondence between standard deviation and most investors' understanding of risk is rough at best. Most investors find variability on the downside much less attractive than variability on the upside—and they like uncertainty even less than risk, which they can, or think that they can, measure. Also, when it comes to the distribution of returns, it is not just the average and standard deviation that are of interest to investors. Whether the distribution is Gaussian (normal)—that is, it has the typical bell curve shape—is also important. Distributions that are slightly tilted toward positive returns (as is the case with Assets A and B) are preferable to ones that are negatively skewed. Skewness should also affect preference for distributions with a higher percentage of extreme returns than the normal distribution (i.e. ones with high kurtosis). Preference for higher kurtosis should rise as skewness becomes more positive, and fall as it becomes more negative (i.e. as the probability of large negative returns rises). In fact, in our example, Asset B has positive skewness and higher than normal kurtosis (compared to Asset A's lower than normal kurtosis). Hence, some investors might be willing to trade off higher positive skewness and kurtosis against higher standard deviation in their assessment of the overall riskiness of Asset B. This might be particularly true when, as in the case of some hedge fund strategies, the expected returns on an investment have a distribution that is far from normal. However, many asset allocation methodologies still do not take these trade-offs into account, because they either assume that the returns on assets are normally distributed, or they assume that investors only have preferences concerning standard deviation, and not skewness or kurtosis.

Covariance and correlation

Covariance and correlation are two ways of measuring the relationship between the time series of returns on two or more assets. Covariance is found by multiplying each year's return for Asset A by the return for Asset B, calculating the average result, and subtracting from this the product of the average return for Asset A and by the

"By failing to prepare, you are preparing to fail." Benjamin Franklin

  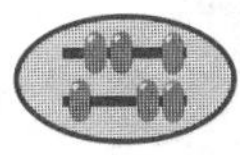 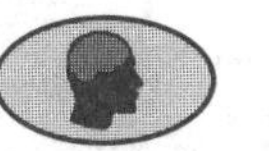  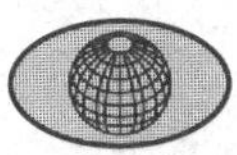   

average return for Asset B—or, more pithily, it is the average of the products less the product of the averages. Correlation standardizes the covariance by dividing it by the product of the standard deviation of Asset A's returns, multiplied by the standard deviation of Asset B's returns. Correlation takes a value between minus one (for returns that move in exactly opposite directions) and plus one (for returns that move exactly together). In theory, a correlation close to zero implies no relationship between the returns on the two sets of returns. Unfortunately, most people forget that correlation only measures the strength of the *linear* relationship between variables; if this relationship is *nonlinear*, the correlation coefficient will also be deceptively close to zero. Finally, covariance and correlation measure the average relationship between two return series; however, their relationship under extreme conditions (i.e. in the tails of the two return distributions) may differ from this average. This was another lesson taught by the events of 2008.

Forming a Portfolio

Let us now combine Asset A and Asset B into a portfolio in which the first has a 40% weight and the second has a 60% weight. The second-to-last row of our table shows the expected arithmetic portfolio return of 5.6% per year. This is simply the weighted average of each asset's expected return. The calculation of the expected standard deviation of the portfolio is more complicated, but it highlights the mathematical logic of diversification. The portfolio standard deviation equals the square root of the portfolio variance. The latter is calculated as follows: [(Asset A weight squared multiplied by Asset A standard deviation squared) plus (Asset B weight squared multiplied by Asset B standard deviation squared) plus (two times Asset A weight multiplied by Asset B weight times the covariance of A and B)]. As you can see, the portfolio standard deviation is 6.1%, which is less than 6.8%—the weighted average of Asset A's and Asset B's standard deviations. The cause of this result is the relatively low covariance between A's returns and B's returns (or alternatively, their relatively low correlation of 0.41). The fact that their respective returns apparently move in less than perfect lockstep with each other reduces the overall expected variability of the portfolio return. However, this encouraging conclusion is subject to two critical caveats. First, it assumes the absence of a nonlinear relationship between A's returns and B's returns that has not been picked up by the correlation estimate. Second, it assumes that the underlying factors giving rise to the correlation of 0.41 will remain unchanged in the future. In practice, however, this is not the case, and correlations tend to be unstable over time. For example, in 2008, investors discovered that despite relatively low estimated correlations between their historical returns, many asset classes shared a nonlinear exposure to a market liquidity risk factor. When liquidity fell sharply, correlations rose rapidly and undermined many of the expected benefits from portfolio diversification.

Expected Portfolio Returns

The last line in our table is an estimate of the geometric or compound average rate of return that an investor might actually be expected to realize on this portfolio over a multiyear period, assuming that we have accurately estimated the underlying means, standard deviations, and correlations and that they remain stable over time (all questionable assumptions, as we have noted). As you can see, it is less than the expected arithmetic annual return. Unfortunately, too many asset allocation analyses make the mistake of assuming that the arithmetic average return will be earned over time, rather than the geometric return. In the example we have used, for an initial investment of $1,000,000 and a 20-year holding period, this difference in returns results in terminal wealth that is lower by $370,358, or 12.5%, than the use of the arithmetic average would have led us to expect. This is not a trivial difference.

ASSET ALLOCATION: ADVANCED TECHNIQUES

The basic methodology we have just outlined can be used to calculate asset weights that maximize expected portfolio return for any given constraint on portfolio standard deviation (or other measure of risk, such as value-at-risk). Conversely, this approach can be used to minimize one or more portfolio risk measures for any given level of target portfolio return. These are all variants of the asset allocation methodology known as mean–variance optimization (MVO), which is an application of linear programming (for example, as found in the SOLVER function in an Excel spreadsheet). Although MVO is by far the most commonly used asset allocation methodology, it is, as we have shown, subject to many limitations.

Fortunately, there are techniques that can be used to overcome some, if not all, of the problems highlighted in our example. We will start with alternatives to the MVO methodology, and then look at alternative means of managing errors in the estimation of future asset class returns, standard deviations, covariances, and other model inputs.

Alternative Approaches to Portfolio Construction

The simplest alternative to MVO is to allocate an equal amount of money to each investment option. Known as the $1/n$ approach, this has been shown to be surprisingly effective, particularly when asset classes are broadly defined to minimize correlations (for example, a single domestic equities asset class rather than three highly related ones, including small-, mid-, and large-cap equities). Fundamentally, equal weighting is based on the assumption that no asset allocation model inputs (i.e. returns, standard deviations, and correlations) can be accurately forecast in a complex adaptive system.

Another relatively simple asset allocation methodology starts from the premise that, at least in the past, different investment options perform relatively better under different economic scenarios or regimes. For example, domestic and foreign government bonds and gold have, in the past, performed relatively well during periods of high uncertainty (for example, the 1998 Russian debt crisis and the more recent subprime credit crisis). Similarly, history has shown that inflation-indexed bonds, commodities, and commercial property have performed relatively well when inflation is high, whereas equities deliver their best performance under more normal conditions. Different approaches can be used to translate these observations into actual asset allocations. For example, you could divide your funds between the three scenarios in line with your subjective forecast of the probability of each of them occurring over a specified time horizon, and then equally divide the money allocated to each scenario between the asset classes that perform best under it.

When it comes to more quantitative asset allocation methodologies, research has shown that—at least in the past—some variables have proven easier to predict and are more stable over time than others. Specifically, relative asset class riskiness (as measured by standard deviation) has been much more stable over time than relative asset class returns. A belief that relative riskiness will remain stable in the future leads to a second alternative to MVO: risk budgeting. This involves allocating different amounts of money to each investment option, with the goal of equalizing their contribution to total portfolio risk, which can be defined using either

  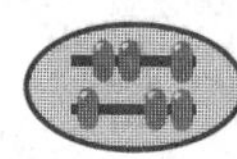   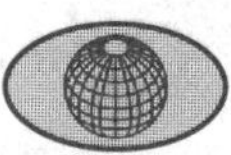   

standard deviation or one or more downside risk measures (for example, drawdown, shortfall, semi-standard deviation). However, as was demonstrated by the ineffective performance of many banks' value-at-risk models during 2008, the effectiveness of risk budgeting depends on the accuracy of the underlying assumptions it uses. For example, rapidly changing correlations and volatility, along with illiquid markets, can and did result in actual risk positions that were very different from those originally budgeted.

The most sophisticated approaches to complicated multiyear asset allocation problems use more advanced methodologies. For example, rather than a one-period MVO model, multiperiod regime-switching models can be used to replicate the way real economies and financial markets can shift between periods of inflation, deflation, and normal growth (or, alternatively, high and low volatility). These models typically incorporate different asset return, standard deviation, and correlation assumptions under each regime. However, they are also subject to estimation errors not only in the assumptions used in each regime, but also in the assumptions made about regime continuation and transition probabilities, for which historical data and theoretical models are quite limited.

Rebalancing Strategies

Multiperiod asset allocation models can also incorporate a range of different rebalancing strategies that manage risk by adjusting asset weights over time (for example, based on annual rebalancing, or maximum allowable deviations from target weights). When it comes to identifying the best asset allocation solution for a given problem, these models typically incorporate sophisticated evolutionary search techniques. These start with a candidate solution (for example, an integrated asset allocation and rebalancing strategy), and then run repeated model simulations to assess the probability that they will achieve the investor's specified objectives. An evolutionary technique (for example, genetic algorithms or simulated annealing) is then used to identify another potential solution, and the process is repeated until a stopping point is reached (which is usually based on the failure to find a better solution after a certain number of candidates have been tested or a maximum time limit is reached). Strictly speaking, the best solutions found using evolutionary search techniques are not *optimal* (in the sense that the word is used in the MVO approach)—meaning a unique solution that is, subject to the limits of the methodology, believed to be better than all other possible solutions. In the case of computationally hard problems, such as multiperiod, multiobjective asset allocation, it is not possible to evaluate all possible solutions exhaustively. Instead, much as for real life decision-makers, stochastic search models aim to find solutions that are robust—ones that have a high probability of achieving an investor's objectives under a wide range of possible future conditions.

ESTIMATING ASSET ALLOCATION INPUTS

A number of different techniques are also used to improve the estimates of future asset class returns, standard deviations, correlations, and other inputs that are used by various asset allocation methodologies. Of these variables, future returns are the hardest to predict. One approach to improving return forecasts is to use a model containing a small number of common factors to estimate future returns on a larger number of asset classes. In some models, these factors are economic and financial variables, such as the market/book ratio, industrial production, or the difference between long- and short-term interest rates. Perhaps the best known factor model is the CAPM (capital asset pricing model). This is based on the assumption that, in equilibrium, the return on an asset will be equal to the risk-free rate of interest, plus a risk premium that is proportional to the asset's riskiness relative to the overall market portfolio. Although they simplify the estimation of asset returns, factor models also have some limitations, including the need to forecast the variables they use accurately and their assumption that markets are usually in a state of equilibrium.

The latter assumption lies at the heart of another approach to return estimation, known as the Black–Litterman (BL) model. Assuming that markets are in equilibrium enables one to use current asset class market capitalizations to infer expectations of future returns. BL then combines these with an investor's own subjective views (in a consistent manner) to arrive at a final return estimate. More broadly, BL is an example of a so-called shrinkage estimation technique, whereby more extreme estimates (for example, the highest and lowest expected returns) are shrunk toward a more central value (for example, the average return forecast across all asset classes, or BL's equilibrium market implied returns). At a still higher level, shrinkage is but one version of model averaging, which has been shown to increase forecast accuracy in multiple domains. An example of this could be return estimates that are based on the combination of historical data and the outputs from a forecasting model.

When it comes to improving estimates of standard deviation (volatility) and correlations, one finds similar techniques employed, including factor and shrinkage models. In addition, a number of traditional (for example, moving averages and exponential smoothing) and advanced (for example, GARCH and neural network models) time-series forecasting techniques have been used as investors search for better ways to forecast volatility, correlations, and more complicated relationships between the returns on different assets. Finally, copula functions have been

▸▸ MAKING IT HAPPEN

- Using broadly defined asset classes minimizes correlations and creates more robust solutions by reducing the sensitivity of results to deviations from assumptions about future asset class returns, which are the most difficult to forecast.
- Equal dollar weighting should be the default asset allocation, as it assumes that all prediction is impossible.
- However, there is considerable evidence that the relative riskiness of different asset classes is reasonably stable over time and therefore predictable. This makes it possible to move beyond equal weighting and to use risk budgeting. There is also evidence that different asset classes perform better under different economic conditions, such as high inflation or high uncertainty. This makes it possible to use scenario-based weighting.
- Techniques such as mean–variance optimization and stochastic search are more problematic, because they depend on the accurate prediction of future returns. Although new approaches can help to minimize estimation errors, they cannot eliminate them or change the human behavior that gives rise to bubbles and crashes. For that reason, all asset allocation approaches require not only good quantitative analysis, but also good judgment and continued risk monitoring, even after the initial asset allocation plan is implemented.

"A man who does not think and plan long ahead will find trouble right at his door." Confucius

  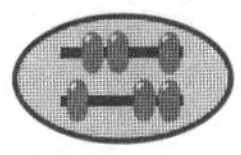   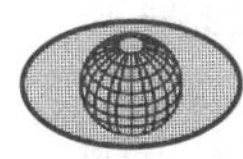  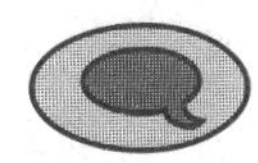 

employed with varying degrees of success to model nonlinear dependencies between different return series.

CONCLUSION

In summary, although they are improving and becoming more robust to uncertainty than in the past, almost all quantitative approaches to asset allocation still suffer from various limitations. In a complex adaptive system this seems unavoidable, since their evolutionary processes make accurate forecasting extremely difficult using existing techniques. This argues strongly for averaging the outputs of different methodologies as the best way to make asset allocation decisions in the face of uncertainty. Moreover, these same evolutionary processes can sometimes give rise to substantial asset class over- or undervaluation that is outside the input assumptions used in the asset allocation process. Given this, relatively passive risk management approaches such as diversification and rebalancing occasionally need to be complemented with active hedging measures such as going to cash or buying options. The effective implementation of this process will require not only paying ongoing attention to asset class valuations, but also a shift in focus from external performance metrics to achieving the long-term portfolio return required to reach one's goals. When your objective is to outperform your peers or an external benchmark, it is tempting to stay too long in overvalued asset classes, as many investors painfully learned in 2001 and again in 2008.

▸▸ MORE INFO

Books:

Asset Allocation:

Bernstein, William. *The Intelligent Asset Allocator: How to Build Your Portfolio to Maximize Returns and Minimize Risk*. New York: McGraw-Hill, 2001.

Darst, David M. *The Art of Asset Allocation: Principles and Investment Strategies for Any Market*. 2nd ed. New York: McGraw-Hill, 2008.

Fabozzi, Frank J., Petter N. Kolm, Dessislava A. Pachamanova, and Sergio M. Focardi. *Robust Portfolio Optimization and Management*. Hoboken, NJ: Wiley, 2007.

Ferri, Richard A. *All About Asset Allocation: The Easy Way to Get Started*. New York: McGraw-Hill, 2006.

Gibson, Roger C. *Asset Allocation: Balancing Financial Risk*. New York: McGraw-Hill, 2000.

Michaud, Richard O., and Robert O. Michaud. *Efficient Asset Management: A Practical Guide to Stock Portfolio Optimization and Asset Allocation*. 2nd ed. New York: Oxford University Press, 2008.

Swensen, David F. *Pioneering Portfolio Management: An Unconventional Approach to Institutional Investment*. New York: Free Press, 2009.

Forecasting:

Mlodinow, Leonard. *The Drunkard's Walk: How Randomness Rules Our Lives*. New York: Pantheon Books, 2008.

Osband, Kent. *Iceberg Risk: An Adventure in Portfolio Theory*. New York: Texere, 2002.

Rebonato, Riccardo. *Plight of the Fortune Tellers: Why We Need to Manage Financial Risk Differently*. Princeton, NJ: Princeton University Press, 2007.

Taleb, Nassim Nicholas. *The Black Swan: The Impact of the Highly Improbable*. New York: Random House, 2007.

Articles:

There are many academic papers on asset allocation and portfolio construction methodologies. The best single source is www.ssrn.com. SSRN is also a good source for papers on markets as complex adaptive systems by authors including Andrew Lo, Blake LeBaron, Cars H. Hommes, and J. Doyne Farmer.

Websites:

In addition to web-based tools based on mean–variance optimization, there are many vendors of more sophisticated asset allocation software. All of the following employ advanced techniques beyond simple MVO:

AlternativeSoft: www.alternativesoft.com

EnCorr: corporate.morningstar.com/ib/asp/subject.aspx?xmlfile=1221.xml

New Frontier Asset Allocation Suite: www.newfrontieradvisers.com

SmartFolio: www.smartfolio.com

Windham Financial Planner: www.windhamcapital.com

"It is a bad plan that admits of no modification." Publilius Syrus

  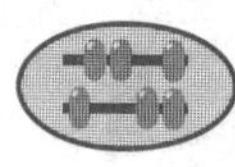  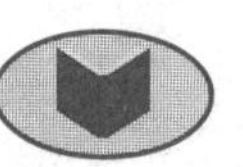 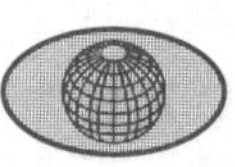   

Booms, Busts, and How to Navigate Troubled Waters by Joachim Klement

EXECUTIVE SUMMARY

- We review the typical anatomy of financial market bubbles and subsequent crashes.
- We show that financial innovation has often triggered exuberant market developments, leading to unjustified market optimism and catastrophic losses for many investors.
- We emphasize the role that psychology and behavioral biases play in market dynamics before, during, and after a crash.
- We provide tips on how to navigate volatile markets more effectively in the inevitable bubbles and crashes of the future—inevitable because of the very nature of investor psychology and financial markets.

A BRIEF HISTORY OF BUBBLES AND CRASHES

For many, the tech bubble of the late 1990s is probably the most prominent example of a stock market boom and bust. Figure 1 shows the exuberance in the Nasdaq Composite stock market index, which includes a significant proportion of technology and telecommunications stocks, compared to the S&P500 Index of the 500 large-cap stocks from traditional sectors like industrials, transportation, utilities, and financials. As the internet and information technology spread throughout society, investors became ever more optimistic about the growth prospects and profit potential of companies involved in IT.

But irrational exuberance, as former Fed Chairman Alan Greenspan called it, is not a phenomenon of the information age. It has taken hold of financial markets time and again throughout history. Table 1 summarizes a selection of stock market slumps after periods of irrational exuberance in the United Kingdom and the United States since 1800. Two observations stand out: Bubbles and crashes are not rare, reoccurring at intervals of 10 to 30 years, and the subsequent market declines typically eliminate from 15% to 50% of the peak market value. Assets such as commodities, sovereign bonds, and currencies have also frequently shown signs of irrational euphoria followed by a severe correction.

THE ANATOMY OF A CRASH

A closer examination of asset price bubbles reveals that the behavior of markets often follows a common pattern that comprises at least four stages:

Innovation

A common ingredient in market bubbles, innovations are often based on concepts that are difficult for a lay person to understand, like the information technology boom, or the biotech bubble at the end of the 1990s. Investors cannot assess the true potential of an innovation for a company's earnings growth or productivity. Innovation in a favorable economic environment increases company earnings, but these initial successes may ultimately have limitations that may be unknown to investors. Since no historical evidence is available about possible risks, market participants may underestimate risks and project excessively high initial growth rates, ignoring the inherent limitations of growth for a new technology.

Figure 1. The tech bubble at the end of the 1990s. (*Source*: Bloomberg and UBS Wealth Management Research as of July 25, 2008.)

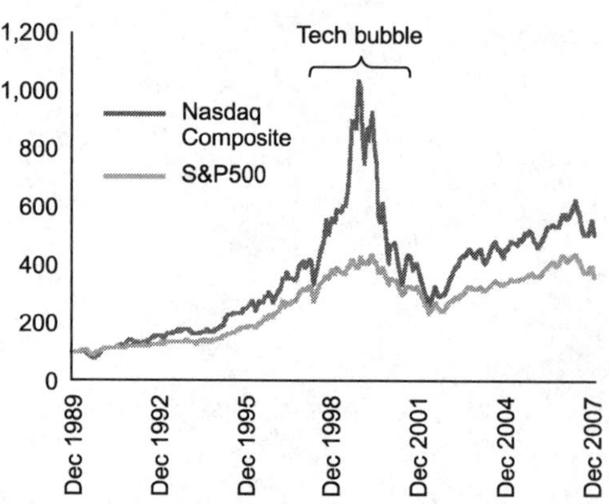

Exuberance

In a second stage, the presumed benefits of innovation and a new economic era are increasingly overestimated. Prices of stocks or houses continue to rise steadily and markets tend increasingly to ignore risks. Often, risks are only acknowledged after they materialize in the real world. This is the time when euphoria begins and investors clamor to get into the market "because prices can't go down" and "this time it's different", or "this is a new era." High profits attract new investors, and this in turn leads to higher returns as cash pours into these markets. A lack of liquidity in the markets may lead to further exuberance when demand becomes much bigger than potential supply. Especially in illiquid assets like houses, short-term demand can drive prices far from fundamentally justified values.

Crash

The positive feedback loop cannot last forever. At some point fundamental forces lead to a trend reversal. The result is often a rapid and steep decline in asset prices as the bubble bursts and the market crashes. The consequent loss in wealth can lead to lower consumption or investments in the real economy and can even destabilize the financial system. The effects can include recessions, or banking and currency crises as we witnessed in 2008. Here, a lack of liquidity can increase the fall in asset prices when sellers want to unload their investments at any price and illiquid investments may have to be sold at the worst possible time. In the financial crisis of 2008 it was the forced selling by hedge funds, private equity funds, and other investors that partially contributed to the sell-off of stock markets in the second half of 2008.

Regulation

A crash frequently is followed by increased regulation to prevent similar events from happening again. It is interesting to note that as a result of regulation and the lessons learned from a market crash, the exact same events are indeed very unlikely to

"I grew up with a lot of brothers and sisters. I did all I could do to really stand out and that nurtured a lot of confidence and drive and ambition." Madonna

     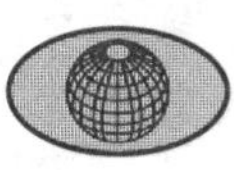   

Table 1. Selected UK and US stock market booms and busts since 1800. (*Source*: M. Bordo, 2003, UBS Wealth Management Research, as of July 25, 2008)

	US boom and bust events		
	Boom (stock market increase, %)	Correction	Decline from peak (%)
Latin America mania	1822–1824 (+78%)	1824–1826	−37.3%
American boom	n.a.	1835–1839	−23.4%
Railroad boom	1840–1844 (+52%)	1844–1847	−34.1%
European financial crisis	n.a.	1874–1878	−31.0%
Roaring twenties	1920–1928 (+137%)	1928–1931	−60.3%
Housing boom	1931–1936 (+110%)	1936–1940	−50.1%
Go-go years	1965–1968 (+67%)	1968–1970	−18.9%
Tech boom	1994–2000 (+89%)	2000–2002	−24.8%
	UK boom and bust events		
	Boom (stock market increase, %)	Correction	Decline from peak (%)
Railroad boom	n.a.	1853–1859	−50.6%
Railroad boom	1875–1881 (+51%)	1881–1885	−26.7%
Rich man's panic	1899–1902 (+30%)	1902–1904	−16.3%
World financial crisis	1903–1906 (+52%)	1906–1907	−19.4%
Roaring twenties	1920–1929 (+168%)	1929–1932	−73.4%
Post-war slump	1941–1945 (+90%)	1946–1949	−10.8%
Go-go years	1965–1968 (+31%)	1968–1970	−15.7%
Tech boom	1994–2000 (+130%)	2000–2002	−27.7%

recur and financial market stability is increased. But, as time passes, the positive effects of regulation fade. Market participants tend to forget about the causes and consequences of past bubbles. Who today considers the lessons of the go-go years of the 1960s, or even remembers them? Every generation can repeat the mistakes of previous generations, as is confirmed by the emergence of bubbles roughly every 20 to 30 years.

A BEHAVIORAL FINANCE VIEW OF THE CURRENT HOUSING CRISIS

We recognize several behavioral biases when reviewing the US housing bubble and the current credit crisis:

- **Selective perception**: House prices tend to be overestimated, and people buying houses as an investment tend to believe that house prices always increase. Information pointing at an overdue correction was ignored and the focus was on affirming news.
- **Herding behavior**: Investors who initially were skeptical about innovative structured credit products started buying them because everyone seemed to be investing and returns were higher than from traditional bonds.
- **Anchoring**: When assessing the risk of losses, past house price corrections were used as an anchor value for possible future corrections. The higher risk of subprime mortgages and the impact of the new mortgage structures were not properly considered, while the possibility of sharper corrections than seen in the past was also grievously underestimated.
- **Loss aversion**: In early 2007, when the first signs of losses from subprime mortgages appeared, mortgage-related structured products incurred minor losses. Even investors who were concerned about a further decline in the housing market held their positions to avoid selling at a loss. This bias also applies to investors who have not sold any stocks since the market peak in July 2007.
- **Cognitive dissonance**: Once an investment incurs a big loss, we tend to blame the wrong investment decision on someone else. Among those blamed for the credit crisis and its losses in affected assets are the mortgage originators, investment banks, real estate speculators, rating agencies, and regulators. We note that investors who were willing to invest in products they did not fully understand simply because they hungered for additional yield are usually not blamed for bubbles and the subsequent crises.

HEED THE WARNING SIGNS

It is extremely difficult to predict when a bubble will burst. Sometimes it is even impossible to judge if there is a bubble at all. We identify some warning signs that can signal excessive exuberance:

- Bubbles are frequently fueled by the procyclical nature of credit supply: Credit increases when the economy booms and vanishes once risks emerge, thus intensifying the bust. When financing becomes very cheap or "free"—that is, nominal interest rates are close to inflation rates—overinvestment is sure to follow. Market participants grow less careful when selecting investments and fuel an evolving boom. Ask yourself: Is the cost of financing unusually cheap? Is credit being used to finance investments, or has some new form of leverage even become the latest innovation?
- By definition, a bubble involves an unsustainable pattern of price changes or cash flows. If returns have been good for a few years, and are possibly even accelerating, ask yourself if this is sustainable. If not, you are in a bubble. If your reaction is that higher returns with lower risks are possible due to some new financial innovation, again, look for a bubble. Financial innovation can never make risks disappear—it can merely redistribute them. If it seems that total risks are lower, the financial innovation is probably opaque or poorly understood at best, and you might be taking on more risk than you thought.
- Have you seen a friend get rich? Are you considering trying something similar? Once nonprofessional investors start putting money where high returns have become self-evident, the bubble is probably well on its way. The emotions we feel when returns are stellar in a market we are not in are nicely described by Charles P. Kindleberger: "There is nothing as disturbing to one's well-being and judgment as to see a friend get rich."[1] Unfortunately, these emotions can mislead, enticing us to enter a bubble at a late stage.

A FINAL WORD

Bubbles appear again and again, and it is extremely difficult to know when one will burst. Our desire to be part of the chase, and our jealousy when seeing others gain, often make us poor investors in times of exuberance. Most of the time, we know a bubble only after it bursts—to our detriment.

However, exuberance works both ways. After a bubble bursts, anything that fueled the bubble is broadly condemned and, once again, underlying fundamentals are ignored. Looking at the credit crisis, we see that the useful innovation of securitization was poorly understood. On the other hand, sudden sell-offs often result in mispricing that can offer significant investment opportunities. The lesson from behavioral finance is probably best reflected in the words of Warren Buffett: "Be fearful when others are greedy and greedy when others are fearful."

"I don't think that ambition is a bad word if you work hard yourself." Lynn Forrester

  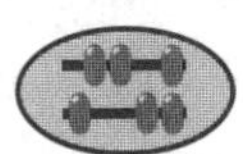   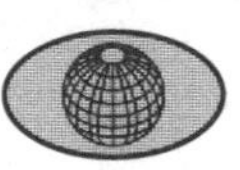   

▸▸ MAKING IT HAPPEN

Even if we recognize a bubble, we often are unable to judge how long prices will keep rising. Also, staying out of a booming market is frustrating. So how should we behave if we have identified a possible bubble? Here are some useful principles:

- Don't sell everything when you identify a bubble—you can take the ride as prices go up. That does not mean that we think we can time the markets, and that one has to be able to know when markets top out to ride the bubble. We think that one can stay invested in a bull market but that one should always have a safety net ready that limits the downside risks of a potential investment—even though this might typically come at additional cost or limited upside potential. For example, the booming asset will take up an ever larger share of your portfolio as it grows in value faster than the rest of your portfolio. It is essential to regularly adjust your exposure to this asset by selling a certain share. Decide on a target allocation, say 5% of the portfolio, and regularly rebalance your portfolio to this target once prices have risen. This also locks in profits.
- If an asset or market has rallied for, say, more than three years, consider investing with downside protection, for example, through protective put options.
- Don't try to get the timing right. Just as around 75% of licensed car drivers think their driving skills are better than average, investors also tend to believe that they can judge market changes better than the rest. History has shown that the largest inflows into markets occur just before the bubble bursts. Emotions and behavioral biases tend to make investors poor market-timers.
- Limit losses through stop-loss orders. This is particularly useful for stocks; however, stop-loss orders can be ineffective in a market crash. Once a bubble bursts, prices often fall sharply as buyers flee the market. Whereas large-cap stocks are usually kept liquid by market makers, small-cap stocks, emerging markets, corporate bonds, derivatives, funds, and structured credit products can turn illiquid overnight. Not being able to sell a position is a real risk in a crisis and investors should consider this when allocating funds to such investments. One remedy here can be guaranteed stop-loss orders, where available. In this case stop-loss limit prices are guaranteed by the broker at the cost of a somewhat higher spread for the transaction. When investing in fixed-income products, a buy-and-hold perspective is recommended.
- Seize opportunities that open up during a crash. Crashes create opportunities through mispricing, and when credit becomes scarce, promising opportunities can arise for investors with spare liquidity.
- Buy only what you understand.

▸▸ MORE INFO

Books:

Kindleberger, Charles P., and Robert Aliber. *Manias, Panics, and Crashes: A History of Financial Crises*. 5th ed. Hoboken, NJ: Wiley, 2005.

Mackay, Charles. *Extraordinary Popular Delusions and the Madness of Crowds*. Radnor, PA: Templeton Foundation Press, 1999.

Nofsinger, John R. *The Psychology of Investing*. 3rd ed. Upper Saddle River, NJ: Prentice Hall, 2007.

Plous, Scott. *The Psychology of Judgment and Decision Making*. New York: McGraw-Hill, 1993.

Shiller, Robert J. *Irrational Exuberance*. 2nd ed. New York: Doubleday, 2006.

Website:

Behavioral finance resources: www.behaviouralfinance.net

NOTES

1 Kindleberger and Aliber, 2005.

"Men do not desire to be rich but to be richer than other men." John Stuart Mill

  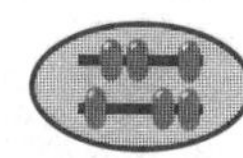   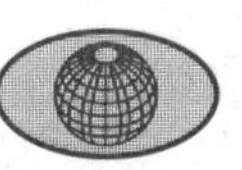   

Carrying Out Due Diligence on Hedge Funds

by Amarendra Swarup

EXECUTIVE SUMMARY

- Due diligence should be the cornerstone of any hedge fund investment program.
- Hedge funds are a complex and volatile asset class, and poor selection will greatly increase the chances of fraud and poor performance.
- Due diligence is about identifying the best hedge fund manager for your investment goals and risk appetite.
- Due diligence is proactive risk management that seeks to generate superior returns while minimizing risk.
- Performance alone is meaningless.
- You need to understand how and why a hedge fund makes money.
- Dig deep and understand all the risks in all possible markets.
- If in the slightest doubt about a fund, just walk away.

INTRODUCTION

Hedge funds have often been cited as valuable additions to any institutional portfolio, thanks to their typically uncorrelated returns to traditional asset classes over the long term, and superior risk-adjusted returns. However, they are also a complex and volatile asset class, and since their ascent onto the investment podium, both institutional and private investors have found themselves burned at regular intervals by embarrassing and costly blowups. The oft-cited collapse of Long-Term Capital Management in 1998 and Amaranth Advisers in 2006, the litany of hedge fund managers wrong-footed by the credit crunch, and, most recently, the uncovering of the $50 billion Ponzi scheme run by Bernie Madoff are but some of the stark reminders of the minefield investors navigate in their quest for absolute and consistent returns.

The reason is simple: Today's increasingly complex asset markets make it more difficult than ever for investors to peer under the bonnet and select the best hedge funds. Many make the naïve decision to invest based solely on a strong track record, little realizing that the simple effort of conducting a thorough investigation into the fund prior to investment can often save them considerable financial pain in the future.

Due diligence is the most important aspect of investing in hedge funds, and often also the most ignored part. It's a bizarre oversight—most people would not buy a house without learning first about the area, local schools, and amenities, conducting structural surveys, investigating the state of the housing market, and so on. Yet when most institutional investors allocate to hedge funds, the lack of simple questions as to honesty, competence, and future potential reduces most investments to the ignoble status of a crapshoot.

DUE DILIGENCE: A DEFINITION

Due diligence is the process of identifying the best hedge fund manager for your investment goals and thereafter continually reevaluating them at regular intervals to ensure that they continue to meet your requirements. In so doing, it looks across the entire gamut of the fund—its investment strategy, performance, personnel, legal structure, risk management, documentation, operational infrastructure, service providers, counterparties, and client base. In essence, it is a proactive risk management approach that successfully balances the twin goals of any investment: generating superior returns while minimizing risk.

Looking at past performance alone is often meaningless in the hedge fund world. Performance tells you nothing about the underlying strategy, its advantages and disadvantages, management's skill, the use of leverage, the impact of different market conditions, and so on. Further, selection bias means that most investors will naturally gravitate toward those strategies and funds that have performed well in the past. Any successful hedge fund strategy will seek in principle to deliver targeted returns within the confines of some defined risk constraints. Yet, while quantitative measures such as volatility capture the riskiness of performance, it does not tell investors how robust the fund's underlying risk management is and how it may react to leaner times in the future.

In contrast, careful due diligence provides a valuable insight into the quality of the fund's strategy, personnel, systems, and, vitally, their risk management. Investors know what to expect in good and bad times, and are able to approach their investment in a rational manner without worrying over every inevitable jitter.

The questions you ask are driven ultimately by your investment goals and the constraints on your balance sheet, such as your investment horizon and the need to maintain an optimal liquidity profile commensurate with your cash flow requirements. While no two investors are likely to have the same set of questions, there are fundamental areas that any proper due diligence process needs to cover.

INVESTMENT STRATEGY

There are over 8,000 hedge funds today, and most claim to have a unique edge over the rest. Further, they are scattered among a myriad of strategies and substrategies—all with very different risk and return profiles that profit during varying market conditions. For example, long/short equity funds are very liquid and target absolute performance irrespective of stock market direction, by going both long and short shares. In contrast, event-driven strategies are more catalyst-driven, focusing on changing corporate structures, mergers and acquisitions, and distressed investing. Arbitrage funds might exploit perceived pricing anomalies to eke out small, steady gains, while strong commodity, currency, and interest rate trends could be harvested by momentum-driven strategies such as those used by CTAs (commodity trading advisers) and global funds. There is no shortage of managers playing across different financial instruments, different sectors, and different geographies—all with their own unique traits, opportunities, and risks.

It's a daunting prospect for any investor looking to pick the right funds, and the two key questions in any due diligence process are:

- How does the fund make its money?
- Why does the fund make its money?

It may seem almost facile, but true outperformance and differentiation from the crowd comes from identifying trading talent and potential, and knowing how to time those investments.

To answer the first question, you need to understand and document the hedge fund's basic investment strategy and trading style. What markets does the manager operate in, and what instruments are used? What are the potential returns, and what is the downside if someone makes the wrong

"Performance alone is meaningless."

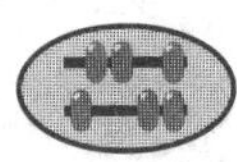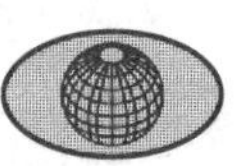

call? What is the outlook given today's markets?

Finding a strategy that matches your investment needs and risk appetite is important. Changing market conditions favor different instruments and strategies. For example, CTAs invest in listed financial and commodity markets as well as in currency markets through options and futures, giving them a wide and often highly liquid market. They are highly directional as they pick trends in momentum-driven markets, and can also lose significantly when these suddenly reverse.

The strategy also needs to sit well within your broader portfolio and balance sheet. For example, despite their volatility, CTAs can be a valuable addition to a broadly diversified portfolio, providing stability and an often rare stream of positive returns at times of negative market stress. Equally, if a company is involved in the energy sector, it is unlikely to want to invest in a long/short equity hedge fund specializing in natural resources.

MORE QUESTIONS TO ASK

The first hurdle crossed, we come on to a more troubling question—what edge does the manager have, if any? Manager selection will contribute far more to your portfolio's performance than broad strategy allocation. True talent lies not in doubling your money in a bull market but in consistently growing it in all markets—good and bad. And ultimately, that's what you're paying those hefty fees for.

Two managers operating the same strategy may look ostensibly the same in terms of style and performance. But one may simply be lucky—a beta jockey riding some market wave for all it's worth, with an inevitable and costly crash looming somewhere on the horizon—while the other may be genuinely skilled, capable of producing consistently good returns irrespective of the wider market (or "alpha" in hedge fund parlance).

How do you tell the difference? The answers are all hidden within their portfolios and in how they generate and implement their ideas.

- *Who are the people?* A veteran manager who has proven his ability to make consistent money in many different environments is often preferable to the newbie who's churned out spectacular returns using an otherwise unfamiliar strategy for the last couple of years.
- *Where do the ideas come from?* A manager who grabs ideas off golfing buddies and follows the herd means that you could find yourself in the same position as many others, greatly increasing the chances of large losses in stressed situations.
- *Are the people who developed the strategies and models still there?* Or is the fund now relying solely on a mysterious oracle for guidance? Models may work fantastically, but they all have limitations—and inevitably stop working without constant research.
- *How is the investment process implemented?* Ideas need to be robustly examined and debated to ensure not only that the potential rewards are worth the risk, but that the downside is amenable. They also need to be compared to what's already there—a portfolio with 20 great pharmaceutical stocks probably doesn't need a twenty-first.
- *How have they performed?* Were all their returns based on a couple of great trades, or do they consistently make money on the majority? Astoundingly good performance may be just as suspicious as bad performance.
- *What's the capacity of the strategy?* Every strategy has an optimal size beyond which returns will begin to suffer as the market gets too crowded. Some strategies, such as global macro, invest around the world across many asset classes—their limitations are likely in the billions. Others, such as those investing in niche emerging markets, may find the constraints considerably tighter.
- *Is the manager a jack of all trades?* The best managers are those who stick to what they know. Sticking your finger into every pie that comes by is likely to become very messy—both for managers and their investors.
- *What happens when the markets turn?* Does the trading strategy have the ability to adapt? Knowing how the fund might perform when the environment suddenly changes is vital. Every strategy will inevitably make losses, but the extent, duration, and how the manager bounces back says a lot about their skill. But going down in the past whenever the broader market does is a worrying sign—that's not what you signed up for, and perhaps that perceived skill was just an extended lucky run at the roulette wheel.

RISK MANAGEMENT

Implicit in the answers to the last two questions is the quality of risk management at the hedge fund. A dynamic risk-monitoring process aimed at reviewing positions and reallocating precious capital is the key to ensuring that portfolios are nimble and always a step ahead of any downturn. The more comprehensive the risk process, the more comfortable you can feel about your assets.

Most importantly, the risk management needs to be independent, with the right of veto. A fund where management can choose to overrule or ignore risk warnings is one that's not worth investing in, no matter how good the returns are. Once past that, there are innumerable other questions regarding the strength of the control framework around the compelling investment strategy that is presented to you.

- *How are positions and exposures sized? Are there any limits?* It's a simple question, but many an eager manager has been caught out by betting the bank on a guaranteed winner—right up to the point where they failed.
- *How is risk actually measured?* Volatility is one measure, value-at-risk another, stress tests a third. Does the manager attempt to capture the unique risks within the investment strategy and actively watch out for them?
- *What are the fund's exposures on the long and short sides?* An equity long/short with mostly long positions and token shorts is likely to be a closet long-only fund, looking to make a bit extra from fees by masquerading as a hedge fund, and unlikely to do well in a downturn.
- *How large is the leverage?* Are there limits, and is it secured on a long-term basis? Some strategies, such as arbitrage, need leverage, but in a downturn this can quickly magnify losses. Equally, with too much leverage, returns could be due to leveraging substandard returns rather than any genuine talent.
- *What about noninvestment risks such as liquidity?* Are there plans in place if this suddenly dries up? If positions need to be liquidated quickly, this may impact the fund adversely and significantly, as shown by the experience of hedge funds trading asset-backed securities during the recent credit crunch.
- *What about counterparties with whom the fund trades or relies on for derivative contracts?* Are there safeguards against defaults, and are contracts watertight?

FINAL HURDLES

Assuming that these questions are all answered to your satisfaction, the due diligence can move on to more mundane but equally important topics, such as the fund's operational infrastructure and checking the legalese in the fund prospectus. Many a brilliant fund manager

"The lack of simple questions as to honesty, competence and future potential can reduce most investments to the ignoble status of a crapshoot."

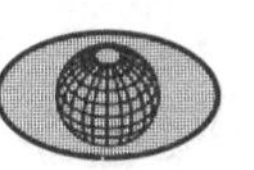

has been undone by a sloppy pricing process and poor systems, and many a fraud has been perpetrated on an unsuspecting investor who didn't check the clauses in the contract until after they had signed.

- *Are the fund managers invested in the fund themselves?* Nothing brings manager and client together as close as knowing you're both rowing the same boat.
- *How long have the people been there?* Having staff on a revolving door policy is likely to cause instability and poor performance.
- *What are the fees?* Talented managers have their price but, no matter how brilliant, there is always a point where you may feel that what you pay to access their skill is simply too high to justify. Moreover, if you're handing over enough cash, you may well be able to negotiate more advantageous fees.
- *How long will your money be locked up for, and how quickly can you get it back?* It is important that the liquidity offered by the fund is consonant with your own circumstances and investment horizons. Equally, the liquidity of the investments made by the manager needs to match or be better than that offered to investors. Otherwise, there may be problems if the fund hits a lean patch and everyone rushes for the exits—as happened with many hedge funds in 2008.
- *Does the manager have reliable references who can tell you honestly about their past experiences?* Ultimately, you have to trust the people you hand your money over to.
- *Visit their offices.* See how they work and interact. Try out some of their systems for yourself.

Potentially, there are hundreds of minor questions. The selection—in both qualitative and quantitative terms—of a successful fleet of hedge fund managers is an exhausting process, at the heart of which is an attempt to best capture trading talent. And even when complete, it's an exercise that is worth repeating every year for every hedge fund you choose to invest in.

CONCLUSION

The ultimate aim of the due diligence process is to convince you that the fund you select is genuinely suited to your investment needs. If there is any niggling doubt, the answer is simple: No matter how good it may seem in other respects, walk away.

The catastrophic demise of Amaranth is a case in point. Amaranth performed in stellar fashion for several years, and its reputation as a stable multi-strategy fund with attractive risk-adjusted returns attracted many institutional investors.

Yet its collapse in September 2006 was not the result of some unavoidable fraud. Rather, the warning signs were there for those investors who chose to look, particularly in the last year or two. Amaranth began to unilaterally change its liquidity terms to make it harder for investors to exit quickly, adopted a burdensome fee structure that passed expenses through to the investor, and morphed into a complex corporate structure which included self-administration.

Strong performances throughout the summer of 2005 flagged a rapidly increasing exposure to volatile energy markets such as natural gas futures. The size of this grew to the extent that to all intents and purposes, Amaranth effectively became the market.

Trapped eventually in a liquidity vice of its own making, its failure serves as a salient example of how active due diligence can avoid these market events. The management of Amaranth was always forthcoming in explaining strategies and exposures, and investors received exposure information continuously through the website and monthly letters. Thorough due diligence would have identified the problems, as well as revealed style drift, operational changes, and inadequate risk systems, all failing to control concentration of exposures and an ever increasing value-at-risk.

It's a powerful lesson. The hedge fund industry thrives because of the freedom offered by the lack of constraints on its activities. However, this freedom is also a double-edged sword that can make the allocation of assets to hedge funds a hazardous exercise.

A thorough due diligence process offers the best chance of avoiding fraud and incompetence, while identifying the best hedge fund managers for your investment goals. Properly carried out, due diligence gives a high probability that the managers you choose will live up to your investment goals and provide a bulwark against the inevitable downturn.

➤➤ MORE INFO

Websites:

Alternative Investment Management Association (AIMA): www.aima.org

Chartered Alternative Investment Analyst (CAIA) Association: www.caia.org

"If there is any niggling doubt, the answer is simple: no matter how good it may seem, walk away."

     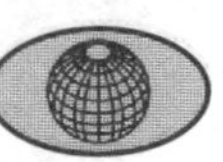   

Carrying Out Due Diligence on Private Equity Funds by Rainer Ender

EXECUTIVE SUMMARY

- Private equity fund due diligence is the first step in an investment process. The goal of due diligence is to identify the risk/return profile of a fund offer.
- A well-structured due diligence process contains a top-down macro and a bottom-up manager analysis, allowing the investor to filter the most promising funds.
- A consistent framework for fund and fund-manager assessment is essential. This assessment must address quantitative and qualitative aspects, and focus on the manager's "ingredients for success".
- At first sight, fund offerings may appear attractive from a pure return perspective. It is crucial that the investment has an attractive risk/return balance.

INTRODUCTION

The term "due diligence" covers a broad range of different due diligence types. These can be grouped into three major types; financial, legal/tax, and business due diligence. The goal of this article is to shed light on business due diligence for investing in private equity funds. Due diligence is commonly defined as "the process of investigation and evaluation, performed by investors, into the details of a potential investment, such as an examination of operations and management, the verification of material facts".[1] "It is a requirement for prudent investors and the basis for better investment decisions."[2] Private equity fund evaluation faces specific challenges; the private character of the industry makes it inherently difficult to obtain the relevant information; furthermore, the investment decision reflects a commitment to a fund manager to finance future investments rather than a straightforward purchase of specific assets. Therefore, common evaluation techniques used to assess public equity investments are not appropriate within the private equity asset class.

The private equity market has enjoyed extraordinary growth rates in the past, and private equity investments showed strong returns, supported by a booming economy and an expanding debt market. The current financial crisis will have a significant impact on the private equity market; a shake-out of fund managers is to be expected over the coming years. Managers who can demonstrate how they created value in the past, beyond just benefiting from favorable market developments, and who are able to make a compelling case for future value creation will continue to raise capital successfully.

Before investing in a private equity fund, an investor should have sufficient comfort regarding:

- Strategy perspective: the investment strategy of the fund.
- Return perspective: evidence that the manager stands out compared to his/her peer group.
- Risk perspective: assurance that risk is mitigated to the level required by the investor.

The relative youth of the private equity industry, data paucity, as well as benchmarking difficulties within and across asset classes are just a few elements that indicate why the investor has to rely on qualitative aspects and judgment during the due diligence process of private equity funds.

STRUCTURAL SET-UP OF A DUE DILIGENCE PROCESS

The Overall Framework

A solid due diligence framework contains a top-down review as a first step. This review must assess the attractiveness of the various private equity sub-segments and regions. The assessment includes various evaluation criteria, such as investment opportunities in the segment, capital demand and supply, the quality of the fund manager universe, entry and exit prices, and the future development potential of the sub-segments. Furthermore, it is important that the investment strategy of a fund manager is not only attractive on a stand-alone basis, but also within the overall context of the investor's total portfolio.

Generating a complete overview of the relevant fund manager universe is the second step. Worldwide, there are about 3,000 private equity fund managers to be considered, making the creation of this overview a very demanding task. It is crucial not to assess the managers who provide you with their fund offering passively, but proactively to benchmark all relevant fund managers for a proper peer-group comparison.

> "The current financial crisis will have a significant impact on the private equity market; a shake-out of fund managers is to be expected over the coming years."

The third step of the framework is to ensure that risks related to the potential commitment are mitigated through an in-depth due diligence process. For all identified issues, due diligence steps must be taken in order to clarify the situation. An investment should only be considered if a sufficient level of comfort is achieved on all issues.

Example of a Due Diligence Process

A clear, well-structured due diligence process, which is tailored to the context of the fund manager, with concrete steps and tools, is an important prerequisite for a comprehensive and consistent

Figure 1. Example of a proven due diligence process structure

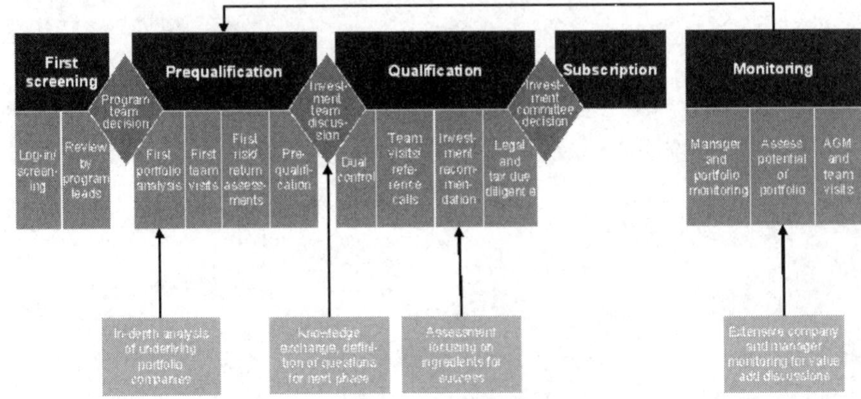

fund-manager evaluation. Below, we describe a process structure that is the result of continuous improvements over the past 25 years.

The first screening of the fund offering addresses the track record, strategy, team, and fit with the portfolio. This analysis can be performed by junior professionals, but it is important to have an experienced senior professional reviewing the screening and taking the final decision on whether to conduct further due diligence. This ensures that the senior has the full picture of the deal flow and the market dynamics.

The prequalification phase starts with a detailed portfolio analysis of all past investments made by the fund manager. Interactions with the fund manager are used to clarify the impact on the value contribution of the manager to past and future investments. Putting these insights into a structured risk-return framework (see next section detailed below), combined with peer-group benchmarking, allows the identification of fund offerings with a promising risk-return potential. It is beneficial to broadly discuss fund offerings within the investment team to identify critical aspects, residual risks, and external referencing possibilities. This knowledge exchange defines questions for the qualification phase.

The qualification phase is divided into four steps:

1 Dual control: the project worker starts working with an independent devil's advocate. The goal of this step is to identify all potential weaknesses that could be discovered by a pair of fresh eyes, and to ensure the quality of the process. It also helps specify further tailored action steps that need to be addressed, and to clarify open issues.
2 The second step is to review the fund manager's governance structures and processes, with the goal of identifying operational and team dynamic risks.
3 The third step is the verification of the assessment through third-party referencing. Well-prepared reference calls with past and present key people from underlying companies are an extremely helpful resource for verifying your current impression of the fund manager. Reference calls provide the opportunity to check the contribution of the fund manager to the value creation and the investment sourcing. If external referencing confirms the current assessment and does not lead to new questions, the investment opportunity fulfils all three evaluation levels: appealing strategy, return potential, and controlled risk.
4 The last step is the legal and tax due diligence.

The investment decision and subscription: having a formalized investment approval mechanism, for example through an investment committee, rounds off the due diligence process, which, as a last step, includes the subscription process to the fund.

Thorough monitoring must be put in place once a long-term investment is made. Monitoring is needed to ensure that active measures can be taken where needed, in order to maximize value for the investor. Monitoring is also an integral part of the due diligence for the investment decision regarding the fund manager's next fund (typically after three to four years). Due diligence represents a deep monitoring effort on prior fund investments.

Risk Return Framework

A clear fund-manager evaluation framework provides consistency among different manager evaluations, and allows for proper benchmarking of managers within a specific peer group. A scoring system that is appropriate for the qualitative and quantitative analyses on a fund manager has proven useful. By constantly applying the system, the scoring becomes well

Table 1. Framework for a manager evaluation addressing risk and return aspects with a scoring system

Return assessment criteria	*Score*	*Risk assessment criteria*	*Score*
Historical performance • Quality of past performance • Aggregate deal performance over time	X.XX	**Historical performance** • Quality of past performance • Deal by deal volatility	X.XX
Deal sourcing • Quality of deal flow • Involvement in deal origination	X.XX	**Operations/team risk** • Governance structure • Process quality	X.XX
Value creation • Operational competence • Level of active involvement in deals	X.XX	**Investment strategy risk** • Investment discipline • General risk elements	X.XX
Exit capacity • Track based on many deals vs single hit • Corporate buyers network	X.XX	**Aggregate company financing risk** • Milestone vs upfront financing • Quality of syndication partners	X.XX
Portfolio return considerations • Common characteristics of individual companies supporting return potential	X.XX	**Portfolio return** considerations • Common characteristics of individual companies supporting risk potential	X.XX
Total return score	**X.XX**	**Total return score**	**X.XX**

CASE STUDY

Fund Due Diligence for the MCAP Fund[3]

MCAP is a newly formed, European, first-time fund manager launching a €250 million fund specialized in development capital and small buyout investments in a single industry. The key person for the fund has deep industry experience. He successfully founded and grew a company operationally superior to more mature, competitive companies. Subsequently, the company was acquired by an international corporation, where he then became the CEO. After stepping down, he formed MCAP. Besides him, there are two other partners who also left their high caliber jobs to launch MCAP. The additional team members previously worked together in various positions; however, none of them has a track record as an investment professional.

A standard due diligence process focused mainly on the historic performance of the fund would pass on this fund after the first screening. The risk-return framework has a different approach:

- The industry targeted by the fund is not covered by existing fund managers. The industry appears to be attractive for backing small, flexible, and dynamic companies with high technological and operational excellence. MCAP could, therefore, be a promising complementary investment.
- The fund manager's ingredients for success from a deal-sourcing and value-creation perspective are in place through the extensive networks of MCAP's partners, and their in-depth industry expertize. Exit capability has only been proven in the sale to the international corporation; there is neither a proven track record, nor an established competitor. Nevertheless, the risk return assessment framework can be applied to benchmark this new fund against other funds with a single industry focus. Reference calls are important sources for validating the reputation and the competency of MCP's team.

"The impulse to acquisition, pursuit of gain, of money, of the greatest possible amount of money, has in itself nothing to do with capitalism. . .One may say that it has been common to all sorts and conditions of men at all times and in all cultures of the earth, wherever the objective possibility of it is or has been given." Max Weber

     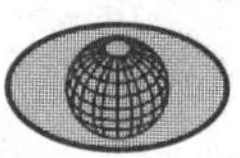   

calibrated. Furthermore, it allows for best-practice manager benchmarking across geographies and segments. Due to the qualitative nature of private equity, the focus of the assessment must be on the "ingredients for success" within the future competitive landscape.

In order to enable the ranking of fund managers within a peer group, a quantitative benchmarking that looks at the return and risk aspects helps to put the full due diligence findings into an aggregate picture. We have applied the framework shown in Table 1 during the past decade.

CONCLUSION

Private equity fund due diligence is a work-intensive undertaking. It requires a clear top-down assessment of investment segments and geographies that, based on fundamental drivers, appear attractive for investment. For the bottom-up fund manager evaluation, a proper due diligence process with clear milestones must be established. This process must be supported by tools that allow a structured assessment of a fund offering, and ensure comparability of different funds. When working in a broad team, special attention is also needed to make certain that all professionals apply the same framework, and that evaluations by different people lead to comparable results.

Finally, it must be emphasized that, while there appear to be many promising investment opportunities, the most important element for due diligence is to identify the risk behind each opportunity.

- Risk mitigation for the investor is the most challenging aspect of the due diligence in this case. The management firm is in formation, and the concept is to operate like an industry holding company, managing five investments with deep operational involvement. It is evident that the fund operation will be loss-making, and that the partners are pre-financing this initiative substantially. They are well aligned with the investors in the fund. Close interaction with the manager, and legal terms allowing intervention by investors, should MCAP drift off course, are prerequisites for reaching the level of comfort needed to make a fund commitment.

MAKING IT HAPPEN

The foundation of a successful due diligence process is a structured process, a proven evaluation framework, and an experienced team. Some valuable aspects are:

- In-depth knowledge of past fund investments, their business and investment performance, and the fund manager's value creation is crucial for the evaluation and the understanding of a private equity fund's offering.
- Broad sharing of the investment project work among all investment team members ensures the quality of the due diligence process, and a consistent investment philosophy across the firm.
- Well-prepared reference calls provide an excellent perspective on how a fund manager creates value.
- An experienced senior professional acting as devil's advocate on an investment project provides valuable, internal challenging and risk mitigation.

MORE INFO

Books:

Mayer, T., and Mathonet P.-Y. *Beyond the J-Curve: Managing a Portfolio of Venture Capital and Private Equity Funds*. Chichester, UK: Wiley, 2005.

Probitas Partners. *The Guide to Private Equity Investment Due Diligence*. London: PEI Media, 2005.

Report:

Kreuter, B., and O. Gottschalg. "Quantitative private equity fund due diligence: Possible selection criteria and their efficiency." Paris: HEC, 2006.

NOTES

1 Sood, V. "Investment strategies in private equity." *Journal of Private Equity* (Summer 2003).

2 Mayer and Mathonet (2005).

3 Fictitious fund example, based on actual cases.

"Ambition should be made of sterner stuff." William Shakespeare

  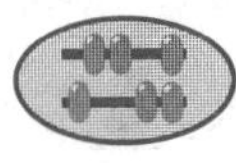   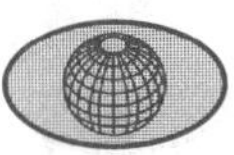   

Viewpoint: Anthony Bolton Savings is a Growth Industry

INTRODUCTION

Anthony Bolton managed one of the UK's most successful and largest mutual funds, Fidelity Special Situations, from 1979 to 2007. Over that period the fund generated an annualized return of 20% (against some 8% for the FTSE All-Share Index). He graduated from Cambridge University with a degree in engineering and entered the City as an investment analyst at investment bank Keyser Ullman. In 1979, Bolton was hired by Fidelity, the Boston-based investment group, as one of its first London-based investors, and has since pursued a contrarian and bottom-up approach to investing with immense success. In surveys of professional investors, he is regularly named the fund manager most respected by his peers, and earned the sobriquet "the quiet assassin" for his role in preventing Michael Green from becoming chairman of the newly merged ITV in 2003. Since stepping down from day-to-day fund management in December 2007, Bolton has focused on mentoring Fidelity's younger fund managers and analysts and overseeing its investment process. In his spare time, he composes classical music using the Sibelius function on his laptop computer.

What is the future for the investment management business? How do you think that it is going to evolve?

Hedge funds have suffered a really hard blow, which is going to set them back quite a few years. However, I don't think that they're going to disappear altogether. The fittest will survive and do well.

There was a bubble in the hedge fund business, which also affected private equity and other alternative asset classes. A huge amount of money flowed into hedge funds in the bubble years, partly the result of investment consultants advising institutional investor clients such as pension funds to put 15% to 20% of their portfolios into alternatives. As always happens in such situations, this meant that less good quality talent was sucked into the hedge fund sector.

Hedge funds are also having to contend with a sudden loss of leverage. Prior to the Lehman Brothers collapse, they had access to almost limitless amounts of leverage and were able to borrow on very good terms from their prime brokers. Since the Lehmans collapse, that has disappeared, and I suspect it will take a while to come back. You're also seeing big redemptions; funds are either being closed down or having to impose restrictions on redemptions. The troubles facing the hedge fund sector cannot be anything other than good news to long-only managers.

We're also seeing a blurring between long-only funds and hedge funds. One example I give is that the Fidelity Special Situations fund, which I managed until December 2007, was given new powers under the EU's UCITSIII regulations, which meant we could short-sell for the first time. More and more long-only funds will take on such powers, which implies a further blurring of the boundaries between long-only funds and hedge funds. Most fund managers are, over the next five years or so, going to have to become as proficient in being short as in being long.

Asset management groups are going to be offering investors a range of products—some pure long-only, some pure hedge funds, and then some that bridge the two. Within that you'll also see a convergence in fees. The traditional 2 and 20 model used by hedge funds is going to come under increasing pressure, while there may also be some upward movement of the very low fees seen in long-only.

Are you confident about the outlook for traditional long-only asset management groups?

Yes I am. The long-term trends are positive because populations are ageing, which means people are going to need to save more. That makes savings a growth industry. There's also a short-term boost because of what's going on in the hedge fund area. Another aspect is that boutiques, small specialist asset management groups, are falling out of fashion. People had fallen in love with boutiques, but there is now much more of a focus on counterparty risk and size. That is playing into the hands of the larger groups.

Will investment banks face tighter regulation?

Until 2004, the investment banks were more tightly controlled—especially where their use of leverage, their balance sheet gearing, was concerned. However, the US authorities lifted some of those controls in 2004, permitting the investment banks to raise their leverage ratios up to 50 or 60 times. Previously the regulated limit was about 10. In future, I suspect that we're going to see a return to the sort of controls in existence prior to 2004.

Should the Glass–Steagall Act, which prevented commercial banks from owning investment banks or vice versa, be reenacted?

In fact, we are moving in the opposite direction. The Federal Reserve allowed both Goldman Sachs and Morgan Stanley to convert themselves into "bank holding companies" at the height of the financial crisis in September 2008. One reason was to give them access to deposits. However, given what has happened, it is essential that controls are once again imposed on their leverage. In the absence of controls on leverage, allowing them to become deposit takers could be very dangerous indeed.

Is it time derivatives were more tightly regulated?

I think that we're going to see tighter regulation of over-the-counter instruments, including a lot of derivatives and credit default swaps. The ones that are not regulated are inherently more dangerous because there's no central clearing organization.

Accountancy and banking regulation are moving in a pro-cyclical direction. Is this a good or a bad thing?

  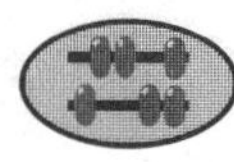  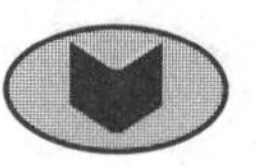 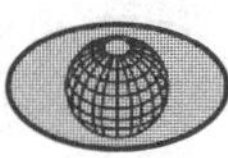   

Both accountancy and bank regulation have been moving in that direction, and it's partly in response to Basel II. But in my view both accountancy and the regulation of bank capital ratios have become far too pro-cyclical. It requires banks and other financial institutions to have their minimum financial ratios at the height of the economic booms and their maximum ratios in the depths of recessions. Some of the banks have complained this isn't even linear, meaning that the effect is multiplied as they enter recessions. It's fairly obvious that regulators have got this the wrong way around. It is going to have to be reversed, which implies some real questions about whether Basel II can survive.

Having high capital ratios as you go into a recession makes sense, but to require even higher ones at the bottom of a recession makes no sense at all; at times like that banks should be permitted to have much lower capital ratios.

Does this mean that what Sir David Tweedie, chairman of the International Accounting Standards Board was arguing for, is being unwound?

The current trend away from mark-to-market, or fair value, accounting is actually quite dangerous. What the world needs now is greater transparency.

Perhaps mark-to-market is a bit like short-selling. Most of the time it is fine and well, but when you get into extreme circumstances—as we had during the banking and financial crisis of 2008—it is correct that you curtail the ability of people to short-sell financial stocks. Otherwise there's real danger that such activity becomes self-fulfilling.

Likewise with mark-to-market accounting; I believe we should have it, but perhaps there are certain circumstances where it can be dangerous.

Occasionally, when you get into a position where the entire capitalist system is at risk, as we had with the Latin American debt crisis of the early 1990s, it might be sensible to temporarily suspend it. At times like that, mark-to-market can have seriously negative repercussions. If mark-to-market had been rigorously applied during the Latin American debt crisis, a great many banks in the US and Europe would have struggled to trade their way out of the crisis and failed.

French president Nicolas Sarkozy is trying to torpedo moves for fair value accounting to be adopted across Europe. If he succeeds, is there a danger that accounting will return to being totally opaque?

Yes, there is and that could be very dangerous. It would take us back to the bad old days when financial institutions were able to hide and disguise everything. I would be strongly opposed to that.

As a consequence of MiFID, stock markets are likely to see a loss of trading business to alternative trading platforms, including Project Turquoise, Chi-X, and Plus Markets. Is this good or bad for investors?

This is an interesting topic and one that is evolving very quickly. The barriers to become a trading venue are now much lower, so it's all about technology, having a robust process, and attracting consistent flows from different investors.

We have seen a proliferation of new venues and I believe this will continue. Flows into dark pools (where prices do not have to be shown and flows can be hidden) are also on the increase. Institutional investors, such as the investment banks, are very much behind the growth of these exchanges, particularly as they are less expensive that the traditional stock exchanges. The success of these new venues will be determined by the business they can attract. A good example is Chi-X, that has 5% market share but makes little profit at this present time.

Do you support further consolidation among international stock exchanges, as we have seen with NYSE, Euronext, and Liffe?

There are arguments for and against. I think that having bigger pools of liquidity is a positive thing, providing that the investor is protected. But there is also a danger that transnational players could use their dominant or monopoly positions to hurt investors, for example by substantially increasing fees. I think this is why we are seeing traditional exchanges also changing and creating different platforms to compete with new entrants.

What is the future for the markets? Should investors think about buying equities again?

I was more cautious earlier than most, from about 2006. However I am now more optimistic. When everyone else is very negative, that's a positive signal to me. When no one wants to buy into rights issues because they believe the stocks concerned will continue to fall, that's a positive to me. When cash positions are high, it means people have already done their selling, which is another positive to me. When the majority of commentators are pessimistic, I am optimistic.

The nature of stock markets is that at the top, everything looks brilliant and at the bottom everything looks terrible. So, you've got to rely on indicators that measure this pessimism and this optimism if you are going to decide when to invest in the market.

▸▸ MORE INFO

Books:

Bolton, Anthony. *Investing Against the Tide—Lessons from a Life Running Money*. FT Prentice Hall, 2009.

Bolton, Anthony, and Jonathan Davis. *Investing with Anthony Bolton: Anatomy of a Stock Market Winner*. 2nd ed. Petersfield, UK: Harriman House, 2006.

"Before anything else, preparation is the key to success." Alexander Graham Bell

  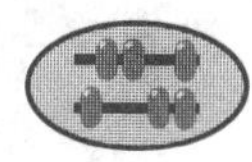   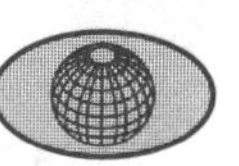 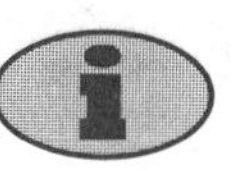  

The Case for SMART Rebalancing by Arun Muralidhar and Sanjay Muralidhar

EXECUTIVE SUMMARY

- Once investment managers establish a long-term strategic allocation or benchmark, fund managers must decide how to manage the fund's ongoing allocation.
- Daily market movements can result in constant drifts of actual portfolio allocations from the strategic benchmark.
- Traditionally, experts advised "static rebalancing" wherein simple rules bring the allocations back to the benchmark if some allocation limit is breached or some calendar date is reached.
- Static rebalancing strategies are risky, as the investors take an implicit bet to be either long or short an asset without really focusing on the view on the markets.
- While static rebalancing is often better than drift, this article describes how SMART (Systematic Management of Assets using a Rules-based Technique) can be a better tool for investors.
- By using market factors and managing allocations proactively within rebalancing ranges (i.e., no change in overall policy), investors can improve performance and risk management.
- SMART rebalancing is essential for good governance.

BACKGROUND

Every fund manager has to deal with a vexing issue—namely, how to manage the rebalancing process as the returns from this activity impact the total portfolio performance. There is a wealth of information on these strategies, and many papers have been written on this topic.[1] Nersesian (2006) does an excellent job of introducing a process to help determine the ideal rebalancing policy and examine the considerations in selecting the appropriate approach. Most rebalancing policies (periodic, range, or threshold) first focus on minimizing the tracking error or absolute standard deviation of the portfolio as the key measure of risk (either directly or by targeting the highest Sharpe ratio), and then attempt to manage the trade-off relative to the transactions costs that more frequent rebalancing generates.[2]

Many portfolio managers manage their asset allocation decisions by adopting a rebalancing policy which typically involves returning the asset allocation to the target allocation or strategic asset allocation (SAA) at calendar intervals (monthly, quarterly, or annually). Alternatively, portfolio managers may use a "range-based" approach whereby the trigger points or ranges are typically 3–5% from the target, based on the volatility of asset classes. Variations of this approach rebalance to somewhere within these allocation ranges or use periodic cash flows to move the asset allocation of the various assets closer to what a rebalancing action would attempt to do. Often these approaches are a move toward a practical maintenance of the strategic weights, trading off between managing transactions costs and tracking error relative to the benchmark. These approaches can be called "static rebalancing" because the limits are set. However, the portfolio still drifts within the bands, as most policies are silent about what actions staff should take within the bands. This is demonstrated in Figure 1.

THE ALLURE OF REBALANCING

Rebalancing is attractive because it is simple to understand and to execute, is explicit and transparent, allowing portfolio managers to put in place the exact policy to be followed and be assured that it is being followed, and avoids the appearance of "do-nothing" or "buy-and-hold." Furthermore, discipline provides a decision regime that can be modeled to quantify the historical risk and return profile. Finally, most analyses suggest that a rebalancing policy is better than doing nothing (or letting the portfolio drift), and that has been good enough for most investors.

THE PROBLEM WITH STATIC REBALANCING

Despite the low tracking error relative to their benchmarks, static rebalancing policies can be problematic owing to the large absolute and relative drawdowns (or declines in the value of the fund). Therefore, when US and European equity declined dramatically from 2000 to early 2003, rebalancing would have done little to reduce the pain of the portfolio and would have caused the rebalanced portfolio to plummet as well. While static rebalancing is attractive in up markets, the analogy in down markets would be to tying your leg to the anchor of a sinking ship.

The larger questions that this article addresses in the new rebalancing paradigm are:

- What are the appropriate performance and risk measures in determining the best asset allocation approach? Additional risk measures like the drawdown in the portfolio (maximum decline in the absolute or relative value of the fund), and success ratio (number of months that you outperform the benchmark) are utilized as these better capture the concept of practical portfolio management risk as opposed to standard deviation. After all, a low tracking error relative to a benchmark may be worthless if the fund is bankrupted by a large drawdown in absolute value.
- Is there a better way to manage asset allocation decisions than static rebalancing?
- Can other approaches preserve the advantages that rebalancing policies

Figure 1. The implicit bet in traditional rebalancing policies

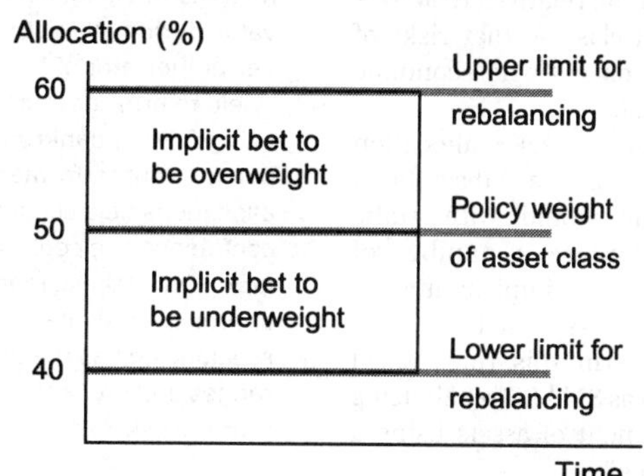

"Ambition, madam, is a great man's madness." John Webster

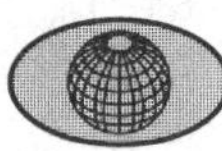

have, namely the ability to have explicit, transparent, and disciplined asset allocation decisions?

INFORMED OR SMART REBALANCING

The more sensible way to make asset allocation decisions is by a process called "informed rebalancing." Informed rebalancing is simply about making asset allocation decisions among the various assets in a portfolio to take advantage of the higher returns in the attractive assets, while underweighting the less attractive assets commensurately. The case for informed rebalancing was made very successfully in Muralidhar (2007), though McCalla (1997) had hinted at a somewhat different approach. This is done by identifying the factors that affect which assets in your portfolio will perform well and which will perform poorly during any given regime/cycle/period. This approach, therefore, involves the following steps:

- Identify all the asset allocation decisions being made in the portfolio.
- Develop investment rules to guide the desired asset allocation tilts in the portfolio. These rules will define the assets that should be overweighted or underweighted relative to the target allocation based upon the levels of certain market or economic factors, typically sources from finance or academic journals. These factors will be measures of valuation (whether an asset class is over- or undervalued), economic activity (different economic conditions favor different asset classes), seasonality, momentum, market sentiment (volume, volatility, risk aversion, fund flows, etc.).
- Quantify the historical performance of such an asset allocation approach to understand the risk/return profile of each factor model and possibly fine-tuning the selection of the various factor-based rules to ensure that they meet the investment objectives or constraints.
- Combine many such factor-based rules into a diversified strategy that provides a net indication of the relative attractiveness of each asset class so that risks of making decisions on a single economic factor are mitigated.
- Implement these asset allocation recommendations in a disciplined way (just as one would with static rebalancing). There are a number of ways to carry out such implementation that will be discussed separately.

For simplicity, we term this rules-based systematic approach as SMART rebalancing (systematic management of assets using a rules-based technique).

ADVANTAGES OF SMART REBALANCING

The SAA is normally derived from one of two types of optimization. The first method models assets and liabilities (ALM) to find the long-term asset allocation that has the best chance of meeting the liability (in the case of an individual, this would be the desired retirement income) requirement. The second method uses a mean-variance approach that makes assumptions of future asset returns and risk (often based upon historical performance) and finds an "efficient frontier" asset allocation with the highest return for an acceptable level of risk or the least risk for a given required return.

The attendant shortcomings of these optimizations aside—the most glaring being the need for an assumption of expected return/risk—this allocation is to be interpreted as the target allocation that over a very long period offers the best chance of meeting the fund objectives expressed in return/risk or funding terms. There is nothing in these mean-variance optimizations that reacts to market conditions in intervening periods. Again, to use a sailing analogy, naïve rebalancing is

CASE STUDY

Analysis of Buy-and-Hold, Static Rebalancing and SMART Rebalancing

A simple case study indicates how a hypothetical portfolio, highlighted in Figure 2, could be managed using such investment rules. We assume a simple portfolio with a strategic investment in four core assets: US Equity (benchmarked to the S&P 500), International Equity (benchmarked to the MSCI EAFE Index), US Fixed Income (benchmarked to the Lehman Brothers Composite Index) and Commodities (benchmarked to the Goldman Sachs Commodity Index). Rules are developed for each set of assets using multiple factors and are combined to create a diversified strategy to manage the allocation across these assets. The performance of this informed rebalancing portfolio is compared with a simple buy-and-hold option and a quarterly rebalanced portfolio. The portfolio target assets and allocation are shown in Table 1.

Further, this analysis was backtested over the period from January 1990 through October 2008, so that it covers a few different market regimes, the technology boom of the late 1990s, the subsequent correction of the early 2000s, the subsequent bull market post-2003, and the more recent decline through 2008. We include transactions costs of 20 bps round trip for all assets, though actual experience suggests much lower costs are incurred.

The performance analysis is restricted to a few key metrics in Table 2 in order to facilitate this discussion, but these results are confirmed over a broader set of risk and return parameters.

As indicated in Table 2, the range rebalancing alternative represents a meaningful improvement over the buy-and-hold strategy and is consistent with most prevailing studies. However, when compared with SMART rebalancing, the only advantage of range rebalancing is a slightly lower standard deviation. However, the lower standard deviation, which is what most professionals use as a proxy for risk, comes at the expense of a 0.5% lower annualized return and therefore a return/risk ratio of 0.67 versus 0.79 for the SMART rebalancing! Notice, though, that this performance and risk advantage comes with very narrow ranges around the strategic asset allocations and hence with ±5% ranges which are more typical, the excess returns and risk management advantages will be much more significant.

More important, in reviewing alternative risk and quality of returns measures—namely *maximum drawdown*, *success ratio*, and *confidence in skill*—the results are more compelling. *Maximum drawdown* measures the maximum decline in the portfolio value during the historical period—to many a more important measure of risk as it is a better indicator of the fund's solvency. This statistic is humorously referred to as the "yield to fire," as it measures how much and for how long one can lose money before being fired or bankrupt. The *success ratio* represents the percentage of months that the portfolio outperformed its benchmark (or a comparable passive portfolio with the target allocations held constant), and the *confidence in skill* is a statistical measure of confidence one could have that these returns were the product of skill as opposed to luck.[3] On all these measures, SMART rebalancing performed much better than the other approaches. While past returns are no guarantee of future returns, essentially SMART rebalancing has the ability to take corrective action to asset allocation within the policy ranges and prevent bad asset allocation decisions from impacting performance and thereby risk.

"If you join a big corporation, you have to aspire to getting as far as you can." Tony Trahar

  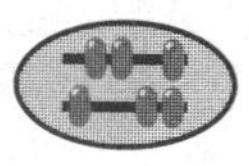  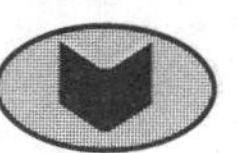 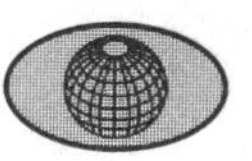   

Figure 2. Investment structure of hypothetical US pension fund

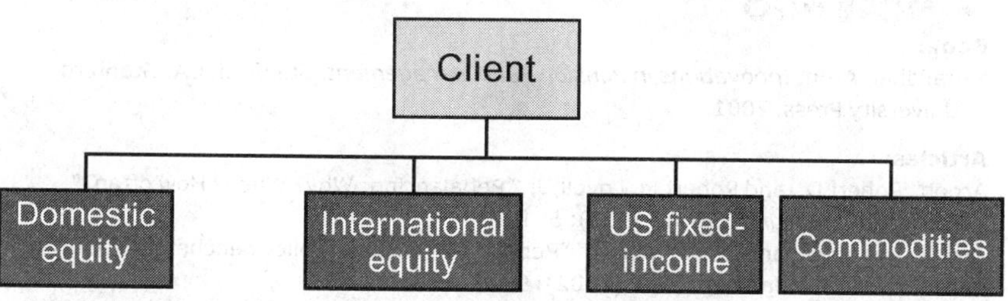

Table 1. Portfolio structure and target allocation

Asset class	*Benchmark asset*	*Target allocation (%)*	*Range (%)*
US Equity	S&P 500	31	2.86
International equity	MSCI EAFE	30	2.92
Fixed income Composite	Lehman Brothers US	33	2.80
Commodities	GSCI	6	1.50

Table 2. Comparing return and risk of informed rebalancing versus buy-and-hold and quarterly rebalancing

	Buy-and-hold (%)	*Range rebalancing (%)*	*SMART rebalancing (%)*
Annualized return	6.2	6.4	6.9
Standard deviation	9.3	8.6	8.7
Return/risk ratio	0.67	0.75	0.7
Maximum drawdown	−31.9	−33.1	−31.7
Success ratio	51.8	51.1	55.3
Confidence in skill	31.1	18.7	99.9

like setting the rudder in the direction of the destination without adjusting for wind direction, tides, or choppy seas, and without considering potentially faster ways of reaching the destination with less risk of drowning. SMART rebalancing, on the other hand, would involve making the appropriate adjustments.

Most importantly, as modern portfolio theory has taught us, the assets included in this portfolio are ideally uncorrelated with each other (or at least have low correlation). The logical extension of this assumption of low correlation is that in any given period (whether determined by market regimes, economic cycles, or calendar periods), some of these assets will perform better than others in the portfolio, and some will outperform their expected returns, while others will underperform these expectations. The static rebalancing approach to asset allocation assumes (or hopes) that these pluses and minuses will even out over time and should not be a concern in the ongoing asset allocation decisions. Moreover, there are many ongoing asset allocations that are necessary as a result of cash flows generated by the portfolio by way of dividends, coupon payments, and contributions, and disbursements to meet ongoing obligations.

SMART rebalancing takes the view that low correlation alone demands that responsible asset managers make asset allocation decisions to position their portfolio for these regimes/cycles/market conditions best and, by doing this well and systematically, can greatly improve the return per unit of risk. After all, most investors expect the same process from their external asset managers/mutual fund managers, and it is logical to demand this same responsibility, process, and governance at one decision level up from the portfolio's managers.

Markets are dynamic and asset returns are going up or down daily, resulting in new changes in the weights of assets changing each day. Many investors feel that if they do not take an explicit decision about an asset weight, they do not have a bet on the markets. However, quite the opposite is true! When applied to the decision on assets that have drifted in allocation above the long-term strategic weight because of strong recent performance, to not rebalance implies a view that this asset will continue to outperform. Similarly, triggering an automatic rebalancing decision to reduce (or increase) the weight on an asset back to its benchmark weight at the end of the quarter because a particular day has been reached, implies a view that this asset will do worse (or better) than other assets. Otherwise, to make such a decision would seem somewhat contradictory. In addition, a rebalancing decision makes the assumption that the benchmark allocation is the most desirable at all times (under all market conditions), and hence managing back to this asset allocation is best for the portfolio regardless of current market

▸▸ MAKING IT HAPPEN

The key to this approach is that while it does involve a little more work than implementing (or recommending) a rebalancing policy, it has similar advantages.

- Simplicity. Once the rules are articulated (and typically these are either explained by fundamental arguments, well-researched trends or common intuition) they can be easily followed and implemented. This simplicity also allows investors to track a few key factors consistently and act on them with confidence.
- *Explicitness and transparency*. By definition, this approach requires a clear definition of the market factors (signals) that will be followed, how these will be used to make asset allocation decisions for the fund, and the policy controls operating on this decision-making process (frequency, asset bandwidths, etc.). Investors then will be able to analyze and vet these decisions thoroughly prior to approving them. This then allows them to execute what is now a disciplined and systematic set of decisions.
- *Superiority*. This approach is superior to the static/naïve rebalancing approaches because it recognizes the limitations of the SAA, makes implicit decisions explicit (what gets monitored gets managed), and operates in the area where the SAA is of limited value. Further, it is both responsible and responsive to current information, which is always more relevant and up-to-date than that used as an input for the SAA decision. Implementation of SMART rebalancing is very similar to static rebalancing and would be implemented in exactly the same way that a current rebalancing program would. In our experience, both programs are easily implemented using futures contracts, so this performance is very easy to achieve and hence does not have any impact on the rest of the portfolio.

"The idea was to prove. . .that you were one of the elected and anointed ones who had the right stuff and could move higher and higher and. . .join the special few at the very top." Tom Wolfe

     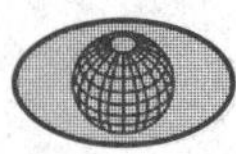   

conditions. So, all asset managers must realize that every decision—whether to overweight, underweight, or continue to allow assets to drift—is an active decision, whether it is made explicitly or implicitly. In short, all these approaches are tactical in nature, even though they are not labeled as such and are often even cloaked as just the opposite!

CONCLUSION

This article has described how the SMART rebalancing approach can meaningfully improve the performance of the investment portfolio. All decisions to change the asset allocation—whether to let the portfolio drift or rebalance on some static policy or to make informed rebalancing decisions—are active asset allocation decisions. Therefore, it is best to make such decisions in an explicit, disciplined, and informed manner by using the various measures that one should constantly be tracking for other investment decisions (economic, valuation, momentum, and market factors). In the current return environment, every bit of performance is needed to meet investment objectives. SMART rebalancing has the advantage of working on the entire asset base, with the added benefit that it can be implemented in addition to other things that may be done in the portfolio.

▸▸ MORE INFO

Book:

Muralidhar, Arun. *Innovations in Pension Fund Management*. Stanford, CA: Stanford University Press, 2001.

Articles:

Arnott, Robert D., and Robert M. Lovell, Jr. "Rebalancing: Why? When? How often?" *Journal of Investing* (Spring 1993): 5–10.

Arnott, Robert D., and Lisa M. Plaxco. "Rebalancing a global policy benchmark." *Journal of Portfolio Management* 28:2 (2002): 9–22.

Bernstein, William J. "Case studies in rebalancing." *Efficient Frontier* (Fall 2000). Online at: www.efficientfrontier.com/ef/100/rebal100.htm

Buetow, Gerald W., Jr, Ronald Sellers, Donald Trotter, Elaine Hunter, and Willie A. Whipple, Jr. "The benefits of rebalancing." *Journal of Portfolio Management* (Winter 2002): 23–32.

Graham, Benjamin, and David Dodd. "Investment link tutorial: Asset allocation." *Just for Funds* blog (May 26, 2007). Online at: www.justforfunds.blogspot.com/2007/05/jff-link-tutorial-asset-allocation.html

Leland, Hayne E. "Optimal asset rebalancing in the presence of transactions." Working paper (August 1996). Online at: papers.ssrn.com/sol3/papers.cfm?abstract_id=1060

Masters, Seth J. "Rules for rebalancing." *Financial Planning* (December 2002): 89–93.

McCalla, Douglas. "Enhancing the efficient frontier with portfolio rebalancing." *Journal of Pension Plan Investing* 1:4 (Spring 1997): 16–32.

Muralidhar, Sanjay. "A new paradigm for rebalancing." *The Monitor* 22:2 (March/April 2007): 12–16. Online at: www.mcubeit.com/Mcubesite/web/pdf/research/A_New_Paradigm_for_Rebalancing.pdf.

Nersesian, John. "Active portfolio rebalancing: A disciplined approach to keeping clients on track." *The Monitor* 21:1 (January/February 2006): 9–15.

Website:

Mcube Investment Technologies: www.mcubeit.com/Mcubesite/web/Books_Articles.html

See Also:

★ Asset Allocation Methodologies (pp. 281–285)
★ Money Managers (pp. 357–359)
✔ Mean-Variance Optimization: A Primer (p. 941)
✔ Understanding Asset-Liability Management (Full Balance Sheet Approach) (p. 889)
Harry Markowitz (p. 1175)
William Sharpe (p. 1193)
Portfolio Theory and Capital Markets (p. 1310)

NOTES

1 See for example Arnott and Lovell (1993), Arnott and Plaxo (2002), Donohue (2003), Bernstein (2000), Buetow *et al*. (2002), Masters (2002), Leland (1996).

2 Leland (1996).

3 Muralidhar (2001), Chapter 9.

"Don't waste your effort on a thing which ends in a petty triumph unless you are satisfied with a life of petty issues." John D. Rockefeller

     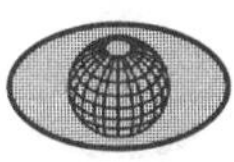   

The Changing Role and Regulation of Equity Research by Simon Taylor

EXECUTIVE SUMMARY

- Equity research provided by investment banks, broker dealers, and independent researchers has an important influence on share prices.
- Research analysts are a very important constituency for the managers of quoted companies.
- Many major investment banks were accused of publishing biased research during the 1990s stock market boom to win higher-margin corporate finance business.
- Regulatory changes, starting in the United States and copied internationally after 2003, restricted contact between analysts and bankers and prevented analysts being paid on the basis of banking fees.
- Analysts are now more likely to offer unbiased opinions and to be more critical of companies.
- Company managers need to be careful to build good relationships with analysts through clear and consistent publication of information.

WHAT IS EQUITY RESEARCH?

Equity research is the publication by analysts of reports, notes, and emails that offer an investment recommendation on the quoted stock of a company (typically buy, sell, or hold). The recommendation is supported by an investment case, financial forecasts, and a valuation. Reports vary enormously, from short updates of a page or less to substantial documents that analyze whole industries and companies in great detail.

Equity research is also done privately by some buy-side institutional investors and hedge funds, but this is not published externally.

WHO PROVIDES IT AND WHY?

Public equity research is provided by three main types of supplier:

- Integrated investment banks that also offer equity broking and trading services plus a wide range of trading in other financial instruments, capital raising, and advisery services to companies.
- Broker dealers that offer equity broking and trading, but not corporate advisery services.
- Pure research providers.

The largest research departments are those in the global investment banks, which employ several hundred analysts each in a wide range of locations, and cover the majority of the world's liquid stocks. Some cover the less liquid smaller-cap stocks too—though these are often covered by smaller investment banks and broker dealers who specialize in particular sectors (especially technology) or regions (especially emerging or frontier economies). These specialist areas require more local and specific knowledge, which niche providers may be better able to provide.

HOW IS RESEARCH PAID FOR?

Research is normally paid for entirely through commissions charged by equity traders. Research is best thought of as a service rather than a product, and consists of both the written output of analysts and access to the analysts themselves through phone calls, emails, and face to face meetings. The service is provided free at the point of delivery. Reports can be provided at an almost zero marginal cost to a very large number of potential clients. But the analyst's time is far more valuable and is allocated only to those clients who are expected to pay for it.

Payment is made indirectly when the investor puts a buy or a sell trade through the firm for which the analyst works. The investor periodically informs the firm how much of the commission was allocated in compensation for the research service provided (as opposed to the pure cost of executing the trade), and for which analyst in particular. The research manager at the firm can then judge the commercial value of the analyst's service and compensate him or her appropriately.

Pure research providers that do not trade receive a cash payment. Typically this is part of the commission earned by a separate bank or broker dealer, and is paid to the research firm on the instructions of the investor who wishes to use the research. Rarely do investors themselves pay for or commission research on a cash-fee basis.

An analyst's provision of a research service to an investor client is not necessarily or even typically linked to commission received in trading in the stocks on which the analyst provides advice. The process of attributing the commission received during a year or quarter to the actual service provided by an analyst is therefore complicated, and the data are often poor.

Investment banks also have other motives for publishing research:

- *To attract equity capital-raising business.* Analyst coverage of a sector may be essential to win IPO (initial public offering) and other equity capital-raising business from companies in that sector. Good research helps to signal that the bank understands the equity markets in those sectors, and that the analyst would likely offer research on a company after its IPO, although the analyst is free to make the shares a "sell."
- *To advertise other higher-margin advisery services.* Banks seeking to attract companies to use their advisery services, especially in M&A, may see research as a form of advertising; good-quality research may reflect well on the less public capabilities of the firm.
- *To promote the general brand and credibility of the bank.* Global investment banks in particular wish to be seen as credible commentators on all the main financial markets, products, and matters of the day.

CONFLICTS ARISING FROM INVESTMENT BANKING COVERAGE

The fundamental conflict of interest in any investment bank or other firm that offers services both to investors and to corporate clients is that raising capital involves dealing with the buyer *and* the seller. In an IPO, the bank is contracted to advise the owners of a company how best to sell their equity to investors. A high price is good for the owners, but not for the investors. But the investors are also clients of the firm, and the firm's relationship with the investors is the main justification for their being competent to execute the IPO. Banks deal with this conflict in two ways:

- By segregating information flows behind "Chinese walls," which strictly limits access to nonpublic and proprietary information.
- By segregating incentives: Staff dealing with the investor clients are compensated mainly, if not entirely, by their ability to offer a good service to them; the bankers who deal with the corporate clients are evaluated quite separately and according to how they have served them.

A second potential conflict arises in the publication of research by any broker

     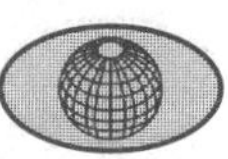   

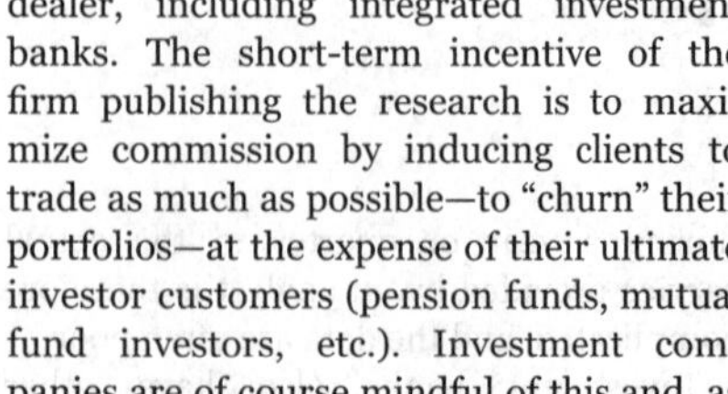

dealer, including integrated investment banks. The short-term incentive of the firm publishing the research is to maximize commission by inducing clients to trade as much as possible—to "churn" their portfolios—at the expense of their ultimate investor customers (pension funds, mutual fund investors, etc.). Investment companies are of course mindful of this and, as professionals in the wholesale market, should be able to look after themselves.

THE GLOBAL SETTLEMENT AND OTHER REGULATORY CHANGES IN 2002–2004

In the late 1990s stock markets reached high levels on the back of a general enthusiasm for technology, media, and telecom (TMT) stocks. Many companies were listed on the stock market as IPOs. This business was very profitable for the sponsoring investment banks. When the stock market fell sharply in 2000–2001, many investors became concerned that the research on these companies had been biased and that analysts had knowingly recommended companies they secretly didn't really value.

In 2001, Eliot Spitzer, District Attorney for the State of New York, started an investigation into allegations that analysts at the investment bank Merrill Lynch misrepresented their views because of the investment banking fees in which they would share. Emails were disclosed that led to a wider investigation of all the leading investment banks.

The bankruptcy of Enron in December 2001 led to the passing of the Sarbanes–Oxley Act on July 30, 2002. Among other provisions, it enabled the Securities and Exchange Commission (SEC) to limit the supervision of and compensation decisions concerning analysts to certain officials, essentially excluding corporate financiers from the process. The Act was followed by rule changes by the National Association of Securities Dealers (NASD) and the New York Stock Exchange, which managed the disclosure of conflicts of interest by research analysts.

In February 2003 the SEC introduced analyst certification, whereby analysts individually attested to the independence of their research and recommendations. There followed in April 2003 the Global Settlement, in which ten large investment banks signed a legal contract to undertake to insulate analyst compensation and evaluation from corporate finance influence, among other measures, and to pay a joint fine of US$1.4 billion. The banks were: Bear Stearns, Credit Suisse First Boston, Deutsche Bank, Goldman Sachs, JPMorgan Chase, Lehman Brothers, Merrill Lynch, Morgan Stanley, Salomon Smith Barney, and UBS Warburg.

The key regulatory changes, including the separation of research analysts from the corporate finance business, were copied in rule changes by stock market regulators around the world. For example, in July 2004 the UK regulator—the Financial Services Authority (FSA)—introduced a rule that required firms producing research to tell their clients whether it met the FSA rules on impartiality. In the same year the European Union introduced the Market Abuse Directive, which required full disclosure of conflicts of interest concerning analysts.

CURRENT PRACTICE AND NEAR TERM PROSPECTS

Research commissioned by the stock market regulators and done by independent academics broadly suggests that the recommendations of analysts are now less likely to be influenced by investment banking considerations. In particular, the distribution of buy and sell recommendations is much less unequal than it was in the late 1990s, when outright sell recommendations were extremely rare on Wall Street. There remain more buys than sells at most banks, but this is likely explained by a combination of analyst optimism and the commercial fact that there are always more opportunities for a buy (anybody can buy) than for sells (only existing holders can sell).

Investment professionals no longer complain about biased or tainted equity research, although they may still doubt the quality or commercial value of much of the research that is produced.

COMPANIES AND EQUITY RESEARCH ANALYSTS

Analysts, no longer facing incentives to be kind about companies with which their corporate finance colleagues do business, are correspondingly able to be more critical of companies. Analysts' opinions influence investors and can raise or lower a company's cost of capital. Companies are well advised to try to keep analysts onside. They are not advised to copy the lawsuit by LVMH (Moët Hennessy Louis Vuitton) against Morgan Stanley in 2002. A French court initially ruled that a Morgan Stanley analyst had allegedly denigrated the company, and fined the bank €30 million. In 2006, the Paris Court of Appeal overturned most of the original findings and canceled the damages.

Any remaining bias in analysts' views results from the desire not to offend a company's management and risk exclusion from corporate events and meetings. But legally companies must disclose material information in a fully public way, so excluding an analyst is either impossible or largely symbolic. Well-established and influential analysts therefore feel emboldened to write candidly about their views of companies and their management, though most are careful to avoid gratuitous offence. Companies can best deal with equity research analysts by being frank, consistent, and helpful.

▸▸ MAKING IT HAPPEN

- Leaders of stock market quoted companies need to take analysts very seriously because they influence investor perceptions of companies.
- Analysts value transparency, clarity, consistency of disclosure, and as much operating information as can be given without compromising a company's commercial position.
- They also value access to senior management—not just the CFO—and appropriate site visits that provide real information about a company's business.
- Long-term credibility with analysts is built by stating and repeatedly referring to key targets and candid accounts of reasons for failing to hit them. That credibility translates into a lower cost of capital and higher stockholder value.

▸▸ MORE INFO

Websites:

Most investment banks and brokerages that provide research restrict access to clients, but are normally happy to include companies in their distribution lists and to provide access to their web portals.

Standard & Poors is a large, independent, nonbank provider of research and has some useful resources on its website. Choose your region and select "Equity Research" from the "Products & Services" dropdown menu: www.standardandpoors.com

A very useful resource on the theory and practice of equity valuation is the home page of Aswath Damodaran of New York University: pages.stern.nyu.edu/~adamodar

Details of the Global Settlement are available at: www.sec.gov/news/speech/factsheet.htm and www.finra.org/Industry/Enforcement/DisciplinaryActions/2003GlobalSettlement

  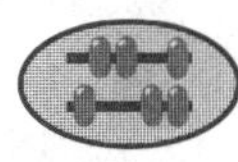   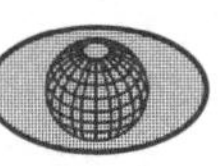   

Corporate Covenant and Other Embedded Options in Pension Funds by Theo Kocken

EXECUTIVE SUMMARY

- The various contingent claims in a pension fund, such as the parent guarantee (corporate covenant) or conditional indexation, can be valued with the same techniques that are used to value options on stocks.
- An application to a real life pension case shows how risk absorption by employers and beneficiaries varies widely, depending on such variables as asset allocation and rating of the sponsor.
- This valuation technique is an indispensable tool for improving pension fund risk management, redesigning pension contracts, and supporting Chief Financial Officers in their decision-making process with regard to mergers or acquisitions.

INTRODUCTION

Pension funds in their defined benefit (DB) form and the alternative structures that have evolved over time are among the most complex risk-sharing institutions ever created, not least because they involve many stakeholders (such as employers, retirees, and employees), all of whom assume different risks.

The employers assume some of the risks by, for example, being obligated to replenish any shortfall in the pension fund. The pensioners and actives assume some of the risk via, for example, partial (instead of full) compensation for inflation.

Unlike with a corporate balance sheet, where it is clear who owns the equity (and hence takes the highest risk and first loss accordingly) and who owns senior debt, there is little agreement on ownership within pension funds. In fact, there is little knowledge about the risks assumed by each stakeholder. Usually, risk is measured for the pension funds as a whole and is typically expressed in terms of the risk of funding shortfall. However, this does not equal the risk that each of the stakeholders may face.

A better quantification of the risks that the various parties assume, which would enable more effective risk management, would prove very valuable. It could be used to negotiate pension contracts and to agree on any entitlements that stakeholders may have to the potential upside (surplus) in the pension fund. As a further illustration, Chief Financial Officers (CFOs) are interested in the specific share of risk that they assume—and the value of those risks—when acquiring a firm with a DB pension fund. With the knowledge provided by the embedded option technique, the CFO could assess what kind of policy measures applied to the pension fund would result in acceptable risks when a target firm—including the firm's obligation to the pension fund—is acquired.

The single most objective way of dealing with multi-stakeholder risk situations that arise in pension funds is the embedded options approach. The risks various stakeholders assume in a pension fund are formulated in terms of options—contingent claims—which stakeholders have written to the pension fund. These options have a certain value that can be determined by employing the same techniques as are applied in the financial markets to price financial options. Since most of the variables relevant to the pension fund have a basis in financial markets (riskless assets such as government bonds, risky assets such as equity and corporate bonds, and interest rate-related liabilities), this is an approach that provides reliable market-consistent values.

Determining the value of these embedded options can be well worth the effort. As will be shown in the analysis below, the contingent claims that stakeholders have in pension funds can easily exceed 20% or 30% of total liabilities in a pension fund. Considering that the estimated value of, for instance, the joint liabilities of UK and Dutch pension funds alone already exceeds 2,000 billion euro, the value of the embedded options is at least hundreds of billions of euros.

IDENTIFYING THE VARIOUS EMBEDDED OPTIONS

To start with, some of the most significant embedded options identified in pension funds are discussed. One of the most important embedded options the employer writes to the pension fund is the so-called parent guarantee, also known as the sponsor covenant. This is the guarantee to support the pension fund in case of funding shortfalls. This option depends on, among other factors, the exact trigger levels at which the parent will pay, as well as (from the perspective of the pension fund) the development of the default probability of the parent company over time.

Two important options that the beneficiaries write to the pension fund are the indexation option and the pension put.

CASE STUDY

The following case is based on a Dutch risk-sharing pension fund with a sponsor that provides the guarantee to the nominal pension obligations, beneficiaries who accept conditional indexation as well as the possibility of a default by the employer (translated into the pension put described above). The contribution rate is fixed to simplify the case.

For expository reasons, the pension fund case applies a simple asset allocation of 50% risk-free government bonds and 50% equity investments. The funding ratio equals 100.[4] The values in the table are expressed as a percentage of the value of the liabilities at $t = 0$. The sponsor's debt is assumed to be BB-rated. Table 1 gives values of embedded options for three different kinds of risk sharing. The second column from the left shows a situation with beneficiaries assuming no risk at all: The sponsor has provided a guarantee and is assumed to be default-free (or a pension protection vehicle such as the PBGC in the United States or the PPF in the United Kingdom exists that in its turn is assumed default-free). In this column, the beneficiaries are entitled to full inflation indexation of their liabilities under all scenarios. They simply bear zero risk. In the third column, the BB rating of the sponsor is taken into account, putting slightly more risk on the beneficiaries' plate through the pension put. In the fourth column, beneficiaries are confronted with the potential default of the employer as well as indexation cuts in situations of low funding ratios.

What does this information tell us? First of all that for this specific situation, the parent guarantee has a value that is close to 30%, in case the possibility of default of the parent is excluded. While this specific result reveals a significant level of risk, it should be noted that it may vary from fund to fund, depending on many factors such as the

"**Investing in stocks is an art, not a science, and people who've been trained to rigidly quantify everything have a big disadvantage.**" Peter Lynch

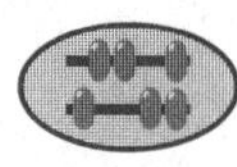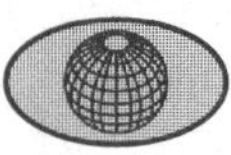

The *indexation option* is the right the pension fund has to waive indexation in case of, say, an insufficient funding level.[1] In case of a very low funding ratio, this implies that the beneficiary's maximum value loss compared to full indexation is roughly the expected inflation multiplied by the duration of his contract.

The *pension put* is the occurrence of a joint "default" event (i.e. a deficit of the pension fund's funding and at the same time a default of the sponsor). Such a joint event will imply writeoffs of the pension entitlements, which is defined as the "payout" of the embedded option. The value of the option depends on, among other things, the (assumptions made with respect to) default probability as a function of time, recovery rates, and correlation between financial markets and the default probability.

Many pension funds have additional embedded options, such as the option to increase contributions (paid by employers and often also partially by the employees) in case of a low funding ratio.[2] And in exceptional cases, such as BAE Systems' pension fund, even longevity options are written by active employees to the pension fund, allowing the fund to reduce pension entitlements in case of an unanticipated rise in longevity. Many other embedded options are implicitly present in pension funds, although the set described above covers the majority of options in DB funds.

The embedded options described above can be explicitly calculated using market-consistent valuation. The values of the embedded options in this article are measured using arbitrage-free option pricing techniques and assuming complete markets. Monte Carlo simulations are used because of the complex nature of the options. It is outside the scope of this essay to discuss these valuation techniques and their underlying assumptions in further detail, since literature is abundant.[3]

APPLICATIONS

How can we use this information to improve risk management and pension design?

The methodology can be applied in many different decision-making situations, among which are:

- evaluating the impact of policy adjustments in a pension fund on the various embedded options and, if necessary, trying to steer with different policy instruments (asset allocation, contribution rate policy, etc.) to make the changes acceptable to all stakeholders;
- actively hedging the complex interest

funding ratio and volatility of the assets. However, it is interesting to see the impact of corporate default risk, and especially explicit risk-sharing such as the possibility of indexation cuts. In the case at hand, the beneficiaries assume almost half of the risks (45%) by accepting conditional indexation and the default risk of the sponsor.

The option values depend on various parameters, such as the composition (and hence the volatility) of the asset mix and the credit rating of the sponsoring company. Table 2 provides some insight on the effect of asset allocation on the embedded option values, with lower equity (higher bonds) and higher equity (lower bonds) allocations.[5] Table 3 provides insight on the effect of variations in credit rating on the option values.

Table 2 reveals that more risk-taking in the pension fund in this case requires that more additional risk be assumed by the employer, by comparison with the beneficiaries, both in absolute and in relative terms. Table 3 explains the importance of credit risk and its effect: If the employer has a low credit rating, the amount of risk beneficiaries are taking is higher in embedded option value terms than the risk assumed by the employer. This picture is completely reversed in the case of a supporting employer with a high credit rating.

Many other variables determine the value of these options, a key one being the actual funding ratio. Table 4 compares the various option values at different funding ratios.

It is clear from Table 4 that at very low funding levels, far below fully funded status, the risk assumed by the corporate is relatively high by comparison with the beneficiaries' risk absorption. This is due to the fact that the indexation option cannot increase that much with lower funding levels (you can only lose your indexation, irrespective of the shortfall level), where the corporate sponsor has to complete the entire shortfall.

Table 1. Values of the embedded options for different kinds of risk sharing (% liability value)

Type of pension fund	*Full indexation + default-free sponsor*	*Full indexation + "default-risk" sponsor*	*Conditional indexation + "default-risk" sponsor*
Parent guarantee (sponsor covenant)	29.7%	28.6%	17.8%
Pension put	-	4.8%	3.1%
Indexation option	-	-	11.3%
Sponsor share (as percentage of total risk)	100%	86%	55%

Table 2. Option values (% of liability value) as a function of asset mix composition

Type of option	*Equity % in total assets*		
	30%	*50%*	*70%*
Parent guarantee	15.2	17.8	22.7
Pension put	2.5	3.1	3.8
Indexation option	12.3	11.3	10.4
Sponsor share (as percentage of total risk)	51%	55%	61%

Table 3. Option values (% liability value) as a function of employer's credit rating

Type of option	*Employer's credit rating*		
	CCC	BB	A
Parent guarantee	8.7	17.8	21.3
Pension put	10.0	3.1	0.3
Indexation option	12.1	11.3	11.0
Sponsor share (as percentage of total risk)	28%	55%	65%

Table 4. Option values (% liability value) as a function of actual funding ratio

Type of option	*Current (nominal) funding ratio*		
	80%	*100%*	120%
Parent guarantee	34.0	17.8	9.1
Pension put	3.4	3.1	2.6
Indexation option	13.4	11.3	6.4
Sponsor share (as percentage of total risk)	67%	55%	50%

"Ah, were I courageous enough. To shout *Stuff your pension!* But I know, all too well, that's the stuff. That dreams are made on." Philip Larkin

     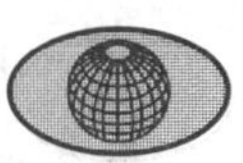   

rate and inflation risks that arise from conditional or capped indexation;

- determining the economic value employers should pay into a pension fund when they want to retreat as risk takers in the pension fund and transfer the risks to the beneficiaries;
- determining the entitlements of the different stakeholders to a potential future surplus in the pension fund, in proportion to the risks they assumed;
- determining the claim a pension fund has on a corporate when considering a merger.

MAKING IT HAPPEN

Implementing the embedded option approach requires various adjustments in the asset and liability management (ALM) models applied by the pension fund. The main steps are:

- The ALM model used should be able to cope with risk-neutral scenarios. Though this may be quite a tedious exercise, a first rough indication can be obtained by setting the risk premia in the system to zero.
- The various option payoffs need to be recognized in the ALM model. Usually this can be achieved via simple adjustments, since all the relevant variables (funding ratio, level of indexation) are available in the model.
- The present value of the risk-neutral payoffs in the previous steps represents the embedded option value.

The reading suggestions below provide some support in executing these steps.

MORE INFO

Books:

Bodie, Zvi. "Pension guarantees, capital adequacy and international risk sharing." In *Frontiers in Pension Finance*. D. Broeders, S. Eijffinger, and A. Houben (eds). Cheltenham, UK: Edward Elgar, 2008.

Kortleve, N., T. Nijman, and E. Ponds. *Fair Value and Pension Fund Management*. Oxford: Elsevier, 2006.

Articles:

Hoevenaars, R. P. M. M. "Strategic asset allocation and asset liability management." PhD thesis, Maastricht University, 2008. Online at: arno.unimaas.nl/show.cgi?fid=9679

Kocken, T. "Curious contracts. Pension fund redesign for the future." PhD thesis, Free University of Amsterdam, 2006.

Website:

Though not much literature is available online, the Social Science Research Network (SSRN) sometimes provides good help on this topic. Visit www.ssrn.com and search for "embedded options." Most applications are related to guarantees in life insurance contracts, bonds, etc., but it may prove useful given the similarities with pension funds' embedded options.

See Also:

Fischer Black (p. 1155)
Myron Scholes (p. 1190)

NOTES

1 Different kinds of embedded options exist related to indexation. The example given here relates to indexation conditional on the level of the funding ratio, as applied in the Netherlands. In the United Kingdom, indexation cuts are linked to the inflation level itself (indexation is capped at a certain level, for example 2.5% or 5%), though introducing "Dutch-type" conditional indexation is high on the United Kingdom's political pension agenda as well.

2 And often also the option to reduce contribution rates in case of a high funding ratio.

3 For the assumptions underlying the case in the text, see Kocken, 2006.

4 Discounted against the nominal swap curve.

5 The credit rating of the sponsor in Table 2 is BB; the funding ratio is again 100%.

"Any time you take a chance you better be sure the rewards are worth the risk because they can put you away just as fast for a ten dollar heist as they can for a million dollar job." Stanley Kubrick

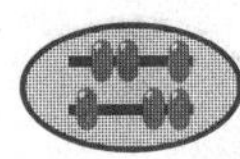
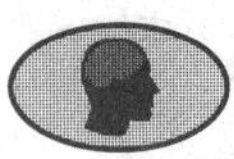

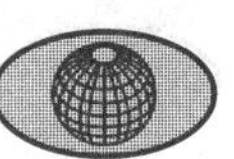

Ethical Funds and Socially Responsible Investment: An Overview by Chendi Zhang

EXECUTIVE SUMMARY

- Ethical funds, also known as socially responsible investment (SRI) funds, have experienced rapid growth around the world. Issues such as global warming, corporate governance, and community involvement have gained significant attention from governments and investors.
- Maximization of stockholder value often conflicts with the interests of other stakeholders in a firm. Corporate social responsibility (CSR) plays a role in reducing the costs of such conflicts.
- Empirical research shows that the following components of CSR are associated with higher stockholder value: good corporate governance, sound environmental standards, and care of stakeholder relations.
- Existing studies hint, but do not unequivocally demonstrate, that SRI investors are willing to accept suboptimal financial performance to pursue social or ethical objectives.
- Given the growing social awareness of investors and the increasingly positive regulatory environment, we expect SRI to continue its growth and relative importance as an asset class.

THE RISE OF SRI

Ethical funds, often also called socially responsible investment (SRI) funds, integrate environmental, social, and governance (ESG) considerations, or purely ethical issues, into investment decision-making. SRI has experienced a phenomenal growth around the world. According to the Social Investment Forum, the professionally managed assets of SRI portfolios in the United States, including retail and, more importantly, institutional funds (for example, pension funds, insurance funds, and separate accounts), reached $2.7 trillion in 2007, or approximately 11% of total assets under management in that country. The European SRI market is also growing rapidly. In 2007, SRI assets in Europe amounted to €2.7 trillion, representing 17% of European funds under management (European Social Investment Forum).

Although ethical investing has ancient origins that were based on religious traditions, modern SRI is based more on the varying personal, ethical, and social convictions of individual investors. Issues such as environmental protection, human rights, and labor relations have become common in the SRI investment screening process. In recent years, a series of corporate scandals has turned corporate governance and responsibility into another focal point of SRI investors. Hence, criteria such as transparency, governance, and sustainability have emerged as essential in SRI screening.

Over the past decade, a number of national governments in Europe have passed a series of regulations on social and environmental investments and savings. For instance, the United Kingdom was the first country to regulate the disclosure of the social, environmental, and ethical investment policies of pension funds and charities. The Amendment to the 1995 Pensions Act requires the trustees of occupational pension funds to disclose in the Statement of Investment Principles "the extent (if at all) to which social, environmental and ethical considerations are taken into account in the selection, retention and realization of investments." This has contributed considerably to the growth of the SRI industry.

SHOULD COMPANIES BE SOCIALLY RESPONSIBLE?

Finance textbooks tell us companies should maximize the value of their stockholders' equity. In other words, a company's only responsibility is a financial one. In recent years, corporate social responsibility has become a focal point of policymakers (and the public), who demand that corporations assume responsibility toward society, the environment, or stakeholders in general. SRI investors thus aim to promote socially and environmentally sound corporate behavior. They avoid companies that produce goods which may cause health hazards or exploit employees (negative screening), whether in developed or developing countries. They select companies with sound social and environmental records, and with good corporate governance (positive screening). In general, SRI investors expect companies to focus on social welfare in addition to maximizing value.

At the heart of the SRI movement is a fundamental question: Is a firm's aim to maximize *stockholder* value or *social* value (where social value is defined as the sum of the values generated for all stakeholders)? Classical economics (for example, Adam Smith's "invisible hand" and the social welfare theorems) states that there is no conflict between the two goals: In competitive and complete markets, when all firms maximize their own profits (value), resource allocation is optimal and social welfare is maximized. However, modern economic theory also tells us that in some circumstances, namely when some of the assumptions of the welfare theorems do not hold, profit-maximizing behavior does not necessarily imply social welfare-maximizing outcomes. One of such circumstances is the existence of externalities that arise when the costs and benefits of an agent's action are affected by the actions of other (external) agents in the economy. Jensen (2001) gives a simple example of externalities, where a fishery's catch is impaired by the pollution of an upstream chemical plant.[1] When the chemical plant maximizes its profit by increasing pollution (as the costs of pollution are not borne by the chemical plant), the fishery downstream suffers through catching fewer fish and social welfare—which in this case is equal to the sum of the profits of the two stakeholders—is not maximized.

In practice, the maximization of stockholder value often conflicts with the social welfare criterion represented by the interests of all stakeholders of a firm, including employees, customers, local communities, the environment, and so forth. By maximizing stockholder value, firms may not take care of the interests of other stakeholders. Economic solutions to the externality problem are based on the principle of internalizing externalities, for example, by imposing regulations (such as quotas, or taxes on pollution) and creating a market for externalities (such as the trading of pollution permits). Furthermore, in continental European corporate governance regimes, a stakeholder approach is more common than in Anglo-Saxon countries.

"The social responsibility of business is to increase its profits." Milton Friedman

  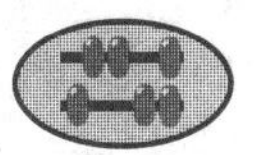   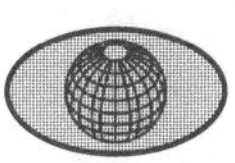   

STOCKHOLDER VALUE VERSUS STAKEHOLDER VALUE

One of the main arguments in favor of CSR and the stakeholder model is that it is consistent with stockholder value maximization. For instance, by anticipating and minimizing the potential conflicts between corporations and society, CSR plays a role in reducing the cost of conflicts. CSR may soften competition in product markets and lead to higher firm value, signal a firm's product quality and improve reputation, and help to attract motivated employees.

Critics of stakeholder value maximization argue that CSR, and the stakeholder theory, have problems in terms of accountability and managerial incentivization. According to the stockholder value concept, managers are expected to invest in a project if its expected return exceeds the cost of capital. In the stakeholder value story, managers are asked to balance the interests of all stakeholders to the point that aggregate welfare is maximized. Still, the stakeholder theory does not define how to aggregate welfare and how to make the trade-off between stakeholders. If the social value of firms can be maximized, society will by definition benefit. However, the question is whether this goal is achievable and how economic efficiency and managerial incentives are affected by the maximization of stakeholder value (including social and environmental value).

Furthermore, CSR and the stakeholder model are also subject to Friedman's (1962)[2] arguments: Companies should only care about profits and, therefore, their stockholders, while governments deal with the provision of public goods and the existence of externalities. If CSR lowers firms' profits due to compromises with stakeholders, firms should not implement CSR strategies as it is more efficient if they charge lower prices and allow consumers to make their own charitable contributions based on personal social and ethical values. This critique also has important implications for SRI: If SRI underperforms conventional portfolios, it would be more efficient for SRI investors to invest in better-performing conventional funds and use part of the returns to comply with their personal convictions by donating money to good causes.

PORTFOLIO CONSTRAINTS AND MARKET (IN)EFFICIENCIES

SRI applies various screening processes to retain stocks complying with specific CSR criteria on social, corporate governance, environmental, and ethical issues, which imposes a constraint on the investment universe available to non-SRI investors. SRI screens may therefore limit the diversification possibilities, and consequently shift the mean–variance frontier toward less favorable risk–return trade-offs than those of conventional portfolios. In addition, believers in the efficient market hypothesis argue that it is impossible for SRI funds to outperform their conventional peers. Screening portfolios based on public information such as CSR issues cannot generate abnormal returns.

However, it is also possible that SRI screening processes generate value-relevant information which is otherwise not available to investors. This may help fund managers to select securities and consequently generate better risk-adjusted returns than conventional mutual funds. In this case, investors may do (financially) well while doing (social) good, i.e. investors earn positive risk-adjusted returns while at the same time contributing to a good cause. For instance, empirical research on CSR shows that portfolios constructed with reference to corporate governance, environmental, and social criteria may outperform their benchmarks.

A key assumption underlying the above hypothesis is that the stock markets misprice information on CSR in the short run. For instance, they may undervalue the costs of litigation that may have to be met by

CASE STUDY

Calvert Social Investment Fund

Calvert is one of the largest families of SRI mutual funds in the United States. Social investment research analysts at Calvert examine corporate performance in the following broad areas, in addition to financial criteria:

- *Governance and ethics*: Including disclosure of policies and procedures, board independence and diversity, executive compensation, and attention to stakeholder concerns.
- *Workplace*: Including labor diversity, labor relations, and employee health and safety. Calvert monitors the quality of policies and programs, compliance with national laws and regulations, and proactive management initiatives.
- *Environment*: Focusing on corporate environmental performance, responsiveness to incidents, and compliance with environmental regulations.
- *Product safety and impact*: Selecting companies that produce safe products and services, in accordance with federal consumer product safety guidelines.
- *International operations and human rights*: Avoiding investment in companies that have a record of serious and persistent human rights problems or that directly support governments that systematically deny human rights.
- *Indigenous peoples' rights*: Avoiding companies that have a pattern and practice of violating the rights of indigenous peoples around the world.
- *Community relations*: Investing in companies that have built solid relationships with the local communities in which they operate.

▸▸ MAKING IT HAPPEN

In order for CSR/SRI to become a workable concept, the following key issues of performance yardsticks should be considered:

- Do you adopt the stockholder value maximization criterion or the stakeholder value maximization criterion? Even if you opt for the stockholder value criterion, it is important to consider the welfare of all stakeholders (employees, community, environment, etc.) as firm behavior induces important externalities. The long-run market value of a firm cannot be maximized if any important stakeholders are mistreated.
- Is corporate social/environmental performance measurable? A lack of precisely formulated corporate goals and measures in respect of CSR/SRI may destroy firm value in the long run. The long-run value of a firm remains the single most important performance measure for management. Maximizing long-run firm value is consistent with maximizing social welfare.
- Are you seeking a competitive advantage for your company by implementing CSR/SRI strategies? Empirical research shows that the following components of CSR are associated with higher stockholder value: good corporate governance, sound environmental standards, and care of stakeholder relations.
- Are investors willing to pay a price for CSR/SRI? If SRI underperforms conventional funds, it could be more efficient for SRI investors to invest in better-performing conventional funds and use part of the returns to comply with their personal convictions by donating money to good causes.

"An inconvenient truth: global warming." Al Gore

   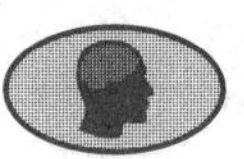  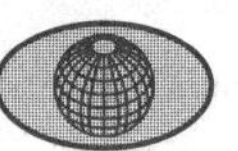   

socially irresponsible corporations, while socially responsible firms may be better protected against such costs. As a result, SRI may outperform conventional funds in the long run. This outperformance hypothesis is also at odds with the efficient market hypothesis. If SRI screening processes do generate value-relevant information, conventional portfolio managers could easily replicate the screens, and the performance edge of SRI over conventional investments should then diminish.

The question as to whether SRI creates stockholder value is ultimately an empirical one. Empirical findings on the performance of SRI are mixed. Although there is little evidence that the average performance of SRI funds in the United States and the United Kingdom is different from that of conventional funds, SRI funds in many continental European and Asia-Pacific countries underperform their benchmarks.[3] Existing studies hint, but do not unequivocally support, that investors are willing to accept suboptimal financial performance if their personal values on social responsibility are satisfied.

CONCLUSION

SRI has experienced rapid growth around the world, reflecting investors' increasing awareness of social, environmental, and governance issues. In recent years issues such as global warming, the Kyoto Protocol, corporate governance, and community investing have gained significant attention from governments and investors around the world. In addition, governments in Western countries have taken many regulatory initiatives to stimulate SRI. Given the growing social awareness of investors and the increasingly positive regulatory environment, we expect SRI to continue its growth and relative importance as an asset class.

▸▸ MORE INFO

Book:

UNEP Finance Initiative. *Values to Value: A Global Dialogue on Sustainable Finance*. United Nations Environment Programme, 2004.

Article:

Renneboog, Luc, Jenke Ter Horst, and Chendi Zhang. "Socially responsible investments: Institutional aspects, performance, and investor behavior." *Journal of Banking and Finance* 32:9 (2008): 1723–1742.

Websites:

Association for Sustainable and Responsible Investment in Asia: www.asria.org
European Social Investment Forum (Eurosif): www.eurosif.org
Social Investment Forum: www.socialinvest.org

NOTES

1 Jensen, Michael C. "Value maximization, stakeholder theory, and the corporate objective function." *Journal of Applied Corporate Finance* 14:3 (2001): 8–21.

2 Friedman, Milton. *Capitalism and Freedom*. 40th anniversary edition. Chicago, IL: University of Chicago Press, 2002.

3 Renneboog, Luc, Jenke Ter Horst, and Chendi Zhang. "The price of ethics and stakeholder governance: The performance of socially responsible mutual funds." *Journal of Corporate Finance* 14:3 (2008): 302–322.

"Social business will be a new kind of business introduced in the market place with the objective of making a difference in the world." Muhammad Yunus

  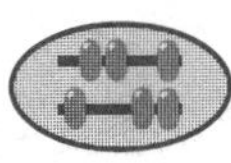   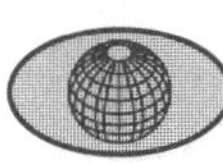   

Forecasting Default Rates and the Credit Cycle by Martin Fridson

EXECUTIVE SUMMARY

- The benefit to corporate bond investors of staying a step ahead of the credit cycle has stimulated interest in models for forecasting one of the cycle's best markers, the default rate.
- A market-based forecasting model can complement actuarial and econometric models, which have inherent limitations.
- This article describes a market-based default-rate forecasting model, based on the distribution of outstanding high-yield bonds between the distressed and non-distressed categories, and the respective, historical default rates of those categories.
- The actual default rate tracks the market-based model's year-ahead forecast fairly closely, although the forecast can overshoot under extreme market conditions.

THE NATURE AND IMPORTANCE OF THE CREDIT CYCLE

Cycles play a major role in analysis aimed at achieving superior investment returns. Stock market participants base their valuations on corporate earnings, which fluctuate with the business cycle. The interest rate cycle strongly influences the performance of high-quality fixed-income assets, such as government bonds and mortgage-backed securities. Similarly, investors in corporate bonds, for which the risk of default is a material factor, can benefit from anticipating turns in the credit cycle.

At the beginning of the credit cycle, lenders perceive the risk of default to be low. They gladly extend loans even to low-quality borrowers, and accept small risk premiums (measured by yield differentials over risk-free rates). Inevitably, some borrowers incur more debt than they are able to support when the business cycle turns down. They consequently default on their obligations, which causes lenders to turn more conservative in their credit extension policies. As it becomes more difficult to borrow, other borrowers fail as a result of being unable to refinance their maturing debts. Finally, as the default wave subsides, lenders regain confidence and a new cycle begins.

The link between the comparative liberality of credit extension risk and premiums on debt is illustrated in Figure 1. In a quarterly survey conducted by the Federal Reserve, senior loans officers of major money center banks indicate whether they are currently raising or lowering the quality standards that corporate borrowers must satisfy to obtain loans. As banks make it harder to qualify for loans, the average risk premium rises in the investment grade corporate bond market.

Risk premiums, in turn, are closely connected with default rates. Figure 2 documents this linkage over the past two US credit cycles. The trailing 12-months default rate on speculative grade issuers reached cyclical highs in June 1991 and January 2002. Roughly coinciding with these peaks were the cyclical maximum points of the option-adjusted spread on the Merrill Lynch High Yield Master II Index, in January 1991 and June 2002.

APPROACHES TO FORECASTING THE DEFAULT RATE

One outgrowth of investors' interest in understanding the credit cycle is an effort to develop a model for forecasting one of its best markers, the default rate.[1] Credit market analysts have worked extensively on this problem since the early 1990s (see More Info for key articles). Three types of

Figure 1. Bank lending standards and risk premium, Q2 1990–Q3 2008, quarterly. (*Sources*: Merrill Lynch & Co., US Federal Reserve)

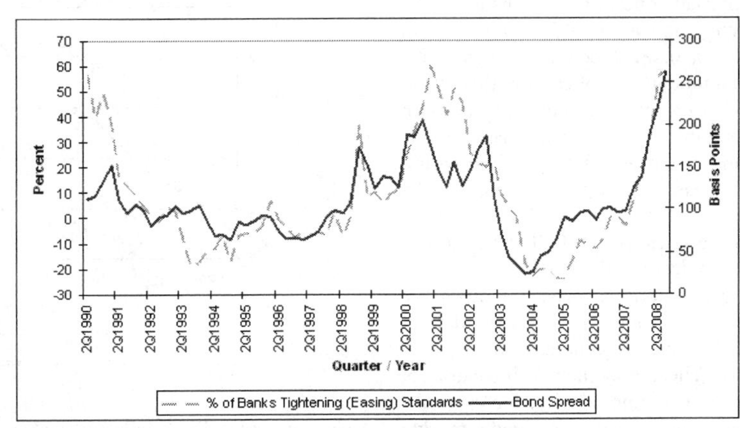

Figure 2. Default rate and risk premium, default rate (global speculative-grade, by issuer) and high yield spread-versus-treasuries, Q1 1989–Q3 2008, quarterly. (*Sources*: Merrill Lynch & Co., Moody's Investors Service)

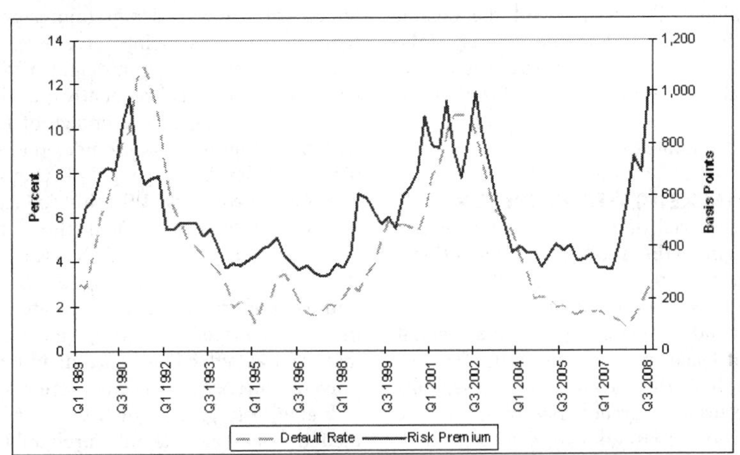

"Eventually, either financing costs rise or income comes in below expectations, leading to defaults on payment commitments." Hyman Minsky

default rate forecasting models have emerged from the research—actuarial, econometric, and market-based.[1]

The actuarial approach derives from empirical data documenting the relationship between bond ratings and the historical incidence of default over stated periods. For example, based on statistics compiled for the period 1983–2007, Moody's Investors Service reports that on average, issuers rated Aa had a 0.009% probability of defaulting within one year and a 0.183% cumulative probability of defaulting within five years. The corresponding figures for issuers rated Caa are 15.371% and 45.803%. Actuarial models apply the rating-specific default rates to the distribution of speculative grade issuers within the rating categories (Ba, B, Caa, and Ca-C), to generate forecasts of the default rate for the speculative grade category as a whole.

A fundamental limitation of the actuarial method is that rating-specific default rates vary substantially from year to year, as a function of variation in economic and credit market conditions. For instance, the B category had a 1.983% default rate in 1997 and a 9.340% default rate in 2001. Actuarial models do not capture this effect, although they typically take into account another period-related variance, namely that an issue's probability of default within a given year is partly a function of the number of years elapsed since issuance. (The curve rises for the first three to four years, then declines thereafter.)

The econometric approach models the speculative grade category's default probability as a function of several variables. These may include indicators of aggregate economic activity, for example, interest rates, measures of credit market conditions, and the variables employed in actuarial models. Generally, the economic indicators employed in such models are forecast, rather than historical, variables. Accordingly, the accuracy of the default rate forecast depends on the accuracy of the forecasts of such items as gross domestic product (GDP) and factory utilization. To put it mildly, errors are not uncommon in macroeconomic forecasting.

Table 1. One-year default rate forecast, October 16, 2009. (*Source*: Merrill Lynch & Co.)

*** Discrepancies in the default rate forecast due to rounding**

		Distribution of High Yield Universe (%)		Annual Default Rate (%)		Weighted Average (%)*
Distressed		63.91	x	23.53	=	15.04
Non-Distressed	+	36.09	x	1.23	=	0.44
Error Correction Term	+			1.12	=	1.12
Default Rate Forecast					=	16.60

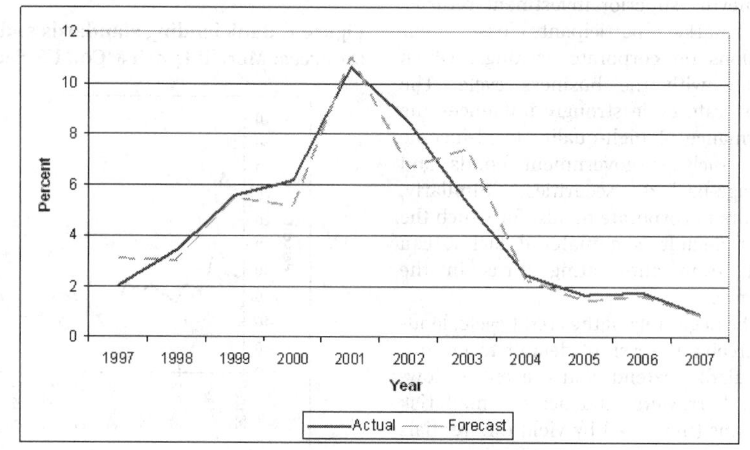

Figure 3. Default rate predictor, actual versus forecast, annually, 1997–2007. (*Sources*: Merrill Lynch & Co., Moody's Investors Service)

THE MARKET-BASED PREDICTOR

Both actuarial and econometric forecasts shed light on the credit cycle, but additional insight into the future default rate can be obtained from the debt market. Day by day, bond investors gauge the default risk of each outstanding issue. To the extent that their consensus assessments are accurate, a cyclical rise or fall in the proportion of issuers judged to be at high risk of default will be followed by a corresponding rise or fall in the actual incidence of default.

The author of this study introduced a now widely used definition of distressed bonds as those with risk premiums greater than 1,000 basis points (10 percentage points) above the rate on default risk-free US Treasuries. He subsequently introduced the distress ratio, or percentage of issues within the high-yield bond index quoted at distressed levels, a gauge of prevailing corporate credit risk. With his colleagues, the author later calculated the average one-year default rate on distressed bonds (Fridson, Covey, and Sterling, 2008). This finding confirmed that, separate from the judgments of the rating agencies, the market was effective in subdividing the universe of speculative grade credits into a higher-risk group (distressed, with a median one-year default probability of 23.53%), and a lower-risk group (non-distressed, with a median one-year default probability of 1.23%). These tools can be combined to create a one-year default rate forecasting model.

As in the actuarial approach, the year-ahead forecast is a function of expected default rates for specified categories, and the universe's breakdown among those categories. The difference is that, unlike rating categories, which are deliberately not fully adjusted to reflect cyclical variation in economic and financial market conditions, market assessments shift in response to short-term changes in issuer-specific default risk. Consequently, the default probability of an individual bond deemed distressed by the market is fairly high in any given year, regardless of the economy-wide level of default risk. As for how it differs from the econometric approach, the market-based predictor's accuracy does

"Under the right circumstances, groups are remarkably intelligent, and are often smarter than the smartest people in them." James Surowiecki

     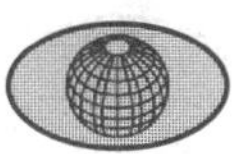   

not depend on accurate predictions of difficult-to-forecast underlying economic variables.

DETAILS OF THE MODEL

To generate a year-ahead forecast of the trailing 12-months default rate, we calculate a weighted average of the distressed and nondistressed default rates, as shown in Table 1. In addition, a positive or negative adjustment factor is required, based on whether the default rate series is in the rising or declining phase of the cycle. This factor is the average amount by which the simple weighted average underestimates the default rate on the way up (1.12 percentage points), and overestimates it (0.74 percentage points) on the way down. These systematic, but correctable, errors arise from the fact that as the distress ratio rises from the preceding month, the number of expected defaults also rises. Some of the incremental expected defaults will probably occur within the 12-month forecast period of the previous month's forecast. This dynamic reverses itself in the default rate cycle's downleg.

Figure 3 confirms that the market is astute in estimating default rates one year in advance. The actual default rate series tracks the year-earlier forecast fairly closely. Comparatively large divergences partly reflect spikes and dips in the series arising from the required switchovers from positive to negative (or vice versa) adjustment factors. In absolute terms, the mean monthly error is 0.37%. From a practitioner's standpoint, this degree of accuracy makes the market-based default rate predictor a useful tool for analyzing the credit cycle.

A caveat is that, under extreme conditions, the predictor may overstate the prospective default rate. Retrofitting the analysis to November 1990, we find that the prevailing distress ratio indicated that the default rate would escalate to 16%. As it turned out, the rate rose no higher than 13% in the succeeding 12 months. The probable explanation was forced selling by high-yield mutual bond funds as a consequence of large and persistent redemptions by fund shareholders. These liquidations evidently pushed prices down to distressed levels on a number of issues that did not truly have a one-year default probability in the neighborhood of 23.53%.

CONCLUSION

The default rate predictor is useful to investors in projecting future returns, which are influenced by fluctuations in default rates and risk premiums. Market timers can exploit it as well, because peaks and troughs in the default rate can represent major turning points in performance of the high-yield asset class. Finally, the default rate predictor can be used as a valuation tool. When the predictor indicates a default rate higher than the rates forecast by econometric models, a possible inference is that some issues are undeservedly priced at distressed levels. That may signal an opportunity to scoop up bargains, in the form of bonds with greater risk premiums than their risk truly warrants.

▸▸ MAKING IT HAPPEN

- The market-based model helpfully corroborated early 2009 econometric forecasts of a rise in the default rate to a level not observed since the Great Depression, a conclusion that many market participants found difficult to accept.
- During the financial crisis that began in 2008, comparing the market-based and econometric models became a way to determine when risk premiums were overstated, making speculative-grade corporate bonds attractive on a risk–reward basis.
- The practical benefits of the market-based default rate forecasting model have parallels elsewhere in the investment world, for example, election markets, and bookmakers' odds on events expected to affect security prices.

▸▸ MORE INFO

Books:

Fridson, Martin, M. Christopher Garman, and Sheng Wu. "Real interest rates and the default rates on high yield bonds." In Theodore M. Barnhill, Jr, William Fr. Maxwell, and Mark R. Shenkman (eds). *High Yield Bonds: Market Structure, Portfolio Management, and Credit Risk Modeling*. New York: McGraw Hill, 1999: 164–174.

Moyer, Stephen G. *Distressed Debt Analysis: Strategies for Speculative Investors*. Boca Raton: J. Ross Publishing, 2005.

Articles:

Fons, Jerome S. "An approach to forecasting default rates." *Moody's Special Report* (August 1991).

Fridson, Martin, Kevin P. Covey, and Karen Sterling. "Performance of distressed bonds." *Journal of Portfolio Management* 34:3 (Spring 2008): 56–62.

Helwege, Jean, and Paul Kleiman. "Understanding aggregate default rates of high yield bonds." *Journal of Fixed Income* 7:1 (June 1997): 55–61. (Also published in *Current Issues in Economics and Finance* (May 1996): 1–6.)

Jónsson, Jón G., and Martin S. Fridson. "Forecasting default rates on high yield bonds." *Journal of Fixed Income* 6:2 (June 1996): 69–77.

Keegan, Sean C., Jorge Sobehart, and David T. Hamilton. "Predicting default rates: A forecasting model for Moody's issuer-based default rates." *Moody's Special Comment* (August 1999).

Metz, Albert, and Richard Cantor. "A cyclical model of multiple horizon credit ratings transactions and default." *Moody's Investors Service* (August 2007).

NOTES

1 Forecasting the aggregate default rate is distinct from estimating individual default probabilities for individual bond issuers, a problem that has generated an extensive literature in its own right.

"Look at market fluctuations as your friend rather than your enemy; profit from folly rather than participate in it." Warren Buffett

  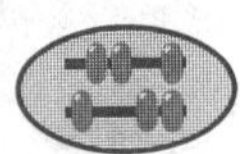   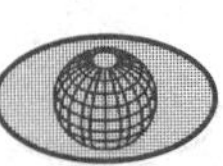   

Viewpoint: Javier Estrada

Investing in a Volatile Environment: A Black Swan Perspective

INTRODUCTION

Javier Estrada, who is Professor of Financial Management at Barcelona-based IESE Business School, was a tennis coach in his native Argentina before moving to live and work in Spain in 1993. He set the cat among the pigeons in global investment circles with his ground-breaking research, "Black swans and market timing: How not to generate alpha," which conclusively revealed that investors who seek to time the market are unlikely to reap rewards. His research focuses on risk, portfolio management, investment strategies, emerging markets, and insider trading. The founding editor of *Emerging Markets Review*, he holds visiting professorships in Scandinavia and Latin America. As wealth management adviser at Sports Global Consulting, Estrada advises professional sports-players on their investments. His favorite football team is Club Atletico River Plate. A fan of hard-rock bands, including Queen, Kansas, and Led Zeppelin, he plays electric guitar in his spare time. His first degree, a BA in economics, was from the National University of La Plata in Buenos Aires, and he also holds MSc and PhD degrees from the University of Illinois at Urbana–Champaign.

We all know that eating properly is essential for our health. Most of us are aware that certain types of food are good for us while others are best avoided. We are also aware of the trade-off between the desirable long-term goal of being fit and healthy and the pain associated with denying ourselves foods that we really like. We also know that patience and discipline are required.

What does healthy eating have to do with investing, you may well ask? Arguably, there are plenty of similarities. Anyone who has gone into a bookstore in search of a book on healthy eating will have been confronted by rows and rows of books, each outlining a different miracle diet.

Anyone looking for a book on investing has a similar experience. Shelf after shelf bulges with with books outlining "high-return, low-risk" strategies. Each gives the impression that all we need do is to follow the indicated path to instant riches. If only life were as easy! If it was, I would not be writing these lines and you would not be reading them—we would probably both be enjoying the Caribbean sun.

A BALANCED DIET

Most of us recognize that eating healthily is going to require a long-term commitment and the making of certain sacrifices (we must kiss goodbye to all those tasty 600-calorie blueberry muffins), and that there is no such thing as a painless shortcut. The same applies to investing.

In reality, the only way to generate high long-term investment returns is to endure some risks in the short term, with the associated pain that comes from sleepless nights as our portfolio value bounces about. There is no such thing as a "high-return, low-risk" strategy. Sadly, the same "no pain, no gain" rule applies both to eating and to investing.

And yet, when it comes to investing, many investors are seduced by "get rich quick" schemes. They often get blinded by the lights of easy money and delude themselves into thinking that gain can be achieved without pain.

For the purpose of this article, I would like to group the investment strategies people are offered into two types: in one group are the "exciting" active investment strategies, which usually promise high returns but claim to achieve them with little or no risk; in the second group are the more boring and conservative passive strategies, which usually promise no gain without pain.

The two approaches can be evaluated from several standpoints, not all of which lead us to the same conclusions. I will evaluate them here through the prism of my own recent research into the so-called "black swans" in financial markets.

BLACK SWANS

A black swan is an event that has three main attributes: First, it is an outlier, lying outside the realm of regular expectations because nothing in the past can convincingly point to its occurrence; second, it carries an extreme impact; and third, despite being an outlier, plausible explanations for its occurrence can be found after the fact, thus giving it the appearance of being both explainable and predictable. In summary, a black swan has three characteristics: rarity, extreme impact, and retrospective predictability.

The black swan perspective of investing is based on three main ideas. The first is that an extremely small number of trading days have a disproportionate impact on long-term investment performance—this is an empirical fact. The second is that, although being invested on the good days and not invested on the bad days would yield extraordinary returns, investors are extremely unlikely to get the timing right. And third, because attempts to time the market are doomed to fail in the long term (in fact, their main consequence is likely to be higher transaction costs), investors are better off holding a properly diversified investment portfolio for the long term.

A PATH TO POVERTY?

Curiously, this is exactly the same recommendation that is put forward by advocates of the efficient market theory of investment. However, the black swan perspective assumes neither market efficiency nor normally distributed returns. Instead, it argues that return distributions have very fat tails and are therefore far from being normal. It also argues that mistakenly assuming that returns are normally distributed can lead to a massive destruction of wealth, as it leads investors to underestimate risk substantially.

Let's first examine the facts. My own research (Estrada, 2008) reveals that a tiny

"Forecasting returns is a mix of art and science, with a fair share of sorcery. In fact, the smaller the number of assets in the portfolio, and the shorter the period for which forecasts are made, the bigger the role played by this last factor." Javier Estrada

     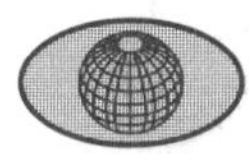   

number of days can have an exceptional impact on long-term portfolio performance.

Across 15 developed markets, being out of the market on the ten days when the biggest stock market rallies occurred would have resulted in portfolios being 51% less valuable than if the money had been passively invested. Not being invested in these markets during their ten worst days would have resulted in portfolios being 150% more valuable than a passive investment would have been.

Given that these ten days represent less than 0.1% of the days in the average developed market I considered, the conclusion is obvious: A negligible proportion of days determines a massive creation or destruction of wealth, and the odds of successfully and consistently predicting the right days to be in and out of the market are nil.

In emerging markets, a tiny number of days have an even bigger impact on portfolio performance. My own research (Estradra, 2009) reveals that across 16 emerging markets, missing the ten best days would have resulted in portfolios being 69% less valuable than if the money had been passively invested. Not being invested on the ten worst ten days would have resulted in portfolios being 337% more valuable than a passive investment would have been. Given that ten days represent 0.15% of the days in the average emerging market I considered, the conclusion is again stark: The probability of successfully and consistently getting the timing right is negligible.

At times of high stock market volatility, like those we experienced during 2008, investors are often tempted to try and take advantage of large daily swings. In such turbulent times many investors attempt to capture outsized returns by frequently jumping in and out of the market, or from one market to another. But investors who engage in this sort of active trading, particularly in a volatile environment, are largely relying on luck rather than on a sound financial strategy.

Investors should bear in mind that the odds are heavily stacked against them; they should also remember that, while the additional transaction costs of their active trading strategy are certain, outsized returns are, at best, a hope.

I run a program on portfolio management for individuals (as opposed to institutions) that aims to give unsophisticated investors some basic tools with which to manage their savings. In this program I tell participants about the two "sad truths" of financial markets. I call them sad truths because these are two statements that most investors would prefer were false. Unfortunately, however, both are true.

PATIENCE IS A VIRTUE

The first statement is that the higher the required return, the greater must be the exposure to risk. The second is that the higher the exposure to risk, the longer must be the investment horizon. Deep inside, participants know that these statements are true, but a part of each of them would prefer to go on believing in painless shortcuts.

In the program, I also tell participants that they should stop focusing on forecasting. I give them many reasons why they should forget about trying to second-guess the market, which stock to buy or sell, or which currency is going to appreciate. I give them plenty of reasons why they should start focusing on asset allocation instead. As with the "sad truths," they instinctively know this advice to be right, but more often than not their next question is whether I think the dollar is going to appreciate or the market is going to fall. Oh, well. . .

Some investors may well question the wisdom of being passively invested in the current environment, since markets are displaying exceptional levels of volatility and apparently going nowhere but down. But hindsight is 20:20. It is very easy to say now that we should have cashed out at the beginning of 2008, but it did not look that obvious at the time. Trends, in fact, are not obvious until they are well in place. Black swans are unpredictable, and we only know when one has hit us after the event.

As mentioned at the beginning, eating healthily and investing have much in common; in both, the long-term goal is desirable, but the "getting there" is the problem. Most investors know what they have to do along the way; most know that pain is a part of the process; most know that patience and discipline are essential; and yet most are tempted into shortcuts ("miracle diets" or "high-return, low-risk" strategies), even though they probably recognize that these may ultimately be dead ends. When it comes down to healthy eating or investing, there is simply no gain without pain.

Black swans do exist, both in the natural world and in the financial markets. Those in nature are just a curiosity, but those in financial markets have critical implications for investor behavior. Volatile markets invite investors to engage in a losing game. And yet, at the end of the day, black swans render market timing a goose chase.

▶▶ MORE INFO

Books:

Estrada, Javier. *Finance in a Nutshell: A No-nonsense Companion to the Tools and Techniques of Finance*. Harlow: FT Prentice Hall, 2005.

Mandelbrot, Benoit B., and Richard L. Hudson. *The (Mis)Behavior of Markets. A Fractal View of Risk, Ruin and Reward*. London: Profile Books, 2005.

Taleb, Nassim Nicholas. *The Black Swan. The Impact of the Highly Improbable*. New York: Random House, 2007.

Articles:

Estrada, Javier. "Black swans and market timing: How not to generate alpha." *Journal of Investing* (Fall 2008): 20–34.

Estrada, Javier. "Black swans in emerging markets." *Journal of Investing* (Summer 2009): 1–7.

See Also:

★ Viewpoint: Javier Estrada (pp. 312–313)

The Black Swan: The Impact of the Highly Improbable (p. 1227)

"Investors think of risk differently from the way it is defined in modern portfolio theory. Both the standard deviation and beta give equal weight to upside and downside fluctuations. Investors, however, do not."

Javier Estrada

  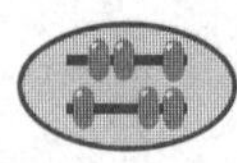   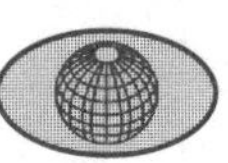   

Funds of Hedge Funds versus Single-Manager Funds by Steve Wallace

EXECUTIVE SUMMARY

- The process of selecting a fund of hedge funds (FoHF) is very different from that of constructing a portfolio of single managers.
- Deciding which investment route to use generally depends on two primary factors: How much money you have to invest, and the resources (expertise, knowledge base, financial resources, human capital, IT systems, etc.) at your disposal.
- The extra fee layer you pay when using a FoHF is generally imposed to meet the cost of sourcing and selecting fund managers.
- It is important that your own investment objectives and those of the FoHF you choose should be compatible.
- A number of other factors need to be considered beside those mentioned above—the decision between a single-manager fund and a FoHF is not a black and white one.

INTRODUCTION

Funds of hedge funds have caused heated debate over the years. The debate revolves around two main issues:

- **Fees**: Having to pay for something which at the time seems intangible or is difficult to value tends to be a cause for concern. To many, it looks like there is a doubling of fees—those charged at the underlying manager level and then again at the FoHF level.
- **Control**: The realization that you must pass control of the underlying fund selection to a FoHF manager can be difficult for some. These people would prefer to retain control as, even if they don't achieve the result they hope for, this is preferable to a result, good or bad, that isn't of their own making.

The initial driver of the decision to choose between FoHF and single manager should be a look inside the firm for the knowledge, expertise, and experience required to source and select the underlying managers. In this article we will look at the elements of the decision to invest either in a basket of single managers or in a FoHF product.

A DEFINITION

A fund of hedge funds, as the name implies, is a fund that invests in a collection of hedge funds. The collection of funds is constructed to balance risks and returns to achieve its mandate. It should be noted that the FoHF portfolio construction process applies not only to hedge funds but also to other products, such as long-only managed funds—funds of funds (FoFs).

The basic premise of a FoHF is that a portfolio can be constructed to generate a return with lower volatility than might occur if the investors constructed the portfolio themselves. FoHF managers are therefore claiming that they have the ability to source, research, and select funds which, when brought together to form a portfolio, can satisfy investors' requirements while reducing volatility.

The two most frequently cited risks that a FoHF aims to reduce are manager risk and downside risk, which in any case are inextricably linked. Manager risk is reduced by the simple expedient of having more than one manager. Merely by having more managers, you reduce the risk to your portfolio that any one manager will fail, whether operationally, performance wise, or in terms of strategy. The other main risk—downside risk—is the possibility that an investment will fall in value. Arguably, one of the main benefits of a FoHF is not that it will "shoot the lights out" in terms of performance, but that it will at least manage the downside risk.

INVESTOR TYPES

Generally, individual investors have traits that make them more likely to invest via a FoHF than in a selection of single managers, and vice versa. In addition there are emotive factors such as fear, a desire for control, and an overconfidence in one's abilities.

Generally speaking, the greater the monetary value of the portfolio, the more likely it is that an investor will go down the single-manager route. But this leaves out one crucial element—the ability to select managers and construct a portfolio using a mix of managers to achieve a return target while minimizing risk.

Looking at Figure 1, we can draw certain conclusions as to whether an investor should favor a FoHF or a single-manager strategy when investing in hedge funds.

The x axis represents the ability of the investor to source and select individual managers. The sourcing aspect is important because there are thousands of different funds to invest in, but the ability to source a list of funds for further consideration is an important part of the process and should not be taken for granted. The "select" element of the x axis brings in the research part of the process. This is where you have managed to source a list of appropriate funds and are able to research them to the same level as a hedge fund research professional. I use the prefix "hedge fund" in front of research professional because the sort of due diligence you apply to hedge funds, whatever the strategy, is very different from that for long-only funds (where only buy–sell decisions are made).

The y axis represents the amount of money that the investor is seeking to allocate to hedge funds. The smaller this is, the less likely you will be able to invest in the number of single-manager funds necessary to satisfy diversification needs as well as meeting minimum investment requirements.

The descriptions of each of the four boxes in the diagram are not mutually exclusive—there is overlap, and other components will come into the decision. I have simply selected two of the primary drivers for the purposes of discussion.

A: At this point the size of the allocation to hedge funds is low and the investor doesn't have the ability to source and select single managers to build the portfolio.

B: This is the point where issues occur. Since the size of the allocation is high, it would appear to indicate that single-manager funds should be selected. However, a look at the x axis suggests that the ability to source and select managers

Figure 1. Hedge fund selection strategy

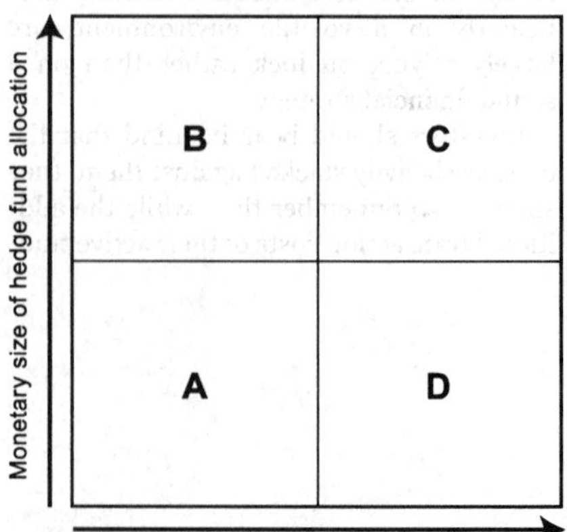

"**First learn the meaning of what you say, and then speak.**" Epictetus

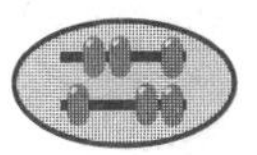
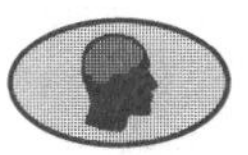

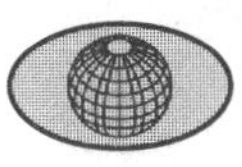

remains relatively low. Therefore, investors in this situation should try to increase their expertise before allocating to single managers.

C: This stage is clearly where the single-manager route makes sense. Here you have the intersection of a large allocation of funds matched by a strong ability to source and select single hedge fund managers.

D: Here we come up against the situation where the investor may have the ability to build a portfolio of single-manager hedge funds to meet their allocation requirements but may not have enough capital to meet the minimum investment requirements of some funds.

ADVANTAGES AND DISADVANTAGES

Below are some of the main advantages and disadvantages of the two hedge fund investing options. Note that this is by no means an exhaustive list.

Fund of Hedge Funds

Advantages

- Managers of the underlying hedge funds are professionally selected.
- Manager diversification.
- Reduced volatility.
- Ease of access.
- Low minimum investment requirements. (In most cases, the minimum investment in one FoHF would be less than the aggregate minimum investments in, say, 20 single-manager funds.)
- Fees can be negotiated.
- Ability to invest in funds that are closed.

Disadvantages

- Not custom-made to your requirements.
- May not fit within your overall portfolio as well as carefully chosen single-manager funds.
- The additional layer of fees means that the performance return needed to break even is higher. (However, the investor is getting something for this extra fee—expertise in manger selection, the FoHF structure, and so on. What value this translates to depends on your circumstances.)

Single-Manager Fund

Advantages

- The portfolio is completely custom-made.
- The ability to dovetail the hedge fund allocation with the overall portfolio.
- The transparency of the overall portfolio.

Disadvantages

- Cost of the expertise required to build a professional portfolio of single managers.
- The investment required to ensure an appropriately diversified hedge fund portfolio.
- Overconfidence in your ability, or that of your team, to select single-manager funds.
- The potential for large losses by any one manager.

▸▸ MAKING IT HAPPEN

People often remark about a FoHF's ability to invest in up-and-coming hedge funds that will generate significant returns as they grow from start-up. This comes back to expertise, since not all FoHFs have the expertise to invest in emerging hedge funds because investment in such funds involves a much more complex due diligence process.

If you are a novice, the risk to the value of your portfolio is high if you invest in hedge funds, whether they are single-manager or FoHF. You should also note that if you do decide to go into hedge funds via a FoHF, you cannot abdicate responsibility completely. A whole other area of FoHF due diligence comes into play here.

The best way forward is to go back to basics—i.e. what was the rationale for investing in hedge funds in the first place? Once you're clear on that, you can ask yourself the next question: Do I have the knowledge required either to invest in a FoHF or to construct a portfolio of single-manager hedge funds? If you don't have that knowledge, there are a number of ways you can obtain it—whether by educating yourself through the Chartered Alternative Investment Analyst program (see under Websites below), discussion with peers, use of hedge fund advisery consultants, or other routes.

Following these suggested actions will guide you down the single-manager or FoHF path. As mentioned earlier, however, if you have the experience to construct a portfolio using single-manager hedge funds but not enough funds to gain diversification benefits, it would be foolhardy to invest in single-manager funds.

▸▸ MORE INFO

Books:

Anson, Mark J. P. *The Handbook of Alternative Assets*. 2nd ed. Hoboken, NJ: Wiley, 2006.

Ineichen, Alexander M. *Asymmetric Returns: The Future of Active Asset Management*. Hoboken, NJ: Wiley, 2007.

Jones, Chris. *Hedge Funds of Funds: A Guide for Investors*. Hoboken, NJ: Wiley, 2007.

Lhabitant, François-Serge. *Handbook of Hedge Funds*. Hoboken, NJ: Wiley, 2006.

Scharfman, Jason A. *Hedge Fund Operational Due Diligence: Understanding the Risks*. Hoboken, NJ: Wiley, 2009.

Travers, Frank J. *Investment Manager Analysis: A Comprehensive Guide to Portfolio Selection, Monitoring, and Optimization*. Hoboken, NJ: Wiley, 2004.

Websites:

Albourne Village—website for the hedge fund and private equity community: www.village.albourne.com

All About Alpha—information service for the asset management and hedge fund industries: www.allaboutalpha.com/blog

Alpha magazine (Institutional Investor): www.iimagazine.com/alpha

Alternative Investment Management Association (AIMA): www.aima.org

Chartered Alternative Investment Analyst (CAIA) Association: www.caia.org

Hedge Fund Matrix: www.hedgefundmatrix.com

Hedge Fund Standards Board (HFSB): www.hfsb.org

Opalesque—News service for participants in the alternative investment sector: www.opalesque.com

  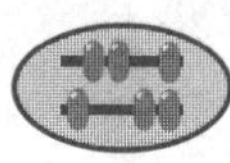   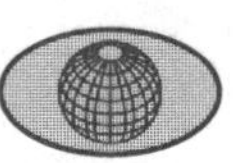   

Hedge Fund Challenges Extend Beyond Regulation by Kevin Burrows

EXECUTIVE SUMMARY

- The loss of liquidity and its impact on hedge fund performance.
- Redemption issues and their impact on future practice.
- Management challenges and sector performance.
- The threat from alternatives to hedge funds.
- How the crash changed the rules of the game.
- The dilemma of a global regulator.

INTRODUCTION

Victim Rather Than Villain

The hedge fund sector has been vilified by some politicians, both in Europe and in the US, as if it were a significant contributor to the banking collapse and subsequent global recession. In reality, the hedge fund industry was very much a victim of the banks during the latter half of 2008, and there are some significant litigation actions pending, in which hedge funds are suing investment banks for alleged misdealings in their collateralized debt obligation (CDO) products and credit default swap (CDS) transactions.

However, potential misdealings aside, it is clear that the dreadful performance turned in by many hedge funds in 2008 was precipitated not just by stock market and property price collapses, but also by the total loss of liquidity in all risky markets, a direct consequence of the massive deleveraging by banks. At the same time as they were reducing the size of their balance sheets, numerous banks closed or drastically slimmed down their proprietary trading desks, leaving hedge funds with no bidders for any instrument that had any degree of complexity about it.

Adding insult to injury, many banks forcibly withdrew previously agreed lines of credit to hedge funds, forcing any hedge fund manager running a leveraged strategy to liquidate their positions as fast as possible. Finally, their clients, disappointed by the lack of "absolute returns" that they were implicitly promised by the hedge funds, became extremely nervous, and many decided to turn their investments back into cash, even though they often had nowhere to put the cash (as banks themselves posed a risk for any significant cash holding), and had no clear alternative investment strategy in sight.

THE IMPACT OF REDEMPTIONS

Faced with the perfect storm of poor performance and severe redemption pressure, hedge fund managers were forced to close funds or suspend redemptions, in order to protect values for those investors remaining with the fund. What the sector experienced during 2008, in other words, was less a performance issue, with strategies failing to work, than a bank run caused by their liquidity mismatch. Money that fund managers thought was "sticky money" (i.e., money that would stay with the fund for the medium term, and so give the fund's investment strategy a chance to work) turned out to be "on demand" money that investors urgently wanted returned to them.

It did not appear to matter, in these circumstances, whether the hedge fund was invested in assets that the investors could expect to be highly liquid, such as equities or government bonds, or whether the fund had a very illiquid strategy, such as asset-based lending, where there was effectively no liquidity or secondary market for those loans. In the latter situation, if a significant proportion of the investors run for the exit at the same time, the fund management has very few options. They can either halt redemptions or run the risk of paying out all of the remaining liquidity at the expense of those opting to stay. Or they can simply liquidate the fund.

MANAGEMENT CHALLENGES AND SECTOR PERFORMANCE

In reality, the way the hedge fund sector as a whole managed the difficult circumstances that characterized the second half of 2008 and the opening months of 2009 was highly commendable. As a generalization, portfolios were managed in a way that protected the interests of as many investors as possible. As a fund-of-funds manager, we were often on the phone to our hedge fund managers saying that, on behalf of our investors, we did not want the fund attempting to pay out all redemptions by liquidating the portfolio at fire-sale prices, as that hurts everyone. We wanted to see redemptions frozen and value preserved.

What the hedge fund sector has learned from this whole experience is that there is a definite price to pay for liquidity, or the lack of it. Investors clearly value the ability to convert their investment back into "cash at hand" in a reasonably short time frame. That ability has a significant value, so in future we will see that option priced into the contract between investor and fund. Moreover, for investment strategies that are largely liquid, the dealing terms will be forced to become more liquid to match the underlying instruments. As a consequence, we will see more monthly dealing hedge funds, with perhaps only a month's notice or even less for withdrawals. We will also witness the continued development of many more daily dealing UCITS III type funds, trading in long-only and long-short strategies, in response to this new-found desire on the part of the investor community for highly liquid products. (The caveat to this, as we shall see in a moment, is that in the current investing environment, it is not clear that hedge fund managers have that much more added value to offer, even in this new format, versus passive investments such as an exchange-traded fund or ETF, where the units can be traded at any time, and where the unit charges are vastly lower than hedge fund fees.)

While the near-liquid funds move to highly liquid redemption terms, strategies that legitimately need a longer investment period to realize their returns, such as distressed debt and structured credit, will move their terms to something more akin to a private equity structure, with anywhere from a two-to-five-year lock-up, and no option for investors to get their money out early. The "middle ground," which used to be comprised of hedge funds with 90-day exit clauses, but where the strategy was, in reality, rather more liquid that this conveys, will come under huge pressure to improve its liquidity terms. It will not be possible for managers to seek to hold assets just to control them; rather, they will have to match the liquidity terms of the clients to the liquidity terms of the assets. That will be a very significant change for the industry.

THE THREAT FROM ALTERNATIVES TO HEDGE FUNDS

The resolution of the liquidity mismatch is only one of a number of changes that the sector is going to have to deal with. Another challenge, which ironically arises naturally

"Nothing arouses ambition so much in the hearer as the trumpet clang of another's fame." Baltasar Gracian

from the current dislocation of the markets, is that a large number of investment opportunities today do not require a hedge fund strategy to generate very acceptable levels of return. This is a point that is hard to overemphasize in terms of its potential impact on the sector—at its moment of maximum client distrust, the hedge fund industry must contend with the fact that many of the best returns available today may lie outside of their hedged strategies.

As an example, take the present dislocation in convertible bonds. An investor today can buy long-only convertible bonds, and be satisfied to simply earn the market beta (which is to say, the performance delivered by the market itself, rather than any outperformance, or alpha, delivered by the skill of the hedge fund manager). That beta has a very good chance of delivering a return on a mixed portfolio of investment-grade and high-yield bonds, in excess of 10–12%. Faced with those levels of expected return, there is little incentive for an investor to seek to gain another 3% by investing with a hedge fund manager promising 15% returns with the traditional hedge fund fee structure of 2/20 (2% management fee and 20% performance fee), but which also comes with all the liquidity, regulatory, and potential fraud risks that hedge fund investing entails. What this means is that it has become much more difficult for hedge fund managers to justify their alpha fee than it was in an era where market beta was delivering very low single-digit returns.

Two further areas of competition for hedge funds, apart from the fact that investors can build their own long-only portfolios with relative ease, come from ETFs, and from the synthetic hedge fund replicators now being offered by the likes of Goldman Sachs, State Street, and Merrill Lynch.

There is now a substantial body of research on hedge fund performance that suggests that about 80% of a hedge fund manager's income stream can be attributed to "alternative beta" factors rather than to management skill. Alternative beta factors refers to market risk characteristics such as equity risk, term structure, credit risk, small cap equity, and emerging markets equity, as well as nonlinear returns such as trend-following strategies. It is now possible to replicate a significant part of hedge fund returns through investing in an appropriately designed futures, ETF and/or options strategy. As they are using liquid instruments as their building blocks, these replicators have no hedge fund fee structure associated with it, and provide complete liquidity, full transparency, no fraud risk, and the opportunity for investors to trade in and out as they require.

Of course, it is true that there are limits to how much of a good hedge fund manager's strategy can be replicated in such structures, and the remaining 20% of manager alpha cannot be captured through these products. However, just as ETFs are taking market share from the actively managed long-only fund industry, I believe the hedge fund replicators now being developed by the former investment banks, among others, will attract sizeable flows of pension fund money that would, in the past, have gone directly into hedge funds.

HOW THE CRASH CHANGED THE RULES

What all this amounts to is that, quite apart from the coming wave of regulation that hedge funds are going to have to deal with, the rules of the game have already changed as a result of the crash. While they were evolving anyway, as they do whenever an industry matures, the market meltdown of 2008 has definitely speeded up this process.

One such change we were seeing just before the crash was a convergence between the active managers in the long-only space, now that the UCITS III rules allow them to take short positions in some circumstances, and hedge funds. This has put a further strain on hedge fund fees, as investors are only willing to pay above-average fees if it gives them access to real investment skill that they cannot tap into at a lower fee structure. Asset allocators (funds of funds, pensions, endowments, etc.) are becoming much more skilled at separating their beta market exposure from their alpha (the value added brought through skill), putting real pressure on hedge fund managers to prove that what they are providing is not simply a leveraged market return. Sophisticated investors are quite capable of leveraging their own positions; they do not need a hedge fund manager to do that for them. So, if on careful analysis a hedge fund's perceived outperformance over the relevant benchmark turns out to be simply a return due to leverage, then that is no longer going to be accepted as the creation of genuine alpha through investment skill.

It is now becoming quite widely recognized just how much the performance of some hedge fund strategies owed simply to leverage. However, ETFs have been created that are leveraged two to five times, which investors can access directly if they want leveraged plays, so that game by the hedge funds has gone. One must also recognize that leverage was a strategy for a buoyant market where liquidity and credit was cheap. Similarly, if the hedge fund strategy was based largely on short-selling, there are short-leveraged ETFs that investors can now use. Again, this is yet more pressure on hedge fund managers to demonstrate to investors just where their alpha performance comes from. Much has been said about the scalability or otherwise of hedge-fund strategies. As successful hedge funds attract a flood of investor money, it inevitably pushes them towards a multi-strategy approach to be able to deploy a large amount of capital effectively. With real skill this can continue to be effective, so another dynamic in the market is that we see the larger, more established and institution-like hedge funds becoming multi-strategy funds, while at the same time the smaller, more niche funds, with assets under management of £100–250 million, are seeking to limit their growth. As managers are paid based on the amount of assets under management, remaining small takes real discipline, but the penalty for not doing so is poorer performance if you grow larger than the opportunity set in which you are investing.

As an added dynamic, there is tremendous pressure on politicians and regulators to "do something," so more regulation now looks certain. However, the irony of this is that the market itself has forced hedge funds to become much more transparent and open, anyway. Following the Madoff fraud, no hedge fund manager can expect to operate an opaque structure on a "trust me" basis.

AN INTERNATIONAL COLLEGE OF REGULATORS?

There are real dangers, however, lying in wait for regulators as they seek to move into the hedge fund space. What would the shape of such regulation look like? One view seems to be favoring the formation of an international college of regulators who would somehow have oversight across the highly complex investment strategies and positions of some 3,000–7,000 hedge funds around the world. The data requirements necessary to enable such oversight are absolutely huge. If one remembers that the individual investment banks themselves did not know or understand what was on their own balance sheets, and it took some of them many weeks with an army of staff to begin to put some numbers to their exposures, it is well-nigh impossible to see how a single regulatory body could have meaningful oversight of the risk exposures of the entire financial industry. And if it saw what it deemed to be too much risk, how would it address this? By sending

a mass email to everyone saying "cut all X exposures by Y percent?" Or would they focus on just the largest funds, thereby giving smaller funds a competitive advantage in the market?

CONCLUSION

Any intervention by a global regulator would be likely to have a tremendous distorting effect in the market. As hedge fund managers live and breathe market distortions, gaming the regulator to produce distortions would become a very viable strategy in its own right. Political rhetoric is easy. Implementing meaningful regulation for a sector that has already become vastly more transparent to investors is much harder. Is the additional gain in transparency and stability that is being sought really worth the huge effort and expense that would be entailed, remembering that the current crisis was precipitated by loose credit standards and the bursting of an asset bubble, events in which hedge funds were only a minor player? These are questions regulators will have to ponder as they look to extend their sway over the hedge fund sector.

▸▸ MORE INFO

Articles:

Andrew Baker. "Shorting—An essential endangered hedge." *Financial Times* (June 8, 2008). Online at: www.ft.com/cms/s/0/41a64588-33f1-11dd-869b-0000779fd2ac.html

Websites:

Alternative Investment Management Association (AIMA): www.aima.org

"Majority of hedge fund assets under management now from institutional investors" (AIMA press release): www.aima.org/en/media_centre/press-releases.cfm/id/987F627D-9924-46E0-B74F58CFF3F43DD9

See Also:

★ Carrying Out Due Diligence on Hedge Funds (pp. 289–291)
✔ Hedge Funds: Understanding the Risks and Returns (p. 938)
ℹ Hedge Funds, Fund Management, and Alternative Investments (pp. 1641–1643)

"Managerial intellect wilted in competition with managerial adrenaline. The thrill of the chase blinded pursuers to the consequences of the chase." Warren Buffett

     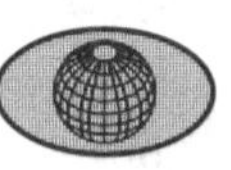   

How Stockholders Can Effectively Engage With Companies by James Gifford

EXECUTIVE SUMMARY

- The Executive Director of the United Nations-backed Principles for Responsible Investment shares his experience of working with and researching stockholders who actively engage with the companies in which they invest.
- He argues that the effectiveness of such engagement is driven by 12 key factors. These include the business case behind a stockholder request, the values of the target company managers, the assertiveness and persistence of the stockholder, and the policy environment in which the engagement takes place.
- Above all, the most influential factor may be whether the company itself wants to change.

INTRODUCTION

How many social workers does it take to change a light bulb? One. But the bulb has got to *want* to change. This is also the theme of this essay on stockholder engagement—the practice of investors seeking to influence corporate behavior for the better.

Institutional investors are increasingly engaging in dialog with companies for the purpose of improving some aspect of a company's environmental or social impact, corporate governance, or strategic performance. This practice is widely known as "stockholder engagement." As of early 2009, the UN-backed Principles for Responsible Investment (PRI), which contain commitments to active ownership, had over 470 signatories representing more than $18 trillion in assets under management. Surveys of these signatories show that more than half engage in dialog with companies, either directly or as part of broader investor collaborations, to influence corporate behavior.

If stockholders want to influence corporate behavior, the company has got to *want* to change. Unless the stockholder has a large stake in a company, they are simply one of many stakeholders in the firm. If the stockholder wants the company to change, the company's managers must be convinced that it is in the best interests of the company to do whatever it is the stockholders are asking.

THE ESSENTIALS OF EFFECTIVE ENGAGEMENT

So what makes for successful engagement? There are 12 key factors that stockholders should consider when seeking to influence a company.

The Values of the Company's Managers Should Be Broadly Aligned with the Premise of the Investors' Request

When an investor engages in a dialog with a company, each of the participants in the conversation must understand from where the other is coming. They should not be too far apart. If, for example, there is a CEO who simply doesn't believe that climate change exists, then it is likely that a request to enhance disclosures of greenhouse gas emissions will fall on deaf ears. If the company's managers are on an entirely different wavelength, it may be wise to expend resources elsewhere, or focus on a topic where the differences are not so great. That said, these companies may well be those where management is so out of touch that it is causing severe damage to the company's prospects. In such cases, the stockholder needs to weigh up the costs and benefits of a long and protracted effort to get the message through.

Strong Business Case

Stockholders need to present a very strong business case, ideally backed up by some kind of evidence. There are many issues that companies have not considered in detail, and in many cases companies are unaware of best practices followed by peers in their industry. The stronger the business case for companies to do something differently, the more likely they are to recognize that the investor has a point.

Assertiveness and Persistence

The UK government-commissioned Myners Report stated that "merely meeting senior management and expressing polite reservations about strategy is not sufficient if it is not effective." CalPERS' legendary 1990s CEO Dale Hanson stated that "kinder, gentler, is not working" when referring to the fund's escalation of activism by its stockholders. But again, assertiveness needs to be appropriate, as the company has got to *want* to change, and if a stockholder is too assertive, it may lead to greater resistance by the company.

Persistence is another important attribute that contributes to effective stockholder engagement. Companies are often slow-moving beasts, and paradigms take time to change. Stockholders need to hang in there for the long term, as engagements can take up to three years to bear fruit. For example, a group of US funds, including Domini and Calvert, successfully encouraged Gap to release its first social responsibility report after two years of dialog.

Building Coalitions with Other Stockholders and Stakeholders

One investor alone, even if it is a large pension fund, has limited capacity to engage with a company. Many large funds hold thousands of companies in their portfolios. It is important that, to promote changes in company behavior, stockholders work together to pool resources and influence. Many investors have the same concerns about particular companies or sectors. In addition, it is more efficient for companies to have a deeper and more comprehensive dialog with well-informed representatives from a group of investors, than having the same superficial conversation with many different stockholder representatives.

There are also opportunities for stockholders to collaborate with other stakeholders, such as NGOs and public policy-makers. Again, it is important that these collaborations are constructive and not seen as ganging up on the company. In many cases, NGOs can provide considerable expertise to companies about managing complex sustainability issues, and many of these organizations work with companies on a routine basis. For example, Insight Investment teamed up with the World Wide Fund for Nature (WWF) to conduct a benchmark of UK-listed house building companies, a process which led to the establishment of the Next Generation benchmark, a multi-stakeholder initiative supported by the house building sector itself.

Going Public

There is no doubt that in certain circumstances it can be useful for a stockholder to up the ante and go public with his or her

"The directors of such joint-stock companies, however, being the managers rather of other people's money than of their own, it cannot well be expected, that they should watch over it with the same anxious vigilance with which the partners in a private copartnery frequently watch over their own." Adam Smith

     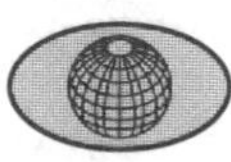   

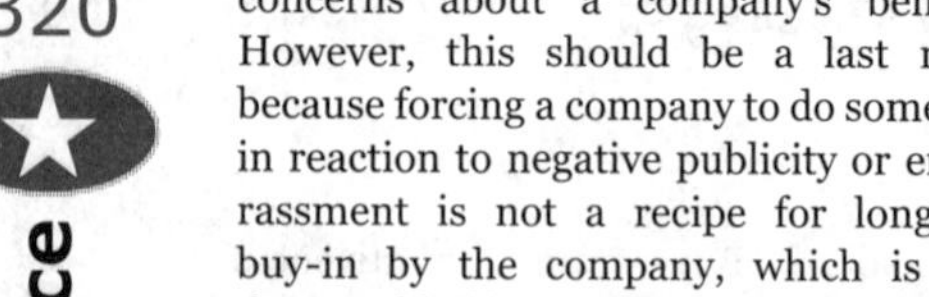

concerns about a company's behavior. However, this should be a last resort, because forcing a company to do something in reaction to negative publicity or embarrassment is not a recipe for long-term buy-in by the company, which is what the stockholder really wants. Again, the company has got to *want* to change.

Alignment with the Interests of the Company, and Being Internally Consistent

For a company to *want* to change, the managers have to feel that the stockholder genuinely has its interests at heart. There may be many points of disagreement, at least initially, but if the company and the stockholder both share a common commitment to the company's long-term success, it will make the engagement much more constructive.

Stockholder organizations also need to be internally consistent. The equities analysts in a fund management organization are often not closely linked with the ESG (environmental, social, governance) people, and they send mixed signals to companies. For example, in their discussions with companies the analysts, may be focusing on short-term financial factors, while the ESG or governance people are talking about longer-term ESG or structural issues. The stockholder organization needs to ensure that it is joined up internally and is sending consistent signals to those companies with which it interacts.

Supportive Political and Policy Environment

If stockholders mirror the political and policy environment, they are more likely to gain a positive response from companies. Regulators are the most powerful stakeholders in a firm. Where there is regulatory momentum on an issue, or clear indications from public policy-makers that they would like companies to move in a certain direction, this provides fertile ground for stockholders to give companies a push along. There is also a very persuasive argument for companies to be well ahead of the regulatory curve.

Make Sure that Your People Are Credible, Senior, Experienced, and Knowledgeable

Company managers know more about their companies than anyone else. Stockholder representatives need to have the expertise and knowledge to add value to the conversation with the company.

Use of Voting and Stockholder Resolutions

Voting against management and filing stockholder resolutions at company AGMs is another tool in the stockholder engagement toolbox. Companies will go to some lengths to avoid embarrassing votes against management or the filing of stockholder resolutions. But again, stockholder resolutions should be used as a last resort as, being seen as hostile acts, they can undermine the legitimacy of stockholders in the eyes of the company.

Societal Legitimacy

It is helpful, though not essential, that the issue on which the investor is engaging is also one that has strong support within the community. It is more likely that a company will recognize the importance of addressing an issue where there is some momentum for change, and it is likely that regulation, NGO pressure, or consumer pressure will emerge in the future.

An Implicit or Explicit Threat of Divestment?

Companies spend significant resources on investor relations, presumably because they value the marginal buyer or seller of their stock. If a stockholder is a large one, a threat of divestment can increase a company's motivation to work with that stockholder to address the issue of concern.

However, divestment is a two-edged sword, and once a stockholder has sold out, it no longer has a relationship with that company. That said, a number of pension funds, such as the Norwegian Government Pension Fund, continue their discussions with divested companies, keeping open the possibility of reinvesting.

Does Size Matter?

It would seem intuitive that large investors would have a greater ability to influence companies. However, while this might be true to an extent, it does not mean that small investors cannot be very influential. For example, Calvert, a US-based sustainable and responsible investment (SRI) fund, played an important role in encouraging Dell to implement a computer take-back and recycling scheme. This was because Calvert brought with it significant experience on these issues and became a trusted adviser to Dell on this process. Dell also saw Calvert as a key stakeholder with which it could have a constructive relationship.

CONCLUSION

Some of the factors identified above are related to the legitimacy of the investor and their case in the eyes of the company (specifically, the credibility of the stockholder representatives, the business case, and the political support for an issue). Some of the factors are power-related, that is, they seek to force the company to do something it doesn't want to do (going public and filing stockholder resolutions). If investors want the company to *want* to change, they should focus on those approaches that build legitimacy and good

CASE STUDY

Collaborative Stockholder Engagement

Morley Fund Management (now Aviva Investors) led a collaborative engagement in 2008 focused on the UN Global Compact, a set of ten principles of corporate responsibility. Working closely with the UN-backed Principles for Responsible Investment, a coalition of 20 investors representing approximately US$2.13 trillion in assets was developed. The coalition sent letters to company chief executives focused on adherence to the disclosure requirement of the UN Global Compact, which is known as a Communication on Progress (or COP).

Without adequate reporting on progress, signing up by companies to the Global Compact's ten principles represents little more than a statement of good intentions. While an engagement focused on reporting is only a part of the process of improvement advocated by the UN Global Compact, it represents the most obvious initial area in which investors have the most potential leverage and influence.

Depending on whether the company was a leader or a laggard in meeting this COP disclosure requirement, the coalition either welcomed good practice or challenged the company to achieve full participant status. In total, the investors wrote to the CEOs of 103 companies in more than 30 different countries, with 25 companies receiving the group's congratulations, and 78—the laggards—being asked to improve their adherence to the Compact. The engagement resulted in over 32% of the companies identified as laggards subsequently submitting a communication on progress and improving their involvement with the UN Global Compact.

The success of the exercise also played a part in stimulating the launch in October 2008 of the "Seoul Initiative"—a collaboration among 52 PRI signatories asking almost 9,000 listed companies to join the UN Global Compact.

"I wasn't satisfied just to earn a good living. I was looking to make a statement." Donald J. Trump

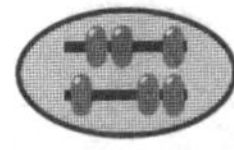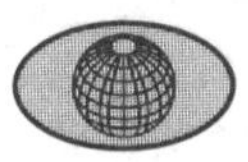

relationships with the company and only use the power-oriented tools when all else fails.

And what if the company simply doesn't want to change? If the issue is crucial to the stockholder, then there needs to be a willingness to dig in over the long term, build coalitions with other stockholders, make public statements, file stockholder resolutions, and, where necessary, take legal action to ensure that stockholders' interests are protected.

▸▸ MORE INFO

Books:

Davis, Stephen, Jon Lukomnik, and David Pitt-Watson. *The New Capitalists: How Citizen Investors Are Reshaping the Corporate Agenda*. Watertown, MA: Harvard Business School Press, 2006.

Hebb, Tessa. *No Small Change: Pension Funds and Corporate Engagement*. Ithaca, NY: Cornell University Press, 2008.

Kiernan, Matthew J. *Investing in a Sustainable World: Why Green is the New Color of Money on Wall Street*. New York: AMACOM, 2008.

Krosinsky, Cary, and Nick Robins (eds). *Sustainable Investing: The Art of Long Term Performance.* London: Earthscan, 2008.

Sullivan, Rory, and Craig Mackenzie (eds). *Responsible Investment.* Sheffield, UK: Greenleaf Publishing, 2006.

Websites:

Principles for Responsible Investment (UNEP Finance Initiative and UN Global Compact): www.unpri.org

Responsible Investor: www.responsible-investor.com

Social Investment Forum: www.socialinvest.org

UNEP Finance Initiative: www.unepfi.org

UN Global Compact; www.unglobalcompact.org

"Man is the only creature that strives to surpass himself, and yearns for the impossible." Eric Hoffer

  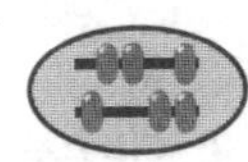   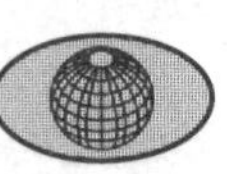   

How to Set the Hurdle Rate for Capital Investments by Jon Tucker

EXECUTIVE SUMMARY

- There exists a wide range of approaches to setting the hurdle rate for capital investments.
- It is essential that we do not set the hurdle rate too high, thereby foregoing valuable investment opportunities, or too low, thereby destroying value for shareholders.
- While academics tend to advocate a series of, at times, complex adjustments, most CFOs settle for a relatively simple approach, and allow for complexity instead in their cash flow projections.
- The most common approach is to employ a CAPM-based equity cost as an input to a WACC calculation.
- A company-wide hurdle rate is typically employed by companies, although adjustments are made for projects of atypical risk.

INTRODUCTION

Chief financial officers are charged with the task of maximizing shareholder wealth. They do this by pursuing two key goals: Maximizing the stream of future cash flows, and minimizing the company's cost of capital. Cognizant of the separation theorem, we tend to separate one goal from the other. However, both are of strategic importance—a healthy stream of cash flows can actually destroy value (and hence reduce shareholder wealth) if the company suffers from a high cost of capital. In a very real sense, then, a company's cost of capital represents an important "hurdle," which its portfolio of projects must exceed in order to create wealth for shareholders. Clearly, the cost of capital, as implied by the company's financing mix, is a good starting point when arriving at the hurdle rate for capital investment appraisal (capital budgeting), but the way in which the company arrives at this cost of capital, and the adjustments made thereafter to arrive at the hurdle rate, warrant further explanation.

HURDLE RATE: A DEFINITION

The hurdle rate is the required rate of return on investment appraisal, above which an investment project is worth pursuing. We know when computing a project's net present value (NPV) that if the discount rate exceeds the project's internal rate of return (IRR), then we should not proceed with the project. The starting point for the hurdle rate is, then, the company's cost of capital, to which a company may then decide to make some adjustment for that project's specific risk, perhaps adding a risk premium. The difficulty for practitioners is that there exists a wide variation of approaches to arriving at the hurdle rate—even academics cannot agree on the best way forward.

Some examples of the difficulties involved are: How do we arrive at the cost of equity capital? How do we arrive at the cost of debt and other financing components? Do we employ the weighted average cost of capital (WACC), or some other metric, to arrive at the cost of capital? If we do employ the WACC, how do we weight the cost of each financing component? What additional adjustment do we make for risk? We will tackle each of these issues in turn, and explore the broad alternative approaches available to the CFO.

THE COST OF EQUITY

There are a variety of ways in which CFOs tend to compute the cost of equity capital. The most prominent and widely employed approach is the capital asset pricing model (CAPM):[1]

$$r_e = r_f + \beta\,(r_m - r_f)$$

where:
r_e = the expected cost of equity capital for a company;
r_f = the risk-free rate of return;
β = the share beta;
r_m = the return on the market portfolio;
$(r_m - r_f)$ = the expected premium offered by the market portfolio over and above the risk-free rate.

However, we encounter a number of difficulties with this approach in a practical setting. Which risk-free rate should be employed—a three-month Treasury bill rate, or a long-term government bond rate? Most academics would suggest the latter, although in practice, the three-month rate is often employed. Should CFOs compute their own beta coefficient, or employ a beta computed by data agencies such as Bloomberg? This is a matter of personal choice, although in practice most companies probably employ an externally published source. What equity risk premium should be employed, and is it realistic in terms of expectations? We could apply an average historical risk premium here, or even estimate the rate implied by current asset prices. Further, if we compute our own average historical premium figure, then applying the geometric average premium is probably the best approach. Each of these issues could warrant a chapter to itself—in the real world, CFOs arrive at a CAPM-based equity cost of capital after much debate within the company, and consultation with their external corporate advisers (such as investment banks). Academics have extended the CAPM to a multi-factor framework to better capture equity risk, adding size and book-to-market factors, although in practice it is unlikely that companies employ such models extensively.

An alternative approach is to employ an earnings model to arrive at the cost of equity capital, that is, to compute the price-to-earnings (PE) ratio (or earnings yield) for a company. This is a relatively simple procedure, given the wide availability of PE ratios, and the broad understanding and use of asset yields in the financial media, although it is most appropriately employed for non-growth companies. The cost of equity, then, is equal to the inverse of the PE ratio:

$$r_e = \left(\frac{E}{P}\right)$$

where:
r_e = the company's cost of equity capital;
E = the company's earnings;
P = the company's share price.

A further alternative is to arrive at the cost of equity capital by means of a simple dividend model. When we rearrange the dividend model, the cost of equity capital equals the expected dividend yield (D_1/P_0) plus the constant compound growth rate of dividends, the latter often based on past trends as a proxy for growth expectations:

$$r_e = \left(\frac{D_1}{P_0}\right) + g$$

where:
r_e = the company's cost of equity capital;
D_1 = the dividend in year 1;
P = the company's share price in year 0;
g = the growth rate of dividends.

In the real world, CFOs should probably compute a cost of equity using all three

"In short, the required rates of return on corporate investments are set not by management but in the financial markets." Alan C. Shapiro and Sheldon D. Balbirer

     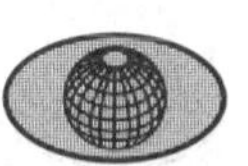   

approaches, benchmark their rate with other companies in their industry (which are likely to have similar betas, business models, and enjoy similar access to financial markets), and only then settle on a suitable figure. In the case of pure equity-financed companies, the cost of equity capital is, by definition, the pivotal figure in arriving at the hurdle rate.

THE COST OF DEBT

A minority of companies set their overall cost of capital at the cost of debt. However, even the cost of debt presents a number of interesting issues to the CFO. First, do we employ the historical cost of debt, or the more meaningful expected cost of debt? Do we look at the cost of total debt, thereby including the cost of short-term debt, or do we focus upon the cost of long-term debt? Regardless of these variations, we certainly need to take into account the tax advantage to debt arising from the deductibility of debt interest payments (whereas equity enjoys no such advantage). Even here, we face an added complication—do we apply a tax advantage based upon statutory corporate tax rates, or marginal rates? Many CFOs will, in practice, employ a long-term debt rate, expressed after tax, based on the marginal corporate tax rate. Further, for the purposes of economic consistency, debt should also include lease obligations. If a company is bond-financed, and there is an active market for those bonds, then the yield to maturity is the appropriate rate, whereas with non-traded debt (such as bank loans) the stated interest rate is the appropriate rate.

THE WEIGHTED AVERAGE COST OF CAPITAL

The WACC is simply the average discount rate applied by the debt-holders and equity-holders of the company to its future cash flows. Discounting the stream of a project's future cash flows by the WACC gives us the capitalized value of that project, whereas so doing for the company's total cash flows gives us the capitalized value of the entire company.

We compute the WACC as follows:

$$\text{WACC} = \left(\frac{D}{D+E}\right) r_d (1 - T_c) + \left(\frac{E}{D+E}\right) r_e$$

where:
WACC = the weighted average cost of capital;
D = the market value of debt;
E = the market value of equity;
r_d = the company's cost of debt capital;
r_e = the company's cost of equity capital;
T_c = the corporate tax rate.

The WACC for a company, then, is simply the cost of the company's financing components (r_d and r_e), weighted by the proportion of those components in the company's capital structure ((D/D+E) and (E/D+E), respectively). We can easily extend this expression for additional forms of financing by weighting them by their proportion in the company's capital structure. The correct approach to weighting here is to compute the market value of each component as a proportion of the total market value of all claims against the company. Note that the cost of debt is effectively reduced by virtue of the fact that there is a tax advantage to debt, as discussed earlier, hence the cost is not r_d but r_d $(1 - T_c)$. This merely reflects the calculation of the corporate tax liability after debt interest costs have been deducted. Employing the WACC as the basis for the hurdle rate makes intuitive sense, as the company must ensure that it is exceeding, on average, the average rate of return required by all of its claimholders. If it is not, then it is destroying value for shareholders.

DEALING WITH RISK

As a general rule, the company should consider investing in projects that generate returns which are higher than the company's hurdle rate. Further, the hurdle rate should be higher for riskier projects than for safer projects.

How do we adjust for risk then? We could adjust the hurdle rate for numerous project characteristics, including: The size of the project, the division within which the project is located, whether the project will be at home or overseas, whether the project is new or existing, and so on. The simplest approach is to apply a company-wide cost of capital as the hurdle rate. The dangers of this approach, however, are that the project under consideration may be more or less risky than the "average" risk of the company's portfolio of investment projects. Large projects are often scrutinized more carefully than smaller projects, given their more material impact on the company's cash flows, and a premium for risk is added to the cost of capital figure to arrive at an appropriate hurdle rate. Most companies add a premium over and above the domestic project hurdle rate for foreign investments. New projects are more risky than existing projects, and should therefore reflect a premium over and above the observed earnings yield of an existing project investment. Ventures such as mergers are more risky still, and thus their returns should exceed a much higher hurdle rate before being sanctioned. Some companies employ a sliding scale of discount rates, depending on a project's nature—discount rates increase as we move from equipment upgrading, through expansion of existing business lines, through new project investments, to more speculative projects.[2]

In the real world, some practitioners argue that we cannot expect the hurdle rate to "take all of the strain" when adjusting for risk. Instead, many argue that the project cash flows themselves should be adjusted for risk to achieve a more realistic estimation of a project's IRR or NPV. Project risk will have a differential impact on the range of cash inflows and outflows and, therefore, a risk-adjusted hurdle rate does not always adequately deal with risk—it can be too blunt an instrument. A carefully computed hurdle rate, in conjunction with risk-adjusted cash flows, and a comprehensive scenario analysis, might be the best way forward, taking care not to double-count risk in the process.

However, presuming that we do indeed employ a hurdle rate which captures risk in some objective and appropriate manner, one way of assuring a more robust approach to capital investment appraisal is to accept only those projects with the highest IRRs, that is, those that exceed the hurdle rate by the highest margin. This may be necessary for most companies in the real world, anyway, in the presence of limited investment funds, and capital rationing.

FREQUENCY OF REVISION

Given the real-world complexity and strategic sensitivity of the hurdle rate figure, it is likely that most companies do not revise the rate on a very frequent basis, often maintaining the same figure for months, or even as long as a year. Events which may encourage CFOs to take another look at the company-wide hurdle rate might include changes in the returns required by investors (such as interest-rate changes), the consideration of major projects, and the prospect of corporate restructuring. Major corporate restructuring has an impact not only on the profile of future cash flows, but also on the returns required by both existing and new claimholders in relation to those cash flows. Given the strategic importance of the hurdle rate, it is typically decided at the level of the board of directors, who take the advice of the CFO, and his/her advisers (consultants, bankers, and so on).

CONCLUSION

In the real world, most practitioners have little appetite for adjusting the hurdle rate for the multitude of factors advocated so fervently by academics. Excepting the all-equity financed case, company CFOs

"Most firms consider risk in the process of investment analysis, but there are wide differences in the techniques used." Aswath Damodaran

  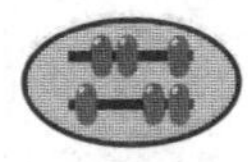   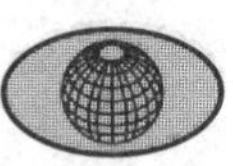   

should typically pursue a CAPM-based weighted average cost of capital, and then make sensible and consistent risk adjustments to determine project hurdle rates. All capital structure components should be expressed at market values, and all costs should be forward looking. A company-wide hurdle rate is probably adequate for many investment projects, although the figure should always be reviewed when dealing with more material, large-scale projects, or indeed corporate restructuring.

CASE STUDY

Determining the Hurdle Rate For a Food Retailer

Company X plc is a FTSE 100 food and drug retailer, listed on the UK stock exchange. The market value of its capital structure components is £12 billion for equity, and £8 billion for debt. The β computed by a reputable data agency is 0.9. The UK 3-month Treasury bill rate is 4.5%, and you estimate that the market tends to pay a premium over and above this rate, of 4.7%. The UK corporate tax rate is 30%, and the rate paid by the company on its 10-year bonds is 5.5%.

We start by computing X plc's cost of equity capital:

$$r_e = r_f + \beta\,(r_m - r_f)$$
$$r_e = 4.5\% + 0.9\,(4.7\%) = 8.73\%$$

We then compute the proportions of debt and equity in the company's capital structure:

$$\frac{D}{(D+E)} = 40\% \text{ and } \frac{E}{(D+E)} = 60\%$$

We can then compute its weighted average cost of capital:

$$WACC = \left(\frac{D}{D+E}\right) r_d\,(1 - T_c) + \left(\frac{E}{D+E}\right) r_e$$
$$WACC = (40\% \times 5.5\% \times (1 - 0.30)) + (60\% \times 8.73\%) = 6.78\%$$

Company X plc applies a hurdle rate of 6.78% to projects of average risk, but adds a margin for projects of higher risk such as an investment in a new product line (+ 5%) or a company acquisition (+10%).

➤➤ MORE INFO

Book:

Bierman, H., Jr, and S. Smidt. *The Capital Budgeting Decision: Economic Analysis of Investment Projects*. 9th ed. New York: Routledge, 2006.

Articles:

Bruner, R., K. Eades, R. Harris, and R. Higgins. "Best practices in estimating the cost of capital: Survey and synthesis." *Finance Practice and Education* 8:1 (Spring/Summer 1998): 14–28.

McLaney, E., J. Pointon, M. Thomas, and J. Tucker. "Practitioners' perspectives on the cost of capital." *European Journal of Finance* 10 (April 2004): 123–138.

NOTES

1 See Sharpe, W. F. "Capital asset prices: A theory of market equilibrium under conditions of risk." *Journal of Finance* 19 (1964): 425–442, and Lintner, J. "The valuation of risk assets and the selection of risk investments in stock portfolios and capital budgets." *Review of Economics and Statistics* 47 (1965): 13–37.

2 A useful discussion of the cost of capital, and how we deal with risk, can be found in Brealey, R. A., S. C. Myers, and F. Allen. *Principles of Corporate Finance*. New York: McGraw Hill/Irwin, 2008: 239–240.

"Since it is not an accounting concept, calculation of the cost of capital should be based on market rather than accounting data." Pierre Vernimmen, Pascal Quiry, Maurizio Dallocchio, Yann Le Fur, and Antonio Salvi

  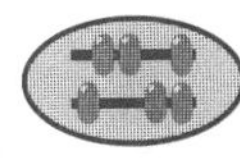 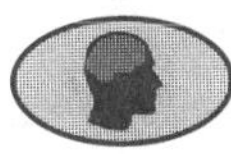  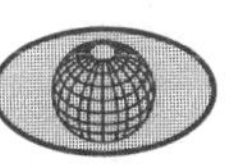   

The Impact of Index Trackers on Shareholders and Stock Volatility by Martin Gold

EXECUTIVE SUMMARY

- Indexes and index-tracking strategies are an increasingly important feature of the contemporary investment environment.
- Index tracking has become a risk-averse strategy for institutional investors, and its popularity has grown strongly, especially within developed capital markets where it is considered difficult to outperform the market reliably.
- Indexes (and indexed portfolios) are actively managed instruments which are constructed according to objective criteria. Their performance typically depends on the market capitalization (size) of stocks.
- Index membership literally confers "investment grade" on firms because numerous managed funds are benchmarked to, or directly invested in, these stocks. Index membership also increases institutional investor ownership levels, trading liquidity, and research coverage by market analysts.
- Index changes can have dramatic effects on stock prices and trading volumes, especially over the short to medium term; longer-term effects remain unclear.

INTRODUCTION

Stock indexing, where investment portfolios mimic or replicate market indexes, has profound implications for both firms and investors. The practice stems from theoretical research which suggests that markets are informationally efficient. Since security prices generally reflect all public information, there is no point in employing active fund management and paying for investment research if there is no prospect of reliably beating the market. Whether or not you believe that beating the market is achievable—and this remains a perennial debate within academic and practitioner circles—the reality is that institutional investors make portfolio allocations with close reference to market indexes. The essential issue for investors and financial managers, therefore, is to be aware of how indexes are managed and to understand the implications for stocks arising from index tracking.

WHAT IS THE "MARKET"? A PRIMER ON INDEXES

This is a seemingly innocuous question, but one that is seldom asked by investors, financial managers, and consumers alike, although they closely scrutinize the fortunes of the Dow Jones in New York or the FTSE100 in London. These important yardsticks affect decision-making in financial markets and also in the real economy. Every day trillions of dollars in capital expenditure/project evaluation, risk modeling, and executive remuneration are all directly linked by market indexes. Investment managers also frequently use index derivatives as a simple and efficient alternative to buying and selling physical constituents.

In financial literature and everyday usage, indexes are given the status and importance of scientific instruments although they are far from being the precise or universal constants which exist in fields such as engineering or physics. A market index simply measures the performance of a basket of securities that is constructed in accordance with the index publisher's methodology. Consequently, an index is a "branded" measure of market performance, where the "market" is whatever the publisher deems it to be.

Although index publishers operate in a competitive marketplace, their index construction methodologies are often similar. Commonly, indexes are weighted according to market value (or capitalization) of their constituent stocks. This weighting scheme is generally regarded as the most accurate reflection of the economic outcomes experienced by all investors in a stock market. This means that once the firms are selected as being representative of the industries in the stock market covered, index performance is calculated using a sum of the individual stocks' returns weighted according to their size. For example, a stock which has a 5% return and represents 10% of the market capitalization will generate 0.5% of the index return for the period. Other schemes which can be used are equally weighted (where each stock has the same weight and performance contribution to the index return) or price weighted (where higher-priced stocks of have a larger index impact, and vice versa).

Although the performance of competing market indexes may appear to be correlated, these outcomes can mask significant differences in the index construction methodologies used. For example, although the S&P500 Index and the Dow Jones Industrial Average may show similar performance for the US stock market, the former is a capitalization-weighted, broad market index comprising 500 constituents, while the latter is a price-weighted index covering only 30 stocks.

Indexes are typically rebalanced periodically to reflect changes to the stock market and corporate actions which can affect constituent firms (known as "index events"). For example, if an index constituent is acquired by another firm, it will be removed from the index and replaced with a new constituent. The index publisher may review the composition of the index to make sure it remains representative of the market it covers. Indexes are also subject to ad hoc changes arising from market events: for example, when a firm goes into bankruptcy.

In the early 2000s, most global index publishers introduced a "free float" calculation methodology. This reduces a stock's weighting in an index (and therefore its contribution to the market's performance) where the availability (or "float") of securities is restricted due to cross-holdings (a corporation's holdings of another company's stock), or untraded ownership stakes held by governments or founders. The adoption of a free float methodology (originally used by the International Finance Corporation for the calculation of its emerging markets indexes in the 1990s) was in part precipitated by the dot com market crash. At that time, many new issues were being included in indexes at their full market capitalization, despite the reality that sometimes less than 20% of the issued shares were actually available to investors for trading in the market.

HISTORY AND RATIONALE FOR INDEXING-TRACKING STRATEGIES

Since the late 1960s, researchers have been examining the performance of professional fund managers using risk-adjusted measures, and they have found that the majority have not outperformed the market averages, even before management fees are taken into account.[1] This empirical literature, known as the "active versus passive debate" in academic and practitioner circles, provides persuasive evidence of

  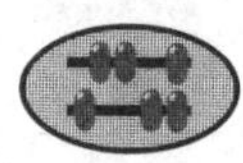   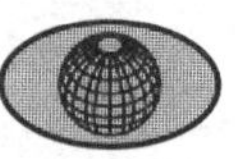   

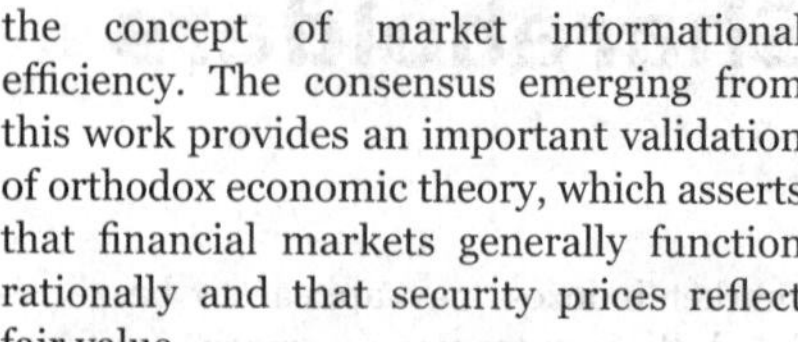

the concept of market informational efficiency. The consensus emerging from this work provides an important validation of orthodox economic theory, which asserts that financial markets generally function rationally and that security prices reflect fair value.

These research findings also spawned the development of so-called passive or index-tracking strategies in the 1970s. The first index-tracking strategy was created in 1971 by Wells Fargo (now Barclays Global Investors) for a single pension sponsor (Samsonite) and used an equally weighted portfolio. In 1973, it created a comingled fund for its trust department clients which tracked the S&P500 Index. In 1976, the Vanguard Group launched the first US index mutual fund (the Vanguard S&P500 Index Fund). Today there are numerous indexes and index-tracking products, covering stock markets, industry sectors, hedge funds, and commodities. According to Standard & Poor's, $4.85 trillion was benchmarked to its US indexes at December 31, 2007: This figure includes $1.5 trillion directly indexed to the S&P500.

The prudent investment standards which govern many pension funds and institutional investors in Anglo-Saxon economies have, since the late 1980s, largely endorsed the benefits (broad diversification with lower operating costs) of investment indexation compared to active portfolio management. In fact, the general intellectual acceptance of market efficiency has effectively reversed the traditional onus on pension fund trustees and other financial fiduciaries to employ active portfolio management strategies that seek to outperform the market while minimizing risks to capital.

Although index publishers disclaim indexes as being measures of investment merit, market pundits and academic researchers have paid surprisingly little attention to the suitability of market indexes for investment purposes, concerning themselves instead with tests of market efficiency. It is also important to note that indexes are themselves actively managed instruments: Index tracking is therefore not a passive, "buy-and-hold" investment strategy, familiar to most personal investors.

MARKET IMPACTS: PRICE AND VOLUME EFFECTS OF INDEX CHANGES

Although indexes have evolved as market measures, they form the underlying basis for index-tracking strategies whose portfolios are managed mechanistically using either full replication (where all constituents are held in their index proportions) or partial replication (a subset of stocks) techniques. Index-tracking strategies are compelled to alter portfolio holdings in accordance with changes announced by index publishers. Significant trading costs (as distinct from operating costs such as brokerage and taxes)—also known as market impact or frictions—can also arise from constituent changes when index funds (and many funds have active managers who also track market benchmarks for active portfolios) rebalance their portfolios.

Because index-tracking strategies involve no judgment or market timing, unlike active portfolio management disciplines, their transactions are price-insensitive. Thus, the growth in the scale of indexed portfolio assets has brought opportunities for arbitrageurs to profit from the potential volatility and liquidity imbalances which are caused by index reconstitution events. For example, arbitrageurs may purchase (or sell) securities due to be included in (or removed from) the index prior to the date of the index event. Index-tracking funds are compelled to buy (or sell) "at any cost" to rebalance their portfolios to the revised index composition.

The direct implications of index reconstitution events have been examined in the academic literature since the mid-1980s. In 1986, Harvard economist Andre Shleifer highlighted the price and volume effects' implications for stocks in the S&P500 Index.[2] He concluded that index tracking created downward sloping demand curves due to the price inelasticity of demand created for these stocks. Several subsequent studies in the United States and the United Kingdom have also documented significant price and volume effects for stocks added and deleted from stock market indexes. Other research, however, has found that prices subsequently reverse over longer time horizons. These findings do not acknowledge the costs of price volatility experienced by investors.

In response to the practical concerns of clients and stakeholders, index publishers announce index changes in advance of the actual index reconstitution events. This has had the effect of bringing forward the volatility associated with these changes from the actual index event date.

CASE STUDY

News Corporation's Inclusion in the S&P500 Index

News Corporation is an integrated and diversified media company with assets of approximately $62 billion as at September 30, 2008. The company has global operations but earns the bulk of its income in the United States. In April 2004, its chairman and CEO Rupert Murdoch announced that the company was seeking shareholder approval to consolidate the ownership of its Australian businesses and to move the company's legal domicile from Australia to the US state of Delaware.

In explaining the change of domicile to shareholders, the directors highlighted the important benefits that were expected to accrue from inclusion of the company in the leading US equity benchmarks, especially the S&P500 Index. They noted that this would:

- correct the "under investment" by US institutions, which only held approximately 52% of its shares compared to peer firms such as Disney (72%), Time Warner (78%), and Viacom (87%);
- increase demand from US institutions that were currently prevented from buying non-US stocks;
- increase trading in the company's shares, which should narrow the gap between the prices of its voting common stock and nonvoting common stock;
- lower the costs of raising equity in a deeper market: the S&P500 Index's total market capitalization exceeded US$10 trillion, 20 times larger than the Australian market benchmark, the S&P/ASX 200 Index.

On November 3, 2004, the company announced that its reincorporation had received court approval and that the New York Stock Exchange would become its primary listing. On November 17, 2004, Standard & Poor's preannounced that News Corporation would be included in the S&P500 index (at the close of trading on December 17, 2004) and that the stock would be removed from its Australian indexes in three additional equal installments. On the date of News Corporation's reincorporation announcement, and on the days it was phased out of the Australian market benchmark, over 195 million shares worth approximately Aus$4.6 billion were traded on the Australian Stock Exchange—approximately one-third of this turnover occurring on the day of the reincorporation announcement alone. Since changing its domicile, the company has raised $5.15 billion in debt securities and started a $6 billion stock repurchase program.

"You can increase your brain power three to fivefold simply by laughing and having fun before working on a problem." Doug Hall

     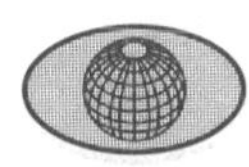   

CONCLUSION

Indexes are an essential tool for measuring financial market performance characteristics. Because there has been a dramatic increase in the scale of funds that directly track market indexes and relative performance monitoring by actively managed portfolios, gaining and maintaining membership of an "index club" is a critically important goal for financial executives.

Compared to nonconstituents, firms included in market indexes have the potential for preferential access to capital, significantly greater research coverage in the investment community, and trading liquidity. Index inclusion can increase demand and stock prices. On the downside, firms excluded from indexes typically lose institutional ownership and can experience considerable price declines in their stocks especially in the short term. The case study shows how the phenomenon of index events creates substantial stock turnover and volatility, despite the reality that no significant changes have occurred in a company's business operations.

▸▸ MAKING IT HAPPEN

- Be index-aware: Membership of the "index club" is important because it confers higher demand for stocks and trading liquidity arising from institutional ownership.
- Find out which stock market indexes cover your firm or your market. What are the inclusion and exclusion criteria used by the publishers, and how is your firm classified in terms of its market value and industry representation? Even if your stock is not included in a broad market index, it may be a potential constituent in an industry-specific or customized index.
- Financial managers need to make sure that index publishers are well informed about their business operations and ownership structures. They should also be aware that index publishers are generally reluctant to delete firms from indexes because this creates excessive index turnover.
- Given that indexes are generally market capitalization-weighted, are profitable merger and takeover opportunities available which will increase the equity base (and thus index size) of the firm?

▸▸ MORE INFO

Books:

Ali, Paul, Geof Stapledon, and Martin Gold. *Corporate Governance and Investment Fiduciaries*. Sydney, Australia: Lawbook, 2003.

Levy, Haim, and Thierry Post. *Investments*. Harlow, UK: Pearson Education, 2005.

Malkiel, Burton G. *A Random Walk Down Wall Street: The Time-tested Strategy for Successful Investing*. 9th ed. New York: W. W. Norton & Company, 2007.

Report:

Gold, Martin. "Fiduciary finance and the pricing of financial claims: A conceptual approach to investment." PhD thesis, University of Wollongong, 2007.

Websites:

FTSE Group/ Financial Times indices: www.ftse.com/Indices

Morgan Stanley Capital International indexes: www.msci.com

Standard & Poor's indexes: www.sandp.com

See Also:

Burton Malkiel (p. 1174)

A Random Walk Down Wall Street: A Time-tested Strategy for Successful Investing (p. 1313)

NOTES

1 For a review of this literature and the debate, see Gold (2007).

2 Shleifer, A. "Do demand curves for stocks slope down?" *Journal of Finance* 41:3 (1986): 579–90.

"It depends on how we look at things, and not on how they are in themselves." Carl Gustav Jung

     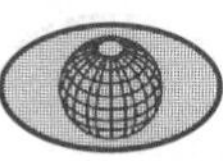   

Viewpoint: Mark Mobius

Emerging Markets: Reflecting on 2008 and Looking Ahead to 2009[1]

INTRODUCTION

Mark Mobius, PhD, Managing Director, joined Templeton in 1987 as President of the Templeton Emerging Markets Fund, Inc. He currently directs the analysts based in Templeton's 15 emerging markets offices and manages the emerging markets portfolios. Dr Mobius has spent more than 30 years working in emerging markets all over the world. He was appointed Joint Chairman of the World Bank and Organization for Economic Cooperation and Development's Global Corporate Governance Forum Investor Responsibility Taskforce.

Dr Mobius has received the following awards: Emerging Markets Equity Manager of the Year 2001 from International Money Marketing; Ten Top Money Managers of the 20th Century in a survey by the Carson Group in 1999; Number One Global Emerging Market Fund in the 1998 Reuters Survey; 1994 First in Business Money Manager of the Year from CNBC; Closed-End Fund Manager of the Year in 1993 from Morningstar; and Investment Trust Manager of the Year 1992 from the *Sunday Telegraph*.

Dr Mobius earned bachelor's and master's degrees from Boston University, and a PhD in economics and political science from the Massachusetts Institute of Technology. He is the author of the books *Trading with China*, *The Investor's Guide to Emerging Markets*, *Mobius on Emerging Markets*, and *Passport to Profits*.

BULL AND BEAR MARKETS

2008 was the year that ended a long bull run in emerging markets. The MSCI Emerging Markets index declined 53% in $ terms in 2008, after surging an astonishing 400% in the preceding five years. During that five-year period, some regions performed even better with the BRIC (Brazil, Russia, India, China) and Latin American indices jumping as much as 700%, while Eastern European markets soared 500%. The recent fall is part of the natural cyclicality of public markets, which experience both bull and bear periods. The important point to remember is that bull markets last longer than bear markets and bull markets go up more in percentage terms than bear markets go down. Since we started the first emerging market fund in 1987, there have been nine bull and bear periods. The average length of the bear markets was six months, while the average for bull markets was 22 months. While the average decline of the bear markets was 32%, the average increase in the bull markets was 113%. We expect these patterns to be sustained in the coming decades.

GLOBAL FINANCIAL CRISIS

Global financial markets during 2008 have been the most volatile since the 1930s. The last serious bear market originated in Asia in 1997, but the 2008 crisis originated in the US. Most critical for 2008 was the unraveling of the highly leveraged derivative structure of subprime mortgages in the US. This has resulted in global financial panic. Extreme risk aversion has led to a drying up of liquidity, tight credit conditions, problems for companies based on highly leveraged finance models, and the collapse of several major financial firms in the US and Europe, as well as high volatility in global emerging markets.

CURRENCIES

During 2008, emerging market currencies weakened against the dollar as a result of the rush to the dollar and US Treasury instruments. Investors sought "safe havens" and US Treasuries were considered the safest haven. US corporations were faced with a liquidity squeeze and sold assets overseas to remit funds home. The fall in emerging market currencies, however, is quite different from the currency crises in the 1980s and 1990s. At those times, emerging market currencies were impacted by poor fundamentals such as balance of payment crises, excessive debt, underdeveloped banking systems, and heavy dollar borrowing. At that same time, the US economic fundamentals were good. The situation is now reversed and the weakening of emerging market currencies was caused by the rush into the dollar by global investors. However, with a higher return on capital and higher growth prospects, emerging markets should eventually attract capital again.

GOVERNMENT INTERVENTION

The major difference between the current global environment and the Great Depression in the 1930s has been the earlier and rapid proactive approach of global governments to take unprecedented actions to support their economies and financial systems.

Recognizing the severity of the credit crunch, in October 2008 major developed and emerging central banks lowered interest rates in an unprecedented globally coordinated monetary policy effort. This was followed by the implementation of fiscal stimulus measures and loosening monetary policies from governments and central banks in developed as well as emerging markets. Thus far in 2009, more than $1 trillion had been pledged by governments around the world to rejuvenate their domestic economies, including China, the US, Germany, the UK, Taiwan, Spain, Japan, South Korea, Russia, France, Australia, Hong Kong, Singapore, and Malaysia.

FRONTIER MARKETS

In addition to emerging markets, frontier markets also present attractive investment opportunities. Frontier markets include economies at the lower end of the development spectrum. They are generally smaller and less developed than other emerging markets but have the potential to grow at a fast pace and could become tomorrow's emerging markets. They are where many emerging markets were 20 years ago when

"**If you look at life one way there is always cause for alarm.**" Elizabeth Bowen

     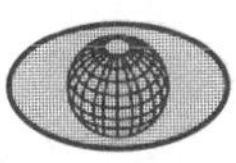   

we started our first emerging markets fund. By offering investors the opportunity to invest in a "younger generation of emerging markets," frontier markets provide an attractive investment opportunity. Many of the characteristics that have made emerging markets fascinating to investors are now becoming increasingly evident in frontier markets. These characteristics include positive economic trends such as high growth, high potential for capital market development, as well as the presence of attractively valued companies.

SMALL CAP COMPANIES

Another interesting area is emerging market small capitalized companies which have the potential to deliver substantial capital appreciation as they transition to becoming well-established, large-sized companies. Identifying them early and investing in them with a long-term perspective can be highly rewarding. Many emerging markets have relatively higher GDP growth, trade surpluses, high foreign reserves, as well as strong investment and domestic demand —an environment where well-run, small cap companies can flourish.

BRIC COUNTRIES

We expect the BRIC economies to continue to be a key driver of global economic growth. They are among the fastest growing economies in the world. The four markets together account for more than 40% of the world population. Domestic demand growth also remains robust. Moreover, Brazil and Russia are resource-rich countries and, although there has been a recent fall in commodity prices, the longer trend for commodity prices is up and these countries will benefit from global demand for oil, steel, aluminum, pulp, and other commodities. China continues to take great strides towards becoming a major global player. Its foreign reserves recently surpassed $1.9 trillion. India continues to be a key center for major sectors such as pharmaceuticals and software.

"3 Cs" INVESTMENT THEMES

Within this environment, we have focused on the "3 Cs" investment themes: Consumer, commodities, and convergence. With rising per capita income and strong demand for consumer and other goods, the earnings growth outlook for consumer-oriented stocks remains positive. We continue to like commodity stocks because many of them have declined significantly below their intrinsic worth, and we expect the global demand for commodities to continue its long-term growth. Additionally, convergence between global economies will continue to provide good opportunities for financially strong companies, which will take larger market shares and consolidate their industries globally.

DECOUPLING

2008 has showed us that the developed markets of the US, UK, and Europe cannot be considered to be "safe" and less volatile. However, that is not to say that emerging markets were not and will not be hit by the developments taking place in developed markets. While there has been much talk about emerging markets "decoupling" from the US market, the reality is that in this day and age decoupling is not possible given the tremendous improvements in communications, money transfers, and world trade. There has been a move in recent decades towards more intense globalization and interdependence between world economies. But, whereas in the past the US was the center as the largest economy in the world, the US economy's dominance is waning, as other economies continue to grow at much faster rates. This has especially been the case in the emerging market countries, where we are seeing new centers of economic wealth and growth. China, Russia, Brazil, and India are clear examples. Moreover, there is a great deal of new growth taking place in the world today.

EMERGING MARKETS REMAIN ATTRACTIVE

Given the steep market decline, investors have begun to shift their focus to the increasingly attractive valuations in emerging markets. Many markets are trading at single-digit price-to-earnings ratios, with many companies trading at below their net asset value. Stock prices rebounded in December 2008 as investors sought to benefit from the attractive investment opportunities in the asset class, allowing emerging markets to rebound from the year-low in October 2008.

While we believe that the longer-term outlook for emerging markets remains positive due to the relatively strong fundamental characteristics and faster growth rate than their developed counterparts, 2009 is expected to be challenging. We can expect more volatility in view of slowing growth and recession concerns in major world economies, volatile exchange rates and commodity prices, and a global credit crunch. While inflation was a major concern in 2008, a correction in commodity prices eased fuel and food prices in many economies, which allowed inflation to subside in the latter part of the year. This has enabled emerging market countries to not worry about higher inflation but take measures to stimulate growth by lowering interest rates and take other fiscal measures.

The perception of risk in emerging markets is now beginning to shift as investors realize that: (1) emerging markets have become net creditors with vast holdings of foreign exchange reserves; (2) emerging markets continue to record much higher economic growth compared to the developed countries; and (3) the debt levels of many emerging market countries are lower than that of developed countries. China now has $1.900 billion in foreign reserves, Russia has $437 billion, South Korea's total is $200 billion, Taiwan has $281 billion, and India has $246 billion. The average economic growth in 2009 for emerging markets is expected to be 3.8% compared to a 0.8% decline for developed countries. For example, while China is expected to grow by 8.1%, the US economy is expected to contract by 0.6%. The total debt to GDP ratio of emerging countries averages 94%, while the ratio for developed countries is 233%. Japan's ratio is 365%, the US is 240%, while the ratio for China is 130%, and Brazil is 90%.

Furthermore, we have already seen corrections in global equity markets, including emerging markets, bringing markets down to even more attractive levels. In most cases, the undemanding valuations in emerging markets have already discounted the weaker earning prospects, and thus a return of bargain investors could see stock prices rebound in the future. While no one can predict the absolute bottom of a market, history has shown us that the best time to buy is when everyone is despondently selling. This enables us to pick up stocks at more appealing prices.

NOTES

1 All figures correct as of December 31, 2008.

"What is of first importance is not the religious or non-religious character of the work done, but the inner attitude in which it is done." Sri Aurobindo

  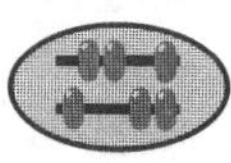   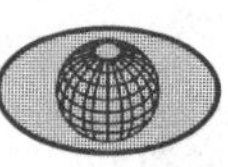   

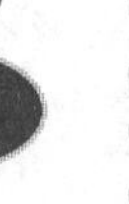

Interdependence of National and International Markets: The Foreign Information Transmission (FIT) Model

by Boulis M. Ibrahim and Janusz Brzeszczynski

EXECUTIVE SUMMARY

- International financial markets transmit signals to each other through direct and indirect channels. Those processes can be analyzed for volatility of prices as well as for returns.
- Transmission channels exist across different geographical regions and various asset classes.
- The "meteor shower" effect is the transmission of signals across markets in different regions, usually in sequences in which they trade. The "heat wave" effect is the transmission of return or volatility signals within the same market over time.
- Information about the existence of meteor showers and heat waves, such as their sign, strength, direction, stability, and statistical and economic significance, can lead to better and more profitable designs of investment strategies on stock, currency, and other financial markets.

INTRODUCTION

The interdependence of national and international financial markets, both in returns and volatility, is well documented in the finance literature. Twenty-four-hour markets, such as the currency market, and less-continuous ones, such as stock markets, are known to exhibit correlation in returns and volatility both over time and across countries or regions. In many cases, such correlation has been increasing in recent decades. This apparent integration has been rationalized by increasing globalization, intensified international capital flows and investments, faster information transfer, harmonization of international regulations, increasing trade and market order flow, as well as enhanced alignment of economic scope, scale, and policy.

Engle, Ito, and Lin, in 1990, introduced the financial equivalent to the astronomical and meteorological phenomena of meteor showers and heat waves, as the interregional and region-specific persistence in volatility. The "meteor shower" (MS) effect refers to the transmission of information, as captured by volatility, across markets (when they trade in different regions and time zones). The "heat wave" (HW) effect is the transmission of information internally within the same market. The MS and HW effects are not mutually exclusive and, hence, during any period of time both of them can co-exist, even though one may dominate.

The MS persistence, or clustering, of volatility has been initially documented between only a few pairs of international stock markets, and for major foreign exchange rates in the currency market. Recently, however, evidence from the currency market has been extended, and innovative new methodology enabled wider and more thorough analyses of stock markets.

INTERDEPENDENCE IN CURRENCY MARKETS

There exists strong empirical evidence that information signals in the shape of volatility are transmitted, or "spill over," in the currency market. Some studies have analyzed foreign exchange rates in five distinct regions of trading activity over the entire 24-hour day, namely: Asia, Asia–Europe overlap, Europe, Europe–America overlap, and America. Based on such time scales and geographical delineation, regional volatility models have been developed, in which volatility in one region is allowed to be a function of previous volatility in that region ("heat wave effect"), and volatility in other regions ("meteor shower effect"). The resulting evidence from empirical tests using historical data shows that in the currency market, the HW effect of own-region volatility spillover over time is usually statistically stronger, and more economically important than the MS effect across regions.[1]

Some of those studies use indicative trading quotes made by currency dealers, while others analyze unique proprietorship data of actual currency transactions reported by the main computer trading centers in London, Tokyo, and New York. They also investigate information linkages as measured by four variables beside volatility; namely, exchange rate return, direction of return, trading activity, and order flow.

In returns and return direction, there exist small informational linkages across trading regions, but not sufficiently significant to be of economic importance. Neither the HW nor the MS effects seem to explain much of the variation over time in the returns of major exchange rates.

These effects, however, seem to explain much more of the variation of volatility over time of these currency pairs. This statistical significance is also economically important, but the economic significance of the HW effect is much larger than that of the MS effect. As far as the smaller MS effect is concerned, it is much more pronounced between the trading region in which the shock originated and the next region in the chronological sequence of the 24-hour trading day, than between regions that are not chronologically sequential.

HW and MS also manage to explain some of the variation in trading activity, with economic significance having the same pattern as that of volatility. In order flow, which is often used as a proxy for information about economic fundamentals, HW and MS effects are detectable, too; however, economic significance can be attributed only to meteor showers.

INTERDEPENDENCE IN STOCK MARKETS

There is documented evidence of linkages, contagion effects, and transmission of signals at times of financial crisis between international stock markets. During periods of financial turmoil correlations between the returns of various assets tend to increase significantly. Such a phenomenon is called the contagion effect, because the shock from one market in financial crisis is transmitted to other markets around the globe, which often results in a similar price reaction as the one observed in the market first affected by the crisis. This happens frequently even when the macroeconomic fundamentals in the countries to which the signals are trans-

  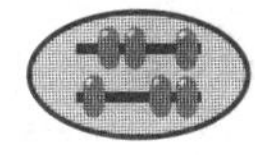   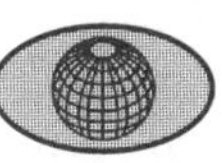   

mitted are healthy. For example, the "Asian Flu" of 1997, the "Russian Virus" of 1998, and the American "Credit Crunch" of 2007, which are names of local financial crises, have spread far beyond the local markets of the countries where the financial turmoil originated. Such situations are often explained by financial or economic interdependence, and the herding behavior of international investors, as well as by other behavioral finance theories.

There is also some evidence that larger stock markets transmit information to smaller or emerging ones. The New York Stock Exchange, for example, seems to transmit news, in the form of return signals, to Europe and Asia, while no single foreign market seems able significantly to explain the movements of the US market. Moreover, earlier empirical evidence suggested that the MS effect between international stock markets situated in specific global regions is stronger than the HW effect that exists between markets of the same region.

Such evidence, in the main, has been reported by analyses that use methodologies blighted with considerable shortcomings. Correlations between international stock market returns have been the main measure of integration, or strength of signal transmission. Linear regressions and similar techniques of measuring association mainly produced static estimates that reflect average values over time, even if the variables involved are incorporated with methodology that takes into account variations over time. For example, parameter coefficients of the commonly used econometric models are usually assumed to be static or constant over time, and so are the parameter coefficients involved in capturing time variations in volatility in popular models of volatility clustering—the phenomena that high volatility tends to be followed by high volatility, and low volatility by low volatility, and the modeling of which had won Robert Engle the Nobel Prize in Economics in 2003. These, now traditional, methodologies do not reveal clearly the changing nature of market integration, the varying degree of signal strength, or the changing sensitivity of markets to information from the same region or other regions. Consequently, we could gain some knowledge of the direction of relationships between markets on average over time, but had no good way of knowing the changing strength of these relationships, their stability over time, or what factors affect strength and stability.[2] It is akin to attempting to measure the amplitude of sea waves by putting a straight rigid measuring rod, such as a ruler, horizontally across the waves.

What are the implications of the knowledge about the nature of transmission effects around the international financial markets? First, investors and financial analysts can produce better forecasts of financial assets prices. Second, trading strategies based on such predictions can be made smarter by, for example, varying the magnitude of financial leverage that can be applied, depending on the strength and direction of transmission relationships. Third, investments based on such knowledge may lead to much higher profits than other strategies that ignore the information about the interdependence of international markets.

FOREIGN INFORMATION TRANSMISSION (FIT) MODELS

This new methodology, introduced by Ibrahim and Brzeszczynski (2009), ushers a solution to the shortcomings of static techniques, and offers means by which answers could be found to questions that static techniques are unable to handle.

In order to present such models and illustrate their capabilities, consider equation (1). This is a regression of y on x (which could be, for example, the returns of two different financial assets, such as returns of the DJIA and NIKKEI indices) and with an intercept alpha, α, and slope beta, β, that can vary over time. The time subscript, t, can be thought of as daily intervals. The innovation in this methodology is in how changes over time in alpha and beta are modeled. This is formalized in equations (2) and (3). The second equation models the daily deviation from average of the intercept alpha, and the third equation models the daily deviation from average of the slope beta. They relate to tomorrow's deviations to today's value, and to the degree to which these values relates to news from another variable z (deviations in variable z). The variable z could be, for example, the return of one more stock market index, such as the FTSE. In this setup, the parameter coefficients a and c capture the extent of autocorrelations over time in intercept and slope deviations, while the parameter coefficients b and d capture the effect of autocovariances in intercept and slope with news (deviations) from the variable z. This type of model is estimated using a combination of a linear projection statistical technique called the Kalman Filter and Maximum Likelihood, and the parameter coefficients that are estimated are α^{-}, β^{-}, a, b, c, d and variances of the error terms w, v_{α}, and v_{β}.

$$y_t = \alpha_t + \beta_t x_t + w_t \quad (1)$$

$$(\alpha_{t+1} - \alpha^{-}) = [a + b(z_t - z^{-})](\alpha_t - \alpha^{-}) + v_{\alpha,t+1} \quad (2)$$

$$(\beta_{t+1} - \beta^{-}) = [c + d(z_t - z^{-})](\beta_t - \beta^{-}) + v_{\beta,t+1} \quad (3)$$

CASE STUDY

The FIT model is estimated for the case where the variables y, x, and z represent daily returns of the Dow Jones Industrial Average (DJIA) of the New York Stock Exchange, NIKKEI 225 of the Tokyo Stock Exchange, and the Financial Times Stock Exchange (FTSE) 100 index of the London Stock Exchange, respectively.

In the historical sample period, from January 4, 1995 to September 2004, the only significant parameter estimates are as follows: $\beta^{-} = 0.082$, $a = -0.741$, $b = 32.276$, and $d = 31.899$ (0.002, 0.232, and 0.010 are the standard deviations of the error terms w_t, v_{α}, and v_{β}, respectively).

These values indicate a significant "meteor shower" effect from the NIKKEI to the DJIA, and that changes over time in both the level and intensity of this "meteor shower" are affected significantly by "foreign" news or signals transmitted from FTSE. In particular, good news of a unit magnitude in London (i.e., a positive signal of unit deviation from average in FTSE returns) is expected to affect the intensity of the NIKKEI–DJIA "meteor shower" by a factor of 31.899.

This factor and its estimate would not be available from conventional models, such as an ordinary least squares regression of returns of the DJIA on those of the NIKKEI 225.

This type of knowledge will obviously have strategic benefits. Traders are informed about the direction of the forecast for the DJIA index (which tells them if the market in New York is likely to go up or down), and its strength based on the signal from the NIKKEI. This signal can be additionally strengthened (or weakened) by what happens with the market that trades in the intermediate time, which, in this example, is the FTSE. Such knowledge allows traders to decide whether to open long or short positions in the DJIA market, and benefit from varying the financial leverage, because the information about the strength of the signal enables a proper assessment of the probability that the forecast's direction will be correct. In such cases, varying the leverage can lead to significantly higher profits.[4]

"J. P. Morgan, when asked what the stock market will do, replied, 'It will fluctuate'." Unknown source

  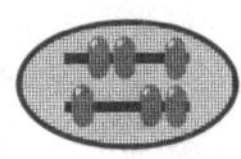   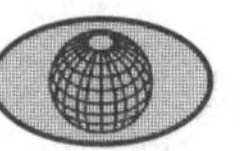   

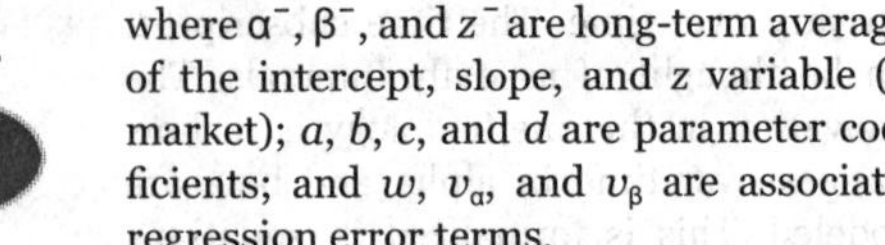

where $\bar{\alpha}$, $\bar{\beta}$, and $\bar{z}$ are long-term averages of the intercept, slope, and z variable (or market); a, b, c, and d are parameter coefficients; and w, v_α, and v_β are associated regression error terms.

In order to put this methodology in a financial context, let the variables y, x, and z represent returns of major stock markets in the three main regions or time zones, namely Asia, Europe, and America. Also, adjust the time subscript t to properly account for the chronological sequence in which markets in these regions trade. In this context, the estimated long-term average intercept and slope parameters $\bar{\alpha}$ and $\bar{\beta}$ measure the nature of the direct relationship between stock markets in Europe and Asia. Other parameters in equations (2) and (3) measure the degree to which deviations from that relationship are sensitive to the preceding day's values. In other words, they capture the degree of daily persistence of "meteor showers" between Europe and Asia. These parameters also measure the impact of news from America on the daily persistence of the MS between these two regions.

If the variable x is made to represent the previous day's returns in Asia, instead of returns in Europe, then $\bar{\beta}$ measures the average intensity of the effect of past Asian returns on contemporary returns in the same region, i.e., the intensity of HW in Asia. In this context, the estimated parameters a and c measure the degree of daily persistence of HW in Asia, and the estimated parameters b and d measure the impact of news in America on this persistence in Asian heat waves. In other words, the FIT model gives knowledge about changes over time in the intensity of heat waves and meteor showers.

Another important, new feature of the FIT methodology is its ability to distinguish between direct and indirect channels of information transmission. In contrast to the above allocation of regions to variables, in which $\bar{\alpha}$ and $\bar{\beta}$ measured the direct relationship between stock markets in Europe and Asia, let the returns of European markets enter the equations as variable z instead of x. In this instance, the estimated parameters b and d will measure the indirect impact of European news on Asian markets through the effect this news has on the direct relationship between Asian markets (the y variable), and American markets (now the x variable). Therefore, the FIT model can measure both the direct and indirect effects of markets on others.[3]

CONCLUSION

There exists evidence that international financial markets transmit signals to each other through direct and indirect channels. The relationships of this type have been identified for different assets and various geographical regions.

Knowledge about such transmission mechanisms, their statistical and economic significance, sign, strength, direction, and stability, can lead to the construction of profitable investment strategies for stocks, currencies, and other financial instruments.

▸▸ MAKING IT HAPPEN

- Models of signal transmission across financial markets (both in returns and volatility) can be used to build complex investment strategies. For example, the FIT model can be applied to forecast the indices of international stock markets, and such forecasts can be then converted into signals giving the trader information necessary to decide whether to open long or short positions (i.e., to buy or to sell given financial asset), and in what leverage.
- In practice, such signals can be used to trade index futures, since trading in derivatives is a less costly environment than that of trading the shares that compose the index itself. Recently, a few spread-betting platforms have started to offer bets on the direction of change of financial instruments. They have relatively low costs of trading, but there is no guarantee that their prices will always perfectly reflect the movements of the prices of the corresponding assets in the real markets.
- Models such as FIT allow investors to profit from both directional (up or down) movements of the price of financial assets. Their major advantage is forecasting the direction of change of financial instruments' value (and some of them, such as FIT, also assess the strength of the signal given the deviations from steady states, which provides additional benefit in the form of information about the likelihood or probability, which can directly help traders to decide on the degree of financial leverage they should apply to their trades).
- Every investment strategy based on the signal transmission models should be accompanied by additional tools, such as properly optimized stop-loss (SL) and take-profit (TP) orders, filters on the signaling variables, and others.

▸▸ MORE INFO

Articles:

Cai, F., E. Howorka, and J. Wongswan. "Informational linkages across trading regions: Evidence from foreign exchange markets." *Journal of International Money and Finance* 27:5 (2008): 1215–1243.

Engle, R. F., T. Ito, and W.-L. Lin. "Meteor showers or heat waves? Heteroscedastic intra-daily volatility in the foreign exchange market." *Econometrica* 59:8 (1990): 525–542.

Ibrahim, B. M., and J. Brzeszczynski. "Interregional and region-specific transmission of international stock market returns: The role of foreign information." *Journal of International Money and Finance* 28:2 (2009): 322–343.

Ito, T., R. F. Engle, and W.-L. Lin. "Where does the meteor shower come from? The role of stochastic policy coordination." *Journal of International Economics* 32:3–4 (1992): 221–240.

Melvin, M., and B. Peiers Melvin. "The global transmission of volatility in the foreign exchange market." *The Review of Economics and Statistics* 85:3 (2003): 670–679.

See Also:

- Eugene Fama (p. 1164)
- How The Stock Market Works (p. 1274)

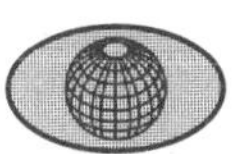

NOTES

1 "Stronger" statistical significance indicates larger and more statistically significant parameter estimates. Economic significance in the reviewed studies is assessed by using impulse response analysis. This is a "sensitivity analysis" technique that measures the effect on significance if shocks in the determinants are introduced (i.e., if the determinants are increased or decreased by a few percentages).

2 The classical approach of dealing with changing intercepts and slopes (beta coefficients) often makes use of dummy variables to test time-related aspects, such as structural breaks and robustness over various subperiods. These are obviously limited by the empirical estimation requirement that the number of "breaks" that could be analyzed or subperiods in which a series could be divided cannot be equal to the number of observations (for example, one cannot analyze the dynamics, and hence dynamic forecasts, of daily movements in intercepts and slopes using dummy variables of daily or lower frequency).

3 This feature is different, and in many ways superior, to the use of interaction terms, or the omission of one variable to check whether another captures a combined effect. The difference is that the FIT model does not simply capture the impact of one variable on another, and how this impact changes over time, but allows for testing which factors have an impact on this impact.

4 Ibrahim and Brzeszczynski (2009) present numerical results of the superior profitability of similar trading strategies based on the FIT model, over those based on a conventional OLS regression model. Average daily profits (net of transaction costs at 0.15%) of 0.17% in excess of that provided by strategies based on conventional OLS regressions are reported for daily trading strategies over a period of one month. Profitability results over periods longer than a month, and at transaction cost levels other than 0.15%, are also reported in Ibrahim and Brzeszczynski (2009).

"Drop the idea that you are Atlas carrying the world on your shoulders. The world would go on even without you. Don't take yourself so seriously." Norman Vincent Peale

  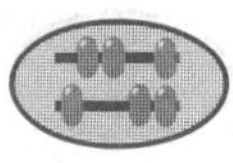   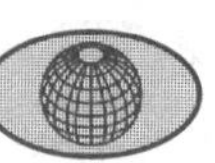   

Investing Cash: Back to Basics
by Mark Camp and Emma Du Haney

EXECUTIVE SUMMARY

- Have regard to risk and security when deciding where to invest.
- A guarantee is only as good as the giver. There is no such thing as an absolute guarantee.
- When investing cash:
  - use internal resources if there is a fully functioning professional treasury;
  - use your clearing bank or custodian;
  - use a specialized investment manager;
  - use suitable pooled funds (money market funds), perhaps through a treasury portal.
- Money market funds offer different yields and returns. Before investing, prioritize between yield, security, and liquidity, and carry out detailed due diligence.
- Simplicity and transparency are key factors.
- The current crisis has highlighted the importance of liquidity and credit.

LESSONS FROM RECENT EXPERIENCE IN FINANCIAL MARKETS

It has become crystal clear that cash must be treated as a separate asset class. This means taking care when considering how, and with whom, cash should be held and invested.

It is equally clear that risk is a very relevant factor for cash. Institutional investors have discovered in the past year that so-called safe cash investments have not been as secure as they thought. For many years, investors have ignored the fundamental principle that extra yield is associated with extra risk. It is now clear that the especially attractive rates paid by Icelandic banks came with significant additional risk.

In times of plenty we tend to overlook or downplay risks and concentrate on the rewards. All we tend to think about is who is top of the league table so that I can maximize my interest income. What can be all too easily forgotten is that the return *of* your money is always more important than the return *on* your money.

A flight to quality, or perceived safety, can quickly become an unstoppable tsunami that can take the good with the bad; witness the ever-lengthening queue outside Northern Rock (a British bank) last September, and the subsequent effect on confidence in all British banks. Everyone now wants a guarantee, and an absolutely safe investment.

What does "guarantee" itself mean? We now know that it is only as good as the counterparty that gives it. Having to worry about counterparty risk is something most of us thought was the thankless and purely box-ticking task of compliance officers, or the credit committee. Now we know better. It must be stressed that it is very unusual for an institutional investor to receive a specific guarantee on a cash placement, except to the extent that a bank, or investment product, receives overt support from a relevant authority that one trusts.

What no one wants to say is that, ultimately, there is no absolute guarantee. This may seem more obvious now, after a year in which we have seen that AAA credit ratings do not guarantee security, and that even a government guarantee is only as good as the economic strength of the country that gives it.

The whole financial world is built on confidence, and if that is fatally cracked then the whole pack of cards can come down, with disastrous economic consequences for us all. That is why all the major governments and central banks, in both West and East, finally acted as decisively as they did toward the end of 2008, coughing up some $6.75 trillion to save the world. This is equivalent to some 10% of the entire $65 trillion global economy [CIA World Factbook 2007], and has been used to recapitalize banks, buy up toxic assets (including subprime-related assets), make loans to financial institutions, and give state guarantees to get the wholesale markets moving again. Even with the size of this unprecedented rescue, risks remain in the financial system according to a recent Bank of England financial stability report.

SO WHAT CHOICES DOES A TREASURER HAVE WHEN INVESTING CASH?

Very large treasury operations. The very largest holders of cash can afford to run a well-resourced internal treasury, including a fully functioning cash desk. Aside from the major banks, however, such entities are few in number, as you have to be investing very large amounts on a daily basis to do this properly.

Treasuries with small or intermittent balances. At the other end of the scale, if one has cash balances that arise only intermittently, or if they are less than $1.5 million, leaving them with your main clearing bank(s) (having done appropriate due diligence and negotiated the best available rates) is probably the best approach.

Netting and pooling are a must. It is assumed that any treasurer will have already maximized any pooling, netting, and aggregating possibilities, across currencies if necessary, as these always offer the best value operationally and economically—and usually in terms of security too.

For treasuries in the middle ground the main strategic options are as follows.

1. Utilize Internal Resources

This has been an attractive option in the past, often because it is considered a low-cost option. But what are the risks involved with this approach? Even if one hires a good cash specialist, where is the backup if he or she falls under the proverbial bus? Where is the backup for the credit specialist? It is no longer good enough to rely solely on the credit rating agencies, or review the agreed counterparty list once a year. Instrument and counterparty credit ratings are just one of the guides to utilize, and they can, and should, be challenged from time to time. Certainly, just calling your friendly money broker from time to time for advice cannot now be considered best practice.

2. Outsource to a Specialist Provider/Treasury Portal

The bank. The first option is to see what your clearing bank, or custodian (if relevant), can provide, especially if cash can be automatically swept on a daily basis. The problem here is risk concentration with just one, or only a handful, of counterparties. A good example of this type of situation is a hedge fund with a single prime broker. Not only does the fund have a serious risk with the prime broker as the derivative counterparty, but the cash margin/collateral would typically be held with the same party, doubling the counterparty risk. Before the Bear Stearns and Lehman Brothers

"**Successful investing is anticipating the anticipations of others.**" John Maynard Keynes

     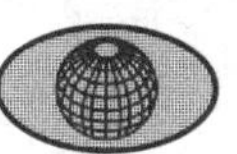 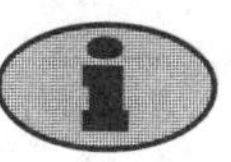 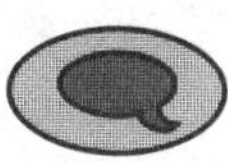 

troubles, the main global prime brokers were considered too big to fail; this is not the position now.

Investment manager. If an institution has large and relatively stable cash balances to invest, then an investment manager can be approached to run a segregated cash mandate. The advantage of this approach is that you get to choose the investment manager, and you can also specify the investment parameters and benchmark, and in that way control risk. Invested cash should also be held with a third-party custodian, thus ring-fencing the assets from the investment manager. The downside is that it is a relatively cumbersome and expensive process to set up in the first place, and it is not very flexible. A serious bespoke cash investment manager will usually require a large minimum investment balance ($150 million plus), and/or minimum fees. Frequent redemption, or movements generally in the mandate, will not be welcomed, as they can materially affect investment strategy and performance. Such arrangements best suit long-term investment cash, and not volatile cash investment.

Pooled funds. Money market funds have been invaluable to many corporate and institutional treasurers in recent years; freeing them from the task of spreading their funds around the various banks. However, money market funds come in many guises, and, as some investors have found to their cost, some of these funds have invested in assets that have proved to be far from low risk.

Treasury portals. Use of portals is extensive in the United States, and brings operational efficiencies if one is a multi-fund user. Such portals are now available in Europe.

MONEY MARKET FUNDS

Let's remind ourselves why money market funds became so attractive. They now account for some 40%, or $4 trillion, of all cash held in the United States. This reflects a 25% rate of growth over the last 12 months, as investors have generally seen SEC registered (Rule 2a-7) money market funds as a safe haven, in spite of a few funds exhibiting obvious stress that has required promoter support, and the well-publicized failure of both "The Reserve" and the "Lehman Funds". However, what this overall growth disguises is a clear move by US institutional investors away from traditional so-called "prime" funds, to US Treasury and government-backed security money market funds, even though the yields on such funds are very low, and even went negative for a short period.

This trend has been much less noticeable with European-domiciled money market funds, although there are now a small number of euro-denominated government securities, and one sterling government fund that has been recently launched. Demand for these new funds has largely been from European subsidiaries of US multinationals, and it remains to be seen whether such funds catch on with European institutional investors.

European money market funds now account for some €420bn ($500 billion) equivalent in the three main currencies, and this includes around £100bn ($145bn) plus of sterling funds.[1] The last decade has seen a very rapid growth for such funds, and although there are recent signs that growth has checked among institutional investors, it seems that high net worth investors are now taking up any slack as they move out of enhanced funds that have contracted sharply or been closed down.

However, Not All Cash Funds Are the Same

Typically, "liquidity" or "treasury-style" funds are managed to a short-dated benchmark such as 7-day Libid (London Interbank bid rate). They offer daily liquidity, carry AAA ratings, and have a constant net asset value (or stable pricing). First of all, they offer diversification—by issuer, instrument, and maturity—and to a greater degree than most institutions could achieve on their own.

Other variants of money market funds, often called cash plus or enhanced cash funds, would typically be managed to 3-month Libor (London Interbank offered rate) or similar, have two-day or longer settlement, and a variable net asset value (i.e. daily market pricing). Such funds can carry an AAA rating, but often they are lower rated. Their attraction is that they should carry a higher yield or return, because they can invest further out along the money market curve (given different benchmark and settlement requirements), and can invest in a wider range of credit instruments, including derivatives and asset-backed paper. All this depends on the extent to which they are "enhanced."

It may seem obvious now, but going forward investors will need to decide what their priorities are from an investment perspective. Security, liquidity, and yield should all be part and parcel of a money market fund, but there has to be a trade-off between yield and the first two. With the credit ratings agencies somewhat discredited, it is all the more important to seek out a professional manager who has the resources to carry out detailed credit analysis on names and instruments.

It is also worth confirming that an offshore fund is run under the IMMFA (Institutional Money Market Funds Association) Code of Practice, as this is a useful "kite mark" to have. IMMFA currently has over 20 active members, and reads like a Who's Who for the money market fund industry.

Going forward, simplicity is also going to be key. Historically, floating-rate instruments, asset-backed securities, medium-term notes and repos may have seemed ideally suited to a money market portfolio. That has proved costly for some, particularly as far as liquidity is concerned. For a pure liquidity fund, the only really acceptable instruments are deposits with reputable counterparties, certificates of deposits (CDs) issued by solid bank names, and short-dated government issued debt. Conventional floating-rate notes or CDs may play a part in some funds, but for those with liquidity as priority, the poor secondary market in these instruments needs to be factored in. The commercial paper market, meanwhile, has all but dried up, removing it as an investible option for many funds.

CURRENT ISSUES IN THE CASH WORLD

Finally, a few comments about the current state of the interbank markets. Liquidity has become a huge issue amid the ongoing financial crisis. Even instruments such as CDs with well-rated banks, which would normally be completely liquid, have become difficult to trade—indeed, the market has even been shut at times. In the United States, the Federal Reserve has recently announced that it is now giving Rule 2a-7 (treasury-style) money market funds access to the Fed window to provide them with liquidity to meet outflows, especially if these are abnormally large. The Bank of England is now committed to providing a similar facility and the European Central Bank may do something similar. A further plan to support funds is to set up a deposit insurance scheme for retail investors similar to that for bank deposits.

As a defensive move, in late September 2008 most funds increased their overnight liquidity (in sterling it was probably in the region of £20–£30 billion, or $30–$45 billion), and this dislocated the interbank markets even more, exacerbating the gap between overnight rates and Libor rates. However, this exercise came at a cost to performance, especially for those funds with a higher proportion of less liquid

"If investing is entertaining, if you're having fun, you're probably not making any money. Good investing is boring." George Soros

securities like floating-rate notes and commercial paper, whose managers' therefore felt that the funds they managed had to hold an even greater proportion in overnight investments, at a time when overnight rates were collapsing.

Sterling and Euro money market funds generally seem to have weathered the storm for now, but of late the disparity between different fund performances has been much greater than usual, as has the gap against their respective fund benchmarks. This is an area worth exploring, as it can tell you a lot about how the fund has been managed and what issues have arisen. It will be interesting to see how funds cope with the recent downturn in interest rates globally. Usually funds are at their most competitive when interest rates are falling.

It is clear that Regulators both in the US and Europe will be reviewing whether, and how, money market funds should be specifically regulated. Watch this space, but in the meantime expect funds to be mcuh more conservatively managed and operated.

MAKING IT HAPPEN

- It is important to have a clear strategy and credit procedures.
- The days of do it yourself are probably numbered, unless you can gear up to run a fully functioning, professional cash desk.
- Your bank, custodian, or financial adviser should be the first port of call.
- Longer term cash can always be placed in a segregated mandate with a specialist cash investment manager.
- There is now a viable choice of pooled funds, as long as you do the appropriate due diligence and get comfortable with the fund and the provider's credentials.
- Treasury-style money market funds can provide professional cash management at low cost with a smoothed return, and give the operational flexibility that is essential for working cash balances. Portals can offer operational advantages for the multi-fund user.
- You do have a choice, and best practice demands careful consideration of all the available options.

MORE INFO

Book:

Treasury Today. *Corporate and Institutional Money Market Funds in Europe*. Best Practice Handbook. London: Treasury Today, 2008. www.treasurytoday.com

Article:

Treasury Management International (*tmi*). Issue no. 167 (July/August 2008), "Seeking Investment Returns." Online at: www.treasury-management.com/articles.php?pubid=1&issueid=109

Websites:

Association of Corporate Treasurers (ACT): www.treasurers.org
Fitch Ratings: www.fitchratings.com
The Institutional Money Market Funds Association (IMMFA): www.immfa.org
Treasury Management (*tmi*) on-line: www.treasury-management.com
Treasury Today. Publisher and provider of treasury info: www.treasurytoday.com

See Also:

Peter Bernstein (p. 1154)

NOTES

1 "fund figures as at 13th March 2009 from iMoneyNet with exchange rates as at 23rd March 2009.

"Rule No.1: Never lose money. Rule No.2: Never forget rule No.1." Warren Buffett

     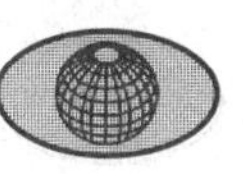   

Investing in Structured Finance Products in the Debt Money Markets by Moorad Choudhry

EXECUTIVE SUMMARY

- A number of structured finance investment products are available in money markets that offer investment options for cash-rich investors.
- Products include asset-backed commercial paper, total return swaps, and collateralized committed repo liquidity lines.
- The returns available for cash-rich investors differ according to asset credit quality, with higher yields on lower-rated assets.
- Returns also differ by product type.
- Investors should assess the liquidity of an instrument type as well as its credit risk.

INTRODUCTION

The application of synthetic securitization and structured finance techniques in debt capital markets has made a range of asset classes available to investors who would not otherwise have access to them. Thus banks, fund managers, and cash-rich corporate institutions can choose from a wide variety of investment options for their funds. This article introduces a sample of money market products that present alternatives for the investment of surplus funds. In each case we consider the basic product structure, and we look at the different yields across products.

The global credit and liquidity crunch in 2007–08 resulted in a widespread "flight-to-quality" as investors became excessively risk-averse. Yield spreads widened considerably and certain asset classes and products were no longer viable. We review here only instruments that remain practical products for both investors and borrowers. The products considered are:

- Asset-backed commercial paper;
- Total return swap funding, or synthetic repo;
- Collateralized committed repo liquidity lines.

ASSET-BACKED COMMERCIAL PAPER

The application of securitization technology in the money markets has led to the growth of short-term instruments backed by the cash flows from other assets, known as "asset-backed commercial paper" (ABCP). Securitization is the practice of using the cash flows from a specified asset, such as residential mortgages, car loans, or commercial bank loans as backing for an issue of bonds. In the case of ABCP the assets are funded in the commercial paper market. The assets themselves are transferred from the original owner (the "originator") to a specially created legal entity known as a "special purpose vehicle" (SPV), so as to make them separate and bankruptcy-remote from the originator. In the meantime, the originator is able to benefit from capital market financing charged at a lower rate of interest than that earned by the originator on its assets.

Figure 1 illustrates a generic securitization transaction for the debt capital markets, issuing asset-backed securities (ABS). The originator has set up the SPV, which then buys the assets from it. The SPV funds itself in the debt capital markets by issuing ABS.

Generally securitization is used as a funding instrument by companies for three main reasons: It offers lower-cost funding than traditional bank loan or bond financing; it is a mechanism by which assets such as corporate loans or mortgages can be removed from the balance sheet, thus transferring the default risk associated with those assets to investors; and it increases a borrower's funding options. For investors it offers a class of assets that would not otherwise be available to them directly, thus widening their return options and potentially diversifying the sources of risk in their portfolio. Equally, issuing ABCP enables an originator to benefit from money market financing that it might otherwise not have access to, perhaps because its credit rating is not sufficiently strong.

When entering into securitization, an entity may issue term securities against assets into the public or private market, or it may issue commercial paper via a special purpose legal entity known as a "conduit." These conduits are usually sponsored by commercial banks. ABCP trades as a money market discount instrument. Investors purchase it from a number of ABCP dealers who work on behalf of the conduit. The return available on ABCP is a function of the credit rating of the issuer, which is dependent on the credit quality of the underlying assets. Conduits often pay a fee to be backed by a line of credit, known as a "liquidity line," which is supplied by a bank. The credit quality and standing of the liquidity bank also drive the credit rating of the conduit.

The assets that can be funded via a conduit program are many and varied; to date they have included:

- trade receivables and equipment lease receivables;
- credit card receivables;
- auto loans and leases;
- corporate loans, franchise loans, and mortgage loans;
- real-estate leases;
- investment grade-rated structured finance bonds, such as asset-backed securities (ABS).

Figure 2 illustrates a typical conduit structure for ABCP issued to the US and European commercial paper markets. (The difference in yields available on ABCP rated A1/P1 compared to bank-issued commercial paper of the same rating is

Figure 1. Securitization structure

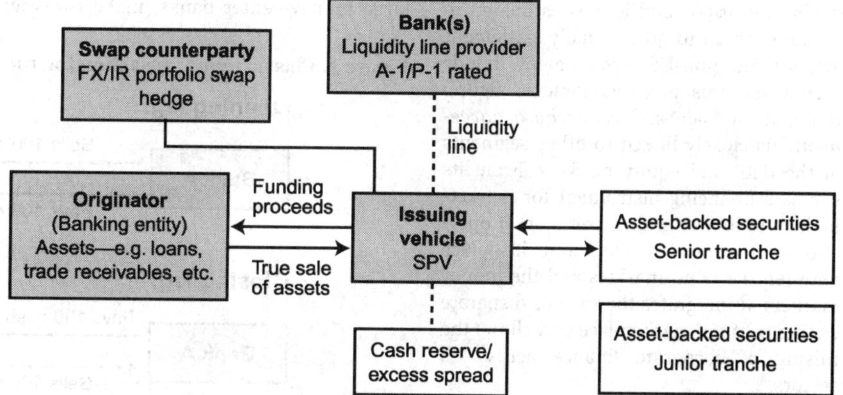

"**Business is not financial science, it's about trading. . .buying and selling. It's about creating a product or service so good that people will pay for it.**" Anita Roddick

Figure 2. Typical conduit structure for ABCP issuance

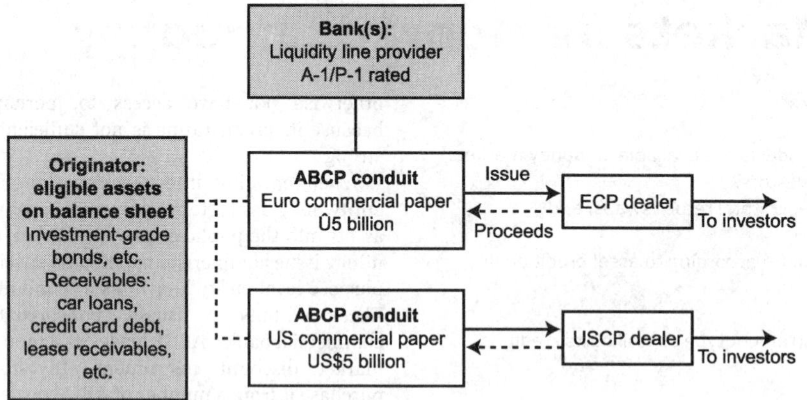

illustrated in Table 2. The higher yield on ABCP reflects investor perception of the higher associated credit risk.)

REPO AND SYNTHETIC REPO

A repo is a transaction in which one party sells securities to another, and at the same time and as part of the same transaction commits to repurchase those securities on a specified date at a specified price. The seller delivers securities and receives cash from the buyer. The cash is supplied at a predetermined rate of interest—the repo rate—which remains constant during the term of the trade. On maturity, the original seller receives back collateral of equivalent type and quality, and returns the cash plus repo interest. Although legal title to the securities is transferred, the seller retains both the economic benefits and the market risk of owning them. This means that the seller will suffer loss if the market value of the collateral drops during the term of the repo, as the seller retains beneficial ownership of the collateral. The buyer in a repo is not affected in profit/loss account terms if the value of the collateral drops.

The repo market is a vital element of the global capital and money markets. The market experienced substantial growth during the 1990s and is now estimated to account for up to 50% of daily settlement activity in non-US government bonds worldwide; this is a phenomenal figure. Repo, from "sale and *repurchase agreement*," is closely linked to other segments of the debt and equity markets. From its use as a financing instrument for market-makers to its use in the open market operations of central banks, and its place between the bond markets and the money markets, it integrates the various disparate elements of the marketplace and allows the raising of corporate finance across all sectors.

Across the world, including financial centres in the North American, European, and Asia-Pacific region, repo is a well-established investment product, utilized by fund managers, hedge funds, corporate treasuries, and local authorities. The practicality and simplicity of repo means that it can be taken up even in capital markets that are still at an emerging stage as well as by a wide range of participants.

What we have described is in effect a secured loan, but one with added flexibility for use in a variety of applications. Market participants enter into a classic repo because they wish to invest cash, for which the transaction is deemed to be *cash-driven*, or because they wish to finance the purchase of a bond or equity that they have bought. Alternatively, they may wish to borrow a stock that they have sold short, which is known as a "reverse repo." However the reverse repo trader is also lending cash. So the trade might be cash-driven or *stock-driven*. The first and most important thing to state is that repo is a secured loan of cash, and it is categorized as a money market yield instrument. Note that every repo is also a reverse repo, depending on which counterparty viewpoint one looks at the transaction from.

Repo market-makers, which include the large money-center banks, make two-way prices in repo in the major currencies. This means they will trade both repo and reverse repo, lending and borrowing cash, against either receiving or supplying collateral, according to customer need. A generic type of collateral, such as government bonds, is known as "general collateral" and refers to a trade in which any specific bond that fits the general collateral type can be supplied as collateral.

Repo is traded under a standard legal agreement termed the Global Master Repurchase Agreement (GMRA). Such an agreement executed once between two parties governs all subsequent trades between them.

Plain Vanilla Repo

Let us say that the two parties to a repo trade are Bank A, the seller of securities, and Bank (or corporate entity) B, which is the buyer of securities. On the trade date the two banks enter into an agreement whereby on a set date, the "value" or "settlement" date, Bank A will sell to Bank B a nominal amount of securities in exchange for cash. The price received for the securities is the market price of the stock on the value date. The agreement also demands that on the termination date Bank B will sell identical stock back to Bank A at the previously agreed price; consequently, Bank B will have its cash returned with interest at the agreed repo rate.

The basic mechanism is illustrated in Figure 3.

Synthetic Repo Via the Total Return Swap

Synthetic repo, undertaken for the purposes of funding a portfolio or investing against a credit-linked instrument, is common in the market. The repo is in the form of a total return swap (TRS), which is classified as a credit derivative; however, when traded for funding or stock borrowing purposes it is identical in economic terms to a classic repo.

A TRS has similarities to an interest rate swap in that it consists of two payment legs,

Figure 3. Classic repo transaction for 100-worth of collateral stock

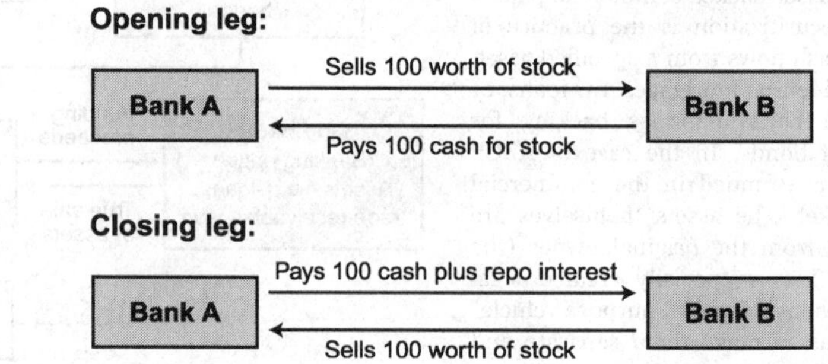

"Whenever there is a financial crisis, it is always the banks that get hit." Gordon Wu

     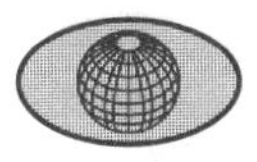   

one the "total return" and the other an interest payment linked to Libor. As a credit derivative, a TRS enables a market participant to access the total return on an asset such as a bond without actually buying it. The return is in the form of the bond's coupon and any capital appreciation during the term of the trade. For an existing investor that is already holding a bond, entering into a TRS enables it to transfer the credit risk associated with the bond to the TRS counterparty.

TRS contracts are used in a variety of applications by banks, and are discussed in detail by Choudhry (2004). When used for funding purposes, a TRS is more akin to a synthetic repo contract. To illustrate this application, we describe here the use of a TRS to fund a portfolio of bonds, as a substitute for a repo trade. This is shown at Figure 4, where counterparty A is the investor lending funds and receiving a Libor-based return. The counterparty to the trade is investing cash against a credit-linked return, which, depending on the credit quality of the linked assets, may be substantially above Libor.

Consider a bank that has a portfolio of assets on its balance sheet for which it needs to obtain funding. These assets are investment grade-rated structured finance bonds such as credit card ABS and investment grade-rated convertible bonds. In the repo market, it is able to fund these at Libor plus 200 basis points. That is, it can repo the bonds out to a bank or non-bank financial counterparty, and will pay Libor plus 200 bps on the funds it receives.

Assume that for operational reasons the bank cannot fund these assets using repo. Instead it can fund them using a basket TRS contract, provided that a suitable counterparty can be found. Under this contract, the portfolio of assets is "swapped" out to the TRS counterparty, and cash is received from the counterparty. The assets are therefore sold off the balance sheet to the counterparty, which may be a corporate treasury or an investment bank. The corporate or investment bank will need to fund this itself—it will either be cash-rich or have a line of credit from another bank. The funding rate the investor charges will depend to a large extent on the rate at which it can fund the assets itself. Assume that the TRS rate charged is Libor plus 220 bps—the higher rate reflecting the lower liquidity in the basket TRS market for non-vanilla bonds.

> "As a credit derivative, a TRS enables a market participant to access the total return on an asset such as a bond without actually buying it."

Assume that at the start of the trade the portfolio consists of five euro-denominated ABS bonds. The parties enter into a three-month TRS, with a one-week interest rate reset. This means that the basket is revalued at one-week intervals. The difference in value from the last valuation is paid (if higher) or received (if lower) by the lender to the borrowing bank; in return the borrowing bank also pays one-week interest on the funds it received at the start of the trade. The bonds in the reference basket can be returned, added to, or substituted. So if any stocks have been sold or bought, they can be removed or added to the basket on the reset date.

Example of a TRS

Table 1 shows a portfolio of five securities that were invested in via a TRS trade between a bank and a non-bank, cash-rich financial institution, which is the investor. The trade terms are shown below.

Trade date	January 8, 2009
Value date	January 12, 2009
Maturity date	April 13, 2009
Rate reset	January 19, 2009
Interest rate	2.445% (one-week euro Libor fix of 2.225% plus 220 bps)
Market value of reference basket	€100,002,300.00

Figure 4. Total return swap as a synthetic repo

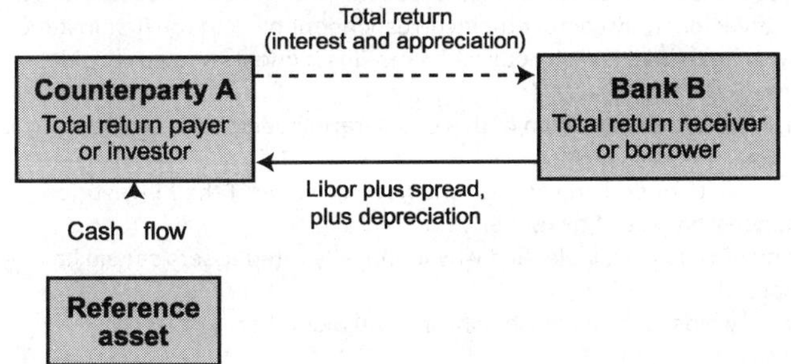

At the start of the trade, the bonds in the basket are swapped out to the lender, who pays the market value for them. On the first reset date, the portfolio is revalued and the following calculations are confirmed:

Old portfolio value	€100,002,300.00
Interest rate	2.445%
Interest payable by borrower bank	€47,542.76
New portfolio value	€105,052,300.00
Portfolio change in value	€ +5,050,000.00
Net payment: borrowing bank receives	€ +5,002,457.24

The existing bonds had not changed in price; however, a new security was added to the portfolio and there has been a week's accrued interest, thus increasing the portfolio's market value. This trade has the same goals and produced the same economic effect as a classic repo transaction on the same basket of bonds. The investor is lending three-month floating money, and is receiving a higher return than from the repo market in the same securities. The cash flows are shown in Table 1.

START OF LOAN	
Portfolio additions	€0.00
Loan amount	€100,002,300.00
Interest rate (Libor + 220 bps)	2.445000%
ROLL-OVER PAYMENTS	
Interest	
Rate	2.445000%
Principal	€100,002,300.00
Interest payable	€+47,542.76
Performance	
Portfolio additions	€5,000,000.00
Accrued interest	€50,000.00
Price movements	€0.00
New portfolio value	€105,052,300.00
Old portfolio value	€100,002,300.00
Performance payment	€+5,050,000.00
Net payment	
Borrower receives from bank/investor	**€+5,002,457.24**
NEW LOAN	
New loan amount (€)	€105,052,300.00
New interest rate	1-week euro Libor + 220

COMMITTED LIQUIDITY LINE FUNDING

The standard bank liquidity line is a standing credit facility set up for a borrower that may be drawn on at any time. Lines are usually reviewed on an annual basis, so they represent a maximum 364-day facility.

"What is high finance? It's knowing the difference between one and ten, multiplying, subtracting and adding. You just add noughts. It's no more than that." John Bentley

  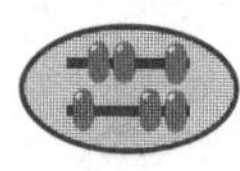   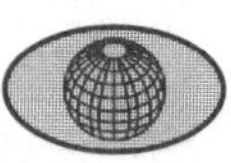   

Table 1. TRS trade ticket, showing portfolio value at start of trade, interest cash flows, and value at end of trade

TRS TICKET					
1-week euro Libor	2.225%				
Name	**Currency**	**Nominal**	**Price**	**Accrued**	**Consideration**
ABC Telecoms 6.25%	Euro	15,000,000	98.00	0.000000	14,700,000.00
SAD Bros 7.50%	Euro	12,000,000	105.00	0.000000	12,600,000.00
DTI 5.875%	Euro	37,000,000	108.79	0.000000	40,252,300.00
Bigenddi 8.25%	Euro	15,000,000	78.00	0.000000	11,700,000.00
BanglaBeat plc 9%	Euro	50,000,000	41.50	0.000000	20,750,000.00
Jackfruit Funding ABS	Euro	5,000,000	100.00	0.000000	5,000,000.00
(addition to basket at roll-over)					
			Portfolio value at start:		**100,002,300.00**
			Portfolio value at rollover:		**105,002,300.00**

Table 2. US dollar lending rates against different instrument types, January 2009. (*Source:* Bloomberg; market counterparties)

Instrument	**1-month**	**3-month**	**1-year**
Bank commercial paper			
A1-P1	0.50%	0.95%	
A2-P2	1.95%	3.56%	
Asset-backed commercial paper			
A1-P1	0.75%	1.30%	
Repo			
US Treasury	0.25%	0.30%	
AAA MBS*	0.85%	2.35%	
Total return swap			
AAA MBS*	0.95%	2.50%	
Liquidity line†			
A1 borrower			
Standing fee	20 bps		
Borrowing fee	Libor + 100 bps		
A2 borrower			
Standing fee			50 bps
Borrowing fee			Libor + 220 bps

*Triple-A rated mortgage-backed securities. †This is a one-year committed liquidity line, drawn against investment grade-rated collateral.

A structure offered by banks to clients that desire longer-term funding is the "evergreen" committed line, which is in theory a 364-day tenor but which is formally "renewed" on a daily basis. This enables the borrower to view the line as longer-dated funding because it is always 364 days away from maturity. Liquidity credit facilities attract a Basel regulatory capital weighting if they are committed to the client. It is common for any borrowings on the line to be collateralized. This turns the liquidity into a committed repo line.

A liquidity facility is an avenue for a bank to invest surplus cash and carries two charges:

- the standing charge, usually calculated as a fixed fee in basis points and payable monthly or quarterly in advance;
- the actual borrowing cost (an interest rate charge) when the line is drawn on.

The standing fee is a function of the credit quality of the borrower. A recent development, widely used by ABCP vehicles, has been the replacement of part or all of the liquidity line with a "committed repo" facility (or committed TRS facility), which carries with it a lower fee and thus saves on costs. Under the committed repo a bank will undertake to provide a repo funding facility using the vehicle's assets as collateral. Thus, in the event that commercial paper cannot be repaid, the vehicle will repo out its assets to the repo provider, enabling it to meet maturing commercial paper obligations.

> "The global credit and liquidity crunch in 2007–08 resulted in a widespread "flight-to-quality" as investors became excessively risk-averse. Yield spreads widened considerably and certain asset classes and products were no longer viable."

YIELD MATRIX

The different products available in money markets mean that there is a range of risk-reward profiles for investors to consider. Table 2 illustrates the variation in yields available in US dollars during January 2009. Investors expect a different return profile for different credit ratings, with higher yields on lower-rated assets. This is confirmed in Table 2. The rates in the table also confirm that returns differ for different instrument types, with a greater yield offered by TRS funding of AAA-rated structured finance securities than by repo of the same collateral.

Structured finance instruments are an alternative investment option for cash-rich long-only investors in the money markets, and in certain cases they can offer a higher return for the same theoretical credit risk. This often reflects liquidity factors, which should be factored into any investment analysis.

▸▸ MAKING IT HAPPEN

Commercial and retail banks all have dedicated repo, commercial paper, and corporate banking desks that provide investment products for other banks as well as cash-rich investors. Investors may contact their correspondent bank in the first instance.

Those wishing to invest in structured finance instruments should consider the following:

- Their risk/reward profile, from both a credit-rating perspective and a value-at-risk perspective.
- The exposure to underlying assets, and how the value of their investment changes with changes in value of the underlying assets.
- The range of yields available, and why identically rated assets should have different credit spreads.
- Reviews of yields, such as those published by Bloomberg.

"The social object of skilled investment should be to defeat the dark forces of time and ignorance which envelope our future." John Maynard Keynes

▸▸ MORE INFO

Books:

Bhattacharya, Anand K., and Frank J. Fabozzi (eds). *Asset-backed Securities*. New Hope, PA: Frank J. Fabozzi Associates, 1996.

Choudhry, Moorad. *Structured Credit Products: Credit Derivatives & Synthetic Securitisation*. Singapore: Wiley, 2004.

Choudhry, Moorad. *Fixed Income Markets: Instruments, Applications, Mathematics*. Singapore: Wiley, 2005.

Choudhry, Moorad. *Bank Asset and Liability Management: Strategy, Trading, Analysis*. Singapore: Wiley, 2007.

Fabozzi, Frank J., and Steven V. Mann (eds). *Securities Finance: Securities Lending and Repurchase Agreements*. Hoboken, NJ: Wiley, 2005.

Fabozzi, Frank J., Steven V. Mann, and Moorad Choudhry. *The Global Money Markets*. Hoboken, NJ: Wiley, 2002.

Martellini, Lionel, Philippe Priaulet, and Stéphane Priaulet. *Fixed-income Securities: Valuation, Risk Management and Portfolio Strategies*. Chichester, UK: Wiley, 2003.

Websites:

Bloomberg on rates and prices: www.bloomberg.com

Investopedia on structured finance: www.investopedia.com/terms/s/structuredfinance.asp

YieldCurve market research: www.yieldcurve.com

"**The most important thing for a young man is to establish a credit ... a reputation, character.**" John D. Rockefeller

Measuring Company Exposure to Country Risk by Aswath Damodaran

EXECUTIVE SUMMARY

- Following the piece on "Measuring Country Risk" (pp. 345–347), we focus on a related question: Once we have estimated a country risk premium, how do we evaluate a company's exposure to country risk?
- In the process, we will argue that a company's exposure to country risk should not be determined by where it is incorporated and traded.
- By that measure, neither Coca-Cola nor Nestlé are exposed to country risk. Exposure to country risk should come from a company's operations, making country risk a critical component of the valuation of almost every large multinational corporation.

INTRODUCTION

If we accept the proposition of country risk, the next question that we have to address relates to the exposure of individual companies to country risk. Should all companies in a country with substantial country risk be equally exposed to country risk? While intuition suggests that they should not, we will begin by looking at standard approaches that assume that they are. We will follow up by scaling country risk exposure to established risk parameters such as betas, and complete the discussion with an argument that individual companies should be evaluated for exposure to country risk.

THE BLUDGEON APPROACH

The simplest assumption to make when dealing with country risk, and the one that is most often made, is that all companies in a market are equally exposed to country risk. The cost of equity for a firm in a market with country risk can then be written as:

Cost of equity = Riskfree rate + Beta (Mature market premium) + Country risk premium

Thus, for Brazil, where we have estimated a country risk premium of 4.43% from the melded approach, each company in the market will have an additional country risk premium of 4.43% added to its expected returns. For instance, the costs of equity for Embraer, an aerospace company listed in Brazil, with a beta[1] of 1.07 and Embratel, a Brazilian telecommunications company, with a beta of 0.80, in US dollar terms would be:

Cost of equity for Embraer = 3.80% + 1.07 (4.79%) + 4.43% = 13.35%

Cost of equity for Embratel = 3.80% + 0.80 (4.79%) + 4.43% = 12.06%

Note that the risk-free rate that we use is the US treasury bond rate (3.80%), and that the 4.79% figure is the equity risk premium for a mature equity market (estimated from historical data in the US market). It is also worth noting that analysts estimating the cost of equity for Brazilian companies, in US dollar terms, often use the Brazilian ten-year dollar-denominated rate as the risk-free rate. This is dangerous, since it is often also accompanied with a higher risk premium, and ends up double counting risk.

THE BETA APPROACH

For those investors who are uncomfortable with the notion that all companies in a market are equally exposed to country risk, a fairly simple alternative is to assume that a company's exposure to country risk is proportional to its exposure to all other market risk, which is measured by the beta. Thus, the cost of equity for a firm in an emerging market can be written as follows:

Cost of equity = Risk-free rate + Beta (Mature market premium + Country risk premium)

In practical terms, scaling the country risk premium to the beta of a stock implies that stocks with betas above 1.00 will be more exposed to country risk than stocks with a beta below 1.00. For Embraer, with a beta of 1.07, this would lead to a dollar cost of equity estimate of:

Cost of equity for Embraer = 3.80% + 1.07 (4.79% + 4.43%) = 13.67%

For Embratel, with its lower beta of 0.80, the cost of equity is:

Cost of equity for Embraer = 3.80% + 0.80 (4.79% + 4.43%) = 11.18%

The advantage of using betas is that they are easily available for most firms. The disadvantage is that while betas measure overall exposure to macroeconomic risk, they may not be good measures of country risk.

THE LAMBDA APPROACH

The most general, and our preferred, approach is to allow for each company to have an exposure to country risk that is different from its exposure to all other market risk. For lack of a better term, let us term the measure of a company's exposure to country risk to be lambda (λ). Like a beta, a lambda will be scaled around 1.00, with a lambda of 1.00 indicating a company with average exposure to country risk and a lambda above or below 1.00 indicating above or below average exposure to country risk. The cost of equity for a firm in an emerging market can then be written as:

Expected return = R_f + Beta (Mature market equity risk premium) + λ (Country risk premium)

Note that this approach essentially converts our expected return model to a two-factor model, with the second factor being country risk, with λ measuring exposure to country risk.

Determinants of Lambda

Most investors would accept the general proposition that different companies in a market should have different exposures to country risk. But what are the determinants of this exposure? We would expect at least three factors (and perhaps more) to play a role.

1 *Revenue source:* The first and most obvious determinant is how much of the revenues a firm derives from the country in question. A company that derives 30% of its revenues from Brazil should be less exposed to Brazilian country risk than a company that derives 70% of its revenues from Brazil. Note, though, that this then opens up the possibility that a company can be exposed to the risk in many countries. Thus, the company that derives only 30% of its revenues from Brazil may derive its remaining revenues from Argentina and Venezuela, exposing it to country risk in those countries. Extending this argument to multinationals, we would argue that companies like Coca-Cola and Nestlé can have substantial exposure to country risk because so much of their revenues comes from emerging markets.

2 *Production facilities:* A company can be exposed to country risk, even if it derives no revenues from that country, if its production facilities are in that country. After all, political and economic turmoil in the country can throw off production

"Every man will speak of the fair as his own market has gone in it." Laurence Sterne

  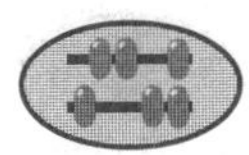   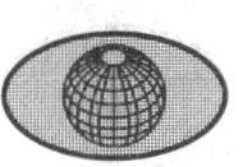   

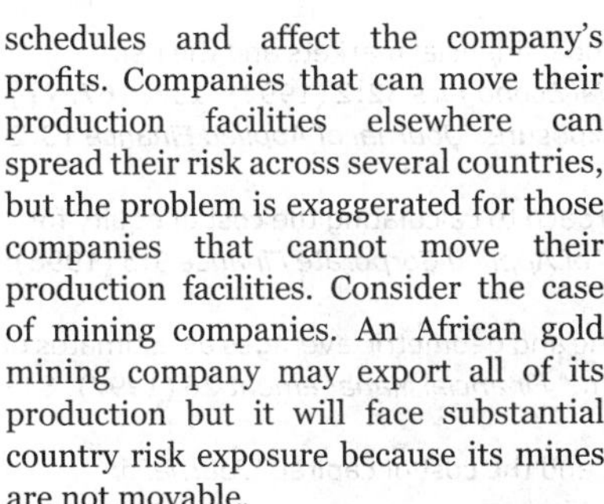

schedules and affect the company's profits. Companies that can move their production facilities elsewhere can spread their risk across several countries, but the problem is exaggerated for those companies that cannot move their production facilities. Consider the case of mining companies. An African gold mining company may export all of its production but it will face substantial country risk exposure because its mines are not movable.

3 *Risk management products:* Companies that would otherwise be exposed to substantial country risk may be able to reduce this exposure by buying insurance against specific (unpleasant) contingencies and by using derivatives. A company that uses risk management products should have a lower exposure to country risk – a lower lambda – than an otherwise similar company that does not use these products.

Ideally, we would like companies to be forthcoming about all three of these factors in their financial statements.

Measuring Lambda

The simplest measure of lambda is based entirely on revenues. In the last section, we argued that a company that derives a smaller proportion of its revenues from a market should be less exposed to country risk. Given the constraint that the average lambda across all stocks has to be one (some one has to bear the country risk!), we cannot use the percentage of revenues that a company gets from a market as lambda. We can, however, scale this measure by dividing it by the percentage of revenues that the average company in the market gets from the country to derive a lambda.

$$\text{Lambda}_j = \frac{\text{(\% of revenue in country}_{\text{Company}})}{\text{\% of revenue in country}_{\text{Average company in market}}}$$

Consider the two large and widely followed Brazilian companies – Embraer, an aerospace company that manufactures and sells aircraft to many of the world's leading airlines, and Embratel, the Brazilian telecommunications giant. In 2002, Embraer generated only 3% of its revenues in Brazil, whereas the average company in the market obtained 85% of its revenues in Brazil.[2] Using the measure suggested above, the lambda for Embraer would be:

$$\text{Lambda}_{\text{Embraer}} = \frac{3\%}{85\%} = 0.04$$

In contrast, Embratel generated 95% of its revenues from Brazil, giving it a lambda of

$$\text{Lambda}_{\text{Embraer}} = \frac{95\%}{85\%} = 1.12$$

Following up, Embratel is far more exposed to country risk than Embraer and will have a much higher cost of equity.

The second measure draws on the stock prices of a company and how they move in relation to movements in country risk. Bonds issued by countries offer a simple and updated measure of country risk; as investor assessments of country risk become more optimistic, bonds issued by that country go up in price, just as they go down when investors become more pessimistic. A regression of the returns on a stock against the returns on a country bond should therefore yield a measure of lambda in the slope coefficient. Applying this approach to the Embraer and Embratel, we regressed monthly stock returns on the two stocks against monthly returns on the ten-year dollar-denominated Brazilian government bond and arrived at the following results:

$$\text{Return}_{\text{Embraer}} = 0.0195 + 0.2681\ \text{Return}_{\text{Brazil dollar-bond}}$$

$$\text{Return}_{\text{Embratel}} = -0.0308 + 2.0030\ \text{Return}_{\text{Brazil dollar-bond}}$$

Based upon these regressions, Embraer has a lambda of 0.27 and Embratel has a lambda of 2.00. The resulting dollar costs of equity for the two firms, using a mature market equity risk premium of 4.79% and a country equity risk premium of 4.43% for Brazil are:

$$\text{Cost of equity for Embraer} = 3.80\% + 1.07\,(4.79\%) + 0.27\,(4.43\%) = 10.12\%$$

$$\text{Cost of equity for Embratel} = 3.80\% + 0.80\,(4.79\%) + 2.00\,(4.43\%) = 16.49\%$$

What are the limitations of this approach? The lambdas estimated from these regressions are likely to have large standard errors; the standard error in the lambda estimate of Embratel is 0.35. It also requires that the country have bonds that are liquid and widely traded, preferably in a more stable currency (dollar or euro).

Risk Exposure in Many Countries

The discussion of lambdas in the last section should highlight a fact that is often lost in valuation. The exposure to country risk, whether it is measured in revenues, earnings, or stock prices, does not come from where a company is incorporated but from its operations. There are US companies that are more exposed to Brazilian country risk than is Embraer. In fact, companies like Nestlé, Coca-Cola, and Gillette have built much of their success on expansion into emerging markets. While this expansion has provided them with growth opportunities, it has also left them exposed to country risk in multiple countries.

In practical terms, what does this imply? When estimating the costs of equity and capital for these companies and others like them, we will need to incorporate an extra premium for country risk. Thus, the net effect on value from their growth strategies will depend upon whether the growth effect (from expanding into emerging markets) exceeds the risk effect. We can adapt the measures suggested above to estimate the risk exposure to different countries for an individual company.

We can break down a company's revenue by country and use the percentage of revenues that the company gets from each emerging market as a basis for estimating lambda in that market. While the percentage of revenues itself can be used as a lambda, a more precise estimate would scale this to the percentage of revenues that the average company in that market gets in the country.

If companies break earnings down by country, these numbers can be used to estimate lambdas. The peril with this approach is that the reported earnings often reflect accounting allocation decisions and differences in tax rates across countries.

If a company is exposed to only a few emerging markets on a large scale, we can regress the company's stock price against the country bond returns from those markets to get country specific lambdas.

CONCLUSION

A key issue, when estimating costs of equity and capital for emerging market companies relates to how this country risk premium should be reflected in the costs of equities of individual companies in that country. While the standard approaches add the

▸▸ MORE INFO

Book:

Falaschetti, Dominic, and Michael Annin Ibbotson (eds). *Stocks, Bonds, Bills and Inflation*. Chicago, IL: Ibbotson Associates, 1999.

Articles:

Booth, Laurence. "Estimating the equity risk premium and equity costs: New ways of looking at old data." *Journal of Applied Corporate Finance* 12:1 (1999): 100–112.

     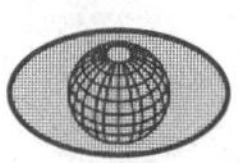   

country risk premium as a constant to the cost of equity of every company in that market, we argue for a more nuanced approach where a company's exposure to country risk is measured with a lambda. This lambda can be estimated either by looking at how much of a company's revenues or earnings come from the country—the greater the percentage, the greater the lambda—or by regressing a company's stock returns against country bond returns—the greater the sensitivity, the higher the lambda. If we accept this view of the world, the costs of equity for multinationals that have significant operations in emerging markets will have to be adjusted to reflect their exposure to risk in these markets.

Chan, K. C., G. A. Karolyi, and R. M. Stulz. "Global financial markets and the risk premium on U.S. equity." *Journal of Financial Economics* 32:2 (1992): 137–167.

Damodaran, A., "Country risk and company exposure." *Journal of Applied Finance* 13:2 (2003): 64–78.

Godfrey, S., and R. Espinosa. "A practical approach to calculating the cost of equity for investments in emerging markets." *Journal of Applied Corporate Finance* 9:3 (1996): 80–90.

Indro, D. C., and W. Y. Lee, "Biases in arithmetic and geometric averages as estimates of long-run expected returns and risk premium." *Financial Management* 26 (1997): 81–90.

Stulz, R. M. "Globalization, corporate finance, and the cost of capital." *Journal of Applied Corporate Finance* 12:3 (1999): 8–25.

Report:

Damodaran, A. "Measuring Company Risk Exposure to Country Risk." Working Paper, SSRN.com, 2008. Online at: pages.stern.nyu.edu/~adamodar/pdfiles/papers/ERPfull.pdf

NOTES

1 We used a bottom-up beta for Embraer, based upon an unlevered beta of 0.95 (estimated using aerospace companies listed globally) and Embraer's debt-to-equity ratio of 19.01%. For more on the rationale for bottom-up betas, read the companion paper on estimating risk parameters, "Measuring Country Risk" (pp. 345–347).

2 To use this approach, we need to estimate the percentage of revenues both for the firm in question and for the average firm in the market. While the former may be simple to obtain, estimating the latter can be a time-consuming exercise. One simple solution is to use data that are publicly available on how much of a country's gross domestic product comes from exports. According to the World Bank data in this table, Brazil got 23.2% of its GDP from exports in 2008. If we assume that this is an approximation of export revenues for the average firm, the average firm can be assumed to generate 76.8% of its revenues domestically. Using this value would yield slightly higher betas for both Embraer and Embratel.

"A spirit of national masochism prevails, encouraged by an effete corps of impudent snobs who characterize themselves as intellectuals." Spiro Agnew

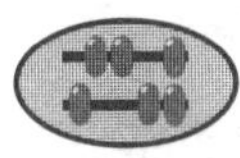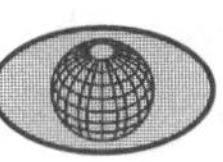

Measuring Country Risk by Aswath Damodaran

EXECUTIVE SUMMARY

- As companies and investors globalize and financial markets expand around the world, we are increasingly faced with estimation questions about the risk associated with this globalization.
- When investors invest in Petrobras, Gazprom and China Power, they may be rewarded with higher returns, but they are also exposed to additional risk.
- When US and European multinationals push for growth in Asia and Latin America, they are clearly exposed to the political and economic turmoil that often characterize these markets.
- In practical terms, how, if at all, should we adjust for this additional risk? We review the discussion on country risk premiums and how to estimate them.

INTRODUCTION

Two key questions must be addressed when investing in emerging markets in Asia, Latin America, and Eastern Europe. The first relates to whether we should impose an additional risk premium when valuing equities in these markets. As we will see, the answer will depend upon whether we view markets to be open or segmented and whether we believe the risk can be diversified away. The second question relates to estimating an equity risk premium for emerging markets.

SHOULD THERE BE A COUNTRY RISK PREMIUM?

Is there more risk in investing in Malaysian or Brazilian equities than there is in investing in equities in the United States? Of course! But that does not automatically imply that there should be an additional risk premium charged when investing in those markets. Two arguments are generally used against adding an additional premium.

Country risk can be diversified away: If the additional risk of investing in Malaysia or Brazil can be diversified away, then there should be no additional risk premium charged. But for country risk to be diversifiable, two conditions must be met:

1 The marginal investors—i.e., active investors who hold large positions in the stock—have to be globally diversified. If the marginal investors are either unable or unwilling to invest globally, companies will have to diversify their operations across countries, which is a much more difficult and expensive exercise.

2 All or much of country risk should be country specific. In other words, there should be low correlation across markets. If the returns across countries are positively correlated, country risk has a market risk component, is not diversifiable, and can command a premium. Whereas studies in the 1970s indicated low or no correlation across markets, increasing diversification on the part of both investors and companies has increased the correlation numbers. This is borne out by the speed with which troubles in one market can spread to a market with which it has little or no obvious relationship—say Brazil—and this contagion effect seems to become stronger during crises.

Given that both conditions are difficult to meet, we believe that on this basis, country risk should command a risk premium.

The expected cash flows for country risk can be adjusted: This second argument used against adjusting for country risk is that it is easier and more accurate to adjust the expected cash flows for the risk. However, adjusting the cash flows to reflect expectations about dire scenarios, such as nationalization or an economic meltdown, is not risk adjustment. Making the risk adjustment to cash flows requires the same analysis that we will employ to estimate the risk adjustment to discount rates.

ESTIMATING A COUNTRY RISK PREMIUM

If country risk is not diversifiable, either because the marginal investor is not globally diversified or because the risk is correlated across markets, we are left with the task of measuring country risk and estimating country risk premiums. In this section, we will consider two approaches that can be used to estimate country risk premiums. One approach builds on historical risk premiums and can be viewed as the *historical risk premium plus approach.* In the other approach, we estimate the equity risk premium by looking at how the market prices stocks and expected cash flows – this is the *implied premium approach.*

Historical Premium Plus

Most practitioners, when estimating risk premiums in the United States, look at the past. Consequently, we look at what we would have earned as investors by investing in equities as opposed to investing in riskless investments. With emerging markets, we will almost never have access to as much historical data as we do in the United States. If we combine this with the high volatility in stock returns in such markets, the conclusion is that historical risk premiums can be computed for these markets, but they will be useless because of the large standard errors in the estimates. Consequently, many analysts build their equity risk premium estimates for emerging markets from mature market historical risk premiums.

$$\text{Equity risk premium}_{\text{Emerging market}} = \text{Equity risk premium}_{\text{Mature market}} + \text{Country risk premium}$$

To estimate the base premium for a mature equity market, we will make the argument that the US equity market is a mature market and that there is sufficient historical data in the United States to make a reasonable estimate of the risk premium. Using the historical data for the United States, we estimate the geometric average premium earned by stocks over treasury bonds of 4.79% between 1928 and 2007. To estimate the country risk premium, we can use one of three approaches:

Country Bond Default Spreads

One of the simplest and most easily accessible country risk measures is the rating assigned to a country's debt by a ratings agency (S&P, Moody's, and IBCA all rate countries). These ratings measure default risk (rather than equity risk), but they are affected by many of the factors that drive equity risk—the stability of a country's currency, its budget and trade balances and its political stability, for instance.[1] The other advantage of ratings is that they can be used to estimate default spreads over a riskless rate. For instance, Brazil was rated Ba1 in September 2008 by Moody's and the ten-year Brazilian ten-year dollar-denominated bond was priced to yield 5.95%, 2.15% more than the interest rate (3.80%) on a ten-year US treasury bond at the same time.[2] Analysts who use default spreads as measures of country risk typically add them on to the cost of both equity and debt of every company traded in that country. If we assume that the total equity risk premium for the United States and other mature equity markets is 4.79%,

  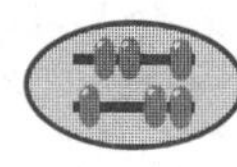   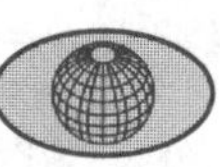   

the risk premium for Brazil would be 6.94%.[3]

Relative Standard Deviation

There are some analysts who believe that the equity risk premiums of markets should reflect the differences in equity risk, as measured by the volatilities of equities in these markets. A conventional measure of equity risk is the standard deviation in stock prices; higher standard deviations are generally associated with more risk. If we scale the standard deviation of one market against another, we obtain a measure of relative risk.

$$\text{Relative standard deviation}_{\text{Country X}} = \left(\frac{\text{Standard deviation}_{\text{Country X}}}{\text{Standard deviation}_{\text{US}}}\right)$$

This relative standard deviation when multiplied by the premium used for US stocks should yield a measure of the total risk premium for any market.

$$\text{Equity risk premium}_{\text{Country X}} = (\text{Risk premium}_{\text{US}} \times \text{Relative standard deviation}_{\text{Country X}})$$

Assume, for the moment, that we are using a mature market premium for the United States of 4.79%. The annualized standard deviation in the S&P 500 between 2006 and 2008, using weekly returns, was 15.27%, whereas the standard deviation in the Bovespa (the Brazilian equity index) over the same period was 25.83%.[4] Using these values, the estimate of a total risk premium for Brazil would be as follows:

$$\text{Equity risk premium}_{\text{Brazil}} = 4.79\% \times \left(\frac{25.83\%}{15.27\%}\right) = 8.10\%$$

The country risk premium can be isolated as follows:

$$\text{Country risk premium}_{\text{Brazil}} = 8.10\% - 4.79\% = 3.31\%$$

While this approach has intuitive appeal, there are problems with comparing standard deviations computed in markets with widely different market structures and liquidity. There are very risky emerging markets that have low standard deviations for their equity markets because the markets are illiquid. This approach will understate the equity risk premiums in those markets.

Default Spreads and Relative Standard Deviations

The country default spreads that come with country ratings provide an important first step, but still only measures the premium for default risk. Intuitively, we would expect the country equity risk premium to be larger than the country default risk spread. To address the issue of how much higher, we look at the volatility of the equity market in a country relative to the volatility of the bond market used to estimate the spread. This yields the following estimate for the country equity risk premium.

$$\text{Country risk premium} = \text{Country default spread} \times \left(\frac{\Sigma}{\varsigma_{\text{Country bond}}}\right)$$

To illustrate, consider again the case of Brazil. As noted earlier, the default spread on the Brazilian dollar-denominated bond in September 2008 was 2.15%, and the annualized standard deviation in the Brazilian equity index over the previous year was 25.83%. Using two years of weekly returns, the annualized standard deviation in the Brazilian dollar denominated ten-year bond was 12.55%.[5] The resulting country equity risk premium for Brazil is as follows:

$$\text{Additional equity risk premium}_{\text{Brazil}} = 2.15\% \left(\frac{25.83\%}{12.55\%}\right) = 4.43\%$$

Unlike the equity standard deviation approach, this premium is in addition to a mature market equity risk premium. Note that this country risk premium will increase if the country rating drops or if the relative volatility of the equity market increases. It is also in addition to the equity risk premium for a mature market. Thus, the total equity risk premium for Brazil using this approach and a 4.79% premium for the United States would be 9.22%.

Both this approach and the previous one use the standard deviation in equity of a market to make a judgment about country risk premium, but they measure it relatively to different bases. This approach uses the country bond as a base, whereas the previous one uses the standard deviation in the US market. It also assumes that investors are more likely to choose between Brazilian government bonds and Brazilian equity, whereas the previous approach assumes that the choice is across equity markets.

Implied Equity Premiums

There is an alternative approach to estimating risk premiums that does not require historical data or corrections for country risk but does assume that the market, overall, is correctly priced. Consider, for instance, a very simple valuation model for stocks:

$$\text{Value} = \frac{\text{Expected dividends next period}}{(\text{Required return on equity} - \text{Expected growth rate})}$$

This is essentially the present value of dividends growing at a constant rate. Three of the four inputs in this model can be obtained externally—the current level of the market (value), the expected dividends next period, and the expected growth rate in earnings and dividends in the long term. The only "unknown" is then the required return on equity; when we solve for it, we get an implied expected return on stocks. Subtracting out the risk-free rate will yield an implied equity risk premium. We can extend the model to allow for dividends to grow at high rates, at least for short periods.

The advantage of the implied premium approach is that it is market-driven and current, and it does not require any historical data. Thus, it can be used to estimate implied equity premiums in any market. For instance, the equity risk premium for the Brazilian equity market on September 9, 2008, was estimated from the following inputs. The index (Bovespa) was at 48,345 and the current cash flow yield on the index was 5.41%. Earnings in companies in the index are expected to grow 9% (in US dollar terms) over the next five years, and 3.8% thereafter. These inputs yield a required return on equity of 10.78%, which when compared to the treasury bond rate of 3.80% on that day results in an implied equity premium of 6.98%. For simplicity, we have used nominal dollar expected growth rates[6] and treasury bond rates, but this analysis could have been done entirely in the local currency. We can decompose this number into a mature market equity risk premium and a country-specific equity risk premium by comparing it to the implied equity risk premium for a mature equity market (the United States, for instance).

- Implied equity premium for Brazil (see above) = 6.98%.
- Implied equity premium for the United States in September 2008 = 4.54%.
- Country specific equity risk premium for Brazil = 2.44%.

This approach can yield numbers very different from the other approaches, because they reflect market prices (and views) today.

CONCLUSION

As companies expand operations into emerging markets and investors search for investment opportunities in Asia and Latin America, they are also increasingly exposed to additional risk in these countries. While it is true that globally diversified investors can eliminate some country risk by diversifying across equities in many countries, the increasing correlation across

"Forget about winning and losing; forget about pride and pain. Let your opponent graze your skin and you smash into his flesh; let him smash into your flesh and you fracture his bones; let him fracture your bones and you take his life. Do not be concerned with escaping safely - lay your life before him." Bruce Lee

markets suggests that country risk cannot be entirely diversified away. To estimate the country risk premium, we considered three measures: the default spread on a government bond issued by that country, a premium obtained by scaling up the equity risk premium in the United States by the volatility of the country equity market relative to the US equity market, and a melded premium where the default spread on the country bond is adjusted for the higher volatility of the equity market. We also estimated an implied equity premium from stock prices and expected cash flows.

▸▸ MORE INFO

Book:

Falaschetti, Dominic, and Michael Annin Ibbotson (eds). *Stocks, Bonds, Bills and Inflation*. Chicago, IL: Ibbotson Associates, 1999.

Articles:

Booth, Laurence. "Estimating the equity risk premium and equity costs: New ways of looking at old data." *Journal of Applied Corporate Finance* 12:1 (1999): 100–112.

Chan, K. C., G. A. Karolyi, and R. M. Stulz. "Global financial markets and the risk premium on U.S. equity." *Journal of Financial Economics* 32:2 (1992): 137–167.

Indro, D. C., and W. Y. Lee, "Biases in arithmetic and geometric averages as estimates of long-run expected returns and risk premium." *Financial Management* 26 (1997): 81–90.

Report:

Damodaran, A. "Equity risk premiums: Determinants, estimation and implications." Working Paper, SSRN.com, 2008. Online at: pages.stern.nyu.edu/~adamodar/pdfiles/papers/ERPfull.pdf

NOTES

1 The process by which country ratings are obtained is explained on the S&P website at www.ratings.standardpoor.com/criteria/index.htm

2 These yields were as of January 1, 2008. While this is a market rate and reflects current expectations, country bond spreads are extremely volatile and can shift significantly from day to day. To counter this volatility, the default spread can be normalized by averaging the spread over time or by using the average default spread for all countries with the same rating as Brazil in early 2008.

3 If a country has a sovereign rating and no dollar-denominated bonds, we can use a typical spread based upon the rating as the default spread for the country. These numbers are available on my website at www.damodaran.com

4 If the dependence on historical volatility is troubling, the options market can be used to get implied volatilities for both the US market (about 20%) and for the Bovespa (about 38%).

5 Both standard deviations are computed on returns; returns on the equity index and returns on the ten-year bond.

6 The input that is most difficult to estimate for emerging markets is a long-term expected growth rate. For Brazilian stocks, I used the average consensus estimate of growth in earnings for the largest Brazilian companies which have ADRs listed on them. This estimate may be biased as a consequence.

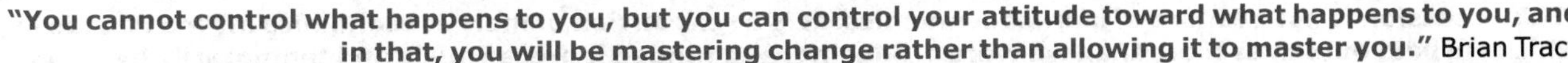
"You cannot control what happens to you, but you can control your attitude toward what happens to you, and in that, you will be mastering change rather than allowing it to master you." Brian Tracy

  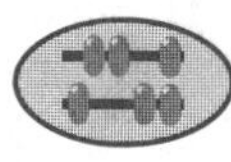   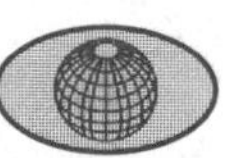   

Viewpoint: James Montier

Only White Swans on the Road to Revulsion

INTRODUCTION

James Montier, an expert in behavioral finance, argues that investors would have a greater chance of spotting the formation of bubbles if they could only brush up on their history and have a greater awareness of human psychology. Co-head of global strategy at Société Générale, Montier has been described as an "enfant terrible" by Frankfurter *Allgemeine Zeitung*, an "iconoclast" by the Financial *Times*, a "maverick" by the *Sunday Times* and "a prophet" by Fast Company. Montier, who formerly worked as an equity strategist at Dresdner Kleinwort Wasserstein, NatWest Markets, and Bankers Trust, has been a top-rated strategist in the annual Extel survey for the last five years. He began mining behavioral economics, then an emerging discipline, to explain investors' irrational behavior during the dotcom bubble. He is a visiting fellow of Durham University and a Fellow of the Royal Society of Arts. When not reading, writing, or speaking, Montier can usually be found swimming with sharks and blowing bubbles at fishes.

The destruction of the US economy, its housing market, its credit markets, its commodity market, and its equity markets has frequently been blamed on or described as a "black swan."

My friend Nicholas Nassim Taleb defines a black swan as a highly improbable event that has three main characteristics: (1) It is unpredictable; (2) It has a massive impact, and (3) *ex post*, explanations are concocted that make the event appear less random, and more predictable than it was.

However, it is wholly wrong to characterize what happened to the US economy and markets as a black swan. To do so is, in fact, an abdication of responsibility. If these extraordinary events were totally unpredictable, then there would have been nothing we could have done to prevent them.

The events of 2003–2008 were not black swans at all. They were "predictable surprises." The term was first coined by Michael Watkins and Max Bazerman. A predictable surprise also has three characteristics: (1) At least some people are aware of the problem; (2) The problem intensifies over time, and (3) Eventually the problem explodes into a crisis, much to the "shock" of decision-makers. As Bazerman says: "The nature of predictable surprises [is that] while uncertainty surrounds the details of the impending disaster, there is little uncertainty that a large disaster awaits."

What evidence do I have that the current mess was a predictable surprise? The *New York Times* ran a fascinating article in mid-December 2007. This noted that, seven years earlier, Edward Gramlich, a governor of the Federal Reserve, had warned that a fast-growing new breed of lenders was luring many households into risky mortgages they couldn't afford. The article also cited the Herculean efforts of Sheila C. Bair, a senior Treasury official, to persuade subprime lenders to adopt a code of practice and to let external monitors verify whether they were complying with these standards.

Robert Shiller, a professor at Yale and founder of the investment management firm MacroMarkets, even went so far as to re-issue his 2000 book, *Irrational Exuberance*, with a special chapter dedicated to the US housing market. Even yours truly (not renowned for having my finger on the pulse) wrote a note on June 20, 2005, entitled *Pictures of a Mania?—US Housing Special* which concluded "All the criteria of a speculative mania seem present to me." So a cacophony of Cassandras were clearly warning of dangers, and these dangers clearly existed.

All this discussion about "foreseeing" future risks might seem odd coming from someone who is known to be openly hostile to the notion of forecasting (see The Folly of Forecasting, Chapter 9 of Behavioral Investing). However, I think a clear line can be drawn between analysis and forecasting. As Ben Graham, the original proponent of value investing, stated: "Analysis connotes the careful study of available facts with the attempt to draw conclusions there based on established principles and sound logic."

So the big question is this: What prevented us from reacting to the predictable surprise? I can think of five major psychological hurdles that hampered us in this regard. Firstly, there is an ever-present over-optimism. Everyone assumes that they are less likely than average to have drinking problems, to get divorced, or be fired, etc. It is highly likely that the same over-optimism applies when it comes to predictable surprises; we expect them to affect others but not us.

In addition to over-optimism, we suffer from the illusion of control. This refers to people's belief that they have influence over the outcome of uncontrollable events. For instance, E. Langer has shown (1975, "The illusion of control," *Journal of Personality and Social Psychology*, 32) that people will pay four and half times more for a lottery ticket that contains numbers they choose rather than a random draw of numbers.

The same study demonstrated that people will bet more on a coin toss before the coin is actually tossed, rather than after. Perhaps they believe they can influence the spin of the coin in the air! The illusion of control is exacerbated by information. The more you think you know, the more likely you are to suffer the illusion of control.

So-called risk management techniques have clearly fostered the illusion of control. The idea that, if we can quantify risk, we can also control it is deeply flawed. In fact, we can neither measure nor control risk. Simply by providing a number, we fool ourselves into thinking we are in control.

The third psychological barrier to recognizing predictable surprises is self-serving bias. This is the innate desire to interpret information and act in ways that are supportive of our own interests.

So estate agents are unlikely to tell you that real estate is too expensive, just as companies will always tell you that everything is fine and dandy. A classic example of self-serving bias can be found in a recent Bloomberg story on the ratings agencies

"This recession is not a failure of market economics. It is a reassertion of market economics after a decade in which we paid ourselves more than we were producing, and funded it precariously and temporarily by complicated credit instruments that it took a while for the market to rumble ..." Matthew Parris

  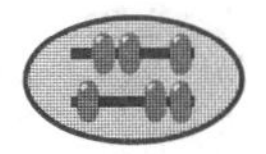   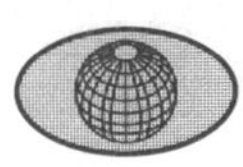   

Moody's and Standard & Poor's. None of the 80 'AAA' securities in the ABX indices meets the criteria that S&P themselves define. Yet only one of these bonds had been downgraded by S&P, and none were downgraded by Moody's.

The penultimate hurdle is myopia (or "hyperbolic discounting," if you happen to be a geek). This reflects the idea that consequences, which occur at a later date, tend to have much less bearing on our choices the further into the future they fall.

This can be summed up as "Eat, drink and be merry, for tomorrow we may die." Of course, this ignores the fact that on any given day we are roughly 26,000 times more likely to be wrong than right with respect to making it to tomorrow. Or, if you prefer, this myopic bias can be summed up by Saint Augustine's plea: "Lord, make me chaste, but not yet." In a world in which short-term profits are so highly prized, it is exceptionally difficult to focus on the longer-term picture.

The final barrier to spotting predictable surprises is inattentional blindness. This refers to the fact we don't see the things we don't look for. The classic experiment in this area concerns watching a video of two teams playing basketball. One is dressed in black, the other in white, and a person is asked to count the number of times the players in white pass the ball amongst themselves. Half way through the video, a man in a gorilla suit walks on, beats his chest and then walks off. Whilst watching the video, around 80% of people fail to spot the gorilla. Why? Because they were distracted with the task of counting the ball passes.

Bubbles are a by-product of human behavior, and human behavior is (sadly) all too predictable.

The details of bubbles change, but the general patterns remain very similar. Such events are clearly not black swans. Of course, the timing of the eventual burst remains as uncertain as ever, but the events themselves are all too predictable. We have long been proponents of the Kindleberger and Minsky framework for analyzing bubbles. Essentially, this model breaks a bubble's rise and fall into five phases as shown below.

Displacement
↓
Credit creation
↓
Euphoria
↓
Critical stage/Financial distress
↓
Revulsion

1. Displacement—The Birth of a Boom

Displacement is generally an exogenous shock that triggers the creation of profit opportunities in some sectors, while closing down profit availability in other sectors. As long as the new opportunities created are greater than those that get shut down, investment and production will pick up to exploit these new opportunities. Investment in both financial and physical assets is likely to occur. Effectively, we are witnessing the birth of a boom.

2. Credit creation—The Nurturing of a Bubble

Just as fire can't grow without oxygen, so a boom needs liquidity on which to feed. Minsky argued that monetary expansion and credit creation are largely endogenous to the system. That is to say, not only can money be created by existing banks ("'inside money"), but also by the formation of new banks, the development of new credit instruments, the use of leverage, and the expansion of personal credit outside the banking system ("outside money").

As J. K. Galbraith writes: "As to new financial instruments, however, experience establishes a firm rule . . . that financial operations do not lend themselves to innovation. What is recurrently so described and celebrated is, without exception, a small variation on an established design . . . The world of finance hails the invention of the wheel over and over again, often in a slightly more unstable version."

3. Euphoria—The Acceptance of the Bubble as Norm

Everyone starts to buy into the new era. Prices are seen as only capable of ever going up. Traditional valuation standards are abandoned and new measures are introduced to justify the current price. A wave of over-optimism and over-confidence is unleashed, leading people to over-estimate potential gains, underestimate the risks, and generally deceive themselves into thinking they can control the situation.

4. Critical Stage/Financial Distress

The critical stage is often characterized by insiders cashing out, and is rapidly followed by financial distress, in which the excessive leverage built up during the boom becomes a major problem. Fraud often emerges during this terminal stage of the bubble's life.

5. Revulsion

This is the final stage of a bubble's lifecycle. Investors are so scarred by the events in which they participated that they can no longer bring themselves to participate in the market at all. Revulsion is characterized by exceptionally cheap asset prices and bargain basement valuations, often bought about by forced sellers.

A through understanding of history and human psychology should better equip investors to understand the warning signs, the opportunities, and the pitfalls associated with the formation of bubbles. But as J. K. Galbraith notes: "There can be few fields of human endeavor in which history counts for so little as the field of finance."

▸▸ MORE INFO

Books:

Galbraith, John Kenneth. *A Short History of Financial Euphoria*. London: Penguin Books, 1994.

Graham, Benjamin. *Security Analysis*. 6th ed. Maidenhead, UK: McGraw-Hill.

Montier, James. *Behavioral Investing: A Practitioner's Guide to Applying Behavioral Finance*. Chichester, UK: Wiley, 2007.

Montier, James. *Behavioral Finance: Insights into Irrational Minds and Markets*. Chichester, UK: Wiley, 2000.

Shiller, Robert. *Irrational Exuberance*. 2nd ed. New York: Broadway Books, 2006.

Watkins, Michael, and Max Bazerman. *Predictable Surprises: The Disasters You Should Have Seen Coming, and How to Prevent Them*. Cambridge, MA: Harvard Business Press, 2004.

Article:

Langer, E. J. "The illusion of control." *Journal of Personality and Social Psychology* 32:2 (1975): 211–328.

See Also:

★ Booms, Busts, and How to Navigate Troubled Waters (pp. 286–288)
★ Viewpoint: Leigh Skene (pp. 238–241)
★ Viewpoint: Todd Buchholz (pp. 189–190)
The Black Swan: The Impact of the Highly Improbable (p. 1227)

"An army of experts assured us on a daily basis that this boom couldn't possibly crash like previous booms because this boom was still going on whereas all previous booms had ended." Mark Steel

  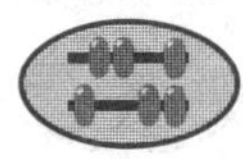   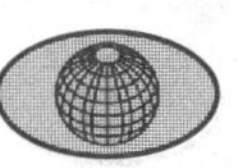   

Minimizing Credit Risk by Frank J. Fabozzi

EXECUTIVE SUMMARY

- Credit risk encompasses credit default risk, credit spread risk, and downgrade risk.
- Market participants typically gauge credit default risk in terms of the credit rating assigned by rating agencies.
- Factors that are considered in the evaluation of a corporate borrower's creditworthiness are: the quality of management; the ability of the borrower to satisfy the debt obligation; the level of seniority and the collateral available in a bankruptcy proceeding; and covenants.
- Credit risk transfer vehicles allow the redistribution of credit risk.
- Securitization is a credit risk transfer vehicle for corporations that is accomplished by selling a pool of loans or receivables to a third-party entity.
- Credit derivatives are a form of credit risk transfer vehicles.

INTRODUCTION

Financial corporations and investors face several types of risk. One major risk is credit risk. Despite the fact that market participants typically refer to "credit risk" as if it is one-dimensional, there are actually three forms of this risk: credit default risk, credit spread risk, and downgrade risk.

Credit default risk is the risk that the issuer will fail to satisfy the terms of the obligation with respect to the timely payment of interest and repayment of the amount borrowed. This form of credit risk covers counterparty risk in a trade or derivative transaction where the counterparty fails to satisfy its obligation. To gauge credit default risk, investors typically rely on credit ratings. A *credit rating* is a formal opinion given by a company referred to as a *rating agency* of the credit default risk faced by investing in a particular issue of debt securities. For long-term debt obligations, a credit rating is a forward-looking assessment of the probability of default and the relative magnitude of the loss should a default occur. For short-term debt obligations, a credit rating is a forward-looking assessment of the probability of default. The nationally recognized rating agencies include Moody's Investors Service, Standard & Poor's, and Fitch Ratings.

Credit spread risk is the loss or underperformance of an issue or issues due to an increase in the credit spread. The credit spread is the compensation sought by investors for accepting the credit default risk of an issue or issuer. The credit spread varies with market conditions and the credit rating of the issue or issuer. On the issuer side, credit spread risk is the risk that an issuer's credit spread will increase when it must come to market to offer bonds, resulting in a higher funding cost.

Downgrade risk is the risk that an issue or issuer will be downgraded, resulting in an increase in the credit spread demanded by the market. Hence, downgrade risk is related to credit spread risk. Occasionally, the ability of an issuer to make interest and principal payments diminishes seriously and unexpectedly because of an unforeseen event. This can include any number of idiosyncratic events that are specific to the corporation or to an industry, including a natural or industrial accident, a regulatory change, a takeover or corporate restructuring, or corporate fraud. This risk is referred to generically as *event risk* and will result in a downgrading of the issuer by the rating agencies.

FACTORS CONSIDERED IN ASSESSING CREDIT DEFAULT RISK

The most obvious way to protect against credit risk is to analyze the creditworthiness of the borrower. In performing such an analysis, credit analysts evaluate the factors that affect the business risk of a borrower. These factors can be classified into four general categories—the quality of the borrower; the ability of the borrower to satisfy the debt obligation; the level of seniority and the collateral available in a bankruptcy proceeding; and restrictions imposed on the borrower.

In the case of a corporation, the quality of the borrower involves assessing the firm's business strategies and management policies. More specifically, a credit analyst will study the corporation's strategic plan, accounting control systems, and financial philosophy regarding the use of debt. In assigning a credit rating, Moody's states:

"Although difficult to quantify, management quality is one of the most important factors supporting an issuer's credit strength. When the unexpected occurs, it is a management's ability to react appropriately that will sustain the company's performance."[1]

The ability of the borrower to meet its obligations begins with the analysis of the borrower's financial statements. Commonly used measures of liquidity and debt coverage combined with estimates of future cash flows are calculated and investigated if there are concerns. In addition, the analysis considers industry trends, the borrower's basic operating and competitive position, sources of liquidity (backup lines of credit), and, if applicable, the regulatory environment. An investigation of industry trends aids a credit analyst in assessing the vulnerability of the firm to economic cycles, the barriers to entry, and the exposure of the company to technological changes. An investigation of the borrower's various lines of business aids the credit analyst in assessing the firm's basic operating position.

A credit analyst will look at the position as a creditor in the case of a bankruptcy. The US Bankruptcy Act comprises 15 chapters, each covering a particular type of bankruptcy. Of particular interest here are Chapter 7, which deals with the liquidation of a company, and Chapter 11, which deals with the reorganization of a company. When a company is liquidated, creditors receive distributions based on the *absolute priority rule* to the extent that assets are available. The absolute priority rule is the principle that senior creditors are paid in full before junior creditors are paid anything. For secured creditors and unsecured creditors, the absolute priority rule guarantees their seniority to equity holders. However, in the case of a reorganization, the absolute priority rule rarely holds because in practice unsecured creditors do in fact typically receive distributions for the entire amount of their claim and common stockholders may receive something, while secured creditors may receive only a portion of their claim. The reason is that a reorganization requires the approval of all the parties. Consequently, secured creditors are willing to negotiate with both unsecured creditors and stockholders in order to obtain approval of the plan of reorganization.

The restrictions imposed on the borrower (management) that are part of the terms and conditions of the lending or bond agreement are called *covenants*. Covenants deal with limitations and restrictions on the borrower's activities. Affirmative covenants call on the debtor to make promises to do certain things. Negative covenants are those that require the borrower not to take certain actions. A

"Great uncertainty about the values of financial assets, particularly more complex and opaque assets, has made investors extremely reluctant to bear credit risk." Ben Bernanke

     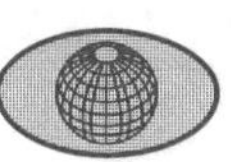   

violation of any covenant may provide a meaningful early warning alarm, enabling lenders to take positive and corrective action before the situation deteriorates further. Covenants play an important part in minimizing risk to creditors.

CREDIT RISK TRANSFER VEHICLES

There are various ways that investors, particularly institutional investors, can reduce their exposure to credit risk. These arrangements are referred to as *credit transfer vehicles*. It should be borne in mind that an institutional investor may not necessarily want to eliminate credit risk but may want to control it or have an efficient means by which to reduce it. The increasing number of credit risk transfer vehicles has made it easier for financial institutions to reallocate large amounts of credit risk to the nonfinancial sector of the capital markets.

For a bank, the most obvious way to transfer the credit risk of a loan it has originated is to sell it to another party. The bank management's concern when it sells corporate loans is the potential impairment of its relationship with the corporate borrower. This concern is overcome with the use of *syndicated loans*, because banks in the syndicate may sell their loan shares in the secondary market by means of either an *assignment* or a *participation*. With an assignment, a syndicated loan requires the approval of the obligor; that is not the case with a participation since the payments by the borrower are merely passed through to the purchaser, and therefore the obligor need not know about the sale.

Two credit risk vehicles that have increased in importance since the 1990s is securitization and credit derivatives. It is important to note that the pricing of these credit risk transfer instruments is not an easy task. Pricing becomes even more complicated for lower-quality borrowers and for credits that are backed by a pool of lower-quality assets, as recent events in the capital markets have demonstrated.

SECURITIZATION

Securitization involves the pooling of loans and/or receivables and selling that pool of assets to a third-party, a special purpose vehicle (SPV). By doing so, the risks associated with that pool of assets, such as credit risk, are transferred to the SPV. In turn, the SPV obtains the funds to acquire the pool of assets by selling securities. When the pool of assets consists of consumer receivables or mortgage loans, the securities issued are referred to as *asset-backed securities*. When the asset pool consists of corporate loans, the securities issued are called *collateralized loan obligations*.

The process of securitization is described in "Securitization: Understanding the Risks and Rewards" (pp. 576–578). A major reason why a financial or nonfinancial corporation uses securitization as a fund-raising vehicle is that it may allow a lower funding cost than issuing secured debt. However, another important reason is that securitization is a risk management tool. Although the entity employing securitization retains some of the credit risk associated with the pool of loans (referred to as retained interest), the majority of the credit risk is transferred to the holders of the securities issued by the SPV.

CREDIT DERIVATIVES

A financial derivative is a contract designed to efficiently transfer some form of risk between two or more parties. When a financial derivative allows the transfer of credit exposure of an underlying asset or assets between two parties, it is referred to as a *credit derivative*. More specifically, credit derivatives allow investors to either acquire or reduce credit risk exposure. Many institutional investors have portfolios that are highly sensitive to changes in the credit spread between a default-free asset and a credit-risky asset, and credit derivatives are an efficient way to manage this exposure. Conversely, other institutional investors may use credit derivatives to target specific credit exposures as a way to enhance portfolio returns. Consequently, the ability to transfer credit risk and return provides a tool for institutional investors; the potential to improve performance. Moreover, corporate treasurers can use credit derivatives to transfer the risk associated with an increase in credit spreads (i.e., credit spread risk).

Credit derivatives include credit default swaps, asset swaps, total return swaps, credit linked notes, credit spread options, and credit spread forwards. In addition, there are index-type or basket credit products that are sponsored by banks that link the payoff to the investor to a portfolio of credits. Credit derivatives are over-the-counter instruments and are therefore not traded on an organized exchange. Hence, credit derivatives expose an investor to counterparty risk, and this has been the major concern in recent years in view of the credit problems of large banks and dealer firms who are the counterparties.

Credit derivatives also permit banks to transfer credit risk without the need to transfer assets physically. For example, in a collateral loan obligation, a bank can sell a pool of corporate loans to a special purpose vehicle (SPV) in order to reduce its exposure to the corporate borrowers. Alternatively, it can transfer the credit risk exposure by buying credit protection for the same pool of corporate loans. In this case, the transaction is referred to as a *synthetic collateralized loan obligation*.

An understanding of credit derivatives is critical even for those who do not want to use them. As Alan Greenspan, then the Chairman of the Federal Reserve Board, in a speech on September 25, 2002, stated: "The growing prominence of the market for credit derivatives is attributable not only to its ability to disperse risk but also to the information it contributes to enhanced risk management by banks and other financial intermediaries. Credit default swaps, for example, are priced to reflect the probability of net loss from the default of an ever broadening array of borrowers, both financial and non-financial."[2]

CONCLUSION

While market participants typically think of credit risk in terms of the failure of a borrower to make timely interest and principal payments on a debt obligation, this is only one form of credit risk: credit default risk. The other types of credit risk

CASE STUDY

A *credit-linked note* (CLN) is a security, usually issued by an investment-grade-rated corporation, that has an interest payment and fixed maturity structure similar to a standard bond. In contrast to a standard bond, the performance of the CLN is linked to the performance of a specified underlying asset or assets as well as that of the issuing entity. There are different ways that a CLN can be credit linked, and we will describe one case here.

British Telecom issued on December 15, 2000, a CLN with a coupon rate of 8.125% maturing on December 15, 2010. The terms of this CLN stated that the coupon rate would increase by 25 basis points for each one-notch rating downgrade of British Telecom below A–/A3 suffered during the life of the CLN. The coupon rate would decrease by 25 basis points for each rating upgrade, with a minimum coupon set at 8.125%. In other words, this CLN allows investors to make a credit play based on this issuer's credit rating. In fact, in May 2003, British Telecom was downgraded by one rating notch and the coupon rate was increased to 8.375%.

"I am far more interested in avoiding risk than I am in capturing every opportunity. My philosophy says that loss of opportunity is preferable to loss of capital." Joseph DiNapoli

are credit spread risk and downgrade risk. When evaluating the credit default risk of a borrower, credit analysts look at the quality of the borrower, the ability of the borrower to satisfy the debt obligation, the level of seniority and the collateral available in a bankruptcy proceeding, and covenants. Credit risk transfer vehicles include securitization and credit derivatives. Credit derivatives include credit default swaps, asset swaps, total return swaps, credit linked notes, credit spread options, credit spread forwards, and baskets or indexes of credits.

▸▸ MAKING IT HAPPEN

Controlling credit risk requires not just an understanding of what credit risk is and the factors that affect a borrower's credit rating but other important implementation issues. These include:

- establishing the credit risk exposure that a corporation or institutional investor is willing to accept;
- quantifying the credit risk by using the latest quantitative tools in the field of credit risk modeling;
- understanding the various credit risk transfer vehicles that can be employed to control credit risk;
- evaluating the merits of different credit risk transfer vehicles to determine which are the most appropriate for altering credit risk exposure.

▸▸ MORE INFO

Books:

Anson, Mark J. P., Frank J. Fabozzi, Moorad Choudhry, and Ren-Raw Chen. *Credit Derivatives: Instruments, Pricing, and Applications.* Hoboken, NJ: Wiley, 2004.

Fabozzi, Frank J., Moorad Choudhry, and Steven V. Mann. *Measuring and Controlling Interest Rate and Credit Risk*. 2nd ed. Hoboken, NJ: Wiley, 2003.

Articles:

Fabozzi, Frank J., and Moorad Choudhry. "Originating collateralized debt obligations for balance sheet management." *Journal of Structured Finance* (Fall 2003): 32–52.

Fabozzi, Frank J., Henry A. Davis, and Moorad Choudhry, "Credit-linked notes: A product primer." *Journal of Structured Finance* (Winter 2007): 67–77.

Lucas, Douglas J., Laurie S. Goodman, and Frank J. Fabozzi. "Collateralized debt obligations and credit risk transfer." *Journal of Financial Transformation* 20 (2007): 47–59.

Websites:

DefaultRisk.Com—for credit risk modeling and measurement: www.defaultrisk.com

Vinod Kothari's credit derivatives website: www.credit-deriv.com

See Also:

★ Securitization: Understanding the Risks and Rewards (pp. 576–578)

NOTES

1 Moody's Investor Service. "Industrial Company Rating Methodology." *Global Credit Research* (July 2008): 6.

2 Speech titled "World Finance and Risk Management," at Lancaster House, London, United Kingdom.

"Through the fat years, the bankers were always right there by our side. But in bad times they backed off in a hurry." Lee Iacocca

  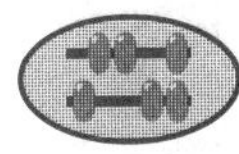 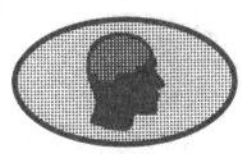  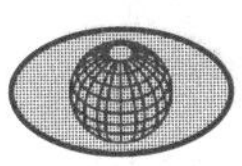   

Mixflation by Giles Keating

EXECUTIVE SUMMARY

- Mixflation is the deflation or rapid disinflation of one large and important block of prices, occurring simultaneously with the rapid inflation of another similarly large block. The collapse of manufactured good prices and surge in commodity prices over much of the last 10 years is a key example. This has now reversed rapidly, suggesting that monetary policy is a crucial driver of mixflation, and not just structural forces (urbanization, industrialization).
- We take a stylized description of global monetary policy (inflation targets, plus output for the Fed, in developed countries and exchange rate targets in emerging countries). We argue this encouraged excess investment in manufacturing etc., and insufficient consumption, in emerging countries. This exaggerated the divergence between manufactured and commodity prices, and created a savings glut, depressing long-term interest rates, and leading to excess risk-taking and asset price bubbles globally, which have now burst.
- A new global monetary regime is needed, with developed countries explicitly targeting asset price volatility alongside inflation, and emerging countries accepting a flexible system for adjusting exchange rates to avoid growing imbalances.

INTRODUCTION

Previous eras—viewed through the simplifying lens of history—seem often to fall into periods of inflation and deflation: the great falling-price boom of the 1880s; The deflationary slump of the 1930s; the inflationary 1970s. But modern times are more mixed. Over much of the last 10 years, manufactured goods prices have fallen while commodity prices soared. During 2008, this bifurcation seemed to briefly give way to a more generalized inflation, until the intensifying credit crisis suddenly instead suggested the risk of deflation. Meanwhile, for the second time within a decade, asset prices have moved in wild gyrations between boom and slump. We could describe this modern era as a phase of mixflation.

A LONGER-TERM PERSPECTIVE

There is considerable evidence to suggest that the experience of the last 10 years in relative price movements has been markedly greater than the preceding decades. Figure 1 shows the Reuters CRB commodity index, deflated by the US CPI and covering the period since the First World War. This shows a far larger percentage rise from the start of the current decade until the peak in July 2008 than recorded at any earlier point. This has been followed by a percentage decline that is also the largest on this data set.

Figure 2 provides evidence of increased volatility in real US house prices. It shows median US house prices (Census Bureau data, one family homes), deflated by core CPI. Following a sharp surge in the 10 years to the late 1970s, there was a period of some two decades of relative stability. Then, in the decade to 2008, there was a major surge. This took the peak growth to its highest peak in this data set. Moreover, it was followed by a sharp reversal down.

Looking at equity markets, Figure 3 shows the total real return (calculated using headline US CPI) on the US S&P 500 index and its predecessors, back to the middle of the 19th Century, and expressed as a deviation from trend. This illustrates that movements in real equity returns over the last 10 years have been more extreme than the past in certain respects. During the dotcom bubble, the index showed its highest ever deviation to the upside, in early 2000. The crash, partial recovery, and then renewed crash since then have taken the index close to the most extreme downside deviations previously recorded. The peak to trough movement is also the largest recorded apart from one event during the Great Depression.

ANALYSIS: MIXFLATION AND MONETARY POLICY

Why are we now living in times where rapidly rising prices in one major part of the economy coexist with falling prices in another, and where inflation can switch so suddenly to deflation? One driving force is global structural change, as demographic expansion in lower-income countries, and the logical and natural move of such countries to higher living standards, puts upward pressure on the prices of natural resources, especially when those had previously seen two decades of decline (see Figure 1). But while such long-term forces

Figure 1. Reuters CRB commodity index, deflated by US CPI

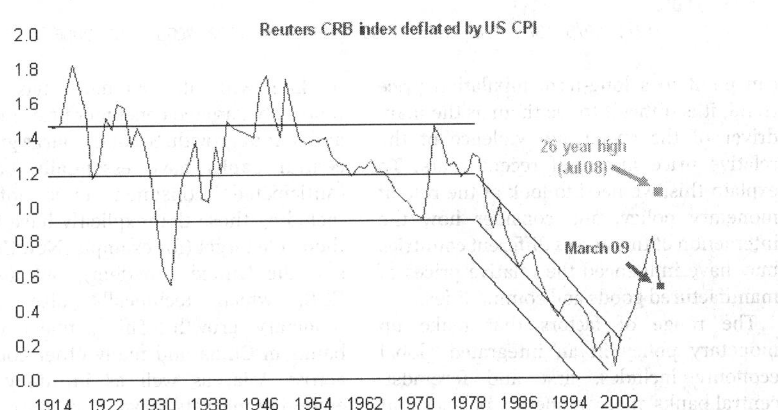

CASE STUDY

A few key figures will help to illustrate the recent experience of mixflation. Over the 10 years to December 2008, US manufactured consumer import prices (excluding autos) fell by a compound rate of 0.1% per annum, while prices of traded commodities (CCI index) rose by 6.6% annually. During the same period, US core consumer prices increased at a rate of 2.2% (and the headline rate by 2.8%) annually.

There were also very wide gyrations in share prices. Over the 10 years to the end of 2008, the US S&P 500 index changed relatively little (its annual return was –3%). However, there were two calendar years when it fell more than a fifth (2002 and 2008 with 23% and 38% falls, respectively) and one year when it rose more than a fifth (2003 with a 26% rise).

"I've come to the belief that banks are not in the business of banking. They're in the business of collecting fees." Patrick C. Kelly

   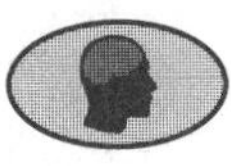  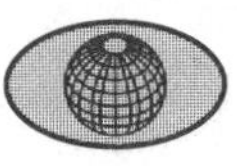  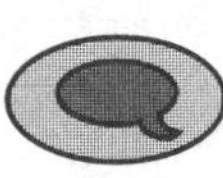 

Figure 2. US house prices relative to core CPI

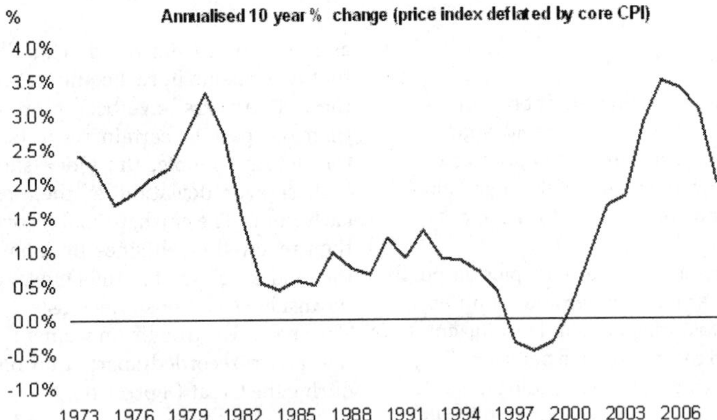

Figure 3. US real equity returns—deviation from trend

Note: green square represents latest available low-point (March 9, 2009)

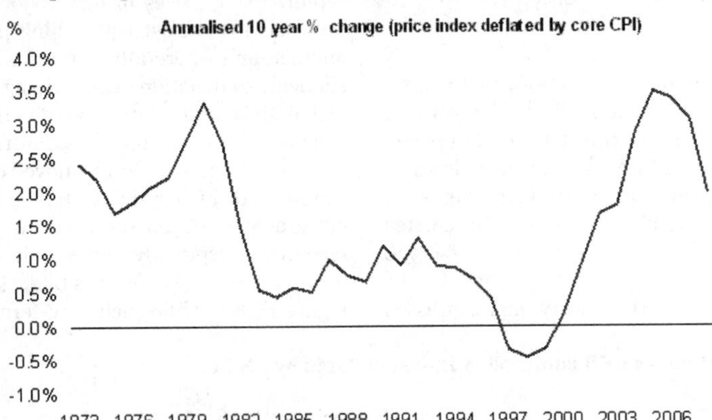

can point to a long-term mixflation price trend, it is difficult to see them as the main driver of the speed and violence of the relative price moves of recent years. To explain this, we need to look at the role of monetary policy, and consider how the interaction of this across different countries may have influenced the relative prices of manufactured goods and commodities.

The range of factors that make up monetary policy in an integrated global economy includes, first and foremost, central banks' macromonetary policies, but the context in which these operate is also critical. This includes financial regulation, fiscal policy, and exchange rate policy (including capital controls). The context also includes other key variables, influenced by past policy actions: The structure of the financial industry; the pace of financial innovation; the pattern of global capital flows; and the risk appetite of investors.

Looking back over the last decade, central banks' macromonetary policies can be divided into, broadly, three types, varying across countries. First, the US Fed, in line with its mandate, has simultaneously targeted consumer price inflation and output growth. Second, a large group of central banks have essentially targeted (anticipated) consumer price inflation, including those that explicitly have this as their sole target (for example, New Zealand and the United Kingdom), but also the ECB, which technically also targets monetary growth. Third, many central banks in China and many other countries across Asia, as well as in many other emerging markets, have, in practice, based monetary policy around an explicit or implicit exchange rate target. The Bank of Japan, wrestling with deflation for a decade, does not fit neatly into this framework, but can perhaps be described as nominally targeting price stability while *de facto* targeting an exchange rate characterized by long phases of depreciation or (more recently) stability, punctuated by occasional violent appreciations.

While these policy regimes were individually based on objectives that were sensible from a national perspective, when interacting together they have caused a range of outcomes that are highly undesirable.

In particular, exchange rate targets were typically set at a relatively low level, so the countries concerned saw high levels of net exports, and supernormal returns on real estate and industrial investment projects. The resulting distortions seem to have been one of the major causes of mixflation. The high rates of net exports boosted the global supply of (mainly lower-end) manufactured products, putting downward pressure on their prices. Simultaneously, the prospect of high returns encouraged large and arguably excessive investment in factories, infrastructure, and real estate, which in turn boosted demand for many commodities, ranging from base metals like copper through to oil and other energy sources. This contributed to surges in their prices, providing the other half of the mixflation phenomenon.

These policies also had distortive effects on international capital flows. Buoyant net exports, combined with large net capital inflows encouraged by the high investment returns, implied a large surplus on basic balance for many of these fast-growing emerging countries. The same occurred in Japan for slightly different reasons, with the basic balance surplus there mainly reflecting depressed consumption. To prevent these surpluses causing unwanted currency appreciation, the local central banks accumulated large foreign exchange reserves, much of which was invested in US government debt or near substitutes. This drove down yields on government debt to levels that appeared low on a theoretical basis (for example, if compared to trend nominal GDP growth).

These low yields were unattractive to many investors, including those like pension funds and insurers with clear future liability streams. Such investors responded by switching into higher-risk, lower-credit quality investments, including tranches of securitised structures with apparently good credit ratings. This lowered the cost and increased the availability of credit, which underpinned the expansion of subprime mortgages and general consumer credit in the United States and, to a varying extent, in many other countries, including the United Kingdom. It also fueled consumer booms and worsened trade deficits in these countries, as well as gradually boosting equity prices. With consumer prices kept under control by mixflation, being the main target of central banks, interest rates were set at a low enough level to accommodate this credit-induced boom, rather than ending it.

"There may be no greater challenges and no greater opportunities for the banking industry than those presented by rapidly changing technology. No industry is more suited to garnering the benefits of e-commerce." Gary Gensler

  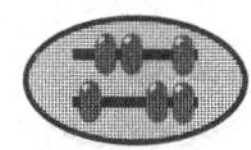   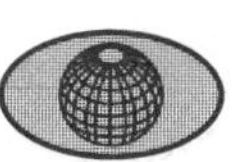   

This boom has now started to unwind. House prices, equity markets, and many credit assets rose to unsustainable levels and then collapsed; many individuals took on excessive loan commitments; banks took on high levels of risk and, eventually, public confidence in them began to be threatened as the extent of losses became clear. At the time of writing, the dollar remains reasonably robust, but this seems to reflect a number of short-term flow effects, and over time it may well come under substantial downward pressure.

Much of the commentary on the credit crisis has focused on issues such as the regulatory framework and capital requirements for banks, the possible perverse remuneration incentives for bank officers, and the role of the rating agencies. The above description suggests that each of these may have played some role, but it also implies that their importance was secondary, compared to the much more fundamental issue of global monetary policy having quite the wrong objectives. On the one hand, a key cause of the credit crisis was that emerging countries and Japan had their monetary policies influenced or dominated by exchange rates. This generated mixflation and perverse capital flows, which then made it inappropriate to focus monetary policy on consumer price inflation in the United States and elsewhere.

There are several rationales for targeting consumer prices, rather than variables, with the potential to be more forward looking (asset prices, credit, or money growth, etc.). First, the forward information content of such variables is meant to be difficult to quantify, especially as institutions change, and indeed some variables tend to become less relevant, precisely because they are targeted. Second, consumer prices are meant to be the ultimate anchor for asset prices. Third, central banks target forecasts of future consumer prices, rather than current levels, allowing them in principle to incorporate forward-looking indicators as appropriate. Fourth, there have been instances (the 1987 stock market crash being an example) where violent movements in key asset prices have occurred with apparently very little impact on the real economy, or on the general price level.

However, as the credit crisis has illustrated, asset price movements often do embed information about the future, even if the signal is not straightforward. For example, a high price for equities or debt may not be signaling robust income streams ahead as a simple time discount model might imply, but instead may be indicating a severe excess demand that over time will become unstable. Extracting this information certainly cannot be done by a crude rule but, nevertheless, it may be very important. Moreover, the path of asset prices clearly does matter in certain circumstances. Some assets (often the case with equities) are held by unleveraged end investors, or on their behalf by entities like pension funds, against very long-term future liabilities. In this case, rather substantial fluctuations may have relatively little feedback to the real economy. But other assets (such as many credit instruments) are held by highly leveraged institutions such as banks, which typically in the modern world have a ratio of assets to equity capital of 30 times or more. Fluctuations in the prices of such assets can clearly have major feed-through to the real economy.

APPENDIX: REVIEW OF LITERATURE

While the term "mixflation" has not been used in the academic literature, it has long been acknowledged that monetary policy may have to be set against the background of widely divergent price signals, especially when consumer prices and asset prices are behaving in a very different way.

The feedback between asset price fluctuations and real economic activity has long been acknowledged by economists (for example, Fisher 1930, Keating 1987), but it has tended to be argued that their influence on monetary policy should, at most, be secondary and indirect. Bernanke and Gertler (2000) suggest that while there is a case in principle for monetary policy to respond directly to "nonfundamental" moves in asset prices, in practice such effects are difficult to identify and therefore asset prices should be used only as an indirect input, via their impact on inflation projections. Subsequent debate has sometimes leant to a greater role for asset prices, with, for example, Borio (2005) advocating that policy be based on multi-year inflation projections, where asset prices play a greater role, while Ingves (2007) gives a practioner's description of (limited) targeting of asset price volatility at the Sveriges Riksbank.

For emerging market monetary policy, it has long been understood that the ability to set domestic interest rates and the exchange rate independently depends inversely on the amount of capital account mobility, and recent work (for example, Saxena 2008) provides some empirical estimates. Such discussions tend to assume that the countries involved are small, relative to the global financial system, but Greenspan (2007) notes that the savings glut in larger emerging countries was large enough to force down long-term US

▸▸ MAKING IT HAPPEN

The implication is that a new regime for central bank monetary policy is needed. For emerging countries, a global initiative should aim to de-politicize the delicate issue of exchange rate targets. It should establish the principle that the short-term gains to one country from an undervalued currency are outweighed over time by the pressures that build up, and should agree a flexible system for adjusting rates on a technical rather than political basis.

For the developed countries, consumer price forecasts should be only one pillar of a broader targeting, which should also include a mandate to dampen extreme fluctuations in asset prices. This mandate should not attempt to define asset price level targets, but rather should have a broad set of targets that included a range of valuation measures, and a range of measures of speed of movement. In short, it should acknowledge that there are severe limits to the signal, which can be extracted from asset prices, while at the same time making use of the crucial information that does lie buried in the noise. Such an approach immediately faces the criticism that it is not a clear and simple rule, but unfortunately we do not live in a simple world, and in any event, existing approaches, based on consumer price inflation, include complex modeling processes. Moreover, in determining the points at which verbal or actual exchange rate intervention is applied, central banks around the world already have experience in operating a regime with some of these characteristics, since the intervention points are often based on a combination of level and rate of change.

With hindsight, the era of mixflation, and the credit crisis with which it is intimately linked, seems to have been driven by unforeseen interactions between monetary policies in different countries across the world. There are powerful structural trends, tending to drive up commodity prices from the low relative levels they reached at the start of this decade. But they have been exaggerated, distorted, and reversed, probably temporarily, by the effects of monetary policy. A new regime is now needed to allow the mixflation era to resume in a more sustainable and ordered way.

"Bankers need a political sense, a second vision, just as sailors need a meteorological sense." Fritz Stern

  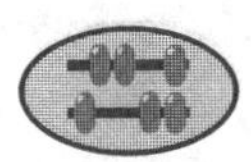 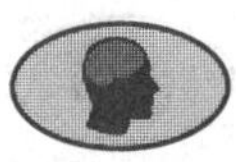  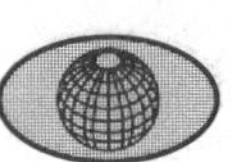   

government bond yields (so that a crucial asset price was influenced by, in Bernanke's terminology, a "nonfundamental" factor). A number of studies have looked at this "conundrum," for example, Warnock and Warnock (2006) conclude that it may have depressed yields by up to 90 basis points. Finally, a recent analysis by Frankel (2006) finds a clear empirical link between real interest rates and commodity prices, and concludes that the latter should be a key monetary condition indicator.

▸▸ MORE INFO

Books:

Frankel, J. "The effect of monetary policy on real commodity prices." In J. Campbell (ed). *Asset Prices and Monetary Policy*. Chicago, IL: University of Chicago Press, 2008.

Greenspan, A. *The Age of Turbulence, Adventures in a New World*. New York: Penguin Press, 2007.

Articles:

Bernanke, B., and M. Gertler. "Monetary policy and asset price volatility." National Bureau of Economic Research, Working paper 7559, 2000.

Borio, C. "Monetary and financial stability: So close and yet so far?" *National Institute Economic Review* 192:1 (2005): 84–101.

Fisher, I. "The debt-deflation theory of great depressions." *Econometrica* 1 (1993): 337–357.

Ingves, S. "Housing and monetary policy: A view from an inflation-targeting central bank." Remarks at the Federal Reserve Bank of Kansas City's Economic Symposium, Jackson Hole, Wyoming, 2007: 433–443.

Keating, G. "A two-good model with capital accumulation and a real balance effect." *Oxford Economic Papers* 39 (1987): 481–499.

Saxena, S. "Capital flows, exchange rate regime and monetary policy." In *Transmission Mechanisms for Monetary Policy in Emerging Market Economies*, BIS Papers No 35, January (2008): 81–102.

Warnock, F., and V. Warnock. "International capital flows and U.S. interest rates." National Bureau of Economic Research, Working Paper 12560, 2006.

NOTES

The author would like to thank Antonios Koutsoukis who provided invaluable assistance in preparing data and material for this paper.

"The distinctive function of the banker begins as soon as he uses the money of others." David Ricardo

  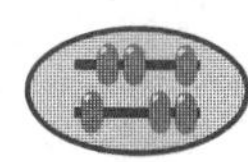   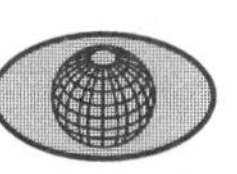   

Money Managers by David Pitt-Watson

EXECUTIVE SUMMARY

- Money managers invest trillions of dollars on behalf of millions of individuals.
- Investments primarily involve the holding and trading of shares.
- Money managers that own equities have a powerful role in the governance of companies, should they choose to exercise it.
- Active stockholders can be of great influence on how, and by whom, companies are managed.

A VAST AND DIVERSE INDUSTRY

Money managers (also known as fund managers or investment managers) manage money on behalf of other people. In most Western countries more than half the population will, directly or indirectly, have a money manager working for them. The managers find suitable investments, and are usually given the discretion by clients to make investments on their behalf.

It is usually the client who owns the investment and takes the risk that it will do well or badly. Therefore placing money with a money manager is different from putting it in a bank account. The bank offers a given return on your money, and it takes the risk on any loan or investment it may make.

The biggest money managers are household names; often they are part of banks or insurance companies. Examples are Fidelity, Vanguard, Barclays Global Investors, Nippon Life, Generali, Allianz, AXA, and Legal and General. Each of these companies manages hundreds of billions, and sometimes over a trillion dollars of people's savings. They have both individual clients and large institutional clients, such as pension funds, who will in turn represent many thousands of savers.

There are literally hundreds of money managers. Sometimes one money manager will use the funds they have under management to invest in another money manager's fund if they feel that gives them access to particular investment skills. And each may offer scores of different funds, each one designed to attract the savings of a particular type of investor.

Money managers invest in all sorts of things, from property to commodities, from government bonds to exchange rate futures. But their largest investments are in the shares and bonds issued by large companies, typically publicly traded companies, whose securities can be easily bought and sold should the need arise.

Money managers are hugely significant in large and developed capital markets. More than 80% of public company shares in the United Kingdom are owned through money managers. In the United States, Japan, and much of Continental Europe, the figure is around 70% and growing.[1]

SOME HISTORY AND CONTEXT

The growth of these financial giants is a comparatively modern phenomenon. In the early days of the Industrial Revolution most companies were both owned and managed by the founders and their families. Over the generations these families had less interest in management and wished to realize the value of their stockholding. One way to do so was to sell some of their shares on the stock market. And being quoted on the stock market had other advantages, in particular, access to a large pool of capital for companies needing finance.

Thus was born the significant stock markets that have now developed in most modern economies.

However, to manage investment in these companies requires a degree of expertise. First, to choose appropriate companies in which to invest. Second, to manage the administration of the various financial transactions that companies undertake, from paying dividends, to rights issues, share splits and repurchases, voting, and other rights given to stockholders.

By the 1950s, money managers had emerged as separate entities, often out of brokerage or other advisery businesses. However, the greatest fillip to their growth came with the development of the private pensions industry and its decision to invest in company securities, including company shares. In most developed capital markets in the 1950s, money managers might have held 15–30% of a company's shares—today it is nearer to three-quarters.[2]

Further, money managers have expanded globally as their investors have sought global investment opportunities. In most European countries, upwards of 40% of shares are owned by foreign investors, usually through a multinational money manager.

The development of an honest and ethical money management industry requires considerable regulation, oversight, and professionalism. After all, these people control trillions of dollars of other people's savings. In most jurisdictions, strict rules are applied on the custody of securities held on behalf of others. Investment mandates make specific rules on what sort of investments and risks can be taken, and regulators insist on systems for the management of conflicts of interest. Nevertheless such conflicts do occur, and they continue to raise issues for the money management industry.

WHAT MONEY MANAGERS DO

So what does a typical money manager do? This, of course, depends on the particular investment mandate they have been given. They may, for example, specialize in Japanese company equities, or in US government bonds, and so on.

However, the usual process of deciding how, say, a pension fund will be managed would be as follows:

- First, the fund will allocate its investments among different types of asset, to maximize return while minimizing risk. So money may be allocated to bonds, equities, property, and other more specialized asset classes.
- Each of these investments has particular characteristics. A bond will give a certain financial return, provided that it is held for its entire life. An equity will give a less certain return but may yield more over the long term, and it is less likely to have its value eroded by inflation.
- Often, a significant investor will choose a specialized money manager for each asset class.
- Usually the money manager will be set a benchmark against which their performance will be judged. So a US equities manager may be compared to the performance of the US stock market. They aim to outperform this benchmark, usually by buying shares which they believe to be cheap, and selling them when they feel they are relatively expensive.

A whole industry of brokers and information providers has grown to serve this trading. Accountants prepare financial statements on company performance. Credit rating agencies decide whether or not a bond is likely to default. Others provide information on the management, the governance, or the social and environmental performance of companies.

In turn, fund managers often specialize in increasingly arcane and complex

"For most large companies it is the money management industry which will represent their shareholders."

  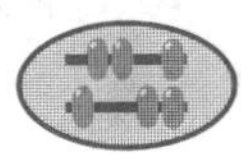   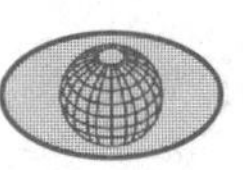   

products, usually with the aim of beating the benchmark. In the fund management world, the average return achieved by the market is known as the beta return. Any additional return is known as the alpha return. Hence, fund managers are focused on seeking the alpha.

EQUITY FUND MANAGEMENT

For most CEOs or boards of companies which are not in crisis, the most significant fund manager is likely to be the one that owns the equities, or shares, in their company. It is therefore worth reviewing some of the different styles of equity fund manager.

The classic mandate is that of the active fund manager. Their aim is to spot companies whose share price is low or high relative to what the money manager believes the ultimate value will prove to be. Active fund managers therefore have a great interest in gaining insight into a company in advance of other investors. In doing this they have to avoid receiving insider information. This is information that is known to people who have access to privileged company information but not known or readily knowable to all stockholders. To avoid abuse of one stockholder by another, it is against the regulations to trade shares if you are "inside" (i.e. in receipt of insider information). However, there are many sources and combinations of sources that active funds use to help them outperform. These can vary from long-term analysis of a company's prospects, to short-term predictions of a company's announcements, and the likely reaction to them. Some managers use quantitative models of a company's behavior, and complex statistics, to try to predict whether its share price is likely to rise or fall. Since it is the trading of shares which determines the price, this often means that money managers try to guess how other money managers are likely to behave.

Some active fund managers seek mandates that encourage them to take significant risks. Others will make only marginal bets to ensure that their performance is never too bad. The latter are known as closet tracker funds.

During the 1970s, researchers studied active fund managers to see whether they were able to beat the market. They discovered that the success of those who did beat the market could be attributed to luck as much as to skill. For that reason, many investors decided that they would stop hiring managers to buy and sell shares and instead hire them to track the market, or the market index. These funds, known as index tracker funds, now account for a significant part of the equity market.

In the last 10 to 15 years, the growing sophistication of derivatives markets has opened new possibilities for fund managers. Rather than simply investing in a security (long-only investing), they can invest in options to buy or sell, or contracts for difference. They can borrow a share and sell it on, so that they will benefit if the share price goes down (known as shorting). Or they can go long in some stocks and short in others, which they believe will allow them to maximize the value of their research into companies and hedge the risk that all company stocks will rise or fall. Such sophisticated investment strategies are often undertaken by hedge funds.

By owning a share in a company, a fund manager also becomes entitled, in most jurisdictions, to vote for who will be on the board of directors and on other issues where there is a need to protect owners' interests. Overt use of these powers lies behind the growth of stockholder activist funds. These invest in companies where they think the management is not creating value as it ought, and they seek to use stockowner powers to bring about a change in the management, the strategy, or the finances of the company.

DIFFERENT TYPES OF EQUITY MANAGER

Money managers have developed different legal forms or vehicles through which to carry out their work. One simple form would be to create a segregated account to handle an investor's funds. Or they may suggest that the investor puts their money in a pooled account. In different countries there are different vehicles through which fund managers operate, often in response to legal and taxation rules. These can include pension and life insurance funds, open- and closed-end funds, mutual funds, and others. More recently there has been a huge growth in exchange-traded funds, which reflect the value of a particular market or index and can be bought or sold at a price reflecting that index.

Depending on their investment philosophy and their mandate, fund managers have a different influence on company management. Active fund managers, who trade shares, determine the share price of a company. If this falls too low it may well attract another company wishing to make a bid. Even if no bid is forthcoming, the failure of a company to maintain a strong return for its stockholders will reflect very badly on management.

Active stockholders are very concerned with the news flow of the company. They will aim to meet the management of the company on a regular basis following company profit announcements. A large company may send their CEO to 50 or more private meetings with money managers following the annual profit announcement. Often their analysts will build complex models of the company's finances and be keen to test assumptions. However, their response to poor management by the company is more often to sell the shares than to agitate for change. Index tracking managers, on the other hand, have few resources to quiz companies. Their strategy will be to hold the shares provided that the company forms part of the index.

Activist stockholders are a different breed. They are keen to influence management decisions. Sometimes this is done in private discussion, but often companies find that their discussions with activists have been leaked to the press, since this is one way that a stockholder, who holds only a limited amount of the company's equity, can put pressure on management.

INFLUENCE OF COMPANY MANAGEMENT

Different fund managers will therefore seek to influence company behavior in different ways, depending on the mandate they have been given by their investors. We have already discussed active and activist managers. Passive managers take only modest interest in day to day performance, but may be more interested in longer-term issues of governance and corporate social responsibility. Some hedge funds may even be in the position where it is in their economic interest for a company to do badly—for example if they are "short" the shares.

Many directors also complain that, since fund managers are often measured on short-term performance, they encourage companies to take action that will cause a short-term rise in the share price but which will damage the company in the longer term, by which time the money manager may have sold his stake. Whatever the truth of these criticisms, it is clearly against the interests of the company and its continuing stockholders to sacrifice a good long-term future for short-term gain.

Directors should also be aware that money managers have multiple sources of information about their companies, from brokers, voting agencies, credit rating agencies, accountants, and many other providers of information. Therefore, as well as briefing money managers who own their shares, they also need to put considerable effort into briefing others who will opine on company performance.

"Different money managers will seek to influence company behaviour in different ways."

  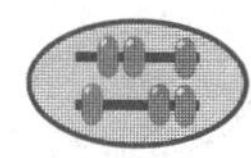   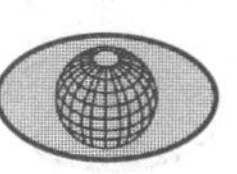   

▸▸ MAKING IT HAPPEN

Finance directors should remember that it is their role to ensure that the company strategy creates value for stockholders. If money managers trust this to be the case, and they enjoy equal access to information about the company, this will usually stand a company in good stead. In dealing with investors, companies will discover managers keen to learn about their company. Finance managers may wish to enquire about the style of the manager's investments, and hence their motivation in investing.

Finance directors are often one of the principle points of contact for money managers. If their company is well run, and if they give appropriate ownership information, they are likely to find relations good. However, if information is unreliable, or inconsistent, or if the company is ill managed, this can cause enormous problems. After all, it is the stockholders for whom the company should be run, and in most countries it is the stockholders who decide who should be on the board of directors.

▸▸ MORE INFO

Book:

Davis, Stephen, Jon Lukomnik, and David Pitt-Watson. *The New Capitalists: How Citizen Investors Are Reshaping the Corporate Agenda.* Boston, MA: Harvard Business School Publishing, 2006.

See Also:

- Gary Brinson (p. 1156)
- George Soros (p. 1197)
- The Alchemy of Finance: Reading the Mind of the Market (p. 1218)

NOTES

1 Davis, Lukomnik, and Pitt-Watson, 2006, p. 4*ff.*

2 *Ibid.*

"Finance managers may wish to inquire about money manager's motivation in investing."

  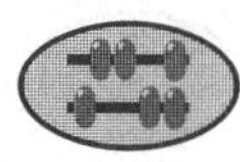 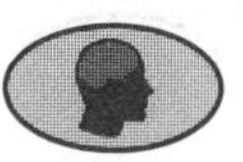  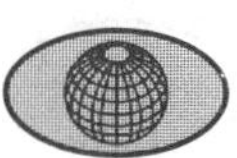   

The Performance of Socially Responsible Mutual Funds by Luc Renneboog

EXECUTIVE SUMMARY

Socially responsible investment funds employ negative and positive screens to select firms for their portfolios. These screens are based on environmental, social, or ethical criteria.

Trade-off: SRI funds could perform better than conventional ones as SRI funds comprise more carefully and actively selected firms. However, SRI funds could perform worse as the screening reduces the diversification potential which comes at a cost.

SRI performance measurement should involve an asset pricing model that captures investment styles. The Fama–French–Carhart model includes the market, firm size, growth opportunities, and share price momentum. In addition, the performance of SRI funds should be compared with the performance of conventional (non-SRI) funds.

Recent research shows that the performance SRI funds around the world is below the expected performance (measured by, for instance, the Fama–French–Carhart model). Furthermore, SRI funds do not outperform their conventional counterparts.

INTRODUCTION

Over the past decade, socially responsible investment (SRI), frequently also called ethical investment or sustainable investment, has grown rapidly around the world. SRI is a process that integrates social, environmental, and ethical considerations into investment decision making. Unlike conventional types of investment, SRI funds apply a set of investment screens to select or exclude assets based on ecological, social, corporate governance, or ethical criteria, and SRI often engages in the local communities and in shareholder activism to further corporate strategies towards the above aims.

WHAT TYPE OF INVESTMENT SCREENS DO SRI FUNDS EMPLOY?

Table 1 presents a summary of the SRI screens used by ethical funds around the world. Usually, SRI mutual funds apply a combination of the various types of screens. 64% of all socially screened mutual funds in the United States use more than five screens, while 18% of SRI funds use only one social screen (Renneboog, ter Horst, and Zhang, 2008a). These screens can be broadly classified into two groups: negative screens and positive ones.

Negative Screens

The oldest and most basic SRI strategy is based on negative screening. These filters refer to the practice that specific stocks or industries are excluded from SRI portfolios based on social, environmental, and ethical criteria. A typical negative screen can be applied on an initial asset pool such as the S&P 500 stocks from which the alcohol, tobacco, gambling, and defense industries, or companies with poor performance in labor relations or environmental protection, are excluded. Other negative screens may include irresponsible foreign operations, pornography, abortion, poor workplace conditions, violation of human rights, and animal testing. After performing a negative SRI screening, portfolios are created via a financial and quantitative selection. Some SRI funds only exclude companies from the investment universe when these firms' revenues derived from "asocial or unethical" sectors exceed a specific threshold, whereas other SRI funds also apply negative screens to a company's branches or suppliers. A small number of SRI funds use screens based on traditional ideological or religious convictions: for instance, they exclude investments in firms producing pork products, in financial institutions paying interest on savings, and in insurance companies insuring unmarried people.

Positive Screens

SRI portfolios are nowadays also based on positive screens, which in practice boils down to selecting shares that meet superior corporate social responsibility (CSR) standards. The most common positive screens focus on corporate governance, labor relations, the environment, sustainability of investments, and the stimulation of cultural diversity. Positive screens are also frequently used to select companies with a good record concerning renewable energy usage or community involvement. The use of positive screens is often combined with a "best in class" approach. Firms are ranked within each industry or market sector according to CSR criteria. Subsequently, only those firms in each industry which pass a minimum threshold are selected.

Combining Negative and Positive Screens

Negative and positive screens are often referred to as the first and second generation of SRI screens respectively. The third generation of screens refers to an integrated approach of selecting companies based on the economic, environmental, and social criteria comprised by both negative and positive screens. This approach is often called "sustainability" or "triple bottom line" (on account of its focus on people, planet, and profit).

Shareholder Activism

The fourth generation of ethical funds combines the sustainable investing approach (third generation) with shareholder activism. In this case, portfolio managers or the companies specialized in granting ethical labels attempt to influence the company's actions through direct dialogue with the management or by the use of voting rights at Annual General Meetings.

> "The main reason why SRI investors may be willing to pay such a price for ethics or social responsibility is based on aversion to corporate behavior which is deemed unethical or asocial."

DOING WELL BY DOING GOOD?

The fact that SRI funds apply screens that limit the full diversification potential may shift the mean-variance frontier towards less favorable risk–return tradeoffs than those of conventional portfolios. For instance, excluding part of the stock market (firms producing alcohol, tobacco, pornography) may negatively influence the risk–return tradeoffs of SRI funds. By this logic, SRI funds are expected to generate a weaker performance than conventional funds for two reasons. First, SRI funds underinvest in financially attractive investment opportunities, as some of these opportunities are excluded from the investment universe because they do not contribute sufficiently to the SRI objectives of the fund. Second, more intense

"The life of money-making is one undertaken under compulsion, and wealth is evidently not the good we are seeking; for it is merely useful and for the sake of something else." Aristotle

  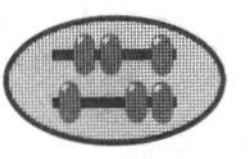   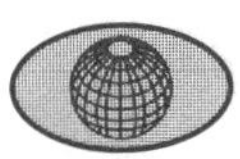   

Table 1. SRI screens. (*Source*: Renneboog, ter Horst, and Zhang, 2008b)

Screens	*Definitions*	*Pos. or Neg. screen*
Tobacco	Avoid manufacturers of tobacco products.	–
Alcohol	Avoid firms that produce/market alcoholic beverages.	–
Gambling	Avoid casinos and suppliers of gambling equipment.	–
Defense/weapons	Avoid firms producing weapons.	–
Nuclear power	Avoid manufacturers of nuclear reactors and firms operating nuclear power plants.	–
Irresponsible foreign operations	Avoid firms with investments in firms located in oppressive regimes such as Burma or China, or firms that mistreat the indigenous peoples of developing countries.	–
Pornography/Adult entertainment	Avoid publishers of pornographic magazines; production studios that produce offensive video and audio tapes; companies that are major sponsors of graphic sex and violence on television.	–
Abortion/Birth control	Avoid providers of abortion; manufacturers of abortion drugs and birth control products; insurance companies that pay for elective abortions.	–
Labor relations and workplace conditions	Seek firms with strong union relationships, employee empowerment, and/or employee profit sharing. Avoid firms exploiting their workforce and sweatshops.	+ –
Environment	Seek firms with proactive involvement in recycling, waste reduction, and environmental cleanup. Avoid firms producing toxic products, and contributing to global warming .	+ –
Corporate governance	Seek companies demonstrating "best practices" related to board independence and elections, auditor independence, executive compensation, expensing of options, voting rights and/or other governance issues. Avoid firms with antitrust violations, consumer fraud, and marketing scandals.	+ –
Business practice	Seek companies committed to sustainability through investments in R&D, quality assurance, and product safety.	+
Employment diversity	Seek firms pursuing an active policy related to the employment of minorities, women, gays/lesbians, and/or disabled persons who ought to be represented amongst senior management.	+
Human rights	Seek firms promoting human rights standards. Avoid firms which are complicit in human rights violations.	+ –
Animal testing	Seek firms promoting the respectful treatment of animals. Avoid firms with animal testing and firms producing hunting/trapping equipment or using animals in endproducts.	+ –
Renewable energy	Seek firms producing power derived form renewable energy sources.	+
Biotechnology	Seek firms that support sustainable agriculture, biodiversity, local farmers, and industrial applications of biotechnology. Avoid firms involved in the promotion or development of genetic engineering for agricultural applications.	+ –
Community involvement	Seek firms with proactive investments in the local community by sponsoring charitable donations, employee volunteerism, and/or housing and educational programs.	+
Shareholder activism	The SRI funds that attempt to influence company actions through direct dialogue with management and/or voting at Annual General Meetings.	+
Unmarried	Avoid insurance companies that give coverage to unmarried couples.	–
Healthcare/ Pharmaceuticals	Avoid healthcare industries (used by funds targeting the "Christian Scientist" religious group).	–
Interest-based financial institutions	Avoid financial institutions that derive a significant portion of their income from interest earnings on loans or fixed-income securities (used by funds managed according to Islamic principles).	–
Pork producers	Avoid companies that derive a significant portion of their income from the manufacturing or marketing of pork products (used by funds managed according to Islamic principles).	–

screening intensity further reduces the investment universe, which may further weaken performance.

However, there are two arguments supporting the alternative hypothesis that states that SRI funds outperform conventional funds. First, sound social and environmental performance signals high managerial quality, which translates into favorable financial performance. Second, social, ethical, and environmental screening may reduce the high costs that emerge during corporate social crises or environmental disasters. If financial markets tend to undervalue such costs, portfolios based on corporate governance, social, or environmental criteria may outperform their benchmarks.

HOW TO MEASURE THE PERFORMANCE OF SRI FUNDS

The performance of ethical (versus conventional) funds is measured by time-series returns of an equally weighted portfolio of funds. One can evaluate the performance of the fund portfolios on a country basis from a local investor perspective: The country portfolios of mutual funds are in local currency, evaluated against local benchmark factors while using local risk-free interest rates. Alternatively, one can assess fund performance from the perspective of an international investor by using international indices as benchmarks.

A first performance measurement method is based on the capital asset pricing model (CAPM):

$$r_t - r_{f,t} = \alpha_1 + \beta_{MKT}(r_t^m - r_{f,t}) + \varepsilon_t$$

where r_t is the return on an equally weighted portfolio of funds in month t, $r_{f,t}$ is the return on a local risk-free deposit (i.e. the one-month treasury bill rate or the interbank interest rate), r_t^m is the return of a local equity market index, β_{MKT} is the factor loading on the market portfolio, and ε_t stands for the idiosyncratic return. α_1 is Jensen's alpha; if alpha is positive, the funds do better than anticipated, whereas a negative alpha indicates underperformance.

"Invest with your brain and heart. Invest for our planet. . .The Funds give investors the ability to unite their financial goals with environmental progress." Sierra Club Funds prospectus

  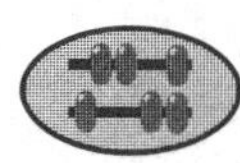   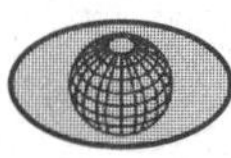   

A more robust evaluation method consists of the four-factor model, which includes the market, size, book-to-market, and momentum factors (this is also called the Fama–French–Carhart model). This model controls for the impact of investment styles on performance:

Table 2. SRI fund performance around the world. (*Source*: Renneboog, Ter Horst, and Zhang, 2008a)

		α_4
Europe		
Belgium	SRI	−5.26
Conventional		−0.78
Difference		−4.48
France	SRI	−5.96*
Conventional		−1.87
Difference		−4.08*
Germany	SRI	−0.62
Conventional		−1.35
Difference		0.73
Ireland	SRI	−6.14*
Conventional		0.55
Difference		−6.69*
Italy	SRI	−2.82
Conventional		0.86
Difference		−3.69
Luxembourg	SRI	−3.34
Conventional		0.11
Difference		−3.45
Netherlands	SRI	−4.10**
Conventional		−2.59*
Difference		−1.50
Norway	SRI	−4.20
Conventional		−1.12
Difference		−3.09
Sweden	SRI	−6.46*
Conventional		0.51
Difference		−6.97**
Switzerland	SRI	−3.01
Conventional		−0.91
Difference		−2.10
United Kingdom	SRI	−2.22*
Conventional		−1.14
Difference		−1.08
North America		
United States	SRI	−3.37*
Conventional		−2.48*
Difference		−0.89
Canada	SRI	−5.35*
Conventional		−2.24*
Difference		−3.11
Asia-Pacific		
Australia	SRI	−2.59
Conventional		−0.38
Difference		−2.21
Japan	SRI	−5.03*
Conventional		0.81
Difference		−5.84*
Malaysia	SRI	−2.99*
Conventional		0.44
Difference		−3.43
Singapore	SRI	−5.71
Conventional		0.95
Difference		−6.66

*Statistical significance

$$r_t - r_{f,t} = \alpha_4 + \beta_{MKT}(r_t^m - r_{f,t}) + \beta_{SMB} r_t^{smb} + \beta_{HML} r_t^{hml} + \beta_{UMD} r_t^{umd} + \eta_t$$

where r_t^{smb}, r_t^{hml}, and r_t^{umd} are the small-versus-big (SMB), high-minus-low (HML) and momentum (UMD) factors, β_{MKT}, β_{SMB}, β_{HML}, and β_{UMD} are the factor loadings on the four factors, and γ_t stands for the idiosyncratic return. α_4 is the four-factor-adjusted return of ethical fund portfolios; if this alpha is positive, the funds do better than anticipated by this asset pricing model, whereas a negative alpha indicates underperformance.

More complex asset pricing models that allow for time-varying risk loadings can be implemented, but these are beyond the scope of this article.

Do SRI Funds Outperform?

- *Performance measure 1:* Is the alpha of the above asset pricing model positive? (Do SRI funds perform better than anticipated by a general asset pricing model that controls for the conventional investment styles?).
- *Performance measure 2:* Is the alpha of SRI funds higher than the alpha of conventional funds? (Do SRI funds outperform the reference group of conventional, non-SRI, funds?).

THE SRI RETURNS

For all SRI funds around the world over the period 1992–2003 (see More Info), some striking results are obtained. SRI funds in all countries on average underperform the stock market index, and SRI funds in all countries on average underperform conventional (non-SRI) funds.

Table 2 shows that:

- α_4 is negative for the SRI funds in all countries. Thus, SRI funds underperform the benchmarks: the market, size, book-to-market, and momentum factors (although it should be noted that some negative returns are not statistically different from zero).
- The conventional funds do not succeed in outperforming the market. The reason is simple: Active funds usually do not succeed in consistently beating the market.
- SRI funds on average underperform conventional funds.

CONCLUSION

Ethical, social, environmental, or governance considerations influence the stock prices, and investors pay a price for the use of SRI screening by funds. The main reason why SRI investors may be willing to pay such a price for ethics or social responsibility is based on aversion to corporate behavior which is deemed unethical or asocial. Investors of SRI funds may thus explicitly deviate from the economically rational goal of wealth-maximization by pursuing social objectives. SRI funds in many European, North-American and Asia-Pacific countries strongly underperform domestic benchmark portfolios (such as the Fama–French–Carhart factors). When comparing the alphas of the SRI funds with those of matched conventional funds, the SRI returns are lower than those of conventional funds, but there is little statistically significant evidence that SRI funds underperform their conventional counterparts in most countries (exceptions being France, Ireland, Sweden, and Japan).

CASE STUDY

In relation to the ethical fund of a major Dutch insurance company, we use the independent services of the Ethical Investment Research Service (EIRIS) to screen the suitability of shares for ethical investment. Shares are also screened by our in-house ethical research team.

Examples of the type of companies not suitable for ethical investment include companies that:

- provide animal testing services or which manufacture or sell animal tested cosmetics or pharmaceuticals;
- have any involvement in intensive farming and that operate abattoirs or slaughterhouse facilities;
- are producers or retailers of meat, poultry, fish, dairy products, or slaughterhouse byproducts;
- manufacture armaments, nuclear weapons, or associated strategic products;
- provide critical services to, or are owners or operators of, nuclear power facilities;
- provide adult entertainment services.

  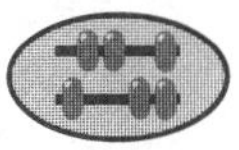 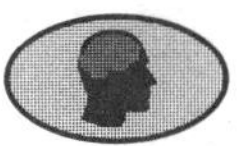  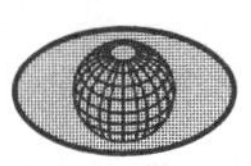   

▸▸ MAKING IT HAPPEN

- Decide whether you are an ethical investor: Do you care about the environment, the social responsibility of firms, human rights, or other social responsibility issues?
- If yes, are you willing to accept a return from an SRI fund that is less than that of conventional (non-SRI) funds?
- If yes, choose the type of fund by reading about the SRI of the fund. Select the screens that you deem most important—for instance, investment in producers of alternative energy; investment in firms with a good human rights record in the developed and developing world; no investment in weapons manufacturers.
- Choose the investment style of the fund: Do they use negative screens or a best-of-class approach on firms that pass the SRI filters?
- Compare the management and load fees of the selected SRI funds.

▸▸ MORE INFO

Books:

Schepers, Donald. *Socially Responsible Investing*. London: Routledge, 2009.

Vogel, David. *The Market for Virtue: The Potential and Limits of Corporate Social Responsibility*. Washington, DC: Brookings Institution Press, 2006.

Articles:

Renneboog, L., J. ter Horst, and C. Zhang. "Is ethical money financially smart?" Finance working paper 117/2006, European Corporate Governance Institute, 2006. Online at: ssrn.com/abstract=887162

Renneboog, L., J. ter Horst, and C. Zhang. "The price of ethics and stakeholder governance: The performance of socially responsible mutual funds." *Journal of Corporate Finance* 14:3 (2008a): 302–322.

Renneboog, L., J. ter Horst, and C. Zhang. "Socially responsible investments: Institutional aspects, performance, and investor behavior." *Journal of Banking and Finance* 32:9 (2008b): 1723–1742.

Websites:

Social Investment Forum: www.socialinvest.org

Sustainable Investment Research International (SiRi): www.siricompany.com

See Also:

★ Ethical Funds and Socially Responsible Investment: An Overview (pp. 306–308)

Muhammed Yunus (p. 1205)

i Social Responsibility of Management (pp. 1735–1737)

"Our joint objective is that bankers should become uniformly acceptable as wise counsellors and friends of the community as a whole and not merely as associates of particular sections of society." Indira Gandhi

  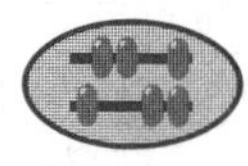  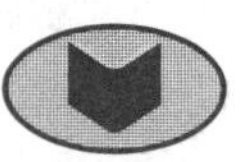 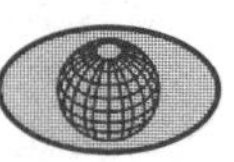   

Price Discovery in IPOs by Jos van Bommel

EXECUTIVE SUMMARY

- When a company goes public, the issuer's intermediating investment bank (aka underwriter, bookrunner, or lead manager) expends efforts and resources to discover the price at which the firm's shares can be sold.
- Buy-side clients also expend effort and resources to value the firm. The market price will be a weighted average of the many resulting value *estimates*.
- To discover the price, the issuer helps buy-side clients with their analysis by providing a prospectus and meeting with their analysts during road show meetings.
- To extract the newly produced information from the market, the issuing team asks selected buy-side clients for indications of their interest.
- Investment banks compensate buy-side clients for their costly analysis by setting the price at a discount from the expected market price.
- In addition, investment banks allocate more shares to those buy-side clients who are more helpful in the price discovery exercise. Because of the repeated interaction between banks and their clients, free riding is curtailed, and price discovery is optimized.

PRICE DISCOVERY

The most important, yet most difficult, part of the initial public offering (IPO) process is setting the offer price. In an IPO, the issuer, aided by an intermediating investment bank, plans to sell a relatively large number of shares of common stock in which there is at that point no market. However, they know that soon after the IPO process the secondary market will impute all the information in the market in an efficient manner. Investors who believe the price to be too high will sell; investors who believe the price to be too low will buy. The key outcome of this competitive trading is the *market price* of the stock.

Naturally, the issuing team (the issuer and its adviser(s)) would like to know the market price in advance. If they had a crystal ball, they would set the price at a small discount (say 3%) to the future market price, so as to generate sufficient interest from buy-side clients. In fact this is exactly what issuers do when they sell securities which already have a market price. Unfortunately, there is no secondary market for IPO shares, and neither are there crystal balls.

To estimate the market price as best as they can, issuers and their advisers conduct a costly analysis to estimate the value of the firm. We call this process *price discovery*.

Note that not only do the issuer and its investment bank analyze the firm. Prospective investors also conduct costly analysis to predict the future market price. Naturally, a good estimate of the future market price gives them a substantial advantage in their dealings with the issuer: If they have strong indications that the offer price is set too high, they stay away from the offering. If they believe the price to be below the future market price, they sign up for IPO shares enthusiastically.

ENTERPRISE VALUATION

There are two main methods to estimate the market value of the firm: multiple analysis, and discounted cash flow (DCF) analysis.

Multiple Analysis

When employing the multiple method, analysts gather performance measures of the firm. A popular measure is *earnings* or *net income*. They multiply these performance measures using *multiples*. The appropriate multiple for a firm's earnings is the *price–earnings ratio*, or P/E. The multiples are obtained from similar firms, (so-called *proxies*, or *pure-plays*). For example, if listed paper manufacturers trade at an average P/E of 9, and we want to estimate the value of an unlisted paper company that recently reported a net income of \$1 million, we would estimate the market price to be \$9 million. Because this single estimate is bound to be imprecise, analysts collect *many* performance measures so as to get *many* estimates. Popular accounting performance measures are earnings, sales, operating income (EBIT), and cash flow (EBITDA). Apart from these, analysts use industry-specific performance measures such as passenger miles (for airlines), overnight stays (for hotels), or page visits (for internet companies). By employing more and more multiples, analysts aim to arrive at an ever more precise estimate of the market price.

Discounted Cash Flow Analysis

A more fundamental valuation method is discounted cash flow analysis. In an efficient market, securities should be worth the present value of the future cash payments that accrue to the shareholders. Since cash today is always more valuable than cash tomorrow, investors discount projected future cash flows at the opportunity cost of capital. For example, if investors want to value a one-year promissory note of \$100, and the one-year interest rate is 10%, they conclude that the note is worth \$100/1.10 = \$90.91. If future cash flows are uncertain (risky), investors use a higher discount rate (see p. 896 to see how the discount rate depends on risk).

Apart from deciding on an appropriate discount rate, investment analysts forecast the company's *free cash flows*, which are defined as the cash generated by operations less the cash dedicated to new investments. Often, young companies do not distribute cash flows to their financiers, but instead solicit cash from the financial markets. In fact, this is an important reason for doing an IPO in the first place. Naturally, the investments are expected to add to the future cash flows. Hence, analysts often predict negative free cash flows early in life, but expect them to become positive as the firm matures.

Forecasting a firm's free cash flows is difficult. To obtain reasonable conjectures, analysts make a *model* to project the revenues, expenses, and investments. Analysts' models can be very sophisticated. They analyze the products or services that the company provides, conduct industry analysis to gauge where the company stands vis-à-vis its competitors, consult market forecasts (of the firm's products and production costs), interview the firm's executives and other employees (as far as this is allowed by the laws that govern financial markets), and conduct sensitivity analysis.

Whatever method investment analysts use to estimate the market value of as yet untraded securities, valuing financial securities is a task that requires skill and effort.

ESTIMATES ARE OFTEN WRONG

Being an investment analyst does not just require hard work, it is also a risky job. After all, despite our best efforts, estimates often turn out to be wrong. That is the nature of *estimates*.

Each valuation is different. Analysts use different multiples, different proxies, and give different weights to individual multiple estimates. DCF valuations are highly sensitive to the many assumptions incorporated into a model, and to the

"Banking establishments are more dangerous than standing armies." Thomas Jefferson

discount rate used to arrive at a present value. Clearly, if we have many independent estimates, the highest estimate is likely to be too high and the lowest estimate is probably too low. If we assume that the estimates are unbiased, the true market value will lie somewhere in the middle.

Hence, there are two ways to engage in price discovery. The first is to help analysts to make more precise estimates. To do this, the issuer and its intermediaries (investment bank, auditor, legal advisers) provide buy-side analysts with a detailed prospectus, which explains the structure of the issue (for example, how many shares are sold), describes the company's business, and presents recent financial performance. In addition, they invite analysts to information sessions on the firm's products and managers. During such road-show presentations, the company presents its business plan, its managers, and its products to prospective investors. An important part of the road-show meetings is the question and answer session, during which analysts can pepper the issuing team with questions so as to fine-tune their models and estimates.

The second way to improve the price discovery is to involve more buy-side clients and more analysts. A statistical property called the *law of large numbers* says that if we have more estimates, the average of these will be closer to the true value. The problem, however, is that if we invite too many prospective investors, it will adversely affect the incentives to produce information.

SOUNDING OUT THE MARKET

When buy-side clients have done their analysis and have become "informed," issuers will find it easier to sell them their securities. However, there are still important differences in opinion among clients. Extracting these opinions is not a straightforward task. Clearly, buy-side clients will be reluctant to part with their hard-earned information. Nevertheless, issuers can *sound out the market* by individually targeting large and well-informed buy-side clients. They do this by ringing them up, and asking them for their opinions and indications of interest. The investment bank writes down indicative orders in a book of orders. This exercise is called *book-building*. Indicative orders can take three main forms. First there are *strike orders*, which indicate a demand that independent of the price. Second, there are *limit orders*, such as "I sign up for 150,000 shares as long as the price is not higher than $10." Finally, there are *step* orders, which are combinations of several limit orders. For example, "If the price is set at $9 or below, we want 130,000 shares; if it is set at $10 or less, we want 80,000 shares; and if you set it higher, we don't want any shares."

After one or two weeks of making phone calls, the bookrunner will have compiled a book of orders, which forms a downward sloping demand curve (see Figure 1). Naturally, this demand curve represents very valuable information for the price discovery process.

SETTING THE PRICE

One would think that the issuing team can now simply set the price so that demand equals supply. If all orders were genuine, this would be the optimal strategy. However, the new shareholders would feel fooled if, after expending significant efforts to analyze the firm, they received no surplus in return. To reward large and sophisticated buy-side clients for their analysis of the firm, investment banks set the offer price at a discount from the expected market price. Historically, the average discount, which translates into an average *initial return* (the return from the offer price to the market price) has been around 15%. Initial returns have been extensively studied. Average discounts differ between countries and time periods. All studies, however, find that smaller and more difficult to value IPO firms tend to be discounted more, which is consistent with the "compensation for analysis efforts" story.

The promise of a discount can be made credible because of the investment bank's reputation and its repeated interaction with the market's buy-side. For example, because Fidelity knows that Goldman Sachs will price IPO shares at a discount, they are willing to expend effort to analyze the IPO firm.

The problem with setting the offer price at a discount is that it attracts "free riders." It seems that investors who simply signed up for all IPOs would, on average, make a profit because of the discount. For this reason, investment banks only invite large and sophisticated investors to submit orders in the book. From experience and repeated interaction, investment bankers know whose indicative orders are most informative. Still, even among the invited bidders there is a temptation to overbid. Because they know that the shares will be set at a discount, buy-side clients want to bid for as many shares as possible. In other words, even the orders of the repeat clients may not be entirely genuine. An important task for the investment bank is to distinguish the *real* demand from the *book* demand (Figure 1). They can never do this perfectly, but, through skill and judgment, experienced bookrunners can assess the seriousness of book orders. So, after closing the book, the issuer compiles the book demand curve, gauges where the real demand is, and then sets the price at a small discount.

The price is set during the *pricing meeting*, which typically takes place on the evening before the actual floatation. During the pricing meeting the issue is officially underwritten, so that the bookrunner becomes legally liable for placing the shares. By scheduling this important

Figure 1. Example of an order book. During book-building, the lead manager calls up prospective buy-side clients and asks them for indicative orders. This results in an aggregate demand curve. Due to "gaming," the bookrunner knows that not all indications of interest are equally sincere, and he or she has to gauge what the *real demand* is—i.e. the demand that is not determined by overbidding (due to anticipated rationing). If the book is as shown in the diagram, and the offer size, including the over-allotment option, is 60 million shares, the underwriter may suggest an offer price of $9.50.

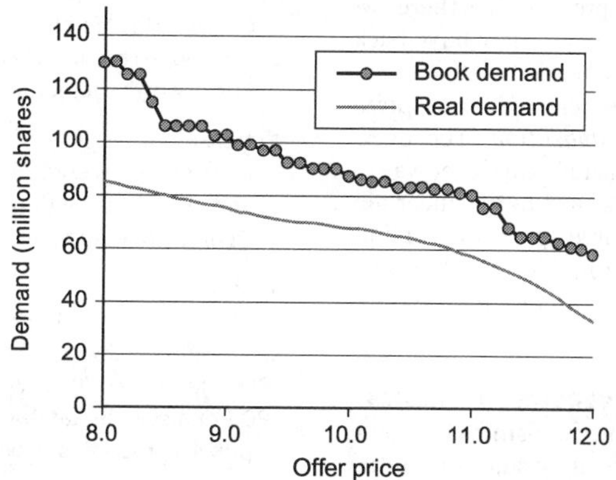

"I sincerely believe that banking establishments are more dangerous than standing armies, and that the principle of spending money to be paid by posterity, under the name of funding, is but swindling futurity on a large scale." Thomas Jefferson

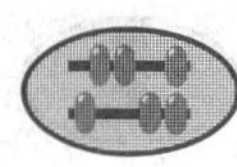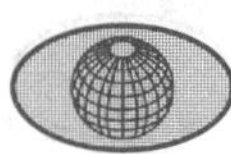

meeting shortly before the actual selling day, the bookrunner reduces the risk of being stuck with IPO shares on its books.

ALLOCATING THE SHARES

As mentioned, the IPO process is a repeated game for buy-side clients and investment banks. Both parties to the price discovery process develop long-term relationships. Investment bankers know which buy-side analysts provide the most accurate indications of interest, and reward them with higher allocations. One way to gauge the quality of the buy-side analysts is to monitor their order submission strategy and their trading behavior after the IPO. Strike orders may indicate poor analysis, while limit or step orders are better signals for price discovery. If a client often asks for large allocations, but then quickly sells ("flips") its shares in the secondary market, this is an indication of poor analysis. Orders that are submitted in the early stage of the book-building indicate confidence and informed decision-making. Hence, it is not surprising that we see that clients who put in limit or step orders early, and do not flip their shares in the secondary market, receive higher allocations on average.

THE OVER-ALLOTMENT OPTION

Almost all IPOs have an *over-allotment option*, also known as a *greenshoe*, named after the company that first used this mechanism. The over-allotment option gives the bookrunner the right to buy a specified number of additional shares from the issuer and sell them on to the buy-side. Or, they have the right to *over-allocate*. Typically, the option is for 15% of the offering size. In practice, the underwriter always over-allocates, so that after the offering the bank is technically "short": they have sold shares they do not yet own. The bookrunner will exercise the over-allotment option if the price in secondary market trading increases beyond the offering price, which is usually the case. If, however, the price in the secondary market comes under pressure (i.e. there is a lot of flipping), the underwriter buys back the shares in the open market.

This is sometimes referred to as *price support* or *price stabilization*. The over-allotment option is therefore a clever way to adjust the supply of shares to the uncertain demand for shares. By keeping track of flippers, bookrunners can monitor buy-side clients and gauge their quality for the price discovery process.

BOOK-BUILDING VERSUS AUCTIONS

The book-building mechanism has become the standard way of selling shares in initial public offerings. The characteristic difference from other IPO mechanisms is the close and personal interaction between relatively few players on both sides of the transaction. These cozy relationships, and the subsequent preferential allocations, sometimes make small investors, issuers, and regulators uneasy about the book-building mechanism. Naturally there is the chance that investment banks and buy-side clients collude to set the offer price low and share the profits of large initial returns. Although there certainly have been instances of doubtful allocations of conspicuously underpriced shares, the book-building mechanism has survived and is widely accepted. The key advantage is that it results in more *information production*.

An obvious alternative to book-building is the auction. Due to its fair and transparent nature, the auction mechanism has been used in several countries, including the United Kingdom, Denmark, and France. However, evidence shows that they are less effective in achieving a high price and a liquid aftermarket. Empirical studies have found that book-built IPOs have, on average, lower initial returns, especially if they were floated by prestigious investment banks.

The Google IPO and a stylized example (see Case Studies) further illustrate how targeted information exchange between relatively few informed players may be more effective for price discovery than an impersonal auction.

CASE STUDIES

The Google IPO

When Google went public in August 2004, it announced upfront that the price would be determined by a competitive Dutch auction in which everybody could participate on equal terms. Large and small investors were invited to submit their limit and step orders through the internet. The price would be set at the point where the 19.6 million shares could be sold. Large institutional investors openly grumbled at the "cheap" way Google was selling its shares, saying that they would not bother to get out of bed for an auction.

The result was that, due to the lack of a targeted information exchange, the market price was not fully discovered. The auctioneers set the offer price at $85, which was at the low end of expectations. When secondary market trading began, the price shot to above $100 within days, and above $200 within months, which suggested that Google did not get the true value for its shares. Many industry watchers (and the author of this article) believe that if Google had opted for a standard book building method, its shares would have fetched a higher price in the primary market.

Illustration of Targeted Information Exchange

Imagine that you receive a surprise inheritance from a distant uncle. The inheritance is a trunk full of foreign coins. Most are post-war coins from various countries, but your seven-year-old son has spotted some gold, silver, and very ancient coins. You are not much of a coin collector and are strapped for cash, so you decide to sell the coins. To do this you go to a coin collectors' fair. At the fair there is an auction session where you could put your coins up for sale. Alternatively, you could approach the three largest collectors, let each have a close look at your collection, explain your situation, and ask them for their offer. If your collection is difficult to value (as a company is), the second route may well get you a higher price.

▸▸ MORE INFO

Books:

Draho, Jason. *The IPO Decision: Why and How Companies Go Public*. Cheltenham, UK, Edward Elgar Publishing, 2006.

Gregoriou, Greg N. *Initial Public Offerings: An International Perspective*. Oxford: Butterworth-Heinemann, 2006.

Article:

Benveniste, Lawrence M., and Walid Y. Busaba. "Bookbuilding versus fixed price: An analysis of competing strategies for marketing IPOs." *Journal of Financial and Quantitative Analysis* 32:4 (1997): 383–403.

Websites:

IPOfinancial (IPOfn) news, analysis, and resources: www.ipofinancial.com

IPO Monitor—Coverage of IPOs and secondary equity offerings: www.ipomonitor.com

IPO-related searches: www.ipo.com

IPO Renaissance Capital— research and investment management services on newly public companies: www.ipohome.com

"A banker is a man who lends another man the money of a third man." Guy de Rothschild

  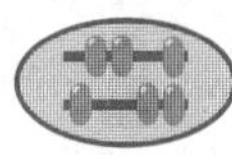   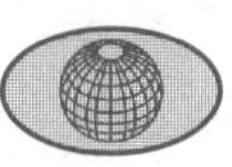   

Private Equity Fund Monitoring and Risk Management by Rainer Ender

EXECUTIVE SUMMARY

- Private equity fund monitoring is a continuous screening of the fund manager's development and the fund's progress, within the context of a top-down and bottom-up market analysis.
- Once implemented, a well-structured private equity monitoring framework, composed of qualitative and quantitative elements, facilitates an assessment addressing two dimensions; the manager and the fund.
- A consistent set of monitoring and benchmarking elements is essential for a coherent assessment of both the single funds and the aggregate portfolio, forming the basis for risk management.
- A functioning monitoring process enables investors to keep control over their private equity portfolio, and take appropriate action where needed. Early risk identification and active involvement are crucial in order to secure maximum value for their investments.

INTRODUCTION

Private equity fund commitments tend to be long-term investments of approximately 12 years. The fund's life consists of three general phases:

- Investment phase: deal origination, due diligence, investments;
- Value creation phase: (re-)positioning the investments for success;
- Harvesting phase: divesting portfolio companies.

Private equity monitoring is a continuous process of tracking the fund's progress and the fund manager's development. The goal of the process is to maximize the investment value and the relationship with the fund manager. Monitoring the current investment is an integral part of due diligence for the investment decision regarding the fund manager's next fund. Due diligence also has a deep monitoring effort on prior fund investments.

An effective private equity monitoring framework is a fine-tuned combination of quantitative and qualitative monitoring elements, based upon the systematic gathering of information and intelligence, supported by a robust IT platform. The information gathering and evaluation must be embedded in an overall monitoring framework. That framework must address concern/comfort levels with regards to funds and fund managers, and trigger which related actions are to be taken by the investor.

A MULTI-DIMENSIONAL PRIVATE EQUITY MONITORING FRAMEWORK

The monitoring process of private equity fund commitments is at the fund level, and is focused on the progress of the portfolio companies and financial performance. At the fund manager level, the investor concentrates on the manager's structural and behavioral developments, such as adherence to the strategy, governance structures, compliance with the terms of the partnership agreement, and the value contribution to the underlying portfolio companies.

It is important to highlight that monitoring involves far more than simple performance control. Monitoring identifies needs for action, and takes the measures needed to secure the best interest for the investor. A simple "traffic lights" concept relating to fund and fund manager illustrates the structured monitoring approach.

Four different monitoring situations can emerge from a private equity fund investment.

1. There is no reason for concern on both fund and fund manager level. The fund is developing on or above plan, and there are no disturbing developments from the manager side. The investor has a sufficient level of comfort on both aspects.
2. Concern about the fund but comfort with the fund manager. This situation can emerge due to negative external market effects/shocks. The impact of the negative effects on the underlying portfolio has been identified, analyzed, addressed, and communicated proactively by the fund manager in a timely manner. Nevertheless, a first escalation level for the monitoring activity is appropriate in such a situation, and can be summarized as follows. Actively support the fund manager to correct deviation. An intense dialogue with the manager and corrective measures are needed. When close interaction with the fund manager provides sufficient assurance that the required measures are taken, no special action may be needed beyond closer monitoring of the development.
3. Comfort with the fund, concern with the fund manager. This often occurs in the context of team issues at manager level, or deviation from the strategy (as a fund or as a manager). The future of the fund is at risk; this triggers the second level of escalation. Put pressure on the fund manager to take corrective actions.
4. Concern with the fund, concern with the fund manager. This development represents the worst situation. The fund appears to develop below plan, and the investor has clear indications that the manager does not cope with the situation properly. The third escalation level is the most rigorous escalation step. Mitigate

Figure 1. "Traffic lights" monitoring concept relating to fund and fund manager development

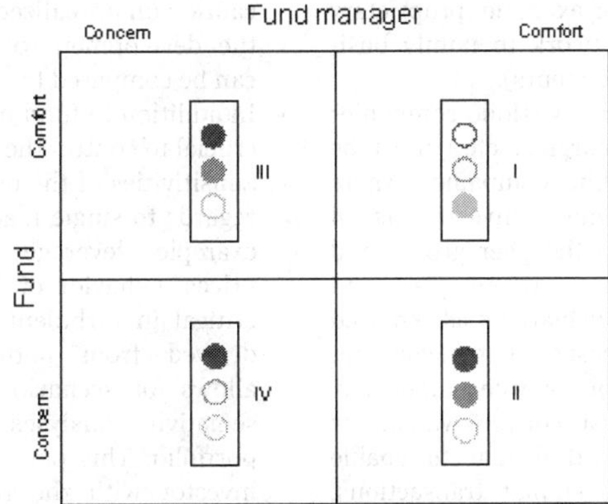

"Quite a few banks have cleaned up their act rather than risk public exposure. In the process, they have discovered that there is profit to be made in lending to residents in underserved neighborhoods." Ralph Nader

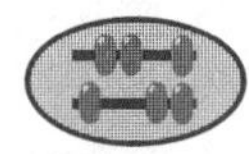

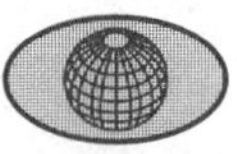
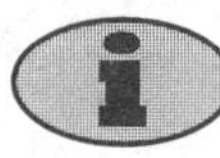

open risks and reduce exposure, for example join forces with a sufficient base of investors, and limit the fund size.

During a fund's lifetime, the emphasis and focus of the monitoring process shifts through phases, due to the changing information requirements and the change in options for actions.

Investment phase: the main focus is on the current and future investments, and whether they are aligned with the declared strategy and value contribution concept of the fund manager. Furthermore, the developments of the fund manager (such as team broadening), and the progress in the older portfolio are important elements for fund-manager monitoring.

Value creation phase: the fund monitoring emphasis shifts towards the progress in the portfolio companies, their valuations, and the resulting interim performance. Manager monitoring focuses on value contribution to the portfolio companies, and the resources made available to support the companies.

Harvesting phase: during the fund's lifetime, this is the real "moment of truth." Fund monitoring focuses on the success of the divestment process for portfolio companies, and related up- or down-valuations relative to the book value. Manager monitoring during this phase concentrates on the peer-group comparison, especially on performance benchmarking in a risk/return context.

Figure 2. Key elements for fund and fund monitoring and benchmarking

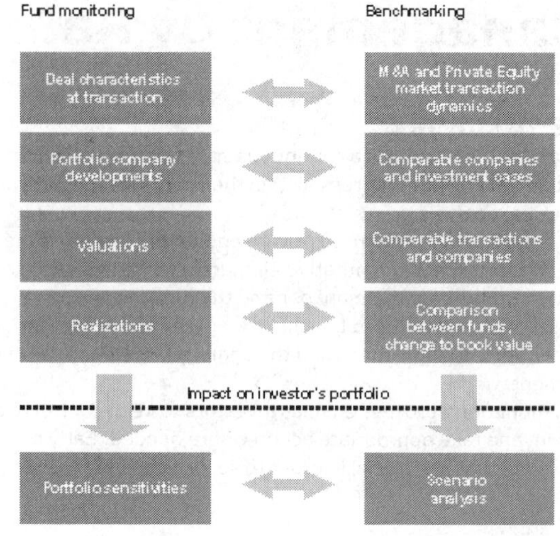

Figure 3. Illustrative recurring due diligence and monitoring activity loop

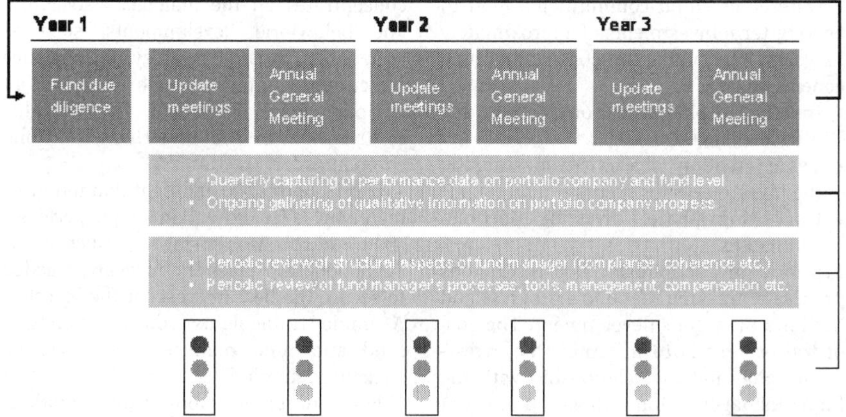

KEY FUND MONITORING AND BENCHMARKING ELEMENTS

The key fund monitoring elements can be structured along the value chain of a single company investment.

- Deal characteristics are evaluated and compared to the overall mergers and acquisitions (M&A) market (for example, entry price, debt financing structure, new investment themes), the private equity market (such as source of transaction) and the declared strategy of the fund manager (for example, proprietary sourcing from network to family businesses and entrepreneurs).
- Development of the portfolio companies (such as sales, margins, etc.) must be compared to public companies where applicable, to similar investments of fund managers in the peer group, and to the original investment plan and strategy. Interim valuations as reported on a quarterly basis are typically not directly comparable between managers. The investor must convert valuations into a standardized format to enable comparisons with similar transactions, public company valuations, or comparable investments of other private equity fund managers.
- In order to review the fund manager's valuation practice, realizations must be tracked against book values prior to the sale. Realizations are the "moment of truth" for a fund performance. Although benchmarking should be applied with caution on unrealized values (see above), the development of fund distributions can be compared to competitive funds.
- In addition to fund monitoring, it is also crucial to control the aggregate portfolio. Sensitivities of the overall portfolio with regards to single macro risk factors (for example, leverage ratios, commodity prices, behavior of US consumers) are critical in turbulent markets. Key data derived from bottom-up monitoring allows for scenario analyses and risk-sensitivity analyses for the complete portfolio. This perspective provides the investor with the required knowledge and information to assess potential rebalancing or risk-mitigating activities within the overall private equity investment program (such as through secondary sales).

THE FUND AND MANAGER MONITORING PROCESS

A best practice is for fund and fund-manager monitoring to be a continuous process with semi-annual, in-depth review across the portfolio.

Figure 3 shows a recurring three-year timeline of a due diligence and monitoring activity loop, based on the assumptions that the fund manager launches a successor fund every three years.

Process and interaction responsibilities must be defined and assigned for all existing fund manager relationships in order to ensure ongoing monitoring and risk management. The monitoring requirements must be clearly specified with regards to bottom-up information needed to create

"The new technology has put some truly sharp teeth in the long-standing effort to prevent banks from adopting lending practices that deprive minority and low- and moderate-income neighborhoods of credit."
Ralph Nader

   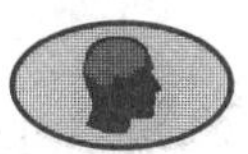  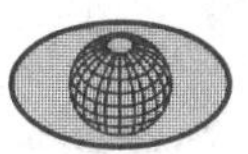  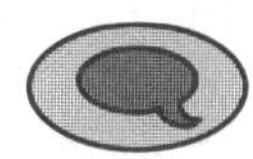 

the aggregate view of the overall portfolio. The responsible professionals continuously monitor developments at the level of both the fund manager and the underlying portfolio companies. Information is compiled from various sources including quarterly reports from the fund, presentations from the annual general meeting (AGM), information from commercial information providers, and broad intelligence activity from interaction with market participants. An aggregate portfolio review should be performed semi-annually, based on the outcome from well-prepared, open, one-on-one meetings with individual fund managers.

CONCLUSION

The fund commitments typically lock in a 12-year business relationship with a fund manager. Therefore, it is not a luxury but a bare necessity to actively monitor developments at both the fund manager and the fund portfolio level. A well-functioning monitoring concept, framework, and process are indispensable for an investor to keep watch over their private equity portfolio. Taking action as specified through the monitoring framework enables the investor to minimize risks and maximize future performance.

CASE STUDY

A well-established venture-capital fund manager with an IT focus started to show below-standard portfolio progress in a subsector, which triggered concern with respect to fund level monitoring. More in-depth analysis provided clear indications that the two persons responsible for the subsector were underperformers compared to their peer group. The rest of the firm had a strong portfolio in the firm's core industry. The concern was actively addressed with the managing partner of the firm, and led to a constructive process resulting in the firm refocusing on its core and separating from the two underperforming partners way before the fund was fully invested. In this case, the fund manager reacted responsively and rigorously. In other cases, the investors would face the following options to push harder for corrective action:

- Indicate plan to decline follow-on fund if there is no change;
- Attempt to pool investors behind the concern and to increase pressure for change on fund manager;
- Enforce an investment stop or a fund size reduction, in line with the legal agreement of the fund through sufficient investor votes, and avoid throwing good money after bad money.

MAKING IT HAPPEN

The following are a few aspects that have proven beneficial to the overall monitoring work of a private equity investor.

- Monitoring requires a coherent concept, framework, and process that serves as day-to-day guidance for the monitoring work.
- Adequate internal or external resources are needed for the start, implementation, and execution of a continuous monitoring process.
- An investor should willingly take action in case of any concern, in order to effectively manage the risk identified through the monitoring work performed.
- Regular interaction with the fund manager is key for the long-term business relationship with the fund manager, and to ensure a proper monitoring outcome.
- Being a value-adding investor with constructive feedback and criticism to the fund manager is part of monitoring. Providing help and support to the fund manager contributes to a positive impact on the fund result for the investor.

MORE INFO

Books:

Mayer, T., and Mathonet P.-Y. *Beyond the J Curve: Managing a Portfolio of Venture Capital and Private Equity Funds*. Chichester, UK: Wiley, 2005.

Müller K. *Investing in Private Equity Partnerships. The Role of Monitoring and Reporting*. Heidelberg, Germany: Gabler Verlag, 2007.

"To the chagrin of banks and other financial corporations, public interest groups. . .are using the new technology to plow through mountains of data to detect who gets mortgage loans and who gets shut out."

Ralph Nader

  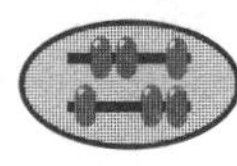 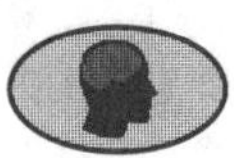  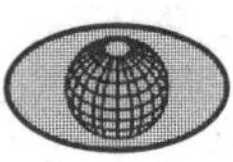   

Viewpoint: Peter Zollinger and John Schaetzl

A Silver Lining to the Credit Crisis

INTRODUCTION

Peter Zollinger, Senior Vice-President at the environmental and social governance consultancy SustainAbility, believes the best way for companies to enhance their reputation and achieve business success is through responsibility, fairness, and integrity. Here he argues that there is a silver lining to the financial crisis, that investors will in future be more likely to align their thinking with human needs. Zollinger's clients include Aracruz (Brazil), Credit Suisse, MasterCard, Rabobank, Standard Chartered Bank, and UBS. Before joining SustainAbility, he was involved in the setup of the Business Council for Sustainable Development (now WBCSD) and AVINA, which invests in sustainability and social entrepreneurs in Latin America. He was educated at the University of St.Gallen, Switzerland, and speaks five languages.

John Schaetzl has a breadth of experience within the healthcare sector. Most recently, he was a portfolio manager at GE Asset Management, where he had a broad research responsibility in this sector. Prior GE, he held marketing and planning roles at Bayer/ Miles Laboratories. He was a consultant to the pharmaceutical industry at Healthcare Forecasting Inc. and Scott Levin Associates. He has taught and held administrative positions at several universities. He is a non-executive director of SustainAbility and Columbus House. He is the co-author of *Practical Politics and American Government* (MacMillan, 1976) and *Project 18: Effectively influencing political decisions* (Edinburgh 1973). Schaetzl has an MA from the University of Pennsylvania and a BA from Harvard College.

HOW CURRENT PAIN CAN BECOME INVESTORS' GAIN

Maps will be redrawn once the current trembling in the financial system subsides. All around the capitalist world continents have been shifting, and releasing massive pent-up pressure. Volcanoes have been erupting everywhere, covering cities and redirecting financial flows. But the citizens of this disturbed world will overcome their shock and their pain and learn a valuable lesson.

As we start to rebuild, we will see a huge opportunity to do better. We will not place our cities in the same locations as before, nor will we design the same faulty edifices and infrastructure.

The current crisis offers the world an opportunity to rethink how to invest for the long term. The era of cheap and supposedly risk-free money is over. Investors—private and institutional—who strived for ever-higher returns and were told that their related exposure can be limited through the use of derivatives and structured products suffered painful losses.

As a consequence, it is again acceptable to pay a lot more attention to the sort of fundamentals which were deemed old-fashioned until not long ago, including the valuation and quality of underlying assets, and long-term financial health of relevant business models. The false promise of spectacular returns through clever financial engineering is being replaced by the quest for sound investments which offer modest, but real, steady and surer, returns.

What could be more promising than the returns on investments fuelled by global mega-trends affecting all societies and the environment? On the economic front, and as we have moved into a global recession, with the ghost of this worsening into a genuine depression, strengthening the demand is the economic paradigm of the hour.

The roots of such additional demand can be found where challenges, such as climate change, access to health care or affordable and healthy nutrition, are being effectively addressed.

This is our argument. But let us explain before you shout and object that the valuations in fields like energy, water, or clean-technology are currently sinking faster than your stomach.

"It will be different this time," is one of the most dangerous phrases in the investor's lexicon. But we cannot help wondering if it may not actually be true this time. For are we not witnessing a long overdue transformation, or at least the end of a 30-year anomaly, and a return to a more sound period of investing?

How did we get where we are? Beginning with Bretton Woods and the opportunity to trade currencies, through three decades of global deregulation and a golden period for investment in which the financial community prospered enormously.

FUND MANAGERS' GOLDEN AGE

Investment bankers and hedge fund managers became the new celebrities in this golden age of finance, often accorded as much of the limelight as sports, movie, and pop stars—or perhaps as much as the robber barons of old. In the United States, over the past 15 years, financial-service firms' share of the S&P's market capitalization soared from 5% to 25%.

New creative investment "derivatives" offered higher returns plus (of course) the associated higher risk. Investors' time-frames and the criteria for selecting one area of investment over another also changed. The quicker and higher returns from guessing quarterly earnings or speculating on all-or-nothing outcomes crowded out the slower long-term returns,

"Financial institutions such as insurance and banking were a powerful presence in the American economy at the turn of the century, and women. . .became office workers in record numbers between 1870 and 1930."
Angel Kwolek-Folland

  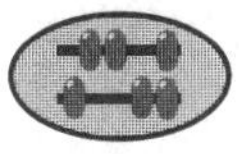   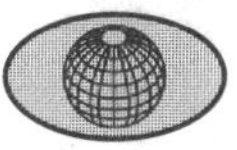   

associated with sound business practices and prudent investment.

The huge amounts of leverage and risk, and the high returns associated with this approach to "investing" ended—as we all knew it must—with a "correction."

Assets are now being appropriately repriced to match their associated risk profiles and, while current holders have suffered, potential buyers are benefiting. A correction is also an opportunity, possibly the opportunity of a lifetime, to buy those assets that have fallen the most from grace in the hope of seeing them return in the direction of their former glory.

One spanner in the works is that a great many structural changes are required before the expected recovery can take place.

Are such changes on the agenda? Policy makers have only started to reshape regulation, including the imposition of new limits on those responsible for investing "other people's money." But we have already seen the bleeding edge.

In the first instance, investment banks no longer exist. Ten years ago there were 14 significant such banks on Wall Street—and almost as many in the City of London. They were the Rodeo and the World Cup rolled into one. Unregulated—with no reserve requirements—they were vehicles promising huge returns but they were also carrying immense risks. Morgan Stanley and Goldman Sachs were the last survivors of this buccaneering breed, until last year they agreed to be reclassified as ordinary commercial banks, with all the limitations, red tape and rigidity that implies.

Secondly, hedge funds are either closing or becoming less "hedgy." Once upon a time it seemed these unregulated vehicles would replace investment banks as the main arena of risk and return. The best and the brightest were lured away from Wall Street thanks to the massive earning power that a 2% and 20% fee structure seemed to make possible. However, half of all hedge funds are either closed or closing, while new ones are having to moderate their fees significantly. It could be a death knell.

In such a vacuum, the drivers behind global sustainability are going to become pivotal forward-looking investors' thinking. New markets and business models designed to address sustainability challenges offer the prospect of real assets, steady growth, and less volatile cash flows. How so, you ask?

SUSTAINABLE PROFITS

Imagine the market opportunity that awaits anyone who is able to find a new way of delivering health services and pharmaceuticals to the billions of patients worldwide, who are today unable to afford so-called blockbuster drugs. Or, bearing in mind all the hype that surrounded last year's launch of the Nano (dubbed the people's car) by Tata Motors, can you imagine the prize that awaits the investors who back a winning "formula" to deliver affordable and sustainable mobility to the masses?

Climate change is today one of the defining global concerns, and it is one that is likely to be with us for generations. The International Energy Agency says it will take US$45 trillion in additional clean-technology investments between now and 2050 to reduce CO2 emissions by 50% from current levels (and that reduction is nowhere near enough, as we now know). That's a phenomenal 1.1% of average annual global GDP over the period.

Or take water, another environmental mega-trend with the potential for global conflicts: it is estimated that investments of US$1 trillion a year in existing water technologies will be needed to meet demand for all water uses through 2030.

At a national level, every country or region has a number of potentially vast and fast-growing markets-in-waiting. In Europe and the United States, the decarbonization of the economy will rank particularly high on the agenda. China is facing massive energy and broader environmental challenges, and the relevant economic sectors should be poised for stable and long-term growth. The myriad of social and environmental challenges facing India offer tremendous opportunities for businesses capable of finding and delivering appropriate solutions.

In general terms, the investments with the greatest long-term potential will be those where capital is directed into ventures that provide products and services that are genuinely needed by the markets.

A scan of the globe quickly reveals that there are a series of massive "divides"—between the haves and have-nots, the educated and the illiterate, the wealthy and the poor, and so on. These ought to provide a powerful leading indicator for any investor who needs to tune their radar. At SustainAbility we think of ten great divides:

1 Demographic
2 Gender
3 Nutritional
4 Environment and resources
5 Educational
6 Health
7 Digital and information
8 Security
9 Governance
10 Wealth

The task is of Herculean proportions: to align all human activity with what Planet Earth can actually bear. But this ought to be the starting point for mainstream investors, putting a different light on the arguments for long-term investing with embedded sustainability. Could anything be more certain than the returns available from investments that acknowledge and help address these global needs?

Thus, the new landscape emerging after the global tremor will see capital flows being redirected through smarter infrastructure and institutions that are better able to resist the next burst of seismic activity. Their final destination will be steadier, longer-term investments, among which will feature a growing percentage that address society's concerns about sustainability. May this positive prospect help us to stay calm while the ground is still shaking.

▸▸ MORE INFO

Books:

Krosinsky, Cary, and Nick Robins (eds). *Sustainable Investing—The Art of Long-Term Performance*. London: Earthscan, 2008.

Lye, Geoff, and Francesca Muller. *The Changing Landscape of Liability: A Director's Guide to Trends in Corporate Environmental, Social and Economic Liability*. Zurich, Switzerland: SustainAbility, 2004.

Reports:

International Finance Corporation and SustainAbility. "Market movers—Lessons from a frontier of innovation." 2007. Online at: www.sustainability.com/downloads_public/MarketMovers/SustainAbility_MarketMovers.pdf

Nelson, Jane, Alok Singh, and Peter Zollinger. "The power to change—Mobilising board leadership to deliver sustainable value to markets and society." SustainAbility/IBLF, 2001. Online at: www.iblf.org/docs/PowertoChange.pdf

SustainAbility. "Risk & opportunity: Best practice in non-financial reporting." 2004.

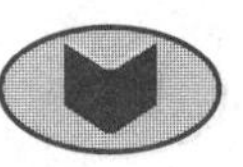
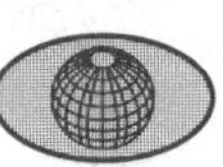

The Role of Commodities in an Institutional Portfolio by Keith H. Black and Satya Kumar

EXECUTIVE SUMMARY

- Institutional investors, including public and corporate pension plans, endowments, and foundations, are rapidly increasing the portion of their assets allocated to commodity investments.
- Investments in commodity futures may improve the reward-to-risk ratio for investment portfolios, as the low correlation between commodity futures and equity and fixed-income investments reduces portfolio volatility.
- Over long periods of time, investments in commodity futures have a risk–return profile similar to that of stocks, which means that there can be substantial gains or losses in any given month or year.
- Commodity futures have a positive correlation with inflation, which can be attractive for pension plans that are required to pay inflation-adjusted benefits to their beneficiaries.
- The best way for institutional investors to access the commodity markets is by identifying skilled and active managers in the futures markets. Investing in commodity index funds, physical commodities, or equity securities are suboptimal solutions.

THE CASE FOR COMMODITIES

The case for commodities is based largely on their historical tendency to offer returns that exhibit a low correlation with those of stock and bond market indices. Although commodities may be volatile, their low correlation with traditional investments can result in a significant diversification benefit. Table 1 shows the correlation between two commodity indices—the Standard & Poor's GSCI (S&P GSCI) and the Dow Jones–AIG Commodity Index (DJ-AIG)—and traditional investments and inflation indices since 1991. Over the last 18 years, a small allocation to investments in commodity futures would have substantially reduced portfolio volatility.

Table 1. Correlation matrix for two commodity indices with traditional investments and inflation indices, January 1991 to September 2008

Correlation with	*S&P GSCI*	*DJ-AIG*
DJ Wilshire 5000 Index	0.04	0.10
Lehman Aggregate Bond Index	0.03	0.02
Consumer Price Index (CPI)	0.18	0.15
Treasury Inflation-Protected Securities (TIPS)	0.16	0.17

Historically, investments in commodity futures have offered their strongest returns during times of below-average returns from traditional stock and bond market investments. Figure 1 shows the performance of commodity futures sorted by the return of the Wilshire 5000 stock market index during the period.

From 1991 to the third quarter of 2008, the Wilshire 5000 index declined by an average of –8.2% during the 20% of calendar quarters with the largest stock market declines. During these quarters of sharp stock price corrections, the S&P GSCI averaged a total return of 4.0%, while the Dow Jones–AIG Commodity Index returned 2.1%. In the second quintile, in calendar quarters when the stock market return was 0.0%, commodity indices earned their highest returns, at 6.1% and 4.8%. Each commodity index experienced its largest gains during times of below-average stock market returns. Conversely, the only periods in which the commodity indices consistently experienced losses were those in which the stock market indices posted their largest gains.

Figure 2 tells a similar story, comparing the returns of commodity indices with those of the Lehman Brothers Aggregate Bond Market Index. In the 20% worst quarters for bond markets, the Lehman Aggregate returned –1.0% and inflation-linked bonds (TIPS) fell by 0.6%. During these quarters of weak bond markets, the commodity indices offered their highest returns: 5.4% for the S&P GSCI, and 3.5% for the DJ-AIG.

Historically, commodities have served in a defensive role, as commodities have earned their highest return in times of weak stock and bond prices. Should these correlations persist in the future, a small allocation to commodities may serve to reduce portfolio risk by increasing returns in times of falling stock and bond prices.

COMMODITY FUTURES INDICES

The two most commonly used commodity futures indices are the S&P GSCI and the Dow Jones–AIG Commodity Index. Table 2 shows the allocation of each index to various commodity markets. Note that the energy markets represent 76% of the GSCI. In contrast, the DJ-AIG index intentionally limits exposure to any single sector to around 33%. Investors may prefer the DJ-AIG index to gain a potential improvement in the risk–reward tradeoff, as the overweight given to energy commodities in the GSCI has historically resulted in higher volatility without a corresponding boost in returns. Since 1991, the GSCI has earned an average total return of 7.1% with a standard deviation (volatility) of 18.4%, while the DJ-AIG averaged an annual return of 8.1% with a lower standard deviation of 12.3%. Earlier, Table 1 showed that the two commodity indices share similar

Figure 1. Performance of commodity futures sorted by return of Wilshire 5000 Stock Market Index, 1991 to third quarter of 2008

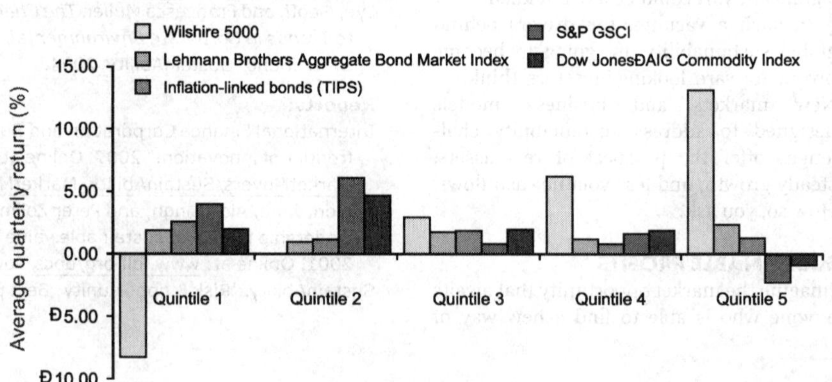

"**Behind all its global responsibilities and impersonal style banking is still a people business. . .it may be the most personal business of all for it always depends on the original concept of credit, meaning trust.**"
Anthony Sampson

  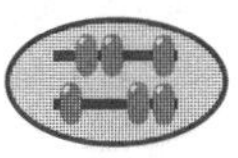 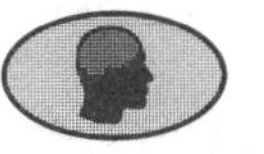  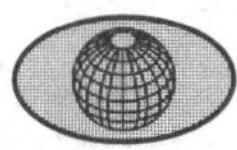   

Figure 2. Comparison of commodity index returns with returns of Lehman Brothers Aggregate Bond Market Index

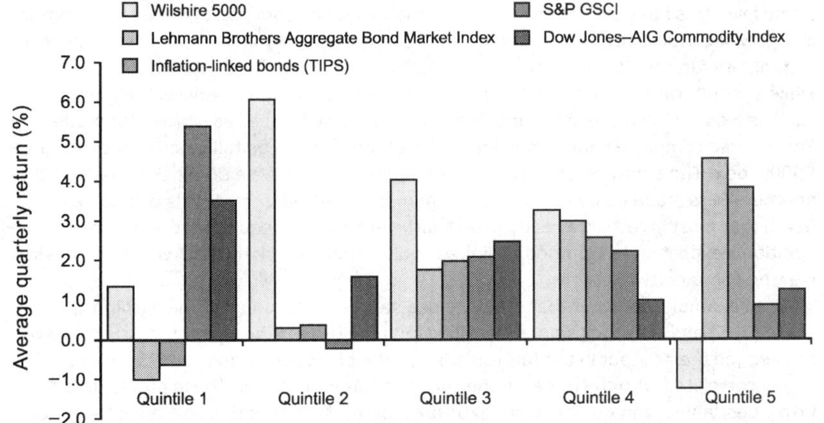

Table 2. Composition (%) of S&P GSCI and DJ-AIG indices as of September 30, 2008

Commodity sector	*S&P GSCI*	*DJ-AIG*
Energy	76.0	35.1
Precious metals	2.2	10.2
Industrial metals	6.2	17.8
Agriculture	12.0	28.4
Livestock	3.6	8.5

correlations with traditional stock and bond investments and inflation.

The total return to a commodity futures index consists of three components: spot return, roll return, and yield. The spot return is the return to an investment in physical commodities. The roll return is earned in the process of passively trading (rolling) futures contracts as they mature and must be replaced. The yield is the interest earned on a short-term fixed-income investment that is pledged to the futures exchange in order to maintain the collateral required to back the futures investments. Table 3 breaks down the total returns from spot, roll, and yield.

Table 3. Decomposition of S&P GSCI returns, 1970 to September 2008

	Annualized return (%)
S&P GSCI Total Return Index	11.8
S&P GSCI Spot Return Index	4.8
S&P GSCI Excess Return Index	5.3
Roll return	0.5
Three-month Treasury Bill yield	5.6

Figures 3 and 4 show some interesting characteristics of the returns on owning physical commodities. Most notably, spot commodity markets have underperformed inflation and cash over long periods of time: while the GSCI spot index earned an annual return of 4.8% since 1970, cash returned 5.6% and the US Consumer Price Index (CPI) increased by 4.6% per year over the same period. Commodity price increases have not exceeded the rate of inflation over long periods of time. As new natural resources are discovered, production technologies improve, and research advances in areas such as crop engineering and alternative energy, commodity prices tend to decline in real (after-inflation) terms.

How, then, could commodities futures have offered a total return since 1970 rivaling that of equities if the ownership of physical commodities does not offer a return that exceeds inflation? The answer is in the roll return and the collateral yield, as shown in Figure 3. (The roll return is approximated by the difference between the excess return and the spot return of the GSCI.) The roll return and collateral yield can only be earned when investing in commodity futures. The return on commodity futures investments, then, has significantly exceeded that of a direct investment in physical commodities over the last 37 years. An extended discussion of roll yield, and the relationship to contango and backwardation term structures in the futures markets, can be found in Black and Kumar (2008).

Figure 3. Ratio of cumulative wealth normalized to cash, 1970 to September 2008

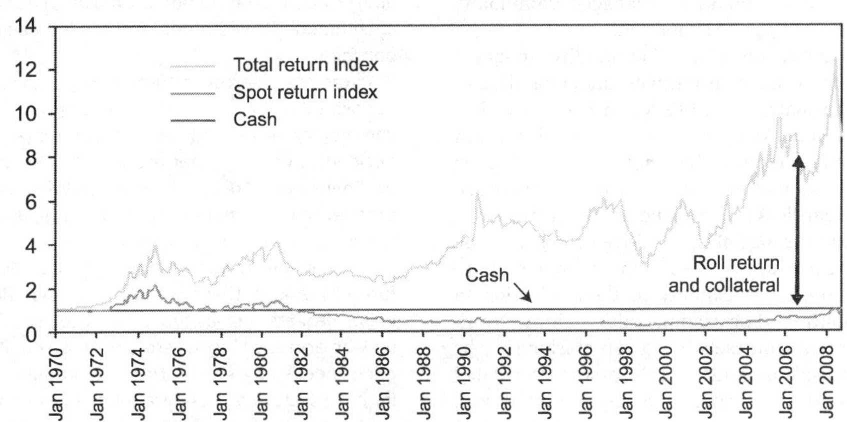

Figure 4. Ratio of cumulative wealth of spot returns normalized to cash, 1970 to September

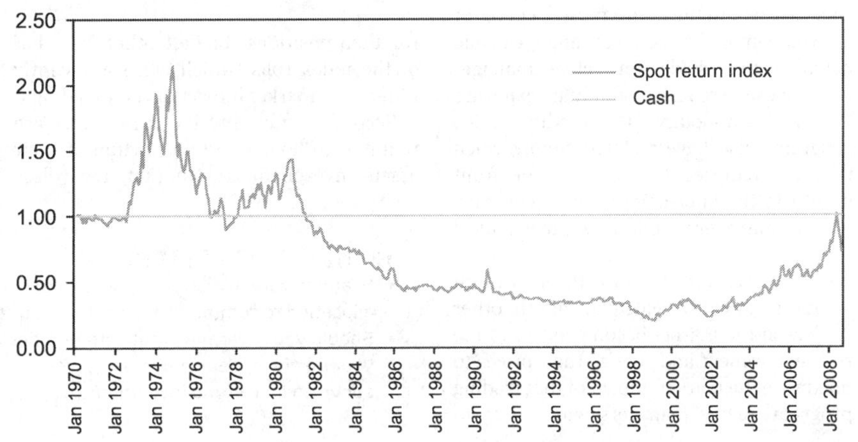

  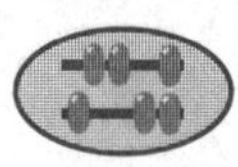   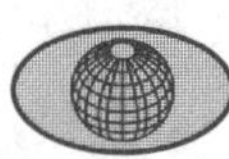   

Not every investor will choose to make use of commodities in their portfolio. It can be difficult to value commodities, as their characteristics don't neatly follow classical valuation models. Commodities do not generate a cash flow, so they can't be valued using discounted cash flow methodologies. Because commodities have a near-zero correlation to equity indices, their beta is also near zero, which disallows use of the capital asset pricing model. Variables such as political strife and weather can have a significant impact on both long- and short-run commodity prices. These exogenous variables are extremely difficult to predict, and they create systemic risks that are not priced in traditional return forecasting models.

ACTIVELY MANAGED COMMODITY FUNDS

Active management has a number of advantages over allocating assets to a commodity index fund. There are several ways in which an active commodity manager can add value relative to an investment in a commodity index. Should a manager demonstrate skill in these areas, an allocation to its managed commodity product can be supported.

First, an active commodity manager should have an intimate understanding of the shape of the futures curves in a variety of commodity markets. Commodity index funds require that investors hold long positions in the near-dated contract, regardless of the shape of the futures curve and the size of the positive or negative roll yield. Active managers, however, have significant flexibility in their selection of contract. For example, although the front-month contracts in a given market may be priced to result in roll losses, later-dated contracts, perhaps at a 12-month maturity, may be priced in such a way that investors may earn a profit from the roll. This flexibility can significantly increase the potential for a return from the futures roll. In a case where the entire futures curve for a given commodity is in contango, causing negative roll yields, an active manager may choose to reduce or eliminate exposure to that commodity. Commodity index programs also have a stated timing when they are required to roll from the front month to the later-dated futures contract. When managers follow a mechanical strategy, such as rolling 20% of their position in each of the fifth through ninth business days of the calendar month, other traders in the market become aware of the roll requirement and change their prices to maximize the market impact of that trading program. Active managers will choose to roll their positions at a date other than that of the index rolls, which can significantly reduce the market impact of their trading.

Second, commodity index investors are required to hold a certain portion of their assets in each futures market, regardless of the fundamental drivers of the spot commodity price. Active commodity managers should be able to show skill in their analysis of the supply and demand dynamics in each market. Ideally, the active manager will implement a long position

CASE STUDY

Commodity Stocks versus Commodity Futures

Some investors have chosen to implement their views on commodity prices by investing in equity securities. The prices of these stocks may be somewhat correlated with those of commodity futures. Metals firms include, for example, Alcoa, and Anglo American, while agricultural firms include Archer Daniels Midland. In the energy sector, stocks such as Exxon-Mobil, Chevron, and ConocoPhillips may be used as a proxy for crude oil. These three companies alone make up 4.6% of the market capitalization of the Wilshire 5000 index. The energy sector as a whole comprises 11% of the US stock market, and another 4% is made up by metals, food, chemicals, and other materials companies. Given that most investors already have a large allocation in equity securities, an additional allocation to commodity-linked equities may not be the best way to express a view on commodity prices.

As an example, consider that the price of a stock is the product of the earnings per share (EPS) and the stock's price/earnings multiple (P/E). When commodity firms have not hedged their output in the futures market, the profits of a firm (i.e. EPS) will be highly correlated with the prices of the commodities it produces. These profits give the firm a desirable commodity market exposure (beta), such that this portion of the stock price is responsive to changes in commodity prices. However, each firm also has a P/E ratio, which can vary with the level of the stock market. This introduces a potentially undesirable stock market beta into the commodity portfolio. This sensitivity to stock prices is unwelcome, as a key reason for investing in commodities is to experience returns that are uncorrelated with those of equity markets. In fact, commodity stocks are likely to underperform commodity futures during times of high inflation. When inflation and commodity prices are rising, stock prices are typically declining. Should the price/earnings ratio of commodity stocks decline in a bear market, the investor may not realize the anticipated benefit of the commodity firm's profits in terms of stock price appreciation. Commodity futures are a more direct way to earn the diversifying benefits of commodity investments without increasing the stock market risk of the overall portfolio.

In the first quarter of 2008, energy stocks and commodity futures indices moved in opposite directions. Even though oil prices were increasing (commodity beta) and commodity futures indices rose as much as 18% in the quarter, the stock market was decidedly negative. Energy stocks fell 8% during the quarter, as the US stock market declined nearly 10% in the quarter. While energy stocks had a higher return than the broader market, there remained a large gap between the performance of commodity stocks and commodity futures.

Though energy, metals and agricultural commodities are well represented in the futures markets, there are other commodities for which futures markets do not currently exist. Markets such as those for water, coal, steel, chemicals, and renewable energy can only be accessed by investors through equity securities. Firms that produce capital goods needed for exploration and production, or to maintain ownership, of commodities in these sectors represent a relatively small part of the equity market, and futures contracts are not available. Although investment in commodities through stocks in the energy, metals, and agricultural sector is not advocated, investors who desire exposure to these other commodity markets may do so using stocks.

➤➤ MAKING IT HAPPEN

- Examine your investment portfolio to determine the potential value added by an allocation to commodity futures investments.
- Should you determine that commodities would improve the risk–return tradeoff of your portfolio, begin your search for an actively managed portfolio that can add value above an index fund investment.

"They have a right to censure that have a heart to help." William Penn

     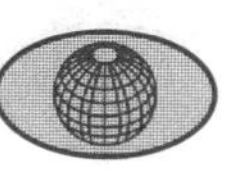   

only in markets where demand is likely to grow faster than supply, while avoiding or selling short in markets with less favorable supply–demand dynamics. While index investors only take long positions in commodity markets, active managers may choose to take no position or a short (negative) position in commodity markets where their analysis predicts a low probability of price increases.

Given the significant opportunities to enhance the returns from spot returns and roll investments in the futures markets, active managers who show skill in these areas may be viewed as an attractive investment opportunity. While active managers may choose to maintain significant short positions in certain commodity markets, funds that maintain a long bias in each of the major market sectors, including energy, metals, and agriculture maximize the diversification effect of the commodities investment. For commodities to play their role as a portfolio diversifier, the fund needs to maintain long positions during times of commodity price increases.

CONCLUSION

Over the last 18 years, commodities have served as an excellent portfolio diversifier. Because of the historical tendency for commodity futures to have a high correlation with inflation, they typically offer higher returns than stocks, bonds, and even Treasury Inflation-Protected Securities during times of market stress. Commodities tend to be a defensive asset class and, as such, tend to underperform during bullish equity markets. Should these trends continue, investors can reduce their portfolio risk by allocating a small portion of their portfolio to commodity futures.

▸▸ MORE INFO

Books:

Fabozzi, Frank J., Roland Füss, and Dieter G. Kaiser (eds). *The Handbook of Commodity Investing*. Hoboken, NJ: Wiley, 2008.

Till, Hilary, and Joseph Eagleeye (eds). *Intelligent Commodity Investing: New Strategies and Practical Insights for Informed Decision Making*. London: Risk Books, 2007.

Articles:

Erb, C., and C. R. Harvey. "The strategic and tactical value of commodity futures." *Financial Analysts Journal* 62:2 (2006): 69–97.

Gorton, Gary B., and K. Geert Rouwenhorst. "Facts and fantasies about commodity futures." *Financial Analysts Journal* 62:2 (2006): 47–68.

Journal of Indexes issue "Inside commodities." November/December 2008. Online at: www.indexuniverse.com/publications/journalofindexes.html (use "Browse archives" link).

Reports:

Black, Keith, and Satya Kumar. "The role of commodities and timberland in an institutional portfolio." Chicago, IL: Ennis Knupp & Associates, 2008. Online at: www.ennisknupp.com/Portals/57ad7180-c5e7-49f5-b282-c6475cdb7ee7/Commodities%20in_an_Institutional_Portfolio.pdf

Black, K. "The role of institutional investors in rising commodity prices." Chicago, IL: Ennis Knupp & Associates, 2008. Online at: www.ennisknupp.com/Portals/57ad7180-c5e7-49f5-b282-c6475cdb7ee7/institutionsandcommodities%20final.pdf

Websites:

Dow Jones–AIG Commodity Indexes: www.djindexes.com/aig

Standard & Poor's: www.standardandpoors.com

Websites:

Jeremy Siegel (p. 1193)

Portfolio Selection: Efficient Diversification of Investments (p. 1309)

Mining (pp. 1525–1527)

Oil and Gas (pp. 1527–1529)

"By blaming others, we fail to find the real solutions to our problems and we do not carry out our own responsibilities." Jeb Bush

  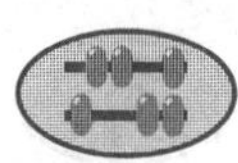   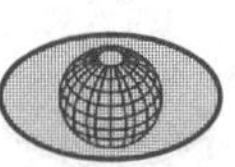   

The Role of Short Sellers in the Marketplace by Raj Gupta

EXECUTIVE SUMMARY

- This article examines the role of short sellers in the marketplace. Short selling involves three major participant groups: Lenders, agent intermediaries, and borrowers.
- First, the history of short selling is discussed. This includes the enactment of the Securities Exchange Act of 1934, the adoption of the uptick rule in 1937, and the relaxation of that rule in 2007.
- Next, the short-sale process is described. Five categories of short position are identified: General collateral, reduced rebate, reduced rebate and fail, fail only, and buy-in.
- Third, the borrowers are identified and their activities discussed. They include hedge funds, mutual funds, exchange-traded fund (ETF) counterparties, and option market-makers.
- Fourth, the lenders are identified and their motivations for lending are discussed. The primary lenders include mutual funds and pension funds.
- Fifth, historical statistics on the universe of lendable securities and the percentage of loaned equities are presented. A dramatic increase in the level of loaned securities is observed.
- Finally, the academic literature on short selling is briefly reviewed.

INTRODUCTION

The terms "short selling" or "shorting" are used to describe the process of selling financial instruments, such as equities or futures, that the seller or holder does not actually own but borrows from various sources. If the value of the instrument declines, the short seller can repurchase the instrument at a lower price and cover the loan.

Short sellers have long played the crucial role of price discovery in financial markets. If short selling were not allowed, traders with negative views of certain stocks would, at best, avoid those stocks. However, short selling allows them to generate returns based on their views if they are correct, hence making short selling an important aspect of price discovery. Companies in certain countries where short selling is not allowed may also list in the exchanges of countries where short selling is allowed.

After the crash of 1929 the United States Congress created the Securities and Exchange Commission (SEC) by enacting the Securities Exchange Act of 1934. The SEC, following an inquiry into the effects of concentrated short selling during the market break of 1937, adopted Rule 10a-1. Rule 10a-1(a)(1) stated that, subject to certain exceptions, a listed security may be sold short:

- at a price above the price at which the immediately preceding sale was effected (plus tick); or
- at the last sale price if it is higher than the last different price (zero-plus tick).

This implied that short sales were not permitted on minus ticks or zero-minus ticks, subject to narrow exceptions. The operation of these provisions was often described as the "tick test." Both the New York Stock Exchange (NYSE) and the American Stock Exchange (Amex) had elected to use the prices of trades on their own floors for the tick test. In 2007, the SEC voted to adopt amendments to Rule 10a-1 and Regulation SHO (which seeks to limit abusive naked short selling by reducing failures to deliver securities) that removed Rule 10a-1 as well as any short-sale price test of any self-regulatory organization (SRO). In addition, the amendments prohibited any SRO from having a price test. The amendments included a technical amendment to Rule 200(g) of Regulation SHO that removed the "short exempt" marking requirement of that rule.

On July 15, 2008, the SEC issued an emergency order related to short selling securities of 19[1] substantial financial firms which took effect July 21, 2008. This order stated that any person executing a short sale in the publicly traded securities of 19 financial firms, using the means or instrumentalities of interstate commerce, must borrow or arrange to borrow the security, or otherwise have the security available to borrow in its inventory, prior to executing the short sale. On September 19, 2008, the SEC, acting in concert with the UK Financial Services Authority, took temporary emergency action[2] to prohibit short selling in 799 financial companies to protect the integrity and quality of the securities market and strengthen investor confidence. This ban was lifted on October 8, 2008.

In this article we will examine the role of short sellers. Short sellers include hedge funds and other speculators, proprietary desks of bank holding companies, options market-makers, and, in recent years, mutual funds that execute 1Xo/Xo strategies. We will discuss the academic literature on short sales, illustrate the short-sale process, examine the role of various participants in the process, including lenders such as mutual funds and pension funds, agent intermediaries such as prime brokers, and borrowers such as hedge funds, mutual funds, and options market-makers, and present statistics on the universe of lendable and loaned securities. It will be seen that the level of securities loaned versus the total universe of lendable securities has increased dramatically in recent years.

THE SHORT SALE PROCESS

There are generally three groups of players in the short-sale process. The groups are securities lenders, securities borrowers (short sellers), and agent intermediaries.

- **Securities lenders**: Securities lenders are institutions with securities portfolios of sufficient size to make securities lending worthwhile. Generally these institutions include mutual funds, insurance companies, pension funds, and endowments. The lending activities of these groups are discussed in greater detail later.
- **Securities borrowers**: Securities borrowers are institutions that engage in short selling either as part of their trading strategies or to hedge their risk exposures. These institutions include hedge funds, mutual funds, ETF counterparties, and option market-makers. We will examine these groups in detail in the next section.
- **Agent intermediaries**: Agent intermediaries are institutions that facilitate the lending and borrowing of securities. These institutions may include custodian banks, broker-dealers, and prime brokers. We will examine the functions of these groups later.

The process illustrated in Figure 1 works well if there are plenty of shares available to borrow. However, one must consider another possibility: What if shares desired

"I wonder how anyone can have the face to condemn others when he reflects upon his own thoughts."
W. Somerset Maugham

     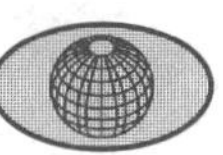  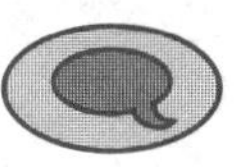 

Figure 1. The short-sale process

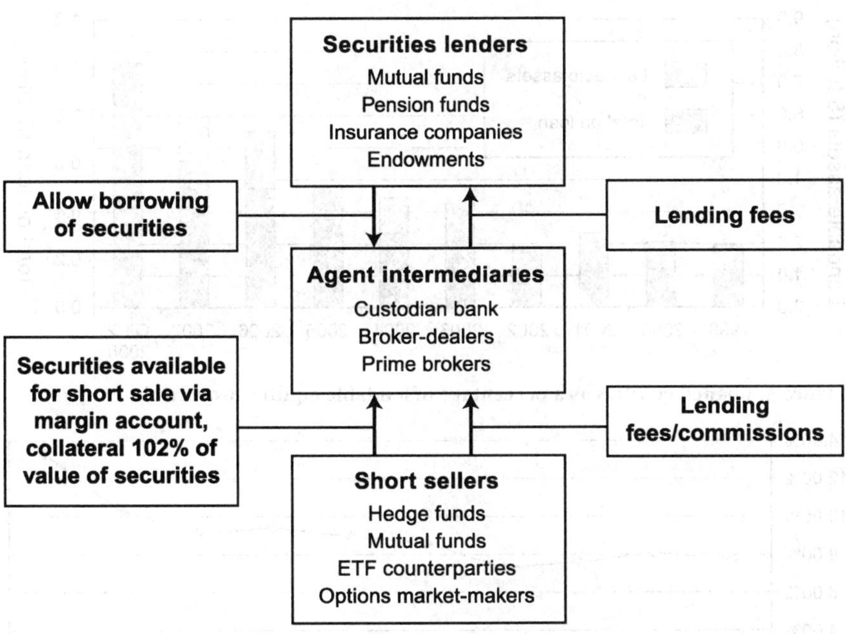

for borrowing purposes are unavailable? Several academic articles have examined impediments to the short-selling process. Evans, Geczy, Musto, and Reed (2008) categorize short positions from an unnamed options market-maker into five types: General collateral, reduced rebate, reduced rebate and fail, fail only, and buy-in. These categories as defined in their database are as follows:

- *General collateral* indicates that a stock has been loaned at the normal rebate rate, i.e. the stock is easy to borrow.
- *Reduced rebate* indicates that the rebate rate is below the general collateral rate—i.e. the stock is special.
- *Reduced rebate and fail* indicates that some shares have been borrowed at a reduced rebate and that the market-maker failed to deliver some shares that were sold short.
- *Fail only* indicates that the market-maker failed to deliver any of the shares in this short position.
- *Buy-in* indicates that the counterparty of the short-sale transaction is forcing delivery on some or all of the shares in the short position.

One would expect a significant majority of short positions to fall into the general collateral category. More than 90% of the short positions in the database used by Evans, Geczy, Musto and Reed (2008) fell into that category.

THE KEY SHORT SELLERS

In this section, we will examine the key short sellers. While certain participants may engage in short selling because of their trading strategy, others may do so to hedge their risk exposures (see Figure 1 for an illustration of the short-sale process). We will examine in detail each of these groups below.

Hedge Funds and Other Speculators

Several hedge fund strategies employ the shorting of stocks as part of their strategy. In the case of convertible arbitrage, the arbitrageur generally takes long positions in convertible bonds and sells short the underlying stock. In the case of equity strategies, managers may use fundamental or quantitative analysis to sell stocks short. Long/short equity strategies generally comprise the bulk of the hedge fund universe, both in terms of assets under management as well as of number of funds. In the case of merger arbitrage, managers sell short the acquiring company, while short-biased strategies engage in short selling of seemingly overvalued stocks.

Bank Holding Companies

Prior to the recent requests by Goldman Sachs and Morgan Stanley to change their status to bank holding companies, investment banks borrowed stock for their proprietary trading desks. However, these and other banks will continue to borrow stock for their proprietary trading desks and other functions.

Short and Ultra-Short Exchange-Traded Funds

In recent years, several exchange-traded funds (ETF) have been established that offer either the inverse or twice the inverse of the returns on a certain index. These exchange-traded funds are generally referred to as short-ETF or ultra-short ETF. The funds generally achieve their short exposure using derivatives such as swaps. While these funds generally do not short underlying stocks, they retain the ability to do so if necessary.

ETF Counterparties

One of the primary instruments that the short- and ultra-short exchange-traded funds use to achieve their exposures is swaps. The counterparty in the swap transaction may choose to hedge their exposures by shorting stocks.

Mutual Funds

In recent years several firms have launched 1X0/X0-type funds. Generally, the equities owned by the fund equal 1X0% of its net asset value, while the equities shorted equal X0% of the fund's net asset value. While a vast majority of the 1X0/X0-type funds are offered through separate accounts, several mutual funds are available to the public.

Option Market-Makers

Options market-makers short sell securities on a regular basis for hedging purposes. They are, however, exempt from locating shares before short selling.

THE KEY EQUITY LENDERS

In this section we will examine the key lenders. These institutional lenders include mutual funds, pension funds, insurance companies, and endowments. Generally, the lending activities take place through an intermediary agent such as a custodian bank or a broker-dealer. These intermediary agents pool securities from various lenders who are unable to lend securities directly. Most broker-dealers combine their security lending activities with their prime-brokerage operations. We will examine each of these groups next.

Mutual Funds

The US mutual fund industry managed around $12 trillion in assets as of year-end 2007. Stock mutual funds accounted for 54% of the total mutual fund industry. In light of the actions of the SEC relating to the banning of short sales on the securities of 799 financial firms, two major mutual funds, Vanguard Group, and State Street Corporation, imposed additional restrictions that halted the lending of their shares.[3] However, lending fees received by mutual funds can be substantial and

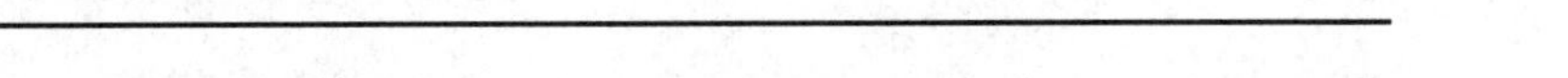
"Those see nothing but faults that seek for nothing else." Thomas Fuller

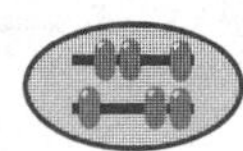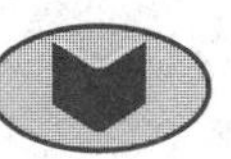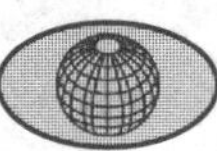

permanent restrictions may impact revenues.

Pension Funds

Equities form a major component in the asset allocation of defined contribution plans. According to Pensions & Investments online,[4] over 50% of assets in corporate defined contribution plans are allocated to equities, while significant percentages are allocated by public and union defined contribution plans as well. Defined benefit plans have a significant percentage of assets allocated to equities as well. Pension funds participate significantly in the equity lending market.

The reasons to lend securities include not only offsetting custody and administrative costs but also the generation of revenue. The infrastructure to support securities lending varies from lender to lender. Lenders sometimes impose credit restrictions. As noted earlier, certain lenders imposed restrictions on borrowing activities in light of the SEC rules prohibiting short selling.

SUMMARY DATA ON SHORT SALES

In previous sections we examined the various aspects of the short-sale process and the key players. In this section we will examine the data on short sales. Figure 2 presents statistics on total lendable equities worldwide. The data were obtained from the Risk Management Association.[5]

The universe of lendable equities ("lendable assets" in Figure 2) denotes the total dollar value of equities available for lending worldwide. These include North American, European, and Pacific-rim equities (including Australia), and other equities not included in the aforementioned categories. The figures are reported as aggregate assets without consideration of client- or bank-imposed guidelines. Not surprisingly, North American and European equities represent a significant portion of the total dollar value of lendable equities worldwide.

The universe of loaned assets ("total on loan" in Figure 2) represents the total dollar value of equities loaned worldwide. Again the total dollar value of loaned North American and European equities represents a significant portion of the universe. One of the interesting aspects is the growth in the universe of lendable assets from around $2 trillion in 1999 to over $7 trillion at the end of the second quarter of 2008. Expectedly, the universe shrank between 2001 and 2002, and then experienced a steady increase. The level of loaned assets worldwide has followed a similar pattern. However, the level of loaned assets experienced a dramatic increase from less than $600 billion at the end of 2006 to over $1 trillion at the end of the second quarter of 2008. In percentage terms, loaned equities increased from 8% of lendable assets worldwide to 13% by the second quarter of 2008. This is shown in Figure 3.

Figure 2. Lendable equities versus loaned equities worldwide

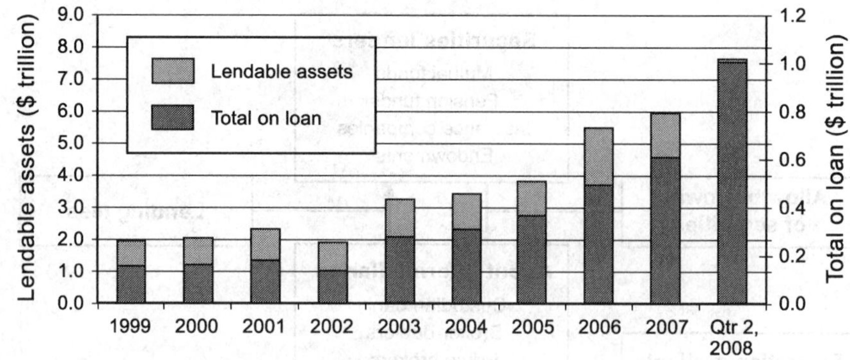

Figure 3. Loaned equities as a percentage of lendable equities worldwide

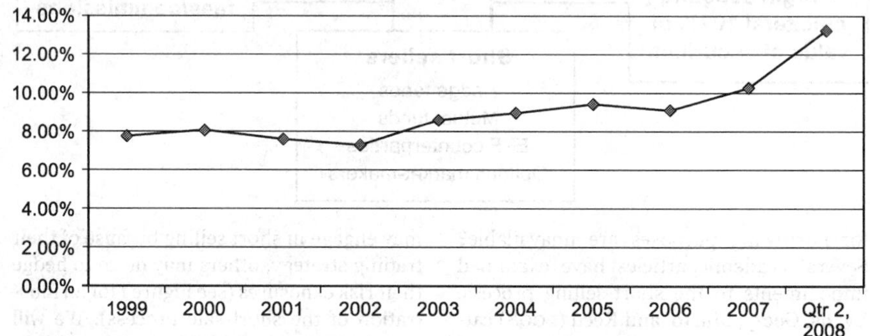

The significant increases in the levels of loaned equities in the years 2006–08 suggest a negative outlook on the stock market by certain traders. In fact, the first signs of the subprime debacle can be traced back to early 2007. Stock prices of bond insurers such as Ambac and MBIA recorded all-time highs in early 2007, before declining precipitously to 15-year lows in 2008, when they lost more than 90% of their value. The stock prices of erstwhile investment banks such as Bear Stearns and Lehman Brothers followed similar patterns before the former merged with JP Morgan and the latter filed for bankruptcy. Further, Fannie Mae, Freddie Mac, American International Group (AIG), Merrill Lynch, Citigroup, Wachovia, and American Express among many others also witnessed precipitous declines in the value of their equities. These numbers, as well as media reports, suggest that short-biased traders such as certain hedge funds correctly predicted the decline of these companies, thus generating enormous capital appreciation for their investors (such as pension funds, endowments, and foundations).

LITERATURE REVIEW

A plethora of academic articles have examined various aspects of short selling. In this section we will examine some of these articles and their contribution to the literature.

Seneca (1967) examined the net effects of large short positions using data between 1946 and 1965. The article finds that short sales act as a predictor of stock prices. Baron and McDonald (1973) explored the risk–return patterns of reported short positions. Using data from the NYSE over the period 1961–66, they found that stocks with more idiosyncratic risk have higher short interest. Brent, Morse, and Stice (1990) examined increases in short interest over the period 1974–86. They found that stocks with convertible securities, options, and high betas tend to have more shares held short. Further, Webb and Figlewski (1993) examined the effects of options on short sales. Using data obtained from CRSP and IDC over the period 1969–85, they found that options facilitate short selling.

More recently Geczy, Musto, and Reed (2002) have examined short-selling costs and constraints. Using data from an

  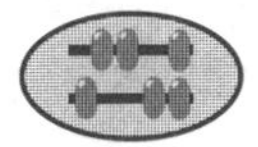   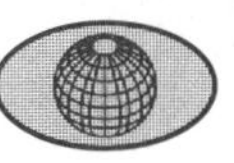   

unnamed custodian bank over the period 1998–1999, they found that short-selling frictions appear strongest in merger arbitrage. Bris, Goetzmann, and Zhu (2007) looked at short sales and market efficiency in world markets. Using data from various investment banks[6] over the period 1990–2001, they found that markets where short selling is prohibited display significantly less negative skewness. Boehmer, Jones, and Zhang (2008) explored whether short sellers are informed. Using data from CRSP and NYSE over the period 2000–04, they found that short sellers are well informed and contribute to efficient stock prices. Diether, Lee, and Werner (2008) studied trading strategies used by short sellers. Using data from various exchanges for 2005, they found that short sellers in both NYSE and NASDAQ stocks increased their short-selling activity after periods of positive returns. Finally Evans, Geczy, Musto, and Reed (2008) looked at whether options market competition tends to oligopoly as stocks become difficult to short. Using data from a large options market-maker over the period 1998–99, they found that market-makers profit when they fail to deliver stock.

CONCLUSION

In this article we have examined the role of short sellers in the marketplace. We showed that short selling involves three major participant groups: The lenders, the agent intermediaries, and the borrowers. We discussed the history of short selling, including the enactment of the Securities Exchange Act of 1934, the adoption of the uptick rule in 1937, and the relaxation of that rule in 2007. We then discussed the short-sale process and identified five categories of short positions. Further, we discussed the profile of borrowers and lenders and provided historical statistics on loaned equities as a proportion of lendable securities. We saw that there has been a dramatic increase in the level of loaned securities. Finally we presented a brief review of the academic literature on short selling.

▸▸ MORE INFO

Articles:

Baron, D., and J. McDonald. "Risk and return on short positions in common stocks." *Journal of Finance* 28:1 (1973): 97–107.

Boehmer, E., C. Jones, and X. Zhang. "Which shorts are informed?" *Journal of Finance* 63:2 (2008): 491–527.

Brent, A., D. Morse, and E. Stice. "Short interest: Explanations and tests." *Journal of Financial and Quantitative Analysis* 25:2 (1990): 273–289.

Bris, A., W. Goetzmann, and N. Zhu. "Efficiency and the bear: Short sales and markets around the world." *Journal of Finance* 62:3 (2007): 1029–1079.

Diether, K., K. Lee, and I. Werner. "Short-sale strategies and return predictability." *Review of Financial Studies* 22:2 (2008): 575–607.

Evans, R., C. Geczy, D. Musto, and A. Reed. "Failure is an option: Impediments to short selling and options prices." *Review of Financial Studies* (2008). Online at: rfs.oxfordjournals.org/cgi/content/abstract/hhm083v1

Geczy, C., D. Musto, and A. Reed. "Stocks are special too: An analysis of the equity lending market." *Journal of Financial Economics* 66:2–3 (2002): 241–269.

Seneca, J. "Short interest: Bearish or bullish." *Journal of Finance* 22:1 (1967): 67–70.

Webb, G., and S. Figlewski. "Options, short sales, and market completeness." *Journal of Finance* 48:2 (1993): 761–777.

Websites:

Australian Securities Lending Association (ASLA): www.asla.com.au

High short interest stocks: www.highshortinterest.com

International Securities Lending Association (ISLA): www.isla.co.uk

NASDAQ short interest: www.nasdaqtrader.com/asp/short_interest.asp

Pan Asia Securities Lending Association (PASLA): www.paslaonline.com

Risk Management Association: www.rmahq.org/RMA

Securities Industry and Financial Markets Association (SIFMA): www.sifma.org

ShortSqueeze.com short squeeze stock short interest (short selling) data: www.shortsqueeze.com

See Also:

★ Private Investments in Public Equity (pp. 560–561)
✔ Hedging Credit Risk— Case Studies and Strategies (p. 862)
✔ Hedging Foreign Exchange Risk— Case Studies and Strategies (p. 863)
✔ Hedging Interest Rate Risk— Case Study and Strategies (p. 864)
✔ Swaps, Options, and Futures: What They Are and Their Function (p. 882)
✔ Trading in Equities on Stock Exchanges (p. 947)
✔ Understanding Hedge Ratios (p. 892)
George Soros (p. 1197)
The Alchemy of Finance: Reading the Mind of the Market (p. 1218)

NOTES

1 These companies include BNP Paribas Securities Corp (BNPQF or BNPQY), Bank of America Corporation (BAC), Barclays PLC (BCS), Citigroup Inc. (C), Credit Suisse Group (CS), Daiwa Securities Group Inc. (DSECY), Deutsche Bank Group AG (DB), Allianz SE (AZ), Goldman Sachs Group Inc. (GS), Royal Bank ADS (RBS), HSBC Holdings PLC ADS (HBC and HSI), JPMorgan Chase & Co., (JPM), Lehman Brothers Holdings Inc. (LEH), Merrill Lynch & Co., Inc. (MER), Mizuho Financial Group, Inc. (MFG), Morgan Stanley (MS), UBS AG (UBS), Freddie Mac (FRE) and Fannie Mae (FNM).

2 For more information visit: www.sec.gov/news/press/2008/2008-211.htm

3 See Kerber, Ross. "2 mutual fund firms act to halt short sales." *Boston Globe* (September 23, 2008).

4 For more information visit: www.pionline.com

5 For more information visit: www.rmahq.org/RMA

6 The term "investment bank" ceased to exist in 2008 when the last two remaining investment banks, Goldman Sachs and Morgan Stanley, asked the Federal Reserve to be converted to bank holding companies following the failures of Bear Stearns and Lehman Brothers and the announcement of the merger of Merrill Lynch with Bank of America.

"To accuse is so easy that it is infamous to do so where proof is impossible." Zoë Akins

  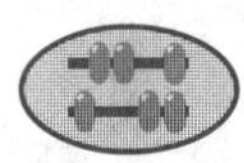   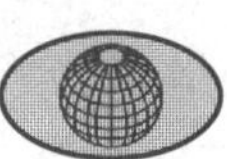   

Understanding the Role of Diversification by Guofu Zhou

EXECUTIVE SUMMARY

- Diversification is a way to reduce risk by investing in a variety of assets or business ventures.
- Systematic risk is not diversifiable, while idiosyncratic risk can be reduced or even eliminated.
- Portfolio diversification depends on risk-aversion and time horizon, and the portfolio mix must be rebalanced periodically.
- Overdiversification/"diworsification" can occur under certain conditions. Business diversification relies on endogenous opportunities, whose value depends on how flexibilities such as timing and expansion options are managed.

INTRODUCTION

To diversify is to do things with variety in order to improve well-being. Diversification is thus a common and fundamental concept in both daily life and business. However, the practice is primarily known as a way of reducing risk by investing in a variety of assets or business ventures. Buying one utility stock in the East coast and one in the West will minimize local shocks, while maintaining roughly the same return as buying either of the two alone. A shop at a resort selling both umbrellas and sunglasses clearly will have a less variable income whether a sunny or a rainy day comes up.

To obtain the optimal strategy of diversification, the risk must be defined and the associated investment opportunities modeled. In addition, the utility or investor's risk tolerance and investment horizon must be specified. In terms of asset allocation and portfolio choice, the risk is usually defined as the standard deviation of the portfolio return. This measures the variability of the return relative to the expected value of the return. Given a fixed level of expected return, the strategy that generates the minimum variance is preferred. To achieve this, the optimal diversification among the assets will usually be required. The risk tolerance of an investor determines the trade-off between return and risk, as well as the level of risk to take.

MODERN PORTFOLIO THEORY

Without a formal framework, *naive diversification* calls for an allocation of an equal amount of money across N assets, and thus it is also known as the $1/N$ rule. This rule goes back to as early as the fourth century, when Rabbi Issac bar Aha suggested: "One should always divide his wealth into three parts: a third in land, a third in merchandise, and a third ready to hand." Naive diversification is clearly not optimal in general. For example, when investing in a money market and a stock index, few investors will allocate 50% to the money market.

In 1951 Markowitz published his famous portfolio theory, which provides the optimal portfolio weights on a given N risky assets (stocks) once the expected returns, covariances, and variances of the assets are given, along with the investor's risk tolerance, in a quadratic utility function. The resulting optimal portfolio is a full diversification with money invested in all of the risky assets. The benefits of diversification depend more on how the assets perform relative to one another than on the number of assets you want to invest. The more the assets do not behave alike—that is, the lower the correlations among them—the more the risk can be minimized by holding the right mix of them.

The optimal portfolio is not risk-free. It is simply the one that has the minimum risk among all possible portfolios of the assets for a given a level of expected return. For any asset, one can decompose its total risk into two components, systematic/market-wide risk and idiosyncratic risk. The optimal portfolio has only market risk, because idiosyncratic risk is diversified away. As a result, there is no point in taking any idiosyncratic risk. But market risk is unavoidable. Intuitively, the return on a suitable portfolio of all stocks in the market has only the market risk, and will not be affected by bad news from some companies, which is likely be offset by good news from others. However, a war, a national disaster, or a global crisis will likely affect the entire portfolio in one direction.

With leverage, the optimal portfolio can theoretically be designed to obtain any desired level of expected return by taking certain necessary risk. The greater the desired expected return on the optimal portfolio, the higher is the risk. Without borrowing and short selling, the diversified portfolio must have an expected return between the highest and the lowest of the asset expected returns. However, the risk is often much smaller than the lowest risk of all the assets.

An efficient portfolio is one that offers either the highest expected return for a given level of risk or the lowest level of risk for a given expected return. The efficient frontier represents that set of portfolios that has the maximum expected return for every given level of risk. No portfolio on the efficient frontier is any better than another. Depending on the investor's risk

CASE STUDY

A Stock Investment

Consider an investment in General Motors, or IBM, or the diversified S&P500 Index for 50 years from 1957 to 2007. Examined at a monthly frequency, and based on all the 50 years of data, the estimated expected return on the three assets are 1.12%, 0.84%, and 0.69% per month, and the estimated monthly standard deviations are 7.01%, 7.59%, and 4.13%, respectively. IBM has the highest expected return, with return per unit of risk of 0.16. Although the market has the estimated lowest expected return, its return per unit of risk is higher, 0.17. On the risk-adjusted basis, the market is the best of the three.

In practice, good firms like IBM are not easy to identify ex ante. If one randomly picks a single stock, the average expected return is almost the market return but with much higher risk. The same is true if one randomly chooses a small group of stocks. In fact, back in 1957, IBM, GM, and Eastman Kodak were all blue chip stocks in the famous Dow Jones Index. Eastman Kodak has long gone from the index, and GM it seems is on the verge of being the next to go, with its value drops of more than 75% up to October, 2008. In addition, many firms have gone bankrupt, merged, or been bought over the years. Hence it is important to hold a diversified portfolio and to manage it over time.

  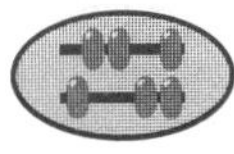   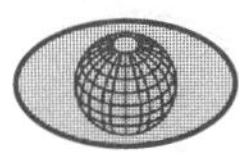   

tolerance, the investor chooses theoretically one, and only one, efficient portfolio on the frontier.

The investment opportunity set is static in the mean–variance framework underlying the Markowitz portfolio theory. As investment opportunities change over time, many argue for *time diversification*—that the risk of stocks diminishes with the length of the investment horizon. While this is debatable, the benefit of diversification across assets, and much of the mean–variance theory, carry through into dynamic portfolio choice models with changing investment opportunities. However, due to incomplete information (such as parameter and model uncertainties), trading costs (such as learning and transaction costs), labor income, and solvency conditions, it can be optimal theoretically to *underdiversify*—to not invest in all assets. Diversification purely for the sake of diversification can cause unnecessary diversification or *overdiversification*, to end up *diworsification* i.e. worsening off from bad diversification.

BUSINESS DIVERSIFICATION: REAL OPTIONS

With competition, the margin of any business diminishes over time. It is therefore vital for a company to make constant innovations and take on good growth opportunities. All of these activities are closely related to diversification. To enhance existing businesses, a company can diversify geographically in its production and R&D, and diversify vertically to take on more of the functions of the businesses previously run by others. While this increases efficiency and reliability, it also increases the risk exposure of the existing business. A company can, however, diversify horizontally by making new products and opening new markets.

Business diversification is, however, much more complex than stock investment diversification. First, the diversification possibilities are not obvious and have to be studied and developed with resources. Second, the risk and return on a new business are endogenously determined by how it is managed. Third, the benefits of diversification may not show up at the start. This is because existing businesses can be weakened when both management and financial resources are switched to diversification. Also, the new business will typically experience higher risk since the firm's management has less experience in running it.

Business diversification is almost always sequential. For any project, there are usually many embedded options, such as when to start, whether to expand, and how to switch. Optimal exercise of the options can enhance the value significantly, and so they should be analyzed carefully. Various risk management practices in a company can also be viewed as diversification whereby, to reduce risk, investments are made in financial assets or derivatives to offset the occasional negative payoffs of businesses. However, business diversification can be counterproductive if funds are inefficiently allocated across divisions, if division managers are self-interested, or if the conglomerates, created through mergers of already inefficient firms perhaps, remain inefficient. In addition, diversification typically provides consistent performance with less upside surprises. Academic research finds a *diversification discount*—that a diversified firm usually trades at a discount relative to a comparable matched portfolio of single-segment firms.

CONCLUSION

For asset investments, diversification is an effective tool in reducing the risk of investments in stocks, bonds, and other securities. Utilizing the correlation structure among the assets, idiosyncratic risk can be reduced or even eliminated. For businesses, diversification is a strategic decision. It is vital for a firm's long-term value creation to identify and manage growth opportunities. Diversification is an important way to manage these opportunities well, reducing risk and ensuring success.

▶▶ MAKING IT HAPPEN

For asset investments, while money managers can apply modern portfolio theory to diversify the risk with a desired level of return, individual investors can make use of the theory indirectly by investing in portfolios managed by the money managers. In practice this can be done via mutual funds and exchange traded funds. Large and wealthy investors can diversify even more with alternative asset classes such as hedge funds, collectibles (like art works), and exotic investment vehicles sold by large banks. They can diversify over various investment styles, managers, and brokerage accounts. For businesses, diversification means putting managerial and financial resources from your primary business into other opportunities. A small investment in strategic planning and diversification can pay off handsomely later. Vertical diversification may be the first to be started, though horizontal vehicles can be pursued at the same time. Diversification can increase the risk of the existing business but reduce the total risk exposure of the firm. However, the various flexibility options in diversification, such as timing and switching, must be valued carefully and managed efficiently to obtain the maximum diversification benefit.

▶▶ MORE INFO

Books:

Bodie, Zvi, Alex Kane, and Alan J. Marcus. *Investments*. 8th ed. New York: McGraw-Hill, 2009.

Campbell, J., and L. Viceira. *Strategic Asset Allocation*. Oxford: Oxford University Press, 2002.

Markowitz, H. M. *Portfolio Selection: Efficient Diversification of Investments*. Hoboken, NJ: Wiley, 1991.

Articles:

Liu, Hong. "Portfolio insurance and underdiversification." Washington University, 2008. Online at: ssrn.com/abstract=932581

Tu, Jun, and Guofu Zhou. "Being naive about naive diversification: Can investment theory be consistently useful?" 2008. Online at: ssrn.com/abstract=1099293

Website:

Guofu Zhou's references on diversification: www.olin.wustl.edu/faculty/zhou/ReferencesOnDiversification.pdf

See Also:

Portfolio Selection: Efficient Diversification of Investments (p. 1309)

"**Diversification: the only free lunch on Wall Street.**" Anonymous

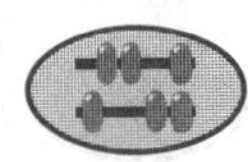

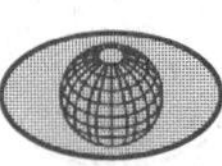

Valuation and Project Selection When the Market and Face Value of Dividends Differ by Graham Partington

EXECUTIVE SUMMARY

The dividends are off the pace
Their value is below their face
So our models we must bend
Towards the valuation end

- When the market and face valuation of dividends differ, the valuation models used for valuing shares and selecting investment projects are likely to result in valuation errors.
- Where valuations are undertaken across different tax jurisdictions, different valuation models may be required.
- Where adjustments are made to discount rates rather than cash flows, this increases the likelihood of error.
- All these problems can be resolved by a simple modification of the standard valuation models.
- The approach, called the *q* method, provides a convenient and simple valuation model with almost universal application.

INTRODUCTION

Suppose that a company declares a cash dividend of $1, then the face value of the dividend is $1. The market value, which is what that dividend trades for in the market, may, or may not, be the same as the face value. Traditional approaches to valuation, such as the discounted dividend model (see p. 963), usually assume that the market value and the face value of dividends are the same. When this is not the case you hit problems in valuation and in making investment decisions using traditional capital budgeting techniques.

A common approach to valuing a share is to discount the expected selling price of the share and then add the discounted value of the dividends that you expect to receive before you sell. This approach is the foundation of the discounted dividend model used to estimate the value of shares. The expected price is by definition a market value, but the dividends are at face value. If the market and face value of dividends differ, adding share prices and dividends together is like adding apples and oranges and calling the total apples. The foundation of the discounted dividend model is therefore decidedly shaky if the market value and face values differ.

Whether the face and market values of dividends differ is a much debated question among finance academics, but there is plenty of evidence that they do. One reason for the difference is taxation. If the company gives you a dollar of dividends and then the government takes away $0.25 in tax, you might well value that dividend at less than a dollar. As it turns out, capital gains taxes also play a role. If instead of paying you $1 of dividends the company keeps that cash in the company, your shares have more asset backing. Consequently your shares are more valuable and you end up paying more gains tax.

The market value of dividends relative to their face value then depends on the relative taxation of dividends and capital gains. In many jurisdictions dividends have a tax disadvantage. This is because returns in the form of price changes are taxed at concessional capital gains tax rates, whereas dividends are taxed as income. In other jurisdictions dividends are tax-advantaged. For example, in imputation tax systems the shareholders receive a refund of corporate tax along with their dividend.

The problem raised by the divergence between the market and face value of dividends also extends to traditional discounted cash flow techniques for capital budgeting (see p. 1099). This is because the use of these techniques is based on their equivalence to the discounted dividend model, as was shown by the Nobel Prize winners Merton Miller and Franco Modigliani.[1]

THE SOLUTION IS *q*

One solution to the problem is to make the discounted values for prices and dividends consistent by adjusting the discount rate. For example, the capital asset pricing model, or CAPM (see p. 1083), a popular model for estimating discount rates, can be extended to allow for differential taxation of dividends and capital gains. The reality, however, is that these after-tax versions of the CAPM have been little used because of the additional complexity that they involve and because of difficulties in implementation. There is a further problem that different models are needed for different tax jurisdictions.

An alternative solution to the problem involves adjusting the cash flow, and it also requires a small change in the definition of the discount rate.[2] This alternative approach is called the *q* method. The advantage of the *q* method is that it is both simple and general in its application. It works whether dividends have a tax disadvantage or a tax advantage (as under an imputation tax system). The approach also allows the face value and market value of interest payments to differ. Thus, whatever tax jurisdiction the valuation is being conducted under, the *q* method can be used without modification. The method also works just as well if the face and market value of dividends differ for reasons other than taxes.

An attractive feature of the *q* method is that the main adjustment is to the measurement of cash flows. One advantage of adjusting the cash flow is that the adjustment is clearly visible, and therefore executives are alerted to the assumptions that are being made. In contrast, where adjustments are buried in the discount rate, it is often a case of out of sight, out of mind. Cash flow adjustments, therefore, are less likely to lead to errors.

The key to the *q* method is to let the market do the work and express everything in market prices. To do this it is first necessary to define the return on equity in terms of the expected growth in share prices, R_{price}. This is done as follows:

$$R_{\text{price}} = \frac{(P^{\text{cum}}_{t+1} - P^{\text{ex}}_t)}{P^{\text{ex}}_t}$$

where P^{cum}_{t+1} represents the expected cum-dividend share price in the next period (at time $t + 1$) and P^{ex}_t represents the ex-dividend share price that we observe now (at time t.[3]) When prices are in equilibrium, R_{price} is the return that investors require on their investment in the shares. In determining their required return R_{price},

"Taxes can cause the market and face value of dividends to differ."

     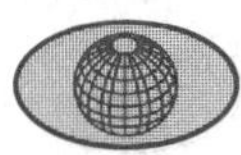   

investors will factor in the effect of any capital gains taxes that they may have to pay.

Next, we decompose the expected cum-dividend price into the expected ex-dividend price next period (P^{ex}_{t+1}) and the market value of dividends. The market value of the dividend is obtained by multiplying the face value of the next period's expected dividend (DIV_{t+1}) by q. The q factor is the ratio of the market value of dividends to the face value of dividends. The q factor, just like the famous Tobin's q, measures the ratio of market value to replacement cost. This is because the cost of replacing the cash paid out as a dividend equals the face value of the dividend. Thus, if the market value of dividends is $0.75 per $1.00 of face value, the q factor is 0.75. The resulting decomposition of the expected cum-dividend price is:

$$P^{cum}_{t+1} = P^{ex}_{t+1} + q(DIV_{t+1})$$

Everything is now expressed in terms of market value. No further adjustments for taxes on dividends or on capital gains are required. This is because the effects of these taxes are fully captured in q and R_{price}. From the two definitions above it is simply a matter of algebra to derive a set of equations for valuation and the cost of capital. We can omit the algebra and go straight to the results.

USING THE *q* METHOD

We begin with the discounted dividend model for today's ex-dividend price. This looks very like the traditional discounted dividend model except that the dividend is multiplied by q and the discount rate is R_{price}:

$$P^{ex}_t = \frac{q(DIV_{t+1})}{(1 + R_{price})^{t+1}} + \frac{(P^{ex}_{t+1})}{(1 + R_{price})^{t+1}} = \sum_{t=t+1}^{\infty} \frac{DIV_t\, q}{(1 + R_{price})^t}$$

The term on the extreme right-hand side says that the value of the share is the present value to infinity of future dividend payments expressed in market values. The model is very similar to the standard discounted dividend model, except that the face value of dividends is multiplied by q to get market values and the discount rate is a rate applicable to discounting market values. If q is equal to one, then the model above becomes identical to the standard discounted dividend model.

Turning to capital budgeting, in using the discounted cash flow approach it is traditional to value a project by discounting the unlevered after-tax cash flow of the project using the weighted average cost of capital (WACC). Three modifications are required when the market and face value of dividends differ. First, multiply the unlevered cash flows by q, thus expressing the cash flows in terms of market values. Second, convert the WACC to a discount rate appropriate for discounting market values. This is done by using R_{price} for the cost of equity and multiplying the cost of debt, r_{debt}, by q. Given a corporate tax rate T_c, the resulting equations are as follows:

$$\text{project value} = \sum_{t=1}^{N} \frac{(\text{unlevered after-corporate-tax cash flow}_t)\, q}{(1 + WACC)^t}$$

$$WACC = \frac{\text{equity value}}{\text{firm value}} R_{price} + \frac{\text{debt value}}{\text{firm value}} r_{debt}(1 - T_c) q$$

At first sight the scaling of the cost of debt by q may seem strange.[4] It arises directly from the algebra used to derive the model for project valuation, and an intuitive interpretation is that it captures the tax-effectiveness of debt relative to equity. If q is less than one, this enhances the tax-effectiveness of debt relative to equity, and if q is more than one, this makes debt less tax-effective. If q is equal to one, then both the project value and WACC equations are exactly the same as those used in the traditional approach to capital budgeting.

A third adjustment may be required when computing the increase in company value created by the project (the net present value, NPV.) This adjustment is only needed if the project is financed from retained earnings that could otherwise be distributed as dividends. Let us suppose that the market value of dividends is $0.75 per dollar of face value; then, if the firm retains $1.00 of earnings rather than paying it as a dividend, investors are only foregoing $0.75 of market value ($q$ = 0.75.) Therefore, the firm only needs to earn its cost of capital on $0.75 of value—or, to put it another way, the opportunity cost of retained earnings is $0.75 per dollar of face value retained. Consequently, if the firm retains $1 million to fund a project, the cost in terms of market value is only $750,000.

Given the project value obtained from the valuation equation above, the NPV is computed as:

$$NPV = \text{project value} - \text{initial investment}$$

Where part or all of the initial investment is funded from retained earnings, the initial investment needs to be converted to market values. The resulting equation for the NPV becomes:

$$NPV = \text{project value} - (\text{external finance} + q \times \text{retained earnings})$$

When q is less than one, this makes retained earnings an attractive source of finance. However, in some jurisdictions, such as countries with imputation tax systems, q can be considerably greater than one. For example, evidence from the German and Australian imputation systems suggests that q can be as high as 1.2, and in some cases higher. In such cases external financing is more attractive than using retained earnings.

One final attractive feature of the q method is that it gives rise to a very simple after-tax version of the CAPM that encompasses the other after-tax CAPMs that have been proposed. Indeed it is so simple that it looks very like the standard CAPM. Given the volatility of the return on a share relative to the overall capital market, measured by beta (β), the risk-free interest rate (r_f), and the q factor for interest payments (q_{debt}), the after-tax CAPM is written as:

$$R_{price,\,i} = r_f\, q_{debt} + \beta(R_{price,\,M} - r_f\, q_{debt})$$

where the subscripts i and M indicate the return on the share and the return on the market, respectively. If bonds and shares are taxed in the same way, and bond and share markets are not segregated, q and

Figure 1. Comparison between old and new shares with different dividend entitlements for Coca-Cola Amatil

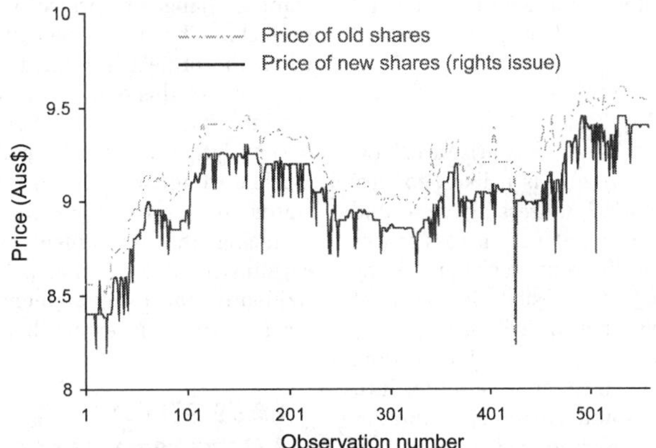

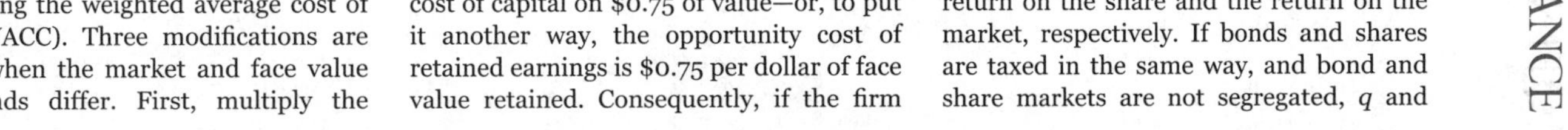

"Using the *q* method of valuation is easy, just make some simple changes to the standard valuation model."

  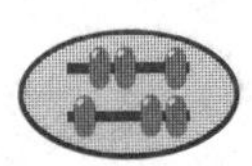   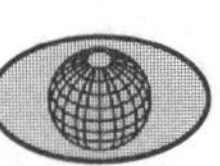   

q_{debt} should be the same. However, where bonds and shares are taxed differently, or where different investors set prices in bond and equity markets, then q and q_{debt} can differ.

MEASURING *q*

Two questions that naturally arise are: How do you measure q, and is it likely to vary much across stocks? Addressing the second question first, q might vary across stocks if the prices of different stocks are set by different types of investor. However, it seems unlikely that q will vary greatly across stocks in a given tax jurisdiction. This is because substantial variation in q across stocks would create opportunities for profitable arbitrage. Substantial variation in q across stocks therefore requires different dividend clienteles to hold different stocks and also calls for substantial barriers to arbitraging the valuation differences created by these clienteles.

Several methods exist for measuring q, and improved methods are being developed. One common approach is to look at the change in the price when the stock changes from trading cum-dividend to trading ex-dividend. Since the dividend detaches from the stock on the ex-dividend day, the change in the value of the stock is a measure of the market value of the dividend. Unfortunately, however, several other factors influence the price change, so this measurement can often be inaccurate as an estimate of dividend value. For example, the stock trades one day at the cum-dividend price and then trades the next day at the ex-dividend price. Thus, the price change reflects both the detaching of the dividend and the effect of news items released in the time between the observations of the two prices.

The price impact of the news often swamps the price impact of the stock going ex-dividend. It is, therefore, much better to simultaneously observe stock prices with and without entitlement to the dividend. One case where this happens is when a company makes a new share issue and the new shares are not entitled to the current dividend.

CONCLUSION

The errors in valuations that arise from assuming $q = 1$ when this is not the case are highly variable depending on the pattern of project cash flows, the life of the project, the cost of capital, and how the project is financed. However, even small deviations from a value of $q = 1$ can result in substantial changes to project value for some projects. The most benign cases arise when the project is funded from retained earnings. In this case there are errors that tend to offset each other. For, example if $q = 0.75$ but is assumed equal to one, the market value of each cash flow is overstated by 25%. However, the cost of financing the investment with retained earnings is also overstated by 25%. Consequently, the overstatement of the cash flows is to some extent balanced by the overstatement of the cost of the investment. Unfortunately, we can't rely on these offsetting errors to always be of similar magnitude.

The moral for senior executives is clear: Whether the market value of dividends is equal to the face value is important. If you believe that the face value and market value of dividends are equal ($q = 1$), carry on using the traditional models; if not, use the q method. If you are uncertain about the magnitude of q, use the valuation equations in this chapter to analyze the sensitivity of the valuation to the size of q.

CASE STUDY

A Measurement of *q*

In mid-1995 Coca-Cola Amatil, an Australian company, made a rights issue in which the newly issued shares were not entitled to the next dividend. The dividend had a face value of Aus$0.095. Figure 1 plots the prices of the old and the new shares, which were matched to be no more than one minute apart. It was possible to observe these prices from 26 July to 30 August. After this time, the old shares went ex-dividend and the old and the new shares became identical.

As can be seen from Figure 1, movements in the price of the old and new shares follow each other closely and there is a more or less constant difference in the price of the two shares. This difference represents the market value of the dividend. Over the cases where each trade involved at least 100 shares, the average difference was 1.53 times the dividend. In other words, q was 1.53 and the average price difference was about Aus$0.145. The dividend had a market value greater than its face value because it had tax credits attached. The tax credits had a face value of Aus$0.049 per share, so adding the tax credit to the dividend gives a grossed up value of Aus$0.144, which is very close to the estimated market value. Clearly, a big difference in valuation would result from assuming $q = 1$, as against the value of $q = 1.53$ that is suggested by the data.

➤➤ MAKING IT HAPPEN

- The first step is for top management to consider whether the market value and face value of dividends are likely to differ for the firm. In other words, is q for dividends equal to one? For some firms, as in the mini-case for Coca-Cola Amatil above, there will be direct evidence on the value of q for the firm. In other cases, published research may provide evidence on market-wide values of q. In most cases the firm value for q is likely to be close to the market-wide value. In some cases management may need to commission a special study to estimate q.
- A precise estimate of q may be difficult to obtain, but imprecise estimates are a common feature of many of the input variables in valuation and capital budgeting. Consequently, imprecision is not a reason for ignoring the impact of q. It is a reason for doing a sensitivity analysis.
- Given a value of q not equal to one, then capital budgeting and valuation procedure manuals need to be updated to include the formulae presented in this chapter. Treasury staff and divisional mangers will need to be trained in the use of these formulae. Top management should provide divisional managers with the value of q, or the range for q to be used in sensitivity analysis. This will eliminate the temptation for managers to use varying estimates of q in gaming the budget.
- It should be emphasized that q impacts not only on the value of cash flows and the cost of capital, but also on the cost of using retained earnings. It also feeds into the measurement of performance using techniques such as EVA, since such techniques rely on measuring the capital invested and the cost of capital.

"Using standard valuation methods when *q* is not equal to 1 can result in substantial valuation errors."

  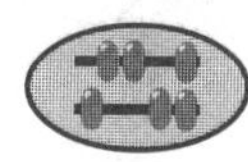   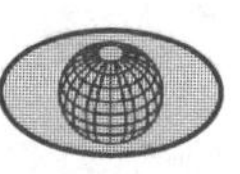   

▸▸ MORE INFO

Book:

Armitage, S. *The Cost of Capital: Intermediate Theory*. Cambridge, UK: Cambridge University Press, 2005.

Articles:

Dempsey, M. "The cost of equity capital at the corporate and investor levels allowing a rational expectations model with personal taxations." *Journal of Business Finance and Accounting* 23 (1996): 1319–1331.

Dempsey, M. "The impact of personal taxes on the firm's weighted average cost of capital and investment behaviour: A simplified approach using the Dempsey discounted dividends model." *Journal of Business Finance and Accounting* 25:5–6 (1998): 747–763.

Dempsey, M. "Valuation and cost of capital formulae with corporate and personal taxes: A synthesis using the Dempsey discounted dividends model." *Journal of Business Finance and Accounting* 28:3–4 (2001): 357–378.

Dempsey, M., and G. Partington. "Cost of capital equations under the Australian imputation tax system." *Accounting and Finance* 48:3 (2008): 439–460.

NOTES

1 Miller, M. H., and F. Modigliani. "Dividend policy, growth, and the valuation of shares." *Journal of Business* 34 (1961): 411–433.

2 For a rigorous exposition of the *q* method, see the early work of Dempsey (1998) and the later work of Dempsey and Partington (2008). Full citations of both works are given above.

3 The stock goes ex-dividend on a particular date, and shares bought after this date are not entitled to the current dividend. Shares bought prior to this date are referred to as cum-dividend and are entitled to the current dividend.

4 In deriving the project valuation model, the interest payments are initially scaled by q_{debt}, but this term cancels out in the derivation and so does not appear in the cash flow.

"The *q* book and the *q* method provide a key to correct valuations."

  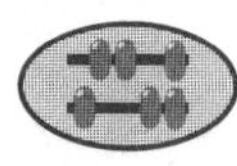   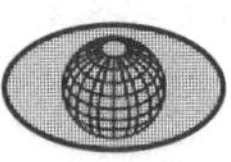   

When Form Follows Function: How Core–Satellite Investing Has Sparked an Era of Convergence by Christopher Holt

EXECUTIVE SUMMARY

- Core–satellite investing involves the separation of portfolios into a passively managed "core" (conforming to a strategic asset allocation framework) surrounded by actively managed "satellites" made up of active long-only funds and alternative investments.
- While this structure yields operational benefits, it stops short of its full potential as a portfolio construction rubric since it deals only with superficial labels (asset classes). Instead, institutional investors are beginning to think in terms of alpha (skill-based) returns and beta (index-based) returns.
- The separation of *alpha* and *beta*, regardless of their source, is a more accurate way to view core–satellite investing.
- This bifurcation has recently led to major changes in the way some pension portfolios are managed and in the way that asset managers service their clients. Asset classes once treated as separate or distinct are now converging into one integrated alpha/beta paradigm.
- Though challenges remain, there is little doubt that core–satellite investing has unleashed a wave of change that is reshaping asset management.

INTRODUCTION

"It is the pervading law of all things organic and inorganic. . .that form ever follows function."

Nineteenth century Chicago architect Louis Sullivan famously observed that a building's design must follow from its functional use. The same might be said about the design of modern portfolios and their management entities (pensions, endowments, asset managers, etc.). After emerging over the past decade as a simple portfolio management rubric, core–satellite investing is leading to a wholesale reengineering of the investment management function.

Core–satellite investing can generally be described as the separation of beta-centric (core) investing from alpha-centric (satellite) investing. However, the term has become stretched and overused. Today, "core" often refers to any number of passive asset classes and even to actively managed mandates. But a more literal definition of core as pure beta and satellite as pure alpha helps to shed light on one of the most significant underlying trends in asset management today—*convergence*.

HISTORY

Prior to modern portfolio theory little effort was made to distinguish between active and passive investing. All investing was simply seen as *active*. Then, in the 1960s, the capital asset pricing model (CAPM) revealed that security and portfolio values could be expressed in terms of two distinct concepts: beta and alpha.

Still, the CAPM remained primarily an analytical technique until the 1990s, when index mutual funds and, soon afterwards, exchange-traded index funds (ETFs) provided investors with an efficient way to invest in the market passively. Advocates of the efficient markets hypothesis saw ETFs as a way to rid themselves of the scourge of active management. But, as evidenced by the continuing interest in mutual funds, many investors were not willing to give up on active management altogether. They wanted both active and passive returns, and they wanted them in a flexible and interchangeable format.

Alternative investments (hedge funds, private equity, real estate, infrastructure, and commodities), it turned out, were the ideal complement to these pure beta funds since their returns had a very low correlation with markets. Thus, a combination of a passively managed ETF and an actively managed alternative investment could be made essentially to approximate a traditional actively managed portfolio. And so the institutional example of core–satellite investing, "portable alpha," was born.

Portable alpha generally refers to a more efficient construction of sponsor portfolios that involves access to market returns (beta) synthetically via futures or swaps, and access to manager skills (alpha) separately, usually via an allocation to a hedge fund. Separating these two sources of returns provided institutional investors with greater flexibility than ever before.

In response to this trend, the asset management industry began to bifurcate into providers of "high alpha" and "cheap beta." As one industry supplier put it at the time:[1]

"The separation of Alpha from Beta is expected to shift profit away from traditional long only active funds toward the extremes of unconstrained Alpha-

Figure 1. A "converged" approach to asset management combines aspects of both the traditional and alternative investment models

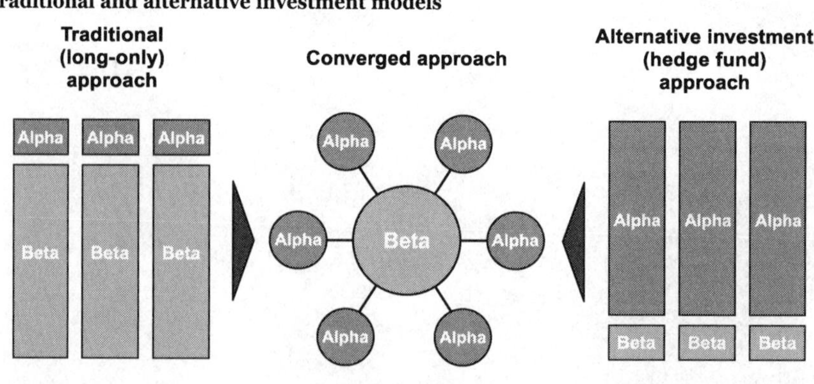

Traditional (long-only) approach
Converged approach
Alternative investment (hedge fund) approach
Alpha
Beta
Alpha
Beta
Alpha
Beta
• Fees based on assets under management;
• Hierarchical structure;
• Stable investment theses;
• Robust operations;
• Well-evolved risk management systems;
• Mature regulatory environment.
• Hybrid fee structures;
• Matrix organizational structure;
• Retooled operational environment;
• Robust yet highly extensible risk management systems;
• Quickly evolving regulatory environment.
• Fees based primarily on performance;
• Flat structure;
• Often long or short same names/theses;
• Nascent operations;
• Evolving risk management systems;
• Weak regulatory environment.

"Things that are done, it is needless to speak about. . .things that are past, it is needless to blame." Confucius

  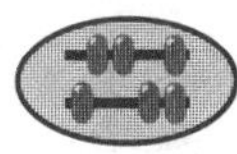 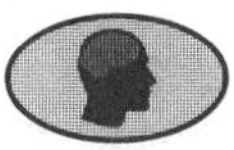  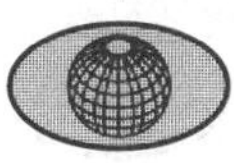  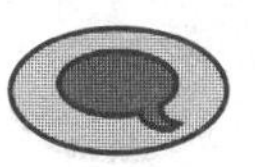 

CASE STUDY

Sweden's AP7 Pension Fund

At the end of 2007, Sweden's national pension system managed approximately US$190 billion. The system comprises seven separate "buffer" funds. Funds one through six manage assets for the system's defined benefit program, while the seventh (AP7) is the default fund for the system's defined contribution plan. About one third of the system's assets are managed in the defined contribution plan, with AP7 managing slightly more than US$14 billion.

Traditionally, the AP7 fund sought beta returns in the form of passive mandates in mature (informationally efficient) markets such as US large-cap equities and alpha returns in the form of active mandates in informationally inefficient markets such as Asian equities. Alpha was also sought via a separate and distinct class for hedge funds and private equity.

But in 2005, after poor performance from its traditional active managers, AP7 decided to restructure the fund in order to "improve the alpha opportunities for traditional long only portfolios." Vice-president Richard Grottheim described the program in AP7's 2007 annual report:[12]

"Separating the alpha management (active management) from the beta management (index management) has been discussed for years in the fund industry and among academics. But few have ever tried it in practice. At the AP7 Fund we decided three years ago to test this approach in our internal management of our equities portfolio."

In 2008 Grottheim and his colleagues described some of the challenges they faced and benefits they saw by implementing such a program:[13]

- *Organizational change*: Management described the most significant change as being a "complete specialization approach in the daily investment operation."
- *Risk measurement*: While AP7 measured the risk of long-only managers using tracking error, this was not possible for pure alpha managers with no apparent benchmark.
- *Portfolio management*: Alpha managers were provided with no net capital, only a "notional amount" used as a baseline for risk measurement. As a result, AP7 management found it difficult to communicate and gain approval for the approach from traditional managers.
- *Fees*: AP7 also found it difficult to agree on an appropriate fee structure. There were no actual assets under management (AUM) amount for calculating management fees, and many had never charged performance-based fees before.
- *Benefits*: According to senior management, the change from traditional long-only portfolios to alpha/beta management has yielded several benefits for both investors and AP7:
  - *Expanded universe*: The fund is now able to "search for skilled managers wherever they exist, even in asset classes outside the strategic allocation."
  - *Fewer investment constraints*: Unlike in traditional long-only mandates, "unnecessary constraints are removed allowing the full insight of active managers to be reflected in portfolio positions."
  - *Fee transparency*: Separating alpha returns from beta returns let AP7 "capture the full economies of beta management and pay active management fees that reflect a manager's skill and ability to add value." While the total fees charged for alpha managers were higher than traditional active managers, they were lower than true hedge funds.

generating investing (more volatile pools, such as certain types of hedge funds and private equity) and passive investing (index funds, exchange-traded funds and certain types of derivatives)."

CONVERGENCE WITHIN INSTITUTIONAL PORTFOLIOS

By placing the major components of the strategic asset allocation in the "core" and more active alpha-generating investments in the "satellite," institutional investors gained flexibility and achieved cost reductions (Figure 1). For example, transitions between active managers (in the satellite) could be executed without incurring the costs of liquidating the core or hiring a transition manager. Also, by removing the benchmark constraint from satellite managers, they are free to implement a greater portion of their investment ideas.

While innovative, this view of core satellite investing still relied on traditional asset class labels (large cap, small cap, hedge fund, etc.), and not on the underlying characteristics of these mandates identifying them as alpha or beta.

Since their introduction in 1949, hedge funds had been viewed by investors as a separate and distinct asset class. But by the early years of the 21st century, the separation, manipulation, and recombination of alpha and beta had begun to attract the interest of large institutional investors. These investors saw alternative investments as *alpha delivery vehicles* first and foremost.

Innovative public pension plans such as Sweden's AP7 (see case study) went a step further, ignoring labels such as "traditional" and "hedge fund," and reoriented their portfolios and organizations along the lines of alpha and beta *regardless of their respective sources.*

As a result, asset classes that have been managed separately are now converging into one business model whose salient parts are alpha and beta, not "traditional" and "hedge fund."

CONVERGENCE WITHIN THE GREATER ASSET MANAGEMENT INDUSTRY

Faced with the headwind of a bull market between 2003 and 2007 and targeting the huge assets under management by traditional asset managers, many hedge funds launched long-biased (even long-only) funds during the past decade.

At the same time, traditional asset managers began to buy hedge fund companies, clearly attracted by their relatively high fees. In 2005, there were 30 major M&A transactions involving alternative investment managers.[2] The next year, the number doubled to 60, then rose again to 76 in 2007. These transactions rose from 20% of the total transaction volume for all asset management deals in 2005 to 32% only two years later.

By 2007, both hedge fund managers and long-only managers saw so-called "130/30" funds as a fertile middle ground between their two business models. Estimates of the potential size of this converged market quickly ranged up to $2 trillion.[3]

Throughout this time, many mutual fund companies also launched long-short or market-neutral funds and marketed them alongside traditional mutual funds. Although these funds tended to underperform *bona fide* hedge funds, they *outperformed* their traditional mutual fund peers. Researchers attributed this to the more flexible investment strategies used by these so-called "hedged mutual funds."[4]

Today, most major traditional asset management firms run some form of hedge fund. And while many hedge fund

   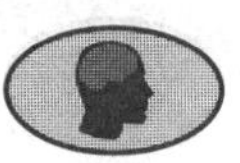  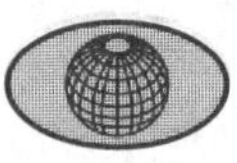   

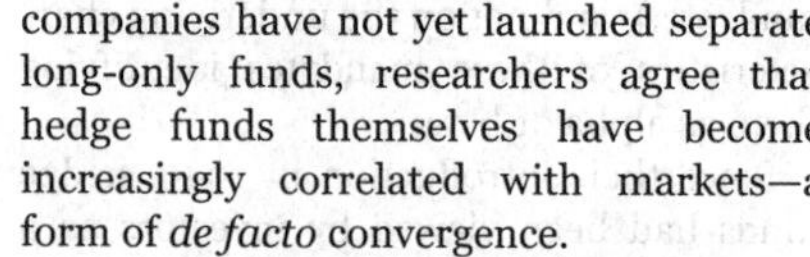

companies have not yet launched separate long-only funds, researchers agree that hedge funds themselves have become increasingly correlated with markets—a form of *de facto* convergence.

KEY IMPLEMENTATION CHALLENGES

Convergence has now become the defining trend in the traditional investment management sector. The need to develop a convergence strategy is nowhere more apparent than within the executive suites of traditional investing's entrenched leadership. As the head of one $800 billion asset management firm told the *Financial Times*:[5]

> "On one side, you have exchange-traded funds and, on the other, you have [private equity firm] Blackstone and the hedge funds. It leaves firms like ours, traditional long-only buy-side firms, needing to make some very tough decisions."

Recent market calamities have required many financial institutions to sell off their asset management divisions to raise capital. Doing so has only accelerated the forces that are driving hedge funds and long-only funds into each others' arms. But although we are well on our way to a "converged" industry, many business model challenges remain.

Some key implementation challenges are described below.

Fee Convergence

Chief among these challenges are the conflicting fee models used by traditional and alternative managers. According to a study by McKinsey & Company, the average hedge fund fee paid by an institutional investor in 2007 was 174 bps. The average fee paid for a domestic (US) equity mandate was 40 bps.[6]

But, beneath the surface of the posted fee rates, convergence is slowly but surely occurring. One study of US equity funds, for example, revealed that while the posted fees for many leading mutual funds were approximately 1% per annum, the effective fee per unit of active management was actually many times higher. If the beta portion of returns was assumed to be replicated by a low-cost ETF, the fees *per unit of active management* were 5% or more. Thus, a hedge fund with a 2% management fee, a 20% performance fee and a low market correlation could easily have the same fee as a traditional mutual fund.[7]

Cultural Convergence

In part due to this contrasting fee model, traditional asset managers have often faced challenges getting (traditionally higher-paid) hedge fund managers to work alongside (traditionally lower-paid) long-only managers.

Portfolio Management Convergence

Hedge fund managers are quick to say that short selling requires a skill set not readily available in a traditional long-only organization. Whether or not this is true, the management of two parallel funds with dramatically different fee structures can raise potential conflicts of interest for portfolio managers. For example, managers can have an incentive to allocate profitable trades to the fund with the performance fee.

But although such conflicts may exist, researchers have discovered that mutual funds managed alongside hedge funds actually perform better than mutual funds managed on their own. The opposite was not found to be true, however. Hedge funds managed alongside mutual funds perform on par with those managed alone.[8]

Operational Convergence

Due in part to industry consolidation, some hedge fund managers have now become so large that their administrative and operational capabilities eclipse those of many mid-sized mutual fund companies. Well over half of the world's hedge fund assets are now managed by companies with at least three billion dollars of assets under management. Many of these firms are diversified financial institutions with many tens of billions of dollars in assets under management.

The varied success of hedge fund initial public offerings (IPOs) has revealed the importance of converged business models. As one M&A advisery firm put it:[9] "Public market investors like the growth story that alternative asset managers present, but they also want to see characteristics more akin to the broadly diversified fund managers they trust."

Risk Management Convergence

Hedge funds emerged from an environment of less regulation and proportionately traditional funds. Cognizant of this, institutional hedge fund investors are often more likely to demand complex risk analysis and exposure reporting from hedge funds than they do from their traditional managers.

Regulatory Convergence

Regulators such as the US Securities and Exchange Commission have long sought to bring hedge funds under the same regulatory umbrella as traditional investment advisers (although its efforts have been punctuated by intermittent setbacks).

The reports published by the President's Working Group on Financial Markets[10] in the United States and the Hedge Fund Working Group[11] in the United Kingdom make it clear that increased regulation—whether government-sponsored or self-imposed—is on its way. Short position disclosure requirements implemented by several regulators in October 2008 have simply added an exclamation mark to this trend.

Summary

This is only a brief list of the business issues arising from convergence in the asset management industry. Convergence will play out in unpredictable ways over the next decade as the investment management industry undergoes a fundamental realignment. This will require institutional investors, hedge funds, and traditional managers to retool their capabilities, to reorganize their structures, and to reinvent themselves. The new organizational form that emerges from the convergence of alternative and traditional investing will have characteristics associated with both models.

What began as a simple framework for organizing a portfolio has sparked a revolution in the way institutional investors and asset managers manage both their portfolios and their organizations. As Louis Sullivan declared, form has once again followed function.

▸▸ MORE INFO

Books:

Callin, Sabrina. *Portable Alpha Theory and Practice: What Investors Really Need to Know*. Hoboken, NJ: Wiley, 2008.

Dorsey, Alan H. *Active Alpha: A Portfolio Approach to Selecting and Managing Alternative Investments*. Hoboken, NJ: Wiley, 2007.

Reports:

Engstrom, Stefan, Richard Grottheim, Peter Norman, and Christian Ragnartz. "Alpha–beta-separation: From theory to practice." Working paper, May 2008. Online at: ssrn.com/abstract=1137673

     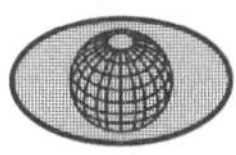   

Hubrich, Stefan. "An alpha unleashed: Optimal derivative portfolios for portable alpha strategies." Working paper, January 2008. Online at: ssrn.com/abstract=1015327

Miller, Ross M. "Measuring the true cost of active management by mutual funds." Working paper, June 2005. Online at: ssrn.com/abstract=746926

Thomas, Lee R. "Engineering an alpha engine." PIMCO, February 2004. Online at: faculty.fuqua.duke.edu/~charvey/Teaching/BA453_2006/Thomas_Engineering_an_Alpha.pdf

NOTES

1 IBM Institute for Business Value. "The trader is dead, long live the trader! A financial markets renaissance." Online at: www-935.ibm.com/services/us/imc/pdf/g510-6270-01-trader.pdf

2 Defined as "minority transactions, recapitalizations and IPOs." www.putnamlovell.com/services/white-papers/AllShookUp.pdf

3 Tabb Group. "Asset flows move from long-only equities to hedge funds and active-extension funds in heightened search for alpha, says TABB Group." September 2007. Online at: www.tabbgroup.com/PageDetail.aspx?PageID=16&ItemID=178

4 Agarwal, Vikas, Nicole M. Boyson, and Narayan Y. Naik. "Hedge funds for retail investors? An examination of hedged mutual funds." Working paper, June 2007. Online at: papers.ssrn.com/sol3/papers.cfm?abstract_id=891621

5 Brewster, Deborah. "Equity fund outflows bring need to adapt." *Financial Times* (April 27, 2008). Online at: www.ft.com/cms/s/0/0e887ecc-1480-11dd-a741-0000779fd2ac.html

6 Hunt, David, *et al*. "The U.S. asset management industry: Smooth sailing gives way to choppy seas." McKinsey & Co. Financial Services, October 9, 2008. Online at: fs.mckinsey.com/Display.aspx?id=c176b052-384d-4df5-86fa-0c5e75559a89

7 Miller, 2005.

8 Zhi Jay Wang, Lu Zheng, and Tom Nohel. "Side by side management of hedge funds and mutual funds." Working paper, March 2008. Online at: ssrn.com/abstract=1107675

9 Putnam Lovell Strategic Analysis. "All shook up: M&A and capital markets activity in global fund management 2007." February 2008. Online at: www.putnamlovell.com/services/white-papers/AllShookUp.pdf

10 Asset Managers' and Investors' Committee: www.amaicmte.org

11 Hedge Fund Working Group: www.hfwg.co.uk

12 *7 Sjunde AP-Fonden Annual Report 2007.* Online at: www.ap7.se/dokument/redovisning/2007/Arsredovisning2007-En.pdf

13 Engstrom, 2008.

"Good men prefer to be accountable." Michael Owen Edwardes

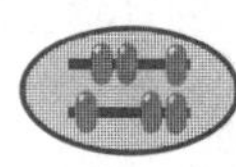
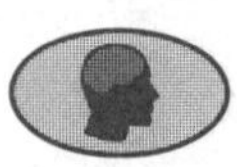

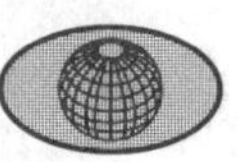

Acquisition Integration: How to Do It Successfully by David R. Sadtler

EXECUTIVE SUMMARY

- Successful integration of an acquisition by the acquiring company is often the most important determinant of the overall success of the acquisition process.
- Gaining financial control of the acquired company and tight cash management are essential from the start.
- Integrating management processes and systems can be difficult and time-consuming, but it is essential if the newly acquired management team is to be involved and empowered.
- Use all available sources of information to make key management appointments as quickly as possible.
- Ensure that the key drivers of value creation are known to all involved in the project, and that the process of searching, negotiating, and integrating reflects the most important of them.
- Move as quickly as possible when integrating.

INTRODUCTION

Acquisitions of any size are a major undertaking for both the acquirer and the target. Substantial returns—in particular returns in excess of the cost of capital employed in the entire initiative—are required not only to create stockholder value, but also to justify the enormous investment of managerial time and effort that goes into a takeover. Many acquisitions succeed. Indeed, many corporate acquirers do a large number of deals and become really good at it. Making money through acquisition, for them, is a key skill to be nourished and developed. But, as repeated studies have demonstrated all too well, many acquisitions—according to some, the vast majority—fail to justify the investment involved.

The success or otherwise of acquisitions is a much studied field, and we can therefore readily identify the principle causes of failure and disappointment.[1] Among them are the payment of excessive prices, missing problems during the due diligence phase, and even the use of faulty financial logic. But perhaps the biggest contributor to the failure of acquisitions is inadequate attention to the process of integrating the newly acquired business.

MAJOR CAUSES OF FAILURE

- Paying too much—especially likely in an auction.
- Targeting the wrong company because the value creation logic is inadequate.
- Power struggles among top management and disagreement about who is to be the boss.
- Cultural obstacles, especially in cross-border deals.
- Incompatibility of IT systems.
- Applying obsolete strategic rationales such as sector diversification, vertical integration, financial synergy, and gap-filling.
- Resistance by regulatory authorities and pressure groups.
- Use of faulty financial logic—i.e. getting the numbers wrong.
- Sloppy due diligence.
- Poorly planned and executed acquisition integration.

Successful integration requires that four tasks be done well. The more attention and skill that is marshaled for this purpose, the better the result is likely to be. The four tasks are: assuming financial control, integrating processes and systems, making key managerial appointments, and ensuring that the value creation logic for the acquisition drives the whole process. Inattention to any of them can cause big trouble.

THE FOUR KEY TASKS OF SUCCESSFUL INTEGRATION

1. Assume financial control

Serious acquirers know that it is essential to assume immediate control over financial performance and cash management. In some cases, the target may have been left vulnerable to acquisition by poor financial management. Such businesses will need special attention in this area.

This phase involves steps such as installing corporate financial reporting procedures and clarifying expenditure-level authority. In some cases it may also involve more frequent reporting of critical cash flow components, until the required systems are bedded in and the management team of the acquired business becomes familiar with what is expected of it. For example, weekly sales figures may temporarily require early scrutiny to ensure that commercial performance has not deteriorated owing to the demands of the acquisition experience. This phase lends itself to detailed checklists and procedures, constructed with expert help and developed and honed through corporate experience.

2. Integrate processes and systems

If the newly acquired business is to play its part in the larger organization, its principal managerial processes—business planning, budgeting, capital expenditure approval, and human resource management—must be integrated with those of the acquirer, so that the target can begin to function as part of the larger whole as quickly as possible. The sooner operational managers can become familiar and comfortable with the new process requirements, the better able they will be to concentrate their efforts on securing competitive advantage and on realizing the benefits expected from the combination of the two organizations.

A major and sometimes seemingly overwhelming aspect of this phase of integration is that of bringing together IT systems. In recent years the IT structures of large organizations have become more all-embracing and, in the case of so-called enterprise systems, may even constitute the digital backbone of the entire business. In such circumstances the criticality of ensuring that the target's systems are quickly and effectively integrated with those of the acquirer is obvious. But sometimes the process is simply too difficult. A number of mergers and acquisitions in the so-called bancassurance sector have floundered because of IT integration problems. The prime rationale for such mergers is usually that of cross-selling—selling the products of the acquirer to the customers of the acquired company and vice versa. This is a difficult goal to achieve at the best of times, and one that is critically dependent on the effective interfacing of the merging organizations' IT systems. When this does not happen, the merger is bound to be a financial disappointment.

3. Make key appointments

The aim here is to do the best possible job in the shortest possible time by putting the right people in charge of the newly acquired business and moving aside those who have not made the cut. Some will say it is not pos-

  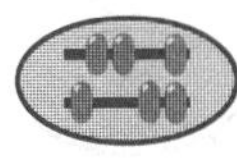   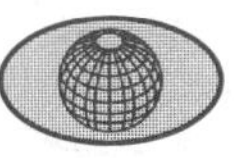   

sible for corporate overseers to know which managers are best for the key jobs until they have been observed in action for some time. The existing management team—the same people who perhaps failed to perform well enough to keep their business independent—may thus be left in place.

Typically, the most demanding step in this phase is the decision about who is to run the new business. Who is to be the boss? All possible sources of information about prospective candidates must be pressed into service. Managers who have experienced prior dealings with the candidate should be interviewed, the directors of the acquired business surveyed, and even individual performance reviews scrutinized. Getting this right is perhaps the most important task of all. If the right candidate is appointed, delays and failures in other areas are more likely to be remedied to everyone's satisfaction. But the wrong appointment can result in long-lasting problems and disappointment.

The object must be to find the right trade-off between speed and the effectiveness of the managerial appointment process. This may mean acting with less certainty, as opposed to delaying the decision until everyone is completely satisfied with the selection.

4. Ensure the primacy of value creation

Most of all, acquirers must be crystal clear about the value creation rationale for the acquisition, and they must ensure that this thinking drives the entire acquisition process, including that of integration. All involved in the acquisition—analysts, negotiators, professional advisers, the top management of the acquiring company, and those who will be responsible for integration—must be clear about how the acquisition is to make money for the stockholders of the acquirer, and must be constantly reminded of this throughout the process.

The value creation rationale is first proposed, clarified, agreed, and approved when acquisition criteria are developed and target candidates are identified. The thinking behind how the combination with the prospective target is to enhance competitive advantage and thus generate superior returns must be clear. That rationale should drive the contract-negotiating process and the due diligence work which backs it up, so that the important drivers of value creation continue to be reflected along the way.

Finally, the small number (perhaps only two or three) of initiatives that will create the value must be given the highest priority when it comes to integrating the new business. The sooner these initiatives are successfully completed, the greater the payoff, owing to the greater present value of the cash flows achieved.

OTHER FACTORS THAT CONTRIBUTE TO SUCCESS

Finally, a comment about speed. There is widespread agreement among serial acquirers that moving as quickly as possible is best. It may be tempting to keep the pressure off the acquired organization, at least temporarily, because they have been through a demanding and possibly anxious time. But momentum can be lost, benefits delayed, and the acquired management team even led to believe that the acquirers are less than serious about achieving the projected financial benefit. Speed is best.

One major UK retailer got this one wrong. To its credit, it was quite clear about its value creation rationale for the acquisition, which was that of implementing its proven EPOS (electronic point of sale) systems in the acquired company. It saw from its observation of the company—and confirmed this during the diligence process—that introducing its technology would impart major operational benefit to the target company. Inventories would be reduced, stockouts would decline, and overall customer satisfaction would increase. But it delayed implementation, reasoning that steps to integrate the target into its organization and enabling the new employees to become comfortable in their new surroundings were necessary for good morale. Sensing a lack of commitment to change, the acquired company's supply chain and IT specialists took the initiative to bolster their systems and make it hard for any subsequent changeover—along with the potential for staff reductions in the process. Operational integration was delayed for over a year and the financial benefits suffered accordingly. The corporate development director, who had been the project manager for the acquisition, commented that this was the biggest mistake in the entire process and that it would never happen again.

In larger organizations, and especially those that regard acquisitions as a key source of future growth and competitive advantage, specialists are often developed to perform the tasks of integration. Dedicated teams can reduce the possibility of delays of the kind described above. Smaller companies, and those with less experience, may not have the luxury of maintaining a dedicated staff, but if deals become a way of life, it is probably advisable that a specialized group be formed to capture the company's experience and institutionalize emerging best practice.

CONCLUSION

Integration is a tough and demanding job, but one that frequently spells the difference between success and failure in an acquisition. The task must be treated as one of the highest priority and responsibility apportioned to the people best suited to doing it. If this is done, and if the four tasks enumerated above are handled quickly and effectively, the chances of financial, strategic, and operational success will be that much higher.

▸▸ MAKING IT HAPPEN

- Design the entire acquisition process to focus on the key drivers of value creation, and ensure that the integration process deals with each as a high priority.
- Prepare a complete plan to action the four key areas—financial control, the introduction of new processes and systems, key appointments, and the pursuit of value creation—as soon as ownership changes hands.
- Develop a cadre of specialists to speed the acquisition process so that operational managers can focus on the business itself.
- Don't delay. Move fast.

▸▸ MORE INFO

Books:

Galpin, Timothy J., and Mark Herndon. *The Complete Guide to Mergers and Acquisitions: Process Tools to Support M&A Integration at Every Level.* San Francisco, CA: Jossey-Bass, 2007.

Sadtler, David, David Smith, and Andrew Campbell. *Smarter Acquisitions: Ten Steps to Successful Deals.* Harlow, UK: Pearson Education, 2008.

NOTES

1 The major causes of acquisition failure are dealt with at some length in Sadtler, Smith, and Campbell, *Smarter Acquisitions* (2008).

"Price is what you pay. Value is what you get." Warren Buffett

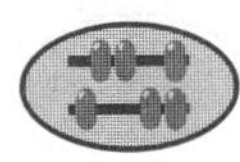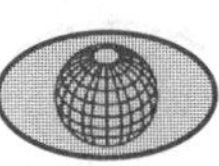

Coping with Equity Market Reactions to M&A Transactions by Scott Moeller

EXECUTIVE SUMMARY

- Overall, stock returns to acquirers tend to be negative or insignificant—in contrast to target companies, where stockholders can benefit greatly.
- Companies that believe they may be targets can influence the value of an ultimate acquisition through the design of defensive techniques and by how they react to bids when they occur. Similarly, acquirers can influence the target share prices through their actions prior to the bid.
- Most acquirers are overconfident in their ability to conduct acquisitions successfully.
- Careful planning, including a robust internal and external communications plan, is required to mitigate the impact on equity markets of acquirers.
- Many factors influence equity market reactions to an M&A bid, including how friendly or hostile the bid is, the financing structure of the bid, the relative size of the two companies, and whether the transaction is a merger or an acquisition.
- Deals conducted in the most recent merger wave appear to have taken some of these issues into account and show better relative performance (relative to the market) than deals conducted in the 1980s and 1990s.

INTRODUCTION

It would be nice if the markets were to react consistently in response to the announcement of M&A deals. But they don't. At least not always. But you can depend on one thing: In the short run, shareholders of target companies benefit more than those of the acquiring company.

It is important to know how to cope with the likely equity market reaction to the announcement of a deal. First of all, you need to understand what those likely reactions will be . . . and then to work out whether there is anything that can be done to influence the market. Bidders can mitigate the likely negative market reaction to their share price, and targets may be able to provoke even higher bids.

This article discusses public companies only—as these are naturally the only ones with an "equity market reaction." However, one can properly extrapolate their experience to private companies as well. While most advisers and principals in privately held companies take into account the experience of publicly held companies, the reaction of the equity markets regarding the bidder's share price is not dependent on whether the target is public or private. Either way, the shareholder value of bidders declines, on average, following the announcement of a large acquisition.

> "Most mergers fail. If that's not a bona fide fact, plenty of smart people think it is. McKinsey & Company says it's true. Harvard, too. Booz Allen & Hamilton, KPMG, A.T. Kearney—the list goes on. If a deal enriches an acquirer's shareholders, the statistics say, it is probably an accident."
> *New York Times*, February 28, 2008

EQUITY MARKET REACTIONS FOR TARGETS

Relatively few deals make money for the bidding company's shareholders. The market rather consistently shows that bidding companies lose money for their shareholders, or at best break even around the time of the announcement of a takeover, whereas target companies attract offer premiums that typically range from 20% to 40%. Stock prices often rise above the offer price if a competing bidder is anticipated.

These returns are relatively consistent in the United States and the United Kingdom, with the data for other countries less clear but indicating similar results. When the bidder and target returns are combined, the overall shareholder wealth effects are typically found to be insignificant over the short term and positive over the longer term.

In the absence of a competing bid, when a takeover is announced the target company's stock price typically rises to a level *below* the offer price, but slowly rises to approach the bid price as time approaches the closing date when the final deal is consummated, which for most deals is 3–6 months after the announcement date (Figure 1). This is because there is some risk that the deal will not go through or will be repriced (usually lower) because of negative information that the bidder finds while conducting due diligence on the target (see "Due Diligence Requirements in Financial Transactions" (pp. 398–401) for a discussion of the best ways to conduct due diligence in M&A deals).

Figure 1. Movement of target company share price

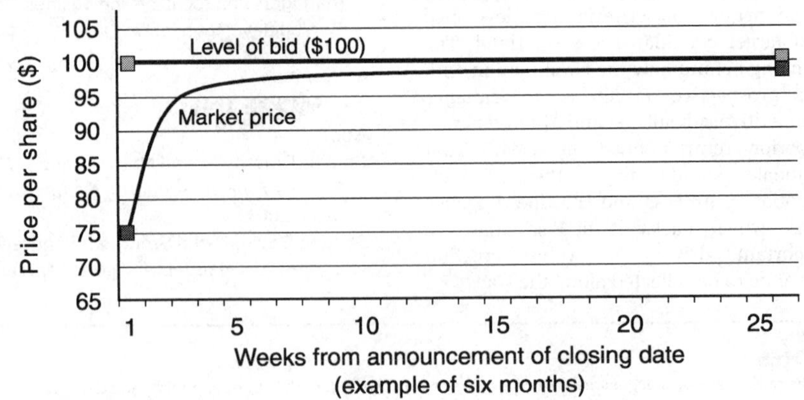

INFLUENCING TARGET COMPANY STOCK PRICES

The target company itself can have an influence on the potential price offered in a number of ways:

- By having a strong defense in place to protect the company from an unsolicited takeover bid. Such defenses can include so-called poison pills (including underfunded pension plans), shares owned by insiders or in friendly hands, golden and silver parachutes not just for senior management but for a wider group of employees (often called "tin parachutes"), and a history of successfully fending off hostile bidders. Research has shown that these defenses, especially poison pills, do result in higher premiums for target companies.
- Most of these defenses are put in place to make it more difficult (that is, expen-

"Equity markets will respond to the announcement of a deal and often NOT the way management expects."

  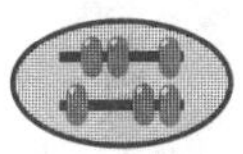   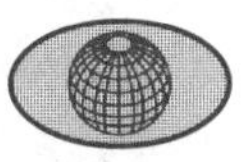  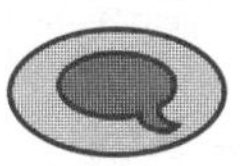 

sive), but not impossible, to be purchased. For example, Mellon Bank put in place tin parachutes for all its employees following an unsuccessful hostile bid by the Bank of New York in 1998; when later, in 2006, a friendly deal was proposed and accepted by Mellon Bank, the senior managers and employees were requested to waive their golden, silver, and tin parachute rights in order to put them on an equal footing with the Bank of New York employees, who had no such employment provisions.

- By letting the market know that a high threshold premium value will be required for any unsolicited bid before the board of directors will recommend it to the shareholders. Yahoo! used this technique when it successfully fended off an unwelcome bid from Microsoft in early 2008 that had a 62% premium associated with it (a so-called "bear hug" offer, which designates an offer above the typical premium range of 20–40%).
- By encouraging competing bids. By opening up the purchase of the company to an auction, the directors admit that the company is for sale and will likely lose its independence, but that they are actively seeking the highest possible price. After Morrisons, the supermarket chain in the United Kingdom, made a formal offer to purchase Safeway for £2.4 billion in January 2003, an auction for Safeway ensued with competing bids from Asda (controlled by Wal-Mart) and J. Sainsbury. There was a feeding frenzy that included Tesco, retail magnate Sir Philip Green, and venture capitalists Kohlberg Kravis Roberts. The price that Morrisons ultimately paid for Safeway was £3.0 billion.

Bidders can also influence the target company's share price, naturally wanting to keep the price of the target down. The most common technique is to conduct a "street sweep," whereby the target company's shares (or a controlling interest in the target) are purchased in a blitzkrieg that gives the market and the target's management no time to react before the takeover is effectively complete. This is very difficult to conduct in practice, and is most successful when a small number of shareholders control a large percentage of the target's shares or where the bidder already has a large ownership in the target. Thus, for example, Malcolm Glazer, who for a long time had been holding 28% of the publicly listed football club Manchester United, purchased a similarly sized holding from Cubic Expression in May 2004, and thus in one purchase came to control the club.

Many bidders, when purchasing their toeholds in potential targets, will publicly announce that they have no interest "at this time" in making a bid for the entire company, maintaining that their holding is a financial interest only "because the shares represent an attractive investment." This was the position declared by Malcolm Glazer in the Manchester United case from the time he first disclosed a 3% ownership in the club in March 2003 up until the time he bought the shares that gave him control in 2005. In his case, the market expected a bid for the entire company, but his public position nevertheless may have lowered the price he ultimately had to pay for that controlling interest.

In all of these situations, it must be noted that proper legal advice must be taken in order not to fall foul of the many regulations and laws that prohibit market manipulation.

EQUITY MARKET REACTIONS FOR BIDDERS

The shareholders of acquiring companies are not as fortunate as those of the targets. On average, their shares decline in value around the time the company announces its intention to take over another company. Thus, in the example above, when Morrisons launched its surprise bid for Safeway (at a 30.3% premium to the prior day's close), its shares declined 14.3%, and when J. Sainsbury entered with its competing bid, its own share price declined on the day by 3.5%. The shareholders of neither bidder benefited, in distinct contrast to Safeway's shareholders.

Because of the relative consistency over time of stock market movements in response to deal announcements, the market will assume that future deals will do the same, including that only 30-40% of all deals are successful, that mid- and long-term shareholder wealth declines by 10-35%, and that the share prices for acquirers and targets move within certain ranges (on average) around the announcement day. Merger arbitrageurs—whether in hedge funds or investment banks—take large positions knowing that bidders' share prices tend to drop immediately after a deal announcement and that targets will see share price appreciation. This then becomes a virtuous (or vicious, for the bidder) cycle, where the movement in the share prices is magnified by this arbitrage activity.

In many cases these movements in share price can lead to extreme changes in share ownership. For example, when the Deutsche Börse (the largest stock exchange at the time in mainland Europe) made a bid for the London Stock Exchange in 2004, the Anglo-American arbitrageurs rapidly became the largest group of shareholders, displacing the long-term German shareholders, whose ownership was reduced to only a third. It was these arbitrageurs who forced the Deutsche Börse CEO to drop the bid in March 2005, leading to a 30% price rise in the Deutsche Börse shares as it became less and less likely that the deal would succeed.

As with the Deutsche Börse CEO who didn't anticipate this change, most managers seem to be oblivious to facts which appear to be obvious to those outside the company. A DLA Piper survey in 2006 showed that 81% of corporate respondents rated their M&A experience as fairly or highly successful, and over 90% of venture capitalists felt the same, yet we know that 60–70% of all deals fail.

INFLUENCING THE STOCK PRICE OF THE BIDDER

In most M&A situations, the bidder controls the timing of when the bid is publicized. The notable exception to this is when there is a market leak, but even in these situations the leak either happens early in the negotiations when it is easier to deny to the press that any deal is pending (as the negotiations have not progressed sufficiently far for a deal to be in place) or late enough in the proceedings that an emergency communication plan should already be in place for just such a situation.

The announcement event is therefore not a surprise to the bidder. Through proper planning and the use of external advisers (including investment banks, but also specialist public relations firms), positive spin on the deal can be delivered to the market: Benefits to all stakeholders are emphasized; new markets are announced; product innovations are forecast. Support from clients, suppliers, and even outside parties (such as local government) can be rallied. Potential problems will have been anticipated, and strategies to neutralize these will have been developed and disclosed.

Nevertheless, to paraphrase Robert Burns, "The best laid plans of mice and men / Go oft awry." In M&A deals, there are ultimately just too many individuals involved and there is just so much that can go wrong that much often does. Therefore, the press turns negative, equity analysts forecast too much dilution of earnings, cash flow declines, and clients, suppliers, employees, and even managers become very worried about their positions—and naturally assume the worst.

"Shareholders of acquirers tend to lose money; target company shareholders almost always gain."

  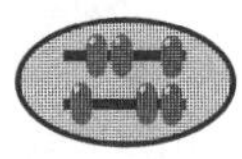 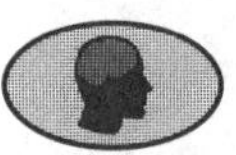  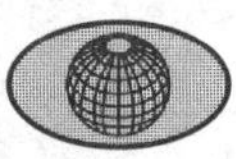   

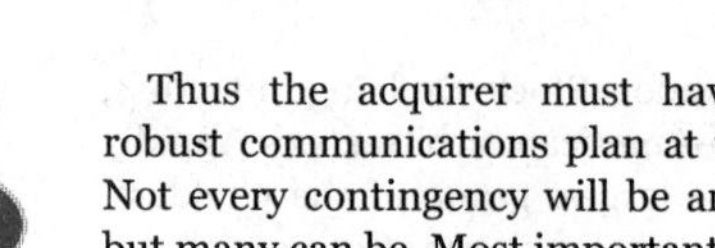

Thus the acquirer must have a very robust communications plan at the ready. Not every contingency will be anticipated, but many can be. Most important is to have teams in place to be able to respond quickly to any false rumors and to replace immediately any such gossip with fact. The company needs to stay in control—as best it can—during the entire deal process. The most effective way to do this is to have a continuous stream of positive stories prepared for periodic, if not even daily, release. Constant communication with the staff of both bidder and target can go a long way towards allaying anxiety and even panic.

One must remember that those who can benefit from the flip side will be acting accordingly as well: these include competitors who see opportunities to grab market share and even valued staff, and trading arbitrageurs who have made bets in the market that the share price will fall. These arbitrageurs certainly have been very successful in pushing down the price of acquirers in many deals, as in the above example where the Deutsche Börse was forced to drop its bid for the London Stock Exchange.

OTHER FACTORS AFFECTING EQUITY VALUES

The above discussion "averages" the results for many companies. Individual deals and individual companies will show different results and provide different returns over time from these averages, and takeover and defensive tactics will also need to be customized for each situation.

There are also other factors that will impact on the equity markets for both the target and bidder's share price. When cash is used to finance the deal instead of issuing more shares, the returns to the bidder are usually higher. In countries such as the United States, where tender offers (often hostile) are common, these do better than friendly mergers. The smaller the target is in relation to the acquirer, the more likely it is that the bidder's share price will not decline relative to the market.

There are also differences in short- and long-term shareholder value effects. This article has looked principally at the short-term effects around the time of deal announcement, but if a longer-term perspective is taken (more than six months), then the negative returns to the bidder are reduced, although still typically remaining negative. Also, one can look at the combined returns when the bidder and target are taken together over the longer term: in this case as noted earlier, history shows that the overall shareholder wealth effects are typically positive.

CONCLUSION

Despite the doom and gloom of the analyses that have looked at the success of companies that merge or acquire, there is some hope: Several recent studies (from Towers Perrin/Cass Business School, McKinsey, and KPMG) have shown that acquiring companies since 2003 are doing better with their deals. Not much, but at least measurably so. Some of the suggestions we've made in this article have been recently more widely adopted by the market. There *is* more focus on careful deal selection and corporate governance. Post-merger integration *is* receiving attention even before the deal closes, and sometimes even before announcement. There is hope—and evidence—with some of these recent studies that perhaps equity markets may start to award an equity premium to companies that acquire well.

▸▸ MAKING IT HAPPEN

The Key Factors

- Understand that the premium offered to the target is only one aspect of the deal's success, and that it is often overshadowed by other factors, especially people issues.
- Formulate a plan for addressing surprises. Try to identify all the ways that the deal could fail . . . and then look for still more ways it could go wrong.
- Do not be overconfident in your ability to integrate an acquisition successfully. Prior experience is helpful, but not sufficient. Each deal is different.
- Proper legal advice should always be taken.
- Plan for a dynamic deal process where changes will need to be made to the acquisition strategy.
- Incorporate a robust communications plan into any deal.

▸▸ MORE INFO

Books:

Gaughan, Patrick A. *Mergers, Acquisitions, and Corporate Restructurings*. 4th ed. Hoboken, NJ: Wiley, 2007.

Moeller, Scott, and Chris Brady. *Intelligent M&A: Navigating the Mergers and Acquisitions Minefield*. Chichester, UK: Wiley, 2007.

Sudarsanam, S. *Creating Value from Mergers and Acquisition: The Challenges*. Harlow, UK: FT Prentice Hall, 2003.

"The best laid plans of mice and men / Go oft awry." Robert Burns

  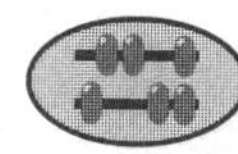   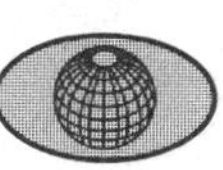   

Cultural Alignment and Risk Management: Developing the Right Culture
by R. Brayton Bowen

EXECUTIVE SUMMARY

- Organization culture may vary in definition from country to country, but it is essentially the sum total of the behaviors and styles of the people who drive the system.
- Organizations that properly align organization culture with business goals and objectives can realize up to 40% improvement in performance compared to peer and competitor organizations.
- Generally, 80% of acquisitions and mergers fail to perform to management's expectations, in most instances, because of a failure to understand and manage organization culture.
- Organizational members have an innate knowledge of what is and is not working within the culture of the organization and, therefore, must be engaged in the process of building the right culture.
- Culture changes within an organization require total mastery of the change management process.
- Organization culture ultimately impacts the financial performance and long-term success of an enterprise.

INTRODUCTION

The goal was to beat Microsoft at its own game. After rebuffing a takeover attempt by the giant corporation, Novell Nouveau went on an acquisition binge of its own. The strategy was to acquire a premier word-processing company that could rival Microsoft, and Microsoft's "Microsoft Word" in particular. So, in 1994, Raymond Noorda, CEO for the then second-largest software company, acquired WordPerfect Corp. for US$1.4 billion in stock. Novell was to become a "software powerhouse," delivering "stand-alone, software suites, groupware, and network applications that were to define new capabilities for information systems", according to WordPerfect's leading executive. Two years later, WordPerfect was sold for less than one-seventh of its original purchase price. The reason for the failed strategy: "The cultures were very, very different," as reported by Novell's successor CEO, Robert Frankenberg (*The Wall Street Journal*, 1996).

Taking the role of the dominator, management of Novell Nouveau assumed their ways and methods to be superior to those of WordPerfect. They eliminated the sales force, assuming the Novell Nouveau organization could assume the sales and marketing function, and went on to make a host of other mistakes. Indeed, their experience was similar to those of the majority of acquiring firms. Generally, 80% of acquisitions and mergers fail to perform to management's expectations, and the overarching factor in most instances is a failure to understand and manage organization culture.

ALIGNING ORGANIZATION CULTURES

What is Culture?

Culture can be thought of as the organizational context in which behaviors can be characterized and assessed. It is the environmental code that prompts people to act in certain ways to "fit in" at different levels and perform in "expected" ways. For example, customers entering a fine dining establishment understand they are expected to dress appropriately, deport themselves in a dignified manner, wait to be seated at an assigned table, and ultimately, pay a high price for the experience. Yet, there are usually no formal rules that are posted stating how guests are supposed to dress or how they are to behave. Once seated at their table with friends or other guests, they can adjust their behaviors to a more relaxed and interactive mode. This analogy equates to organizational cultures, wherein the overarching culture may prompt people to act one way, whereas once they settle into their own departments or business units, their behavior may change somewhat from the corporate norm. Bringing about change on an organization-wide basis requires considerable understanding of what is needed and why; and it requires superior change-management ability.

Elements of organization culture include: How people work together; how responsible they feel for the success of the enterprise; how ethically they behave; how people behave toward customers; how they feel about the quality of the company's goods and services; how prideful they feel about the mission of the enterprise; and ultimately, how fulfilled people feel in having a say in the business or making a difference in people's lives as a result of the work they perform. In the end, highly constructive and productive cultures lead to optimum outcomes.

Why Change?

More corporations are coming to appreciate that relationship marketing is leading to increased sales, as compared to transactional marketing. To effect a shift of such magnitude requires a carefully planned migration of both structural and cultural change. Companies such as Globus, the German based hypermarket; DM-Drogeriemarkt, a retail chemist; Southwest Airlines and Lufthansa, both commercial airline companies; and Ikea, the Swedish multinational home furnishing retailer—all have created cultural environments that have enabled them to be enormously profitable compared to their industry counterparts. In each of these organizations, employees work as teams. Management provides prescriptive guidance rather than restrictive direction. Employees are entrusted to do the right thing and encouraged to be the best at what they do, namely, providing customers not only with quality goods and services but also with great customer experiences.

Up to 40% improvement in performance can be achieved by changing organization culture. According to Stanford Business School professor, Jeffery Pfeffer, providing training, status equalization, employment stability, and strong recognition and reward programs can propel any number of organizations to enviable levels of success.

To remain viable and competitive, even service sector entities, for example utilities, financial institutions, and government services, are recognizing the need to shift from transaction-based systems to ones that are more relationship-focused. Such changes require enormous changes in organization culture, as well as in supporting structures, i.e., operational, technological, and policy structures. Because

     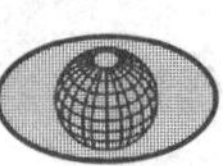   

"structure follows strategy", it is virtually impossible to make shifts in organizational culture unless changes in structure occur, as well, to support such seismic shifts.

When Is Change Necessary?

Nowhere is the need for cultural alignment more evident than in the case of acquisitions and mergers. What usually happens is that the acquiring entity assumes its culture to be superior to that of the entity being acquired, as in the case of Novell Nouveau, cited earlier. Rather than identifying and optimizing the most constructive aspects of the acquired organization's culture, the culture of the acquirer subsumes the culture of the acquired organization. Consequently, the outcome is not unlike that of Novell Nouveau's in acquiring WordPerfect. Equally, compelling circumstances exist when organizations are pummeled by downturns in the economy or paradigm shifts in industry standards and/or customer preferences. Organizational transformations are required to jumpstart the business concept or power-charge employees, propelling them in a new direction. Out of the ashes of the past must arise a new phoenix, if the organization is to transform itself into a vital resource for meeting, if not exceeding, customer needs and marketplace demands. Today, Starbucks, the international brand, roaster and specialty coffee retailer, which operates in 43 countries with approximately 15,000 stores, is being assailed by competitors offering cheaper alternative products. Under Howard Schultz, returning to the company as chairman and CEO, the company is adopting a turnaround strategy of providing customers not only with the distinctive Starbucks "experience," and new innovations, but also, a can-do employee attitude. "Welcome to Starbucks! What can I get started for you?" is the greeting welcoming every customer. While it is still early in the game, the emphasis is on reigniting the emotional attachment customers have had in the past with the product and the people who are the face of the company.

Similarly, when organizations determine their focus must shift from product sales to customer satisfaction and retention, a significant change in organization culture is required. Employees need to be trained and empowered to improve the quality of goods and services, solve problems, and earn the respect and, ultimately, the loyalty of their customers. For example, in 1993, when CEO Louis Gerstner took the reins of IBM, the company had just lost US$8 billion. His challenge was to transform IBM from a stodgy, centralized, mainframe computer company, where customers were expected to come to "Big Blue" and turf wars among departments abounded, to a fast-paced, customer-focused, well-oiled machine, where employees were expected to work as a team to meet and exceed the needs of their customers. In *Who Says Elephants Can't Dance*, Gerstner wrote, "Culture isn't just one aspect of the game. It *is* the game. In the end, an organization is nothing more than the collective capacity of its people to create value."

As organizations continue to grow globally, it becomes a virtual impossibility for management to be ever-present, critically focused on day-to-day operations. Instead, organization cultures must be designed that are conducive to teamwork, self-direction, ethical decision-making, and the achievement of outstanding results. Team members throughout the organizational system must share a vision and a passion that can only come from an organization culture that is carefully designed and ardently nurtured.

A MODEL FOR THE IDEAL CULTURE

Organizational Awareness

Ask any employee about his or her organizational culture, and chances are the words chosen to describe the environment will range from "political," "highly competitive," "collaborative," and "team-like" to "stressful," "mission driven," even "rewarding." The collective wisdom of organizational members represents a sort of meta-knowledge about the behaviors exhibited as a result of the cultural context in which they function. These descriptors, in essence, paint a picture of how functional or dysfunctional an organization's culture is and, in turn, how successful or unsuccessful the organization is as a whole in the way it operates. Moreover, it is this collective conscience, or meta-knowledge, that contains the answers as to how the organizational culture could and should be ideally.

Dimensions of Culture

Various models exist for assessing the culture of an organization. Perhaps the most widely used survey instruments have been developed by Human Synergistics International. Their Organizational Culture Inventory®, for example, measures 12 thinking and behavioral styles, which make up three groupings, termed the "constructive," "passive-aggressive," and "passive-defensive" styles. An "ideal" culture is "constructive" when the dominant organizational styles are "self-actualizing," "achieving," "humanistic and encouraging," and "affiliative." Summary results from completed assessments enable organizations to understand how their cultures operate and where improvements can be made to improve outcomes in a variety of areas, including employee / labor relations, customer relations, organizational performance, and profitability.

Blueprint for Change

The benefit of using such assessments as described above is that organizational leadership is better able to target areas for change. Knowing how the present organizational culture impacts on performance, and where enhancements can be made to improve performance can form the basis of a master plan, or blueprint for change. Moreover, by tapping into the collective

▸▸ MAKING IT HAPPEN

Culture change requires a strategic perspective on why culture is important to the organization, and how it will make a significant difference in the strategic positioning and success of an enterprise. The process begins with articulation of the vision and mission of the organization. To achieve optimum performance, the culture of the organization needs to be aligned with the vision, mission, and strategic goals and objectives of the organization. The behaviors of senior leadership must model the new standard, and the change and implementation process must begin with senior leadership.

- Conduct a system-wide assessment of the organization's current culture.
- Determine where change is necessary and why.
- Profile the desired culture of the organization, ensuring that the targeted profile will bring out the best in the organization.
- Engage organizational members in the processes of assessing the current culture, profiling the desired culture, and implementing needed change.
- Incorporate the desired behavioral styles into the performance planning and management process for both individual members, and the business as a whole.
- Continue to assess progress versus plan. Be certain to obtain feedback from key stakeholders such as customers, vendors, and investors, and make adjustments as needed to improve results.

"Keep alive the light of justice, and much that men say in blame will pass you by." Euripides

conscience of the organization and enlisting the involvement of organizational members, leadership can manage the change process more effectively—simply put, it becomes a holistic process or a "bottoms-up-top-down" approach. In the end, the change effort is sustainable, because all organizational members understand what is needed and how to make it happen—more importantly, they become collaborators in the change process rather than victims or passive spectators. Any number of corporations, including American Eagle Outfitters, Disney, Men's Wearhouse, and Hewlett Packard, have focused on organizational culture as a means of optimizing performance, while sparking the commitment and active engagement of their employees. They have adopted that strategy from day one, and it has been the foundation for success.

Further Implications

In addition to profiling the culture of an organization, management can extend the evaluative process to assessing the individual behavioral styles of organizational members. Consistent with the notion that "a chain is only as strong as its weakest link," the behavior of every member of the organizational "chain" must be aligned with the desired profile of the organization's ideal culture to ensure optimum results. Further, individual performance plans should be honed to include the behavioral norms expected of organizational members, and periodic reviews conducted to help determine how well behaviors are aligned, and where improvement in individual behavioral styles is needed.

CONCLUSION

In a global economy that is becoming more complex and conflicted, there is little room for error, and even less room for guess work. Organizational culture is as critical an element in managing a business as information technology, or financial controls. Indeed, it is more elusive but equally powerful to ensuring the success of an enterprise. The experience of a Novell Nouveau and WordPerfect proves how costly the neglect of organizational culture can be to the financial performance of a business. By way of contrast, those organizations that consciously tend to the process of building the right organizational culture have reaped rewards well beyond those achieved by their peer and competitor organizations.

▸▸ MORE INFO

Books:

Bowen, R. B. *Recognizing and Rewarding Employees*. New York: McGraw-Hill, 2000.

Cameron, K. S., and R. E. Quinn. *Diagnosing and Changing Organizational Culture: Based on the Competing Values Framework*. San Francisco, CA: Jossey-Bass, 2005.

Driskill, G. W., and A. L. Brenton. *Organizational Culture in Action: A Cultural Analysis Workbook*. Thousand Oaks, CA: Sage Publications, 2005.

Gerstner, L. V. *Who Says Elephants Can't Dance: Leading a Great Enterprise Through Dramatic Change*. New York: HarperCollins, 2002.

Hennig-Thurau, T., and U. Hansen (eds). *Relationship Marketing: Gaining Competitive Advantage Through Customer Satisfaction and Customer Retention*. New York: McGraw-Hill/Irwin, 2000.

Pfeffer, J. *The Human Equation: Building Profits by Putting People First*. Boston, MA: Harvard Business School Press, 1998.

Schein, E. H. *Organizational Culture and Leadership*. 3rd ed. San Francisco, CA: Jossey-Bass, 2004.

Articles:

Barriere, M. T., B. R. Anson, R. S. Ording, and E. Rogers. "Culture transformation in a health care organization: A process for building adaptive capabilities through leadership development." *Consulting Psychology Journal: Practice and Research* 54:2 (2008): 116–130.

Clark, D. "Novell nouveau: Software firm fights to remake business after ill-fated merger." *Wall Street Journal (Midwest ed)* 76:62 (January 12, 1996): A1, A6.

Kavita, S. "Predicting organizational commitment through organization culture: A study of automobile industry in India." *Journal of Business Economics & Management* 8:1 (2007): 29–37.

Websites:

The Howland Group, Inc.: www.howlandgroup.com

Human Synergistics International: www.humansynergistics.com

   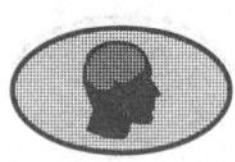  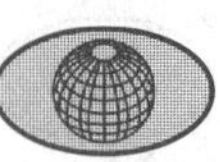   

Due Diligence Requirements in Financial Transactions by Scott Moeller

EXECUTIVE SUMMARY

- There is an urgency for companies to conduct intensive due diligence in financial deals, both before announcement (when it should be easy to call off the deal) and after.
- Traditional due diligence merely verifies the history of the target and projects the future based on that history; correctly applied due diligence digs much deeper and provides insight into the future value of the target across a wide variety of factors.
- Although due diligence does enable prospective acquirers to find potential black holes, the aim of due diligence should be this and more, including looking for opportunities to realize future prospects for the enlarged corporation through leveraging of the acquiring and the acquired firms' resources and capabilities, identification of synergistic benefits, and postmerger integration planning.
- Due diligence should start from the inception of a deal.
- Areas to probe include finance, management, employees, IT, legal, risk management systems, culture, innovation, and even ethics.
- Critical to the success of the due diligence process is the identification of the necessary information required, where it can best be sourced, and who is best qualified to review and interpret the data.
- Requesting too much information is just as dangerous as requesting too little. Having the wrong people looking at the data is also hazardous.

INTRODUCTION

This is not your father's due diligence.

Due diligence is one of the two most critical elements in the success of an Mergers and Acquisitions (M&A) transaction (the other being the proper execution of the integration process) according to a survey conducted in 2006 by the Economist Intelligence Unit (EIU) and Accenture. Due diligence was considered to be of greater importance than target selection, negotiation, pricing the deal, and the development of the company's overall M&A strategy.

But not even a decade ago, when due diligence was conducted in financial transactions, the focus was almost always limited to financial factors, pending law suits, and information technology (IT) systems. Today, those areas remain important, but they must be supplemented during the due diligence process by attention to the assessment of other factors: management and employees (and not just their contracts, but how good they actually are in their jobs), commercial operations (products, marketing, strategy, and competition—both existing and potential), and corporate culture (can the companies actually work together when they're merged?). But even these areas are now mainstream when due diligence is conducted. Newer areas of due diligence are developing rapidly: risk management, innovation, and ethical (including corporate social responsibility) due diligence.

The 2006 EIU/Accenture survey also found that although due diligence is considered as a top challenge by 23% of CEOs in making domestic acquisitions, this rises to 41% in the much more complex cross-border transactions, which make up the majority of financial transactions, even in today's depressed markets.

ORGANIZING FOR DUE DILIGENCE

It's a two-way street: Buyers must understand what they are buying; and targets must understand who's pursuing them and whether they should accept an offer.

To be successfully conducted, due diligence must have senior management involvement and control, often assisted by outside experts such as management consulting firms, accountants, investment banks, and maybe even specialist investigation firms.

To quote from a Pricewaterhouse-Coopers report issued in late 2002: "We always have to make decisions based on imperfect information. But the more information you have and the more you transform that into what we call knowledge, the more likely you are to be successful."

That said, there is only a certain amount that can be handled by the number of people involved, the time restrictions under which they are working, and the quality and variety of resources available to them. Moreover, there is the danger of being overloaded by too much information if those involved do not have good management and analytical methods they can deploy.

By and large, it is not the quantity of information that matters so much as its quality and how it is used. Although diligence may not be cheap (as a result of fees charged for often highly complex work by professional services firms), the alternative of litigation or the destruction of stockholder value (as a consequence of having been "penny wise and pound foolish" in the execution of the due diligence process) may prove far more costly in the long run.

THE DUE DILIGENCE PROCESS

Although due diligence may be only one part of an acquisition or investment exercise, in many ways it is by far the most significant aspect of the M&A process. Done properly, acquirers should be better able to control the risks inherent in any deal, while simultaneously contributing to the ultimate effective management of the target and the realization of the goals of the acquisition.

As an instrument through which to reveal and remedy potential sources of risk, due diligence—by confirming the expectations of the buyer and the understanding of the seller—enables firms to formulate remedies and solutions to enable a deal to proceed. In many ways, due diligence lends comfort to an acquirer's senior management, the board, and ultimately the stockholders, who should all insist on a rigorous due diligence process, which provides them with relative (though not absolute) assurance that the deal is sensible, and that they have uncovered any problems pertaining to it that may derail matters in the future.

Ideally, due diligence should start during the deal conception phase, and initially it can use publicly available information. It should then continue throughout the merger process as further proprietary information becomes available. Full use of the due diligence information collected would mean that it is not just used to make a go/no-go decision about whether the acquisition should proceed and to determine the terms of the deal, but that the findings from due diligence should also be incorporated in the planning for the postmerger integration.

Clearly it is easier to obtain high-quality data if the deal is friendly; in unfriendly deals due diligence may never progress

"Know thy enemy and know thyself; in a hundred battles you will never be in peril." Sun Tzu

  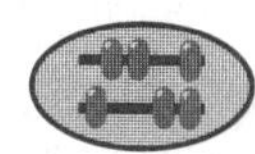   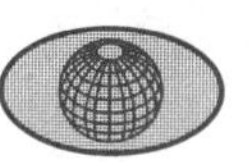   

further than publicly available data. This lack of access to internal information has scuppered many a deal—for example, the takeover attempt by Sir Philip Green of Marks & Spencer in 2004.

THE SCOPE OF DUE DILIGENCE[1]

Before undertaking due diligence—given the typical time, cost, and data constraints—it is important to focus on areas that are likely to have the most impact on value. Thus, due diligence should be tailored to:

- the type of transaction
- the motivation for doing the deal
- plans for the target once acquired
- the impact on the existing operations of the acquirer

Some basic questions to ask include:

- Is the acquirer a strategic or a financial buyer?
- How fully integrated will the target be once acquired, and in what time frame?
- Is the whole company being acquired?
- Does the target represent new product lines, marketing channels, or geographic territories, or is there overlap with the acquirer's existing operations?
- Will certain functional operations of the target be eliminated?
- Will the IT systems of the target be retained?
- How will the rating agencies respond to the transaction?

TYPES OF DUE DILIGENCE INFORMATION

Each industry has its own special due diligence requirements. For example, an insurance company will need a review of major policies, actuarial assumptions, and sales practices, whereas the purchase of a bank would require a review of its marking policies and risk management systems.

As noted above, one starts with external sources. Although these rarely provide a sufficient overview of an organization at the level required to obtain a proper understanding, secondary sources do equip management with valuable information, allowing them to strategize and develop honed and more focused questions for their further internal due diligence on the prospective acquisition.

In spite of the centrality of financial, legal, cultural, and other areas of due diligence, examples abound of transactions that were completed without effective due diligence being done through lack of time or because management was overconfident in its ability to understand the target, resulting in devastating losses of stockholder value.

Financial Due Diligence

Financial due diligence enables companies to obtain a view of an organization's historical profits, which can then be used as a canvas on which to paint a picture of the company's financial future. Developed around an array of building blocks—including auditing and verifying financial results on which an offer is based, identifying deal breakers, reviewing forecasts and budgets, pinpointing areas where warranties or indemnities may be needed, and providing confidence in the underlying performance (and therefore future profits) of a company—financial due diligence allows the bidder to make the proper offer for the target, or perhaps uncover reasons for not proceeding with the deal.

Legal Due Diligence

As companies expand into hitherto commercially less experienced parts of the world in search of new markets and products (such as China, Vietnam, or certain countries in the Middle East and Africa), the requirement to conduct effective and sufficient legal due diligence work can prove more trying, and in certain cases near impossible. Nevertheless, the need to check title over assets that are being sold, and to ensure that the entity being acquired is legitimate and free of any contractual or legal obstacles which might derail the M&A process, will undoubtedly remain pivotal to the due diligence process no matter where the target resides. Governmental regulatory concerns (such as monopolies, employment law, taxes, etc.) will also be investigated as part of the legal due diligence.

Commercial Due Diligence

Given that companies are bought not for their past performance but for their ability to generate profits in the future, acquirers must use commercial due diligence to obtain an objective view of a company's markets, prospects, and competitive position. As noted by Towers Perrin in a discussion of operational due diligence, there is a "need to look at all the relevant sources of value to avoid unpleasant surprises."[2] This means a deeper query into certain operations that heavily determine a target's ultimate value to the acquirer—i.e. growth opportunities and resulting future income.

Whether obtained to reduce risk associated with the transaction, help with the company valuation, or plan for postmerger integration, commercial due diligence enables acquirers to examine a target's markets and performance—identifying strengths, weaknesses, opportunities, and threats. Focused on the likely strategic position of the combined entity, commercial due diligence, by reviewing the drivers that underpin forecasts and business plans, concentrates on the ability of the target's businesses to achieve the projected sales and profitability growth post acquisition.

Despite the seemingly obvious pivotal benefits that commercial due diligence can bring to acquiring organizations, *Competitive Intelligence Magazine* reported in 2003 that "only 10% of respondents to an

CASE STUDY

Failure in Due Diligence: VeriSign's Purchase of Jamba

In June 2004, VeriSign acquired privately held Berlin-based Jamba for US$273 million. VeriSign was an internet infrastructure services company which provided the services that enabled over 3,000 enterprises and 500,000 websites to operate. Through its domain name registry it managed over 50 million digital identities in more than 350 languages. Revenues exceeded US$1 billion dollars in the previous year. VeriSign had extensive experience with acquisitions, having made 17 acquisitions prior to Jamba, including four that were valued at more than this particular purchase.

Jamba had millions of subscribers and was the leading provider of mobile content delivery services in Europe. It was best known for the Crazy Frog character used in the most successful ring tone of all time.

But, beneath the surface, trouble was brewing that could easily have been uncovered by even the most rudimentary due diligence: complaints to regulators had noted that Jamster, the UK and US rebranding of Jamba, was targeting children, despite the fact that Jamster's mobile content services were intended for adult customers only. Perhaps more disturbingly, only days before the acquisition VeriSign discovered that a significant portion of Jamba's profits came from the distribution of adult content in Germany—despite a VeriSign policy of not supporting adult or pornographic companies. There were backlashes in Germany over other issues and Jamba was forced to make a declaration of discontinuance regarding many of its contracts. Other legal actions were pending in Germany and the United States.

Unsurprisingly, Jamba's revenues peaked early the following year.

     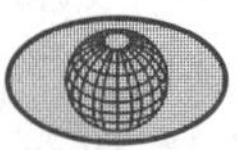   

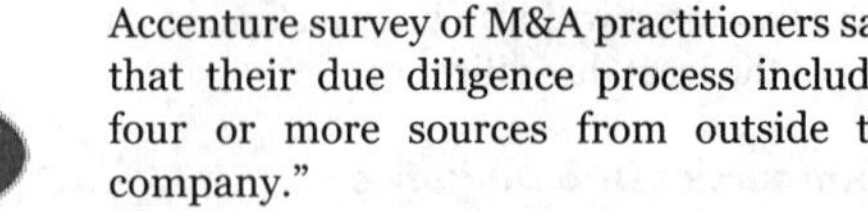

Accenture survey of M&A practitioners said that their due diligence process included four or more sources from outside the company."

Innovation Due Diligence

Linked closely to commercial risk but meriting special attention is the due diligence of the research and development (R&D) process. This is more than just an analysis of intellectual property rights. Many nonindustrial companies may not have explicit R&D groups, but still remain dependent on the development of intellectual property to maintain their business growth. It must be understood how this is encouraged.

Management Due Diligence

Naturally, acquirers need to perform discrete investigations in order to evaluate both the competence of the target's management and the quality of their past performances, and to ensure that the management of the target and acquirer are compatible. One would think that this would be recognized by any acquirer today, but one acquisition team recently told us that their senior management felt confident enough in their own ability to conduct their management due diligence that they could do this "over a cup of tea," basically, by eyeing the management team from across the table. Nevertheless, in the rush to do deals in the peak merger year of 2007, many of the largest deals properly included extensive management surveys, including 360 degree appraisals, psychometrics, and even investigative reporting.

Cultural Due Diligence

Since one of the more difficult areas for integrating two companies concerns combining their corporate cultures, due care needs to be applied to ensure cultural fit. Indeed, cultural fit is so important that 85% of underperforming acquisitions blame different management attitudes and culture for the poor performance of the combined entities, as reported at a conference in 2006 by Towers Perrin and Cass Business School. Thus, by assessing soft factors such as a company's leadership style, corporate behavior, and even dress code, an acquirer may be able to build an accurate picture of a target's values, attitudes, and beliefs, and so determine if there will be a good cultural fit within their own organizational structure.

Ethical Due Diligence

There is an emerging area, best described as ethical due diligence, that overlaps in many ways with management and cultural due diligence but is not to be confused with legal due diligence. The most obvious requirement of ethical due diligence is to determine whether management have engaged in unethical professional acts (as defined, usually, by the ethical standards of the acquiring company), but it also necessarily includes assessment of the corporate social responsibility activities of the company.

Risk Management Due Diligence

It is critical to understand how the target reports and monitors its inherent business risks. The events in financial and real estate markets in the past several years highlight the need to check carefully not just all risk management systems, but also the *culture* of risk in a company.

CASE STUDY

No Cultural Fit for Sony in the Movie Industry

In 1988, Sony (a Japanese electronics manufacturer) acquired Columbia Pictures (an American moviemaker) for US$3.4 billion. With cultures that could scarcely have been more different, the acquisition—which involved little consideration of cultural fit between the two entities—failed to live up to commercial expectations, with Sony famously writing down US$2.7 billion on the deal by 1994.

CONCLUSION

According to the EIU/Accenture survey, only 18% of executives were highly confident that their company had carried out satisfactory due diligence. This is probably due to the lack of attention given to this critical aspect of a deal, or to the view that it is merely a box-ticking exercise conducted by outside advisers.

In short, the probing of a wide variety of due diligence areas should provide a counterbalance to the short-termism of traditionally limited financial and legal due diligence, helping acquirers to understand how markets and competitive environments will affect their purchase, and confirming that the opportunity is a sensible one to undertake from a commercial and strategic perspective, especially in cross-border deals.

▸▸ MAKING IT HAPPEN

Key factors in conducting informative and timely due diligence are:

- Identifying the critical areas to probe: financial, legal, business, cultural, management, ethical, risk management, etc.
- Identifying the most important information to collect in those areas, as there is never enough time to look at everything in as much detail as one might want.
- Identifying the right sources for the desired information.
- Identifying the right people to review the data: this should include those who know most about that area and also those who will be managing the business post acquisition.

Due diligence should not be a mere confirmation of the facts. Bridging the strategic review and completion phases of any merger or acquisition exercise, the due diligence process allows prospective acquirers to understand as much as possible about the target company, and to make sure that what it believes is being purchased is actually what is being purchased. The due diligence process digs deeper *before* the point of no return in consummating a deal.

▸▸ MORE INFO

Books:

Howson, Peter. *Due Diligence: The Critical Stage in Mergers and Acquisitions.* Aldershot, UK: Gower Publishing, 2003.

Moeller, Scott, and Chris Brady. *Intelligent M&A: Navigating the Mergers and Acquisitions Minefield.* Chichester, UK: Wiley, 2007.

Sudarsanam, Sudi. *Creating Value from Mergers and Acquisition: The Challenges.* Harlow, UK: Pearson Education, 2003.

"Few things are impossible to diligence and skill." Samuel Johnson

  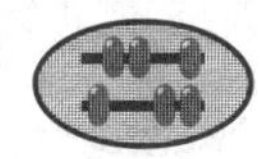   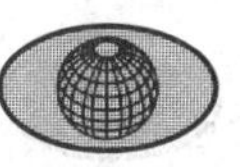 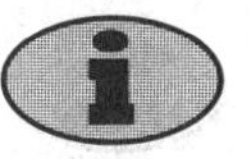  

Article:

May, Michael, Patricia Anslinger, and Justin Jenk. "Avoiding the perils of traditional due diligence". *Outlook Journal* (July 2002) Online at: Accenture: http://tinyurl.com/c4quzw.

Website:

Intelligent Mergers—Scott Moeller's blog site: www.intelligentmergers.com

NOTES

1 Adapted from Fell, Bruce D. "Operational due diligence for value." *Emphasis* no. 3 (2006): 6–9. Online at: tinyurl.com/d7w36t

2 *Ibid*.

"The pursuit of alibis for poor industry performance is one of the great Australian art forms." John Button

  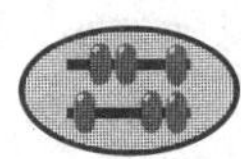 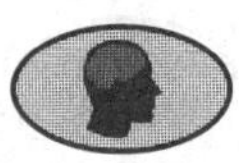  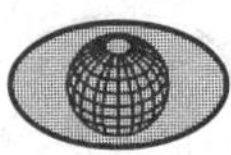   

Identifying and Minimizing the Strategic Risks from M&A by Peter Howson

EXECUTIVE SUMMARY

- The high failure rate of acquisitions can be mitigated considerably by dealing with the strategic risks that are present at every stage of the acquisition process.
- It is best to start with a well-developed business strategy, a clear idea of the place of mergers and acquisitions (M&A) in this strategy, and an acquisition target that furthers strategic aims.
- Before embarking on negotiations, acquirers should avoid the risk of overpaying by setting a price above which they will not go.
- Before negotiating the final details, due diligence should be used as a final confirmation of the strategy and the target's fit.
- The most important thing is to make sure that the post acquisition plan is put together early and in as much detail as possible. Acquirers need to add value, and they can only do this if they are clearly focused on the sources of extra value and how to realize them right from the very start.

INTRODUCTION

M&A is extremely risky. Studies carried out over the last 30 years suggest that the failure rate is above 50% and probably close to 75%. However, by identifying and acting to minimize the strategic risks early on in the process, the rewards can be spectacular.

There are four stages in the M&A process:

- acquisition strategy
- due diligence
- negotiation
- post-acquisition integration

Strategic risks are present in each.

Acquisition Strategy

M&A is glamorous. Market analysts see M&A as a sign of a dynamic management and mark up share prices accordingly. For management, M&A can be a means of bolstering short-term performance and/or masking underlying problems. It is hardly surprising that the failure rate is so high when the mystique of M&A encourages acquirers to rush into acquisitions.

M&A Is a Strategic Tool

This brings us to the first strategic risk—a failure to recognize that M&A is a strategic weapon. Strategy is all about giving customers what they want, and to do it better or more cheaply than anyone else. It is about competitive advantage gained through superior capabilities and resources. M&A should fit into this framework.

Given the high risk of failure, acquirers should ask themselves if acquisition is the best means of achieving aims. There will generally be a tradeoff between risk and time. Acquisition is the highest-risk route to corporate development, but it is often the quickest. Acquisition should be examined alongside all the other options—organic development, joint venture, merger, etc.

Is the Timing Right?

Implementation is the key to successful strategy and this is the clue to the next strategic risk—is this the right time to be acquiring? Getting the transaction done and integrating it afterwards will take up a disproportionate amount of time, resource, and expertise. This means making sure that there is:

- a strong base business (if existing operations are struggling, acquisitions will only add to the problems);
- the resources to add value (where there are insufficient resources to manage an acquisition, the chances of adding value are slim).

Select the Right Target

The next risk may sound obvious, but one of the biggest ever M&A disasters stemmed in part from selecting the wrong target. In 1991 AT&T, the US telecommunications company, bought NCR for $7.48 billion. AT&T was implementing a so called "3Cs strategy" where communications, computers, and consumer electronics were expected to coalesce into a new market. It bought NCR to provide a capability in computers. But NCR was not a computer company. Its core business was in retail transaction processing and banking systems, and it happened also to manufacture a range of "me too" personal computers. While this may be an extreme example, it is not uncommon for buyers to misunderstand the target company's capabilities.

Due Diligence

The strategic risks in due diligence all stem from making the focus of due diligence too narrow.

The success of any acquisition depends on buyers creating value. Due diligence presents a potential buyer with the access and information it needs to confirm that a

CASE STUDY

In 1996, Federal-Mogul, a US auto parts company, appointed a new Chairman and Chief Executive, Dick Snell, whose view was that in the automotive industry, a firm must be big.

Automobile makers were focusing on assembly, branding, and marketing, and were encouraging parts manufacturers to play a bigger role in the design and development of components. They were also encouraging the larger suppliers to supply modules and systems rather than components.

Federal-Mogul's "growth by acquisition" strategy had the simple aim of increasing sales from $2 billion to $10 billion in six years. The company already made gaskets and seals, but not enough to market a full engine or transmission-sealing package. Federal-Mogul also made engine bearings, but did not have the ability to market the bearings as a system complete with pistons, piston rings, connecting rods, and cylinder liners.

Federal-Mogul first bought T&N plc (in 1997), a supplier of engine and transmission products and Europe's leading supplier of gaskets. With sales of $3 billion, T&N was bigger than Federal-Mogul itself. Soon after (in 1998), Federal-Mogul paid $720 million for privately held Fel-Pro Inc., of Skokie, IL. Fel-Pro was a leading brand of replacement sealing products. Following these two acquisitions, Federal-Mogul had a $1 billion global sealing business and the basis for providing an integrated engine package. Later that year, Federal-Mogul went on to buy Cooper Automotive for $1.9 billion. Cooper added three completely new product areas (see Table 1).

In July 1998, Federal-Mogul's share price was $72. By September 2001 it was $1. On October 1, 2001, the company filed under Chapter 11 of the US Bankruptcy Code. What went wrong?

"The benefits of many mergers have been lost during the integration phase." Richard Corzone

transaction can be a long-term success. This means using due diligence not just as an input to the sale and purchase agreement but, more importantly, also to confirm both the robustness of synergy assumptions and their deliverability. As people will deliver the extra value, buyers should also make sure that due diligence covers cultural and people issues.

Negotiation

In negotiation, the strategic risk is overpaying. Buyers are almost certainly going to have to pay a premium for the control of a company. The challenge is to make sure that the synergies are big enough to cover both the premium and the deal costs. Work out a price in advance and, as it is all too easy to get carried away, always set a maximum walk away price before negotiations begin.

Post-Acquisition Integration

The major cause of acquisition failure is poor integration. Integration is poorly carried out because it gets forgotten. Doing the deal may be sexy, but integration is where the real money is made or lost. The strategic risks stem from not starting work on the integration plan early enough in the process. As integration is central to valuation, the integration plan must be put together well before negotiations begin, and the other golden rules of acquisition integration also demand an early plan:

- Integrate quickly to minimize uncertainty. In particular, integration changes related to personnel need to be made as soon as possible; early communication is paramount; and there should be early victories to demonstrate progress.
- Do not neglect the soft issues. The culture of a company is the set of assumptions, beliefs, and accepted rules of conduct that define the way things are done. These are never written down, and most people in an organization would be hard pressed to articulate them. However, they can substantially increase post-acquisition costs or hold back performance
- Manage properly. Buyers should appoint an integration manager. Like any other big project, acquisitions need one person to be accountable for the project's success.

Overambitious Strategy

Following the Fel-Pro acquisition, the logical thing would have been to continue building the engine and transmissions business. Instead, Federal-Mogul kept its electrical businesses and the friction businesses acquired with T&N, and went on to add three entirely new product ranges. Focusing only on revenue and growth rarely, if ever, produces a strong organization and financial results over the long term.

Problems Picked Up in Due Diligence Not Acted On

T&N had at one time manufactured building products containing asbestos, and for years it paid out an increasing number of compensation claims for asbestos-related diseases. Following the takeover, the number of asbestos claims against T&N and its former subsidiaries exploded. In October 2001 there were 365,000 asbestos claims pending. By the end of 2001, Federal Mogul had paid out $1 billion in claims.

While Federal-Mogul was aware of the asbestos issue, Federal-Mogul leaders did minimal due diligence, failed to appreciate just how serious it was, and believed that, because it operated in the United States, it would be able to manage the litigation better.

Poor Integration

Federal-Mogul paid a high price for T&N and the other big acquisitions, promised too much, and failed to deliver. Federal-Mogul leadership repeatedly promised the market that integration would bring tens of millions of dollars worth of synergies. In fact, according to a stockholder class action, the company's integration activities destroyed the acquired businesses. The class action claimed that, "After an acquisition, the Company would slash sales staff at the acquired company, close manufacturing and warehouse facilities, reduce investment in research and development, reduce customer service and implement aggressive sales practices."

Federal-Mogul's management lacked an understanding of how international businesses operate. It was obsessed with the Detroit Big Three and dismissive of the other vehicle assemblers, yet the strategic logic of acquiring parts manufacturers should be to broaden geographic reach and bring closer relationships with vehicle assemblers.

Federal-Mogul management also failed to appreciate that the rest of the world was not like the United States and, in particular, that Europe was not like a group of US states. Federal-Mogul centralized all its operations, including customer service. When Federal-Mogul moved aftermarket operations to the United States, it was surprised that its telecom ordering system did not recognize overseas telephone numbers. In contrast, T&N had given a great deal of autonomy to its regions.

Finally, Federal-Mogul lost key staff by insisting that anyone who stayed had to move to Detroit. Most former T&N leaders opted to take the money. While it is not impossible to buy a company larger than yourself, it is difficult to manage something the size of T&N without retaining most of the management team—and T&N was actually quite good at managing asbestos claims.

Federal-Mogul emerged from Chapter 11 bankruptcy on December 27, 2007 after a financial reorganization designed to protect it from asbestos claims.

Table 1. Federal-Mogul's acquisitions

	Existing operations (as of 1996)	*1997: T&N acquisition*	*1998: Felpro acquisition*	*1998: Cooper Automotive acquisition*
Engine and transmission				
Engine Bearings	X	X		
Pistons and piston rings		X		
Seals	X	X	X	
Camshafts	X	X		
Other				
Lighting	X			
Fuel pumps	X			
Friction (brake and clutch pads)		X		
Powdered metals		X		
Ignition				X
Chassis				X
Wiper blades				X

     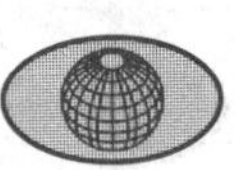   

▸▸ MAKING IT HAPPEN

- Think of M&A as a means to gain competitive advantage rather than short-term improvements in financials.
- M&A is the most risky form of corporate development, so be sure to consider alternatives such as organic growth or joint ventures.
- M&A will divert resources from the existing business, so make sure it is strong before embarking on acquisitions.
- Be sure to understand the target company—what it does, how it operates, how it makes money—and be able to articulate why it fits the strategy.
- Do not neglect soft issues like management and culture. Do not assume that "they are just like us," because they won't be.
- Prepare a detailed integration plan in advance.
- Keep the due diligence scope wide. Always use it to confirm the sources of added value identified and quantified in the integration plan.
- Never be lured into overpaying. Set a clear walk-away price and do not exceed it.
- Once the deal is done, communicate immediately, clearly, consistently, and abundantly to everyone concerned. Do not forget external parties, above all customers.
- Implement changes quickly and smoothly and do not underestimate the size of the task.

▸▸ MORE INFO

Books:

Camp, J. *Start with NO: The Negotiating Tools that the Pros Don't Want You to Know*. New York: Crown Business, 2002.

Carey, Dennis, *et al*. *Harvard Business Review on Mergers & Acquisitions*. Boston, MA: Harvard Business School, 2001.

Cleary, P. J. *The Negotiation Handbook*. Armonk, NY: M. E. Sharpe, 2001.

Freund, James C. *Smart Negotiating: How to Make Good Deals in the Real World*. New York: Fireside, 1993.

Howson, Peter. *Due Diligence: The Critical Stage in Acquisitions and Mergers*. Aldershot, UK: Gower Publishing, 2003.

Howson, Peter. *Commercial Due Diligence: The Key to Understanding Value in an Acquisition*. Aldershot, UK: Gower Publishing, 2006.

Howson, Peter. *Checklists for Due Diligence*. Aldershot, UK: Gower Publishing, 2008.

Howson, Peter, with Denzil Rankine. *Acquisition Essentials*. London: Pearson Education., 2005.

Hubbard, Nancy. *Acquisition: Strategy and Implementation*. Basingstoke, UK: Palgrave Macmillan, 1999.

Hunt, J. W., S. Lees, J. J. Grumbar, and P. D. Vivian. *Acquisitions: The Human Factor* London: London Business School and Egon Zehnder International, 1987.

Lajoux, Alexandra Reed, and Charles Elson. *The Art of M&A Due Diligence: Navigating Critical Steps and Uncovering Crucial Data*. New York: McGraw-Hill, 2000.

Rankine, Denzil. *Why Acquisitions Fail: Practical Advice for Making Acquisitions Succeed*. London: Pearson Education, 2001.

Article:

Davy, A. J., *et al*. "After the merger: Dealing with people's uncertainty." *Training and Development Journal* 42 (November 1988): 57–61.

Report:

KPMG. "Unlocking shareholder value: Keys to success." London: KPMG, 1999. Online at: www.imaa-institute.org/docs/m&a/kpmg_01_Unlocking%20Shareholder%20Value%20-%20The%20Keys%20to%20Success.pdf

Websites:

Commercial due diligence—AMR International: www.amrinternational.com

Financial due diligence—BDO Stoy Hayward: www.bdo.co.uk

See Also:

★ Acquisition Integration: How to Do It Successfully (pp. 390–391)

★ Merger Integration and Transition Management: A New Slant for Finance Executives (pp. 415–417)

"The role of takeovers is to improve unsatisfactory companies and to allow healthy companies to grow strategically by acquisitions." James Goldsmith

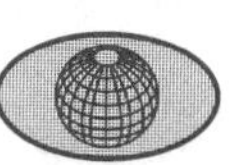

Leveraged Buyouts and Recession

by Louise Scholes and Mike Wright

EXECUTIVE SUMMARY

- After unprecedented levels of deal activity in 2007, the descent into recession in 2008 has presented both challenges and opportunities for the buyout and private equity market.
- We will likely see higher failure rates of buyouts as a consequence of highly leveraged transactions running into difficulties.
- Private equity-backed and larger buyouts appear less likely to fail than other buyouts. Secured creditors on average recover about 60% of their loans in failed buyouts.
- The increase in general business failure associated with recession introduces opportunities for buyouts to rescue and turn around these failing firms, with retail sector deals especially prevalent in recent years.
- Private equity firms can take advantage of the increased supply of failing firms provided that they have the necessary means (financial and management skills) to turn the businesses around.
- Private equity firms have been less in active in recent years in buying failed firms, though there have been some significant transactions.
- Buyouts of failed firms are disproportionately more likely to fail again than buyouts from other vendor sources.

THE BUYOUT MARKET IN EUROPE

The buyout market in Europe involves management buyouts and buyins of firms with or without the assistance of private equity. A management buyout is the purchase of a business by its own management, whereas a management buyin involves the purchase of a business by an external management team. Buyouts are economically very important in terms of business regeneration and survival in Europe and the United States. In the United Kingdom, buyouts account for about half of all M&A activity. According to the European Private Equity and Venture Capital Association (EVCA), investments in buyouts accounted for 79% of all private equity and venture capital investments in Europe in 2007. The buyout market in Europe reached a record €175 billion from almost 1,500 transactions by the end of 2007 Figure 1. The UK buyout market is by far the largest contributor to this total, with €67 billion from 670 buyouts, with public to privates and secondary buyouts having a particularly high profile.

However, following the boom that ended in 2007, buyout market conditions have been changing markedly. As the recession begins to bite, there is a rise both in failures of buyouts and in buyouts of failed firms. The private equity industry may struggle as investments fail or underperform, but potentially it can restore the balance by buying and reviving failing companies. The industry has survived despite the recessions of the past and, provided it can adapt, will survive the current recession.

BUYOUT FAILURES

The numbers of buyouts that have entered receivership (the UK corporate bankruptcy regime) over the past two decades are shown in Figure 2. Over the two decades 1985–2006, CMBOR data show that 1,480 of the total of 12,923 UK buyouts completed (11.5%) had entered receivership by end 2006. Numbers reached a peak in 1991 and again in 2002 (Figure 2). There is also some evidence of an increase in the number of buyout receiverships in 2007. These peaks coincide with the greatest falls in GDP in the United Kingdom, as shown in Figure 3.

The sharp build up in buyout receiverships during the last major recession in the early 1990s is particularly striking and indicates a likely future trend in the recession now unfolding. It is also notable that those buyouts completed during 1988–90, the peak years of the first buyout wave, had the highest failure rate. As overall buyout activity in the second wave was considerably above that of the first wave, receivership numbers during the current recession will likely be higher. Leverage in the second wave may have been offset by lower interest rates than in the first wave, but inflation was also lower. Although the Bank of England is reducing

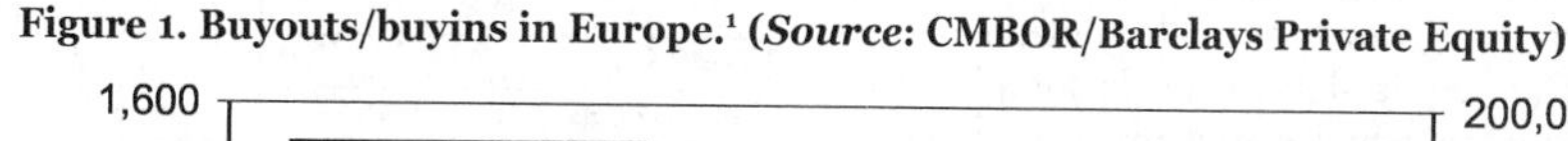
Figure 1. Buyouts/buyins in Europe.[1] **(*Source*: CMBOR/Barclays Private Equity)**

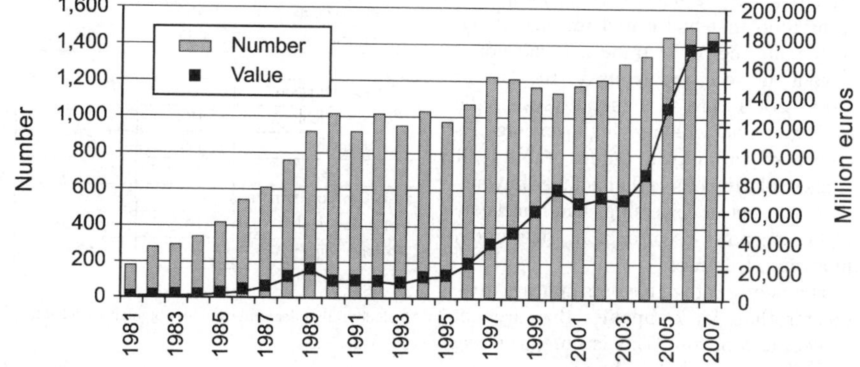

Figure 2. Receiverships of buyouts/buyins in the United Kingdom. (*Source*: CMBOR/ Barclays Private Equity)

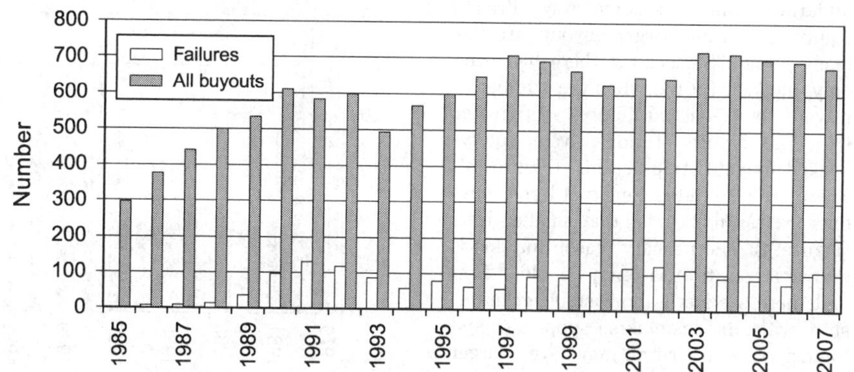

"**Blameless people are always the most exasperating.**" George Eliot

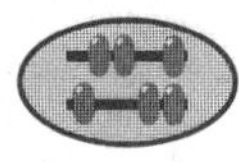

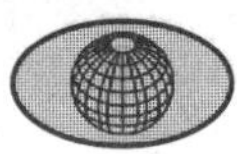

Figure 3. Receiverships in the United Kingdom versus GDP. (Source: CMBOR/Barclays Private Equity/OECD)

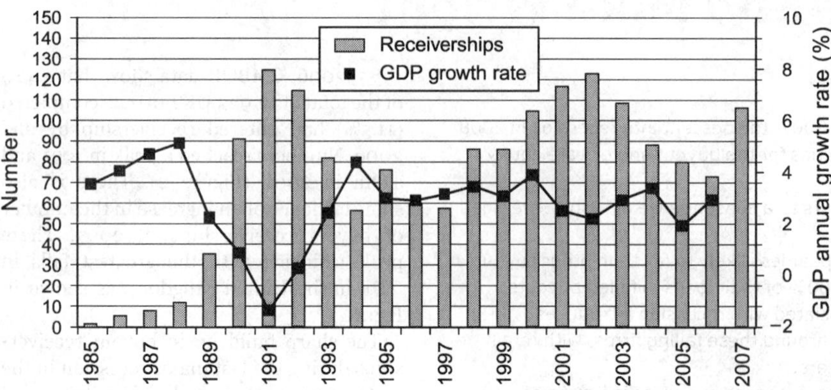

interest rates in the hope of kick-starting the economy, the outlook for the survival of buyout firms in these turbulent conditions is somewhat uncertain.

Periods of economic recession can exacerbate the problems of servicing highly leveraged financing structures if cash flows are hit. Studies of larger US buyouts completed during the first buyout wave of the 1980s and of the whole UK buyout market up to the early 1990s provide strong evidence that higher amounts of debt were associated with an increased probability of business failure or need for restructuring. More recently, our examination of the 719 UK private equity-backed deals completed from 1996 that had exited through initial public offering (IPO), trade sale, secondary buyout, or receivership up to the end of June 2008 provides some systematic indication of whether high leverage is associated with buyout failure (Table 1). It is particularly notable that smaller buyouts that entered receivership had markedly higher proportions of debt in their initial financing structures.

The failure rate of buyouts appears to be greater than for companies that are not subject to a buyout. This is not surprising since companies that are bought out are not a random subset of the population but are usually firms that have been identified as underperforming in some way. Private equity-backed and larger buyouts are less likely to fail. Since 2001 there has been only one year (2003) when the number of private equity-backed failures was greater than the failure of non-private equity-backed buyout transactions (Figure 4). There are also indications that larger buyouts are less likely to fail than smaller deals (Figure 5). The primary reason for this is that a larger firm is often an older firm and therefore has a more stable relationship with its customers, suppliers, and financiers. A larger firm may have a larger portfolio of related products and may have diversified into unrelated products, thus reducing the risk of failure if sales in certain areas fall. A larger firm may also contain more separable assets that can be disposed of to generate cash to pay down debt and help restructure the core business.

Table 1. Debt and receiverships in the United Kingdom. (*Source*: CMBOR/ Barclays Private Equity)

Deal size range	*No. of buyouts*	*Total debt* as % of total financing*
Up to £9.9 million		
All exited deals	366	48.9
Receiverships	110	53.7
£10–49.9m		
All exited deals	454	46.9
Receiverships	83	54.3
£50–99.9 million		
All exited deals	124	61.0
Receiverships	13	51.2
£100 million or more		
All exited deals	141	63.6
Receiverships	5	65.0

£1 = US$1.5

*Includes senior debt, mezzanine debt, high-yield debt, and vendor loans.

US$1.5.

An important issue for financiers of buyouts that eventually fail is the share of their investment that can be recovered. In UK buyouts completed in the period 1990–95 that subsequently defaulted, secured creditors recovered on average 62% of their investment, and many of these companies were eventually restructured and sold as going concerns. In comparison with the general population of small firms, buyouts appear to experience fewer going-concern realizations from receivership (30%), make a lower average repayment to secured creditors, and make fewer 100% repayments to these creditors.

BUYOUTS AS A MEANS OF FIRM SURVIVAL

Failing companies can also be rescued through a management buyout. In times of recession there has been an increase in the number of buyouts from failed companies (Figure 6). Buyouts from firms in receivership peaked in the depth of the recession of the early 1990s, with 107 deals in 1991 accounting for 18.4% of the deal volume. A second, lower peak occurred in the much shallower recession of the early 2000s, with 76 deals completed in 2002, accounting for 11.9% of deal volume. Within the onset of recession, the number of buyouts of failed firms is expected to rise significantly in the immediate future.

The total value of transactions involving buyouts from receivership peaked slightly later in 2003 at £332 million, with an average deal value of £4.1 million. More recently, the total value of buyouts from receivership has so far peaked in 2007 at £336 million for an average deal size of £10.8 million. Most of these buyouts from receivership involve the purchase of parts

Figure 4. Private equity and receiverships in the United Kingdom. (*Source*: CMBOR/ Barclays Private Equity)

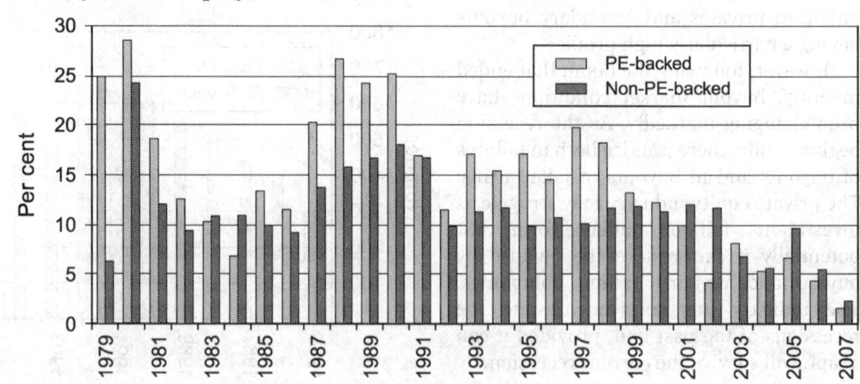

  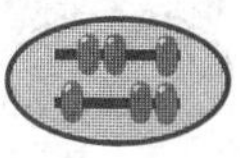   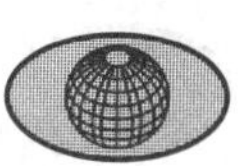   

Figure 5. Receiverships in the United Kingdom by initial deal size. (*Source*: CMBOR/ Barclays Private Equity)

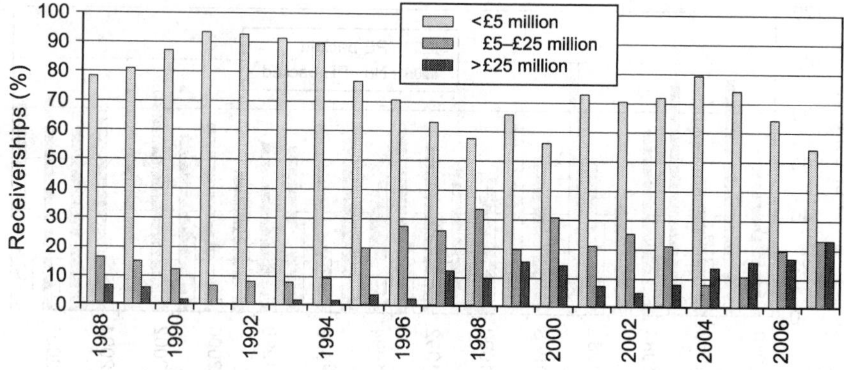

Figure 6. Sources of buyouts in the United Kingdom versus GDP. (*Source*: CMBOR/ Barclays Private Equity/OECD)

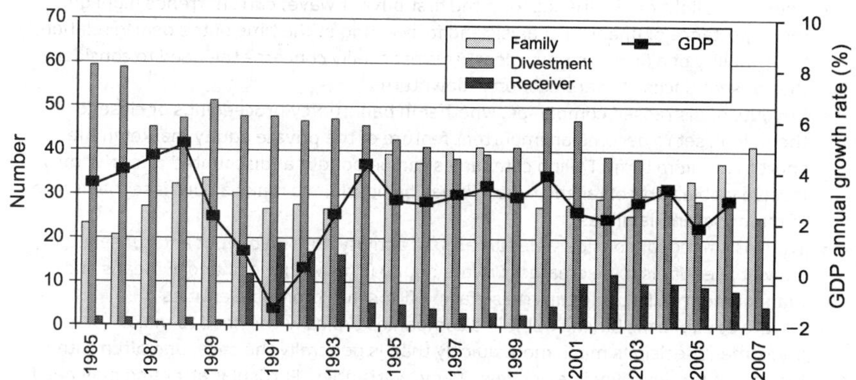

of failed groups rather than attempts to rescue whole firms (see for example the Denby mini-case study below).

Buyouts of firms in receivership have occurred across a wide range of industries, being most numerous over the last decade in manufacturing, followed by business and support services, retail, and technology, media, and telecommunications (TMT) (Table 2). However, there are notable differences between the earlier and later parts of the last 10 years. Reflecting the collapse of the dot.com boom, the number of buyouts from failed firms in TMT was far higher in the 1999–2004 period than in the more recent five-year period. In contrast, buyouts of failed firms in the retail sector have been particularly prevalent in the 2004–08 period compared to the previous five years.

Private equity firms were most active in buying failing firms during the recessions of the 1990s and 2000s, when there was a good supply of firms in receivership and where bargains were to be found (Figure 7). At other periods, most noticeably the last six years, private equity firms have not been the main purchasers of these target firms. As the current recession bites, private equity firms can take advantage of the situation by buying failing companies.

Although it is too early to assess the effects of buyouts from receivership in the current recessionary period, our survey evidence from the last deep recession of the early 1990s, using a representative sample of 64 buyouts from receivership, showed that major restructuring activities were needed to turn around the business. Almost two-thirds (64%) had appointed new directors, 56% had not appointed existing directors, 48% had reduced debtor days, 38% had reduced their vehicle fleet, and 34% had cash flow problems post-buyout. The average employment level fell from 202 on buyout to 158 at the time of the survey. However, some 63% had not made job redundancies on buyout. Subsequently, 36% had reduced employment, 36% had not changed employment, and in 19% of cases employment was above pre-buyout levels. On a cautionary note, evidence from deals completed in the recession of the early 1990s shows that buyouts of firms in receivership are more likely to fail again than buyouts from other vendor sources.

Table 2. Sector distribution of buyouts/ buyins in the United Kingdom by number. (*Source*: CMBOR/Barclays Private Equity)

Sector group	*1999–2003*	*2004–08**
Business and support services	24	24
Financial services	7	4
Food and drink	15	16
Healthcare	4	2
Leisure	10	20
Manufacturing	106	88
Paper, print, publish	20	15
Property and construction	4	9
Retail	14	35
TMT	33	13
Transport and comms	3	6
Others	16	26

*2008 figures are for first nine months only.

CASE STUDIES

Ethel Austin

This case provides an example of how a buyout can run into difficulty when (1) the product is not selling because the competition does it better, (2) the product is not selling because of economic conditions beyond the firm's control, and (3) the firm has a large debt to service (the percentage of senior debt is much greater than the average, as shown in Table 1). It also provides an example of how a firm can be rescued by someone who has expertise in that particular area of business and who therefore has a chance of rejuvenating the company.

Ethel Austin is a discount fashion group founded by Ethel and George Austin in 1934 in Liverpool, England. At its peak at the beginning of 2008, the company had about 300 stores, 2,800 employees and a turnover of £150 million. The firm has had two management buyouts in its recent past. The first was in 2002, when the Austin family sold the business to its management team, supported by Lloyds Development Capital, for £55 million (64% of which was senior debt); and the second was in 2004, when the business was sold again to ABN AMRO for £122.5 million (57% senior debt).

Ethel Austin was put into administration in April 2008, when it was claimed that it had been struggling because of competition from rival budget chains such as Primark and Matalan and the big supermarkets. More than 450 jobs were axed and 33 stores were closed by the administrators, Menzies Corporate Restructuring. Elaine Gray, the previous chief executive and joint owner of MK One, bought Ethel Austin from the administrator in April 2008, saving 2,500 jobs and 260 stores in the

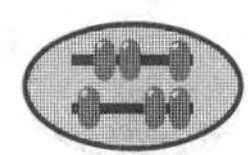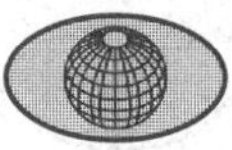

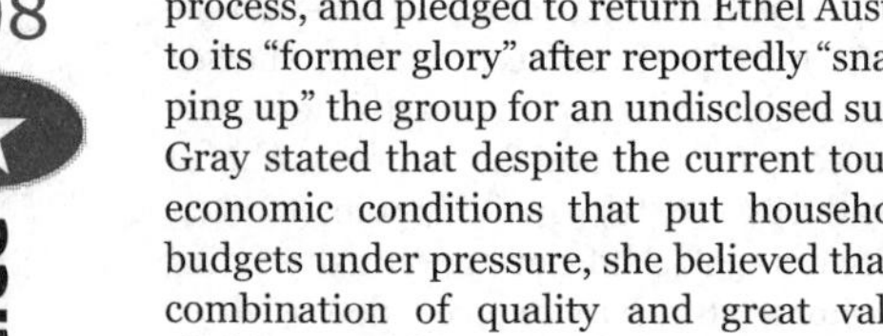

process, and pledged to return Ethel Austin to its "former glory" after reportedly "snapping up" the group for an undisclosed sum. Gray stated that despite the current tough economic conditions that put household budgets under pressure, she believed that a combination of quality and great value clothing could make Ethel Austin a retail success story once again.

Denby

The case of Denby highlights what can happen when a large organization goes into receivership. A management buyout provides a means by which more viable divisions can survive. Denby is a world famous British pottery manufacturer based in Denby, Derbyshire, which started producing pottery in 1809. In June 1990, Coloroll, Denby's parent company, went into receivership and Denby was purchased by its own management, backed by 3i (a private equity group), for a total of £7.4 million. Denby's managing director and three associates invested £140,000 for a 55% stake in the company, while 3i held the balance.

The firm began to sell its products in the United States, and by the time it floated on the London Stock Exchange in 1994 it was valued at £43.4 million. It used some of the proceeds of the sale to repay its debts and continued its expansion abroad, updated its range of products, and opened a visitor center complex at Denby. The center became a major tourist attraction, with 300,000 visitors a year by the end of the century. The company has since undergone two more management buyouts: The first in 1999 for £40.7 million involved a delisting from the stock exchange; and the second in 2004 for £48 million was a management buyout. Denby has added glassware and porcelain to its product range and continues to flourish.

Figure 7. Buyouts from the receiver in the United Kingdom. (*Source*: CMBOR/Barclays Private Equity)

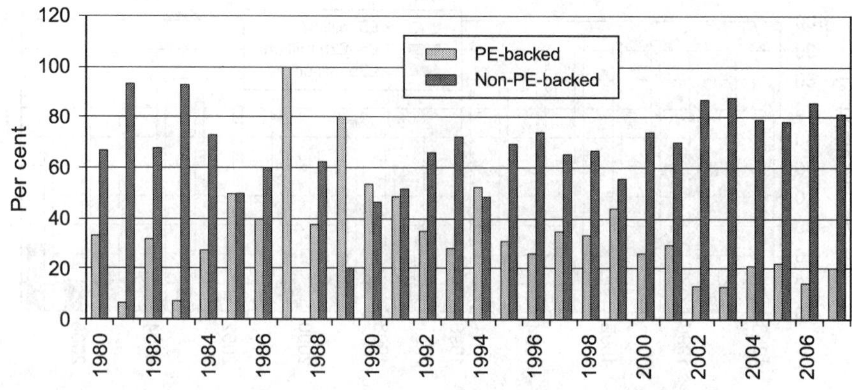

⏩ MAKING IT HAPPEN

- Seen in the light of experience from the first buyout wave, current trends highlight the importance of financial analysis and forecasting at the time of the deal in relation to the ability of a firm to service debt. This especially concerns the need to consider the consequences of sharp economic downturns.
- Buyouts of distressed companies, whether in bankruptcy proceedings or close to them, look set to become an important feature of the private equity market in the short to medium term. Failing companies can be bought at discounted prices. If they involve viable parts of failed groups, it may be possible to make a purchase that is free of major parent liabilities.
- There is a need for considerable turnaround activity both on buyout and subsequently if a viable entity is to be created. Private equity firms with the financial means and management skills could turn these failing firms into profitable entities.
- Private equity firms buying out failed companies typically will need to make investment decisions much more quickly than is generally the case, and often with less scope for due diligence and few, if any, warranties. Particular attention may need to be given to ensuring that suppliers and customers will remain committed to the company.
- There is a premium on private equity firms having expertise in a particular sector and in having done distress deals that enable rapid assessment of prospective risks and returns. It is also important to assess the caliber of incumbent management. If they are not a contributory factor to failure, their knowledge of the business may be crucial in avoiding the pitfalls due to the contracted deal process noted above.

⏩ MORE INFO

Reports:

Gilligan, John, and Mike Wright. "Private equity demystified: An explanatory guide." London: ICAEW, Corporate Finance Faculty, November 2008. Available free at: www.cmbor.com

Wright, Mike, Andrew Burrows, Rod Ball, Louise Scholes, Miguel Meuleman, and Kevin Amess. "The implications of alternative investment vehicles for corporate governance: A synthesis of research about private equity firms and 'activist hedge funds'." Paris: OECD, July 2007. Available free at: www.cmbor.com

Websites:

British Private Equity and Venture Capital Association (BVCA): www.bvca.co.uk

Centre for Management Buy-out Research (CMBOR), Nottingham University Business School: www.cmbor.com

European Private Equity and Venture Capital Association (EVCA): www.evca.com

NOTES

1 Europe is defined here as Austria, Belgium, Denmark, Finland, France, Germany, Ireland, Italy, The Netherlands, Norway, Portugal, Spain, Sweden, Switzerland, and the United Kingdom.

"It is the fate of those who toil at the lower employments of life. . .to be exposed to censure, without hope of praise." Samuel Johnson

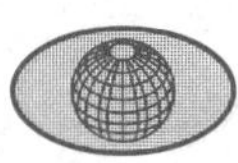

Leveraged Buyouts: What, Why, When, and How by Scott S. Johnson

EXECUTIVE SUMMARY

- A leveraged buyout (LBO) is the acquisition of a company financed by debt.
- The use of debt multiplies both the potential return and risk.
- LBOs require active and liquid credit markets.
- Stable, mature businesses with predictable—and ideally recurring—revenues are generally the best LBO targets.
- LBO returns are maximized by buying low and selling high, properly capitalizing the buyout, and maximizing profitable and high-quality growth during the hold period.

WHAT

A leveraged buyout (LBO) is the acquisition of a company financed by debt. It is not unlike the typical purchase of a residence where the majority of financing is derived from a mortgage, and the balance from cash (equity) contributed by the buyer.

The use of debt in an LBO leverages the equity return, providing the equity holder with the possibility of higher returns at the cost of higher risk. Debt levels have averaged 72% of total capital from 1996 to 2008, according to Standard & Poor's. Debt levels vary due to numerous factors, including the vibrancy of credit markets, the ability of the company to support debt, and the strategy of the given LBO.

Although select transactions that could be considered LBOs occurred prior to the 1980s, this acquisition strategy grew in popularity in the 1980s when ample debt financing became available, in particular with the rise of the sub-investment grade, or "junk" debt market. Over the past decade, the strategy has seen even more activity with more than US$100 billion raised by private equity funds. Buyouts have, in fact, become a material element in mergers and acquisitions. From 2004 to 2008, US buyout volume was US$1 trillion, according to Standard & Poor's.

LBOs can involve the acquisition of an entire company or a division of a company. In some cases, management, usually with the financial backing and transactional expertise of a private equity group, buys out its own entity, which is then more specifically referred to as a management buyout (MBO). Yet another permutation is leveraged recapitalization, whereby some equity plus debt are used to provide liquidity to shareholders, either to buy their shares outright, or provide cash to them (not unlike a residential mortgage refinancing).

WHY

Although the leveraged buyout entails risk, given the challenges of servicing debt, significant returns are possible without the need for material growth.

Furthermore, the need to generate sufficient cash flow for debt service imposes discipline.
Companies that, pre-LBO, were inefficient, or overloaded with expenses are forced to streamline their operations and cost structure to succeed. At the same time, the need to service debt can generate short-term decision-making that may not always be in the best long-term interest of the business. However, the World Economic Forum's "Global impact of private equity report 2009"[1] estimated that the extra productivity from 1,400 private equity transactions of US manufacturing concerns raised output by US$4 billion, to US$15 billion per year from 1980 to 2005 (expressed in inflation-adjusted 2007 dollars).

WHEN

LBOs are most commonly considered when a candidate company can support the required leverage, and credit markets can provide such leverage.

Good LBO candidates operate in relatively stable businesses with consistent business models. These are generally mature companies with positive cash flow, and an established operating and profitability history. Earlier-stage companies, or those that require continued cash investments to achieve their objectives are generally not good candidates.

Furthermore, companies with a cyclical business, or those materially exposed to major exogenous risks such as technological obsolescence or fashion risk, are

CASE STUDY

How Debt Can Magnify Both Returns and Risk

Let's take a company with US$10 in profit and assume it is acquired for 6x profit, or US$60. In the LBO of this company, US$40 of the purchase price is financed with debt and US$20 is an equity investment, so equity is one-third of the total capital. In the unleveraged scenario, US$60 of equity—100% of the consideration—is used to acquire the company.

If the company is sold at the end of five years, and profits have grown at a compound annual growth rate of 10% to US$16 (a cumulative growth of 60%), and the purchase price multiple remains 6x, the business is sold for US$97. In the unleveraged scenario, the annual return is equal to the profit growth, i.e., 10% per annum and 60% on a cumulative basis.

On the other hand, the LBO equity return is much higher. In the LBO, the company sale price value (its enterprise value, or EV) is still US$97. Of the US$97, the first US$40 is returned to the debt holders to pay off their principal, leaving US$57 for the equity. Unlike the unleveraged case, where the sale price is 60% greater than the investment, here the US$57 is 183% greater than the US$20 investment.

The annual return in the LBO is more than double the unleveraged deal: 23% vs. 10% (See Figure 1). Please note that this scenario is an oversimplification, with numerous factors such as transaction costs, working capital, and annual cash flow generation excluded (even when those factors are included, the LBO continues to outperform the unleveraged deal approximately 2:1).

Our case study also illustrates the risks of the leveraged buyout strategy. Without any interest expense or debt principal due, the unleveraged company in our simplified example can weather substantial declines in operating profit, and still maintain positive cash flow. Conversely, if the leveraged company sees a decline of profits of just 25%, its profits after interest expense fall three times that level, or 75%. If the leveraged company had material levels of capital expenditures, or debt principal repayments (which are both post-tax items), it may not be able to service its cash needs. The likely result would be a cash squeeze, which would have negative or potentially disastrous implications (See Figure 2).

"Leverage is a very sharp, double-edged sword." Richard Bernstein

   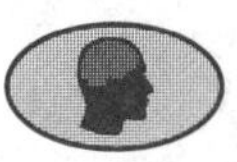  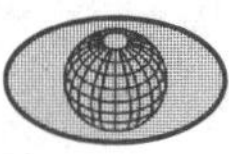   

Figure 1. Case study: Sample LBO vs all equity acquisition

	LBO	All equity
Initial acquisition		
Profit	$10	
Multiple	6.0 ×	
Value	$60	
Capitalization		
Debt	4.0 ×	0.00 ×
	$40.0	$0.0
Equity	2.0 ×	6.00 ×
	$20.0	$60.0
Return after year-5 sale		
Value	$96.63	
Less: debt	($40.00)	$0.0
Equity value	$56.63	$96.63
Annual return	23.1%	10.0%
Return on capital	1.8 ×	0.6 ×
Profit after five years:		
Annual growth	10.0%	
Cumulative growth	161.1%	
Year-5 profit	$16.11	
Year-5 sale price:		
Year-5 profit	$16.11	
times multiple of	6.0 ×	
gives sale price	$96.63	

Note: Excludes transaction and closing fees and assumes no principal amortization or cash generated.

also less-optimal buyout candidates. Explicitly recurring revenue businesses (i.e., contractual) or implicit (for example, regularly repurchased consumables) are good targets. Sectors that often exhibit these characteristics and have yielded successful buyouts include consumer, business services, defense, and media.

HOW

LBO returns can be generated from five factors as follows:

1 **Buying low**. The lower the entry valuation level, the greater margin of safety provided for investors. Furthermore, a company acquired at a lower valuation will require less debt to achieve the optimal debt-to-capital mix. On the other hand, higher quality and larger companies often have greater growth prospects, are generally more stable, and thus usually sell for higher valuations. When valuations are high, buyers take the risk that even if the business is properly capitalized and shows good growth, exit valuation levels could be lower and will not be sufficient to generate an acceptable return. While careful analysis can help determine if the steps below are to be a success, entry valuation is critical, as it is a factor that is controllable at the beginning of the LBO.

2 **Maximizing equity returns by minimizing equity investment to prudent levels**. An LBO investor must first decide the maximum leverage the business can support, and then try to finance the deal to that level, but not more. In strong credit markets, LBO investors should resist the temptation to overleverage their portfolio companies. In weak credit markets, investors need to ensure that, at lower debt levels, they can still achieve their minimum return hurdles (often accomplished by "buying lower").

What is the appropriate debt level? This clearly varies. Two helpful benchmarks to consider are the overall leverage, and the ability of the company to support its debt, and other obligations. Debt levels are often measured as a multiple of earnings before interest, taxes, depreciation, and amortization (EBITDA), a simplified proxy for cash flow. Debt-to-EBITDA levels for buyouts have historically varied by year, largely as a function of the state of the debt markets. In 2007, average debt to EBITDA was 6.0x, but fell to 4.8x in 2008, and averaged as low as 3.5x in 2001, according to Standard & Poor's.

LBO investors will also be concerned with their buyout's ability to service its debt. The fixed-charge covenant ratio (FCCR) is a common measure used to measure debt service levels. The FCCR is the ratio of a company's cash flow to its fixed charges, which typically include taxes, interest, capital expenditures, and debt principal payments. Lenders often seek minimum FCCR levels of 1.10–1.35x.

Debt levels also vary due to the structure of the debt offered. In larger transactions, publicly traded bonds, which often form the bulk of the financing, do not typically carry principal amortization, allowing for greater debt capacity. In smaller transactions, debt is typically provided in two tranches: senior debt, typically from banks, and "mezzanine debt," which is subordinate to the senior debt and carries higher rates of interest and sometimes includes equity participation in the form of warrants. Senior debt in such structures often includes principal amortization, which can impose material burdens on a company.

Thus, the financing structure makes a material difference in the level of debt a company can support. In particular, debt capital structures that have less (or no) principal amortization are more conducive to higher debt levels, as the total debt servicing costs are much lower (especially when it is considered that debt principal repayments are post-tax obligations).

Debt levels are also a function of the strategy of the buyout group. Some groups tend to use comparatively less debt, so they have "dry powder" to finance any shortfall or add-on acquisition.

3 **Maximizing quality organic growth before exit**. Generally, the more growth that occurs during the holding period, the more valuable the company will be at exit. However, a company must be care-

Figure 2. Case study: Effect of profit decline

	LBO	All equity
Base profit	$10.00	
Decline in profit	25%	
New profit	$7.50	
Interest	$5.00	$0.00
Profit after interest	$2.50	$7.50
Decline in profit after interest	-75.0%	-25.0%
Debt	$40.00	
Interest rate	12.5%	
Interest expense	$5.00	

⏩ MAKING IT HAPPEN

- Do your diligence. While confirmatory diligence to verify financial and operating assumptions is critical, exploratory diligence is often not given enough focus. The buyout investor should, in particular, understand the sustainability of a company's competitive advantages, and make sure they understand not just the recent history of a company's sector, but the sector's outlook, and what underlying threats may exist to that sector.
- Debt structure. While the price of debt is critical, equally if not more important are the terms of that debt. Key areas worth considering include the maturity date of the debt, the level of principal amortization, if any, and how a given lender may act as a partner (especially if results are poor, and covenants are violated).
- "Skin in the game." While a buyout investor can provide management equity upside, through the use of stock options, having a management team invest their own cash in the deal—putting "skin in the game"—confirms management's confidence in the opportunity, and binds them to both the upside and downside.

"When things go wrong you have to pass the blame along the line, like pass-the-parcel, till the music stops."
Tom Stoppard

   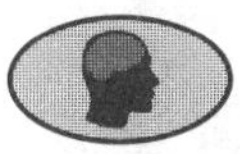  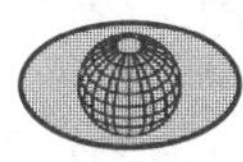   

ful to focus on generating "good" revenue. While "good" revenue may vary from company to company, it generally entails business that preserves or bolsters a company's competitive advantages and margins, does not create unnecessarily high customer concentration, is ideally of a recurring nature, still yields a good return on investment net of capital expenditures and working capital requirements, and is the type of business that would appeal to a potential buyer. To achieve these goals, the buyout group relies on its partnership with management. Furthermore, the buyout investor must carefully use the correct management incentives to generate the desired results. These programs usually revolve around the use of longer-term equity incentives that help shape management's overall motivation, and minimize short-term decision-making. For a typical buyout CEO, the annual compensation will be lower than a corporate position, but if the buyout is successful, the payout can be much higher than what would have been possible as a corporate employee.

4 **Making profitable add-on acquisitions or divestitures as appropriate**. Buyout investors may seek to grow a business through acquisition, or sell off divisions as appropriate. The buyout investor must carefully weigh the return on capital that will be generated by incremental investment, as well as the cash that could be generated from a divestiture, which would likely be used to deleverage the business.

5 **Selling high**. After an investment holding period of typically three to seven years, a buyout firm will seek to exit its investment, so that the proceeds may be returned to its own investors. If growth has been positive and consistent, and industry trends and valuation levels are favorable, the buyout firm should achieve a good return on its investment. However, the reality is that valuation levels years after a deal is consummated are well outside of the control of the buyout firm, so having a flexible timetable, entering the deal at a reasonable valuation level, improving the performance of the company during the holding period, and appropriately capitalizing the company are essential to executing a profitable LBO.

▸▸ MORE INFO

Websites:

The Association for Corporate Growth, the predominant industry association for the middle market buyout industry: www.acg.org

The Deal, magazine and online resource: www.thedeal.com

The Private Equity Analyst, a periodical published by Dow Jones: www.fis.dowjones.com/products/privateequityanalyst.html

The Private Equity Council: www.privateequitycouncil.org

Standard and Poor's Leveraged Commentary and Data, "A Guide to the Loan Market:" www.lcdcomps.com/press/LoanMarketguide.pdf

See Also:

★ Leveraged Buyouts and Recession (pp. 405–408)
★ Viewpoint: Jon Moulton (pp. 214–215)
Barbarians at the Gate: The Fall of RJR Nabisco (p. 1223)

NOTES

1 www.weforum.org/pdf/cgi/pe/Full_Report2.pdf, p. 44.

     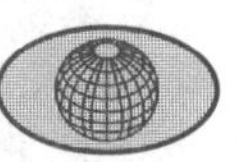   

Maximizing Value when Selling a Business by John Gilligan

EXECUTIVE SUMMARY

- *Advisers advise, principals decide*. Advisers may not understand industry-specific risks and are therefore badly placed to make judgments on some risk issues. Be prepared to debate with your own advisers and to overrule them if your knowledge is superior, no matter how much they are being paid.
- *Don't buy a dog and bark yourself*. Corporate sales are complex and risky. Appoint experienced advisers and get them to manage the process under your control.
- *Information*. The importance of information cannot be overemphasized. Buyers are motivated by fear and greed: The quality, tone, and flow of information critically impact both motives.
- *Valuation*. Agree what the walkaway price is with your advisers before starting a process, review it constantly, and be prepared to walk away if necessary.
- *Competitive tension*. The best deals are achieved where more than one buyer with cash (but not an uncontrollable host) wants to purchase a business. Use this rivalry to maximize the bids received and to eliminate risks that might prevent the buyer from delivering the deal.
- *Blunderbuss versus rifle shot*. Most businesses have a limited target population of buyers who may pay a strategic premium. The approach when marketing needs to favor those most likely to pay the best price.
- *Financial bidders are active*. In the past 20 years more businesses worldwide have probably been sold to private equity firms than any other type of acquirer. Use them to create competitive tension.
- *Auctions have to be managed*. Theory and practice suggest that many tactics in auctions are counterintuitive. Think through what you are going to do and clearly communicate it to potential purchasers.
- *Say nothing*. There are always matters that are uncertain in any deal. Staff are always unsettled by uncertainty. It is best to say nothing at all to them, but if you do decide to explain what is happening, you must be completely honest. But remember, any ambiguity is interpreted negatively.
- *Only the fittest survive*. Transactions are long and often tedious. Do not let boredom, fatigue, or lack of patience deflect you from your final goal, especially when the winning line is near.
- *The one that got away*. The world is full of people who nearly did the best deal ever. To achieve success, you need to give and take; it is not a war, it is a negotiation.

INTRODUCTION

All corporations seem complex to those looking in from the outside. The cocktail of relationships, contracts, and assets coming together to generate value is different in every company, and the process of realizing the value embedded in that cocktail requires planning, foresight, and pragmatic judgment. Failure to sell a business that has been publicly put up for sale can destroy huge amounts of value. Each situation is unique and no text can provide a comprehensive guide, any more than you could write the complete guide to sailing in all weathers. This article will deal with general principles and strategies, not technical details. Furthermore, it will address the question of *how* to sell a business, not *why* you should sell a business.

ADVISERS—WHAT THEY DO, WHAT THEY DON'T DO

It would be perverse not to believe that corporate finance advice is valuable. Here is one casual, empirical data point that supports this view: Private equity firms, many themselves ex-corporate financiers, and whose core business is buying and selling companies, almost always use advisers. The question is not *whether* to appoint advisers; it is what should they be tasked with doing, and what is the limit of their role. Their role is not to make decisions. They are there to limit the number of decisions the vendor has to make regarding the key commercial factors that make deals happen. Good advisers should be prepared to debate decisions and use their experience to guide their clients toward the paths of least resistance. However, only the owners can make the final decisions.

Having described what advisers don't do, the natural question is: So what *do* they do? The answer to this is—pretty much everything except making the final commercial decisions. Expect advisers to prepare, collate, and analyze data that will be presented to potential purchasers. They should project manage every aspect of the sale process, providing a clear and coherent strategy to achieve a successful outcome with an acceptable level of risk. This is the necessary skill set of any adviser and it enables the company to concentrate on delivering to its customers, not preparing itself for sale. As the saying goes, "Don't buy a dog and bark yourself."

The added value in corporate finance comes in three ways. First is the ephemeral thing called judgment. As one partner of a major British practice used to describe it, having a good "bullshit detector" helps. Second is the ability to take the burden away from the client. Advisers should do all the heavy lifting, leaving their clients to concentrate on the business itself and the key decisions. Finally, and of crucial importance in many deals, advisers need to be able to access the right people in the right places who may wish to acquire the business.

INFORMATION—WHAT YOU SAY, AND HOW YOU SAY IT

In 2001 three US economists, Akerlof, Steiglitz, and Spencer shared the Nobel Prize in economics. Their body of work deals with an area formally known as "information asymmetry," or more colloquially: What do you do when I know things you don't know? This section tries to answer a simple question: If a purchaser can't tell a good car from a bad car, how can a seller get a premium for a good car? The same problem arises when you are selling a company, only more so. Companies are the most complex things that are traded, and selling one may transfer all the future and historical risks and rewards to the new owner. If you cannot persuade the new owner that the net value of those risks and rewards is quantifiable and positive, you won't sell the business. This is one of the commonest areas in which transactions fail. A failure to think through the strategy of managing and transmitting information results in transactions falling apart further down the line, as purchasers narrow the information asymmetry in due diligence and find that what they were told origin-

"It's far better to buy a wonderful company at a fair price than a fair company at a wonderful price." Warren Buffet

  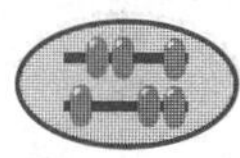 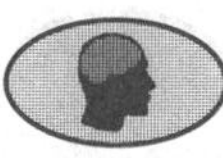  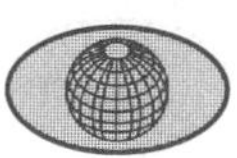   

Figure 1. Typical business sale process

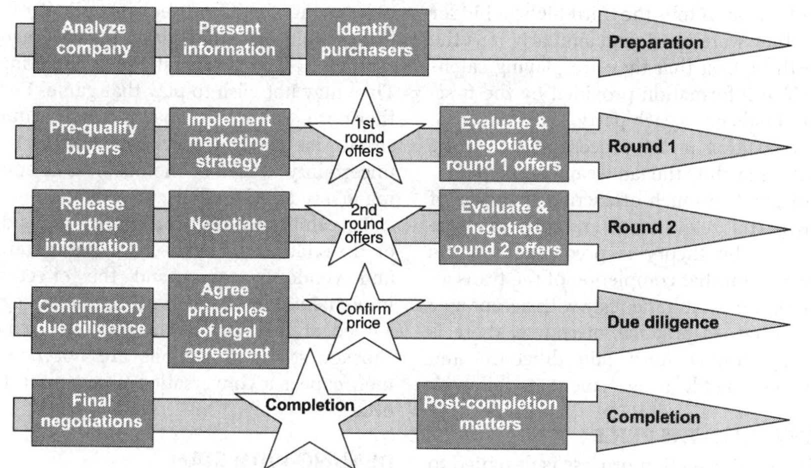

ally is not what they found to be true subsequently.

There are a number of ways to deal with information asymmetry. The simplest and crudest solution is to ignore the issue entirely. Provide limited data and tell purchasers to rely on their own judgment. In essence, this is what happens in an unsolicited hostile takeover, and may well be the reason that so many hostile approaches subsequently turn out to be failures.

To bridge the asymmetry you can either transmit information (under a suitable confidentiality agreement) or agree to take residual risks away from the purchaser by, for example, giving warranties. At the extremes, the negotiating positions are either: "We will give you access to do whatever due diligence you like, but we are not warranting anything," or "We will warrant that the information we give to you is materially correct, but you are not getting any more access than that." The approach to this question needs to be decided early on since it flows through the entire transaction approach and materially influences the form of legal agreement that will emerge at the end of the process. It is also important to communicate your approach to purchasers clearly and consistently. If you do not, they will impose their view on you and purchasers will seek both a belt and suspenders: full access, and full warranties.

VALUATION. . .IS IN THE EYE OF THE BEHOLDER

In theory, the value of any asset is the present value of its future cash flows. To maximize value, you need to show the maximum future cash flow and the minimum cost of capital. This leads to the infamous "hockey stick" projections—projections that reverse a declining trend and rise thereafter. These are fed into a spreadsheet and out pops a valuation. The danger of believing your own propaganda is that you set unrealistic targets. You must aim high, but not every attempt can be a world record.

In addition to DCF (discounted cash flow) valuations, advisers should prepare a variety of analyses. Comparable transactions that have occurred recently and analysis of comparable quoted companies valuations are the most frequently seen.

Another way to discover what advisers think your business is really worth is to look at where their fee proposal starts to generate significant uplift. Where fees are correlated to value, you can often work out the implicit valuation of any adviser from their fee proposal.

It is frequently contended that the most important output of the theoretical valuation process is not the maximum number calculated, but that it validates a "walkaway" price—the price at which the vendor will simply stop the process and refuse to sell. This number needs to be at the forefront of your mind in any negotiation. It also needs to be refreshed periodically if the prospects for the business or its markets change materially.

It is also important to remember that all these analyses are simply checking out the potential valuation. To actually achieve a transaction at a particular valuation, you normally need competitive tension or a compelling strategic premium.

COMPETITIVE TENSION—CREATING FEAR, ENCOURAGING GREED

Once you have surveyed the landscape, the task is to identify and communicate with those purchasers most likely to place a valuation on the business that they can afford to pay and which exceeds the walkaway price. When considering the number of parties to approach to create a market, again there are two extremes: blunderbuss or rifle shot.

The blunderbuss approach says that since you never know who might be looking for a business like yours, you should maximize the probability of hitting the target by firing as widely as possible. The downside is that circulating information widely makes a confidential process most unlikely.

The rifle shot approach targets a limited number of buyers, maximizing the probability of reaching those specific purchasers wishing to acquire the business. You risk missing a purchaser that you don't know of, but the process can be managed much more efficiently in a small and tightly controlled market.

Whichever approach is used, maximum tension requires only a few, well-funded potential purchasers to emerge from the initial marketing. There is not much to gain from an auction with seven purchasers compared to an auction with six, but it is much harder to efficiently manage a large number of parties. The number of parties taken into the final process needs to be consistent with the information strategy adopted. It's no use offering open access with no warranties to a large number of bidders; it is unmanageable in practice.

The special case of a market with one buyer presents different challenges. Here there are different ways to motivate a deal. In a market of one, you have to adopt either the "takeaway sale," or enter a courtship.

The takeaway sale is a tactic used by realtors and used car salesmen across the globe. You quickly show your wares and then you rapidly remove them. The message is clear: It is a once in a lifetime opportunity to buy this house/car/company, and it won't come again; act quickly. This is a risky approach. If the purchaser doesn't believe you, your negotiating position can be seriously undermined if they react with a studied show of indifference to the opportunity presented. However when it does work, it can produce spectacular results because a strategic premium is paid by the purchaser.

Courtship is subtler and has its own risks and rewards. It involves exploring possibilities and exchanging information and plans to build a consensus on the way forward and what that means in terms of valuation. When the logic of bringing two companies together is compelling, two questions often arise: First, which is the diner and which is the dinner? Second, even if the

"Before everything else, getting ready is the secret of success." Henry Ford

     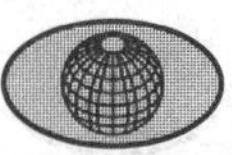   

cake is bigger, you still have to negotiate how it is going to be shared. A courtship strategy requires a significant investment of senior management time and emotion.

The biggest risk in a failed courtship is, as we all know, the effect of a broken heart. The impact on corporations of a failed courtship should not be underestimated: It can paralyze a corporation just as surely as it can turn a teenager into a gibbering wreck.

FINANCIAL PURCHASERS—ELEPHANTS OR DUNG BEETLES

Financial buyers come in many forms and provide liquidity to many different markets. The private equity (PE) industry contains both large strategic purchasers (elephants) and opportunists, who seek to snap up companies when no strategic purchaser emerges (dung beetles). Whichever strategy they are pursuing, and despite being much misunderstood and maligned, over the past 20 years financial purchasers have acquired more companies than trade acquirers. Any vendor who does not consider the PE market as a potential purchaser may be missing, at a minimum, a valuable source of competitive tension, and possibly the optimal purchaser.

AUCTIONS—THEORY AND PRACTICE

In a traditional, so-called English auction, bidding stops when the last but one bidder drops out. The vendor receives fractionally more than the second highest bidder was willing to pay. There are various ways to attempt to capture the value that the highest bidder might have paid. For example, a reverse auction (also known as a Dutch or clock auction) operates by the price declining until it is accepted by a bidder. This results in the so-called winner's curse—the only thing that the purchaser knows for certain is that they paid more than anyone else would have.

A counterintuitive solution to the problem was proposed by US economist William Vickrey. In a Vickrey auction, sealed bids are received and the asset is sold to the highest bidder, but at the price bid by the second highest bidder. This system ensures that each bidder bids their own true valuation, rather than speculating on the possible bids of other parties. The theoretical underpinnings are outside the scope of this chapter, but Vickrey was (jointly) awarded the 1996 Nobel Prize in economics for his work in this area.

Information from the first round of bids can be used to intensify informed competitive tension in subsequent rounds. For example, in a group of four second-round bidders, all the bidders might be informed of the value of the third highest bid received in round one. This tells the two highest bidders that they were one of two, but not who was highest. It tells the third highest bidder that they were third, and similarly tells the fourth highest that they are playing catch-up. The information provided by the first-round bids gives each party a clear steer on their position in the process and a strong guide regarding the landscape of the bids.

In practice much of auction theory is of only partial relevance to any corporate sale because the theory is predicated on the assumption that completion of the transaction occurs simultaneously with acceptance of the bid. In practice, of course, there is usually confirmatory due diligence and negotiation of legal agreements to follow.

DEFENDING THE PRICE

Whereas the auction process is designed to drive up the price, the period between accepting an offer and completion is usually defensive. The purchaser may try to find a justification to "chip" the price, and will rarely give any credit for positive variances against any plans they have relied on in the bid. The standard negotiating position of any purchaser when faced with positive information is, "We anticipated improvements in our original bid."

Negative variances are rarely anticipated in a bid and often result in variations to the terms of the indicative offer. Be aware that the legal status of an indicative offer varies from country to country. Whereas most UK and US acquirers view indicative offers relatively lightly, many non-Anglo-Saxon countries view the making of any offer, however qualified it may be, as significant and, in some jurisdictions, potentially legally binding. It helps to understand this when judging both the offers received and the ability to meet any timetable that you might have set for purchasers.

A contract race may alleviate exposure to price chipping, but it requires purchasers to risk paying significant fees in pursuit of a transaction that they have (on average) around a 50% possibility of completing. They may not wish to play that game. Furthermore, the process may increase acquisition risk for the purchaser due to the uncertainty caused to the business, resulting in a reduced final price.

The ability to defend the price depends on the relationship between the purchasers' and vendors' teams, and the effective implementation of the information strategy agreed at the start of the process. If the "hockey stick" projections are not being met, expect a conversation about price to occur.

DEALING WITH STAFF

Companies are possibly the only assets you can sell where the value of the asset is dependent on the goodwill of the people employed in the business. It is extremely difficult to maintain complete secrecy in any transaction. The requirement to collate information not routinely produced often causes questions to be asked. Similarly, e-mails and telephone calls from unfamiliar advisers may trigger suspicion. Uncertainty invariably causes discontent, and transactions involve great uncertainties. Against this background, it is generally advisable to say nothing to staff unless required to do so. Any ambiguous information is often interpreted negatively, causing even more speculation and disruption. The alternative is to communicate honestly, including all the unknowns and uncertainties, giving legitimacy to the speculation but fanning the uncertainty.

Once a deal is certain, communication with staff must form a key part of the post-transaction integration plan.

▸▸ MAKING IT HAPPEN

Any transaction involves extensive amounts of work and lengthy negotiations peppered with key decisions. There are periods of little apparent activity followed by periods characterized by long meetings that often drag into the night. Transactions are done by people, not by processes, and it is of utmost importance that the key decision-makers do not let boredom, frustration, or fatigue cloud their judgment. Many deals have failed because the principals or their advisers could not keep their head when the finish line was in sight.

Risks often seem more significant when you stare at them for too long. At the end of any transaction there are often negotiations regarding matters that no senior manager would normally consider material. Principals need to use commercial judgment to cut through any of these issues that are holding up a deal.

Finally, the world of mergers and acquisitions (M&A) is full of people who nearly did the best deal ever. M&A is often spoken about using the language of conflict, with winners and losers. In fact, it is about negotiation, a process that requires give and take. There is no point in beating your "opponent" at the negotiating table if all you end up with is a large bill for an aborted transaction.

"In modern business it is not the crook who is to be feared most, it is the honest man who doesn't know what he is doing." William Wordsworth

  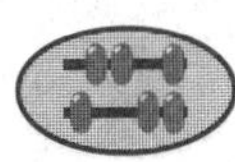   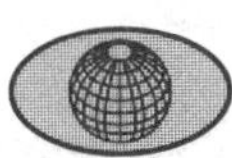   

Merger Integration and Transition Management: A New Slant for Finance Executives by Price Pritchett

EXECUTIVE SUMMARY

- Negotiating a good deal is a dangerous act if management isn't solidly prepared to make the deal work.
- Mergers are a fast-growth strategy—and they require fast management.
- The pre-close period is the staging platform for effective integration.
- A merger is always based on a financial proposition, but success invariably rests on the human proposition.

INTRODUCTION

Merger success—defined as value creation—depends heavily on how well conceived the deal was to begin with. But a good outcome is even more dependent on having a well-designed and carefully implemented integration strategy. To put it simply, no deal is a good deal if management can't make it work. Studies over the past several decades prove, however, that far too often companies lack the ability to design and execute a viable integration plan. Over half of all mergers end up as disappointments or outright failures that destroy shareholder value.

Many things contribute to the high casualty rate, but the myriad risk factors can be greatly reduced and in some cases eliminated. The odds of success dramatically improve when management adheres to some fundamental rules for effective integration.

Nevertheless, merger and acquisition (M&A) remains a high stakes game that is undertaken in pursuit of uncommon growth. As such, it calls for uncommon management.

TRANSITION MANAGEMENT SHOULD BEGIN EARLY

The merger transition period starts long before the deal gets final approval and actually closes. Weeks and months can pass as negotiations, due diligence, and the regulatory approval process proceed. Problems, however, don't wait around on management to close the deal. As soon as people pick up the scent that their company is in play, they begin to think and act differently. Their attitudinal shifts and behavior changes create leadership challenges that are unique to mergers. This explains why status quo management stops working.

The troublesome organizational dynamics that kick into gear need immediate attention, so transition management and integration planning should begin at least as soon as the deal becomes public knowledge. The pre-close period is a crucial phase. It's the mobilization zone for merger success where you set the stage for an informed, well- executed integration.

Particularly during the pre-close period, there are far more questions than answers, so the major workforce issue that needs to be addressed is *uncertainty*. People in leadership roles will need the merger management skills necessary to:

- navigate uncertainty and prepare for change;
- deal with people's negativity and resistance;
- keep employees engaged and retain talent;
- protect productivity and client relations.

A lot of damage can occur even before the deal papers are signed if managers at all levels don't respond appropriately to the new organizational dynamics.

GOVERNANCE OF THE INTEGRATION PROCESS

The transition management infrastructure should be set up, staffed, and functioning prior to the closing date. One person—a credible, experienced senior manager—should be appointed as integration manager with responsibility for overseeing integration planning and implementation. This position provides a single point of accountability for integration success. Given the unique demands of the job, the integration manager needs to possess a high energy level, strong sense of urgency, tolerance for ambiguity, and strong project management skills. The role also calls for in-depth knowledge of the business, good communication skills, plus the ability to create structure and process.

Typically a project management office is established to support the integration manager in running the integration effort. This will consist of a small group of people who meet daily, or at least weekly, to facilitate work streams, set priorities, coordinate schedules, etc., to ensure that the project runs in a disciplined manner.

An executive oversight body ordinarily serves as a steering committee. Members of this group (some drawn from the acquired company) might include the CEO, president, legal counsel, CFO, a senior level human resources executive, a senior communications officer, plus the integration manager. The steering committee designs the high-level merger integration strategy, sets timelines, and decides on synergy targets. Additionally, this group removes roadblocks, resolves sensitive merger issues, and serves as the final sign-off authority on expenditures and key staffing decisions.

A number of merger integration teams should be formed to conduct the analysis and integration planning for combining the various functional areas. Also, additional teams usually are needed to address cross-functional issues or company-wide matters such as communications, culture integration, etc.

In small mergers with limited staff, integration planning and execution is ordinarily handled by the managers who are accountable for the various functional areas. But even in small deals the integration should be conducted with strict project management discipline and a single person in charge as integration manager.

Of course, legal restrictions or the realities of competition can limit merging companies' ability to plan and organize prior to finalizing the deal. But preparation pays huge dividends, so management should make maximum use of the pre-close period.

Day 1—that point on the calendar when the merger goes live—is a day of reckoning. The acquirer's "opening moves" reveal the quality of pre-close planning and make a defining statement about management's ability to execute. Day 1 activities also are scrutinized for what they might imply about the future, so what's said and done should be carefully orchestrated to manage people's expectations appropriately.

FIVE GROUND RULES FOR EFFECTIVE INTEGRATION

There are two sides to the merger integration coin: project management and people management. Project management deals

"Things will probably come out all right, but sometimes it takes strong nerves just to watch." Hedley Donovan

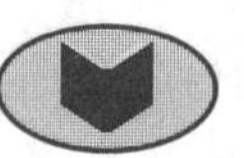
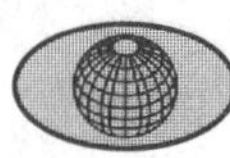
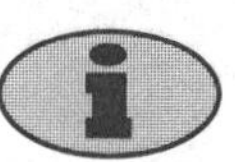

with the *mechanics*—that is, the administrative, operational, and technical matters involved in consolidating two organizations. People management deals with the so-called *soft stuff*, the highly-charged political, cultural, and personal issues that surface during a merger. It's generally agreed that "the soft stuff is the hard stuff," meaning that people management is more difficult than project management in mergers and acquisitions.

Actually, both aspects of integration management are complicated. But the following ground rules can help the merger process go smoothly and greatly improve the odds of success.

1. Remember—the first word in merger is "me"

Employees, first and foremost, are concerned about themselves. The question they want answered is "How will I personally be affected by the merger?" Until the individual gets answers to the "me issues," you're going to have only half an employee even though you're paying full salary. People can adjust to tremendous amounts of change, and they can deal with disappointment, but they hate to be left hanging in the wind wondering how they'll be affected in the shakeout. Provide closure as soon as possible.

2. Tighten up the integration timeframe

The longer you take to integrate, the closer you live to the edge. You are in a race—a race against the organizational problems and risk factors that are generic to mergers. . .a race against competitors who are building counterstrategies. . .and a race against the merger critics who would love to see you fail. The integration period is a destabilized, perilous time, and speed is your friend. As the saying goes, "Skate fast over thin ice."

3. Promise problems

Mergers are designed to strengthen organizations, but invariably things get worse before they get better. You need to predict this. And you should explain why it happens. Otherwise, the merger critics will point to the normal side effects of change as proof that the deal was ill-advised or that it is being poorly executed. You can preempt the critics, protect management's credibility, and actually make the merger less stressful by straightforwardly telling people what to expect.

4. Educate your workforce on how to perform during the merger

The integration period is a time of ambigu-

CASE STUDY

Merger of Chicago Mercantile Exchange with Chicago Board of Trade

CME and CBOT competed against each other for more than a century, first in agricultural commodities and later in futures and options trading. By acquiring CBOT Holdings for roughly US$8 billion, CME created a combined company valued at approximately US$25 billion. The merger produced the world's largest financial exchange with a market reach that encircles the globe.

The diagram below shows the integration management framework that was designed to transition the two firms into a single organization.

CME invested substantial time and money in laying the groundwork for effective integration. For example, managers in both companies were given briefings on best practices in mergers. Also, a day-long kickoff meeting for integration team leaders was designed to:

- work through the team charters;
- review regulatory guidelines on information sharing;
- provide an orientation regarding the integration planning approach, rules of engagement, expectations, etc.;
- define the scope and boundaries for each planning work stream;
- share information about each other's business;
- begin building cross-company relationships.

Overall, the CME–CBOT merger followed a disciplined integration process and adhered to an urgent timeline for completion.

Figure 1. Integration framework for the CME–CBOT merger

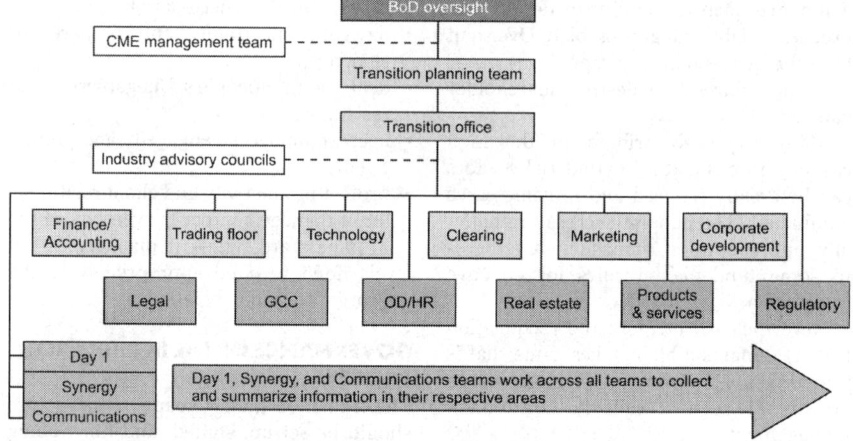

▸▸ MAKING IT HAPPEN

Integration planning and execution typically take shape through a financial lens, and appropriately so. The problem with this, however, is that many of the heavy-duty merger success factors revolve around the "soft stuff," which doesn't lend itself readily to hard financial metrics in the *predictive* sense. Of course, *after the fact*, the costs of poorly handling these people management issues may be obvious and easily calculated.

- Financial executives, perhaps even more than the people in human resources, should be champions for an integration effort that respects the influence and monetary impact of cultural, political, and personal issues.
- Calculate the potential costs associated with *not* managing the "soft stuff" effectively. Studies prove that people/cultural issues can wreck a deal.
- Culture problems are conveniently blamed when mergers go bad, but usually executives give culture little more than lip-service during integration. Treat culture as a make-or-break issue from the beginning, and make the investment of money and true expertise needed to deal appropriately with cultural differences.
- Engineer some "early wins." Defuse the critics and resistors by showcasing evidence that the merger is rapidly bringing benefits.

"Trying to squash a rumor is like trying to unring a bell." Shana Alexander

     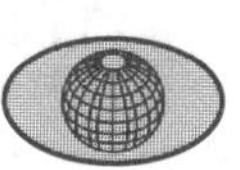   

ity, instability, and stress. It's not business-as-usual. Train your managers in the unique challenges of mergers, and provide guidance on how to lead during large-scale change. Give all employees an orientation on the basics of being acquired and merged—explain how organizations are affected, the difficulties that can be expected, how people react, and how they personally can have a positive influence on the merger process. If you fail to tell the workforce what's coming, or if you don't coach them on how you want them to handle it, why should you expect people to perform the way you'd like?

5. Communicate, communicate, communicate

People crave information and answers. If your communication efforts fail to satisfy their curiosity, the rumor mill will fill the void. Remember, "The more unpleasant the message, the more effort should go into communicating it." But give it to people straight—the good, the bad, and the ugly. Don't shave the truth, and don't slip into a propaganda mode with too much "happy talk" about the merger. Communication problems spawn all kinds of additional problems, so feed a steady stream of accurate and helpful information to all key stakeholders.

CONCLUSION

Mergers represent unconventional growth, and they produce a highly predictable set of "growing pains." But while all mergers are alike in this regard, every merger is different in that each brings its own idiosyncratic problems, which may be very unpredictable.

There's no excuse for failing to prepare merging organizations for the generic challenges. And, for that matter, management also should "expect the unexpected" and be fully prepared to improvise. If people have been trained properly, and if the appropriate transition management infrastructure is in place, the integration effort should succeed in spite of the inevitable surprises.

▸▸ MORE INFO

Books:

Pritchett, Price. *The Employee Guide to Mergers and Acquisitions*. Dallas, TX: Pritchett, 1986.

Pritchett, Price. *Making Mergers Work: A Guide to Managing Mergers and Acquisitions*. New York: McGraw-Hill, 1987.

Pritchett, Price. *The Employee Handbook for Shaping Corporate Culture: The Mission Critical Approach to Culture Integration and Culture Change*. Dallas, TX: Pritchett, 2002.

Pritchett, Price. *The Unfolding: A Handbook for Living Strong, Being Effective, and Knowing Happiness During Uncertain Times*. Dallas, TX: Pritchett, 2006.

Pritchett, Price. *Deep Strengths: Getting to the Heart of High Performance*. New York: McGraw-Hill, 2008.

Pritchett, Price, Donald Robinson, and Russell Clarkson. *After the Merger: The Authoritative Guide for Integration Success*. 2nd ed. New York: McGraw-Hill, 1997.

Journal:

Journal of Mergers & Acquisitions. Online at: www.iupindia.org/ijma.asp

Websites:

Association for Corporate Growth (ACG): www.acg.org

Mergers Unleashed: www.mergersunleashed.com

The Deal: www.thedeal.com

  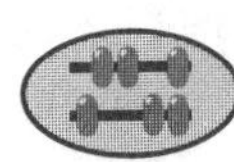   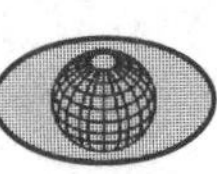   

Mergers and Acquisitions: Patterns, Motives, and Strategic Fit by Siri Terjesen

EXECUTIVE SUMMARY

- Mergers and acquisitions (M&A) are two broad types of restructuring through which managers seek economies of scale, enhanced market visibility, and other efficiencies.
- A merger occurs when two companies decide to combine their assets and liabilities into one entity, or when one company purchases another.
- An acquisition describes one company's purchase of another—for example, the absorption of a smaller target firm into a larger acquiring firm.
- The nature and scope of M&A activity has changed over time, with a growing trend to cross-border transactions.
- M&As are motivated by the expectation of financially rewarding synergies in terms of reduced fixed costs, increased market share, cross-sales, economies of scale, lower taxes, and more efficient resource distribution.
- At the individual level, executives may pursue M&As because of psychological drivers such as empire-building, hubris, fear, and mimicry.
- There are five broad types of strategic fit: overcapacity, geographic roll-up, product or market extension, research and development, and industry convergence.
- M&A execution can be hampered by incompatible corporate cultures, with failure to achieve synergies, high executive turnover, and too much focus on integration at the expense of customers.
- Before the deal, managers should formulate a clear and convincing strategy, preassess the deal, undertake extensive due diligence, formulate a workable plan, and communicate to internal and external stakeholders.
- After the deal, managers should establish leadership, manage culture and respect employees, explore new growth opportunities, exploit early wins, and focus on the customer.

INTRODUCTION

Mergers and acquisitions are two broad types of restructuring through which managers seek economies of scale, enhanced market visibility, and other efficiencies. A merger occurs when two companies decide to combine their assets and liabilities into one entity, or when one company purchases another. The term is often used to describe a merger of equals, such as that of Daimler-Benz and Chrysler, which was renamed DaimlerChrysler (see case study). The term "acquisition" simply refers to one company's purchase of another—as when a smaller target firm is bought and absorbed into a larger acquiring firm.

PATTERNS

The worldwide M&A market topped US$4.3 trillion and over 40,000 deals in 2007. Figure 1 depicts the growth of M&A activity, quarter by quarter, over the last five years.

The nature and scope of M&A activity has changed substantially over time. In the United States, the Great Merger Movement (1895 to 1905) was characterized by mergers across small firms with little market share, resulting in companies such as DuPont, Nabisco, and General Electric.

More recently, globalization has increased the market for cross-border M&As. In 2007 cross-border transactions were worth US$2.1 trillion, up from US$256 billion in 1996. Transnational M&As have seen annual increases of as much as 300% in China, 68% in India, 58% in Europe, and 21% in Japan.[1] The regional share of today's M&A market is shown in Figure 2.

MOTIVES

Mergers and acquisitions are often motivated by company performance, but can also be linked to executive decision-makers' empire-building, hubris, fear, and tendency to copy other firms.

The dominant rationale used to explain M&A activity is that acquiring firms seek improved financial performance through synergies that enhance revenues and lower costs. The two companies are expected to achieve cost savings that offset any decline in revenues. Then Hewlett-Packard CEO Carly Fiorina justified the merger with Compaq at a launch effort on September 3, 2001: "This is a decisive move that accelerates our strategy and positions us to win by offering even greater value to our customers and partners. In addition to the clear strategic benefits of combining two highly complementary organizations and product families, we can create substantial shareowner value through significant cost-structure improvements and access to new growth opportunities."[2]

The formula for the minimum value of the synergies required to protect the acquiring firm's stockholder value (i.e. to avoid dilution in earnings per share) is:

$$\frac{\text{(pre-M\&A value of both firms + synergies)}}{\text{post-M\&A firm number of shares}} = \text{pre-M\&A firm stock price}$$

Managers may be motivated by the potential for the following synergies:

- *Reduced fixed costs*: Duplicate departments and operations are removed, staff often made redundant, and typically the former CEO also leaves.
- *Increased market share*: The new larger company has increased market share and, potentially, greater market power to set prices.
- *Cross-sales*: The new larger company will be able to cross-sell one firm's products to the other firm's customers, and vice versa.
- *Greater economies of scale*: Greater size enables better negotiations with suppliers over bulk buying.
- *Lower taxes*: In some countries, a company that acquires a loss-making firm can use the target's loss to reduce liability.
- *More efficient resource distribution*: A larger company can pool scarce resources, or might distribute the technological know-how of one company, reducing information asymmetries.

At the individual decision-making level, M&A activity is also linked to the following:

- *Empire-building*: M&As may result from glory-seeking, as managers believe bigger is better and seek to create a large firm quickly via acquisition, rather than through the generally slower process of organic growth. In some firms, executive compensation is linked to total profits rather than profit per share, creating an incentive to merge/acquire to create a firm with higher total profits. Furthermore, executives often receive bonuses for completing mergers and acquisitions, regardless of the resulting impact on share price.
- *Hubris*: Public awards and increasing praise may lead an executive to overestimate his or her ability to add value

"...we can create substantial shareowner value through significant cost-structure improvements and access to new growth opportunities." Carly Fiorina

  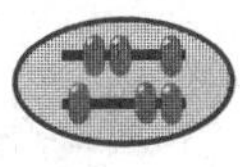   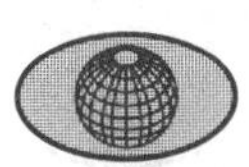   

Figure 1. Global M&A activity 2002–07. (*Source*: Thomson Financial, Bain & Company analysis)

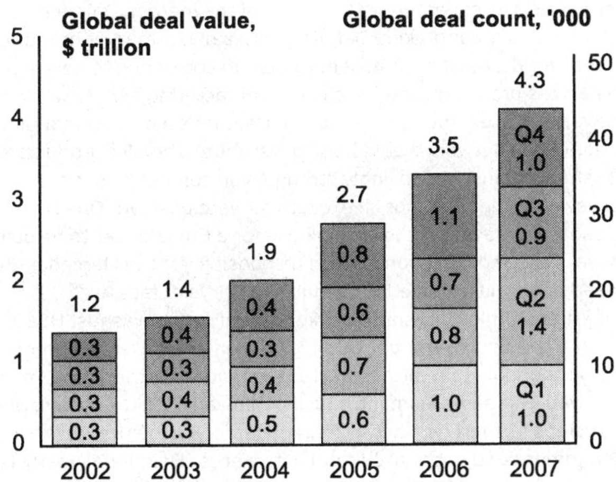

to firms. CEOs who are publicly praised in the popular press tend to pay 4.8% more for target firms. Hubris can also lead executives to fall in love with the deal, lose objectivity, and overestimate expected synergies.

- *Fear*: Managers' fear of an uncertain environment, particularly in terms of globalization and technological development, may lead them to believe they have little choice but to acquire if they are to avoid being acquired.
- *Mimicry*: If leading firms in their industry have merged or acquired others, executives may be more likely to consider the strategy.

Executives may overpay for a target firm. Microsoft has acquired more than 128 companies, but recently withdrew a US$44.6 billion offer of cash and stock for Yahoo. Microsoft CEO Steve Ballmer commented on the logic of the decision: "Despite our best efforts, including raising our bid by roughly $5 billion, Yahoo! has not moved toward accepting our offer. After careful consideration, we believe the economics demanded by Yahoo! do not make sense for us, and it is in the best interests of Microsoft stockholders, employees, and other stakeholders to withdraw our proposal."[3]

STRATEGIC FIT

Regardless of their category or structure, all M&As share the common goal that the value of the combined companies will be greater than the sum of the two parts. M&A success depends on the ability to achieve strategic fit. Harvard Professor Joseph Bower identifies five broad types of strategic fit, based on the relationship between the two companies and the synergies sought: overcapacity M&A, geographic roll-up M&A, product or market extension M&A, M&A as R&D, and industry convergence M&A.[4]

Overcapacity M&A

In this horizontal M&A, the two companies often competed directly, with similar product lines and markets. The new combined entity is expected to leverage synergies related to overcapacity by rationalizing operations (for example, shutting factories). This often one-time M&A can be especially difficult to execute as both companies' management groups are inclined to fight for control.

Geographic Roll-Up M&A

In a geographic roll-up the new entity seeks geographic expansion, but often keeps operating units local. For example, Banc One purchased many local banks across the United States in the 1980s. Banc One was, in turn, acquired by JPMorgan Chase & Co. in 2004.

Product or Market Extension M&A

Market-based roll-up focuses on extending a product line or international coverage. Often the two companies sell similar products but in different markets, or different products in similar markets. Brands are often a key motivation. Philip Morris purchased Kraft for US$12.9 billion—four times its book value. Philip Morris CEO Hamish Marshall justified the premium: "The future of consumer marketing belongs to companies with the strongest brands."[5]

M&A as R&D

A fourth type of strategic fit is research and development. Companies may acquire or merge with others to access technologies. Microsoft has aggressively pursued this strategy, acquiring smaller, entrepreneurial firms such as Forethought, which had presentation software that would eventually be known as PowerPoint.

Industry Convergence M&A

Finally, the new entity may be motivated by a "bet" that a new industry is emerging and the desire to have a position in this industry. For example, Viacom purchased Paramount and Blockbuster in the expectation that integrated media firms controlling both content and distribution were the wave of the future.

Figure 2. Global M&A market 2007—share by region. (*Source*: Thomson Financial)

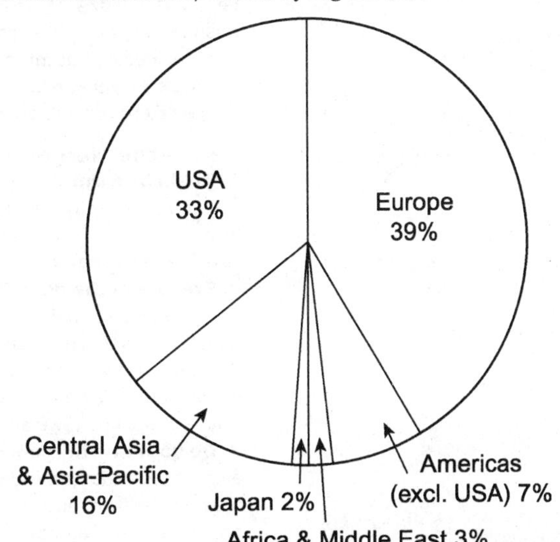

"...for as long as I'm responsible for the Mercedes-Benz brand, only over my dead body will a Mercedes be built in a Chrysler factory." DaimlerChrysler executive

  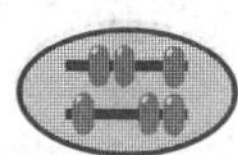   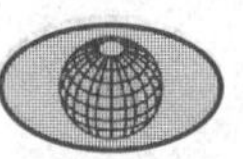 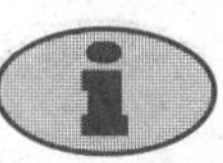  

CONCLUSION

Mergers and acquisitions can be accretive in that they increase financial performance, or dilutive in the reverse case, where a measure such as earnings per share (EPS) actually falls. It is a fact that 70% of mergers and acquisitions actually destroy value.

In implementation, M&As typically face the following critical issues:

- *Incompatible corporate cultures*: The cultures of the two companies may be inconsistent, resulting in resources being diverted away from the focal synergies.
- *Business as usual*: The target company may allow redundant staff and overlapping operations to continue, thwarting efficiency.
- *High executive turnover*: The target company may lose critical top management team leadership. A recent study reports that target companies lose 21% of their executives each year for at least ten years following an acquisition (twice the turnover experienced in nonmerged firms).
- *Neglect business at hand*: A recent McKinsey study reported that too many companies focus on integration and cost cutting, and neglect the daily business at hand and customers.

CASE STUDY

The Failed Merger of DaimlerChrysler

Germany's Daimler and the United States' Chrysler merged in 1988, creating the world's largest commercial auto manufacturer. At the time of the merger, Daimler's CEO claimed that the merger of a luxury car maker (Daimler) with a mass-market brand (Chrysler) would become the world's most profitable auto manufacturer due to new economies of scale and scope across brands, product niches, manufacturing expertise, and distribution networks. For example, it was hoped Daimler's high-end manufacturing expertise and worldwide network would help to distribute Chrysler products and compete successfully against increasingly strong Asian competitors, especially Toyota and Honda. However, at the time, not all executives were positive. One DaimlerChrysler executive was quoted as saying, "It is unthinkable for a Chrysler car to be built in a Mercedes-Benz factory, and for as long as I'm responsible for the Mercedes-Benz brand, only over my dead body will a Mercedes be built in a Chrysler factory."[6]

By the end of 2003 DaimlerChrysler's market capitalization was just US$38 billion, significantly lower than the pre-merger US$47 billion in 1998. Despite product costs, DaimlerChrysler was unable to realize expected synergies. Furthermore, many competitors followed Chrysler's lead, introducing minivans, pickup trucks, and SUVs that eroded Chrysler's formerly attractive market share. Further barriers to success came with management and national cultural differences: Daimler's mostly German management used approaches that did not go down well with Chrysler managers. By early 2003 most of Chrysler's top executive team had left the firm.

Seven years after the merger the picture became more positive, with Chrysler contributing one-third of the company's earnings in the first half of 2005. Dieter Zetsche was promoted to chairman of DaimlerChrysler's board. By August, market capitalization reached US$54 billion and worldwide sales of the newly launched Mercedes were up 9%. Still, the American market proved difficult, with the three major American auto manufacturers experiencing significantly declining sales. Meanwhile, Toyota and Honda sales were up 16% and 10% respectively, gaining in the upscale market DaimlerChrysler had hoped to dominate.

In the summer of 2006, DaimlerChrysler sought to make a positive out of a negative in its US television advertisements, with Zetsche presented as an amusing cultural misfit to America. Still the company faced high labor and health care costs and soaring fuel costs. By April 2007, DaimlerChrysler confirmed that buyers were being sought, as German investors declared "this marriage made in heaven turned out to be a complete failure." In fact, some suggested that Daimler could itself become a takeover target if it did not sell Chrysler. By May, DaimlerChrysler had paid Cerberus Capital Management, a private equity investment firm, US$650 million to end its exposure to health care and other costs as well as to ongoing operational losses.

▸▸ MAKING IT HAPPEN

Despite the grim statistics, several companies are skilled M&A executors. For example, General Electric has integrated as many as 534 companies over a six-year period, and Kellogg's delivered a 25% return to stockholders after purchasing Keebler.[7] The following are key steps to facilitating a successful process before and after a merger:

Before the Merger

1. Begin by formulating a clear and convincing strategy. Strategists must first develop a compelling and sustainable strategy. Key questions include: What is your firm's strategy? What role does the M&A play in this strategy? What is the vision of the strategy of the new entity?

2. Preassess the deal. Prior to signing a memo of understanding, managers should examine operational and management issues and risks. Seek answers to the following questions: Is this the right target? What is the compelling logic behind this deal? What is the value? How would we communicate this value to the board of directors and other key stakeholders? What will our strategy be for bidding and negotiations? How much are we willing to spend? If we are successful, how can we accelerate integration?

3. Do your due diligence. Executives must acquire and analyze as much information as possible about potential synergies. In addition to managers across key functional areas in the firm, outside experts can be brought in to help appraise answers in the preassessment, and especially to challenge assumptions, by asking questions such as:

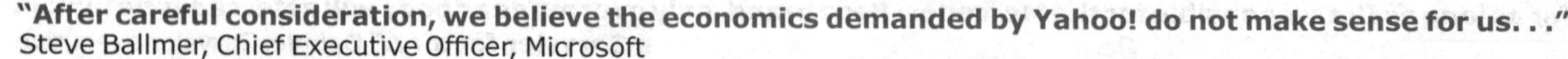

"After careful consideration, we believe the economics demanded by Yahoo! do not make sense for us. . ."
Steve Ballmer, Chief Executive Officer, Microsoft

  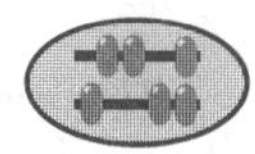 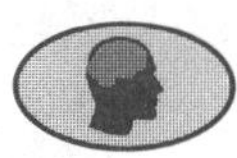  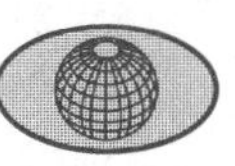   

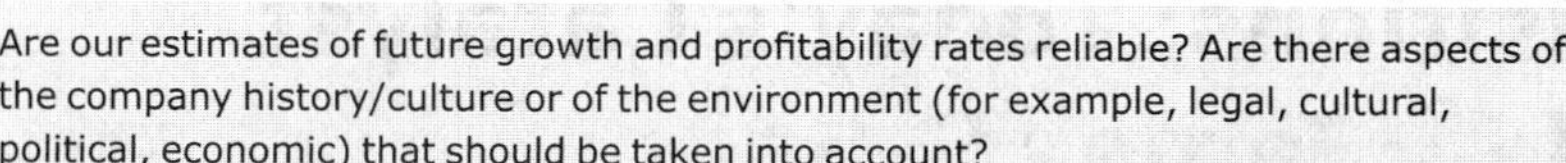

Are our estimates of future growth and profitability rates reliable? Are there aspects of the company history/culture or of the environment (for example, legal, cultural, political, economic) that should be taken into account?

4. Devise a workable plan. Formulate plans that take into account some of the following: What is our new entity's organizational structure? Who is in charge? What products will be taken forward? How will we manage company accounts? What IT systems will we use?

5. Communicate. M&A transactions tend to be viewed favorably when executives can convincingly discuss integration plans, both internally and externally. Managers should be prepared to answer the questions identified above, as well as: How can we prepare our people psychologically for the deal? What value will be created? What are the priorities for integration? What are the primary risks? How will progress be measured? How will we address any surprises?

After the Deal

6. Establish leadership. The new entity will require the quick identification and buy-in of managers, especially at top and middle levels. Ask: Who will lead the new entity? Do we have buy-in and support from the right people?

7. Manage the culture and respect the employees of the merged/acquired company. An atmosphere of respect and tolerance can aid the speed and ease of integration. Executives should formulate plans that address the following concerns: How can we encourage the best and brightest employees to stay on in the new entity? How can we build loyalty and buy-in?

8. Explore new growth opportunities. Long-run performance is linked to identifying and acting on both internal and external growth opportunities. Managers should seek out any untapped growth opportunities in the new entity.

9. Exploit early wins. To build momentum, the new entity should actively seek early wins and communicate these. To identify them, consider whether there early wins in sales, knowledge management, or the work environment.

10. Focus on the customer. To survive, firms must create value for customers. Managers must continue to ask: Are we at risk of losing customers? Are our salespeople informed about the new entity? Can our salespeople get our customers excited about the new entity?

▸▸ MORE INFO

Books:

Bruner, Robert F. *Deals from Hell: M&A Lessons That Rise Above the Ashes.* Hoboken, NJ: Wiley, 2005.

Galpin, Timothy J., and Mark Herndon. *The Complete Guide to Mergers and Acquisitions: Process Tools to Support M&A Integration at Every Level.* San Francisco, CA: Jossey-Bass, 2007.

Miller, Edwin L. *Mergers and Acquisitions: A Step-by-Step Legal and Practical Guide.* Hoboken, NJ: Wiley, 2008.

Sadtler, David, David Smith, and Andrew Campbell. *Smarter Acquisitions: Ten Steps to Successful Deals.* Harlow, UK: Pearson Education, 2008.

Websites:

Google Scholar articles—search on terms "mergers and acquisitions" or "M&A": scholar.google.com

Yahoo! Finance M&A news: biz.yahoo.com/topic/m-a

NOTES

1 Firstbrook, Caroline. "Transnational mergers and acquisitions: How to beat the odds of disaster." *Journal of Business Strategy* 28:1 (2007): 53–56.

2 Quoted on ThinkExist.com: thinkexist.com/quotation/this_is_a_decisive_move_that_accelerates_our/346964.html

3 Smalley, Tim. "Microsoft withdraws from Yahoo! acquisition." *Bit-tech.net* (May 5, 2008).

4 Bower, J. L. "Not all M&As are alike—and that matters." *Harvard Business Review* 79:3 (2001): 92–101.

5 Biggar, J. M., and E. Selame. "Building brand assets." *Chief Executive* 78 (1992): 36–39. Cited in Bahadir, S. Cem, Sundar G. Bharadwaj, and Rajendra K. Srivastava. "Financial value of brands in mergers and acquisitions: Is value in the eye of the beholder?" *Journal of Marketing* 72:6 (2008): 147–154.

6 Waller, David. *Wheels on Fire: The Amazing Inside Story of the Daimler–Chrysler Merger.* London: Hodder & Stoughton, 2001, p. 243.

7 Perry, Jeffrey S., and Thomas J. Herd. "Mergers and acquisitions: Reducing M&A risk through improved due diligence." *Strategy & Leadership* 32:2 (2004): 12–19.

"Some M&As can be quite profitable, for example, Kellogg's acquisition of Keebler delivered a 25% return to the shareholders."

     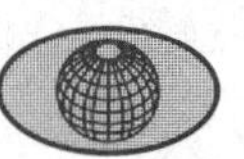   

Mergers and Acquisitions: Today's Catalyst Is Working Capital by James S. Sagner

EXECUTIVE SUMMARY

- In developed economies M&As are now used to acquire balance sheet assets, particularly cash hoards and other working capital; previously, M&A was oriented to strategic diversification or integration.
- Although the volume of deals is down due to global economic conditions, the premiums paid for companies remain robust.
- Acquirers appear to understand the risk inherent in these transactions, including the threat of investigation by US, EU, and Japanese regulators.
- Until the recent problems with lines of credit provided by banks, many companies held excessive amounts of liquidity, making them vulnerable to unfriendly takeovers.
- Various consulting companies have international practices in working capital management, including advising on mergers and assisting management to achieve efficiencies after the deal is completed.
- Global M&A looks for the following characteristics: a high current assets-to-revenue relationship; a holding of cash that is not likely to be applied to business operations; and a proven income stream that should provide adequate cash flow to pay down borrowings used to provide financing for an acquisition.

INTRODUCTION

Merger and acquisition (M&A) activities in developed countries once focused on strategic transactions for diversification or for vertical or horizontal integration. While that continues to be the situation in the developing economies, the M&A game in the United States, Western Europe, and Japan is often either to gain balance sheet assets, particularly hoards of underperforming cash, or to improve the acquired company's working capital management. It's a complete revolution in the way companies and investment bankers look at candidates for M&A. What's going on?

CHANGES IN THE M&A LANDSCAPE

Although the first half of 2007 saw $2.7 trillion in worldwide M&A activity, the various credit problems in the United States and Europe saw a significant reduction in total activity for the year.[1] Some deals have been announced in the first half of 2008, with many focusing on growth through the acquisition of competitors. The most recent twelve months (through October 2008) show $3.7 trillion in global M&A activity, which is lower than the previous two years and roughly equivalent to 2005.[2] The premiums being paid for companies remain strong, with deals averaging about 25% above the publicly traded share price.[3] The weak American dollar has brought several foreign buyers to the United States in the search for access to attractive markets and technologies.

Some of the past M&A hype has been tempered by a better understanding of the risk of these transactions, as documented by such publications as *BusinessWeek*[4] and as experienced in the loss of value to investors.[5] The lure of expanding markets, product lines, technologies, and customer bases drove much of M&A through the last three decades of the 20th century. Many of these hopes turned out to be illusory as mergers underperformed or failed due to incompatibilities between the marketing, production, engineering, financial, and systems functions of the participants.

Some mergers came under investigation by one or more US regulatory agencies, and were delayed, rejected, or abandoned. For example, the Federal Trade Commission has acted against "threats" of raised concentration in markets for frozen pizza, carburetor kits, urological catheters, and casket parts. The Justice Department hit mergers threatening to raise concentration in markets for frozen dessert pies, artificial Christmas trees, vandal-resistant plumbing fixtures used in prisons, local towel rental services, drapery hardware, and commercial trash hauling in Dallas.[6] The European Commission has been even more rigorous in its merger reviews than the two US agencies.

Research by Towers Perrin and the Cass Business School finds that the most recent era of M&A deals has created value, rather than led to its destruction as in earlier periods.[7] The emphasis has switched to the execution of the deal and a focus on improved financial performance.

Although strategic expansion will continue to be of interest despite the threat of antitrust review, future M&A practice will likely focus on two completely different attractions that avoid the regulators' microscope:

- underused liquidity on balance sheets, offering opportunities for the acquirer to redeploy cash in productive activities;
- inefficient working capital management, leading to opportunities to improve the utilization of current assets and liabilities.

UNDERUSED LIQUIDITY

Recent studies illustrate the predicament that many businesses currently face: too much money on balance sheets and too few attractive capital investments. The Association for Financial Professionals (AFP) conducted a recent study which reported that 36% of respondents held larger amounts of short-term investments than six months earlier, that is, from November 2006 to May 2007.[8] Furthermore, the expectation was that these balances would grow over the subsequent year. A second study reports that cash balances have expanded 50% in eight years, with the total of cash and short-term investments at $5.25 trillion at year-end 2007.[9]

As of mid-2008, the typical public company had a weighted average cost of capital of just over 10%; see Table for the calculation. A company with cash or near-cash investments can only earn about 2% pre-tax on these assets at the current rates available,[10] or about 1% after tax. Thus, companies holding cash incur a direct *loss* of nearly 9% on that asset without receiving any possible strategic gain. Acquirers can use this cash to pay down debt, acquire stock in the open market, increase dividends, or expand business operations. In fact M&A deals are often financed by loans made against the assets and cash flow of the acquired company. For example, the 2006 deal involving the hospital company HCA Inc. involved only $5.5 billion in cash,

Table 1. Illustration of cost-of-capital calculation

	Balance sheet portion	After-tax costs	Weighted component costs
Debt	40%	0.056*	0.022
Equity	60%	0.140†	0.084
	100%		0.106

* Pre-tax 8% less corporate tax rate.

† 12% growth + 2% dividend.

"The eighties was an era when many companies were asset rich and cash poor." Nicola Horlick

  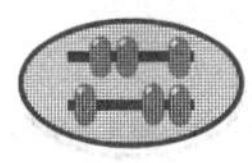   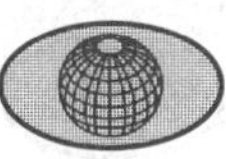   

with the balance of the $33 billion price financed by the cash and future income of HCA.

INEFFICIENT WORKING CAPITAL MANAGEMENT

Working capital (WC) is defined as current assets less current liabilities; in this section we will focus on current assets other than cash. In the last four decades of the previous century, the percentage of WC as a percentage of sales declined by three-fourths.[11] Although this represents a significant improvement in the management of these balance sheet accounts, estimates are that the total of excess WC may still exceed $600 billion.[12]

There are merger opportunities in acquiring companies with excess WC and managing these accounts so that it approaches as close to zero as possible. The concept of WC as a hindrance to financial performance is a complete change in attitude from the conventional wisdom before the turn of the 21st century. However, WC has never contributed to a company's profits; instead, it just sits on the balance sheet awaiting disposition. The Checklist box gives some ideas for working capital management.

Various consulting companies have developed international practices in working capital management, including advising on mergers and assisting management to achieve efficiencies once the deal has been completed. For example, REI is a US-based advisery services organization that has developed a global brand in WC services. REI has enabled clients in more than 60 countries to free up over $25 billion through optimization of working capital in the last 10 years alone. FTI Consulting offers an array of services designed to help companies address critical issues and improve performance prior to engaging advisery services for acquisitions, divestitures, and recapitalizations. There are several other firms that support M&A analyses while assisting the new management to squeeze efficiencies out of the current asset and/or current liability portions of the balance sheet.

CHECKLIST OF WORKING CAPITAL IDEAS

Accounts Receivable

The credit and collection process, no matter how aggressive, inevitably results in some uncollectable amounts. When faced with the cost of the credit review process, bad debt expenses, and the cost of credit and collections, some businesses outsource their collection activities to a factor. Factors purchase or lend money on accounts receivable based on an evaluation of the creditworthiness of prospective customers of the business calculated as a discount from the sale amount, usually about 3 to 4%. That is, the factor will receive the entire sales amount, the selling company having received 96 to 97% at the time that the buyer was accepted by the factor.

Receivables Collateralization

In collateralization, a receivables package is offered as a security to investors. The critical element is a periodic, predictable flow of cash in payment of debts, such as credit cards, automobile loans, equipment leases, healthcare receivables, health club fees, and airline ticket receivables.

The market for public collateralizations is in the hundreds of billions of dollars, which has driven the required interest return to investors to become competitive with bank lending arrangements. Initial costs are higher than bank loans because the services of several professionals are required: attorneys; commercial and/or investment bankers; accountants; rating agencies (when ratings are required); and income servicers. However, the advantage of receivables collateralization is substantial—the transformation of receivables into cash.

Inventory

Just-in-time (JIT) requires that required materials be in the place of manufacture or assembly at the appropriate time to minimize excess inventory and to reduce wastage and expense. JIT succeeds when there are: a limited number of transactions; few "disturbances" due to unscheduled downtime, depending instead on periodic maintenance; the grouping of production processes to reduce the movement of work-in-process; and a significant focus on quality control (QC). QC minimizes downtime and the holding of buffer or safety stock to replace defective materials.

In traditional JIT, the company owns the inventory of components and parts, assuring access as the next production operation begins. JIT as currently practiced places the materials at the manufacturing or assembly site, but title remains with the vendor until production begins. This relationship requires suppliers to optimize the stock of inventory, holding only those items that have been specified or are known to be required based on a statistical analysis of purchasing history. Both the provider and the user of materials are forced to develop a strong partnering attitude and minimize the adversarial stance often observed between purchasing counterparties.

Accounts Payable

Inefficient payables pervade US business. Invoices presented for payment should be matched against purchase orders and receiving reports to determine that the vendor has met the terms and conditions of the order, and that materials were received in good condition and in the correct amount. In practice, invoices are often paid without ascertaining that all requirements have been met. In about one-third of all payables situations, no purchase order was ever issued, nor was there a contract or other written agreement as to price or specifications.

A substantial number of companies have inadequate policies regarding appropriate purchasing and accounts payables practices. For example:

- Should the payment be released on the due date or some specified number of days after the due date?
- Are all cash discounts to be taken, or only those that provide a stipulated discount?
- Can the requesting business unit choose the supplier, or does purchasing have the authority to select vendors so as to maximize volume pricing?
- Has purchasing determined that approved vendors are legitimate businesses, with a suitable record of providing goods and services to the business community?

LET'S LOOK AT A DEAL

The $90 billion hostile takeover by Pfizer of Warner-Lambert (Warner), completed in 2000, was hyped as a traditional horizontal integration of two powerful pharmaceutical companies. Clearly, Pfizer was acquiring a significant asset in Lipitor, Warner's cholesterol-lowering drug, and established cost savings through headcount reductions. Stock analysts even made statements to the effect that the deal was strictly "...for strategic reasons—for Lipitor, for the therapeutic enhancements Warner-Lambert brings, and for the sheer marketing clout..."[13]

However, the merger was motivated in large part by financial considerations. In 1999 Warner reported cash and short-term investments of $1.943 billion, equivalent to 17.0% of total assets of $11.442 billion, versus 13.8% for the industry. Pfizer was buying the cash hoard, which was $360 million more than the rest of the industry required for the assets carried. Pfizer was also buying an excellent balance sheet, including a current ratio of 1.5 times and current assets as a percentage of sales of 44.0%. And Warner earned $2.441 billion before taxes in 1999, a very healthy 18.9% of sales versus 9.6% for the industry.

"The very best takeovers are thoroughly hostile. I've never seen a really good company taken over. I've only seen bad ones." James Goldsmith

     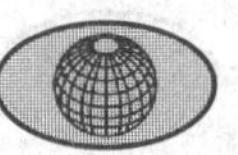   

TIPS FOR CFOS ON FUTURE M&A DEALS

The flood of US dollars in foreign ownership continues to grow due to the persistent balance of payments deficits in the United States. Global investors looking for properties will be looking at public companies with the following characteristics:

- a high current assets-to-revenue relationship, particularly where the current ratio exceeds the average for the industry;
- a cash (and near-cash) hoard that is not likely to be applied to business operations and is unlikely to be used for dividends or stock repurchases;
- a proven income stream that should provide adequate cash flow to pay down borrowings used to provide partial financing for an acquisition.

Furthermore, there is a trend toward M&A that is not strategic within an industry, meaning that a hostile or friendly approach can come from anywhere at any time.

Too many companies hoard cash while waiting for capital projects with superior returns. In fact, those opportunities may never appear. Financial analysts are beginning to recognize that worthwhile capital investments are unusual and are likely to be short-lived. In other words, the reality of international competition shortens any competitive advantage a company may gain, unless protected by patents or other exclusive arrangements. To quote a leading finance text:

> "It is a basic principle of economics that positive NPV [net present value] investments will be rare in a highly competitive environment. Therefore, proposals that appear to show significant value in the face of stiff competition are particularly troublesome, and the likely reaction of the competition to any innovations must be closely examined."[14]

Savvy outsiders can analyze the financial statements of targeted companies and, with the help of their investment bankers, take friendly or hostile action to seize a financially inefficient business.

▸▸ MORE INFO

See Also:

★ Acquisition Integration: How to Do It Successfully (pp. 390–391)
★ Coping with Equity Market Reactions to M&A Transactions (pp. 392–394)
★ Mergers and Acquisitions: Patterns, Motives, and Strategic Fit (pp. 418–421)
✔ Achieving Success in International Acquisitions (p. 954)
✔ Acquiring a Company (p. 955)
✔ Acquisition Accounting (p. 956)
✔ Planning the Acquisition Process (p. 959)
✔ Structuring M&A Deals and Tax Planning (p. 962)
✔ Using IRR for M&A Financing (p. 964)
✔ Using the Market-Value Method for Acquisitions (p. 966)

NOTES

An earlier version of this article appeared as "Why working capital drives M&A today." *Journal of Corporate Accounting & Finance* 18:2 (2007): 41–45. Used by permission of John Wiley & Sons, Inc.

1 *Weekly Corporate Growth Report* (December 24, 2007).

2 Thomson Reuters, as reported in "Investment banking deals." *The Economist* (November 8, 2008): 118.

3 Data from June 2008; see "M&A premiums up despite slowdown" at www.businessweek.com/investing/insights/blog/archives/2008/06/despite_the_ma.html

4 David Henry, "Mergers: Why most big deals don't pay off." *BusinessWeek* (October 14, 2002). Online at: www.businessweek.com/magazine/content/02_41/b3803001.htm

5 According to *BusinessWeek*, 61% of acquirers in a merger destroyed their stockholders' wealth (*ibid.*).

6 These situations were noted by Frederick M. Rowe on pp. 1512–13 of "The decline of antitrust and the delusions of models: The Faustian pact of law and economics." *Georgetown Law Journal* 72:5 (1984): 1511–1570. For a review of American antitrust policy, see James S. Sagner. "Antitrust as frontier justice: Is it time to retire the sheriff?" *Business and Society Review* 111 (March 2006): 37–54.

7 At www.innovations-report.com/html/reports/economy_finances/report-112476.html (June 17, 2008). Towers Perrin is a global consulting firm that specializes in human capital strategy, program design and management, and risk and capital management.

8 AFP in conjunction with Citigroup. *2007 AFP liquidity survey: Report of survey results.* Online at: www.afponline.org/pub/pdf/Liquidity_2007.pdf

9 See: www.treasurystrategies.com/resources/pressReleases/08CorpLiquidityPR.pdf

10 Commercial paper rates for up to 120 days were 2.50% in mid-June 2008 according to the *Wall Street Journal* (rates are from June 10, 2008, as quoted on page C10).

11 Standard and Poor's *Financial Analyst's Handbook*, 2002.

12 Tim Reason. "Capital ideas: The 2005 working capital survey." *CFO Magazine* (September 1, 2005). Online at: www.cfo.com/article.cfm/4315504?f=related

13 Comment by Martyn Postle, Cambridge Pharma Consultancy (UK), reported in David Shook. "Pfizer-Warner: One drug merger that might just deliver." *BusinessWeek* (May 17, 2000). Online at: www.businessweek.com/investor/content/eemi/emi0517a.html?chan=search

14 Ross, Stephen A., Randolph W. Westerfield, and Bradford D. Jordan. *Essentials of Corporate Finance*. 5th ed. Boston, MA: McGraw-Hill/Irwin, 2007, p. 275.

"Chief executives seem no more able to resist their biological urge to merge, than dogs can resist chasing rabbits." Philip Coggan

  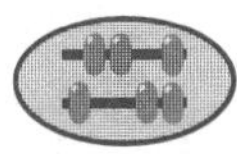   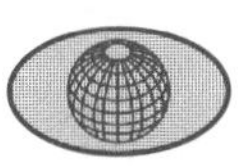   

Valuing Start-Ups by Aswath Damodaran

EXECUTIVE SUMMARY

- Young and start-up companies pose the most problems in valuation, for a variety of reasons.
- Start-ups have a limited history, are generally not publicly traded, and often don't survive to become successful commercial enterprises.
- Faced with daunting estimation challenges, analysts often fall back on simplistic forecasts of revenues and earnings, coupled with high discount rates, to capture the high failure rate.
- In this article I suggest that traditional valuation models can be used to yield better estimates of the value of these firms.

INTRODUCTION

Although the fundamentals of valuation are straightforward, the challenges in valuing companies shift as they move through their life cycle: from the initial idea and start-up business, often privately owned, to young growth companies, either public or on the verge of going public, to mature companies with diverse products and serving different markets, and finally to companies in decline, marking time until they disappear. At each stage we may be called on to estimate the same inputs—cash flows, growth rates, and discount rates—but with varying amounts of information and different degrees of precision.

DETERMINANTS OF VALUE

If we accept the premise that the value of a business is the present value of the expected cash flows from its assets, there are four broad questions that we need to answer in order to value any business:

1. What are the cash flows generated by existing assets?

If a firm has significant investments that it has already made, the first inputs into valuation are the cash flows from these existing assets. In practical terms, this requires estimates of: how much the firm generated in earnings and cash flows from these assets in the most recent period; how much growth (if any) is expected in these earnings/cash flows over time; and how long the assets will continue to generate cash flows.

2. How much value will be added by future investments?

For some companies, the bulk of the value will be derived from investments they are expected to make in the future. To estimate the value added by these investments, you have to make judgments on both the magnitude of these new investments relative to the earnings from existing assets; and the quality of the new investments, measured in terms of excess returns, i.e. the returns the firm makes on the investments over and above the cost of funding them.

3. How risky are the cash flows, and what are the consequences for discount rates?

Neither the cash flows from existing assets nor the cash flows from growth investments are guaranteed. When valuing these cash flows, we have to consider risk somewhere, and the discount rate is usually the vehicle we use. Higher discount rates are used to discount riskier cash flows, and thus give them a lower value than more predictable cash flows.

4. When will the firm become mature?

The question of when a firm is mature (i.e. when the growth in earnings/cash flows is sustainable forever) is relevant because it determines the length of the high-growth period and the value we attach to the firm at the end of the period (the terminal value). It is a question that may be easy to answer for a few firms, including larger and more stable firms that are either already mature businesses or close to it, and firms that derive their growth from a single competitive advantage with an expiration date (for instance, a patent).

A framework for valuing any business that takes into account these four considerations is shown in Figure 1.

Although these questions may not change as we value individual firms, the ease with which we can answer them may change, not only as we look across firms at a point in time, but also across time—even for the same firm.

VALUING YOUNG COMPANIES

Every business starts with an idea stimulated by a market need that an entrepreneur sees (or thinks that he or she sees) and a way of filling that need. Although many ideas go nowhere, some individuals take the next step of investing in the idea.

The capital to finance the project usually comes from personal funds (from savings, friends, and family), and if things work out as planned the result is a commercial product or service. If the product or service finds a ready market, the business will usually need more capital, and the providers of this are often venture capitalists, who provide funds in return for a share of the equity in the business. Building on the most optimistic assumptions, success for the investors in the business may ultimately be manifested as a public offering to the market or sale to a larger entity.

ESTIMATION ISSUES

At each stage in the process we need estimates of value. At the idea stage, the value may never be put down on paper, but it is the potential of realizing this value that induces the entrepreneur to invest time and money in developing the idea. At subsequent stages of the capital-raising process, valuations become more important because they determine what share of ownership the entrepreneur will have to give up in return for external funding. At the time of the public offering, the valuation is key to determining the offering price.

From the template for valuation that we developed in the last section, it is easy to see why young companies also pose the most daunting challenges. There are few or

Figure 1. The fundamental questions in valuation

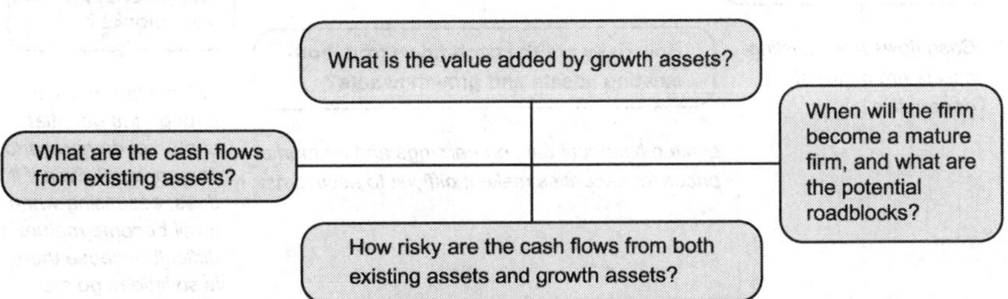

What is the value added by growth assets?
What are the cash flows from existing assets?
When will the firm become a mature firm, and what are the potential roadblocks?
How risky are the cash flows from both existing assets and growth assets?

  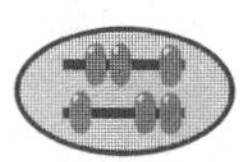   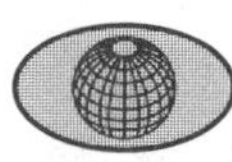   

no existing assets, and almost all of the value is based on the expectations of future growth. The current financial statements of the firm provide no clues about the potential margins and returns that may be generated in the future, and there are few historical data that can be used to develop risk measures.

To complete our consideration of estimation problems, we should remember that many young firms do not make it to the stable growth stage. Estimating when this will happen for firms that do survive is difficult. In addition, these firms are often dependent on one or a few key people for their success, and losing them can have a significant effect on value.

Figure 2 summarizes these valuation challenges.

Given these problems, it is not surprising that analysts often fall back on simplistic measures of value, guesstimates, or on rules of thumb to value young companies. In the process, though, they risk making serious valuation errors.

MEETING THE ESTIMATION CHALLENGE

Given the challenges we face in estimating cash flows and discount rates for the purpose of valuing young companies, it should come as no surprise that many analysts use shortcuts, such as applying multiples to expected future earnings or revenues, to obtain dubious estimates of value. We believe that staying within the valuation framework and making the best estimates of cash flows is still the best approach.

CASH FLOWS AND GROWTH RATES

For many young companies, the biggest challenge in estimating future cash flows is that there is no historical base of any substance to build on. However, we can still estimate expected cash flows using one of two approaches:

Top-Down Approach

In this approach, we begin with the potential market for the firm's products and services and work backwards:

- Estimate the share of this market which the firm hopes to gain in the future and how quickly it can reach this share; this gives expected revenues in future years.
- Make a judgment on the profit margins the firm should see once it attains the targeted market share; this provides the earnings that it hopes to generate each period.
- Finally, evaluate what the firm needs to invest to accomplish this objective; this represents the capital that it has to reinvest in the business, which is a cash drain each year.

Generally, as the firm's revenues grow and it moves toward the target margins, we should expect to see losses in the earlier years become profits in the later ones. With high growth, it is entirely possible that cash flows will stay negative even after profits turn the corner, since the growth will require substantial reinvestment. As growth subsides in the later years, the reinvestment will also decline and cash flows will become positive.

The key to succeeding with this approach is getting the potential market share and target margin right, and making realistic assumptions about reinvestment needs.

Bottom-Up Approach

For those who believe that the top-down approach is too ambitious, the alternative is to start with what the young company can generate as output, given its resource constraints, and make estimates of the revenues and profits that will be generated as a consequence. This is more akin to a capital budgeting exercise than to a valuation, and the valuation will depend on the quality of the forecasts of earnings and cash flows.

The projected earnings and cash flows from both approaches are dependent on the promoters of the company not only being able to come up with a product or service that meets a need, but also that they can adapt to unexpected circumstances at the same time as delivering their forecast results.

Figure 2. Estimation issues for young and start-up companies

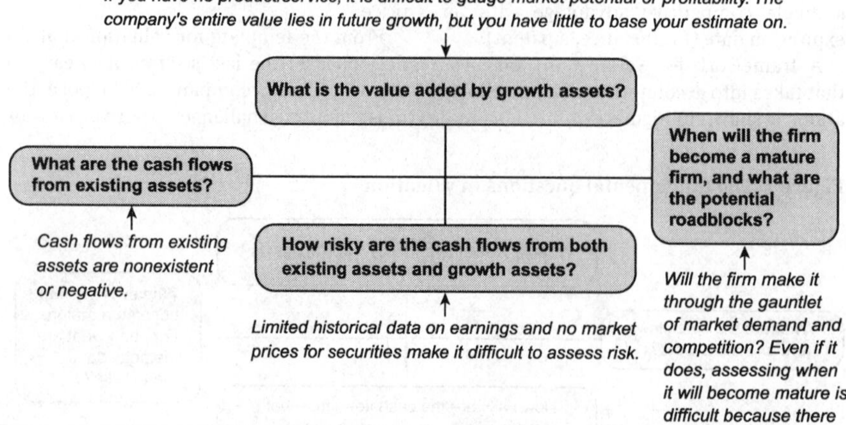
Making judgments on revenues/profits is difficult because you cannot draw on history.
If you have no product/service, it is difficult to gauge market potential or profitability. The company's entire value lies in future growth, but you have little to base your estimate on.
What is the value added by growth assets?
What are the cash flows from existing assets?
When will the firm become a mature firm, and what are the potential roadblocks?
Cash flows from existing assets are nonexistent or negative.
How risky are the cash flows from both existing assets and growth assets?
Limited historical data on earnings and no market prices for securities make it difficult to assess risk.
Will the firm make it through the gauntlet of market demand and competition? Even if it does, assessing when it will become mature is difficult because there is so little to go on.

DISCOUNT RATES

The absence of historical data on stock prices and earnings makes it difficult, but not impossible, to analyze the risk of young companies. To make realistic estimates of discount rates, we need to be able to do the following:

Assess Risk from the Right Viewpoint

The risk in an investment can vary, depending on the point of view that we bring to the assessment.

- For the founder/owner who has his or her entire wealth invested in the private business, all risk that the firm is exposed to is relevant risk.
- For a venture capitalist who takes a stake in this private business as part of a portfolio of many such investments, there is a diversification effect, where some of the risk will be averaged out in the portfolio.
- For an investor in a public market, the focus will narrow even more, to only the risk that cannot be diversified away in a portfolio.

As a general rule, the discount rates we obtain using conventional risk and return models, which are built for the last setting, will understate the risk (and discount rates) for young companies, which are usually privately held.

Focus on the Business/Sector, Not on the Company

Since young firms have little operating history and are generally not publicly traded, it is pointless trying to estimate risk parameters by looking at the firm's history. We can get a much better handle on risk by looking at the sector or business of which the firm is a part and evaluating the riskiness of publicly traded firms in the same sector at different stages in the life cycle.

  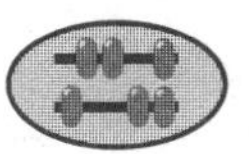 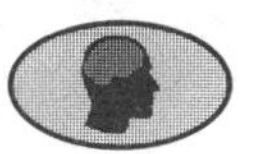  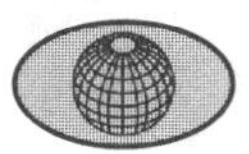   

Adjust Risk Measures and Discount Rates as the Firm Matures (At Least in the Projections)

Our task in valuation is not to assess the risk of a young firm today, but to evaluate how that risk will change as the firm matures. In other words, as revenues grow and margins move toward target levels, the risk that we assess in a company and the discount rates we use should change consistently: lower growth generally should be coupled with lower risk and discount rates.

TERMINAL VALUE

In most discounted cash flow valuations, it is the terminal value that delivers the biggest portion of the value. With young firms this will be doubly so, partly because the cash flows in the early years are often negative and partly because the anticipated growth will increase the size of the firm over time.

Consider Scaling Effects and Competition

When firms are young, revenue growth rates can be very high, reflecting the fact that the revenues being grown are small. As revenues grow, the growth rate will slow, and assessing how quickly this will happen becomes a key part of valuing young companies. In general, the speed with which revenue growth will decelerate as firms get larger will depend on the size of the overall market and the intensity of competition. In smaller markets, and with more intense competition, revenue growth will decline much more quickly and stable growth will approach sooner.

Change the Firm's Characteristics to Reflect Growth

As a firm moves from start-up to stable growth, it is not just the growth rate that changes, but the other characteristics of the firm as well. In addition to the discount rate adjustments we mentioned in the last section, mature firms will also tend to reinvest less and have lower excess returns than younger firms.

Consider the Possibility That the Firm Will Not Make It

Most young firms do not make it to become mature firms. To get realistic estimates of value for young firms, we should consider the likelihood that they will not make it through the life cycle, either because key employees leave or because of capital constraints.

CONCLUSION

It is far more difficult to estimate the value of a young company than a mature company. There is little history to draw on and the firm's survival is often open to question. However, that should not lead us to abandon valuation fundamentals or to adopt fresh paradigms. With a little persistence, we can still estimate the value of young companies. These values may not be precise, but the lack of precision reflects real uncertainty about the future of these companies.

▸▸ MAKING IT HAPPEN

To value young growth companies:

- Assess the potential market and the company's likely market share (if successful).
- Estimate what the company has to do (in terms of operations and investments) to get to this market share.
- Estimate the cash flows based on these assessments.
- Evaluate the risk in the investments and also how it will change as the company goes through the growth cycle, and convert the risk into discount rates.
- Value the business and the various equity stakes in that business.

▸▸ MORE INFO

Books:

Damodaran, Aswath. *The Dark Side of Valuation; Valuing Old Tech, New Tech, and New Economy Companies*. Upper Saddle River, NJ: Prentice Hall, 2001.

Gompers, Paul, and Josh Lerner. *The Venture Capital Cycle.* 2nd ed. Cambridge, MA: MIT Press, 2006.

Metrick, Andrew. *Venture Capital and the Finance of Innovation*. Hoboken, NJ: Wiley, 2007.

Guidelines:

Multiple authors. "International private equity and venture capital valuation guidelines." October 2006. Online from: www.privateequityvaluation.com

Website:

Damodaran Online: www.damodaran.com

"I'm a single, straight billionaire in Manhattan. What do you think? It's a wet dream." Michael Bloomberg

  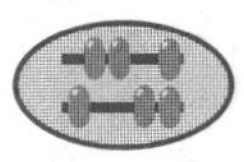   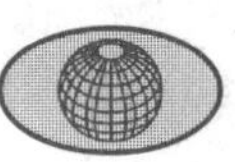   

Why Mergers Fail and How to Prevent It by Susan Cartwright

EXECUTIVE SUMMARY

- Mergers and acquisitions (M&A) are increasing in frequency, yet at least half fail to meet financial expectations.
- The United States and the United Kingdom continue to dominate M&A activity. As the number of cross-border deals increases, however, many other national players are entering the field, further highlighting the issue of cultural compatibility.
- Financial and strategic factors alone are insufficient to explain the high rate of failure; greater account needs to be taken of human factors.
- The successful management of integrating people and their organizational cultures is the key to achieving desired M&A outcomes.

INTRODUCTION

The incidence of M&A has continued to increase significantly during the last decade, both domestically and internationally. The sectors most affected by M&A activity have been service- and knowledge-based industries such as banking, insurance, pharmaceuticals, and leisure. Although M&A is a popular means of increasing or protecting market share, the strategy does not always deliver what is expected in terms of increased profitability or economies of scale. While the motives for merger can variously be described as practical, psychological, or opportunist, the objective of all related M&A is to achieve synergy, or what is commonly referred to as the 2 + 2 = 5 effect. However, as many organizations learn to their cost, the mere recognition of potential synergy is no guarantee that the combination will actually realize that potential.

MERGER FAILURE RATES

The burning question remains—why do so many mergers fail to live up to stockholder expectations? In the short term, many seemingly successful acquisitions look good, but disappointing productivity levels are often masked by one-time cost savings, asset disposals, or astute tax maneuvers that inflate balance-sheet figures during the first few years.

Merger gains are notoriously difficult to assess. There are problems in selecting appropriate indices to make any assessment, as well as difficulties in deciding on a suitable measurement period. Typically, the criteria selected by analysts are:

- profit-to-earning ratios;
- stock-price fluctuations;
- managerial assessments.

Irrespective of the evaluation method selected, the evidence on M&A performance is consistent in suggesting that a high proportion of M&As are financially unsuccessful. US sources place merger failure rates as high as 80%, with evidence indicating that around half of mergers fail to meet financial expectations. A much-cited McKinsey study presents evidence that most organizations would have received a better return on their investment if they had merely banked their money instead of buying another company. Consequently, many commentators have concluded that the true beneficiaries from M&A activity are those who sell their shares when deals are announced, and the marriage brokers—the bankers, lawyers, and accountants—who arrange, advise, and execute the deals.

TRADITIONAL REASONS FOR MERGER FAILURE

M&A is still regarded by many decision makers as an exclusively rational, financial, and strategic activity, and not as a human collaboration. Financial and strategic considerations, along with price and availability, therefore dominate target selection, overriding the soft issues such as people and cultural fit. Explanations of merger failure or underperformance tend to focus on reexamining the factors that prompted the initial selection decision, for example:

- payment of an overinflated price for the acquired company;
- poor strategic fit;
- failure to achieve potential economies of scale because of financial mismanagement or incompetence;
- sudden and unpredicted changes in market conditions.

This ground has been well trodden, yet the rate of merger, acquisition, and joint-venture success has improved little. Clearly these factors may contribute to disappointing M&A outcomes, but this conventional wisdom only partly explains what goes wrong in M&A management.

THE FORGOTTEN FACTOR IN M&A

The false distinction that has developed between hard and soft merger issues has been extremely unhelpful in extending our understanding of merger failure, as it separates the impact of the merger on the individual from its financial impact on the organization. Successful M&A outcomes are linked closely to the extent to which management is able to integrate members of organizations and their cultures, and sensitively address and minimize individuals' concerns.

Because they represent sudden and major change, mergers generate considerable uncertainty and feelings of powerlessness. This can lead to reduced morale, job and career dissatisfaction, and employee stress. Rather than increased profitability, mergers have become associated with a range of negative behavioral outcomes such as:

- acts of sabotage and petty theft;
- increased staff turnover, with rates as high as 60% reported;
- increased sickness and absenteeism.

Ironically, this occurs at the very time when organizations need and expect greater employee loyalty, flexibility, cooperation, and productivity.

PEOPLE FACTORS ASSOCIATED WITH M&A FAILURE

Studies like the one conducted by the Chartered Management Institute in the UK have identified a variety of people factors associated with unsuccessful M&A. These include:

- underestimating the difficulties of merging two cultures;
- underestimating the problem of skills transfer;
- demotivation of employees;
- departure of key people;
- expenditure of too much energy on doing the deal at the expense of postmerger planning;
- lack of clear responsibilities, leading to postmerger conflicts;
- too narrow a focus on internal issues to the neglect of the customers and the external environment;
- insufficient research about the merger partner or acquired organization.

DIFFERENCES BETWEEN MERGERS AND ACQUISITIONS

In terms of employee response, whether the transaction is described as a merger

"The benefits of many mergers have been lost during the integration phase." Richard Corzone

  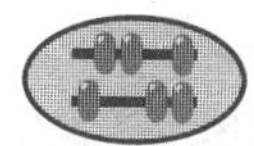   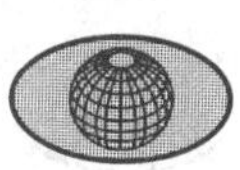   

or an acquisition, the event will trigger uncertainty and fears of job losses. However, there are important differences. In an acquisition, power is substantially assumed by the new parent. Change is usually swift and often brutal as the acquirer imposes its own control systems and financial restraints. Parties to a merger are likely to be more evenly matched in terms of size, and the power and cultural dynamics of the combination are more ambiguous. Integration is a more drawn-out process.

This has implications for the individual. During an acquisition there is often more overt conflict and resistance, and a sense of powerlessness. In mergers, however, because of the prolonged period between the initial announcement and actual integration, uncertainty and anxiety continue for a much longer time as the organization remains in a state of limbo.

CULTURAL COMPATIBILITY

The process of merger is often likened to marriage. In the same way that clashes of personality and misunderstanding lead to difficulties in personal relationships, differences in organizational cultures, communication problems, and mistaken assumptions lead to conflicts in organizational partnerships.

Mergers are rarely a marriage of equals, and it's still the case that most acquirers or dominant merger partners pursue a strategy of cultural absorption; the acquired company or smaller merger partner is expected to assimilate and adopt the culture of the other. Whether the outcome is successful depends on the willingness of organizational members to surrender their own culture, and at the same time perceive that the other culture is attractive and therefore worth adopting.

Cultural similarity may make absorption easier than when the two cultures are very different, yet the process of due diligence rarely extends to evaluating the degree of cultural fit. Furthermore, few organizations bother to try to understand the cultural values and strengths of the acquiring workforce or their merger partners in order to inform and guide the way in which they should go about introducing change.

CASE STUDY

Paul Hodder was involved as director of human resource management in the formation of Aon Risk Services, a merger of four rather different retail-insurance-broking and risk-management companies. A major theme of their integration process was the formation of a series of task groups to review and identify best practice. Another part involved an organization-wide training program to provide individuals with life skills to help them initiate and cope with change, to improve teamwork, and to develop support networks. Enthusiasm for the program provided several hundred change champions to lead change projects and assume support and mentoring roles. Good communication of early wins and successes has reassured organizational members that the changes are working and are beneficial.

MAKING IT HAPPEN

Making a good organizational marriage currently seems to be a matter of chance and luck. This needs to change so that there is a greater awareness of the people issues involved, and consequently a more informed integration strategy. Some basic guidelines for more effective management include:

- extension of the due diligence process to incorporate issues of cultural fit;
- greater involvement of human resource professionals;
- the conducting of culture audits before the introduction of change management initiatives;
- increased communication and involvement of employees at all levels in the integration process;
- the introduction of mechanisms to monitor employee stress levels;
- fair and objective reselection processes and role allocation;
- providing management with the skills and training to sensitively handle M&A issues such as insecurity and job loss;
- creating a superordinate goal which will unify work efforts.

CONCLUSION

Despite thorough pre-merger procedures, mergers continue to fall far short of financial expectations. The single biggest cause of this failure rate is poor integration following the acquisition. The identification of the target company, the subsequent and often drawn-out negotiations, and attending to the myriad of financial, technical, and legal details are all exhausting activities. Once the target company has been acquired, little energy or motivation is left to plan and implement the integration of the people and cultures following the merger. It seems nonsensical to waste all the resources and energy that have gone into the merger through inadequate planning of the integration stage of the process, yet all too often organizations do just that. Without a properly planned integration process or its effective implementation, mergers will not be able to achieve the full potential of the acquisition.

›› MORE INFO

Books:

Cartwright, Susan, and Cary L. Cooper. *Managing Mergers, Acquisitions and Strategic Alliances*. 2nd ed. Woburn, MA: Butterworth-Heinemann, 1996.

Cooper, Cary L., and Alan Gregory (eds). *Advances in Mergers and Acquisitions*. Vol. 1. New York: JAI Press, 2000.

Stahl, Gunter, and Mark E. Mendenhall (eds). *Mergers and Acquisitions*. Stanford, CA: Stanford University Press, 2005.

See Also:

John D. Rockefeller (p. 1185)

"When it comes to mergers, hope triumphs over experience." Irwin Stelzer

     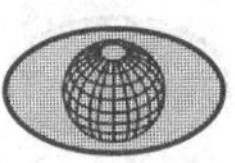   

Building Potential Catastrophe Management into a Strategic Risk Framework by Duncan Martin

EXECUTIVE SUMMARY

Most organizations recognize the need for a strategic risk framework. Such a framework typically identifies and analyzes the key strategic risks faced by the organization, such as competitive, regulatory, technological, demographic, or environmental changes. Adopted at the highest level of the organization, effective strategic risk frameworks drive resource allocation and, consequently, the ability of the organization to achieve its goals.

However, many organizations do not integrate the potential impact of catastrophes into the strategic risk framework. This can result in an organization suffering large unexpected losses from a catastrophe despite investing significant time and energy into a risk management framework. For example, a business might foresee–and mitigate–the entry of a new competitor into their market, but be caught off guard by a major flood that causes equal disruption and loss in value.

To avoid being blind-sided in this way, best practice risk management builds catastrophe risk management into the same framework as strategic (and other) risks. In this way, the full spectrum of risks is measured and managed consistently, and resources are directed at those risks that pose the greatest threat to the organization. Such optimal resource allocation underpins long run organizational success.

DEFINITIONS

What is catastrophic risk? Catastrophic risk is: Stuff happens. Some unexpected, perhaps unexpectable, natural event occurs. Half a world away from its source in southern China, SARS kills 38 people in Toronto; a nuclear reactor at Chernobyl is driven into a state its designers never even imagined, even as its operators disable critical safety features, and it explodes; events in the Middle East cause Britons to blow themselves up on the London Underground.

Strategic risk is also stuff happening, but from a business point of view. An ailing computer manufacturer trounces established consumer electronics firms by producing the killer portable music device, and then follows up with a mobile phone that is both revolutionary and beautiful; tiny car firms constrained by post-war, small island scarcity eliminate waste by worshipping quality, end up reinventing the entire manufacturing process, and brutally upend incumbents; Wall Street's best and brightest simulate endless market disruption scenarios, except the one that finally happens–no bids and no offers; total paralysis.

Beyond strategic and catastrophe risk, financial and operational risk are equally necessary if less glamorous parts of a fully functional risk framework. Only through the consistent identification, measurement, and management of the full spectrum of risks can an organization ensure that it meets its objectives successfully.

CORE CONCEPTS

More formally, there are four core concepts in risk: Frequency, severity, correlation, and uncertainty.

An event is frequent if it occurs often. Most catastrophes are, mercifully, infrequent. Historically, there is a severe earthquake (seven or greater on the Richter scale) about once every 25 years in California. Hence, the frequency of big earthquakes in California is 1/25 or about 4% each year.

An event is severe if it causes a lot of damage. For example, according to the US Geological Survey (USGS), between 1900 and 2005 China experienced 13 earthquakes which, in total, killed an estimated 800,000 people. The average severity was 61,000 people.

Most people's perception of risk focuses on events that are low frequency and high severity such as severe earthquakes, aircraft crashes, and accidents at nuclear power plants. Strategic risk also focuses on low frequency/high severity changes, such as disruptive technologies or new entrants. However, a fuller notion of risk includes two additional concepts: Correlation and uncertainty.

Events are correlated if they tend to happen at the same time and place. For example, the flooding of New Orleans in 2005 was caused by a hurricane; the 1906 earthquake in San Francisco also caused an enormous fire.

Estimates of frequency, severity, and correlation are just that: Estimates. They are usually based on past experience, and as investors know well, past performance offers no guarantees for the future. Similarly, the probabilities, severities, and correlations of events in the future cannot be extrapolated with certainty from history: They are uncertain.

The rarer and more extreme the event, the greater the uncertainty. For example, according to the US National Oceanic and Atmospheric Administration, in the 105 years between 1900 and 2004 there were 25 severe (category four and five) hurricanes in the US. At the end of 2004, you would have estimated the frequency of a severe hurricane at 25/105, or about 24% per year. However, there were four severe hurricanes in 2005 alone. Recalculating the frequency at the end of 2005, you would end up with about 27% per year (29/106). That's a large difference, and would have a material impact on preparations.

Which estimate is correct? Neither, and both: Uncertainty prohibits "correctness." Uncertainty is the essence of risk and coping with it is the essence of risk management.

Both catastrophic and strategic risk management are then predicting and managing the consequences of rare, severe, and potentially correlated events under great uncertainty.

THINK, PLAN, DO

Integrating catastrophe risk into strategic risk management requires a common conceptual framework. Best practice risk management is—always and everywhere—a three step process: Think, plan, do (Figure 1).

Figure 1. Think, plan, do

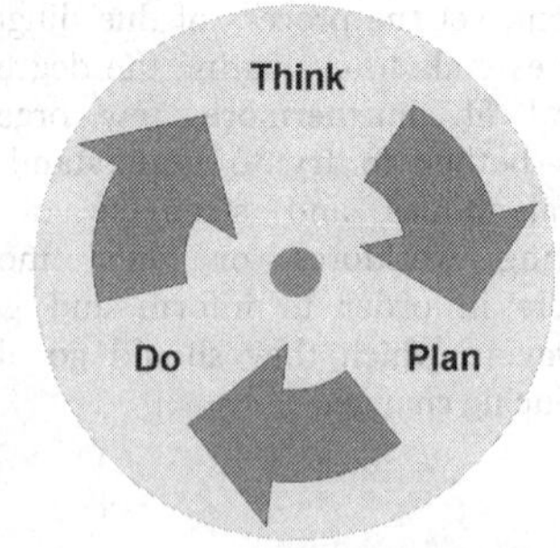

Think

Thinking comes first. Before being able to manage risk, risk managers must know how much is acceptable to themselves and their organization, and conversely at what stage to cut any losses.

"I buy when other people are selling." J. Paul Getty

  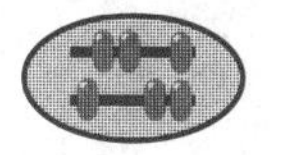 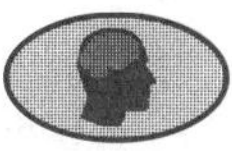  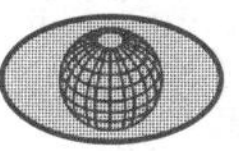 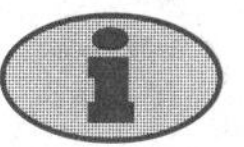  

This risk appetite is not self-evident. It is a philosophical choice, an issue of comfort with the frequency, severity, and correlation of, and uncertainty around, potential events. Different individuals and organizations have different preferences.

Some people enjoy mountain climbing. They are comfortable with the knowledge that they're holding onto a small crack in a wet rock face with their fingertips and it's a long way down. Others prefer gardening, their feet firmly planted on the ground, their fingertips on their secateurs and not far from a cup of tea. Similarly, some organizations aspire to blue chip, triple-A solidity, others the rough and tumble of start-ups and venture capital, with the added drama of the San Andreas fault under their feet.

For strategic risk, managers attempt to simplify risk appetite down to how much money an organization is prepared to lose before it cuts its losses and changes objectives. For catastrophes, it is the frequency with which a certain event results in death–the frequency and severity of fatal terrorist attacks in London for example. In some cases it is defined externally. For example, on oil rigs in the North Sea it is defined through legislation. Events that cause death more often than once in 10,000 years are not tolerable, and rig operators must mitigate the risk of any event with worse odds than this.

CASE STUDY

Morgan Stanley was until recently a leading American investment bank. Investment banking is not for the faint-hearted, as it involves taking very large financial risks. Consequently, Morgan Stanley invested very large amounts in financial risk management. In general, this worked well and the firm was mostly profitable through the 1990s.

Managing financial risk was merely par for the course for investment banks though. One of the things that set Morgan Stanley apart from its peers was its assessment of catastrophe risk at one of its major operational hubs: The World Trade Center (WTC) in downtown New York. Their corporate security manager, a decorated former soldier named Rick Rescorla, predicted the 1993 WTC bombing and had been able to convince the firm that such an attack would happen again. The firm had committed to move out at the end of their lease in 2006. On September 11, 2001, Morgan Stanley had 37 hundred employees in the WTC. All but six—one of the Rescorla—got out alive, a direct result of constant practice and calm execution.

The integration of catastrophe risk into the strategic risk framework of the firm saved many lives. Few cases are this dramatic, but the point is the same: Risks are risks, regardless of source. The way we label them is entirely arbitrary. If, because of that labelling, we fail to treat all risks consistently, the consequences can be serious.

Plan

Planning is next. There are two parts: A strategic plan that matches resources and risks; and a tactical plan that assesses all the major risks identified, and details the response to each one.

The first part is the big picture risk appetite. If, for example, an organization decides that the frequency, severity, and uncertainty of flooding in London is too great, the big picture is that the organization needs to leave London, incurring whatever costs this requires.

The strategic big picture also has to make sense. For example, although low cost airlines need to be cheap, they cannot afford to cut corners on safety. Valujet discovered this when it was forced to ditch its brand following a catastrophic crash in 1996, as did Spanair in 2008. Similarly, although the high command of the US Army Rangers recognizes that they operate in very dangerous environments–occasionally catastrophically so, such as Mogadishu, Somalia–and hence will on occasion lose soldiers, they have adopted a policy of "no man left behind." This helps to ensure that in combat Rangers are less likely to surrender or retreat, perhaps as a result winning the day. Consequently, airlines spend a lot on safety, and armies spend a lot on search and rescue capabilities.

The next stage is detailed tactical planning. First, identify all the risks, strategic and catastrophic, financial and operational, all the things that might go wrong. Then, assess and compare them to see which ones are the most likely and the most damaging. Finally, figure out what to do, who's going to do it, and how much that's going to cost.

California's state-wide disaster planning process is an excellent template for responding to catastrophes, mostly likely because there's plenty of opportunity to practice: All manner of major incidents there–earthquakes, tsunamis, floods, wildfires, landslides, oil spills–occur relatively frequently. State law specifies the extent of mutual aid obligations between local communities and requires each community to appoint a state-certified emergency manager. Each emergency manager creates a detailed disaster management and recovery plan for his or her local community, reflecting local issues and needs. These plans are audited by state inspectors and rolled up into a state-wide plan. The plan is input to the state budgeting process in order to obtain the necessary resources.

Critically, risk aversion does not necessarily make you safer. Many people or communities express a low risk appetite but baulk at the expense of reducing their risk to match their risk appetite. They don't put their money where their mouth is, and instead simply hope that the rare event doesn't happen. However, in the end, even rare events occur. The results of mismatching risk appetite and resources were devastatingly demonstrated recently as Katrina drowned New Orleans.

Conversely, a large risk appetite is not the same thing as recklessness. Technology venture capital firms quite deliberately "bet the farm" on a few firms in narrow technology domains that they believe will be highly disruptive, and hence profitable. This is high risk for sure, but the extensive deliberation and diligence of the investment and management processes mitigate the risk.

Do

Doing is a combination of activities. Before an event, *doing* means being prepared. This consists of acquiring and positioning the appropriate equipment, communications systems, and budget; recruiting, training, and rehearsing response teams; and ensuring that both the public and the response teams know what to do and what to not do. After an event, *doing* means keeping your wits about you while implementing your plan, managing the inevitable unexpected events that crop up, and, to the extent possible, collecting data on the experience.

Once the epidemic has broken out or the earthquake has hit, the key is not to panic. Colin Sharples, a former acrobatic pilot and now the head of training and industry affairs at a British airline, observes that instinctively "your mind freezes for about 10 seconds in an emergency. Then it reboots." Frozen individuals cannot help themselves or others. To counter this instinct, pilots are required go through a continuous and demanding training programme in flight simulators which "covers all known scen-

"What is more mortifying than to feel that you have missed the plum for want of courage to shake the tree."
Logan Pearsall Smith

  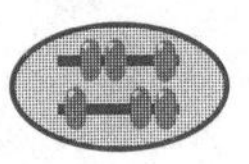 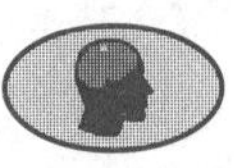  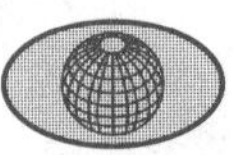 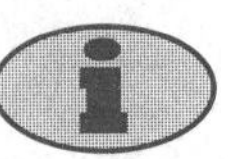  

arios, with the more critical ones, for example engine fires, covered every six months. Pilots who do not pass the test have to retrain."

Most environments where catastrophes are possible have similar training programmes, albeit usually without the fancy simulation hardware. As Davy Gunn of Glencoe Mountain Rescue puts it: "Our training is to climb steep mountains in bad weather, because that's what we do [when we're called out]." In addition to providing direct experience of extreme conditions, such training also increases skill levels to the point where difficult activities become routine, even reflexive. Together, the experience and the training allow team members to create some "breathing space" with respect to the immediate danger. This breathing space ensures that team members can play their part and in addition preserve some spare mental capacity to cope with unexpected events.

The importance of this "breathing space" reflex reflects a truth about many extreme situations: They don't usually start out that way. Rather, a "chain of misfortune" builds up where one bad thing builds on another and the situation turns from bad to critical to catastrophic. First, something bad happens. For example, first a patient reports with novel symptoms and doesn't respond to treatment. Then they die . . . then one of their caregivers dies too. Then one of their relatives ends up in hospital with the same symptoms . . . and so on. A team with "breathing space" can interrupt this chain by solving the problems at source as they arise, allowing them no time to compound. For example, a paranoid and suspicious infectious disease consultant (the best kind) might isolate the patient and implement strict patient/physician contact precautions before the infection was able to spread.

Close the Loop

When the *doing* is over and situation has returned to normal, risk managers must close the loop and return to *thinking*. The group has to ask itself "so how did it go?" Using information collected centrally and participants' own experience, each part of the plan is evaluated against its original intention. This debrief can be formal, or informal, depending on what works best. Sometimes it might even be public, such as the Cullen enquiry into the disastrous Piper Alpha North Sea oil platform fire in 1989 that cost one 165 deaths.

Where performance was bad, the group must question whether the cause was local–training, procedures, and equipment –or strategic–the situation was riskier than the organization wants to tolerate, or is able to afford. These conclusions feed into the next round of *thinking* and *planning*.

Pitfalls

The main pitfall in the integration of catastrophe risk into strategic risk management is an insufficiently holistic process. Usually this stems from the separation of strategy development, risk management, and in many cases insurance. In many organizations strategy development is the sexiest assignment, and is jealously guarded by its departmental owners. As a result, in some cases strategic plans can be insufficiently informed by risk assessment. Risk management departments often do not help themselves, since they tend to communicate in jargon and equations. Separately–and strangely in this author's view–insurance is sometimes not part of the risk management organization. Rather, it is part of the finance area, and an obscure part at that. Consequently, decisions on which risks to cover and to what degree can be taken in complete isolation of the organization's overall risk appetite. Such disjoints between different parts of the risk assessment process lead to a lack of integration, and ultimately to inconsistent treatment of risks and misallocation of scarce resources.

▸▸ MAKING IT HAPPEN

In terms of implementation, there are five key principles. First, integration can only come from the top down. Only an organization's senior management can both view the full holistic picture and require compliance further down. Second, the integration has to be genuinely "lived" by the senior managers. If employees feel that integration is merely lip service, they will not participate and the experiment will fail. Third, since risk appetites tend to be low with respect to very severe events, the resultant scarcity of events may drive hubris: It hasn't happened for a while, therefore it probably won't or can't happen again. In industrial settings, researchers have observed that the odds of a serious accident increase with the time elapsed since the last one. Avoiding this complacency is critical. Fourth, conversely, is the balance between sounding the alarm and having people respond. The more often an alarm sounds, the more likely it is that individuals will assume it's just a drill, or faulty, and tune it out. However, if an alarm never sounds, no one will know what to do. There is no specific right answer to either of these points, except the first two: A genuine, heartfelt impetus from the top down. Finally, many risk issues are amenable to sophisticated mathematical and computational treatments. There is a temptation to assume that just because a risk is measured, it is managed. It isn't.

▸▸ MORE INFO

Books:

Abraham, Thomas. *21st Century Plague: The Story of SARS*. Baltimore, MD: Johns Hopkins University Press, 2005.

Cullen, W. Douglas, Lord. *The Public Inquiry into the Piper Alpha Disaster*. London: HMSO, 1990.

Junger, Sebastian. *The Perfect Storm*. London: Harper Perennial, 2007.

Martin, Duncan. *Managing Risk in Extreme Environments*. London: Kogan Page, 2008.

Perrow, Charles. *Normal Accidents*. Princeton, NJ: Princeton University Press, 1999.

Pyne, Stephen. *Year of the Fires*. London: Penguin, 2002.

Singer, Peter. *Corporate Warriors: The Rise of the Privatized Military Industry*. Ithaca, NY: Cornell University Press, 2004.

Article:

Stewart, James. "The real heroes are dead." *The New Yorker* (February 11, 2002).

Websites:

California Office of Emergency Services: www.oes.ca.gov

London Resilience: www.londonprepared.gov.uk

"At some point a good leader with inadequate data will say, Ready, fire, aim—and if it doesn't work we'll correct it, but at least the timing is right to start with what we have." Robert Townsend

     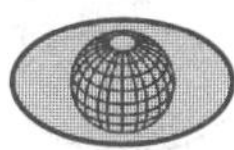   

Business Continuity Management: How to Prepare for the Worst by Andrew Hiles

EXECUTIVE SUMMARY

- No organization is immune from disaster.
- Business continuity management (BCM) is an integral part of corporate governance.
- A business continuity plan (BCP) can protect your brand, reputation and market share.
- The prerequisite discipline of risk and impact assessment reveals critical dependencies and threats to them, enabling preventative measures to be taken.
- Risk and impact assessment identifies and prioritizes mission-critical activities and the timeframe in which they must be resumed; it can also provide new risk insights to improve your business performance.

INTRODUCTION

Over five years even a well-managed organization has an 80% chance of suffering an event that damages its profits by 20%.[1]

The cause could be equipment downtime, failure of utilities or supply chain, terrorism, fire, flood, explosion, or adverse weather. Whatever the cause, without a BCP, the result is the same: damage to reputation, brand, competitive position, and market share. Sometimes this damage, and subsequent losses, are severe enough to lead to permanent closure.

Yet such loss can be minimized, or even avoided, by implementing a business continuity management (BCM) system which includes developing a business continuity plan (BCP).

Quite simply, those organizations that have a BCP tend to survive a major adverse incident, while those without a BCP tend to fail.

WHAT IS BCM?

According to one definition, BCM is: a "holistic management process that identifies potential impacts that threaten an organisation and provides a framework for building resilience and the capability for an effective response which safeguards the interests of its key stakeholders, reputation, brand and value creating activities."[2]

Information and communications technology (ICT) disaster recovery is an important and integral part of BCM—but only one part. BCM covers all mission-critical activities (MCAs)—operations, manufacturing, sales, logistics, HR, finance, etc.—not just the technology.

THE BC PROJECT

BCM starts as a project, but, once the BCP has been developed, audited and exercised, it becomes an ongoing program needing regular maintenance and exercise.

The project activities are illustrated in Figure 1.

MAKING IT HAPPEN

Phase One

The BC project should start with a clear understanding of the needs of the stakeholders and the support of the board. BC policy needs to be set.

A high-level steering group needs to be set up to decide priorities and define the scope of the project. For instance, is the objective to be "business as usual"—or will it just cover the 20% of goods or services that generates 80% of the profits? Will it cover all customers, or just the most important ones? Does it embrace all locations, or just head office? How far does it go down into the supply chain? Will it cover only local disasters, or is it to cope with wide area disasters—hurricanes, major floods, etc.?

Figure 1. BCP project structure

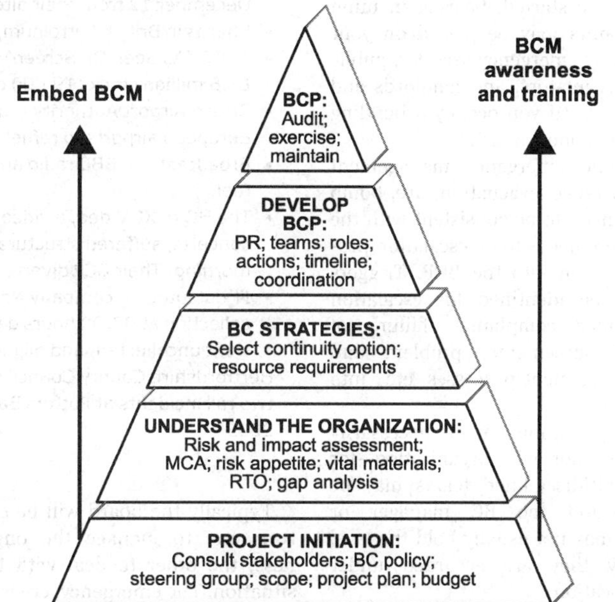

Next, a project plan should be developed, identifying the milestones and deliverables of the project. These include:

- risk and impact assessment;
- agreeing BC strategies;
- developing the BCP and implementing contingency arrangements;
- audit and exercising the BCP.

A budget can be established for Phase One from a knowledge of how many sites are to be covered, how many people are to be interviewed, how many processes are to be included at each site, and an assessment of time for research and report writing.

Risk and impact assessment can be broken down into subactivities:

- identification of assets and threats to them;
- weighting threats for probability and impact (in cash and noncash terms);
- identification of MCAs and their dependencies;
- establishing the recovery time objective (RTO) for each (the maximum acceptable period of service outage);
- establishing the recovery point objective (RPO) for each (the timestamp to which data and transactions have to be recovered);
- identifying the resources needed for recovery and the timeframe in which they are required;
- identifying any gaps between the RTO, RPO, and actual capability (for example,

"Just because the river is quiet does not mean the crocodiles have left." Malay proverb

   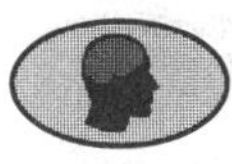  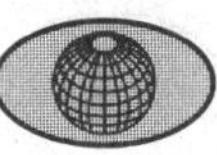   

the IT backup method may not permit recovery within the RTO);

- establishing the organization's appetite for risk;
- making recommendations for risk management and mitigation;
- making recommendations to close any gaps revealed.

The risk and impact assessment is usually conducted by analysis of building plans and operational layouts; review of reports on audit, health, safety, and environmental and operational incidents; interview of key personnel; and physical inspection.

Once these activities have been completed, possible contingency arrangements can be considered. The instinctive reaction is to replicate existing capability—but there may be more cost-effective options.

Holding buffer stock could cover equipment downtime. Increased resilience and "hardening" of facilities may reduce risk to an acceptable level. Items or services could be bought in, rather than undertaken in-house. Contracts could be placed with commercial BC service vendors for standby IT, telecommunications and work area recovery requirements.

The risk and impact assessment then forms the basis for a cost–benefit analysis of the contingency options and allows a BC strategy to be recommended and agreed.

This report, incorporating the findings and recommendations from the risk and impact assessment, forms a natural close to Phase One. Usually there is a natural break while recommendations are considered and the budget for Phase Two is agreed.

Phase Two

Once the BC strategy has been agreed, the BC plan can be started, bearing in mind what constraints may be placed on your organization by emergency services, public authorities, regulators, and landlords and other occupants (if you occupy a building with more than one tenant).

Incident and emergency management plans (for instance, evacuation, fire, bomb threat, etc.) need to be consistent with the BCP, and there needs to be escalation processes from them into the BCP. Triggers should also be identified for escalation from customer complaints, failure of service-level agreements, problem and incident management processes, etc., into the BC process.

The BC organization may not necessarily mirror the normal organization—for instance, multidisciplined teams may be appropriate—and the BC manager or coordinator may not usually hold the level of authority they are accorded under disaster invocation.

CASE STUDY

Buncefield

Buncefield Oil Storage Terminal supplied fuel to London Heathrow from pipelines transporting fuel from the north of England. It was owned by Hertfordshire Oil Storage Ltd, a joint venture between Total and Texaco. Other businesses were attracted to the site—Marylands Industrial Park—because of its low cost.

Around 06:00 hours on Sunday, December 11, 2005, an explosion occurred, measuring 2.4 on the Richter scale, it was heard as far away as France and the Netherlands.

The Buncefield incident was the biggest explosion, and the accompanying fire was the biggest fire, in peacetime Europe. Twenty-five different fire services tackled the blaze with 600 fire fighters.

The explosion and subsequent fire:

- destroyed some 5% of UK petrol stocks and destroyed 20 fuel tanks;
- Injured 200 people; 2,000 were evacuated;
- damaged more than 300 houses and required 10 buildings to be demolished;
- caused all the schools in the county to be closed;
- cost local businesses and local authorities £1 billion: it impacted 600 businesses and prevented 25,000 staff from getting to work;
- disrupted global air traffic schedules and local transport;
- caused businesses to suffer disruption of supply;
- caused many organizations to invoke their BC plans;
- made big retailers re-assess their supply chain issues;
- forced companies to make public statements to protect their share value;
- created major environmental impact from millions of gallons of burning oil which required more than three million gallons of contaminated firewater with up to 40 different contaminants to be disposed of; it took 500 tankers five weeks to move it.

Other impacts were equally devastating:

- By January 10, 2006, data recovery and communications restoration was still ongoing.
- By January 11, 2006, 75 businesses employing 5,000 people were still unable to use their premises.
- Insurance cover was inadequate to cover losses.
- In August 2006, 2,700 claimants sued for a billion pounds in a case that will cost £61 million.
- Supermarket chain Sainsbury's closed three stores damaged by fire;
- Brewers Scottish & Newcastle lost £10 million of stock.
- Retailer Marks & Spencer closed a food depot, disrupting deliveries to retail outlets.
- Fujifilm, 3Com Corporation, and Alcom buildings were damaged.
- Andromeda Logistics' distribution centre was evacuated: operations resumed on December 12 from their alternative distribution center.
- Shares in British Petroleum, a bystander, briefly dived.
- ASOS (As Seen On Screen), an online fashion retailer, lost its new warehouse with £5.5 million stock (19,000 orders were refunded).
- British Airport Authority rationed aviation fuel at Heathrow: airlines diverted to other European airports to refuel.
- Broadcasts on BBC radio and television news urged motorists to avoid panic buying of fuel.
- The HQ of XL Video, a video producer for trade shows, events, television, and concerts, suffered structural damage. They had 12 projects to load on the Monday morning. Their BCP diverted projects: all shows were shipped on December 12.
- IT outsourcing company Northgate Information Solutions Ltd had backups ready for collection at 07:00 hours daily, but the fire happened at 06:00. Local tax payments went uncollected, and billing information for utility companies was lost.

Hertfordshire County Council's crisis management plan worked: it had been used at the two rail incidents at Potters Bar and Hatfield and been thoroughly tested in October 2005.

Typically the board will be separated in two: one to manage the ongoing business, the other to deal with the disaster situation. The emergency, crisis or business continuity management team (BCMT) will include board-level decision-makers. These include members from business and support units, and the BC manager

"The tendency of an event to occur varies inversely with one's preparation for it." David Searles

     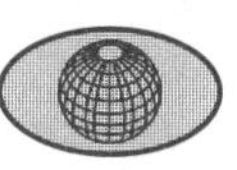   

(effectively the project manager for recovery) will report to them.

Business and support unit teams, including ICT, will report on recovery progress and seek clarification, information and support from the BC manager. The BC manager will resolve any priority clashes within his or her authority and refer others to the BCMT.

The overview at Table 1 needs to be amplified by detailed action plans covering each BC team.

The BCP coordinator is not necessarily the same person who will be BC manager once the BCP is completed. The BCP coordinator's role is to ensure that all BCPs are completed consistently and comprehensively.

The BCPs should not be scenario-based, since the disaster is unlikely to fit neatly into any scenario envisaged. Instead, they should be based on a worst-case scenario: total loss of MCAs. However, if they are developed in a modular fashion, if a lesser disaster happens, only that part which is relevant can be invoked.

The BCP coordinator will draft a BCP for the BCMT and for his or her BC activities, including BCP invocation procedure, and will provide advice and guidance to the business and support unit BC coordinators.

Next, a template BCP should be developed that can be used for each team. Once they have had training, BCP development coordinators for each business and support unit complete these. A support program can be created for their guidance as they develop their BCPs.

Each BCP should spell out assumptions so they may be challenged (for example, an assumption that more than one site will not suffer a disaster at the same time; or that skilled people will be available post-disaster).

The minimum content should include:

- prioritized MCAs and a credible action plan for their recovery within RTO and RPO;
- lists of team members, alternates, roles, and contacts;
- resource requirements and when and how they are to be obtained;
- contact details of internal and external contacts;
- information on relevant contracts and insurance;
- reporting requirements;
- instructions on handling the media;
- any useful supporting information (such as damage assessment forms; maps and information about alternate sites; detailed technical recovery procedures).

Table 1. BC organization partial example

BC Management team	IT team	Base site recovery team
Leader: BC management team leader Alternate	*Leader:* TBD Alternate: TBD	*Leader:* TBD Alternate: TBD
Members: CFO Alternate COO Alternate P RO Alternate Marketing director Alternate Estates manager Alternate: TBD Admin support: TBD	*Members:* Applications manager Alternate PC Servers/LAN manager Alternate Data/voice communications manager Alternate: TBD Admin support: TBD	*Members:* Office services manager Alternate PC Servers/LAN Alternate: TBD Data/voice communications Alternate: TBD Damage assessment/salvage Alternate Loss adjuster: TBD Admin support: TBD
Reports: BC manager Alternate	*Roles:* Recovery of all platforms, systems applications and data at standby site: TBD Data/voice communications recovery at standby site: TBD	*Roles:* Damage assessment, limitation and salvage Recovery at base site Recovery of operational capability at base site IT, data/voice communications recovery at base site
Roles: Consider group (corporate) impacts. Manage recovery. Coordinate all team action. Consider safety and security and environmental issues. Decide on priorities. Reassure media and authorities.		

TBD – to be determined

Once the BCPs have been developed they can be audited, reviewing each BCP for comprehensiveness, clarity, and accuracy. This also ensures that interrelationships between BCPs are reflected in the counterparty BCP.

Rigorous exercises probe BCP effectiveness under different disaster scenarios and provide realistic training for BC team members.

Lessons from BC audit and tests should be incorporated into the BCPs. Where this has not yet been done, a list should be provided at the beginning of the BCP stating what weaknesses were found to exist; who is responsible for rectifying them; and the timeframe for doing so.

The BCP may take many forms: hard copy; handheld devices; memory sticks, etc. Whatever the format, it should be kept secure, and steps should be taken to ensure that only the current version can be held.

CONCLUSION

Wise executives have long known the importance of risk and impact assessment and the need for contingency planning. With today's threats, this has never been more important. Buncefield proved the need to:

- develop a BCP to protect reputation, brand, and share value and market share;
- communicate to key stakeholders;
- communicate to emergency services and staff;
- keep investors and customers informed;
- have alternative sites for operations and for a control center;
- read and understand the emergency plans of the local authorities;
- ensure that key standby resources are in place, such as information (status, contacts); accommodation (operations and work area); and reserves (stock, spare equipment, etc.).

Buncefield cost local businesses £70 million, much of it uninsured. It is imperative to check insurance cover. The impact of a major disaster could last for months, or even years.

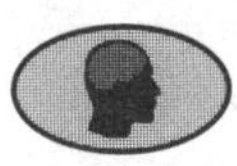

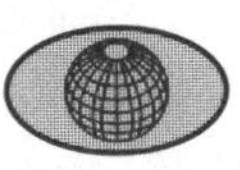

▸▸ MORE INFO

Books:

Hiles, Andrew. *Business Continuity: Best Practices—World-class Continuity Management*. Brookfield, CT: Rothstein Associates, 2007.

Hiles, Andrew. *The Definitive Handbook of Business Continuity Management*. 2nd ed. Chichester, UK: Wiley, 2007.

Hiles, Andrew N. *Enterprise Risk Assessment and Business Impact Analysis: Best Practices*. Brookfield, CT: Rothstein Associates, 2002.

Von Roessing, Rolf. *Auditing Business Continuity—Global Best Practices*. Brookfield, CT: Rothstein Associates, 2002.

Websites:

Association of Contingency Planners: www.acp-international.com

Business Continuity Institute: www.thebci.org

Continuity Central: www.continuitycentral.com

Disaster Recovery Institute International: www.drii.org

Standards:

BS 25999 Business Continuity Management (UK)

HB 221 Business Continuity Management (Australia)

NFPA 1600 Emergency Management and Business Continuity (USA)

GLOSSARY

BC: Business continuity

BCM: Business continuity management

BCP: Business continuity plan

BIA: Business impact assessment

DRP: A plan for the continuity or recovery of information and communications technology (ICT)

MCA: Mission-critical activities

Risk appetite: The level of loss that an organization is prepared to tolerate

RTO: Recovery time objective

RPO: Recovery point objective (of data or transactions)

NOTES

1 Oxford Metrica, www.oxfordmetrica.com

2 British Standards Institute/Business Continuity Institute Publicly Available Specification 56.

"One cannot leap a chasm in two jumps." Winston Churchill

  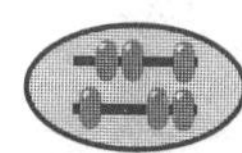   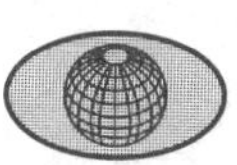   

Countering Supply Chain Risk by Vinod Lall

EXECUTIVE SUMMARY

- Business strategies such as outsourcing, lean manufacturing and just-in-time lead to efficiency gains but at the same time expose the supply chain to higher risks.
- There are different sources of risk in a modern supply chain. Recognizing and appropriately managing these risks is necessary for a glitch-free functioning of the supply chain.
- Supply chain risk management strategies must be holistic and integrated with the whole supply chain environment.
- Firms must have dedicated budget line items for supply chain risk management activities.
- Failure mode effects analysis (FMEA) can be used to assess supply chain risks.

INTRODUCTION

In March 2000, a fire at a Philips semiconductor factory damaged some components used to make chips for mobile phones. Ericsson and Nokia—two of Philips' major customers—responded to the event in very different ways. Ericsson decided to let the delay take its own course, while supply chain managers at Nokia monitored the situation closely and developed contingency plans. By the time Philips discovered that the fire had contaminated a large area that would disrupt production for months, Nokia had already lined up alternative suppliers for the chips. Ericsson used Philips as a sole supplier and faced a severe shortage of chips, leading to delay in product launch and huge losses to its mobile phone division.

Today's global supply chains are complex and lean while efficiently delivering products and services to the marketplace. These supply chains involve a rigid set of transactions and decisions that span over longer distances and more time zones with very little slack built into them. As a result they are susceptible to several types of risk. These risks include operational risk due to demand variability, supply fluctuations and disruption risk due to natural disasters, terrorist attacks, pandemics, and breaches in data security. Such risks disrupt or slow the flow of material, information, and cash, and put billions of dollars at stake due to stock market capitalization, failed product launches, and the possibility of bankruptcies. In the above example, Ericsson lost 400 million euros after the Philips semiconductor plant caught fire; another example occurred when Apple lost many customer orders during a supply shortage of memory chips after an earthquake in Taiwan in 1999. Supply chain executives and managers must visualize and have a clear understanding of these risks along the entire supply chain, starting from the sourcing of raw materials to the delivery of the final product or service to the consumer. Once these risks are identified, they need to be scored on the likelihood of occurrence, and their impact must be quantified. Resources must then be used to mitigate or eliminate elements of high risk.

TYPES OF SUPPLY CHAIN RISK

Supply chain risks can be classified into different types depending on their origin. These include supply risk, demand risk, internal risk, and external environment risk.

Supply risk: These are the risks on the supply/inbound side of the supply chain. Supply risk may be defined as the possibility of disruptions of product availability from the supplier or disruptions in the process of transportation from the supplier to the customer. A supplier may be unavailable to complete an order for a number of reasons, including problems sourcing necessary raw materials, low process yield due to increased scrap, equipment failure, damaged facilities, or the need to ration its limited product among several customers. Transportation disruptions occur while products are in transit and add to the delivery lead time. They may be caused by delays in customs clearance at borders, or problems with the mode of transportation, such as the grounding of air traffic.

Demand risk: Demand risk is the downstream equivalent of supply risk and is present on the demand/outbound side of the supply chain. It may be due to an unexpected increase or decrease in customer demand that leads to a mismatch between the firm's forecast and actual demand. Increase in customer demand leads to depletion of safety stocks, resulting in stock-outs, back orders, and the need to expedite. A fall in customer demand leads to increased costs of holding inventory and, inevitably, price reductions. Other sources of demand risk are dependence on a single customer, customer solvency, and failure of the distribution logistics service provider.

Internal risk: This is the risk associated with events that are related to internal operations of the firm. Examples include fire or chemical spillage leading to plant closure, labor strikes, quality problems, and shortage of employees.

External environment risk: These risk elements are external to and uncontrollable from the firm's perspective. Examples include blockades of ports or depots, natural disasters such as earthquakes, hurricanes or cyclones, war, terrorist activity, and financial factors such as exchange rates and market pressures. These events disrupt the flow of material and may lead to plant shut-down, shortage of high-demand items, and price increases.

STRATEGIES FOR SUPPLY CHAIN RISK MANAGEMENT

Strategies for managing risk must be a part of supply chain management and must include processes to reduce supply chain risks that at the same time increase resilience and efficiency. Firms typically use basic strategies of risk-bearing, risk avoidance or risk mitigation, and risk transference to another party. The goal of risk-bearing is to reduce the potential damage caused by the materialization of a risk, and to be successful requires that early warning systems be installed along the supply chain. The main goal of risk avoidance is to reduce the probability of occurrence of a risk by being proactive, while under risk transfer the potential impact of risk is transferred to another organization such as an insurance company.

"Strategies for managing risk must be a part of supply chain management and must include processes to reduce supply chain risks that at the same time increase resilience and efficiency."

MITIGATING SUPPLY CHAIN RISKS

A firm could use strategic and tactical plans under four basic approaches to mitigate the impact of supply chain risks. These approaches include supply management, demand management, product management, and information management. The task of managing supply chain risk is difficult as approaches that mitigate one risk

"Educated risks are the key to success." William Olsten

     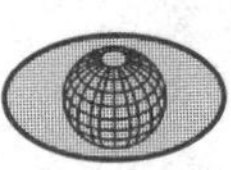   

element can end up exacerbating another. Also, actions taken by one partner in the supply chain can increase the risk for another partner.

Supply Management

Supply risks can be reduced by building a web of internal and external sources. Strategically, firms should focus their core competencies on new products and ideas and the engineering necessary to reduce time-to-market. They should continue to manufacture strategic, high-value, long-life products that have relatively low demand volatility while outsourcing non-strategic, low-value manufacturing and logistics services. It is important to be very selective in building a strong web of vendors and closely managing the vendor network. For each new product, the firm must capitalize on the varying expertise of its vendor network and use expected time-to-market, quality level and price to select a vendor from the network.

Tactical plans under supply management focus mostly on supplier selection and supplier order allocation. For this firms should develop a profile of their supply bases to get a more complete picture of the supply side of the chain. This profile should include a wide range of supplier information including the total number of suppliers, the location and diversity of suppliers, and flexibility in the volume and variety of supplier capacities. Analysis of these data will help firms identify vulnerabilities in their supply chains so they can strategize, create contingency plans, conduct trade-off analysis of issues such as single sourcing, and, if needed, identify and line up backup sources.

Demand Management

Strategic plans under demand management focus on product pricing, while tactical plans are used to shift demand across time, across markets, and across products. One product pricing strategy is called the "price-postponement strategy," whereby the firm decides on the quantity of the order in the first period and then determines the price in the second period after observing updated information about demand. Shifting demand across time is known as "revenue management" or "yield management," whereby firms usually set higher prices during peak seasons to shift demand to off-peak seasons. One technique for shifting demand across markets is called "solo-rollover by market;" this involves selling new products in different markets with time delays, leading to non-overlapping selling seasons. To shift demand across products, firms use pricing and promotion techniques to entice customers to switch products or brands.

As with the supply side, firms must also develop a profile of the demand side to analyze the outbound side of the supply chain. Analysis of the demand side will identify dangers such as those associated with overreliance on a single distribution center to serve a large market, or the risks of having a highly concentrated customer base.

Supply Chain Reserves Management

Firms can deal with supply chain risks by holding reserves of inventory and capacity in the supply chain. Managers must decide carefully on the optimal location and size of these reserves as an undisciplined approach may lead to increased costs and hurt the bottom line.

Product Management

Firms can look at their internal networks and develop a profile of their products, processes, and services. Analysis of data in this profile can help to determine if there is a good mix of products and services and if there are risks in processes such as those used for fulfilling orders.

Information Management

Information technology tools can be used to understand and manage risk better by providing visibility into planned events and warnings for unplanned events in the entire supply chain. Firms must manufacture low-risk products first and use improved forecasts to produce the riskiest products very close to the selling season. This requires the use of reliable data and better forecasting methods. Key members in the supply chain must have easy and timely access to accurate information on such measures as inventory, demand, forecasts, production and shipment plans, work in process, process yields, capacities, backlogs, etc. This offers more opportunities to all parties to respond quickly to sudden changes in the supply chain and requires the implementation of information technology solutions that interface business data and processes end to end.

The collaborative planning, forecasting, and replenishment (CPFR) model is often used to induce collaboration and coordination through information sharing between supply chain partners such as retailers and manufacturers. Under CPFR, the manufacturer generates an initial demand forecast based on market intelligence on products, and the retailer creates its initial demand forecast based on customer response to pricing and promotion decisions. Both parties share their initial demand forecasts and reconcile the differences to obtain a common forecast. Once both parties agree on the common forecast, the manufacturer develops a production plan and the retailer develops a replenishment plan.

▸▸ MAKING IT HAPPEN

It is critical to have an easy-to-use tool to identify and manage supply chain risk. FMEA is a well-documented and proven risk management tool that is used to evaluate the risk of failures in product and process designs. It can be used to evaluate supply chain risk using the following process steps:

- **Step 1**. Identify the categories of supply chain risk.
- **Step 2**. Identify potential risks in each category.
- **Step 3**. Use a rating scale of 1–5 to rate the opportunity, probability, and severity for each risk. The opportunity score for a risk is the frequency with which it occurs. One-time risk events receive an opportunity score of 1, while commonly occurring risk events are assigned an opportunity score of 5. The probability score is the score for the expected likelihood that a risk event will actually happen, so high probability scores are used when the probability of a risk event occurring is large. The severity score indicates the level of impact if the risk materializes. Low-risk events cause a minimum impact on the supply chain and receive a low severity score. Risk events that have a significant impact on the supply chain in terms of cost, time, and quality are assigned a high severity score.
- **Step 4**. For each potential risk, calculate the risk priority number (RPN) as RPN = opportunity × probability × severity.
- **Step 5**. Use Pareto analysis to analyze risks by RPN. Pareto analysis is a formal technique used where many possible courses of action are competing for the attention of the problem-solver. The problem-solver estimates the benefit delivered by each action and then selects the most effective action.
- **Step 6**. Develop action plans to mitigate risks with high RPN.
- **Step 7**. Use another cycle of FMEA to reassess the risks.

"Everything is sweetened by risk." Alexander Smith

  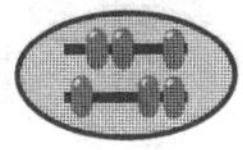 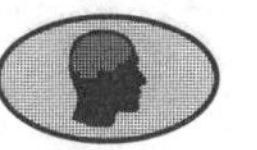  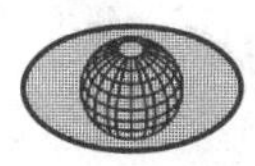   

CONCLUSION

The pursuit of new markets for products and of new sources for components is making supply chains longer and more complex. With this expansion comes increased risk, which may result in disruptions to the supply chain. These disruptions may be unexpected and statistically rare, but they must be understood, identified, and managed.

▸▸ MORE INFO

Books:

Chopra, Sunil, and Peter Meindl. *Supply Chain Management: Strategy, Planning & Operations*. 3rd ed. Upper Saddle River, NJ: Prentice Hall, 2006.

Sheffi, Yossi. *The Resilient Enterprise: Overcoming Vulnerability for Competitive Advantage.* Cambridge, MA: MIT Press, 2007.

Websites:

Council of Supply Chain Management Professionals: cscmp.org

Supply-Chain Council: www.supply-chain.org

See Also:

Michael Porter (p. 1182)

"Great successes never come without risks." Flavius Josephus

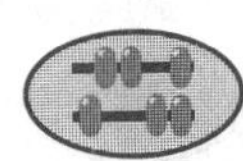

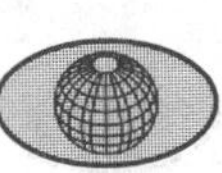

Dealing with Cybersquatters by Shireen Smith

EXECUTIVE SUMMARY

- It is advisable to seek legal advice when dealing with a cybersquatter. A good lawyer will invariably save you time and frustration and will also probably lead you to a better outcome than if you attempt to deal with the problem yourself.
- Collect as much evidence as you can on the domain name and the website at the domain name.
- Have a good business strategy in place to minimize the risk of cybersquatting.
- You can choose whether to take the cybersquatter to court or to arbitration. Each has its own advantages.

INTRODUCTION

Cybersquatting is to be distinguished from the business of domaining. Domainers legitimately own a large number of domain names. They use them to earn money from advertising which they place on the pages that people visit and by selling the domains later on. This use of domain names is completely legitimate.

Cybersquatters will also use domains in similar ways to domainers. The main difference between the two is that cybersquatters do not have legitimate claims to the name. Very often they will email a company and tell it that they have a domain name that the company would want and will only transfer that name for a large sum of money.

It is important to avoid responding with angry emails. If the domain is not too important to you, consider waiting awhile. Once the cybersquatter realizes that the domain is not valuable to you, and if the website at the domain doesn't get many hits, the cybersquatter will probably not renew it. If you decide to wait it out, then register the domain for a snapback service which will automatically purchase the domain name for you when it becomes available.

THE "HOTMAIL" APPROACH

Many companies, in order to avoid legal costs, will try the "hotmail approach" when they discover that someone owns a domain name they want. They register a fake email account and approach the domain name owner asking to buy the domain name for a small fee. Many times the domain name can be purchased for less than the cost of launching a legal complaint. Be careful when trying this to not reveal who you are at any time nor to tell them what you need the domain name for.

This technique is also best saved for a website that you will not actually use; you do not want the cybersquatter to realize you are paying out for websites as it only encourages them to engage in more of this behaviour. They are likely soon after to register a bunch of domain names similar to your trademark.

If you successfully acquire a domain name in this way it is best to make sure you use a third party as the registrar or use a privacy service. You should probably also use an escrow service for transfer of the money. There have been several cases where money was paid but the domain was never transferred.

However, many domain owners are increasingly becoming aware of this technique, and realize that domain buyers are not who they say they are, or if they are, that they are buying on behalf of another entity. If you are dealing with a knowledgeable domain owner, expect them to be very cautious. They will want to know as much about the potential buyer as possible in order to either maximize the sale or to prevent a UDRP (see "Arbitration" section below) action against them later. Companies are known to use the domainer's willingness to sell as evidence of bad faith in a UDRP simply because the owner names a price that he would sell at.

STEPS FOR DEALING WITH CYBERSQUATTERS

Dealing with cybersquatters tends to be frustrating, time consuming, and expensive. Often a company that has been trading for years suddenly realizes someone else has a domain name with their company or product name in it.

The first step is to collect evidence, such as a printout of the domain's website. Keep evidence of any references on the website to you or to your competitors. Also be very careful when approaching a cybersquatter, and keep copies of all communications.

The next step is to check the "whois." This is a facility that can be used to find out who owns a domain name. Many websites use it to offer this service. Be sure to use a reputable site such as www.domaintools.com. There has been a recent controversy about disreputable whois services that collect information on users or are involved in what is known as domain tasting. In domain tasting, once a domain has been searched, a registration provider will buy the domain name to see if it is lucrative and will return it at the end of the free taster period if it is not.

Do not be surprised if the domain is registered to a fictitious name or if the registrant is using a name shield (discussed below). At this stage it is important to check the date when the domain was registered to the current owner. If they registered the domain name before you began your business, the case is much more difficult to prove, and your options for recourse are more limited.

CASE STUDY

Microsoft

Cybersquatting was becoming a serious problem for Microsoft, so in 2006 it launched legal actions against a number of cybersquatters in the United States and the United Kingdom. It publicly denounced the typosquatters who had registered slight variants of its brand and had been earning money from adverts which they placed on the pages that people mistakenly visited.

In the United States, Microsoft filed six lawsuits against typo-squatters and settled with an untold number. One of these lawsuits was to reveal the identities of 54 domain name owners. In the end, it was able to recover thousands of domain names and an untold amount of damages. In one case in California, Microsoft was awarded $1 million in damages in a case against a cybersquatter who had registered 85 infringing domain names. Microsoft was also successful in the United Kingdom where it launched five legal actions which allowed it to recover over 6,000 domain names.

It hopes to take further action in other countries against other cybersquatters. Aaron Kornblum, senior attorney for Microsoft, said "We hope that our stance and activity on this issue will help motivate and empower other companies whose brands are abused to take action."

"In this electronic age your domain name is as important as the sign above your company's front door." Gordan Philip

  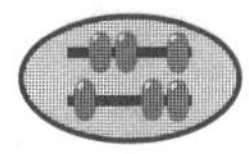   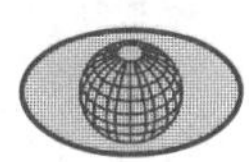   

LEGAL RECOURSES

There are many complex legal issues that arise in retrieving domain names through legal channels. It is essential to do some research on the registrant to find out who you are up against. Often, however, you will discover that cybersquatters use false details or a name shield to protect their identity.

A name shield means that the registrant's name is displayed as "Whois Guard" or similar. This will make it more difficult to determine the identity of the real registrant, but it will not prevent you from getting transfer of the domain names in either court or arbitration.

If the name is not shielded, find out whether there have been previous UDRP proceedings against the owner. Evidence of their having lost previous arbitration proceedings will be useful in your own case since it is evidence of bad faith. Some country-level domains (such as .uk) even have special rules for registrants who have had several decisions made against them, and in such cases the cybersquatter will have a much higher burden of proof to prevent the transfer of the domain.

Lawyers will then write to the owner to state your claims and demand transfer of the domain. If the registrant of the domain is a legitimate domainer they are more likely to agree to settle with you for fear of being labeled a cybersquatter in a judgment. Once lawyers get involved, some cybersquatters even agree to sign an undertaking not to do this again.

When dealing with cybersquatters the rule of thumb is to be prepared for almost anything. One common practice is known as cyberflight where the registrant, soon after being contacted, quickly transfers the domain to another party or another name. If this happens before you have filed your arbitration or lawsuit, then you will generally have to serve another letter on the new registrant unless there is good evidence that it is the same registrant. You can usually tell this by assessing whether the website has changed and whether there have been other changes, such as the website's server.

Once you file suit in arbitration or court, the domain is locked. However, cyberflight can occur during the time lapse between your filing suit and the domain name being locked. If it occurs during this period, you will probably be able to amend the complaint rather than having to start from scratch, because courts or tribunals tend to regard the complaint as having the same registrant.

Benefits of Litigation

One of the benefits of litigation is that there a large number of remedies available, including damages. It is also possible to get an undertaking from the squatter not to register any names in the future which infringe against your trademark rights. Additionally, in these types of cases cybersquatters often have to pay damages and legal fees in addition to transferring the domains.

ARBITRATION

The UDRP stands for the Uniform Domain-Name Dispute-Resolution Policy and is used for disputes over all top-level domain names (.com, .net, etc.) Country-level domain names like .us or .uk are governed by very similar policies.

Two of the benefits of arbitration over litigation are that it is generally cheaper and faster. The filing fees are lower, and you will not need to go to the expense of having a trial. To win in this type of arbitration you will need to prove three elements—that you have prior rights in the name; that the owner does not have rights in the name; and that the domain name was registered and is being used in bad faith.

The main limitation of the UDRP is that you only will be awarded transfer of the domain name. The tribunal does not have the power to award any money, so you will not get any damages or legal costs.

However, transfer of the domain may be all you can realistically achieve. This is especially true in cases where the registrant is based in a jurisdiction that is out of your reach for enforcement of court orders or is using a cloaked identity. Service of process under domain name arbitration requires only proof that you tried to contact the registrant using their whois details.

CONCLUSION

Dealing with cybersquatting can be difficult. It is best to develop a long-term strategy for dealing with cybersquatting as well as other internet infringements.

▸▸ MAKING IT HAPPEN

Cybersquatting is a complex area of law, so it is generally best to seek legal advice rather than attempting to deal with the problem on your own.

- Prevention is one of the most important steps in the fight against cybersquatting. Securing top-level and country-level domain names for the territories in which you trade or intend to trade reduces the risk of cybersquatter problems.
- Another preventative step is to have a good administrative domain management system in place to ensure that domains are renewed on time.
- A distinctive name helps a lot. Generic brand names like "Apple" inevitably mean that cybersquatters and other legitimate domain name owners will be able to claim rights in brand names you may regard as more rightfully yours.
- Make sure your brand is adequately protected on the internet by registering trademarks and seeking legal advice on internet law and copyright.

▸▸ MORE INFO

Book:

Bettinger, Torsten, Tony Willoughby, and Sally Abel (eds). *Domain Name Law and Practice: An International Handbook*. New York: Oxford University Press, 2005.

Websites:

DomainTools, includes a whois checker: www.domaintools.com

Internet Archive has archived versions of websites: www.archive.org

Martindale, for specialists in domain name and intellectual property law: www.martindale.com

World Intellectual Property Organization (WIPO) for domain name dispute resolution and cases: www.wipo.int/amc/en/domains

"Unfortunately, online criminals and scam artists find the Internet full of opportunities to line their pockets at the expense of leading brands and customer trust." Irfan Salim

     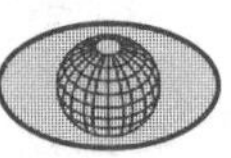   

Dispute Resolution: The Forum Selection Clause

by Elisabeth de Nadal and Víctor Manuel Sánchez

EXECUTIVE SUMMARY

- The forum selection clause in a contract determines the process by which the parties to the contract will have their disputes resolved and the venue for such dispute resolution. These processes generally take the form of litigation in a national court, arbitration, or other dispute resolution process such as mediation.
- The forum selection clause provides certainty to the parties in the often uncertain arena of international commercial transactions, where the uncertainty is due to the different countries and jurisdictions involved.
- The specific forum selection clause that best meets the interests of the parties should be decided on the basis of several considerations, which will differ from case to case.
- Given the relevance of the clause, and the legal consequences involved in the decision, it is advisable for managers to consult lawyers when such clauses are negotiated and drafted.

INTRODUCTION

When two companies start a business relationship, they do not wish future conflict or discrepancies to arise; company managers are human beings, and most human beings begin relationships confident that they will work out well.

However, as with all human relationships, it is natural that differences may occur. This is why contracts should include dispute resolution clauses and a forum selection clause—sometimes just called a forum clause. More importantly, it is why managers should negotiate the choice of forum clause for a contract as seriously and thoroughly as any other clause in the contract.

WHAT IS A FORUM CLAUSE? WHAT IS ITS PURPOSE?

The forum clause is the clause in a contract that sets out the process whereby the parties will seek a resolution to any dispute that may arise between them, as well as the venue where the dispute is to be resolved.

Unless there is a reason to the contrary, contracts should contain a forum selection clause to give the parties certainty in national and international trade. Negotiating a forum clause gives the parties the opportunity to agree on the method they will use to resolve disputes that meets the specific needs of the parties and the business contracted, as well as the most convenient place.

When deciding the forum clause, major goals should be to ensure that: the clause fits the needs of both parties; the clause is valid and enforceable; the method chosen will allow enforcement of the court or arbitration decision.

HOW TO NEGOTIATE THE FORUM CLAUSE

The following tips should be taken into account when negotiating a forum selection clause:

- Managers should view the possibility of litigation as par for the course in a commercial relationship (as it is preferable to failure of the relationship).
- The choice of a forum clause deserves the same attention and energy from negotiators as clauses setting the price, the representations and warranties, and any other material aspect of the contracted business.
- Due to the complexity and legal technicalities of the various options open to the parties, it is always advisable to have a lawyer present when negotiating this clause.

CIRCUMSTANCES TO CONSIDER

When negotiating the forum clause to be included in a contract, several circumstances must be considered so that the interests of the parties are best served in the event that a dispute arises. First we consider two important general points.

If a contract contains no forum clause, national courts will ensure jurisdiction by default. Thus, litigation will take place in a venue defined by domestic or international regulations. This venue might be totally unknown to the parties when executing the contract.

The specific national court that ensures jurisdiction will be determined by international rules and conventions, or by the internal laws of the country in which the statement of claim is filed. For negotiation purposes, in commercial contracts the plaintiff tends to have more options open to it in influencing which national court will have jurisdiction, based on factors such as the defendant's place of residence, where the contract is performed, and generally a close connection of the contract with a specific national court, etc. In view of the multiplicity of options open to the plaintiff, as a general principle it is not advisable to leave a contract without a forum clause. Having no agreed clause would amount to playing a football match without knowing in advance the rules of the game and the place where the game is to be played.

When the parties have decided to include a forum clause, the next decision is whether to opt for litigation before a national court or for some other means of dispute resolution. If the first option is chosen, the clause must refer to the courts of a specific country or city; if the second, the clause must refer to a specific dispute resolution method—for example arbitration or mediation. In the case of arbitration or mediation, certain particulars of the dispute resolution method must also be identified, such as the institution that will manage the arbitration or mediation, the procedure for appointing arbitrators, the place where the arbitration or mediation is to be held, the language in which the proceedings are to be conducted, how costs are to be allocated, and so on.

Other circumstances to be borne in mind to ensure that a satisfactory choice of forum clause is made are the following:

The parties' nationalities and the need for neutrality: If the parties have different nationalities and one party is able to litigate in its home country, the other party may be disadvantaged by lack of knowledge of the legal system, in terms of procedural and material law applicable, the judges' competence, and the legal culture and expectations of the outcome. General disadvantages relating to language and physical distance are other considerations, as are fears that a local judge may tend to protect national litigants and concerns about corruption; whether or not these have any basis in fact, the provisions of a forum clause should seek to allay such concerns. These are some of the reasons why international contracts include a forum selection clause that ensures neutrality for both parties by referring to the courts of a third country or to arbitration.

Complexity of the matter: The field and specific issue that may be the subject of a potential dispute, and thus the specialist competencies of courts and judges, are

"Good people do not need laws to tell them to act responsibly, while bad people will find a way around the laws." Plato

  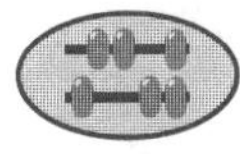   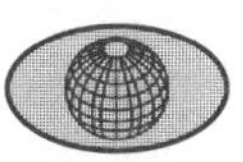   

relevant. In national courts it is not possible to ensure that a person with specific competence in a certain field will judge a dispute. Some countries have courts that specialize in particular issues, and these may be able to resolve a contract problem, but other countries do not. Therefore arbitration may be a more suitable choice as it allows the parties to choose the most suitable independent arbitrators with expertise in the relevant field.

Amount at stake and costs: The amount involved and/or the strategic importance of the business contracted will also influence the decision. Litigating in the national courts of one country may be more costly than in others. On the other hand, litigating in national courts is generally less costly than arbitration.

Flexibility and speed: It is impossible for the parties to influence the flexibility and speed of a national court system (since the procedural rules that apply are mandatory), but other forms of dispute resolution such as arbitration allow the parties to design the way any proceedings will develop and enable them to build in flexibility to meet their needs.

Final decision: The system of appeals until a decision is rendered final is different in each country. Arbitration awards cannot be appealed, and can only be set aside on the basis of very restricted grounds.

Recognition and enforcement of the decision: If a court or arbitration decision made in one country will need to be recognized and enforced in another country, issues to consider are whether both countries are parties to international or bilateral conventions that allow the enforcement of decisions, and the internal rules of enforcement of decisions made in foreign countries in the target countries.

COURT JURISDICTION

A forum selection clause that specifies a national court for the resolution of disputes should be negotiated on the basis of the factors discussed above. Before deciding on this option, and deciding on the courts of one particular country, advice on and knowledge of the following issues is relevant, and law professionals should be consulted on these issues:

Enforceability of the Forum Clause

National rules in the countries involved and international conventions set the circumstances under which an express submission to a particular national court can be made. If none of the conventions apply, then the specific country's internal rules determine the validity of the forum clause in favor of the specific national courts.

In most of the European Union, the rules of jurisdiction are set out in Regulation 44/2001. According to this, the national court chosen by the parties is competent in contractual matters when there is a forum clause in its favor and/or when one of them is resident in a member state, except when proceedings relate to real estate. Although superseded in most cases, the Brussels Convention, 1968, and the Lugano Convention, 1988, should also be residually taken into account.

In the United States, this issue is regulated through case law. In general, forum clauses that "are prima facie valid and should be enforced unless enforcement is shown by the resisting party to be unreasonable under the circumstances" (Bremen v. Zapata Off-Shore Co 407 U.S. 1 (1972)) are enforced.

China also tends to allow the enforcement of forum clauses, unless the dispute involves real estate, harbor operations, or foreign investment enterprises, in accordance with the Civil Procedure Law (CPL) of the People's Republic of China, dated April 4, 1991.

Procedural Rules

An important consideration is the procedural rules of the specific country, namely the number of instances and system of appeals until a judgment is rendered definitive, as the time required to resolve disputes depends largely on the national courts.

Specialized or Generalist Courts

A real understanding of the issues and the quality of the judgment made by a court may depend on whether a country has specialized courts.

Immediate Enforceability

Another consideration is whether judgment is immediately enforceable or whether enforcement may be delayed pending the conclusion of an appeals procedure.

Rules for Taking Evidence, Internally and Internationally

If the evidence on which a party relies is obtained in the country where the lawsuit takes place, the internal rules of that country will prevail. However, if the evidence is to be taken abroad, then international conventions and bilateral conventions will apply.

The Hague Convention, 1970, on taking evidence abroad in civil or commercial matters is widely admitted in the international arena in the matter of obtaining evidence in one signatory state and presenting it in another. In the European Union, Regulation 1206/2001 on cooperation between the courts of member states in taking evidence in civil or commercial matters facilitates these matters greatly. In the United States and some countries of the American continent, the Inter-American Convention, 1975, on taking evidence abroad applies.

Enforceability Abroad

If it is likely that a judgment will have to be enforced in a foreign country, it is necessary to find out whether there is an international convention or a bilateral treaty that facilitates such enforcement; if there is not, it will be necessary to ascertain the quality of the legal regime set by the internal rules of the country where the judgment is to be enforced.

EU Regulation 44/2001 regulates the recognition and enforcement in an EU member state of a judgment rendered in another member state. The Brussels Convention, 1968, and the Lugano Convention, 1988, should also be considered for residual issues.

There is no convention or bilateral agreement between the United States and any other country for reciprocal recognition and enforcement of judgments. The United States relies on state law for the enforcement of foreign judgments, which generally requires a lawsuit to give effect to the foreign judgment.

In China there is a twofold procedure: the claimant petitions the courts, or the court directs a petition to recognize and enforce the judgment. Treaties, mandatory Chinese law, and the principle of reciprocity are taken into account.

ARBITRATION

Arbitration is a mechanism to resolve disputes outside courts. With arbitration the dispute is adjudicated by one or more arbitrators, who reach a decision known as an award. Arbitration is a popular choice in international commercial transactions and investment. When deciding whether arbitration is the right choice, parties should consider the following:

Neutrality

Arbitration overcomes the disadvantages of litigating in another party's country. The parties choose the place of arbitration, the nationality and number of arbitrators, and the language and other particulars of the proceedings.

Final and Binding Award

An arbitral award cannot be appealed. It

may only be challenged in the state where the arbitration takes place (the so-called submission for nullity), or in the country where the award is to be enforced (opposition to the enforcement). The grounds for nullity and opposition are very limited.

Confidentiality

Arbitration is private. Unlike proceedings in most national courts, arbitration hearings and awards are not public. This can be important when sensitive issues are at stake in a dispute.

Complexity

Parties may choose the arbitrators they deem appropriate to solve a complex matter, provided that they are impartial and independent.

Costs

Parties must pay the arbitrators' fees and the administrative fees of the institution in charge of the arbitration. As a general rule, this makes arbitration more expensive that litigation in national courts.

Recognition and Enforcement

The recognition and enforcement of arbitration awards benefit from an international regime that is more secure, rapid, and certain than that applying to court decisions.

The Convention on the Recognition and Enforcement of Foreign Arbitral Awards 1958 (New York Convention) has been signed by 143 countries (as at February 2009) and sets a straightforward and well-defined regime to which all signatory states adhere. In Europe, most EU countries are also parties to the Geneva Convention on International Commercial Arbitration of 1961, which is even more favorable for the recognition and enforcement of awards. In the Americas, the Inter-American Convention on International Commercial Arbitration 1975 (which applies to members of the Organization of American States (OAS)) is also relevant.

Institutional or Ad Hoc Arbitration

Arbitration can be conducted under the auspices of an international organization or on an ad hoc basis. The former type is subject to regulation, and the institution chosen assumes the procedural issues related to the arbitration. In ad hoc proceedings, the arbitrators are in charge of the administration and the proceedings.

MEDIATION

Mediation is a dispute resolution process whereby the parties attempt, by themselves and on a voluntary basis, to reach a settlement of the dispute with the assistance of a third party (mediator). The settlement agreement is as valid as any contract entered into by the parties. Parties to contracts frequently choose to have a mediation stage as a prior step to arbitration or litigation.

CONCLUSION

Forum selection clauses in contracts provide the parties with certainty about the method that they will use to resolve disputes and the venue where any such proceedings will be held. Negotiating and drafting these clauses therefore deserves the same careful attention as any other clause in a contract.

Given the many different circumstances that have to be considered when deciding on a forum clause that best fits the interests of the parties, it is advisable not to negotiate them without a lawyer or other professional adviser.

▸▸ MAKING IT HAPPEN

- It is important to include in a contract a well-drafted forum selection clause that demonstrates clearly the parties' intentions to resolve disputes arising from the contract by means of a specified process or mechanism.
- In multicontract situations it is essential to coordinate the forum clauses contained in different documents or contracts that are part of one global transaction. This is necessary to avoid inconsistencies that may impair the efficacy and enforceability of judgments, and also to avoid opportunistic behavior by one party, such as a motion for lack of jurisdiction.
- Particular attention should be paid to a problem that arises frequently when the following contractual structure has been used: The main contract contains an arbitration clause but is accompanied by an ancillary agreement that does not contain an arbitration clause and in which a third party also participates—generally guaranteeing the debt arising from the main obligations or establishing an escrow agent in charge of releasing the amounts set as variable prices of the main contract.
- Include the same forum clause in all the different contracts that cover the transaction. In particular, if arbitration is selected, reference should be made to the same institution, the same place of arbitration, and same number of arbitrators in all the arbitration clauses in all the contracts.

▸▸ MORE INFO

Books:

Bühler, Michael W., and Thomas H. Webster. *Handbook of ICC Arbitration: Commentary, Precedents, Materials*. 2nd ed. London: Thomson/Sweet and Maxwell, 2008.

Fawcett, James, and Janeen M. Carruthers. *Cheshire, North and Fawcett: Private International Law*. 14th ed. Oxford: Oxford University Press, 2008.

Gaillard, Emmanuel, and John Savage (eds). *Fouchard Gaillard Goldman On International Commercial Arbitration*. The Hague: Kluwer Law International, 1999.

Global Legal Group (GLG). *The International Comparative Legal Guide to: International Arbitration*. London: GLG, 2007.

Grubbs, Shelby R. *International Civil Procedure*. The Hague: Kluwer Law International, 2003.

Law Business Research. *Global Arbitration Review 100 – 2009*. London: Law Business Research, 2009.

Websites:

American Arbitration Association: www.adr.org

American legislation on private international law (US State Department website): www.state.gov/s/l/c3452.htm

Cairo Regional Centre for International Commercial Arbitration: www.crcica.org.eg

Center for Effective Dispute Resolution: www.cedr.co.uk

European legislation on private international law (Europa website): europa.eu/scadplus/leg/en/s22003.htm

International Chamber of Commerce, arbitration section: www.iccwbo.org/court/arbitration/id4398/index.html

International Institute for Conflict Prevention & Resolution (CPR): www.cpradr.org

London Court of International Arbitration: www.lcia.org

"A rock pile ceases to be a rock pile the moment a single man contemplates it bearing within him the image of a cathedral." Antoine de Saint-Exupéry

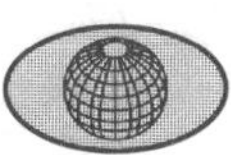

Electronic Invoicing in the European Union by Hansjörg Nymphius

EXECUTIVE SUMMARY

This article examines the following issues:

- the EU Expert Group on e-invoicing and the European framework
- the goals – more effective value chains and streamlined information flows
- the current state of e-invoicing
- EDI as a precursor to e-invoicing
- growth in the supplier market
- issues with current models of e-invoicing

INTRODUCTION

Europe is entering a crucial stage in the development of electronic invoicing. The European Commission (EC) has made the development of e-invoicing an objective in both the 2002 and the 2005 eEurope Action Plans.[1]

The invoice, just to summarize, consists of an itemized account of goods shipped, services performed or work done, an amount expended or owed, and a demand for payment. It may contain a range of other administrative or logistics information, and usually will state applicable taxes payable. It is the crucial link, or perhaps the pivot, between the physical and financial supply chains and, accordingly, has been described as the "queen" of commercial documents. It is important to note that in traditional invoicing all these features are derived from a single paper document, often with the word "invoice" on it.[2]

Two years ago the EC formed an Expert Group on e-invoicing with the aim of establishing a Europe-wide framework that allows for the standardized exchange of e-invoices by all market participants, particularly those involved in purchase and supply. Studies indicate that implementing electronic invoicing on a Europe-wide basis could reduce supply-chain costs by €243 billion, by streamlining business processes and driving innovation.

The Expert Group initiative emerged from the EC's "Broad-Based Innovation Strategy," launched in September 2006, which recognized that "Europe cannot compete unless it becomes more inventive, reacts better to consumer needs and preferences, and innovates more." This in turn goes back to the Lisbon Treaty, which aims to enhance the efficiency of Europe through installing innovation at all levels and by implementing modern democratic institutions. "E-government, or the ready availability of government services over the internet, including online payment and online invoicing—which equates to e-invoicing—is seen as a natural part of this progression. The Lisbon Treaty aims to make Europe the most competitive and dynamic knowledge-based economy in the world by 2010."

In recognizing and reacting to the competitive challenge facing Europe, two aspects emerge as the basis for improving European competitiveness in a global economy: Efficiency and certainty. More efficient value chains reduce cost; improving the certainty of the environment in which they operate makes them more competitive.

Streamlining the flow of information in any value chain will reduce inefficiencies, improve certainty, and reduce costs. As Europe moves to adopt the Single Euro Payments Area (SEPA), it is logical that this is linked to the business processes that settle a vast majority of business-to-business (B2B) and business-to-government payments. SEPA is expected to contribute significantly to the Lisbon agenda.

Electronic invoicing involves the replacement of manual paper-based routines with new integrated systems and processes. Expected benefits include the creation of integrated supply chains which are more cost-effective, less error-prone, faster, and simpler to manage. Other benefits include improved customer care (typically, as the joint EBA/Innopay report, "E-invoicing 2008," points out, nearly half of customer queries relate to invoicing) as well as improved risk management. Cross-selling and up-selling opportunities can also enabled through electronic invoicing, the report notes.

The outlook for these developments is promising despite obvious barriers to initial adoption. The European Banking Association (EBA), as a force for collaboration in the European payments industry over many years, is strongly committed to working with all stakeholders to identify practical solutions and to working closely within the European Electronic Invoicing Framework (EEIF) as it develops.

Today e-invoicing in Europe across all organizations, from government to the private sector, has a relatively low penetration, just as in North America and the Asia–Pacific region. There were some 28 billion invoices (paper and electronic) in 2006 in Europe. Approximately 50% of these invoices were B2B and the remaining 50% were business-to-consumer (B2C). However, the growth in e-invoicing is rapid, as would be expected from a low base, and annual rates of growth of 60%–100% are mentioned, with some markets growing at an even faster rate. So far the various country-specific e-invoicing initiatives amount to between 2% and 3% of the total invoices issued, with the total number of e-invoices issued in Europe being around 490 million in 2006 and, when the statistics have been finalized, are expected to be around 710 million for 2007. The leaders are the Nordic countries and Switzerland, with adoption rates of around 10% in B2B invoicing. The Swedish government, for example, decided that all government agencies had to be capable of handling invoices electronically by July 2008, a move that is expected to generate savings of around €400 million over the next five years.

EDI AS A PRECURSOR TO E-INVOICING

Electronic data interchange (EDI) was a precursor to e-invoicing. EDI is a standard for the dematerialization of trade-related documents between trading partners, and invoices are a part of this standardization effort. However, in some countries, even an EDI electronic invoice requires a paper summary to meet national legislation requirements. So far, EDI adoption around the world has largely happened with large companies with well-defined supply chains.

There are a number of studies which show that it costs between four and 70 euros to process a paper invoice, with cross-border invoicing being the most

"At some point a good leader with inadequate data will say, Ready, fire, aim—and if it doesn't work we'll correct it, but at least the timing is right to start with what we have." Robert Townsend

  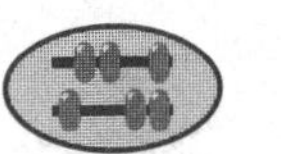   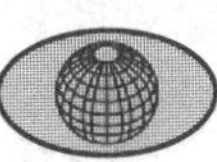   

expensive. This estimate includes the cost of handling and receiving the invoice, matching against orders and deliveries, and approving payment. Accounts payable automation can significantly reduce the cost of handling these inbound invoices. There have also been successful total invoice management initiatives, with suppliers becoming outsource providers of both accounts payable and accounts receivable functions. Scanning, optical character recognition, and data mapping techniques support the dematerialization of paper documentation across parties.

Online banking is a major driver for the adoption of e-invoicing around the world. Countries with high rates of online banking adoption also show high e-invoicing adoption rates. Large companies have adopted EDI. However, online banking has appealed strongly to medium-sized firms, who often use their bank's e-invoicing offerings to pay clients.

We are also witnessing many government initiatives to promote e-invoicing. The European Commission website, ec.europa.eu, lists a number of examples, including an interesting one in Slovenia which has the potential to involve neighboring countries.

The business of service providers in the e-invoicing market is to add value to invoice senders and/or invoice receivers. Such value-added services can be categorized from exchange and conversion services (mainly focused on creation of an exchange network) to complete sourcing of accounts payable or accounts receivable management services. In Europe, there are a large number of service providers and service solutions with a huge variety of product features and business models. This, in part, is a reflection of the variety of countries, languages, commercial practices, service concepts, legal environments, and implementations of relevant EU directives. Many of the generic models are similar to practices carried out in North America and elsewhere.

GROWTH IN THE E-INVOICING SUPPLIER MARKET

The overall number of service providers involved in the e-invoicing market has grown from 160 in 2006 to 260 in 2007. Some commentators suggest a continued growth in the number of service providers, whilst others are expecting a major consolidation. Critical mass for an e-invoicing service provider is believed to be around 1.5 million invoices per year. The e-invoicing sector is worth around €1 billion per year.[3]

A number of banks have entered the market, competing directly to offer a bundle of supply chain services, typically to large corporations. There are collective schemes with a community of banks cooperating to provide a service based on a common set of rules, standards, and agreed terminology.

A key functionality to these service models and providers is the ability to exchange electronic documents between a sender and a receiver. There are four models for this exchange:

1 **Bilateral model**: Buyers and sellers in a one-to-one relationship.
2 **Three-party model**: Senders and receivers are connected to a single central hub. This model's limitation is that senders and receivers can only reach other senders or receivers attached to that hub. So one sender committed to e-invoicing might have to become a member of multiple hubs. To solve this "limited reach" problem in the three-party model, the concept of "roaming" has been introduced.
3 **Roaming Model**: Emerging model which looks to a "hub of hubs," or a network of hub-to-hub connections to provide real cross-border reach.
4 **Four-party model**: Senders and receivers of invoices are supported by their own consolidator service provider (for the sender) and aggregator service provider (for the receiver). A network usually based on open standards provides connectivity and the facilities for the secure, trusted exchange of invoices and/or other business documents. In the four-party model, the consolidator and aggregator roles are often two different service providers.

BARRIERS TO E-INVOICING

As the EEI Expert Group's interim report on e-invoicing points out, while the current legislative environment across Europe has a foundation that underpins the integrity and authenticity of an e-invoice, and that will serve for a Europe-wide e-invoicing solution, there are legislative hurdles. E-invoicing lies at the crossroads of several areas of legislation, including VAT, accounting, payment, authentication, company transparency, and data retention. There are complexities for both supplier and buyer, and for service providers.

Securing European compliance for an e-invoicing solution is complicated. VAT issues will require unanimity from member states, and requirements on archiving and other processes will also take time to resolve.

The operational barriers to e-invoicing largely depend on trust and technical interoperability issues. In some respects, e-invoicing suffers from the fact that some believe that it will progress more easily once we have a universally open, fully secure, and interoperable internet-based B2B network across Europe. In reality, this is likely to be challenging and a pragmatic approach may yield better and faster results, based on emerging "best practice" models.

The EU informal Task Force report noted that standardization of e-invoices is currently fragmented, with many specifications in use both in the EU and abroad. Further standardization work is required. There is a strong school of thought that recommends that any solution should be global, not simply an EU solution. Steps are being taken to get the major international standards-setting bodies, such as the UN's CEFACT and the ISO's Technical Committee on Financial Services, to work together for the development and delivery of an international e-invoicing standard.

Others argue that the absence of a global standard is not as big an inhibitor as many believe. The history of XML has shown that it is possible for standards to be communicated and managed through a variety of technical means, including translation services working on an "any format in, any format out" basis.

Overall, most view the absence of a uniform global standard for e-invoicing as not being a "showstopper." However, any improvements in this direction will certainly help market development in the long run.

ISSUES WITH BUSINESS AND COOPERATION MODELS

End-users and businesses tend to be reluctant to choose a particular model or solution, because often that model only addresses one subset of their requirements and solves only one particular issue. Many experts feel that the current industrial structure has too many players, excessive market fragmentation, and a lack of interoperability. The current collaboration model between the various stakeholders is felt to be inadequate, and there is evidence of a degree of contention/defensiveness for market positions. More clarity is needed on an agreed definition of the cooperative versus competitive space. The prize in terms of market expansion from the creation of a platform for appropriate and targeted collaboration, for example in the area of interoperability, could be very large indeed.

"**Corporate risk takers are very much like entrepreneurs. They take personal risks to make new ideas happen.**"
Gifford Pinchot

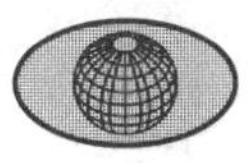

MORE INFO

Reports:

de Boer, Tonnis, *et al.* "E-invoicing 2008: European market description and analysis." Euro Banking Association/Innopay, February 2008. Online at: www.abe-eba.eu/Repository.aspx?ID=54942e07-ad65-4dc4-920e-09c7cce51497

Koch, Bruno. "E-invoicing and EBPP: European market overview." Billentis, February 2009. Online at: www.billentis.com/ebilling_e-invoicing_European_Market_Overview_2009.pdf

NOTES

1 eEurope 2005: An Information Society for All: ec.europa.eu/information_society/eeurope/2005/index_en.htm

2 de Boer, Tonnis, *et al.* (2008).

3 Figures cited from a speech by Bruno Koch, a recognised authority on e-invoicing; see www.billentis.com

"Be bold, be bold, and everywhere, Be bold." Edmund Spenser

Employee Stock Options by Peter Casson

EXECUTIVE SUMMARY

- Employee stock options are call options on the employer company's common stock, and are usually not transferable.
- Most employee stock options have a vesting period, during which the holder is not unconditionally entitled to the option, with options vesting at the end of the period if performance conditions are met.
- Employee stock options may be used by companies to recruit, retain, and provide incentives to employees and executives. Companies with weak cash flows that cannot afford to pay employees the market rate entirely in cash may use stock options in lieu of cash.
- Companies may use employee stock options to capture tax or accounting benefits associated with them.

INTRODUCTION

Employee stock options are a component of the compensation package of many employees and executives. As well as providing a mechanism for linking pay with the performance of the company's stock price, stock options can facilitate the recruitment and retention of employees. The effectiveness of stock option compensation derives from the basic characteristics of options and from particular features found in many employee stock options. This article describes the essential features of employee stock options and explores the ways in which they are used by companies.

CHARACTERISTICS OF EMPLOYEE STOCK OPTIONS

Employee stock options are call options granted by an employer on the company's common stock. Call options are contracts that give holders the right, but not the obligation, to acquire stock at a specified price (the exercise price), either on a specified date or over a specified period. The fair value of a call option has two components. The first, known as intrinsic value, is the amount that the holder would receive were the option to be exercised today. This amount, which cannot be negative, is the greater of zero and the difference between the fair value of the underlying stock and the exercise price of the option. The second, known as time value, is the difference between the fair value and the intrinsic value of the option.

The fair value of a call option on a company's common stock is sensitive to changes in:

- The fair value of the underlying stock—the value of the option rises with increases in the fair value of the stock.
- The expected volatility of the returns on the underlying stock—the value of the option increases with increases in expected volatility.
- The risk-free rate of interest—the value of the option increases with increases in the risk-free rate.
- The time until the option expires—the value of the option decreases as time to expiry decreases.
- The dividends expected to be paid on the underlying stock over the life of the option—the value of the option decreases with increases in the expected dividend payments.

Stock options granted to employees usually have an exercise price equal to the fair value of the underlying stock on the date the option is granted, and have a life of seven to ten years. Stock options generally have additional features that affect their fair value. First, there is usually an initial period, often three years, after the grant of the option (the vesting period), during which the employee is not unconditionally entitled to the option. Rather, the employee's entitlement to the option at the end of the vesting period only comes about if performance conditions are met. The performance condition for employees is usually to remain in the employment of the grantor company during the vesting period. Options, especially those granted to senior executives, may have additional performance conditions relating to company and/or personal performance. Second, once vested, options are usually forfeited if the employee leaves the grantor company. However, it is usual for employees to be able to exercise options within a period, often 90 days, after leaving the company. The forfeiture provision normally means that employees are forced into an early exercise of in-the-money options. Third, employee stock options are usually nontransferable, which means the employees can only realize value by exercising the option and selling the stock. In so doing, they forego the time value of the option.

WHY COMPANIES USE EMPLOYEE SHARE OPTIONS

Companies grant stock options to attract, retain, and motivate employees and executives. In addition, start-up companies and companies with weak cash flows may grant stock options to compensate for the below-market cash wages that they can afford. Finally, options may be granted to capture taxation and/or accounting benefits.

CASE STUDY

BG Group plc[1]

BG Group plc is a UK-listed company engaged in the discovery, extraction, transmission, distribution, and supply of natural gas. BG has about 5,000 employees, more than 60% of whom are located outside the United Kingdom. The company operates two stock option schemes, a company share option scheme (CSOS) and a sharesave scheme. The CSOS is open to UK and overseas employees above a certain grade. The number of CSOS options granted to individuals depends on their past performance and their expected contribution to the company. The CSOS scheme aims to "drive real earnings growth over the long term." Options granted under this scheme, which have an exercise price equal to the fair value of the company's shares at the time of grant, have a vesting period of three years, and vested options may be exercised at any time until the tenth anniversary of the grant. Options vest to the extent that there has been real growth in earnings per share (EPS) over the vesting period. All the options will vest if EPS growth over the vesting period is at least 30% more than growth in the retail prices index (excluding mortgage payments) (RPIX), and half the options will vest if EPS growth is at least 15% more than RPIX growth.

The sharesave scheme, which is approved by the UK tax authority, allows eligible employees to acquire shares in the company using the proceeds of a tax-exempt monthly savings plan. BG Group uses the scheme as a way of encouraging share ownership in the company.

  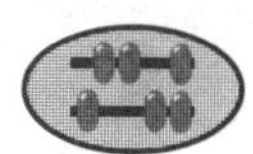   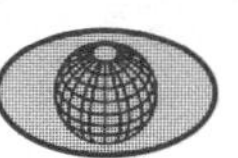   

Stock options attract employees and executives for the following reasons. First, individuals whose abilities match the needs of the company may be attracted by stock options because they believe that their abilities will improve company performance and that this will be reflected in an enhanced stock price. Second, the offer of stock options may attract those employees who are most optimistic about the company's future prospects. Their optimism may lead them to overvalue the options, so reducing the company's overall employment costs. Finally, stock options may attract relatively less risk-averse employees who meet the needs of the company.

Employee stock options can be used as a way to increase employee retention. The vesting conditions usually found in the options encourage employees to remain with the company until the options become exercisable. In addition, employees will forego the time value of vested options if they are forced into early exercise by leaving the company. Finally, as employees build up a portfolio of options over time, it becomes more costly for a competitor to attract the company's employees, as the competitor may have to compensate them for the value foregone from forfeiting unvested options or from suboptimally exercising options.

Holders of employee stock options have an incentive to act in a way that increases the value of the options. The fair value of employee stock options is, as described above, sensitive to the company's stock price, the expected volatility of the stock, and the dividends expected to be paid on the stock during the life of the options. Employees may act, through enhanced performance, to increase company performance, and that in turn may be reflected in the stock price. Although grants of stock options to CEOs and senior executives may be effective in increasing company performance, the incentive effects of grants to other employees are questionable, as there are significant free-rider problems. The other incentive effects are confined to options held by senior executives, especially CEOs. Senior executives holding stock options may make riskier investment decisions and/or increase the company's leverage with a view to increasing the expected stock volatility. Stock options may also reduce the dividend on the company's stock.

Stock options may be used by start-up companies and companies experiencing cash constraints. Here employees may sacrifice part of their cash compensation in exchange for stock options. Although financial institutions are usually seen to be in a better position than employees to bear the risks associated with lending, employees may be willing to do so because: (1) options attract risk-seeking individuals, who, if the company fails, will move to another company; (2) they possess superior knowledge and so perceive the risk differently to financial institutions; or (3) they do not understand the risks.

Companies may use stock option compensation because of preferential tax policies, although this depends on the tax regime of the country in which the employee and the company are resident. Stock option compensation may, depending on the jurisdiction, be taxed at the time of grant, or at the time the option is exercised, or when the stock acquired on the exercise of the option is subsequently sold. Employees may be charged either to income tax or to capital gains tax on their stock option compensation. Finally, stock option compensation by the company may or may not be tax-deductible. A country's tax regime may offer favorable tax treatment to stock option schemes that have particular features. In such cases, the provisions of the tax regime may shape the option schemes that companies use.

Stock option compensation may also be used because of the way it is accounted for in company financial statements. The accounting treatment of stock options was seen in the past to be advantageous when stock options were recorded at their intrinsic value at the time of grant. As options are usually granted with an exercise price equal to the fair value of the stock on the date of grant, the intrinsic value of the option is zero. This meant that there was no charge against income. However, both international and US accounting standards now require companies to charge the fair value of stock options, as measured at the time of grant, against income.

CONCLUSION

The structure of employee stock options facilitates their use by companies to attract, retain, and motivate employees and executives. In particular, the vesting provisions provide incentives for employees to remain with the company. Employee stock options have a role in aligning employees' and executives' interests with those of stockholders. Performance conditions attached to the vesting of some stock options may also align the objectives of employees with those of the company. The structure of stock options may be shaped to take advantage of tax and/or accounting rules.

▶▶ MAKING IT HAPPEN

The decision to establish stock options schemes usually rests with the board of directors, and it may require stockholder approval. In designing a scheme it is necessary to consider:

- Why the company wants an employee stock option scheme.
- Which employees should be included within the scheme.
- The characteristics of the stock options. This includes consideration of the exercise price, the vesting period (if any), vesting conditions, the forfeiting of vested options if the employee leaves the company, and the life of the option.
- The tax and accounting implications of the scheme.

▶▶ MORE INFO

Book:

Wheeler, Peter R. *Stock Options + Grants: The Executive's Guide to Equity Compensation*. Sunnyvale, CA: AdviserPress, 2004.

Article:

Hall, B. R. "Six challenges in designing equity-based pay." *Journal of Applied Corporate Finance* 15:3 (2003): 49–70.

Website:

National Center for Employee Ownership (NCEO): www.nceo.org

NOTES

1 Information from BG Group plc Annual Report 2007.

"People love to recognize, not venture. The former is so much more comfortable and self-flattering."
Jean Cocteau

     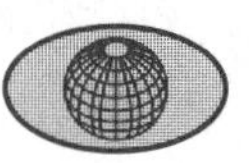   

Essentials for Export Success: Understanding How Risks and Relationships Lead to Rewards

by Paul Beretz

EXECUTIVE SUMMARY

- The global business environment can present opportunities for rewards for the exporter if international risk attributes can be determined and mitigated.
- Exporters who want to succeed should be able to identify and evaluate their "IQ" (international qualities).
- The risk elements of country, currency, and culture can significantly impact global business transactions.
- Relationship-building and the ability to sustain those relationships are necessary qualities for reaping rewards.

INTRODUCTION

More and more, companies located throughout the world are recognizing that the way to sustain long-term growth is not by continuing to emphasize local, in-country markets. Whether it be for better or worse, global business is a factor that can provide businesses with the opportunity to consider new and challenging markets. In 2008, we saw that severe credit and financial issues could spread quickly, and that no part of the world was immune. Therefore, an understanding of the key risk factors that can lead to rewards is essential.

How should a business assess world markets? One initial approach for exporters is to determine their "IQ," or international qualities, before either entering or expanding their overseas markets.

RATING YOUR COMPANY'S "IQ"

The "IQ" test shown in Figure 1 will address your company's readiness to compete in the global marketplace. For each question, give your company a letter grade (A–F, or U for "Unknown") and state the reason(s) for your grade. Grade A = 90–100%, B = 80–89%, and so on.

RISKS FACING THE EXPORTER

An exporter will face many risks once the decision to sell in overseas markets is made. Key risk areas, in particular, are known as the "three Cs"—country, currency, and culture.

Country Risk

Figure 2 outlines the dimensions of country risk when goods or services are sold globally. Exporters may wish to use the chart to classify the major risk issues and attributes of each risk by country.

Theses are the questions to ask when determining the dimensions of country risk:

- What currency will you be selling in? Is the decision a competitive one? Are you equipped internally to deal in multi-currencies?
- Do you know the laws in specific countries? (For example, a joint venture in China must balance imports with exports, or else it could be barred by the government from obtaining hard currency.)
- What is the recent political history (that could influence the availability of funds or internal stability)? This will include government takeover of properties, whether with or without compensation, operational restrictions, or damage to property or personnel.
- What is the current economic environment in the country? Have there been local currency devaluations recently?
- Have there been border disputes that could escalate military readiness and therefore impact the availability of hard currency, both within the country's borders and as funds leaving the country? If the exporter's customer base is expanding through direct investment abroad, will there be access to the invested capital and will earnings be able to be repatriated? This could impact cash flow and the ability to meet its trade obligations.

Figure 1. The "IQ" test

"IQ" question	Grade	Reason
What percentage of your revenues do you expect from the country(ies) you will be exporting to?		
What do you expect as your market share and industry ranking in that/those country(ies)?		
Will you establish direct sales relationships with your major customers?		
Will you ever expect to be considered a company that is "part" of the country you are exporting to?		
Have you analyzed all the cultural, currency, and country issues you will encounter in exporting to a particular country?		
What is your knowledge of the market for your product in a given country?		
What is your knowledge of the economic structure and the current state of the economy in a new country?		
Have you analyzed the legal system in a new country for the legality of your contracts or relationships? Can you cancel a relationship with a distributor or an agent if necessary? Is your documentation of sale legally binding?		
Once the sale is made, and payment is not forthcoming, what are your options in achieving payment? Practically, culturally, and legally, what are the norms?		

Currency Risk

Exporters have to consider selling in foreign currencies to offshore customers. In this competitive environment, an exporter needs flexibility in determining the currency that is billed to the customer. In a volatile global economy, however, billing a buyer in a currency that differs from the seller's own currency can be fraught with risk: When payment is due, has the value of the currency fallen in value against the seller's currency?

"It is simply too easily forgotten that when it comes to economic activities, one of the greatest virtues a country or community can have is a culture of tolerance." Thomas Friedman

  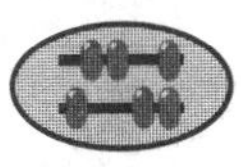 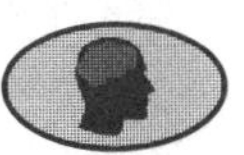  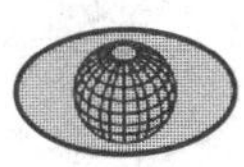   

Figure 2. Dimensions of country risk

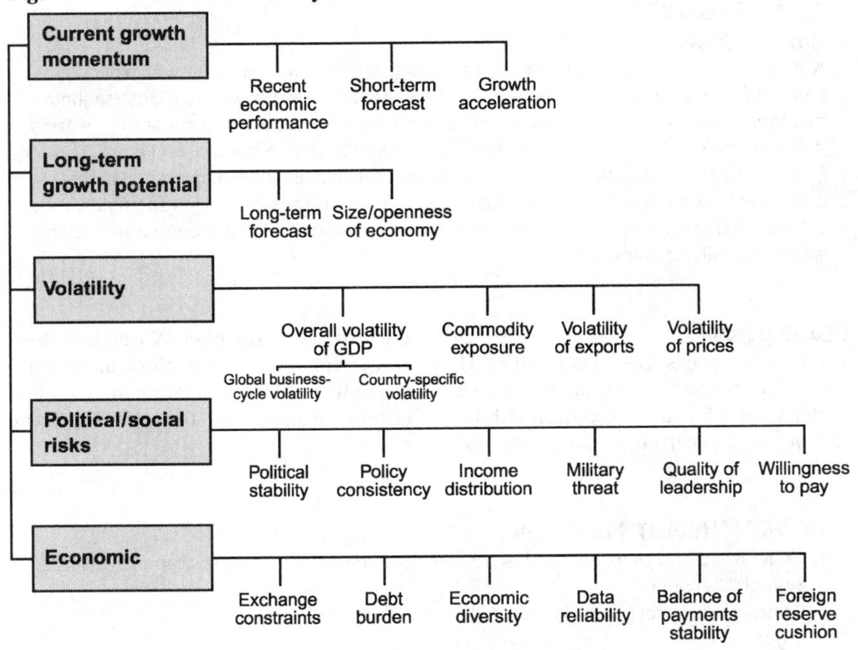

One approach for the exporter is to deal in the foreign exchange (FX) market, which is an enormous, sophisticated, and efficient global communications system operating around the clock to enable international transactions. Large commercial banks are the dominant players in the FX market, serving as intermediaries between supply and demand; corporations are the principal end-users. FX transactions are speculative by nature and thus can be volatile, thereby increasing risk.

Three basic transactions for managing FX risk are *spot transactions, forward transactions* and *options*. *Spot transactions* are purchases or sales of foreign currency for "immediate" delivery. *Forward transactions* carry a specified price and stipulated future value date for the exchange of currencies. They are used most often to cover future foreign currency payables and anticipated receipts. *Options* are a more suitable tool for "hedging" risk when a foreign customer's commitment is not firm. Buyers pay a premium for the option to exchange foreign currency at a predetermined rate ("strike price"). Options are bought and sold on the "exchange-traded" (less flexible, less expensive) and "over the counter" (more flexible, more expensive) markets, and they allow buyers to take advantage of favorable changes in currency rates while guarding against adverse changes.

The prudent financial manager recognizes that currency risk is a major factor in the export decision.

Culture Risk

The proactive, truly globally oriented exporter living in today's competitive marketplace understands that business decision making is a form of art as much as a science. All the evaluation tools available cannot take the place of experience. It is essential to possess a fundamental, analytical approach to the export selling process. The "art" form of today's global business process includes an understanding of how the cultures and negotiation processes of different countries become part of the arsenal of tools in making an intelligent decision. How the culture of each country or region impacts the risk is material to the ultimate business decision.

A lack of awareness—whether it be intentional or not—can impact the business relationship, impede the negotiations, and end the opportunity to complete the business transaction. Does the exporter understand customs and practices regarding whether or not to shake hands and what clothes to wear? Does the exporter know about presenting business cards (in different languages)—and not writing on the card? Mistakes that involve eating and drinking have been known to end a business opportunity; many Westerners do not know that in certain Chinese provinces the act of putting chopsticks in a rice bowl means "death" to the person on the other side of the table. In many world cultures, the customer expects the eldest representative of the exporter to be involved in negotiations (such elders are known as the "gray-haired gods"), even if this person is not the most astute.

HOW RELATIONSHIPS CAN LEAD TO REWARDS FOR THE EXPORTER

Awareness, attitude, and anticipation are crucial. In the global business environment, the observant exporter should know how to

CASE STUDY 1

Country Risk

A large forest products company based in the United States had solid business relations with five distributors located in a Latin American country. These distributors, in total, owed US$10 million to the exporter, all within payment terms. When the central bank of the country froze all payments leaving the country, the government bank instructed all vendors selling into the country that they would have to wait five years for any repayment of debt. The country manager of the forest products company, who had developed excellent relations with several key executives at the central bank over the years, was able to discount the US$10 million debt with a global bank located outside the country. The result? The exporter was paid 95 cents on the dollar within 60 days. In addition, future sales were paid through an escrow account with the same bank. What is the moral of the story? Even though the five customers were well financed and deemed extremely creditworthy, a country calamity impacted their ability to process business normally. Without the relationship the forest products country manager had developed, the exporter would have had to wait five years for payment.

CASE STUDY 2

Currency Risk

Tyco International, Ltd., based in Bermuda, with headquarter operations in Princeton, NJ, US, is a maker of safety, industrial, and construction products. According to a *Wall Street Journal* article of November 12, 2008 ("Tyco warns currencies, costs will hit earnings"), the company said that in September and October 2008, it saw about a 20% devaluation in currencies of foreign countries where the company did business. The chief executive estimated that these exchange rate fluctuations could reduce fiscal revenue in 2009 by about $2 billion and reduce annual earnings by about 38 cents a share. Tyco generates about 50% of its revenue abroad.

"When tolerance is the norm, everyone flourishes—because tolerance breeds trust, and trust is the foundation of innovation and entrepreneurship." Thomas Friedman

     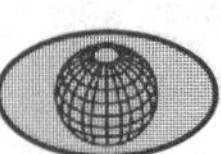   

watch and listen, rather than expect the transaction to happen "now." Relationship building is not only critical with offshore customers, but also imperative with a company's own "internal" customer—the branch office or agent in that country of business. Many exporters demonstrate hubris in their belief that how they do business in their own country is how it is best to do business in the country of the potential importer.

The proactive, successful exporter desiring to succeed in other lands will study behavior, learn about verbal and nonverbal differences that exist, and often will use a "go-between" in order to create the desired relationship. The person who is the intermediary may be one's own country manager; or it could be a banker, business owner, or government employee in a key position in the country who understands how to help achieve the connection between the two parties. Any person-to-person relationship, especially in the business world, has a better chance of succeeding when trust is both understood and established. This need for relationship means that a feeling of complete trust and confidence must exist, not only that the other party will not take advantage of them, but also that they can presume upon the indulgence of the other.

Trust, as part of relationship-building, is paramount in much of the negotiating process. In China, *guanxi* literally means "relationships" and is understood as the network of relationships among various parties that cooperate together and support one another. In Japan, *shokaijo* can mean a letter of introduction, indicating that the status of the exporter is confirmed with the Japanese customer or contact, as opposed to a "cold" call. It provides more of a "guarantee" that the exporter is connected to the business process in Japan. *Jeito* (in Brazil) is the way a businessperson, though local contacts and experiences, is given the chance to succeed.

CASE STUDY 3

Culture Risk

A large chemical company had been negotiating a licensing agreement with a Middle-Eastern country for close to a year. As the final meeting was drawing to a close, a junior member of the exporter's team asked the customer's executives present at the meeting if everything was "OK" and, at the same time, made the gesture shown in Figure 3.

In the customer's culture this hand signal was an insulting and vulgar sign, so the customer took offense and walked out of the meeting. It took numerous apologies from the exporter and another six months to restore the relationship before the transaction was eventually consummated.

CONCLUSION

The exporter needs to evaluate their "IQ." Once that process is completed, the exporter should identify the critical risk factors of country, currency, and culture with the business transaction. Woven into these risk factors are the attributes of relationships. By carefully evaluating the risks and ensuing relationships, an exporter can reap rewards.

▸▸ MAKING IT HAPPEN

To understand how to navigate both the risks and the relationships to reap the rewards, the exporter should:

- Be proactive in determining the ("IQ") international qualities of their own organization.
- Evaluate the risk dimensions of the particular country (or countries) where they want to do business.
- Know enough about how to assess currency risks to know when to call the experts.
- Study, study, and study some more the cultural mores of the countries in which they do business.

▸▸ MORE INFO

Books:

The Handbook of Country Risk 2007–2008. London: Coface & GMB Publishing Ltd., 2007.

Morrison, Terri, Wayne A. Conaway, and Joseph J. Douress. *Dun & Bradstreet's Guide to Doing Business Around the World*. Paramus, NJ: Prentice Hall, 2000.

Websites:

Country risk—Investopedia: www.investopedia.com/terms/c/countryrisk.asp
Culture risk—Wise GEEK: www.wisegeek.com/what-is-a-faux-pas.htm
Currency risk—Investopedia: www.investopedia.com/terms/c/currencyrisk.asp
FCIB (an association of executives in finance, credit and international business): www.fcibglobal.com/reports/country_reports.shtml
International Education Systems: www.marybosrock.com/faux_pas.html

"The policy of being too cautious is the greatest risk of all." Jawaharlal Nehru

  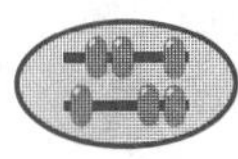   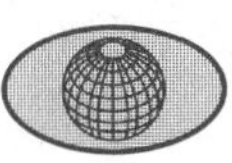   

Exporting Against Letters of Credit

by Buddy Baker

EXECUTIVE SUMMARY

- A letter of credit is a great way for exporters to protect themselves against nonpayment risk, as long as they are prepared and able to present the documents called for. If they don't, the issuing bank might not pay.
- The exporter should provide the importer with explicit guidelines for what the letter of credit is to include.
- The exporter should refuse a confirmation added to a letter of credit by a branch or subsidiary of the issuing bank.
- Exporters can centralize their letter of credit business by insisting on freely available letters of credit and using "silent confirmation" when in need of protection against country risks.
- Discrepancies should and can be avoided by reading every credit in advance, getting amendments when necessary, and preparing the documents exactly as specified.
- Payment can be obtained almost immediately and at lower cost, even when documents are discrepant, by working with one's relationship bank and using shippers' indemnities.
- Letters of credit also serve as a vehicle for very inexpensive financing.

INTRODUCTION

Letters of credit (LofCs) are a time-honored means of payment for international shipment of goods. Although the vast majority of letters of credit get paid when drawn upon, it is a mistake to think of them as guarantees. Rather, LofCs have specific rules governing how payment works. If sellers do not comply with these rules, they risk not being paid when shipping goods—which is precisely the risk that letters of credit are supposed to guard against.

In addition to providing risk protection, LofCs serve as a vehicle of payment. A knowledgeable seller can obtain LofCs that provide immediate funds.

THE PURPOSE OF LETTERS OF CREDIT

When selling goods, a seller must take into account and manage the risk of not being paid. In the case of exported goods, these risks include not just the risk that a buyer will not have enough cash to pay, or will dispute their liability to pay, but also the risk that something will happen in the buyer's country that prevents payment. Letters of credit were developed as a means of payment that, when properly structured and drawn upon, sidesteps these risks.

HOW LETTERS OF CREDIT WORK

A letter of credit is a bank's own engagement to pay a specified amount of money to the named beneficiary upon presentation to the bank of specified documents. In a transaction involving a sale of goods, the contract of sale will specify that payment is to be made by means of a letter of credit. The buyer will then ask their bank to issue an LofC naming the seller as beneficiary for the amount of the order. The bank undertakes in the LofC to pay the seller, not specifically upon shipment of the goods the buyer has ordered, but upon presentation of the documents specified in the credit. A bank would be hard-pressed to verify that goods have actually been shipped in accordance with a contract of sale, but has little trouble checking documents for compliance with stated content requirements. The buyer tells the bank what documents to call for and agrees to reimburse the bank for the payment when made to the seller. The bank does not really care what documents the buyer wants them to pay against as they are just going to pass the documents along. To the buyer, however, since the purpose of the LofC is to pay for goods when shipped, it is important that the documents provide evidence that the goods have been shipped as agreed.

When the seller receives the LofC, they should read it carefully to determine whether the LofC requirements can be complied with. Besides the list of documents, these include such information as how soon the transport document must be issued (evidence of when the goods were shipped), how soon the documents must be presented, and where the documents must be presented. Among other things, the seller should make sure that:

- the credit amount is sufficient to cover the shipment (particularly if the terms are cost, insurance and freight (CIF) or cost and insurance paid to (CIP));
- the documents required will be available and can be presented before the expiry date of the credit;
- the latest shipment date (if there is one) specified in the letter of credit can be met.

If the requirements are not acceptable, the seller should request the buyer to get the credit amended. To avoid the time and expense of amendments, it is highly recommended that the seller provide the buyer with letter of credit instructions up front so that the buyer knows what documents and other requirements are acceptable to the seller.

ROLES OF THE ADVISING AND NOMINATED BANKS

In international transactions, it is almost unheard of for the seller to deal directly with the issuing bank. The issuing bank will arrange for a bank in the country of the seller to deliver the LofC to the seller, and the LofC will provide for the seller to present documents to a bank in the seller's country (see Figure 1). The bank that delivers the LofC is called the "advising

Figure 1. How international letters of credit work

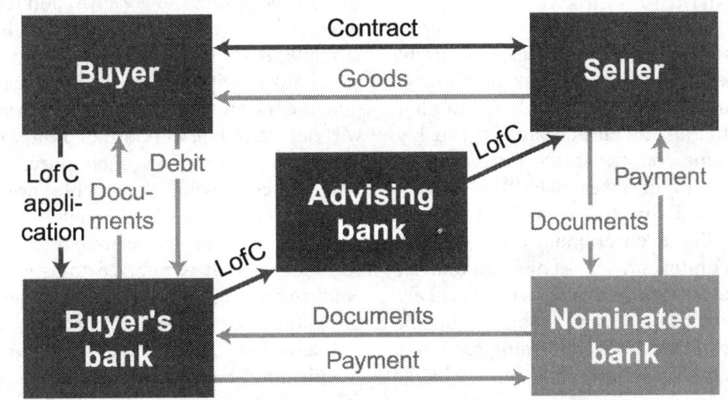

bank" and the bank to which the seller is to present documents is called the "nominated bank." The advising bank is responsible for the accuracy of the information it delivers. The rules governing letters of credit require that the advising bank take steps to verify the authenticity of the credit as well, but an advising bank is not responsible for payment.

Oftentimes, the advising bank is also the nominated bank, but it is also fairly common for letters of credit to state that they are "available with any bank." This allows the seller to present documents to a bank of their own choosing. The nominated bank examines the documents and collects payment from the issuing bank. By insisting that LofCs be freely available, sellers gain the freedom to present documents to their own bank regardless of who played the role of advising bank. The seller's own bank may be willing to provide discount pricing and special services to the seller, like expedited processing, assistance with correcting discrepancies in the documents, or loans against documents in the process of collection.

CONFIRMED LETTERS OF CREDIT

Confirmed letters of credit work a bit differently. A confirmed letter of credit is one where the advising bank has added its own engagement to pay to that of the issuing bank. The advising bank becomes a party to the credit, and it must be invited by the issuing bank to add its confirmation. As a party to the LofC, it has the right to reject amendments. And, in order to take advantage of a bank's confirmation of a letter of credit, the seller must present documents to that bank.

> "The seller receives the same protection [with a "silent confirmation"] as with a regular confirmation, but also has the freedom to choose the "confirming" bank."

The purpose of getting a letter of credit confirmed is to shift the risk of nonpayment from the buyer's bank to another bank. After all, the buyer's bank is probably in the same country as the buyer, and if a country event takes place that affects the buyer's ability to get funds out of the country, like a government-imposed payment moratorium or a new system of exchange controls, the buyer's bank is likely to be caught in the same problem. Thus, it is important that the confirming bank not be just a foreign branch of the buyer's bank, lest it, too, get caught in the same problem. Even foreign branches are subject to regulations imposed by their home countries.

The issuing bank will not ask the advising bank to add its confirmation unless requested to do so by its customer, the buyer. The buyer will not request that the LofC be confirmed unless the seller tells them to. Thus, it is the seller who states, probably in the contract of sale, that payment is to be by means of a confirmed letter of credit. Unfortunately, the seller cannot dictate to the issuing bank which advising or confirming bank it must use. The issuing bank considers it their own prerogative to choose advising and confirming banks. First, the advising bank must be an established correspondent of the issuing bank in order that they may verify the authenticity of the letter of credit as part of the advising process. If the LofC is to be confirmed, the advising bank must also have a credit line established for the issuing bank. It is very embarrassing to a bank to request that another bank confirm one of their letters of credit and then be declined. So the issuing bank may well use its own choice of advising and confirming banks even when the seller has specified another bank. Indeed, some issuing banks are known to choose their own branches and subsidiaries, which, as previously described, does not provide the protection expected to come with confirmation.

A BETTER ALTERNATIVE: SILENT CONFIRMATION

Due to the difficulties of getting letters of credit confirmed by acceptable banks, sellers should consider alternative structures for protection against country risks. One very effective structure is what is known as a "silent confirmation." A silent confirmation is not actually a confirmation at all, but a structure built upon the afore-described structure of freely available letters of credit. At the point where the seller receives a freely available LofC, they should take it to their own bank to verify that it is willing to receive and collect payment for documents once shipment is made. If so, the seller may inquire as to the bank's willingness to purchase the documents and the underlying receivable without recourse, supported by a written commitment to effect such purchase as long as complying documents are presented to the seller's bank. Such a commitment to purchase documents without recourse is what is referred to as a "silent confirmation." The seller receives the same protection as with a regular confirmation, but also has the freedom to choose the "confirming" bank. To the bank, the risk is the same as if it had confirmed the LofC, with the exception that it has no right to reject amendments. By providing in the commitment to purchase documents that the commitment is revoked if the seller accepts any amendments without the bank's approval, the bank achieves the same result.

PRESENTING DOCUMENTS

Whether or not the LofC is confirmed, the seller is entitled to payment only if they comply with the requirements of the credit. Many LofCs authorize the nominated bank to charge the issuing bank's account upon presentation to it of compliant documents. The issuing bank is entitled to ask for the money back if, when it receives the documents, it determines that the documents are not compliant. The nominated bank must therefore examine the documents and will pay the seller only upon the presentation of documents which it feels certain will not be refused by the issuing bank. Because any discrepancy is grounds for refusal, the nominated bank will insist that the documents comply strictly with the terms of the letter of credit. In fact, over 75% of letter of credit documents are found to contain discrepancies.

AVOIDING DISCREPANCIES

While the documents required under letters of credit may vary, most LofCs commonly call for the presentation of a draft, commercial invoices, and transport documents. The nominated bank is expected to examine these and any other specified documents with care, to be certain they appear on their face to comply with the terms and conditions of the credit. The Uniform Customs and Practice for Documentary Credits provides a set of guidelines banks use for examining documents. (See the article "Understanding the UCP600" for further information.)

These are some of the most common discrepancies found in LofC documents:

- Documents contain inconsistent data.
- Documents were presented more than 21 days after date of shipment (or other presentation period specified in the LofC).
- Full set of transport documents was not presented or other required documents are missing.
- Draft is drawn incorrectly or for the wrong amount.
- Draft is not signed or not endorsed.
- Invoice does not describe merchandise in exact accordance with the letter of credit. *Note:* If the letter of credit describes merchandise in a foreign language, then the seller must describe the merchandise

  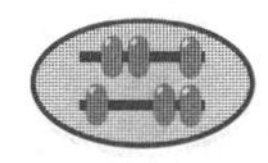   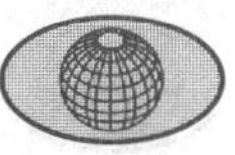   

in that language on the invoice; translations are not acceptable.

- Invoice does not show the same shipping terms as specified in the LofC.
- Invoice includes charges inconsistent with the shipping terms in the LofC.
- Invoice is not made out in the name of the applicant shown in the LofC.
- Insurance coverage is insufficient or does not include the risks specified by the LofC.
- Insurance certificate or policy is not endorsed.
- Insurance certificate is dated later than the shipment date (acceptable if coverage is stated to be warehouse-to-warehouse).
- Transport document is not clean (defective condition of goods or packaging is indicated).
- Transport document does not clearly indicate the name and capacity of the signer and who the carrier is (must be signed "ABC Co. as carrier" or "XYZ Co. as agent for ABC Co., the carrier").
- Transport document is not consigned correctly or is not endorsed (if endorsement is required).
- Multimodal transport document was presented when LofC calls for a bill of lading (acceptable if an "on board" notation has been added that includes the name of the vessel and the port of loading).
- Multimodal transport document was presented when shipping terms are FOB (i.e., port to port) and does not indicate inland freight has been prepaid or otherwise fails to meet requirements for port-to-port shipment.
- Transport document is not marked "freight prepaid" or "freight collect" as required under the credit or in agreement with the invoice and shipping terms.
- Not all documents show license numbers, letter of credit numbers, or other identification required in the credit.
- Documents are not signed in accordance with LofC terms (any document called a "certificate" must be signed).

DEALING WITH DISCREPANCIES

If the seller's documents contain discrepancies that cannot be corrected, there are a few alternatives available to still try to collect payment. It should be noted, however, that the seller has lost a key element of the letter of credit: the issuing and confirming banks' obligation to pay. The most common course of action, despite the fact that it is expensive and time consuming, is that the seller asks the nominated bank to cable the issuing bank requesting a waiver of the discrepancies. As long as the buyer's credit condition is still good, the issuing bank is likely to agree to contact the buyer regarding the discrepancies. If the buyer agrees to pay despite the discrepancies, the issuing bank will then cable the nominated bank to provide its waiver.

Instead of cabling for a waiver of discrepancies, an alternative approach the seller can take is to ask the nominated bank to forward the documents to the issuing bank for approval. If the seller is comfortable that there is no real danger of the buyer refusing the documents, they may further request that the nominated bank go ahead and pay against the seller's indemnity. Under such an arrangement the seller agrees to cover any loss or damage the nominated bank may sustain in the unexpected event documents are refused by the issuing bank. Although the use of such "shippers' indemnities" varies by country, banks are generally willing to accept such indemnities from their own customers so long as the credit standing of the customer is satisfactory.

Even though 75% of documents have discrepancies, less than one letter of credit drawing in 1,000 actually gets refused. (This is due to the fact that buyers who can obtain letters of credit to begin with are normally good credit risks, they want the merchandise that was shipped and will therefore agree to pay even though documents do not comply, they wish to remain on good terms with their suppliers, and, unless the underlying contract of sale has been violated, they are legally obligated to pay anyway.) The use of shippers' indemnities is highly recommended as a way to obtain payment days or weeks sooner as well as avoid cable expenses. Because indemnities will be accepted only by banks with whom the seller has credit lines, sellers wishing to make use of such arrangements should present documents to their own banks rather than following the common, but often unfavorable, practice of submitting documents to the advising banks.

> "...over 75% of letter of credit documents are found to contain discrepancies."

CASE STUDY

Vinmar International

With 26 offices in 20 countries, Vinmar International, Ltd., is one of the world's premier petrochemicals marketing, distribution, and project development companies. Letters of credit are an important part of Vinmar's risk management strategy. Tom Wells, Managing Director of Vinmar Finance, indicates that 40–50% of the company's sales are made against letters of credit. Altogether, this amounts to some 4,000 sets of documents a year, with values ranging from 50,000 to 10 million US dollars. Vinmar sells to the same buyers on a repetitive basis and so does not use an LofC instructions form but has instead adopted the practice of requiring buyers to submit a draft of each letter of credit in advance, before the buyer applies for the LofC to be opened. Somebody who understands LofCs must review and approve each draft and then each LofC when it is received, and request appropriate amendments before shipment is made. Shipments are made from all over the world. After shipment, Vinmar uses a staff of people in India with strong letter of credit experience to prepare the documents. Says Tom, "If you're using letters of credit and then you don't comply with the requirements, you might as well be selling on cash-against-documents terms. You're just wasting time and money and fooling yourself about the risk." Tom's advice: "Make sure the people preparing the documents know what they are doing; hire a company that specializes in letter of credit document preparation if you don't have the volume to maintain internal expertise."

Tom is a proponent of developing relationships with banks that are active in and have expertise in the trade finance business. The company's preference is to work with banks in their credit facility, but Tom finds that some banks are more willing than others to confirm LofCs in certain parts of the world. He has therefore also developed relationships with a few "niche players" that can handle places like Africa and Pakistan. Vinmar always asks for freely available LofCs and, when necessary, it also uses silent confirmation. This permits Vinmar to present documents to its relationship banks even when the letters of credit have been advised by someone else. Because buyers are repetitive, Tom finds that the issuing banks will then act to open correspondent arrangements with Vinmar's banks for future transactions.

Another best practice Vinmar has adopted is to always discount time letters of credit to take advantage of the low interest rates. In fact, Vinmar readily offers buyers 30-day terms for letter of credit sales—"it takes 10 to 20 days to put documents together and present them anyway" says Tom.

     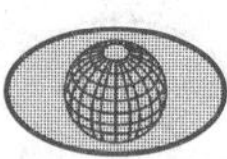   

FINANCING THE TRANSACTION

Once the nominated bank is satisfied that the documents comply with the LofC requirements (or has a satisfactory indemnity from the seller), it will trigger the payment mechanism outlined in the credit. Payment may be expected in a few days, for a letter of credit payable at sight, or a few months, for a credit available against time drafts or by deferred payment. If the seller is a relationship customer, the nominated bank may be willing to advance funds to him prior to receipt of payment from the issuing bank. It is even likely the seller can sell the receivable to the nominated bank without recourse (similar to the silent confirmation structure described before, but without the commitment in advance) and take the receivable off their books. This practice is referred to as "discounting," since the bank deducts its interest charges from the amount paid. The interest rate for discounting such bank obligations is usually much less than the company's normal borrowing rate (often even lower than the US Federal Funds and international LIBOR rates at which banks lend money to each other), making it very attractive to accept such financing.

CONCLUSION

Although letters of credit are viewed as the next best thing to cash, they don't always get paid. It is important for the exporter selling on letter of credit terms to understand and comply with the letter of credit requirements. It is a good idea to tell the buyer in advance what documents the seller intends to present and then to read the letter of credit to make sure the documents specified can indeed be presented in the time frames indicated.

This article provides some tips for avoiding discrepancies, but, if they do occur, it is often possible to get them waived. When shipment has been made and documents have been presented, it is often easy and inexpensive to finance the transaction for the time remaining until payment is collected.

Export letters of credit are flexible tools for credit risk mitigation and financing, but it is important to know how to use them.

▸▸ MAKING IT HAPPEN

The way a company manages its letter of credit activity can be improved by:

- developing an LofC instructions form;
- requiring freely available LofCs;
- using silent confirmation;
- centralizing activity with a relationship bank;
- putting a shipper's indemnity program in place.

These procedures are not difficult, but they require that a point person be nominated and given authority to get them running. In most companies the logical point person is the credit manager, who already makes the decision of when to require letters of credit and frequently is also responsible for collecting payment from customers. Someone from treasury should be involved in the determination of the best way to finance receivables. Whether the designated person is the credit manager or someone else, that person should attend letter of credit training classes to become familiar and comfortable with how letters of credit work and the concepts described here. The person should write the company policy for letters of credit, document what has been decided, and provide internal training for others within the firm, from credit, treasury, and sales departments, and should also be involved in all discussions with the company's banks regarding export services used by the company.

▸▸ MORE INFO

Book:

Baker, Walter (Buddy), and John F. Dolan. *Users' Handbook for Documentary Credits under UCP600*. (Publication number 694.) Paris: International Chamber of Commerce, 2008. Available as eBook online at: www.iccbooksusa.com

Websites:

The International Chamber of Commerce Commission on Banking Technique and Practice: www.iccwbo.org/policy/banking

The ICC Business Bookstore: www.iccbooksusa.com

See Also:

★ Essentials for Export Success: Understanding How Risks and Relationships Lead to Rewards (pp. 450–452)
★ International Arbitration: Basic Principles and Characteristics (pp. 479–481)
✔ Administering Contracts Successfully (p. 967)
✔ Practical Techniques for Commercial Mediation (p. 1001)
✔ The Principles of Litigation (p. 1002)

"**In civil business: what first? Boldness; what second, and third? Boldness.**" Francis Bacon

  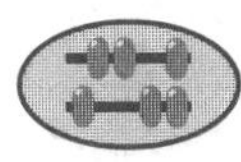   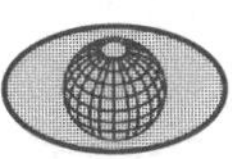   

Viewpoint: Thierry Malleret

Understanding Global Risks for the Corporate

INTRODUCTION

Thierry Malleret is a managing partner at Rainbow Insight, an advisery boutique that provides tailor-made intelligence to high-net-worth individuals and investors.

Until April 2007, Thierry headed the Global Risk Network at the World Economic Forum, a network that brings together top-end opinion, policymakers, CEOs, and academics to look at how global issues will effect business and society in both the short and long term.

Thierry has organized the Davos annual forum and has spoken at global, industry, and regional events for several consecutive years. Prior to that, he worked in investment banking (as chief economist and strategist of a major Russian investment bank), think tanks, and academia (both in New York and Oxford), and in government (with a three-year spell in the prime minister's office in Paris).

Thierry has written several business and academic books. He has appeared on numerous network television programs (including CNN and CNBC), and published in: the *International Herald Tribune*, the *Wall Street Journal*, and *Time* magazine. His next book, *Global Risks: Business Success in Turbulent Times*, was published in 2007.

He was educated at the Sorbonne and the École des Hautes Études en Sciences Sociales in Paris, and St Antony's College in Oxford. He holds a PhD in economics.

In the past century, a multinational company might have dealt with a major catastrophe once every 20 years or so. Today, a global business deals on average with about 10 global risks simultaneously.[1] Why? Because global risks are today's risks; they are an integral part of our world characterized by ever greater complexity and accelerating change, a world so interdependent that most risks which occur at the local level are likely to entail a "cascading" or "domino" effect. In such a world, global risks are becoming more relevant and more pervasive than ever.

WHAT IS A GLOBAL RISK?

A global risk is defined by its global character and its potential to impact upon many different groups or industries in different countries and regions, often simultaneously. Risks are by nature idiosyncratic as their definition depends on who you are; but it is safe to say that risks as different as terrorism, emerging fiscal crises, disruptions in oil supplies, climate change, Islamic radicalism, pandemics, or a sudden decline in a major country's growth all qualify as global risks. When it unfolds, a global risk has far reaching consequences for our global society and global economy. From the standpoint of a business entity, a global risk is quintessentially a nonbusiness risk, which has nonetheless the potential to impact decisively on the P&L or the reputation of a business.

In our increasingly interdependent world, global risks often make the headlines: terrorism, failed and failing states, the utilization of the internet to launch cyber attacks, natural disasters, tsunamis and tropical cyclones possibly caused by climate change. Currently, all these dominate our perception of the risk landscape. Others have not yet penetrated public consciousness, but can have a devastating impact on particular industries. The risk of identity theft, for example, can have dramatic implications for financial services as the sanctity of contract and interpersonal trust are all critical ingredients of the success of a business. In today's world where no country is an island, nobody can hide from global risks.

Businesses executives and all those in charge of mitigating risks cope well with "familiar" business risks, which are traditionally within the canvas of the firm (project risks, competitive risks, industry risks, currency risks and the like). However, they often find themselves far less equipped to deal with a set of new, less familiar, potentially more dangerous, global risks. Why is this? Mainly because we live in a world in which risks are mutating into uncertainties. Technically, a risk can be defined as a probabilistic event (which, in turn, means it can be priced), while an uncertainty is non-probabilistic (and therefore cannot be priced). With a few significant exceptions (such as natural disasters), most global risks are not of a quantifiable nature. This difference matters enormously because as human beings we are fundamentally uncomfortable with the notion of something that cannot be measured. Whether we are a CEO, CFO, or CRO is irrelevant in that respect. This notion, that we deny uncertainty because we dislike it, has been captured by the so-called Ellsberg paradox; in which people's choices violate the expected utility hypothesis, which is normally taken as evidence for ambiguity, or uncertainty aversion.

THE WORLD IS CHANGING: THE PROPERTIES OF GLOBAL RISKS

Global risks are a determining feature of today's highly interdependent world. All elements of the global system are so highly and intrinsically intertwined that the occurrence of any particular global risk is almost sure to have a cascading effect and to lead to another global risk. Let us consider the following example; Hurricane Katrina struck New Orleans, Louisiana, as a category 4 storm on August 29, 2005. Costal storms are common, but this one was the costliest natural disaster in the history of the United States, inflicting total damage estimated at US$100 billion. However, perhaps more significant (and shocking) was the collateral damage inflicted by hurricane Katrina beyond its immediate physical impact; the sequence of events—the domino effect—that the natural disaster put into motion. Katrina had an impact on the Bush presidency, already weakened by difficulties in Iraq, on race relations in the United States, on global oil prices, and on the assessment of US power and capacity in many parts of the world. The same observation about the unforeseeable permutations that the occurrence of a global risk may cause also applies to the terrorist attacks of September 11th and many others. In a

"Challenging the status quo has to be the starting point for anything that goes under the label of strategy."
Gary Hamel

  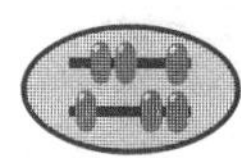   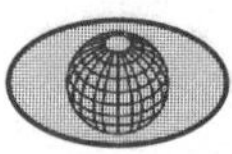   

world characterized by uncertainty, complexity, volatility, turbulence, asymmetry, and time compression, global risks increasingly matter.

As verified by the financial debacle and global recession that started in 2008 (derivatives appeared on top of a list of global risks compiled for a book that I wrote for MacMillan in 2006), global risks travel fast and have the annoying habit of reproducing themselves unexpectedly and in the most improbable places. They have also a tendency to provoke "tipping points," with which they share three main characteristics:

1 contagiousness—like ideas and products, in today's globalized world, global risks spread like epidemics;
2 relatively minor causes can have major effects—see the "small" sub-prime crisis turning into a full blown financial crisis of major proportions;
3 changes tend to happen dramatically rather than gradually.

Global risks have the particularity that they cannot be predicted—a similarity they share with "black swans" (very low probability, very high-impact kinds of events). However, even if one cannot predict the future, one can prepare for it.

How to Mitigate Global Risks Effectively and Seize Opportunities

When dealing with global risks, like any kind of risk, it is important to remember that a risk always represents both a threat and an opportunity. In most minds, a risk is often associated with the fear of a loss, but it does not have to be that way. Why is it that a few succeed while the majority fail? In the end, it is very much a question of character. In the words of Churchill: "an optimist sees an opportunity in every danger, while a pessimist sees a danger in every opportunity." Global risks are no different, but are certainly more difficult to grasp. There is no magic formula for managing them, but there are certain sensible measures, which must be taken to avert failure. Some are organizational; a set of well-defined policies that must be implemented by any company if it is to survive external shocks. They include among others the (1) alignment of risk assessment, management, and communication, (2) the systematic assessment of vulnerabilities, (3) the stress-testing of some scenarios, (4) the inclusion of risk thinking in the culture of the company etc. They also depend on mistakes that must not be made, such as relying too much on mechanistic risk-models (VaR, for example, has not served financial institutions too well...).

But most importantly, what differentiate's companies that excel at dealing with global risks from those which fail are the attitudinal traits of the leadership. They are much less tangible than the organizational attributes, but can be a source of lasting competitive advantage. Three attitudinal traits are essential:

1 The capability of the leadership to use networks, which constitute the most effective organizational response to complexity. If they are sufficiently diverse and allow for a wide range of opinions, networks provide an excellent way of aggregating information and meaningful insights. Business executives can use them as effective early-warning systems to alert them to global risks that are far out on the horizon or just over it, and to understand how they might affect their business.
2 The awareness of the cognitive biases that affect our decisions made under conditions of uncertainty. In particular, one of our greatest human failings is the tendency to see the future like the past. The world is changing fast and the "like the past" fallacy is often associated with the inability of the leadership to question underlying assumptions and to keep going as if "all things being equal, not much will change." More generally, smart people are more likely to do stupid things when they insulate themselves from advice and criticism.
3 The ability to puncture denial. This looks like a very mundane recommendation, and it is yet the most effective factor for dealing with global risks successfully. As Jack Welch, the former CEO of GE, often said: it is one the most difficult challenges decision makers face because people "love the status quo." The automotive industry is a case in point: some companies, like Toyota, understood the significance of climate change and took action to transform this global risk into an opportunity well before their competitors. Others, in particular, the US automotive industry, were in denial and failed to adapt to a changing global environment in time.

The thread that transcends these global risks and makes us understand how one might be hit by them or how one might profit from them is quite obvious; only those business executives who are conscious of the universe and the significance of the prevailing global risks can successfully mitigate them. "Be prepared" is the name of the game; he or she who comprehends and masters the context in which he or she operates, grasps the trends, and thus better understands the risks, will be optimally positioned to act and react promptly and pertinently to them. The great insight from the current crisis (applicable to all other global risks) is that those who emerge on top will have shown themselves able to act swiftly and decisively. As the French scientist Louis Pasteur once said: "Chance favors the prepared mind."

➤➤ MORE INFO

Books:

Cleary, S., Malleret, T. *Global Risk: Business Success in Turbulent Times*. New York: Palgrave Macmillan, 2007.

Taleb, N. *The Black Swan: The Impact of the Highly Improbable*. New York: Penguin, 2007.

Website:

Global Risk program of the World Economic Forum: www.weforum.org/en/initiatives/globalrisk/index.htm

NOTES

1 These numbers are based on anecdotal evidence gathered when the author was the head of the Global Risk Network at the World Economic Forum. In that capacity, he interviewed hundreds of CEOs of large international companies.

"Be bold; everywhere be bold; but be not bowled over." O. Henry

  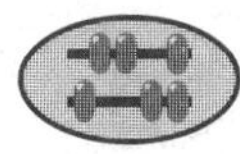   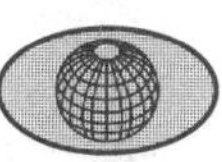   

Financial Techniques for Building Customer Loyalty by Ray Halagera

EXECUTIVE SUMMARY

- Given that one of the three key determinants of customer loyalty is the total cost of owning a company's product or using their service, financial techniques can play a significant role in building customer loyalty, and ultimately the company's profitability.
- Some of the financial techniques that can be used to build customer loyalty include:
  - discounting;
  - frequent buyer programs;
  - loyalty programs;
  - special terms for prepurchasing;
  - enhanced credit terms;
  - bundling of goods or services;
  - discounts on purchasing related goods or services.
- Since all markets are not the same, not all financial techniques have the same impact across markets. Whether the market consists of consumer or business buyers is the biggest determinant of how effective a financial technique is in building customer loyalty.
- Implementing a technique to build loyalty with customers may not have a short-term payoff, and in certain markets it can actually create problems that cost the company more than the increased profitability attributable to increasing the period of time the customer is retained.

INTRODUCTION

Every organization knows that in order for it to survive, let alone grow, it has to acquire and then retain profitable customers. And it is loyal customers that generate increasing profits for each additional year they are retained.

- Acquiring new customers can cost five times more than retaining current customers.[1]
- A 2% increase in customer retention has the same effect on profits as cutting costs by 10%.[2]
- A 5% reduction in customer defection can increase profits by 25–85%.[3]
- The customer profitability rate over the life of a retained customer tends to increase annually by up to 20%.[4]
- Extensive and continuing research into customer loyalty has concluded that it is driven by the customer's ongoing perception of value, which is a combination of:
  - what the customer receives;
  - how the product or service is sold, delivered, and supported;
  - how much the product or service costs—that is, the price or total cost of ownership.

Finance professionals can deploy a wide range of techniques that can impact the customer's total cost of owning their company's product or using their company's service, which in turn impacts customer loyalty and ultimately the organization's profitability. Not only do financial managers need to be aware of the many techniques under their control, but they also need to be aware of some of the problems, where relevant, that may be encountered in implementing a specific technique.

TWO PROVISOS

First, a financial manager's primary goal is to maximize the organization's profitability by accounting, analyzing, and reporting the financial implications of actions taken or which it is proposed to take. And they are usually expected to make a recommendation based on their findings. Because many of the suggested financial techniques to increase customer loyalty have short-term benefits that may not cover the short-term costs, financial managers may be reluctant to recommend many of the techniques if they lose sight of the longer-term benefits of customer loyalty and subsequent long-term retention.

Second, not all markets and customers are the same, and, accordingly, not all financial techniques will have the same impact on building customer loyalty. The major determinant as to whether or not a specific financial technique will impact customer loyalty is whether the customer is in a consumer market or a business market.

In selling to a consumer market (business to consumer, or B2C), the market attributes include:

- the value of a transactions is usually small;
- the number of buyers is large;
- the selling cycle is short;
- the product, and even the service, can be mass-produced;
- the selling effort is focused on the end user.

Selling to a business market (business to business, or B2B) requires taking into account attributes that include:

- the value of transactions is usually larger than for B2C;
- there are fewer buyers than in B2C;
- the selling cycle can be long, complex, and involve an ongoing relationship between the seller and whoever is in charge of purchasing decisions;
- the product or service often needs to be customized;
- the selling effort is often directed toward a decision-maker who is not the end user.

The above attributes can render a technique for building customer loyalty in a B2C market inappropriate for a B2B market, and vice versa. These differences will be noted where appropriate.

A RANGE OF FINANCIAL TECHNIQUES FOR BUILDING CUSTOMER LOYALTY

As discussed above, total cost of ownership is one of three drivers of the customer's perceived value of a good or service, with perceived value determining how loyal the customer will be to the seller. Accordingly, any financial technique that can positively impact the customer's perceived total cost of ownership will build customer loyalty. Of the multitude of financial techniques that are in use, the following are the more prevalent.

A Discounted Price Over a Contracted Time Period

The seller offers a lower price for a good or service in return for the buyer committing to purchase the good or service for an extended period of time, usually two to three years, thereby locking in the customer's business over that period.

Potential problem: The less unique the product or service is compared to those offered by competitors, the more likely it is that the buyer will use the proposed lower price to negotiate an even lower price under similar terms with one or more competitive suppliers, and then to negotiate a still lower price with the supplier that originally proposed the discounted price.

"A 5% reduction in customer defection can increase profits by 25–85%." Frederick F. Reichheld

   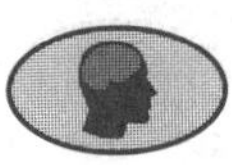  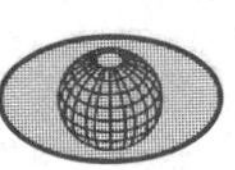   

Accordingly, the less unique or customized the good or service is (which usually applies to B2C markets), the less viable this financial strategy is for building customer loyalty.

A Discounted Price for a Committed Volume Purchase with Variance

The seller offers a lower price for a good or service in return for the buyer committing to purchase a certain volume over a period of time. The seller and buyer further agree that if the buyer purchases a certain percentage less than the agreed amount by the end of the period (usually 95% or less), the buyer will pay a premium at the end of the period for the smaller amount purchased, with the premium equaling the difference between the contracted discounted price and the higher price associated with the lower volume times the number of units purchased.

Potential problem: Like the problem arising with a discounted price over a period of time, the buyer may use the proposed lower price and terms to negotiate a better price and terms with a competitive supplier. Accordingly, this financial technique is more viable with unique or customized goods or services, and is therefore more appropriate for a B2B market.

Frequent Buyer Program

The seller offers the buyer a rebate or free goods or services subsequent to the buyer purchasing a certain dollar or unit volume. Coffee house chains such as Kaldi's in St Louis, Missouri, provide a Coffee Club card that is punched every time a cup of coffee is purchased, with the card holder receiving a free cup of coffee after ten purchases.

Potential problem: Competitors may decide to offer their own frequent buyer programs, and may even increase the value of the rebate, rendering this an ineffective technique for persuading customers to stay with the supplier and not utilize the competition.

Loyalty Program

The seller offers preferential treatment or certain services free to buyers who enroll in a loyalty program. National Car Rental's Emerald Club allows its members to bypass the rental counter and even to select any rental vehicle that is available in their rental class on the lot. Avis' Preferred allows its members to bypass the rental counter and go straight to the rental cars. Loyalty programs such as American Airlines' AAdvantage program offer increasing levels of benefits for members who increase their air miles over a given time period, with Platinum members given preferential seating and boarding over Gold members.

Potential problem: The added cost of the preferential treatment or benefits may not be offset by the profitability that is expected to be generated by repeat usage by a loyal customer if competitive suppliers offer comparable preferential treatment and benefits, especially if enrollment in a loyalty program is at no cost or low cost. In such a situation the buyer will enroll in multiple competitive loyalty programs and purchase the lowest-priced goods or services.

Prepurchase/Buy Forward

The seller offers a discounted price to a buyer who pays in advance for an amount of goods or services to be delivered at some future date or over a certain time period, with the discount rate being greater than the interest rate paid on money placed in a low-risk investment. The benefit of this technique to the seller is that it locks in the buyer's business over a certain period. The benefit to the buyer is that it eliminates any price increases during the contracted period.

Potential problem: The buyer may try to secure comparable terms with a competitive supplier and then use those terms to negotiate better terms with the original supplier, or the buyer may give the business to the supplier offering the best terms.

Enhanced Buyer Credit Terms

The seller offers to finance the buyer's purchases at an interest rate and terms equal to or better than the buyer would receive from a third-party commercial source of credit.

Potential problem: The buyer may try to secure comparable terms with a competitive supplier. Furthermore, the seller needs to ensure that the buyer is creditworthy.

Bundling Goods or Services

The seller includes ancillary goods or services at no cost to the buyer when a primary or major good or service is purchased. Personal computer manufacturers such as Dell and HP bundle printers, monitors, and even 24-hour help services with the price of the computer. Express oil change services such as Jiffy Lube include topping off all fluids and

CASE STUDY

Use of Financial Incentives to Secure a Customer's Loyalty

Career Systems International (CSI) is a company that provides training to managers on developing behavior conducive to engaging and retaining their direct reports. CSI successfully used a number of financial techniques to negotiate a multi-year contract for its training programs and services with a major hospitality chain that sought to reduce the high turnover rate of its employees. The financial techniques that were deployed to create a loyal customer who not only accepted the multi-year contract but also agreed to extend the contract at the time of renewal included:

- *A discounted price for a committed volume purchase with variance*. The price per participant taking the training program was discounted in return for the hospitality chain agreeing to put 5,000 managers through the program over a two-year period. The buyer agreed that if fewer than 4,500 managers took the program during the two-year period, it would pay a premium of $20 for every participant who did go through the training program.
- *Prepurchase/buy forward*. The hospitality chain buyer was offered and took an additional 10% discount on the total cost of training the 5,000 managers by paying one-third of the total amount of the training fees at the time of signing, one-third at the first anniversary of the contract date, and the remaining third at completion of the two-year contract.
- *Bundling goods or services*. CSI offered, at no cost to the buyer, a website providing suggestions, articles, chat rooms, online coaching, and other information related to management behavior conducive to retaining employees, with the website accessible only to managers who had completed the CSI workshop.
- *Customization*. The seller also provided, at no charge to the hospitality chain, customization of the workshop to include the buyer's terminology, reference to its management practices, and an assessment instrument which the buyer had been using.

The above actions built customer loyalty by reducing the buyer's total cost of ownership for the training initiative once the buyer was willing to make a commitment to buy the training materials and services and ancillary online support, over first a two-year time period, and then for a subsequent two-year period under the same conditions.

"The customer profitability rate over the life of a retained customer tends to annually increase by up to 20%."
Frederick F. Reichheld

     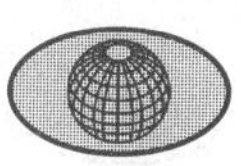   

checking tire pressure in the price of an oil change.

Potential problem: The seller needs to have good cost accounting of the services or goods bundled in with the primary good or service to ensure that profit margins are not needlessly eroded by including certain goods or services in the bundled package.

Discounts on Related Goods

The seller offers a discount on additional units of an item or other items it sells and which are purchased at the same time as the first unit is purchased. This technique for creating customer loyalty is often found in grocery stores where an item is advertised at some percentage off the price of the second unit purchased.

Potential problem: Competitors may implement the same pricing strategy and thereby remove any incentive for the buyer to be loyal to the seller that initially implements the strategy.

Trade-Ins

The seller offers to buy back its durable goods at prices better than the buyer can secure on the open market if he or she replaces the goods with another version of the seller's durable goods. This financial technique for building customer loyalty has been deployed by sellers ranging from automobile dealers to clothing retailers.

Money-Back Guarantees or Penalty Payments

The seller commits to buying back the good or refunding fees for a service delivered if the good or service doesn't meet the performance standards established at the time of the sale. During its formative years Domino's Pizza grew in large part through loyal customers retained by its promise "pizza delivered to your house in 30 minutes or it's on us."

Benefit Sharing

The supplier offers the buyer a good or service at a highly discounted price under the condition that the buyer share any cost savings or revenue generated from using the good or service. A select number of companies that provide sales training sell their training programs at deep discounts to buyers who agree to share a portion of the increased revenue attributable to their sales people going through the training.

▸▸ MAKING IT HAPPEN

Customer loyalty is one path to increased profitability for an organization. In any organization, marketing, customer service, and/or sales take the lead role in building customer loyalty. However, since the total cost of ownership is one of the three elements that determine the level of a customer's loyalty, the financial function has the potential to significantly impact customer loyalty. For finance to play a key role in building customer loyalty, certain questions need to be addressed:

- Is our organization aware of the increased profitability that is attributable to customer loyalty and subsequent customer retention? What information do I need to present to build the case for taking action to improve customer retention?
- Does my company sell to consumers, or does it sell to businesses? The markets we sell to will determine both the short- and long-term viability of certain financial techniques. Some techniques may require nonfinancial elements to position us as preferable to our competition over the long run.
- How unique are our goods or services in customers' eyes? The more our good or service is perceived as being no different to that of our competitors, regardless of the market we are in, the more likely it is that a financial technique which reduces the price paid by the customer will not increase customer loyalty because our competitors will copy it.
- What techniques can we use that reduce the total cost of ownership as perceived by the buyer but do not require us to cut our effective price for the good or service or add a good or service that would reduce our gross margin on the sale? Money-back guarantees? Trade-ins? Loyalty programs?
- Understanding that the profits from a loyal customer increase the longer we retain the customer, what technique can we use that avoids a price cut (though it may reduce our immediate gross margin) but which will increase the lifetime profit from the customer? Bundling goods or services? Discounts on related goods or services?
- In considering price-cutting techniques to build customer loyalty—such as a discounted price over a contracted time period, or prepurchase—are we cost-competitive enough that the competition will not be able to profitably match our price-cutting techniques?

▸▸ MORE INFO

Books:

Gitomer, Jeffrey. *Customer Satisfaction is Worthless, Customer Loyalty is Priceless: How to Make Them Love You, Keep You Coming Back, and Tell Everyone They Know*. Austin, TX: Bard Press, 1998.

Johnson, Michael D., and Anders Gustafsson. *Improving Customer Satisfaction, Loyalty, and Profit: An Integrated Measurement and Management System*. San Francisco, CA: Jossey-Bass, 2000.

Reichheld, Frederick F. *Loyalty Rules: How Today's Leaders Build Lasting Relationships*. Cambridge, MA: Harvard Business School Press, 2003.

Reichheld, Frederick F, with Thomas Teal. *The Loyalty Effect: The Hidden Force Behind Growth, Profits, and Lasting Value*. Cambridge, MA: Harvard Business School Press, 2001.

Websites:

American Management Association (AMA): www.american-management-association.org

American Marketing Association: www.marketingpower.com

Net Promoter, for a loyalty metric: www.netpromoter.com

Professional Pricing Society (PPS): www.pricingsociety.com

Strategic Pricing Group (SPG): www.strategicpricinggroup.com

Word of Mouth Marketing Association (WOMMA): www.womma.com

NOTES

1 Murphy, Emmett C., and Mark A. Murphy. *Leading on the Edge of Chaos: The 10 Critical Elements for Success in Volatile Times*. Paramus, NJ: Prentice Hall, 2002.

2 *Ibid*.

3 Reichheld, Frederick F., and W. Earl Sasser, Jr. "Zero defections: Quality comes to services." *Harvard Business Review* 68:5 (1990): 105–111.

4 Reichheld, Frederick F. *The Loyalty Effect* (2001).

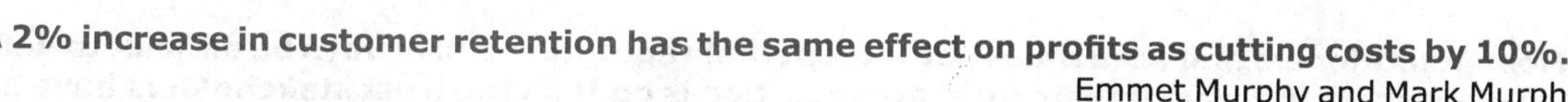

"A 2% increase in customer retention has the same effect on profits as cutting costs by 10%."
Emmet Murphy and Mark Murphy

  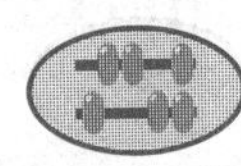 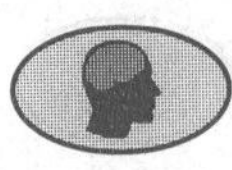  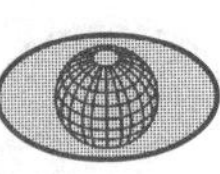   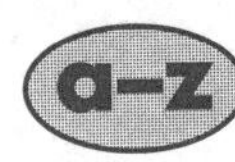

Fraud: Minimizing the Impact on Corporate Image by Tim Johnson

EXECUTIVE SUMMARY

- Fraud is a threat faced by all organizations, regardless of their size or sector, that can easily plunge any organization into crisis, real or perceived.
- The key to crisis management—particularly when trust in business remains very low—is to set the agenda, communicate robustly, and not allow speculation or rumor to run rife.
- Robust communication strategies require organizations to consider their *message*, their *audience*, and the *medium* theywill use to communicate their message.
- In cases of fraud, such messages should center on *concern*, *control*, *commitment*,and *containment*.

INTRODUCTION

The threat of fraud is faced by all organizations regardless of their size or sector. From the perspective of reputation management, controlling the impact of fraud is particularly challenging for two reasons:

1 That an organization has become a victim of fraud suggests either that someone in the organization is corrupt, or that the organization and its compliance systems are vulnerable. Neither possibility inspires confidence.

2 The word "fraud" has a wide range of meanings. It can refer to a sustained, systemic failure that can bring an organization to its knees. Or it can refer to low-level compliance failure that, while regrettable, is unlikely to lead to long-lasting damage.

If fraud has been committed or is suspected, how can an organization's reputation be protected? First, we need to understand what reputation is and its importance. We also need to understand the rudiments of crisis reputation management.

REPUTATION AND WHY IT IS IMPORTANT

Reputation is hard to define. Famously, there are numerous definitions. Put simply, it is the sum total of what our stakeholders feel about a company and how they act as a result of that feeling. This sounds woolly, and indeed it is. Over the years, many attempts have been made to try and measure organizational reputation in quantifiable and, preferably, hard financial terms. Some progress has been made. But you still won't find a line on the asset—or liability—side of your balance sheet that refers to your organization's reputation.

Most practitioners and academics now accept that reputation will always be difficult to define and quantify. However, there is broad agreement that reputation is built on the trust stakeholders have in an organization, and that trust is far from woolly. On the contrary, trust brings hard commercial benefits: it helps to build strong brands, launch new products, secure licensing deals, recruit the best staff, and avoid intrusive regulation. Few would disagree that protecting that trust, and thus reputation, is critical to the business.

However, that's easier said than done because trust is a rare commodity—particularly in light of high-profile incidents, such as the rogue trading which led to the collapse of Barings Bank and, more recently, the Enron scandal. In 2006, Ipsos MORI found that only 31% of those surveyed in the United Kingdom trusted business leaders to tell the truth. This lack of trust manifests itself in many ways, including a surge in the numbers of nongovernmental organizations, a breakdown in accepted societal structures, and the growth of antiglobalization sentiment that is often fueled by an aggressive 24/7 media. Even during times of "business as usual," reputation management is not an easy business.

So what should be done to protect organizational reputation during a crisis prompted by, for example, a case of fraud?

CRISIS COMMUNICATIONS

When something goes wrong, the natural instinct is to want to fix the problem behind closed doors. This is perfectly understandable, and in an ideal world the issue would be attended to and the relevant stakeholders told about the actions taken to rectify the problem—if anyone needs to be told at all.

However, in a world of citizen journalists and social networking, even problems such as *suspected* fraud become harder to contain within an organization. News often leaks to the wider world long before the organization has found a solution. Sometimes, news can reach the outside world even before it reaches management.

In such circumstances, the key to reputation management is to be ready and willing to communicate about the problem, outlining what has happened, the extent of the situation, and, critically, what the organization is doing to put it right. The organization must establish itself as the authoritative source of information about the situation, crushing harmful speculation and robustly deflecting the vicious rumors that inevitably accompany such stories.

In developing such a communication plan, an organization needs to consider the following factors:

- *Message*: What it will say about the situation and when.
- *Audience*: Who it will say it to and in what order.
- *Medium*: The platform it will use to say it.

Each crisis situation is different, but in cases of fraud organizations should consider the following.

Key Considerations

Messaging

Fraud can be brought to an organization's attention in many ways (for example, internal audit, whistleblower, media inquiry, etc.). Regardless of how the news reaches an organization, holding messages are required immediately. These are for use until an investigation is complete.

In cases of fraud, the "4Cs" should be applied:

- *Concern* (for what's happened): The incident is being treated extremely seriously.
- *Control* (of the situation): The claim is being investigated thoroughly.
- *Containment* (of the consequences): While regrettable, this will not have a material impact on the organization.
- *Commitment* (to compliance): "If this is the first time such an allegation has been made, initiate organizational compliance procedures over and above what is required."

It is often helpful when considering how to communicate *containment* to try to contextualize the message. For example, "This allegation relates to less than 0.0001% of turnover in just one of 30 markets we operate in." However, it is important not to downplay the alleged

"**Most practitioners and academics now accept that reputation will always be difficult to define and quantify. However, there is broad agreement that reputation is built on the trust stakeholders have in an organization, and that trust is far from woolly. On the contrary, trust brings hard commercial benefits.**" Warren Buffett

  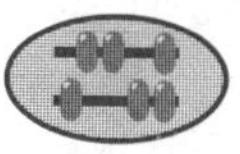 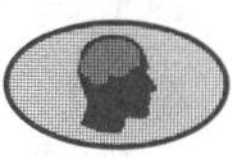  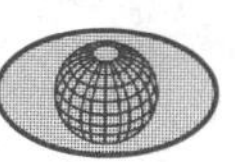   

Figure 1. Stakeholder mapping—Matrix to plot which audiences should receive proactive communication in a crisis

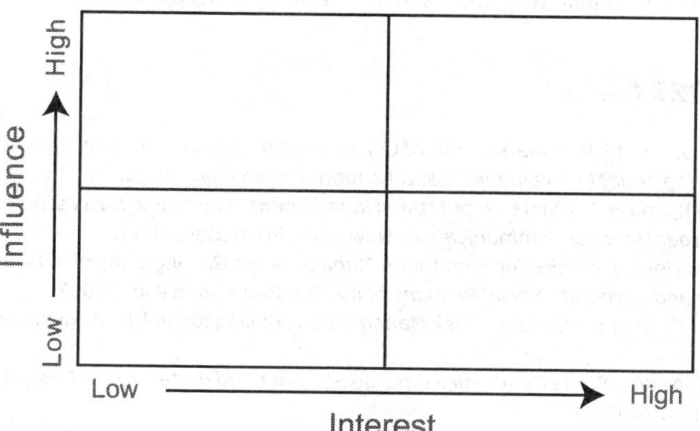

fraud if it may materially affect the organization.

Audience

Although an organization should be prepared to use this interim messaging widely and rapidly, if news of the alleged fraud is successfully contained, it may only be necessary to communicate it to a limited number of stakeholders.

To help identify which stakeholders should be proactively notified with these messages, an organization must consider which of its audiences have an interest in the problem (often the same as those who are affected) and those who may have some influence on its resolution. This can be plotted on a simple matrix (see figure 1).

Stakeholders in the top right-hand corner should be identified and a stepwise briefing process should be implemented. Clearly, this takes judgment and this is where external reputation management advisers can prove extremely valuable. When identifying your stakeholders, it is important to be as precise about them as possible:

- "Staff" is not a useful stakeholder category. A specific level of management in a specific department is more useful and will focus the process.
- There may be regulatory procedures to follow (for example, stock market announcements), and these must be adhered to.

Finally, it is worth noting that through an organization's ongoing "peacetime" reputation management program, solid relationships with these key stakeholders should already be in place. This is known as banking "relationship credit." The more relationship credit you have banked in peacetime, the easier it will be to draw on that credit in times of crisis, and the more forgiving stakeholders are likely to be.

Medium

Organizations should form a small senior team to manage the situation and use it to brainstorm how these messages will be delivered—for example, in person, by written letter, or via the media. However, it is important not to overcomplicate this part of the process. It is simply a case of considering those who are being notified and thinking about how they might be approached. For example, the head of a regulatory agency may appreciate it if the organization's CEO/MD delivers these messages in person.

There are three additional considerations:

- It is often useful (with legal advice) to put things in writing to stakeholders. However, always assume that whatever is written may be leaked or will be subject to compulsory disclosure in court. As a rule, an organization should not write anything that it wouldn't want to see in a newspaper or hear repeated in front of a judge.
- Putting a human face on things should never be underestimated. Even hardened regulators and authorities respond better to a one-to-one interaction than they do to a statutory written communication. An organization should consider who should make that interaction. If a minor regulatory infringement is involved, using the CEO to deliver the message is not appropriate. But if potentially it's a major issue, the chair of the board is the only appropriate person.
- Everyone will have their own agenda. The regulators and authorities may decide that they want to showcase an organization or defend any possible allegations that they were "asleep at the wheel." It can't stop the latter, but it is better that those stakeholders know your side of the story.

CASE STUDY

Société Générale

In January 2008, French bank Société Générale, one of Europe's biggest financial services companies, revealed that it had lost €4.9 billion in an incident of fraud involving a single futures trader.

Société Générale managed the incident very well. It was required to respond quickly, and it did: Two days after suspicions were aroused concerning unusual trading activity, the bank's chairman, Daniel Bouton, informed the governor of the Bank of France and suspended the trader in question, Jérôme Kerviel. The company successfully contained the incident and did not attempt to play down its potential magnitude.

As soon as Société Générale had complied with regulatory reporting, it moved from interim messages to release its first public statement, establishing itself as the authoritative source of information. The bank successfully communicated its containment of the crisis—despite admitting that it would need significant new capital to offset the losses, it reassured the financial community that it was still on course to make a good profit. It continued to give information to the authorities before releasing a candid statement about the incident: who Kerviel was, arbitrage activities, the method behind the fraud, how it was uncovered, and measures taken since the event.

The crisis required a human face, and the frontline response came from Daniel Bouton, whose resignation as executive chairman was rejected by the board early on but who eventually stepped down to nonexecutive chairman.

At the time of writing, Jérôme Kerviel is facing charges of breach of trust, computer abuse, and falsification. He has denied any wrongdoing and claims that the bank knew of his actions but let him continue as long as he was making money. The ongoing investigation and a €4 million fine imposed by France's banking regulator clearly makes it difficult for Société Générale to draw a line under the incident. However, the bank has laid the groundwork with strong actions to back up its messages (such as internal investigations into compliance) that have demonstrated its determination to stakeholders and built trust in the process.

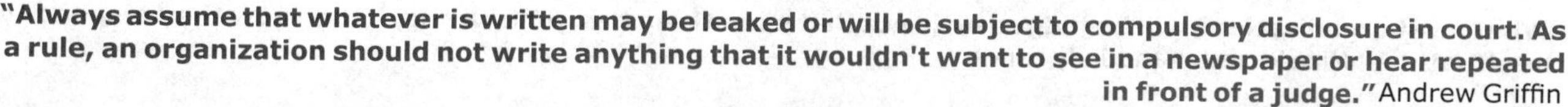

"Always assume that whatever is written may be leaked or will be subject to compulsory disclosure in court. As a rule, an organization should not write anything that it wouldn't want to see in a newspaper or hear repeated in front of a judge." Andrew Griffin

   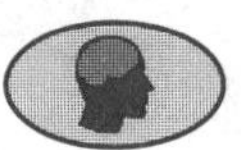  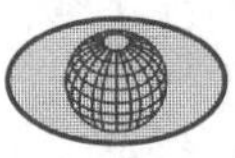   

DRAWING A LINE UNDER THE SITUATION

Once the investigation has been completed, you should be prepared to draw a line under the situation. To some extent, doing this depends on how public the situation has become. If developments have been highly publicized and commented on by a wide range of stakeholders, then a wide-ranging outreach plan should be developed to communicate how the organization intends to move on. If the situation has been relatively contained, the outreach plan may be far less reaching.

Irrespective of the reach of the communications plan, some underpinning messages will be required. The 4Cs formula outlined above can be revisited and revised. And it is important that messages are backed up by action. With stakeholders now less trusting than they were, an organization needs to *show* its audience that it has moved on, not just *tell* them.

For example, if an organization says that it is committed to compliance, can it allow the person accused of fraud to stay in their position? If an organization says it is confident that the situation is now under control and cannot recur, what tangible steps or changes can it point to as evidence that it really has acted to prevent a recurrence?

The more tangible the evidence underpinning the message, the firmer and more convincing the line the organization will be able to draw under the situation.

CONCLUSION

Everyone accepts that things go wrong from time to time. What most organizations will be judged on is not that something has gone wrong, but on how they respond to the situation.

Although every situation has its own dynamics, by following some of the broad guidelines outlined above organizations that are victims of fraud will go a long way toward protecting themselves from some of the reputational fallout they may suffer. Ultimately these guidelines should also help to maintain that all-important trust from their stakeholders.

▸▸ MORE INFO

Books:

Alsop, R. J. *The 18 Immutable Laws of Corporate Reputation: Creating, Protecting and Repairing Your Most Valuable Asset*. London: Kogan Page, 2006.

Doorley, J., and H. F. Garcia. *Reputation Management: The Key to Successful Corporate and Organizational Communication*. New York: Routledge, 2005.

Griffin, A. *New Strategies for Reputation Management: Gaining Control of Issues, Crises and Corporate Social Responsibility*. London: Kogan Page, 2007.

Larkin, J. *Strategic Reputation Risk Management*. Basingstoke, UK: Palgrave MacMillan, 2003.

Mitroff, I. A. *Why Some Companies Emerge Stronger and Better from a Crisis*. New York: Amacom, 2005.

O'Hanlon, Bill. *Thriving Through Crisis: Turn Tragedy and Trauma Into Growth and Change*. New York: Perigee, 2005.

Regester, M., and J. Larkin. *Risk Issues and Crisis Management in Public Relations: A Casebook of Best Practice*. 4th ed. London: Kogan Page, 2008.

Ulmer, R., T. Sellnow, and M. W. Seeger. *Effective Crisis Communication: Moving from Crisis to Opportunity*. Thousand Oaks, CA: Sage Publications, 2006.

van Reil, C. B. M., and C. J. Fombrun. *Essentials of Corporate Communication: Implementing Practices for Effective Reputation Management*. New York: Routledge, 2006.

Articles:

Ettenson, R., and J. Knowles. "Don't confuse reputation with brand." *MIT Sloan Management Review* 49:2 (2008). Online at: sloanreview.mit.edu/the-magazine/articles/2008/winter/49213.

Gardberg, N., and C. Fombrun. "The global reputation quotient project: First steps towards a cross-nationally valid measure of corporate reputation." *Corporate Reputation Review* 4:4 (2002): 303–307.

MacMillan, K, Kevin Money, Steve Downing and Carola Hillenbrand. "Giving your organisation SPIRIT: An overview and call to action for directors on issues of corporate governance, corporate reputation and corporate responsibility." *Journal of General Management* 30:2 (2004): 15–42.

See Also:

★ CSR: More than PR, Pursuing Competitive Advantage in the Long Run (pp. 147–149)
★ How Internal Auditing Can Help With a Company's Fraud Issues (pp. 646–650)
★ Understanding Reputation Risk and Its Importance (pp. 514–516)
★ What Is the Range of the Internal Auditor's Work? (pp. 732–735)
✔ Understanding Internal Audits (p. 1053)
✔ What Is Forensic Auditing? (p. 1057)

"What most organizations will be judged on is not that something has gone wrong, but on how they respond to the situation." Mike Regester and Judy Larkin

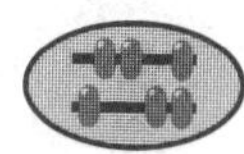

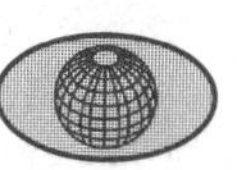

Political Risk: Countering the Impact on Your Business by Ian Bremmer

EXECUTIVE SUMMARY

- Business decision-makers must understand the political dynamics within the emerging market countries in which they operate.
- We can measure a state's stability—the ability of its government to implement policy and enforce laws despite a shock to the system.
- Essential to managing any type of risk is the development of a detailed and effective hedging strategy.
- Companies should not accept too much risk exposure within any one country or region.
- Rules of the game can change quickly in developing countries, and the cultivation of "friends in high places" isn't always a strong enough hedge.
- Operating in some developing countries comes with reputational risks at home.
- Too many companies have historically relied for insight into local politics and culture on employees who have lived in a particular country for only a short time—or have even merely traveled there.
- Those doing business in developing states need to have credible emergency response plans in place when events outside their control shut down supply chains, prevent local workers from coming to work, or otherwise disrupt operations.
- Developing strategies to recruit and train local managers serves several useful purposes.
- Devoting a share of profits to investment in local schools and universities, infrastructure, and charities can generate stores of goodwill, which is sometimes essential for cooperation with local workers and government officials.
- In some countries, foreign companies should be wary of transferring proprietary information to local partners or developing it inside the country.
- A foreign firm must look beyond what its local competitors are capable of producing today. It must anticipate how those capabilities are likely to develop over time.
- Conditions sometimes force companies to cut their losses and head for the exit. Ensuring that process is as painless and inexpensive as possible forms a crucial part of any sound risk mitigation strategy.
- Political risk can be managed. It should not be avoided altogether.

INTRODUCTION

Over the past several years, and across a broad range of companies, corporate decision-makers seeking opportunities overseas have learned that it is not enough to have a knowledge of a foreign country's economic fundamentals. They also have to understand the forces and dynamics that shape these countries' politics. This is especially true for emerging markets, where politics matters at least as much as economic factors for market outcomes. Of course, understanding that political risk matters is one thing. Knowing how to use it is another.

STABILITY

Starting with the basics, when committing a company to risk exposure in an emerging market country, it's essential to understand how political risk impacts the underlying strength of its government. There are two key elements to consider: stability and shock. Shocks are especially tough to forecast, because there are so many different kinds and because shocks are, by definition, unpredictable. We can't know when an earthquake will strike Pakistan, an elected leader will fall gravely ill in Nigeria, or a previously unknown group will carry out a successful terrorist attack in Indonesia.

But we can take the measure of a state's stability, which is defined as a government's ability to implement policy and enforce laws despite a shock to the system. The global financial crisis, a potent shock, has inflicted heavy losses on Russia's stock market. But Prime Minister Vladimir Putin has amassed plenty of political capital over the past several years, and President Dmitry Medvedev, his handpicked successor, basks in Putin's reflected glow. Neither need fear that large numbers of Russian citizens will turn on them anytime soon. In addition, a half-decade of windfall energy profits has generated more than $500 billion in reserves, ready cash that can be used to bail out stock markets, banks, and, if necessary, an unpopular government. That's why, for the near-term, Russia will remain stable.

Pakistan is a different story. The country's newly elected government has a range of rivals and enemies. Inflation, power shortages, and a wave of suicide attacks have undermined the ruling Pakistan Peoples Party's domestic popularity. The financial crisis leaves the country at risk of debt default, forcing the government to negotiate a loan package with the International Monetary Fund that could impose austerity measures—the kind that helped topple civilian governments in Pakistan in the 1990s. The country is less stable than Russia, because it is much more vulnerable to the worst effects of shock.

President Luiz Inácio Lula da Silva has bolstered Brazil's stability over the past several years by quelling fears of left-wing populism with responsible (and predictable) macroeconomic policies. The Chinese Communist Party's ability to generate prosperity at home via three decades of successful economic liberalization has helped its leadership to build durable near-term stability.

But Nigeria's future stability remains at the mercy of President Umaru Yar'Adua's failing health as historical tensions between northern Muslims and southern Christians combine with ongoing security challenges in the oil-rich Niger Delta region to prevent his government from building a national reputation for competence, vision, and strength. Iran's theocrats and firebrand president Mahmoud Ahmadinejad have effectively used the international conflict over the country's nuclear program to shore up support for the government in the face of high inflation and gasoline rationing. Underlying political factors in all these countries have a substantial impact on stability—and, therefore, on the country's business climate.

DIVERSIFY

Yet it is not sufficient to possess broad insights into state stability. If corporate decision-makers are to design a credible business strategy that mitigates political risk and maximizes profit opportunities, they have to look deeper at the vulnerabilities that are peculiar to each country, each province, each community. Essential to managing any type of risk is the development of a detailed and effective diversification strategy. Given the political volatility within many developing world

     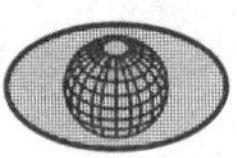   

states—countries that will generate a large share of global growth over the next several decades—this kind of strategy is especially important. Even within a country as relatively stable as China, a closer look at internal political dynamics can identify various kinds of risk.

Two years ago, US officials worried publicly over a spike in sales of Russian arms to China. Dire predictions of a developing Russian–Chinese military axis became commonplace. But in 2007, sales of Russian arms to China fell by some 62%. Was it because the two governments had some sort of behind-the-scenes falling out? Did the Chinese leadership suddenly doubt the quality of Russian-made products? In reality, the arms sales slowed because China had mastered the design of many of the weapons, and Chinese companies began to produce them in sufficient quantities that demand for foreign-made weaponry fell sharply.

This is a cautionary tale, one that reminds us that any company betting heavily on long-term access to Chinese consumers (or to customers in many other developing countries) may be making a big mistake. There is plenty of money to be made in China for the next several years, but putting too many eggs in a single basket remains as risky as ever. For businesses with supply chains in China and other developing states, it's also important to build redundancies that are not overly exposed within any one region within these countries.

There are other, less obvious, components of a solid diversification strategy. Multinational companies should use all the leverage that their home governments and international institutions can provide to ensure that the governments of the countries in which they accept risk exposure protect their intellectual property rights, enforce all local laws intended to safeguard their commercial interests, and maintain open markets. Rules of the game can change quickly in developing countries, and the cultivation of "friends in high places" isn't always by itself an effective plan.

KNOW THE COUNTRY

Gaining insight into a country's political, economic, social, and cultural traditions is essential for a successful risk mitigation strategy. Where should this insight come from? Too many companies have historically relied on employees who have lived in a particular country for only a short time—or may even have done no more than travel there. Turning to the guy who backpacked through country X during college for useful information about its politics and culture—not as rare a phenomenon as you might think—is no substitute for the knowledge that can be gained from local workers themselves and from trained political risk analysts.

DESIGN AN EMERGENCY RESPONSE

Generally speaking, emerging market countries are more vulnerable than rich world states to large-scale civil unrest, public health crises, and environmental disasters. Those doing business in developing states need credible emergency response plans in place when events outside their control shut down supply chains, prevent local workers from coming to work, or otherwise disrupt operations. Some businesses have designed technology plans that allow workers to work from home. In cases when circumstances force foreign workers to leave the country, locals should have the necessary training and skills to assume their responsibilities for an extended period. The added expense and time for training are well worth the cost. In some countries, they're essential.

INVEST IN LOCAL WORKERS

Developing strategies to recruit and train local managers serves several useful purposes. First, it gives the host country government an investment in the success of a foreign-owned business. Every job created by a foreign firm is one that local government doesn't have to create. All governments want to keep unemployment at a minimum. Second, it gives local citizens a stake in the foreign company's success and helps to build solid relationships within the community. Some multinational firms have formed mutually profitable partnerships with local colleges and universities that give companies a fertile recruiting ground and ambitious students opportunities for work.

INVEST IN THEIR COMMUNITIES

Devoting a share of profits to investment in local schools and universities, infrastructure, and charities can generate stores of goodwill, which is sometimes essential for cooperation with local workers and government officials. Yet, sensitivity to the local culture matters too. In many developing states, suspicions that Western (especially American) companies have a political or ideological agenda can undermine efforts to promote trust. Contributions to local quality of life should be seen to come without strings attached.

PROTECT INTELLECTUAL PROPERTY

In some countries, foreign companies should be wary of transferring proprietary information to local partners or developing it inside the country. Forging alliances with local partners in joint ventures often serves as an effective risk mitigation strategy, but today's partner can become tomorrow's competitor, and a foreign firm can't always count on local courts or officials to safeguard its assets. Ironically, some foreign multinationals with long-term plans to remain inside a particular emerging market country have invested in local innovation. In the process, they have given locals an incentive to press their own government for stronger legal protections for intellectual property rights. Others have pooled their lobbying efforts with both local businesses and other foreign firms. When lobbying a government, strength in numbers can make a difference.

KNOW THE LOCAL COMPETITION

Successful firms understand their comparative advantages. But a foreign company must look beyond what its local competitors are capable of producing today. It must anticipate how those capabilities are likely to develop over time. Identifying the markets in which a firm's core competencies are likely to deliver profits for the foreseeable future is essential for long-term risk mitigation strategies.

In many emerging market countries, local companies are often better at large-scale efficient manufacturing than at designing products, marketing them, and delivering them to the customer. Knowing how quickly the local competition can climb the value chain helps with the design of an intelligent, long-term business strategy.

KNOW WHERE TO FIND THE EXITS

Many companies have made lots of money in emerging markets. But as Wall Street veterans like to say, "Don't confuse brilliance with a bull market." Some companies have gotten away with ignoring the need for solid risk-management strategies and have simply ridden the wave produced by the inevitable rise of emerging market economies.

Yet, as skepticism of globalization grows in some developing countries, as their governments respond to domestic political pressure by rewriting rules to favor local companies at the expense of their foreign competitors, and as the challenges facing multinational companies operating inside these countries become more complex, it's important to have an exit strategy. There are plenty of developing states that are now open for business and investment. They have different strengths and vulnerabilities. Too much risk exposure in any one of them

"If we begin with certainties, we shall end in doubts; but if we begin with doubts, and we are patient with them, we shall end in certainties." Sir Francis Bacon

  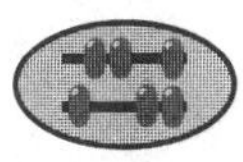   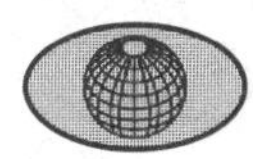   

can create unnecessary risks. Conditions sometimes force companies to cut their losses and head for the door. Ensuring that this process is as painless and inexpensive as possible forms a crucial part of any sound risk mitigation strategy.

DON'T FORGET THE POWER OF PERCEPTION

Operating in some developing countries comes with reputational risks at home. Several US companies have faced tough domestic criticism for doing business with governments that are accused of violating international labor, environmental, and human-rights standards. For a company's leadership, clearly communicating what the company will and won't do to gain market access in certain countries—and strict adherence to these standards of conduct—can help to minimize this risk.

POLITICAL RISK INSURANCE

As a last resort, a firm can purchase political risk insurance from providers like the Multilateral Investment Guarantee Agency, an arm of the World Bank, or the US government's Overseas Private Investment Corporation. But this should be a last resort strategy, because high premiums, substantial transaction and opportunity costs, and the complexities of establishing a valid claim have taught many companies that it is far more cost-effective to prevent or preempt bad outcomes than to rely heavily on plans to cope with their aftermath.

A LITTLE TOLERANCE IS A GOOD THING

It's useful to remember that having a good exit strategy does not require you to use it. Doing business in developing states comes with risk. But refusing to enter these markets or pulling out at the first sign of trouble comes with a high cost to opportunity. Foreign companies will be earning solid profits within emerging market states for many years to come. Political risk can be managed. It should not be avoided altogether.

›› MORE INFO

Books:

Bracken, Paul, Ian Bremmer, and David Gordon (eds). *Managing Strategic Surprise: Lessons from Risk Management and Risk Assessment*. New York: Cambridge University Press, 2008.

Howell, Llewellyn D. (ed.). *Handbook of Country and Political Risk Analysis*. 3rd ed. East Syracuse, NY: Political Risk Services Group, 2002.

Moran, Theodore H. (ed.). *Managing International Political Risk*. London: Blackwell Publishing, 1999.

Moran, Theodore H., Gerald T. West, and Keith Martin (eds). *International Political Risk Management: Meeting the Needs of the Present, Anticipating the Challenges of the Future*. Washington, DC: World Bank Publications, 2007.

Wilkin, Sam (ed.). *Country and Political Risk: Practical Insights for Global Finance*. London: Risk Books, 2004.

Articles:

Bremmer, Ian, and Fareed Zakaria. "Hedging political risk in China." *Harvard Business Review* 84:11 (2006): 22–25.

Henisz, Witold J., and Bennet A. Zelner. "Political risk management: A strategic perspective." Online at: www.management.wharton.upenn.edu/henisz/papers/hz_prm.pdf

"Insuring against political risk." *The Economist* (April 4, 2007). Online at: www.economist.com/finance/displaystory.cfm?story_id=8967224.

"Integrating political risk into enterprise risk management": Online at: www.pwc.com/extweb/pwcpublications.nsf/docid/EAB01AC994713716852570FF006868B6

Stanislav, Markus. "Corporate governance as political insurance: Firm-level institutional creation in emerging markets and beyond." *Socio-Economic Review* 6:1 (2008): 69–98.

Websites:

Eurasia Group, global political risk advisery and consulting firm: www.eurasiagroup.net

Multilateral Investment Guarantee Agency (MIGA)'s Political Risk Insurance Center: www.pri-center.com

PricewaterhouseCoopers: www.pwc.com. Enter "political risk" in search box to find articles and resources.

See Also:

★ How to Manage Emerging Market Risks with Third Party Insurance (pp. 468–470)
★ Measuring Company Exposure to Country Risk (pp. 342–344)
★ Measuring Country Risk (pp. 345–347)
★ To Hedge or Not to Hedge (pp. 100–102)
★ Viewpoint: Thierry Malleret (pp. 457–458)
✔ Comparative and International Financial Regulation (p. 923)
✔ International Comparisons of Company Law (p. 991)
✔ Understanding and Calculating RORAC, RAROC, and RARORAC (p. 1006)

     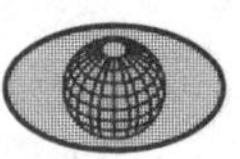   

How to Manage Emerging Market Risks with Third Party Insurance by Rod Morris

EXECUTIVE SUMMARY

- Emerging markets present significant noncommercial political risks.
- Political risks can be mitigated through insurance products known as political risk insurance (PRI).
- PRI is a vehicle designed to help both equity investors and financial institutions to mitigate the losses that can result from a foreign government's substantive violation of the terms and conditions that originally attracted the foreign investment.
- More than 40 insurers, both private and public sector, offer such coverage.
- This article gives a comparative overview of the features of the public and private sector approaches.

INTRODUCTION

There are numerous issues that investors and companies must consider when contemplating an investment in a foreign country. Take for example, cultural differences, the tax regime, foreign currency exchange restrictions, the regulatory and legal environment, the judicial system, and security requirements for both assets and employees. For emerging markets in particular, each of these factors can be further complicated by the potential for politically motivated interference, or changes in the government's attitude to foreign investment.

Foreign governments, especially those without an effective system of checks and balances, can create a favorable investment climate and then reverse or alter it quickly and dramatically. The results can be devastating to a foreign investor's ability to survive. A government's abrogation or unilateral alteration of an investor's licenses or agreements, new and onerous regulations or taxes, confiscation of property, and so on can happen, do happen, and will continue to happen, even if an investor hires an entire team of international and local lawyers and does everything right. None of that will matter when the local political environment takes an abrupt turn, which can happen for any number of reasons, including financial crisis, coup, or regime change. Nor will it be much use if terrorists or organized crime factions create an untenable atmosphere of insecurity.

There is also a growing trend known as "resource nationalism," in which governments have tried to grab a bigger share of the control and profits derived from diminishing supplies of, or increasing demand for (and therefore increasing prices of), their country's commodities such as tin, gold, and oil. Some governments are forcing unilateral restructuring of contracts and concessions, or even forcing a change in ownership that flips the foreign investor from a majority to minority position. The trend is particularly notable in Russia, Latin America, and Africa. Even if an investment is experiencing no problems with the sovereign government, there is no guarantee that it will be safe from interference from increasingly militant local governments, local judges interpreting local laws, or activist community organizations, which can frustrate or destroy a project just as effectively as an outright confiscation.

It is therefore essential that any potential investor makes a study of the current and likely economic and political risks of a country. Countries with developing or struggling economies and immature or undemocratic political structures can offer significant opportunities but at the same time pose significant risk. Much of that risk can be described as political, and many of these political risks can be mitigated through insurance products, known generically as PRI (political risk insurance). Assessing these risks may require some outside assistance, and there are a number of organizations that can help (see the More Info section).

WHAT IS PRI?

Political risk insurance is a broad term that includes a variety of coverage options for losses that have as their cause some kind of political motivation—whether by those in government or by others acting against it. PRI is designed to help both equity investors and financial institutions to mitigate the kinds of losses that can result from a host government's substantive violation of the terms and conditions which attracted the original investment. For equity investors, PRI can indemnify them for losses of their assets and/or interruption of their business income resulting not only from politically inspired violence, but also from the type of governmental actions that go beyond the normal, prudent, reasonable, and responsible exercise of governmental authority. For financial institutions, PRI provides the aforementioned coverage, as well as additional benefits such as the ability to increase capacity for international loans; the ability to offer clients more attractive financial terms; risk management of country, region, or sector concentrations; and protection against payment defaults by a governmental entity.

PRI products insure a wide range of risks or causes of loss, but, for the sake of simplicity, the coverage options generally fall within three broad categories: expropriation, inconvertibility, and political violence.

Expropriation (CEN)

Expropriation is the most commonly purchased political risk coverage. It is also referred to as confiscation, expropriation, and nationalization (CEN) coverage. Essentially, it insures against wrongful interference by a foreign government that deprives investors of their fundamental rights to proceeds or ownership. Such actions can include not only outright confiscation or nationalization, but also breach of contracts, abrogation of licenses, changes that result in unfairly discriminatory treatment in regulation, taxes, tariffs, and/or impairment of the ability to pass costs through to consumers. Coverage can apply to a single discrete action, such as the seizure of assets, plants, or equipment by the government, or a series of actions that ultimately make the investment no longer economically viable—usually referred to as "creeping expropriation."

Although it does not fit well within the category of expropriation, there is a related product that is referred to as "nonhonoring of a sovereign guarantee." Briefly, this protects financial institutions and exporters against a payment default guaranteed by a sovereign, sub-sovereign, or in some cases a sovereign-owned enterprise.

Inconvertibility (T&C)

Also known as transfer and convertibility (T&C) insurance, inconvertibility coverage insures earnings, return of capital, principal and interest payments, and technical assistance fees against the imposition of new currency restrictions or controls that prevent conversion from local currency to

  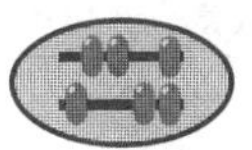   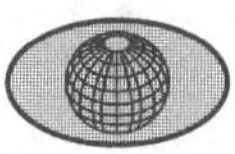   

hard currency and/or the transfer and repatriation of funds. It does not protect against currency fluctuation, devaluation, or any preexisting restrictions on conversion or transfer.

Political Violence

This coverage protects against a loss of assets or income due to events such as terrorism, sabotage, revolution, insurrection, war, civil war—essentially, any politically motivated act of violence. This coverage is a much broader protection than is normally afforded under property and casualty insurance policies, which typically exclude perils such as war, or offer very limited protection against terrorism and sabotage. *No one can afford to assume that they are immune from potential loss due to terrorism and violence.* The number of terror attacks worldwide continues to rise, and emerging markets are at greater risk than Western Europe or the United States. According to the regional breakdown shown in Table 1, there are almost 15,000 terrorist attacks per year. It is unlikely that the world will see a sudden reversal of this trend. Far from it.

Table 1. Terror attacks 2005–07. (*Source*: US National Counterterrorism Center)

Year	Africa	East Asia	Europe and Eurasia	Middle East	South Asia	Western Hemisphere	Total
2005	256	1,005	780	4,222	4,022	868	11,153
2006	422	1,036	659	7,755	3,654	826	14,352
2007	835	1,429	606	7,540	3,607	482	14,449

PRI INSURERS

A web search will produce a number of hits for both insurers and intermediaries (brokers and consultants) offering PRI products. Such a search, however, provides no clear evidence of the competence, capabilities, or financial strength of these companies. There is, nevertheless, an association of over 40 of the most reputable PRI carriers in the world, both private and public, known as the Berne Union. You can access a list of its members at www.berneunion.org.uk and be confident that you will find a responsible insurer. Although Lloyd's syndicates are not members, they are equally excellent.

PRI insurers fall into two categories: government-sponsored (public) and private. Government-sponsored programs are offered by many developed countries to encourage trade and investment in emerging markets. Such programs would include not only those sponsored by single governments (for example, EFIC of Australia, NEXI of Japan, OPIC of the United States, Sinosure of China), but also multilateral organizations (for example, ADB, the Asian Development Bank; ICIEC, of the Islamic Development Bank; and MIGA of the World Bank) that are funded and supported by multiple countries.

In general, private-market insurers such as Lloyd's, AIG, Chubb, and Zurich are unwilling to assume as much risk or offer terms, limits, or policy periods that are as expansive as the public insurers such as OPIC and MIGA. This can present significant practical problems not only for investors, but also for intermediaries such as brokers, as evidenced by the case study below.

COMPARISON OF PRI FROM PUBLIC AND PRIVATE INSURERS

A detailed comparison of the differences between individual programs is not possible here, but some general comments on some of the more significant considerations as between the private and public markets may be informative. Generalities are never quite fair, but they can provide some basic insight into what to expect when seeking cover. For government-sponsored programs, the references below are to OPIC and MIGA since they are the largest and most experienced. When referring to private insurers, the commonalities of programs from companies such as AIG, Zurich, and Lloyd's are used.

Capacity: The private market offers less per project/investment than government-sponsored programs. The capacity of private insurers has increased over the years, but it is still considerably less than MIGA's $200 million and OPIC's $250 million policy maximum, with the ability to exceed even this ceiling under extremely unusual circumstances.[2]

Term: Private insurers usually cover contracts for no longer than 15 years, whereas MIGA offers 15–20 years, and OPIC has offered 20-year contracts for a very long time.

Eligibility: Private insurers are basically unrestricted, while MIGA is restricted

CASE STUDY

Sempra Energy: A Cautionary Tale

Sempra Energy, a Fortune 500 energy services holding company, successfully bid to participate in the privatization of the Argentine gas sector in the 1990s. Sempra then became interested in purchasing PRI for its investment, and hired Marsh USA to act as its broker in finding an appropriate product. Argentina's spotty and inconsistent handling of foreign investment justified the company's concern, and it believed that Marsh would survey the market and identify the best choice. Marsh chose a policy from National Union, an AIG affiliate. In January 2002, the government of Argentina was in the midst of a financial crisis that resulted in the enactment of, *inter alia*, the Emergency System Act, which converted and froze public utility tariffs in pesos rather than the agreed US dollar amounts.

Sempra filed a claim with National Union, but compensation was denied. Sempra took the denial to arbitration and lost because, in fact, National Union's contract was not sufficiently broad to provide coverage under the particularly confusing chain of facts. In its arbitral opinion, however, the panel pointed out that an OPIC policy would, in fact, have provided coverage. Considering that Marsh had selected the National Union policy over the OPIC policy, Sempra then filed suit[1] in July of 2007 in the Los Angeles Superior Court alleging that Marsh had failed "to obtain an insurance policy that provided the coverage it promised to procure for Sempra." It accused Marsh of negligence, breach of oral and written contracts, breach of fiduciary duty, and negligent misrepresentation. Sempra was awarded US$48.5 million in damages.

This case illustrates a number of lessons but, suffice to say, investors should review carefully their approach to emerging market investments: Analyze the country risk, and make an informed decision about mitigating the risk through insurance or some other approach; carefully evaluate any intermediaries; vet the reasons and justifications for PRI recommendations; and carefully evaluate the recommended product to be certain that it is sufficiently broad to cover the types of claims or problems that might arise.

Notwithstanding the events in the case study, it has to be said that private insurers can often be more flexible in terms and conditions and quicker to execute contracts, and they are not encumbered by statutes or covenants that restrict eligibility or require a lot of information. Additionally, public carriers do not like to be seen as competing with the private market. Their preference is that investors only approach them when the private market is inadequate or unavailable.

"Only the dead have seen the end of war." Plato

     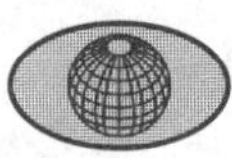   

to insuring investors from member countries, and OPIC is restricted to investors with significant US ownership.

Rates: Private insurers price for profit, while the public market prices to be self-sustaining. Low-risk situations favor the private market, but, as risk increases, any such advantage tends to disappear. Also, much more than government-sponsored insurers, private insurers increase price based on demand and their own country concentrations. OPIC's rates are based only on risk and are guaranteed for the full term of the contract.

Appetite: OPIC and MIGA are designed to be markets of last resort (i.e. an investor is expected to try the private market first), yet they may very well be the only viable or affordable market in high-risk situations—for example, Afghanistan, Pakistan, and much of Africa.

Small business: Private insurers find it difficult to make money on policies for small amounts. Government-sponsored carriers, on the other hand, assist small investors as a matter of public policy.

Financial strength: Certainly Lloyd's and all of the Berne Union insurers are A-rated or equivalent. Because it is a US government agency, OPIC is not rated, but a rating is unnecessary as it is backed by the full faith and credit of the US government.

Coverage: OPIC has a history and reputation of being a product innovator but is sometimes constrained by its authorizing statute. With respect to political violence, however, only OPIC covers losses resulting from chemical, nuclear, and biological events. In today's world, that is not an insignificant difference. OPIC is the only carrier in the world that has been offering such broad coverage, and they have been doing it for decades.

Loss avoidance: Government-sponsored insurers have the ability to bring considerable pressure to bear on foreign governments when there is advance indication of a potential problem.

Claim payment histories: For many reasons, private insurers reveal almost no information about the number, type, or amounts of paid claims, denied claims, or claim determinations that are in dispute or arbitration. The same is not true of OPIC, which is the only carrier in the world whose records are open to the public both with respect to individual claim determinations and to aggregate numbers, which convey some interesting stories and patterns.

Ease of doing business: Without question, it is easier to do business with private market insurers. Public carriers require more information, both at the time of application and throughout the term of the contract. They need additional information in order to report to their governing bodies that they are fulfilling their missions, by supporting investments which help both the country of investment as well as its people by protecting worker and human rights and the environment, while doing no harm to the US economy or jobs.

CONCLUSION

Investment in emerging markets is replete with risk. A thorough vetting should be done not only of the risk factors, but also of the tools that can be used to mitigate those risks. Political risk insurance is one of the best tools for mitigating these risks and it is available from a growing and capable population of insurers, both private and public.

MAKING IT HAPPEN

The always quotable American baseball player, Yogi Berra, said: "If you don't know where you're going, chances are you'll wind up someplace else." Without a clear perspective on the political, judicial, regulatory, and social climate for foreign investment, one can easily make a mistake. Even with full knowledge of current conditions, the climate for investment can change very quickly. It is always prudent to consider options in mitigating the substantial risks that can arise and overtake you.

- Consider the use of firms that provide expert analysis of emerging market risks.
- Compare and contrast the advantages of the private and public PRI carriers for the needs of your specific investment.
- There are many advantages to using an insurance broker but, especially for the public PRI carriers, they are not required.
- Insist that the insurance broker thoroughly explains all your options and the reasons for their recommendations to satisfy yourself that the recommendations fulfill your needs rather than theirs.

MORE INFO

Brokers:

Aon: www.aon.com/uk/en/risk_management/political-risk

Lloyd's: www.pri-center.com/directories/partner_specific.cfm?pgid=5&orgnum=34313

Marsh: global.marsh.com/risk/politicalRisk

Willis: www.willis.com/Client_Solutions/Services/Political_Risk

Sovereign Ratings and Other Info:

Fitch Ratings: www.fitchratings.com

IMF: www.imf.org/external/country

Moody's (registration required): www.moodys.com

S&P—Find "Sovereigns" from the home page: www.standardandpoors.com

Other Sources:

Berne Union: www.berneunion.org.uk

CountryRisk.com guide to country research on the internet: www.countryrisk.com

Economist Intelligence Unit: www.eiu.com

Eurasia Group: www.eurasiagroup.net

Global Insight: www.globalinsight.com

Oxford Analytica global strategic analysis: www.oxan.com

NOTES

1 Sempra Energy v Marsh USA Inc. et al., case no. cv07-5431 in US District Court, Central District of California.

2 Having greater limits available from one carrier is always an advantage when the alternative is to piece cover together from a number of different carriers with the potential for gaps in cover or tenor that may require yet another contract to cover the "Difference in Conditions" (DIC).

"Only the dead have seen the end of war." Plato

  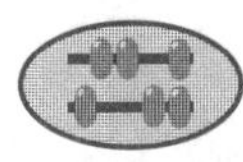   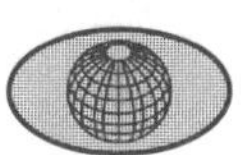   

Human Risk: How Effective Strategic Risk Management Can Identify Rogues by Tom McKaig

EXECUTIVE SUMMARY

- Corporations and high-level risk management are built around the people in organizations—and people are fallible.
- The need to evaluate human risk is clear: Stories abound of rogue employees in large and small organizations who have destroyed their entire firm.
- At the extreme, rogue firms, such as Enron, can destroy shareholder value and employees' lives.
- Building a quality-based organization helps to drive out rogues, but that's not the only way.
- Control measures need to be in place.
- Legal measures, the spotlight of publicity, and backing up corporate policies with firm action are all effective tools.

INTRODUCTION

Best practices in strategic risk management are intended to prevent weaknesses within corporations causing damage or even pulling down the firm. However, effective strategic risk management tools and techniques became harder to implement as business operations grow, become more complex, and operate in multiple locations. The controls that might have once been deemed acceptable in keeping employees within corporations on the same page begin to be less effective in cases of corporate restructurings that split businesses into smaller business units, and where employees are prodded into making deeper contributions to the bottom line.

Technology has not necessarily been a savior in this type of situation. Although technology has provided a platform for enhancing competitive advantage for business, it has also been a tool used by smart, capable, yet ill-intentioned employees to steal and distort overall results.

In the age of managerial cutbacks and increased workloads, a lot of things can happen that go unnoticed by overburdened managers. Interview techniques intended to keep rogues out of the workplace are—in spite of all the high-end questionnaires and intensive interview techniques that may be used—oftentimes ineffective, as potential employees are extremely savvy about modern interview techniques. Players in the job market are often familiar with the drill. Job hunters pass through many revolving interview doors, allowing them to hone their skills on how to dupe the interview process. Some interviewers may be incompetent or show poor judgment. HR departments are not foolproof, and it is only realistic to accept the fact that rogues in the workplace are here to stay. HR people will sometimes catch potential wrongdoers at the gatepost through psychological tests and other forms of due diligence involving intuition and criminal checks. But don't count on it.

Newspapers are full of stories about accountants who pad the books and give kickbacks to friends and family. Unhappy workers can damage product on the assembly line. A fired employee can show up at the workplace intent on payback for the injustice he or she feels they have suffered (in the United States this is called "going postal"). A multinational manager away from the watchful eyes of the home office can withhold information and deliver selective reports. Expense accounts can be padded. Goods can be pilfered from warehouses.

Given the current economic and political shocks, the last thing a company needs is to find itself in the news on account of the excessive creativity of one or more of its employees. Managers must face the fact that rogues will enter their organizations. So the question becomes: What can be done about it before the damage is done?

Keep in mind that human risk is about more than employees stealing from a firm; it can include individuals making unsound business decisions because nobody told them otherwise. Mistakes can be just as bad as deliberate fraud, as the following case shows.

CASE STUDY

An Invitation to Rogue Employees

The example of a small Costa Rican bank serves to illustrate this point. At the height of the opening of Costa Rica's financial markets to foreign financial institutions in 1995 there was a rush to change operations practice. In the pre-free market era, Costa Rican banks could do as they pleased and were immune to punishment even when there were banking scandals and losses that were large for Costa Rica's fragile economy during the 1980s and 1990s. Old-style banks, accustomed to getting away with providing poor customer service and having lax internal controls, found that their business environment was changing with the pending legislative changes, set to open Costa Rica's financial markets to the world.

With poor leadership at the helm, and a lack of almost any strategic management initiative, employees were forced to take on new and undefined roles in their bank. Most of these were ill-suited to employees who were given inadequate training and guidance for their new tasks.

As part of rising to the challenge of this expected competition from foreign banks, and in light of the assumed effectiveness of recently ordered ATM machines, the bank we are considering decided that a (ill-informed) lean and mean policy of rampant firing would be an acceptable cost-saving measure. Half of the bank's staff lost their jobs, and those who remained quickly became demoralized. The newly installed bank machines did not function properly. Friday afternoon payday waits grew to two hours from the already unacceptable 15–30 minutes.

Internal communications broke down. In place of the usual courteous conversations, vitriolic emails flew from one cubicle to the next—seeding the environment for "surprise actions" from a growing league of unhappy, overworked, and demoralized employees. With no controls in place, an inexperienced bank teller authorized a loan of $US 1 million to a long-standing customer—based solely on the fact that the teller liked the man and felt that he could be trusted with the money. For a small bank with a net worth of $37 million, this inappropriate loan decision was the start of a string of poor management decisions that led to its implosion. Throughout this process the business culture undermined any attempts to implement benchmarking studies or best-practice management solutions. The "generous" employee was not fired and kept his duties with a severe reprimand. The future of the bank was sealed, and eventually it went down.

"However, quality leadership can also be lost through some catastrophic change."
In Juran and Gryna (eds) (1988)

  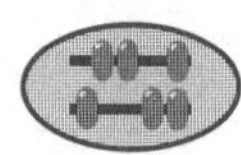   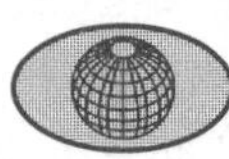   

AT THE EXTREME

At the extreme end of the spectrum, there is a widespread pattern of "pushing the boundaries" of everything from accounting rules to disclosure rules for public companies, lax internal controls, managements that focus on doing deals rather than managing, outright fraud and theft, and incentive systems that reward the wrong actions.

Enron followed this pattern. The case of Enron shows how a combination of intellectual laziness and groupthink by a large number of employees, consultants, and analysts allowed a group of greedy and ambitious individuals to get away with massive fraud. Enron was not a case of one or two people at the top undertaking a complex scheme unbeknown to others, but rather a case of many individuals who knew what they were supposed to do, but didn't do it. This was a case of analysts who never really questioned how Enron made its money, of accountants who didn't ask simple questions, and of employees and board members who saw dubious things but were afraid to stand up and ask the questions they should have.

STRATEGIC RISK MANAGEMENT: A VIEW

What is risk management, and how does it apply to the actions of employees? According to Kent D. Miller, " 'risk' refers to variation in corporate outcomes or performance that cannot be forecast *ex ante*."[1] The key element here is to recognize that there is true uncertainty about human risk, or indeed any risk. The fact that an organization has survived to today without major scandal does not guarantee that it is safe in the future.

So what to do? According to Miller, effective risk management responses frequently include avoidance (which we have noted is almost impossible with the case of human risk), control (to be addressed in a moment), and cooperation and imitation (which can be achieved through quality initiatives).

QUALITY INITIATIVES CAN HELP

An organization is only as good as its parts—in this case the human parts. One fractured link in the chain means one vulnerable corporation. The quality aspect of management can be evoked to work hand in hand with problem prevention, but it is all too often overlooked.

Typically quality applies to (but is not limited to) reducing or eliminating defects in manufactured products. Beyond this, management also needs to invoke quality principles that smooth the internal environment. When intra-corporate communication channels are damaged, the ensuing misinformation may foster rogue behavior within the organization. Many quality experts cite training, transparency, empowerment, and clear communication as vital steps in building a quality organization.

Whether dealing with production issues or those relating to customer service, quality initiatives espoused by management thinkers like Armand V. Feigenbaum, J. M. Juran, Philip B. Crosby, and Frank Gryna can help a business. Firms that include quality as a core value, and reinforce this value through everyday practice, have experienced reductions down to zero of defects on production lines, lower worker turnover, higher levels of worker empowerment through training, more worker satisfaction, greater productivity, and a positive outlook on the company. Valuing people as the key drivers of both quality and performance is important to a firm and can go a long way toward identifying rogues and frustrating their efforts.

Quality starts with managers. Being an ethical role model is a key function of any leader. And the good news is that nothing special has to be done to become such a positive model. However, when leadership falters it can open the door to a rogue hit, doing as much damage to the corporation as a rogue wave can do to a ship at sea. You have to work at good leadership.

But the emphasis on quality alone is not enough. Control mechanisms, including both financial and performance audits, are important for preventing and uncovering potential problems. The really effective tools are punishment and brandishing the legal arsenal available to the company. Such measures reassure the public. A corporation just can't hunker down to avoid embarrassment. Swift and fair measures will fill the void of those strategic management initiatives that fail to catch rogue employees and will serve as a heavy reminder to others who may be about to embark on a negative course of action.

To many, the idea of punishment seems to be a return to management's dark past in the days of command and control. This is not the case. Taking corrective action, including negative reinforcements and punishments, is a legitimate function of managers, just as much as positive reinforcements are. Corrective actions can include firings, admonishments, wage deductions, and suspension without pay. People in authority are chary about digging in their heels to fight for what is ethically and obviously right for fear of being politically incorrect, or worse, manifestly insensitive. Many in decision-making positions prefer a course of inaction because they lack the gumption required to stay the course. If a manager has documented proof (paper or electronic) of wrongdoing by an employee, and particularly in a unionized environment, there is little that a union can do to "rescue" the employee from receiving the appropriate reprimand, short of the union condoning such rogue behavior.

CONCLUSION

A manager faces many risks—from industry-wide risks such as currency and interest rate risks, to department-specific risks such as accounting and treasury risks. Most of these risks can be quantified, though we are finding out that many of the numbers assigned to these risks are little more than educated guesses. Unfortunately the identification, measurement, and quantification of human risk are difficult and challenging. In spite of our best efforts, and in spite of pundits who spout an arsenal of "proof" to the contrary, reliable numbers cannot be assigned to human risk. Nor can risk be completely eliminated from an organization. But quality initiatives and control mechanisms can go a very long way to minimize exposure.

▸▸ MAKING IT HAPPEN

- Learn to live with the uncertainty of any risk, especially human risk.
- Place renewed emphasis on what is already being done, including audits (financial and performance), internal financial controls, and clear financial reporting.
- Vigilantly tweak and enforce the control mechanisms already in place. Think about expanding and/or adding controls.
- Revisit your own role as a highly visible manager. Are corporate controls short-sighted, or are they clearly structured so as to prevent deceit, fraud, and rogues from doing future damage?
- Identify high-risk areas in your firm—from inventory to treasury areas. Think about safety and security measures in addition to internal controls.

"Total-quality-control programs thus require, as an initial step, top management's reemphasis of the respective quality responsibilities and accountabilities of all company employees." Feigenbaum (2004)

  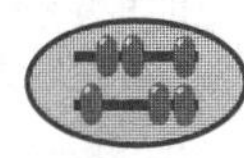 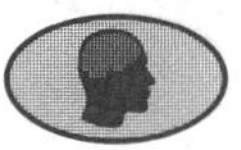  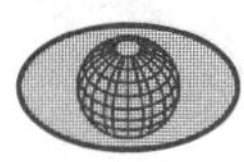   

▸▸ MORE INFO

Books:

Crosby, Philip B. *Completeness: Quality for the 21st Century*. New York: Penguin (Dutton), 1992.

Feigenbaum, Armand V. *Total Quality Control*. 4th ed. New York: McGraw-Hill, 2004.

Gryna, Frank, M. *Quality Planning & Analysis: From Product Development Through Use*. 4th ed. New York: McGraw-Hill, 2000.

Hill, Charles W. L., and Thomas McKaig. *Global Business Today*. 2nd Canadian ed. Whitby, ON: McGraw-Hill Ryerson, 2009.

Juran, J. M., and Frank M. Gryna (eds). *Juran's Quality Control Handbook*. 4th ed. New York: McGraw-Hill, 1988.

Mintzberg, Henry. *Managers Not MBAs: A Hard Look at the Soft Practice of Managing and Management Development*. San Francisco, CA: Berrett-Koehler Publishers, 2004.

Articles:

Becker, David M. "Testimony concerning new regulatory tools to control the activities of rogue individuals in the financial services industries." Given before the Subcommittee on Oversight and Investigations and the Subcommittee on Financial Institutions and Consumer Credit US House of Representatives, March 6, 2001. Online at: www.sec.gov/news/testimony/ts042001.htm

Boak, Joshua. "Rogue trader rocks firm: Huge wheat futures loss stuns MFGlobal." *Chicago Tribune* (February 29, 2008). Online at: archives.chicagotribune.com/2008/feb/29/business/chi-fri_traderfeb29

Clark, Andrew. "From ethical champion to rogue interloper—BP's American nightmare: Accidents and allegations of market fixing destroy environmentalist image." *The Guardian (London)* (November 16, 2006). Online at: www.guardian.co.uk/business/2006/nov/16/ethicalbusiness.oilandpetrol

Gunther, Will. "In the crosshairs: Limiting the impact of workplace shootings." *Risk Management* 55 (November 2008). Online at: findarticles.com/p/articles/mi_qa5332/is_11_55/ai_n31162724

Johnston, David Cay. "Staff says I.R.S. concealed improper audits and rogue agent." *New York Times* (May 1, 1998). Online at: tinyurl.com/aqf9tr

KPMG. "An approach to mitigating rogue trading risks." KPMG LLP, 2008. Online at: www.us.kpmg.com/Rutus_Prod/Documents/12/19429NSS_RogueTrader_screen.pdf.

Malakian, Anthony. "Internal controls need to be tightened." *Bank Technology News* (April 2008). Online at: www.americanbanker.com/btn_article.html?id=20080327QJ4HD229

Prince, C. J. "To catch a thief: Employee fraud hits growing businesses hardest. Here's what you can do to make sure there's not a thief among you." *Entrepreneur Magazine* (September 2007). Online at: www.entrepreneur.com/magazine/entrepreneur/2007/september/183068.html

Website:

CBC News coverage of the Conrad Black affair: www.cbc.ca/news/background/black_conrad

NOTES

1 Miller, Kent D. "A framework for integrated risk management in international business." *Journal of International Business Studies* 23:2 (1992): 311–331.

"The extent to which the task of the worker is adequately planned reflects the degree to which the worker is placed in a state of self-control. The plan, do, check, act cycle is often called the 'Deming cycle.'" Gryna (2000)

     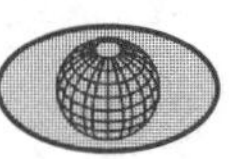 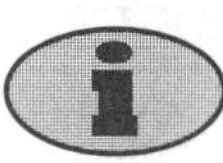  

The Human Value of the Enterprise

by Andrew Mayo

EXECUTIVE SUMMARY

- People are often spoken of as assets but are generally treated as costs, because we have no credible system of valuing them.
- The problem is that in today's knowledge-based organizations value is driven more by people than by any other factor.
- There are five main approaches to building a measurement system for people, or human capital.
- The attempt to value people financially has not been successful; however, an index of value factors provides a necessary balance with seeing people as costs.
- Current best practice looks at connecting the value of people in terms of their characteristics (and the value they produce in both financial and nonfinancial terms) via measures of their engagement and motivation.

INTRODUCTION

Our people are our most important asset. This frequent statement from chief executives is often received with justifiable cynicism. The problem is that people within an organization do not always experience decisions and policies in their everyday work life that support such a belief. The accountant who once described people to me (admittedly with a smile) as "costs walking about on legs" is often closer to the reality of organizational experience. The very term "human resources" reinforces this concept of people. Organizations that are driven by an often understandable drive for increased efficiency and minimized costs see "headcount" as the easy target.

There are many reasons for this. One is the domination of management by current targets for bottom line results—often resulting in a very short-term mindset. Such single-mindedness is illogical because it is out of balance; the desired final outcomes are driven by satisfying other demands that generally get much less attention. A powerful system of financial processes and targets dominates the life of most managers. Measures of intangibles, such as employees' capabilities or customers' loyalty may exist, but they are frequently excluded from appearing in the monitoring and control systems in any serious way.

Another problem is that people do not fit the strict financial definition of an asset. They cannot be transacted at will, their contribution is individually distinctive and variable (and subject to motivation and environment), and they cannot easily be valued according to traditional financial principles. However if we view "assets" as value-creating entities, and in an era where knowledge and its application is the key competitive advantage, we will arrive inevitably at the foundational role people play. Organizations do employ some just for "maintenance," but the vast majority are value adding. Some indeed should be seen as investments rather than costs—but management accounting rarely recognizes this.

Perhaps the greatest problem is the lack of credible measures that relate to people and their value. We know in detail what they cost; we have no balancing quantity for their value. We feel it when it has been lost, but often too late.

THE VALUE OF PEOPLE

Is There a Problem to Be Solved?

There is indeed a major problem. The valuation of companies has progressively changed over the last 20 years, putting a much higher weight on intangible assets like knowledge, competence, brands, and systems. These assets are also known as the *intellectual capital* of the organization. The problem is that we have no comparable system of measurement that enables us to give these the same balanced attention we give to financial matters. The result is that decisions about investment and resources are not necessarily in the long-term interest of the stockholders, even though they may appear to be at the time they are made. A classic case is the laying off of key people, particularly after mergers and acquisitions, only to hire them back when the value they contributed is suddenly recognized.

David Norton, coauthor of *The Balanced Scorecard*, says of his experiences in working on performance management that "the worst grades are reserved for the typical executive team for their understanding of strategies for developing human capital. There is little consensus, little creativity, and no real framework for thinking about the subject. Worse yet, we have seen little improvement in this over the past eight years. The asset that is the most important is the least understood, least prone to measurement, and hence the least susceptible to management".

People-Related Measures

No standardized approach has become widely accepted as yet, but the various ways in which systematic measurement has been applied to people can be summarized as follows.

- *Attempting to value people financially as assets: human resource (or asset) accounting*. This will be discussed in more detail below.
- *Creating an index of good HR practices and relating them to business results.* Researchers including Mark Huselid of Rutgers University and consulting firms such as Watson Wyatt have shown positive correlation between investment in HR management and stockholder value.
- *Statistically analyzing the composition of the workforce and measures of employees' productivity and output.* The best-known proponent here is Jac Fitz-enz of the Saratoga Institute, California, who has extensively deployed ratios of all kinds and conducts a worldwide benchmarking practice.
- *Measuring the efficiency of HR functions and processes and the return on investment for people initiatives and programs.* Dave Ulrich of the University of Michigan is the champion of a measurement-orientated HR function, and Jack Philips is the leading proponent of RoI for HR initiatives and programs.
- *Integrating people-related measures through a performance management framework.* These are frameworks that look for balance in performance measures between the needs of the different stakeholders, or in relation to the component parts of the total intangible assets. The best known is Kaplan and Norton's *Balanced Scorecard*. An alternative approach comes from Karl-Erik Sveiby of Sweden, whose *Intellectual Capital Monitor* chooses a small number of measures for three kinds of intellectual capital—customer, structural, and human.

The most comprehensive approach to the human dimension is found in Mayo's *Human Capital Monitor*. This links three areas of measurement:

"Everywhere in the world the industrial regime tends to make the unorganized or unorganizable individual, the pauper, into the victim of a kind of human sacrifice offered to the gods of civilization." Jacques Maritain

     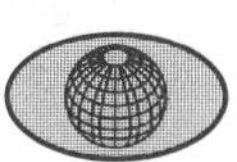   

- the human capital that people lend to organizations in exchange for the value added to them;
- the financial and nonfinancial value for stakeholders that this human capital produces;
- the motivation and commitment of the people, which depend primarily on the environment in which they work.

Valuing People as Assets

There are three criteria for defining any asset:

- It must possess future service potential.
- It is measurable in monetary terms.
- It is subject to the ownership and control of the company, or it is rented or leased.

Traditional methods of coming to a valuation include:

- *Cost-based.* This method typically looks at acquisition or replacement cost. The costs of recruiting an employee can be assessed and then depreciated over the expected future service of the person hired. Alternatively the person's gross remuneration can be used as a base.
- *Market-based.* The price to be paid in an open market must be a reflection of the value of a person. Value is very difficult to assess, however, and does not take account of the value of service continuity in itself.
- *Income-based.* The cash inflows expected by the organization related to the contribution of the human asset, calculated as the present value of the expected net cash flows. This is good for individuals whose efforts are directly related to identifiable income.

Human resource accounting, or human asset accounting, has been primarily developed in the United States under the guidance of Professor Eric Flamholz. He sees the value of a person as the product of two interacting variables—his or her conditional value and the probability that the person will stay with the organization for *x* years. *Conditional value* is the present worth of the potential services that could be rendered if the individual stayed with the organization, and is a combination of productivity (performance), transferability (flexible skills), and promotability. The latter two elements are heavily influenced by the first. This figure is then multiplied by a *probability* factor: the probability that the person will stay for the *x* years. This gives the *expected realizable value*, which is a measure of the person's worth. There are a number of difficulties with this approach, not least of which is the estimation of potential future services. It also leads to lower values for older and more experienced people who have less time to render future services. This is not necessarily the reality.

The truth is that this is not a well-known discipline, and it has not been generally adopted by either the financial or HR communities.

A more useful approach was originally developed by UK researchers W. J. Giles and D. F. Robinson in 1973. They developed a factor called the human asset multiplier, which is applied to gross remuneration. This reflects a number of intrinsically valuable attributes of individuals. Mayo, in his 2001 book, came to similar conclusions, namely that although it would be really helpful if we could have a realistic, generally accepted, absolute financial formula, this is unlikely to be achieved. But it would be a major step forward if we could at least enable people's relative values to be compared against their costs. He proposed a formula for what he called the human asset worth (HAW), where

$$\text{HAW} = \text{EC (employment cost)} \times \frac{\text{IAM (individual asset multiplier)}}{1{,}000}$$

(The divisor of 1,000 is used so that the resulting number does not look like a financial one.)

The *individual asset multiplier* is designed to reflect the relevant factors that make individuals valuable in their current context. These factors are not universal and vary for each group of employees sharing a common value output. Examples, however, include:

- specialized knowledge, skills, and experience;
- personal skills and behaviors;
- contribution to stakeholder value;
- potential to grow and contribute at a higher level;
- personal productivity in relation to stakeholder value;
- alignment with organizational values.

Each of these factors can be assessed on a scale, weighted for importance, and then added together to give the multiplier.

Such a formula can lead to tools such as a *human asset register*, which can monitor changes and compare teams and units. The process of analyzing the individual components may lead to strategies for change in the organization. It can be argued strongly that such tools are at least as important as those used for cost management.

A Framework of Measures

The following characteristics are suggested as criteria for a framework of people-related measures:

- with the exception of workforce statistics, measures should not stand alone but be connected to other outcomes for the organization—particularly the value created for stakeholders;
- a framework should be *useful* for the users. These might be external (investors, analysts, benchmarking) or internal (managers, other functions). Their needs are different, so more than one framework may be needed. Usefulness means informing actions to be taken;
- the underlying collection, definitions, and presentation of data need to be valid and reliable, and have credibility with the users;
- they should not be compiled through the lens of an accountant. Quantification does not equate necessarily with dollars. Value added can be both financial *and* nonfinancial.

None of the approaches described above meets all these criteria. An attempt to do so is found in Mayo's *Human Capital Monitor*. This links three areas of measurement for specific groups of employees:

- the human capital that people lend to organizations in exchange for the value added to them. This is measured by the Human Asset Worth approach;
- the motivation and engagement of the people, which depend primarily on the environment in which they work. Outcome measures are used, such as attrition, absenteeism, opinions, and management judgment—and also "input" measures of the factors that make a difference to the group under study;
- the financial and nonfinancial value for stakeholders that this human capital produces—often measured as a productivity factor.

This provides a tool for managers which stands alongside their financial statements and informs them about people-related actions.

CONCLUSION

The term *human capital* can be used to describe the asset value of your people. Maximizing human capital through acquisition, retention, growth (and sometimes retention) should be a major priority of all executives, not an area left to the HR department alone. It is the area in which measurement is least well understood.

This is all about sustainable stockholder (or public sector beneficiary) returns. People are the one factor of value growth that drives all others. The value that a company creates results from the way that people apply their skills, energies, and expertise to the capital and raw materials that customers want. Of all the business

"Microsoft's only factory asset is the human ingredient." Fred Moody

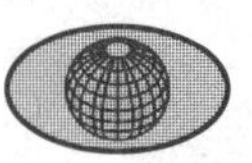

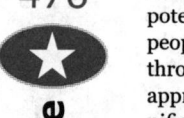

levers available to leaders, the greatest potential to build value is offered by people. It is time indeed to recognize this through demanding a rigorous and credible approach to both valuing this most significant asset, and linking that value meaningfully to the benefits for stakeholders. What gets measured gets managed—and we need reality behind the rhetoric about our people.

▶▶ MORE INFO

Books:

Becker, B. E., Mark Huselid, and David Ulrich. *The HR Scorecard: Linking People, Strategy, and Performance*. Cambridge, MA: Harvard Business School Press, 2001.

Davenport, Thomas O. *Human Capital: What It Is and Why People Invest It*. San Francisco, CA: Jossey-Bass, 1999.

Fitz-enz, Jac. *The ROI of Human Capital*. New York: AMACOM, 2000.

Flamholtz, Eric G. *Human Resource Accounting: Advances in Concepts, Methods, and Applications*. 3rd ed. New York: Kluwer, 1999.

Mayo, Andrew. *The Human Value of the Enterprise: Valuing People as Assets—Monitoring, Measuring, Managing*. Naperville, IL: Nicholas Brealey, 2001.

Phillips, J., *et al*. *The Human Resources Scorecard: Measuring the Return on Investment*. Oxford: Butterworth-Heinemann, 2001.

See Also:

★ Corporate Responsibility in a Global World: Marrying Investment in Human Capital with Focus on Costs (pp. 144–146)

★ CSR: More than PR, Pursuing Competitive Advantage in the Long Run (pp. 147–149)

★ Risk Management: Beyond Compliance (pp. 510–513)

★ Value Creation—Perspectives and Implications (pp. 834–838)

✔ Calculating Return on Investment in Human Resources (p. 975)

✔ Performing a Skills Gap Analysis (p. 998)

Gary Becker (p. 1153)

"**. . . the reason for the turn to temporary workers is perfectly straight forward. They can be treated as goods, as material goods.**" Noam Chomsky

  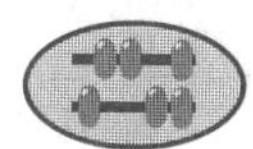   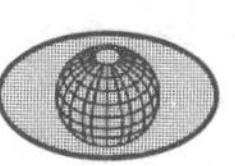   

Intellectual Capital by Thomas A. Stewart

EXECUTIVE SUMMARY

- Intellectual capital is knowledge that transforms raw materials and makes them more valuable.
- Conventional accounting fails to measure the value of intellectual capital, but markets clearly reward it.
- Intellectual capital includes the talent of staff, the value of proprietary knowledge and processes, and the value of relationships with customers and suppliers.

INTRODUCTION

Intellectual capital is just that: a capital asset consisting of intellectual material. To be considered intellectual capital, knowledge must be an asset able to be used to create wealth. Thus, intellectual capital includes the talents and skills of individuals and groups; technological and social networks and the software and culture that connect them; and intellectual property such as patents, copyrights, methods, procedures, archives, etc. It excludes knowledge or information not involved in production or wealth creation. Just as raw materials such as iron ore should not be confused with an asset such as a steel mill, so knowledge materials such as data or miscellaneous facts ought not to be confused with knowledge assets.

INTELLECTUAL CAPITAL AS AN ASSET

From the standpoint of traditional accounting, intellectual capital frequently does not fit the definition of an asset. Generally, under accounting rules, an asset must be tangible; it must have been acquired in one or more transactions, so that it has a known cost or a market value; and it must be under [illegible]

[illegible] businesses from seeing, managing, or building knowledge assets. This in turn inhibits companies' ability to compete and prosper in an economy in which knowledge has become an important source of profits. The intellectual capitalists use a looser definition: an asset is something that transforms raw material into something more valuable. It is a magician's black box. Inputs get put in—a few handkerchiefs, say; the asset does something to transform them; and out come outputs worth more than the inputs—rabbits, maybe. The question of ownership and control matters less than the question of access. A corporation might not own scientific expertise (in the form of a cadre of employees, for example), but it has the use of it and can exert a quasi-proprietary influence over how it is used.

Intellectual capital, then, is knowledge that transforms raw materials and makes them more valuable. The raw materials might be physical—knowledge of the formula for Coca-Cola is an intellectual asset that transforms a few cents' worth of sugar, water, carbon dioxide, and flavorings into a dollar's worth of refreshment. The raw material might be intangible, like information. Knowledge of the law is an intellectual asset; a lawyer takes the facts of a dispute (raw material), transforms them through his knowledge of the law (an intellectual asset), to produce an opinion or a legal brief (an output of higher value than the facts by themselves).

Though financial accounting does not measure intellectual capital, markets clearly do. Stock in companies in the pharmaceutical industry, for example, generally trade at a high premium over the book value of their assets, and the companies' return on net assets is abnormally high; but if their spending on research and development is added to their capital, both their market-to-book ratios and their returns on assets come to [illegible]

[illegible] larly Denmark, are leaders in the field.)

Indeed, it was the unusual behavior of the equities of knowledge-intensive companies that first drew the attention of analysts to intellectual capital. The term seems to have been employed first in 1958, when two financial analysts, describing the stockmarket valuations of several small, science-based companies, concluded that "The intellectual capital of such companies is perhaps their single most important element," and noted that their high stock valuations might be termed an "intellectual premium." (Morris Kronfeld and Arthur Rock, "Some Considerations of the Infinite," *The Analyst's Journal*, November 1958, p. 6.) The idea lay dormant for a quarter of a century. In the 1980s, Walter Wriston, the former chairman of Citicorp, noted that his bank and other corporations possessed valuable intellectual capital that accountants (and bank regulators) did not measure.

INTELLECTUAL CAPITAL ANALYZED

Karl-Erik Sveiby, a Swede, intrigued by the anomalous stockmarket behavior of knowledge-intensive companies, began an investigation that produced the first analysis of the nature of intellectual capital. Sveiby, his colleagues, and *Affärsvärlden*, Sweden's oldest business magazine, noticed that the magazine's proprietary model for valuing initial public offerings broke down for high-tech companies. Sveiby concluded that these companies possessed assets not described in financial documents or included in the magazine's model. With a like-minded group of associates, he sat down to puzzle out what these might be. In "Den Osynliga Balansräkningen Ledarskap" ("The Invisible Balance Sheet"), 1989, they laid the foundation stone for much of what has come after by producing a taxonomy for intellectual capital. Knowledge assets, they proposed, could be found in three places: the competencies of a company's people, its internal structure (patents, models, computer and administrative systems), and its external structure (brands, reputation, relationships with customers and suppliers).

After some tinkering by others—the pieces are now usually called human capital, structural (or organizational) capital, and customer [illegible]

[illegible] executive at the Swedish financial services company Skandia, persuaded his management to appoint him "Director, Intellectual Capital"; Skandia became the business world's most conspicuous laboratory for intellectual capital studies.

Ideas whose time has come flower everywhere at once. Ikujiro Nonaka and Hirotaka Takeuchi in Japan began investigations of how knowledge is produced that resulted in "The Knowledge-creating Company" (*Harvard Business Review*, November–December 1991), and Thomas A. Stewart synthesized U.S. research in intellectual capital in "Brainpower: How Intellectual Capital is Becoming America's Most Important Asset" (*Fortune*, June 3, 1991).

Every company or organization possesses all three forms of intellectual capital.

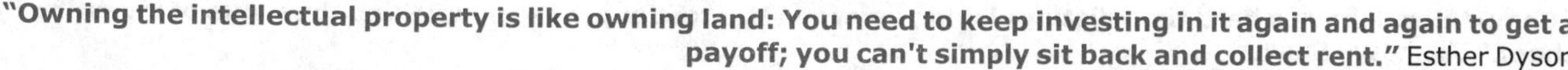
"Owning the intellectual property is like owning land: You need to keep investing in it again and again to get a payoff; you can't simply sit back and collect rent." Esther Dyson

     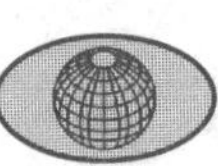 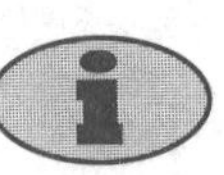  

Human capital consists of the skills, competencies, and abilities of individuals and groups. These range from specific technical skills to "softer" skills, like salesmanship or the ability to work effectively in a team. An individual's human capital cannot, in a legal sense, be owned by a corporation; the term thus refers not only to individual talent but also to the collective skills and aptitudes of a workforce. Indeed, one challenge faced by executives is how to manage the talent of truly outstanding members of their staff: how to use it to the utmost without becoming overdependent on a few star performers, or how to encourage stars to share their skills with others. Skills that are irrelevant to a company's business—the fine tenor voice of an actuary, for example—may be part of the individual's human capital, but not of his employer's.

Structural capital comprises knowledge assets that are indeed company property: intellectual property such as patents, copyrights, and trademarks; processes, methodologies, models; documents and other knowledge artifacts; computer networks and software; administrative systems; and so forth. A data warehouse is structural capital; so is the decision-support software that helps people to use the data. One knowledge-management process is converting human capital—which is usually available to just a few people—into structural capital, so it becomes shareable. This happens, for example, when a team writes up the "lessons learned" from a project so that others can apply them. Some structural capital can be said to be owned in common; open-source software is an example. In general, however, proprietary assets, whether intellectual or otherwise, are of more strategic value than assets equally available to competitors.

Customer capital is the value of relationships with suppliers, allies, and customers. Two common forms are brand equity and customer loyalty. The former is a promise of quality (or some other attribute) for which a customer agrees to pay a premium price; the value of brands is measurable in financial terms. The loyalty of a base of customers is also measurable, using discounted cash flow analysis. Both are frequently calculated when companies are bought and sold. In a sense, all customer capital should eventually reflect itself either in a premium price or a sticky buyer–seller relationship.

Every organization possesses intellectual capital in all three manifestations, but with varying emphasis, depending on its history and strategy. For example, a chemical company might have as a knowledge asset the ability to concoct custom chemical compounds that precisely match its customer's needs. That asset might be people-based, residing in the tacit knowledge of dozens of skilled chemists; it might be structural, found in an extensive library of patents and manuals, or databases and expert systems; it might be relationship-based, found in the company's intimate ties to customers, suppliers, universities, etc. Most likely, of course, the asset—skill at making custom chemicals—is a combination of the three. A company that takes a strategic approach to intellectual capital will examine its business model and the economics of its industry to manage the combination of human, structural, and customer capital in such a way as to create value that competitors cannot match.

At least three characteristics of intellectual capital give it extraordinary power to add value. First, companies that use knowledge assets deftly can reduce the expense and burden of carrying physical assets, or can maximize their return on them. For example, transportation companies can use information networks and skill in logistics and load management to maximize their utilization of assets like rail cars and containers. Second, it can be possible to get enormous leverage from knowledge assets. The value of an aircraft can be realized over just one route at a time, whereas that of an airline's reservation system is limited only by the number of people in the world. In a study of the chemical industry that examined 83 companies over 25 years, Baruch Lev, professor of accounting at New York University, found that R&D spending (one form of investment in intellectual capital) returned 25.9% pretax, whereas capital spending earned just 15% (about 10% after tax, approximately the cost of capital).

Third, human and customer capital are the primary sources of innovation and customization. The increasing sophistication of machinery and information technology has led to the automation of more and more repetitive tasks. These manufacturing economies of scale are sources of competitive advantage in industrial processes. At a certain point, however, their value diminishes: the more it is possible to do a task the same way twice, the harder it is for one company to differentiate its offerings from its competitors'. When this happens the value of innovation, customization, and service increases; all are highly dependent on intellectual capital.

▸▸ MAKING IT HAPPEN

- Treat knowledge as an asset only if it is capable of yielding an economic return.
- Build human capital by developing the skills, competencies, and abilities of individuals and groups who deliver value to customers.
- Convert human capital into structural capital by organizing the exchange and sharing of knowledge.
- Optimize customer capital—the value of relationships with suppliers, allies, and customers—by building brand equity and customer loyalty.
- Use knowledge assets to reduce the expense and burden of carrying physical assets, or to maximize return on those assets.
- Look for competitive advantage from innovation, customization, and service rather than from economies of scale.

▸▸ MORE INFO

Books:

Davenport, Thomas H., and Laurence Prusak. *Working Knowledge: How Organizations Manage What They Know*. Cambridge, MA: Harvard Business School Press, 2000.

Edvinsson, Leif, and Michael S. Malone. *Intellectual Capital*. New York: Harper Business, 1997.

Mayo, Andrew. *The Human Value of the Enterprise: Valuing People as Assets—Monitoring, Measuring, Managing*. Naperville, IL: Nicholas Brealey, 2001.

Stewart, Thomas A. *Intellectual Capital: The New Wealth of Organizations*. New York: Doubleday, 1997.

Stewart, Thomas A. *The Wealth of Knowledge: Intellectual Capital and the Twenty-First Century Organization*. New York: Doubleday, 2003.

Sullivan, Patrick H. *Value Driven Intellectual Capital: How to Convert Intangible Corporate Assets into Market Value*. New York: Wiley, 2000.

Teece, David J. *Managing Intellectual Capital*. New York: Oxford University Press, 2002.

Website:

Intellectual Capital Startpage, a truly global website with links to dozens of IC resources: www.intellectualcapital.nl

"Companies. . .have a hard time distinguishing between the cost of paying people and the value of investing in them." Thomas A. Stewart

  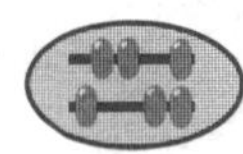   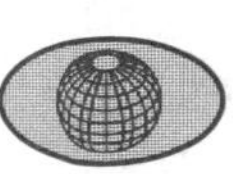   

International Arbitration: Basic Principles and Characteristics by Stavros Brekoulakis

EXECUTIVE SUMMARY

- International arbitration is a contractually based dispute resolution mechanism that offers an alternative to national courts.
- International arbitration has experienced a remarkable growth in the last three decades, due to its unique advantages over litigation.
- The advantages of arbitration include privacy and confidentiality of proceedings, procedural flexibility, and high rates of enforceability of arbitral awards.
- Despite its many advantages, there is growing concern that arbitration is becoming increasingly expensive and time-consuming. This concern, although not unfounded, is often overplayed. Ultimately, it is down to the users of arbitration to draft effective arbitration agreements and to put an effective arbitration procedure in place.
- To arrive at a successful resolution of disputes through arbitration, the parties involved should pay particular attention to the choice of arbitrators and the arbitration institution, and, most importantly, give due consideration to the drafting of the arbitration agreement.

DEFINITION AND DISTINCTIVE FEATURES OF ARBITRATION

International arbitration can be defined as a specially established mechanism for the final and binding determination of disputes concerning a contract between two or more parties that has an international element. The disputes are determined by independent arbitrators in accordance with standards and procedures chosen by the parties involved in the dispute.[1]

The distinctive feature of arbitration is that it is a *private* dispute resolution mechanism, which nevertheless provides arbitrators with *judicial* power. More specifically:

- arbitration is a private dispute resolution method, in which the arbitrators' mandate to resolve a dispute derives from a *contract* (i.e., an arbitration agreement or arbitration clause).
- arbitrators have the *power* to deliver an award that finally resolves the dispute that is binding on the parties.

The above characteristics of arbitration distinguish it from the following.

Litigation proceedings before national courts. In litigation, national courts are an expression of state power and they are bound to apply the rules and procedures of the state they are attached to. National judges owe allegiance to their state and they have limited or no discretion to deviate from the procedural codes and rules of that state. By contrast, in arbitration parties are free to determine how the proceedings are to be conducted, subject only to minimum safeguards (due process). Party autonomy is a fundamental principle in arbitration, which gives the parties the opportunity to tailor the proceedings in accordance with their commercial needs and the special characteristics of the case. Arbitrators are private judges whose mandate is determined by the arbitration agreement concluded by the parties, and who owe allegiance to the parties that have appointed them rather than to a state.

Alternative dispute resolution (ADR) methods. Despite the fact that their authority derives from a contract, arbitrators have the power to grant an award, which is a final decision that is binding on the parties. Arbitral awards are enforceable in the same way that national judgments are. Therefore, arbitration must be distinguished from other forms of ADR, such as mediation. Here, as in arbitration, a third party (mediator) is involved in the resolution of the dispute between the two commercial parties. However, the mediator has no power to impose a decision on the parties. Mediators work with the parties to resolve their dispute by an agreement; they cannot issue a binding decision. Thus, the outcome of a successful mediation is a settlement rather than an enforceable award.

DIFFERENT FORMS OF ARBITRATION

There are two basic types of arbitration: *ad hoc* and *institutional*. Parties are free to choose between these two types in their arbitration agreement. If the parties fail to specify in their agreement which type of arbitration they prefer, the arbitration will be presumed to be *ad hoc*.

Ad hoc arbitration is an arbitration that is specifically designed by the parties for a particular dispute. Here there are predetermined rules for the arbitrators to rely on when conducting the proceedings (although sometimes the United Nations Commission on International Trade Law (UNCITRAL) arbitration rules are used). Thus, it is up to the parties to determine the proceedings and to the arbitrators to fill any gaps. Ad hoc arbitration is more flexible than institutional, as the parties are completely free to adapt the proceedings to the particulars of the case. It can also be less expensive than institutional arbitration, as the parties avoid the fees of the institution and they can negotiate the fees of the arbitrators. However, for an ad hoc arbitration to work, the parties must have provided for a clear set of proceedings in advance, as there are no institutional rules to fall back on if they disagree on the arbitration process after the dispute arises.

Institutional arbitration is an arbitration that is conducted under the auspices of a particular arbitration institution and in accordance with the rules of that institution. Institutional arbitration is more popular among international parties.[2] This is because the parties feel more comfortable with experienced institutional administrators (known as "case managers") who are willing to take care of any issue that might arise during the proceedings. Parties are also attracted by the reputation and the strong brand name of many established arbitration institutions, which, as many parties believe, increases the enforceability of an arbitration award. The most popular institutions are the International Chambers of Commerce (ICC), the London Court of International Arbitration (LCIA), the American Arbitration Association (AAA), and the Stockholm Chamber of Commerce.[3]

ADVANTAGES OF INTERNATIONAL ARBITRATION

International arbitration has experienced a remarkable growth in the last three decades, and it is now perceived as the natural dispute resolution mechanism for disputes arising out of international transactions.

The remarkable growth of arbitration is due to the following advantages compared to national litigation and other ADR methods:

Privacy and confidentiality: Unlike litigation proceedings that take place in public, arbitration proceedings are private and, unless the parties agree otherwise, they remain confidential. Thus, the existence of the arbitration, the evidence and the documents exchanged in the arbitration, and the final award cannot be divulged to third

     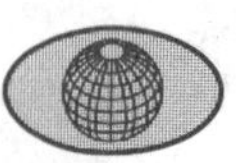   

parties. The duty of confidentiality is binding on the arbitrators, the parties, and their counsel, and it is considered an important commercial advantage of arbitration.

The parties appoint the arbitral tribunal: Unlike litigation, where the dispute is determined by national judges appointed by the state, in arbitration the parties have the opportunity to appoint those who will decide on the dispute (i.e., the arbitrators). Usually, arbitral tribunals consist of either one arbitrator, who is chosen by both parties, or three arbitrators, where each party appoints one arbitrator and a chairman is then chosen by the two party-appointed arbitrators. The fact that the parties may participate in the constitution of the tribunal enhances their confidence in the arbitration process, as they can appoint arbitrators who are familiar with their legal or cultural background. It also gives the parties the opportunity to select arbitrators who have the expert knowledge required by the particular characteristics of the dispute. For example, an engineer or an architect is often appointed as an arbitrator to determine a complex construction dispute.

Enforceability of arbitral awards: International arbitration awards are more easily enforceable than national judgments. This is due to the 1958 New York Convention on the Recognition and Enforcement of Foreign Arbitral Awards, which has now been signed and ratified by 143 countries. The New York Convention has thus established an internationally harmonized regime for the enforcement of arbitral awards, where recognition and enforcement are only exceptionally disallowed on limited grounds. By contrast, there is no international convention that enables the enforcement of national judgments.

Procedural flexibility: Arbitration proceedings are determined by the arbitration agreement of the parties. Thus, the principle of party autonomy provides parties with considerable liberty to tailor their own dispute resolution process in accordance with their needs and the particulars of their dispute. Therefore, procedural flexibility and party autonomy make arbitration the most suitable dispute resolution mechanism for international commercial transactions.

Neutrality: Arguably this is the most attractive feature of international arbitration. Proceedings generally take place in a country with which neither party has links; the dispute is determined in accordance with transnational rules, or according to the national law of a neutral country; and arbitrators are appointed from different countries and with different nationalities. Neutrality is of utmost importance in the context of international arbitration, where each party wants to avoid a national court of its co-contractor.

AREAS OF CONCERN

Arbitration has always been considered a quicker and less expensive means of dispute resolution than national courts. Although in theory and in many cases this is still so, there is growing concern that arbitration proceedings are becoming increasingly costly and time-consuming. International arbitration is now widely perceived to be even more expensive than litigation.[4] The international arbitration community is concerned about these issues, and arbitration institutions have issued guidelines for the parties and the arbitrators to reduce the time and cost of arbitration proceedings.

Costs related to arbitration can be divided into two groups: Fees for the counsel; and arbitration costs, which include the fees of the arbitrators, the administrative fees of the institution (if the arbitration is institutional), and expenses related to the hearings (hiring the venue, translation costs, traveling costs for the witnesses, fees for the experts appointed by the tribunal, etc.).

Ultimately, arbitration is a party-led mechanism, and therefore it is up to the parties, who also are the fee payers, to take the necessary steps for the proceedings to take less time and money.

INCREASING THE CHANCES OF SUCCESSFUL ARBITRATION

Here are some of the factors that parties should consider to arrive at a successful resolution of their disputes through arbitration:

Appoint the right arbitrator: Parties should look for arbitrators who are available to embark on the proceedings quickly. Many arbitrators have a busy schedule, which inevitably will lead to delays in the hearings and the issuance of the final award. Parties are advised to do thorough research before selecting their arbitrators. Nowadays it is general practice for parties to interview potential arbitrators and gather information relating to their previous work. The number of arbitrators appointed may also impact the cost of the proceedings. A panel of three arbitrators will normally improve the quality of the award and reduce the risk of an arbitrary decision. However, three-arbitrator tribunals will generally be more expensive and time-consuming as it is more difficult to convene meetings, arrange hearings, or reach a final agreement when three arbitrators are involved.

Choose the right arbitration institution: Parties should be aware that while in ad hoc arbitrations parties may negotiate the arbitrators' fees, in institutional proceedings fees are calculated in accordance with predetermined rules. Different institutions

CASE STUDY

Ill-Drafted Arbitration Clauses Result in Further Litigation

The parties in *Lucky Goldstar v Nag Moo Kee Engineering* (High Court of Hong Kong, 1993) had included the following arbitration agreement in their contract: "Any dispute or difference arising out of this contract shall be arbitrated in a 3rd Country, under the rule of a 3rd Country and in accordance with the rules of procedure of the International Commercial Arbitration Association."

This was a "pathological" arbitration clause that made no sense, for the following reasons:

- The institution provided for in the clause, namely the "International Commercial Arbitration Association," did not exist.
- No seat of arbitration was specified; the rather ambiguous reference to "a 3rd Country" made no sense; and there was no indication which this "3rd Country" might be.

Therefore, when a dispute arose over the contract, the parties could not commence arbitration proceedings as there was no arbitration institution to which the parties could submit their dispute. Inevitably, therefore, the parties had to resort to a national court, which came up with a rather creative interpretation of the ambiguous arbitration clause in order to give effect to the parties' original intention to submit their dispute to arbitration. The High Court of Hong Kong held that since there was no "International Commercial Arbitration Association," the parties should be referred to the best-known international arbitration institution, which it judged to be the ICC.

It is, of course, fortunate in this specific case that the national court managed to give meaning to and enforce this ill-drafted arbitration agreement. However, the parties eventually lost time and money, as they had first to resort to a national court before finally starting arbitration proceedings.

"International arbitration may be defined as the substitution of many burning questions for a smoldering one." Ambrose Bierce

  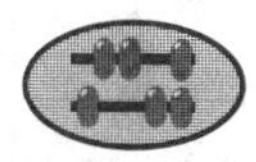   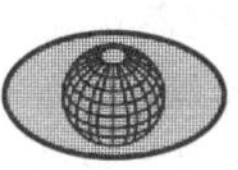   

have different methods for calculating arbitrators' fees. For example, the LCIA's rules set out a recommended range of hourly rates which may only be deviated from in exceptional circumstances, while under ICC rules the arbitrators' fees are calculated as a proportion of the sum in dispute (the so-called *ad valorem* method). Thus, parties are advised to look into the methods that different institutions use to calculate arbitrators' fees before deciding which institution they should submit their dispute to.

Draft efficient arbitration clauses: Parties often focus on the substantive clauses of their contracts but pay little attention to the arbitration clauses. Arbitration clauses are usually the last provisions to be incorporated in a contract, and they are drafted without debate or much consideration of the specific needs of the particular contract. Ambiguous arbitration clauses will most likely result in lengthy litigation, causing delays and increasing the cost of the arbitration proceedings. Parties are advised to draft clear arbitration clauses that set out an effective and rapid set of arbitration proceedings (see the Making It Happen section).

Make use of technology: As mentioned above, arbitration proceedings are flexible and can be specifically designed to suit the particular case. There is no need for the hearings to be conducted in person at a particular venue. Arbitrators and parties are advised to make use of technology in order to reduce the costs of the proceedings. For example, arbitration hearings, including witness and expert examination, may be conducted via video-conference; and documents, including the submissions of the parties, may be communicated by email or other convenient means.

▸▸ MAKING IT HAPPEN

Drafting Effective Arbitration Clauses

Ill-drafted arbitration clauses can prolong litigation proceedings and thwart the resolution of a dispute in a quick and efficient way. In order to draft effective arbitration clauses, parties should consider the following points carefully:

- The intention to arbitrate must be clearly and unambiguously stated in the arbitration clause. Avoid permissive language such as "parties *may* submit any dispute to arbitration."
- It should be stated clearly whether the arbitration is to be ad hoc or institutional. If the parties opt for an institutional arbitration, it is very important that unambiguous reference is made to an arbitration institution that exists (see the Case Study). If ad hoc arbitration is chosen, the seat of the arbitration must be clearly stated.
- The safest solution is for the parties to use one of the arbitration clauses recommended by well-known arbitration institutions. However, parties should not attempt to modify these set arbitration clauses, as there is a risk that the clause will be rendered unenforceable.
- Here, for example, is the arbitration clause recommended by the ICC: "All disputes arising out of or in connection with the present contract shall be finally settled under the Rules of Arbitration of the International Chamber of Commerce by one or more arbitrators appointed in accordance with the said Rules."

▸▸ MORE INFO

Books:

Born, Gary. *International Arbitration and Forum Selection Agreements: Planning Drafting and Enforcing*. 2nd ed. The Hague: Kluwer Law International, 2006.

Lew, Julian D. M., Loukas A. Mistelis, and Stefan Kröll. *Comparative International Commercial Arbitration*. The Hague: Kluwer Law International, 2003.

Redfern, Alan, and Martin Hunter, with Nigel Blackaby and Constantine Partasides. *Law and Practice of International Commercial Arbitration*. 4th ed. London: Sweet & Maxwell, 2004.

Websites:

American Arbitration Association: www.adr.org
ICC Commission on Arbitration: www.iccwbo.org/policy/arbitration/id2882/index.html
London Court of International Arbitration: www.lcia-arbitration.com
School of International Arbitration, Queen Mary University of London: www.schoolofinternationalarbitration.org
United Nations Commission on International Trade Law (UNCITRAL): www.uncitral.org

NOTES

1 Lew, Mistelis, and Kröll, *Comparative International Commercial Arbitration* (2003), para 1-1.

2 In a survey conducted by the School of International Arbitration, Queen Mary University of London, and PricewaterhouseCoopers, entitled "International arbitration: Corporate attitudes and practices 2006," it was found that 76% of parties prefer institutional arbitration to ad hoc arbitration. This study and a second published in 2008 are available online at: www.pwc.com/arbitrationstudy.

3 See the above study for a list of the popularity of the various arbitration institutions.

4 In the 2006 survey mentioned in note 2, it was found that 65% of respondents perceived arbitration to be more expensive than litigation.

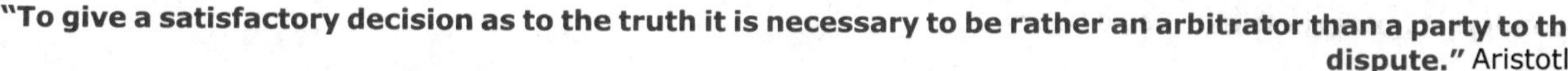

"To give a satisfactory decision as to the truth it is necessary to be rather an arbitrator than a party to the dispute." Aristotle

  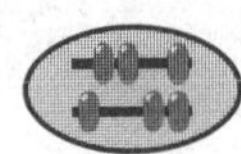   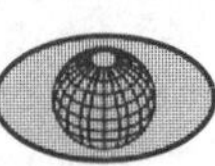   

Managing Intellectual Capital by Leif Edvinsson

EXECUTIVE SUMMARY

- Intellectual capital is already gaining significantly in recognition and acceptance as a means of valuing and developing the key intangible assets of a business.
- Surveys indicate that two-thirds of all US companies have started to look proactively for new ways to collect and report nonfinancial data, including intellectual capital.
- At least a third of the current investment decisions by US companies are considered partly on the basis of intangibles. Statistics suggest that greater reliance on nonfinancial measures results in more accurate earnings forecasts.

INTRODUCTION

Intellectual capital (IC) is an offspring of the knowledge era. It is still in its formative phase, having first been formally recognized in 1991 when the large Swedish corporation, Skandia, started implementing a comprehensive set of innovative knowledge practices to account for its intangible assets. This pioneering initiative, championed by Jan Carendi and Bjorn Wolrath, resulted in Leif Edvinsson being appointed as the world's first Director of Intellectual Capital (IC).

How will business assets be evaluated over the next decade—will they take account of those assets that are frequently and simultaneously both the most important and the most intangible? It is worth considering:

- why just a handful of the millions of companies started since 1900 achieved solid growth for two decades, and why most of them failed within less than five years;
- why managers try to achieve results by imposing financial goals and controls while knowing next to nothing about their company's products, technologies, and customers;
- how managers succeed without having any idea of the return on investments in network relationships, the costs of seeking information, or the state of their IC index.

UNDERSTANDING INTELLECTUAL CAPITAL

How Intellectual Capital Has Developed

The roots of the IC concept run deep. Norris Kronfeld and Arthur Rock wrote about it in an article featured in the November 1958 edition of *The Analyst's Journal*. The economist John Kenneth Galbraith discussed the term "intellectual capital" in 1969, and Peter Drucker spoke about "knowledge workers" before that. Though systems for recording IC are now proliferating, the concept is still mysterious to most wage earners.

The Importance of Nonfinancial Measures

The importance of nonfinancial measures is self-evident. W. Edwards Deming, legendary creator of the quality circles concept, has criticized managers in the United States for spending over 97% of their time analyzing figures, and less than 3% on the intangibles that really matter. In other words, they spend 97% of their time trying to figure out 3% of what is going on.

Every third Nordic company now takes these "soft values" into account. The IC network plays its part in this global value evolution. We work with hundreds of consultants and researchers along two mainstream lines: we assist organizations that are installing IC routines, and we cultivate and improve our tools by developing IC ratings and using intellectual labs like the growing net of Future Centers.

Powerful institutions, like the US Federation of Accounting Standards Board (FASB) and the Securities and Exchange Commission (SEC) in Washington, are now endorsing supplementary accounts. The influential Brookings Institution explores the issue systematically. In Denmark a government proposal has made it a matter of legislation. When the international magazine *Business Week* ranks business schools, it features indicators of intellectual capital. Since present financial indicators just refer to the past, they create perilous gaps between the bottom line and long-term goals. They offer a frail groundwork for the strategies of leading-edge companies. Clearly, the key to future productivity is to recognize the interplay of psychological, sociological, and political values in entrepreneurship.

To the extent that customers get involved as co-producers, knowledge that used to be external and distant becomes ever more internal and intimate. Obviously, such changes cannot be handled by traditional accounting practices.

Monetary economies and accounting practices have provided mankind with efficient tools for complex social organization. The present challenge is to make them more multidimensional. Instead of being just black boxes, they could become compasses for charting the course toward tomorrow. The bottom line may be useful when a bank considers lending money to a company. It is not useful for running a company. Cash is only the beginning and the icon of the value-creating process. It is a wonderful enabler, but it can make us forget the reasons for doing something, for creating meaning.

It takes patience, perseverance, and painful re-examinations to make a vision like IC consistently operative. To date, it has been mainly the large and lucrative companies that have taken intangibles into account. Unfortunately, some of them seem to get it all wrong. Instead of using the indicators to advance employee competence or increase surplus and stockholder value, they often exploit them chiefly as seminar exercises for top management.

This is dangerous, since the emerging talent war has triggered a brain drain from large companies to small and medium-sized enterprises. Future business battles will be about ideas and nontraditional thinking, turned into knowledge innovations.

Certainly, figures cannot be faked as easily as words and symbols. Some people fear that before global standards are established, IC audits will open the gates for arbitrary, even fraudulent practices. Probably, yes. But in the absence of IC, vast areas of corporate reality remain in the dark, just visible to insiders. You might as well argue that IC is just what the doctor ordered to restore public confidence in the stock and securities markets.

A corporate rush to cut the brain's lead times is the name of the competitive game now. One way to win is to start learning before new skills are required. To make qualified guesses, and invest in the supposed future. Buying such intellectual options will be a key strategy in the knowledge economy.

The internet now defies the established control of distribution channels and intellectual property. It undermines anyone whose status depends on privileged access to information. It leverages IC by offering extraordinary opportunities to start new businesses and see prompt returns. It is doing all that, and is likely do it much better and faster tomorrow. Maybe it is time to replace Adam Smith's famous

     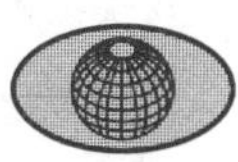   

metaphor of the market—the invisible hand—and talk about the invisible brain.

Though stock market booms and busts distract attention from what is really happening, the industrial laws of gravity are being supplanted by rules dictated by knowledge. As the costs of copying and distributing products approach zero, old value chains will break or become obsolete.

There is much to be done before IC standards achieve the sophistication and reliability required to earn general respect. Nevertheless, they are already worth their weight in gold. As financial capital becomes ever more questioned and volatile, sustainable earnings capabilities and new wealth will tip the scales in favor of IC.

CONCLUSION

How will economic assets be distributed if the main social distinction is between those who know things and those who do not, rather than between owners of capital and employees? IC may not be a sufficient answer to that question, but it might provide us with instruments to handle it with.

IC is not just any fashionable management fad, like benchmarking, reengineering, or quality circles. It is not something you can choose to apply or not as conditions and feelings change. It is more generic.

Classic cost management and accounting was not widely practiced in the business world until the fifties. Let's call these approaches the first generation of knowledge management tools. The costs of failing to change them into second-generation IC tools may assume massive proportions. To trade knowledge according to the old financial scorecards is like navigating an airplane just using the fuel meter and ignoring data about altitude, position, etc.; like accounting for the cost of a check while ignoring the loss of the capital it draws from; or as awkward as building with Lego bricks while wearing boxing gloves.

Jack Welch, the former CEO of General Electric, said that we must globalize our intellectual capital, and one way to achieve this is to work toward an international IC system. The key challenge for corporate and political leaders who want to make a difference is not only to develop contexts for future growth. It will take more than communicating intangibles to stakeholders in a repetitive, auditable, and trustworthy way. In the face of coming institutional failures, social entrepreneurship will be a critical concern. The real future space—the IC of nations—will demand significant knowledge innovations.

▸▸ MAKING IT HAPPEN

There are a variety of approaches to managing intellectual capital, and as a starting point it may be helpful to consider the following questions:

- **Can you identify your intangible assets, and do you understand what they contribute to your organization?** It is worth considering that stockholders and other stakeholders value them, and they affect market perceptions of the business's value. There is therefore a powerful reason for measuring and actively managing your portfolio of intangible assets.
- **How might you measure and monitor the value of your intangible assets, your intellectual capital?** You can't manage what you can't measure, and given the importance of IC it should be continuously valued and developed.
- **How could you manage and develop the value of your intellectual capital?** At a time of commodity production and information overload, intellectual capital is a major source of competitive advantage, a key differentiator, and this can deliver significant benefits in terms of customer retention, acquisition, and innovation.

It is valuable to audit your intellectual capital, understanding its place and significance in the fragmenting value chain, and helping to decide a strategy for managing it. The key to making it happen is to nurture your reputation, people, and other key assets, focusing on how these resources can be fully employed and also developed and grown.

▸▸ MORE INFO

Books:

Cusumano, Michael A., and Constantinos C. Markides (eds). *Strategic Thinking for the Next Economy*. San Francisco, CA: Wiley, 2001.

Edvinsson, Leif. *Corporate Longitude*. Englewood Cliffs, NJ: FT Prentice Hall, 2002.

Marr, Bernard. *Perspectives on Intellectual Capital: Multidisciplinary Insights into Management*. Woburn, MA: Butterworth-Heinemann, 2005.

Stankosky, Michael. *Creating the Discipline of Knowledge Management: The Latest in University Research*. Woburn, MA: Butterworth-Heinemann, 2005.

See Also:

★ Intellectual Capital (pp. 477–478)
★ Protecting Your Intellectual Property—Nonregistered Rights (pp. 495–496)
★ Protecting Your Intellectual Property—Registered Rightss (pp. 497–498)
★ The Value and Management of Intellectual Property, Intangible Assets, and Goodwill (pp. 109–112)
✔ Intellectual Property—Copyright (p. 988)
✔ Intellectual Property—Patents—An International Overview (p. 989)
✔ Intellectual Property—Registered Designs and Trademarks (p. 990)
C. K. Prahalad (p. 1183)
Intellectual Capital: The New Wealth of Organizations (p. 1279)

"It is better to err on the side of daring than the side of caution." Alvin Toffler

     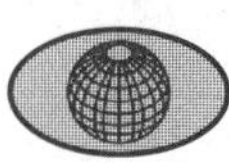   

Managing Operational Risks Using an All-Hazards Approach by Mark D. Abkowitz

EXECUTIVE SUMMARY

- Operational risk management (ORM) enables an enterprise to understand, prioritize, and control risks that threaten its well-being and the livelihood of its partners.
- Although traditionally stove-piped within an organization, different operational risks share many common elements, providing an opportunity to consolidate ORM into a single all-hazards approach, one that is holistic and systematic.
- The key to effective ORM is to recognize and mitigate those risk factors that erode our margin of safety, so allowing situations to spiral out of control.
- A key first step is for an organization to perform an ORM physical, enabling the identification of reasonably foreseeable risks, benchmarking the current status of the ORM program, revealing gaps where the organization is vulnerable, and developing cost-effective strategies to address these gaps.
- Based on recent historical events and changing conditions in our world, bringing ORM to the forefront of an organization is more important now than ever before.

OPERATIONAL RISK MANAGEMENT: A DEFINITION AND A STRATEGY

For the purpose of this discussion, Operational Risk Management (ORM) is considered to be the policies, methods, practices, and institutional culture that enable an enterprise to understand, prioritize, and control risks that threaten the well-being of the organization, its business partners, communities in which it operates, and society at large.

The cost of *poor* operational risk management can be excessive, considering that the occurrence of undesirable events can lead to fatalities and injuries; property loss; business interruption; clean-up, remediation and disposal; fines and penalties; future inspections; new regulations; long-term human health effects; environmental degradation; damaged investor, insurer, supplier, and customer relations; and loss of public confidence. By contrast, the cost of *good* operational risk management may be limited to investment in risk management benchmarking and needs assessment; resources allocated to control high-priority risks; and ongoing costs associated with ORM performance monitoring and evaluation.

THE NEED FOR AN ALL-HAZARDS APPROACH

In many organizations, the approach to dealing with operational risks is stove-piped, with different entities having responsibility for different hazards. For example, environmental health and safety worries about toxicity exposure, legal is concerned with liability, human resources focuses on occupational health, executive management has its eye on business continuity, risk management addresses insurance, and research and development cares about design failure. As a result each group has its own priorities, separate resources are used to address each problem, and there is limited coordination. Yet, while each threat may seem quite different, when one takes a closer look at how these events evolve, there is remarkable similarity; that is, a pattern or "recipe" for disaster emerges. This situation begs for the adoption of a single "all-hazards" ORM approach, a process that is holistic and systematic in nature.

RISK FACTORS

Within a recipe for disaster, each ingredient can be thought of as an underlying risk factor that erodes our margin of safety. Once this margin of safety is exceeded, the situation is liable to spiral out of control. Therefore, management control of risk factors is at the crux of an effective ORM program. In attempting to manage these risk factors within an organization, it is helpful to group them into the following categories:

Design and construction flaws: If there is a flaw in the design process and it is not discovered in time, the system is prone to failure. Even when the design is valid, problems can still arise if the materials used to fabricate the system components are faulty or the components are not assembled properly.

Deferred maintenance: It is human nature to choose to deal with problems at a later time, especially if the system is not actually malfunctioning. Unfortunately, decisions to defer maintenance often lead to the failure of a key system component before the repair can be made, causing a serious accident to occur.

Economic pressures: Organizations typically manage a limited budget. When these resources are too scarce or spending is not controlled adequately, pressure intensifies to implement strict cost-cutting measures. This can lead to shoddy workmanship, the purchase of inferior quality materials, elimination of the use of backup operating and safety equipment, or management ignoring problems that arise.

Schedule constraints: When a deadline has been imposed, and the activity has fallen behind schedule, pressure to make up ground can cause the responsible party to turn a blind eye to important details. This situation often leads to the elimination of critical tasks, personnel trying to accomplish tasks in parallel that should be done in sequence, or not pursuing certain considerations in sufficient depth to fully understand their impact on safety.

Inadequate training: Because of a lack of adequate training, individuals who are prone to make mistakes may be placed in positions of responsibility. This in turn can either initiate or intensify a crisis situation. When there are personnel shortages, individuals may be thrown into an important decision-making role while covering for others, performing a function for which they were not properly trained. Because individuals tend to forget what they were originally taught and since processes change over time and require new learning, lack of retraining can also be a problem.

Not following procedures: When engaged in a repetitive activity, complacency can set in, and individuals tend to drift away from following formal protocols. Consequently, they either neglect to perform certain steps or invent other ways to accomplish the same task, often not considering the possible safety hazards caused by their actions. Failing to follow procedures can create a hazardous situation, one that is exacerbated by coworkers whose actions are based on assuming that those procedures are being followed.

Lack of planning and preparedness: Because of the luxury of time and the fact that a disastrous event may not have been experienced in recent memory, people tend to place a low priority on being adequately prepared for a crisis situation. All too often, little forethought is given to the variety of disaster scenarios that could reasonably occur and how to deal with

"We must dare to think unthinkable thoughts. We must learn to explore all the options and possibilities that confront us in a complex and rapidly changing world. We must learn to welcome and not fear the voices of dissent." J. William Fulbright

them effectively. Even in circumstances where significant effort has been devoted to planning and preparedness, the product of this effort can be a written plan that is not practiced or updated, rendering it of little value when a calamity arises. Lack of planning and preparedness is one of the most common risk factors at play when something goes wrong.

Communication failure: Communication failures can occur at various stages, altering an outcome in different ways. When communication fails between members of the same organization, critical information is not shared, such as when one group decides to shut down a critical protection system for maintenance while another group is carrying out a dangerous experiment. Poor communication between organizations is also problematic. Finally, lack of communication with the public or the provision of inaccurate information can place people at risk either because they do not know the hazards they are facing, or because they are not properly advised on how to protect themselves. Along with lack of planning and preparedness, communication failure is the most common risk factor at play when something goes wrong.

Arrogance: Arrogance can rear its head in many forms, but usually appears as either the person in charge being driven to succeed for individual gain without sufficient regard for the safety of others, or an experienced individual who has become overconfident in his or her ability to deal with any problem that might present itself. In either form, arrogance can have serious repercussions.

Stifling political agendas: Government policies can have a powerful effect on the propensity for disasters. If these political agendas are hard-nosed, with little room for dialog and compromise, affected parties can feel that they have little recourse other than to resort to extreme and often hostile measures.

It is important to note that we, as humans, are involved in each and every one of these factors. While this implies that we contribute to the cause or impact of every disaster, it also means that we have an opportunity to control these factors more effectively to achieve a better future outcome.

GETTING STARTED

A key first step is for your organization to have an *ORM physical*, essentially a comprehensive review of how operations are performed, what risks are present in performing these operations, and how these risks are presently being managed . This engages the organization in identifying "reasonably foreseeable" risks, benchmarking the current status of the existing ORM program, identifying program gaps where the organization carries the greatest liability, and suggesting strategies and tactics that can be implemented to close these gaps. Having a risk physical is important regardless of whether the organization's ORM program is relatively new or fairly mature.

CASE STUDIES

ORM Failures and Successes

There are several historic events that bring the failures and successes of operational risk management into focus. How could the event have been prevented? What could have been done to mitigate the impacts? What management controls have been implemented since the event occurred? Could it happen again? These are all legitimate ORM questions that, through hindsight, allow us to learn from experience and apply these lessons to deploying more effective ORM in the future.

Hurricane Katrina

During August 2005, Hurricane Katrina slammed into the United States, hitting the coastal areas of Florida, Louisiana, and Mississippi. A combination of storm surge, wave action, and high winds resulted in the destruction of buildings and roads in the affected areas. The impact of Katrina on New Orleans was unusually severe; portions of the city were left under 20 feet of water due to failure of the earthen levees and floodwalls that had been constructed to safeguard the city from this type of event. Hurricane Katrina caused nearly 2,000 fatalities and an estimated economic loss of $125 billion, in addition to displacing hundreds of thousands of people from their homes and workplaces. The destruction and loss of life in New Orleans, while initiated by the storm itself, cannot be attributed entirely to Katrina. Numerous failures of the city's flood protection system due to poor design and construction, deferred maintenance, and a lack of funding left New Orleans susceptible to a hurricane of Katrina's magnitude. As the city filled with water, the hurricane's effects were compounded by insufficient emergency planning and preparedness, and the inability of responders to communicate.

Alaska Pipeline and Denali Earthquake

A major earthquake struck the Alaska mainland on November 3, 2002, along the Denali fault, which passes directly under the Trans-Alaska Pipeline. Had the pipeline ruptured, it would have resulted in spillage of up to a million barrels of crude oil a day in an environmentally sensitive area. Yet not a drop of oil was released. This potential catastrophe was averted due to successful ORM in both the design of the pipeline system and the quality of the maintenance, surveillance, and emergency preparedness. The pipeline design team, using extensive field data, devised a system such that it could survive a major earthquake should one occur during the pipeline's projected 300-year operating period. As a result, a $3 million up-front investment in geological studies and corresponding design considerations helped to prevent an environmental disaster that could easily have topped $100 million in remediation costs. Concurrently, a comprehensive surveillance and maintenance system was implemented, capable of identifying problem locations in real time and dispatching crews accordingly. Moreover, emergency response was facilitated by a well-organized incident command system, contingency planning, and a training program.

►► MAKING IT HAPPEN

- Designate ORM as a core business practice within the organization by establishing the program at the vice-president level. The VP should be responsible for defining ORM policies and procedures, and for providing oversight of program activities.
- Organize an ORM committee, which reports to the VP, with membership that includes representatives from each element of the organization that has a designated ORM responsibility.
- Perform an ORM physical, and use it as a basis for defining program priorities, allocating resources, and implementing management control strategies.
- Monitor and evaluate ORM performance to determine whether program objectives are being met.
- Maintain ORM as a living process that is part of the culture of the organization.

CONCLUSION

We can ill afford not to recognize the new age of operational risk management, one based on a holistic and systematic approach to identifying reasonably foreseeable risks, establishing priorities, and adopting practical, achievable, and cost-effective control strategies. As history has taught us, we remain vulnerable to the occurrence of catastrophic events whose prevention or mitigation is within our control. Moreover, changing conditions in our world are posing new challenges that will require making tough risk-related choices. Adopting an all-hazards ORM approach does not mean that we will never suffer another tragedy. However, the prospect of that happening is less likely to occur once investments in prevention and mitigation have been made. The bottom line is that we can, and should, do much better at being a master rather than a victim of risk. All it takes is a more organized approach to takes the risks that affect our daily lives, coupled with a greater tolerance for unfortunate events that will sometimes occur no matter how hard we try to avoid or prevent them.

▸▸ MORE INFO

Books:

Abkowitz, Mark D. *Operational Risk Management: A Case Study Approach to Effective Planning and Response*. Hoboken, NJ: Wiley, 2008.

Garrick, B. John. *Quantifying and Controlling Catastrophic Risks.* San Diego, CA: Elsevier, 2008.

Websites:

Risk World: www.riskworld.com

Society for Risk Analysis: www.sra.org

See Also:

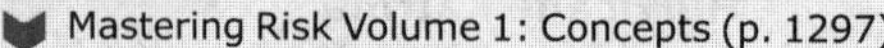

Mastering Risk Volume 1: Concepts (p. 1297)

  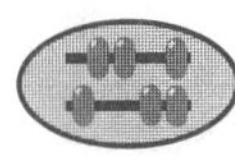   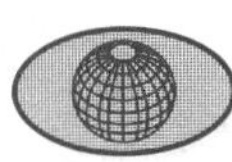   

Viewpoint: Aldo Mareuse
The Evolving Role of the CFO

INTRODUCTION

Aldo Mareuse, 44, has been chief financial officer of Orascom Telecom Holding, the Middle East's most successful mobile telecoms group since 2002. Based in Cairo, Egypt, Orascom Telecom is listed on the Cairo and London stock exchanges. Aldo Mareuse is also CFO of Weather Investment SpA, a private company that owns a majority stake in Orascom Telecom. Weather also owns Wind, Italy's third largest mobile operator, and Wind Hellas, the third largest such operator in Greece. Prior to joining Orascom Telecom, Frenchman Mareuse worked in various positions and locations for the investment bank Credit Suisse First Boston. His last role was as managing director of CSFB's investment banking division, telecommunications group, where he focused on advising telecom players in M&A, equity and debt financing. He holds an engineering degree from École Centrale de Lyon and is married with three children. When he is not traveling between Islamabad, Cairo, Rome or New York in the winter, he enjoys back country skiing in the Alps or in the Rockies, and in the summer he likes to cruise on the Mediterranean.

How has the CFO role evolved in the past five to 10 years?
The whole pace has stepped up a gear. Capital markets have evolved dramatically in the past five years and continue to evolve. As a result, the capital markets function has become much more central to the CFO role. Financings have become much more sophisticated and the products used for raising capital—including equity, debt, and a range of other instruments—have a much shorter lifetime. So the CFO has to be much more aware of his products and able to make decisions more quickly. In the old days, you could plan something six months ahead. That's no longer possible.

Has Orascom Telecom been actively raising capital in recent times?
Even though it is a private company, Weather Investments SpA is much bigger than Orascom. Like Weather, we have raised a substantial amount of debt, across the spectrum including bank debt, bonds and mezzanine finance. So we have covered the capital markets spectrum and have been extremely active in the last three to four years.

Have you found that raising capital became more difficult since the credit crisis erupted in August 2007?
Basically the market has been frozen. So it hasn't been difficult; it's been non-existent. This has meant that, in the short term, the CFO role has been much more about looking at cost reduction and free cash flow optimization, rather than the capital market activities, which have been shut down. The CFO role has become a much more inwardly focused function than a year or so ago.

How do you predict the CFO role will evolve over the next five or 10 years? Will we return to a more outward-looking function and more active in capital markets?
I don't think the capital markets will be nearly as active as they were in the period between 2003 and 2007. They're going to be much slower for a very long period of time. It's going to be much more difficult and expensive to raise finance. And the focus will be more on the cash flow a company generates, rather than raising it externally from third parties.

Will that make the CFO's job more boring and/or more difficult?
I don't know if it will become more boring, but it will certainly become more difficult. During the period of easy credit, you could simply put up your hand and five banks would come offering you whatever you wanted. It had become slightly artificial, slightly surreal. It's back to basics now.

What other factors are driving change in the way finance departments must function?
As a result of Sarbanes-Oxley, we have an odd situation where corporates are obliged to be very transparent. They have to publish earnings releases quarterly, disclose numbers every quarter, and respond openly to detailed questions from investors. Yet, the hedge funds and long-only investors who are asking these questions are under no obligation to tell you how many shares they own, or indeed if they have any at all. There's an un-level playing field in transparency. Investors want all this transparency, but they're not being transparent themselves. I always laugh when I sit down with an investor and he asks me why my profit margin fell from 43.5% to 43.2% in a given quarter; I then ask him if he holds any shares and he says, "Sorry, I can't tell you."

Do you think that ought to change?
There's so much pressure for hedge funds to be more transparent; yes, I think that this will definitely change.

How can finance managers, including CFOs, add value to their organizations and ensure standards of corporate governance are improved? What attributes do CFOs need to achieve this?
The best tools the CFO has in his armory are the financial results themselves. However, there's lots of leeway in terms of how you present these results. You can present the same set of figures to the same accountancy standards. However, one version could be made so opaque that hardly anybody understands it, and another could be written so transparently that everybody instantly understands the issues.

What's the temptation as a CFO? Is it to produce the opaque type or the transparent type?
That is a very, very important question, and I don't really have the answer. If you disclose too much, and you don't know the agenda of the investor, who is across the table from you, you could really suffer. In

"Creditors have better memories than debtors." Benjamin Franklin

the past, I would always have advocated full transparency, but I've discovered that this can work against you.

Can you give me an example of how that could work against you?
Well, let's say a corporate does an attractive financing. Let's say the terms of this financing are based on the share price. If you were to disclose all the terms, some investors—and particularly hedge funds—are going to play against you.

Do you mean by pushing the share price up or down?
Yes, depending on whether your financing is built on the share price going up or down. With the derivatives tools that are available now, you can do whatever you want in terms of financing. And obviously people can play against you and they don't have to tell anyone. If someone is a short-seller of your stock, he doesn't have to tell you that he's a shorter; yet, he's going to ask you exactly the same sorts of questions that a long-only investor would ask you. It can be quite frustrating.

Would you say that part of it is trying to second guess these guys whenever you're preparing how to release information to the market?
Exactly. Whenever you're preparing financial statements and other reports, it's difficult because these documents are going to be published and could be read by anybody.

What about ethical values? How do they sit in all this?
At the end of the day, what you always carry with you is your reputation. As a CFO, this is arguably the most important asset you have. Therefore, you need to maintain it at any price. Frankly speaking, I am not a big fan of all these Sarbanes-Oxley rules. I have been a board member of a company listed in the US and which has to abide by all these rules. It's a lot of paperwork; it makes a lot more money for the lawyers, but it doesn't increase transparency at all.

Did the use of "fair value" accounting exacerbate the recent financial crisis?
It definitely did. The US banks ran into trouble much faster than the European banks, because the European banks had more leeway in terms of not marking assets to market. That put the US banks in a very tight spot. I wouldn't be surprised if there are still further big blowouts among European banks. I am not sure that forcing banks to mark to market immediately is a particularly good idea. It just intensifies the nervousness and panic in the market.

Should CFOs be more cognizant of nonfinancial performance indicators, including the environmental and social impact of their business, over and above their existing focus on financial performance?
As CFOs, we are not currently equipped to do this. However, in principle, I believe that the CFO should worry more about these things. In future, companies are going to have to properly allocate resources to measure all that.

What sort of relationship should the CFO have with the CEO, other board members and with investors?
At the end of the day, the CEO and the board decide on the allocation of capital.

The allocation of capital is an easy task if you've got good tools, and the CFO is there to provide these tools, both to the board and to external investors. Obviously, reporting to the CEO, the CFO has to provide all the relevant numbers and ensure these are robust, reliable and transparent, for the benefit of the entire board as well as investors.

In terms of the training required for a CFO, the traditional route is for them to first qualify as accountants, work in private practice and then move into the industry. Is this a sensible career path?
Accountants tend to be good at recording what has happened in the past but they are generally pretty clueless when it comes to thinking about the future. In today's market, it's more important to be able to raise funds. If you're able to raise funds, you can talk to investors and you can probably also do a budget. These three functions are critically important. Because I was an investment banker at CSFB before becoming Orascom's CFO, I found it easy to do the financing part, the investor relations part, the budget part, and the treasury part. It was more of a challenge for me to do the accounting part.

What is your view of the quality of audits provided by the "big four" accountancy firms PricewaterhouseCoopers, Ernst & Young, KPMG, and Deloitte?
There is substantial room for improvement in the quality of the audit reports. They don't really understand the commercial issues. And, if you don't understand commercial issues, you don't understand risk. They're just playing by the book. They are too focused on rules, and they often don't understand the bigger picture. Accountancy firms and rating agencies need to improve their understanding of the issues before they can provide more added value. They're more into preservation, acting as a safety net to ensure companies don't do things that are completely stupid.

So what can be done to improve the quality of auditing?
I think audit firms should employ higher caliber people, which would make auditing more expensive.

But you, as a company, would be happy to pay more if you were getting better quality auditing?
If the entire industry was doing it, yes. It would enhance the quality of all companies' financials and give investors less incentive to question the figures all the time. So, at the end of the day, yes.

A few years ago there were suggestions that it was somehow inappropriate for a Cairo-based group to acquire a mobile phone company in developed countries. Does that sort of prejudice still exist?
When we bought Italy-based Wind, people were saying, "What is Italy doing? They're selling a mobile phone company to an Egyptian!" There was an assumption that we would turn up on camels wearing djellabas! Likewise, eyebrows were raised when Mittal bought Arcelor. Now, however, everybody understands that an Indian, Chinese or Asian company can manage assets in Europe or the US better than the Europeans or Americans. Whilst the credit crisis caused emerging markets to become less fashionable, in the long term, the growth is going to be these markets. Everyone understands they have disciplined management teams, who are capable of running assets anywhere in the world.

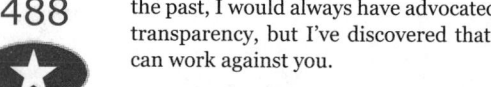

▸▸ MORE INFO

Books:

Bainville, Jacques, and Hamish Miles (trans). *Napoleon*. Paperback ed. Safety Harbor, FL: Simon Publications, 2002.

Carnegie, Dale. *How to Win Friends and Influence People*. New ed. London: Vermillion, 2007.

Gallo, Max. *Louis XIV: Le Roi Soleil*. Paris: XO Editions, 2007.

Minc, Alain. *Une Histoire de France*. Paris: Éditions Grasset & Fasquelle, 2008.

"The attitude of disrespect that many executives have today for accurate reporting is a business disgrace. And auditors...have done little on the positive side. Though auditors should regard the investing public as their client, they tend to kowtow instead to the managers who choose them and dole out their pay." Warren Buffett

  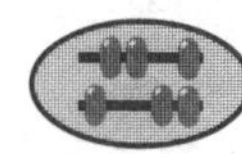   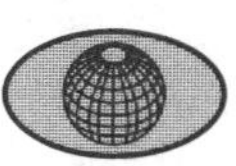   

Managing Retirement Costs by Beverly Goldberg

EXECUTIVE SUMMARY

- The large generation of baby boomers born in the years after World War II is nearing retirement age, and the generation that follows is far smaller.
- Although the aging of the workforce may not affect every business, or every area of a business, management should, at the very least, conduct demographic surveys of their workforces, discover the retirement plans of older employees, and explore the skills needed to remain productive.
- The costs of recruiting and training new workers must be evaluated and measured against the costs of programs aimed at retaining older workers to decide what approach, or mix of approaches, should be taken to ensure that major problems do not develop.
- If necessary, retention programs aimed at convincing employees with needed skills to remain longer should be put in place. Among the programs already being used across the G7 nations (with varying degrees of success) are phased retirement, flexible hours, working from home, temporary work, job sharing, and consulting.

INTRODUCTION

The industrialized nations of the world are getting grayer. In the United States some 76 million individuals, known as the baby boomers, were born between World War II and 1964, wheareas the generation that followed numbered only 66 million. One-fifth of current workers in the United States will reach retirement age by 2020, and some industrialized nations, such as Japan, are graying even faster. This means that the number of people in the workforce available to replace the boomers as they reach retirement is much smaller than the number that will be leaving the workforce. Moreover, the trend to smaller families, which means smaller populations of younger people available to employers, has been continuing (Table 1), indicating that the problem of fewer replacements for retiring workers is one that will not disappear.

Although some analysts dismiss the warning that labor shortages will be a major problem—citing increased productivity and immigration as mitigating factors—others predict that the lack of skilled workers to replace retirees, a phenomenon that is often called the "boomer brain drain," will be devastating. The truth is that the retirement of this huge cohort of workers will affect different nations, different regions within nations, different industries, and different companies in different ways.

Table 1. Fertility rates* in the industrialized nations. (*Source*: United Nations Population Division)

Country	*1960*	*2000*
Canada	3.6	1.6
France	2.9	1.8
Germany	2.5	1.3
Italy	2.5	1.2
Japan	2.0	1.4
United Kingdom	2.8	1.7
United States	3.3	2.0

*Average number of children born to a woman over her lifetime

Unfortunately, in large organizations, human resources and personnel managers—who were the first to feel the effects of this trend—have found it difficult to convince senior management of its importance, primarily because the problem is not immediate. In smaller organizations, where dealing with issues about employees may be in the hands of the finance department, the issue often does not surface as a problem, because hiring is done on an individual basis by those needing to find replacements for employees who leave. In the case of large organizations, the head of human resources should ask the CFO to help by conducting an in-depth analysis of the actual costs of an older workforce, as well as the costs of recruiting replacements. In smaller organizations, the CEO, COO, and CFO should work together to determine whether they are facing problems due to the age and composition of the workforce.

WILL BOOMER RETIREMENTS ADVERSELY AFFECT YOUR BUSINESS?

When matched to a skills survey, a demographic profile of your organization as a whole, and of specific departments and teams, will help to determine whether or not it needs to develop programs to forestall major problems. For example, in the United States, according to a recent Hay Group study, "a substantial number of mission-critical employees in the utilities industry from the executive suite down to the lineman are rapidly approaching retirement age in the next four years." As a result, according to a Hay Group spokesman, "The electric and gas industries could easily collapse if they don't put a plan in place for staffing, retention, recruitment, and training."[1] In the United Kingdom, a similar report to the Scottish Parliament indicates that there are likely to be recruitment problems in the electro-technical sector because there are not enough qualified workers to replace those who are due to retire in the next few years.[2]

In general, the companies that should be most concerned about the fact that a fifth of current workers will reach retirement age by 2020 are those that have the highest concentration of older employees, such as utilities, manufacturing, health care, and retail. All companies, however, may have certain groups of employees whose skills may not be easy to replace. Or they may have large numbers of employees in certain functional areas who may be eligible for retirement at about the same time.

So the sensible approach is to assemble a profile of the ages of the current workforce, the skills needed by workers in each job category, and the retirement plans of older workers to determine when they plan to retire, as well as what it might take to entice them to stay. At the same time, companies should examine whether younger people in the region are acquiring the skills that will be needed when older workers retire. If they find that this is not happening, companies must see what measures they can take to induce the current workforce to undertake additional skills training and to convince high school students to pursue those skills and vocational schools and colleges to provide training in them.

ASSESSING THE COSTS OF RETIREMENT

Companies facing the loss of employees to retirement must factor in the costs of hiring workers to replace those who leave when deciding how to deal with the issue of retirement. Among the costs to be analyzed are:

- lost productivity during the time it takes to find a suitable replacement;
- the costs of finding a replacement for the departing worker;
- the time needed for the new employee to adapt to the culture and become fully proficient at the job;
- ancillary costs due to productivity losses by colleagues of the retiring employee as

"**Failure to investigate or recognize the issues surrounding the maturing workforce will pose a threat to future growth and productivity.**" Conference Board, New York

     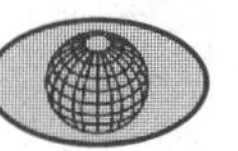   

they adjust to the departure and then to working with the new hire.

Measuring the costs of lost productivity during the search for a replacement requires having records (or management knowledge) of the amount of work usually completed by employees in the same position over a given period. Management then must look at the amount of work not being done by the person leaving to determine how much can be taken over by others in the department. In addition, it may be necessary to hire temporary workers from an agency to do much of the work until the replacement is found. Taken together, the loss of completed work, the overtime put in by others in the department, and the cost of temporary workers provides a measure of the costs of the lost productivity.

Analyzing the costs of finding the replacement includes examining the costs of advertising the job opening; agency fees, or bonuses for referrals from current employees; time spent by managers on interviews; and, sometimes, costs of relocation (usually for highly skilled workers).

In general, the cost of replacing an experienced worker averages about 50% of the employee's annual salary, but that proportion (and cost) rises dramatically for those with specialized skills. For example, according to *InformationWeek* magazine, "IT employee replacement costs are 2.5 times the annual salary of an IT professional leaving the organization."[3] In addition, this rule of thumb understates the cost of lost productivity when many employees in any given functional area must be replaced over a short period.

Some observers contend that the costs of replacing older workers may be largely or wholly offset by younger workers' lower pay and benefits (although that assumes that younger workers with the needed skills are available). While some costs, such as higher salaries due to seniority, more accrued vacation time, and larger contributions to pension plans (and in the United States higher health care premiums) are real, many others that are given as reasons not to retain older workers are myths.[4] For example, some claim that older workers take more sick days than younger workers. According to the US Bureau of Labor Statistics, in 2007 the absence rate of full-time workers aged 25 to 54 was 3.2 per 100, and workers aged 55 and over were absent at only a marginally higher rate: 3.6 per 100.

PROGRAMS AIMED AT RETAINING OLDER WORKERS

Solutions to the problem posed by the likelihood that large numbers of baby boomers will retire simultaneously include keeping a portion of these would-be retirees in the workforce by modifying traditional work rules. A Towers Perrin survey of workers in the G7 countries found that, while about 40% of workers over age 50 indicated that they plan to retire from their current positions in the next five years, almost the same number stated that they plan to work in some capacity after retiring from their current jobs.[5]

The same study found that almost half of workers nearing retirement find the possibility of part-time work and flexible work for their present company enticing, while a little more than a third would be attracted by the possibility of working from home. About a fourth of those planning to retire say they would stay on if they were offered retention bonuses, credits to pension benefits for delaying retirement, or the ability to collect partial pensions while working. The same proportion would be interested in returning as contractors.

Many companies that already have encountered problems due to retirements have instituted programs both to develop replacements and to hold on to some older workers, including:[6]

- training programs for younger workers who have the basics they need to acquire the specific skills that will be lost;
- mentoring programs to transfer specialized knowledge from retiring workers to younger staff;
- phased retirement policies that enable employees to reduce the number of days they work each week gradually over a period of years;
- flexible work options that would allow employees to job share (two older workers sharing a single job) or to work on a reduced schedule;

CASE STUDY

A Midwestern US Nursing School

One of the major causes of the general nursing shortage in the United States is the shortage of nursing faculty to train those who wish to enter the field. This shortage is the result of both the retirement of older tenured faculty and the lack of interest of nurses with advanced degrees in teaching rather than nursing, primarily because nurses with specialized skills earn more than nursing faculty.

In the case of this Midwestern state university-based nursing school, the problem was particularly severe because of the aging of the state's population: like many other states in the northern Midwest, the population in general is older, with a consequent increase in the demand for nurses. The university's board of regents asked the nursing school to increase the number of nurses they graduated each year and made available some funding for the effort.

After careful examination of the issue, a program was developed that included the following actions:

- Recruiting recently retired faculty to teach as adjuncts at a salary higher than that usually paid to part-time university faculty.
- Working with hospital administrators in the region to find out which current older nurses were planning to retire in the next two to five years because the work had become too physically demanding. These nurses were offered scholarships for advanced degrees in exchange for promises to join the faculty for a given number of years.
- Meeting with principals of high schools in the region to see whether they knew of older teachers, especially science teachers, who were planning to retire because of burnout or boredom. Such teachers were offered scholarships for degrees that would enable them to pursue a new career teaching nursing students (a more dedicated and mature student body), again in return for a promise to teach at the university's nursing school.
- Running advertisements in other regions promoting the advantages to nursing teachers of relocating to the region and offering them relocation expenses and recruitment bonuses.

Each of these approaches had some degree of success. Only a small number of new faculty were recruited as the result of seeking adjuncts and placing advertisements in other regions. However, the number of soon-to-retire nurses and teachers who applied for and were granted scholarships gives promise that the needed expansion of the faculty will occur over the next five years. The time frame is longer than expected because those who accepted are, for the most part, attending school only part time. The reason for this is that the scholarships only provide tuition and do not cover such things as living expenses.

"Work needs to be made a more attractive and rewarding proposition for older workers." OECD

  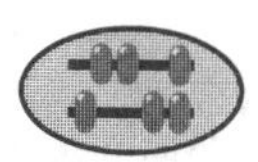   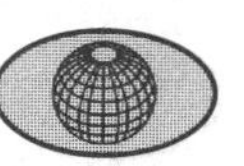   

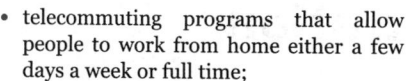

- telecommuting programs that allow people to work from home either a few days a week or full time;
- consulting and contracting arrangements that can be used to increase staff at the busiest time of the year;
- keeping in touch with retirees and offering them special bonuses for returning in some capacity after sampling retirement.

CONCLUSION

Senior managers cannot bury their heads in the sand when it comes to the issue of the approaching retirement of baby boomers, which will begin in earnest in 2010. Analyzing the possibility of shortfalls of needed skills now will give businesses time to put in place programs to prevent the loss of employees with those skills and to develop plans that will ensure that new employees with those skills will be available when needed.

MAKING IT HAPPEN

Because senior management often dismisses the issue of the aging of the workforce, the CFO, along with the heads of human resources and personnel, must formally evaluate the likelihood that major problems will develop and estimate the costs of programs aimed at addressing such problems. Only by presenting hard evidence will they be able to convince senior management to take action aimed at eliminating these threats to the long-term success of the business. Such evidence should include:

- a general demographic profile of employees, as well as profiles of various divisions, functional areas, and teams;
- a catalog of specialized skills and educational levels of current employees in various divisions, functional areas, and teams;
- the retirement plans of current employees, matched to their areas and skills;
- when these analyses indicate a future skills shortfall, a further analysis should be carried out to determine:
  - recruitment costs when it comes to difficult-to-replace skills;
  - the general availability of people with those skills;
  - the costs of training people in those skills;
  - the costs of various programs aimed at retaining retirees with those skills for a period of time.

MORE INFO

Books:

DeLong, David W. *Lost Knowledge: Confronting the Threat of an Aging Workforce.* New York: Oxford University Press, 2004.

Dychtwald, Ken, Tamara J. Erikson, and Robert Morison. *Workforce Crisis: How to Beat the Coming Shortage of Skills and Talent.* Boston, MA: Harvard Business School Press, 2006.

Goldberg, Beverly. *Age Works: What Corporate America Must Do to Survive the Graying of the Workforce.* New York: The Free Press, 2000.

Report:

Towers Perrin. *Perspectives of employers, workers and policymakers in the G7 countries on the new demographic realities.* September 2007. Online at: www.aarp.org/research/work/employment/intl_older_worker.html

Websites:

Aging Workforce News for developments, tools, and resources for managing older workers and boomers in the workplace: www.agingworkforcenews.com

American Association of Retired Persons, now just AARP: www.aarp.org. See especially the section on employee retention: www.aarp.org/money/careers/employerresourcecenter/retention; and the Towers Perrin report listed above.

NOTES

1 Hay Group. "Study says utility industry faces severe manpower shortage as majority of its workforce plans retirement": www.jobbankusa.com/news/business_human_resources/utility_industry_faces_severe_manpower_shortage.html.

2 Submission by National Electrotechnical Training (NET): www.scottish.parliament.uk/business/committees/historic/x-enterprise/inquiries-01/lli-submissions/ell-010.pdf.

3 Luftman, Jerry with Rajkumar Kempaiah. "Tips for recruiting and retaining IT talent." *Information Week*: www.informationweek.com/news/management/trends/showArticle.jhtml?articleID=201807942.

4 Grossman, Robert. "Keep pace with older workers." *HR Magazine*: www.shrm.org/hrmagazine/articles/0508/0508grossman.asp.

5 Towers Perrin, 2007.

6 Goldberg, 2000.

"Keeping our people around will help cut down on our recruiting expense and help us manage costs while leveraging experienced workers." Marie McCarthy

     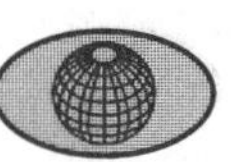   

Multiparty and Multicontract Arbitration

by Stavros Brekoulakis

EXECUTIVE SUMMARY

- Multiparty arbitration involves several actions between several parties to different contracts.
- Multicontract arbitration involves several actions arising out of several contracts between the same two parties.
- In both multiparty and multicontract arbitrations the issue is whether the several actions and several sets of proceedings can and should be consolidated.
- Consolidation of several sets of arbitration proceedings might be beneficial as it would prevent the risk of having conflicting arbitral awards and it would reduce time and cost.
- However, consolidation of several sets of arbitration proceedings might violate the consensual nature of arbitration.
- Thus, multiparty and multicontract arbitrations may only be achieved if all the relevant parties have expressly provided so in their arbitration agreements.

MULTIPARTY ARBITRATION

Contemporary international transactions are extremely complicated and very often require the participation of several parties in the delivery of a single project. For example, a typical construction project will usually involve—apart from a client and a main contractor—an engineer and/or an architect, several subcontractors, suppliers, financiers, and possibly additional commercial parties. Therefore, a dispute that might arise between the client and the main contractor would most likely affect the legal or financial position of the subcontractor, the engineer, or the supplier, who would thus have an interest in participating in any proceedings between the client and the main contractor. Thus, in litigation proceedings, provision is invariably made for parallel interrelated proceedings between different parties to be consolidated in order to prevent the risk of having conflicting decisions, and to reduce time and cost.

However, in contrast to litigation, arbitration is a dispute resolution mechanism that is based on a contract—i.e. an arbitration agreement. Only those persons who have unequivocally consented to and signed an arbitration agreement can participate in arbitration proceedings and be bound by the resulting arbitral award.

The contractual basis of arbitration is thus a double-edged sword: On the one hand, it makes arbitration a very flexible dispute resolution mechanism, allowing the parties to design the arbitration proceedings in accordance with their commercial needs. This has proved to be a significant advantage of arbitration over litigation, and has contributed to the increasing popularity of the former amongst members of the international commercial community, particularly in the last 30 years. On the other hand, its contractual basis makes arbitration unsuitable to accommodate multiparty projects, and it frequently leads to unfavorable results.

Thus, in the above example of a typical multiparty construction project, the usual practice will be for a client and a main contractor to sign a bilateral arbitration agreement. Consequently, it will not be possible for a subcontractor, an engineer, or a supplier (the "third parties") to participate in the arbitration proceedings between the client and the main contractor (the "original parties"). These persons will remain third parties to the arbitration proceedings even if they have played an active role in the actual business project and, therefore, have an interest in the outcome of the dispute between the original parties.

The prevailing view is therefore that multiparty proceedings in arbitration are not possible unless all the relevant parties have consented to arbitration.

MULTIPARTY ARBITRATION AND CONSENT

Parties may provide consent for multiparty arbitration either in one multiparty arbitration agreement or in several identical arbitration agreements that make express references to each other.

Single Multiparty Arbitration Agreement

Multiparty arbitration agreements are typically found in multiparty contractual arrangements, such as join ventures and consortium agreements. Thus, for example, where a dispute arises between two of the parties involved in a consortium, other consortium members may intervene in the arbitration proceedings between the original parties. Similarly, multiparty arbitration proceedings may result from an arbitration agreement inserted in the articles of association of a corporation, so that all the shareholders will be bound by that arbitration agreement.

Several Identical Bilateral Arbitration Agreements

Consent for multiparty proceedings may be ascertained from several contracts with arbitration clauses that first, provide for arbitrations with identical characteristics and second, make express references to each other (so-called "back-to-back" arbitration agreements). For example, a client and a main contractor should agree on an arbitration agreement that would provide for the same arbitration institution, seat of the arbitration, and applicable law as those provided in the arbitration agreement included in the subcontract between the same main contractor and a subcontractor.

MULTIPARTY PROCEEDINGS IN ARBITRATION LAWS AND RULES

Even if the parties fail to provide for multiparty proceedings in their arbitration agreements, multiparty arbitration may still result from the applicable arbitration laws and rules. However, the majority of institutional rules and arbitration laws do not make any provisions for multiparty proceedings. This leaves the exclusive decision on such a delicate issue to the parties. For example, no relevant provision is found in the respective Rules of the International Chamber of Commerce (ICC) (1998), the International Centre for Dispute Resolution (ICDR) of the American Arbitration Association (AAA) (2008), the United Nations Commission on International Trade Law (UNCITRAL) (1976), the Stockholm Chamber of Commerce (2007), or the China International Economic and Trade Arbitration Commission (CIETAC) (2005). Even when institutional rules provide for multiparty arbitration, they provide for the self-evident, namely that multiparty proceedings require the consent of all the relevant parties. This is, for example, the case with the Vienna Rules or the Netherlands Arbitration Institute Rules.

There are only a few exceptions to the principle of requiring the consent of all the relevant parties for multiparty arbitration. For example, in some institutional rules—such as those of the London Court of Inter-

"**To give a satisfactory decision as to the truth it is necessary to berather an arbitrator than a party to the dispute.**" Aristotle

  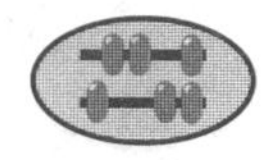 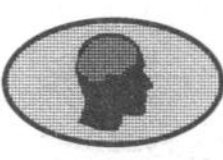  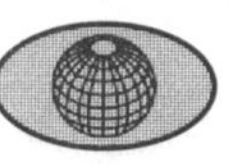   

national Arbitration (LCIA), the Belgian arbitration and mediation organization CEPANI, or the Swiss Rules—the consent of all the relevant parties is not required for the consolidation of two pending arbitrations between several parties, or the joinder of a third party. In these cases, the decision for the consolidation or the joinder is entrusted either to the arbitral tribunal or the administration body. This approach is more prevalent in arbitration rules related to specific industries, such as construction,[1] commodities,[2] securities,[3] or maritime.[4]

National arbitration laws also opt for party autonomy, the majority of which avoids the inclusion of any fall back provisions, let alone mandatory ones, for third-party mechanisms. Indeed, no relevant provisions can be found in the US Federal Arbitration Act, the Swiss Private International Law Act (PILA), the French New Code of Civil Procedure (NCCP), the German Code of Civil Procedure (ZPO), or the Model Law.

Only as a rare exception do arbitration laws deviate from the consensual approach, and provide for compulsory multiparty proceedings ordered exclusively by national courts, even without consent of all the relevant parties. The classic example here is the Netherlands Code of Civil Procedure art.1046, which provides for compulsory consolidation to be ordered by the President of the Amsterdam District Court.

THE "GROUP OF COMPANIES" DOCTRINE IN ARBITRATION

Issues relating to multiparty arbitration often arise in the context of several companies operating within the same group. It is an established practice for large multinational groups to operate through several subsidiaries, associated or holding companies. Often the parent company will play a decisive role in a contract formally signed by a subsidiary (the signatory party). In this context, there have been several arbitral awards holding that an arbitration agreement signed by the signatory subsidiary can be "extended" to the nonsignatory parent company when the following conditions are met:

- Both the signatory and the nonsignatory party belong to the same group of companies.
- The nonsignatory party played an active role in the negotiations, performance, or termination of the contract, including the arbitration agreement.

The theory of extending an arbitration agreement to nonsignatory companies of a group was first applied in the celebrated arbitration case of Dow Chemical versus Isover Saint-Gobain (ICC award 1982). Two subsidiaries of the Dow Chemical Company group entered into two separate distribution contracts with Isover Saint-Gobain. Both distribution agreements contained an ICC arbitration clause. When a dispute arose out of the distribution agreements, the two Dow Chemical subsidiaries alongside their parent company and another subsidiary of the same group initiated arbitration proceedings against Isover Saint-Gobain. The respondent challenged the jurisdiction of the tribunal on the basis that the parent company and the third subsidiary of the claimants were not parties to either of the two arbitration agreements incorporated in the distributions contracts. However, the ICC tribunal held that the parent company and the third subsidiary were bound by the arbitration agreement signed by the other companies of the group. The tribunal noted that the arbitration agreement had in fact been extended to all companies of the group that had been actively involved in the conclusion and performance of the contract signed by the original subsidiaries.

Despite the fact that since the Dow Chemical award the "group of companies" theory has been applied by several awards and has been upheld by several national courts, some jurisdictions are still reluctant to accept it. For example, a relatively recent decision of English Courts annulled an award that had extended arbitration agreement to the nonsignatory parent company (see Peterson Farms Inc. versus C & M Farming Ltd, 2004).

MULTICONTRACT AND MULTICLAIM DISPUTES

In contrast to multiparty arbitration that involves several parties, multicontract proceedings involve several claims arising out of several contracts between the same two parties. For example, two parties may enter into a purchase agreement and, at the same time, agree first on a finance agreement (where the seller finances the purchase) and second on a security agreement (to secure the finance of the purchase). In other words, the same two parties enter into three different interrelated agreements. Let us assume here that the parties provide for an arbitration agreement in the purchase agreement but fail to provide for an arbitration agreement in the other two contracts. In such a case, if different disputes arise out of the several contracts, it is questionable whether the several disputes between the same two parties can be brought before a single arbitration forum and determined in a single set of proceedings.

Here, the advantage of consolidating the several disputes before a single forum would be to prevent conflicting arbitration awards and to save time and money. Again as in the case of multiparty arbitration, the consent of the two parties to consolidate the several disputes arising out of interrelated contracts is required. However, unlike multiparty arbitration, multicontract arbitration does not give rise to issues relating to the violation of confidentiality or violation of equal treatment of the several parties (see the Dutco case below).

The best time to deal with multicontract

CASE STUDY

Multiparty Arbitration and Equal Treatment of the Several Parties

It is important to keep in mind that in multiparty arbitration proceedings each of the several parties must be given equal rights in the constitution of the tribunal, otherwise the award will be open to annulment. This was the clear message sent by the French Supreme Court in the case of Siemens AG versus Dutco Construction Co. (1992). Here, a dispute arose out of a consortium agreement for the construction of a plant. The contract contained an arbitration clause for ICC arbitration by three arbitrators. Dutco, one of the consortium parties, brought a claim against the other two consortium members, Siemens and BKMI. Dutco appointed its own arbitrator, while the ICC asked the two co-respondents (Siemens and BKMI) to jointly appoint one arbitrator (the third arbitrator would then be appointed by the two party-appointed arbitrators, as is the usual case). Siemens and BKMI refused to jointly appoint a single arbitrator, arguing that they had divergent interests despite being co-respondents. They argued that each one of them should have been given the right to appoint its own arbitrator. Upon threats by the ICC Court to appoint an arbitrator on behalf of the two co-respondents, Siemens and BKMI finally jointly nominated an arbitrator, but they reserved their right to challenge the appointment procedure. The highest court of France indeed annulled the ICC award holding that in multiparty proceedings each of the several co-respondents had the right to appoint its own arbitrator, otherwise the principle of equality of the parties would be violated.

"International arbitration may be defined as the substitution of many burning questions for a smoldering one."
Ambrose Bierce

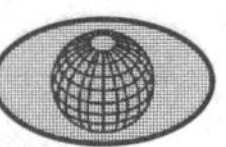

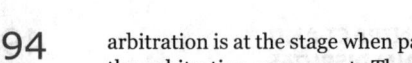

arbitration is at the stage when parties draft the arbitration agreement. There are several possible courses of action:

- The parties may provide for a single framework arbitration agreement that expressly covers any dispute that might arise out of the several interrelated contracts between the parties. Thus, in the Dutco example, the parties may provide for an arbitration agreement in the main contract (the purchase agreement) expressly providing that this arbitration agreement would also cover any other dispute arising out of the finance and the security agreement between the two parties.
- The parties may insert an identical arbitration agreement in each of the several contracts, which expressly refers to the possibility for consolidating the several disputes.
- Another way for the parties to deal with multiparty arbitrations is to adopt institutional rules that provide for consolidation of the several claims arising out of the several contracts. Such rules include the ICC Arbitration Rules, Art. 4(6) or the Swiss Rules Art. 4(1).

▸▸ MAKING IT HAPPEN

Drafting Tips

When several parties to several contracts want to provide for multiparty proceedings, the several arbitration agreements should make express references to each other. For example, in the context of several construction contracts, the arbitration agreement in the main contract should provide that: "In case a dispute arises out of the contract between the client and the contractor, the subcontractor may be joined in the arbitration proceedings."

Moreover, a similar provision should be included in the subcontract between the contractor and subcontractor, providing that: "In case a dispute arises out of the contract between the contractor and the subcontractor, the client may be jointed in the arbitration proceedings."

Other Practical Solutions

Instead of formal consolidation of the several sets of proceedings, parties may opt for a de facto consolidation. This can be achieved either if the parties appoint the same arbitrator(s) in all the sets of arbitration or if the different sets of arbitration proceedings hold concurrent hearings.

▸▸ MORE INFO

Books:

Hanotiau, B. *Complex Arbitrations: Multiparty, Multicontract, Multi-Issue and Class Actions*. The Hague: Kluwer Law International, 2006.

Lew, Julian D. M., Loukas A. Mistelis, and Stefan Kröll. *Comparative International Commercial Arbitration* (Chapter 16). The Hague: Kluwer Law International, 2003.

Websites:

American Arbitration Association: www.adr.org

International Chamber of Commerce: www.iccwbo.org

NOTES

1 See the AAA Construction Industry Arbitration Rules and Mediation Procedures (including Procedures for large, complex construction disputes) R-7 (consolidation).

2 See the US National Grain and Feed Association, s.5 (e)–(f).

3 See the New York Stock Exchange Arbitration Rules, s.612 (d).

4 For example, the London Maritime Arbitration Association, s.14 (b).

"**At all events, arbitration is more rational, just, and humane than the resort to the sword.**" Richard Codben

  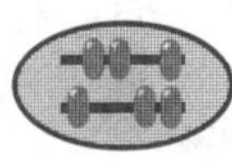   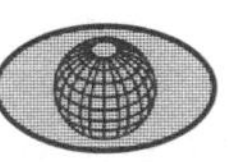   

Protecting Your Intellectual Property—Nonregistered Rights by Jeremy Phillips

EXECUTIVE SUMMARY

- Copyright, database rights, and some countries' design rights—as well as rights covering confidential information, know-how, trade names, and get-up—are intellectual property rights that do not depend on an application process that results in registration.
- If a right is not registered, third parties may find it impossible to identify either the ownership and/or the extent to which the unregistered right is protected.
- Statutory unregistered rights are generally vested with the characteristics of property and may be assigned, licensed, and used as collateral, whereas nonstatutory rights may not possess these qualities.
- The most legally and commercially significant nonregistered intellectual property right is copyright, a broad term that encompasses many different types of right. Some unregistered designs are also accorded protection.
- Rights involving confidential information and trade secrets are generally recognized, although the manner in which the law protects them may differ substantially between different jurisdictions.
- Unregistered rights in trade names and get-up, variously protected by laws of unfair competition and passing-off, serve to reinforce the registered protection provided by trademark and registered design law.

INTRODUCTION

While patents, trademarks, and some other intellectual property rights require registration following a process of application and examination or deposit, other rights (such as copyright or some design rights) automatically come into being either when a work is created or as a consequence of a relationship. Examples of the latter are the rights in confidential information that arise from the relationship of a person who communicates information to a specific person or persons, and rights in the goodwill in a trading name that result from the relationship between a trader and his customers.

Nonregistered intellectual property rights are just as important as registered rights. Examples of extremely valuable nonregistered rights include J. K. Rowling's copyright in the *Harry Potter* books and the formula for the Coca-Cola syrup. Both nonregistered and registered rights may exist together in the same object, whether serially or simultaneously. Thus an invention, which is vulnerable until the patent right is granted, is protected as a trade secret until it is disclosed to the public. Equally, a computer program that satisfies the appropriate criteria for patentability is also protected by copyright.

PROBLEMS ARISING FROM NONREGISTERED RIGHTS

Without registration, it is not easy to identify the rights holder of, in particular, a copyright work. It is dangerous to rely on information contained in a copyright notice in a published work or on a web page, since title to the copyright may have passed on more than once since the notice was originally published. Often a work is considered to be an "orphan work" if the author or copyright owner cannot be identified or traced at all. Some businesses are prepared to take the risk of using an orphan work without permission on the assumption that, if no author or copyright owner can be found, that use will remain undetected.

For practical reasons, it is not possible to provide a registration system for confidential information and technical know-how. A licensee of the use of such information may therefore unwittingly be paying for the right to use information that is already available in the public domain and which, with effort, the licensee could have found and used without payment. The party possessing such information will be reluctant to warrant its secret nature since it too has no means of verifying whether this is so.

As for trade dress (the visual appearance of a product), trade names, and logos, internet search engines have now facilitated identification of their existence and the extent and geographical scope of their use. Instances of accidental use of a trade name or trade dress that closely resembles that of a competitor have therefore fallen sharply. The same applies to unregistered designs of products whose shape is distinctive.

NONREGISTERED RIGHTS AS PROPERTY

Although details vary between different countries, copyright, database rights, and designs are generally protected by statute that specifically accords them the status of property that can be assigned, licensed, mortgaged, or left to someone in a will or on death. Rights in respect of confidential information, know-how, trade dress, get-up and the like are generally said to be *in personam*. This means that those rights can only be enforced against others when they are infringed in certain circumstances, but they do not constitute property as such. Commercial practice in most countries, however, is to treat the latter category of rights as though they were property when assigning them (whether together with the business from which they originated or separately).

Because of its variety and longevity, copyright in a single work may be simultaneously the subject of many separate property transactions. For example, the right to publish a work of fiction in book form may be assigned to A for 20 years, the right to serialize it in a newspaper may be exclusively licensed to B for six months, and the right to reproduce it in cartoon form for the full copyright term may be nonexclusively licensed to D. An option to purchase the movie rights, exercisable for 10 years, may be bought by E, and the right to produce a computer game based on it may be pledged to F as collateral for a loan which enables the copyright owner to pay for its translation into French so that it may be published in that language by G for 50 years. Since assigned rights may themselves be disposed of by the assignee, and many licenses permit the grant of sublicenses, a party that is not aware of all these transactions may struggle to establish precisely who controls which rights to a given work.

In principle, the owner of copyright, database right, or design right is the party that initially creates it. Rules which vary from country to country regulate issues relating to ownership where the creator is employed by another or is commissioned by another as an independent contractor.

"In a human capital-intensive environment, all you bring to the table is your own intellectual property. You will not share this precious resource with others unless you trust them to reciprocate." Francis Fukuyama

  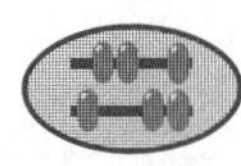   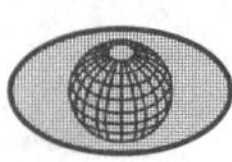   

COPYRIGHT, DATABASE RIGHT, AND UNREGISTERED DESIGNS

In general, copyright extends to original literary, dramatic, artistic, and musical works and movies, sound recordings, broadcasts, and transmissions, but there may be substantial national variations. Thus, some countries' copyright laws protect original perfumes, while others protect new published editions of old works and the first publication of a hitherto-unpublished work after expiry of the normal copyright term. The term of protection for original authors' works generally contains a substantial *post-mortem* element, while media that contain or transmit works are protected for a shorter, fixed period. Complex rules relate to normally unauthorized uses of others' works that are permitted for news reporting, criticism and review, freedom of speech, and, in some jurisdictions, transformative use that results in the creation of a substantially new work.

Where a copyright work is created by an identifiable human author, that author may be entitled to exercise moral rights in addition to normal commercial rights. Moral rights may include the right to be known as the author, the right to object to pejorative alterations, the right to decide when the work is finished, and the right to withdraw it from circulation. In addition, in some countries a nonauthor has a corresponding right not to be falsely identified as author. These rights may be commercially insignificant, but if ignored can add delay, expense, and ill-will to any commercialization of an affected work.

Database right protects compilations of data where there has been substantial investment in their creation or acquisition but that fail to satisfy the criterion of originality for copyright in an author's work. This 15-year right is provided in the national law of each European Union member state but has not yet been accepted as an international norm.

Many countries protect original or novel designs under an unregistered design right, either in place of or in addition to a regime for registration of designs. In the European Union, the harmonized national unregistered design right provides protection for three years—usually sufficient to assist a product based on a novel design concept at the earliest stages of its marketing.

RIGHTS IN CONFIDENTIAL INFORMATION AND KNOW-HOW

Depending on the jurisdiction, confidential information is generally protected by principles of civil law or by equitable rules that govern unreasonable conduct. Where the relationship of confidentiality between discloser and disclosee is contractual (as in the case of the licensing of trade secrets or technical know-how), the nature and extent of protection against wrongful use or disclosure are governed by the terms of the contract. If the confidentiality relates to personal rather than technical or commercial information, a further level of protection may be imposed by obligations to protect personal privacy under the Universal Declaration of Human Rights, the European Convention on Human Rights, or under local laws.

Where the confidentiality of information is lost through a wrongful act, the accused party may face both a claim for damages and an injunction to prevent it obtaining advantage from the fact that the information is no longer secret.

RIGHTS IN COMMERCIAL GET-UP, TRADE NAMES, AND THE LIKE

Even where no trademark right is registered, any sign, emblem, or get-up identified with one trader may not be used by another with a view to diverting custom. This is achieved by rules relating to unfair competition, or passing-off, or by statutes that prohibit specific unfair marketing practices. To invoke this protection, injured parties must generally prove that the allegedly infringing item is associated with them by their customers. Such evidence can be expensive to obtain and, where obtained by survey evidence, may be rejected as methodologically flawed.

Although this relief is invoked with decreasing frequency as the scope of registrability of trademarks widens, it remains important. It may be the only relief where, for example, the plaintiff's trade name or get-up is not registrable as a trademark, or where the activity objected to does not fall within the legal definition of trademark infringement but nonetheless interferes with the plaintiff's trade.

▸▸ HYPOTHETICAL CASE STUDY

Fancy-Fry

Calorie Corporation develops a fast-food concept that it wishes to develop as a business format franchise. Following confidential discussions with external consultants and key officers, the corporation creates a manual containing descriptions of the various concepts that will comprise the new franchise, together with sketches and guidance on operating, reordering stock, accounting, and advertising. Each element of the manual is protected by copyright as well as by confidentiality.

Calorie next produces a model for the restaurant, including furniture and design concepts, which it trials at a nearby location. Now the existence of the restaurant becomes public knowledge, though the contents of the manual do not. Members of the public give their reactions, which are favorable, to the ambience and décor, which, collectively, constitute the restaurant's get-up. The name Fancy-Fry is chosen for the concept. This cannot initially be registered as a trademark since it is descriptive of the restaurant's fare. However, the name catches on and generates goodwill among local diners.

A disgruntled ex-employee surreptitiously obtains a copy of the format manual, which he photocopies and returns. Using it, he opens up the Fancy-Free restaurant across the street from Fancy-Fry. The ambience and get-up of the two restaurants cause diners to assume that they belong to the same franchise.

Calorie can sue for injury to its confidential information, infringement of its unregistered trademark and its copyright, for misappropriation of its trade dress, and can force Fancy-Free to change or close—all without the assistance of any registered intellectual property rights.

▸▸ MORE INFO

Books:

Derclaye, Estelle. *The Legal Protection of Databases: A Comparative Analysis*. Cheltenham, UK: Edward Elgar Publishing, 2008.

Milgrim, Roger M. *Milgrim on Trade Secrets*. New York: Matthew Bender, 1967. Current copies looseleaf to order with additions and revisions.

Wadlow, Christopher. *The Law of Passing Off: Unfair Competition by Misrepresentation*. 3rd ed. London: Sweet & Maxwell, 2004.

Website:

The IPKat weblog: www.ipkat.com

"Owning the intellectual property is like owning land: You need to keep investing in it again and again to get a payoff; you can't simply sit back and collect rent." Esther Dyson

  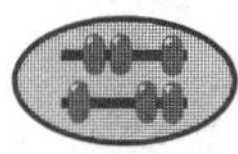   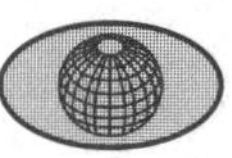   

Protecting Your Intellectual Property—Registered Rights by Jeremy Phillips

EXECUTIVE SUMMARY

- There are many types of intellectual property right, only some of which are registrable; those that are registrable have little in common other than their registrability.
- Registration of intellectual property rights provides objective and verifiable legal protection against competitors.
- Registration provides national or regional protection and can be costly, requiring careful budgeting.
- Failure to register a transaction involving an intellectual property right may have adverse legal consequences for the beneficiary of the transaction.
- Once registered, an intellectual property right is presumed to be valid until the contrary is established, thus providing a powerful strategic weapon for controlling a market.
- Registered intellectual property rights may be expensive to maintain, incurring renewal fees and, in some cases, regular policing against unauthorized use.

INTRODUCTION

Although some intellectual property rights come into existence on the creation of their subject matter, most intellectual property rights are not recognized by law until a process of registration is completed. Patents for inventions, trademarks, and some types of design are generally subject to registration systems.

Patents protect inventions that are new, nonobvious, and industrially applicable. Trademarks protect words, names, logos, product packaging, and shapes, among other things, that enable the consumer to distinguish the goods or services of one business from those of another. Designs protect the aesthetic and not totally functional elements of the shapes of manufactured products.

Registration of each of these rights enables others to ascertain: the nature of the right protected; legal entitlements of owners and users of the right; and information from which the expiry date of that right can be calculated.

Registration is not synonymous with examination: It may follow a rigorous, often interactive application procedure over a period of months or years—this is usually the case for patents and trademarks—or it may only require a deposit, as in the case of some designs.

REGISTRATION AND CERTIFICATION

Proof of registration of any interest in an intellectual property right is necessary if that interest is invoked in litigation. In patent and trademark infringement proceedings, for example, a court will accept a certificate of entitlement to that right as evidence. Registration helps a prospective licensee of a right to identify who must be approached for a license request. When a business is acquired, registration enables a due diligence search to find out which of the assets used by the target business are owned by it. Where the information recorded on the register does not accord with reality, it may be necessary to seek rectification of the register, a process that may be both slow and costly.

In some circumstances the state of the register will not accord with reality because of the length of time taken by the registry in question to record an assignment or license. Sometimes the information on the register may be up to two years out of date, or more. Local practitioners should be able to advise, in any given jurisdiction, on the state of the register.

INTERNATIONAL, REGIONAL AND NATIONAL REGISTRATION

With some exceptions, patents, trademarks, and designs are rights granted under national law; the scope of their exercise is thus coextensive with national borders. The owner of the rights must therefore factor into any business plan the identity and number of countries in which protection of the registered right is needed. More than 200 countries provide some form of intellectual property protection, but the cost of obtaining registration in each of them is often prohibitive for even the wealthiest corporations (the cost of truly international patent protection can easily exceed US$2 million, and many new products and processes incorporate several separate patentable concepts). Therefore, proprietors have to balance the cost of formalities in protecting the right against the potential value of exploiting that right in a particular country. In all cases, the intellectual property owner incurs official fees as well as those of local professional representatives. In the case of patents, further expense is incurred in searches of the patent records and technical literature to see whether an invention has been anticipated by an earlier patent, and by the cost of translating the patent into the language of each country in which protection is sought (this may exceed 85% of the total cost). For trademarks, additional expense is incurred in finding out whether the mark to be registered would be likely to cause confusion to consumers or damage an earlier mark.

The World Intellectual Property Organization (WIPO) administers facilitative systems that enable an applicant to seek registration of a patent, trademark, or design in a multiplicity of countries through a single application that is processed by WIPO and then forwarded to the granting office of each target country. These schemes (the Patent Cooperation Treaty, the Madrid System for trademarks, and the Hague scheme for designs) reduce the cost and bureaucracy of international protection but do not remove the obstacles to registration that exist at national level.

Not all registered rights are limited by national borders. As an alternative to national registration, the European Union has introduced pan-European trademark and design rights that confer protection via a single registration throughout the 27 EU member states, and the African Intellectual Property Organization offers a single patent that covers 16 francophone African nations. The European Union does not yet have a pan-European patent; the European Patent Office, which processes and examines patent applications for up to 35 European countries, is not an organ of the European Union.

CONSEQUENCES OF FAILURE TO REGISTER AN INTEREST

The initial grant of a patent, trademark, or design is automatically recorded on the register. Subsequent transactions involving these rights require registration in most countries, and this requires action on the part of the party that acquires the right or gains permission to use it.

Where registration is not effected, the purchaser of a registered right may not be able to assert its entitlement against a later

"Owning the intellectual property is like owning land: You need to keep investing in it again and again to get a payoff; you can't simply sit back and collect rent." Esther Dyson

     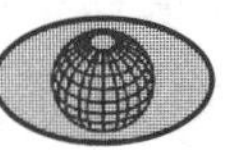   

purchaser of the same right from the same seller. The holder of a nonregistered right may also be penalized when suing an infringer, either through a prohibition on the recovery of damages or through a bar on the recovery of legal costs.

STRATEGIC VALUE OF A REGISTERED RIGHT

Once an intellectual property right is registered, its strategic value to the proprietor is enormous. Because a certificate of registration is presumptive evidence of the validity of the registered right, a court will take the validity of an asserted right at face value in proceedings for its enforcement. This is particularly valuable where the proprietor of the right seeks interim relief against an allegedly infringing act, such as the manufacture, importation, or sale of an infringing product, by having that activity stopped until a full trial can take place, often more than a year later. Even if a patent is later held to be invalid, the fact that it is presumed valid until the contrary is proved can block a competitor from entering the market for the patented product for long enough to force the competitor to abandon its plans altogether. Although the patent term may for up to 20 years, most patents do not remain in force for more than half that period. Since their commercial currency may be short, even a short period of interim relief may be crucial.

The law does provide checks and balances against abuse of the power wielded by the intellectual property right's owner. For example, where an interim order prevents a competitor from performing an act which, following the full trial, turns out never to have infringed the right, the competitor may be entitled to receive compensation. Many jurisdictions also provide that the making of an unwarranted threat to commence infringement proceedings is itself a civil wrong. In most developed and developing economies, competition and antitrust rules prevent uses of intellectual property rights that are deemed to be an abuse of their proprietor's dominant position or a means of distorting the normal operation of a competitive market.

MAINTENANCE OF A REGISTERED RIGHT

Although details vary across the jurisdictions, most registered rights incur renewal fees which, if not paid, result in the lapse of the right. Some countries provide for late renewal or even the resuscitation of lapsed rights on payment of the appropriate fee, so it is prudent for any business that does not have its own in-house intellectual property administration to outsource its renewals to a specialist in the field.

Trademarks in most countries run for a 10-year period that is renewable indefinitely so long as the renewal fee is paid. In some jurisdictions, renewal is contingent on proof of use of the trademark, so the proprietor should make sure that samples proving use of the trademark in the form in which it is registered, and for the goods or services for which it is registered, are preserved. In many countries, nonuse of a registered mark for a continuous period, usually three or five years, will expose it to the risk of revocation for nonuse.

The registration of a trademark is vulnerable to "genericity," when, by virtue of the use made of the trademark by competitors or by consumers, the mark has ceased to function as a means of distinguishing the goods of one business from another and has become the name of a product itself. Trademarks such as Aspirin, Caterpillar, Hoover, Thermos, and Walkman have at times been threatened by their own popularity—in some cases losing registration in certain jurisdictions while preserving it in others.

HYPOTHETICAL CASY STUDY

Nimboshave

Nimbo Corporation devised a three-in-one product, being a combination bottle opener, corkscrew, and electric razor. Following consultation with its patent lawyer, the corporation was advised that the product as a whole was not patentable, being a combination of known parts each of which performed its normal function. However, the process of affixing the bottle opener to the outer casing of the electric shaver involved a novel technical solution that was patentable. Nimbo decided to apply for patent protection in jurisdictions in which electric razors were made or widely used but not to seek patent protection in jurisdictions in which males favored the growth of beards or those in which the consumption of alcohol was illegal.

The casing of the electric razor had to be shaped to accommodate the fixture of the corkscrew when it was not in use and to provide a comfortable grip for the corkscrew when opening bottles. This shape was not merely functional but possessed a substantial aesthetic appeal, on the basis of which it appeared to be registrable as a design in certain markets. Initially, Nimbo did not consider it worth registering a design right, but it later discovered that the cost of design registration was very small and that the nuisance effect of design registration might deter prospective competitors.

Nimbo Corporation elected to brand the product as "Nimboshave." A search of the Bulgarian register revealed that another company already held an earlier registration of the word mark Nimboshave for a conventional wet-shave apparatus. Suspecting that Nimboshave had not been used for a continuous period of more than five years, Nimbo proposed to apply to have the mark revoked to clear the way for registration of its own mark. The proprietor of the earlier mark proposed to resist this application. After a brief negotiation, Nimbo agreed not to challenge the earlier mark, took an exclusive license to use Nimboshave in Bulgaria for a trivial royalty, registered its interest as exclusive licensee of that mark, and then imported and sold Nimboshave products there.

▸▸ MORE INFO

Books:

Bently, Lionel, and Brad Sherman. *Intellectual Property Law*. 3rd ed. Oxford: Oxford University Press, 2008.

Chisum, Donald. *Chisum on Patents*. New York: Matthew Bender, no date. 27 volumes, looseleaf, updated with revisions.

McCarthy, J. Thomas. *McCarthy on Trademarks and Unfair Competition*. 4th ed. New York: West Publishing, 1998–2008. Binder/looseleaf.

Websites:

United States Patent and Trademark Office: www.uspto.gov

World Intellectual Property Organization (WIPO): www.wipo.int

See Also:

★ Protecting Your Intellectual Property—Nonregistered Rights (pp. 495–496)

✔ Intellectual Property—Registered Designs and Trademarks (p. 990)

C. K. Prahalad (p. 1183)

"**Both Apple and Pixar. . .Their product is pure intellectual property. Bits on a disk.**" Steve Jobs

  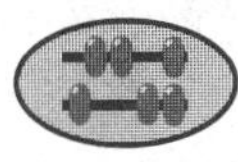   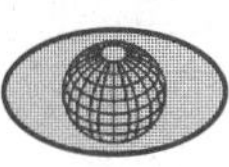   

Reducing Costs and Improving Efficiency by Outsourcing and Selecting Suppliers

by Paul Davies

EXECUTIVE SUMMARY

- Start outsourcing by constructing the exit clause; this will tell you and your outsource partner what you are focused on and will save you time and expense if things go wrong.
- Focus on the downsides first and understand the management changes required, the communication strategy, the training needs, and your regular engagement with the outsourcer.
- Outsourcing is a process, not an event. What and how you outsource will change over time.
- Outsource chore and focus on core. Keep value creation for your clients in-house.
- In general, outsource a process as is. Let your outsource partner reengineer processes.
- Do not manage your outsource partner; rather, monitor, review, and reassess.
- Choose a partner, not a supplier—one that you can work with through good and difficult times.
- The lowest-priced outsourcer will usually be the most expensive in the long term.
- Outsourcing can not only save money and increase efficiency, but can also rejuvenate your business by refocusing your attention on what makes you great.

INTRODUCTION

As a tool for the CFO, outsourcing has an important role to play in reducing costs and improving efficiency. It is important, however, to bear in mind that in addition to the direct and indirect benefits of outsourcing, there are also direct and indirect disadvantages. Outsourcing isn't the answer on its own, and it has to be part of a holistic analysis to be successful.

START WITH THE EXIT CLAUSE

Without putting a damper on the idea, whenever you contemplate outsourcing always consider how you will exit. This may seem curious, but over the years I have found it to be absolutely essential. If outsourcing does not deliver what you expected, if your strategy changes, if the outsource partner decides on a different business model, or if the whole market turns in a different direction—all of which can happen—you need to be able to regain control of what is often a vital, if not mission-critical, process. In such circumstances, you will need to be able to take it back yourself or pass it to another outsourcing company.

Think carefully about this because what you take back won't be what you outsourced. There may well be new IT systems being used, and certainly the processes won't be as you left them. If you haven't an exit agreement, working out who owns the intellectual property underlying the new processes is very difficult and is just one example of the problems that can occur.

The moment to decide how you want to be able to exit is before it becomes a necessity and, preferably, when you are negotiating the contract. If this sounds obvious, many companies fail to do so and suffer as a result.

Understanding your exit strategy will also tell you a great deal about what you want from the outsourcing process. You may be rightly seduced by the idea of not having to spend management time on human resource back-office processing, or by the advantages of not having to worry about expense account processing. If at this same moment you think rationally about what would prompt you to exit from the contract, you will understand most clearly what your business drivers for outsourcing are. If, for example, you put in the exit clause that you have the power to terminate if the proposed savings are not realized, you know what your real objective is. It may be that you insist on a range of triggers and if, for example, you focus on service levels and your end clients' satisfaction with your overall service, you have the same knowledge about your objectives and, more importantly, so does the outsource provider.

In short, brainstorm why you might want to get out of the contract—preferably together with the company that you intend to outsource to—and you will find that not only do you have the comfort of being able to get out of the contract effectively, but that you are also much less likely to have to do so. You will have a much better sense of the advantages and disadvantages of working with your outsourcing partner—and that company will better understand you.

DISADVANTAGES AS A POINTER TO THE BENEFITS

Let us continue by considering the disadvantages of outsourcing, and, by doing so—paradoxically perhaps—you will better understand what you have to do to be successful. You will discover, despite your efforts to communicate, that your current employees do not fully understand why you are taking the outsourcing route. They will probably be fearful that their roles are next, and this can harm performance. In addition, you will lose the sense of immediate control that you had and, instead of going down to the relevant office, you have to go through a process to achieve something that was very simple. You may find that your outsource partner doesn't give you the service you thought you were buying and, without proper review processes, correcting this can waste time and effort. You may find that the insights that cross-departmental meetings and discussions bring are no longer informed by the different perspective that the outsourced department brought. Some of the drawbacks will be relatively obvious, but others will come into your perspective just at the wrong moment, such as when you can't make sense of some information just prior to a board meeting.

These disadvantages point up how your approach to outsourcing must be holistic and built on solid communications.

One area that nearly always gets less attention than it needs is training. It is a significant extra cost that rarely makes itself known until after the deal is signed off. Typically, you will focus on the training of the staff of the outsourcing company, only to discover that your own people have largely been ignored. There will have been a communication to your existing staff about what is going on, but very little to show them how to get, for example, HR support now that it has been outsourced beyond a telephone number.

To get the best out of the new arrangements, you have to train your staff how to

"Think carefully about how you will exit because what you take back won't be what you outsourced."

  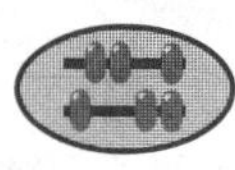   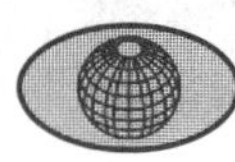   

Figure 1. Reasons for outsourcing—CFOs' responses. (*Source*: Computerworld and InterUnity Group, Inc.)

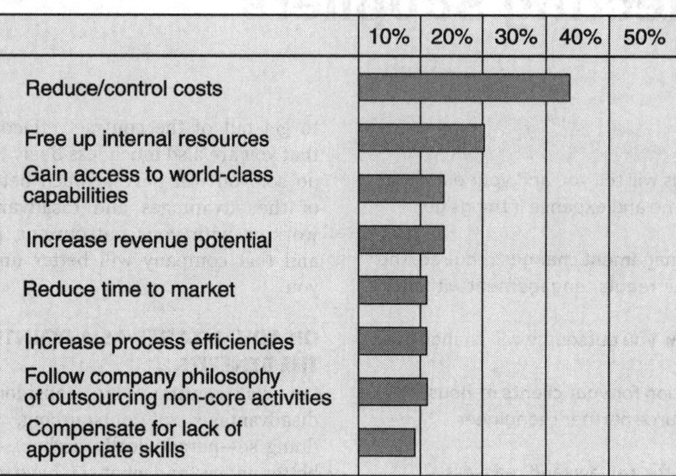

deal with accounts payable now that it is remote. Your managers have to move beyond control and micromanagement into monitoring. That can be very difficult to achieve.

You will have noted the focus on communication—and this, as in any serious business reengineering, has to be well thought through and effective. The best way to achieve this is to ensure that there is a feedback mechanism both on the information and the quality of the way it is presented, not to say its timeliness.

OUTSOURCING IS A PROCESS

Outsourcing is often presented as an event that you get right once. When you find that the service isn't delivering what you thought you were paying for, you will be grateful that you included in the review mechanisms not just a focus on whether the service level agreement (SLA) has been met, but a real, hard look at the SLA itself. Your review process, including market testing on a periodic basis, is more important and should be given more attention than you may at first imagine.

If you have a clear-eyed perspective on the downsides, it will help you appreciate the benefits of outsourcing. If you have outsourced a process to your outsourcing partner, the amount of management time devoted to that process can be reduced—and refocused. You can devote the time you spent agonizing over the process to instead considering the outputs and, more importantly, the outcomes. That is probably the greatest benefit of outsourcing, but you will have to train yourself and your organization to get there.

CORE AND CHORE

Choose carefully what you outsource. Think of core and chore. Ask yourself what the focus of your business is, what gives you competitive edge, and what gives you your unique qualities. Anything fitting that description is core to you—and should only be considered for outsourcing as a last resort.

Another way of deciding whether a process or processes can be outsourced is to ask yourself how close the process is to value creation; that is, how essential it is to your relationship with your customers. To appreciate the distinction, look at the difference between sales, which is generally very customer-focused and vital to your value proposition, and marketing, which is equally focused on your customers, but at one stage removed from value creation. You may well, for example, already use a marketing agency, which is a form of outsourcing, and you may use a logistics company to fulfill your orders. They both touch your customers, but what they do doesn't have the immediate effect of a salesperson.

That is not to say that sales cannot be outsourced, and I have seen very successful franchise arrangements, again a form of outsourcing. You just have to be pretty sure that the real value in your goods and services isn't affected by outsourcing sales.

There is a strong line of research that says that outsourcing your core business processes can be very detrimental to your business. You should analyze this carefully, with particular attention to concerns such as impacts on customer satisfaction.

Chore, on the other hand, includes all processes that make precious little difference to your effectiveness in the marketplace. By outsourcing them to a specialist company you gain from economies of scale, as the outsource company will provide the service to more than one company. To you, saving 30 seconds on processing an expense claim is probably neither here nor there. To an outsourcing company, it can mean the difference between profit and loss, with savings also passed to you.

What you will find over time is that you are presented with an incredible, shrinking core. What you initially regarded as a

CASE STUDY

A property management company wanted to expand, but also wished to minimize disruption and stay in the same offices. Through our discovery phase, we identified that by outsourcing some of the chore—rent collection, invoicing, accounting—not only could they do that and save money, but they could release their experienced staff to address higher-value business opportunities. These included, for example, identifying additional properties, working more closely with their clients, and increasing the range of services.

We achieved these major aims—and reduced the cost per property managed. Over a relatively short period, what was outsourced expanded to include insurance policy processing, legal secretarial work, and, as the property development side of the business came into the picture, land development applications. From the company's retail interests, the back-office processing of accounts receivable and accounts payable was brought into the contract.

The key was the relationship between the property company and the outsourcer—and the trust that was built up—so that either side could suggest further areas for outsourcing.

Finally—and this might be an interesting challenge for CFOs—the company's CFO realized that his function, as currently understood, had almost entirely been taken over. He was faced with a dilemma. His alternative, however, was to take a more strategic role, which was what the company wanted, and he was persuaded to view the role differently and become the strategic planner rather than a deliverer of information.

"Typically, you will focus on the training of the staff of the outsourcing company, only to discover that your own people have largely been ignored."

  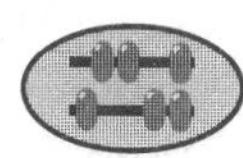   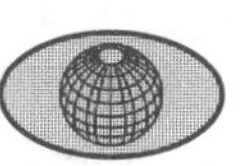   

fundamental element in your value proposition can be broken down into smaller processes, and those from which you are not directly gaining value can be outsourced. In the IT world, for example, it is normal for programming to be outsourced. The work of system specification remained in-house, until it was realized that value creation resides in the business analysis that underpinned the specification. In turn, the business analysis was really only a service, parts of which could be outsourced, as the real value lay in understanding the client and the client's business model. It should be no surprise, then, that in the IT world major corporations keep only two things in-house: sales and strategy.

You may not choose that route for your business—and imagine the exit strategy needed if you ever brought it all back in-house. But part of your internal debate once you have started outsourcing processes has to be focused on what is next, and if there is nothing else that you want to consider outsourcing, why not?

AS IS OR REENGINEER FIRST?

Consider next the major stumbling block to decisions on outsourcing. Most internal debates, once you are persuaded that outsourcing will achieve cost savings and efficiency gains, focus on whether you should outsource your processes as is, or whether you should reengineer them first. There is no absolutely right answer, but in practice allowing a fresh pair of eyes to reengineer your processes usually produces immediate benefits. Just ensure that the contract allows you to share in your outsourcing partner's gains! The real message is that you shouldn't allow such debates to delay any decisions on outsourcing. So the best course usually is to outsource as is. You didn't reengineer your cleaning or your security before you outsourced them, and yet your outsourcing partner will have done so and provided a better service.

Choosing a company with which to outsource your processes is clearly a major decision. You should be looking for a partner. While you may think that outsourcing your cleaning will not require a solid partnership, devoting time to working with your outsourcer—in HR processes, in accounts payable and receivable, in expenses administration, in property management—is essential. If there is one rule about outsourcing, it is that you should not outsource and forget. Outsource and review; outsource and monitor; outsource and work with your outsource provider as a partner, exploring what should be outsourced next, what should come back in house, and what is needed to be even more successful.

If you do that, it becomes obvious that you need to select a company to take on your processes that you can work with as a partner, taking formal time to meet and review regularly. Selecting such a company relies on matching your company's culture, sharing an explicit set of values, and relying on their integrity and honesty. You need a company that you can say no to and one that you can discuss your exit requirements with when there is no intention of doing anything but signing the contract.

This is a challenge to your procurement department—but one that will pay real dividends. The short-term lowest price is always the most expensive route in outsourcing, because a low-price provider will usually be one that hasn't built in the time required to continually partner with you or find new and better ways to serve you more efficiently.

REJUVENATION

Outsourcing can, as one of our clients said to us, rejuvenate your business, reduce your costs, and increase your efficiency—and remind you why you are in business.

▸▸ MAKING IT HAPPEN

- Understand your exit issues and strategy.
- Identify core, and only outsource chore.
- Don't manage your outsourcer—monitor.
- Have formal and regular reviews of SLAs as well as assessing performance against them.
- Don't outsource and forget.
- Outsource and create added value.
- Work in partnership with your outsource supplier.
- Understand the training requirements in full.
- Communicate—before, during, and after—with every stakeholder, and evaluate how well your communication strategy is working.

▸▸ MORE INFO

Books:

Benn, I., and J. Pearcy. *Strategic Outsourcing: Exploiting the Skills of Third Parties*. London: Management Consultancies Association, 2002.

Halvey, J. K., and B. M. Melby. *Business Process Outsourcing: Process, Strategies, and Contracts*. Hoboken, NJ: Wiley, 2000.

Reports:

Syntel on service level agreements: "The keys to successful service level agreements: Effectively meeting enterprise demands." Online at: www.syntelinc.com/uploadedFiles/Syntel_SLA(1).pdf

Whitaker, Jonathan, Mayuram S. Krishnan, and Claes Fornell. "Does offshoring impact customer satisfaction?" May 2008. Online at: papers.ssrn.com/sol3/papers.cfm?abstract_id=1010457

(See also Wharton Business School for incisive research into outsourcing, including: "Globalization and Outsourcing: Integration with India and China." April 2007. Online at: www.wharton.upenn.edu/alumni/wharton125/events/finale/panels.cfm?panel=panels%5Cday1%5Csession1%5Cpanel5.xml)

Websites:

National Association of Software and Services Companies, India: www.nasscom.in

National Outsourcing Organisation, UK: www.noa.co.uk

Outsourcing Institute, USA: www.outsourcing.com

The Wharton Business School has incisive research into outsourcing. Search on "outsourcing" at: www.wharton.upenn.edu

See Also:

Cost and Effect: Using Integrated Cost Systems to Drive Profitability and Performance (p. 1244)

"You will gain from focused expertise on something that you do as part of your operations but at which they work hard to achieve greater efficiency."

  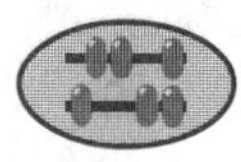 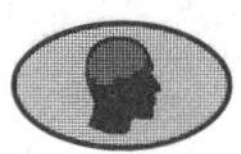  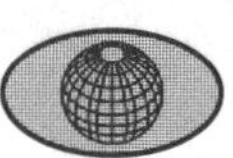 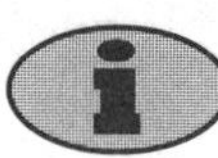  

Reducing Costs through Change Management by Beverly Goldberg

EXECUTIVE SUMMARY

- When senior management decides to move a business in new directions or adopt new methods, processes, and/or technologies in order to remain competitive, it must work to prepare its employees for the changes that will take place as a result.
- Making formal change management programs a part of the process of change from its inception is necessary to ease employees' uncertainty and anxiety about the effects of the coming changes in their jobs. This can create resistance to change, slowing or even derailing the adoption of what is new.
- The board and CEO must make it clear to everyone in the company that they fully support the planned changes, explaining the danger that the business will face if it does not change.
- The CFO must ensure that change management programs are part of the financial planning for every new process and/or technology that a business intends to adopt, which requires recognizing the time change management programs take and the personnel needed to implement such programs, including staff from various departments such as public relations and human resources as well as outside consultants.

INTRODUCTION

Today, globalization, technological advances, scientific developments, and new business theories and processes are forcing businesses to make changes over and over again, often introducing yet another change before the last round undertaken has been implemented. The changes that must be made to ensure success in so highly charged a business environment requires changes in the work that people do, the way they do it, the environment they work in, and/or the skill sets they have. Unfortunately, change often meets resistance because it threatens the security and comfort of employees at all levels and in all areas of the business. Senior management must take responsibility for seeing to it that this natural resistance to change is planned for and that programs are put in place to overcome it before it can delay or even derail the new direction the business is taking.

> "The CFO is responsible for making certain that plans for managing change and the costs of doing so are included in proposed budgets for implementing new processes and new technologies."

Change management may be described as a process for opening an enterprise's culture to new ways, gaining individual employee buy-in, and training employees to be a part of the new and better enterprise. If management fails to anticipate the need for change management, projects will inevitably cost more than anticipated—or fail. The CFO is responsible for making certain that plans for managing change and the costs of doing so are included in proposed budgets for implementing new processes and new technologies. By reducing resistance to what is new from the start, costly delays in implementation can be avoided and projects are far more likely to be finished on time and on budget.

CHANGE MANAGEMENT HAS CHANGED

In the past, change management theory involved three stages:[1]

- first, unfreezing the current culture by making people understand that there would be a new way of doing things and that management was behind the change and would brook no arguments about it;
- second, introducing what was new and providing training and education to open employees to the new processes and/or technologies;
- third, refreezing the culture once the change was made.

Now that change seems to come about every twenty days rather than every twenty years, a different approach is necessary.

Although the first step in successfully implementing change remains explaining to employees that the organization is changing and senior management wholeheartedly endorses and supports the changes being made, it also requires:

- providing people with information about the new ways of doing things;
- convincing them of the validity of the new approach;
- showing them the personal as well as corporate benefits that the change will bring.

The second stage begins when employees are brought to understand that in order to gain a competitive advantage or keep abreast of competitors, the company has to adopt new processes and new technologies. They also are shown that if they do not learn new ways to work, they will join the ranks of the unskilled. Putting those two facts together, they are helped to realize that if the company they work for suffers because it cannot produce as quickly and inexpensively as its competitors, they will be in the uncomfortable position of seeking employment without having the skill sets that are becoming the standard in their industry.

Then, breaking with the classic idea of refreezing the culture as a final stage, the culture is moved to a dynamic stage where people become comfortable with the new machines, processes, and/or technologies but await—and even anticipate—the next changes that will be made. In other words, openness to change and anticipating change become the organizational mindset, thus lowering the costs and time involved in subsequent changes.

COMMUNICATION: THE KEY TO CHANGE MANAGEMENT SUCCESS

Successful change management programs involve intensive communication efforts. Internal company media are used to present the determination of senior management to make the changes and explain its reasons for doing so in terms of long-term profitability. Frequent meetings are used to:

- discuss similar moves being made by competitors;
- explain the training that will be provided;
- convey to employees their roles in the newly shaped organization.

By helping employees understand what is happening early on, frequent communications prevent the anxiety created by rumor and speculation that may lead a company's most valuable employees to leave, exactly the ones who are likely to learn the new system or process most easily. By communicating the news that change is taking place, explaining the nature of the process,

"Nothing endures but change." Heraclitus

     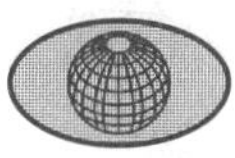   

assuring employees that training in the new skills will be available, and that those skills are leading edge, potential problems can be eliminated.

Effective communication efforts can:[2]

1 Stop rumors from creating turmoil by easing anxiety and quelling speculation, both of which reduce productivity and create groups determined to band together to foil change.
2 Make employees aware of what is happening in the outside world so that they understand that the company will become less competitive unless the planned changes are made.
3 Help employees to understand what will be going on, making it easier for them to adjust to the requirement of the new reality.

> "When evaluating the proposed budgets of programs that will bring change, CFOs must raise the issue of the need for change management from the outset, the point at which such programs will be most effective in lowering the total costs of a project."

4 Convey management's commitment to the planned change by explaining that what is going to happen is part of the business's new mission, perhaps in the form of a specific *mission statement* for the team most involved in the change (the mission statement should be presented as equivalent to a constitution that can neither be overthrown nor rewritten).
5 Assure employees that training will be available when they need it and explain that such training reflects the organization's commitment to *continuous learning*.
6 Achieve buy-in at all levels of the organization, which is critical because experience shows that top-level acceptance of change is not enough.
7 Develop *change agents* from those employees who demonstrate an eagerness to try new things. (When embarking on a specific change, be certain to select at least a few such employees to take part, even if they may not have been your first choice based on seniority or skill sets.)
8 Break down the barriers between employees. *Cross-functional relationships* are necessary to realize the benefits of the new technologies and processes, because these usually require employees from different functional areas to work together.
9 Ensure that the change management program builds flexibility into the organization's culture by continually reminding everyone, once the change has been made, of the successes achieved and keeping them abreast of other changes on the horizon in their industry.

CONCLUSION

Most people are comfortable with the way things are and tend to resist change because they fear the unknown. As a result, when businesses decide to adopt new methods, processes, and/or technologies, a variety of problems tend to emerge, ranging from rumors of staff cuts that result in the loss of the best employees to other organizations, to employees who fail to engage fully in or try to sabotage training programs slowing the implementation of the change. Unfortunately, management too often fails to anticipate these problems until the change they are trying to make runs into some of these obstacles to success. At that point, a decision is made to set up formal

CASE STUDY

A Major US University Press

A major university press in the United States renowned for its books on art also publishes many scholarly books in other fields. It has long been known for the beautiful interior design and covers of all its books, even those on arcane subjects that were projected to sell as few as six hundred copies. Because of recent budget constraints imposed as a result of cuts in financial support from the university, the head of the press decided that books that were not about art or that did not involve numerous illustrations (such as books about philosophy) would in the future be produced by desktop typesetting in order to reduce costs. Knowing that this decision would be resisted by many of the press's long-time employees, he brought in a change management team to help ease the transition to the more cost-effective system.

The change management team began by having the director of the press and the CFO meet with senior managers to explain the need for budget cuts and the scope of the financial losses incurred by many of the books they published. The presentation to the managers included projections of how many fewer books they would be able to publish in the future if the current production methods were not changed. The managers realized that publishing fewer titles would result in a need for fewer employees. Included in the materials distributed at the meeting were some books produced on desktop systems and a set of job listings posted by other publishers showing that experience in desktop publishing was becoming a part of the requirements for design and production jobs. At the end of the meeting, the managers were encouraged to tell those on their staffs who were likely to be most resistant to the planned change what they had learned.

A few days later, those employees who had been forewarned (who were among the most talented and experienced) took part in a meeting that gave them the opportunity to discuss their concerns and helped them see that the appearance of those books of value primarily to small groups of scholars were of less importance than making them available. The goal was, at the very least, to prevent this group of employees from banding together to try to influence others against the new system.

An organization-wide assembly was then held to announce the change to desktop typesetting and design and to present the opportunity for anyone interested in learning the new systems to volunteer for a pilot project. When two senior designers indicated their interest, a number of younger employees joined them in volunteering. The senior designers soon became change agents for the project.

The pilot project was set up in a central room that almost everyone in the organization walked by at some point during the day. People were encouraged by the trainers to come in and watch, creating interest in and comfort with the desktop system. Showing the ease with which those in the pilot project were adapting was critical because the next change, which was already in the planning stage, was to speed production and further cut costs by moving away from editing texts on paper to online editing.

The openness of the process and the influence of the change agents eased the transition. (Although some very senior designers left, those who remained were able to take on the design of more art books because they no longer worked on other titles; the result was that the inevitable staff reduction was relatively painless.) The following year the press produced the usual number of titles, almost within the parameters of the new budget, and the change in the editing process—aimed at bringing costs down to where they needed to be—was launched.

change management programs. The costs of those programs—in addition to the costs in time and money that result from the delays because of resistance—can create enormous budget overruns. That is why, when evaluating the proposed budgets of programs that will bring change, CFOs must raise the issue of the need for change management from the outset, the point at which such programs will be most effective in lowering the total costs of a project.

MAKING IT HAPPEN

If new methods, processes, and/or technologies are needed, the importance of the planned changes and the organization's commitment to them must be made clear to employees at all levels by senior management, especially the board and CEO. The CFO's role includes assessing and then explaining the financial benefits of the changes, making certain that the costs of change management programs as well as training are including in the costs of the what is being planned, and, when it comes to new technologies, he or she may be responsible for the change management programs needed to overcome the tendency of people to resist change, which can slow implementation. Such change management programs must:

- Relate the proposed change to strategic business objectives to ensure buy-in and support for the new initiative.
- Communicate evidence that direct competitors are implementing such changes and present examples from other industrial sectors that have made gains from making similar changes.
- Present strong financial data showing the benefits of the proposed change to the organization in terms of increased efficiency and lower costs and/or more sales or increased revenue.
- Explain what is likely to happen to employees as a result of the changes; for example, there will be a reduction in the number of employees, but it will be less than the number of cuts that would take place if competitors who make the changes win a certain percentage of customers.
- Provide early evidence, even if only projections, of the benefits of the change being made, so that the importance of change becomes clear and gains increasing support as it proceeds.

MORE INFO

Books:

Hughes, Mark. *Change Management*. London: Chartered Institute of Personnel and Development, 2006.

Jellison, Jerald, M. *Managing the Dynamics of Change: The Fastest Path to Creating an Engaged and Productive Workplace*. New York: McGraw-Hill, 2006.

Kotter, John. *Leading Change*. Boston, MA: Harvard Business School Press, 1996.

Website:

Change Management Learning Center: www.change-management.com

See Also:

Cost and Effect: Using Integrated Cost Systems to Drive Profitability and Performance (p. 1244)

NOTES

1 Schein, Edgar. *Organizational Culture and Leadership*. 3rd ed. San Francisco, CA: Jossey-Bass, 2004.

2 Goldberg, Beverly, and John Sifonis. *Dynamic Planning: The Art of Managing Beyond Tomorrow*. New York: Oxford University Press, 1994.

"There is nothing more difficult to plan. . .nor more dangerous to manage, than the creation of a new system."
Machiavelli

  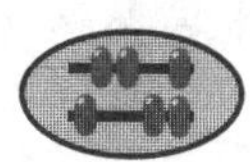   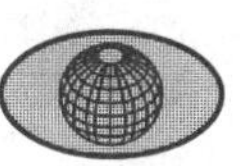   

Reducing Costs through Production and Supply Chain Management by Vinod Lall

EXECUTIVE SUMMARY

- There are numerous drivers of production and the supply chain, and there are several processes under each driver. These processes are associated with high overheads and offer opportunities for cost reduction.
- Cost reduction requires a complete knowledge and mapping of all costs, cycle times, purchases, inventories, suppliers, customers, logistics, and other service providers throughout the supply chain.
- Cost reduction in the supply chain often requires trade-off analysis amongst conflicting alternatives using the total cost approach.
- Successfully achieving supply chain cost savings requires the use of cross-functional teams with representation from marketing, design, procurement, production, distribution, and transportation employing an organized approach.

INTRODUCTION

IKEA, the Swedish home products retailer, is known for its good-quality, inexpensive products, which are typically sold at prices 30–50% below those of its competitors. While the price of products from other companies continues to rise over time, IKEA claims that its retail prices have been reduced by a total of 20% over the last four years. At IKEA, the process of cost reduction starts at product conception and continues throughout the process of design, sourcing of materials and components, production, and distribution. For example, the "Bang" mug has been redesigned many times to realize shipping cost savings. Originally, 864 mugs would fit into a pallet. After redesign a pallet held 1,280 mugs, and with a further redesign 2,024 mugs could be squeezed into a pallet, reducing shipping costs by 60%.

Organizations today are looking for opportunities to improve operational efficiencies and reduce cost without having a negative effect on customer service levels. Production and supply chain management can help to reduce costs by connecting every unit in the supply chain, fostering collaboration among supply chain partners, and offering visibility into the demand and supply side of the chain.

Production and supply chain management involves a number of drivers through which acquired raw materials are converted into finished goods for sale to customers. In turn, these drivers involve several processes that offer opportunities for cost reduction. Common drivers include procurement, design of the supply chain, inventory, transportation, warehousing, and collaboration. Cost reduction requires timely and improved decision-making for common processes under each driver.

PROCUREMENT

Procurement, also known as purchasing, is the process of acquiring raw materials, components, products, services, and other resources necessary either for the production processes themselves or for the support of production processes. Procurement processes ensure that supplies are available in the right place, in the right quantity, and at the right time. Buyers can play a major role in reducing supply chain costs by taking actions to reduce costs incurred in the flow of products from the suppliers to the ultimate customers. Some of the actions are discussed below.

Buyers must increase the flow of information throughout the supply chain, from the customer to the manufacturer and on to the supplier. This will make each entity in the chain aware of the inventory carried by the others and work towards the reduction of inventory without sacrificing customer service levels. Buyers must also take action to reduce cycle times, which will make the supply chain more responsive. To achieve a reduction in lead times, buyers must track and measure supplier lead-times, analyze trade-offs that result from lead time reduction, and then negotiate shorter lead times. Another action buyers can undertake to reduce supply chain cost is to select suppliers on the basis of their total supply chain capability and not just price, lead time, and quality levels.

DESIGN OF SUPPLY CHAIN

There are several principles under design of the supply chain that can help to reduce costs. These include component commonality, component modularity, and postponement.

Component commonality: The principle of component commonality focuses on the design and use of common components for families of products. When there are a large number of products in a supply chain, the inventory of components will naturally be large. Component commonality calls for the use of common components in a variety of products. This reduces costs not only by reducing inventory cost but also through reduced material cost, reduced production cost, and reduced product obsolescence. For example, a computer manufacturer can design common components such as memory and disk drives and use different combinations of these components to produce different finished products.

Component modularity: The principle of component modularity recommends that common subsystems be designed as modules to meet a broad range of feature requirements. This reduces the number of components that must be produced, kept in materials and repair parts inventory, and integrated into the product during the production process. This reduces procurement, manufacturing, and inventory costs, leading to a lower supply chain cost. Manufacturers of electronic products, for example, use the principle of modularity to design and assemble printers, computers, and so on.

Postponement: Postponement means delaying the bringing of products into their final form until close to the point of sale, when customer demand is known with greater accuracy. This results in a better match between supply and demand, leading to reduced costs mainly through inventory reductions. For example, a traditional garment manufacturer might dye the thread before knitting it into sweaters, whereas a garment manufacturer using postponement would postpone dying until the last point in the supply chain, when customer color preferences are known with a greater degree of certainty.

INVENTORY

Inventory resides at several locations in a supply chain, and the goal of inventory management is to reduce or eliminate inventory wherever it exists in the supply chain. This increases the velocity of movement of material through the chain, reducing the time from the point where material enters to the point of final consumption or sale. Slow movement of material leads to higher average inventories throughout the supply chain and results in

"Compromise is but the sacrifice of one right or good in the hope of retaining another, too often ending in the loss of both." Tryon Edwards

higher inventory carrying costs. Techniques that can help reduce these costs include the following.

The first technique is to use models such as vendor-managed inventory (VMI) and drop-shipments to reduce the number of locations where inventory is stored. With VMI the buyer of a product provides certain information to a vendor of that product, and the vendor takes full responsibility for maintaining an agreed level of inventory of the material, usually at the location where the buyer uses it.

Second, the same strategy should not be used to manage and control all inventory items regardless of their value. Instead, use ABC analysis (not the same as activity-based costing) to classify inventory into different classes and to maintain appropriately safe stock levels based on the class. ABC analysis makes use of Pareto's Law and classifies inventory into classes A, B and C. A-class items are high in value and low in number, requiring tight control, while C-class items are low-value, high-number items that can be loosely controlled. Items classed as B include medium-value, medium-number items and typically require a blanket policy for control.

Other inventory management techniques include reducing the amount of transportation/pipeline inventory, and application of lean and just-in-time techniques to reduce or eliminate waste.

TRANSPORTATION

Transportation is used to move products from one location in the supply chain to another and is a significant component of the supply chain cost. A responsive transportation system can help to lower supply chain costs by achieving a high level of product availability at a reasonable price. A common technique for making a transportation system responsive is "cross-docking." Under cross-docking, products from a supplier are aggregated into trucks that arrive at distribution centers. At these centers the process of cross-docking means that products are exchanged between different trucks so that each truck leaving for a given retail location is loaded with products from several suppliers.

Transportation planners can reduce supply chain costs by reducing transportation costs by selecting low-cost modes of transport and using software to plan optimal routes and delivery schedules. The various modes of transport include water, rail, truck, intermodal, and air, and package carriers such as DHL, FedEx, and UPS. Having a low-cost supply chain depends closely on the selection and use of an appropriate mode of transport. Water is typically the least expensive, although slowest, whereas air is the most expensive and fastest. Transportation planners often use the approach of total cost analysis to select the best mode. This requires finding the total cost for each mode of transportation and using the mode that has the lowest total cost. The total cost is made up of, and considers, the trade-off between the cost of transport, cost of inventory at the origin, cost of inventory in the pipeline, and cost of inventory at the destination. Several companies develop and provide software that helps planners to construct transportation routes and schedules. Planners also use satellite-based global positioning systems to lower costs while still maintaining a responsive transport system.

WAREHOUSING

Warehouses are locations in the supply chain to and from which inventory is transported. Supply chain planners can help to reduce costs by making good decisions about warehousing strategies, such as the location and capacity of warehouses, and operational decisions such as the functions to be performed at the warehouse, the order-fulfilment methodology to be used, etc.

When deciding on the location of warehouses, planners use a trade-off analysis to choose between a large centralized location, which is more efficient, and multiple decentralized locations that offer a higher level of responsiveness. A number of factors including the quality, cost and availability of the workforce, tax effects, and proximity to customers are used in the analysis. Capacity decisions typically involve decisions on the need for and amount of extra capacity. Warehouses with excess capacity offer flexibility at a cost, while those with little excess capacity are more efficient. Trade-off analysis is also used to make decisions on warehouse capacity. Operational decisions deal with day-to-day processes such as stock placement, stock picking, and cycle counting. Warehouse planners use warehouse management system (WMS) software to plan and execute these processes.

COLLABORATION

Collaboration in a supply chain focuses on joint planning, coordination, and process integration between the firm and its suppliers, customers, and other partners such as the logistics providers. In addition to cost reduction, collaboration offers the advantages of business expansion to other areas, increased return on assets, improved customer service, reduced lead times, increased reliability and responsiveness to market trends, and a shorter time to market. Several options are available for achieving collaboration in a supply chain. These include:

- systems that transmit information between partners using technologies such as fax, e-mail, electronic data interchange (EDI), or extensible markup language (XML);
- systems such as electronic hubs and portals that facilitate the procurement of goods or services from electronic marketplaces, catalogs, and auctions;
- systems such as collaborative planning, forecasting and replenishment (CPFR) that permit shared collaboration rather than just a simple exchange of information amongst the supply chain partners.

CASE STUDY

Transportation Analysis Pays Off for Computer Products Firm

A leading US manufacturer of computer accessories makes many products in China and then funnels them into a single distribution center on the West Coast that serves hundreds of retail clients. The company contracted with various freight services to send the products to retail customers using different modes of transportation, including small-package air, small-package ground, less-than-truckload, truckload, and heavy-weight air freight. The company wanted to have a better understanding of transportation processes and to control transportation costs. To do so, it hired the services of UPS Consulting (UPSC).

UPSC undertook a careful analysis and helped the manufacturer to reduce its domestic transportation costs by approximately 30% by the following means:

- negotiation of better rates with new freight service providers;
- setting up a returns program with a single carrier that picks up and returns the product using the most cost-effective transportation mode;
- development of a user-friendly one-page guide to carrier and mode selection that matches the weight and size of a parcel shipment with the preferred shipping method;
- helping employees to understand shipping parameters;
- establishing a compliance system that requires weekly meetings to review shipping activities and handle any special issues that arise.

"It's easy to make good decisions when there are no bad options." Robert Half

  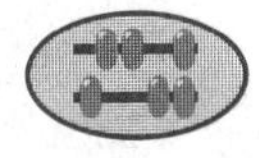   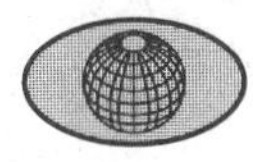   

The three systems identified above offer different levels of benefits and are associated with varying levels of expected costs. Organizations need to examine and quantify the benefits and costs of the alternative systems before selecting an appropriate system.

CONCLUSION

This article has explored major sources of cost savings in a production and supply chain and identified some techniques used by supply chain personnel such as buyers, inventory managers, and transportation planners. The techniques identified were discussed by grouping supply chain processes under the common supply chain drivers of procurement, design of the supply chain, inventory, transportation, warehousing, and collaboration.

▸▸ MORE INFO

Books:

Chopra, Sunil, and Peter Meindl. *Supply Chain Management: Strategy, Planning & Operations*. 3rd ed. Upper Saddle River, NJ: Prentice Hall, 2006.

Jacobs, F. Robert, and Richard B. Chase. *Operations and Supply Management: The Core*. Boston, MA: McGraw-Hill/Irwin, 2008.

Websites:

Council of Supply Chain Management Professionals: cscmp.org

Supply Chain Council: www.supply-chain.org

UPS Supply Chain Solutions: www.ups-scs.com

See Also:

★ Countering Supply Chain Risk (pp. 437–439)
★ Financial Techniques for Building Customer Loyalty (pp. 459–461)
★ Profitability Analysis Using Activity-Based Costing (pp. 801–804)
★ Reducing Costs and Improving Efficiency by Outsourcing and Selecting Suppliers (pp. 499–501)
✔ Business Process Reengineering (p. 974)
✔ Performing Total Cost of Ownership Analysis (p. 999)
✔ Understanding Pareto's Law (p. 1063)
Michael Porter (p. 1182)
Igor Ansoff (p. 1151)
Reengineering the Corporation: A Manifesto for Business Revolution (p. 1314)

"If two lines on a graph cross, it must be important." Ernest F. Cooke

     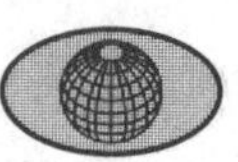   

Return on Talent by Subir Chowdhury

EXECUTIVE SUMMARY

- The performance of an organization is determined by the performance of its employees.
- Organizations must therefore measure return on talent as well as return on investment.
- Knowledge is one of the most important factors for business success. If knowledge assets are increased, related factors such as sales will also increase.
- Talent—or intellectual capital—has fast become one of the most significant areas of business activity and competition.

INTRODUCTION

The performance of an organization is entirely determined by the performance of its employees. This bold statement deserves further study. If the determinant of corporate performance is not its employees, what is? Is it strategic intent? Core competencies? Manufacturing? Is it proprietary technologies? The best equipment and laboratories? A visionary CEO? Yes, it's all of these things. And all of these things are created and constantly improved by employees. Talented employees are the agents of change. Good employees join in to help implement new initiatives. Others follow at various times, depending on when they can break the bounds of their comfort zone to enter the area of change, uncertainty, and opportunity. They fall by the wayside because they were in the wrong job.

It is broadly recognized that past performance is not a reliable indicator of potential or future success. Yet many organizations continue to use past performance to identify high-potential employees. How much true talent is overlooked by this practice? Overlooked and misplaced high-potential employees stagnate. The problem of identifying, positioning, and compensating high-potential employees spans all disciplines and levels, from the loading dock to the boardroom. Lost and underused employees represent enormous, largely unreckoned financial loss. A second problem is the difficulty of measuring the financial contribution of employees beyond global measures such as revenues per employee.

To focus a successful organization, managers must use a new tool called return on talent (ROT). Most organizations focus on return on investment (ROI), and fail to understand the key strategy of how to increase ROI by increasing ROT.

HARNESSING TALENT

ROT has the power to revolutionize business. ROT is calculated by dividing the knowledge generated and applied by the investment in talent. You need to address the dilemma of how to measure an intangible asset and how to generate high ROT value. For decades, organizations have used key metrics like ROI and ROA (return on assets) to determine value. But increasingly an effective new-economy organization will use ROT. Current business measurements merely measure the use of capital, but ROT is expressed as follows:

$$\text{ROT} = \frac{\text{Knowledge generated \& applied}}{\text{Investment in talent}}$$

If you have talented people, knowledge is just one component. The generation of knowledge is the most important thing talent can provide. Now you may realize that knowledge generated by the talent doesn't equal knowledge applied, right? And if knowledge isn't applied, the company loses most of the market value of that knowledge. Whatever knowledge a person generates in a year divided by how much is invested in that particular person is the value.

If an employee generates many innovative ideas but never implements any of them, that person fails to generate any value because the return to the company is zero. Knowledge generated does not necessarily mean knowledge applied. So value is knowledge generated *and* applied. Knowledge becomes an asset only when it's captured and used effectively; if it isn't effectively applied, it can't generate any yield or ROI. Generating a lot of knowledge within organizations doesn't add any value unless that knowledge is used in effective strategy formulation. Knowledge assets, like money or equipment, are worth cultivating only in the context of strategy. You can't define and manage intellectual assets unless you know what you are trying to do with them. This is the backbone of the knowledge economy; success in this field depends on mastery of talent, just as success in manufacturing relies on the skilful employment of plant and supply chains.

THE VALUE OF KNOWLEDGE

Return on Talent

The value of knowledge generated increases with its effective deployment. Effective knowledge generated means high ROT. It leads to a creative workforce, innovations, smooth processes, continuous product improvements, and improved communications. It helps management to be flexible, to capitalize on opportunities, and to keep pace with the changing business climate. Talented people influence those around them, and their knowledge is shared over time. Top knowledge generators should be rewarded. If managers expect top talents to achieve their maximum performance and produce maximum return, they must not place them in routine jobs.

ROT measures the payback from investment in people; it shows whether managers are hiring the right people and how effectively they use them to achieve business success. It can be a quantitative or qualitative measurement, based on management's viewpoint. Are managers getting the maximum payback on their investment? If managers want to see quantitative results, they need to put a price on knowledge generated, based on the results achieved. Talent generates knowledge, which is one of the greatest assets in the global economy. True knowledge brings creativity and innovation, and adds value to the company. Knowledge has become a key production factor, along with traditional resources such as raw materials, buildings, and machinery. Companies that measure the knowledge generated and applied by their talent can make their investments in talent more profitable. Further, companies cannot improve what they do not measure.

Effective managers use ROT measurements to make their investments in talent more profitable. ROT measurements help monitor performance, forecast opportunity, and determine the profitability of their investment in talent. To make their investment more profitable, management must constantly measure ROT, continuously improve ROT, and nurture, develop, and refresh talent.

Return on Knowledge

Return on knowledge generated and applied is more difficult to calculate and track. Knowledge creates real wealth through multiple applications, for example, repeating the same application pervasively through a corporation, or finding new applications to new situations. Knowledge

"**There is no such thing as great talent without great will-power.**" Honoré de Balzac

     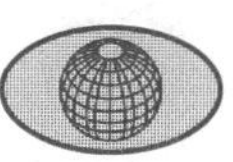   

applications have breadth (across organizations) and length (in time). Years may pass between the generation of knowledge and its first application, let alone subsequent applications.

In order to properly account for the value of knowledge generated, initial estimates need to be made and refined yearly as applications appear on the horizon and then are realized. Leading indicators of return are based on projections of the probability of each anticipated application and the monetary value of each application summed over all anticipated applications.

Forward-looking projections and backward-looking allocations are both judgments, and there's no reason to believe that one is any better than the other. Indeed, projections made while focusing on the knowledge generated may be the more reliable of the two. It is certain that the combination of early projections, after-the-fact allocations, and annual updating and tracking between knowledge generated and the first of a series of applications, greatly improves the capability to measure and link return on knowledge generated and applied, and investment in talent.

CONCLUSION

Organizations that constantly improve ROT grow at a rapid rate. Management can monitor the performances of individuals as well as teams. Knowledge is one of the most important factors for business success. If knowledge assets are increased, then all other related factors like production and sales will be automatically increased. Consequently, organizations should try to improve ROT continuously to sustain sales growth. ROT is a superb key performance indicator, and one that is set to be measured and managed in much the same way as financial issues.

▸▸ MAKING IT HAPPEN

- **Build a team focused on developing talent.** To reach high ROT scores, you need a talent team. Often you find one or two good people who can generate knowledge and perhaps even apply that knowledge, but you don't have a talent team that can leverage their ideas. Most of the individual talent in a company can be innovative if the team dynamics are right. If you have a low ROT score, you may have a dysfunctional team. ROT scores are not fixed; they change over time.
- **Measure and monitor ROT.** If you are a manager who hires and invests in talent, you need to monitor ROT closely. In a company the size of General Motors or General Electric, you probably view salaries as a regular fixed cost that is standard. The portion that may vary is how much you invest in certain ideas. If you see that certain employees are not generating enough knowledge and success relative to your investment in them, that should be a big red flag because your ROT value might become negative, or much lower than your competitor's ROT value.
- **Decide how to increase ROT throughout the organization.** If you were hired to manage talent with a low ROT score (perhaps even a negative value), you need to do some things to boost the ROT fast. How do you turn around an organization and achieve higher ROT scores? You do it person by person, function by function. You have to assess the talent on your team and find out who and what is bringing the most profit to the company, who and what is winning and keeping the best customers. Your first task is to perform talent diagnostics. You might easily spend six months identifying all your talent and determining which ones you can work with to turn the company around. But usually you don't have six months to do talent diagnostics. So you need to do it faster, even in a large company. There is much to be said for focusing on quick, high-profile actions that build support and momentum behind the need to increase ROT.

Many managers assess employees' talent intuitively—they don't necessarily need a measurement tool. Every manager, however, benefits from having a tool to measure and monitor ROT. Apple soared when Steve Jobs was CEO, and faded when he left. It soared again when he returned as Apple's CEO. It doesn't mean that Jobs was a good or bad person. He was a very effective person in that environment. Many good CEOs fail in environments in which there is no structure. They go by intuition. After you identify the key talents, give them the authority and resources to boost the ROT team score. The talent diagnostic may show that in one division you have a lot of talented people, while in a different division you have very few. You have to cross functions, making sure you balance the talent according to the needs of the organization, and then challenge each talent and team to reach a financial goal.

▸▸ MORE INFO

Books:

Becker, Brian E., Mark A. Huselid, and Richard W. Beatty. *The Workforce Scorecard: Managing Human Capital to Execute Strategy*. Cambridge, MA: Harvard Business School Press, 2005.

Brockbank, Wayne, and David Ulrich. *The HR Value Proposition*. Cambridge, MA: Harvard Business School Press, 2005.

Chowdhury, Subir. *The Talent Era: Achieving a High Return on Talent*. Upper Saddle River, NJ: Financial Times Prentice Hall, 2002.

Kaplan, Robert S., and David P. Norton. *Alignment: Using the Balanced Scorecard to Create Corporate Strategies*. Cambridge, MA: Harvard Business School Press, 2006.

"All our talents increase in the using, and every faculty, both good and bad, strengthens by exercise."
Anne Brontë

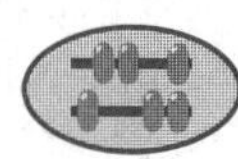

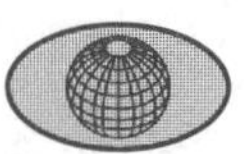

Risk Management: Beyond Compliance by Bill Sharon

EXECUTIVE SUMMARY

- The boundaries between risk management and compliance have eroded over the past decade, to the detriment of both functions.
- The definition of risk should be expanded to include opportunities and uncertainties, not just hazards.
- The context for assessing operational risk is business strategy.
- The role of risk managers needs to expand so that they become coordinators of the risk information that is readily available in operational and business units.
- The perception of risk is dependent on one's organizational responsibilities, and the convergence of those perceptions is the central focus of the management of risk.

INTRODUCTION

Over the past decade the line between risk management and compliance has been blurred to the point where, in many organizations, it is impossible to determine if they are not one and the same. In part, this confusion between the two functions was initiated and then exacerbated by the passage of the Sarbanes–Oxley Act of 2002 and the implementation of Basel II. Both of these events consumed a great deal of resources, and many consulting firms labeled these efforts "risk management." They are, in fact, compliance requirements designed to protect stakeholders and, in the latter case, ensure the viability of the financial system. They are not designed for, and nor can their implementation achieve, the management of risk in individual companies or financial institutions.

This confusion between compliance and risk management has led to a defensive posture in dealing with the uncertainties of the competitive business environment. Risk has been confined to the analysis of what could go wrong rather than what needs to go right. Risk management organizations have become the arbiters of what constitutes risk and have assumed an adversarial relationship with business managers, particularly in capital allocation exercises. Failures and scandals are met with calls for more regulation, the implementation of regulations becomes the province of risk management organizations, and the execution of strategy (arguably the area in most need of risk management) becomes further separated from any kind of disciplined analysis.

AN EXPANDED DEFINITION OF RISK

As Peter Bernstein tells us in his book *Against the Gods: The Remarkable Story of Risk*, the word risk comes from the old Italian *risicare*, which means "to dare." Daring is the driving idea behind business, the idea that a product or a service can achieve excellence and value in the marketplace. Strategy necessarily incorporates risk from the perspective of those actions which are required for its success.

In 1996 Robert G. Eccles, a former Harvard Business School professor, and Lee Puschaver, a partner at Price Waterhouse (now PricewaterhouseCoopers), developed the concept of the "business risk continuum." They argued that organizations that were successful in managing risk were those that focused on uncertainties and opportunities as much as they did on hazards. The context for evaluating risk in this manner is business strategy. This idea—that the definition of risk should be expanded to include those actions that an organization needed to embrace to achieve its goals—was revolutionary and codified what some companies were already beginning to initiate. Unfortunately, the narrow view of risk has prevailed for the past decade, and Eccles' and Puschaver's work has essentially been ignored.

The overwhelming emphasis of most risk organizations today is on the hazard end of the scale. Dot.com, Enron, and now subprime, along with the increased focus on terrorism, cataclysmic natural disasters, and the potential for pandemic diseases, have most complex organizations in a defensive posture. The problem with this approach is that risk driven from the hazard perspective is experienced as overhead in the operational disciplines and business units; it's a cost of business, not an activity that enhances value or improves the possibility of success.

By expanding the definition of risk (or returning to its original meaning) companies can harness the inherent risk management abilities and information available throughout their organization and develop a predictive process to address mission-critical tasks. Understanding how risk is perceived and how people react to those perceptions is an essential step in managing the opportunities and uncertainties inherent in implementing a business strategy.

ORGANIZATIONAL ROLES AND THE PERCEPTION OF RISK

Daniel Kahneman and Amos Tversky, the authors of "Prospect Theory," conducted a variety of experiments on the perception of risk and the responses that people had to identical information presented in different contexts. Among their conclusions they determined that:

1 emotion *always* overrides logic in the decision-making process,
2 people suffer from cognitive dysfunction in making decisions because they never have enough information,
3 people are not risk-averse, they are loss-averse.

While these conclusions may be unsettling to those involved in quantitative risk analysis, all three are useful assumptions around which to build a proactive risk management process. Emotion is at the core of any business—the desire to produce the best product, offer the best service, and compete in the marketplace comes from passion, not analytics. Managing risk is about managing emotion, not eliminating it.

From an organizational perspective, the perception of risk is colored by one's responsibilities. In the operational environment, technologists see opportunities in deploying software and hardware. HR professionals define success as the attraction and retention of high-performance employees. In the business units, opportunities require risks to be taken in order to capture market share or evolve a product line to the next level. Often these business leaders are unaware of the operational capabilities and capacities on which they must rely to achieve their goals. Operational managers often lack clarity on the business models they support. Individually, these perceptions of risk tell only part of the story and require the balance of all of the organizational perceptions in order for the cognitive dissonance to be managed and mitigated.

In this context, risk managers become coordinators of business intelligence rather than arbiters of what is and is not a risk. The management of risk is a communication process that is central to the success of

"**Real commitment is rare in today's organization. . .90% of the time what passes for commitment is compliance.**"
Peter Senge

     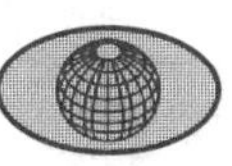   

the enterprise rather than an overhead process that compliance so often becomes. Participation in risk management is equivalent to participating in the development of business strategy. The desire not to lose (rather than the misguided view of being averse to "daring") is the underlying motivation for the process.

THE RISK PERCEPTION CONTINUUM

The risk perception continuum (Figure 1) summarizes the categories of risk and how they can be placed in an operational context. Using Eccles and Puschaver's concept of the three categories of risk, an organization can assign one of three different perceptions to determine the source and value of risk information:

- *What Should Be* is the perception of risk that comes from external standards. These are "best practices" for both operational and business managers. The measures involved determine the degree to which an organization is aligned with these practices in the context of what the organization wants to achieve. For example, alignment with "best practices" for a data center is likely to be more important for a financial institution than an advertising agency.

  It is tempting to place compliance functions in this area and track these issues as hazards. This is a mistake on two levels. First, the risk management process is central to the success of the organization and needs the oversight of the audit function. Putting them in the same unit creates a conflict of interest, one that is clearly identified in the Committee of Sponsoring Organization's (COSO) enterprise risk management framework. Second, compliance is a legal and regulatory function. One does not assess the risk of not complying. The primary audiences for this information are regulators and external auditors, and the ability to adhere to these requirements is really the baseline for participating in the marketplace.
- *What Is* comprises the uncertainty of the operating environment of the organization. This is the area where quantitative analysis and hedging are done to determine the upside and downside of a deal. It is here that both business and operational managers have the greatest impact on the management of risk, and it is here that the communication of the different perceptions of risk is most critical. The convergence of these perceptions constitutes valuable business intelligence.

  The classic example of managing risk in this manner is the HR hiring process.

Figure 1. The risk perception continuum

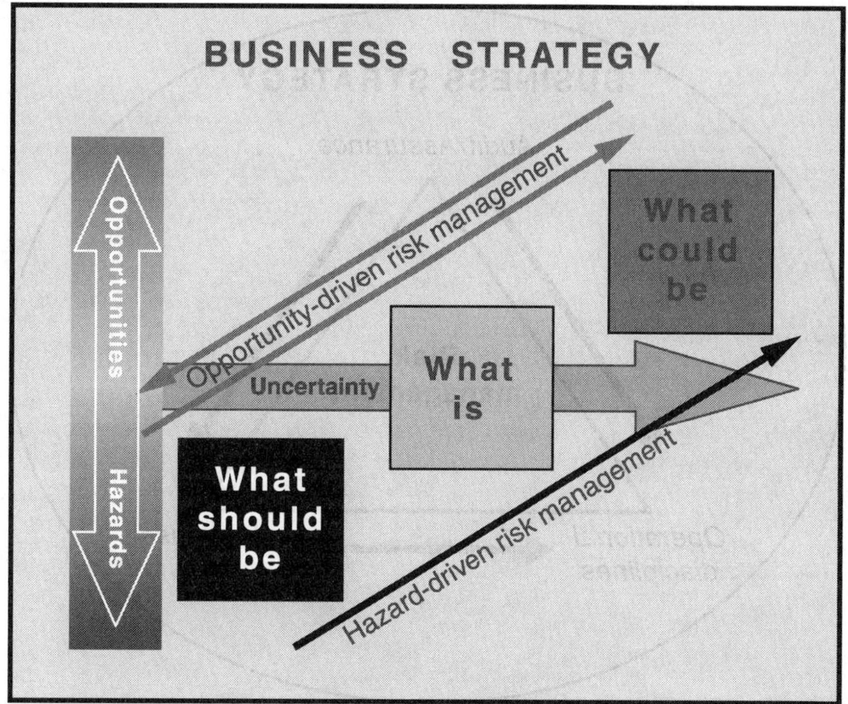

The MD of equity trading in an investment bank may have an urgent need for a large number of junior traders. The human resources department has a responsibility to ensure that the people the MD wants to hire have actually attended the universities claimed on their resumés and that they have passed a strenuous background check. The tension between these two perceptions is satisfied by the candidates signing a letter accepting their immediate dismissal should they be found to have misrepresented their qualifications. The organization embraces the risk that the contributions to the strategy will outweigh the potential for any damage that might be done during a relatively small window of time.

- *What Could Be* is the repository of the strategy of the organization and the perception of what risks need to be taken for it to be achieved. This perception is dynamic and responds to the demands of the marketplace, as well as the capabilities of the operating environment.

  Perhaps the best known example of how strategy drives the management of risk in an organization is the behavior of the US space agency, NASA, following John F. Kennedy's announcement that there would be an American on the moon by the end of the 1960s. In recently released tapes of meetings between Kennedy and James Webb, the director of NASA, the impact of strategy on operational capabilities is well illustrated. Webb advises Kennedy of the vagaries of space and the need to expand the space program to include a number of interim steps necessary to gain a better understanding before anyone can go to the moon. Kennedy listens and then tells Webb that he doesn't care about space, he wants to get to the moon before the Russians.

  What's interesting about this exchange is that Kennedy was defining a strategic goal that had no near-term likelihood of being achieved. He was also using that strategic goal to redefine the risk. The technical risk was unknowable at the time, but the political risk was quantifiable. Strategy organizes the operational environment and focuses it in specific directions. It requires operational managers to converge their perceptions of risk with the goals of the organization.

Figure 1 also demonstrates the difference between driving risk management from the opportunity or strategy perspective as opposed to the hazard perspective. The latter approach tries to force standards up through the organization. Operational managers experience this as an audit process and, other than quarterly reports from the audit committee, very little of this information receives much attention from the senior executives responsible for implementing strategy.

Alternatively, risk management driven

"We sort out all the hygiene factors, get all the control and risks battened down, then look for the sizzle."
Guy Hands

     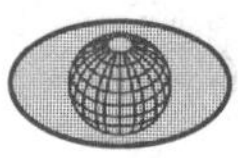   

Figure 2. Converging the perceptions of risk

from the opportunity perspective creates a communications vehicle for the entire organization. This is a bi-directional process because, as the strategy is communicated into the operating environment, the organization responds with business intelligence.

IMPLEMENTING A RISK MANAGEMENT PROCESS

Using the organization's strategy as the context (rather than "best practices" or regulatory requirements), the first step in the process is to ask operational managers to identify the risks that must be embraced in order to achieve this strategy (operational disciplines are defined as those organizational units that do not generate income, i.e. finance, HR, IT, PR, etc.). Once identified, these activities are assessed—usually using a RAG (red, amber, green) rating—to determine the likelihood of their being achieved.

There are two important steps in this first stage of the process that are often lacking in risk management programs.

1 Operational managers are asked to predict a risk rating, usually on a quarterly basis, for the next four quarters. This provides the organization with more valuable data than point-in-time risk assessments, whose shelf-life tends to be quite short. It also provides operational managers with the ability to communicate anticipated challenges in the future and/or illustrate how current challenges will be positively addressed over time.
2 Operational managers are also asked to note whether the activities they believe must be undertaken have sufficient funding. Once this information has been collated, the organization has a map of where it is investing in managing risks central to the strategy and where it is not.

Operational managers are then asked to complete an actual vs. planned assessment at the end of each quarter. This is not an exercise to assess competency, but rather another channel for communication in the risk management process. Strategy may change, requiring a new perception of risk. Operational awareness of greater or lesser challenges may impact the original risk rating. Departures from the original assessment are expected and should be viewed as business intelligence rather than as a scoring of prescient abilities.

Once the process is established with the operational managers, the second stage of the risk management process can be implemented. Here, business managers are asked to contribute their perceptions of risk to the mission-critical operational activities that have been identified. For example, if the IT department identified the rollout of a new operating system as a risk that needed to be embraced and rated it as an amber or a red given the exposure in maintenance and security, the business managers might rate it as a green as they have no clear knowledge of the technical issues. Differences in the perception of risk are expected and provide an opportunity to understand risk across operational and business disciplines.

The third stage (figure 2) in the risk management process is the audit review, which not only validates the process itself, but also uses the risk assessments as a source for audit oversight of specific operational activities. The convergence of perception between operational and business managers and the audit function provides the risk management process with the widest possible range of understanding of risks to the strategy.

Once this process is established, metrics can be applied to risk ratings, operational

CASE STUDY

JP Morgan—Managing the risk of outsourcing

The risk management process can be scaled to encompass the entire organization, a specific business unit, or a large project. A year prior to outsourcing 40% of its technology, JP Morgan initiated a predictive risk management program that converged the perceptions of technology and business managers and established an IT risk profile for each business unit.

- The IT self-assessment process was conducted quarterly on a global basis, and provided the bank with a portfolio view of IT operational risk across all business units.
- The risk profiles allowed the bank to negotiate service levels based on an understanding of where the internal IT group was supporting the business strategy and where improvements were necessary.
- The IT self-assessment process was transferred to the successful vendors and the business units continued to contribute their perceptions, resulting in a shared process between the vendors and the bank.
- Perhaps the most important result of the process was a better understanding in the business units of IT capabilities and capacities. The organization gained an understanding of the technology that provided competitive advantage (and should therefore be retained in the bank) and of the infrastructure and shared applications that could be turned over to external vendors.

"If a man will begin with certainties, he shall end in doubts; but if he will be content to begin with doubts, he shall end in certainty." Francis Bacon

  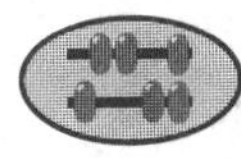 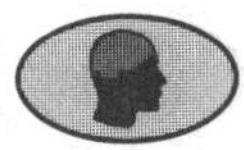  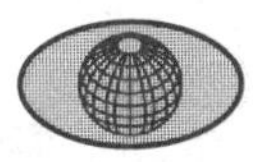   

disciplines can be weighted in importance by business unit, and portfolio views of risk can be developed across business units.

CONCLUSION

No risk management function can ensure that negative events won't happen. The complexity of the markets and the speed of change create exposures that are difficult to predict. Managing risk as a process that engages the entire enterprise in the achievement of the business strategy does, however, create a resilient organization that can better respond to difficulties that always arise.

▸▸ MAKING IT HAPPEN

The operational risk management process described in this article begins with the business strategy but ultimately engages the entire organization. Senior management needs not only to endorse the process but also to participate in and use it on a continuing basis. The early stages of the process require patience, and some care should be taken in the initial implementation.

- There is often confusion in the operational disciplines about what is a risk to the business strategy and what is a best-practice or compliance requirement. Risk managers will likely need to assist operational managers in this distinction.
- Simplicity is key in the early stages of the risk management process. Many efforts collapse under their own weight when organizations attempt to accomplish too much in a short period of time. Risk management is about leveraging existing expertise; complex metrics can be applied once the system is robust.
- Using the risk management process as a communication process, not only for challenges but also for capacities and creative solutions, is essential in making it a robust vehicle for the generation of business intelligence.

▸▸ MORE INFO

Book:

Bernstein, Peter L. *Against the Gods, The Remarkable Story of Risk*. New York: Wiley, 1996.

Article:

Kloman, Felix. "Risk management and Monty Python, Part 2." *Risk Management Reports* 32:12 (2005).

Report:

Puschaver, Lee, and Robert G. Eccles. "In Pursuit of the upside: The new opportunity in risk management." Leading Thinking on Issues of Risk, PricewaterhouseCoopers, 1998.

Websites:

COSO (Committee of Sponsoring Organizations of the Treadway Commission): www.coso.org

Prospect theory: prospect-theory.behaviouralfinance.net and www.sjsu.edu/faculty/watkins/prospect.htm

Risk Metrics: www.riskmetrics.com

Strategic Operational Risk Management Solutions (SORMS): www.sorms.com

See Also:

★ The Effect of SOX on Internal Control, Risk Management, and Corporate Governance Best Practice (pp. 620–622)
★ Managing Operational Risks Using an All-Hazards Approach (pp. 484–486)
★ Risk—Perspectives and Common Sense Rules for Survival (pp. 811–814)
★ A Total Balance Sheet Approach to Financial Risk (pp. 103–105)
✔ Applying Stress-Testing to Operational Risk Exposure (p. 970)
✔ Basel II—Its Development and Aims (p. 920)
✔ Establishing a Framework for Assessing Risk (p. 1034)
✔ Sarbanes–Oxley: Its Development and Aims (p. 1047)
Amos Tversky (p. 1202)
Mastering Risk Volume 1: Concepts (p. 1297)

"Risk occurs when you don't know what you're doing." Warren Buffett

     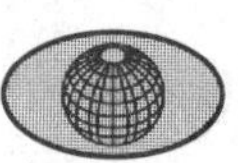   

Understanding Reputation Risk and Its Importance by Jenny Rayner

EXECUTIVE SUMMARY

- Reputation is a critical intangible asset; it is an indicator of past performance and future prospects.
- Reputation is based on stakeholders' perception of whether their experience of a business matches their expectations.
- Knowing your major stakeholders, how they perceive you, and what they expect of you is vital in managing reputation risk.
- Everyone working for an organization bears some responsibility for upholding its reputation.
- Reputation risk is anything that could *impact* reputation—either negatively (threats) or positively (opportunities).
- Risks to reputation should be integrated into the business's enterprise risk management (ERM) framework so that they receive attention at the right level and appropriate actions are taken to manage them.

INTRODUCTION

Reputation is the single most valuable asset of most businesses today—albeit an intangible one. A 2007 global survey[1] rated damage to reputation as the top risk, although half the respondents admitted that they were not prepared for it. Hard-earned reputations can be surprisingly fragile in the globalized, technologically interconnected 21st century. The trust and confidence that underpin them can be irrevocably damaged by a momentary lapse of judgment or an inadvertent remark.

That is why understanding reputation risk has become a key focus for businesses in all sectors. It is now recognized that reputation risks need to be managed as actively and rigorously as other more quantifiable and tangible risks.

REPUTATION AND ITS VALUE

Reputation is an accumulation of perceptions and opinions about an organization that reside in the consciousness of its stakeholders.

An organization will enjoy a good reputation when its behavior and performance consistently meet or exceed the expectations of its stakeholders. Reputation will diminish if an organization's words and deeds are perceived as failing to meet stakeholder expectations, as illustrated by the reputation equation below.[2]

Reputation – Experience = Expectations

Reputation has intrinsic current value as an intangible asset. Although reputation will not appear as a discrete balance sheet item, it represents a significant proportion of the difference between a business's market and book values (less any quantifiable intangibles such as licenses and trademarks). Since intangibles usually represent over 70% of market value, reputation is often a business's single greatest asset.

Reputation also plays a pivotal role in a business's future value by influencing stakeholder behavior and, hence, future earnings potential and prospects. A good or bad reputation can affect stakeholder decisions to maintain or relinquish their stake—be they investors, customers, suppliers, or employees. The "corporate halo" effect of a reputable business can help to differentiate products in a highly competitive sector, may allow premium pricing, and can be the ultimate deciding factor for a prospective purchaser of services. A strong reputation can help to attract and retain high-quality employees and can deter new competitors by acting as a barrier to market entry. Reputation can also shape the attitude of regulators, pressure groups, and the media towards a business and can affect its cost of capital.

Perhaps the greatest benefit of a good reputation is the buffer of goodwill it provides, which can enable a business to withstand future shocks. This "reputational capital," or "reputation equity," underpins stakeholder trust and confidence and can persuade stakeholders to give a business the benefit of the doubt and a second chance when the inevitable unforeseen crisis strikes.

DEFINING REPUTATION RISK

Reputation risk should be regarded as a generic term embracing the risks, from any source, that can *impact* reputation, and not as a category of risk in its own right. Regulatory noncompliance, loss of customer data, unethical employee behavior, or an unexpected profit warning can all damage reputation and stakeholder confidence.

Reputation risk is not only about downside threats, but also about upside opportunities. Climate change, for example, is a potential business threat, but many firms have spotted and exploited the flip-side opportunity for competitive

CASE STUDY

Citigroup

In September 2004 the Financial Services Agency (FSA), Japan's bank regulator, ordered Citigroup to close its private banking business in the country following "serious violations" of Japanese banking laws. An FSA investigation found that inadequate local internal controls and lack of oversight from the United States had allowed large profits to be "amassed illegally." The bank had failed to prevent suspected money laundering and had misled customers about investment risk. The punishment meted out by the FSA was particularly severe as a previous inspection in 2001 had exposed similar compliance weaknesses, which Citigroup had not corrected.

Citigroup's then chief executive, Charles Prince, visited Japan in October 2004 in an attempt to repair the company's tarnished image. Bowing, he apologized for the activities of his senior staff, saying that they had put "short-term profits ahead of the bank's long-term reputation." He pledged to improve oversight, change the management structure, increase employee training on local regulations, and set up an independent committee to monitor progress. He said: "Under my leadership, lack of compliance and inappropriate behavior simply will not be tolerated and we will take direct action to ensure that proper standards are upheld and that these problems do not reoccur."

That same month French retailer Carrefour fired Citigroup as a financial adviser on the sale of its Japanese operations to prevent its own reputation from being tarnished by association.

"It takes twenty years to build a reputation and five minutes to ruin it. If you think about that you'll do things differently." Warren Buffett

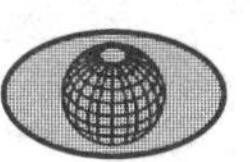

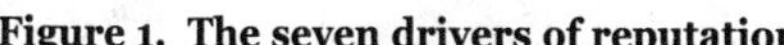
Figure 1. The seven drivers of reputation

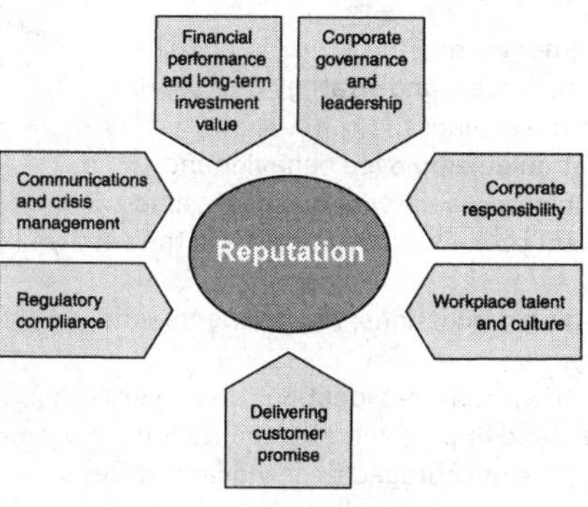

advantage by developing green technologies and promoting themselves as environmentally friendly, thereby enhancing their reputation.

Reputation risk can therefore be defined as:

"Any action, event or situation that could adversely or beneficially impact an organization's reputation."

IDENTIFYING REPUTATION RISKS

The most crucial stage of the reputation risk management process is *identifying* the factors that could impact reputation. Risks have to be recognized and understood before they can be managed. Considering the seven drivers of reputation is a useful starting point, as these are also fertile sources of threats and opportunity to reputation (see figure above.[3])

Businesses should consider not only the risks under their direct control, but also risks in the "extended enterprise" relating to suppliers, subcontractors, business partners, advisers, and other stakeholders. Could the values, business practices, or activities of its partners expose the business to reputation risk by association?

One way of approaching this is to consider the expectations of each major stakeholder group against the drivers of business reputation to develop a "heat map" of potential trouble spots and zones of opportunity. Major mismatches between expectations and experience can be analyzed to highlight areas where action is needed to bridge the gaps.

Asking the following questions may also help to uncover reputation risks:

- What newspaper headline about your business would you least (or most) like to see? What could trigger this?
- What could threaten your core business values or your license to operate? Such risks can seriously damage reputation and lead to an irreversible loss of stakeholder confidence.
- Could there be collateral risk arising from the activities of another player in your sector? If so, the reputation of your own business may be vulnerable and come under intense stakeholder scrutiny.
- Could reputation risk exposure arise from an acquisition, merger, or other portfolio change? A mismatch of values, ethos, culture, and standards resulting in inappropriate behavior could seriously damage reputation. Conversely, if the acquisition target enjoys a superior reputation, it could provide a competitive edge.

EVALUATING, RESPONDING TO, MONITORING, AND REPORTING RISKS

Once risks to reputation have been identified, they can be evaluated, appropriate risk responses developed, and the risks monitored and reported.

Risks to reputation can be *evaluated* in the usual way by considering the likelihood of the risk occurring and the impact if it does. The reputational impact of such risks should be considered explicitly, alongside financial or other impacts. This can be done by the use of a word model which explains reputational impact in a way that is relevant and meaningful for a given business. The table below provides an example of a four-point reputation impact scale that caters for both threats and opportunities.

In assessing reputational impact, the view of relevant stakeholders should be considered to ensure that the impact is not underestimated. That is why understanding stakeholders and what they regard as current and emerging major issues lies at the heart of reputation risk management.

Reputational impact can sometimes be quantified in monetary terms—for example, expected reduced income resulting from loss of customers or license to operate; or impact on share price, or on brand value. The true ultimate impact can be difficult to estimate as the immediate consequence may be only a relatively small financial penalty (for example, a fine for pollution). However, the event may, over time, have an insidious effect which erodes the business's reputation (for example, because of a perception that the business is not concerned about the environment).

Response plans should be developed to manage the more significant risks that present unacceptable exposure to the business. The gap between experience and expectation can be bridged by improving the business's performance or behavior and/or by influencing stakeholder expectations so they are more closely aligned with what the business can realistically deliver. As reputation is based on stakeholder perception, focused and clear communication to stakeholders is vital so that their perception will accurately reflect business reality.

A business may have done everything possible to anticipate and guard against reputational threats, but if a crisis strikes and the business response is inappropriate, its reputation may still end up in tatters. Having an effective and well-rehearsed generic crisis management plan that can be quickly adapted and implemented to suit specific circumstances is therefore a key component of an effective reputation risk management strategy.

Once risks to reputation have been identified and responses agreed and implemented, the risks can be regularly *monitored* by management to ensure that responses are having the desired effect. Finally, the up-to-date status of the risks should be *reported* at the right level to inform decision-making and enable external disclosure to stakeholders.

ROLES AND RESPONSIBILITIES

The board of a business is the ultimate custodian of a business's reputation. However, managing reputation risk successfully

Table 1. Sample reputation impact assessment criteria

Low	*Moderate*	*High*	*Very high*
Local complaint or recognition Minimal change in stakeholder confidence Impact lasting less than one month	Local media coverage Moderate change in stakeholder confidence Impact lasting between one and three months	National media coverage Significant change in stakeholder confidence Impact lasting more than three months Attracts regulator attention or comment	National headline/ international media coverage Dramatic change in stakeholder confidence Impact lasting more than 12 months or irreversible Public censure or accolade by regulators

     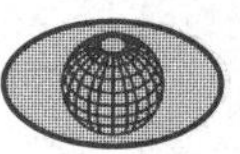 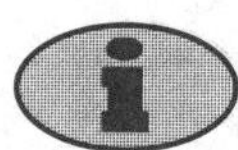  

requires a team effort across the business from executive and nonexecutive directors, senior and middle managers, public relations staff, risk and audit professionals, and key business partners.

Everyone employed by and indirectly working for a business should be expected to uphold the business's values and bear some responsibility for spotting emerging risks that could impact reputation. The telltale signs of an imminent crisis are often missed because personnel are not risk-aware: a spate of customer complaints, safety near-misses or supplier nonconformances, a sudden rise in employee turnover, or pressure group activity. These can act as crucial early warning indicators which allow a business to take corrective action and avert disaster.

CONCLUSION

A good reputation hinges on a business living the values it claims to espouse and delivering consistently on the promise to its stakeholders. Being "authentic," being "the real thing," has never been so important. Pursuing short-term gain at the expense of long-term business reputation and stakeholder interests is no longer acceptable practice.

Successfully managing reputation risk is both an inside-out and an outside-in challenge. The inside-out component requires business leaders to establish an appropriate vision, values, and strategic goals that will guide actions and behaviors throughout the organization. The outside-in component requires the business to continuously scan the external environment and canvass stakeholder opinion to ensure it is on a track that will secure the continuing support, trust, and confidence of its stakeholders.

Active and systematic management of the risks to reputation can help to ensure that perception is aligned with reality and that stakeholder experience matches expectations. Only in this way can a business build, safeguard, and enhance a reputation that will be sustainable in the long term.

▸▸ MAKING IT HAPPEN

The key components of reputation risk management are:

- Clear and well-communicated business vision, values, and strategy that set the right ethical and stakeholder-aware tone for the business.
- Supporting policies and codes of conduct that guide employee behavior and decision-making so that goals are achieved in accordance with business values.
- Extension of the business's values and relevant policies to key partners in the supply chain.
- Dialogue and engagement to track the changing perceptions, requirements, and expectations of major stakeholders continuously.
- An effective enterprise-wide risk management system that identifies, assesses, responds to, monitors, and reports on threats and opportunities to reputation.
- A culture in which employees are risk-aware, are encouraged to be vigilant, raise concerns, highlight opportunities, and act as reputational ambassadors for the business.
- Transparent communications that meet stakeholder needs and build trust and confidence.

▸▸ MORE INFO

Books:

Atkins, Derek, Ian Bates, and Lyn Drennan. *Reputational Risk: Responsibility Without Control? A Question of Trust*. London: Financial World Publishing, 2006.

Fombrun, Charles J., and Cees B. M. van Riel. *Fame and Fortune: How Successful Companies Build Winning Reputations*. Upper Saddle River, NJ: FT Prentice Hall, 2003.

Larkin, Judy. *Strategic Reputation Risk Management*. Basingstoke, UK: Palgrave MacMillan, 2003.

Rayner, Jenny. *Managing Reputational Risk: Curbing Threats, Leveraging Opportunities*. Chichester, UK: Wiley, 2003.

Article:

See articles in *The Geneva Papers on Risk and Insurance Issues and Practice* 31:3 (July 2006). Find issue in "Archive" at: www.palgrave-journals.com/gpp

Reports:

Coutts and Company. "Face value: Your reputation as a business asset." London: Coutts and Company, 2008.

Economist Intelligence Unit. "Reputation: Risk of risks." White paper, 2005.

Resnick, Jeffrey T. "Reputational risk management: A framework for safeguarding your organization's primary intangible asset." Opinion Research Corporation, 2006. Online at: www.carma.com/Reputational_Risk_White_Paper.pdf

Websites:

The John Madejski Centre for Reputation, Henley Business School at the University of Reading—search on "Madejski" at: www.henley.reading.ac.uk

Reputation Institute: www.reputationinstitute.com

See Also:

★ CSR: More than PR, Pursuing Competitive Advantage in the Long Run (pp. 147–149)
★ Fraud: Minimising the Impact on Corporate Image (pp. 462–464)
★ Internal Auditors and Enterprise Risk Management (pp. 680–682)
★ The Value and Management of Intellectual Property, Intangible Assets, and Goodwill (pp. 109–112)
✔ Defining Corporate Governance: Its Aims, Goals, and Responsibilities (p. 907)
✔ Understanding Crisis Management (p. 919)

NOTES

1 Aon's Global Risk Management Survey, based on responses from 320 organizations in 29 countries.

2 Oonagh Mary Harpur in Chapter B4 of *Corporate Social Responsibility Monitor*. London: Gee Publishing, 2002.

3 Rayner, 2003.

"The way to gain a good reputation is to endeavor to be what you desire to appear." Socrates

  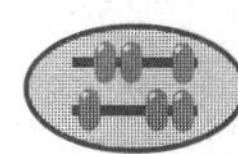   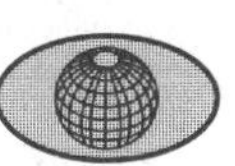   

Acquiring a Secondary Listing, or Cross-Listing by Meziane Lasfer

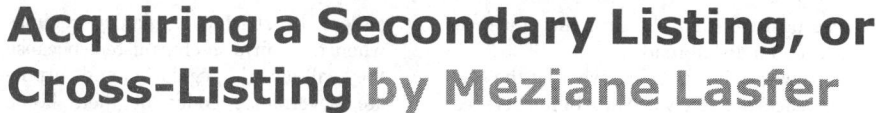

EXECUTIVE SUMMARY

- Over the last three decades an increasing number of companies have sourced their equity capital in foreign countries by listing their stock abroad.
- This strategy of parallel listing on both domestic and foreign stock exchanges, referred to as "cross-listing," is used by companies from both developed and emerging markets.
- In 2008, for example, 121 companies from BRIC countries (Brazil (7), Russia (24), India (24), and China (66)) were listed on the London Stock Exchange Alternative Investment Market (LSE-AIM), an equivalent to NASDAQ in the United States.
- Although the major stock markets for cross-listing are in the United States (NYSE and NASDAQ) and London (LSE and LSE-AIM), with a 43% market share in 2007, firms are also likely to cross-list in other markets of the world, such as the Singapore, Euronext, Hong Kong, and Mexico stock exchanges.
- According to the Bank of New York Mellon, during the first half of 2008 more than $2.4 trillion of depository receipts (DRs) traded on US and non-US markets and exchanges, up 85% from the previous year.

INTRODUCTION

Cross-listing is controversial and raises a number of academic and practitioner questions, particularly: Why and how does a firm cross-list, and does cross-listing create additional value for existing stockholders? The purpose of this article is to discuss the institutional framework of cross-listing, the classification of depository receipts (DRs), the types of DR available in the United States, the reasons why companies list abroad (by contrasting the advantages and disadvantages of raising equity capital in foreign markets), and the cross-listing process.

INSTITUTIONAL BACKGROUND

Companies cross-list by issuing depository receipts. These are certificates that are first issued by the company to a bank in a foreign country, which in turn issues the certificates to investors in that country. Indirectly, DRs represent ownership of home market shares in the overseas corporation. The underlying shares remain in custody in the home country, and DRs effectively convey ownership of those shares. DRs are quoted and normally pay dividends in the foreign country's currency (for example, US dollars or euros). DRs can be established either for existing shares that are already trading, or as part of a global offering of new shares. Each DR normally represents some multiple of the underlying share. This multiple allows the DR to possess a price per share that is appropriate for the foreign market, and the arbitrage normally keeps foreign and local prices of any given share the same after adjustment for transfer costs. DRs can be exchanged for the underlying foreign shares, and vice versa.

CLASSIFICATIONS OF DEPOSITORY RECEIPTS

There are a number of classifications of depository receipts, two of which are:

- *Trading location*: Global depositary receipts (GDRs) are certificates traded outside the United States; American depositary receipts (ADRs) are certificates traded in the United States and denominated in US dollars.
- *Sponsorship*: A sponsored ADR is created at the request of a foreign firm that wants its shares to be traded in the United States. In this case, the firm applies to the Securities and Exchange Commission (SEC) and to a US bank for registration and issuance. In contrast, an unsponsored ADR occurs when a US security firm initiates the creation of an ADR. Such an ADR would be unsponsored, but the SEC still requires all new ADRs to be approved by the firm itself.

TYPES OF LISTING

In the United States there are four types of depositary receipt: Levels 1 and 2 apply to cases where the DR is created using existing equity; Levels 3 and 4 apply to cases where new equity is issued, such as an initial public offering (IPO).

Level 1 is the least costly, as the DRs are traded over the counter in the United States, in the pink sheet market. There is little additional disclosure requirement, apart from the translation of the home country's financial statements into English. On average, about 56% of the approximately 1,500 DR programs are classified as Level 1.

Level 2 is relatively more costly. The DRs are traded on the NYSE, NASDAQ, and AMEX exchanges, with greater cost as the initial fee can exceed US$1 million. A cross-listed firm must also reconcile to US GAAP, report quarterly, and meet the listing requirements of the US exchange on which it trades.

Level 3 is similar to Level 2 for existing quoted companies, except that it applies to IPOs; the firm raises new equity capital in a public offering and trades on the NYSE, NASDAQ, or AMEX. A company must meet full SEC disclosure requirements, comply with US GAAP, report quarterly, and meet the listing requirements of the exchange.

Level 4, now referred to as 144A, applies to firms that raise new equity capital through a private placement. The securities are not registered for sale to the public; rather, investors follow a buy and hold strategy. Firms that use this method are exempt from disclosure requirements of a new equity issue in the United States, such as the SEC disclosure and the US GAAP. In April 1990 the SEC approved Rule 144A, which permits qualified institutional buyers to trade privately placed securities without SEC registration. These securities are traded on a screen-based automated trading system known as PORTAL, established to create a liquid secondary market for those private placements.

In other countries, the requirements depend mainly on the type of markets in which the company is going to be cross-listed. For example, requirements to list on the London Stock Exchange Official List are more extensive than those for the Alternative Investment Market.

The choice between listing in the United States (ADR) and in other markets through GDR depends on a number of factors. In particular, companies are likely to prefer listing in the United States through ADRs only if their objective has a powerful appeal to US retail investors and they are able to cover the significant cost of Sarbanes–Oxley compliance and major exposure to liability for management and board of directors. ADRs are also useful if they can benefit by selling new shares at a premium. Cross-listing through GDR may be cheaper, quicker, and could achieve the same purpose with fewer downsides. For example, cross-listing in the London Stock

"There has long prevailed a conventional wisdom rationalizing why firms pursue overseas listings."
Karolyi, 2006

     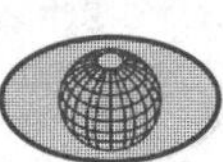   

Exchange involves two main rounds, where the firm receives comments from the UK Listing Authority (UKLA) in about two weeks. Furthermore, since July 2005, the UKLA no longer requires 25% of GDR issues to be distributed to European investors.

As an alternative to depository receipts, companies can have "Euroequity public issue." Under this method, instead of listing a share on the home market and then cross-listing, shares are issued simultaneously in multiple markets. The term Euroequity has nothing to do with Europe *per se*. Euroequity public issue simply refers to equity issues that are sold globally. Often these are used for very large equity issues, and different tranches are sold in different markets.

WHY DO COMPANIES CROSS-LIST?

In general, companies cross-list when the size of their financial needs exceeds their domestic market capacity. There is a limited liquidity in the domestic market, and the price of stock may be more attractive in a foreign market, especially if there is market segmentation and DRs offer diversification benefits to investors. The existing domestic investors also benefit, since cross-listing is likely to mitigate the agency conflicts with their managers. A company becomes more visible internationally, and the share prices are likely to be more efficient (known as price discovery), because trading happens in two or more markets and more financial analysts follow the cross-listing. However, some costs make cross-listing less attractive. This section provides a summary of the benefits and costs of cross-listing.

Benefits of Cross-Listing

The most widely cited benefit is the reduction in the cost of capital. Cross-listing is likely to reduce the cost of capital, because in close domestic markets the efficient frontier is determined only by the set of domestic assets. Therefore, the equity cost of capital depends on the risk premium of the domestic market portfolio. However, if the firm is cross-listed it can reach foreign investors who will be able to invest in both foreign and domestic firms, and the market risk premium will be lower because the level of diversification that investors can attain in an open capital market is far greater. As a result, a cross-listed firm's cost of capital will be lower. Karolyi (1998) reports that the cost of capital of UK cross-listed firms in the United States decreases by 2.64%, from 15.56% before to 12.91% after cross-listing. The market reaction is also positive when the firm announces the decision to list abroad.

However, it is not clear whether the market reacts positively because of the decrease in the cost of capital or whether it is driven by one or more of the additional benefits of cross-listing. These are:

- Improved liquidity of existing shares and broadening of the stockholder base, with, as a result, a reduced probability of takeovers.
- Establishment of a secondary market for shares used in acquisitions.
- An increase in the firm's visibility and political acceptability to its customers, suppliers, creditors, and host governments.
- Creation of a secondary market for shares that can be used to compensate local management and employees in a foreign subsidiary.
- The recently developed bonding hypothesis, which suggests that managers will adhere to stricter regulatory regimes when their firm is cross-listed, because they will face the regulation and corporate governance codes of their home country as well as the foreign market.

Costs of Cross-Listing

The positive market reaction to cross-listing could also reflect the trade-off between the benefits of cross-listing discussed above and some potential costs, namely disclosure costs. In cross-listing and selling equity abroad, a firm faces two barriers: an increased commitment to full disclosure and a continuing investor relations program. Non-US firms must think twice before cross-listing in the United States. Not only can the disclosure requirements be onerous, but timely quarterly information is also required by US regulators and investors. Costs are likely to be higher for firms that have been accustomed to revealing far less information.

▸▸ MAKING IT HAPPEN

Over the last few years, an increasing number of firms have listed their shares in foreign markets. The decision to cross-list is strategic and involves the following issues:

- Where to cross-list: Companies can go to the United States and issue American depository receipts (ADRs), or to other non-US stock exchanges by issuing global depository receipts (GDRs).
- The choice of a particular market depends on a number of factors. In particular, the firm needs to know whether its stock is attractive to US investors, and whether it can comply with all the requirements of listing, including stronger information disclosure, before it issues ADRs.
- A firm also needs to understand the reasons for cross-listing before issuing depository receipts. The most fundamental is often financing needs, and the inability of the firm to cover this from the domestic market.
- In general, cross-listing leads to an increase in share prices on the announcement date. Such market reactions are likely to be driven by a number of factors, including a reduction in the cost of capital, a wider geographical range of stockholders, an increase in visibility and financial analysts' coverage, and the adoption of stricter corporate governance codes.

▸▸ MORE INFO

Articles:

Baker, H. K., J. R. Nofsinger, and D. G. Weaver. "International cross-listing and visibility." *Journal of Financial and Quantitative Analysis* 37:3 (2002): 495–521.

Coffee, J. C., Jr. "Racing towards the top? The impact of cross-listings and stock market competition on international corporate governance." *Columbia Law Review* 102 (2002): 1757–1831.

Dobbs, Richard, and Marc H. Goedhart. "Why cross-listing shares doesn't create value." *The McKinsey Quarterly* (November 2008). Online at: www.mckinseyquarterly.com/Corporate_Finance/Performance/Why_cross-listing_shares_doesnt_create_value_2253

Doidge, C. A., G. A. Karolyi, and R. M. Stulz. "Why are foreign firms listed in the U.S. worth more?" *Journal of Financial Economics* 71:2 (2004): 205–238.

Doidge, C. A., G. A. Karolyi, and R. M. Stulz. "Has New York become less competitive in global markets? Evaluating foreign listing choices over time." Working paper 2007-03-012, Fisher College of Business, Ohio State University, 2007.

"A fundamental benefit of cross-listing is the enhancement of investor protection." Lasfer, 2009

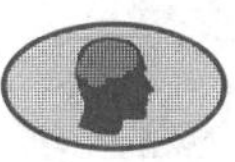

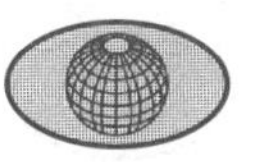

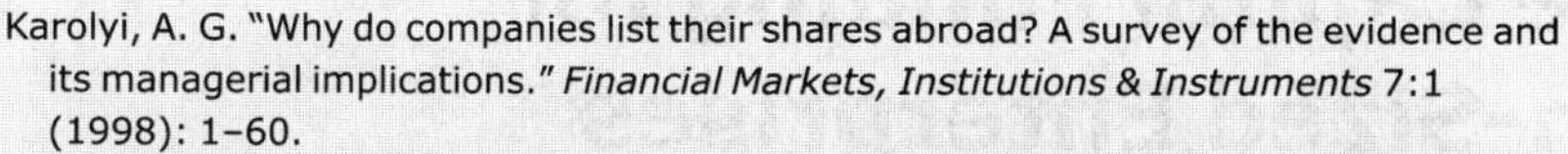

Karolyi, A. G. "Why do companies list their shares abroad? A survey of the evidence and its managerial implications." *Financial Markets, Institutions & Instruments* 7:1 (1998): 1–60.

Karolyi, A. G. "The world of cross-listing and cross-listings of the world: Challenging conventional wisdom." *Review of Finance* 10:1 (2006): 99–152.

Korczak, A., and M. A. Lasfer. "Does cross listing mitigate insider trading?" Working paper, Cass Business School, City University, London, 2009.

Leuz, C. "Cross listing, bonding and firms' reporting incentives: A discussion of Lang, Raedy and Wilson (2006)." *Journal of Accounting and Economics* 42:1-2 (2006): 285–299.

Leuz, C. "Was the Sarbanes–Oxley Act of 2002 really this costly? A discussion of evidence from event returns and going-private decisions." *Journal of Accounting and Economics* 44:1-2 (2007): 146–165.

Licht, A. N. "Cross-listing and corporate governance: Bonding or avoiding?" *Chicago Journal of International Law* 4 (Spring 2003): 141–164.

Pagano, M., A. A. Roell, and J. Zechner. "The geography of equity listing: Why do companies list abroad?" *Journal of Finance* 57:6 (2002): 2651–2694.

Sarkissian, S., and M. J. Schill. "The overseas listing decision: New evidence of proximity preference." *Review of Financial Studies* 17:3 (2004): 769–810.

Websites:

Bank of New York Mellon press releases 2008: www.bnymellon.com/pressreleases/2008/pr071408b.html

Crosslisting.com: www.crosslisting.com

London Stock Exchange: www.londonstockexchange.com

The Open University learning module on cross-listing: openlearn.open.ac.uk/mod/resource/view.php?id=193754

US Securities and Exchange Commission: www.sec.gov

See Also:

★ The Cost of Going Public: Why IPOs Are Typically Underpriced (pp. 531–533)
★ Financial Steps in an IPO for a Small or Medium-Size Enterprise (pp. 540–542)
★ IPOs in Emerging Markets (pp. 545–547)
★ Price Discovery in IPOs (pp. 364–366)
✔ Merchant Banks: Their Structure and Function (p. 929)
✔ Raising Capital by Issuing Shares (p. 1021)
✔ Stock Markets: Their Structure and Function (p. 1025)

"To last, a company must strive to add long-term value rather than going for the quick buck...it must be guided by the desire for continued relations with its principal constituencies—employees, customers, suppliers, stockholders." Charles G. Koch

  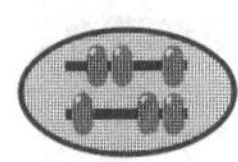   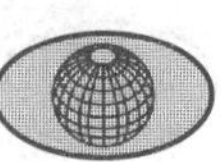 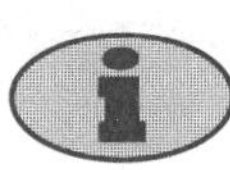  

Assessing Venture Capital Funding for Small and Medium-Sized Enterprises by Alain Fayolle and Joseph LiPuma

EXECUTIVE SUMMARY

- Entrepreneurs and small and medium-sized enterprise (SME) managers capitalize their firms with debt equity investments, or a combination of both.
- Equity investments such as venture capital can erode executive control but can enable access to the investor's knowledge, advice, and networks.
- Venture capital can be provided by business angels, independent venture capital firms (IVCs[1]), corporations, or universities.
- The sources' differing investment objectives, backgrounds, and control mechanisms deliver varying levels of added value to the SME.
- Companies seeking venture capital should select investors whose objectives, potential to add value, and expectations of control mesh most closely with those of the entrepreneur.

INTRODUCTION

Entrepreneurs and SME managers face two key choices when financing their ventures: debt or equity. Debt in the form of personal loans (including credit cards) and bank loans, key sources for most nascent ventures, gives efficient incentives for managers to exert effort and allow entrepreneurs to maintain control. The availability and utility of debt vary significantly with economic conditions, which, in turn, will have an impact on the supply and cost of capital. To a lesser extent, entrepreneurs rely on equity financing,[2] in which parties external to a venture obtain partial ownership (and control) in exchange for financial capital, thus diluting managers' incentives to expend effort. Equity financing is particularly important for high-growth ventures, since the amount of debt financing available may not permit sufficiently rapid growth in volatile industries (for example, technology). Objectives and incentives that are well aligned between investor and manager are the most efficient and facilitate additional value for the venture.

VENTURE CAPITAL

Venture capital (VC) refers to independently managed, dedicated pools of capital which the providers channel into equity or equity-linked investments in privately held, high-growth companies.[3] Worldwide, more than \$30 billion is invested annually as venture capital,[4] with the most intensive use in the United States, Europe, and Israel (with \$28 billion, \$6 billion, and \$.7 billion invested respectively in 2007).[5] Venture capital represents a bundle of productive, value-adding resources, comprising the human capital (knowledge and experience) and social capital (network) of the venture capitalist—who oversees the investment—in addition to the financial capital. The value and productivity of these non-financial aspects of VC can be significant, influencing a venture's offering, geographic diversity, and growth. Venture capitalists can help to professionalize a new venture through representation on the board of directors, executive recruiting, or by exerting rights of control (over, for example, cash flow and liquidation) in exchange for capital. Despite modest levels of investment,[6] venture capital-backed companies[7] accounted for over ten million jobs and \$1.8 trillion in revenue in the United States in 2003[8]—approximately one-sixth of GDP.

Venture capital can come from business angels, independent VC firms (IVCs), corporate venture capital (CVC) programs, and universities. The different ways in which these are funded, investments are managed, and partners are compensated (see Table 1[9]) result in varying allocations of control rights between the investor and the venture capitalist. Angel investors, for example, rarely require representation on corporate boards, whereas IVCs generally do seek directorships. Investment objectives influence the nature of companies in which VCs invest and, correspondingly, the value they are able to add. Independent VC firms invest solely for financial reasons and may best add value to SMEs by helping them to recruit key executives or access additional capital. Corporations that provide CVC often invest for strategic reasons, frequently in ventures with complementary offerings. These corporations are generally multinational, enabling them to add more value in the development of foreign networks of customers, suppliers, and partners. However, CVC investors generally do not invest in early-stage ventures, usually waiting until an IVC invests before committing their resources.

Table 1. Characteristics of the different providers of venture capital

	Angel	*IVC*	*CVC*	*UVC*
Typical background	Ex-entrepreneur	Ex-entrepreneur or financial	Large, tech-savvy multinational	Patent holder
Motivation	Financial and "giving back"	Financial	Strategic and financial	Commercialize patents
Fund source	Self	Limited partners	Corporate	University, government
Investment method	Direct	Direct	Direct and indirect	Direct and indirect
General partner compensation	Gain from exit or early buy-out	Percentage of valuation increase	Salary plus bonus	Salary plus bonus
Average invested per venture	~\$10,000[a]	~\$8 million[b]	~\$4.5 million[c]	<\$250,000[d]

[a] Allen, Kathleen A. *Launching New Ventures: An Entrepreneurial Approach*. Boston, MA: Houghton Mifflin Company, 2006.

[b] PricewaterhouseCoopers/National Venture Capital Association, "MoneyTree™ report." Data: Thomas Reuters.

[c] *Ibid.*

[d] Miles, Morgan P., John B. White, and Eve White. "University sponsored venture capital: An exploratory study." *Journal of Business and Entrepreneurship* 13:1 (2001): 129–134.

"The creation of new ventures is the economic engine that drives regional and international economies."
Harry J. Sapienza

  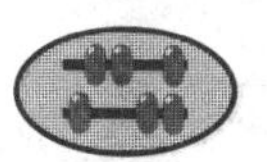   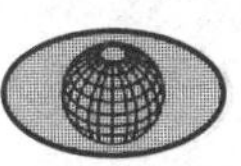 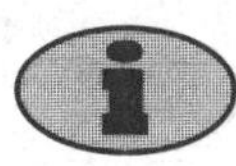  

SELECTING THE RIGHT TYPE OF VC

Though only a small percentage of companies receive venture capital,[10] those that do can usually choose its source and should therefore select investors whose objectives, added-value potential, and expectations of control are most in accord with those of the business owner. Since the process of pitching ventures to investors and negotiating terms can be time-consuming, especially for SMEs and young ventures, it is crucial to establish your objectives and target VC sources early on. This may also help to avoid later contract issues, optimize venture capitalist contributions, and increase the venture's value. Questions to consider are:

What stage are we at? At the seed or startup stage, angel financing is best because it comes with fewer strings attached and is easier to "buy out." Angel investors are good stewards and may take active, informal roles in the company. Corporations generally do not invest at early stages, so IVC is most likely at the next stage, with CVC most used in expansion stages.

How big a VC provider do you need? While this answer often depends on capital needs, prestigious or "big name" IVC providers bring broad and helpful networks, in addition to status, that can help when exiting via a public offering or acquisition. However, prominent VCs often require more control over cash flow, voting, board representation, and liquidation. Such rights are often contingent on observable performance measures. If the venture does badly, VCs obtain more control, whereas if the venture does well, VCs relinquish most control and liquidation rights.

Do I need a specialized VC provider with specific industry knowledge and contacts? Industry specialization helps VC firms to develop skills for vetting and selecting investments, and for developing relevant industry knowledge and networks. Generalist firms are able to thrive and grow as industries evolve and ebb, and they have cross-industry experience and networks that may benefit nascent ventures.

How much capital do we need, and what do we need the funds for? If funds are needed for initial technology development, CVC, with the associated corporate technology knowledge, may provide access to technical skills. In addition to supplying capital of their own, IVCs are good at helping companies in which they invest to obtain access to other funds because of their legitimacy and the networks they have.

Are we planning to enter foreign markets? The VC industry is globalizing,[11] and since VC providers tend to invest in ventures that are geographically proximate, there is limited foreign investment. In addition, some VC providers tend to eschew investments in internationalized ventures, since they cannot easily monitor their activities. CVC associated with a multinational enterprise may provide foreign market knowledge and assist in market penetration, and permit access to foreign customers, suppliers, and partners who can help to monitor the internationalized venture.

How vulnerable is my intellectual property? Working with a VC provider requires an exchange of detailed information about development projects, product specifications, and marketing plans. Corporations often invest for strategic reasons based on industry or market congruity with new ventures. Such congruity suggests that the investor could easily appropriate the intellectual property of the SME. Research suggests that receiving investments from multiple corporations may limit that risk.

CONCLUSION

SMEs and young ventures that receive capital investments can often choose their source. The boundary-spanning role of investors, as both advisers and links to external networks, places VCs in a unique position to add value to a venture. The potential for investors to aid in the growth and development of such ventures demands that entrepreneurs and SME managers make their choice in a considered manner that is consistent with their overall strategy. Careful consideration of investor types can lead to an efficient selection process that provides value throughout the life of the venture.

CASE STUDY

Tessera Enterprise Systems

Tessera Enterprise Systems, a custom software developer, was founded in Boston in 1995 by an executive team that had previously worked together for three years. Tessera's target market included some of the largest American retail and financial companies, such as Eddie Bauer and Charles Schwab. The founders provided initial funding for the venture, but after one year it was decided that venture capital was required to expand the company. Tessera, however, secured an investment offer from Greylock Management, a prominent Boston-based IVC. Greylock's status added legitimacy to the fledgling venture, permitting it to obtain contracts with target companies such as Charles Schwab, Eddie Bauer, and other prominent clients. Subsequent expansion and third-stage funding from two other prominent IVCs solidified Tessera in the market and led to a corporate expansion to San Francisco. At the same time, Tessera considered establishing an office in Switzerland to serve potential European clients. One of the VC providers likened internationalization to loading an airplane with stacks of cash and opening the doors while flying over the Atlantic.

Tessera nevertheless pursued its foreign market entry strategy and, while it slowly obtained some European contracts, it did so without the involvement or aid of its IVC investors. Had Tessera sought investment from a technology corporation such as Oracle (on whose products its offerings were often based), it might have been better able to leverage its investor's networks and knowledge to the benefit of its foreign business. A modest capital round was provided by IVCs and a private investor in preparation for an exit. Tessera, originally planning on a public offering and broad foreign expansion, was acquired in 2001 by iXL, an Atlanta-based internet services provider company with offices in San Francisco and London.

▸▸ MAKING IT HAPPEN

Since VC has the potential to change the nature of resources in an SME so dramatically, entrepreneurs must approach it with a strategic view of how it may best add value, and source it accordingly. At the same time as they assess their financial capital needs, SME managers should do the following:

- Carefully consider the type of advice, information, and network access you want from an investor in the light of current needs and strategic direction.
- Identify VC providers that have great reputations for providing value in a manner consistent with your willingness to cede some control.
- Ask others who have undertaken VC-backed ventures about their experience with investors—both IVC and CVC—and the success and problems they encountered.
- Identify companies that had exits—IPOs and acquisitions—most consistent with your goals and ask about their investors.

"...entrepreneurs do not stop soliciting interest from venture capitalists after receiving one offer, but rather attempt to establish a market for their companies' shares." Gordon Smith

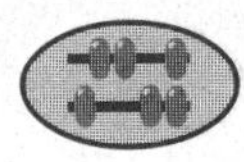

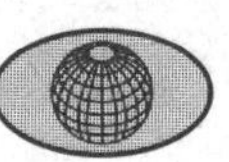

▸▸ MORE INFO

Books:

Gompers, Paul A., and Josh Lerner. *The Venture Capital Cycle*. Cambridge, MA: MIT Press, 1999.

Maula, M., and G. C. Murray. "Corporate venture capital and the creation of US public companies: The impact of sources of venture capital on the performance of portfolio companies." In Michael A. Hitt, Raphael Amit, Charles E. Lucier and Robert D. Nixon, (eds). *Creating Value: Winners in the New Business Environment*. Oxford: Blackwell Publishing, 2002.

McNally, Kevin. *Corporate Venture Capital: Bridging the Equity Gap in the Small Business Sector*. London: Routledge, 1997.

Articles:

Maula, M. V. J., E. Autio, and G. C. Murray. "Corporate venture capitalists and independent venture capitalists: What do they know, who do they know and should entrepreneurs care?" *Venture Capital* 7:1 (2005): 3–22.

Sapienza, Harry J., Allen C. Amason, and Sophie Manigart. "The level and nature of venture capitalist involvement in their portfolio companies: A study of three European countries." *Managerial Finance* 20:1 (1994): 3–17.

Smith, Gordon. "How early stage entrepreneurs evaluate venture capitalists." *Journal of Private Equity* 4:2 (2001): 33–45.

Van Osnabrugge, Mark, and Robert J. Robinson. "The influence of a venture capitalist's source of funds." *Venture Capital* 3:1 (2001): 25–39.

Websites:

National Venture Capital Association (NVCA): www.nvca.org

European Private Equity and Venture Capital Association (EVCA): www.evca.eu

NOTES

1 We wish to emphasize that the acronym "IVC" here refers to formal venture capital investments by independent firms specialized for this purpose. Other literature uses "IVC" to refer to informal venture capital investments.

2 For example, in the United States fewer than 7% of companies obtain outside equity financing, whereas 45% take on outside debt Alicia Robb and David T. Robinson, "The capital structure decisions of new firms: Second in a series of reports using data from the Kauffman firm survey," Kansas City, MO: Kauffman Foundation (2008). New Zealand businesses are almost six times more likely to seek additional debt financing than equity financing (www.stats.govt.nz), whereas nearly 20 times more Canadian companies sought debt financing than equity financing (www.sme-fdi.gc.ca).

3 Gompers and Lerner, (1999).

4 Ernst & Young Fourth Annual Venture Capital Insight Report, "Exits set to increase worldwide as venture capital industry continues to globalize." London: Ernst & Young, May 3, 2006.

5 PricewaterhouseCoopers/National Venture Capital Association, "MoneyTreeTMreport." Online: www.pwcmoneytree.com/MTPublic/ns/index.jsp, Data: Thomas Reuters, Accessed 5March2009; www.evca.com; and www.investinisrael.gov.il respectively.

6 From 1999 to 2002, less than 0.5% of GDP was invested via venture capital in the United States (OECD report).

7 This includes those that are now public companies, such as Intel, Microsoft, eBay and Home Depot.

8 Global Insight, "Venture impact 2004: Venture capital benefits to the U.S. economy." www.nvca.org/pdf/VentureImpact2004.pdf.

9 Note that this table is based on examples from the United States. In Europe, for example, research institutes often take the place of universities in conducting research and formulating approaches to the commercialization of intellectual property.

10 For example, in the United States fewer than 0.1% of all companies founded in the 1990s received venture capital (authors' analysis of US data from the NVCA). In Europe, the probability of receiving VC is approximately 0.07% (Eric Achtmann, "Getting a view of VC in Europe. . .from the centre," 4th Annual MIT VCPI Conference, Cambridge, MA, December 1, 2001).

11 See, for example, Hall, G., and C. Tu. "Venture capitalists and the decision to invest overseas." *Venture Capital* 5:2 (2003): 181–190, and Manigart, S., *et al.*. "Human capital and the internationalization of venture capital firms." *International Entrepreneurship and Management Journal* 3:1 (2007): 1–125.

"Failure is more frequently from want of energy than want of capital." Daniel Webster

  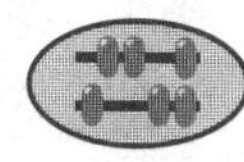   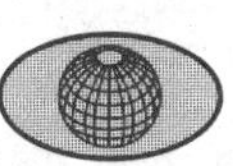   

Attracting Small Investors by Wondimu Mekonnen

EXECUTIVE SUMMARY

- Small investors are individuals who purchase small amounts of stocks for themselves, as opposed to institutional investors such as pension funds.
- Small investors can deposit money in banks and building societies to earn interest on their savings.
- Although it has been the traditional belief that money deposited in a bank or building society is safer than an investment in stock, the recent crises experienced by these High Street institutions have eroded that trust.
- Investments in company stock involves risk, but the rewards can be much greater than from a deposit or savings account.
- In dealing with small investors, CEOs and CFOs are advised to implement various incentives to keep existing investors and attract new ones.

INTRODUCTION

A company is financed by various sources, such as short-term borrowings, long-term debt, and owner's equity—ordinary shares, preference shares, and reserves. Small investors can participate in most of these. A significant portion of funds finds its way into the bond or stock markets through financial institutions that are the repositories of household savings. Therefore, the size of resources available for financing a company's activities depends to a large extent on household savings. Small investors are usually individuals who purchase small amounts of stocks for themselves, in contrast to the large institutional investors such as pension funds. Small investors are sometimes referred to as individual, or retail, investors.

In 2005, the Investment Company Institute reported that 91.1 million household investors in the United States held US$56.9 million of various types of equities.[1] This constituted 50.3% of all households. The growing number of small investors gives the market depth.

BANKS AND BUILDING SOCIETIES

Banks and building societies depend primarily on household savings, of which they are the main custodians. The amount of interest they offer on deposits and savings accounts can be an incentive to small investors. For their very survival, therefore, it is vital that such institutions understand how to deal with small investors. They have to design incentives to encourage people to save. One way they do this is by offering savings accounts with a variety of earning structures and conditions. The Halifax's fixed saving term option[2] and Abbey's Individual Savings Accounts (ISAs) offer the kinds of incentives that may encourage household savings.

Companies can raise money by selling bonds to investors. Although in theory, small investors could buy corporate bonds and hold them, they play little role in the primary market. Simply put, bonds tend to be bought and sold in a closed circle of insiders and experts.

INVESTMENT IN SHARES

More and more small investors have become shareholders, and share dealing is no longer a job reserved for city slickers. In the United Kingdom, the Building Societies Act 1986 allowed building societies to demutualize and become public limited companies instead of mutually owned organizations (i.e. owned by the customers who borrowed and saved with the society). A case in point is when the Halifax Building Society announced that it was to merge with the Leeds Permanent Building Society and convert to a plc. The Halifax floated on the London Stock Exchange on June 2, 1997, making more than 7.5 million customers of the Society shareholders in the new bank—the largest extension of shareholders in UK history. Of the new shareholders, 2.1 million were small investors. That is about one-third of all the investors in the Halifax (Snowdon, 2008). A report published in May 2008 reveals that small investors hold a combined total of 770 million shares worth almost £4 billion in HBOS, as the group is now known. Their average holding is 375 shares.

Another example was when Abbey National (now Abbey) was demutualized in 1989, in which 1.7 million small investors held 200 to 300 shares. Abbey was eventually taken over by the Spanish bank Santander (Papworth, 2005). £400 million of Bradford & Bingley's funds come from small investors (Treanor, 2008),[3] who form more than a third of its lenders. The recent nationalization (government takeover) of Bradford & Bingley will mark the end of the line for the last independent former building society to take on bank status.

Risk-taking investors may not wish to be limited to the small amount of interest they can earn on a deposit account, but prefer to take the risk of investing in company stocks. With such investments they can reap the reward if prices rise, although they have to suffer the consequences if prices fall. When markets are rising, what a saver might make in three years from a savings account can be made in a year, or even in months, in the stock markets. Thus, the reward for taking risk can tempt small investors to invest in shares. Companies should therefore make every effort to tap into this potential source of finance.

Anyone can trade in shares by him- or herself or through an agent, called a stockbroker. The quality and speed of market information has improved tremendously. Newspapers, especially the *Financial Times*, and various websites report movements in share prices. Using the internet, up to date information on share prices can be obtained instantly in the comfort of one's home. The London Stock Exchange home page[4] provides continuous reporting on market movements in the FTSE indices. Similarly, the New York Stock Exchange,[5] the largest in the world, provides information on various indices including S&P500, AEX, and Euronext 100 online. As a result, the number of small investors trading in shares has been steadily increasing. Figure 1 shows the growth in equity ownership by US households between 1983 and 2005.[6]

THE CREDIT CRUNCH AND SMALL INVESTORS

Although household savers are one of the most important sources of funds for investment, negative news about a financial institution that acts as a custodian of their savings can cause panic and a rush on banks or building societies to withdraw their money. This can bring the financial market tumbling down. Financial institutions such as banks and mortgage lenders need to understand the risks associated with being the custodians of the wealth of individual investors. The recent crisis that started in the US banking sector ended by engulfing the world, prompting panicking savers almost to pull down even giant healthy banks and mortgage lenders and initiating a worldwide financial crisis.

"The biggest competitive advantage that individual investors have is that we can afford to hold stocks for five years or more. Most Wall Street pros can't do that." Tim Hanson

     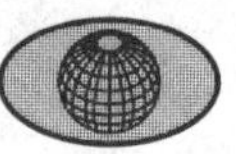   

Figure 1. Equity ownership by US households. (*Sources*: The Investment Company Institute/the Securities Industry Association (ICI/SIA) equity ownership surveys; Federal Reserve Board Survey of Consumer Finances; US Census Bureau)

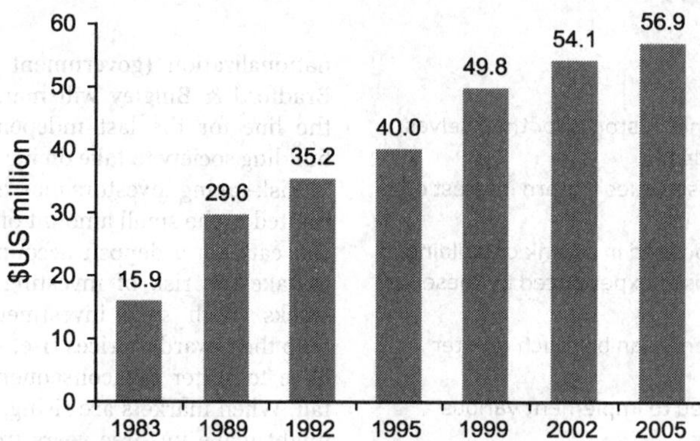

The first such panic took place in the United Kingdom in September 2007 and involved a bank called Northern Rock. When depositors started queuing to withdraw their money, the Bank of England made an unprecedented and dramatic move to save the collapsing bank. The *Guardian* newspaper of Friday September 14, 2007, reported that this intervention by the Bank was agreed between its governor, Mervyn King, the chancellor, Alistair Darling, and the Financial Services Authority. Northern Rock customers were urged to stay calm—but it did little to help. It was reported that the Northern Rock sought the funding because of a cash shortage caused by the month-long crisis in global credit markets that began with the collapse of the subprime mortgage market in the United States. At the time, depositor's money in Northern Rock amounted to more than £100 billion. The unfortunate chain of events did not stop there. The next casualties of the panic attack were the Halifax-Bank of Scotland (HBOS) Group and Bradford & Bingley, and even Barclays Bank was affected. The bad news spread among small investors like wildfire. The large-circulation tabloids in particular fed the panic, causing more confusion. For example, the *Sun* newspaper of November 27, 2008, wrote:

> "Britain's biggest mortgage lender, whose funding position has been in the spotlight in the wake of the Lehman Brothers collapse, saw its stock suddenly plunge 30 per cent despite starting the session up around seven per cent higher."

These events in the United Kingdom were followed by similar losses of confidence affecting IKB in Germany, BNP Paribas in France, and other banks throughout the world.

Times Online (the online version of *The Times* and the *Sunday Times*) of August 14, 2008, explained what underlay the crises as follows. "Years of lax lending inflated a huge debt bubble as people borrowed cheap money and invested it into property. Lenders were free with their funds, especially in the United States, where billions of dollars of so-called Ninja mortgages—no income, no job or assets—were sold to people with weak credit ratings." The low interest rates and easy access to mortgages sent property prices spiralling up. And whenever the borrowers ran into trouble with their repayments, rising house prices allowed them to remortgage their properties. Eventually, interest rates—which had been low in 2004—began to rise quickly, US house prices started to fall, and borrowers began to default on mortgage payments. This sparked trouble. The banks became too nervous to lend money to individuals any more—and even to each other. When they did lend, it was at higher rates of interest to cover the risk. It was the last straw that broke the camel's back. Thus began the credit crunch that hit the United States and the world. Lehman Brothers filed for bankruptcy on September 15, 2008. Together with the problems faced by Merrill Lynch and AIG, this caused a sharp drop and turmoil in the global stock markets, a chilling harbinger of the world economic crisis to follow.

HANDLING SMALL INVESTORS

Small investors need assurance from CEOs and CFOs that they will not ignore them or overlook their interests when times get tough. A good way of doing this is to turn managers into shareholders. Managers must be perceived as being ready to make sacrifices in the interests of the company's investors. In tough times small investors want to see that those in charge are not losing just their jobs but also their own investment in the company, because managers faced with such a prospect can be expected to work hard to turn the business around to save their own skins. They must be seen as having an incentive to put their blood and sweat into the business to avoid a personal hit if the venture fails.

Small investors think about risk. They would like to see that a company is well secured by holding a well-diversified portfolio of various shares. Small investors like to see steady growth in the profitability of a company and its subsidiaries, with a corresponding rise in the share price.

The way existing shareholders are treated can attract potential small investors. Rights issues to existing shareholders instead of dividends are one way of attracting potential investors. Preference shares can also be attractive to small investors. Preference shares offer a guaranteed stream of fixed income whether the company makes a profit or not, although it is riskier than debt in terms of priority if the company goes bankrupt and into liquidation.

Turning workers into shareholders is another way of creating small investors. And of course that is on top of the improvement in corporate performance it may bring about. Six per cent of German employees, for example, own stock in the

➧ MAKING IT HAPPEN

Actions that can be taken to maintain small investors' confidence to continue investing include the following:

- Make managers shareholders, and let the small investors know about it.
- Protect your company against any possible financial risk by holding a well-diversified portfolio of various shares.
- Keep the existing shareholders happy, well treated, and looked after. They will bring in more investors.
- Turn your workers into shareholders. Workers with a financial stake in a company work more efficiently when the company's success results in a rise in the share price.
- Create a stable and conducive environment that encourages people to save and prosper.

"A few years from now, don't be surprised if some blogger in his boxer shorts brings down the next Enron."
Michael Brush

     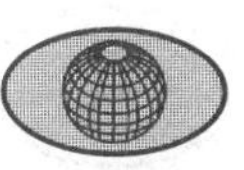  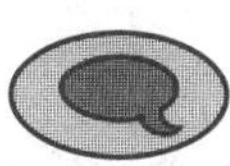 

company they work for,[7] and the plan is to increase their stake.

Keeping small investors interested in saving and investing is vital for the protection of the financial interests of companies. It is therefore important to create a stable and conducive environment that encourages people to save and prosper.

CONCLUSION

In conclusion, dealing with small investors can be a tricky business. Banks, building societies, and other institutional investors and mortgage lenders all depend on household savings and small investors. Between them, the millions of small investors can raise substantial funds that are a vital source of economic growth and stability. However, it is important to win and hold the trust of small investors so that they are encouraged to save and invest. Even a whisper of negative comment about an organization they have entrusted their money to may make them panic and rush in their millions to withdraw their cash. This can create a liquidity problem so severe that it can bring down the largest of corporations. In dealing with small investors, therefore, various techniques should be implemented to encourage them and to maintain their confidence.

▸▸ MORE INFO

Books:

Lindahl, David. *Trump University Commercial Real Estate 101: How Small Investors can get Started and Make it Big*. Hoboken, NJ: Wiley, 2008.

Stowe, John D., Thomas R. Robinson, Jerald E. Pinto, and Dennis W. McLeavey. *Equity Asset Valuation*. Hoboken, NJ: Wiley, 2007.

Articles

Brush, Michael. "A revolution for small investors." MSN Money (April 30, 2008). Online at: tinyurl.com/cjhbq9

Hanson, Tim. "Secret advantages for small investors." The Motley Fool (January 9, 2006). Online at: tinyurl.com/cdjlo5

Lease, Ronald C., Wilbur G. Lewellen, and Gary G. Schlarbaum. "The individual investor: Attributes and attitudes." *Journal of Finance* 29:2 (1974): 413–433.

Lian, Tan Kin. "Protecting the small investors." The Online Citizen (blog site), Singapore (September 22, 2008). Online at: theonlinecitizen.com/2008/09/protecting-the-small-investors

Luo, Jar-Der. "The savings behavior of small investors: A case study of Taiwan." *Economic Development and Cultural Change* 46:4 (1998): 771–788.

Malmendier, Ulrike, and Devin M. Shanthikumar. "Are small investors naïve about incentives?" *Journal of Financial Economics* 85:2 (2007): 457–489. Online at: www.people.hbs.edu/dshanthikumar/AreSmallInvestorsNaiveAboutIncentives.pdf

Papworth, Jill. "Investors should lose Abbey habit." *Guardian (London)* (January 22, 2005). Online at: www.guardian.co.uk/money/2005/jan/22/abbey.jobsandmoney

Snowdon, Ros. "HBOS cash call sets poser for small investors." *Yorkshire Post* (April 30, 2008). Online at: www.yorkshirepost.co.uk/news/HBOS-cash-call-sets-poser.4033854.jp

Treanor, Jill. "Small investors threaten to derail B&B fundraising." *Guardian (London)* (June 28, 2008). Online at: www.guardian.co.uk/business/2008/jun/28/bradfordbingleybusiness.banking

Varian, Hal R. "Economic scene; despite the recovery in stocks, some of the forces behind the internet bust are still lurking." *New York Times* (July 3, 2003). Online at: tinyurl.com/agkjuj

Wilson, Graeme. "Halifax in a fix." *Sun (London)* (September 17, 2008). Online at: www.thesun.co.uk/sol/homepage/news/money/article1699151.ece

Websites:

Investment Company Institute: www.ici.org

The Motley Fool investment community: www.fool.com

MSN Money: moneycentral.msn.com

Securities Industry and Financial Markets Association (SIFMA): www.sifma.org

See Also:

Jack Welch (p. 1204)

NOTES

1 Investment Company Institute, Washington, DC, and Securities Industry and Financial Markets Association, New York, *Equity Ownership in America, Fall 2005*.

2 www.halifax.co.uk/savings/personalrates.asp

3 theonlinecitizen.com/2008/09/protecting-the-small-investors

4 www.londonstockexchange.com/en-gb

5 www.nyse.com

6 As note 1.

7 David Hudson. "Toward a shareholder society." *Spiegel Online* (March 30, 2000). Online at: www.spiegel.de/politik/deutschland/0,1518,71070,00.html

"The problem established firms seem unable to confront successfully is that of downward vision and mobility, in terms of the trajectory map." Clayton M. Christensen

  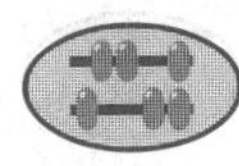 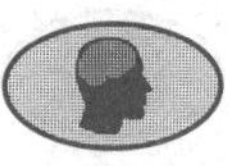  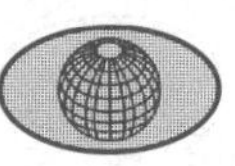   

Capital Structure: A Strategy that Makes Sense by John C. Groth

EXECUTIVE SUMMARY

- Perfect capital markets prescribe an optimal capital structure.
- Imperfect capital markets, the seasonal and cyclical aspects of an economy, and the variability of market conditions argue that a company should have a target capital structure and an operating capital structure range.
- Managers should be sensitive to changes in the business risk of a company, as these alter the optimal capital structure.
- Maintaining good debt capacity makes sense and may favorably influence stock price.
- Using bad debt capacity does not make sense from the viewpoint of stockholders and primary creditors.
- Projects with good economic returns restore debt capacity and reduce the debt/equity (D/E) ratio. Bad projects that do not have attractive economic returns will have an adverse effect on capital structure, increase the D/E ratio, and eventually decrease the optimal D/E ratio.
- Managers may adjust capital structure quickly or gradually. Whether quickly or gradually hinges on a variety of factors.
- Capital structure is important for privately held firms.
- Stock repurchase programs call for sensitivity and possible adjustment of debt capital so that one attains and/or preserves the desired capital structure.
- Leveraged buyouts often distort capital structure. The decision to accept abnormal capital structures originates with those promoting the buyout and their perceptions about gains relative to personal capital at risk.
- Issues related to control may influence the choice of capital structure.

INTRODUCTION

Perfect capital markets enjoy an array of assumptions, including no cost to bankruptcy, infinitely divisible financial assets and liabilities, no transaction costs, etc. Pursuing a selected optimal capital structure would allow minute adjustments, the issuance or redemption of small amounts of capital, and other conveniences. We would simply strive for the optimal debt/equity ratio depicted in Figure 1. Indeed, in this unreal world one would keep all the equity for control and to maximize wealth—and employ massive amounts of debt.[1]

Imperfect Capital Markets

The rudeness of imperfect markets prompts us to adopt a reasonable strategy that allows one to benefit from the tenets of capital structure theory while respecting the reality of markets and economies. Imperfect capital markets, bankruptcy costs, and that a company with financial flexibility may have attractive opportunities during periods of adverse market conditions argue for a strategy for the management of capital structure. Additionally, capital market participants may value a company with the financial flexibility that would allow it to pursue opportunities even (or especially) during periods of high market stress. A company with financial flexibility may find bargains during periods of distress.

In this article we first address background issues. Then we will move to recommendations. We will see that the suggested strategy does not seek to have the theoretical optimal debt/equity (D/E) ratio.

Good and Bad Debt Capacity

A company that has a less than optimal D/E ratio has unused good capacity. Normally a company with "good" debt capacity can borrow quickly on favorable terms to pursue an attractive opportunity. Thus, it can obtain capital quickly without the delays or possible undesirability of an equity offering.

Exceeding the optimal D/E ratio results in the company using "bad" debt capacity. History tells us that it is possible to do stupid things. Occasionally, we also see agents taking actions that promote their own interests, rather than acting in a way that benefits owners and creditors. Bad debt capacity adversely affects the weighted cost of capital, limits flexibility, and decreases stock price.

ISSUES AND STRATEGY

Interrelationships

The *expected* streams of cash flows that originate in the business or operating side of a company service the sources of capital, including short-term liabilities such as accounts payable. Choices on the asset side of the company, and how successfully the company operates assets and interacts with the markets for goods and services, precipitate effects on the financing side of the company.

Although EBITDDA (earnings before interest, taxes, depreciation, depletion, and amortization) is not necessarily a cash flow in a period of time, for reasons explained in my article "Accounting and Economics—Critical Perspectives" (see qfinance.com), let us for simplicity assume that it *is* a cash flow. Those who have provided financing for the company have a keen interest in the level of expected cash flows, and the timing and the uncertainty of those cash flows. Hence, what the company chooses to do (its investments) and how well it employs those assets to generate cash flows (production, sales, collections, etc.) influence the business risk of the company.

The business risk, and factors such as tax rules and rates, influence the optimal financing for the company and, in turn, the financial risk of the company. Let us share some summary comments.

MANAGING AND ADJUSTING CAPITAL STRUCTURE

The company might select a gradual, a lumpy, or a quick process for adjusting capital structure. For discussion, we will assume that the company has the ratio D/E = C in Figure 1, a level which is less than the optimal D/E = O. Its WCOC is higher than it need be, and the value of the company and equity are lower than they could be.

We will examine different ways of altering the D/E ratio. Our discussion will explain ways to either increase or decrease the D/E ratio to show how different variables influence the ratio. Later we will suggest how this sample company might move towards the optimal point. Shortly we will explain why normally we probably *don't* want to move to the optimal point.

Possible Gradual Process Steps

To move the D/E ratio to the left (which is not our objective for the company in Figure 1), do one or more of the following:

- If a dividend-paying company, have a payout ratio of less than 100%. To adjust the payout ratio, one can increase dividends at a slower rate than the growth in earnings.
- Pay off some of the principal of the debt

  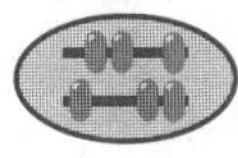 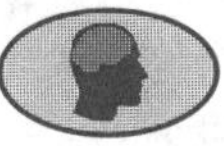  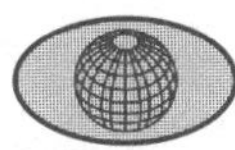   

Figure 1. Adjusting capital structure

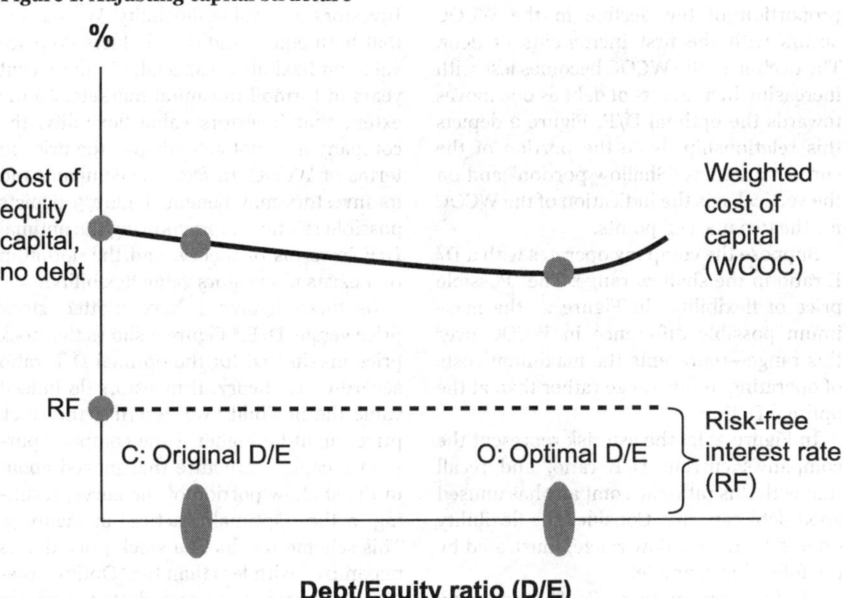

using cash flow from operations and/or from the sale of assets.

- Do both.

To move the D/E to the right, towards the optimal ratio:

- Increase the payout ratio.
- Delay, if without penalty and with explanation to the market, the retirement of principal on debt.[2]

The Lumpy Approach

The borrowing of chunks of money for corporate use, such as capital projects, will result in a jump to the right in the D/E ratio. Employed wisely in projects that have good economic results, the freshly raised capital generates fresh additions to equity. The D/E gradually moves back to the left.

The Quick Process

Adjusting capital structure quickly is relatively easy if the company has less than the optimal amount of debt and wants to increase its D/E ratio. The tactic calls for arrangement for, and announcement of, the borrowing of the appropriate amount of money for the purpose of using the proceeds to repurchase some of its stock *to adjust the capital structure to an optimal level.* Explaining the purpose for the borrowing gives notice to all stockholders and offers a positive reason for stock repurchase, thus avoiding arguments of possible negative signaling associated with stock repurchase.

To increase the D/E ratio quickly, one might borrow a chunk of capital (again with explanation to the market) and declare a special cash dividend. This approach requires careful consideration of tax preferences of the stockholders in tax environments where dividends are taxed at a high rate.

As part of an acquisition strategy—though not as a reason for acquisition—the company might acquire another company that has too much debt. The combined companies could have a capital structure closer to the optimum. This is shown as follows. If the acquiring company has a less than optimal D/E ratio, its stock price will be depressed. If the acquired company has a D/E ratio greater than the optimal, its stock price will also be depressed. A combination of two companies with the "correct" proportions will result in an increase in value traceable to the movement towards a more optimal capital structure.

This improvement in stock value could be realized *without the acquisition* by just adjusting the capital structure of both companies. We mention this only because capital structure considerations and adjustments are sometimes important in acquisitions.

If a company has more than the optimal amount of debt, adjusting capital structure may not be as easy, or at least not as advisable, under certain market conditions. Even if capital markets are in turmoil, some theorists will argue for the following approach: announce the issuance of common stock, with the proceeds dedicated to retiring some debt. The market's knowledge of this act of moving towards the optimal debt ratio should favorably affect the price of the stock.

Practitioners might suggest that such a change could have adverse effects if the company is under duress or when markets are in tumult. Some would argue that the funds realized from the equity offering make this a poor strategy. Instead, the company should ride out the bad times or bad markets and make adjustments to its capital structure at a later date.

ISSUES CONCERNING CONTROL

A company may alter its capital structure for reasons of control. Equity holders—except for certain classes of stock found in some markets—have voting rights. Assume that some current equity holders value control. We will term these the "control group." The nature and manner of altering the capital structure may influence control in one or more ways:

- The company repurchases some of its stock. Repurchased shares, or "treasury stock," do not confer voting rights. Those in the control group do not sell any stock. The control group now has a larger percentage of ownership. The D/E moves to the right.
- The company issues new stock with a rights offering. The D/E moves to the left. Members of the control group exercise their rights and buy the shares. If not all other stockholders exercise their rights, one or both of the following may occur:
  – Some do not exercise rights at all: the control group's proportion of ownership increases.
  – Some sell rights to others, who exercise the rights and buy stock, leading to dispersion of stockholder ownership. Dispersion of ownership may increase the effective control of the control group, even with the exercise of all rights.[3]

OTHER ISSUES

Risk Preferences and the Choice of D/E Ratio

Recall a fundamental principle of the valuation of risky assets. *Markets* value assets, not management or the board of directors. The implications of this fundamental principle are straightforward—and important. *Do what the markets like.* The risk preferences of market participants, rather than the personal preferences of management, should guide decisions and influence the choice of capital structure. Select a target capital structure based on market inputs.

Capital Structure and Privately or Closely Held Organizations

Decisions and strategies for privately/closely held taxable companies rest on the same principles. However, the tax scenario for the corporation as well as its tax pos-

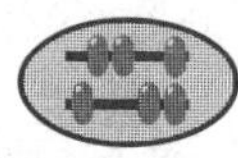

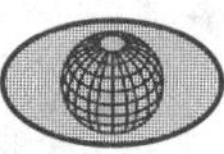

ition with respect to the other taxable entities owned by the same people—and the resultant consolidated tax position—may suggest different strategies.

For example, owners with deep pockets who are willing and ready to provide infusions of equity in bad times may argue for a more aggressive D/E ratio for the company in the hope of garnering greater tax benefits. Additionally, different risk preferences influence choice. If one "owns the store" and *currently* has no concern about market valuation, the choice of capital structure will anchor to personal tax circumstance and risk preferences. The issues are complex and very sensitive to the particular consolidated tax position, as well as to personal risk preferences and attitudes towards debt.

Agency Costs

Investors should guard against a form of management agency costs, namely, the use of bad debt capacity to further management's objectives and interests at the expense of stockholders, and possibly creditors. For example, management may employ excessive debt to protect against takeover, and thus preserve its position. In another example, a management might use excess debt rather than raise equity, because raising equity would dilute its equity position, including the proportion of votes it controls—which is important in preserving board/management control. This dilution could occur for one or both of the following reasons: managers own the stock but are not willing to purchase the correct proportions of the new equity; ownership of stock is dispersed in a way such that newly issued shares are held by those who are less supportive of management.

A RECOMMENDATION FOR CAPITAL STRUCTURE STRATEGY

Transaction costs associated with the issuance of securities, changes in economic and market conditions, the "lumpiness" of capital investments, and the arrival of misfortune despite the best planning, the potential for unexpected opportunities, as well as other factors prompt us to suggest a particular strategy for capital structure.

Strategy

Pursue a capital structure that garners a substantial portion of the benefits of an optimal capital structure. Preserve flexibility for the company. Explain the strategy to the markets. Hope—and we think it will—that markets value the strategy.

In my article "Capital Structure—Perspectives" (pp. 31–34), Table 1 depicts the behavior of the weighted cost of capital as one alters the D/E ratio. A substantial proportion of the decline in the WCOC occurs with the first increments of debt. The decline in the WCOC becomes less with increasing increments of debt as one moves towards the optimal D/E. Figure 2 depicts this relationship. Note the portion of the curve marked as "Shallow portion" and on the vertical axis the indication of the WCOC for the two marked points.

Suppose the company operates with a D/E ratio in the shallow range. The "Possible price of flexibility" in Figure 2—the maximum possible difference in WCOC over this range—represents the maximum costs of operating in this range rather than at the optimal D/E.

In Figure 2, let the asterisk represent the company's current D/E ratio, and recall that with this ratio the company has unused good debt capacity. Consider the flexibility offered by the shallow range, illustrated by the following example.

Markets are in turmoil. The company recognizes an opportunity. The good debt capacity allows it to borrow money quickly to pursue the opportunity. The borrowing moves the asterisk to the right by a chunk, but not past the optimal D/E ratio. The good economic results of the project generate equity and move the D/E back to the left, restoring the good debt capacity. This occurs because good projects increase the value of equity (and we measure D/E in market values), and such projects generate returns to equity. As the company generates cash flow, it may also pay off principal on the debt, accelerating the movement of the D/E to the left.

Figure 2. Capital structure versus WCOC

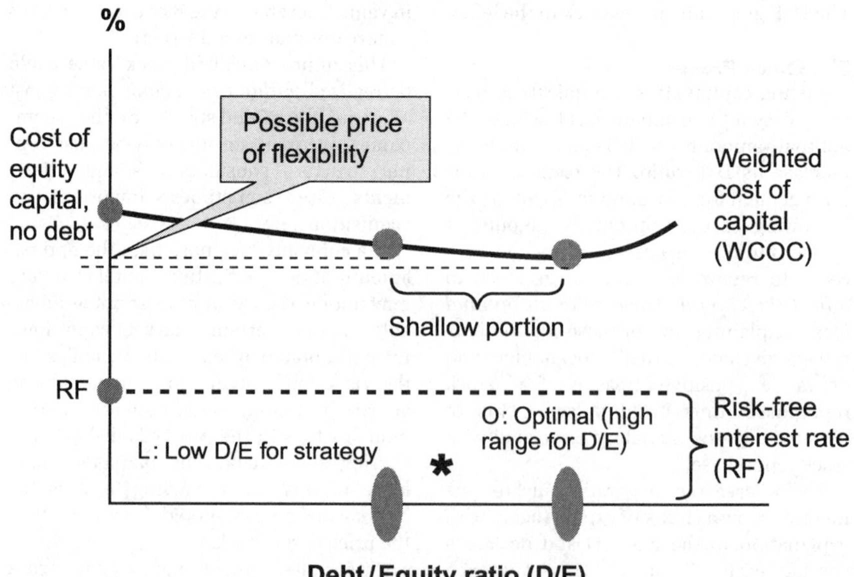

The Value of Flexibility

Investors may value flexibility. We suspect that both equity and debt holders do place value on flexibility, especially in the recent years of turmoil in capital markets. To the extent that investors value flexibility, the company may not actually pay the price in terms of WCOC. In fact, the company and its investors may benefit. Figure 3 depicts possible relationships, showing the optimal D/E in terms of theory, and the optimum that exists if investors value flexibility.

In these figures I have plotted stock price versus D/E.[4] Figure 3 shows the stock price maximized for the optimal D/E ratio according to theory. If investors do indeed value the flexibility we describe, the stock price might be higher if the company pursued a capital structure that moved about in the shallow portion of the curve, resulting in the "Optimal practice" in Figure 3. This scheme results in a stock price that is maximized with less than the "Optimal theory" D/E ratio. The heavy dotted curve for stock price intentionally has a slightly higher maximum stock price—a speculation on our part. We caution that many theorists would not agree with this conclusion. On the other hand, a number of practitioners as well as investors might find the assertion reasonable.

CONCLUSION, IDEAS, AND ACTIONS

Theory is important. Common sense is powerful. Strategy benefits from theory and common sense. The time horizon for strategy depends on a variety of factors, including the dynamics of the social, polit-

"Markets operate under uncertainty. It is therefore crucial to market performance that participants manage their risks properly. . . the answer, as it always has been. . .less debt, more equity, and hence a larger buffer against adversity." Alan Greenspan

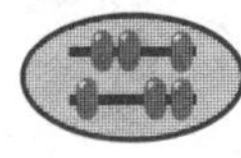

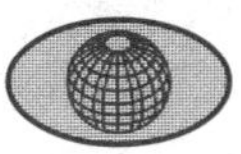

Figure 3. Flexible capital structure and value

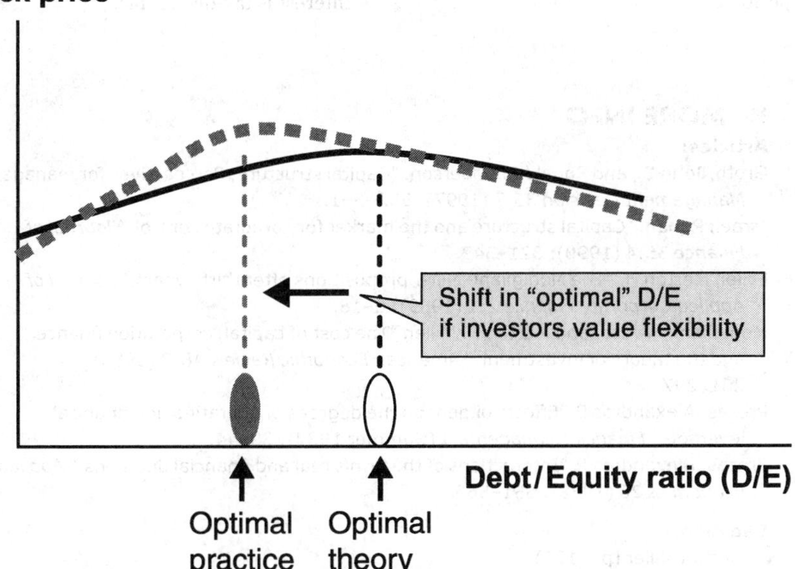

ical, economic, and technology environments. Tactics should be consistent with short-term success and long-term opportunities.

Here are some suggestions that might fare well in dynamic environments and prepare you to survive on a favorable basis in periods of high economic uncertainty and market turmoil.

- Estimate your current optimal capital structure.
- Many (all) economies enjoy/suffer the effects of cycles. When times are good, and as the tide moves to flood, pay down some debt. Move to the left on the shallow portion of the capital structure curve, rather than remain in the region of theoretical optimal debt. Increasing good unused debt capacity not only helps in survival, but also may allow for harvesting opportunities when the falling tides have carried others to peril.
- Operate in the shallow part of the WCOC curve. Leave a reasonable chunk of unused debt capacity, enough to allow rapid financing of unusual opportunities.
- Compare the current D/E to the target D/E and the shallow curve range for the D/E. If it lies within the shallow curve range, you don't need major adjustments now. Continue to track and anticipate how the company will "walk about" in the shallow curve range.
- If the company is outside the shallow curve range, decide on the strategy to move to the target range. The choice of how to move to a more optimal debt/equity ratio hinges on a number of factors, including the expected internally generated cash flows, the expected internal generation of equity, the principal repayment/refunding schedule, cash flow relative to capital investments, dividend policies, and external market conditions.
- Compare the business risk of actions you anticipate taking with your current business. Recognize and react to a change in the business risk of the company. If the business risk of the company increases/decreases as a result of good investment choices that are of higher risk, adjust financial risk by decreasing/increasing the target debt/equity ratio.
- If you currently have significant unused good debt capacity, recognize that this good debt capacity is of potential interest to a company seeking acquisitions. The buying company can use your unused good capacity as a way of financing the acquisition, or to move the combined company capital structure to a more favorable range.
- Changing from the use of bad debt capacity might involve one or several different actions, including the acquisition of a company that has unused good capacity. Do not buy a company for this reason alone! However, recognize this potential effect in acquisition strategies.
- Evaluate whether control issues are important or even dominant; control is often a concern for private or closely held companies. We assert that, for public companies, efforts by management to protect management's position and issues of control should rarely if ever determine the correct course of action.
- Decide on a strategy for capital structure that is consistent with the corporate strategy.
- Communicate your capital structure target and strategy to markets. Separately from the choice of D/E and the strategy, effective communication reduces the uncertainty in investors' minds. Here is a sample statement:
  – "Given our intended investments, likely market conditions, and the tax environment, our target D/E is about 25%. To allow us to take advantage of favorable opportunities during different phases of economic cycles, we will typically maintain a working D/E capital structure. in the 15% to 25% range."
  – "This strategy allows us to employ good debt capacity to obtain funds quickly to pursue attractive opportunities, regardless of economic conditions and capital market circumstances"
  – "We feel that investors value a flexible financing policy that allows their company to maintain choice of action and to avoid ever being forced to take particular actions."
- Behave consistently with your strategy. Demonstrated behavior builds and sustains credibility. Increased credibility reduces investor uncertainty and enhances stock prices.
- Remember that an increase/decrease in the corporate tax rate increases/decreases the value of using debt. Changes in tax rates should prompt a review and adjustment of capital structure.

SUMMARY

The prudent use of debt in financing *if interest is tax-deductible* offers the prospect of increasing firm value.

Issues of control also influence the use of debt versus equity.[5] For publicly owned companies, managers might, inappropriately, use too much debt as a means of perpetuating management's control or to promote management's interests. Making D/E choices to perpetuate control is defensible (although perhaps not wise) to maintain control of private and/or family-owned firms.

Perfect capital markets with the tax-deductibility of interest argue for an optimal debt/equity ratio. The presence of imperfect capital markets, seasonal and cyclical business cycles, a change in the nature and risks of investments, and human behavior suggest a strategy for the management of capital structure.

Finance the company in the shallow

"If you don't have some bad loans, you are not in business." Paul Volcker

     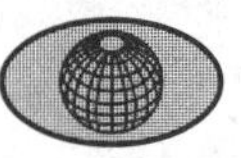   

segment of the weighted cost of capital curve. Leave some unused good debt capacity to allow the company to pursue opportunities even if capital market conditions are unfavorable, or to use as an emergency reserve. The emergency reserve concept rests on the common sense perspective that a company should never be forced into a course of action—but should be able to *choose* to follow a course of action.

Operate with a debt/equity ratio that is lower than the optimal ratio. This posture provides flexibility, allows practical management in raising capital, and keeps the company away from the steeply increasing WCOC that occurs above the optimal D/E. This position of creditworthiness allows one to raise a chunk of capital from debt to fund an opportunity independent of the conditions in capital markets.

Investing the raised capital in good investments will generate cash flow and increase the equity base, with a resultant decrease in the D/E ratio, moving it back to the left. Good projects that are managed well restore good debt capacity and will allow one to repeat the process in future periods.

In summary: capital structure makes a difference in an environment in which interest is tax-deductible.

▸▸ MORE INFO

Articles:

Groth, John C., and Ronald C. Anderson. "Capital structure: Perspectives for managers." *Management Decision* 35:7 (1997): 552–561.

Israel, Ronan. "Capital structure and the market for corporate control." *Journal of Finance* 36:4 (1990): 321–349.

Miller, Merton H. "The Modigliani–Miller propositions after thirty years." *Journal of Applied Corporate Finance* 2:1 (1989): 6–18.

Modigliani, Franco, and Merton H. Miller. "The cost of capital, corporation finance and the theory of investment." *American Economic Review* 48:3 (1958): 261–297.

Prezas, Alexandros P. "Effects of debt on the degrees of operating and financial leverage." *Financial Management* (Summer 1987): 39–44.

Prezas, Alexandros P. "Interactions of the firm's real and financial decisions." *Applied Economics* 20 (1988): 551–560.

See Also:

- Merton Miller (p. 1177)
- Franco Modigliani (p. 1178)

NOTES

1 Since in perfect capital markets one has no costs and bankruptcy has no undesirable consequences.

2 We want the market to understand that the delay in repayment of principal is part of altering the capital structure—to avoid any perception that the company is unable to make the payments of principal. This delay approach is only to avoid debt issuance costs for fresh debt.

3 Depending on circumstances, the structuring of the rights offering can almost certainly ensure that some shareholders not in the control group do not exercise their rights.

4 In many presentations and discussions the plot/discussion is total firm value versus D/E.

5 Managers and boards of directors that make capital structure decisions to protect their position or influence their rewards generate agency costs borne by stockholders and, in some circumstances, also by creditors.

"This is a world inhabited not by people who have to be persuaded to believe but by people who want an excuse to believe." J. K. Galbraith

  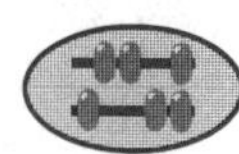   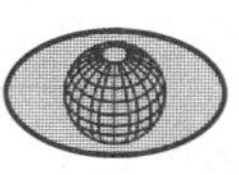   

The Cost of Going Public: Why IPOs Are Typically Underpriced by Lena Booth

EXECUTIVE SUMMARY

- The underpricing of initial public offerings (IPOs) is an indirect cost of going public that is borne by the issuing firm. Its magnitude varies across IPOs with different issue characteristics, allocation mechanisms, underwriter reputations, and general financial market conditions.
- Commonly used share allocation methods in IPOs are auction, fixed price, and book-building. Book-building is the most popular method, and it allows smaller, less known companies to go public.
- IPOs are underpriced to signal issue quality, mitigate adverse selection problems, reward investors for truthfully revealing information, lessen underwriters' potential legal liabilities, allow underwriters to curry favor with their clients, promote ownership dispersion for liquidity and control, and attract media attention/publicity.
- Issuing firms can attempt to reduce underpricing by engaging reputable underwriters and auditors, having frequent disclosures, waiting until they possess desirable characteristics, and/or using the auction method if they are of high quality.

INTRODUCTION

When firms go public, they incur direct and indirect costs associated with the initial public offering (IPO) process. Direct costs are fairly predictable—they include registration, underwriting, and attorney and auditing fees. The indirect cost, commonly known as IPO underpricing, is one of the most perplexing puzzles in finance. It is observed in almost every financial market in the world and across all procedures of share allocation. IPOs are, on average, underpriced by 18–20% in the United States. During the hot issue period, underpricing was much higher, as many of the IPO firms did not have strong financials or growth potential and simply rode the wave to go public. In countries where regulations and restrictions are imposed in the IPO market, underpricing is higher as well.

WHAT IS IPO UNDERPRICING?

Underpricing refers to the price run up of the IPO on the first day of trading. It is also known as the initial return or first-day return of the IPO.

$$\text{Underpricing} = \frac{\text{(First-day closing price} - \text{Offer price)}}{\text{Offer price}} \times 100\%$$

The first-day closing price represents what the investors are willing to pay for the firm's shares. If the offer price is lower than the first-day closing price, the IPO is said to be underpriced and money is left on the table for new investors. Since existing shareholders settle for a lower offer price/proceeds than what they could have got, money left on the table represents the wealth transfer from existing shareholders to new shareholders.

$$\text{Money left on the table} = \text{(First-day closing price} - \text{Offer price)} \times \text{Number of shares}$$

On average, the amount of money left on the table is about twice the amount of direct underwriting fees, and for many IPO firms it can equal several years of operating profit.

Although most IPOs are underpriced, the level of underpricing varies across IPOs with different issue characteristics, allocation mechanisms, underwriter reputation, and general financial market conditions. For example, the level of underpricing is reduced for larger IPOs, those underwritten by prestigious investment banks, firms with a longer operating history or more experienced insiders on the board, and those which intend to use the proceeds to repay debt. On the other hand, technology firms, firms backed by venture capital, firms with negative earnings prior to the IPO, or firms that went public during a bull market experience greater underpricing.

SHARE ALLOCATION IN IPOS

IPO underpricing happens regardless of whether issuers use the auction, the fixed-price, or the book-building method to go public. In the auction method, investors submit their desired price and quantity bids. The offer price that will allow the firm to sell all its shares is determined after bids are submitted, and hence incorporates the demand for the shares. A maximum price is usually chosen as well, so that unrealistic bids (bids well over the clearing price) can be eliminated. This is done to prevent investors from placing very high bids to ensure that they are allocated shares. Shares are then allocated, on a pro rata basis, to all the investors who placed bids between these two prices. In a uniform price auction, all the investors receiving shares will pay the same market clearing price. In the less common discriminatory price auction, investors pay the prices they bid for.

In a fixed-price offer, the issuer and the underwriter jointly determine the offer price, and investors place orders for shares at this price. If the issue is oversubscribed, shares are either allocated through lottery or on a pro rata basis.

In the book-building method, the underwriter promotes the IPO by disseminating information about the issuing firm via road shows. They gather indications of interest by soliciting from potential investors their desired prices and quantities for the issue. The underwriter then uses this information to determine the final offer price. Under this method the underwriter has complete discretion on the allocation of new shares.

Of the three allocation mechanisms, evidence has shown that IPOs under the auction method show the lowest average underpricing. However, firms that choose the auction method sometimes fail to go public because bids for their shares are insufficient. This problem is especially common for smaller, less known companies, which require substantial information production and dissemination by the underwriters. For these firms, the book-building method might be the only option that will allow them to go public. It is therefore not surprising to see the book-building method, a method that is used predominantly in the United States, gaining popularity around the world.

WHY ARE IPOS UNDERPRICED?

IPO underpricing continues to be a global phenomenon despite a vast amount of research that attempts to explain it. Theories based on information asymmetry suggest that high-quality issuers deliberately underprice their IPOs to signal their quality to outside investors, hoping that it will be too costly for low-quality issuers to mimic. Underpricing also helps to overcome adverse selection problems. Since uninformed investors tend to get a higher allocation of overpriced shares, they will stop participating in IPOs if issues

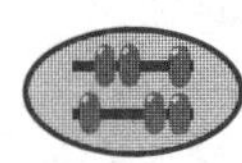

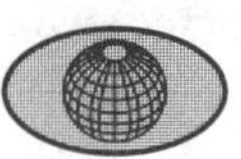

are not, on average, underpriced. In the book-building framework, the theory of partial adjustment suggests that investment banks only partially adjust IPO offer prices upward when they receive positive information about the value of the issue. They purposely leave money on the table to reward investors who truthfully reveal their information about the issue and threaten access to future deals for those that do not.

Some studies suggest that investment banks underprice IPOs to protect their reputation. When new issues are priced lower than they should be, investment bankers reduce their legal liability by lowering the chance of price declines. There is also evidence that greater underpricing leads to more aftermarket trading volume, which increases the revenue of investment bankers when they subsequently become the market-makers for these IPO firms. Investment bankers also benefit from underpricing because it allows them to curry favor with their clients in exchange for their loyalty and continued business. These explanations do not make it clear why issuing firms approve underpricing as it only benefits the investment banks.

There are explanations of underpricing that are based on information production and ownership dispersion which will benefit the issuing firms. If issuing firms want to have a more dispersed ownership, they need to underprice their IPOs so that more investors will be induced to produce information about the issue and subsequently buy the shares. Dispersed ownership increases liquidity and aftermarket trading, and also helps existing owners to retain control of their firms. These explanations predict a positive relationship between underpricing and aftermarket liquidity. However, there is also an explanation that predicts an inverse relationship between these two variables. When aftermarket trading for an IPO is expected to be thin, investors face higher aftermarket trading costs associated with asymmetric information; thus, they demand a higher level of underpricing to compensate them for the liquidity risk.

It has also been argued that underpricing is a substitute for marketing expenditure. Hugely underpriced IPOs tend to receive a disproportionate amount of media attention and publicity. Research shows that an extra dollar left on the table reduces other marketing expenditure by about the same amount. Higher underpricing also attracts more analyst coverage post IPO.

CONCLUSION

Underpricing comes at the expense of the original owners and venture capitalists of

CASE STUDY

The Google IPO

Google, the world's most widely used search engine, filed for an IPO in April 2004. Founded in 1998 by Sergey Brin and Larry Page, Google grew rapidly in the internet space, due mainly to its superior search technology. With a core business in selling search-based advertising, by 2004 Google had shown impressive sales growth and handsome profit margins. According to its filing, Google generated US$961.9 million of revenue and US$106.5 million of net profit in 2003. It had been profitable since 2001.

Google decided to use the auction method to go public, a deviation from the book-building method that is primarily used in the United States. According to Brin and Page, an auction would provide a fair process for all investors and help to determine the share price that reflected a fair market valuation of Google. They believed that auction mitigates problems associated with unreasonable speculation, which can result in boom–bust cycles that may hurt investors in the long run. They also wanted their shares to be within reach for any investors, unlike book-built IPOs, which are available only to those who have special relationships with the underwriters. The lead underwriters of the Google IPO, Morgan Stanley and Credit Suisse First Boston, helped to decide on a preliminary price range of US$108 to US$135 a share. That range was later revised to US$85–95, and the number of shares offered was reduced after it became apparent that the IPO wasn't as popular as expected.

Google successfully went public on August 19, 2004, at US$85 per share, selling 19.6 million shares. The first-day closing price was US$100.34, resulting in an underpricing of 18.05% and US$300.7 million left on the table. The underpricing of 18% was about average compared to other US IPOs but low relative to other internet IPOs, especially those that went public during the bubble period of 1999–2000. Google managed to go public using the auction method because it waited six years until it was well established, became a household name, and had a record of positive earnings.

However, many industry watchers felt that Google did not fare well in its IPO because it chose the auction method. It started as a hot IPO, yet had to reduce its filing price range due to insufficient demand at the higher price range that was originally proposed. Some attributed the low demand to lack of participation by institutional investors. Others claimed that Google was sabotaged by investment bankers, who prevented their clients from bidding because it had chosen a method that offered them little benefit. Could Google have got a higher offer price and larger issue proceeds if it had used the book-building method? It is a question we cannot answer but which will leave us wondering for a long time.

▸▸ MAKING IT HAPPEN

Although underpricing may be inevitable due to certain risk and liquidity constraints, there are ways in which issuing firms can reduce it if they want to. Here are some suggestions:

- *Engage reputable underwriters and auditors*: Prestigious underwriters use their reputation capital to certify the value of the firm and reduce investor uncertainty about the value of the issue, and that consequently lowers the level of underpricing. Reputable auditors are better able to certify the accuracy of the financials and reduce uncertainty as well. From a partial adjustment perspective, prestigious underwriters are expected to have more future deals to compensate investors. They do not have to pre-commit a large underpricing for each issue and thus are expected to underprice less.
- *Frequent disclosure*: Issuing firms can also reduce underpricing by voluntarily and frequently disclosing information about themselves in the press, provided that the quiet period rule is not violated. Frequent disclosures reduce asymmetric information, and hence lower the information production costs incurred by investors.
- *Issuer characteristics*: IPO underpricing is lower with certain issuing firm characteristics. If issuing firms can wait until they are larger in size, have a longer operating history, and possess a record of positive earnings before going public, they are likely to reduce the level of underpricing. Underpricing can also be reduced if there are more experienced insiders sitting on the board of the issuing firm.
- *Use the auction method if feasible*: As noted above, many explanations of underpricing were derived from the book-building framework. To reduce underpricing, issuers in IPO markets in which the auction mechanism is available

"There is no system in the market, and there are many approaches that work." Adam Smith

the issuing firm. However, these insiders typically do not strongly oppose or even attempt to avoid it, because they generally do not sell their shares until about six months later, after the lockup period expires. To them, underpricing creates excitement that could help create sustainable interest in the firm's shares, thus keeping demand strong until they are ready to sell. Additionally, insiders are so contented with their new-found wealth that they do not mind leaving some money on the table for new investors. Underpricing is simply viewed as an inevitable cost of going public.

might want to go public that way. However, the auction method works only if the issuing firm is a superior quality firm that has high investor awareness. Also, if the issuing firm is concerned more about factors other than underpricing—for example, price stabilization and post-IPO analyst coverage provided by investment banks—book-building may be a better choice.

▸▸ MORE INFO

Book:

Jenkinson, Tim, and Alexander Ljungqvist. *Going Public: The Theory and Evidence on How Companies Raise Equity Finance*. 2nd ed. Oxford: Oxford University Press, 2001.

Articles:

Derrien, François, and Kent L. Womack. "Auctions vs. book-building and the control of underpricing in hot IPO markets." *Review of Financial Studies* 16:1 (2003): 31–61.

Ritter, Jay R., and Ivo Welch. "A review of IPO activity, pricing, and allocations." *Journal of Finance* 57:4 (2002): 1795–1828.

Websites:

IPO data—Jay R. Ritter's page of IPO links: bear.cba.ufl.edu/ritter/ipodata.htm

IPOresources.org: www.iporesources.org

See Also:

Banking and Financial Services (pp. 1500–1502)

     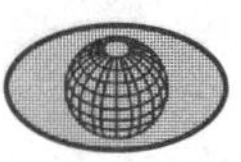   

Credit Ratings by David Wyss

EXECUTIVE SUMMARY

- A credit rating is an opinion from a credit rating agency about the creditworthiness of an issuer or the credit quality of a particular debt instrument.
- Primarily, the rating opinion considers how likely the issuer of the debt instrument is to meet its stated obligations, and whether investors will receive the payments they were promised.
- A failure to meet such payments may be considered a default.

INTRODUCTION

There are three major international rating agencies in the United States: Standard & Poor's Ratings Services (a unit of The McGraw-Hill Companies), Moody's Investors Service, and Fitch Ratings (a unit of Fimalac SA). In addition, there are many regional and niche rating agencies that tend to specialize in a geographical region or industry. The major agencies state that their opinions of the credit quality of securities are based on established, consistently applied, and transparent ratings criteria. Although the agencies use different criteria, definitions, and rating scales, they each state a view on the probability that an entity or security will default. Some rating agencies also assess the potential for recovery—how likely the investors are to recoup their investment in the event of default.

Issuers of most fixed-income securities issued in world financial markets request and receive a credit rating from a rating agency. Although credit rating evaluations are not always required, they may increase the marketability of a debt instrument by providing investors with an independent opinion about the instrument's relative credit quality.

WHY DO CORPORATIONS REQUEST A CREDIT RATING?

A credit rating opinion is often required by investors before they purchase securities. Many investors want to see an established opinion about the credit quality of a security that is not from the issuer or underwriter. In addition, some funds have made it a requirement for their investment guidelines or as part of what they have promised their investors. Issuers who are not well known or who are trying to sell into international markets may benefit from a rating from a recognized rating agency.

The rating provides market participants with an opinion on the credit quality of a particular investment. Ratings from the major credit rating agencies have a strong track record, as reported in their default and transition studies. Over the long run, securities with a higher credit rating have consistently had lower default rates than securities with lower ratings. Ratings are just opinions, however, and there have been certain periods when highly rated securities in a specific sector ultimately performed worse than other securities rated in the same category. Accordingly, ratings do not remove the need for the investor to understand what he or she is buying.

The Standard & Poor's rating scale is a simple and easy-to-understand shorthand for its credit opinions. A more detailed analysis is typically available from Standard & Poor's, including the rationale behind the rating opinion. Investors are encouraged to read the detailed analysis carefully to understand why an agency assigned a particular rating.

Having a rating may be useful even if a corporation elects to raise money privately rather than through a public bond issue. Obtaining a rating may make it easier for a company to seek funding from a private lender or bank. Although not every company needs a credit rating, most medium-sized or larger firms find it useful.

HOW A RATING IS ASSIGNED

Credit rating agencies assign ratings to issuers, including corporations and governments, of debt securities, as well as to individual issues such as bonds, notes, commercial paper, and structured finance instruments. The agencies rate an issuer by analyzing the borrower's ability and willingness to repay its obligations in accordance with their terms. The agency's analysts consider a broad range of business and financial risks that may interfere with prompt and full payment.

Most rating agencies use a mix of quantitative and qualitative analysis. Typically, analysts who consider qualitative factors contact management at the firm being rated to obtain additional information that may help them to arrive at an informed opinion. In some cases, they will ask for information that is not available to the general public, such as details of business plans, strategies, and forecasts. Agencies generally also examine the company's audited financial reports to analyze credit strengths and weaknesses.

A rating can apply to an individual issue, although the issuer may also be assigned an underlying rating based on its overall financial strength. An individual issue is usually given an evaluation based on information provided by the issuer or obtained from other reliable sources. Key considerations include:

- the issue's legal structure, including terms and conditions;
- the seniority of the issue relative to the other debt of the issuer;
- the existence of external support or credit enhancements, such as letters of credit, guarantees, insurance, and collateral—which are protections that are designed to limit the potential credit risk.

When an issuer requests a rating, it generally supplies the rating agency with its audited financial statements. In most cases, the rating agency will also meet with the issuer to discuss any questions that the agency may have and to learn about any business plans or other factors considered to be important. Frequent issuers will often have a longer-term contractual relationship with the rating agency that may include rating all new debt issues.

Credit ratings from the major rating agencies are normally paid for by the issuer of the securities, and are made public immediately thereafter, although in some cases issuers or investors may request a "private" rating on a security. When ratings are requested by parties other than the issuer, and without direct access to the issuer for questioning, they are usually marked as "public information" or given similar subscripting by the rating agency. The issuer-pays model has two hallmarks: First, the major rating agencies make ratings public (and if they didn't, *that* news would quickly become public), so it is hard to get investors to pay for what they can get for free on the news. Second, issuing a rating often involves access to the company's confidential data, which is not permissible under a subscriber-pays model.

In some circumstances, most agencies will rate some securities without any consultation with the issuing firm. In these cases the ratings are based only on public data, and are normally indicated as such.

Ratings are generally published at the time they are issued. However, sometimes a private rating may be issued for an individual investor or group of investors, usually for a security that is not intended for

public trading. Many firms want a confidential rating for management purposes and as a second opinion on the credit quality of a loan.

Ratings are not static, and rating opinions can change (or transition) if the credit quality changes in ways that were not expected at the time the security was issued. Ratings may be reviewed and updated on a regular basis, or when a significant change occurs in the performance of the issuer, the markets, or the economy. The acquisition or divestiture of a company, a political threat to (or from) the government, or erosion in the economy or credit markets can cause a rating to be adjusted. Normally, warning of a likely change is provided through an "outlook" or "credit watch" that states the direction in which a rating may move. However, sometimes a sudden deterioration may force a shift in a rating with little warning.

RATING SCALE

Each credit rating agency uses its own criteria and methodology to evaluate creditworthiness. The process may be predominantly quantitative or qualitative, but is usually a blend of the two. Once an agency completes the analysis, it issues a rating based on its own scale. Ratings are typically expressed as a grade, such as AAA, BB, or CC, with AAA (or equivalent) denoting the strongest and D (or its equivalent) the weakest (i.e. that a default has already occurred). Note that the rating scale for short-term instruments such as commercial paper is different from the long-term scale. For example, at S&P the top long-term rating is AAA, while the highest short-term credit rating is A-1+. D stands for default in both scales.

Although a rating scale is relatively straightforward, the assumptions, considerations, and judgments behind the opinions can be complex. Most agencies explain their rationale in published documents that may be read by investors. Among others, the risk factors include the financial performance of the firm, the characteristics of the economy and industry it operates, and the quality of its management. Standard & Poor's credit ratings strive to be forward-looking, focusing not just on the past but also on the likely future state of the industry and the firm.

Standard & Poor's ratings are intended to be consistent across all issuers and debt instruments. Over the very long term, all instruments with the same (say, A) rating are expected to have similar default experience. However, the short-term behavior of these instruments may be very different. Different industries respond differently to economic and credit cycles.

Credit ratings are not exact measures of the default probability of an issue or issuer, but an opinion about relative credit risk. In assigning ratings, agencies rank relative credit risk from strongest to weakest, based on relative creditworthiness and credit quality within the rated universe. Actual default probabilities may change over time.

RECOVERY

Some credit rating agencies incorporate the potential for recovery into their opinions, while others may give a recovery rating that is separate from the credit rating. Recovery prospects after default are an important component in evaluating credit quality, particularly in evaluating more risky debt issues.

ISLAMIC CREDIT

Mounting demand for *shariah*-compliant financial products and services has fueled the rapid expansion of the Islamic banking industry. More and more banking clients are choosing to invest in a broadening range of Islamic financial instruments (IFI) through long-established banks in the Gulf Cooperation Council (GCC) and Malaysia. The model has spread beyond the Gulf to the Maghreb and Muslim Asia, as well as to Muslims in predominantly non-Muslim countries in the West, Asia, and Africa.

Demand for *shariah*-compliant instruments has risen sharply as a result of strong economic growth within the Islamic world and the large surpluses of the oil-producing countries. The volume of *shariah*-compliant instruments outstanding is estimated at over $500 billion, with *sukuk* (an Islamic financial certificate) issuance reaching $100 billion. Islamic banks have focused on the retail segment in the Arab world and Malaysia but are expanding to other countries. North Africa has been a recent region of strong growth, with Tunisia and Morocco authorizing Islamic banks for the first time in 2007. The central bank of Morocco became a shareholder in the International Financial Services Board (based in Malaysia), which serves as a transnational regulatory body to harmonize regulation and supervision for Islamic banks.

Islamic securities such as *sukuk* are rated by agencies employing the same fundamental analysis as are used for rating other issues. The rating provided does not, however, express an opinion regarding the *shariah* compliance of any Islamic financing instrument, institution, or debt issue. It is the responsibility of the *shariah* board of the originating institution to rule on compliance with Islamic law. The agency rates the security based on its analysis of the willingness and ability of the issuer to make the agreed payments, as specified in the security.

RATINGS AND INVESTMENT

Although credit quality is an important element in an investment decision, it is not the only or even the most important element. Ratings opinions are not investment recommendations. In making any investment, the investor should consider the trade-off between risk and reward. Credit quality is only a partial measure of one of those trade-offs.

A security's price is generally one of the most important considerations for an investor. If the price is low enough, almost any investment becomes desirable; if the price is too high, any investment becomes unattractive. The price determines the long-run return on the investment, assuming that it pays as scheduled.

As a minimum, three other factors besides price and credit quality should be considered. First, what is the downside risk or likely recovery if the security defaults? Second, what is the liquidity of the investment—how easy is it to sell if it must be disposed of before its maturity date, and how responsive is pricing to changes in interest rates or the market environment?

An important issue for investors buying outside their home country is the potential for exchange rate change or government interference with the ability to collect payment. Fortunately, foreign exchange controls have become very rare outside of a few very weak emerging economies, but foreign

▸▸ MAKING IT HAPPEN

- Ratings can be obtained from a variety of agencies. Consider who will be your likely investors before deciding to go with a global or a local rating agency.
- Have your financial and business plans in order and fully audited by a reputable firm before trying to get a rating.
- Ratings are opinions about credit risk, and not investment advice or opinions on pricing.
- Work with your banker on determining which agency to use and whether a rating is desirable.

  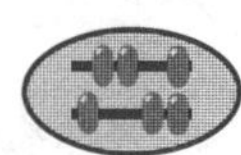 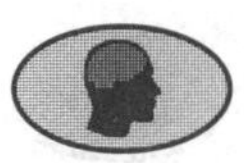  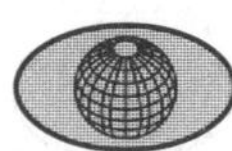   

exchange risk is very real. The US dollar/euro exchange rate went up 20% in early 2008 and then down 20% over the next three months.

CONCLUSION

Credit ratings may be used by investors and other market participants in making investment and business decisions that are aligned with their risk tolerance or credit risk guidelines. Credit ratings are opinions about the perceived credit risk of a particular debt issue. In general, the greater the credit risk, the higher the return investors may expect for assuming that risk. For that reason, credit ratings may be useful for both issuers and investors when a debt issue is first issued in the primary markets and continues to be so for investors who trade securities in secondary markets.

▸▸ MORE INFO

Books:

Duffie, Darrell, and Kenneth Singleton. *Credit Risk: Pricing, Measurement, and Management*. Princeton, NJ: Princeton University Press, 2003.

Fuchita, Yasuyuki, and Robert E. Litan (eds). *Financial Gatekeepers: Can They Protect Investors?* Baltimore, MD: Brookings Institution, 2006.

Langohr, Herwig M., and Patricia T. Langohr. *The Rating Agencies and Their Credit Ratings: What They Are, How They Work, and Why They Are Relevant*. Chichester, UK: Wiley, 2008.

Levich, Richard M., Giovanni Majnoni, and Carmen Reinhart (eds). *Ratings, Rating Agencies and the Global Financial System*. Norwell, MA: Kluwer Academic, 2002.

Article:

Cantor, Richard. "An introduction to recent research on credit ratings." *Journal of Banking & Finance* 28:11 (2004): 2565–2573.

Websites:

The main sources of information on ratings are the websites of the three major rating agencies: www.moodys.com, www.standardandpoors.com, and www.fitchratings.com. A good discussion of ratings trends is found in the "Guide to credit rating essentials" produced by Standard & Poor's (2008, 20 pages): www2.standardandpoors.com/spf/pdf/fixedincome/SP_CreditRatingsGuide.pdf

"You can't manage what you don't measure." W. Edwards Deming (probably apocryphal)

  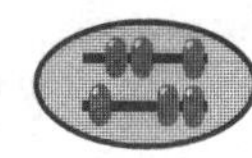   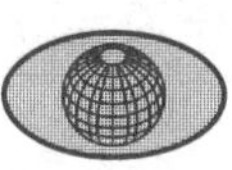   

Equity Issues by Listed Companies: Rights Issues and Other Methods by Seth Armitage

EXECUTIVE SUMMARY

- A rights issue is a method by which a listed company can issue new shares. The principle of a rights issue is that stockholders are offered new shares in proportion to their existing holdings. If stockholders do not want to buy the new shares, they can sell their rights on the stock market.
- The main alternative issue methods are the firm-commitment offer, the private placement or placing, and the open offer. These methods have been replacing rights issues in several countries.
- The average reaction of a company's share price to firm commitments is negative, but it is positive for placements and open offers. The reaction to rights issues varies by country.
- The aim for a company is to have a smooth issue that raises the intended amount of capital for a competitive fee and at a minimum discount.

INTRODUCTION

This article is about issues of shares to investors by companies that are already listed on a stock exchange. Such issues are often called rights issues, although in fact the rights issue is only one of several issue methods used. Other methods will also be discussed here. A generic term for issues by listed companies is seasoned equity offers (SEOs).

TYPES OF OFFER

Rights Issue

The principle of a rights issue is that the company offers the new shares to its existing stockholders in proportion (pro rata) to the number of shares owned by each stockholder. In most countries this is a requirement of company law. The stockholder's right of first refusal over the new shares is known as the preemption right. If a stockholder does not want to buy some or all of the new shares to which he or she is entitled, he or she can sell the rights to them on the stock market during a prescribed offer period. In the United Kingdom this period is three weeks.

The offer price of the new shares is usually set at a large discount to the market price of the existing shares just before the issue is announced. This discount means that the rights are likely to be worth something during the offer period. A numerical example is helpful in understanding the rights issue mechanism:

Company X:

Number of existing shares	10 million
Number of new shares	5 million
Price of existing shares before offer is announced	\$12
Offer price	\$9

In this example, Company X is issuing one new share for every two existing shares in what is known as a "one-for-two" issue. The new equity to be raised is \$45 million. The offer period starts on the ex-rights date, when the existing shares cease to carry the one-for-two entitlement to the new shares. If the underlying value of the company does not change, the share price will fall to the theoretical ex-rights price (TERP) on the ex-rights date. The TERP is the weighted average value of the old and the new shares. In the example, the TERP is \$11:

$$\frac{((10 \text{ million} \times \$12) + (5 \text{ million} \times \$9))}{15 \text{ million}} = \$11$$

At this market price, each right to one new share will be worth \$2; that is, \$11 − \$9.

An important point about rights issues is that a stockholder is as well off whether or not he sells the rights. If he does not sell, and he buys the new shares, he loses \$10 per old share when they go ex-rights, but gains \$2 per new share because the offer price is \$2 below the market price ex-rights. If he sells the rights, he still loses \$10 per old share but gains \$2 in cash per new share. However, this ignores the cost of selling rights, which can be substantial if the company's shares are illiquid.

The majority of rights issues are underwritten. This means that the investment bank arranging the issue will find sub-underwriters, usually investing institutions, to buy the shares at the offer price, or will buy them itself if necessary. The deeper the discount, the less likely it is that the underwriters will be called upon.

Firm-Commitment or Public Offer

In the United States, rights issues by commercial companies (as opposed to investment companies) have been rare since the 1970s. The standard method for larger issues is the firm-commitment offer. After the issue is announced, there is a book-building period of about one month, during which a syndicate of investment banks invites applications for the new shares and the share registration document is finalized. With a shelf offering, the new shares will already have been registered with the Securities and Exchange

CASE STUDY

Bradford and Bingley's "Rights Reissue," May–June 2008

The rights issue of Bradford and Bingley plc, a British mortgage bank, was among the most extraordinary in living memory. On May 14, 2008, Bradford and Bingley announced that it was to raise £300 million via a 19-for-25 issue at an offer price of 82p—a discount of 48% on the preannouncement share price. However, on June 4, 2008, while the offer period was still running, the bank unexpectedly announced a profit warning, the resignation of its chief executive, and a restructuring of the issue. In particular, the offer price was cut to 55p to avoid the share price dropping below the offer price after the profit warning. A price cut mid-offer is extremely rare, but without it the underwriters would have been left holding much of the issue at a loss, and they might have sought to escape their obligations by invoking the "material adverse change" clause in the underwriting agreement.

In a further twist, Bradford and Bingley arranged for Texas Pacific Group (TPG), a private equity investor, to buy shares at 55p via a placing, acquiring a 23% stake and two seats on the board. TPG's shares were not offered to existing stockholders and were therefore not part of the rights issue proper. TPG's involvement as a potentially active investor was generally welcomed. At the same time, some institutional stockholders were annoyed at not being given the chance to invest more at 55p. As one said, "If there was no TPG, the whole thing would have collapsed. But it comes at a huge price for investors."[1]

"Steel prices cause inflation like wet sidewalks cause rain." Roger Blough

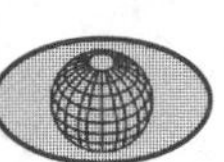

Commission. There is no pro rata offer to existing stockholders.

The offer price is set the day before the shares are issued. The offer price used to be the same as, or very close to, the prevailing market price. But, during the 1990s, it became common to set the offer price at a discount to the market price of about 2.5%. Firm-commitment offers are underwritten by the syndicate of investment banks that market the issue. Non-underwritten public offers are known as "best efforts" offers. Both rights issues and firm commitments are accompanied by a prospectus—a marketing document and memorandum that contains information required by the relevant regulatory authority.

Private Placement or Placing

A third type of offer is the private placement. In the United States, private placement refers to the sale of a block of shares by private negotiation, usually to one or two investors only and for a fairly small amount (a few million dollars). Placements are less onerous to arrange than firm commitments, because the shares are not offered to investors in general and no prospectus is required. Most placements are made at a discount, the average being around 15% in the United States. In the United Kingdom the term "placing" is used for any sale of shares that does not involve a pro rata offer to existing stockholders. Larger placings will have 20 or 30 placees.

Open Offer

An open offer combines a pro rata offer to existing stockholders with a private placing. Although stockholders retain their preemption rights, the rights cannot be traded and are therefore worthless unless the stockholder chooses to buy new shares. This type of offer is now standard in the United Kingdom but appears to be unique to that country.

ASPECTS OF PRACTICE

Market Reaction to SEOs

The share price of US industrial companies falls by around 3% on average when a firm-commitment offer is announced. The stock market reaction to rights issues is mixed; it is negative in some countries and positive in others. A negative reaction is surprising on the face of it, since a company would not be expected to go to the expense of a share issue unless it had a good use for the money, i.e. a positive net present value investment.

The leading explanation (Myers and Majluf, 1984) is that news of an SEO indicates that the issuer is more likely to be overvalued than undervalued. An undervalued company is one in which the market value of the equity is less than the managers' assessment of its value. If the managers are correct, issuing shares when the company is undervalued means that existing stockholders who do not buy will lose out to new investors, who will obtain shares at below the full-information price. Some undervalued companies will choose not to issue as a result, even if they need the money for a worthwhile investment. Therefore, companies that choose to issue are more likely to be overvalued, and the market price will fall as a result.

However, the market reaction to private placements, placings, and open offers is positive on average. These issue methods potentially involve detailed investigation of the issuer by placees or underwriters, who have access to private information about the company. So one explanation for the positive reaction is that the willingness of these well-informed agents to buy or underwrite certifies a minimum value for the issuer. Another explanation is that in some placements an active placee is introduced, i.e. an agent who brings know-how or an intention to intervene in the company, and the market reacts positively to news of a placement to such an investor.

Decline of the Rights Issue

The decline of rights issues in the United States, the United Kingdom, Japan, and elsewhere is somewhat puzzling. The firm-commitment method that replaced them in the United States is more expensive and does not offer an obvious advantage. Most placings are made at a sizeable discount, which means that stockholders who are not invited into the placing lose out. Possible disadvantages of rights issues include the cost of selling large blocks of rights, delays in the issue process compared with placings, and less effective certification of value than in an open offer or placing.

Rights issues work best when most of the new shares will be bought by existing stockholders willing to take up their rights. There is then little need to find other buyers. They are therefore frequently used by family-controlled firms. Rights issues also work well for the largest companies, with very liquid shares, because it is cheap and easy to sell rights on the market.

Long-Run Underperformance Following SEOs

Companies that raise new equity tend to underperform in relation to other companies matched by industry, size, and risk over a three- to five-year horizon. This underperformance occurs for both returns on the shares and operating profit. The same finding applies to companies that make or have made an initial public offer. One explanation is that, on average, companies successfully time their issue for when they are overvalued.

Issue Costs

The total cost of a firm-commitment offer in the United States is, on average, 7% of the amount raised, ignoring any discount. The cost of a rights issue or open offer in the United Kingdom is 6% on average. Much the largest components of the cost are the fees to the lead bank and to the underwriters. The cost is relatively more for smaller companies, partly because there are clear economies of scale and partly because they are riskier.

Discounts

Discounts to the market price are a cost to nonsubscribing stockholders, except in a rights issue. Why are discounts needed? First, investors tend to buy large blocks, which could be costly to sell in future. There is a strong empirical relationship between depth of discount and the bid–ask spread of the issuer's shares. Second, the value of many issuers is rather uncertain;

›› MAKING IT HAPPEN

- An equity issue is an expensive process and time-consuming for senior management.
- Key practical aspects include the choice of lead investment bank and other professional-service firms (for example, lawyers), the type of issue, the size and timing of the issue, whether to have it underwritten, the content of the prospectus, the level of fee, the offer price discount, and who the main buyers (future stockholders) will be.
- Companies are largely in the hands of the lead investment bank once the issue process is under way, but they can (and do) shop around when selecting the lead bank. When making the choice and negotiating the terms of the issue, company managers should be aware of the terms on which recent SEOs have been made by companies of a similar size. The fees and discount should be competitive.
- The company should aim for a smooth issue that raises the intended amount and is sold to a group of investors who are, or plan to be, long-term holders of the shares.

"I see nothing in the present situation that is either menacing or warrants pessimism. . .I have every confidence that there will be a revival of activity in the spring, and that during this coming year 1930 the country will make steady progress." Andrew William Mellon

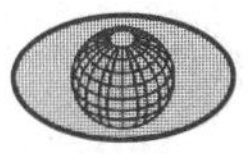

in the academic jargon, there is high information asymmetry. There was a major shift in the 1990s in the type of company listed on stock exchanges, away from well-established companies with a successful track record, toward smaller firms that are still in the product development stage. The discount could also provide compensation for costs of investigating the issuer, or for future costs of active monitoring.

▸▸ MORE INFO

Book:

Eckbo, B. E., R. W. Masulis, and ø. Norli. "Security offerings." In B. E. Eckbo (ed). *Handbook of Corporate Finance: Empirical Corporate Finance*. Vol. 1. Amsterdam: Elsevier, 2007, 233–373. A thorough review of research on SEOs.

Article:

Myers, S. C., and N. S. Majluf. "Corporate financing and investment decisions when firms have information that investors do not have." *Journal of Financial Economics* 13:2 (1984): 187–221.

Report:

Myners, Paul. "Pre-emption rights: Final report." UK Department of Trade and Industry, February 2005. Online at: www.berr.gov.uk/files/file28436.pdf. The pros and cons of rights issues from a practitioner's perspective.

NOTES

1 *Financial Times* (June, 6, 2008).

"A depression is either a 12 percent unemployment rate for nine months or more, or a 15 percent unemployment rate for three to nine months." Alan Greenspan

  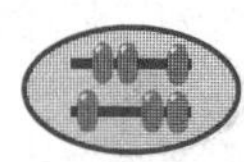 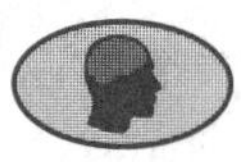  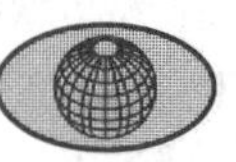   

Financial Steps in an IPO for a Small or Medium-Size Enterprise by Hung-Gay Fung

EXECUTIVE SUMMARY

- The firm forms an underwriting syndicate by selecting a lead underwriter and co-managers. Typically, for small and medium-sized firms underwriters charge a fee of 7% of the issue value. In the United States, a firm registers with the Securities and Exchange Commission (SEC) for the IPO issue, and when it has received approval it distributes a preliminary prospectus, known as a "red herring," to the public.
- The firm has to select an exchange on which to list its stock.
- The firm and the underwriter arrange road shows to promote the issue and to find out more about market demand; later this will provide useful information for setting the offer price and determining how many shares should be issued.
- After the IPO trading, the lead underwriter provides market research on the issue and other relevant information.

WHY AN IPO?

An initial public offering (IPO) of stocks is a share offering to the public by a small or medium-sized enterprise (SME) undertaken to raise additional cash for future growth or to enable existing stockholders to cash out by selling part of their holdings. Among other things, a successful IPO will provide a company with an objective valuation of its stock, create a good public image of the company—thus lowering its cost of borrowing—and provide it with a pool of publicly owned shares for future acquisitions of other companies. However, there are also drawbacks to being a public company, such as loss of freedom (including costly disclosure requirements and close monitoring by the public and government) and, if a takeover is threatened, potential loss of control.

TYPES OF IPO

There are many types of IPO, illustrating the different management and owner compensation contracts in firms.

- The *plain vanilla IPO* is undertaken by a privately held company, mostly owned by management, who want to secure additional funding and determine the company's fair market value.
- A *venture capital-backed IPO* refers to a company in which management has sold its shares to one or more groups of private investors in return for funding and advice. This provides an effective incentive scheme for venture capitalists to implement their exit strategy after they have successfully transformed a firm in which they invested so that it is financially viable in the market.
- In a *reverse-leveraged buyout*, the proceeds of the IPO are used to pay off the debt accumulated when a company was privatized after a previous listing on an exchange. This process enables owners who own majority shares to privatize their publicly trading firms, which are undervalued in the market, thus realizing financial gains after the public was informed of the high intrinsic value of the private firm.
- A *spin-off IPO* denotes the process whereby a large company carves out a stand-alone subsidiary and sells it to the public. A spin-off may also offer owners of the parent firm and hedge funds the opportunity to capitalize mispricing in both the subsidiary and parent if the market is not efficient enough. An interesting example in the United States was the spin-off of uBid by Creative Computers in 1998, which enabled arbitragers to capitalize the mispricing between the two listed companies.

THE IPO PROCESS

Overview

The first task of management is to select the underwriters who will be responsible for the new issue. This is done roughly three months before the IPO date. The underwriters provide the issuing firm with procedural and financial advice. Later they will buy the stock and then sell it to the public. The company, with the aid of lawyers, accountants, and underwriters, submits a registration statement to a regulatory body (such as the Securities and Exchange Commission (SEC) in the United States) for approval of the public offering. The registration statement is a detailed document about the company's history, business, and future plans. Specifically, the SEC requires information on the details of the company (form S-1), its financial history (form S-2), and expected cash flows (form S-3). The company must be able to back up the information provided to the SEC.

In the United States, about six weeks prior to the IPO issue the SEC reviews and approves the content of the disclosure to the public; this becomes the preliminary prospectus and is also called the "red herring." In December 2006, the SEC set new rules on what information must be included about a public company's executive compensation, including the level of executive pay, the benchmark used, and what quantitative or qualitative methods are employed in determining that pay.[1] The prospectus is a legal document describing the securities to be offered to participants and buyers. It is advised on and distributed by the underwriters, and provides information such as the types of stock to be issued, biographies of officers and directors with detailed information about their compensation, any litigation in place, and any other material information.

After publication of the prospectus the company, with the help of the underwriting syndicate, prepares for roadshows to meet potential investors—primarily institutional investors in major cities like New York, San Francisco, Boston, Chicago, and Los Angeles. Roadshows may sometimes be arranged for overseas investors. After the SEC approves registration of the IPO, the underwriters and the company will agree on the amount and price of the issue. On the day prior to the IPO issue the exact price of the shares to be issued is announced by the underwriter. After the IPO, the lead underwriter provides stock liquidity and research coverage.

The IPO date is followed by a "lockup" period, the duration of which varies across different issues and markets, but is in the region of 180 days for a typical issue. After this "insiders," who include the underwriters, are allowed to sell their shares. Insiders may or may not hold on to stock they own depending on their motives and objectives. However, the lockup period appears to exert no control on those who bought shares at the market-offered IPO price, although there are regulatory restrictions on the types of clients to whom the firm can sell stock.

Selection of Underwriters

The board of a firm planning to launch an IPO will first meet with potential candidates for underwriters among investment

"The economic depression that struck Europe in the fourteenth century was followed ultimately by economic and technological recovery. But the depression we have moved into will have no end. We can anticipate centuries of decline and exhaustion." Jean Gimpel

  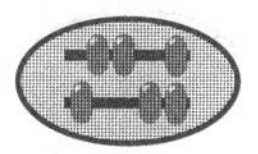 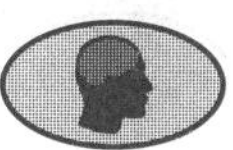  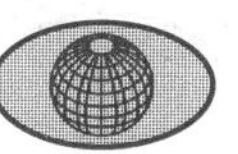   

banks and then select the lead underwriter. The choice of underwriter is based on criteria that include: a preliminary valuation of the firm based on its financial information; and the characteristics of the underwriter, such as previous IPO experience, strengths and weaknesses, client network, research capabilities, and support for post-IPO issues. Discounted cash flow analysis and earnings multiples (such as the price/earnings ratio) are typically used to come up with the preliminary value of the company.

Citigroup was ranked first among underwriters in 2007, arranging $617.6 billion of offerings, and JPMorgan Chase was second with $554.1 billion. Deutsche Bank was ranked third and Merrill fourth in underwriting volume.[2] Citigroup has been top of the list for the past eight years. As a result of the global recession that began in 2008 the underwriting volume has declined, while fees have increased.

Types of Underwriting

The management of the IPO firm selects the underwriters and decides on the type of underwriting it wants. There are two types of underwriting: *firm commitment*, and *best efforts*. If the underwriter enters a firm commitment with the company, the underwriter is confident about the issue and is willing to buy all the shares if there is insufficient demand. In a firm commitment offering, the underwriters will buy the IPO shares at a discount in the range 3.5–7.0% and then sell them on to the public at the full offer price.

In a best efforts case, the investment bank will only do as much as it reasonably can to sell the shares and will return unsold equity to the firm. This practice is common for less liquid securities. However, if there is excess demand, the bank will ask for a "greenshoe" option, allowing it to buy additional stock from the IPO firm. Typically, a lead underwriter asks other investment banks to form an underwriting syndicate to take care of the IPO issue before final approval by the SEC. The syndicate serves to expand the marketing of the company's stock issue and to reduce the overall risk of the lead bank. The syndicate members are involved in the underwriting either through a commitment to sell the shares or just in marketing of the shares.

Underwriters may face legal consequences if a new issue goes wrong. Therefore, they have to present accurate and fair facts about the firm to investors, because otherwise they may be sued for misrepresentation, or for failing to carry out due diligence. Some underwriters may allocate stocks of popular new issues to their important corporate clients; this is known as "spinning," and is deemed to be unethical and illegal.

Underwriters charge different spreads, and domestic and overseas spreads may differ. The average underwriting fee (spread) runs between about 3.3% and 7% in the United Kingdom and the United States (Brealey, Myers, and Allen, 2008).

Selection of an Exchange

Different exchanges have different listing requirements. In general, they require minimum levels of pretax income, net tangible assets, and number of stockholders. For example, a New York Stock Exchange listing requires an income of either US$2.5 million before federal income taxes for the most recent year or US$2 million pretax for the each of the preceding two years. The firm must have been profitable in the two years before a listing.

The NASDAQ (National Association of Securities Dealers Automated Quotations), the largest electronic screen-based equity securities trading market in the United States, has lower listing requirements than the NYSE. Other markets, such as the NASDAQ Small Cap Market and the American Stock Exchange, offer even lower listing requirements (www.inc.com/guides/finance/20713.html). Thus, an IPO firm needs to assess its own strengths and weaknesses in order to pick the right exchange on which to list its shares.

A firm also needs to select a trading symbol for use on the exchange. For example, Microsoft trades as MSFT. A fee, which varies for each exchange, has to be paid for the services provided.

Subscription Procedure

IPO shares are distributed in different ways to investors. One approach is an open auction, where investors are invited to submit bids stating the number of shares they wish to purchase and the price they will pay for them. The highest bidders get the securities. The Google IPO of US$1.7 billion in 2004 and the Morningstar IPO of US$140 million in 2005 used this open auction method.

The bookbuilding method is the most commonly used in the United States today and is gaining popularity and dominance across the globe (Degeorge, Derrien, and Womack, 2007). During the roadshows, the investment banker asks institutional investors and individual clients about their intention to buy the shares. Each bid indicates the number to be purchased, and may include a limiting price. Such information is recorded in a "book," from which the name bookbuilding is derived. These indications of interest provide valuable information, because all bids are compiled to ascertain the market demand for the security. Although these bid indications are not binding, the investment banker can utilize the information to set the final offer price, which is made known on the day before the actual issue (Cornelli and Goldreich, 2003).

The appeal of the bookbuilding method, despite its higher underwriting costs, is that investment banks provide better promotion and research coverage of the IPO than other IPO issuing procedures. Thus, the networking of the bank with clients helps to enhance the image of the issuing firm. Chief financial officers appear to prefer this approach to IPOs despite the higher cost.

IPO COST AND PRICING

Underpricing

Besides the substantial underwriting cost and direct costs of lawyers, printers, accountants, etc., the IPO firm has to bear notional losses due to the underpricing of the issue—i.e., the IPO price is less than the true price of the stock. If the offering price is less than the true value of the issue, original stockholders effectively provide a bargain to the new investors. The finance literature shows that investors that buy at the issue price on average realize high returns (for example, 18%) over the following days. This high return from underpricing is common across the world—especially in China, which provides the highest return of 257% (Loughran, Ritter, and Rydqvist, 1994).

Underpricing, which is most likely to be seen with the bookbuilding method, can be justified as follows. First, a low offer price makes it probable that shares will later be traded at a higher price in the market, thus enhancing the firm's ability to raise capital in future. That is, underpricing ensures that the IPO is successful and that those who want to buy the issue will follow the same underwriter among those in the market. Second, it is a way to avoid the winner's curse—the feeling of investors that they have paid too much. Simply, underpricing makes it more likely that an IPO will be successful. It appears that stockholders of the IPO firm focus more on likely gains in wealth from later stock price increases than on any short-term loss from underpricing (Loughran and Ritter, 2002).

New Price and Stock Issue

Suppose that an IPO firm has 10 million shares with a current valuation of $100 million, that it wants to raise $70 million for

"We have gone from boom to bust faster than at any time since the oil shock. When you screech to a halt like that, it feels like getting thrown through the windshield." Stephen S. Roach

     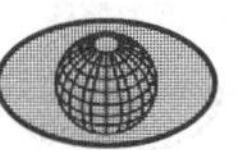   

the issue, and that it has to pay $4.9 million for the direct cost of issuance, which is in general about 7% of the issue value (Hansen, 2001). The post-issue price, P_{new}, which includes underpricing, and the number of new shares to be issued, N, will be determined simultaneously. That is, the dollar amount of the new issue will cover the fund required and the direct cost to be paid, while the augmented value of the firm will include the old and new assets of the firm. P_{new} and N can be determined as follows:

$$P_{new} \times N = \$70{,}000{,}000 \text{ (new fund)} + \$4{,}900{,}000 \text{ (issue cost)} \quad (1)$$

$$(10{,}000{,}000 + N) \times P_{new} = \$100{,}000{,}000 \text{ (old assets)} + \$70{,}000{,}000 \text{ (new assets)} \quad (2)$$

Solving these two equations (1) – (2) yields the new price of the IPO, P_{new} = $9.51. The number of new shares to be issued, N = 7,875,920

MAKING IT HAPPEN

- An IPO is a time-consuming process.
- The success of an IPO depends on the successful selling of the firm to the investment banks, to the regulator, to the analysts, and to the public.
- During the six-month IPO process the firm's operations need to be on autopilot cruise control as management will be totally tied up during this time.

MORE INFO

Books:

Brealey, Richard A., Stewart C. Myers, and Franklin Allen. *Principles of Corporate Finance*. 9th ed. New York: McGraw-Hill, 2008.

Killian, Linda, Kathleen Smith, and William Smith. *IPOs for Everyone: The 12 Secrets of Investing in IPOs*. Hoboken, NJ: Wiley, 2001.

Articles:

Cornelli, F., and D. Goldreich. "Bookbuilding: How informative is the order book?" *Journal of Finance* 58:4 (2003): 1415–1443.

Degeorge, Francois, Francois Derrien, and Kent L. Womack. "Analyst hype in IPOs: Explaining the popularity of bookbuilding." *Review of Financial Studies* 20:4 (2007): 1021–1058.

Hansen, Robert S. "Do investment banks compete in IPOs? The advent of the '7% plus contract.'" *Journal of Financial Economics* 59:2 (2001): 313–346.

Loughran, Tim, Jay R. Ritter, and Kristian Rydqvist. "Initial public offerings: International insights." *Pacific-Basin Finance Journal* 2 (1994): 165–199.

Loughran, Tim, and Jay R. Ritter. "Why don't issuers get upset about leaving money on the table in IPOs?" *Review of Financial Studies* 15:2 (2002): 413–444.

Websites:

Hoover's IPO Central: www.hoovers.com/global/ipoc

Inc. magazine articles on IPOs: www.inc.com/guides/finance/20713.html

Investopedia IPO definition: www.investopedia.com/terms/i/ipo.asp

NOTES

1 See *Wall Street Journal*, December 8, 2008.

2 See *International Herald Tribune*, January 1, 2008.

"Does the consumer really know who you are, or are they buying the brand that is being promoted this week?"
Robert Evans

  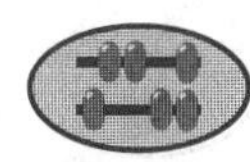   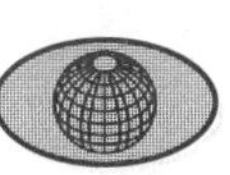   

How and When to Use Nonrecourse Financing by Thomas McKaig

EXECUTIVE SUMMARY

- Nonrecourse financing is debt where the loan is completely secured by collateral, which is often real estate. In case of default, the borrower is not liable because the lender is limited to collateral pledged for that loan—the lender has "no recourse" to the borrower's other assets.
- Nonrecourse financing is typically found in infrastructure projects such as the construction of toll roads and bridges. In this case, the borrower (a large construction company) is under no obligation to make payments on the loan if the revenue generated from the project on completion (the bridge or the toll road when built) is insufficient to cover the principal and interest payments on that loan.
- Although the benefits of such financing are obvious (the borrower is not using its balance sheet for the loan and can therefore undertake more leveraged projects than it could otherwise), such financing comes at a cost. Lenders often seek other credit guarantees and will almost certainly charge more for the loan than with more traditional, recourse financing.
- Nonrecourse financing does not mean "no risk," and some companies may undertake projects that have a riskier profile than they should otherwise assume, as will be shown in a case study.

INTRODUCTION

When companies are negotiating loans from lenders, there are many clauses that are important points for negotiation over and above the amount of the loan and interest charged. These items can include assignment of the loan (on the part of either the borrower or the lender), future fund advances, and prepayment capability. Another key clause is the nonrecourse clause, under which the lender agrees not to hold the borrower (the company) liable in the event of default on the loan.

Typically, therefore, nonrecourse financing is different from personal loans, such as mortgage loans, where the lender holds the borrower personally responsible for the sum borrowed if the value of the item being financed (the house) is insufficient to repay the total amount of the loan. Such loans are often called *recourse loans*. On the corporate side, most small business start-up loans are recourse loans—if the business fails, the owner is still liable to repay the loan amount in full.

Not all nonrecourse financing is the same—the phrase itself is very broad. Nonrecourse clauses in loan agreements, for example, may state the specific conditions under which the lender will not hold the borrower personally liable in the event of default. If these conditions are not met, then the borrower becomes liable. Such financing is sometimes referred to as *limited-recourse financing*.

It is also important to remember that, while nonrecourse loans relieve the borrower of corporate liability, they do not release whatever property is used as collateral for the loan—the lender still has an interest in the property as security for the loan.

Nonrecourse financing is the norm in the world of project financing for major projects that are government or quasi-government sponsored (infrastructure projects such as toll roads, hospitals, or power-generating plants). It is so much a part of project financing that many textbook definitions of "project finance" specify that it is a key component: a project is financed based on, and secured by, the project itself, with the lender being repaid out of the project's cash flow, rather than the project being secured by the general assets or creditworthiness (the balance sheets) of the sponsors (the engineering companies, the construction companies, or even the government bodies) of an infrastructure project. In most of these cases, the companies undertaking the project are either not sufficiently creditworthy, or else are unwilling to assume the high debt loads associated with traditional financing for large, multibillion dollar projects. Nonrecourse financing is also the norm in the commercial real estate world for the construction of major projects such as office buildings or shopping malls.

The benefits of nonrecourse financing to the borrower are obvious. Borrowers are able to enter into agreements that they could not afford under traditional

CASE STUDY

Nonrecourse Does Not Mean No Risk

The early 1990s were a tough time for real estate investments in North America and throughout much of the world. But it was preceded by many profitable years of highly speculative construction and development of office buildings and retail facilities. This long building boom also encouraged all parties in the development process to stretch themselves and become more exposed to the overall project, which everyone agreed could only increase in value. Lenders soon became co-owners of projects. Developers, who used to sell a project on completion, wished to keep a portion of the development for themselves, and tenants wondered why they should pay rent when they could explore co-ownership arrangements.

Consider the example of a mid-size real estate asset management firm that became tired of managing the assets of others, and wanted a piece of the pie for themselves. Their plan was to obtain a nonrecourse loan for the construction of a major shopping mall. The real estate company would make money during the construction process (as construction managers) from ongoing mall management and from a small equity stake in the mall, which the managers would keep for themselves. And with a nonrecourse loan, the real estate firm wouldn't be liable for interest payments if things went badly. It was a "no lose" situation.

However, no liability is not the same as having no exposure. The real estate manager, aided by the thought that nonrecourse meant no possibility of loss, staked all of its time and effort on this one project, rather than diversifying among many real estate holdings, as other managers had done. When the lender eventually took over the half-finished project, it was true that the real estate manager had no further financial liability for this project. However, because the lender stopped the project, the construction fees to the manager stopped, their own minority equity stake shrank to zero, and they didn't survive long enough to benefit from the ongoing mall management contract. The project was eventually completed many years later, but neither the original lender nor the real estate asset manager remained in business to enjoy the eventual profit.

"The benefits of nonrecourse financing are not free." Ling and Archer

  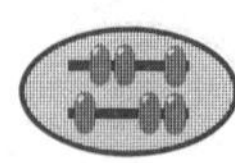   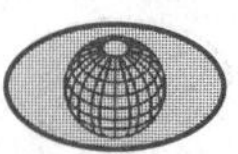   

financing methods. Project financing deals are also highly leveraged, allowing borrowers (more accurately called "the sponsoring parties" to the agreement) to put fewer of their own funds at risk. Furthermore, depending on the structure of the loan agreement, borrowers may not be required to report any of the project debt on their balance sheet.

> "Not all nonrecourse financing is the same—the phrase itself is very broad. Nonrecourse clauses in loan agreements, for example, may state the specific conditions under which the lender will not hold the borrower personally liable in the event of default."

A large firm undertaking a project may use nonrecourse debt as a way of limiting its risk exposure by effectively isolating a new project. For example, a large university might use nonrecourse financing to fund the construction of a new building because the institution as a whole would not want to put its balance sheet at risk to fund the construction of one building.

However, some dangers accompany this increased exposure to risk. "Non-recourse" is not a synonym for "no downside risk," though some companies may come to believe that. The Case Study illustrates some of the dangers when companies forget about increased risk exposure.

CONCLUSION

There are some real advantages to nonrecourse financing for the borrower. In some cases, such as large project financing agreements, it allows projects to be completed that might not otherwise have broken ground if more traditional financing methods were used. But, as the economists say, there is no such thing as a free lunch. Be sure to take into account the costs of this financing before rushing into a nonrecourse deal.

Costs

In any negotiation—especially a loan negotiation—no concession, such as a nonrecourse clause, comes free. In many cases, the lender may seek to mitigate its increased risk from writing a nonrecourse loan by seeking additional guarantees or warranties from the borrower, from other parties that are part of the project finance group, or even from third parties such as governments or quasi-governmental agencies. Such "credit enhancement" can produce an end result where the borrower ends up with exposure that is very similar to a recourse loan. In still other cases, additional equity has to be pledged by the borrower to cover the lender's risk. Once again, if the borrower is pledging assets worth 110% or more of the loan amount, it is wise to question what you have to gain from having a nonrecourse loan.

Borrowers also pay for the nonrecourse clause in a loan agreement. This can either come about in the form of higher interest rates for the loan, or higher up-front financing costs and fees to arrange the loan, or both. Nonrecourse financing may also result in a shorter list of lenders (and therefore a less competitive and higher-priced marketplace) than recourse loans. The final cost comes from the greater amount of time needed to both negotiate and, ultimately, structure a nonrecourse financing agreement. Legal costs and time costs associated with these more complex financing arrangements must be considered in the overall financing equation. Selling property that is encumbered by a nonrecourse loan will often give rise to a more complex tax situation (depending on the country the company is operating in), which is another factor to consider.

▸▸ MAKING IT HAPPEN

- In any loan negotiation ask yourself, "Can I afford to have nonrecourse financing?"
- When any loan is coming up for renewal, ask yourself if nonrecourse financing is appropriate for your firm.
- When circumstances at your firm change (for example, if your balance sheet strengthens), examine the appropriateness of nonrecourse financing.
- Also consider the appropriateness of nonrecourse financing when circumstances in the world change (for example, the credit market is looser/tighter, or a project is nearing completion so its risk profile changes) and you are renegotiating a loan.
- Government-backed programs can often stand between a lender and a firm, offering nonrecourse loans to the firm but providing a government guarantee if things go wrong, thereby offering a service to the lender as well. These programs vary by country and usually apply to specific, targeted industries—small business, agriculture, or protected industries. Check what programs apply to your firm, both now and in the future.

▸▸ MORE INFO

Books:

Brueggeman, William B., and Jeffrey Fisher. *Real Estate Finance and Investments*. New York: McGraw-Hill, 2005.

Liaw, K. Thomas. *The Business of Investment Banking*. New York: Wiley, 1999.

Ling, David C., and Wayne R. Archer. *Real Estate Principles: A Value Approach*. 2nd ed. New York: McGraw-Hill, 2006.

Slee, Robert T. *Private Capital Markets: Valuation, Capitalization, and Transfer of Private Business Interests*. Hoboken, NJ: Wiley, 2004.

Tjia, John. *Building Financial Models: A Guide to Creating and Interpreting Financial Statements*. New York: McGraw-Hill, 2004.

Websites:

Collaboratory for Research on Global Projects at Stanford University: crgp.stanford.edu

International Project Finance Association (IPFA): www.ipfa.org

National Council for Public–Private Partnerships (NCPPP): ncppp.org

Project Finance Magazine: www.projectfinancemagazine.com

Project Finance Portal, Harvard Business School: www.people.hbs.edu/besty/projfinportal

Public Financial Management blog, International Monetary Fund: blog-pfm.imf.org/pfmblog/2008/02/a-primer-on-pub.html

Urban Land Institute (ULI): www.uli.org

"To obtain a nonrecourse provision, lenders will usually require an additional fee and/or higher interest rate as compensation for this lesser amount of loan security." William B. Brueggeman and Jeffrey Fisher

  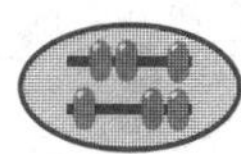   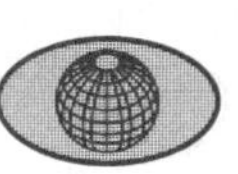   

IPOs in Emerging Markets
by Janusz Brzeszczyński

EXECUTIVE SUMMARY

- IPO activity in emerging markets depends strongly on the macroeconomic environment, business cycles, and stock market phases.
- The number of IPOs increases during bull markets and decreases during bear markets.
- Companies launching IPOs during bull markets can count on raising more capital than if they go public in a bear market.
- There is usually a time lag of about a year between changes in stock market index returns and the subsequently observed IPO activity.

INTRODUCTION

An initial public offering (IPO) is the sale of a company's shares to the public for the first time, leading to a stock exchange listing. This process is known also as a public offering, or "going public."

The main reason for IPOs is the need for fresh capital to finance various business activities, such as the development of new products or expansion into new markets. Most IPOs are launched by relatively small but dynamic companies, which grow too fast to be financed in traditional ways only such as by bank loans. Nevertheless, many big privately owned companies also elect to become publicly traded.

Decisions about an IPO are predominantly based on the actual capital requirements and the expansion plans of the management, but the timing of the IPO is very strongly determined by the current macroeconomic environment, business cycles, and stock market phases.

IPOs are considered to be risky for both the issuers and the investors. The issuers may miscalculate the value of the company and choose the wrong time to go public. In this event, the amount of capital raised from the IPO will be less than expected, and control of the company may be lost by diluting the shares of previous stockholders in the new ownership structure after the IPO. However, when an IPO is successful, a company can raise more capital than anticipated, and the original stockholders may still be able to control the company.

As for the risks faced by the investors, first, they may make errors in assessing the company value, and second, it is very difficult to predict how the share price will behave once the company is listed on the stock exchange. Investors normally have access to limited historical data only, which makes the valuation and the appraisal of the firm's financial situation rather difficult. Moreover, the majority of IPOs are companies that are experiencing a transitory growth stage. This creates even more uncertainty about their value in the future. Last but not least, the stock market before and after an IPO may behave in an erratic way and exhibit high volatility, which in a short period of time may lead to either unexpected profits or unexpected losses.

INITIAL PUBLIC OFFERINGS

The main advantage of an IPO is that the company is not obliged to return the capital raised from the investors. The downside is that new stockholders are entitled to a share of future profits (usually in the form of a dividend). The stockholdings of the existing owners will be diluted in the new ownership structure, and in many cases they may even lose control over the company. However, they expect their shares to become more valuable after the IPO, when the company should be able to generate higher profits from the capital raised in the IPO process.

In an IPO the issuers are usually assisted by underwriting firms, such as investment banks, which help to decide on the best offer price and the timing of the offer. They also deal with the legal aspects of the entire process. Furthermore, the underwriter approaches investors with offers to sell the shares of the IPO company.

The sale of shares in an IPO may take place using different methods. These are: Dutch auction, firm commitment, best efforts, bought deal, or self-distribution of stock. When the IPO is successful and the underwriters sell the shares, they are rewarded by a commission calculated as a certain percentage of the value of the shares issued and sold.

The number of new IPOs in any market always depends on business cycles. One of the best examples is the dot-com bubble in the United States during the 1990s, when share prices were rising sharply and many young companies from the high-tech sector were seeking capital through IPOs. After the companies were listed on the stock market, their share prices skyrocketed—and continued to do so until the bubble burst.

The value of the IPO of a company is usually relatively high in comparison to alternative methods of financing such as bank loans. The largest IPOs in history so far have been: Industrial & Commercial Bank of China ($21.6 billion) in 2006; NTT Mobile Communications ($18.4 billion) in 1998; Visa Inc. ($17.9 billion) in 2008; and AT&T Wireless ($10.6 billion) in 2000.

PRICING OF PUBLIC OFFERS

In order to sell a large number of new shares and raise significant amounts of capital, an IPO has to offer investors a strong incentive to buy. That is why most IPOs tend to be underpriced. On the one hand, a consequence of this is that investors who buy the shares at the offering price can earn substantial returns, and this tends to happen over a relatively short period of time. On the other hand, when an IPO is severely underpriced the result may be what is known as "money left on the table." This term is used to describe the situation when the company experiences a relative loss of capital, i.e. the loss of money that could have been raised from the market in an IPO if the shares had been offered and sold at a higher price.

If the shares are overpriced, the underwriters may not be able to sell all of them. They then face the problem of acquiring the shares themselves—which is even more troublesome when the current market price is lower than the issuing price.

The public offering price (POP) is the price at which IPOs are offered to the public by an underwriter. Several factors affect this price, including data about a company's financial situation (past, current, and forecasted), macroeconomic conditions and stock market trends (current and predicted), as well as information about investors' confidence.

A preliminary registration statement filed with the securities commission, which describes a new IPO, is called a "red herring." It does not include the price or issue size and it may be updated many times before it becomes the final prospectus. The process of soliciting orders to buy an IPO before its registration is approved by the securities commission is known as "gun jumping." An advertisement published by the underwriters giving information about the details of an IPO is called a "tombstone." The first recommendation issued by an underwriter for an IPO is known as the "booster shot." Its aim is to promote the new shares of the IPO company and to increase the chance of its successful sale to the public. The underwriters cannot, however, promote the IPO during the "quiet period," which is the interval of time following the filing with the securities commission and before the registration statement. The term "quiet period" refers also to a certain number of days after an IPO is listed on the stock market, during which the company and those underwriters directly engaged in the IPO are not allowed to issue any financial forecasts or recommendations for the company concerned.

IPOs IN EMERGING MARKETS

In many emerging markets the term "going public" may seem confusing. In countries that did not have free-market economies in the past, and where government ownership was dominant over private ownership, most companies that launched IPOs were in fact privatized, because they were sold by the government to *private* investors through the stock market. Hence, they were in fact *going private* rather than *going public*.

A problem in emerging market financial systems is that many small, young private firms that have good investment opportunities can show little evidence of past business and financial performance. They therefore face serious problems when they want to attract external finance for new ventures. This is because in these countries either firm financing is intermediated or the capital markets are underdeveloped. Furthermore, in many emerging markets the legal and regulatory environment is rather weak, and financial intermediaries tend to give priority to large companies that have a relevant track record and own a certain value of physical assets which can be used as collateral for loans. There is also a danger that intermediaries may favor firms controlled by politicians. In emerging markets, the development of public equity markets has been found to be beneficial for the financial systems. It is believed that public capital markets are more immune to the influence of politicians and other lobbying groups.

The development of capital markets in emerging market countries, combined with their dynamic macroeconomic growth in recent years, has triggered IPO activity on their stock exchanges. However, it is worth distinguishing between the various sources of capital that are being invested in IPOs. In many emerging markets the limited availability of capital has been a major problem. Even though the economic growth of emerging countries in recent years has helped in the accumulation of capital from domestic sources, much of the capital invested in IPOs has its origin in developed countries. An important role here is played by venture capital companies, which often use an IPO as their exit strategy. However, the activity of venture capital funds may differ from country to country—it is, for example, traditionally higher in Asian markets and lower in the emerging market countries in Europe.

A typical IPO process in an emerging market starts when a company enters a high growth phase and the management decides that there is a momentum in the firm's life during which a relatively large amount of new capital can be raised for further expansion. It is then that the shares can be sold via an IPO at prices that result in high multiples of the most commonly used financial ratios, such as price/earnings ratio (P/E), or price/bookvalue ratio (P/BV). Other typical reasons why companies decide to become public in emerging markets and launch an IPO are easier access to capital in the future, increased liquidity of their shares, and, last but not least, visibility and prestige when they are listed on the stock market.

The number of IPOs in emerging markets is variable over time and depends on many key factors, among which the macroeconomic environment and the rate of growth of the economy are the dominant ones. There is evidence to show that IPO activity in emerging markets is related to phases of the stock market, which in turn

Figure 1. New IPOs *versus* stock market returns in Poland in the period 1997–2008. (*Source*: Warsaw Stock Exchange and author's calculations. The data exclude the NewConnect market segment)

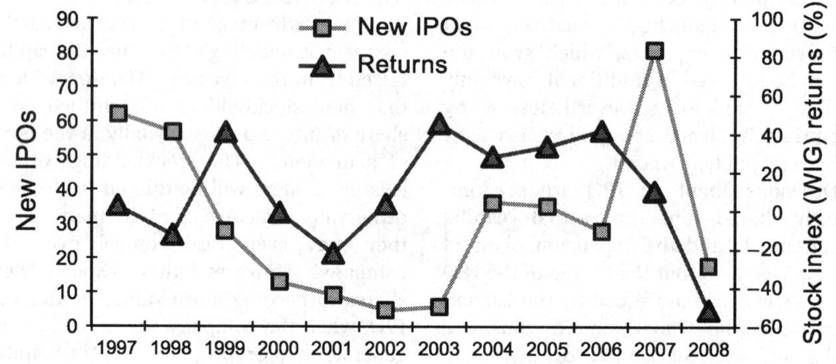

CASE STUDY

IPOs in the Emerging Market in Poland

Figure 1 shows the number of new IPOs and the main stock market index (WIG) returns for the Polish stock market over a period of 12 years from 1997 to 2008. An important feature of this graph is the one-year shift of new IPOs relative to the situation in the stock market, where the pattern of volatility of index returns clearly leads the IPO activity. The correlation coefficient between those two variables is only 0.0244 (2.44%) when IPOs and stock market index returns are analyzed simultaneously, but increases to as high as 0.5683 (56.83%) when the WIG returns are lagged by one year.

Following the period 2003–2006, during which the WIG index increased at an annual rate of nearly 40%, in 2007 the number of new IPOs jumped to 81 from an annual average of less than seven in 2001–2003 and 33 in 2004–2006. When global stock markets collapsed in 2007 and continued to seek new bottoms in 2008 (events that were reflected in the returns of the Polish market index WIG), the number of new IPOs in 2008 fell more than fourfold to less than 20 from the peak of just over 80 the year before.

This finding shows that decisions about IPOs are strictly dependent on stock market phases and that IPOs tend to increase when share prices are rising and to decrease when they fall. The relationship is not simultaneous, with some lagged effect being observed that may be linked to the length of time decision-makers need to assess the profitability of a new IPO, given the financial environment and predictions of how much capital can be raised from the stock market at current prices.

     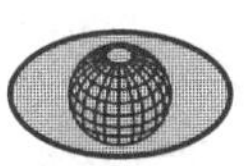   

are connected to business cycles. Bull and bear market periods always depend on the macroeconomic indicators and the prospects of economic growth.

Macroeconomic activity also affects the degree of underpricing of IPOs. Although this effect tends to be more pronounced in emerging market countries than in developed economies, it is in fact always time-varying in its nature, and depends periodically on macroeconomic conditions. Nevertheless, there are cases in which the underpricing was so severe that the share price on the first day of listing reached a level more than 100% higher than the offer price in the IPO—in well-established markets the underpricing is typically below 20%.

CONCLUSION

The number of IPOs in emerging markets and the profitability of the public offers are related to macroeconomic conditions (both global and local), business cycles, and stock market activity. In most emerging market countries there is a time lag between movements of the stock market index and decisions to launch new IPOs.

The correct timing of an IPO is very important for a company that plans a public offering. An IPO may raise different amounts of capital from investors depending on whether stock markets are in a bull or a bear phase.

▸▸ MAKING IT HAPPEN

- Emerging markets are not immune to trends in global financial markets. Hence, it is important for company executives who plan IPOs in these countries to have a good understanding of the global macroeconomic environment and of the financial linkages with developed countries.
- There are research institutes that sell forecasts of future macroeconomic trends and predictions of stock market performance. Forecasts of the world economy are also offered by such institutions as the World Bank, the International Monetary Fund, and the United Nations, as well as by central banks and the finance ministries of individual countries.
- Any decision to launch an IPO should be very carefully analyzed using not only past financial data for the company, but also macroeconomic forecasts. These may provide valuable information about future economic growth, which is likely to impact stock market activity and share prices directly.
- Timing an IPO correctly may lead to substantial gains if the IPO shares sell at a high price. Poor timing may result in the loss of capital if stock market prices are too low.

▸▸ MORE INFO

Articles:

Beck, Thorsten, Asli Demirgüç-Kunt, and Vojislav Maksimovic. "Financial and legal constraints to firm growth: Does firm size matter?" *Journal of Finance* 60:1 (2005): 137–177.

La Porta, Rafael, Florencio Lopez-de-Silanes, and Guillermo Zamarippa. "Related lending." *Quarterly Journal of Economics* 118:1 (2003): 231–268.

Rajan, Raghuram G., and Luigi Zingales. "The great reversals: The politics of financial development in the 20th century." *Journal of Financial Economics* 69:1 (2003): 5–50.

Shleifer, Andrei, Rafael La Porta, Florencio Lopez-de-Silanes and Robert W. Vishny. "Legal determinants of external finance." *Journal of Finance* 52:3 (1997): 1131–1150.

Websites:

International Monetary Fund (IMF): www.imf.org

United Nations: www.un.org

World Bank: www.worldbank.org

  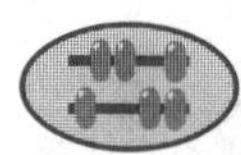 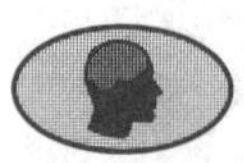  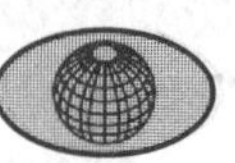   

Islamic Modes of Finance and the Role of *Sukuk* by Abdel-Rahman Yousri

EXECUTIVE SUMMARY

- Islamic finance modes are based on profit/loss sharing because of *riba* (interest) prohibition.
- *Murabaha* has been responsible since the 1970s for the employment of about 80–90% of Islamic banks' resources. The bank provides commodities on a "cost plus profit" price formula to customers who pay back their debt in installments.
- *Ijarah* ranks next in importance after *murabaha* and implies a promise by the bank (lessor) to gift or sell the leased asset at a nominal price to the lessee by the end of the leasing period.
- *Diminishing musharaka* is a new product whereby the bank provides capital to a customer/partner whose share in partnership is increased gradually by repaying the principal in installments, plus a share of the realized profits to the bank.
- *Salam* entitles instant cash to a bank customer against its commitment to deliver prescribed commodities at a future date. *Parallel salam*, on the other hand, is practiced by banks to hedge their *salam* operations.
- In *istisna* the bank finances the manufacturing of a commodity for a customer who pays its price in installments. It is practiced mostly in Gulf countries.
- Islamic financial institutions, in the form of the limited liability joint stock company, rely totally on "ordinary shares" for raising their capital.
- *Multiple-party mudaraba* has enabled Islamic banks to work as partner/investor on a profit/loss basis for large numbers of capital owners whose deposits take the form of investment accounts.
- Islamic financial institutions have recently extended their activities in capital markets, and *sukuk* (Islamic bonds) are playing an important role in mobilizing resources.
- Because of *riba* prohibition, securitization (for *sukuk* purposes) should neither include *murabaha*, *istisna*, and *salam* assets, which are debt arrangements, nor allow for guaranteed regular payment to *sukuk* holders. Yet, *sukuk* experience, though it has been successful in terms of resources mobilized, shows deviation from these rules.
- If *sukuk* do not maintain strict *shariah* rules they are bound to be confused with conventional bonds.

INTRODUCTION

Broadly speaking, Islamic modes of finance can be divided into two types: Either they provide direct finance as capital funds through partnership (*musharaka* and *mudaraba*) or they provide indirect finance through leasing (*ijarah*) and sale contracts (*murabaha, bai ajil, salam,* and *istisna*). All modes are based on the principle of *riba* (interest) prohibition, and all seek to maintain Islamic business ethics (freedom and leniency of transactions, recognition of and regard for private property, and justice).

MODES OF FINANCE

Musharaka

Musharaka (partnership) is practiced by Islamic banks either on a "permanent" or on a "diminishing" basis. In both cases capital is provided by the bank in return for a share in the realized profit (or the loss if a loss occurred). In *diminishing musharaka,* which is a new Islamic product, the bank is entitled to receive, in addition to its share in realized profits, an extra payment that is specifically assigned for the purpose of reducing its share in the company's capital until this is fully paid off by the partner. Diminishing *musharaka* has mostly been used to finance small and medium-size enterprises, but it has also been employed in the financing of several big projects in some Arab Gulf countries (Kuwait, Bahrain, and Emirates).

Murabaha

Among all the modes of Islamic finance, *murabaha* has played the most important role. Banks' annual reports reveal that since the 1970s *murabaha* has been steadily responsible for the employment of about 80–90% of Islamic banks' resources. *Murabaha* in traditional *fiqh* (Islamic jurisprudence) is a spot sale contract where the price is based on a cost plus profit margin formula. The contract has been modified to include *bai ajil* (deferred payment sale) and renamed as "Murabaha to the Order of the Purchaser". According to the new contract, the bank's customer orders the purchase of a prescribed commodity that is available in the domestic or the foreign market. If the customer's creditability is satisfactory, the bank buys the commodity, adding its markup to the market price. The bank accepts payment for the commodity in installments, which normally stretch over one year or more. When *murabaha* purchase is made by means of importation from foreign markets, letters of credit and foreign conventional banks are involved, and necessary *shariah* precautions are taken to avoid payment of "interest" at any step.

Murabaha, which has established a flexible mechanism for extending interest-free trade credit on short- and medium-term bases to households and firms, has also played a significant role in financing small and microenterprises (for example Faisal Bank's Um Dorman branch in Sudan). Banking risk involved in *murabaha* operations is significantly reduced by customers undertaking to fulfill the contract once the commodity is purchased and by collaterals in the form of mortgage rights given to the bank over the purchased commodity until its price is fully paid.

The practice of *murabaha* has been the subject of criticism. It is held against Islamic banks that they are frequently guided by prevailing interest rates in determining their profit margin (markup) when they should instead consider market conditions for deferred payment sale, as intended in *shariah.* Also, banks have sometimes (for instance in Pakistan) not acted as purchasers and have merely financed customers in equivalent cash to the ordered commodity price plus markup. In this case the markup charged by the bank above the commodity price is no different from interest, which is prohibited.

Salam

Salam is the sale of a prescribed commodity for deferred delivery in exchange for immediate and full payment of its price. *Salam* is permissible in *shariah* to meet the instant cash needs of a seller who undertakes the future delivery of the commodity. *Salam* sale is absolutely forbidden in currencies, gold, silver, and all quasi-money assets, since gain in this exchange is *riba.* The objects of *salam* are commodities (or services) that are normally available in the market and can be specifically defined in terms of quantity, and quality. The exact

"**Opportunities pass by as the passing of the clouds, thus seize the opportunities of goodness.**"
Imam Ali ibn Abi Taleb

  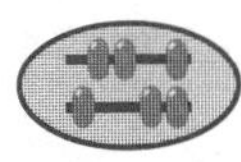   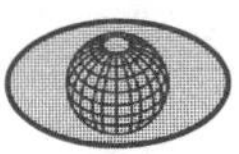   

date and place of delivery must be specified in the contract to avoid any problem. Thus, banking finance is extended to firms or individuals against their commitment to deliver commodities at future dates.

To hedge the *salam* operation banks also practice *parallel salam*. This involves making counter deals with other parties whereby they obtain immediate cash payments against a commitment to deliver commodities of similar quantity and quality to those in the *salam* contracts at some future date. Islamic banks in Pakistan, Sudan, and in some Arab Gulf countries have practiced *salam* transactions.

Istisna

Istisna is a manufacturing contract, treated in traditional *fiqh* as a special sale contract. A household that wishes to build a house, or a firm that needs to construct a building, or to manufacture equipment with particular specifications, would approach the bank for this purpose. The bank has to estimate the economic viability of the operation and the creditability of the customer. If the response is favorable, an *istisna* contract will be signed between the two parties. The customer submits a down payment and undertakes to pay the remaining part of the manufacturing price, as mutually agreed with the bank, in installments over a given period of time. The Islamic bank would then sign a *parallel istisna* contract whereby it extends finance to a firm that agrees to manufacture the requested object according to specification and to deliver it at an agreed future date. Islamic banks in the Arab Gulf countries have used this type of contract successfully to finance big operations, particularly in the construction sector and infrequently in the industrial sector.

Ijarah Muntahia Bittamleek

Ijarah muntahia bittamleek (lease ending with ownership) ranks next in importance after *murabaha* as an employment mode. The Islamic bank purchases *real assets* for leasing as requested and specified by its customers. The bank (lessor) and the client (lessee) will mutually agree on the leasing period, rent, and terms of payment. Maintenance and insurance of the leased asset are the bank's responsibility, whereas the lessee has to bear the running costs as well as any repair costs in the case of misuse. As *shariah* does not allow for the combination of leasing and ownership in one single contract, *ijarah muntahia bittamleek* implies a promise on the part of one party—namely the bank—to gift or to sell the leased asset at a nominal price to the lessee by the end of the leasing term. *Ijarah muntahia bittamleek* has opened the door for successful leasing activities by the Islamic banks, particularly in the housing sector. *Ijarah* of houses gives to the bank the advantage of keeping the title of property until the end of leasing period, and to the lessee the benefit of subleasing rights.

MODES FOR MOBILIZING INTEREST-FREE FINANCIAL RESOURCES

Musharaka and *mudaraba* have, since the 1970s, been responsible for the mobilization of interest-free financial resources. More recently, *sukuk* (Islamic bonds) have also played an increasingly important role.

Islamic banks and insurance companies (*takaful*) have depended on *musharaka*, which took the form of the limited liability joint stock company, to obtain and raise their capital. New *shariah* rules approved in the 1970s stated that the modern corporation was allowed to rely only on ordinary shares; it could not issue preference shares or interest-based bonds. Trade in shares of Islamic financial institutions is restricted by certain *shariah* rules that ordinary Muslim investors cannot easily recognize. This limits their circulation in secondary markets.

Mudaraba has been the most suitable and practical mode for mobilizing financial resources to Islamic banks. The traditional dual-partnership *mudaraba* contract between the *rub-ul-mal* (capital owner) and the *mudareb* (the active partner who manages the investment) has been replaced by a multiple-partnership contract to enable the Islamic bank to function as *mudareb* for large numbers of capital owners. Unlike depositors in conventional banks, these capital owners are "partners" in Islamic banks, and their funds are deposited in investment accounts. According to *shariah*, they are liable to loss if this occurs, and they are not promised any returns by the bank except a share in any profit realized. Holders of investment accounts trust the Islamic bank to pool their resources (possibly combined with its own investable funds) and to use them directly or indirectly in different investment projects, within *shariah* boundaries, for the sake of profit. Against traditional *shariah* rules, Islamic banks have imposed no restrictions on withdrawals from the investment accounts at any time during the *mudaraba* operations. Islamic banks within a dualistic banking system have to submit to the central banks' secular regulations and to meet the competition from conventional banks that normally allow withdrawals from time deposits at any time.

Irregular withdrawals from investment deposits would have a negative effect on the flow of financial resources to investment activities, particularly if long-term projects were targeted. This situation has led Islamic banks to offer and operate investment deposits that are accepted for a "specified period," or authorized only for a "specific project." Banks have also issued *mudaraba*, *musharaka*, and investment certificates of different types that have helped to give some stability to funds assigned to investment activities. Nevertheless, these certificates were not negotiable in secondary markets.

THE DEVELOPMENT OF *SUKUK*

Of growing importance, particularly in the last decade, has been the development of *sukuk* (Islamic bonds). *Sukuk* arose as a natural response to the remarkable growth of Islamic financial services and allowed Islamic banks, companies, and sovereigns to raise *shariah*-compliant funds through the market. It is this development in fact which has led to the growth of an Islamic capital market, though trade in shares of Islamic banks, *takaful* companies (or companies whose activities comply with *shariah*) is always feasible.

According to AAIOFI's definition of investment *sukuk* (Shariah Standard 17), there are fourteen possible forms that these can take. However, *sukuk* development meant approval of securitization within Islamic finance. Within the *shariah* framework the scope of assets that can be pooled, designated, and packaged for securitization is comparatively limited. The *ijarah* contract has been widely accepted by *fuqaha* (Muslim jurists) for securitization, since *sukuk* will rightly be backed by physical assets and financial rights over usufruct. Contracts such as *murabaha*, *istisna*, or *salam* cannot be securitized because they are *debt arrangements*. According to *shariah*, debt-based contracts cannot be traded in secondary markets, If this is done it would typically mean trade in money and involvement in *riba*. Yet, the decision of the Organization of the Islamic Conference's Fiqh Academy (Number 5, Fourth Annual Plenary Session, Jeddah, 1988) opened the door for assets in the form of money or debt (for instance, *istisna* and *murabaha*) to be exceptionally securitized if mixed in "minor proportion" with physical assets (*ijarah*).

Under *shariah* principles of interest prohibition and profit/loss sharing, no guarantee can be given in respect of either regular payment to *sukuk* holders or

"Truth is timeless, and returning to truth is better than continuing in falsehood." Umar ibn al-Khattab

redemption of the *sukuk*'s face value. This goes against conventional market practices. Payments to *sukuk* holders should be made from the *actual or realized* cash flow of the investment that is based on the assets in the underlying pool. However, guarantees of performance, collateralization attached to *sukuk*, and their rating by conventional standards (Fitch or Standard & Poor's) imply the existence of mechanisms that secure a regular known flow of income to *sukuk* and redemption of their full face value. For example, in the Islamic Development Bank (IDB) *sukuk* issue of $400 million in 2003, returns were calculated on a fixed-rate basis of 3.635% per annum until their full redemption in 2008. The same principle applies to all the *sukuk* issued by sovereigns, and Salman Syed Ali (2005) observes that "rents payable to *sukuk* holders are not necessarily generated from the use of *sukuk* assets but from general revenues and other earnings of the state enterprise."

All this throws doubt on the genuine submission of *sukuk* to the principle of profit/loss sharing. Besides, the exception made for possible securitization of *murabaha* and *istisna* assets in "minor proportion" with *ijarah* assets has been widely extended. As in the case of IDB's $400 million *sukuk* of 2003, the "minor proportion" of *murabaha* and *istisna* assets reached 49% of total tangible assets. More serious in this case is that under exceptional circumstances the composition of *ijarah* assets can fall temporarily under 51%, but not to a minimum of 25%, of the total pool of assets!

In practice, therefore, the gap between Islamic *sukuk* and conventional bonds has narrowed considerably. In future issues, *sukuk* should stick strictly to *shariah* rules if they are not to be confused in the markets with conventional bonds.

▸▸ MORE INFO

Books:

Hassan, M. Kabir, and Mervyn K. Lewis (eds). *Islamic Finance: The International Library of Critical Writings in Economics.* Cheltenham: Edward Elgar Publishing Ltd., 2007.

Iqbal, Munawar, and Tariqullah Khan (eds). *Financial Engineering and Islamic Contracts.* New York, NY: Palgrave Macmillan, 2005.

Karim, Rifaat Ahmed Abdel, and Simon Archer (eds). *Islamic Finance: Innovation and Growth*. London: Euromoney Books, 2002.

Warde, Ibrahim. *Islamic Finance in the Global Economy*. Edinburgh: Edinburgh University Press, 2007.

Articles:

Ali, Salman Syed. "Islamic capital market products: Developments and challenges." Jeddah: IRTI, Islamic Development Bank (IDB), 2005 (Occasional Paper No. 9). Available online at: www.irtipms.org/PubDetE.asp?pub=213

Yousri, Abdel-Rahman. "Islamic banking modes of finance: Proposals for further evolution." In Munawar Iqbal and Rodney Wilson (eds). *Islamic Perspectives on Wealth Creation: Studies in Honour of Robert Hillebrand*. Edinburgh: Edinburgh University Press, 2005.

Yousri, Abdel-Rahman. "Islamic securities in Muslim stock markets, and an assessment of the need for an Islamic secondary market," *Islamic Economic Studies* 3:1 (1995), 1–37. (Downloadable from www.irti.org)

Reports:

AAOIFI (Accounting and Auditing Organization for Islamic Financial Institutions). "Shari'a standards," 2008. www.aaoifi.com/keypublications.html

Islamic Fiqh Academy of the Organization of Islamic Countries. "Resolutions and recommendations of the council of the Islamic Fiqh Academy 1985–2000." Jeddah: IRTI, Islamic Development Bank (IDB), 2000. Available online at: www.irtipms.org/PubDetE.asp?pub=73

Reports:

Prince Al-Walid bin Talal (p. 1150)

An Introduction to Islamic Finance Theory and Practice (p. 1283)

"Truth is timeless, and returning to truth is better than continuing in falsehood." Umar ibn al-Khattab

  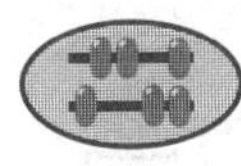 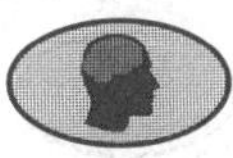  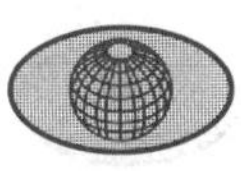   

Issuing Corporate Debt by Steven Lowe

EXECUTIVE SUMMARY

- The Nobel Prize-winning Modigliani and Miller theorem that capital structure does not matter does not reflect the inefficiencies of the real world.
- Taxes, default costs, agency costs, equity dilution issues, credit rationing, and stockholder/debtholder tensions all impact the economists' perfect market.
- Divergent goals between debt and equity holders lead to a number of behaviors, such as decision risk shifting, underinvestment, and asset stripping, which can skew the financing decision. Debt covenants exist to even out the risk/reward structures between debt and equity holders.
- Current economic theory suggests that an optimal capital structure that balances the risk of bankruptcy with the tax savings of debt does exist, although it can be a struggle for individual corporations to hit this target amid the constantly changing influences of the modern operating environment.

INTRODUCTION

The existence and determination of optimal capital structure is an ongoing topic of research in corporate finance. In a perfect market setting, with no frictions, Modigliani and Miller's seminal research in 1958 suggested that the market value of a firm is independent of its capital structure. In other words, capital structure does not matter.

Miller (1991) explained the intuition for this with a simple analogy: "Think of the firm as a gigantic tub of whole milk. The farmer can sell the whole milk as it is. Or he can separate out the cream, and sell it at a considerably higher price than the whole milk would bring." He continued: "The Modigliani–Miller proposition says that if there were no costs of separation (and, of course, no government dairy support program), the cream plus the skim milk would bring the same price as the whole milk." The essence of the argument is that increasing the amount of debt (cream) lowers the value of outstanding equity (skim milk)—selling off safe cash flows to debtholders leaves the firm with more lower-valued equity, keeping the total value of the firm unchanged. Put differently, any gain from using more of what might seem to be cheaper debt is offset by the higher cost of now riskier equity. Hence, given a fixed amount of total capital, the allocation of capital between debt and equity is irrelevant because the weighted average of the two costs of capital to the firm is the same for all possible combinations of the two.

Of course, corporations do not operate in a perfect world, and few if any companies are 100% debt financed. Since Modigliani and Miller's Nobel Prize-winning paper, a host of possible explanations for the relevance of particular financial structures has emerged, centering around the impact of taxes, the costs of default, agency costs, equity dilution, and credit rationing, as well as the differing goals of management and sponsors. Modigliani and Miller have also suggested that firms maintain a reserve borrowing capacity to allow for economic uncertainty. We will look at each of these potential inefficiencies in turn.

IMPACT OF TAXES

Of the most obvious violations of Modigliani and Miller's assumptions are corporate taxes and the tax deductibility of interest payments. Usually, interest payments made to debtholders are deducted from corporate profits before they are taxed. Consequently, the corporate tax saved acts as a subsidy on interest payments. For example, if the tax rate is 34%, then for every dollar paid in interest payments 34 cents of corporate taxes are avoided by the company (although those receiving the interest must pay tax on their interest income). In contrast, if income is paid out as dividends to stockholders, that income is taxed twice, once at the corporate level via corporate taxes, and again as an income tax on the equity holder. Hence, any corporation seeking to minimize its taxes and maximize the revenues available to investors should finance itself entirely with debt.

In a 1977 article, "Determinants of corporate borrowing," Myers showed that considering corporate taxes in isolation does not reflect real world economic interactions. Transferring interest payments to individual bondholders to avoid corporate taxes does not make investors any better off if they then have to pay higher personal taxes on that interest income than the corporation and investors would have owed had the corporation not used debt. Miller argued that because tax rates on capital gains have often been lower than tax rates on individuals' dividend and interest income, the firm might lower the total tax bill paid by the corporation and investor combined by not issuing debt at all. Moreover, taxes owed on capital gains can be deferred until the realization of those gains, further lowering the effective tax rate on capital gains. Because of this interaction, there is an optimal level of debt (less than the 100% suggested above) for corporations as a whole.

DEFAULT COSTS

Costs associated with financial distress and, more obviously, bankruptcy also keep firms from issuing large levels of debt compared to their level of underlying equity finance. These costs can take two forms, being either explicit or implicit. Explicit default costs include the payments made to lawyers, accountants, and other professional advisers in the case of bankruptcy and liquidation, or filing for Chapter 11 protection. These costs can represent a significant portion of total corporate assets, which are lost to investors in the case of bankruptcy. Corporations also need to consider the indirect costs of financial distress that occur as a company moves closer to default and bankruptcy. These can include higher costs from suppliers which fear that the company might not pay its future bills, and the loss of customers who want stable and long-term relationships with their suppliers and counterparties.

Clearly, investors would prefer that firms stay out of default or financial distress so that these costs, both explicit and implicit, are not incurred. However, as a corporation takes on more and more debt, the probability of bankruptcy increases. Hence, the marginal benefit of further increases in debt declines as debt increases. At the same time, the marginal cost increases, so that a firm that is optimizing its overall value will focus on this trade-off when choosing how much debt and how much equity to use for financing. These costs are one of the factors that restrain firms from maintaining very high levels of debt, and are why different industries, with different earnings volatility, can support different levels of debt.

AGENCY COSTS

The decision to issue corporate debt arises from the conflict between competing sources of finance offered by the debt and equity markets. There are large differences between a firm that is 100% owner managed and one in which the equity is

"An appropriate capital structure is a critical decision for any business organization."
Roy L. Simerly and Mingfang Li

  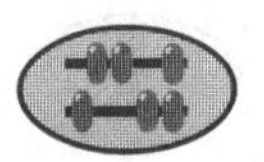   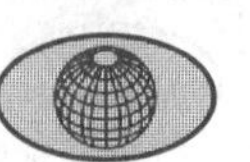   

owned by external stockholders or a mix of the managers and outside stockholders. With external stockholders, the managers act as agent for the ultimate owners. Although these agents should run the firm to maximize its value, they may not be perfect agents for the equity owners as they may make some decisions to further their own interests ahead of the ultimate owners. Agents could award themselves excess pay or benefits, or indulge in empire-building to increase their own reputations. They may even favor the security of the debt-holders rather than the returns of the stockholders. The impact of these agency costs can affect the distribution of financing for a corporate.

CREDIT RATIONING

Traditional economics argues from the standpoint that markets are efficient (as we have seen with Modigliani and Miller's contribution). In 1981 Joseph Stiglitz and Andrew Weiss suggested that markets are only efficient under exceptional circumstances. To reduce potential losses, lenders without perfect knowledge of their counterparties have an incentive not only to charge higher rates to high-risk lenders, but also to ration the provision of credit to them as well. The concern for the lender is that, as it raises the rate of interest charged for its loans, only those firms which are most desperate for finance will take the loans, and these are precisely the corporations that are most likely to go into bankruptcy. If bankruptcy occurs, the corporation is able to walk away from its debt and the lending institution underwrites the cost of failure. This suggests that if a firm is able to obtain a large amount of loan financing, it has a large incentive to undertake higher-risk projects because the risk is asymmetric.

Typically, credit rationing will most often happen with smaller and younger corporations, which are more likely to be owned by their founders, rather than to firms that have a track record or some existing external investors. It is with these owner–managed firms that the risk of imperfect knowledge creates most tension between equity and debt holders. Not only is it likely that the manager/owner of a firm has superior information on his business, but he can also adjust his managerial or investment strategy after concluding a debt contract. Only corporations with riskier projects would be ready to take high interest rate loans, so raising the interest rate without credit rationing would increase the proportion of risky borrowers and reduce the overall profitability of the lender.

EQUITY DILUTION

Myers and Majluf (1984) produced research suggesting that owner-managers use external financing (debt or equity) only when there is insufficient internal financing (i.e. their own money) available for new projects. Indeed, they go as far as to suggest that managers prefer to issue debt over equity. The idea behind this theory is that managers often believe they have a better idea of the true worth of their corporation than potential outside bond or equity investors. Since potential investors cannot adequately value stock, it would generally be sold at a price below the price the managers think appropriate. Rather than sell stock too cheaply, therefore, managers who need external financing will prefer to issue debt. It can be argued that in issuing equity to outside investors, owner–managers might think that the firm is overvalued and that the current owners are taking advantage of this overvaluation. This reinforces the view that debt is likely to be preferred over equity in smaller, private companies.

DIFFERING GOALS OF FINANCIAL SPONSORS

The idea of bondholder and stockholder conflict is widely accepted as a key determinant of financial policy. Bondholders and stockholders often have competing aims and attitudes to risk-taking behavior. Even in highly profitable corporations, stockholders bear most of the investment costs but share the benefits with bondholders. Consequently, bondholders typically value a risk-averse strategy as that will increase the chances of getting all their investment back. Stockholders, on the other hand, are willing to take on riskier projects. If the risky projects succeed, they will get all the profit themselves, whereas if the projects fail the risk is shared with the bondholders.

Another area where these divergent goals are clearly demonstrated is with the problem of underinvestment in times of financial difficulty. Stockholders have little incentive to invest in new projects as corporate default approaches, because the funds they contribute to the enterprise will benefit bondholders and other creditors in the event of default; this is the so-called debt overhang problem. Even if the bondholders would be better off with the investment, equity holders will be unwilling to pay for them. Alternatively, as corporate default approaches, equity stockholders will be willing to invest all their current investment in a very risky project with high potential returns. If the project fails, the bondholders will lose more, but the stockholders can be no worse off because their claims were worthless anyway. If, however, the project succeeds, the stockholders will be the major beneficiaries.

Finally, and perhaps most obviously, stockholders could just pay out all of the firm's assets as dividends to themselves, leaving an empty shell for the bondholders to claim when the firm is then unable to repay its debt. In an effort to prevent this, most debt issues or bank lending will have covenants attached to prevent the equity holders stripping assets, and hence security, away from the corporation that takes on the debt financing. These covenants exist to restrict stockholders' freedom of action, and to try to even out the risk/reward structures between debt and equity holders. However, bond contracts cannot prevent all eventualities.

All of these strategies—risk shifting, underinvestment, paying out large dividends—are more likely the more indebted is the firm. Stockholders may adopt policies that benefit themselves at the expense of the bondholders, and the incentive to do this is strongest when it is

▸▸ MAKING IT HAPPEN

- Economic theory can only help so much in deciding the optimal financing structure for a corporation.
- Modigliani and Miller's seminal work in 1958 suggested that it did not matter whether a corporation was debt or equity financed, but the perfect assumptions on which their theorem rested have proved an unrealistic fit to corporate experience of the real world. Here taxes, the fear of bankruptcy, and the divergent aims of bond and stockholders, particularly in times of financial distress, far outweigh the pull of economic theory.
- The ideal mix of financing for an individual corporation is almost impossible to find because of near constantly shifting debt and equity market sentiment in response to perceived risk and return, and the competitive environment of an individual corporation.
- However, a corporation can benchmark its financing structure against its competitors, similar industries, and the advice of consultants and investors.

"The Modern Theory of capital structure began with the celebrated paper of Modigliani and Miller (1958)."
Wikipedia

  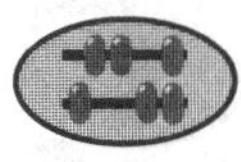 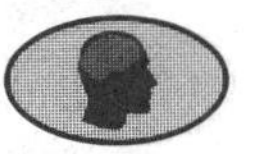  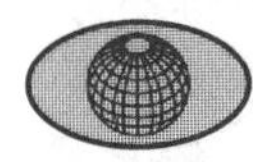   

not clear that the firm will have sufficient cash flow to cover its debt payments.

Potential lenders know this and limit the debt they extend accordingly. Similarly, corporate managers who want to attract lenders and debt funding have to judge how much debt is suitable for a company in a particular industry and state of growth. Young firms in high-growth industries, for example, tend to use less debt, and firms in stable industries with large quantities of fixed assets tend to use more debt.

CONCLUSION

Current economic theory, based on many of the ideas discussed above, suggests that an optimal capital structure exists that balances the risk of bankruptcy with the tax savings of debt. Once established, this capital structure should provide greater returns to stockholders than they would receive from an all-equity firm. However, the complexities of the competitive environment and the huge diversity of corporations and their competitive environments all affect an individual corporation's optimal capital structure.

▸▸ MORE INFO

Books:

Chew, Donald H., Jr. *The New Corporate Finance: Where Theory Meets Practice*. 3rd ed. New York: McGraw-Hill, 2001.

Jaffee, D. M. *Credit Rationing and the Credit Loan Market*. New York: Wiley, 1971.

Articles:

Allen, Franklin, and Douglas Gale. "Optimal security design." *Review of Financial Studies* 1:3 (1988): 229–263.

Donaldson, Gordon. "Financial goals: Management vs stakeholders." *Harvard Business Review* (May–June 1963): 116–129.

Hackbarth, Dirk. "Determinants of corporate borrowing: A behavioral perspective." Paper presented at 14th Annual Utah Winter Finance Conference, February 5–7, 2004.

Harris, Milton, and Artur Raviv. "The theory of capital structure." *Journal of Finance* 46:1 (1991): 297–355.

Jensen, Michael, and William Meckling. "Theory of the firm: Managerial behavior, agency costs and ownership structure." *Journal of Financial Economics* 3:4 (1976): 305–360.

Miller, Merton. "Debt and taxes." *Journal of Finance* 32:2 (1977): 261–275.

Miller, Merton. "Leverage." *Journal of Finance* 46:2 (1991): 479–488.

Modigliani, Franco, and Merton H. Miller. "The cost of capital, corporation finance and the theory of investment." *American Economic Review* 48:3 (1958): 261–297.

Myers, Stewart C. "Determinants of corporate borrowing." *Journal of Financial Economics* 5:2 (1977): 147–175.

Myers, Stewart C. "The capital structure puzzle." *Journal of Finance* 39:3 (1984): 575–592.

Myers, Stewart C., and Nicholas S. Majluf. "Corporate financing and investment decisions when firms have information that investors do not have." *Journal of Financial Economics* 13:2 (1984): 187–221.

Simerly, Roy L., and Mingfang Li. "Re-thinking the capital structure decision: Translating research into practical solutions." Online at: www.westga.edu/~bquest/2002/rethinking.htm

Stiglitz, Joseph E. "On the irrelevance of corporate financial policy." *American Economic Review* 64:6 (1974): 851–866.

Stiglitz, Joseph E, and Andrew Weiss. "Credit rationing in markets with imperfect information." *American Economic Review* 71:3 (1981): 393–410.

Website:

Wikipedia article on capital structure: en.wikipedia.org/wiki/Capital_structure

See Also:

- Merton Miller (p. 1177)
- Franco Modigliani (p. 1178)

"We know very little about capital structure [but] capital structure changes convey information to investors."
Stewart C. Myers

     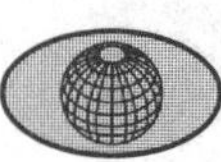   

Managing Activist Investors and Fund Managers by Leslie L. Kossoff

EXECUTIVE SUMMARY

- Organizations not previously of interest to activist investors or hedge funds should prepare to be targeted.
- Be proactive in understanding why investors become agitators, and address their concerns before they escalate.
- Organizational governance—particularly the combined chairman/CEO position—and financial management will be the easiest targets for activists.
- Activists often succeed because they communicate better than management—particularly to tagalong investors who become part of the proxy fight.
- Unlocking stockholder value and simultaneously developing and executing on a long-term strategy will give activists less reason to agitate and less success with tagalongs; executive management will then have a less volatile financial landscape within which to work.

INTRODUCTION

Whether or not your organization has been a target in the past for activist investors and fund managers, you have to plan on it becoming a fact of life from now on—things have changed.

It used to be that only a few organizations were hit by activist investor activity. From the almost prophetic, and beautifully constructed, Benjamin Graham move on Northern Pipeline in 1951, to Carl Icahn's dramatic moves on Yahoo! during the "Microhoo" (Microsoft–Yahoo!) debacle of 2008, activist investors were a rarity—something other organizations had to deal with. A problem for the really Big Boys. Not everyone else. Not you.

Not any longer.

Whether or not you have any known activist investors currently rearing their heads, you'll have to plan for when they show up—because they will. If you work it right, proactively, as well as when the activism hits, you'll manage your way through those very choppy waters and find a safe haven at the end.

WHY INVESTORS BECOME ACTIVIST

Historically, the reason that most activist investors became active was because they saw something wrong with the way things were being managed. The value of the company was not fully represented in the share value. Management was taking the organization in a direction—usually with a direct correlation to falling share value or dividends—that was making the investors unhappy.

But those reasons are historical, and they were retrospective. One of the big changes is that now investors become activists *proactively*. They see things on the horizon that they don't like, and they act accordingly. Not only may they not be happy with what has happened in the past, they're also not happy about what they see coming next.

For management, that is a wake-up call in the best possible way. It puts the onus on you to look at those components of your business that might lead investors to become activist—and take action accordingly. Because if they're seeing something they don't like, either they need to understand why it is the right thing for the business to do, or you need to take a different, objective, look at what they're not liking so that you can determine the relative merit of what they see.

Also, by looking at the organization the way the activists do, you will see other weaknesses—in everything from your strategy, to your operations, to your financial management—that might be the next focus of their attention. You don't want that; you want to make the fix before they ever have the chance to raise their voices.

TOO GOOD AN OPPORTUNITY TO MISS

And then there are those activist investors who get in because they see something that your company has to offer that is just too good an opportunity to miss. It may be because they have a history of being activist and simply see a new opportunity on which to bring their activist skills and financial acumen to bear. Or it may be because your company is such a good target for some other opportunity which you're not considering (like M&A) that they want to get in and make fast money. Whatever the reason, they'll find a way.

Activist investors have a profile. They are identifiable, as is their methodology. Part of that methodology is to get others who own shares in your company to tag along. In most cases, they can't pull off what they want on their own. They need proxy votes. That being the case, they're making a case to their counterparts that you have to counter in its entirety.

Activist investors identify where your organization is exposed. That's where their opportunities lie. Then, once they've got a handle on where, from their perspective, you're going wrong, their next move is to start communicating that shortfall to others they can bring on board. They create the tagalongs. Tagalongs start out knowing nothing more than what they are told. Many of them, on seeing where the activists are going, will become involved in finding out information for themselves—but those tend to be the larger investors who already have analysts working your organization or your sector anyway. If the activists can get enough small investors involved and on side, they'll win.

On your side is that if you can identify those activist investors and fund managers with large stockholdings in your firm, you will be able, with a high sense of assurance, to begin figuring out what their strategy will be. Track their track record.

Then, if you've done your homework and figured out where your exposure lies, you'll be able to address those problems before the activists can take the initiative. You will also be in a stronger position to tell all your investors—especially those proxy candidates—exactly what you're doing, and why the management is on top of the problems and opportunities that everything from economic conditions to global competition are throwing your way.

Activists can't win if management is doing its job—and well.

THE EASY TARGETS

There are some problems which organizations create for themselves that are easy pickings for the activists—and provide some of the highest exposure for management. Now and going forward, corporate governance is the easiest target that activist investors will be able to find.

Since the Sarbanes–Oxley Act of 2002, the question of whether the same person can be both chairman and chief executive officer, and still ensure that the organization is safe for its stockholders, is—and will continue to be—the easiest target of all. It doesn't matter in which country the organization is headquartered. All that matters is that it is publicly traded and that stockholders should not fear that having

"In preparing for battle I have always found that plans are useless, but planning is indispensible."
Dwight David Eisenhower

     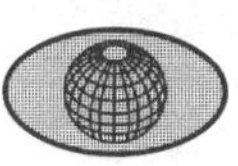   

the same person in the two roles, with their different responsibilities, is creating an increase in risk.

Activist investors and fund managers are looking for situations where the board is perceived as being entrenched. Unfortunately, even if having the same person as your chairman and CEO is the best thing that's happened to your organization in years, from an outside perspective it looks like cronyism on the board. This is a situation that many will associate with lack of transparency and with untrustworthy and inadequately considered decisions.

That puts the onus on the chief executive and the board, *in toto*, to ensure that stockholders see a level of transparency in governance that goes beyond what existed before. Transparency of voting structures—and even a periodic, situational decision to rescue him or herself by the chairman/chief executive—will go far to calm what could otherwise give rise to very contentious criticisms of the board and how the company is managed at the top.

Issues surrounding everything from operational decisions to, most particularly, executive compensation and bonuses will also be fodder for the activists, both now and in the future. The tolerance for perceived cronyism and mismanagement is lower than ever—and is likely to stay that way.

In effect, just as politicians have to deal with a 24-hour news cycle, so too do corporate executives. There is no rest and no hiding from activists once they decide they want to engage.

AVOIDING THE ACTIVISTS' GLARE

A clear-cut corporate strategy for addressing stockholder concerns will do more to avoid the possibility of successful activism than anything else.

First, the stockholders need to see, on an ongoing basis, that the company is dedicated to unlocking stockholder value; that it is committed to finding new ways to make their investment pay off for them—now and in the future.

That is achieved by ensuring that the long-term strategic objectives that are set are not only well communicated, but are also fully executed to the stockholders' satisfaction. By setting and delivering on those long-term objectives, executive management can build long-term investor trust and commitment, leading to a much less volatile financial landscape for the companies operations.

And, finally, it's all about communication. Activists become activists—particularly the successful ones—by doing a better job of getting their message across to stockholders than corporate management does. By working diligently to ensure that stockholders not only have the information they need, but never feel that anything is being withheld from them, the chances of activists getting involved and their capability to bring in others can be severely reduced.

Ultimately it's all about good management, and about thinking like an activist before they can make their arguments stick. By being proactive and objective about the company—and then doing the right things—you'll stop the activists getting a toehold. More importantly, they'll have no reason to try to do so.

CASE STUDY

Microsoft/Yahoo!

It was bad enough for Yahoo! when Microsoft decided to make an unsolicited offer for its takeover. Initially offering $31 per share—a 62% premium over the then share price—Microsoft had decided to expand its internet presence through a big acquisition. This was even though Microsoft, at number three in the search engine business, with Yahoo! in second place, had little or no chance of coming close to the big beast, Google, for the advertising revenues that were there to be had.

When Carl Icahn decided to get into the fray, however, all the rules changed. Buying 5% of Yahoo!, Icahn started actively lobbying for the so-called Microhoo (or Micro-Hoo) deal to go through. He wanted those premiums—especially when Microsoft upped its offer price to $33 per share.

But Jerry Yang, Yahoo!'s chief executive, and Roy Bostock, its nonexecutive chairman, didn't want to sell—at least not at that price. They had other plans, with and without Google. As a result a three-way fight started, but after a while it wasn't altogether clear who was on whose side—especially because so much of the fight was conducted using the business media.

The proxy fight was about to begin. Icahn was fighting to remove all the current members of Yahoo!'s board, including Yang, and to replace them with a completely new set chosen by him. But at that point Microsoft decided that it not only didn't want to pay the price Yahoo! was asking, but also that it wasn't comfortable doing a deal with Icahn tacitly setting the terms. The fight to create Microhoo was over before it began.

For Icahn—who still thought that the Microsoft deal was the best bet (and still had his 5%)—the challenge became how to create an alternate win. He, rightfully, wanted to be able to do something with his shares. The win, then, was a resort to the extent of his and his investors' voices on the Yahoo! board. The outcome was that the Yahoo! board of directors was expanded from 10 seats to 11, with one current board member stepping down, and three new board members—one of which was to be Icahn, the other two selected from his list of alternates—to be added.

The jury is still out on whether there will ever be a deal between Microsoft and Yahoo! But if it's up to Carl Icahn, he'll agitate until he gets the financial win he's looking for.

▸▸ MAKING IT HAPPEN

- Before the activists get the chance, take an objective look at where the business is exposed, and then take action to correct those deficiencies.
- Identify activist investors who already own shares in the company, then research how, and on what particular issues, they have agitated in the past.
- Be proactive in taking steps to address the activists' issues—from leveraging, to corporate governance, management structure, strategy execution, and more—to reduce the activists' opportunities to act.
- Recognize that activism is now future-oriented—not just retrospective and based on the board's previous decisions. Make sure that forward planning and the ability to execute and deliver are sound.
- Message well and continuously to your stockholders, so that it is the company's message that gets the most traction—not that of the activists.

▸▸ MORE INFO

Books:

Burke, Edmund M. *Managing a Company in an Activist World: The Leadership Challenge of Corporate Citizenship.* Westport, CT: Praeger, 2005

Schroeder, Alice. *The Snowball: Warren Buffett and the Business of Life.* London: Bloomsbury, 2008

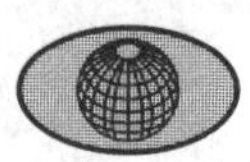

Articles:

Greenwood, Robin, and Michael Schor, "When (not) to listen to activist investors." *Harvard Business Review* 86:1 (2008).

Levin, Timothy W., and Phillip T. Masterson. "Implications of hedge funds as activist investors: No longer flying under the radar." *Investment Lawyer* (October 1, 2006).

Websites:

The Icahn Report: www.icahnreport.com

Investopedia: www.investopedia.com

Websites:

Warren Buffett (p. 1157)

Gary Becker (p. 1153)

"The general who wins a battle makes many calculations. . .ere the battle is fought. The general who loses a battle makes but few calculations beforehand. Thus do many calculations lead to victory, and few to defeat." Sun Tzu

  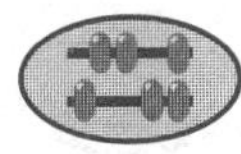   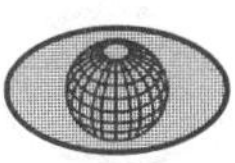   

Optimizing the Capital Structure: Finding the Right Balance Between Debt and Equity

by Meziane Lasfer

EXECUTIVE SUMMARY

- Just over 50 years ago Miller and Modigliani (1958) showed that under a certain set of conditions—namely perfect capital markets with no taxes and agency conflicts—a firm's capital structure is irrelevant to its valuation.
- Their results are controversial and have raised a large number of questions from academics and practitioners.
- This article summarizes the main issues underlying the choice by firms of an appropriate capital structure, taking into account their specific fundamentals as well as macroeconomic factors.
- It presents the benefits and costs of borrowing, describes how to assess these to arrive at the basic trade-off between debt and equity, and examines conditions under which debt becomes irrelevant.

TYPES OF FINANCING

There are three financing methods that companies can use: debt, equity, and hybrid securities. This categorization is based on the main characteristics of the securities.

Debt Financing

Debt financing ranges from simple bank debt to commercial paper and corporate bonds. It is a contractual arrangement between a company and an investor, whereby the company pays a predetermined claim (or interest) that is not a function of its operating performance, but which is treated in accounting standards as an expense for tax purposes and is therefore tax-deductible. The debt has a fixed life and has a priority claim on cash flows in both operating periods and bankruptcy. This is because interest is paid before the claims to equity holders, and, if the company defaults on interest payments, it will be declared bankrupt, its assets will be sold, and the amount owed to debt holders will be paid before any payments are made to equity holders.

Equity Financing

Equity financing includes owners' equity, venture capital (equity capital provided to a private firm in exchange for a share ownership of the firm), common equity, and warrants (the right to buy a share of stock in a company at a fixed price during the life of the warrant). Unlike debt, it is permanent in the company, its claim is residual and does not create a tax advantage from its payments as dividends are paid after interest and tax, it does not have priority in bankruptcy, and it provides management control for the owner.

Hybrid Securities

Hybrid securities are securities that share some characteristics with both debt and equity and include, for example, convertible securities (defined as debt that can be converted into equity at a prespecified date and conversion rate), preferred stock, and option-linked bonds.

THE IRRELEVANCE PROPOSITION

In 1958 Modigliani and Miller demonstrated that, under a certain set of assumptions, the choice between any of these securities (referred to as capital structure or leverage) is not relevant to a company's valuation. The assumptions include: no taxes, no costs of financial distress, perfect capital markets, no interest rate differentials, no agency costs (rationality), and no transaction costs. These assumptions are, in fact, the main drivers of capital structure and gave rise to the trade-off theory of leverage.

THE TRADE-OFF OF DEBT

In this so-called Miller–Modigliani framework, firms choose their optimal level of leverage by weighing the following benefits and costs of debt financing.

Benefits of Debt

There are two main advantages of debt financing: taxation, and added discipline.

Taxation: Since the interest on debt is paid before taxation, whereas dividends paid to equity holders are usually paid from profit after tax, the cost of debt is substantially less than the cost of equity. This tax-deductibility of interest makes debt financing attractive. Suppose that the debt of a company is \$100 million and the interest rate is 10%. Every year the company pays interest of \$10 million. Suppose that the corporation tax rate is 30%. If the company does not pay tax, its interest will be \$10 million and the cost of debt will be 10%. However, if the company is able to deduct the tax on this \$10 million from its corporation tax payment, then the company saves \$10 million × 30% = \$3 million in tax payments per year, making the effective interest payment only \$7 million. If the debt is permanent, every year the company will have a \$3 million tax saving, referred to as a tax shield. We can compute the present value (PV) by discounting annual value by the cost of debt, as follows:

$$\text{PV of tax shield} = \frac{k_d \times D \times t_c}{k_d} = D \times t_c$$

where k_d is the cost of debt, D is the amount of debt, and the product of k_d and D gives the amount of the interest charge. t_c is the corporation tax rate. We simplify the ratio by k_d to obtain the present value of the tax shield as the product of the amount of debt and the corporation tax rate. Thus, the value of a company that is financed with debt and equity (such a company is referred to "levered") should be equal to its value if it is financed only with equity plus the present value of the tax shield. We can write this value as:

$$\text{Value of levered firm with debt } D = \text{Value of nonlevered firm} + D \times t_c$$

These arguments suggest that the after-tax cost of debt can be computed as 10% × (1 – 30%) = 7%.

Added discipline: In practice, the managers are not the owners of the company. This so-called separation of managers and stockholders raises the possibility that managers may prefer to maximize their own wealth rather that of the stockholders. This is referred to as the agency conflict. In general, debt may make managers more disciplined because debt requires a fixed payment of interest, and defaulting on such payments will lead a company to bankruptcy.

Costs of Debt

Debt has a number of disadvantages, including a higher probability of bankruptcy, an increase in the agency conflicts between managers and bondholders, loss of future financial flexibility, and the cost of information asymmetry.

"Smaller companies with significant growth opportunities should make limited use of debt to preserve their continuing ability to undertake positive-NPV projects." Graham and Harvey (2002)

  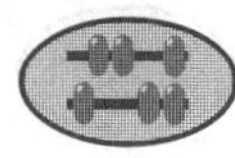   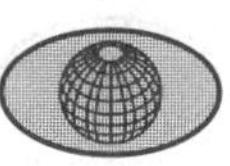   

Expected bankruptcy cost. Given that debt holders can declare a company bankrupt if it defaults on its interest payment, companies that have a high level of debt are likely to have a high probability of facing such a default. This probability is also increased when a company is operating in a high business risk environment. Debt financing creates financial risk. Thus, companies that have high business risk should not increase their risk of default by taking on a high financial risk through their use of debt. Evidence indicates that much of the loss of value occurs not in the liquidation process but in the stage of financial distress, when the firm is struggling to pay its bills (including interest), even though it may not go on to be liquidated.

> "Debt financing creates financial risk. Thus, companies that have high business risk should not increase their risk of default by taking on a high financial risk through their use of debt."

Agency costs. These costs arise when a company borrows funds and the managers use the funds to finance alternative, usually more risky, activities than those specified in the borrowing contract to generate higher returns to stockholders. The greater the separation between managers and lenders, the higher the agency costs.

Loss of future financing flexibility. When a firm increases its debt substantially, it faces difficulties raising additional debt. Companies that can forecast their future financing needs accurately can plan their financing better and may not raise additional funds randomly. In general, the greater the uncertainty about future financing needs, the higher the costs.

Information asymmetry. When companies do not disclose information to the market, their information asymmetry will be high, resulting in a higher cost of debt financing.

Redeployable assets of debt. Lenders require some sort of security when they fund a company. This security is referred to as collateral. Lenders accept assets that can be resold or redeployed into other activities, such as property (real estate), as collateral. In general, the lower the value of the redeployable assets of debt, the higher are the costs.

FINANCING CHOICES AND A FIRM'S LIFE CYCLE

Although companies may prefer to use internal financing to minimize the issuance (transaction) costs, the trend in financing depends critically on the firm's life cycle.

Start-ups are small, privately owned companies. They are likely to be financed by owners' funds and bank borrowings. Their funding needs are high, but their ability to raise external funding is limited because they do not have sufficient assets to offer as security to finance providers. They will try to seek private equity funding. Their long-term leverage is likely to be low as they are mainly financed with short-term debt.

Expanding companies are those that have succeeded in attracting customers and establishing a presence in the market. They are likely to be financed by private equity and/or venture capital in addition to owners' equity and bank debt. Their level of debt is low and they have more short-term than long-term debt in their capital structure.

High-growth companies are likely to be publicly traded, with rapidly growing revenues. They will issue equity in the form of common stock, warrants, and other equity options, and probably convertible debt. They are likely to have a moderate leverage.

Mature companies are likely to finance their activities by internal financing, debt, and equity. Their leverage is likely to be relatively high but will depend on the costs and benefits of debt and their fundamental factors, such as business risk and taxation.

CONCLUSION

This article discussed the different financing methods companies can use and then argued that their choice depends on the costs and benefits of debt financing and the firm's life cycle. For example, whereas start-up companies are likely to be financed with private personal funds, making their leverage low, mature companies tend to have high leverage because they are able to mitigate the costs of debt and gain from the tax benefits. In addition to these factors, in practice firms may choose their financing mix by mimicking comparable firms, or they may adopt the average level of debt of all the companies in their industry. These methods are not highly recommendable as they may result in a suboptimal choice. In other cases they follow a financing hierarchy, where retained earnings are the preferred option, followed by external financing in the form of debt, and then equity. This preference is driven by the transaction and monitoring costs.

▸▸ MAKING IT HAPPEN

The choice of financing is strategic and involves the following issues:

- Both low- and high-debt financing are suboptimal. Companies should aim for the most advantageous level of debt financing, whereby the costs are minimized and the benefits are maximized.
- The costs of debt include a greater probability of bankruptcy, an increase in the agency conflicts between managers and bondholders, a loss of future financial flexibility (including the availability of collateral assets), and information asymmetry costs.
- The benefits relate mainly to tax shields and the added discipline to mitigate the agency conflicts between stockholders and managers.
- This equilibrium applies primarily to mature companies. Start-ups and growth companies are likely to have lower leverage as their borrowing capacity is low. It also applies to companies that normally pay dividends and do not accumulate cash for reinvestment in order to avoid the need to raise external financing.
- The recent financial crisis has highlighted another issue in debt financing, namely liquidity. Leverage concepts were developed mainly in times when debt financing was fully available. In the current credit crisis this is no longer the case. Companies therefore now have to pay an extra liquidity cost to raise additional capital. The question is whether this is a temporary situation or a permanent one, in which case debt will become more costly and leverage will be lower than in the past.
- Another challenge of debt financing relates to the ethics of the use of excessive debt financing, particularly by financial institutions. Pettifor (2006) was able to foresee the current crisis, tracing debt financing back to early times and arguing that religions are against debt because it results in usury. She provides interesting arguments, challenging the whole structure of debt financing, payment of interest, and interest tax deductibility. Possibly a new structure of debt that is linked to the profitability of assets and incurs no interest will emerge from the current crisis.

"The motivation for debt finance appears to be driven by the resolution of the agency conflicts and, in the long-run, by tax savings" Lasfer (1995)

  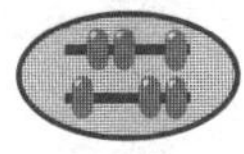   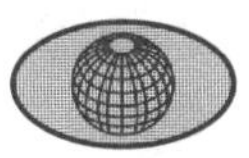   

▸▸ MORE INFO

Books:

Damodaran, Aswath. *Applied Corporate Finance: A User's Manual*. 2nd ed. Hoboken, NJ: Wiley, 2006.

Pettifor, Ann. *The Coming First World Debt Crisis*. Basingstoke, UK: Palgrave Macmillan, 2006.

Articles:

Graham, John R., and Campbell R. Harvey. "How do CFOs make capital budgeting and capital structure decisions?" *Journal of Applied Corporate Finance* 15:1 (2002): 8–23.

Lasfer, M. A. "Agency costs, taxes and debt: The UK evidence." *European Financial Management* 1 (1995): 265–285.

Modigliani, Franco, and Merton H. Miller. "The cost of capital, corporation finance and the theory of investment." *American Economic Review* 48:3 (1958): 261–297.

Websites:

About.com article "Debt financing—Pros and cons": entrepreneurs.about.com/od/financing/a/debtfinancing.htm

Answers.com article "Debt financing": www.answers.com/topic/debt-financing

Washington State University teaching module "Financing sources for ICTs: Debt finance": cbdd.wsu.edu/kewlcontent/cdoutput/TR505r/page31.htm

See Also:

★ Capital Structure: A Strategy that Makes Sense (pp. 526–530)
★ Capital Structure: Implications (pp. 27–30)
★ Capital Structure: Perspectives (pp. 31–34)
✔ Conflicting Interests: The Agency Issue (p. 901)
✔ Investors and the Capital Structure 911
✔ Understanding and Using Leverage Ratios (p. 1027)
✔ Understanding Capital Markets, Structure and Function (p. 1028)
✔ Understanding Capital Structure Theory: Modigliani and Miller (p. 890)
Merton Miller (p. 1177)
Franco Modigliani (p. 1178)

"I'm concerned that some of the basic but important fundamentals of investing are being lost on investors. Or, even worse, simply ignored. Unless investors truly understand both the opportunities and the risks of today's market, too many may fall victim to their own wishful thinking." Arthur Levitt, Jr

     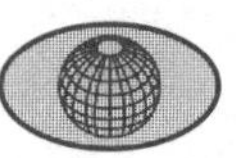   

Private Investments in Public Equity

by William K. Sjostrom, Jr

EXECUTIVE SUMMARY

- A private investment in public equity (PIPE) is a type of public company financing transaction that is prevalent in the United States.
- In a typical PIPE transaction, a public company privately issues common stock or securities convertible into common stock to a small number of sophisticated investors in exchange for cash. The company then registers the resale of the common stock issued in the private placement, or issued on conversion of the convertible securities issued in the private placement (the PIPE shares), with the US Securities and Exchange Commission (SEC).
- Generally, investors must hold securities issued in a private placement for at least six months. However, because the company registers the resale of the PIPE shares, investors are free to sell them into the market as soon as the SEC declares the resale registration statement effective (typically at most within a few months of the closing of the private placement).
- In 2007, companies closed on 1,458 PIPE deals in the United States, raising approximately $84 billion in the aggregate.
- While companies of all sizes have used PIPEs to raise money, PIPE deals have emerged as a vital source of financing for small public companies, with the overwhelming majority of deals being completed by companies with market capitalizations of $250 million or less. This is driven by the reality that PIPEs represent the only available financing option for many small public companies.

TYPES OF PIPE

PIPE transactions are highly negotiable; hence, there is a fair amount of variation from deal to deal with respect to the attributes of the PIPE securities. PIPE securities may consist of common stock or securities convertible into common stock, such as convertible preferred stock or convertible notes, and may be coupled with common stock warrants.

Regardless of the type of securities involved, PIPE deals are categorized as either traditional or structured. With a traditional PIPE, the PIPE shares are issued at a price fixed on the closing date of the private placement. This fixed price is typically set at a discount to the trailing average of the market price of the issuer's common stock for some period of days prior to closing of the private placement. As mentioned above, securities regulations generally prohibit investors from selling PIPE shares prior to the SEC declaring the resale registration statement effective. Thus, because the deal price is fixed, investors in traditional PIPEs assume price risk, which is the risk of future declines in the market price of the issuer's common stock during the pendency of the resale registration statement.

With a structured PIPE, the issuance price of the PIPE shares is not fixed on the closing date of the private placement. Instead, it adjusts (often, downward only) based on future price movements of the issuer's common stock. For example, investors may be issued convertible debt or preferred stock that is convertible into common stock based on a floating or variable conversion price, i.e., the conversion price fluctuates with the market price of the issuer's common stock. Hence, with a structured PIPE, investors do not assume price risk during the pendency of the resale registration statement. If the market price declines, so too does the conversion price, and therefore the PIPE securities will be convertible into a greater number of shares of common stock.

For example, say an investor purchases a $1,000,000 convertible note in a PIPE transaction, and the note provides that the principal amount is convertible at the holder's option into the issuer's common stock at a conversion rate of 90% of the per share market price of the stock on the date of conversion. Thus, if the market price of the issuer's common stock is $10 per share, the note is convertible at $9.00 a share into 111,111 shares of common stock. If the market price drops to $8 per share, the note is then convertible at $7.20 per share into 138,889 shares of common stock. Regardless of how low the price drops, on conversion the investor will receive $1,000,000 of common stock based on the discounted market price of the stock on the day of conversion.

Some structured PIPEs do contain floors on how low the conversion price can adjust downward, or caps on how many shares can be issued on conversion. If a structured PIPE has neither a floor nor a cap, it can potentially become convertible into a controlling stake of the PIPE issuer. Continuing the example from above, if the market price dropped to $0.01, the note would then be convertible into more than 100 million shares, which would constitute a controlling stake unless the issuer had at least 200 million shares outstanding. Hence, structured PIPEs lacking floors or caps are pejoratively labeled "death spirals" or "toxic converts," because investors in these deals may be tempted to push down the issuer's stock price through short sales, circulating false negative rumors, etc., so that their structured PIPEs become convertible into a controlling stake of the issuer.

REGISTRATION REQUIREMENT

The registration requirement of a PIPE transaction can be either concurrent or trailing. With a concurrent registration requirement, investors commit to buy a specified dollar amount of PIPE securities in the private placement, but their obligations to fund are conditional on the SEC indicating that it is prepared to declare the resale registration statement effective. If the SEC never gets to this point, the investors do not have to go forward with the deal. Thus, the issuer bears the registration risk; that is, the risk that the SEC will refuse to declare the resale registration statement effective.

With a trailing registration rights requirement, the parties close on the private placement and then the issuer files a registration statement. Consequently, the investors bear the registration risk. If the issuer never files, or the SEC never declares the registration statement effective, the investors will not be able to sell their PIPE shares into the market for at least six months. As a result, PIPE deals that include such trailing registration requirements typically obligate the issuer to file the registration statement within 30 days of the private placement closing date and require that it be declared effective within 90 to 120 days of such date. If these deadlines are not met, the issuer is obligated to pay the investors a penalty of 1% to 2% of the deal proceeds per month until filing or effectiveness.

PIPE ISSUERS

As mentioned above, companies of all sizes

"It's better to be the head of a chicken than the tail of a cow." Stan Shih have used PIPEs to raise money. Larger companies pursue PIPEs as a quicker and cheaper route to funding than a registered public offering. The vast majority of PIPE deals, however, are undertaken by small public companies. These companies generally pursue PIPEs not because they offer advantages over other financing alternatives, but because the companies have no other financing alternatives. By and large, PIPE issuers are not only small in terms of market capitalization but have weak cash flow and poorly performing stocks. Thus, traditional forms of financing are simply not an option. Few, if any, investment banking firms are willing to underwrite follow-on offerings for small, distressed public companies. Further, these companies lack the collateral and financial performance to qualify for bank loans and the upside potential to attract traditional private equity financing.

Given the distressed status of PIPE issuers, PIPE financing can, of course, be very expensive. Not only does the company typically issue common stock or common stock equivalents at a discount to market price, but PIPE deals often involve other cash flow rights such as dividends or interest (typically paid in kind not cash) and warrants. For example, in August of 2007, Callisto Pharmaceuticals, Inc., a biopharmaceutical company located in New York, raised $11.2 million in a PIPE financing consisting of 1,124,550 shares of Series B Convertible Preferred Stock, and 22,491,000 warrants. The conversion price of the Series B Preferred Stock was set at a 23% discount to Callisto's market price on the day prior to the deal. This compares to a typical discount of 4% for a traditional seasoned equity public offering.

INVESTORS IN PIPES

Hedge funds constitute nearly 80% of the investors in micro-cap PIPEs. Hedge funds invest for the obvious reason: their returns from PIPE investments meet or beat market benchmarks. Hedge funds are able to obtain market-beating returns notwithstanding the poor performance of PIPE issuers through a relatively straightforward trading strategy. They sell short the issuer's common stock promptly after the PIPE deal is publicly disclosed. To execute a short sale, a fund borrows stock of the PIPE issuer from a broker–dealer and sells this borrowed stock into the market. The fund then closes out or covers the short sale at a later date by buying shares in the open market and delivering them to the lender. By shorting stock against the PIPE shares, the fund locks in the PIPE deal purchase discount. With a traditional PIPE, if the market price of the issuer's common stock drops below the discounted price following a PIPE transaction, the fund will take a loss on the PIPE shares, but this loss will be exceeded by gains realized when it closes out its short position because it will be able to buy shares in the market to cover the position at a lower price than it earlier sold the borrowed shares. If the market price of the issuer's common stock rises after the PIPE transaction, the fund will take a loss when closing out the short position, because it will have to buy shares to cover the position at a higher price than it earlier sold the borrowed shares. This loss, however, will be exceeded by an increase in the value of the PIPE shares since they were purchased at a discount to the pre-rise market price.

In addition to short selling, many hedge funds retain up-side potential by negotiating for warrants as part of a PIPE transaction. Hedge funds typically hold on to these warrants even after unwinding their PIPE shares positions so that they can profit further in the event the issuer's stock happens to rise above the warrant exercise price. In sum, hedge funds are able to garner superior returns through PIPE investments because they purchase the PIPE shares at a substantial discount to market, manage their downside risk through short sales and floating conversion prices, retain up-side potential through warrants, and liquidate their positions a relatively short time after closing on the private placement.

▸▸ MAKING IT HAPPEN

- Explore other financing options first; PIPE financing is often very expensive, especially for smaller public companies.
- Retain experienced PIPE counsel (see the league tables at www.sagientresearch.com PIPE agents).
- Retain a PIPE agent to advise on deal structure and locate investors (see the league tables mentioned above.
- If pursuing a structured PIPE deal, insist on a floor on how low the conversion price can adjust downward, or a cap on how many shares can be issued on conversion.
- Consider restricting investors' ability to engage in short selling.
- Consider the amount of dilution existing investors will suffer as a result of the PIPE financing and how to address their complaints.
- Make sure you consult your accountant because, depending on structure, the deal may produce a noncash charge to earnings.

▸▸ MORE INFO

Book:

Dresner, Steven, with E. Kurt Kim (eds). *PIPES: A Guide to Private Investments in Public Equity*. Revised and updated ed. New York: Bloomberg Press, 2006.

Article:

Sjostrom, William K., Jr. "PIPEs." *Entrepreneurial Business Law Journal* 2 (2007): 381. Online at: ssrn.com/abstract=992467

Websites:

The PIPEs Report: News, information, and analysis concerning PIPE deals: pipes.dealflowmedia.com

Sagient Research publishes data on PIPE deals: www.sagientresearch.com

SRFF: Website of leading PIPE issuer legal counsel Sichenzia Ross Friedman Ference: www.srfflp.com

See Also:

★ Equity Issues by Listed Companies: Rights Issues and Other Methods (pp. 537–539)
★ Raising Capital in Global Financial Markets (pp. 566–568)
✔ Raising Capital through Private and Public Equity (p. 1022)
✔ Options for Raising Finance (p. 1017)
Warren Buffett (p. 1157)
The Snowball: Warren Buffett and the Business of Life (p. 1319)

"Chief executives, who themselves own few shares of their companies, have no more feeling for the average stockholder than they do for baboons in Africa." T. Boone Pickens

  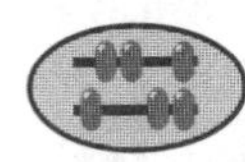   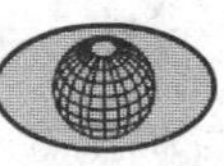   

Public–Private Partnerships in Emerging Markets by Peter Koveos and Pierre Yourougou

EXECUTIVE SUMMARY

- A public–private partnership (PPP) is an "arrangement in which the private sector supplies infrastructure assets and services traditionally provided by governments."
- The public and private sectors have different goals and organizational philosophies and cultures. Reconciling these differences requires a strong commitment, and a clear vision regarding expectations and outcomes.
- The essence of PPP is risk allocation—whether these operations add value depends primarily on how risk is identified, managed, and priced.
- In emerging markets, international partners must address not only the project risk and country risk, but also the risks posed by the lack of local managerial skills, inadequacy of institutions, corruption, lack of transparency, and others.
- Project financing can be used for PPP projects, thus clarifying a key element of the partnership financing structure.
- One of the most significant and interesting global economic developments of the past few years is the emergence of Africa as a competitive region for business.
- The Bujagali Hydropower Project represents the largest mobilization of private financing for a power project in Africa.

INTRODUCTION

Given the state of public sector resources around the world, governments seek to enhance resources by attracting private sector participation. Such participation may be somewhat unstructured, or more formal. The public–private partnership (PPP) is one of the formal approaches to cooperation. PPP, in various forms, is not a new construct. The current frailties of the global economy have forced governments to reduce costs and limit risks. This paper examines the nature of PPP, and describes some of the advantages and disadvantages of PPP. The discussion then focuses on the viability of PPP in emerging markets in general, and African countries in particular. A case study, Bujagali Hydropower Project in Uganda, illustrates many of the major concepts discussed throughout this paper.

DEFINITIONS/NATURE OF PPP

There are many definitions of PPP. Most versions of PPP are very similar, although the degree of control shared by the partners, and several other characteristics of the partnership may receive different emphasis from definition to definition. Thus, PPP is an "arrangement in which the private sector supplies infrastructure assets and services traditionally provided by governments"[1] (Michel). Other terms for PPP include: PPI (private participation in infrastructure); PSP (private sector participation); in the UK, the term used is PFI (private finance initiative); in Australia, the reference is to PFP (privately financed projects); and P3 is commonly used in the US (see Yescombe, 2008). Other variants include the build–transfer–lease (BTL) and build–own–operate–transfer (BOOT) options. In some cases, two or more of the above terms can be used in combination. For example, project financing can be used for PPP projects, thus clarifying a key element of the partnership, financing. Project financing schemes may involve a variety of instruments such as the special-purpose vehicle (SPV), a legal entity with its own assets and obligations. Creation of this joint venture among project sponsors enables the flow of funds. An SPV is typically a highly leveraged company, with limited-recourse debt and limited equity participation. PPP can indeed be very complicated, and requires thorough analysis of associated terms and conditions.

PPP: SOME ADVANTAGES AND DISADVANTAGES

PPP is part of the recent movement of "new public management." PPP is a means through which the two sectors can become interdependent. Managers in each sector must independently answer some basic questions: Why are we participating in this partnership? Where are we going to operate? Who are our partners? How are we going to proceed? What is our exit strategy?

Specific benefits for the public sector include: [2]

- reduces project costs and time, while enhancing its overall efficiency and effectiveness;
- enables access to and learning from private sector resources, technology, and managerial skills;
- credit enhancement and, consequently, access to long-term financing;
- shifts risk to the private sector;
- pursues an integrated approach to project completion;
- involves participation from various partners, and may legitimize the project in the eyes of the citizenry, and other stakeholders;
- PPP may provide greater economic benefits than other forms of cooperation, such as public sector procurement. These extra benefits are usually referred to as value for money (VfM).

For the private sector participant, the analysis is based on the profitability of the project in terms of dollars and cents, and is usually more objective than that conducted by the public sector. Participation in a given project can be analyzed using standard

Figure 1. Bujagali project simplified stockholding structure

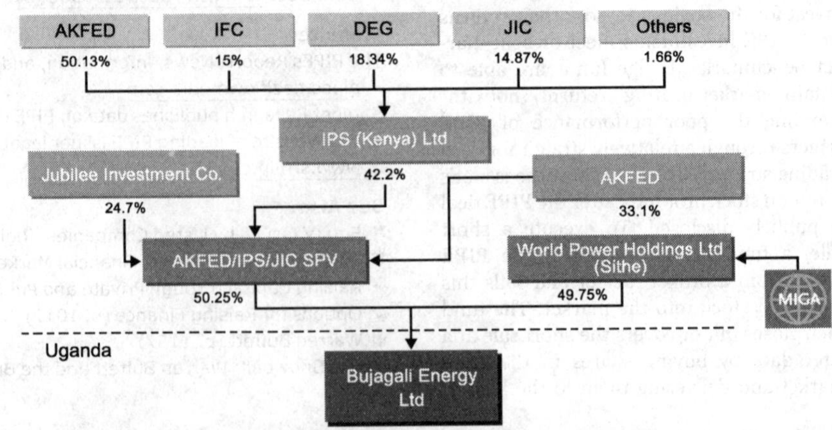

Data adapted from Bujagali Energy Limited for the Private Power Generation (Bujagali) project. "Project appraisal document." World Bank/IFC/MIGA Report No. 3 842 1 –UG, Pages 68 and 72

"Anybody who said that brands were irrelevant in the 1980s will be singing the blues in the next millennium."
Michael Ovitz

  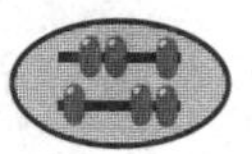   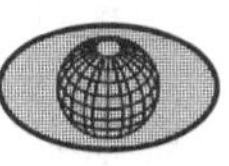   

finance tools. These projects usually involve a great deal of risk, but government backing and involvement of international financial institutions help mitigate risks. The limits of risk–return trade-offs, and the ensuing risk allocation, are even more crucial factors leading to project assessment. A great deal of emphasis is placed on risk management, including the formulation of an exit strategy.

PPP also involves potential disadvantages. PPP entails considerable agency costs, as it must be thoroughly cultivated and managed in terms of planning, monitoring, and acceptance of loss of some control. Private and public sectors often have different goals, and organizational philosophies and cultures. Reconciling these differences in order to bring about the desired project results requires a strong commitment, and a clear vision regarding expectations and outcomes.

The above are especially relevant to public authorities in emerging markets. As emerging markets are so diverse, the analysis must be adjusted to fit the particular country's environment.[3]

EMERGING MARKETS

The term "emerging market" is used to describe countries whose economies are undergoing a significant transition through a series of reforms.[4]

For a private sector firm, operating in an emerging market can be an attractive prospect leading to profit generation, increased market share, and access to growing markets. The firm's ability to access this opportunity depends on how risk is identified, managed, and priced. Business risks exist in every country. Operating in emerging markets, however, may make these risks even more prevalent. The risks include:[5]

- Political risk, defined as a change in government policy that affects foreign companies, is often associated with weak political, legal, and institutional infrastructures. To manage political risk, foreign organizations must be familiar with the political landscape, and learn how to operate in an uncertain and different environment. Property rights, a staple of Western economic institutions, can often be easily undermined. The heavy hand of government can also interfere with a firm's plans and desired outcomes.
- Economic risk. In general, emerging markets exhibit a higher degree of volatility than that shown by developed economies. Even assessing the state of the economy in many of these markets is challenging, as the "official

Figure 2. Bujagali project financing plan

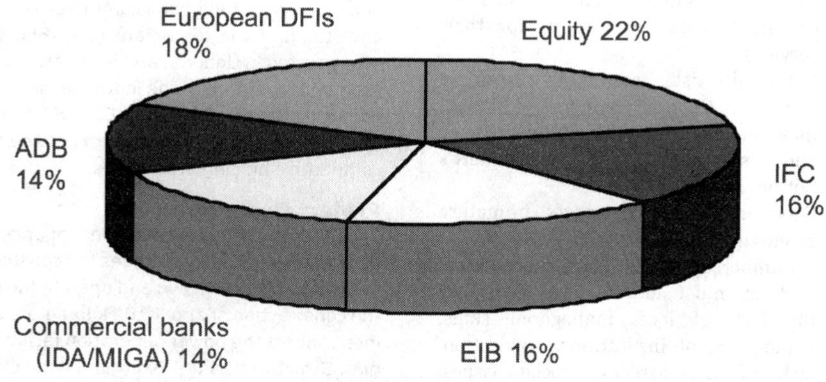

Data adapted from Bujagali Energy Limited for the Private Power Generation (Bujagali) project. "Project appraisal document." World Bank/IFC/MIGA Report No. 3 842 1 –UG, Page 16

Figure 3. Project contractual arrangements

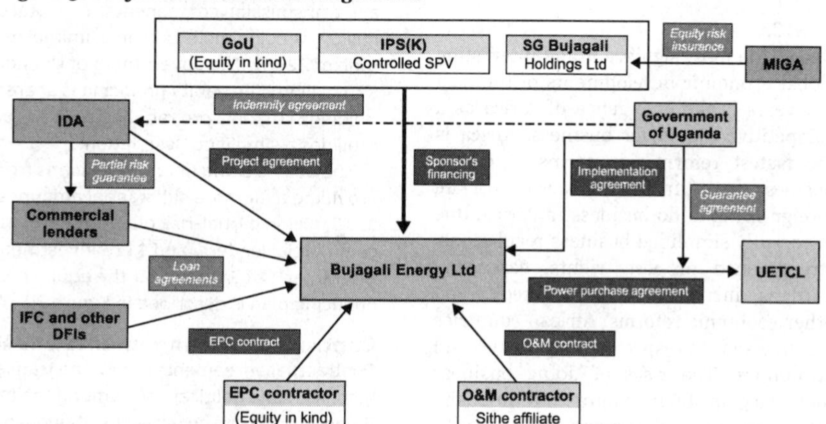

Data adapted from "Project appraisal document" World Bank/IFC/MIGA Report No. 3 842 1–UG, Page 21

CASE STUDY

Bujagali Hydropower Project, Uganda

The Bujagali Project is a private power generation project. The 250 MW run-of-the-river hydro-electric power plant is currently under construction on the Victoria–Nile on Dumbbell Island, Jinja, Uganda. The project achieved its financial closing in December 2007, and is expected to be commissioned in 2011. Bujagali is the first independent power project (IPP) in Uganda, and the largest mobilization of private financing for a power project in Africa. It was named "Africa Power Deal of the Year 2007" by *Project Finance* magazine. Bujagali is a good example of how various international financial institutions can work together with private sector project sponsors to address their financing and risk mitigation concerns, and meet the client country's economic objectives.

Rationale for PPP

According to the World Bank, the severe shortage of electricity in Uganda contributed to a decline in GDP growth to around 5% in 2005/06. Bujagali is an essential part of Uganda's energy-sector strategy to provide a sustainable and affordable source of electricity. The government of Uganda lacks, however, the necessary technical expertise and financing to complete the project on its own. Private sector participation was sought to fill the gap.

Project Partners

The Bujagali project is a public–private partnership between the private sector project sponsors represented by Bujagali Energy Ltd (BEL), the government of Uganda, including the Ministry of Energy and Mineral Development (MEMD) and Uganda

  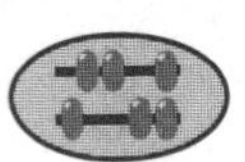 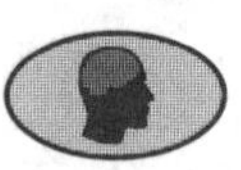  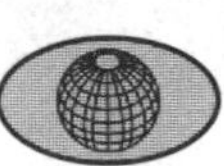 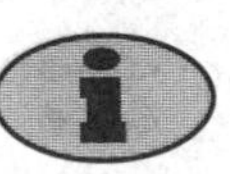  

statistics" may not be accurate. Partners, then, must rely on their own analysis of future market conditions for their services.

- Financial risk, stemming from a country's financial system weakness, may impact on the value of the currency and, subsequently, the company's bottom line.
- Other risks. The country's immature economic infrastructure is vulnerable to a number of disruptions. International partners must address risks posed by the lack of local managerial skills, inadequacy of institutions, corruption, lack of transparency, social issues, income inequalities, pollution, and other elements in the operating environment.

AFRICA

One of the most significant and interesting global economic developments of the past few years is the emergence of Africa as a competitive region for business. Africa is the fastest reformer in terms of easing business entry.[6] It is now easier for private foreign firms to do business in Africa, due to recently simplified business regulations, strengthened property rights, eased tax burdens, increased access to credit, and other economic reforms. African countries are diverse with respect to their politics and economics. The risks of doing business may vary in their nature and intensity from country to country. These risks may emanate from the region's poverty, numerous conflicts, corruption, and health problems, or from the lack of adequate infrastructure. Risks also present opportunities—for example, infrastructure projects are often open to foreign participation. Moreover, many risks can be mitigated through bilateral official insurers (for example, OPIC), multilateral insurers (for example, MIGA) and private risk insurers (for example, AIG). Africa has provided the stage for PPP in such sectors as utilities, energy, minerals, health, tourism, and others.

CONCLUSION

PPP can offer a win–win situation for both the public and the private sectors. Globalization has led to the emergence of new economies. With scarce resources, the public sector in many economies needs private sector partners. PPP is a unique opportunity for the two diverse sectors to learn how to work together. For the public sector, shifting risks and securing financing are important benefits. For the private sector, the environment represents an opportunity to add value to the organization, and act in a socially responsible manner. PPP involves complicated arrangements that require a great deal of expertise and flexibility. The essence of PPP is risk allocation—preparation, and proper risk management and pricing are a must.

Electricity Transmission Company Ltd (UETCL), multilateral and bilateral development financial institutions,[7] and commercial lenders, including Absa Capital (South Africa) and Standard Chartered Bank (UK). BEL, a special-purpose company (SPC), is incorporated in Uganda, and is privately owned by Industrial Promotion Services (Kenya) Ltd (IPS (K)), the industrial development arm of the Aga Khan Fund for Economic Development (AKFED) and SG Bujagali Holdings Ltd (Mauritius), an affiliate of US-based Sithe Global Power LLC. The sponsors were selected through international competitive bidding procedures.

Project Description

The Bujagali project is developed, financed, constructed, and maintained by BEL on a BOOT basis. BEL also manages the construction of the Interconnection Project on behalf of UECTL, which will own and operate the project. The Interconnection Project involves the construction of about 100 kilometers of high-voltage electrical transmission line to interconnect the power generation facility (the Bujagali project) to the national electric grid. Structured as IPP, BEL will sell the electricity to UETCL, Uganda's national transmission company, under a 30-year power purchase agreement (PPA).

Financing

Finance for the project is structured as an integrated package for both the power plant and transmission components. The total cost for the integrated projects, about $800 million, is being mobilized on a limited-recourse basis, through equity and debt in the ratio of 22:78. The government of Uganda provided an in-kind equity contribution of $20 million. The equity financing is shared by the sponsors, IPS (K) and SG Bujagali Holdings Ltd, on a pro rata basis. The equity structure of BEL is complex. Figure 1 provides a simplified description.

The debt is being financed by loans from the group of lenders, the World Bank group providing a far more substantial amount of $360 million ($130 million loan from IFC, $115 million partial-risk guarantee from International Development Association to commercial lenders, and $115 investment guarantee from Multilateral Investment Guarantee (MIGA) to cover the equity position of SG Bujagali Holding Ltd). The project financing plan is described in Figure 2.

Contractual Arrangements and Risk-Sharing Mechanism

Contractual agreements define the transactions and allocation of the commercial, technical, and political risks among the partners. The contractual structure of the Bujagali project is consistent with industry practice for limited-recourse project finance transactions (see Figure 3). The project implementation agreement, also called the concession agreement, signed between the government of Uganda and BEL on December 13, 2005, defines the terms of the concession the government grants to BEL to design, finance, own, operate, and maintain the project. Under the 30-year PPA, BEL agrees to sell exclusively to UETCL all the production, and UETCL agrees to purchase the contracted capacity (i.e., 250 MW), with the government guaranteeing the UETCL's payment obligations. In addition to the implantation agreement and PPA, BEL signed a fixed-price, date certain, turnkey engineering, procurement, and construction (EPC) contract with Salini Costruttori SpA (Italy), and Alsthom Power Hydraulique (France), and an operation and maintenance (O&M) agreement with affiliates of Sithe Global. The EPC contract requires the power plant to be commissioned within 44 months. The EPC contractors were selected through competitive bidding, in accordance with the EIB procurement rules. The O&M agreement reflects BEL's commitments under the PPA.

The contractual structure ensured that the project-related risks, including completion and operation, were borne by the project sponsors and commercial lenders. However, these risks were mitigated by contracts and various insurance arrangements. The risks related to supply/input (hydrology risk), market, political, and natural forces were borne by the government of Uganda under the government guarantee and implementation agreements. The participation of the IFC and the guarantees provided by the World Bank group (IDA and MIGA) are critical in mitigating the completion risk, and to provide Uganda with access to long-maturity commercial loans in favorable terms.

"As the retail trade consolidates, it will look more and more at big fresh brands that are constantly innovating."
Niall Fitzgerald

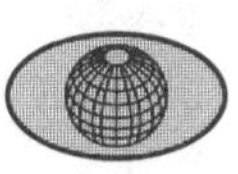

▸▸ MAKING IT HAPPEN

- Conduct a readiness analysis of your organization.
- Know exactly what you want and expect.
- Know what the various partners want and expect.
- Work to build trust among partners.
- Put together a solid risk management process, with clear accountability and understanding of the risks faced, how they are allocated, and how risk is to be priced.
- Be as specific as possible about your role and responsibilities.
- Familiarize yourself with the nature and operations of international financial institutions and agencies, such as the World Bank, its affiliated agencies (IFC, IDA, MIGA), and other cooperating organizations.
- Make sure you do a feasibility study and conduct due diligence.
- Go slow! Learning about PPP is important. Existing relationships could serve as an easier first step.
- Decide on what valuation techniques would be appropriate (for example, internal rate of return, net present value, adjusted present value, and real options).
- Analyze all possible scenarios.
- Review and revize as appropriate.
- Work towards a sustainable relationship, but have an exit strategy.

▸▸ MORE INFO

Books:

Akintoye, Akintola, Matthias Beck, and Cliff Hardcastle. *Public–Private Partnerships: Managing Risks and Opportunities.* Malden, MA: Blackwell Science, 2003.

Grimsey, Darrin, and Mervyn Lewis. *Public Private Partnerships: The Worldwide Revolution in Infrastructure Provision and Project Finance.* Northampton, MA: Edward Elgar Publishing, 2007.

Mobius, J. Mark. *Mobius on Emerging Markets.* New York: Irwin Professional Publishing, 1996.

Osborne, Stephen P. (ed). *Public–Private Partnerships: Theory and Practice in International Perspective.* London: Routledge, 2000.

Yescombe, E. R. *Public–Private Partnerships: Principles of Policy and Finance*. Oxford: Elsevier, 2007.

Article:

Michel Francois. "A primer on public–private partnerships." *Public Financial Management Blog* (February 22, 2008). Online at: blog-pfm.imf.org/pfmblog/2008/02/a-primer-on-pub.html

Reports:

Economist Intelligence Unit. "Operating risk in emerging markets." London: The Economist Intelligence Unit, 2006.

Kennedy, Robert E. "Project valuation in emerging markets." Harvard Business School: Boston, MA, May 14, 2002. Online at: www.hsbp.harvard.edu

See Also:

Joseph Stiglitz (p. 1198)
Energy (pp. 1512–1513)
Mining (pp. 1525–1527)

NOTES

1 See, for example, Yescombe (2007), especially Chapter 2.

2 See Kennedy (2002) for treatment of valuation in these markets.

3 See Mobius (1996), p. 6, and Investopedia.com.

4 See, for example, Mobius (1996), Chapter 9, Grimsey and Lewis (2007), Chapter 9, and The Economist Intelligence Unit (2007).

5 The International Bank for Reconstruction and Development/The World Bank, 2007: www.doingbusiness.org/documents/DoingBusiness2007_FullReport.pdf

6 Bujagali Hydropower Project: www.bujagali-energy.com; www.worldbank.org/bujagali

7 The institutions include the African Development Bank (ADB), European Investment Bank (EIB), the World Bank Group, Agence Française de Développement (AFD), Proparco, Netherlands Development Finance Company (FMO), Kreditanstalt fur Wiederaufbau (KfW), and Deutsche Investitions und Entwicklungsgesellschaft (DEG).

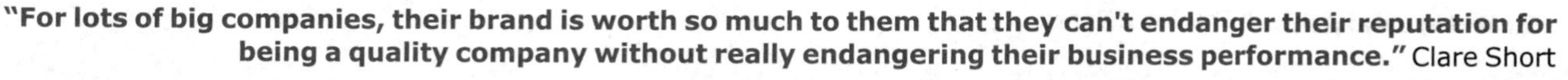
"For lots of big companies, their brand is worth so much to them that they can't endanger their reputation for being a quality company without really endangering their business performance." Clare Short

     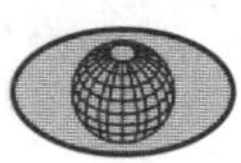   

Raising Capital in Global Financial Markets by Reena Aggarwal

EXECUTIVE SUMMARY

- Major changes are occurring in the capital-raising process in global financial markets. These changes are being driven by:
  - the globalization and consolidation of stock exchanges;
  - the growth of private equity;
  - sovereign wealth funds;
  - the emergence of new regions and countries as financial powers.

INTRODUCTION

During the last decade global financial markets have grown tremendously, becoming large and liquid, and with substantial depth. At the same time, demand for capital has increased significantly, with capital markets continuing to play a dominant role in the allocation of capital.

However, some major shifts are being seen in the roles of the suppliers and users of capital. This article focuses on four such shifts that impact both those global firms which are looking to raise funds and the institutional investors that provide the capital. The four developments that underlie these major shifts are: the globalization and consolidation of stock exchanges; the growth of private equity; the increasing role of sovereign wealth funds as a source of capital; and the emergence of new countries and regions as major financial players.

The recent global financial crisis has clearly highlighted the challenges that companies worldwide face in raising capital. Either funding is just not available or the cost has gone up considerably. The combination of the global economic slowdown and challenges in raising funds in the capital markets has meant that companies are cutting costs, capital investment, and jobs. The financial markets and financial institutions collapsed in a variety of ways, and this will result in structural and regulatory changes that will impact the raising of capital in global financial markets.

THE GLOBALIZATION OF STOCK EXCHANGES[1]

Stock exchanges play a critical role in the capital-raising process. In January 2007 the total market capitalization of all publicly traded companies in the world was US$51.2 trillion and reached US$57.5 trillion in May 2008 before dropping below US$36.6 trillion in October 2008.[2] However, exchanges across the world have undergone major structural changes in the last few years. Starting with the demutualization of the Stockholm Stock Exchange in 1993, the number of financial exchanges that have adopted a for-profit, publicly listed organizational form has grown steadily. This trend can be seen both in the stock exchanges of different countries and in financial exchanges that trade different types of securities.

The rapid organizational transformation of exchanges from member-owned mutual companies to joint-stock companies is unparalleled, and this process is the manifestation of a number of innovations and deregulatory events that have occurred in the last decade. The for-profit structure has allowed exchanges to raise capital and invest in technology that is essential if they are to compete. As public companies, exchanges have needed to increase market share and develop additional sources of revenue. There has been considerable consolidation among the large global exchanges. The New York Stock Exchange acquired Euronext, forming NYSE Euronext; Nasdaq gained control of OMX; and the Chicago Mercantile Exchange merged with its rival, the Chicago Board of Trade.

The globalization of stock exchanges beyond the authority of a single national regulator has meant a rethinking of the regulatory framework. It can be argued that regulatory policy rarely leads, but more often follows, market innovations. As such, the challenge for regulators will be to develop regulatory programs that respond to globalized markets.[3] National regulators are moving in the direction of increased coordination and convergence of regulation in accordance with generally accepted principles. IOSCO, the international organization of securities regulators, has played a key role in promoting greater cooperation and the development of commonly accepted regulatory principles. The financial crisis of 2008 has given added emphasis to the need for global coordination in an environment where capital has no national boundary.

The global consolidation of some of the largest exchanges has been beneficial both for companies raising capital and for investors/traders. This consolidation has made it easier for companies worldwide to raise large sums of capital through public offerings and cheaper for market participants to conduct transactions in deep, liquid markets. In addition to public capital, there has been a tremendous increase in the use of private capital.

GROWTH OF PRIVATE EQUITY

During the last decade private equity firms have become a major source of funds for small and large companies, for firms seeking buyout financing, and for firms in distress. The ten largest private equity firms, ranked by the amount of capital raised for direct private equity investment between 2002 and 2007, are shown in Table 1. Private equity is an investment in the assets of a company in which the equity does not trade in the public markets. Therefore, investment in private equity requires a long-term approach. Institutional investors such as pension funds and endowments are major investors in private equity, and private equity has become accepted as a distinct asset class. During the last decade, there has been considerable allocation by institutions into this asset class, although the current economic crisis has caused them to reevaluate their strategy.

The funds differ with respect to their investment philosophy. For example, the Blackstone Group was founded in 1985,

Table 1. Ten largest private equity firms ranked by capital raised for direct private equity investment between 2002 and 2007. (*Source*: Private Equity International, 2008)

Firm	*Assets (US$ billion)*
The Carlyle Group	52.0
Goldman Sachs Principal Investment Area	49.1
Texas Pacific Group	48.8
Kohlberg Kravis Roberts	40.0
CVC Capital Partners	36.9
Apollo Management	32.8
Bain Capital	31.7
Permira	25.4
Apax Partners	25.2
The Blackstone Group	23.2

     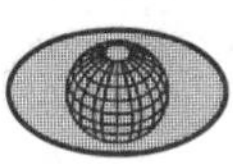   

went public in 2007, and is listed on the New York Stock Exchange. It is diversified into several lines of business that include corporate private equity, real estate, hedge funds, credit, and advisery services. In contrast, Apax Partners is a "pure play" global private equity firm that focuses only on specific sectors. Until recently, private equity activity was focused on investment in the United States and Europe, but now there is increased interest in the emerging markets of Asia–Pacific as a destination for private equity funds. For example, there has been a significant rise in the amount of private equity investment flowing to China, Singapore, South Korea, and India. Global buyout investment has seen considerable expansion in the last few years. Private equity has now become a major source of capital for companies around the world.

SOVEREIGN WEALTH FUNDS AS A SOURCE OF CAPITAL

Another newcomer on the global financial scene is sovereign wealth funds (SWFs). SWFs are government investment funds that invest in foreign companies to earn profits and increase the wealth of the state. These funds have existed for a long time, but the increase in their scope and magnitude has recently made them a major financial player. The source of funding for SWFs varies from export revenues to foreign exchange reserves. In early 2008 the assets controlled by SWFs were estimated to be $3 trillion, and they are expected to rise to $12 trillion by 2012. For comparison, the assets managed by institutional investors like pension funds and endowments amount to $53 trillion. The assets of SWFs are expected to grow at a tremendous rate and become a major provider of funding for companies in both developed and developing markets.[4,5]

Some of these funds have already taken significant positions in a number of foreign companies. As shown in Table 2, the largest sovereign fund is the Abu Dhabi Investment Authority, the investment arm of Abu Dhabi, with $875 billion under management. The fund grew due to the sharp rise in oil prices in early 2008. The fund made an investment of $7.5 billion in Citigroup, has a 4.5% ownership in the home builder Toll Brothers, and also has positions in companies such as EFG Hermes, one of the leading investment banks in the Arab world, and Banque de Tunisie et des Emirats, a Tunisian bank.[6] Similarly, the China Investment Corporation is estimated to have a size of $200 billion, funded by Chinese foreign exchange reserves. The fund has large positions in the private equity firm Blackstone Group ($3 billion) and in the investment bank Morgan Stanley ($5 billion). Other large SWFs include those of Norway, Saudi Arabia, Singapore, and Kuwait.

The growth and size of these funds has attracted considerable attention and discussion. Typically, SWFs make decisions based on sound, long-term investment strategies. Unlike hedge funds, they do not use leverage. Overall, the impact of SWFs is positive in that they invest the resources of a country efficiently. Their investment in companies such as Citigroup, Morgan Stanley, and Barclays has been particularly welcomed, as other sources of capital were unavailable to these companies. For the future, there is concern in some circles whether these funds will remain simply vehicles for financial investment or if they will take an activist role in companies with the objective of gaining political clout for their countries. There is also concern about the lack of transparency and regulation of SWFs.

Table 2. Top ten sovereign wealth funds ranked by assets under management. (*Source*: Sovereign Wealth Fund Institute, October 2008)

Country	Sovereign wealth fund	Assets ($ billion)
UAE: Abu Dhabi	Abu Dhabi Investment Authority	875
Saudi Arabia	SAMA Foreign Holdings	433
Singapore	Government of Singapore Investment Corporation	330
China	SAFE Investment Company	311.6
Norway	Government Pension Fund—Global	301
Kuwait	Kuwait Investment Authority	264.4
China	China Investment Corporation	200
China: Hong Kong	Hong Kong Monetary Authority Investment Portfolio	173
Russia	National Welfare Fund	189.7
Singapore	Temasek Holdings	134

EMERGING FINANCIAL POWERS

In addition to New York, London, and Tokyo, which historically have been the world's financial centers, a number of new regions and countries are catching up and emerging as dominant players. The *McKinsey Quarterly* reports that during the period May 2007 to May 2008, 35 European companies, including Air France, Bayer, British Airways, and Fiat, delisted from the New York Stock Exchange when it became easier to delist.[7] European markets have integrated, the euro has proven itself to be a strong currency, and the region has increased its market share in the last decade. At the same time, the BRIC countries (Brazil, Russia, India, and China) have become new economic powers as their economies grow at much faster rates than developed countries. This growth has resulted in the formation of large

▸▸ MORE INFO

Books:

Dow Jones Financial Information Services. *Galante's Venture Capital and Private Equity Directory*. Dow Jones, 2009. (Also available as an online database. Details at: fis.dowjones.com/products/galante.html)

Harris, Larry. *Trading & Exchanges: Market Microstructure for Practitioners.* New York: Oxford University Press, 2003.

World Economic Forum. *Globalization of Alternative Investments. Working Papers Volume 1: The Global Economic Impact of Private Equity Report 2008.* Geneva: WEA, 2008. Online at: www.weforum.org/pdf/cgi/pe/Full_Report.pdf

Article:

Fenn, G. W., N. Liang, and S. Prowse. "The private equity market: An overview." *Financial Markets, Institutions, and Instruments* 6:4 (1997): 1–105.

Information Service:

Dow Jones Financial Information Services. *Private Equity Analyst.* Online at: www.fis.dowjones.com/products/privateequityanalyst.html

Websites:

Dealogic: www.dealogic.com

Private Equity International (PEI): www.peimedia.com

Sovereign Wealth Fund Institute: www.swfinstitute.org

Thomson Reuters Private Equity Hub: www.thomsonreuters.com/products_services/media/pehub

"Hiccups in the international business scene are not new to us. Wedgwood china has survived upheavals before—the Napoleonic Wars, the Franco-Prussian War, the world wars. We do have a sense of continuity."
Arthur Bryan

   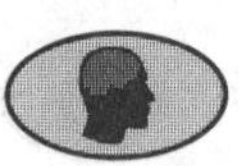  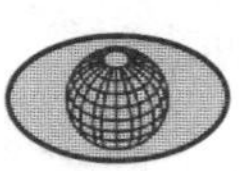   

companies that are competing globally and need large amounts of global capital. Private wealth in these countries has also grown, and the owners of this wealth are becoming another source of capital.

For some years oil-exporting countries benefited tremendously from high oil prices. These countries, among which are Indonesia, Middle Eastern states, Nigeria, Norway, Russia, and Venezuela, became the world's largest source of global capital flows. The *McKinsey Quarterly* estimates that in 2006 $200 billion of petrodollars went to global equity markets and $100 billion to fixed-income investments. It is estimated that even with oil averaging $50 a barrel, net capital outflows from the oil-exporting countries are likely to amount to $387 billion a year through 2012. The future wealth of some of these countries, and hence the capital outflows from them, will depend on oil prices.

CONCLUSION

A number of important changes are taking place in global financial markets that need to be monitored carefully. Stock exchanges have been transformed to become global entities. In addition to the traditional public capital markets, recent years have seen the emergence of private equity and sovereign wealth funds as major players in financial markets. There have also been considerable shifts in regional concentrations of wealth. These changes have impacted the landscape of global financial markets.

NOTES

1 Aggarwal, R., and S. Dahiya. "Demutualization and public offerings of financial exchanges." *Journal of Applied Corporate Finance* 18:3 (2006): 96–106.

2 World Federation of Exchanges, available at www.world-exchanges.org/statistics/ytd-monthly.

3 Aggarwal, R., A. Ferrell, and J. Katz. "U.S. securities regulation in a world of global exchanges." In S. Shojai (ed). *World of Exchanges: Adapting to a New Environment*. London: Euromoney Books, 2007, ch. 7.

4 Simon Johnson, "Straight talk: Emerging markets emerge," *Finance and Development* (IMF) 45:3, September 2008. Online: www.imf.org/external/pubs/ft/fandd/2008/09/straight.htm.

5 Kimmitt, R. M. "Public footprints in private markets: Sovereign wealth funds and the world economy." *Foreign Affairs* (January/February 2008).

6 Thomas, L. Jr. "Cash-rich, publicity-shy, Abu Dhabi fund draws scrutiny." *New York Times* (February 28, 2008).

7 Dobbs, R., and M. H. Goedhart. "Why cross-listing shares doesn't create value." *McKinsey Quarterly* (November 2008).

"This is a violation of the brand and we're not doing it." Lou Gerstner

  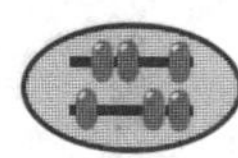   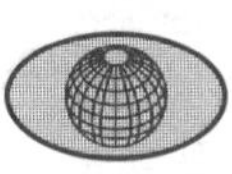   

Raising Capital in the United Kingdom

by Lauren Mills

EXECUTIVE SUMMARY

- It has never been harder to raise capital. The credit crunch means banks are even less willing to lend money to small and medium-sized enterprizes (SMEs). So raising capital is likely to be more time-consuming and costly than before. It is therefore vital you know how much money you need, and what you need it for, before approaching potential backers.
- A lot will depend on whether you are funding a start-up, buying an asset, seeking growth finance, or looking for an exit.
- Whatever stage you are at, you must have a business plan, strong management, and good growth prospects—or potential backers are unlikely to be interested.

INTRODUCTION

Raising capital to grow a business has never been more challenging or time-consuming. While there are still many sources of finance, ranging from government and EU grants, to bank loans, private equity, angel investors, or a stock market flotation, some will be easier to come by than others in the post-credit crunch climate. One of the biggest problems will be deciding which route is best for you.

Before weighing up the pros and cons of each, carry out a ruthless analysis of your business. Start by asking yourself some elementary questions. Do you have strong management in place? Do you have a business plan? Do you know what you need to do to move your business to the next stage? This may sound somewhat elementary, but it is surprising how many companies keep drifting in one direction without knowing whether this is the best route to pursue, or whether the best captain is at the helm.

It is therefore essential to have a clear idea of what you want to achieve and how you are going to achieve it before approaching potential financiers.

GRANTS

In January 2009, the United Kingdom's Business Secretary, Lord Mandelson, announced a new package of financial measures to help businesses with short-term funding issues weather the economic downturn. Help is also available for companies looking to finance the next stage of growth.

The support package consists of loan guarantees and a new Enterprise Fund. It is intended to help companies which are struggling to obtain finance for working capital and investment.

The Government measures include:

- A £10 billion Working Capital Scheme, securing up to £20 billion of short-term bank lending to companies with a turnover of up to £500 million.
- An Enterprise Finance Guarantee Scheme, securing up to £1.3 billion of additional bank loans to small firms with a turnover of up to £25 million.
- A £75 million Capital for Enterprise Fund (£50 million from government, plus £25 million from banks) to invest in small businesses which need equity.

The Working Capital Scheme is a direct response to the constraint on bank lending to ordinary-risk businesses with a turnover of up to £500 million a year. The government has agreed to provide banks with guarantees for 50% of the risk on existing and new working capital portfolios worth up to £20 billion as part of the scheme.

The government guarantee will free up capital, which the banks must use for new lending as a condition of this scheme. This is lending that would otherwise not have been provided, the UK Government has claimed. The first £1 billion guarantee tranche of the scheme is expected to be available in March 2009.

The Enterprise Finance Guarantee is intended to help smaller, credit-worthy companies which might otherwise fail to access the finance they need for working capital or investment finance due to strict lending conditions.

The government will provide £1 billion worth of guarantees to support £1.3 billion of bank lending to smaller firms with an annual turnover of up to £25 million, which are looking for loans of up to £1 million for a period of up to 10 years.

The guarantee, available through high street banks, will apply to loans and can also be used to convert existing overdrafts into loans to enable businesses to free up their current overdraft facilities to meet working capital requirements.

To help businesses raise new long-term finance, the UK Government is also offering to invest in viable companies which have high levels of existing debt through the new Capital for Enterprise Fund.

The government also provides a range of financial support to businesses—including loans and guarantees, grants, and equity—through various "Solutions for Business" products.

To find out more about what is on offer, the best starting point is your local Business Link. This is the government's business advice network, which offers an abundance of information online, over the telephone, or via face-to-face meetings with an adviser.

A new "one-stop shop," easy-to-use web portal has been launched on the Business Link website to direct companies to the most appropriate form of support, and help them assess their eligibility for the various schemes.

There is also a Grant for Business Investment (GBI), which provides capital to support business investment or job creation projects and is part of the Government's Solutions for Business portfolio. The idea is to help businesses grow, become more efficient, modernize, and diversify.

A grant under GBI is for the acquisition of key assets such as buildings, machinery, and equipment, and to help create new jobs or safeguard existing ones. Grants start at a minimum of £10,000 and there is no maximum limit. The final amount will depend on the size and location of the business, and the size and quality of the project. It is also worth bearing in mind that businesses applying for this grant will be assessed according to the level of skills they require within their workforce, and their anticipated productivity improvement. So companies must be clear about what they hope to achieve before applying.

In Scotland, this is called the Grant for Regional Selective Assistance (RSA). Information about this can be found on the Scottish Business Grants website.

In Northern Ireland, it is called the Enterprise NI Loan Fund (ENILF). Information is available on the Enterprise NI website.

Remember, there is a limited pot of cash available, so competition for grant funding is extremely fierce. Furthermore, the application process is often long-winded and arduous. Applicants must complete detailed application forms. They must also demonstrate how they will satisfy

"The name Disney is one of the world's most powerful brands." Michael Eisner

     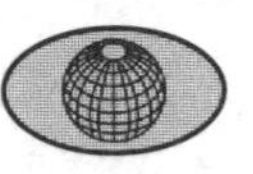   

the funding conditions and requirements of any one scheme. It is essential that you understand the Government's economic objectives in providing grants and tailor your application to meet them.

BANK LOANS

Individuals looking for start-up capital, or small firms seeking finance to pay for assets such as computer equipment, machinery, or cars, could look to their bank or building society for the cash. But lending criteria are far tougher now than before the credit crunch hit.

The advantage of a bank loan—if you can get one—is that it will be for a fixed sum, over a fixed period of time, so you know how much you need to pay back and for how long. In theory, this should make it relatively easy to manage your budgets. And while you will have to pay interest on bank or building society loans, you will not be obliged to hand over a percentage of your profits or a share of your company.

Even before the global financial meltdown there were drawbacks:

- The banks impose strict terms and conditions on most loans. In some cases they may even insist you offer some sort of security. So you may be required to secure the loan against the assets of your business or even your home.
- Bank loans are not very flexible, so you may find yourself paying interest on funds you are not using. You will also have to make regular repayments, which may make it hard to manage cash flow if your customers are not paying their bills on time.

If you feel a bank loan could cover your business needs, then remember to research the market carefully.

A good place to start is the website Money Supermarket, which offers information on business current accounts—which will give you an idea of which banks to approach.

The Institute of Chartered Accountants in England and Wales (ICAEW) reckons nine out of 10 SMEs are likely to be contacted by their banks to discuss the terms of their overdrafts by the end of 2009.

Clive Lewis, SME expert at ICAEW, believes businesses should explore a range of financing alternatives and use "appropriate funding." This, he says, could include asset finance, factoring, hire purchase, invoice discounting, leasing, and equity finance.

Lewis warns of even tougher times ahead. He advises business owners to seek advice on alternatives to bank finance, because there is an estimated £800 billion funding gap between deposits and lending in the United Kingdom. This is because savings levels have dropped off and cheap foreign capital from the wholesale markets has dried up.

PRIVATE EQUITY OR VENTURE CAPITAL

Private equity firms and venture capitalists are still looking to invest in businesses with strong management and good growth prospects. However, they are more likely to invest in companies they have already backed than take on new risk in the current economic climate.

It is worth remembering that private equity investors tend to invest in a business for the medium term, rather than the longer term. In practice this often means from three to five years, although they may invest for far longer or much shorter periods of time.

Unlike lenders, they tend not to have rights to interest or to be repaid at a particular date. But they will want a share of the ownership and in some instances may demand an element of control of the business. They often insist that a non-executive is appointed to the board. This is not necessarily a bad thing. If you do your homework and bring in an external investor with experience in your sector, then you could be adding another dimension to your business by beefing up senior management expertise. And this can be invaluable in terms of brainstorming for new ideas.

Venture capital or private equity financing tends to be best suited to businesses gearing up for a flotation or trade sale—both of which will be hard to achieve while stock markets remain volatile and credit is hard to come by. This is because the investor will need to be able to realize a return for the investment via a well-thought-out exit strategy.

Before approaching potential private equity investors, it is essential to ask yourself how credible your management is. Do you have a solid track record? And do you have the communications skills necessary to sell your story effectively? You will need a strong product or service. And you must be able to show that you can deliver year-on-year growth to realistic targets. Ultimately, you must still be highly ambitious and driven to attract interest from private equity backers.

Once you have completed a serious analysis of your business and its prospects, you must draw up a detailed business plan. It should be written in plain English, without jargon or fluff—private equity professionals have a nose for sniffing out sound ideas from speculative pipe dreams.

The main advantage of private equity financing is that the investor will have a vested interest in your business's success. These types of investors are also often prepared to offer follow-up funding as the business grows.

BUSINESS ANGELS

Business angels are high net worth individuals who invest on their own, or as part of a syndicate, in high-growth businesses. In addition to money, they often make their own skills, experience, and contacts available to the companies they invest in. According to the British Business Angels Association (BBAA), angel investors rarely have a connection with a company before they invest in it. However, they are more than likely to have experience of its industry or sector, so could bring invaluable experience to the table.

The BBAA believes business angels are "an important but still under-utilized" source of money for new and growing businesses.

Typically, business angels invest between £10,000 and £750,000 in an investment, making them an attractive alternative for smaller firms looking to raise smaller sums.

Before investing, business angels will check out factors ranging from management expertise and track record, to a company's competitive edge and compatibility between the management, the business plan, and the business angel's skills and investment preferences.

A good starting point for further information is the BBAA's website.

STOCK MARKET FLOTATION

The number of companies seeking a stock market flotation has plummeted in the wake of the credit crunch. In the first half of 2008, only 333 companies sought to raise finance through an initial public offering (IPO), compared to 702 companies in the same period a year earlier.

Given the turbulent state of the world's equity markets, it is unlikely that IPOs will regain their status as a popular route to new finance in the foreseeable future.

A stock market flotation involves selling shares in your business on one of the stock markets. There are three markets in the United Kingdom. The London Stock Exchange Main Market is mostly populated with larger companies. However, the Alternative Investment Market (AIM) and the PLUS market are both aimed at smaller companies.

If an IPO is a realistic option for your business, it is important to remember it is not an exit—it is the beginning of the next

"When you build a brand it is often tempting to force-fit success—you want it to jump and you want it to jump fast." Ric Simcock

stage of growth. Companies considering a stock market flotation must have strong management, a healthy track record, and excellent growth prospects.

Traditionally, the main advantage of a stock market flotation is ready access to funds. Flotation may also add to your company's credibility and raise its profile. It also provides an opportunity for business owners and other investors, such as private equity backers, to realize their investment. Having your own traded shares may also help you grow your business because you can offer shares as well as cash in any potential takeover bids.

There are disadvantages, however. Costs associated with floating a business can be substantial. There will be higher ongoing professional fees, as you will need advisers to help you comply with the added regulatory burden that floating a business can bring. You will also have to consider the interests of shareholders when running the company—and there will be times when their objectives will differ from yours.

Choosing the right market is vital. London's Main Market is the most stringently regulated and is only suitable for the largest companies. A minimum of 25% of the company's equity must be traded, to ensure liquidity, and companies must have been trading for at least three years. While the main market gives access to the widest possible audience of potential investors, it comes at a price. Professional fees and costs are far higher than for AIM or PLUS.

In contrast to the main market, AIM does not require a company to have a trading record. And while it is part of the London Stock Exchange, it offers a more flexible regulatory environment and is less expensive. There is no minimum percentage of shares that has to be traded, yet AIM-listed companies attract a wide range of investors, including institutional backers. AIM offers tax breaks and incentives for owner–managers, and is a very liquid market. A nominated adviser is required at all times.

PLUS is aimed at smaller companies seeking to raise up to £10 million. While it is regulated, the rules are not as stringent as those of AIM or the Main Market. While the costs associated with floating and running a company on the PLUS market are lower than its larger rivals, the pool of investors is not as deep and is mainly restricted to private investors.

If you think your company is ready for a stock market flotation, then remember that preparing for a float is a challenging and expensive process. It can take months to organize. For businesses that have not been part of a regulated industry before, it can be a cultural shock.

CONCLUSION

Choosing the right type of finance for your business is incredibly important. You must have a thorough understanding of what stage your business is at and what you need the money for before you pursue any one of the options. A lot will depend on whether you are funding a start-up, buying an asset, seeking growth finance, or looking for an exit.

▸▸ MORE INFO

Websites:

British Business Angels Association: www.bbaa.org.uk
Business Link: www.businesslink.gov.uk/realhelp/finance
Enterprise NI Loan Fund: www.enterpriseni.com/Content.asp?nSectionId=4&nSubSectionId=50
Money Supermarket: www.moneysupermarket.com
Scottish Business Grants: www.scottishbusinessgrants.gov.uk/rsa/208.html

"You can get fame quickly but we're building a brand with depth and flavour." Carl Lyons

  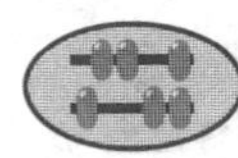   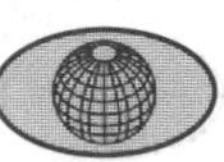   

Role of Institutional Investors in Corporate Financing by Hao Jiang

EXECUTIVE SUMMARY

- Institutional investors have become increasingly important in global capital markets.
- In equity markets, institutional investors tend to prefer liquid stocks with larger market capitalization, higher turnover, and higher price levels.
- Institutional investors particularly favor stocks in popular equity indexes, giving them higher valuations because their performance is typically benchmarked against those indexes.
- In bond markets that are mainly populated by institutional investors, there is a clear clientele effect.
- Private equity funds are an important source of capital for entrepreneurial firms.

INTRODUCTION

Institutional investors have become increasingly important in global capital markets. As of the end of December 2007, total assets under management by major global institutional investors reached US$81.90 trillion. In particular, mutual funds, pension funds, and insurance companies managed US$26.2, 28.2, and 19.9 trillion of assets, respectively, while assets managed by nontraditional managers such as hedge funds, sovereign funds, and private equity funds experienced dramatic growth, reaching US$2.3, 3.3, and 2.0 trillion in 2007 (Figure 1). In comparison, the world equity markets amounted to US$60.8 trillion, and the aggregate value of corporate bonds outstanding in the United States, the largest corporate bond market, was US$5.8 trillion in 2007. Clearly, for any successful corporate managers who raise capital to finance their future growth, it is crucial to understand such institutionalization in the global fund markets.

MAJOR INSTITUTIONAL PLAYERS

Institutional investors are a heterogeneous group of investors that populate the global capital markets. Based on their legal type, institutional investors can be broadly classified into mutual funds, pension funds, insurance companies, sovereign funds, hedge funds, and private equity funds.

A mutual fund is an investment vehicle that buys a portfolio of securities selected by a professional investment adviser to meet a specified financial goal (investment objective). Between 2000 and 2007, the total net assets of mutual funds grew from US$6.96 to 12.02 trillion in the United States, from US$3.29 to 8.98 trillion in Europe, from US$1.13 to 3.67 trillion in Asia-Pacific, and from US$16.92 to 95.22 billion in Africa (Figure 2).

A pension fund is a pool of assets forming an independent legal entity that are bought with the contributions to a pension plan for the exclusive purpose of financing pension plan benefits. Table 1 lists the world's 20 largest pension funds as ranked by *Pensions & Investments.* Insurance companies and banks are also important types of institutional investor that constitute the traditional asset managers.

Paralleling the growth of traditional institutions is the universe of nontraditional institutional investors. Among them, a sovereign wealth fund (SWF) is a state-owned investment fund composed of financial assets such as stocks, bonds, real estate, or other financial instruments funded by foreign exchange assets. Table 2 shows the top sovereign wealth funds across the world.

A hedge fund is an unregulated pool of money managed by an investment adviser, the hedge fund manager, who typically has the right to have short positions, to borrow, and to make extensive use of derivatives. Hedge fund managers receive both fixed and performance fees. Table 3 shows the top ten hedge funds based on assets under management ranked by *Institutional Investor* in 2007.

A private equity fund is a pooled investment vehicle which invests its money in equity securities of companies that have not "gone public" (i.e. are not listed on a public exchange). Private equity funds are typically limited partnerships with a fixed term of ten years (often with annual extensions). At inception, institutional investors such as pension funds and endowments (limited

Figure 1. Assets under management by different types of institutional investors in 2007. (*Source*: International Financial Services London)

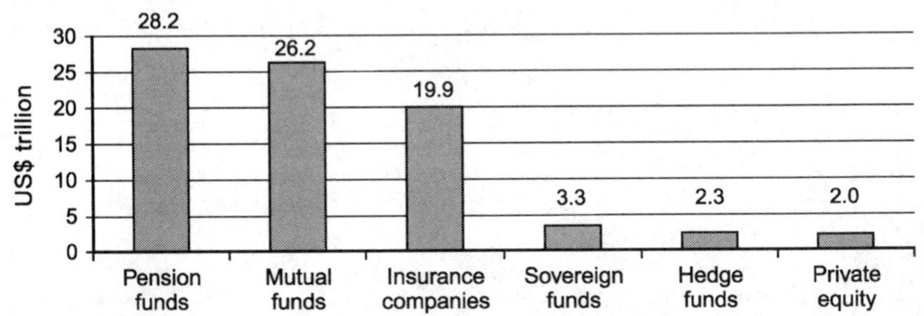

Figure 2. Total net assets of mutual funds around the world. (Source: *2008 Investment Company Fact Book*, Washington, DC: Investment Company Institute, 2008)

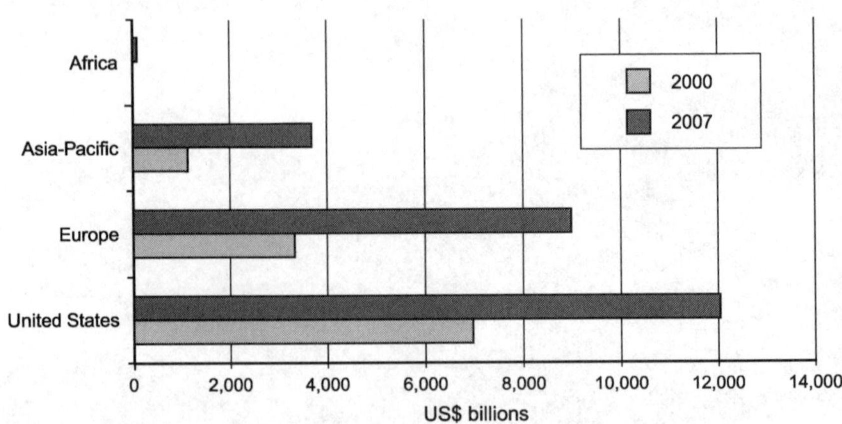

"The growing importance of the institutional sector will continue to have a profound impact on the structure of financial markets." Organization for Economic Co-Operation and Development

     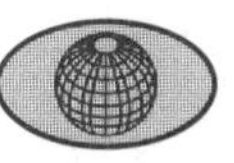   

Table 1. The world's top 20 pension funds based on total assets. (*Source*: *Pensions & Investments*; Watson Wyatt, 2006)

Rank	Fund	Country	Assets (US$million)
1	Government Pension Investment	Japan	870,587
2	Government Pension	Norway	235,849
3	ABP	Netherlands	226,974
4	National Pension	Korea	214,184
5	California Public Employees	US	195,978
6	Pension Fund Association	Japan	183,352
7	Federal Retirement Thrift	US	167,165
8	Local Government Officials	Japan	137,153
9	California State Teachers	US	133,988
10	New York State Common	US	131,861
11	GEPF	South Africa	124,167
12	Postal Savings Fund	Taiwan	117,265
13	Florida State Board	US	114,935
14	General Motors	US	114,271
15	New York City Retirement	US	105,860
16	Ontario Teachers	Canada	99,490
17	Texas Teachers	US	94,384
18	New York State Teachers	US	87,353
19	Public Schools Employees	Japan	85,224
20	PGGM	Netherlands	84,986

partners) commit a certain amount of capital to private equity funds, which are run by the general partners. Table 4 is a list of the ten largest private equity firms in the world as ranked by *Private Equity International* in 2008.

THE ROLE OF INSTITUTIONAL INVESTORS IN CORPORATE FINANCING

Institutional investors supply capital for firms seeking to raise finance from both publicly traded securities markets and from the private domain.

Institutional Investors as Holders of Publicly Traded Securities

Given their large portfolio size, institutional investors naturally become dominant holders of publicly traded securities. According to the 13F filings that institutional investors are required to lodge with the Securities and Exchange Commission (SEC), institutional investors hold over 68% of the total market value of US common stocks. According to the "Flow of Funds" data provided by the Federal Reserve, institutional investors hold approximately 86% of corporate bonds in the US corporate bond markets. Therefore, their investment behavior will have a significant influence on the pricing of these securities. For corporate managers who raise money from capital markets, it is important to understand the demand structure of institutional investors for publicly traded securities.

Despite their apparent heterogeneity, institutional investors share common characteristics because of the legal environment that they face as fiduciaries, and because of the demand for liquidity resulting from the large sizes of their portfolios and the need to reduce transaction costs. As a group, institutional investors exhibit preferences for certain stock characteristics in their equity portfolio. In particular, they tend to prefer stocks with larger market capitalization, higher turnover ratios, and higher levels of price. In other words, institutional investors are willing to pay a higher premium for stocks with these characteristics.[1]

Because most institutional investors benchmark their performance against certain indices, they naturally exhibit preferences for stocks in popular equity indexes. In the US market, when stocks are included into the S&P500 Index, the most prevalent equity index, the prices of those stocks tend to experience a 2–3% increase over a short period of time.

Firms with access to the corporate bond market tend to issue bonds as a means of debt financing. Based on the credit quality of the issue, corporate bonds can be classified into investment-grade and noninvestment-grade (high-yield or junk

Table 2. The world's largest sovereign wealth funds. (Ranking by Sovereign Wealth Fund Institute, 2008)

Country	Fund	Assets (US$billion)	Inception	Origin
UAE: Abu Dhabi	Abu Dhabi Investment Authority	875	1976	Oil
Saudi Arabia	SAMA Foreign Holdings	433.0	n/a	Oil
Singapore	Government of Singapore Investment Corporation	330	1981	Noncommodity
China	SAFE Investment Company	311.6		Noncommodity
Norway	Government Pension Fund—Global	301	1990	Oil
Kuwait	Kuwait Investment Authority	264.4	1953	Oil
China	China Investment Corporation	200	2007	Noncommodity
Russia	National Welfare Fund	189.7	2008	Oil
China: Hong Kong	Hong Kong Monetary Authority Investment Portfolio	173	1998	Noncommodity
Singapore	Temasek Holdings	134	1974	Noncommodity
UAE: Dubai	Investment Corporation of Dubai	82	2006	Oil
China	National Social Security Fund	74	2000	Noncommodity
Qatar	Qatar Investment Authority	60	2003	Oil
Libya	Libyan Investment Authority	50	2006	Oil
Algeria	Revenue Regulation Fund	47	2000	Oil
Australia	Australian Future Fund	43.8	2004	Noncommodity
US: Alaska	Alaska Permanent Fund	39.8	1976	Oil
Kazakhstan	Kazakhstan National Fund	38	2000	Oil
Ireland	National Pensions Reserve Fund	30.8	2001	Noncommodity
South Korea	Korea Investment Corporation	30	2005	Noncommodity
Brunei	Brunei Investment Agency	30	1983	Oil

"Worldwide, mutual fund assets reach $26 trillion." 2008 Investment Company Fact Book

     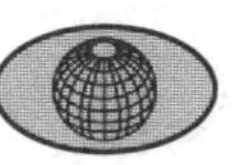   

Table 3. The world's top ten hedge funds. (Ranking by Institutional Investor, 2007)

Rank	Fund	Location	Firm capital (US$ million)
1	JP Morgan Asset Management	New York, NY	44,700
2	Bridgewater Associates	Westport, CT	36,000
3	Farallon Capital Management	San Francisco, CA	36,000
4	Renaissance Technologies Corp.	East Setauket, NY	33,300
5	Och-Ziff Capital Management Group	New York, NY	33,200
6	DE Shaw Group	New York, NY	32,240
7	Goldman Sachs Asset Management	New York, NY	29,206
8	Paulson & Co	New York, NY	28,979
9	Barclays Global Investors	London, UK	26,227
10	GLG Partners	London, UK	23,900

Table 4. The world's ten largest private equity firms. (Ranking by Private Equity International, 2008)

Rank	Firm	Headquarters	Capital raised 2003–2008
1	The Carlyle Group	Washington, DC	$52 billion
2	Goldman Sachs Principal Investment Area	New York, NY	$49.05 billion
3	Texas Pacific Group	Forth Worth, TX	$48.75 billion
4	Kohlberg Kravis Roberts	New York, NY	$39.67 billion
5	CVC Capital Partners	London, UK	$36.84 billion
6	Apollo Management	New York, NY	$32.82 billion
7	Bain Capital	Boston, MA	$31.71 billion
8	Permira	London, UK	$25.43 billion
9	Apax Partners	London, UK	$25.23 billion
10	The Blackstone Group	New York, NY	$23.3 billion

bonds, which are rated Ba and below by Moody's, or BB and below by Standard & Poor's). For corporate bond issuers, it is important to recognize the tendency of different classes of corporate bonds to attract different types of institutional investor—namely the clientele effect—in corporate bond markets.

Institutional investors generally place restrictions on investing in noninvestment-grade bonds. For example, the National Association of Insurance Commissioners (NAIC) imposes on insurance companies an upper limit of 20% of their assets for investment in high-yield bonds. Pension funds often impose limits on the value of a portfolio that can be invested in high-yield bonds. US investment-grade bond mutual funds place a limit of 5% of assets for investments in junk bonds and must sell any security if it falls below a B rating. However, there are institutional investors that specialize in junk bonds such as hedge funds with strategies in distressed assets and high-yield bond mutual funds. A recent study shows that when a bond receives a downgrade from investment to speculative grade there is a persistent price decline of 2%, whereas similar downgrades that do not cross the junk bond threshold do not experience such persistent price drops. This result suggests the importance of investor clientele for the pricing of corporate bonds.[2]

Institutional Investors as Fund Intermediaries for Private Firms

For entrepreneurial firms at the early stage of their life cycle, private equity funds comprise an important source of financing. Two primary categories of private equity funds are venture capital funds and leveraged buyout funds. In particular, venture capital funds provide equity capital for firms that are not yet profitable and lack tangible assets. Typically, such venture capital funds are active investors and play a primary role in shaping the top management team of the companies in which they invest.

Unlike venture capital funds that invest in young, fast growing private companies, leveraged buyout funds invest in established companies and facilitate the process of purchasing an entire company or a controlling part of the stock of a company involving large amounts of debt—a "leveraged buyout." During the past two decades, both types of private equity funds have played an increasingly important role in corporate financing.

CONCLUSION

The dramatic expansion of institutional investors in global capital markets demonstrates the changing savings pattern of households in the global economy. As such, corporate managers who wish to raise funds to finance the growth of their firms must understand such institutionalization in the global fund markets. In equity markets, institutional investors tend to prefer liquid stocks with larger market

CASE STUDY

Hedge Funds and the Turmoil of the Convertible Bonds Market

Convertible bonds, which give holders an option to exchange the bonds for a specified number of shares of common stocks, are an importance source of capital for many firms. Among various reasons, managers favor convertible bonds because they are less costly than a direct share issuance, and because firms to which straight debt and equity are not available can still raise money in the convertible bond market. SEC Rule 144A, effective in 1990, allows firms to issue securities to qualified institutional buyers (QIBs) without having to register these securities. This regulation significantly accelerates the capital-raising process from more than one month in the public market to one or two days in the 144A market from announcement to closing. As a result, nearly all convertible bonds in recent years have been issued via the 144A market.

According to the SDC Global New Issues database, convertible bond issuance amounted to $50.2 billion in 2006, increasing more than sixfold from $7.8 billion in 1992. It is generally believed that hedge funds that conduct convertible arbitrage are the major players in the convertible bond markets, purchasing more than 70% of convertible bonds in the primary market.

In late 2004 and early 2005, large institutional investors in convertible hedge funds, unimpressed with the performance of hedge funds in 2004, started to withdraw capital from those funds. To meet investor redemptions, hedge funds sold convertible bonds, causing their prices to fall relative to their fundamental values, which in turn lowered the returns on convertible hedge funds. From January to May of 2005, the Credit Suisse/Tremont Convertible Arbitrage Hedge Fund Index decreased by 7.2%.[3] The lower returns on convertible hedge funds triggered further investor redemptions and more selling of convertible bonds, forming a vicious cycle. The price of convertible bonds dropped significantly below fundamental values. The maximum discount of convertible bonds was 2.7% in May 2005.[4] A gradual price recovery took place in 2006.

"Private Equity funds have grown from a tiny part of the financial market in the early 1980s to an important global force today." Michael Jensen

     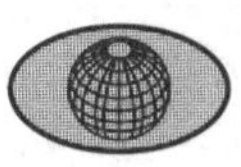   

capitalization, higher turnover, and higher price levels. Because the performance of institutional investors is typically benchmarked against certain indexes, stocks in popular equity indexes are particularly favored by institutional investors and are thus priced at a higher valuation ratio. In bond markets that are mainly populated by institutional investors, there is a clear clientele effect. Banks, insurance companies, pension funds, and investment-grade bond mutual funds place severe restrictions on the holdings of high-yield bonds, whereas hedge funds and high-yield bond mutual funds provide capital for high-yield issuers. Lastly, private equity funds are an important source of capital for entrepreneurial firms.

▸▸ MAKING IT HAPPEN

Institutional investors have dominated global capital markets. As a result, the assets under their management constitute an important source of capital for corporate managers.

- To attract institutional investors in equity markets, liquidity of shares is a major consideration. In particular, larger market capitalization, higher turnover, and higher price levels are important in attracting institutional holdings. Index membership is a strong sweetener.
- In bond markets, investment-grade bonds have a broader institutional investor base, whereas the issuance of high-yield bonds relies on capital providers such as specialized bond mutual funds and hedge funds.
- For entrepreneurial firms that seek both capital and strategic support, private equity funds appear to be increasingly important.

▸▸ MORE INFO

Books:

Davis, E. Philip, and Benn Steil. *Institutional Investors*. Cambridge, MA: MIT Press, 2004.

Jaeger, Robert A. *All About Hedge Funds: The Easy Way to Get Started*. New York: McGraw-Hill, 2003.

Pozen, Robert C. *The Mutual Fund Business*. 2nd ed. Boston, MA: Houghton Mifflin, 2002.

Pratt's Guide to Private Equity & Venture Capital Sources. Thomson Venture Economics, 2008.

Websites:

Dow Jones Financial Information Services *Galante's Venture Capital & Private Equity Directory*: www.fis.dowjones.com/products/galante.html

Institutional Investor: www.institutionalinvestor.com

Investment Company Institute (ICI): www.ici.org

Pensions & Investments: www.pionline.com

Preqin: www.preqin.com

Private Equity International (PEI): www.peimedia.com

Sovereign Wealth Fund Institute: www.swfinstitute.org

Watson Wyatt: www.watsonwyatt.com

NOTES

1 Gompers, P. A., and A. Metrick. "Institutional investors and equity prices." *Quarterly Journal of Economics* 116 (2001): 229–259.

2 Da, Z., and P. Gao. "Clientele change, persistent liquidity shock, and bond return reversal after rating downgrades." Working paper, University of Notre Dame, IN. Online at: ssrn.com/abstract=1280834

3 Based on the author's calculations.

4 Mitchell, M., Pedersen, L. H., and T. Pulvino. "Slow moving capital." *American Economic Review* 97:2 (2007): 215–220.

"Private Equity funds have grown from a tiny part of the financial market in the early 1980s to an important global force today." Michael Jensen

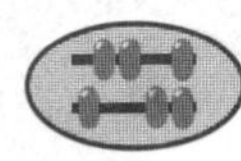

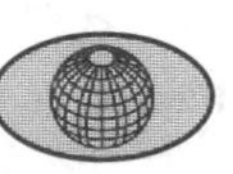

Securitization: Understanding the Risks and Rewards by Tarun Sabarwal

EXECUTIVE SUMMARY

Securitization creates value for organizations, investors, and consumers:

- It separates the funding of receivables from their origination and servicing, and allows origination and servicing revenues to grow without additional balance sheet financing.
- It provides cash flow and balance sheet management benefits.
- It allows for targeted asset liquidation, improvements in asset liquidity, and access to capital markets at rates different from enterprise credit ratings.
- The flexibility in transforming risks permits mutually beneficial matches in targeted market opportunities, both for organizations and investors.
- Deeper capital markets allow for price discovery of illiquid assets, greater access to funds for new firms and consumers, and greater financial innovation.

Securitization creates risks of moral hazard and lack of transparency:

- Separation of funding from origination can create moral hazard, generating higher-than-expected risks and leading to conflicts between investors, firm shareholders, and firm creditors.
- Complexity of structural transformations creates lack of transparency, which, in turn, can lead to greater illiquidity and possible market failure. These effects are worse in globally inter-connected markets.

INTRODUCTION

In broad terms, securitization can be viewed as pooling receivables and selling claims to these receivables in capital markets. For example, a mortgage lender may pool together thousands of mortgages and sell claims on mortgage receivables to investors. Historically, the first securitizations in the 1970s in the United States were those of pools of mortgages. With the success of mortgage-backed securities, other groups of receivables were securitized as well, including auto loan receivables, credit card receivables, and home equity receivables.

Although a majority of securitizations are of receivables on consumer debt[1] (whether mortgage or nonmortgage), in principle, any cash flow receivable can potentially be securitized. There are several so-called "exotic" securitizations—for example, securitization of mutual fund fees, movie revenues, tobacco settlement fees, and even music royalties. Moreover, student loans, manufactured housing loans, equipment leases, and commercial mortgages are also securitized.

SECURITIZATION BASICS

Securitized products have some common characteristics.[2] They typically involve an originator of receivables who forms a pool of receivables that is then sold to a special-purpose entity. This entity in turn issues securities backed by a beneficial interest in the receivables. For a successful securitization, it is important to understand this process in detail.

The originator of receivables identifies a pool of receivables to be securitized. For example, a mortgage lender identifies which loans will form a particular pool for a securitization. As borrower and loan characteristics affect receivables and losses on a loan, the credit quality of the receivable pool is affected by its loan quality.

The originator transfers the receivable pool to a special-purpose entity (SPE), typically a type of trust. Accounting rules govern the balance sheet treatment of such a transfer. For example, if this transfer is classified as a sale, an originator can remove these receivables from its balance sheet, but in the case of a financing, it cannot do so. Moreover, for a transfer of receivables to be a true sale, the ownership of these assets should be separated from the transferor to the extent that in the case of the transferor's bankruptcy, the transferor's creditors should not be able to access these receivables and jeopardize the beneficial interest of the investors in the securities.[3]

The SPE issues securities backed by the collateral of receivables in the pool. Different securities (or tranches) issued on the same collateral pool may have very different risk characteristics, depending on how pool receivables are allocated to securities and depending on credit enhancements. For example, a *senior* tranche may have first access to pool receivables as compared to a *junior* or *subordinate* tranche, and therefore, the *senior* tranche would have a relatively lower risk. Similarly, a credit enhancement, such as third-party insurance of promised cash flows, lowers the credit risk of the security. Therefore, depending on the structure of the transaction, securities issued on the same collateral pool may carry different credit ratings. Over time, securitization structures have evolved in complex ways to take advantage of diverse demands by investors.[4]

The differential risks of these securities may change over the life of the securities. For example, credit risk for issued securities depends on the performance of the underlying collateral pool and on credit enhancements, both of which may vary over time. Important factors affecting pool performance include a lender's underwriting criteria (such as credit score of the borrower, credit history, down payment, loan-to-value ratio, and debt service coverage ratio), economic variables (such as unemployment, economic slowdown, and bankruptcies), and loan seasoning (payment patterns over the age of loans). Credit enhancements affect credit risk by providing more or less protection to promised cash flows for a security. Additional protection can help a security to achieve a higher credit rating, lower protection can help to create new securities with differently desired risks, and these differential protections can help to place a security on more attractive terms. Violation of credit enhancements can trigger an "early amortization" event, which starts prepayments on securities using available SPE resources.

Therefore, pool performance evaluation, security cash flow allocation, and servicing of receivables continue on an ongoing basis. In particular, bond rating agencies assign a credit rating to each security issued by the SPE, and they evaluate this rating periodically. Moreover, for publicly issued securities, periodic financial reports are filed with regulatory agencies. The originator of receivables typically continues to service the receivables (i.e., collect payments on the receivables, manage delinquent accounts, and so on) for a fee.

BENEFITS OF SECURITIZATION

An important idea behind securitization is that it separates the funding of receivables from their origination and servicing. Such a separation can provide cash flow and

"**Greed is all right. . .Greed is healthy. You can be greedy and still feel good about yourself.**" Ivan Boesky

     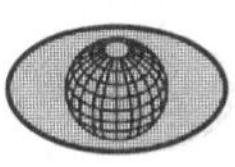   

balance sheet management benefits, structural flexibility benefits, and deeper capital markets.

Cash flow and balance sheet benefits are available to the originator mainly because selling loans in capital markets allows a lender to raise funds to originate more loans, which can again be securitized. As the originator frequently continues to service the securitized receivables, revenue from origination and servicing activities continues to grow. Moreover, as securitized assets can typically be removed from the balance sheet, the net balance sheet effect is zero. In this sense, securitization improves revenues without additional balance sheet financing. A securitization can also improve balance sheet liquidity by converting long-term and illiquid receivables into funds that can be used for additional value-generating investments. A securitization can also help to manage any mismatch between assets and liabilities. Finally, to the extent allowable, selective securitizations of receivables can allow for regulatory capital arbitrage.

Structural benefits from securitization arise from the flexibility available in transforming cash flows and risks of the collateral pool into those of the securities issued on the pool. For example, creative use of credit enhancements allows relatively poor-quality receivables, such as subprime loans, to be transformed into some tranches of high credit quality and other tranches of low credit quality. Similarly, it is possible to carve out long-term, nonrevolving securities from short-term, revolving credit card receivables.

Structural flexibility allows originators and investors to tailor securitizations to their needs. Originators can sell particular assets with greater liquidity if these assets can be transformed creatively into securities desired by investors. Similarly, investors with particular needs may have more choices if different originators innovate to serve their needs.

In principle, deeper capital markets may arise from improved cash flows, better balance sheet management, and greater structural flexibility. A securitization of high-quality assets may allow a relatively young firm or a firm with a low credit rating to access capital market funds at lower cost than would otherwise be available. Securitization may facilitate market price discovery of illiquid assets. It allows for the sale of precisely identified assets to be independent of the asset owner's financial condition. It allows greater financial innovation and better matching of sellers and buyers, and it may allow for deeper debt market penetration by opening newer lending markets, such as subprime lending.

RISKS OF SECURITIZATION

While the unique characteristics of securitizations are capable of providing benefits, they create additional risks as well.

When standard cash flow risks[5] are combined with the separation of funding of receivables from their origination and servicing, this may produce unintended consequences. For example, if repayment behavior is significantly worse than expected, investors may be concerned about moral hazard; that is, receivables in the collateral pool were "cherry-picked," and investors may require additional support for the securities. In extreme circumstances, investors may require the originator to provide an explicit guarantee or to take back poorly performing collateral (sometimes termed moral recourse). As the collateral pool is off the originator's balance sheet, recognizing poorly performing assets jeopardizes the originator's financial condition, and such actions will be resisted by the originator's stockholders and bondholders. Similarly, if the originator is in a poor financial condition, its creditors might consider going after assets that are securitized and off the originator's balance sheet. This can jeopardize investor claims on the collateral pool and question the legitimacy of the bankruptcy-remoteness of the SPE. Moreover, a narrow focus on origination can create an incentive to over-originate (or overextend) loans to marginally less creditworthy borrowers.

The structural flexibility in transforming collateral pool characteristics into very different security characteristics, while arguably a great benefit of securitization, also has the potential to create great risks.

The more complex the structure, the greater is lack of transparency, and the harder it is to analyze and forecast security performance. For example, consider long-term securities collateralized by short-term credit card receivables. These are naturally exposed to amortization risk due to a mismatch between cash flow receipts on the receivables and cash flow payments on the securities.[6] Add to this a senior-subordinated security structure. Now add third-party insurance, and finally add

CASE STUDY

The growth of subprime lending in the United States started around the mid-1990s. A subprime borrower typically has some combination of a blemished credit history, a relatively short credit history, poorly documented income prospects, and an uncertain repayment ability.

Before the 1990s, subprime borrowers typically found it hard to qualify for bank loans. During the second half of the 1990s, in the face of relatively low interest rates, investors were more willing to seek opportunities with higher yields that came with a greater, but manageable, degree of risk.

Securitization of consumer debt receivables helped to connect these two sides, with finance companies serving as intermediaries. Improvements in credit reporting and statistical analyses facilitated the development of risk-scoring models to lend profitably to subprime borrowers. Credit enhancements and structured tranches created securities that addressed investor needs.

The success of initial securitizations fueled rapid growth in securitizations. Debt markets deepened to provide loans to subprime borrowers, finance companies found an attractive source of new financing, and could continue to increase revenues from profitable origination and servicing fees, investors found securities with desirable characteristics, rating agencies generated additional fees, and third-party insurers generated additional premiums.

In a span of about ten years, concerns started to arise as securitized products became exceedingly complex, with the introduction of collateralized debt obligations (CDOs), and of CDOs of CDOs, or "CDO-squared;" lending started to look indiscriminate, with concerns about real estate appraisals, and about lack of adequately documented repayment ability; and real estate prices appeared to defy historical trends. As the US economy slowed and house prices lowered, and as delinquencies and foreclosures on subprime debt rose, the value of securities backed by subprime receivables deteriorated. The complexity and opaqueness of the securitization structures exacerbated the problem by making it virtually impossible to put a reliable value on these securities. This led to a crisis of confidence that paralyzed trade in some of these securities. Markdowns in the value of such securities started to hemorrhage balance sheets of security holders, especially some hedge funds, and led to the first casualty of a titan on Wall Street, Bear Stearns, in March 2008.

"We should never lose sight of the underlying essence of a market—a place where buyers and sellers come together. Every other feature—whether crafted by tradition or technology—exists only to serve that primary purpose." Arthur Levitt, Jr.

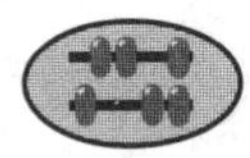

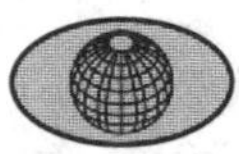

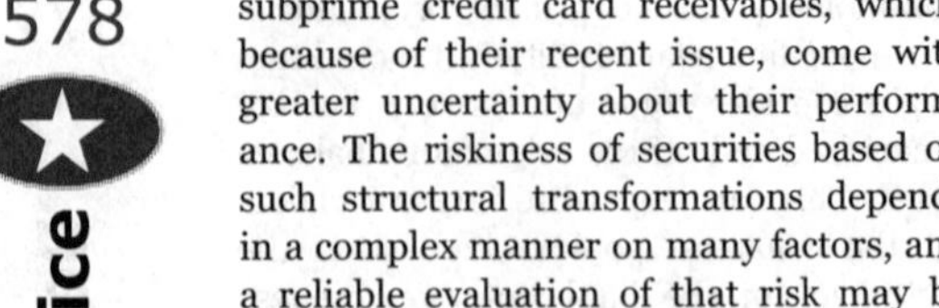

subprime credit card receivables, which, because of their recent issue, come with greater uncertainty about their performance. The riskiness of securities based on such structural transformations depends in a complex manner on many factors, and a reliable evaluation of that risk may be very hard to obtain, if it can be obtained at all.

Lack of transparency is made worse when the collateral pool in a securitization has opaque or otherwise hard-to-value assets. As, in principle, any receivable can be securitized, a security that was created as a result of securitization can be used further in a new collateral pool to issue new securities. As the initial security is hard to analyze, when several such securities are pooled together and then tranched off again,[7] it is not surprising that there are cases where a final security is inscrutable, even with the most sophisticated analysis.

A complex security, by and of itself, is not an insurmountable obstacle to reap the rewards of securitization. But in uncertain times, complexity combined with lack of transparency may throw wrenches in the wheels of smoothly operating markets. In other words, if reliable information is unavailable, market participants may be unwilling to pay high prices for securities that may turn out to be bad investments, and this can lead to a crisis of confidence severe enough that trade in particular securities grinds to a halt. Moreover, interconnected debtors and creditors may serve to exacerbate such a problem by extending it to other securities. Such a dynamic has been mentioned as a core problem resulting in global credit market disruptions that started in the United States in 2007.

CONCLUSION

No doubt, securitization presents new developments and exciting opportunities. Securitization allows for more precise targeting of asset liquidation. It can create value for originators and investors. It can deepen capital markets, thereby providing funds for new borrowers and new businesses. And it can improve market price discovery for illiquid assets.

When a securitization gets beyond the analytical apparatus of market participants, however, it is capable of destroying value. The potential harm is greater in globally inter-connected markets.

▸▸ MAKING IT HAPPEN

Executives may find it useful to keep in mind the following key ingredients to a successful securitization.

- Characteristics of assets to be securitized should be documented well and identified clearly.
- Transfer of assets to a SPE to form a collateral pool should be a true, bankruptcy-remote sale.
- The transformation of collateral pool risks into security risks should be simple enough to provide clear and robust analysis of the dependence of security risks on collateral performance.
- Processes for servicing, and for ongoing monitoring of collateral and security performance, should be well-defined, with some evidence of success under reliability testing.
- Using collateral, securities, and structures with an established history or clear evidence of success provides greater liquidity in security trading, and more reliable analysis of collateral performance.
- Using opaque and exotic structures requires considerable expertise and comes with greater risks.

▸▸ MORE INFO

Book:

Fabozzi, Frank (ed). *The Handbook of Fixed Income Securities*. 7th ed. New York: McGraw Hill, 2006.

Reports:

The Bond Market Association and the American Securitization Forum. "An analysis and description of pricing and information sources in the securitized and structured finance markets." October 2006. Online at: www.sifma.org/research/pdf/Pricing-Informaton_Sources_Study_1006.pdf

European Securitisation Forum. "ESF securitisation data report." Online at www.europeansecuritisation.com/dynamic.aspx?id=194

Websites:

The American Securitization Forum: www.americansecuritization.com

The European Securitisation Forum: www.europeansecuritisation.com

The Securities Industry and Financial Markets Association: www.sifma.org

NOTES

1 Consumer debt is used here in a broad sense, including secured debt (such as home mortgages, auto loans, manufactured home loans, and so on) and unsecured debt (such as credit cards, student loans, and so on).

2 Although the principles outlined here apply to all securitizations, for concreteness, specifics are presented for consumer receivable securitizations.

3 This feature is sometimes termed bankruptcy-remoteness.

4 For additional details on some common securitization structures, see Sabarwal, T. "Common structures of asset-backed securities and their risks." *Corporate Ownership and Control* 4:1 (2006): 258–265.

5 Such risks include underwriting risk, interest rate risk, default risk, prepayment risk, and market risk.

6 This is usually addressed by having a *revolving* period and an *accumulation* period when cash flow receipts are kept aside for use later in making promised payments on the securities.

7 Collateralized debt obligations (CDOs) typically have such a structure.

"There is no human feeling to the US securities markets and sometimes no discernible evidence of human intelligence either. But they work." Robert J. Eaton

     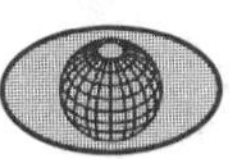   

Sources of Venture Capital

by Lawrence M. Brotzge

EXECUTIVE SUMMARY

- Sources of capital depend on whether it is an early-stage company or a rapidly expanding business that is seeking significant financing.
- Angel investors rather than venture capital funds usually provide seed capital for new companies.
- Use your network to get connected with sources of venture funding, and know your audience before you meet with them.
- Venture capitalists look for high rates of return and have a relatively short time horizon.
- These investors will assist the entrepreneurs with many aspects of their business besides capital.

INTRODUCTION

There are many sources of venture capital. They include:

- friends and family;
- individual angel investors or angel investor groups;
- early-stage venture capital funds (VCs);
- expansion-stage and later-stage VC funds;
- community-based venture funds; these are often run by development agencies, which are usually funded or subsidized by local government funds designed to stimulate business growth.

This article answers a number of questions about obtaining venture capital. When is it appropriate to seek venture funding rather than bank financing? How do you go about finding these funding sources? How do they differ, and what drives their investment decisions? Entrepreneurs and their management team need to understand the role of these investors, what expectations they will have for return on their investment, and over what time frame they will expect to earn those returns.

EARLY-STAGE COMPANIES

Companies are usually started by a single entrepreneur or a small group of entrepreneurs. These founders frequently work for no pay, a situation that is referred to as "sweat equity."[1] The initial cash needed is likely to be provided by the founders, but may be supplemented by money from friends and family members who have a variety of reasons to want to be a part of what the founders are doing. This type of funding is sometimes referred to as "seed capital."[2] The founders may also seek bank financing, but if the bank is willing to extend credit it will probably be based on their personal assets or borrowing capacity. Banks rarely lend to companies that do not have a track record of revenues and profits.

Venture capitalists generally expect to see that the founders have put in a combination of sweat equity and personal cash, and they prefer to see that they have raised some money from friends and family. After exhausting these sources, entrepreneurs may think it is time to approach VCs to raise the funds they need to grow their business. In fact, although VCs did invest smaller amounts in the 1970s and 1980s, they are now much larger funds and tend only to invest when companies need multiple millions. As this transition was taking place, angel investors began to fill the gap between friends and family and VCs.

ANGEL INVESTORS

Typically, angel investors are thought of as wealthy financiers who want to fund startup companies that have a change-the-world idea or invention. They do usually have some wealth, but it is not necessarily the case that they are extremely rich. Successful business men and women may be sought out by entrepreneurs for their particular expertise. These individuals may not have previously thought of themselves as angels, but they may become interested in the business and impressed by the entrepreneurs and decide to invest. On the other hand there are those who regularly look for such opportunities. Angels generally invest in companies in their local area so they can keep an eye on their money.

Beginning in the mid-1990s, angel investors began to realize that there were some disadvantages to being a lone investor. For example, it is unlikely that one or even a couple of people possess all the knowledge necessary to make wise investments. They may have knowledge of many aspects of the business they are considering, but they are not likely to understand everything about the business and how to structure the investment. Additionally, a single investor would have to put a fairly large sum in a single company to have any real say in the business. A group of angels is more likely to have a breadth of knowledge and, by pooling their funds, an impact on the company. Angel investment groups have been forming over the past 10 to 15 years, and there are now several hundred such groups in the United States and Canada.

A 2008 study of US angel investing[3] showed that in 2007 some $26 billion was invested in over 57,000 entrepreneurial ventures and that the number of active investors totaled almost 260,000. It can readily be seen that individual angel investors still make up the lion's share of investors, which creates a challenge for those entrepreneurs trying to connect with them.

Finding angels requires networking. Ask attorneys and accountants, especially those who frequently work with and specialize in startup companies. If your business is technical in nature, you might contact universities, and you should certainly try to make contact with current and retired executives who come from industries related to yours.

VENTURE FUNDS

Some VCs focus on investing in particular industry sectors, or geographies, or stages of a company's life. Some may restrict their investments to local businesses. Some will fund early-stage companies, but others may only entertain investments in what are known as expansion-stage and later-stage companies.

The definition of an early-stage business can vary widely and is not easily defined in terms of revenues. If, for example, it is a service business or software company, it may not require a lot of investment for the company to achieve positive cash flows. At the other extreme, a life sciences business (biotech, pharmaceutical, and medical devices), which involves substantial research and regulatory approval, may be years from any real revenues and will need significant funding along the way. As a general rule, before a company is ready for VC funding a number of events will have taken place, such as completion of proof of concept, development of prototype products, beta testing of the product or service, and, finally, generation of revenues. However, certain types of businesses—most

"Angel investment groups have been forming over the past 10 to 15 years, and there are now several hundred groups in the United States and Canada."

  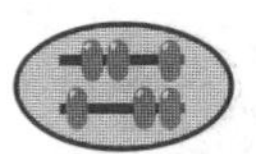   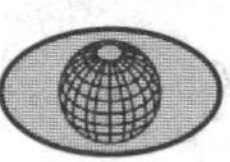   

notably life sciences or other large technical projects—require such large amounts of capital that they are well beyond the capacity of angels. These businesses tend only to be funded by the VC specialists. But for many new businesses there is an overlap between angels and "early-stage" VCs, and it is not uncommon that the two groups will coinvest.

What constitute expansion- and later-stage companies? Expansion-stage companies have customers and proven revenue, and there are good reasons to believe that they are positioned to grow very rapidly, at rates of 30–100% annually. And later-stage companies already have substantial revenues, so the next round of financing is meant to grow the company to a critical mass and attract public financing, or result in a merger or acquisition by another company. In both situations it is likely that this will provide liquidity and at least a partial exit for founders and investors. Many young companies never get to the point of seeking expansion or later-stage VC funding not because they fail, but rather because they determine that an earlier merger or acquisition makes more sense for both founders and investors.

WHAT VENTURE CAPITALISTS LOOK FOR

It makes little difference if it is an angel investor or an early-stage VC, they expect to see a business plan with a detailed description of the business model, marketing plans, competition, etc. This includes financial statements showing past results and a forecast for the next three to five years. Considerable emphasis will be placed on the cash flow forecast, as cash flow is a primary concern with any relatively new business. Investors will want to know how their investment will be put to use—often referred to as "use of proceeds." They tend to look unfavorably on large portions of their funds being used for accrued and unpaid expenses, particularly founders' salaries, or to pay down accounts payable. The prospective investors will perform considerable due diligence, which will include such areas as product reviews; speaking with customers, vendors and distributors; and examining any patent filings and pending legal matters. Primary among their assessments will be evaluating the management team.

The review performed by expansion-stage and later-stage VCs does not differ much from that outlined above; however, their investigations will look more closely at areas such as market conditions. Since at this point the business has a proven market for its product or services, it is far easier to assess future growth projections than when the company was just entering the market. Thus, a reasonably accurate assessment can be made of how fast the business can be scaled up and its ultimate potential. VCs will also reevaluate the company's management. Often the skills needed to launch a business differ from those required to grow it.

All venture investors have one question in common: When will they see a return on their investment? In other words, when will there be a liquidity event—a sale of the company or a public offering of the stock? This is called the exit strategy.[4] Venture capital is not generally meant to be long-term in nature. Most funding assumes that there will be an exit in three to seven years.

RETURN ON INVESTMENT SOUGHT BY VENTURE CAPITALISTS

The earlier in a business's life cycle the investment is made, the greater the risk. Thus, the higher the potential return on investment the venture capitalist will seek. Because there is a risk of total loss on at least some their investments, VCs must be able to see the potential for significant returns on each new investment. This means either quick returns or, if the time frame will be longer, large multiples of their investment. So company founders should not be surprised to learn that venture capitalists would like the opportunity to earn 10 or even 25 times their investment. That means that most venture investors have little interest in businesses that do not have excellent growth and profit prospects.

The terms of the investment will include the financial structure and the "pre-money value,"[5] which is the value placed on the business before the new investors put their cash into the company. Thus, pre-money value is the amount assigned to all investors who have invested in the equity of the company thus far. This determines what percentage the new investor will own. If the pre-money value is $3 million and $1 million is newly invested by VCs, they own 25% of the company.

There are also many considerations as to what security the venture investors will own. They usually require a form of a security that is "senior" to the equity held by founders and small investors. This provides legal protection and authority, even though they may be minority investors (in terms of their ownership share of the company). The instrument often used for this purpose is preferred stock, with a variety of provisions attached that allow some level of control over major business decisions.

For the venture investors to have an opportunity to earn handsome returns on their investment, they focus not only on the pre-money valuation, but also on how many future rounds of fundraising the company might need as it grows. Even if future investments are made on the basis of an increased valuation, the additional capital will dilute prior investors' ownership stake. So while the need for additional funding may be a good indication that the company is growing and needs more working capital to expand, that must trans-

CASE STUDY

Example of the Actual Results of an Early-Stage VC

The investors put in $120 million between 1998 and 2002, which is a typical funding period. This was invested in 31 companies and—although the fund has not yet exited all of these companies—reported results to date, plus a reasonable projection of ultimate exits, show these results:

Number of companies	*Exit as a multiple of the amount invested*
6	0
6	Less than 1x
7	1x to 2x
5	2x to 3x
3	5x to 10x
2	10x to 15x
1	50x plus
31	Average: 3.3x

The internal rate of return (IRR) to the investors will be about 23% on an annualized basis. This table illustrates how results vary by investment, indicates the degree of risk, and demonstrates why the VC must have the potential (often unrealized) to earn very large returns on each investment. In this case, without the three deals that produced very large returns, the overall results would not have been very attractive.

"Often the skills needed to launch a business differ from those required to grow it."

  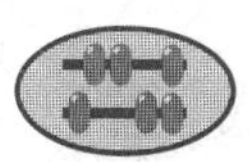   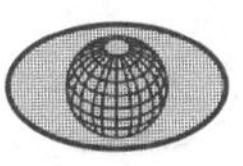   

late to a much higher ultimate liquidation value if each investor group is to see healthy returns on the capital they put at risk. Historically, venture capital internal rates of return (IRR)[6] have averaged between 20% and 30%.

THE ROLE OF VENTURE CAPITALISTS AFTER THEY INVEST

Venture investors are not passive financiers; rather, they foster growth in companies by becoming actively involved with the management team, and in developing strategic and operational plans, marketing plans, etc. They will hold one or more positions on the company's board of directors. VCs see themselves as entrepreneurs first and financiers second.

▸▸ MAKING IT HAPPEN

Companies will encounter lots of competition when seeking venture funding. So be sure to take the right steps to increase your company's chances of success:

- *Where should I be looking for investors?* Be certain to look for help from local organizations that foster new business development in your area, such as local development agencies and funds established to encourage innovation and new technologies, and universities.
- *How do I get connected to the right funding sources?* Talk to all your contacts, ask lots of questions, and remember that it is far better to arrive at a source via a referral.
- *How do I prepare to meet with prospective investors?* Consider getting someone to coach your management team, prepare a first-class, focused business plan, understand your cash flow, and prepare realistic financial projections.
- *What should I know about my audience?* They will be assessing the management team as much as the business. VCs do not invest in businesses that do not have significant growth potential, but you must be realistic and prepared to defend your numbers. They will also be interested in knowing that there are multiple exit strategies.
- *How do I sell our management team?* Show the investors that you are the right people to run the business, and address areas where you need to add missing skills. Remember that founders may not be the best people to run the company, and consider supplementing the team with an advisery board, or ask the VC to assist in identifying advisers.

▸▸ MORE INFO

Book:

Van Osnabrugge, Mark, and Robert J. Robinson. *Angel Investing: Matching Startup Funds with Startup Companies—A Guide for Entrepreneurs, Individual Investors, and Venture Capitalists.* San Francisco, CA: Jossey-Bass, 2000.

Websites:

Angel Capital Association (North America's professional alliance of angel groups): www.angelcapitalassociation.org

Center for Venture Research, Whittemore School of Business and Economics, University of New Hampshire: wsbe.unh.edu/cvr

Kauffman Foundation: www.kauffman.org

National Venture Capital Association: www.nvca.org

See Also:

★ Assessing Venture Capital Funding for Small and Medium-Sized Enterprises (pp. 520–522)
★ Viewpoint: Nenad Pacek (pp. 832–833)
★ Valuing Start-Ups (pp. 425–427)
✔ Dealing with Venture Capital Companies (p. 1011)
✔ Investors and the Capital Structure (p. 911)
✔ Managing Working Capital (p. 872)
✔ Options for Raising Finance (p. 1017)
✔ Using Mezzanine Financing (p. 1031)
Prince Al-Walid bin Talal (p. 1150)

NOTES

1 See "Sweat equity" at www.businessfinance.com/sweat-equity.htm

2 See "Seed capital" at www.businessfinance.com/seed-capital.htm

3 Center for Venture Research. "The angel investor market in 2007: Mixed signs of growth." Online at: wsbe.unh.edu/files/2007%20Analysis%20Report_0.pdf

4 See "Exit strategy: Business plan basics" at www.bizplanit.com/vplan/exit/basics.html

5 See "The pre-money value of a pre-revenue startup" at www.matr.net/article-25906.html

6 For a basic explanation of IRR and a downloadable spreadsheet example, see www.solutionmatrix.com/internal-rate-of-return.html

"Historically, venture capital internal rates of return (IRR) have averaged between 20% and 30%."

  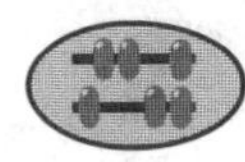 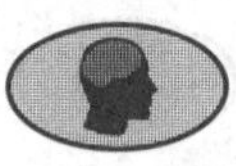  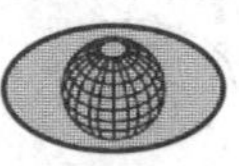   

Understanding and Accessing Private Equity for Small and Medium Enterprises

by Arne-G. Hostrup

EXECUTIVE SUMMARY

- Private equity is an important component of funding for small and medium enterprises (SMEs).
- The goal of securing a company's long-term financing and becoming independent of banks' continuously changing lending behavior is one that preoccupies many enterprises, from foundation to sale.
- Very few companies are familiar with the market structure, processes, framework, and conditions of private equity.
- There are a number of reservations about this type of financing.

DEFINITION OF PRIVATE EQUITY

Private equity is the generic term for all forms of financing through external equity capital in the broader sense. The generic term is often subdivided into:

- *Venture capital* (VC) is made available by business angels (who provide so-called informal venture capital, or IVC) and venture capital companies, usually management companies with a venture capital fund under administration. VC is made use of in a company's early stages—from foundation, market entry, and growth, right down to bridge financing prior to an initial public offering (IPO).
- *Private equity* in a narrower sense is made use of in, for example, expansion, internationalization, MBO/MBI, general reorganization of debt capital financing structures, and turnarounds.

The unequivocal characteristic of private equity in the SME sector is that the investor makes the invested capital available without provision of security and thus participates fully in the entrepreneurial risk of a business. Capital is normally made available over the medium to long term (3–10 years) in the form of liable equity. The forms of investment range from acquisition of a stake under the provisions of company law, with payment of the amount invested into the company's capital reserve, to a completely dormant partnership with no direct relationship under the provisions of company law. A combination of both options is often seen, with the investor becoming a shareholder of the company and making part of his investment as a nonrepayable payment into the capital reserve and another part as a repayable and continuously interest-bearing dormant partnership investment.

As regards the extent of the stakes acquired under company law, the range varies from minority and majority holdings to complete takeovers by the private equity investor. The investor's objective is to sell the acquired shares at a later point in time within the framework of a so-called exit, thereby making as much profit as possible. The exit can take place within the framework of an IPO, a trade sale, or a buy-back by the previous shareholders. Professional private equity investors usually expect a rate of return of more than 30% per annum. The expectations of business angels may differ.

MARKET STRUCTURE AND PARTICIPANTS

As a basic principle, the private equity market can be subdivided into the informal/formal and private/governmental areas. In general, the entire field of business angel financing is regarded as the informal private equity market. Business angels are wealthy private investors who use their own capital to acquire stakes in other companies. The formal private equity market is the entire "regulated area," i.e. usually private equity funds or their management companies. Depending on the investment motive or situation of the company, the market subdivides further, with investors specializing in the following sectors:

- seed-financing (business angels)
- early-stage businesses
- later-stage businesses
- medium-sized businesses
- buy-outs
- corporate venture capital

Within these sectors there are investors who confine themselves to a certain technology or geographic region. Usually, there is an umbrella organization that unites the private equity firms in any major country and, in some cases, major regions. As a rule, umbrella organizations are a good place to find individual investors and to research their respective special interests (see More Info section).

INVESTMENT PROCESS

Business Plan

A substantive business plan is the basic requirement for any involvement of private equity investors. Within the framework of the business plan, the company's strategy and objectives are usually articulated for at least the next five years. In addition, the firm seeking equity capital must highlight all business and financial aspects of a project. At an international level, the following structure is commonly found in business plans:

- executive summary
- product or service
- market and competition
- marketing and sales
- business model, business system and organization
- entrepreneurial team, management, personnel
- implementation schedule
- opportunities and risks
- financial planning and financing
- appendix.

The business plan is the basis for an investor's decision to invest and usually becomes an integral part of a participation agreement. Moreover, the plan is a helpful controlling instrument for management over the following years. The business plan should therefore be compiled with care.

Selecting and Addressing Investors

How do I find and select the right investor for my company? And how do I address this person or fund? Generally, there are three ways in which an SME can identify potential investors:

- research on the internet, followed by a direct approach with submission of the business plan
- presentations at investor conferences
- hiring a corporate finance (CF) consultant.

For smaller or younger companies, direct addressing or presentation at conferences is a common method. In particular, this applies to the entire venture capital segment. Larger or established companies tend to shy away from "publishing" a request for financing in this way and often make use of a corporate finance

"**In order to know what I am worth I should know who is judging me.**" Ernst R. Hauschka

     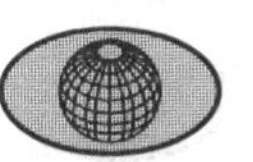   

consultant. The extent of support provided by such a consultant ranges from the simple establishment of contact with investors to comprehensive support for the entire process. For instance, many CF consultants offer support when it comes to compilation of the business plan, then present a list of suitable investors and take charge of directly addressing such investors. Support during the due diligence process and contract negotiations is also customary. Consultants are mainly remunerated on the basis of a fixed daily rate (700–2,000) and a performance-related fee in the event that a private equity investment materializes. The usual commission ranges from 1 to 4% of the investment. The amount varies depending on the agreed fixed remuneration and the support services provided.

Due Diligence

After an investor has voiced interest, he or she begins with the due diligence process. The entire company is "put to the test." Its history, current market and competition, and strategy for the future are closely examined. Some investors prefer to undertake parts of the due diligence themselves, but as a rule the task is passed to external consultants. The due diligence process is often divided into the following parts:

- *Legal*: Fulfillment of the duty to provide information or limitation of liability risks; identification and valuation of legal risks.
- *Product/technique*: Assessment of products/services at the development stage, technical feasibility, market acceptance, etc.
- *Strategic/business*: Description and, if possible, quantification of potential on the market and resource side.
- *Commercial*: Assessment of the future development of the market in which the business operates.
- *Financial*: Assessment of the company's past commercial situation and its future earnings potential.
- *Tax*: Identification of tax-related risks and a tax-optimized design for the transaction.
- *Environmental*: Disclosure of any environment-related liabilities that may impose a heavy cost burden following conclusion of the deal.

In most cases analysis focuses on the financial and strategic/business areas. Depending on the company's age and history, legal due diligence may also become a focal point. The objective is to provide a background for decisions that are in accordance with the investment, based on the performed corporate analysis. Due diligence requires careful preparation by the management of the business to ensure that information and data requested by the investor or his agent are properly and fully presented.

An important factor in preparation and organization of materials for the due diligence process is the selection of a team, and thereby the establishment of responsibilities for the collection and processing of data and making available contact persons for interviews.

Before the start of the due diligence process, the company that is going to be scrutinized should create a "data room" in which all required information is gathered so that it can be accessed and inspected by the examiners. This can range from a simple folder or CD to a professionally designed online platform (these are offered by specialized service providers). With an online platform all the required data are input in electronic form so that they can be checked by external examiners with authorization to access the information. Clearly, the younger a company is, the fewer materials there may be available for examination. In the case of a foundation project, this material is often confined to the business plan.

Practice has shown that the due diligence process can often become protracted, or that there may even be a breakdown of the entire contract negotiations, for the following reasons:

- incomplete documents
- contact persons not available for interviews
- unconvincing budget planning (e.g. unrealistic assumptions, inconsistent planning, poor or incomplete data sources)
- legal disputes with uncertain outcomes in respect of liability, or warranty and patent risks as well as risks related to the legal protection of registered designs
- environmental risks
- tax-related risks
- insufficient recoverability/value of inventories and accounts receivable
- management is unable to convince an investor of its ability to realize the business objectives beyond a limited extent

Company Valuation

Valuation of the company is almost always the most critical issue in contract negotiations, and intended projects frequently fail at this particular point as the parties involved are unable to reach agreement on the price. Company valuation can be based on various internationally recognized procedures, such as:

- discounted cash flow
- multiples like price-earnings ratio or price-cash flow ratio;

CASE STUDY

InkJet

The German company InkJet Ltd., founded in 2000, has developed an innovative and patented inkjet technology for industrial use. During the first two years the company focused on development, and in subsequent years it made a successful entry into the German market. In 2007, with turnover at €4.5 million, InkJet decided to expand its business internationally, with a focus on the European market as a first step. After drawing up the business plan it was known that between €2 and €2.5 million would be needed to finance the expansion. Up to that point the company had been entirely financed by founders' capital and debt. It was very quickly realized that this method of financing would not work for the planned internationalization. The company therefore began to seek out a private equity investor, and found one in 2008.

The investor was a corporate venture capital company that focuses on industrial technology, and is backed by an Austrian enterprise. This company invested €2.5 million in cash. The payment was arranged in three parts, linked to the fulfillment of three technology and finance milestones (for example, a turnover of €12 million in 2010). The VC obtained 35% of the corporate shares for €1.3 million. The other €1.2 million was injected as a silent partnership with a current rate of interest of 10% plus an exit kicker. Furthermore, the founders accepted a subsequent adaptation of the company valuation in favor of the investor if results fall short of the business plan forecasts by more than 10%.

The entire participation process from initial contact to execution of the participation agreements took nine months, of which the pure due diligence process took approximately four months. The rest of the time was used for internal preliminary examinations by the investor, contract negotiations, and coordination processes. Technical and commercial due diligence was carried out by the investor itself, while the tax and legal due diligence was conducted by external consultants.

     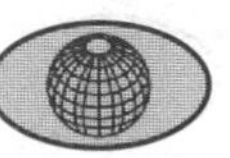   

- asset value procedure;
- exit value procedure.

Which procedure is used depends on many factors, such as the preferences of the investor, the country in which the company's registered office is located, and the age of the company.

When determining a company value that is appropriate for both sides, the following should be borne in mind:

- there is no such thing as a correct value
- although valuation procedures are objectively comprehensible, the range of results they give can be extremely wide
- company valuation is always a reflection of opinions, which can differ widely—especially with young companies. However, a valuation can indicate a plausible value
- in the final analysis, it is offer and demand that determine the value of a company

In conclusion, the general rule is that there is a value, and there is a price.

Contracts

Participation agreements are very extensive contracts, often consisting of several hundred pages. Therefore, a lawyer should *always* be consulted. As a general rule, in the case of participation in a limited liability company, such an agreement has the following components:

- participation agreement
- partnership agreement
- articles of association
- contract on the establishment of a silent partnership
- advisery committee statute
- management board regulations
- managing director employment contract

How individual agreements are allocated among the above-mentioned documents may vary from one investor to another. For instance, certain agreements may be incorporated in the participation agreement by one investor, while another investor may place the same agreements within the partnership agreement.

Participation agreements include a large number of clauses that often raise problems for companies which are seeking private equity for the first time. For instance, investors have comprehensive rights to information and codetermination but, at the same time, the rights of original shareholders regarding the sale of their corporate shares are massively restricted. Within the framework of the entire contract negotiations and the composition of the contract, one main thing should be remembered: Investors and previous shareholders have the same objective—they both wish to make the company as successful as possible.

▸▸ MAKING IT HAPPEN

In summary, the following aspects should be taken into consideration before the decision to finance a company with the help of private equity is executed:

- *Company's business model*: The business model must be checked as to whether it is suitable for private equity. Features to look for are high growth potential, sufficient market size, unique selling propositions, customer benefit, and competitive advantage.
- *Management team*: Complementary talents, professional experience and knowledge of the trade, key positions filled or capable of being filled over the short term.
- *Professional business plan*: Compilation of the business plan is the prime responsibility of the entrepreneur and his management team. It is not delegable to consultants, who only have an auxiliary function. The management, especially the founder, is personally responsible for the business plan's content, and must "sell" and defend it. Attention must be paid to the plan's completeness and formal structure. Beware of exaggerated assumptions with regard to projected sales and capital requirements.
- *Select appropriate investors*: Look for experience, background, track record, potential for adding value, references from the portfolio, team structure, age of the fund, financial resources available for new investments, participation agreements, information, codetermination, and controlling rights.
- *Contacting*: Establishing contact with the selected private equity fund should preferably be done through informal channels.
- *Due diligence*: The management should use the investor's check-up to amend the business plan/business model if required, or to develop it further, and they should be open to criticism and suggestions.
- *Cooperation*: Management should do their utmost to support the due diligence process in an open and honest manner, tell the truth, and submit suitable references. They should not conceal anything from the investor, as he will be the future copartner, able to make the founder personally liable for years to come based on the liability provisions of the participation agreement.
- *If a memorandum of understanding is reached*: Negotiations about company valuation shouldn't start too early: "The longer they check, the hotter they become, the more they are willing to pay"! Founders should not attempt to play off investors against each other, as the various private equity players in any one country usually know each other personally.
- *Consultants*: The advisability of calling in legal and tax consultants to conduct contract negotiations is self-evident. Any money saved by not doing so may well be completely negated by consequent losses or expenses incurred at the exit stage.

▸▸ MORE INFO

Websites:

African Venture Capital Association: www.avcanet.com
Association Française des Investisseurs en Capital (France): www.afic.asso.fr
Australian Private Equity & Venture Capital Association: www.avcal.com.au
British Private Equity and Venture Capital Association: www.bvca.co.uk
China Venture Capital Association: www.cvca.com.hk
European Private Equity & Venture Capital Association: www.evca.eu
German Private Equity and Venture Capital Associations: www.bvkap.de
Indian Venture Capital Association: www.indiavca.org
National Venture Capital Association (US): www.nvca.org

See Also:

★ Due Diligence Requirements in Financial Transactions (pp. 398–401)
✔ Raising Capital through Private and Public Equity (p. 1022)
✔ Understanding Private-Equity Strategies: An Overview (p. 951)

  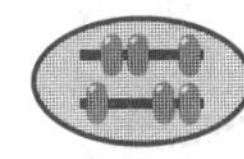   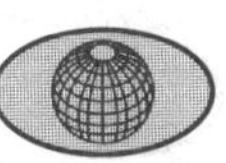   

Understanding Equity Capital in Small and Medium-Sized Enterprises by Siri Terjesen

EXECUTIVE SUMMARY

- Equity capital or financing is funding raised by a business in exchange for a share of the ownership.
- Equity financing enables firms to obtain money without incurring debt, or without needing to repay a specific amount of money at a particular time.
- There are four stages of equity investment: seed, early-stage, expansion, and late-stage financing.
- Equity capital sources differ in terms of timing, amount provided, type of firm funded, extent of due diligence, contract type, expectations of timing and payback, and monitoring of business decisions.

INTRODUCTION

Entrepreneurs may require both debt and equity financing, and often start their firms by financing growth through equity. Equity capital is money invested in the venture with no legal obligation on the entrepreneur to repay the principal amount or to pay interest on it; however, it requires sharing the ownership and profits with the funding source, and possibly also paying dividends to equity investors.

After value has been built, entrepreneurs may consider debt financing, which involves a payback of the funds (with interest) for use of the money. In short, debt places a burden of repayment and interest on the entrepreneur, whereas equity capital forces the entrepreneur to relinquish some degree of ownership and control.

The stages of equity financing are depicted in Figure 1. In the first stage, known as the seed stage, entrepreneurs tend to raise capital from their own savings, though they may also seek informal investment from family, friends, business angels, and public sources. Entrepreneurs may then choose to pursue formal equity capital through rounds of early-stage, expansion, and late-stage financing. This may be followed by an initial public offering (IPO) and, finally, raising of finance from public markets and banks. Summary details of the financing stages are as follows:

- *Seed financing* is the initial funding to develop a business concept, for example by expenditure on research, product development, and initial marketing to reach early-adopter customers. Companies that receive seed funding may be in the process of incorporation, or may have been in operation for a while.
- *Early-stage financing* is sought by companies that have completed the product/service development stage and test marketing but require additional financing to expand.
- *Expansion financing* is provided when the company is poised to grow rapidly. The funds may be used to increase production capacity, marketing, or product development, and/or provide additional working capital.
- *Late-stage funding* refers to pre-IPO investments to strengthen a company's positioning and to gain endorsements from top venture capital (VC) firms as the company prepares to list.

At any stage, equity investment can come from informal or formal sources. However, it is more usual to access informal sources in the seed and early stages, and formal sources in the expansion and late stages.

Figure 1. The stages of equity financing

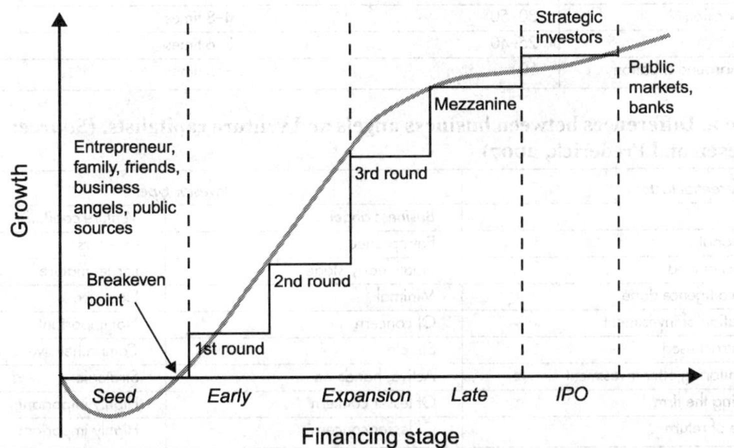

INFORMAL EQUITY SOURCES

Informal and Angel Investment

Informal investment refers to equity provided by individuals. In addition to accessing their own savings and those of family, friends, and even neighbors, entrepreneurs seek informal "angel" investors who provide financial capital as well as business expertise for running a company.

As shown in Figure 2, the rates of informal investment vary dramatically around the world, from a high of 13% in Uganda to a low of 0.5% in Japan. Business owners are approximately four times more likely to make informal investments than are non business-owners (Bygrave and Hunt, 2005). As can be seen in the figure, many informal investors have experience as owners/managers of their own businesses.

Although the profile of angel investors varies, in developed economies, angels tend to have entrepreneurship experience, be retired from their own firm or a corporation, and have net incomes in excess of US$100,000 a year. Most angels invest in companies within a two-hour traveling distance of their home, and therefore the informal investment market is geographically diverse. On average, the angel capital market is approximately ten times the size of the formal venture capital market. Indeed, small firms are eight times more likely to raise finance from business angels than from formal institutions.

Business angels tend not to have any previous relationship with the entrepreneur, and are often more objective. Angel investors can be passive (backing the judgment of others) or active (hands-on, with advice or direct management input to help the business to establish itself). Angels tend to invest as individuals or as part of a larger group, and generally as a part-time interest rather than as a full-time job (as is the case of venture capitalists). In addition

"My biggest challenge in transforming the company was fear. Under socialism, people learned to be afraid to express their opinions." Peter Zwack

  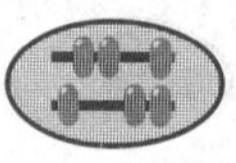   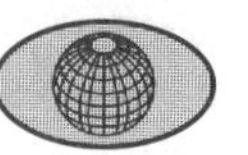   

Figure 2. Rates of informal investment around the world. (*Source*: Global Entrepreneurship Monitor data)

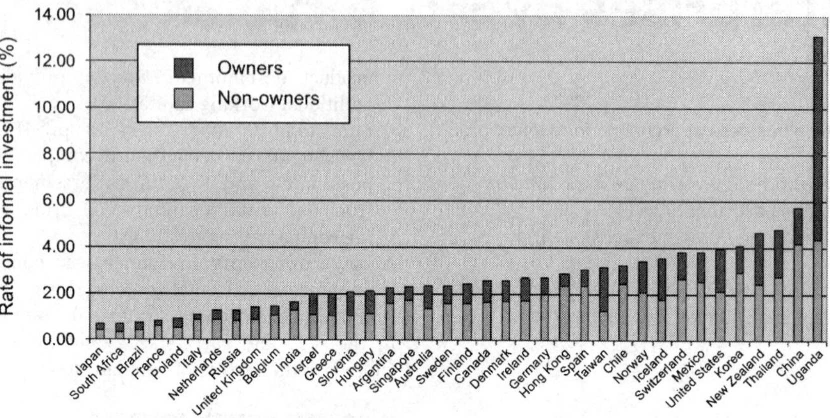

to financial goals, informal investors often seek other, nonfinancial returns, among them the creation of jobs in areas of high unemployment, development of technology for social needs (for example, medical or energy), local revitalization, provision of assistance to indigenous peoples, and just personal satisfaction from the assistance they give to entrepreneurs.

Business angels prefer to fund high-risk entrepreneurial firms in their earliest stages. They fill the so-called equity gap by making their investments in precisely those areas where institutional venture capital providers are reluctant to invest. Angels may also prefer to fund the smaller amounts (within the equity gap) that are needed to launch new ventures, and they invest in almost all industry sectors. Angels tend to be more flexible in their financial decisions, and also tend to have different criteria, longer investment horizons ("patient" money), shorter investment processes, and lower targeted rates of return than venture capitalists. Business angel funding can make a firm more attractive for other sources of finance. However, business angels are less likely to make follow-on investments in the same firm.

FORMAL EQUITY SOURCES

Venture Capital

Venture capitalists can be a valuable and powerful source of equity funding for new ventures, providing, in addition to capital, help with a full range of financial services for new or growing ventures. These include market research, strategy, management consulting, contacts with prospective customers/suppliers/others, assistance in negotiation and with management and accounting controls, employee recruitment, risk management, and counseling on regulations. Venture capitalists tend to have ambitious expectations for both the return on and the increase in their investment, as shown in Table 1.

The process of seeking venture capital financing includes the following four stages:

- Initial screening to assess the firm's ability to meet the VC's particular requirements.
- Detailed reading of the business plan.
- Verbal presentation to the venture capitalist.
- Final evaluation, including visiting suppliers, customers, consultants, and others; the venture capitalist then makes a final decision.

This four-step process screens out approximately 98% of all venture plans, with the remaining 2% receiving some degree of financial backing. Venture capitalists reach a go/no-go decision in an average of six minutes on the basis of the initial screening, and in less than 21 minutes on the basis of an overall proposal evaluation. The main factors in their decision are the firm's expected long-term growth and profitability, although an entrepreneur's background and characteristics are also taken into account.

Venture capitalists tend to agree on an exit strategy at the time of investment, with the following five main mechanisms:

- Trade sale to another company.
- Repurchase of the venture capital shares by the investee company.
- Refinancing or purchase of the venture capital equity by a longer-term investment institution.
- Stock market listing.
- Involuntary exit.

Table 2 summarizes the differences between business angels and venture capitalists.

Initial Public Offering

As the firm grows, managers may consider an IPO, which is when a company's shares are first sold to the public. An IPO is often the first time people outside the company have the opportunity to buy its shares; hence, IPOs are referred to as "going public" or "floating" the company. An IPO has advantages and disadvantages. The advantages are:

- *Amount and efficiency of capital raised*: Selling shares is one of the fastest ways to raise large sums of capital in a short period of time.
- *Liquidity*: A public market provides liquidity for owners, who can readily sell their shares.

Table 1. Typical returns on investment (ROI) and increase on initial investment sought by venture capitalists. (*Source*: Terjesen and Frederick, 2007)

Stage of business	*Expected annual ROI (%)*	*Expected increase on initial investment*
Seed	60+	10–15 times
Early	40–60	6–12 times
Expansion	30–50	4–8 times
Late	25–40	3–6 times
Turnaround situation	50+	8–15 times

Table 2. Differences between business angels and venture capitalists. (*Source*: Terjesen and Frederick, 2007)

Differential factor	*Investor type*	
	Business angel	*Venture capitalist*
Personal	Entrepreneurs	Investors
Firms funded	Small, early-stage	Large, mature
Due diligence done	Minimal	Extensive
Location of investment	Of concern	Not important
Contract used	Simple	Comprehensive
Monitoring after investment	Active, hands-on	Strategic
Exiting the firm	Of lesser concern	Highly important
Rate of return	Of lesser concern	Highly important

     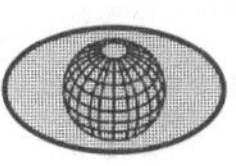   

- *Value*: The market puts a value on the company's shares, which in turn allows a value to be placed on the company.
- *Image*: Publicly traded companies are often perceived to be stronger by suppliers, financiers, and customers.

However, an IPO also has several disadvantages:

- *Cost*: IPO expenses are significantly higher than for other sources of capital due to fees for accounting, legal services, prospectus printing and distribution, and the cost of underwriting the shares. The cost can easily exceed $1 million.
- *Disclosure*: An IPO requires detailed public disclosure of company affairs, but new firms may prefer to keep this information private. Furthermore, the paperwork involved in meeting regulation requirements and providing regular information about performance may drain large amounts of management time, energy, and money that could be better invested in opportunities for company growth.
- *Stockholder pressure*: Stockholders are interested in a strong performance record on earnings and dividends, and so may put pressure on managers to focus on short-term performance. If managers do this, it can be at the expense of long-term growth and improvement.

The advantages and disadvantages of IPO funding are summarized in Table 3.

Should a firm decide to pursue an IPO, it is important that it be aware of laws with respect to securities and investments, which vary across countries but include the following common elements.

Investor information: Firms must provide investors with key information.

Investment banker or underwriter: Most firms select a lead investment banker to sell the new shares, usually at fees of about 7% of the issue value.

Ownership structure: The shares sold in the IPO are designated as primary shares, which are new shares, and secondary shares, which were previously owned by existing stockholders, usually the founders and managers of the firm. The size of the new issue relative to the existing shares and their distribution change the ownership structure. The IPO often results in moving from management by firm founders toward professional management of the firm. The IPO generally occurs when the founder's entrepreneurial activities are coming to an end, but often he or she will play a role in the future of the company.

Lockup provisions: When going public, IPOs almost always commit to a lockup period, whereby insiders (major stockholders, directors, and senior officers) are prohibited from selling shares without the written permission of the lead underwriter until a certain amount of time has passed. On average, the waiting time is 180 days. These lockup provisions control the supply of shares sold during the period after the IPO by insiders or existing stockholders who might have inside knowledge and, thus, unfair advantage.

Table 3. Advantages and disadvantages of IPO funding. (*Source*: Terjesen and Frederick, 2007)

Advantages	*Disadvantages*
Stronger capital base	Pressure for short-term growth
Improves other financing prospects	Disclosure and confidentiality
Better placed to make acquisitions	Costs—initial and ongoing
Diversification of ownership	Restrictions on management
Increased executive compensation	Loss of personal benefits
Increased company and personal prestige	Trading restrictions

CASE STUDY

An Angel in England

Anita Roddick started her own business, The Body Shop, creating and selling beauty products. Roddick was keen to open a second shop in Chichester, but the bank turned down her request for a loan. In desperation, Roddick asked her friend Aidre, who was helping to manage the first store, for help. Aidre had a boyfriend named Ian Bentham McGlinn, who had some spare cash from operating a local garage. Scottish born McGlinn offered Roddick £4,000 in 1976 in return for 50% equity in the business. Anita accepted the offer but wrote to her husband Gordon (who was on a two-year hike in South America) to inform him of the offer. Gordon wrote back suggesting that she "not do it, not give away half the company," but it was too late.

With his equity investment, McGlinn became a business angel and sat on the board of The Body Shop, resigning just before it was floated on the stock market in 1984. At the time of the flotation McGlinn was worth £4 million, but he avoided the press by taking a holiday in Portugal. By 1991, McGlinn's 52 million shares were worth £150 million, though his dividends were worth only £638,000 annually. The Roddicks and McGlinn together owned 56% of The Body Shop, preventing a takeover. In 1996, McGlinn sold 3.5% of the business for £12 million. When L'Oreal took over The Body Shop in 2006, McGlinn's 22% stake was worth £137 million. As of 2007, Ian McGlinn was ranked no. 28 on the *Sunday Times* Rich List, with an estimated worth of £146 million.

▸▸ MAKING IT HAPPEN

When approaching venture capitalists, entrepreneurs must remember that VCs are inundated with potential business opportunities. It is therefore advisable to keep the following in mind.

Do

- Prepare all your materials before soliciting firms.
- Send a business plan and a covering letter first.
- Contact several firms with this material.
- Keep phone conversations brief—prepare a one-minute and a three-minute pitch.
- Remain positive and enthusiastic about your company and its product or service.
- Know your minimum deal and walk away if necessary.
- Negotiate a deal you can live with.
- Investigate the venture capitalist's previous deals and current portfolio structure.

Don't

- Don't expect a response.
- Don't dodge questions.
- Don't give vague answers. Know what you can and cannot disclose before you start talking, so that you do not stumble over awkward questions.
- Don't switch off—be an active listener as you will always learn something.
- Don't hide significant problems.
- Don't expect immediate decisions.
- Don't become fixated on pricing.
- Don't embellish facts or projections.

     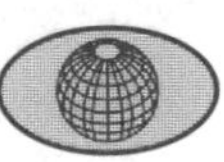   

Presence of venture capitalists: Many firms may be financed by VCs, who take an ownership position and have partial control over the entrepreneurs. The IPO may change this control as the VC distributes the shares to their limited partners. An IPO may be a cheaper form of financing than that provided by VCs, and will certainly provide liquidity to the existing pre-IPO stockholders.

Issue size: With the fixed costs of an IPO to create a liquid market, the number of new shares in the IPO should be large enough to provide sufficient liquidity, but small enough so that the issuing firm does not raise more cash than it can profitably use.

Mechanisms for pricing IPOs: IPOs may be priced through auctions, fixed-price offers, or book-building. In auctions, the market-clearing price is determined after bids are submitted. In a fixed-price offer, the price is set prior to the allocation. If there is excess demand, shares are rationed on a pro rata or lottery basis. In book-building, the investment bankers canvas potential buyers and then set an offer price. Book-building is now the predominant mechanism by which IPO shares are sold around the world.

Prospectus: If a company is raising capital by offering its shares to the public for the first time, it will issue a disclosure document called a prospectus. The prospectus is a formal written offer to sell shares and provides an investor with the information necessary to make an informed decision. All negative information must be clearly highlighted and explained. Some of the specific detailed information that must be presented includes: the history and nature of the company, its capital structure, a description of any material contracts, a description of the securities that are being registered, the salaries of major officers and directors and the price paid for any security holdings they may have, underwriting arrangements, an estimate of and planned use for the net proceeds to be raised, audited financial statements, and information about the competition with an estimate of the probability that the firm will survive.

When considering an IPO, managers should ask the following questions:

- Can the company run without you while you are managing the IPO process? The work leading up to a public offering is time-intensive and can deflect your focus away from everyday operations, ultimately hurting the business. If the company lacks a strong management team, it can be helpful to appoint an interim CFO with experience of taking companies, preferably small, through the rigors of going public.
- Can you get to a market capitalization of $100 million within three years of going public? The value of a public company is a multiple of what it earns. If the result isn't near $100 million, staying private may be best. This number is a good indicator because it is the level of earnings at which the company can attract brokers and investors.
- Are you building a company with high gross and operating margins? High margins are important because they keep companies out of the volume game. For a company to reach critical mass in earnings with low margins, it must generate enormous sales growth.
- Can your business deliver double-digit sales and earnings growth? The competition among public companies, mutual funds, and other investment networks is fierce. Investors won't look twice at a company that doesn't grow fast enough to warrant the use of their time and money.
- Are you building a family business? If the succession plan for the business is set in stone to be passed on to the kids, public may not be the right route. Families measure the success of a business generation by generation. Money movers are interested in the quarter-to-quarter progress.
- Can the business be built inexpensively? The main reason companies go public is to raise initial funds for major growth. As a result, sales and growth need to reflect the use of the first round of financing. If another round of financing is needed to achieve the original plan, investors may look elsewhere.

▸▸ MORE INFO

Books:

Cendrowski, Harry, James P. Martin, Louis W. Petro, and Adam A. Wadecki. *Private Equity: History, Governance, and Operations*. Hoboken, NJ: Wiley, 2008.

Gadiesh, Orit, and Hugh MacArthur *Lessons from Private Equity Any Company Can Use*. Cambridge, MA: Harvard Business School Press, 2008.

Reports:

Bygrave, W. D., and S. Hunt. Global Entrepreneurship Monitor 2004 Financing Report, Babson College and London Business School, 2005.

Global Entrepreneurship Monitor data. Available from www.gemconsortium.org

Terjesen, S., & Frederick, H. 2007. Sources of Financing for Australia's Entrepreneurs. Lulu.

Website:

US Small Business Administration on equity financing: www.sba.gov/services/financialassistance/basics/financing

See Also:

★ Optimizing the Capital Structure: Finding the Right Balance Between Debt and Equity (pp. 557–559)

Damodaran on Valuation: Security Analysis for Investment and Corporate Finance (p. 1245)

"The twentieth-century struggle between capitalism and socialism is, at an ideological level, a fight about the content of progress." John Berger

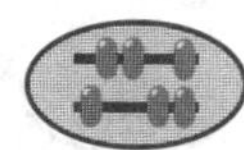

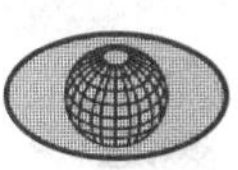

Understanding the True Cost of Issuing Convertible Debt and Other Equity-Linked Financing by Roger Lister

EXECUTIVE SUMMARY

- Convertible securities (CSs) combine debt and equity. In option terms, CSs are a call option on a specified number of shares whose exercise price is the debt claim forgone in exchange for the shares. CSs are also like a stock with a put option whose exercise price is the market value of the convertible.
- Some critics insist that CSs are uneconomic because they address several habitats of investors at the same time. Others say that they comprise flexible, non-dilutive, easily executed, and cheap finance, which appeals to many professional investors including hedge funds.
- The basic formula defines the cost of CSs but ignores tax and dividends. The formula produces a weighted average of the cost of the debt and the cost of a call option on the issuer's shares.
- Management's task is to measure the cost of CSs with the formula while allowing for the real world influences that the basic model ignores.
- Cost-influencing factors include dividends, tax, and resolution of agency costs.

INTRODUCTION

Convertible securities (CSs) and other equity-linked instruments combine debt and equity. Depending on the terms and the issuer's future performance, CSs can range from almost pure equity to an option-free bond. In option terms, a CS can be viewed in two ways. It amounts to a straight bond with a call option on a specified number of shares. It is also effectively a share with a put option whose exercise price is the market value of the convertible.

Some iconoclasts persistently argue that CSs and other equity-linked instruments are essentially uneconomic. Classically championed by Tony Merrett and Allen Sykes, critics maintain that by jointly approaching the equity and fixed interest markets a company must offer costly conversion rights to attract the equity investor while giving virtually the same rights to the fixed interest investor who values them less. Likewise, issuers must give fixed interest investors an acceptable income. In short, CSs contradict the advantage of specialization whereby capital-raising is tailored to habitats of investors. The iconoclasts invoke studies like Ammann, Fehr, and Seiz (2006) to the effect that negative equity returns follow the announcement and issue of CS.

A counterargument is that CSs are flexible, non-dilutive, easily executed, and cheap finance. CSs appeal to professional investors including hedge funds which exploit arbitrage opportunities.

Rating agencies such as Fitch see sense in both viewpoints and hold that the desirability of CSs depends more strongly than other sources of finance on individual corporate circumstances and market context. Fitch (2006) concludes:

"Issuers must find continuing compelling reasons for such issuance...The lower costs of such issuance compared with the cost of issuing equity are certainly supportive, as are the gradual standardisation, transparency and consistency of documentation, market practice and the activities of the agencies. On the other hand, issuers and their advisers must always strive to satisfy several constituencies, including regulators, legal and tax authorities, the agencies and finally, investors. Investor appetite underpinned the buoyant corporate activity of recent years. However, that appetite arose in an environment of low interest rates that will not persist indefinitely."

What is the true cost of CSs? Definition is less difficult than measurement. Having defined the parameters and influences on cost, management must frankly ask whether their measurements are so unreliable as to make them a dubious basis for decision-taking. Of course this applies across financial management, but it is particularly acute for the cost of capital.

THE COST FORMULA

The cost of a CS is a weighted average of the cost of its debt element and the cost of a call option on the issuer's shares, since the investor in a CS is a lender and the holder of a call option on the value of the firm. The difference between a conversion right and a regular call option is that a CS holder gets new shares upon exercise. It follows that if the price at which the CS holder is entitled to shares is below market price, then the value of all corporate equity, including the convertor's, is diluted. This explains why a convertible warrant is worth less than a straight call option on the company's shares whose exercise leaves existing equity intact.

The market will discount each element to the present using appropriate required rates of return. The cost of CS is an average of the rates weighted by each element's share of total market value.

The starting point is the textbook formula (see, for example, Copeland, Weston and Shastri, 2004, Chapter 15) which can be summarized as follows.

These are the essential terms: k_{CV} is the cost of convertible debt; B is the value of debt element; W is the value of equity element, being the value of a call option on the company's shares; $B + W$ is the value of the convertible security; k_b is the required rate of return on debt; and k_c is the required rate of return on a call option on the company's shares. See below.

Using the capital asset pricing model,

$$k_c = R_f + [E(R_m) - R_f]\,\beta_c$$

where k_c is the required rate of return on a call option on the company's shares with the same maturity as the CS; R_f is the risk-free rate of return for a bond with the same maturity as the CS; $E(R_m)$ is the expected rate of return on a portfolio comprising all the shares in the market; β_c is the systematic risk of the call option expressing its correlation with the market. β_c is computed by reference to the β of an underlying share of the company adjusted to option using the Black–Scholes option pricing programme:

$$k_{cv} = k_b\left(\frac{B}{B+W}\right) + k_c\left(\frac{W}{B+W}\right)$$

The basic Black–Scholes option pricing scheme assumes that the issuer pays neither dividends nor tax (see, for example, Berk and DeMarzo, 2007, Chapters 21, 22, 23; Brealey and Myers, 2007, Part 6; and packages like the London Business School's).

FACTORS INFLUENCING COST

In the real world, dividends, tax, and mitigation of agency costs influence the cost of a CS.

"You can't run with the hare and ride with the hounds." English proverb

Dividends: If a company pays dividends then the value of the call option C changes. A call option on a dividend-paying share suffers, since a cash dividend liquidates some corporate value and the proceeds go to shareholders but not option holders. The larger the dividends, the more the option suffers. Option holders who try to anticipate this by early exercise gain dividends but lose interest on the exercise price.

> "Convertible securities are flexible, non-dilutive, easily executed, and cheap finance. They appeal to professional investors including hedge funds which seek to exploit arbitrage opportunities."

Options on dividend-paying stocks with assumed-continuous or, more realistically, discrete dividends can now be valued (Chandrasekhar and Gukhal, 2004), but only with protracted and complex mathematics beyond the present scope.

Tax: The impact of tax on cost is unique for every issuer, holder, and regime. Tax impinges on C, the value of the call, on β, its systematic risk and on k_b, the cost of debt. The impact in any particular case depends on:

- the issuer and holder's tax regime;
- interacting intra-group regimes;
- corporate, inter-corporate, and personal taxes at critical decision points;
- the taxable status of issuer, holder, and associates;
- how issuer and holder prioritize tax allowances.

Some aspects of recent relevant tax regulations for the United Kingdom are illustrative. The issue price is split between debt and equity. The debt element is valued by discounting comparable straight debt at the interest rate that would have been payable had the security contained no equity conversion feature. The difference between this value and the issue price of the security is treated as being either an equity instrument or an embedded derivative, according to whether the company can only issue shares or whether it has the discretion to pay cash. In the former case the conversion right is treated as an equity issue and is disregarded for tax. In the latter case it is in principle taxable as an embedded derivative. If so, a chargeable gain or allowable loss will arise when the company pays cash to the holders. The gain or loss is determined by a formula based on the difference between the book value of the equity element and the amount paid.

Any difference between the deemed issue price of the debt element and the amount payable on its redemption is amortized and is tax-deductible over the life of the security.

A company can get a high and timely tax deduction by paying high interest on a CS with a short life. This reduces k_b, the cost of debt. However if CS holders are taxable, their personal tax may negate the deduction: if debt is tax-inefficient relative to equity, such investors will require compensation by way of a higher return.

Furthermore tax benefits may be truncated by bankruptcy, voluntary conversion by bondholders, or a company decision to force conversion. If cross-border jurisdiction is involved it becomes necessary to examine how CSs would be categorized under relevant tax treaties, EC directives, and double taxation resulting from any inconsistent classification.

Mitigation of agency costs: Agency costs are costs of conflict among different classes of investor and between managers and investors. They reflect opportunities for equity to exploit debt and for managers to invest sloppily, forgo good investments, shirk, and enjoy perks. Endangered parties impose monitoring costs on the shareholders. If the endangered party is a lender, then the cost of debt rises. With CSs an equity sweetener reduces the monitoring costs by aligning the interests of debt and equity.

CSs can reduce the managerial incentive to over-invest in poor, low-return projects. For example, consider the second of two interdependent risky investments, which is only beneficial if the first succeeds. Either finance can be borrowed at the outset for both projects or CSs can be issued that will be sufficient for the first project while providing enough for the second on conversion. If all goes well, the second project will be duly financed by conversion. If the first project fails, the value of the CS will fall, nobody will convert, and management will be able to repurchase the debt at its low value in the open market. Indeed Mayers (2003) has observed a correlation between conversion and spates of corporate investment. If all had been borrowed upfront and if the first project failed, management might be tempted to invest the unused borrowings in easy, unprofitable projects.

A TREND AND ITS REVERSAL

A suitably selected trend illustrates in combination a number of the factors discussed. Such was the boom of 2003 (*Economist*,2003) and the subsequent fall.

The factors that prompted the surge in the early 2000s to issuance to a near-historic high are concerned with cost, capital structure, value, financial mobility, and market context:

- The market had no appetite for equity, and at the same time companies were suffering from unpalatable gearing levels. CSs with a low coupon provided financial mobility and some reassurance to anxious investors and garnered tax advantage.
- Hedge funds were attracted to CSs because they perceived a bargain insofar as the issue price underestimated the volatility of the equity, which meant that the call option, C in the basic formula, was undervalued.
- Hedge funds bought the convertible, sold the debt, and kept the undervalued call option. They then sold shares short to exploit underestimated volatility.

A reversal of the trend came when

- the volatility of equities declined;
- companies grew wise to the excessive cost of CSs that they were suffering;
- for tax reasons dividends increased, and this hurt short sellers who had to pay the dividends to their purchaser.

▸▸ MAKING IT HAPPEN

The decision to issue CSs follows the answers to a series of questions.

- Is there presently a "hot convertible debt window" in the market or are there contraindications?
- Do the causes of the window or the contraindications apply to us?
- What is our debt capacity? If we are near its limits will CSs bust us or will they enable us to stretch our borrowing?
- Can we tailor CSs to our real investment needs? Can we at the same time mitigate agency costs?
- What tax-planning opportunities do CSs offer? Should we prioritize other tax benefits?
- Measurement of the parameters of the cost of capital is notoriously difficult. How reliable are our estimates? For example, how stable is our beta and how reliable is our estimate of volatility?

  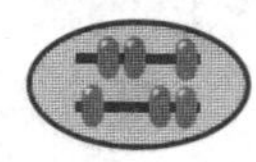   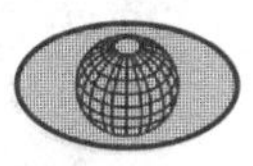   

▸▸ MORE INFO

Books:

Berk, Jonathan, and Peter DeMarzo. *Corporate Finance*. Boston, MA: Pearson Addison Wesley, 2007.

Bhattacharya, Mihir. "Convertible securities and their valuation." In Fabozzi, F. J. (ed). *The Handbook of Fixed Income Securities*. New York: McGraw-Hill, 2005, pp. 1393–1442.

Brealey, R.A., and S.C. Myers, *Principles of Corporate Finance*. 9th ed. New York: McGraw-Hill, 2007.

Copeland, Thomas, Fred Weston, and Kuldeep Shastri. *Financial Theory and Corporate Policy*. 4th ed. Boston, MA: Addison-Wesley, 2004.

Tuckman, Bruce. *Fixed Income Securities: Tools for Today's Market*. 2nd ed. Hoboken, NJ: Wiley, 2002.

Articles:

Ammann, Manuel, Martin Fehr, and Ralf Seiz. "New evidence on the announcement effect of convertible and exchangeable bonds." *Journal of Multinational Financial Management* 16:1 (2006): 43–63.

Asquith, Paul. "Convertible bonds are not called late." *Journal of Finance* 50:4 (1995): 1275–1289.

Campbell, Cynthia J., Louis H. Ederington, and Prashant Vankudre. "Tax shields, sample selection bias, and the information content of conversion-forcing bond calls." *Journal of Finance* 46:4 (1991): 1291–1324.

Chandrasekhar, C.R., and Reddy Gukhal. "The compound option approach to American options on jump-diffusions." *Journal of Economic Dynamics and Control* 28:10 (2004): 2055–2074.

Economist. "Options and opportunities." July 17, 2003. Online at: www.economist.com/finance/displaystory.cfm?story_id=E1_TJNSDRJ

Economist. "Convertible bombs." November 14, 2002. Online at: www.economist.com/finance/displaystory.cfm?story_id=E1_TQQGNJJ

Fitch Ratings. "Guide to hybrid securities." 2006. Online at: www.gtnews.com/feature/138_2.cfm

Laurent, Sandra. "Convertible debt and preference share financing: An empirical study." Working paper, 2005. Online at: ssrn.com/abstract=668364

"If we had launched Orange in the US, which is considered the home of branding, it would never have worked."
Hans Snook

  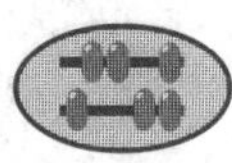 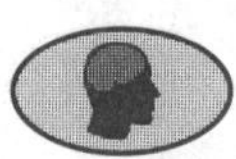  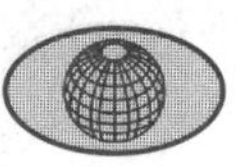   

Using Securitization as a Corporate Funding Tool by Frank J. Fabozzi

EXECUTIVE SUMMARY

- Securitization involves the creation of one or more securities backed by a pool of loans or receivables.
- Securitization is an important vehicle for raising funds that are used by nonfinancial and financial firms.
- The motivation for the use of securitization rather than the issuance of a secured corporate bond is the potential to reduce funding costs, particularly for firms that have a low credit rating.
- Another reason for the use of securitization is to manage corporate risk.
- The securitization process involves the creation of a special-purpose vehicle and the transference of assets to that entity.
- All securitization transactions require one or more forms of credit enhancement to obtain a credit rating.

INTRODUCTION

Securitization is the process of creating securities backed by a pool of loans or receivables. For a corporation, securitization is an alternative fund-raising process to the issuance of secured corporate bonds. The securities issued via the securitization process differ from traditional secured corporate bonds, where it is necessary for the corporate issuer to generate sufficient earnings to repay the bondholders. So, for example, if an equipment manufacturer issues a bond in which the bondholders have a first mortgage lien on one of its plants, the ability of the manufacturer to generate cash flow from all of its operations is required to pay off the bondholders. In contrast, in a securitization transaction, the burden of the source of repayment to those holding the created securities shifts from the cash flow of the corporate issuer to the cash flow of a pool of loans or receivables, and/or to a third party that guarantees the payments if the asset pool does not generate sufficient cash flow.

Although securitization was first used in the late 1960s by US government entities to create mortgage-backed securities, it was not used by nonfinancial corporations (i.e., corporations whose principal activity is the production of goods and nonfinancial services) to raise funds in the public market until March 1985 when Sperry Lease Finance Corporation (now Unisys) issued securities backed by a pool of lease receivables. Despite a major setback in the securitization market due to problems with one asset class—residential mortgage-backed securities backed by subprime borrowers—securitization continues to be an important funding alternative for nonfinancial corporations.

TYPES OF ASSETS SECURITIZED

The types of assets that have been securitized can be divided into four general categories: Mortgage loans, retail loans, wholesale loans, and operating revenue.

The securities created by securitization of a pool of mortgage loans are referred to as *mortgage-backed securities* (MBS). Those backed by a pool of high-quality residential mortgage loans are called *residential mortgage-backed securities*, and those backed by a pool of commercial loans (i.e., mortgage loans for income-producing properties such as apartment buildings, office buildings, and shopping centers) are called *commercial mortgage-backed securities*. These securitized products are typically used as funding vehicles for financial entities such as depository institutions (banks and savings and loan associations) and finance companies. For nonfinancial entities the bulk of securitizations use account receivables.

When securities are backed by a pool of retail loans, they are referred to as *asset-backed securities* (ABS). The major types of retail loans securitized include credit card receivables, home equity loans, automobile loans, and student loans. In fact, the largest sector of the asset-backed securities market is the mortgage-related asset-backed securities market, the sector that saw a major meltdown starting in the summer of 2007. The wholesale market includes commercial loans and bonds. The security created from the securitization of these types of debt instruments is called a *collateralized debt obligation*. Finally, a special area which has been used primarily in Europe is the securitization of operating revenue.

THE SECURITIZATION PROCESS

To explain the securitization process and the parties involved, we will use an illustration of a hypothetical corporation, which we call HCE, Inc., which manufactures heavy construction equipment. Although some of this firm's sales are for cash, the bulk are in the form of installment sales contracts. Effectively, an installment sale contract is a loan to the buyer of the equipment who agrees to repay HCE over a period of time specified in the contract. For purposes of this illustration, it is assumed that the loans are all for four years. The collateral for the loan is the equipment purchased by the borrower. The loan specifies an interest rate that the buyer pays.

The credit department of HCE makes the decision as to whether to extend credit to a customer. It receives a credit application from a customer and, on the basis of criteria established by this manufacturer, decides whether to extend a loan and the amount that will be lent. The criteria for extending credit or a loan are referred to as *underwriting standards*. Because HCE is extending the loan, it is referred to as the *originator* of the loan.

Moreover, HCE may have a department that is responsible for servicing the loan. *Servicing* involves collecting payments from borrowers, notifying borrowers who may be delinquent, and, when necessary, recovering and disposing of the equipment if the borrower defaults on its obligation. The servicer of loans need not be the originator of the loans, but in our illustration we are assuming that HCE is the servicer.

Let us now examine how these loans can be used in a securitization transaction. Figure 1 summarizes the transaction. We will assume that HCE has more than $300 million of installment sales contracts. This amount is shown on the corporation's balance sheet as an asset, or more specifically as a receivable. We will further assume that HCE wants to raise $300 million and that HCE's treasurer decides to raise that amount by securitizing these receivables.

To do so, HCE will set up a legal entity, referred to as a *special-purpose entity* (SPE) or *special-purpose vehicle* (SPV). For now, we'll postpone explaining the purpose of this legal entity, but it will be made clearer later that the SPE is critical in a securitization transaction. Let's assume that the SPE that is set up by our hypothetical manufacturer is Construction Asset Trust (CAT). HCE will then sell to CAT

"A lot of our communications have celebrated what we were not." Rawdon Glover

  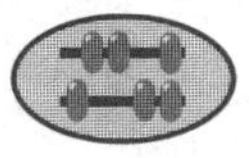   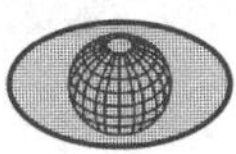   

Figure 1. Illustration of securitization of $300 million of installment sales contracts

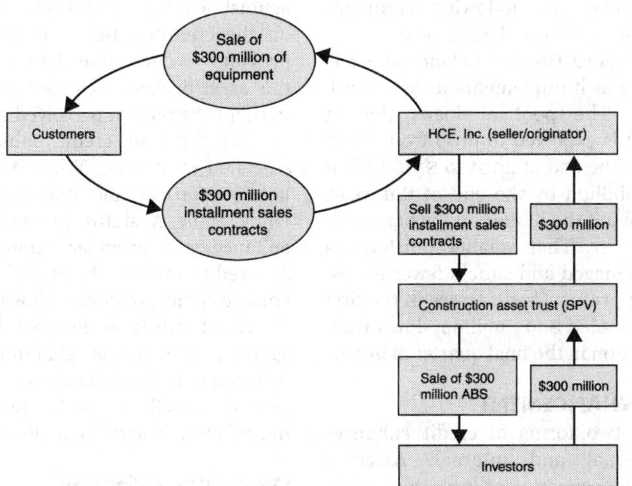

$300 million of the loans and, in exchange, will receive from CAT $300 million in cash, the amount that HCE's treasurer wanted to raise. CAT obtains the $300 million to pay for the pool of loans by selling securities that are backed by the pool of loans acquired. It is these securities issued by CAT that are called asset-backed securities. The asset-backed securities issued in a securitization transaction are also referred to as *bond classes* or *tranches*.

A simple transaction can involve the sale of just one bond class with a par value of $300 million. We will call this Bond Class A. Suppose that 300,000 certificates are issued for Bond Class A with a par value of $1,000 per certificate. Then, each certificate holder would be entitled to 1/300,000 of the payment from the collateral after expenses and fees are paid. Each payment made by the borrowers (i.e., the buyers of the equipment) consists of principal repayment (i.e., amortization) and interest.

The typical securitization transaction has more than one bond class. For example, there can be rules for distribution of principal and interest other than on a *pro rata* basis to different bond classes. It may be difficult to understand why such a structure should be created. What is important to understand is that there are institutional investors who have needs for bonds with different maturities and credit ratings. A securitization transaction can be designed to create bond classes with investment characteristics that are more attractive to institutional investors to satisfy those needs.

An example of a more complicated transaction is one in which two bond classes are created, Bond Class A1 and Bond Class A2. The par value for Bond Class A1 is $130 million and for Bond Class A2 it is $170 million. The priority rule can simply specify that Bond Class A1 receives all the principal that is paid by the borrowers until all of Bond Class A1's $130 million has been paid off, and then Bond Class A2 begins to receive principal. Bond Class A1 is then a shorter-term bond than Bond Class A2.

As will be explained later, there are typically structures where there is more than one bond class but the two bond classes differ as to how they will share any losses resulting from defaults of the borrowers in the asset pool. In such a structure, the bond classes are classified as *senior bond classes* and *subordinate bond classes,* and the structure is referred to as a *senior subordinate structure*. Losses are realized by the subordinate bond classes before there are any losses realized by the senior bond classes. For example, suppose that CAT issued $250 million par value of Bond Class A, the senior bond class, and $50 million par value of Bond Class B, the subordinate bond class. As long as the aggregated defaults in the asset pool do not exceed $50 million, then Bond Class A will be repaid its $250 million in full.

POTENTIAL FOR REDUCING FUNDING COSTS

To understand the potential for reducing funding costs by securitizing corporate assets rather than issuing a corporate bond, consider once again our hypothetical manufacturer, HCE, Inc. Suppose that this corporation's credit rating as assigned by the three major rating agencies (Fitch Ratings, Moody's Investors Service, and Standard & Poor's) is triple B. If HCE's treasurer wants to raise funds of $300 million and it issues a corporate bond, its funding cost would be whatever the benchmark Treasury yield is plus the prevailing yield spread for triple B issuers in the bond market. Suppose, instead, that the treasurer utilizes $300 million of its installment sales contracts as collateral for a bond issue. In that case, the cost will be the same as if it issued a standard corporate bond, because if HCE defaults on any of its outstanding debt, the creditors will go after all of the corporate assets, including the loans to HCE's customers.

Now instead suppose that HCE creates CAT (the SPE) and sells the loans to that entity as explained in the previous section. If the sale of the loans by HCE to CAT is done properly—that is, the sale of the loans is at the fair market value—CAT, not HCE, is then the legal owner of the receivables. This means that if HCE is forced into bankruptcy, its creditors cannot recover the loans sold because they are legally owned by CAT. The implication is that if CAT sells the asset-backed securities that are backed by the pool of loans, investors interested in buying the bonds will evaluate the credit risk associated with the pool of loans independently of the credit rating of HCE. The credit rating that will be assigned to the securities issued by CAT will be whatever CAT wants the credit rating to be! It may seem odd that the issuer (CAT) can get any credit rating it wants, but that is the case. The reason is that CAT will show the characteristics of the collateral for the securities (i.e., the loans it will acquire) to a credit rating agency. In turn, the rating agency will evaluate the credit quality of the loan pool and inform CAT what must be done to obtain a desired credit rating.

More specifically, the issuer will be asked to "credit enhance" the structure. There are various forms of *credit enhancement* that we will review in the next section. Basically, the rating agencies will look at the potential losses from the loan pool and make a determination of how much credit enhancement is necessary for the securities issued to achieve the targeted rating sought by the issuer. The higher the credit rating sought by the issuer, the more credit enhancement a rating agency will require. Thus, HCE, which we assumed is triple B rated, can obtain funding using the loan pool as collateral to obtain a better credit rating for the bonds issued than its own credit rating. In fact, with enough credit enhancement, it can issue a bond of the highest credit rating, triple A.

The key to a corporation issuing bonds with a higher credit rating than the corporation's own credit rating is the SPE. Its role is critical because it is the SPE that legally separates the assets used as collateral from the corporation that is seeking funding.

  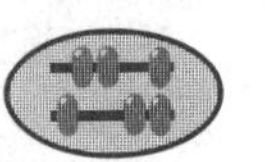   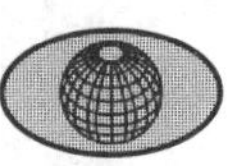   

It would seem natural that a corporate treasurer would always seek the highest credit rating (triple A) for the securities backed by the collateral in a securitization transaction. However, the awarding of a targeted credit rating requires sufficient credit enhancement, and this does not come without a cost. As described in the next section, there are various credit enhancement mechanisms, and they increase the costs associated with borrowing via a securitization. So, when seeking a higher rating, the corporate treasurer must assess the trade-off between, on the one hand, the additional cost of credit enhancing the securities to be issued by the SPE and, on the other hand, the potential reduction in funding cost by issuing a bond with a higher credit rating.

A case study of the use of securitization to reduce funding costs is provided by Ford Motor Company. In 2001, the auto manufacturer was facing the downgrade of its credit rating to that of noninvestment grade status (more popularly referred to as "junk bond" status). As a result, in early 2002 its wholly owned financing subsidiary, Ford Motor Credit (FMC), increased its issuance of asset-backed securities backed by auto loans rather than issue corporate bonds. For example, in the first two weeks of 2002, FMC issued $5 billion in asset-backed securities. In fact, because of the concern with downgrading, from 2000 to mid-2003, FMC increased securitizations to $55 billion (28% of its total funding) from $25 billion (13% of its total funding). Also, while the ratings of the auto manufacturers were downgraded in May 2005, the ratings on several of their securitization transactions were actually upgraded due to high subsisting levels of credit enhancement.

SECURITIZATION AS A TOOL FOR RISK MANAGEMENT

The potential to reduce funding costs is the main reason why nonfinancial corporations will use securitization, but another important reason is that it provides a risk management tool. More specifically, once the loans or receivables are sold to the SPE, the risks associated with those assets are transferred to the SPE and, ultimately, to the owners of the asset-backed securities. One major such risk is credit risk—the risk that the borrower will default.

A case study of how securitization has been used as a risk management tool is once again provided by Ford Motor Credit. Automobile loans are assets on the firm's balance sheet and subject the firm to the risk that borrowers will default on their obligations. On the use of securitization by Ford Motor Credit's chief financial officer, David Cosper, the following comment appeared in a *BusinessWeek* article:

> "Overall, Ford Credit's balance sheet is shrinking as it implements its lower-risk strategy. The pool of loans that it manages is expected to drop from $208 billion at the end of 2001 to $180 billion to $185 billion by the end of this year. 'We have put the brakes on the business,' says Cosper. That smaller portfolio is better managed and suffers fewer losses, boosting profits. Credit losses in the first quarter totaled $493 million, down from $912 million in the final quarter of 2001."

CREDIT ENHANCEMENT

There are two forms of credit enhancement—external and internal. *External credit enhancement* involves third-party guarantees such as insurance or a letter of credit. *Internal credit enhancement* includes overcollateralization, senior subordinated structure, and reserves. Securitization transactions will often have more than one form of credit enhancement. The rating agencies specify the amount of credit enhancement required to obtain a specific credit rating. Based on prevailing market conditions, the issuer must assess each form of credit enhancement to determine the most cost-effective credit enhancement mechanism or combination of mechanisms. In general, when deciding to improve the credit rating on some securities in a structure, the issuer will evaluate the trade-off associated with the cost of enhancement versus the reduction in yield required to sell the security.

Below we describe the various forms of credit enhancement mechanisms.

Third-Party Guarantees

Until the difficulties encountered by monoline insurers, the most common form of third-party guarantee was insurance wherein, for a premium, an insurance provider agrees to guarantee the performance of a certain amount of the collateral against defaults. The rating agencies decide on the creditworthiness of the insurance provider to determine the credit rating of the asset-backed securities to be issued. Perhaps the biggest perceived disadvantage to this form of credit enhancement is so-called *event risk*. Triple A rated bondholders, for example, may only be able to enjoy triple A status for as long as the enhancement provider retains its triple A credit rating status. If the credit enhancement provider is downgraded (i.e., its credit rating is lowered by a rating agency), the bonds guaranteed by the enhancement provider are typically downgraded as well unless the performance of the collateral warrants no downgrade.

Overcollateralization

Overcollateralization, a form of internal credit enhancement, is provided by issuing securities with a par value that is less than the par value of the loans or receivables in the asset pool. For example, if there are $300 million of loans in an asset pool and the issuer wanted to use overcollateralization for credit enhancement to achieve, say, a triple A credit rating for the securities to be issued, the issuer would obtain from the rating agencies an indication as to how much par value of securities it could issue versus the $300 million par value of loans in the asset pool to obtain the target rating. Depending on the characteristics of the loans and their perceived creditworthiness, the rating agencies might allow, say, $285 million of par value of securities to be issued. The cost of this form of credit enhancement is implicit in the price paid for $300 million par value of collateral versus the proceeds of issuing only $285 million par value of securities.

Senior Subordinate Structure

The senior subordinate structure, which was mentioned earlier, involves the subordination of some bond classes for the

▸▸ MAKING IT HAPPEN

Using securitization as a funding vehicle requires an understanding not just of the transactions but also of the implementation issues. These include:

- having the ability to analyze alternative securitization structures in order to maximize the proceeds received from the sale of the loans/receivables (i.e., best execution);
- determining whether, given market conditions, the issuance of secured debt or asset-backed securitization is the better funding vehicle;
- having a relationship with an investment banker that can structure the transaction based on prevailing market conditions and the characteristics of the collateral, as well as negotiating with the rating agencies regarding credit enhancement;
- having the ability to service the loans and report on the assets in the pool, or identifying other entities capable of doing so;
- having an organizational structure and staff that will allow frequent securitizations.

"If I'm Philip Morris or R.J. Reynolds I'd go celebrate, because I know whatever brands I have now will never be seriously challenged by a new product." Clive Chajet

  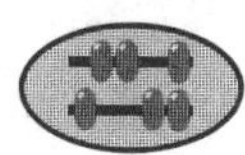 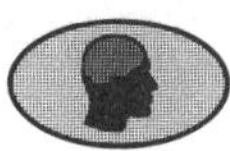  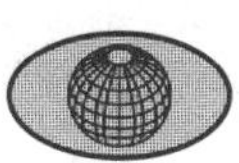   

benefit of attaining a high investment-grade rating for other bond classes in the structure. On the basis of an analysis of the collateral, a rating agency will decide how many triple A bonds can be issued, how many double A bonds, and so forth down to nonrated bonds.

The cost of this form of credit enhancement is based on the proceeds that will be received from selling the bonds, which is in turn determined by the demand for the bonds. The yields that must be offered on the bond classes are affected by the yields demanded by investors. The lower the credit rating of the bond class, the more yield is demanded and the lower will be the proceeds received by the SPE from the sale of the bonds for that bond class.

Reserve Funds

Reserve funds come in two forms: Cash reserve funds and excess spread. *Cash reserve funds* are straight deposits of cash generated from issuance proceeds. In this case, part of the profits from the deal are deposited into a fund and used to offset any losses. *Excess spread accounts* involve the allocation of excess spread into a separate reserve account after paying out the coupon to bondholders, the servicing fee, and all other expenses on a monthly basis.

CONCLUSION

Securitization, the process of creating securities backed by a pool of loans or receivables, has become an important funding source for both financial and nonfinancial corporations. In addition to the potential for reducing funding costs, securitization can be used as a risk management tool. The key in a securitization process is the role played by the SPE. In a properly structured securitization transaction, investors in the securities issued by the SPE, called asset-backed securities, can only look to the cash flow of the loan pool held by the SPE to repay the debt obligation and not to the general assets of the seller/originator of the loans or receivables.

In a securitization transaction, to obtain a credit rating that will allow the sale of the asset-backed securities, the structure must be credit enhanced. Credit enhancement provides protection of varying degrees for the bond classes in the structure. Credit enhancement mechanisms include third-party guarantees such as insurance or a letter of credit (external credit enhancement) and overcollateralization, senior subordinated structure, and reserves (internal credit enhancement).

▸▸ MORE INFO

Books:

Davidson, Andrew, Anthony Sanders, Lan-Ling Wolff, and Anne Ching. *Securitization: Structuring and Investment Analysis*. Hoboken, NJ: Wiley, 2003.

Fabozzi, Frank J. (ed). *Issuer Perspectives on Securitization*. Hoboken, NJ: Wiley, 1999.

Fabozzi, Frank J. (ed). *Accessing Capital Markets through Securitization*. Hoboken, NJ: Wiley, 2001.

Fabozzi, Frank J., and Vinod Kothari. *Introduction to Securitization*. Hoboken, NJ: Wiley, 2008.

Kothari, Vinod. *Securitization: The Financial Instrument of the Future 3e*. Hoboken, NJ: Wiley, 2006.

Peaslee, James E., and David Z. Nirenberg. *Federal Income Taxation of Securitization Transactions*. 3rd ed. New Hope, PA: Frank J. Fabozzi Associates, 2001.

Articles:

Fabozzi, Frank J., and W. Alexander Roever. "Primer on securitization." *Journal of Structured and Project Finance* (Summer 2003): 5–19.

Fabozzi, Frank J., and Vinod Kothari. "Securitization: The tool of financial transformation." *Journal of Financial Transformation* 20 (2007): 34–44.

Websites:

Vinod Kothari's securitization website: www.vinodkothari.com

Federal Income Taxation of Securitization Transactions website: www.securitizationtax.com

See Also:

★ Credit Ratings (pp. 534–536)
★ Securitization: Understanding the Risks and Rewards (pp. 576–578)
✔ The Bond Market: Its Structure and Function (p. 1010)
✔ How to Use Credit Rating Agencies (p. 939)
✔ How to Use Receivables as Collateral (p. 1014)
✔ Understanding Capital Markets, Structure and Function (p. 1028)
✔ Understanding Debt Cover (p. 1029)

"The world is first a Coke world, then an orange world, then a lemon-lime world." Roberto Goizueta

  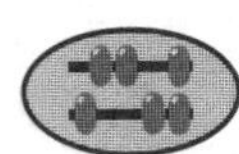   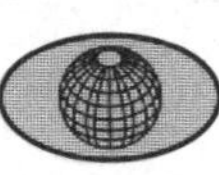   

What the Rise of Global Banks Means for Your Company by Chris Skinner

EXECUTIVE SUMMARY

- Multinational corporations are consolidating their business requirements for financial services into a few core global players.
- Global banks offer a platform for global access to cash management, liquidity, and risk management, thereby improving the methods by which firms can manage their finances.
- Global banks are being driven by their customers, with many multinational businesses moving from local to global supply chains, which has demanded global financial support.
- Global supply chains demand global banking to enable firms to operate effectively across borders with confidence, rather than having to rely on barter or other less reliable forms of value exchange.
- Global banks face a lack of standards across banks and borders, an area that should be addressed and resolved over time.

INTRODUCTION

Over the past decade, it has seemed that big banks have only gotten bigger. This is down to a variety of factors—from mergers and acquisitions through to technological leverage—but the most overriding factor has been the impact of globalization. As corporations and organizations have created global supply chains, so the largest banks have tried to follow their clients' needs by creating global infrastructures. For most firms, this means is that they can now work in partnership with a bank that reflects their multinational capabilities without having to open separate accounts in each of the countries of operation.

WHICH ARE THE GLOBAL BANKS?

A small number of banks provide global coverage and branding. Obvious examples are Bank of America, Bank of Tokyo–Mitsubishi UFJ, Barclays, BNP Paribas, Citi, Deutsche Bank, HSBC, JP Morgan Chase, Royal Bank of Scotland (RBS), and Santander. All are creating global brands and global presence through acquisitive growth, which is why RBS and Santander acquired the global operations of ABN AMRO outside the Benelux in 2007 and why HSBC acquired Crédit Commercial de France (CCF) in France and Household Finance in the United States.

Obviously, the latest liquidity and credit crisis has changed some of the focus of these banks. By way of example, JP Morgan Chase has had to refocus upon domestic American soil after its acquisitions of Bear Stearns and Washington Mutual, as have Bank of America and Citigroup, but the trend is generally toward global presence and support.

HOW DO YOU RECOGNIZE A GLOBAL BANK?

The easiest way to spot a global bank is by its brand, which will typically be just a symbol and a name acronym.

The reason this is worth mentioning is that many global banks are trying to create non-national identities as a pure name and logo. For instance, Deutsche Bank has removed the name from its emblem in many branches and operations, and Santander is often just represented by its logo rather than by its name. For the same reason, these bank brands tend to be emblazoned on panels and ramps in many airport terminals. Have you spotted how many HSBC banners there are as you get on and off an aircraft, each panel providing a global and local message? This is to reinforce the global message. While RBS, Barclays JP Morgan Chase and others operate in over 50 countries, HSBC would claim to be the most globalized, with over 80 countries covered. That is not to deny the existence of competition from other specialist regional players, such as Nordea in the Scandinavian region and Standard Chartered across Asia, but the difference between a regional and global player can be important, especially for firms that want to trade across global borders.

WHAT ADVANTAGES DO GLOBAL BANKS OFFER?

For multinational firms operating across multiple regions, the main advantage of global banks is that they can offer a consolidated view of all finance across all countries of operation. This is becoming a critical factor as firms expand into globalized structures themselves.

For example, a critical discussion that has been taking place amongst these banks is how to provide effective financial support for supply chains. As many businesses are moving services to India and sourcing of product to China and related Asian countries for supply to Europe and America, there is a need for easy transfer of funds and payments for supplies between countries on either side of the planet. Historically, this has been incredibly difficult. For example, at a major banking convention in 2004, Heidi Miller, JP Morgan Chase's Head of the Treasury and Securities Services, asked: "Why do we make things so complicated for our clients? . . . A friend who lives in Europe . . . bought a boat . . . When the boat was ready, he called his bank to arrange payment. And his bank told him it would take about six weeks to transfer the funds."

This example was for a simple payment from the United States to France, and the friend she referred to happened to be the CEO of a major bank. The banking industry now recognizes it has been slow to respond to the need for global financial management and payments. To meet this challenge, many banks are now developing services in this area.

WHAT SERVICES DO GLOBAL BANKS OFFER?

The biggest enhancement that global banks offer is a single, global view of financial flows for their business clients. This is the offering of a single connection to their systems for all the treasury operations of corporations around the world. Therefore, a business operating in over 100 countries can now have a consistent view of its cash, risk, and liquidity for all treasury and finance functions. That view of monetary movements will be the same for the financial manager in New York, San Paolo, Sydney, Tokyo, Frankfurt, and London, because the bank can provide realtime interfaces to the business account on a single platform.

The fact that these banks offer global, realtime cash management is the critical differentiation for them. In fact, it goes further than this, with many banks competing on the basis of the value-added services they believe they can provide.

Value-added services may include the provision of an aggregation capability to all payment processing systems globally. This means that you only need to link to one

"Twenty years ago, I would never have dreamt that we would be the ninth largest bank in the world."
Emilio Botin III

     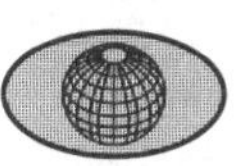   

bank in order to gain access to payment processing via SWIFT, Fedwire, CHIPS, SEPA systems such as the Euro Banking Association's STEP2, and Faster Payments in the United Kingdom through VocaLink, etc. Today, many firms have to create a direct connection with each of these systems through local banks in every country. The difference now is that you need only connect once to gain global connectivity.

Another value-added differentiation these banks claim to have is the ability to provide the total view of other facets of business, such as risk. The current view of risk management is that customers receive intra-day or end-of-day risk reports for their total liquidity management positions. The challenge with this approach is that markets are so volatile today that an intra-day or end-of-day view may result in overexposure to the markets for both the business and the banker to that business. Therefore, realtime liquidity management to avoid these overexposures has become another valued service that global banks can deliver, whilst local banks cannot.

WHY USE A LOCAL BANK?

The fact that global banks offer global services, global payments processing, and global liquidity and risk management is great news if yours is a global business requiring such global services. Global businesses can gain economies of scale and the efficiencies of only dealing with a small number of financial partners. However, a regional or domestic firm with regional or domestic needs may question whether it requires such global structures and operations. Some may say they do, because they source raw materials from overseas and deliver and distribute products in multiple nations. However, if you are a small fish playing in this big pond, you may find you are paying a high price for such services in terms of both fees and the lack of attention you might receive by comparison with a more localized operation.

This is certainly an accusation levelled at many of the large global operators by small businesses. It does not necessarily hold true, but many smaller firms consider that a local bank can provide a better service than a global operator, especially with regard to the advice they can gain access to.

However, every firm seeking a banker has a choice. Local domestic, regional, and global banks all offer services that are appropriate to the clients who want those services, and it is really the choice of the financial leadership within the business to determine whether a local or global service is more appropriate to their needs.

This decision will normally be driven by such questions as:

- Do you operate in more than 20 countries?
- Do you have regular cross-border transactions that require currency transfers?
- Would you find it beneficial if your bank could provide you with a global view of all of your cash and risk positions?
- Do you have revenues of more than $1 billion per annum?
- Are you heavily involved in structured finance and the money markets?
- Do you have extensive internal expertise in financial management?

The list can be extensive, but if you answered "yes" to most of these questions you probably would find it beneficial to work with a global bank. Equally, if you answered "no," then a domestic or regional bank will probably cater to most of your needs.

CONCLUSION

The rise of global banks is driven by businesses that now operate globally. The increasing use of supply chains where goods are sourced from the growth economies of the past decade—Brazil, Russia, India, and China—has led to a rethinking of finance. The fact that banks could not provide global finance has driven an acquisitive emergence of new global bank brands that are now trying to cater for this need. However, the services of these banks will not be appropriate to every organization, and it is therefore necessary to consider carefully the real requirements of a bank provider before placing all of one's financial eggs into a single global basket.

CASE STUDY

HSBC is one of the finest examples of global banking in existence today. This is because HSBC has operations from the Americas through Europe to Asia. During the credit crisis, HSBC found that its American operations, represented by a firm it had acquired, resulted in significant writedowns for the subprime crisis. However, HSBC overcame these issues and still made a considerable profit thanks to its global diversity. This is why HSBC is one of the few banks not to have been hit by the issues of weakened capital base that we have seen with other banks.

In addition, HSBC is able to leverage its global positions. By way of example, HSBC recently spent over $200 million on creating a global banking website service. That's an incredible amount, and far more than other banks could possibly afford to spend on an internet banking services. However, HSBC's internet banking service is now a single global platform that can be tweaked to local demands. Hence, by spending $200 million, HSBC created the world's most powerful internet banking service with 200 variations appropriate to each country of operation. As a result, HSBC deploys the world's best internet banking services for $1 million per country, which, on an economies of scale basis, provides far more efficiency and effectiveness.

▸▸ MORE INFO

Book:

Skinner, Chris. *The Future of Banking in a Globalized World*. Chichester, UK: Wiley, 2007.

Websites:

The Financial Services Club: www.fsclub.co.uk

The Financial Services Club blog: www.thefinanser.com

Independent newswire and information source for the worldwide financial technology community: www.finextra.com

See Also:

★ Business Implications of the Single Euro Payments Area (SEPA) (pp. 20–21)

★ How to Successfully Assess a Company's Global Treasury Needs and Objectives (pp. 66–68)

✔ Retail Banks: Their Structure and Function (p. 930)

"A global brand tends to increase the brand value of those organisations and it has an effect on the share price." Terry Tyrrell

  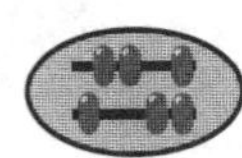   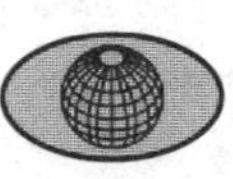   

Accounting for Business Combinations in Accordance with International Financial Reporting Standards (IFRS) Requirements

by Shân Kennedy

EXECUTIVE SUMMARY

The International Accounting Standards Board (IASB) has introduced requirements in the last few years to make those involved in business combinations more accountable for the transactions that have taken place. In particular:

- All business combinations must now be accounted for using the acquisition accounting method.
- The intangible assets arising from a business combination must be identified and recognized separately from purchased goodwill.
- Purchased goodwill is no longer permitted to be amortized; instead, it must be tested for impairment each year.

INTRODUCTION

The accounting for business combinations under IFRS is governed by four key standards:

- IFRS 3, Business Combinations;
- IAS (International Accounting Standards) 27, Consolidated Financial Statements;
- IAS 36, Impairment of Assets;
- IAS 38, Intangible Assets.

IFRS 3 sets out the requirements to be followed in accounting for a business combination. Its introduction in 2004 represented a substantial change from the standard it superseded, IAS 22. IFRS 3 signaled the end of the benign method of accounting for business combinations known as "merger accounting." Instead, all business combinations must be accounted for using the acquisition accounting method. This requires that both acquirer and acquiree are identified for each transaction, that a fair value exercise is performed on the acquiree's assets and liabilities, and that purchased goodwill arising from the transaction is capitalized in the balance sheet.

A further consequence of the introduction of IFRS 3 is that intangible assets must be recognized separately from purchased goodwill instead of being subsumed within purchased goodwill. Purchased goodwill itself is not amortized, but must be reviewed for impairment annually. The performance of the impairment review is covered by IAS 36, Impairment of Assets, and the identification and recognition of intangible assets is covered by IAS 38, Intangible Assets.

The tightening up of business combination accounting was noted by accountants PricewaterhouseCoopers: "The acquisition process will need to become more rigorous, from planning to execution."[1]

The following steps are involved in accounting for a business combination under IFRS 3:

- identification of the acquirer and the acquiree;
- performance of a fair value exercise on the acquiree's assets and liabilities;
- identification and measurement of the fair value of the intangible assets arising;
- measurement of the amount of any non-controlling interest in the acquiree;
- measurement of the amount of goodwill arising from the transaction.

A revised version of IFRS 3 was issued by the IASB in January 2008, and its requirements will be mandatory for accounting periods from July 2009 onward. While the revision is quite comprehensive, it does not change the overall approach set out above. The revision is part of the Convergence Program underway between the IASB and the Financial Accounting Standards Board (FASB), aimed at reducing the number of differences between IFRS requirements and US Generally Accepted Accounting Principles (US GAAP). In addition to tightening up certain areas, the revision developed the previous IFRS 3 by:

- providing additional guidance regarding the recognition and fair value measurement of the acquiree's assets and liabilities;
- changing the requirements for measuring goodwill and the remaining noncontrolling interest when less than a 100% stake in the acquiree is purchased or when an increase in an existing stake is involved.

IDENTIFICATION OF ACQUIRER AND ACQUIREE

IAS 27 demands that the acquirer in a business combination be identified as the party that gains control, with control being defined as "the power to govern the financial and operating policies of an entity so as to benefit from its activities." Control is presumed to exist if one entity owns more than 50% of the voting power of the other, unless it can be demonstrated that this voting power does not constitute control. Conversely, control can be seen to exist when one entity owns less than 50% of the voting rights in the other but controls it through some other means, such as a shareholder agreement. This situation was seen when ABN AMRO was acquired by the Royal Bank of Scotland (RBS)—RBS owns only 38% of the issued share capital of ABN AMRO but is able to control it through a consortium agreement with the other owners, Fortis and Santander. Thus, RBS consolidates ABN AMRO in its financial statements.

Other guidance provided in IAS 27 for identifying the acquirer includes that, generally, the acquirer is:

- larger than the acquiree;
- the party issuing equity or paying cash as consideration;
- the party that has more seats on the board of directors of the combined entity.

IFRS 3 does, however, also deal with reverse acquisitions in which smaller companies acquire larger ones through the issue of significant amounts of equity.

FAIR VALUE EXERCISE ON THE ACQUIREE'S ASSETS AND LIABILITIES

Consistent with any acquisition accounting exercise, IFRS 3 requires that the acquired assets and liabilities are recognized initially at fair value in the consolidated financial statements of the combined entity. The standard provides some clarification regarding identification of these assets and liabilities. For instance, IFRS 3 prohibits the setting up of acquisition reorganization provisions since these are not liabilities of the acquirer at the acquisition date. Prior to IFRS 3, acquiring companies often set up substantial acquisition reorganization provisions. Costs, such as those relating to redundancy and factory closures, were charged to these provisions post acquisition rather than to the profit and loss account. Now, such costs must be charged to the profit and loss account of the combined entity post acquisition.

IDENTIFICATION AND MEASUREMENT OF THE INTANGIBLE ASSETS ARISING FROM A COMBINATION

IAS 38 defines an intangible asset as "identifiable" if it can be separated from the entity—i.e. can be leased or sold separately from the entity—or if it is secured legally. By defining identifiability in terms of separability as well as legal security, the number of potentially recognizable intangible assets increases. For instance, software technology may not be legally protected by a patent, but this does not prevent it from being licensed or sold to a third party. Consequently, if a software company is acquired, those intangible assets that may be recognized include both patent protected and unprotected software. Since IFRS 3 assumes that the fair value of intangible assets arising from an acquisition can be measured reliably, if in existence such assets must be recognized in the fair value balance sheet.

> "...intangible assets must be recognised separately from purchased goodwill rather than subsumed within purchased goodwill. Purchased goodwill itself is not amortised but must be reviewed for impairment annually"

It is the broadening of the net of intangible assets to include those that are not secured legally, together with the assumption that all identifiable intangible assets arising from a business combination can be measured reliably, that has greatly increased the number of intangible assets recognised separately from goodwill following a business combination.

IFRS 3 clarifies that certain intangible assets might be recognized in the consolidated financial statements but are not recognized in the financial statements of the acquiree. Thus, internally developed brands and customer relationship assets of the acquiree would not be recognized as intangible assets in the financial statements of the acquiree, because the cost of their development would be recorded as an expense. However, provided they satisfy the IAS 38 requirement to be identifiable intangible assets—i.e. if they are intangible, identifiable, controlled by the entity, and expected to give rise to future economic benefits—they are recognized in the consolidated financial statements.

Potentially, a very large number of intangible assets might need to be valued for balance sheet recognition purposes. IAS 38, however, allows the preparer of accounts to combine certain complementary intangible assets as a composite intangible asset—a brand—if the fair values of the underlying component intangible assets cannot be determined reliably or if they have similar useful lives. In practice, this concession is often used to reduce the number of intangible assets that need to be valued following a business combination. A proposed amendment to IAS 38 suggests that the concession could be extended to complementary assets other than brands.

An example of the increased number of intangible assets recognized following business combinations can be seen in the results of Yell Group plc.

Table 1. Analysis of Intangible Assets in Yell Group Financial Statements March 2008

Contracts	£47m
Non-compete agreements	£6m
Customer lists	£366m
Brand names	£856m
Software costs	£44m
Total identifiable intangible assets	£1,319m
Goodwill	£3,899m

In contrast, the Yell Group financial statements for March 2005—the last before transition to IFRS—show a goodwill balance of £1,635 million and no identifiable intangible assets.

Neither IFRS 3 nor IAS 38 provides any substantive guidance on determining the fair value of intangible assets. Instead, best practice has developed in the marketplace and tends to be driven by the auditors of the accounts. Many intangible asset valuation consultancies have commented on the difficulty of valuing these intangible assets. One such consultancy, Brand Finance, notes in its website literature: "In many instances the valuation of such assets is a complex undertaking" and "it will be important to demonstrate that best practice techniques are being applied."

In January 2009, the International Valuation Standards Council (IVSC) issued two Exposure Drafts on the valuation of intangible assets generally and on the valuation of intangible assets for IFRS reporting purposes. These set out the key valuation methods that are used and address some of the more complex issues that can arise. They follow their issue, in July 2007, of a Discussion Paper on the topic of the valuation of intangible assets for IFRS reporting purposes.

In response to the IVSC's Discussion Paper, the International Actuarial Association noted "We support the issuance of guidance on valuation of intangible assets for IFRS reporting purposes."

MEASURING THE AMOUNT OF ANY NON-CONTROLLING INTEREST IN THE ACQUIREE

If, as a result of a business combination, the acquirer owns less than 100% of the acquiree, there is a remaining non-controlling interest, previously known as a minority interest, in the acquiree to be recognized. Accounting for this non-controlling interest has changed following the recent revision to IFRS 3. Previously, the non-controlling interest had to be measured at its proportionate share of the identifiable net assets, i.e. excluding its goodwill. The revision introduced the option to measure the non-controlling interest at its fair value and thus include its goodwill. Several commentators were concerned about the difficulty of measuring this fair value, especially where the acquiree company's shares were unlisted, and for this reason the option to measure at fair value was not made mandatory. Under US GAAP, however, the non-controlling interest must be measured at fair value—no option is permitted. This represents a continuing difference between IFRS and US GAAP requirements.

MEASURING THE GOODWILL ARISING FROM A BUSINESS COMBINATION

The revised IFRS 3 requires that goodwill is measured as the following:

The sum of:

- the fair value of the consideration paid;
- the amount of any non-controlling interest measured as described above;
- the fair value of any previously held non-controlling interest in the acquiree;

Less:

- the net sum of the acquisition date assets acquired and liabilities assumed, measured as required by IFRS 3.

It is important to note that goodwill itself is not measured at fair value—it is the residual amount that results from applying the calculation above. As a result of the option with respect to measurement of any non-controlling interest, the amount measured for goodwill may or may not include goodwill in such non-controlling interest.

▸▸ MORE INFO

Reports:

International Valuation Standards Committee (IVSC). "Revised International Guidance Not No. 4, Valuation of Intangible Assets". January 2009.

International Valuation Standards Committee (IVSC). "Proposed new International Guidance Note No. 16, Valuation of Intangible Assets for IFRS Reporting Purposes." January 2009.

Websites:

Company Reporting, comments on the types of intangible asset being recognized in company accounts are regularly made by this UK-based organization: www.comrep.co.uk

International Accounting Standards Board (IASB), from whom copies of the relevant IFRS and technical summaries of each standard can be obtained: www.iasb.org

International Actuarial Association (AAI/IAA): www.actuaries.org

International Valuation Standards Committee (IVSC): www.ivsc.org

NOTES

1 Source: "Acquisitions: Accounting and transparency under IFRS 3." PricewaterhouseCoopers, April 2004. Online at: www.pwc.com/fi/fin/ifrs/pwc_acq_acc_transp_ifrs3.pdf

"Running a media brand is about harnessing the value of people. . .journalists, DJs, editors—all of them are the brand." Vijay Solanki

     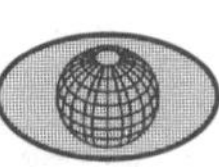   

Accounting for Share-Based Payments under IFRS by Shân Kennedy

EXECUTIVE SUMMARY

- In 2005 the International Accounting Standards Board (IASB) introduced International Financial Reporting Standard, IFRS 2, Share-based Payment, to address the issue of accounting for remuneration paid to employees in the form of equity, derivatives of equity, or cash linked to the price of equity.
- Most awards are made as shares or share options, and are known as equity-settled share-based payments.
- Valuation and accounting issues affect how such awards are reflected in a company's financial statements.
- A valuation exercise is required in respect of the fair value of the awards at the date they were granted.
- An accounting exercise is required in respect of the extent to which the grant-date fair value is charged to the company's profit and loss account.
- These valuation and accounting exercises take full account of any conditions attaching to the earning of the award by the employee.

INTRODUCTION

Share-based payments are often made to employees for the purpose of incentivizing them to remain with a company or to improve their standard of performance and, thus, may be granted subject to certain conditions. IFRS 2, Share-based Payment, analyzes in detail the types of condition that might be applied and how they impact the accounting treatment.

The standard requires that equity-settled share-based payment awards are accounted for using the modified grant-date approach. This requires the measurement of the fair value of the award at the grant date, adjusted to reflect certain types of conditions, known as market conditions and nonvesting conditions. The extent to which this adjusted, i.e. modified, fair value is charged to the profit and loss account is determined according to the extent to which other conditions, known as vesting conditions that are not market conditions, apply and are satisfied. No charge is made on a cumulative basis over the vesting period if such other conditions apply but are not satisfied.

The following steps are involved in application of the modified grant-date approach:

1 Identify whether there are conditions attaching to the award and determine which of the following three categories they fall into:
   - market (vesting) conditions;
   - nonmarket (vesting) conditions;
   - nonvesting conditions.

2 Determine the grant-date fair value of the award, modified if necessary to reflect any market or nonvesting conditions identified.

3 At the end of each reporting period, true up the modified grant-date fair value in respect of the extent to which vesting conditions that are not market conditions, i.e. nonmarket vesting conditions, are expected to be achieved.

When the standard was first introduced, there was concern that it could result in substantial charges to the profit and loss account. Ultimately, however, charges have on average not been as large as originally expected. Accountants PricewaterhouseCoopers are quoted as saying in respect of FTSE 350 companies:[1] "At the median the expense charge represents approximately 2 per cent of profit before tax and before IFRS 2 charge."

The charge varies according to the extent to which entities use share-based payments to incentivize staff, and there is therefore some concentration of charges in particular industries. Accountants PricewaterhouseCoopers are further quoted as saying,[2] "FTSE 250 technology companies. . .incurred average reductions in profits of about 12 per cent to IFRS 2 charges."

CASE STUDY

Example of Service Period Conditions and Truing-Up of Profit and Loss Account Charges

Suppose that an entity with a December 31 year-end granted one share option to each of 150 staff on January 1, 2006, that the options had a grant-date fair value of $3, and that there was a three-year service period condition with no other vesting or nonvesting conditions.

At December 31, 2006, company management expected that two-thirds of the staff would still be employed by them on the vesting date of December 31, 2008, and, hence, that the award would vest for 100 of their staff. Thus, the expected cumulative charge in the profit and loss account over the three-year period would be 100 × $3 = $300.

This $300 would be spread over the three years and, hence, a charge of $100 would be made in the profit and loss account for the year to December 31, 2006.

At the following year-end, December 31, 2007, company management expected that 80% of the original 150 staff would still be employed on December 31, 2008, and hence that the award would vest for 120 staff. Thus, the expected cumulative charge over the three-year period would be "trued up" to 120 × $3 = $360.

This expected cumulative charge of $360 would be spread over the three years and, hence, the cumulative charge after two years would be $240. As $100 was charged to the profit and loss account in the year to December 2006, the balance of $140 would need to be charged to the profit and loss account in the year to December 2007.

Finally, at December 31, 2008, management found that exactly 100 of the original 150 staff were still employed. Hence, the award would have vested for 100 staff. Thus, the required cumulative charge for three years would have finally trued up to $300. However, $240 had been charged cumulatively in 2006 and 2007 and, hence, the remaining balance of $60 would have to be charged to the profit and loss account in 2008.

IDENTIFICATION OF CONDITIONS ATTACHING TO AWARDS

Conditions are classified as either vesting or nonvesting. Vesting conditions are defined as those that determine whether the company has received the services that entitle the employee to receive the award, and they can be either service period conditions or performance conditions. The vesting period is the period during which any specified vesting conditions are to be achieved. Service period conditions require the employee to work for the company for a specified period of time, often three years. Performance conditions require the employee to work for the company for a specified period of time and to achieve a specified performance target.

Performance conditions themselves may include what is known as a market condition. This is a condition that relates to the price of the underlying equity. For instance, share price and total stockholder return (TSR) targets are examples of market conditions. However, profit targets, earnings per share targets, sales targets, and service period conditions are not market conditions as they have no connection with the underlying share price. Generally, market conditions are attached only to awards to relatively senior members of staff, who are considered to be in a position to have some impact on a company's share price.

For instance, a directors' share plan might be granted to all executive directors that entitles them to the award if the share price increases by 50% over a three-year period. A more complex type of award might be that entitlement varies according to a sliding scale and is based on a comparison between the company's TSR over the vesting period and that of a group of, say, 11 peer group entities. If the company's TSR is in the top quartile of that of the peer group, a maximum level of award is made; if the TSR is in the second quartile, a sliding scale of say, 50%, 60%, or 70% of the maximum level of award is made, depending on the precise position within the quartile. If the company's TSR is in the bottom half for the peer group, no award will vest.

Nonvesting conditions are those that determine whether the employee receives the award but not whether he or she has provided the services that entitle him/her to the award. Thus, such conditions may be outside the control of the employee—for instance, they could take the form of an inflation or interest rate target for a country. Alternatively, they may be within the control of the employee but may not relate to whether the employee has provided the services required to earn the reward. For instance, there is a type of award that is common in the United Kingdom—the save as you earn (SAYE) scheme—under which the employee saves a certain amount from his or her salary each month over the vesting period, and he or she may subsequently use the cumulative amount saved to exercise options at the end of the vesting period. In some cases, employees stop saving during the vesting period and withdraw their cash saved to date, thereby losing their entitlement to exercise options at the end of the vesting period; however, this does not mean that the employee has not provided the required services during the vesting period.

Almost all awards include service period conditions. Some relatively straightforward awards do not include any other type of condition.

DETERMINATION OF THE GRANT-DATE FAIR VALUE OF THE AWARD

For awards of shares rather than share options, determination of grant-date fair value is easiest when the shares are listed and actively traded, and there are no market or nonvesting conditions. In such cases, the grant-date fair value is simply the quoted price of the equity, adjusted if appropriate for dividends that may be foregone during the vesting period.

Determination of grant-date fair value is complicated if there are market conditions. In such cases, the value of the shares awarded will be higher if the award vests than if the award does not vest, and this must be factored into determination of the fair value of the award at grant date. The method used most often in such cases to arrive at a value is Monte Carlo simulation, although its application requires a good understanding of statistical distributions.

If the award comprises unlisted shares, a valuation technique will need to be applied to value the unlisted shares at the grant date—again an adjustment will be required in respect of any anticipated dividends during the vesting period.

If share options rather than shares are the subject of the award, an option pricing model will be required to determine their fair value at grant date. IFRS 2 refers to the Black and Scholes model and the binomial model. Although these models are both based on the same underlying share price theory, the Black and Scholes model is formulaic, whereas the binomial model assumes that share prices follow a series of small steps. In practice, the Black and Scholes model tends to be easier to apply but is less flexible than the binomial model.

The inputs to each model are the same and comprise the following:

- share price on the grant date;
- exercise price of the option;
- life of the option;
- risk-free interest rate over the life of the option;
- dividends expected over the life of the option;
- expected volatility of the underlying share price over the life of the option.

The most difficult of these inputs to estimate is the expected volatility, which is a measure of the extent to which the company's share price is expected to go up or down in successive periods.

When the IASB first made clear that option pricing would be necessary in financial statements, there was considerable comment that this could cause difficulties. The *Financial Times* noted in an article in 2005:[3] "The details of IFRS require companies to use complex mathematical models to calculate the fair value of options."

TRUING UP THE PROFIT AND LOSS CHARGE IN RESPECT OF EXPECTED ACHIEVEMENT OF NONMARKET CONDITIONS

As noted earlier, the grant-date fair value is charged to the profit and loss account only to the extent that vesting conditions that are not market conditions are achieved over the vesting period. Thus, at the end of each reporting period after the grant date, an estimate is required of the extent to which any such conditions will be satisfied.

CONCLUSION

Although initially many preparers of accounts were concerned about the implications of the introduction of IFRS 2, most companies have now adjusted to the standard. Some companies have in-house staff able to perform the complex option pricing calculations, while others use external valuation consultants.

▸▸ MAKING IT HAPPEN

There are really two stages to reporting under IFRS 2.

1. The modified grant-date fair value of the award has to be determined.
2. This fair value has to be charged to the profit and loss account over the vesting period of the award according to the extent that nonmarket conditions are expected to be achieved.

The first step is the more complex and may require use of an option pricing model for share options or a valuation technique for unlisted shares. The second step is less complex but may require some clear thinking and a carefully constructed Excel spreadsheet, especially if there are significant numbers of staff involved or the actual and expected achievement of nonmarket vesting conditions to reflect.

"We didn't actually overspend our budget. The Health Commission allocation simply fell short of our expenditure." Keith Davis

  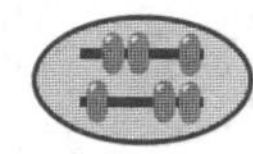   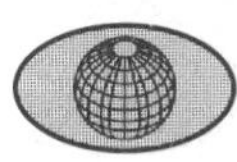   

MORE INFO

Websites:

Various option-pricing calculators are available online that use the Black and Scholes or binomial models. Websites that provide these include:

BloBek AB: www.blobek.com

FinCAD: www.fincad.com

Hoadley Trading & Investment Tools: www.hoadley.net/options/options.htm

There are many valuation advisers that will run any of these models, including valuation advisers from the Big Four accountants, smaller firms of accountants, and valuation consultants or actuaries.

Crystal Ball, add-on to MS Excel for Monte Carlo simulation: www.oracle.com/crystalball

NOTES

1 "Company profits hit by IFRS 2 rules." *Financial Times* (September 18, 2006).

2 *Ibid.*

3 "IT companies fear effect of IFRS stock option rules." *Financial Times* (August 11, 2005).

     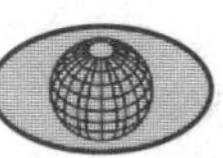   

Aligning the Internal Audit Function with Strategic Objectives by Ilias G. Basioudis

EXECUTIVE SUMMARY

- Due to high-profile scandals at the beginning of the century, regulators and the accounting profession worldwide have put forward a series of initiatives to repair the damage and restore faith in corporate governance.
- Globally, more companies are adopting corporate governance best practice.
- An independent internal audit function is widely recognized as an integral part of a company's strategic objectives, corporate governance, and risk management.
- The internal audit standards issued by the Institute of Internal Auditors serve as authoritative guidance for members of the internal audit profession.
- Internal audit's role is to evaluate the appropriateness and effectiveness of companies' systems and processes, and to identify and manage risks present in the normal course of conducting business activities.

INTRODUCTION

Given today's complex and rapidly changing management climate, companies must implement continuous improvements to achieve efficiency, and assure investors and other concerned parties of solid corporate governance.

The recent scandals at Enron, World-com, Parmalat, and others have raised the profile of corporate governance across the globe. Trust in the process of financial accounting, corporate governance, and auditing has been undermined by these high-profile corporate scandals. In response, regulators and the accounting profession worldwide have put forward a series of initiatives to repair the damage and restore faith in corporate governance. Furthermore, companies must continuously implement improvements to achieve effective and efficient management in order to assure the investors, other stakeholders, and concerned parties in general of its good and sound corporate governance. Globally, more companies, governments, states, and regulators are adopting corporate governance best practice, and placing more emphasis on improving corporate governance in companies, which in turn improves the confidence of investors and stakeholders in companies.

Worldwide legislative initiatives, of which the Sarbanes–Oxley Act (US) and Directive No. 8 (EU) are the most famous, make senior management responsible for establishing, evaluating, and assessing over time the effectiveness of risk management processes, systems of internal control, and corporate governance processes. In tandem, companies play a critical role in the national economy, or economies, in which they have activities. A country's competitiveness, wealth, efficiency, and high level of economic growth may depend on the competitive nature of its companies. There is no doubt that a transparent and reasonable corporate governance structure has a positive impact on a company.

The audit committee is a subcommittee of the board of directors, and is widely recognized as an integral part of a company's corporate governance, and, together with the internal audit function, they contribute towards the company implementing continuous improvements. In fact, one line of thought claims that the audit committee, especially in large organizations, could not possibly be effective without an efficient, effective, and independent-minded internal audit function.

As a result, the internal audit function has the potential to be one of the most influential and value-adding services available to a company's senior management and board of directors. Furthermore, with the growing focus on corporate governance issues, organizations are increasingly exploring the potential benefits to be gained from establishing an effective and efficient internal audit function. Company boards must identify the opportunities, risks, and exposures that can determine success or failure. The establishment of an internal audit function can become an integral part of overall strategy, and assist in achieving corporate objectives.

THE PURPOSE AND ROLE OF INTERNAL AUDITING

According to The Institute of Internal Auditors' (IIA) definition of internal auditing, the internal audit function should provide independent, thorough, timely, and objective results of quantitative and qualitative testing to senior management, and, in essence, help evaluate organizational risk management. Internal auditing assists public and private organizations to meet overall corporate objectives by establishing a systematic and disciplined approach to assessing, evaluating, and improving the quality and effectiveness of risk management processes, systems of internal control, and corporate governance processes. This systematic approach and analysis is implemented across all parts of an organization, and the internal auditor reports directly and independently to the most senior level of management. The role of the internal auditor, therefore, is to provide an overall assurance to management that all key risks within an organization are managed effectively, so that the organization can achieve its strategic objectives.

An internal audit function should be independent and unbiased, and hold a neutral position within an organization. The audit function looks beyond the narrow focus of financial statements and financial risks (although these risks are included in the remit of the internal auditor's job), and it may, for example, involve auditing reputational, operational, environmental, or strategic risks. Reputational risks could involve labor practices in host countries; operational risks include poor health and safety procedures; environmental risks might involve pollution generated by a factory; while a strategic risk might involve the board stretching company resources by producing too many products.

An internal audit function should have the ability itself to define the scope of internal audits (after consultation with the internal audit's primary stakeholders), the authority to obtain information and resources, and have an appropriate reporting structure to senior management. The internal audit team members do not test their own work, or the work of persons that they report to. Any actual or potential conflicts of interest that hinder an honest, independent, and unbiased assessment must be disclosed.

INTERNAL AUDIT STANDARDS

In order to operate an internal audit function that is objective, independent, effective, and useful to an organization, it is essential that the internal audit function complies with the International Standards for the Professional Practice of Internal Auditing, developed by the Institute of Internal Auditors. The International Standards are authoritative guidance for the internal audit profession, and are principles-focused. Implementation

"Corporate insiders...can seldom transform an organization beset by inertia." John P. Kotter

  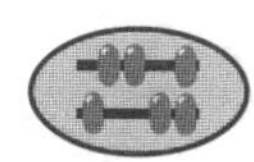   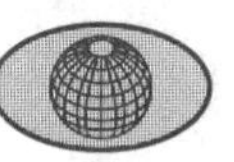   

standards refer to either assurance or consulting activities, and are embedded in the attribute and performance standards. Attribute standards refer to the composition of the audit department in terms of staff expertise and ongoing training, as well as independence and objectivity. Attribute standards also refer to the internal audit department's purpose, authority, and responsibility.

Performance standards refer to how the internal audit function should operate, and how the planning, scope, and reporting activities should be conducted and by whom. The performance standards reflect the purpose of the internal audit function in that they define the activities to be completed, which help make sure that the internal audit function is operating as designed for the benefit of the organization.

Another authoritative guidance issued by the IIA is the Code of Ethics. This is a statement of principles and expectations governing the behavior of individuals and organizations in the conduct of internal auditing, and provides a description of minimum requirements for conduct, and describes behavioral expectations rather than specific activities. The Code of Ethics refers to the integrity, objectivity, confidentiality, and competence of internal auditors.

DESIGNING A STRATEGICALLY FOCUSED INTERNAL AUDIT FUNCTION

How well an organization is able to recognize, understand, and manage its risks plays a critical part in the success, or failure, of the organization, and, consequently, the value it is able to deliver to customers, shareholders, and other stakeholders.

The internal audit function contributes to better overall governance when it operates within a strategic framework established by the audit committee and senior management. Once this strategic framework is in place, the corporation will be well positioned to define the mission, organizational structure, resource model, working practices, and communications protocols for the internal audit function.

Hence, when designing and implementing an effective internal audit function, the corporation's strategic objectives must be followed closely, and not vice versa. In other words, the internal audit's primary stakeholders must determine how the function will deliver the desired value, and what the specified outcomes expected of the new function are to be.

Common internal audit outcomes include:

- assessment of internal control effectiveness and efficiency;
- risk management and control assurance;
- regulatory and corporate compliance assurance;
- legislature readiness assessment and ongoing testing, such as Sarbanes-Oxley Act (US) and Directive No. 8 (EU);
- fostering awareness of risk and control across the organization;
- ability to respond to urgent events.

Once the function is established and the specific outcomes have been identified and defined, the internal audit's stakeholder expectations should be reassessed on a regular basis, and the mission for the internal audit function must be clearly articulated, so that the performance of the function can be evaluated on a regular basis. In addition, a formal mission statement for the internal audit function should be laid out by the head of the audit function, with the cooperation of senior management and the audit committee. The mission statement must also be aligned clearly and directly with stakeholder expectations and the internal audit's specified outcomes, as otherwise it would be of little value and possibly detrimental to achieving corporate strategic performance. Furthermore, the mission statement must be shared and communicated, to achieve full understanding and buy-in among key stakeholders and staff.

Once the mission statement is agreed, a formal strategic plan must be approved. This plan formally defines the value proposition of the new function, the customers it serves, and the value it will create now and into the future. The strategic plan serves as an operational manual of the new function, and as guidance on the key objectives and outcomes of the function, and how they will be achieved. The strategic plan sets a standard against which future decisions and results can be measured. Ideally, the plan should be reviewed at least annually, with changes considered and approved by all primary stakeholders as appropriate. For large companies, a full audit cycle of three years generally may seem appropriate; that is, the whole organization should be audited in an appropriate manner within three years. However, high risk areas should be audited at least annually.

Next, it is critical for the internal audit to develop a systematic process to analyze risk, and ensure that the audit plan is sufficiently broad in scope and executed in a timely manner. Internal auditors should segment the corporation into well-defined, reasonably sized, auditable units (often collectively called the "audit universe"), and then identify, determine, and prioritize/rank the inherent risks in each unit. Even a small business unit is likely to have a range of risks, some of which are higher priority than others. Inherent risks are those present in the normal course of conducting business activities. These include external risks such as changes to global, national, and economic climates, as well as technological, legal, social, and political changes. Inherent risks also include internal factors that warrant special attention, including changes in operating systems, new product launches, entry to new markets, management and organizational changes, and the expansion of foreign operations. Therefore, the risk assessment should evaluate current and prospective risks, particularly where new risks are emerging due to a change in the corporation's strategy or product mix.

The senior management and the audit committee must ensure the risk assessment executed by the audit function is not limited by reference to its own skill sets. In other words, a misalignment must be avoided between the technical competencies necessary to execute the audit plan and the skill sets resident in the internal audit function. An effective way to prioritize processes for audit purposes is to look at a matrix of probability of occurrence versus severity of loss for each of the processes, and develop a risk-based audit plan according to this classification.

Furthermore, other departments and functions within an organization gather intelligence and other important information, and senior management and the audit committee must ensure that the internal auditors are aware of these, and use them accordingly in determining and prioritizing risks. However, it is not necessary that the internal audit's independent view on risks coincide with other functions' perspectives in the organization, and this needs to be recognized and accepted. Senior management and the audit committee should also evaluate whether any "strong" executives or directors outside of the internal audit function, or "strong" business areas within the organization, have played a major role in shaping the internal audit's plan, and, if so, in what way. After the risk assessment is performed and the risk-based audit plan is drawn up, it is then important that timely and comprehensive coverage by the internal audit function is secured in order that the reliability and effectiveness of the internal controls in mitigating the significance and/or likelihood of a risk occurrence are considered. Another step to be taken after the assessment of risks and the audit

plan are completed is the creation of current and longer-term budgets for the internal audit function. Budgets must provide sufficient resources for internal auditors to deliver the developed risk-based audit plan, as well as the flexibility to respond to changing business needs.

Budgets should be aligned with corporate strategies, and look to internal audit benchmarks developed by the IIA or other third parties to establish a budgetary baseline as compared to similar internal audit functions within the same industry. The budget should be projected on a three-to-five-year horizon.

The fieldwork should begin as soon as possible, even prior to having all staffing and infrastructure in place. Key stakeholders in an organization want to see demonstrable progress promptly, so it is important to begin conducting the audits without delay, in order for the internal audit function to create immediate value. In a start-up internal audit department, the first three months are important in completing the audits of three to five known high-risk areas, such as general computer systems and controls, inventory management, and other business areas with known internal control problems and challenges.

> "Internal auditors perform their role by working with boards of directors, audit committees, and senior managers to help them understand the consequences of risks and ineffective processes to manage them."

At times, corporations are impatient for results and, thus, they may choose to outsource all, or nearly all, of the internal audit to a third-party specialist firm. This is in contrast to the IIA's recommendation, which states that internal audit activity should never be fully outsourced, but should be managed from within the organization. Outsourcing can have several advantages, including employing professionals who are more independent as they are not beholden to management for their compensation; access to resources necessary to complete specific high-risk audits; access to an array of technical, up-to-date expertise; and, possibly, knowledge transfer to the organization's employees as the function converts into a full in-house or co-sourced resource model.

On the other hand, full or near-full outsourcing brings with it specific governance challenges for senior management and the audit committee. These problems may include the following: limited communication and level of interaction between the organization and the third-party audit professionals; increased difficulty for the third-party auditors to gain sufficient standing in the corporation; outsourcing is significantly more expensive on a per-hour basis than undertaking the function in-house; and, the corporation has limited ability to influence audit team appointments when the internal audit function is fully outsourced. If some level of dependence on third-party firms for specialist audit skills is necessary for a corporation, then selective use of co-sourcing arrangements should be in place.

By revisiting stakeholder-specified outcomes and the internal audit function's mission statement developed earlier in the start-up process, a balanced staffing model must be adapted to each corporation's needs. Best practice requires corporations to staff their internal audit functions with long-tenured audit career professionals, as well as rotating talented executives from across the organization for two-or three-year rotations in internal audit. Furthermore, the necessary internal audit infrastructure and methodologies should be developed at the same time. These will greatly improve the efficiency, quality, and consistency of the internal audit process, and will provide assurance towards compliance with both the organization's methodologies, policies, and desired outcomes, and the standards developed by the IIA. Corporations should establish routine, robust, and frank lines of communication with their key internal audit professionals. It is imperative that an internal audit function communicates effectively and freely with all its internal stakeholders (and, primarily, with senior management and the audit committee). On a regular, if not daily, basis, the internal audit should seek opportunities for dialogue and communication with the corporation's senior management and the audit committee, creating a strong, clear connection between the internal audit mission and the corporation's strategic issues and risks.

In addition, the external auditors also have a role to play in an organization's corporate governance, and, as such, the audit committee should seek to establish and maintain good links and cooperation between internal and external audits.

Finally, it is important that the internal audit demonstrates results, and its reports are actionable and implemented. The reports should be generated and circulated in a timely fashion after the audit is complete, and senior management and the audit committee should ensure that an effective and timely follow-up to the reports has been implemented.

CONCLUSION

Organizations serve their stakeholders. Senior management's role is to ensure that the organization's resources are managed and applied effectively to meet objectives and responsibilities. A crucial part of this process of governance is the design of appropriate systems and processes in order for them to be able to identify and manage risks effectively and efficiently. Internal audit's role is to evaluate the appropriateness and effectiveness of those systems and processes, whether they are related to finance, IT, brand reputation, health and safety, legal and regulatory compliance, human resources, and/or major projects.

Internal auditors perform their role by working with boards of directors, audit committees, and senior managers to help them understand the consequences of risks and ineffective processes to manage them. They encourage and support managers to

▸▸ MAKING IT HAPPEN

Aligning the Internal Audit Function with Strategic Objectives

- Define stakeholder expectations.
- Articulate the mission, structure, resource model, working practices, and communication protocols for the internal audit function.
- Develop a formal strategic plan and assess company risks.
- Establish short- and long-term budgets for the internal audit function.
- Launch fieldwork quickly and, concurrently, assess any further needed skill sets.
- Develop internally or acquire (by outsourcing) enabling internal audit infrastructure, methodologies, and technologies.
- Determine clear lines of communication between the internal audit function and all company stakeholders (primarily, however, with senior management and the audit committee).
- Measure the results of the internal audit function.

"I have come to view strong corporate governance as indispensable to resilient and vibrant capital markets."
Arthur Levitt, Jr.

have appropriate systems in place. Internal auditors then report to senior management and the audit committee on how effectively these systems of control are operating. In such a way, the corporation succeeds in aligning the internal audit function with its strategic objectives.

▸▸ MORE INFO

Books:

Pickett, K. H. Spencer. *The Essential Handbook of Internal Auditing*. Chichester, UK: Wiley, 2005.

Pickett, K. H. Spencer. *Audit Planning: A Risk-Based Approach*. Hoboken, NJ: Wiley, 2006.

Standard:

"Auditing standard no. 5: An audit of internal control over financial reporting that is integrated with an audit of financial statements." Public Company Accounting Oversight Board (US), July 25, 2007. Online at: www.pcaobus.org/Standards/Standards_and_Related_Rules/Auditing_Standard_No.5.aspx

Websites:

Institute of Internal Auditors, UK and Ireland: www.iia.org.uk

Institute of Internal Auditors, US: www.theiia.org

"...without financial reporting premised on sound, honest numbers, capital markets will collapse upon themselves, suffocate and die." Arthur Levitt, Jr

  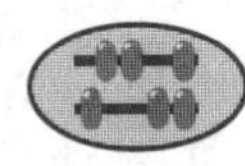   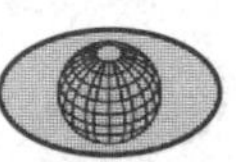   

The Assurance versus Consulting Debate: How Far Should Internal Audit Go?

by Michael Parkinson

EXECUTIVE SUMMARY

- The internal audit function of most organizations contains highly qualified and experienced individuals who, over a number of years, develop a detailed understanding of the organization's risks and operations.
- Thus, when a complex business risk issue emerges, the internal auditors may be well placed to help address it.
- Under these circumstances, does the short-term advantage of using the internal auditors as consultants to address the problem outweigh the longer-term cost of potentially compromising the level of assurance provided to the board and top management?

INTERNAL AUDIT

Internal auditors have described their discipline as an "assurance and consulting activity." Such a definition immediately begs the question: what is the difference, and what should the balance be?

Assurance has been variously defined. The dictionary definition, "a statement or indication that inspires confidence," differs quite considerably from the statement to be found in Assurance Standards (quoted here from the Australian Assurance Standards Board): "[the level of] satisfaction as to the reliability of information provided. The degree of satisfaction achieved is determined by the nature and extent of procedures performed by the auditor, the results of procedures and the objectivity of the evidence obtained." The high standards of evidence and the limited range of reports that flow from this latter definition are a long way from the resource commitment and the kind of reports that most managers want from their internal auditors. Most managers are seeking something more akin to the first definition, but they want to retain the reliability provided by objective, evidence-based reviews.

Consulting, on the other hand, is generally accepted as meaning the provision of professional advice. It implies an underlying professional competence that is used in making judgments about a given situation and relied on by the user of the consultant's advice.

While the description of internal auditing set out above is widely accepted, it is not the only definition to be found. Many internal auditors omit "consulting" from their scope, believing that providing advice impedes their objectivity. Others assess their value to the organization by the volume of consulting requests that they receive from management.

There are two risks to the organization reflected in this issue: excess levels of consulting may compromise the assurance that the organization requires, but prohibiting consulting work may prevent the organization from using the skills and experience of the internal auditors to solve business problems.

ASSURANCE AND CONSULTING

There is a range of internal and external customers for assurance provided by internal audit. The primary customer is, classically, the audit committee of the organization. While it is often the case that internal audit reports elsewhere in the organization, most internal auditors say that they serve the organization through the stewardship of its owners, the board, or its equivalent. (In mature organizations this is reflected in the internal auditor's reporting lines—to the audit committee for functional purposes and to the chief executive for administration.) The audit committee is the board's agent for assurance.

The Audit Committee has three basic sources for the assurance it needs: organizational management, who are resourced to run the organization have (as a group) full knowledge of its operations and have a responsibility to account for their activity; the internal auditor, who should be resourced to examine the critical risks of the organization and is independent of management operations; and external audit, who are resourced to examine the financial statements of the organization and offer an opinion that is independent of both management and internal audit.

The mutual independence of the three arms of assurance is critical. In some circumstances, it is appropriate for the audit committee to seek confirmation from all assurance sources before making critical decisions. Any activity that might impair independence or objectivity will limit the value of the assurance provided and therefore limit the confidence of the audit committee—consulting activity can impair objectivity.

Most of the risks of the organization are beyond the scope of the external auditor. The reliability of the critical control systems for these risks is attested only by management and internal audit. In these circumstances any impairment to internal audit objectivity can be a serious issue.

Assurance

While management might see assurance as little more than a statement of comfort, from the auditor's point of view there are three components: a model of what ought to occur (the normative model); an evidence-based assessment of what is occurring; and an analysis of the difference.

For the internal auditor, identifying the normative model is often an arguable process; it is only occasionally provided by an external authority, such as accounting standards. Frequently the organization has not specified the manner in which it should operate, or even the mechanisms by which performance will be measured. The internal auditor's first task might therefore be to construct a normative model for the organization.

Even when the organization has a model of operation, it is the internal auditor's duty to consider whether that model adequately addresses the organization's risks. Internal auditors are required to apply their own judgment about whether the level of risk being accepted by the organization is appropriate. The assurance that comes from this process has a level of consulting impicit within it.

Many internal audit service providers, perhaps driven by fear of an increasingly litigious society, are unwilling to provide any form of assurance at all. This seems to arise from confusion between "assurance" as used by internal auditors and what an external auditor means by the word.

Consulting

As soon as the internal auditors provide recommendations to management, they have stepped from the area of assurance into that of providing advice. This is, strictly, consulting. Some internal auditors

"My greatest strength as a consultant is to be ignorant and ask a few questions." Peter F. Drucker

     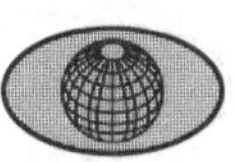   

feel uncomfortable about providing recommendations because they believe that it will impede their independence should they review the same area again. However, when a process fault has been properly analyzed by the internal auditor, the next step—suggesting a solution—is logical. Often the solution will be jointly developed by the internal auditor and responsible members of management, but it still is delivered with the internal auditor's (implicit) approval.

The internal audit function of many organizations is a significant pool of talented individuals. These individuals, by the nature of their roles, can develop a deep understanding of the organization. When the introduction of new systems or processes is contemplated, internal auditors are in a position to provide sound advice, based on their knowledge of the organization and their skill in the analysis of control systems. This type of consulting activity is an extension of the assurance process. While it is in relation to an activity that has not yet commenced, and is in the form of strong advice, the commentary of internal audit should still be regarded as recommendations and not as instructions. Some organizations ask their internal auditors to sign off or approve the implementation of systems or processes. This act moves the internal auditor from the role of adviser to the role of manager and is extremely dangerous; it makes the internal auditor partially responsible for the system or process.

The conduct of consulting activities by internal auditors is still constrained by the internal auditing standards. This has a number of direct benefits, as all the conclusions and observations made by the internal auditor will continue to be based on robust evidence.

These same standards that make the work of the internal auditor valuable also mean that internal audit consulting cannot be a private service. If the internal auditors observe control faults, or risks that would be reported if the project were an assurance review, they are required to report these issues (or make sure that they are reported) to responsible management and the audit committee.

An extreme form of consulting is where an internal auditor is seconded to a line area for a defined period. During this time they are not operating as an internal auditor and the removal of this individual from the internal audit function must be transparently reported. Such a situation encompasses many of the same issues that arise when an internal auditor is given a consulting function.

ASSURANCE VERSUS CONSULTING

The most commonly cited drawback of using internal audit as a consulting service is the threat of self-audit. That is, those who rely on the assurance process ask whether they will be able to get assurance from either the internal auditors or management if the auditors have consulted with management in the development of the process. If the internal audit function has been asked to sign off the process, then this may be a real problem, but it is arguable that the internal auditor would have the same problem if management were to implement an extensive set of recommendations as the result of an assurance review.

This risk, while real, can be managed. The mechanisms devised for internal auditors to manage the impairment that arises from having worked in an area under review can be applied to this situation. The obvious step is to use an alternative internal auditor—either another individual within the function or one obtained from outside the organization. When this cannot be done, the impairment must be declared in the assurance process and the internal audit project should be thoroughly reviewed by someone who was not involved in the original consulting exercise. In this case, although the independence of the internal auditor is impaired, an acceptable level of objectivity can be maintained.

There is a greater difficulty in relation to service providers. It might occur that one unit of a professional services firm is providing consulting services at the same time that another unit is assisting the internal audit function. In this case, the tight financial interdependence of the units means that one unit cannot give objective assurance in relation to the other. In this scenario it may also be difficult to enforce the requirement that internal auditors providing advice must report adverse control findings through the audit committee.

The second serious risk to consider is the impact of consulting activities on the assurance program. An internal audit program will have been approved by the audit committee to achieve a desired level of assurance. If the use of internal audit resources in consulting activities is to effectively reduce the level of assurance provided, the permission of the audit committee should be obtained.

Internal auditors have an underlying responsibility to protect the organization. This does not mean that internal audit has a primary responsibility to management, nor the obligation to respond to whatever management requires. On the other hand, the internal audit function cannot stand outside the organization when it has skills that can be effectively applied to resolving issues. There is a need for the internal auditor to use judgment.

Internal audit consulting can help management make decisions that have the best control consequences for the organization, but following internal audit advice does not mean that the consequences of decisions taken belong to the internal auditors. The consequences, good or bad, of implementing internal audit recommendations belong to management. Internal audit should not take credit for good outcomes, and management should not blame the auditors for the bad ones.

CONCLUSION: FINDING THE BALANCE

Assurance is perhaps directed at minimizing loss, and consulting at maximizing benefit. Both are valuable to an organization. However, consulting can be an excuse for putting internal audit in the position of management, or doing work that management should be doing. This must be avoided; internal audit should provide information, not take decisions.

Finding the right balance requires a conscious strategy. The audit committee must, on behalf of the organization, determine how much assurance is needed, plan it appropriately, and resource it.

The Audit Committee must determine the rules under which consulting will be offered and manage the amount of consulting that Internal Audit does. This involves requiring reports from all the work done by Internal Audit, whether it is consulting or assurance.

▸▸ MAKING IT HAPPEN

The audit committee must determine the rules under which consulting will be offered and manage the amount of consulting that internal audit does:

- Specify the assurance responsibilities of internal auditors in an assurance program;
- Specify, in the internal audit charter, the consulting services that internal auditors may provide, and the circumstances under which they may be provided;
- Require reports to the audit committee for all the work done by internal auditors, whether it is consulting or assurance;
- Monitor achievement of the assurance program.

"An individual without information cannot take responsibility; an individual who is given information cannot help but take responsibility." Wilbert Lee Gore

➤➤ MORE INFO

Books:

Fraser, John, and Hugh Lindsay. *20 Questions Directors Should Ask About Internal Audit*. Toronto, ON: Canadian Institute of Chartered Accountants, 2007.

Reding, K. F., P. J. Sobel, U. L. Anderson, M. J. Head, S. Ramamoorti, and M. Salamasick, with C. Riddle. *Internal Auditing: Assurance and Consulting Services*. Orlando, FL: IIA Research Foundation, 2007.

Reports:

International Auditing and Assurance Standards Board. "ISAE 3000: Assurance engagements other than audits or reviews of historical financial information." International Federation of Accountants, 2003. Online at: www.accountability21.net/uploadedFiles/Issues/ISAE_3000.pdf

Institute of Internal Auditors (IIA). "International standards for the professional practice of internal auditing." Orlando, FL: IIA. Online at: www.theiia.org/guidance/standards-and-guidance/ippf/standards

". . . the responsibility to minimise risks and prevent problems happening in a particular institution lies, first and foremost, with the people who run and own that institution . . . no government should ever be in the business of using public money to protect executives who make the wrong call or bad decisions." Alistair Darling

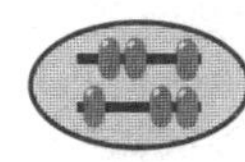

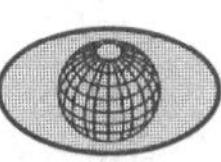

Best Practices in Risk-Based Internal Auditing by Sheryl Vacca

EXECUTIVE SUMMARY

- Agree on a common framework for the risk-based auditing and monitoring program.
- Assess risks across the enterprise and then prioritize them by looking at the likelihood of occurrence and impact for the organization.
- Develop a risk-based auditing and monitoring plan from the identified risk priorities.
- Execute a corrective action plan developed by management to mitigate risks and/or resolve risks.
- Assess the auditing and monitoring process for effectiveness.

GETTING STARTED

In designing risk-based auditing and monitoring activities, it is important that the internal auditor works closely with the organization's senior leadership and the board, or committee of the board, to gain a clear understanding of auditing and monitoring expectations and how these activities can be leveraged together to help minimize and mitigate risks for the organization. These discussions should also include leadership from the legal, compliance, and risk management functions, if they are not already a part of the senior leadership team.

This process should include performing periodic audits to determine compliance with respect to applicable regulatory and legal requirements, and to provide assurance that management controls are in place for the detection and/or prevention of noncompliant behavior. Additionally, risk-based auditing and monitoring should include mechanisms to determine that management has implemented corrective action through an ongoing performance management process to address any noncompliance.

Once the common framework for the risk-based auditing and monitoring program has been established, four key tasks must be performed:

1 Assessment and prioritization of risks, conducted enterprise-wide;
2 Development of a risk-based auditing and monitoring plan;
3 Execution of a corrective action plan developed by management to mitigate risks and/or resolve risks;
4 Periodic assessment of the overall process for effectiveness.

RISK ASSESSMENT

The Committee of Sponsoring Organizations of the Treadway Commission (COSO) helped to define "risk" as any event that can keep an organization from achieving its objectives.[1] According to the COSO model, risk is viewed in four major areas:

- operational (processes and procedures);
- financial (data rolling up to internal/external statements);
- regulatory (federal, state, local, organizational policy);
- reputation (institutional).

There are several ways in which risk assessments in these areas can be conducted. These include the use of:

- focus groups to assist in the identification of risks;
- interviews of key leadership and the board;
- surveys;
- reviews of previous audit findings, external audits conducted in the organization, and identifying what is occurring within the industry and the local market, etc.

Once risks have been identified, a prioritization process is needed to identify the likelihood of the risk occurring, the ability of management to mitigate risk (i.e. are there controls in place for risk, regardless of the likelihood of those risks of occurring?), and the impact of risk on the organization. Risk prioritization is an ongoing process and should include periodic reviews during the year to ensure that previous prioritization methods, when applied in real time, are still applicable for the risk.

It is important that senior leadership participate in, and agree with, the determination of the high-risk priorities for the audit and monitoring plan. This will ensure management buy-in and focus on risk priorities. Also, with managers involved at the development stage of the plan, they will be educated as to the type of activities being planned and the resources needed to conduct these activities. Hence, during the plan year, if there are changes, management will understand the need for additional resources or a change in focus in the plan as the business environment and priorities may change.

DEVELOPING THE PLAN

The International Standards for the Professional Practice of Internal Audit (IIA), Standard 2120 says "The internal audit activity must evaluate the effectiveness and contribute to the improvement of the risk management processes."[2]

This is done through the development and execution of the risk-based auditing and monitoring plan.

Risk assessments and prioritization are important elements in the development of your risk-based auditing and monitoring plan. Considerations related to the plan should also include:

- Review of other business areas in the organization which may be conducting an audit or monitoring activity in this area:
  - If so, could you leverage this resource for assistance in completing the stated activity, or utilize their activity and integrate the results into the overall plan?
- Resources available to implement plan:
  - Do you have the appropriate resources for the subject matter as needed within your department? (If not, is there subject matter expertise somewhere else in the organization?)
  - If subject matter requires outsourcing, budget considerations and overall risk priorities may need to be re-evaluated.
- Hours needed to complete the plan
- Projected timeframes
- Defined auditing or monitoring activities and determination as to whether they are outcomes or process oriented
- Flexibility incorporated into the plan to address changes in risk priorities and possibly unplanned compliance risks/crises which may need an immediate audit or monitoring to occur.

IIA Standard 2120.A1 identifies the focus of the risk assessment process: "The internal audit activity must evaluate risk exposures related to the organization's governance, operations, and information systems regarding the:

- Reliability and integrity of financial and operational information.
- Effectiveness and efficiency of operations.
- Safeguarding of assets;

"It's all papers and forms, the entire Civil Service is like a fortress made of papers, forms, and red tape."
Aleksandr Nikolayevich Ostrovsky

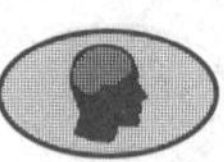

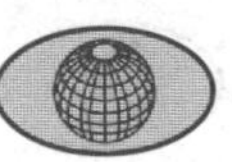

- Compliance with laws, regulations, and contracts.

The process of risk assessment continues through the execution of the plan where the engagement objectives would reflect the results of the risk assessment. Risk-based auditing and monitoring is ongoing and dynamic with the needs of the organization.

EXECUTION OF THE PLAN—MAKING IT HAPPEN

Each activity should have a defined framework which will provide management with an understanding of the overall expectations and approach as you execute the plan. The framework for your activities should include the following actions:

- Set the purpose and goal for the activity (audit or monitoring):
  - Identify the scope from the purpose or goal, but make sure that it is objective, measurable, and concise.
  - Before conducting activities in high-risk priority areas, it is important to consider whether legal advice may be needed in establishing the approach to the activity.
- Conduct initial discussion with the business area for input related to audit attributes, timing, and process:
  - Concurrent vs retrospective status may be determined at this point. (Concurrent is "real time" and before the end point of what you are looking at has occurred. Retrospective is after the end point has occurred, i.e. the claim has been submitted or the research has concluded, etc. Milestones should be determined for rationale as to how far back to go, for example, new law, new system, etc.)
- Finalize the approach and attributes:
  - Sampling methodology will be determined largely by the scope (purpose and goal) of your activity. For example, the sample used in self reporting a risk area to an outside enforcement agency may be predetermined by the precedent that the enforcement agency has set in industry; to determine if education is needed in a risk area, a small sample only may be needed, etc.
  - Consider the audience frame of reference that will receive the results of activity, and then develop an appropriate format for reporting.
- Conduct the activity.
- Identify preliminary findings and observations.
- Provide an opportunity for findings and observations to be validated by the business area.
- Finalize the report.
- Identify processes for the follow-up after management has taken corrective action related to activity findings and observations.
- Data collection and tracking are critical because they provide trend analysis and measurement of progress.
- Determine the key points of activity that may be provided to leadership and/or in reporting to the board.

The overall process of developing the audit and monitoring plan should be documented. This would include a description of

Figure 1. Benefits of an effectively executed risk-based auditing and monitoring plan

NO BIG SURPRISES
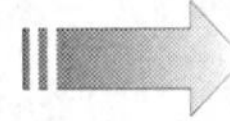

Early warning systems

- Systematically identify, assess, and prioritize risks.
- Avoid unrewarded risks and protect assets in place.

Integrated infrastructure

- Ensure that bad news travels fast internally first Ñhave early warning systems in place.
- Prevent and respond rapidly to potential catastrophic failures.
- Improve ability to anticipate and prepare for change.
- Establish a risk-based culture.
- Provide assurance that key risks and exposures are understood and mitigated.

NO BIG MISSED OPPORTUNITIES

Comprehensive policies and procedures

- Seek growth, but ensure that strategic and tactical risks are mitigated.
- Maximize chances of success of achieving business plan goals.
- Accelerate ability to respond to change and opportunities.

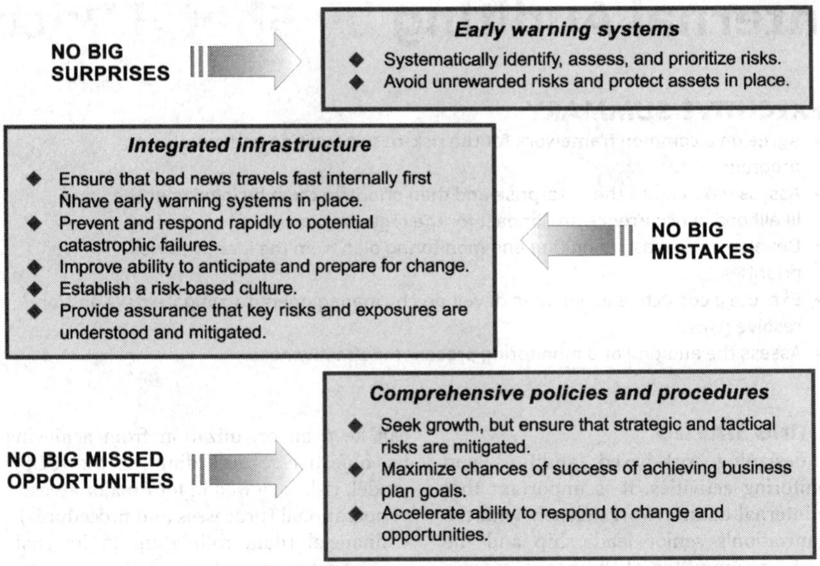

CASE STUDY

Scenario: An organization with multiple businesses in several geographic locations is conducting an enterprise-wide risk assessment. It is noted during the risk assessment that, due to recent financial losses, the organization is going through a consolidation of business units and reduction in force. This has been identified as a high-risk priority area for the auditing and monitoring plan for the next fiscal year.

In planning the audit on the risk area of business consolidation, the following considerations should be included:

- The business consolidation could be impacting the organization in various ways—customer base loss, reduced finances, loss of reputation, loss of workforce resulting in loss of controls, etc.
- The risk-based audit will focus on areas of greatest impact: loss of controls in financial areas due to the reduction in workforce.
- The timing of the audit will be negotiated to bring the most value to the organization. This might involve having a two-part audit. Part I could take place after the business consolidation and reduction in workforce have occurred. This would include assessing the consolidated business unit to determine if there are any gaps in the financial controls. For instance, segregation of duties is commonly found in situations with loss of people and consolidation of functions. Any gaps identified would become actions for management to correct before the Part II audit took place.
- Management may also want to set up its own monitoring system to ensure that its corrective actions have resolved any of the gaps identified.
- Part II of the audit would occur after a negotiated period of time with management and would allow the corrective actions to have been in place long enough for their effectiveness to be determined.

The overall purpose of this type of risk-based auditing is to work with management in "real time," to add value to the organization in regard to its strategic and best business interest, and to provide input on processes before they become "fixed." After management believes it has the "fixes" in place, then the second part of the audit will help to provide assurances that the risks identified are no longer risks and that no new gaps or lack of controls have developed around the process of business consolidation and reduction in workforce.

"Too many diversified companies strangle individual businesses with red tape in the form of financial and bureaucratic guidelines." Kenichi Ohmae

  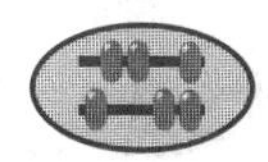 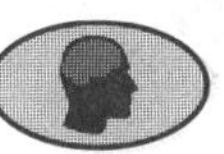  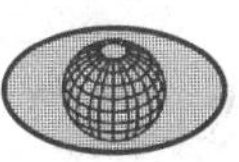 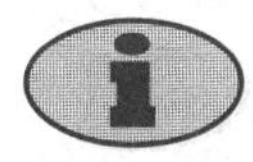  

how the risk assessment was conducted and the methodology for prioritization of risks. Working papers to support the audit findings, reports, and corrective action plans should be documented and filed appropriately. Prior to the audit activity, be sure to define and document what should be considered as part of the working papers.

At the end of each plan year, it is important to conduct an evaluation of the overall effectiveness of the plan. Questions to consider may include:

- Was the plan fully executed?
- Were appropriate resources utilized for the plan's execution?
- Were the activities conducted in a timely manner?
- Did the plan "make a difference" in regard to the organization's strategy and business?
- Did the plan reach the goal of detecting, deterring, and/or preventing compliance research risks from occurring?

Annual evaluations may be conducted through self reviews or independently of the internal audit function by a third party, i.e. peer review conducted with auditors from other organizations, Quality Assessment Review conducted according to IIA standards (every 5 years), etc. However, while self reviews are less resource intensive, it is recommended that a independent review be conducted at least every other year to assess the effectiveness of your auditing and monitoring efforts. Figure 1 helps to identify the benefits of an effectively executed risk-based auditing and monitoring plan.

In summary, effectiveness in the development and execution of the risk-based audit and monitoring plan will be determined by the integrity and characteristics of the overall audit and monitoring process. Effective audit and monitoring activities will assist in the identification of weaknesses in controls, management's action to correct those weaknesses, and follow-up to ensure that timely mechanisms have been put in place to strengthen controls for mitigating the business risks. Additionally, risks will be detected, deterred and/or prevented with effective auditing and monitoring activities.

▸▸ MAKING IT HAPPEN

The development of an effective risk-based auditing and monitoring program includes several key elements:

1. Performing an enterprise-wide risk assessment that includes operational, financial, regulatory, and reputational risk (1-IIA).
2. Prioritizing risks identified through measures such as likelihood and impact for the organization.
3. Developing a risk-based auditing and monitoring plan from the identified risk priorities.
4. Determining that corrective action plans which have been developed by management to mitigate priority risks or ensure controls are in place to lower the risk level for the organization.
5. Conducting follow-up activities that validate, monitor, or audit corrective actions to mitigate and/or resolve the identified risks.
6. Re-evaluating risks on an annual basis through a risk assessment process to ensure that the priority risks of the organization have been addressed.
7. Conducting a periodic third-party review of risk-based auditing and monitoring plan to assess whether:
   - processes are in place to identify risks;
   - appropriate resources are utilized to audit and/or monitor risks;
   - a commitment to reinforcing the need for management to execute plans to mitigate risks is demonstrated by the board and senior management.

▸▸ MORE INFO

Websites:

Federal Sentencing Guidelines, Chapter 8. US Sentencing Commission's webpage's at www.ussc.gov/general.htm (history and overview of the guidelines) and www.ussc.gov/GUIDELIN.HTM (guidelines and manuals). Chapter 8's provisions can be found at www.ussc.gov/2004guid/tabconchapt8.htm

General Accounting Office (GAO): www.gao.gov

Institute of Internal Auditors www.theiia.org

Public Company Accounting Oversight Board (PCAOB): www.pcaobus.org

Sarbanes–Oxley Act 2002: www.soxlaw.com

Securities and Exchange Commission: www.sec.gov

Society of Corporate Compliance and Ethics (SCCE): www.corporatecompliance.org

NOTES

1 The Committee of Sponsoring Organizations of the Treadway Commission. *Enterprise Risk Management Framework: Draft (2003)*. Published in 2004 as *Enterprise Risk Management—Integrated Framework* and available from www.coso.org

2 Institute of Internal Auditors. Professional Practice Standards 2120-Risk Management and Section A1., January, 2009.

  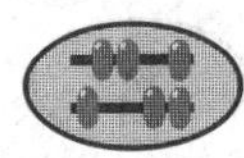 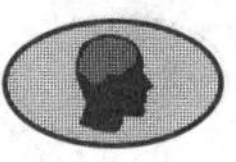  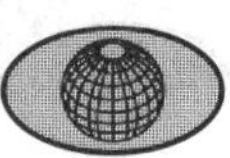   

Classification and Treatment of Leases by Roger Lister

EXECUTIVE SUMMARY

- Accounting bodies, both international and national, require leases to be classified in terms of economic substance rather than legal form.
- Current regulation distinguishes a finance lease from an operating lease. If a lease transfers the risks and rewards of an asset to the lessee, it is a finance lease. Otherwise, the lease is an operating lease. A finance lease appears in the balance sheet; an operating lease may remain off the balance sheet.
- New international and national accounting standards will almost certainly remove the distinction. Except for very short leases, all will go on the balance sheet.
- The change will eliminate a sometimes artificial distinction, but higher reported leverage may have ill effects. Management may avoid otherwise desirable leasing to protect the leverage ratio. Bond covenants may be breached and need to be renegotiated. There may be an incentive to circumvent the standard by taking out a succession of short but renewable leases.
- Tax allowances emphasize legal form, but tax in its detail tends to follow accounting standards. Companies will therefore need to consider the tax impact of the new standard as it solidifies.
- Anti-avoidance tax legislation proliferates daily and will probably increase as governments seek every opportunity to raise revenue in straitened times. At worst, a measure will be retrospective. Planners should monitor discussion and attempt the difficult task of identifying and anticipating the most likely changes, including anti-avoidance legislation.

INTRODUCTION

Lease accounting is nearer than ever to its goal of reporting substance rather than form. International regulators and their national counterparts agree that right-to-use rather than legal title should determine the classification and treatment of leases. The choice is essentially between disclosing a lease as a financial instrument on the balance sheet or as an operating lease on the income statement.

Financial reporting of leases is addressed in the International Accounting Standards Board's International Accounting Standard IAS 17. The International Accounting Standards Board (IASB) benefits from the participation of many countries, including the US Financial Accounting Standards Board (FASB).

Why lease? Management needs to test conventional answers carefully since some have limited relevance, while others are frankly contestable. Leasing is sometimes promoted for its small initial outlay, even as 100% financing. This ignores the fact that a rational lessor like a lender will seek a cushion of equity to protect the finance provided. A more rational answer is that leasing is advantageous if it provides more finance than the borrowing which it displaces. Management is essentially asking how far, for their company, is leasing a substitute for borrowing and how far a complement. Research suggests that leasing tends to be a substitute for borrowing for larger firms and a valuable complement to borrowing for small and medium enterprises (SMEs). Leasing can help to overcome SMEs' difficulty in conveying their quality to would-be financiers.

CLASSIFICATION

Currently, the essential distinction is between the finance and the operating lease, but it is virtually certain that under the revised international financial reporting standard due about 2011 this distinction will disappear. The new classification will equate finance and operating leases. All but the shortest contracts will be treated like finance leases. New national standards will probably anticipate, accompany, or follow the new international standard.

A finance lease transfers substantially all the risks and rewards of asset ownership to the lessee and features accordingly in the balance sheet. An operating lease remains off balance sheet. If a lease satisfies any one or more of certain criteria, then it may be a finance lease. These are:

- Ownership of the asset is transferred to the lessee at the end of the lease term;
- The lease contains a bargain purchase option to buy the equipment at less than fair market value;
- The lease term is for the major part of the economic life of the asset even if title is not transferred;
- At the inception of the lease, the present value of the minimum lease payments amounts at least substantially to all of the fair value of the leased asset;
- The leased assets are of a specialized nature such that only the lessee can use them without major modification;
- Any cancellation losses are borne by the lessee;
- The lessee takes gains and losses on the asset's residual value;
- The lessee can rent for a secondary period for less than the market rent.

The international standard, unlike some national standards, does not focus on a numerical percentage of fair asset value (typically 90%).

"Asset" means the lower of the fair value and the present value of the minimum lease payments (MLP). MLP are discounted at the interest rate implicit in the lease if practicable, or else at the enterprise's incremental borrowing rate. Depreciation has to be consistent with that for similar owned assets. If ultimate ownership is unlikely, the asset has to be depreciated over the shorter of the lease term and the life of the asset. The income statement includes depreciation and the finance charge. Rental payments are recognized as part finance charge and part repayment of the liability to the lessor. Repayments of the obligation reduce the liability in the balance sheet.

In the case of operating leases, periodic rentals are charged in total against income on a straight-line basis, unless another systematic basis is more representative of the time pattern of the user's benefit. Any outstanding rentals are reported in the balance sheet, distinguishing maturities and categories of activity.

> "Why lease? Management needs to test conventional answers carefully since some have limited relevance, while others are frankly contestable."

IAS 17 is further explained in SIC 15, SIC 27 and IFRIC 4 and 12. SIC 15 states that any incentives such as rent-free periods or contributions by the lessor to the lessee's relocation costs should be reported as a reduction of lease income or lease expense. IFRIC (a standard issued post 2001) 4 and 12 consider cases where a right to use, while

"You don't own me." Bette Midler

not a lease in form, may amount to a lease for financial reporting purposes. Examples are outsourcing arrangements, telecommunication contracts that provide rights to capacity, and take-or-pay and similar contracts in which purchasers must make specified payments regardless of whether they take delivery of the contracted products or services.

Current classification and treatment of leasing has already brought financial reporting closer to economic reality, and the new standard will continue this progress. It will break down deceptive barriers between economically similar transactions. However, management needs to recognize potentially perverse effects. Reported leverage will increase if finance and operating leases are both on the balance sheet, possibly causing management to avoid otherwise beneficial leases. Bond covenants may be nominally breached and have to be renegotiated. Without suitable safeguards, companies may circumvent the standard by taking out short but renewable leases that will in practice span an asset's useful life.

In the case of leveraged leasing (not under discussion here), the lessee gains access to the lessor's leveraged capital. The lessor owns the asset but typically provides only some 25% of capital while garnering any tax allowance in full. Institutional lenders provide the balance of the purchase price to the lessor on a non-recourse basis.

An extract from Christian Dior's 2007 accounts illustrates how lease classification appears in practice:"In addition to leasing its stores, the Group also finances some of its equipment through long term operating leases. Some fixed assets and equipment were also purchased or refinanced under finance leases."

SALE AND LEASEBACK

Extra financial reporting issues arise with sale and leaseback. An owner selling and leasing back an asset should in the first instance revise the recorded value of the asset to its economic value. This avoids distortion of the sale and leaseback transactions.

If the asset is sold at fair value and made the subject of an operating lease, any profit belongs in the year's income statement. If the sale is above fair value, the purchaser will charge higher rentals. In this case, the seller's profit on sale must be set against the high rentals by annual installments over the term of the lease or until the time of any rent review if sooner. If the asset is sold at a loss, the loss must be recognized immediately unless the purchaser compensates by below-market rentals, in which case the loss is amortized over the period of use. If the asset is sold at fair value and made the subject of a finance lease, any excess of proceeds over recorded value is amortized over the term of the lease.

CASE STUDY

Coleman

The British Tax Court imposed the strong proof rule on the taxpayer to show that it was entitled to depreciation deductions on a double-dip leasing transaction, even though the transaction was structured to also obtain a UK tax advantage. Coleman involved a cross-border leasing transaction, in which the parties sought to obtain depreciation deductions on certain leased computer equipment for both UK and US tax purposes. The lease and title to the computer equipment were transferred by a dealer to UK lenders, who were able to write off the computers in one year under UK tax law. The dealer retained an interest in the residual of the lease and (to simplify matters greatly) sold a portion of the residual interest to the US taxpayers. These persons claimed to be the owners of the leased computer equipment for US tax purposes and depreciated their bases in the equipment for US tax purposes. The court held that the record failed, under the strong proof standard, to sustain the petitioners' position that they were the owners of the computer equipment, and that the form of the transaction as a financing should be disregarded.

TAX

Significant tax changes will come with new accounting standards and increasing anti-avoidance legislation. Legislators and avoiders dodge and weave around pitfalls and opportunities. Management has to monitor and even try to influence discussion and hope that anti-avoidance provisions will not be retrospective.

In the United Kingdom, current detailed regulations[1] as administered by HM Revenue and Customs tend to look to the accounting standards subject to the fundamental difference that the tax definition of finance lease is based on legal title. Thus, a taxable lessor can still pass the benefits of capital allowances to a nontaxable lessee in the form of reduced rentals. Other points include:

- Finance charges are deductible according to any method that gives the lessor a constant return on rentals outstanding.
- If premature termination occurs, individual circumstances will determine whether any payment is an adjustment of past rentals (revenue expenditure) or a penal charge (capital expenditure).
- Any rebate or further rental arising on the substitution of one finance lease for another in respect of the same asset will also be a revenue item for tax purposes. Where an operating lease becomes a finance lease any transitional payment is treated as a revenue item.
- Rentals on operating leases are tax-deductible.

The above general rules are subject to a continuing stream of anti-avoidance legislation. For example, on November 13, 2008, the UK government announced that it would take action, effective from that date, to prevent a loss of tax on transactions involving the leasing of plant or machinery under long funding leases, on the sale of a company that is an intermediate lessor of plant or machinery, and on rents payable on long funding leases of films.

Anti-avoidance legislation has countered many traditional tax benefits of leasing such as deferral of income, conversion of income into capital, acceleration of capital allowances, and techniques connected with sales and leasebacks. The cat and mouse anti-avoidance game becomes particularly frenetic when it crosses borders. This arises with double-dip leasing, when differing tax treatment of lessor and lessee under different jurisdictions generates allowances in each country. Anti-avoidance has closed off many such opportunities, and the taxpayer's defeat in the Coleman case (see Case Study) illustrates both the complexity of the taxpayer's attempt and the taxpayer's vulnerability.[2]

OPEN ISSUES

Much will be resolved when the new international standards appear, but in the meantime companies should monitor the IASB's discussions of open issues. Sensitive areas under discussion include the following.

Right of Use

The Board favored reporting the lessee's right of use during the term and the accompanying obligation to make specified payments. This seemingly innocuous definition amounts to a preference for a model that does not take account of an obligation to return the physical item. This may be insignificant for a long lease, but is material for a shorter lease.

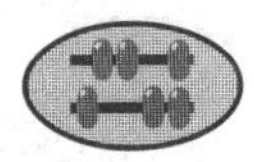

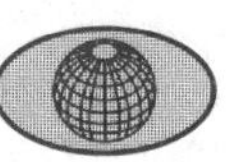

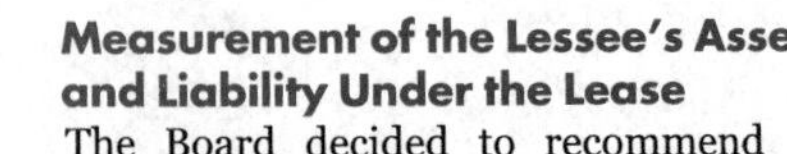

Measurement of the Lessee's Asset and Liability Under the Lease

The Board decided to recommend that right to use should be initially measured at the present value of the "expected lease payments." They noted that these may differ from minimum lease payments if they include contingent rentals. The discount rate used in calculating the expected lease payments should be the secured incremental borrowing rate.

Options to Extend or Terminate a Lease

The Board decided to propose that options to extend or terminate the lease should be based on an assessment of the lease term, but it did not express a preference among the various frameworks for assessment, for example, a probability-weighted approach, or as to whether the estimated lease term should be trued up on a regular basis. There was a consensus that all contractual, non-contractual, financial, and business factors should be taken into consideration when determining the lease term.

Purchase Option

The Board favored inclusion of the purchase option if exercise of the option was the most likely outcome.

Residual Value Guarantee

The Board decided to propose that the lessee's liabilities should include the obligation to make payments under a residual value guarantee.

▸▸ MAKING IT HAPPEN

Classification and treatment should not dominate the leasing decision. They should be integrated with the decision to achieve an optimal capital structure, including optimal financial mobility. Six important lessons emerge from the present review:

- It remains important to choose between an operating and finance lease contract, but discussions regarding the revised international standard and evolving national standards must be carefully monitored to see how best to contract the lease.
- Opportunities should be taken to contribute to the discussions, especially if there is a chance to head off a result that will harm the company's interests.
- The tax impact of a leasing decision under current provisions is crucially important.
- Probable changes of tax treatment in response to the new standard must be monitored.
- Anti-avoidance legislation must be anticipated as far as possible—the content of tax cases may provide a first indication.

▸▸ MORE INFO

Books:

Epstein, Barry J., Ralph Nach, and Steven M. Bragg. *GAAP 2009*. 6th ed. Hoboken, NJ: Wiley, 2008.

International Accounting Standards Board. *International Financial Reporting Standards IFRS 2008: Including International Accounting Standards (IASs) and Interpretations as approved at 1 January 2008*. London: IASB, 2008.

Articles:

Beattie, V., A. Goodacre, and S. J. Thomson. "International lease-accounting reform and economic consequences: The views of U.K. users and preparers." *International Journal of Accounting* 41:1 (2006): 75–103.

Frecka, T. J. "Ethical issues in financial reporting: Is intentional structuring of lease contracts to avoid capitalization unethical?" *Journal of Business Ethics* 80:1 (2008): 45–59.

Henry, E., O. J. Holzmann, and Y. Yang. "Tracking the lease accounting project." *Journal of Corporate Accounting and Finance* 19:1 (2007): 73–6.

Websites:

Equipment Leasing and Finance Association (ELFA): www.elfaonline.org

Finance and Leasing Association (FLA): www.fla.org.uk

HM Revenue and Customs' information about taxation of leases (UK): www.hmrc.gov.uk/manuals/bimmanual/bim61101.htm

International Accounting Standards Board (IASB): www.iasb.org.uk

International Finance and Leasing Association (IFLA): www.ifla.com

QFINANCE

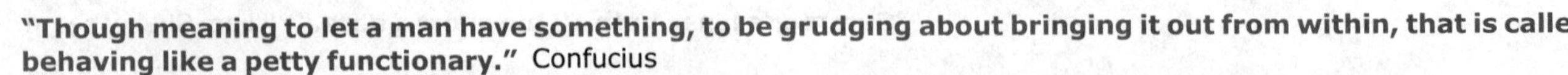
"Though meaning to let a man have something, to be grudging about bringing it out from within, that is called behaving like a petty functionary." Confucius

  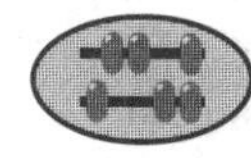 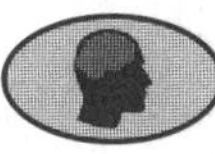  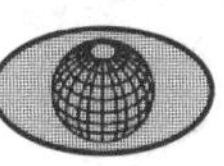   

Costs and Benefits of Accounting-based Regulation in Emerging Capital Markets by Wang Jiwei

EXECUTIVE SUMMARY

- Securities regulation is vital to the development of an efficient capital market.
- Accounting-based regulation embeds accounting numbers as a threshold.
- There are both benefits and costs to accounting-based regulation.
- The costs of accounting-based regulation include opportunistic behavior by management to manipulate accounting numbers, and capital resource misallocation.
- The benefits of accounting-based regulation include the potential to mitigate resource misallocation by preventing poorly performing firms from entering the market and to avoid "adverse selection problems" by managers.
- Recent Chinese regulations on rights offerings and seasoned equity offerings shed light on the costs and benefits of accounting-based regulation in emerging capital markets.

INTRODUCTION

One of the most controversial debates in economic policy is: Should governments intervene in or regulate capital markets? Pure free-marketeers believe that the "invisible hand" can correct all market failures. However, advocates of intervention characterize the regulation process as one in which government intervention corrects market failures and maximizes social welfare. In the case of regulating stock issuance after initial public offerings (IPO), governments in many countries adopt a "disclosure-based approach" with limited government regulation and intervention. No official approval is needed to issue additional shares as long as companies provide adequate disclosure. There is no accounting-based profitability threshold that the company has to meet before making the stock issuance. The rationale is that such thresholds create additional costs for investors.

COSTS OF ACCOUNTING-BASED REGULATION

In a world without transaction costs, parties will naturally achieve an efficient outcome without any form of intervention. Regulation, then, is only bound to worsen the outcome, at the very least by imposing undue costs. Under regulation, governments must devote tremendous resources of money and time to screen new entrants, thus reducing social welfare. The money and time could have been allocated to other government projects that would enhance social welfare. Applicants also incur costs related to compliance. When an accounting-based threshold is embedded in a regulation, there may be agency problems for investors, as explained in the following paragraph.

Regulations based on accounting numbers, such as a minimum return on equity (ROE) threshold, can provide incentives for contracting parties to manipulate accounting data opportunistically to meet these thresholds. The reason for corporate managers to commit this opportunistic behavior is that they believe it will be costly for regulators to "undo" such behavior. If a manager opportunistically manipulates accounting data to meet criteria for issuing additional shares to the public, this action will trigger inefficient allocation of capital resources and hence diminish the welfare of investors.

BENEFITS OF ACCOUNTING-BASED REGULATION

In efficient capital markets, investors are sophisticated enough to weed out poorly performing firms. Hence there is no need for accounting-based regulations to gauge the performance of new entrants. However, situations in emerging markets may be different. In these emerging market environments, accounting-based regulation may bring benefits that exceed the costs. The following three points explain why accounting-based regulations may be needed in emerging markets.

- Emerging markets are typically portrayed as inefficient. At the early stage of capital market development, investors do not have enough sophistication to screen the "good eggs" and "bad eggs" in the market.
- Firms can manipulate the selling price of stocks at a big discount from the ongoing price. This large discount forces existing shareholders to purchase additional shares irrespective of a firm's performance, as otherwise their ownership will be diluted.
- There are severe "adverse selection problems" in emerging markets, especially by comparison to developed markets. That is managers, as insiders, know more than the market about the true value of the firm and have an incentive to issue additional shares when stock prices are overvalued.

These market failures cannot be automatically corrected by the market because the market *per se* is inefficient. Government should act as a "helping hand" and intervene by imposing accounting-based regulation. This regulation is used to help investors to distinguish good and bad firms on the market and can minimize adverse selection by managers. These benefits may exceed the costs associated with the misallocation of capital resources.

Figure 1. The distributions of ROEs in China over two periods in 1992–98

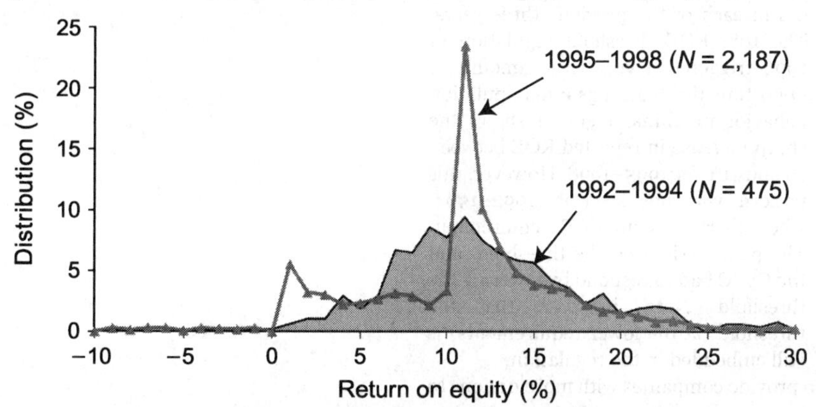

"Letting a hundred flowers blossom and a hundred schools of thought contend is the policy for promoting the progress of the arts and the sciences and a flourishing culture in our land." Mao Zedong

  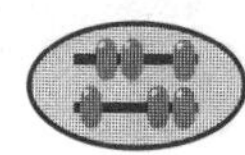 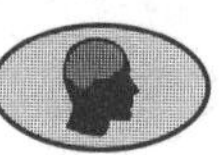  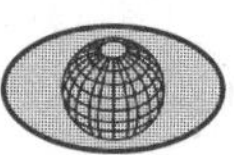   

CASE STUDY

Accounting-Based Regulations in China

The Chinese government has used accounting-based regulation to regulate share issuance by listed companies. China's experience will be considered here because it sheds light on the costs and benefits of accounting-based regulation in emerging capital markets.

In the early 1990s, China's listed companies could only issue additional shares through preemptive rights offered to existing shareholders. Due to the lack of other means of raising capital and the Chinese investing public's insatiable demand for stocks in the early 1990s, rights offerings were excessively abused by listed companies. To curb this activity, the China Securities Regulatory Commission (CSRC) issued a series of regulations to restrict rights issues after November 1993. The following are the major milestones of China's regulations on rights offerings.

- November 1993: Listed companies were allowed to issue rights to existing shareholders if they had been profitable in the previous two years.
- September 1994: The CSRC required listed companies that wished to issue additional shares to have at least three years' profits and a minimum three-year *average* return on equity of 10%. The CSRC found that rights offerings were abused by listed companies in the way they reported profits. In fact it is very simple for companies to manipulate accounting numbers to report a profit.
- January 1996: The CSRC increased the threshold to a minimum ROE of 10% in *each* of the previous three years. Within about 18 months the CSRC found that the accounting-based regulation of 1994 was still not stringent enough to curb the opportunistic behavior of listed companies.
- March 1999: The CSRC lowered the threshold to a minimum three-year average ROE of 10% and a minimum ROE of 6% in each of the previous three years. The 10% ROE threshold regulation of 1996 triggered a very large amount of opportunistic earnings manipulation behavior in China. Figure 1 shows the sharp increase in reported ROE between 10 and 11% for 1995–1998. However, this pattern was not seen in 1992–1994, when there was no ROE requirement. The public criticized the threshold, and the CSRC had to respond by lowering the threshold. Note, however, that the threshold (at the lower requirements) is still embedded in the regulation.

To provide companies with more options to raise additional capital, the CSRC allowed large-scale seasoned equity offerings (SEO) in May 2000 by issuing regulations that were similar to the rights offering regulations of 1993. The CSRC believed that China's capital market had become more efficient during the first seven years and would be able to correct market failures automatically. This regulation did not impose a strict profitability threshold, and any company with profits in the previous three years could apply to the CSRC for SEO authorization. Below we list the major milestones in China's regulations on seasoned equity offerings—it will be seen that they are surprisingly similar to the regulations for rights offerings.

- May 2000: The CSRC issued a regulation that allowed listed companies with three years' profits to apply to the CSRC to conduct seasoned equity offerings.
- March 2001: The CSRC increased the threshold to a three-year average ROE of 6%. This was not a definitive threshold in that companies that did not meet it could qualify under certain conditions—for example, if the management and underwriter provided detailed evidence of the healthy state of the company. Again the CSRC found that the SEO was abused by Chinese listed companies, and therefore increased the threshold to curb excessive abuse.
- July 2002: The CSRC raised the bar to a three-year average ROE of 10% and a minimum ROE of 10% in the previous year. Since the 2001 threshold was not definitive, management and underwriters were able to collude to help poor companies to gain additional market resources. For example, Wuhan Department Store Group Co. Ltd. announced a SEO proposal right after the 2001 Regulation went into effect. Its ROEs in the previous three years (1998 to 2000) had been 3.16%, 2.72%, and 2.41%—all below 6%.

The various regulations on rights offerings and SEOs detailed above imposed at least two types of cost on China's capital markets. The first cost was the earnings "management" needed to achieve the numerical accounting threshold. Managers of poorly performing companies could manipulate accounting numbers to meet the threshold so that they could then raise additional capital from investors. When this happens, investors' capital may be allocated to less efficient projects and their welfare is reduced. The second cost of a numerical threshold was that it had the potential to exclude firms with a potential for good future performance and to allow firms with likely poor future performance to conduct rights offerings or SEOs.

Despite the costs consequent on the adoption of numerical rules, the Chinese government continues to use similar rules to establish rights issues and SEO qualifications. As mentioned above, this accounting-based regulation has two possible benefits: one is that the regulation helps to minimize resource misallocation, and the other is that the regulation can reduce the adverse selection problem in equity offerings.

▸▸ MAKING IT HAPPEN

Governments of emerging economies must have an excellent understanding of the status of their capital markets. The following actions should be considered when policymakers implement accounting-based regulations:

- Promote rigorous capital market research by academics and consultants.
- Understand the demand and supply of capital markets.
- Impose a stringent threshold at the beginning.
- Actively monitor market reactions to government regulations and adjust the regulations accordingly.

"It doesn't matter if a cat is black or white, so long as it catches mice." Deng Xiaoping

  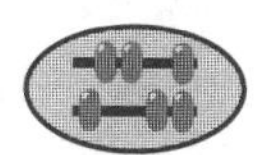   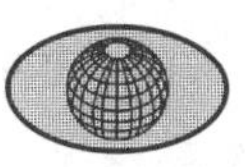   

⏩ MORE INFO

Book:

Pigou, Arthur C. *The Economics of Welfare*. 4th ed. London: Macmillan, 1932. Online at: www.econlib.org/library/NPDBooks/Pigou/pgEW.html

Articles:

Chen, Kevin C. W., and Jiwei Wang. "Accounting-based regulation in emerging markets: The case of China's seasoned-equity offerings." *International Journal of Accounting* 42:3 (2007): 221–236. Online at: dx.doi.org/10.1016/j.intacc.2007.06.001

Zingales, Luigi. "The future of securities regulation." Chicago Booth School of Business Research paper no. 08-27 and FEEM Working paper no. 7.2009, 2009. Online at: ssrn.com/abstract=1319648

Websites:

China Securities Regulatory Commission: www.csrc.gov.cn/n575458/n4001948

US Securities and Exchange Commission: www.sec.gov

"**Bureaucracy emerged out of the organization's need for order and precision and the workers' demands for impartial treatment. It was an organization ideally suited to the values and demands of the Victorian age.**"

Warren Bennis

  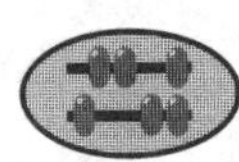 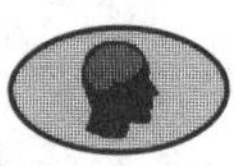  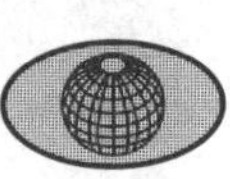   

The Effect of SOX on Internal Control, Risk Management, and Corporate Governance

Best Practice by David A. Doney

EXECUTIVE SUMMARY

- The effect of the Sarbanes–Oxley Act of 2002 (SOX) has been dramatic and global. SOX enhanced the regulatory framework for investor protection and confidence.
- SOX has required or encouraged a variety of best practices related to management accountability, auditor independence, audit committees, internal control reporting, risk management, and improvement of financial processes.
- One of the important contributions of the regulatory guidance is the "top-down risk-based assessment," a robust framework for identifying and assessing financial reporting risks.
- Compliance approaches, benefits, and costs continue to evolve as practice and regulatory guidance change.

INTRODUCTION

The Sarbanes–Oxley Act of 2002 was passed in the context of a series of high-profile corporate scandals, a brief recession, and the events of 9/11. These factors were cited by President George W. Bush as a threat to investor confidence and the US economy overall. He also declared: "This law says to every dishonest corporate leader: you will be exposed and punished; the era of low standards and false profits is over; no boardroom in America is above or beyond the law."[1]

US Senator Paul Sarbanes stated that during the development of the law, a series of Senate hearings with experts from business, government, and academia resulted in a "remarkable consensus on the nature of the problems."[2] These included inadequate oversight of the accounting profession, conflicts of interest involving auditors and stock analysts, weak corporate governance procedures, inadequate disclosure rules, and insufficient funding for the Securities and Exchange Commission (SEC).

The SOX law, corresponding guidance from regulators, and evolving approaches to implementation have resulted in a variety of internal control, risk management, and corporate governance best practices.

HOLD MANAGEMENT ACCOUNTABLE

The law requires that the CEO and CFO sign certifications quarterly and annually attesting that they have reviewed the financial statements and (to their knowledge) believe them to be fair, accurate, and complete. Penalties for fraudulent certification are severe. This requirement has encouraged such best practices as:

- *Disclosure committees*: A cross-functional group of top-level managers that meets to discuss pending public disclosures, including quarterly and annual financial reporting.
- *Representation letters*: To support the certification by the CEO and CFO and ensure that material information is made known to them, a variety of senior finance and operations managers sign representation letters regarding financial reporting matters relevant to their areas of responsibility.
- *Improvement of finance organization*: Many companies expanded the number and quality of financial personnel, particularly with respect to US Generally Accepted Accounting Principles and SEC reporting requirements.

MAINTAIN AUDITOR INDEPENDENCE

Auditors are the primary watchdogs of the corporation. Prior to SOX, auditors performed significant consulting work for publicly traded companies ("issuers") that they audited. Further, auditors often moved into senior financial management positions in the client company. These factors created at least a perceived conflict of interest.

SOX prohibits auditors from providing many types of consulting services to issuers they audit.

The law also prohibits auditors from auditing an issuer if the issuer's CEO or top financial management worked for the audit firm during the past year.

EMPOWER THE REGULATORS

Prior to SOX, the audit industry was self-regulated. SOX also established the Public Company Accounting Oversight Board (PCAOB), a nonprofit, nongovernmental entity, to oversee the audit firms. The PCAOB sets standards and publicly discloses the results of its auditor reviews and any disciplinary action taken.

Critics also argued that the SEC, the regulator tasked with investor protection and corporate disclosure standards, was significantly underfunded and understaffed. The SEC budget was nearly doubled in the wake of SOX and remains at that level today.

ENGAGE AUDIT COMMITTEES

Prior to SOX, former SEC Chairman Arthur Levitt stated that "qualified, committed, independent and tough-minded audit committees represent the most reliable guardians of the public interest."[3] The many scandals that resulted in SOX indicated that audit committees were not performing their financial oversight responsibilities effectively.

SOX mandated that the audit committee, rather than management, be accountable for the relationship with the auditor, including selection, compensation, retention, and review of independence. Issuers are now required to disclose whether or not the audit committee has a financial expert, which has encouraged additional financial expertise on audit committees. Auditors are now required to provide more robust disclosures to the audit committee regarding alternative accounting policies and their discussions with management. Audit committees must also ensure the availability of an anonymous reporting channel for accounting or auditing matters (i.e. a "whistleblower hotline"). The law also expanded protection for whistleblowers and penalties for retaliation against them.

EVALUATE KEY FINANCIAL CONTROLS

The infamous SOX "Section 404" guidance requires both management and the external auditor to provide a report that includes an opinion regarding internal control over financial reporting (ICFR). This is additional to the traditional auditor's opinion on the accuracy of financial statements. It requires management to document and comprehensively test financial controls necessary to address "material misstatement risks."

Any controls that are assessed as not effectively designed (i.e. not capable of addressing the related risk, even if executed) or not operating effectively (i.e. not executed consistently) result in "deficien-

"The board is responsible for the successful perpetuation of the corporation. That responsibility cannot be relegated to management." John G. Smale

cies." More serious deficiencies are categorized as "significant deficiencies" or "material weaknesses" and must be reported to the external auditor and audit committee. Material weaknesses require public disclosure during the quarter they are identified and, if not remediated as of year-end, an unfavorable opinion on ICFR in the issuer's annual report.

The requirement to perform a comprehensive control assessment has resulted in several improvements in the art and science of financial management. For example, controls related to the "tone at the top," incentives, and conflicts of interest were often not formally assessed prior to SOX. Focus on effective controls has significantly improved. Further, the quality of the SOX assessment (for example, project management, technology use, risk assessment, and quality of presentation materials) is a good proxy for "tone at the top" in the organization and the process management skills of the finance team.

In the aftermath of SOX the focus of internal auditing efforts also shifted significantly to financial controls, as opposed to operational processes. Many issuers expanded the staffing and capabilities of their internal auditing teams to absorb incremental SOX responsibilities. The New York Stock Exchange (NYSE) listing standards now require that all listed companies have an internal audit function. Tracking deficiencies to resolution also establishes good discipline for internal audit follow-up of all issue types, as required by internal auditing standards.

IMPROVE RISK MANAGEMENT

Pressure is increasing on businesses to improve risk management practices. This comes from a variety of sources, including regulators, credit rating agencies, and activist shareholders. Further, the subprime mortgage crisis which became apparent in 2007 has (arguably) exposed systemic risk management concerns.

The 2007 guidance from the SEC and PCAOB regarding SOX Section 404 established a comprehensive framework for conducting a "top-down" financial reporting risk assessment. For example, management is required to identify material misstatement risks and related controls, which then must be tested. (See the Case Study for details.)

Techniques used in top-down risk assessment are applicable to other risk categories. Under the COSO Enterprise Risk Management (ERM) framework, risks fall into strategic, operational, legal/regulatory, and financial reporting categories. SOX compliance implies substantial coverage of

CASE STUDY

SIRVA, Inc.—Implementing a Top-down Risk Assessment

SIRVA, Inc., is a decentralized global moving and relocation services company with revenues of $4 billion in 2007. Under new internal audit leadership in 2007, the company implemented a top-down risk assessment, new SOX compliance software, and brought the effort substantially in-house. This resulted in *annual* savings of over $3 million and brought costs into line with benchmark companies.

First, management completed a risk-ranking of each balance sheet account (and certain sub-accounts) to assess the risk of material misstatement. The ranking was also used to identify key process/location combinations ("processes"). For example, revenue and receivables might be significant (i.e. in-scope) for one location but not another.

Second, processes were risk-ranked. Higher-risk processes or topics included entity-level controls, period-end reporting, revenue, and key accounting estimates and judgments. Other transactional processes such as accounts payable, payroll, tax, and treasury were lower risk and received less assessment effort. Nearly 200 material misstatement risks (MMR) were documented by systematically considering key accounting policies and financial statement assertions for each process or account. Risks represented "what could go wrong" in relation to the account or assertion.

Third, the number of key controls tested was reduced from the prior year by 50% (from nearly 1,000 to 500) by including only those entity-level and transaction-level controls needed to address the MMR. In other words, specific risks determined which controls mattered, as opposed to merely large dollar balances, locations, or systems. Management assigned each control a risk-ranking of high, medium, or low. This ranking was based on a combination of account-specific and control-specific factors in the SOX guidance. Sample sizes used in testing were based on the ranking and the frequency of control operation.

Fourth, SOX compliance software was implemented to document the risks, controls, and tests. Comprehensive status and quality reporting was developed and discussed in weekly meetings with the global audit team and management.

Finally, multiple domestic general ledger systems were consolidated into one system. Further, two major operating platforms were consolidated into one, removing an entire financial process.

▸▸ MAKING IT HAPPEN

SOX regulations and implementation have provided a series of best practices to help companies improve risk, control, and governance, even if technically they are not required to comply.

- Identify and remove conflicts of interest that affect your business. These can involve auditors, management, the board, vendors, outside consultants, etc.
- Ensure that your external auditors and internal auditors are independent by having their continuing employment, performance rating, and compensation determined by the audit committee or board.
- Help to ensure that financial disclosures are transparent and fairly describe the organization's performance by using a disclosure committee and management representation letters.
- Insist on a robust top-down risk assessment of financial reporting processes. The extent of testing to perform (the primary cost-driver) can then be determined appropriately.
- Capture risk and control information in compliance database software. User-friendly software that can be customized and administered by non-IT personnel is available at very reasonable prices.
- Establish risk committees at the senior management and board level. These committees can direct risk management efforts and help the audit committee to focus on financial reporting matters.
- Develop reporting of operating metrics that are predictive of financial results and share it with the audit committee and board.
- Communicate periodically to the audit committee any significant deficiencies identified (financial or otherwise) and management's progress towards remediating them.
- Use the financial reporting effort and framework to initiate or improve an ERM program.

  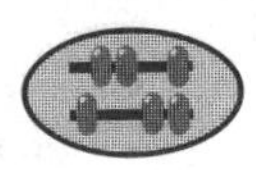 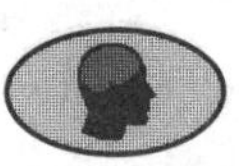  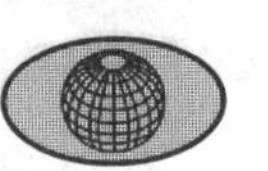  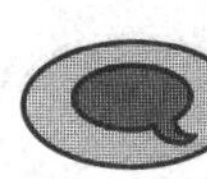 

financial reporting risks. The SOX compliance process also provides a framework that relates processes, risks, and controls, and the network of managers involved, which can be used to help establish an ERM program.

Many companies also use SOX-compliance database software, which may also be useful for retaining risk information to support an ERM program and as an internal audit workflow tool. For example, as internal audits are completed, the amount of risk and control information expands in such a database, across all risk types.

In response to increased expectations around risk, many audit committees have expanded their scope to include overall risk management. With SOX efforts addressing financial reporting risks, they can focus more attention on strategic and operational risks. Some issuers have also created board risk committees to address non-financial reporting matters.

IMPROVE FINANCIAL PROCESSES

The significant cost of the ICFR assessment required under SOX Section 404 represents a "tax" on inefficiency, providing additional incentives for process improvement. Redundant systems, processes, or locations generally require some type of incremental assessment, increasing the scope and cost of compliance. The Financial Executives International (FEI) survey of SOX 404 compliance costs in 2007[4] indicated that, for companies with average revenue of $4.7 billion, the costs in *decentralized* companies averaged $1.9 million, 46% higher than the $1.3 million in *centralized* companies. The difference is likely to be a fraction of the savings available from addressing the underlying process inefficiency.

In addition, manual control procedures involve substantially higher testing costs. For example, a manual control that operates daily may require a sample size of 30 to be evaluated by an expert. However, the same control if automated requires a sample size of just one and does not have to be evaluated each year if certain criteria are met. Leading companies track the number of manual versus automated controls and seek automation opportunities. Reducing the number of manual journal entries is another means of improving the reliability of financial statements and reducing closing-cycle time, while reducing both compliance and personnel costs.

Section 404 is one of the more contentious elements of SOX, due to the significant cost of compliance. According to a survey by FEI that included issuers with an average revenue of $4.7 billion, compliance costs were $1.7 million during 2007, or 0.36% of revenue. The total cost includes internal and external labor and auditor attestation fees.[5]

Compliance costs have continued to decline since 2004, when Section 404 became applicable for most issuers. The 2007 SEC and PCAOB guidance has provided management with additional flexibility in addressing risk and determining the timing, nature, and extent of testing procedures, further reducing costs.

CONCLUSION

SOX has resulted in dramatic changes in internal control, risk management, and corporate governance. Management and audit committees are more focused on financial reporting. The internal control and risk management best practices discussed above continue to evolve in practice. Companies continue to focus and reduce costs in their SOX 404 efforts through top-down risk assessment and compliance software, which have broader applications to other risk management efforts.

▸▸ MORE INFO

Book:

Farrell, Greg. *America Robbed Blind. How Corporate Crooks Fleeced American Shareholders (and How Congress Failed to Stop Them).* Buda, TX: Wizard Academy Press, 2005.

Websites:

Committee of Sponsoring Organizations of the Treadway Commission (COSO): www.coso.org. For *Enterprise Risk Management—Integrated Framework (2004)*: www.coso.org/-ERM.htm

Institute of International Auditors (IIA): www.theiia.org. For *The International Standards for the Professional Practice of Internal Auditing*: www.theiia.org/guidance/standards-and-guidance/professional-practices-framework/standards

Public Company Accounting Oversight Board (PCAOB): www.pcaob.org

PCAOB Auditing Standard No. 5, "An audit of internal control over financial reporting that is integrated with an audit of financial statements and related independence rule and conforming amendments" (2007): www.pcaob.org/Rules/Docket_021/2007-05-24_Release_No_2007-005.pdf

Sarbanes–Oxley. The text of the Act can be found at: fl1.findlaw.com/news.findlaw.com/hdocs/docs/gwbush/sarbanesoxley072302.pdf

US Securities and Exchange Commission (SEC): www.sec.gov

"Commission guidance regarding management's report on internal control over financial reporting under Section 13(a) or 15(d) of the Securities Exchange Act of 1934." Interpretive guidance release 33-8810, etc. (2007): www.sec.gov/rules/interp/2007/33-8810.pdf

NOTES

1 Office of the Press Secretary, The White House. "President Bush signs corporate corruption bill" (Sarbanes–Oxley Act 2002): www.whitehouse.gov/news/releases/2002/07/20020730.html

2 Lucas, Nance. "An interview with United States Senator Paul S. Sarbanes." *Journal of Leadership & Organizational Studies* (June 22, 2004).

3 Levitt, Arthur. "The numbers game." Speech dated September 28, 1998. www.sec.gov/news/speech/speecharchive/1998/spch220.txt

4 Financial Executives International (FEI). News release "FEI survey: Average 2007 SOX compliance cost $1.7 million." fei.mediaroom.com/index.php?s=43&item=204

5 *Ibid.*

A complete cross-referenced index of SEC filers, audit firms, offices, CPAs, services, fees, compliance/enforcement actions and other critical disclosure information can be found at: www.sarbanes-oxley.com

"I have experienced many instances of being obliged, by better information or fuller consideration, to change opinions even on important subjects, which I once thought right, but found to be otherwise." Benjamin Franklin

  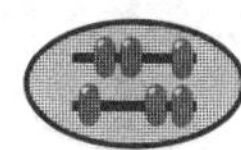   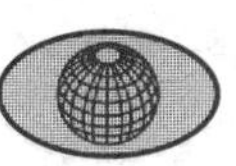   

Effective Financial Reporting and Auditing: Importance and Limitations by Andrew Higson

EXECUTIVE SUMMARY

- There is a debate about the specification of the objective of financial statements.
- Clear specification of this objective is important for the financial reporting standard-setters (so they can produce consistent and coherent standards), users (so they understand the nature and scope of financial reporting), external auditors (so they can say whether the financial statements are "fit for purpose"), and educationalists (so they can teach the next generation).
- The lack of clarity about the objective of the financial statements appears to have created a financial reporting expectations gap.
- Perceived defects in financial statements have resulted in a call for real-time financial reporting, but this may have the effect of creating more volatility in share price movements.

INTRODUCTION

The major problem with financial reporting is that people with limited financial knowledge can look at a set of accounts and, by attempting to interpret the numbers, feel that they understand what is happening in an organization. While in simpler times this may have been true, the scale and complexity of modern business, together with the limitations of what can be portrayed in financial statements, means that today's statements may have the capability to mislead as much as they can inform their users.

A large telecom business may have over two hundred million transactions a day in its accounting records, and such a scale of activity is almost beyond human comprehension. The complexity, and uncertainty, surrounding some transactions and financial instruments make their inclusion in the financial statements problematic to say the least. In the past accounting was defined as "an art of recording, classifying and summarizing in a significant manner and in terms of money, transactions and events which are, in part at least, of a financial character, and interpreting the results thereof."[1] The need for financial reporting came about with the development of permanently invested capital (today's share capital), which required a return to be made to the shareholders for their investment over a period of time (usually annually). The separation of ownership and management, especially in larger organizations, gave rise to the need for the accountability of the managers (agents) to the owners (principals), the financial statements being a convenient basis for this. In some jurisdictions financial statements also form a basis for the calculation of taxation. This subdivision of an organization's life into artificial accounting periods may not sound exciting, but it is important. It may not cover all aspects of an organization's activities, but originally this was never intended.

DECISION-USEFULNESS

Since the 1960s, the function of accounting has been increasingly regarded as "to provide quantitative information primarily financial in nature about economic entities that is intended to be useful in making economic decisions, in making resolved choices among alternative courses of action,"[2] and accounting was seen as a service activity.

On a simplistic level, the decision-usefulness approach may be intuitively appealing, but it could also be conceptually flawed and an example of circular reasoning: just because some people may take decisions based on the financial statements, does this mean that decision-usefulness should be specified as the objective of financial statements? When one takes a decision, one should be looking to the future—yet the financial statements say very little about an organization's future. One should also consider the future economic climate, an organization's competitors, and expected technological developments; financial statements say very little about these things. Often short-term investors are more concerned about taking their decision in *anticipation* (buy long, sell short) of the publication of the financial statements rather than waiting for them to come out, reading them, and then taking a decision.

An important component in the debate about the objective of financial statements has been the vagueness of the nature, scope and purpose of accounting "theory." One would have expected developments in financial reporting to have been built on theory and thus be conceptually robust. The focus on unspecified users taking unspecified decisions, at unspecified times, with unspecified results hardly seems an appropriate basis for the production of consistent and coherent financial reporting standards, and consequently there is a danger that the financial reporting standard-setters have been building on shifting sands rather than on firm foundations.

THE CALL FOR REAL-TIME REPORTING

Given the prevailing emphasis on decision-usefulness, and the perceived limitations of financial statements in this respect, some analysts and other external parties have been calling for companies to make real-time accounting data available to them. The argument is that immediate access to, and a greater quantity of, data about a company should improve users' decision-making ability and thus improve market efficiency. However, if companies were to adopt real-time reporting (this presumably would be the reporting of results on a minute-by-minute basis rather than just putting the annual accounts on the internet), would the results make sense?

There is a danger that there has been a confusion over the "recording" aspect of accounting and the "reporting" aspect of the financial statements. "Raw" accounting data are simply a means of recording in order to keep track of the transactions undertaken by an organization—which is obviously very important for management to do. The periodic financial statements use these accounting data, and related assumptions and conventions, to allocate profit to the appropriate accounting period and to present the financial figures at a point in time (this is after the necessary cut-off adjustments and checks have been made). Given the scale of modern business, one wonders what users would really make of all the data.

To allow outsiders access to real-time "raw" accounting data does raise the question as to how exactly it would lead to greater market efficiency. Indeed, instantaneous access to real-time accounting data may not necessarily result in greater market efficiency—though greater volatility in share price movements would be a distinctly possible consequence.

"No law or ordinance is mightier than understanding." Plato

  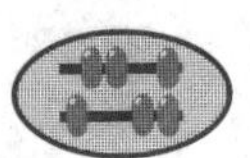   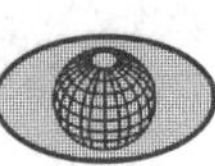 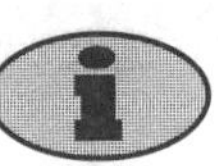  

THE FINANCIAL REPORTING EXPECTATIONS GAP

It is likely there is a financial reporting expectations gap[3] composed of two elements, one being an expectations gap relating to the financial statements, and the other being the audit expectations gap (Figure 1). There has been much discussion of the audit expectations gap (some users of financial statements think that the external auditors are there to detect fraud, that they produce the financial statements, that they check everything recorded by the client's accounting, etc.). The audit expectations gap has been a driving force behind the expansion of the audit report and has focused the debate about the responsibilities of the external auditors. Compared to the discussion about the audit expectations gap, the possibility of a financial statements expectations gap has almost been ignored.

Figure 1. The financial reporting expectations gap. (*Source*: Higson, 2003, p. 13)

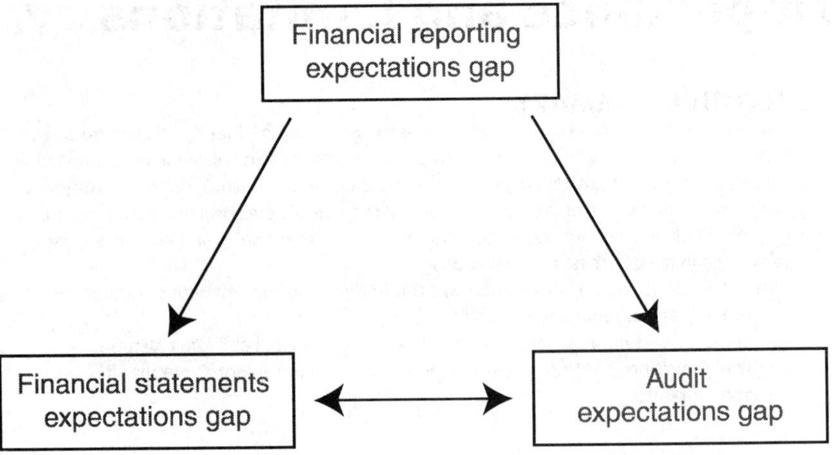

It is suggested that one element is the already discussed focus of the accountancy profession on the decision-usefulness of financial statements. Just because some people do take decisions based on them, it does not mean that they take the right decision. Another problem is the use of financial statements as an assessment of "performance"; this is because the financial statements *per se* say nothing about the economy, efficiency, and effectiveness of the organizations that produce them. There is also the tension between the long-term development of an organization and the short-term results contained in the financial statements. It is easier for users of financial statements to focus on the short-term figures contained in such statements than to try to look long-term. The broadening of the notion of performance could mean that financial statements would then be recognized for what they are—an attempt to allocate profit to the appropriate accounting period and to indicate the financial position at a point in time—and that they would then enable the debate about what constitutes corporate performance to really begin.

IMPLICATIONS FOR THE EXTERNAL AUDITORS

One might assume that the audit report would be saying that the financial statements are "fit for purpose"; however, traditionally the auditors have said nothing about the decision-usefulness of financial statements. Indeed, the Company Law Review Steering Group report[4] stated: "auditors have no liability to existing shareholders who rely on their report for investment decisions (for example to buy or sell shares), or actual creditors of the company who may make similar decisions about maintaining or withdrawing credit, or potential investors whether of equity or debt, or other potential creditors (for example trade creditors), who rely on the audit report for a view of the financial position of the company." It is therefore not surprising that in the United Kingdom, following the Bannerman case[5] in 2003, the auditors added a paragraph to their audit report which included the advice that: "Our work has been undertaken so that we might state to the company's members those matters we are required to state to them in an auditor's report and for no other purpose . . . we do not accept or assume responsibility to anyone other than the company and the company's members as a body, for our audit work, for this report, or for the opinions we have formed."

The auditors say nothing about corporate economy, efficiency, and effectiveness in their audit report. The users have to try to make their own assessment of these things based on the limited amount of data in the financial statements available to them.

It can be seen that the auditors tend to think of themselves as doing what is required of them (i.e. to follow the auditing standards and ensure that the financial statements have been produced by management in accordance with financial reporting standards), but I wonder how many readers of financial statements will understand this and understand what all these standards mean.

CONCLUSION

The challenges of corporate reporting in the twenty-first century can only be met once there is a real understanding about the nature, scope, and limitations of the financial statements and of the role of the external auditors.

Without a strong theoretical basis, the danger is that the financial reporting standard-setters will merely end up pandering to the perceived needs of the supposed users of financial statements.

The word "performance," in a theatrical sense, could be defined as "an act of make-believe aimed at enchanting an audience." The existence of the financial statements expectations gap may mean that this fate has already befallen the phrase "financial performance" (think about Enron's and WorldCom's financial statements!); it is important that it does not befall the phrase "corporate performance."

▸▸ MAKING IT HAPPEN

An Agenda for Developments in Corporate Reporting

- Give consideration to a tighter and arguably more realistic specification of the objective of the financial statements.
- Increase education about the scope and limitations of financial statements and the external audit.
- Conduct a proper debate about the nature of communicating corporate performance and the assessment of corporate economy, efficiency, and effectiveness.
- Reflect on the usefulness of real-time access to corporate accounting data.

"Oft expectation fails, and most oft where most it promises; and oft it hits where hope is coldest; and despair most sits." William Shakespeare

  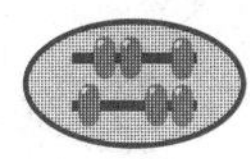   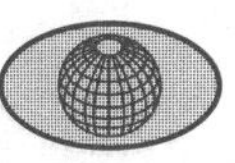   

▶▶ MORE INFO

Books:

Deegan, C., and J. Unerman. *Financial Accounting Theory*. European ed. London: McGraw-Hill, 2006.

Elliott, B., and J. Elliott. *Financial Accounting and Reporting*. 12th ed. Harlow, UK: FT Prentice Hall, 2007.

Harrison Jr, W. T., and C. T. Horngren. *Financial Accounting*. 6th ed. Upper Saddle River, NJ: Pearson, 2005.

Higson, A. *Corporate Financial Reporting: Theory & Practice*. London: Sage Publications, 2003.

Riahi-Belkaoui, A. *Accounting Theory*. 5th ed. London: Thomson, 2004.

Website:

Corporate Financial Reporting, the author's website: www.accounting-research.org.uk

NOTES

1 American Institute of Accountants (AIA), Committee on Terminology (1953). *Accounting Terminology Bulletin* No. 1. New York: AIA, 1953, p. 9.

2 Accounting Principles Board (APB). *Statement No. 4: Basic Concepts and Accounting Principles Underlying Financial Statements of Business Enterprises*. New York: AICPA, 1970, para. 40.

3 Higson, 2003.

4 Company Law Review Steering Group. *Modern Company Law for a Competitive Economy: Final Report*. London: DTI, 2001, para. 8.127.

5 Auditing Practices Board Discussion Paper. *The auditor's report: A time for change?* London: Financial Reporting Council, 2007, pp. 11–12.

"You have to know accounting. It's the language of practical business life. It was a very useful thing to deliver to civilization. I've heard it came to civilization through Venice which of course was once the great commercial power in the Mediterranean. However, double entry bookkeeping was a hell of an invention." Charlie Munger

  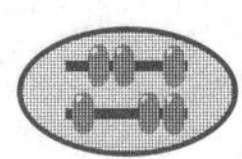 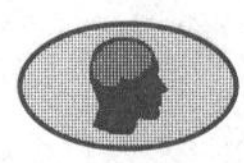  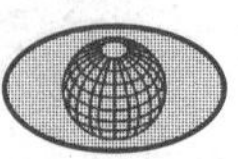   

Engaging Senior Management in Internal Control by Philip Ratcliffe

EXECUTIVE SUMMARY

- Internal control systems must have the backing of senior management to be effective.
- Internal auditors should make management aware of the importance of sound internal controls, and the serious problems that could arise if they are inadequate.
- The benefits of sound internal controls include efficiency and effectiveness, protection against losses and unpleasant surprises, optimum use of assets, and motivated staff—all in all, they make a major contribution to organizational survival and prosperity.
- Key risks resulting from lack of good internal control are fraud, incorrect accounts, inefficiency and ineffectiveness, damage to the reputation of the organization and its management, and a consequent fall in the value of the company.
- Internal auditors should form their own view of the specific risks facing their organization.
- If the internal control system is inadequate, they should meet with senior management to explain the need for strong, sound controls and their benefits for the organization.

HOW TO GET SENIOR MANAGEMENT TO TAKE INTERNAL CONTROL SERIOUSLY

Top managers in any organization have many calls on their time and attention. Vying for their attention will be customers, suppliers, employees, consultants, and many others. Internal controls can easily be squeezed out of their agenda. The problem this can create is that if senior management does not take control seriously, the "tone from the top" will be wrong—and if the people in charge don't care, then why should anyone else in the organization? Rightly or wrongly, this is the message that will be perceived across the organization, and internal control will suffer.

So, as a corporate auditor, how can you push internal control up the priority list? Showing clearly to management the benefits of strong internal control on the one hand, and the consequences of failure of internal control on the other, is one path to this goal.

Benefits of Control

A key message to communicate to management is that effective, active controls give positive benefits as well as avoiding negative outcomes. Having controls that are effective will ensure that the directions of the board and senior management are implemented as intended; that operations and activities are carried out efficiently and meet their objectives; and that the assets used in an organization are not only properly accounted for, but also that they are used effectively and efficiently for the benefit of the organization. Procedures which follow sound control principles enable people to carry out their work in an environment that is orderly and satisfying to work in. Good internal control will also protect an organization and its staff against the temptations of dishonesty, fraud, and theft.

Organizations that have sound internal controls will know where they are, and where they are going, because management information controls will tell the organization's management what they need to know when they need to know it. If the first imperative of most organizations is survival, then good internal control can play a major role in achieving that objective. Additionally, and very importantly, there can also be an efficiency dividend for an organization if good, cost-effective internal control systems are in place; for example, when processes are streamlined and well controlled, fewer people may be needed to do the work.

The Impact of Control Failure Inside the Business

All too often, internal control only becomes a concern to top management after it breaks down. Out of the blue comes the sudden discovery of a massive fraud or a major hole in the accounts, or a business segment that was thought to be profitable is dramatically discovered not to be. There is a myriad of such possibilities. Management discovers, painfully, that when there is such a breakdown of control, almost everything else has to be thrown out of the window while the breakdown is investigated. It has to engage with internal auditors, external auditors, consultants, and specialists to uncover the root causes of the problem, as there is no cure without first making a diagnosis. The managers immediately responsible for the failure must be identified, and a conclusion reached on their degree of culpability. And if someone has to be fired, who is going to take on their responsibilities?

Then, senior managers have to make up their minds what to do about the underlying problem. What changes have to be made to ensure that it can never happen again? Should they commission reviews in other similar parts of the organization to gain assurance that the problem isn't endemic elsewhere? Are major investments in systems or capital items needed to fix things? Should procedures be revised? Do staff need retraining or reorganizing? If so, who is going to implement the changes, and where is the money going to come from?

Control Breakdown Can Have External Implications

Another vital aspect is the impact of a breakdown on external relations. Do investors and the stock markets have to be informed? Is a profits warning necessary? How will stakeholders react? What will

CASE STUDY

When a new chief executive officer joined his company, the chief audit executive arranged an early meeting with him. The CAE discussed the internal controls in the organization, demonstrated his knowledge of their strengths and weaknesses, and explained his view of the importance of controls and the vital role to be played by the CEO in setting an example—the tone from the top. As a result, the CEO agreed to have regular meetings to discuss internal controls and to review the assurance provided by internal audit and any resultant need for action, undertakings he subsequently fulfilled. Expectation that these meetings would take place helped to ensure that management throughout the organization gave high priority to internal control and to responding to internal audit findings.

"Trust is not a substitute for internal control."

     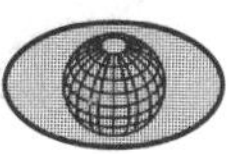   

the (inevitably negative) impact be on the share price, and therefore the value, of the organization? Often such an announcement will create a loss of shareholder value that is many times the original operating loss. At times like these, an executive director may be lucky to keep his job; at the very least, there is a major risk of loss of personal and corporate reputation.

The Opportunity Cost is Great

On top of this, in a serious case the opportunity cost of the time that management will lose in attending to the consequences of an internal control breakdown can be massive. Strategic issues, tactical issues, business development—all these and many more normal concerns of senior management will have to take a back seat until the problem is resolved. Add to this the loss of reputation and of confidence, inside and outside the organization, because news will inevitably leak out however carefully those involved try to prevent it.

The case here has been made in the context of a commercial organization, but similar considerations apply to all other types of organization, whether governmental, private, or in the not-for-profit sector.

GETTING MANAGEMENT BACKING: WHERE TO START

If the benefits of sound controls are so tangible, and the aftermath of a failure of internal control is so dreadful, how does the corporate auditor make a start on obtaining top management's backing for a regime of sound internal control? Corporate governance regulations in many countries, and best practice, now require organizations formally to analyze and record the risks they face. The purpose of this requirement is, first, to ensure that organizations actually understand their risk profile, as only then can they seriously and properly consider whether they have the right mitigation arrangements in place. Often a management team, in making explicit the risks they face, will discover that initially they do not have a common view as to what the risks are. Only when they have a unified vision can they expect to come up with a coherent and balanced response. Only then can they hope to design and develop a comprehensive internal control system that meets the needs of the organization. The corporate auditor can assist by becoming involved in the risk identification process, by emphasizing to senior management the immediate impact of failure to mitigate the risks (for example, by pointing out that the accounts will be incorrect), and the secondary, but possibly even more drastic, consequences (for example, that a profits warning will have to be issued and the share price will nosedive.)

It is not least by confronting management with the consequences of control failure that it can be helped to take internal control seriously. The internal auditor can help to create an understanding and appreciation of the consequences of control failure by making presentations and having one-to-one meetings with influential people, such as the chairman/president, chief executive, chief financial officer, audit committee chair, other board members, and senior managers. The objective is to create an awareness of internal control in the organization and, through that awareness, to change the attitude to it.

While some risks may be external to the organization and not susceptible to internal control, many can be mitigated by internal controls. In some cultures, management is reluctant to accept the need for internal controls, believing that staff should be trusted. Internal auditors should point out to such management that trust is not a substitute for internal control. A proper system of internal controls should be considered a force for moral good, in that it effectively removes temptation from employees by ensuring that undesirable behaviors will be promptly detected and corrected; if employees understand this, they will be less likely to attempt to defraud their employer.

CONCLUSION

Management's role in ensuring effective internal control is vital. Management sets the tone from the top. Unless management engages and commits, the rest of the organization will not take internal control seriously. The internal auditor can help management to appreciate the importance of internal control by demonstrating its value—not least, the efficiency dividend to an organization if good, cost-effective internal control systems are in place—and by making management aware of the consequences of failures of internal control. The internal auditor can further assist management by highlighting the need to set tone from the top, to allocate sufficient resources for internal control, and to ensure that internal control processes are suitably designed for the needs of the business.

▸▸ MAKING IT HAPPEN

- Collect evidence about the state of internal controls and any opportunities that exist for improving them.
- Present the benefits of better controls in terms with which management can identify.
- Review the organization's code of conduct or similar document; if none exists, it is worth raising the issue.
- Seek a meeting with the head of the organization and influential members of the board. Have a clear but short agenda. Aim for some specific goals from your meeting. Go prepared with a succinct presentation and some practical recommendations.
- Use the opportunity to argue for the importance of tone from the top where internal control is concerned; if the top people in the company take internal control seriously, so will everybody else. Ask whether they like unwelcome surprises, and what they are prepared to do to avoid them.
- Point up the risks facing the organization, and show how a well-designed control structure can help to avoid or mitigate the worst consequences.
- Don't expect everything to be achieved with just one meeting. Be prepared to keep going back with the same messages until they are not only accepted, but also acted on.

▸▸ MORE INFO

Book:

Sawyer, Lawrence B., Mortimer A. Dittenhofer, James H. Scheiner, Anne Graham, and Paul Makosz. *Sawyer's Internal Auditing: The Practice of Modern Internal Auditing.* Altamonte Springs, FL: Institute of Internal Auditors, 2003.

Reports:

American Institute of Certified Public Accountants. "Internal control—Integrated framework." 1994. Order online at: www.theiia.org/bookstore

Financial Reporting Council. "The combined code on corporate governance." 2008. Online at: www.frc.org.uk/corporate/combinedcode.cfm

"Ensure that your organization really understands its risk profile."

  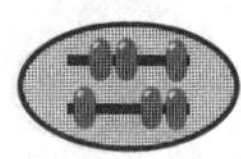   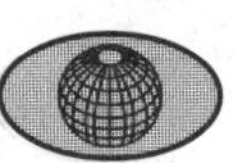   

Enterprise Risk Management and Solvency II by Andrew Davies

EXECUTIVE SUMMARY

The article considers enterprise risk management (ERM) in the light of Solvency II, an updated set of regulatory requirements for insurance firms operating in the European Union. It begins from the perspective that in many organizations ERM is an evolving area that needs to be further developed. We look at:

- The key components of ERM;
- The dangers of overcomplicating processes;
- How policies, risk strategy, and risk appetite are set;
- Capital allocation and management;
- The implications of Solvency II.

INTRODUCTION

There is a great deal that the insurance sector has to come to terms with as it addresses the implications of Solvency II. There are broad general questions such as: What does it all mean? How will it be achieved and its requirements met? How much will it cost both from a capital and a monetary perspective? What resources are required? Then there is the related issue of how the International Financial Reporting Standards will fit with Solvency II.

ENTERPRISE RISK MANAGEMENT: CULTURE IS THE KEY

Rating agencies, analysts, shareholders, and regulators are all taking more interest in capital models and enterprise risk management (ERM). Effective ERM acts as the common thread that links balance sheet strength, operating performance and business profile."[1]

In an ideal ERM model, the risk management group will work with the board and all employees to ensure that their organization has effective ERM. It is fair to say that the majority of companies today have some form of ERM, but it is also true that for many this is an area that needs further development.

ERM is not about finding the perfect model, it is about having a strong risk-management culture which ensures that risk is understood, controlled, and effectively communicated. Effective ERM should be part of an insurance company's DNA.

The key components of ERM are:

- Aligning risk appetite and strategy;
- Enhancing risk response decisions;
- Reducing operational surprises and losses;
- Identifying and managing multiple and cross-enterprise risks;
- Seizing opportunities;
- Improving the deployment of capital.

Management should consider the company's risk appetite in evaluating its strategy, setting objectives, and developing mechanisms to manage related risks. ERM provides the rigour to identify and select alternative responses to risk—such as risk avoidance, risk reduction, risk sharing, and risk acceptance. Through ERM, companies enhance their ability to identify potential events and establish responses, thereby reducing surprises and associated costs or losses.

Every company faces a variety of risks that affect different parts of the organization, and ERM facilitates effective responses to such multiple risks. By considering a full range of potential events, management can identify and proactively realize opportunities.

Finally, obtaining robust risk information allows management to assess overall capital needs effectively and enhance capital allocation.

ERM AND SOLVENCY II

Solvency II is based on three "pillars". Pillar 1 is about capital requirements and the triggers for supervisory action. Pillar 2 focuses on the supervisory activities of regulators, based on organisational and governance requirements. Pillar 3 covers additional disclosures that supervisors may need to carry out their regulatory function. Under Solvency II, the concept of an "internal model" effectively refers to an enterprise-wide risk management framework. It covers both the quantitative requirements of Pillar 1 and the organizational and governance requirements of Pillar 2.

The broad thrust of an internal model is to use an economic capital model, accompanied by the embedding and effective management of risk, driven from the board to the front line.

It is important to remember the context and immediate historical backdrop against which the insurance sector is working. It is undeniable, for example, that the industry has had problems with risk assessment and modelling in recent years. The 2005 hurricane damage payouts and the current credit crisis put significant stress on capital and liquidity requirements for many companies. This makes discussion of capital adequacy regimes a very strong necessity, not just an academic exercise.

However, as insurance company boards try to square up to these issues—and there are many of them—there is a real danger of overcomplicating certain processes and of critical data being obscured by information overload. Having a complex model is no guarantee of success, as the crises experienced by several banks will testify. Instead, what is really critical is to ensure that the insurer's approach to risk management is simple enough for all staff to understand and engage with, and that it is also effective enough to add real value. The concept of "proportionality" is specifically enshrined within the proposed European Directive for Solvency II, so there is regulatory recognition that we do not need to over-elaborate.

Risk management will only be fully effective if people throughout the organization receive clear, consistent messages from leadership and understand what they need to do. It starts at the top, and senior management need to develop a unified view, common language, policies, and appropriate governance structures.

The recent testimony of Paul Moore, former head of Group Regulatory Risk at HBOS, makes clear the importance of culture in risk management. Moore commented that "Being an internal risk and compliance manager at the time felt a bit like being a man in a rowing boat trying to slow down an oil tanker."[2] If the culture is wrong, then even the most sophisticated model will be ineffective.

Markel Corporation, the company for which I work, is a relatively small company with 400 employees.[3] It therefore has a very flat organization structure, enabling close interaction between board and employees. This is very helpful as all employees can be given clear and consistent messages in a common language. We are committed to creating an environment in which risk is managed effectively. The Markel style, which articulates our core values, includes statements that "we will build the financial value of our company," which implies a steady, cautious approach

"The problem is that lots of people in organizations may have vision, but there's absolutely zero meaning. . .They've. . .forgotten why they are there, which is why bureaucracies become stodgy and obsolete and filled with inertia." Warren Bennis

to risk, and "we are encouraged to challenge management. . .we have the ability to make decisions or alter a course quickly," which empowers discussions of strategy. As both US and UK management "walk the talk," this culture facilitates a risk-focused approach for all employees.

Figure 1 highlights that a clear articulation of risk strategy and risk appetite is an essential starting point in embedding risk management across an organization. These statements of corporate objectives act as the fundamental reference point against which all risk-taking and risk-mitigation activity within an organization should be benchmarked. They provide governance and define boundaries within which risk-based decision-making can occur, and provide a clear framework for the selection of one course of action over another.

Policies, risk strategy, and risk appetite are set at board level, and this is embedded into the annual and day-to-day activities of the business. These activities are analyzed through various risk maps, capital models, and sensitivity metrics. In addition, external factors such as market movements and the actions of competitors are communicated to the business. The model at Markel that is shown in Figure 2 splits the business into two components—underwriting and investing. As a consequence there are several key committees and meetings. These are:

- IBNR (incurred but not reported losses) and P&L meetings, at which all aspects of underwriting and reserving are discussed.
- Investment Committee meetings, where all aspects of the company's investment performance and strategy are discussed.
- And in the middle there are the Capital and Risk Committees, which look at the company's risk and capital management.

The IBNR and P&L meetings are crucial to the way Markel operates. A thorough and robust reserving process is the cornerstone of a successful organization. It is important that underwriters and management agree on the IBNR results as this ensures that there is one version of the truth. Having two sets of numbers causes confusion, wastes time, and results in poor decision-making.

The meetings need to be held on a consistent and regular basis. At Markel, IBNR meetings are held quarterly, and the P&L meetings are held on a monthly basis. The IBNR packs and P&L statements show the combined ratio and the required return on risk-adjusted capital by line of business. They include all allocated expenses so that the underwriters understand the full cost of writing their business.

Figure 1. Insurer of the future with integrated model

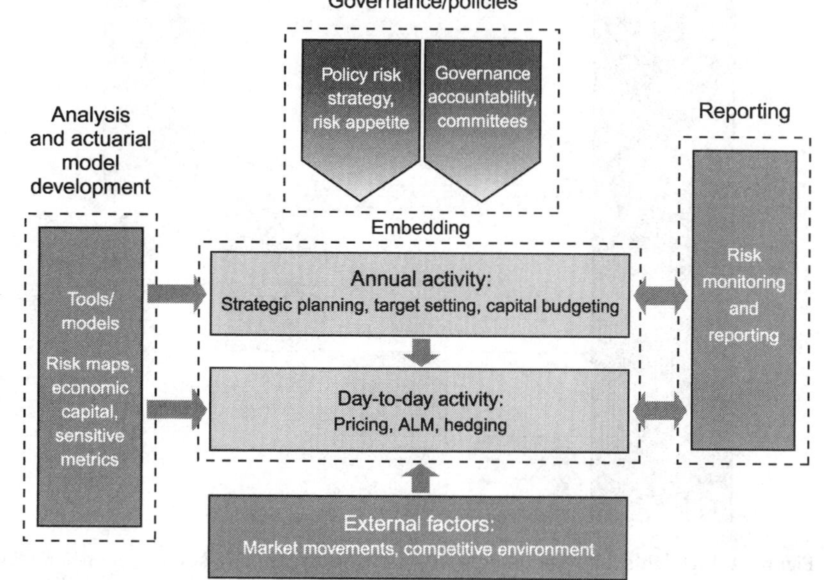

Figure 2. Model used at Markel

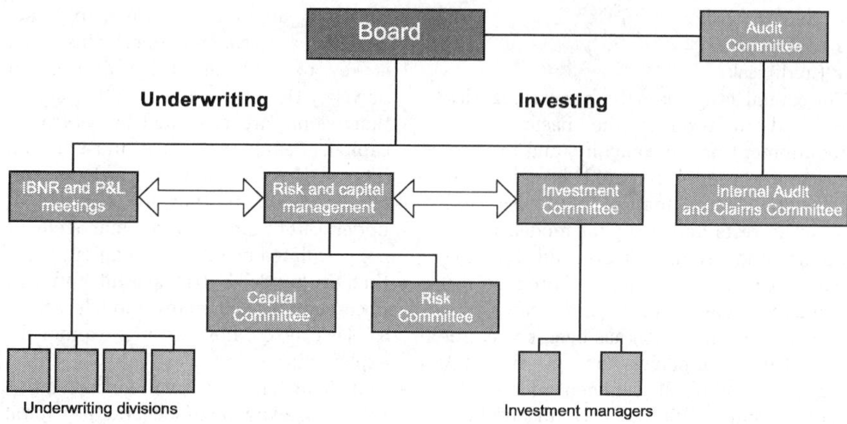

The IBNR and P&L meetings are attended by senior management and underwriters and are a crucial part of the business culture at Markel. They are used to identify lines of business that are not achieving profitability and required return on capital targets so that appropriate action can be taken at the earliest opportunity.

It is crucial that the results of all these meetings are embedded in the management and financial reporting and also in the capital management of the business.

Finally, the activities and results of the business are fed back to the board through effective risk management and reporting.

The results are a key driver in deciding the remuneration of underwriters. Part of our underwriters' remuneration is phased over a period of years, which thus provides a safeguard against underwriting strategies that appear profitable in the short term but ultimately deteriorate. The alignment of risk management with remuneration strategy is an essential part of the effective embedding of ERM.

CAPITAL ALLOCATION AND MANAGEMENT

The standard model for the majority of companies in the United Kingdom today is a product of the Individual Capital Assessment (ICA) regime, introduced by the Financial Services Authority while it waited for Europe to refine and introduce Solvency II. The implementation of ICA has been a significant step forward in delivering more risk-based capital management and has gone a good way to help meet the challenges of Solvency II.

"Bureaucracy. . .carries much of the function in modern industrialized society that was carried by the extended family, the village and the surrounding community before the industrial revolution." Elliot Jacques

     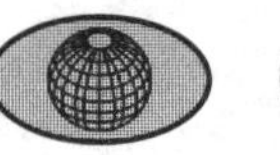   

Figure 3. Capital allocation

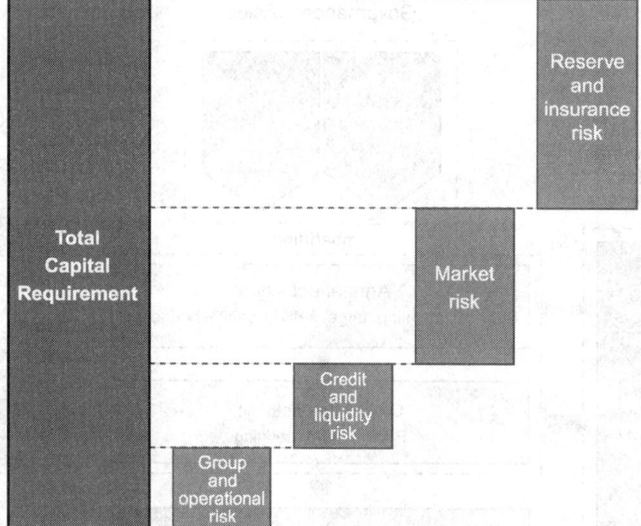

Figure 3 highlights that for a nonlife company the basic capital requirement is split into four risk categories:

- Insurance risk;
- Liquidity risk;
- Market risk;
- Credit risk.

The capital assigned to these risk categories is used to produce the basic capital requirement of the company, and in most cases the capital required is calculated through a combination of stress and scenario tests and a capital model. Operational and group risk are added to the basic capital requirement to produce the company's total capital requirement.

Although this model has been successful in getting companies through the ICA regime, it will not be sufficient to meet the requirements of Solvency II. In addition, ICA models suffer from the fact that for the most part they have been developed and owned by the finance and actuarial departments in companies. As a consequence, there has been minimal embedding into the rest of the business. At Markel, our ICA process has always been multi-disciplined, with a number of stakeholders involved. However, we are embedding the process further. Individual members of the Capital and Risk Committee work with the Board, underwriters, and investment managers to ensure that they understand the capital being allocated to them and the risk-adjusted returns required.

The key to effective capital management is to ensure:

- that it drives the decision-making process, ensuring optimal use of capital;
- that it is embedded into the business. It needs to be a key driver in strategy and planning, acquisitions, new lines of business, and legacy claims management. This is an area that needs a considerable amount of effort, but the benefits are considerable. This area is key to achieving the objectives of Solvency II;
- that people are rewarded by return on capital. People will take more of an interest if their bonuses are dependent on it, so ensure that the bonuses of underwriters and senior management are calculated by return on capital;
- that the model is transparent and well documented. Too many models act as a black box whose results cannot be explained;
- that financial and nonfinancial information used by the model and the capital management team is consistent with the information used by the business. Different information causes confusion, wastes time, and will result in poor decisions being made. An organization cannot have a model that operates with stand-alone information—it needs to be embedded into all aspects of the business.

The goal should be to minimize group and operational risk through effective ERM. A prudent approach is to have minimal appetite for credit and liquidity risk and a reasonable appetite for market risk.

The last and most significant risk is reserve and underwriting risk. A sound approach here is to split the capital required for reserve and underwriting risk into two components: prior-year reserve risk and current business risk. Here one allocates capital to cover the uncertainty on prior-year insurance reserves. Again, one can try to reduce this capital requirement by establishing prudent case and IBNR reserves so that reserves are more likely to be redundant than deficient.

Capital is also allocated to underwriting the current business. This capital is allocated to each product line, enabling management to set combined ratio targets that achieve the required return on risk-adjusted capital. These combined ratio targets will vary according to the volatility, length of tail, and reinsurance usage of the product line. In addition, the combined ratio target will take into consideration diversification with other classes of business.

The combined ratio targets are used to benchmark underwriting performance, and they act as a key driver in the setting of underwriter and management bonus targets.

WHAT ARE THE IMPLICATIONS OF SOLVENCY II?

The three-pillar approach of Solvency II works as follows. Pillar 1 deals with the quantitative capital requirements. It ensures that the valuation of assets and liabilities, and the calculation of capital requirements, are standardized. The areas covered are:

- Valuation of technical provisions;
- Minimum capital requirement;
- Solvency capital requirement;
- Investment rules

Pillar 2 deals with the qualitative side of Solvency II and focuses on

- The principles of internal control and risk management;
- Individual risk and capital assessment;
- The supervisory review process.

Pillar 3 deals with disclosure requirements discipline and covers:

- Transparency and disclosure and the support of risk-based supervision through market mechanisms.

So what are the implications of Solvency II for capital management? Already we can see that there are problems.

Within Pillar 1 it is clear that the technical provision under Solvency II and IFRS (International Financial Reporting Standards) is calculated differently. This difference will be a potent source of confusion, additional cost, and wasted effort—and it needs to be resolved.

It is also clear that the communications effort required to implement Pillar 1 will not be trivial. How are the new technical provisions to be communicated and embedded in the business? How do you explain to underwriters that their loss ratio reflects discounting and a cost-of-capital

"The manifest picture of bureaucratic organizationorganisation is a confusing one." Elliot Jacques

   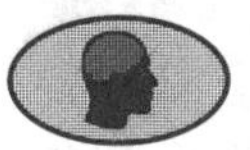  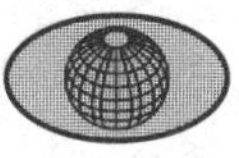   

adjustment? It took a long time for underwriters to understand combined ratios, so this will be a challenge.

The minimum capital requirement (MRC) set out in Solvency II fails to reward appropriate risk management due to its formulaic approach. It is also clear that in the majority of cases an internal capital model produces a lower solvency capital requirement, which means that there is a significant advantage to an organization in having its model approved. Finally, there are also significant implications for IT and data collection.

With Pillar 2 it is crucial that a company can demonstrate that it has effective ERM and that it is embedded in the business. Meeting the embedding or "use test" requires significant time and resources.

The main focus of Pillar 3 is disclosure, and therefore the implications of these disclosures need to be carefully thought through. These disclosures will include a report on:

- Governance and risk management;
- Valuation principles applied for solvency purposes;
- The internal model: methodologies, assumptions, and validation;
- Capital requirements, with an account of the company's minimum capital requirement and solvency capital requirement (SCR) and any breaches during the year, plus a breakdown of the SCR standard formula and internal model calculations.

CONCLUSION

So how does the road ahead look? It is clear that the sector has a number of challenges to overcome and that a period of hard work lies ahead. An effective ERM model, as we have argued through this piece, should be fundamental to any approach to implementing Solvency II and will, of itself, bring tremendous benefits to organizations that work to embed ERM in their organization.

MAKING IT HAPPEN

- A strong management culture will ensure that risks are understood, controlled, and effectively communicated. Effective ERM is a key driver in Solvency II.
- It is crucial that capital and risk management are embedded in the business. These are the DNA of an insurance company.
- Return on risk-adjusted capital should be a key driver in the remuneration of underwriters and management.
- Considerable resources and expense are still required to develop a fully integrated model; however the capital benefits of doing so will be significant.

MORE INFO

Websites:

European Commission collection of documents on various aspects of Solvency II: ec.europa.eu/internal_market/insurance/solvency/index_en.htm

Financial Services Authority (FSA) section on Solvency II: www.fsa.gov.uk/pages/About/What/International/solvency/index.shtml

Solvency II Association training and presentations: www.solvency-ii-training.com

NOTES

1 A. M. Best. "Risk management and the rating process for insurance companies." January 25, 2008. Online at: www.ambest.com/ratings/methodology/riskmanagement.pdf

2 Paul Moore, HBOS, "man in a rowing boat"

3 Markel International comprises the international operations of Markel Corporation, a US property casualty company listed on the New York Stock Exchange. It writes a variety of property, casualty, and marine insurance and reinsurance business through its two London-based platforms, Markel International Insurance Company and Markel Syndicate 3000.

"Bureaucracy is. . .a potentially powerful force in the direction of freedom and justice in industrial society, by acting to ensure openness and social mobility." Elliot Jacques

  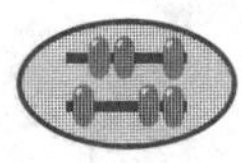   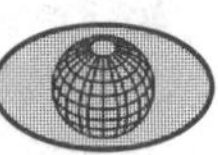   

Viewpoint: Viral Acharya and Julian Franks

Regulation after the Crash

INTRODUCTION

Julian Franks is Professor of Finance and Academic Director at London Business School's Centre for Corporate Governance. Here he reflects on the shape of future regulation of the financial services sector. His research focuses on bankruptcy and financial distress and corporate ownership and control, a field in which he has won two international prizes. He served as a member of a UK government working party reviewing the insolvency code and advised (with LBS professor Richard A. Brealey) the Office of Constitutional Affairs on the issue of outside equity for law firms and is an adviser to the regulator, Ofcom, and BAA. His qualifications include a BA (Sheffield), an MBA (Columbia), and PhD (London).

Viral V. Acharya is Professor of Finance at London Business School and New York University Stern School of Business, Academic Director of the Coller Institute of Private Equity, and a research affiliate of the Centre for Economic Policy Research (CEPR). He joined LBS in 2001 following a PhD in finance from Stern School of Business and bachelor degrees in computer science and engineering from the Indian Institute of Technology, Mumbai. His research interests are in the regulation of banks and financial institutions, corporate finance, credit risk, the valuation of corporate debt, and asset pricing with a focus on the effects of liquidity risk and he has won a string of awards for his academic papers. He was appointed as a Senior Houblon-Normal Research Fellow at the Bank of England in summer 2008 to conduct research on the efficiency of the interbank lending markets.

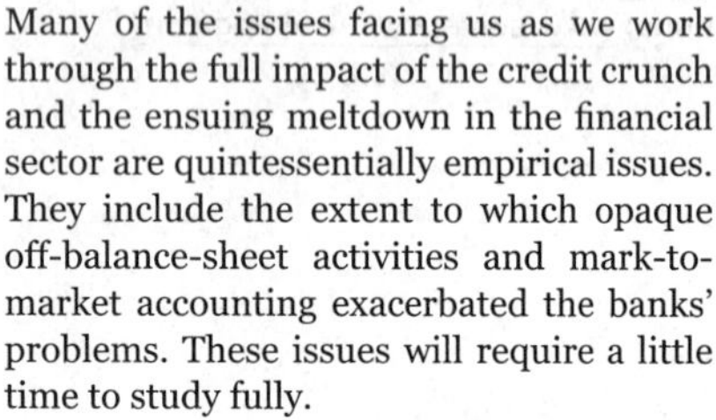

Many of the issues facing us as we work through the full impact of the credit crunch and the ensuing meltdown in the financial sector are quintessentially empirical issues. They include the extent to which opaque off-balance-sheet activities and mark-to-market accounting exacerbated the banks' problems. These issues will require a little time to study fully.

There is, therefore, a real danger that the many temporary measures we see being taken by governments around the world will be set in concrete before the issues involved have been fully digested and their implications and lessons understood. One has to hope that wisdom will prevail and that temporary solutions will remain temporary until we are all a great deal clearer as to what has happened and how we can fix it.

Here we raise a number of points that we believe are worth considering. For example, one thing that is emerging from the current downturn is that this recession is really going to test insolvency procedures, both in the United Kingdom and across Europe. There are two elements to this, namely insolvencies for traditional companies and insolvency procedures for banks and financial institutions. We shall confine our comments to the latter.

Our view is that we could benefit greatly by extending the insolvency provisions that apply to utilities to the financial services sector. In the event of a utility company failing, a special administrator regime can be applied, taking control of the company and reorganizing it in a way that takes account of stakeholders other than creditors and shareholders. At present, our insolvency laws require administrators to focus only on the needs of these two groups. However, in the special utility regime, customers come first and the regulator has the freedom to arrange matters to prioritize continued service to customers.

We are seeing a de facto move in this direction with the nationalization of the banks. However, this is not quite the same as the "ring fencing" of the utility assets. When Enron imploded, because of the special utilities regime, the assets of Wessex Water, which was wholly owned by Enron, were ring-fenced from the company's nonregulated assets. The special administrator was able to take control of those assets and run them not just for the shareholders and creditors, but also to the benefit of water consumers. This created a significantly different set of circumstances to those with which a traditional insolvency practitioner deals.

This kind of regime dates back to the 19th century, where the United Kingdom passed special administration rules for railways that prevented creditors from tearing up the railway lines to recoup their losses from railways that had gone bust.

The United States did not follow suit and in the end the US government had to step in and break contracts to stop creditors from ripping up the tracks. Similarly, today, with busted utility companies, creditors are unable to recoup their losses by digging up the pipes for scrap.

Policymakers should give some thought to these special insolvency regimes when contemplating the future of the banking sector. The question is: what kind of bankruptcy regime do we need, going forward, for financial services companies, and to which organizations should such a regime apply? Banks? Insurance companies? Investment Banks? All of them or just a select few?

Another aspect of regulation that will have to be thought about very carefully is regulatory arbitrage. Because deposit

"The development of the modern form of the organization of corporate groups in all fields is nothing less than identical with the development and continual spread of bureaucratic administration." Max Weber

  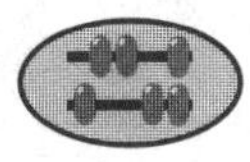   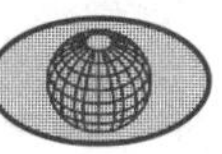   

insurance makes the cost of deposits for banks lower, what you really want to prevent, in these circumstances, is banks using the finance raised within the regulatory regime to subsidize the purchase of assets somehow that are (or, at least should be) outside the regime.

So, how do we prevent banks from using assets which are partially or fully guaranteed and which therefore have a relatively low cost of capital, from competing unfairly in other markets? How can a regulatory regime ensure that, in the event of subsidized funds being used outside the ring fence that the conventional—i.e., the unguaranteed—cost of capital is fully recognized?

One way of solving the problem would be for central banks to charge banks a risk-based, "marked-to-market" fee for their government guarantees. It would ensure that banks would face the full cost of capital once they moved outside the ring fence of protected assets. If the central bank does not charge a fee, or charges too low a fee, then the regulator (and ultimately government) has to ask itself how it is preventing regulatory arbitrage.

Another crucial point, of course, concerns off-balance-sheet assets. There is no question but that off-balance-sheet assets such as Credit Default Swaps (CDSs) and Collateral Loan Obligations (CDOs) have been very serious causal contributors to the present crisis. Regulators, for reasons we and many others do not fully understand, have allowed this to happen in an uncontrolled way, and that game is now over. Already we are seeing the implementation of central clearing houses for CDSs.

The more subtle point is that banks were able to keep certain types of assets off their balance sheets because these assets were deemed to be "nonrecourse" assets by regulators. However, in most of the asset-backed commercial paper conduits there was, in fact, explicit recourse in the form of close to 100% liquidity and credit enhancement by sponsoring banks.

Even in the case of SIVs, where such enhancement was not complete, it is clear that the sponsoring bank stood behind those assets as far as its reputation was concerned. This is why so many of the SIVs whose assets lost liquidity during the subprime crisis were taken back by banks onto their balance sheets.

Thus, the so-called "credit risk transfer" innovations employed during 2003 to the second quarter of 2007 were aimed at gaming regulation and taking on excessive leverage and risk, rather than generating economic efficiency. This is a very important point for regulatory authorities to get to grips with and we suspect that, when they do, it will lead to a much tighter definition of what banks can and cannot do. Once this happens, or even looks as if it is on the cards, you will get a predictable hue and cry about "the dead hand of regulation stifling innovation in the financial sector."

THE FUTURE OF REGULATION

There are two sensible options for the future of regulation. One is to take the existing regulatory framework and to look to improve it in a variety of ways. Or the regulatory authorities can go down a different route. They can look to ring-fence the activities of banks and move the proscribed activities into other institutions that are also regulated, but that do not carry the same systemic risk (since banks occupy such a critical place in the economy). A third option is for the regulator to try to do a mix of both options. That route, in our opinion, leads to some very serious policy traps and errors for regulators.

As things stand, most governments and bank regulators are determined to avoid a depression or a profoundly deep recession. And they want to put a regulatory regime in place that will mitigate these problems if they arise again. These are laudable aims and one does not want to underestimate the scale of the issues with which governments are grappling.

Our guess is that banking activities will end up being narrowed substantially. We cannot allow banks to take on the huge risks that they have been taking on, at the same time as having their liabilities guaranteed by government. What rationale is there, for example, for guaranteeing the deposits of an institution whose revenues largely come from making markets in derivatives? So we would expect commercial banks—the deposit-guaranteed banks—to be shorn of at least some of the ability to do investment banking. Already, we have seen the big US investment banks hurrying to shed their investment banking status because they were being massively disadvantaged by the guarantees being offered to commercial banks.

It is now beyond argument that we need effective regulation and the mechanisms and structures that enable effective regulation to take place. With hindsight we can all see that it was very unfortunate that there was not a clearing house for some of these derivative products. One thinks particularly of the CDSs market and the CDOs.

If there had been a clearing house where all these deals were registered, it would have been much clearer, at a much earlier stage in the proceedings, just who owed what to whom, how they would settle, and what the losses on specific transactions were likely to be. It is now virtually axiomatic that where you have large markets in products, and the CDS market is absolutely enormous, being valued variously at between US$40 trillion and US$60 trillion, you really do need a clearing house. There are already a number of moves to regulate and further standardize the CDS market and that is, of course, desirable.

In the United Kingdom the major commercial banks have been heavily involved over the last 20 years or more in the leveraged buyout market (LBO). Our view here is that, though we will see a high level of defaulting in the LBO market through the current downturn, the defaults are likely to be triggered through breaches of covenants at a level well above the liquidation value of the assets. Losses, therefore, to the banks should be limited. As consumer spending tightens, we are seeing some major retailing names fold, but this has tended to be because the underlying business models were not sufficiently robust.

MARKETS' GROWING AWARENESS

A vigilant debt market can be very useful in forcing companies to face up to their weaknesses much earlier in the cycle of decline. This does not, of course, detract from the misery of the people being made unemployed. What we are seeing though, is a growing awareness that the prices many businesses paid for acquisitions were far too high and the financial institutions that provided debt funding for those acquisitions were not careful enough. There was many a deal done from which they should have walked away. Banks were chasing market share, rather than profitability and that is costing them—and the rest of the economy—dearly now.

In principle there is no argument but that banks have to be adequately capitalized, and it is equally clear that the current crisis has shown that they were not adequately capitalized for the level of risk that they were running. The regulatory regime, especially Basel requirements, failed and failed badly.

It is now a moot point whether Basel II is salvageable. Clearly we need some sort of global agreement to which everyone signs. It would be a nightmare having different jurisdictions setting reserve capital values. Basel II was 10 years in the making and yet it clearly did not work. On some fronts, it did better than Basel I but on others, it fared much worse. Can we reconvene and mend it? That question still remains to be worked through.

What is clearly a problem with Basel II is

"Bureaucratic administration means fundamentally the exercise of control on the basis of knowledge."
Max Weber

that it is far too dependent on the banks' own assessments of risk taking. We knew about the off-balance-sheet vehicles but we decided to leave it to the banks to decide whether these vehicles carried any risk to the bank and for what risk they should be accounting. People who defend the modeling approach say that it was not the model's fault, but the fault of the bankers. But that is the point. Capital requirements cannot be designed solely based on statistical objectives of quantifying risks; their design must also account for bankers' incentives to "game" the requirements.

INTERNATIONAL REGULATORY POWER

That there will have to be some international agreement at the end of all this seems inevitable. Banking has become too globalized for purely local, national decisions. Ultimately this throws up the issue of global coordination and burden-sharing during significant crises. Currently the variability of regulation across countries is significant, yet as we have seen in the current crisis, when banks fail in one country, taxpayers in other countries can find themselves being expected to pick up the bill. The UK taxpayer was not responsible in any way for the adventures undertaken by the Icelandic banks, but they still paid the price.

The ratings agencies too, have come out of things extremely badly. Products were given a Triple A rating that were by no stretch of the imagination Triple A. The people who set up these products thought the risks were diversifiable, with low correlation between the various classes of risk. In point of fact, the risks were highly correlated. To be precise, they became highly correlated during a systemic downturn. People just did not give sufficient weight to the idea of such systemic risk.

A company providing earthquake insurance must ask itself whether, in the worst case, it can meet the losses it is insuring. It is now clear that institutions such as AIG did not bother to pose this question to themselves at all. Provided there is no earthquake, selling earthquake insurance looks like free money. But it is absolutely fatal to assume that one will never happen. Of course, if you are too big to fail, the costs are primarily borne by taxpayers. And, this is why, regulation after the crash will need to focus primarily on pricing government guarantees right and precluding large-scale regulatory arbitrage by the financial sector.

▸▸ MORE INFO

Books:

Acharya, Viral and Matthew Richardson. *Restoring Financial Stability: How to Repair a Failed System*. Hoboken, NJ: Wiley, 2009.

Bagehot, Walter. *Lombard Street: A Description of the Money Market*. Chichester, UK: Wiley, 1999.

Bebchuk, Lucian, and Jesse Fried. *Pay without Performance: The Unfulfilled Promise of Executive Compensation*. Cambridge, MA: Harvard University Press, 2004.

Dewatripont, Mathias, and Jean Tirole. *The Prudential Regulation of Banks*. Cambridge, MA: MIT Press, 1994.

Kindleberger, Charles P., and Robert Aliber. *Panics, Manias and Crashes: A History of Financial Crises*. 5th ed. Basingstoke, UK: Palgrave Macmillan, 2005.

Rochet, Jean-Charles. *Why Are There So Many Banking Crises*. Princeton, NJ: Princeton University Press, 2008.

See Also:

Alan Greenspan (p. 1169)

The Age of Turbulence: Adventures in a New World (p. 1217)

Banking and Financial Services (pp. 1500–1502)

"The purely bureaucratic type of administrative organization. . .is superior to any other form in precision, in stability, in the stringency of its discipline, and in its reliability." Max Weber

  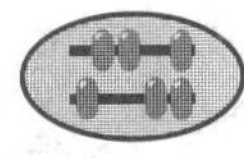 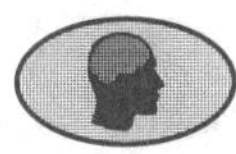  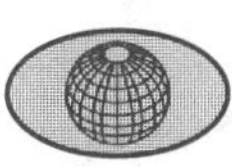   

Fair Value Accounting: SFAS 157 and IAS 39 by Kevin Ow Yong

EXECUTIVE SUMMARY

- Fair value accounting is increasingly being adopted by many countries across the world.
- When financial instruments are not traded in active markets, fair value accounting involves subjective estimations based on valuation models.
- There are many measurement considerations that managers need to be aware of when making subjective valuation estimates of their firms' financial instruments.
- Understanding these measurement issues aids managers in considering how best to manage their firms' assets and liabilities in a fair-value-driven accounting regime.

INTRODUCTION

Recent initiatives by both the International Accounting Standards Board (IASB) and the US Financial Accounting Standards Board (FASB) have increased the use of fair value accounting for financial reporting across many jurisdictions around the world. There are many issues surrounding fair value accounting. This article outlines the main measurement issues contained in the fair value accounting standard used by the FASB (SFAS 157), and that used by the IASB (IAS 39).

THE RATIONALE FOR FAIR VALUE ACCOUNTING

The increasing use of fair value accounting in financial reporting came about because accounting standard setters have debated, and come to the conclusion that fair value appears to meet the conceptual framework criteria better than other measurement bases (for example, historical cost, amortized cost, among others). Notwithstanding this rationale, a major issue with fair value accounting is the difficulty of measurement ("subjective estimates") when financial instruments do not trade in active markets. Both SFAS 157 and IAS 39 provide measurement guidance as to how firms should compute fair value estimates in such a situation.

FAIR VALUE ACCOUNTING BASED ON SFAS 157

SFAS 157 details the framework for measuring fair value for firms reporting their financial statements based on US GAAP. Prior to this standard, there were different definitions of fair value, and limited guidance in the applications of those definitions. SFAS 157 provides a consistent definition of fair value, outlines several types of valuation techniques that can be used to measure fair value, and requires firms to disclose their valuation inputs (the "fair value hierarchy"), in order to increase consistency and comparability in fair value measurements.

The standard defines fair value as "the price that would be received to sell an asset or paid to transfer a liability in an orderly transaction between market participants at the measurement date" (paragraph 5). This definition focuses on the price that would be received to sell the asset or paid to transfer the liability ("exit price"), not the price that would be paid to acquire the asset or received to assume the liability ("entry price"). An orderly transaction assumes that the firm has sufficient time to market the asset. Hence, fair value estimates should not be estimated as in a forced liquidation or distress sale, contrary to some misconceptions about fair value accounting.

SFAS 157 states three valuation techniques which can be used for estimating fair values. They are the market approach, income approach, and/or cost approach (paragraph 18). A market approach typically uses quoted prices in active markets, but other valuation techniques consistent with the market approach include the use of market multiples derived from a set of comparables, and matrix pricing that allows a firm to value securities without relying exclusively on quoted prices.

The second approach is the income approach. The income approach uses valuation techniques to convert future amounts (cash flows or earnings) to a single present value amount. Examples of such valuation techniques include present value discounted cash flows, option pricing models (for example, the Black–Scholes–Merton formula, or a binomial model), and the multi-period excess earnings method. Finally, the cost approach is based on the amount that would be required to replace the service capacity of an asset. From the perspective of a seller, the price that would be received for the asset is determined based on the cost to a buyer to acquire or construct a substitute asset of comparable utility, adjusted for obsolescence such as physical, functional (technological), and economic (external) obsolescence.

SFAS 157 establishes a fair value hierarchy that prioritizes the inputs to valuation techniques that are used to measure fair value. Broadly speaking, inputs refer to the assumptions that market participants would use in pricing the asset or liability, including assumptions about risk. The standard specifies the use of valuation techniques that maximize the use of observable inputs (i.e., based on market data obtained from sources independent of the firm), and minimize the use of unobservable inputs (i.e, inputs that reflect the firm's own assumptions as to how market participants would price an asset or liability) (paragraph 21).

Specifically, a firm is to use Level 1 inputs (unadjusted quoted prices in active markets) on the assumption that a quoted price in an active market provides the most reliable evidence of fair value. It shall be used whenever available (paragraph 24), except when it is available but not readily accessible (paragraph 25), or when it might not represent fair value at the measurement date (paragraph 26). If observable prices are not available, the firm can value its assets based on Level 2 inputs (observable inputs other than quoted prices included within Level 1). Level 2 inputs are inputs such as (i) quoted prices for similar (but not identical) assets or liabilities in both active and inactive markets, and (ii) inputs other than quoted prices such as interest rates and yield curves, credit risks, default risks, and other inputs that can be derived principally from observable market data by correlation, or other means (market-corroborated inputs). A Level 2 input must be substantially observable for the full term of the asset or liability.

Finally, to the extent that observable Level 2 inputs are not available (for example, situations in which there is little market activity for the asset or liability at measurement date), Level 3 inputs can be applied. These are the firm's own assumptions about how other market participants would price the asset or liability. To ensure that there is information that will enable financial statement users to assess the quality of inputs used to estimate these fair value measurements, the standard requires

"Capitalism. . .strongly tends to foster the development of bureaucracy. . .Conversely, capitalism is the most rational economic basis for bureaucratic administration and enables it to develop in the most rational form."
Max Weber

  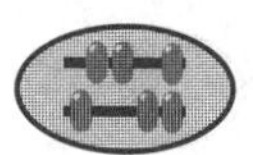 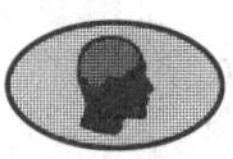  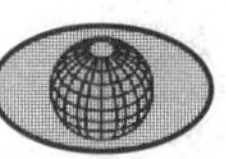   

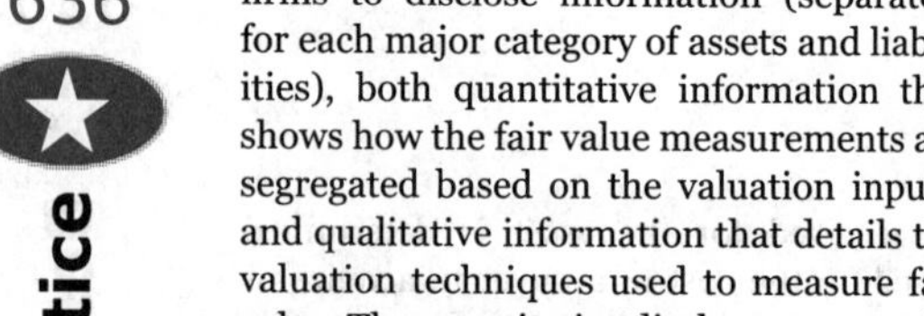

firms to disclose information (separately for each major category of assets and liabilities), both quantitative information that shows how the fair value measurements are segregated based on the valuation inputs, and qualitative information that details the valuation techniques used to measure fair value. The quantitative disclosures are to be presented in tabular format. An example is given in the Case Study.

FAIR VALUE ACCOUNTING BASED ON IAS 39

IAS 39 details the principles for recognizing and measuring financial instruments for firms that report their financial statements under IFRS. IAS 39 defines fair value slightly differently from SFAS 157. Fair value is defined as "the amount for which an asset could be exchanged, or a liability settled, between knowledgeable, willing parties in an arm's length transaction" (paragraph 9).

There are some subtle language differences between the fair value definition in SFAS 157 versus that in IAS 39. SFAS 157's definition is explicitly based on the concept of an "exit price," whereas IAS 39's definition is based neither on "exit price," nor "entry price." SFAS 157 uses the "market participants" view whereas IAS 39's definition uses the concept of "willing buyer and seller." SFAS 157 states that the fair value of a liability is the price that will be paid to transfer a liability, whereas IAS 39 defines the fair value of a liability as the amount for which it can be settled. The IASB has asked for respondents' views on these differences.

As with SFAS 157, IAS 39 states that fair value estimation is not the amount that a firm would receive or pay in a forced transaction, involuntary liquidation, or distress sale (paragraph A69). Also consistent with SFAS 157, IAS 39 regards the best evidence of fair value as quoted prices in an active market (paragraph 48). Finally, while IAS 39 does not explicitly classify valuation inputs into Level 1, Level 2, and Level 3 categories as specified in SFAS 157, it does specify that the chosen valuation technique should make maximum use of market inputs and rely as little as possible on firm-specific inputs.

Regarding the measurement issues relating to fair value estimation, IAS 39 provides three classifications: Active markets for which quoted prices are available, inactive markets for nonequity instruments, and inactive markets for equity instruments. For financial instruments trading in active markets, the appropriate quoted market of an asset held (or liability to be issued) is the current bid price, whereas for assets to be acquired (or liability held), it is the current ask price. When current bid and ask prices are unavailable, the price of the most recent transaction can be used provided that there has not been a significant change in economic circumstances since the time of the transaction. Furthermore, quoted prices can be adjusted if the firm can demonstrate it is not fair value (for example, distress sales).

In the absence of an active market for a nonequity financial instrument, IAS 39 specifies that the preferred valuation technique to be used is the valuation technique that is shown to be commonly used by market participants to price the instrument (for example, if the valuation technique has been demonstrated to be able to provide reliable estimates of fair value obtained in actual market transactions). The chosen valuation technique needs to be consistent with established economic methodologies for pricing financial instruments, and the firm needs to calibrate the valuation technique periodically by testing it for validity using prices from any observable current market transactions in the same instrument (or based on any available observable market data).

Finally, for equity instruments (and any linked derivatives) that do not have a quoted market price in active markets, IAS 39 specifies that these instruments are to be measured at fair values only if the range of reasonable fair value estimates is not significant, and the probabilities of the various estimates can be reasonably assessed. Otherwise, the firm is precluded from measuring these instruments at fair value.

FURTHER CONSIDERATIONS

Recent illiquidity in some financial markets due to the subprime crisis has highlighted to standard setters the need to provide additional guidance in the measurement of fair value of financial instruments in markets that are not active. The IASB formed an expert advisery panel in mid-2008 to discuss specific issues encountered in the current adverse market environment. Likewise, the FASB issued FSP FAS 157-3, *Determining the fair value of a financial asset in a market that is not active*, to clarify how management's internal assumptions and observable market information should be considered when measuring fair value in markets that are not active, as well as how market quotes such as broker quotes should be considered in measuring fair value.

First, while broker quotes may be an appropriate input when measuring fair value, they are not necessarily determinative if an active market does not exist for the financial market. Thus, the firm should not automatically conclude that a particular transaction price is determinative of fair value. In markets that are not active, managerial judgment is required to evaluate whether individual transactions are forced liquidations or distressed sales.

Having said that, it is also inappropriate to automatically conclude that an inactive market implies the presence of forced transactions. The determination of whether a transaction is forced requires a comprehensive understanding of the circumstances of the transaction. Examples of what may constitute a forced transaction include a legal requirement to transact

CASE STUDY

Two examples are given that show how financial assets and liabilities are disclosed, as reported by HSBC Finance Corporation, which is incorporated in the US, and HSBC Bank plc, a UK entity. Evidently, HSBC Finance Corporation categorized and reported the fair values of its assets and liabilities based on the nature of valuation inputs (Note 15 to the accounts). For example, the firm reported US$3,136 million of available-for-sale securities, of which US$354 million were fair value estimates from quoted prices in active markets (Level 1), US$2,743 million were fair value estimates from Level 2 inputs and US$39 million originated from Level 3 valuation inputs.

In contrast, HSBC Bank plc has traditionally reported its fair values by measurement basis (for example, £427,329 million as trading assets) in its Notes on the Financial Statements (Note 15: Analysis of financial assets and liabilities by measurement basis). To provide additional disclosures that are similar to SFAS 157's disclosure requirements, HSBC Bank plc disaggregated its £427,329 million of trading assets into fair value estimates that were derived from quoted prices (£234,399 million), versus those fair value estimates that were based on valuation methods using observable inputs (£185,369 million), and significant nonobservable inputs (£7,561 million).[1]

"There is something about a bureaucrat that does not like a poem." Gore Vidal

  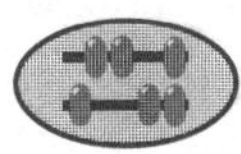   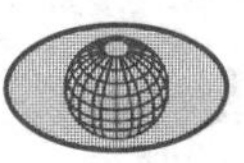   

regardless of market conditions, or a necessity to dispose an asset immediately, even if there is insufficient time to market that asset to be sold. Hence, the presence of an inactive market may simply reflect an imbalance between supply and demand (i.e., more sellers than buyers), and not represent evidence of forced transactions (or distress sales).

Finally, the standard setters also clarify that, regardless of the valuation technique used to estimate fair values, a firm should always include appropriate risk adjustments that take into account credit and liquidity risks. This is because a fair value estimate that does not take into account all factors that market participants would consider in pricing the instrument does not represent a fair estimate of a current transaction price on the measurement date.

GOING FORWARD

The IASB is currently working on several long-term projects that will further clarify guidance on fair value measurements. First, the IASB is working to establish a single source of guidance for all fair value measurements required or permitted by existing IFRSs, so as to reduce complexity, and improve consistency in their application. This project is similar in intent to SFAS 157, although it might differ in its requirements and wording. Publication of the exposure draft is expected in the second quarter of 2009, and the effective date to publish the standard is projected to be in 2010.

Second, the IASB is currently working to simplify and improve IAS 39. The board recognizes the need to improve the reporting of financial instruments, and to reduce the complexity of that reporting. In March 2008, the IASB published a discussion paper, *Reducing Complexity in Reporting Financial Instruments*. Going forward, the IASB plans to issue an IFRS to simplify financial instrument reporting, although no specific timeline has been set.

Third, the financial crisis has raised concerns that users need further information on how firms estimate the fair value of their financial instruments when there are only limited market data to support those estimates. In October 2008, the IASB published an exposure draft, *Improving Disclosures about Financial Instruments*, that proposes amendments to IFRS 7 (*Financial Instruments: Disclosures*). The exposure draft proposes disclosure requirements that are similar to the disclosure requirements in SFAS 157, such as having the three-level, fair value hierarchy. Depending on the comments received, the board will deliberate whether to proceed with amending IFRS 7.

Similarly, the FASB has also announced the addition of new FASB agenda projects intended to improve both the application guidance used to determine fair values, and the disclosure of fair value estimates. These projects were added partly in response to recommendations contained in the December 2008 Securities and Exchange Commission's (SEC) report on mark-to-market accounting. The SEC report recommended against suspension of fair value accounting standards, and reaffirmed that investors generally believe fair value accounting increases financial reporting transparency. The FASB anticipates that the project on application guidance will be completed by the end of the second quarter of 2009, and the project on improving disclosures in time for 2009 year-end financial reporting.

CONCLUSION

The trend toward fair value accounting appears to be irreversible. Fair value accounting requires recognition of balance sheet amounts at fair value, and changes in fair values to have an impact on the income statement, or via stockholder equity. Managers should be aware of the various measurement issues involved in valuing the financial instruments in their companies, especially when subjective fair value estimates are involved.

MAKING IT HAPPEN

Managers need to consider some important considerations when implementing fair value accounting. For example:

- The availability of observable market inputs, and how that would affect the estimation of fair values;
- The validity of valuation models used to estimate subjective fair values, given that valuation models might overlook certain key assumptions;
- The possible impact of increased volatility in their firms' earnings, and/or valuations as a result of fair value accounting, and how best to mitigate the increased volatility;
- The potential of systemic risk (or contagion risk) during periods of rapidly falling markets.

▸▸ MORE INFO

Reports:

FASB. "FASB staff position no. FAS 157-3. Determining the fair value of a financial asset when the market for that asset is not active." October 10, 2008. Online at: www.fasb.org/pdf/fsp_fas157-3.pdf

FASB. "Summary of statement no.157: Fair value measurements." Online at: www.fasb.org/st/summary/stsum157.shtml

IASC Foundation. "Technical summary. IAS 39 Financial Instruments: Recognition and Measurement." Online at: www.iasb.org/NR/rdonlyres/339C384D-045B-47D7-AA8E-8D26DFA726FB/0/IAS39.pdf

IASB Expert Advisery Panel. "Measuring and disclosing the fair value of financial instruments in markets that are no longer active." October 2008. Online at: www.iasb.org/NR/rdonlyres/0E37D59C-1C74-4D61-A984-8FAC61915010/0/IASB_Expert_Advisery_Panel_October_2008.pdf

US Securities and Exchange Commission. "Report and recommendations pursuant to Section 133 of the Emergency Economic Stabilization Act of 2008: Study on mark-to-market accounting." Online at: www.sec.gov/news/studies/2008/marktomarket123008.pdf

Websites:

Financial Accounting Standards Board (FASB): www.fasb.org
International Accounting Standards Board (IASB): www.iasb.org

NOTES

1 Case study references:

HSBC Finance Corporation 10-Q filing for period ended September 30, 2008
Note 15 to consolidated financial statements (unaudited) – Fair value measurements (pp 33–36)

HSBC Bank plc Annual Report 2008
Note 15 on the financial statements: Analysis of financial assets and liabilities by measurement basis (pp 392–395)

HSBC Bank plc Annual Report 2008
Report of the directors: Impact of market turmoil (pp 144–187)

All reports available online at: www.hsbc.com/1/2/financialresults

"In an information society, neither governments nor corporations will rely exclusively on formal, bureaucratic rules. . .Instead, they will have to decentralize and. . .rely on the people over whom they have nominal authority to be self-organizing." Francis Fukuyama

  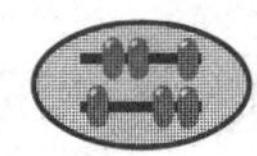   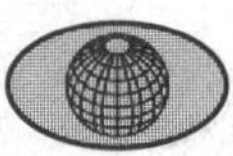   

Has Financial Reporting Impacted on Internal Auditing Negatively? by Andrew Chambers

EXECUTIVE SUMMARY

- At the turn of the millennium, the internal auditing profession sought to formally broaden its role for internal audit by embracing "consulting services" that went beyond its traditional assurance role. This move was almost immediately challenged by the collapse of Enron and other large corporations, which led to stockholders and boards demanding more focus not only on the internal audit assurance role but also, more specifically, on the assurance of internal control over financial reporting—at the expense of assurance on operational effectiveness and efficiency and assurance on compliance with laws, regulations, and policies.
- Since then, internal audit has often been commandeered into discharging what should be management's role—for instance, to comply with Section 404 of the Sarbanes–Oxley Act (2002)—whereas the proper internal audit role should be to audit the compliance work that management has done. A better balance is now being achieved, not least as the Sarbanes–Oxley compliance requirements become bedded into companies as well as becoming slightly less onerous.
- The storm that hit the US corporate sector at the turn of the millennium was a salutary reminder of the importance of effective assurance auditing and the need for this to be done in depth. However, it is not only (or even primarily) in financial and accounting matters that assurance is needed. Entities achieve their objectives mainly in the operational areas of their businesses, and they need assurance that operations are effective and efficient. They also need assurance that laws and regulations are being complied with, for instance with regard to the security of personal data in IT.
- Entities can also benefit from the consulting services that internal audit is able to offer, but internal audit is still neglecting these activities by focusing disproportionately on the internal control of financial reporting.

INTERNAL AUDIT'S CONSULTING ROLE

It was unfortunate that the Institute of Internal Auditors (IIA) released its first consulting *Standards*, to add to its already existing assurance *Standards*, at exactly the time when Enron collapsed. "Implementation Standards" set out how the "Attribute Standards" and "Performance Standards" should be applied in the context of either assurance or consulting work. In 2007 the IIA announced that it had no plans to release further sets of "Implementation Standards."[1]

In spite of its bad timing, the release of the consulting *Standards* was a natural development in the evolution of internal auditing, albeit not one that gained universal approval. This development was the principal driver behind the release in 2000 of a completely revamped set of *Standards* (effective January 1, 2002) to replace the IIA's original *Standards* that had remained unaltered, except in one or two minor details, since their release in 1978. The main need for new *Standards* arose from a widely held perception that the old *Standards* had ceased to describe either what constituted contemporary best practice in internal auditing or, indeed, how internal auditors spent much of their time. Faced with this challenge, the IIA set out to determine the nature of internal auditing as it currently was. Prior to developing the new *Standards* the IIA invested much effort, including two exposure drafts, in achieving an agreed new definition of internal auditing. The new *Standards* were then modeled around this new definition (see Optimizing Internal Audit, (pp. 694–696)):

> "Internal auditing is an independent, objective assurance and consulting activity designed to add value and improve an organization's operations. It helps an organization accomplish its objectives by bringing a systematic, disciplined approach to evaluate and improve the effectiveness of risk management, control, and governance processes."[2]

Prior to this definition and prior to the new *Standards*, internal auditing had been perceived as an assurance service, but now "consulting activity" was added. Some say this definition gives the consulting role equal weight to the assurance role (for example, "the definition gives equal consideration to both assurance and consulting activities")[3]. The fundamental challenge was to determine whether all the non-assurance activities that engaged internal auditors' time should continue to be regarded as noninternal audit work or whether they should be brought within the definition of internal auditing. The latter was decided upon. This was hardly surprising as throughout the 1990s there had been some skepticism as to the value of internal auditors' assurance work and a view that their role in providing consulting services was much more constructive and added much more value.

SWING TO MORE EMPHASIS ON THE ASSURANCE ROLE

Then came the spectacular collapses of Enron, Tyco, Worldcom, and others. Almost immediately the pendulum in the internal audit role swung away from offering consulting services toward providing stronger assurance. Audit committees and boards arrived at the painful realization that they had been starved of the independent assurance they needed and they looked to their internal auditors, among others, to provide them with that assurance.

The IIA's Global Auditing Information Network (GAIN) survey found that 36% of a total of 341 respondents fully supported the idea of internal auditors doing consultancy work. Of the remainder, 41% agreed with the statement: "consulting is usually the way to go, but you have to be careful; sometimes it is not a good idea," 7% considered that internal auditors should rarely or never do consulting work, and 16% thought that in theory consulting sounded good, but in practice it was a bad idea more often than not.

"In spite of its bad timing, the release of the consulting *Standards* was a natural development in the evolution of internal auditing, albeit not one that gained universal approval."

An *AuditWire* article[4] quoted two contrasting views about the place of consultancy services in the internal auditor's repertoire:

Against:

> "The Andersen debacle drove home the risks to maintaining our independence when we auditors neglect or stray from our primary mission, which should be providing internal control assurance.

"Time spent on any item of the agenda will be in inverse proportion to the sum involved." C. Northcote Parkinson

When my audit team is approached by management for a consulting project, four red flags are raised in my mind:

—If management is asking the audit group for help, there must be a control concern. As an auditor, my first responsibility is to decide whether an audit or investigation is warranted.

—If there is no control concern, I must wonder whether the manager considers the project too risky for his or her own people to do or whether it's of too little value to engage a third party on the project.

—If it's too risky for the manager's own people to tackle, does this indicate that the manager has the wrong people on staff or not enough people? If the project has insufficient value to warrant hiring a third party, why would I want to associate our audit group with the project?

—Finally, I must ask myself whether I believe that I have been so successful in my assurance role that internal auditing has no other risk-based priorities to pursue. If so, the audit group must be overstaffed."

> The Sarbanes–Oxley Act of 2002, itself a direct result of the Enron debacle, has turned the screw further as far as internal audit is concerned.

In favor:

"Consulting is one of the most important services we provide for management. We have found a direct correlation between our time spent on consulting and the decrease that we have in investigations. So, when I do my audit plan at the beginning of the year, I save a certain amount of time to do the consulting projects that aren't part of the risk-based audit program . . .

We have an incredibly wonderful, comfortable relationship [with management]. People see the audit staff as peers and feel very comfortable calling and asking them questions . . .

In the next couple of months, I'll be developing an online conflict-of-interest training course, which our federal researchers will be required to take. We'll be doing that with our new whistleblowers policy as well."

The corporate governance debacles at the turn of the millennium, of the United States in particular but of Europe and elsewhere too, therefore heralded a relative swing away from an internal audit emphasis on consulting services back to the more traditional assurance role. Indeed there are many internal audit functions, including some of the largest, that reject a consulting role entirely. The heavily revised 2009 *Standards* of the IIA will make that harder, if not impossible, to sustain while still applying the *Standards*.

INTERNAL AUDIT FOCUS ON ASSURANCE OVER FINANCIAL REPORTING

The impact of the corporate governance debacles has been even more extreme than stated above: Not only have management and the audit committee tended to place more stress on the assurance role of internal audit, but beyond that, they have often required internal audit to focus on assurance about financial and accounting matters rather than assurance on operational and other matters. The standard definition of internal control gives three objectives of internal control, and internal audit functions have recently been asked to focus more on providing assurance on the second of these:

"Internal control is broadly defined as a process, effected by the entity's board of directors, management and other personnel, designed to provide reasonable assurance regarding the achievement of objectives in the following categories:

—Effectiveness and efficiency of operations;

—Reliability of financial reporting;

—Compliance with applicable laws and regulations."[5]

and

"Internal control can be judged effective in each of the three categories, respectively, if the board of directors and management have reasonable assurance that:

—They understand the extent to which the entity's operations objectives are being achieved.

—Published financial statements are being prepared reliably.

—Applicable laws and regulations are being complied with."[6]

That the assurance needs of boards extend across all three objectives of internal control and also risk management is illustrated well by a provision within the United Kingdom's corporate governance code:

"The board should, at least annually, conduct a review of the effectiveness of the group's system of internal controls and should report to shareholders that they have done so. The review should cover all material controls, including financial, operational and compliance controls and risk management systems."[7]

CASE STUDY

This case illustrates how internal audit focus has been skewed by recent demands for extra assurance of internal control over financial reporting.

One of the top ten global multinationals came to Sarbanes–Oxley compliance rather later than it should have done. At the time it already had difficulties with the regulatory authorities, in particular the SEC. It was determined not to fail in its compliance with Section 404, having already risked the ire of the SEC with respect to its disclosures under Section 302. The multinational's approach to Section 404 compliance was to set up a dedicated Section 404 compliance team within its internal audit function. The head of this team, recruited from outside, had been a partner at one of the "Big Four" accountancy firms. Worldwide, the company had some 250 internal auditors and 70 became Section 404 specialists, many being recruited from outside. In addition, the company bought in supplementary Section 404 compliance resources from one of the Big Four. These overhead costs for management compliance with Section 404 did not of course include the extra fees paid to the external auditors for their own attestation work under Section 404. Typically, Section 404 has doubled the cost of the external audit.

The team's approach was first to develop a plan, with dates, for rolling out the project. It then identified and documented all the processes that could have a material impact on the multinational's financial statement assertions. This included identifying and documenting the key controls within these processes, and then developing and documenting a program to test the functioning of these controls. The results of all this work were recorded in process maps, narrative writeups and spreadsheet-based control registers.

Following the successful implementation of this part of Section 404 compliance, the emphasis then become to transfer this compliance work to line management, so that line managers themselves became responsible for running the compliance program in the future.

     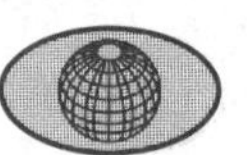   

IMPACT OF SARBANES–OXLEY ON INTERNAL AUDITING

The Sarbanes–Oxley Act of 2002, itself a direct result of the Enron debacle, has turned the screw further as far as internal audit is concerned. It has been emulated outside the United States with equivalent laws now in Canada and Japan. The Sarbanes–Oxley Act catches US quoted companies, overseas subsidiaries, and operating units of US quoted companies and companies registered elsewhere with secondary listings in the US. Draconian criminal sanctions contained within the Act mean that the criminalization of breaches of corporate governance has arrived in a serious way, and executives across the world are mindful of the global reach of the US Department of Justice. Section 906 on "Corporate Responsibility for Financial Reports" of the Sarbanes–Oxley Act sets out criminal penalties with fines of up to one million dollars or imprisonment of up to 10 years, or both, for chief executive officers and chief financial officers (or equivalent thereof) who certify financial reports in the knowledge that they do not comport with all the requirements; or if the false certification were willful, the penalties may be up to five million dollars or imprisonment for up to 20 years, or both (see Implementing an Effective Internal Controls System, (pp. 661–664)).

The key certification requirement is set out in Section 404. Subsection (a) requires that each annual report contain an internal control report, which states the responsibility of management for establishing and maintaining an adequate internal control structure and procedures for financial reporting. The annual report must also contain an assessment by management, as of the end of the most recent fiscal year of the issuer, of the effectiveness of the internal control structure and procedures of the issuer for financial reporting. Subsection (b) requires that, with respect to that internal control assessment, each registered public accounting firm that prepares or issues the audit report for the issuer shall attest to, and report on, the assessment made by the management of the issuer in accordance with *Standards* for attestation engagements issued or adopted by the Public Companies Accounting Oversight Board (PCAOB). Such an attestation shall not be the subject of a separate engagement. Section 302 of the Act requires a similar assessment and certification by management of internal control over other disclosures made in the annual report.

> "The Sarbanes–Oxley Act was designed in a panic and rushed through in a blinding fervour of moral indignation."
> *The Economist*

> "Sarbanes–Oxley has provided a bonanza for accountants and auditors, the very professions thought to be at fault in the original scandals."
> Tony Blair[8]

Very frequently, internal audit has been drafted in to undertake much of the assessment work on behalf of management with respect to Sections 302 and 404 compliance, diverting internal audit from other work. This was particularly the case when companies were initially seeking to comply with the Sarbanes–Oxley Act. Over time, companies have been endeavoring to transfer this compliance work to line management, freeing up internal audit to provide assurance that this work is being done effectively rather than doing the work itself.

Measures by the SEC and PCAOB[9] (in 2007), sometimes termed "SOX-Lite," have helped to make compliance less onerous. The definitions of "significant deficiencies"[10] and "material weaknesses"[11] in internal control—both of which have to be reported by management—have been relaxed, and the so-called "triple audit" by the external auditors under Section 404 has now become just a "double audit," though it is the least costly element that has been abandoned under PCAOB Auditing Standard No. 5.[12]

Following the delisting of British Airways in the United States, and thus the end of its requirement to comply with the Sarbanes–Oxley Act, the company's annual report for the year ended 31 March 2008 showed a reduction in external audit fees from £4.3 million to £3 million, and further savings of £1.27 million associated with other costs primarily pursuant to complying with the Sarbanes–Oxley Act.

▸▸ MAKING IT HAPPEN

Key "learning" points for finance professionals, as well as ideas and issues for action or further consideration:

- Take compliance requirements seriously.
- Consider the costs of compliance when deciding whether to list or delist in the US.
- Don't leave new compliance requirements to the last moment.
- Consider using your internal audit function in the initial stages of implementing new compliance obligations.
- Remember that internal audit should be independent of the activities upon which it provides assurance.
- In time, transfer compliance responsibilities to line management and away from internal audit.
- Accept that internal audit adds value when assurance over operational efficiency and effectiveness along with assurance of compliance with laws, regulations, and policies are both "in scope"—not just assurance of control over financial reporting.
- Accept that internal audit also adds value when it is available to provide consulting services to management.
- Consider whether internal audit is sufficiently independent of management to provide valuable assurance to the board and its audit committee.

NOTES

1 Further sets might, for instance, have been in the areas of fraud investigations, IT auditing, governmental internal auditing, and auditing in financial institutions.

2 The IIA's definition of internal auditing, to be found within its *Standards*.

3 Christina Brune, "Consulting: Friend or Foe?" *AuditWire* 25:1 (January–February 2003).

4 Christina Brune, in "Consulting: Friend or Foe?" *AuditWire* 25:1 (January–February 2003), quotes Peter Rodgers (vice president and general auditor of BISYS Group Inc. in Columbus, Ohio) as being against consulting services, and Geraldine Gail (director of internal audit, the University of California, Santa Cruz) as being in favour.

5 Committee of Sponsoring Organizations (COSO) (www.coso.org). *Internal Control—Integrated Framework*. AICPA,1992. (Available at www.cpa2biz.com).

6 Executive Summary to *Internal Control—Integrated Framework*, p. 4.

7 Financial Reporting Council (2008): The Combined Code on Corporate Governance, June 2008, Code Provision C.2.1 (www.frc.org.uk).

8 Speech on compensation culture delivered at the Institute of Public Policy Research, University College, London, on May 26, 2005. www.number10.gov.uk/output/Page7562.asp.

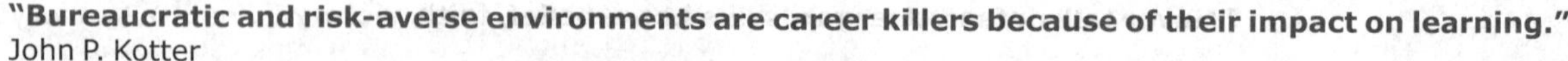

"Bureaucratic and risk-averse environments are career killers because of their impact on learning."
John P. Kotter

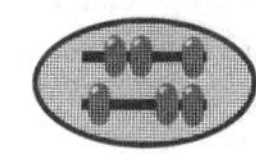

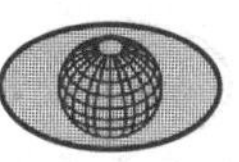

▸▸ MORE INFO

Reports:

Financial Reporting Council. "The Combined Code on Corporate Governance." June 2008. Online at: www.frc.org.uk/documents/pagemanager/frc/Combined_Code_June_2008

Financial Reporting Council. "Internal control—Revised guidance for directors on the Combined Code." October 2005. Online at: www.frc.org.uk/documents/pagemanager/frc/Revised%20Turnbull%20Guidance%20October%202005.pdf

Financial Reporting Council. "The Turnbull guidance as an evaluation framework for the purposes of Section 404(a) of the Sarbanes–Oxley Act." December 2004. Online at: www.frc.org.uk/documents/pagemanager/frc/draft_guide.pdf

Public Companies Accounting Oversight Board (PCAOB). "Auditing Standard No. 5: An audit of internal control over financial reporting that is integrated with an audit of financial statements." 2007. Online at: www.pcaobus.org/Standards/Standards_and_Related_Rules/Auditing_Standard_No.5.aspx

US Securities & Exchange Commission. "Commission guidance regarding management's report on internal control over financial reporting under Section 13(a) or 15(d) of the Securities Exchange Act of 1934." June 20, 2007. Online at: www.sec.gov/rules/final/2007/33-8809.pdf

Website:

The Institute of Internal Auditors: www.theiia.org

This Florida-based website is a fund of information. In particular: *Sarbanes–Oxley Section 404: A Guide for Management by Internal Controls Practitioners* (2nd ed., January 2008) at www.theiia.org/download.cfm?file=31866. The Institute's bimonthly membership newsletter, *AuditWire*, is available in electronic form to IIA members and subscribers on its website and via e-mail. The IIA runs Global Audit Information Network (GAIN)—a very effective and economic online benchmarking service for internal audit functions. More information at www.theiia.org/research/benchmarking/gain/?search=GAIN

9 In particular, PCAOB Auditing Standard No. 5 replacing the more demanding Standard No. 2.

10 PCAOB Auditing Standard No. 2 (2004): "A control deficiency (or a combination of internal control deficiencies) should be classified as a *significant deficiency* if, by itself or in combination with other control deficiencies, it results in more than a remote likelihood of a misstatement of the company's annual or interim financial statements that is more than inconsequential will not be prevented or detected." This statement has been replaced by PCAOB Auditing Standard No. 5 (2007): "A *significant deficiency* is a deficiency, or a combination of deficiencies, in internal control over financial reporting that is less severe than a material weakness, yet important enough to merit attention by those responsible for oversight of the company's financial reporting."

11 PCAOB Auditing Standard No. 2 (2004): "A significant deficiency should be classified as a *material weakness* if, by itself or in combination with other control deficiencies, it results in more than a remote likelihood that a material misstatement in the company's annual or interim financial statements will not be prevented or detected." This has been replaced by PCAOB Auditing Standard No. 5 (2007): "A *material weakness* is a deficiency, or a combination of deficiencies, in internal control over financial reporting, such that there is a *reasonable possibility* that a material misstatement of the company's annual or interim financial statements will not be prevented or detected on a timely basis . . . A material weakness in internal control over financial reporting may exist even when financial statements are not materially misstated."

12 Until 2007, the PCAOB interpreted Section 404 as requiring a "triple audit"—(1) the traditional audit of the financial statements, (2) an attestation that management have done what they are required to do under SEC rules to assess and certify the effectiveness of internal control over financial reporting, and (3) the external auditor's own assessment of the effectiveness of internal control over financial reporting. In fact, a careful reading of Section 404 indicates that the Act only required (1) and (2). Post 2007 requirements under the SOX-Lite regime mean that PCAOB Auditing Standard No. 5 continues with (1) and (3) (above)—a surprising interpretation by PCAOB, but one that preserves a maximum of the extra fee-earning opportunity that Section 404 has given external auditors.

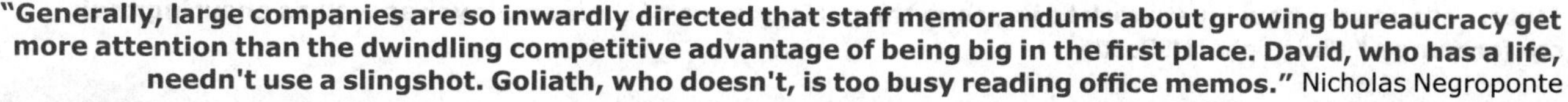
"Generally, large companies are so inwardly directed that staff memorandums about growing bureaucracy get more attention than the dwindling competitive advantage of being big in the first place. David, who has a life, needn't use a slingshot. Goliath, who doesn't, is too busy reading office memos." Nicholas Negroponte

     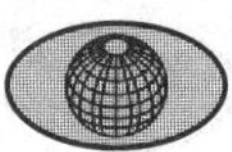   

How Can Internal Audit Report Effectively to Its Stakeholders? by Andrew Cox

EXECUTIVE SUMMARY

- Internal audit has a range of stakeholders who rely on its work, seeking assurance that the organization is running well and that there are effective controls in place.
- Internal audit has a responsibility to its stakeholders to provide reports on the operation of the organization's risk management, control, and governance processes. It also has a responsibility to justify the value of its work and the organization's spending on internal audit resources.
- Internal audit can report on its work to its stakeholders by:
  - reporting on the outcomes of its internal audit work;
  - reporting on the quality of its internal audit work.
- Together, these elements combine to provide stakeholders with an overall view of the effectiveness of internal audit; one without the other will only provide a partial reporting structure.

INTRODUCTION

Internal audit has a variety of stakeholders who rely on its work. These include: the board of directors; the audit committee; the chief executive officer; senior executives such as the chief financial officer, chief information officer, chief risk officer, etc.; the external auditors; in some cases, regulatory bodies; and stockholders—who, in the case of government organizations, could be the public.

All these stakeholders are seeking assurance that the organization is running well, and that effective controls are in place and operating properly. Internal audit has an important role to play in providing assurance to these stakeholders, but the trick is how to report the results of its work to them effectively.

ASSURANCE MODELS

Assurance can be equated with the term governance, the four pillars of a good corporate governance framework being—according to the Institute of Internal Auditors—executive management, the audit committee, external audit, and internal audit. Each of these elements relies to an extent on the others, and they all need to be operating effectively to provide overall assurance to stakeholders.

The board of directors will generally want to see a combined assurance model in place for the organization that provides three lines of defense, as shown in Table 1. This demonstrates the interdependencies between the four pillars of good corporate governance and the three lines of defense that go to make up a combined assurance model.

REPORTING ON THE OUTCOMES OF INTERNAL AUDIT WORK

A model for reporting the outcomes of internal audit work could be based on the following four elements: internal audit reports, recommendations for improvement, a communication strategy, and an annual internal audit report. These are discussed below.

Internal Audit Reports

Internal audit reports are the most important part of the work of an internal audit function. The report is the culmination of the effort directed toward an audit of a part of the organization. Internal audit can be a costly resource, so reports of its work should demonstrate its value to the organization. Internal audit reports need to be:

- Timely: reports should be issued in a timely manner.
- Accurate: reports should contain accurate information.
- Logical: reports should be logical and valid.
- Clear: reports should be clearly written and easily understood.

Table 1. Combined assurance model with three lines of defense

	Key performance indicator	*Measure*	*Target*	**Frequency**
	1 Completion of *Internal Audit Plan*			
1.1	Complete planned internal audits as per the approved *Internal Audit Plan* (subject to approved plan amendments)	% of planned internal audits completed within the financial year	95%	Annually
1.2	Complete special and ad hoc management-initiated internal audits and investigations in addition to scheduled internal audits (an allowance for this is contained in the *Internal Audit Plan*)	% of allowance utilized for unplanned ad hoc and management-initiated internal audits and investigations	95%	Annually
1.3	Approved *Internal Audit Plan* to be completed within the approved internal audit budget	% variance from approved budget for the financial year	5%	Annually
	2 Implementation of internal audit recommendations			
2.1	Internal audit recommendations accepted by management	% of recommendations accepted by management (subject to internal audit independence being maintained)	95%	Annually
2.2	Monitor the implementation status of internal audit recommendations by management and report outcomes to the audit committee	Updated status obtained from responsible managers and reported to the audit committee	Quarterly status reports delivered	Quarterly
	3 Formal survey feedback			
3.1	Result of customer feedback surveys following each internal audit	% of survey responses of good or better (averaged)	90%	Annually
3.2	Result of annual feedback survey of members of the audit committee	% of survey responses of good or better (averaged)	90%	Annually
	4 Independent quality review of internal audit			
4.1	Result of external quality assessment of internal audit in accordance with *The International Standards for Professional Practice of Internal Auditing*	Report issued detailing results of review	Consistent with better practice	Five-yearly

"Internal auditors now must work to improve the performance of their employer as well as ensuring their conformance." Christopher McRostie

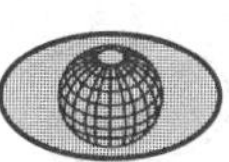

- Purposeful: reports should state why the internal audit was performed.
- Written with the audience in mind: reports should be written to suit the intended reader.

The power of a tick cannot be underestimated—it provides balance to an internal audit report. People do not go to work to do a bad job, and they appreciate recognition of good work. What they do not appreciate is an audit report that is negative by exception, says nothing positive, and effectively just gives them stick. So, acknowledge good work, and always say something positive in the report—and not begrudgingly.

Internal audit reports need to tell a story and be insightful. Merely telling people what is wrong cannot be seen as a good use of internal audit resources. That is the easy work, and does not reflect well on internal auditing as a profession. The real value of the work of internal audit comes from an emphasis on cause and effect. It is easy work to find the effect, but much more difficult to ascertain the root cause. Because of this, many internal auditors take the easy way out and just report on what has been found to be operating ineffectively.

Many internal audits could provide additional value to the organization if there was more emphasis on efficiency, effectiveness, economy, and organizational outcomes, with a view to assisting the organization further to improve and streamline business processes.

Recommendations for Improvement

Internal audit reports need to contain recommendations for improvement if they are to have any point. And the recommendations need to be targeted at correcting the root cause.

Locating the cause provides information on accountability relationships, and provides the basis for making improvements. It is important not just to find that something is wrong, but to work out what caused it to be wrong. This can prevent similar problems from happening again. Each recommendation needs to include:

- Whether it is agreed with or not by the audit customer (and if not, why not).
- What the audit customer is going to do about it (action plan).
- By what date the action will be implemented and completed.
- Who will be responsible for implementing the recommendation.

Recommendations contained in internal audit reports also need to be risk rated. In this way, management with the responsibility to implement remedial action will know which recommendations are most important and should be implemented first.

An important task of the internal audit function is to ensure that agreed recommendations arising from internal audit reports are satisfactorily actioned within a reasonable time-frame. If this is not done, its work will be virtually worthless. Many internal audit functions adopt an approach whereby:

- Agreed recommendations from internal audit, external audit, and regulatory bodies are entered into a tracking system and monitored on an ongoing basis by internal audit and the audit committee.
- Management responsible for implementing the recommendations is required to advise internal audit when this is complete, or to provide periodic reports on progress where this may be over a longer period of time.
- Overdue recommendations are reported to the audit committee.
- Internal audit periodically follows up to ensure that implementation has occurred as reported by management. This can be by 100% follow-up, by following up only those recommendations of higher risk, or by following up on a sample basis. A full follow-up audit is not generally necessary.

One point worthy of consideration is the necessity to cover off risks if recommendations are not actioned within a reasonable time-frame. Where a recommendation relates to a higher-risk problem and is not dealt with quickly, the chief audit executive should ask:

- Why has it not been actioned?
- Should the risk rating assigned to the recommendation be increased?
- What fall-back or interim risk management procedures have been put in place to mitigate the risks associated with non-implementation of the recommendation?
- Should management make a statement accepting the risk associated with non-implementation of the recommendation?

This information should be reported to each meeting of the audit committee.

Communication Strategy

To develop and maintain a profile within an organization, internal audit should take steps to improve its communication in order to make itself more visible to the wider organization. Some ways in which internal audit might do this include:

Raising awareness

- Have information about internal audit and its achievements posted on the organization's intranet.
- Distribute a small brochure about internal audit, what it does, and its achievements.
- Further develop relationships with stakeholders by making presentations on the work of internal audit to groups within the organization's corporate environment.
- Prepare an annual internal audit report on its activities.

Engaging management

- Consult with internal audit customers prior to the commencement of each internal audit, and request their input to the objectives and scope of the audit.
- Facilitate a risk workshop with internal audit customers in the planning phase of each internal audit.
- When conducting internal audits, internal auditors should spend most of their time in the work areas of their internal audit customers, rather than in the internal audit work area.
- At the completion of internal audit fieldwork, hold a workshop with the audit customer to discuss and agree possible improvement options.
- Provide a balanced reporting format by reporting on what management is doing well, in addition to identifying opportunities for improvement.

CASE STUDY

Measurement of the Internal Audit Function

The chief audit executive of an organization in Brisbane Australia was seeking ways to measure the work of his internal audit function. He knew that internal audit was doing a good job, but he did not have the evidence to prove it. In thinking how to address this problem, he designed KPIs against which his internal audit function could demonstrate its performance to the audit committee and the organization (Table 2). After all, internal audit assesses the performance of other areas of the organization, so why should it be exempt from having its own performance examined?

The chief audit executive considered these to be the KPIs the audit committee would be interested in to provide an overall assessment of the work of internal audit, and when he asked the audit committee, they agreed. He discounted KPIs such as the number of internal audit recommendations, or the number of internal audit hours delivered, since these can be manipulated and would therefore have little credibility with the committee.

"Internal audit needs to prove its value to its organization. Otherwise what is the good of it?" Nigel Morgan

Providing value-add

- Plan for each internal audit with a wider view by encompassing objectives relating to efficiency, effectiveness, economy, and organizational outcomes.
- Have involvement in working groups related to strategic developments within the organization in an observer/adviser capacity. It is considered best practice for internal audit to contribute to such forums by providing opinions, and ensuring that controls are considered and built-in to projects and systems under development, rather than after the event via post-implementation reviews, without necessarily compromising the integrity of later audits.

Annual Internal Audit Report

In some organizations, best practice extends to providing the audit committee and management with an annual report of internal audit activities featuring:

- Achievements in the year.
- Analysis of systemic issues identified through the work of internal audit.
- An opinion on the organization's overall risk management, control, and governance environment.

This can provide additional assurance to the audit committee, as well as being beneficial in alerting management to issues and risks identified in internal audits but which may also be occurring in other business areas.

REPORTING ON THE QUALITY OF INTERNAL AUDIT WORK

A model for reporting on the quality of internal audit work could be based on the following four elements: a quality assurance and improvement program, performance measures, review by external audit, and review by regulatory bodies.

Quality Assurance and Improvement Program

The "International Standards for the Professional Practice of Internal Auditing" issued by the Institute of Internal Auditors requires every internal audit function to operate a quality assurance program:

> "The chief audit executive must develop and maintain a quality assurance and improvement program that covers all aspects of internal audit activity."

A quality assurance and improvement program is designed to enable an evaluation of internal audit's conformance with the Definition of Internal Auditing and the Standards, and an evaluation of whether internal auditors apply the Code of Ethics. The program also assesses the efficiency and effectiveness of internal audit and identifies opportunities for improvement.

Table 2. KPIs prepared by the chief audit executive to assess internal audit

First line of defense	Second line of defense	Third line of defense
Management controls	**Management of risk**	**Independent assurance**
Real-time focus	Real-time focus + review focus of 1st line	Review focus of 1st and 2nd line
Elements Policies and procedures Internal controls	***Elements*** Risk management Legal department	***Elements*** External audit Internal audit
Role Review compliance Implement improvements	***Role*** Confirm compliance Recommend improvements	***Role*** Independently confirm compliance Recommend improvements

Source: National Australia Bank, with amendment.

This program should include both internal and external assessments. Internal assessments comprise: ongoing monitoring of the performance of the internal audit activity; and periodic reviews performed through self-assessment or by other persons within the organization with sufficient knowledge of internal audit practices.

External assessments must be conducted at least once every five years by a qualified, independent reviewer or review team from outside the organization. The chief audit executive must discuss with the board the need for more frequent external assessments; and the qualifications and independence of the external reviewer or review team, including any potential conflict of interest. The chief audit executive must communicate the results of the quality assurance and improvement program to senior management and the board.

Performance Measures

Best practice in internal auditing suggests that, like most business units in an organization, internal audit should have performance measures or key performance indicators (KPIs) in place to demonstrate its own level of performance. Best practice also suggests that performance measures need to be specific (clear and concise), measurable (quantifiable), achievable (practical and reasonable), relevant (to users), and timed (having a range or time limit). For more on this, see the case study.

Review by External Audit

As part of its annual external audit of an organization, the external auditors will usually assess the internal audit function on such matters as its organizational status, scope of function, technical competence, and due professional care exercised in its work.

Review by Regulatory Bodies

In many countries, regulatory bodies review the competency and work of internal audit as part of their periodic regulatory review of an organization. These are generally restricted to particular industry groups, for example financial institutions.

CONCLUSION

Internal audit has a responsibility to its stakeholders to provide reports on the operations of the organization's risk

▸▸ MAKING IT HAPPEN

The chief audit executive should develop effective reporting mechanisms with the audit committee and other stakeholders. Key reporting tools include:

- Insightful internal audit reports.
- Monitoring of internal audit recommendations, and periodic follow-up to ensure that recommendations have been implemented effectively and in a timely way.
- An internal audit communication strategy.
- An annual internal audit report that covers achievements in the year, an analysis of systemic issues identified through the work of internal audit, and an opinion on the organization's overall risk management, control, and governance environment.
- A quality assurance and improvement program that incorporates both internal and external assessments.
- Key performance indicators measuring the performance of internal audit.
- Periodic review of internal audit by external auditors and, where applicable, regulatory bodies.

"The process of developing and monitoring metrics for internal audit can serve as an effective marketing tool for the internal audit function." *Internal Auditor* magazine

  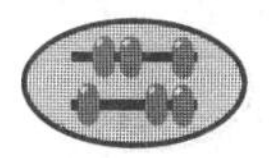   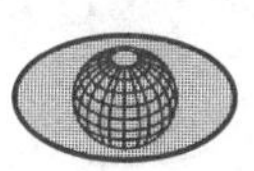   

management, control, and governance processes. It also has a responsibility to justify the value of its work and the organization's spending on internal audit resources.

Internal audit can do this in two ways:

- By reporting on the *outcomes* of its internal audit work.
- By reporting on the *quality* of its internal audit work.

▸▸ MORE INFO

Books:

Australian National Audit Office (ANAO). *Public Sector Internal Audit—An Investment in Assurance and Business Improvement*. Canberra: ANAO, September 24, 2007. Online at: www.anao.gov.au/director/publications/betterpracguides.cfm

Reding, K. F., *et al. Internal Auditing: Assurance and Consulting Services*. Altamonte Springs, FL: Institute of Internal Auditors Research Foundation, 2007.

Sawyer, Lawrence B., Mortimer A. Dittenhofer, and James H. Scheiner. *Sawyer's Internal Auditing: The Practice of Modern Internal Auditing*. Altamonte Springs, FL: Institute of Internal Auditors, 2003.

Standards:

The Institute of Internal Auditors (IIA). "International standards for the professional practice of internal auditing," Altamonte Springs, FL: IIA, 2009. Online at: www.theiia.org/guidance/standards-and-guidance/ippf/standards/?search=standards

Websites:

The Institute of Internal Auditors: www.theiia.org

The Institute of Internal Auditors—Australia: www.iia.org.au

See Also:

★ The Assurance versus Consulting Debate: How Far Should Internal Audit Go? (pp. 608–609)
★ Engaging Senior Management in Internal Control (pp. 626–627)
★ Implementing an Effective Internal Controls System (pp. 661–664)
★ Internal Audit and Partnering with Senior Management (pp. 668–671)
★ Internal Auditors and Enterprise Risk Management (pp. 680–682)
★ Managing the Relationships between Audit Committees and the CAE (pp. 685–687)
★ New Assurance Challenges Facing Chief Audit Executives (pp. 691–693)
★ Optimizing Internal Audit (pp. 694–696)
✔ Requirements of the UK Combined Code on Corporate Governance (p. 913)
✔ Understanding Internal Audits (p. 1053)

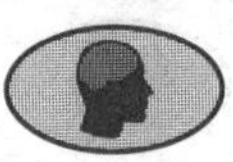

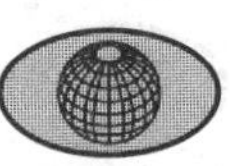

How Internal Auditing Can Help With a Company's Fraud Issues by N. Gail Harden

EXECUTIVE SUMMARY

- Fraud risk exposure should be assessed periodically by an organization to identify specific potential schemes and events for which it needs to have controls in place to mitigate risks.
- Internal audit serves as a critical defense against the threat of fraud, with a focus on assessing and monitoring controls designed to prevent and detect fraud.
- Internal auditors can be part of fraud deterrence by examining the adequacy of the system of internal controls.

INTRODUCTION

Regulatory oversight is increasing, as are penalties. A passive attitude in an organization toward oversight and the topic of fraud, antifraud programs, and controls would be a strong indicator of a significant deficiency in its system of internal controls.

Economic factors can increase the occurrence of fraudulent practices. When the economy is in a downturn the risk of fraud increases due to personal financial pressures, the stagnation of compensation, and corporate stabilization strategies.[1] Problems associated with corporate stabilization strategies include:

- fewer personnel and fear of downsizing;
- increased workloads;
- less accuracy;
- less time to make decisions;
- shortcuts taken to circumvent controls;
- low morale;
- likelihood of "cooking the books" to meet performance goals.

Additionally, corporations expand into foreign markets to reduce costs, which can lead to less transparency, stretched resources, and corrupt practices.

FRAUD AND FRAUD RISK ASSESSMENT DEFINED

Fraud is defined as the use of dishonesty, deception, or false representation in order to gain a material advantage or injure the interests of others. Types of fraud include false accounting, theft, third party or investment fraud, collusion between employees, and computer fraud. Fraud risk assessment is a structured approach to identify and analyze fraud risk and controls in an organization, and to assess whether those controls are working as intended. PricewaterhouseCoopers (PwC) explained:

> "Fraud risk assessment expands upon traditional risk assessment. It is scheme and scenario based rather than based on control risk or inherent risk. The assessment considers the various ways that fraud and misconduct can occur by and against the company. Fraud risk assessment also considers vulnerability to management override and potential schemes to circumvent existing control activities, which may require additional compensating control activities."[2]

WHY SHOULD INTERNAL AUDIT PERFORM FRAUD RISK ASSESSMENT?

The Institute of Internal Auditors (IIA) sets forth professional standards that require internal auditors to assess the risks facing their organizations. Furthermore, internal audit is expected to evaluate whether the company's controls sufficiently address identified risks of material misstatement in financial reporting due to fraud.

Internal audit participates in fraud deterrence by examining and evaluating the adequacy of internal controls. By merely asking such questions, internal audit makes it known that it is on the lookout for possible fraud schemes. Internal audit reports to the audit committee and management on the functioning of internal controls in relation to fraud risk, thus facilitating adherence to financial reporting and corporate governance responsibilities.

The audit committee has responsibilities of fiduciary oversight to consider:

- the process utilized to identify, document, and evaluate fraud risk;
- types of fraud identified;
- the level of likelihood and significance of fraud;
- appropriate action taken to close any gaps in the existence and operation of controls;
- opportunities for override of controls by management.

Figure 1. The fraud risk assessment process

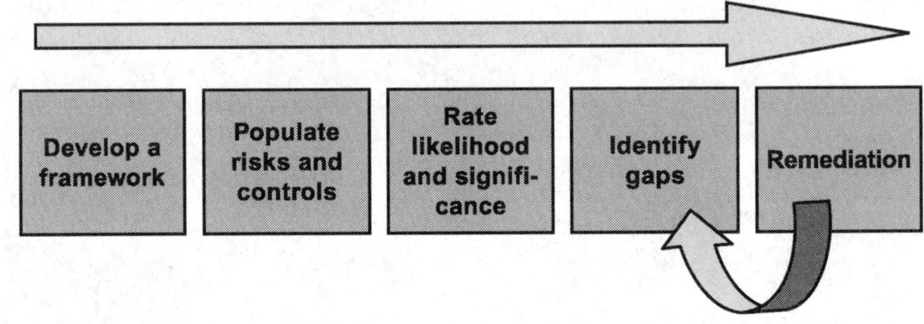

Figure 2. Rating the likelihood and significance of risks

Likelihood and significance
(gray = higher risk)

Risks

#1 – Shell company scheme
#2 – Overpayment scheme
#3 – Phony contractor scheme
#4 – Personal travel expenses
#5 – Fraudulent auditor/inspector expenses
#6 – Check tampering
#7 – Orders for personal supplies

Significance		#6			
				#4	
			#1		
		#2		#5	
	#7				
	Likelihood				

"Always do right. This will gratify some and astonish most." Mark Twain

  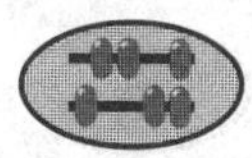   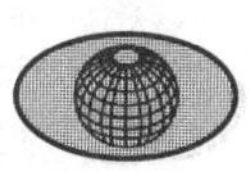   

Table 1. Example of a fraud risk assessment framework

Fraud Risk Assessment			*Accounts Receivable*			*Process Owner <Insert Process Owner Name>*		
Fraud Risk	*Likelihood*	*Significance*	*Control Activity*	*Preventive or Detective*	*Has Audit tested Control?*	*Date tested*	*Result*	*Action Plan*
Theft of cash receipts and written off as bad debts.	High	High	Reconciliation of bad debt expense reserve with supervisory review.	Detective	Yes	1/10/06	OK	
Person posting receivables does not also have system access to make journal entries to bad debt expense.				Preventative	Yes	1/10/06	OK	
Procedure exists and is followed to turn over delinquent accounts to a third-party collections agency.				Preventative	Yes	1/10/06	OK	
Accounts receivables reconciled to the general ledger by individual with no conflicting duties.				Detective	Yes	1/10/06	OK	
Accounting Manager authorization required to write off uncollectible accounts.				Preventative	Yes	1/10/06	OK	
Rebilling of past due items to change the number of days past due (To change DSO's for example).	Medium	Medium	Policy disallows cancelling and rebilling invoices unless the original was billed to the wrong client, or some other extenuating circumstances.	Preventative	Yes			
All credits require the use of a request form and approval from management according to an authorization matrix.				Preventative	Yes	1/10/06	OK	
Duties to input billing and credits to the AR system, approvals for credits, and collections activities are segregated.				Preventative	Yes	1/10/06	OK	
Kitting – writing checks against insufficient funds or unavailable funds and hoping the funds are deposited or become available before the checks clear the account.	Medium	Low	The Accounting Manager has a "cash card" where cash receipts and disbursements are logged. He monitors the cash level and transfers money from savings when necessary to cover disbursements. The Controller approves the disbursement batches and also has access to monitor the daily cash position.	Preventative	Yes	1/10/06	OK	
ZBA Accounts – type of bank account where funds are transferred from a deposit account to a disbursement account as disbursements are presented for payment.				Preventative				Company does not currently use ZBA accounts.
Positive pay set up with the bank. This is a practice where the company sends a file to the bank of all the disbursements generated and the bank will only pay those that are on the file.				Preventative				Company is in progress to set up this type of arrangement.

   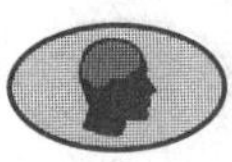  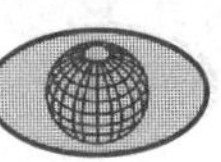   

Table 2. Identifying control gaps and recommending remediation plans

Control Activity	Preventive or Detective	Has Audit Tested Control?	Date tested	Result	Action Plan
Reconciliation of bad debt expense reserve with supervisory review.	Detective	Yes	1/10/2006	Failed	No supervisory review, effective April 11, 2008, now have supervisory review.
Person posting receivables does not also have system access to make journal entries to bad debt expense.	Preventive	Yes	1/10/2006	OK	
Procedure exists and is followed to turn over delinquent accounts to a third-party collections agency.	Preventive	Yes	1/10/2006	OK	
Accounts receivable reconciled to the general ledger by individual with no conflicting duties.	Detective	Yes	1/10/2006	Failed	AR account reconciled but contained variances. Account to be reconciled and reviewed by August 31, 2008. Owner: Corporate Controller.
Accounting manager authorization required to write off uncollectible accounts.	Preventive	Yes	1/10/2006	OK	
Policy disallows cancelling and rebilling invoices unless the original was billed to the wrong client, or some other extenuating circumstances.	Preventive	No			

PROCESS OVERVIEW

The fraud risk assessment process is a structured method to identify possible fraud schemes, identify internal controls that help to prevent or detect identified fraud schemes, document the results of testing the controls, and implement corrective action plans where needed. The objective of this process is to identify the existence of controls and how they operate, not necessarily to seek out fraud. Adequate controls reduce the opportunities for fraud to be committed. The assessment considers the various ways in which a company can be subjected to fraud and misconduct, along with its vulnerability to management override and other potential schemes to circumvent existing controls.

Fraud risk assessment is a continuous process, as shown in Figure 1.

Process Steps

The steps in the process are:

- develop a framework (i.e. a format);
- identify risks and controls;
- rate the likelihood and significance of the risks;
- identify gaps;
- plan and implement remedial measures.

The process should follow the approach recommended by the Committee of Sponsoring Organizations (COSO).[3] This includes:

- setting the "tone at the top," instituting a code of ethics, and setting up a whistleblower hotline;
- monitoring effectiveness;
- communication;
- identifying risks;
- linking risks and controls.

OTHER FRAUD PREVENTION & DETECTION ACTIVITIES

The following control activities meet the COSO element of "tone at the top," a code of ethics, and whistleblower hotlines:

CASE STUDY

To understand the process better, consider the following approach taken by a specific company.

Develop a Framework

Development of a framework consists of selecting the business processes to assess, determining the automation tool to use, and setting up the layout using such a tool. The layout should include the identified potential fraud schemes, an evaluation of the likelihood and significance of the risks, controls to prevent or detect the risks, the type of control, whether the control has been tested, the date of the test and the results, and corrective action plans. Table 1 shows an Excel worksheet utilized by the company in our case study.

The business processes assessed by this company were financial reporting, business development, sales, billing, accounts receivable, cash receipts, purchasing, accounts payable, payroll, inventory and shipping, officers' expenses, and entity level controls. Revenue recognition and management override controls are of particular concern, and they fall under financial reporting controls. All processes were also assessed and organized according to the business location to which the processes have been decentralized.

Balance sheet and expense accounts should be identified as they relate to each of the business processes. Mapping accounts to the processes can be useful in determining the financial impact of a particular process by business location. For example, locations with higher revenue have a higher financial impact on the Revenue Recognition Process.

Identify Risks and Controls

The next step is to populate the framework with fraud schemes (risks) and controls. To identify potential fraud schemes and best practice controls requires extensive research. Examples of resources are, but are not limited to, seminars and conferences, articles and white papers from experts such as the Institute of Internal Auditors, Deloitte, KPMG (or other CPA (certified public accountant) firms—these were used in the case example), business periodicals and journals, and the American Institute of Certified Public Accountants (AICPA).

It is important to choose controls that can be tested. For example, a third-party control cannot be tested. Reliance on external audit to find an error, or customer complaints, are examples of inadequate controls. No controls exist that provide absolute assurance against fraud. Individuals who are sufficiently motivated will find a way to override or circumvent controls. Even so, controls are a vital part of fraud deterrence. Auditors should continually ask themselves: "How could someone get around this control?" The general expectation of internal auditors is that they have sufficient knowledge to identify indicators of fraud, but they are not expected to have the expertise of a person whose primary responsibility is detecting and investigating fraud.

"It is always right to detect a fraud, and to perceive a folly; but it is very often wrong to expose either. A man of business should always have his eyes open, but must often seem to have them shut." Philip Stanhope

  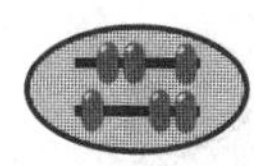 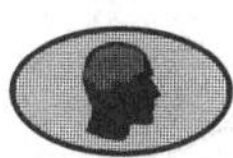  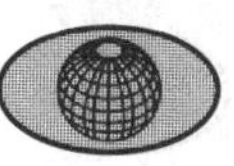   

- company ethics and anti-fraud policy/program;
- fraud response policy and procedure;
- active participation and support from management and the board of directors;
- conducting background investigations prior to employment for senior and sensitive positions;
- ethics and fraud awareness training.

These topics and other related controls constitute what is referred to as "entity level controls." Table 3 shows the fraud risk assessment for entity-level controls.

CONCLUSION

An article in *Business Finance* in May 2008 (Skalak, 2008) stated that the average cost of one incident of fraud is US$3 million. Fast-growing companies are more susceptible to fraud. As they expand into new markets, acquire new operations, and enter joint ventures these companies become more vulnerable.

Internal audit is in a key position to lead the fraud risk assessment process as it has extensive knowledge of the company and direct lines of communication with management and the audit committee, as well as experience, training and a structured approach to identify and evaluate. Internal audit has a responsibility to assist the audit committee to carry out its fiduciary duties. Fraud risk is a key area of responsibility of the audit committee. According to a PwC white paper:

> "For internal audit, this environment poses both opportunities and challenges. Corporate auditors who move quickly to develop antifraud action plans will find ample ways to provide added value to their organizations. Conversely, internal audit directors who fail to address rising stakeholder expectations jeopard-

Rate the Likelihood and Significance of Risks

Risks should be rated by likelihood and significance. The objective of a risk rating is to narrow down and prioritize the controls to test. Process owners/managers should be interviewed or surveyed to evaluate risk ranking.

Likelihood can be assessed based on three levels: "remote," "more than remote/reasonably probable," and "probable." Likelihood could be evaluated based on previous experience and past audit results.

Significance can be determined by using the standards "inconsequential," "more than inconsequential," and "material." Materiality can be based on financial impact, reputation risk, and/or shareholder or lender considerations. Management determines the organization's risk appetite—the amount of risk the company is willing to accept as a consequence of doing business.

In our case study, the described levels equated to "low," "medium," and "high."

In our case study, the company rated likelihood and significance on a scale of 1 to 5, 1 representing the least risk or significance. The chart shown in Figure 2 was used to display the rating results graphically. Risks falling in the gray blocks require higher priority. In this example, risk #7, Orders for personal supplies, had a rating of 1 for likelihood and 1 for significance, thus placing it in the lower left-hand corner. Risk #4 had a rating of 4 under likelihood and 4 for significance, and so on. Risks falling closer to the top right-hand corner are the highest risks and should receive highest focus and priority.

Identify Control Gaps

Risks and controls have been identified and populated into the spreadsheet. The next step is to identify control gaps and weaknesses. Identifying control gaps and weaknesses meets the COSO element of "monitoring effectiveness." Generally, the information needed to document whether the controls exist and are working as intended comes from operational internal audits, external audits, direct testing, or any other regulatory testing.

Remediation

Remediation plans meet the COSO element of "communication." Missing controls, or controls not working as intended and the related corrective action plans, are communicated to the process owners and company management, as well as to the audit committee. The case example tracks all the corrective action plans utilizing a Microsoft Access database. Action plans not completed by the due date are reported to the audit committee.

Refer to Table 2 for an example of the section of the fraud risk assessment worksheet (Table 1) related to the testing of controls and setting out corrective action plans for remediation.

Table 3. Fraud risk assessment for entity-level controls

Fraud Risk Assessment		*General Fraud Controls – "Entity Level"*		*Process Owner Board of Directors*	
Control Activity	*Preventive or Detective*	*Has Audit tested Control?*	*Date tested*	*Result*	*Action Plan*
Code of Ethics – communicated, training, monitoring	Preventive	Yes	2/1/2007	OK	
Background investigation when hiring	Preventive	Yes	2/1/2007	OK	
Ethics hotline and whistleblower program	Detective			OK	
Defined process for investigation of alleged fraud	Detective				
IT controls – system access, fraud detection & monitoring, controls to prevent inappropriate computer modifications and overrides by IT	Both	Yes	Annual	NI	IT Strategic Plan
Documented antifraud policies and procedures, Code of Ethics/Conduct, and hiring and promotion standards	Preventive		2/1/2007	OK	
Promoting antifraud programs through the organization's communication programs	Preventive				
Segregation of duties	Preventive				
Audit Committee is actively overseeing fraud prevention programs and incident investigations	Preventive	Yes	2/1/2007	OK	
Internal Audit assesses and tests controls for fraud risk in the organization	Detective	n/a	n/a	n/a	

"Some cursed fraud of enemy hath beguiled thee, yet unknown, and me with thee hath ruined." John Milton, *Paradise Lost*

   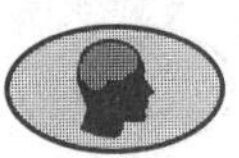  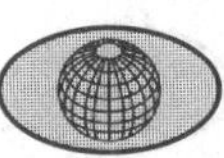   

ize their relevance and imperil their job security."[4]

Internal audit's work on fraud risk assessment can add value to the organization. The following comment was cited in a *Business Finance* article in August of 2007. Larry Harrington, Vice-president of Internal Audit at Raytheon, was quoted as saying:

> "We're building relationships within the engineering, supply chain, contracts, and other areas of the company that we might not otherwise have worked with that often, and folks who did not work with us that often might have had a perception of internal audit as the people who stab the wounded and beat up the dead. When you work with the rest of the business on a project like this, they see our talent, energy, and passion in a much more positive light."[5]

Ongoing Monitoring

In order to meet the COSO element of "monitoring effectiveness," the content of the framework should be regularly revisited to determine whether there are any new weaknesses, risks, or controls, and to take into account any changes in the internal and external environments. In conjunction with operational audits and other testing of controls, current data are entered for test results and corrective action plans.

▸▸ MAKING IT HAPPEN

The following are keys for success:

- A planned and documented approach, based on COSO recommendations, that integrates fraud risk assessment with operational and other audits.
- Active involvement from management.
- Consideration of specific potential fraud schemes for each business process and for general ledger accounts.
- Mapping of fraud risks and schemes to control activities.
- Assessment of fraud risks by likelihood and significance.
- Making fraud risk assessment an ongoing process.

▸▸ MORE INFO

Articles:

Deloitte Forensic Center. "Ten things about fraud control: How executives view the 'fraud control gap'." Deloitte, November 2007.

KPMG. "Fraud risk management: Developing a strategy for prevention, detection, and response." KPMG International, 2006.

Krell, Eric. "The awakening." *Business Finance* (August 1, 2007).

PricewaterhouseCoopers. "Key elements of antifraud programs and controls." PwC White paper, November 2003.

PricewaterhouseCoopers. "Key elements of antifraud programs and controls." PwC White paper, 2003.

PricewaterhouseCoopers. "The emerging role of internal audit in mitigating fraud and reputation risks." PwC, 2004.

Skalak, Steven. "Up for grabs." *Business Finance* (May 1, 2008). Online at: businessfinancemag.com/article/grabs-0503

Wells, Joseph T. "New approaches to fraud deterrence: It's time to take a new look at the auditing process." *Journal of Accountancy* 197 (Feb 1, 2004).

Websites:

AICPA antifraud/forensic accounting resources: fvs.aicpa.org/Resources/Antifraud+Forensic+Accounting

Deloitte "Dbriefs" webcasts (US): www.deloitte.com/dtt/section_node/0,1042,sid%253D5456,00.html. Especially those on "Fraud detection, deterrence, and prevention: Are you doing enough?" (April 11, 2006) and "Fraud risk management: Whose job is it anyway?" (April 9, 2007).

IIA Member Exchange: www.theiia.org/memberexchange

PricewaterhouseCoopers: www.pwc.com

Protiviti risk and business consulting: www.protiviti.com

NOTES

1 "Financial fraud: Does an economic downturn mean an uptick?" Deloitte webinar, July 16, 2008.

2 "Key elements of antifraud programs and controls." PwC, December 11, 2003, p. 12.

3 The Committee of Sponsoring Organizations of the Treadway Commission (COSO) is a US private-sector initiative, formed in 1985. Its major objective is to identify the factors that cause fraudulent financial reporting and to make recommendations to reduce its incidence. COSO has established a common definition of internal controls, standards, and criteria against which companies and organizations can assess their control systems.

4 "The emerging role of internal audit in mitigating fraud and reputation risks." PwC, March 16, 2004, p. 3.

5 "The awakening." *Business Finance* (August 2007).

"The internet was not always the top priority in Microsoft's strategy. Its arrival changed our business and became the biggest unplanned event we've ever had to respond to." Bill Gates

     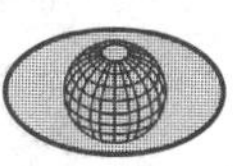   

How Much Independence for Supervisors in Financial Market Regulation? by Marc Quintyn

EXECUTIVE SUMMARY

- The degree of political independence that financial supervisors should enjoy is a hotly debated topic.
- This is because financial supervisors are a "one of a kind" breed of regulatory agency. They supervise the sector that is at the heart of the allocation of capital in any society, and therefore attract much political interest, not only in normal times, but even more so in times of crisis.
- While a fair degree of independence is justified—institutionally, in their regulatory and supervisory work, and financially—independence alone will not establish the right incentive structure for supervisors.
- Agency independence is not a goal in itself. It is just one institutional arrangement that should assist in establishing a governance framework that provides the regulatory agency with the right incentives to discharge its delegated powers. The other three elements are accountability, transparency, and integrity.
- Accountability arrangements ensure that the agency maintains legitimacy towards its stakeholders. This legitimacy will support independence, as will accountability.
- Transparency and integrity arrangements play an important role in making independence and accountability effective.
- These four elements of regulatory governance keep each other in equilibrium, and together establish the right incentives for the agency to fulfill its mandate, and for its stakeholders to refrain from interfering.

INTRODUCTION

The concept of independence, and, in particular, political independence is loaded. In a principal–agent relationship, it is associated with (more) power for the agent and a loss of power or grip for the principal. While the notion of an independent central bank is now more or less generally accepted in democratic societies, the broader notion of independent regulatory agencies (IRAs)—agencies that regulate and monitor important parts of social and economic life on behalf of government—is slowly gaining acceptance.

Financial sector supervisors are a "one of a kind" regulatory agency among these IRAs, and the debate about their independence is fairly recent, i.e., since the late 1990s and the turn of the century. Financial supervisors possess some unique features among IRAs that complicate the discussion about their degree of political independence. They are close to the central banks in that they contribute to preserving a country's financial stability by monitoring the health of individual institutions. Yet they differ from most other IRAs (central banks, competition regulators, and utilities regulators) in a number of crucial ways. Most importantly, they monitor a sector that fulfills a central role in the economy as allocator of capital, and as a source of governance for the corporate sector. For these very reasons, the sector has always generated much attention from the political class. This political interest, which is also eagerly exploited by the sector itself, opens the door to constant attempts at political interference and lobbying.

Add to this uniquely distinguishing feature (i.e., the nature of the sector they supervise) a number of other specific characteristics in the content of their supervision job, and it is clear why the independence of financial supervisors is such a much-debated issue. These other characteristics are:

- their mandate contains a great number of contingencies;
- given the sensitivities inherent in the workings of the financial system, transparency in their supervisory operations needs to be weighed against confidentiality more than in any of the other types of regulators;
- they wield wide-ranging judicial powers which include "the coercive power of the state against private citizens," which is more far-reaching than for any other type of IRA.

These features lead to two conclusions regarding their independence. First, a fair degree of regulatory and supervisory independence is needed to insulate them from both political *and* industry interference and lobbying. Second, and equally important, given their job content, the granting of independence alone is most unlikely to provide the right incentive structure to financial supervisors. In order to fulfill their mandate properly, independence arrangements need to be designed in coordination with other features, which together establish a regulatory governance structure that provides the right incentives to the supervisors, as well as to the other stakeholders, in particular their political masters.

Such an incentive-compatible governance structure for financial supervisors should be built around elements of independence, accountability, transparency, and integrity. These four ingredients of a governance framework, if designed properly, tend to reinforce each other, as we shall demonstrate. In the next section, we substantiate the need for supervisory independence, and the subsequent section presents an incentive-compatible regulatory governance framework.

ESSENTIAL ELEMENTS OF INDEPENDENCE

The need for regulatory and supervisory independence in the financial sector stems broadly from the same sources as central bank independence, and finds its origin in the literature on time inconsistency in economic policy.[1] Time inconsistency occurs when the government's optimal long-run policy differs from its optimal short-run policy, leading to situations where the government in the short run reneges on its long-term commitments. Thus, time inconsistency emphasizes the need for a credible and binding precommitment to a particular mandate that prevents violations *ex post*. In the case of monetary policy, Rogoff (1985) argued that one way to achieve policy credibility is to place it in the hands of a person or institution who weighs inflation deviations more heavily than in the social welfare function—the "conservative central banker" whose preferences will differ from those of the government. The need for agency independence follows from this: For the central banker to have a different reaction function, they need to be independent from government.

The analogy with supervisory independence is straightforward. Bank liquidations are typically politically unpopular, as they can result in genuine hardship for depositors and other creditors, many of who will also be voters. Vote-maximizing politicians with short time horizons may be concerned about the short-term costs of bank closures,

  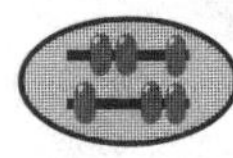   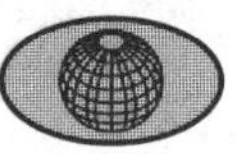   

whether fiscal, in terms of lost votes, or in terms of lost campaign contributions, and will be sensitive to the demands of these groups, particularly if these are politically well organized. Politicians may be tempted, as a result, to put pressure on supervisors to organize a bailout or exercise forbearance to avoid short-term costs. However, short-term forbearance may be the cause of higher longer-term resolution costs. Accordingly, politicians face the same incentives in relation to failing banks as they do in relation to the goal of price stability. Hence the need for independent regulators whose reaction function differs from that of their political masters.

Let us now define ways in which this independence could be made operational. For financial supervisors, there are actually four dimensions to it—institutional, regulatory, supervisory, and budgetary independence.

Institutional Independence

Institutional independence is achieved if the agency as an institution is separate from the executive and legislative branches of government. Institutional independence encompasses three critical elements:

- the terms of appointment and dismissal of its senior personnel should be clearly defined to avoid political interference, and thus ensure security of tenure;
- the agency's governance structure should favor decision-making by a commission, as opposed to vesting all responsibilities in the chairperson, to reduce external influences;
- decision-making should be as open and transparent as possible, to minimize the risk of political interference.

Regulatory Independence

Regulatory independence refers to the ability of the agency to have an appropriate degree of autonomy in setting prudential rules and regulations for the sectors under its supervision. Autonomy in setting prudential regulations will help in ensuring that the regulatory framework is stable and predictable, complies with international best practices, and is not contaminated with political considerations.

Supervisory Independence

Supervisory independence refers to the degree of independence with which the agency is able to exercise its judgment and powers in such matters as licensing, on-site inspections and off-site monitoring, sanctioning, and enforcement of sanctions (including revoking licenses), which are the supervisors' main tools to ensure the stability of the system.

Supervisory independence is the most difficult of the four dimensions of independence to guarantee. To preserve its effectiveness, the supervisory function typically involves private ordering between the supervisor and the supervised institution. However, the privacy of the supervisory process makes it vulnerable to interference, from both politicians and supervised entities. Political interference (and interference from the industry itself) can take many forms, and can indeed be very subtle, making it difficult to shield the supervisors from all forms of interference.

As the supervisory process starts with the act of licensing a financial institution, supervisors should ideally have the final word on who can enter the system. A typical situation that may lead to problems is one where the government has the final say over the licensing of individual banks and may—either out of self-interest or lack of technical ability to assess business plans—license unviable projects. The same degree of autonomy should apply to exit procedures, based on the same argument that supervisors are in the best position to decide on the viability of individual institutions. Decisions to close or not close an institution that are taken on political, rather than technical, grounds may result in the prolongation of the life of insolvent or corrupt institutions, thus ultimately increasing resolution costs. Moreover, if the power of license revocation is not in the hands of the supervisor, the threat by the supervisor can be empty, and their other powers undermined.

To strengthen supervisory independence, it is recommended that (i) supervisors enjoy legal protection in the performance of their duties. The absence of proper legal protection in many instances has a paralyzing effect on supervision; (ii) supervisors enjoy appropriate salary levels to attract better qualified individuals who may be less prone to bribery; (iii) rules-based system of sanctions and interventions be applied (see Rules Versus Discretion Supervisory Intervention Finacial Institutions).

Budgetary Independence

Budgetary independence refers to the ability of the regulatory agency to determine the size of its own budget, and the specific allocations of resources and priorities that are set within the budget. Regulatory agencies that enjoy a high degree of budgetary independence are better equipped to withstand political interference (which might be exerted through budgetary pressures), to respond more quickly to newly emerging needs in the area of supervision, and to ensure that salaries are sufficiently attractive to hire competent staff.

FROM REGULATORY INDEPENDENCE TO GOVERNANCE

"...governance is an effort to craft order, thereby to mitigate conflict and realize neutral gains. So conceived a governance structure obviously reshapes incentives."[2]

Independence for supervisors is a necessary but insufficient condition when establishing the proper incentive structure for meeting their mandate. When allowed to operate at arm's length of the government, the challenge is to endow them with the right incentive-compatible governance attributes. Following Williamson's definition of governance, the aim of the model of governance arrangements elaborated in this section is exactly to:

- craft order, internally in the agency, and between the agency and its stakeholders (for instance, by identifying mechanisms to avoid capture, see below);
- mitigate conflict between the agency and its stakeholders;
- assist in realizing gains for all stakeholders, i.e., to ensure that the delegation of power to the financial supervisor is a socially optimal solution.

Making Williamson's definition operational, Das and Quintyn (2002) identified four essential pillars of good regulatory governance: Independence, accountability, transparency, and integrity. If well designed, these four pillars can underpin most of the key elements of internal and external governance arrangements for regulatory agencies. They lay down principles for dealing with shareholders (the government) and stakeholders (regulated and supervised entities, customers of the regulated entities, and the public at large), and for setting up *internal* governance arrangements in support of the *external* ones. They underpin mechanisms for attaining the agency's stated objectives and for monitoring its performance.

Although references to these four principles are rare in the corporate governance literature, some parallels can easily be made: The need for an arm's length relationship between managers and shareholders in the corporate sector finds its parallel in the need for independence for the regulator from the share- and stakeholders (government and regulated industry, respectively). Independent regulators have a fiduciary relationship with their stakeholders. To be effective, these fiduciary responsibilities need to be complemented with accountability arrangements towards the stakeholders. Further-

"The real problem for any government coming to power is to control the civil servants. They will all explain why it is quite impossible to do things other than the way they are currently done." Milton Friedman

  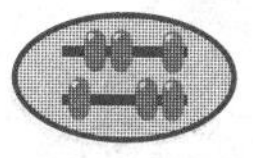 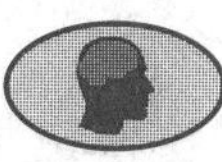  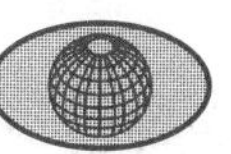   

Figure 1. The four pillars of regulatory governance

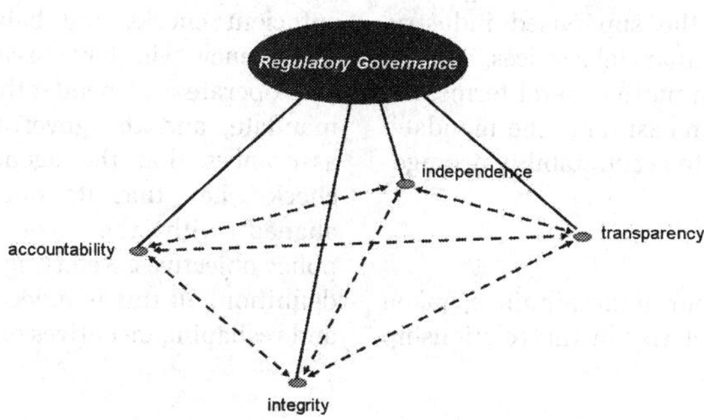

more, transparency mechanisms facilitate accountability, and integrity measures minimize conflicts of interest. As can already be observed from this overview, a major feature of this foursome is that they reinforce each other (Figure 1). Weakening one of them tends to undermine the effectiveness of the others, and, in the end, the quality of the agency's governance.

Accountability

Accountability is the indispensable, other side of independence. Yet it is a problematic one, because policy makers and agencies seem to have trouble getting a practical grasp of its workings. One of the problems is that many scholars still tend to refer to narrow concepts of accountability, more or less equivalent to reporting. Another problem is that the line between accountability and control remains very thin, leading to misunderstandings about the true meaning and content of accountability. The purpose of designing accountability arrangements is to put in place a combination of monitoring arrangements and instruments, so as to arrive at a situation where no one controls the agency directly, but the agency is nonetheless under control, i.e., it can be monitored—not just by the government, but by other stakeholders as well—to see if it fulfills its fiduciary obligations.

Modern interpretations of accountability as a mechanism of checks and balances stress that it fulfills at least four functions.

1 To provide public oversight. This is the classical role of accountability.
2 To maintain and enhance legitimacy of the agency. The actions of an agency with delegated power need to have legitimacy in the eyes of the other stakeholders, in order to enjoy the granted independence effectively. If the agency's actions are perceived as lacking legitimacy, its independence will not be long lasting. Legitimacy can be generated through various accountability mechanisms and relations. Once it has been accepted that accountability generates legitimacy, and legitimacy supports independence, it becomes clear that the relationship between accountability and independence does not imply a trade-off, as is often stated, but is one of complementarities. In other words, properly designed independence and accountability arrangements lead to a virtuous interaction between both pillars of governance.
3 To enhance the integrity of regulatory governance. Besides political and industry capture, independent agencies face a third type of capture: Self-interest capture. There are situations in which the powers of the regulatory agency are captured by individual staff pursuing their own self-interest, which may not be consistent with social welfare. Regulatory self-interest can take a variety of forms including, in highly corrupt societies, the abuse of regulatory powers to extract rents. Less blatant, but potentially just as damaging, is the motivation of "not on my watch," i.e., the desire of regulators to delay the emergence of problems until after they have left office. Agency accountability provides society with assurances that regulation is not being manipulated or subverted by private interests.
4 To improve agency performance. Accountability is not only about monitoring, blaming, and punishing. It is also about enhancing the agency's performance. By giving account to the executive and legislative branches of government, the agency provides input to the government as to how to (re)shape its broader economic and financial policies, and receives feedback from the government. In this sense, accountability stimulates coordination with the government and enhances the agency's legitimacy, without encroaching on its independence. Accountability also enhances agency performance by avoiding that the independent agency becomes uninformed and loses touch with the (political) reality of the nation. Accountability forces the agency into a dialogue with all stakeholders, with positive effects on its performance.

Transparency

Transparency refers to an environment in which the agency's objectives, frameworks, decisions and their rationale, data and other information, as well as terms of accountability are provided to the stakeholders in a comprehensive, accessible, and timely manner.

Transparency has increasingly been recognized as a "good" in itself, but it also serves other purposes related to the other components of governance. As a good in itself, policy makers have been recognizing that it is a means of containing market uncertainty. In addition, transparency has become a powerful vehicle for countering poor operating practices and policies. It has become a main conduit of accountability to a large number of stakeholders.

Integrity

Integrity is often the forgotten pillar. Yet it is an essential one, as it provides several underpinnings for good internal governance in support of the external elements. Integrity refers to the set of mechanisms that ensure that agencies' staff can pursue institutional goals without compromising them as a result of their own behavior or self-interest. Integrity affects staff of regulatory agencies at various levels. Procedures for appointing heads, their terms of office, and criteria for removal should be such that the integrity of the board-level appointees (policy-making body) is safeguarded. Second, the integrity of the agency's day-to-day operations is ensured through internal audit arrangements, which ensure that the agency's objectives are clearly set and observed, and accountability is maintained. Ensuring the quality of the agency's operations will maintain the integrity of the institution and strengthen its credibility to the outside world. Third, integrity also implies that there are standards for the conduct by officials and staff of their personal affairs, to prevent conflicts of interest. Fourth, assuring integrity also implies that the staff of the regulatory agency enjoy legal protection while discharging their official duties.

Mutual Reinforcement

A key feature of these four pillars is that they hold each other in balance and

   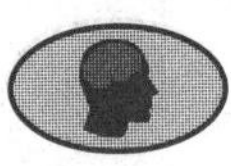  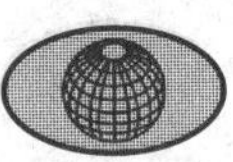   

reinforce each other as governance pillars. The previous paragraphs have already illustrated this, and a few more examples will reinforce the point. Independence and accountability are two sides of the same coin. Independence cannot be effective without proper accountability. Without accountability, agencies (or their heads) can lose their independence easily in disputes with the government. Transparency is a key instrument to make accountability work. It is also a vehicle for safeguarding independence. By making actions and decisions transparent, chances for interference are reduced. Transparency also helps to establish and safeguard integrity, in the sense that published arrangements provide even better protection for agency staff (against themselves). Independence and integrity also reinforce each other. Legal protection of agency staff, as well as clear rules for the appointment and removal of agency heads, support both their independence and integrity. Finally, accountability and integrity also reinforce each other. Because of accountability requirements, there are additional reasons for heads and staff to keep their integrity. Together, they reduce the risk of self-interest capture.

Accountability is extremely important in the case of a financial supervisor. As stated before, this agency's mandate is much less measurable (such as "to maintain a sound financial system" often in conjunction with other goals such as "consumer protection," "prevention of money laundering," etc.), and cannot be very specific because of all the contingencies involved in financial sector regulation and supervision. Some authors have argued that such a vague mandate precludes proper accountability, and, therefore, that these agencies should not be granted too much independence from government.

The argument developed here states that, on the contrary, these agencies should be able to operate at arm's length from the government (and the industry) for the reasons discussed in the literature, but that accountability arrangements should be such that the agency remains "in check." Given the wide range of contingencies in financial regulation and the large number of stakeholders in financial regulation and supervision, a "360 degree"-type of accountability is required, involving arrangements towards the three government branches, the supervised industry, the customers of financial services, and the public at large. In more general terms, the less specific and measurable the mandate, the more elaborate accountability arrangements should be.

CONCLUSION

In sum, these four underpinnings, taken together, create clarity in the relationship between the financial supervisors and the government (and other stakeholders). With sufficient checks and balances in place, the agency will have assurances that it can operate independently to pursue its mandate, and the government will have assurances that the agency remains "in check," i.e., that its operations remain aligned with the government's broad policy objectives. Referring to Williamson's definition, all this is indeed about shaping and reshaping incentives on both sides.

▸▸ MORE INFO

Books:

Bovens, Mark. "Public accountability." In E. Ferlie, L. Lynne, and C. Pollitt (eds). *The Oxford Handbook of Public Management*. Oxford: Oxford University Press, 2004.

Das, Udaibir, and Marc Quintyn. "Financial crisis prevention and crisis management—The role of regulatory governance." In Robert, Litan, Michel Pomerleano, and V. Sundararajan (eds). *Financial Sector Governance: The Roles of the Public and Private Sectors*. Washington, DC: Brookings Institution Press, 2002.

Quintyn, Marc, and Michael Taylor. "Robust regulators and their political masters: Independence and accountability in theory." In Donato Masciandaro, and Marc Quintyn (eds). *Designing Financial Supervision Institutions: Independence, Accountability, and Governance*. Cheltenham, UK: Edward Elgar, 2007.

Articles:

Hüpkes, Eva, Marc Quintyn, and Michael Taylor. "The accountability of financial sector supervisors: Theory and practice." *European Business Law Review* 16:6 (2005): 1575–1620.

Kydland, Finn, and E. Prescott. "Rules rather than discretion: The inconsistency of optimal plans." *Journal of Political Economy* 85:3 (1977): 473–491.

Majone, Giandomenico. "Strategy and structure: The political economy of agency independence and accountability." *Designing Independent and Accountable Regulatory Agencies for High Quality Regulation: Proceedings of an Expert Meeting in London, Organization for Economic Cooperation and Development, January 10–11, 2005*: 126–155.

Quintyn, Marc, Silvia Ramirez, and Michael Taylor. "Fear of freedom—Politicians and the independence and accountability of financial sector supervisors." IMF Working Paper 07/25, Washington, DC: International Monetary Fund, 2007. Also in Donato Masciandaro, and Marc Quintyn (eds). *Designing Financial Supervision Institutions: Independence, Accountability, and Governance*. Cheltenham, UK: Edward Elgar, 2007.

Quintyn, Marc. "Governance of financial supervisors and its effects—a stocktaking exercise." SUERF Studies (2007/4): 64

Rogoff, Kenneth. "Optimal degree of commitment to an intermediate monetary target: Inflation gains versus stabilization costs." *Quarterly Journal of Economics* 100 (1985): 1169–1189.

Williamson, Oliver. "The new institutional economics: Taking stock, looking ahead." *Journal of Economic Literature* 38:3 (2000): 595–613.

See Also:

Banking and Financial Services (pp. 1500–1502)

NOTES

1 Kydland and Prescott (1977).

2 Williamson (2000).

"It is a characteristic of committee discussions and decisions that every member has a vivid recollection of them and that every member's recollection differs violently from every other member's recollection."
Jonathan Lynn

  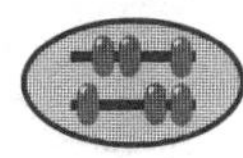   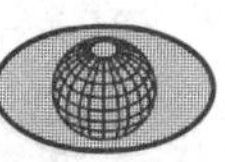   

How to Implement a Standard Chart of Accounts Effectively by Aziz Tayyebi

EXECUTIVE SUMMARY

A chart of accounts (COA), represents a unique set of codes to consistently record all an entity's transactions, is therefore a well recognised, fundamental accounting need. Whether it concerns a complex organization with numerous divisions, or an individual applying basic cash accounting, it is essential to be able to collate financial information that is relevant, both for internal management and external parties. This article considers some questions that management should take into account when implementing a standard COA, such as:

- Why update a COA? An organization may need to adopt a new COA if its industry or country adopts a new set of specific accounting standards. Furthermore, as organizations evolve, it is vital that the COA keeps pace and stays relevant to management.
- What are the options when implementing a COA? Implementing a new COA can improve an existing system, or involve a completely new development. Management should take care to incorporate all useful accounts from older systems.
- What are the practical consideration when designing a COA? Management must consider user needs, detailed design specifications, logistics, cost/benefit analysis, and legal requirements.

INTRODUCTION

A chart of accounts (COA) is essentially a set of codes for the consistent classification of financial information. This allows for the systematic production of decision-useful accounting information for management, such as budgeting, monitoring, and management reporting. Similarly, a standard COA helps to ensure comparability in external financial reporting.

The COA facilitates the recording of all transactions, which are filtered into a unique account code, based on certain criteria. While these criteria are influenced both by internal management needs as well as regulatory requirements, many common types of codes would always be expected, such as revenue, expenses, assets, liabilities, and equity.

WHY UPDATE A CHART OF ACCOUNTS?

A standard COA represents an integral part of an overall financial information system. A COA takes inputs from source accounting documents and journal entries, and allocates that information to a prescribed set of accounts, ultimately producing financial reports, which in turn enable users of that information to track the performance of the business, in a format that best suits their needs.

External Decisions

COAs can change for a number of reasons, including an industry-wide move to standardize accounting terminology. An example of this was the development of a standard COA for not-for-profit organizations (NPOs) in Queensland, Australia. In 2002, Queensland University of Technology (QUT) and Queensland Treasury commenced a project to develop a standard COA for small NPOs that received government funding. The project was commissioned because, at the time, Australia did not provide specific national accounting standards for NPOs. As a result, there was tremendous inconsistency in accounting categories and terms required by government departments in their funding relationships with such organizations. Research from QUT indicated that these inconsistencies created a heavy compliance burden on NPOs when acquitting grants, with many additional costs being incurred in the reporting process . Thus, through an extensive consultation process, a standard COA was launched in Queensland in 2006. The success of the COA, both for NPOs and the funders, through reducing simplification of the reporting process, increasing understanding, and consistency of accounting practices, led to other Australian jurisdictions subsequently commencing similar projects.[1]

A significant number of companies around the world have recently implemented International Financial Reporting Standards (IFRS). For many of those companies, the IFRS implementation was mandated in national legislation. The transition to IFRS involves significant practical and logistical challenges, especially in upgrading and adapting IT systems across the organization. A report issued by KPMG[2] in 2008 indicated that, "IT costs are generally over 50 per cent of the cost of IFRS conversion," and that changes to the COA are inevitable.

Other key regulatory requirements, which can have an impact on the COA, revolve around taxation. For larger companies with overseas subsidiaries that will be using the same general ledger system, it is important to consider country-specific requirements when completing the COA, while providing as much consistency as possible.

Organizational Decisions

More commonly, businesses are likely to go through restructuring, make a strategic decision to implement a new IT system, or simply acknowledge that the current COA is not fulfilling the information needs of the business. Whatever the reasons are for change, management needs to assess both the new business requirements, as well as any that were not being met previously.

Similarly when considering the implementation of new reporting systems, it is essential to ensure that the individual components of the financial system, such as invoicing, stock management, and disbursements, are providing the appropriate support to the wider business objectives. This is often why ERM packages are so useful, as they allow information from a common source to be shared across previously disparate departments of the business.

OPTIONS WHEN IMPLEMENTING A CHART OF ACCOUNTS

Essentially, an organization is faced with three choices.

1 Keep the COA from the legacy system in place;
2 Supplement the existing COA with some additional ones;
3 Overhaul the COA and implement the new, changed structures.

From a practical point of view, moving away from the existing COA also has the significant advantage of offloading redundant codes and accounts which unnecessarily congest it.

In practice, especially when a comprehensive system such as an ERP package is being implemented, the organization faces limited choices. The chances are management will have to consider a whole-scale overhaul of the current system. Thus,

"I despise bureaucrats. I despise administrators. . .There has been an overgrowth of an arrogant master class of administrators. . .who regard themselves as being in charge and everyone else as being their lackeys."
Camille Paglia

it is also essential to ensure that, while this is an opportunity to cleanse the current COA, it is also vital to ensure that the new COA reflects the realities of the business. All-round general ledger systems are, by their nature, more sophisticated, linking various sets of data. Designing an appropriate COA is a complex process.

PRACTICAL CONSIDERATIONS WHEN DESIGNING A NEW CHART OF ACCOUNTS

As previously described, the COA is only one element in the information system (manual and automated) which aids management decision-making. The COA is, however, a key part, bringing together financial information held within the general ledger, and filtering it into a format that can be used by managers.

The general considerations for implementing a new COA are, unsurprisingly, akin to those that would be assessed when making any significant system changes. Considerations include an assessment of user needs, a detailed design, potential impact assessment and testing, and simulations prior to final running. By thoroughly considering these basic procedures, it should be possible to complete a relatively risk-free, "big bang" approach to the adoption of the new COA. However, in the case of an overall system change, management may decide to run both systems for a period of time in order to ensure that all data are being captured. While costly and time-consuming, the old COA is then still available for cross-reference.

User Needs

Again, reiterating the main reason for having a standard COA, the initial phase of implementation must begin with a thorough analysis of the organization's information requirements. Thus management will need to consider the existing outputs resulting from their present COA, and ensure that all potential stakeholders, within and outside the finance department, are involved in the process.

Understanding the current condition should ensure that relevant COAs are included in the new version, and that shortcomings are remedied. A simulation of the revised COA can then be produced, allowing the stakeholders to preview the resulting information. The main aim of this phase is not to determine what the final reports may look like, but to confirm that the required information is being generated.

Logistical Consideration

Business analysts tend to want as much information as possible, and then decide which information they really need at any given time. This desire, coupled with the wide range of internal and external stakeholders, may make it tempting to include excessive fields in a COA. However, it is generally the case that by widening the net of accounts, the likelihood of error, as well as underutilized codes, will be greater too. Thus, it is also vital to strike the right balance between the user's often-exhaustive demands, and the limitations of an efficient data-capture system.

Typically management may be interested in analyzing performance based on:

- individual product basis and product class;
- separate cost centers;
- geographical segments;
- legal entities.

However, it is the needs of the business that should ultimately dictate the scope of data requirements.

It is also possible that the difficulty and cost of generating some information might ultimately mean that it is not worthwhile. The tendency is that future preparers of information may find it too difficult to provide the inputs regularly, and, therefore, these accounts would again become vacant. Thus, it is imperative to conduct a careful analysis of the process for data capture. While much reporting information can easily be extracted from basic input data from invoices, etc., the consistent splitting of costs and revenues by appropriate cost and activity centers is more challenging.

In order to maintain a consistent application of the COA, it is also important that a thorough guide is in place, outlining how information should be captured and recorded. Again, a regular review of these guidelines should be conducted.

Manual or Electronic Conversion?

In practice, the choice of manual or electronic conversion will be dictated by the type of system being implemented. If a totally new package is introduced, then the standard COA is already inbuilt, and only the process of identifying and/or adding new accounts is required, as discussed above. If the organization is simply implementing a new standard COA only, then the organization is faced with either a manual or an electronic change. Usually, electronic downloading into the accounting software is straightforward—the relevant file is downloaded from the data file into the existing accounting package, which then essentially overlays the existing COA.

A manual conversion requires a thorough comparison between the new standard COA and the existing COA. The process of identifying relevant accounts is, again, critical, although by virtue of the fact that this is not automated, it can be lengthier. A constant review of output reports, such as trial balances, is required.

If the company's financial statements are audited, it is important to consider any requests from auditors, regardless of whether the process is manual or electronic. It is, therefore, important to document any changes to the COA, with an appropriate audit trail in place.

Balancing Cost-Center Demands and Legal Entity Requirements

Many large organizations have a number of subsidiaries that are legal entities in their own right. While management may

▸▸ MAKING IT HAPPEN

A correctly structured COA should support the financial and management reporting process, enabling the organization to evaluate its performance in a manner that uses information systems efficiently. Ultimately, a good understanding of the business and its future direction ensures that an optimum COA is developed. It is essential that managers are involved throughout the implementation process. At the centre of the considerations should be:

- Appraising the current system, including the relevance of outputs and accessibility of information, by bringing together managers from relevant departments.
- Understanding the current and potential information needs of the organization and focusing on the overall business strategy and processes, while taking into account external reporting and regulatory requirements.
- Designing and assessing the potential impact of the new COA against those user needs, and adopting an appropriate strategy to move from the old chart.
- Balancing the benefits of numerous financial information demands with the finite resources, both time and costs, required to capture that information, and ensure its accuracy.
- Putting in place a robust framework for operating the COA, including guidance on use (for future employees), regular review of outputs, and methodology for inputs.

"Administrative purpose usually outruns the facts. Indeed the administrative official's ardor for facts usually begins when he wants to change the facts!" Mary Parker Follett

make business decisions on quite different aspects, the financial reporting process demands that a COA is able to meet all external reporting requirements, such as statutory and tax reporting. The COA must be set up so that a full trial balance for that individual entity can be obtained.

This can lead to possible conflicts and difficulty, especially where corporate cost centers are managed across a number of reporting entities. It may be that, at a cost-center level, additional detail is required on income-statement accounts, but limited detail is required for balance-sheet classifications—there is no compromise on statutory requirements.

Management should carefully consider how best to set up an accounting company, or a cost center for COA purposes. Typically, when businesses have their own general ledger systems or are legal reporting entities, a separate accounting company approach is the optimal solution. A cost-center approach is more appropriate when an organization is reviewed on the basis of divisional performance, which is supervised by individual mangers themselves.

While a standard COA should be comprehensive enough to allow for all divisional requirements, it should not compromise the compliance requirements of statutory reporting, either for the local entity, or the group as a whole.

CONCLUSION

Changing a COA involves a thorough understanding and analysis of the existing business requirements. However, it is equally important to realize that most businesses constantly evolve, and management information needs may also change. It is, therefore, essential that the implementation process includes a clear vision for future years, and makes the most of available technologies such as eXtensible Business Reporting Language (XBRL), for example. XBRL can benefit the dissemination of financial information from various sources, including various charts of account.

Finally, it is important to be mindful that there is no ideal standard COA. What fits the needs of one organization, and indeed one manager within an organization, may be considerably different for another. What is vital is that a thorough investigation of the needs of the organization as a whole is conducted.

▸▸ MORE INFO

Book:

Douglas A. Potter. *The Automated Accounting Systems and Procedures Handbook*. New York: Wiley, 1991.

Websites:

Queensland University of Technology, experiences of implementing a standard chart of accounts (SCOA): www.bus.qut.edu.au/research/cpns/seminarevent/ExperiencesofimplementingthestandardchartofaccountsSCOA.jsp

Queensland University of Technology, chart of accounts research project: www.bus.qut.edu.au/research/cpns/whatweresear/chartofaccou.jsp

NOTES

1 Queensland University of Technology, research programme, website

2 KPMG, The Effects of IFRS on Information Systems, 2008

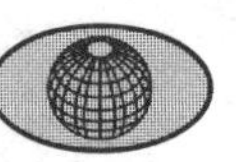

Identifying the Main Regulatory Challenges for Islamic Finance by Bilal Rasul

EXECUTIVE SUMMARY

- Harmonization and standardization within the Islamic financial industry, as well as with the conventional banking and finance industry, are the biggest regulatory challenges.
- *Shariah* rulings in *Fiqh* should be harmonized by central Islamic authorities such as the Islamic Fiqh Academy.
- Pursuit is toward uniform regulatory frameworks which restrict *shariah* arbitrage.
- *Shariah* advisers and advisery boards are indispensable in the regulation of Islamic financial institutions, but there is a dearth of expertise and there are not enough advisers to match the growing demand.
- *Shariah*-compliant securities are relatively few and not liquid.
- The Islamic Financial Services Board's Ten-year Master Plan for Islamic financial services is a good starting point to tackle the regulatory challenges.

INTRODUCTION

Globally, Islamic finance has exhibited its potential through the ever-increasing number of Islamic financial institutions (IFIs). Unofficial estimates figure Islamic financial assets of the IFIs at nearly a trillion dollars. The Islamic financial industry is still growing and is finding its niche in many Muslim as well as non-Muslim countries. The growth is swift, but it is accompanied by regulatory issues and challenges which will need to be addressed in order to facilitate and coordinate the innovation and diversity that it brings.

ISLAMIC FINANCE: THE FUNDAMENTAL DIFFERENCE

In order to understand Islamic finance it must be known that the underlying theme of Islamic finance is the *niyah* or "good intention"—the element that drives the Islamic socio-economic system for ensuring the enhancement of the welfare of society. The *niyah* may represent the Islamic philosophy of conducting life and business, but it is not restricted to Muslims. The tenet pertains to justice and fairness which can be practiced by all, Muslim and non-Muslim alike. The Islamic financial system, therefore, hinges on the *niyah* as an essential ingredient for every contractual transaction that is executed.[1]

For the layman, the fundamental difference between Islamic finance and conventional finance is the feature in the latter to put a cost on money in financial transactions, i.e. interest, or *riba* as it is known in the Islamic financial world. Basically, whatever is borrowed has to be returned but with an increment.

In Islamic finance one of the questions most often visited is: "Money has time value; how can it not have a cost?" The simplest answer is that in Islamic finance there is no concept of money as a commodity: There is always an underlying contract in the form of a partnership or venture that is entered into between the lender and the borrower, with the profits or losses and the risks all being shared. Therefore, a fixed return *per se* cannot be assured. This perspective of Islamic finance confers a "soul" to business activity. The motives are the welfare of the people; an egalitarian society; the opportunity for all to benefit without being exploited. Islamic finance covers the social aspect of being in enterprise. Above all, it is trust-based.

ISSUES

Harmonization and Standardization

The contracts prescribed in Islamic law provide a significant part of the principles and procedures explicitly laid down in the *Fiqh* or Islamic jurisprudence which must be observed for *shariah* compliance. For instance, the Qur'an is replete with passages that denounce *riba* as exploitative and against the norms of fairness. The problem arises where the principles and procedures for specifics are not so easily found and therefore have to be derived from the *fatwas*, or interpretations of the *shariah* scholars. The *fatwas* awarded on financial transactions differ amongst scholars and across jurisdictions, which produces the problem of pluralism in *shariah* interpretations.[2] There are mainly five schools of thought in Islamic jurisprudence for example, *Hanafi, Shafei, Hanbali, Maliki,* and *Ibadi* amongst others. Each school of thought has its own set of *muftis* (scholars) on Islamic financial issues which, more often than not, creates conflict and ambiguity in decisions on the veracity of a transaction in terms of its compliance with the *shariah*. In this context the Quran states "As for those who divide their religion and break up into sects, thou hast no part in them in the least: their affair is with Allah: He will in the end tell them the truth of all that they did." Al-Qur'an, Surah 6 (Al-Anaam) Ayat 159

So, the biggest challenge faced by the regulators of Islamic finance is harmonizing and standardizing these interpretations into a consistent and efficient regulatory framework that will ensure unimpeded Islamic financial intermediation amongst the participants.

The process of harmonization and standardization of transactions across and within borders is undoubtedly a daunting one and has to be comprehensive. In some jurisdictions certain transactions are considered *shariah*-compliant while in others they may not be accepted as so. It is extremely difficult to adjudge as to which is the closest to *shariah*. Consensus in the *fatwas* may be overcome by the centralization of the *shariah* rulings in a central Islamic authority such as the Islamic Fiqh Academy of the Organisation of the Islamic Conference (OIC), which is recognized by a large majority of scholars. In the event of disagreement the Academy can give its verdict.

The pursuit should be toward uniform regulatory frameworks based on principles and standards designed by universally accepted organizations such as the Islamic Financial Services Board (IFSB) and the Accounting and Auditing Organization of Islamic Financial Institutions (AAOIFI). The adoption of the guidelines drafted by these institutions is the panacea for the *shariah* arbitrage that exists otherwise.

Not secondary to this issue is the problem of emulating the conventional financial system and applying the BASEL II principles.[3] Effective risk management measures applied to the conventional financial system need to be applied to Islamic finance, but with certain modifications and adaptations. The Islamic financial industry has to be adept with techniques and competitive products to improvise and emulate the conventional banking and finance industry. Only then can IFIs compete with the conventional giants and access the international markets while maintaining their Islamic identity.

"While the industry regulators and supervisors are in the front line facing this challenge, in fact the challenge is much wider, and confronts the firms competing in the industry at the micro level and the governmental and legislative authorities in the host countries at the macro level." *The Regulatory Challenge*

  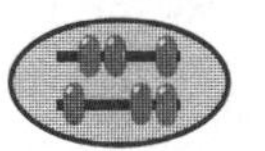 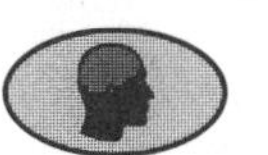  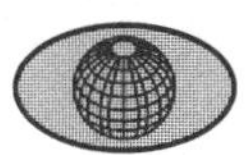   

SHARIAH EXPERTISE

The lack of *shariah* expertise is also one of the challenges that face the regulators of the Islamic financial industry. Due to the infancy of the system, very few institutions have produced the desired skill set for the Islamic financial and banking industry. While there are plenty of Islamic jurisprudence experts, there is a dearth of Islamic financial experts with a knowledge of the dynamics of conventional finance and its transformation to an Islamic/*shariah*-compliant system. Due to the regulatory obligation of instating *shariah* oversight, IFIs employ less-experienced *shariah* scholars, as only a limited number of professionals are available, and they are usually attached to more than one IFI concurrently.

The transition to Islamic finance is highly technical and complex. A balance has to be maintained in order to provide, on the one hand, an adequate return and to remain, on the other hand, within the boundaries of the Qur'an and Sunnah, which cannot be done without quality *shariah* supervision. In order to achieve this, regulators of the capital and money markets will have to encourage the development of educational institutions that offer programs and syllabi for Islamic financial technical skills. INCEIF (International Centre for Education in Islamic Finance) in Malaysia is an example that has designed an outstanding course—namely, CIFA (Chartered Islamic Financial Analyst), which prepares the student for a specialized course in Islamic finance.

Shariah-Compliant Securities

The limited number of *shariah*-compliant securities emanates from the lack of both harmony and Islamic financial prowess, and poses yet another problem in the development of the industry. Due to the paucity of available instruments in the market, investors are constrained to take their funds elsewhere. The limited choices also affect the liquidity of the securities as there is a limited market for them. The buying and selling of such securities is not as lively as in the conventional securities market, possibly due to their non-speculative nature. Nevertheless, investors are eager to place their funds in *shariah*-compliant securities, even for a comparatively lower return, provided that a reasonable degree of assurance can be given with regard to their nearness to *shariah*. The market for *shariah*-compliant securities, in terms of buyers and sellers, quite certainly exists, but it awaits the introduction and innovation of new Islamic instruments. Much of the apprehension that exists in the market with regard to *shariah*-compliant securities, or Islamic banking and finance for that matter, is owed to the slow pace of development of products and awareness-creating endeavors. In this context, the Liquidity Management Centre and the International Islamic Financial Market (IIFM) have a huge mandate and are vigorously involved in bridging the gaps in terms of investment of surplus funds of IFIs and creating Islamic financial markets.

> "The combination of services offered by operating IFI and the prevailing practices compound the difficulties of designing a regulatory framework to govern them."[4]

CONCLUSION

A purely Islamic financial system would be ideal—one in which the *niyah* and trust are predominant so that a self-perpetuating regulatory system prevails. There would be minimal regulatory interference—only for transparency and disclosure. In such a system, issues of compliance diminish directly with the prevalence of a coherent and trustful financial environment in which profits and risks are authentically disclosed and equitably distributed.

While a conventional financial system cannot evolve into an Islamic one overnight, praiseworthy efforts are being made in terms of bringing the diverging interpretations to a common platform and attempting to accord them congruence. In this context, the contributions of AAOIFI and the IFSB, as conduits for bringing solutions to the problems of standardization and harmonization, and as cornerstones of change and adaptation, must not be undermined in any way. The IFSB's Ten-year Master Plan for Islamic Financial Services is an excellent precursor to the type of regulatory environment that should prevail in jurisdictions offering Islamic finance.

CASE STUDY

The Case of *Sukuk*

Sukuk, the plural of *suk* meaning Islamic bond, are a case that particularly highlights the divergence in views of Islamic scholars. One of the most popular Islamic financial instruments, the *sukuk* have questions looming over them. The renowned *shariah* scholar Sheikh Muhammad Taqi Usmani believes that the guarantee to pay back the invested capital in *sukuk* undermines the tenets of the *shariah* by compromising on the risk and profit/loss sharing philosophy. Sheikh Usmani contends that the investment must be consequential to the investor where profits and losses both have to be anticipated. The views of Sheikh Usmani are difficult to oppose, but in giving impetus to the Islamic financial industry certain exemptions are in order, for which AAOIFI may well have the solution.[5]

▸▸ MAKING IT HAPPEN

The solution to the harmonization problem is to design regulatory frameworks that are standard. Thus, all criteria relating to the formation of Islamic financial institutions, the induction of *shariah* experts, the risk management measures, and the various codes should conform with a standard document, such as an enabling Islamic financial services law, which prescribes common Islamic financial accounting standards, corporate governance practices, and prudential regulations for risk management for the industry, and which interfaces with the IFSB's Ten-year Master Plan for Islamic Financial Services.

To bolster the Islamic securities market, companies listed on the stock exchanges (financial or manufacturing) should be encouraged to pursue *shariah* compliance. To achieve these objectives the role of the regulator(s) is emphasized.

▸▸ MORE INFO

Books:

Karim, Rifaat Ahmed Abdel, and Simon Archer. *Islamic Finance: The Regulatory Challenge*. Singapore: Wiley, 2007.

Mirakhor, Abbas. "General characteristics of an Islamic economic system." In Baqir al-Al-Hasani, Bakir, and Abbas Mirakhor (eds), *Essays on Iqtisad*. Silver Spring, MD: NUR Corp., 1989, pp. 45–80.

Venardos, Angelo M. *Islamic Banking and Finance in South-East Asia: Its Development and Future*. 2nd ed. Singapore: World Scientific Publishing, 2006.

"Government proposes, bureaucracy disposes. And the bureaucracy must dispose of government proposals by dumping them on us." P. J. O'Rourke

  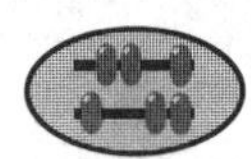   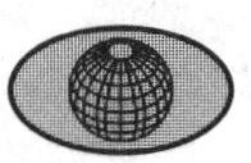   

Articles:

Ainley, Michael, Ali Mashayekhi, Robert Hicks, Arshadur Rahman, and Ali Ravalia. "Islamic finance in the UK: Regulation and challenges." Financial Services Authority, November 2007. Online at: www.fsa.gov.uk/pubs/other/islamic_finance.pdf

Akhtar, Shamshad. "Islamic finance: Its sustainability and challenges." *Journal of Islamic Banking and Finance* 25:1 (2008).

El-Hawary, Dahlia, Grais Wafik, and Zamir Iqbal. "Regulating Islamic financial institutions: The nature of the regulated." World Bank Policy Research Working Paper 3227 (March 2004).

Thomas, Abdulkader, and Sheikh Muhamed Becic. "Are *sukuk* Islamic?" *Islamic Business and Finance* 26 (2008). Online at: www.cpifinancial.net

Websites:

Islamic Financial Services Board: www.ifsb.org

Securities and Exchange Commission of Pakistan: www.secp.gov.pk

See Also:

- John Kenneth Galbraith (p. 1166)
- Alan Greenspan (p. 1169)
- An Introduction to Islamic Finance Theory and Practice (p. 1283)

NOTES

1 Mirakhor (1989).
2 Venardos (2007).
3 Basel Committee on Banking Supervision (BCBS). "Consultative document—Overview of the new Basel Capital Accord." Bank for International Settlements, April (2003). Online at: www.bis.org/bcbs/bcbscp3.htm
4 El-Hawary *et al.* (2004), p. 36.
5 Thomas and Becic (2007).

"The speed with which bureaucracy has invaded almost every branch of human activity is something astounding once one thinks about it." Simone Weil

  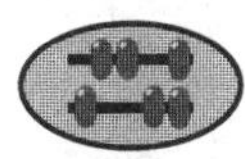   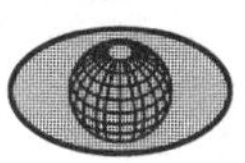   

Implementing an Effective Internal Controls System by Andrew Chambers

EXECUTIVE SUMMARY

- Effective internal control gives reasonable assurance, though not a guarantee, that all business objectives will be achieved. It extends much beyond the aim of ensuring that financial reports are reliable. It includes the efficient achievement of operational objectives and ensuring that laws, regulations, policies, and contractual obligations are complied with.
- There is growing appreciation that effective internal control does not evolve naturally. It requires concerted effort on an ongoing basis.
- Often initially stimulated by the requirements of the Sarbanes–Oxley Act (2002), many more businesses are now systematically documenting, testing, evaluating, and improving their internal control processes. We show how to do this.
- In a large organization this more rigorous focus on internal control is likely to encourage greater standardization of similar processes in use in different parts of the organization.
- More effective internal control does not necessarily cost more. Aside from reducing costly risks of avoidable losses and business failures, it is often no more costly to organize business activities in ways that optimize control.
- Better internal controls may enable a business to engage safely in more profitable activities that would be too risky for a competitor without those controls.

INTRODUCTION

In some jurisdictions law or regulation may require effective systems of internal control, with serious penalties for irresponsible failure. The Sarbanes–Oxley Act (2002) requires CEOs and CFOs of companies with listings in the United States to certify their assessment of the effectiveness of internal control over reported disclosures (s302) and financial reporting (s404), with penalties of up to $1 million and ten years imprisonment for unjustified certification, or up to $5 million and 20 years imprisonment for wilful breach of the requirements (s906). The Public Companies Accounting Oversight Board's Auditing Standard No. 5 (2007) requires the company's external auditors themselves to assess the effectiveness of their client's system of internal control over financial reporting, in order to meet the audit requirements of s404 of the Sarbanes–Oxley Act.

Japan and Canada have laws broadly similar to the Sarbanes–Oxley Act. Although not reinforced by the risk of criminal sections, provision C.2.1 of the United Kingdom's Combined Code on Corporate Governance (2008) requires that the board of a company listed on the main market of the London Stock Exchange should, at least annually, conduct a review of the effectiveness of the group's system of internal controls and should report to shareholders that they have done so. The review should cover all material controls, including financial, operational, and compliance controls, and risk management systems. In addition, the UK Financial Services Authority's Disclosure and Transparency Rule DTR 7.2.5 R requires companies to describe the main features of the internal control and risk management systems in relation to the financial reporting process (see Schedule C).

WHAT "EFFECTIVE" MEANS

Although similar requirements exist in many countries, the principal driver for implementing an effective internal controls system should be the enlightened self interest of the company.

Effective internal control is intended to give reasonable assurance of the achievement of corporate objectives at all levels. An internal control framework should be used for the design and evaluation of an internal control system. The COSO framework is the most widely applied of three published frameworks.[1] COSO (the Committee of Sponsoring Organizations of the Treadway Commission) defines internal control as follows:

"Internal control is broadly defined as a process, effected by the entity's board of directors, management and other personnel, designed to provide reasonable assurance regarding the achievement of objectives in the following categories:

1 Effectiveness and efficiency of operations.
2 Reliability of financial reporting.
3 Compliance with applicable laws and regulations."

Other definitions of internal control categorize the objectives of internal control differently, but fundamentally, effective internal control gives reasonable assurance that all of management's objectives will be achieved. For instance, the King Report[2] defines internal control as follows:

"The board should make use of generally recognized risk management and internal control models and frameworks in order to maintain a sound system of risk management and internal control to provide a reasonable assurance regarding the achievement of organizational objectives with respect to:

1 Effectiveness and efficiency of operations;
2 Safeguarding of the company's assets (including information);

CASE STUDY 1

A multinational company took the requirement to comply with s404 of the Sarbanes–Oxley Act as an opportunity to assess the effectiveness of its internal control generally, not just internal controls over financial reporting.

First, the accounting processes that could lead to financial misstatements were identified. Second, mission critical operational processes were identified where there were significant risks of not achieving business objectives and/or risks of misstatement. These accounting and operational processes were documented in process maps (flowcharts), using distinctive symbols to denote what were considered to be key s404 controls, other key financial controls and key operational controls. These controls were described in a spreadsheet-based control register, supplemented where necessary by further process narrative. From this understanding of each process, deficiencies in control procedures were identified and corrected. Using predetermined, documented test scripts, each key control within a process was then tested for compliance prior to drawing a conclusion about internal control effectiveness of the process.

Initially this work was done by the internal audit function, before being transferred to become an ongoing responsibility of management, working to an annual cycle.

"If companies view the new laws as opportunities—opportunities to improve internal controls, improve the performance of the board, and improve their public reporting—they will ultimately be better run, more transparent, and therefore more attractive to investors." William Donaldson

  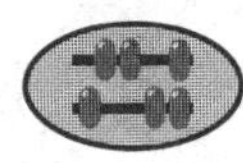   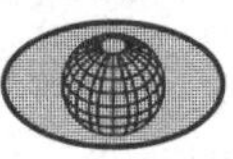 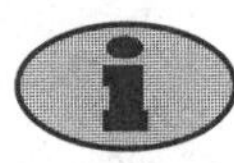  

3 Compliance with applicable laws, regulations and supervisory requirements;
4 Supporting business sustainability under normal as well as adverse operating conditions;
5 Reliability of reporting;
6 Behaving responsibly towards all stakeholders."

Before a conclusion can be reached that internal control is effective, both *results* and *processes* must be considered. For the former, the test is whether there have been any known outcomes attributable to significant breakdowns in internal control. Absence of these does not lead automatically to the conclusion that internal control is effective: it is possible that there may have been breakdowns of internal control yet to be discovered; it is also possible that serious weaknesses exist within the system of internal control that have not yet been exploited. So the second test must also be applied, which is to assess the quality of the control processes or "components."

DESIGN CHARACTERISTICS OF AN EFFECTIVE INTERNAL CONTROLS SYSTEM

The COSO internal control framework recognizes five essential components of any effective internal control system:

- *The control environment:* Values and culture; tone at the top; policies, organizational structure.
- *Information and communication:* Reliability, timeliness, clarity, usefulness.
- *Risk assessment:* Identification, measurement, and responses to threats.
- *Control activities:* Procedures followed for a control purpose.
- *Monitoring:* Review of internal control arrangements.

A common failing in designing and evaluating a system of internal control is to focus almost exclusively on control activities, vitally important though they are, overlooking that the other components are also essential. The Securities and Exchange Commission's rule for management's implementation of s404 of the Sarbanes–Oxley Act requires that a recognized internal control framework is applied. Usually it is the COSO framework that is used, and the framework comprises all of these five as being essential components of an effective system of internal control.

General hallmarks of an effective system of internal control include that controls:

- are designed to meet objectives which are clear;
- have regard to competitive issues;
- enable and ensure that performance is measured;
- result in unsatisfactory performance being rectified;
- ensure that activities are completed in a timely way;
- are cost effective;
- are placed as early in the process as is practical, so that thereafter there is control;[3]
- are "preventative" rather than merely "permissive";
- have no more movements, or steps than are necessary.

Control activities can be categorized as follows:

Preventive controls: *To limit the possibility of an undesirable outcome being realized.* The more important it is that an undesirable outcome should not arise, the more important it becomes to implement appropriate preventive controls. Examples are when no one person has authority to act without the consent of another, or limitation of action to authorized persons (such as only those suitably trained and authorized being permitted to handle media enquiries).

Corrective controls: *To correct undesirable outcomes that have been realized.* Examples are the design of contract terms to allow recovery of overpayment, or contingency planning for business continuity/recovery after events which the business could not avoid.

Directive controls: *To ensure that a particular outcome is achieved or an undesirable event is avoided.* Examples are a requirement that protective clothing be worn, or that staff be trained with required skills before working unsupervised.

Detective controls: *To identify undesirable outcomes "after the event."* Examples are stock or asset checks which detect unauthorized removals, or post-implementation reviews to learn lessons.

Performance controls: *To orientate and motivate the organization's people to focus on the achievement of targets that*

CASE STUDY 2

To be useful, process narrative on internal control must be sufficiently specific to indicate whether control is effective. In the three examples below, only the third is adequate. The reader of the first and second examples will be unclear as to whether it is merely the narrative that is inadequate, or that internal control is inadequate.

Control Documentation Poor

A report on duplicate invoices is produced before payments are made. It is looked at and approved by someone who plays no other part in the order processing and invoicing procedures.

Control Documentation Average

Each day, before the payments processing run, the senior creditors clerk (SCC) investigates a report on possible duplicate invoices. The SCC signs and dates this report when the check has been completed, and sends the report to James Smith for second review and final approval. James signs and dates the report to indicate completion of his review and approval of the SCC's investigation.

Neither James nor the SCC has access to the purchase order or invoice processing SAP modules or the manual parts of those subsystems.

Control Documentation Good

Daily, before the IT-based processing of payments, the SCC personally prints out a possible duplicate payments report from the payables module in SAP (SAP report code 9VDFZ3). This report may indicate five possible types of duplicate (refer to details in the process narrative).

The SCC investigates the possible duplicate invoices as indicated in the report by checking the accuracy of invoice data captured in the SAP accounts payable module against original invoices, making sure that each invoice is valid by reference to source documentation such as purchase orders as necessary.

The SCC has no responsibility for other elements of this system, not having any involvement in, or other access to, the processing of purchase orders or invoices—these access rights are blocked to the SCC by the accounts payable module.

When the SCC has completed the investigation, he signs and dates the possible duplicate payments report to indicate that the investigation has been completed. His manager then reviews the possible duplicate payments report, together with the relevant, supporting evidence and comments from SCC's investigation. If the manager is satisfied by the investigation and supporting evidence, he signs and dates the possible duplicate payments report to indicate approval of the SCC's investigation.

"Cars have brakes so that they can go faster." Anonymous

  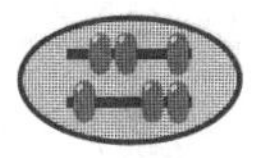 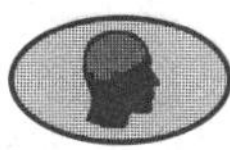  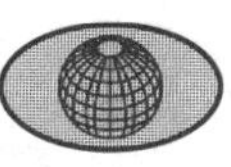   

are appropriate for the achievement of objectives. Examples are despatching all orders on day of receipt of order, or allowing that less than 2% of production should fail quality control checks.

ASSESSING INTERNAL CONTROL EFFECTIVENESS

A widely followed approach to assessing and improving internal control effectiveness has been developed that comprises these steps (see case study 1):

1 Determine the documentation to be used, such as process maps (flowcharts), control registers, and process narratives.
2 Identify the objectives to be achieved.
3 Determine the processes that are key to the achievement of objectives.
4 Learn about each key process, documenting it in narrative, spreadsheet, and/or flowchart form.
5 Within a key process, identify and document the key controls.
6 Judge the potential of each key control to be effective, if followed as intended. Modify the control approach if necessary.
7 Design and document tests to be conducted to assess compliance with each control.
8 Conduct these tests.
9 Interpret the results of these tests. Where necessary, ensure better compliance or modify the control approach if satisfactory compliance is judged impractical.
10 Interpret the control significance of unwanted outcomes that have occurred.
11 Consider the adequacy of the control environment, information and communication, risk assessment, control activities, and monitoring.
12 Conclude on the effectiveness of internal control at the process level.

TESTING INTERNAL CONTROLS

The extent of testing is a compromise between the need for thoroughness and the testing resources available, and will vary according to the criticality of the controls that are being relied upon, the potential for the controls to be circumvented, and the results of initial testing. For controls designed to operate at intervals (such as at week, month, or year ends), initial sample sizes may be as in Table 1. For controls that apply to individual transactions Table 2 may be appropriate, which can also be used for interval controls that are used in multiple locations or on multiple occasions.

ONGOING MAINTENANCE OF AN INTERNAL CONTROLS SYSTEM

Changing business requirements will result in modified business processes and the risk that controls within those processes may be abandoned or made less effective. Each modified business process that is key to the achievement of a business objective should be reassessed, applying steps 3 to 6 (above), prior to releasing the new or modified business process for operational use.

For established processes, performance criteria should be established to monitor the quality of performance and the extent to which controls fail.

Table 1. Sample sizes to be used if the control operates at the frequencies shown

Frequency of control	*Sample size*
Annually	1
Quarterly	2
Monthly	2
Weekly	5
Daily	20
Many times a day	25

Table 2. Sample sizes for transaction controls

Population size	*Sample size*
1–3	1
4–11	2
12–50	3
51–100	5
101–200	15
201–300	20
Above 300	25 max

⏩ MAKING IT HAPPEN

The approach to follow:

1 Adopt and understand a recognized internal control framework.
2 Engage the board, management, and other personnel in the ownership of internal control.
3 Identify the mission critical business processes.
4 Consider standardizing processes across the business.
5 Document those processes, highlighting the key controls.
6 Consider the effectiveness of the key controls and improve where necessary.
7 Design tests to confirm satisfactory compliance with key controls, and take remedial action as required.
8 In addition to control activities, consider whether the other essential components of an effective system of internal control are sound—for example, the control environment, information and communication, risk assessment and monitoring.
9 Draw overall conclusions.
10 Use the results from this process as a continuous improvement tool to improve the internal control system.

⏩ MORE INFO

Books:

American Institute of Certified Public Accountants (AICPA). *Internal Control over Financial Reporting: Guidance for Smaller Public Companies.* Institute of Internal Auditors (IIA) Research Foundation, 2006. Order from: www.theiia.org/bookstore

Chambers, Andrew. *Tolley's Internal Auditor's Handbook.* 2nd ed. London: LexisNexis Butterworths, 2009. See especially chapter 6.

Committee of Sponsoring Organizations of the Treadway Commission (COSO). *Internal Control—Integrated Framework.* 2 vols, 1992. Order from: www.coso.org/IC-IntegratedFramework-summary.htm

COSO. *Guidance on Monitoring Internal Control Systems.* To be published in 2009. See exposure/review link at: www.coso.org

Articles:

Sneller, Lineke, and Henk Langendijk. "Sarbanes Oxley Section 404 costs of compliance: A case study." *Corporate Governance: An International Review* 15:2 (2007): 101–111.

Wagner, Stephen and Lee Dittmar. "The unexpected benefits of Sarbanes–Oxley." *Harvard Business Review* (April 2006). Online at: hbr.harvardbusiness.org/2006/04/the-unexpected-benefits-of-sarbanes-oxley/ar/1

Reports:

Canadian Institute of Chartered Accountants: A number of publications in the series *Control Environment—Guidance on Control*,including the COCO internal control framework,online at: www.rmgb.ca/3/0/8/3/index1.shtml

"In short, if you are looking for leniency you had better be able to show that you cared about preventing corporate misconduct before you discovered it occurred." Cynthia A. Glassman

  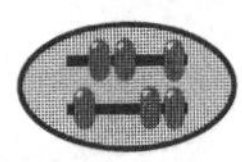 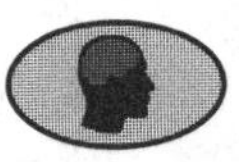  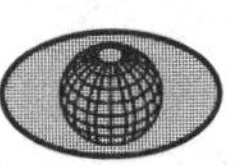   

COSO. "Enterprise risk management—Integrated framework." 2004. Summary and print requests online at: www.coso.org/ERM-IntegratedFramework.htm

Financial Reporting Council (FRC), UK. "The Turnbull guidance as an evaluation framework for the purposes of Section 404(a) of the Sarbanes–Oxley Act." 2004. Online at: www.frc.org.uk/documents/pagemanager/frc/draft_guide.pdf

FRC. "Internal control: Revised guidance for directors on the Combined Code." October 2005. Online at: www.ecgi.org/codes/code.php?code_id=178

HM Treasury, UK. "The orange book: management of risk—Principles and concepts." October 2004. Online at: www.hm-treasury.gov.uk/d/3(4).pdf

Institute of Internal Auditors (IIA). "Sarbanes–Oxley Section 404: A guide for management by internal controls practitioners." 2nd ed. January 2008. Online at: www.theiia.org/download.cfm?file=31866

Public Company Accounting Oversight Board (PCAOB). "Auditing standard no. 5: An audit of internal control over financial reporting that is integrated with an audit of financial statements." July 2007. Online at: www.pcaobus.org/Standards/Standards_and_Related_Rules/Auditing_Standard_No.5.aspx

Securities and Exchange Commission (SEC). "Commission guidance regarding management's report on internal control over financial reporting under section 13(a) or 15(d) of the Securities Exchange Act of 1934." June 2007. Online at: www.sec.gov/rules/interp/2007/33-8810.pdf. Subject to amendment issued August 2007: www.sec.gov/rules/final/2007/33-8809.pdf

Website:

Institute of Internal Auditors: www.theiia.org

See Also:

★ The Effect of SOX on Internal Control, Risk Management, and Corporate Governance Best Practice (pp. 620–622)
★ Engaging Senior Management in Internal Control (pp. 626–627)
★ How Can Internal Audit Report Effectively to Its Stakeholders? (pp. 642–645)
★ Internal Audit and Partnering with Senior Management (pp. 668–671)
★ Optimizing Internal Audit (pp. 694–696)
★ What Is the Range of the Internal Auditor's Work? (pp. 732–735)
✔ Sarbanes–Oxley: Its Development and Aims (p. 1047)
✔ Understanding Internal Audits (p. 1053)
Managing Financial Resources (p. 1294)

NOTES

1 Other recognized internal control frameworks are the Canadian "CoCo" framework, and the United Kingdom's Turnbull framework.

2 King Report on Corporate Governance for South Africa (March 2002), "King II," Institute of Directors in Southern Africa. "King III" is to be published in 2009.

3 For instance, incoming cash should be controlled at the point and time of entry into the business.

"Bureaucracy is ever desirous of spreading its influence and power." Herbert Hoover

   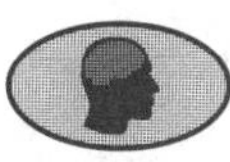  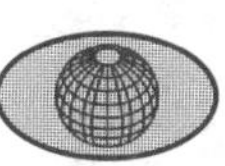   

Incorporating Operational and Performance Auditing into Compliance and Financial Auditing by Andrew Cox

EXECUTIVE SUMMARY

- Almost every audit can also be an operational or performance audit.
- With a bit of creativity, it is not too difficult to include a value-adding element to a compliance or financial audit.
- Operational and performance auditing can provide added value to your organization.
- Including an operational or performance auditing element in your audits can enhance the image of auditing for those being audited and also for management.
- Auditors can increase their job satisfaction through operational and performance auditing.
- The 3Es of economy, efficiency, and effectiveness should be integral components of the internal auditor's work.

INTRODUCTION

"The truth is, "audit gets no respect." Quite frankly, if the audit department in question is using yesterday's approach in today's company, has not manoeuvred top management and the board into focusing on the company's top five or ten risks, has not caused management to quantify these risks, and has not succeeded in developing authorized bounds of risk tolerance, then it doesn't deserve any respect."

Larry Small, President, Fannie Mae, 2000

This is a great quote, but what a pity it was not applied in recent times when this company got into serious financial difficulty. Perhaps a greater focus on operational and performance auditing might have helped.

What are the big risks for management? Are they likely to be immaterial accounting mistakes, a missing signature on a form, an immaterial asset that cannot be located, people not following a procedure exactly, or perhaps petty cash missing?

Or maybe management is more concerned with making sure the organization is running properly, which means focusing on economy, efficiency, and effectiveness—better known as the 3Es.

OPERATIONAL AND PERFORMANCE AUDITING

What is the difference between operational and performance auditing?

- **Operational audit**. Sometimes called program or performance audits, these examine the use of resources to evaluate whether those resources are being used in the most efficient and effective ways to fulfill an organization's objectives. An operational audit may include elements of a compliance audit, a financial audit, and an information systems audit. This term is mainly used in the private sector.
- **Performance audit**. This is an independent and systematic examination of the management of an organization, program, or function to identify whether the management is being carried out in an efficient and effective manner and whether management practices promote improvement. This term is mainly used in the public sector and may be the same as or similar to an operational audit.

While there may be purists who will argue there is a difference, the reality is that they seek to achieve the same objective. Although operational and performance auditing are generally applied to public sector auditing, and operational auditing is usually applied to private sector auditing, both seek to achieve organizational improvement of the 3Es.

THE AUDIT CONTINUUM

The audit continuum is shown in Figure 1. As we move from basic compliance auditing to more complex forms of auditing such as operational and performance auditing, the complexity of the audit and the difficulty in getting agreement to the audit objectives from the audit customer increases.

THE DIFFERENCES

The differences between operational and performance auditing, and compliance and financial auditing, are shown in Table 1. The real difference is that operational and performance auditing will genuinely add value and seek to improve the bottom line of an organization. Compliance and financial auditing cannot make this assertion, since their focus is generally on whether things are being done in accordance with legislation, regulations, policies, and procedures. Important though this aspect may be, it is unlikely to have the same improvement objective as operational and performance auditing.

Figure 1. The audit continuum

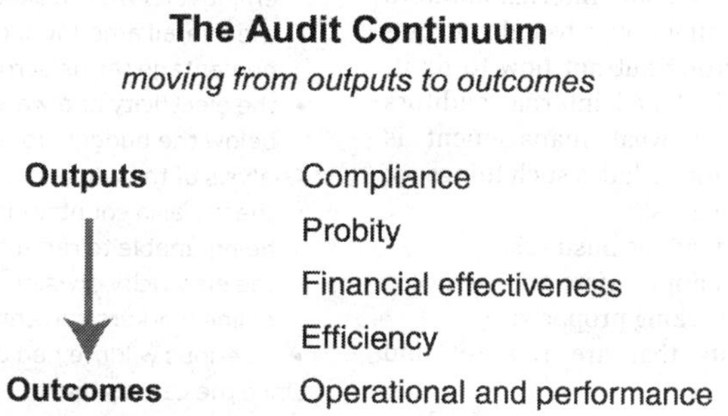

Table 1. Differences between operational and performance auditing, and compliance and financial auditing. (*Source*: The State Audit Institution of the United Arab Emirates)

	Operational and performance auditing	Compliance and financial auditing
Purpose	Does performance meet the 3Es?	Is there compliance?
Focus	The organization and its objectives	Accounting transactions
Academic base	Economics, political science, sociology, etc.	Accounting
Methods	Methods vary from audit to audit	Standardized methods
Assessment criteria	Unique for each audit	Standardized criteria
Reports	Varying format	Standardized format

"The new business environment requires an equally new vision for internal audit." KPMG

  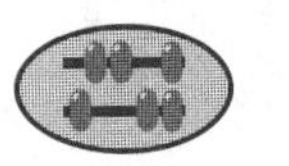   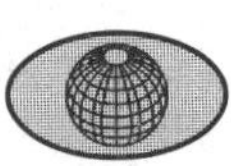   

ECONOMY, EFFICIENCY, AND EFFECTIVENESS

What are we seeking to achieve by using performance and operational auditing? The aim is to find out whether business operations are being managed in an economic, efficient, and effective manner; whether procedures for promoting and monitoring the 3Es are adequate; and, importantly, whether improvements can be made.

Economy is concerned with minimizing the cost of resources used (people, materials, equipment, etc.), having regard to the appropriate quality required: i.e., keeping the cost of inputs low without compromising quality. An example could be where healthcare supplies or services of a specific quality are purchased at the best possible price.

Efficiency is concerned with the relationship between goods and services produced (outputs) and the resources used to produce them (inputs): i.e., getting the most from available resources. An example could be where the cost of providing healthcare has been reduced over time. Efficiency is about "doing things right."

Effectiveness is concerned with achieving predetermined objectives (specifically planned achievements) and having the actual impact (output achieved) compared with the intended impact (objective): i.e., achieving the predetermined objective. An example could be where disease rates have fallen as a result of the healthcare provided. Effectiveness is about "doing the right things."

WHAT MANAGEMENT WANTS

Although there are many internal auditors who still believe their job is to tell management what is wrong but not how to fix it, many more enlightened internal auditors have worked out what management is really seeking. This includes such things as:

- help in reducing risk;
- help in improving the business;
- assurance that appropriate governance is in place and working properly;
- internal audits that are relevant and timely;
- internal audits that genuinely add value;
- more value for the money spent on internal audits.

THE STEPS IN PERFORMING AN OPERATIONAL OR PERFORMANCE AUDIT

The sequence of an operational or performance audit is likely to be:

- establish what should be done;
- establish what is being done;
- compare "what should" with "what is";
- investigate significant differences;
- assess the effects of the differences;
- determine the cause of the differences;
- develop audit findings and value-adding options and recommendations.

While the initial steps may not be very different from a compliance or financial audit, the crucial and value-adding steps are: determining the cause of the differences; and developing audit findings and value-adding options and recommendations.

These are the difficult parts. Most compliance or financial auditors can work out an effect, but trying to isolate the cause can be much harder. Hence, many internal auditors find it easier just to report on what is wrong and avoid trying to identify the root cause of a problem.

Often an internal audit recommendation will be something like "Employees should follow the procedures." This is lazy internal audit work and not a particularly enlightened recommendation—it is more of a

CASE STUDY

It is not difficult to turn a compliance audit into a performance audit. In fact, almost every audit can also be an operational or performance audit. And, by being creative, internal auditors can make their internal audit work more interesting and satisfying.

This case study comes from an internal audit conducted in a utilities company that provides electricity, gas, and water to the community. In this company, field staff work overtime. (Overtime is time worked beyond an established limit: i.e, hours worked in excess of the working hours prescribed in the employment agreement.)

The objectives of the audit were to:

- determine who had responsibility for overtime and assess whether this arrangement was working effectively;
- identify the key risks involved with overtime and the mitigation strategies and controls currently in place to manage those risks;
- identify the extent of overtime worked and test whether the key controls were working effectively to manage the identified risks;
- ascertain whether overtime requirements were being effectively communicated to managers and staff;
- review whether management regularly received and acted on feedback on the need for overtime and periodically examined cost-effective alternatives.

The audit covered all the regular auditing matters such as compliance with policy and procedures, sampling and testing overtime calculations, etc., as you would expect in a compliance audit. Since it found that overtime payments were being made correctly in accordance with policies and procedures, the audit was a nonevent. But, with some extra work, analysis of the data showed that:

- most overtime was worked in the electricity division;
- overtime was being worked by around a third of employees, with the number of employees who worked overtime increasing;
- the overall amount of overtime had been steadily increasing in absolute and payroll percentage terms across the organization over the previous four years;
- the electricity and water divisions had overtime budgets for the next year that were below the budgets for the current year (almost certainly optimistically).

Analysis of the causes revealed that:

- there was a countrywide shortage of line workers, resulting in the electricity division being unable to recruit sufficient numbers of people with these skills;
- the electricity division pole replacement program was difficult to run with the number of line workers currently employed by the organization;
- a serious wildfire had destroyed substantial electricity assets.

Once the causes had been identified, the audit recommendations suggested that the organization consider such things as:

- developing a longer-term perspective when formulating future industrial plans for the workforce;
- extending human resources employee self-service to the field employees;
- extending mobile computing to the field for human resources activities and job costing;
- further annualizing salaries to include an overtime component;
- changing the rostering of work crews to true shift work arrangements over 24/7/365.

This added real value to the audit, rather than being a simple compliance audit approach—which would have merely reported that overtime calculations were being made correctly.

"We will make an impact when we understand and anticipate stakeholder needs, use our core competencies to highlight weaknesses in a timely manner, and provide meaningful recommendations that solve the 'big problems'." Head of Internal Audit in an Australian Government department

     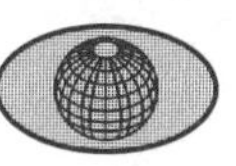   

throwaway line. There may be many reasons why an employee is not following procedures. But not many employees will deliberately disobey a procedure unless it is a bad procedure, or something else is preventing them from complying with it.

PARTNERING WITH MANAGEMENT

There are a number of ways in which internal auditors can promote their services—in particular the benefits of operational and performance auditing. These may include:

- Develop an engagement model and get management buy-in.
- Closely align your internal auditing with the business.
- Plan a risk-based internal audit program developed with management.
- Aim to become an integral part of the organization and to help management improve the business.
- Plan each internal audit with management.
- Facilitate a frank risk assessment with management and stakeholders for each internal audit.
- Formulate insightful objectives for each internal audit, not just "throwaway lines."
- Ask management to agree and sign off the terms of reference for each internal audit.
- Consider using technical experts where internal auditors may not have all the necessary skills for an internal audit.
- Facilitate a workshop with management and stakeholders at the conclusion of an audit to discuss and agree possible improvement options.

REPORTING

As mentioned previously, the real value in an internal audit report is in determining the cause of the differences between "what is" and "what should be," and developing audit findings and value-adding options and recommendations. This is the essence of what operational and performance auditing is all about.

By working closely with management and stakeholders at the conclusion of the audit to discuss improvement options, possibly using a facilitated workshop approach, a much better outcome can be achieved. After all, the people doing the job know a lot more about it than the internal auditor!

CONCLUSION

With a bit of creativity, it is not too difficult to include a value-adding element in a compliance or financial audit:

- Almost every audit can also be an operational or performance audit.
- You can do operational and performance auditing to provide added value to your organization.
- Including an operational or performance auditing element in your audits can enhance the image of auditing with the people being audited and with management.
- You can increase your job satisfaction through operational and performance auditing.

▸▸ MAKING IT HAPPEN

- Develop an engagement model for your internal auditing, and get management buy-in.
- Closely align your internal auditing with the business, plan a risk-based internal audit program developed with management, and aim to become an integral part of the organization in order to help management improve the business.
- Plan each internal audit with management, and facilitate an up-front risk assessment with management and stakeholders at the commencement of each internal audit—this is a quick and cost-effective way to determine the business processes, risks, and control procedures in place, as well as getting management buy-in.
- Ask management to agree and sign off the terms of reference for each internal audit—be sure that the objectives of an operational or performance audit are insightful and are not just throwaway lines.
- Consider using experts in technical subject areas where internal audit may not have all the skills required for an internal audit.
- Measurement criteria need to be developed; this is much more difficult than a compliance or financial audit and needs to be objective, understandable, comparable, complete, and acceptable.
- Learn the difference between "hard controls" (existence of policies and procedures, documents, payment approvals, segregation of duties, etc.) and "soft controls" (focus on ethics, integrity, competency, relationship building), and learn how to audit soft controls.
- Go outside the organization to get information and consult with external stakeholders.
- Keep the audit focused and timely, if not properly managed operational and performance audits can take on a life of their own and can end up taking a long time to complete.
- Engage and communicate with management throughout the internal audit.
- Convene a peer review challenge session within internal audit for the draft report; also do this for service providers who perform internal audits for you.
- Get the report "as right as it can be" before taking a draft to management.
- Facilitate a workshop with management and stakeholders at the conclusion of the audit to discuss and agree possible improvement options.

▸▸ MORE INFO

Books:

Reding, K. F., P. J. Sobel, U. L. Anderson, M. J. Head, S. Ramamoorti, and M. Salamasick, with C. Riddle. *Internal Auditing: Assurance and Consulting Services*. Orlando, FL: IIA Research Foundation, 2007.

Sawyer, L. B., M. A. Dittenhofer, J. H. Scheiner, and Lawrence B. Sawyer, with A. Graham, and P. Makosz. *Sawyer's Internal Auditing*. 5th ed. Orlando, FL: IIA Research Foundation, 2003.

Report:

Institute of Internal Auditors (IIA). "International standards for the professional practice of internal auditing." Orlando, FL: IIA. Available from: www.theiia.org

Websites:

Australian National Audit Office (ANAO): www.anao.gov.au

International Organization of Supreme Audit Institutions (INTOSAI): www.intosai.org

Institute of Internal Auditors (IIA): www.theiia.org

Office of the Auditor-General of Canada: www.oag-bvg.gc.ca

Training Courses and Postgraduate Qualifications:

Graduate Certificate in Performance Audit and Evaluation, University of Canberra. Details online at: www.canberra.edu.au/courses-units/gc/gcpae

Institute of Internal Auditors (IIA): "Performance auditing in the public sector." Details online at: www.theiia.org/training/index.cfm?act=seminar.onsitedetail&semID=76

Institute of Internal Auditors (IIA): "Operational auditing." Details online at: www.theiia.org/training/index.cfm?act=seminar.onsitedetail&semID=209

"Almost every audit can also be an operational or performance audit." Andrew Cox

  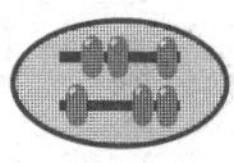 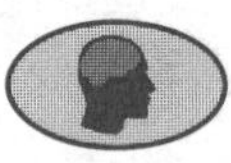  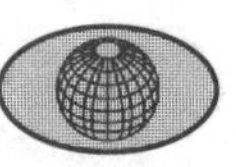   

Internal Audit and Partnering with Senior Management by Bruce Turner

EXECUTIVE SUMMARY

- The business world is constantly changing. Internal auditors increasingly need to embrace ongoing changes to the business. They also need to understand changes to key drivers, such as the regulatory environment, the profession, and the social and political landscape.
- To do so, internal auditors must maintain a meaningful dialog with senior management, so as to understand their changing needs and expectations.
- An internal audit work plan that aligns neatly with the primary risk concerns of senior management and other key stakeholders ensures that the audit effort is directed at the areas that are likely to add the greatest value to the organization.
- Because of the increasing complexity associated with running an organization, internal auditors must ensure that their recommendations translate into improved business processes and effective risk management, governance, and control arrangements.
- Internal auditors need to have the capability to deliver a product that meets or exceeds the expectations of senior management.
- Internal auditors must also be able to tell their story to maintain their influence, relevance, and credibility within the organization.

THE CHANGING ENVIRONMENT

"The internal audit function has evolved from corporate cop to that of a savvy in-house consulting service."[1]

Internal auditing in the twenty-first century imposes even greater demands on the professional internal audit staff, whose role has expanded to combine both an assurance and a consulting service to management. Internal audit charters have been broadened considerably to reflect these demands.

The chief executive of the Institute of Internal Auditors in Australia (Christopher McRostie) has reflected:

"In rapidly changing and increasingly complex business and regulatory environments the internal audit function has evolved from corporate cop to that of a savvy in-house consulting service that not only reports problems, but that also gives constructive suggestions to line managers about how to improve the performance of the business."[2]

Internal audit staff are being increasingly relied on to provide organizational expertise in risk management, internal control, and governance processes as a consequence of the emergence of stronger corporate governance demands across the world. Internal auditors need to have strategies in place that allow them to remain abreast of trends and emerging issues within their organization and the broader business community.

Contemporary internal auditing practitioners need to apply a strategic approach to understanding the key organizational value drivers and positioning themselves to meet the expectations of senior management.

Internal auditors are well placed to influence senior management in setting the right tone at the top. This, in turn, is a powerful way to nurture an organizational culture that is consistent with the values, risk tolerance, and strategies of senior management and the board.

WHAT SENIOR MANAGEMENT WANTS

"The Chief Audit Executive should effectively manage the internal audit activity to ensure it adds value to the organization."[3]

Senior management trusts internal auditors to "tell it as it is" by reporting without fear or favor. One company chairman[4] observed that "senior management want much more immediate and informal input on how the corporation is doing . . . I'd rather have the internal auditor on my doorstep telling me what I need to know so I can act on it now." His main suggestions for internal auditors were:

- Don't be distracted from good business practice.
- Understand your customer.
- Avoid being too production-oriented.
- Prioritize your activities and coordination role.
- Speak up when others may not.

Senior management is looking for assurance that current business activities meet regulatory and legislative obligations. They are also looking for ideas that drive better business performance in line with their overarching strategies and business model.

Internal auditors are best placed to meet senior management's expectations when they apply a sense of urgency to their work, apply a win–win mindset, and consistently deliver on commitments made. It is imperative that the integrity and credibility of their activities is undoubted, and that they nurture a professional and constructive relationship. The chief audit executive should undertake surveys of senior management to measure the quality of the service and determine how well the internal audit activity is serving their needs.

See below for a perspective on senior management's priorities in one organization in relation to internal auditing.

SENIOR MANAGEMENT PRIORITIES

- Accurate reporting, which reflects a business perspective, is well-written, easy to follow, and is consistent with the facts.
- Practical, constructive, and actionable recommendations.
- Proper consideration of business concerns and perspectives.
- Clear communication of objectives and scope at the start of the audit.
- Disruption to daily business operations is minimized.

The chief audit executive ought to maintain regular conversations with senior management with the objective of understanding their business perspectives and expectations of the internal audit activity. This helps to shape the planning, objectives, and scope of individual audits. The relationship should be based on cooperation, collaboration, and mutual respect.

A structured stakeholder relationship program is a useful mechanism to ensure that regular contact is maintained and that the conversations and commitments are appropriately tracked. It needs to be tailored for the business environment by recognizing the areas that need the greatest level of contact.

By way of example, a three-tier stakeholder relationship program schedule might have:

- Quarterly contact with senior managers, such as the chief financial officer and chief risk officer.

"The internal audit function has evolved from corporate cop to that of a savvy in-house consulting service."
LexisNexis

- Half-yearly contact with business leaders in remote locations.
- Annual contact with managers of relatively low-risk activities like marketing.

Because of the heavy workload of many senior managers, it may be difficult to get time in their diaries. Get to know who their gatekeepers are and build relationships with them. That can sometimes help to unlock the doors in a more timely manner.

Some larger agencies establish audit liaison officers or champions across their business lines or regional offices as contact points for the internal audit activity. These people can also facilitate audit planning and the conduct of audits, and provide periodic updates on the status of previous audit recommendations.

> "Internal audit staff are being increasingly relied on to provide organizational expertise in risk management, internal control, and governance processes as a consequence of the emergence of stronger corporate governance demands across the world."

There are benefits in establishing an internal auditor alumni. Most internal auditors retain their passion for the profession when they leave the area. They represent a fertile avenue across the organization for keeping abreast of what is really going on in the business.

PLANNING THE INTERNAL AUDIT EFFORT TO DELIVER VALUE

"Begin with the end in mind."[5]

The internal audit effort is underpinned by effective planning that directs audit effort to the higher-risk areas of the business. It is imperative that senior management and other key stakeholders are engaged in the development of the internal audit plan to ensure that it is relevant and consistent with the organization's risk profile.

In addition to looking for feedback on the adequacy and effectiveness of risk management, governance, and internal controls, senior management want recommendations that help to improve business processes. They are no longer satisfied with receiving just the results of individual audits, though these remain important. Senior management are increasingly looking for the internal auditors to provide additional analyses of the results of audits to identify systemic issues and provide insights into the corporate culture of the organization. One way of meeting these expectations is to set "themes" for the various audits contained in the internal audit plan. This facilitates high-level reporting to senior management against each of the themes.

Internal auditors can provide the greatest value to senior management when they:

- Align their activities to their organization's goals and objectives, and periodically review the role of internal audit in the light of changes to the business and global events.
- Understand the business, the key drivers, the impact of developments on the organization's risks, and the mood of senior management.
- Consult effectively with senior management, staff, and other key stakeholders, and contribute ideas and advice on an ongoing basis.
- Elevate the focus of their activities to strategic decision-making and broader risk management strategies and mitigation, while maintaining an appropriate balance with traditional compliance and operational and financial auditing.
- Provide broader information and a deeper insight into emerging governance, risk, and control issues in a timely manner.
- Deliver what they promise.

MAXIMIZING INTERNAL AUDIT'S CAPABILITY

"The vision of the director of auditing and the high expectations of management are merely wistful wishes without the right staff to do the job."[6]

It is the capability of internal audit staff that often determines the level of credibility, trust, and respect that the internal audit activity has within the organization.

Ensure that senior management and the audit committee are kept apprised of the talent within the internal audit activity. Periodically produce a staff profile that sets out the skills, experience, qualifications, and years of audit experience of the internal auditors. This helps to establish or retain credibility, especially when it is combined with benchmarking of other internal audit activities.

At a time in our history when there is a global shortage of professional internal audit practitioners, coupled with a broader internal audit charter, it is imperative to position the internal audit activity as an employer of choice.

To attract the right people, use the results of the periodic external quality assessment reviews to differentiate your internal audit activity from others (these reviews are mandatory under professional internal auditing standards).

Elements that could be considered in building greater internal capability include the following.

- Develop a recruitment strategy based on a skills gap analysis. This will ensure that you have the right multidisciplinary capability to undertake the broad range of audits in the internal audit plan.
- Establish internal audit as a learning environment and encourage innovation. This is a point of differentiation from others that will help to cater for the needs of talented and ambitious individuals.
- Produce a professional development plan for internal auditors that incorporates both a top-down and a bottom-up approach. There are typically three elements: develop the current capability; extend the capability to broaden the circle of influence; and identify future disciplines. The top-down analysis will help to close the gap between current and future staff capability needs. It should

CASE STUDY

Misguided auditing efforts

On reviewing the audit coverage of the retail loan portfolio of a commercial bank, an auditor discovered that there was broad coverage of personal loans which averaged about US$30,000. The auditors were doing a very thorough audit of the personal loans in line with the content of the internal audit plan, their sampling techniques were effective, their work papers were well-constructed, and the resultant audit report was well written.

However, the auditor also found that there was absolutely no audit coverage of foreign currency loans, although the average loan was around US$750,000 and had a far greater inherent risk. The reason was simple. Foreign currency loans had been introduced the previous year, and internal audit planning had not kept pace with the changing loan product and risk profile of the commercial bank. Consequently, the internal audit effort was misdirected and proved to be of little value to senior management in the overall context of their loan portfolio.

also promote continuous learning by encouraging postgraduate studies and the pursuit of professional certifications. The bottom-up element reflects the specific developmental needs of individual internal auditors.

- Recognize that internal auditors must have exceptionally strong communication skills across all areas (especially written, reading, oral, listening, body language, and presentation).
- Promote professional internal auditing standards. Use the results of the periodic external quality assessment reviews to differentiate your internal audit activity from others.
- Build greater awareness of the internal audit activity across the organization, as this will help to attract fresh talent to the area. For instance, many large organizations have a structured graduate recruitment program, which is potentially a rich breeding ground. But graduates often do not understand the nature of internal auditing beyond the basic technical aspects they learned at university.
- Establish a policy that encourages subject matter experts to spend some time in internal audit on a secondment (typically three to six months). Tailor this to attract people with high potential, on the basis that what they learn in internal audit will help them throughout their career.

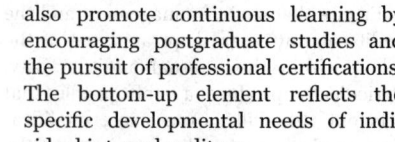

> "The internal audit activity influences the business in many different ways, quite apart from producing the traditional audit reports. To this end, it is important that the chief audit executive takes the time to tell the internal audit story."

TELLING THE INTERNAL AUDIT STORY

"The balanced scorecard can help internal auditing directors achieve superior performance by focusing on value-added services, corporate strategies and priorities."[7]

The internal audit activity influences the business in many different ways, quite apart from producing the traditional audit reports. To this end, it is important that the chief audit executive takes the time to tell the internal audit story.

The balanced scorecard is a contemporary reporting structure that helps to paint a picture of how effectively the internal audit activity is partnering with senior management and driving value for the organization. In addition to periodic reporting throughout the year, the balanced scorecard approach provides a solid foundation for producing an annual report on internal audit aimed at better informing internal stakeholders. The balanced scorecard typically focuses on four elements: partnering with the audit committee; supporting senior management; managing internal audit processes; and managing people and their development.

There is an emerging interest in what internal audit is doing outside the organization. A recent trend has been to include a section in the balanced scorecard on professional outreach (for example, activities with professional associations, presentation of papers at external conferences, and published articles).

There are a range of communication channels that the chief audit executive can use to help build the "audit brand." The strategies will vary depending on the size of the organization. A good starting point is to develop a marketing plan or communication strategy. The intention is to influence people across the organization to embrace appropriate governance and risk management techniques, and to promote an effective control environment. In doing so, it helps to raise awareness about the internal audit activity, which, in turn, helps to garner cooperation and support for internal auditors in the conduct of their work.

Elements that could be included in a communication strategy include:

- Active participation in presenting key messages at the organization's induction, training, and other corporate programs.
- Articles in staff newsletters.
- An interesting, useful, and informative internal audit intranet site.
- Establishment of a network of business unit champions as a conduit for regular communications on audit matters.
- Taking an interest in the organization's graduate programs, so as to help promote ambassadors for internal audit in future leaders.
- Brochures on the internal audit activity.

ELEMENTS OF AN ANNUAL REPORT ON INTERNAL AUDIT

The content of an annual report will be dictated by the needs of senior management and the nature of the internal audit charter. Typical headings include:

- Foreword;
- Summary of internal audit activities;

▸▸ MAKING IT HAPPEN

The chief audit executive must set the right direction for the internal audit activity in consultation with the audit committee and senior management. This will be reflected in an internal audit charter that outlines the role and responsibilities of the internal audit activity, as well as its vision and mission. The internal audit plan will reflect where internal audit resources are best applied.

At a time when the expectations of senior management and other stakeholders are getting higher, successful internal auditing demands the right people. These people will be intelligent, passionate, and innovative. They will have the knack of communicating well with senior managers and other stakeholders and responding to their needs, without compromising their independence of mind. Their research will alert them to the "next big risk."

Ideas for Further Consideration

There is a strong parallel between factors that result in highly credible internal auditing and those at the heart of a successful small business. Internal auditors will be well placed to partner with senior management when they think like a manager and apply business concepts similar to those outlined below. They are nine easy steps that underpinned a successful franchise business:[8]

- Try different things.
- Try to do everything you do better, and improve what you do in every possible way.
- Try to be more cost-effective.
- Try to keep overheads down.
- Try to give better service to your clients, make them happy, and focus on them.
- Be persistent and never give up.
- Look after your customers obsessively and worry about how you can look after them better.
- Give maximum service for the least cost.
- Listen a lot. Listen all the time. Listen. Listen. Listen.

  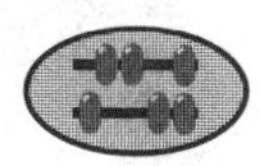   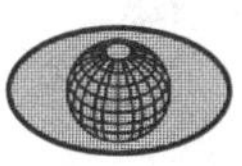   

- Overall conclusion;
- Activity headings.

For each balanced scorecard element there should be:

- A performance summary;
- A meeting attendance summary;
- Highlights;
- Areas for continuing focus.

MORE INFO

Books:

Australian National Audit Office (ANAO). *Public Sector Internal Audit: An Investment in Assurance and Business Improvement.* Better Practice Guide. Canberra: Australian National Audit Office, 2007. Available from: www.anao.gov.au

Covey, Stephen R. *The 7 Habits of Highly Effective People: Powerful Lessons in Personal Change.* London: Simon & Schuster, 2004.

Fraser, John, and Hugh Lindsay. *20 Questions Directors Should Ask About Internal Audit.* Toronto, ON: Canadian Institute of Chartered Accountants, 2004.

Frigo, Mark L. *A Balanced Scorecard Framework for Internal Auditing Departments.* Altamonte Springs, FA: Institute of Internal Auditors Research Foundation, 2002.

Pickett, K. H. Spencer. *The Internal Auditor at Work: A Practical Guide to Everyday Challenges.* 2nd ed. Hoboken, NJ: Wiley, 2004.

Sawyer, Lawrence B., *et al. Sawyer's Internal Auditing: The Practice of Modern Internal Auditing*. 5th ed. Altamonte Springs, FA: Institute of Internal Auditors, 2003.

Websites:

Australian National Audit Office: www.anao.gov.au
Canadian Institute of Chartered Accountants: www.cica.ca
Corporate Executive Board: www.audit.executiveboard.com
Institute of Internal Auditors: www.theiia.org

See Also:

★ Engaging Senior Management in Internal Control (pp. 626–627)
★ Financial Reporting: Conveying the Message Down the Line (pp. 162–164)
★ Incorporating Operational and Performance Auditing into Compliance and Financial Auditing(pp. 665–667)
★ Internal Audit Planning: How Can We Do It Better? (pp. 672–673)
★ The Internal Audit Role—Is There an Expectation Gap in Your Organization? (pp. 677–679)
★ New Assurance Challenges Facing Chief Audit Executives (pp. 691–693)
✔ Corporate Governance and Its Interpretations (p. 902)
✔ Defining Corporate Governance: Its Aims, Goals, and Responsibilities (p. 907)
✔ Requirements of the UK Combined Code on Corporate Governance (p. 913)
✔ Understanding Internal Audits (p. 1053)

NOTES

1 LexisNexis. *Risk Management* Issue 48 (2008): 12.
2 *Ibid.*
3 Spencer Pickett, K. H. (2004), pp. 60–61.
4 Thomas, R. L. "A chairman's view of internal audit." *Bank Management Journal* (May/June 1996): 28–29.
5 Covey, Stephen R. (2004), chapter on habit 2.
6 Sawyer, Lawrence B. *Sawyer's Internal Auditing*. 3rd ed. IIA, 1988, p. 785.
7 Frigo, Mark L. (2002), pp. 43, 50 (slightly edited).
8 Meltzer, G. "Someone else's slip-ups—Minding their own business." *Daily Telegraph (Sydney, Australia)* (October 16, 2001): 34 (edited).

"The vision of the director of auditing and the high expectations of management are merely wistful wishes without the right staff to do the job." Lawrence B. Sawyer

  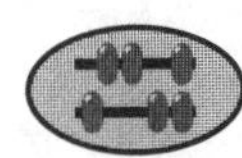   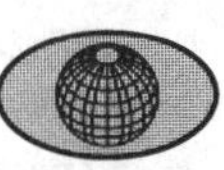   

Internal Audit Planning: How Can We Do It Better? by Michael Parkinson

EXECUTIVE SUMMARY

- Internal auditing is widely promoted as a critical component in the governance of organizations. Yet many directors and top managers are concerned that they are not getting maximum value from this resource.
- Although in many organizations internal audit is under-resourced or under-qualified, the most common problem is that it is poorly used by the organization.
- Poor planning leads to application of internal audit activity in the wrong places and the delivery of irrelevant reports.

INTRODUCTION

Internal audit is an information service. Internal auditors do not—indeed, must not—make decisions for the managers of organizations. They are a highly skilled and expensive resource that exists to serve the best interest of the organization and yet, on the surface, they do not directly contribute to organizational performance. They examine processes and produce reports; they attempt to capture good practice and identify poor; and they design controls to address identified risks. It is the information they convey to the managers of an organization that makes internal auditors valuable.

Information is valuable when it is reliable and relevant. To be reliable it must be objectively based on evidence and well argued. The internal auditing standards provide the basis for the production of reliable information, as they require the application of appropriate techniques by suitably qualified individuals. Reliability comes from discipline and competence.

Relevance means providing information that is needed, when it is needed. Relevance can only be achieved by sound planning—planning that identifies the needs of the organization and enables the delivery of internal audit results at a time when they can be acted on. Planning is a process that must involve not only the professional input of the internal auditor, but also the strategic input of the board and top management of the organization.

Internal auditing will be ineffective if it does not ask, or is not asked, the right questions.

GAINING CONTEXT: A STRATEGY FOR INTERNAL AUDIT

The top level of planning for internal audit needs to consider the users of the information that internal audit is to provide. The users might include a wide range of interests: clearly, the direct managers of areas reviewed will use the reports, but users will also include top management, the audit committee, and, in many cases, a variety of stakeholders external to the organization.

Two levels of program planning are warranted:

- a strategy for internal audit developed as part of a wider strategy for assurance;
- an annual program of internal audits that considers both the requirements for strategic assurance and the need for more immediate advice.

Focus on Risk

Internal audit must address the risks the organization faces. These are of two basic kinds—risk to conformance and risk to performance—and neither type should be addressed to the exclusion of the other. Setting the balance is a crucial strategic decision that must be taken at board level.

The most useful information usually relates to the most significant risks that an organization faces. Some organizations still use rotational programs (programs that consider each part of the organization in turn), but these are of limited value as the assumption is that the risks are static. Planning of internal auditing must be based on a current assessment of the organization's risks.

An internal audit might develop ways of better addressing a risk, might provide assurance that a significant risk is being well controlled, might advise that a significant risk is not being well controlled, or might advise that risks have been misrepresented. During the internal auditor's strategic planning process, the issue to consider is whether a particular risk is important to the organization. Whether organizational management believes the risk to be well controlled is a lesser issue. False belief—that a significant risk is well controlled—can be a dangerous assumption.

It is not the role of internal audit to second-guess management, but it can be its role to hold a mirror to management representations. Internal audit has a role to challenge assumptions and to test processes. In this context it can be healthy for disagreements about risk exposures or appropriate levels of control to be fully explored.

The chief audit executive (CAE), in consultation with the audit committee and top management, should design an assurance strategy that meets the assurance requirements of the organization and its stakeholders. This strategy should consider: mechanisms for delivery of assurance across the full set of organizational risks; the structure of the organization; reasonable restrictions on available resources; and the contribution of the full range of possible assurance providers.

While an unacceptable risk might be the responsibility of management, internal audit might have skills that can assist in addressing it. Such a risk cannot wait for attention from a routine assurance program (there may be little assurance to provide), and internal audit may have the skills and experience to contribute to the design and implementation of improved controls. The assurance strategy should, therefore, allow for the application of internal audit resources to such issues. This type of activity needs careful handling within the organization—the internal auditing standards warn against allowing the approved assurance program to be compromised by diversion of resources into management activity.

Coordinating with Other Review Bodies

The internal auditing standards require the CAE to coordinate internal audit review activities with other assurance providers. This is responsible use of resources and involves confirming the quality of the activity of other internal review activities and then appropriately relying on their results. It also involves considering the extent to which internal auditing can, without compromising the integrity of its work, support the activity of external review bodies. It must be remembered here that the scope of activity of the internal auditor is much wider than the area of interest of the financial statement auditor or any regulator.

Internal reviews that should be considered include regulatory compliance

"The success of a project will depend critically upon the effort, care, and skill you apply in its initial planning."
Gerald M. Blair

  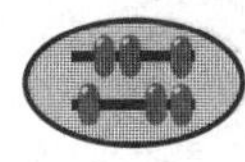   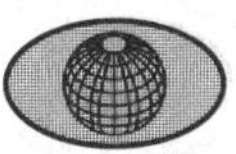   

activities, control self-assessments, and quality assurance activities such as ISO 9000 processes. In a well-coordinated assurance environment the work of the internal auditor can contribute to the maintenance of an organization's formal quality certifications. On the other hand, internal audit should not *become* the quality assurance program. This wastes the skills of the function and allows line managers to abrogate their supervision and management responsibilities.

A coordinated set of review programs ensures that overlap of review activity is deliberate and contributes to improved assurance rather than wastes resources. Ideally, this coordination is achieved as part of strategic planning, but some will inevitably be a response to particular circumstances.

Getting it right requires awareness and flexibility within a well-structured framework. The organization must be sure that the assurance provided by internal audit is sufficient in the context of other assurance providers and the needs of the organization, and must ensure that resources are sufficient to provide all necessary coverage.

APPLYING INTERNAL AUDIT RESOURCES: THE INTERNAL AUDIT WORK PLAN

At least once each year the CAE should develop a work program from the assurance strategy. It has been traditional to do this once a year, but it is increasingly being undertaken more regularly. A balance between responsiveness and planned coverage must be maintained. An internal audit program driven by short-term issues risks missing underlying problems with longer-term implications.

This work program will be informed by the current risk profile of the organization. If an organization has a mature risk management regime in place, this information will be readily available; in its absence the internal auditor will be reliant on advice from line managers and budget bids. An organization with a formulaic approach to the internal audit budget may provide resources based on history, or on an average organization, rather than on real needs. This will not provide an optimal result.

Activities that warrant immediate or proactive attention from the internal audit activity will be planned for the organization. The provision of proactive advice enables an organization to design processes correctly before implementing them. This is significantly more effective than relying on *post-hoc* criticism, which can lead to a requirement to modify processes after implementation. In particular, it has been established that changes made to computer systems become more expensive as development proceeds. A fundamental control fault detected after the implementation of such a system can be extremely costly.

Internal audit activity must be scheduled and resourced to allow work to be completed while the information is still relevant. This requires close cooperation between management and the internal audit activity. There is little value in keeping the internal audit work plan secret; making it public allows, and should oblige, managers to keep internal audit aware of issues that might be relevant to the timing of the review activity.

The CAE must have scope within the work plan to respond to issues as they arise. This enables organizational management to obtain advice about issues that concern them, and allows the internal audit work plan to respond to issues of concern as they are identified. This, clearly, should not be a license for the CAE to do as he or she wishes, and departures from the approved plan should be reported to the audit committee for their ratification.

The Individual Internal Audit Project

Scope and objectives for an internal audit project are likely to have been approved by the Audit Committee a considerable time before the review commences. They should not be adopted without consideration of changes in conditions since the planning. Often, the initial scope of the project will be broadly stated and needs to be further developed and expanded as the internal audit is conducted.

The CAE must have scope within the project to modify its focus. There will be issues of particular concern to the line manager; there will be matters that, in the judgement of the CAE, need attention. The internal audit must remain the instrument of the Audit Committee but it needs to address the realities of the organisation.

As planning for the project proceeds, the internal auditor will consider the risks of the process in greater detail. Risk registers maintained by the organisation facilitate this process, but the internal auditor needs to validate this information. It is also useful to involve relevant management in this risk assessment process. In this way, any differing views about risks, and the controls to address them, can be identified early in the project.

To be sure that there is no ambiguity in the final scope, the internal auditor might consider phrasing the information to be obtained as a question. A focusing question enables the internal auditor to know whether the results of the internal audit have been achieved – they will be able to answer the question.

Disciplined planning ensures that internal audit activity is directed at review objectives. Working from a question to be answered makes the relevance of any proposed audit procedures absolutely clear.

Complex questions are analysed during planning to produce simpler questions that remain relevant to the outcome. A focusing question enables the auditor to differentiate activity that is relevant – ie contributes to answering the question – from that which is not. The internal auditor can identify the information needed to answer the questions and can determine whether expert help is needed to do this.

Inability to phrase the internal audit scope as a question suggests that the task has been defined ambiguously. Scope ambiguity leads to waste and failure.

▸▸ MAKING IT HAPPEN

The steps to success are:

- Formally align internal audit with risk management activity.
- Build a strategy to address the assurance needs of the organization.
- Build a medium-term internal audit work plan that is both consistent with the strategy and aligned to current needs.
- Clearly state the information outcomes needed from internal audit projects.

▸▸ MORE INFO

Book:

Picket, K. H. Spencer. *Audit Planning: A Risk-Based Approach*. Hoboken, NJ: Wiley, 2006.

Article:

Parkinson, Michael. "A strategy for providing assurance: Audit committees can gain assurance from many places." *Internal Auditor* (December 2004).

"Plans are only good intentions unless they immediately degenerate into hard work." Peter F. Drucker

Reports:

Australian National Audit Office. *Public sector internal audit: An investment in assurance and business improvement.* Better Practice Guide. Canberra, Australia: Australian National Audit Office, 2007. Online at: www.anao.gov.au/uploads/documents/Public_Sector_Internal_Audit.pdf

Institute of Internal Auditors (IIA). "International standards for the professional practice of internal auditing." Orlando, FL: IIA. Available from: www.theiia.org

Professional Accountants in Business (PAIB) Committee. "Enterprise governance: Getting the balance right." New York: International Federation of Accountants, 2004. Available from the IFAC website: www.ifac.org

Standards Australia. "HB 158–2006: Delivering assurance based on AS/NZS 4360:2004 risk management." Sydney, Australia: Standards Australia, 2006. Available from: www.saiglobal.com/shop

"A committee is a thing which takes a week to do what one good man can do in an hour." Elbert Hubbard

  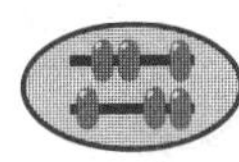   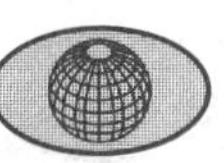   

Viewpoint: Ernst Ligteringen

No More Room for "Business as Usual"

INTRODUCTION

Ernst Ligteringen, Chief Executive of the Global Reporting Initiative, argues that having common global standards for reporting companies' nonfinancial performance is going to be an essential part for economic recovery. He believes that reporting environmental and social performance is not less important than reporting financial profit and loss. Ligteringen has run the GRI since it was established as an independent organization in 2002, including having overall responsibility for secretariat operations and the coordination of a global network of stakeholders. A Dutch national, Ligteringen previously worked for a number of international organizations, including the International Federation of Red Cross and Red Crescent Societies, Oxfam, and Terres de Hommes in Africa, the Caribbean, Latin America, Asia, the Middle East, and Europe.

As markets and regulation are redefined over the coming decade, transparency and accountability are going to the buzzwords. As we seek to rebuild the global financial system following a collapse that was, at least in part, brought about by opaque financial dealings, markets and regulators will be looking to clear the glass.

Intangibles have been accorded growing importance in financial analysis for some time—and their greater inclusion in valuations is likely to have a significant impact on the future of investment analysis. Research indicates that in the late 1970s intangibles accounted for just 5% of the total market valuations of companies in the FTSE 350 index. Today this has risen to nearer 80%, and the figure is even higher in the case of certain major global brands.

As the first decade of the 21st century draws to a close, enormous changes are underway in terms of global demographics and lifestyles. The United Nations (UN) estimates the world's population will grow by up to 50% over the next 30 years to reach nine billion people. More and more people around the world are now, quite understandably, expecting to have or, indeed, already have lifestyles which until recently were the preserve of people in Western countries. These changes are fueled by, and dependent, on the availability of resources and the ability to use the environment as a dumping ground, both of which have clearly defined limits. The resulting changes—in global ecosystems and economic disparities within and between countries—will alter the world, so that "business as usual" is no longer going to work in terms of providing the world with sustainable prosperity. And there is a growing awareness of this, by consumers, regulators, and others.

One key intangible that is going to require in-depth analysis in the years to come is how well-positioned companies are to handle these changes. Transparency on how a company addresses a range of economic, environmental and social concerns is going to become paramount in gauging how it is positioned to maintain a strong reputation and brand, and its ability to offer products and services that meet the new needs arising from a changing world.

A FULLER TOOLKIT

Speaking at the 2006 conference of the Global Reporting Initiative (GRI), former US vice-president Al Gore explained how the way in which corporate accounts are presented colors our perception of results.

Gore quoted from the eminent US psychologist Abraham Maslow, who famously said if a hammer is our only tool, we are likely to see all problems and opportunities as nails. Gore then discussed the consequences of relying on financial data alone to assess a company's results. The actual value of natural resources and human capital wrapped up in a company simply cannot be captured in the conventional balance sheet. This leaves significant blind spots that negatively affect companies' as well as the public's interest.

More and more investment analysts are recognizing these shortcomings and have started to use a more sophisticated toolkit. Rather than just rely on financial indicators, they are actively seeking out so-called "nonfinancial" information.

The asset managers who have signed up to the United Nations Principles for Responsible Investment have committed to analyzing the "environmental, social and governance" (ESG) aspects of companies in their investment universe. The signatories represent over US$18 trillion of assets under management. The numbers involved means this group is one of ever-growing importance for companies.

The investors, as well as others in government and regulatory agencies worldwide, have recognized that current accounting practice is obsolete. Traditional financial disclosures do not capture the true cost, or the true value, of products and services. As we saw with America's subprime fiasco, what seems to make economic sense in the short term can cause immense harm in the longer term.

The narrow perspective of conventional business reporting will inevitably lead to further market failures through the overexploitation of essential natural resources such as fisheries, forestry, and finite fuel resources. Conventional forms of business reporting will neither give the market, individual companies nor society adequate warning signals of what is to come and which companies are most exposed to these changes.

In this context, investors are continuing to push for a new model of reporting, one that informs us not only about a company's impact on the environment and society, but also about how those impacts might come back to haunt the company.

THE NEW MODEL

In the mid-1990s, a group of asset management firms with an interest in "socially responsible investment" (SRI) began to discuss how they might obtain better data from companies to inform their dialogue and, ultimately, their investment decisions. Driven by this group's interests, the idea of a global framework was born. The idea was that this would provide a platform for

  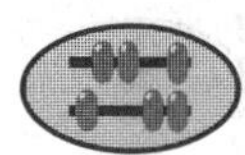 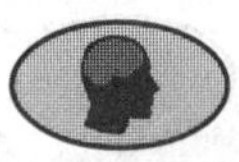  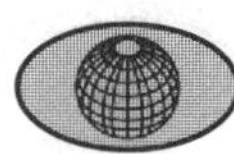  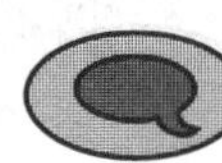 

transparent sustainability reporting, and ultimately gave rise to the launch of the Global Reporting Initiative in 1997.

Twelve years on, and great progress has been made in developing a common framework for sustainability reporting. As a global network organization GRI brings business leaders together with investors, accountants, civil society organizations, trade unions, and academics in developing the guidance for corporate disclosure of economic, social, and environmental performance.

Working groups comprised of these stakeholders meet to outline what the guidance should be. Their proposals are then opened up to global consultation. In this way, the GRI framework represents the best current thinking on the critical sustainability issues facing people, planet, and prosperity.

The GRI guidelines contain guidance for companies and organizations in general regarding reporting principles and key indicators to measure and disclose economic, environmental, and social performance.

The guidelines are made freely available as a public good for companies and other organizations globally, irrespective of their size, sector or country.

Because they facilitate the transparent disclosure of sustainability information, the GRI guidelines provide the basis for like-for-like comparison between companies and, just as importantly, allow for change to be effected from within the company.

The investment management firms that have signed up to the UN's Principles for Responsible Investment are advised that persuading companies to use GRI guidelines is one of the key actions they can take in implementing the principles.

GROWING ACCEPTANCE

Today, the GRI's latest version of the Sustainability Reporting Guidelines (G3) provides the world's most widely used framework for sustainability reporting.

Of course, there are still some skeptics around, but their voices are fewer as companies realize the value they can gain from measuring and disclosing how they are positioned to meet the challenges of sustainability.

A recent survey by KPMG, published towards the end of 2008, happily confirmed that GRI Guidelines have become the global norm for sustainability reporting. It revealed that nearly all of the world's largest 250 companies disclose data on their sustainability performance and some 80% use the GRI framework as the basis for their reporting. That's a very encouraging start but reporting on economic, environmental and social performance is still far from universal. Smaller firms and companies based in emerging markets still need further encouragement.

There is no room for complacency and GRI intends to continue to engage a wide range of stakeholders in the development of sustainability reporting to ensure that the framework continues to represent the best current thinking on sustainability. GRI's multi-stakeholder, consensus-seeking approach has proved to be the most valuable way to deliver reporting guidance that is universally applicable, and responds to the changing needs and expectations of a dynamic environment and society.

Investors remain one of GRI's key stakeholder groups and, likewise, GRI has an essential role to play in ensuring that there is consistent, material, and reliable information on sustainability performance available to the financial markets. Without standardized information, investors and the financial markets will be unable to integrate environmental and social factors into their decision-making. And, as we've seen, these factors are going to be of increasing importance.

The Financial Accounting Standards Board in the United States was born of the stock market crash of 1929 and the ensuing Great Depression. In order to regain trust following the slump 80 years ago, it was felt that greater transparency was needed through the provision of more robust data.

Eighty years on we find ourselves once again reexamining the reporting landscape against the backdrop of a financial and economic catastrophe. Arguably the stakes are even higher this time round.

▸▸ MORE INFO

Reports:

Global Reporting Initiative. "G3: Global Reporting Initiative sustainability reporting framework." 2006.

Investor initiative in partnership with UNEP Finance Initiative and the UN. "Global compact PRI progress report: Principles for responsible investment." 2008.

KPMG. "International survey of corporate responsibility reporting." 2008.

KPMG and SustainAbility, commissioned by the Global Reporting Initiative. "Count me in: The readers' take on sustainability reporting." 2008.

SustainAbility, UNEP, and Standard & Poor's. "Tomorrow's value: The global reporters' 2006 survey of corporate sustainability reporting." 2006.

"Being good is good business." Anita Roddick

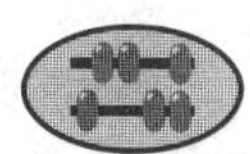

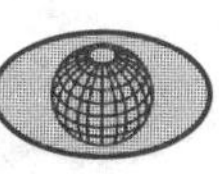

The Internal Audit Role—Is There an Expectation Gap in Your Organization? by Jeffrey Ridley

EXECUTIVE SUMMARY

- Every internal audit role should be established with a charter approved and reviewed annually at board level.
- The internal audit charter should describe the internal audit role in the organization it serves, including its purpose, authority, responsibility, and relationships with external organizations.
- The internal audit charter should be promoted across the organization at all levels and as appropriate across its supply chains and to its stakeholders.
- Internal audit should have measures in place to demonstrate its level of performance to the organization.
- Expectation gaps at organization and individual customer levels should be identified, and all performance measures continuously monitored if the full added value of the internal audit role is to be achieved.
- New dimensions of the internal audit role in an organization should be continuously explored to ensure that it is at the cutting edge of its professional attributes and in its performance.

INTRODUCTION

Establishing the internal audit role in any organization requires formality to ensure that it is understood not only by the board and management but also by its customers across the organization and, where necessary, those external to the organization. The internal audit assurance and consulting role should be explained clearly in a charter to minimize any expectation gaps at board and organization levels. When the role is being established, it is important that internal audit management should have an input into the formal process through discussion with the board and senior management.

The Institute of Internal Auditors (IIA), as the global professional body representing internal auditing in every country, has always recommended and now requires in its *International Standards for Professional Practice of Internal Auditing* (or *Standards*) that "the purpose, authority and responsibility of an internal audit activity . . . should be formally approved and kept under review at the highest level in an organization." In some sectors this may also be a requirement of one or more of an organization's stakeholders, such as government or a sector's regulator.

PURPOSE, AUTHORITY, AND RESPONSIBILITY OF THE INTERNAL AUDIT ROLE

Purpose

The purpose of professional internal audit is described in the IIA's 2009 definition as:

*"Internal auditing is an **independent objective assurance and consulting activity** designed **to add value and improve** an organization's operations. It helps an organization accomplish its objectives by bringing **a systematic, disciplined approach to evaluate and improve** the effectiveness of **risk management, control, and governance processes**."*

Key to this definition of internal auditing are the words in bold:

- Independence of the internal audit and its objectivity are critical for all dimensions of the role practiced by the internal auditor.
- The value it adds to improve an organization's operations should be measured and reported continuously.
- All its services require systematic and disciplined processes.
- It requires a wide and deep knowledge and understanding of risk management, control and governance within the organizations it serves, across their supply chains, and with all their stakeholders.

Writers on internal auditing have been promoting its independent assurance and consulting roles since the first statement of responsibilities of the internal auditor was published by the IIA in 1947. Consultancy and training were never mentioned as such in the IIA's statements but were implied by its scope of responsibilities. The best evidence for this is in the "objective and scope of internal auditing" in its 1957 statement:

"The overall objective of internal auditing is to assist all members of management in the effective discharge of their responsibilities, by furnishing them with objective analyses, appraisals, recommendations and pertinent comments concerning the activities reviewed. The internal auditor therefore should be concerned with any phase of business activity wherein he can be of service to management. The attainment of this over-all objective of service to management should involve such activities as:

- *Reviewing and appraising the soundness, adequacy and application of accounting, financial and operating controls.*
- *Ascertaining the extent of compliance with established policies, plans and procedures.*
- *Ascertaining the extent to which company assets are accounted for, and safeguarded from losses of all kinds.*
- *Ascertaining the reliability of accounting and other data developed within the organization.*
- *Appraising the quality of performance in carrying out assigned responsibilities."*

The 1971 revision to this statement changed the fourth activity from "accounting and other data" to "management data," and added a sixth activity—"Recommending operating improvements." This widened the scope of internal audit into all operations. In 1981, the statement was further changed to state that internal auditing is a service to the "organization," not just to "management." This brought the board and all operating levels in the organization into the internal auditing market place.

Lawrence Sawyer[1] supported the role of internal auditors as consultants (and trainers) in his 1979 writings. He draws vivid pictures of "problem-solving internal auditors" providing reviews, appraisals, communications and advice on management: "the [internal] auditor has a duty to know the functions of management as thoroughly as the manager does." He discusses various consulting opportunities for internal auditors in the services they can provide, and he also gives recognition to internal auditors as teachers: "the internal auditor's role as a teacher is little known, insufficiently practiced, and generally not believed or accepted."

As the IIA scope statement was being revised, practicing internal auditors were

"Professional internal auditors are experts in governance and skilled in the strategic, tactical and operational aspects of risk assessment and audit planning." Cutting Edge Internal Auditing, 2008, p. 4

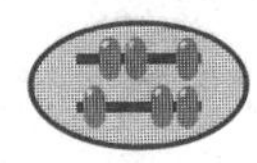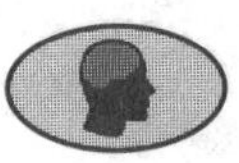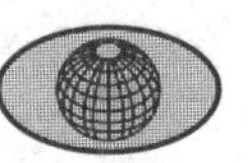

broadening their services by increasing the number of dimensions in the role they provided in their organizations. Dr James Wilson and Dr Donna Wood[2] researched the behavioral dynamics of internal auditing, recognizing seven dimensions and conflicts in the internal auditor's role at that time (1985):

1 Accountant
2 Policeman
3 Watchdog
4 Teacher
5 Consultant
6 Communicator
7 Future Manager

These dimensions and conflicts still exist in internal auditing. They should all be addressed at board level and, as appropriate, be clearly seen in its charter. They are currently seen in the IIA's definition of internal auditing and in its *Standards*.[3] The two roles in the definition—assurance and consultancy—are defined thus:

- **Assurance services** involve the internal auditor's objective assessment of evidence to provide an independent opinion or, conclusions regarding . . . a process, system or other subject matter . . .
- **Consulting services** are advisery in nature, and are generally performed at the specific request of an engagement client . . .

The other dimensions can all be seen in these roles in practice and in the *Standards* and supporting guidelines.

Authority

The authority of internal audit should always lie at board level, evidenced by its reporting lines to the board and senior management and reviews of its performance at these levels. That authority may include reporting lines to the chair of an audit committee and presence at its meetings. It should also include open access to all an organization's employees, operations, systems, records, and property.

Responsibility

The responsibility of internal audit should clearly state the scope of its work in the organization and its reporting requirements to the board, senior management, and customers. In some organizations this may also include reference to the internal audit role in the organization's training programs, code of conduct, procedure for dealing with whistleblowing, and fraud prevention, detection, and investigation processes.

PROMOTING THE INTERNAL AUDIT ROLE

The internal audit charter approved by the board is only the beginning of the promotion of the internal audit role throughout an organization. It has to be visible to all its customers in the services it provides and in its planning and engagement processes. Internal auditing has developed many ways to do this through the publishing of internal brochures, intranet websites, and even organization websites. Examples of each can be found in many internal auditing text books.

Cindy Cosmas (1996)[4] studied how internal auditing in North America marketed itself within the organizations to which it provided services. She concluded that it required some initial planning and formality, but that it brought significant benefits:

"A marketing program, or plan, is essential for every internal auditing department. A well-devised plan will direct internal auditors in their quest to provide valuable services to their organization."

Cosmas goes on to say that such a plan should consist of specific objectives, a well-developed customer base, effective promotional tools, a plan of action, and a way to monitor success: in other words, a business strategy. It is not about internal auditing living on an island in an organization, separated from its customers! She discusses internal auditing marketing its creativity in her chapter on internal audit participation in management teams:

CASE STUDY

Nine Important Points to Avoid Internal Audit Expectation Gaps[8]

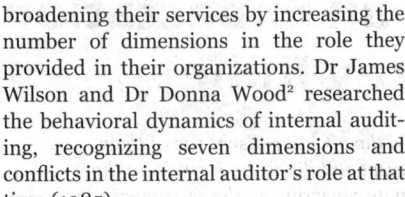

More and more organizations are beginning to benefit from professional internal audit practice. This can be seen from the growing number of internal auditors in Europe that can be found in all sectors, public and private. This growth has been accelerated by legislation and regulation that requires organizations to demonstrate the effectiveness of their governance, risk management, and internal control processes because it is clear that an internal audit activity is uniquely positioned to support management. In the detailed paper,[8] we set out what we consider to be best practice in internal auditing and how organizations should use internal auditing to help achieve good governance and risk management practice. The most important points are:

1 Professional internal auditors will apply and uphold the IIA's *Code of Ethics* in all circumstances.
2 The audit committee will ensure that the mandate and responsibility of the internal audit activity is formalized in a charter that it approves.
3 The audit committee will ensure that the internal audit activity has a direct reporting line to the chief executive of the organization and an open and direct communication line to the board and itself, in order that it maintains its independence.
4 The chief audit executive will support the board and executive management in fulfilling its responsibilities for the systems of governance, risk management, and internal control.
5 The audit committee will ensure that the internal audit activity is adequately resourced and competently staffed by investing in their qualification and their continuing professional development. The promotion of qualifications, endorsed by the profession of internal auditing, will be central in this approach.
6 The chief audit executive will develop and maintain a quality assurance programme that covers all aspects of the internal audit activity, monitoring its effectiveness by using both internal assessments and assessments by appropriate external review bodies.
7 The chief audit executive will plan the internal audit work on the basis of the risks facing the organization, will make relevant and timely reports to other participants in the governance process, and will follow-up internal audit recommendations to enable the drive for continuous improvement in the organization to be successful.
8 The internal audit activity will promote internal controls that effectively mitigate risks in all activities of the organization.
9 The audit committee and the chief audit executive will work to improve the cooperation between all those active in the field of governance, in particular, optimizing cooperation with statutory auditors to ensure the comprehensive audit of all activity.

Consider

1 Are these nine points all reflected in your internal audit role and charter?
2 Are there any expectation gaps in your organization concerning these nine points?

"It is important that there is agreement in an organization on the roles internal auditors undertake. . ."
Cutting Edge Internal Auditing, 2008, p. 69

"Utilizing creative instincts is one of the internal auditor's most powerful marketing tools." She recognized at the time the growing participation by internal auditors in team projects across organizations, working closely with operating staff and management. Seeing internal auditing creativity as an important part of the marketing, she writes:

"As a marketing tool, audit participation on project teams has been beneficial overall in winning management's praise and support. Internal auditing brings a unique perspective to project teams through their background and training."

MEASURING THE INTERNAL AUDIT EXPECTATION GAP

Cindy Cosmas also saw the marketing of internal auditing services as one of its key indicators for success and an important performance measure for assessing its continuous improvement: "The primary purpose of a performance measurement system is to support continuous improvement," and "To improve a process we must know how our customer intends to use the process outcome." Knowing what the internal auditing customer wants is fundamental to a good marketing plan. Knowing whether the customer understands the internal audit services approved by its charter is also very important.

A current performance measurement tool with many internal audit activities is the use of a questionnaire during its engagements to seek feedback from its customers on the service it provides. Such a questionnaire is an effective way to seek views on how the customer understands the internal audit's role in the organization and whether it is perceived to be as written in its charter. Another practice is to use discussion and training groups within the organization to spread the purpose, authority, and responsibility of the internal audit role.

One example of an expectation gap in the internal auditing role is in the prevention, detection, and investigation of fraud. This is too often not always clear and can cause different perceptions across an organization at all levels. Chambers (2005)[5] recognizes this:

"There is undoubtedly an expectation gap for internal auditors in the area of fraud. . .Other parties expect. . .internal auditors to be effective at detecting significant fraud. . .[and] preventing significant fraud. . .Much effort is needed by the chief audit executive to explain internal audit's interface with fraud."

Today's New Image for Internal Auditing

In my book *Cutting Edge Internal Auditing* I cite an article published in 2005[6] in which I wrote:

"By the late 90s some different aspects of the internal auditor's role were identified in new IIA research—assurers of control, risk facilitators, in-house consultants, business analyst, fraud detectors, innovators, quality advocates, advisers on governance. Later research in the UK[7] in 2002 supported these aspects; showing internal audit in the UK is currently adding value in the following six elements of the governance process, ranked in order of perception by those it serves:

- *Assurance that the internal control framework is operating effectively.*
- *Assurance that major business risks are being managed appropriately.*
- *Detection and prevention of fraud and irregularities.*
- *Improving business performance by sharing knowledge of best practices.*
- *Identification of new business risks.*
- *Use of knowledge and experience to tackle urgent issues.*

The first three are the traditional approaches to internal audit work. Most board members and management recognise these. The last three require a participative teamwork approach and for some internal audit functions are still relatively new services: in some internal audit activities they have been provided for many years. Today's professional internal auditors should be well trained and competent to add all of these values in their organizations. A measure of their professionalism is whether they can and do. Board and audit committee members should expect and ensure that all are well provided."

Since 2005 these new services have changed the internal audit role in many organizations and continue to do so, encouraged at board level and by management. They have also been pioneered by many internal auditors as they develop their professional attributes and practices to increase their value.

▸▸ MAKING IT HAPPEN

The internal audit role has a variety of independent professional dimensions, created and approved at board level to meet management, risk management, control, and governance needs at all levels in an organization, and across its supply chains. To minimize any expectation gaps in the services it provides it is important that:

- the purpose, authority, and responsibility of the role are clearly established in a charter;
- that charter is promoted at all levels across the organizations it serves;
- customer perceptions and expectations of the internal audit role are measured continuously;
- expectation gaps are identified and monitored;

▸▸ MORE INFO

Websites:

European Confederation of Institutes of Internal Auditing: www.eciia.org
Institute of Internal Auditors: www.theiia.org
Institute of Internal Auditors UK and Ireland: www.iia.org.uk

NOTES

1 Sawyer, Lawrence B. *The Manager and the Modern Internal Auditor*. New York: Amacom, 1979.
2 Wilson, James A., and Donna J. Wood. *Managing the Behavioral Dynamics of Internal Auditing.* Altamonte Springs, FL: IIA Research Foundation, 1985.
3 Anderson, Urton, and Andrew J. Dahie. *Implementing the Professional Practices Framework*. 2nd ed. Altamonte Springs, FL: IIA Research Foundation, 2006.
4 Cosmas, Cindy E. *Audit Customer Satisfaction: Marketing Added Value* Altamonte Springs, FL: IIA Research Foundation, 1996.
5 Chambers, Andrew. *Tolley's Internal Auditor's Handbook*. 2nd ed. Edinburgh, UK: LexisNexis Butterworths, 2009.
6 "Is internal auditing's new image recognized by your organization?" In Chapter 4 of *Cutting Edge Internal Auditing*, Jeffrey Ridley. Chichester: Wiley, 2008.
7 *The Value Agenda*. London: Deloitte & Touche and IIA, 2002.
8 *Internal Auditing in Europe—Position Paper*. Brussels: European Confederation of Institutes of Internal Auditors, 2005.

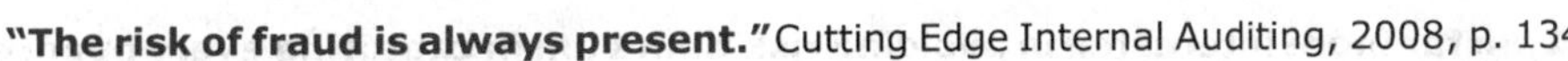
"The risk of fraud is always present." Cutting Edge Internal Auditing, 2008, p. 134

  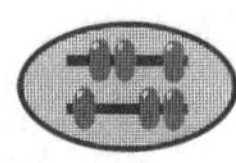   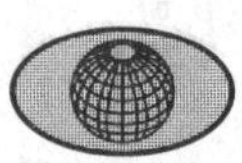   

Internal Auditors and Enterprise Risk Management by Ian Fraser

EXECUTIVE SUMMARY

- Organizations should implement effective risk management as a component of good corporate governance.
- Internal audit has a natural affinity with risk due to its centrality to audit and auditor expertise in monitoring and systems review.
- The key issue for determination is the parameters of the internal audit responsibility in the risk management area. Is internal audit best focused on a monitoring and review role, or might this extend to risk identification and the establishment of risk management systems?
- There is no one "best-fit" solution, and much will depend on organizational size, safeguards to protect objectivity, and the range and scope of available internal auditor expertise.

INTRODUCTION

Traditionally, internal auditors have been "policemen," and their efforts have been concentrated on the more detailed, and arguably less appealing, aspects of financial auditing within organizations. Often, therefore, internal auditors have been regarded in the past as the poor relations of their external auditor cousins. This no longer applies, however, as the purpose of many internal audit functions has evolved over time.

From a concern with (arguably) low-level financial audit, internal auditors have progressed to systems audit and an involvement with economy, efficiency, and effectiveness (the 3Es), to their contemporary focus on enterprise risk management. I generalize here, of course; not every internal audit function in every organization has been involved with each of these areas. In the public sector, for example, there has tended to be more involvement with the 3Es. This chapter is concerned with the internal audit role in connection with how enterprises manage risk.

INVOLVEMENT OF INTERNAL AUDIT WITH RISK

To an extent, the traditional role of internal auditors in connection with financial auditing gave them an initial knowledge base with which to get involved with risk management. Financial auditing has a concern with the risk of financial misstatement, whereas (although this burden falls primarily on the external auditors) audit risk is primarily concerned with the risk of issuing a wrong opinion on the financial statements. The recent external audit phenomenon of business risk auditing has pinpointed that effective financial audit (whatever the ostensible audit methodology employed) has to engage with business risks. The rationale for the latter assertion is, of course, that entity business risks, of whatever nature, ultimately affect the risk of misstatement in the financial statements. There is, therefore, a clear link between business risk and audit risk.

Thus, in one sense, it is natural for auditors (whether internal or external) to be concerned with the management of risks within organizations. External auditors tend to be involved with organizations on an occasional, rather than an ongoing, basis, and so it is difficult for them to have anything other than a relatively superficial appreciation of the business risks. Indeed, this is a valid criticism that has been made of "business risk auditing" as an external audit methodology. Arguably, therefore, there is a ready-made role for internal auditors in connection with risk.

Undoubtedly, however, the UK Turnbull Report (henceforth "Turnbull") on corporate governance was an important catalyst in the process of involving internal auditors with risk management. The Turnbull emphasis on the adoption by corporations of risk-based approaches to the establishment of internal control systems, and on the subsequent monitoring of these systems' effectiveness, created a role for high-level monitoring agencies within organizations. Internal audit functions were the clear beneficiaries of this, and Turnbull provided an opportunity for internal auditors to align their work to real business issues and to make an impact at board level. There was a clear opportunity for internal auditors to enhance their (in many cases) erstwhile humble status and to expand their jurisdiction as a professional interest group.

THE INTERNAL AUDIT RISK ROLE—WHAT SHOULD IT BE?

While it is now probably fairly uncontroversial to argue that internal auditors certainly have a role to play in relation to risk management, the parameters of the role are far less easily defined. Are internal auditors executive managers specializing in risk management, or, alternatively, are they concerned primarily with the monitoring of organizational risk management systems? There has certainly been a tendency, post-Turnbull, for internal audit functions to gravitate toward the former role. The intention of Turnbull, however, was primarily that the internal audit role should largely be focused on the *evaluation* of risk management and the monitoring of internal control effectiveness. While the post-Turnbull era has seen some companies assign ownership of risk management to internal audit, there is recognition of the pitfalls involved in this. With most internal auditors still receiving what is primarily a financial training, there may be a danger of non-financial risks receiving inadequate consideration.

There is also a real danger of internal audit departments losing their independent status within organizations if they evolve into risk management functions. There is evidence that when risk management initially became a priority for organizations, many internal audit heads were assigned responsibility for risk management audit. This, however, has not always been the case as distinct functions for internal audit and risk management have been established in some organizations.

In brief, the internal audit role might be summarized as: "The provision of objective assurance to corporate boards and senior management on risk management effectiveness; specifically, to ensure that key risks are managed appropriately and that internal control systems are operating effectively."

This is a general definition, though, and might be interpreted in various ways as far as the fine detail of responsibilities is concerned.

PROFESSIONAL GUIDANCE AND POTENTIAL DIFFICULTIES

The available professional guidance goes into more detail by emphasizing the distinction between the risk *management* and *monitoring* roles. The Institute of Internal Auditors (IIA), for example, suggests (in its

"I am far more interested in avoiding risk than I am in capturing every opportunity. My philosophy says that loss of opportunity is preferable to loss of capital." Joseph DiNapoli

position statement *The Role of Internal Audit in Enterprise-Risk Management,* available on the IIA website) that internal auditors should be responsible for:

- "Providing assurance on the design and effectiveness of risk management processes, providing assurance that risks are correctly evaluated, evaluating risk management processes, evaluating the reporting on the status of key risks and controls, and reviewing the management of key risks, including the effectiveness of the controls and other responses to them."

But not for:

- "Setting the risk appetite, (the willingness of an organization to accept a defined level of risk), imposing risk management processes, providing assurance to the board and management, making decisions on risk responses, implementing risk responses on management's behalf, accountability for risk management."

The IIA suggests that internal functions may be responsible for the following functions as long as safeguards are put in place to protect internal independence:

- "Championing the establishment of Enterprise Risk Management (ERM) within organizations, developing risk management strategy for board approval, facilitating the identification and evaluation of risks, coaching management on responding to risks, coordinating ERM activities, consolidating the reporting on risks, maintaining and developing ERM frameworks."

It's when we come to this last category, however, that delineation of responsibilities may be unclear. This may be especially the case with the distinction between monitoring and advice by internal auditors on the one hand, and the exercise of a management role on the other. There has arguably been a tendency for some internal auditors to assume more executive-type roles in the ERM area as a way of enhancing their professional jurisdiction. The Institute of Chartered Accountants in England and Wales (ICAEW) takes a broadly similar line to the IIA by emphasizing the internal audit role in assessing the various processes by which risks are *identified,managed, controlled,* and *reported.*

Overall there is certainly not one "easy-fit" solution. Various legitimate approaches to delineating responsibilities might be taken. For example, internal audit would normally be responsible for such functions as the evaluation and monitoring of risk management processes and controls. It would never normally be regarded as appropriate for internal audit to assume ownership of organizational risks or to set the risk appetite.

CONCLUSION

Effective risk management is a necessity for all organizations and is an important component of good corporate governance. Internal audit needs to be involved in the process—at a minimum it has an important role to play in the monitoring of risk management systems. In many cases there may be sound arguments for extending this to functions such as developing reporting frameworks for risk management and facilitating the identification of risks. The size of the organization, independence safeguards, and the range of internal audit expertise are all important issues requiring consideration when determining the boundaries of external audit responsibilities.

CASE STUDY

Tonko—Shaping the Internal Audit Role through Experience

- Tonko is a large conglomerate group, with around 50,000 employees. It operates in several international geographies over several industrial sectors. Tonko is based in the United Kingdom and has had a strong internal audit function operating from the home country for around 25 years.
- The corporate governance and risk agendas of the 1990s saw the profile of risk management being enhanced significantly within the group, with responsibility for the area being given initially to the group internal audit function. This appeared to be the natural home for risk management because of the prominence given to internal audit by Turnbull and by other authoritative corporate governance pronouncements. This worked well.
- Internal audit established business risk management systems and reporting mechanisms that flowed up from business units to divisions and ultimately fed into the group risk strategy. Internal audit carried out the usual monitoring role on these, making sure, first, that risks (and changes in these) were being reported on, and, second, that action was taken as appropriate.
- Internal audit also ran risk workshops at various levels to facilitate the identification of risks. Line management subsequently took action to control and mitigate the risks identified.
- Internal audit was involved in a two-way facilitation process. It was first ensured that business unit and divisional risk concepts and appetites were aligned with those of the group. At the same time internal audit made sure that lower-level concerns fed into the overall group risk evaluations and group risk register where appropriate.
- While this system worked quite well and could have continued indefinitely, some confusion was expressed about the internal audit role. It was unclear whether the internal auditors were acting as facilitators/risk identifiers or as monitors/assessors. There was also some loss of focus on basic controls in the work of internal audit.
- As a result a separate group of risk specialists was established with the remit of working with group business units and divisions in identifying risks and to prioritize these. Internal audit retained responsibility for the review and monitoring of risk management systems and for making sure that there was alignment of concepts and priorities at all group levels.
- It is not suggested that the Tonko experience is a template that should be followed by all organizations. Smaller entities, in particular, sometimes find that the combined approach works best. The size, and available skill set, of the internal audit function will be important determinants of the process.

►► MAKING IT HAPPEN

- Whatever the responsibilities of the internal audit (or, if it exists, risk management) function, the board has to get involved by setting the "risk appetite" of the organization and by assigning broad functional responsibilities.
- It's important that in a large or diversified organization individual divisions and business units feel involved in the process.
- It will generally be appropriate for internal audit, at a minimum, to be responsible for evaluating and monitoring risk management processes and for providing assurance on the adequacy of risk evaluation and reporting.
- *If* the independence and objectivity of internal audit are protected, and *if* the internal audit function has access to the appropriate range of expertise, *then:*
- The internal audit role might be extended to the facilitation of risk identification and the development of risk reporting frameworks.

  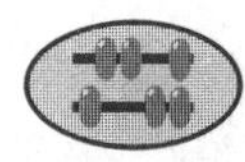 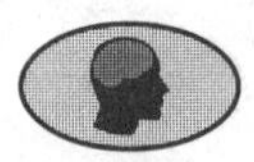  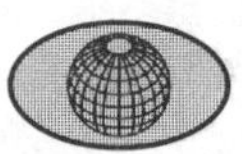   

▸▸ MORE INFO

Books:

Fraser, Ian A. M., and W. M. Henry. *The Future of Corporate Governance: Insights from the UK*. Edinburgh, UK: Institute of Chartered Accountants of Scotland, 2003.

IFAC. *Enterprise Governance: Getting the Balance Right*. New York: Professional Accountants in Business (PAIB) Committee, International Federation of Accountants, 2004.

Pickett, K. H. Spencer. *Auditing the Risk Management Process*. Hoboken, NJ: Wiley, 2005.

Pickett, K. H. Spencer. *Audit Planning: A Risk-Based Approach*. Hoboken, NJ: Wiley, 2006.

Websites:

The Committee of Sponsoring Organizations of the Treadway Commission provides guidance on organizational governance, business ethics, internal control, enterprise risk management, fraud, and financial reporting: www.coso.org

Personal website by David M. Griffiths introducing risk-based internal auditing: www.internalaudit.biz

The Institute of Internal Auditors, for internal auditing standards and other professional pronouncements: www.theiia.org

See Also:

★ The Assurance versus Consulting Debate: How Far Should Internal Audit Go? (pp. 608–609)
★ Best Practices in Risk-Based Internal Auditing (pp. 611–613)
Peter Bernstein (p. 1154)
Mastering Risk Volume 1: Concepts (p. 1297)

"Experienced traders control risks, inexperienced traders chase gains." Alan S. Farley

  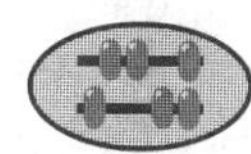   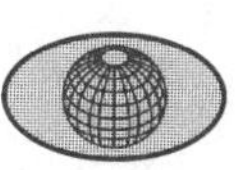   

The LIFO Conundrum: Convergence of US GAAP with IFRS and Its Implications on US Company Competitiveness by William C. White IV

EXECUTIVE SUMMARY

- The long-term goal of the SEC and the International Accounting Standards Board (IASB) is to establish one set of financial reporting standards for all publicly owned companies to follow.
- IFRS does not permit the use of LIFO as an inventory valuation method.
- The switch to a permitted inventory valuation method under IFRS for US businesses employing LIFO could result in the acceleration of payments for deferred tax liabilities affiliated with the companies' LIFO reserve.
- In many cases, the tax obligations generated by the adoption of IFRS could result in significant, unplanned cash outflows putting US businesses at a distinct competitive disadvantage, relative to their peer companies, and lowering their market valuations.
- The change from LIFO to FIFO or weighted average cost, both accepted IFRS methods of inventory valuation, typically results in higher-ending inventory balances, lower cost of goods sold, and higher earnings per share (EPS) in a rising cost environment.
- Some of the possible solutions the US Treasury Department should explore are eliminating the current LIFO conformity rule, and enabling companies adopting IFRS to extend the period over which the tax liabilities generated by the switch from LIFO to FIFO can be settled.
- IFRS adoption would be required for companies whose equity is traded on public markets; however, smaller companies may simply keep LIFO and never adopt these standards.
- Adoption of IFRS would mean that financial statement users would need to adapt to the new method of inventory valuation, and its impact on earnings, cashflow, assets, and equity.

INTRODUCTION

Since August 2008, when former Securities Exchange Commission (SEC) chairman, Christopher Cox, presented a timeline for public companies to transition away from US GAAP (generally accepted accounting principles) to (IFRS) international financial reporting standards, many executives and policy-makers have been concerned about the implications of the differences between the two standards of reporting. The goal of the SEC and the International Accounting Standards Board (IASB) is ultimately to put both US and other international public companies on a consistent, comparable financial reporting basis. This, in turn, would enable analysts, shareholders, and company management to evaluate financial performance among industry competitors, no matter where they are domiciled around the globe.

However, as Mary Smyth, Controller for United Technologies Corp., warned in *CFO Magazine* recently, "The transition from US GAAP to IFRS is not an accounting-standard adoption exercise, but rather a global project, impacting every facet of a company's operations." One of those facets is the method of inventory valuation used by US companies. Under US GAAP, US companies are allowed to use an inventory valuation method referred to as LIFO (last in, first out). Under IFRS, LIFO is not permitted as a basis for valuing inventory for financial reporting purposes. This has many implications for US businesses that currently employ LIFO, one of the most significant of which is the potential acceleration of deferred tax liabilities that have accumulated on their balance sheets over many years of operations.

LIFO DEFINED

LIFO implies that as inventories turn over, companies using this method to account for their inventory transactions will use their most recent purchases of inventory to sell first. This enables companies to deduct the most recent costs associated with their inventory from their sales proceeds. Consequently, companies using LIFO better match current revenues with current costs. This concept rarely reflects that actual flow of inventory. Most companies prefer to sell their oldest purchases of inventory first—called FIFO (first in, first out). LIFO has been permitted for US companies since the early 1970s. During this period of high inflation in the United States, many companies adopted LIFO to lower their taxable earnings, and thereby, lower their then-current tax payments. Under current IRS tax regulations, a company that uses LIFO for tax reporting must also use it for financial reporting purposes. This is referred to as the LIFO conformity rule.

The computation of cost of goods sold (COGS) is:

COGS =
Beginning Inventory + Purchases – Ending Inventory

When valuing their ending inventory using LIFO, most companies start with the inventory valued on a FIFO basis, then use a method called dollar-value LIFO to revalue their inventory to LIFO. This approach uses a cost index, similar to the US Consumer Price Index, to value pools of like inventory items, versus revaluing individual inventory items, at current costs. In times of rising costs, this restatement typically drives up COGS, and, therefore, lowers the cost of ending inventory. On the balance sheet, inventory is typically stated on a FIFO basis with an offsetting contra-asset account, called a LIFO reserve, that nets inventory to a LIFO value.

THE CONUNDRUM

All companies compete for capital in the world equity markets. To survive and grow, companies have to have access to the cheapest money available. By migrating to IFRS, many executives believe they will be better able to attract foreign investment for growth. For companies using LIFO, however, the road to adoption of IFRS is fraught with potential cash penalties.

A recent study performed at the Georgia Tech Financial Analysis Lab examined the tax effect, among other impacts, of changing from the LIFO valuation of inventory to FIFO. It revealed that 36% of US companies use LIFO in valuing all or a portion of their inventories. Further, the study reviewed a sample of 30 companies with the largest percentage of LIFO reserves to total assets, and found that their pretax income would be higher on average by 10% and 12% in 2006 and 2007, respectively, if they used FIFO in valuing their inventories. More importantly, the study revealed that these same companies would have more than US$15 billion of cumulative federal income taxes due if

"There are risks and costs to a program of action. But they are far less than the long-range risks and costs of comfortable inaction." John F. Kennedy

  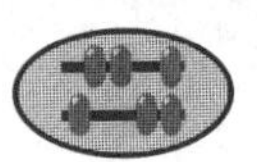 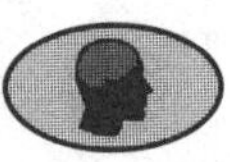  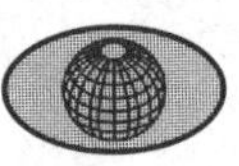   

they switched from LIFO to FIFO. Under current IRS regulations, most of these companies would be allowed to spread their tax payments over four years. This seems fair and equitable at first glance, until one realizes the gravity of these tax payments. For example, Exxon Mobil Corporation had a LIFO reserve balance of US$25.4 billion at the end of its fiscal year 2007. At a 35% effective tax rate, the company would be forced to pay the IRS approximately US$2.2 billion a year for four years (approximately US$8.9 billion in total, or 4% of its total assets).

The switch from LIFO to FIFO, or to moving average cost, another permissible inventory valuation method under IFRS, has other counterintuitive effects. The change typically results in higher-ending inventory, lower COGS, and higher earnings per share (EPS) in a rising cost environment. One would infer that higher EPS would mean higher valuations for the companies making these changes. However, the underlying impact of higher cash payments for taxes owed has the opposite effect—lower valuations for companies making the switch, i.e. cash paid for tax liabilities means less cash for working capital, advertising and promotion, or oil exploration, in the case of Exxon Mobil Corporation. These impacts on firm value and competitiveness mean companies that employ LIFO are reluctant to adopt IFRS.

While many LIFO-based company executives, shareholders, and lenders are against adoption of IFRS due to its impact of increasing taxable income, and, consequently, the associated tax payments, many policy-makers challenge the validity of LIFO. They believe that LIFO has been used for years by companies to defer income and tax payments, and doesn't truly reflect the flow of inventory through an enterprise. Eliminating LIFO through convergence with IFRS provides lawmakers with a way to clean up the current tax laws, and provides a source of sorely needed tax revenues.

POTENTIAL SOLUTIONS

There are many potential solutions that could provide companies with more of an incentive to adopt IFRS. If the US Treasury Department were to eliminate the conformity rule, this would allow companies to continue using LIFO for tax-reporting purposes, and use FIFO or weighted average cost for IFRS. Another possibility would be to enable companies adopting IFRS to extend the period over which the tax liabilities generated by the switch from LIFO to FIFO could be settled. For example, instead of spreading the tax payments over four years, they could be spread over 10 years. Another suggested approach is the possible use of net operating loss carrybacks and carryforwards to offset the tax liabilities. All of these would require compromises on behalf of company executives, shareholders, boards of directors, and policy-makers.

As IFRS adoption is most critical for companies whose equity is traded in the public markets, smaller companies may simply keep LIFO and never adopt these standards. If no compromises are reached, larger companies may gradually and voluntarily have to lower their ending inventories over the adoption period, to minimize the impact of the tax liabilities represented by their LIFO reserve. By lowering inventory levels, the historical costs imbedded in the inventory valuation are finally realized. This is called LIFO liquidation, meaning the LIFO reserve is taken back into income, due to the physical reduction in ending inventory relative to prior periods. This can sometimes be impossible to achieve, given the necessary safety stock that is required to meet product demand.

CONCLUSION

There are many advantages to adopting IFRS for public companies. Convergence of US GAAP and IFRS has evolved over the past three years, as the result of collaboration between the IASB and the US Financial Accounting Standards Board (FASB). Recent FASB standards have harmonized the treatment of many accounting transactions, including the treatment of goodwill and intangibles on the balance sheet. However, the adoption of IFRS by LIFO-based companies represents a huge test for all stakeholders. The current SEC chairperson, Mary Shapiro, has indicated that she will not be held to the timetable outlined by her predecessor, and has challenged the quality of the rules underlying IFRS.

Adoption would mean that financial statement users—analysts, shareholders, lenders, and others—would also need to adapt to the new method of inventory valuation, and its impact on earnings, cashflow, assets, and equity. The change would result in the recalibration of performance ratios typically used by rating agencies, debtholders, banks, and analysts to determine liquidity, financial stability, and profitability of the adopting firm. Additionally, compensation committees of the boards of directors would need to realign their incentive compensation structure and expectations to reward executives for performance, and not for the accounting impact of the inventory valuation change.

▸▸ MAKING IT HAPPEN

- Stay abreast of the developments and SEC timeline for IFRS adoption by consulting your public accountant, and the sources outlined below.
- Consult and advise your national lawmakers on your position on IFRS adoption.
- Analyze the financial impact a potential switch away from LIFO would have on current earnings and tax obligations.

▸▸ MORE INFO

Articles:

Bloom, Robert, and William J. Cenker. "The death of LIFO? Changing inventory method requires managing the accounting-tax differences." *Journal of Accountancy* (January 2009).

Johnson, Sarah. "SEC pushes back IFRS roadmap." *CFO.com* (February 4, 2009). Online at: www.cfo.com/article.cfm/13056185

Mulford, Charles W., and Eugene E. Comiskey. "The potential consequences of the elimination of LIFO as part of IFRS convergence." report, Georgia Institute of Technology, December 2008. Online at: www.smartech.gatech.edu/handle/1853/26316.

Websites:

IFRS: www.ifrs.com

Report on the consequences of the elimination of LIFO: www.mgt.gatech.edu/fac_research/centers_initiatives/finlab/finlab_reports_2008.html

FIFO and LIFO explained: en.wikipedia.org/wiki/FIFO_and_LIFO_accounting

See Also:

Financial Accounting and Reporting (p. 1256)

"The reasonable man adapts himself to the world; the unreasonable one persists in trying to adapt the world to himself. Therefore all progress depends on the unreasonable man." George Bernard Shaw

  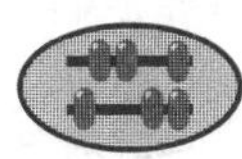   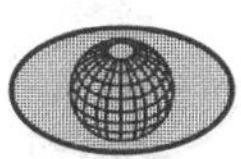   

Managing the Relationships between Audit Committees and the CAE by Richard E. Cascarino

EXECUTIVE SUMMARY

- Audit committees are a fundamental part of the proper governance of any organization, together with executive management and internal as well as external audit.
- An audit committee can only be as effective as is permitted by the information it receives.
- The relationship between the committee and the chief audit executive (CAE) is critical to the successful functioning of the audit committee.
- The relationship will be effective in an environment of mutual trust and common understanding.
- Of all the committees involved in the management and control of an organization, perhaps the audit committee has the most significant impact on the life of the CAE.
- Although, in general, all audit committees fulfill a similar function within the organization, the nature of the organization itself can prescribe a particular emphasis in the working of the audit committee. This, in turn, affects the nature of the relationship between the CAE and the committee as a whole.

THE ROLE OF THE AUDIT COMMITTEE

The audit committee is intended, overall, to assist an organization to achieve an effective internal control structure derived directly from the tone at the top. The authority of an audit committee is drawn from the board of directors, the rules and regulations of the organization, and any relevant governance legislation of the country or countries within which the organization operates.

This role, of necessity, involves ensuring that the risk management process remains both comprehensive and ongoing instead of the annual process that is implemented in many organizations. Corporate policies regarding legal compliance, compliance with corporate codes of conduct, and conflicts of interest must be maintained and policed. In addition, the audit committee has a duty to review both current and pending legislation as it relates to corporate governance within the country or countries wherein it operates. Communication is the key to good governance and includes ensuring that the financial statements presented to the shareholders are both understandable and reliable, and facilitating internal communication with senior management and internal audit. Communication with internal audit should go beyond the scheduled committee meetings, and the CAE should be encouraged to communicate with the chair of the audit committee directly. The audit committee, as a whole, should meet privately with the CAE at least annually to seek assurances about the independence of the internal audit function.

To ensure effective use of internal auditing, the audit committee would normally review internal audit plans as well as reports and significant findings. It would seek to ensure that internal auditing is carried out by professionals with a comprehensive understanding of the business systems and processes as well as of the corporate culture within the organization.

The audit committee relies on the internal audit function to provide objective opinions, information, and, when necessary, education to the audit committee, while the audit committee in turn will provide oversight and validation to the internal audit function. In today's environment this could include the outsourcing or co-sourcing of all or part of the internal audit function; however, the audit committee should ensure that the role of the CAE remains within the organization itself.

INTERNAL AUDIT REPORTING STRUCTURE

In order to ensure transparency and to prevent undue influence internally, the Institute of Internal Auditors (IIA) recommends that the CAE maintain a dual reporting relationship. Typically, this would involve the CAE reporting to executive management at as high a level as possible for administrative purposes to ensure alignment with corporate direction, support at a managerial level, and the normal administrative support required for a staff function. The second relationship, with the audit committee, is for operational and functional purposes, to ensure that independence and objectivity is maintained. The audit function's independence and reporting structure are normally laid out in the internal audit charter, which specifies the dual reporting structure as well as the internal auditors' right of access to personnel and records without hindrance or impediment, a critical part of their independence. The charter would normally be signed by both the chief executive and the chair of the audit committee.

The audit committee should provide oversight, strategic direction, accountability, and enforcement where required. Part of such oversight includes ensuring that the internal audit function is properly positioned, resourced, and supported. This involves reviewing and approving:

- the internal audit activity's charter, and mission statement where appropriate, to ensure they meet the needs of the organization;
- the annual work plan to ensure that all significant risk areas are being addressed and that no restrictions are placed on the scope of internal audit activities;
- the resources, skill levels, and budget to ensure that the work plan is achievable within the appropriate time;
- internal audit activities, performance, and recommendations.

At the same time, the audit committee is responsible for providing input into the appointment, dismissal, evaluation, compensation, and succession planning of the CAE. This is a critical activity of the audit committee since the CAE will, of neccessity, have a high degree of interaction with the audit committee. The committee will typically seek to ensure that candidates for a CAE position have distinguished themselves professionally. They would normally have an advanced degree, the appropriate professional designation, and several years experience in an audit supervisory role. Typical professional designations could include the Certified Internal Auditor (CIA), Certified Government Auditing Professional (CGAP), Certified Financial Services Auditor (CFSA), or Certified Information Systems Auditor (CISA) among others.

The committee is also responsible for ensuring that a continuous quality assurance and improvement program exists within internal audit and that full disclosure of the results be made to the audit committee.

"Audit committee duty entails significant time and effort and requires accountability when things go wrong."
Curtis C. Verschoor

    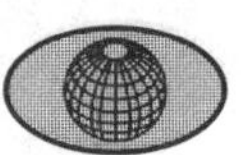   

THE RELATIONSHIP WITH INTERNAL AUDIT

The audit committee chair can foster a healthy relationship with the internal auditors, and particularly the chief internal auditor, by keeping communication channels open, getting to know the CAE as a person, frequently touching base between meetings, and taking an interest in and caring about the internal audit function. It is also a good idea for the audit committee chair to meet with the entire senior internal audit staff from time to time to get to know some of the individuals who report to the CAE, and to thank them for their efforts.

It is critical that the internal audit function be positioned well within the organization so that the internal auditors are not limited in what they can review, and that they, and the recommendations they propose, are respected by line management. It should always be remembered that the accountability for, and ownership of, good internal controls are the responsibility of management—not of the internal auditors and not of the audit committee. The internal auditors, nonetheless, must recognize that theirs is a unique yet critical role.

The CAE needs to be up to date on best practices and trends in governance, as well as on "emerging issues," and the audit committee will seek reassurance in this area. The audit committee also needs assurance that the internal auditors understand the corporate strategy and have the professional judgment to identify all forms of risk at an early enough opportunity to allow management to take appropriate action. In order for the audit committee to be appropriately assured in these areas, performance assessment of both the CAE and internal audit will be required.

MUTUAL TRUST

Most critical to the relationship between the audit committee and the internal audit activity is trust. The audit committee chair needs to be sure that the CAE understands and shares the committee's concerns and priorities. In addition, the CAE must be willing to communicate results and opinions without fear or favor and regardless of who is involved. Due to its unique position and the sensitivity of information passing through its hands, the audit committee needs assurance that the internal audit activity maintains the highest level of integrity and values.

The committee needs to be able to trust that, when confronted with management resistance or a failure of management integrity, the CAE will make the right decision and take appropriate action. By the same token, the CAE must be able to rely on the support and backing of the chair of the audit committee, and the committee as a whole. This ensures that the "internal audit activity [is] free from interference in determining the scope of internal auditing, performing work, and communicating results" (IIA Standards).

Two Cases in Point

In one government department, accusations of corruption were made against the chief executive. The CAE who reported to the chief executive took the accusations directly to the audit committee chair. Although the responsible Minister was notified, it was the audit committee, acting independently, that commissioned an external forensic investigation into the allegations. The external route was chosen so that, regardless of the outcome, the CAE would be able to continue to function effectively within the department. In the event, the allegations proved unjustified, but it was the trust between the CAE and the audit committee chair which made it possible for such allegations to be brought forward without fear of reprisal. In a contrasting case involving a pension fund, allegations of abuse of power by the chief executive were brought to the attention of the CAE. These were taken to the chair of the audit committee, who immediately called the chief executive to discuss them privately. There was no follow-up. The trust between the audit committee and the CAE was destroyed, ultimately resulting in the resignation of the CAE.

ASSESSING PERFORMANCE AND PLANNING AHEAD

The *International Standards for the Professional Practice of Internal Auditing*[1] promulgated by the Institute of Internal Auditors requires that an external assessment, performed by appropriately qualified reviewers and carried out to professional standards, be conducted every five years. This is designed to give the audit committee assurance that the work of the internal audit function is being conducted to internationally accepted standards.

In addition, the CAE is required to ensure quality on an ongoing basis. The CAE may utilize benchmarking to develop an internal auditor balanced scorecard for the audit committee to use for assessing the performance of the internal audit function. An objective evaluation would, nevertheless, include such areas as audit scope and coverage (including financial, compliance, operational, IT, and fraud auditing), audit capabilities, independence, objectivity, supervision, and internal audit assignment quality control. In addition to ensuring the quality of the work of the internal audit function, the audit committee chair will also seek assurance on the performance of the audit committee itself. The CAE can assist in benchmarking the committee's performance in terms of committee structure and composition, the role of audit committee members, and leadership of the committee against standards such as The Board Institute's Audit Committee Index[2] on behalf of the chair of the audit committee. The European Corporate Governance Institute (ECGI) has produced an excellent paper on such benchmarking.[3] This presents an opportunity for the audit committee to review and discuss all areas of its performance, as well as to bring to the table items that committee members feel should be covered in the future, and training opportunities that would enhance performance.

It is critical that proactive succession planning for the internal audit function and the CAE be an important area of focus and support by the audit committee. Many organizations use internal audit as a training ground for future executive managers and rotate candidates through the internal auditing function. While this is beneficial to the organization in terms of managers who understand internal control, it can be devastating to the effectiveness of the

▸▸ MAKING IT HAPPEN

In Order to Manage the Relationship the CAE Must:

- Keep the audit committee informed on risks faced by the organization. Monitor the risk environment for new/changed risks which need to be brought to the audit committee's attention.
- Check that the audit committee's charter, activities, and processes are appropriate. Periodically review the audit committee's practices against international standards and "best practices" on behalf of the chair of the audit committee.
- Educate the audit committee on the internal audit team's charter, role, and activities. The CAE should seek to obtain management and audit committee buy-in on internal auditing's goals, objectives, risk assessments, and audit plan by demonstrating their appropriateness and relevance.

"Audit committees are only as good as the information they receive." Committee of University Chairmen

  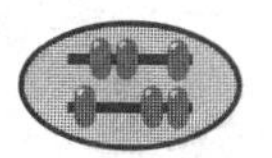   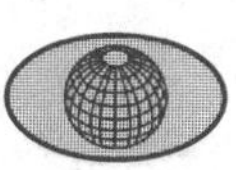   

internal audit function if carried out to excess. One internal audit function lost seven out of eight senior auditors in a six-month period as they were head-hunted by operational areas of the organization. Succession planning is intended to ensure that, while some of the current team may get appropriate and substantive positions in the organization as rotations end, the effectiveness of the internal audit function is not impacted. Professional, career-oriented internal auditors form the backbone of the function and they must see career opportunities with internal audit itself. In addition, succession planning is critical to the organization's ability to attract the right talent into the internal audit activity.

CONCLUSION

The mere existence of the audit committee does not necessarily translate into an effective monitoring body over corporate governance. By the same token, the existence of an internal audit function, in-sourced or out-sourced, does not guarantee the effectiveness of the system of internal controls. It is the combination of the two, both acting in a professional manner for the benefit of the organization as a whole, which contributes significantly to the achievement of sound corporate governance.

Audit Committee Characteristics

- independence
- financial knowledge and experience
- frequency of meetings
- involvement in CAE appointment and dismissal
- reviewing internal audit program and processes
- ensuring internal audit quality

Internal Audit Function Characteristics

- independence and objectivity
- availability of adequate resources
- internal audit staff expertise
- use of external subject matter experts where appropriate

- Ensure that the internal audit function is responsive to the needs of the audit committee and the board. Meet frequently with the audit committee chair to ensure that the committee's needs are fully understood and met.
- Ensure open and effective communication with the audit committee and its chair. Effective communication is one of the best tools for understanding organizational priorities and reinforcing the benefits and value of internal auditing.
- Provide training, when appropriate, to audit committee members on the topics of risk and internal control. Not all committee members will initially be up to speed on the changing needs and legislation.
- Confirm the quality of the services provided. Internal auditing should provide quality performance indicators to show that it complies with the IIA's *International Standards for the Professional Practice of Internal Auditing* and the IIA's *Code of Ethics* and that it adds value on an ongoing basis.
- Provide feedback on the internal audit function's achievement of its operational plans and objectives.

▸▸ MORE INFO

Books:

Braiotta, Louis, Jr. *The Audit Committee Handbook*. 4th ed. New York: Wiley, 2004.

Burke, Frank M., and Dan M. Guy. *Audit Committees: A Guide for Directors, Management, and Consultants*. 2nd ed. New York: Aspen Law & Business, 2002.

Cascarino, Richard E., and Sandy van Esch. *Internal Auditing: An Integrated Approach*. 2nd ed. Lansdowne, South Africa: Juta Academic Publishers, 2006.

Moeller, Robert. *Brink's Modern Internal Auditing*. 6th ed. Hoboken, NJ: Wiley, 2005.

Ruppel, Warren. *Not-for-Profit Audit Committee Best Practices*. Hoboken, NJ: Wiley, 2005.

Articles:

Collier, P. A. "Audit committees in major UK companies." Managerial Auditing Journal 8:3 (1993): 25–30.

Goodwin, J. "The relationship between the audit committee and the internal audit function: Evidence from Australia and New Zealand." International Journal of Auditing 7:3 (2003): 263–278.

Reports:

Australian National Audit Office. "Public sector audit committees." Canberra, Australia: Australian National Audit Office, 2005.

Blue Ribbon Committee on Improving the Effectiveness of Corporate Audit Committees. "Report and recommendations of the blue ribbon committee on improving the effectiveness of corporate audit committees." New York: New York Stock Exchange and National Association of Securities Dealers, 1999.

European Corporate Governance Institute (ECGI). "Institutional position paper: a benchmark for audit committees." November 2002. Online at: www.ecgi.org/codes/documents/auditcom_final_paper.pdf

Institute of Internal Auditors. Practice Advisery 1110-2: "Chief audit executive (CAE) reporting lines." Altamonte Springs, FL: IIA, December 2002.

Institute of Internal Auditors. Practice Advisery 2060-2: "Relationship with the audit committee." Altamonte Springs, FL: IIA, December 2002.

Institute of Internal Auditors. "A Global Summary of the Common Body of Knowledge 2006." Online at (free to IIA members): www.theiia.org/research/common-body-of-knowledge/download/

Websites:

Audit Committee Effectiveness Centre: www.aicpa.org/audcommctr/homepage.htm

Securities and Exchange Commission: www.sec.gov

NOTES

1 Available from the Institute of Internal Auditors: www.theiiahttp.org

2 See: www.theboardinstitute.com/web/products.asp?f=prod_acix

3 PDF download: www.ecgi.org/codes/documents/auditcom_final_paper.pdf

"Don't let the complexity of a large company mask the need for performance. Bureaucracy is a conspiracy to bring down the big. And it can. You may need to be large to compete in the world stage, but you need to find ways to avoid allowing that size to mask poor performance." Donald Rumsfeld

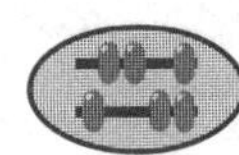
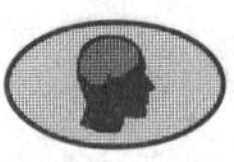

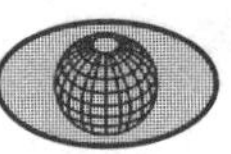

The Missing Metrics: Managing the Cost of Complexity by John L. Mariotti

EXECUTIVE SUMMARY

- Despite the best efforts in many areas, the accounting and finance systems currently in use overlook the costs of complexity.
- The costs are hidden in the operating statements of a company until the period-end results show the adverse effects.
- It is time to recognize that these costs exist, identify them, and develop new metrics in the place of those that are missing.

INTRODUCTION

Accounting systems have come a long way in the past decades. Activity-based costing revealed where costs were being incurred and what was driving them. The blizzard of regulations following the debacles involving Enron, WorldCom, and others led to the passage of the Sarbanes–Oxley Act (in the United States) and many other new regulations. Although these are burdensome, they impose much-needed disciplines on finance and accounting.

In spite of this, one area remains unmeasured, untracked, and unmanaged: costs caused by complexity. I began studying this area in earnest shortly after the dot-com collapse. When an area comes under intense scrutiny, some details are discovered that have thus far gone unnoticed. This is the case with the costs of complexity.

As far back as 2001, Oracle CEO Larry Ellison described a "War on Complexity" in computer software. There were simply too many systems that were not integrated, and others that were very difficult to integrate. This fragmentation of systems caused huge complexity, duplication of effort, and waste (which Ellison's Oracle Corporation hoped to solve).

VARIETY CAN ADD VALUE—IF MANAGED PROPERLY

On the other hand, there are instances when complexity—properly managed—can be a source of great competitive advantage. Structure, systems, and processes must be carefully designed to minimize transaction cost and complexity. One example of the productive use of complexity is the web retailer Amazon, whose breadth of offering is extensive, thus making it a "one-stop shopping" site for millions. While Amazon's distribution system is always at risk of being overburdened by complexity, its front end handles the huge variety of goods seamlessly.

Similarly, US sandwich seller Subway assembles sandwiches to order from about thirty containers of meat, cheese, and vegetables, using just a half-dozen varieties of bread. It can make millions of sandwich (and salad) combinations, to customer preferences, with minimal waste. There are many other examples like these two. All depend on the right systemic design to keep complexity from growing out of control, causing waste and inefficiency.

COMPLEXITY COSTS ARE HIDDEN

When I first began to research why complexity costs remained unmeasured in nearly all companies, I discovered that it was because these costs are, by their nature, hidden in accounting systems. To bring this problem into perspective, let's consider how complexity occurs and what kinds of waste it causes. It will become apparent why financial systems simply "overlook" complexity's costs until the end-of-period reporting shows the detrimental effects.

There is no doubt that complexity's effects are readily apparent in month-end, quarter-end, and year-end results, where they adversely affect both the income statement and the balance sheet. Unfortunately, the only place where they are visible is on the bottom line, or on a few lines of the balance sheet. Even then, there's no indication of how these costs were incurred, or what might have been done to manage them.

SEEKING HIGH GROWTH IN LOW GROWTH MARKETS

Much of complexity that goes unmeasured and unmanaged is created with the best of intentions, in search of revenue growth. Many wealthy developed countries (the United States, most of Europe, Japan, etc.) are growing very slowly, both in population and in their economies. When companies seek growth in these mature markets, they usually resort to proliferation, which leads to complexity. The gain in revenue is redistributed across a broader range of products and services, with only modest increases in total. The many resulting new products, customers, markets, and suppliers add much more in complexity costs than in profit.

Mergers and acquisitions are another source of complexity. If either of the two combined companies is already burdened with complexity, this will transfer to the merger. If both are thus burdened, real trouble is likely. Simply combining the "DNA" of two companies is a daunting task, as illustrated by the troubled combination of Alcatel (France) and Lucent (United States). There are issues of product and customer overlap, duplications of organization and facility, systems redundancies, and large cultural conflicts that must be sorted out. This is perhaps one of the main reasons why mergers seldom lead to long-term growth in shareholder value.

Less developed countries are typically growing at much higher rates (China, India, Brazil, etc.). Emerging consumer societies and favorable balances of trade fuel their economic growth. There's a different complexity problem here: most of these countries save more and spend less—both as consumers and as governments. Further, these countries are less familiar to sellers who operate in developed countries, and therefore marketing and operating mistakes are made. These mistakes also lead to proliferation, often due to errors in targeting or serving the desired markets and customers.

PROFITS ARE PROPORTIONAL TO REVENUES; COSTS ARE PROPORTIONAL TO TRANSACTIONS

Thus, either approach to growth adds to complexity, but for different reasons. Profits are derived from increased revenues, but costs are incurred from increased transactions. Therein lies the root of the problem. A few simple reports can expose the problem. First, calculate sales per customer, per product, per location, etc., and track the trends. They are typically declining, indicating more transactions for less revenue. Next, sort the annual sales, profits, etc., for customers and products, in descending order of value, and compute a cumulative column. Now look at the bottom of the list. There is always page after page of "losers" with few sales and low or negative profits.

Few accounting systems calculate a couple of simple, yet important, measures. What is the cost to process a customer

"Everything should be made as simple as possible, but not simpler." Albert Einstein

  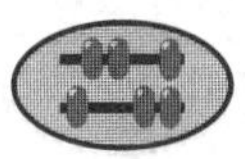   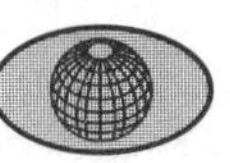   

order from "end to end"—from receipt of the order until the payment is in the bank? Few, if any, companies know the answer to this question. One US study, performed by Sterling Commerce, calculated it at about $50. Consider the following quick calculation to show how complexity adds cost and waste.

Average companies make about 5% net profit (after tax) on sales revenue. That means they must get $20 of sales to make $1 of net profit. If processing an order costs $50, they must get a $1,000 order to earn the equivalent of what it costs to process the order. If that type of customer orders every week, $50,000 worth of annual sales is barely generating net profit that equals the cost of processing the orders.

This dramatically illustrates how customer orders that are small and frequent can add complexity cost, and yet this cost can remain undetected as a drain on profit. A similar comparison could be made for the cost to process purchase orders, or the expense to set up and maintain documentation for a product or service. Nowhere are these costs gathered—or managed. Most companies have a few departments that perform these functions. Therefore, totaling those departmental expenses and dividing that sum by the total number of orders processed will yield an approximation of how much each order costs to process. Yet, few or no companies do this calculation or consider its impact.

Complexity costs are also insidious because most of them are hidden in "catch-all" accounts such as variances, allowances and deductions, and so forth. Extra effort is needed to reveal the origin of such entries (more on that later). First, let's consider a simple example of how easily complexity can occur and grow.

A SIMPLE EXAMPLE: ONE WHITE COFFEE MUG

Imagine a product: a coffee mug offered in one style, color, size, and type of packaging. It is sourced from one supplier, packaged and stocked in one location, and offered for sale to one customer. You can easily compute the "standard cost" of this mug in terms of material, labor, and overhead (an older way), or in terms of material plus cost of acquisition, plus fixed and variable conversion costs (a newer way). If the mug's total landed cost is $1 and it sells for $2, this yields a 50% gross profit margin.

Because the mug is successful, the company has decided to expand the line to four styles, four colors, two sizes, and two package options. There are now sixty-four different mug variations, which lead to increased complexity in forecasting, buying, controlling, and managing raw materials, inventory, etc. The "standard cost," however, is still computed in the same way as before, which yields apparently accurate results: cost = $1 (assuming a good job of purchase negotiation), price = $2, and gross profit margin = 50%. *But something is wrong*. Intuitively, you know that there are complexity costs that the old metrics don't capture—at least, not assigned to the product line. The true profitability is not the same as before.

Expand the product line again: Purchase from two suppliers, package and stock in three locations, and sell into (just) three different countries. Assuming there are no differences in purchase cost or productivity, the standard cost, price, and gross profit margin remain the same. But now, the combinations and permutations have grown to over a thousand, and the company must take into account different marketing materials, purchasing errors (due to forecast errors and demand volatility), and more. Now the profitability is clearly lower.

On top of all this, there are color mixes and assortments of the product that vary according to market, customer, production plant, distribution center, and country. Consequently the warehouse begins to fill up with products in the wrong colors or styles, wrong package sizes, etc. Something must be done with these oddments, so they are repacked (at a cost variance) and sold at discounts (at a price variance), and new replacements are flown in (at huge freight expense variances) to meet customer service needs. More of the profits disappear into those "catch-all" accounts.

As noted earlier, many of the extra costs reside in accounts like deductions, allowances, premium freight costs, or variances. Complexity creates noticeable increases in overhead and administrative expenses; impacts the reserve available for inventory obsolescence; or incurs additional labor to rework, repack, and remark inventory. Few, if any, of these costs impact the standard cost of sales and the standard gross margin. Thus, the product still appears to be nicely profitable, and the complexity costs remain hidden in undifferentiated accounts—or result in "non-recurring charges," which, mysteriously, seem to "recur" from time to time. At the end of accounting periods, the true costs hit with full impact, in many cases wiping out all profit.

A COMPLEXITY CRISIS CALLS FOR METRICS

I call this sequence of events "a complexity crisis." The finance and accounting metrics, intended to help track the results of the company do so—eventually. Unfortunately, the complexity remains unmanaged and the missing metrics do not reveal the problems until after the fact. Complexity strikes like a robber. The money is gone. Clues to the crime are few, and the perpetrators plead innocence. Only a knowledgeable accountant, with help from supply chain or marketing staff can unearth the clues and track the waste back to its root causes.

The solution for this is evident: to devise and implement the "missing metrics." Many of these are easy to create; some are already in use. In other instances they will require whole new initiatives. If new metrics were in place and tracked regularly, such losses would be found much sooner. Then corrective actions could be started sooner as well. Major public accounting companies could help by sanctioning such metrics, to provide some uniformity. Unfortunately, thus far, they have been unresponsive to those needs.

Typical Missing Metrics

- Sales per product stock keeping unit (SKU);
- Sales per product category;
- Sales per customer;
- Sales per location;
- Sales per employee (hourly, including full-time equivalent, salaried, and total);
- Sales per part number (components, materials, work in process, and finished goods (FG)).

- Gross profit per product SKU;
- Gross profit per product category;
- Gross profit per customer;
- Gross profit per location.

- Purchases per vendor;
- Purchases per commodity type;
- Production (output value) per person-hour (or equivalent measure of labor input);
- Total number of SKUs by division or business unit and company total;
- Number of SKUs added and dropped during the last time period (quarterly, semiannually or annually).

- Cost to process a customer order (end to end);
- Cost to process a purchase order (end to end);
- Cost to set up and maintain a product SKU;
- Cost to serve by customer (including freight, handling, and order processing costs).

"I keep six honest serving men. They taught me all I knew. Their names are What and Why and When and How and Where and Who." Rudyard Kipling

  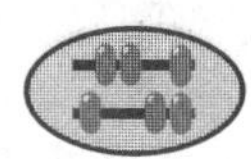   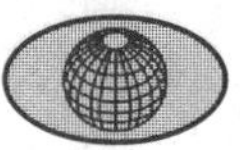   

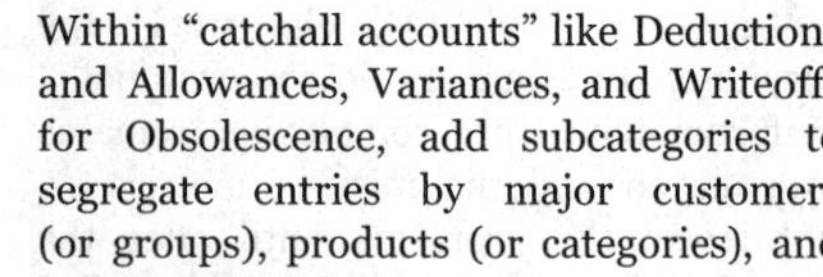

Within "catchall accounts" like Deductions and Allowances, Variances, and Writeoffs for Obsolescence, add subcategories to segregate entries by major customers (or groups), products (or categories), and locations (divisions).

- Expenses per product line or category;
- Expenses per customer, and/or by customer type/category;
- Expenses per location;
- Percentage of sales per product line or category;
- Percentage of sales per customer, and customer type or category.

PLUS A TOTALLY NEW METRIC—THE COMPLEXITY FACTOR (CF)

Obviously, there is a common overall purpose among these metrics. Remember that the objective of new metrics is to reveal where the costs of complexity are hiding and are wasting time and money. Choose among those, or devise your own that measure similar complexity-related outcomes. Finally, an overall Complexity Factor can be calculated by means of the following formula (where "locations" are meaningful facilities and "countries" are places where legal entities exist):

$$\frac{(\text{No. of suppliers} + \text{No. of customers} + \text{No. of employees}) \times (\text{No. of FG SKUs}) \times (\text{No. of markets served}) \times (\text{No. of locations}) \times (\text{No. of countries})}{\text{Total annual sales revenue (in the company currency of choice)}}$$

The resultant number provides a "benchmark," called a Complexity Factor (CF), for the business (or subunit) whose data were used to calculate it. Obviously, a CF can be calculated for each business unit, division, geographical unit, etc. *and* for the entire company. It can also be customized to a company's specific situation to make it more relevant, varying the terms in the ideal context.

While this may seem like a large number of new metrics, the data to compile them should already exist. Different parts of the business should use and manage CFs based on various metrics that are relevant to their activities. Not all parts need use all metrics.

WHAT GETS MEASURED, GETS MANAGED; WHAT DOESN'T, DOESN'T

The mere presence of metrics doesn't mean management will do anything different. On the other hand, the absence of metrics virtually assures that nothing will be done. The old line "What gets measured, gets managed," is true. The opposite, "If you can't—or don't—measure it, you can't—or don't—manage it," is also likely to be true.

Measurement alone doesn't solve any problems. It merely points to the effects of those problems. To manage them requires a series of steps. First, use Pareto's Principle (the 80-20 rule). Sort products and customers in descending order of annual revenues and profits, and carefully analyze the bottom of the list. Most of these are "losers" with a few strategically important "potential winners" scattered about. Getting rid of the losers is imperative.

Upgrading some "losers" into "winners" (top 20%) is possible, but for most, it is impractical. In the middle group careful analysis can help in upgrading potential winners and downgrading imminent losers. There are newly devised, powerful tools and techniques to help in sorting, selection, and optimization of complex instances, but describing these goes beyond the scope of this discussion. (See More Info for Sixth Sense and Emcien.)

THE TIME FOR NEW METRICS IS NOW

Now is the time for accounting and finance organizations around the globe to recognize the huge cost of complexity and how poorly managed it is. It is also time to introduce new metrics that track down, quantify, and help to manage the rampant complexity that plagues so many companies.

The waste of time and money due to "missing metrics" and the failure to track and manage complexity are immense. Correcting these problems is not always easy, but the starting point is as simple as the two basic rules of problem solving: First, identify the problem; second, solve the problem. Once the "missing metrics" have been devised and implemented, it's time to take action and put them into use. The results will be surprising in terms of both speed and magnitude, and that is a very rewarding outcome for all stakeholders.

▸▸ MORE INFO

Books:

George, Michael L., and Stephen A. Wilson. *Conquering Complexity in Your Business*. New York: McGraw-Hill, 2004.

Mariotti, John. *The Complexity Crisis: Why Too Many Products, Markets, and Customers Are Crippling Your Company—And What to Do About It*. Avon, MA: Adams Media, 2008.

Articles:

Gottfredson, Mark, and Keith Aspinall. "Innovation versus complexity: What is too much of a good thing?" *Harvard Business Review* 83:11 (2005): 62–71.

Heywood, Suzanne, Jessica Spungin, and David Turnbull. "Cracking the complexity code." *McKinsey Quarterly* (May 2007): 85–95. Online at: www.euromed-management.com/blog/Articles/McKinsey.pdf

Berlind, David. "Oracle: Misquoted, misunderstood." *ZDnet Tech Update* (September 6, 2001). Online at: techupdate.zdnet.com/techupdate/stories/main/0,14179,2810851,00.html

Reports:

AT Kearney. "Waging war on complexity: How to master the matrix organizational structure." 2003.

Sixth Sense Partners has a private white paper on how to use customer engagement in sorting winners and losers: www.sixthsensepartners.com

George Group and Knowledge@Wharton. "Unraveling complexity in products and services." Special report, 2006. Online at: knowledge.wharton.upenn.edu/special_section.cfm?specialID=45

Website:

Emcien: Optimization tools for complex solutions: www.emcien.com

"In theory there is very little difference between theory and practice; in practice there is a lot of difference."
John Mariotti

  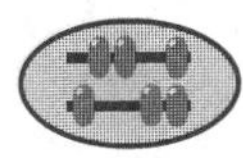   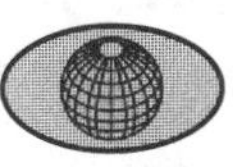   

New Assurance Challenges Facing Chief Audit Executives by Simon D'Arcy

EXECUTIVE SUMMARY

- Internal audit's raison d'être is to provide assurance on the effectiveness of the management and control of significant risks.
- Assurance can only ever be reasonable but not absolute—continuing corporate failure due to inadequate risk management and control challenges the value of such reasonable assurance.
- Chief audit executives can use objective criteria to demonstrate the integrity of their reasonable assurance propositions.
- Objective criteria include completeness, frequency, future orientation, explicitness, objectivity, and subject matter knowledge.
- A key challenge for CAEs is that of a shift of mindset away from just doing audits, to auditing actually providing assurance of demonstrable integrity.

INTRODUCTION

Looking back over the last 15 to 20 years, it does seem that at one time the biggest challenge facing the profession of internal auditing was whether the unique scope and contribution of internal audit was clearly defined, understood, or indeed actually needed. Much of the thought leadership around internal auditing in recent years has focused on this challenge. Two publications by PricewaterhouseCoopers in 2007,[1] and a heads of internal audit summit "The Future of Internal Auditing Starts Here" in May 2008[2] jointly facilitated by the Institute of Internal Auditors and Deloitte, have all concluded that internal audit's primary role is clearly to provide assurance on the effectiveness of risk management. In fact, in many organizations internal audit already clearly does this, as demonstrated in Protiviti's June 2007 publication *Internal Auditing Around the World*.[3] It is clear—and has been since Turnbull (1999),[4] if not before—that boards have a duty to get themselves assured on the effectiveness of their systems of internal control. There is no doubt that chief audit executives see that their raison d'être is to provide such assurance, and many will claim, with some justification, that they have provided and will continue to provide this assurance. Therefore, on the face of it, CAEs have responded to their most fundamental challenge.

THE PROBLEM WITH ASSURANCE

If Turnbull (1999) marks the turning point in corporate governance, it has nevertheless not marked a turning point in the steady stream of corporate failures and disasters, which are often due to ineffective risk management and control. The role of internal audit in these scenarios has been, if not quite exonerated, then at least found not liable, by virtue of one of the basic precepts of internal audit assurance—that it can only ever be reasonable and not absolute.

However, with the market turmoil of 2007 and 2008, the steady stream of failures has become a torrent of biblical proportions—initially, at the time of writing (September 2008), sweeping away the foundations of some major global financial institutions and likely to spread to other sectors as systemic market and recessionary risks crystallize. Accompanying the unfolding disasters is a damning commentary from governments and media on the hopelessly inadequate risk assessment and management capability of those corporates. The spotlight has been on the managers of risk and the attitude of senior executives to the assessment and management of risk. However, it will not be long before the spotlight moves toward the assurers of the effectiveness of risk management, and whether those assurers were in any way culpable. Rightly or wrongly, many will assume that reasonable assurance from internal audit should have identified and reported on the inadequacies of the risk management process, or at least been capable of doing so.

There is now a new challenge facing CAEs—that they are able to demonstrate that their assurance propositions have integrity and can withstand scrutiny against some key criteria. Internal audit assurance involves judgment, and there is an inherent imperfection in a process that relies on judgment. However, there is a difference between an omission or oversight based on accepted fallibility, and one where the scope of assurance was too narrow, where assurance conclusions lacked clarity, or were delivered too infrequently, or where work undertaken lacked sufficient knowledge or objectivity. Assurance delivered on the basis of a flawed proposition is indeed unreasonable assurance.

Therefore, in rising to meet that challenge, CAEs have been aspiring to create assurance propositions that are:

- *Complete*: They cover all significant risks.
- *Frequent*: They provide assurance with sufficient frequency.
- *Explicit*: They give assurance outcomes that are clear and unambiguous.
- *Future-oriented*: They offer assurance that controls will continue to be effective in the future, not just that they have been effective in the past.
- *Objective*: They provide objective assurance based on sound knowledge.

DEMONSTRATING THE INTEGRITY OF ASSURANCE IN A POST-CREDIT-CRUNCH WORLD

Most CAEs I have spoken with on the topic are in agreement that the above are valid criteria against which to assess assurance to demonstrate that the assurance given has integrity. However, there is no formulaic result or correct answer that the assessment should derive. Some CAEs are quite clear that their current risk-based methodologies score quite favorably in the assessment. The following is an amalgam of my own thoughts, assessments, and actual solutions, developed across four financial services organizations in the past decade in trying to respond to the challenge.

Completeness

First, were all significant risks in scope for my internal audit function? How sympathetic would or should a stakeholder be if the explanation was "sorry, out of scope" for not providing any assurance coverage on a significant risk area where a major issue had arisen. The default position is for "everything" to be in scope, because that is where assurance adds the most value. However, my experience is that "everything" means different things to different people, and it still leads to mismatches between expected assurance coverage and actual audit coverage. The cry of "where were the auditors?" when something goes wrong is less rhetorical and more actual than you might imagine. It served my function to define "everything" up front, rather than have to explain omissions retrospectively. This is becoming even more sensible in an environment where many point to the least tangible risk areas, such as strategy, sustainability, and culture, as those where assurance is most needed.

"**Increasingly, boards are turning to the profession for assurance.**" Mervyn King

     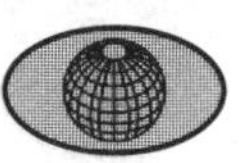 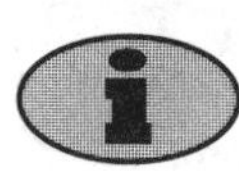  

(In fact, many respected observers are pointing to poor culture and behavior as being what has led to the economic meltdown, rather than policy or process failure.) If something is going to be agreed as out of scope, it is better to be in a position to have clearly defined and agreed it, even if by doing so you are reducing the value of your assurance proposition.

The best method I have found for creating an assurance universe, and to use as a basis for an assurance contract with the organization, is to list the significant risks (there are normally around 20, and such a list is often referred to as a risk map or significant risk register) as recognized and agreed by the board. What is clear is that the significant risk register must include all financial, strategic, and operational risks as a minimum, including liquidity and sustainability risks. The internal audit profession is now turning its attention to the new paradigm risks that have been made painfully clear by the credit crunch—systemic/globalization risk, behavioral risks, and supply chain risks.

Frequency

The Combined Code on Corporate Governance, which sets the rules for FTSE-listed companies and is also recognized as a benchmark by nonlisted and public sector companies in the United Kingdom, implies a minimum annual assessment of the effectiveness of internal control (as a proxy for the effectiveness of management of significant risks).

However, a once-a-year assessment—even if it is about all the risks—does not appear to be frequent enough. The organizations for which I have worked have generally used a very compelling risk-based approach that prioritizes the assurance requirement over three years. But with this scenario it seemed to me that even a once-a-year assessment can only cover one-third of the assurance requirement (accepting that it would always include the highest-priority areas). I have posed the frequency question many times to senior managers, board members, and audit committee chairs. Their answer tends to be in the negative—i.e., it would be unreasonable that a major risk management breakdown should go unnoticed by internal audit until it was too late because the CAE's view of that risk was out of date, because it had not been looked at for six months or more, and was not due to be looked at again for another six months or more.

In fact, the best frequency would be if CAEs were in a position to provide a complete opinion all of the time. Logistical and practical constraints make this impossible. However, I have been able to produce more frequent assessments by focusing on each of the risk categories for which assurance is required and creating a strategy for delivering the outputs that I need so that I can stand in front of an audit committee once a quarter and deliver conclusions that have demonstrable integrity. Such strategies comprise combinations of continuous assessment techniques, ongoing reviews, and revisions of conclusions previously arrived at, as well as baseline assessments.

REVIEWS AND ASSESSMENTS

Baseline reviews are undertaken where management of the risk is relatively stable. These are time-framed, in-depth reviews of established controls and processes. The conclusions from such reviews may have a long shelf life and, if stability continues, may only need a light refresh to remain valid.

Continuous assessments involve regular or continuous reviews of a range of information and activity that indicate whether controls are operating as intended. They are used where conclusions have previously been established but more certainty is required to ensure that those conclusions remain valid between baseline reviews. They include a review of the output of other risk and control functions—for example, compliance.

Ongoing reviews are used where projects and other business initiatives may bring changes to the risk and control framework and reduce the value of reviewing preexisting processes and controls, or where control environments are unstable/immature and action is being undertaken to establish or remediate controls.

Orientation

In thinking about frequency challenge, I also started to think about the orientation of assurance. By orientation, I mean whether the assurance is just focused retrospectively, on things that have happened in the past, or whether it can and should look to the future. The Combined Code implies that the annual assessment will be a retrospective view of the previous year, much like the external auditor's opinion on the financial statements. However, in much the same way as external auditors consider the going concern aspects of firms, it seemed to me that my conclusions should have some element of future proofing.

Again, I considered the value of assurance that was anchored in the past (especially when it could refer to an event as long as 364 days in the past). If a risk had already crystallized, any assurance was old news and irrelevant. If controls were effective, for how long would they continue to be effective? I felt that my assurance would be more reasonable if I could "future proof" it.

But how much future proofing can and should be given? I achieved this by attaching a shelf life to quarterly conclusions. This is a concept where I vary how long my assurance conclusions are likely to remain valid, depending on certain broad criteria. For example, if the control environment is either currently unstable or will be subject to some major change in the near future, the validity of any conclusions will be short-lived. If the area is stable and likely to remain so, then a long shelf life can be given—and easily refreshed using the continuous assessment technique. In the organizations where I have employed this approach, in any set of quarterly conclusions the shelf lives given have varied considerably across risk categories. In fact, the more I have used this approach, the more I find that the fact that an explicit view on shelf life has been given has become as important as the actual length of time which is stated.

Explicitness

The requirement (by boards) for CAEs to give opinions on the effectiveness of the system of internal control and risk management is one of the biggest areas of debate and challenge facing the profession at the moment. Because of the legal implications of opinions, many CAEs will not give them, and will only report issues as they arise. Some CAEs who are prepared to give opinions do so without much thought of the consequences, or do so in the vein of "everything is effective apart from the following issues."

Setting aside the legal status argument, in my experience such approaches are potentially flawed. The default position of the recipients of assurance is one of assuming that all other controls and risk management activities across the enterprise are effective and will continue to be so, unless they have specifically been told otherwise. Unless that was truly the intended message, the assurance that is being provided is misleading. That is why I have worked on providing separate conclusions (as opposed to opinions, to avoid the legal connotation) for each significant risk category (and sometimes at a risk subcategory level) each quarter. My preference has been to go for a binary conclusion, where "this risk is effectively managed" is signaled by a green symbol, and "this risk is not effectively managed" is represented by a red one.

For a "green" conclusion nothing further is required in the way of explanation other than an indicator of the breadth and depth of coverage used to reach the conclusion.

"External audit doesn't give you the sort of review and assurance over risk and controls across the spectrum of financial and non-financial aspects of the organization but a good internal auditor does." Lord Smith of Kelvin

  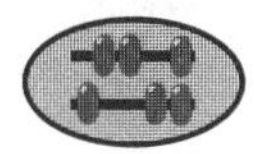   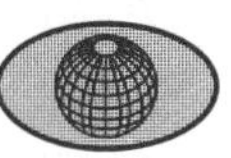   

For a "red" conclusion the list of supporting issues, as well as the reliability indicator, are described.

My experience is that the binary approach is a step too far for some, so I have also employed a three-level and a four-level approach, where the conclusions range from "well controlled," through "acceptable level of control" and "controls require improvement," to "insufficient control." The point is that it is the explicitness of the conclusion (at the level of significant risk) and the reliability indicator which provide the assurance that is intended, rather than the summary of issues reported. The approach encourages much greater challenge and scrutiny—but I have found that to be a good thing.

Objectivity and Subject Matter Expertize

These are not new concepts or challenges for CAEs, but the challenge is to rethink them in the framework of the new assurance paradigm. Many cite independence of opinion as an end in itself, but it is only valuable if it enhances objectivity. After all, in any walk of life, not just in internal audit, we tend to be more convinced by the conclusion of someone who has no vested interest in what that conclusion is. Similarly, we tend to be more convinced by a conclusion if it is given by someone who really knows the subject to which it relates. Therefore, regardless of the completeness, frequency, future orientation, or explicitness of a conclusion, it can only provide reasonable assurance if we have confidence in the objectivity and expertize in the subject matter of the person giving it. Therein lies the challenge, as sometimes one element can only increase at the expense of another. In meeting this challenge, I have found that it is the recognition of the dynamic relationship between objectivity and subject matter expertize which allows dynamic management of it.

CONCLUSION

In common with many disciplines, the challenge for CAEs is not one of technique or technical development, but one of focus. In many ways, the biggest challenge is one of a shift of mindset away from planning to deliver some audits, toward planning to deliver an assurance outcome of demonstrable integrity. However, I believe it is a challenge that must be met, so that assurers have a stronger chance of helping their organizations to avoid corporate calamity due to risk management and control failure.

▸▸ MAKING IT HAPPEN

- It is most important that you have a solid anchor or hook on which to hang your assurance. Ideally this should be the board-defined risk exposures. If your organization does not have these, help your organization to define them.
- It will take several quarters to build rhythm and momentum, and up to 18 months to achieve a baseline assurance for all of the risks of equivalent requisite quality.
- If you already know something, and are confident in that knowledge, do not waste valuable resources on proving something you already know. Reliable knowledge, however gained, contributes to your assurance.
- If you set off down this path, there will be many naysayers. They will challenge whether you can realistically deliver all the work that is necessary, claiming that you can only scratch the surface. Stay focused. The best way to convince naysayers is with the outputs and outcomes. The number of audit man-days has always been, and always will be, an input measure, and is no guide to whether good, bad, or indifferent assurance is produced.
- Less—in terms of number of issues—is definitely more. The number of audit issues in any one organization should genuinely reflect the competence of risk management and not the number of auditors
- You will need to spend as much—if not more—time converting your own people to the cause. Old habits die hard. The only way to do this is to be persistent and unwavering in your assurance strategy. Be prepared to repeat. . .and repeat and repeat.
- Make use of early converts and use them shamelessly to help spread the message.

▸▸ MORE INFO

Periodicals:

Internal Auditing, monthly magazine of the Institute of Internal Auditors UK and Ireland: www.iia.org.uk/en/Publications/IA_and_BR_Magazine

Internal Auditor, monthly periodical of the IIA, Florida: www.theiia.org/intauditor

Articles:

Chambers, Andrew. "The board's black hole—Filling their assurance vacuum: Can internal audit rise to the challenge?" *Measuring Business Excellence* 12:1 (2008): 47–63.

D'Arcy, Simon. "Bubble trouble—The wrong attitudes to risk." *Mortgage Finance Gazette* (February 4, 2009). Online at: www.mfgonline.co.uk/article/Bubble-trouble-the-wrong-attitudes-to-risk-228895.html

Perry, Michelle. "Weathering the storm." *Financial Services Review* (May 2008): 10–12. Online at: tinyurl.com/djcazk

Piper, Arthur. "A matter of opinion." Interview with Alec Richmond, then President of IIA UK and Ireland. *Internal Auditor* (June 1, 2007). Online at: www.thefreelibrary.com/Internal+Auditor/2007/June/1-p5634

Report:

Turnbull, N. "Internal control: Guidance for directors on the combinal code." The Institute of Chartered Accountants in England and Wales, September 1999

NOTES

1 PricewaterhouseCoopers (PwC), "Internal audit 2012: A study examining the future of internal auditing and the potential decline of a controls-centric approach." PwC (2007); also "State of the internal audit profession study: Pressures build for continual focus on risk." PwC (2007). Both downloadable from www.pwc.com (search on titles).

2 Institute of Internal Auditors (UK and Ireland) in association with Deloitte, "Towards a blueprint for the internal audit profession." London: IIA (2008). Online from: www.iia.org.uk.

3 Protiviti, *Internal Auditing Around the World*. Four volumes published between 2005 and 2008 with profiles of internal audit functions at leading international organizations. The series tells the stories of 16 successful internal audit functions and examines common denominators that separate these leaders from their peers. Available from the Protiviti website: www.knowledgeleader.com.

4 *Internal Control: Guidance for Directors on the Combined Code* (the Turnbull Guidance) was originally published by the Institute of Chartered Accountants in England and Wales in 1999 and was followed by a number of subsequent revisions.

"Internal audit could be well placed to provide continuous, 360° independent assurance; but significant changes to the internal audit paradigm will be needed." Andrew Chambers

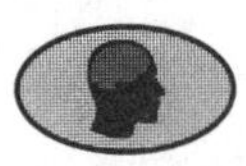

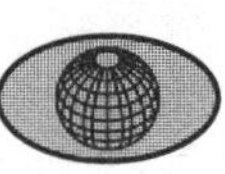

Optimizing Internal Audit by Andrew Chambers

EXECUTIVE SUMMARY

To optimize an internal audit function it is necessary to:

- conform with the International Professional Practices Framework of the global Institute of Internal Auditors;
- define the role, responsibilities, and authority of the internal audit function within a formal charter approved by the board;
- report to the board;
- embrace both assurance and consulting roles within the internal audit mission;
- function independently;
- ensure that no business areas are "off-limits" to internal audit;
- plan future audit engagements based on the chief audit executive's risk assessment;
- be committed to continuous improvement of the internal audit function.

INTRODUCTION

Internal auditing is defined by the Institute of Internal Auditors (IIA) as follows:

> "Internal auditing is an independent, objective assurance and consulting activity designed to add value and improve an organization's operations. It helps an organization accomplish its objectives by bringing a systematic, disciplined approach to evaluate and improve the effectiveness of risk management, control, and governance processes."[1]

It is widely accepted that whether or not the staff of an internal audit function are affiliated to the IIA, if the internal auditing corresponds to the above definition, best-value internal auditing will only result when generally accepted internal auditing standards are applied. Internal auditing should be a valued part of the total assurance process. To be so it requires independence from the activities it audits and it needs to report independently to all those who rely on the assurance that internal audit provides.

Today, internal audit is a service for management and also for those, such as boards and audit committees, charged with governance. Particular internal audit functions may also have certain obligations to report to outside parties, such as regulators. It is important that the roles, responsibilities, and authority of internal audit are clearly set out and supported within the organization.

ESSENTIAL PREREQUISITES FOR INTERNAL AUDITING

Clear ground rules must be kept to if internal audit is to add best value to both its assurance and consulting roles. In any entity, these should be set out in the internal audit charter, which must be approved by the board or by the board's audit committee on behalf of the board. The most senior level that relies on the assurance given by internal audit needs to be confident that internal audit is not subordinating its judgment on professional matters to that of anyone else. Usually, at its most senior level internal audit reports to the audit committee of the board. Compromised professional judgment may occur with respect to:

- determining the planned programme of audits;
- accessing information and personnel necessary to properly conduct an audit;
- deciding the content of internal audit reports.

While it may appear that the chief audit executive is reporting directly to the audit committee, as indeed should be so, that reporting is of little value if it is in effect censored by senior management before it reaches the audit committee.

Internal audit is both an audit *for* management and also an audit *of* management *for* the board through the board's audit committee. If internal audit is compromised professionally, then it is essential that those who rely on the assurance that internal audit gives are fully cognizant of this. An audit committee needs to have time alone with the chief audit executive, with other executives not being in attendance; this can take place in a 15-minute session at the start of each audit committee meeting. Audit committees should also be involved in advance in decisions relating to the appointment, reappointment, dismissal, and remuneration of heads of internal audit.

Organizationally it is preferable that the internal audit function does not belong to the finance/accounting function of the organization as this makes it harder for internal audit to audit financial and accounting matters with sufficient independence and objectivity. It also makes it more difficult for internal audit to be welcomed as having a valuable contribution to make when it audits the operational areas of the business. Ideally, internal audit should report directly to the chief executive or, alternatively, to someone, or to a committee, outside of the main functional areas of the business.

> "The chief audit executive must report to a level within the organization that allows the internal audit activity to fulfill its responsibilities. The chief audit executive must confirm to the board, at least annually, the organizational independence of the internal audit activity."[2]

THE SCOPE OF INTERNAL AUDIT

Contemporary internal auditing provides assurance to management and to the board, and also offers consulting services. The nature of both these services should be set out in the internal audit charter. The two services overlap: an assurance audit is likely to lead to advice on making improvements; consulting work may reveal issues that have to be taken up by internal audit in the context of its assurance role. Of the two, assurance is the core role, but some would argue that not to offer consulting services would now be inconsistent with professional internal auditing standards and would miss an opportunity to add value.

There should be no no-go areas for internal audit assurance as this limits the assurance that internal audit is able to provide; where there are no-go areas

CASE STUDY 1

Management and internal audit of a multinational company knew about an overstatement of oil reserves for some two years before the board and the board's audit committee learnt about it. Executive directors are said to have met before board meetings to agree a common line to be taken at the board. Reports from the chief audit executive passed across the desk of the chief financial officer before going to the audit committee. The chief executive, director of exploration, and chief financial officer left the company; when the company next appointed a new chief audit executive, the company sought an external candidate for the first time.

"Objectivity requires internal auditors not to subordinate their judgment on audit matters to others."
IIA, Glossary to *Standards*

     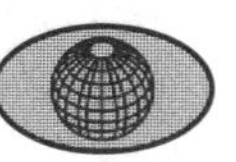   

CASE STUDY 2

The independent chairman of the board of a bank fired the bank's chief executive. The inside story was that the in-house chief audit executive used his direct access to the chair of the audit committee to contact that chair, by phone, between audit committee meetings, to discuss his concerns about apparent misconduct by the chief executive.

The chair of the audit committee, which comprised exclusively independent directors, convened a special meeting of the committee to follow this up. No executives other than the chief audit executive, who was invited to attend part of the meeting, knew that it was taking place. At the meeting the audit committee asked internal audit to investigate the matter further and report the findings directly to the committee. The chief audit executive timed the audit fieldwork to coincide with the annual vacation of the chief executive. The internal auditors gathered evidence which showed that the chief executive was using company resources for his personal benefit. Hence, when the chief executive returned from vacation, the chairman of the board dismissed him.

Had the chairman of the board not been independent, it would have been harder for the company to deal with this matter effectively. His independence meant that the chairman of the audit committee was able to keep him "in the loop" throughout, without risk that the confidentiality of the enquiry would be jeopardized.

Had internal audit been outsourced to an external service provider, it might have been less likely to learn about the alleged misconduct by the chief executive. However, internal audit is often identified as a point where concerned employees may blow the whistle, and this can be so whether or not internal audit is in-house.

(i.e. restrictions of scope) the implications need to be clearly understood by those who rely on the assurance that internal audit gives.

Unlimited scope for internal audit includes the authority to audit across the operational areas of the business, not just within accounting and finance, and at all levels. An emerging issue is whether internal audit is able to provide assurance to boards themselves that the policies of boards are being implemented by management and that there are no banana skins round the corner, unknown to the board, on which the company may slip in the future.

Consulting services by internal auditors may include the provision of counsel and advice, of facilitation (such as facilitating control self-assessment workshops of managers and staff), or of training services. Internal auditors avoid assuming any management responsibilities as part of their consulting services, neither would they take on responsibility for designing processes except in an advisery capacity. One reason is that internal auditors need to be independent of management processes in order to be able to audit those processes objectively.

Internal auditors will undertake consulting work only when both internal audit and the client consider this to be justified. On the other hand, the management of a business activity should not be allowed to prevent an assurance audit from taking place.

"The chief audit executive should consider accepting proposed consulting engagements based on the engagement's potential to improve management of risks, add value, and improve the organization's operations. Accepted engagements must be included in the plan."[3]

More and more heads of internal audit are being asked not just to report the results of individual audits but also to provide *overall assurance opinions*, annually or more frequently, to top management and to boards or their audit committees. This makes it more important that internal audit optimizes the utilization of its scarce internal audit resources—in order to maximize the reliability of the overall opinion that internal audit gives.

Internal audit should plan its program of audits annually, based on a risk assessment which makes use of inputs from management and from the board or the board's audit committee. Internal audit should map its plan of audits to management's own risk map or risk register. But a proportion of internal audit time should be set aside to "look round the corners" that top management are not looking around in case there are major unnoticed or concealed risks.

While the future plan of audits will be determined annually, the internal audit function should have a longer perspective on audit coverage that takes into account audit work done over previous years and earmarked to be done over the next three years or so. The chief audit executive should consider the extent to which work done in earlier years can be utilized in coming to the overall assurance opinion.

PROFESSIONAL BODIES AND SUPPORT

The internal auditing profession is organized globally, as is appropriate for a function that so often operates transnationally. The IIA, established in the United States in 1941 and headquartered in Florida, now has many members outside of North America, belonging to 250 chapters and affiliated institutes in 165 countries. Membership has grown from 100,000 in 2004 to over 160,000 in 2008, of whom about 75,000 are fully professionally qualified certified internal auditors (CIAs). The IIA also offers the following specialist qualifications:

- Certification in Control Self-Assessment (CCSA);
- Certified Government Auditing Professional (CGAP);
- Certified Financial Services Auditor (CFSA).

Exams for the IIA's professional certifications can be sat at 90 sites throughout the world and in 18 languages. They can be taken at times of the candidate's choosing, rather than at two set dates during the calendar year. If a candidate fails an exam, he or she may retake the exam when at least 90 days have elapsed.

All members of the IIA commit to observe a common *Code of Ethics*, which

CASE STUDY 3

Following a fatal, high-profile explosion at one of its oil refineries and a number of environmental failures, the board of a multinational oil company commissioned an enquiry by an outside panel. It must have appeared to the board that the board's policy that the company should be a green and safe oil multinational was not being implemented by management. The board agreed to the panel's recommendation that the panel should appoint an external expert to provide independent assurance to the board on health and safety matters for at least five years.

Two questions arise from this. First, whether (and if not, why not) the board had been receiving sufficient internal assurance that the policies of the board were being implemented by management; and second, the extent to which internal audit could be relied on to provide the board with that assurance. The panel's solution addressed the board's needs for assurance only in the area of health and safety.

"The internal audit activity must be independent, and internal auditors must be objective in performing their work." IIA Standard 1100, Independence and Objectivity

   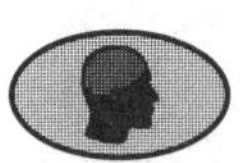  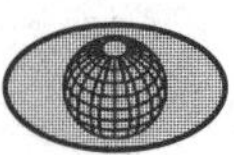   

includes an obligation to apply the *Standards* of the IIA.[4] There are approved translations of the *Standards* in 32 languages. The global Association of Chartered Certified Accountants (ACCA) has recently endorsed the IIA's *Standards* as applicable to ACCA members working as internal auditors, and the 2009 version of the United Kingdom's HM Treasury *Government Internal Audit Standards* is modeled on the IIA's *Standards*. The International Professional Practices Framework of the IIA, which includes the *Standards* as well as the *Code of Ethics*, practice adviseries and practice guides, has been significantly revised, with the revised version published on January 1, 2009. The revised *Standards* themselves, to be conformed to from January 1, 2009, were released on the IIA's website on October 1, 2008, to give sufficient time for internal audit functions to align themselves with the modified requirements.

QUALITY ASSURANCE ASSESSMENTS AND INTERNAL AUDIT MATURITY FRAMEWORKS

An effective opportunity to ensure optimum quality internal auditing is to be found in the quality assurance requirements of the *Standards* of the IIA. These require that there should be annual internal assessments of each internal audit function, and independent, external quality assessments at least once every five years. The benchmark to be used is the *Standards* of the IIA. These standards represent the approach to internal auditing that should be followed if an organization is to obtain optimum value from its investment in internal audit. Internal audit maturity frameworks are now being applied to assess the quality of internal audit functions.[5]

▸▸ MAKING IT HAPPEN

Key guidance to get best value from your internal audit function:

1. Develop a charter for your internal audit function, approved by the board or by your audit committee of the board.
2. Staff your internal audit function with professionally qualified people and those in the process of becoming qualified.
3. Require adherence to relevant internal auditing standards.
4. Ensure a scope for internal audit that includes assurance and consulting work.
5. Don't ever ask your internal audit function to subordinate its judgment on professional matters to anyone else.
6. Benchmark your internal audit function against others.
7. Take seriously the need for both internal and external quality assurance assessments of your internal audit function.
8. Support your internal auditors and ensure that they are properly resourced.

▸▸ MORE INFO

Websites:

AuditNet, a US information and resources site developed for the benefit of the internal audit profession by Jim Kaplan. There are a number of discrete areas on AuditNet. The IIA now hosts this site, which has links to and from its own: www.auditnet.org

The Institute of Internal Auditors: www.theiia.org

The IIA's Florida-based website is a fund of information. It carries the internal auditing *Standards* and *Code of Ethics* as well as, for members, the rest of the International Professional Practices Framework. Also on this site is the IIA's excellent bookstore on internal auditing.

The IIA Inc.'s Research Foundation has sponsored the development of an Internal Auditing Capability Maturity Model (IA-CMM), published late 2008. Lead researcher and author is Elizabeth (Libby) MacRae.

The IIA runs the Global Audit Information Network (GAIN), a very effective and economic online benchmarking service for internal audit functions. More information at: www.theiia.org/research/benchmarking/gain/?search=GAIN

United Kingdom HM Treasury website: www.hm-treasury.gov.uk

This has a wealth of guidance on internal auditing including:

- *"The Orange Book"—Management of Risk: Principles and Concepts*: www.hm-treasury.gov.uk/media/C/6/1104_orange_book.pdf
- *Internal Audit Quality Assessment Framework*, including the Treasury's own internal audit maturity model: www.hm-treasury.gov.uk/media/D/8/iaqaf.pdf
- *Government Internal Audit Standards*: www.hm-treasury.gov.uk/media/6/6/GIAS_2001(272Kb).pdf

NOTES

1 Institute of Internal Auditors (IIA). *International Standards for the Professional Practice of Internal Auditing* ("*Standards*"). Altamonte Springs, FL: IIA, 2009. Can be downloaded from www.theiia.org, along with the *Code of Ethics*, Practice adviseries and Position papers. See "Websites" in "More Info."

2 IIA (2009). Standard 1110: Organizational Independence.

3 IIA. Standard 2010.C1.

4 See note 1.

5 For example, the UK HM Treasury's *Internal Audit Quality Assessment Framework*, which includes its internal audit maturity model (see "Websites" in "More Info"); or the IIA Inc. Research Foundation's Internal Auditing Capability Maturity Model (IA-CMM), to be published late 2008.

"Is the internal audit function robust enough to challenge senior management? Clearly if the internal control function is too weak to effectively challenge those responsible for determining the organisation's operations, it has little value in its role of risk control." John Tiner

  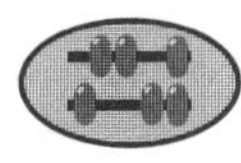   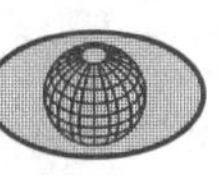   

Performance Reporting under IFRS

by Peter Casson

EXECUTIVE SUMMARY

- International Accounting Standard 1 (revised), "Presentation of financial statements," requires companies to report their performance in a statement of comprehensive income.
- The International Accounting Standards Board (IASB) and the US Financial Accounting Standards Board (FASB) have agreed to converge their financial reporting standards.
- As part of the convergence, the IASB and FASB are developing a new standard that is likely to affect the way in which performance is reported in the future.

INTRODUCTION

Financial statements prepared under International Financial Reporting Standards (IFRS) include a statement of comprehensive income which, together with associated notes, report a company's performance for the accounting period. The International Accounting Standards Board (IASB), an independent body, sets the IFRS. The IASB took over responsibility for setting international accounting standards from the International Accounting Standards Committee (IASC), which issued International Accounting Standards (IAS). The IASB adopted the then existing IAS when it took over from the IASC, and the acronym IFRS is now used to include both IFRS and IAS, as well as the interpretations developed by the International Financial Reporting Interpretations Committee or the former Standing Interpretations Committee.

The presentation of a company's financial performance under IFRS is dealt with in IAS 1 (revised) "Presentation of financial statements." Revisions to the standard in 2007, which are in effect for accounting periods beginning on or after January 1, 2009, include the requirement for reporting entities to present a statement of comprehensive income.

The development of IFRS is shaped by an agreement reached between the IASB and the US Financial Accounting Standards Board (FASB) to make their existing financial reporting standards compatible and to coordinate work programs. The IASB and FASB are collaborating on a project entitled "Financial statement presentation," which may lead to further changes in the way entities report performance.

This article describes the essential features of reporting performance under IAS 1 (revised), possible future changes to performance reporting standards, and non-IFRS performance measures.

REPORTING PERFORMANCE UNDER IAS 1

IAS 1 (revised) "Presentation of financial statements" sets out the basis for the presentation of financial statements so as to achieve comparability of a company's financial statements over time and across the financial statements of different companies.

The revised standard, issued in 2007, requires a "statement of comprehensive income," where only an income statement was previously required. This change increases the comparability with the US standard FAS 130 "Comprehensive income." Comprehensive is defined in FAS 130 as "the change in equity [net assets] of a business enterprise during a period from transactions and other events and circumstances from nonowner sources. It includes all changes in equity during a period except those resulting from investments by owners and distributions to owners."

Comprehensive income is more inclusive than profit or loss for a period because, although a company is generally required to recognize all income and expenses in the period in profit or loss, some IFRSs either require or permit otherwise. Items that should/may be excluded from profit or loss include: (1) correction of errors from prior periods; (2) changes in accounting policies; (3) revaluation surpluses; (4) gains and losses arising on the translation of the financial statements of a foreign operation; and (5) gains and losses on remeasuring available-for-sale financial assets. Such items, which are excluded from profit or loss, represent components of other comprehensive income as they result in a change in equity.

In looking at the reporting of performance under IFRS it is useful to consider: The general features of reporting under IFRS; the presentation of comprehensive income; the way in which expenses may be analyzed. It is also useful to look at the specific issues related to discontinued operations and exceptional items.

General Features of Financial Reports under IFRS

IAS 1 (revised) identifies a set of general features for the reporting of financial performance. The first requirement is the fair presentation of a company's financial performance. This requires that the effects of a company's transactions and other events are faithfully represented in its statement of comprehensive income. It is generally presumed that a company will achieve this through the application of IFRSs. However, in some rare instances, it is necessary to depart from IFRSs in order to achieve a fair presentation. Other general features identified in IAS 1 (revised) are:

- *Going concern*: A company should prepare its statement of comprehensive income on the assumption that it will continue its operations into the indefinite future.
- *Accrual basis of accounting*: A company should include income and expenses when they meet definition and recognition criteria.
- *Materiality and aggregation*: A company should present each material class of item separately.
- *Offsetting*: A company cannot usually offset items of income and expense.
- *Frequency of reporting*: A company should usually publish its financial statements at least annually.
- *Comparative information*: A company should disclose comparative information for the previous period.
- *Consistency of presentation*: A company is required to present and classify items in its statement of comprehensive income on a consistent basis from one period to the next.

Presentation of Comprehensive Income

Companies are required to present a statement of all income and expenses recognized in an accounting period. This may be reported either in a single statement of comprehensive income or in two statements—an income statement showing the components of the profit or loss for the period, and a statement of comprehensive income that includes the components of other comprehensive income.

"A company's ethical conduct is something like a big flywheel. It might have a lot of momentum, but it will eventually slow down and stop unless you add energy." William Adams

  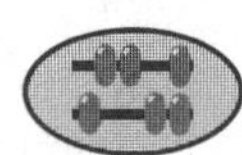   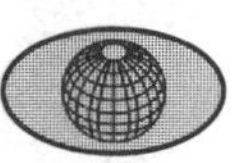   

IAS 1 (revised) requires that the following 10 categories should, as a minimum, be presented in the statement of comprehensive income:

- Revenue.
- Finance costs.
- Share of the profit or loss of joint ventures and associates, i.e., companies over which the reporting company exercises significant influence but which are not subsidiaries or joint ventures.
- Tax expense.
- The post-tax profit or loss on discontinued operations, together with the post-tax gain or loss on the disposal of the assets of the discontinued operations.
- Profit or loss.
- Each component of other comprehensive income.
- Total comprehensive income.

Where a reporting company is a parent company presenting a consolidated statement of comprehensive income, it is necessary to show the allocation of:

- Profit or loss for the period attributable to: Holders of the stock of the parent company; and minority interests, i.e., holders of the subsidiary companies' common stock other than the stock held directly, or indirectly, by the parent company.
- Total comprehensive income for the period attributable to: Stockholders of the parent company; and minority interests.

Analysis of Expenses

A company is required to present an analysis of its expenses. The analysis may take one of two forms:

- The "nature of expense" method requires the company to classify expenses according to their nature—for example, expense groups such as raw materials and consumables, depreciation, employment costs, and advertising costs.
- The "function of expense" or "cost of sales" method requires the company to aggregate expenses according to their function—for example, cost of sales, distribution costs, and administrative expenses.

Management is required to select the method which, in its view, is most reliable and relevant. Where a company uses the "function of expense" method, it must provide additional information on the nature of the expense.

IAS 1 (revised), as noted above, requires companies to distinguish between continuing and discontinued operations in its reporting of performance. A discontinued operation is a major part of the company (e.g., line of business or geographical area of operation) that has either been disposed of or is held for sale.

When items of income or expense are material, a company is required to disclose their nature and amounts separately. These include: Write-downs of inventories and of property, plant, and equipment; restructuring costs; disposals of items of property, plant, and equipment; disposals of investments; litigation settlements.

PERFORMANCE REPORTING UNDER IFRS IN THE FUTURE

The IASB and the FASB agreed in 2004 to conduct a joint project on the presentation of financial statements with a view to developing a standard on the organization and presentation of information in such statements. As part of this project, the IASB and FASB issued a joint discussion paper, "Preliminary views on financial statement presentation," in 2008.[1]

In the discussion paper, the IASB and FASB propose a classification of items within a statement of comprehensive income. This classification first distinguishes between continuing and discontinued operations, and then further classifies continuing operations into business and financing, with further subclassifications of business and financing. As a result, the statement of comprehensive income would present the following components of comprehensive income:

Business:

- Operating income and expenses;
- Investment income and expenses.

Financing:

- Financing asset income;
- Financing liability expenses;
- Income taxes on continuing operations (business and financing);
- Discontinued operations (net of tax);
- Other comprehensive income.

The statement would also include a subtotal for profit or loss and a total for comprehensive income for the period. Under the proposals, all companies would be required to present a single statement of comprehensive income.

ALTERNATIVE PERFORMANCE MEASURES

Companies frequently report additional performance measures to those required under IFRS. Such additional measures may be designed to reflect the particular circumstances of the company and/or special features of the period being reported. In some cases these alternative performance measures are derived directly from a company's audited financial statements. This includes such measures as EBIT (earnings before interest and tax) and EBITDA (earnings before interest, tax, depreciation, and amortization). Sometimes the measures require adjustments to the figures reported under IFRS, such as "non-IFRS income" and "non-IFRS earnings per share." While some companies define and explain the alternative performance measures they use, others do not.

There are two explanations for the publication of alternative performance measures. The first is that company managers are providing additional information in order to reduce information asymmetry. For example, accounting information is adjusted for items that are regarded as transitory. The alternative explanation is that managers report these numbers with the intention of misleading readers of financial reports. Regulators have therefore attempted to address potential abuse. For example, the Committee of European Securities Regulators (CESR) issued recommendations on the use of alternative performance measures in 2005.

CONCLUSION

IAS 1 (revised) requires companies to present a statement of comprehensive income which includes the profit or loss for the period together with other components of comprehensive income. The IASB assumes that compliance with the

▸▸ MAKING IT HAPPEN

- The preparation of a statement of comprehensive income, together with the accompanying notes, requires compliance with IAS 1 (revised) and the application of IFRS with the overall objective of fairly representing the transactions and other events of the reporting entity.
- There may be circumstances in which a company needs to depart from IFRS in order to provide a fair representation.
- Users of financial statements should be aware of the accounting standards, and of any departures from standards, in their analysis of the statement of comprehensive income.

"To know how to dissimulate is the knowledge of kings." Cardinal Richelieu

  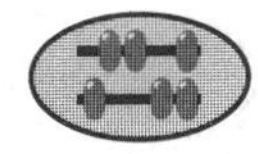 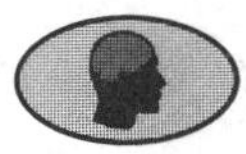  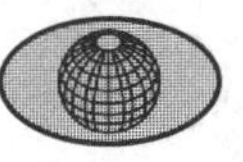   

provisions of the standard should ensure that companies provide users of financial reports with key information that informs economic decisions.

▸▸ MORE INFO

Book:

Ernst & Young. *International GAAP® 2009*. 2 vols. Chichester, UK: Wiley, 2009. Online at: www.wiley.com/legacy/igaap09

Websites:

Deloitte—IAS Plus: www.iasplus.com

International Accounting Standards Board (IASB): www.iasb.org

NOTES

1 FASB/IASB, "Discussion paper, preliminary views on financial statement presentation," October 16, 2008. Online at: www.fasb.org/draft/index.shtml.

"There's nothing wrong with big companies. A lot of people think big business in America is a bad thing. I think it's a really good thing. Most people in business are ethical, hard-working, good people. And it's a meritocracy." Steve Jobs

   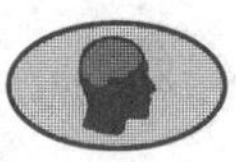  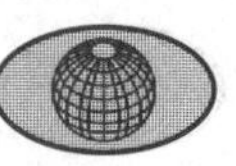   

Principles versus Rules in Financial Supervision—Is There One Superior Approach? by Marc Quintyn

EXECUTIVE SUMMARY

- Financial liberalization, which started in the 1970s, has altered the nature of financial operations dramatically. In contrast with the pre-1970s, often called the period of financial repression, good financial institution governance is now critical for the soundness of the individual financial institution, and, by extension, the stability of a country's financial system.
- In response to these deep and far-reaching changes in the financial sector, financial regulation and supervision has become much more important than ever before, and the nature of its business has been changing in equally dramatic ways.
- Supervisors were likened for the longest time to compliance, or box-ticking officers. Now, in this governance-driven financial environment, they have become "governance supervisors," monitoring the operations of the financial institutions on behalf of the diffused and ill-informed deposit-holders of these institutions.
- Since the start of this transformation of the supervisory approaches, debates have been conducted about the optimal way to supervise the financial systems. Some jurisdictions believe in a principles-based approach, while others swear by a rules-based approach.
- The discussion is about guiding, or keeping in check, financial institutions through broad-based principles versus well-defined, specific rules. Practice shows that life is too complex for any of these two extremes alone. Both systems have their pros and cons, and best practice seems to go in the direction of a supervisory approach that offers a balance of principles, supported by guidelines and rules. In the aftermath of a crisis, all sides call for more rules; in quiet times, all sides think that they can steer the course with principles. As normal times inherently carry the seeds of a crisis within them, any supervisory system should balance rules and principles.

INTRODUCTION

The Challenging Nature of Financial Supervision

Two things can be stated with certainty about financial sector supervision. First, that few professions have changed so dramatically in recent years, in form, approach, scope, and substance. Second, that the task of supervisors, when compared to several other domains of public policy, has become extremely complex, and that no end is in sight with regard to this process. These fundamental changes are taking place in response to the equally dramatic changes that we are witnessing in the sectors they are mandated to oversee.

Financial Liberalization

It all started with financial liberalization, which took hold in the 1970s. Between World War II and the 1970s, all financial systems around the globe were heavily regulated, or mainly in government hands. It had become common to describe the government's approach to handling the system as "financial repression." From the mid-1970s on, first domestically, and subsequently internationally, liberalization triggered many changes that profoundly altered the face of the financial system and the nature of its operations. Financial liberalization, in turn, unleashed competitive forces, first within the banking systems, subsequently within other subsectors, and finally among all of them, leading to a blurring of boundaries among previously clearly delineated subsectors, such as banking, securities markets, and insurance. Fierce competition pressurized financial institutions to take on more risks to outpace competitors and ensure lasting profitability. Major advances in information and communication technologies further propelled this process forward—provisionally, until a few years ago when the system collapsed under the weight of too many incorrectly assessed risks and too much leverage.

Adequate risk management requires high-quality governance of financial institutions in order to preserve financial sector stability in this new environment. In sharp contrast with the financial repression period—when financial sector behavior was largely prescribed, and financial institution governance, therefore, was left with only a few degrees of freedom —financial institution governance has become a crucial variable in guaranteeing the success of these liberalized and globalized financial systems.

Reorientation of Financial Supervisors' Work

Such dramatic changes in the way the financial sector operates have required major adjustments in the supervisor's regulatory and supervisory frameworks, and in the ways they enter into dialogue with the supervised entities.[2] Thus, supervisors had to metamorphose from compliance, or box-ticking, officers in the old, repressed systems, to what we would call now "governance" supervisors. They needed to replace their reactive approach with forward-looking, proactive ways of doing business with financial institutions. Under this new paradigm, the task of the supervisor is mainly to monitor and guide financial institutions to implement comprehensive risk management and internal control frameworks suitable for their particular institutional risk profiles, subject to prudential standards.

This view of regulation and supervision is closely aligned with Dewatripont and Tirole's (1994) "representation hypothesis" of regulation. Prudential regulation "...is primarily motivated by the need to represent the small depositors and to bring about an appropriate corporate governance for banks" (p.35). Managers of financial institutions have a fiduciary responsibility towards their shareholders, but the feature that distinguishes financial institutions from the rest of the corporate sector in the economy is that they also have a very large and diffuse group of stakeholders (or debtholders), many of them not well-informed about their financial institution. So, the above view sees the supervisor as performing the role of one important stakeholder in the financial institutions' corporate governance, representing the set of diffuse stakeholders, i.e., the depositors. From this follows that bank regulation and supervision have become part of the overall corporate governance regime of financial institutions.

In such a framework, financial institution governance consists of two parts: The regulators ensure debt governance, and shareholders ensure equity governance. As a result, bank managers have to serve two masters, the shareholders and the

"Businesses should play to win, but they should also play by the rules. It is in our own interests that our social norms put common interests above the interests of the individual." George Soros

     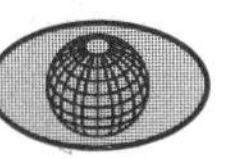   

regulators, the latter representing the bulk of the uninformed stakeholders. These governance arrangements thus induce, or force, management to internalize the welfare of all stakeholders, not just shareholders. In recent years, this role has gained even more prominence because financial liberalization has also led to a "privatization of risk," whereby savers are increasingly dependent on financial markets to determine their future financial security. This development requires more attention from the supervisors to risks that customers take upon themselves when confronted with an opaque financial system.

An Ongoing Process

So, there is broad agreement on the rationale—financial regulation and supervision are needed—and on the objectives—soundness of the individual institutions to preserve financial sector stability. But how about the best approach to get from starting point to objective? This is where most of the debate has taken place in recent years, and is most likely to continue for several years, as the discussions in the aftermath of the 2007–2008 financial crisis are amply demonstrating. As the debate about the best supervisory approaches continues, discussions are frequently presented in the form of dichotomies such as "principles-based versus rules-based supervision."

This debate is about the best approach for ongoing, day-to-day supervision of financial institutions. Typically, "either/or" discussions attract a lot of attention and often have a tendency to misrepresent the extreme concepts. We will therefore present the origins of the debate, clarify the concepts and review their merits, and see how close or how far we are from best practices in financial supervision.

PRINCIPLES-BASED VERSUS RULES-BASED SUPERVISION

Financial liberalization has put the onus of preserving financial institution soundness, and by extension financial system stability, on the governance of the financial institutions. A financial world where corporate governance has been given a much greater responsibility than before, for innovation, progress, and risk management, is inconsistent with a box-ticking supervisory approach. Supervisors need to be "governance supervisors," which means that they monitor financial institution governance, and intervene where necessary to keep it within the agreed framework. In this context, greater emphasis on "principles" than on "rules" is a natural and consistent transformation.

The Financial Services Authority (FSA), the United Kingdom's unified supervisor since 1997, has advertised itself most explicitly as a "principles-based" supervisor. According to the British unified supervisor, a principles-based regulatory regime specifies desired outcomes and allows financial institutions to chart their own paths to those results. Thus, the main features of such a supervisory regime can be summarized as follows.

- The regulator defines a set of principles (11 in the case of the FSA—see Box 1) regarding the conduct of a financial institution's business. These principles are general by nature, and set normative goals with respect to, for instance, integrity, adequacy of financial resources, and proper standards of market conduct.
- By definition, these principles are outcomes-oriented. They are meant to leave the supervised institution a lot of freedom to achieve the outcomes by the ways that it deems most adequate.

It should not come as a surprise that principles-based supervision is being promoted by a UK-based supervisor. Historically, there was no legal basis for the activities of the Bank of England (the supervisor until 1997), either in regard to its central bank or supervisory functions. For the longest time, the British banking system was managed as a small gentlemen's club through the use of "moral suasion." The system perfectly matched the needs of the City of London and the British authorities, and moral suasion was considered by both sides as "best practice" to guide and supervise the system. In that regard, this system of supervision was uniquely British and has never been replicated elsewhere.

Significant changes in the institutional composition of London's financial markets in a more recent period, integration in the European financial markets, as well as a number of financial scandals have made this approach gradually obsolete, and have led to a legal formalization of the British system. Nonetheless, the roots have never entirely disappeared, and have resurfaced under the form of a preference for "principles" to guide the financial system, rather than a strictly rules-based system. The rest of the world seems more critical, or even skeptical, towards this British love for principles. So, let us look at the advantages of both approaches in the current context.

Principles-Based Supervision

Principles-based supervision leaves bank managers great freedom to pursue the outcomes set by the supervisors in ways that they deem most suitable, given the realities of their own institution. Interference from supervisors is minimal. Rules, on the other hand, tend to divert managers' attention from the big picture by keeping them focused on details and on compliance, rather than on the spirit of the principle.

Principles leave the markets in general a lot of freedom to be creative and innovative, as long as they respect the boundaries set by the principles. Strict rules tend to kill initiative, creativity, and innovation.

> "When everyone is calling for more regulation, e.g. as now, just after a crisis, it is not needed at all, since bank managers are timid and risk-averse. When regulation is needed, no one wants it, because asset prices are rising, there is a boom, everyone is optimistic, and regulation just gets in the way. [1]"

Principles open the door to a productive dialogue between supervisor and supervised, leading to better mutual understanding (this is also part of the spirit of Pillar 2 under Basel II). Too much reliance on rules tends to keep alive the image of the supervisor as the policeman, associated with the compliance officer from the earlier days.

Financial systems are nowadays so complex that all-encompassing principles work better than rules. It is simply impossible to have rules to govern each and every activity of a financial institution.

Rules-Based Supervision

- Rules provide clarity and certainty for financial institution managers. Principles often lack these features, and, as a result, may yield opposite results from what they intended. Indeed, if uncertainly with respect to the interpretation of the principle prevails, the supervised manager may err on the conservative side and actually interpret the principle as a rule. Such behavior would defeat the purpose of the principles.
- Rules provide transparency for bank managers and ensure more fairness. They know exactly what they can expect from the supervisors. Principles are open for interpretation, and uncertainty. Lack of transparency can even lead to obstructing a level playing field.
- Rules are more operational than

   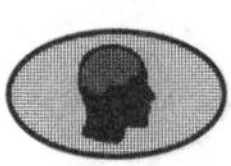  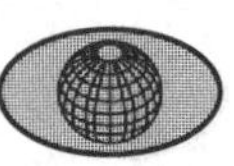   

principles. Principles need to be supported by guidelines or rules to become operational.

- The financial system is so complex—and becoming more complex every day—that rules or guidelines are needed in support of the broad principles, to explain the principles or direct their implementation.

Towards a Principles-cum-Rules System

Reliance on supervisory principles has a lot of appeal in our modern, governance-driven financial industry. However, putting the advantages and disadvantages of both approaches side by side leads us fairly easily to the conclusion that this discussion of principles versus rules is a false discussion. Neither approach alone would be superior and effective, and best practice would probably be a supervisory system that promulgates a number of principles that are supported by a set of prudential standards or rules. In fact, the FSA, for all the talk about principles-based supervision, is quick to state that its 11 principles are backed up by a 8,500-page rulebook. And the rule book is growing in the wake of the 2007–2008 crisis.

Thus, the best way to design supervision of the financial system is to provide financial institution governance with the right incentives by setting out a number of principles, but to back these principles with a set of prudential rules and standards, and guidelines to further align managers' and supervisors' incentive structures. The current financial crisis, in particular, has shown that the financial system cannot survive on principles alone, without rules, which sometimes will take the form of guidelines, and sometimes need to be prescriptive. Without rules and standards, the incentives of financial institution managers will never be aligned with those of the supervisors. This seems to be the nature of the game in the financial system.

A very illustrative example of aligning incentives through rules where principles fall short, is the generalized call, in the wake of the 2007–08 financial crisis, for forms of dynamic (or countercyclical) provisioning mechanisms. Most countries' supervisory frameworks impose provisioning rules in case assets become nonperforming. These provisions need to be formed at the time the asset becomes nonperforming, i.e., when the economy goes into a downturn and pressure on bank capital increases (i.e., capital shortages occur). The idea behind countercyclical provisioning is that (part of the) provisions be set aside in the good times, when the loans are made. This exercises a dampening effect on the bank's profitability in the short run, and sounds, therefore, counterintuitive. However, it forces bank managers to align their incentives with those of the supervisors who protect the banks' stakeholders. Spain is one of the few countries that went into the 2007–08 financial crisis with a version of such a system in place, and most analysts agree that it has protected the Spanish banking system compared to many other countries.

Now, part of the confusion in the principles versus rules discussion also stems from the fact that many commentators still see rules as the pre-liberalization instrument. Under the financial repression epoch, rules prescribed and governed all sides of the operation of financial institutions, such as price-setting, credit allocation, and the like. When we think of rules nowadays, we have in mind prudential rules—rules that guide the behavior of the financial institutions. They are sometimes prescriptive (risk-based capital ratios, or limits on off-balance sheet activities), but more often serve as guidelines for prudent bank behavior (such as rules about connected lending, exposure to a single borrower, foreign exposure limits, loan classification rules, and loan provisioning rules). This type of prudential rule is perfectly consistent with the establishment of governing principles.

So a further convergence toward a system that sets out a number of overriding principles that are supported by rules and guidelines seems to go in the direction of a best practice for financial sector supervision. The transition to such a balanced supervisory approach needs to be supported by some important changes in the governance of supervisors and supervised institutions as well. In general, as already mentioned, the dialogue between supervisor and supervised institution is critical. More dialogue leads to better mutual understanding of each other's motives and incentives. For supervisors, this transition also implies more attention to accountability and transparency in their own governance. A system that is based, to some extent, on principles gives a great deal of power to the supervisor. At the end of the day, the supervisor decides whether the institutions act in the spirit of the principle. To avoid the use of dual standards, and therefore to avoid undermining a level playing field among financial institutions, supervisors will benefit from accountability arrangements whereby the supervisor can explain to all stakeholders (government, supervised entities, public at large) why they took the decisions that they took.

THE FSA'S 11 PRINCIPLES

1 A firm must conduct its business with integrity.
2 A firm must conduct its business with due skill, care, and diligence.
3 A firm must take reasonable care to organize and control its affairs responsibly and effectively with adequate risk management systems.
4 A firm must maintain adequate financial resources.
5 A firm must observe proper standards of market conduct.
6 A firm must pay due regard to the interest of its customers and treat them fairly.
7 A firm must pay due regard to the information needs of its clients, and communicate information to them in a way which is clear, fair, and not misleading.
8 A firm must manage conflicts of interest fairly, both between itself and its customers, and between a customer and a client.
9 A firm must take reasonable care to ensure the suitability of its advice, and of discretionary decisions for any customer who is entitled to rely on its judgment.
10 A firm must arrange adequate protection for its client's assets when it is responsible for them.
11 A firm must deal with its regulators in an open and cooperative way, and must disclose to the FSA appropriately anything relating to the firm of which the FSA would reasonably expect notice.

Source: Financial Services Authority

▸▸ MORE INFO

Books:

Dewatripont, Mathias, and Jean Tirole. *The Prudential Regulation of Banks*. Cambridge, MA: MIT Press, 1994.

Norton, Joseph. "Selective bank and environmental developments: Supervisory trends upon entering the twenty-first century." In International Monetary Fund (eds). *Current Developments in Monetary and Financial Law*. Washington, DC: IMF, 2003.

"If you must play, decide on three things at the start: the rules of the game, the stakes, and the quitting time."
Anonymous

     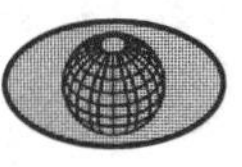 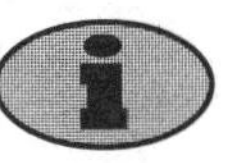 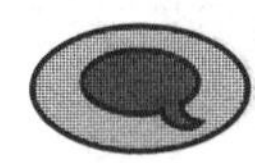 

Articles:

Geneva Reports on the World Economy. "The fundamental principles of financial regulation." Preliminary conference draft, 2009.

Gould, Ronald. "Financial regulation—Flattering misconceptions." Conference presentation, AEI, March 29, 2007. Online at: www.aei.org/event1483

Kydland, Finn, and E. Prescott. "Rules rather than discretion: The inconsistency of optimal plans." *Journal of Political Economy* 85:3 (1977): 473–491.

Quintyn, Marc. "Governance of financial supervisors and its effects—A stocktaking exercise." SUERF Studies, 2007/4.

Schwarcz, Steven. "The 'principles' paradox." Duke Law School Legal Studies, Research Paper No. 205, March 2008.

Wallison, Peter. "Fad or reform: Can principles-based regulation work in the United States?" AEI for Public Policy Research, June 2007.

See Also:

★ How Much Independence for Supervisors in Financial Market Regulation? (pp. 651–654)

★ Viewpoint: Jay W. Lorsch (pp. 150–151)

★ Viewpoint: Viral Acharya and Julian Franks (pp. 632–634)

★ Why Organizations Need to be Regulated—Lessons from History (pp. 736–738)

✔ Principles of Financial Services Regulation (p. 1045)

✔ Understanding Internal Capital Adequacy Assessment Process (ICAAP) (p. 1051)

NOTES

1 Geneva Reports on the World Economy (2009).

2 The oversight of the financial system consists of two elements: Regulation and supervision. Both functions might be performed by one and the same person, but they are different—respectively, rule-setting and rule-implementation and enforcement. Even within the financial system, there are differences in emphasis. For instance, in the securities area, the term "regulator" is used more frequently than "supervisor," because in their tasks, the regulatory aspect dominates. In this article, we prefer to use the word "supervisor," mainly for the sake of conciseness. However, when we refer to the regulatory function specifically, we will use that term.

"There are three secrets to managing. The first secret is have patience. The second is be patient. And the third most important secret is patience." Chuck Tanner

  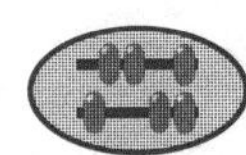 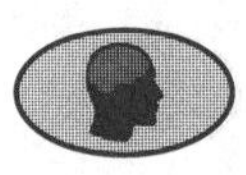  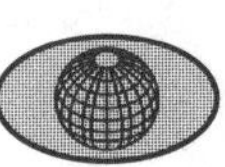   

Procedures for Reporting Financial Risk in Islamic Finance by Daud Vicary Abdullah and Ramesh Pillai

EXECUTIVE SUMMARY

- Uncertainty is a defining feature of the economic environment. Economic agents' perceptions of risk, together with their willingness and ability to bear it, fundamentally shape decisions, transactions, and market prices. Well-considered decisions should be based on information that helps to highlight existing risks and uncertainties. An important component of the information system of an organization or economy is financial reporting, through which an enterprise conveys information about its financial performance and condition to external users, often identified with its actual and potential claimants. It stands to reason, therefore, that financial reporting should provide a good sense of the impact of those risks and uncertainties on measures of valuation, income, and cash flows.
- It is important to reconcile the perspectives of accounting standard setters on the one hand, and prudential authorities on the other, on what information should be reported, and on how it should be portrayed. The final goal is a financial reporting system that is consistent, as far as possible, with sound risk management and management practices and that can serve as a basis for well-informed decisions by outside investors as well as prudential authorities.
- Outside investors, be they equity or debt holders, would normally require certain information about the financial performance of a firm so as to guide their decisions. First, they would surely wish to form a view about the firm's past and current profitability, solvency, and liquidity at a given point in time. Second, they would probably also like to develop a picture of the risk profile of those attributes over time and, hence, of their potential future evolution. Third, they might additionally wish to gain a sense of how reliable or accurate those measures are. Combined, these three elements would provide the raw material to inform views about expected returns properly adjusted for risk and for the inevitable uncertainties that surround measurement. These three types of information correspond to the key categories into which the ideal set can be divided—namely, first movement, risk, and measurement error—and they are equally applicable to financial reporting in an Islamic finance environment.

INTRODUCTION

The key elements of Islamic finance can be summarized as follows:

- Materiality and validity of transactions: There is no profit sharing without risk taking, and earning profit is legitimized by engaging in economic venture. Money is not a commodity but a medium of exchange, a store of value, and a unit of measurement.
- Mutuality of risk sharing: Clearly defined risk and profit sharing characteristics serve as an additional built-in mechanism. There are clearly laid out terms and conditions.
- Avoidance of *riba* (interest), *maysir* (gambling), and *gharar* (uncertainty).

The key elements of Islamic financial risk can be summarized as follows:

- The reporting of financial risk in an Islamic financial institution (IFI) requires greater transparency and disclosure than does its conventional counterpart.
- This is particularly true with respect to additional *shariah* governance and some risk areas that are unique to Islamic finance.
- IFIs have greater fiduciary duties and responsibility to their stakeholders than do conventional institutions.
- The additional duties and responsibilities of IFIs are overseen by the IFI's *shariah* board.

First-movement information describes income, the balance sheet, and cash flows at a point in time. It is the type of information with the longest tradition by far in accounting.

Risk information is fundamentally forward looking. Future profits, future cash flows, and future valuations are intrinsically uncertain. Risk information is designed to capture the prospective range of outcomes for the variables of profit as measured at a particular point in time.

Measurement error information designates the margin of error or uncertainty that surrounds the measurement of the variables of profit, including those that quantify risk. The need for this type of information arises whenever these variables have to be estimated. For instance, measurement error would be zero for first-movement information concerning items that were valued at observable market prices for which a deep and liquid market existed. But it would be positive if, say, such items were marked to model and/or traded in illiquid markets, since a number of assumptions would need to be made to arrive at such estimates.

There has been a wide array of change and development in Islamic finance in recent years. The Accounting and Auditing Organization for Islamic Financial Institutions (AAOIFI) has tackled several of the pertinent issues in its Financial Accounting Standards (FAS). In particular, FAS 1 relates to general presentation and disclosure in the financial statements of Islamic banks and financial institutions. FAS 5 relates to the disclosure of bases for profit allocation between owners' equity and investment account holders. FAS 17 concerns Investment. FAS 22 and FAS 23 deal with segment reporting and consolidation, respectively. AAOIFI Governance Standards 1–6 also provide relevant guidance. In particular, Governance Standard 6, Principles of Governance Section 7, gives guidance in respect of risk management.

Understanding Islamic Banking Risk

Islamic financial institutions are exposed to all the risks that a conventional one is. However, there are some fundamental differences, particularly in the aspect of *shariah* compliance, where noncompliance can lead to reputational risk and worse.

Typical banking risk exposure includes the following:

- *financial:* balance sheet, capital adequacy, credit, liquidity;
- *operational:* fraud, product, business services, system failure, delivery, and process management;
- *business:* country, reputational, regulatory, legal, macropolicy;
- *event:* political, banking crisis, contagion.

BASIC RISK ANALYSIS

Ratios and analytics are in a constant state of evolution in order to reflect the growing

"Only through international recognition and consistent application of these (AAOIFI) standards will the Islamic banking and finance industry realize the full benefits of accurate and transparent financial reporting." Mohamad Nedal Alchaar

     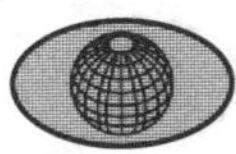   

challenges of Islamic finance and the constant stream of new products. In particular, the convergence of international supervisory standards, initiated by the Islamic Financial Services Board (IFSB) since its inauguration in 2002, have contributed to this developing landscape. Typical ratios relate to liquidity, capital adequacy, insider and connected financing, financing portfolio quality, large exposures, and foreign exchange positions

Peer group benchmarking is a relevant measurement criterion. Here the behavior of an individual institution can be measured against peer group trends and industry norms. Significant areas such as profitability, product risk, the structure of the balance sheet, and capital adequacy come to mind. Any significant deviations of the individual institution from what is considered to be the norm must be investigated and understood, as they may well represent an early warning for negative trends in both the IFI and the industry.

What's Different in an IFI?

Islamic contracts and the allocation and sharing of risk: The analysis described above should also include the nature of the Islamic contracts included in the balance sheet and a basic understanding of how the risk is allocated or shared. Therefore a fundamental understanding of the IFI's balance sheet is required.

Liabilities: These include equity capital, reserves, investment accounts (*mudarabah* and *musharakah*) and demand deposits (*amanah*). Money is deposited in investment accounts in the full knowledge that the deposit will be invested in a risk-bearing project, where the profit will be divided between the institution and the depositor on a prearranged profit-sharing ratio. The depositor is also exposed to the risk of loss if the projects invested in do not perform. In many ways these types of deposit have a similarity with an equity investment in the bank, and it is this lack of clarity between shareholders and investors/depositors that can lead to a perception of increased riskiness. IFSB and AAOIFI guidelines have provided significant help in clarifying this issue.

Assets: These include short-term trade finance (*murabahah* and *salam*), medium term financing (*ijarah* , *istisna*, etc.), long-term partnerships (*musharakah*) and fee-based services (*kifala*, etc.).

These asset and liability contracts carried in the balance sheet of an Islamic financial intermediary give a clear indication of two fundamental differences between Islamic financial intermediaries and their conventional counterparts. First, the relationship between the depositors and the bank is based on profit and loss sharing principles; and second, the asset side of the bank may include "risky" assets such as *mudarabah* and *musharakah* that a conventional bank may not carry.

KEY ELEMENTS OF GOOD CORPORATE GOVERNANCE

Good corporate governance is defined by the set of relationships between the institution's senior management, its board, its shareholders, and other stakeholders:

- *Corporate strategy* defines how success can be measured.
- *Responsibilities* include assignment and enforcement.
- *Strong financial risk management* should be independent of the business, with good internal control and separation of duties.
- *Good values and a code of conduct* should be well articulated and maintained, especially in the area of related parties.
- *Proper incentives* must be consistent with objectives, performance, and values
- *The roles of stakeholders* must be clearly set out.

The Roles of Stakeholders

- *Regulators* monitor the statutory environment and help to create an enabling environment
- *Shariah boards* protect the rights of all stakeholders in accordance with the principles of *shariah.*
- *The board of directors* sets the direction of the bank and ensure its soundness.
- *The executive management* executes the direction of the board and has sufficient competence and knowledge to manage the financial risks.
- *The board audit committee and internal audit* are logical extensions of the board's risk management function. They assist executive management in identifying and managing risk areas.
- *External auditors* are responsible for validating the results and providing assurance that appropriate governance processes are in place.
- *Market participants* should accept responsibility for their own investment decisions. They therefore need transparent disclosure of information from financial institutions
- *Shareholders* can appoint officers in charge of the governance process, subject to appropriate screening on related party transactions.

THE ROLE OF *SHARIAH*

Shariah boards are unique to IFIs. They have a responsibility to monitor the activities of the financial institution and to ensure compliance with *shariah* principles. As such, the *shariah* board acts as a governance body to protect the rights of the stakeholders in the IFI.

In some jurisdictions, national *shariah* boards have been formed, which work closely with regulators and supervisors in protecting the rights of all investors.

TRANSPARENCY AND DISCLOSURE

Practices in IFIs have improved significantly in recent years, but there is still room for improvement in a number of areas:

- Quantitative methods for the measurement of risk still need improvement. AAOIFI is driving changes in this area.
- The decisions and methodology of the *shariah* boards should be disclosed more publicly. This will enhance the credibility of IFIs and also help to educate the public on the *shariah* decision-making process.
- There needs to be a clear demarcation between equity and depositors' funds.
- The financial information infrastructure requires constant improvement to ensure that a "virtuous cycle" of information continually forces practitioners to adopt sound corporate governance practices.
- Standardized reporting practices throughout IFIs would significantly assist in improving the collectability and analysis of data from them.

▸▸ MAKING IT HAPPEN

Good financial risk management is about changing behaviors and attitudes. Boards and executive management are responsible for setting the implementation process, and regulators are responsible for creating a conducive environment. For example:

- The board must set the direction.
- Regulators must ensure a supportive environment that encourages transparency and good market discipline, thereby creating a virtuous cycle.
- The market must value good financial discipline and risk management and must reward compliant companies accordingly.
- All stakeholders must recognize their responsibilities.

"As Islamic Finance becomes an integral part of the international financial system, it will be increasingly tested by developments such as the current international financial crisis. The key for the Islamic financial industry is to ensure that it will not be a source for such financial instability." Zeti Akhtar Aziz

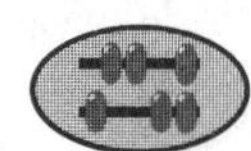

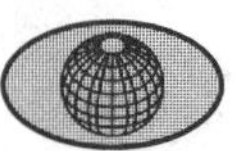

CONCLUSION

There are many similarities between conventional and Islamic risk management, as well has some significant differences, which have been highlighted above. The risk management process itself in an IFI does not differ much from conventional banking practices. However, it is the analysis and the identification of the risk environment that differ.

The balance sheet of the IFI needs to be structured in a way that will allow the easy identification of risk, particularly in the area of sources of funding and in the application of those funds for financing purposes.

The role of the *shariah* board is significant in protecting the rights of all stakeholders and ensuring that the business of the IFI is conducted in accordance with the principles of *shariah*.

▸▸ MORE INFO

Books:

Greuning, Hennie Van, and Sonja Brajovic Bratanovic. *Analysing and Managing Banking Risk: A Framework for Assessing Corporate Governance and Financial Risk Management.* Washington, DC: World Bank, 2000.

Karim, Rifaat Ahmed Abdel, and Simon Archer (eds). *Islamic Finance: The Regulatory Challenge*. Singapore: Wiley, 2007. See in particular Sundararajan, V. "Risk characteristics of Islamic products: Implications for risk measurement and supervision," pp. 40–68.

Article:

Grais, Wafiq, and Zamir Iqbal. "Corporate governance challenges of Islamic financial Institutions." Paper presented at Seventh Harvard University Forum on Islamic Finance, 2006.

Websites:

AAOIFI (Accounting and Auditing Organization for Islamic Financial Institutions): www.aaoifi.com

IFSB (Islamic Financial Services Board): www.ifsb.org

PRMIA (Professional Risk Managers' International Association): www.prmia.org

See Also:

★ Identifying the Main Regulatory Challenges for Islamic Finance (pp. 658–660)
★ Islamic Modes of Finance and the Role of *Sukuk* (pp. 548–550)
✔ Business Ethics in Islamic Finance (p. 900)
✔ Key Islamic Banking Instruments and How They Work (p. 927)
✔ Key Principles of Islamic Finance (p. 928)
✔ An Overview of *Shariah*-Compliant Funds (p. 942)
✔ The Role of the *Shariah* Advisery Board in Islamic Finance (p. 931)
An Introduction to Islamic Finance Theory and Practice (p. 1283)

"It is while Islamic Finance is still in the early stage of development that the opportunity has been taken to strengthen its foundations and put in place the prerequisites that will pave the way for its development and safeguard the stability of the system." Ulanddy Uyob

  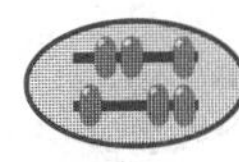   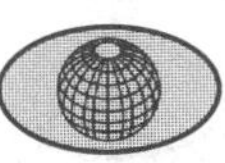   

Viewpoint: Sir John Stuttard
Days of Reckoning

INTRODUCTION

Sir John Stuttard has spent his career with accountants, PricewaterhouseCoopers, of which he is now a vice-chairman. He has focused on auditing, acquisitions, stock exchange listings, and privatizations for UK, US, and Scandinavian companies. He was made a Knight, and then a Commander, of the Order of the Lion of Finland, and has been Chairman of the Finnish–British Chamber of Commerce. He served in the Cabinet Office for two years and spent five years in China as PwC executive chairman. He has also been a director of the China Britain Business Council. He is currently a trustee of Charities Aid Foundation and of Morden College, a governor of King Edward's School, Witley, and on the board of other charities. He served as Sheriff of London in 2005–2006 and Lord Mayor in 2006–2007.

THE BLAME GAME

When something goes wrong, regrettably, I'm afraid it's human nature to point the finger at someone else. All too rarely does one admit responsibility and a share of the blame.

Back in the late summer of 2007, when it was clear that many financial institutions were facing difficulties, the first group to be attacked was the credit rating agencies. In September that year, European Union Commissioner Charlie McCreevy criticized credit rating agencies such as Moody's and Standard & Poor's for their conflicts of interest and poor methodologies. European Central Bank president Jean-Claude Trichet joined in.

Then the focus switched to the regulators, particularly after Northern Rock in the United Kingdom had to be bailed out by the government. It was unusual and refreshing, therefore, to witness the United Kingdom's Financial Services Authority publish two separate internal reports criticizing itself for shortcomings caused by frequent changes in senior staff, inadequate review and discussion of findings, and failure to engage properly with Northern Rock.

Towards the end of 2008 and during the first two months of 2009, the criticism has been directed at bank executives, with their large bonuses, and to the non-executive directors who, it is alleged, should have exercised better corporate governance.

So who actually is to blame for what happened and what needs to be done to limit the possibility of it happening again? To begin with, we should all have seen it coming. Large trade surpluses in China and the Gulf countries generated huge foreign exchange reserves, which were typically invested in US Treasury bonds and Eurobonds, leading to inflated credit in the global financial system and the lowering of real interest rates.

This cheap, available money led to an extension of credit around the world. At the same time, investors were searching for higher yield and financial institutions became even more imaginative at creating new financial instruments. Financial activity exploded with, for example, the value of outstanding credit default swaps increasing from almost nothing in 2000 to over US$60 trillion in 2007. Gearing by financial companies increased tenfold in the period 1987 to 2007 and household debt doubled.

Was it surprising, therefore, that the bubble eventually burst? When there is too much credit in the system and when the price of borrowing does not reflect the intrinsic risk, there is bound to be a day of reckoning. And the fallout has been simply devastating for many.

Our global institutions, our governments, and many economists seemed content to allow agreeably high levels of economic growth to continue without spotting the thunder clouds gathering. And the media, usually so quick to criticize, didn't blow the whistle either. We were all riding on a cloud of hubris.

THE ROLE OF THE REGULATORS

And what of the regulators? A major problem is that our financial companies have become global, whereas financial regulators are, for understandable national reasons, predominantly national. And they each have their own structures and methodologies when it comes to regulation, just like different religions.

For example, in the United States there are many regulators for different parts of the financial sector and there is an insurance regulator in each state. In Britain, there is just one, the FSA, and in many other countries, such as China, there are three.

But the philosophies and methodologies are also very diverse. The French, the Germans, and the Chinese are very prescriptive. Their form of regulation is rules-based. Yet, America was very liberal and flexible in its approach. In his book *The Age of Turbulence*, completed in June 2007 when the crisis was brewing but not yet fully upon us or recognized, Alan Greenspan, formerly Chairman of the Federal Reserve, wrote: "Public sector surveillance is no longer up to the task," and "We have no sensible choice other than to let markets work."

I was concerned to read this. While the capabilities of financial regulators to provide oversight have indeed diminished in recent years because of the complexity of financial markets, regulators are appointed by governments to protect people and to protect economies from systemic failure, as well as fraud.

But then much of the blame must be laid at the door of those banks that took the greatest risk or did not test their strategies and their business models, or made acquisitions at high prices. Lehmans is no longer with us and others such as the Royal Bank of Scotland are, effectively, in state ownership. Bankers have apologized. The finger has also been pointed at nonexecutive directors for allowing such risks to be taken on their watch.

THE RESPONSIBILITIES OF GOVERNMENTS

At the end of the day, governments must

  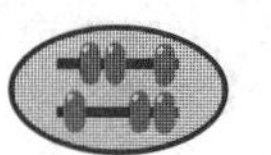 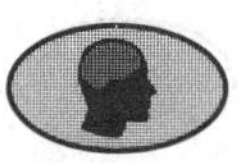  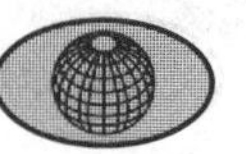 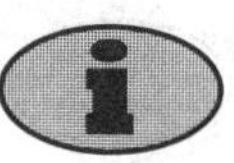  

take responsibility for the effective management of the economy. They are expected to ensure economic growth, reasonable levels of employment, limited inflation and the health of the various sectors (not least the financial sector to provide a payments system), credit for investors, as well as opportunities for savers to invest for retirement. After all, if things go wrong, governments have to step in, as we have witnessed throughout the world in recent months.

At present, the conflicting needs of deleveraging banks yet encouraging bank lending represent a real dilemma for any government seeking to recover after the credit bubble has burst.

The priority must be to prevent hardship. Yet this should not be at the expense of long-term remedies or driven by short-term political expedience. The world's political leaders have an opportunity to put forward simple propositions.

To try anything too complicated would not work. After all, there are as many views globally about the form and manner of regulation as there are faiths, and it is inconceivable that there will ever be one world religion.

The goals should be very clear. The politicians should encourage a world body —possibly the IMF—to monitor global trends and influence national governments. They should establish a global College of Regulators to share best practice, establish clear responsibilities, and ensure better communication between regulators.

PRINCIPLES FOR BEST PRACTICE

They need to develop a set of principles (not rules) for best regulatory practice, based around improvement in risk assessment, risk management, closer relations between regulators and those regulated, and recruitment of higher caliber staff in the regulatory bodies. That means rejecting the laissez-faire approach as represented by the phrase: "We have no sensible choice other than to let markets work."

Regulators should be encouraged to be more interventionist with financial institutions when identifying risky strategies or high-risk product areas and request directors to cease these activities. Regulators also need to control the shadow banking system and to focus more on risk. But we don't want more box-ticking. Instead, we should adopt the maxim of "one in, one out" when it comes to new regulations. We need better regulation, not more regulation.

Finally there should be a review of accounting rules on off-balance sheet credit and securitized intermediation, to ensure that arrangements to remove potential risks from balance sheets are correctly communicated to shareholders and others. That however does not mean giving in to suggestions that we should turn the clock back on "mark-to-market", since to do so would hide the truth and delude those who rely on corporate reports.

In most countries, with the exception of China, there is a need to reduce debt and to encourage savings. We cannot keep living beyond our means. That is unfair on future generations as well leading, inevitably, to financial and economic hardship.

CORPORATE GOVERNANCE

Action is also required by companies and their directors. During the last decade, banks have merged with investment banks and have become hugely innovative. There have been suggestions that the financial sector has become too innovative, driven by high remuneration and encouraging bonuses. New instruments have become so complex, prompting Warren Buffet to say in 2002 that "derivatives are financial weapons of mass destruction, carrying dangers that, while now latent, are potentially dangerous".

There is anecdotal evidence that many senior executives did not fully understand what their bright young things had cooked up. There is further evidence that nonexecutive directors did not fully understand the complexities of the business and did not fully appreciate the risks.

So it is necessary to examine and change remuneration systems to put a greater emphasis on risk assessment and risk management, at the same time preserving innovation and managed risk-taking.

Equally important is strengthening corporate governance yet further, by supporting nonexecutive directors more, so that they perform their job better. They need comprehensive information about the business, about new business areas, about potential risks, about plans to innovate, and manage risks. They need more, independent assessments of business trends, of management performance, and of prices to be paid for major acquisitions.

We know from experience that things go wrong when a dominant, enthusiastic chief executive is not subject to challenge from a strong chairman and a talented, informed board. The wrong strategies are chosen, inflated prices are paid for acquisitions, and frauds often result.

In the United States, there is a need to separate the roles of chief executive and an independent chairman. In the United Kingdom we believe that we have the right corporate governance framework in place, but it doesn't always work in practice as well as it might.

It has been suggested that chief financial officers should be more independent from their chief executives by, for example, arranging for them to report jointly to the independent chairmen—and that chairmen should also be involved in selecting and assessing the performance of chief financial officers.

Another proposal is for nonexecutive directors to have a dedicated corporate executive to advise them on particular issues and to commission independent valuations of proposed major acquisitions.

It is also important that nonexecutive directors do not take on too many directorships. That means they will be able to devote more time to the companies on whose boards they sit—and, to facilitate this, ensure that they are properly paid, given their knowledge, expertise, and expected time commitment.

Credit rating agencies also need to review their practice to ensure that conflicts of interest are managed and that they are seen to be independent. Attacks on these agencies are reminiscent of the attacks on auditors about a decade ago—and remedies have been found in my profession, with which governments, investors, and commentators have confirmed that they are now satisfied.

REBUILDING TRUST AND CONFIDENCE

But a further and final thought is the need to rebuild trust and confidence in the financial system. We, here in London, have long prided ourselves in our integrity where the phrase "my word is my bond" was in common parlance. A high standard of ethics is the bedrock of professionalism in banking, share dealing, and trading, as it is in medicine. Perhaps one outcome of the financial crisis is a greater awareness of rebuilding such fine values in the global financial system.

We need to rediscover Adam Smith's concept of socially responsible capitalism. This is a debate in which we should all be engaged—to minimize the chances that the current financial crisis will recur.

➧➧ MORE INFO

See Also:

John Kenneth Galbraith (p. 1166)

"One of the most striking differences between a cat and a lie is that the cat has only nine lives." Mark Twain

  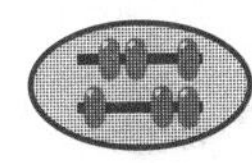   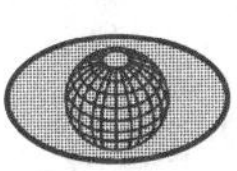   

The Rationale of International Financial Reporting Standards and Their Acceptance by Major Countries by Véronique Weets

EXECUTIVE SUMMARY

- Differences in accounting systems create inefficient transfers of information that have a negative impact on the allocation of resources, efficiency of capital markets, and tax harmonization.
- International financial reporting standards (IFRS) are standards published by the International Accounting Standards Board (IASB), which is committed to develop a set of high-quality, global standards that require transparent and comparable information in general purpose financial statements.
- The IASB is a private organization that has no legal power to enforce the application of its standards.
- After the implementation of the 4th, 7th, and 8th directives, the European Union decided in 2002 to oblige the use of standards published by the IASB as from 2005 for the preparation of the consolidated financial statements of entities listed on a European market.
- Foreign registrants in the United States no longer have to reconcile their financial statements to US GAAP if they apply IFRS.
- Local amendments of IFRS reduce the comparability of IFRS financial statements, one of the objectives of the IASB.

INTRODUCTION

Why Financial Reporting Needs to Be Harmonized

Although basic accounting principles such as the accrual basis and the going-concern assumption are widely accepted, the application of these principles in different economic and cultural environments has led to significant differences in how accountants report similar transactions. Local differences exist in, for example, the treatment of goodwill, the definition of a group, treatment of borrowing costs, measurement of impairment, and the treatment of deferred taxes.

For entities that are globally active, these differences in financial reporting requirements create extra complications in terms of preparing, consolidating, auditing, and interpreting financial statements. This is because financial statements have to be reconciled before consolidated financial statements can be prepared, the analysis of potential acquirees in a foreign country increases the costs of the mergers and acquisitions department because they have to familiarize themselves with a foreign accounting system, and investors have to be informed about differences in financial reporting. In general, the differences in accounting treatments create non-optimal information for users of financial statements, which in turn leads to less than optimal allocation of resources.

The need for a harmonized, high-quality set of accounting rules is not new. Several initiatives have been taken to arrive at a globally accepted set of financial reporting standards. An important player in this is the European Union. Since the 1970s it has made serious efforts to harmonize the national accounting rules within Europe, resulting in several directives and regulations. Other organizations concerned with international aspects of accounting, active since the 1970s, are: the International Federation of Accountants (IFAC), the Accountants' International Study Group, the International Organization of Securities Commissions (IOSCO), the Fédération des Experts Comptables Européens (FEE), the Inter-American Accounting Association (IAAA), and the Organisation for Economic Co-operation and Development (OECD).

HARMONIZATION WORK BY THE IASB

In 1973 the predecessor of the International Accounting Standards Board (IASB), the International Accounting Standards Committee (IASC), was founded by the professional accounting organizations of nine countries: Australia, Canada, France, Japan, Mexico, the Netherlands, the United Kingdom (together with Ireland), the United States and Germany. The IASC was operational until 2001, and published 41 International Accounting Standards (IAS), some of which were later replaced or amended. The objectives of the IASC were to develop a single set of high-quality, global accounting standards that require transparent and comparable information in general purpose financial statements.

In 2001 the IASC was succeeded by the International Accounting Standards Committee Foundation (IASCF). The organization within the IASCF that publishes standards and interpretations is the IASB. One of the changes was that new standards were no longer called International Accounting Standards (IAS) but International Financial Reporting Standards (IFRS). This means that the current list of IFRS consists of a series of IAS, standards originally published by the IASC before 2001 (although some were amended afterwards), and a number of IFRS, which were published by the IASB after 2001. Table 1 gives a list of standards published by March 31, 2009.

Although the IASB cooperates with national accounting standard-setters to achieve convergence, it is a private organization with no legal power to enforce the application of its standards. Financial support is received from the major accounting firms, private financial institutions, and industrial companies throughout the world, central and development banks, and other international and professional organizations.

ACCEPTANCE OF IASB STANDARDS BY THE MAJOR COUNTRIES

At the moment nearly 100 countries require or accept financial statements that are presented in accordance with IFRS. Figure 1 gives an overview.

Europe was one of the first regions to require the application of IFRS. In 2002 it published the IAS Regulation (EC)1606/2002, which required listed entities to use IFRS for the preparation and presentation of their consolidated financial statements as from 2005. EU member states were allowed to enlarge this obligation to unlisted entities and/or individual financial statements. Since the legislation takes the form of a regulation (as opposed to a directive), member states do not have to translate the requirements to their national legislation. To ensure that current and future standards do not act to the detriment of European interests, an endorsement mechanism was established. At this moment the difference between the standards of the IASB and the endorsed standards concerns only hedge accounting (this is called the "carve-out"). Once a standard

"The US GAAP is an unsustainable Tower of Babel." Sir David Tweedie

   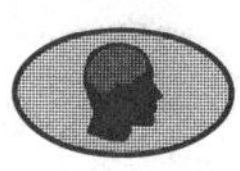  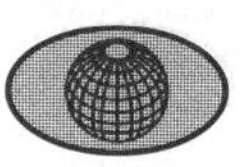  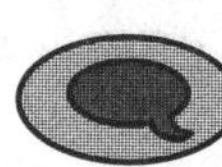 

Table 1. International Standards published 31 March 2009

IAS	Topic	Comment
1	Presentation of financial statements	
2	Inventories	
3*	Consolidated financial statements	Superseded by IAS 27 and IAS 28
4*	Depreciation accounting	Withdrawn in 1999
5*	Information to be disclosed in financial statements	Superseded by revised IAS 1
6*	Accounting responses to changing prices	Superseded by IAS 15
7	Statement of cash flows	
8	Accounting policies, changes in accounting estimates, and errors	
9*	Research and development costs	Superseded by IAS 38
10	Events after the balance sheet date	
11	Construction contracts	
12	Income taxes	
13*	Presentation of current assets and current liabilities	Superseded by revised IAS 1
14*	Segment reporting	Superseded by IFRS 8
15*	Information reflecting the effects of changing prices	Withdrawn in 2003
16	Property, plant and equipment	
17	Leases	
18	Revenue	
19	Employee benefits	
20	Accounting for government grants and disclosure of government assistance	
21	The effects of changes in foreign exchange rates	
22*	Business combinations	Superseded by IFRS 3
23	Borrowing costs	
24	Related party disclosures	
25*	Accounting for investments	Superseded by IAS 39 and IAS 40
26	Accounting and reporting by retirement benefit plans	
27	Consolidated and separate financial statements	
28	Investments in associates	
29	Financial reporting in hyperinflationary economies	
30*	Disclosures in financial statements of banks and similar financial institutions	Superseded by IFRS 7
31	Interests in joint ventures	
32	Financial instruments: presentation	
33	Earnings per share	
34	Interim financial reporting	
35*	Discontinuing operations	Superseded by IFRS 5
36	Impairment of assets	
37	Provisions, contingent liabilities and contingent assets	
38	Intangible assets	
39	Financial instruments: recognition and measurement	
40	Investment property	
41	Agriculture	
IFRS	**Topic**	**Comment**
1	First-time adoption of international financial reporting standards	
2	Share-based payment	
3	Business combinations	
4	Insurance contracts	
5	Non-current assets held for sale and discontinued operations	
6	Exploration for and evaluation of mineral resources	
7	Financial instruments: disclosures	
8	Operating segments	

* Superseded or withdrawn.

or interpretation is endorsed (a process that can take a year or more), it is published in the official journal of the European Union and is applicable in all member states.

Since the publication of the Norwalk Agreement in 2002, both the Financial Accounting Standards Board (FASB), the regulator in the United States, and the IASB have published new and changed standards in order to converge US Generally Accepted Accounting Principles (US GAAP) with IFRS. Examples are IFRS 5/SFAS 144, IFRS 8/SFAS 131, and the new version of IFRS 3. In November 2007 the US Securities and Exchange Commission (SEC) voted to allow foreign companies to submit financial statements to the Commission using IFRS as adopted by the IASB (with a temporary exception for the European carve-out) without having to include a reconciliation of the IFRS data to US GAAP. The next step would be to allow US companies to use IFRS for the preparation of their financial statements. It is estimated that this will be possible as from 2011.

The Australian Accounting Standards Board issued 40 accounting standards applicable for financial years beginning on or after January 1, 2005. Those standards are sometimes referred to as Australian equivalents to International Financial Reporting Standards (A-IFRS). Considerable differences from IFRS remain.

In February 2006, the China Accounting Standards Committee (CASC) adopted a comprehensive set of New Chinese Accounting Standards (CAS) that took effect as of the 2007 financial reports of listed companies in China. Unlisted companies are also encouraged to use the new CAS. These cover nearly all the topics under the current IFRS and, with a few exceptions, are substantially in line with IFRS. Since then, both mandatory interpretations and less formal guidance for application of the new standards have been issued.

Other countries like Brazil that require the application of IFRS for the preparation of consolidated financial statements of listed entities as of 2010, Canada that requires the application of IFRS for publicly accountable profit-oriented entities as of 2011, India that will require the application of IFRS by listed entities as well as banks, insurance companies and large companies as of 2011 are currently also in the process of implementing IFRS for the preparation of financial statements. India has indicated that it might amend IFRS to take into account "Indian conditions." Japan is involved in a convergence project with the IASB.

CONCLUSION

Differences in accounting methods create information costs for the preparers, auditors, and users of financial statements. Several organizations recognized the need to harmonize financial reporting, and the European Union was one of the first to publish directives to reduce differences in the reporting of similar transactions.

The IASB is a private organization that

"Before you can really start setting financial goals, you need to determine where you stand financially." David Bach

     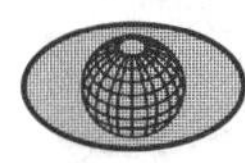   

publishes standards and interpretations for global acceptance. More and more countries allow or insist on the use of IFRS for the preparation of financial statements. However, some countries or regions appear to believe that these IFRS must be adapted to their specific needs—for example, Australia with the creation of A-IFRS, Europe instituting a "carve-out" for hedge accounting, and India looking to adapt the standards to an Indian context. These local interpretations of IFRS might give a false impression of comparability and lead to erroneous conclusions if the local differences are not known by the user of the information. The United States, by contrast, has stated that foreign registrants that use IFRS instead of US GAAP must apply IFRS as published by the IASB. Users of the European carve-out are encouraged to comply with full IFRS as soon as possible, and within a maximum of two years.

Figure 1. The global move towards IFRS. (© Cethys, 2008)

▸▸ MORE INFO

Books:

IASCF. *International Financial Reporting Standards (IFRSs)*. London: IASCF Publications, 2008.

Nobes, Christopher, and Robert B. Parker. *Comparative International Accounting*. 10th ed. Harlow, UK: FT Prentice Hall, 2008.

Websites:

The International Accounting Standards Board (IASB) website gives access to all IASB standards and interpretations: www.iasb.org

Deloitte's site IAS Plus has daily updates on what is happening in the IFRS world and information on almost all IASB standards: www.iasplus.com

IAS Plus also gives information on the acceptance of IFRS in nearly 200 jurisdictions on this page: www.iasplus.com/country/country.htm

The website of the European Financial Reporting Advisery Group (EFRAG) has information on the endorsement of standards in Europe: www.efrag.org

See Also:

- Financial Accounting and Reporting (p. 1256)
- ★ Accounting for Business Combinations in Accordance with International Financial Reporting Standards (IFRS) Requirements (pp. 598–600)
- ★ Accounting for Share-Based Payments under IFRS (pp. 601–603)
- ★ Effective Financial Reporting and Auditing: Importance and Limitations (pp. 623–625)
- ★ Has Financial Reporting Impacted on Internal Auditing Negatively? (pp. 638–641)
- ★ UnderstandingtheRequirementsforPreparingIFRSFinancialStatements(pp. 723–724)
- ✔ IFRS: The Basics (p. 1036)
- ✔ Key Accounting Standards and Organizations (p. 1038)
- ✔ The Ten Accounting Principles (p. 1050)
- ✔ Understanding the Key Components of GAAP: The Continuing Concern Concept (p. 1054)

"Any informed borrower is simply less vulnerable to fraud and abuse." Alan Greenspan

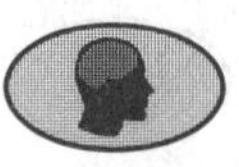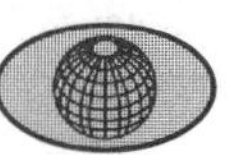

Revising Basel II—But at What Cost?

by Vishal Vedi

EXECUTIVE SUMMARY

This article examines:

- Why Basel II is now seen as too pro-cyclical.
- The unfortunate timing which saw the implementation of Basel II taking effect just as the global recession took hold.
- The Basel Committee is already reshaping Basel II to take account of the weaknesses discovered so far.
- The future of securitization in the post crash world is now under consideration.
- The shape of regulation to come.

INTRODUCTION

Pro-cyclicality and its Issues

The future regulation of banking is currently a major area of focus for supervisors and policy-makers, in particular, with the G20 recently committing to strengthening how banks are regulated. There seems to be consensus among stakeholders that additional capital, of the right quality, is required in the system. There is also concern that the existing Basel II requirements are too pro-cyclical to continue to act as the blueprint for bank regulatory capital guidance, without some revision. This is not a new insight. A number of senior figures in the industry have long been concerned that the models behind Basel II might well be pro-cyclical.

A pro-cyclical measure has the unfortunate effect of reinforcing the direction of a particular cycle. In boom times, for example, the models perceive less risk, with banks having to hold a lower amount of regulatory capital for a typical exposure. This, in turn, frees up capital, which allows the banks to pour more credit into the financial system. Other things being equal, this process will continue as long as the economy remains in upswing. Similarly, when the cycle turns negative, at precisely the point when bank lending is freezing and governments are trying to restart economies, the models perceive higher levels of risk and suggest that banks should hold higher reserves, exacerbating lending difficulties.

Because of this, the Basel Committee took action to try to manage the pro-cyclicality of the Basel II framework, for example, by stressing loss-given defaults and probability of defaults to see how these parameters would potentially behave in a downturn, and to suggest corrections. However, the extent of the pro-cyclicality issue was, nevertheless, difficult to gauge, and, with hindsight, it is now clear that the implications are potentially far more severe than was thought when Basel II was originally being implemented.

A CASE OF BAD TIMING

One of the peculiarities of the global crisis, in the context of Basel II, is the timing. After a lengthy gestation, beginning 10 years ago, the regulations began to be implemented in the European Union in 2007, with full implementation the following year. The United States, by contrast, only introduced Basel II on a mandatory basis for its 10 or so largest banks, reasoning that as these banks accounted for the vast majority of overseas business done by US banks, and, as the Basel Committee designed Basel II primarily with internationally active banks in mind, it made sense to restrict implementation to these. Implementation costs were also a major consideration. US implementation commenced on a phased basis this year.

At the same time, the credit crunch began in summer 2007, which means that Basel II had not been implemented to any great extent beforehand. This is an important point to grasp, because the events that brought about the present global financial slowdown were in preparation for many years prior to 2007. Basel II, then, is not responsible for the crash, and it is not a failure because of the crash. However, its continued implementation and adoption has now become much more problematic. It is clear that there are a number of areas, for example, the way risks interact, that the models did not fully capture, and which Basel II arguably did not encompass, not least because of its focus on individual firms rather than, in addition, considering system-wide effects.

There were also issues with credit-rating agencies. The difficulties with the rating agencies are now well documented. The ratings for a range of structured credit products were shown to be unreliable in the credit-crunch environment, and some form of international regulation of rating agencies now seems inevitable. However, in defense of the rating agencies, it could be argued that the credit default swap market was commonly understood as being relatively safe, and we now know that the instruments were incorrectly premised, that the exposures they brought with them were not fully understood, and that the hedges that banks put in place turned out to be ineffective when they were needed, not least because of the extent of the movement in the underlying asset (US property prices) on which so many of them were based.

At the time, though, a bank with a large CDO book, all of which was AAA-rated by leading rating agencies, and where any exposure the bank had was hedged out, or thought to be hedged out, did not look risky. With hindsight, it is clear that the risks were significant, and furthermore, because of the linkages between exposed positions, the hedges were being backed by organizations which themselves were massively exposed. The result was a freezing of liquidity right across the market.

THE BASEL COMMITTEE RETHINK

Where things stand at present is that the Basel Committee is working to revise its accord. Some areas of focus include the trading book, treatment of securitization and resecuritization, pro-cyclicality, and the quality of capital. Basel II, of course, is not a legislative body, but a committee of national supervisors, historically from the G7 plus a handful of other countries, but recently expanded to include countries such as China, India, and Russia. It will be down to national governments to implement the new regulations. Within the European Union, this will be driven at a European level.

Already, as we have seen in the United Kingdom from the report on the banking crisis from Lord Turner, the head of the Financial Services Authority (FSA), which was released in mid-March, the UK regulations on liquidity and bank capital requirements are likely to be toughened up. Whereas previously a degree of "gaming" of the rules by banks was apparent, it is likely that in future there will be less tolerance for this. Already, commentators are talking about the need for greater simplicity in regulatory mechanisms, on the grounds

"Fashion is something barbarous for it produces innovation without reason and imitation without benefit."
George Santayana

     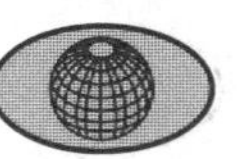   

that complexity makes the system inherently more difficult to monitor and understand. The difficulty with this, though, is that simplicity is potentially achieved at the cost of setting much higher capital ratios for banks, as well as curbing their activities.

RECOVERY FOR BANKS COULD BE MORE DIFFICULT UNDER NEW RULES

While the latter might be viewed as desirable to some market commentators, it will mean that banks may become less profitable and may, therefore, take longer to repair their balance sheets. Holding additional regulatory capital will have an impact on banks' ability to lend, just as governments are doing their utmost to free up frozen credit markets. There is also an issue about the effectiveness of simple rules, which will not be well aligned to differentiations in risk, and may, therefore, encourage "gaming", albeit perhaps in new forms.

The depth of the difficulties the market is now in is also related to the way in which some banks moved a great deal of their risk portfolio off their books, and into special investment vehicles (SIVs), perhaps as a means of funding positions in a more capital-efficient fashion. During the crisis, a number of banks were faced with either having to bring some of these portfolios back on balance sheet, or providing support to off-balance-sheet SIVs. Going forward, one can see much stricter regimes coming into play around SIVs, and banks in general will be focused much more closely on off-balance-sheet risk, even when this takes the form of exposures that they are not legally obliged to meet.

THE FUTURE REGULATION OF SECURITIZATION

It has to be remembered that while offering high loan-to-value mortgages to those of limited means was one cause of the US subprime mortgage collapse, the problems were exacerbated by the fact that banks and financial institutions went on to leverage this risk through the securitizations that they put in place on residential mortgages. In all of this, it is very difficult to distinguish between what was intrinsically a bad business model, and what was the bad execution of an intrinsically sensible idea.

In principle, collateralized debt is a good thing for the sector, in that it frees up capacity on the originator's books and stimulates investment. However, lending on the assumption that markets can only ever go up is not good business, and, if the originators then write CDOs on the back of these, the resulting creation can be a tremendously toxic asset, if its risk/return characteristics and vulnerabilities are not fully understood. It seems clear that once the dust has settled, securitization will not be abandoned by the market entirely, even if it, in future, follows a different path. For the originator, it is a very useful tool to have available and there are sound, prudent ways of dealing with the objection that securitization creates moral hazard by moving risk away from the originator.

The rethinking of Basel II is likely to mean that regulators will demand that banks hold more and better quality capital, particularly in good times, although they will only be asked to increase their capital ratios slowly, as the world works its way through the recession. The overall framework is likely to remain largely unchanged, but the treatment of particular product types and risk classes will change, particularly so far as the trading book is concerned, into which too many positions were placed that did not, in the event, have sufficient liquidity to be treated in this way.

THE SHAPE OF REGULATION TO COME

What the industry has today is some visibility on the direction of the elements of change in the Basel II framework. Charges for market risk will increase. Additional capital will be set aside as the world economy recovers. There will be much more rigorous stress testing of the elements that go to make up capital adequacy. And liquidity guidelines will be seen as an essential complement to the capital regime. The FSA, for example, has issued liquidity guidelines that it wants to see implemented by early 2010. These are major proposals and have the potential to have impact on governance models, business models, and bank business activities. There is some cloudiness because these proposals and their implications are still being worked through, but it is clear that the industry agrees that liquidity merits more detailed regulation, although there remains much debate about the specific details of the regulation.

It is also clear that banks are going to need to revisit some essential components of their strategy and business models. The changes being proposed may well result in pressure for more restricted business models than we have seen for banks, and for operating models that offer less incentive for risk-taking. It must be said that these models are not really geared to encouraging more lending, which is what governments want, at least in the short term.

CONCLUSION

In conclusion, we can already see the nature of the coming changes, but what is also clear is that while they should ultimately make for a banking system that is less prone to systemic liquidity and capital issues, the changes do little in and of themselves to get the economy out of the present recession. Other policy tools are needed to achieve this.

▸▸ MORE INFO

Reports:

European Central Bank. "Financial integration in Europe." April 2009. Online at: www.ecb.int/pub/pdf/other/financialintegrationineurope200904en.pdf

Financial Services Authority. "The Turner review: A regulatory response to the global banking crisis." March 2009. Online at: www.fsa.gov.uk/pubs/other/turner_review.pdf

Website:

Basel Committee: www.bis.org/bcbs

See Also:

Alan Greenspan (p. 1169)

The Age of Turbulence: Adventures in a New World (p. 1217)

"We have corporate CEOs who raise their pay 20 percent or more in years when they lay off thousands of people. It's obscene." Charles Handy

     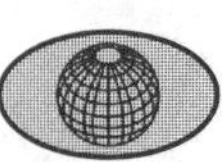   

Solvency II—A New Regulatory Framework for the Insurance Sector by Paul Barrett

EXECUTIVE SUMMARY

This article examines:

- The aims of Solvency II.
- Challenges to the self-regulatory principle.
- The role of misunderstanding and therefore mispricing risks as one of the key casual factors in creating the crash is now much better understood.
- The minimum capital requirement proposals in Solvency II continue to be a topic of debate.
- The role of the "group of 12" in challenging Solvency II has been to delay its implementation.
- The roadmap to completion.

INTRODUCTION

In July 2007, the European Union (EU) introduced the Framework Directive for Solvency II, which aims to be a "modern, risk-based, supervisory framework for the regulation of European insurance and reinsurance companies."

The aim is for the directive to be enacted into law in member countries by October 2012. In the words of the UK's Financial Services Authority (FSA), the directive "aims to establish a revised set of EU-wide capital requirements, valuation techniques, and risk management standards" to replace the current Solvency I regime. It will apply to all insurance companies across the EU with a gross premium income exceeding €5 million.

One of the features that those new to the Solvency II directive tend to find confusing is the "three pillars" approach. Pillar One involves insurance companies demonstrating that they have adequate resources to support the business that they are writing. Pillar 2 is about systems of governance, while Pillar 3 focuses on the reporting requirements of the directive, and covers such matters as the firm's risk management framework and functions, capital add-ons, and supervisory reporting.

The most important feature of Solvency II is its risk-based character: Capital requirements are related to the risk profile of an insurance entity, instead of being set in an arbitrary way on a country-by-country basis by the national regulators and legislators. Higher risks will lead to a higher capital requirement.

A second feature of the Solvency II framework is a greater focus on insurance groups (as opposed to separate legal entities). The existing Solvency I regime, being on a state-by-state basis, finds it impossible to consider groups operating on a pan-European basis, from the perspective of group capital adequacy.

A third feature is the market-consistent valuation for both assets and liabilities. Finally, Solvency II explicitly allows for the use of internal modeling for the calculation of capital requirements.

This very brief summary raises one immediate thought in the light of the current credit crunch. With respect to the banks, we have seen that the Basel II regulatory framework has been rendered rather spectacularly irrelevant, being unable to predict or prevent the banking collapses that have characterized the present credit crunch.

As the Association of British Insurers (ABI) Director General, Stephen Haddrill, said in a recent speech on Solvency II, there are those who now question whether the insurance sector would be better turning away from developing advanced modeling techniques to help the sector run its businesses, as advanced modeling did not help the banks or the banking regulators.

The wisdom of aligning regulatory requirements with management's own internal targets and priorities, as reflected in an organization's creation of its own risk-assessment models, is also now being challenged. In a speech made in October 2008, Thomas Huertas, head of banking regulation at the FSA, said: "The broad assumption underlying the Basel capital accord—that regulators around the world could rely on firms' own risk models as the basis for capital requirements—has not turned out to be correct, at least for the trading book."

What is now under scrutiny is the application of the self-assessment principle across financial markets, including insurance. The principles that underpinned Basel II were initially similar, and now appear to be moving apart. Basel II, while still not finalized in its amended form, appears to be moving in the direction of more prescriptive regulation. Solvency II, on the other hand is, for the moment, sticking with the idea of firms assessing their own risks and setting capital requirements, then getting regulators to sign off on the assumptions involved. We can expect considerable pressure for Solvency II to move into line with Basel II, which would ensure a consistency of fundamental principles across the sector with respect to setting capital levels for risk-taking financial institutions. However, the impact will almost inevitably be to increase capital reserve requirements.

A "LIVING FRAMEWORK"

It is important to point out that another alternative to Solvency II would be a return to the old style, more cautious and traditional approaches to regulation, where national markets were largely closed, and were closely controlled by national authorities and local regulators setting out rigid and often simplistic regulatory targets and standards. That is clearly not a serious and credible approach for the sector in the 21st Century. In that sense, it would be better for Solvency II to be a "living framework" like Basel II, and evolve in line with it in terms of first principles.

In fact, the events of the past year have served to emphasize most emphatically the importance of properly understanding risks, and of having the appropriate systems in place to respond to changing circumstances. The credit crunch was caused not by a failure of the models run by the banks, but rather by the failure to properly understand the risks involved, the failure to rigorously test the assumptions underpinning those models, and the failure to consider the appropriate stress scenarios when developing the business model. Above all, it has become clear that many firms simply did not collect and check the right amount and quality of data, without which no model will work.

Any regulatory failure that occurred was closely linked to the absence of a fully risk-based regime, and an incomplete understanding by regulators and others about the interaction of risks and how these should have been managed. Solvency II, by way of contrast, aims to bring a far more sophisticated, integrated, and transparent regime to insurance markets.

The FSA has already indicated that, for UK insurers, it will expect to see a cross-functional team involved in implementing

"I think we are in danger of a populous backlash. I think it will be against big institutions of all kind, government and big business." Rosabeth Moss Kanter

  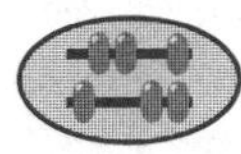   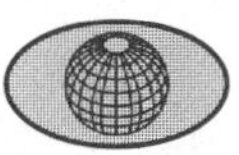   

and maintaining the internal models for the risk/capital requirement calculations. The team will probably comprise finance, actuarial, risk, and IT functions as a core team, plus subject-matter experts in investment, tax, and reinsurance. The regulator will also expect the firm's senior management and board members to be able to demonstrate an understanding of the development of the firm's internal model, as well as its processes and outputs. The regulator will expect to see a commitment to embed the internal model into the firm's actual business decision-making.

SETTING NEW GLOBAL STANDARDS

In short, Solvency II is an opportunity to set new global standards in the quality and sophistication of regulation. To this end, the ABI believes that Solvency II must be bold and innovative, to support insurers in adopting economic capital modeling and advanced risk management, and to reward them for doing so. It needs to recognize the reality of cross-border insurance groups, and it should help them to compete effectively across the European single market and beyond.

A better regulated, more efficient, and more competitive insurance industry will also be better placed to meet the needs of its customers, providing the protection they need at a price they can afford.

One of the most important innovations of Solvency II is the recognition that what matters is groups rather than separate legal entities. So, where an organization has operations in many European countries, each of which are separate legal entities, regulation is done at the group rather than the national level, with the national regulators being represented in "colleges of regulators," who, together, will develop a supervisory plan for the pan-national group entity.

The ABI supports the idea of the Committee of European Insurance and Occupational Pensions Supervisors (CEIOPS), which has had a major role in shaping Solvency II, acting as the appeal court in the case of any dispute arising among regulators at the national and pan-national levels. This will open the regulators up to a high level of scrutiny, and will resolve issues in a transparent manner.

There is still considerable debate on the minimum capital requirement (MCR) proposals in Solvency II. These concerns address the issue of the MCR required from an insurance company at a given risk exposure. There is still argument about the best way of calculating the MCR. It is crucial, if the industry is to avoid sliding back to the nonrisk-based, arbitrary constraints of the past, that the MCR is group- and risk-based. The industry does not want to get to a position where, say, some two-thirds or more of the capital in a group is tied down and isolated in each legal entity in the group. This would considerably reduce the capacity of the group to absorb shocks, and would push up capital requirements artificially, so increasing costs and, ultimately, having an adverse impact on the competitiveness of European insurers.

Although current plans are to implement Solvency II from October 31, 2012, for UK insurance companies and groups planning to use internal models, the Financial Services Authority has set target dates starting in the first half of 2009.

The directive itself has been in development over a number of years, beginning with the publication of the first draft in July 2007. By October 2008, the European Parliament had voted broadly in support of the Commission's proposals, and both the Association of British Insurers and the European insurance industry are strongly supportive. However, Europe as a whole, considered as all 27 member states, is not yet united on the directive.

A minority, led by Spain and Poland—sometimes referred to as the "group of 12" (although their number and degree of support varies)—have opposed the proposals in Solvency II for a radical overhaul of group supervision, which would allow group capital structures and diversification effects to be properly recognized using "group support" as a capital instrument. Instead, such countries prefer to look back towards solo supervision by a single national regulator, and solo capital requirements set by the regulator and the member state concerned.

This runs contrary to the intention of the single market, and undermines one of the key proposals of Solvency II. However, this "group of 12" has been very effective in standing firm and marking out its position as a blocking minority under EU rules.

Recent events in the financial markets have made governments and supervisors more cautious. This means we are likely to have a compromise. Although the details will be crucial, as Solvency II offers many advantages, it is not a deal to be done at any price.

There is also an issue over the treatment of equity risk and asset risks more generally. While the specifics tend to affect life insurers more than nonlife (and are highly significant for UK annuity companies), it has been a major roadblock in the negotiations. France has been pressing for a very liberal approach to equity risk, but has failed to produce any detailed proposals, nor has it been able satisfactorily to answer the genuine concerns raised by supervisors across Europe. This intransigence had the most serious consequences for the negotiations on Solvency II in the second half of 2008, as France held the presidency and controlled the drafting and amendment process for the council.

If Solvency II is to remain on track, a deal must be reached which both the council and the European Parliament can accept before May 2009, when the European Parliament is dissolved for elections. If a deal is not reached by then, it is likely that Solvency II will be delayed by at least a year, with the risk of even more delay.

The FSA have run qualitative impact studies to calculate possible changes in a firm's capital reserve under Solvency II, and the latest (known as QIS4) shows Solvency II will be a significant step forward for insurers' solvency. The study covered 88% of the nonlife companies represented by market share. In total, 11 small, 29 medium, and 20 large firms took part.

CONCLUSION

We remain hopeful that a deal will be reached before May 2009, with consultation on the detailed implementing measures expected to follow almost immediately on any approval of the directive. Provided key elements such as group supervision and group support are not undermined, and the robustness of the capital calculations is adhered to, Solvency II will allow insurers to remain resilient, even in difficult times.

It should help to protect policy holders' interests by making it much less likely that there will be a failure of a major insurance company. This will also reduce the chances of market disruption. Furthermore, by moving to a pan-European, group-based approach for judgments on solvency, the directive will simplify the current patchwork of local standards that have been put in place to support the earlier directive, Solvency I.

▸▸ MORE INFO

Websites:

Association of British Insurers *Solvency II Bulletin*: abi.org.uk/Display/default.asp?Menu_ID=773&Menu_All=1,773,0&Child_ID=779

European Union guidelines on Solvency II: www. ec.europa.eu/internal_market/insurance/solvency/index_en.htm

"Just to the windward of the law." Charles Churchill

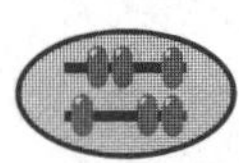
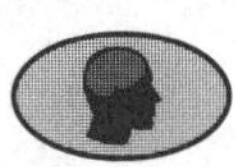

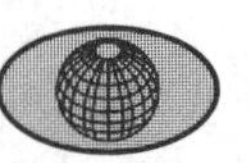

Starting a Successful Internal Audit Function to Meet Present and Future Demands by Jeffrey Ridley

EXECUTIVE SUMMARY

- Starting an internal audit function requires a clear and inspiring vision to provide the right direction for its success.
- The services provided by the internal audit role must add value and meet the needs of all its customers, at every level in the organization. This demands a wealth of knowledge and experience of risk management, control, and governance processes in the function.
- The internal audit charter approved at board level must state the professional standards expected from all staff in the function.
- Internal auditors in the function should be trained to ask the right questions and advise on the impact of present and future change at all levels in the organization, from strategic to operational.
- Quality of performance in the function and its continuous improvement requires a total commitment, measured and reported at board level through key performance indicators, and feedback from its customers.
- The function should contribute to implementation of quality policies in the organization it serves by using its own experience of achieving performance quality.

INTRODUCTION

In 1998 on the occasion of the fifty-year celebration of the establishment of the Institute of Internal Auditors (IIA)'s five chapters in the United Kingdom, I wrote:[1]

> "We need to be seen as innovators in the world of regulation, control and auditing. Creativity, innovation and experimentation are now key to our professional success. They must be the vision of all internal auditing functions. This means improving old and developing new products and services for delighted customers, with a focus on their objectives. This means being at the leading edge in all the markets in which we sell our internal auditing services. This means beating our competitors and knowing who these are. This means having the imagination, and foresight into what our organizations will require from us, not just in the year 2000, but also in 2005 and beyond.
>
> In this 50th year celebration of our national institute's past and present teamwork, all IIA-UK [and Ireland] members should continue to set their sights on being inventors of an improved and new internal auditing, to delight all their customers ... and increase its status as an international profession."

Establishing a successful internal audit function requires more than just support and resources approved at board and senior management levels; or an external requirement by government and regulators; or encouragement by external auditors. These are all important drivers and influences for creating the function and setting the boundaries in which it will operate and provide services. But the present and future demands of a successful function require a clear and inspiring vision for the direction of its services, which can only be provided by those who work in the function. It demands their knowledge and experience of risk management, control, and governance processes; their professionalism; their imagination, innovation, and creativity to manage change in what is and will be required from their services. All these attributes are needed if these service providers are to delight all their customers by the quality of their performance. They are needed whether internal auditing is resourced by staff in-house, outsourced, or co-sourced.

CLEAR AND INSPIRING VISION

A vision statement is key to the mission of any organization or function. In 1991 Richard Whitely wrote some inspirational words on vision statements:[2]

- A good vision leads to competitive advantage.
- One way to define vision is ... a vivid picture of an ambitious, desirable state that is connected to the customer and better in some important way than the current state.
- How does this vision represent the interests of our customers and values that are important to us?
- A vision has two vital functions, and they're more important today than ever before. One is to serve as a source of inspiration. The other is to guide decision making, aligning all the organization's parts so that they work together.
- If your vision is not an impetus to excellence, then it has failed.
- When a company clearly declares what it stands for and its people share this vision, a powerful network is created—people seeking related goals.
- Constantly communicate your vision for your organization to those who work with you and for you. Don't let a day go by without talking about it.

This advice has not dated. It can be seen in many vision statements used by organizations today and will be tomorrow. An inspirational vision for internal auditing in an organization can have a significant impact on those who provide and receive the service. It should be aligned with its organization's vision, creating direction for all its resources, promotion, planning, engagements, and reporting. From the vision should flow the strategic mission of the internal audit role and its business plan, which will set the scene for the resources needed for its achievement. Following the creation of an internal auditing vision statement, all internal auditing staff and senior management should be involved in its development. Seek total organization commitment and board approval for its direction. That direction will set the scene for the services it will provide.

KNOWLEDGE AND EXPERIENCE OF RISK MANAGEMENT, CONTROL, AND GOVERNANCE PROCESSES

No internal audit function can be successful unless it is expert in the principles and practices of management, risk management, control, and governance in the sector in which it works and across the supply chains developed by its organization. This expertise demands not only knowledge of what these processes require but also an understanding of the principles on which they are based, experience of how they operate at all levels within an organization, and how they are reported to all stakeholders. This expertise has to be at the management level of internal auditing and with all internal auditors.

"A team approach to managing knowledge needed for professional internal auditing is essential when planning its services..." *Cutting Edge Internal Auditing*

  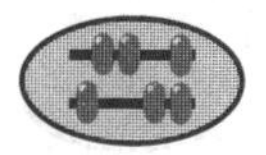   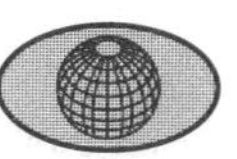   

Successful organizations assess and manage their economic, environmental, and social risks, mitigating these through appropriate strategies and controls. Successful internal audit functions focus on this corporate social responsibility and its "triple bottom line"[3] in all their engagements—across the entire range of an organization's strategies, policies, processes, and reporting. In many organizations internal auditing is seen as a facilitator in the assessment and management processes addressing these risks. To be successful today, the planning of internal audit engagements and the conducting of assurance and consulting reviews must always be linked to risks and controls in an organization's "triple bottom line."

In 1991, the US Committee of Sponsoring Organizations (COSO) published its integrated control framework exposure draft. This became its risk and control guidance for management and auditors worldwide, published in 1992.[4] Its five integrated elements of "*control environment, risk assessment, control activities, monitoring, and information and communications*" are basic requirements in all risk and control processes. It defines control as a process "designed to provide reasonable assurance regarding the achievement of [effectiveness and efficiency of operations] objectives." Importance of the COSO control elements and key concepts is significant for the mitigation of risks. These have been adopted as best practices by many regulators and organizations. Their importance is even more evident today as organizations embed risk management in their processes, from strategy setting to the achievement of objectives at every level in every operation.

In 2004[5] COSO further developed its framework into an Enterprise Risk Management (ERM) model providing further guidance for the management of risk and control across all levels of an organization. Based on its 1992 control framework, this model demonstrates the importance of embedding each of the 1992 integrated framework elements in the strategic, operations, reporting, and compliance decision-making processes across the whole enterprise. Understanding the description of each of the elements in the ERM model is a good test for management and all auditors in any organization. Such understanding is essential for internal audit success.

The IIA Inc. (2006),[6] in its overview of organizational governance, discusses the internal auditors' role, recommending that "they act as catalysts for change, advising or advocating improvements to enhance the organization's governance structure and practices." Possible steps for the internal auditor to be successful in an organization's governance processes are seen as [*my comments in brackets*]:

1 Review all the relevant internal and external audit policies, codes, and charter provisions, pertaining to organizational governance. [*Look for the key words and phrases about governance.*]
2 Discuss organizational governance with executive management or members of the board. The objective of these discussions is to ensure internal auditors have a clear understanding of the governance structure and processes from the perspective of those responsible for them, as well as the maturity of these processes. [*In these discussions relate direction and control in the organization to the achievement of its vision, mission, and key objectives.*]
3 Discuss options for expanding the role of internal auditors in organizational governance with the board chair, board committee chairs, and executive managers. These discussions could involve explaining the potential actions internal auditors could take and the resources required, as well as the possibility of an assurance gap between the board's assurance requirements and the organization's practices, if internal auditors did not assist in this area. Ensure the internal audit charter is consistent with the expanded role being considered. [*Consider providing education programs on governance for all board, management, and employee training programs.*]
4 Discuss organizational governance topics with other key stakeholders including external auditors and employees of the organization's departments such as legal, public affairs corporate secretary office, compliance, and regulatory affairs. During these discussions, explore their current and future activities as well as how an expanded internal audit role could coordinate with their activities. [*This should also be in every internal audit, not only in the organization but also across all its external relationships.*]
5 Develop a broad framework of the organization's governance structure by identifying potential areas of weakness and concern. [*A real opportunity to be creative in thinking and design.*]
6 Draft a multi-year plan to develop the

CASE STUDY

Scope and Types of Work in Successful Internal Audit Functions[10]

The scope of internal auditing covers all the activities of an organization, without regard for internal boundaries or geographical restrictions. It encompasses the adequacy and effectiveness of governance, risk management, and internal control processes in identifying and responding to all the risks facing the organization. The following are examples of the different types of work that internal audit may undertake:

- giving assurance to the board that the organization's risks have been properly identified and managed in accordance with the approved risk appetite;
- reviewing the activities undertaken by management to implement the ethical policy across the whole organization;
- giving assurance that business continuity and disaster recovery planning, including for mission-critical information systems, are adequate given the risks facing the organization and the risk appetite;
- giving assurance that the purchase process includes adequate controls to ensure agreed levels of competitiveness, cost savings, and quality performance;
- assisting the management team in evaluating the actual return on investments over a given period of time;
- carrying out an internal audit to verify an organization's compliance with labor laws and regulations;
- giving assurance that measures are properly designed and working effectively to address health, safety, and environmental risks on industrial sites;
- verifying that all purchase and sales contracts comply with the organization's policies;
- giving an opinion on the efficiency and effectiveness of the customer complaints process;
- providing advice to management on the design and implementation of risk management processes.

Consider

- How many of these examples of types of work exist in your internal audit function?
- Have you promoted all of these services in your internal audit charter?

"If governance in an organization is defined As direction and control then to be at the cutting edge today internal auditing must be involved with both, either independently or in partnership with management."

Cutting Edge Internal Auditing

   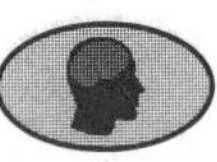  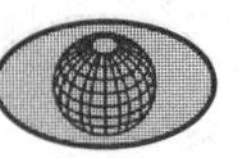   

internal audit role in organization governance areas methodically [*Another opportunity to be creative.*]

7 Perform a pilot audit in one of the areas noted above. Select a single, well-defined, manageable topic and assess the adequacy of the design and execution of the activities related to the topic. Performing a pilot audit will allow the internal auditor a chance to gauge the organization's response to his or her expanded role and learn how to coordinate more effectively with other stakeholders. [*This should only be the start. It should lead the internal auditor along many paths in many different dimensions.*]

Note how these recommendations link in to the guidance for success in this article.

PROFESSIONALISM

Professional attributes and performance requirements for internal auditing are clearly set out in the IIA's *International Standards for Professional Practice of Internal Auditing*. These *Standards* and their supporting guidelines have been continuously developed internationally since the 1970s. They represent "best practice" internal auditing and will continue to be revised by international teams to reflect both the needs of internal auditors and the organizations in which they provide their services. All internal auditing charters should require the internal audit role to comply with these standards: not all do! Yet every board would expect its external auditors to comply with developed international standards for external auditing. Why should internal auditing be different?

The *Standards* set out requirements and guidance for internal auditing attributes and performance of work. All are based on defined principles of *Integrity*, *Objectivity*, *Confidentiality*, and *Competency* in its *International Code of Ethics*, first published in 1968 and since revised to meet current and future internal auditing needs for all its members and those who have achieved the status of its qualification *Certified Internal Auditor*.[7]

MANAGING CHANGE

All operations in an organization have a past, a present, and a future. This must be recognized in the planning of all internal auditing services and in each of its engagements. What has happened before and what is happening today will influence what will happen in the future. What happens in the future will also be influenced by more change, not only in the organization but also externally, by many of its stakeholders and events beyond its control. Every test and observation in an internal audit engagement needs to be considered in this scenario of past, present, and future change. Future change is change that can be forecast during the engagement, and change that might be hinted at by events leading to "beyond the horizon." Beyond the horizon is not always an easy prediction to make, but it should be attempted by the internal auditor studying events and issues surrounding the operations being reviewed, and in discussion with board members and management at all levels.

QUALITY OF PERFORMANCE

To be successful an internal audit function must have a total commitment to the quality of its performance and continuous improvement. This is a requirement of the IIA *Standards*. Such commitment will be strongly influenced by its collective knowledge, experience of risk management, control, and governance; its professionalism of service; and its ability to question change in the past, present, and future. This can be seen in the cutting-edge internal auditing framework in the figure, developed within the chapters of my book *Cutting Edge Internal Auditing*.[8]

In Figure 1, each of the directional lines demonstrates an importance in the management of internal audit. Each touches and influences the quality of performance in an internal audit function:

- The horizontal line represents the level of knowledge and experience of risk management, control, and governance in the function across the organization's supply chains—*supplier* through *operations* to *customers*, related today to economic, social, and environmental issues and risks. The wider the line the better the service provided by the function and greater the impact on the vertical and diagonal lines and the quality of its performance.
- The vertical line represents the compliance of the function with The IIA *International Standards*. The deeper the line, the better the compliance and greater the impact on the horizontal and diagonal lines and the quality of its performance.
- The diagonal line represents the function's ability to question change across time past, present, and future, and into beyond the horizon. The wider the line, the greater the involvement of the function in the organization's risk management processes; and the greater the impact on the horizontal and vertical lines and the quality of its performance.

A total commitment to quality by the staff in the function can create opportunities for it to contribute to the organization's quality culture. Gupta and Ray[9] show that "internal auditors can leverage their knowledge of business processes and play an active role in the development and implementation of [the] Total Quality Improvement process." Their research describes the complete range of quality management tools and techniques used by organizations to implement and measure quality improvement programs showing how a knowledge of these and experience in their use can improve an internal audit activity's services and processes. Their research identifies seven steps (Table 4-22, p.104) to be under-

Figure 1. Cutting-edge internal auditing framework

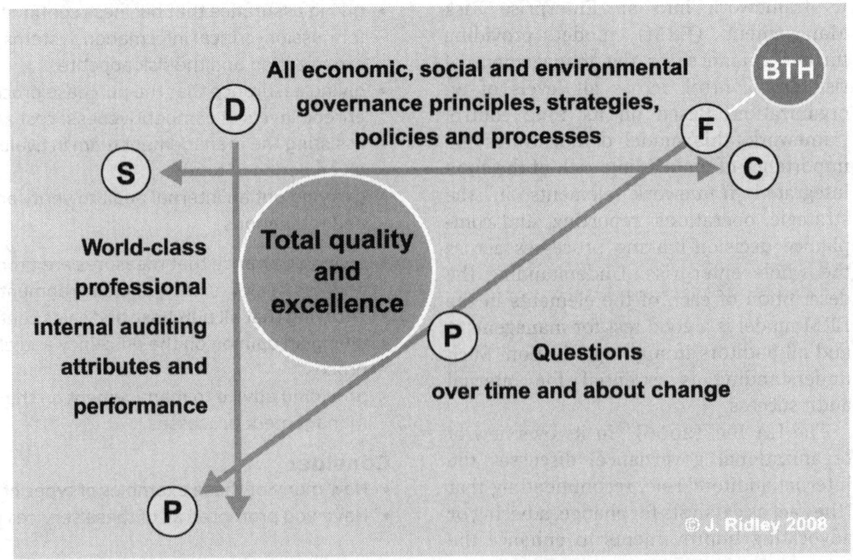

"...quality schemes and governance each strengthen the other in all supply chains, internal and external."
Cutting Edge Internal Auditing

taken to implement Total Quality Improvement in internal auditing:

1 Development of Mission and Vision Statements and establishing internal audit department objectives.
2 Establishment and implementation of performance measures for various stages of the internal auditing process.
3 Identification of customers of internal auditing departments.
4 Development and implementation of internal auditing customer satisfaction surveys and feedback systems.
5 Benchmarking with other internal auditing departments.
6 Introspective self-analysis.
7 TQM training and education of the internal auditing staff.

Note how these steps have been woven into the guidance in this article for establishing a successful internal audit function to meet present and future needs for all its customers.

▸▸ MAKING IT HAPPEN

Starting a successful internal auditing function requires a chief audit executive who is experienced in the implementation of professional internal auditing processes and has a full understanding of the principles and practices of management, risk management, control, and governance. That experience and knowledge must be used to educate the board and senior management in the role that internal auditing should assume to add best value to the organization. That role should be written into a charter, approved at board level, showing its purpose, authority, and responsibility. Once established, the internal auditing function should:

- create an inspiring vision linked to its aimed success;
- develop a plan to achieve its vision, focused on adding value;
- employ and train competent qualified professional staff;
- focus all its engagements on changes in the past, present, future and beyond the horizon;
- report its findings on a timely basis to appropriate management and the board;
- continuously measure and improve the quality of its services and delight its customers.

▸▸ MORE INFO

Websites:

Committee of Sponsoring Organizations of the Treadway Commission: www.coso.org
European Confederation of Institutes of Internal Auditing: www.eciia.org
Global Reporting Initiative: www.globalreporting.org
Institute of Internal Auditors: www.theiia.org
Institute of Internal Auditors, UK and Ireland: www.iia.org.uk

See Also:

★ The Assurance versus Consulting Debate: How Far Should Internal Audit Go? (pp. 608–609)
★ Best Practices in Corporate Social Responsibility (pp. 123–126)
★ Best Practices in Risk-Based Internal Auditing (pp. 611–613)
★ Incorporating Operational and Performance Auditing into Compliance and Financial Auditing (pp. 665–667)
★ Internal Audit and Partnering with Senior Management (pp. 668–671)
★ Internal Auditors and Enterprise Risk Management (pp. 680–682)
★ New Assurance Challenges Facing Chief Audit Executives (pp. 691–693)
★ Optimizing Internal Audit (pp. 694–696)
✔ The IIA Code of Ethics (p. 1037)

NOTES

1 Ridley, J. "IIA—UK celebrates 50th." *Internal Auditing* (March 1998): 12.
2 Whiteley, Richard C. *The Customer-Driven Company: Moving from Talk to Action*. London: Basic Books, 1991, pp. 21, 26–28, 32, 37.
3 *Sustainability Reporting Guidelines* 2000–2006.
4 Committee of Sponsoring Organizations. *Internal Control—Integrated Control Framework*. New York: American Institute of Certified Public Accountants, 1992.
5 Committee of Sponsoring Organizations. Enterprise Risk Management - Integrated Framework, New York: American Institute of Certified PublicAccountants, 2004.
6 *Organizational Governance: Guidance for Internal Auditors*. Altamonte Springs, FL: Institute of Internal Auditors, 2006.
7 See the IIA website (www.theiia.org) for details of this and other internal auditing qualifications.
8 Ridley, Jeffrey. *Cutting Edge Internal Auditing*. Chichester, UK: Wiley, 2008.
9 Gupta, Parveen P., and Manash R. Ray. *Total Quality Improvement Process and the Internal Audit Function*. Altamonte Springs, FL: IIA Research Foundation, 1995.
10 *Internal Auditing in Europe—Position Paper*. Brussels: European Confederation of Institutes of Internal Auditors, 2005.

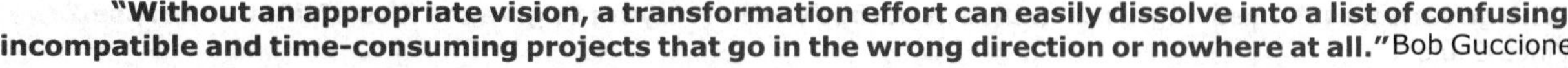
"Without an appropriate vision, a transformation effort can easily dissolve into a list of confusing, incompatible and time-consuming projects that go in the wrong direction or nowhere at all." Bob Guccione

     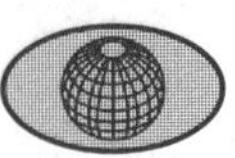   

Tripping over Prudence—Ideas for a Sensible Fix for Basel II by Samuel Sender and Noel Amenc

EXECUTIVE SUMMARY

- Why the combination of government bail-out money and retained capital ratios is flawed
- The feedback loop involved in marked-to-market amplifies book risk in a downturn and distorts management and regulatory responses
- The importance of creating a buffer
- Floor and target capital levels generate substantial advantages in providing banks with more flexibility in a crisis
- Off-balance sheet disclosures will be addressed by the new regulatory requirements as part of the risks on which banks will have to manage and report.

INTRODUCTION

One of the great ironies of the present crisis, given the prevailing consensus that it was too much easy, low-cost credit that caused the US housing bubble, and sent investors off in search of higher returns, is the way the crisis has been exacerbated by undue regulatory prudence. For this, Basel II, as it currently stands, must take some of the blame, as must regulators around the world, who have failed so far to take sensible action to mitigate the effects of Basel II.

Certainly, governments around the world have been taking action, often fairly dramatic action, to pump money into the banking system, and this might look anything but prudent when considered from the standpoint of the long-term debt that countries are generating for future generations. Yet the iron hand of prudence remains, in that there has, at the time of writing (mid-March 2009), as yet been no relaxing of bank capital ratios.

AN UNHAPPY COMBINATION

This combination of government bail-out money and retained capital ratios does not stand up well to analysis. It is only necessary to grasp the scale of total assets in the global banking system for the point to emerge. Total bank assets are as great as the combined total of the stock-market capitalization of all the world's exchanges added to total public-debt securities. This is more than twice the size of total global pension-fund assets, and more than 40% larger than world GDP. It follows that 8–10% of this total is a very big number indeed, which is what the Basel II capital-adequacy ratios demand banks retain as, basically, unusable capital in their capital reserves.

One of the issues here is that Basel II mandates that banks raise capital or cut lending as their risks are perceived to increase. That this is pro-cyclical is a point that has been made many times. It constrains banks precisely when a cure for the global predicament is for them to lend (reasonably prudently) to corporates, municipalities, and housing markets.

When bank assets suffer large depreciations, and suppliers of capital are not present in the market, the lack of the ability of banks to restore capital ratios means that their desire to cut lending halts the economy. For this reason, regulators need to allow banks to have temporarily lower capital ratios during downturns. In the present case, it took more than six months, after the Lehman bankruptcy, for the Basel Committee simply to admit that they were prepared to take action to alleviate the pro-cyclical nature of Basel II, and to state it would not advocate raising capital requirements during this period of economic stress. Whereas, an immediate reaction was needed, at least from national regulators, given the lack of a global supervisor at that time. National regulators and supervisors had the chance to define more precisely the buffers expected under Pillar II, without formally departing from the Basel accord, because buffers above the 4% minimum Tier I requirement are only defined in a qualitative manner in the Basel accord.

During the recent downturn, Basel II has, instead of easing the banking situation and freeing up capital to support lending, forced yet more funds to be locked up in capital reserves, thus deepening the downward cycle (the meaning, of course, of being pro-cyclical).

The point has also been made many times that marked-to-market accounting rules, as introduced by the International Financial Reporting Standards, exacerbate the impact of Basel II on bank capital ratios, by amplifying notional book risk, which raises the capital ratio and further constrains liquidity, in a vicious feedback loop. The direct result is the appearance of systemic risk in the global banking sector, which only governments appear to have the necessary "deep pockets" to resolve—hence the general decision by national governments to pour money into the system. Because of delays in government decisions, this also involves the risk of inefficient public intervention: while governments were fixing the bank capital ratios, the economy was experiencing a large downturn; now that they are trying to support the economy, rising default rates mean bank capital ratios are hit for the second time.

This policy also runs some very severe fiscal risks. It may well weaken both the banking system and public finances. The *Financial Times*, for example, recently likened the government's underwriting of UK bank debts to the predicament of a python engaged in trying to swallow a hippopotamus. In this analogy, an investor might feel uneasy betting their house on the snake's digestive capacity, and, in fact, the markets have rendered their judgment in the downward spiral of both bank share prices and ratings for sovereign debt (including sovereign CDS spreads).

THE IMPORTANCE OF CREATING A BUFFER

There is a very good argument for why bank capital adequacy ratios should be allowed to fluctuate. In a fair-value world, asset values fluctuate over the business cycle. This is inevitable. In banking, this has an impact on capital ratios, either via reduced Tier 1 capital, or via the increased cost of risk. It is clear, as we have already shown, that the banking sector is far larger than any other institutional investor, so the capacity of long-term unregulated investors, such as sovereign wealth funds, to absorb bank assets or to supply them with capital is limited. It follows that the financial system can be stabilized only if capital adequacy ratios are allowed to fluctuate. This is even more the case when a greater share of the economy has been financed with capital-market instruments rather than with traditional loans that are much less sensitive to changing market prices.

The major point here is that the main thrust of Basel II, which mandates raising capital requirements in a crisis, is wide of the mark, as it was not a lack of capital that led to the crisis. If, on the other hand, capital requirements were allowed to

"The government increasingly resembles somebody who is trying to give the kiss of life to a corpse."
Vince Cable

  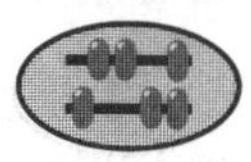   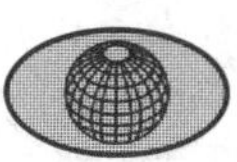   

flex, they could then function as shock absorbers, or buffers, in times of crisis.

This pragmatic approach follows the same line of thinking as that set out in the Solvency II framework for insurance companies. It defines two capital requirements: a floor, or minimum capital requirement, beneath which banks would be declared legally and unquestionably insolvent, and a flexible, upper target level that is equivalent to the average capital requirement over the cycle (remembering that under Basel II, capital follows risk, but risk varies through the cycle). As the average would be less than the maximum capital requirement, this would release very significant sums for use by the banks.

In this model, the difference between the minimum, or floor, ratio and the average ratio is the buffer. It needs to be kept large enough to keep banks from having to seek capital urgently during an economic crisis, when they might be expected to have difficulty accessing new capital. It should also be managed countercyclically. Banks should increase their reserves during periods of great profitability (not decrease them, as they would under Basel II, when risk modeling generates lower capital-ratio requirements).

This, in itself, would have a positive impact in helping to prevent speculative booms in scarce assets. In periods of crisis, falling below the target, or upper buffer level, would be permitted once the regulators had approved the bank in question's plan for recovery over the medium term.

By bringing about this distinction between the target and the floor, it becomes possible to limit the banking sector's contribution to the formation of speculative bubbles. In the very short term, it would limit the need for injections of public funds into banks. Given the current poor financial health of many banks, capital requirements under this proposal would be lowered in many instances to the point where many recapitalization plans would be unnecessary, saving the taxpayer huge sums in debt and leaving the government free to concentrate resources on stimulus programs for other sectors of the economy.

A system of floor and target capital levels means that the banking system is able to absorb shocks immediately, and may avoid panic like that which has followed the Lehman bankruptcy. It also makes sure that the market will not demand that banks increase their capital levels in anticipation of higher regulatory capital requirements over the short term. One may, however, note that the large deterioration in the economy will result in time in increased default rates and future write-downs on structured credit products that banks have exposure to, so that even with flexible capital requirements, public injections may be necessary in some banks.

This proposal does not conflict with an analysis that shows that average capital requirements for banks may well need to rise over the medium term, but it gives time to prepare for the recapitalization of banks, without secondary effects on the economy.

Average capital requirements for banks may need to rise, as regulatory analyses have shown that, for several reasons, capital requirements should rise to reflect risk more accurately: liquidity and off-balance sheet risks will probably be taken into account more explicitly; the fall in capital requirements resulting from the transition from Basel I to Basel II may be offset with the rise in required Tier I ratios; and trading-book risks may require additional capital as well. In addition, higher capital requirements may help reduce bank leverage.

Already, one thing that has emerged very clearly out of the present global banking crisis is that it is chiefly in the area of liquidity that banks need to work to analyze, measure, and manage risk more effectively. It is important to note here that there is currently no direct capital requirement for liquidity risk in existing banking regulations. The reason for this is that people thought that offsetting liquidity risk with capital would be inefficient—if you had the capital, then liquidity would not be an issue, and setting aside the capital could create the problem artificially. Going forward, we can definitely expect liquidity risk management, as well as its supervision, to be reinforced. There will be a much more vigorous stress-testing regime, looking at the effects and implications of a prolonged drought in market liquidity.

RISKS IN THE TRADING BOOK AND OFF-BALANCE SHEET DISCLOSURES

Bank trading books include all activities linked to derivatives, structured products, and trading accounts; most credit risk was initially thought to be excluded, but the increasing use of structured credit products and their classification, for accounting purposes, as held for trading, have meant that an ever-greater share of credit risk is dealt with in the trading book. Capital requirements are calculated with a historical value-at-risk (VAR) of the daily profit and loss of the trading book, with a holding period of 10 days that assumes market liquidity is sufficient to sell trading assets within 10 days.

As this assumption has been proven to be too optimistic, capital requirements in the trading book should rise to reflect risk more accurately. Possible changes include an additional capital requirement for liquidity risk (in the trading-book module or in a liquidity module); more modern principles for the valuation of less-liquid securities, such as structured credit risk (for instance, a market value margin could be used so that the balance sheet reflects high trading prices only with caution); and volatility assumptions that assume stressed market conditions, as opposed to average past market conditions, and that result in a rise in VaR numbers. Capital requirements for off-balance sheet exposures are expected to increase, in particular in the event of additional explicit or implicit commitments from banks that sponsor special-purpose vehicles.

THE IMPACT OF MARKET EXPECTATIONS OF BANKS

After the bankruptcy of Lehman Brothers, the market essentially demanded higher capital ratios from banks, both as a protection against further bankruptcies, and because the market, in general, anticipated rising prudential capital requirements. If this was where the regulators were going, then banks had to demonstrate to the market that they could cope with this. As a result, the market has penalized banks that complied with current capital requirements, but possibly not with anticipated (upward) changes in capital requirements. This, in turn, led to plunging bank share prices, which prompted massive government intervention. To date, the commitment of governments represents approximately 3.5% of banks' total risk-weighted assets—again, a very big number. In other words, all banking shareholders' equity has been wiped out by losses and write-offs, and governments are stepping in to replace most of banks' shareholder equity.

The arguments advanced in this article, so far, suggest that if governments had, instead, undertaken a more complete revision of banking regulation, with a clear distinction between target capital requirements and minimum capital requirements, buffers would have been automatically created that would have made the first wave of public funds, invested between October 2008 and early 2009, unnecessary.

Had such an improvement been made earlier, banks would not have had to raise additional capital during the crisis. This step, even if taken late, could have avoided much of the distress experienced by the banking sector in recent months. Raising capital is the regulators' reaction to perceived weaknesses in the banking sector.

"The private market has screwed itself up and they need the government to come help them unscrew it."
Barney Frank

  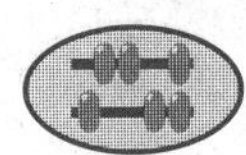 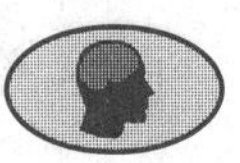  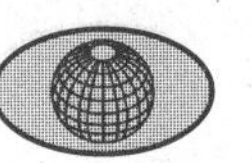 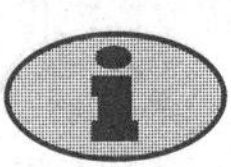  

However, regulators must be aware that market participants judge the solvency strength of an institution by comparing its capital base to regulatory requirements, so raising requirements, in effect, undermines the banking sector's strength over the short run. As an immediate rise in capital requirements when market liquidity has dried up is obviously dangerous, it is crucial to distinguish between the average, or target, capital requirements and the current capital requirements (knowing that current capital requirements will be closer to minimum capital requirements during times of stress). It should be clear, from all that has been said, that it is only when this distinction is made that regulators can start to think of increasing average capital requirements.

In fact, our analysis shows that a tolerance for Tier 1 capital ratios just 1% lower during downturns would have made public funds unnecessary, and prevented much of the recent instability. Total capital raised by banks as of September 2008, estimated at US$434 billion, represents 1.2% of risk-weighted assets (RWAs). The US$250 billion of public funds injected since October 2008, not accounting for those invested in bankrupt institutions, represent approximately 1% of RWAs. Had regulators authorized Tier 1 capital of 3%, instead of a minimum of 4%, this, in itself, would have obviated much of the need to inject public money.

Governments are now taking a second look at all the requirements surrounding the banking sector. As a result, it may yet not be too late to implement this suggested distinction between target capital and a floor, or minimum capital level, to give the sector the buffer it needs.

▶▶ MORE INFO

Articles:

Sender, Samuel. "Banking: Why does regulation alone not suffice? Why must governments intervene?" edhec-risk.com (October 28, 2008). Online at: www.edhec-risk.com/latest_news/featured_analysis/RISKArticle.2008-10-28.1714/view

Amenc, Noël. "Financial crisis or regulatory crisis? An interview with Noël Amenc." edhec-risk.com (February 10, 2009). Online at: www.edhec-risk.com/Interview/RISKArticle.2009-02-10.2517/view

Website:

EDHEC's Risk analysis site, EDHEC-Risk Asset Management Research: www.edhec-risk.com

See Also:

★ The Crash and the Banking Sector—Laying the Foundations (pp. 187–188)
★ Revising Basel II—But at What Cost? (pp. 712–713)
★ Viewpoint: Viral Acharya and Julian Franks (pp. 632–634)
✔ Basel II—Its Development and Aims (p. 920)
✔ Understanding Internal Capital Adequacy Assessment Process (ICAAP) (p. 1051)
Alan Greenspan (p. 1169)
The Age of Turbulence: Adventures in a New World (p. 1217)
Banking and Financial Services (pp. 1500–1502)

"For as long as I can remember the slogan has been ... the federal government ought to behave more like families, because families balance their budgets. It turns out that families looked around and said, 'You know what? Let's behave more like the government!'." George Will

  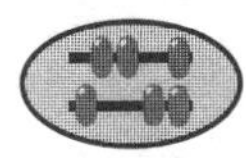   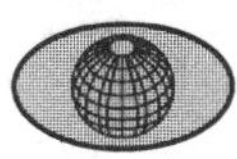   

Understanding the Requirements for Preparing IFRS Financial Statements by Véronique Weets

EXECUTIVE SUMMARY

- Financial statements made according to International Financial Reporting Standards (IFRS) have to comply with 37 standards and 26 interpretations.
- The standards are principle-based.
- An important qualitative aim of IFRS is to achieve comparability.
- Under IFRS, a complete set of financial statements comprises statements of: financial position; comprehensive income; changes in equity for the period; and cash flows. Accompanying notes should summarize significant accounting policies and provide other explanatory information.
- IFRS guidelines are primarily oriented towards the statement of financial position (formerly called the balance sheet). Those preparing financial statements should start from the definitions of the elements of the statement of financial position and the statement of comprehensive income and check whether the elements meet the recognition criteria.
- A number of different measurement bases are used to determine the monetary thresholds at which the elements of financial statements must be disclosed and appear in the statement of financial position and the statement of other comprehensive income.

INTRODUCTION

International Financial Reporting Standards (IFRS), drawn up and published by the International Accounting Standards Board (IASB), are rapidly becoming the most globally applied set of accounting standards. Approximately 9,000 public companies in the European Union had transferred to IFRS reporting as of 2005. Russia, China, Canada, Japan, Australia, and many other countries, including those in the Middle East, are adopting IFRS or have plans to converge their national standards with IFRS. There is therefore a growing need for a better understanding of these standards.

Since its inception in 1973 as the International Accounting Standards Committee, the IASB, as it became in 2001, has issued almost 3,000 pages of standards (excluding superseded ones) along with their interpretations. These treat various topics from first-time application of IFRS to property, plant and equipment, financial instruments, mineral resources, income taxes, and so on. At this moment financial statements prepared under IFRS have to comply with 37 standards and 28 interpretations. Many topics have not yet been covered, so the IASB is continuously improving the current standards and publishing new standards. The Board's current project timetable plans the publication of 24 new consultation documents and 23 final pronouncements between now and 2011. These will include six discussion papers, 18 exposure drafts, 22 final IFRS and one final guidance document. As a result, people involved with application of the standards will be obliged to invest considerable time in keeping their knowledge up to date.

BASIC PRINCIPLES

Because IFRS are a principle-based set of standards, the IASB avoids setting benchmarks to determine the appropriate accounting treatment. For example, unlike in *SFAS 13—Leases*, the US standard applying to lease arrangements, the equivalent IASB standard, *IAS 17—Leases*, sets no benchmarks to determine whether a lease is a finance lease or an operating lease. The person responsible for preparing a financial statement is thus required to use his judgment to give a faithful representation of the situation that is in accordance with the substance of the transaction and economic reality and not merely with its legal form.

Alongside that, great importance is given to the overall comparability of financial statements, both in a single period (across entities) and from period to period (within the same entity). This means that accounting policies should be applied consistently, and benchmarking within industries is encouraged. Furthermore, comparative information is required for at least the preceding accounting period. Financial statements should be prepared at least annually.

The general features of IFRS financial statements (fair representation and compliance with IFRS, along with a going-concern, accrual basis of accounting, materiality and aggregation, offsetting, frequency of reporting, the provision of comparative information, and consistency of presentation) are described in *IAS 1—Presentation of Financial Statements* (revised in 2007). The qualitative characteristics of financial statements (relevance, faithful representation, comparability, verifiability, timeliness, and understandability) are dealt with in the *Conceptual Framework for Financial Reporting* (a discussion paper to improve the framework, published in 2008).

PRESENTATION AND DISCLOSURE

The purpose of IFRS financial statements is to provide information about the reporting entity that is useful to all stakeholders of the entity. The IASB considers capital providers to be the primary users of financial statements as they provide risk capital. The IASB believes that the provision of financial statements that meet the needs of this special interest group will also meet the needs of a broad range of other users.

In order to fulfil this objective, financial statements have to provide information about an entity's assets, liabilities, equity, income and expenses (including gains and losses), contributions by and distributions to shareholders, and cash flows. Therefore a complete set of IFRS financial statements comprises:

- A statement of the financial position (formerly called the balance sheet) that presents the assets, liabilities, and equity of the entity. Although there are some minimum requirements, the entity has to use its judgment to decide on what additional items it should include depending on the nature of the business. In most cases entities will present current and non-current assets and current and non-current liabilities as separate classifications.
- A statement of comprehensive income that includes all non-owner changes in equity. Comprehensive income consists of profit or loss for the period and other comprehensive income, i.e. gains and losses that are not presented in profit or loss (for example, exchange differences on translating foreign operations, available-for-sale financial assets, cash flow hedges, gains on property revaluation, actuarial gains and losses on

"Before, you could look at accounting standards every 10 years, now something happens every month." Stig Enevoldson

  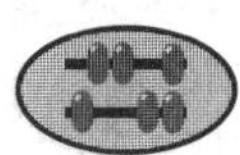   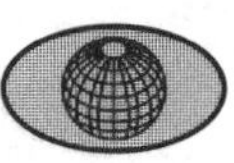   

defined benefit pension plans, share of other comprehensive income of associates).

- A statement of changes in equity in which total comprehensive income for the period, effects of retrospective applications or restatements, and transactions with owners in their capacity as owners are presented.
- A statement of cash flows for the period, making a distinction between cash flows from operating, financing, and investing activities.
- Notes summarizing the significant accounting policies used, along with any other explanatory notes that may be required.

RECOGNITION AND MEASUREMENT

IFRS financial statements are oriented towards statement of financial position. Most of the current standards address elements that are recognized in the statement of financial position; next to that there are some standards on disclosures (segment reporting, related parties, financial instruments), and only one about the statement of other comprehensive income (IAS 18—Revenue). For most transactions those preparing statements start from the definitions and recognition criteria of items to be included in the statement of financial position and derive the elements of profit or loss from the changes in assets and liabilities.

- An asset is defined as a resource controlled by the entity as a result of past events and from which future economic benefits are expected to flow to the entity.
- A liability is a present obligation of the entity arising from past events, the settlement of which is expected to result in an outflow from the entity of resources embodying economic benefits.
- Equity is the residual interest in the assets of the entity after all its liabilities have been deducted.

Items that meet the definition of an element should be recognized if it is probable that any future economic benefit associated with the item will flow to or from the entity and the item has a cost or value that can be reliably measured.

Measurement of the elements of the statement of financial position depends on the specific guidelines for the element. Measurement methods include: historical cost, current cost, realizable (settlement) value, present value, and fair value. The newer standards often use fair value (the amount for which an asset could be exchanged, or a liability settled, between knowledgeable, willing parties in an arm's length transaction) as a basis for measurement of, for example, financial instruments, investment property, net assets of an acquiree in a business combination, and so on. But for most entities the most important part of their statement of financial position (property, plant and equipment, intangibles, inventories, receivables, trade payables, ordinary bank loans) is still measured at a value that relates to the historical cost. Often more than one measurement basis is used (for example inventories are measured at the lower of cost and net realizable value). Past entry price (cost), accumulated past entry price, allocated past entry price, amortized past price, combined past price, current exit price, value in use, future net exit price, and most likely future amount are all measurement bases used to measure the elements of an IFRS statement of financial position.

CONCLUSION

At the moment IFRS consist of 37 standards and 28 interpretations, which will be subject to significant changes in the near future. Understanding financial statements made in compliance with IFRS therefore imposes a large expenditure of effort in keeping up to date with these accounting changes.

Being principle-based and oriented towards the statement of financial position, deciding on the appropriate accounting treatment in accordance with IFRS means that preparers of such statements analyze whether elements meet the definition of an asset or a liability and then test whether the recognition criteria are met. A long list of measurement bases is currently used to determine the monetary threshold above which an element should be included in the statement of financial position.

Although the use of fair value as a measurement base has increased over the last years, for most companies it is not the most important measurement base.

In order to inform the users of financial statements about their financial position, financial performance, and changes in their financial position, entities have to prepare a statement of financial position, a statement of comprehensive income, a statement of changes in equity, and a statement of cash flows, along with notes explaining the significant accounting policies that have been used. The preparation and presentation of the financial statements is oriented towards capital providers since the IASB believes that by meeting their financial information needs, statements prepared for these users will also meet the information needs of other users, such as employees, banks, suppliers, and governments.

▸▸ MAKING IT HAPPEN

Preparing IFRS financial statements requires a change in mindset toward principle-based thinking from a statement of financial position perspective. This means that the standards give clear principles for the elements that have to be recognized in the statement of financial position; changes in the value of these elements, or elements that do not meet the definition of such elements, are recognized in the statement of other comprehensive income. In addition to the need to familiarize oneself with the requirements imposed by IFRS, the preparation of high-quality financial statements in accordance with the standards requires further effort to keep up to date with modifications and new standards. The nature of the disclosures required under IFRS calls for the involvement of all departments in a company: the human resource department has to provide information about employee benefits (pensions, option plans, bonuses), engineers and technical people have to give information allowing estimation of the useful life of property, plant, and equipment, the sales department must give information on sales terms and conditions, and lawyers may be needed to provide estimations so that obligations can be measured.

In order to achieve that goal the following questions are key:

- Are key managers aware of the initial and subsequent costs and effort necessary to be fully up to date with IFRS guidelines?
- Do you have the support and commitment of other departments?
- Are changes needed in your financial reporting information systems?
- Do you have an adequate reporting pack to receive timely and correct information from associates, subsidiaries, joint ventures, etc.?
- Are you supported by valuation experts for the measurement of pensions, financial instruments, share option plans, etc.?

"The extent to which companies had to use fair value is a myth." David Cairns

  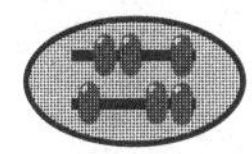 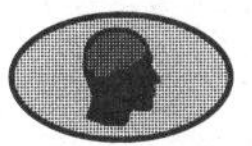  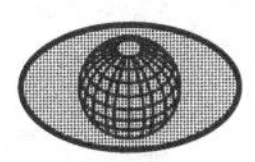   

▸▸ MORE INFO

Books:

IASCF. *International Financial Reporting Standards (IFRSs)*. London: IASCF Publications, 2008.

Alfredson, Keith, Ken Leo, Ruth Picker, Paul Praeter, Jenny Redford, and Victoria Wise. *Applying International Financial Reporting Standards*. Enhanced ed. Milton, Australia: Wiley, 2007.

Websites:

The International Accounting Standards Board (IASB) website gives access to all the IASB's standards and interpretations: www.iasb.org

Deloitte's site IAS Plus has daily updates on what is happening in the IFRS world and information on almost all IASB standards: www.iasplus.com

"Accountancy is the language of business, and it really has to reflect what's happened." Sir David Tweedie

  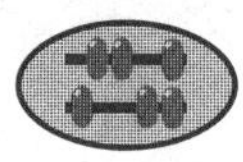   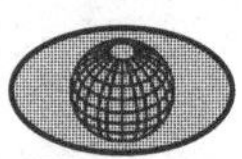   

US Financial Regulation: A Hopeless Tangle, or Complexity for a Purpose? by Lawrence J. White

EXECUTIVE SUMMARY

- The US financial services sector is heavily regulated.
- The regulatory structure is quite complicated, with a myriad of regulatory agencies and overlapping responsibilities.
- This structure is daunting and confusing, and it has its costs and complications.
- However, a great advantage to this complicated and duplicative system is that it gives someone with an innovative idea more than one place to turn; there is no monopoly regulator.
- Although there are periodic calls for simplifying the system, a major cost from simplification would be this reduced choice, and consequent reduced innovation.

INTRODUCTION

The US system of financial regulation has received heightened scrutiny recently, because of the financial debacle of 2007–2009. No observer can come away from that scrutiny without being overwhelmed by the complexity of financial regulation in the United States. Many are convinced that this system's complexity is somehow responsible, at least in part, for the debacle; and, in any event, they would argue that the system must be reformed and simplified.

Any enterprise that enters the US financial services industry must immediately confront this regulatory system and its complexity. The reasons for having financial regulation—and at least some of the reasons for the system's complexity—are certainly worth understanding. That there are actually strengths and advantages to that complexity should be understood as well.

FINANCE IS SPECIAL

Finance is special, for at least four reasons.

1. Finance is ubiquitous. Every individual, enterprise, organization, or government requires finance, even if it is self-finance, to smooth income and expenditure flows, and to provide the basis for investment. The payments system of a modern economy—cash, checks, credit and debit cards, electronic transfers—involves finance as well.
2. Finance involves an unavoidable time sequencing that creates special problems: Finance always involves an initial conveyance of funds—a loan, an investment—and then a later reversal of the flow of funds—the loan repayment (plus interest), a stream of dividends, etc.[1] Because of this time sequencing, the lender or investor has to be worried about the prospects of being repaid. But asymmetric information problems between the lender and the borrower (or between the investor and the enterprise) will adversely affect the lender's (investor's) ability to determine the prospects for repayment.
3. Many individuals have difficulties understanding finance and its complexities.
4. At least partly because of reasons 1, 2, and 3, the financial sector is heavily and extensively regulated;[2] financial regulation, too, is ubiquitous.

CATEGORIES OF REGULATION

Despite its ubiquity, financial regulation is not an undifferentiated mass of governmental intervention in the provision of financial services. There are a few important categories that can help in the understanding of the whys and the wherefores of financial regulation.

- Prudential regulation. This type of regulation is reserved primarily for depository institutions (i.e., commercial banks, savings institutions, and credit unions), insurance companies, and defined-benefit pension plans (i.e., those in which a company has promised a retiree a specified monthly or annual sum).[3] The goal of prudential regulation of these institutions is to maintain their solvency, so that their claimants will remain whole[4] and so that the institutions themselves can function as major providers of credit to the rest of the US economy. The important comparison between a healthy (solvent) bank and an insolvent bank, shown in Tables 1 and 2, illustrates the goal of prudential regulation: Maintain banks in the condition shown in Table 1, and avoid having banks incur losses so as to arrive in the condition shown in Table 2.
- Consumer safety regulation. This encompasses prudential regulation (as consumers often have their savings in banks, etc.) but goes substantially beyond, and includes disclosure requirements, limits on what can and cannot be sold, and licensing requirements for who can do the selling. Such requirements can apply to financial advisers, brokers, dealers, and accountants, as well as to the banks and other financial institutions.
- "Economic" regulation. This usually involves limits on prices and/or profits and/or entry or exit. Examples include usury limits (i.e., a maximum interest rate that can be charged on a loan), limitations on where a bank can establish locations, and restrictions on what kinds of products or services a bank (or other financial institution) can offer. The motives underlying "economic" regulation are usually complex, sometimes encompassing anti-trust and consumer protection considerations, but sometimes also just reflecting the successful lobbying of incumbents who fear competition (but who usually "dress up" their arguments in the language of consumer protection).

THE REGULATORY AGENCIES

Here is where complexities truly do arise. The reasons for the complexities are partly rooted in the United States system of decentralized federalism, whereby the 50 states have a considerable degree of sovereignty and autonomy alongside the federal government, and partly in a patchwork of regulatory agencies (at the state and federal levels) that have been legislated into existence as new financial institutions and new problems have arisen. This complexity is illustrated by the following:

- There are five federal regulators of depository institutions, as well as one or more regulator in each of the 50 states. The states also regulate lenders and

Table 1. The balance sheet of a solvent (healthy) bank or thrift

Assets	*Liabilities*
US$100 (loans, bonds, investments)	$92 (deposits) $8 (net worth, owners' equity, capital)

Table 2. The balance sheet of an insolvent bank or thrift

Assets	*Liabilities*
$80 (loans, bonds, investments)	$92 (deposits) –$12 (net worth, owners' equity, capital)

"There are only two kinds of men: those righteous who believe themselves sinners; the other sinners who believe themselves righteous." Blaise Pascal

   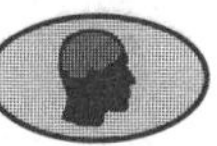  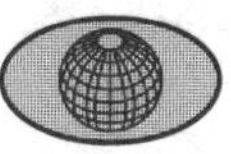   

mortgage originators that are not depositories.

- There is a separate federal agency that has the responsibility for regulating Fannie Mae, Freddie Mac, and the Federal Home Loan Bank System.
- There are two federal regulators of the securities markets and financial instruments, as well as 50 state regulators (and 50 state attorneys general, who are prepared to bring lawsuits against securities firms on behalf of their respective states' citizens).
- The regulation of insurance companies is exclusively the domain of the 50 states.
- Pension funds are regulated by two federal agencies, and, again, the 50 states also have a say.
- Consumer fraud in financial products can be the responsibility of yet another federal agency, as well as the 50 states.

There are overlapping responsibilities and jurisdictional disputes throughout this framework. For example, federal bank regulators and the 50 state bank regulators are constantly struggling for jurisdiction with respect to consumer protection issues. As another example of regulatory complexity, a commercial bank's holding company is usually regulated by the Federal Reserve, while the primary safety-and-soundness regulator for the bank itself will be the federal Office of the Comptroller of the Currency, or one of the 50 state bank regulators; but if the "bank" is a savings institution, then the regulator of its holding company will be the federal Office of Thrift Supervision (OTS), and the regulator of the savings institution itself will either be the OTS or one of the 50 state regulators. It is surely no exaggeration to claim that a diagram of these multiple agencies and their responsibilities looks considerably more complicated than a 1930s radio wiring diagram.

IS SIMPLER BETTER?

It is easy to see why this crazy-quilt pattern—and its extra costs—would provide the ammunition for periodic proposals to reorganize and simplify the architecture of the US regulatory system, even in the absence of a financial crisis. Such proposals stretch back at least to the 1970s; the most recent major proposal, "Blueprint for a Modernized Financial Regulatory Structure," emerged from the US Treasury Department in March 2008, but the Treasury initiated its efforts on this proposal a few years earlier, even before the current debacle was a specter on the horizon. The current debacle will surely give birth to many more such proposals.

But is simpler really better? Before arguing against simplification, I will concede a few obvious points: The current system is extremely complicated. The complications and duplications can delay regulatory decisions and increase costs, and a competitive regulatory "race to the bottom" is a risk.[5] If the regulatory system were being designed on a "clean sheet," with no history or legacy, it would probably not be designed with these complications and duplications.[6]

But, also, there is no credible argument that links this complexity to the current debacle. So, why might complexity and duplication actually be preferable? Fundamentally, the presence of multiple regulators is more likely to encourage innovation in the financial sector. Just as a monopoly in the private sector can be an impediment to the implementation of new ideas, so can a monopoly in regulation. For someone with a good idea—whether it's a better financial instrument, or a better way to regulate—the initial answer of "No!" by a sole regulatory agency might well mean the demise of that idea. By contrast, if there are multiple regulators, an initial "No!" to the innovator need not be a death sentence, as other regulators may have different viewpoints.

The three historical case studies illustrate this point.

WHAT ABOUT THE FINANCIAL DEBACLE OF 2008–2009?

It is clear that excessively lax prudential regulation of depository institutions, and of large complex financial institutions more generally (for example, investment banks, financial holding companies, Fannie Mae, and Freddie Mac), along with inadequate consumer protection regulation with respect to mortgage originations in the US, can explain much of the financial turmoil of 2008–2009. And, at the center of the

CASE STUDY 1

Exchange-Traded Financial Derivatives

In the 1970s, the introduction of exchange-traded financial derivatives happened in Chicago, on exchanges that had previously handled agricultural and minerals futures, and under the jurisdiction of the US Commodities Futures Trading Commission (CFTC). This was not a coincidence. These instruments were seen as competitive to the stocks and bonds that were traded primarily in New York, and that were under the jurisdiction of the US Securities and Exchange Commission (SEC). The latter agency was usually sympathetic to the concerns and arguments of the New York-based brokerage community. Had there been only one regulator—which surely would have been the SEC—the development and flourishing of these innovative instruments would surely have been restricted and delayed.

CASE STUDY 2

Breaking the Grip of Regulation Q

A legacy of the 1930s that was still in full force in the late 1960s was the legal requirement that the Federal Reserve (through its "Regulation Q") maintain ceilings on the interest rate that banks (and, starting in 1966, savings institutions) could pay on deposits. The Congressional intent was to restrict banks' competition for deposits, which had (mistakenly) been thought to have encouraged unprofitable lending by banks, and to have contributed to the wave of bank failures in the early 1930s.

The consequences of "Reg Q" for a roughly competitive banking (and savings institution) industry was exactly what is taught in Economics 101 to freshmen: A shortage of supply (of deposits) by households and businesses, and an excess of demand, and less-efficient ways of inducing households to bring and keep their deposits in the bank—such as offering them toasters and other gifts, which began in response to Reg Q.

The breaking of this gridlock started with a different regulator: The National Credit Union Administration (NCUA), which in the early 1970s placed no restrictions on the interest rates that credit unions could pay to their depositors. This competition then put pressure on savings institutions, which lobbied their regulator (the Federal Home Loan Bank Board) for greater latitude in pricing deposits; after some exemptions were granted, greater competitive pressures were next experienced by banks, which pressured for and then received some exemptions. Finally, in the early 1980s, most of the provisions of Reg Q were repealed (although a vestige remains in the prohibition on banks and savings institutions from paying interest on business checking accounts). The competition inspired by the NCUA surely hastened the demise of this inefficient regulatory restriction.

   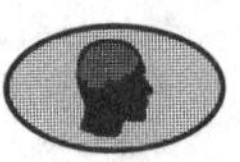  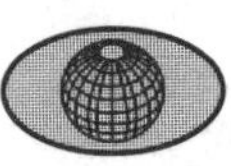  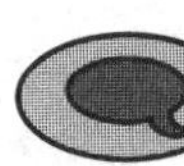 

turmoil were the financial innovations of a variety of mortgage derivatives that were based on subprime mortgage loans.

However, it is hard to claim that this regulatory laxity was due to the complexity of the US regulatory structure; equivalently, it is far from clear that a more unified and simplified regulatory structure would have prevented the debacle. For example, the more unified regulatory structures that exist in the United Kingdom and the rest of Western Europe have not been appreciably better at shielding their financial systems from the turmoil.

Further, the financial innovations, if used responsibly (as they were before the US housing boom turned into a bubble around 2004–2005), could have achieved the usual results of useful innovations: Better and/or more varied products at lower costs that could benefit participants, and thereby could be socially beneficial. For a complex set of reasons, which mostly involve the problems of asymmetric information involving the multi-tiered participants in the vertically disintegrated mortgage process (and even some vertically integrated participants), the innovations were abused. But, again, the complexity of the US regulatory system was not a cause or abettor of this abuse.

CONCLUSION

In Robert Bolt's *A Man for All Seasons*, Sir Thomas More asks his son-in-law (William Roper), "What would you do? Cut a great road through the law to get after the devil?" When Roper replies affirmatively, More responds, "Oh? And when the last law was down and the devil turned 'round on you, where would you hide, Roper, the laws all being flat?"

A monopoly regulator need not be the devil. Still, the cause of financial innovation, and even regulatory innovation, will be better served in a more diverse environment.

Financial firms are often in the forefront of lobbying for regulatory simplification, including the consolidation of duplicative agencies. If the arguments concerning innovation that are advocated here are correct, such efforts are shortsighted. The adage, "beware what you wish for, because you might get it," is surely appropriate here.

CASE STUDY 3

Regulatory Expertise with Respect to Interest Rate Risk

After the savings and loan debacle of the 1980s, federal regulators realized that they needed better methods of measuring and regulating the interest rate risks that were embedded in the long-lived, fixed-rate mortgages held by savings institutions and, increasingly, by commercial banks. As of the early 1990s, the US Office of Thrift Supervision (OTS), which regulated savings institutions, had far better knowledge of the problems, and better regulatory procedures for dealing with interest rate risks than did the other federal regulators of depository institutions. It took a while for the latter to catch up.

▸▸ MORE INFO

Books:

Acharya, Viral V., and Matthew Richardson. *Restoring Financial Stability: How to Repair a Failed System*. Hoboken, NJ: Wiley, 2009.

White, Lawrence J. "The partial deregulation of banks and other depository institutions." In Leonard W. Weiss, and Michael W. Klass (eds). *Regulatory Reform: What Actually Happened*. Boston, MA: Little, Brown, 1986: 169–204.

White, Lawrence J. *The S&L Debacle: Public Policy Lessons for Bank and Thrift Regulation*. New York: Oxford University Press, 1991.

Articles:

Gramm, Wendy L., and Gerald D. Gray. "Scams, scoundrels, and scapegoats: A taxonomy of CEA regulation over derivative instruments." *Journal of Derivatives* 1 (Spring 1994): 6–24.

White, Lawrence J. "Bank regulation in the US: Understanding the lessons of the 1980s and 1990s." *Japan and the World Economy* 14 (April 2002): 137–154.

Websites:

Commodity Futures Trading Commission (US): www.cftc.gov

Federal Deposit Insurance Corporation (US): www.fdic.gov

Federal Reserve (US): www.federalreserve.gov

Office of the Comptroller of the Currency (US): www.occ.treas.gov

Securities and Exchange Commission (US): www.sec.gov

NOTES

1 Insurance involves a similar time sequencing, where the initial event is the commitment to provide insurance, and the later event is the payout if/when the insured-against event occurs.

2 This is true in virtually all countries.

3 This contrasts with a defined-contribution pension plan, in which employees contribute specified sums (sometimes matched by employer contributions), which are then invested in financial instruments that are selected by the employee.

4 Deposit insurance and other forms of back-stopping are also present for these institutions and their liability claimants, to protect the claimants against insolvencies that occur despite prudential regulatory efforts. With deposit insurance (or some other guarantee) in place, the details of prudential regulation can be considered as analogous to the rules that insurance companies establish to protect themselves.

5 A regulatory race to the bottom can occur when financial institutions seek regulators that are the most lax. The regulators compete in laxity, so as to maintain or enlarge their regulatory domains; and laxity is a problem because the regulation really is serving a worthy social purpose (rather than just protecting incumbents or otherwise distorting beneficial outcomes).

6 However, as is argued below, in an important sense the duplication of regulatory agencies is a protection against a form of regulatory failure; and complex systems are often designed with deliberate redundancies and duplication to protect against unexpected failures.

"Natural resources are morally neutral. As such they can be a source of great good. . .or dreadful ill. The key element is not the resource itself, but how it is exploited." Nicky Oppenheimer

  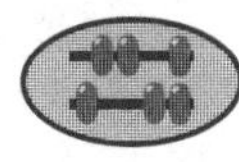   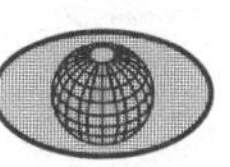   

What are the Leading Causes of Financial Restatements? by F. Todd DeZoort

EXECUTIVE SUMMARY

- Financial restatements are serious corporate reporting failures that have the potential to undermine stakeholder confidence and decisions.
- The quality of corporate governance, risk management, and compliance systems is critical in controlling financial restatement risk within organizations.
- The number of financial restatements increased consistently after the Sarbanes–Oxley Act until 2007, when the number and magnitude of restatements started to decrease.
- The research literature in accounting and finance provides useful evidence about the leading causes of financial restatements, including accounting complexity, transaction complexity, human error, and fraud.
- The effects of restatements are widespread and contingent on the cause of the restatement. Possible restatement effects include negative market reactions, reduced credit access, and turnover within management and the board of directors.

INTRODUCTION

Both the International Accounting Standards Board (IASB) and the Financial Accounting Standards Board (FASB) in the United States highlight the importance of "reliability" as a primary qualitative characteristic necessary to make accounting information useful to users making economic judgments and decisions. Reliability in this context refers to a quality of financial reporting that makes it a verifiable, faithful representation of transactions and events that have occurred within an organization.[1]

Financial restatements represent reporting failures where companies admit that previous financial representations are not reliable. Such reporting failures have various potential causes and effects that can undermine company health and raise questions about the expertise and integrity of individuals that affect reporting, operations, and compliance. In the post-Sarbanes–Oxley era, financial report users (for example, investors, creditors, analysts) have seen an explosion in the number of restatements, giving rise to questions about why so many companies find it difficult to produce accurate information.

UNDERSTANDING FINANCIAL RESTATEMENT TRENDS

Companies face daunting challenges when compiling financial reports that users rely on when making economic decisions. For example, managers preparing financial reports work in highly competitive business environments, where they face: complex business transactions; the need to comply with complex accounting rules, regulations, and laws; pressure to control reporting and compliance costs; and powerful incentives to report results in the best possible light. Given the diversity and magnitude of these challenges, huge emphasis has been placed on the importance of quality governance, risk assessment, and compliance (GRC) systems to help companies achieve their objectives and ensure accountability among key players in the financial reporting process.

Financial restatements must be made when financial GRC systems fail and companies file annual or quarterly reports that are not in conformity with generally accepted accounting principles (GAAP). Companies filing misstated financial statements must restate and correct previous reported results. For example, US public companies that file inaccurate reports are required to provide a formal restatement announcement in 8-K filings with the Securities and Exchange Commission (SEC).[2] Further, the SEC highlights that "the restatement process, which may take longer than 12 months, imposes significant costs on investors as well as preparers. During that process, companies often go into a "dark period" and issue very little financial information to the public."[3] Some companies attempt to avoid alarming users by providing "stealth restatements" that are disclosed in quarterly or annual reports without formally filing an 8-K.

Although restatement numbers in the United States increased prior to 2000, the passage of the Sarbanes–Oxley Act of 2002 (SOX) prompted a dramatic increase in the number of financial statements filed each year. The Act (such as in Section 404 on internal controls) created significant focus on the quality of financial governance by management, audit committees, internal auditors, and external auditors.

Interestingly, Figure 1 indicates that the number of financial restatements in the United States dropped in 2007 for the first time since the passage of the SOX, although over 1,200 restatements were still filed. The recent decrease in number of restatements has been accompanied by recent decreases in the average number of issues per restatement and the average income effect. Table 1 also reveals that the average income decrease per restatement in 2005 was over $21.3 million; in 2006 the average income decrease was $17.8 million. In 2007, the average income decrease dropped to only $3.6 million.

These trends raise questions about whether financial reporting is actually improving or whether regulators are simply becoming more lenient in their approach.

Figure 1. Number of restatements in the United States, 2001–2007. (*Source*: Audit Analytics, 2008)

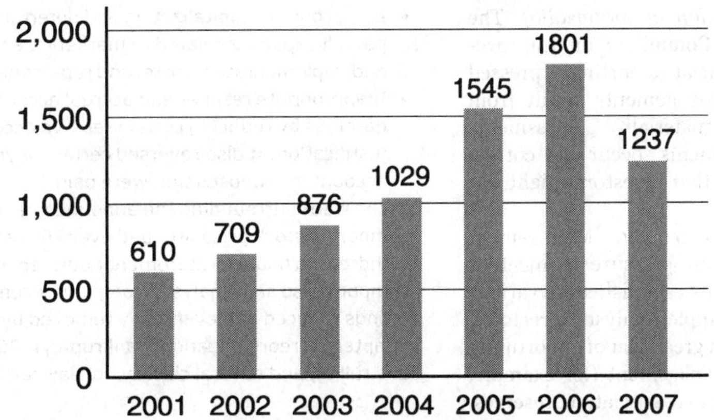

Table 1. Restatement characteristics. (*Source*: Audit Analytics, 2008)

	Average income effect	Average number of issues	Average restatement period
2005	–$21.33 million	2.41	746 days
2006	–$17.81 million	1.97	710 days
2007	–$3.64 million	1.87	643 days

CAUSES AND EFFECTS OF RESTATEMENTS

The causes of financial restatements vary considerably across cases. However, the accounting research literature (for example, Plumlee and Yohn, 2008; Scholz, 2008) and existing restatements highlight a number of potential causes of restatements, including:

- *Complexity of accounting standards and/or transactions.* Although there is a growing push to emphasize principles-based standards, companies in the United States still face demands related to rules from an array of authoritative bodies. GAAP involve hundreds of rules provided by IASB for most countries and FASB in the United States.
- *Weak financial governance and controls.* Contemporary corporate governance frameworks highlight the importance of management, the board of directors/audit committee, internal auditors, and external auditors in ensuring financial reporting reliability. Weak governance and internal controls over financial reporting increase the likelihood of financial reporting failure and restatement.
- *Increased auditor and audit committee conservatism.* The SOX created a number of new demands on auditors and audit committees. Increased regulation, scrutiny, and legal exposure for auditors and audit committees increase their motivation to be conservative and revisit management's judgments when evaluating financial reporting and specific accounting issues.
- *Broad application of materiality.* The SEC Advisery Committee on Improvements in Financial Reporting expressed concern that restatements result from overly strict materiality assessments where restatements occur to correct misstatements that investors might not find important.
- *Earnings management.* Management faces tremendous pressure to meet or beat expectations established by various groups (for example, analysts, directors). GAAP provide a great deal of opportunity for earnings management (for example, in areas related to depreciation, reserves, asset valuation) that is subject to abuse that can lead to restatement.
- *Lack of transparency.* In complex reporting environments, companies often fail to provide disclosures that are complete and understandable in compliance with GAAP. For example, footnotes that fail to provide clear, sufficient descriptions of company activities and policies undermine financial reporting reliability.
- *Fraud.* The largest frauds are due to financial reporting schemes where individuals intentionally misstate companies' financial statements.

Plumlee and Yohn (2008) conducted an empirical study of over 3,700 restatements during the period 2003–06, to identify the leading causes of financial restatements. They classified restatement causes as due to either a basic company error, an intentional manipulation, a transaction complexity, or some characteristic of an accounting standard. Their results revealed that over half of the restatements analyzed during the four-year period were due to "basic internal company errors" rather than to the complexity of the transaction or accounting standard.[4]

A closer look at prominent causes of restatements reveals a wide variety of accounting problems, including (but certainly not limited to) expense recognition, revenue recognition, misclassification in financial statements (for example, cash flows), executive compensation (for example, stock options), valuation of estimates (for example, liabilities, reserves), and business combinations (for example, mergers, acquisitions) and reorganizations.

While not necessarily causal, the research literature also provides evidence that highlights a variety of factors that are associated with financial restatements. Research indicates a positive link between short-term incentive compensation (for example, bonuses, stock options) for officers and audit committee members and the likelihood of restatements.[5] Such findings raise critical questions about the use and nature of incentive compensation for management and directors to motivate behavior in the interests of shareholders.

The effects of financial restatements are difficult to pinpoint precisely given the difficulty in controlling for other events (for example, company, industry) that affect companies during the period when restatements occur. However, the research literature provides some overall insights into the types of effects that restatements can have. For example, investors react negatively when their companies announce financial restatements. Studies consistently show a negative market reaction around restatement dates, although evidence suggests that the strength of the reaction depends on a variety of factors (for

CASE STUDY

Safety-Kleen Corporation

Safety-Kleen is a North American waste management company that issued a major financial restatement in 2001. In 2000, the company's board of directors initiated an investigation of possible accounting fraud within the company. The next year, Safety-Kleen restated (reduced) previously reported net income by $534 million for the period 1997–99.[7] The restatement issues included:

- Improper revenue recognition involving contingent contract claims, property sales, and other contingent revenue.
- Inappropriate recognition of gain on derivatives transactions. Safety-Kleen management violated GAAP by inappropriately using cash generated by derivatives transactions to increase interest income and to reduce interest and other operating expenses.
- Inappropriate capitalization and deferral of operating expenses, including capitalizing payroll expenses related to marketing and start-up activities, software development and implementation costs, and repair and maintenance expenses for company trucks.
- Inappropriate reserve and accrual accounting. Company management increased earnings by reducing certain reserve account balances without sufficient justification. It also reversed certain payroll expense accruals that had been made to account for bonuses that were paid.

In the week surrounding the announcement of Safety-Kleen's investigation, the company's stock price dropped over 70% and its auditor, PricewaterhouseCoopers, withdrew its financial statement audit reports for the previous three years. The company also saw analysts' company recommendations downgraded and its credit ratings reduced and eventually removed by some agencies. Safety-Kleen filed for Chapter 11 (reorganization) bankruptcy in 2000, and underwent a formal SEC investigation and ruling, and several class action lawsuits from external stakeholders.

  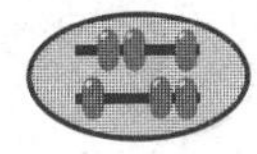 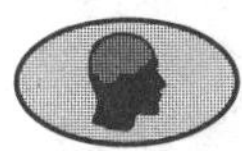  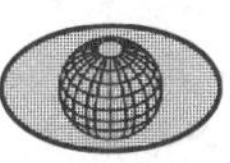   

example, restatement cause, issue).[6] Further, market reactions appear to be less severe in the post-SOX era than they were pre-SOX, suggesting that markets have become more "comfortable" with the restatement environment.

Beyond capital market responses, restatements have the potential to affect companies' efforts to secure credit, with evidence suggesting that restatements are associated with higher interest rates and stricter borrowing terms for restating companies.[8] The research literature also links restatements (and restatement effect on income) to turnover in top management and the board of directors. For example, Srinivasan (2005) finds a positive relation between the magnitude of income-reducing annual restatements and the likelihood of independent director turnover.

CONCLUSION

Financial restatements are reporting failures that have a variety of potential causes and effects on markets, organizations, and individuals. Though the number of restatements has been declining in recent years after steady growth post-SOX, a number of events create questions about what the number and nature of restatements will look like in the future. For example, the SEC's Advisory Committee on Improvements to Financial Reporting developed recommendations to consider alternative approaches to assessing materiality to reduce the number of "unnecessary" restatements that investors do not seem to care about. Alternatively, the impending shift to International Financial Reporting Standards in the United States will likely provoke a new wave of restatements because of confusion and abuse related to the transition from the current rules-based approach to accounting and reporting using a more principles-based approach. Ultimately, stakeholders interested in minimizing financial restatement risk need to invest heavily in GRC frameworks that prioritize financial reporting reliability.

▸▸ MAKING IT HAPPEN

Managing the risk of financial restatements requires strong commitment to a long-term focus on financial reporting governance and internal controls. These processes should prioritize active involvement among a variety of internal and external stakeholder groups that collaborate to address key questions in the area. For example:

- Is financial restatement risk evaluated formally within the company? If so, who is involved in the risk assessment? Explicit periodic restatement risk assessment should include the audit committee, management, internal audit, and external audit.
- What are the key financial restatement risks within the company and industry? Does the organization have a plan for managing the consequences of financial restatements if they occur?
- Are cutting-edge GRC frameworks and practices being implemented around a culture of integrity and expertise to ensure that the design and operation of internal controls over financial reporting are effective?

▸▸ MORE INFO

Articles:

Archambeault, D. S., F. T. DeZoort, and D. R. Hermanson. "Audit committee incentive compensation and accounting." *Contemporary Accounting Research* 25:4 (2008): 965–992.

Graham, J. R., S. Li, and J. Qiu. "Corporate misreporting and bank loan contracting." *Journal of Financial Economics* 89:1 (2008): 44–61.

Srinivasan, S. "Consequences of financial reporting failure for outside directors: Evidence from accounting restatements and audit committee members." *Journal of Accounting Research* 43:2 (2005): 291–334.

Reports:

Audit Analytics. "Financial restatements: A seven year comparison." February 2008. For purchase online at: www.auditanalytics.com

Audit Analytics. "Financial restatements and market reactions." March 2008. For purchase online at: www.auditanalytics.com

Glass, Lewis & Co. "Restatements: out of sight, out of mind." May 30, 2008. Available from Glass, Lewis & Co. by subscription from: www.glasslewis.com

Government Accountability Office. "Financial restatements: Update of public company trends, market impacts, and regulatory enforcement activities." Washington, DC: US Government Accountability Office, 2007. Online at: www.gao.gov/new.items/d06678.pdf

Plumlee, M., and T. L. Yohn. "An analysis of the underlying causes of restatements." Working paper, 2008. Online by search at: www.ssrn.com

Scholz, S. "The changing nature and consequences of public company financial restatements 1997–2006. Department of the Treasury, 2008. Online at: www.imanet.org/pdf/USTR.PDF

Securities and Exchange Commission. "Final report of the Advisery Committee on Improvements to Financial Reporting to the United States Securities and Exchange Commission." Washington, DC: SEC, 2008.

NOTES

1 Financial Accounting Standards Board. FASB Concepts Statement No. 2, "Qualitative characteristics of accounting information," May 1980.

2 The SEC requires companies to file form 8-K to report the occurrence of material events and changes (for example, bankruptcy, change in control of the company, change of audit firm, change in the board of directors).

3 SEC Advisory Committee on Improvements to Financial Reporting. *Final Report of the Advisery Committee on Improvements to Financial Reporting to the United States Securities and Exchange Commission*, August 1, 2008, p. 6.

4 Plumlee, M., and T. L. Yohn. "An analysis of the underlying causes of restatements." Working paper, March 1, 2008.

5 Archambeault, *et. al.* 2008.

6 Bhattacharyya, A. "Time for us to consider restatements." *Business Standard (New Delhi)* (February 25, 2008).

7 United States General Accounting Office (GAO). *Financial Statement Restatements: Trends, Market Impacts, Regulatory Responses, and Remaining Challenges*. Washington, DC: GAO, October 2002.

8 Graham, *et. al.* 2008.

  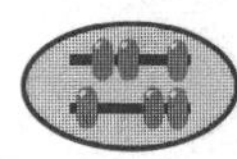   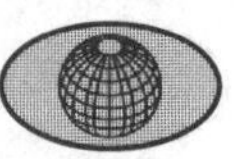   

What Is the Range of the Internal Auditor's Work? by Andrew Cox

EXECUTIVE SUMMARY

The range and type of the internal auditor's work depend on a number of factors:

- The mandate for internal audit contained in the internal audit charter.
- What the audit committee and management want internal audit to do.
- To whom the chief audit executive (head of internal audit) reports.
- The capability and skills of the internal auditors.
- Any legislative or regulatory requirements of internal audit.

But it's a bit like Forrest Gump when he said "Life is like a box of chocolates—you never know what you're gonna get." Internal auditing is a bit like that box of chocolates as the range and quality of the services are variable—and, indeed, often you really don't know what you're going to get.

INTRODUCTION

Internal auditing is an evolving profession. It has been around for a very long time, probably since the pharaohs in Egypt. But it wasn't until 1947—when the foremost professional body for internal auditing, the Institute of Internal Auditors (IIA), was formed—that internal auditing was set on its path to emerging as a profession.

Subsequently, professional standards and a code of ethics for internal auditing have been established, and in 1974 professional certification for internal auditing was created, with the designation Certified Internal Auditor. Over that time, the scope of internal auditing has changed significantly.

THE EVOLUTION OF INTERNAL AUDITING

The evolution of how internal audit determined what it would audit can be tracked in Table 1:

Table 1. The evolution of internal auditing—up to the 1990s

Then (up to the 1990s)	*Advantages*	*Disadvantages*
Areas for internal audit identified on a functional basis from historic information.	Often cyclical (every year).	Done in isolation of the business.
Set of one-dimensional risk factors applied (high, moderate, low).	Well known to internal auditors.	Time-consuming.
Input into a model and prioritization based on risk rankings.	Safe approach.	Focus on functional areas.
3- or 5-year strategic internal audit plan based on risk rankings.		May not be timely, relevant, or responsive.
Annual internal audit plan based on available resources.		Correlation between risk rankings and internal audit plan often weak. Assumed a static organization.
Presented to the audit committee (but not always).		

Nowadays, Table 2 could be the best representation:

Table 2. The evolution of internal auditing—1990s–2008

Now (1990s–2008)	*Advantages*	*Disadvantages*
Areas for internal audit identified on a functional, cross-organizational, and strategic basis—may use the organization's risk register.	Well known to internal auditors.	Can be challenging.
	Done in consultation with the business.	Time-consuming.
Discussed with senior management— additional internal audit areas may be added.	Broader scope that considers business risks.	May not be timely, relevant, or responsive.
Set of risk factors applied, input into a model, and prioritized based on risk rankings.	Facilitates integration of internal audit, risk management, and strategic planning.	
3-year strategic internal audit plan based on risk rankings.	Requires strong understanding of the business.	
Annual internal audit plan based on available resources.		
Presented to the audit committee.		

In the future Table 3 would be more accurate.

The point is this: The range of an internal auditor's work will generally be related to where the he or she is currently placed in regard to these three evolutionary phases of the internal audit continuum. As we move into the more difficult methods of operating an internal audit function, the complexity of internal audit work increases, and the capability and skills of the internal auditor need to be greater. Many internal auditors are still in the early evolutionary phases of internal auditing, because the future is seen as too difficult and daunting.

WHAT DO THE STANDARDS SAY?

The internal auditing standards we will consider here are those issued by the Institute of Internal Auditors (IIA, 2007). The internationally accepted definition of internal auditing issued by the IIA is:

> "Internal auditing is an independent, objective assurance and consulting activity designed to add value and improve an organization's operations. It helps an organization accomplish its objectives by bringing a systematic, disciplined approach to evaluate and improve the effectiveness of risk management, control, and governance processes."

This was a step up from the previous definition, which concentrated on assurance. This definition expanded the role of internal audit to encompass consulting services. To understand the difference between assurance services and consulting services, we need a couple of definitions:

"The internal audit function needs to change from the department of 'No' to the department of 'Did you know?'" Linda Bardo Nicholls

  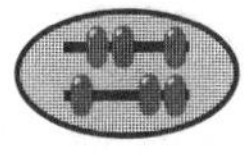 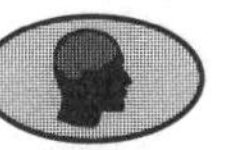  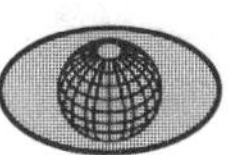   

Table 3. The evolution of internal auditing—2008 onward

Future (2008 onward)	*Advantages*	*Disadvantages*
Areas for internal audit identified on a functional, cross-organizational, and strategic basis using the organization's risk register and other relevant information.	Done in consultation with the business.	Requires strong commitment from senior management.
Develop base audit plan.	Timely, relevant, and responsive.	Requires discipline to ensure that the internal audit consultation process is effective.
Discuss with senior management, including facilitated workshops—additional audit areas may be added.	Broader scope taking into account business risks.	May not be well known to internal auditors.
Develop annual or longer-term assurance plan.	Facilitates integration of internal audit, risk management, and strategic planning.	
Develop flexible, rolling internal audit consulting plan to provide timely, relevant, and responsive services. Present to audit committee.		

Assurance: An objective examination of the evidence for the purpose of providing an independent assessment of risk management, control, or governance processes for an organization. Examples may include financial, performance, compliance, system security, and due diligence engagements.

Consulting: Advisery and related client service activities, the nature and scope of which are agreed with the client, and which are intended to add value and improve an organization's governance, risk management, and control processes without the internal auditor assuming management responsibility. Examples include counsel, advice, facilitation, and training.

It should be noted that the definitions of internal auditing and the standards focus on risk management, control, and governance:

Risk management: Internal audit should assist the organization by identifying and evaluating significant exposures to risk and contributing to the improvement of risk management and control systems.

Control: Internal audit should assist the organization in maintaining effective controls by evaluating their effectiveness and efficiency and by promoting continuous improvement.

Governance: Internal audit should assess and make appropriate recommendations for improving the governance process in its accomplishment of the following objectives:

- Promoting appropriate ethics and values within the organization.
- Ensuring effective organizational performance management and accountability.
- Effectively communicating risk and control information to appropriate areas of the organization.
- Effectively coordinating the activities and communicating information among the board, external and internal auditors, and management.

WHAT TYPE OF WORK?

So, what should be the range and type of work carried out by internal audit for an organization? The IIA believes that the work and methods of internal audit should encompass:

- Conducting enterprise risk assessment.
- Utilizing risk and control self-assessment.
- Using internal control processes based on COSO (Committee of Sponsoring Organizations) guidelines.
- Partnering with management.
- Integrating corporate governance into practice.
- Increasing staff performance.
- Communicating more effectively.
- Developing staff, both personally and professionally.
- Using technology to increase staff efficiency.
- Establishing an assurance function.
- Providing consulting services.
- Conducting audits in emerging areas.
- Utilizing performance measures.

This leads to the types of internal audit provided by the internal audit function, which may include some or all of the following:

Compliance audit: The review of both financial and operating controls and transactions to see how they conform with established laws, standards, regulations, and procedures.

Financial audit: The examination of the financial records and reports of a company to verify that the figures in the financial reports are relevant, accurate, and complete. The general focus is on making sure that all assets and liabilities are properly recorded on the balance sheet, and that the statement of income and expenses is correct.

Information technology (IT) audit: A review of the controls within an entity's technology infrastructure. These reviews are typically performed in conjunction with a financial statement audit, internal audit review, or other form of attestation engagement.

On-demand audit: A request for an internal audit initiated by the board, audit committee, or management in response to their particular concerns, and which has not been scheduled in the internal audit plan of work. It may also be known as a management-initiated review.

CASE STUDY

Designing a Comprehensive Internal Audit Plan

A large public sector organization with a significant commitment to internal auditing provided sufficient funds to resource an internal audit function of 25,000 audit hours each year. The audit committee wanted an annual internal audit plan of work that provided assurance and examined how well the organization was operating, but which was also responsive to the changing needs and risks of the organization. The risk-based annual internal audit plan of work to achieve this designed by the chief audit executive is summarized in Table 4.

Rather than have a static annual internal audit plan, the plan shown in the table was designed to cover an 18-month period with a refresher every six months so that workflows could be smoothed and work allocated to internal auditors continuously. The plan encompassed the following areas:

- *Cyclical 12 months scheduled*: For high-risk areas worthy of annual internal audit attention.
- *Rolling 6 months scheduled*: Higher-risk areas scheduled for periodic or one-off internal audits.
- *Rolling 3 months reserve*: Areas held in reserve in case of postponement or cancellation of other internal audits.
- *Rolling 3 months unassigned*: Reserved for on-demand internal audits initiated by management for emerging business issues and risks.

"Internal auditors should be out there winning friends and influencing people." David Lawler

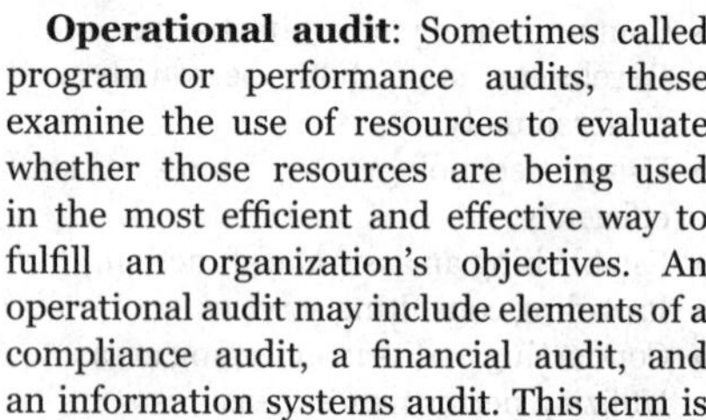

Operational audit: Sometimes called program or performance audits, these examine the use of resources to evaluate whether those resources are being used in the most efficient and effective way to fulfill an organization's objectives. An operational audit may include elements of a compliance audit, a financial audit, and an information systems audit. This term is mainly used in the private sector.

Performance audit: The independent and systematic examination of the management of an organization, program, or function for the purpose of identifying whether the management is being carried out in an efficient and effective manner, and whether management practices promote improvement. This term is mainly used in the public sector, and a performance audit may be the same as or similar to an operational audit.

Quality audit: The systematic examination and evaluation of all activities related to the quality of a product or service, to determine the suitability and effectiveness of the activities to meet quality goals.

Value for money (VFM) audit: An examination of how resources are allocated and utilized. The audit is concerned with interrelated concepts of efficiency, effectiveness, economy, and organizational outcomes. VFM audits are more common in the public sector than the private sector since the profit criterion is lacking in the public sector, and they may be the same as or similar to a performance audit.

Table 4. The chief audit executive's risk-based annual internal audit plan

Audit type	*Cyclical 12 months scheduled hours*	*Rolling 6 months scheduled hours*	*Rolling 3 months reserve hours*	*Rolling 3 months unassigned hours*	*Annual total hours*
Compliance *Assurance*	6,000	0	0	0	6,000
Consulting	0	0	0	0	
Financial *Assurance*	750	2,500	1,000	500	5,000
Consulting	250	0	0	0	
IT *Assurance*	3,000	0	0	0	6,000
Consulting	3,000	0	0	0	
Performance *Assurance*	0	0	0	0	5,000
Consulting	500	2,500	1,000	1,000	
Internal audit planning	500	0	0	0	500
Audit monitor and follow-up recommendations	500	0	0	0	500
Audit committee	500	0	0	0	500
External audit coordination	1,500	0	0	0	1,500
					25,000

WHAT INFLUENCES THE TYPE OF WORK?

The range and type of the internal auditor's work depend on a number of factors:

The mandate for internal audit contained in the internal audit charter: This is what the audit committee and the organization want internal audit to do. Although ideally this should include both assurance services and consulting services, it is true to say that some audit committees and management believe that internal audit should not stray from its roots of providing assurance, so in some organizations the internal audit charter has focused only on the provision of assurance services. This attitude peaked following the corporate collapses of the 1990s. However, more enlightened audit committees and management of today seek a more comprehensive internal auditing service for the organization. This has the potential to add a lot of value, rather than just reporting what is wrong in compliance and financial areas.

To whom the chief audit executive reports to: The chief audit executive should report to the audit committee functionally and for operations, and to the chief executive officer for administration. Where a chief audit executive may have other reporting arrangements—for example to a chief executive officer for operations and administration, or worse, to a chief financial officer—there is a risk that internal audit may lose a measure of its independence. This has a potential to impact negatively on the range and type of work to be performed by internal audit.

The capability and skills of the internal auditors: As the work of internal audit moves toward more difficult methods of operating, the complexity of internal audit work increases. This means that the capability and skills of the internal auditor need to be greater, and many internal auditors see this as a quantum leap so great

▸▸ MAKING IT HAPPEN

Chief audit executives should look to his or her audit committee and management for guidance on the range and type of work to be performed by the internal audit function. However, the chief audit executive, as an internal audit professional, should be using his or her knowledge and experience to identify and influence the formulation of a risk-based internal audit plan of work that best provides for the needs of the organization. This is likely to be a blended plan of internal audit work that encompasses both assurance services and consulting services:

Assurance Services

- Part of the overall internal audit plan of work.
- Annual or longer-term focus.
- Risk-based.
- May include cyclical internal audits of higher-risk areas.
- Need to consider legislative and regulatory requirements.
- Need to consider external audit to avoid duplication of audit effort.
- Estimated hours for audit topics assessed from previous internal audits (structured gut feel).
- Focus on compliance, financial issues and risks, financial controls, and IT reviews.

Consulting Services

- Part of the overall internal audit plan of work.
- Flexible, rolling focus—rather than fixed in time.
- Risk-based and customer-focused.
- If limited previous data are available, estimate hours needed for internal audit topics on the basis of the best available information and past experience (unstructured gut feel).
- Focus on current and emerging business issues and risks, and system under development reviews.

"**Internal audit needs to have the right direction, the right people, and to be properly equipped.**" Bruce Turner

that they prefer to remain comfortable where they are.

Any legislative or regulatory requirements of internal audit: The work of internal audit will nearly always have a role to provide assurance of legislative and regulatory compliance; this is an important role that should never be forgotten.

CONCLUSION

The range and type of the internal auditor's work depend on a number of factors:

- The mandate for internal audit contained in the internal audit charter.
- What the audit committee wants internal audit to do, and how enlightened it is.
- What management wants internal audit to do.
- To whom the chief audit executive (head of internal audit) reports.
- The capability and skills of the internal auditors.
- Any legislative or regulatory requirements of internal audit.

➡ MORE INFO

Books:

Australian National Audit Office. *Public Sector Audit Committees: Having the Right People is the Key*. Canberra: Australian National Audit Office, 2005.

Australian National Audit Office. *Public Sector Internal Audit—An Investment in Assurance and Business Improvement*. Canberra: Australian National Audit Office, 2007.

Picket, K. H. Spencer. *Audit Planning: A Risk-Based Approach*. Hoboken, NJ: Wiley, 2006.

Reding, Kurt F., Paul J. Sobel, Unton L. Anderson, Michael J. Head, Sridhar Ramamoorti, and Mark Salamasick. *Internal Auditing: Assurance and Consulting Services*. Altamonte Springs, FL: IIA Research Foundation, 2007.

Sawyer, Lawrence B., Mortimer A. Dittenhofer, and James H. Scheiner. *Sawyer's Internal Auditing: The Practice of Modern Internal Auditing*. 5th ed. Altamonte Springs, FL: IIA Research Foundation, 2003.

Standards:

Institute of Internal Auditors (IIA). *International Standards for the Professional Practice of Internal Auditing*. Altamonte Springs, FL: IIA, 2007. Online at: www.theiia.org/guidance/standards-and-guidance/ippf/standards

Website:

The Institute of Internal Auditors: www.theiia.org

"The worker is the slave of the capitalist society, the female worker is the slave of that slave."
James Connolly

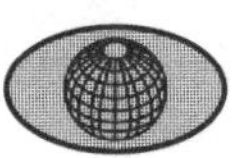

Why Organizations Need to be Regulated—Lessons from History by Bridget M. Hutter

EXECUTIVE SUMMARY

- Organizations both create and manage risk on a global scale, but their capacities to manage risk vary enormously.
- Since the origins of crises in organizations are well documented, anticipating risks and preparing for their control have become an essential part of risk regulation regimes.
- Regulation, which is often formulated in response to a crisis, targets the risks that organizations can pose to the stability of the macroeconomy, to fair competition, and to consumer protection.
- Typically regulation is state-based, but there has been a move to include transnational organizations.
- Regulation is about managing risk, not elimination of the underlying activities.

INTRODUCTION

As far back as the Middle Ages, history provides plenty of lessons on the effects of the failure of financial institutions, of consumer ignorance being exploited through the sale of inappropriate securities, pension plans, and mortgages, and of high and opaque charges for financial products and services. Arguably, regulation has become imperative today, given the increasingly transnational nature of financial markets. Another factor is the growth of large multinational organizations, now possibly more powerful than some nations. They pose particular risk and regulatory problems because they can both create and manage risks, sometimes on a global scale. Crises can have catastrophic effects nationally and internationally. Anticipating risks and organizing for their control have thus become an integral part of risk regulation regimes, which aim to influence the risk management practices of organizations. Their objectives are to make sure that organizations give high priority to risk management, to shape motives and preferences, and to influence organizations' objectives and practices accordingly.

ORGANIZATIONS AND RISKS

The capacities of financial organizations to identify and manage risks vary according to many factors. Financial organizations are often reliant on risk modeling, which itself relies on the availability of good quality data. But the past is not always a good predictor of the future (particularly where data are drawn from a period of benign economic conditions), and data may be incomplete, poorly collated, and historically limited. Moreover, staff will vary in their ability to interpret these data. Organizations need to be open to identifying new risks and understanding that circumstances and personnel change, and these may well change the risks an organization faces. Stress testing—assessing the potential impact of alternative scenarios—can usefully supplement risk modeling by introducing risks that may not be evident from past data. Organizations tend to run these stress tests by assuming that the shocks are specific to them rather than systemwide, and they find it difficult to translate the results into positive action. They may fail to recognize that specific shocks can generate contagion and other externalities. These are some of the lessons of 2007, when liquidity dried up across the financial system. Risk modeling had been undertaken in a period of economic optimism and firms overestimated their ability to identify and control the risks associated with the innovative new products they were developing.

The routines and practices of different groups and people within the organization also require consideration. For example, risk-taking may be made to seem normal, or it may be unwittingly incentivized, as in the Barings and Société Générale cases. Or organizations may deny the severity of a risk and thus inhibit their ability to deal with underlying problems. This is typically done by blaming individuals or part of an organization for something that is much more systemic and dangerous. Again, the Barings case is illustrative—the rogue trader was blamed and the responsibility of the organization in permitting and supporting his risky activities were initially ignored. Remuneration incentives based on short-term sales performance are an integral part of the rogue traders' stories. The 2007–2009 crisis has continued to demonstrate that the excessive risk-taking such bonuses can incentivize has not led to organizations learning lessons.

The organizational origins of crises are well documented. In 1984 Charles Perrow coined the term "normal accidents" to emphasize the inevitability of something going wrong.[1] He focused on complex systems where the interaction of unexpected multiple failures can lead to catastrophe, this being most likely where the system is tightly coupled and has no slack to cope with such eventualities. Opinions differ about organizations' ability to prevent and contain risks, but most agree that large, complex, transnational organizations give rise to distinctive difficulties of risk detection, proof, responsibility, and power. This is well exemplified by the cases of AIG and UBS in 2008, where varying risk management practices in different parts of their transnational organizations led to financial crisis. One commentator remarked "AIG has 125,000 employees. Basically, 80 of them tanked the firm."[2]

RISK REGULATION

The rationales for regulating financial organizations focus on three main areas: the risk they can pose to the stability of the macroeconomy, fair competition, and consumer protection. Safeguarding the stability of the broader financial system means that concern is usually focused on risks that might arise following the failure of a financial institution. Of particular concern are the contagion effects on confidence in other financial firms, disruption to the functioning of financial markets, and the difficulties faced by customers in transferring their business to other firms. Competitive concerns focus on providing a level playing field for entry to markets and also the negative impacts that may follow for consumers. There are wider concerns about the imbalance of power arising from the asymmetry of information between firms and consumers. As a result, consumers may not have the information or understanding they need to protect themselves when choosing financial products and services. In some jurisdictions there may be a requirement to guarantee the availability of a quality product at a fair price, or even to supply a basic financial product to the entire population.

Risk regulation is often a reaction to crisis. Crises and disasters can give a major

"AIG has 125,000 employees. Basically, 80 of them tanked the firm." Jeremy Siegel

  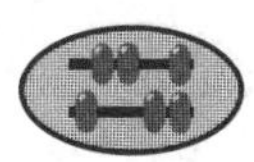   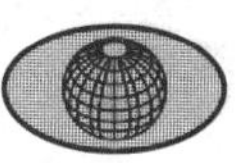   

impetus to new regulations, increased supervision, and more intense monitoring, as we have seen in the wake of the Wall Street crash, the East Asian financial crisis, Barings, and the world financial crisis of 2007–2009. Operating at state level, or that of business organizations, insurers, and professional bodies, regulatory reorganizations try to avoid repetition of the original incident. How suitable such reorganizations are may sometimes be questioned. There may be overcompensation and amplification of reactions that may in themselves be risky and become the source of new risks.

The classic definition of regulation views it as the use of the law to constrain and organize economic activity. The emphasis is on rules enacted by the state, backed by sanctions which are typically administrative/criminal, and are usually accompanied by the creation of administrative agencies to implement the rules. Increasingly, the concept of regulation has embraced governmental and nongovernmental sources, so financial risks and their management may involve numerous "regulatory" organizations. These include, for example, state risk regulation regimes, multinational businesses, trade organizations, and transnational regulators. Hybrid forms of regulation have emerged that involve a mix of state and corporate regulatory efforts. A notable example would be enforced self-regulation, involving a mix of state and corporate regulatory efforts. Simply put, the government lays down broad standards which companies are then expected to meet. This requires companies to develop risk management systems to secure and monitor compliance. Where compliance is not being achieved, companies are expected to have procedures in place to deal with noncompliance. Regulatory officials oversee this process. They undertake monitoring themselves and can impose public sanctions for noncompliance. An example of this is principles-based regulation, whereby a regulator sets the high-level outcomes and leaves firms (plus a potential role for trade bodies in setting codes, etc.) flexibility in how to achieve those outcomes.

It is important to understand that regulation is about the management of risk and not the elimination of the underlying activities. It tries to be enabling and to balance risk against other factors, such as costs, competitive position, and innovation. It does so in the interests of markets, firms, shareholders, and consumers, as well as national economies and the global economy. These entities may not always share common objectives. Decisions need to be made about how much uncertainty is acceptable and what levels of risk are tolerable. Making these decisions involves a complex process of risk assessment and risk management whereby risks are identified, estimated, and evaluated; decisions are then made about what to do about the risks. This process is itself fraught with many risks for both regulators and the regulated. For example, regulatory and financial organizations face the risk of either not regulating serious problems or overregulating for small risks. Organizations' risk appetites might incline state regulators to be risk-averse and businesses to be more inclined to risk-taking. At the micro level, neither may be able to identify and control risks sufficiently.

The enforcement of regulation is crucial, but the tensions and ambiguities surrounding regulation are often reflected in the sanctioning system, where most fines are smaller than the profits made by breaching the regulations, which therefore may not constitute a deterrent to risk-taking. The main deterrent may be the stigma attaching to being caught and sanctioned, but the evidence that these have any significant effect is contradictory.

CONCLUSION

History teaches us that organizational risk will always be present, not least because of the difficult problem of balancing risks and risk management against other organizational objectives. Organizations vary widely in their ability and willingness to manage risk, and increasingly their failures have had global impact. Traditional arguments for regulation have been

CASE STUDY

The UK Financial Services and Markets Act 2000

The Financial Services and Markets Act 2000 brought about a major reorganization of regulation in the United Kingdom. It exemplifies many of the key reasons for regulating financial organizations. For example:

- It was a reaction to regulatory problems caused by crises that suggested an apparent inability of current regulatory regimes to cope. An underlying objective was to restore confidence to the regulatory system following a series of unrelated financial embarrassments, such as BCCI, Barings, and the sale of inappropriate pension plans.
- It aimed to simplify a diverse, complex, and fragmented regulatory system that had evolved piecemeal over time and was inefficient and costly. The Act amalgamated nine regulatory agencies, which employed over 2,000 staff and regulated many thousand authorized firms and registered individuals, into one organization, the Financial Services Authority.
- It responded to changes in the regulatory environment, namely a changing industry and a "global" world. Integrated regulation was seen as a response to a financial world marked by diversification, increased complexity, and new management approaches. For example, the financial services industry had become more complex and had adopted new management structures to organize and manage its businesses on a group-wide basis.
- Financial services are important to the economy, and the Act was designed to maintain confidence in this sector. There was a belief that supervision was essential to the competitiveness of the financial sector, both domestically and internationally.
- In addition to improving consumer protection, the new regulator was mandated to raise the financial capability of the consumer by requiring the consumer to be given more information.

➤➤ MAKING IT HAPPEN

There are three main lessons here for organizations:

- The first is the importance that needs to be attached to the setting out by their boards and senior management of a clear risk policy and to making sure that this is fully embedded in the controls and culture of the organization.
- The second is the importance of taking a wider view of risk management, embracing alternative scenarios and the possibility of system-wide shocks.
- The third is taking responsibility for the risks these pose.

For the authorities, the challenges include:

- Working together effectively on a global scale.
- Introducing proportionate responses to financial crises.
- Finding a way to translate global risks into the regulation of individual organizations.

"Regulation is about managing risk, not elimination of the underlying activities." Bridget Hutter

reinforced by the failures of corporate governance and risk management that were brought into stark relief by the financial crisis beginning in mid-2007. These arguments include the global and interlocking nature of the financial system, the importance of recognizing the impact of system-wide shocks on individual firms, and the need for organizations to understand the risks they pose. Ideally, regulation is a cooperative effort involving the state, individual organizations, and other influential players such as insurance companies, industry associations, and consumer groups. Increasingly, this needs to involve transnational collaboration.

▸▸ MORE INFO

Books:

Braithwaite, John, and Peter Drahos. *Global Business Regulation*. Cambridge, UK: Cambridge University Press, 2000.

Hutter, Bridget, and Michael Power (eds). *Organizational Encounters with Risk*. New York: Cambridge University Press, 2005.

MacKenzie, Donald. *An Engine, Not a Camera: How Financial Models Shape Markets*. Cambridge, MA: MIT Press, 2008.

Sparrow, Malcolm K. *The Character of Harms: Operational Challenges in Control*. New York: Cambridge University Press, 2008.

Taleb, Nassim Nicholas. *The Black Swan: The Impact of the Highly Improbable*. London: Penguin Books, 2008.

Report:

UBS. "Shareholder report on UBS's write-downs." Zurich: UBS, April 18, 2008. Online at: www.ubs.com/1/g/investors/shareholderreport.html

Websites:

Centre for Analysis of Risk and Regulation, London School of Economics and Political Science: www.lse.ac.uk/collections/CARR

Risk Management and Decision Processes Center, Wharton School, University of Pennsylvania: grace.wharton.upenn.edu/risk

NOTES

1 Perrow, Charles. *Normal Accidents: Living With High-risk Technologies*. New York: Basic Books, 1984.

2 Knowledge@Wharton. "Lesson one: What really lies behind the financial crisis?" Article discussing Professor Jeremy Siegel's ideas, January 21, 2009. Online at: knowledge.wharton.upenn.edu/article.cfm?articleid=2148

"The final task of industry, therefore, is to organizeorganise participation in these activities, even in the most backward communities and countries." James Mooney

  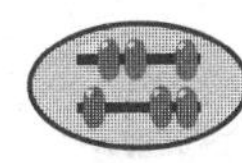   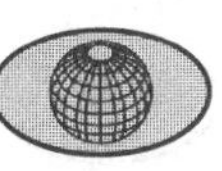   

Aligning Structure with Strategy: Recalibrating for Improved Performance and Increased Profitability by R. Brayton Bowen

EXECUTIVE SUMMARY

- Aligning organizational structure with corporate strategy requires financial "rethinking".
- In difficult economic times, it is not unusual for organizational leaders to demand across-the-board cuts of some arbitrary percentage to achieve bottom-line results.
- Unfortunately, that approach often cuts into the "muscle" of critical functions that are vital to the successful performance of the enterprise and its future viability.
- As an alternative, activity-based cost accounting quantifies the cost of specific work activities throughout organizational systems.
- This approach to redesign helps the organization recalibrate how and where work can be better aligned with corporate direction.
- The enterprise can achieve not only better organizational performance with this method, but also bottom-line efficiencies that improve financial results.

INTRODUCTION

Phlebotomy—the ancient practice of bloodletting—seemed logical when medical science centered on the belief that four humors made up the human body: yellow bile, black bile, phlegm, and blood. It was thought at the time that an ailing person could be brought to good health by vomiting, purging, starving, and bloodletting. Unfortunately, in the latter instance, any number of the sick bled to death! By today's medical standards, the practice is considered quackery. Now when a patient is ill, the condition is diagnosed extensively until the source of the problem is identified. If an operation is required, the repair is made with surgical precision.

Oddly enough, phlebotomy continues to be practiced on the body "corporate" in any number of organizations, where the four key elements are considered to be: capital, equipment, product (services), and people. A poor-performing organization, like an ailing patient in ancient times, is "bled" of its people resource. If the economy turns down, more blood is let, until the enterprise either recovers, or dies. In rough economic times, it is not unusual for organizational leaders to demand across-the-board cuts of some arbitrary percentage to achieve bottom-line results—not unlike phlebotomy, where cuts were made on almost all parts of the body. Unfortunately, that approach often cuts into the "muscle" of critical functions that are vital to the successful performance of the enterprise, and its future viability. And, the reality is that once an organization goes through a major bloodletting, a.k.a., "downsizing", "rightsizing", or "rationalizing", management will resort to doing it again and again. Invariably, the organization fails to achieve its performance objectives, and the scars of phlebotomy serve only to remind the employees who remain that they too may be the subjects of such savagery in the future. Trimming excess resource is certainly necessary from time to time, but keeping trim and fit on a regular basis should be the norm.

DESIGNING FROM THE OUTSIDE IN

Why Are We in Business?

Ask anyone why he or she is in business, and the answer ultimately is "to make money." Certainly, that should be the final result, but the mission is "to serve customers," and the outcome should be "customer satisfaction." Without customers, there is no business. Consequently, the design of an organization must be built from the outside in. In other words, it must begin with the end-customer in mind. Adrian Slywotzky makes the point in *The Profit Zone:* "The value of any product or service is the result of its ability to meet a customer's priorities" (p. 23). Structuring a business strategically requires a careful analysis of what the customer priorities are. To design from the outside in, it is important to know what the customer values: does the customer have a need, either actual or perceived? How much is the customer willing to pay? How quickly does he or she want delivery? Does the customer expect ongoing support? Does the product (service) fulfill a lifestyle or ego need? Does the customer wish to participate in an interactive process of design and fabrication? Will the customer return for replacement and/or enhanced products (services)? When businesses make across-the-board cuts without regard to customer priorities, it is as though they have compromised the outcome for the customer and jeopardized the integrity of the relationship for the future. Entire industries have reneged on their promises of product quality and customer commitment, for example General Motors promised a unique customer relationship with its Saturn division; now it is selling the line to save money. Delta Airlines has continuously cut services and increased fees, reportedly to survive, while management has continued to receive generous compensation and pension benefits; today is it merging with Northwest. Circuit City, a big box retailer, lost its way with customers a long time ago. Today, it is out of business. Cost-cutting measures for all these businesses were applied without regard to the ultimate value proposition for the customer.

WHAT IS THE "ESSENCE" OF THE BUSINESS?

Continuous realignment requires the ongoing process of taking time out of the design, fabrication, and delivery cycles. Time savings equal cost savings. Increasing the value proposition for customers and shareholders requires the ongoing process of assessing the cost of doing business, as well as the return on investment. But, downsizing structure for the sole purpose of reducing cost, in and of itself, is not a sustainable strategy. Form must follow function. Structure must follow strategy. Consequently, any restructuring must begin with outcomes in mind, and the quintessential outcome in business is the value proposition for the customer. So, recognizing that businesses change constantly, how does one go about the process of continuous realignment? Rather than across-the-board cutting—like phlebotomy—consider the alternative: activity-based costing, more commonly referred to as "ABC" accounting. This approach more accurately assigns value to discrete activities, business functions, cross-organizational processes, and, ultimately, specific products and services. It even identifies the cost of what is not being done, like "waiting for instructions" or "idling in traffic." Indeed, it is a process that encourages long-range thinking and strategic decision-making rather than short-term, knee jerk reacting.

"**Design is not just what it looks like and feels like. Design is how it works.**" Steve Jobs

  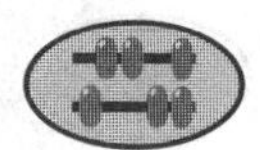   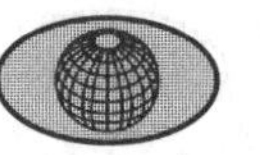   

STRUCTURAL REDESIGN

Begin with Outcomes in Mind

Establish expectations from the outset by beginning with the outcomes to be realized, for example:

- The proposed redesign will be aligned with the organization's vision, mission, values, and major strategies;
- The overall design will enhance the value proposition for the customer;
- Opportunities for income generation will be identified, and a more effective allocation of resources will be proposed according to the income opportunities identified;
- The new structure will be at least 80% aligned with the primary, value-adding initiatives of the organization;
- Organizational members will be empowered to work in self-directed work teams to enhance the exchange of diverse opinions and the sharing of ideas and solutions;
- The number of organizational levels will be reduced to facilitate the rapid transference of information;
- Quality assurance and continuous improvement will be built into the collective cognition and processes of the new organizational design.

Of course, one of the expected outcomes might be a targeted reduction in the cost of people resources; but even if it is not a stated outcome, typically an organization will realize a 10% reduction in the cost of human resources as a result of more efficient and effective organizational design.

Once outcomes have been established, the next step is to identify all work activities.

TAKING STOCK OF WORK ACTIVITIES AND THEIR IMPORTANCE

Taking stock requires identification of every work activity performed throughout the organizational system. For example, in the area of finance (partial list):

- Accounts payable;
- Accounts receivable;
- General accounting.

In the area of manufacturing (partial list):

- Requisitioning materials;
- Assembling parts;
- Testing finished products.

The next step is to identify those activities that are "primary," i.e. value-adding and essential to the organization's primary mission; and those that are "secondary," albeit important, but, nevertheless, ancillary to the core mission of the organization. Hence, for a marketing firm, an example of a primary activity would be "advertising layout," while an example of a secondary activity would be "accounting." (If an enterprise is in the business of advertising, it is not in the business of accounting; therefore, accounting is a secondary activity.) In the final stage of design, it is important to retain 80–90% of the primary activities for the integrity of the organization. Only the most important support activities should be retained, roughly 10–20%. The remaining support activities would be targeted for outsourcing and/or elimination. In this way, the essence of the organization is preserved and, indeed, strengthened.

THE PROCESS OF REDESIGNING

To ensure acceptance of proposed changes in the new structure and to enhance the effectiveness of the design itself, utilization of a cross-organizational/cross-functional design team is recommended. Using the inventory of activities suggested above, the design team proceeds with surveying the organization to determine what activities are being performed by people throughout the organizational system, as well as the amount of time expended in performing each activity. This survey feedback is integrated with a reporting system that contains a comprehensive listing of all positions, and the payroll associated with each person. The process is also effective in capturing non-productive time. Once data collection is complete, and the data are integrated with the payroll reporting system, reports can be generated that allow the design team to assess what work is being done currently, where it is being done, who is doing it, and what the associated costs are. Armed with this knowledge, the design team can go on to look at design alternatives that better align with the outcomes expressed at the outset of the process.

SAMPLE REPORTS

Data can be arrayed in several formats to provide the right information to facilitate the redesign process for the team.

The Activity Costs by Function report (Table 1) allows team members to see the actual cost of each function within the organization. The High to Low Activity Costs report (Table 2) gives an instant snapshot of where the organization is spending its money. In the example shown, 80% of the payroll cost is being expended on 27% of the total activities performed within the system. And, finally, Table 3, identifying Primary and Support work, provides a ready assessment of how aligned organizational activities are with the primary mission, vision, and strategies of the organization. Ideally, primary activities account for 80–90% of all the activities in the organization. Typically, at the start of a redesign process, it is not unusual to see only 55–65% alignment. The difference between the actual and ideal allocation constitutes the "gap" in alignment that then has to be addressed in the redesign process.

Table 1. Activity costs by function

Code	Activity description	Cost US$ (000)	Cost %	FTE	Avg. time
0400	*Finance*	*238.3*	*16.1*	*12.36*	*26.3*
0401	Accounting	88.9	6.0	5.02	15.2
0249	Accounting–general	7.7	0.5	0.35	5.8
0250	Accounting–revenue	4.3	0.3	0.10	5.0

Table 2. Activity costs—High to low

Code	Activity description	Cost US$ (000)	Cost %	Cumulative %	FTE people	Avg. time
0001	Managing	179.8	12.1	12.1	2.55	14.2
0356	Marketing	75.1	5.1	37.3	2.20	44.0
0534	Customer service	68.0	4.6	41.9	4.38	24.3
	...	...	...	...	...	...
	# OF ACTIVITIES: 29	1,186.2			46.44	

27% of 109 activities cost 80% of payroll

Table 3. Activity costs by primary and support designation

Code	Activity description	Cost US$(000)	Cost %	FTE	Avg. Time
0100	*Primary work*	*606.6*	*40.9*	*24.63*	*58.6*
0315	Product development	161.2	10.9	6.20	36.5
0356	Marketing	75.1	5.1	2.20	44.0
	...	...	...	...	...
0200	*Support work*	*876.6*	*59.1*	*32.97*	*55.9*
0249	Accounting–general	7.7	0.5	0.35	5.8
0250	Accounting–revenue	4.3	0.3	0.10	5.0
	...	...	...	...	...

"If you don't know where you are going, any road will take you there." George Harrison

  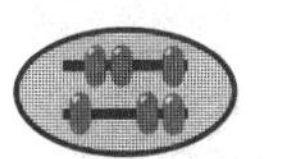   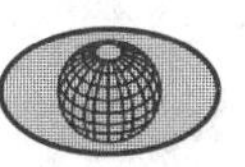   

CONTINUOUS REDESIGN

Building quality into the system means incorporating the ability of organizational members to redesign continuously—taking time and cost out of organizational processes, while imbedding flexibility and resiliency into the fabric of the corporate being. Embracing this competency and cultivating its continuous application can potentially stave off the need for major restructuring in the event of severe economic downturns, or increased competitive forces in the marketplace. Indeed, as many times as GE's Appliance Division faced potential closing, continuous reengineering and structural redesign prevented the threat from ever being realized.

CONCLUSION

In a global economy flexibility, adaptability, and quick response times are critical attributes for any organization that wishes to compete in today's competitive environment. Traditional accounting methods and other management metrics fail to capture the true cost of organizational processes, "hidden work," and even "non-work." Activity-based cost accounting provides a level of accountability and transparency that is not achievable with more traditional systems. Moreover, the team-based approach suggested here not only builds relationships among organizational members and understanding throughout the organizational system, it also facilitates the management of change, as design team participants prepare themselves for the implementation of changes in organizational structure they have designed. And, finally, this approach allows for continuous and systematic analysis of the organization and its processes to ensure the ongoing alignment of organizational structure with the strategic goals and desired outcomes of the enterprise.

▸▸ MAKING IT HAPPEN

Aligning organizational structure with strategic goals and objectives requires intelligent planning and detailed analysis. The benefits of an ABC approach to organizational design far exceed those realized as a result of executive fiats or corporate bloodletting. The following steps are needed to ensure optimum results:

- Determine the desired outcomes of any restructuring—begin with the end in mind.
- Plan to design from the outside-in, by identifying customer needs and expectations.
- Assemble a cross-organizational and cross-functional team to conduct the analysis and propose structural change.
- Identify and catalog the unique work activities that exist throughout the organizational system.
- Conduct a comprehensive analysis of the work that is being done, capturing cost, people units, and time quantities.
- Compare the feedback with personnel data, specifically pay and hours worked.
- Generate meaningful management reports that will allow intelligent analysis by the team.
- Train the team in organizational design concepts that will result in a more horizontal organization and self-direction.
- Secure management approval of the changes and encourage continued analysis of organizational processes and related structures.

▸▸ MORE INFO

Books:

Kaplan, R. S., and W. Bruns. *Accounting and Management: A Field Study Perspective*. Boston, MA: Harvard Business School Press, 1987.

Ostroff, F. *The Horizontal Organization: What the Organization of the Future Actually Looks Like and How It Delivers Value to Customers*. Oxford: Oxford University Press, 1999.

Pfeffer, J. *The Human Equation: Building Profits by Putting People First*. Boston, MA: Harvard Business School Press, 1998.

Slywotzky, A. J., and D. J. Morrison. *The Profit Zone: How Strategic Business Design Will Lead You to Tomorrow's Profits*. New York: Times Books, 1997.

Websites:

BNET, the go-to place for management: www.bnet.com

The Howland Group, Inc.: www.howlandgroup.com

"Form follows function—that has been misunderstood. Form and function should be one, joined in a spiritual union." Frank Lloyd Wright

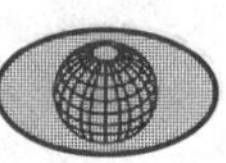

Assessing Opportunities for Growth in Developing Countries of Micro, Small, and Medium-Size Enterprises by Montague J. Lord

EXECUTIVE SUMMARY

- The density of micro, small, and medium-size enterprises (MSMEs) is a good indication of positive or negative changes that are occurring in an economy, as high and upper-middle-income countries have a greater proportion of these types of enterprises than do low-income countries.
- Value chains are widely considered to be the main engine for MSME growth in developing countries, because they can provide access to markets and technology, encourage business linkages, facilitate the upgrading of skills, and create links with international companies.
- Value chains should not, however, be viewed as a panacea for MSME development, as linkages to large companies are easily broken during periods of sluggish growth and market contractions, and, more generally, MSMEs are often unable to integrate into large-scale business relationships because they lack international standards, and quality controls.
- Business development service (BDS) centers have proven successful in upgrading MSMEs, and facilitating their entry into value chains. As such, they should become an integral part of the MSME development process; the challenge is to make BDS centers self-sustainable. A model that combines a cost-sharing facility (CSF) with a credit guarantee facility (CGF) can provide a means of ensuring that sustainability.

INTRODUCTION

The predominance of micro, small and medium-size enterprises (MSMEs) in the business activities of countries generally reflects the magnitude of growth, employment, competition, and poverty within those countries. The density of MSMEs, measuring their number per 1,000 persons, is greater in high-income countries such as the United States and members of the European Union than in middle- and low-income countries such as Malaysia and Bangladesh (Figure 1). The same relationship exists between microenterprises and income levels: high and upper-middle-income countries have a greater proportion of these types of enterprises than do low-income countries. The density of MSMEs is, therefore, a good indication of positive or negative changes that are occurring in an economy.

From an economic policy perspective, development of MSMEs can be a means of promoting growth and development in a country, although the causal direction is not always clear: in some cases, the MSME sector can be the driving force behind economic growth and poverty reduction, as it was in some Asian newly industrialized economies (NIEs, or "Tigers") during the "Asian Miracle" of the 1980s, while in others it follows the growth of export-oriented large enterprises. In nearly all cases, however, large foreign and domestic enterprises have played a key central role in the growth process, with MSMEs linked closely to them as downstream suppliers, and subcontracting between MSMEs providing business linkages that have enhanced sector efficiency, and productivity. In the current global financial crisis, increasing attention is now being paid to the role of value chains in promoting growth, innovation, and cross-border investments as a means of efficiently exploiting existing MSME capacities to renew growth in the emerging economies of Asia, Latin America, and Eastern Europe.

Figure 1. MSME density in country income groups. (*Source*: Derived from data in International Finance Corporation (IFC), World Bank Group, MSME database online)

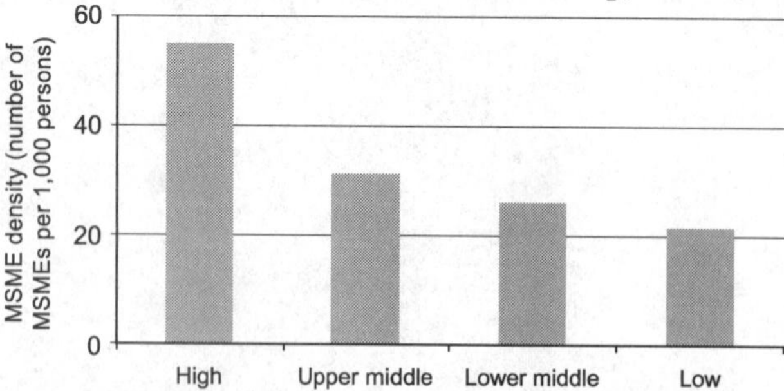

Note: MSME density refers to the number of MSMEs per 1,000 persons in a country.

DEFINING MICRO, SMALL, AND MEDIUM-SIZE ENTERPRISES (MSMEs)

There is no single standard for defining the size of MSMEs. Most countries use the following definitions based on the number of employees:

- **Microenterprises**: 1–9 employees
- **Small-size enterprises**: 10–49 employees
- **Medium-size enterprises**: 50–199 employees

Note: The greatest variation in definition occurs in the upper end of medium-size enterprises, and can range from 99 to 499 employees.

MSMEs AND GLOBAL VALUE CHAINS

Value chains are widely considered to be the main engine for MSME growth in developing countries. They can provide those enterprises with access to markets and technology, encourage business linkages, facilitate the upgrading of skills, and create links with international companies. By integrating their activities into international chains of production at various stages of added value, MSMEs can reap the potential benefits of global trade.

With the growth of regional trade arrangements among developing and transition economies, value chains have the added advantage of geographic proximity of MSME linkages to large companies in neighboring countries, as distance is one of the most stable determinants of successful value-chain relationships. In that sense, buyer–supplier relationships in cross-border value chains are replacing cross-border trade based on market-determined transactions. The changing regional and international context, and the growing role of value chains in

"From an economic policy perspective, development of MSMEs can be a means of promoting growth and development in a country, although the causal direction is not always clear."

     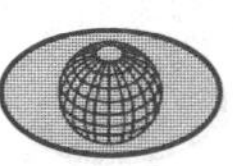   

production and trade suggest that much of the potential growth for MSMEs is situated in or around integrated cross-border production systems.

The experience of developing and transition economies, however, shows that value chains are not, in and of themselves, a panacea for MSME development. First, MSME-related value-chain activities in some countries have flourished during periods of rapid national and international market growth, but linkages to large companies have been broken during periods of sluggish growth and market contractions. During periods of cyclical or structural downturns, large companies cut costs by downsizing business activities through cuts in personnel and elimination of suppliers, a process that is often unplanned and unorganized. The role of MSMEs is then to become a buffer for absorbing unemployed workers from large firms, and prepare new entrepreneurs for eventual graduation into large firms when the economy recovers.

Secondly, under the current global financial crisis, many companies are tightening their supply chains. Countries are adopting strategies to mitigate supply-chain risks by adopting performance-based contracts with suppliers or service providers, establishing closer collaborative relations with trading partners, developing multi-sourcing strategies, and using redundant suppliers. Closer collaborative relations are now reflected in increased near-shore sourcing and manufacturing activities, as companies favor regions such as Eastern and Central Europe over China, and other East Asian countries. The situation is compounded in many countries by weakening export growth and softening industrial production, as well as falling prices for high-value-added products in agriculture.

Finally, MSMEs are often unable to integrate into large-scale business relationships because they lack international standards and quality controls. Most of these enterprises operate without any type of certification, which greatly reduces their prospects of developing backward linkages with large enterprises. Their ability to develop domestic and international commercial activities by improving quality standards through, for example, the adoption of just-in-time management systems is equally limited, and often requires both the adoption of best business practices within firms, and support from outside sources such as business organizations, large company affiliates, and the public sector. These best business practices are outlined in the next section.

BEST PRACTICES FOR PROMOTING BUSINESS LINKAGES

Good business practices for MSME linkages to large enterprises are generally recognized to follow established guidelines:

- Improve products and services of local suppliers, through technology transfer and skills upgrading that give local suppliers the ability to meet international production and quality standards. Access to product-related technology and design specifications can help suppliers meet specifications of international standards.
- Implement policy initiatives that promote an enabling environment for the private sector, emphasizing taxation, infrastructure, red tape reduction, intellectual property protection, competition policy, finance, and measures that impact on the overall competitiveness of an economy.
- Strengthen the supply capacity of local MSMEs in different fields, ranging from technical skills in production processes to management competences. Business support services can conduct training sessions with suppliers and distributors on quality control, international standards in producing for exports, and methods to improve management practices.
- Improve access to finance and non-financial business services with specialized competencies in different fields. The section that follows discusses ways to foster special credit facilities and advance payment mechanisms in

CASE STUDY

Coffee in Laos is grown by small producers or stakeholders in the southern part of the country. Production is mostly organic, as the cost of fertilizers is outside their reach, and infrastructure and access to transportation limits their access to agricultural inputs. Despite its high quality, Laotian coffee farmers have been unable to take advantage of their organic product for several reasons:

1. without extension services, farmers have poor on-farm technical skills, and poor post-harvest handling, all contributing to low yield, poor quality control, poor product quality, and limited volume of a marketable product;
2. lack of marketing facilities prevents them from linking with key buyers in the international coffee market;
3. branding of Laotian coffee has not occurred;
4. the Coffee Growers Association of Laos lacks the capacity to promote its organic coffee and reap higher prices.

Existing constraints have also given rise to a number of weaknesses in the supply-chain process:

1. high formal and unofficial transaction costs;
2. lack of organization among producers;
3. weak linkages between Laotian exporters and international markets, due to the widespread use of coffee traders;
4. dominance of one company in the supply chain;
5. lack of organizational capacity among the main coffee actors;
6. dominance of the Coffee Growers Association over all coffee-exporting activities.

A recent Asian Development Bank team working on an agricultural sector loan identified supply-chain opportunities for Laotian coffee farmers with Doi Tung Development Corporation in Thailand. Doi Tung is now exploring ways to establish supply-chain systems that promote market-oriented transactions, and ensure involvement of producers in all stages of coffee processing (especially for arabica-type coffee). They are also working with Laotian producers to create coffee post-harvest facilities, and improve export delivery facilities to lower the price penalty currently applied to Laotian coffee because of the unreliability of deliveries.

As part of these developments, efforts are being made in the following areas:

- Financing public investment on extension services and rural infrastructure that will improve physical infrastructure to facilitate access to agricultural inputs, and reduce the cost of transporting coffee from farm to processing location and markets.
- Improving market information systems to reduce spread between producer and market prices, as well as strengthening market distribution channels for accessing agricultural inputs, and ensuring producers' quality requirements are met for particular markets.
- Establishing mechanisms for determining quality standards as well as grading, classification, and quality grading, to differentiate product pricing.
- Enhancing investment financing mechanisms and export credit guarantee facilities.

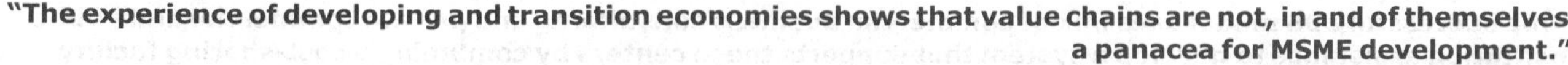
"The experience of developing and transition economies shows that value chains are not, in and of themselves, a panacea for MSME development."

     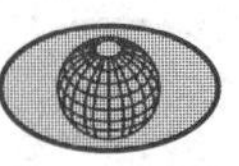   

support of MSMEs, by linking those facilities to business support services, and providing guarantees for suppliers taking out loans from banks.

- Promote development of industrial clusters that generate economies of scale and agglomeration, which can help to develop a network of firms cooperating in complementary areas of specialization. One way to promote those clusters is by promoting their local presence, through cluster-focused subcontracting promotion programs that diffuse information on infrastructure and financial facilities. The programs can be combined with international seminars to attract potential foreign and domestic suppliers.

UPGRADING MSMEs FOR BETTER BUSINESS LINKAGES

Business development service (BDS) centers have proven successful in upgrading MSMEs in a way that facilitates their entry into value chains. These centers provide a wide range of services covering management and vocational skill training, consultancy and advisery services, marketing assistance, access to information, technology development and transfer, and business linkage promotion, that allow enterprises to take advantage of value chains.

Financing these services has, however, proven difficult as many businesses are unable or unwilling to pay for the services, with the result that BDS centers go out of business within a few years. Moreover, because the medium and upper range of small businesses is more capable of paying for these services, business consultants usually target those enterprises rather than micro and small enterprises. As a result, the largest and most important sector of these enterprises do not benefit from the services.

One successful BDS model uses a mix of commercial business consultants and private, commercial, and public institution assistance to develop a system that supports these centers by combining a cost-sharing facility (CSF) with a credit guarantee facility (CGF). The challenge is to make BDS centers self-sustaining within a period of, for example, five to seven years from their inception. The CSF is a fund, normally managed by the BDS center, that provides matching grants to businesses using the BDS services. To overcome the resistance of small businesses in paying for the services, the business portion of the cost is taken from a part of a loan offered to the businesses. Those loans are supported through a credit guarantee facility that selectively backs loan applications by MSMEs to commercial banks. The financial guarantee agency is normally represented by a commercial insurance company acting as a guarantor to the borrowers.

Examples of the application of this model range from a multi-pronged SME development project in India, supported by a US$120 million loan by the World Bank, to similar projects in Bhutan and the Maldives, financed by the Asian Development Bank (ADB), and a Danish-funded SME development project for the agricultural sector in Tanzania. In all these cases, BDS centers are being created with the combined use of CSFs and CGFs, to ensure the sustainability of SME development and financial services. Under these mechanisms, a direct relationship is created between the guarantor and the borrower, as the former needs to assess loan applications, and selects the ones to be guaranteed. This process reduces the probability of moral hazard on the part of the commercial bank during the screening process. While other BDS models may be more appropriate for some particular sector or country, this model is being successfully implemented in a number of Asian countries. Whatever the form of the BDS service, it is important to recognize that its success will depend on a mix of both MSMEs and large enterprises, commercial BDS and companies, financial institutions, and public and donor-assisted interventions.

CONCLUSION

The focus of MSMEs has shifted from the development paradigm targeting niche markets, to one directed at the establishment of member networks operating along a value chain. Developing and transition economies offer access to mineral and agricultural resources, as well as low-cost labor. Likewise, the development of clusters of competitive suppliers in Latin America has made it possible for domestic suppliers of automotive parts and components in Argentina and Brazil, and electronics components in Mexico to become first-tier suppliers in global value chains.

But the value-chain model should not be viewed as a panacea for MSME development. Not only are linkages to large companies easily broken during periods of sluggish growth and market contractions, but MSMEs are often unable to integrate into large-scale business relationships because they lack international standards and quality controls. The rewards of such a business model are only likely to be gained by those enterprises that are able and willing to take the necessary steps to establish sustainable business linkages. For suppliers, it means adopting specific policies to attract foreign direct investment, building their capacity to upgrade their skills and competitiveness, and taking proactive measures to improve their capacity to supply the market. For large local firms or multinationals, it means creating available information and opportunities for business linkages, organizing trade fairs, participating in business-matching events, and developing outreach programs to MSMEs that support BDS services as a means of establishing business linkages.

▸▸ MAKING IT HAPPEN

For MSMEs in developing countries, the establishment of business linkages with large local or transnational companies offers a way to access international markets, finance, technology, management skills, and specialized knowledge. Key actions for creating those linkages include the following:

- Identifying the gap between the supply capacity of the local enterprise, and the requirements of large companies, or foreign affiliates;
- Strengthening supply capabilities by developing skills in different fields, ranging from technical skills in production processes to management competencies that focus on technical and managerial skills;
- Gaining access to networks of suppliers by locating in industrial parks and special economic zones, or, where size limits access, through industrial complexes specifically geared towards smaller enterprises;
- Improving access to non-financial business services through BDS centers, as well as financial services, by participating in credit guarantee facilities;
- Promoting public-private partnership programs that support an enabling environment for business linkages, especially in countries where market systems are still in their infancy;
- Networking with other suppliers to create a critical mass of enterprises for backward linkages to occur, especially able to link up with several large companies, rather than relying on a single one that may break relations during market downswings, or periods of sluggish growth.

"One successful BDS model uses mix of commercial business consultants and private commercial and public institution assistance to develop a system that supports these centers by combining a cost-sharing facility with a credit guarantee facility."

  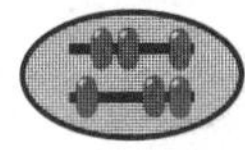   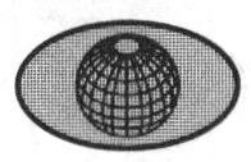   

▸▸ MORE INFO

Articles:

Ayyagari, Meghana, Thorsten Beck, and Asli Demirgüç-Kunt. "Small and medium enterprises across the globe." World Bank, March 2005.

Mugione, Fiorina. "Good practices and policy options in the promotion of TNC-SME business linkages". Trade and Development Board Commission on Enterprise, Business Facilitation and Development Expert Meeting on Best Practices and Policy Options in the Promotion of SME-TNC Linkages. Geneva, November 6–8, 2006.

UNCTAD Secretariat. "Developing business linkages." Trade and Development Board, Commission on Enterprise, Business Facilitation and Development, Expert Meeting on Best Practices and Policy Options in the Promotion of SME-TNC Business Linkages. Geneva, November 6–8, 2006.

Websites:

Comprehensive database on micro, small, and medium-size enterprises: www.rru.worldbank.org/Documents/other/MSMEdatabase/msme_database.htm

Doing business database for countries: www.doingbusiness.org

"Business development service (BDS) centers have proven successful in upgrading MSMEs in a way that facilitates their entry in value chains."

  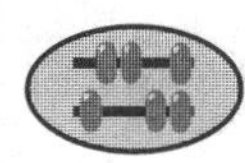   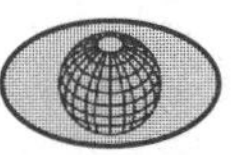   

Assessing Opportunities for Growth in Small and Medium Enterprises by Frank Hoy

EXECUTIVE SUMMARY

- The growth stage of a small or medium-size enterprise (SME) typically requires more resources than the company commands.
- In order to grow in their competitive environments, SMEs should proactively engage in identifying opportunities.
- The management team should have criteria and procedures for assessing opportunities, as only the most promising and suitable should be pursued.
- Exploiting opportunities includes obtaining resources to implement the business's growth strategy.
- The long-term health and survival of SMEs depends on their ability to recognize, evaluate, and pursue growth opportunities in competitive environments.

INTRODUCTION

Many companies experience rapid growth at some stage of their life cycle. For some, this may happen soon after they are launched. Others have multiple spurts, followed by a leveling-off period or even a decline. A consistent characteristic of the growth stage is that demands exceed existing resources. Consequently, business owners must be creative in acquiring and managing the resources needed to seize growth opportunities.

Successful entrepreneurs are astute at, first, identifying opportunities and, second, taking action to pursue those opportunities. The idea behind starting a business may have been spontaneous. It may come from prior experience or personal preference. It may have resulted from loss of employment. Although bankers, investors, and educators often emphasize the need for planning in advance of opening an enterprise, the evidence is that most venture creators did not prepare a business plan before they started. For a small or medium-size enterprise (SME) that has been operating for some time, however, a planning process is essential to any assessment of whether to take up a growth opportunity.

IDENTIFICATION OF OPPORTUNITIES

Opportunity recognition is at the core of an entrepreneurial venture. The founder of a company with growth potential will identify and seek to satisfy unmet customer needs. Creativity, new technologies, and new marketing approaches are all characteristics of growing enterprises. A key word in this stage is *flexibility*. The leaders of the company are finding new markets, sometimes on the international scene. Growth may come not only from sales of products and services, but also through acquisition. The growing firm gains recognition for its brand name and builds customer loyalty.

Robert Ronstadt coined the term "corridor principle" to explain how small and medium business owners identify opportunities that a prospective entrepreneur does not recognize.[1] At the time an individual opens his or her first enterprise, it is as if the budding entrepreneur is inside a room consisting of his or her life experiences and observations. Starting the business is the equivalent of opening a door, stepping out, and discovering a corridor. Up and down the corridor are other doors, each representing a new opportunity. If the first door—i.e., starting the business—is not opened, none of the other doors will be seen. Launching the business allows the owner to enter new networks, obtain access to information, and otherwise make discoveries that would never have happened without going into business.

From the strategic management literature, we learn about "environmental scanning" as a technique for being alert to new events, trends, and changes that may result from legislation and regulation, competitor initiatives and reactions, customer tastes, technological developments, and many other occurrences. Some business executives look at environmental disruptions as threats, but those disruptions are invariably viewed as opportunities for entrepreneurial small and medium business owners. Rita McGrath and Ian MacMillan proposed formalizing the scanning procedure by

CASE STUDY

Spira—Six Billion Customers?

Andrew B. Krafsur, CEO of Spira Footwear, Inc., contends that everyone on the planet is a potential customer for his company's shoes. Formed in January 1999, Spira was initially funded through loans from the founder and his wife. In the spring of 2001, the company sold common stock through a private placement, obtaining proceeds of US$1,155,000. Spira introduced its shoes to the market in December 2001.

The critical competitive component that Spira offered was a patented "WaveSpring" technology. According to the company website, "WaveSpring technology stores and disburses energy with every step."[4] The spring involved is laterally stable, lightweight, and compact. It can fit in both the heel and forepart of the shoe.

In July of 2007, Spira issued a private placement memorandum seeking a total of US$4,000,000 from accredited investors—i.e., individuals with net worth of at least US$1,000,000 or an annual income of at least US$200,000. The funds were to be used to reduce debt, to increase inventory, and for market expansion, including in international markets. Over the next year negotiations with the primary targeted investment group proved slower than expected. Less than US$1,000,000 was raised, leading the executive team to seek other sources of financing. An additional half million dollars was raised from the owning family of a department store chain, and an angel investor committed a US$1,000,000 loan that could be later converted to equity.

General economic conditions throughout 2008 made fundraising efforts difficult. During that period, the number of initial public offerings in the United States fell drastically and bank lending was reduced. Spira's financing efforts were delayed and met with multiple challenges, causing, in turn, delays in the implementation of growth strategies. By early 2009, Spira was positioned to license its technology to other manufacturers and to enter selected markets in Europe. The global recession that began in 2008 limited Spira's ability to obtain financing. Additionally, growth projections were adjusted to take into account reduced consumer buying power. The management team continued to focus on sales growth, including leveraging an alliance with the Walt Disney Company.

"Copying other organizations' activities sounds like industrial espionage to some people, but the truth is that benchmarking is perfectly legal and ethical." Warren Bennis

  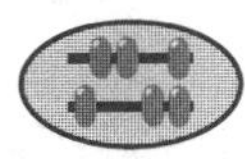   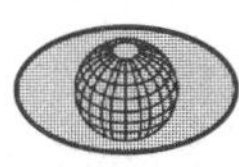   

devising a register in which opportunities could be categorized as one or other of the following:[2]

- redesign of products or services
- redifferentiation of products or services
- resegmenting of the market
- reconfiguring of the market
- development of breakthrough competencies

ASSESSMENT OF OPPORTUNITIES

Enterprises that have been functioning for a period of time have strategies that were either formulated or which emerged. The first test of whether to seize an opportunity is to evaluate whether it is consistent with the firm's strategy, as the risk and cost of failure can be high if there is a mismatch. On the other hand, if the business is in decline, an opportunity that requires a change in strategy may be the key to renewal and growth.

Before pursuing the opportunity, firm managers should ascertain the conditions that produced it. Will they persist? Is there a market of sufficient size to make the opportunity attractive? And what resources are required to succeed in exploiting the opportunity?

Failure to consider this last question can lead to disaster. Many small and medium enterprises do not have the resource base to embark on high-growth trajectories. Such growth may demand significant capital infusions. Smaller firms may not have access to traditional sources of capital. They may not have collateral or credit lines for borrowing and are not likely to be publicly traded, so they can't seek equity investment. Financing at this stage requires creativity. It is not unusual for business owners in the early growth stages to rely first on their own resources—personal savings, home mortgages, pension funds, etc.—followed by funding from family and friends. A family member with a steady income and solid credit record may be the cosigner on a bank loan. For some companies, financing may not be available at all. In such situations, "bootstrapping" may be the appropriate course of action. This term is derived from the notion of pulling oneself up by the bootstraps, i.e., being self-reliant. It involves finding ways of achieving goals when capital is limited, minimizing the need for outside financing, maximizing the impact of the entrepreneur's investment, and/or optimizing cash flow.[3]

Some additional criteria that SMEs use to screen opportunities include:

- the competitive environment and profit potential of the industry;
- general and local economic conditions;
- the ability of the firm to achieve a sustainable competitive advantage;
- the competence of the management team;
- the prospects for wealth creation and the feasibility of harvesting that wealth.

EXPLOITATION OF OPPORTUNITIES

There are numerous triggers that may enable a small firm to seize a growth opportunity:

- the firm finds an unexploited market niche, and the newly tapped demand launches the growth stage
- the firm overcomes the "liability of newness" factor as customers, suppliers, and creditors conclude that it will survive and they increase the level of business which they are willing to conduct
- the management team travels up the learning curve, becoming more competent, perhaps even redefining the nature of the business
- the founder faces a crisis and is forced to reinvent the business
- a change of leadership brings in new ideas and perspectives
- the business acquires and exploits skills it did not previously have
- alliances are formed with partners that may help the firm to enter new markets or introduce new products
- managers recognize that the company has entered a gradual decline that must be reversed if the business is to survive

Because growth opportunities typically exceed the capacity of the small or medium enterprise, creative approaches may be needed to obtain the finance that will build such capacity. Immediate sources of equity or debt are most likely to be the owners themselves and other management team members. This is typically followed by family members who are willing to accept risk in support of their relatives. The willingness of banks to provide financing is usually a function of the credit history of the firm and economic conditions. In the case of SMEs, banks often look to the assets of the owner rather than the revenue-generating ability of the firm.

Numerous alternative organizations engage in lending practices, however. Credit unions have become aggressive in business lending. For minority and disadvantaged populations, a variety of microlenders provide financial assistance. For those firms whose growth phase has true value-creating potential, wealthy individuals known as business angels may be a source of funds. Angel investors often bring the added benefit of business management expertise, and may serve in formal or informal advisery capacities with an enterprise to which they provide money.

CONCLUSION

Creativity and an ability to identify opportunities are seen as characteristics of entrepreneurs at the time they start their companies. Enterprises that prosper and grow must continue to identify and pursue opportunities. In an existing small or medium business, structuring the process for recognizing and exploiting opportunities prevents the management team from slipping into routines that worked in the past but may not keep the firm competitive in the future. Enterprise managers must be able to:

▸▸ MAKING IT HAPPEN

The growth of an enterprise is often accompanied by increased bureaucratization. When a company is founded and in the start-up stage, the owner is involved with everything. As the firm grows, even small businesses develop policies, procedures, and guidelines. As these rules develop, the management team must be diligent to prevent them from stifling further growth. Such diligence should lead to an organizational culture that encourages the assessment and pursuit of opportunities. Actions that can be taken to promote this include:

- familiarizing new employees with the history and traditions of the enterprise, especially introducing them to the sacrifices that were made and the initiatives taken;
- investing in continuing education for all employees, not just on specific job requirements, but also on improving communication and other interpersonal skills;
- providing information about industry conditions and forecasts, technological developments, and other topics;
- engaging in team-building efforts, particularly those that hone opportunity identification and assessment skills.
- Devising a system that reinforces experimentation and innovation.

"To take a simple example, a construction company is, on the face of it, a perfectly appropriate investment. But if a great deal of its activity involves the building of casinos, then it is not for an Islamic investor."
Hasnita Dato Hashim

1 identify opportunities;
2 assess whether those opportunities are appropriate for their firms;
3 devise strategies to exploit the opportunities.

These steps require more planning than entrepreneurs generally engage in at the time they create their ventures. And the management team should always keep in mind that implementing the plans will be different from formulating them.

▸▸ MORE INFO

Books:

Bhidé, Amar V. *The Origin and Evolution of New Businesses*. New York: Oxford University Press, 2000.

Harvard Business Review on Entrepreneurship. Boston, MA: Harvard Business School Press, 1999.

Hitt, Michael A., *et al.* (eds). *Strategic Entrepreneurship: Creating a New Mindset*. Oxford: Blackwell, 2002.

Websites:

Capital Formation Institute: www.cfi-institute.org

National Association of Seed and Venture Funds (NASVF; US): www.nasvf.org

US Small Business Administration: www.sba.gov

NOTES

1 Ronstadt, Robert. "The corridor principle." *Journal of Business Venturing* 3:1 (1988): 31–40.

2 Gunther McGrath, Rita, and Ian MacMillan. *The Entrepreneurial Mindset: Strategies for Continuously Creating Opportunity in an Age of Uncertainty*. Boston, MA: Harvard Business School Press, 2000.

3 Cornwall, Jeffrey. *Bootstrapping*. Upper Saddle River, NJ: Prentice Hall, 2009.

4 spirafootwear.com, accessed February 14, 2009.

"Every falling-away from species virtue, every crime against one's own nature, every evil act, every one without exception records itself in our unconscious, and makes us despise ourselves." Abraham Maslow

  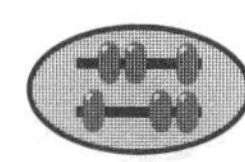   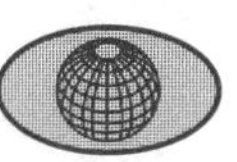   

Avoiding the Mistakes of the Past: Lessons from the Startup World by James E. Schrager

EXECUTIVE SUMMARY

Congratulations if you didn't personally feel the hardship of the dot-com implosion. Many millions went to their demise but at least left behind a legacy of what not to do. Fear not if you won't be using the internet in your next venture. Many of these lessons generalize well beyond their former faulty incarnations. For those of you with a new product, technology, or division to launch, most translate into corporate organizations.

INTRODUCTION

Failure is a wonderful teacher. The new-economy revolution had many of the trappings of a genuine economic revolt: vast fortunes forged in a fortnight, dashing young heroes and heroines, rotten institutions brought to their knees. It held such great promise, yet today even the dreams feel thoroughly eviscerated. What to learn from the revolution that never was? What lessons can be applied to new ventures?

There is no better place to look for historical clues than the business plans presented by aspiring business managers. These serve as the revolutionary documents of record, holding within their propositions the seeds of ultimate success or failure. We will reassess these pillars of revolutionary wisdom.

THE LESSONS TO LEARN

We Will Establish First-Mover Advantage

The problem with this mantra is that first mover by itself means little; what matters instead is the power of your strategy. The first team to execute a dumb idea has accomplished nothing. In some cases, when you have an exceptional new technology, being first brings power. In other cases—say, when your strategy is nothing more than another way to sell books—being first has little effect. Post-revolution, you can safely ignore the first-mover boasts. Instead, worry about the inherent strength or weakness of the business strategy.

Amazon was concerned with being the first big player selling books on the Web. However, Amazon's profit struggle has shown that being first made little difference. If you have an invention, for example, the xerographic copy process, being first is wonderful. But note the difference: Xerox got a patent for its process, thereby making it not only the first, but also the only company to offer a plain-paper copier. Since no one could duplicate its service, it was able to charge a premium. Amazon will never be the only seller of books, so its margins will always be subject to pressure. First mover is fine when defensible, but meaningless without a way to stop competitors entering the market.

We Will Be the Technology Leader

Venture capitalists (VCs) are at their best when making carefully calibrated bets on technology companies. They have mostly ignored the rough-and-tumble world of retail business on their way to investments in computer memory chips, software codes, medical devices, pharmaceuticals, genomics, magnetic storage media, telecom satellites, optical bandwidth, and truly new technologies. In each case, tech-company founders had to produce something new and wonderful that worked as promised, would be in great demand, and could be protected via patents, trade secrets, or switching costs. Internet retailers may claim to have some bits of technology in a one-click purchase screen or real-time chat lists, but these are hardly protectable. As such, e-retailing cannot be the basis of a technology strategy.

Claims of new technologies that cannot be protected are not worth much. Instead, strategies may center on building a brand; however, this is expensive to construct and requires constant maintenance to remain viable.

We Will Create a Powerful Image

Instead of worrying about technology that can be protected, retailers concentrate on the precise construction of a tailored image to appeal to a consistently fickle public. Priceline discovered how expensive it is to spend for a national audience and capture just a tiny slice. The overreach inherent in most mass-media advertising makes it a very dull tool for carving a startup's image. So how will the image be created? Post-revolution business plans need to find a more efficient way than simply throwing money at the problem! Your marketing plan must also develop a carefully conceived media approach to allow for your image to be built in an economically efficient manner.

We Will Attract the Best VCs—With Their Reputations We Can't Fail

As long as VCs can sell the idea to Wall Street, they'll build the company. When they cannot, they'll do their best to be long gone. Post-revolution, VCs who dabbled in e-commerce look just like other Wall Street pawns, appearing to be infallibly brilliant when the market goes up and hapless fools when the market collapses.

The final customer for your product rarely cares who was behind the financing. It's clearly better to have a brilliant idea funded by people no one has ever heard of than a specious idea promoted by a well-known VC shop.

We Plan a Full-Scale National Rollout to Leverage Our First-Mover Advantage and Ensure Our Ability to Grow

An accurate market test is your very best insurance against a giant belly flop. But don't think you'll impress anyone by faking it. For example, a pacemaker distributor in Japan gauged demand for a new product by displaying it to its current customers. Even though the doctors involved in the test showed overwhelming approval of the new device, it didn't meet sales projections once launched. In looking at why the test failed, the distributor noticed that the new device sold almost exclusively to existing customers. The distributor failed to realize the extent to which doctors are brand-sensitive. Make it a real test or don't bother.

We Will Form Alliances with Key Players

This is a fine idea, except that in the early days no one knows who will win. In times of rapid change, even an alliance with a leading company may not deliver the promised advantages. The underlying business strategy, not just its alliances, must be more carefully understood. Very few partnerships in which the giving and taking aren't balanced will survive.

The internet Changes Everything

Well, not really. The information superhighway is certainly here to stay, and we'll use it more and more, but gone are the stories of TheStreet.com buying Dow Jones, e-STEEL buying Bethlehem, and Amazon buying Wal-Mart. Other than Wall Street bonuses, the immediate changes wrought by the internet were fairly modest and will play out over a much longer period than the

"The mistakes of the great, promulgated along with the discoveries of their genius, are apt to work havoc."
Erwin Schrödinger

  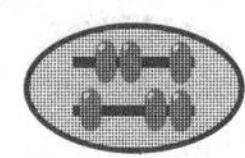 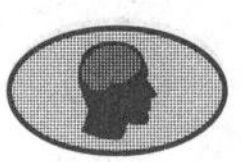  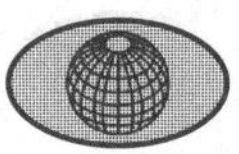   

matter of weeks we were promised at the outset.

In fact, it's comforting to know that the internet won't change everything overnight. The pace of change continues, even though not all change is progress. The internet does enable very rapid access to information and the rather carefree exchange of e-mail messages. If either of these two attributes can drive your business plan further or faster, by all means use the internet to get there. But what the internet will not do is take people out of the center of the business process.

CONCLUSION

The basic rules of business strategy remain intact and do indeed apply to the internet. Like selling things in a store, selling products on a computer screen isn't about technology. A technology business develops something new that cannot be easily imitated. This is the great lesson of the internet failures. New businesses can be understood by looking at success and failure patterns of the past. A careful review of the strategy you propose can help.

MAKING IT HAPPEN

- Protect any new technology with patents or trademarks—create barriers to market entry.
- Determine your strategy, then your goals (growth isn't a strategy; it's a goal).
- Aim to reach your target market in an economical way.
- Promote your marketable idea, not your financial backers.
- Stage an accurate market test.
- Use the internet if it can drive your business plan further or faster.
- Be realistic: by all means consider different scenarios, but do not lose sight of reality.

MORE INFO

Books:

Gupta, Udayan (ed). *Done Deals: Venture Capitalists Tell Their Stories*. Cambridge, MA: Harvard Business School Press, 2000.

Slywotzky, Adrian, *et al*. *Profit Patterns: 30 Ways to Anticipate and Profit from Strategic Forces Reshaping Your Business*. New York: Random House, 1999.

See Also:

Nicholas Negroponte (p. 1180)
E-Commerce (pp. 1508–1510)
Information Technology (pp. 1522–1523)

"The man who makes no mistakes does not usually make anything." E. J. Phelps

  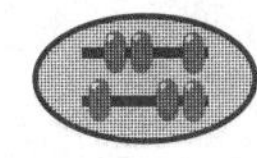 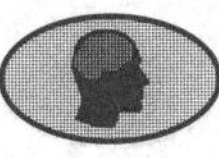  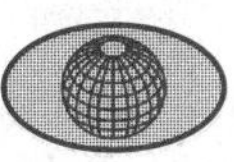   

Viewpoint: Rajiv Dogra

India Today and Tomorrow

INTRODUCTION

Rajiv Dogra is a diplomat by profession, engineer by training, writer by choice and an artist by inclination. He is currently he is based in New Delhi and is a well-known commentator and columnist. He became a member of the Indian Diplomatic Service in 1974. During the course of a wide ranging professional career he was India's Ambassador to Italy, Romania, Moldova, Albania and San Marino . He was also India's Permanent Representative to the United Nations Agencies in Rome (FAO, WFP and IFAD), and India's last full time Consul General in Karachi. He is the author of two novels; Footprints in Foreign Sands and Almost an Ambassador. Amongst the honours received by him is an Honorary Doctorate.

A TENTATIVE POWER

India has long been the object of myths. The early Romans believed that this phenomenally rich country was guarded in the north by a solid wall of ivory, while Pliny the senior worried that India's huge trade surplus would bankrupt the Roman Empire. More recently, in the 18th century, India accounted for 22.6% of global trade.

Today, however, with close to 18% of the world's population, India's GDP is barely 1% of the global total. This modest rating seems natural for a country which has spent much of its independent existence in a mode of self-preservation, a principal priority for a nation that was subjugated under numerous invaders for centuries before its bloody rebirth in 1947.

It is little surprise then that apprehension defined many of India's early policies. Nonalignment was essentially an astute institutional mechanism to keep the eastern and western blocs at bay. The same wariness was responsible for an inward-looking approach to economic development, and domestic monopolies encouraged this fear of the foreign.

As a result, India was fatalistically wedded to an austere rate of growth till the early 1990s. It was content with this soul satisfying, but bare-to-the-bones performance, as long as it validated its part socialist, part capitalist, agonizingly plural, and noisily democratic experiment in nation building.

As in the past, the proudest achievement in its post independence history has been reinscribing into the national ethos the value of tolerance. Consequently, everything is possible and all avenues are open. That is why India continues to pursue a firmly secular line, adopting all religions. This spirit of accommodation also leads again and again to foreign policy choices that can best be termed as those of a soft power, not that of a smart power.

This idealism has also led India to technological choices where it has sought gain through pain by insisting on reinventing the wheel, terming that struggle "appropriate technology." It established its own technological and business universities to rival those in the West, and started on its own torturously slow course to enhance its technological capabilities. This set it apart from others in the region, and also paved the way for an educated, ambitious middle-class that today equally powers Silicon Valley and Bangalore's call centers.

In part, this self-imposed grind is a principled position—an application at all levels of its motto that truth alone should triumph, even if that truth needs to be technologically carved out by its own efforts. There is even a label for this painful quest: *swadeshi* or self-reliance.

In contrast, China has taken a different, more pragmatic route, choosing instead to harness the technological revolutions in the West for its growth. This same difference in approach between India and China can also be witnessed when they tackle the issue of future prosperity. China has a foreign exchange reserve of US$2 trillion and sits happily on it. India has a little over US$250 billion and worries constantly.

But managing large foreign exchange reserves is the lesser of India's worries in the coming years. There are larger, more fundamental challenges that lie ahead, and how India handles them will determine its place on the global stage. In particular, the litmus test is whether India, or rather its democracy, can deliver in a country that is largely poor, suffers a scarcity of food and water, and is governed by coalition governments whose partners often pull in different ideological directions. Can India continue to avoid a million mutinies as it sets forth on a new, faster paced agenda?

BOOM, BUST, AND PROMISE

There is no doubt that India broke out of its long self-imposed slumber in the early 1990s. Two important changes took place almost simultaneously. First, a new generation began to step into decision-making positions within the government and industry. This ambitious leadership was no longer encumbered by the neuroses of a colonial past. It was instead confident and bubbling with ideas for India's place in a new technological world. Second, the 1990s also marked the beginning of the end of a deep held suspicion about the private sector, a major shift in attitude.

On a practical level, however, caution was still the watchword and its mantra make haste slowly. Reforms arrived warily and with limitations, but the doors of the Indian economy had definitely creaked open and investor confidence increased correspondingly.

Previously, Indians settled abroad remitted funds to their families back home on an as needed basis. Now, they began to park their funds in high yielding financial instruments, hoping to tap into this prosperous new India. Investments in new start-ups grew dramatically, and, by 2007, inward remittances to India had reached an annual figure of US$25 billion, the highest in the world. International investors also began looking for trophy acquisitions in Indian industry, actively adding the "Indian option" to their portfolios.

In the early 2000s, as Indian software companies leveraged off their success in preparing for the feared millennium bug, it seemed that the sky was no longer the limit.

Year after year, the Indian economy began posting 8–9% GDP growth. Superlatives such as *India Rising*, *India Shining*, and *Incredible India* rolled in routinely. The international media was besotted and began to laud India, regardless of its warts. For a few years, it looked as if India was truly everywhere.

In line with the recent economic record, 2008 started magnificently with India finally within sight of double digit economic growth. At a societal level, secular India was now increasingly ambition driven rather than separated by religion. The stock market was booming and the flood of foreign capital was assuming embarrassingly large proportions.

But the turmoil in the financial markets through the year soon provided a sharp reminder that this new paradigm brought not only opportunities, but also the real risk of a sharp economic downturn. India could not avoid the debris of the Western financial meltdown and this revived the idea that perhaps India's earlier phobia of anything external was not unwarranted.

The slowdown has also brought home the growing realization that as an economic power, India has many problems in its own backyard. Ideally, the subcontinental region around India should be in intense engagement with itself—an eminently sensible approach as the alternative is strife.

Viewed dispassionately, the region shows tremendous potential. China, India, Pakistan and Bangladesh together contain a population of almost 2.8 billion people, a little over 41% of the global total. This is a formidable human resource, with history-shaping possibilities as a market. Properly harnessed, one could only imagine the boost this could give to regional industry and trade. In today's context of an increasingly globalized economy, it also represents an incredible new opportunity for the wider world.

THE GEOPOLITICAL LANDSCAPE

That's the theoretically feasible part. The reality, unfortunately, is ridden with roadblocks. India is surrounded by a number of neighbors who are unlikely to see it progress with a friendly eye. So, the illusion that it could make others in the region partners in its progress is likely to be stumped by a rude reality check.

If the European Union is the largest example of a stable economic and political union, South Asia presents the picture in reverse. From one country, it devolved into three—India, Pakistan, and Bangladesh. Economic integration may provide a useful slogan occasionally at regional meetings in South Asia, but businessmen who value their money are unlikely to take it seriously for a very long time yet.

India lives in a tough neighborhood. The countries to its west are particularly fragile. Pakistan is a failing economy, riven with terror and drugs. Under an almost constant military thumb from its inception, it is poised presently between naïve optimism and harmful self-destruction. Further up, Afghanistan is in historical hemorrhage. Every so often, it finds itself a new reason to bleed, with the Taliban providing the latest iteration of a thousand cuts.

To the south, Sri Lanka is finally emerging from a bloody civil war. But its disparate society will take a long time to settle. To India's east, Myanmar lurches between being a forbidden state and a forbidding entity thanks to its military junta. Bangladesh has episodic experiments with democracy before a general whimsically decides that enough is enough. In the north, Nepal has transitioned quickly from a self-serving monarchy to stultifying Maoists, Nepal's current ideological inspiration, and its neighbor, China, is in an all weather monochromatic mode.

By their very nature, dictatorships do not encourage the spirit of enquiry that is so essential to the evolution of a nation. Like human beings, nations must reinvent themselves constantly to succeed. But such churning is only possible in a democracy, and it seems that India may remain an isolated island of democracy in the region for some time to come.

The other reality that India must remain conscious of is the fact that its weaknesses are no longer only internal. It is true that there are plenty of internal tensions: regional disparities, social inequality, shoddy infrastructure, and poor healthcare, to name just a few of the issues that keep people angry. But the ability to shout democratically lets off some steam continually and, more recently, there is also the assurance that the idea of growth is working and is broadly inclusive.

The larger and more serious challenges for India are external. Terror remains the biggest security concern. The lack of democracy elsewhere in the region will keep adding to large-scale migration into India. Moreover, the economy will continue to be sensitive to global cues. Therefore, ignoring these external factors would be poor policy and India's greatest advances in the future will likely come from its ability to manage them.

THE FUTURE?

In this, it should be served well by the fact that nearly 50% of India's population is below the voting age. Just as the youthful generation of the 1990s did not carry the baggage of post-colonial prejudices, the new crop of leaders do not have bitter memories of economic deprivation from the 1950s and 1960s. Instead, they have been brought up on a diet of liberalization and have seen innovation pay rich dividends. These young men and women will influence the important decisions that need to be made on transformational issues, such as development and India's place in the new world architecture.

There is no doubt that India wants to participate with greater vigor on the global stage and feels it has a justifiable claim. There is also a growing recognition by the outside world that the changed global realities necessitate that a large country like India must not remain on the sidelines. The reasons are unambiguous: it has the second largest population in the world, and is the largest democracy which actively promotes secularism as its governing article of faith. Moreover, with its growing intellectual, economic, and technological participation in the world, it can contribute meaningfully in shaping a post-credit crunch global order.

But the passage to the global high table is not going to be smooth. Leaving aside regional prejudices, the Big Five—the United States, United Kingdom, Russian Federation, China, and France—still maintain the heart of the United Nations as an exclusive preserve. Not all of them retain the global status today they once had, and so are likely to resist any expansion till the last possible moment. India may, therefore, find itself waiting at the door-step of the UN Security Council for a long while yet.

However, it may receive an invitation from the G8 within the year. This pragmatic offer will be an important first step for India, along with others, such as Brazil and South Africa, to interact annually with the leaders of the current G8. That invitation may also set in motion a chain of events, where India could find itself participating more actively on issues of global governance.

The recent global financial turmoil has brought about the belated recognition that the world urgently needs a more effective regulatory system, if it is to avoid any more painful shocks of this magnitude. Here, India's record of a prudently run and mostly unscathed banking system stands out, though events such as the recent Satyam fiasco—India's Enron—shows that no system is immune to human ingenuity.

Over the next few decades, as its profile becomes larger and more complex, the challenges for India will multiply also.

"Business doesn't have to choose between making profit and protecting the environment, between economic success and ethical responsibility, between satisfying the customer and meeting the demands of other stakeholders. In other words, we don't have to make a choice between profits and principles." Jeroen Van der Veer

  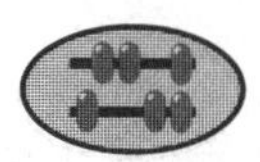   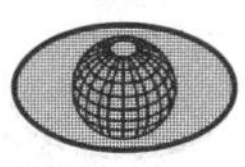   

From ancient times, India has fascinated visitors by its abstraction and bewildered them with its variety. Now, and increasingly in the future, outsiders will seek a more comprehensible India and one with which they can do business.

India's challenge lies in putting up that modern face.

▸▸ MORE INFO

Books:

Nilekani, Nandan. Imagining India: The Idea of a Renewed Nation. New York: Penguin Press, 2009.

Sen, Amartya. *The Argumentative Indian: Writings on Indian History, Culture and Identity.* New York: Farrar, Straus and Giroux, 2005.

See Also:

★ Geopolitical Risk: Countering the Impact on Your Business (pp. 465–467)
★ Globalization and Regional Business Strategy (pp. 769–771)
★ Middle East and North Africa Region: Financial Sector and Integration (pp. 254–257)
★ Viewpoint: Hamish McRae (pp. 789–790)
★ Viewpoint: Mark Mobius (pp. 328–329)
India (pp. 1404–1406)

"Patents on life. . .the enclosure of the intellectual and biological commons." Vandana Shiva

  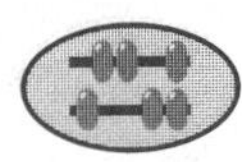 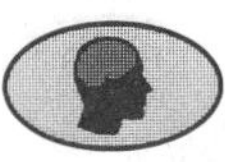  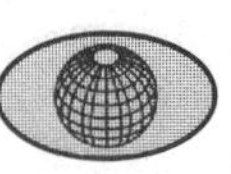   

Corporate-Level Strategy by David R. Sadtler

EXECUTIVE SUMMARY

- The parent company should add more value than other owners could.
- The skills at the center need to match the improvement opportunities in the businesses.
- Geographic and sectoral diversification are to be avoided; there are other ways to grow.
- Vertical integration is unlikely to succeed.
- When value added no longer seems feasible, demerge or break up completely.
- Good central managers never stop demanding real and substantial value added.

INTRODUCTION

Implementing a successful corporate-level strategy has become an urgent priority for all corporations. Parent companies must demonstrate that they are creating stockholder value by their own actions and initiatives, and not just reaping the profits of the businesses in their charge. The sanctions for being seen to fail in this challenge can be severe. At the very least, stock prices will suffer; at the other extreme, predators will force a breakup.

A FRAMEWORK

The challenge of corporate-level strategy is to ensure that value is being added to every business in the company's portfolio. That value must, of course, exceed its cost. Corporations with good corporate strategies do even better: they add more value than other companies in the same businesses.

Ensuring that this value-added process is productive requires several actions by top management:

1. It must identify ways in which each business can be helped. This help must make possible a major improvement in business performance. Without an understanding of where improvement potential exists, the search for value added cannot be real and substantial. These improvement opportunities should be identified and agreed on through managerial dialog and business-planning systems.
2. Central management must make sure that it possesses the skills to provide the help needed. Different kinds of improvement opportunities require different forms of help. Management must see that it has those capabilities.
3. It must construct a portfolio of businesses in which this constructive fit—useful skills attuned to the needs of the businesses—exists. How businesses can be helped is bound to change over time. The strength of the fit must be continually reappraised.
4. Management must ensure that it is sufficiently familiar with the requirements for the success of each business and that it will not damage that business, whether by approving the wrong investment proposals, appointing the wrong general managers, or giving poor strategic guidance.

QUESTIONS FOR MANAGEMENT

The pursuit of added value often presents managers with challenging issues to resolve.

How can we grow if our core business is limited in terms of further expansion? This question arises when management has divested businesses that didn't fit and is left with one core business. If it has a commanding market share, competes in a nongrowing market, and has little opportunity for overseas expansion, the dilemma can be a real one. This is especially true in an era in which capital markets reject diversification and demand that companies stick to their knitting.

Capital markets are wary of any form of corporate diversification. They are simply being pragmatic: experience has shown them that diversification doesn't work well. What is the single-business company to do to find growth opportunities? There are four possible answers:

1. Seek a way to reinvent the business by looking for new customers, new markets, new ways to present the product, and a better package of customer value to offer. Even commodity products can be differentiated by offering them in a different service context. First, make certain that growth limits really have been reached.
2. Consider moves into related businesses that share existing resources and skills. Such initiatives should possess the same requirements for success. If not, the management skills both at the business-unit level and in the parent company may be inadequate to the challenge.
3. Operate a nursery of new ideas. Business unit managers are always on the lookout for new products and markets. The more promising should be regarded as new-product research and development initiatives. Those that offer promise can then receive modest investment until there is a persuasive reason to make a serious commitment.
4. Although unconventional in today's environment, it may be smart simply to operate the existing low-growth business for cash flow, eschewing major growth aspirations. Mature industries can often be sustained for a long time without heavy investment and achieve above-average returns.

What's wrong with vertical integration as a way of extending the opportunities for a stagnant business? In other words, why shouldn't we acquire our customer to guarantee an outlet for our products?

Vertical integration has increasingly lost favor among thoughtful managers. While it may seem like a sensible proposition to guarantee a supply of raw materials or markets for your products, vertical integration frequently exhibits three major shortcomings:

1. When one division sells products to another division, disagreement often arises about transfer pricing and product and service quality. The selling division realizes it has a captive customer and often works less hard to retain the business. Much time is wasted resolving such intramural issues.
2. Entry into new upstream or downstream businesses often involves competing with your existing customers. Several corporate breakups have been the result of the realization that this problem was insoluble under the existing ownership arrangements.
3. Entry into new businesses often involves dealing with differing requirements for success; it thus requires a new range of managerial skills and capabilities, both at the business-unit level and in the parent company. Mistakes are made, and the business suffers competitively.

Is it wise to limit the number of eggs in our basket? Management teams often seek positions in different industrial sectors simply to spread risk. They reason that when one sector is unattractive owing to a cyclical market turndown, other sectors can take up the slack. While this can give comfort to management teams, it's an unwise strategy in today's markets. Capital

"The art of reaching business targets is not to aim at the impossible, but to aim at the championship level."
Charles Forte

  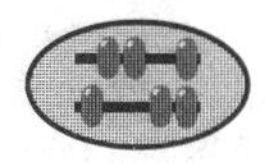 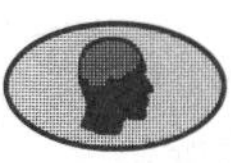  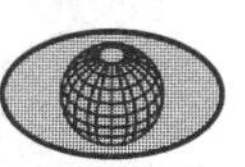   

markets will say: "We can spread our own risk; you do what you know how to do." The management team that focuses its effort and investment on areas in which it has demonstrable skills will be rewarded appropriately in capital pricing. The same caution should be applied to overseas diversification. Some management teams intentionally direct investment to different parts of the world in order to limit exposure in any one area. Unless such geographic expansion is initiated to strengthen one's competitive positioning in a particular global marketplace, the investment community is likely to scorn this form of expansion. There are simply too many downsides to investment abroad to undertake it without a solid competitive business rationale. Currency exposure, entry into alien market environments, and bone-wearying travel all represent significant costs of expanding internationally.

The pressures to build a bigger company are enormous: managers are taught to believe that their enterprise must grow or die; ambitious executives want new challenges—they expect to get paid more when the company gets bigger, and they may believe that economies of scale are always the reward from sheer size. But the pressures of bureaucratic cost, operating manager motivation, decision-making complexity, internal competitive conflicts, suspicion of remote top managers inequitably enriching themselves, and the like all represent potential downsides to great size. To be responsible stewards of stockholder interest, directors and top managers must continually examine and manage this implied trade-off. Failure to do so can be the ultimate destroyer of value-added strategy.

DEMERGER AND BREAKUP

When it becomes clear that a failed corporate strategy is in place—when you recognize that substantial and discernible value is not being added—the question of portfolio changes arises. In some cases this may involve simply a trade, sale, or demerger of the business for which there is no fit. Sometimes, when the value-added formula has substantially dissipated, total breakup is indicated: the company ceases to exist in its entirety and breaks into several pieces.

Successful corporate strategists believe in the primacy of value added. They constantly seek out ways to provide the kind of help the businesses in the corporate portfolio need. They continually search for major improvement opportunities among the businesses. They adjust both their portfolio of businesses and the capabilities of the parent company to provide a continuing match between the needs of the business units and what the parent can provide. And when the businesses need no further help of the sort they can offer—and this often happens—they wish them Godspeed and release them into the outside world.

CASE STUDY

The UK conglomerate Hanson Trust offers a superb example of how to do it right. During the 1970s and 1980s it built a portfolio of low-tech, mature businesses by means of acquisition and disposal. It sought out undermanaged companies with major positions in mature businesses that were looking for opportunities to strengthen their competitive position by tight, disciplined management. When its acquisitions brought in businesses that didn't fit Hanson's profile, they were disposed of. Hanson was clear about its value-added formula: it found businesses whose fortunes could be dramatically improved through tight financial discipline and strong general management motivation. It worked well and stockholders benefited greatly.

In the 1990s it became apparent that the formula no longer had much to offer stockholders. Major opportunities for the Hanson treatment were waning, especially in the United Kingdom and the United States. All the fat targets had been exploited. At the same time computer-facilitated financial control systems made Hanson's approach an ordinary corporate capability. Finally the businesses in the Hanson stable became so well run that there was little improvement potential left. Realizing that the value-added formula had become obsolete, the company broke itself up into five pieces, each of which has thrived competitively on its own.

▸▸ MAKING IT HAPPEN

- Make sure that value is being added to every business in the portfolio by identifying ways in which each can be helped to achieve major improvements in performance.
- Restrict the portfolio to activities in which a constructive fit—useful skills attuned to the needs of the businesses—exists at the center.
- If growth prospects appear limited, try reinvention, moves into related businesses, new ideas, or a cash-cow strategy.
- Focus effort and investment on areas in which you have demonstrable skills: don't diversify into unknown areas.
- When substantial and discernible value is not being added, change the portfolio.

▸▸ MORE INFO

Books:

Galbraith, Jay R. *Designing Organizations: An Executive Guide to Strategy, Structure, and Process*. San Francisco, CA: Jossey-Bass, 2002.

Goold, Michael, *et al. Corporate-Level Strategy*. New York: Wiley, 1994.

Kare-Silver, Michael de. *Strategy in Crisis*. New York: New York University Press, 1998.

Kraines, Gerald A. *Accountability Leadership: How to Strengthen Productivity through Sound Managerial Leadership*. Franklin Lakes, NJ: The Career Press, 2001.

Mintzberg, Henry. *The Rise and Fall of Strategic Planning*. New York: Prentice Hall, 1994.

Useem, Michael. *Leading Up: How to Lead Your Boss So You Both Win*. New York: Crown Business, 2001.

"The essence of strategy is not the structure of a company's products and markets, but the dynamics of its behavior." Tom Peters

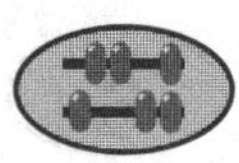

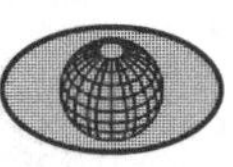

Creating Value with EVA by S. David Young

EXECUTIVE SUMMARY

- Economic value added (EVA) can serve as the cornerstone of a value-based management system.[1]
- EVA is more than a performance metric. It also represents a mindset that focuses management attention on the value-creation imperative.
- EVA is profit as economists think about profit. It differs from the conventional accounting-based approach in that it imposes charges for the use of all capital, including equity.
- The value of the firm equals capital employed, plus the present value of future EVAs. By motivating managers to increase future EVA, companies can promote value-creating behavior.
- When managers are evaluated and paid on the basis of EVA, they have stronger incentives to improve operational and capital efficiency, dispose of unprofitable business, achieve more optimal capital structures, and invest in value-creating projects.

INTRODUCTION

The value-based management movement is based on two assumptions. The first is that the main aim of any business in a market economy is to maximize shareholder value. The second is that markets are too competitive for companies to create such value by accident. They must plan for it. And that means having the right culture, systems, and processes in place so managers make decisions in ways that deliver better returns to shareholders.

At the very least, corporate functions must be informed by value-based thinking—planning, capital allocation, operating budgets, performance measurement, incentive compensation, and corporate communication. EVA is a tool for achieving this. EVA is a measure of performance, but its uses extend further. When implemented properly, and especially if tied to management compensation, it is a powerful way to promote shareholder value.

EVA: A DEFINITION

EVA is a measure of profit. Not the accounting profit we are accustomed to seeing in a corporate income statement, but profit as economists define it. Both are measured net of operating expenses; they differ only in the treatment of capital costs. While income statements recognize only the interest paid to bankers and bondholders, EVA recognizes all capital costs, including the opportunity cost of shareholder funds.

The difference between accounting profit and economic profit can be seen in Figure 1. On the left side is profit as it appears on the typical income statement, where EBIT is earnings before interest and tax (a popular term for pre-tax operating income), I is interest expense, T is income taxes, and IC is invested capital. Net income is simply operating income, with interest and taxes removed. Note that the only capital cost included in the profit measure is interest expense (the amount of debt multiplied by the interest rate).

EVA, or economic profit, also starts with EBIT. Income taxes are subtracted to produce net operating profit after tax, or NOPAT. But instead of subtracting interest, EVA charges for the use of *all* capital, including equity finance. While accounting profit charges only for the cost of debt, capital charges for the calculation of EVA equal the product of invested capital and the cost of capital (COC). The cost of capital, popularly known as the weighted-average cost of capital (WACC), is a function of the cost of debt and equity weighted for their relative proportions in the company's capital structure.

Economic profit is based on an idea generated by the English economist Alfred Marshall in the late 19th century: for investors to earn true economic profits, sales must be sufficient to cover all costs, including operating expenses (such as labor and materials) and capital charges. Such economic profits are the basis of value creation. Indeed, as management guru Peter Drucker has written, "EVA is based on something we have known for a long time: what we generally call profits, the money left to service equity, is usually not profit at all. Until a business returns a profit that is greater than its cost of capital, it operates at a loss."[2]

It can be mathematically proven that the worth of a business must equal invested capital—the sum of fixed assets, cash, and working capital—plus the present (or discounted) value of future EVA. Value determined in this way is mathematically equivalent to the value estimates produced by discounted cash flow models. The upshot: as capital market expectations of corporate EVA increase, so do share prices. Companies can thus use EVA targets to motivate managers to deliver the financial results that capital markets want. This approach is especially useful for executives one or two levels below top management, managers who have little direct influence over share price and for whom stock options are less effective.

EVA-DRIVEN COMPANIES AND FINANCIAL PERFORMANCE

So, what exactly have EVA companies done to improve financial performance and deliver superior returns to shareholders? The clues can be seen in the definition of EVA. EVA equals after-tax operating profit minus capital costs, with capital costs equal to invested capital multiplied by the WACC.[3] However, EVA can be expressed in a different, yet equivalent, way.

When operating profit is divided by invested capital, it yields a measure called return on invested capital (ROIC). The difference between ROIC and WACC,

Figure 1. Accounting profit (EBIT) versus economic profit (EVA)

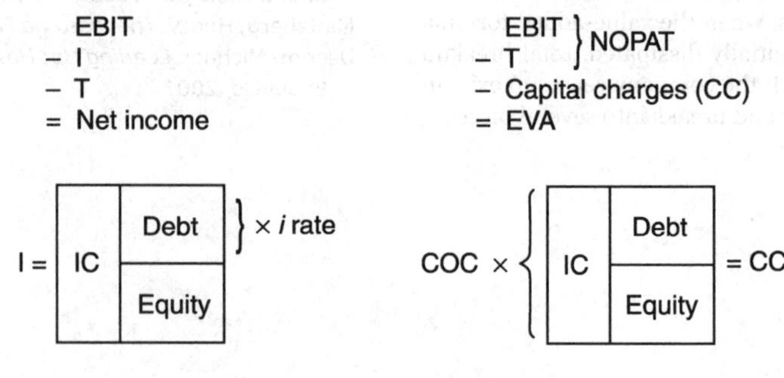

"Annual income twenty pounds, annual expenditure nineteen nineteen six, result happiness. Annual income twenty pounds, annual expenditure twenty pounds ought and six, result misery." Charles Dickens

multiplied by capital employed, equals EVA:

EVA = (ROIC – WACC) × Capital employed

Holding other variables constant, EVA increases when ROIC increases; when WACC decreases; when capital employed increases (assuming profitable growth); or when capital employed decreases (in the case of money-losing assets). Evidence from EVA adopters shows several ways to achieve improvements:

- *Increasing asset turnover*. For example, EVA companies are more likely to drive reductions in inventory and speed up the collection of receivables.
- *Repairing assets*. Many companies discover that managers on EVA incentive plans are inclined to overhaul existing assets rather than request capital to buy new ones. Also, when additional capacity is required, managers are more likely to acquire used assets.
- *Structuring deals that require less capital*. For example, Armstrong, an American plastics and floor products company, had always insisted on a controlling stake in any acquisition. After adopting EVA, the company began to define the minimum amount of capital it could put into a deal and still get what it wanted.
- *Disposing of unprofitable businesses*. Well-managed companies have always done this, but EVA-driven bonus plans create a sense of urgency to use assets more efficiently by, for example, shedding chronic money-losing operations.
- *Increasing debt financing*. Senior managers tend to "underlever" their businesses, which means they rely too much on equity finance and not enough on debt. As a result, companies fail to take advantage of valuation tax shields that can increase after-tax cash flows to capital providers. EVA changes such behavior because, when managers are charged for capital, they have powerful incentives to design capital structures that minimize the cost of capital. For the underlevered company, this means taking on debt, which is precisely what many companies have done after adopting EVA.
- *Investing in profitable growth*. The net present value (NPV) of future cash flows for a proposed capital investment is mathematically equivalent to the present value of incremental EVAs. Therefore, future EVA will increase to the extent that investments are made in projects with positive NPV. However, because the short-term effect of investment may be to cause EVA to decline, companies must take special care to ensure that senior managers have long-term incentives to create value. This need explains, in part, why companies continue to rely on stock options. Equity participation, if structured properly, provides incentives for managers to seek out investments that will boost EVA in the future even if short-term results are compromised.

The first three of the above actions increase EVA through improvements in ROIC. Disposing of unprofitable businesses increases EVA, provided that improvements in the spread between ROIC and WACC more than compensate for the reduction in invested capital. Increasing financial leverage increases EVA by reducing the WACC, assuming that the company is underlevered when it begins taking on more debt. Investing is profitable, and increases EVA, as long as the ROIC for new investments exceeds the WACC.

EVA AND MANAGERIAL COMPENSATION

Although EVA is a potentially powerful tool for creating value-creating incentives, there are some limitations and drawbacks to its use. For example, capital charges might compel managers to forgo potentially value-creating projects out of fear that short-term EVA will suffer. Simply put, because EVA is a single-period measure of performance, managers with EVA-linked bonuses may willingly sacrifice long-term competitiveness in the interests of pursuing short-term targets. Another potential drawback is found in attempts to bring EVA into levels of the firm below the level of strategic business units. Inevitably, contentious and arbitrary cost allocations and transfer prices are required to calculate EVA. In such cases, even the most ardent proponents of EVA have found that performance indicators that represent components or predictors of EVA are more appropriate than EVA itself for incentivizing behaviour.

CONCLUSION

Great business leaders, past and present, have always known about EVA without calling it that. EVA reveals to the rest of us the insights the best business managers have always had at a deep intuitive level. To make the most of this powerful tool for value creation, managers should know that EVA is much more than a measurement system. It's also an instrument for changing managerial behavior. Implementing value-based principles requires acceptance and understanding among all managers, who not only must appreciate why value creation is so important but also must grasp the fundamental concepts underlying value creation. One of the great virtues of EVA is that it makes sound finance theory accessible, so that operating managers, including those with no background or experience in accounting or finance, can incorporate insights from these disciplines into the way they run their businesses.

CASE STUDY

SPX—Corporate Transformation through EVA

SPX is a large US auto parts and industrial products company. It was a chronic underperformer in the early 1990s, with low profits and a languishing share price. After a change of CEO in 1995, the company adopted EVA as the centerpiece of its change program. By the end of the following year a dramatic improvement in performance was evident.

After adopting EVA, SPX engaged in a broad range of actions, all with one overriding purpose: the creation of shareholder value. For example:

- In the first year after adopting EVA, inventories were cut by 15%, despite higher sales.
- SPX's portfolio of businesses underwent important changes. Several business units were sold, not because they were unprofitable but because strategic reviews revealed that the businesses were worth more to other companies. Meanwhile, several key value-enhancing acquisitions were made.
- Divisions were consolidated for greater operating efficiency. Substantial cost savings were realized.
- Several finance-based initiatives were undertaken. For example, the quarterly dividend was eliminated in favor of stock repurchases, a more tax-efficient way of returning cash to shareholders.

The above actions were neither unusual nor dramatic. Any good executive knows what they are. What makes this company's experience so instructive is that it was able to create a business culture that put value creation at the center of all key management processes and systems. Most critically, senior management bonuses were linked to EVA improvement. It's this link that provided managers with the incentive to aggressively pursue value-creating initiatives. Perhaps the key issue in any business is not whether its managers are capable of creating value, but whether they are motivated to do so.

"I just never got involved with the cash flow thing. My attitude was creativity will see me through." Adrienne Landau

  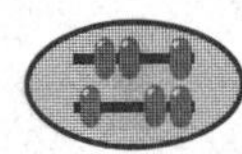 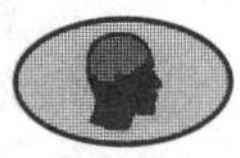  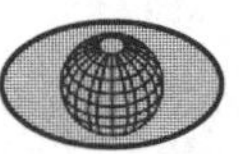   

MAKING IT HAPPEN

Because EVA is really about changing behavior and attitudes, the implementation process must begin with the board and the CEO. However, the CFO's advice and counsel will carry a lot of weight on several key implementation issues. For example,

- How will EVA be calculated? Some companies choose to make adjustments to the standard EVA measure. Finance professionals must decide which adjustments, if any, are appropriate for their own business.
- Are changes needed to the company's accounting and IT systems? Often, significant upgrades are needed to deliver divisional EVA figures in a timely fashion.
- How far down the organizational hierarchy will EVA be calculated? The rule of thumb in most companies is to limit EVA to large business units. Of course, EVA can be calculated at lower levels, but the measurement process will likely be compromised by the arbitrary nature of transfer pricing and overhead allocation practices. Instead, companies tend to rely on other key performance indicators.
- Which managers will have bonuses linked to EVA? Most users limit EVA-linked bonuses to senior managers for the same reasons noted above (i.e., the difficulty of calculating EVA below the level of strategic business units).
- Who will need training in EVA and how will the training needs be executed? Anyone whose performance evaluation or pay is affected in any way by EVA needs to understand the measure—how it's constructed and the steps they can take to improve it.

MORE INFO

Books:

Koller, Tim, Marc Goedhart, and David Wessels. *Valuation: Measuring and Managing the Value of Companies*. 4th ed. Hoboken, NJ: Wiley, 2005.

Martin, John D., and William J. Petty. *Value Based Management*. Boston, MA: Harvard Business School Press, 2000.

Young, S. David, and Stephen F. O'Byrne. *EVA and Value Based Management: A Practical Guide to Implementation*. New York: McGraw-Hill, 2001.

Website:

Value-Based Management: www.valuebasedmanagement.net/methods_eva.html

See Also:

★ Capital Budgeting: The Dominance of Net Present Value (pp. 23–26)
★ Comparing Net Present Value and Internal Rate of Return (pp. 40–42)
★ Multinationality and Financial Performance (pp. 796–797)
★ Value Creation—Perspectives and Implications (pp. 834–838)
★ Viewpoint: Ravi Nedungadi (pp. 815–816)
★ Why EVA is the Best Measurement Tool for Creating Shareholder Value (pp. 843–844)
✔ Assessing Business Performance (p. 1059)
✔ Managing the Time Value of Money (p. 871)
✔ Understanding and Calculating RORAC, RAROC, and RARORAC (p. 1006)
✔ Understanding the Weighted Average Cost of Capital (WACC) (p. 897)
The EVA Challenge: Implementing Value-added Change in an Organization (p. 1250)

NOTES

1 EVA is a registered trademark of Stern Stewart & Company.

2 Peter Drucker, *Classic Drucker*, Boston, MA: Harvard Business School Press, 2008, p. 107.

3 Some companies prefer to calculate EVA on a pre-tax basis, especially for division performance measurement.

"Forecasting by bureaucrats tends to be used for anxiety relief rather than for adequate policy making." Nassim Nicholas Taleb

  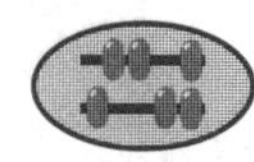 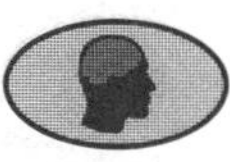  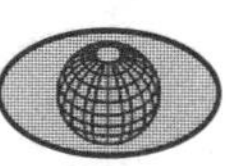   

Enhance Competitive Performance via Critical Key Performance Indicators (KPIs)

by Zahirul Hoque

EXECUTIVE SUMMARY

- Measuring performance is a fundamental part of every organization, whether it is run by a private sector or a government sector.
- Performance measures are used to evaluate organizational as well as managerial performance.
- A key performance indicator (KPI) is a quantitative value that can be scaled and used for performance evaluation.
- Organizations should use both financial and nonfinancial KPIs when measuring employee as well as firm performance.
- KPIs should be aligned with business strategy, work environment, and employee incentives.
- Too many KPIs should be avoided, to maximize their usage by employees in their day-to-day operations.
- "It is much more difficult to measure non-performance than performance."

INTRODUCTION

Measuring performance is a fundamental part of every organization, whether it is run by a private sector or a government sector. A performance measurement system (PMS) highlights whether the organization is on track to achieve its desired goals. Performance measures are primarily used to evaluate organizational, as well as employee performance. A PMS develops key performance indicators (KPIs), or metrics, depending on the nature and activities of the organization. KPIs can serve as the cornerstone of an organization's employee incentive schemes. KPIs are used as guidelines and incentives to facilitate the coordination of managers' and business unit's goals with those of the overall corporation, that is, they encourage goal congruency. Through these metrics, the organization communicates how it wishes the employees to behave, and how this behavior will be judged and evaluated. Effective organizational managers rely on KPIs to set direction, make strategic decisions, and achieve desired goals.[1]

It has been suggested that, in today's competitive and global financial crisis environments, organizations need to be masters at anticipating customers' needs, devising radical new product and service offerings, and rapidly deploying new production technologies into operating and service delivery processes.[2] For several decades, performance measurement has been used as an internal informational tool to evaluate business units' operations, and make program and budgetary decisions.

PMS AND KPIS: DEFINITIONS

A PMS typically comprises systematic methods of setting business goals, together with periodic feedback reports that indicate progress against those goals.[3] Within a PMS, an organization develops some key performance metrics or indicators. A KPI can be defined as "a quantitative value that can be scaled and used for purposes of comparison."[4] There is also the view that "KPIs are quantifiable performance measurements used to define success factors, and measure progress toward the achievement of business goals."[5] The PMS literature classifies performance measures into two major groups: financial and nonfinancial. Financial measures may include return on investment (ROI), earnings per share (EPS), revenue (sales) growth, profit margin, etc. Nonfinancial measures may include customer satisfaction, employee satisfaction, production efficiency, quality, customer services, etc.

BALANCED SCORECARD MEASURES

In today's competitive environment, one that encompasses fierce global competition, advancing technology, and increased customer awareness, traditional KPIs such as ROI and EPS can be inadequate for a business organization. Traditional KPIs, although they can aid in detecting weaknesses with respect to the use, or non use of individual investment or assets, and focus management's attention upon earning the best profit possible on the capital available, tend to avoid isolating individual business units, in that it may not be reasonable to expect the same ROI for each unit. If the unit sells its respective products in markets that differ widely, with respect to

CASE STUDY

Aligning KPIs and Strategy[6]

Omega is a water utility company that provides five core services to its customers, namely bulk water supply, water purification, reticulation of water and wastewater treatment, and wastewater disposal. On average, Omega provides services to more than 157,000 residential properties. In July 2003, Omega introduced a multidimensional PMS to improve accountability, and to communicate to organizational members the objectives and targets of the entity. As shown in Table 2, Omega developed a total of 33 KPIs for each of its six major activities. Table 2 shows this new KPI system, which, consistent with the balanced scorecard, combines a series of nonfinancial and financial KPIs. According to Omega's senior management, one of the advantages of adopting a multidimensional PMS is that it gives a better indication to employees of the long-term organizational priorities. It also helps to communicate any crisis to all of Omega's divisions, which was important to ensure that any impact is minimized. Each KPI is tailored, not to a division but to one of the five major activities of Omega, consistent with its attempts to become more outcome-focused. For instance, the percentage of lost working days or absentees is aimed at measuring Omega's ability to be a chosen employer. Similarly, the return on net operating assets is a new KPI, which is used to measure the commercial sustainability of Omega. In setting the KPIs, Omega employees suggested that it was common when the information was available to benchmark against other water entities, to ensure that the divisions are providing a service at a similar standard as their private and public counterparts, so that they are not seen to be performing poorly when the contractual period ends. Some of Omega's subdivisions also suggested that this had put the division under pressure to improve its performance.

  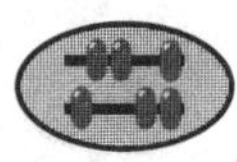   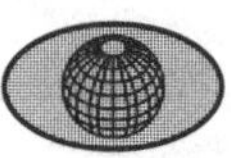   

Table 1. KPIs in a PMS within a manufacturing setting

Perspective	*KPIs*
Financial	Operating income Sales growth Return on investment Earnings per share
Customer	Market share Customer response time On-time delivery Number of customer complaints Number of warranty claims Customer satisfaction survey Sales return due to poor quality
Internal business processes	Material efficiency variance Ratio of good output to total output at each production process Rate of material scrap loss Number of new patents Number of new product launches
Employee learning and growth	Employee satisfaction survey Employee education and training Employee health and safety

product development, competition, and customer demand, lack of agreement on the optimum rate of return might discourage managers who believe the rate is set at an unfair level.

> "For several decades, performance measurement has been used as an internal informational tool to evaluate business units' operations, and make program and budgetary decisions."

For the sake of making the current period performance measure look good, be it ROI or EPS, managers may be influenced to make decisions that are not in the best long-run interests of the firm. A major concern with traditional KPIs is that these performance metrics focus on results largely internal to the firm. During the last decade, there has been an overemphasis on the use of financial KPIs to measure firm performance. This has resulted in organizations losing sight of important indicators which measure levels of customer satisfaction, process flexibility, or adaptation in response to changing needs. A strategy which concentrates on financial criteria is too closely related to short-term profit maximization. Broader measures such as customer-based measures, product and process measures, and continual improve-

Table 2. KPIs of Omega

Major strategic focus	*KPIs*
Customer focus	% Customer satisfaction % Compliance with verbal service-request response times Number of water supply interruptions per 1,000 properties Number of planned water supply interruptions per 1,000 properties Number of unplanned water supply interruptions per 1,000 properties % of water and wastewater service interruptions within 5 hours Number of customer complaints per 1,000 properties Number of water quality complaints per 1,000 properties Number of odor complaints per 1,000 properties % of meters installed within 14 days from date of payment
Chosen employer	% lost working days Training expenditure versus total operating expenditure (%)
Environmental sustainability	% tests meeting WWTP EPA license criteria Quantity of treated water supplied per property, not seasonally adjusted Number of uncontained wastewater spills % of wastewater spilt per wastewater treated % effluent reused
Commercial sustainability	Combined operating costs per property % expended of revenue-funded capital expenditure Water and wastewater renewals expenditure as a percentage of current replacement cost of system assets % unaccounted water Operating profit Return on turnover (net profit after tax/sales) Return on net operating assets (EBIT/total net assets) Debt-equity ratio (total interest-bearing debt/total equity) Total financial distribution to council (as a % of post-tax profits)
Quality water service provision	% tests meeting NHMRC (1996) bacteria criteria % tests meeting NHMRC (1996) chemical criteria Water main breaks per 100km of water main Sewer chokes per 100km of wastewater main Wastewater main (gravity and pressure) breaks per 100km of main
Accountability	% Compliance with wastewater spillage procedure (ensures spillages are properly reported and remedied) Maintenance of ISO 9000 and 14000 third-party certification

▸▸ MAKING IT HAPPEN

Developing KPIs is a critical decision-making process for any organization. Effective KPIs are those that help the organization to achieve its desired outcomes. Performance indicators must advocate the firm's internal and external environment. However, for many firms the difficulty is that there are too many KPIs, ones that are outmoded, and that are not harmonious. KPIs should observe changes in the market environment, determine and assess progress towards business strategies and goals, and affirm achievement of performance goals. This is elaborated in turn. Robert Simon at Harvard University developed three tests to assess whether a measure or metric is suitable to support a performance goal.

1 Does the KPI align with business strategy?
2 Can it measured effectively (that is, metrics should be objective, complete and responsive)?
3 Is the measure linked to economic value?[8]

According to Robert Simon (2000, p.239): "To be effective as communication devices, managers must use measures to focus attention. As you all know, what gets measured gets managed."

Linking KPIs to Business Strategy and Competitive Environments

Strategy plays an important role in the choice of KPIs, and effective KPIs must be able to assess the organization's progress on strategic priorities. Business strategy has been broadly conceptualized as a continuum spectrum between two extreme orientations: at one extreme, prospector or differentiator firms; and at the other end, defender or cost-leader firms. However, some business units may stand between both defenders and prospectors, which are often refereed to as "analyzers."[9]

"In all businesses, there is a constant tension between profit, growth, and control." Robert Simon

ment and innovation measures, enable the organization to establish longer-term improvements which further effective competition.

Further, the imperative for improved performance measures cannot be ignored with today's worldwide competition and advancing technologies. Once new technologies are introduced, major organizational changes are required, as the interaction between people and technology is essential to ensure business processes become more and more effective, and, therefore, performance measures which focus only on financial criteria will not reflect the new technological and competitive environments. New performance measures, if devised strategically, will profoundly influence business performance. Thus, more attention also needs to be placed on generating suitable nonfinancial performance measures to be a successful competitor, given today's global financial crisis. Significant attention is now being given by academics and managers to building a more extensive and linked set of measures for appraising and directing corporate and divisional performance, influenced largely by Kaplan and Norton's notion of the "balanced scorecard."

The balanced scorecard approach focuses on both financial and non-financial measures. The financial measures indicate if improvements in financial performance resulted from sacrificing investments in new products, or on-time delivery. The balanced scorecard includes financial measures that slow the results of actions already taken. Kaplan and Norton suggest that financial measures should not be eliminated altogether, because a well-designed financial performance measurement system can actually enhance, rather than inhibit an organization's management program. The balanced scorecard supplements the financial measures with operational measures on customer satisfaction, internal processes, and the firm's innovation and improvement activities. Kaplan and Norton's balanced scorecard comprises the following four dimensions:

- Financial—applying appropriate financial performance measures to ascertain whether the company is profitable.
- Customer—assessing customer satisfaction (the customer perspective). In a competitive market, customers must be content, or market share will drop. Customers care about price, faster and reliable deliveries, design, quality, and level of services.
- Internal business processes—tracking interorganizational indicators to determine whether the business units are efficiently using resources, and ascertaining competitive performance in developing "next generation" products.
- Learning and growth dimension—this measures such things as training and development, information systems, employee satisfaction, employee productivity, etc.

Kaplan and Norton suggest that the use of the balanced scorecard may motivate breakthrough improvements in critical activity areas such as products, processes, customers, and market developments. They further suggest that, while traditional financial measures report on what happened in the last period without indicating how managers can improve performance in

As defender or cost leaders focus on searching for new ways to reduce production and distribution costs, to cut marketing expenses, and to improve product quality, short-term, retrospective financial and efficiency indices (for example, cost control, internal business processes, quality and efficiency, operating profit, cash flow from operations, return on investment, etc) are relatively informative KPIs of performance. In contrast, as prospectors or differentiators compete in a broad product market domain by introducing new products and developing new markets, KPIs for focuses such as these would necessarily come from knowing what the customer wants, the level of staff involvement in creativity, and the ability of the organization to produce and market new products. Hence, a greater usage of non-financial KPIs (for example, new product development, market share, and customer satisfaction), as opposed to short-term financial indicators, would be prominent in this type of firm.

Analyzer strategies combine both defender and prospector strategies. As a result, an analyzer firm's organizational problem is how to accommodate both stable and dynamic areas of operations. The first concentrates on being efficient, and the second concentrates on watching its competitors closely, so as to determine the possibility of introducing new products or services as rapidly as possible. In relation to the first area, analyzers may tend to emphasize stability, defense of the firm's position in the market, and to earn the best profit possible. The key rationale being that too many firms are able to provide the same product at the same price, hence the incentive to increase sales, or the profit margin, is to ensure its internal processes are acting as efficiently and cost-effectively as possible. As a result, analyzers may place emphasis on short-term, financial KPIs. The second area focuses on new market opportunities by developing new brands in response to emerging environmental trends. Consequently, the level of uncertainty would be high in organizations pursuing analyzer strategy. Consistent with this strategic position, analyzers are also likely to rely more on non-financial KPIs. Thus, since analyzers operate in two combined market areas, these firms would then be more prone to incorporate a much broader range of KPIs, such as that required by the balanced scorecard. It is felt that for analyzers, four dimensions of the balanced scorecard, as outlined above, can be regarded as meeting organizational performance measurement requirements, as they provide useful insights into the firm's performance evaluation paradox in one report. In conclusion, different types of strategy will require different types of PMS and KPIs, and an appropriate fit between PMS and strategy is likely to enhance a firm's performance.

Aligning KPIs and Incentives

Are KPIs linked to employee incentives? If KPIs are not linked to employee incentive schemes they tend to be overlooked by employees and therefore they are likely to result in no desired outcomes. KPIs must be aligned with employees' individual goals and job descriptions. As a rule of thumb, Robert Simon suggested a maximum of 10 KPIs for each individual; otherwise individuals may suffer from information overload. With a reasonable number of KPIs, at the individual level, employees use KPIs to track their performance against agreed targets. Further, when developing KPIs for individuals, financial indicators should integrate nonfinancial or operational indicators on customer satisfaction, internal processes and the firm's innovation and improvement activities.

Implementation of KPIs

Organizations also need to place greater emphasis on implementation issues when designing and implementing a PMS, and relevant KPIs. A recent study in Australia identified several factors (such as top management support, adequate technology, greater employee involvement in the design stage, adequate staff training and education, and linking PMS and KPIs with other financial control models) that impact on the successful implementation of a new PMS.[10]

"Performance is your reality. Forget everything else." Harold S. Geneen

  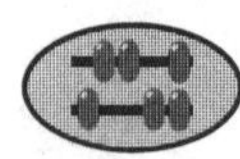 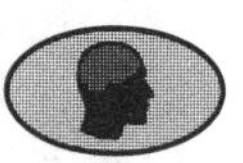  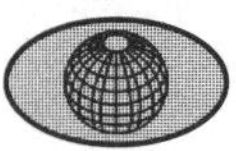   

the next, the balanced scorecard functions as the cornerstone of a company's current and future success.

Table 1 provides examples of widely used KPIs within a PMS in a manufacturing setting.

CONCLUSION

An English-born American communications executive, who was president and CEO of ITT, suggests that, "the best way to inspire people to superior performance is to convince them by everything you do and by your everyday attitude that you are wholeheartedly supporting them."[7] This short article suggests that measuring performance is important for all businesses. However, it is much more difficult to develop KPIs for each area of performance within the organization which can be measured effectively. Effective KPIs are those that enhance business performance in all areas of businesses—financial and nonfinancial. Harold Green remarks: "Performance stands out like a ton of diamonds. Non-performance can always be explained away." KPIs need to be developed to fit to the business process flow, and focus attention on the critical success factors of the business.

▸▸ MORE INFO

Books:

Hoque, Z. *Handbook of Cost and Management Accounting*. London: Spiramus, 2005.

Hoque, Z. *Strategic Management Accounting: Concepts, Processes and Issues*. 2nd ed. Sydney, Audtralia: Pearson Education, 2003.

Johnson, H. T., and R. S. Kaplan. *Relevance Lost, the Rise and Fall of Management Accounting*. Boston, MA: Harvard Business School Press, 1987.

Kaplan, R. S., and D. P. Norton. *The Balanced Scorecard: Translating Strategy into Action*. Boston, MA: Harvard Business School Press, 1996.

Lynch, R. L., and K. F. Cross. *Measure Up!* Cambridge, MA: Blackwell Publishers, 1991.

Niven, P. R. *Balanced Scorecard Step by Step: Maximizing Performance and Maintaining Results*. New York: Wiley, 2000.

Simon, R. *Performance Measurement & Control Systems for Implementing Strategy*. Upper Saddle River, NJ: Prentice Hall, 2000.

Articles:

Ittner, C. D., D. F. Larcker, and M. V. Rajan. "The choice of performance measures in annual bonus contracts." *Accounting Review* 72:2 (1997): 231–255.

Kaplan, R. S., and D. P. Norton. "The balanced scorecard—Measures that drive performance." *Harvard Business Review* (January–February 1992): 71–79.

Kaplan, R. S., and D. P. Norton. "Putting the balanced scorecard to work." *Harvard Business Review* (September–October 1993): 134–147.

Nanni, A. J., Jr, J. R. Dixon, and T. E. Vollmann. "Integrated performance measurement: Management accounting to support the new manufacturing realities." *Journal of Management Accounting Research* 4 (1992): 1–19.

Websites:

Website of Better Management: www.bettermanagement.com

Website of the Balanced Scorecard Institute: www.balancedscorecard.org

NOTES

1 Simon (2000), p.3.
2 Kaplan and Norton (1996).
3 Simon (2000), p.7.
4 *Ibid*., p.234.
5 See www.bettermanagement.com/topic/subject.aspx?f=11&s=704, accessed on February 11, 2009.
6 Based on Moll, J., and Z. Hoque. "New organizational forms and accounting innovation: The specifier/provider model in the Australian public sector." *Journal of Accounting & Organizational Change* 4:3 (2008): 243–269.
7 See www.thinkexist.com/english.Author/x/Author_3037_1htm, accessed on February 19, 2009.
8 For further details, refer to Simon (2000), pp.234–238.
9 Miles, R.E., and C.G. Snow, (1978) *Organizational Strategy, Structure, and Process*. New York: McGraw Hill, 1978.
10 Hoque, Z., and C. Adams. *Measuring Public Sector Performance: A Study of Australian Government Departments*. Melbourne: CPA Australia.

"Biopiracy is the Columbian discovery 500 years after Columbus." Vandana Shiva

   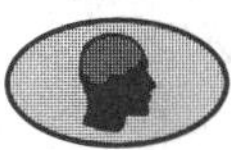  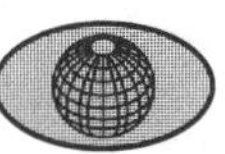   

Viewpoint: Frank Feather

China 2020: Double and Quadruple Happiness

INTRODUCTION

Frank Feather is a business futurist, with a remarkably accurate 30-year forecasting track record that often defies conventional wisdom. He is ranked as one of the "Top 100 Futurists of All Time" by Macmillan's *Encyclopedia of the Future*. A best-selling author and dynamic keynote speaker, Feather was born in the UK but is now based in Toronto, Ontario, Canada. He has consulted to companies including Ericsson, IBM, Ford, Nokia, and Shell. Continuously since 1984 he has been special adviser to China on economic modernization and market reforms, and he has seen many of his ideas implemented there. He previously worked for Barclays Bank, Toronto-Dominion Bank and CIBC.

China has a remarkable and unmatched 30-year track record of doubling and quadrupling its gross domestic product. In 1978, the country's GDP was US$147 billion and falling, per capita income was only US$190 a year, and more than 250 million people were living in abject poverty. Adjusted for inflation, the country's per capita output in 1977 was no higher than it had been in 1957.

Undaunted, China set itself some audacious goals. It aimed to quadruple its GDP between 1980 and 2000, something it had achieved by 1996. It then determined to double its output between 2000 and 2010. Again, the goal was achieved ahead of schedule. The country's next goal is to quadruple GDP between 2000 and 2020 and to achieve "moderate prosperity." China's long-term 70-year goal, laid down in 1978, is to boost its per-capita GDP to that of medium-income countries by 2050, a goal which it will almost certainly surpass before the self-imposed deadline.

WAVE-LIKE ECONOMIC DEVELOPMENT

China's overall economic strategy is simple. It is based on the "third wave" concept developed by the futurist Alvin Toffler in his book by the same title, published coincident with reforms in 1980. The book was translated into Chinese and read by every mainland Chinese politician and academic and "third wave" became part of the vocabulary.

Toffler's three waves are agriculture, industry, and services. China set about modernizing each of these sectors, shifting workers from the first to the second, and then on to the third wave. Since 1979, the mix of workers engaged in each type of activity has been transformed: the percentage of the workforce in farming has fallen from 47% to 11%; the percentage in manufacturing has fallen marginally from 39% to 49%; while the percentage engaged in services has soared from 14% to 40%. By comparison, the number of service workers in the US economy surpassed those in manufacturing in 1950, and the third wave service sector now employs 82% of the US workforce.

On my first lecture tour to China in 1984, I was asked: "What comes after the Third Wave?" In response, I developed a six-wave model, which China now uses. While client privilege prevents me from divulging how China applies this, I broke the burgeoning third wave sector into two waves (services and high-tech) and added two new waves (leisure/tourism and outer space). These six waves are described in my book *Future Consumer.com*, which was also published in China.

China's strategy is to develop these six waves, in order to build a post-industrial society. It also aims to become energy self-sufficient and to clean up its environment. Today's emphasis is to further modernize industry, to grow the high-tech, service, and tourism sectors, and to continue with the push into aerospace.

FOCUS ON INNOVATION AND CONSUMERS

To reduce its dependence on exports, China is also putting greater emphasis on original research and development (R&D), rather than simple manufacturing and assembly. We are going to see some impressive innovations emerge from China in various high-tech sectors in coming years. For example, the country has just test flown its first regional jet and has launched an initiative to compete in full-size passenger airplanes by 2020. China is also going to become a major global player in automobiles.

There is also a big push to grow the consumer economy. China has one of the highest savings rates in the world. While this major strength creates a massive pool of investment funds, Chinese consumers have a natural reluctance to spend, contributing only 35% to GDP (versus more than 70% in the United States). This is changing, with new-found affluence and the marketization of the housing and other sectors, encouraging consumers to make a bigger contribution to economic output.

Retail sales are growing at an impressive pace—more than 20% a year—and this is taking up some of the slack caused by the drop in exports to recession-hit global economies. It is estimated that in the next four years, almost half a billion units of refrigerators, washing machines, color television and cell phones will be sold in rural areas alone.

ECONOMIC FORECASTS TO 2020

There are several recent, if diverse, forecasts of China's long-term growth prospects. According to the accountancy firm PricewaterhouseCoopers, China could match US GDP in absolute terms by 2025 and surpass it by 30% by 2050. The Carnegie Endowment forecasts that China's economy will overtake the United States by 2035, and it will be twice its size by 2050.

Of course, these studies were completed before the current global recession. So how has the recession affected China's prospects?

During the past 30 years, China has had economic slowdowns. It also has a nine-year cycle, similar to that of Western economies. However, the slowdowns in China seem to precede those of the West, by at least a year, and China also weathers these slowdowns comparatively well, largely thanks to Beijing's excellent macroeconomic control.

"It is not by force and violence that His Majesty intends to establish a commercial intercourse between his subjects and China; but by other conciliatory measures so strongly inculcated in all the instructions which you have received." Arthur Wellesley Wellington

China's GDP growth rate slowed in 1980–1981 (versus 1981–1982 in the West), in 1988–1990 (versus 1991–1992), and in 1997–1999 (versus 2000–2001). The first of these downturns was triggered by the initial farm price reforms and a budget deficit. Despite the recent "opening up" of its economy, China at the time remained largely detached from the wider global economy. The second downturn was again caused by overheating and inflation, which then fed into the Tiananmen Square incident of 1989. Yet, this did not cause a full-blown recession. The third downturn was caused somewhat by the 1997 Asian financial crisis, which China helped to bail out, and also by urban price and housing reforms.

In each case, however, China was back in recovery mode as the West slowed down. I believe that we will see a similar scenario in 2009–2010. China has deliberately cooled its torrid growth rate (its economy has grown by more than 10% in each of the last five years), and it was retooling its manufacturing and consumer sectors before it got slammed with a sharp downturn in exports in 2008.

As mentioned, consumers are taking up the slack, buying more durables, and I believe China will still record 9% economic growth in 2009. That will lift GDP to about US$3.7 trillion on an exchange rate basis, and to US$7.7 trillion on a purchasing power parity (PPP) basis. That is more than half the size of the US economy.

In addition, the Chinese government is rolling out a massive four trillion Yuan (US$600 billion) stimulus package, aimed at infrastructure and other major initiatives. As this kicks in, I forecast that GDP will grow by 10% in 2009 and 2010, before settling back to a more manageable 8–9% annual rate. I expect that to be sustained until around 2017, when another slowdown cycle will cause growth to fall to 7–8%, a slowdown which I predict will again precede the next slowdown in the West, which I forecast for around 2019. By then, China will be in recovery mode again, ending the decade with an average GDP growth rate of 9%.

Based on these figures and their underlying assumptions, China's GDP will be about US$11 trillion (exchange rate basis) and could be at least US$25 trillion (on a PPP basis) by 2020.

This will ensure that China remains the second largest economy, with the United States retaining top dog position. But it will have at least quadrupled and will be positioned to overtake that of the United States in the 2020–2040 timeframe. Per capita income will still be relatively low, at around US$12,000 on a purchasing comparative basis, with millions of people well below that level. But China will be a relatively modern, well-off society, and it will be a major player in the commercial aircraft, automobile and computer hardware and software sectors, as well as the world's leading tourist destination.

BASICALLY RECESSION-PROOF

China has shown itself to be basically recession proof. Even in the 1989–1990 downturn, it still managed to grow industrial output by around 4%. It took the 1997 Asian crisis in its stride, and appears likely to weather the current global recession. This can be put down to several strengths.

The main strength comes from foreign investment, which was initially attracted by the strategy of the special economic zones (SEZs) that China set up in 1980. Since then, more than four-fifths of the Fortune 500 companies have invested in China, with some 800 R&D centers set up by those and other foreign firms.

Overall, more than 500,000 foreign companies have established operations of various sizes in China. Total foreign direct investment (FDI) at the end of 2007 was US$759 billion and this could exceed US$1 trillion by the end of 2010. This investment is not going to go away. Indeed, despite the recession, FDI continues to flood in, with new projects announced daily.

Second, China is extremely cash rich. It has a 40% savings rate (that of the United States is basically zero) and has amassed US$2 trillion in foreign exchange reserves. The country has a huge balance of trade surplus, even in the downturn, and a healthy balance of payments position.

Thirdly China is rich in terms of its people. Its vast workforce gives it a tremendous competitive advantage, despite stories that it is being priced out of the global market. What these stories overlook is that China still has a vast and undeveloped interior. This allows it to shift factories inland, allowing the services, high-tech, and tourism sectors to grow in the coastal regions.

Fourth, as noted, China also is a vast consumer market that could single-handedly drive reasonable economic growth for at least the next couple of generations. China is also developing significant intellectual capital that will drive innovation, making it more efficient at creating real value added. Even the country's ageing population is not a significant handicap, just as it has not been to Europe. Rather, the ageing population will fuel rapid growth in the health care, housing and tourism sectors.

So, while there's no denying that China faces significant challenges in resource availability and the environment, as well as in creating millions of jobs every year, there appears little to stop it from achieving its ambitious ongoing objective of further quadrupling its GDP.

⏩ MORE INFO

Books:

Feather, Frank. *Future Consumer.com*. Toronto, ON: Warwick, 2000.

Toffler, Alvin. *The Third Wave*. New York: Random House, 1980.

Articles:

The Economist. "China's reforms: The second long march." (Dec 11, 2008). Online at: www.economist.com/research/articlesbysubject/displaystory.cfm?subjectid=478048&story_id=12758848

Xiaoping, Deng. "Build socialism with Chinese characteristics." *People's Daily (Beijing)* (June 30, 1984).

Reports:

Keidel, Albert. "China's economic rise—Fact and fiction." Carnegie Endowment for International Peace, 2008. Online at: www.carnegieendowment.org/files/pb61_keidel_final.pdf

PricewaterhouseCoopers. "The world in 2050: Beyond the BRICs—Brazil, Russia, India and China." 2008. Online at: www.pwc.com/extweb/pwcpublications.nsf/docid/146E4E4D52487154852573FA0058A179/$file/world_2050_brics.pdf

Websites:

Asia Development Bank, China pages: www.adb.org/PRC

China National Bureau of Statistics (NBS): www.stats.gov.cn/english

CIA World Fact Book, China page: www.cia.gov/library/publications/the-world-factbook/geos/ch.html

See Also:

✔ China (pp. 1374–1375)

"Without establishing the appropriate networks in China, it will be virtually impossible to penetrateva market that is significantly different from that in the Western world." Rosalie L. Tung

  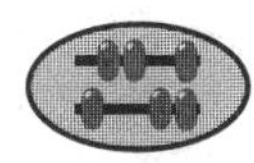   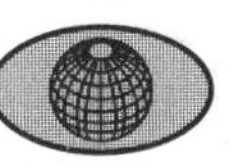   

Everything You Need to Know About Benchmarking by Robin Mann

EXECUTIVE SUMMARY

- Benchmarking is much more than a comparison of performance.
- Benchmarking focuses on learning from the experience of others and can be defined as "identifying, adapting, and implementing the practices that produce the best performance results."
- Benchmarking is a powerful method for breakthrough thinking, innovation, and improvement, and for delivering exceptional bottom-line results.
- New benchmarking methodologies aim to ensure that benchmarking projects result in major benefits, both financial and nonfinancial.
- New tools available on the internet make benchmarking easier.

INTRODUCTION

Organizations are constantly looking for new ways and methodologies to improve their performance and gain a competitive advantage. As they seek improvements to their own business processes, many organizations recognize the importance of learning from best practices that have been achieved by other organizations. By removing the need to reinvent the wheel and providing the potential to adopt proven practices, benchmarking has become an important methodology for providing a fast track to achieving organizational excellence.

TYPES OF BENCHMARKING

It is useful to distinguish between the main types of benchmarking.

First, there is *informal benchmarking*. This is a type of benchmarking that most of us do unconsciously at work and in our home life. We constantly compare and learn from the behavior and practices of others—whether it is how to use a software program, cook a better meal, or play our favorite sport. In the context of work, most learning from informal benchmarking comes from the following:

- Talking to colleagues and learning from their experience (coffee breaks and team meetings are a great place to network and learn from others);
- Consulting with experts (for example, business consultants who have experience of implementing a particular process or activity in many business environments);
- Networking with people from other organizations at conferences, seminars, and internet forums;
- Websites, online databases, and publications that share benchmarking information provide quick and easy ways to learn of best practices and benchmarks.

Second, there is *formal benchmarking*, of which there are two types: performance benchmarking, and best practice benchmarking.

Performance Benchmarking

Performance benchmarking describes the comparison of performance data obtained by studying similar processes or activities. Comparisons of performance may be undertaken between companies, or internally within an organization. It is useful for identifying strengths and opportunities for improvement. Performance benchmarking may involve the comparison of financial measures (such as expenditure, cost of labor, cost of buildings/equipment, cost of energy, adherence to budget, cash flow, revenue collected) or nonfinancial measures (such as absenteeism, staff turnover, the percentage of administrative staff to front-line staff, budget processing time, complaints, environmental impact, or call centre performance).

Most people equate benchmarking to performance benchmarking. This is unfortunate, because performance benchmarking on its own is of limited use. Too often performance benchmarking data are collected (often at significant cost) and no further action is taken after the data have been obtained. While performance benchmarking enables a performance gap to be identified, it does not provide the idea, best practice, or solution as to how performance can be improved and the gap closed.

Best Practice Benchmarking

Best practice benchmarking describes the comparison of performance data obtained by studying similar processes or activities *and identifying, adapting, and implementing the practices that produced the best performance results.* Best practice benchmarking is the most powerful type of benchmarking. It is used for learning from the experience of others and achieving breakthrough improvements in performance. Best practice benchmarking focuses on "action"—i.e. doing something with the comparison data and learning why other organizations are achieving higher levels of performance.

Best practice benchmarking projects typically take from two to four months to identify best practices. The practices then need to be adapted and implemented. The time taken for the whole project varies depending on the project's scope and importance, and on the resources used. Projects are usually resource-intensive (in terms of the project team's time), and so care needs to be taken that they focus on issues of high strategic importance that will deliver major bottom-line benefits.

POPULARITY OF BENCHMARKING

Research by the Centre for Organisational Excellence Research (COER), on behalf of the Global Benchmarking Network, identified the popularity of benchmarking in comparison to other business improvement tools.[1] This research was based on a survey that was completed by over 450 companies from more than 20 countries.

Figure 1 shows the results in terms of the popularity of 20 business improvement tools. *Mission and vision statements* and *Customer (client) surveys* were the most popular (used by 77% of organizations), followed by *Strengths, weaknesses, opportunities, and threats* (72%), and *Informal benchmarking* (68%). *Performance benchmarking* was used by 49% and *Best practice benchmarking* by 39%.

WHAT IS THE PAYBACK FROM BENCHMARKING

This depends on the type of benchmarking used. For informal or performance benchmarking it is difficult to assess as these types of benchmarking are focused on organizational learning and/or better decision-making, and usually the benefits are not quantified by organizations that employ these techniques. However, it can be assumed that these methods, and benchmarking in general, are very important if an organization wishes to compete nationally and internationally—it makes sense for an organization to have management processes and systems of a similar

"Fools say 'Learn from your mistakes.' I prefer to learn from the mistakes of others." Otto von Bismarck

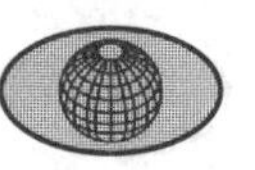

Figure 1. Use of business improvement tools worldwide. (From study by COER, 2008[2])

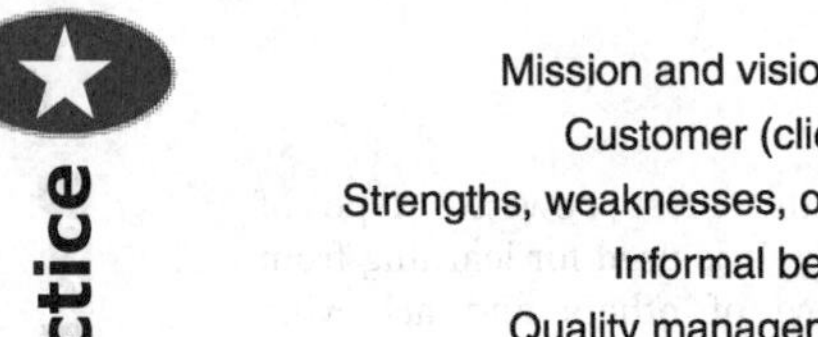
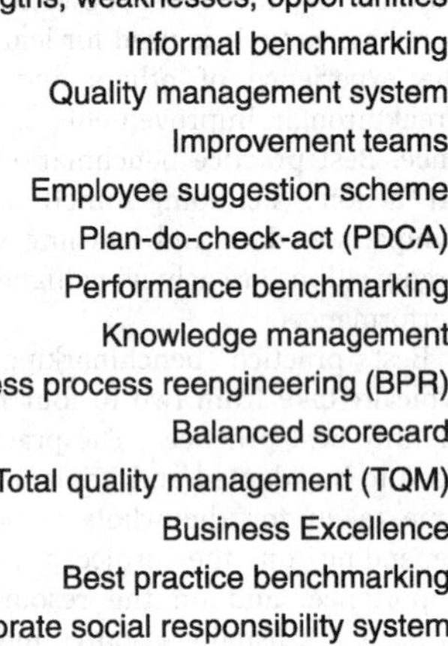
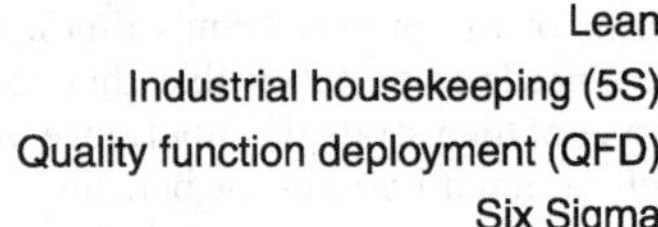
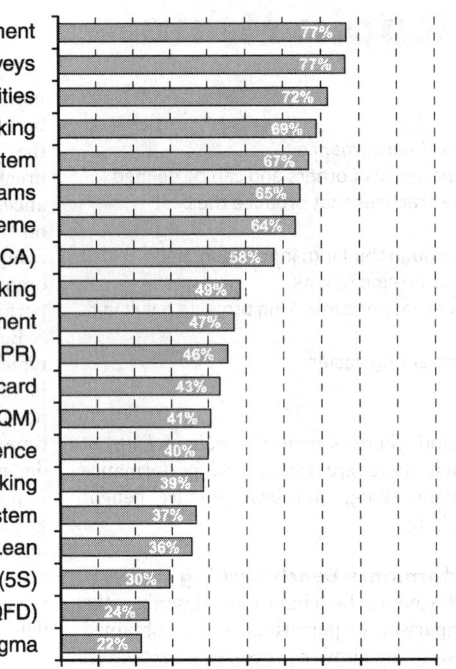

Figure 2. TRADE best practice benchmarking methodology

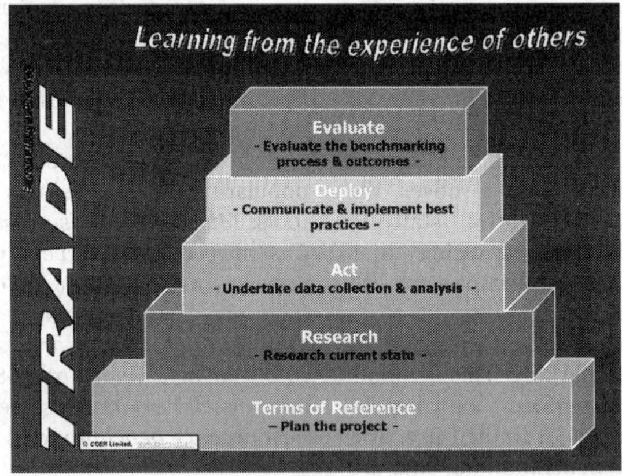

or better standard than competitors. Certainly, business excellence models, which are used in over 80 countries to encourage companies to apply the principles of business excellence, have as a core element the need for organizations to benchmark, identify performance gaps, and learn from others. The most popular business excellence models are the Baldrige Criteria for Performance Excellence (developed in the United States), where benchmarking accounts for approximately 50% of the model score, and the European Foundation for Quality Management (EFQM) Excellence Model. For further details, see under Websites at the end of the article.

For best practice benchmarking, the payback can be calculated on a project by project basis. Payback, from a financial perspective, is likely to vary depending on the specific aims of the project. If projects are carefully selected, planned, and managed, there is no reason why major benefits (financial and nonfinancial) should not be obtained. A study of 30 organizations that used best practice benchmarking indicated an average financial return of $100,000 to $150,000 per project, with some reaping benefits of more than $1,000,000 per project.[3]

There are many case studies that focus on the success gained through benchmarking. The best known of these describe the experience of Xerox, which was the pioneer in applying benchmarking concepts (Dr Robert Camp, previously of Xerox, wrote the first book on benchmarking in 1989). It was in the late 1970s and early 1980s that Xerox, faced with ruin due to more efficient Japanese competitors, first undertook some performance benchmarking, and the findings were astonishing. The results showed that:

- Xerox's ratio of indirect to direct staff was twice that of the direct competition;
- It had nine times the number of production suppliers;
- Assembly line rejects were in the order of ten times worse;
- Defects per 100 machines were seven times worse;
- Product time to market was twice as long.

To address this crisis, Xerox developed its benchmarking approach to identify not only performance gaps but also to learn why other organizations were performing better. Much of this learning came from studying the practices of organizations from outside their industry, as this often resulted in identifying breakthrough practices. For example, Xerox benchmarked L.L. Bean, a Maine outdoor sporting goods retailer, because of their excellent warehouse procedures (which are now the standard at most companies). In total, over a period of ten years, almost 230 performance areas were benchmarked. This resulted in Xerox becoming an industry leader and recognized as world class. Xerox won the Malcolm Baldrige National Quality Award in the United States in 1989.

METHODOLOGIES FOR BEST PRACTICE BENCHMARKING

There is no single benchmarking methodology that has been universally adopted. The wide appeal and acceptance of benchmarking has led to the emergence of a range of benchmarking methodologies. TRADE is one such methodology. The TRADE benchmarking methodology (Figure 2) focuses on the exchange (or "trade") of information and best practices to improve the performance of processes, goods and services. TRADE consists of five stages:

- Terms of reference: Plan the project (aims, objectives, scope, resources, cost/benefit analysis);

"We cannot solve problems with the same thinking we had when we created the problems." Albert Einstein

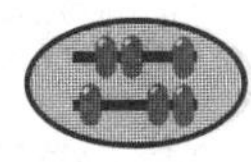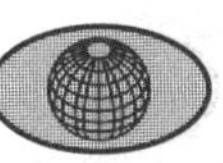

- **R**esearch: Research the current state/performance;
- **A**ct: Undertake data collection and analysis to compare against others;
- **D**eploy: Communicate and implement best practices;
- **E**valuate: Evaluate the benchmarking process and outcomes to ensure that the project has achieved its aims.

Benchmarking projects should be targeted at a process area or activity that will deliver the best value to an organization. The project aim can be broad, or it can be specific. The aim may relate to improving the performance of a process, activity/task, business improvement tool, equipment, strategy, or behaviour. Examples of project aims are:

- To improve a customer complaint management process to world-class standard;
- To identify and implement best practices in the application of the balanced scorecard;
- To become an industry leader in ways of providing financial information to clients;
- To develop a winning team culture;
- To reduce the time taken to recruit new staff.

Once a project aim is set, the process or activity to be studied should be broken down into its component parts and current performance measured. Benchmarking partners to learn from can then be identified for the component parts and their practices studied through surveys or site visits. An analysis is then conducted to determine which processes or activities should be adopted and, after any necessary adaptations, implemented.

Figure 3. Business Performance Improvement Resource (www.BPIR.com)

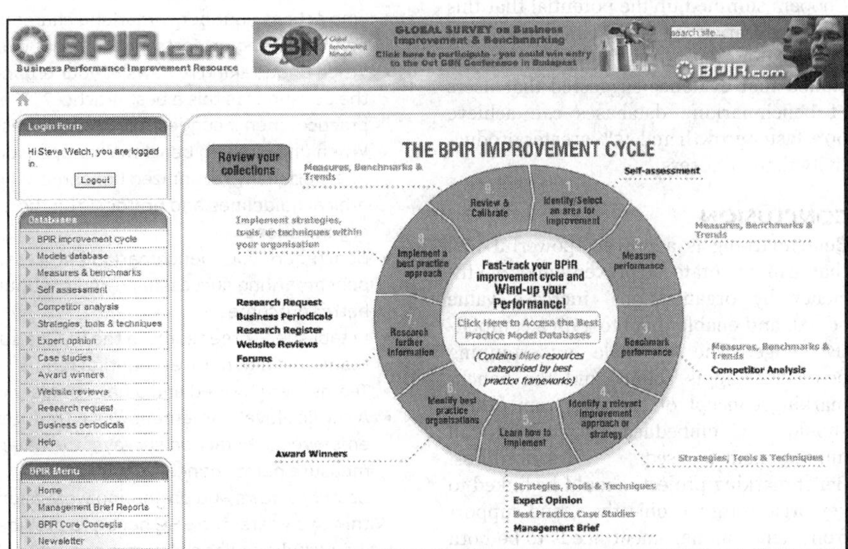

The Business Performance Improvement Resource (BPIR; see under Websites at the end of the article) is one of the new resources that are a valuable support to benchmarking projects. The BPIR (Figure 3) is a vast knowledge repository containing databases with thousands of benchmarks, measures, best practices, benchmarking partners, case studies, and studies/trends that cover virtually every aspect of business. The resource can help to improve any business practice, from handling customer complaints, through undertaking performance appraisals, to improving strategic

CASE STUDY

Benchmarking Leads to Cost Reduction of the Finance Function

An Australian company conducted a global benchmarking exercise on its finance function and found that it had an outdated infrastructure that cost more than 4% of company revenues to run, that staff spent more than half of their time collecting data, and that the information did not meet its global business information needs. A reengineering team redesigned the company's business processes and proposed that the company create a shared services centre (SSC) to process common transactions, drive down costs, and improve the quality of the service delivery. The company achieved the following:

- Selected a location for the SSC based on the quality/skill/cost/flexibility of the workforce, taxation, communications costs and infrastructure, real estate cost, travel accessibility, political stability, language suitability, and company infrastructure;
- Established three teams in the SSC: a supplier process team, a customer process team, and a general accounting team;
- Teams were trained and a new mind-set was developed to service the business units;
- A service level agreement was introduced and customer satisfaction surveys, employee satisfaction surveys, the balanced scorecard, and Six Sigma were used to measure performance;
- Salary reviews and promotion were aligned with performance.

THE USE OF TECHNOLOGY TO MAKE BENCHMARKING EASIER

In the 1980s and 1990s benchmarking was mainly confined to large, successful, private sector organizations with projects that tended to be extremely costly but brought in very high returns. Today's technological advancements have transformed communications and opened up a whole new information-based world. Any organization can now access low-cost internet-based benchmarking services and opportunities such as consortia, surveys both on- and off-line, virtual common interest groups such as forums, and best practice information resources. These resources are a real boon to organizations that want to access best practices and expert advice/opinion but do not have the resources for full-scale benchmarking projects.

⏩ MAKING IT HAPPEN

Benchmarking—learning from the experience of others—makes common sense. How should this technique be used to reap the most benefits? Here are some tips:

- Undertake a self-assessment (a business excellence self-assessment is best) or quality audit, or have a brainstorming meeting to identify key opportunities for improvement in your organization. For those key practices or processes that require improvement, undertake a best practice benchmarking project to seek out best practices. If you do not have the resource to do this, search for benchmarks and best practices using a literature or website search.

"Benchmarking is the process of identifying, understanding and adapting superior practices from organizations locally and worldwide to help your organization improve its performance and achieve priority business results." Robert Camp

     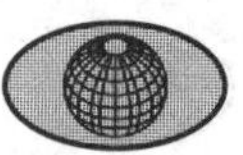   

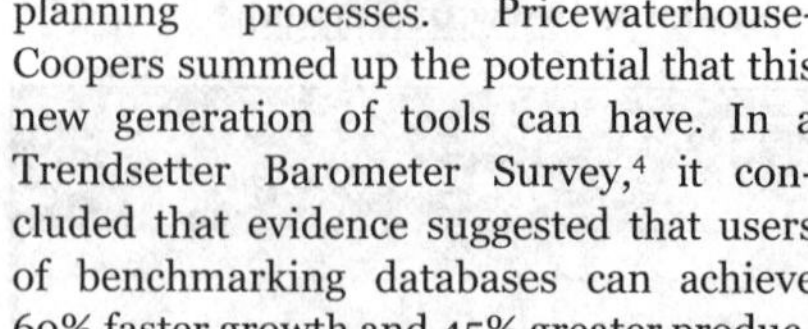

planning processes. PricewaterhouseCoopers summed up the potential that this new generation of tools can have. In a Trendsetter Barometer Survey,[4] it concluded that evidence suggested that users of benchmarking databases can achieve 69% faster growth and 45% greater productivity than nonusers.

CONCLUSION

Benchmarking is a proven, powerful tool that can facilitate improvements to efficiency by organizations, increase value added, and enable them to gain a competitive edge. The rationale underpinning benchmarking is sound, and the benchmarking concept of learning from others should be embedded throughout all improvement-focused organizations. Benchmarking projects should be linked to key organizational objectives, and support from senior management needs to be both strong and visible.

There is little doubt about the potential and versatility of benchmarking as a tool. It has been successfully applied by organizations of different sizes and in different industry sectors and has become one of the most popular management tools. However, it is thought that most organizations use performance benchmarking (comparing performance) rather than the more powerful but resource-intensive approach of best practice benchmarking (comparing and learning from others and implementing best practices). Using best practice benchmarking methodologies, such as TRADE, and website resources, such as the BPIR website, will help more organizations to reap the benefits of benchmarking.

- Have at least one person within your organization who is trained in benchmarking and who acts as your benchmarking champion. This person can help to facilitate your benchmarking projects and/or conduct benchmarking research.
- When undertaking reviews of your organization's processes and practices, always ask the question "Is this a best practice?" If evidence is not forthcoming that it is a best practice, then it suggests that the process or practice will benefit from benchmarking.
- When undertaking benchmarking, ensure that your organization follows an internationally recognized benchmarking code of conduct.[5] A code of conduct provides ethical guidelines and protocols on the exchange of information between organizations.
- Benchmark your benchmarking process. Learn from others how to conduct benchmarking successfully, and continually strive to refine your process to achieve better outcomes.
- Established three teams in the SSC: a supplier process team, a customer process team, and a general accounting team;
- Teams were trained and a new mindset was developed to service the business units;
- A service level agreement was introduced and customer satisfaction surveys, employee satisfaction surveys, the balanced scorecard, and Six Sigma were used to measure performance;
- Salary reviews and promotion were aligned with performance.

Within two years, the SSC began to provide high value-added services to the business units, including financial reporting and analysis, treasury management, tax and legal consulting, and credit and collection management. The cost of running the SSC was less than 1% of sales revenue and achieved world-class standards. The SSC reduced the cost of the finance function globally by more than 50%.

➤➤ MORE INFO

Book:

Camp, Robert C. *Benchmarking: The Search for Industry Best Practices That Lead to Superior Performance.* Portland, OR: Productivity Press, 1989.

Websites:

Baldrige National Quality Program, on the National Institute of Standards and Technology (NIST) website. A US government website that promotes the Baldrige Criteria for Performance Excellence: www.quality.nist.gov

Business Performance Improvement Resource (BPIR) has a large collection of information and resources on benchmarking and best practice: www.bpir.com

Centre for Organisational Excellence Research (COER), a New Zealand-based research and consultancy organization headed by the author. The website provides information on business excellence and TRADE benchmarking projects: www.coer.org.nz

European Foundation for Quality Management (EFQM), developers and custodians of the EFQM Excellence Model: www.efqm.org

Global Benchmarking Network (GBN) provides a listing of the main promoters/experts in benchmarking from over 20 countries: www.globalbenchmarking.org

See Also:

Michael Porter (p. 1182)
Balanced Scorecard: Translating Strategy Into Action (p. 1221)

NOTES

1 Centre for Organisational Excellence Research (COER). *Report on the Global Use of Business Improvement Tools and Benchmarking* COER Report. Palmerston North, New Zealand: Massey University, November 2008. Available from: www.coer.org.nz

2 *Ibid.*

3 *Ibid.*

4 PricewaterhouseCoopers (PWC). "Fast-growth companies that benchmark grow faster, are more productive than their peers." Barometer Surveys, May 1, 2002. Online at: www.barometersurveys.com, go to "Trendsetter Barometer," and download from "Archives."

5 Global Benchmarking Network (GBN). *Benchmarking Code of Conduct.* Berlin: GBN Secretariat, 2008. Available from: www.globalbenchmarking.org/download_archive

"Leave the beaten path occasionally and dive into the woods. You will be certain to find something you have never seen before" Alexander Graham Bell

  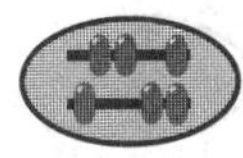   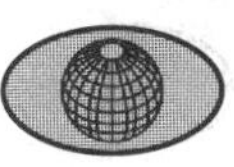   

Globalization and Regional Business Strategy by Alan M. Rugman

EXECUTIVE SUMMARY

- Globalization is misunderstood—it does not, and has never, existed in terms of a single world market with free trade.
- Triad-based business is the past, current, and future reality.
- Multinational enterprises operate within triad markets and access other triad markets; they have regional, not global, strategies.
- National governments strongly regulate most service sectors, thereby limiting free market forces; the extent of regulation is not decreasing.
- Businesses need to think local and act regional; they should forget global.

INTRODUCTION: THE MYTH OF GLOBAL STRATEGY

Recent research suggests that globalization is a myth. Far from taking place in a single global market, most business activity by large firms takes place in regional blocks. There is no uniform spread of US market capitalism, nor are global markets becoming homogenized. Government regulations and cultural differences divide the world into the triad blocks of North America, the European Union, and Japan. Rival multinational enterprises from the triad compete for regional market share and so enhance economic efficiency. As a result, top managers now need to design triad-based regional strategies, not global ones. Only in a few sectors, such as consumer electronics, is a global strategy of economic integration viable. For most other manufacturing sectors (automobiles, for example) and for all services, strategies of national responsiveness are required, often coupled with integration strategies.

The real drivers of globalization are the network managers of large multinational enterprises. But their business strategies are triadic, or regional, in scope and are responsive to local consumers; they are not global and uniform.

The specialty chemicals business and the automobile industry are triad-based, not global. There is no global automobile; more than 90% of all automobiles produced in Europe are sold in Europe, and regional production and predominantly local sales are also the norm in North America and Japan. Successful multinationals now design strategies on a regional basis; unsuccessful ones pursue global strategies.

SOME COMMON GLOBAL MISUNDERSTANDINGS

Globalization has been defined in business schools as a process of economic integration that facilitates the production and distribution of products and services of a homogenous type and quality on a worldwide basis.[1] Simply put, it involves providing the same output to countries everywhere. And, in recent years, it has become increasingly common to hear business executives, industry analysts, and even university professors talk about the emergence of globalization and the dominance of international business by giant, multinational enterprises (MNE) that are selling uniform products from Cairo, Illinois, to Cairo, Egypt, and from Lima, Ohio, to Lima, Peru.[2]

> "The real drivers of globalization are the network managers of large multinational enterprises. But their business strategies are triadic, or regional, in scope and are responsive to local consumers; they are not global and uniform."

To back up their claims, these individuals often point to the fact that foreign sales account for more than 50% of the annual revenues of companies such as Dow Chemical, Exxon, Hewlett Packard, IBM, Johnson & Johnson, Mobil, Motorola, Procter & Gamble, and Texaco.[3] (For more on these firms, see UNCTAD's *World Investment Report*.) These are accurate statements, but they fail to explain that most of the sales of so-called global companies are made on a triadic or regional basis. For example, most MNEs that are headquartered in North America earn the bulk of their revenue within their home country or by selling to members of the broad triad: The North American Free Trade Agreement (NAFTA), the European Union (EU), or Japan, and a small group of nations in Asia and Oceania.[4] Recent research gives ample supporting data:

- More than 85% of all automobiles produced in North America are made in North American factories owned by General Motors, Ford, Daimler–Chrysler, or European or Japanese MNEs. More than 90% of the cars produced in the European Union are sold in the EU. More than 93% of all cars registered in Japan are manufactured domestically.
- In the specialty chemicals sector, over 90% of all paint is made and used regionally by triad-based MNEs. The same is true for steel, heavy electrical equipment, energy, and transportation.
- In the services sector, which now employs approximately 70% of the workforce in North America, Western Europe, and Japan, business activity is all essentially local or regional.[5]

Another misunderstanding about globalization is the belief that MNEs are globally monolithic and excessively powerful in political terms. Research shows this is not so. MNEs are not monolithic; in fact, the largest 500 multinationals are spread across the core triad. Of these 500 companies, 151 are headquartered in the United States and another 170 in the European Union. Sixty-four have headquarters in Japan, with a further 29 in China, 15 in Korea, eight in Australia, seven in India, and six in Taiwan, giving some 129 in the largest economies of Asia.[6] Further, these triad-based MNEs compete for global market share and profits across a wide variety of industrial sectors and trade services. And this process of regional competition erodes the possibility of sustainable long-term profits and the possibility of building strong, sustainable political advantage.[7]

A third misunderstanding about globalization is the belief that MNEs develop homogeneous products for the world market, and through their efficient production techniques are able to dominate local markets everywhere. In truth, multinationals have to adapt their products for local markets. For example, there is no global automobile. Instead there are regionally based North American, European, and Japanese factories supported by local regional suppliers who provide steel, plastic, paint, and other necessary inputs for producing automobiles for their respective geographic triad regions. Car designs that are popular in one region of the world are often rejected by customers in other

     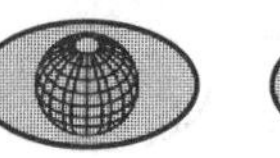   

geographic areas. The Toyota Camry that dominates the US market is a poor seller in Japan. The Volkswagen Golf, which was the largest selling car in Europe, failed to make an impact in North America. Even pharmaceutical companies, which manufacture medicines that are often referred to as universal products, have to modify their goods to satisfy national and state regulations, thus making centralized production and worldwide distribution economically difficult.

WORLD TRADE IS HIGHLY REGIONAL

World trade provides a good example of just how regional MNEs are. The amount of trade in terms of exports and imports has grown rapidly over the last decade, but it continues to be dominated by the core triad of the United States, the European Union, and Japan.[8] The latest data show that in 2005 these three groups accounted for 51% of world exports and 59% of world imports. The percentage of exports that each group sends to the others is quite small. For example, the United States exports approximately 21% of its total to the EU and 6% to Japan, but the largest export market for the United States is Canada, which takes 23%, with another 13% going to Mexico. An analysis of imports reveals the same general picture. The United States receives 18% of its imports from the EU and 8% from Japan, but 17% from Canada and 10% from Mexico. In 2005 the United States took 16% of its imports from China.

Simply put, with the recent exception of China, the core triad members do not rely on each other for most of their exports or imports. So on whom do they rely? The answer is: On other members of their own triad. For example, as shown in Table 1, over 66% of all exports by EU countries go to other members of that triad. The core triad members can be expanded by adding Canada and Mexico to the United States, which gives us NAFTA, and then constructing a group of countries for Asia. The Asian group consists of Japan, Australia, New Zealand, China (including Taiwan and Hong Kong), India, Indonesia, Malaysia, the Philippines, Singapore, and Thailand, along with the smaller Asian Pacific economies. This gives us the broad triad. The results confirm that the world's trade is dominated by the triad.

According to data for 2005 66% of EU exports are internal. The EU exports relatively less to NAFTA and to Asia. The internal NAFTA trade, at 56%, is surprisingly high, given that Canada is only one-twelfth the economic size of the United States and Mexico only about one-twentieth the economic size of the United States. Most Asian trade is also intra-regional, at 53%.

Table 1. Intra-regional trade in the triad, 1980–2005. (*Source*: Author's calculations based on the IMF, *Direction of Trade Statistics Yearbook*, 2006 and 1985)

Intraregional exports			
Year	*EU*	*NAFTA*	*Asia*
2005	66.4%	56.0%	53.1%
2000	67.2%	58.1%	42.4%
1980	53.5%	33.6%	27.3%
Cumulative average annual change			
1980–2005	0.01	0.02	0.03
2000–2005	–0.00	–0.01	0.06

Data for Asia were calculated using information for exports from Japan, China, India, Indonesia, South Korea, Malaysia, Singapore, Thailand, and Australia to the Asian region and the world. Data for the EU are for intra-EU exports in 2000 and 2005 and intra-EEC exports in 1980.

In summary, the majority of world trade in the European and Asian triads is within their internal markets, and for North America just over half of its trade is also intra-regional. Most of the rest of world trade is between triad members. Given the dominance of the triad in world trade (and direct investment data show the same picture), the appropriate strategies for individual multinationals need to be regional rather than global.

CONCLUSION

It is possible to offer some practical strategies for managers who want to increase their company's international revenues and profits. Some of the most useful lessons are these:

"In summary, the majority of world trade in the European and Asian triads is within their internal markets, and for North America just over half of its trade is also intra-regional."

- Be prepared to design strategies which take into account regional trade and investment agreements such as NAFTA and the single market of the EU.
- Also learn to deal with different cultures and become nationally responsive when necessary.
- Develop new thinking and knowledge about regional business networks and triad-based clusters, and assess instead of always developing pure global strategies.
- Make alliances and foster cross-cultural awareness in your senior managers.
- Develop analytical methods for assessing regional drivers of success rather than globalization drivers; regional drivers may be more useful in the future in gaining and holding market share.
- Encourage all your managers to think regional, act local—and forget global!

▸▸ MORE INFO

Books:

Friedman, Thomas L. *The World is Flat: A Brief History of the Twenty-first Century*. Updated and expanded ed. New York: Farrar, Straus & Giroux, 2006.

Giddens, Anthony. *Runaway World: How Globalization is Reshaping our Lives*. New York: Routledge, 2003.

Rugman, Alan M. *The End of Globalization: Why Global Strategy is a Myth & How to Profit from the Realities of Regional Markets*. New York: AMACOM, 2001.

Rugman, Alan M. *The Regional Multinationals: MNEs and "Global" Strategic Management*. Cambridge, UK: Cambridge University Press, 2005.

Rugman, Alan M., and Simon Collinson. *International Business*. 5th ed. London: FT Prentice Hall, 2009.

Rugman, Alan M., and Joseph R. D'Cruz. *Multinationals as Flagship Firms: Regional Business Networks*. Oxford: Oxford University Press, 2000.

Yip, George S. *Total Global Strategy II*. 2nd ed. Upper Saddle River, NJ: Prentice Hall, 2003.

Article:

Rugman, Alan M., and Alain Verbeke. "A perspective on regional and global strategies of multinational enterprises." *Journal of International Business Studies* 35 (2004): 3–18.

Website:

UNCTAD *World Investment Report*: www.unctad.org/WIR

See Also:

Globalization and Its Discontents (p. 1270)

"We continue to struggle with the old question. . .of whether to obey a superior even when the order is unjust."
John Ralston Saul

  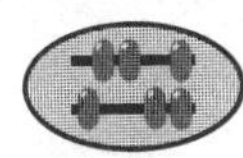   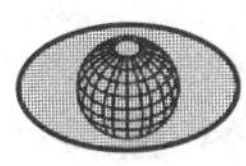 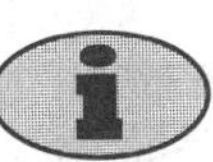  

NOTES

1 See Rugman and Collinson (2009), Chapter 1. The definition of "globalization" is a subject of intense academic debate. Most business school scholars would adopt the definition of economic integration used here, where integration across national borders yields the potential for firm-level economies of scale and/or global brand name products. Contingent on this definition of "pure" economic globalization is the need for products to be uniform across markets. A much broader definition of globalization is used by other writers, such as Anthony Giddens, a sociologist. He defines globalization as "the worldwide interconnection at the cultural, political and economic level resulting from the elimination of communication and trade barriers," and he states that "globalization is a process of convergence of cultural, political and economic aspects of life" Giddens (2003). Again, convergence (of cultures, tastes, regulations, etc.) is an extreme version of homogeneity of products and services. The thesis of this article is that such convergence and homogeneity has not occurred; instead of globalization we observe regional/triadic production and distribution. Therefore, MNEs do not need global strategies; regional strategies are more relevant.

2 Yip (2003) and Friedman (2006).

3 For more on these firms, see "The world's top non-financial 100 TNCs, ranked by foreign assets," *World Investment Report*, New York: United Nations, annual. Available from: www.unctad.org

4 NAFTA consists of the United States, Canada, and Mexico. The European Union is now made up of 27 countries, but the data used here are for the EU's 15 members up to 2003, namely Belgium, France, Italy, Luxembourg, the Netherlands, Germany, Great Britain, Denmark, Greece, Ireland, Portugal, Spain, Austria, Finland, and Sweden. The 12 major Asian economies included here are Australia, China, India, Indonesia, Malaysia, New Zealand, the Philippines, Singapore, South Korea, Taiwan, Thailand, and Japan.

5 Rugman (2001), Chapter 1.

6 Data adapted from "The World's Largest Corporations (2008) *Fortune*, Vol. 158, No. 2, pp. 165–182.

7 Rugman (2005) and Rugman and D'Cruz (2000).

8 This analysis is based on Rugman (2001), Chapter 7.

"Ethical conduct is not a matter of conformity to some preset plan. It is more concerned with acceptable and desirable parameters of conduct." Damian Grace

   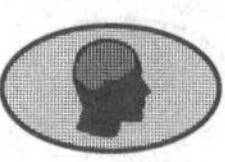  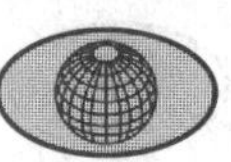   

Growing and Maximizing SME Profitability Without Compromising ROI by Neil Marriott

EXECUTIVE SUMMARY

- Small and medium-sized enterprises (SMEs) are increasingly important to long-term regional, national, and global economic prosperity.
- While growing, many SMEs encounter periods that require investment in assets and/or research and development (R&D) in advance of any resulting increase in turnover and associated profits.
- During this period, known as the "valley of death," key performance indicators such as return on investment (ROI) can be adversely impacted and limit the scope for future investment.
- To manage growth, SMEs must determine the right timing and response to customer demands.
- To recover ROI, SMEs must control costs and balance long-term prospects with short-term profitable opportunities.

INTRODUCTION

Small and medium-sized enterprises (SMEs) are, more than ever, the lifeblood of regional and national economies. The structural shift from goods to service sectors favors the creation of more small firms, where a smaller size is an economic choice for a business vehicle. This shift was exacerbated by technological changes such as the extensive use of microchip technology, which now makes smaller-scale production more economically viable.

SMEs can be more flexible and responsive to new market opportunities and economic recessions. In periods of high unemployment many former employees start their own enterprises, relying on their experience, education, and managerial skills. Furthermore, large firms increasingly place part of their work outside the organization—providing a further incentive for the creation of new small firms, since subcontracting and outsourcing can reduce production costs. However, as SMEs grow and develop, they face strains on their profitability that impact on a key performance indicator—return on investment (ROI). Furthermore any deterioration in ROI will compromise a firm's ability to obtain finance for further expansion.

DEFINITION OF RETURN ON INVESTMENT

Return on investment, often abbreviated to ROI, is a ratio that takes the firm's profit for a given accounting period (normally one year) and divides this by its invested capital, as measured by the balance sheet. The capital invested is calculated as stock and long-term debt. ROI is a measure that demonstrates the effectiveness of the management to use the capital available to generate profit, and hence a return for those investing in the company. The higher the ROI, the better the performance, and the happier existing investors will be. A higher ratio will also improve the company's ability to find new investors.

THE VALLEY OF DEATH

A problem occurs for SMEs during their growth and development phase, when expenditures on asset acquisition and R&D need to be funded and financing obligations must be serviced. Debt finance, in particular, adversely impacts profitability because interest payments reduce the net profit available for distribution to equity investors. This difficult period, known as the "valley of death," or "death valley curve" (see Figure 1), is experienced by all SMEs as their need for funds increases and they rack up large accumulated losses before profits from sales can be realized. SMEs that engage in technology transfer and new product development face the greatest difficulties in making it through these challenging times.

GROWING AND MAXIMIZING SME PROFITABILITY WITHOUT COMPROMISING ROI

So how can SMEs grow and maximize their profitability without compromising ROI? The first rule is that growth must be carefully managed, with expansion financed through a series of stages. DeepStream had backers with deep pockets and a lot of patience. Venture capitalists are in it for the long term, but many companies are financed by debt provided by banks, who expect their interest and capital payments to be made on time, regardless of the firm's position on the death valley curve.

Instead of diving headlong into expansion at all costs, SMEs need to manage their customers' aspirations, planning where they want to be and when. In this way the size of the valley can be limited and it will be possible to return to a profitable position far sooner than would otherwise be the case. It is far better to have a series of planned growth phases between which ROI can be allowed to return to acceptable levels. This will demonstrate to potential equity investors that management is in control of the company's destiny and that it is not being controlled by any unrealistic demands from customers.

The second rule is to manage your costs, as it can be quite easy for SME managers to

Figure 1. The valley of death. (*Source*: Osawa and Miyazaki, 2006)

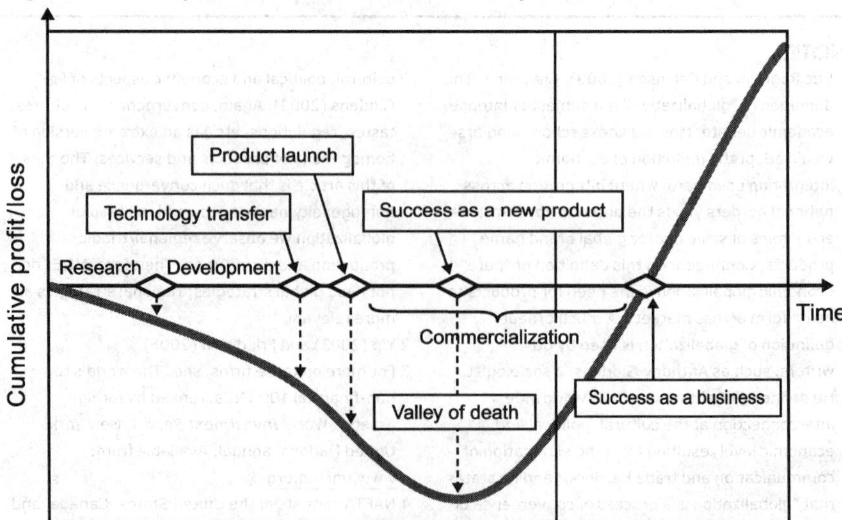

"As a small businessperson, you have no greater leverage than the truth." John Greenleaf Whittier

accept the loss-making situations that are experienced as a company expands and to lose control of expenditure. Debt blindness sets in as the figures become ever larger and managers lose sight of the original business plan.

Finally, focus on the more short-term profitable options available to the business. Long-term contracts are fine and can keep investors happy, but economic conditions may change and a bird in the hand is worth two in the bush. The contentedness of investors will quickly change if the long-term contracts fail to come to fruition because customers go bankrupt or file for administration.

CASE STUDY

DeepStream Technologies

UK-based DeepStream Technologies was founded in May 2003 by chief executive Mark Crosier, along with ten other people. They worked unpaid for almost a year to realize their ambition for the product and the company, designing and manufacturing intelligent embedded sensors for remote service enablement in, for example, energy management and building efficiency applications.

Early in 2004, DeepStream secured a total £2.8 million (then US$5.2 million) investment, raised between Doughty Hanson Technology Ventures and the company founders. Later that year DeepStream was awarded two contracts for over US$15 million to design and supply contracts for miniaturized electronic protection modules for switchgear products. A number of business awards followed in 2005. Second tier funding was obtained in September 2006—£5 million (then US$9.5 million) from 3i, a world leader in private equity and venture capital, and a further £2.8 million (then US$5.3 million) from initial investor Doughty Hanson; additionally, they were awarded government grants of £1.5 million (US$2.9 million).

More success came when DeepStream was named a 2007 Technology Pioneer by the World Economic Forum[1] in Davos, and Mark Crosier was named Ernst & Young's Science & Technology Entrepreneur of the Year for the United Kingdom's northern region. In July 2007 employee numbers reached 60. Further long-term contracts were obtained in 2008 and employee numbers expanded to 80, with a new production facility opened as the company announced plans to double in size by 2010.

This case study is of a company that is a huge success story, but what do the figures say about this SME during its growth and expansion phase? The large contracts, though headline-grabbing, are long term, and realized annual sales over the period 2004–07 averaged less than £0.3 million (US$0.6 million). During this time, the costs of expansion continued to rise until by March 31, 2007, the company had accumulated a total loss of £7.8 million (US$15 million). The effect on ROI was devastating, with negative returns reported, and yet the long-term prospects for the company are good, the investors are content, and the credit rating of the firm is measured as stable.

►► MAKING IT HAPPEN

- Control the growth of your company; don't let its growth control you.
- Who is in charge—the management or the customers? Sure you have to respond to customer needs, but they are not going to deal with the bank manager when your overdraft exceeds the agreed limit.
- Keep the costs under control and according to plan. Don't think that because you are investing in a growing company you can't keep on top of purchases and investments.
- Don't chase the end of the rainbow. Some large orders may appear very attractive and profitable in the long term, but would you really be able to cope in the meantime?
- Take smaller strides forward and allow profitability to return. Let the business catch its breath, and then take the next steps to further growth and development.

►► MORE INFO

Books:

Murphy, L. M., and P. L. Edwards. *Bridging the Valley of Death: Transitioning from Public to Private Sector Financing*. Golden, CO: National Renewable Energy Laboratory, 2003. Online at: www.cleanenergystates.org/CaseStudies/NREL-Bridging_the_Valley_of_Death.pdf

O'Berry, Denise. *Small Business Cash Flow: Strategies for Making Your Business a Financial Success*. Hoboken, NJ: Wiley, 2007.

Scarborough, Norman M., Douglas L. Wilson, and Thomas W. Zimmerer. *Effective Small Business Management: An Entrepreneurial Approach*. 9th ed. Upper Saddle River, NJ: Prentice Hall, 2008.

Article:

Osawa, Yoshitaka, and Kumiko Miyazaki. "An empirical analysis of the valley of death: Large-scale R&D project performance in a Japanese diversified company." *Asian Journal of Technology Innovation* 14:2 (2006): 93–116.

"The manager has his eye on the bottom line; the leader has his eye on the horizon." Warren Bennis

     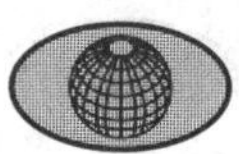   

Websites:

European Business Angel Network (EBAN): www.eban.org
Institute for Small Business and Entrepreneurship (ISBE): www.isbe.org.uk
International Network for SMEs (INSME): www.insme.org
National Venture Capital Association (NVCA): www.nvca.org
US Small Business Administration (SBA): www.sba.gov

NOTES

1 The World Economic Forum is an independent international organization committed to improving the state of the world by engaging leaders in partnerships to shape global, regional, and industry agendas.

"Ask five economists and you'll get five different answers—six if one went to Harvard." Edgar R. Fiedler

  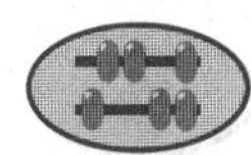   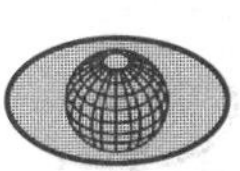   

The Impact of Climate Change on Business

by Graham Dawson

EXECUTIVE SUMMARY

- The impact of climate change on business—or the monetary value of the costs that may be incurred by affected parties and the benefits that they may accrue—is difficult to assess with any degree of precision.
- The Stern Review and the United Nations Intergovernmental Panel on Climate Change (IPCC) have reported the results of running complex computer models that integrate climate science and economics with the aim of predicting the economic impact of climate change far into the future.
- There is no agreement concerning the appropriate discount rate or the monetary value of effects where market prices are not available.
- Uncertainty also surrounds the rate, and carbon-intensiveness, of the growth of the world economy for decades and even centuries ahead, while the hypothesis of anthropogenic climate change itself continues to be controversial.

THE GLOBAL IMPACT OF CLIMATE CHANGE ON PEOPLE

The standard approach to assessing the economic impact of climate change on business requires giving a monetary value to the costs that may be incurred by those affected and the benefits that may accrue to them.

The most comprehensive attempt to do this is the Stern Review (2007), commissioned by the UK government, which predicts severe impacts from an average global temperature rise of 2–3°C within the next 50 years or so. These impacts include an increased risk of flooding from melting glaciers, followed by disruption to water supplies, affecting up to one-sixth of the world's population, mainly in the Indian subcontinent and parts of China and South America. In higher-latitude areas, such as Northern Europe, agricultural yields may increase with a temperature increase of 2–3°C, but declining yields, especially in Africa, could leave hundreds of millions of people without sufficient food. Increased mortality from heat-related deaths and the spread of tropical diseases is predicted, although there will be fewer deaths from exposure to cold. With warming of 3–4°C, thermal expansion of the oceans is predicted to cause rising sea levels, which could lead to inundation of low-lying coastal land, displacing "tens to hundreds of millions" of people. The risks are greatest for Southeast Asia (Bangladesh and Vietnam), small islands in the Caribbean and the Pacific, and large coastal cities, such as Tokyo, New York, Cairo, and London. Extreme weather events may become more frequent.

MODELING THE COSTS OF CLIMATE CHANGE

It is easy enough to put a monetary value on some of these impacts. For example, there is a lot of expensive real estate with known market prices in major coastal cities such as London, New York, and Tokyo. Moreover, without offices or factories for people to work in, or homes for them to live in, output would fall, at least for a while. Declining crop yields (adjusted for higher prices) and also fish stocks would reduce the value of world output. Standard practice is to estimate the loss of output consequent upon people's incapacity for paid and unpaid work.

Quantifying these predicted impacts of climate change in monetary terms requires degrees of certainty and precision that may not be attainable. Both the science and the economics of climate change are subject to considerable uncertainty and are therefore deeply controversial.

The impacts of climate change on business depend on the magnitude of temperature changes associated with different concentrations of CO_2 and other greenhouse gas (GHG) emissions, according to the scientific hypothesis of anthropogenic climate change. The earliest studies of the economic impact of climate change assumed a doubling of atmospheric concentrations of CO_2 by 2050, and estimated the costs of the resulting increase in global mean surface temperature at approximately 2% of world gross domestic product (GDP).

Subsequent modeling of the economic impact of climate change has sought to integrate scientific models of the global climate and economic models of future world economic growth. The anthropogenic hypothesis holds that most of the observed rise in temperature has been caused by GHG emissions from fossil fuel use in economic activity. The future path of GHG emissions depends on the rate of growth of world economic activity and how that growth is divided between more and less carbon-intensive processes. So predicting the future path of GHG emissions, and hence the impact of climate change on business, involves modeling the rate of growth of the world economy well into the future.

The United Nations Intergovernmental Panel on Climate Change (IPCC) occupies a near-monopoly position in disseminating climate science to policy makers throughout the world. It does not predict future temperature increases and their impacts but prepares a number of illustrative outcomes, using integrated assessment models (IAM). Models of world economic growth and consequent GHG emissions are combined with climate science models,

CASE STUDY

What Would This Mean for Business Activity in, for example, the United States?

If predictions such as those reported by Stern prove to be accurate, business will be forced to adapt to changes in climate. Adaptation would involve a range of measures of varying cost. In the United States, temperature increases of up to 2–3°C might cause the wheat belt to shift northward into Canada; US farmers in the Midwest would have to plant new crop varieties, a fairly routine adjustment. In northern areas, winter deaths from exposure to the cold would fall and tourism might increase. Further south, the melting of snow could make the water supply to California and the Mississippi basin more erratic, causing more acute problems for agriculture. Deaths from exposure to heat and the cost of air conditioning and refrigeration would increase. At higher temperatures, southern parts of the United States would see an increased risk of extreme weather events, requiring substantial investment to defend low-lying cities, such as New Orleans and New York, from flooding.

"You cannot control what happens to you, but you can control your attitude toward what happens to you, and in that, you will be mastering change rather than allowing it to master you." Brian Tracy

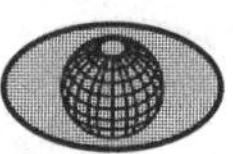

showing the links between those GHG emissions and temperature change.

The Stern Review used PAGE2002, an IAM designed by the UK government in 2000 and modified two years later. Stern claims that the overall costs and risks of business-as-usual (BAU) climate change would be equivalent to losing 5–20% of global GDP each year, "now and forever," but this may not be as apocalyptic as it sounds.

Stern explains the different stages by which this estimate of the economic impact of climate change was reached. The model is run to simulate a period of 200 years or more and "produces a mean warming of 3.9°C relative to pre-industrial in 2100." The first stage indicates that the costs and risks of climate change that can be quantified in terms of market values (basically, lost output) would be equivalent to losing at least 5% of global GDP each year, "now and forever."

At this point, Stern departs from most other models by adding in "non-market" impacts on the environment and human health. Nonmarket impacts are those that cannot be given a monetary value by referring to a market price (for instance, the price of land lost to coastal flooding). The costs of disease or of lost agricultural land in subsistence economies, for example, do not have a market price. Including this second stage increases the total cost from 5% to 11% of global GDP. These estimates are highly controversial. Since standard practice is to estimate health impacts in terms of lost output from incapacity to work, applying this and other techniques to estimate the cost of nonmarket impacts is subject to considerable uncertainty. It has also been argued that the degree to which both disease and casualties from natural disasters are related to income rather than environmental factors is not taken into account.

The third stage adds amplifying feedback effects, including the risk of catastrophic climate change, which increase the potential total cost from 11% to 14% of global GDP. Finally, Stern considers the view that a disproportionate burden of climate change would fall on poor regions. If this were given a stronger relative weight, the total cost of global warming could increase to "around 20%" of global GDP. Stern arrives at such a large adjustment for poor regions because he assumes that vulnerability to climate change is independent of development, but it seems more likely that such vulnerability depends on the capacity to adapt and hence on the level of development.

UNCERTAINTIES IN THE ECONOMIC VALUATION OF IMPACTS

"Now and Forever"

The phrase "now and forever" invites examination. The effects of climate change are expected to occur year by year over a very long period of time. The Stern Review calculates the present value of the costs of climate change by averaging the total costs over the number of years the model runs at a rate of discount. Nordhaus ran the Stern model to calculate the costs of climate change, including nonmarket and catastrophic impacts that take Stern's estimate up to 14% of world output, for each year the model covers. According to Nordhaus, the model projects a mean loss of only 0.4% of world output in 2060, rising to 2.9% in 2100 and 13.8% in 2200. Losses averaging about 1% over the period 2000–2100 become about 14% "now and forever" because the losses in the distant future are extremely high (and a low discount rate is used). Nordhaus argues that, "using the [Stern] *Review*'s methodology, more than half of the estimated damages now and forever' occur after the year 2800."

Discounting

For most people, $100 is worth more today than $100 next year because there is a degree of uncertainty about what might happen between now and next year; they would prefer to have $100 to spend right now to having it at some point in an uncertain future. In other words, the *present value* of that $100 payable to you in 10 years is less than $100 paid to you now. Similarly, the expected future costs, no less than the benefits, of an event or occurrence should be discounted, i.e. reduced in value, in order to estimate their present value.

Since many economic impacts of climate change are not expected to occur until decades or even centuries into the future, their occurrence is inevitably subject to a degree of uncertainty. The impacts of catastrophic climate change may never happen, so economists discount, or reduce the value of, their costs. As you add up the costs of climate change year by year, you might want to adjust downward those expected in later years—that is, you might want to *discount* them to reflect the uncertainty of their occurrence. The higher the rate at which you discount such costs, the lower will be their present value.

The discount rate used may influence the results of a model more than any other parameter or value used in the model. There is no agreement about the appropriate rate of discount to use, and Stern argues that any discount rate greater than zero unfairly devalues the interests of future generations. He sets the "pure time preference rate" at zero, on the grounds that a future generation has the same claim on our ethical attention as the current one. Based on a zero pure time preference rate, the discount rates used in Stern's running of PAGE2002 are lower than those used in most other models and do much to explain why Stern's "baseline" cost of 5% of world GDP is higher than the results of other models (typically 1–2% of world GDP). Other ethical approaches are at least as convincing. For example, agent-relative ethics holds that agents naturally value people who are linked to them by kinship or proximity above strangers who are remote in space or time. This approach implies a higher discount rate, which would reduce the loss from "business as usual" in Stern's model substantially below 5% of world GDP.

The estimate is an annual average for an indefinite future; losses are low for the first 50 years or so, and using unusually low discount rates produces a high present value for the catastrophic losses predicted for 2200 and beyond. By that time, given rates of world economic growth sufficient to cause the projected carbon emissions and climate change, it is reasonable to assume that most people will be very much better off than the current generation, although not quite as much better off as they would have been in the absence of climate change.

Scenarios of Future World Economic Growth

How much better off would these future generations be, and which groups of people would gain most? What will the world economy look like 100 years from now? Wisely, the IPCC has demurred from making any such prediction, offering instead six illustrative scenarios of possible future courses that the world economy might take. In 2007 the IPCC reported the "best estimates and likely ranges for global average surface air warming for six... emissions marker scenarios." The best estimate for the low scenario is 1.8°C, and the best estimate for the high scenario is 4.0°C. The important point here is that scenarios are descriptions of possible outcomes to which no probability can be attached. Of the six scenarios, the IPCC asserts that that: "All should be considered equally sound." If it is impossible to assess the risk of any of the associated impacts, there is radical uncertainty.

It is widely believed that the impact of an increase in global temperature of less than 2°C will be mild, and that cereal yields will

"The times they are a-changin'." Bob Dylan

  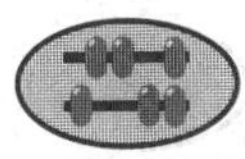   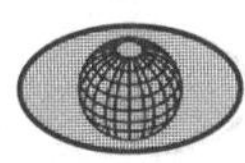   

actually increase in temperate regions. With a global temperature increase of 4°C, the impacts are projected to be catastrophic, with up to 80 million people exposed to malaria, and up to 300 million more affected by coastal flooding each year, with rising risks of extreme weather events. But, on the IPCC's own admission, it is impossible to say whether the impact of climate change will be mild or catastrophic.

Uncertainty in Climate Science

Uncertainty also surrounds the science of climate change. In its most recent report, the IPCC claims that there is 90% certainty that most of the increase in global mean temperature since the middle of the twentieth century has been caused by the observed increase in greenhouse gas concentrations in the atmosphere. This is actually a rather cautious and vague claim, because it is consistent with a significant role for natural causes being the reason for the rise in global temperature. In the decade since 1998 global temperature has not risen, and critics of the IPCC argue that the scientific evidence for dangerous change is far from overwhelming.

Conclusion

The impact of climate change on business, or the monetary value on the costs that may be incurred by affected parties and the benefits that they may accrue, is difficult to assess with any degree of precision.

The Stern Review and IPCC have reported the results of running complex computer models that integrate climate science and economics with the aim of predicting the economic impact of climate change into the remote future. However, there is no agreement concerning (i) the appropriate discount rate and (ii) the monetary value of effects where market values are unavailable. Uncertainty also surrounds the rate, and carbon-intensiveness, of the growth of the world economy for decades and even centuries ahead, while the hypothesis of anthropogenic climate change itself continues to be controversial.

▸▸ MAKING IT HAPPEN

Business may be affected by policies to mitigate climate change as much as by climate change itself. In the negotiations for the Kyoto Protocol, which seeks to establish a global framework for reductions in GHG emissions, the fossil fuel producers and users resisted aggressive reductions, while insurance companies and renewable energy producers were more favorably disposed toward them. It is not clear whether aggressive mitigation policies will survive the financial crisis of 2008, with many policy makers more concerned to reduce the effects of the expected global recession than the more distant threats posed by climate change.

▸▸ MORE INFO

Books:

Lawson, N. *An Appeal to Reason: A Cool Look at Global Warming*. London: Duckworth, 2008.

Nordhaus, W. D. *The Challenge of Global Warming: Economic Models and Environmental Policy*. New Haven, CT: Yale University Press, 2007.

Singer, S. F., and D. T. Avery. *Unstoppable Global Warming: Every 1500 Years*. Lanham, MD: Rowman & Littlefield, 2006.

Stern, N. *The Economics of Climate Change: The Stern Review*. Cambridge, UK: Cambridge University Press, 2007.

Articles:

Beckerman, W., and C. Hepburn. "Ethics of the discount rate in the Stern Review." *World Economics* 8:1 (2007): 187–210.

Brittan, S. "On climate change and good sense." *Financial Times* (February 9, 2007).

Byatt, I., *et al.* "The Stern Review: A dual critique. Part II: Economic aspects." *World Economics* 7:4 (2006): 199–232.

Carter, R. M., *et al.* "The Stern Review: A dual critique. Part I: The science." *World Economics* 7:4 (2006): 167–198.

Tol, R. S. J., and G. W. Yohe. "A review of the Stern Review." *World Economics* 7:4 (2006): 233–250.

Reports:

Goklany, I. M. "Death and death rates due to extreme weather events: Global and US trends 1900–2006." In *Civil Society Report on Climate Change*. London: International Policy Press, 2007, pp. 47–60. Online at: www.csccc.info/reports/report_20.pdf

House of Lords. "The economics of climate change." HL Paper 12-1, Select Committee on Economic Affairs 2nd Report of Session 2005–06. London, 2005.

Intergovernmental Panel on Climate Change, Working Group 1: The Physical Science Basis of Climate Change, 4th Assessment Report (IPCC WG1 AR4 Report), "Summary for policymakers." IPCC Secretariat, c/o WMO, Switzerland, 2007. Online at: ipcc-wg1.ucar.edu/wg1/wg1-report.html

Reiter, P. "Human ecology and human behaviour: Climate change and health in perspective." In *Civil Society Report on Climate Change*. London: International Policy Press, 2007, pp. 21–46. Online at: www.csccc.info/reports/report_20.pdf

US Climate Change Science Program (CCSP), Annual Report to Congress. *Our Changing Planet: The US Climate Change Science Program for Fiscal Year 2009*. Online at: www.climatescience.gov/infosheets/ccsp-8

Websites:

Global and Development Environment Institute at Tufts University: www.ase.tufts.edu/gdae

Intergovernmental Panel on Climate Change (IPCC): www.ipcc.ch

Science and Environmental Policy Project: www.sepp.org

United Nations Environment Programme (UNEP) climate change pages: www.unep.org/themes/climatechange

US Climate Change Science Program (CCSP), integrating federal research on global change and climate change: www.climatescience.gov

"The unprecedented impact of climate change transforms the very purpose of government. Once quality of life meant the pursuit of two objectives: economic growth and social cohesion. Now there is a trinity of aims: prosperity, fairness and environmental care." Gordon Brown

   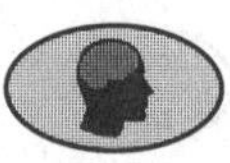  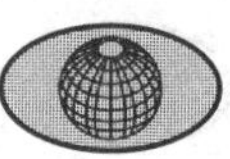   

Viewpoint: Graeme Leach

Corporate Taxation and its Impact on Foreign Direct Investment

INTRODUCTION

Graeme Leach is Chief Economist and Director of Policy at the Institute of Directors, which he joined in August 1998. He is also visiting professor of economic policy at the University of Lincoln.

A frequent conference speaker and media commentator on the UK and global economy, in recent years he has spoken at conferences in the US, Canada, China, Germany, Italy, France, Spain, Sweden, Ireland, Belgium, Greece, Taiwan, and Zimbabwe.

In 2006 he was appointed to the Conservative Party's Commission for Tax reform.

Prior to joining the IoD he was economics director at the Henley Centre, analyzing future economic and social change. This included editorship of The Henley Centre's UK economic forecasts, global macroeconomic outlook and consumer and leisure futures services. As part of this consulting, he has recently produced *Tomorrow's Work, a Report Into the Future of the Way We Work*, and is currently researching for a forthcoming book entitled *The Future of the West*.

In 1998 he was awarded the WPP Atticus Award for original published thinking on futures issues.

Previously, Graeme worked as economic adviser to the Scottish Provident Investment Group, and as a senior economic consultant with Pieda.

The burden of corporate taxation obviously influences the volume and location of foreign direct investment (FDI) for the simple reason that it determines after tax returns from investment. In a globalize world economy with footloose investment, multinational enterprises have the capacity to shift their location and/or taxable income across borders. There is also an asymmetry to the impact of taxation and FDI. Small differences in the tax burden may have little or no impact on FDI as the location decision is based on a number of factors and a small discrepancy in one area is unlikely to swing the location decision. In contrast, a large divide in the tax burden can become the tipping point issue, elbowing aside other influences. Even where a country had a significant advantage in tax competitiveness, which has then eroded, it may still lead to relocations. An example of this would be where a country was traditionally weak say in the competitiveness of its transport and education systems, but had enjoyed a real competitive advantage in its tax system. If the tax advantage falls, even when remaining positive, it could highlight deficiencies in other areas and thereby trigger a relocation elsewhere.

Consequently, a competitive corporate tax system is a necessary but not sufficient condition to attract FDI. Possessing a low tax burden and very little else will not attract FDI. Afghanistan has a zero rate of corporate income tax but is clearly not in receipt of massive private sector investment. The UAE, in comparison, also has a zero rate of corporate income tax which when combined with other influences has achieved huge inward FDI.

The Organisation for Economic Co-operation and Development (OECD) has recently stated that: "there is a broad recognition that international tax competition is increasing and that what may have been regarded as a competitive tax burden on business in a given host country at one point in time may no longer be so after rounds of tax rate reductions in other countries."

So what drives inward and outward FDI and what is the role of corporate taxation in this process? FDI, like competitiveness, is not determined by a single driver. Many factors intervene in this process, such as market size, market growth, proximity to market, access to market, labor supply, transport infrastructure and the quality of the physical infrastructure.

Taxation is but one of many influences on inbound FDI but how important is it in comparison to other primary influences? These are the issues to which we now turn.

WHICH MEASURE OF TAXATION DO COMPANIES LOOK AT?

When assessing the impact of corporate tax on FDI a very real obstacle emerges at the outset. When multinational companies look at an overseas investment how do they define the tax rate they are likely to pay?

Is it the headline rate of marginal tax or is it the average rate of corporate taxation? Does it include or exclude employer social insurance contributions? Or do companies think in terms of the effective rate of taxation based on an assessment of prospective reliefs and allowances for which they will be eligible? How significant is the burden of indirect, energy and environmental taxes? To what extent is the decision based on the complexity of the tax system and the resources required to achieve compliance? To what extent does consistent application of tax law—or lack of—influence overseas investors? To what extent is the decision made on the basis of personal rates of income tax?

There are also significant differences in terms of the relationship between different types of FDI (manufacturing, service sector, advanced economy versus emerging market) and the tax system. Another huge issue of course is the role of transfer pricing within multinational organizations and the scope it provides for evading or reducing tax liabilities.

Tax planning clearly matters but it is difficult to allow for all these influences in cross country comparisons. The relative importance of each factor will almost certainly differ depending on the nature of the FDI decision.

PricewaterhouseCoopers (PwC) publish annual data on corporate tax rate, labor tax rate and other tax rates in order to estimate

"Unless managers are aware of ethical issues. . .they will fail to institutionalise ethics in corporate life. Ignorance can be as pernicious as malice." Damian Grace

  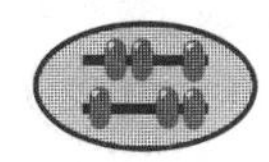   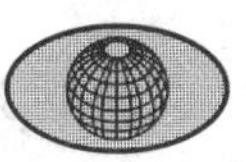   

a total tax rate (TTR). PwC place the UK 59th in the world based on its TTR ranking. The complexity of the analysis is well illustrated by France. France's TTR ranks 160th in the world, below Zimbabwe at 156. Nobody would surely suggest this made Zimbabwe a better investment than France. A range of reliefs and allowances mean that France has a low effective rate of corporate tax, but very heavy payroll taxes result in a high overall TTR.

TAX IS BECOMING THE TIPPING POINT FOR FDI DECISIONS

Recent OECD research has suggested that the impact of taxation on FDI is increasing—FDI is becoming more sensitive. One reason is that the nontax barriers to capital movement have been reduced over recent decades, and consequently tax has shifted up the agenda of considerations—illustrated by the decision of WPP to move its tax base to Ireland.

Of course, there is variation across different sectors and countries but a rule of thumb is that FDI decreases by up to 5% following a one percentage point rise in the tax rate on FDI.

In response to these pressures, many countries have lowered their rate of corporate income tax. This is a headline grabbing and obvious means to signal a lower tax burden to potential inward investors. Such reductions have tended to involve measures to broaden the tax base. Indeed, in the UK, Conservative proposals to reduce corporate income tax are funded by the withdrawal of various reliefs and allowances.

HOW BIG AN ISSUE IS TAX COMPETITIVENESS?

Should we be concerned about comparative tax systems given that the Nordic economies have been successful with high tax burdens? The answer is yes. Many of the Nordic economies have been successful over the past 10 to 15 years, but part of the explanation is that they have been reducing their tax burdens—albeit from very high levels. Over the past 15 years Sweden has reduced its tax to GDP ratio by around 6% of GDP, Finland by around 5% of GDP and Denmark by just 1% of GDP. In addition, one also has to consider the counterfactual argument. The Nordic economies could have performed even better than they have, if their tax burdens had been lower.

The damaging potential impact of taxation on FDI is best understood with the concept of deadweight loss. When examining the impact of taxation we do not look at the tax burden alone, we also need to examine the excess burden or deadweight loss of taxation. The deadweight loss of taxation is the loss of output which would have occurred in the absence of the tax—a loss of economic welfare above and beyond the tax revenues collected. Deadweight loss is the ultimate stealth tax.

Deadweight costs (losses) go unnoticed, even by those who pay them, because instead of taking from companies what they already have, they take from companies what they would have had, but will never get. No one sees the extra output that would have been created by FDI decisions made in the absence of higher taxes.

To summarize, there is likely to be an increase in the sensitivity of FDI to tax systems over the coming years. As the world economy weakens, companies will face even greater pressure to maintain, after tax, returns in the face of much weaker pretax returns. There will also be increased emphasis on clearly defining the nature of the tax burden (marginal rates, average rates, effective rates etc.) and what it means for individual enterprises.

The most successful economies will marry the lowest tax burdens with strong performance in other key drivers of FDI such as market size, growth, labor supply and transport infrastructure.

"If there is no conception that a decision entails ethical considerations, and if there is no adequate conceptual vocabulary to make sense of ethical requirements, then reasonable ethical standards in business become a matter of luck." Damian Grace

  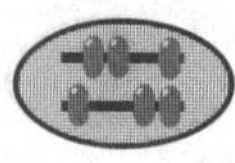   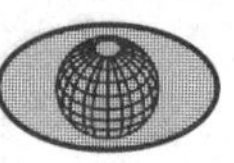   

The Impact of Demographics on Business and the World Economy by Gabriel Stein

EXECUTIVE SUMMARY

- Over the past 10 years, the world has become divided into savers and spenders. The solution to the global financial crisis requires the savers to become spenders and vice versa.
- This transition will be helped by demographic factors as the populations in most saving countries are aging, whereas in most spending countries they are young.
- The transition will be most dramatic in the United States—which, as a result, is likely to move into a sustainable, though not permanent, current account surplus.

THE COMING US CURRENT ACCOUNT SURPLUS

A World Divided Into Savers and Spenders Who Need to Change Places

One of the key causes behind the global financial crisis of 2007/08 has been the division of the world into "savers" (countries with a savings surplus) and "spenders" (countries spending someone else's surplus). The problem with this division is that it is asymmetrical. There is no theoretical limit to how much people can want to save. But spending someone else's savings involves getting into debt, and there is certainly a limit to how much debt anyone can take on. By 2007/08, it was clear that American households had amassed a debt burden they could no longer service at normal interest rate levels, and that households in some other countries, like the United Kingdom and Australia, were not far behind.

Thus, in order to eliminate global financial imbalances, there has to be a shift between savers and spenders. Households in the spending countries need to save to bring down their debt burden, whereas households in saving countries need to spend more—not least so that the former spender economies can grow by exporting to the former savers. It is possible that this will not happen—that spenders will begin to save but the savers will continue to save at current rates. However, by definition world investments have to equal world savings. If everyone attempts to raise their savings to income ratio, investments will by default suffer and world activity will slow even more.

This may seem a tall order. But there are reasons to expect that over the next five years there will be a sea change in world saving and spending patterns. The reason for this is demographic. As it happens, many of the saving countries are among those with the oldest populations. This means that large cohorts of their populations will imminently change from saving (for retirement) to spending (their retirement savings). Equally, a number of the spending countries have somewhat better demographic profiles, but because of their tendency not to save, they need to start saving considerably more in the near future. This pattern is not true for all countries, but it is true for a large number. Notably, one key development over the medium term is likely to be a shift in the United States from a persistent current account deficit to a sustained, though not necessarily long-lasting, current account surplus.

At first glance some of these developments seem counterintuitive. We are used to some countries being regular surplus countries, with large excess savings. But, in theory, countries with aging, but not yet retired, populations, should have a savings surplus as the working-age cohorts save up for retirement. This is generally the case, as Figures 1 and 2 show.

Figure 1 shows the old age dependency ratio—the number of people aged 65 or above relative to those aged 15–64, in a number of countries in 2005 and 2050. Figure 2 shows the change in this dependency ratio.

Figures 1 and 2 should be read together with Figure 3, which shows current account balances in 2007. As is clear from Figures 2 and 3, the countries facing the greatest deterioration in their dependency ratio are generally also those with current account surpluses (i.e., excess savings). There are exceptions to this rule: Spain is a deficit country, yet one with the prospect of a substantial demographic deterioration over the next 45 years. So, to a lesser extent, are Italy and France. These countries are likely to face substantial difficulties as their populations age—especially Italy, where the population and the labor force are already shrinking and aging fast.

As households increase their spending, some other sector will have to save more. This must be either companies (i.e., they must become less profitable), or governments (by moving into deficit, or further into deficit), or foreigners (i.e., countries whose households are increasing their spending must move further into current account deficit). In other, saving countries—for example, Germany, Korea, Japan, Singapore, to take those with the worst demographic profile—the switch from household saving to spending can be more easily accommodated, since it will simply require a smaller current account surplus—which, as it so happens, is exactly what is needed for these countries from a global economic perspective.

THE UNITED STATES WILL SEE THE MOST DRAMATIC DEVELOPMENTS

The most dramatic development is likely to take place in the United States. This is because the United States is in very many ways an exceptional country. Although it has a far better demographic future than many other countries, it is nevertheless an aging economy. Yet, as is well known, US households are not saving. For most of the post-war period until the early 1990s, the US household savings rate was somewhere between 8% and 12% of income. However, it then began to drop rapidly, falling below 5% in the mid-1990s and turning negative by mid-2005.

Arguably, this is not a correct measure of savings. If US households' financial or real assets appreciated enough in value to compensate for a lower savings rate, it would make financial sense to depend on such assets, rather than to save. But this necessitates a constantly rising stock market and/or housing market. Admittedly, household net housing wealth rose from 0.8 times personal disposable income in 2000, to 1.2 times in early 2006. Although this is not insignificant (particularly as disposable income also has risen over this time), it is more or less in line with the long-term average. Moreover, as the US housing boom turned to bust, the ratio slipped back to 0.8 times by 2008. Moreover, household financial wealth, at 4.1 times disposable income, is still less than the 5.1 times reached at the peak of the high-tech boom.[1]

Traditionally, one of the ways in which US (and other) pensioners have financed their retirement is to end their working life

"In a human capital-intensive environment, all you bring to the table is your own intellectual property. You will not share this precious resource with others unless you trust them to reciprocate." Francis Fukuyama

Figure 1. Dependency ratios (people aged 65+ per person aged 15–64) in selected countries in 2005 and 2050. (*Source*: US Census Bureau)

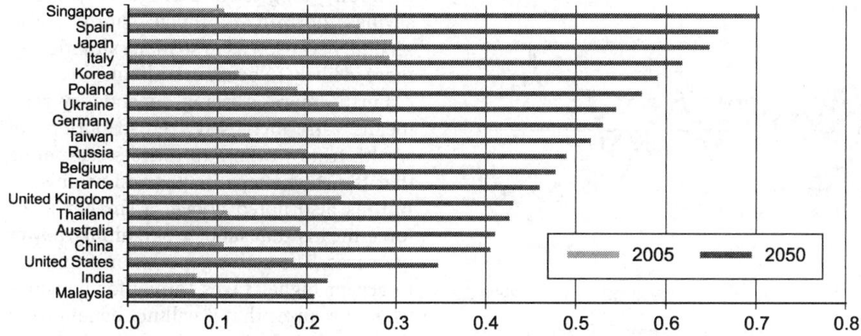

Figure 2. Change in the dependency ratio 2005–2050. (*Source*: US Census Bureau)

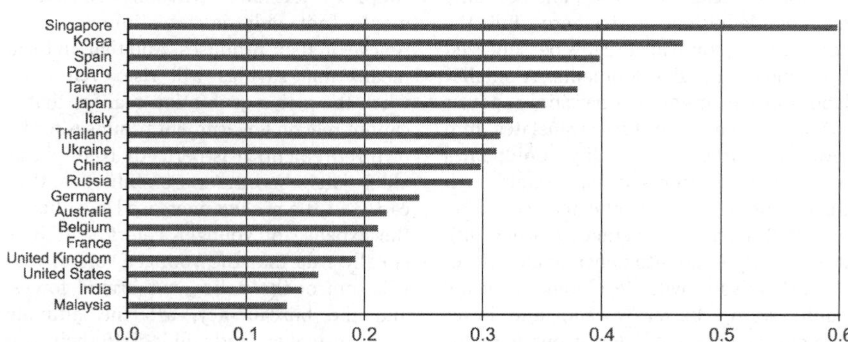

Figure 3. Current account balances in 2007 (US$ billion). (*Sources*: IMF *World Economic Outlook, October 2008*; DataStream)

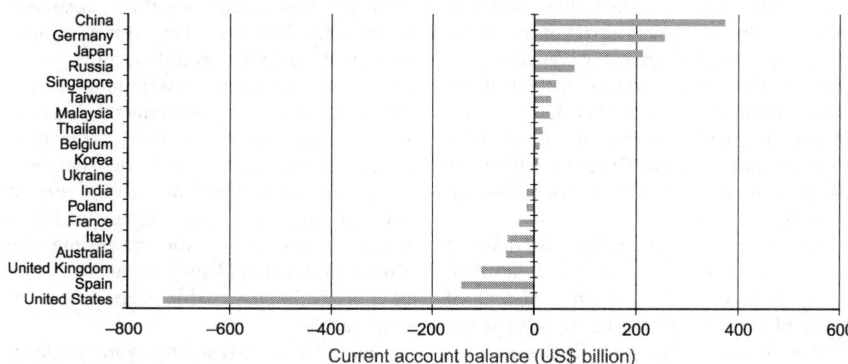

with a mortgage-free home. The home would then be exchanged for something smaller, with the balance providing the means for retirement. But in a situation where the country has just gone through a protracted housing boom, it may not be possible to realize the necessary funds. Even less so as a situation in which a large segment of the population tries at (roughly) the same time to sell their houses is likely to put substantial downward pressure on house prices. Adding to the financial pressure, US households' pension assets, though impressive at $12.3 trillion in the second quarter of 2008, still only average about $80,000 per person in the labor force. (Obviously, the average pension fund is larger, as many people do not hold pension funds.) Assuming a life expectancy of 20 years at retirement, a 5% interest rate, and a complete drawdown of the fund over the expected life, this gives a pension of just under $4,200 per annum!

THE BABY-BOOMERS ARE DUE TO RETIRE—BUT CAN'T

In theory, the first cohort of baby boomers, those born in 1946, are due to retire in 2011. But the upshot of the argument above is that, some time between now and 2011, two things are likely to happen. The first is that the 1946 cohort are going to realize that they cannot afford to retire—at least not if they expect to continue to enjoy anything like the standard of living they have gotten used to. Hitherto, this realization has been masked by strong rises in asset prices—financial assets in the 1990s, and then, fortuitously, real assets (houses) in the 2000s. But the values of both shares and houses are now falling, with the loss needing to be replaced by further savings. That is not necessarily a bad thing, as it means that a large group of people with substantial experience will continue to work, which will benefit output growth. Moreover, it also means that they remain savers, rather than switching to being spenders, which is also good news.

But the second point, about later retirement, has a less positive side. It also means that the 1946 cohort, having realized that it must continue to work because it lacks the wherewithal to retire on, is going to start saving in earnest. Although people of this age group can continue to work, they will nevertheless be acutely aware of the fact that their remaining working life is limited—five years, maybe 10, very unlikely more than that. And it is during this limited period of time that they will have to build up the savings to live on when they eventually do retire.

Furthermore, once this realization has hit the 1946 cohort, it won't stop there. It will—and probably rather faster—also hit the 1947 cohort, and then the 1948 and 1949 cohorts, etc. In other words, large groups headed for retirement will realize they have to save.

Such a development would provide a sharp contrast to what has recently been the case. For many years the US household and government sectors have been reacting to events from abroad, notably from Europe and Asia. Because most of the rest of the world has a savings surplus, the US domestic sectors have been forced into deficit. Meanwhile, within the United States the corporate sector has clawed its way back to a surplus after a protracted period in deficit in the mid- to late 1990s. This put further strain on the other two sectors, as their deficits had to widen. However, an increase in US household savings would suddenly reverse these roles. Notably, the US household sector would go from being the passive recipient of excess savings from the rest of the world to being the active exporter of increased US savings. There may well be—indeed, there almost certainly will be—effects on the other

     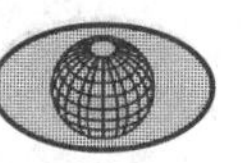   

Figure 4. US financial balances by sector as percentage of GDP, 1958–2008. Note that the current account balance equals the foreign sector balance, but with reverse sign

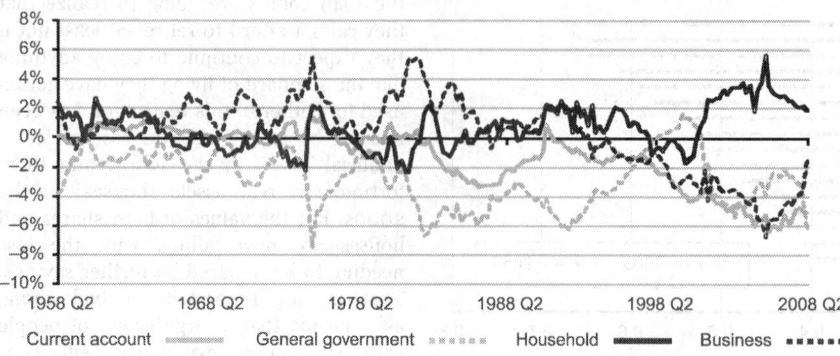

sectors as well. But the net effect is still likely to be on the foreign sector.

As it happens, this will tie in with what is happening in the rest of the world. Aging populations all over Europe, as well as in the Far East, will turn populations now intent on saving into spenders. This will reduce their current account surpluses, and possibly even turn them into deficits. In other words, just as Americans begin to save more, the rest of the world will be prepared to accommodate that increased saving.

This also means that the narrowing of the US trade deficit—a natural consequence of greater saving—will occur much faster than is currently assumed. The United States will not only import less (a consequence of increased savings) but will also export more—a consequence of diminished savings in the rest of the world.

By how much will US household savings rise? This is obviously impossible to gauge. But the long-term (since 1952) average of the household sector financial balance has been a surplus of ½% of GDP. By the third quarter of 2005, it had dropped to a deficit of just under 7% of GDP (Figure 4). By the second quarter of 2008, it had risen back to a deficit of 1½% of GDP, although this was entirely due to households ceasing to invest in housing; up to that point savings had not yet risen. Further, we have to assume that the savings of near-retirees are likely to be above, rather than below, the long-term average. A conservative assumption is therefore that the financial balance of the US household sector at the very least will revert to its long-term average.

IF US HOUSEHOLDS SAVE MORE, SOMEONE ELSE HAS TO SAVE LESS

Increased US household savings have to be balanced by a reduction in some other sector's savings. This is because the sum of sectoral financial balances in any economy has, by definition, to be zero. But the corporate sector will already be squeezed by demographic developments. A smaller labor force means greater bargaining power for labor, which in turn translates into lower corporate profitability. Companies are likely to try to resist this. So, although the corporate sector surplus may well drop back to its long-term average (½% of GDP), it is unlikely to go into deficit again. Moreover, this ties in with developments in the public sector. Fewer workers and lower corporate profits mean lower public sector revenues. At the same time, demographic changes will put increased pressure on public sector expenditure. For the moment, the public sector deficit has widened substantially under the impact of the global financial crisis. But this is a cyclical development. Here too, therefore, there is likely to be resistance to any further deterioration of the financial balance. Moreover, over time the public sector financial balance is likely to move back toward its long-term average of around 3%.

The adjustment therefore becomes a matter of arithmetic. If the household sector balance swings from a deficit of 1½% of GDP to a surplus of ½%; if the corporate sector defends its balance as vigorously as it can; and if the public sector balance reverts to its structural mean, then the foreign sector surplus must narrow. In this case, the implied domestic movements amount to approximately 5% (households +2%, public sector close to +4%, and corporate sector around –1%). To put it in more familiar terms, the US current account deficit must reduce by 5%. As it happens, the deficit was 5% in the second quarter of 2008, meaning that the required shift essentially eliminates it.

Moreover, so far the argument has assumed that the financial balance of the household sector only reverts to its long-term average. In fact, that is an unlikely development. First, because (as noted above) households are likely to save more than any long-term average since their savings horizon is much shorter. And second, because—as in so many situations—there is likely to be an overshoot.

Furthermore, a rising dependency ratio means an increased redistribution of wealth from workers to retirees (assuming that the state keeps its pension promises). But, as also noted above, a smaller labor force means that labor's bargaining power increases. The active generation is unlikely to accept higher taxes to pay for pensions when it realizes that it will not benefit from them. This is likely to reinforce the trend toward a higher retirement age, probably coupled with lower pensions as governments (not only in the United States) renege on their promises. And that, in turn, means that savings will rise even more when the active generation realizes that it cannot rely on government promises for its own retirement. It is perfectly true that as older voters become more numerous, they can vote themselves increased benefits at the expense of younger voters. But it is equally true that the younger voters, who will control the police, the armed forces, and the bureaucracy, are the ultimate decision-makers and will look to their own welfare.

The time frame is uncertain. But the direction is not. Beginning some time over the next five years, and within a relatively short span, the US is likely to move into a sustained current account surplus. Note, sustained. . .but not necessarily long-lasting. Because once the baby-boomers do begin to retire, some five to 10 years later than expected, they revert to being spenders. Some time down that line, the US current account surplus will once again turn into deficit. However, in the meantime the United States should see a number of years of a perfectly sustainable current account surplus.

This switch carries important implications for the US economy over the same period. US households have already grasped the need to deleverage, i.e., to reduce their debt burden. This in itself will badly hit household spending and slow GDP growth. But the demographic developments and the need to save for retirement mean that, even when debt levels have been brought down to a sustainable level, US households will continue to save and, crucially, will not embark on another borrowing and spending spree. An aging and saving population means that US output growth will have to become more reliant on exports than it has been for decades.

"Rather than comparing war to art, we could more accurately compare it to commerce, which is also a conflict of interests and activities." Karl von Clausewitz

  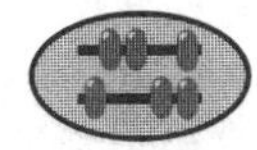 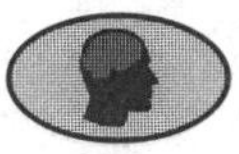  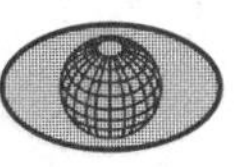   

▸▸ MORE INFO

Books:

International Monetary Fund (IMF). *World Economic Outlook October 2008: Financial Stress, Downturns, and Recoveries*. Washington, DC: IMF, 2008. Online at: www.imf.org/external/pubs/ft/weo/2008/02/pdf/text.pdf

Reserve Bank of Australia (RBA). *Demography and Financial Markets*. Proceedings of a Conference held in Sydney July 23–25, 2006. Sydney, NSW: RBA, 2006. Online at: www.rba.gov.au/publicationsandresearch/Conferences/2006/

Sterling, William, and Stephen Waite. *Boomernomics: The Future of Your Money in the Upcoming Generational Warfare*. New York: Ballantine Books, 1998.

Websites:

United Nations Department of Economic and Social Affairs, Population Division: www.un.org/esa/population

US Census Bureau, International Data Base: www.census.gov/ipc/www/idb

World Bank Data and Statistics, population statistics: go.worldbank.org/WIEXLO9J10

See Also:

Joseph Stiglitz (p. 1198)

United States (pp. 1493–1495)

NOTES

1 US Flow of Funds, published quarterly by the Board of Governors of the Federal Reserve Bank of the United States; latest data available used.

"Ethical traps are more common now than a generation ago. . .In a volatile world, it is easy to step over moral boundaries." John P. Kotter

   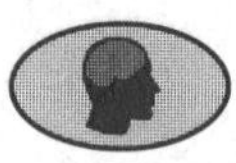  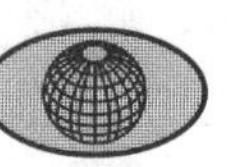   

Increasing the Profitability of Small and Medium Enterprises—A Practical Guide by Tom Brown

EXECUTIVE SUMMARY

- A company's survival depends on more than just revenue generation. Revenues must always exceed costs.
- Managers must know in detail exactly how revenues were generated for the past three years; this analysis should classify revenue by product line, customer, geography, and in any other way that helps to paint a well-defined picture of the true sources of business income.
- There are important distinctions between probable and possible future revenues. Probable revenues hinge on maintaining the business already in place; possible revenues come from managing your business with greater expectations.
- Managing costs are often the starting point for increasing profits. Before cutting costs, it's important to exercise the same level of analysis as was used to pinpoint revenues for the past three years.
- The three most likely places to start with cost cutting are worker or manager costs, inventory costs, and overhead or processing costs.
- Increasing revenue without increasing costs disproportionately is the best way to grow a stellar business.

INTRODUCTION

Many managers too often forget that business income should always exceed the cost of doing business. Deni Tato is a good example. She started her Cincinnati-based business, Contract Interiors, in 1986; by 1992, the business needed a large warehouse for the hundreds of chairs and desks in inventory. Contract Interiors employed some 50 employees. Yet in 2000 the company's $15 million in revenue was generated against the backdrop of an economic downturn; all that inventory, payroll, and operational cost amounted to a level of overhead that strangled profits. In short order, Deni formed alliances with other local companies and transferred some of her employees to their payrolls, while also offloading her warehouse and delivery trucks. Contract Interiors became a sales and marketing company with a smaller, tightly focused staff of 18 while sustaining revenue levels and boosting profitability.

THE BOTTOM LINE

When people talk about the top line and bottom line, they are talking about the difference between revenues at the top of the income statement and what remains at the bottom of the spreadsheet after all costs have been subtracted. The bottom line is the number that represents a company's profitability.

No matter where a company's bottom line is today, its managers should—and most probably *can*— boost its profitability. How? They must ask, first, whether the business can generate higher revenues reasonably, and then whether it can cut costs efficiently.

GENERATING HIGHER REVENUES

A manager who is unwilling to settle for the same results year after year should ask how the company can increase revenue without disproportionately increasing costs. This business hurdle, of course, can't be fully addressed until the manager has a detailed list of company sales for (at least) the last three years, projected revenue for the current year, and an estimate of sales for the next three years. Past tax statements can be examined to determine the reported income. But profitability thinking requires that a manager categorize past revenues in as many ways as he can: by year, individual product, product line, customer, geography, sales channel—even by selling technique (for example sales representative, direct mail, online). Pinning down a crisp outline of how the company generated every sales dollar for the last three years is important because it helps to delineate current and future revenues.

Starting with the detailed revenue analysis for the past three years, the manager can then look at current-year performance to see if last year's numbers will hold or slide. The current year's analysis should then be tested using the same, or very similar, reference categories. In looking back over three years, it's easy to allow wishful thinking to permeate projections. For example, it's easy to project that a company's largest customer in the past will double in size and, happily, will double orders with all vendors. But that thinking doesn't take into account the possibility of competitors taking away contracts now in place. It also doesn't take account of a large customer moving in an entirely new direction, removing the need for goods and services it may have been buying for years. In short, a manager must list past, present, and future revenue numbers, and then consider projections for present sales—and especially future sales—with intense scrutiny. Every projection should be challenged. When a manager has settled on a set of numbers that is (a) conservative, (b) justified, (c) rational, and (d) supportable, the probable near-term revenues for his business have been plotted. Only now is he ready to ask how his business can *increase* those revenues.

This increase can be called *possible* revenues. Probable revenues come from managing the status quo responsibly so a business doesn't go backward. Possible revenues come from managing your business with greater expectations. A manager would be wise to ask:

Can this company profitably expand what it makes? Large corporations such as Apple Computer were not always billion-dollar enterprises. Yet Apple is a good example of how, time after time, this question drove its business to new heights. First Apple focused on providing a desktop computer with a small footprint, then on computers that could be carried in a briefcase, then on computers that could be handheld while playing music (the iPod line), then on computers that could make phone calls (the iPhone) while doing thousands of other assorted personal chores, such as managing calendars, finding restaurants, even reading books. Apple learned that each product could be the springboard for another product. It didn't invent the wheel, but the company surely reinvented it over and over, much to the benefit of Apple's bottom line.

Can this company profitably expand how it sells? Brian Scudamore simply wanted a summer job. In 1989, he was a university student in Vancouver looking for seasonal work. Not finding any, Scudamore started "The Rubbish Boys" by buying a truck for $700 and offering to haul away anything that the trash services would not. His business grew. Then Scudamore asked himself if there were a way to do this online, in essence to become the "Fedex" of junk. Today, that expansion from a look-us-up-in-the-phone-book company to an internet business has made 1-800-GOT-JUNK a huge success story, now operating in 300 locations in three different countries.

Can this company profitably expand its customer base? Joe Steffick started tying fishing flies back in 1954. He became very good at it—so much so that he began selling them as a sideline to his job at a plate glass factory. Then he started selling his flies through a sporting goods store, then a hardware store, then a department store chain. In time, his nascent company grew to the point that Joe's Flies are now sold in small and large stores as well as online. There are many keys to this success story; but, at the heart, there is one key driver: Steffick and his associates kept asking who else might want to use their products. The answers—from local sportsmen to department store shoppers to fly-fishing enthusiasts buying equipment online—have helped the business to serve an ever widening array of customers.

CUTTING COSTS

When discussing profitability, some experts advise managers to start by cutting costs, yet generating higher revenues is often the most overlooked way to increase profits. Nonetheless, managers should keep in mind that expanding a business is only wise if it can be done profitably. That means that the costs of expansion must not weigh down or, worse, erase any increased revenues.

Managing costs requires the same kind of intensive numerical analysis that was suggested for past, present, and future revenues. However, with costs, a manager has to know the *exact* cost for every strand of the process for manufacturing an item or providing a service: the raw materials and machinery needed, personnel required, space to store or operate equipment, transportation expenses, even the costs of sending out an invoice — a manager needs to know each and every cost variable. Only then can he begin to cut costs.

But the exercise can pay off handsomely. In fact, a company can increase profitability simply by maintaining current revenues and lowering costs. It can do this by focusing on one or more of the following techniques.

Reducing worker or manager costs: The reason that every layoff makes the headlines is twofold. First, a layoff affects employees, the people side of the business. Second, layoffs usually augur an immediate boost to the bottom line. Any time a business can find a way to generate the same productivity using fewer man hours of labor or management (employee costs are often a large percentage of the operating costs of any business), the closer it comes to higher profitability.

Reducing inventory costs: Inventory requires storage. Lots of inventory requires lots of storage. And, if that inventory is not being used quickly, that storage has a cost in and of itself. No matter the line of business, from auto parts to printing, when a business has to keep a large quantity of items on hand it must of necessity buy or rent space to do so. Thus, when companies can find faster ways to turn raw materials into marketable products, the cost of inventory goes down. This is not just because the inventory has to be stored for less time; it is also because inventory is being converted into billable invoices at an ever faster rate.

Reducing overhead or processing costs: Every business has a production line, whether for a product as small as a fishing lure or as large as a jumbo jet. For a services business—say, a janitorial service, there's still a production line consisting of the acquisition of cleaning implements and materials, going to the cleanup site, performing the work, and going to the next site. Yet, above and beyond the production costs, every company has a cost of doing business. For example, if it takes three employees two hours to put together one invoice, there's room to reduce costs by introducing technology to speed up the work, streamlining how invoices are generated, or expanding the productivity of any one of those three employees by teaching more efficient work practices. Any work involved in the production of an item (or service performed) can be considered a processing cost. And all such costs must be judged for the value they add to the bottom line; if there's no value added, it's waste.

CONCLUSION

To think about increasing profitability simply by raising revenues or cutting costs really misses the opportunity to consider profit as a barometer of business vitality. For it is *increasing revenue without disproportionately increasing costs* that truly grows a stellar business. If a company that has solid numbers for the previous three years boldly decides to sell its products across an entire region, hires employees, rents warehouses and builds factories, adds to its transportation fleet, and doubles its advertising budget, that may be sheer genius or sheer lunacy depending on the ratio of new sales to new costs.

Nothing succeeds more in the business world than a simultaneous focus on expanding what, how, and for whom a business operates, while focusing on ways to reduce per-unit production, delivery, or per-sale costs.

▸▸ MAKING IT HAPPEN

- Rigorously determine how the company has generated revenues in the past, how it plans to make sales this year, and how it plans to grow in the future.
- Explore three questions: Can the business profitably expand what it makes? Can the business profitably expand how it sells? Can the business profitably expand whom it serves?
- Realize that expansion of business revenue only makes sense if concomitant costs don't exceed projected revenue.
- Recognize that the three most effective ways to reduce costs are to minimize the amount of labor or management needed, reduce the inventory-to-invoice cycle, and pare wasteful overhead or processing costs.

▸▸ MORE INFO

Book:

Kubinski, Ron. *Building a Breakthrough Business Through Significant New Business Growth and Profitability*. Houston, TX: American Productivity & Quality Center, 2004.

Articles:

Altitude Communications. "The top 5 ways to increase your business' profitability." May 15, 2008. Online at: www.altitudecommunications.com.au/?process=views/article.php&articleId=4002

Business Link. "Increase your profitability." Online at: www.businesslink.gov.uk/bdotg/action/layer?topicId=1079681521

Gillman, Steve. "Increase business profits." Online at: articles.directorym.co.uk/Increase_Business_Profits-a966199.html

  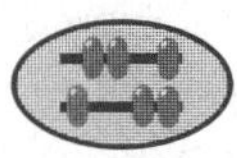 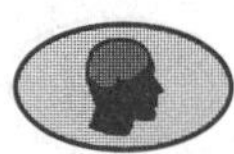  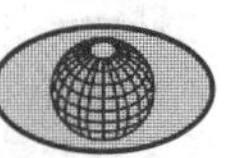   

Innovation and the Path to Growth, Profitability, and Competitiveness by John Milton-Smith

EXECUTIVE SUMMARY

- Disciplined managerial leadership and teamwork are keys to innovation.
- Innovation should be driven by the end customer, not by R&D.
- Aim to create unique market space and make competition irrelevant.
- The 7Es innovation framework identifies seven essential stages in the innovation process.
- The Cochlear case provides an instructive example of a structured innovation process.
- Organic growth based on innovation is the surest path to sustainable growth and profitability.
- Mergers and acquisitions (M&A) are a high-risk substitute for innovation strategy.
- Innovation should be managed as an open process involving a variety of partners.

INTRODUCTION

As management guru Peter Drucker pointed out, entrepreneurial management and innovation were the drivers of the exceptional employment and profit growth in the United States during the 1970s and 1980s. Drawing on insights from this period, Drucker argued that innovation is due more to purposeful, systematic hard work rather than simply "a flash of genius". It is, therefore, important to distinguish innovation from invention.[1] Whereas creative ideas and discovery are at the heart of invention, innovation involves the creative management and application of invention. As companies such as 3M and IBM have demonstrated, innovation should be treated as a standard organizational function responsible for finding new sources of customer value.[2]

There are three major categories of innovation. According to Christensen, two of the categories—sustaining innovation and disruptive innovation—are complementary, but significantly different. Sustaining innovation is incremental, and reflected in continuous improvements to the safety and efficacy of pharmaceutical drugs, whereas disruptive innovation includes major breakthroughs, such as the automobile and digital photography.[3] Some of the most successful disruptive innovations are products, services, processes, and experiences that apply or combine existing elements in different ways to produce radically new customer benefits and experiences. Examples include Apple iPod, YouTube, Star Alliance, and Starbucks.

The third category is "business concept innovation". Because of the intensity of competition and turbulence in the market environment, Hamel argues that "companies must adopt a radical new innovation agenda", and apply systematic innovation "design rules".[4] This view is endorsed by Bill Gates, who, warning of the risks confronting complacent incumbents, has claimed that "Microsoft is always two years away from failure".[5]

Neither the iPod nor YouTube rely on disruptive technology, yet both have created new global markets. Whereas the iPod offers a unique experience through the quality of its design, customer interface, and product extensions, YouTube has invited millions of people worldwide to become amateur broadcasters by creating and sharing original videos. In the case of Star Alliance, a group of otherwise competing airlines collaborates to provide passengers with seamless global routing options, ticketing arrangements, and loyalty benefits. Starbucks, on the other hand, reinvented the traditional Italian coffee shop to create a global coffee culture and experience, based on market development, line extension, and mass customization.[6] Once the focus is on the end-customer, every element in the design and delivery of the value chain becomes a potential opportunity for innovation. As in the examples given above, radical innovation lies in the bundling and branding of multiple value-adding elements, rather than in any single element.[7]

Service and experience innovation—easily the biggest generators of wealth-producing added value—are the areas most neglected by R&D communities and the "innovation industry". Kim and Mauborgne (2005) use Cirque du Soleil as an example of a company which has created "the blue ocean of new market space", and made competition irrelevant. In "achieving both differentiation and low cost by reconstructing elements across industry boundaries", Cirque du Soleil invented a unique, live entertainment experience, involving elements of circus, theater, opera, and ballet. It is different from traditional circuses. There are no animals or star performers, and the target audience is sophisticated adults rather than children. New shows tour the world regularly, partly financed by regional sponsors and a loyal customer base.[8]

THE 7Es INNOVATION FRAMEWORK

Innovation is complex, involves risk, and cannot be reduced to simple templates.[9] However, a systematic and disciplined innovation strategy has a number of common elements. Under the direction of a CEO who is strongly committed to organic growth and innovation, there should be an "open market for ideas, capital, and talent".[10] Innovation project team leaders should be given responsibility for critical functions and processes, including the following, which, the sake of convenience, could be designated "the 7Es":

- **Explore** by generating and vetting ideas from a wide variety of internal and external sources;

CASE STUDY

Cochlear: The Triumph of Organic Growth Strategy

Cochlear Limited provides an excellent demonstration of the innovation processes listed above. Cochlear is a Sydney-based medical technology business with a long-standing mission to help the hearing-impaired. Despite humble beginnings, Cochlear produces the world's best-selling hearing implant. By early 2009, it had a global market share of 70%, and approximately 2,000 employees in more than 20 countries.

Cochlear was built on the entrepreneurial drive and single-minded passion of Professor Graeme Clark. Even as a young ear, nose, and throat specialist in Melbourne in the 1960s, his father's deafness drove him to explore new ways of overcoming hearing impairment. In order to win over skeptics, Clark was extremely careful to evaluate his experiments with the utmost rigor. In fact, the early tests were unsuccessful. Finally, he concluded that an implant with single-channel stimulation of the inner-ear auditory nerves would not lead to speech understanding in deaf people.

"Management's total loyalty to the maximization of profit is the principal obstacle to achieving higher standards of ethical practice." Kenneth R. Andrews

  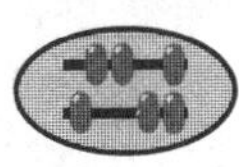   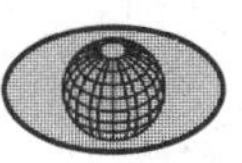   

- **Evaluate** by assessing and prioritizing options, making a selection and giving feedback;
- **Extend** by involving and co-opting partners and opinion leaders, and progressively demonstrating "small wins";
- **Experiment** by designing, testing, demonstrating, and reviewing a prototype or pilot study;
- **Engage** by winning the management's support for a proposed business model;
- **Evangelize** by publicizing, showcasing, celebrating, and involving all stakeholders;
- **Execute** by implementing the business model, including launch and marketing strategies.

THE CRITICAL LINK BETWEEN INNOVATION, GROWTH, AND COMPETITIVENESS

The synergistic relationship across innovation, growth, and competitiveness demonstrated in the Cochlear case is well documented. For example, there is a significant body of research confirming that a record of ambitious organic growth is the main determinant of a company's stock-market value. Investors regard strong organic growth as a reliable indicator of a sound business model. Furthermore, commitment to the discipline of organic growth is evidence that managers think strategically about the future, believe that innovation is the key to competitive advantage, and stay focused on creating value for customers.[14]

The sustained growth and market capitalization performance of companies such as GE, Google, Samsung, Dell, and Procter & Gamble (P&G) further underline the importance of innovation-driven organic growth. For example, between 2004 and 2006, soon after adopting a radical "connect and develop" open innovation model, more than 100 of P&G's new products had elements which originated outside the company.[15] More recently, in 2008, A. G. Lafley, P&G's CEO confirmed the transformation, stating that, "P&G has delivered, on average, 6% organic sales growth since the beginning of the decade, virtually all of it driven by innovation".[16]

In a comprehensive study of corporate growth conducted over a ten-year period, Hess found that the companies most committed to organic growth outperformed the S&P 500 by a factor of 10. He concluded that, in the long term, "the companies that succeeded to a greater degree than their peers were found to follow an organic growth strategy". By contrast, attempts to generate growth through M&A failed to

The bionic ear concept emerged gradually, and involved the integration of research from numerous disciplines. Clark consolidated and extended his research while undertaking a doctorate, and after becoming chair of a new department at the University of Melbourne. During this time, Clark partnered with a leading expert in sound quality and a small local company experimenting with heart pacemakers. Finally, he confirmed that multi-channel stimulation was a feasible option, and began to pursue it with vigor.

Clark's major experimental phase began in the 1970s. The lengthy delay was due largely to the indifference of the medical community, and the lack of financial support. Fundraising continued to be a major obstacle, and the leading Australian research bodies repeatedly rejected Clark's applications for research grants. Forced to operate outside the normal research channels, and adopt a direct crusading approach, Clark became a full-time evangelist, undertaking a hectic round of fundraising lunches and meetings.

After more than seven years of struggle, Clark's first major breakthrough came in 1974, when he persuaded the proprietor of a new television channel to conduct a telethon to finance the first prototype. When the telethon money ran out, Clark persuaded Prime Minister Malcolm Fraser to help. However, it was not until 1982 that Cochlear Limited finally floated on the stock exchange, and the systematic execution of Clark's vision began.

Because of the strict regulation of medical technology, and notwithstanding the enormous credibility which Cochlear has earned, there is no respite for top management. They will always need to be evangelists. In recent years, 13 new territory outreach specialists have been added to the US field force to help educate hearing-aid professionals, a training and education center has been established in Beijing, and a Cochlear Awareness Network has been created so that volunteers can be enlisted to provide information to potential implant recipients.

Most of Cochlear's growth took place during 2003–2008.This period was marked by consistent annual growth in sales, revenue, and net profit, while gross margin increased to 72%.Whereas in April 2002, there were 35,000 cochlear implant users worldwide, by 2008 this figure had more than tripled to more than 120,000. Since 2003, the company has been reinvesting 12–13% of revenue into continuing R&D activities, and set up partnerships with more than 80 universities worldwide.[11] According to Cochlear's half-yearly results, reported on February 11, 2009, the growth trajectory has been maintained, despite the global financial crisis, with a further net profit increase of 22%.[12]

Even as a relatively small SME, Cochlear continued to pursue a global strategy based on organic growth and strong branding. Despite the general preference for growth by M&A, Cochlear remains committed to the philosophy that you get bigger by being better. There is still a huge unserved market. According to its latest annual report, Cochlear estimates that there are about 278 million people with moderate to profound hearing loss in both ears, and this figure will rise as the population ages and life expectancy increases. Apart from upgrades and repairs, Cochlear is also developing specialized products for different types and degrees of hearing loss.[13]

▸▸ MAKING IT HAPPEN

The practical action steps for implementing an innovation-based organic growth strategy are as follows:

- Top management focuses on mission-driven organic growth, treats M&A with great caution, and aims to create strongly branded, unique market space.
- The CEO becomes a highly visible innovation leader and champion, stimulates the discussion of new ideas, and encourages information sharing and learning.
- Innovation is at the center of the mission statement, strategic goals, job descriptions, performance targets, etc.
- The CEO provides innovation leadership, and, with a top-level team, approves and supports major innovation projects.
- Cross-boundary innovation project teams operate throughout the organization.
- All innovation projects demonstrate how they will contribute added value in providing a unique experience to the end-customer.
- The initial criterion for an innovation project is "possibility", not "probability" but projects that fail an initial feasibility study are killed off quickly.
- The operating protocols for all innovation project teams specify criteria for an open process, including suppliers, customers, and other partners.

     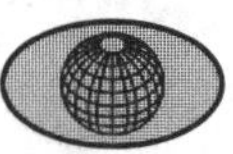   

achieve their objective, indicating that M&A is opportunism rather than strategy and frequently involves a "quick fix" approach to expansion and market share.[17]

STRATEGIC PARTNERSHIPS FACILITATE INNOVATION AND GROWTH

As opposed to M&A, strategic alliances and partnerships are increasingly successful organic growth options, as the Cochlear case demonstrates. Open innovation, working closely with customers, suppliers, service providers, and other firms, is generally the most cost-effective method for identifying value-creating opportunities, sharing knowledge, expanding into new markets, and lifting competitiveness.

According to Lendrum (2003), the benefits of partnerships relate not only to increased growth and profits for shareholders and other stakeholders, but also include improvements in leadership effectiveness, workplace relations, and innovation capability. Based upon his extensive research, Lendrum concludes that innovation "is a key factor in the evolution and revolution of partnering/alliance relationships, and the driving force behind the process".[18]

The link between partnerships and innovation is critical. Indeed, "the more radical the innovation, the more deeply and broadly must other players, especially customers, be involved".[19] Market leaders such as Philips, IBM, and Toyota have hundreds of inter-firm partnerships, which have played a major role in their growth and competitiveness. Groupings such as science parks and clusters (geographic concentrations of interconnected companies) offer the same potential partnership benefits to SMEs, which tend to be nimbler and more innovative than their larger counterparts. Successful replications of the so-called "Silicon Valley Effect" can now be found in most parts of the world, including Tromso in Norway, Cambridge in England, the Emilia-Romagna region of Italy, Malaysia's Cyberjaya, and Doha's Education City.

▸▸ MORE INFO

Books:

Hess, E. *The Road to Organic Growth: How Great Companies Consistently Grow Market Share from Within*. New York: McGraw-Hill, 2007.

Kim, C., and R. Mauborgne. *Blue Ocean Strategy. How to Create Uncontested Market Space and Make the Competition Irrelevant*. Boston, MA: Harvard Business School Press, 2005.

Lendrum, T. *The Strategic Partnering Handbook*. New York: McGraw-Hill, 2003.

Article:

The McKinsey Quarterly. "How companies approach innovation: A McKinsey global survey." October 2007. Online at: www.mckinseyquarterly.com/How_companies_approach_innovation_A_McKinsey_Global_Survey_2069

Websites:

Asian Productivity Organization: www.apo-tokyo.org

Cambridge MIT Institute: www.cambridge-mit.org

The Conference Board: www.conference-board.org

Hay Group: Your Challenges: www.haygroup.com/ww/challenges

Knowledge@Wharton Innovation and Entrepreneurship: knowledge.wharton.upenn.edu/category.cfm?cid=12

PricewaterhouseCoopers Center for Technology and Innovation: www.pwc.com/extweb/service.nsf/docid/D9A4C1B3A70E44F885256F8800743B91

See Also:

Michael Porter (p. 1182)

Reengineering the Corporation: A Manifesto for Business Revolution (p. 1314)

NOTES

1 Drucker, P. F. *Innovation and Entrepreneurship*. New York: Harper Business, 1993, pp. 30–36, 138, 150.

2 O'Connor, G. C., R. Leifer, A. C. Paulson, and L. L. Peters. *Grabbing Lightning: Building a Capability for Breakthrough Innovation*. Hoboken, NJ: Wiley, 2008, pp. 169–170, 202–203, 259.

3 Christensen, C. M. *The Innovator's Dilemma*. New York: Harper Business, 2000, pp. xv, 10–19.

4 Hamel, G. *Leading the Revolution*. Boston, MA: Harvard Business School Press, 2002, pp. 59–118, 251–282.

5 Hamel, G. "The challenge today: Changing the rules of the game." In Leibold, M., G. J. B. Probst, and M. Gibbert (eds). *Strategic Management in the Knowledge Economy*. New York: Wiley-VCH, 2005, p. 119.

6 Winter, S. G. "Appropriating the gains from innovation." In Day, G. S., and P. J. H. Shoemaker (eds). *Wharton on Managing Emerging Technologies*. New York: Wiley, 2000, pp. 245, 256.

7 *Ibid*.

8 Kim, W.C., and R. Mauborgne. (2005), p. 18.

9 Lord, M. D., D. deBethizy, and J. Wager. *Innovation that Fits*. Upper Saddle River, NJ: Prentice Hall, 2005, pp. 18, 134, 230.

10 Hamel. 2002, *op. cit*, 299–302.

11 Cochlear Limited, *Annual Report 2008,* Sydney: 8–20.

12 Ooi, T. "Dollar's decline boosts Cochlear hopes." *The Australian Business* (February 11, 2009): 1.

13 Cochlear Limited. *op. cit*. See also World Health Organization. "Deafness and Hearing Impairment." *Fact Sheet No. 300*. New York: March, 2006: 1.

14 Day, G. S. 2006. "Closing the growth gap: Balancing 'big I' and 'small I' innovation." *Knowledge@Wharton,*February 1, 2006: 1. Online at: knowledge.wharton.upenn.edu/papers/1333.pdf

15 Huston, L. and N. Sakkab. "Connect and develop: Inside Procter and Gamble's new model for innovation." *Harvard Business Review* (March 2006): 1–3.

16 Lafley, A. G. "P&G's innovation culture." *Strategy+Business Enews* (August 28, 2008): 2–10.

17 Hess, E. D. (2006), 1–3, 27.

18 Lendrum, T. (2003), pp. 5, 39, 155–156.

19 Moore, J. F. *The Death of Competition. Leadership and Strategy in the Age of Business Ecosystems*. Chichester, UK: Wiley, 1996, p. 61.

"I would constructively rebel by changing the rules but, once agreed, I would observe them." Howard Davies

  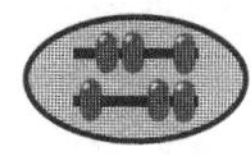   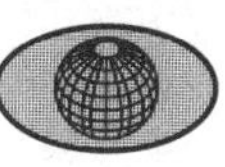   

Viewpoint: Hamish McRae

Economic Ebb and Flow, a World of Challenges and Opportunities

INTRODUCTION

Hamish McRae is the principal economic commentator of *The Independent* and *The Independent on Sunday*.

He is the author of the acclaimed work *The World in 2020: Power, Culture and Prosperity*, first published in 1994 and translated into more than a dozen languages.

His other books include *Capital City—London as a Financial Centre*, co-authored with Frances Cairncross, and *Wake-up Japan*, co-authored with Tadashi Nakamae.

In 2007 he won Communicator of the Year at the 2007 Business Journalist Awards, in 2006 he won Business and Finance Journalist of the Year at the British Press Awards and in 2005 he won the David Watt Prize for outstanding political journalism. Mr McRae is a visiting Professor at the School of Management at Lancaster University and a council member of the Royal Economic Society.

He was deputy editor of *The Banker* and editor of *Euromoney* before becoming financial editor of *The Guardian* in 1975. In 1989 he moved to *The Independent* where he is now associate editor. He was educated at Fettes College, Edinburgh and has an MA in Economics and Political Science from Trinity College, Dublin.

The world economy is shaped by a mix of long-term trends and cyclical influences. During a downturn there can be too much emphasis on the economic cycle, and we tend to lose sight of the longer-term. That is a pity for several reasons. An obvious one is that the best way to prepare for the next upturn is to take advantage of our knowledge and assessment of long-term social and economic trends. Another is that the downturn actually speeds up some of these trends, most notably the shift of economic power away from Europe, and to a lesser extent North America, towards Asia. Still another is that these trends will have "soft" effects, changing our society in profound ways, and understanding these is a key to understanding how to benefit from seismic social changes.

So what are these shifts? I find it most helpful to think in terms of these five key forces for change:

- **Demography**—the developed world will have a higher proportion of older people than any previous human society, but parts of the developing world will remain young. This creates great tensions both between countries and within them. The better the developed world copes with ageing, the more it will be able to defuse such tensions.
- **Resources and the environment**—we are catching a glimpse of the end of the oil-driven world economy and are becoming far more concerned about the environmental consequences of poor energy practice. That will not only change the balance of power in the world, but it will also create huge new opportunities for firms that can develop appropriate new technologies as well as those that can help mediate and manage rising environmental concerns.
- **Globalization**—the world economy is measurably more global than ever before and the key characteristic is the rise of the BRIC countries, the clever acronym invented by Goldman Sachs to describe Brazil, Russia, India and China. Within the past year China has passed Germany to become the worlds' third largest economy. But globalization is changing direction, moving from physical shipment of goods to trade in services, foreign direct investment and international movements of the highly skilled. Globalization naturally creates great opportunities, but the progress will need to be managed carefully if it is not to give rise to greater resistance. There are already signs of concern about the consequences of globalization, including in The United Kingdom the Prime Minister's call for "British jobs for British workers" and in the United States a requirement in the Federal stimulus package that financial institutions that get taxpayers' money should not use these funds to employ foreign workers. The danger is that these measures will lead to more overt protectionist ones, which might curb global trade and investment.
- **Technology**—we are living through one of the periodic bursts of technological advance, particularly in telecommunications. What makes the communications revolution so special is not just its capability, but also its reach. The world has near-zero cost telecommunications and the lead of the West over the rest of the world is diminishing every week.
- **Government and social change**—governments will tax less and regulate more. That seems likely to happen despite the surge in intervention in response to the banking meltdown because government revenues are being cut away by international competition. Just as the corporate world will need help in coping with regulation, so will the governments in framing it. Business is increasingly mobile, able to move not just its production facilities, but also its tax domicile; therefore light but effective regulation will become a key competitive issue.

There are obviously different levels of certainty attached to these shifts. We know a great deal about demography, for changes happen only slowly. We also know something about energy trends, but are less sure about the consequences for the global climate—and we know nothing at all about oil prices, at least in the short term.

As far as the shift of power to the BRIC countries is concerned, while the Goldman Sachs' project gives a set of predictions as to the size of the various world economies in the years ahead, there is an obvious uncertainty as to whether the present headlong advance of these countries will be maintained. For example, the model suggests that China will pass the US in the late 2020s to become the world's largest economy. But, of course, that might happen a few years earlier in the middle 2020s, or maybe a bit later. However, for China *not* to become the largest economy by say 2050 would require some sort of radical shift in its performance or some unknowable global economic or environmental catastrophe.

With technology too, it is easy to be wrong about the detail, but harder to be wrong about the general direction. The kit of the communications revolution—the computers, the internet routers, the fiber optic cables and so on—is already here. We can see the hardware now. However, it is harder for us to envisage the software and the social consequences of that. The way Google has become a transitive verb, as in "I Googled you," shows how global behavior has shifted as a result of one piece of clever maths.

Changes in government and society are the hardest to predict. Who could have forecast at the beginning of 2006 that within two years the UK government would have nationalized or part-nationalized much of the British banking system? But I think we can see that governments will be under financial pressure, from stagnant tax revenues, and will also face increasing demands from the financial and physical needs of an ageing population. That is going to be very difficult and they will need help from the business community to try to satisfy those demands.

This changing world will lead to implications for the business community. There seem to be at least half a dozen long-term issues that businesses will need to confront. The key ones are:

- The likelihood that at least the developed world will experience slower growth than it has been used to. This is partly a natural consequence of falling workforces, a phenomenon already evident in Japan and Germany. But it is also a function of the difficulty in increasing productivity in the service industries. This has proved much harder to achieve than it has been in manufacturing and, as the balance of output shifts from goods to services, the problem will become harder still.
- Continued and persistent concern about environmental practices. Customers will want companies to be "green" or at least as green as is practicable. Moreover, people will want to work for employers with a reasonable reputation, and those with a bad one will find it hard to recruit good people.
- The growing influence from the fast-growing economies in Asia on the ideas of the West. We are used to a world where the liberal democracies have had a monopoly of ideas as to how the world economy should be ordered. We have, so to speak, set the rules in a host of areas including corporate governance, accounting practices, work-practice standards and so on. That dominance will not disappear suddenly, but it will gradually diminish as the preferences of India, China and other emerging economies become relatively more important.

> "There are obviously different levels of certainty attached to these shifts. We know a great deal about demography, for changes happen only slowly. We also know something about energy trends, but are less sure about the consequences for the global climate—and we know nothing at all about oil prices, at least in the short term."

- The ability of technology to level the global playing field and to enable centers of excellence to distribute their output worldwide. Thus a computer expert in Bangalore is able to compete with other people with similar skills anywhere in the world on a level basis. In that sense the world has become flatter. But Bangalore can achieve global reach, creating an industry that competes effectively against similar (but higher cost) centers in the US and Europe. This means that centers of excellence can compete much more effectively than before so the world is not flat at all.
- Companies will have to interact more closely with government. Regulation may or may not become more onerous, but it will certainly become more complicated. So companies will have to become better at making their case to the electorate, reaching over the heads of the politicians. Governments are local in the sense that they have jurisdiction over a geographic area; companies are or can become global, so they will have to project their influence in many different jurisdictions.
- Then there is trust. Each of the points above mirrors the long-term trends outlined earlier. But the downturn has raised another matter, the extent to which the business community is trusted. Financial services naturally have seen their reputation devastated, and other businesses will be damaged too. The prizes will go to the corporations that emerge from the downturn with a solid support from their customers for doing what they say they will do—not always easy, but vital in the longer run.

There is no magic wand that can guide companies, or governments, or people to select the most important global trends and then get on the right side of them. But there is hope. There are some things we can say about the future with reasonable confidence and the more we can bolt down what we know, the easier it becomes to create a nimble strategy for coping with the things we cannot know. That goes for cyclical trends too. We know there is an economic cycle—it is just extraordinarily difficult to remember in the middle of a serious downturn that there will be a recovery. . .or that there will be a downturn when tails are up.

▸▸ MORE INFO

See Also:

- Joseph Stiglitz (p. 1198)
- Brazil (pp. 1364–1365)
- China (pp. 1374–1375)
- India (pp. 1404–1406)
- Information Technology (pp. 1522–1523)
- Russian Federation (pp. 1461–1463)

"A solid business must build on justice, fairness, and transparency." Gaston Vizcarra

  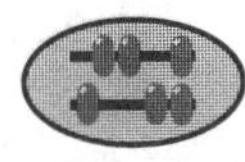 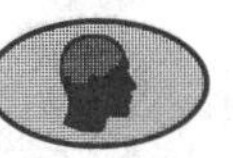  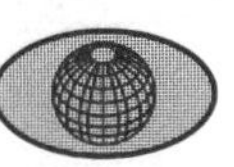   

Maximizing a New Strategic Alliance by Peter Killing

EXECUTIVE SUMMARY

- Over 60,000 strategic alliances have been formed in the past decade. About half were joint ventures. Only 40% meet or exceed their partners' expectations.
- To be successful with strategic alliances you must be clear about your objectives, get the alliance design right, and manage the alliance effectively after it is formed.
- There is an important difference between shallow and deep alliances, and you should know which type you need and why.
- Alliance success depends in large part on skilled managers who are good with people, have a high tolerance for ambiguity and conflict, and are patient yet persistent.
- The clearest sign of alliance success is growing trust between the partners.

INTRODUCTION

More than 60,000 strategic alliances were formed in the 1990s. About half of these were joint ventures. The other 50% were nonequity arrangements such as technology licensing agreements, joint marketing arrangements, and joint research or development projects. Most of these alliances were international, so it's no surprise to learn that the world's largest multinationals are heavy alliance users: IBM (254 alliances), General Motors (138), Mitsubishi (233), Toshiba (147), Philips (207), and Siemens (200) are just some examples.

Clearly the ability to create and manage strategic alliances is an important skill for most management teams. If you cannot make effective use of alliances in today's world, you will be at a serious competitive disadvantage.

GETTING IT RIGHT

A 1999 study by Andersen Consulting indicates that only 40% of alliances achieve or exceed the initial expectations of their partners, which suggests there's a lot of room for improvement. One of the reasons for the relatively low success rate is that there are many different aspects of the design and management of alliances that you need to get right, from clearly understanding your objectives, to managing the alliance after it is formed. They can be grouped into three sequential steps:

- **Clarify objectives.** What do we need and for how long? Is an alliance the best way to get what we need?
- **Design the alliance.** What type of alliance should we create? What should our role be?
- **Manage after the deal is done.** How do we effectively manage the alliance? Can we build trust?

Clarify Objectives and the Need for the Alliance

The first challenge is to be clear about what your company needs to fulfil its strategy, which may be different from what others in your industry need. The second challenge is to decide whether an alliance is the best way to get what you need. Three common reasons for forming alliances are:

- **To enter new markets.** One of the classic purposes of joint ventures is to enter foreign markets. Typically the foreign company finds the local market attractive but does not feel confident enough to enter without local knowledge, and so takes a local partner. In some countries the government insists on such a relationship. In China, for example, joint ventures between foreigners and local companies are prevalent. Often, as foreign companies gain confidence in their ability to operate locally, they end the joint venture by buying out their local partner and creating a wholly-owned subsidiary. In this case the alliance is a step on the road to something else.
- **To create new technology and set industry standards.** In technology-intensive industries like computing and telecommunications, companies often use alliances to attempt to create a new technology that will become the industry standard. An example is Symbian, a joint venture formed in 1998 by Psion, Ericsson, Nokia, and Motorola. Symbian's objective is to create an operating system for wireless devices to exchange information efficiently. Microsoft has also shown an interest in this area and has considered building its own alliance around its CE operating system with partners including NTT DoCoMo and British Telecom. The competition has shifted from company versus company to alliance versus alliance.
- **To shape consolidation.** In consolidating industries such as airlines, telecoms, and the automotive industry, alliances are often formed between companies that fear they are too small to continue independently (and that do not want to be taken over) and those that intend to play a dominant role in the consolidation. The alliance between Fiat and GM was formed for precisely this reason. This deal involves cross-ownership holdings between the two companies, two 50–50 joint ventures, and a variety of smaller cooperative arrangements. Fiat also had an option to sell itself to GM (before agreeing a "divorce" worth $2 billion in 2005). The immediate motives behind such alliances are to gain economies of scale and global reach, to eliminate excess capacity, and to keep the smaller company out of the hands of predators.

Why Use an Alliance?

Alliances are often the least-preferred choice of the companies that enter them. Many companies would rather enter a new market themselves, or perhaps make an acquisition. GM, for example, would probably have preferred to buy Fiat, but the company was not for sale. Alliances are often seen as difficult to manage, ambiguous in terms of control and decision-making (and as a result slow moving), and requiring an extraordinary amount of management time and attention. The usual motives, positive and negative, for proceeding with an alliance are:

Positive

- to harness the partner's energy and knowledge;
- to set an industry standard by involving partners;
- to learn something;
- to gain economies of scale or global reach;
- to reduce risk;
- to gain speed.

Negative

- government insists on alliance;
- acquisitions are too expensive or not available;
- it's the only financially affordable alternative;
- the company fears being acquired;
- an alliance will prevent a competitor's acquisition of, or alliance with, the partner;
- closing the business is too expensive;

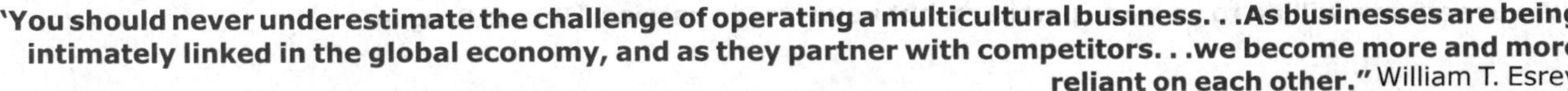

  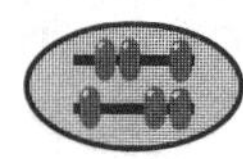   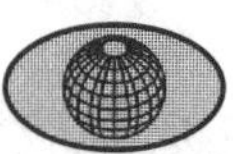   

an alliance provides a more graceful exit.

You should be clear on your own motives as well as your partner's. There are no data on this issue, but alliances formed for positive motives may have a higher success rate.

Design the Alliance

There are many types of alliance. The simplest are straightforward license agreements and shared marketing deals; the most complex are multipart arrangements such as cross-ownership positions, joint ventures, and cooperative projects between partners. Faced with an abundance of choice, managers entering an alliance need to make a key decision: whether they want a shallow alliance or a deep alliance.

Shallow Alliances—Traveling Light

A shallow alliance might be thought of as a flirtation—a low-commitment alliance that doesn't have a lot of resources devoted to it and that can be broken on short notice. As an example, think of current airline alliances such as the Star and One World alliances, which seem to feature new partners every month. Or consider Cisco and its internet-related businesses. Cisco often cannot judge if a young company's fledgling technology will prove to be important a year later. The shallow alliance solution is to buy 10% of the company's stock in a friendly transaction and get a seat on the board and an option to buy the remainder of the equity. The assigned board member can then assess the company's management, its market prospects, and its technology. If it looks good, they buy the rest of the company. If not, they leave. Shallow alliances thus create options for companies in fast-changing industries in which the way ahead is not clear. The alliances are not usually intended to be permanent.

Deep Alliances—Commitment

At the other end of the spectrum are deep alliances involving high levels of financial and managerial commitment by the partners. Deep alliances feature many links between the partners, usually including one or more seats on the board of directors, cross-ownership positions, at least two or three joint ventures, and many less formal but important cooperative projects. Deep alliances are generally slower-moving than shallow alliances, more difficult to manage, and more difficult to end. The benefits of success can be high, but so can the costs of failure. Deep alliances are not for the timid.

Manage After the Deal Is Done

Once you've formed an alliance, you'll sooner or later discover that you have brought together partners with different ways of doing things and somewhat different objectives, priorities, and performance standards. These differences make the management of alliances a difficult task. The single most important thing you can do to maximize the probability of success is to assign some of your very best people to work on it. "Best" means managers with excellent people skills, cross-cultural sensitivity, and a tolerance for ambiguity and frustration. Alliance managers need to be patient, yet persistent.

Six months into the life of your alliance you should look closely at the relationship between the partners. Is trust starting to develop? If not, why not? Where are the trouble spots? Many texts advise that when choosing a partner you should choose someone you trust. This is difficult to do unless you have worked together before. The real question is whether or not you can develop trust over time. The best predictor of the future performance of any alliance is the current level of trust between the partners.

Finally, don't assume that the alliance is done when the deal is signed. This is just the beginning. Be flexible and open to change and learning. There will be plenty of opportunity for both.

▸▸ MAKING IT HAPPEN

Strategic alliances are increasingly popular, even necessary; however they are often a high-risk strategy. It is worth viewing the alliance in three distinct phases:

- **Before the deal is struck:** The vital period when goals are considered, resources prepared, and partners considered. Internal agreement on the goals, strategy, and resources to be used is important, as is choosing the right partner and evaluating them thoroughly through due diligence.
- **Negotiating the deal:** The terms of the agreement and, significantly, the expectations of each partner and the *spirit* of the agreement, will be decisive in determining the effectiveness of the alliance.
- **Post-agreement management:** Successful agreements are those that are consistently and attentively resourced, managed, and valued. If they are not, they are unlikely to survive normal commercial pressures.

Some key questions to consider include:

- Have you formally assessed the aims and benefits of the strategic alliance?
- How does the alliance fit with your overall commercial strategy?
- Who needs to be informed of the alliance—and when?
- Have you sought the advice of professional advisers?
- Have you taken time to understand the target and the commercial implications?
- To what extent should the alliance be integrated into your existing business? Who will lead this?
- Do you have a fully costed and resourced plan for managing the alliance? What are the targets and success criteria for the alliance?

▸▸ MORE INFO

Books:

Cauley de la Sierra, M. *Managing Global Alliances: Key Steps for Successful Collaboration*. Reading, MA: Addison-Wesley, 1995.

Doz, Yves L., and Gary Hamel. *Alliance Advantage: The Art of Creating Value through Partnering*. Cambridge, MA: Harvard Business School Press, 1998.

Lewis, Jordan D. *Trusted Partners: How Companies Build Mutual Trust and Win Together*. New York: Free Press, 2000.

Website:

Alliance Strategy offers resources and readings on alliance strategy and management. It is maintained by Ben Gomes-Casseres, author of *The Alliance Revolution*: www.alliancestrategy.com

"We are always willing to be trade partners, but never trade patsies." Ronald Reagan

  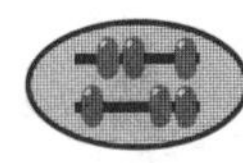 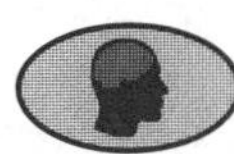  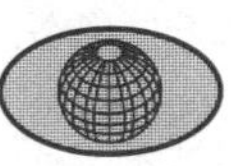   

Multidimensional Performance Measurement Using the Balanced Scorecard by Priscilla Wisner

EXECUTIVE SUMMARY

- An organization's financial performance results from decisions made by its managers and employees.
- Managers and employees need operational performance metrics that are aligned with the daily decisions being made, rather than a high-level set of financial metrics that are reported on a monthly or a quarterly basis.
- The Balanced Scorecard (BSC) represents a set of financial, customer, operational, and organizational metrics that capture multidimensional aspects of performance.
- Using a BSC, top management can signal strategic objectives to managers and employees. Top management can then gather data that shows whether or not performance at the individual and the strategic business unit levels is aligned with the strategic objectives of the firm.

INTRODUCTION

For generations, many businesses have measured organizational success based on a narrow set of financial performance measures, such as operating and net profit, return on investment, and earnings per share of stock. Financial performance measures are valuable in that they capture the economic consequences of business decisions; however, they tend to be "lagging" indicators of performance that report the financial effects of operational business decisions weeks or months after the decisions have been implemented.

Organizational managers and employees typically manage their work in terms of physical flows and other nonfinancial resources. For example, sales managers focus on market size, sales volume, share of wallet, customer satisfaction, and similar measures. Production managers concentrate on production capacity, throughput time, quality, and productivity metrics. Human resource managers are responsible for hiring appropriately skilled personnel, maintaining a safe and legal workplace, and organizational development outcomes. Managers and employees throughout the organization make decisions and use resources that eventually impact the financial outcomes of the firm; to do so effectively, they need performance feedback that links the outcomes of their decisions to the strategic and financial goals of the firm. This feedback is most useful when it is a "leading" performance indicator, or one that is closely related to the work being performed. The Balanced Scorecard (BSC) was developed as a management tool to help managers better understand and link customer, operational, and organizational decisions to financial outcomes, and to the strategy of the organization.

BSC BASICS

While General Electric has been credited with developing one of the first balanced scorecard performance models,[1] the BSC concept was first described by Dr Robert Kaplan and David Norton in a series of *Harvard Business Review* articles in the early 1990s, and was subsequently expanded upon in books and articles by these and other professionals. The BSC as a management tool has gained widespread acceptance in the corporate world. In a survey of more than 700 companies operating in five continents, Bain and Company reported that 62% of the respondents used the BSC.[2]

BSC perspectives typically include financial, customer, operational (internal business processes), and organizational (learning and growth) aspects. By identifying key performance measures within each of these perspectives, top management signals strategic objectives and organizational goals to managers and employees. By receiving feedback on achieved outcomes for each of these measures, management is able to evaluate how closely performance is meeting strategic objectives.

As shown in Figure 1, the four traditional BSC perspectives are interlinked, and are linked to the overall vision and strategy of the organization. Each perspective reflects a focus area for the implementation of strategy and, therefore, for performance measurement:[3]

- Financial perspective—focuses on financial aspects of performance, and links strategic objectives with financial impacts. Balance sheet, income statement, and cash flow performance measures are often included in this dimension. Some firms include alternative measures of financial performance, such as economic value added, recycling income, and sales growth by channel.
- Customer perspective—contains measures that reflect how the firm is creating customer value. Customer satisfaction measures are typical, but leading firms will include measures such as share of mind and share of wallet, consumption per capita, customer retention, and product accessibility measures.

Figure 1. Linking of BSC perspectives

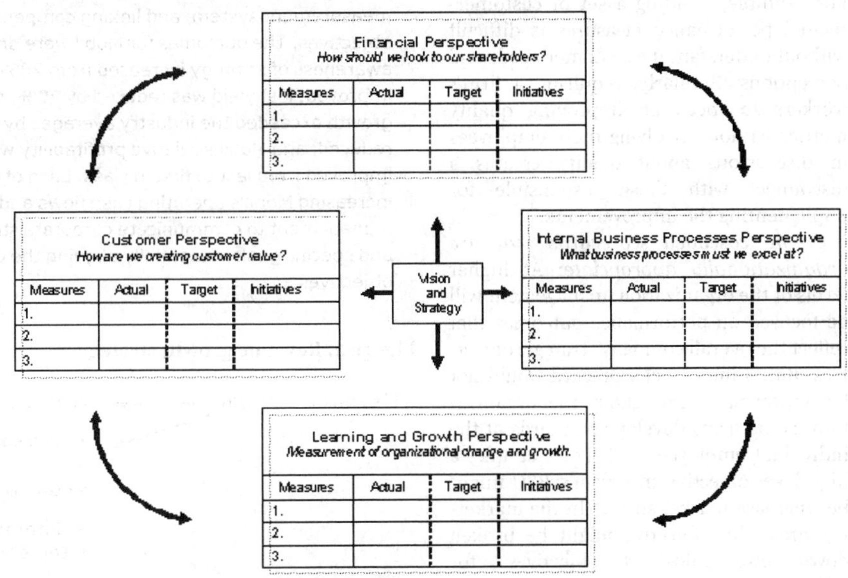

"**Markets reduce everything, including human beings and nature, to commodities.**" George Soros

  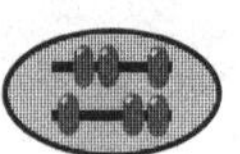   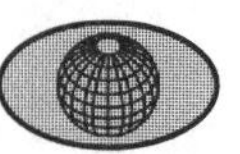   

- Internal business processes perspective—focuses on how a company is performing through an operational lens. Internal business processes encompasses many facets of operations, including engineering design, purchasing, manufacturing, distribution, and environmental and social performance. In a customer service organization, measures might include response time, process quality, employee productivity, and bridge to sales ratios.
- Learning and growth perspective—assesses how well the organization is preparing itself and its employees for the future. This perspective often includes measures of organizational practices, employee development and satisfaction, and systems development and deployment. Aspects commonly measured in this perspective include employee turnover, diversity, promotions from within, training hours or expense by employee, innovation measures, and surveys of corporate climate.

IMPLEMENTING A BSC

The BSC is not a "one size fits all" management tool. Each BSC is unique to the strategy, objectives, and culture of the individual organization. However, the following guidelines are important to any successful BSC implementation.

Stakeholder participation in BSC development: Every top management team employing a BSC must carefully translate the organization's strategy into meaningful and actionable performance measures. This process requires the participation and input of the organizational stakeholders who are either impacted by the strategy or responsible for implementing the strategy. For example, building a set of customer-related performance measures is difficult without understanding customer needs and perceptions. Similarly, requiring a firm's workers to focus on improving quality metrics without involving these employees in discussions about quality creates a disconnect with those responsible for implementing the improvements.

Create cascaded scorecards that are organizationally appropriate: At higher levels of the organization, management will be focused on performance outcomes that reflect the overall company strategic objectives. But, a high-level scorecard would not be appropriate throughout the organization. Some firms develop scorecards at the individual employee level. For example, a high-level objective in a firm's BSC might be "increase market share." In the marketing area, this objective might be broken down into mid-level objectives, for example, "increase market share in Europe," "increase market share in Asia," or "increase market share of customers aged 18–25 years old." At the individual level, this objective could be further defined in a way that reflects the responsibilities of that marketer, such as "increase market share in France" or "increase market share in China." Alternatively, the objective might be related to a specific product or service. The goal of cascading is 1) to translate the strategic objective into specific objectives for the hundreds and thousands of employees throughout the organization that carry out the day-to-day work; and 2) to link the work of each employee and strategic business unit to the overall strategic goals of the organization by defining measures appropriate to the employee and business unit.

Define linkages between measures: Value creation in any organization is accomplished by understanding and creating synergies between the various aspects of organizational performance. Increasing sales without having the corresponding production or service capabilities will likely lead to loss of value rather than a

CASE STUDY

Mobil Corporation

In the early 1990s, Mobil Corporation's North America Marketing and Refining group (Mobil) implemented a strategy that resulted in an increased return on capital from 6% to 16%, and an improved operating cash flow of over $1 billion per year.[4] This dramatic improvement in financial results was achieved in just three years, and was aided by a BSC implementation to help focus and align the organization.

In 1994, Mobil began a BSC project as a means to help communicate and implement a strategic organizational change. Mobil's new strategy was twofold: 1) increase volume and revenues of premium products; and 2) reduce costs and improve value chain productivity. Mobil began by defining its high-level financial objectives—return on capital employed and net margin—and then disaggregated these objectives into specific objectives related to its revenue growth and productivity strategies. An example of Mobil's objectives in relation to its revenue growth strategy is shown in Figure 2.

After developing the financial perspective of the BSC, Mobil's managers developed the customer, internal, and learning and growth perspectives. The customer perspective focused on customer satisfaction and dealer relationships, using specific performance measures to capture achievement on each objective. The largest set of measures were the internal business processes measures, which included new product volume and profitability, dealer quality, refinery performance, inventory management, order quality, and safety measures. In the learning and growth perspective, the firm focused on measures such as an employee climate survey, core competency achievements, and the availability of strategic information.

Each perspective contained a small set of focused and interlinked measures that were keys to achieving corporate strategy. The development of the BSC was accompanied by a realignment of organizational structures, the use and communication of the new measurement system, and linking compensation with meeting the explicit goals and objectives. The outcomes for Mobil were dramatic—surveys showed that employee awareness of strategy increased from 20% to 80%, safety and environmental statistics improved, lost yield was reduced by 70%, new products were being introduced, volume growth exceeded the industry averages by over 2% annually, cash expenses were reduced, and Mobil's relative profitability within the North American oil industry improved from last to first in class. Each of these improvements had an impact on increasing Mobil's operating cash flows and return on capital employed. The BSC helped management to communicate corporate strategy through a set of strategic objectives and specific goals, essentially aligning the organization toward a common set of objectives.

Figure 2. Revenue growth strategy

Revenue Growth → Nongasoline revenue
- Increase nongasoline revenues and margins

Premium brands revenue
- Improve volume of premium (versus industry)
- Increase percentage of premium mix

"I think that the best companies are companies that have a real purpose." Marjorie Scardino

long-term increase in value. Increasing production output at the cost of reducing product safety and reliability will negatively affect quality, costs, and reputation. An effective BSC explicitly shows the cause and effect linkages between key performance indicators. A leading insurance company was concerned about its market stock price. By evaluating company data, company managers determined that the amount of time it took a claims adjuster to contact the customer following an accident could influence market stock price. How was this so? The study showed that the length of contact time influenced customer satisfaction, which influenced policy renewal rates, which led to revenues from premiums, which ultimately influenced operating income and stock price.

Choose a small set of focused measures: Each BSC should contain a small set of performance measures, generally with not more than 15–20 recommendations for any single BSC. Developing a limited set of measures is challenging, but forces managers to focus on the most important aspects of organizational performance. Having too many measures tends to create "noise" in the process, both for the managers and for the employees who are working toward the stated goals, leading to uncertainty about which measures are key drivers of success.

Create balance in the scorecard: To be "balanced" does not mean to be equal in all dimensions. A balanced scorecard is one that contains:

- multiple perspectives of performance;
- leading and lagging measures;
- internally focused and externally focused measures;
- short-term and long-term measures;
- quantitative and qualitative measures.

Link the BSC to employee compensation: An effective BSC sends a message to employees that "strategy is everyone's job." If this is the case, then firms need to reward employees for carrying out the strategic intent of the organization. If the objectives and measures within the BSC are aligned in such a way that value is created by carrying out these actions, then employees should be rewarded for increasing the firm's value proposition. Organizational development research has shown that linking reward systems to explicit and controllable expectations creates strong linkages between employee behaviors and the achievement of organizational goals.

CONCLUSION

The BSC is a powerful concept that enables organizational change. The BSC is not just a performance measurement tool, but a multidimensional system that requires management to define strategy in operational terms, and to understand and communicate the cause and effect relationships between the work performed at all levels of the organization and the high-level strategic goals. An effective BSC communicates strategy throughout the organization, thereby signaling to the employees what achievements are needed to implement strategy. A BSC also serves to communicate results back to management, using measures that link into specific strategic objectives. By having such a detailed map of strategic intent and accomplishments, both managers and employees can become more effective in their work.

▸▸ MAKING IT HAPPEN

- Top management involvement is key—The BSC is a strategic management system that is used to change organizational culture, making strategy everyone's job. This change cannot happen without the involvement of top management.
- Translate strategy into operational terms—Strategic objectives must be linked to specific operational perspectives, objectives and indicators. In effect, the BSC "tells the story of the work."
- Link measures within and between the perspectives—All measures should lead to increasing value for the organization. Management should be able to articulate the cause and effect relationships between the measures, and the paths by which the measures link to each other and to organizational value.
- Cascade the BSC throughout the organization—BSCs can be created for each strategic business unit, for departments within each business unit, and, ultimately, for each employee. These cascaded BSCs help to define the performance objectives into meaningful metrics that link the work being performed at all levels of the organization to the strategic goals of the firm.
- Link the BSC to compensation—By rewarding employees for specific performance outcomes that are linked to strategic objectives, alignment is created between the work being done and the broader strategic goals of the firm. There is a cause and effect relationship between "what gets measured, gets managed" and "what gets rewarded, gets attention." By rewarding the specifically defined actions that create value, management is assuring that employees are focused on doing the right things.

▸▸ MORE INFO

Books:

Epstein, Marc J., and Bill Birchard. *Counting What Counts: Turning Corporate Accountability to Competitive Advantage.* Reading, MA: Perseus Books, 1999.

Kaplan, Robert, and David P. Norton. *The Balanced Scorecard: Translating Strategy into Action*. Boston, MA: Harvard Business School Press, 1996.

Kaplan, Robert, and David P. Norton. *The Strategy-Focused Organization: How Balanced Scorecard Companies Thrive in the New Business Environment*. Boston, MA: Harvard Business School Press, 2001

Websites:

Balanced Scorecard Institute: balancedscorecard.org

Balanced Scorecard Report: harvardbusinessonline.hbsp.harvard.edu/b02/en/newsletters/news-bsr_home.jhtml

Management and Accounting Web: www.maaw.info

Optima Media Group Business Intelligence. See the "Performance Measurement Portfolios" for BSC information: www.business-intelligence.co.uk

NOTES

1 Hendricks, Kevin, Larry Menor, and Christine Wiedman. "The Balanced Scorecard: To adopt or not to adopt?" *Ivey Business Journal* (November/December 2004).

2 *Ibid.*

3 Adapted from: Kaplan, R.S., and D.P. Norton. "Using the Balanced Scorecard as a strategic management system." *Harvard Business Review* 74:1 (January–February 1996): 75–85.

4 Data from this case study was reported in: Kaplan, R.S., and D.P Norton. *The Strategy-Focused Organization*. Boston, MA: Harvard Business School Press, 2001.

"You show me a capitalist, I'll show you a bloodsucker." Malcolm X

  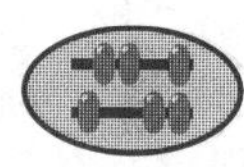 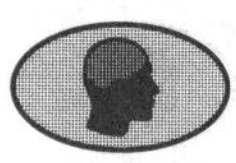  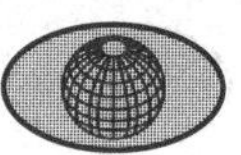   

Multinationality and Financial Performance by Alan M. Rugman

EXECUTIVE SUMMARY

- Senior executives, especially finance officers, need to be aware that standardized metrics to evaluate international performance are only applicable when firms operate globally. Now that research shows that large firms actually operate regionally, it is necessary to use new regional metrics to measure performance.
- Regional variables are important new measures that supplement the traditional measures of multinationality; indeed, the regional measure is a superior measure of the financial performance of multinational enterprises (MNEs).
- There is evidence that MNEs perform in an intraregional manner, on the basis of both sales and assets; there are strong intraregional effects across all industry sectors.
- Analysis of multinationality and financial performance needs to take into account the new metrics available on regional sales and assets, and the return on foreign assets.

INTRODUCTION

Most of the world's 500 largest firms have extensive international operations; indeed, these firms average 35% of their sales in other countries. Finance officers and senior executives involved in strategic management usually assume that such firms are operating globally. This is a bad mistake, since recent academic research has demonstrated that the vast majority of the foreign sales of these firms are actually made within the firm's home region of the broad triad of the European Union, North America, and Asia–Pacific. In other words, the world's largest firms are actually operating regionally rather than globally.

The regional nature of business means that the traditional financial and accounting metrics used to evaluate international performance need to be revised. These measures assume that firms operate globally, such that financial performance can assume standardized operations across the world. (Globalization is usually defined as worldwide economic integration leading to standardization and commonality.) Instead, financial performance needs to be measured within the home region and not globally. Large firms face additional risks in expanding operations beyond their home region. Such additional risks need to be compensated by a better performance on interregional sales in contrast to the less risky intraregional sales. In this article we outline the nature of regional activity and the new regional metrics required to measure the financial performance of large firms.

THE REGIONAL DIMENSION OF MULTINATIONALITY AND PERFORMANCE

Recent empirical research has established that MNEs operate regionally rather than globally. It was shown by Rugman and Verbeke (2004) that only nine of the world's 500 largest firms operate globally, i.e., in all three regions of the broad triad of North America, Europe, and Asia–Pacific. In contrast, of the 380 firms that provide data for the year 2001 on the geographic scope of their sales, 320 average 80% of such sales in their home region. In Rugman (2005) some 60 cases were examined to establish the robust nature of this regional effect. It was also demonstrated that whenever data on assets were provided by firms, these upstream production data also revealed a regional rather than a global effect. The implications are that the MNEs are more likely to source through regional clusters than through a global supply chain. However, robust testing of the asset data remains to be undertaken.

We shall now present data on both sales and assets. These data are presented for the five-year time period 2001–05. The purpose of these data will be to demonstrate that the regional effect is applicable over time and that there appears to be no trend towards globalization. Rather, these data indicate that there is a longitudinal argument that regionalization is now a stable phenomenon.

Table 1 reports data on intraregional sales and assets for the period 2001–05. This is for a set of the world's largest 500 firms. Among 500 firms, geographic sales and assets data are available for 386 firms during this period. The data are compiled from the annual reports of these publicly traded companies. These annual reports are now available on the internet under each company's name. This table updates and supplements the data for 2001 reported in Rugman and Verbeke (2004) and in Rugman (2005). In Table 2 data are reported for the ratio of regional to total sales (R/TS) and also for the ratio of regional to total assets (R/TA). In addition, the table reports the conventional measure of multinationality in previous empirical research. This is (F/TS), i.e., the ratio of foreign (F) to total (T) sales. The table also reports the ratio of foreign to total assets (F/TA). For more detail, see Rugman (2007).

The table reports that the average (R/TS) for the world's largest firms is 75.7%. There is almost no variation over time. Next, the table reports that the average (R/TA) is 76.7%. Again, there is very little variation over time. These data suggest that the world's largest firms are slightly more regional on assets than on sales. Table 2 also reports that the average (F/T) for sales is 35.2%, while the average (F/T) for assets is 32.5%.

> "thought leaders need to know that recent academic research demonstrates that the financial performance of multinational firms can only be properly assessed using metrics that reflect the regional, not global, nature of their activities."

CHOOSING THE CORRECT METRICS

There is an interesting variation by triad region. In Table 2 the (F/TS) for Europe is 55.5%, and for assets it is 52.1%. This partly reflects the historical lag in statistical data collection whereby the 27 member states of the European Union still record trade, foreign investment, and foreign sales data across country borders. In practice, the European Union is now an integrated internal market with common political institutions, a uniform judicial system, and

Table 1. Foreign and intraregional sales and assets of large firms, 2001–05

	Sales		Assets	
	F/TS (%)	R/TS (%)	F/TA (%)	R/TA (%)
2001	33.6	75.6	31.2	77.2
2002	34.9	75.8	32.1	76.9
2003	35.5	75.8	32.7	76.4
2004	35.8	75.2	33.2	76.4
2005	36.4	75.2	33.1	76.5
Average	35.2	75.7	32.5	76.7

"The evidence is that most of the world's largest firms are stay at home multinationals. The world of international business is a regional one not a global one." Alan M. Rugman

Table 2. Foreign and intraregional sales and assets of large firms by regional origin, 2001–05

	Sales		Assets	
	F/TS (%)	R/TS (%)	F/TA (%)	R/TA (%)
N. America	26.9	78.0	27.0	76.5
Europe	55.5	70.8	52.1	72.9
Asia	27.4	77.2	21.1	81.6
Average	35.2	75.7	32.5	76.7

one with a common currency for most of the member states. Thus, scholars need to be careful in using data on (F/T), since the international aspect of both sales and assets is exaggerated for Europe. In contrast, the regional variable is stable across the three regions of the triad. The distortionary effect of Europe does not appear in the average of (R/TS) of 75.7% and (R/TA) of 76.7%. It can be concluded that the (R/T) variable is more stable and, perhaps, more reliable than the traditional (F/T) variable.

Both variables are preferable to the "scope," measure, which simply counts the number of foreign countries in which an MNE has subsidiaries. This gives only a vague indication of geographic sales (or asset) dispersion, and it is probably very misleading as it misses the magnitude of sales (or assets) across countries and triad regions. For example, for a UK firm to have a subsidiary in the US is much more significant than for it to have 12 subsidiaries in the new member states of the European Union. Yet the scope measure would count the UK firm as 12 times more internationalized in Europe than in North America.

CONCLUSION

It has been shown here that large firms, including the vast majority of the world's multinational enterprises (MNEs), operate regionally rather than globally. The 500 largest firms average about 75% of their sales in their home region of the triad. They also have most of their assets in their home region. It is reasonable to assume that smaller firms are even less global and more local in their operations. Indeed, small firms are often associated with large MNEs in localized clusters and act as key suppliers and distributers in partnership with the MNEs. In other words, the world's largest MNEs act as strategic leaders (flagships) in determining the regional nature of business around the world.

For financial officers, the key implication of the evidence that large firms perform regionally is that new metrics are required to evaluate firm performance. It is no longer appropriate to consider the aggregate ratio of foreign to total sales since interregional sales are more risky than intraregional sales. Rather, it is necessary to use the ratio of regional to total sales. Data have been presented in this article for both types of metrics. It is apparent that the regional sales metric provides important new information to financial officers. New academic work is being undertaken to assess financial performance of large firms using the regional metric rather than the aggregate metric for multinationality. Initial results demonstrate that the financial performance of a firm is better explained by the regional metric than by the old multinationality metric. In the future, business practice and performance metrics for MNEs must be better aligned to the new academic research which has demonstrated the lack of globalization and the regional nature of business activity.

CASE STUDY

The relationship between multinationality (M) and performance (P) is a traditional topic in the areas of international business and the financing of multinational enterprises (MNEs). In this literature, *P*, as a dependent variable, is broadly determined by the degree of multinationality, *M*, where *M* is usually proxied by the ratio of foreign to total sales or assets, i.e., (*F/T*). There is either a linear, quadratic, or cubic (*S*-curve) fit, allowing for controls such as size of the firm, industry grouping, and organizational learning effect over time, etc. (see Rugman (2007)). Recently, this *M* and *P* literature has included regional aspects of (*F/T*) and performance—for example, performance now includes return on foreign assets (ROFA).

There are now better and more detailed data on the geographic dispersion of activities.

The new accounting standards affecting most of the world's MNEs now make it possible to adopt both a new dependent variable (for performance) and a new independent variable (for multinationality):

1 Performance can now capture the return on foreign assets (ROFA), not just the return on total assets (ROTA).
2 Multinationality is now available on a regional basis, i.e., the ratio of regional (R) to total (T) sales (*R/T*). This offers better information on the strategic performance of an MNE, in comparison to the traditional metric of the return of foreign-to total sales or assets (*F/T*).

Further, it is possible to calculate the performance of MNEs using Tobin's *q* as a performance measure. While this is restricted to examining the performance of the consolidated MNE, Tobin's *q* permits us to modify the accounting data reported by the firms with a stock market capitalization measure. The Tobin's *q* captures both the stock market valuation of the firm along with key elements of accounting-based rates of return. In a recent paper Tobin's *q* has been explained both by traditional (*F/T*) measures of multinationality and by the regional variable (*R/T*). These results are reported in Rugman (2007).

▸▸ MAKING IT HAPPEN

Finance professionals need to keep up to date about academic research on the financial performance of multinational enterprises (MNEs). These firms disclose accounting information in their annual reports. Traditionally they disclose their degree of multinationality, usually the ratio of foreign (F) to total (T) operations. Thus it is relatively easy to calculate the F/T for sales and/or assets. The average F/T ratio is approximately 35% for sales and slightly less for assets. Large firms also disclose aspects of their financial performance, including return on assets (ROA). Academic studies traditionally examine the impact of F/T on ROA.

Recently, both variables have been modified. First, we can now assemble data on the ratio of regional (R) to total (T) operations. Most of the world's largest 500 firms have R/T ratios of over 70% for both sales and assets. Second, many large firms now report the ROFA. This allows us to calculate the performance of foreign subsidiaries. This is a finer-grained performance measure than the traditional ROA. These data showing the impact of ROFA on R/T have been reported in Rugman (2007) and by Rugman, Yip, and Jayaratne (2007).

"The semiglobalized state of the world is far removed from either complete localization or complete integration, and it is a better basis for company strategy." Pankaj Ghemawat

     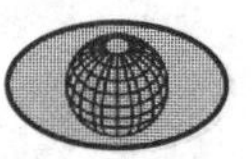   

MORE INFO

Books:

Rugman, A. M. *The Regional Multinationals: MNEs and "Global" Strategic Management*. Cambridge, UK: Cambridge University Press, 2005.

Rugman, A. M. (ed). *Regional Aspects of Multinationality and Performance*. Oxford: Elsevier, 2007.

Articles:

Rugman, A. M., and A. Verbeke. "A perspective on regional and global strategies of multinational enterprises." *Journal of International Business Studies* 35:1 (2004): 3–18.

Rugman, A. M., and A. Verbeke. "Liabilities of regional foreignness and the use of firm-level versus country-level data: A response to Dunning et al." *Journal of International Business Studies* 38:1 (2007): 200–205.

Rugman, A. M., George S. Yip, and S. Jayaratne. "A note on return on foreign assets and foreign presence for UK multinationals." *British Journal of Management* 19 (2008): 162–170.

See Also:

Lou Gerstner (p. 1167)

Multinational Business Finance (p. 1301)

"Some companies inadvertently or knowingly have overinternationalized so that a negative effect on performance is seen." Farok Contractor

  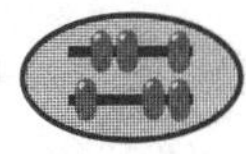   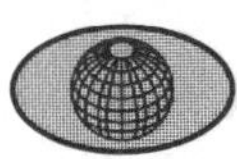   

Viewpoint: Mike Moore

Globalization, Challenges, and Threats—Where Will the WTO and Free Trade Go?

INTRODUCTION

Mike Moore is the Special Adviser to the UN Global Compact for Business and Development. He was Prime Minister of New Zealand in 1990 and Director-General of the World Trade Organization (WTO) from 1999 to 2002.

He has had a distinguished career in politics and was the driving force behind important changes in the WTO. His term at the WTO coincided with momentous changes in the global economy and multilateral trading system. He is widely credited with restoring confidence in the system following the setback of the 3rd Ministerial Conference held in Seattle in 1999.

While maintaining the organization's focus on trade liberalization, Mike also gave particular attention to helping poor countries participate effectively in the multilateral trading system. He introduced initiatives to enhance the WTO's image and deepen its relations with civil society resulting in 10 new members joining the WTO during his tenure.

Mike was the youngest Member of Parliament elected in New Zealand in 1972. He was an active participant in international discussions on trade liberalization. As Minister of Overseas Trade and Marketing, he played a leading role in launching the Uruguay Round of GATT negotiations.

Mike is a distinguished author and recipient of many global honours.

The past 60 years have seen more wealth created than the rest of history put together. The United Nations Development Programme reports that poverty throughout the world has been reduced more in the past 50 years than the previous 500 years. The past decade has been the most successful in human history by sustained economic development. Why, then, is globalization so controversial? Because those with privileges seldom surrender them without a fight. The Doha Development round and China joining the World Trade Organization were the high points of my time as Director-General of the WTO. The Doha round would add well over one trillion dollars annually to the world economy, and it would be producers in poor countries and consumers in rich countries who will do the best.

Agricultural subsidies in the EU, US, and Japan are a simple wealth transfer from the poorest consumer to the richest producers; these subsidies hurt Africa and Latin American growers the most. Rich countries spend one billion dollars a day to make food dearer. Competition and trade not only allocate resources more efficiently, but are major contributors to driving out corruption by exposing crony, phony capitalists who always prosper when they get close to politicians and bureaucrats. Competition and efficiency are important drivers, by using resources more wisely to help the environment. Where foreign investment is encouraged, evidence abounds that investment creates more and better paid jobs, and raises revenue for government. When there's so much evidence of these virtues, it's not time for us to lose our nerve.

The global economic crisis has brought leaders together and they have urged that the Doha Development round progress. Good. But well-meaning words and communiqués are not enough. It sounds grand to tell ministers and ambassadors in Geneva to work harder—what needs to change are the instructions from capitals. Agriculture, as always, is the problem. The now famous G20 Meeting in Washington, DC, was heralded as a sign of the shift in power, with creditor nations like India, Russia, Saudi Arabia, and China, at last getting a seat at the table and given the respect they deserve. It's laughable that Belgium has more influence at the IMF than China. It's dangerous, too. Some talk of another Great Depression coming out of this crisis. Not so, not in the same way. World trade collapsed by 70% in the late 1920s, now we have the WTO which prevents such extreme immediate populist action. In the 1930s, there were a series of destabilizing devaluations. It's impossible to imagine France putting up tariffs on German exports, or Italy preventing currency movements. We have the EU and the Euro. So far, so good.

The World Trade Organization has played a major role in building a predictable, rules-based system that's helped drive the global economy forward, creating and spreading wealth.

The generation that emerged from the devastation of the Second World War and the Great Depression pledged "never again." They dreamed of creating a new kind of global order based on common and universal values—of law, co-operation, shared prosperity, and individual rights. They launched the Marshall Plan where, for the first time in modern history, the victors rebuilt their former enemies—the opposite of what had happened under the ill-fated Treaty of Versailles. They created international institutions that, a half-century later, are a bedrock of our global order: the UN, the IMF, the World Bank, and the GATT, now the WTO. This system was the embodiment of a revolutionary idea. That free markets, the free co-existence of nations and peoples—were the surest guarantee of peace. And that a free world could, in turn, only be built on the foundations of the international rule of law. It is sometimes easy to forget, when even the Cold War is a fading memory, how spectacularly successful that idea has been.

National governments cannot ensure clean air, and a clean environment, run an airline, organize a tax system, attack organized crime, solve the plagues of our age—AIDS, poverty and genocide—without the co-operation of other governments and international institutions.

Just joining, and the process of joining,

     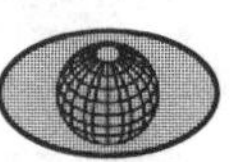   

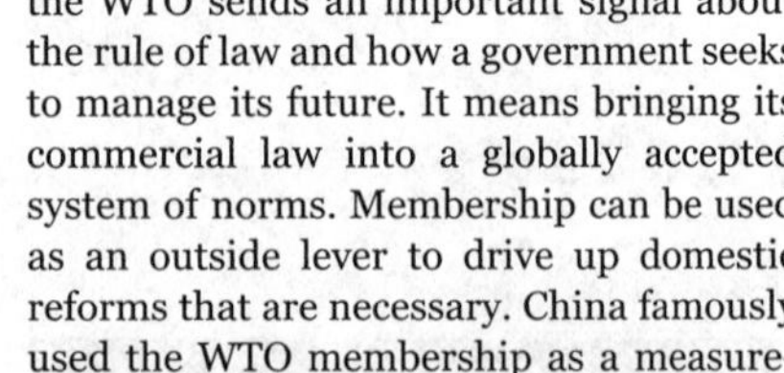

the WTO sends an important signal about the rule of law and how a government seeks to manage its future. It means bringing its commercial law into a globally accepted system of norms. Membership can be used as an outside lever to drive up domestic reforms that are necessary. China famously used the WTO membership as a measurement, a step-ladder, to lift its economy, and cement in its rules and systems.

The WTO is not imposed on countries. Countries choose to participate in an open, rules-based, multilateral trading system for the simple reason that it is overwhelmingly in their interest to do so. The alternative is a less open, less prosperous, more uncertain world economy—an option few countries would willingly choose.

The multilateral trading system's expansion is remarkable. It began with just 23 members in 1947. The WTO now has nearly 150 members, including, recently, China. This also explains why members have repeatedly agreed to widen and deepen the system's body of rules. The multilateral trading system was initially concerned mainly with trade in goods, and it was based not on a permanent organization but on a provisional treaty, the General Agreement on Tariffs and Trade (GATT). By the end of the Uruguay Round in 1994, the system contained sweeping new rules for services, intellectual property, subsidies, textiles, and agriculture. It was also established on a firm institutional foundation, the new WTO, with a strengthened mechanism for settling disputes. The most recent round, launched in Doha in November 2001, has development issues at the center. No other international body oversees rules that extend so widely around the world, or so deeply into the fabric of economies. Yet at the same time, no other body is as directly run by member governments, or as firmly rooted in consensus decision-making and collective rule. The multilateral trading system works precisely because it is based on persuasion, not coercion—rules, not force. That's why it's difficult and painfully slow.

Two fundamental principles underpin the equal rights of WTO members. One is the principle of nondiscrimination. The WTO treats all members alike, be they rich or poor, big or small, strong or weak. Central among these rules is the "most-favored nation" obligation—which prevents WTO members from discriminating between foreign goods, or treating products from one WTO member better than those from another—and the "national treatment" rule—which obliges governments to treat foreign and domestically produced products equally. Nondiscrimination has been key to the multilateral trading system's success. Preferential trade blocs and alliances, by definition, exclude and marginalize nonmember countries. This not only hurts the countries themselves, but can be harmful for the system as a whole. The multilateral trading system—based on a uniform set of international rules under which all countries are treated equally—was designed precisely to avoid a world of inward-looking trade blocs and self-destructive factionalism. From a national perspective, the principle of nondiscrimination has also allowed countries to liberalize their economies and integrate into the world trading system at their own pace and space.

The WTO has a binding dispute settlement system—a "world trade court"—with a possibility of appeal. No other global institution has a system of managing differences by a binding legal system. It works; no government, mighty or modest, has ever ignored a ruling.

This is a jewel in the multilateral architecture that is sidelined at great cost. Trade will always advance and the large numbers of bilateral and regional deals being struck are a direct response to failure to advance the current Doha round. They are not free trade agreements, but "preferential" trade agreements. They offer privileges to some and discriminate against others, creating trade diversion, e.g. US beef into Korea, but not Uruguay beef.

They create new inefficiencies, new rules; none have really addressed agriculture, all have dangerous exemptions and none have a binding disputes mechanism. Dangerously, some have put into play, rules that they couldn't get at the WTO.

The WTO talks failed in Geneva in 2008, in part because of the demand of some big developing countries to have rules against export surges. That's without proof of damage to local production, no disputes system. What small countries can stand up to India, China, Japan, or the US and EU when they insist on selfish conditions in a bilateral or regional situation? Especially if a competitor nation gives in. It puts dangerous powers, new levers, in the hands of politicians. How can I explain that Australia could do a deal with the US but not New Zealand? Because the US didn't appreciate our foreign policy? The global economic crisis may make leaders and governments re-think. At the time of writing, they are calling for movement over the Doha round. Let's see. This is a work in progress, failure or reversal is just too dreadful to contemplate.

  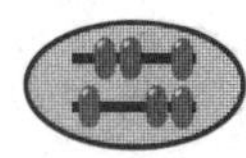   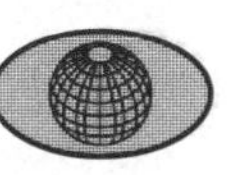   

Profitability Analysis Using Activity-Based Costing by Priscilla Wisner

EXECUTIVE SUMMARY

- Traditional cost allocation methodologies in firms can provide misleading information about the profitability of products, product lines, customers, and markets.
- Activity-based costing (ABC) provides more meaningful information about the drivers of costs, the activities performed in a firm, and the relationship between costs and products, customers, markets, and segments.
- In addition to supplying more detailed and better cost and profitability information, an ABC analysis enables managers to evaluate processes from an activity viewpoint, leading to identification of non value-adding activities and process inefficiencies.
- ABC does not change overall profitability in a firm; it better aligns cost assignment to the *causes* of those costs.
- With better information, better decisions can be made in a firm to improve profitability—this is the power of ABC.

INTRODUCTION

Cost allocation in firms can provide misleading information about the profitability of products, product lines, customers, and markets. Traditional cost allocation practices allocate all manufacturing overhead costs using a single driver such as direct labor hours, direct labor dollars, or machine hours. Sales-related costs are typically ignored. While technically accurate, in most complex organizations a single overhead cost driver is not sufficient to accurately assign the pool of overhead costs to the products that are being produced or the customers that are being served.

Many firms—from manufacturing to medical and healthcare to banking and financial services to hospitality and not-for-profit organizations—have benefited from designing and implementing ABC allocation systems. Using ABC tools has helped these organizations to understand profitability more clearly, and has provided meaningful information about processes and costs associated with delivering goods and services. A well-designed and implemented ABC system is a powerful aid to management evaluation and decision-making, thereby improving organizational performance.

TRADITIONAL COST ALLOCATION

Factory overhead costs in a manufacturing organization are varied and complex. These costs consist of indirect labor, indirect materials, and other indirect factory support costs. Factory support personnel include process design engineers, supervisors, maintenance workers, inspectors, purchasing agents, security personnel, and administrative workers such as accountants and human resource personnel. Indirect materials are those materials that cannot be individually associated with a product—such as drill bits, shop supplies, paper goods, and maintenance supplies. Other indirect costs include utilities for the plant, depreciation of the machinery, training costs, and technology to run the production systems.

Using a traditional cost allocation methodology, factory overhead costs are allocated to products using a single driver, often direct labor hours. Sales, general, and administrative costs are typically ignored in a traditional costing methodology, since they are not part of the production process and are not considered in the cost of goods sold equation.

Overhead costs have grown substantially in the past decades, as a result of factors such as globalization, technology, product customization, security concerns, and regulatory oversight. In the past, when overhead costs were a smaller proportion of factory costs and direct labor was a larger proportion, it made sense to allocate overhead costs to products using a traditional methodology. The direct labor base was a large proportion of costs, and overhead support costs were a relatively small proportion of total costs. As shown in Figure 1, direct labor costs have declined as a percentage of total costs, while overhead costs have grown.

Figure 1. Total costs over time

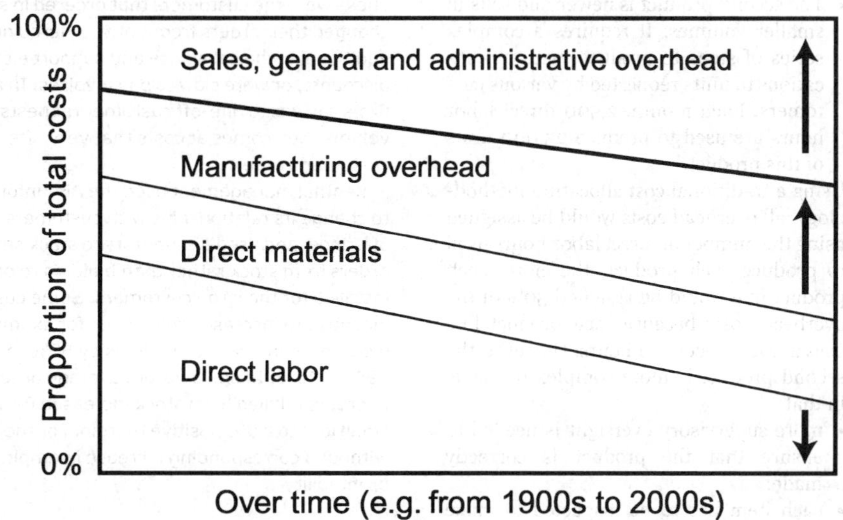

The increased complexity of manufacturing operations makes the traditional methodology obsolete. What is needed to improve the understanding of costs is, first, to associate costs with the activities that are causing the resources to be used, and then to associate these activities with the products that are being produced. This way, products that require a complex set of activities or a high-cost set of resources as part of the production process will be allocated the costs associated with these activities and resources.

IS YOUR COST ALLOCATION SYSTEM FAULTY?

There are various indicators that a cost allocation system is not providing accurate information. You need a new cost system when:

- *The volume of production increases but profitability declines.* This often happens when management cannot accurately determine the cost of activities and resources associated with production processes.

"**Because business equates success or failure with profitability, the superficial conclusion is that profit is the sole objective. . .the difficult decisions. . .are those involving the conditions under which profit may be realized.**"
Crawford H. Greenewalt

- *The product mix changes from lower- to higher-margin products, but profitability declines.* This situation indicates that the "high-margin" product was actually using more resources than it was being allocated in the cost system. As the firm makes more of this product, more resources are consumed and profitability decreases.
- *Managers do not trust the numbers from the accounting system and sometimes build their own cost systems.* Functional managers often have good process knowledge about the organization. For example, when the sales group ignores accounting information in pricing products and instead uses its own calculations, it is an indication that the accounting system is not supplying accurate information.
- *The firm produces a mix of higher-volume standardized products or services and lower-volume customized products or services, yet the cost allocation system uses a single driver to assign overhead costs to products.* A single driver ignores variation in overhead costs and variation in process activity, resulting in an average number. As complexity increases in a firm, averages distort information at a segment level.

ABC: HOW IT WORKS

Consider an organization with two primary products:

- The first product is well established in the marketplace, sells in high volumes, and is made from a relatively small number of components. In sum, it is a relatively simple product to make and support. Each month, 2,500 direct labor hours are used to produce 100,000 units of this product.
- The second product is newer and sells in smaller volumes. It requires a complex series of steps to produce, with modifications to units requested by various customers. Each month, 2,500 direct labor hours are used to produce 25,000 units of this product.

Using a traditional cost allocation methodology, all overhead costs would be assigned using the number of direct labor hours used to produce each product; therefore, each product line would be assigned 50% of the overhead costs because each product line uses 2,500 direct labor hours. However, the second product is more complex to make, in that:

- more supervisory oversight is needed to ensure that the product is correctly made;
- each item has to be inspected to make sure that the modifications have been correctly done;
- the shipped batches are much smaller in size.

Each of these resources—supervision, inspection, packing, and shipping—costs money, and the need for them is increased by the second product line. An ABC allocation would more accurately associate their costs with the product lines that consumed them, thereby assigning more supervision, inspection, and pack-and-ship costs to the second product line. The data in the following example compare a traditional costing outcome with an ABC outcome for the two products.

BENEFITS OF ABC

An ABC analysis provides management with a wealth of financial and operational information. The benefits of ABC include the following:

- Costs are associated with activities that create those costs.
- Profitability can be calculated from multiple perspectives, such as product line, customer, or market.
- It provides information about "hidden" losers and winners, i.e. which product lines/customers/markets have lower profit margins than was originally thought and which give better profit margins.
- It provides cost rates for organizational activities that are helpful for benchmarking and making process decisions.
- It aligns with business process reengineering work by helping managers to put a price tag on non value-added activities, such as waste or rework.
- Attention is focused on process costs and how they interact with profitability segments. Armed with explicit measurements of the costs of activities and

CASE STUDY

ABC Used to Improve Processes and Evaluate Customer Profitability

Kanthal[1] is a global producer of electrical heating material and elements that are used in industries including electronics, chemical, ceramics, medical, and appliances. Headquartered in Sweden, Kanthal sells its products throughout the world. In the mid-1980s, Kanthal implemented an ABC project to help it realize its strategy for higher growth and profitability. The specific goals of the company were to:

- achieve profit objectives by division, product line, and market;
- determine order and sales support costs, so that the sales force could make better decisions about customer requests;
- increase sales without increasing overhead costs.

At the time of the initial analysis, Kanthal had about 10,000 customers and produced about 15,000 items.

The ABC analysis showed that, of Kanthal's total Swedish customer base, 30% contributed the majority of the profits, about 40% were break even, and 30% were not profitable. The analysis also showed that two of the largest customers were among the least profitable for the firm.

An activity analysis helped to focus on the root causes of the low-margin customers. These were the customers that ordered in small order sizes or in unpredictable amounts, changed their orders frequently, ordered nonstocked or customized products, required additional technical advice and support either pre- or post-sale, demanded large discounts, or were slow to pay invoices. In a culture that focuses on building sales, many firms say yes to one-off customer requests and demands; however, the additional sales volume then comes at costs that very often are not directly associated with the customer's order.

Kanthal management used the ABC information to change internal processes and also to change its relationships with customers. The firm reduced the variation in product offerings, and used distributors to stock smaller-volume items, enabling it to meet more orders from stock rather than building to order. On-line order entry systems were installed for the large customers. Some customers were given a small discount as an incentive to increase order sizes; for example, when one customer was given a 5% discount to increase order lines by 50%, profitability for that customer increased from 19% to 45%. In one division, average order size increased by over 60%, the percentage of orders fulfilled from stock increased from 36% to 63%, and profitability went from a small loss to a 9% positive margin. For the company as a whole, sales increased by 20% without a corresponding increase in employees, leading to a 45% increase in profitability.

"Enterprises are paid to create wealth, not control costs." Peter F. Drucker

  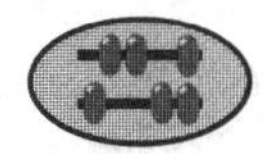   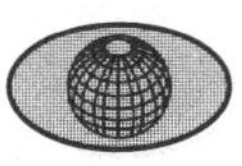   

processes, management can communicate that paying attention to these factors is important. In other words, what gets measured gets managed.

CONCLUSION

An ABC analysis requires an in-depth evaluation of an organization's processes and activities, which in turn enables an allocation of costs that better reflects resource usage. Conducting an ABC analysis provides financial and operational information to management that facilitates more effective decision-making, thereby leading to improved financial outcomes.

Table 1. Comparison of traditional and ABC costings for the same product lines

Example:		*Direct labor*	**Supervision**	**Inspection**	**Pack & ship**	**Total overhead**
	Units	*hours*	*% of effort*	*Inspect hours*	*# shipments*	
Product 1	*100,000*	*2,500*	*40%*	*200*	*30*	
Product 2	*25,000*	*2,500*	*60%*	*800*	*50*	
Overhead costs by activity:			$100,000	$50,000	$40,000	$190,000
Traditional costing (single overhead cost pool)						
Overhead rate (190,000 Ö Direct labor hours (5,000)) =					$38.00	
Product 1 overhead:	(2,500 direct labor hours x $38) =					$ 95.000
Product 2 overhead:	(2,500 direct labor hours x $38) =					$ 95,000
						$190,000
Activity-based costing (multiple cost pools)						
Each cost pool is allocated according to the activity used by each product						
			Supervision	**Inspection**	**Pack & ship**	**Total overhead**
		Activity rate:	*Proportional allocation (% of effort)*	*$50.00 per inspection hour*	*$500.00 per shipment*	
Product 1 overhead:			$40,000	$10,000	$15,000	$ 65,000
Product 2 overhead:			$60,000	$40,000	$20,000	$125,000
						$190,000

▸▸ MAKING IT HAPPEN

To conduct an ABC analysis, organizational data are needed about costs incurred, work performed, and the cost objectives (for example products, customers, markets) of the analysis. An ABC analysis can be done for one department, for an entire manufacturing operation, or for the whole organization. However, it is often an advantage to start with a smaller-sized project (a single department or a plant) as the learning curve is steep.

1 Gather the cost data from the general ledger or other financial records. Segment the data into cost pools, whereby each cost pool represents a related set of costs. For example, a maintenance cost pool might consist of maintenance labor costs, supervision, tools and equipment used for maintenance, and training costs for maintenance workers.

2 Define the activities of the business (*what work is performed*), using the following framework:

- *Facility-level activities:* Those related to overall operations (for example management, human resources, security, legal).
- *Cost-object level activities:* Activities that support a product (for example design, testing, engineering), or a customer (for example order processing, shipping, technical support), or a market (for example advertising, sales support).
- *Batch-level activities:* Activities related to a batch, equally and at the same time (for example set-up, material handling, inspection).
- *Unit-level activities:* Activities performed for each unit of activity (for example direct labor).

Once the activities of work are determined, assign the resource costs to the activities.

3 Assign the activity costs to the cost objectives (product lines, customer, markets, etc.) according to the cost object's use of each activity. Determining the allocation basis requires process knowledge and transactional data; often statistical analysis can be used to verify relationships between transactions performed and costs incurred.

▸▸ MORE INFO

Books:

Bleeker, Ron R., and Kenneth J. Euske (eds). *Activity-based Cost Management Design Framework: Getting It Right the First Time.* Austin, TX: Consortium of Advanced Management, International, 2004.

Cokins, Gary. *Activity-based Cost Management: An Executive's Guide*. New York: Wiley, 2001.

Kaplan, Robert S., and Steven R. Anderson. *Time-driven Activity-based Costing: A Simpler and More Powerful Path to Higher Profits.* Boston, MA: Harvard Business School Press, 2007.

"Watch the costs and the profits will take care of themselves." Andrew Carnegie

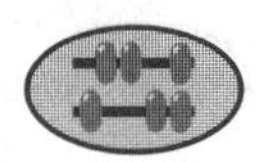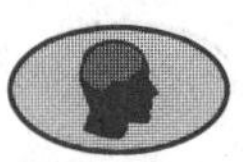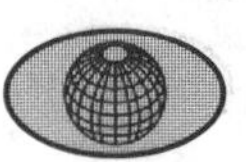

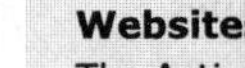

Websites:

The Activity Based Costing Benchmarking Association (ABCBA) is a group of ABC practitioners who share data and best practice information: www.abcbenchmarking.com

The Consortium of Advanced Management, International (CAM-I), is an international consortium of business, government, and academic leaders who work collaboratively on cost, process, and performance management issues: www.cam-i.org

The Institute of Management Accountants (IMA) is a global organization that "provides a dynamic forum for management accounting and finance professionals to develop and advance their careers through certification, research and practice development, education, networking, and the advocacy of the highest ethical and professional practices": www.imanet.org

The International Federation of Accountants (IFAC) is a global consortium of accountants that promulgates standards and publishes articles and papers on topics of interest in the accounting and finance disciplines: www.ifac.org

The Management and Accounting Web is dedicated to education, research, and the practice of management and accounting disciplines. Contains links to dozens of management accounting and finance resources: maaw.info

NOTES

1 Data for this mini-case were reported in Robert S. Kaplan, *Kanthal (A)*, Harvard Business School Case 190-002, 1995.

"Watch the costs and the profits will take care of themselves." Andrew Carnegie

  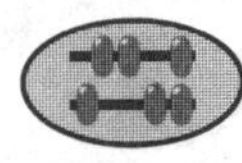   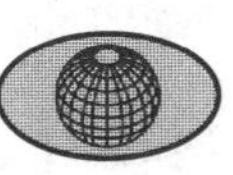   

Project Planning Techniques for Small and Medium Enterprises by Damian Merciar

EXECUTIVE SUMMARY

- Establish agreement on which project to undertake.
- Consider the project management (PM) theories: Is your project predominately process or operational in nature?
- Be careful to manage risk during the implementation of your project.
- Never separate cost and schedule considerations in a project.
- Empower team members.
- Be consistent in application of PM techniques. Profit enhancement and cost savings are just two areas where improvements can be made.

DEFINITION OF A PROJECT

One working definition of a project would be that it is a one-off job that has a known start time, a planned end time, and an intended outcome, and that it would include a defined scope of work, a budget, and personnel assigned to carry out the work. What distinguishes a project from regular work is that it is multi-task in nature—it is not a single job repeated.

This is where the *Project Management Institute Body of Knowledge* (PMBOK) comes to the fore (Project Management Institute, 2004). PMBOK is the guide setting out what is generally agreed to be best practice in the world of project management. The guide was the first to recognize the five basic phases of a project fully: initiating, planning, executing, controlling and monitoring, and closing. Using its methods, projects are completed by dividing them up into processes, or stages. A project is distinct from a process, primarily in that it is a collection of a series of processes.

Likewise, project management is not just a schedule of works that has to be completed. All the sophisticated and intricate software available will not make a project manager. Indeed, the bulk of this software is primarily focused on scheduling. Let us not forget the management element and all that implies—from office politics over resource allocation to managing distinct and different personalities. This role successfully combines the "what" and the "how" of a job: *what* being the scope and desired end result, and *how* being the process and control structure that you use to get there.

PERFORMANCE, COST, TIME, AND SCOPE

Performance refers to both operational and specialist requirements—operational being what it is that the project is aiming to achieve or do, and specialist referring to the specific characteristics that apply to the output or deliverable: color, speed, dimensions, etc. Cost in the service sector is predominately the labor cost required to complete the job. This cost itself will typically also contain an element to "keep the lights on"—office rental, property taxes, facilities management, etc. For manufacturing firms, material and capital equipment costs are accounted for separately.

Time is the time required to complete the project, and scope is the magnitude (and by implication the limitation) of the work to be undertaken. The relationship between these variables is key and can be shown as:

$$\text{Cost} = f(\text{Performance, Time, Scope})$$

In other words cost is a function, f, of the performance, time, and scope of the project. It is not necessarily important to note that if you know three of these variables the fourth can be determined. Rather, it is more important to note that any project has a scope, a cost, a time, and a quality as constraints, and it is vital that these are balanced and progressed toward the outcome, which is completion of the project. The combination of these variables represents the performance of the project. You cannot assign arbitrary values to these four elements; doing this may be useful in a control situation where additional resources are required, but a director will not release them to his project manager and will tell him instead just to get the job done. (Presenting the director with a particular constraining factor or factors, possibly—if not preferably in this instance—identified using scheduling software, will help to influence a decision to grant additional resources.)

PROJECT METHODOLOGY

Project methodology must be explicit and include the five basic processes: initiating, planning, executing, controlling and monitoring, and closing. *Initiation* can range from a single employee recognizing a fault at factory level, to a global CEO deciding to change a product offering. *Planning* is typically done by the equivalent of middle management, with notable exceptions. *Executing* the project can either be done by an in-house team or by retained professionals, while *controlling* will always lie finally with the client. *Monitoring* is the micromanagement of the project's keeping to its brief. *Closing* includes an assessment of fitness for purpose: whether a project has achieved its stated aims. If a project slides or becomes nonviable, the project manger will not usually be the person who decides whether to reschedule or discontinue a project—he or she would normally require sign-off at a higher level. The whole project team needs to be aware of accountabilities and limits to authority.

This area is not limited to ISO 9001 and its application. Quality management, assessment, audit potential, and control are important parts of project management, though they are not the defining ones. A useful methodology needs to be efficient and not onerous: it is supposed to be a framework for process delivery—making it easier to complete the project.

Many software packages are available for the project manager, from the complexity and comprehensiveness of Oracle's Primavera (typically beyond the scope of most SMEs) to commercial open-source applications such as those available from Project.net. One of the most widely known and available packages is Microsoft Project 2007 (MSP, 2007). Again, one must not rely solely on such software; they are tools to help facilitate projects and their limitations need to be understood.

CRITICAL PATH ANALYSIS VERSUS PERT

A critical path is a route through a project that has no slack, and is the longest path to completion of the work. A "float" is any path shorter than the critical path; it may be shorter because it separates distinct tasks that can be done at the same time, allowing some slack in the project. Slack is essential as otherwise there is no room for contingencies or significant changes of plan. If resources allow, tasks can of course be run concurrently, or "parallel" in software terminology, thereby shortening the critical path.

A Gantt chart is a bar chart that shows progress along a given axis. The axis almost always represents time. However, the original Gantt charts did not display information relating to dependency—that is, the completion of one task of a project being dependent on the successful completion of an earlier task. Ability to display this relationship was developed in the 1950s using arrow diagrams, and resulted in the critical path method (CPM) and the performance evaluation and review technique (PERT). Both techniques determine the critical path in a project. PERT is slightly more useful as it uses considered task duration and allows probabilities of completing the work to be included. This is a measure of actual time taken, rather than only a rigid expected time given for a project. This probabilistic method allows for three time estimates: pessimistic, most likely, and optimistic. CPM only uses considered, and therefore more rigid, task duration. Both use some form of notation, either on completion of a task ("activity on node") or on the action path ("activity on arrow"). The purpose of the arrows is to show whether a particular item of work can be begun and whether the task on which it is dependent has been completed—bar charting alone does not make this clear.

EARNED VALUE ANALYSIS

Earned value analysis or learned value management (EVA or EVM) is about the integration of cost and schedule tracking. For example, if a project has a budget of $1,000 and you have spent $200, from a cost perspective you are 20% through your project. However, if you have only completed 10% of the work, you are in line to double both the time required and the cost of the finished project. EVA gives three measurements that allow you to tell exactly where a project is: a measurement of what is supposed to be done, what has actually been done, and the amount of cost spent doing it.

Continuing this example, let us say that you have fully utilized your S1,000 budget. This figure is also called the *budgeted cost of work scheduled* (BCWS). However, you have only completed $800 worth of the work in the original planned budget schedule—this figure is called the *budgeted cost of work performed* (BCWP). BCWP is also known as "earned value" To finish the project therefore will require another $200—or *actual cost of work performed* (ACWP). From these figures we can identify:

Schedule variance = BCWP – BCWS = $800 – $1,000
= –$200

Cost variance = BCWP – ACWP = $800 – $1,200
= –$400

Budget variance = BCWS – ACWP = $1,000 – $1,200
= –$200

These figures are important. For instance, the cost variance shows that you actually have $800 worth of work completed, and that in nominal terms it will take another $400 to complete the project on the basis of this assessment of the worth of your present position. A company director might conclude from these figures that the project was running 50% over budget. In fact, in this instance it would be more accurate to use the budget variance figure of $200, which is only 20% over budget.

Most reasonable software packages allow you to show EVA in spreadsheet format.

CRITICAL RATIO

The critical ratio (CR) is a performance index that itself is the product of two other indices. The first is the *schedule performance index* (SPI). The second is the *cost performance index* (CPI). These are given by:

$$SPI = \frac{BCWP}{BCWS} \qquad CPI = \frac{BCWP}{ACWP}$$

BCWP/BCWS is the work you have actually accomplished divided by the work you were supposed to accomplish, so SPI is a measure of work, or project, efficiency. CPI is the work you have completed divided by what it actually cost, and so represents a measure of spending efficiency. If these two ratios are combined, the outcome is the critical ratio:

$$CR = SPI \times CPI$$

As with all ratios that illustrate performance, the value will equal 1.0 if work is going exactly as planned. In our example this happens if you complete $1,000 worth of work for $1,000 scheduled and $1,000 actual cost. It will be less than 1.0 if the project is performing worse than planned, and greater than 1.0 if performing better.

Statistics can further refine these figures to arrive at measures of deviation. This will typically be beyond the scope of the SME project manager, and as an executive tool for reporting to directors a flag can be inserted into the software to report to management if the CR falls below a specified figure—say 0.7.

CAPACITY MANAGEMENT

For the SME, project management need not be too complicated. There do not need to be large numbers of variables in the spreadsheets and project management software. As often as not, managing the process of project management can itself become a challenging job. Therefore, as a director

CASE STUDY

Project Management in Competitive Exports

An Indian firm involved in the export market, predominantly to the United States, was a manufacturer of telecoms and switching equipment. An efficient and competitive firm, if not the largest, it used the best quality components and was the first company in its industry to regularly export such technical equipment to the West. However, times were changing: overall, component quality had improved greatly and the company now faced competition from recently acceded countries to the European Union and from the economic and technological superpower that is China. Margins at the company were relatively tight and costs were not always stable as a large part of the raw materials were volatile commodities, such as metals, bought on the international market. Many of the managers had been educated both at Western universities and at India's top universities, with a biased representation, naturally, from engineering and technical disciplines.

After some years of stiff competition, the company lost out on a contract to supply the key US export market to a South Korean company. After much reflection—their quality assurance process was first rate, their manufacturing process efficiency standards were leading edge, and their own supplier contracts were as tightly negotiated as possible—managers began to think about applying project management to the whole product life cycle. Detailed costs were identified and allocated. Responsibility for different stages of the process were more clearly demarcated and the concept of team ownership of specific projects was used for the first time. Reward and incentive schemes were initiated and internal team competitions established. Benchmarks for delivery were created that were more closely related to cost and schedule, as opposed to previously when the emphasis had been toward quality and reliability. Within a year the firm had won back that export contract and improved efficiency enough to bid for another, without increasing the headcount.

  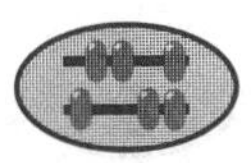   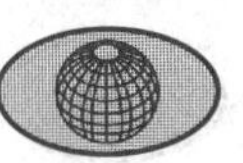   

one needs to be aware of the capacity of the individual who is doing the project management. Too many projects and too much complexity can easily overwhelm the project management, leading to sub-optimal performance and projects that come in under par. As a rule of thumb, two or three small projects are all that one person should manage. Don't overlook the ancillaries that go with projects—attending meetings, preventing bottlenecks, and defending one's turf from rival managers who are aware of the fixed resources available at company level. These can easily detract from the successful completion of a project.

PROJECT REVIEW AND CHANGE

It may be thought this section is self-evident. It isn't—in fact project review and project change are vital components of both successful and unsuccessful projects. If a project is going wrong, there has to be a clearly defined set of criteria that set out *exactly* what must be done and whose responsibility it is to do it. Typically it will be a director who decides whether to abort a current project or significantly change the path the project is on. However, detailed reporting rules need to be agreed on by all team members to ensure that management is aware of the precise status of a project.

CONCLUSION

Management and Leadership

These two are inextricably linked: just as manufacturing control is only a small part of project management, project management is itself only a small part of running a company. Leadership is key here: not every manager is a leader, nor is every leader a successful manager—quite often the two attributes are very separate. Leadership is for another chapter, but it is essential if a project manager is to "buy in" the team doing the work he or she requires of them to his or her vision of why they are doing it. The subtle difference between management and leadership alone can shift the bottom line either way by tens of thousands.

MAKING IT HAPPEN

- Project management can be a huge specialism, so understand your project and your contribution to it.
- Distinguish between the various theories of project management and discover which best fits your situation.
- Do not lose sight of the importance of process control.
- Review your project path and be prepared to change it if not doing so could jeopardize successful implementation.

MORE INFO

Books:

Kendall, Gerald I., and Steven C. Rollins. *Advanced Project Portfolio Management and the PMO: Multiplying ROI at Warp Speed*. Boca Raton, FL: Ross Publishing, 2003.

Kerzner, Harold. *Project Management: A Systems Approach to Planning, Scheduling, and Controlling*. 8th ed. Hoboken, NJ: Wiley, 2003.

Lewis, James P. *Project Planning, Scheduling, & Control: A Hands-on Guide to Bringing Projects in On Time and On Budget*. 4th ed. New York: McGraw-Hill, 2005.

Project Management Institute (PMI). *A Guide to the Project Management Body of Knowledge* (PMBOK® Guide). 3rd ed. Newtown Square, PA: PMI, 2004. Available from: www.pmi.org

Websites:

Association for Project Management (UK): www.apm.org.uk
International Project Management Association: www.ipma.ch
Project Management Institute: www.pmi.org
SME Toolkit: www.smetoolkit.org
SME Blog: www.sme-blog.net

Resources Mentioned in the Text:

Oracle's Primavera project management software: www.primavera.com
Commercial open-source project management resources: www.project.net
Microsoft Project (MSP) 2007: www.microsoft.com/smallbusiness/products/project

  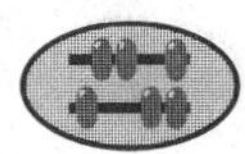 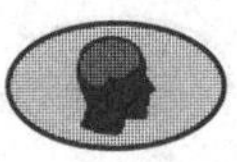  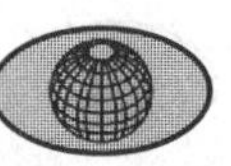  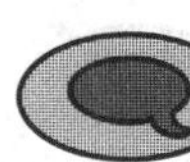 

Real Options: Opportunity from Risk

by David C. Shimko

EXECUTIVE SUMMARY

Real options arise from the ability of economic agents to adjust their behavior to maximize the values of their assets or contracts.

- Common examples are the right to make, expand, contract, defer, or cancel an investment or contract.
- Value real options by considering the value of the asset or contract with and without the ability to adjust.
- In some cases, the Black–Scholes model can be used to approximate the value of real options directly.
- Real options generally increase in value as uncertainty about the future increases.
- Real options can be proprietary or shared, simple or compound, restructurable or not.
- Real options have real value; many corporate valuations cannot be explained except for the presence of real options.

WHAT IS A REAL OPTION?

The origin of the term "real option" derives from financial options. For example, the right to buy a house for a fixed period of time at a fixed price is a call option,[1] except that the underlying asset is a real asset, not a financial asset. Business people and economists discovered that many business processes involve options, and that financial mathematics can be brought to bear to value those options. Some popular examples include:

- the right to make an investment, such as the option to build a plastics plant in China;
- the right to expand or contract an investment based on changes in market conditions, such as a plant design that accommodates changes in production rates at very low cost;
- the right to defer an investment, such as the right to wait for better market conditions to develop a property;
- the right to accelerate an investment;
- the right to cancel a contract;
- the right to produce or not to produce a product, such as the right of a petroleum refinery or electricity power plant to produce or not produce fuel or power;
- the right to choose how to undertake an investment, such as a gold producer's right to choose the mining strategy that maximizes its value.

"Option" and "optimize" share the same root, the word "opt"—meaning, of course, "to choose." Therefore, the value of a real option can be thought of as the value of any right to choose, when compared with following a strategy where no such right is conferred. This suggests the mathematical relation:

Value of real option =
Value of strategy with decision rights –
Value of strategy without decision rights

In some cases, the option value may be computed directly, as shown in Example 1.

Example 1

A company has a one-year option to acquire an oil-producing property for $100 million. The present value of the drilling profits is currently estimated to be $100 million, and the oil reserves are currently being depleted at the rate of 2% per year. The present value assessment varies according to the price of oil, with a percentage volatility (standard deviation) of 15% per year. If the interest rate is 4%, what is the value of the option?

To value the option, it is helpful to see how the real option resembles a standard financial call option. The owner of an equity call option has the right to buy a stock at a predetermined price (the strike price) for a predetermined period of time. The stock pays dividends which the option holder will not receive if the option is unexercised. Stock volatility makes the option valuable—the more volatile the stock, the greater the value of deciding to buy later at a fixed price. In the case of the oil option, the "stock value" is the present value of the profits, the "volatility" is the percentage variation in the present value, the "strike price" is the acquisition price of the property, and the "dividend" is the depletion of the oil reserve.

As a first approximation, an analyst might use the Black–Scholes formula of stock option pricing to value the real option. Using any online calculator, and the inputs below, the resulting call option value is $6.82 million.

Stock price	US$100
Dividend	2%
Exercise price	US$100
Volatility	15%
Interest rate	4%
Time	1 year
Call option value = US$6.82	

Some real options fit the Black–Scholes framework nicely, but most real options have degrees of complexity that are not captured by the option pricing model.

Example 2

A developer owns a piece of land that is currently used as a parking lot. The present value of the parking lot revenues is $5 million. He can convert the land into an apartment building and net an additional $5.5 million in present value. Or he can convert the parking lot into an office building and net an additional $6 million in present value. What is the value of the property in this case?

(1) US $5 million, since it currently being used as a parking lot.
(2) US$11 million, since the office project is more profitable than the apartment project.
(3) The value of the highest current net present value (NPV) usage of the land.
(4) None of the above.

The answer is clearly not (1); a parking lot is worth more than the present value of its current income since it has demonstrated valuable alternative uses. Answer (2) is tempting, but it is wrong if there are any other projects more valuable. Answer (3) may be correct, but also could be incorrect because of the use of the word "current." It may have a more valuable use in the future and, under some conditions, it would be worthwhile to wait to develop the land until that possibility materializes.

The correct answer is generally (4), since the value of the land is equal to *or higher than* its current value in the highest use. The reason for this is that conditions change over time. If the property owner waits a year, they may find that residential real estate grows faster than commercial, or vice versa. At some point, however, it is optimal to make the irreversible decision as to how to convert the property. In those cases, the value of waiting is zero.

Because the property owner has the right to wait to invest, this confers additional

"The real options approach. . .provides important insights about businesses and strategic investment. These insights are more vital than ever, given the rapid pace of economic change." Michael Mauboussin

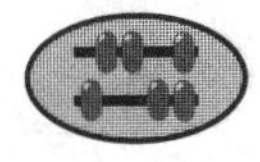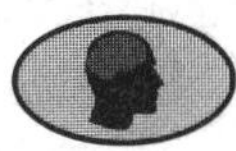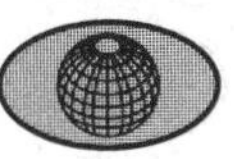

value to investment until the moment when it is no longer optimal to wait, and the option is exercised.

PROPERTIES OF REAL OPTIONS

In many situations, increased project risk reduces project value. This is particularly true when a company has constrained capital and increased risks put the company's survival in jeopardy.

Real options have the opposite effect. Like financial options, they generally increase in value the more uncertain the values of the underlying variables. They generally increase in value the longer the time an option can be deferred. And they increase in value as the cost to exercising falls.

Real options also tend to mitigate project risk, since the project owner has the right to modify strategy midcourse. This can help avoid the worst outcomes for the project, providing a kind of operational hedge against downside risk.

VALUING REAL OPTIONS

When an option pricing formula cannot be applied, there are two other ways to value real options: One using backward induction (best for decision trees) and one using simulation (best for problems with continuous input price changes). As an example of option valuation using backward induction, consider the following game, similar to the American television show *The Price is Right*.

Backward Induction

The contestant is given $50 and has to make a decision whether to keep the $50 or pay $50 to choose one of three boxes. One box has a valuable prize worth $100, but the other two boxes have nothing. After choosing a box, the host reveals an empty box and offers the contestant a chance to switch. What is the value of the player's option to switch?

The tree in Figure 1 summarizes the decision problem.

If the contestant always keeps their box of choice, the expected value is 33.33 since there is a ⅓ chance of getting US$100. If they switch after seeing an empty box, there is a ⅔ chance they changed an empty box for a valuable one, and a ⅓ chance they changed a valuable box for an empty one.

Using backward induction, we confirm that switching is the best strategy, and since the value of that is greater than $50, the value of the game is US$66.67. The value of the game without the right to switch is US$50, since it is optimal not to play the game. Therefore, the value of the

Figure 1. Decision problem summary

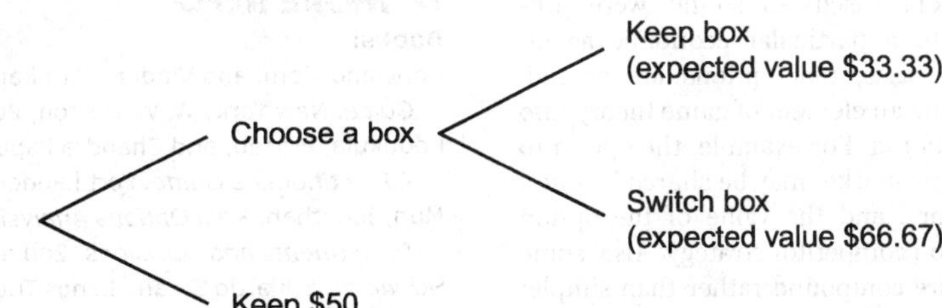

option to switch in this case is US$16.67 (= 66.67 – 50).

Simulation

More generally, real options are valued using stochastic modeling and some form of optimization theory. For example, plastics can be produced from natural gas or from naphtha. To value a plant that has the option to choose its feedstock, it is necessary to simulate price fluctuations in natural gas and naphtha and determine how the company would optimize its feedstock strategy depending on the prices realized. This problem is complex because switching is costly and cannot be accomplished instantaneously.

Clearly, there is always value in having the ability to switch feedstocks; however, that value may be very small if the costs of switching are high or the volatility of feedstock prices is low. Generally we can say that the value of the switching option is the difference in value between the plant that can switch its feedstock and the value of the plant that cannot.

NPV AND REAL OPTIONS

Many companies make avoidable NPV mistakes. According to the textbook approach, for example, a manufacturing firm should update its production methods if the present value of the benefits exceeds the present value of the costs. This is not necessarily correct. If new and better innovations are being made available over time, management may find an even better renovation alternative. If they repeatedly renovate every time they make a small gain, they will have lost the opportunity to have made a big gain on the best possible renovation.

For this reason, the NPV rule must consider the value of the option to wait to renovate. The NPV rule can be adjusted by including the lost option as a cost or by requiring the present value of benefits to exceed a predetermined multiple of the present value of the costs. This problem was first analyzed rigorously by McDonald and Siegel (1986).[2]

CASE STUDY

In 1998, the NYSEG's Homer City power plant, an 1,884 megawatt coal-fired plant located on the border of New York and Pennsylvania, sold for a price of $955 per kilowatt of capacity. Similar plants, Dunkirk and Huntley, sold for about a third of that price. What was the difference? Was it a problem of irrational exuberance on the part of the bidders, or was there something else going on?

It turns out that because of its location, the Homer City plant had the option of delivering power into New York, and into Pennsylvania and Ohio, giving it the opportunity to benefit from price discrepancies in the three regions. At one hour's notice, the plant could decide to sell in whichever market had the higher price. This real option owned by the NYSEG accounted for roughly two thirds of the market value of the plant. This case was analyzed by Robert Ethier.[3]

▸▸ MAKING IT HAPPEN

- Identify an aspect of a business where managers respond differently to different market conditions. It may be evidence of the existence of a real option.
- Value the option by considering how the company behaves with and without the flexibility.
- Evaluate the cost/benefit of increases or reductions in flexibility using the same framework.
- Apply this methodology to other corporate situations, and the valuation of acquisitions and divestitures.

"Real options represent what is possible beyond the current business operations. Investors can ignore real options, try to find real option value for free, or consciously seek out companies that have abundant real option value." Zeke Ashton

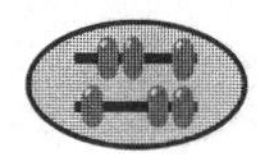

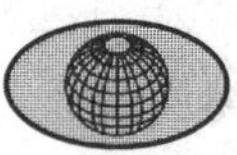

ADVANCED REAL OPTIONS

The options discussed so far were proprietary to a particular economic agent. In some cases, real options are shared, introducing an element of game theory into their valuation. For example, the option to enter a new market may be shared by one's competitors, and the value of the option depends on competitor strategy. Also, some options are compound rather than simple; in these cases, one exercises an option to obtain another option, which adds a layer of analytical complexity, but the financial intuition remains the same.

➤➤ MORE INFO

Books:

Copeland, Tom, and Vladimir Antikarov. *Real Options, Revised Edition: A Practitioner's Guide*. New York: W. W. Norton, 2001.

Kodukula, Prasad, and Chandra Papudesu. *Project Valuation Using Real Options: A Practitioner's Guide*. Fort Lauderdale, FL: J. Ross Publishing, 2006.

Mun, Jonathan. *Real Options Analysis: Tools and Techniques for Valuing Strategic Investments and Decisions*. 2nd ed. New York: Wiley, 2005.

Schwartz, Eduardo S., and Lenos Trigeorgis. *Real Options and Investment Under Uncertainty: Classical Readings and Recent Contributions*. Cambridge, MA: MIT Press, 2001.

Trigeorgis, Lenos. *Real Options: Managerial Flexibility and Strategy in Resource Allocation*. Cambridge, MA: MIT Press, 1996.

Website:

Links to articles, papers, and other resources on real options: www.puc-rio.br/marco.ind/ro-links.html

NOTES

1 A financial call option is the right to buy a security at a predetermined price for a predetermined time period. A put is the right to sell a security at preset terms.

2 McDonald, Robert, and Daniel Siegel. "The value of waiting to invest." *Quarterly Journal of Economics* 101:4 (1986): 707–728.

3 Ethier, Robert G. "Valuing electricity assets in deregulated markets: A real options model with mean reversion and jumps." February 1999. Viewable on the New York State Library website at www.nysl.nysed.gov.

"We know the good but we do not practice it." Euripides

  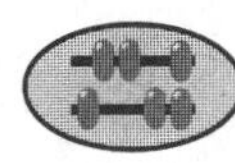 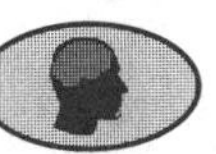  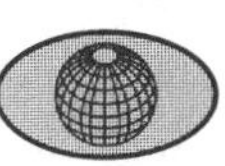 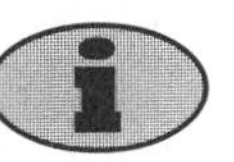  

Risk—Perspectives and Common Sense Rules for Survival by John C. Groth

EXECUTIVE SUMMARY

- "Risk" generally implies the potential for loss (gain), an unfavorable (favorable) outcome, or danger (safety).
- Uncertainty is different. Many characterize "uncertainty" as the doubt as to the outcome. Uncertainty may stem from lack of knowledge about a potential outcome, or from variability in the outcome that has nothing to do with available knowledge.
- People argue over the definition of risk and what kind of risk is relevant in the pricing of assets. Our approach defines risk as whatever risk influences investor behavior and the resultant pricing of assets.
- An increase in the perceived risks of any asset results in a decline in its value. Most economic models view this as a nonlinear relationship.
- There are "controllable" and "uncontrollable" risks. Managers need to identify the uncontrollable risks and make conscious decisions concerning exposure to such risks.
- "Unnecessary risk" is risk that can be eliminated without adversely affecting expected returns. Exposing your company to unnecessary risks garners no reward and adversely affects company value.
- Managers should employ common sense rules of risk management for survival. Esoteric models should supplement rather than displace these rules.
- Survival in an uncertain environment with exposure to risk argues for a strategy of preserving the right of choice and commitment, and avoiding positions that force a course of action.
- Managers will benefit from awareness of and a strategy for risk and uncertainty resolution versus capital commitment with time.

INTRODUCTION

We are fortunate to live in a world characterized by risk and uncertainty. Absent risk and uncertainty, with work, diligence, and access to information we could know each event that was to transpire. We would lose the opportunity for expectations, dreams, surprises, good fortune, and much more. We might as well have these "good" things, since in a certain world we presumably would still have "bad" events. Conceptually, in an uncertain world we can in fact choose to avoid *some* risks and bad events, or at least mitigate the effects of these events.

Common sense guidelines or rules will assist in garnering the benefits of bearing risk, allow us to make decisions that make sense, and protect us from unacceptable consequences. For simplification, we will consider a risk relative to a situation—for example, a new product, surgery, oil exploration, negotiating the release of hostages—and refer to the whole as a "project."

First, let's look at essentials, then some common sense rules, and after that ideas for action. Surprisingly, we admit that historically people have benefited—and in the future they will continue to benefit—from ignoring everything we say here. People have taken risks without conscious evaluation or without regard to risk–return relationships. Sometimes the results have been incredibly beneficial or rewarding. On other occasions the results have been disastrous.

SOME FUNDAMENTALS

People differ in their views concerning risk and uncertainty. "Risk" generally implies the potential for loss (gain), an unfavorable (favorable) outcome, or danger (safety). A number of investors would think of risk in a semivariance or asymmetric sense: It's only risk "if it comes out bad." More generally, one thinks of risk as an outcome that may vary (favorably or unfavorably) as a result of the underlying process(es) that will generate the outcome. With respect to investments, many define risk as the chance of variability in the outcome.

Some characterize "uncertainty" as the doubt concerning the outcome. Uncertainty may stem from lack of knowledge about a potential outcome, or from variability in the outcome that has nothing to do with available knowledge.

An "outcome" that occurs at a point in time may result from chance, the influence of variables (for example a force), or a combination of both. Often the risk of a venture may have its origin in one or more factors. In a dynamic rather than a purely mechanistic environment, the inherent risk of an investment may vary with time. Alterations in the origins of risk result from changes in the array or level of influence of variables that affect outcomes.

One can sometimes limit risk by influencing or even eliminating the influence of certain variables on outcomes. Generally, these efforts have costs that will affect the net outcome of circumstance.

For ease of discussion, we will combine risk and uncertainty in a practical way: With risk and uncertainty, we don't know for sure what will happen. Additionally, we will define "risk resolution" as the emergence of reality, the resultant impact on the variables that influence the outcome, and the event and the consequences that occur.

Core principle: *We do not live probabilities or expected values, or predicted or modeled outcomes. We live the events of reality that arrive with time.*

The demise of Long Term Capital Management (LTCM) in 1998, creating global financial panic, tells us that even the legends of Wall Street and the incredible talents of Nobel laureates cannot alter this principle. Shirreff (2004) illuminates a host of issues related to LTCM and other aspects of risk. The subprime debacle, as well as certain derivatives, shows that some continue to ignore fundamental principles, or harvest returns while foisting the risk and consequences of poor decisions on others. These and other historical events prompt us to share perspectives and common sense rules on risk.

COMMON SENSE RULES

Since we live events, not distributions or probabilities, applying some common sense rules will enable us first to survive, and second, to survive on favorable terms.

Identify All Sources of Risk[1]

Turn over every rock to unearth factors that may influence the outcome of the contemplated course of action. Sources of risk fall into major categories:

- *Inherent in the project*: For example, the ability to complete a project as anticipated, the outcome of events related to pursuit of the project, whether the oil is there or not, and technical issues.
- *External to the project*: For example, political and market factors that will influence the realization of the project and/or the benefits it brings. External factors may influence whether the project proceeds as planned (denied permits, blocked access, nonavailability of materials) and/or the realization of

"I feel very strongly that, in the short run, the market is illogical, capricious, wanton and wild in the way that it prices financial assets. It behaves just as you would expect any mechanism driven by fear and greed to behave." Robert G. Kirby

  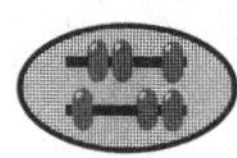   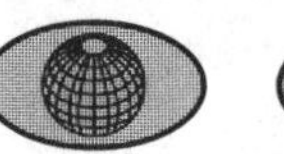   

expected benefits even if the project itself is brought to completion as expected (changes in energy prices or taxation, expropriation, etc.).

- *External–inherent effects*: Forces external to the project may affect the course of the project or its outcome. A rise in the cost of ingredients used in a food processing/marketing venture with consequent effects on markets and margins is an example.
- *Inherent–external effects*: For example, the outcome of a project may alter the external environment, as when a project changes the efficiency and economics of microchip manufacturing, with a major impact on applications and markets.

Never Bear Risk Unintentionally

Under the right circumstances the conscious bearing of risk offers opportunity. Having a source of risk that "surprises" us offers the prospect of various outcomes ranging from good, through unfavorable, to bad—perhaps uncontrollably bad or even disastrous.

Remember that risk allows the possibility of good as well as bad outcomes. An outcome that stems from the unconscious bearing of risk might offer an incredibly good reward. Recognizing the possibility of good/bad outcomes is quite different from doing well accidentally. Unfortunately, danger lurks in bearing risk unconsciously—we do not get to choose if the outcome is good or bad. Absent an awareness of the risk, unless we have succeeded in getting another party to bear all known and unknown risks, the impact of unfavorable consequences falls on us.

Overlooking or inadvertently ignoring certain risks can have a disastrous impact on outcomes. A recent disclosure suggests that a major manufacturer of aircraft may have failed to consider consciously the risks attendant on signing sales contracts denominated in one currency while having significant exposure on the input and production side in another currency. Importantly, the choice to accept such risk is logical and defensible even if the subsequent chain of events proves unattractive. *To overlook risk when making decisions differs considerably from the choice to accept a risk.*

Choose, Rather than Be Compelled, to Bear Risk

Historically, the decision to assume risk, coupled with the events that transpired, has resulted in some very beneficial outcomes. *In risk exposure, the issue is choice rather than the level of risk.* We purposely offer an example from outside economics. In 1928, a daring surgeon and a patient—the true equity in the venture—took a huge risk when the surgeon performed the first hemispherectomy on a human.[2] Individuals have taken extraordinary risks in many fields and under many circumstances so that others might benefit, and we later accord them accolades or see them as an intrepid explorer or hero.

Consciously deciding to bear a risk if there is sufficient potential benefit is logical. Inadvertently bearing risk due to a lack of diligence fails the test of judgment.

Returning to the arena of business, *recognizing and accepting* the risk inherent in exposure to multiple currencies differs considerably from discovering later that one failed to consider the risks and potential consequences of bearing this risk.

Only Take On Risk You Can Afford to Bear

Regardless of the expected return, bear risk only if the consequences of an adverse outcome are tolerable.

Common sense argues that we avoid risks with potential outcomes that *to us* are unacceptable given circumstances. Consciously accepting the risk of bankruptcy and ruin *to oneself* is acceptable. Indeed, a personal choice "to pursue the dream" in the face of huge risk has played an important role in the world, and it will always do so. To lose your own mind capital, or financial or physical capital, or even your life by electing exposure to certain risks seems defensible—and the world has benefited from such risk-takers.

In contrast, exposing *others* to a risk who cannot tolerate that risk or its potentially catastrophic outcome fails the test of common sense. More importantly, exposing others to risk they do not knowingly choose to bear fails the test of decency and morality.

Clearly Understand Who Is Bearing Risk

Knowledge of the origins and nature of the elements of risk is essential to follow this rule. Whatever the risk at a point in time for a particular project, someone is bearing the risk—either singly or divided in some fashion amongst more than one party. To illustrate, a company may feel it should not bear the collective risks of several projects during a particular time window or during certain phases of the projects. Consequently, the company may share this risk with other parties, with this shedding of the risks either permanent or transitory.

Protect Against the Reversion of Risk

If you intend to transfer risk to another party, ensure that the transfer in fact occurs. Second, protect yourself against the possibility that the risk will revert to you without your permission, or if it does, without compensation. In addition, you must assess that the party accepting the risk can tolerate/survive the risk, and also not escape the risk in a manner that transfers it back to you.[3]

The burdens of responsibility extend beyond legality. If the risk effectively reverts back to you and you accept the consequences because of your sense of social responsibility, or moral stance, or to protect your reputation, then we commend you. Rather than become the risk-bearer of last resort, instead carefully transfer the risk to those that can and will bear the risk. After all, a default on the bearing of risk defeats the objective of transferring the risk.[4]

For various reasons, a plan for risk management across time, or during the progression of events, might include the shifting of certain risks among/between parties at different points in time or with respect to particular events and outcomes. For

Figure 1. Capital invested versus time and risk resolution

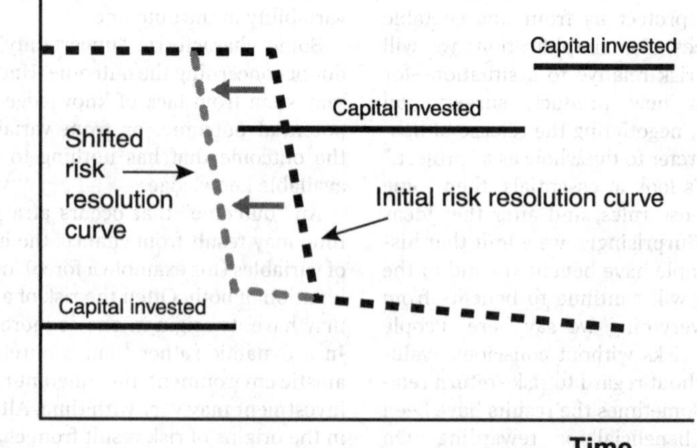

"To be a leader in this new economy, you have to love risk—which means patterning your life on the heroic, not on the strategic. Acting boldly is better than acting knowingly." Harriet Rubin

  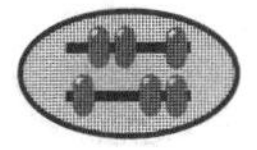 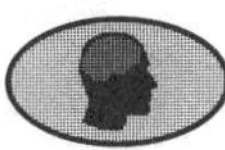  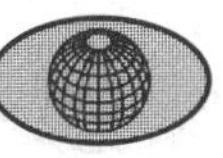   

instance, a company may choose to avoid certain risk factors during the construction of a new facility by resorting to a turnkey contract. Naturally, confidence that the party accepting the risk can comply and deliver is of paramount importance to avoid risk reversion.

Evaluate Risk Resolution with Events and/or Time

The outcome of one or more events associated with the progress of a project can have a profound effect on the level of the resolution of risk and the remaining risk for the rest of the project path. The successful synthesizing of a substance at the laboratory level and repeated replication of the synthesis can greatly alter the remaining risk in the project. Subsequent success in attaining the expected output and quality from a pilot plant would resolve more risk and cause a drop in the residual risk of the project.

Figure 1 depicts the general notion of risk resolution with events/time, without discussion of alternative scenarios and details. However, we share an example of a core issue: the commitment of capital at risk versus the resolution of risk. This example illustrates the shifting of a major risk-reduction event to an earlier point in time to resolve a major portion of uncertainty before committing the next chunk of capital. The initial risk resolution curve is shown in the figure.

As you might expect, shifting the resolution curve to the left, as indicated by the gray arrows, often entails additional costs. The analysis and decision to pursue this path should capture the relationship between those incremental costs, the chance of an unfavorable outcome, the investment schedule, and the cost of failure.

Other approaches to coping with the pattern of investment versus time versus risk resolution exist that are important if it is impossible, or prohibitively expensive, to shift the resolution curve. For example, one party desiring to participate in the venture might find it possible to take or create an option that allows it to participate if later on risk is resolved in a favorable manner. For example, a pharmaceutical company might take an option on another small company in the situation represented by the initial resolution curve, the relative bargaining positions obviously influencing the nature and terms of the option.

Divide Return and Risk Disproportionately

In many models of valuation, changes in cash returns have a linear effect on value.

Table 1. Value and changes in cash flow versus discount rate

	Year 10 cash flow	Change in cash flow	Discount rate	Present value	Change in value
A	$900		0.15	$222.47	
		($100)			($24.72)
B	$1,000	Base	0.15	$247.18	
		$100			($24.72)
C	$1,100		0.15	$271.90	
D	$1,000		0.14	$269.74	
					$22.56
E	$1,000	Base	0.15	$247.18	
					($20.50)
F	$1,000		0.16	$226.68	

Changes in the required rate of return have a nonlinear effect on value. Table 1 illustrates these relationships with a present value problem. A to B to C involve changes in cash flow, with the same dollar effect on value—up or down $24.72 as the cash flows increase or decrease from the base value–highlighted with solid line boxes.

The discount rate reflects the risk of cash flows. D, E, and F illustrate the asymmetric effects of changes in the discount rate, with different dollar effects on value. An equal increase or decrease of 1% in the rate yields an unequal change in value ($22.56 vs. $20.50).

Know the Way Out

The best analysis will not overcome the reality that we don't know what the future holds. Even if we choose a course of action that passes all the common sense tests, we still should always ask: How do I get out of here if. . .?

We hope we will not have to escape a particular circumstance. Giving some thought to that possibility will prepare us for such an undesirable outcome—even though we may take an entirely different path from those identified in this process. People are remarkably resilient and creative. Thinking through things ahead of time somehow

▸▸ MAKING IT HAPPEN

Applying the common sense rules for risk suggests the following:

- *Assess the origins of risk that may influence the potential course of action*. Classify those risks as controllable, partially controllable, or uncontrollable.
- *Focus first on the uncontrollable elements of risk*. If these factors potentially have such dire consequences as to make the outcome unacceptable, the decision is relatively simple: Get someone else to bear this risk, or abandon this course of action. Make sure that the party accepting the risk is fully able to take it on, as you don't want it to revert to you.
- *Identify the potential expected benefits of taking on the risk*. Segregate these benefits into two categories: those that are easy to quantify, and those that are hard to quantify.
- With the expected benefits identified, for controllable risks decide if you wish to bear, hedge, or transfer the risks. For partially controllable risks, evaluate whether you can afford exposure to the residual risks.
- *The quantum effect*. If you feel you have a course of action that offers the possibility of disproportionate returns—a quantum leap in terms of good effects or outcome—but you cannot rationalize the action in a risk–return context, then ignore everything I've said. Accept that you are moving from logic to feelings and commitment—and do it anyway.
- Reflect and decide if the contemplated course of action makes sense.
- Follow the common sense rules offered here.

"If a man will begin with certainties, he shall end in doubts; but if he will be content to begin with doubts, he shall end in certainty." Francis Bacon

  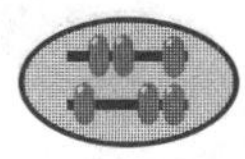 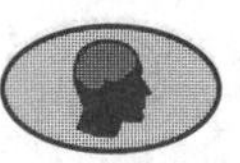  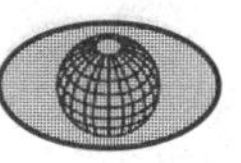   

prepares the mind to work at its best, no matter what happens.

The Common Sense Test

A final step in the analysis of a decision to be taken is the power of an important question: *Does the contemplated course of action make sense?* Step back from the details of analysis, and from any obsession with the project, and weigh it up from the perspective of an independent observer.

OTHER ISSUES

Capital at Risk

Give attention the nature of the capital at risk: financial or tangible capital—or, more importantly, human capital. Care and diligence in exposing human capital to risk are critical, for example in pharmaceutical trials or new methods of treatment. Creatively determine how to minimize human capital at risk until events/time resolve risk in a manner that assures attractive expected benefits/risks for individual human capital at risk.

Avoid Unnecessary Risk

Unnecessary risk is risk one can eliminate without adversely affecting expected returns. Capital markets will not reward one for bearing risk that one can avoid.

Normally unnecessary risk, if present, resides on the operating side of a company. For example, in a manufacturing setting we intend that specific events with specific outcomes should occur. That unintended events or outcomes occur often arises from poor management, poor design, or choice of inappropriate technology, process design, and so on.

SUMMARY

We will enjoy or endure the events that actually occur in the future—not probabilities, distributions, or expected values. Common sense rules of risk management will protect one from many adverse consequences. Ignoring these rules, and making poor judgments, may yield disastrous outcomes, as illustrated only too well by the current debacle in subprime mortgages.

Models, derivatives, financial engineering, and any array of esoteric methods or practices do not overcome the fundamental fact that we live in an uncertain world. What others do will deprive us of choice, but we ourselves can increase the uncertainty of outcomes by our own behavior and the choices we make. Great care should therefore be taken to follow the common sense rules of risk management.

▸▸ MORE INFO

Book:

Shirreff, David. *Dealing with Financial Risk.* Princeton, NJ: Bloomberg Press, 2004.

Articles:

Groth, John C. "Common-sense risk assessment." *Management Decision* 30:5 (1992): 10–16.

Groth, John C. "Environmental risk: Implications of rational lender behaviour." *Journal of Property Finance* 5:3 (1994): 19–32.

NOTES

1 Groth (1992) offers practical details on identifying and classifying risk factors.

2 The date of the first hemispherectomy on a human as well its classification as success or failure is a matter of debate, fed by issues such as the extent of the procedure as well as measures of success. The first human hemispherectomy, in 1923, is attributed to Walter Dandy, but the first complete procedure, also by Dandy, was performed in 1933. The procedure is primarily used to treat epilepsy.

3 A social conscience dictates that one not knowingly transfer risk to a third party that, because it cannot bear or tolerate the adverse outcome of the risk, or through intent, defaults and transfers the adverse outcome to society.

4 As the reader is well aware, some parties may "accept" risk for compensation with the *intent* of defaulting on the bearing of the risk and garnering (stealing) unearned returns, i.e. taking the returns without actually bearing the risk.

"The mission of a manufacturer should be to overcome poverty, to relieve society as a whole from misery and bring it wealth." Konosuke Matsushita

  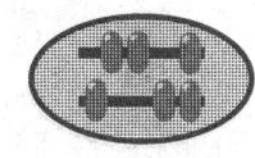 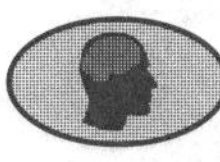  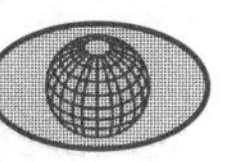 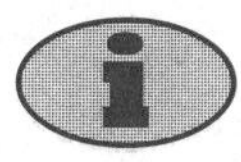  

Viewpoint: Ravi Nedungadi

The CFO and the Sustainable Corporation

INTRODUCTION

Ravi Nedungadi, President and group CFO of United Breweries Group, has steered the India-based brewing and aviation group through a number of major acquisitions. He is proud to have resisted the hard-sell tactics from investment bankers to get into exotic derivatives before their valuations tumbled. He was the youngest student ever to qualify in the final of the chartered accountancy exam at the age of 20. Early positions at industrial companies were followed by a move to UB Group in 1990 as corporate treasurer. Two years later, Nedungadi transferred to London as finance director of the group's international businesses. Appointed president and group CFO in 1998, he has led the way to sharpening the group's focus on areas of core competence and global reach. Under his leadership the market capitalization of the three principal group companies has grown to US$7.7 billion, up from US$145 million three years earlier. He has many awards, including the Udyog Ratan Award; CNBC TV18's CFO of the Year M&A (2006); the CNBC Award for India's best CFO in the FMCG & Retail Sector (2007), and the IMA Award for CFO of the year (2007). He lives in Bangalore, India, with his wife and two children.

Success means different things to different CFOs. This is because the solutions finance directors come up with are largely determined by the strategic goals of their organization, and the particular challenges of the sector and markets in which they operate.

In our own case, managing rapid growth in India's burgeoning economy over the past two decades has given our finance function some sharp lessons and made us acutely aware of the importance of remaining focused on customer satisfaction.

In the light of the spectacular implosions of some previously highly respected institutions in the banking sector and elsewhere over the course of 2008 and 2009, the importance of putting customer satisfaction—rather than the pursuit of short-term profits—at the center of the organization's business processes has been highlighted in the most dramatic way.

When our organization first began to develop an international dimension 20 years ago, it was a conglomerate. One of my first lessons was the importance of achieving a sharp focus for management and strategic thinking, since it is next to impossible to devise a coherent group-wide strategy for a conglomerate. The importance of thinking about what was core and what was noncore, and deciding where your strengths as an organization lie, were very obvious in that sort of structure.

After I became group CFO, we set about selling off noncore assets and focusing on two very clear business lines: alcoholic beverages and Kingfisher Airlines. Both are positioned in the consumer arena.

There were two major lessons from these changes. The first concerns the importance of establishing and maintaining strong brands. The second is that you will get the behavior you reward.

Regulators around the world are now taking on board the fact that what undoubtedly helped to create last year's banking disasters was a reward structure based on a very short-term and partial view of profits. If you reward exuberant greed, you get exuberant greed.

REWARDING BEHAVIORS

Ten years ago, we found that some of our drinks businesses had a long history of being focused on volumes. What mattered above all else was how many millions of liters we could ship; we lost sight of the costs of producing, selling, and shipping the product. The reward matrix and definitions of success were all about volume. The irony was that, as you competed for more and more volume, you inevitably slipped down the market to where margins were increasingly thinner, as that is where the large volumes are to be had.

So the reward matrix entrenched management behavior that was actually destroying economic value rather than creating it, since it was geared to tying up more and more resources in less and less profitable market segments.

Now the metric that really matters to me is economic value-added. It is not rocket science. It is about knowing what it costs you to make something and get it to market and knowing that you are achieving the appropriate returns to justify that effort. Our solution—one that I commend to others—is to analyze and completely recast our reward matrix to bring them into line with our strategy, which is to seek to grow margins in core markets.

We gave a tremendous degree of autonomy to senior management in our various business units, but the reward structure emphasized economic value-added, and it is focused on long-term performance over three to five years with an emphasis on driving margin improvements.

If you are aiming at the consumer market, it is impossible to overestimate the importance of establishing a strong brand. In an emerging market such as India, it is the difference between success and failure. The Indian market has been characterized by 50 years of deprivation and, as the country's economy has been growing strongly, there is a huge appetite for new experiences and for a bit of what one might call "conspicuous consumption." The pent-up demand in the young, relatively well-paid professional and semi-professional workforce is massive. But this does not mean you can take the consumer for granted.

You have to challenge your assumptions and quality standards continuously. When we chose to launch a new airline, a winning play for us was to recognize that we were not seeking to create just another transportation company. It was not going to be about volumes and filling seats. It had to be about the quality of the passenger experience from the moment they arrive at the kurbside of the airport to when they leave the airport at their destination.

None of this is about short-term thinking or short-term profits. If you look at the era of exuberant greed that characterized Wall Street for most of the last decade, you will look in vain for anything resembling a long-term strategy. The key desire was to make as much money in as short a time as possible. The client's best interests were assumed to be served by chasing the upward spiral as hard as one could. So questions about the levels of risk that clients, and ultimately the organizations themselves, were being subjected to, vanished from the radar.

RESISTING WALL STREET'S SALESMEN

People just forgot that a two decades long bull run has to end some time. In fact, one heard plenty of arguments to the effect that we had reached a point where valuations, whether of property or stocks and shares, could only ever go up. In the sheer testosterone rush of being in the thick of it all, people forgot about fundamentals.

"Our whole economy is based on planned obsolescence." Brooks Stevens

   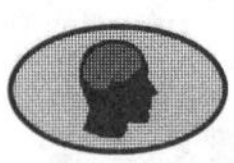  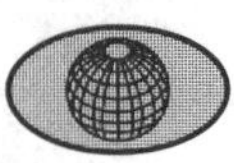   

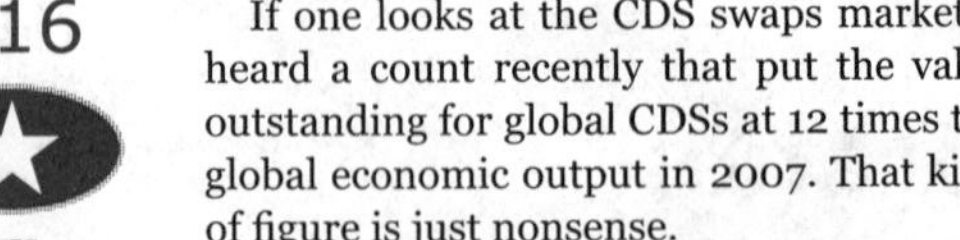

If one looks at the CDS swaps market, I heard a count recently that put the value outstanding for global CDSs at 12 times the global economic output in 2007. That kind of figure is just nonsense.

As a CFO I was contacted again and again by bankers before the crash. All of them had a similar story to tell. I was shown complex derivatives products that we were told were guaranteed to turn our treasury function into a massive profit center for the company. However, we have always taken a very prudent view of the treasury function. For us, it is essentially a defensive function, hedging us against interest rate and currency risks. That is what a properly run treasury function is supposed to do and we resisted all the instruments the bankers tried to sell us.

In retrospect, it turns out that those instruments were devised by professors of mathematics who had no idea of the real economy and were being sold by sales people who had no grasp of what they were selling.

We avoided falling into this trap not because we "saw through" the products, but because we recognized that we did not understand them. We took the decision many years ago that we would only do what we understood as an organization, and that we would look at everything else only in so far as it was necessary defensively.

So we budget for a particular exchange rate, and we hedge our position to make sure we achieve that rate, but we certainly do not look to turn a profit out of derivatives and hedge mechanisms. We look at our hedging efforts as insurance. This, in my view, is very much what the CFO should be about, preventing the organization, whatever it is, from getting into territory that management does not understand.

This does not necessarily mean being passive. We have done more acquisitions in the last 10 years than many companies around the world. I am completely supportive of the idea that a company should grow through acquisition when it sees the right opportunities. However, you have to follow the discipline of knowing why you are doing it and that your operations people are fully committed to delivering measurable results from the acquisition.

The moment an acquisition is something that some external M&A team has dreamed up for you and talked you into is the moment that you risk destroying value in your organization.

M&A THAT PAYS

When we bought our biggest competitor in the Indian drinks business for one and a half times our market capitalization at the time, it was a tremendously large venture for us. But we knew why we were doing it and what we needed to do to make it work. As a result, the acquisition delivered unprecedented returns and allowed us to grow our market capitalization 10 times in a few years.

But not every acquisition is going to be easy and, where there is a real cultural divide, it will almost certainly prove difficult. Before making acquisitions, my advice to CFOs is to devote plenty of time to understanding the target before pulling the trigger. Thereafter, once you have ensured that the right structures are in place, you should resist the temptation to swamp the acquired business with your own people. Their main role should be the temporary one of ensuring that all the reporting and other systems are what you want them to be.

What attracted us to the Scotch whisky group Whyte & Mackay, which we acquired for £600 million in May 2007, was that it gave us an opportunity to bring our brand creation strength to bear on an organization that was strongly focused on bulk Scotch. Whyte & Mackay is today selling far more branded whisky than it did in the last several years combined. The moral of the story is—know where you are strong and where you can bring your strengths to bear.

Governance in India and other emerging economies will be hugely helped by the global adoption of International Financial Reporting Standards. One of the really good things about IFRS is that it moves away from an accounting perspective based on following formal rules, which companies then "game," to prioritizing substance over form.

Of course, IFRS has its problems. Among other things, mark-to-market accounting has been criticized as having contributed to the credit crunch. There is no doubt that mark-to-market in mayhem conditions is really mark-to-meltdown, and that helps no one. But the enduring strength of IFRS is that is that it can and does constantly push one to look for substance over form, and that has to be a good thing.

Markets across the emerging economies are increasingly rewarding transparency and coherence. As companies perceive this, they will move to bring their practices in line with what the market is rewarding. When I started my career, corporate governance in India did not really exist. However, for some time now, audit committees in India have been taking it very seriously indeed.

One example is one of India's larger IT companies, which recently tried to do a related-party transaction without transparency. The institutional shareholders strongly resisted, forcing the company to reverse its stand. In the process, the company lost nearly 60 % of its market capitalization over a matter of a few days. If the markets are going to punish senior management misbehavior like this, then inappropriate or idiosyncratic management behavior that is not designed to enhance shareholder value will disappear.

▸▸ MORE INFO

Books:

Bernstein, Peter L. *Against the Gods: The Remarkable Story of Risk*. Chichester, UK: Wiley, 1998.

Bossidy, Larry, and Ram Charan. *Confronting Reality: Doing What Matters to Get Things Right*. London: Crown Business, 2004.

Charan, Ram. *Profitable Growth is Everyone's Business: 10 Tools You Can Use on Monday Morning*. London: Crown Business, 2004.

Huntsman, Jon M. *Winners Never Cheat: Everyday Values We Learned As Children*. Philadelphia, PA: Wharton School Publishing, 2005.

Middleton, Julia. *Beyond Authority: Leadership in a Changing World*. Basingstoke, UK: Palgrave Macmillan, 2007.

Taleb, Nassim Nicholas. *Fooled by Randomness: The Hidden Role of Chance in Life and in the Markets*. 2nd ed. London: Random House, 2008.

See Also:

India (pp. 1404–1406)

"The meek shall inherit the earth, but they'll never increase market share." William G. McGowan

  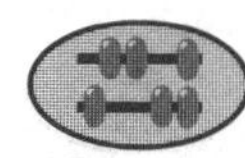   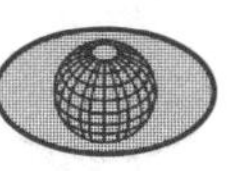   

Statistical Process Control for Quality Improvement by Priscilla Wisner

EXECUTIVE SUMMARY

- Statistical process control (SPC) is a management philosophy that relies on straightforward statistical tools to identify and solve process problems.
- By systematically identifying potential problems in process control, managers can proactively make corrections before quality outcomes suffer.
- SPC methods are useful in helping managers to measure whether their processes and products conform to design specifications, and they also help organizations to improve productivity and reduce waste.
- SPC methods are used extensively in manufacturing settings but are also relevant in the service sector.

INTRODUCTION

Statistical process control (SPC) is an optimization philosophy centered on using a variety of statistical tools to enable continuous process improvement. Closely linked to the total quality management (TQM) philosophy, SPC helps firms to improve profitability by improving process and product quality. Although initially used in manufacturing, SPC tools and methods work equally well in a service environment.

SPC methods are used extensively by organizations to enable systematic learning. Using methods developed in the 1920s by Walter Shewhart and subsequently enhanced by quality consultants William Edwards Deming and Joseph Juran, organizations are able to use a set of straightforward statistics to find out whether or not their processes conform to expectations. Furthermore, the use of SPC methods can help to identify instances of process variation that may signal a problem in the process. By identifying process variation and potential nonconformance with design expectations early in the production or service environment, managers can proactively make corrections before the process variation negatively impacts quality and customer perceptions.

AN OVERVIEW

Although SPC is enabled with statistical analysis, the management philosophy that underlies SPC is much broader than a set of statistics. To improve a process systematically, managers must first identify key processes and key variables of interest. Every organization has hundreds, if not thousands, of processes and variables that can affect product and service outcomes, and one challenge is to focus on the processes and variables that are of key concern. SPC tools can be useful in identifying areas that need attention, but managerial insight is needed to use the SPC tools strategically.

Managers can directly influence organizational performance using SPC practices. Their choice of key processes and performance variables creates a feed-forward signaling device to the organization about key performance indicators. This causes attention to be paid to these processes and variables. Feedback is then received through the SPC information, enabling evaluation of the data and an opportunity for corrective actions to be taken. Thus, SPC is not merely a set of statistical tools, but a management philosophy that helps organizations to improve performance through feed-forward and feed-back loops.

SPC TOOLS

The SPC toolkit contains a number of tools to help managers to evaluate processes. Many of the tools were first identified as essential to continuous quality improvement by Kaoru Ishikawa, a Japanese quality expert. This section describes a number of the tools that are commonly used by organizations to evaluate and improve quality performance. To learn more about how to construct each of these and other SPC tools, refer to the More Info section at the end of this article, where details and links are given.

Flowcharts

Flowcharts depict the progress of work through a series of defined steps. They can be used to communicate a process to employees who are being trained for the work, and management can use them to evaluate process flows, constraints, and gaps. The symbols used in flowcharting are standardized; some of the more commonly used are rectangles (activities and tasks), diamonds (decision points), rectangles with a wavy base (documents), cylinders (files), and arrows (linkages). The flowchart in Figure 1 demonstrates an order entry process.

Figure 1. Flowchart for an order entry process

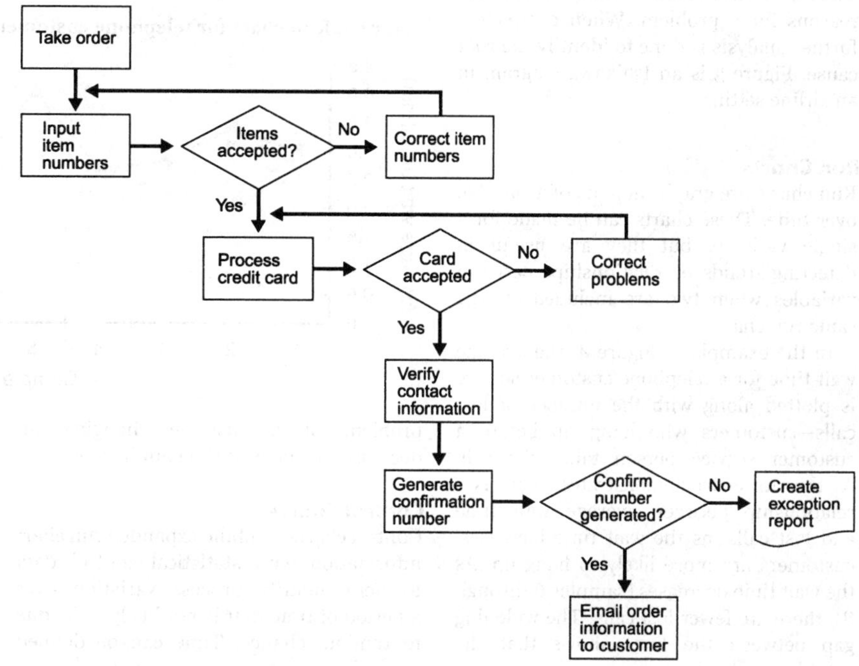

"Not everything that can be counted counts; and not everything that counts can be counted." George Gallup

Pareto Charts

Pareto charts are graphical demonstrations of occurrences, with the most frequently occurring event to the left and less frequent occurrences to the right. Pareto charts are named after Vilfredo Pareto, an Italian economist who identified that 80% of the wealth is held by a relatively small share of the population. This has been translated into the Pareto principle, which says that about 80% of outcomes are typically created by about 20% of causes. By constructing a Pareto chart, managers can quickly see what problems are most prevalent in their organizations.

The Pareto chart in Figure 2 shows the occurrences of accidents in a manufacturing organization; 58% of the accidents in the plant are falls, followed by broken bones at 21%. The managers can see that these two types of accident are the most prevalent, and they are perhaps related.

Figure 2. Pareto chart of accidents in a manufacturing plant

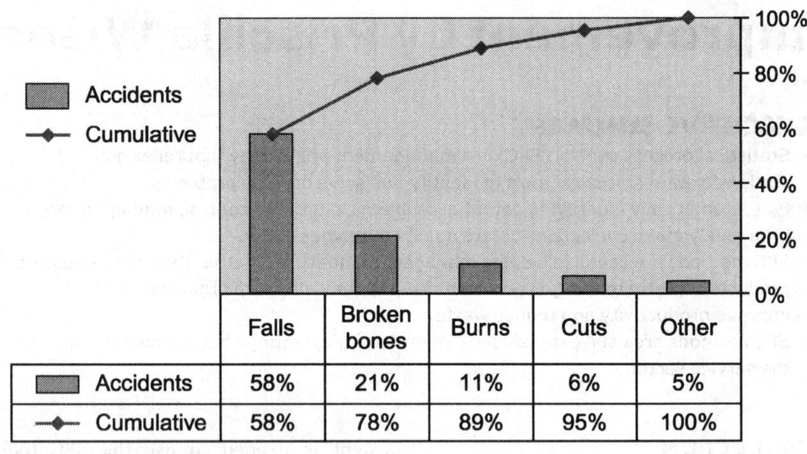

	Falls	Broken bones	Burns	Cuts	Other
Accidents	58%	21%	11%	6%	5%
Cumulative	58%	78%	89%	95%	100%

Ishikawa Cause-and-Effect or Fishbone Diagrams

These diagrams depict an array of potential causes of quality problems. The problem (the head of the fish) is displayed on the right, and the bones of the fish—representing the potential causes of the problem—are drawn to the left. Potential causes are often categorized as materials, equipment, people, environment, and management. Other categories may be included as appropriate. Useful in brainstorming the causes of problems (including potential problems) from multiple perspectives, these diagrams should include all possible reasons for a problem. When completed, further analysis is done to identify the root cause. Figure 3 is an Ishikawa diagram in an airline setting.

Figure 3. Ishikawa diagram prepared for investigation of cause(s) of delayed flight departures

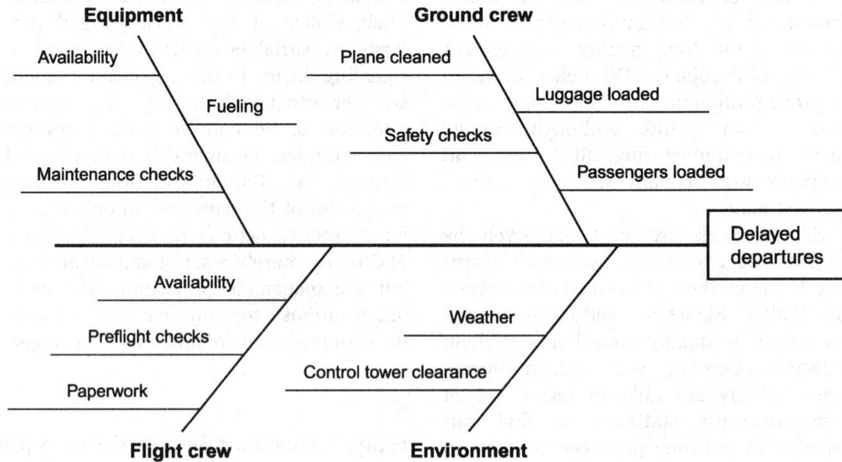

Run Charts

Run charts are graphical plots of a variable over time. These charts can be made for a single variable, but they are useful in detecting trends or relationships between variables when two are included on the same run chart.

In the example in Figure 4, the average wait time for a telephone customer service is plotted along with the number of lost calls—customers who hang up before a customer service person takes the call. As the run chart demonstrates, there is a relationship between average wait time and lost calls: as the wait time increases, customers are more likely to hang up. As the wait time decreases (samples 6 through 8), there are fewer lost calls. The widening gap between the lines shows that the problem of a customer hanging up decreases as the wait time diminishes.

Figure 4. Run chart for telephone customer service

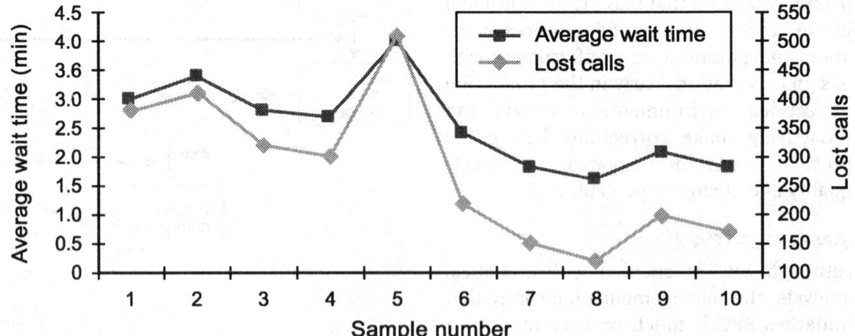

Control Charts

Control charts combine expanded run chart information with statistical control data to help identify process variation over a period of time that is not likely to be due to random chance. Time can be defined as a production run, a series of batches, a day's activities, or any relevant time period that captures the process being evaluated. Useful in manufacturing, administrative, and service functions, control charts provide rapid feedback on key variables of interest. Control variables of interest might include those listed in Table 1.

  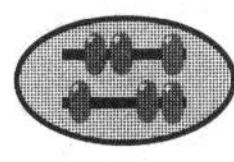 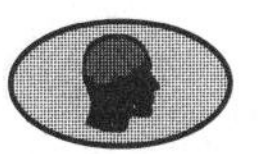  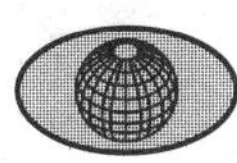   

Table 1. Examples of control variables in different business sectors

Manufacturing environment	Service environment
Liters of liquid in a container	Wait time in a bank line
Thickness of a coating	Delivery time for packages
Tension in a coil	Temperature of a restaurant entrée
Direct labor time per unit	Time lag between a customer request and a service response
Changeover time between batches	Infection rates in a medical setting
Defect rates	Loan approval time
Overhead costs	

Control charts are used to show when a process is in, or out of, statistical control. Statistical control does not imply zero variation—some degree of variation is normal and it is unrealistic to expect zero variation. However, the control chart is able to demonstrate data patterns that indicate that a process is out of control, and it is useful as a tool for making continuous improvement by reducing variability. The most commonly employed control charts are the mean chart and the range chart, often referred to as X-bar and R-charts.

The Mean Chart

The mean chart (X-bar chart) shows the variation in a process by plotting the actual mean values of a set of sample data. Each set of sample data consists of multiple observations of the process that's being evaluated. These data are plotted against the background of the mean of all the samples taken and the upper and lower control limits for the data. These limiting bounds are each three-sigma limits, meaning that almost all (99.73%) of the variation in the process is expected to fall within a six-sigma limit. Sigma, represented by the Greek symbol s, is the standard deviation of a distribution.

Signals from a mean chart that a process is out of control include the following:

- Data points that fall above the upper control limit or below the lower control limit.
- Eight or more consecutive data points that fall above or below the mean line.
- Two out of three consecutive points in the lower or upper third of the chart.
- Six or more consecutive data points that trend up or down within the chart, as this indicates a trend or drift of the variation in the process.
- Fourteen or more points that alternate in an up or down direction, indicating that there may be too much variation in the process.

Figure 5 is an example of a mean control chart, constructed for a month's sample data. The chart shows that samples 2, 9, and 16 are all above the upper control limit, indicating a problem. Interestingly, each of these samples was taken on the same day of the week (each is seven days apart). Another problem highlighted by the chart is the set of daily sample means recorded after day 20. Starting on that day, a series of sample means falls below the mean for the set of data. Although these data points are all within the control limits, they indicate a potential problem in the process because more than eight consecutive points fall below the mean.

The Range Chart

The range chart (R-chart) is similar to the mean chart in having upper and lower (three-sigma) control limits, but the data plotted for each sample are now the *range* between the largest and the smallest value in the sample. By plotting the range of values, variation within each sample is more apparent.

Signals from a range chart indicating that a process is out of control are similar to those for the mean chart and include the following:

- Data points that fall above the upper control limit or below the lower control limit.
- Eight or more data points in succession that fall above or below the mean.
- Six or more consecutive data points that trend up or down, as this indicates

Figure 5. Mean control chart for a production process (y axis represents mean values)

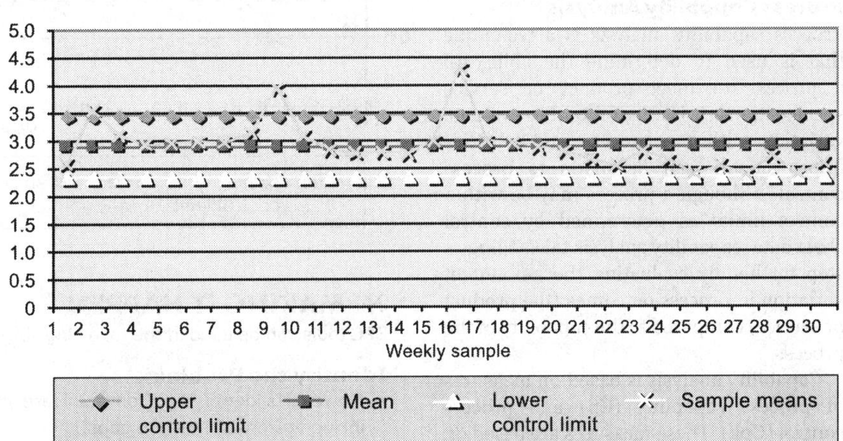

CASE STUDY

Graco Children's Products[1]

Graco Children's Products, a US manufacturer of children's equipment such as high chairs, baby swings, and car seats, set itself the goal of improving product quality in the design phase of operations. By identifying problems early in the design process, the firm expected to reap benefits in manufacturing performance, product quality, and customer satisfaction.

Using SPC tools, Graco managers were able to analyze multiple design options efficiently. For example, in the plastics injection molding area there were more than 30 variables of interest to evaluate. One analysis was done for a plastic grip handle on a child carrier seat. The handle had a problem with warping, which caused too much curvature in the part, making later assembly of the carrier seat difficult. Eight machine variables were identified as potential causes of the problem. By using SPC analysis data, Graco determined that three variables—hold time, cure time, and material temperature—significantly impacted warping. By modifying these processes, the organization was able to correct the problem and reduce associated costs. The SPC analysis also showed that cooling temperatures did not significantly impact quality outcomes, which led to a decision not to invest in expensive cooling equipment. By using SPC tools to focus attention on process variables that could be controlled in the design phase of the product, Graco managers improved process and product quality, which resulted in savings for the organization.

  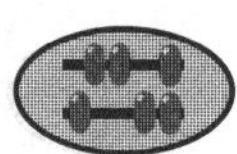   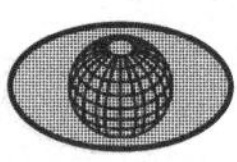 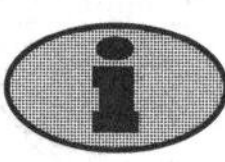  

- a trend or drift of variation in the process.
- Fourteen or more points that alternate in up and down directions, indicating that there may be too much variation in the process.

The range chart in Figure 6, which has been constructed for the same set of data as the mean chart, demonstrates that there is wide variation in the sample data. As in the mean chart, the three data points that fall outside the upper control limit indicate a process that is not in control. The strong variability in consecutive data points also indicates potential problems in process control. As a general rule, although data points may fall within the control limits, variations from the norm can be pointers to performance problems, product returns, possible lawsuits, loss of customer loyalty, and loss of reputation. All of these risks can be costly for an organization.

Process Capability Analysis

Process capability analysis is a technique that is used to determine the ability of a process to meet product or service specifications. It is a useful tool to evaluate variation within a process and whether improvements can be made to process control. Although a process may be within control limits as determined by control chart data, capability analysis takes things a step further by evaluating the amount of variation in process outcomes (the product or service) compared to the capability of the process.

Capability analysis is based on measures of process capability (Cp) and process control (Cpk). These measures are based on the means and standard deviations of a process variable and are indicators of the aptitude, or capability, of the process to perform. Similarly, measures of actual process performance (Pp) and process control (Ppk) demonstrate how a process is actually performing. A comparison of the actual process control data (Ppk) with the process capability data (Cpk) helps managers to evaluate numerically how much variation there is in an in-control (within control limits) process, and whether modifications of the process will reduce variation. Refer to the iSixSigma website for details of process capability calculations and uses.

Taguchi Loss Function

The Taguchi loss function is based on the assumption that all variation has a cost, even when the variation does not violate the data patterns defined by control charts. This concept is most useful where deviations from expectation are expected to be costly. Taguchi posited that all deviations from target values ultimately result in customer dissatisfaction. The Taguchi loss function enables organizations to calculate the financial consequence of process variability, making it useful in reaching design decisions.

CONCLUSION

Statistical process control benefits organizations by providing a systematic method for the monitoring and evaluation of process variation. Too often, managers do not notice changes and problems in processes until either the output is inspected or customers make complaints.

By proactively identifying potential process problems and using SPC tools to evaluate process outcomes and improve process control, organizations are able to direct their resources more efficiently and can focus management time and attention on the most pressing problems.

Figure 6. Range chart for same process data as in Figure 5 (y axis represents difference between largest and smallest values within a sample of data)

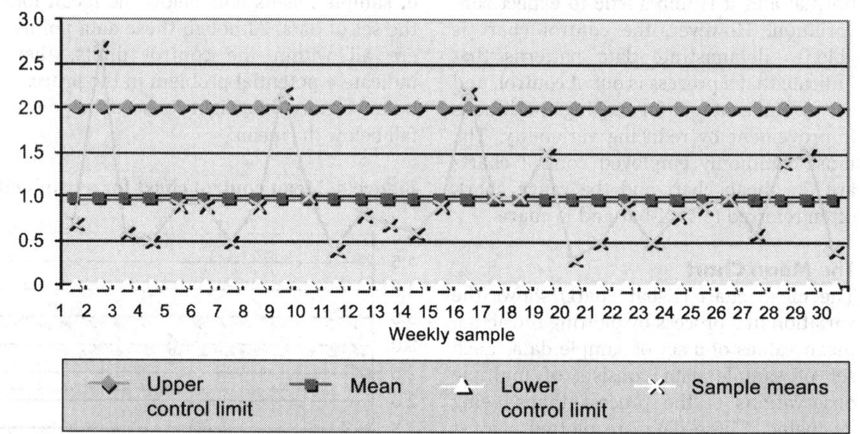

▸▸ MAKING IT HAPPEN

SPC tools can be used in the following stages of process evaluation and improvement:

Identify the Problem

- Flowcharts identify and communicate information about the flow of a process, including constraints and gaps.
- Pareto analysis identifies the issues that are causing most of the problems.

Identify the Reasons for the Problem

- Use Ishikawa cause-and-effect diagrams to brainstorm the causes of a problem from a multidimensional perspective.

Analyze the Data

- Run charts show the variability in data over time and the potential relationships between multiple variables.
- Control charts identify process variation using a set of statistical tools, enabling the identification of out-of-control variation.
- Process capability analysis is used to show the amount of variation in an in-control process, and can be useful in improving a process.
- The Taguchi loss function assigns an economic value to variation, helping to make trade-off decisions in process and product design.

"That action is best, which provides the greatest happiness for the greatest numbers." Francis Hutcheson

  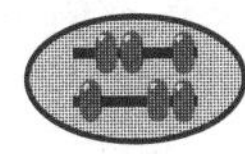 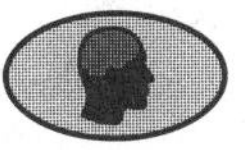  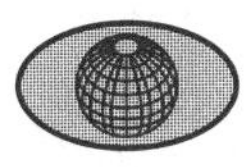   

▸▸ MORE INFO

Books:

Amsden, Robert T., Howard E. Butler, and Davida M. Amsden. *SPC Simplified: Practical Steps to Quality*. 2nd ed. New York: Productivity Press, 1998.

Crossley, Mark. L. *The Desk Reference of Statistical Quality Methods*. 2nd ed. Milwaukee, WI: ASQ Quality Press, 2007.

Pyzdek, Thomas. *The Six Sigma Handbook: The Complete Guide for Green Belts, Black Belts, and Managers at All Levels*. New York: McGraw-Hill, 2003.

Websites:

American Society for Quality (ASQ), a professional association dedicated to learning about quality and the improvement of quality in organizations. ASQ administers the prestigious Malcolm Baldrige National Quality Award. Membership is available to individuals or organizations: www.asq.org

iSixSigma, an online forum and extensive statistical process control resources: www.isixsigma.com

Management and Accounting Web (MAAW), dedicated to education, research, and the practice of management and accounting disciplines. Contains links to dozens of management and finance resources: www.maaw.info

Managers-Net, an archive of articles and examples of management topics. Click on "Contents" and then on "Index to the complete Technical Archive" for an alphabetical list of topics: managers-net.com

Quality America, Inc., has resources for implementing SPC tools, including articles, an encyclopedia, technical references, and interpretation guides for SPC analysis: qualityamerica.com

See Also:

★ Profitability Analysis Using Activity-Based Costing (pp. 801–804)
★ Reducing Costs and Improving Efficiency by Outsourcing and Selecting Suppliers (pp. 499–501)
★ Reducing Costs through Change Management (pp. 502–504)
★ Reducing Costs through Production and Supply Chain Management (pp. 505–507)
★ Turning Around Financial Performance (pp. 825–827)
The Six Sigma Way: How GE, Motorola and Other Top Companies are Honing Their Performance (p. 1317)

"**These capitalists generally act harmoniously and in concert to fleece the people.**" Abraham Lincoln

   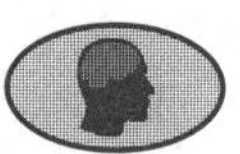  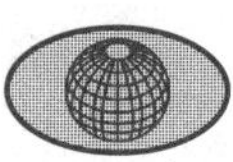   

Toward a Total Global Strategy by George Yip

EXECUTIVE SUMMARY

- Globalization has become a goal for many companies.
- But simply spreading activities around the globe is not enough; companies need coherent global strategies.
- In the past, multinationals tailored their products and services to local markets. This represented a multi-local rather than global approach.
- The challenge now is to develop truly integrated global strategies that leverage competitive advantage across all markets.

INTRODUCTION

In the 1980s and the 1990s, many companies were still debating whether they should globalize. For most, this debate has now ended. Companies assume that they should globalize unless they can find very good reasons not to.

The spread of the internet and the Web provides one compelling reason. Any company that creates a website has instant global reach, with corresponding demands for delivery and service. In addition, evidence shows that companies that globalize achieve better competitive and financial performance.

But globalizing, in the sense of spreading activities around the world, is not enough. Companies also need to be globally integrated. They need globally coherent strategies, global networks, and the ability to maximize profits on a global basis. However, turning a collection of country businesses into one worldwide business that has an integrated, global strategy is not easy. It presents one of the stiffest challenges for managers today. Developing and implementing an effective global strategy is the acid test of a well-managed company.

THE CASE FOR GLOBALIZATION

Whatever the anti-globalization protestors may say to the contrary, a range of forces is driving companies around the world to globalize. Many managers view this as expanding their participation in foreign markets. But companies also need to globalize in another sense. They need to integrate their worldwide strategy. This contrasts with the traditional multinational approach.

In the past, multinationals have tended to set up country subsidiaries that design, produce, and market products or services that were tailored to local needs. But this model is now in question. Increasingly, the multinational approach is seen as a "multilocal strategy" rather than a truly global strategy.

Today, a growing number of managers are asking, if they are in a global industry, whether their business should have a global strategy. Better questions are: how global is our industry, and how global should our business strategy be? This is because virtually every industry has aspects that are global or potentially global. But some industries have more aspects that are global, and more intensely so.

Similarly, a strategy can be more or less global in its different elements. An industry is global to the extent that there are inter-country connections. A strategy is global to the extent that it is integrated across countries. Global strategy should not be equated with any one element—standardized products, or worldwide market coverage, or a global manufacturing network. Instead, global strategy should be a flexible combination of many elements.

BEYOND THE MULTINATIONAL MODEL

Recent and coming changes make it likely that in many industries a global strategy will be more successful than a multilocal one. Indeed, having a sound global strategy may well be the requirement for survival as the changes accelerate. These changes include: the increasing convergence of consumer tastes across countries; the reduction of tariff and non-tariff barriers; technology investments that are becoming too expensive to amortize in one market only, and competitors who are moving from country-by-country competition to global competition.

CASE STUDIES

Gillette

Gillette, the US shaving products company, provides one of the most aggressive examples of globally standardized strategy. While many corporate strategies still regard local adaptations as essential to their success in foreign markets, Gillette minimizes adaptation for cultural differences. The company sells the same products, uses the same production methods, enforces the same corporate policies, and uses the same advertising in every country where it conducts business.

The results are impressive. The company now dominates the shaver market with a 70% market share worldwide. The main advantages of this business model are scale and flexibility, most notable in research and development costs and leveraging intellectual capital across the globe. In addition, the company is more nimble. This was demonstrated during the Asian crisis in the late 1990s. Rather than maintain advertising expenditures in an area with flat to negative growth, Gillette chose to shift its marketing funds to Eastern Europe, where better sales growth was forecast. It is because the company treats the world as one region that it has such flexibility in its operations.

Toyota

Toyota is another company that has benefited from an integrated global approach. It recognized early that in the automobile industry, where some local customization is essential, a global strategy requires multi-regional production. In the late 1990s, Toyota spent over $10 billion on global expansion in an aggressive effort to become the first truly globally organized car manufacturer. The company developed manufacturing hubs in the three major markets—North America, Europe, and Asia—with the ability to customize vehicles for regional markets.

Such extensive coverage now allows Toyota to react quickly to local tastes, bypass regional trade barriers, and utilize locally based suppliers to increase cost efficiencies. The company set up an assembly plant in the United States as early as 1987 and continued expansion at a number of sites there and in Canada throughout the 1990s.

In Europe, by 2001, Toyota had a regional parts center in Belgium, and manufacturing plants in the United Kingdom, France, and Turkey (another is scheduled to open in Poland in 2002). This local production allows Toyota to bypass tariffs and locally produce Toyota's "Europe Car." In Asia, a local network of suppliers and assembly hubs allows Toyota to build sturdy, simply designed, low-priced cars that appeal to the Asian consumer.

"It's ridiculous to call this an industry—it's not. This is rat eat rat, dog eat dog." Ray Kroc

In the 1990s, the world saw greater convergence in customer needs and tastes; the drastic reduction of many government barriers to free trade and investment; an acceleration of enablers in communications, and a surge in globally applicable new technological products and services. All this does not mean that every industry has become entirely global. But today, nearly every industry has a significant global segment in which customers prefer products or services that are much more global in nature.

Around the global segments, however, regional, national, or sub-national niches still exist. The size of the global segment varies, from very large in the personal computer industry, to relatively small in many parts of the food industry. But the global segment is increasing in size in nearly all cases.

TUMBLING BARRIERS TO TRADE

Around the world, trade barriers continue to fall. The most important examples include: the North American Free Trade Agreement among the United States, Canada, and Mexico; the continuing integration of the European Union; the formation of the new World Trade Organization in 1995, and China joining that body in 2001. The Asian Crisis of 1997 to 1999 has also helped to open up economies such as Japan and South Korea.

At the same time, the rise of the newly industrializing countries (NICs) such as Hong Kong, Taiwan, South Korea, Singapore, Thailand, Malaysia, Mexico, and Brazil has increased the number of viable sites for sophisticated manufacturing operations with low labor costs. Even China and India are beginning to join the industrialized world and the global market economy.

Almost every product or service market in the major world economies now has foreign competitors. They compete to sell everything from computers, to fast food, or medical diagnostic equipment. Increasing foreign competition is itself a reason for a business to globalize in order to gain the size and skills to compete more effectively. But an even greater spur to globalization is the advent of new global competitors who manage and compete on an integrated global basis.

THE GLOBAL REVOLUTION

In the 1980s these global competitors were primarily Japanese. Their central approach to global competition was one of the factors that allowed Japanese companies to conquer so many Western markets. In the 1990s, American and European companies

▸▸ MAKING IT HAPPEN

So how can companies create truly global strategies? For most, there are three separate stages involved.

1 Developing the core strategy: this is the basis of sustainable strategic advantage. It is usually, but not necessarily, developed for the home country first. Without a sound core strategy to build upon, a global strategy cannot be successful.

2 Internationalizing the core strategy: this stage involves the international expansion of activities, and adaptation of the core strategy. Companies need to have mastered the basics of international business before they can attempt a global strategy (because the latter often involves breaking the rules of international business).

3 Globalizing the international strategy: this involves integrating the strategy across countries to leverage the company's total global potential.

Multinational companies are usually adept at the first two steps. What they are less familiar with is the third stage. For one thing, total globalization runs counter to the accepted wisdom of tailoring for national markets. Yet, it is this third step that is vital to creating a successful total global strategy.

The first step towards a global strategy, then, is the creation of a viable core strategy. This involves several key elements:

- selection of the type of products or services that the business offers;
- the types of customers that the business serves;
- the geographic markets served;
- major sources of sustainable competitive advantage;
- functional strategy for each of the most important value-adding activities;
- competitive posture, including the selection of competitors to target;
- investment strategy.

At the second stage, a business expands outside its home market and needs to internationalize its core business strategy. The key to internationalizing is to select the geographic markets in which to compete. This choice has much more importance for an international business than for a national business.

For most businesses, international market selection presents issues that are much more challenging. These include the role of barriers to trade—such as import tariffs and quotas, and foreign ownership rules—as well as differences from the home country in laws, language, tastes, and behavior. Other aspects of internationalization strategy involve how to adapt products and programs to take account of foreign needs, preferences, culture, language, climate, and so on.

Typically, the end result is that the company ends up with strategies and approaches that involve large differences among countries. These differences can then weaken the company's worldwide cost position, quality, customer preference, and competitive leverage.

This is where a global strategy comes in. It involves strategic integration across all markets to leverage competitive advantage.

A key issue here is: what aspects of strategy should be globalized? Managers can answer this question by analyzing industry conditions or "industry globalization drivers." This provides the basis for evaluating the benefits and costs of globalization, and creates a clearer understanding of the different ways in which a globalization strategy can be used through the use of "global strategy levers."

Industry globalization drivers are externally determined by industry conditions or by the economics of the business. They fall into four groups—market, cost, government, and competitive drivers.

Taken together, these represent the industry conditions that determine the potential and need for competing with a global strategy. Each group of drivers is different for each industry and can also change over time.

Global strategy levers, on the other hand, are the choices available to the business. They operate along five dimensions:

- market participation—involves the choice of country markets, and the level of activity;
- products/services—involves the extent to which business offers the same or different products in different countries;
- location of value-adding activities—involves the choice of where to locate each of the activities that comprise the entire value-added chain, from research to production to after-sales service;
- marketing—involves the extent to which a business uses the same brand names, advertising and other marketing elements in different countries;

     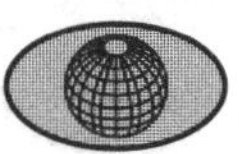   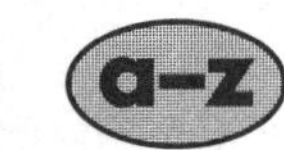

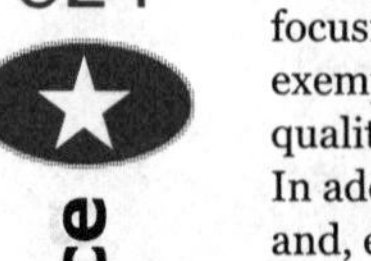

responded to the Japanese challenge by focusing much more on quality. This was exemplified by the adoption of "six-sigma" quality by General Electric and Motorola. In addition, a growing number of American and, especially, European companies began to develop new models of globalization that were more flexible than the centralized Japanese approach. Companies such as Asea Brown Boveri, for example, developed networked models that combined the benefits of both global integration and national responsiveness.

In recent years, the communications and information revolution has also made it much easier to apply a globally integrated approach to management. Improvements in air travel, computers, satellites and telecommunications make it much easier to communicate with, and control, far-flung operations. Today, in a world where e-mail has become pervasive, it is easy to forget the dramatic impact of the humble facsimile machine. Its immediacy plugged every executive's desk into the global market. The internet and the Web completed this revolution.

- competitive moves—involves the extent to which a worldwide business makes competitive moves in individual countries as part of a global competitive strategy;

A global strategy should aim to ensure that all global strategy levers are optimally positioned relative to the industry drivers, and relative to the position and resources of the business and its parent company. In this way, a company ensures that the global whole is greater than the sum of its local parts.

MORE INFO

Books:

Yip, George S. *Total Global Strategy II*. Harlow, UK: Prentice Hall, 2002.

Yip, George S. *The Asian Advantage: Key Strategies for Winning in the Asia-Pacific Region*. Cambridge, MA: Perseus, 2000.

See Also:

- Igor Ansoff (p. 1151)
- Lou Gerstner (p. 1167)
- Corporate Strategy: An Analytic Approach to Business Policy for Growth and Expansion (p. 1243)

"**We have been finely duped. . .full of courtesy, full of craft.**" Maria Edgeworth

     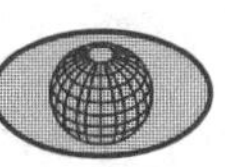   

Turning Around Financial Performance by David Magee

EXECUTIVE SUMMARY

When financial performance lags, a full-scale, company-wide plan of action is required to get the best and longest-lasting results. Merely dictating cost reductions is not enough to foster true change within the organization. At Nissan, CEO Carlos Ghosn, who now runs both Nissan and Renault, implemented a grass-roots process designed to force employees to find cost-saving solutions. Ghosn drastically turned around the company's performance over a span of two years using the following tools:

- cross-functional teams
- identifying root problems
- eliminating costs the customer does not see
- investing in product design

INTRODUCTION

No business, big or small, is immune from needing to address and correct financial performance. Often the reason is obvious, such as when a once-reliable bottom line turns negative, placing employee jobs, ownership equity, and product or service quality at risk. Sometimes, however, the need and potential benefits are not so obvious.

Take General Electric as an example. This stalwart American blue-chip corporation, in business for more than 100 years, was considered one of the world's best-managed companies when Jack Welch took over as company chairman and CEO in 1981. GE was profitable, but the period was recessionary in the United States, and the stock had languished for years. So, Welch made the assumption that good was not good enough.

He began drastic cost-cutting measures across the board, eliminating more than 100,000 jobs and millions of dollars in costs. At the same time, Welch put processes in place to strengthen the organization from within, focusing on human resources development, while investing heavily in leadership training. By the end of the 1990s, GE's stock was recognized for its consistently high returns, and Welch was known as one of the 20th century's top business leaders.

LISTEN DEEPLY

Typically, the need to address financial performance comes when that of a business has fallen below acceptability, either losing money or is not up to normal bottom-line standards. Such was the case with Japanese automaker, Nissan, in the late 1990s. A one-time industry leader, Nissan was losing millions of dollars annually, and teetering near bankruptcy, when French automaker Renault took a controlling stake in the company. Renault infused Nissan with much-needed capital, but that was the least of its contributions to the company.

A young, relatively unknown leader named Carlos Ghosn became the CEO of Nissan, and his mission was to turn around financial performance in three months. The company's demise had taken years, so there were many skeptics, yet Ghosn formulated a turnaround strategy designed to deliver quick and lasting results.

First, he traveled to all of Nissan's factories and facilities, spending most of his time with middle-management workers, asking questions about their jobs and facilities, and listening deeply. Management, he assumed, did not have the answers. He needed to listen to the core employee group of the company. Then, Ghosn returned to Nissan and implemented a plan designed to cultivate solutions to the company's problems from the ground up.

Creating nine cross-functional teams to assess each area of the business, including purchasing, research, administrative, and finance, Ghosn challenged them to find, within 90 days, cost-cutting solutions worth hundreds of millions of dollars. Each team was assigned a top company vice-president as a member, but that person was not placed in charge, as Ghosn believed lower-level employees would not

CASE STUDY

Nissan's position as a profitable and viable global automaker was in complete default by 1999. The once-strong company had lost money for six of seven consecutive years, beginning in 1992. Its global market share was in decline and the company was losing, on average, US$1,000 per vehicle sold in the United States. Carlos Ghosn knew that regeneration of the company product was imperative, but the product alone would not save the company. Thus, he devised a cost-saving strategy to improve financial performance, allowing Nissan to ramp up its product development, thereby saving the company and sending it on a path to profitability.

The reasons identified by Ghosn, and the team he charged with solving the company's financial crisis, included:

- lack of profit orientation;
- lack of cross-functional communication and teamwork;
- no sense of urgency;
- protection of long-standing, nonbeneficial relationships;
- lack of shared vision and long-term goal orientation.

Through the deployment of problem-solving, cross-functional and cross-company teams (Renault had just became the owner of Nissan), Ghosn and Nissan arrived at a solution. Cost savings would be achieved through the following tactics:

- changing relationships with suppliers (none were off-limits);
- reducing staff overheads;
- closing nonviable plants and eliminating nonprofitable products;
- debt reduction;
- establishing clear pay-for-performance guidelines for all employees, including executives;
- establishing a clear leadership succession plan for the long term.

The results, implemented in all their aspects, led to immediate financial improvement, allowing Nissan to invest more in the product while giving more to shareholders. The Nissan Revival Plan was completed one full year early, with better-than-expected outcomes. Profits soared to record heights (more than US$3.8 billion in 2002), although market share remained relatively flat.

then speak up enough. Instead, middle- and upper-middle-level employees were named as pilots, charged with guiding the team on its mission.

Ghosn's reasoning for creating a cross-functional structure for the task was simple: by creating teams with employees from different disciplines, members would be forced to challenge one another objectively and give answers honestly. And by forcing the teams to work to a tight deadline, he gave them less time to find excuses.

"Three months was the longest time I could imagine," said Ghosn. "Multitask work is simply a question of exercise. If you work on trying to act quickly, you will be good at it. When you know that time is important, you learn to work faster."

Many believed Nissan could not be fixed, because the company was part of Japan's interlinked business network, or *keiretsu*, which dictated many banking and supplier relationships that were not necessarily in the company's best interest, yet nobody wanted to break the long-held ties. For instance, the company had literally hundreds of bank accounts, spreading its wealth throughout its *keiretsu*, but finance had previously refused to consolidate them, thus saving costs, arguing it would end vital cross-company relationships. Ghosn did not buy that argument, however, giving the cross-company teams a firm directive: "No sacred cows, no taboos, no constraints," he said.

SEND TEAMS BACK TO THE DRAWING BOARD

In the beginning, the cross-functional teams were hesitant, and the process did not go as fast as Ghosn had hoped. Most members did not know each other well, if at all, so at first, they had to find ways of working with one another. Ghosn asked for weekly updates, and for the first few weeks recommendations were not at all aggressive, shying away from what they thought was not possible. Ghosn pushed them back to the drawing board, urging them to go and see for themselves when necessary, to find the root cause of problems.

If, for example, bolts used in car manufacturing were costing the company more than they should, the team needed to find out why, and recommend eliminating the problem. If banking costs were too high, the team should benchmark (a point of reference for measurement) against other companies and other industries to find a standard. Then, Nissan should recommend cost-cutting to meet that standard, regardless of long-standing company relationships. Similarly, even though Japan practiced "jobs for life," if the company needed to eliminate positions to restore financial credibility, the teams were responsible for providing that information.

By the end of the 90 days, Nissan's cross-functional teams had made considerable progress. Ghosn had instructed them to present him with two sets of numbers:

1 recommended cuts, those they deemed were sufficient to meet the aggressive demands;
2 stretch cuts, the highest conceivable number they could come up with.

He assessed each of the recommendations himself, line by line, and reached a firm decision.

IMPLEMENT TO THE MAXIMUM LEVEL

There are many benefits from using cross-functional teams to solve a company's financial woes. Nissan employees say they experienced dramatic professional and personal growth, for instance. However, the company as a whole benefits the most, perhaps because solutions are provided from within, not from above. Certainly, Ghosn was orchestrating the teams' direction in response to his own deep learning before the process. He was not, however, simply placing demands upon employees who did not believe in the cuts. Had Ghosn ordered drastic cuts without the teams having found solutions themselves, for example, most would never have bought into them. By forcing them to find solutions, however, he showed them possibilities, thus increasing the odds of successful implementation.

When presented with the findings, involving some 2,000 areas that the nine teams assessed before making recommendations, Ghosn decided some changes and cuts would not be nearly as effective as all the changes and cuts. "It was a tough call," said Ghosn, "but I decided to go for it completely. . .the maximum level."

Ghosn did more than just announce the cuts, however. He personally took responsibility, saying that if the company was not profitable again within a year, he and the entire company board of directors would quit. Other board members did not know about this, yet Ghosn made the comment to show employees he stood with them in the drastic action, which broke up Nissan's *keiretsu* relationships, eliminated jobs, and closed factories.

INVEST IN PRODUCT

Cost reductions alone are not enough to transform a company's bottom line, however. Ghosn believed cuts must be made in conjunction with product or service enhancement, providing plan sustainability instead of just a one-off impact on the profit-and-loss statement. So, just as the cost-cutting plan was announced, Nissan revved up its product investment, ramping up the number of automobiles it built, and spending millions on redesign, with an emphasis on customer-recognized functionality and flair. In other words, as the organization the customer never sees was de-engineered through the cost-saving plan, the product reaching the customer was enhanced across the board, increasing sales and raising the company's brand image.

One year after Nissan implemented the plan, the company was profitable again, so Ghosn did not have to quit his job (he was named Nissan's CEO, and several years later became CEO of Renault as well, in a dual-leadership capacity). Purchasing costs were reduced by 11% in one year, manufacturing plant utilization rates increased from 51% to 74%, and sales increased. Within three years of implementing the plan, Nissan posted its best-ever profits for a full year, and began a second-phase revival strategy, cutting more costs and investing more in a new and redesigned product. Today, Nissan is considered one of the healthiest of all global automotive manufacturers, far from its position a decade before when bankruptcy was an option.

▸▸ MAKING IT HAPPEN

Cross-functional teams are established under the premise that solutions to a company's problems lie within the organization. In establishing team rules, make nothing off-limits to explore or discuss—nothing. Teams should not be hindered by tradition or sensitive corporate issues. Teams should have no decision-making power, only the ability to make powerful recommendations. Teams should include one to two leaders from top company ranks, but the power to run meetings should rest with a pilot from middle management. Membership of the team should be made up of five to nine members from different disciplines, and they should have different leadership qualities. Subteams can be established in larger companies to facilitate information and solution finding.

  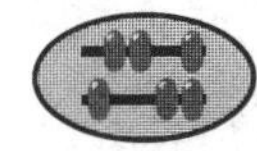 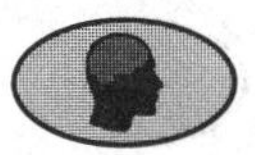  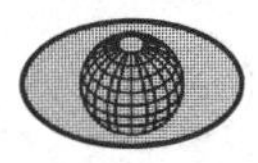   

⏩ MORE INFO

Books:

Ghosn, Carlos, and Philippe Riès. *Shift: Inside Nissan's Historic Revival*. New York: Currency/Doubleday, 2005.

Magee, David. *Turnaround: How Carlos Ghosn Rescued Nissan*. New York: HarperBusiness, 2003.

Article:

Ghosn, Carlos. "Saving the business without losing the company." *Harvard Business Review* (January 2002). Online at: hbr.harvardbusiness.org/2002/01/saving-the-business-without-losing-the-company/ar/1

"Not property is wrong, not profits are wrong, nor money or gain, but the swollen disproportionate gain that can turn a monied group to be the bosses of their fellow men." Stephen Leacock

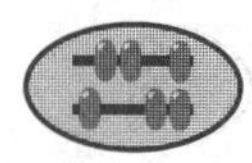
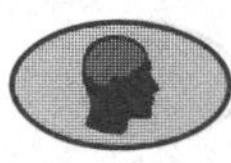

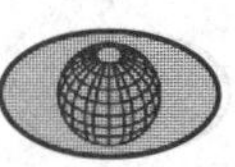

Using Decision Analysis to Value R&D Projects by Bert De Reyck

EXECUTIVE SUMMARY

- Valuing R&D projects is a critical component of project portfolio management.
- Traditional methods for valuing financial assets cannot be easily used for valuing R&D projects, as they are very different in nature.
- Decision analysis is widely used for valuing projects in R&D-intensive industries such as pharmaceuticals and energy.
- Using decision trees, one can determine a project's expected net present value (eNPV) and downside risk, two essential ingredients for determining whether or not to proceed with the project.

INTRODUCTION

Project portfolio management, the equivalent of financial portfolio management but focused on R&D projects rather than financial assets, often relies on decision analysis methods to value projects rather than traditional financial valuation methods such as net present value (NPV). In finance, the idea of managing portfolios of assets goes back a long time, with the first formal methods being developed in the 1950s. Simply put, assembling a portfolio of stocks, bonds, and other financial instruments balances the risk a manager is taking with any one of the investments. Over time, this same idea has also taken hold for managing a portfolio of R&D projects, where it is referred to as *project portfolio management.*

Project portfolio management considers the company's set of projects in a holistic way, providing an overview of the potential value, as well as the inherent risks of both the projects a company is currently engaged in and those it plans to initiate in the future. By means of project portfolio management, risks can be reduced through diversification of the product portfolio and value enhanced by identifying synergies between projects. Companies in the pharmaceutical and energy industries, for instance, have long recognized the value of project portfolio management, and they are using sophisticated methods and software tools to support this process.

Project portfolio management comprises the following functions:[1]

- determine a viable project mix;
- balance the portfolio;
- monitor the projects in the portfolio;
- analyze and enhance project performance;
- evaluate new opportunities against the current portfolio, taking into account capacity and funding capabilities;
- provide information and recommendations to decision-makers.

THE DIFFERENCE BETWEEN FINANCIAL AND R&D PORTFOLIO MANAGEMENT

Financial portfolios and project portfolios are very different in nature. The main characteristics of investing in financial instruments include:

Divisible investments: Financial instruments allow investment in small portions of an asset, rather than being all or nothing.

Simple interdependencies: The interrelationships between different investment opportunities can typically be captured by: The correlation between the assets' returns; and their financial value, as established by the financial markets.

Passive participation: Investing in financial instruments is typically a passive form of participation: The decision is mainly whether or not to invest, and how much.

Availability of information: Much information is available about financial assets in the form of historical performance and fundamental analyses concerning the future outlook.

Tradability: Most financial instruments are tradable assets, resulting in agreed-on valuations and opportunities to sell assets that do not fit your portfolio.

Clear objectives: The main objective is to maximize the risk–return performance of your portfolio.

Contractual clarity: Clearly defined terms exist for investing in a financial instrument, outlining the rights of the parties involved relying on established market rules.

These characteristics are not shared by a portfolio of R&D projects, which can be characterized as follows:

Discrete investments: Investments in projects are nondivisible, increasing the impact of an investment decision on your portfolio.

Complex interdependencies: Complex interdependencies and interactions exist between projects. Project outcomes are subject to synergies—for example, through the sharing of proprietary knowledge—and investment decisions may affect the options available in related projects.

Active participation: Investing in projects requires active management. Besides making a go/no-go decision and setting a budget, numerous decisions will have to be made during the project lifetime that will impact the outcome.

Lack of information: Since projects are largely unique, not much information is available on related past projects or for the prediction of future performance.

Nontradability: Projects cannot be easily sold, resulting in a lack of valuation information and lock-in situations.

Fuzzy objectives: Projects are typically governed by a multitude of objectives, both financial and nonfinancial, and typically include qualitative objectives.

Contract ambiguity: Project investments may result in disagreement concerning who is entitled to which benefit, with multiple stakeholders holding different views.

As a result, conclusions derived from finance cannot simply be transferred to other areas, nor can their methods be used without adaptation. That is why a variety of approaches have been proposed for valuing R&D projects, which is *the* central issue in managing a portfolio of R&D projects. The most commonly used is *decision analysis*, in which decision trees are used to represent the project's potential outcomes and their likelihood.

DECISION ANALYSIS: A DEFINITION

A central component in decision analysis is the concept of a decision tree. An example of a decision tree is given in Figure 1. In the figure:

- The squares, circles, and triangles represent points in time, which proceeds from left to right.
- The squares, or *decision nodes*, indicate decisions to be made, and the circles, or *chance nodes*, indicate the time when the result of an uncertain event becomes known. The triangles, or *end nodes*, indicate the end of the time horizon.
- The branches indicate the stage that follows, depending on which decision is made or which scenario unfolds.
- A probability is given on top of each branch that emanates from a chance node. This indicates the likelihood of that particular outcome materializing, given that all the preceding steps have

"It ain't what you don't know that gets you into trouble. It's what you know for sure that just ain't so."
Mark Twain

  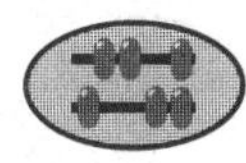 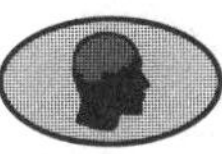  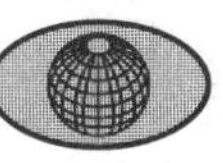   

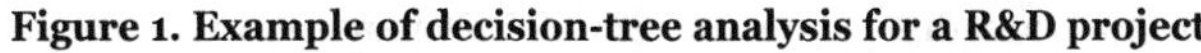

already happened. These uncertainties are outside your control. The probabilities of all the branches emanating from a chance node sum to one.

- Below each branch that emanates from a decision or chance node a monetary value can be added to indicate the cash in- or outflows associated with that particular decision or outcome.
- To the right of the end node two numbers are shown, the upper one representing the likelihood of ending up in that particular scenario, and the lower one the cumulative monetary value.

A key insight resulting from a decision-tree analysis is the so-called *expected value*. Starting at the right of the tree and working back to the left, we perform two types of calculations:

- At each chance node (circle), we compute an expected value as the sum of the probability-weighted expected values associated with the successor nodes.
- At each decision node (square), we determine the highest expected value of the successor nodes. The branch(es) resulting in the highest expected value are indicated by "TRUE," the others by "FALSE," indicating a preferred set of actions based on maximizing the expected value of the project.

Continuing this process, we arrive at the root node of the tree with the *expected value* of the decision tree. The term "expected value" is rather confusing, however, as this value should never be *expected*. In fact, it may even be impossible to obtain, and is merely a probability-weighted average of all the potential outcomes.

USING DECISION ANALYSIS TO VALUE R&D PROJECTS

Decision trees are a natural tool to value R&D projects, as these projects typically consist of several phases. Each project phase can be associated with a stage-gate, a point at which one decides whether or not to continue with the project, depending on the results of the earlier phases and new information obtained about the future. The results of each stage can be represented by a chance node in a decision tree, with the option to abandon the project as a decision node. Other chance nodes can be added to represent possible competitor actions, legislation uncertainties, and global economic conditions. Decision nodes can be added to represent different possible actions, including the injection of more funds and resources in case of favorable developments, accelerating the project to bring forward its market launch date, etc.

As R&D projects typically take several years to complete, it is essential that the

Figure 1. Example of decision-tree analysis for a R&D project

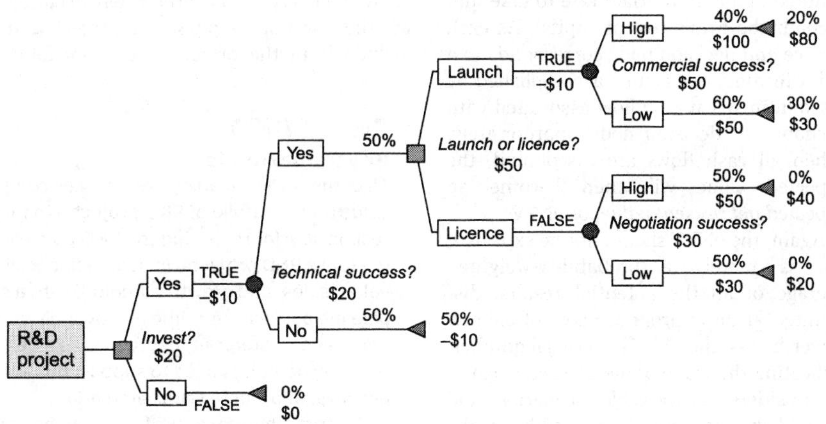

Figure 2. Decision tree for the Phytopharm project

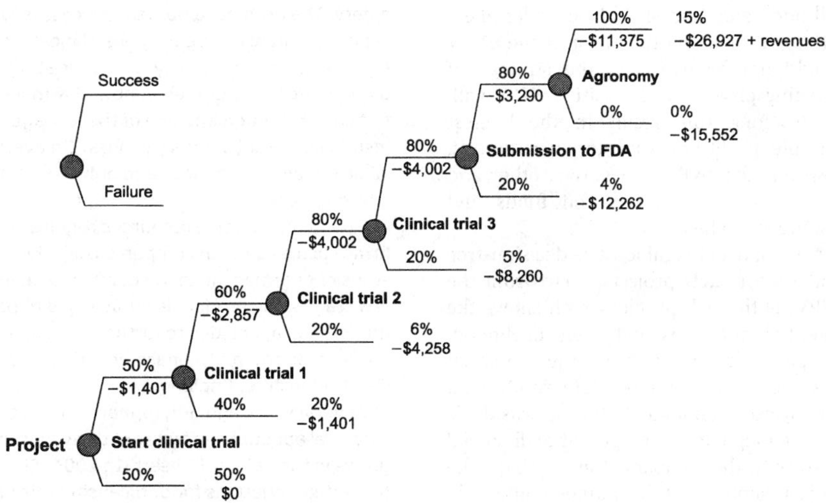

Figure 3. Example of a tornado diagram

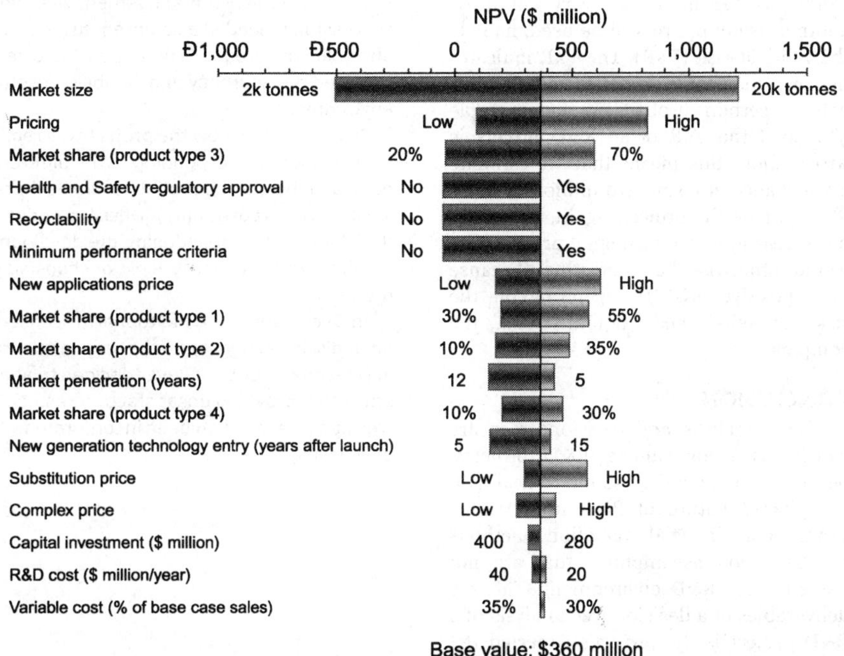

"If a man will begin with certainties, he shall end in doubts, but if he will be content to begin with doubts, he shall end in certainties." Francis Bacon

cash flows in the decision tree are discounted at an appropriate rate to take into account the firm's cost of capital. As each chance and decision node corresponds to a point in time, this can be accomplished by discounting each cash flow associated with a chance or decision node appropriately. When all cash flows are discounted, the expected value will then become an *expected net present value*, or eNPV.

Again, the eNPV should not be expected, but is merely a probability-weighted average of all the potential results, discounted at an appropriate cost of capital. Nevertheless, the eNPV is a crucial number, indicating the value of the project, because it considers all possible scenarios and how likely they are. In principle, if the eNPV of a project is positive, the project will add value and should be undertaken. Although for a one-time project the eNPV should not be expected, the strategy of pursuing projects with positive eNPV will, in the long run, result in the highest possible profit for your organization. If, however, the eNPV is negative, other and better uses for the required funds and resources can be found.

A second deliverable of a decision-tree analysis for R&D projects, apart from the eNPV, is the risk profile, which shows the potential outcomes and their likelihood. Of particular interest is the potential downside, the worst possible result with a nonzero likelihood. If this downside is large enough to cause potential financial distress to the company, then perhaps the project should not be pursued after all, despite a potential positive eNPV. If the worst-case scenario is very unlikely, another useful metric can be used, namely the value-at-risk (VaR). The VaR indicates the loss that could result from a project with a certain probability, for example 5%. So if the VaR of an R&D project is $10 million, this means that we estimate a 5% chance of losing $10 million or more if we pursue the project. Again, this could be a reason for rejecting a project that would otherwise be interesting (because of a positive eNPV), depending on the risk appetite and liquidity of the company.

CONCLUSION

Decision analysis and decision trees are widely used for valuing R&D projects, because they are ideally suited to deal with the phased nature of R&D investments. Traditional financial valuation methods are based on assumptions that are not realistic in a R&D environment. The key deliverables of a decision-tree analysis of a R&D project is the project's expected net present value (eNPV) and its value-at-risk (VaR), two crucial criteria when deciding whether or not to pursue a project and include it in the organization's portfolio. The general rule is that the eNPV should be positive, and the VaR not so high that it may cause financial distress in case of an unfavorable outcome.

CASE STUDY

Phytopharm plc

All of the world's leading life sciences companies use decision-analytic approaches to value their portfolio of R&D projects. In fact, many have a decision-analysis group, responsible for reviewing the R&D portfolio. They typically use a wide variety of criteria to assess R&D projects, including financial value measured by the projects' net present value, sales, and growth potential, with a special focus on potential blockbusters, pipeline balance over time and over different therapeutic areas, risk, unmet medical need, and strategic fit, expressed as a desire to build strength in certain therapy areas. An array of tools is used to support this analysis, including net present value, decision analysis, and Monte Carlo simulation.

Before a pharmaceutical drug can be approved for production and marketing, stringent scientific procedures must be followed in several stages to ensure patient safety. The drug development process is typically composed of basic research (approximately two years), pre-clinical testing (approximately three years), clinical trials (approximately six years, consisting of phases I, II, and III), followed by a review by regulatory authorities. A new pharmaceutical drug that is being investigated can fail to make it through any one of these stages due to potential harmful side effects or insufficient proof of effectiveness. On average, only one in five medicines that enters clinical trials is launched; and only 1 in 10,000 compounds in the research phase makes it to the market.

Due to the massive resources required to perform the late-stage clinical trials, smaller firms such as biotech companies or university spin-offs typically only perform the first steps of pharmaceutical research and development. If the product passes these first few stages, the product is outlicensed to partners with the financial, R&D, and marketing capabilities to further develop and launch it in the market. This was the case for Phytopharm plc, a pharmaceutical and functional food company based in Cambridgeshire, England.

Several years ago, Phytopharm acquired the exclusive license to develop and market a natural appetite suppressant derived from the *Hoodia gordonii* succulent, a cactus that grows in the Kalahari Desert. In 2004, Phytopharm's senior management was preparing to start negotiations for outlicensing this product, which had shown promise in early pre-clinical and clinical trials and successfully passed proof-of-principle. Although Phytopharm's senior management was confident that the product could be very successful, it needed a comprehensive and flexible methodology to rigorously predict and value the product's potential. A choice was made to use decision analysis as it provided transparency and flexibility, useful characteristics in a negotiation environment.

Figure 2 shows how the project was represented as a decision tree, with the different chance nodes corresponding to the different stages that had to be successfully navigated before the product could be marketed (all numbers are disguised and for illustrative purposes only). Decision nodes (not shown) could be added to represent decisions such as abandoning the development in case of unfavorable clinical trial results or commercial outlook, or choosing between different alternative technologies or markets.

In December 2004, Phytopharm licensed the product to Unilever for $40 million and an undisclosed royalty on the sales of all products containing the extract. Unfortunately, in November 2008, Unilever decided to abandon the product due to a recent clinical study that provided unsatisfactory results. This possibility was foreseen in the decision-tree analysis, and had been incorporated when calculating the project's value at the time of licensing[2].

"Profits arise out of the inherent, absolute unpredictability of things." Frank Knight

  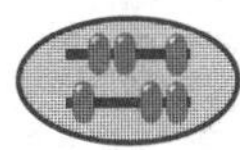   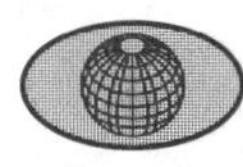   

▸▸ MAKING IT HAPPEN

There are several challenges when using decision trees for valuing R&D projects. For example:

- Which discount rate should be used? Traditional finance theory suggests that a discount rate should be used that reflects the cost of capital of a typical project. The question, however, is what to do when a project is not very typical. And what if the risk changes profoundly over the life cycle of the project? These issues are currently the topic of heated debate, both in R&D organizations and business schools. Note, however, that since the possibility of failure is already explicitly included in a decision-tree analysis, this risk should not be used to further increase the discount rate used to evaluate the project. The only risk that should be considered is the nondiversifiable market risk of the project, i.e., the correlation of the project and market returns.
- When a project contains many stages, with numerous uncertainties and possible decisions, a decision tree can easily "explode" and become unwieldy. Therefore, it is recommended that before carrying out a decision-tree analysis, a sensitivity analysis is performed to determine the main causes of uncertainty, which can then be incorporated in the decision tree. A so-called tornado diagram, which visualizes the key risks in a horizontal bar chart that resembles a tornado, can be used to determine these key risks. An example is shown in Figure 3.
- The validity of any conclusions drawn from a decision analysis depends heavily on the quality of the information used in the analysis. The principle "garbage-in-garbage-out" applies in this context. A common issue that has been observed is the tendency for people to be overconfident, in the sense that we all typically underestimate the magnitude of risks that we are facing. This has led to many criticizing the value-at-risk concept for performing a financial risk assessment, as none of these models could predict the magnitude of the current financial crisis. Therefore, it is essential that sufficient attention is paid to the quality of the data used in the analysis.
- A chance node in a decision tree can distinguish several possible outcomes, but it cannot specify a continuous range of outcomes. This, of course, can be approximated by defining numerous separate outcomes, but doing this will result in the tree "exploding." A better approach is to combine decision-tree analysis with a Monte Carlo simulation, which is ideally suited for analyzing risks with a continuous range of potential outcomes.

▸▸ MORE INFO

Books:

Savage, Sam L. *Decision Making with Insight*. 2nd ed. Cincinnati, OH: South-Western College Publishing, 2003.

Winston, Wayne L., and S. Christian Albright. *Practical Management Science*. 3rd ed. Cincinnati, OH: South-Western College Publishing, 2006.

Websites:

Decision Analysis Society, a subdivision of the Institute for Operations Research and Management Science (INFORMS): decision-analysis.society.informs.org

Palisade Corporation, a provider of decision-analysis software, used to create the examples in this article: www.palisade.com

Strategic Decisions Group, a strategy consulting firm specializing in decision analysis and founded by, among others, the father of decision analysis, Professor Ronald A. Howard of Stanford University: www.sdg.com

See Also:

✔ Applying Cost–Benefit Analysis to Project Appraisal (p. 968)
✔ Costing a New Project (p. 980)
i Project Finance (pp. 1711–1713)
A Behavioral Theory of the Firm (p. 1225)

NOTES

1 Kendall, Gerald I., and Steven C. Rollins. *Advanced Project Portfolio Management and the PMO: Multiplying ROI at Warp Speed*. Boca Raton, FL: J. Ross Publishing, 2003.

2 More details on this case study can be found in: Crama, Pascale, Bert De Reyck, Zeger Degraeve and Wang Chong. "R&D project valuation and licensing negotiations at phytopharm Ltd."

"Chance favors only the prepared mind." Louis Pasteur

  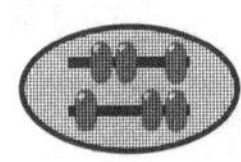 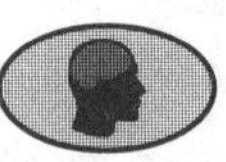  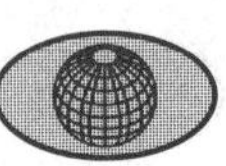 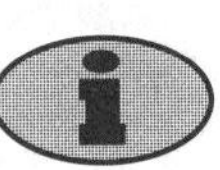  

Viewpoint: Nenad Pacek

Corporate Strategies in Central and Eastern Europe (CEE) from 2009 to 2011

INTRODUCTION

Nenad is Vice President of Corporate Network, Economist Group's business advisery service for multinational companies. Nenad is the lead author of the best selling book Emerging Markets: lessons for business success and outlook for different markets. He advises global and regional managers of multinational companies on how to make the best strategic and operational choices regarding international expansion and how to interpret economic and business environments on all continents, particularly in Central Eastern Europe, Middle East and Africa. nenadpacek@economist.com

The CEE region, together with emerging Asia, was the best region for corporate growth from between 1999 and 2008. The years 2006 and 2007 were record years for multinational companies operating in CEE, when economic growth exceeded 7% for the first—and probably last—time. As the global economic crisis spread during 2008, sales growth in CEE slowed, particularly in the second half of the year.

As we enter 2009, it is clear that 2009 and 2010 will be very difficult for any multinational corporation operating in CEE. The region is unable to escape the global slowdown. As I argued even back in the autumn of 2007 in regular papers to our clients, the decoupling theory has always seemed like nothing but a silly myth, because it assumed that CEE region and other emerging markets were on another planet.

The key strategic pillars for multinationals operating in CEE over the last decade, and especially in the last three to four years, have been:

- Steady increase in corporate resources that are solely dedicated to developing business in CEE.
- Sharp increase in local presence everywhere, but also in small, perhaps non-strategic markets.
- Using the region as a European, and sometimes even global, manufacturing site.
- Desire and action to take control over the business, and not leave business and brand-related items to local distributors.
- To move from an opportunistic approach to the region to a more systematic business development.
- Reluctance and refusal, rightly so, to merge CEE operations into a pan-European structure (where CEE would be managed by the same person who runs Western Europe).
- Understanding that success comes from a steady increase in focus, attention, and upfront business investment (which is hard to do in a pan-European organizations).
- To look increasingly at CEE as an appropriate site for European and global R&D initiatives, European shared services, and logistics.
- To expand sharply to Russia and view it as a strategic market in the medium to long-term.
- To expand product portfolios to address not only the top tiers of the market, but also to move to the middle and the bottom of the segmentation pyramid. This came as a response to international and local competitive pressures.
- To keep hunting for good acquisitions of local competitors.
- To be responsive increasingly to local market needs when it comes to attracting and retaining talent.
- To gain full material and moral backing of the CEO and top corporate officers for CEE expansion and strategy.
- To create subregional clusters in order to keep fixed costs under control. For example, back-office functions for four or five markets would be in one country, not all of them.
- To learn to avoid a "Catch 22" situation when the CEO says: "I will give you more resources when you prove there is more business in country X." This has been the fastest way to failure.
- Not to assume that if you are a market leader in the developed world, this would be repeated in CEE without strong business development and brand building investment;
- To decentralize decision making increasingly and to give more accountability and responsibility to country managers.
- To follow the corporate structure model where geographic priority comes first, followed by business unit priority with functions serving geography and business units. In other words, the model where a regional director drives all business units in CEE has proved to be very successful and more so than a business model driven by global heads of business units (which may not have interest in CEE because he or she is busy focusing on larger volume markets).
- To learn to manage usually inflated expectations about the region, although this remains a big managerial headache for which there is ammunition.
- To nurture speed and flexibility and to avoid knee jerk reactions if one has a bad month or a quarter.
- To invest a huge amount of money into training on typically excellent CEE staff, and to promote CEE managers to senior regional roles.
- To learn to differentiate between markets and appreciate that the region, while having many similarities, is not homogenous in terms of commercial maturity levels, economic development and risks/opportunities.
- To appreciate that friendship and close relationships matter more than in the developed world, and building them often precedes business.

Multinational companies that have used most of the above points during the last decade have built significantly better market positions than their competitors. They are also better positioned to ride through the current global storm of weak demand, uncertainty, and doom.

"**No plagiarist can excuse the wrong by showing how much of his work he did not pirate.**" Learned Hand

I have been observing the above international business principles over the last two decades and they will remain relevant for years to come, not just in CEE, but in the rest of the emerging market world. But, in the current uncertain environment, businesses also need other principles.

As we enter a sharp slowdown, it is exceptionally important not to lose a strategic perspective of the market. Like other crises in history, this one will eventually pass too and companies that do not panic will end up in good market positions for the future. And the future does remain bright once we get out of the global slump. CEE is an emerging market that is more predictable and more sustainable than virtually any other emerging market region. The education levels are high and social structures (roofs above heads, basic social services) are still strong enough to allow low taxation, which will attract capital investment and encourage entrepreneurship. The quality of people, their educational background, and desire to get wealthier will surely be drivers of economic development in the next decades.

Markets that are likely to bounce back faster after the crisis include Poland, Czech Republic, Slovakia, Slovenia and Russia. Despite the current slowdown, they have solid fundamentals with low financing requirements, low levels of debt, and solid reserves. These are the markets that should, just, avoid a recession in 2009.

But markets such as Hungary, Romania, Bulgaria, Estonia, Latvia, Lithuania, Ukraine, Croatia, and Serbia will take longer to bounce back. They have financed their fast growth in 2006 and 2007 with mountains of leverage (at private, corporate, and government level) and will take time to correct their yawning deficits. Some, or maybe all, will be rescued by the IMF, which will impose the usual mantra of tighter fiscal and monetary policies. This will help their fundamentals over time, but it will also push them into a prolonged U-shaped recession or no-growth phase that will be frustrating for business. Also, their currencies remain exposed to depreciations and those that run currency pegs might have to break them in case of prolonged global credit crunch.

In an environment of slow growth over the next two years and some recovery in year three, I expect to see two types of multinational companies.

The first, a larger group of multinationals, will be companies that have low cash positions globally, fairly high debt/equity ratios and run their business very much according to the quarterly earnings cycle (and they give analysts expectations about the next quarter). These companies' primary goals will be to protect the bottom line in the short-term. They will lay off people quickly, cut all kinds of costs sharply, stop investments—all with the aim to preserve profitability and to come at least a little closer to previously promised earnings estimates.

The second, a smaller group of multinationals, will be those that have better cash positions, senior management that is thinking about the next five to 10 years, lower debt exposure, and a mindset that seeks opportunities when others panic.

This group includes a minority of my clients who are now, in addition to all the key strategic pillars, thinking about the following:

- I want to buy that local competitor who is now either trading at a discount on the local stock exchange or the private owner is desperate for cash and wants to sell for the amount that he or she would never have agreed to during the boom times;
- I want to buy some of those distributors that have been good to us, but they were never perfect, and we want to take more control of the business anyway;
- I will not lay off people because this will increase loyalty and we can use the turmoil to actually build market share by investing more in business development and promotion;
- I will use the current environment to renegotiate various cost items with my landlord or with media vehicles that we use for our promotional activities;
- We will look to buy land which is trading at a discount for our future manufacturing expansion;
- We will seek to buy companies which governments still own but, because they are desperate for cash, it will be cheaper and easier to get hold of some companies previously seen as family silver.

Not everyone can afford this approach, but those companies that can will build larger market share that will, in good times, feed the bottom line. As markets mature, increasing market share becomes harder and more expensive.

"You are not here to merely make a living. You are here in order to enable the world to live more amply, with greater vision, with a finer spirit of hope and achievement. You are here to enrich the world, and you impoverish yourself if you forget the errand." Woodrow T. Wilson

  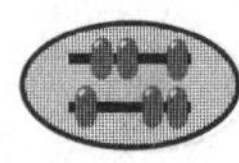   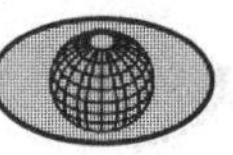   

Value Creation—Perspectives and Implications by John C. Groth

EXECUTIVE SUMMARY

- Cultural perspectives and respect for differences are important in a global economy. "Value" is viewed in different ways in different economies and cultures.
- The forms of capital include human, tangible, and financial. Human capital divides into physical and mind capital. We are living in the era of mind capital.
- A holistic view of an economy and an operating company allows one to recognize the origin of value in a competitive environment.
- Analysts and decision-makers benefit from thinking in terms of the opportunity costs of capital and the implications of employing capital.
- The economic returns *of* capital are very distinct from returns *on* capital.
- Invested capital, flowing capital, idle capital, and opportunities related to these variables are core to decisions that seek to create value.
- Idle human capital in an organization becomes lost capital with each passing minute.
- Lost capital represents an unfavorable, and even potentially disastrous, event for a company and for society.
- Value creation is consistent with the wise use of resources. Thus it provides an important perspective for executives who live in a world that is giving increased attention to the use of resources in the context of social responsibility, sustainability, and environmental concerns.

INTRODUCTION

This article focuses on the creation of value by a company or organization. We assume a competitive environment in the sense that the end user of a product or service has the right to buy or not to buy, to use or not to use a product or service. Although the discussion and examples focus on value creation in terms of economic measures—for example, an increase in share price—we recognize that other important measures of value exist. Quality of life is one such indicator—and even this measure varies with culture and circumstance. Such cultural differences and perspectives are important and should command our respect. At the end of the article, we will assert that at the local level competitive environments do allow individuals to make choices, determine what is of value, and subsequently influence the use of resources and the rewards or punishments for the use or misuse of those resources.

FORMS OF CAPITAL

Capital has three forms: tangible, financial, and human. Human capital has two forms: physical capital, and mind capital. We live in an era of mind capital—with mind capital offering profound opportunities.

Employing capital wisely leads to the creation of value. The unwise use of capital destroys value. The creation of value accrues to the firm or organization and to society. The destruction of value takes from the organization and from society.

A HOLISTIC VIEW OF AN ECONOMY

In a working economy, the production process uses resources—tangible, human, and financial—to fulfill human needs. Figure 1 illustrates the discussion.

Need fulfillment occurs at the point of value, where individuals choose to exchange money or some other form of exchange/store of value in expectation of fulfilling a need. *A person buys a product or service not to be nice, but to satisfy needs, wants, and desires.* In a competitive environment the customer *chooses* to select or reject the offered product or service. The ability to choose the best alternative in a competitive market is essential to wise resource use and the potential creation of value, taking into account the long-term implications of short-term choices.

Figure 1. The value cycle

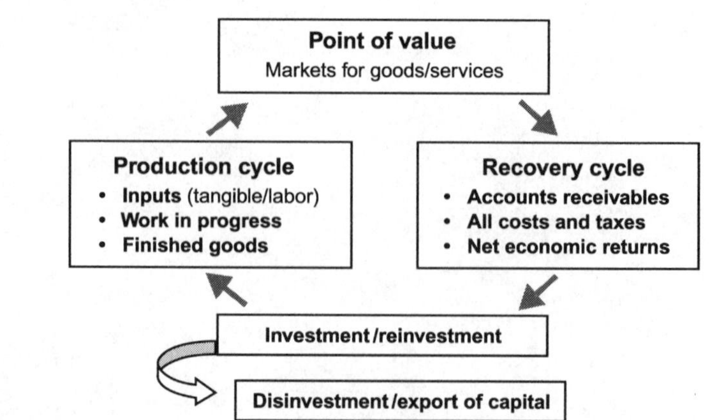

Fulfilling human needs when a customer buys a product is essential to *potential* value creation. The production cycle converts inputs of capital into a product or service. Selection of the product brings need fulfillment to the customer, fulfillment that is possible because we converted capital of one form into another form, or made available a product (for example food) otherwise not easily accessible to the customer.

THE COMPANY'S PERSPECTIVE

For the company, the fundamental processes of the value cycle are: convert capital of one form into capital of another form (i.e. convert inputs of production into finished goods); sell the product; collect on sale; pay all costs, including the cost of capital and taxes; have a positive economic return net of capital costs; reinvest in the cycle and repeat the process.

Investment in working assets, and often capital assets and land, supports the operation of the cycle. Working assets often include those shown in Figure 1—for example, raw materials inventories. Capital assets such as plant, equipment, and land often support the operating cycle. Capital assets are tangible or physical assets with an expected useful life that extends beyond the current operating period.

Various financing arrangements fund the working and capital assets that support the value cycle.

Reinvestment of the recovered capital, and possibly of net margins, and allowing it to circulate through the cycle again occur if the *expected* returns of repeating the cycle appear attractive compared to the opportunity cost of capital. The opportunity

"The substitution of monetary values for all other values is pushing society toward a dangerous disequilibrium." George Soros

  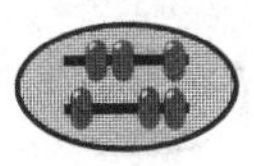   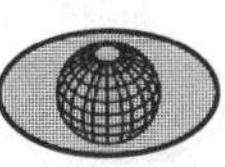   

cost of capital represents the expected returns on the next best alternative with the same risk.

In valuation we refer to cash or economic returns, not accounting returns. Second, investments/disinvestments represent capital opportunities; for example, if I reduce my investment in finished goods inventory, the amount of capital I release or disinvest opens an opportunity for investment elsewhere.

When the cycle works, resources are used to deliver need fulfillment. In a competitive environment in which the customer chooses to buy from us, we *earn* the return—we do not extract or exploit the return. Value creation occurs if this return exceeds all costs, including the cost of capital. *Value creation signals an approval of our use of resources.*

In a competitive environment, if the person selects your product or service rather than an alternative, currently you enjoy a competitive advantage. Without a sale, your capital stops circulating, becomes idle, declines in value during this idle period, and may even become lost capital. We will address these issues shortly.

LIFE VALUE CYCLE AND RELATIONSHIPS

Let's identify the factors that drive value creation in this cycle. Then we will share an example of how change in one variable alters the value creation process. To focus on concepts and relationships, we will hold some factors constant. For example: increasing cash inflows at a point in time will increase value, other factors constant; in a dynamic world the price of bearing risk is not constant, and a change in the price of bearing risk could negate the impact of the increased cash flows. Nevertheless, the increased cash flows would still have yielded a benefit in that relative performance is better.

Costs. In this cycle costs include those that will occur and become a cash cost if we make a change. These are variable costs. A company also has fixed costs, both cash and noncash in nature.

Contribution margin. The contribution margin (sales price less variable costs) from operating this cycle must cover fixed costs to achieve breakeven. The margin also must cover taxes, fees, and, hopefully, the cost of capital. A net positive return above all of these costs signals an addition to value since the company has earned a net return in excess of the cost of capital.

Invested capital. Operating the cycle requires capital to be invested in the assets in the cycle—for example, the money value of the asset cash, raw materials inventory (RMI), work in process inventory (WIPI), finished goods inventory (FGI), and the value of the accounts receivables (A/R). Here is a hypothetical case to illustrate.

A company keeps 20,000 units in finished goods inventory (FGI), each at a variable cost of \$1.00; sells 2,000 units per day; production rate equals sales rate. Thus the FGI represents 10 days of unit sales. During the year, we always see 20,000 units in FGI, representing an investment all year of \$20,000. The actual physical units in inventory change during the year as units are sold and replaced by new production.

There are also investments in cash, raw materials, work in process, and accounts receivables. As for FGI, for each of these assets we can calculate the "number of days" in the asset. For example, if the time from start of production to completion of a product is 7.5 days, then WIPI is 7.5 days.

For simplicity: Let the number of days in cash, RMI, WIPI, FGI, and A/R total 60 days. This means that it takes 60 days from the time a dollar leaves the asset cash until it comes back to the same point. Variable costs are \$1.00 per unit, and sales price is \$1.05 per unit. We'll use these data in the following discussion.

Circulating capital. In the example, it takes 60 days for money to complete one trip through the cycle. Using a 360-day year for convenience, we could circulate *the same* money six times during the year. Many call this a "turnover" of 6.0. If we take money out of cash and send it through the cycle, we are circulating the capital. Obviously, *circulation only occurs if a customer buys the product and pays for the purchase.* The gross cash flow during the year for each dollar circulated six times is:

Turnover × Margin = 6 × \$0.05 = \$0.30

Return of capital. When the customer pays the \$1.05, \$1.00 of this represents a return *of* capital—i.e. the same dollar that we put into the cycle coming back.

Return on capital. The \$0.05 is a gross return *on* capital, gross because we have not yet covered fixed costs and taxes and the cost of capital.

Forms of capital and risk. Note that after the \$1.00 leaves cash to proceed through the cycle, the *form* of the capital changes as one transforms it from cash to raw materials, labor, energy, work in process, finished goods, accounts receivables—and back to cash when the customer pays.

A fundamental principle is that *changing the form of capital changes the risk of that capital.* To illustrate, work in process carries higher risk than raw materials. FGI has lower risk than WIPI since the risk of production has passed. The risk of sale remains. Hence, A/R are generally (if we granted credit wisely) of less risk than FGI since the risk of sale is over. Just the risk of collection remains.

Idle capital. A product that sits idle between steps in production during work in process, or product held in finished goods inventory before sale, are examples of idle capital. Idle capital is capital standing still.

Idle capital loses value at a minimum rate since one could employ the capital elsewhere in the world and earn a return. At a minimum, the capital could earn the risk-free rate of interest. The opportunity cost of capital is the more appropriate estimate of the decline in value. Idle capital might also face the risk of obsolescence or spoilage. For example, a restaurant prepares a food item in anticipation of a purchase. Freshness and value decline with time. At some point the restaurant has to remove the unsold item from inventory, and the money equivalent to the investment in the food item and the return that capital could have earned become lost capital. Lost capital is discussed below.

On occasions, inflationary rises in the price of inputs captured in the product might offset declines in value of idle capital. However, holding tangible capital, for example, raw materials as a hedge against inflation, should reflect a conscious choice. This choice, and its potential outcome, differ greatly from inadvertently holding idle capital.

Lost capital. Lost capital is capital depleted of value which one can never employ again. To illustrate, we make an automobile tire. After the production process is over, we discover that the tire is defective. The resources invested in the tire and disposal costs less any salvage represent lost capital.

Lost capital is a bad outcome for your company—and for society. In the context of the \$1.00 example, the company destroys the \$1.00 net of recovery or disposal costs. For example, if a tire fails quality tests, the company loses not only the \$1.00, but also the cost of disposing of the defective tire.

Importantly, the loss of capital also results in another loss. If we make a product no one wants, or a product that is defective, the capital employed becomes lost capital. No one can ever again use lost capital to fulfill a human need. *Hence, the use of resources without fulfilling human needs takes from your organization and*

"Running a media brand is about harnessing the value of people . . . journalists, DJs, editors—all of them are the brand." Vijay Solanki

society and eliminates the future use of resources. In financial jargon, one loses the present value of all future returns that one could have realized had the capital been preserved for repeated use.

Human capital—the special case. Idle and lost human capital has special import. *Idle human capital always becomes lost capital.* With the passage of time, the human capital disappears—forever. People can never again have the day just lived. Minute by minute, idle human capital turns into lost capital.

VALUE CREATION—CONCEPTS TO APPLICATION

We move to application by making a simple change in our hypothetical case, reducing variable costs from $1.00 to $0.99 per unit—while maintaining *actual* value and the value *perceived* by the customer. This $0.01 reduction in cost is a 1% change relative to the original cost of $1.00.

Maintaining *actual* value is important so that we do not later have higher product returns or warranty claims, or suffer damage to brand name or company reputation. Maintaining or increasing the customer's *perceived* value is necessary to maintain sales as well as customer satisfaction—which are both crucial in the longer term. We don't want to do things in the short term that have adverse effects long term.

Let's examine the changes that will result from lowering the cost to $0.99. The changes will occur during an adjustment period (i.e. as units in FGI that have $1.00/unit invested are replaced by units with $0.99/unit invested) and culminate in a new steady state.

Disinvestment of capital from the cycle. For example, in FGI, replacement of 20,000 units at $1.00 with 20,000 units at $0.99, with the asset cash increasing by 20,000 × $0.01 = $200.00. Likely, the investments in WIPI and RMI decrease. Also, investor capital invested in the A/R changes. Previously, each $1.05 in A/R had $1.00/unit of money invested, but now only has $0.99/unit invested.

The net effect is a reduction in total capital invested in the working assets other than cash. The disinvestment results in an increase in the asset cash. If we had sufficient cash before this change, we can take the excess cash out of the cycle—reducing total assets at work in the cycle.

Generation of capital. The company now circulates $0.99 to collect a $0.06 margin rather than $1.00 to harvest a $0.05 margin. The contribution margin increases from $0.05 to $0.06 per unit. The cash generated increases, breakeven is lowered, and profits grow at a faster rate once past breakeven. Note that the gross cash flows per $0.99 circulated six times during the year generate:

$$\text{Turnover} \times \text{Margin} = 6 \times \$0.06 = \$0.36$$

Recognize that one now circulates less capital but generates more cash contribution margin. The contribution margin from sales will cover fixed costs sooner and, after taxes, the contribution margin per unit of sales is greater.

Improvement in margins and changes in invested capital may stem from a variety of actions. Chickens and eggs provide a practical way to visualize relationships. Let's say, for example, that genetics, selection, and management of chickens for egg production raise yearly output from 280 to 300 eggs per chicken—with obvious effects on returns. At the same time:

- production benefits from a reduction in the number of "idle days" for the hen;
- less capital needs to be invested in the form of chickens to generate a given number of eggs;
- less has to be invested in chicken houses and land;
- fewer chickens are needed to breed replacement hens for the egg production facility;
- fewer resources are at work, such as crop land, to support the process;
- energy usage is lower;
- and so on.

Cycle turnover. Reducing the time to complete a pass through the cycle represents opportunity. Going back to our initial example, suppose that one reduces the time for work in process and the total time through the cycle declines from the original 60 days to 52 days. Now one can circulate capital through the cycle more than six times a year (360/52 = 6.92) and generate more cash. Often a reduction in cycle time also reduces capital invested in the cycle—an added benefit since now one has greater cash flow on less capital invested at risk.

Numerous examples of reducing cycle length could be cited. Continuing with chickens, reducing the time from the hatch of a chicken to when it is used for meat is one example. Decreasing days from planting to the harvest of beans is another.

Improvements in cycle time often yield other advantages. In the case of the bean plants, the shortened time to harvest: reduces the days the crop is at risk of damage from weather and pests; reduces the time capital has to be invested; may also allow more crops during the annual season, resulting in more contribution margin per year; reduces the idle time of the land and equipment employed to support the operation.

There is also a reduction in risk associated with the invested capital since noncash risky assets decline, the less risky asset cash increases, and cash flow generation is greater.[1] The risk of the company declines since it has lower variable costs, generates more cash, has less risk exposure in assets, and achieves breakeven sooner.

Capital demands. Since variable costs of sales are lower, the company needs less capital to support growth. For example, to add to FGI to support increased sales requires less investment.

Returns, risk, capital. The elasticity of demand *may* allow the company to lower prices, increase volume, and generate more contribution margin relative to invested capital—selling more product units at a lower cost but spawning greater economic returns. Success at this increases the need fulfillment of people and reduces inflationary pressures in the economy. Furthermore, cash flow returns relative to invested capital increase and the risk of these cash flows decreases.

Cost of capital. Capital markets are sensitive to how well a company performs. In efficient capital markets, a reduction in risk, improvement in cash flows, and reduced capital exposed to risk result in a reduction in the cost of capital. This in turn increases the net economic margin (the economic returns less the cost of capital), with enhancement of value.

Value. The joint effects of the above events distill to an increase in value, with the following general relationships at work.[2]

- A change in expected cash flows results in a linear effect on value.
- A change in perceived risk associated with cash flows results in a nonlinear, exponential effect on value.
- A decrease in investors' perceptions of risk results in decline in the required rate of return, other market factors held constant. An increase in perceived risk causes an increase in the cost of capital.
- A decline in cost of capital has a greater dollar impact on share value than an equal increase in cost of capital—this relationship arising from the nonlinear effect inherent in discounting.
- Increasing cash flows, less risk in the cash flows, less risk due to a lower breakeven, and less capital at risk, all result in increases in value.

DISINVESTMENT FROM A COMPANY OR ECONOMY

The global economy and interrelationships, the relationship of a company's cycle to an

"Organizational values always derive from individual values—especially those of the founding fathers and of the very top executives." S. K. Chakraborty

economy, and the relationship of cycles across economies are important to the manager. Future choices of investments/disinvestments will hinge on identifying the relative attractiveness of investments across economies.

Note in Figure 1 the block that occurs with disinvestment/export of capital. For a company and/or an economy, if the *expected* returns given risk are no longer attractive compared to capital at risk, the company does not reinvest in the circulation of capital. The company may remain stagnant and leave current capital in place. Alternatively, it may disinvest and use the capital on other opportunities in the economy or outside the economy. Some specific observations follow.

Human capital may leave a company or an economy—with potentially unfavorable or even disastrous consequences in the longer term. Both mind and physical human capital have a critical role in translating ideas of value into actions that create value. In the modern world, the products of mind capital can and do leave one economy and go to another. With the communications available this can now be done quite easily.

A company that maintains a *status quo* in an economy does not grow. It may dispose of harvested margins through the payment of dividends, or remove the contribution margins generated from sales and take these outside of the economy. Companies don't disinvest for no reason, or to be cussed. Decision-makers understand economics and move capital to environments that offer better risk conditions or expected returns on capital.

The export of capital obviously depletes capital from the economy. Often the export of capital results in a decrease in the fulfillment of human needs, increased social dissatisfaction, and attendant increases in social and political risk—all of which increase the cost of capital to the economy. The burdens of these movements of capital fall on the members of the economy.

Companies that reinvest in the value cycle in an economy continue to assist in the fulfillment of human needs. If growth opportunities exist, a portion or the entire harvested net margin from the previous value cycle is returned through the cycle and can support growth. The process generates and keeps capital in an economy—and contributes to the delivery of products and services to consumers.

Fulfilling human needs generally fosters social and economic stability, both of which distill to lower political risk. A decline in political risk improves the availability of capital to the economy and lowers the cost of capital. These factors jointly increase the value of economic earnings streams and assets.

An American President once said something like this (paraphrased since what he actually said is debated): "A rising tide raises all boats." This is certainly a true statement. However, a rising tide is a peril to those who do not have a boat. Creating value in an organization creates value in an economy. It brings boats to more people.

Thinking as a marketer: Improving the opportunities for people in an economy increases our chance of having them as customers. The success of a company's customers is in the interest of customers and the company.

Making decisions and managing for economic value benefits the organization. At the same time, such actions are very compatible—and in fact essential if society is to benefit from the use of resources.

SUMMARY

In a competitive local environment people can choose how to use resources to deliver products and services which other people in that environment value. Value creation that results from the delivery of need fulfillment clearly signals the wise use of resources.

In some cultures and economies, value may be defined as an economic measure of opportunity or wealth. In others, people may see value differently, and act differently. To illustrate, some may decide to preserve a local habitat and forgo the consumption of goods and services that would have been possible if they had sold their land. We recognize that being forced to sell to survive is not a choice, but necessity. In contrast, deciding to preserve elements of life rather than exchange them for consumption represents an important element of choice: people do make decisions based on a value frame of reference.

▸▸ MAKING IT HAPPEN

- If making a decision with the intent of creating economic value, employ economic, not accounting, measures.[3]
- Use the value cycle when you examine a contemplated action and capture in an analysis: the impact of invested, flowing, idle, and potentially lost capital; the turnover and margins; the risk; the influence of variables such as costs and risks.
- Decisions and actions intended to create value (both economic and social) should rest on analysis and even, when appropriate, on gut feelings. Don't let decisions and actions be dictated by accounting. Accounting should account for, not compel or dictate, a particular course of action. For example, you do it if it is the "correct thing to do," rather than because it is a tax-deductible expense.
- Consider wider social, political, and economic forces, trends, developments, and implications as you make decisions on deploying capital. Decisions of companies made from a short-term perspective may have profound implications over the longer term.[4] Second, the consumer's own decisions, often made in the context of immediate circumstances, also have both short-term and long-term implications.
- Making decisions that have social and other value not measurable by economic measures is important. In such analysis, focus on these social and other issues *separately* from the economics. Do not mix up accounting or economic analysis in an effort to justify the decision. *People do good things because those actions are important and meaningful—even if they do not have a measurable economic return or favorable impact on reported earnings.*
- Identify all forms and amounts of capital invested in a course of action. Identify expected returns on this employment of capital, including returns on human capital.
- For expected returns, minimize invested capital at risk.
- Increase the circulation of capital in the value cycle.
- In making long-term investments, seek economies in which you feel that social and political risk will decline. Interestingly, some leading indicators of such a trend have anchors in the arena of human capital. Economies that respect human capital, allow for its development, and allow the accumulation by the individual of returns on human capital will experience increases in need fulfillment, a reduction in social risk, and a decline of political risk. The protection of intellectual and real property rights is critical to fostering an environment and behavior that nurtures human capital to yield the benefits of human capacity. The net effects will be:
  - A better life for individuals.
  - An improvement in the standard of living.[5]
  - An increase in the value of expected cash flows originating in that economy.
  - An appreciation in the value of tangible assets in that economy.

     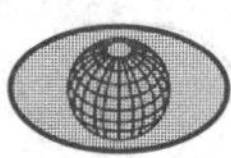   

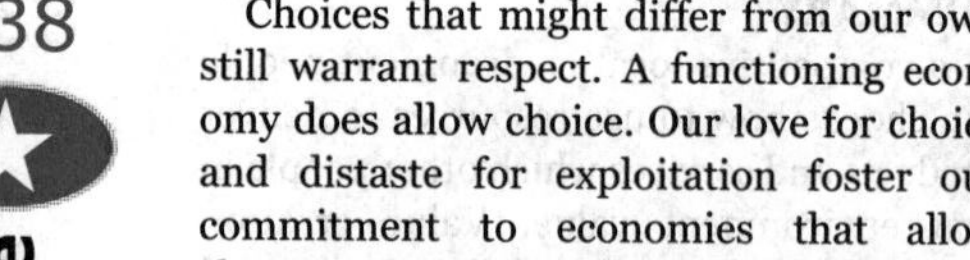

Choices that might differ from our own still warrant respect. A functioning economy does allow choice. Our love for choice and distaste for exploitation foster our commitment to economies that allow choice rather than compel acceptance.

The value cycle portrayed here, and the variables in the relationships that influence value creation, are the bedrock for mangers intent on making decisions that garner value in an economy.

MORE INFO

Articles:

Byers, Steven S., John C. Groth, Malcolm R. Richards, and Marilyn K. Wiley. "Capital investment analysis for managers." *Management Decision* 35:3 (1997): 250–257.

Byers, Steven S., John C. Groth, and Marilyn K. Wiley. "Managing operating assets to create value." *Management Decision* 35:2 (1997): 133–142.

Groth, John C., and Clair J. Nixon. "Financial information, risk, and share value." *Management Decision* 30:7 (1992) 30–37.

Groth, John C., Steven S. Byers, and James D. Bogert. "Value management: Capital, economic returns and the creation of value." *Management Decision* 34:6 (1996): 21–30.

Video:

Charlie Rose interviews GM CEO Rick Wagoner (August 18, 2008). Online at: www.charlierose.com/view/interview/9225

See Also:

★ Comparing Net Present Value and Internal Rate of Return (pp. 40–42)
★ Creating Value with EVA (pp. 756–758)
★ CSR: More than PR, Pursuing Competitive Advantage in the Long Run (pp. 147–149)
★ The Human Value of the Enterprise (pp. 474–476)
★ Managing Intellectual Capital (pp. 482–483)
★ The Value and Management of Intellectual Property, Intangible Assets, and Goodwill (pp. 109–112)
✔ Calculating Return on Investment in Human Resources (p. 975)
✔ Managing the Time Value of Money (p. 871)
Warren Buffett (p. 1157)
The Six Sigma Way: How GE, Motorola and Other Top Companies are Honing Their Performance (p. 1317)

NOTES

1 In an economy with inflation, holding cash assets may be very risky compared to, for example, holding commodities in raw materials inventory.

2 My article "Risk—Perspectives and Common Sense Rules for Survival" (pp. 811–814) includes more detail on the relationships that follow.

3 My article "Accounting and Economics—Critical Perspectives" (see qfinance.com) addresses related issues.

4 I am indebted to an anonymous reviewer for accenting and offering an example that illustrates the importance of "getting it right" and adding value versus "getting it wrong" and destroying capital in an economy. Portions of an interview with a CEO of a large company illustrate how the interplay of variables and resultant choice can promote short-term decisions and behavior that have long-term implications. See Rose interview with Rick Wagoner (2008).

5 We should recognize that different societies define and view standard of living in different ways—and not necessarily with measures employed in other cultures. Using resources wisely in the context of a particular society will depend on that society's values.

"Human beings possess the potential to be educated for values." S. K. Chakraborty

  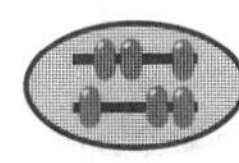   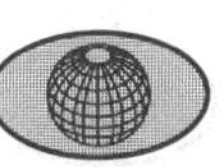   

What Entrepreneurs and Small Business Owners Can Do to Increase Their Chances of Success in the Global Economy by Neuman Pollack

EXECUTIVE SUMMARY

- Advances in technology, communications, and transportation have transformed the world into a global village, and small and medium-size enterprises (SMEs) can take advantage of this.
- Beyond any short-term gains they may make, SMEs also gain experience in performing on a larger stage.
- Entrepreneurs and SMEs often go global in response to the state of their domestic market environment.
- To be successful, SME managers and entrepreneurs who engage in international trade must demonstrate high levels of passion, motivation, competence, and advocacy support.
- Development of an international perspective, or *global mindset,* facilitates engagement in international business.
- From a practical perspective, entrepreneurs and SME managers must broaden their horizons and sharpen their skills to successfully engage with the international arena.

INTRODUCTION

Entrepreneurs and small business owners are motivated to solve problems or deliver services better, faster, cheaper than others in the market. Entrepreneurs harness creativity and innovation to seize opportunities and offer alternatives in the marketplace. Successful entrepreneurs manage risk by closely monitoring business processes and financial obligations, as well as by focusing intently on their market and the challenges of building market share. With democracy encircling the globe and once-rigid barriers to free trade being eroded, the entrepreneur in many industry sectors seeks opportunities beyond his/her local region or country in a worldwide market. Adopting a global strategy can enable a small company to enhance its growth in the face of increased competition. In some instances, a global strategy is necessary, especially when facing competition from abroad. Today's more open world business environment is not risk-free; indeed, no market strategy is risk-free. Small and medium-size enterprises (SMEs) must recognize that doing business internationally involves added dimensions of uncertainty and risk, such as fluctuation in world currencies, global (regional) economic and political unrest, and inconsistencies in the global supply chain.

The US Small Business Administration estimates that approximately 25% of all US export volume (in dollars) is attributable to small businesses.[1] In terms of the number of US companies engaged in international trade, "97 percent of all exporters are small and medium size companies."[2] A recent survey of SME CEOs revealed that 56% look favorably on engaging in international business, with fewer than 20% considering it a threat.[3] Among countries in geographical proximity, as in Europe, the prevalence in terms of both the value of international trade and participation by SMEs is infinitely greater. It must be remembered that international trade is a two-way street. Indeed, import activity among American companies is far greater than export activity, a fact that shows up in the year-on-year trade deficits recorded by the United States in recent decades.

INTERNATIONAL TRADE: GROWTH AND CHALLENGES

The recent acceleration of international trade provides greater opportunities for SMEs. Government efforts around the world promote and assist small businesses in expanding the value of their international operations. Advances in technology, communications, and transportation have transformed the world into a global village. SMEs can penetrate markets by relying on the ubiquity of telecommunications, increasing access to the global supply chain, and engaging with world markets. Language, once a barrier to small firms in the international arena, is no longer an issue, with the widespread acceptability of English as the global language of business. The growth of trade alliances, such as NAFTA, CAFTA, ASEAN, and Mercosur, the expansion of the European Union, and efforts to consolidate currencies across national boundaries, such as the adoption of the euro by a dozen Western European countries and of the US dollar in Ecuador facilitate integration in the international community. The sheer growth of China, India, Brazil, and Russia, as well as other states of the former Soviet Union, provides both great opportunities and risks for SMEs around the globe. Global telecommunications have greatly reduced the technical barriers to trade, with even the smallest firms able to operate in a virtual 24/7, 24 time-zone environment.

The key to success for SMEs, however, is learning how to overcome the many *internal* barriers that exist. SMEs face a lack of resources related to acquiring and understanding information, managerial knowledge and experience, short time horizons, and inadequate planning.[4]

Yet, despite such limitations, many SMEs engage in international trade with varying degrees of success. At best, international trade activities can be risky for all firms due to regional and global political instability, exchange rate fluctuations, climatic and other environmental uncertainties, the pace of change in telecommunications and transportation, shifting markets, and new entrants (competition) in those markets. Some understanding of these factors and adopting the right mode and timing of internationalization—for example, whether to export directly or through intermediaries—can minimize the inherent risks. The worldwide economic downturn in 2007–08 presented a particularly difficult set of circumstances for SMEs around the world.

> "The key to success for SMEs, however, is learning how to overcome the many *internal* barriers that exist."

Firms that view their initial foray into international trade as part of a business learning curve or as an investment in their future are more apt to succeed in the long term, especially compared to firms that are monetarily or psychologically unprepared or are unwilling to adopt a long-range view.[5] Indeed, research has long suggested that, for firms that are developing a capacity to operate abroad, success in the

"Economic globalization places pressure on small and medium-sized firms to participate in international business." William J. Burpitt and Dennis A. Rondinelli

   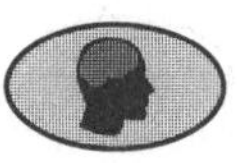  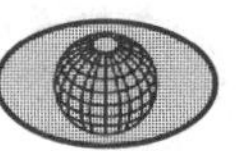   

international arena depends on proceeding gradually. This gradualism is often referred to as staged or incremental internationalization.[6] Enhanced knowledge and an incremental approach, however, are not sufficient for success, particularly for SMEs with limited resources. SME managers also need to develop an outlook based on contextual factors[7] and their inherent operating environment, industry structure, and marketing strategy.[8]

Beyond the short-term gains, SME managers also gain confidence and experience by performing on a larger stage. Horizons are broadened, and they become sensitive to economic and geopolitical changes to which they formerly paid scant attention. This learning can affect manager's perspectives and strategies more than short-term financial success, reinforcing the decision to engage in international trade. As SME managers gain more experience, their knowledge increases, enhancing their confidence to further expand international activities. This learning not only provides reassurance, but it also reinforces their decision-making.[9]

As a group SMEs differ from large, established firms in terms of complexity and formality. Small, entrepreneurial firms are generally more flexible in developing their strategies and are swift to embrace the global environment as a learning opportunity. However, SMEs will only be successful if they are able to manage the multitude of dimensions associated with globalization. For example, success in the international arena correlates with an ability to engage in highly complex relationships.[10] These may include the establishment of subsidiaries and joint ventures, or the initiation of subcontracting and materials importation as core elements of the business plan. SMEs learn and benefit from such activities, but they become successful *only* if they take advantage of them. Mastering the learning curve reduces the complexity of doing business globally, enhancing the prospects of financial success.

ENGAGING THE INTERNATIONAL ARENA AND DEVELOPING A GLOBAL MINDSET

Entrepreneurs and SMEs may go global in response to the state of their domestic market environment.[11] If domestic conditions are good, SME managers are less likely to take on the risks associated with overseas activity. Conversely, if there are few prospects for growth in the domestic market, they have more inclination to accept such risks. In going global, SME managers tend to choose an entry mode that minimizes risk. The least risky, least costly, and most frequent entry mode is the export of finished goods. More complicated modes involve sourcing, manufacturing, equity, and partnership arrangements. However, SME managers will engage in more complex and costly entry modes as an alternative to simply exporting if they need to exercise greater

CASE STUDY

The Great American Hanger Company[15]

The Great American Hanger Company was founded by 25-year-old entrepreneur Devon Rifkin in 1999. Rifkin's vision was to create a company dedicated solely to providing solutions for clothes-hanging needs. The company supplies a broad range of hanger products in both wood and metal, some with fabric overlays, to leading hotels and also sells directly to wealthy individuals worldwide. The company grew from an idea to a US$100 million firm in less than 10 years.

Design, marketing, and distribution of an extensive product line is coordinated at the company's corporate headquarters in Miami, Florida. Manufacturing, however, takes place at several sites in Asia, initially in India and now also in China. Rifkin established his first Asian link over the internet through the sourcing website Alibaba.com. The Wooden Enterprises and Trading Cooperative in India was able to produce his wooden and metal designs with high quality at low cost, enabling Rifkin to grow his company rapidly by being highly competitive.

The Great American Hanger Company now uses Hong Kong as its sourcing hub. Rifkin is able to meet suppliers, view finished products, and schedule follow-up visits to manufacturing facilities in a time- and cost-effective manner. He was quoted in the *Hong Kong Trader* as crediting much of the growth and success of his company to this strategy: "The air that we breathe, so to speak, has everything to do with our suppliers and our supply from China, and our relations through Hong Kong as the door that opens for us to the rest of our supply world. I give Hong Kong and China single-handedly the credit for allowing me the opportunity to grow my business as successfully as we have thus far."

Once the supply chain was firmly established, the key to success has been the focus on a single product category—hangers. Growth was based on marketing to selective targets—hotels, retail stores, and now celebrities and other wealthy individuals—both domestically and internationally. This is a good prescription for any entrepreneur to follow.

⏩ MAKING IT HAPPEN

From a practical perspective, entrepreneurs must broaden their horizons and sharpen their skills if they are to engage successfully in the international arena. They will have already navigated barriers to entering their own domestic market, as well as economic, social and political hazards. They now must learn to navigate international barriers, such as tariffs, quotas, and embargos, along with the economic, political, social, and cultural challenges associated with doing business across oceans, continents, and hemispheres. Specific points that entrepreneurs and SME managers must consider are:

- Research the feasibility of engaging in international business.
- Assess the firm's competitive advantage in target countries or regions.
- Calculate the market value of the firm's products or services.
- Establish the true financial costs associated with importing and/or exporting.
- Be mindful of differing business, social, political, and cultural mores.
- Be cognizant of legal standards to safeguard investments and intellectual property.
- Preplan activities, leaving no loose ends to be determined later.
- Develop strong relationships with foreign partners, employees, and clients.
- Adopt a *global mindset* for themselves and their firm.
- Transform the firm into a global enterprise.

As in all business enterprises, a key factor associated with both strategy and operations is the leaders, managers, and rank and file personnel. People make the all difference. Thus, it is more than just necessity and opportunity that drive the internationalization of SMEs; it is also the wisdom and familiarity that can be acquired through the desire to expand beyond local and domestic environments. Today's entrepreneurs are highly educated; they manage risk by gaining understanding and developing experience. To be successful, they must think global and act global.

"Capital as such is not evil; it is its wrong use that is evil. Capital in some form or other will always be needed."
Mahatma Gandhi

  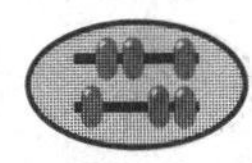   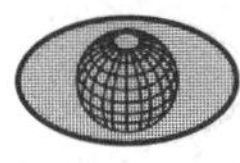   

control over foreign resource availability or over their access to foreign markets. Similar strategies may be followed in sourcing (importing) raw materials or components for further fabrication, or finished products for direct sale.

While these decisions are the result of some strategic thinking, the underlying basis for international trade activity and the degree to which it is pursued are related more to economic necessity than to opportunity. Although a high percentage of SMEs in developed economies engage in some form of international business, such activity is not necessarily maintained on a continuous basis. Firms that are only marginally engaged in international activities tend to disengage, often due to a "lack of strategic planning" and commitment.[12] Such firms may redirect their efforts back to their domestic markets when the business climate is once again supportive. Increasingly, though, this can be a perilous decision, leading to competitive disadvantage in their home markets.

Sustainable international engagement and success require:

- Understanding the market for one's products or services;
- Delivering quality in the design, manufacture, and distribution of products or services;
- Demonstrating a commitment to outstanding customer service;
- Maintaining capable and dedicated personnel;
- Operating with financial and ethical integrity.

Not surprisingly, these are the same factors that are essential for success in the domestic market. SMEs engaging in international trade must demonstrate high levels of passion, motivation, competence, and support in order to succeed.[13] Indeed, it is as much the "soft side" of business engagement that leads to success as the "hard side" of technical know-how. Balancing these factors is essential for success. If the entrepreneur or SME owner is not personally able to provide this balance, he or she must be prepared to share the responsibility for the success of the firm with others.

Firms can be characterized as either "born global" or "late starters." A born global firm is one in which the entrepreneur engages in international trade from the onset of operations. For these entrepreneurs, *being global* is simply their *state of being*. The late starter is an existing firm that begins to engage in international business some time after inception. The development of an international perspective, or *global mindset*, provides a foundation and supporting commitment to embrace the global market as permanent player. The *global mindset* is characterized by a realization that domestic boundaries are not a limit and that the entrepreneur must adopt a virtual "locus of control" beyond his or her immediate environment. By adopting this perspective, entrepreneurs and SMEs enhance their potential for success. External enablers, such as the European Union, NAFTA, CAFTA, Mercosur, ASEAN, and other free-trade arrangements among countries, set the stage for engagement. SMEs operating with a *global mindset* will develop a competitive edge over their domestic competitors as a result of the knowledge gained from international trading partners, as well as their broadened perceptions and attitudes.[14]

▸▸ MORE INFO

Websites:

There are many useful resources that entrepreneurs and owners of SMEs can readily access. Articles, books, and information guides are produced by academics and practitioners alike. In addition, governmental, nongovernmental agencies, organizations, and consulting groups provide valuable information through their websites and web-based newsletters. The following listing provides some resources that will be useful to entrepreneurs and owners of SMEs in the United States and around the globe.

Alibaba is the world's leading B2B e-commerce company serving SMEs in China and around the world: www.alibaba.com

Entrepreneur Press is a provider of books, information, and guidance for entrepreneurs and small business on all aspects of business: www.entrepreneurpress.com

Entrepreneurship.org is the website of the Ewing Marion Kaufman Foundation and the US Commerce Department's International Trade Administration's public–private partnership. The focus is on encouraging best practices in entrepreneurial leadership, to promote economic growth around the world, and to assist all nations in developing the environment to allow entrepreneurs to organize and operate business ventures, create wealth, and employ people: www.entrepreneurship.org

International Entrepreneurship provides entrepreneurs from around the world with access to import and export information, general business data, financing sources, and entrepreneurial success stories for over 100 countries. Links to domestic entrepreneur help sites are provided for each country: www.internationalentrepreneurship.com

MarketResearch.com has the world's largest and continuously updated collection of market research, with more than 160,000 market research reports from over 600 leading global publishers. Country reports provide strategic insight into geographic, political, and business environments and their effects on economic performance and potential: www.marketresearch.com

The Indus Entrepreneurs' (TiE) mission is to foster conscious entrepreneurship globally by educating, mentoring, and networking: www.tie.org

World Franchising's website provides a comprehensive directory of franchise opportunities, leading you to the most up-to-date franchise information available on the internet: www.worldfranchising.com

See Also:

Michael Porter (p. 1182)

Balanced Scorecard: Translating Strategy Into Action (p. 1221)

"In the capitalist urban milieu. . .the routinisation of day-to-day activities is stripped away from tradition. . .they become matters of habit or of dull economic compulsion." Anthony Giddens

NOTES

1 Gatewood, E. J. "External assistance for startups and small businesses." In William D. Bygrave and Andrew Zacharakis (eds). *The Portable MBA in Entrepreneurship*. 3rd ed. Upper Saddle River, NJ: Wiley, 2004, p. 239.

2 Burpitt, W. J., and D. A. Rondinelli. "Small firms' motivations for exporting: To earn and learn?" *Journal of Small Business Management* 38:4 (2000): 1–14.

3 Grant Thornton International Business Owners Survey 2006. "Focus on the global market." Online at: www.internationalbusinessreport.com/files/ibos_2006_global_markets.pdf

4 Ali, A., and P. M. Swiercz. "Firm size and export behavior: Lessons from the Midwest." *Journal of Small Business Management* 29 (1991): 71–78; Baird, I. S., M. A. Lyles, and J. B. Orris. "The choice of international strategies by small businesses." *Journal of Small Business Management* 32:1 (1994): 48–59; Karagozoglu, N., and M. Lindell. "Internationalization of small and medium-sized technology-based firms." *Journal of Small Business Management* 36 (1998): 44–59; Li, L., D. Li, and T. Dalgic. "Internationalization process of small and medium-sized enterprises: Toward a hybrid model of experiential learning and planning." *Management International Review* 44:1 (2004): 93–116; and Naidu, G. M., and V. K. Prasad. "Predictors of export strategy and performance of small and medium-sized firms." *Journal of Business Research* 31 (1994): 107–115.

5 Burpitt, W. J., and D. A. Rondinelli. "Small firms' motivations for exporting: To earn and learn?" *Journal of Small Business Management* 38:4 (2000): 1–14.

6 Johanson, J., and F. Weidersheim-Paul. "The Internationalization of the firm—Four Swedish cases." *Journal of Management Studies* 12:3 (1975): 305–322; Johanson, J., and J.-E. Vahlne. "The internationalization process of the firm—A model of knowledge development and increasing foreign market commitments." *Journal of International Business Studies* 8:1 (1977): 23–32; and Li, L. D. Li, and T. Dalgic. "Internationalization process of small and medium-sized enterprises: Toward a hybrid model of experiential learning and planning. *Management International Review* 44:1 (2004): 93–116.

7 Welch, L. S., and R. K. Luostarinen. "Inward–outward connections in internationalization." *Journal of International Marketing* 1:1 (1993): 44–56; Jones, M. V. "The internationalization of small high-technology firms." *Journal of International Marketing* 7:4 (1999): 15–41; and Roberts, J. "The internationalization of business service firms: A stages approach." *Service Industries Journal* 19:4 (1999): 68–88.

8 Turnbull, P. W. "A challenge to the stages theory of the internationalisation process." In P. J. Rosson and S. D. Reid (eds). *Managing Export Entry and Expansion*. New York: Praeger, 1987, pp. 21–40.

9 Burpitt, W. J., and D. A. Rondinelli. "Small firms' motivations for exporting: To earn and learn?" *Journal of Small Business Management* 38:4 (2000): 1–14.

10 Kalantaridis, C. "Internationalisation, strategic behaviour and the small firm: A comparative investigation." *Journal of Small Business Management* 42:3 (2004): 245–262.

11 Rasheed, H. S. "Foreign entry mode and performance: The moderating effects of environment." *Journal of Small Business Management* 43:1 (2005): 41–54.

12 Crick, D. "The decision to discontinue exporting: SMEs in two U.K. trade sectors." *Journal of Small Business Management* 40:1 (2002): 66–77.

13 Shooshtari, N. H., and J. Reece. "Global business and the smaller company." *Montana Business Quarterly* 38:2 (2000): 17–20.

14 Spears, M. C., D. F. Parker, and M. McDonald. "Globalization attitudes and locus of control." *Journal of Global Business* 15:29 (Fall 2004): 57–64.

15 Material for this case study was obtained from the company's website: www.hangers.com; Bianchi, Alessandra. "Take your business global." FORTUNE Small Business Open Forum, October 15, 2007. Online at: www.openforum.com/leadership/article_takebusinessglobal.html; and Anon. "Effective business hub gets deals done." *Hong Kong Trader* (January 2, 2008). Online at: www.hktrader.net/200801/trade/products-hanger200801.htm

"Experiential learning may be viable for the SMEs that intend to explore foreign market opportunities but lack relevant international knowledge and competence. . ." Li, Li, & Tevfik

  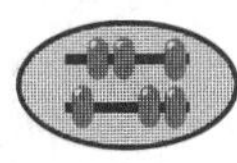   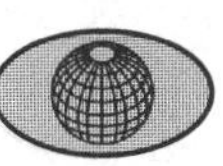   

Why EVA Is the Best Measurement Tool for Creating Shareholder Value by Erik Stern

EXECUTIVE SUMMARY

- Economic value added (EVA) has transformed the corporate finance scene and business practice by transferring modern business theory from classroom to boardroom.
- Traditional metrics, with their roots in accounting, distort economic reality. For example, crucial long-term intangible investments often fall foul of traditional metrics.
- If stockholder value is the goal, then the key to any metric must be the cost of capital, or stockholders' required return.
- At its best EVA is not just a financial metric, it is a complete management system focused on value creation.
- Incentive-based EVA uniquely aligns the interests of managers, employees, and stockholders. Studies show that EVA companies, after implementation, have increased their market value over peer by some 50% over five years.
- Bold implementation of EVA signals the beginnings of transparency and accountability, though it is too often the subject of lip service. Implementing EVA half-heartedly or without incentives spells disappointment.
- A balanced scorecard demands EVA as the balancing mechanism. EVA covers everything managers can influence, and therefore all drivers of value.

INTRODUCTION

Financial measuring tools are many and varied. The media and equity analysts focus on financial accounting metrics such as sales and sales growth, margin, operating profit and operating profit growth, bottom-line earnings and its partner earnings per share (EPS), market value, return on equity, and return on assets or cash flow.

Each of these metrics is flawed. Neither sales nor operating profit accounts for the financial requirements necessary to achieve them, in terms of either annual expenses or capital invested. Bottom-line profits and EPS take no account of the fact that equity has a cost. Market value ignores the capital employed to create it—invest more, and of course market value rises, without necessarily creating value. And yet each is popular.

Why is so fundamental a series of misapprehensions so widespread? The answer lies in the past. Accounting operating profit is conservative—literally. It focuses on collateral, or at least what would be left of a company after bankruptcy. This is a more than adequate measure for a bank, but it is misleading for an investor. The theory of modern business is founded on the blindingly simple insight that business is primarily about economics, not accounting.

THE PROBLEMS WITH EXISTING CORPORATE FINANCE MEASURES

Debt-inspired measures are misleading because they *expense*—write off as expenses—aspects of business that are becoming increasingly important. Long-term intangible investments (training, brand building, and so on), in particular, create much of the value of companies today. Yet traditional accounting procedures expense these rather than treating them as investments. Additionally, investments in acquisitions (goodwill) and in restructuring (extraordinary items) are expensed. This is a mistake. A focus on value demands that long-term investments should appear on the balance sheet for the current year, taking the cost of capital into account.

Unless they take into account the cost of capital, return measures can become inflated. Furthermore, concentrating on percentages can lead to a misguided focus—for example, reducing capital investments (especially intangibles) calculated to create profits in the future.

If the hurdle rate for returns is very high, increases may discourage optimal creation of value. If the hurdle for returns is very low, increases may destroy value. If return objectives are above the required returns of investors—the right benchmark—then managers may forgo investments that create value. If returns are the objective and an increase fails to meet this required return, value destruction results.

Of other measures, cash flow will not provide the right answers in growing businesses. When Wal-Mart was growing rapidly, new stores cost more than the existing cash flow, yet no one demanded that the company stop investing and growing. Furthermore, the net present value of free cash flow emphasizes success in the terminal value of the equation rather than the horizon that managers can visualize and experience. Free cash flow, in other words, is not a flow measure.

MVA

The best measure of corporate performance is market value added (MVA), because this measure differentiates between the total market value, including debt and equity, and the total capital invested: MVA is the difference. (MVA may also be viewed as management value added—the value managers have added to a company.)

The problem is that MVA is strongly affected by stock price, which is notoriously independent of senior executives. This makes MVA less useful for encouraging the creation of value, since it has limited operational use.

THE NEED FOR A MEANINGFUL FINANCIAL MEASURE

An alternative is necessary, one that focuses on what managers can influence rather than what they cannot. The measure should differentiate between financial inputs—what enters a company over time—and outputs—the value created. Clearly our choice should not be a driver of value such as the financial accounting metrics that managers can influence. Consider instead output, on an annual basis, as operating profit after tax, with certain adjustments for intangible and other long-term investments and other accounting anomalies, and input as the annual rental charge on the total capital employed, both debt and equity. The rental charge or required return, known alternatively as the hurdle rate for investments or the weighted average cost of capital, is the true benchmark against which all investments and management should be measured. This is economic value added (EVA).

UNDERSTANDING EVA

EVA covers all that managers can influence, all drivers of value. This is seen more easily if we view EVA as the capital investment multiplied by the difference between the actual return and the required return. If we think in addition about the required return as a mix of business risk and financial risk (where financial risk, or debt level, has a potential benefit also), then we have four

"In our view, derivatives are financial weapons of mass destruction carrying dangers that, while latent, are potentially lethal." Warren Buffett

of the major components of market value as defined by Merton Miller and Franco Modigliani. These are:

- the cost of capital for business risk
- the amount of debt
- the current level of operating profit
- capital expenditure

The other components look at future EVA (investor expectations for future growth) in the current level of EVA—what we call FGV, or future growth value. They are the expected return on new investment, and the time horizon for excess growth in profitability or EVA. Managers can influence more or less imperfectly the debt, operating profit, capital expenditure, and future returns. They influence the horizon and business risk little, if at all.

The Value and Scope of EVA

EVA covers profit and loss and the balance sheet, differentiating intangibles and growth, and thus all factors of production. Growing or improving EVA is the goal, with historic investments viewed as sunk. Hence, managers should focus on growing when the returns are greater than the cost of capital, redeploying capital when the returns are less than the cost, and improving returns on existing capital, as well as having an optimal capital structure (debt versus equity).

If value creation is key, then EVA is the answer, and improvement of EVA is the goal. How managers achieve this or choose to accomplish this depends on what they think is success for their business. Of course the answer may depend on the state of the economy. In reality, investing and containing costs are crucial everywhere in the economic cycle. However, criticism thrives in a falling market and falters in a rising one. A falling market puts failing companies under the microscope, and a rising market forgives all but the worst performers.

In other words, containing costs increases current and near-term EVA, and is always crucial. But investing determines near-term and future EVA and is also always crucial, if the cash is available.

Performance measurement is the bedrock of business. Since people manage what they measure, EVA can form the foundation for a more transparent and accountable management system, especially when combined with powerful incentives to improve EVA at every level, in every activity, across all functions, and independent of geography. With rights to make decisions accurately allocated, a fair system of transfer pricing in place, information flowing freely, and the appropriate tools and training offered, responsibility joins transparency and accountability through robust control and performance evaluation. Pay for the right performance, and value-based management results.

Under EVA, budgeting gives way to long-term planning. Control of the ends and the means is relinquished respectively to externally and objectively determined investor expectations, and to management choice and opportunity that allow managers to bet their own success on their meeting or beating stockholder requirements.

CONCLUSION

EVA is, in short, the best measurement tool for creating stockholder value. A balanced scorecard of metrics allows for a big-picture view, but what is the balancing mechanism? If value creation over the long term is the goal (and if it isn't, stockholders should run), then EVA must be the balancing mechanism. Sales, margin, operating profit, and bottom-line profit simply fall short. Market value lacks levers. Return measures give the wrong answers. Only EVA can change companies.

Indeed, EVA correlates better with stock price than any other measure: by 50%, compared with up to 30% for other metrics. Since EVA charges for all the factors of production, continuous improvement in EVA always furnishes investors with an increase in value.

Clearly, if an organization pays lip service to EVA and blindly measures it without thinking about the behavioral consequences and the need to balance simplicity and accuracy, or else provides poorly considered or misguided incentives to create EVA, the outcome will disappoint. However, a robust system that's adhered to in times of boom and bust will provide the foundation of sound decision-making and business practices.

MAKING IT HAPPEN

- Start using EVA as the key financial measure: subtract input (annual rental charge on the total capital employed) from output (adjusted operating profit after tax).
- Employ EVA as the foundation of a more transparent, responsible, and accountable management system, with robust control and performance evaluation.
- With the right to make decisions accurately allocated, put a fair EVA-based system of transfer pricing in place.
- Couple continuous restructuring of existing businesses to milk value with cautious investment in future businesses.
- Focus managers on growing where returns exceed cost of capital, and on redeploying capital where returns are less than its cost.
- Insist on improving returns on existing capital as well as on having an optimal capital structure (debt versus equity).

MORE INFO

Books:

Bloxham, Eleanor. *Economic Value Management: Applications and Techniques*. Hoboken, NJ: Wiley, 2003.

Stern, Joel M., and John S. Shiely. *The EVA Challenge: Implementing Value-Added Change in an Organization*. New York: Wiley, 2004.

Young, David, and Stephen F. O'Byrne. *EVA and Value-Based Management: A Practical Guide To Implementation*. New York: McGraw-Hill, 2000.

Website:

A site set up by Stern Stewart, the global consulting company which pioneered the development of the EVA framework: www.eva.com

See Also:

★ Creating Value with EVA (pp. 756–758)
★ Reinvesting in the Company versus Rewarding Investors with Distributions (pp. 172–173)
✔ Calculating Total Shareholder Return (p. 936)
Jack Welch (p. 1204)
The EVA Challenge: Implementing Value-added Change in an Organization (p. 1250)

"**One of the soundest rules to remember when making forecasts in the field of economics is that whatever is to happen is happening already.**" Sylvia Porter

  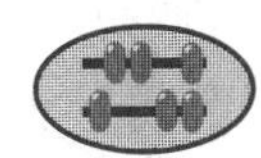 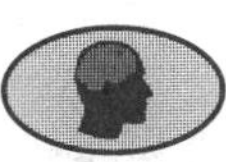  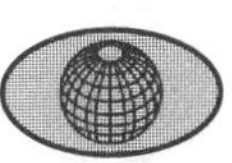   

Winning Commercial Tenders by Damian Merciar

EXECUTIVE SUMMARY

- Winning commercial tenders is a key component of success for professional services firms.
- In order to win, your firm must invest time and resources in gaining knowledge that provides a competitive edge.
- Relationships are vital: remember that you are not aiming just to win one contract, but to establish a long and mutually beneficial partnership with your client.
- Use tendering strategically; when successfully deployed, tendering can be the catalyst for developing new skills and exploring new markets.
- Understand the power and scope of your pricing principles. These can garner greater profit than simple pricing techniques and exploit market positioning for the bidder.

This article refers primarily to professional services firms, though the application lends itself more widely across the commercial, if not the manufacturing, sectors. The article will follow the headings of an appreciation of what it is that the client is after, followed by an analysis of the market and then the competition. Vendor selection will be discussed and of key consideration, the role of price in formulating a bid.

DETERMINE THE DESIRED OUTCOME

Before a vendor or bidding contractor can consider whether his or her deliverable output is aligned with the client's desired outcome, the client must fully understand what it is they want to achieve by the project. A clearly defined project will greatly assist the vendor in removing the element of second-guessing the client.

Fundamentally, the scope of a project comes down to three things:

- *Understanding the client*: Appreciate where the client is relative to his or her competitors, and where, with existing resources, he or she would like to be.
- *A plan*: To get them from their current position to where they would like to be—even if the aim of the project itself is simply to gain greater knowledge of the competitive marketplace. Such insight could be a development milestone and lay the groundwork for implementation.
- *Implementation of the results*: the application of the operational and strategic recommendations that arise from successful completion of a project.

Of course, the fact-finding may result in a fuller understanding of the client's environment, and so a better proposition than the client originally requested. Firms that are able to outline this additional benefit are more likely to be selected by potential clients.

ANALYZE THE CLIENT

Knowing all about the buyer is crucial—have they been in the market for this type of project before and, if so, who did they use last time? Did they act on the vendor's recommendations? Is the client easy to bid for? Are they likely to have clear expectations, or is the initial bidder selection going to be a time-wasting process because the client has left areas open to interpretation? Do you, as vendor, know how receptive the client may be to recommendations? Is there scope for the client to use your services further—for example to implement the project or to identify and develop an additional plan?

Of all these questions, this last is the most important. Time spent bidding for contracts is vital to winning new work, but time misspent in bidding for the wrong contracts can waste valuable resources and distract attention from more appropriate and winnable contracts.

> "What are the tactical considerations in putting together a sales pitch: should you make it learned and cultured, or experienced and savvy, and do you have the people who can do either convincingly? More fundamentally, are you the right contractor to be making a bid?"

ANALYZE THE COMPETITION

Develop a comprehensive database of your competitors' activities. Find out the number of bids they place and their success rates. Knowing the client and the brief, would you expect to see your company on a list of bidders? Aim for objectivity—seen through the eyes of a competitor, how would you rate your company's chances of success? Do you have employees who have worked for companies on your list of other bidders, and if so, can they be mined for tactical advantage?

If not, search through public information about the competitors you expect to be bidding against. Break down the search by

CASE STUDY

Niche Consultancies—Bidding to Win

A niche consultancy practice in England that specializes in business economics and management received an invitation to tender from a large national telecoms company in Europe. The client was a new one, as was the sector specialism. The time allowed to complete the project was four months, and the potential contribution to that year's fees was £500,000. The managing director was keen to win the project as it would show his company in a favorable light, add intellectual capital, and generally increase the firm's prestige. This would likely help to secure future contracts.

In this project, the relation between fixed telephony and wireless was critical to understanding the client's commercial offering. The MD set about learning all about the sector and the geography in which the telecoms company operated, and he began to put his bid calculations together. He included his best consultants and contacted external contractors to be included in the submission. After pricing for travel, hotels, and currency fluctuation, he stripped down his margin by 15% so that the bid would be seen as evidently competitive. The bid was submitted—only to fail. Genuinely disappointed, the MD requested a debriefing and was told that he had been beaten by an established competitor with greater experience of the intended project.

The client, however, had noted the professionalism of the submission and the obvious care and thought that went into it, and also was impressed by how the MD interviewed over the phone. The next year, when the same client published a follow-up invitation to tender, the MD again submitted a proposal—and won, despite this time excluding the 15% discount. The strategy of bidding carefully and thoroughly, and doing so again after a disappointment, paid off and the learning process had been worth it.

"What they fail to realize is that the quality of the implementation often depends on the quality of the plan."
Freed, Freed, and Romano

   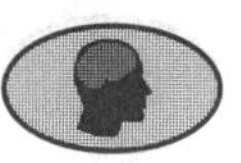  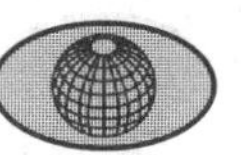   

industry sector and by geography. If time permits, take a calculated view and include an outlier on your shortlist: new companies come to the fore for a reason—can you spot who may be on the ascendant? Include reputation and reliability, cost, and a view on their persuasiveness as a vendor. Do you know how many clients have acted on his or her respective recommendations?

VENDOR SELECTION

Frequently, vendors are disqualified for not following the brief—the college mantra of "answer the question" applies here. *Have* you answered the question? Consider simple but decisive issues such as proofreading your document for clarity and presentation. Are you going to get it done on time? Be comprehensive—do you cover everything fully in the terms of reference, expression of interest, or invitation to bid?

The qualifications of your team need to be part of how you persuade a potential client to use you. Have you got the right people, and if not, can you get them? If you can get them, does it make commercial sense to do so—how will it affect your margin? Using external contractors presents both risks and rewards: at what stage do you decide which is a risk and which an inspired choice? Is there scope for bringing in additional people or swapping people once the project is underway? Can the project be used as a testing ground for potential collaborators? Are those collaborators part of your potential future revenue stream, bringing additional contacts and likely insights with them?

Present the strengths of your team members to the vendor. Promote their relevant experience in a way that will appeal to the client. If necessary, rewrite team member's résumés, concentrating on what they can deliver—this is easier said than done, but it can be worth the time spent. Simple visual tricks, such as leading the eye with paragraph alignment, can help to highlight these skills. Remember that you may have just seconds to stand out.

PRICE CAREFULLY

This section is split into a discussion of the initially appraised price for the tender and the price that is actually submitted after careful and comprehensive consideration.

Initial Price

The bidder's initial price is likely simply to be a function of the expected benefits to the client, how long he has known the client, and the estimated likelihood of winning. In basic economic terms, this is necessary, but not sufficient, information. Your company needs to decide first on a basic pricing strategy:

- *Value-based pricing*: This is where the price to the client is based on an expectation of the value of the product, where the product is typically either a plan or an implementation. This is a difficult, though potentially more lucrative, approach than rate-based pricing and requires a thorough knowledge of the client's business. It also requires an understanding of how they assess their anticipated changes after completion of the project. Useful metrics for an accurate valuation could be based on increases in revenue, increased market share, a change in market position, insights gained, or likelihood of success.
- *Rate-based, or per diem, pricing*: More straightforward, the price here can simply be the number of consultants multiplied by their respective rates, multiplied by the number of days on the project. Expenses should be included.

> "Time spent bidding for contracts is vital to winning new work, but time misspent in bidding for the wrong contracts can waste valuable resources and distract attention from more appropriate and winnable contracts."

Then there are strategic values to winning a tender:

- How much do you wish to work with the client? They may occupy a sector you have specifically targeted.
- Will your competence as a firm increase—for example, by broadening the experience and skills of your consultants?
- Does the project promote a new regional or national presence for your company?
- Is there scope for additional fees or continued work with the client?

Tactical values should also enter into your consideration. For instance, will the project utilize otherwise underused staff? Will it lead to more training for those engaged in consultancy? Could it increase publicity for your firm? Is your firm in a position to negotiate counter offers and to price for subsequent phases with the same client?

Submitted Price

When all these factors have been duly thought through, the bid may be put forward at a high price—we are confident of winning and can clearly show our greater added value than the competition. Or a low price—for our own internal reasons, we wish to make our presence known in this sector, and so shall view our bid as an investment contributing to the likelihood of future contracts. On the client side, typically, their return on investment will be between 5:1 and 10:1—that is, over the three years after the project or implementation they will be seeking returns between five and ten times the cost of utilizing you.

CONCLUSION: THE STRATEGIC VALUE OF WINNING, AND THE ASSOCIATED RISKS

Some of these values have already been touched on—for example, the opportunity to break into new markets and increase the capabilities of your staff. Directly aligned with these values are potential costs. Can your finances support a start on the project—how are payments to be structured? Do you accurately understand the client's requirements, and can you fulfill them? Do all parties agree on the gains from the project? Will pursuing the project result in a conflict of interest for existing clients? Is there an opportunity cost to fulfilling the project? Might it fundamentally alter the direction of your business? Does the cost of *not* pursuing the bid outweigh all the potential for a negative outcome? If the answer to this last point is yes, then go ahead and bid strategically.

▸▸ MAKING IT HAPPEN

- Know your competencies, and where you fit in the market place. Are you certain you have access to the professionals needed to do the job?
- Know your competitors and what their strengths are.
- Understand the requirements of your client—*precisely what* do they want?
- Understand that bidding is both a knowledge-based affair and a tactical affair. Ensure that you know how and where to utilize this knowledge. Fully understand your pricing strategy—and make sure you are able to defend it when challenged.

"A long term contract is usually established at the request of the client, not as a result of a proposal by you."
Alan Weiss (2003)

▸▸ MORE INFO

Books:

Freed, Richard C., Shervin Freed, and Joe Romano. *Writing Winning Business Proposals: Your Guide to Landing the Client, Making the Sale, & Persuading the Boss*. 2nd ed. New York: McGraw-Hill, 2003.

Lewis, Harold. *Bids, Tenders & Proposals: Winning Business Through Best Practice*. 2nd ed. London: Kogan Page, 2007.

Weiss, Alan. *Million Dollar Consulting: The Professional's Guide to Growing a Practice*. 3rd ed. New York: McGraw-Hill, 2003.

Articles and Guides:

Business Link. "Price your product or service." Online at: tinyurl.com/b2q7y5

Small Business Notes. "Value-based pricing." Online at: www.smallbusinessnotes.com/operating/marketing/pricing/valuebased.html

Small Business Notes. "Marketing." Online at: www.smallbusinessnotes.com/operating/marketing.html

UK Trade & Investment. "European Union external aid—Guide to winning business." Online at: tinyurl.com/d9mm9b

Websites:

Business Link—UK government free business advice and support: www.businesslink.gov.uk

Small Business Notes—Information and resources for small business owners: www.smallbusinessnotes.com

See Also:

★ Project Planning Techniques for Small and Medium Enterprises (pp. 805–807)

✔ Costing a New Project (p. 980)

✔ The Objectives of Corporate Planning and Budgeting (p. 877)

CHECKLISTS

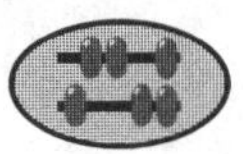

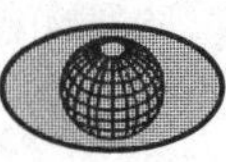

Checklists

Practical solutions for everyday questions and challenges

The Checklists provide you with a comprehensive handbook of practical answers and concepts that appear in business on a daily basis. Each entry reflects current thinking and best management practice, and is designed to give you a practical answer to your problem—fast.

The Checklists provide problem solving via the fast route and cover a variety of subjects from "Setting Up a Key Risk Indicator System" and "Structuring and Negotiating Joint Ventures" to "Understanding and Using Currency Swaps" and "Options for Raising Finance."

Each Checklist includes a definition, a useful list of dos and don'ts, advantages and disadvantages, and action pointers. More information is also included to provide the reader with the opportunity to delve deeper into the subject area.

   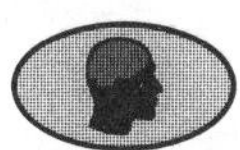  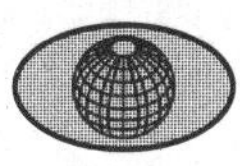   

Contents

Corporate Balance Sheets and Cash Flow

Governance and Business Ethics

Insurance and Financial Markets Including Macroeconomics

  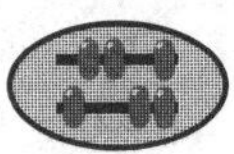 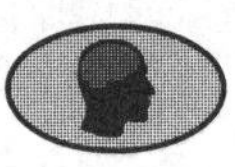  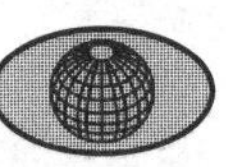   

Making and Managing Investments

Mergers and Acquisitions

Operations Management

Raising Finance

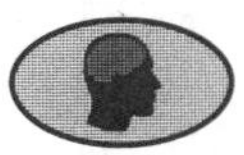

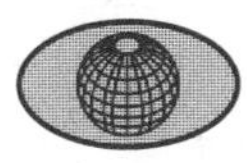

Regulation and Compliance

Strategy and Performance

  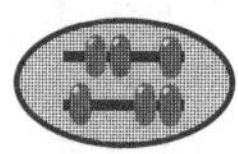  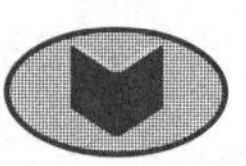 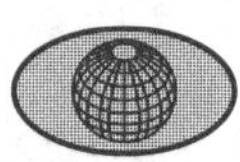   

Assessing Cash Flow and Bank Lending Requirements

DEFINITION

Lack of cash flow is a major cause of a business failing as, even though it may be turning a profit, if the money does not flow in on time the business will not be able to settle its debts. Cash flow is basically the measure of a company's financial health, showing the amount of cash generated and used by a company in any given period. Cash flow is essential to ensure solvency, as having enough cash ensures that creditors and employees can be paid on time. Banks require companies to show the difference between sales and costs within a specified period, which acts as an indicator of the performance of a business better than the profit margins. Sales and costs and, therefore, profits do not necessarily coincide with their associated cash inflows and outflows. Even though a sale has been secured and goods delivered, payment may be deferred as a result of credit to the customer, yet suppliers and staff still have to be paid and cash invested in rebuilding depleted stocks. The net result is that although profits may be reported, the business may experience a short-term cash shortfall.

The main sources of cash flow into a business are receipts from sales, increases in bank loans, proceeds of share issues and asset disposals, and other income, such as interest earned. Cash outflows include payments to suppliers and staff, capital and interest repayments for loans, dividends, taxation, and capital expenditure. Cash flow planning entails forecasting and tabulating all significant cash inflows and analyzing in detail the timing of expected payments, which include suppliers, wages, other expenses, capital expenditure, loan repayments, dividends, tax, and interest payments.

A computerized cash flow model can be used to compile forecasts, assess possible funding requirements, and explore the financial consequences of other strategies. Computerized models can help prevent major planning errors, anticipate problems, and identify opportunities to improve cash flow and negotiate loans.

Banks must ensure that a business is viable, which entails asking pertinent questions. Lenders will insist on up-to-date information on the type of industry, management capabilities and experience, business plans and daily operations, key competition, and PR and marketing plans. They have to know that the business makes sense and can repay a loan, and what security is available in case of insolvency. Companies have to keep within their cash limits regardless of anticipated business. Business factoring is an alternative to bank loans—a factoring company buys your credit invoices and provides you with immediate cash in exchange for a small fee ranging between 1.5% and 5.0%. Factoring is more flexible than a bank loan.

ADVANTAGES

Ensuring good cash flow through a company helps to:

- increase sales;
- reduce direct and indirect costs and overhead expenses;
- raise additional equity;
- gain the confidence of banks and potentially secure more loans.

DISADVANTAGES

- If your profit margins are already low, you might not be able to afford bank fees.
- The banks have a tendency to up fees and charge for late payments.

DOS AND DON'TS

DO

Do understand the way your company works, using a detailed analysis of banking procedure and taking into consideration:

- overdraft facilities and investment accounts;
- the number of monthly transactions;
- the number of written monthly checks;
- how customers pay you;
- the suitability of electronic banking for your business;
- cash access facilities;
- interest income;
- overall expenses and fees.

DON'T

- Don't overestimate sales forecasts.
- Don't underestimate costs.
- Don't underestimate delays in payments.
- Don't forget to check your debtors' credit history carefully.

ACTION CHECKLIST

It is essential to keep track of your cash and not allow any surplus to sit idle. Accounts must be carefully monitored and cash invested to maximize returns. There are many ways to increase cash flow:

- ✔ reducing credit terms for historically slow payers;
- ✔ reviewing customer payment performance;
- ✔ becoming more selective when granting credit;
- ✔ seeking other ways to pay rather than all in one installment, such as deposits or staggered payments;
- ✔ reducing the amount of time of the credit terms;
- ✔ invoicing immediately the work has been done;
- ✔ improving collection systems for billing;
- ✔ adding late payment charges.

➤➤ MORE INFO

Books:

Fight, Andrew. *Cash Flow Forecasting*. Oxford: Butterworth-Heinemann, 2006.

Mulford, Charles W., and Eugene E. Comiskey. *Creative Cash Flow Reporting and Analysis: Uncovering Sustainable Financial Performance*. Hoboken, NJ: Wiley, 2005.

Reider, Rob, and Peter B. Heyler. *Managing Cash Flow: An Operational Focus*. Hoboken, NJ: Wiley, 2003.

See Also:

★ Valuing Start-Ups (pp. 425–427)

✔ Preparing a Cash Flow Forecast (p. 880)

✔ Retail Banks: Their Structure and Function (p. 930)

"The debt is like a crazy aunt we keep down in the basement. All the neighbors know she's there, but nobody wants to talk about her." H. Ross Perot

  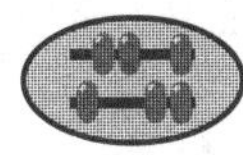 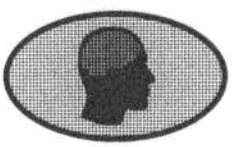  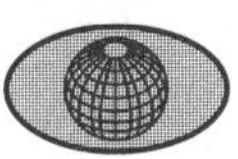   

Building a Forex Plan

DEFINITION

Forex, which is short for "foreign exchange," is the largest trading market in the world, turning over as much as US$1.5 trillion every day. There is no central marketplace for currency exchange, which is done over the counter. Currencies are traded on a global basis 24 hours a day, five days a week. Financial transactions involve one party purchasing a quantity of one currency in exchange for selling a quantity of another. Trading commonly occurs between large and central banks, currency speculators, corporations, governments, and other institutions. Currency prices depend on many factors, but ultimately the price depends upon supply and demand.

Forex markets react to trade levels and trends. Trade and investment flows indicate the demand for goods and services, in turn indicating demand for a country's currency to conduct trade. Trade deficits can have a negative impact on a nation's currency. A currency loses value when a country experiences rising inflation, which erodes demand for that particular currency. As a generalization, the healthier a country's economy, the better its currency will perform. Factors to look out for include economic factors, political conditions, and market psychology.

An effective and proven plan can help a company to exploit the forex currency trading system to its best potential. Customizing a forex plan in line with specific issues and needs can help to manage foreign exchange in the most cost-effective and efficient way. It is customary—and wise—to begin with a simulated forex trading account, which does not need any investment upfront but is used to train beginners in the strategies and fundamentals of forex trading.

A well-considered forex plan needs to take into account various elements. Decide whether you will hedge recorded or future assets and liabilities and how. Choose a trustworthy and competitive forex supplier. Plan the scope of activity taking into account objectives and time frames in which to achieve set goals. Make sure you schedule regular assessments of your forex business and revise any activities as needed. A forex plan should be sustainable, so aim to negotiate transactions at the most favorable prices. Keep track of your forex exposure by implementing methods for data capture. A good plan also has internal controls—consider your business processes and documentation requirements, ensure that you have strict authorization limits, and keep tasks segregated where necessary. Finally, stay familiar with accounting and reporting requirements.

A forex plan should be reviewed at every stage, from the first planning phase and throughout implementation. Senior management should sign off all decisions to ensure that risks are minimized. If the forex plan is of limited duration (for example for a specific project), then a post-implementation review is wise as it can identify areas for improvement and efficiency gains if you decide to enter the forex markets in the future.

ADVANTAGES

- When a company needs to use forex (for example, if it conducts business abroad), a strong forex plan can boost profits if transactions are conducted with care and insight. A good understanding of how to use forex transactions to advantage can also give an edge over business competitors.

DISADVANTAGES

- There is always a risk of losing money and thus profit, especially if you ignore advice and are overconfident about market conditions.

ACTION CHECKLIST

- ✔ Be as informed as you can on how the forex currency trading system operates.
- ✔ Enroll in a reputable forex trading system course online and familiarize yourself with the forex currency market with a simulated trading account.
- ✔ Learn forex investment strategies, including the buy signals that forex charts give traders.
- ✔ Choose the amount you want to make on every forex trade before you begin trading; this is usually more than or equal to the earnings that you can afford to lose in the forex trade.
- ✔ Select your forex suppliers and counterparts.
- ✔ Negotiate forex transactions at more favorable price points.

DOS AND DON'TS

DO

- Watch charts and indicators.
- Work out how much you are willing to risk per trade.
- Review existing general ledger activity in the foreign currency accounts (gain/loss account and other comprehensive income (OCI) accounts).
- Take a sample historical review or monitor current activity to compare forex rates and forex hedge costs.

DON'T

- Don't ignore factors such as government budget deficits or surpluses, inflation levels and trends, economic growth and health, political conditions, long-term trends, technical trading considerations, and domestic, regional, and international political conditions and events.
- Don't be too greedy—don't expect too much too soon.

›› MORE INFO

Books:

Cheng, Grace. *7 Winning Strategies for Trading Forex: Real and Actionable Techniques for Profiting from the Currency Markets*. Petersfield, UK: Harriman House, 2007.

Ponsi, Ed. *Forex Patterns & Probabilities: Trading Strategies for Trending & Range-bound Markets.* Hoboken, NJ: Wiley, 2007.

Websites:

A forex guide for beginners: www.forex-guide.net/beginner-investing.html

Insider's Guide to Forex Trading: forextradingonlinehelp.com

International Financial Services London (IFSL) research report, "Foreign exchange 2007": www.ifsl.org.uk/upload/CBS_Foreign_Exchange_2007.pdf

"We all of us, rich and poor, have to live with the insecurity caused by an out of control global casino with a built-in bias towards instability. Because it is instability that makes money for the money-traders."
Anita Roddick

  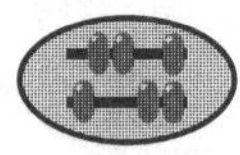 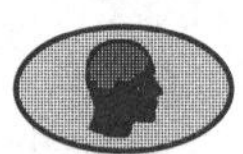  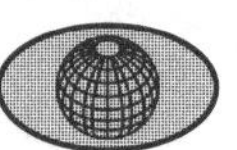   

Creating a Standardized Process

DEFINITION

A standardized process is a process that defines a single method of performing a task. Standardization means that all employees will perform a task in the same way on every occasion that the task is carried out. A standardized process is a repeatable, consistent way of performing tasks that can span organizational boundaries. Examples include processing paperwork for a new employee or carrying out the payroll processing for a business.

Importantly, a standardized process should run as efficiently as possible. Often, good candidates for being outsourced are standardized processes for tasks that would be performed in much the same way across different organizations (new employee and payroll processing are such examples), and where the process adds no unique business value for the organization.

Despite the often dynamic behavior of organizations, they should be thought of as operating a number of interrelated processes. The success of an organization is often dependent on those processes. Yet many companies neglect the area of processes, regardless of the age of the business. Gaining a full understanding of the processes within a company and how to manage those processes remains a challenge for modern organizations.

If a company can break down its operations into a number of discrete and defined processes, it can remove its dependence on the knowledge of individuals. As such, standardized processes need to be documented and should not be the province of individuals, or even groups of employees. Standardized processes must belong to the business. Process modeling applies to procedures, standards, work instructions, and guidelines, as well as business processes.

The challenge is to create accurate, concise, and standardized processes. This is no simple task, especially in larger companies, which may be filled with complexities, buried processes, and difficult communication trails.

Only with a full set of business processes will a company be able to grow and achieve its potential.

DOS AND DON'TS

DO

- Consult as many people in your organization as possible.
- Analyze, map, measure, and document.

DON'T

- Don't make assumptions.
- Don't believe that your business can succeed without standardized processes.

ADVANTAGES

- Implementing standardized processes usually results in lower process overheads and can reduce the complexity of information systems.
- Repeat performance of a task gives the same expected results every time.
- There is less need for personal expertise, and business growth may be enhanced.

DISADVANTAGES

- The main downside to standardizing processes is that staff may become bored.
- There is little or no room for innovation within a standardized process.

ACTION CHECKLIST

- ✔ Break your company down into key business processes to see where it may be possible to standardize.
- ✔ Understand why each process is required.
- ✔ Reduce each process to its least-skilled level.
- ✔ Test each process with staff unfamiliar with that process.

▸▸ MORE INFO

Books:

Harmon, Paul. *Business Process Change: A Manager's Guide to Improving, Redesigning, and Automating Processes*. San Francisco, CA: Morgan Kaufmann, 2003.

Jeston, J., and J. Nelis. *Business Process Management: Practical Guidelines to Successful Implementations*. 2nd ed. Oxford: Butterworth-Heinemann, 2008.

Journals:

Business Process Management Journal. Online at: info.emeraldinsight.com/products/journals/journals.htm?id=BPMJ

International Journal of Business Process Integration and Management. Online at: www.inderscience.com/browse/index.php?journalID=115

Websites:

The Business Process Journal: Jim Reardan's Essays and Observations on Business Strategy and Process Management: www.businessprocessjournal.com

SM Thacker's (UK) website has useful pages of links to business process resources: www.smthacker.co.uk/summary_business_processes.htm

See Also:

- ✔ Business Process Reengineering (p. 974)
- ✔ Inventory—How to Control It Effectively (p. 992)
- ✔ Invoicing and Credit Control for Small and Medium-Sized Enterprises (p. 993)
- ✔ Key Components of an Optimal Enterprise Resource Planning System (p. 870)

"Resolve to perform what you ought. Perform without fail what you resolve." Benjamin Franklin

  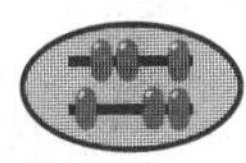   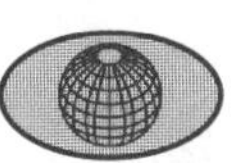   

Dealing with Financial Intermediaries

DEFINITION

A financial intermediary is an individual or a company that acts as a go-between between two or more parties to a financial transaction. One party is usually the provider of a service or product, and the other party is usually the client or customer.

It is usual to think of a financial intermediary as an individual (such as a financial adviser, mortgage broker, or mortgage adviser), but a financial intermediary can also be an institution such as a bank that provides funds to a borrower (the client) but obtains those funds from another financial institution. Most people or entities who deal with any kind of finance do not enter the markets directly themselves but use brokers or intermediaries, with commercial banks being the most common form of financial intermediary.

Using a financial intermediary offers a number of advantages. First, an intermediary has the infrastructure to deal with transactions. They can also diversify to spread their own risk. An individual or small institution would struggle to achieve this. Financial intermediaries also know their particular markets, having built up a wealth of experience. They are also likely to be able to judge accurately which customers present the greatest risk to them and charge them accordingly.

Small-scale financial intermediaries—usually a small brokerage firm or an individual—act as a buffer between the customer and the financial institution, selling their expertise and taking commission on others' financial products. The benefits of using a small-scale intermediary are their experience, knowledge of specific markets, and personal attention.

Bona fide financial intermediaries are usually regulated too, depending on which jurisdiction they are based in. Clients of regulated intermediaries generally have some form of consumer protection.

ADVANTAGES

Financial intermediaries:

- can spread their risk;
- have wide knowledge of financial markets;
- have access to many financial providers and institutions;
- are usually regulated;
- charge a fee, which can often be better value than the commission taken by a bank, which may reduce the amount you have to invest.

DISADVANTAGES

- You have to put your trust in a third party.
- You will be charged for the services they provide.
- You will be at least one step removed from any transaction you enter into.

ACTION CHECKLIST

✔ Search the internet and local directories for financial intermediaries. Asking your own contacts for recommendations can be a wise step.

✔ Talk to more than one intermediary to see what they are offering, what their specialisms are, and if they have the contacts and expertise to carry out the transaction you require.

✔ Work on building a good working relationship with the intermediary so that you can develop mutual trust.

DOS AND DON'TS

DO

- Check out the experience and history of your financial intermediary.
- Check their charges, but be prepared to pay for a good service.
- Check that they are regulated.
- If dealing with an online intermediary (e.g. for trading shares), verify their credentials.

DON'T

- Don't go with the first financial intermediary you talk to.
- Don't use an unregulated intermediary.

⏩ MORE INFO

Book:

Arshadi, Nasser, and Gordon V. Karels. *Modern Financial Intermediaries and Markets.* Upper Saddle River, NJ: Prentice Hall, 1997.

Journal:

Journal of Financial Intermediation. Online at: www.elsevier.com/locate/jfi

Article:

Demirgüç-Kunt, Asli, and Ross Levine. "Stock market development and financial intermediaries: Stylized facts." (World Bank policy research working paper no. 1462). *World Bank Economic Review* 10:2 (May 1996): 291–321.

See Also:

★ IPOs in Emerging Markets (pp. 545–547)
✔ Conflicting Interests: The Agency Issue (p. 901)
✔ Financial Intermediaries: Their Role and Relation to Financial Markets (p. 1012)
✔ Structuring, Negotiating, and Drafting Agency Agreements (p. 1005)

"Commerce, n. A kind of transaction in which A plunders from B the goods of C, and for compensation B picks the pocket of D of money belonging to E." Ambrose Bierce

  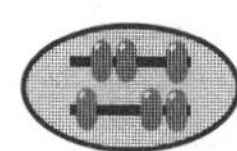 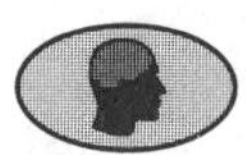  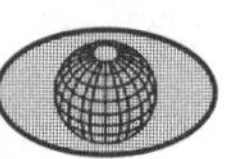   

Defining the Financial Manager's Role

DEFINITION

A financial manager is responsible for providing financial advice and support to colleagues and clients to enable them to make sound business decisions. The role of the financial manager is more than simply accounting; it is multifunctional. Financial managers must understand all aspects of the business so that they are able to adequately advise and support the chief executive officer in decision-making and ensuring company growth and profitability.

Almost every firm, government agency, or other type of organization has one or more financial managers. Financial managers oversee the preparation of financial reports, direct investment activities, and implement cash management strategies. They also implement the long-term goals of their organization.

Many corporations operate multifunctional teams where the financial manager is responsible for a particular division or function, or looks after a range of departments and functions. Financial managers often have specific roles and titles:

Controllers prepare financial reports and analyses of future earnings or expenses that summarize the organization's financial position. Controllers are also in charge of preparing special reports required by regulatory authorities—especially important because of the Sarbanes–Oxley Act, designed in part to protect investors from fraud.

Treasurers and finance officers direct and oversee budgets, monitor the investment of funds, manage associated risks, supervise cash management activities, execute capital raising strategies, and deal with mergers and acquisitions.

Risk and insurance managers administer programs to minimize risks and losses that could arise from financial transactions and business operations.

Credit managers supervise the firm's issuance of credit, fix credit-rating criteria, determine credit limits, and monitor the collection of past-due accounts.

Cash managers supervise and manage the flow of cash receipts and disbursements to meet business and investment needs.

The financial manager's role, particularly in business, is changing in response to technological advances that have significantly reduced the time it takes to produce financial reports. Financial managers now perform more data analysis to offer senior management ideas on how to maximize profits. They play an increasingly significant role in mergers and acquisitions and in related financing, and in areas that require wide-ranging, focused knowledge to diminish risks and maximize profit.

ADVANTAGES

- Financial managers improve business organization and risk management by providing reassurance on the effectiveness and efficiency of operations, financial reporting, and compliance with applicable laws and regulations.
- Financial managers provide management with an in-depth and unbiased understanding of risks that the organization may be facing, allowing for preemptive planning.
- Financial managers give company officers and directors forewarning of ethical and legal issues that may affect the organization.

DISADVANTAGES

- Although they are meant to be independent and impartial, financial managers are paid by the company and are an integral part of the company management; this can lead to conflicts of interest when advising senior management on, for example, investment risk.
- Financial managers' judgments, estimates, and interpretations are not always objective because of their close relationship with the organization for which they work.

ACTION CHECKLIST

- ✔ Has the financial manager worked in related business fields previously and, if so, for how long? What reliable references can be provided?
- ✔ How good is his/her track record on risk assessment and planning for contingencies?
- ✔ In assessing business processes, how up-to-date is he/she with technology controls in auditing?

DOS AND DON'TS

DO

- Consult with the financial controllers where ethical or legal issues may be involved.

DON'T

- Don't forget to consult key stakeholders and managers when evaluating and employing new financial managers, so that areas of competence can be checked.

▶▶ MORE INFO

Books:

Brigham, Eugene F., and Louis C. Gapenski. *Financial Management: Theory and Practice*. 11th ed. Cincinnati, OH: South-Western College Publishing, 2004.

Jorion, Philippe. *Financial Risk Manager Handbook*. 4th ed. Hoboken, NJ: Wiley, 2007.

Shim Jae K., and Joel G. Siegel. *Financial Management*. 2nd ed. Hauppauge, NY: Barron's Educational Series, 2000.

Article:

Varughese, Jess, and Peter Bond. "The ten commandments of integrating an acquisition." *US Banker* (July 2008).

Report:

US Government Accountability Office. "Financial management: Effective internal control is key to accountability." February 16, 2005.

Websites:

Association for Financial Professionals: www.afponline.org

Financial Management Association International (FMA): www.fma.org

See Also:

★ Money Managers (pp. 357–359)

★ Viewpoint: Ravi Nedungadi (pp. 815–816)

✔ Sarbanes–Oxley: Its Development and Aims (p. 1047)

"Capitalism is an art form, an Apollonian fabrication to rival nature. . .Everyone born into capitalism has incurred a debt to it. Give Caesar his due." Camille Paglia

  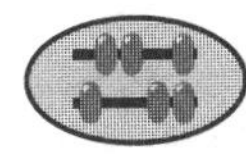   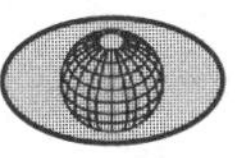   

Developing a Contingency Funding Plan

DEFINITION

A contingency fund is an amount of money that's kept in reserve for use in times when other funding resources have run out. In this way, the contingency fund can help guard against possible losses of important assets. In short, it's about sound budgeting for emergencies and the unexpected.

Historically, banks or companies have generally failed because they had no meaningful contingency plan. Indeed, banks with a sound contingency funding plan are considered much more likely to survive a funding crisis. While no retail bank actually failed during the global credit crunch of 2007–08, the British-based Northern Rock came close after fears over its liquidity caused customers to make a run on its funds and the Bank of England was forced to step in and shore up its finances. Having a credible contingency funding plan enables a bank or organization to forecast its liquidity in various worst-case scenarios.

The sensible realization that at some time in the future things might not be rosy is the first step towards setting up a contingency fund. Financial resources can run dry quickly in an emergency, forcing an organization to look elsewhere for funding. Having a contingency fund can help avoid the need to rely on other entities.

ADVANTAGES

- A contingency fund can help to relieve an organization of financial problems in times of difficulty.
- A contingency fund may even save an organization from going under.

DISADVANTAGES

- Salting away money into a contingency fund can seem like wasting money that could be used elsewhere, for example, for running the business, buying more assets, etc.
- It can be tempting to use the money in a contingency fund for other "emergencies" that are not actually defined for the use of the fund.

ACTION CHECKLIST

- ✔ Decide what the contingency fund will be for. Draw up a list of all possible situations where things might go wrong (worst-case scenarios) that are not covered by your insurance policies and consider under what circumstances you might need to draw on a contingency fund. This will help to define the uses for the fund. Then calculate how much it would cost in total to fund those areas of concern, and start setting aside spare cash in the contingency fund.
- ✔ Establish a set of rules for its use. In what circumstances will it be used? How much of the contingency fund can be used for a particular event or at one time? How long should it last? The uses of a contingency fund should be clearly defined. Veering from the rules for its use could compromise the financial health of the organization should a real need for the fund ever arise. Don't view it as a handy pot of money to dip into whenever needed.
- ✔ Establish a budget. Determine how much money to feed into the fund, and how often.

DOS AND DON'TS

DO

- Establish a budget.
- Decide exactly what the contingency fund will be for.
- Move money into the fund as appropriate.
- Automate saving into the fund so that it is not optional. Set up a standing order at the bank to ensure a regular transfer of money.
- Take advantage of the best savings account available so that the contingency fund earns interest while not in active use.

DON'T

- Don't ignore the rules for the use of the fund.
- Don't miss payments into the fund.
- Don't withdraw from the fund for purposes other than those for which it was set up, or before the end of a predefined period.

▸▸ MORE INFO

Book:

Nissenbaum, Martin, Barbara J. Raasch, and Charles L. Ratner. *Ernst & Young's Personal Financial Planning Guide.* 5th ed. Hoboken, NJ: Wiley, 2004.

Article:

Nelson, Michael. "Establishing a capital contingency fund for utilities." *Public Works* (October 1994).

See Also:

- ✔ Identifying Your Continuity Needs (p. 986)
- ✔ Options for Raising Finance (p. 1017)
- ✔ Understanding Crisis Management (p. 919)

"A crash does not come knocking at the front door by appointment." Jim Slater

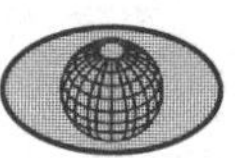

Estimating Enterprise Value with the Weighted Average Cost of Capital

DEFINITION

Enterprise value (EV) is a fundamental metric for measuring a company's market worth and is often used in place of market capitalization. The standard formula for EV is the market capitalization *plus* debt, minority interest, and preferred shares, *minus* total cash and cash equivalents. Because enterprise value is more comprehensive than market capitalization and takes debt into account, it is considered to be a more accurate representation of a company's value and often viewed as the theoretical takeover price.

Estimating enterprise value with the weighted average cost of capital (WACC) also takes the share price into account. WACC is the rate at which a company must pay to finance its assets. It is the minimum return that a company needs to earn from its existing asset base in order to satisfy its creditors, owners, and any other of its capital providers, and to keep its stock price constant.

WACC is used to discount expected cash flows during the excess return period to arrive at the aggregate of the organization's cash flow from operations. The company's residual value is calculated by dividing the net operating profit after tax by its WACC (based on an assumed terminal growth rate of 0%). Enterprise value is the sum of cash flow from operations, the residual value, and the short-term assets.

ADVANTAGES

- Using WACC to calculate a company's enterprise value gives the most accurate figure possible for the value of a company. Some investors follow a value philosophy and look for companies that generate a lot of cash flow compared with their enterprise value. In general terms, businesses that do this are likely to require less additional reinvestment. With plenty of cash, the owners can take the profit out of the business and invest it elsewhere or pay dividends to investors.

DISADVANTAGES

- The main disadvantage is that enterprise value is not as easy to calculate as market capitalization. The latter is a simple multiplication of the number of shares by the share's unit value, whereas enterprise value takes other less tangible factors into account, making the calculation more elusive.

ACTION CHECKLIST

- ✔ Understand the reasons why you want to value a company. Is it to buy the company or to buy the stock?
- ✔ Assess whether you really need very accurate figures. The enterprise value calculation will provide these, but adding in the WACC will give an even more accurate result.

DOS AND DON'TS

DO

- Use enterprise value with WACC if you are considering buying a company.

DON'T

- Don't overcomplicate your calculations if you just want a ballpark figure. In that case, use market capitalization.
- Don't add cash in to the value of a company—take it away.

▸▸ MORE INFO

Books:

Copeland, Tom, Tim Koller, and Jack Murrin. *Valuation: Measuring and Managing the Value of Companies*. 3rd ed. New York: Wiley, 2000.

Koller, Tim, *et al.* *Valuation Workbook: Step-by-Step Exercises and Tests to Help You Master Valuation*. 4th ed. Hoboken, NJ: Wiley, 2006.

See Also:

✔ Acquisition Accounting (p. 956)
✔ Calculating a Company's Net Worth (p. 935)
✔ Understanding the Weighted Average Cost of Capital (WACC) (p. 897)
John D. Rockefeller (p. 1185)
Damodaran on Valuation: Security Analysis for Investment and Corporate Finance (p. 1245)

"**Accuracy, n. A certain uninteresting quality carefully excluded from human statements.**" Ambrose Bierce

  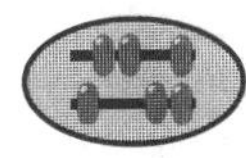   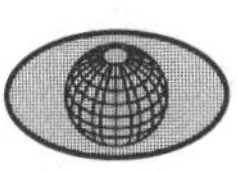   

The Foreign Exchange Market: Its Structure and Function

DEFINITION

The foreign exchange market, also known as the forex, FX, or currency market, involves the trading of one currency for another. Prior to 1996 the market was confined to large corporate banks and international corporations. However it has since opened up to include all traders and speculators. Today, the average daily turnover in forex markets is US$1.9 trillion, according to the Bank of International Settlement's Triennial Survey. The market is growing rapidly as investors gain more information and develop more interest.

In trading foreign exchange, investors bet that one currency will appreciate over another; they profit when they bet correctly and collect the profit in the form of an interest rate spread when they return to the original currency. The profit margins are low compared with other fixed-income markets. Large trading volumes can, however result, in very high profits. Most forex trading takes place in London, New York, and Tokyo, with most trading activity in London, which dominates the market at 30% of all transactions. New York's market share is 16%, and Tokyo's has fallen to 10% due to the growing prominence of Singapore and Hong Kong. Singapore has become the fourth largest exchange market globally, and Hong Kong is the fifth, having overtaken Switzerland. The various players in the foreign exchange market include bank dealers, 16% of which are international investors and speculators. Banks account for almost two-thirds of forex transactions; of the rest, about 20% is mainly attributable to securities firms that operate in the international debt and equity markets.

One type of very short-term transaction is the *spot transaction* between two currencies, delivering over two days and using cash as opposed to a contract.

In a *forward transaction*, the money is not exchanged until an arranged date and an exchange rate is agreed in advance. The time period ranges from days to years. *Currency swaps* are a popular type of forward transaction; these involve the exchange of currency by two parties for an agreed length of time and an arrangement to swap currencies at an agreed later date. Another type is a *foreign currency future*, which is inclusive of interest. A standard contract is drawn up and a maturity date arranged. The time schedule is about three months.

In a *foreign exchange option* (FX option), the most liquid and biggest options market in the world, the owner may elect to exchange money in a designated currency for another currency at an agreed date in the future. This type of transaction depends on the availability of option contracts on an organized exchange. Otherwise, such forex deals may be carried out using an over-the-counter (OTC) contract.

ADVANTAGES

- The forex market is extremely liquid, hence its rapidly growing popularity. Currencies may be converted when bought or sold without causing too much movement in the price and keeping losses to a minimum.
- As there is no central bank, trading can take place anywhere in the world and operates on a 24-hour basis apart from weekends.
- An investor needs only small amounts of capital compared with other investments. Forex trading is outstanding in this regard.
- It is an unregulated market, meaning that there is no trade commission overseeing transactions and there are no restrictions on trade.
- In common with futures, forex is traded using a "good faith deposit" rather than a loan. The interest rate spread is an attractive advantage.

DISADVANTAGES

- The major risk is that one counterparty fails to deliver the currency involved in a very large transaction. In theory at least, such a failure could bring ruin to the forex market as a whole.
- Investors need a lot of capital to make good profits because the profit margins on small-scale trades are very low.

ACTION CHECKLIST

- ✔ Be alert for unanticipated corrections and wild fluctuations in currency exchange rates.
- ✔ Look for volatile markets that offer opportunities for quick profit.
- ✔ Watch out for lost payments, and be aware of delays in payments and money received. There may also be discrepancies between bank drafts received and the original price of the contract.
- ✔ It is wise to exit from the forex market at the point when your profit targets have been achieved as this ensures that you stay within the profit zone.

DOS AND DON'TS

DO

- Make sure when you pick a pair of currencies that you understand their relationship.
- Use a trading system that you can trust with your money.

DON'T

- Don't be greedy: take your profits at the right time.
- Don't be emotional when you trade.

▸▸ MORE INFO

Books:

Archer, Michael Duane. *Getting Started in Forex Trading Strategies*. 7th ed. Hoboken, NJ: Wiley, 2008.

Dicks, James. *Forex Made Easy: 6 Ways to Trade the Dollar*. New York: McGraw-Hill, 2004.

Shamah, Shani Beverly. *A Foreign Exchange Primer*. Wiley Finance Series. Chichester, UK: Wiley, 2003.

Websites:

Easy-Forex is a forex trading platform with learning pages and tools: www.easy-forex.com

FOREX.com is a forex trading platform where you can try a free practice account; also learning and resource pages: www.forex.com

FOREXONTOP provides a ranked list of the most visited forex websites (over 500 sites): www.forexontop.com

"**That realm cannot be rich whose coin is poor or base.**" William Cecil

  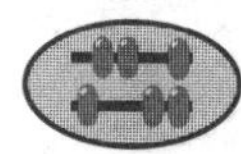   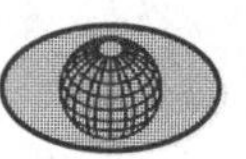   

Hedging Credit Risk—Case Studies and Strategies

DEFINITION

Credit risk is the uncertainty about the ability of a debtor or the counterparty in an agreement to make a payment. Strategies for managing credit risk use traditional credit analysis techniques to screen counterparties and may also take advantage of hedging via derivatives.

Corporations frequently need to estimate the likelihood of defaults, the exposure, and the severity of loss from a default event. Taking into account these factors and market-based inputs, it is possible to estimate both expected and unexpected losses across a portfolio.

Expected credit losses can be statistically estimated over a period of time. Risk-adjusted credit loss provisions can then be set and factored into pricing as part of the normal cost of doing business. Unexpected losses form the basis for the credit risk capital-allocation process.

INSTRUMENTS

There are three main structures of derivative that enable an organization to manage credit risks more effectively.

With a credit default swap (CDS), a buyer purchases a contract and makes regular payments to a seller of credit protection. In the event of a default, the buyer receives compensation from the seller. This is commonly seen as an insurance policy for the buyer. It can, however, be used speculatively as there is no requirement for the buyer to hold any asset or have any potentially loss-making relationship with the so-called "reference entity."

Total return swaps are similar to interest rate swaps. One side makes payments based on the total return from an asset. The other makes floating or fixed payments. The notional amount of the underlying asset is the same for both parties.

A credit linked note (CLN) covers a specific credit risk. Investors receive a higher yield in return for accepting risk relating to a specific event. It provides a hedge for borrowers against an explicit risk. A CLN is created through a trust using very low-risk securities as collateral. Investors are paid a floating or fixed rate throughout the period of the note. At its completion they will either receive par or, if the reference entity has defaulted, the recovery rate value of the note.

CASE STUDY
Credit Default Swap

Although swaps can be used to hedge against any sort of credit risk, they are easiest to explain through a notional case study of an instrument such as a bond. A fund may, for example, hold $8,000,000 of Mega Car Company's five-year bond, and is concerned about the possibility of default due to market conditions arising from rising oil prices, increased government regulation on emissions, or the macroeconomic climate.

The fund decides to buy a credit default swap in a notional amount of $8,000,000 to cover the potential default value. The CDS in this case trades at 150 basis points, so the fund will pay 1.5% of $8,000,000, or $120,000 annually.

If Mega Car Company does not default, the fund will simply receive the full $8,000,000. In this case its return will not be as good as it would have been without the CDS.

On the other hand, if the corporation does default after, say, two years, the fund will receive its $8,000,000 from the seller of the CDS. It could be that the seller will take the bond or pay the difference between the recovery value and the par value of the bond.

Alternatively, Mega Car Company could make a breakthrough in low-emission technology and dramatically improve its credit profile. In that case the fund might decide to reduce its outgoings by selling the remaining period of the CDS.

ADVANTAGES

- Derivatives such as a CDS will reduce or entirely remove the risk of default.

DISADVANTAGES

- The cost of hedging will reduce the return on investment.

▸▸ MORE INFO

Books:

Chacko, George, Anders Sjöman, Hideto Motohashi, and Vincent Dessain. *Credit Derivatives: A Primer on Credit Risk, Modeling, and Instruments.* Upper Saddle River, NJ: Wharton School Publishing, 2006.

Colquitt, Joetta. *Credit Risk Management: How to Avoid Lending Disasters and Maximize Earnings.* New York: McGraw-Hill, 2007.

de Servigny, Arnaud, and Olivier Renault. *The Standard & Poor's Guide to Measuring and Managing Credit Risk.* New York: McGraw-Hill, 2004.

See Also:

★ How the Settlement Infrastructure Is Surviving the Financial Meltdown (pp. 211–213)
★ The Role of Short Sellers in the Marketplace (pp. 376–379)
✔ Managing Your Credit Risk (p. 873)
✔ Swaps, Options, and Futures: What They Are and Their Function (p. 882)
✔ Understanding Hedge Ratios (p. 892)

"There's only one thing to do with loose change of course. Tighten it." Flann O'Brien

  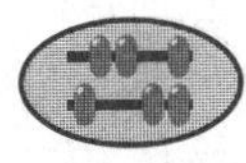   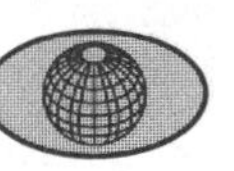   

Hedging Foreign Exchange Risk—Case Studies and Strategies

DEFINITION

A company that imports raw materials, exports finished goods, or has overseas assets or subsidiaries is exposed to fluctuations in exchange rates. Adverse movements can wipe out export profits, while positive changes can increase the price of its products in the foreign market. Equally, the company could benefit from windfall profits as a result of exchange rate fluctuations.

A company trading across national borders therefore has a number of choices. It can take a chance with spot rates, buying currency when required. This leaves it totally at the mercy of exchange rates. The risk can be removed if it books a forward exchange contract that fixes the rate for the date on which it will be needed for a transaction. If the rate improves, however, the company will not be able to take advantage of the improvement.

Using a combination of flexible products allows the company to protect itself against adverse movements while still giving it the ability to profit from improvements. A wide variety of instruments are available that allow companies to pursue this strategy. Which is chosen depends partly on the level of risk and also on the ease of converting the currencies.

CASE STUDIES

The Participating Forward

This product is similar to a forward exchange contract in that it limits risk by offering a worst-case exchange rate for a transaction. If, however, there is a favorable move in exchange rates, the company can take advantage—generally with half its currency. There is usually no premium payable for this product.

Example

A company imports Cava wine from Spain to the United Kingdom. It is April, and a supplier has to be paid €4 million in October in time to catch the Christmas market.

The forward rate is 1.2100, and the company wants the certainty of a worst-case rate but doesn't want to lose out if the rate goes up. The foreign exchange broker offers a rate of 1.1800, with the option to buy half the currency on the spot market two days before completion of the transaction.

Possible Outcomes

Sterling strengthens against the euro and the rate rises to 1.2500. The customer pays £1,694,915 for the first €2,000,000 at the low rate agreed in advance and £1,600,000 for the second €2,000,000 at the spot rate. The average rate is therefore 1.215, slightly better than the forward rate, but not as good as the spot rate.

Alternatively, the euro strengthens against sterling and the spot rate is 1.1600. The company then pays the rate of 1.1800 for the whole transaction.

The advantages of a participating forward are: a guaranteed worst-case rate; total protection against currency falls; a partial benefit from currency gains; and no premium. The disadvantages are: if the currency weakens the rate will not be as good as a forward exchange contract; and the spot rate will be better if there is a positive move in currency.

The Protection Option

With this service a company pays a premium for an option to exchange currency on a fixed forward date at a predetermined rate. If the spot rate on that date is better than the predetermined rate, the company can decide not to exercise its option to sell at the predetermined rate.

Example

A UK company is selling dresses to a customer in the United States. In six months it will receive $4,000,000. The current forward rate for this date is 2.0000. Fearing that sterling is going to strengthen against the dollar, the company opts to buy a protection option at the forward rate.

Possible Outcomes

Sterling does strengthen against the dollar, taking the rate to 2.1500. The company then exercises its right to sell dollars at 2.0000.

The dollar strengthens against sterling. The rate is now 1.85000. The company takes the better rate on the spot market.

The advantages of the protection option are: a guaranteed worst-case rate; total protection against negative currency fluctuations; and the ability to take full advantage of positive currency movements. The disadvantage is that a premium is payable to the foreign exchange trader.

OTHER HEDGING PRODUCTS

There are many other ways for companies to hedge against currency variations using derivatives. Currency markets are extremely volatile, and it makes sense for any organization trading across national borders to protect itself from these fluctuations.

⏩ MORE INFO

See Also:

★ Using Structured Products to Manage Liabilities (pp. 106–108)
✔ Building a Forex Plan (p. 855)
✔ The Foreign Exchange Market: Its Structure and Function (p. 861)
✔ Identifying and Managing Exposure to Interest and Exchange Rate Risks (p. 867)
✔ Understanding and Using Currency Swaps (p. 885)

"When a system of national currencies run by a central bank is transformed into a global electronic marketplace driven by currency traders, power changes hands." Walter Wriston

     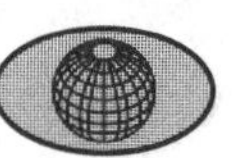   

Hedging Interest Rate Risk—Case Study and Strategies

DEFINITION

Risks arise from the way the value of an investment changes with the level of interest rates. This is most clearly seen in the value of fixed-rate investments such as bonds. If interest rates rise, the opportunity cost from holding the bond falls as it becomes more advantageous to switch to other investments.

Alternatively, a company with a loan at a variable rate of interest may want to adapt its payments to avoid the risk arising from a rise in interest rates. It may also want to aid its financial planning by creating a more even pattern of repayment.

A number of instruments exist to hedge against the risks posed by changing interest rates. For a company that decides to reduce its exposure to rising interest rates associated with variable rate funding there are two main types of derivative.

A cap will ensure that the company does not have to find more than a maximum agreed level of interest. The company will benefit if interest rate levels stay below that level. A cap is paid for up-front. A variation on this instrument is the cap and collar, whereby the company will pay the seller of the product if interest rates fall below an agreed level.

Swaps allow the company to exchange variable-rate payments for a guaranteed fixed rate. Swaps do not generally require any advance payment to the seller.

There are a huge variety of swap instruments, reflecting the international nature of the debt market. For instance, although there would be no advantage in swapping a fixed rate for another fixed rate within the same currency, as the outcome would be known, it may be desirable to swap fixed rates between two currencies. Every variable of currency, floating and fixed exchange rate can be swapped.

CASE STUDY

Vanilla Interest Rate Swap

A company enters into a vanilla interest rate swap with a bank to reduce the risk from fluctuations on a $10 million loan it has taken out on a floating rate. The bank agrees to a fixed rate of, for example, 6% over five years, while the floating rates are based on the six-monthly Libor (London Interbank Borrowing Rate) plus 2%. If the Libor is 4% at the start of the agreement, the amount payable is 6% in both cases, although any percentage could be agreed.

If the Libor rises to 6%, the amount payable every six months would be 8% of $10 million divided by two, or $400,000. The company's agreement with the bank is for a rate of 6%, or a payment of $300,000 in this case. The company will receive the difference of $100,000 from the bank.

The amount of the loan does not change hands and the company may continue to make the variable payments. It will receive cash if interest rates rise, and pay the bank if they fall. The net effect on the company is the same as if it had taken out a fixed-rate loan. Although the obvious route would be for a company to take out a fixed-rate loan, initially this may not be available or it may be too expensive.

Moreover, because the amount of the swap is notional, it is not necessary for the company to match the whole amount of the loan or to ensure that its entire life is covered. There may well be occasions when risk managers expect interest rate rises over the short to medium term. Continuing with a swap arrangement after the rises have peaked could wipe out initial gains.

ADVANTAGES

- A swap is flexible, allowing a company to adjust its maturity, payment frequency, and principal to suit its ongoing financial arrangements.
- Interest rates can be managed independently of financing arrangements.
- There is no requirement for a payment up-front.

DISADVANTAGES

- The arrangement locks the company into a fixed rate that may not be advantageous.
- Early termination may incur a cost.
- There is a slight additional risk of failure from involving an additional financial institution in the swap arrangement.

▸▸ MORE INFO

Book:

Coyle, Brian. *Interest-Rate Swaps*. London: Financial World Publishing, 2004.

See Also:

★ The Role of Short Sellers in the Marketplace (pp. 376–379)
★ Corporate Covenant and Other Embedded Options in Pension Funds (pp. 303–305)
✔ Identifying and Managing Exposure to Interest and Exchange Rate Risks (p. 867)
✔ Understanding and Using Interest Rate Swaps (p. 887)
✔ Understanding and Using the Repos Market (p. 949)

"**The market, whether stock, bond or super, is a barometer of civilization.**" Jason Alexander

  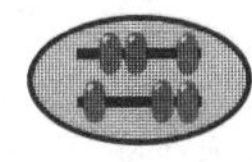   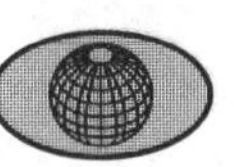   

Hedging Liquidity Risk—Case Study and Strategies

DEFINITION

The concept of "liquidity risk" tends to be very loosely defined. It is used most commonly with reference to the banking and finance industry, but it is an important issue for all companies. Broadly, liquidity risk is the danger that it will be difficult or impossible for an organization to sell an asset in order to provide capital to meet short-term financial demands.

A company needs to remain solvent; the liquidity risk is in the secondary market for its assets, which may not be sellable in time to meet short-term financial commitments, or will be sold at a price considerably below the perceived current market value. The problem may arise as the result of a liquidity gap or mismatch. This means that the dates for inflow and outflow of funds do not match up, creating a shortage.

Systemic liquidity risks arise from external factors. National or international recessions and credit crunches have the largest general impact on liquidity. Capital market disruptions, however, are more common. The collapse of the Russian ruble in 1998, for instance, created a global liquidity crisis, with a capital flight to quality away from the highly speculative Russian stock market.

Generally, liquidity is abundant during times when the economy is booming. During a downturn the impact on companies may increase if they continue with strategies based on the assumption that the high liquidity will continue indefinitely.

CASE STUDY

A company has outgoings of $8,000,000 a month against income from sales of $10,000,000. It faces a number of threats to its liquidity: for example, the price of the commodity it sells has fallen by 25%, leaving its income at $7,500,000 against $8,000,000 outgoings, and it has to find a way to raise the additional $500,000.

Some major customers have axed or cut their orders, leaving the company with a surplus of products to sell on the market. It has lost $4,000,000 in "normal" monthly sales and now has to offload products it is forced to sell, below cost, at 50% of the expected price simply to pay its bills ($6,000,000 in expected sales plus $2,000,000 to meet monthly obligations of $8,000,000).

The company chose to secure its position and iron out liquidity problems in the following ways:

- It held cash to cover some of the shortfall, but it lost the potential income from this capital.
- It set up a line of credit with its bank to help cover the shortfall.
- It sold off some assets in order to meet its financial obligations. This is risky as assets that have to be sold in a hurry may not realize their book price.

All this assumes that the company assessed its liquidity risks accurately and market conditions did not change.

STRATEGIES

Threats to a company's liquidity seldom happen in isolation but are intertwined with other financial risks. If, for example, a company fails to receive a payment, it may be forced to raise cash elsewhere or default on its payments. In this scenario, credit risk and liquidity risk are linked.

The aim of a liquidity management strategy is to minimize the cost of capital, allowing efficient access to capital and money markets at competitive prices during times of "normal" activity. Concurrently, the strategy should provide high levels of liquidity during periods when the financial markets are impaired.

The latter part of the strategy is often described as "life insurance." At a simple level this can mean organizing lines of credit well in advance of market turmoil, which is the cheapest option. However, the activities of a company and the market it operates in are dynamic. There will be periods when it is cash-rich and others when it is cash-poor. As cash is the ultimate liquid asset, there will be periods when it can "self-insure" and times when it will need to approach an external source for insurance.

ACTION CHECKLIST

✔ Examine predicted cash flows for the company. Look for any major negatives. Their impact can be stress-tested by analyzing the effect of a default by the major parties.

✔ Ensure that inflows and outflows match as far as possible.

✔ Assess the risk profile of the company before deciding what measures to put in place. In general liquid assets have a lower rate of return.

✔ Start a process of scenario testing. What happens if there is a default within an income stream?

✔ Ensure that the impacts of rare events are tested too. They may be unusual in isolation, but the more there are, statistically the higher the probability that one will occur.

▸▸ MORE INFO

Book:

Coyle, Brian. *Cash Flow Forecasting & Liquidity*. Risk Management Series: Cash Flow Management. London: Financial World Publishing, 2004.

See Also:

★ Navigating a Liquidity Crisis Effectively (pp. 86–88)
✔ Identifying Weak Points in Your Liquidity (p. 868)
✔ Managing Working Capital (p. 872)
✔ Measuring Liquidity (p. 875)

"**The eighties was an era when many companies were asset rich and cash poor.**" Nicola Horlick

  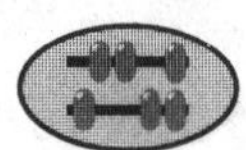   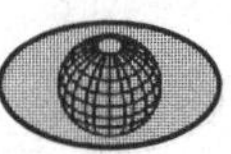   

How to Manage Your Credit Rating

DEFINITION

A credit rating is an assessment of the creditworthiness of an entity such as an individual, a corporation, or even a country. Credit ratings are worked out from past financial history as well as current assets and liabilities, and are used to inform a potential lender or investor about the probability of the entity being able to pay back a loan. However, in recent years credit ratings have been used more widely. They have, for example, been used to make adjustments to insurance premiums or to establish the amount of a leasing deposit.

Credit reference agencies compile credit histories on individuals using information from sources such as electoral registers, court judgments, and lenders. Anyone applying for credit can expect to have their request recorded for the credit agencies to access and use. Financial institutions compile their own credit ratings for companies. The best known credit raters are Moody's and Standard & Poor's, which produce credit ratings for listed companies, banks, and even countries.

Credit reference agencies do not make the decision on whether to offer credit to would-be borrowers. It is for the lenders to reach a decision using information amassed by the credit agencies, combined with their own lending criteria and knowledge.

Having a bad credit rating limits your borrowing options. Court judgments, defaults on payments, and bankruptcy orders will all reduce your credit rating score. This applies equally to individuals and businesses. Where a credit applicant has a poor credit rating, credit may still be obtained through the subprime market, where the borrower is charged much higher rates of interest.

ADVANTAGES

Managing your credit rating can help to:

- ensure that you have access to credit in the future;
- enable you to take out a mortgage or loan; give you peace of mind.

DISADVANTAGES

- Repeated applications for credit (particularly unsuccessful ones) are recorded on your file.
- Repeated checks of your credit rating are recorded on your file.

ACTION CHECKLIST

- ✔ Buy access to your credit history and use it to check your credit rating.
- ✔ Make sure that any spent court judgments are recorded as such on your file.
- ✔ Ensure that any annulled or discharged bankruptcy order is recorded as such on your file.
- ✔ Keep up with all payments.

DOS AND DON'TS

DO

- Understand what your credit rating is.
- Check for errors in your credit rating, and have them amended.
- Work to make your credit history better if it has been poor in the past.
- Ask a potential lender if you fit their profile of a typical successful credit applicant as this may help you to avoid an actual credit check.
- Pay your creditors on time. If you miss a payment, inform your creditor straight away.
- Make sure you are on the electoral register.
- Make sure you complete credit card application forms correctly.
- Make your credit card, store card, loan, and mortgage repayments on time.
- Consider asking a family member or friend with a good credit rating to co-sign for a small loan or credit card. This can help your own rating.

DON'T

- Don't miss any payments.
- Don't check your credit record too often.
- Don't apply for loans too often, especially if you have a doubtful credit record.
- Don't avoid having any credit—no credit record is as bad as a poor credit record.

▸▸ MORE INFO

Books:

de Servigny, Arnaud, and Olivier Renault. *The Standard & Poor's Guide to Measuring and Managing Credit Risk.* New York: McGraw-Hill, 2004.

Ong, Michael K. (ed). *Credit Ratings—Methodologies, Rationale and Default Risk.* London: Risk Books, 2002.

See Also:

★ Corporate Covenant and Other Embedded Options in Pension Funds (pp. 303–305)
★ Credit Ratings (pp. 534–536)
✔ The Bond Market: Its Structure and Function (p. 1010)
✔ How to Use Credit Rating Agencies (p. 939)
✔ Raising Capital by Issuing Bonds (p. 1020)

"Nowhere does history indulge in repetitions so often or so uniformly as in Wall Street." Jesse Livermore

  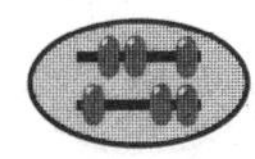 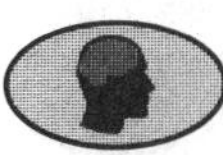  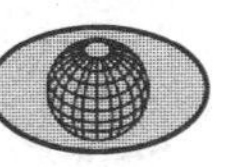   

Identifying and Managing Exposure to Interest and Exchange Rate Risks

DEFINITION

The successful management of a portfolio includes maximizing returns from shifts in exchange and interest rates, which in turn requires an appreciation of the associated exposures. Not knowing the exposure can leave the portfolio open to significant risk.

Exchange rate risk is the risk arising from a change in the price of one currency against another. Companies or institutions that trade internationally are exposed to exchange rate risk if they do not hedge their positions. There are two main risks associated with exposure to exchange rates.

- Transaction risk arises because exchange rates may change unfavorably over time. The best protection is to use forward currency contracts to hedge against such changes.
- Translation risk concerns the accounts, and the level of risk is proportional to the amount of assets held in foreign currencies. Over a period of time, changes in exchange rates will cause the accounts to become inaccurate. To avoid this, assets need to be offset by borrowings in the affected currency.

The significance of the exposure will depend on the portfolio's weightings and operations. Identifying the level of risk in the above exposures should help with selecting a suitable defense strategy.

Interest rate risk relates to changes in the floating rate. Failure to understand exposure to interest rates can lead to substantial risk. The two main areas of concern here should be borrowings and cash investments. The best way of appreciating exposure to changing interest rates is to stress-test various scenarios. How, for example, would a change in rate from 4% to 6% affect your ability to borrow?

MITIGATING THE RISK

Exchange Rate Exposure

Other than the two strategies mentioned above, good strategies for minimizing exchange rate exposure involve employing one or more of the following products.

- **Spot foreign exchange:** An obligation to buy/sell a specified quantity of currency at the current market rate to be settled in two business days.
- **Structured forwards:** Exchange forwards embedded with, generally, more than one currency option. This adaptation allows a more effective hedge and should improve the exchange rate within the client's perception of the market.
- **Currency options:** An option to the right to buy/sell a certain amount of currency at a specific exchange rate on or before a specific future date.

Interest Rate Exposure

Once identified, the risks can be minimized using the following methods:

- **Interest rate swap:** A method for changing the interest rate you earn/pay on an agreed amount for a specified time period.
- **Cross-currency swap:** An exchange of principal and interest payments in separate currencies.
- **Forward rate agreement:** Two parties fix the interest rate that will apply to a loan or deposit.
- **Interest rate caps:** The seller and borrower agree to limit the borrower's floating interest rate to a specified level for a period of time.
- **Structured swap:** An interest rate/cross-currency swap embedded with one or more derivatives. This allows the client to minimize his exposure on his perception of the market.

ADVANTAGES

- The one key advantage to identifying exposure to interest and exchange rate fluctuations is the ability to minimize possible losses in the event that your view of the market is wrong. This approach will also minimize the chance of unexpected events disrupting the investment strategy.

DISADVANTAGES

- As with any hedge strategy, minimizing possible losses also reduces potential gains. Only those who are supremely confident in their forecasts and with a cushion to absorb losses should consider taking any extra risk to maximize returns.

ACTION CHECKLIST

✔ Plan your approach. Establish what your aims are when dealing with exchange rates/foreign currencies. Decide on your strategies for dealing with interest rate exposure. Create risk registers that set out clear procedures for dealing with risks as they arise.

✔ Calculate what losses you can afford, or what profits you need to make, and stick to them.

DOS AND DON'TS

DO

- Set realistic targets.
- Stick to your strategy.
- Research best strategy and implementation.

DON'T

- Don't be overoptimistic.
- Don't alter your strategy midway.
- Don't expose yourself to excessive risk.

➤➤ MORE INFO

Books:

Fornés, Gastón. *Foreign Exchange Exposure in Emerging Markets: How Companies Can Minimize It*. Basingstoke, UK: Palgrave Macmillan, 2009.

Friberg, Richard. *Exchange Rates and the Firm: Strategies to Manage Exposure and the Impact of EMU*. Basingstoke, UK: Macmillan, 1999.

See Also:

✔ Hedging Foreign Exchange Risk— Case Studies and Strategies (p. 863)
✔ Hedging Interest Rate Risk— Case Study and Strategies (p. 864)
✔ Understanding and Using Inflation Swaps (p. 886)

"Better never means better for everyone. . .It always means worse, for some." Margaret Atwood

  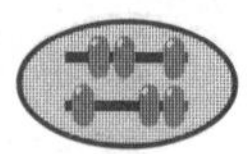 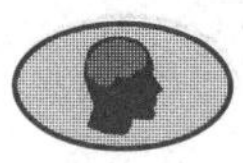  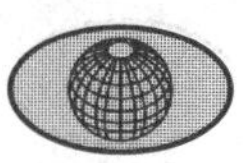   

Identifying Weak Points in Your Liquidity

DEFINITION

The liquidity of an asset is the degree to which it, or a security, can be traded on the market without affecting its price, and how quickly this can be done. Another way of looking at liquidity is to determine how quickly an asset can be converted into cash.

Liquidity became a much-discussed topic during the so-called credit crunch in 2007–08. Following the subprime crisis that started in the United States in 2007, banks all over the world suddenly found themselves unable to borrow money from each other as trust ran out and questions were raised over banks' creditworthiness. This meant that banks had to rely on their own sources of funding, and those with a lack of liquidity suffered. Those that were unable to turn their assets into cash had problems trading.

As a result of the credit crunch, banks had to put new measures in place to identify the weak points in their liquidity. There are companies specializing in liquidity risk management that can help firms to understand and manage their liquidity. A liquidity health check generally involves undertaking a review of processes, systems, and financial reports throughout the company.

When markets are in good health, liquidity is not generally a problem. Liquidity issues tend to become exposed during an economic downturn or recession.

Having liquidity means having the ability to meet obligations as they become due. Liquidity is crucial to the viability, and credibility, of any bank. Even a whiff of a rumor of illiquidity can be enough to trigger a run on a bank—for example, the run on Northern Rock in the United Kingdom in 2007. A liquidity shortfall at a single organization can have systemic repercussions, as the credit crunch of 2007–08 showed. That is why managing liquidity is one of the most important activities for banks to perform well.

ADVANTAGES

Identifying weak points in your liquidity is important because:

- it will enable you better to manage your assets during difficult financial periods as well as during good ones;
- it will ensure that you (as an individual or an organization) have a diverse portfolio of assets and investments that will cover more risk scenarios.

DISADVANTAGES

- The effort involved in identifying weak points in your liquidity may seem superfluous in good times.
- It requires expenditure to create and set up the necessary processes for liquidity management.

ACTION CHECKLIST

- ✔ Analyze your cash flow-based liquidity gap.
- ✔ Carry out scenario-based analyses.
- ✔ Perform liability modeling and stress-testing.
- ✔ Implement a liquidity policy that will identify methods, processes, and responsibilities.

DOS AND DON'TS

DO

- Analyze your liquidity provision.
- Diversify your funds.
- Implement regular liquidity status reporting.
- Consider planning for a contingency fund.
- Make sure your reporting system is accurate, informative, regular, comprehensive, and realistic.

DON'T

- Don't maintain a large number of illiquid assets.
- Don't go too far the other way and turn all your prime assets into cash.
- Don't ignore liquidity when times are good.

▸▸ MORE INFO

Books:

Coyle, Brian. *Cash Flow Forecasting & Liquidity*. Risk Management Series: Cash Flow Management. London: Financial World Publishing, 2004.

Matz, Leonard, and Peter Neu (eds). *Liquidity Risk Measurement and Management: A Practitioner's Guide to Global Best Practices*. Singapore: Wiley, 2006.

See Also:

★ Managing Liquidity in China—Challenging Times (pp. 81–84)
✔ Hedging Liquidity Risk—Case Study and Strategies (p. 865)
✔ Cashflow Reengineering: How to Optimize the Cashflow Timeline and Improve Financial Efficiency (p. 1234)
Measuring Liquidity (p. 875)

"We often discover what *will* do, by finding out what will not do; and probably he who never made a mistake never made a discovery." Samuel Smiles

  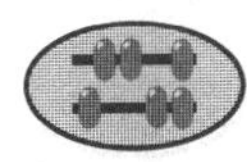   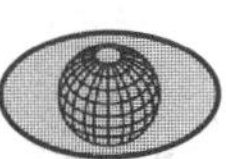   

Insuring Against Financial Loss

DEFINITION

Every business faces a unique combination of exposures. The overall impact of an incident can reach far beyond the immediate damage to property and be far more expensive and harmful to the company than the original loss.

Policies covering these areas are often grouped together as "miscellaneous financial loss" or "contingency" insurance. A combination of policies may be required to cover these consequential losses in tandem with a business continuity plan. It will be necessary for the company to weigh up the risks from self-insuring (i.e. having an emergency fund for such contingencies) or buying cover from an insurer.

CHECKLIST OF FINANCIAL RISKS THAT CAN BE COVERED

Weather

Some types of business, particularly in the construction, leisure, and agricultural sectors, may be adversely affected by unfavorable weather conditions.

Business Interruption

Interruption insurance can fill the gaps in existing policies. It can cover both the continuing and emergency costs faced by the business along with loss of income arising from an enforced shutdown.

Breakdown of Machinery

The failure of specialist machinery can lead to losses considerably greater than the cost of repair if it affects the output of the business.

Credit Insurance

Domestic and export credit risks can be covered through a commercial risks policy. This provides protection against events such as a customer becoming insolvent or defaulting on payment for a prolonged period, or a political event delaying or preventing payment.

Crime

A company can be covered against third party theft, employee dishonesty, forgery, copyright theft, and so on. Particular attention should be paid to ensuring that it is not only forced entry that is included in the policy as a larger proportion of crime is committed by insiders than by third parties.

Theft and Personal Injury

Robbery, attempted robbery, and injuries resulting from these crimes can be covered whether they occur on a company's premises, in or out of working hours, or when cash is being transported from a bank safe or from a company strong room.

Key Man Insurance

Many businesses are reliant on particular individuals. Key man cover protects against losses arising from their death or long-term illness. The types of loss that may be included are profits, the cost of hiring a replacement, and the delay before the replacement starts to make a contribution to profits.

Kidnap, Ransom, and Extortion

This type of cover is particularly relevant to companies operating in certain high-risk territories. Companies are often less than transparent about policies that include ransom insurance for fear that it will be seen to encourage kidnapping and extortion.

License Loss

Establishments such as bars, restaurants, hotels, clubs, and casinos are vulnerable to loss of license. Cover may be available against this eventuality.

Cyber Insurance

In recent years there has been an increasing risk arising from so-called "cyber crime." This includes damage from hack attacks, viruses, and defamation. These can all have an effect on profits as well as costing money to resolve and potentially causing damage to third parties.

Single Project Insurance

Sometimes a company faces a specific collection of risks arising from a single major project. A construction company, for example, that wins a government contract may face a combination of public liability, funding, and penalty risks, cover against which may be rolled into a single, limited-time policy for the duration of the project.

ADVANTAGES

- It is possible to insure against almost every eventuality and business risk.

DISADVANTAGES

- The cost of such cover would be prohibitive. A risk profile should be drawn up to analyze which areas of the balance sheet it is cost-effective and appropriate to insure.

➤➤ MORE INFO

Books:

Gaughan, Patrick A. *Measuring Business Interruption Losses and Other Commercial Damages*. Hoboken, NJ: Wiley, 2003.

Hoffman, Philip T., Gilles Postel-Vinay, and Jean-Laurent Rosenthal. *Surviving Large Losses: Financial Crises, the Middle Class, and the Development of Capital Markets*. Cambridge, MA: Belknap Press, 2007.

See Also:

✔ Corporate Insurance Cover: A Primer (p. 979)
✔ Insuring Against Business Interruption (p. 987)
✔ Stress Testing to Evaluate Insurance Cover (p. 932)
✔ Understanding the Components of an Insurance Contract (p. 934)

"**He's a businessman. . .I'll make him an offer he can't refuse.**" Mario Puzo

     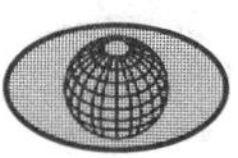   

Key Components of an Optimal Enterprise Resource Planning System

DEFINITION

ERP computerized systems integrate a company's entire business operation. Simply put, an ERP system binds together different computer systems for any large organization, with each department having its own system that communicates and shares information with the rest of the company's systems. ERP integrates all key areas, including accounting, planning, purchasing, inventory, sales, marketing, PR, finance, human resources, and any other areas of importance to a company. Installing an ERP system enables a company to monitor and manage effectively the performance level of equipment, while simultaneously increasing uptime and increasing responsiveness, thus facilitating and fulfilling customer needs as well as streamlining company performance.

Although originally developed for large companies, ERP also benefits small and medium-sized companies and those involved in service rather than manufacturing, with ERP programmers creating a new generation of software that is easier to install, more manageable, and importantly, cheaper. The new systems are more modular, allowing installation to proceed gradually as a company evolves. ERP can also be outsourced, with the ERP manufacturer supplying the technology and the support staff required. This option has proved easier and cheaper than buying and implementing a whole system in-house. Hosted ERP or web-deployed ERP enables a company to run its ERP system through a web-hosted server and access it via the internet. This allows companies to reduce their IT investment in hardware and personnel.

ERP systems have also expanded through the evolution of technology to include new functions such as linking ERP to other software systems that affect the supply chain. This allows companies to view inventory and its status as it moves through the supply chain. ERP has also been adapted to support e-commerce by making order fulfillment and distribution easier and simplifying electronic procurement.

Computer security is included within an ERP to protect against both outsider crime, such as industrial espionage, and insider crime, such as embezzlement.

ADVANTAGES

- Deploying an ERP system can improve efficiency and reduce operational costs.
- New levels of transaction visibility can be gained for all involved in a process.
- Companies can make smarter business decisions, keep up to date with customer requirements, track inventory, implement and maintain industry best practices, and forecast product demand.
- Complex computer applications can be replaced with a single, integrated system.

DISADVANTAGES

- ERP systems require the installation of new technical support and training of staff, and they are expensive.
- They desensitize operations procedures and rely on the whole system working.
- Systems can be difficult to use or too restrictive.
- The system may be overengineered relative to the actual needs of the customer, resulting in lack of personal service.

ACTION CHECKLIST

- ✔ Evaluate all company needs carefully and create a list of business issues that the ERP system has to address.
- ✔ Research potential ERP vendors by talking to other companies that have similar working requirements. Avoid choosing an ERP system vendor too quickly.
- ✔ Check the user-friendliness of the system.
- ✔ Ensure that you can customize the system to meet your requirements comprehensively.

DOS AND DON'TS

DO

- Assess plenty of systems and see how they can work for your company.
- Look at the needs of your company from every angle.
- Check that your personnel are up to the task and, if not, check that you can employ the right personnel.

DON'T

- Don't sign up to an ERP without all the facts.
- Don't expect an ERP to run the business for you without your input.
- Don't be too ambitious and believe that the system will solve any ongoing problems with communication within your company.

▸▸ MORE INFO

Book:

Waldner, J.-B., and W. J. Duffin (trans). *CIM: Principles of Computer-Integrated Manufacturing*. Chichester, UK: Wiley, 1992.

Articles:

Scott, J. E., and L. Kaindl, "Enhancing functionality in an enterprise software package." *Information & Management* 37:3 (2000): 111–122.

Wailgum, Thomas. "ERP definition and solutions." *CIO* (April 17, 2008). Online at: www.cio.com/article/40323

Wei, C. C., and M. J. Wang. "A comprehensive framework for selecting an ERP system." *International Journal of Project Management* 22:2 (2004): 161–169.

Wei, C. C., C. F. Chien, and M. J. Wang. "An AHP-based approach to ERP system selection." *International Journal of Production Economics* 96:1 (2005): 47–62.

Website:

Dos and don'ts of ERP implementation: www.smthacker.co.uk/implementing_ERP_computer_systems.htm

See Also:

★ How to Better Manage Your Financial Supply Chain (pp. 57–59)

✔ Business Process Reengineering (p. 974)

"The biggest opportunity is harnessing our knowledge within the organisation to provide better solutions."
Martin Sorrell

  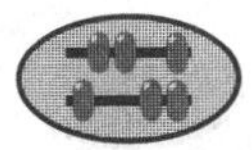   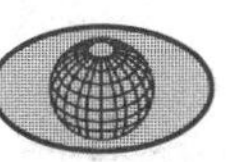   

Managing the Time Value of Money

DEFINITION

The time value of money is based on the premise that most people would choose to receive, say, $10,000 now, rather than the same sum in five years' time. Why? Firstly, because any rational person knows that the $10,000 will almost certainly buy you less in five years' time than it will today. Secondly, there is no certainty that you will actually receive the money five years from now. As the proverb says, a bird in the hand is worth two in the bush.

Businesses use time-value-of-money formulae to make rational decisions on future expectations.

Discounting allows us to understand what we would need to invest today if we wanted to receive a certain amount in the future. Compounding helps us to calculate the sum that we will receive in the future if we invest a certain amount today.

Several other equations can be used to calculate loans, mortgages, the future values of annuities, etc. These equations are frequently combined for particular uses. For example, bonds can be readily priced using these equations. A typical coupon bond is composed of two types of payment: a stream of coupon payments similar to an annuity, and a lump-sum return of capital when the bond matures—that is, a future payment. The two formulae can be combined to determine the present value of the bond.

For an annuity that makes one payment per year, there is an annual interest rate. However, the time frame in years must be converted into the number of periods consistent with the compounding frequency of the rate. For an income or payment stream with a different payment schedule, the interest rate must be converted into the relevant periodic interest rate. For example, if a mortgage requires monthly payments, the interest rate has to be divided by twelve.

The rate of return in these calculations can be either the variable solved or a predefined variable that measures a discount rate, interest, inflation, rate of return, cost of equity, cost of debt, or any number of similar concepts. The choice of the suitable rate is vital to the exercise, and the use of an incorrect discount rate will make the results worthless.

For calculations involving annuities, you must decide whether the payments are made at the end of each period (i.e. ordinary annuity) or at the beginning of each period (i.e. annuity due).

Most formulae are available on financial calculators or can be set up on a spreadsheet.

ADVANTAGES

- Time-value-of-money formulae are generally easy to understand and are widely used.
- The data used by the formulae are readily available.
- Discounting tells us what we would need to invest today if we wanted to receive a certain amount in the future.
- Compounding helps us to calculate the sum that we will receive in the future if we invest a certain amount today.

DISADVANTAGES

- It can often be difficult to identify the appropriate formula without expert help.
- The data on which the initial investment was made often change over the lifetime of the investment.

ACTION CHECKLIST

- ✔ Before you use time-value-of-money formulae, you need to understand the cash flows your business is likely to have and how your cash cycle is calculated.
- ✔ You need to understand how a business manages its working capital as a whole, focusing particularly on how debtors are managed.
- ✔ You must familiarize yourself with the way the banking system and financial markets work—what influences those markets and how a business seeks additional finance when it is required.
- ✔ You must understand what capital expenditure budgeting is and how a business decides whether or not to spend money on a particular project.

DOS AND DON'TS

DO

- Seek help in identifying an appropriate rate for your calculations.

DON'T

- Don't base your planning completely on these formulae, as the data on which the initial investment was made often change over the lifetime of the investment.

▸▸ MORE INFO

Books:

Clayton, Gary E., and Christopher B. Spivey. *The Time Value of Money: Worked and Solved Problem*. Philadelphia, PA: W. B. Saunders, 1978.

Luecke, Richard A. *Manager's Toolkit: The 13 Skills Managers Need to Succeed*. Boston, MA: Harvard Business School Press, 2004.

Tuckman, Bruce. *Fixed Income Securities: Tools for Today's Markets*. 2nd ed. Chichester, UK: Wiley, 2002.

Articles:

Irons, Ann. "Managing finances." *Finance Matters (ACCA)* 60 (August 2004). Online at: www.accaglobal.com/students/publications/finance_matters/archive/2004/60/2210852

Johnson Publishing Co. "Managing your finances." *Jet* (November 2002).

Websites:

NoteWorthy secrets of the time value of money: www.noteworthyusa.com/secrets.html

StudyFinance.com overview of the time value of money: www.studyfinance.com/lessons/timevalue/index.mv

See Also:

★ Creating Value with EVA (pp. 756–758)
✔ Managing Working Capital (p. 872)
✔ Understanding Free Cash Flow (p. 891)

"**Time is an illusion. Lunchtime doubly so.**" Douglas Adams

   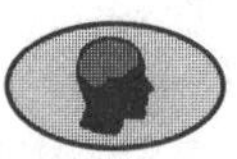  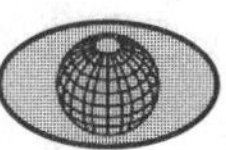   

Managing Working Capital

DEFINITION

Working capital, also known as net working capital, is a measurement of a business's current assets, after subtracting its short-term liabilities, typically short term. Sometimes referred to as operating capital, it is a valuation of the assets that a business or organization has available to manage and build the business. Generally speaking, companies with higher amounts of working capital are better positioned for success because they have the liquid assets that are essential to expand their business operations when required.

Working capital refers to the cash that a business requires for its day-to-day operations—for example, to finance the conversion of raw materials into finished goods that the company can then sell for payment.

Among the most important items of working capital are levels of inventory, accounts receivable, and accounts payable. Working capital can be expressed as a positive or a negative number. When a company has more debts than current assets, it has negative working capital. When current assets outweigh debts, a company has positive working capital.

The requirement for working capital depends on the type of company. Some companies are intrinsically better off than others. Examples include retailers (which have a fast turnover of cash) and insurance companies (which receive premiums before having to settle claims).

Manufacturing companies, on the other hand, can incur considerable upfront costs for materials and labor before they receive payment. For much of the time, these companies spend more cash than they generate.

A company will try to manage cash by:

- identifying the cash balance that allows it to meet day-to-day expenses but minimizes the cost of holding cash;
- finding the level of inventory that allows for continuous production but lessens the investment in raw materials and reduces reordering costs;
- identifying the appropriate source of financing, given the cash-conversion cycle.

It may be necessary to use a bank loan or overdraft. However, inventory is preferably financed by credit arranged with the supplier.

If a company is not operating efficiently, this will show up as an increase in the working capital. This can be judged by comparing the amounts of working capital from one period to another. Slow collection and inventory turnover may signal an underlying problem in the company's operations.

ADVANTAGES

Proper management of working capital gives a firm the assurance that it is able to continue its operations and that it has sufficient cash flow to satisfy both maturing short-term debt and upcoming operational expenses.

DISADVANTAGES

- If a company's current assets do not exceed its current liabilities, then it may run into trouble paying back creditors in the short term.
- A declining working-capital ratio over a longer time period could also be a red flag that merits further analysis. For example, it could be that the company's sales volumes are decreasing and, as a result, its accounts receivable are diminishing.

ACTION CHECKLIST

- ✔ Check the amount of working capital. If a company is not operating in the most efficient manner (for example slow collection), it will show up as an increase in working capital. This can be understood by comparing the working capital from one period to another. Slow collection may signal a fundamental problem in the company's management.
- ✔ Is your `performance indicator' for credit control better than those of other businesses in the same sector?
- ✔ Invoices should always be accurate in every detail and to the penny when quoting amounts. Inaccuracy is an excuse to query and delay payment. Also aim to send out your invoice the day after delivery of the goods.
- ✔ Chase debtors—Money that customers still owe cannot be used meet other obligations.

DOS AND DON'TS

DO

- Check that a company has sufficient working capital, as this is an indicator of the success of the business. Lack of working capital may not only mean that a company is unable to grow, but also that it has too little cash to meet its short-term obligations.

DON'T

- Don't allow working capital to fall below the level at which the company has more debts than current assets.

➤➤ MORE INFO

Books:

Berman, Karen, Joe Knight, and John Case. *Financial Intelligence: A Manager's Guide to Knowing What the Numbers Really Mean*. Boston, MA: Harvard Business School Press, 2006.

Downes, John, and Jordan Elliot Goodman. *Barron's Finance & Investment Handbook*. 7th ed. Hauppauge, NY: Barron's Educational Series, 2006.

Moyer, R. Charles, James R. McGuigan, and William J. Kretlow. *Contemporary Financial Management*. 11th ed. Mason, OH: South-Western/Cengage Learning, 2009.

Articles:

García-Teruel, Pedro Juan, and Pedro Martínez-Solano. "Effects of working capital management on SME profitability." *International Journal of Managerial Finance* 3:2 (March 2007) 164–177.

Nelson Publishing. "Conserving working capital." *Tooling & Production* (June 2008).

Websites:

JP Morgan working capital management: www.jpmorgan.com/tss/Knowledge_Bank_Index/Working_Capital_Management/1106305784457

About.com Investing for Beginners: Investing Lessons & Quizzes: beginnersinvest.about.com/cs/investinglessons

"**Once the *what* is decided the *how* always follows. We must not make the *how* an excuse for not facing and accepting the *what*.**" Pearl S. Buck

  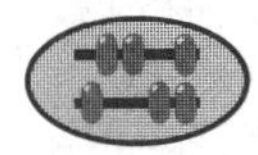 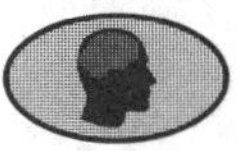 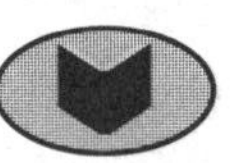 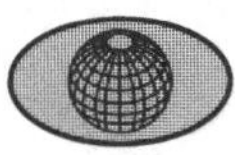   

Managing Your Credit Risk

DEFINITION

Credit risk is the risk of loss caused by a debtor defaulting on a loan or other line of credit, whether the principal, the interest, or both. The sound management of credit risk involves reining in all exposure to financial risk to within acceptable limits. A company's rate of return should always be risk-adjusted to take account of credit risk and other risks.

Good control of credit risk involves managing not only the risk associated with individual deals or transactions, but also that of an entire portfolio (i.e. ensuring that risk is both minimized and evenly spread). Banks in particular need to have a comprehensive policy in place for managing all kinds of risk—credit risk forms the most important part of any such policy. The collapse of Barings Bank in 1995 is a textbook example of what can happen when an organization lacks safeguards for managing credit risk. Loans tend to be the main source of credit risk for many banks. They are, however, exposed to other sources of credit risk, such as in the trading book, or on and off the balance sheet. For all kinds of companies credit risk also exists in other financial instruments, such as interbank or currency transactions, trade financing, equities, and derivatives.

Exposure to credit risk remains a key problem on a global basis. Companies need to learn lessons from high-profile cases such as Barings and Northern Rock. The Basel Committee drew up a set of principles to be used when evaluating a credit risk management system. Although the principles are aimed at financial institutions, they apply equally to all organizations. How a company approaches the issue will vary according to factors such as the supervisory techniques they use, whether they employ external auditors, and the size of the institution. Smaller businesses, in particular, need to ensure they have an adequate risk–return policy in place.

Firms are exposed to credit risk when, for example, they do not insist on advance payment for products or services. By billing after delivery, the company takes the risk that the customer may default on payment, leaving it out of pocket. Many companies quote payment terms of 30 days as standard, and it only takes one large defaulted payment to expose the firm to cash flow problems and possible bankruptcy.

Many firms operate a credit risk department whose role is to assess the financial health of their customers and decide whether to extend credit or not. They may use software to analyze such risks and assess how to avoid, reduce, or transfer any credit risk. Credit rating companies such as Standard & Poor's, Moody's, and Dun and Bradstreet also sell financial intelligence to firms needing external assistance in managing credit risk with their clients.

Companies can lessen their credit risk by, for example, cutting their payment terms to 15 days, limiting the amount of goods or services available on credit per transaction, or even insisting on payment up-front. Strategies such as these cut exposure to risk, but the downside is that they can affect the volume of sales and subsequent cash flow.

ADVANTAGES

- A keen awareness of credit risk that includes processes to identify, measure, monitor, and control credit risk should protect all but the smallest organizations from major problems.

DISADVANTAGES

- Small firms that have only a very few customers find it difficult to manage credit risk due to their vulnerability should a customer turn out to be a late-payer or even default on payment entirely.

ACTION CHECKLIST

Specific credit risk management practices vary among organizations according to the type and complexity of their credit activities. A comprehensive policy for managing credit risk should address the following points:

- ✔ Create an appropriate credit risk environment.
- ✔ Implement a policy that ensures the credit-granting process is sound.
- ✔ Assess the quality of your assets and determine that you have adequate provisions and reserves.
- ✔ Maintain quality procedures for credit administration, measurement, and monitoring processes.
- ✔ Ensure that you have adequate controls in place.

▸▸ MORE INFO

Books:

Bluhm, Christian, Ludger Overbeck, and Christoph Wagner. *An Introduction to Credit Risk Modeling.* Financial Mathematics Series. Boca Raton, FL: Chapman & Hall/CRC, 2002.

de Servigny, Arnaud, and Olivier Renault. *The Standard & Poor's Guide to Measuring and Managing Credit Risk.* New York: McGraw-Hill, 2004.

Duffie, Darrell, and Kenneth J. Singleton. *Credit Risk: Pricing, Measurement, and Management.* Princeton Series in Finance. Princeton, NJ: Princeton University Press, 2003.

See Also:

★ How the Settlement Infrastructure Is Surviving the Financial Meltdown (pp. 211–213)

★ Minimizing Credit Risk (pp. 350–352)

✔ Building an Efficient Credit and Collection Accounts System (p. 972)

✔ Derivatives Markets: Their Structure and Function (p. 924)

✔ Hedging Credit Risk—Case Studies and Strategies (p. 862)

"**Bankruptcy or credit default is not an issue.**" Bernie Ebbers

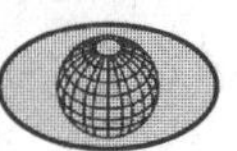

Measuring Financial Health

DEFINITION

When measuring a business's financial health we have to ask a number of questions. What is the source of its revenue? On what does it spend its income, and where? How much profit is it earning? The answer lies in a company's financial statements and by law all public companies have to make these statements freely available to everyone. Financial statements can be broken down into three parts: the profit and loss statement (also called the income statement), the balance sheet, and the cash flow forecast.

The profit-and-loss statement tells us whether the company is making a profit. It indicates how revenue (money received from the sale of products and services before expenses are taken out, also known as the "top line") is transformed into net income (the result after all revenues and expenses have been accounted for, also known as the "bottom line"). A profit and loss account covers a period of time – usually a year or part of a year.

The balance sheet is a snapshot of a business's financial health at a specific moment in time, usually at the close of an accounting period. A balance sheet shows assets, liabilities, and shareholders' equity/capital. Assets and liabilities are divided into short term and long term obligations. The balance sheet does not show the flows into and out of the accounts during the period. A balance sheet's assets should equal liabilities plus owners' equity.

The cash-flow forecast or statement identifies the sources and amounts of cash coming into and going out of a business over a given period. In an established business, an acceptable method is to combine sales revenues for the same period one year earlier with predicted growth.

To survive, the organization's total assets should be greater than its total liabilities. Current assets (such as cash, receivables, and securities) should also be able to cover current liabilities (such as payables, deferred revenue, and current-year loan and note payments). If an organization's cash and equivalents greatly exceed its current liabilities, the organization may not be putting its money to the best use.

ADVANTAGES

- Profit and loss statements track revenues and expenses, so that managers and investors can determine the operating performance of a business over a period of time.
- Balance sheets can be used to identify and analyze trends, particularly in the area of receivables and payables.
- A cash flow forecast shows where cash is employed or tied up. It is an early warning indicator when expenditures are running out of line or sales targets are not being met.

DISADVANTAGES

- Profit and loss statements do not report factors that might be highly relevant but cannot be reliably measured (for example: brand recognition and customer loyalty).
- A balance sheet shows a snapshot of a company's assets, liabilities, and shareholders' equity. It does not show the flows into and out of the accounts during the period

ACTION CHECKLIST

statements to evaluate the overall financial condition of the business. Financial ratios help gauge viability, liabilities, and projected future performance.

- ✔ Use financial ratios on financial
- ✔ Carefully analyze any profit and loss accounts for differences during the reporting period. Anomalies might be due to seasonal or other variations or may indicate deeper problems.
- ✔ Quantify in financial terms how decisions based on the financial statement could impact on business.
- ✔ Financial statements cannot resolve all grey areas. Be prepared to consult and be involved in a long and complicated process of analysis.
- ✔ Consult and question managers and key business stakeholders when evaluating financial statements.

DOS AND DON'TS

DO

- Make sure that you have used the financial ratios when analyzing financial statements. If in doubt, consult an expert analyst.
- Check which accounting principles were used when drawing up the accounts.

DON'T

- Don't assume that all financial statements truly reflect a company's financial position. Measuring and reporting permit considerable discretion and the opportunity to influence results.

MORE INFO

Books:

Koller, Tim, McKinsey & Company, Marc Goedhart, David Wessels, and Thomas E. Copeland. *Valuation: Measuring and Managing the Value of Companies*. Chichester, UK: Wiley, 2005.

Pereiro, Luis E. *Valuation of Companies in Emerging Markets: A Practical Approach*. Chichester, UK: Wiley, 2002.

Reilly, Robert F., and Robert P. Schweihs. *Handbook of Advanced Business Valuation*. Maidenhead, UK: McGraw-Hill Professional, 1999.

Articles:

Lewellen, J. "Predicting returns with financial ratios." *Journal of Financial Economics* (May 2004).

Stein, Neil. "Company financial statements." *ACCA* (April 2003).

Websites

American Accounting Association: www.aaa-edu.org

International Federation of Accountants: www.ifac.org

See Also:

✔ Understanding the Balance Sheet (p. 894)

"Our democratic capitalist society has converted Eros into an employee of Mammon." Octavio Paz

  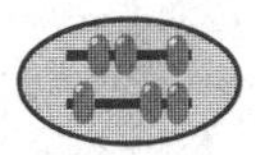 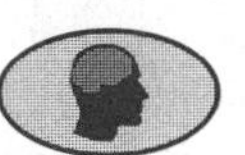  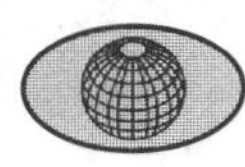   

Measuring Liquidity

DEFINITION

Liquidity refers to the ability of an asset to be easily converted to cash without bringing about a major movement in price and with the lowest loss in value. Liquidity also refers to a company's ability to meet its obligations in terms of possessing sufficient liquid assets.

Various ratios are used to measure liquidity. These include: the current ratio, which is the simplest measure and is calculated by dividing total current assets by total current liabilities; and the quick ratio, calculated by deducting inventories from current assets and then dividing by current liabilities. Although the two ratios are similar, the quick ratio provides a more accurate assessment of a business's ability to pay its current liabilities. The quick ratio cuts out all but the most liquid of current assets. Inventory is the most notable omission, because it is not as speedily convertible to cash.

For example, Table 1 using the quick ratio on the balance sheet.

Total Current Assets ($115,000) divided by Total Current Liabilities ($70,000) = 1.65. Therefore, for every dollar of liabilities, the company has $1.65 in liquid assets to meet those obligations. As a general guide, companies with a quick ratio of greater than 1.0 are considered satisfactorily able to meet their short term liabilities. Liquidity is a measure of the ability of a debtor to pay their debts. It is crucial that a business has enough cash on hand to meet accounts payable, interest expenses, and other bills as and when they become due.

Table 1. Example balance sheet

Cash	$55,000	Accounts Payable	$25,000
Equities/Securities	$15,000	Expenses (accrued)	$20,000
Accounts Receivable	$45,000	Notes Payable	$10,000
		Debt	$15,000
Total Current Assets	**$115,000**	Total Current Liabilities	**$70,000**

ADVANTAGES

- The quick ratio is a reasonable marker of a business's short term liquidity. The quick ratio gauges a company's ability to meet its short term obligations with its most liquid assets. The higher the quick ratio, the better the position of the business.
- A high or increasing quick ratio usually signifies that a business is experiencing above average growth, is rapidly changing receivables into cash, and is able to cover its financial obligations.

DISADVANTAGES

- The current ratio is the simplest measure and is calculated by dividing total current assets by total current liabilities. However, the current ratio does include inventory, which is often not as swiftly redeemable for cash and is often sold on credit.
- Simple liquidity ratios do not give information about the level and timing of cash flows, which really establish a company's ability to pay liabilities when due.

DOS AND DON'TS

DO

- When using liquidity ratios to compare a business with others in an industry, allow for any material differences in accounting policies between the compared company and industry norms.
- Determine whether liquidity ratios were calculated before or after adjustments were made to the balance sheet or income statement. In some cases, these adjustments can significantly affect the ratios.

DON'T

- Don't forget that, although the current ratio is the simplest measure, it does include inventory, which is often not as swiftly redeemable for cash and is often sold on credit.
- Don't forget to take into account factors such as type of industry (long/short cycle), allowances for bad debt, and payment and collection procedures.

ACTION CHECKLIST

- ✔ Check whether a business has a low or decreasing quick ratio. This normally suggests that the business is over leveraged, unable to maintain or increase its sales, settling its bills too quickly, or collecting its receivables too slowly.
- ✔ Capital requirements, which differ from industry to industry, can have an effect on quick ratios. Therefore, make liquidity comparisons among companies within the same industry.
- ✔ Take into account factors such as type of industry (long/short cycle), allowances for bad debt, and payment and collection procedures.

▸▸ MORE INFO

Books:

Bittel, Lester R., and Muriel Albers Bittel. *Encyclopedia of Professional Management*. New York: McGraw-Hill, 1978.

Cengage Learning. *Introduction to Financial Accounting*. Stamford, CT: Cengage Learning EMEA, 1997.

International Monetary Fund, Statistics Department. *Financial Soundness Indicators: Compilation Guid*. Washington, DC: International Monetary Fund, 2006.

Articles:

Latin Trade. "Cash flow" (January 2006).

Scordis, Nicos. "The value of smoothing cash flows." *Risk Management* (January 2008).

Websites:

Financial Accounting Standards Board: www.fasb.org

International Federation of Accountants: www.ifac.org

See Also:

★ How to Successfully Assess a Company's Global Treasury Needs and Objectives (pp. 66–68)

★ Navigating a Liquidity Crisis Effectively (pp. 86–88)

✔ Managing Working Capital (p. 872)

     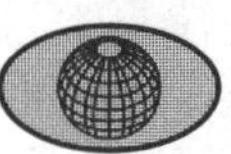   

Methods for Dealing With Inflation Risk

DEFINITION

Inflation risk can be defined as the risk that the value of physical or financial assets will be eroded by inflation. To protect against that loss, investment managers need to employ one or more of several tried and tested methods.

Investors generally choose investments that offer "insurance" against inflation risk. However, it is important to remember that the overall risk of an investment comes from all risk sources, not just the risk of inflation.

Inflation hedging, which takes into account the co-movements of inflation rates and asset returns from period to period, is one of the most commonly used methods for managing inflation risk. The less influence the rate of inflation has on the real return of an investment, the more effective the inflation hedge will be for the investment. Popular hedges against inflation include property, equities, or commodities that generally have a rising value. Studies of periods of high inflation in the 1970s and 1980s show that, in the mid-term, earnings and the dividend growth rates of equities at least kept pace with inflation.

A popular method for managing inflation risk is the use of inflation protection, which examines the inflation risk of an asset and assesses whether that asset's real return will be lower than a specific target return (such as zero) at the end of a determined investment period. One downside to using this risk metric is that it only takes into consideration the probability of negative deviations from the target return, but not the amount of them.

The third main method is the inflation swap. Here, the swap involves the use of inflation derivatives (or inflation-indexed derivatives) to transfer inflation risk from one party to another and protect against future liabilities. The derivatives used may be over-the-counter or exchange-traded derivatives.

ADVANTAGES

- Taking practical steps to deal with inflation risk minimizes both the possibility of real losses and any losses themselves should they occur.

DISADVANTAGES

- There is no guarantee that any methods used will protect completely against inflation, and there will always be a degree of risk. The real return of an investment is always uncertain, even for safe assets such as default-free zero-coupon bonds that have a maturity equal to the length of the investment period, even though the nominal cash flow is guaranteed.

ACTION CHECKLIST

- ✔ Check that the dividend yields and payout ratios of your chosen method are suitably high and at least in line with inflation.
- ✔ Assess each method thoroughly to determine which is likely to give your assets the best protection against inflation.
- ✔ Run full risk management scenarios that take into account all risks, not just inflation.

DOS AND DON'TS

DO

- Take into account all risk factors, not just the risk of inflation.
- Calculate the probability and amount of any shortfall when making inflation-proof investment decisions.
- Review your decisions if the global economy starts shifting unexpectedly, as you may need to adjust your portfolio for the best protection.

DON'T

- Don't assume that traditionally inflation-proof investments such as property are a safe haven. For example, during the credit crunch of 2007–08, the real value of both property and equities fell steeply while inflation rose sharply.

▸▸ MORE INFO

Books:

Baumol, William J., and Alan S. Blinder. *Macroeconomics: Principles and Policy*. 11th ed. Cincinnati, OH: South-Western College Publishing, 2008.

Brice, Benaben (ed). *Inflation-linked Products: A Guide for Investors and Asset & Liability Managers*. London: Risk Books, 2005.

Brigo, Damiano, and Fabio Mercurio. *Interest Rate Models—Theory and Practice, with Smile, Inflation and Credit*. 2nd ed. Berlin: Springer-Verlag, 2007.

Deacon, Mark, Andrew Derry, and Dariush Mirfendereski. *Inflation-indexed Securities: Bonds, Swap & Other Derivatives*. 2nd ed. Chichester, UK: Wiley, 2004.

Mishkin, Frederic S. *The Economics of Money, Banking, and Financial Markets*. 8th ed. Boston, MA: Addison-Wesley, 2006.

Walmsley, Julian. *The Foreign Exchange and Money Markets Guide*. 2nd ed. New York: Wiley, 2000.

Article:

Federal Reserve Bank of Boston. "Understanding inflation and the implications for monetary policy: A Phillips curve retrospective." 53rd Economic Conference, June 9–11, 2008, Chatham, MA. Presentations online at: www.bos.frb.org/phillips2008

See Also:

★ The Globalization of Inflation (pp. 206–207)
✔ Hedging Interest Rate Risk—Case Study and Strategies (p. 864)
✔ Swaps, Options, and Futures: What They Are and Their Function (p. 882)
✔ Understanding and Using Inflation Swaps (p. 886)
✔ Understanding Asset–Liability Management (Full Balance Sheet Approach) (p. 889)

"Inflation is as violent as a mugger, as frightening as an armed robber, and as deadly as a hit man."

The Objectives of Corporate Planning and Budgeting

DEFINITION

Finance departments are always under pressure, the more so in a climate of economic uncertainty. Increasing accountability and shorter budgeting cycles result in organizations seeking new ways to manage the budgeting process and developing solutions that meet the exact needs of their clients as well as match their own business attributes.

Corporate planning is defined as the process of drawing up detailed action plans in order to achieve the aims and objectives of an organization. It takes into account organizational resources and the environment within which a company operates.

Corporate planning is the responsibility of senior management, and there should be a structured approach to achieving objectives and implementing corporate strategy. Good corporate planning and budgeting should reduce the cost of the overall budgeting process and the time taken to complete the budgeting cycle, as well as improve both data integrity and security. Corporate planning should also take into account corporate or enterprise objectives, structures, and functions. Results and performance solutions are built into a corporate business structure, to record actual business data based on resulting value, capital worth, and performance costs.

E-budgeting solutions are becoming more popular as they completely automate the development of a company's budget and forecast. Web-based enterprise budgeting systems are centrally administered and provide flexible tools for budget planners, allowing constant monitoring, updates, and modeling. They also free up time in the finance department for strategic decision-making rather than paper-pushing.

Budgeting is about responsible money management. The overriding purpose of a budget is to stop overspending, which can be done by monitoring cash flow, and to prevent any existing or future debt from becoming an unmanageable mess. Good budgeting ensures that a company's cash flow is monitored and assessed regularly, that funds are available for payments out, and expansion, and that the business does not spend beyond its capabilities.

Companies should assess whether their spending is growing and why, and identify measures to reduce it. It is vital to ensure that the budget is in alignment with corporate objectives, and it is useful to measure budgets by activity and/or project, and not just by department.

ADVANTAGES

- Strong financial planning ensures that a company can keep track of revenues, expenditure, cash flows, capital, and investments, as well as make accurate financial forecasts.
- Good budgeting calculates capital needed for business organization, human resources, facilities and equipment, and management strategy.
- Corporate planning should assess, monitor, and prioritize liabilities, focus on profitable opportunities, and involve regular reassessment of the company's business practices. It also helps to locate all of a company's concerns, such as money, products, employees, systems, and customers, under one roof.

DISADVANTAGES

- Rigid corporate and financial planning may be inappropriate for some smaller firms, which may benefit from a more fluid approach.
- Larger corporations risk becoming fixed in their outlook by adhering strictly to planning—it's important to maintain a flexible approach and reassess plans if necessary.

ACTION CHECKLIST

- ✔ Define the goals and communicate a clear company-wide strategy.
- ✔ Customize plans and models to fit the business needs.
- ✔ Spend less time on processes and more on analysis.
- ✔ Enable participation by everyone involved in the company.
- ✔ Streamline workflow management.

DOS AND DON'TS

DO

- Ensure that the traditional financial view generated by your financial system reflects a robust cost model.
- Develop a portfolio inventory listing all existing applications and systems.
- Identify the business "owner" of each application or project.

DON'T

- Don't forget to review and revise budgets on a regular basis.
- Don't view corporate plans as fixed eternally.

▸▸ MORE INFO

Books:

Barnes, N. M. L. (ed). *Financial Control*. London: Thomas Telford, 1990.

Reider, R., and P. B. Heyler. *Managing Cash Flow: An Operational Focus*. Hoboken, NJ: Wiley, 2003.

Thierauf, R. J. *A Problem-finding Approach to Effective Corporate Planning*. Connecticut, MA: Greenwood Publishing Group, 1987.

See Also:

★ Capital Budgeting: The Dominance of Net Present Value (pp. 23–26)
✔ Basic Steps for Starting a Business (p. 971)
✔ Preparing a Budget (p. 879)
Management Accounts: How to Use Them to Control Your Business (p. 1291)

"Co-operative capitalism does not spontaneously emerge from free markets—it needs to be designed."
Will Hutton

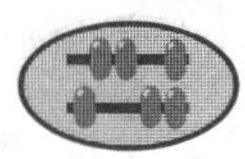

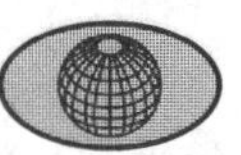

Obtaining an Equity Value Using the Weighted Average Cost of Capital (WACC)

DEFINITION

Equity value is a market-based measure of the value of a company. In mergers and acquisitions, equity value is a more accurate measure of the value of a company than is market capitalization because equity value incorporates all equity interests in a firm. In contrast, market capitalization is calculated by multiplying the number of common shares currently outstanding by the share price.

WACC influences the calculation of equity value because the cost of financing any debt will reduce the company's nominal value. Valuation of a business using WACC means using the market value of equity, not its book value.

The example below shows how using WACC to calculate the debt value actually reduces the value of the debt and therefore reduces the company's overall equity value.

EXAMPLE

Let us assume that a company has five million shares outstanding and that each share has a current market value of $8. The market capitalization of this company is thus 5,000,000 × $8 = $40,000,000.

Now let us assume the company has a debt value of $10 million and a WACC of 15%. The WACC equity value is calculated as follows:

equity value = market capitalization
+ [debt value × (1 − WACC)]
= $40,000,000 + [$10,000,000 × (1 − 0.15)]
= $40,000,000 + $8,500,000
= $48,500,000

If WACC were not used in this calculation, the equity value of the company would simply be the sum of market capitalization and the debt value—that is, $50 million.

WACC is particularly used in acquisitions or financing business operations, and is also the method used to determine the discount rate for valuing a company using the discounted cash flow method.

ADVANTAGES

- Calculating equity value using WACC takes into account the market capitalization *plus* the debt *plus* the cost of financing that debt.

DISADVANTAGES

- WACC is not easy to obtain because of the different types of data that have to be found. It is a complicated measure that requires a lot of detailed company information.

ACTION CHECKLIST

- ✔ A company with an investment return that is greater than its WACC is creating value. Conversely, a company with a return less than WACC is losing value and investors should look elsewhere.
- ✔ WACC should be recalculated annually in order to maintain correct figures.

DOS AND DON'TS

DO

- Use the market value of equity to value a business.
- Use the WACC if you are considering buying a business or if you are a value investor.

DON'T

- Don't use the book value of the equity to value a business.
- Don't invest in a company with a rate of return less than the WACC.

▸▸ MORE INFO

Books:

Loos, Nicolaus. *Value Creation in Leveraged Buyouts: Analysis of Factors Driving Private Equity Investment Performance*. Wiesbaden, Germany: Deutscher Universitäts-Verlag (DUV), 2006.

Stewart, G. Bennett, III. *The Quest for Value: A Guide for Senior Managers*. 27th ed. New York: HarperCollins, 1991.

Articles:

Miles, J. A., and J. R. Ezzell. "The weighted average cost of capital, perfect capital markets and project life: A clarification." *Journal of Financial and Quantitative Analysis* 15:3 (1980): 719–730.

Yee, Kenton K. "Earnings quality and the equity risk premium: A benchmark model." *Contemporary Accounting Research* 23:3 (2006): 833–877.

"**Successful capitalism demands a fusion of co-operation and competition and a means of grafting such a hybrid into the soil of the economic, political and social system.**" Will Hutton

Preparing a Budget

DEFINITION

Many businesses that are under pressure overlook budgeting, because with already tight schedules they feel they can do without extra work that may seem to be unproductive. In fact, budgeting can save time, as it helps you to prepare for the future and anticipate problems before they occur.

A budget is basically a translation of your business plan into numbers. In its simplest form, a budget is a detailed plan of future receipts and expenditure. You can use your budget to confirm the activities you have planned for the coming year. Can you afford additional staff? Do you need to expand? When should you start a new sales campaign? When are the slow periods, when making ends meet is a challenge? There are no fixed time periods for budgets, but generally they coincide with the financial year. Businesses normally divide the budget into manageable areas, for example sales, production, materials purchasing, marketing, etc.

The **sales budget** is normally calculated by multiplying the expected number of sales by the selling price of the product.

The **production budget** will be made for the proposed flow of stock, using unit numbers instead of financial figures.

The **materials purchasing budget** will use the figures proposed on the production budget to determine the amount of raw materials needed to manufacture the necessary number of units.

The **staff budget** determines how many staff you will need for the operations of the business.

The **overheads budget** can be compiled either by apportioning the overheads to each product/service or by keeping the overheads as a single budget.

The **capital expenditure** budget covers the purchase of land or buildings, the hire of equipment, etc.

These individual budgets all come together to create the master budget. You can use this to compare actual results with anticipated goals. If some of your expenses are higher than you expected, do you need to look for ways to cut them, or is it because business has increased? If your sales aren't on track, what has caused the difference? Use the information constructively, so that you can make adjustments immediately, if needed, and improve your next budget.

Knowing what all your business activities will cost, and when such expenses will occur, will help prevent any unexpected surprises that could lead to financial problems down the road.

ADVANTAGES

- Budgeting can help save time, because it helps you to prepare for the future and anticipate problems before they occur.
- Your budget can be used to assess whether your present profit is adequate. In a small business, the profit should be large enough to make a return on your investment and a return on your own work.
- Being aware of what business activities will cost, and when such expenses will occur, will help to prevent any unexpected surprises that could lead to financial problems down the road.

DISADVANTAGES

- Protracted budget evaluation could divert key resources away from core business activities, potentially resulting in the business overlooking valuable opportunities.
- Some numbers depend on judgments, estimates, and interpretation, because certain factors might be highly relevant but cannot be reliably measured.

ACTION CHECKLIST

✔ Use your budget to validate the activities you have planned for the coming year. Will you be able to afford to expand your facilities or equipment? Can you employ new staff? When would be the best time to launch a new product?

✔ Do you have times when sales are slow? If so, how can you meet that challenge?

✔ Compare your budgeted figures with your actual results. Then, ask yourself why the numbers are different. If some of your expenses are higher than you expected, do you need to look for ways to cut them, or has the volume of business increased? If your sales are not on track, what has happened to cause the difference? Use the information constructively, so that you can make adjustments immediately, if needed, and improve your next budget.

DOS AND DON'TS

DO

- Use your budget as a benchmark to check your progress toward your business goals.

DON'T

- Don't overlook budgeting. Being unaware of what all your business activities will cost, and when such expenses will arise, could lead to problems.

▸▸ MORE INFO

Books:

Kemp, Sid, and Eric Dunbar. *Budgeting for Managers: A Briefcase Book*. New York: McGraw-Hill, 2003.

Longenecker, Justin C., Carlos W. Moore, J. William Petty, and Leslie E. Palich. *Small Business Management: An Entrepreneurial Emphasis*. 13th ed. Mason, OH: Thomson South-Western, 2006.

Articles:

Adams, Paul E. "Corporation bookkeeping for your small business budgeting." *MoreBusiness.Com* (April 1, 2002). Online at: www.morebusiness.com/running_your_business/financing/d1017621920.brc

SBOCTeam. "Accountant in a box." *Small Business Online Community* (November 2007). Online at: smallbusinessonlinecommunity.bankofamerica.com/blogs/AccountingAndBudgeting/2007/11/15/accountant-in-a-box

SBOCTeam. "Get what's coming to you." *Small Business Online Community* (April 2008). Online at: smallbusinessonlinecommunity.bankofamerica.com/blogs/AccountingAndBudgeting/2008/04/17/get-whats-coming-to-you

Website:

Microsoft Small Businesses Centre: www.microsoft.com/smallbusiness/resources/startups

"Watch the costs and the profits will take care of themselves." Andrew Carnegie

     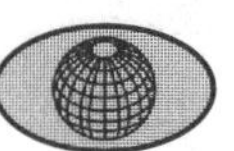   

Preparing a Cash Flow Forecast

DEFINITION

A cash flow forecast aims to predict a company's future financial liquidity over a specific period of time, using tried and tested financial models. While cash normally refers to the liquid assets in a company's bank account, the forecast usually estimates its treasury position, which is cash plus short-term investments minus short-term debt. The cash flow itself refers to the change in the cash or treasury position from one period to the next. The cash flow forecast is an important way to value assets, work out budgets, and determine appropriate capital structures. It will provide a good indicator of a company's financial health for potential investors.

Several methods are generally used to forecast cash flow—one direct, and three indirect. The direct method is most suitable for short-term forecasts of anywhere from 30 days up to a year, since it is based on actual data from which the projections are extrapolated. The data used are the company's cash receipts and disbursements (R&D). Receipts primarily include accounts from recent sales, sales of other assets, proceeds of financing, etc. Disbursements include salaries, payments for recent purchases, dividends, and debt servicing. Many of the R&D entries are based on projected future sales.

The other methods all use a company's projected income statements and balance sheets as their basis. The first method is adjusted net income (ANI), which first examines the operating income (EBIT or EBITDA), then looks at changes on the balance sheet such as receivables, payables, and inventory to forecast cash flow. The pro forma balance sheet (PBS) method looks at the projected book cash account—if the projections for all other balance sheet accounts are correct, then the cash flow will also be correct. Both these methods can be used to make short-term (up to 12 months) and long-term (multiple year) forecasts. Since they use the monthly or quarterly intervals of a company's financial plan, they must be adjusted to account for the differences between the book cash and the actual bank balance, and these may be significantly different.

The third method uses the accrual reversal method (ARM), which reverses large accruals (revenues and expenses that are recognized when they are earned or incurred, disregarding the actual receipt or dispersal of cash) and calculates the cash effects based on statistical distributions and algorithms. This allows the forecasting period to be weekly or even daily. It can also be used to extend the R&D method beyond the 30-day horizon because it eliminates the inherent cumulative errors. This is the most complicated of all methods and is best suited for medium-term forecasts.

ADVANTAGES

- Cash flow projections offer a useful indicator of a company's financial health.
- Cash flow forecasts enable you to predict the peaks and troughs in your cash balance, helping you to plan borrowings, and they tell you how much surplus cash you may have at a given time. Most banks insists on forecasts before considering a loan.

DISADVANTAGES

- A cash flow forecast never tells the whole story about a company's financial situation and should not be relied on as the sole indicator.

ACTION CHECKLIST

- ✔ Be realistic when inputting your estimates. An acceptable method is to combine sales revenues for the same period 12 months earlier with predicted growth.
- ✔ Choose suitable accounting software to help you prepare a cash flow forecast. Check that it will enable you to update your projections if there is any change in market trends or your company's fortunes. Good software simplifies planning for seasonal peaks and troughs and can also calculate for "what if" scenarios.

DOS AND DON'TS

DO

- Use the most appropriate method, depending on how long you want your forecasting horizon to be.
- Remember that a cash flow forecast can only determine the short-term sustainability of a company. The longer the forecast horizon, the higher the chance of an inaccurate projection.
- Bear in mind that the forecast is dynamic—you will need to adjust it frequently depending on business activity, payment patterns, and supplier demands.

DON'T

- Don't rely solely on a cash flow forecast to determine a company's financial stability—look at the other financial statements and forecasts, such as an income statement and a balance sheet, to see what's actually going on.
- Don't forget to incorporate warning signals into your cash flow forecast. For example, if predicted cash levels come close to your overdraft limits, this should sound an alarm and trigger action to bring cash back to an acceptable level.

▸▸ MORE INFO

Books:

Coyle, Brian. *Cash Flow Forecasting and Liquidity*. London: Global Professional Publishing, 2001.

Fight, Andrew. *Cash Flow Forecasting*. Burlington, MA: Butterworth-Heinemann, 2005.

Loscalzo, William. *Cash Flow Forecasting: Guide for Accountants and Financial Managers*. Maidenhead, UK: McGraw-Hill, 1982.

See Also:

✔ Preparing Financial Statements: Balance Sheets (p. 1043)
✔ Preparing Financial Statements: Profit and Loss Accounts (P&Ls) (p. 1044)
✔ Understanding Free Cash Flow (p. 891)
Financial Control for Non-Financial Managers (p. 1257)

"If you're trying to create a healthy organization, one that can sustain itself over time, simply legislating and dictating behavior and outcomes doesn't work at all." Walter Wriston

  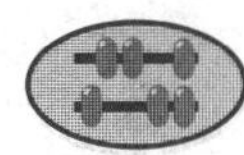   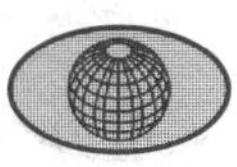   

Setting Up a Dividend Policy

DEFINITION

A dividend is a payment made to a stockholder by a company from any earned profits (i.e. not from any other surplus). Companies generally use profit for two things—to reward stockholders for investing in the company or to reinvest in the business (known as retained earnings). Most companies generally reinvest a portion of the profit and pay out the rest in dividends. From the company's perspective, the payment of dividends is the division of an asset among stockholders.

Dividends are paid out on after-tax income, although the dividends received by stockholders are usually treated as taxable income for tax purposes, depending on their country of residence. Dividends are usually settled on a cash basis, although payment often is in the form of a check. However, many companies pay dividends in the form of additional shares or offer a dividend reinvestment program that enables stockholders to use the cash dividend to buy more shares in the company.

The dividend is normally paid out as a fixed amount per share. Thus, each stockholder receives a dividend in proportion to his or her holding. Most companies pay dividends on a fixed schedule, such as quarterly, half-yearly, or annually. However, a company can declare a dividend whenever it chooses—this is usually known as a special dividend to distinguish it from the regular payouts.

When setting up your dividend policy, key decisions will be how frequently to pay out, what percentage of profit to distribute among stockholders, and whether you will offer them other options, such as stocks in lieu of cash. Once the policy is in place, it needs to be communicated clearly to all stockholders so that they know how often and in what form dividends will be distributed. Policies can always be amended. For example, if the company's profits are badly hit one year, the board may decide not to pay dividends but to reinvest all the profit in the hope of better subsequent profits.

It is usual to publish the policy as a distinct corporate document for distribution in printed form. Many companies also publish the dividend policy on their websites. Amendments to the policy should be distributed in the same way.

ADVANTAGES

- Having a clear and transparent policy is essential for attracting stockholders. They are putting trust into a company by investing in it, and the company returns that trust by being open about what investors can expect to receive in return.
- It is also important that any changes to the dividend policy, whether temporary or permanent, are communicated clearly and in a timely fashion to stockholders.

DISADVANTAGES

- The only real disadvantage of a dividend policy is that some stockholders may be exposed to double taxation. In such a situation, stock repurchases may be more efficient if the tax rate for capital gains is lower.

ACTION CHECKLIST

✔ Determine how frequently you will pay out dividends. Be realistic about this—don't announce quarterly dividends if you know the cash flow patterns mean that a payout can only be made half-yearly.

✔ Have your policy written up professionally by someone experienced in the field.

✔ Ensure that the policy document is checked for compliance with all relevant financial regulations and laws in your territory of jurisdiction.

DOS AND DON'TS

DO

- Keep the dividend policy up to date and ensure that stockholders receive regular mailings about any changes.
- Inform stockholders well in advance of each payment date what percentage of profit the payout will be.

DON'T

- Don't amend dividend policy without good reason or telling your stockholders why.

▸▸ MORE INFO

Books:

Frankfurter, George M., and Bob G. Wood, with James Wansley. *Dividend Policy: Theory and Practice*. San Diego, CA: Academic Press, 2003.

Lease, Ronald C., *et al. Dividend Policy: Its Impact on Firm Value*. Boston, MA: Harvard Business School Press, 2001.

Manos, Ronny. *Capital Structure and Dividend Policy: Evidence from Emerging Markets*. Saarbrücken, Germany: VDM Verlag, 2008.

See Also:

★ Dividend Policy: Maximizing Shareholder Value (pp. 152–155)

★ Reinvesting in the Company versus Rewarding Investors with Distributions (pp. 172–173)

✔ An Overview of Stockholders' Agreements (p. 1019)

✔ Using Shareholder Value Analysis (p. 953)

"They seldom pretend to understand anything of the business of the company. . .but receive contentedly such half yearly or yearly dividends, as the directors think proper to make them." Adam Smith

  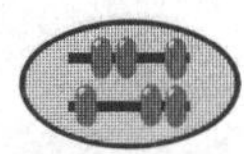   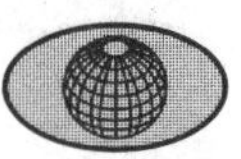   

Swaps, Options, and Futures: What They Are and Their Function

DEFINITION

A swap is a derivative in which two parties agree to exchange a set of cash flows (or leg) for another set. A notional principal amount is used to calculate each cash flow; these are rarely exchanged by the parties. A swap is usually used to hedge a risk, such as an interest-rate risk, or to speculate on a price change. It may also be used to access an underlying asset in order to earn a profit or loss from any change in price while avoiding posting the notional amount in cash or collateral.

An option is a financial instrument that gives the holder the right to engage in a future transaction on an underlying security or futures contract. The holder is under no obligation to exercise this right. There are two main types of option. A call option gives the holder the right to purchase a specified quantity of a security at a fixed price (the strike price) on or before the specified expiration date. A put option gives the holder the right to sell. If the holder chooses to exercise the option, the party who sold, or wrote, the option is obliged to fulfil the terms of the contract.

Futures are traded on a futures exchange and represent an obligation to buy or sell a specified underlying instrument on a specified date (the delivery date or final settlement date) in the future at a specified price (the futures price). The settlement price is the price of the underlying asset on the delivery date. Both parties to a futures contract are legally bound to fulfil the contract on the delivery date. If the holder of a futures position wishes to exit their obligation before the delivery date, they must offset it either by selling a long position or buying back a short position. Such an action effectively closes the futures position and its contractual obligations.

ADVANTAGES

- The use of derivatives means that some financial risks can be transferred to other parties who are more willing or better suited to take or manage those risks and can thus be a useful tool for risk management.
- Purchasing derivatives can be a safer choice if there is a possibility of a looming bear market as they are hedged, unlike equities.
- Buying now at a future price can be cheaper than buying at market price in the future, bearing in mind that the spot price could be less expensive.
- A long call option requires no obligation when it is due.

DISADVANTAGES

- If the market changes dramatically, it is possible to lose financially if the derivatives are being used as a speculative instrument.
- If you hold the put option on a derivative, you are obliged to adhere to it if the holder of the call chooses to exercise their right to sell or buy.

DOS AND DON'TS

DO

- Take time to consider which derivative is most suitable for the transaction you have in mind.
- Consult a financial intermediary or seek other expert guidance if you are unsure.

DON'T

- Don't enter into a contract that will lock you in if there's the slightest possibility that you may need to exit before its expiration date.

▸▸ MORE INFO

Books:

Arditti, Fred D. *Derivatives: A Comprehensive Resource for Options, Futures, Interest Rate Swaps, and Mortgage Securities*. Financial Management Association Survey and Synthesis Series. Boston, MA: Harvard Business School Press, 1996.

Cox, John C., and Mark Rubinstein. *Options Markets*. Englewood Cliffs, NJ: Prentice Hall, 1985.

Hull, John C. *Options, Futures, and Other Derivatives*. Prentice Hall Series in Finance. 7th ed. Upper Saddle River, NJ: Prentice Hall, 2008.

Redhead, Keith. *Financial Derivatives: An Introduction to Futures, Forwards, Options and Swaps*. London: Prentice-Hall, 1996.

Articles:

Black, Fischer, and Myron S. Scholes. "The pricing of options and corporate liabilities." *Journal of Political Economy* 81:3 (1973): 637–654.

Cox, J. C., S. A. Ross, and M. Rubinstein. "Options pricing: a simplified approach." *Journal of Financial Economics* 7 (1979): 229–263.

Moran, Matthew. "Risk-adjusted performance for derivatives-based indexes—Tools to help stabilize returns." *Journal of Indexes* (4th Quarter 2002): 34–40.

Schneeweis, Thomas, and Richard Spurgin. "The benefits of index option-based strategies for institutional portfolios." *Journal of Alternative Investments* (Spring 2001): 44–52.

See Also:

★ The Role of Short Sellers in the Marketplace (pp. 376–379)

✔ Hedge Funds: Understanding the Risks and Returns (p. 938)

✔ Derivatives Markets: Their Structure and Function (p. 924)

Futures, Options, and Swaps (p. 1268)

Option Volatility and Pricing: Advanced Trading Strategies and Techniques Sheldon Natenberg (p. 1306)

"Derivatives are financial weapons of mass destruction." Warren Buffett

  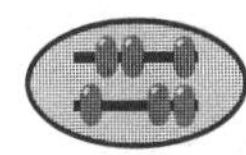   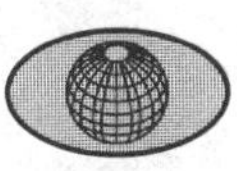   

Understanding and Calculating the Total Cost of Risk

DEFINITION

Risk exists virtually everywhere in business; from the obvious, easily insurable risks such as cover for property assets to more obscure, yet not insignificant, risks such as the loss of key employees to illness. However, in an effort to cover as many bases as possible, some companies channel resources into their risk management operations, potentially raising questions over whether these units are delivering good value for stakeholders in the company. The total cost of risk (TCOR) is a tool for measuring the overall costs associated with the running of the corporate risk management operation, including all insurance premiums, risk control and financing costs, administrative costs, and any self-retained losses incurred, relative to other key measures such as overall company revenues, total headcount, and its asset base. Over time, TCOR therefore provides a yardstick to assess how a company's risk-related costs are changing relative to the overall growth rate of the business. In turn, management can then explore potential ways to assess how the company's TCOR is changing relative to industry benchmarks, typically with the use of data derived from of managing key risks vary widely between different industries—e.g., "physical" risk research conducted by trade groups and industry organizations. Given that the costs considerations are uppermost in the oil distribution business, yet food producers may focus more on liability insurance risks—working with these industry bodies can be the best way to obtain relevant and comparable risk-related cost data.

ADVANTAGES

- Calculating the total cost of risk can help companies to highlight inconsistencies in their approach to risk management.
- The process can also identify areas where the cost of managing a particular risk may be excessive relative to risks elsewhere, potentially leading to reallocation of some elements of the risk management budget.
- By highlighting inefficiencies in the risk management process, TCOR can also generate direct cost savings.

DISADVANTAGES

- Truly comparable TCOR data can be difficult to access, though trade bodies can help. However, prized data on direct competitors—such as a key rival also pushing into a new, high-growth market segment—is plainly sensitive and therefore not generally available.
- TCOR analysis can be mistakenly seen purely as a cost-cutting exercise.

DOS AND DON'TS

DO

- Remember that industry benchmarks may not always be truly comparable with your company in every aspect.
- Consider whether some minor risks could be covered in-house.
- Make use of specialist software to help you arrive at decisions on issues such as risk retention, as risk management budgeting is by nature complex.

DON'T

- Don't ignore the value added by the risk management function when making budgeting decisions. This is a mistake. Risk management should not be seen purely as a cost.
- Don't expect that TCOR analysis will lead to immediate cost savings. This could lead to disappointment. Be prepared to invest in risk management tools which will deliver financial benefits over time.
- Don't see the management of risk-related costs as an issue for which all possible solutions lie within the company. Explaining your objectives and priorities to external risk management specialists and insurance brokers could be very productive.

ACTION CHECKLIST

- ✔ Use a basic framework to breakdown costs into component categories such as risk financing, risk administration, risk compliance costs, and self-insured losses.
- ✔ Identify existing costs for each category, expressed as a percentage of overall company revenues.
- ✔ Use any available data from industry bodies for comparison with your existing TCOR figures in each category.
- ✔ Consider possible reasons for differences between your company's numbers and industry-wide figures.
- ✔ Establish targets for each category for future years.

►► MORE INFO

Books:

Frenkel, Michael, Ulrich Hommel, Gunter Dufey, and Markus Rudolf. *Risk Management: Challenge and Opportunity*. 2nd ed. Berlin: Springer, 2005.

Merna, Tony, and Thaisal F. Al-Fani. *Corporate Risk Management: An Organisational Perspective*. Chichester, UK: Wiley, 2008.

Articles:

McDonald, Caroline. "Cost of risk hits 10-year low." *National Underwriter Property & Casualty—Risk & Benefits Management* (January 2001).

Tilley, Keith. "Cost versus risk." *Strategic RISK* (November 2004).

Website:

Risk and Insurance Management Society (RIMS): www.rims.org

See Also:

★ Risk Management: Beyond Compliance (pp. 510–513)
★ Risk—Perspectives and Common Sense Rules for Survival (pp. 811–814)
✔ Understanding and Calculating RORAC, RAROC, and RARORAC (p. 1006)
Mastering Risk, Volume 1: Concepts (p. 1297)

"Economic acquisition is no longer subordinated to man as the means for the satisfaction of his material needs. This. . .is evidently as definitely a leading principle of capitalism as it is foreign to all peoples not under capitalist influence." Max Weber

  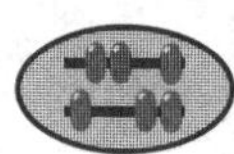   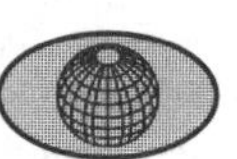   

Understanding and Using Carry Trades

DEFINITION

The term "carry" refers to the practice of borrowing a low-yielding currency and lending a high-yielding currency. The trader attempts to capture the difference between the rates, which can often be substantial, depending on the amount of leverage the trader chooses to use.

Carry trading correlates with global financial and exchange rate stability. It is less commonly used when there are global liquidity shortages. The risk in carry trading is that foreign exchange rates may change unfavorably for the trader, who must then pay back a more expensive currency with a less valuable currency. Carry trades can weaken the target currency because traders sell the borrowed sum and convert it into other currencies. Historically, commercial banks exploited the carry trade by borrowing cheaper short-term funds in their domestic credit markets. They would then lend at longer maturities in the same domestic credit market by making loans to corporate or individual customers or by buying government or corporate bonds. This spread between short-term and long-term funding costs made it a very attractive way of creating credit.

In order to curtail monetary growth as inflation picked up, central banks got into the habit of raising short-term rates, but in recent years this practice of raising rates has spread from domestic banks to a broader range of international financial institutions. Two factors have helped to create this cross-currency carry trade. First has been the growing efficiency of credit markets, thanks to the development of information systems such as computer-driven trading systems with automated stop-loss options, and the diffusion of these trading techniques. Second, the improvement in macroeconomic management techniques over the last 15 years has played a major part in reducing volatility in a range of markets, and this has encouraged investors to take risks across more asset classes.

Monetary policies in the first half of the 2000s led to the yield curves in most major economies becoming flat or inverted. As a result, the scope for funding carry trades narrowed down to the Japanese yen and the Swiss franc. By early 2007, it is estimated that US$1 trillion was staked on the yen carry trade. However, Japanese inflation was much weaker in 2008, implying a possible return to deflation and meaning that the Bank of Japan will not be able to raise interest rates very much. Thus the yen will remain low yielding and will continue to be an attractive funding currency for international carry traders in the short term.

During the economic turmoil of 2008, investors became increasingly desensitized to the measures that were introduced domestically and internationally, and banks became reluctant to lend to each other. With aggressive selling in the euro/yen and sterling/yen carry trades, those in euro/dollar and sterling/dollar have come under pressure.

ADVANTAGES

- Carry trades are profitable as long as the prices of the assets that are bought rise in value or if the price of the liability (domestic currency) does not increase.
- Assets need to be highly liquid—for example quoted equities, commodities, bonds, higher-yielding currencies.

DISADVANTAGES

- The uncertainty of exchange rates makes the carry trade risky.
- A small movement in exchange rates can result in huge losses unless the money is hedged appropriately.
- In slumping economies interest rates tend to fall, which encourages lower-valued and lower-yielding currency.

ACTION CHECKLIST

✔ Ensure that there are low-yielding currencies available to be borrowed to finance the trade.

✔ Check that the current business cycle is perceived to be still in the expansion phase.

✔ Watch out for low-volatility conditions.

✔ Borrow in the low interest rate currency (yen, Swiss franc, offshore yuan).

✔ Invest in the high interest rate currency (US dollar, NZ dollar, Australian dollar, Korean won, Indian rupee).

DOS AND DON'TS

DO

- Take your cash out of the market if you can.
- Keep a careful eye on the currencies of the countries in which you are investing.

DON'T

- Don't expect a fast return on your money.
- Don't assume that the markets will recover quickly in times of economic difficulty.

▸▸ MORE INFO

Book:

Thomas, Lee R. *Carry Trade Opportunities in Non-dollar Markets*. Goldman, Sachs & Co., 1988.

Articles:

Gagnon, Joseph E., and Alain P. Chaboud. "What can the data tell us about carry trades in Japanese yen?" FRB International Finance Discussion Paper no. 899, July 2007. Online at: www.federalreserve.gov/pubs/ifdp/2007/899/default.htm

Galati, Gabriele, Alexandra Heath, and Patrick McGuire. "Evidence of carry trade activity." *BIS Quarterly Review* (September 2007): 27–41. Online at: www.bis.org/publ/qtrpdf/r_qt0709e.pdf

See Also:

✔ Building a Forex Plan (p. 855)

✔ The Foreign Exchange Market: Its Structure and Function (p. 861)

✔ Hedging Foreign Exchange Risk— Case Studies and Strategies (p. 863)

✔ Understanding and Using Currency Swaps (p. 885)

"Capitalism is truly miraculous. What other system enables us to cooperate with millions of other people. . .in an incredible, complex web of commercial transactions?" Steve Forbes

  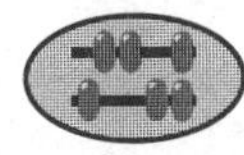   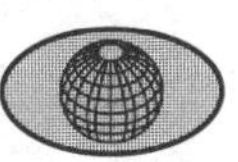   

Understanding and Using Currency Swaps

DEFINITION

A currency swap is a foreign exchange transaction in which two or more parties agree to exchange a set amount of one currency for another for a specified period of time. At the end of the determined timespan, each party returns to the other the original sum swapped. Currency swaps are a useful tool for legitimately bypassing foreign exchange controls. Currency swaps are typically negotiated for any period of time up to 30 years' maturity.

Under international accounting rules, a currency swap is not considered to be a loan and therefore does not usually appear on a company balance sheet. Rather, it is accounted as a foreign exchange transaction (the short leg), with the requirement to close the swap (the far leg) being accounted as a forward contract. All cash flows associated with the swap are paid—the initial receipt/payment of loaned principal, the payment/receipt of interest (in the same currency), and the ultimate return/ recovery of the principal upon maturity.

It is not uncommon for a company to shop around to reduce the amount needed to service a debt. By borrowing at a lower cost in a particular currency and then exchanging it for a debt in the currency the company really desires, both parties can improve the condition of their debt while also maximizing their cash flows.

ADVANTAGES

The main advantage of entering into a currency swap is its flexibility—the maturity of a swap is usually negotiable for at least 10 years. Entering into a currency swap can help both parties limit or manage their exposure to fluctuations in interest rates or to obtain a lower interest rate—a foreign company is unlikely to have access to better rates than a domestic company. As companies service their swap obligations with cash flow generated in a foreign currency, they thus also reduce their exchange rate risk exposure. An additional benefit to engaging in a currency swap is the reduction of counterparty risk, as evidenced by the bid–ask spread.

By definition currency swaps are also combined with an interest rate swap in two currencies. The terms of a swap may be drawn up to have fixed versus floating payments in different currencies beyond fixed rates.

DISADVANTAGES

- Any benefit of entering into a currency swap must be balanced against the costs of the transaction and managing risks such the pre-settlement risk and the settlement risk. However, the chief risk in engaging in a currency swap is that the other party may fail to meet its obligations either during the period of the swap or upon maturity. Should one party wish to exit the swap before maturity, the exiting party must secure the consent of its counterparty before pursuing a mutually agreed exit strategy, much as in the case of selling an exchange-traded futures or option contract before maturity. Some exit routes include the following:
  1. Entering into an offsetting swap. For example, the exiting party could enter into a second swap, this time receiving a fixed rate and paying a floating rate.
  2. Selling the swap to a third party. As swaps have a calculable value, one party may sell the contract to a third party, with the permission of the counterparty.
  3. Purchasing a "swaption." This allows a party to set up, but not enter into, a potentially offsetting swap at the time they execute the original swap.

▸▸ MORE INFO

Books:

Hull, John C. *Options, Futures, and Other Derivatives*. 7th ed. Prentice Hall Series in Finance. Upper Saddle River, NJ: Prentice Hall, 2008.

Redhead, Keith. *Financial Derivatives: An Introduction to Futures, Forwards, Options and Swaps*. London: Prentice Hall, 1996.

Walmsley, Julian. *The Foreign Exchange and Money Markets Guide*. 2nd ed. Wiley Frontiers in Finance Series. New York: Wiley, 2000.

See Also:

★ To Hedge or Not to Hedge (pp. 100–102)
★ A Total Balance Sheet Approach to Financial Risk (pp. 103–105)
✔ Building a Forex Plan (p. 855)
✔ The Foreign Exchange Market: Its Structure and Function (p. 861)
✔ Hedging Foreign Exchange Risk— Case Studies and Strategies (p. 863)

"One of the dynamics of capitalism is that because it's in constant change, there are always people who feel they're going to be hurt by change and are going to resist it." Steve Forbes

     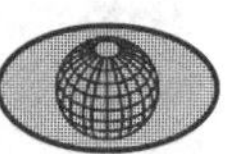   

Understanding and Using Inflation Swaps

DEFINITION

An inflation swap involves the use of inflation derivatives (or inflation-indexed derivatives) to transfer inflation risk from one party to another. The derivatives used may be over-the-counter or exchange-traded derivatives. Inflation swaps have become increasingly popular since the turn of the century as pension funds, for example, recognize the need for inflation-linked assets that match future liabilities. Conversely, borrowers such as governments or large corporations understand that inflation-linked assets or revenues can be funded by inflation-linked debt. Inflation swaps frequently include real rate swaps, such as asset swaps of inflation-indexed bonds. Inflation swaps are simply a linear form of such derivatives. Real rate swaps consist of the nominal interest swap rate minus the corresponding inflation swap.

There are three main types of inflation swap. In a standard interbank inflation-linked swap, or zero-coupon inflation-linked swap, cash flow is exchanged on the maturity date. This swap pays out the exact value of the cumulative inflation for a fixed capital sum over a determined period. This is a good option for investors, particularly pension funds, seeking an investment mix aimed at compliance with long-term, inflation-related obligations.

In a year-on-year inflation-linked swap, inflation is used on an annual basis rather than a cumulative one. This structure is suitable for investors seeking to protect cash flow. Typically, an inflation swap is priced on a zero-coupon basis, with payment exchanged upon maturity. One party pays the compound fixed rate, while the other pays the actual inflation rate for the term of the swap. In Europe, inflation swaps are typically paid on a year-on-year basis where the year-on-year rate of change of the price index is paid. In the United States, payment is more typically on a month-on-month basis, although the inflation rate used is still the year-on-year rate.

In an inflation-linked income swap two cash flows are exchanged, each of which follows the inflation index. One party pays a fixed inflation increase annually over the period of the contract. The other party pays the actual inflation over the period of the contract. The swap itself consists of a series of zero-coupon swaps.

Other traded inflation derivatives include caps, floors, and straddles, which are usually priced against year-on-year swaps. The inflation derivatives market in the United Kingdom is substantial, although the equivalent market in the eurozone is many times bigger.

ADVANTAGES

Public authorities, and companies dealing in utilities, real estate, and distribution all benefit from high inflation as it brings bigger profits. Conversely, insurers, pension funds, and private investors fare better when inflation is low, as otherwise they face a shrinking margin. Thus, there is a potential market for selling or buying inflation. The key advantage of entering into an inflation swap is being able to hedge against future price rises or diminishing margins. By selling inflation in an inflation-linked swap, future income linked to inflation can be protected.

DISADVANTAGES

The main disadvantage of participating in an inflation swap is the risk that inflation rates may change drastically as a result of unexpected shifts in the global economy. Such changes can expose parties to loss of profit or negative equity.

▸▸ MORE INFO

Books:

Brice, Benaben (ed). *Inflation-linked Products: A Guide for Investors and Asset & Liability Managers*. London: Risk Books, 2005.

Brigo, Damiano, and Fabio Mercurio. *Interest Rate Models—Theory and Practice, with Smile, Inflation and Credit*. Corrected 3rd printing. Berlin: Springer, 2007.

Deacon, Mark, Andrew Derry, and Dariush Mirfendereski. *Inflation-indexed Securities: Bonds, Swap & Other Derivatives*. 2nd ed. Wiley Finance Series. Chichester, UK: Wiley, 2004.

Hull, John C. *Options, Futures, and Other Derivatives*. 7th ed. Prentice Hall Series in Finance. Upper Saddle River, NJ: Prentice Hall, 2008.

Redhead, Keith. *Financial Derivatives: An Introduction to Futures, Forwards, Options and Swaps*. London: Prentice Hall, 1996.

Walmsley, Julian. *The Foreign Exchange and Money Markets Guide*. 2nd ed. Wiley Frontiers in Finance Series. New York: Wiley, 2000.

Website:

Website dedicated to the topic of inflation derivatives: www.inflationderivatives.com

See Also:

★ A Total Balance Sheet Approach to Financial Risk (pp. 103–105)

✔ Derivatives Markets: Their Structure and Function (p. 924)

✔ Methods for Dealing With Inflation Risk (p. 876)

✔ Swaps, Options, and Futures: What They Are and Their Function (p. 882)

Futures, Options, and Swaps (p. 1268)

"The ideology of capitalism makes us all connoisseurs of liberty—of the indefinite expansion of possibility."
Susan Sontag

  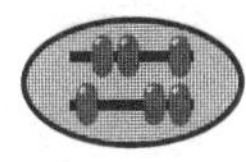   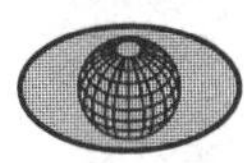   

Understanding and Using Interest Rate Swaps

DEFINITION

An interest rate swap is a popular, highly liquid derivatives instrument in which one party exchanges its stream of interest payments for another party's stream of cash flows. Interest rate swaps are used by hedgers to manage their fixed or floating assets and liabilities, and by speculators to profit from changes in interest rates.

There are various types of interest rate swap, the most common being where one party agrees to pay a fixed rate (the swap rate) to the other party, which in return pays a floating rate to the first party. The rate is usually denominated in a particular currency, which is then multiplied by a notional principal amount (for example, US$1 million). The notional amount is generally used only to calculate the size of cash flows to be exchanged. The floating rate is usually pegged to a reference rate such as the Libor, and the interest payments are settled net. When the swap is initiated, it is priced so that its net present value is zero.

Other popular swap types are fixed–fixed, floating–floating, or a combination including different currencies (interest rate swaps are often combined with currency swaps).

ADVANTAGES

The chief advantage of an interest rate swap is that it limits a company's exposure to interest rate fluctuations, and thus reduces risk. By swapping interest rates, a firm is able to alter its interest rate exposures and bring them in line with management's appetite for interest rate risk.

Where there is a positive quality spread differential, a further benefit is the opportunity for arbitrage. This enables each party to take advantage of the other's credit-worthiness in the swap.

Other pluses include increasing the certainty of an issuer's future obligations, saving money should interest rates decline (here, the party paying a floating rate will be the beneficiary of a rate drop), the option of revising your debt profile to benefit from anticipated future market conditions, and reducing the amount of debt service.

Interest rate swaps generally involve minimal cash outlay. It is usual that on a payment date only the difference between the two payment amounts is paid to the entitled, rather than an exchange of the full amount of interest.

DISADVANTAGES

The downside to participating in an interest rate swap is the exposure to risk, typically interest rate risk and credit risk. The interest rate risk occurs when there are changes in the floating rate. In a standard fixed-for-floating swap, the party paying the floating rate benefits if rates fall but is exposed if rates rise, in a similar fashion to holding a long bond position. The credit risk remains whether the swap is in-the-money or not. If one party to the swap is in-the-money, then the risk is their exposure to the other party defaulting.

▸▸ MORE INFO

Books:

Arditti, Fred D. *Derivatives: A Comprehensive Resource for Options, Futures, Interest Rate Swaps, and Mortgage Securities*. Financial Management Association Survey and Synthesis Series. Boston, MA: Harvard Business School Press, 1996.

Hull, John C. *Options, Futures, and Other Derivatives*. 7th ed. Prentice Hall Series in Finance. Upper Saddle River, NJ: Prentice Hall, 2008.

Redhead, Keith. *Financial Derivatives: An Introduction to Futures, Forwards, Options and Swaps*. London: Prentice Hall, 1996.

Walmsley, Julian. *The Foreign Exchange and Money Markets Guide*. 2nd ed. Wiley Frontiers in Finance Series. New York: Wiley, 2000.

See Also:

★ A Total Balance Sheet Approach to Financial Risk (pp. 103–105)

✔ Hedging Interest Rate Risk—Case Study and Strategies (p. 864)

✔ Identifying and Managing Exposure to Interest and Exchange Rate Risks (p. 867)

✔ Swaps, Options, and Futures: What They Are and Their Function (p. 882)

✔ Understanding and Using the Repos Market (p. 949)

"Capitalism is a hotel. Its penthouse suites are always filled, but not necessarily with the same people."
Paul Samuelson

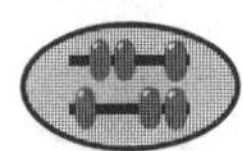

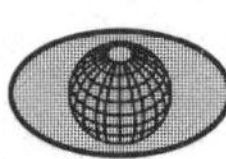

Understanding and Using the Cash Conversion Cycle

DEFINITION

The cash conversion cycle (CCC) refers to the period of time in which a company is able to convert its resources into cash. Resources can include such factors as labor, raw materials, and utilities. This metric is used as part of working capital analysis. The cycle can, perhaps, be best defined as the time it takes to collect the cash from sales after paying for the resources purchased by the company. The cycle may consist of up to five separate stages of conversion:

- Resources into inventories
- Inventories into finished goods
- Finished goods into sales
- Sales into accounts receivable
- Receivables into cash

The cash conversion cycle uses a basic formula to calculate the time period, which is always in days, as follows:

CCC = Inventory conversion period (DIO) + Receivables conversion period (DSO) – Payables conversion period (DPO)

Inventory conversion period (DIO) = Inventory / CGS × 365

Receivables conversion period (DSO) = Receivables / Sales × 365

Payables conversion period (DPO) = Accounts payable / CGS × 365

where CGS is cost of goods sold, DIO is days of inventory outstanding, DSO is days of sales outstanding, and DPO is days payable outstanding.

The above formulae should be adjusted to take into account any reduction in requirements due to delaying payment for purchases. The formulae are also based on averages and do not take account of seasonality, or trends in growth, or decline of the business.

The cash conversion cycle is important for both retailers and manufacturers as it measures how quickly a company can convert sales into hard cash. Companies should aim to have the shortest possible cycle as it means capital is tied up for less time, making the bottom line stronger.

Economists cite the CCC as one the most accurate metrics for the real financial health of a company, as it is not only easy to calculate but it also reflects the dynamic situation on a day-to-day basis when you input the data.

ADVANTAGES

- In a short cash conversion cycle, capital is freed up for investment purposes or capital expenditure.

DISADVANTAGES

- In a long cash conversion cycle, capital is locked into core operations and cannot be used for anything else.

ACTION CHECKLIST

✔ Note that often both sales and purchases are made on credit rather than with cash—this difference should be accounted for when calculating the cycle. Special attention should also be given to the length of the receivables processing period: A shorter period is generally best, but in certain circumstances it can sometimes be offset by an increase in that for accounts payable by paying creditors more slowly, although this may be viewed as irresponsible.

✔ Note that the receivables days look backward (debtors arise out of sales that have already been made), whereas the inventory days look forward (inventory is held in order to meet future sales).

✔ The cash conversion cycle can be used as part of a company's strategy. For example, a firm aiming to be the lowest-price supplier on the market will probably tailor its inventory and receivables days accordingly, with tight payment times and a willingness to accept stock-outs in order to avoid holding excessive inventory. Conversely, a high-end supplier would be more likely to extend generous credit terms, and hold more lines of inventory, to reflect a business model that charges higher prices to its customers.

DOS AND DON'TS

DO

- Remember that some businesses will have a smaller CCC, such as those selling goods for cash, which therefore have no receivables, or those selling services, which therefore have no inventory.
- Remember that the cycle may be negative if a company settles with its creditors immediately after purchasing raw materials, manufacturing the goods, and selling them for cash.

DON'T

- Don't run any of the formulae without first making the specific adjustments applicable to your business.

▸▸ MORE INFO

Book:

Hilton, Ronald W. *Managerial Accounting*. 7th ed. McGraw-Hill, 2006.

See Also:

★ How to Better Manage Your Financial Supply Chain (pp. 57–59)
✔ Building an Efficient Credit and Collection Accounts System (p. 972)
✔ Choosing the Right Payment Policy (p. 976)
✔ How to Optimize Stock Control (p. 985)

"Market fundamentalism undermines the democratic political process and the inefficiency of the political process is a powerful argument in favor of market fundamentalism." George Soros

  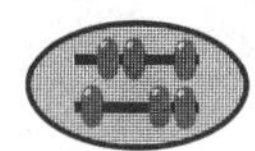   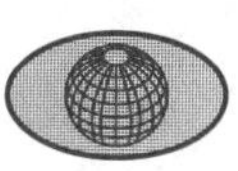   

Understanding Asset–Liability Management (Full Balance Sheet Approach)

DEFINITION

Asset–liability management, or ALM, is a means of managing the risk that can arise from changes in the relationship between assets and liabilities. ALM was originally pioneered by financial institutions in the 1970s as interest rates became increasingly volatile. This volatility had dangerous implications for financial institutions. Some, for example, had sold long-term guaranteed interest contracts—some guaranteed rates of around 16% for periods up to 10 years. However, when short-term interest rates subsequently fell, these institutions, such as the equitable in the US, were crippled. Prior to the 1970s, interest rates in developed countries varied little and thus losses accruing from asset–liability mismatches tended to be minimal.

Following the experience of equitable and other institutions, financial firms increasingly focused on ALM, whereby they sought to manage balance sheets in order to maintain a mix of loans and deposits consistent with the firm's goals for long-term growth and risk management. They set up ALM committees to oversee the ALM process. Today, ALM has been adopted by many corporations, as well as financial institutions. ALM now seeks to ascertain and control three types of financial risk: Interest rate risk, credit risk (the probability of default), and liquidity risk, which refers to the danger that a given security or asset cannot be traded quickly enough in the market to prevent a loss (or make a predetermined profit).

But ALM also now seeks to address other risks, such as foreign exchange risks and operational risks (covering areas such as fraud and legal risks, as well as physical or environmental risks). The techniques that are now applied by ALM practitioners have also developed, reflecting the growth of derivatives and other complex financial instruments. ALM now includes hedging, for example, whereby airlines will seek to hedge against movements in fuel prices and manufacturers will seek to mitigate the risk of fluctuations in commodity prices. Meanwhile, securitization has allowed firms to directly address asset–liability risk by removing assets or liabilities from their balance sheets.

ADVANTAGES

- ALM can help protect a financial institution or corporation against a variety of financial and nonfinancial risks.
- The mere process of identifying risks enables businesses to be better prepared to deal with these risks in the most cost-effective way.
- ALM ensures that a company's capital and assets are used in the most efficient way.
- It can be used as a strategic and business tool to improve earnings.

DISADVANTAGES

- ALM is only as good as the people on the ALM committee and the operational procedures that they follow.
- ALM can prove costly in terms of both the time required of employees and the investment required in management tools such as IT and techniques such as hedging.

ACTION CHECKLIST

- ✔ Establish an ALM committee to oversee the process.
- ✔ Ensure the committee has the necessary tools and techniques for measuring and managing rate, credit, and funding risk. This should include a computer system that enables the monitoring of funding sources and credit exposures.
- ✔ Acquire a managerial accounting system that can control the information fed into the computer system.
- ✔ Establish a reward and penalty system to manage those employees who are taking rate, credit, funding and other risks.

DOS AND DON'TS

DO

- Talk to one of the many consultancy firms that specialize in ALM, and that can advise on establishing an ALM committee and improving its performance.
- Ensure those appointed to the ALM committee have the necessary knowledge and experience to perform their tasks.
- Constantly monitor the performance of your committee.

DON'T

- Don't seek to cut costs in terms of investing in management tools and personnel.
- Don't forget that risks are constantly changing and developing. Make sure your ALM committee has the skills to deal with the latest developments.

▸▸ MORE INFO

Books:

Buckley, Adrian. *Multinational Finance*. 5th ed. Harlow, UK: FT Prentice Hall, 2003.

Dermine, Jean, and Youssef F. Bissada. *Asset and Liability Management: The Banker's Guide to Value Creation and Risk Control*. 2nd ed. Harlow, UK: FT Prentice Hall, 2007.

Tilman, Leo M. (ed). *Asset Liability Management of Financial Institutions: Maximising Shareholder Value through Risk-Conscious Investing*. London: Euromoney, 2003.

Articles:

Blommestein, H. J., and F. K. Kalkan. "Sovereign asset and liability management—Practical steps towards integrated risk management." *Bank- en Financiewezen/Revue Bancaire et Financière* Issues 6–7 (2008): 360–369.

Buehler, Kevin, and Anthony Santomero. "How is asset and liability management changing? Insights from the McKinsey Survey." *The RMA Journal* 90:6 (March 2008): 44–49.

Detemple, Jérôme, and Marcel Rindisbacher. "Dynamic asset liability management with tolerance for limited shortfalls." *Insurance: Mathematics and Economics* 43:3 (December 2008): 281–294.

Website:

Institute of Risk Management: www.theirm.org

"This is called capitalism. We create a product called Windows. Who decides what's in Windows. It's the customers who buy Windows." Bill Gates

     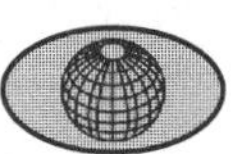   

Understanding Capital Structure Theory: Modigliani and Miller

DEFINITION

The Modigliani–Miller theorem states that, in the absence of taxes, bankruptcy costs, and asymmetric information, and in an efficient market, a company's value is unaffected by how it is financed, regardless of whether the company's capital consists of equities or debt, or a combination of these, or what the dividend policy is. The theorem is also known as the capital structure irrelevance principle.

A number of principles underlie the theorem, which holds under the assumption of both taxation and no taxation. The two most important principles are that, first, if there are no taxes, increasing leverage brings no benefits in terms of value creation, and second, that where there are taxes, such benefits, by way of an interest tax shield, accrue when leverage is introduced and/or increased.

The theorem compares two companies—one unlevered (i.e., financed purely by equity) and the other levered (i.e., financed partly by equity and partly by debt)—and states that if they are identical in every other way the value of the two companies is the same.

As an illustration of why this must be true, suppose that an investor is considering buying one of either an unlevered company or a levered company. The investor could purchase the shares of the levered company, or purchase the shares of the unlevered company and borrow an equivalent sum of money to that borrowed by the levered company. In either case, the return on investment would be identical. Thus, the price of the levered company must be the same as the price of the unlevered company minus the borrowed sum of money, which is the value of the levered company's debt. There is an implicit assumption that the investor's cost of borrowing money is the same as that of the levered company, which is not necessarily true in the presence of asymmetric information or in the absence of efficient markets. For a company that has risky debt, as the ratio of debt to equity increases the weighted average cost of capital remains constant, but there is a higher required return on equity because of the higher risk involved for equity holders in a company with debt.

ADVANTAGES

- In practice, it's fair to say that none of the assumptions are met in the real world, but what the theorem teaches is that capital structure is important because one or more of the assumptions will be violated. By applying the theorem's equations, economists can find the determinants of optimal capital structure and see how those factors might affect optimal capital structure.

DISADVANTAGES

- Modigliani and Miller's theorem, which justifies almost unlimited financial leverage, has been used to boost economic and financial activities. However, its use has also resulted in increased complexity, lack of transparency, and higher risk and uncertainty in those activities. The global financial crisis of 2008, which saw a number of highly leveraged investment banks fail, has been in part attributed to excessive leverage ratios.

▸▸ MORE INFO

Books:

Brealey, Richard A., Stewart C. Myers, and Franklin Allen. *Principles of Corporate Finance*. 9th ed. Boston, MA: McGraw-Hill/Irwin, 2008.
Stewart, G. Bennett. *The Quest for Value: The EVA Management Guide*. New York: HarperBusiness, 1991. (Also published by HarperCollins under the title *The Quest for Value: A Guide for Senior Managers*.)

Articles:

Miles, J., and J. R. Ezzell. "The weighted average cost of capital, perfect capital markets, and project life: A clarification." *Journal of Financial and Quantitative Analysis* 15 (1980): 719–730.
Modigliani, Franco, and Merton H. Miller. "The cost of capital, corporation finance, and the theory of investment." *American Economic Review* 48:3 (1958): 261–297.
Modigliani, Franco, and Merton H. Miller. "Corporate income taxes and the cost of capital: A correction." *American Economic Review* 53:3 (1963): 433–443.

See Also:

★ Capital Structure: Perspectives (pp. 31–34)
★ Optimizing the Capital Structure: Finding the Right Balance Between Debt and Equity (pp. 557–558)
✔ Investors and the Capital Structure (p. 911)
Merton Miller (p. 1177)
Franco Modigliani (p. 1178)

"The dynamics of capitalism is postponement of enjoyment to the constantly postponed future."
Norman O. Brown

  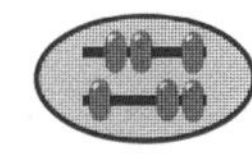   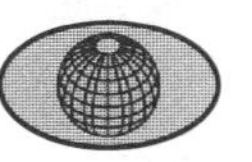   

Understanding Free Cash Flow

DEFINITION

Free cash flow is a measure of financial performance and is defined as cash flow available for distribution among any parties that hold security in a company. It comprises the net income plus depreciation and amortization minus capital expenditure and any changes in working capital. The free cash flow is the cash that a company has available for use after paying out the necessary expenditure to maintain or expand its asset base. It matters, as it is a means for a company to boost shareholder value through, for example, mergers and acquisitions, R&D, paying dividends, or reducing debt. It can thus be viewed as an alternative bottom line.

Unlike earnings, free cash flow represents real cash. It is a very useful way to assess the financial health of a company as it is what is left after all the accounting assumptions built into the earnings have been stripped away. A company may seem to be generating high earnings, but only free cash flow indicates whether any real money has been generated in a designated period. Ultimately, the stock market's estimate of how much free cash flow a company will generate in the future is reflected in the share price.

Even a profitable concern may have a negative cash flow. This does not necessarily signal financial problems—it may indicate that the company is making large investments with potentially high returns. Shareholders may agree to forgo dividends one year or longer if they believe that such a strategy will produce better returns in the long term.

Free cash flow can, of course, vary from year to year, depending on the capital expenditure (usually referred to as capex) and any changes in working capital. Thus, no accounting year can be described as normal when measured purely by free cash flow. However, a company that has stable capex should in the long term have free cash flow that is roughly equal to its earnings.

It is important to remember that how a company uses its free cash flow matters a lot. A company using its free cash flow on share buy-backs (for example, when the share price has fallen below its intrinsic value) or to pay out dividends is more attractive to investors. Conversely, a company that pays out more of its free cash flow in dividends than it is generating is overstretching its spare cash.

ADVANTAGES

Rising free cash flow often indicates that increased earnings lie ahead. And when free cash flow booms as a result of revenue growth, cost-cutting, or debt reduction, a company is in a position to reward its investors promptly. This why analysts generally view free cash flow as a reliable metric for assessing value.

DISADVANTAGES

Free cash flow is not immune to manipulation in the accounts as there are no regulatory standards for determining it. A company with a high free cash flow may be underreporting its capex, for example, or stretching out its payments. However, any impact is likely to be only temporary. Also important to note is that a company may have trouble sustaining earnings growth if free cash flow is poor, and it may be forced to increase its debt. In the worst-case scenario, insufficient free cash flow could tip a company into a situation of illiquidity.

▸▸ MORE INFO

Books:

Brealey, Richard A., Stewart C. Myers, and Franklin Allen. *Principles of Corporate Finance*. 8th ed. McGraw-Hill/Irwin Series in Finance, Insurance, and Real Estate. Boston, MA: McGraw-Hill/Irwin, 2005.

Stewart, G. Bennett, III. *The Quest for Value*. New York: HarperBusiness, 1991.

Article:

Jensen, Michael C. "Agency costs of free cash flow, corporate finance, and takeovers." *American Economic Review* 76:2 (1986): 323–329.

See Also:

★ Why EVA is the Best Measurement Tool for Creating Shareholder Value (pp. 843–844)
✔ Assessing Business Performance (p. 1059)
✔ Measuring Financial Health (p. 874)
✔ Preparing a Cash Flow Forecast (p. 880)

"The pursuit of modern life is economic and the fundamental principle of economic production is individual independence." Chen Duxiu

  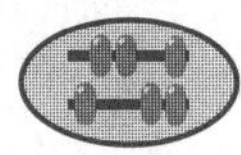   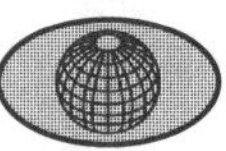   

Understanding Hedge Ratios

DEFINITION

Hedging is the art of reducing or eliminating financial risk by entering into a transaction that will protect against loss through a compensatory price movement.

A hedge ratio, therefore, is a mechanism for calculating the number of options or other derivatives, or amount of currency, needed to hedge against the risk of loss in a portfolio of shares or other derivatives. It is also known as a delta.

A delta is commonly used to compare the value of a position protected by a hedge with the size of the actual position. For instance, you need to calculate the number of options necessary to offset a change in value resulting from a price change in 100 shares of common stock at a given point in time. If you need two options to offset the change, the delta is 2. To give a practical example, if you have a call option on shares for a particular company, a delta of 0.50 means that for every $1.00 increase in the share price, the option price rises by $0.50.

The hedge ratio can also identify and help to minimize any risks in futures contracts. Thus, it may be used to compare the value of a futures contract with the value of the underlying instrument (for example a cash commodity or shares) that is being hedged. Indeed, a hedge ratio can be used to hedge any kind of financial instrument.

The formula for a hedge ratio is as follows:

$$H = -1$$

where

$$\text{hedge ratio} = \frac{\text{total delta equivalent}}{\text{total stock value}}$$

No matter what instrument is being hedged against, the formula for the hedge ratio remains the same: H = −1.

Delta values change constantly, according to how the specific financial instrument is performing on the markets. The rate of change of a delta's underlying asset price is called the gamma. In order to maintain a hedge ratio of H = −1, it must be adjusted regularly. This process is known as dynamic hedging. When a position has a hedge ratio of H = −1, it is known as delta neutral.

The value of a delta is usually equal to a one-point change up or down in the underlying security over a short time period. If an option has a high delta, it is usually more profitable to purchase the derivative, as the greater percentage movement relative to the price of the underlying security offers better leverage. For derivatives with a low delta, the reverse is true and it is better to sell.

▸▸ MORE INFO

Articles:

Black, F. "Universal hedging: Optimising currency risk and reward in international equity portfolios." *Financial Analysts Journal* 45:4 (1989): 16–22.

Gardner, G. W., and T. Wuilloud. "Currency risk in international portfolios: How satisfying is optimal hedging?" *Journal of Portfolio Management* 21:3 (1995): 59–67.

Harris, Richard, and Jian Shen. "Robust estimation of the optimal hedge ratio." *Journal of Futures Markets* 23:8 (2003): 799–816.

Qian, Edward, and Stephen Gorman. "International benchmarks: In support of a 50% hedge ratio." *Journal of Investing* 9:2 (Summer 2000).

Shafer, Carl E. "Hedge ratios and basis behavior: An intuitive insight?" *Journal of Futures Markets* 13:8 (1993): 837–847.

See Also:

★ Carrying Out Due Diligence on Hedge Funds (pp. 289–291)
★ The Role of Short Sellers in the Marketplace (pp. 376–379)
★ To Hedge or Not to Hedge (pp. 100–102)
✔ Hedge Funds: Understanding the Risks and Returns (p. 938)
✔ Hedging Credit Risk— Case Studies and Strategies (p. 862)

"While there are successes of market economies, there are also needs for supplementation in other fields in terms of public intervention, in terms of political participation, and so forth." Amartya Sen

   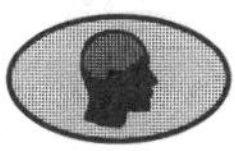  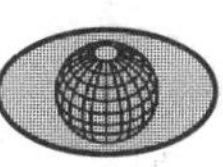   

Understanding Key Financial Terms and Statements

DEFINITION

Publicly traded companies are under an obligation to deliver regular trading updates to the market, ensuring that at all times they present a reasonable reflection of their actual trading performance. However, the terms commonly used in trading statements range from the readily understood, such as "sales" to the more complex and obscure such as "EBITA." While audited accounts are intended to ensure that the company's interim and full-year trading statements provide a truthful assessment as to how the company has fared during the specified trading period, investors frequently pay particular attention to the "outlook" or "prospects" section of a company review, on the basis that stock valuations are heavily geared to perceptions of future earnings. Given that many stocks typically trade on multiples of 10 or more of earnings, stocks are, therefore, highly sensitive to the perception of how future earnings could vary from existing market forecasts. How a company's results compare to the market's consensus expectations is usually the major driver for the stock's direction following a trading update. For example, should a company announce record results, the stock is actually likely to decline should even these results fail to match the market's even more optimistic expectations.

When reporting their performance, companies present four kinds of financial statements:

1 balance sheet—a breakdown of the company's assets and its liabilities at a fixed date;
2 income statement—details of how much money the company earned and what it spent during the period;
3 cash flow statement—how cash moved in and out of the company during the period;
4 stockholders' equity statement—a statement summarizing the opening balance, additions to and deductions from, and the closing balance of the stockholders' equity account, over a stated period.

While the purpose of each of these statements is relatively easy to understand, some of the terminology contained in company reports can be confusing without some accountancy knowledge. The following paragraphs present a small selection of examples of commonly misunderstood terms used by companies in their trading updates:

- EPS—Earnings per stock. The figure represents the company's total net income during the period, minus dividends to be paid to preferred stockholders (i.e. guaranteed dividends), divided by the number of stocks in issue. As the latter can change during the review period, many companies use a weighted average stock count figure for the review period as a whole.
- EBIT—Earnings before interest and tax. This figure represents the total income from all sources before interest payments and taxes are taken into account.
- Working capital—Trading current assets less trading current liabilities.
- Retained earnings—This figure refers to the total of net earnings—revenues after all expenses, taxes, and interest deductions—that the company has built up.
- Return on capital employed—Also known as ROCE, this is a measure of the returns that a business is achieving from the capital employed, usually expressed in percentage terms. Typically used as a guide as to how efficiently a company is using the money invested in it, ROCE can be expressed as the ratio of operating profits achieved to the total amount of operating capital invested (i.e. both equity and debt) in the business.

ADVANTAGES

- Understanding financial terms and statements helps investors to make more informed decisions.
- During extended periods of volatility in financial markets, investment news becomes mainstream news, so an understanding of the terms used becomes even more beneficial.

DISADVANTAGES

- Some of the terminology used in finance and investment can be complex.
- Detailed analysis of statements and company-specific financial number crunching requires knowledge and considerable resources, so it is best left to expert analysts.

ACTION CHECKLIST

✔ Keeping abreast of general economic and financial news can add a greater sense of perspective when looking at financial statements.

DOS AND DON'TS

DO

- Take advantage of freely available investment research when making investment decisions.
- Be prepared to contact companies' investor relations departments with any queries you may have.

DON'T

- Don't be afraid to seek advice. Attempting to study company trading statements in detail is best reserved for those with accounting expertise.
- Don't focus exclusively on one company's results without reference to factors that may be impacting on the wider industry.

▸▸ MORE INFO

Books:

Becket, Michael Ivan H. *How the Stock Market Works: A Beginner's Guide to Investment.* 2nd ed. London: Kogan Page, 2004.

Taparia, Jay. *Understanding Financial Statements: A Journalist's Guide.* Oak Park, IL: Marion Street Press, 2004.

Website:

US Securities and Exchange Commission's (SEC's) "Beginners' guide to financial statements": www.sec.gov/investor/pubs/begfinstmtguide.htm

"One of the things about the free enterprise capitalism system is that life is brutal." Bernard Cornfeld

     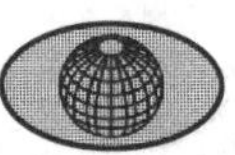   

Understanding the Balance Sheet

DEFINITION

In financial accounting, the balance sheet is one of four standard financial statements and is a summary of a company's financial position at a given point in time. The balance sheet normally is broken down into three main elements—assets, liabilities, and net equity—to show what the company owns and owes on that date. It is usual to include intangible assets such as goodwill alongside tangible assets such as property. Typically, a balance sheet is published at the end of the company's financial year when the accounts have been audited, but it may also be produced at the end of a quarter, half-year, or other specified period.

Of the three elements on the balance sheet, the assets are normally listed first, followed by any liabilities. The difference between the two is the equity, or worth, of the company. The equity may be referred to as net assets, shareholders' equity, or net worth. The equity will always equal the assets minus the liabilities, or, conversely, the assets must equal the liabilities plus the equity:

Equity = Assets – Liabilities

OR

Assets = Liabilities + Equity

The balance sheet is always drawn up so that the assets are presented in one section with the liabilities and equity in the other, and they must match each other, or balance (hence the title "balance sheet"). Double-entry bookkeeping is used to record the value of each line on the balance sheet. Because a corporate balance sheet tends to be lengthy and complex, it is usually published in the company's annual report, typically with that of the previous year alongside for comparative purposes.

The International Accounting Standards Committee is responsible for drawing up guidelines for corporate balance sheets. Accounts published to this standard are usually marked as IAS compliant. There are also a number of country-specific bodies that draw up accounting guidelines, and, depending on the country where a company is based, such standards may be obligatory.

The assets on a balance sheet typically include the following items: current assets such as inventory, accounts receivable, cash and cash equivalents, and prepaid expenses; long-term assets such as property, plant and equipment; investment property such as real estate held for investment purposes; intangible assets, which includes goodwill, patents and intellectual property; and other financial assets.

The liabilities are usually items such as: accounts payable, provisions for warranties or court decisions, financial liabilities (excluding the two previous items) such as promissory notes and corporate bonds, liabilities and assets for current tax, and deferred tax liabilities and tax assets.

The last element on the balance sheet is the equity, or net worth. Theoretically, the shareholders' equity actually forms part of a company's liabilities, as the shares in fact represent monies owed to the shareholders after payment of all other liabilities. In practice, however, the liabilities on the balance sheet exclude the shareholders' equity. Thus, the equity by definition is equal to the assets minus the liabilities, i.e. the difference between the two.

On the balance sheet equity typically includes: the total number of shares authorized, issued and fully paid, and issued but not fully paid; the par value, i.e. face value, of the shares; a reconciliation of shares outstanding at the beginning and the end of the period covered by the balance sheet; a list of any rights, preferences, or restrictions of the shares; treasury shares, including those held by subsidiary or associated companies; and any shares reserved for issuance under options and contracts.

▸▸ MORE INFO

Book:

Williams, Jan R., Susan F. Haka, Mark S. Bettner, and Joseph V. Carcello. *Financial & Managerial Accounting: The Basis for Business Decisions*. 14th ed. Boston, MA: McGraw-Hill/Irwin, 2008.

Websites:

American Institute of Certified Public Accountants: www.aicpa.org
Financial Accounting Standards Board: www.fasb.org
International Accounting Standards Board: www.iasb.org
Institute of Chartered Accountants in England and Wales: www.icaew.co.uk

See Also:

★ The Missing Metrics: Managing the Cost of Complexity (pp. 688–690)
★ Understanding the Requirements for Preparing IFRS Financial Statements (pp. 723–724)
★ Valuing Pension Fund Liabilities on the Balance Sheet (pp. 113–115)
✔ Preparing Financial Statements: Balance Sheets (p. 1043)
✔ Understanding Asset–Liability Management (Full Balance Sheet Approach) (p. 889)

"Capitalism still possesses quite substantial and far from exhausted resources." Konstantin Ustinovich Chernenko

  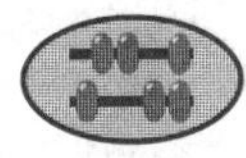   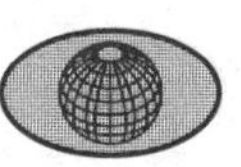   

Understanding the Cost of Capital and the Hurdle Rate

DEFINITION

The cost of capital is the rate of return that an investor expects to earn on his or her investment. If an investment is to be worthwhile, the expected return on capital must be greater than its cost. In other words, the *risk-adjusted* return on capital (that is, incorporating not just the projected returns, but the probabilities of those projections) must be higher than the cost of capital.

Cost of capital is made up of two elements: debt and equity. The cost of debt is, in the simplest terms, the amount of interest paid on the debt. The interest cost is historical, but investor expectations may also influence the actual cost (i.e. investors may accept a higher cost in the short term where the long-term gains are better). Other factors may also affect the cost of debt. The interest rate usually includes the risk-free rate plus a risk component, which takes into account the probability of default on the debt.

The cost of equity is more complex. The traditional calculation used is that of dividend capitalization, whereby the dividends per share are divided by the current market value of the stock plus the dividend growth rate. Thus, the cost of equity is equal to the compensation demanded by the market in exchange for ownership of the asset and bearing the risk of ownership.

The cost of capital is often used as the discount rate, i.e. the rate at which the projected cash flow is discounted to determine the net present value.

The weighted average cost of capital (WACC) is a method of measuring a company's cost of capital. The total capital is taken to be the value of a company's equity (if there are no outstanding warrants and options, this is equal to the company's market capitalization) plus the cost of its debt (this must be continually updated as the cost of debt changes every time there is a change in the interest rate). When calculating the WACC, the equity in the debt-to-equity ratio is the market value of all equity, rather than the shareholders' equity on the balance sheet.

The hurdle rate is the minimum rate of return, when applying a discounted cash flow analysis, that an investor requires before they commit to an investment. A company may apply it when deciding whether to undertake a project, or a bank when extending loans. It must be equal to the incremental cost of capital. It is known as the hurdle rate because the amount of return determines if the investor is "over the hurdle" and ready to invest.

ADVANTAGES

Using a hurdle rate can help take the emotion out of making a decision on investment by focusing purely on the financial aspects. When an investment looks exciting, it can be easy to overlook the risks or a potentially poor rate of return. A risk premium can be appended to the hurdle rate if evaluation of the investment shows that specific opportunities inherently contain high levels of risk.

DISADVANTAGES

A major downside to using a hurdle rate is that, inevitably, some profitable projects will be rejected. Additionally, if the hurdle rate is too high, a company may only favor projects that are profitable in the short term rather than taking a long-term view. Thus it can make companies seem conservative and deter them from investing in innovation where the returns are uncertain.

▸▸ MORE INFO

Book:

Ross, Stephen A., Randolph W. Westerfield, and Jeffrey Jaffe. *Corporate Finance*. 8th ed. Boston, MA: McGraw-Hill, 2008.

Articles:

Modigliani, F., and M. Miller. "The cost of capital, corporation finance and the theory of investment." *American Economic Review* 48:3 (1958): 261–297.

Yee, Kenton K. "Aggregation, dividend irrelevancy, and earnings-value relations." *Contemporary Accounting Research* 22:2 (2005): 453–480.

See Also:

✔ Appraising Investment Opportunities (p. 1058)
✔ Assessing Cash Flow and Bank Lending Requirements (p. 854)
✔ Understanding the Relationship between the Discount Rate and Risk (p. 896)
✔ Understanding the Weighted Average Cost of Capital (WACC) (p. 897)
Robert Merton (p. 1176)

"I do believe that capitalism is inherently Darwinian and that a totally free market is ultimately inhumane, because you'll have what happened in the 19th century—a kind of piling up of profits at the very top. . .we should not tolerate, in an affluent society, extreme levels of poverty or deprivation." Camille Paglia

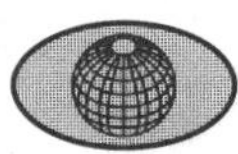

Understanding the Relationship between the Discount Rate and Risk

DEFINITION

The discount rate is the percentage by which a discounted cash flow (DCF) valuation is reduced in each time period beyond the present. Estimating a suitable discount rate is difficult and is an uncertain part of DCF. The problems are magnified by the fact that small changes in the interest rate can cause large changes in value for the final result down the line.

The discount rate used in financial calculations is commonly taken to be equal to the cost of capital. Adjustments can be made to the discount rate to take into account associated risks for uncertain cash flows. Examples of discount rates applied to various types of companies show a wide range:

Start-up companies seeking new money	50–100%
Early start-ups	40–60%
Late start-ups	30–50%
Mature companies	0–25%

High discount rates apply to more risky companies, for a number of reasons:

- Stocks are not traded publicly, so there is a reduced market for ownership.
- The number of willing investors is limited.
- The risk that start-ups will fail is higher.
- Forecasts by the business owners may be overoptimistic.

When a business has made a profit and is deciding whether to reinvest it in the business or pass it to stockholders, it must consider the discount rate. In an ideal world, reinvestment now guarantees larger profits later, and the amount of extra profit required by stockholders in the future, so that they will agree to reinvestment now, based on the stockholder's discount rate. The capital asset pricing model (CAPM) is a way of estimating stockholders' discount rates. These rates are usually applied by businesses to their decisions on reinvestment by calculating the net present value of the decision. If a company uses the CAPM to work out the discount rate, it must first determine the equity cash flows that are subject to this rate.

The capital asset pricing model takes three variables into account when calculating a discount rate:

Risk-free rate: This is the return (as a percentage) from investing in risk-free securities, for example government bonds.

Beta: Beta is a measurement of how the stock price of a company reacts to a change in the market. A beta figure greater than 1 means that the stock price of the company changes more than the rest of the market. A beta below 1 means that the stock price is stable and does not respond wildly to changes in the market. A beta of less than zero means that the stock price moves in the opposite direction to the market, taking leveraging effects into account.

Equity market risk premium: This is the return on investment above the risk-free rate that investors require.

The discount rate is calculated as follows:

Discount rate = Risk-free rate + Beta × Equity market risk premium

The relationship between the discount rate and risk needs to be considered when performing a DCF analysis because any adjustment of the discount rate needs to allow for risk in future cash flows, and investors need to understand the trade-off between the amount of risk and expected future returns. A higher expected return is usually accompanied by a higher risk. Risk-averse investors usually prefer to hold a risk-free asset that has an expected return that is lower than that of a risky asset. Thus the discount rate would have to rise in order to attract risk-averse investors.

ADVANTAGES

- Applying risk to discount rates gives a better understanding of risks and returns.
- Considering the risk associated with a company gives an investor a better chance of understanding the risk associated with the investment.

DISADVANTAGES

- Many low-level investors may not wish to consider the complexity of the relationship of discount rates to risk.
- Becoming too concerned about risk could mean missing out on a spectacular future return.

ACTION CHECKLIST

When considering an investment, consider the position of the company:

✔ What are the expected rates of return?

✔ What are the risks involved?

✔ Do the rates of return compensate for those risks?

DOS AND DON'TS

DO

- Ensure that the risks associated with the expected returns are taken into account and understood.
- Understand the calculations involved in determining discount rates.
- Understand the nature of the company that is seeking inward investment—i.e. its level of maturity.

DON'T

- Don't ignore the risks.

⏩ MORE INFO

Books:

Bailey, Martin J., and Michael C. Jensen. "Risk and the discount rate for public investment." In M. C. Jensen (ed). *Studies in the Theory of Capital Markets*. New York: Praeger, 1972.

Pannell, David J., and Steven G. M. Schilizzi (eds). *Economics and the Future: Time and Discounting in Private and Public Decision Making*. Cheltenham, UK: Edward Elgar Publishing, 2006.

See Also:

★ Valuing Pension Fund Liabilities on the Balance Sheet (pp. 113–115)
✔ Preparing a Cash Flow Forecast (p. 880)
✔ Understanding the Cost of Capital and the Hurdle Rate (p. 895)

"Sometimes it's tough for African Americans to embrace capitalism." Deborah Wright

  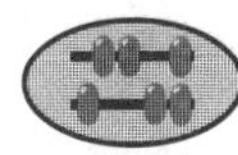   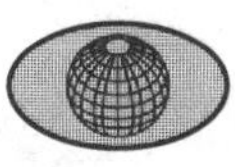 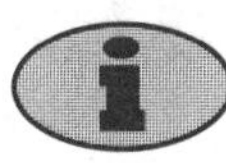  

Understanding the Weighted Average Cost of Capital (WACC)

DEFINITION

The weighted average cost of capital (WACC) measures the capital discount of a company's income and expenditure. It is a component of the formula used for calculating the expected cost of new capital and it represents the rate that a company is expected to pay to finance its assets. It is thus the minimum return that a company must earn on its existing asset base to satisfy its creditors, owners, and other providers of capital.

WACC is calculated by taking into account the relative weight of each component of a company's capital structure. The calculation usually uses the market values of the components, rather than their book values, which may differ significantly. Components may include equity (both common and preferred), debt (straight, convertible, or exchangeable), warrants, options, pension liabilities, executive stock options, and government subsidies. More exotic sources of financing, such as convertible/callable bonds or convertible preferred stock, may also be included in a WACC calculation if they are present in significant amounts as the cost of these is usually different from plain vanilla financing methods. For a company with a complex capital structure, calculating WACC can be a time-consuming exercise.

The equation used to calculate WACC uses the cost of each capital component multiplied by its proportional weight as follows:

$$WACC = E/V \times R_e + D/V \times R_d \times (1 - T_c)$$

where R_e is cost of equity, R_d is cost of debt, E is market value of the firm's equity, D is market value of the firm's debt, V = E + D, E/V is percentage of financing that is equity, D/V is percentage of financing that is debt, and T_c is corporate tax rate.

To determine the value of each component it is assumed that the weight of a source of financing is simply its market value (rather than the book value, which may be significantly different) divided by the sum of the values of all the components. The easiest component to calculate is the market value of the equity of a publicly traded company, as this is simply the price per share multiplied by the number of outstanding shares. Likewise, the market value of preferred shares is easy to determine and is calculated by multiplying the cost per share by number of outstanding shares. The market value of a company's debt is also easy to discover if a company has publicly traded bonds. However, many companies have debt in the form of bank loans, whose market value is not easily found. However, the market value of debt is often fairly close to the book value, at least for companies that have not experienced significant changes in credit rating. Thus, calculation of WACC typically uses the book value of any debt.

On the cost side, the cost of preferred shares is calculated by dividing the periodic payment by the price of the preferred shares. The cost of ordinary shares is typically determined using the capital asset pricing model. The cost of debt is usually the yield to maturity on the company's publicly traded bonds, or the rates of interest charged by the banks on recent loans. The cost of debt can be cut further as a company can usually write off taxes on the interest it pays on the debt. Thus, the cost of debt is calculated as yield to maturity multiplied by (1 minus the tax rate).

Because governments usually allow tax to be deducted from interest, there is an inherent bias towards debt financing. However, the cost of financial distress, such as bankruptcy, tilts any bias towards equity financing. In theory, therefore, the ideal debt-to-equity ratio in a company is usually the point at which any tax benefits accrued by debt financing are outweighed by the costs of financial distress.

⏩ MORE INFO

Books:

Armitage, Seth. *The Cost of Capital: Intermediate Theory*. Cambridge, UK: Cambridge University Press, 2005.

Johnson, Hazel. *Determining Cost of Capital: The Key to Firm Value*. London: FT Prentice Hall, 1999.

Pratt, Shannon P., and Roger J. Grabowski. *Cost of Capital: Applications and Examples*. 3rd ed. Hoboken, NJ: Wiley, 2008.

Website:

Formularium for a simple practical (auto) calculation of WACC: formularium.org/en/10.html?go=96.169

See Also:

★ Creating Value with EVA (pp. 756–758)
★ Using Decision Analysis to Value R&D Projects (pp. 828–831)
✔ Investors and the Capital Structure (p. 911)
✔ Understanding the Cost of Capital and the Hurdle Rate (p. 895)
Robert Merton (p. 1176)

"Predatory capitalism created a complex industrial system and an advanced technology; it permitted a considerable extension of democratic practice and fostered certain liberal values, but within limits that are now being pressed and must be overcome." Noam Chomsky

     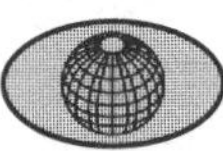   

Understanding Yield/Revenue Management

DEFINITION

Originally developed and refined in the airline industry in the 1970s, yield management ("YM" or revenue management as it is also known) is a tool that aims to capitalize on a full understanding of customer buying behavior, in order to maximize the benefit that can be derived from providing a limited-life product or service.

Sophisticated PC-based YM models harness a range of inputs to help create a pattern of projected demand, and then look to help the provider to match the demand with goods or service provision at the optimal level, using pricing as the key mechanism to help shape the demand pattern. The "perishable" element of the product or service is very important for both the buyer and the seller as it heightens the need for a transaction to be struck within a particular time frame. YM seeks to exploit the passage of time in order to maximize revenues for the provider, though this "perishability" element can, of course, be a double-edged sword in that unsold goods essentially expire with a lost opportunity cost to the seller. Yield/revenue management techniques also rely on the essentially limited supply of the product or service, and an acceptance from buyers that prices paid can vary over time and between different buyer categories. The tools are at their most valuable in situations where the fixed cost related to the provision of the perishable goods or service far outweighs any variable costs.

Through the study of consumer buyer behavior, YM can generate sales of essentially identical goods or services to different customers at different prices. A straightforward example in the sale of airline tickets would be a low fare offered to a client booking weeks in advance, with this client potentially finding him/herself sitting next to another passenger who exhibited different buying behavior, perhaps buying his/her ticket only the day before travel, thereby paying a huge premium to the early booker. YM can also discriminate on the basis of time in other ways. A supermarket, for example, could heavily discount fresh goods as they approach their "best before" dates, or could even vary the displayed price of goods on LED screens at different times of the week in an attempt to manage demand, perhaps making goods more expensive on busy Friday evenings/weekends and cheaper on quieter weekday mornings, in an effort to encourage some shoppers to adjust their shopping times.

Under some circumstances, however, there can be an ethical argument against excessive use of YM techniques. Just as price discrimination can be based on inputs such as time, prices can also be varied according to factors such as the buyer's location, financial profile and frequency of previous transactions. This could, for example, create the basis for a potential client to be quoted a higher price based on past customer buying patterns which might suggest that clients from a particular geographic location are prepared to pay more than those from elsewhere. However, this can create situations in which a relatively poor retail client who happens to reside in a particular area can be penalized. Above all, attitudes to the acceptability of some aspects of YM techniques vary between industries and countries.

ADVANTAGES

- YM helps companies to enhance revenues or profits through understanding of customers' buying behavior.
- YM models can also help companies to plan their output to capitalize on the predicted demand patterns.
- The tool can help lower the chances of "opportunity loss" for both buyers and sellers when perishable goods or services go unsold.
- YM has a long, proven track record of giving a significant marketing advantage over rivals not implementing YM method.

DISADVANTAGES

- The techniques can be inappropriate for goods or services available in virtually unlimited supply, those which are not time-sensitive or perishable in nature, or where variable costs of provision are large in relation to fixed costs.
- YM can raise ethical issues related to varying prices for the same goods or services between different customers.
- Some customers could react badly to perceived injustices related to the principle of price discrimination, potentially resulting in a public relations issue.

ACTION CHECKLIST

- ✔ Ensure you have some flexibility to respond to variations in demand.
- ✔ Assess how any segmentation within your market breaks down.
- ✔ Consider the range of input factors you would apply to your YM model, for example, advance booking discounts.
- ✔ Discuss how you will inform customers of the new pricing structures.
- ✔ Be prepared to go back and make regular adjustments to your YM system for optimization purposes.

DOS AND DON'TS

DO

- Ensure that employees are trained in the benefits of YM systems—some key insights about buyer behavior may be gleaned from employees with direct customer contact.
- Utilize information about buyer behavior patterns to help shape the development of your product offering, rather than using it purely as an input for pricing.
- Assess the potential impact of a poorly received YM system—some customers may react badly if the new charging structure is perceived to be unfair compared to legacy fixed-pricing structures.

DON'T

- Don't assume that the introduction of YM systems will be universally approved. Consider the risk of alienating long-standing core customers.
- Don't send out confusing messages to customers—it's important to understand your market segmentation.
- Don't assume that YM systems are only commercially viable for industry leaders. The potential benefits of such systems may out weigh implementation cut offs.

▸▸ MORE INFO

Article:

Jarvis, Peter. "Introducing yield management into a new industry." *Journal of Revenue and Pricing Management* 1:1 (May 2002): 67–75.

Websites:

Revenue management system providers, IDeaS: www.ideas.com; JDA Software: www.jda.com; and Revenue Management Systems: www.revenuemanagement.com

"Much of what we took for granted in our free-market system was not nature at all, but culture. The dismantling of the central planning function did not, as some had supposed, automatically establish market capitalism." Alan Greenspan

  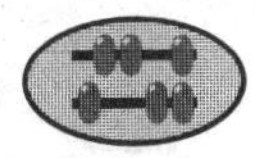   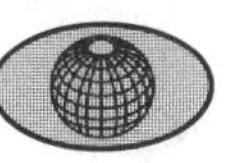   

The Board's Role in Executive Compensation

DEFINITION

Salary is just one of many elements that collectively form executive compensation. Bonuses (sometimes performance-related or even guaranteed), stocks, stock options, pension contributions, medical provisions, and even the use of chauffeured cars all contribute toward the compensation that company executives enjoy.

Setting the appropriate level of compensation for executives can be a considerable challenge for the company board. Set the level too low, and key decision-makers could be tempted away by rival firms. Set the level too high, and the board is left open to the charge that executive performance has failed to deliver value for shareholders. So, in setting compensation levels, the company must seek to attract and retain executive talent while satisfying itself that management is delivering returns appropriate for the level of investment made in the company by stockholders.

Given the scope for executive mobility between firms, the levels of executive compensation in any one firm are frequently compared with those of other companies. Cultural factors play a role in the level of executive mobility between companies and society's general acceptance of executive remuneration. In Japan, for example, executive compensation is typically a more modest multiple of average salaries than in countries such as the United States, where executive compensation, boosted dramatically by the impact of stock options, tends to tower far above the pay and benefits of the average worker.

As levels of executive compensation have risen sharply over recent years, particularly in the United States, pressure on company boards has resulted in increased use of independent parties to help set an appropriate level of remuneration. These typically take the form of a remuneration committee or an independent nonexecutive director charged with the responsibility of creating a "Chinese wall" between those deciding remuneration and those benefiting from it.

ADVANTAGES

- Linking executive pay to the achievement of clearly defined performance targets incentivizes managers while still delivering value for stockholders.
- Establishing and supporting an impartial and independent remuneration committee ensures that the board cannot be accused of "feathering their own nests" by awarding themselves excessive benefits.
- The board can delegate all responsibilities relating to pay and terms of employment for senior staff, freeing resources for other matters relating to the success of the business.

DISADVANTAGES

- The correlation between improvement in a company's overall performance and the precise contribution of any single executive can be difficult to quantify. This could result in an underperforming executive receiving excessive remuneration relative to better-performing colleagues.
- Some chief executives take the view that they should retain the power to decide the level of remuneration of senior executives, arguing that they are in a strong position to judge individual contributions.

ACTION CHECKLIST

✔ The remuneration committee should be a committee of the board composed of independent nonexecutive directors.

✔ The board must ensure that the executive remuneration committee is widely acknowledged to be truly impartial and independent. Any doubts over the committee's independence could cause damage to the firm's reputation among the investment community.

✔ The chairman of the board should ensure that the independent remuneration committee has access to external compensation expertise, such as independent benefits consultants. However, to avoid conflicts of interest, the committee should not use consultants with professional links to the board.

DOS AND DON'TS

DO

- Disclose executive remuneration, as proper reporting improves accountability. Listed companies should detail directors' compensation in the remuneration section of the company's annual report.
- Allocate space in the annual report for a statement from the remuneration committee to facilitate direct communication with stockholders on matters such as remuneration policies and service contracts.

DON'T

- Don't permit the chairman of the remuneration committee to be also the chairman of the pension fund trustees, as this could present potential conflicts of interest.
- Don't expect use of a remuneration committee to put an end to all criticism of executive pay.

▸▸ MORE INFO

Books:

Ellig, Bruce R. *The Complete Guide to Executive Compensation*. 2nd ed. New York: McGraw-Hill, 2007.

Reda, James F., Stewart Reifler, and Laura G. Thatcher. *The Compensation Committee Handbook*. 3rd ed. Hoboken, NJ: Wiley, 2007.

Articles:

Bruce, Alistair, Trevor William Buck, and Brian G. M. Main. "Top executive remuneration: A view from Europe." *Journal of Management Studies* 42:7 (2005), 1493–1506.

Hill, Jennifer. "Regulating executive remuneration: International developments in the post-scandal era." Vanderbilt law and economics research paper no. 06-06. *European Company Law* 3 (2006): 64–74.

Website:

Mercer, global remuneration consultants: www.mercer.com

See Also:

✔ Creating a Sustainable Development Policy (p. 905)

"Be content with your wages." Luke 3:14, New Testament

  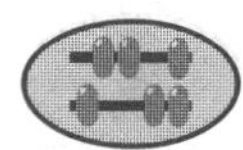 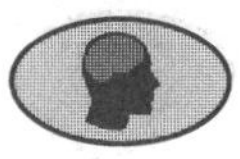  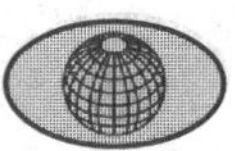   

Business Ethics in Islamic Finance

DEFINITION

The overarching principles of Islam set the operating framework for every aspect of how business is conducted in the Muslim world. While the shifting boundaries of acceptable behavior in conventional Western business are set by laws, regulations, and corporate governance guidelines, Islamic business is governed by divine principles covering values such as fairness, equality, and morality dating back over a thousand years. More specifically, Islamic finance adopts a long-term partnership approach between businesses, often based on investors essentially taking an equity stake in businesses. *Shariah* law outlaws the charging of interest of any kind, while in the wider context the use of money to generate interest is not permitted. Speculation of any kind is also forbidden, while investments are required to deliver social benefits to the community. Islam also forbids activities in prohibited areas such as gambling or alcohol, instead specifying that *shariah*-compliant businesses should focus on legitimate trade-based activities.

The ethical standards to which Islamic businesses operate reflect the same standards and principles of the Qu'ran, which every Muslim is expected to follow in every aspect of their lives. Therefore, Islamic businesses must operate on a basis of fairness and integrity, while also treating everyone equally. The need for honesty, truthfulness, and fair dealing is also inherent in Islamic business, requirements which have wide-ranging implications across the full spectrum of business activities, from advertising to after-sales customer service. Islamic companies must also respect the principle of trusting others to be as good as their word. However, this puts the responsibility on businesses to cover their liabilities promptly, honoring their word with timely payment, given the exclusion of credit facilities. The emphasis on the partnership approach to business is further underlined by the need for companies to look after their investors' interests, thus protecting them whenever possible from *dharar* (any kind of harm). The "stakeholder" element of Islamic financing is reflected in the onus on working in tandem with other businesses whenever possible, while markets should generally be free and prices competitive. For example, attempting to squeeze suppliers on price would be unacceptable behavior, as would any attempt to capitalize on others' misfortune by raising selling price, excessively should, for example, the supply of goods be temporarily interrupted.

ADVANTAGES

- Business ethics in Islamic finance reflect the moral principles and standards which every Muslim must follow in every aspect of their lives.
- Islamic business encourages a long-term partnership approach, based on mutual interest and a spirit of cooperation.
- Honestly, integrity, and a sense of genuine fair play are ingrained in the operating principles of Islamic business.

DISADVANTAGES

- Muslim businesses may be less able to capitalise on short-term market opportunities given that speculative activities are not permitted by Islamic ethical standards.
- Islamic business managers do not enjoy the same financial incentives which drive managers of many mainstream Western businesses, though they are motivated by moral objectives and standards.
- Given the moral and ethical goals of Islamic businesses—rather than the pursuit of pure profit—less efficient businesses (in purely financial terms) could hamper the development of newer, more entrepreneurial, customer-focused start-ups.

ACTION CHECKLIST

- ✔ In view of the increasing global influence of Islamic finance, companies aiming to do business with *shariah*-compliant organizations should gain some understanding of their guiding principles and ethics.
- ✔ Understand the importance for Islamic business of building long-term partnerships, rather than the pure pursuit of short-term profit.
- ✔ Compliance with Islamic principles may create complications for non-Muslims in the short term. However, it is important to understand that Islamic business aims to bring collective benefit to wider society.

DOS AND DON'TS

DO

- Recognize the importance that Islamic business ethics place on high moral values, while bringing collective benefit to the wide community, rather than the objective of making short-term profits.
- Appreciate that while high ethical standards are enshrined in the principles of Islamic businesses, the interpretation of the conformity of some financial products to *shariah* law may vary slightly between institutions.

DON'T

- Don't make the mistake of thinking that conventional Western business ethics are fully compatible with the ways of Islam—managers shouldn't enter into partnerships with Islamic businesses without first understanding and appreciating how attitudes to the pursuit of profit differ.
- Don't adopt a pick-and-mix approach to business ethics—the way Muslim businesses operate reflects their owners' deep-rooted attitudes, beliefs, and commitment to the principles of Islam.

▸▸ MORE INFO

Books:

Ayub, Muhammad. *Understanding Islamic Finance*. Chichester, UK: Wiley, 2007.
Iqbal, Zamir, and Abbas Mirakhor. *An Introduction to Islamic Finance: Theory and Practice*. Singapore: Wiley, 2007.

Articles:

Parvez, Zahid. "Lack of business responsibility: an Islamic perspective". *International Journal of Business Governance and Ethics* 3: 1 (January 2007).
Rice, G. "Islamic ethics and the implications for business". *Journal of Business Ethics* 18: 4 (February 1999).

Website:

International Institute of Islamic Business & Finance: www.netversity.org

"Between the capitalist and communist systems of society lies the period of the revolutionary transformation of the one into the other. . .the revolutionary dictatorship of the proletariat." Karl Marx

  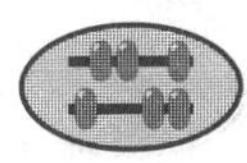 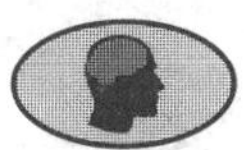  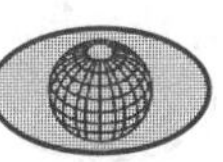   

Conflicting Interests: The Agency Issue

DEFINITION

Those running a company should be committed to delivering maximum returns to its stockholders. However, vested interests can sometimes play a role in decision making, frequently managers' personal interests. The way in which a company's stock is dispersed across various stockholder groups can also have a significant bearing on the nature of the specific corporate governance issues it faces. In many developing countries, as well as in some parts of Europe, company stock ownership can be concentrated within a relatively narrow group of investors—certainly when compared with the wider stock-ownership base that is typical in the United States. This concentration of ownership can heighten the risk that the company board is pressurized to make a particular decision—for example, by a powerful industrialist or oligarch with widespread interests and considerable influence, who attempts to steer a company's board down a particular route, potentially to the detriment of other stockholders.

Even in countries where stockholder bases are generally more diversified, conflicts of interest can still arise between company principals and boards of directors in cases where those making decisions are influenced by self-interest. Managers should in all cases inform the board of any potential conflict of interest between themselves and stockholders in advance. Stakeholders can then be made aware of the potential conflict of interest through a disclosure statement, while the board should take appropriate action to ensure that the interests of stockholders are not compromised. This could involve independent monitoring of management decision making or the insistence that the relationship behind the potential conflict of interest is severed.

ACTION CHECKLIST

- ✔ The establishment of an independent remuneration committee is often an important step toward adequately rewarding top-performing executives and satisfying large institutional stockholders that the company's resources are being used appropriately.
- ✔ Aim to align executive compensation with stockholders' interests by granting managers stock options.
- ✔ Other elements of executive compensation can be linked to factors such as sales or earnings growth.
- ✔ The establishment of a management monitoring program can help to counter the risk of pressure from dominant external stockholders and protect the interests of other stockholders by scrutinizing executives' decisions.

ADVANTAGES

- Correctly anticipating potential conflicts of interest gives corporate governance professionals the scope to instigate procedures that will ensure probity and help to protect stockholders.
- A well-diversified stockholder base and thorough research by investment analysts into a company's decision making can help to remind managers that any actions they take to put their own interests ahead of the wider stockholder base could be exposed, making them vulnerable to removal from their positions.
- Companies seen to be operating in an inappropriate manner can rapidly lose stockholder support, exposing them to the risk of a hostile takeover. This risk can create an element of "self-policing" by managers who would otherwise be tempted to put their own interests ahead of those of the wider stockholder base.

DISADVANTAGES

- Aiming for complete protection against the impact of the agency issue is unrealistic. Steps can be taken to try to address the main risks, but in practice major stockholders may still hold considerable influence.
- Striking the balance between rewarding top-performing managers and allowing them excessive influence over their own remuneration levels can be difficult.
- Operating an effective and robust corporate governance program can be expensive, with the costs ultimately carried by the stockholders.

DOS AND DON'TS

DO

- Ensure that executive remuneration is set by an independent committee with an understanding of competitors' compensation levels.
- Be prepared to permit the remuneration committee to grant stock options to managers to incentivize them to deliver maximum returns for stockholders.

DON'T

- Don't see scrutiny by external investment analysts as a threat: the greater threat to a company's stock price could come from suspicions that managers are feathering their own nests, rather than working to deliver maximum stockholder value.
- Don't skimp unnecessarily on the costs of establishing appropriate structures to oversee executive remuneration and decision making. Disquiet over the probity of decision making can trigger a loss of confidence among key institutional stockholders. In terms of executive remuneration, excessive levels could trigger a stockholder revolt, while companies that under-remunerate executives risk the upheaval of losing key talent to rivals.

▸▸ MORE INFO

Books:

Sullivan, John D., Jean Rogers, Catherine Kuchta-Helbling, and Aleksandr Shkolnikov (eds). *In Search of Good Directors: A Guide to Building Corporate Governance in the 21st Century*. 3rd ed. Washington, DC: Center for International Private Enterprise, 2003.

Luo, Yadong. *Global Dimensions of Corporate Governance*. Malden, MA: Blackwell Publishing, 2007.

Organisation for Economic Co-operation and Development (OECD). *OECD Principles of Corporate Governance*. Paris: OECD, 2004. Online at www.oecd.org/daf/corporateaffairs/principles/text

Website:

International Corporate Governance Network: www.icgn.org

"Nobody is sure anymore who really runs the company (not even the people who are credited with running it), but the company does run." Joseph Heller

   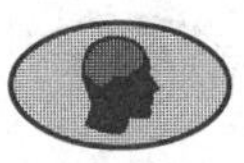  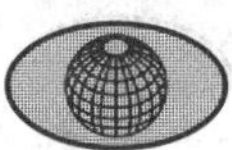   

Corporate Governance and Its Interpretations

DEFINITION

Corporate governance is the system by which organizations are directed and controlled. The defects of poor corporate governance have recently been very visible in financial institutions around the world. Since the endorsement of Sarbanes–Oxley, companies have set up audit committees, added financial experts to their boards, improved financial whistle-blowing capacity, and enhanced corporate transparency in financial statements and shareholder disclosures. However, are there any benefits from all of these requirements and best practices, and do they pay any dividends?

For good corporate governance to work, open and honest communication is necessary, with transparent policies and practices, clear lines of authority, and strong internal controls and audit functions, backed by a board that can act with clear independence from management.

A board has to identify with the business and its competition, focus on strategic problems and risk management, and establish high, yet pragmatic, standards of performance. The board directs the plans of the company but does not manage the company. The board must pick first-rate people to run the business while retaining its role to confront, evaluate, and hold managers accountable.

To do this, the board must develop and approve a strategic plan, establish specific and measurable goals, establish risk parameters (which should be reviewed regularly in light of the strategic objectives), encourage and preserve open lines of communication, select competent management, measure managers' performance, and hold management responsible using compensation and continued employment.

In contrast, management has the responsibility to implement the board's strategy, risk tolerances, and policies; keep directors fully informed; deal with the day-to-day operations of the business and its staff; and operate the information systems, procedures, and reports that keep the lines of communication open.

The costs of poor corporate governance have been very evident in the present financial crisis. Firms that engage in unscrupulous and risky behavior will generally fail, while those that have enhanced corporate governance will have higher valuations, greater profitability, and better sales. The recent market turmoil suggests that buying shares in firms that score highly in corporate governance may yield positive returns.

ADVANTAGES

- Good corporate governance is part of good risk management. It brings problems and concerns to light, allowing them to be addressed promptly.
- Good corporate governance helps businesses to focus on strategic issues and risk management, and establishes realistic standards of performance.
- Decision-making is improved by thorough analysis under good corporate governance. Management is held accountable, and management compensation is linked to shareholder value.
- The board can select good managers to run the business while maintaining its role to challenge, measure, and hold managers responsible.

DISADVANTAGES

- A board that lacks independence may not be willing to address poor performance by a line of business or even hold the management accountable.
- The dual loyalty that many board members feel to the management and to the institution is normally resolved in favor of the institution.

ACTION CHECKLIST

- ✔ Risks need to be reviewed periodically in light of the strategic objectives and margins of the business.
- ✔ How strong is the audit committee, and does the audit committee charter reflect the committee's areas of competence?
- ✔ Conduct a self-assessment periodically to help match expectations and actions.
- ✔ How effective is the risk-assessment program, how successful is the internal governance control, and are managers held accountable?
- ✔ Does the board and/or audit committee receive adequate and timely information from the internal and external audit staff?
- ✔ Does the relationship between board and management reflect their independent roles?

DOS AND DON'TS

DO

- Set up an effective and independent corporate governance program.

DON'T

- Don't cut back on good corporate governance programs because of reduced margins—objective opinions may help to resolve problems.

›› MORE INFO

Books:

Colley, John L., *et al. What is Corporate Governance?* New York: McGraw-Hill Professional, 2005.

Mallin, Chris A. *Corporate Governance.* 2nd ed. Oxford: Oxford University Press, 2007.

Monks, Robert A. G., and Nell Minow. *Corporate Governance*. Malden, MA: Blackwell Publishing, 2004.

Articles:

Causey, Dawn. "The worth of good corporate governance." *Community Banker* (August 1, 2008).

PR Newswire. "Icahn launches campaign to improve corporate governance." *PR Newswire* (18 September 2008).

Websites:

UK Financial Services Authority: www.fsa.gov.uk

US Securities and Exchange Commission: www.sec.gov

See Also:

★ Improving Corporate Profitability Through Accountability (pp. 170–171)

✔ Defining Corporate Governance: Its Aims, Goals, and Responsibilities (p. 907)

Governance and Risk: An Analytical Handbook for Investors, Managers, Directors, and Stakeholders (p. 1271)

"Wisdom lies neither in fixity nor in change, but in the dialectic between the two." Octavio Paz

  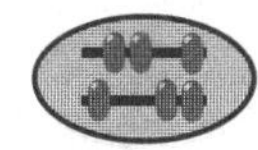   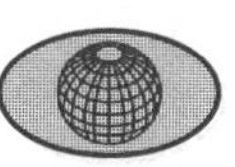   

Corporate Governance Practices in Private Equity-Owned Firms

DEFINITION

The relative ease with which acquisition funds can be raised from the capital markets and global investors' push for higher rewards from specialized forms of investment have significantly raised the profile of private equity companies. As leading private equity players have capitalized on opportunities to expand their investment portfolios, their disclosure and other corporate governance responsibilities have also grown, with reforms such as the Sarbanes–Oxley Act (2002) increasing the costs associated with meeting regulatory requirements for listed companies. However, such higher costs may actually have played a role in the growth of the titans of the private equity industry. While the regulatory costs associated with the acquisition of medium-sized, medium-growth companies could lessen the attraction of these deals for smaller private equity firms, the largest private equity houses can use their fund-raising clout to capitalize on the effective regulatory economies of scale achievable through the acquisition of much larger industry players. The elimination of costs associated with regulatory requirements can also be very significant among smaller companies, such as those merged into larger entities owned by private equity firms.

There is no shortage of evidence that the combined benefits of active ownership and the improved corporate governance approach taken by private equity firms are important drivers of the success of private equity-driven deals. From a governance perspective, the representation of private equity firms at the board level is an important mechanism for improved effectiveness, while the streamlining of management structures can help to address agency issues. Private equity firms are also frequently able to call on external governance experts with experience of potential conflicts of interest at other companies in the same industry. The higher management incentives created by private equity houses can help to accelerate change by sweeping away long-standing inefficient working practices, creating an enhanced performance culture and generally improving the transparency of decision making.

ADVANTAGES

- Private equity firms can use their board-level representation to improve corporate governance standards.
- Improved governance can be an important driver of the improved financial returns resulting from private equity firms' investment in underperforming companies. Most private equity deals are also heavily levered with the view of reducing the cost of capital to enhance returns.
- The improved performance associated with better governance standards can also be implemented at the subsidiaries of a conglomerate acquired by a private equity company.

DISADVANTAGES

- Despite evidence that the involvement of private equity specialists strengthens acquired businesses and creates new jobs over the medium term, private equity companies are sometimes still regarded as "asset strippers."
- The poor perception of private equity companies among such bodies as trade unions could slow the pace of change in countries where union representation on company boards is commonplace.
- Unless they are subject to a heavily discounted valuation, smaller businesses in mature, slower-growth markets are generally unattractive to private equity companies, with the result that the private equity route to improved governance is rarely an option.

ACTION CHECKLIST

- ✔ Private equity firms do not regard corporate governance improvements as merely a "bolt-on" measure after the acquisition. Governance considerations should begin as early as the due diligence process, so that the benefits can be realized as early as possible.
- ✔ Every effort should be made to achieve consistency in corporate governance standards across a private equity firm's investment portfolio. Plainly, some acquired companies are likely to require more reform than others.

DOS AND DON'TS

DO

- Be transparent on governance issues, notably executive incentives, to help build trust and ease lingering suspicions about the motives of the private equity industry.
- Take account of cultural and social considerations when implementing change in acquired companies. It can be helpful to retain the support of the workforce when introducing structural reform to improve efficiency and raise governance standards.

DON'T

- Don't wait for regulations to be imposed on the private equity industry on issues such as accountability for decisions taken and transparency in areas such as management remuneration. The best approach is to be proactive.
- Don't overlook the need to inform all stakeholders of progress made in improvements to corporate governance structures. Investors in private equity firms, such as pension funds and sovereign wealth funds, are likely to take an active interest in reforms introduced in companies within the private equity firms' portfolios.

▸▸ MORE INFO

Books:

Cendrowski, Harry, James P. Martin, Louis W. Petro, and Adam A. Wadecki. *Private Equity: History, Governance, and Operations*. Hoboken, NJ: Wiley, 2008.

O'Brien, Justin. *Private Equity, Corporate Governance and the Dynamics of Capital Market Regulation*. London: Imperial College Press, 2007.

Article:

Cumming, Douglas, Donald S. Siegel, and Mike Wright. "Private equity, leveraged buyouts, and governance." *Journal of Corporate Finance* 13:4 (September 2007): 439–460.

"As in law so in war, the longest purse finally wins." Mahatma Gandhi

  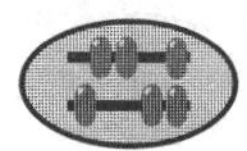   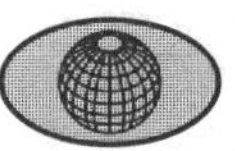   

Creating a Comprehensive Audit Committee Evaluation Form

DEFINITION

After the revelation of corporate fraud at Enron and evidence of management largesse at Tyco early in the new millennium, a lack of investor confidence in the veracity of some corporate earnings reports and questions over the integrity of some leading global executives sparked demands for dramatic improvements in global corporate governance. In the United States, the Sarbanes–Oxley Act (2002) required reforms to corporate governance practices, including the establishment of auditing and related attestations, ethics, and independence standards. Pressure grew elsewhere in the world for companies to tighten their corporate governance standards to meet the rising expectations of stockholders, to whom company boards and audit committees ultimately answer.

Given the elevated demands made by stockholders, activist investors, investment analysts, regulators, and journalists, many companies have sought to stay ahead of the curve by implementing formal measures to help verify the effectiveness of audit committees. Indeed, New York Stock Exchange proposals for improved listing standards have included the suggestion that companies should instigate formal evaluation processes for the entire board and for the board's major committees, not least the audit committee.

There are many different approaches to ensuring audit committee effectiveness. The evaluation form method has rapidly gained favor, although this is most effective as part of a broader program that includes processes to secure the independence and objectivity of members. In general terms, the scope of the audit committee should encompass the full range of the company's activities, rather than simply amounting to a box-ticking exercise relating to compliance with existing regulations.

ADVANTAGES

- Self-evaluation measures such as the evaluation form can help audit committee members focus on ways to improve existing processes.
- The evaluation form approach enables interested parties to provide a frank assessment of the audit committee's effectiveness on an anonymous basis.
- This method also provides a forum for participants to raise issues that members of the audit committee themselves may not have considered.

DISADVANTAGES

- Given the differences between company cultures and practices, no standard approach will consistently deliver major improvements in the effectiveness of all audit committees. However, the evaluation form can be a useful means of gauging the views of internal stakeholders.
- The approach is only truly effective if the form is compiled in a way that elicits unbiased feedback from participants. Phrasing questions to prompt responses that the compilers favor is certain to undermine the process.

ACTION CHECKLIST

- ✔ Agree on the evaluation process to be used and identify an individual to be charged with the overall responsibility for its coordination.
- ✔ Consider the main elements of the evaluation form, such as organizational factors, the overseeing of the reporting process, and routes to possible improvement. The evaluation form can then be compiled, inviting participants to grade the effectiveness of all aspects of the committee and its activities.
- ✔ Determine how communication should be handled with the main audit committee and other relevant individuals, such as the board chairman, independent auditor, and in-house legal heads.
- ✔ Give the evaluation forms to all relevant parties, and then compile the results. Compare the results from different categories of participants to determine how perceptions of the audit committee's effectiveness vary between different areas of the business.

DOS AND DON'TS

DO

- Maximize the effectiveness of this approach by carrying out the process annually.
- Leave space on the evaluation form for participants to add further comments on issues that may not have been considered when creating the form.
- Obtain the advice of company legal experts on how the results of the evaluation process should be recorded and filed.

DON'T

- Don't regard the evaluation form as merely a means of demonstrating compliance with existing industry regulation. To do so could mean missing out on a real opportunity to improve the effectiveness of the audit committee.
- Don't use this evaluation approach as the sole means of improving the effectiveness of the audit committee. Rather, use this method of internally driven improvement in conjunction with other industry-wide best-practice methods to provide an externally driven element for further improvement.

▸▸ MORE INFO

Book:

Verschoor, Curtis C. *Audit Committee Essentials*. Hoboken, NJ: Wiley, 2008.

Articles:

Braiotta, Louis, Jr. "Corporate audit committees: An approach to continuous improvement." *The CPA Journal* (July 2002).

Smith, L. Murphy. "Audit committee effectiveness: Did the blue ribbon committee recommendations make a difference?" *International Journal of Accounting, Auditing and Performance Evaluation* 3:2 (2006): 240–251.

Websites:

KPMG's Audit Committee Institute: www.kpmg.com/aci

The American Institute of Certified Public Accountants (AICPA) provides an audit committee toolkit: www.aicpa.org

"The worldwide movement towards fiscal rectitude and the creation of an economic environment which is transparent and rewards efficiency is no longer a matter of choice but one of necessity." Deepak Lal

  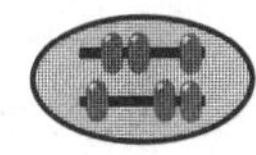   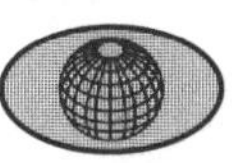   

Creating a Sustainable Development Policy

DEFINITION

The Brundtland Commission coined what has become the most often quoted definition of sustainable development as being development that "meets the needs of the present without compromising the ability of future generations to meet their own needs."

A sustainable development policy is a model of resource use that aims to meet human requirements while preserving the environment, so that these needs can be met not only in the present but also for the indefinite future. It is a means of trying to resolve the conflict between various competing goals, and it involves the simultaneous pursuit of economic prosperity, environmental quality, and social equity.

Businesses are becoming increasingly interested in sustainable development, and many companies are taking steps to ensure that they conduct themselves in a socially responsible manner. Some are even introducing codes of conduct for their suppliers, to ensure that other companies' policies or practices do not tarnish their own reputation.

The positive outcomes that can arise when businesses adopt a policy of social responsibility include:

- enhanced brand image and increased sales and customer loyalty;
- greater productivity and quality;
- improved ability to attract and retain employees;
- possible improved financial performance, with lower operating costs;
- reduced regulatory oversight;
- access to capital;
- product safety and reduced liability.

The payback to the community and the general public includes:

- improved charitable contributions;
- more employee volunteer programs;
- business involvement in community welfare, education, and employment programs;
- product safety and quality;
- greater material recycling;
- better product durability and functionality;
- greater use of renewable resources.

Whereas traditional business models were all about profit, sustainable development recognizes that without happy, healthy people to staff a business and the natural environment able to sustain those people, the supply of resources for the business is simply unsustainable over the long term. Therefore, environmental management tools—including life-cycle assessment and costing, environmental management standards, and eco-labeling—are now commonly integrated with business plans in enterprises worldwide.

ADVANTAGES

- "At the most fundamental level, the sustainability of human societies is a function of the relationship between ecosystem energy production, human energy expropriation and the ecosystem transformations that result from human withdrawals of energy and matter and additions of waste and pollution." (Freese, 1997).

DISADVANTAGES

- Although it is possible to replace some natural resources, it is unlikely that it will ever be possible to replace ecosystem benefits, such as the protection provided by the ozone layer.
- The evolutionary loss of some biodiversity is irreversible.
- The use of fossil fuels, for example, is not sustainable. But how does society plan to eliminate the use of petroleum products?
- Under sustainable development, all resources must be regulated and controlled in order to meet the needs of the present generation as well as those of all future generations. How do you plan to regulate and control the use of resources by all individuals, families, and businesses?
- Sustainable development is for rich nations. When you don't have enough to eat, you don't worry about sustainability.

ACTION CHECKLIST

✔ If you are considering integrating environmental projects with business plans, carefully study the potential business risks and obtain as much information from as many sources as you can before committing to an expensive process.

✔ Encourage an environment of openness about the kinds of risk facing the business from sustainable development policies. Some risks are obvious, but managers of individual business units may sometimes know more about hidden risks.

✔ Involve key business stakeholders in the evaluation of sustainable development and the alternative solutions.

DOS AND DON'TS

DO

- Carefully plan and implement the integration of sustainable development policies.

DON'T

- Don't make the mistake of being attracted to sustainable development policies without being sure that the conversion process has been thoroughly understood.

➤➤ MORE INFO

Books:

Mawhinney, M. *Sustainable Development: Understanding the Green Debates*. Oxford: Blackwell Publishing, 2002.

Organisation for Economic Co-operation and Development. *Sustainable Development: Critical Issues*. Paris: OECD Publishing, 2001.

Schmandt, J., and C. H. Ward. *Sustainable Development: The Challenge of Transition*. Cambridge, UK: Cambridge University Press, 2000.

Articles:

Business Publisher. "Magazine on sustainable development for business." *Business Publisher* (June 17, 2008).

Christianson, L., A. Bhandari, and B. Steward. "Embracing sustainable development as a profession." *Resource: Engineering & Technology for a Sustainable World* 15:7 (October 2008): 21–23. Online: www.asabe.org/resource/08octcontents.pdf

Websites:

DMOZ Open Directory Project: www.dmoz.org/Science/Environment/Sustainability

International Institute for Sustainable Development (IISD): www.iisd.org

  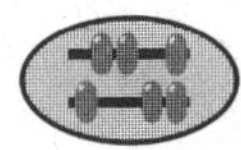   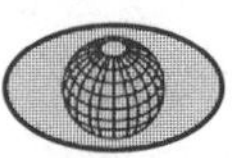   

Creating Executive Compensation

DEFINITION

The level of executive remuneration has risen sharply in many of the World's developed economies over recent decades, with the pay gap between those at the top of the corporate tree and those at the bottom growing ever wider. While this growing divide may trouble some on ideological grounds, the need to set compensation levels at the right level to attract and to retain talented executives has never been greater. Moves to link executive remuneration to performance have found increasing favor over recent years. The objective is to reward executives on the basis of their achieving predetermined measures of the success of the business. While middle-ranking managers may benefit from bonuses linked to relatively simplistic targets such as annual sales increases, the performance-related element of top executives' remuneration can often be more complex, depending on a variety of factors that include company earnings, outright share price performance, and share price performance relative to the company's peer group.

In the United States, executives can expect to benefit from a combination of salary, bonus, stock options, stock grants, and a range of long-term incentive contracts. Over recent years executives have increasingly benefited from a shift to offer stock options.

Specialist independent remuneration committees have increasingly been established by leading listed companies wishing to strike the balance between rewarding top talent and making sure that shareholders' interests are well served. This approach typically stands up well to shareholder scrutiny by distancing executives from the role of effectively setting their own levels of remuneration.

Cultural factors can also have a considerable influence over the acceptable boundaries for top-level managerial pay. Remuneration packages which aggressively leverage private-sector executive remuneration to performance have been widely accepted in countries such as the United States for several decades, though in more conservative countries such as Japan the link between pay and performance has historically been more tentative. However, recent moves by activist investors to extract better shareholder returns in Japan have seen the performance culture penetrate through to boardroom salaries. In other countries such as the United Kingdom, elements of performance-related pay have also percolated into the remuneration packages of senior public service workers as a result of the need to compete with the increasingly incentive-driven private sector for top managerial talent.

ADVANTAGES

- A balanced, well-structured executive remuneration package can help to attract and retain key decision makers.
- Transparency in executive remuneration can find favor with institutional shareholders and is an important element in sound corporate governance.
- A mix of short and long-term performance-related elements can provide further incentives for executives to deliver success. Granting longer-term share options can help to further align executives' and shareholders' interests.

DISADVANTAGES

- The perception that executives may be excessively rewarded for moderate or poor performance can be very damaging to morale among lower-ranking employees.
- Poorly conceived incentive schemes can skew performance toward particular targets that may not necessarily align with the success of the business.
- During boom years, the pay scales in remuneration structures can be compete to attract recognized industry talent. This potentially leaves companies committed to paying excessive rewards for apparent failure during leaner times.

ACTION CHECKLIST

- ✔ Gain a full understanding of how existing remuneration policies operate before rushing to implement changes.
- ✔ Study the remuneration arrangements employed by the wider market and compare those used by your own company.
- ✔ Consider the cultural factors within your company which could effectively limit acceptable multiples between the potential remuneration of executives and that of lower-ranking employees.
- ✔ Introduce some element of performance-related pay to avoid alienating key workers at lower levels of the corporate structure.
- ✔ Consider how the performance strength of individual executives can be judged in relation to the overall performance of the company or division.

DOS AND DON'TS

DO

- Make sure that any new proposed executive reward scheme is in keeping with the culture of the company.
- Target consistency and fairness in creative executive compensation. Inflated remuneration to tempt talent from rivals could generate ill-feeling.
- Consider the tax implications before introducing changes to remuneration policies.

DON'T

- Don't underestimate the resources needed to effectively develop and manage executive remuneration policies.
- Don't aim for a remuneration structure which incentivizes managers to shift focus to hitting short-term targets. Opportunities to deliver long-term benefits could be missed.

▸▸ MORE INFO

Book:

Berger, Lance A., and Dorothy R. Berger. *The Compensation Handbook*. 4th ed. New York: McGraw-Hill, 2000.

Article:

Cahill, Miles B., and Alaina C. George, "Executive compensation incentives in a volatile market." *American Economist* 49:2 (Fall 2005): 33–43.

Website:

Mercer Consulting Executive Remuneration Perspective: www.mercer.com/perspective

"We're overpaying him, but he's worth it." Samuel Goldwyn

  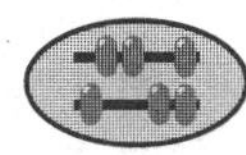   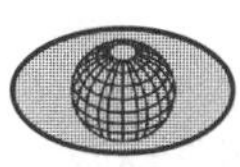   

Defining Corporate Governance: Its Aims, Goals, and Responsibilities

DEFINITION

In order for a company to exist, it has to be set up and registered with the appropriate company authority. Once registered, the company is regarded as a legal person, with legal rights and obligations. A company's existence and organization are continuously scrutinized through a well-established set of rules, laws, and policies that govern the way in which the company is run and controlled. This is known as corporate governance.

Companies can be private or public. Public companies, under certain circumstances, can choose to list their shares on a stock exchange or alternative investment markets. The corporate governance rules apply to every company, whether private or public. However, the larger and more complex a company is, the more closely its decisions are scrutinized. For multinational companies corporate governance has extended internationally, with rules and regulations that cooperate at cross-border levels.

Corporate governance exists to protect the shareholders of a company. It also aims to preserve the reputation of a company and its business against any fraudulent acts committed by its directors and officers. The directors of a company must always make decisions objectively, in the best interests of the company's business and its shareholders. They have the responsibility to run the company successfully and bring in profits for the shareholders. They have to do this ethically, within the framework of laws and regulations that govern the running of a company.

Companies must file yearly accounts that are subject to public notice. Accounts and the auditing of accounts by independent auditors are important aspects of corporate governance. They ensure the smooth running of the business and its good reputation.

ADVANTAGES

- A system of corporate governance gives the shareholders confidence that a company is well monitored and that its directors are acting in the best interests of the company and its shareholders.
- Corporate governance guards against defrauding of shareholders and the company's business.

DISADVANTAGES

- The bigger the company, the more it will be scrutinized. The need to comply with numerous corporate governance requirements is expensive and can deter the directors from their main priority, which should be running the business in the best interests of the shareholders.
- Too much supervision could restrict the independence of a company in the way it runs its business.

ACTION CHECKLIST

✔ Be well informed about any corporate governance rules.

✔ Be prepared to put in place a thorough system of auditing and risk management.

DOS AND DON'TS

DO

- Obtain advice from your legal advisers and accountants regarding the best system of auditing and risk management to put in place and the consequences of a breach of the rules.

DON'T

- Don't ignore compliance with the rules of corporate governance. The consequences could be not only financial penalties for the company but also criminal responsibility for the directors.
- Don't overlook the importance of setting up proper procedures to deal with the consequences of a breach.

▸▸ MORE INFO

Books:

Keasey, Kevin, Steve Thompson, and Michael Wright. *Corporate Governance: Accountability, Enterprise and International Comparisons*. Chichester, UK: Wiley, 2005.

Solomon, Jill. *Corporate Governance and Accountability*. 2nd ed. Chichester, UK: Wiley, 2007.

Article:

Lee, Soo Hee, Jonathan Michie, and Christine Oughton. "Comparative corporate governance: Beyond 'shareholder value'." *Journal of Interdisciplinary Economics* 14:2 (2003): 81–111.

Websites:

Corporate Board corporate governance magazine: www.corporateboard.com
Financial Reporting Council (UK): www.frc.org.uk
High Beam Research—articles, research, and archives: www.highbeam.com
Institute of Chartered Accountants in England and Wales: www.icaew.co.uk
Institute of Chartered Accountants in Scotland: www.icas.org.uk
PricewaterhouseCoopers: www.pwc.com
Questia online library: www.questia.com

See Also:

★ Improving Corporate Profitability Through Accountability (pp. 170–171)
★ Viewpoint: Jean-Claude Trichet (pp. 252–253)
✔ Corporate Governance and Its Interpretations (p. 902)
✔ Requirements of the UK Combined Code on Corporate Governance (p. 913)
Governance and Risk: An Analytical Handbook for Investors, Managers, Directors, and Stakeholders (p. 1271)

  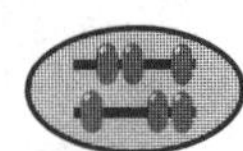   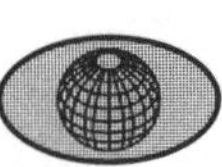   

Directors' and Officers' Liability Insurance

DEFINITION

D&O insurance provides financial security for the directors and officers of a business in the event that they are sued because of their performance or actions undertaken in the course of their duties as they relate to the company.

This type of insurance is sometimes confused with errors and omissions liability insurance. Errors and omissions liability is concerned with performance failures and negligence with respect to products and services and not the performance or duties of management.

D&O insurance normally incorporates employment practices liability and sometimes fiduciary liability. This includes cover against harassment and discrimination suits, which is where there is the most risk. In the United States, employment practice suits comprise the single largest area of claim activity under D&O policies—more than 50% of D&O claims are related to employment practices.

Businesses should have D&O insurance to protect directors and officers against antitrust or unfair trade practice allegations made by stockholders, employees, clients, regulators, and competitors.

Since a director or officer can be held personally responsible for the acts of the company, most directors and officers will stipulate that they are to be protected. If they were not, their own assets would be at risk.

Banks, investors, and venture capitalists will also demand that businesses have D&O insurance as part of their conditions for funding a company.

A common misconception about D&O insurance is that it allows directors or officers to operate in areas, or be employed in acts, that they know to be incorrect. Intentional actions are not covered by D&O insurance.

Due to recent bank failures (for example, Lehman Brothers), banks and other financial institutions that are facing operational or financial challenges are now finding it difficult to obtain D&O insurance.

ADVANTAGES

- The cost of defending lawsuits might exceed the net worth of most private companies and, therefore, judgments can be financially crippling.
- D&O insurance protects the company's assets, as well as those of the company's directors and officers.
- Conflicts of interest may exist, due to the complexity of responsibilities, and companies may have a difficult time attracting qualified individuals to their boards without D&O coverage.
- Banks, investors, and venture capitalists are more willing to fund businesses that have D&O insurance.

DISADVANTAGES

- Premiums can be high, depending on the industry and the size of the risk.
- It is impossible for insurance to cover all eventualities.

ACTION CHECKLIST

- ✔ Analyze the risks your business may be facing, their probability, and their likely impact.
- ✔ Consider how existing D&O policies insure against multiple minor claims as well as more significant/catastrophic single incidents. Examine whether any particular exclusion clauses could leave your business exposed to risks you thought were covered.
- ✔ Try to quantify in financial terms how falling foul of various risks could affect your business. Only once an actual liability figure is available can you expect an insurance supplier to be able to provide a D&O quotation to cover that risk.
- ✔ Be prepared to seek the advice of specialist risk consultants. The field of commercial insurance can be far more complex than its consumer equivalent, and risk consultants can help companies to understand and evaluate both risks and potential solutions. Industry-specific experts from specialist risk-management companies can help you to devise custom solutions to protect against potential D&O liabilities.

DOS AND DON'TS

DO

- Update risk-assessment frameworks regularly, to help keep management informed of the constantly changing business environment and its hazards.

DON'T

- Don't make the mistake of basing a decision purely on price. D&O insurance is a highly complex area and insurance solutions are many and varied.

▸▸ MORE INFO

Books:

Hoffman, D. G. *Managing Operational Risk: 20 Firmwide Best Practice Strategies.* Hoboken, NJ: Wiley, 2002.

Mathias, J. H., *et al. Directors and Officers Liability: Prevention, Insurance, and Indemnification.* Looseleaf ed. New York: Law Journal Press, 2000.

O'Leary, M., and American Bar Association. *Directors and Officers Liability Insurance Deskbook*. 2nd ed. Chicago, IL: American Bar Association, 2007.

Articles:

Engen, J. R. "Rising cost of liability protection." *Bank Director* (2nd Quarter, 2008). Online at: www.bankdirector.com/issues/articles.pl?article_id=11947.

Read, M. J. "Resting insured." *Community Banker* (August 1, 2008). Online at: www.highbeam.com/doc/1P3-1545226651.html.

Websites:

American Insurance Association (AIA): www.aiadc.org

Association of British Insurers (ABI): www.abi.org.uk

See Also:

✔ Corporate Insurance Cover: A Primer (p. 979)
✔ Sound Business Judgment and Immunity from Liability (p. 916)
✔ Stress Testing to Evaluate Insurance Cover (p. 932)
✔ Understanding the Components of an Insurance Contract (p. 934)

"There is nothing more difficult to take in hand, more perilous to conduct, or more uncertain in its success, than to take the lead in the introduction of a new order of things." Niccolò Machiavelli

  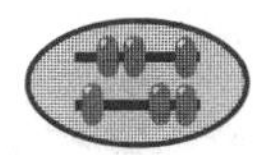   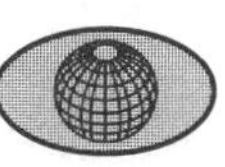 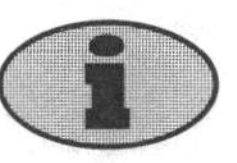  

Directors' Duties: A Primer

DEFINITION

Directors have important and powerful positions in a company. The stockholders entrust them with the running of the company, and this is why the law requires directors to comply with certain duties.

Directors have a duty to act within their powers for a proper purpose, which is underlined in the bylaws of the company. They also have a duty to promote the success of the company and, in doing this, must balance the interests of the stockholders, employees, suppliers, and customers of the company. The law does not define success, but in general this is agreed to mean increasing the value of the company and its business.

The directors are required to exercise independent judgment when making their decisions. They also have a duty to exercise reasonable care, skill, and diligence in the performance of their duties. An experienced director will be expected to exercise a higher degree of care, skill, and diligence in the performance of his or her activities.

Directors have a duty to avoid conflicts of interest. What constitutes a conflict of interest is a complex issue, but in general it refers to transactions between a director and third parties, rather than between a director and the company. Directors have a duty not to accept benefits from third parties if they give rise to a conflict of interest. Benefits in this sense include money and benefits in kind, such as corporate hospitality. It is advisable to obtain specific legal advice in respect of conflicts of interest, as this subject can be quite controversial and difficult to assess.

Directors have a duty to declare any interest in proposed transactions or arrangements with the company. They must disclose any such interest to the board of directors and, in certain circumstances, obtain the approval of the stockholders. This includes transactions involving the director or any person connected with the director, such as a spouse or children, and the company.

ADVANTAGES

- Directors' duties enhance the role of a company's directors and guide their direction of the company's business.
- These duties also reduce the risk of fraud and nonperformance, in the interests of the stockholders.
- The duties give stockholders and investors the confidence to invest in companies and enable them to follow the directors in the performance of their responsibilities.

DISADVANTAGES

- Compliance with directors' duties can be expensive in terms of both time and money. It requires an active training program and professional advice.

ACTION CHECKLIST

✔ When accepting an appointment as a director of a company, make sure you understand the consequences of the appointment. Obtain specific information about the company itself and the duties imposed upon directors by the bylaws of the company, as well as the company laws in the country where the company is incorporated.

✔ If necessary, obtain legal advice regarding the consequences of your appointment, and the duties, obligations, and responsibilities you will have as a director under the law.

✔ Most jurisdictions require a transparency in any personal interest a director may have in the company, and it will oblige the director to declare any conflict of interest it may have with the business of the company.

DOS AND DON'TS

DO

- Put in place a good training program that will keep the directors up to date with their duties.
- Obtain legal and professional advice regarding any changes in the legislation governing directors' duties.

DON'T

- Don't ignore the importance of complying with directors' duties and responsibilities. Doing so could be damaging both to the directors in question and to the company.
- Don't underestimate the need for proper training of directors and professional advice to help them fulfill their duties.

▸▸ MORE INFO

Books:

Loose, Peter, Michael Griffiths, and David Impey. *The Company Director: Powers, Duties and Liabilities*. 10th ed. Bristol, UK: Jordan Publishing, 2008.

Mitchell, Philip. *Tolley's Directors' Duties*. Croydon, UK: Tolley Publishing, 2007.

Webster, Martin (ed). *The Director's Handbook: Your Duties, Responsibilities and Liabilities*. 2nd ed. London: Kogan Page, 2007.

Article:

Cooke, Peter. "Duties of directors in new Companies Act 2006: Legal Q&A." *Personnel Today* (May 2007). Online at: www.personneltoday.com/articles/2007/05/08/40470/duties-of-directors-in-new-companies-act-2006-legal-q.html

Websites:

UK Institute of Directors: www.iod.com

US National Association of Corporate Directors: www.nacdonline.org

Websites:

★ Reinvesting in the Company versus Rewarding Investors with Distributions (pp. 172–173)

✔ The Board's Role in Executive Compensation (p. 899)

✔ Business Process Reengineering (p. 974)

✔ Creating Executive Compensation (p. 906)

✔ Regulatory Responsibilities of Executive and Nonexecutive Directors: An International Overview (p. 912)

"The one predominant duty is to find one's work and do it." Charlotte Gilman

  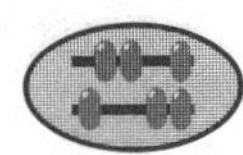   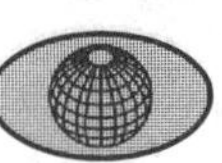   

Governance Practices in Family-Owned Firms

DEFINITION

Corporate governance practices have come under greater scrutiny in recent years, particularly in the wake of the 2001 corporate debacle that was the collapse of the energy trader Enron. Even at the opposite end of the capitalization spectrum, family-owned businesses have not entirely escaped some suspicious investors' attention, leading to increased pressure for reform. Many businesses owned largely by families have responded by making the governance practices more formal, while generally increasing the transparency of their operations.

Family ownership of listed companies is commonplace, with wealthy families continuing to own large stakes in listed companies. In some European countries, powerful families effectively control their family-owned companies using voting rights that exceed their actual economic stake in the business.

Family-owned businesses benefit from a stronger personal bond between the owners and the actual business, and between the owners and employees, with the result that the family owners can be less focused on short-term earnings growth and more on long-term strategic development. However, governance structures within family businesses typically evolve with the development of the business—a process formalized in the model of family-business growth and governance developed in the late 1990s by Kelin Gersick, John Davis, Marion Hampton and Ivan Lansberg. This widely accepted model identifies three stages of transition of family businesses:

1. Founder or controlling owner stage

Management and ownership are in the hands of one individual or a couple benefiting from the input of close advisers such as accountants and legal professionals. Governance is typically informal, although the personal attitudes of the owner(s) are often reflected in the way the business operates.

2. Sibling partnership stage

With the approaching retirement of the founder(s), control passes to the next family generation. Governance is frequently complicated by the involvement of a wider base of stakeholders than at the founder stage. Some governance needs are best overseen by a board of directors or a separate advisery body.

3. Cousin consortium

Control of the business becomes further diversified as the siblings pass control of the business to their own children. Some may exit the business completely, potentially selling their stake to outsiders and conceivably diluting the family interest to the extent that the business may no longer be regarded as a family operation. In other cases, some siblings may seek to concentrate control by buying out other stakeholders. The need for an independent governance structure increases considerably.

ADVANTAGES

- Greater transparency can improve the public perception of how family-controlled businesses hope to serve the needs of all stakeholders.
- Understanding the development pattern of a business can help to identify how its governance needs are changing.
- The centralized nature of family ownership can help to keep the costs of corporate governance lower than is the case for firms with wider public share ownership.

DISADVANTAGES

- Some investors may be skeptical as to how committed family-run businesses are to equally serving the interests of all shareholders.
- Some growing family businesses can be slow to recognize the need to put in place measures to satisfy outsiders.
- Liquidity in family-owned companies is often tighter than in other companies, with some families creating legal barriers to the disposal of stock. This can lead to greater resistance to the transparency demanded by modern corporate governance standards.

ACTION CHECKLIST

- ✔ Family businesses should play to their greatest strength—the ability to pursue a strategy for longer-term gain.
- ✔ Family-owned businesses should also resist short-term industry fads and instead focus on building a long-term market presence.
- ✔ It is necessary to be aware of the risk that some stakeholders in family businesses might languish in the comfort zone away from mainstream shareholder pressure and instead pursue their personal goals on the business's time and at the expense of other stakeholders.

DOS AND DON'TS

DO

- Recognize how governance needs evolve over time.
- Appreciate that an external perspective can help family members better understand the need for more formal governance procedures to reassure non-family investors.
- Understand that accepting the accountability to an independent governance board can bring real advantages to the business.

DON'T

- Don't fall into the trap of thinking that corporate governance only amounts to protecting the reputation of the family.
- Don't ignore the benefits that external accountability can bring, such as an increased incentive to drive the company's strategy.

▸▸ MORE INFO

Articles:

Steier, Lloyd P., James J. Chrisman, and Jess H. Chua. "Entrepreneurial management and governance in family firms: An introduction." *Entrepreneurship Theory and Practice* 28:4 (June 2004): 295–411.

Ward, John L. "Governing family businesses." *eJournal USA* (February 2005): 38–41.

Website:

IFC Corporate Governance: www.ifc.org/corporategovernance

"I avoided the company because I wanted the opportunity to have a track record of starting a business where you are not the boss's son." James Murdoch

  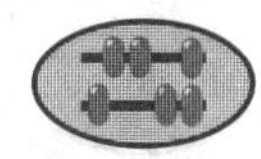   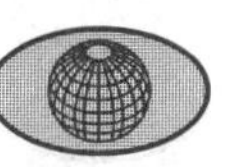   

Investors and the Capital Structure

DEFINITION

A company's capital structure is determined by its long-term financing arrangements, including a combination of common stock, debentures, preferred stock, long-term debt, and retained earnings. The capital structure, which is also known as the capitalization structure, differs from the financial structure in that the latter reflects short-term liabilities and accounts payable.

To better understand the nature of a company's capital structure, it is worth considering the comparative levels of equity and debt. Companies with relatively high levels of debt are said to have higher "gearing." However, a company's gearing outlook is not always as simple as it may appear at first glance. Convertible bonds, for example, are classed as debt at the time of issue but could subsequently become equity. Conversely, preference shares are by nature equity, but they have a fixed-return element that gives them certain debt-like characteristics.

At a simplistic level, a company's choice of capital structure should have no impact on the company's total value, as represented by the sum of equity and debt. This theory is sometimes known as "capital structure irrelevance" or the "Modigliani–Miller theory." Promulgated in the 1960s by Franco Modigliani and Merton Miller, who later collected the Nobel Prize for Economics, the basis of the theory is that all investors in the company ultimately benefit from the total cash flows enjoyed by the company. Changes to the overall balance between equity and debt have no effect on the cash flows, only on how they are effectively divided up between different types of investor. However, more advanced financial models subsequently demonstrated the limitations first recognized by Modigliani and Miller: factors of relevance include the impact of taxation and agency issues, i.e. conflicts of interests between executives, equity investors, and bondholders.

ADVANTAGES

- A basic understanding of a company's capital structure, particularly its level of gearing, is a useful starting point when considering an investment in the company.
- Investors in companies with capital structures based on equity would expect to receive returns on their investment via dividends. Capital growth is also likely when the company is performing well. However, one advantage of this structure from the company's perspective is that payment of dividends is optional, giving the company the right to make no dividend payments during challenging trading periods.

DISADVANTAGES

- A company with a capital structure based largely on debt is required to pay interest to the debt holders, regardless of how the company is performing. However, there may be tax advantages associated with debt repayments.
- Careful thought needs to be given to capital-structure decisions, based on factors such as expected rate of investment return and cost of capital. Ill-judged capital-structure decisions can lead to serious financial problems.

ACTION CHECKLIST

- ✔ Be clear about the differences between capital structure and financial structure—terms that are often confused. Capital structure is the equity/debt balance of a company's long-term finances, whereas financial structure also includes short-term funding arrangements, as represented in the current liabilities on the company's balance sheet.
- ✔ Aim to understand the factors behind companies' choice of capital structure. There are many considerations behind these decisions, including cash flow projections, possible taxation benefits, funding availability, industry factors, risk considerations, and cash management.

DOS AND DON'TS

DO

- Consider the benefits of buying a combination of shares and debt when making an investment in a company. This approach would effectively lower the gearing of the investment opportunity relative to a shares-only purchase.
- Bear in mind that, while differences between rival companies' capital structures can seem significant, research based on extensions of the Modigliani–Miller theory has suggested that the benefits of adjustments to companies' capital structures are frequently limited.

DON'T

- Don't ignore a company simply because of its capital structure. An investor looking for a more highly geared proposition could buy shares in the company, then lend against them.
- Don't ignore the possible impact of agency problems when analyzing companies. Conflicts of interest can occur in many forms, even between stockholders, debt holders, and executives.

» MORE INFO

Books:

Kühn, Christian. *Capital Structure Decisions in Institutional Buyouts*. Wiesbaden, Germany: DUV, 2006.

Riahi-Belkaoui, Ahmed. *Capital Structure: Determination, Evaluation, and Accounting*. Westport, CT: Quorum Books, 1999.

Articles:

Brounen, Dirk, Abe de Jong, and Kees Koedijk. "Capital structure policies in Europe: Survey evidence." *Journal of Banking and Finance* 30:5 (May 2006): 1409–1442.

Talberg, Magnus, Christian Winge, Stein Frydenberg, and Sjur Westgaard. "Capital structure across industries." *International Journal of the Economics of Business* 15:2 (2008): 181–200.

See Also:

★ Capital Structure: A Strategy that Makes Sense (pp. 526–530)

✔ Understanding Capital Structure Theory: Modigliani and Miller (p. 890)

"Bond investors are the vampires of the investment world. They love decay, recession—anything that leads to low inflation and the protection of the real value of their loans." Bill Gross

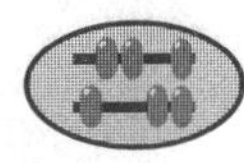
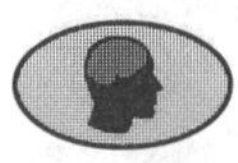

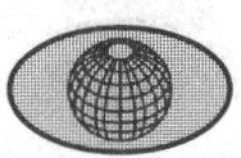

Regulatory Responsibilities of Executive and Nonexecutive Directors: An International Overview

DEFINITION

From a legal point of view, there is no difference between the executive and nonexecutive directors in terms of their responsibilities towards the company and its stockholders. It is recognized, however, that executive directors have an active role in directing the company's affairs for the benefit of, and in the best interests of, the stockholders. The executive directors—and especially the managing director—have overall responsibility for the performance of the company's business. The nonexecutive directors have a supervisory and balancing role, controlling the activities of the executive directors and the board in general.

The directors are responsible for the company's books and accounts and are responsible to stockholders and investors for the company's activities and results. They must act in good faith, in the best interests of the company's business and stockholders. Any conflict of interest with the company's business must be declared and approved by the board and, in certain circumstances, by the stockholders at a general meeting.

Directors must always act with due skill and care and must keep up to date with the needs of the company and its business. They must also consider the needs of the company's employees.

Directors have a responsibility to establish the company's objectives and policies and, once these have been established, to monitor their development and progress. They also appoint the company's senior management.

Directors have an active duty to comply with money-laundering regulations, which are now established internationally. In certain circumstances (when, for example, nonexecutive directors supply their services to the company via another business), they will have to register with certain government departments for the purposes of the money-laundering regulations.

ADVANTAGES

- Regulatory responsibilities enhance the role of a company's directors and guide their direction of the company's business.
- These responsibilities also reduce the risk of fraud and nonperformance, in the interest of the stockholders.
- The regulations give stockholders and investors the confidence to invest in companies and enable them to follow the directors in the performance of their responsibilities.

DISADVANTAGES

- Compliance with the regulatory responsibilities can be expensive in terms of both time and money. It requires an active training program and professional advice.

ACTION CHECKLIST

✔ Make sure that you appoint the right individuals as executive and nonexecutive directors. Executive directors will have an active role in the day-to-day running of the company while the nonexecutive will play more of a guiding role.

✔ Stress to your chosen appointees that all directors, executive and nonexecutive, have, in view of the law, equal duties and responsibilities.

✔ Establish training programmes that will allow the directors to keep up to date with any changes in the law in respect of the running of the company, their duties and responsibilities.

DOS AND DON'TS

DO

- Put in place a good training program that will keep the directors' skills up to date with their regulatory responsibilities.
- Obtain legal and professional advice regarding any changes in the legislation governing directors' responsibilities.

DON'T

- Don't ignore the importance of complying with the regulations governing directors' duties and responsibilities.
- Don't underestimate the need for proper training of directors and professional advice to help them fulfill their responsibilities.

▸▸ MORE INFO

Books:

Loose, Peter, Michael Griffiths, and David Impey. *The Company Director: Powers, Duties and Liabilities*. 10th ed. Bristol, UK: Jordan Publishing, 2008.

Mitchell, Philip. *Tolley's Directors' Duties*. Croydon, UK: Tolley Publishing, 2007.

Smithson, John. *The Role of the Non-executive Director in the Small to Medium Sized Business*. New York: Palgrave Macmillan, 2003.

Webster, Martin (ed). *The Director's Handbook: Your Duties, Responsibilities and Liabilities*. 2nd ed. London: Kogan Page, 2007.

Wilson, Andrew. *The Importance of Being Ethical: Business Ethics and the Non-Executive Director*. Berkhamsted, UK: Ashridge Management College, 1993.

Article:

Cooke, Peter. "Duties of directors in new Companies Act 2006: Legal Q&A." *Personnel Today* (May 2007). Online at: www.personneltoday.com/articles/2007/05/08/40470/duties-of-directors-in-new-companies-act-2006-legal-q.html

Websites:

Institute of Directors: www.iod.com

National Association of Corporate Directors: www.nacdonline.org

See Also:

★ Boardroom Roles (pp. 130–131)

✔ Directors' Duties: A Primer (p. 909)

"If one is going to change things, one has to make a fuss and catch the eye of the world." Elizabeth Janeway

     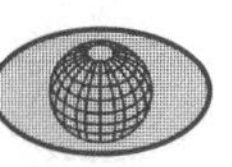   

Requirements of the UK Combined Code on Corporate Governance

DEFINITION

All companies incorporated in the United Kingdom that are listed on the main market of the London Stock Exchange must comply with the Listing Rules, which require them to account for the application of the Combined Code. The Combined Code was first issued in 1998 and has been updated regularly, the most recent update being in June 2008.

The Code establishes main and specific principles of corporate governance, dealing with four broad areas: directors and the board; remuneration of directors; accountability and audit; and the relationship with shareholders. Each area of the code establishes principles and guidelines for the companies that come under its rule.

According to the Code, a company's board of directors is responsible for its success. The board's role is to put in place effective controls that will identify and manage the risks for the business. The decisions made must be objective and in the best interests of the company's business. The Code distinguishes between executive directors, who are involved in the day-to-day running of the company, and nonexecutive directors. Nonexecutive directors should decide the level of remuneration of executive directors.

The Code requires a clear division of responsibilities between the chairman, who is in charge of the board, and the chief executive of a company, whose main preoccupation should be running the business. These two roles cannot be fulfilled by the same person. The Code also deals with the procedure for the appointment of the board, the requirement to improve their skills, their reelection, and their evaluation. The directors should have a level of remuneration that is sufficient to attract, retain, and motivate them.

The Code also establishes the financial reporting principle, under which the board must present a balanced and understandable assessment of the company's financial position and its prospects. The board must also maintain a sound internal control that will protect the company's assets and shareholders' investments. The board must appoint an auditing committee and maintain an appropriate relationship with the company's auditors. The board must also maintain dialog with shareholders of the company.

ADVANTAGES

- The Code gives shareholders confidence that a company is well run and that there is transparency in the way the board makes its decisions.
- It establishes what is known as the "comply or explain" attitude. Companies that come under its rule must comply with, or explain why they have not complied with, its principles and requirements.

DISADVANTAGES

- The need to comply with numerous corporate governance requirements is expensive and can deflect directors from their main priority, which is running the business in the best interests of the shareholders.
- Some maintain that too much supervision could bring a lack of independence to the way a company runs its business.

ACTION CHECKLIST

✔ Be well informed when it comes to the Combined Code and its contents.

✔ Be prepared to put in place a thorough system that guarantees that each one of the principles of the Code is understood and complied with. If not, be prepared to explain why compliance is not necessary.

DOS AND DON'TS

DO

- Obtain advice from your legal advisers and accountants to find out and understand the best system to put in place and the consequences of any breach of the Code.

DON'T

- Don't ignore compliance with the rules of corporate governance. The consequences could not only be financial penalties for the company but also criminal charges for the directors.
- Don't overlook the importance of setting up proper procedures to deal with the consequences of a breach.

▸▸ MORE INFO

Websites:

Financial Reporting Council (UK): www.frc.org.uk
Financial Services Authority (UK): www.fsa.gov.uk
Institute of Chartered Accountants in England and Wales: www.icaew.co.uk
Institute of Chartered Accountants in Scotland: www.icas.org.uk

See Also::

★ Improving Corporate Profitability Through Accountability (pp. 170–171)
★ What Are the Leading Causes of Financial Restatements? (pp. 729–731)
✔ Corporate Governance and Its Interpretations (p. 902)
✔ Corporate Governance Practices in Private Equity-owned Firms (p. 903)
✔ Sarbanes–Oxley: Its Development and Aims (p. 1047)

"Human beings were held accountable long before there were corporate bureaucracies. If the knight didn't deliver, the king cut off his head." Alvin Toffler

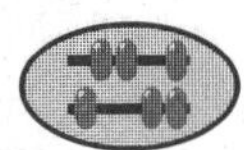

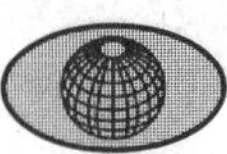

The Responsibilities of Trustees

DEFINITION

A trust or charity can be set up either to benefit particular persons or for any charitable reason. "Trustee" is the legal word that bestows on a person or institution legal title to hold property on behalf of a recipient, such as a trust or charity. Trustees are generally selected because of their personal reputation or professional status. They are given independent authority to make decisions according to their best judgment or professional criteria, and are empowered to act on behalf of the beneficiary.

The great majority of trustees serve as volunteers, and receive no payment for their work. Their responsibilities and duties are generally to:

- accept ultimate responsibility for directing the trust's affairs, and ensure that it is solvent, well run, and delivers the outcomes and benefits for which it was set up;
- ensure that the trust complies with law, and prepare reports on what it has achieved, and annual returns and accounts as required by law;
- ensure that the trust does not breach any of the requirements or rules set out in its governing document and that it remains true to its purpose and goals;
- comply with the requirements of legislation and other regulations that govern the activities of the trust;
- act with integrity, and avoid any personal conflicts of interest or misuse of funds or assets;
- ensure that the charity is and will remain solvent (duty of prudence);
- use charitable funds and assets reasonably, and only in furtherance of the trust's objectives;
- avoid undertaking activities that might place the trust's funds, assets, or reputation at any undue risk;
- use reasonable care and skill in the role of trustee, using personal skills and experience as needed to ensure that the trust is efficiently managed (duty of care);
- obtain independent professional advice on all matters where there may be material risk to the trust, or where the trustees may be in breach of their duties.

As a rule, all the trustees—acting as a team—take all decisions. However, decisions need not be unanimous, and a majority decision is sufficient unless the charity's governing document states otherwise.

Different jurisdictions regard a trustee's duties in different ways. Normally, however, the legislation follows the general body of elementary fiduciary law that is found in most common-law jurisdictions.

ADVANTAGES

- Trustees are chosen for their independence, personal repute, and professional standing.
- Most trustees serve as volunteers, receive no payment for their work, and are collaborating for altruistic reasons.
- Because of their commitment to create positive change in society, trustees should do their utmost to ensure that the charity or trust succeeds in its aims.

DISADVANTAGES

- As trustees are volunteers and receive no recompense, it may sometimes be difficult to find people with the management skills necessary to run what may be a complex organization.

ACTION CHECKLIST

✔ Look for an in-depth analysis of particular jurisdictional differences between countries before setting up a trust or charity and consult independent specialists in fiduciary law.

✔ When selecting trustees, find out what specialist skills they can bring. Most modern charities need skilled support in areas such as management, advertising, public relations, and fund raising, which are highly specialized.

✔ Set up a professional, formal selection procedure when looking for trustees to ensure that you have the right balance of skilled candidates.

✔ Seek legal advice from specialists when setting up the charters or governing documents.

DOS AND DON'TS

DO

- Spell out in clear terms the goals of the trust, their probable impact, and the effort that may be required.

DON'T

- Don't take on the job of a trustee unless you are sure that you have skills to offer and the time required to do the job properly.

▸▸ MORE INFO

Books:

Claricoat, J., and H. Phillips. *Charity Law A to Z: Key Questions Answered*. 2nd ed. Bristol, UK: Jordan Publishing, 1998.

Gaudiani, C. *The Greater Good: How Philanthropy Drives the American Economy and Can Save Capitalism*. New York: Times Books/Henry Holt, 2003.

Thompson, K. W. (ed). *Philanthropy: Private Means, Public Ends*. Lanham, MD: University Press of America, 1987.

Articles:

Harrison, R. "Trustees new casualties of law." *Pensions Week* (July 24, 2006).

M2 Presswire. "Launch of consultation on Criminal Records Bureau checks of trustees of charities." February 2007.

Websites:

American Institute of Philanthropy (AIP): www.charitywatch.org
Charity Trustee Network (CTN): www.trusteenet.org.uk

See Also:

✔ Defining Corporate Governance: Its Aims, Goals, and Responsibilities (p. 907)
✔ Selecting the Board and Evaluation Process (p. 915)
✔ Understanding Decision-Tree Analysis (p. 1061)

"It is change. . .that is the dominant factor in society today. No sensible decision can be made without taking into account not only the world as it is, but the world as it will be." Isaac Asimov

  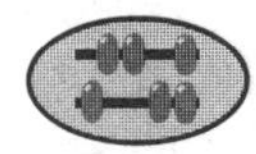   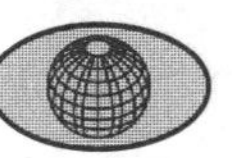   

Selecting the Board and Evaluation Process

DEFINITION

The role of a company's directors and board is to ensure the prosperity of the business and to manage the company in the best interests of its stockholders.

The law and the bylaws of a company usually establish the minimum number of directors that should be appointed to the board—from one in small companies to dozens in more complex public listed companies. They will also specify the composition of the board, in terms of executive and nonexecutive directors. There should be a minimum number of independent directors. These are people who have independence from any party with influence over the board, the company, or its business.

In general, appointing directors to the board is an objective and formal process. Following recent international scandals involving directors and a lack of control exercised by the board, the rules of corporate governance of selection and appointment of the board have been tightened. The role of the nonexecutive director has become more important than ever.

Directors are appointed by a company's stockholders or by its board. However, the dismissal of a director can only be done by the stockholders.

The appointed directors have a position of trust towards the company, its business and its stockholders. The appointment of a board involves a thorough selection process. The executive directors must have the right level of professional experience and skills to be able to run, enhance and develop the business of the company. The nonexecutive directors are not involved in the day-to-day running of the business but must be able to give enough time to the supervision and running of the board. Their role in supervising the activities of the board and executive directors has become increasingly important. Nonexecutive directors are usually businesspeople with significant experience in the running of businesses and boards.

The bylaws of a company usually require the board to appoint a chairperson. The chairperson supervises board meetings and procedures and has a casting vote in the event that the board cannot come to an agreement. (The board normally makes decisions based on a majority of votes.) This means that the chairperson's decision is final.

ADVANTAGES

- Putting in place a good selection process for directors, and selecting an appropriate board, will enhance the performance of the company.
- A well-selected board, which can work in harmony, will not only be enjoyable to work with but will also produce the most efficient results.

DISADVANTAGES

- Selecting the right board can be time consuming.
- Attracting the right directors can be expensive, because it means paying them competitive salaries.
- It is sometimes necessary to use a specialist headhunting agency to help with the selection of directors. This can be very expensive.

ACTION CHECKLIST

✔ Thoroughly research potential appointees to join the board of the company. Look at their credentials, résumé and experience, and also discuss their suitability with them. It is essential that the appointment will work in the interest of the board and the company's business overall.

✔ Highlight the implications of being a director in the company; what is expected of the individual, how the company operates, how you expect the decisions to be made.

✔ Assess how the individuals who will form part of the board will work together. Determine who would be best in an executive directorship and who would be better as a nonexecutive member. Consider if their experience is relevant in view of the aims of the company.

DOS AND DON'TS

DO

- Always select a board through a thorough process of interviews and evaluation.
- Obtain relevant information regarding the experience and skills of each member of the board before appointment.
- Research the market carefully before deciding whom to invite to be a board member.
- Make sure that each member of the board—especially the nonexecutive directors—can dedicate to the company as much time as is required.
- If necessary, be prepared to use specialist recruitment consultants, who will be able to help you find the right members of the board.

DON'T

- Don't rush into appointing someone as a member of the board on the sole basis of their reputation. A good reputation and the right credits are important, but they may not be sufficient for the needs of the company. Interview and get to know the people you will be appointing to the board.
- Don't underestimate the need for proper research and professional advice when selecting the right board.

▸▸ MORE INFO

Books:

Loose, Peter, Michael Griffiths, and David Impey. *The Company Director: Powers, Duties and Liabilities*. 9th ed. Bristol, UK: Jordan Publishing, 2007.

Mitchell, Philip. *Tolley's Directors' Duties*. Croydon, UK: Tolley Publishing, 2007.

Webster, Martin (ed). *The Director's Handbook: Your Duties, Responsibilities and Liabilities*. 2nd ed. London: Kogan Page, 2007.

Article:

Cooke, Peter. "Duties of directors in new Companies Act 2006: Legal Q&A." *Personnel Today* (May 2007). Online at: www.personneltoday.com/articles/2007/05/08/40470/duties-of-directors-in-new-companies-act-2006-legal-q.html

Websites:

Business resources and directories: www.business.com

Institute of Directors: www.iod.com

FT site for nonexecutive directors and trustees: www.non-execs.com

"I get many invitations but I only join the boards of companies where I admire the management and believe in the company." Jill Ker Conway

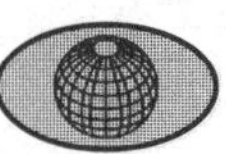

Sound Business Judgment and Immunity from Liability

DEFINITION

Sound business judgment and immunity from liability is a legal principle under common law that makes directors, officers, managers, and other representatives of a firm immune from responsibility for losses acquired in dealings that are within their competences to make when there is satisfactory evidence to demonstrate that the actions were made in "good faith." The ruling originated in the United States in 1945 and functions by application of precedent, because it is not enacted in legislation.

This judgment allows for a strong presumption of immunity in favor of the board of directors of a business, liberating its members from possible liability for decisions that result in harm or damage to the business. The presumption is that "in making business decisions not involving direct self-interest or self-dealing, corporate directors act on an informed basis, in good faith, and in the honest belief that their actions are in the corporation's best interest."

The directors and managers of a business have the responsibility to run and direct the business. Frequently they face difficult decisions, such as purchasing another business or property, expanding into other areas of industry, or issuing shares or paying dividends. To face these tasks without fear of liability, courts have given substantial leeway to directors and managers. As part of their duty of care, directors and managers have a duty not to misuse the business's assets by undercharging or overpaying for goods and services.

The 1945 ruling specifies that courts will not assess the business decisions of directors who have performed their duties:

- in good faith;
- with all the due care that an ordinarily prudent person in a similar situation would exercise under comparable circumstances;
- in a manner which the directors reasonably believe to be in the best interests of the corporation.

The sound business judgment and immunity from liability rule is very tricky to overturn and the courts will generally not interfere unless there is incontrovertible evidence of fraud or misappropriation.

ADVANTAGES

- Business decisions must sometimes be made, with high stakes and under considerable time pressure, in circumstances in which detailed information is not available.
- Sound business judgment and immunity promote optimal corporate governance without compromising directors' flexibility and innovation.
- The ruling protects honest directors and officers from the risks inherent when unsuccessful decisions are reviewed in hindsight.
- It prevents the stifling of risk taking and enterprising business activity.

DISADVANTAGES

- The principle gives directors and managers substantial leeway and absolves part of their ethical concern for the management of the business.

ACTION CHECKLIST

✔ Check to see how the principle of sound business judgment and immunity from liability functions in your country or jurisdiction before relying on it to avoid prosecution.

✔ Review risks periodically in the light of strategic objectives. Analyze the risks your business may be facing, their probability, and their likely impact.

✔ Seek the advice of specialist legal and risk consultants, who can help you to understand and evaluate complex risks and potential pitfalls.

DOS AND DON'TS

DO

- Set up an effective and independent corporate governance program to help keep management informed of the constantly changing business environment and its risks.

DON'T

- Don't rely on demonstrating "good faith" in sound business judgment to give you immunity from liability.

➤➤ MORE INFO

Books:

Emerson, Robert W. *Business Law*. 4th ed. Hauppauge, NY: Barron's Educational Series, 2004.

Kelly, David, Ann Holmes, and Ruth Hayward. *Business Law*. 5th ed. New York: Routledge Cavendish, 2005.

Marsh, Stanley Bryan, and J. Soulsby. *Business Law*. 8th ed. Cheltenham, UK: Nelson Thornes, 2002.

Articles:

Black, Bert, and Robert L. Whitener. "Director liability for bad judgment and bad faith: The business judgment rule and many states' 'director shield statutes' protect corporate directors from liability. . ." *Trial* (June 1, 2007). Online at: www.accessmylibrary.com/coms2/summary_0286-31345067_ITM

Epstein, Richard A. "A New Year's resolution for CEOs: No special deals." *Chief Executive* (December 2006).

Websites:

American Bar Association: www.abanet.org

The Law Society (UK): www.lawsociety.org.uk

See Also:

★ Booms, Busts, and How to Navigate Troubled Waters (pp. 286–288)

✔ Directors' and Officers' Liability Insurance (p. 908)

"There are plenty of recommendations on how to get out of trouble cheaply and fast. Most of them come down to the same thing. Deny your responsibility." Nancy Peretsman

The Triple Bottom Line

DEFINITION

Traditional accounting models are all about profit and more profit, whereas triple bottom line accounting recognizes that, without content, healthy people to run a business, and the natural environment to sustain those people and resources the business is simply unsustainable in the long term. Triple bottom line accounting means expanding the traditional reporting framework to take into account environmental and social factors as well as financial performance.

The idea proposes that an organization's license to operate in society comes not just from rewarding shareholders through enhanced profits (the economic bottom line), but by improving its environmental and social performance. As such, it includes environmental responsibility, social awareness, and economic profitability.

The triple bottom line is sometimes referred to as "TBL" or "3BL." Triple bottom line can also be simply summarized as People, Planet and Profit:

People

People are also known as *human capital.* The people aspect means treating employees, the community, and the region in which a corporation conducts its business correctly. In this part of the TBL, business not only ensures a fair day's work for a fair day's pay but also reinvests some of its profits into the surrounding community through education, sponsorships, or donations, or helping in projects that promote the common good.

Planet

Under the planet principle, or *natural capital*, a business will endeavor to minimize its ecological impact in all areas—from obtaining raw materials, through production processes, to shipping and management. It is a "cradle to grave" attitude, and in some cases "cradle to cradle," i.e. taking responsibility for goods after they've been sold by, for example, offering a recycling or return program.

Profit

TBL is about making a principled profit, rather than earning a profit at any cost. In other words, the profit made should be in accord with the other two principles of People and Planet.

The TBL concept is important because it is not just about commerce; it is an ongoing process that helps a company to run a more sustainable and greener business and demonstrates to the community at large that the company is working not just for profit but also for the members of the community. On balance, without people and planet, there would be no profit to be made.

ADVANTAGES

- A TBL business endeavors to benefit the natural order as much as possible—or at least do no harm and curtail environmental impact.
- TBL manufacturing businesses conduct a life-cycle assessment of products to determine their true environmental cost, from the growth and harvesting of raw materials to manufacture, and then from distribution to eventual disposal by the end user.
- TBL companies make an effort to reduce their ecological footprint by vigilantly managing the consumption of energy and nonrenewables and reducing manufacturing waste, as well as rendering waste less toxic before disposing of it in a safe and legal manner.

DISADVANTAGES

- Quantifying this bottom line is a relatively new task. Therefore, it is sometimes problematic and often subjective.
- The types of problems that occur in social and environmental realms do not lend themselves to a measure that would allow for clear-cut accounting. How, in financial terms, do you measure the two factors of People and Planet?

ACTION CHECKLIST

- ✔ If you are considering TBL, carefully study any potential downsides and obtain as much information from as many sources as you can before committing to an expensive process.
- ✔ Will the TBL model suit your business, and how will you measure the People and Planet principles?
- ✔ Support an atmosphere of openness about the kinds of problems the business will face if it adopts TBL.
- ✔ Involve key local stakeholders in the evaluation of how a TBL program could benefit the local community.

DOS AND DON'TS

DO

- Involve both your accountants and lawyers in the evaluation of the risks and potential benefits of TBL.

DON'T

- Don't make the mistake of being attracted to TBL because it is politically advantageous. Implementation could be expensive and time-consuming, with potentially unpredictable results.

▸▸ MORE INFO

Books:

Elkington, J. *Cannibals with Forks: The Triple Bottom Line of 21st Century Business*. Gabriola Island, BC: New Society Publishers, 1998.

Henriques, A., and J. Richardson. *The Triple Bottom Line, Does It All Add Up? Assessing the Sustainability of Business and CSR*. London: Earthscan, 2004.

Savitz, A. W., and K. Weber, *The Triple Bottom Line: How Today's Best-run Companies are Achieving Economic, Social, and Environmental Success—And How You Can Too*. San Francisco, CA: Jossey Bass, 2006.

Willard, B. *The Sustainability Advantage: Seven Business Case Benefits of a Triple Bottom Line*. Gabriola Island, BC: New Society Publishers, 2002.

Articles:

Colman, R. "Triple bottom line benefits." *CMA Management* 78:1 (2004): 3.

Henderson, L. "Triple bottom line: The conceptual frontier." *Bellingham Business Journal* (April 2008).

Websites:

Ethical Investment Association (EIA): www.ethicalinvestment.org.uk

SustainAbility: www.sustainability.com

"I am captivated more by dreams of the future than by history of the past." Thomas Jefferson

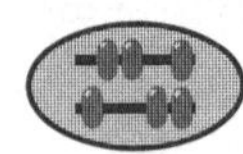
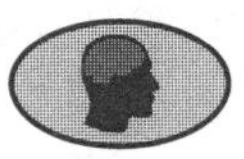

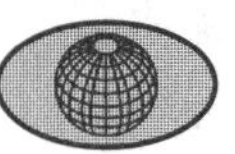

Understanding Anti-Takeover Strategies

DEFINITION

Anti-takeover strategies come in a number of different guises. Terms such as "shark repellent" and "poison pill" are used to describe the defensive methods or tactics that companies use to attempt to prevent mergers, i.e. the joining of two or more businesses into one, or hostile takeovers, when a business is acquired against the management's or shareholders' wishes.

Anti-takeover strategies are designed to make a company unattractive to predators. They do this in the following ways:

- A shareholder rights plan or poison pill has two different strategies. The "flip-in" allows existing shareholders to purchase more shares at a discount in order to dilute the value of the shares, while the "flip-over" allows shareholders to purchase the bidder's shares at a discount.
- A provision in the company's charter or articles allows shareholders to sell their shares to the bidder for more than the market price.
- A company takes on sufficient debts to make it unattractive, as a bidder would be responsible for those debts.
- The business issues bonds that have to be redeemed at a higher price if the company is taken over.
- The company offers its employees stock options, high bonuses, and exceptional severance pay that would cost a bidder dearly.
- Staggered elections to the board of directors over a period of years can mean that a potential bidder is faced with a hostile board of directors until new elections can be held.

In some jurisdictions, such as the United Kingdom, anti-takeover strategies are illegal or some control on their use is mandated. However, in the United States, where they are legal, the recent economic decline and fear of becoming an acquisition target have renewed interest in anti-takeover strategies in all their forms.

ADVANTAGES

- Anti-takeover strategies are useful when a company feels that its stock has become undervalued and that it may become the target for a takeover.
- Anti-takeover strategies are useful when the predator company's intentions are to acquire the company and then load the company with so much debt that it is unviable.
- Short-term poison pills may help businesses through difficult financial periods when they could be vulnerable as targets.

DISADVANTAGES

- Anti-takeover strategies are sometimes used to entrench management and prevent shareholders from selling their stock and maximizing its price.
- Board members sometimes hide behind poison pills to retain their positions.

ACTION CHECKLIST

- ✔ Check that the use of anti-takeover strategies is legal in the country or jurisdiction in which the company is operating.
- ✔ Determine which method would provide the greatest protection without hurting the company's value.
- ✔ Avoid tying the company to stock options, high bonuses, and exceptional severance pay for employees you might later want to fire.
- ✔ If you are taking on debts or issuing bonds to make the company unattractive, make sure that you can service those debts even if the economy turns down.

DOS AND DON'TS

DO

- Consult with partners, directors, lawyers and accountants before initiating anti-takeover strategies.

DON'T

- Don't use anti-takeover strategies unless you are sure that they won't backfire and leave the company vulnerable.

⏩ MORE INFO

Books:

Gaughan, Patrick A. *Mergers, Acquisitions, and Corporate Restructurings*. 3rd ed. New York: Wiley, 2002.

Peck, Simon, and Paul Temple. *Mergers and Acquisitions: Critical Perspectives on Business and Management*. New York: Routledge, 2002.

Sternberg, Elaine. *Just Business: Business Ethics in Action*. 2nd ed. Oxford: Oxford University Press, 2000.

Articles:

Dolbeck, Andrew. "Investors, IPOs, and shark repellent." *Weekly Corporate Growth Report* (June 28, 2004). Online at: www.allbusiness.com/business-finance/equity-funding-sales-equity-to-public-ipo/997989-1.html

Wellner, Alison Stein. "Golden handcuffs." *HR Magazine* (October 1, 2000).

Websites:

Investopedia: www.investopedia.com

Magazines and resources for CFOs: www.cfo.com

See Also:

★ Leveraged Buyouts and Recession (pp. 405–408)
✔ Understanding Private-Equity Strategies: An Overview (p. 951)
✔ Using the Comparable Net Worth Method in Squeeze Outs (p. 965)
Barbarians at the Gate: The Fall of RJR Nabisco (p. 1223)

"The rapidity of technological change makes the search for facts a permanently necessary feature."
Alfred P. Sloan

  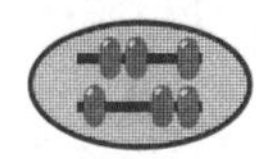   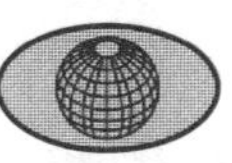   

Understanding Crisis Management

DEFINITION

Although any development that poses a serious threat to a business and/or its shareholders can be thought of as a crisis of some kind, events that require rapid and far-reaching action by management to avert significant damage to the organization require some form of crisis management. All businesses should expect to face major challenges from time to time, but the precise form of possible threats to the survival of an organization are very difficult to predict, with the need for the right solutions to be identified and implemented within a tight timescale often adding to the severity of the crisis.

The immediate threat of bankruptcy is an obvious situation that requires crisis management, though struggling companies in need of urgent corporate restructuring or debt refinancing could also employ crisis management techniques. Similarly, companies facing major problems such as a catastrophic computer systems failure, a large-scale industrial accident, a major product recall, or a sudden collapse in sales due to a health scare can also benefit from the implementation of crisis management strategies.

Though the precise nature of potential crises facing businesses varies considerably according to their operating environment, in all cases crisis management presents significant challenges for senior management. When preparing outline crisis management plans in advance, executives should ensure that appropriate personnel structures are in place to help deal with major events that could threaten the business. Management should also impress on their crisis management teams how the company's core values should be reflected in the methodology employed to steer the organization through the crisis. Additionally, emphasis should be placed on how the organization intends to communicate with parties such as employees, clients, and investors during a possible crisis, bearing in mind that loss of support from any of these could in itself pose a grave threat to the business.

In many cases, companies can also improve their state of readiness to deal with potential future crises by testing the mechanisms they have put in place to handle potential threats such as computer failure or product recalls. However, the procedures employed to handle an immediate crisis should integrate effectively with a strategic plan to help the company's overall recovery plan.

ADVANTAGES

- Robust crisis management plans can equip organizations to withstand threats to their survival better.
- Awareness of potential threats can put an organization in a better position to take early action, often helping to avoid more serious problems.
- Effective crisis management plans can help companies to achieve improved levels of regulatory compliance.
- Appropriate planning for potential industry-wide crises can give a company the upper hand over ill-prepared competitors.
- Effective communications during a crisis can help determine how the company's core values and beliefs have helped it to overcome a major challenge, potentially enhancing public perception of the company.

DISADVANTAGES

- Crisis management planning may seem expensive.
- Attempts to plan exhaustively for every conceivable threat can be counterproductive.
- Excessive focus on potential threats can divert management focus on how to capitalize on growth opportunities for the business.

ACTION CHECKLIST

- ✔ Prepare an overall crisis management plan that encapsulates the company's core values and beliefs.
- ✔ Establish a crisis management team structure and define roles and responsibilities.
- ✔ Define and clarify lines of authority reporting.
- ✔ Ensure that effective structures are in place for communications with key stakeholders.
- ✔ Link the crisis management plan to a business recovery program.

DOS AND DON'TS

DO

- Recognize the increased operating safety levels associated with effective crisis management planning.
- Appreciate that robust planning to deal with major threats can give a company a competitive advantage.
- Plan for business recovery, not just how to handle the immediate crisis.

DON'T

- Don't ignore the potential long-term benefits of effective crisis management in terms of improved corporate reputation, as doing so can be costly.
- Don't become obsessed with every conceivable challenge that faces the business, as this can be counterproductive.

›› MORE INFO

Books:

Devlin, Edward S. *Crisis Management Planning and Execution*. Boca Raton, FL: Auerbach Publications, 2007.

Fink, Steven. *Crisis Management: Planning for the Inevitable*. Lincoln, NE: iUniverse, 2002.

Articles:

Chong, John K. S. "Six steps to better crisis management." *Journal of Business Strategy* 25:2 (2004): 43–46.

Sturges, D. L. "Communicating through crisis: A strategy for organizational survival." *Management Communication Quarterly* 7:3 (1994): 297–316.

Websites:

Federal Emergency Management Agency (FEMA): www.fema.gov

FEMA Emergency Management Institute—Business and industry crisis management: training.fema.gov/emiweb/edu/aem_courses1.asp

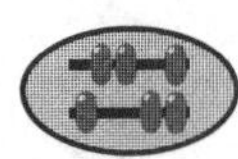

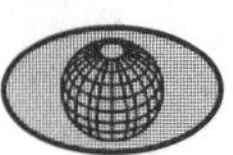

Basel II—Its Development and Aims

DEFINITION

The Basel Accords are recommendations on banking laws and regulations issued by the Basel Committee on Banking Supervision. Basel II, drafted initially in June 2004 and intended to replace Basel I in due course, aims to create an international standard for regulators to use when creating regulations on how much capital banks must set aside to guard against the types of financial and operational risks they face. The theory is that the Basel II international standard would help protect global financial systems from the types of problems that might arise should a major bank, or a series of banks, collapse. This would be achieved by designing and implementing rigorous risk and capital management requirements to ensure a bank holds sufficient capital reserves appropriate to the risk it is exposed to through its lending and investment practices. This implies that the greater the risk to which the bank is exposed, the greater the amount of capital the bank must reserve to safeguard its solvency and overall economic stability.

Basel II aims to ensure that capital allocation is more risk sensitive, to separate operational risk from credit risk and quantify both, and to attempt to align economic and regulatory capital more closely to reduce the scope for regulatory arbitrage. There are three pillars to Basel II.

Pillar I covers the maintenance of regulatory capital (minimum capital requirements) calculated for the three major components of risk that a bank faces: Credit risk, operational risk, and market risk. The credit risk component can be calculated using one of three methods that vary in their degree of sophistication: The standardized approach, the foundation IRB (internal ratings-based) approach, and the advanced IRB approach. Similarly, there are three different approaches for operational risk: The basic indicator approach (BIA), the standardized approach (TSA), and the advanced measurement approach (AMA). For market risk, the preferred approach is value-at-risk (VaR).

Pillar II not only deals with the regulatory response to the first pillar and gives regulators better tools for implementing regulations, it also provides a framework for dealing with the residual risks a financial institution may face, such as systemic, concentration, strategic, reputational, liquidity, and legal risks. This pillar gives a financial institution the power to review its risk management system.

The third pillar concerns market discipline and the promotion of stability in the financial system. The number of disclosures that a financial institution must make is greatly increased, in order to give the market a better picture of the overall risk position of the financial institution, and enables its counterparties to price and deal appropriately.

Since 2004, Basel II has gone through a number of revisions. In July 2008, the US federal banking and thrift agencies (comprising the Board of Governors of the Federal Reserve System, the Federal Deposit Insurance Corporation, the Office of the Comptroller of the Currency, and the Office of Thrift Supervision) issued final guidance outlining the supervisory review process for financial institutions implementing Basel II. This guidance aims to help financial institutions meet certain qualification requirements in the advanced approach rules, which took effect on April 1, 2008.

The implementation of an international agreement such as Basel II can be very complex, requiring the need to accommodate differing cultures, varying structural models, and the complexities of public policy and existing regulation. Basel II is open to interpretation by various countries' legislatures and regulators during implementation. As banks now must deal with multiple reporting requirements for different regulators, including Basel II, according to their geographic location, a number of software applications have been developed to assist, including capital calculation engines and automated reporting solutions.

Regulators around the world are working on implementing Basel II. US regulators have agreed on a joint final approach that enforces the IRB approach for the largest banks, while agreeing that the standardized approach will not be available to anyone. The European Union (EU) has already implemented the accord via the EU Capital Requirements Directives. Many European financial institutions are already reporting their capital adequacy ratios under Basel II requirements. All European credit institutions within the EU were due to have adopted it by 2008. In response to a questionnaire drafted by the Financial Stability Institute (FSI) in 2006, 95 national regulators indicated they would implement Basel II, in one form or another, by 2015.

THE FUTURE

With the impact of the 2008/09 financial crisis still to be fully seen, there is likely to be much discussion on whether Basel II has been a failure. What is not in doubt is that there will be a Basel III.

▸▸ MORE INFO

Books:

Chernobai, Anna S., Svetlozar T. Rachev, and Frank J. Fabozzi. *Operational Risk: A Guide to Basel II Capital Requirements, Models, and Analysis*. Hoboken, NJ: Wiley, 2007.

Gleeson, Simon. *International Regulation of Banking: Basel II, Capital and Risk Requirements*. Oxford: OUP, 2009.

Ozdemir, Bogie, and Peter Miu. *Basel II Implementation: A Guide to Developing and Validating a Compliant, Internal Risk Rating System*. New York: McGraw-Hill Professional, 2008.

Websites:

Basel 2 implementation—Approaches and challenges: www.basel2implementation.com
Basel II Compliance Professionals Association: www.basel-ii-association.com
Best practices for BIS II implementation: bis2information.org

See Also:

★ Risk Management: Beyond Compliance (pp. 510–513)
✔ Comparative and International Financial Regulation (p. 923)
✔ The EU Regulatory Regime (p. 1035)
✔ Principles of Financial Services Regulation (p. 1045)
The Basel Handbook: A Guide for Financial Practitioners (p. 1224)

"Economies of scale are giving way to economies of scope, finding the right size for synergy, market flexibility and, above all, speed." John Naisbitt

  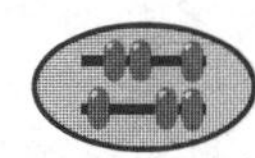   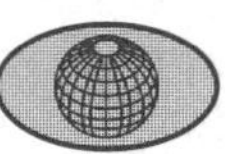   

Calculating Your Total Economic Capital

DEFINITION

Economic capital is the amount of risk capital that a company must have to cover any risks it is facing, such as operational risk, credit risk, or market risk. The amount held is that needed to ensure the business could overcome a worst-case scenario and still survive. Economic capital must be realistically estimated to manage the risks and to budget the costs of regulatory capital that needs to be maintained across the different divisions of the company. It is not the same as regulatory capital, which is a mandatory sum that a company must hold. The sum is determined by the regulators. Financial services should aspire to ensure the amount of risk capital they hold is at least equal to their economic capital.

Economic capital is calculated by determining the amount of capital that a company must have at its disposal to ensure it remains solvent over a defined period of time, taking into account the probability of any risks actually occurring. Thus, economic capital is usually calculated as the value-at-risk (VaR), where VaR is defined as the tipping point for the probability of a mark-to-market loss on the business within the predetermined timeframe, assuming the markets are stable and no trading has occurred. There is no universally accepted method for calculating economic capital.

The full economic scenario (FES) method is an approach that takes into account all possible risks for a company, and is useful where the main goal is to determine the economic capital for all the combined risks. However, the FES approach does not allocate any explicit amount of economic capital to any particular risk. It is calculated by applying a set of economic scenarios to all divisions of the company, then applying assumptions for each scenario. These assumptions usually include interest, equity returns, inflation, defaults, and actual versus expected claims for various products.

ADVANTAGES

- A one year mark-to-market, stress-testing approach to calculating economic capital is probably the easiest and fastest way to quantify a company's risk exposure and achieve quantifiable business benefits.

DISADVANTAGES

- Combining results that have been derived over different time horizons, even where they have been calculated consistently, can present difficulties as it allows risks in one timeframe period to be hedged against other risks in a different timeframe, which may be unjustifiable.

ACTION CHECKLIST

- ✔ First calculate the potential losses for each risk category. The more detailed the calculation, the better, but you may find that you do not have sufficient data to do more than a simple assessment.
- ✔ Next determine the probability and severity of such losses. Use a VaR model for market price risks and self-assessment for operational and strategic risk to generate the possible losses and their distribution across the business. Allow for worst-case scenarios when determining how severe losses could theoretically be.
- ✔ Consider using scenario analysis to determine the risk probabilities of infrequent but severe events, as these are hard to calculate within economic capital.

DOS AND DON'TS

DO

- Remember that the use of economic capital as an internal model for capital adequacy has been driven by regulatory requirements, particularly the Solvency II proposals, which introduce a comprehensive risk management framework for defining required capital levels, and implementing procedures to identify, measure, and manage risk levels.

DON'T

- Don't forget that strategic risks are not usually calculated when determining economic capital, as it makes no sense to calculate a capital charge for this unless a suitable modeling method is used that considers the benefits of the strategic options.

▸▸ MORE INFO

Books:

Porteous, Bruce T., and Tapadar Pradip. *Economic Capital and Financial Risk Management for Financial Services Firms and Conglomerates*. Basingstoke, UK: Palgrave Macmillan, 2005.

van Lelyveld, Iman (ed). *Economic Capital Modelling: Concepts, Measurement and Implementation*. London: Risk Books, 2006.

See Also:

★ Booms, Busts, and How to Navigate Troubled Waters (pp. 286–288)
★ Understanding the Role of Diversification (pp. 380–381)
✔ Measuring Financial Health (p. 874)
✔ Understanding and Calculating RORAC, RAROC, and RARORAC (p. 1006)
✔ Understanding Asset–Liability Management (Full Balance Sheet Approach) (p. 889)

"The mode of production of material life conditions the general process of social, political and spiritual life... changes in the economic foundation lead sooner or later to the transformation of the whole immense superstructure." Karl Marx

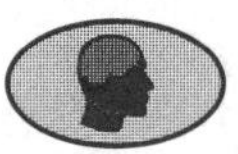

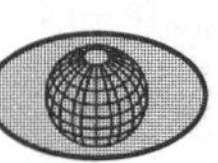

Captive Insurance Companies: How to Reduce Your Costs

DEFINITION

Captive insurance companies are insurance companies that have the specific objective of financing risks from a parent group or its customers. The process is a risk management technique—a company forms its own insurance company subsidiary to finance its retained losses. Captives are of interest to companies when they find that their insurance premiums have risen significantly as they can reduce costs. In addition, companies can gain greater control by owning their own insurance company.

Creating a captive offers a self-financing option for buying insurance. The captive either holds onto the risk of providing insurance or can pay reinsurers to take the risk. Captives are usually based in a country that has a favorable tax regime with more relaxed controls. When a company uses captive insurance, the money buys a service and is invested with a good possibility of a return. Cost savings can be realized through reduced overheads, allowing a larger percentage of the premium to be used for claims payments.

Captives also give access to the reinsurance market, which operates on a lower cost structure than other direct insurers, and there is the potential to earn investment income on unpaid loss reserves.

There are several types of insurance captive:

- *Single-parent captive*: An insurance or reinsurance company formed primarily to insure the risks of its parent or affiliate.
- *Association captive*: Owned by a trade, industry, or service group for the benefit of its members.
- *Group captive*: Jointly owned by a number of companies to provide a vehicle to meet a common insurance need.
- *Agency captive*: Owned by an insurance agency or brokerage firm for the purpose of reinsuring a portion of their clients' risks.
- *Rent-a-captive*: Providing captive facilities, for a fee, to others—often companies that are too small to establish their own captive.
- *Special purpose vehicle/company*: Mostly used for catastrophe bonds and reinsurance "sidecars". They may be formed as a rent-a-captive facility to enable companies that do not have a sufficient volume of insurance premiums to access many of the benefits associated with an offshore captive.

Offshore captive insurers are often more attractive because they enjoy lower tax rates on investment and underwriting income, resulting in reduced expected tax payments. Captives give noninsurers access to reinsurance markets that were previously only accessible to commercial insurance companies. The reasons for creating a captive insurance company are varied, but it may be that the external insurers are charging too much, or that the required coverage is unavailable.

ADVANTAGES

- Premiums paid to a captive insurance company are tax-deductible.
- Insurance can be obtained through the international reinsurance market at a more favorable premium.
- Investment returns can be obtained directly on the invested capital.
- The types of risk that a captive can underwrite include damage to property, public and product liability, professional indemnity, employee benefits, employer's liability, and motor and medical aid expenses. Risks that may be uninsurable or cost-prohibitive can be included.
- Additionally, the parent company's entire family can benefit from group funding of a captive through consolidation of coverage, centralized administrative support, and a significant reduction in insurance expenses.

DISADVANTAGES

- A substantial amount of capital is initially required to ensure that the captive remains financially healthy.
- Third-party dependency on service providers.
- Inadequate loss reserves where actual losses exceed initially expected levels and additional funds need to be allocated. Such a situation could disguise risks to the parent company.
- Reduced availability of other insurance facilities.

ACTION CHECKLIST

- ✔ Create an insurance program based on the needs of your company.
- ✔ Exercise greater control over your cover because you do not have to choose a standard offer from the commercial market.
- ✔ Keep a clean loss record so that premiums do not increase.

DOS AND DON'TS

DO

- Stabilize the cost of insurance and determine your premiums by your company's own loss experience, not by an industry-wide standard.
- Obtain more competitive wholesale quotes from primary insurers.
- Maximize the yield on the portfolio.
- Structure the maturities to meet your cash flow requirements.

DON'T

- Don't cut corners to save costs.
- Don't assume that your company is too small for captive insurance.
- Don't forget to look at renting rather than buying a captive insurance facility.

▸▸ MORE INFO

Books:

Bawcutt, Paul A. *Captive Insurance Companies: Establishment, Operation, and Management*. 4th ed. London: Witherby, 1997.

Klingenschmid, Florian. *Captive Insurance Companies in Risk Management*. Saarbrücken, Germany: VDM Verlag, 2008.

See Also:

✔ Corporate Insurance Cover: A Primer (p. 979)
✔ Understanding the Components of an Insurance Contract (p. 934)
Insurance (pp. 1520–1521)

"So far as power is concerned, does anyone believe the premiums of insurance companies are all almost uniform by accident?" Jimmy Hoffa

  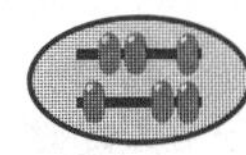   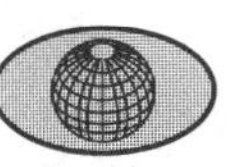   

Comparative and International Financial Regulation

DEFINITION

As financial services has become a global industry, regulators and compliance officers increasingly need to be aware of the regulations—at least on a general level—in other major financial centers, and the broad principles of those regulations. This gives them a context in which to interpret rules and underlying regulatory concepts elsewhere.

Comparative views with other regulatory systems enable regulators to develop a more subjective approach to their own and other systems of regulation. If other financial centers have developed different principles and rules: Why is this? What are their objectives? Could they be integrated at home? How can varying rules be met in different centers?

The current trend is for policies to be developed by international groups, so any regulator taking part in such discussions must have a solid understanding of international principles of regulation, cooperation, and enforcement.

The financial crisis of 2008/09, which had its roots in the 2007 US subprime mortgage crisis, has revealed that current regulation falls well short of what is required to maintain a coherent and stable financial system in individual countries, and around the world. The challenge now is to come up with new rules and new or modified institutions that will reduce systemic risks, yet still allow innovation and keep unnecessary burdens to a minimum.

The speed of change in financial markets has accelerated, with the development of new trading strategies and new products, linking assets, markets, and currencies in new ways around the world, and this has created new risks. Thus, all regulators need to understand the problems and management of systemic risk. Measuring systemic risk requires better information, which, in turn, necessitates the review of company transparency, disclosure and reporting, and data collection from more institutions. The rules themselves must be improved to reduce systemic risk, and there needs to be improvements in the robustness of the financial infrastructure.

Regulators need to increase the levels of international communication and cooperation with other regulatory organizations. International groups include the Basel Committee on Banking Supervision, the International Organization of Securities Commissions, and the International Association of Insurance Supervisors. Standards developed in international forums must be backed by economic analysis to achieve the best regulations. Global standards from these groups are adapted and applied to local markets.

What the financial crisis of 2008/09 showed beyond any doubt is that the financial system is truly global. No large economy was immune to the problems. How could subprime mortgage failure in the United States cause a worldwide economic collapse? The question is rhetorical, but, whatever the answer, the fact remains that it did. No national regulator could have avoided the crisis, even if it had foreseen it. Therefore, it is evident that the financial situation in one country is driven by what happens in others, and it follows that the financial regulations of one country can affect all others. This has underlined the need for far greater coordination among regulators on a global basis in order to avert future worldwide economic disasters.

▸▸ MORE INFO

Books:

Davies, Howard, and David Green. *Global Financial Regulation: The Essential Guide*. Cambridge, UK: Polity, 2008.

Goodhart, Charles, Philipp Hartmann, David T. Llewellyn, Liliana Rojas-Suarez, and Steven Weisbrod. *Financial Regulation: Why, How and Where Now?* London: Routledge, 1998.

Gray, Joanna, and Jenny Hamilton. *Implementing Financial Regulation: Theory and Practice*. Chichester, UK: Wiley, 2006.

Journals:

Financial Regulation International.

Journal of Financial Regulation and Compliance.

See Also:

★ Viewpoint: Sir John Stuttard (pp. 707–708)
✔ The EU Regulatory Regime (p. 1035)
✔ Middle East: Regulatory Structure and Powers (p. 1041)
✔ Principles of Financial Services Regulation (p. 1045)
The Global Financial System: A Functional Perspective (p. 1269)

  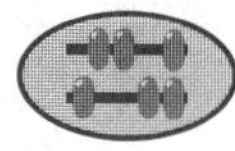   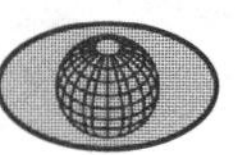   

Derivatives Markets: Their Structure and Function

DEFINITION

Derivatives markets attract three main types of participants: hedgers, speculators, and arbitrageurs. Hedgers reduce the risk that they face in terms of asset prices by using futures or options markets. Speculators focus on future price movements, for which futures and options contracts provide them with extra leverage. Such investors speculate on potential gains and losses and help to make the market more liquid. Arbitrageurs, on the other hand, take advantage of price differences in different markets. For example, they use the discrepancy between cash prices and future prices to make a profit.

The derivatives market can be seen as providing a number of economic benefits. Being speculative in nature, it provides the investor with a perception of the market not only in terms of current prices, but also in terms of the future. A further function is that derivatives markets transfer risks from those who have no appetite for them to those who do. Finally, the underlying cash market enjoys higher trading volumes from more players as a result of risk mitigation.

ADVANTAGES

- The derivatives market is a thoroughly exciting one for certain types of investor. It attracts creative, educated, vibrant, and intelligent investors who make optimal use of the opportunities offered and transfer their enthusiasm to new entrants as well. This perpetuates the entrepreneurial spirit within the economy, and not only creates better and new products but also has a positive effect on the job market.
- Importantly, derivatives markets can be extremely beneficial for both individuals and the overall economy of a country. Entrepreneurial players are energized to create new businesses, products, and concomitant employment opportunities from the profits they make from the derivatives markets. In addition, derivatives markets then also increase savings and long-term investment through the risk-transferring function. In this way, participants in the market can expand the volume of their activity as a result of the wide variety of choices available.

DISADVANTAGES

- The main disadvantage of the derivatives markets arises from the lack of thorough investigation into how to use the risk transfer factor. This can result in difficulty when trying to margin transactions, or to monitor various participants' activities and tailor one's own activity accordingly.
- A lack of thorough research and sound investment may lead to investment losses for which the investor is not prepared. The risk transfer factor therefore needs to be applied in a targeted way in order to ensure that the investor does not take unnecessary risks.
- Several risks may be involved for those who are not thoroughly familiar with speculative markets. Even though risks can be transferred, remember that the derivatives market operates on a paradigm of uncertainty. An investor who is not comfortable with uncertainty in investment might be more comfortable taking on a different type of investment structure.

ACTION CHECKLIST

- ✔ Make sure you have thoroughly investigated your company's ability to take risks and absorb possible losses if you decide to participate in the derivatives market.
- ✔ You must be comfortable with a significant element of speculation.
- ✔ Seek advice and guidance from the relevant professional experts.

DOS AND DON'TS

DO

- Investigate your options in this market thoroughly.
- Ensure that you are fully aware of the risks you will be taking, and of what level of risk you are comfortable with.
- Make an informed choice, particularly where risk is concerned.
- Make sure that you continually review your risk level and modify it if and when necessary.

DON'T

- Don't take unnecessary risks.
- Don't forget to check regularly that you are not exceeding the risk level at which you are comfortable.
- Don't approach the derivatives market with a careless attitude. Make sure that you are always aware of trends and speculations in the market.
- Don't invest if you are not completely comfortable with participating in a speculative market.

▸▸ MORE INFO

Books:

Marthinsen, John. *Risk Takers: Uses and Abuses of Financial Derivatives*. 2nd ed. Boston, MA: Prentice Hall, 2008.

McDonald, Robert L. *Derivatives Markets*. 2nd ed. Boston, MA: Addison-Wesley, 2006.

Taylor, Francesca. *Mastering Derivatives Markets: A Step-by-Step Guide to the Products, Applications and Risks*. 3rd ed. Harlow: Pearson Education, 2007.

See Also:

★ Using Structured Products to Manage Liabilities (pp. 106–108)

★ Viewpoint: Leigh Skene (pp. 238–241)

✔ Swaps, Options, and Futures: What They Are and Their Function (p. 882)

✔ Understanding and Using Currency Swaps (p. 885)

🌐 Banking and Financial Services (pp. 1500–1502)

"When I was young, people called me a gambler. As the scale of my operations increased I became known as a speculator. Now I am called a banker. But I have been doing the same thing all the time." Sir Ernest Cassel

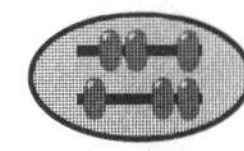
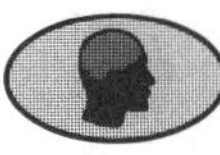

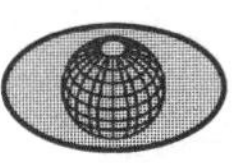

Insolvency/Bankruptcy Regulations in Major Regions

DEFINITION

An individual or legal entity is considered insolvent if he/she/it is unable to pay debts when they are due.

Insolvency procedures differ around the world, but all of them allow debtors to find a solution to their indebtedness and protect them from creditors.

In the United Kingdom, the bankruptcy procedures available to an individual depend on the amount of money that individual owes. If the debts are less than £5,000, an administration order can be obtained. The order is issued by the local county court, which administers the debts. The effect is that the creditors cannot take any legal action against the individual. If the debts are over £5,000 but under £15,000, a debt management plan (DMP) could be suitable if the individual can pay all his/her debts within a five-year period. If an individual has assets to protect or is restricted by his/her employment from bankruptcy, has more than three creditors and debts over £15,000, and can afford to pay £200 per month, an individual voluntary arrangement (IVA) might be appropriate. This is, however, expensive.

Declaring oneself bankrupt is only suitable for someone who has no assets to worry about. Bankruptcy gives that individual the right to protect himself from a crippling level of debt. If there are any assets, they transfer to a trustee, who will administer them and pay off creditors. The debt will be written off, but control of the individual's outgoings and earnings will be in the hands of the trustee. Once declared bankrupt, an individual will find it very difficult to find credit, and his or her reputation will be tarnished.

In the United States, bankruptcy is regulated by the Bankruptcy Code, which was enacted in 1978. This is also known as Title 11 of the United States Code and is recognized as the federal law that governs all bankruptcy cases. Each US district has a bankruptcy court, which deals with the bankruptcy procedure. The court's decisions are made by a bankruptcy judge.

The purpose of bankruptcy is to obtain a bankruptcy discharge, which will release the debtor from personal liability for specific debts and prohibits any creditor from taking action to collect those debts. In the United States there are six types of bankruptcy case, which are known by the numbers of the chapters that apply to them: Chapters 7, 9, 11, 12, 13, and 15.

Chapter 7 covers liquidation, a court-supervised procedure in which a trustee is appointed to take over the assets of a debtor's estate, transform them into cash, and distribute this cash to creditors. Chapters 9 and 11 deal with reorganization, which is used by companies that intend to continue their business while repaying creditors through a court-approved reorganization plan. Chapter 9 deals with indebted municipalities. Chapters 12 and 13 cover the adjustment of debts of an individual with a regular income. The individual can keep his/her main assets, such as a house, and repay debt over a three- to five-year period. The procedure under Chapter 12 applies to farmers or fishermen. Chapter 15 deals with cross-border cases of insolvency.

ADVANTAGES

- Insolvency and bankruptcy regulations protect debtors by allowing them to schedule payment of their debt.
- The regulations prevent a company or individual from acquiring irresponsible and unlimited debt and allow creditors to take charge of the future of an indebted business.

DISADVANTAGES

- Insolvency and bankruptcy regulations are very complex.
- Specialist financial and legal advice is always required when someone is declared bankrupt or insolvent.
- Insolvency and bankruptcy should be used as a last resort and not as a shield or an escape from debt or responsibility to creditors.
- Once declared bankrupt or insolvent, an individual or entity will find it very difficult to obtain credit. Their credit record will be damaged and their credibility undermined.

DOS AND DON'TS

DO

- Carefully weigh up the implications of declaring yourself or a business bankrupt or insolvent. Understand that the consequences can be very serious. Your creditworthiness, reputation, and future can be put in jeopardy.
- Obtain relevant legal and financial advice on any decision to declare yourself bankrupt or the business insolvent.
- Research the consequences carefully before making a decision.

DON'T

- Don't underestimate the need for proper research and professional advice.
- Don't use bankruptcy and insolvency as an escape. It could influence your financial and business dealings for the rest of your life.

▸▸ MORE INFO

Books:

Blum, Brian A. *Bankruptcy and Debtor/Creditor: Examples and Explanations*. 4th ed. New York: Aspen Publishers, 2006.

Israel, J. *European Cross-Border Insolvency Regulation*. Antwerp, Belgium: Intersentia Publishers, 2005.

Article:

Parker, Susan, Gary F. Peters, and Howard F. Turetsky. "Corporate governance and corporate failure: A survival analysis." *Corporate Governance* 2:2 (2002): 4–12.

Websites:

American Bankruptcy Institute: www.abiworld.org
California Bankruptcy Forum: www.calbf.org

See Also:

✔ Comparative and International Financial Regulation (p. 923)
✔ International Comparisons of Company Law (p. 991)
✔ Managing Bankruptcy and Insolvency (p. 997)

"Capitalism without bankruptcy is like Christianity without hell." Frank Borman

  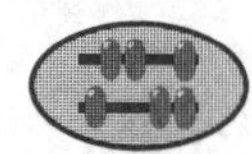   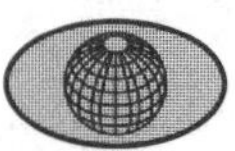   

The Interbank Market: Its Structure and Function

DEFINITION

The interbank market is the market on which individual banks conduct transactions among themselves. It consists primarily of commercial and investment banks that buy and sell currencies. They are obliged to establish set rules and clearly defined lines of credit between themselves before they can trade. The interbank market has the greatest monopoly of all trading, both commercial and speculative. Members can influence supply and demand, and their trading activities can alter the exchange rates at any time. They have most power selling in the foreign currency exchange market.

These banks trade on their customers' behalf, but their other important purpose is to make profits for themselves. They have at their fingertips specialist knowledge and awareness of the market, as well as the skills required to keep an eye on the activities of their co-participants in the market.

Since the early 1980s there have been many important developments in the interbank market. The introduction of Reuters' electronic brokerage system, known as the Monitor Dealing Service, followed by its Dealing 2000-1 system in 1989, are examples. However, the market was entirely transformed by the introduction of Reuters' Dealing 2000-3 system in 1992 and the subsequent launch by FX market-making banks of the Electronic Broking Services (EBS) system, which made possible the automatic matching of quotes from dealers. Since the introduction of electronic systems, dealers have been able to conduct a number of trades simultaneously and can achieve a greater level of efficiency in doing so, along with tighter spreads and lower costs. There is a consequent greater level of transparency, and a greater number of players can now operate alongside the commercial and investment banks.

EBS and Reuters D2/Dealing 3000 are direct competitors—a trader's choice of which system they will use usually depends on the currencies they need to trade. EBS is standard for matching euros, US dollars, yen and Swiss francs with each other, whereas D2 is generally used for all other currency pairings.

ADVANTAGES

- The close interbank relationships described above are valuable in that they give all members access to the cooperating institutions within a relationship. Their combined expertise serves as a useful role model for other lenders, who are monitored by those banks. The interbank system also enables the smaller, less powerful banks to be monitored with regard to their levels of market discipline and compliance.
- Competition between the member banks ensures that there are tight spreads and fair pricing. For individual investors this is the source of their price quotes as the interbank market is dominated by larger players: customers are the large mutual and hedge funds and the big multinational corporations.
- All the member banks can see the best market rates.

DISADVANTAGES

- Smaller banks suffer restrictions in dealing with the larger banks and as a result have less favorable pricing available to them. It is even worse for individual investors, who cannot access the interbank market at all. The lowest quote that banks are able to give is between US$10 million and US$100 million. This means that individuals have to rely on online market-makers for their pricing, which may not be very competitive. Only the big players with plenty of capital really benefit from the interbank market.

ACTION CHECKLIST

✔ Do your homework diligently, accessing as much help as you can in securing as good pricing as possible.

✔ Seek the advice of a skilled financial expert.

DOS AND DON'TS

DO

- Take utmost care with your choice of interbank broker, especially for foreign exchange transactions.
- Be diligent and persevere in obtaining the best deal possible with your broker.

DON'T

- Don't rush into a transaction.
- Don't give in to persuasive selling by your broker.

›› MORE INFO

Book:

Boele, Georgette. *Strategic Market Analysis: EUR/USD Interbank Market as Diversified Organization*. Massapequa, NY: Alan Guinn, 2002.

See Also:

✔ The Foreign Exchange Market: Its Structure and Function (p. 861)
✔ Hedging Foreign Exchange Risk— Case Studies and Strategies (p. 863)
✔ Understanding and Using Carry Trades (p. 884)
✔ Understanding and Using Currency Swaps (p. 885)

"A state without the means of some change is without the means of its conservation." Edmund Burke

  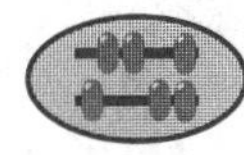   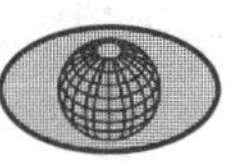   

Key Islamic Banking Instruments and How They Work

DEFINITION

The need to fully conform to *shariah* law has created both challenges and opportunities for financial institutions aiming to serve their growing Muslim client base. Requirements that money cannot be used for the purposes of making money (effectively forbidding the charging of interest), and the need for investments to deliver some form of collective or community benefit, have necessitated a high degree of innovation from Islamic financial institutions to develop a range of new products for customers seeking full compliance with *shariah* law.

Among the leading Islamic banking products are:

Murabaha

A kind of "cost-plus" transaction in which the bank buys the asset then immediately sells it to the customer at a pre-agreed higher price payable by installments. This price is set at a level that takes account of the time value of money until the customer's monthly payments cover the bank's selling price, less any deposit paid. This facility is often used in the way that mainstream banking customers might seek a mortgage when buying property.

Bai Salam

A kind of forward sales contract which requires the buyer to pay in advance for goods that are to be supplied later. *bai salam* contracts are often used in manufacturing; a buyer would expect to receive a more attractive price when paying in advance with funds that can be used in the meantime by the producer.

Istisna

Istisna, another form of forward sales contract, is a longer-term financing mechanism under which a price is agreed before the asset described in the agreement is actually built. Sellers can then either create the asset themselves or subcontract, with buyers also having the option of paying the entire sum due either in advance or as installments during the manufacturing process. *istisna*, meaning "asking someone to manufacture" in Arabic, is a common form of financing in the construction industry.

Ijara

A form of *shariah* law-compliant leasing involving the rights over the use of an asset under which the bank buys the asset then leases it to the customer over a fixed period in return for a pre-agreed monthly price. Provisions can be made for the customer to buy the asset at the end of the agreed period. Thought needs to be given to issues such as the provision of insurance, as the asset is effectively owned by the bank during the lease period.

Mudaraba

A form of investment partnership between a bank and a business that shares the risk and losses/profits between both parties at pre-agreed levels. A *mudaraba* transaction, bringing some of the benefits of a business loan to *shariah*-compliant business customers, effectively requires the bank to take a stake in the business, with clients investing their time and expertise in running the enterprise.

ADVANTAGES

- Islamic banking instruments permit Muslims to benefit from a growing range of financial products in compliance with *shariah* law.
- Some products require a partnership between the client and the bank, encouraging both parties to take a longer-term view.
- Islamic banking dictates that transactions should serve to provide some form of benefit to the community at large, rather than setting pure profit as the aim.

DISADVANTAGES

- With some financial aspects of *shariah* law open to interpretation, some instruments may be offered by some institutions, but not by others.
- Some non-Muslim clients could find that the conditions imposed by Islamic banks prevent them from taking advantage of shorter-term opportunities.

ACTION CHECKLIST

✔ When entering into leasing-style arrangements, ensure that all "grey" areas are covered by the agreement, such as the insurance and maintenance costs of the asset.

✔ Islamic banking is by definition more stable than conventional mainstream banking in that it outlaws involvement in speculation or short-term industry "trends." However, clients must ensure that they are committed to operating within the boundaries set by *shariah* law before using Islamic banking services.

DOS AND DON'TS

DO

- Appreciate that the stability of the Islamic banking sector can come at the price of a slower pace of product innovation.
- Recognize that the rapid growth in Islamic banking globally could present an attractive source of funds for businesses prepared to make a long-term commitment to operation under *shariah* principles.

DON'T

- Don't ignore the aim of Islamic banking to bring a wider benefit to society.
- Don't see Islamic banking institutions as financial services providers for Muslims only; such banks can be valuable long-term commercial partners for a range of individuals and companies.

▸▸ MORE INFO

Book:

Iqbal, Munawar. *A Guide to Islamic Finance*. London: Risk Books, 2007.

Articles:

Patel, Ebrahim. "Fundamentals of Islamic finance." *Accountancy SA* (August 2006).

Wilson, Scott B. "Islamic finance: Origins, emergence and future title." *Illinois Business Law Journal* (September 2007).

Website:

Institute of Islamic Banking and Insurance: www.islamic-banking.com

  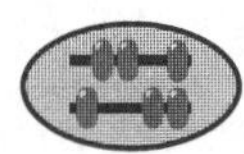   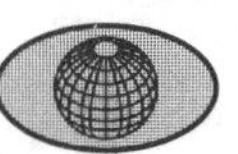   

Key Principles of Islamic Finance

DEFINITION

The principles of Islamic law derive from interpretations of two sources: the Qur'an and the Sunna. The central pillars of Islamic finance are that wealth must be generated from legitimate trade and asset-based investment, while the use of money for the purposes of making money is expressly forbidden. Crucially, the latter means that Islamic finance does not permit the charging or paying of interest (*riba*). Under Islamic principles, investment must also have a social and an ethical benefit to wider society, with short-term speculative investments (known as *masir*) strictly forbidden. Islamic finance also prohibits investment in sectors classified as inappropriate on moral grounds by *shariah* law. These include industries involving alcohol, gambling, or drugs, but can extend well beyond these narrow boundaries. Each Islamic bank's adherence to the principles of *shariah* law is governed by its own *shariah* board, a body charged with the responsibility of overseeing all processes of the bank. While some aspects of *shariah* law may be subject to individual interpretation, the board also has the responsibility to decide which proposed deals are acceptable to the bank on *shariah* grounds, and which are not.

Given that Islamic finance forbids the charging of interest, banks must earn their profits through the provision of fee-based services, or through a kind of partnership with clients in which both the risk and the profits or losses are shared between the bank and the customer, according to pre-agreed conditions. Such arrangements typically allow the client to draw a salary from the business, which is then deducted from profits. *Shariah* law also permits a range of leasing-style agreements under which the bank can buy an asset on behalf of a customer, then charge a regular, pre-agreed rental fee. As in mainstream Western banking, these agreements can be fixed-term operating leases or lease purchases, with the latter obliging the client to buy the asset at the end of the period, at a predetermined price. While some leasing arrangements can be relatively straightforward, others can become more complex, depending on how the asset is originally purchased by the bank. Given that Islamic finance does not permit the charging of interest, a bank originally buying the asset on the basis of a variable interest rate may seek an arrangement by which the rental charge is increased, to effectively compensate any increase it faces in financing costs. However, some *shariah* boards may refuse to sanction such agreements, potentially leaving the bank with exposure to interest rate risk.

ADVANTAGES

- Islamic finance provides a basis for commercial transactions for followers of Islam to enter into, which would be impossible on conventional banking terms.
- The adoption of Islamic finance principles gives banks access to a substantial new customer base.
- The partnership basis on which some Islamic businesses are established with banks ensures that the bank has a direct stake in the success of the venture.
- The rejection of deals involving short-term, speculative activity encourages businesses to invest for the longer term.
- Islamic finance contracts offer flexibility in terms of the applicable legal jurisdiction.

DISADVANTAGES

- Some financial aspects of *shariah* law can be open to interpretation, with the result that some Islamic banks may agree transactions that would be rejected by other banks.
- These "grey" areas, resulting from inconsistencies in interpretation, can create more uncertainty for clients than under conventional banking arrangements.
- Some leasing arrangements can become appreciably more complicated when trying to ensure conformity to Islamic principles.
- Given that the banks are the legal owners of assets under rental or leasing agreements with clients, issues such as liability for insurance and risk can be complications.

ACTION CHECKLIST

- ✔ Non-Muslims should consider how Islamic finance can provide them with access to financial backing from those seeking *shariah*-compliant funds.
- ✔ As more institutions launch products compliant with Shari'ah principles, investors should take time to assess their best choice of potential banking partners.
- ✔ Understand that adherence to interpretations of Islamic principles can create complications over the medium term.

DOS AND DON'TS

DO

- Recognize that the ethical considerations and long-term partnership advantages offered by Islamic finance can come with the price of greater complexity and uncertainty.
- Take professional advice as to the tax treatment of Islamic finance transactions within your particular jurisdiction.
- Appreciate that the prohibition of activities perceived as speculative could limit the business's scope to capitalize on potentially lucrative short-term opportunities.

DON'T

- Don't regard Islamic finance as purely "specialty" banking; the market is fast becoming mainstream with a rapidly expanding range of products available.
- Don't look at Islamic banking in isolation, as deals can be structured with a combination of conventional and *shariah*-compliant finance.

▸▸ MORE INFO

Articles:

Dar, Humayon A., and John R. Presley. "Islamic finance: A Western perspective." *International Journal of Islamic Financial Services* 1:1 (April 1999).

Wilson, Rodney. "An introduction to Islamic finance." *Journal of Islamic Studies* 14:1 (2003).

Websites:

International Institute of Islamic Finance, Inc.: www.iiif-inc.com

Islamic Financial Services Board: www.ifsb.org

"There can be no major change in a complex organization unless there are both sufficient resources and substantial readiness." Robert H. Miles

  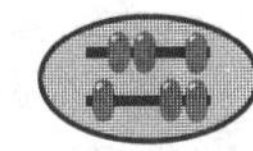   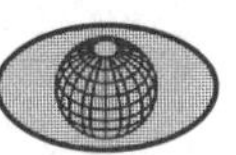   

Merchant Banks: Their Structure and Function

DEFINITION

Merchant banks, also known as investment banks, offer various services in international finance and long-term loans for wealthy individuals, multinational corporations, and governments.

An investment bank is split into the so-called front, middle, and back office functions. The front office deals with investment banking and management, sales and trading, structured products, private equity investment, research, and strategy. The middle office deals with risk management, finance, and compliance. The back office deals with transactions, operations, and technology.

The main function of a merchant bank is to buy and sell financial products. They manage risk through proprietary trading, carried out by special traders who do not interface with clients. The trader manages the risk for the principal after they buy or sell a product to a client but does not hedge their total exposure. Banks also try to maximize the profitability of certain risk on their balance sheets.

Merchant banks manage debt and equity offerings. They assist companies in raising funds from the market. This can include designing instruments, pricing issues, registering offer documents, underwriting support, issue marketing, allotment and refund, and stock exchange listing. They also help in distributing securities such as equity shares, mutual fund products, debt instruments, insurance products, and fixed deposits among others. Merchant banks use a mix of institutional networks—mutual funds, foreign institutional investors, pension funds, private equity funds, and financial institutions—and retail networks, depending on how they interact with specific clients.

Merchant banks offer corporate advisery services to clients for their financial problems. Advice may be sought in such areas as determining the right debt-to-equity ratio, the gearing ratio, and the appropriate capital structure. Other areas of advice may be in areas of refinancing and seeking sources of cheaper funds, risk management, and hedging strategies. Further areas for advice are rehabilitation and turnaround management. Merchant bankers may design a revival package in conjunction with other financial institutions.

Merchant bankers assist clients with project advice, helping them from the project concept stage, through feasibility studies to examine a project's viability, to the preparation of documents such as a detailed project report.

Merchant banks arrange loan syndication for their clients. This begins with an analysis of the client's cash flow patterns, helping to determine the terms for borrowing. The merchant bank then prepares a detailed loan memorandum to be circulated to the banks and financial institutions that are to join the syndicate. Finally, the terms of lending are negotiated for the final allocation.

Merchant banks provide venture capital and mezzanine financing (a hybrid of debt and equity financing that is typically used to finance the expansion of existing companies). In this way they can help companies to finance new and innovative ventures.

Following the global financial crisis of 2008, which saw the collapse of several prominent investment banks in Europe and the United States in September of that year, the viability of using a business model that is based heavily on banks purchasing each others' debts has been severely questioned. Certainly in the United States, the view is that this business model is no longer sustainable and is unlikely to continue in the same form in the future. It remains to be seen how merchant banks will restructure in the aftermath of the financial turbulence of 2008.

ADVANTAGES

- Merchant banks perform functions that cannot be carried out by businesses on their own.
- Merchant banks have access to traders, financial institutions, and markets that companies or individuals could not possibly reach.
- By using their skills and contacts, merchant banks can get the best possible deals for their clients.

DISADVANTAGES

- Merchant banks are really only for large corporate customers, or extremely wealthy smaller businesses owned by individual clients.
- Not all deals carried out by merchant banks meet with unqualified success.
- There is always risk attached to the kinds of deal that merchant banks undertake.

ACTION CHECKLIST

✔ Shop around for a merchant bank.

✔ Understand what the bank is offering and make clear exactly what you expect it to do.

✔ Make sure that the results are fully monitored and reported back to you.

DOS AND DONT'S

DO

- Use a merchant bank with good standing and history.
- Use a merchant bank with a firm financial footing—especially in times of uncertainty about financial institutions.

DON'T

- Don't use a merchant bank if you are a small business.
- Don't use the first merchant bank you find.
- Don't go in blindly without understanding the risks involved.

➤➤ MORE INFO

Books:

Chapman, Stanley. *The Rise of Merchant Banking*. Economic History Series. London: Routledge, 2005.

Young, George Kennedy. *Merchant Banking: Practice and Prospects*. 2nd ed. London: Weidenfeld & Nicholson, 1971.

See Also:

★ Mergers and Acquisitions: Today's Catalyst is Working Capital (pp. 422–424)

✔ Acquiring a Company (p. 955)

Banking and Financial Services (pp. 1500–1502)

"They're just cold-blooded fish sitting at the top of some bloody great building looking at stats—and they've got handbooks." Peter de Savary

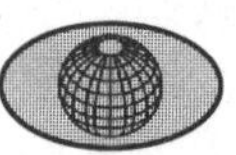

Retail Banks: Their Structure and Function

DEFINITION

Retail banks offer a range of services to individual customers and small businesses, rather than to large companies and other banks. The services can include current accounts, savings accounts, investment advice and broking, and loans and mortgages. Retail banks perform two crucial functions for customers: firstly, they enable customers to bank their money securely, access it easily, and conduct transactions; and secondly, they provide access to additional money to fund large purchases, such as buying a home. In return for holding customers' funds, which they can then invest, banks pay customers interest.

Traditionally, retail banks have provided these services directly to the customer via branches. While many still do this, retail banks now offer their services by telephone and the internet as well. Some operate solely via the internet and do not have facilities to serve customers at physical outlets. Other organizations, such as supermarkets, have now entered the banking sector and also offer a wide range of banking services.

It has become more difficult to identify the traditional retail bank—a bank that funds itself through customer deposits and lending—because retail banks now often combine retail and wholesale banking. It is therefore more relevant to today's banking structure to regard retail banking as a series of processes rather than as an institution.

The intermediation services offered by retail banks (such as looking after customers' money and making loans) and the payment services (allowing customers to make transactions using debit cards, checks, etc.) mean that they have to make funds available to customers at very short or immediate notice. This inevitably means that a retail bank has to manage the risk that more money will be requested by customers than it has available and of customers defaulting on loans. Banks do this by holding stocks of liquid assets, maintaining a cushion of capital, lending to different types of borrower, adjusting interest rates, and screening potential borrowers (credit scoring).

ADVANTAGES

- Your money is much more secure than in a box under your bed and you can buy goods, be paid, and sell things without cash changing hands.
- The bank you are familiar with and which knows you can also offer you a wide range of other services, such as mortgages and insurance. Your bank may be able to offer you competitive deals in return for your loyalty as a customer.
- Retail banks offer a variety of ways you can access your account and manage your money, most notably via internet banking. This means that you can keep a close eye on your finances and avert many potential problems.

DISADVANTAGES

- Banks are a business, and they need to make money from looking after yours. If the bank decides to apply charges to your account (within the terms of the account), you may only find out about it afterwards—for example if you accidentally go overdrawn without permission. If you disagree with a charge, you will need to contest it to recover the money.

ACTION CHECKLIST

- ✔ Think carefully about what you want from a bank account and what is important to you. For example, if you are not concerned about having face-to-face contact with your bank, an internet-only bank may suit you.
- ✔ When choosing an account, check the interest rate offered and how quickly and by what methods you can access your money.
- ✔ When looking for a current or checking account, find out what extra services the bank can offer you, such as a debit card, overdraft facility, free or cheap insurance policies, etc.
- ✔ Does the bank have local branches, or is it internet only? Are you comfortable with the ways in which you can communicate with the bank?
- ✔ Most importantly, find out what charges apply to various transactions and events, such as going overdrawn without the bank's approval.

DOS AND DON'TS

DO

- Compare different banks and their products and services.
- Look for added value, such as free insurance.
- Challenge charges you feel are unfair or wrongly applied to your account.
- Regularly review your savings accounts to make sure you continue to get the best interest rates available.

DON'T

- Don't let financial problems get out of control, and don't put off talking to your bank about them if they do.
- Don't be afraid to move to a new bank if you are not happy with your current one and if, via sound research, you have found something better. The bank you want to move to will be happy to take on the transfer arrangements for you.

▸▸ MORE INFO

Books:

Casu, Barbara, Claudia Girardone, and Philip Molyneux. *Introduction to Banking*. Harlow, UK: Pearson Education, 2006.

Heffernan, Shelagh. *Modern Banking*. 2nd ed. Chichester, UK: Wiley, 2004.

Pond, Keith. *Retail Banking*. London: Global Professional Publishing, 2007.

Websites:

Bank.org.uk reviews all UK banks: www.bank.org.uk

British Bankers' Association: www.bba.org.uk

US Federal Reserve: www.federalreserve.gov

US Treasury Comptroller of the Currency: www.comptrollerofthecurrency.gov

"I've come to the belief that banks are not in the business of banking. They're in the business of collecting fees." Patrick C. Kelly

  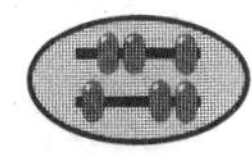   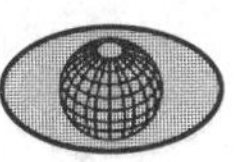   

The Role of the *Shariah* Advisery Board in Islamic Finance

DEFINITION

The *shariah* board is a key element of the structure of an Islamic financial institution, carrying the responsibility of ensuring that all products and services offered by that institution are fully compliant with the principles of *shariah* law. The role of the board also involves the reviewing and overseeing of all potential new product offerings. Additionally, the board may be called on to make a judgment on individual cases referred to it, relating to whether specific customer business requests are acceptable to the institution. Given that *shariah* law is derived from studies of both the Qur'an and the Sunna, inconsistencies can occur in the interpretations of precisely where the boundaries of compatibility lie, with the result that some *shariah* boards may deem unacceptable proposals that may be approved by other boards.

With demand for *shariah*-compliant financial services growing at a faster rate than mainstream banking, the board can also play a vital role in helping to develop new procedures and products to position the institution to adapt to industry trends, and customers' expectations. The board should also be closely involved in overseeing *shariah*-compliant training programs for employees. Board members also participate in the preparation of an annual investors' report on the bank's balance sheet, with particular reference to its compliance with *shariah* principles.

Given the importance of the role of the *shariah* boards in ensuring the conformity of the institution's offerings, boards typically include acknowledged experts, such as contemporary Islamic scholars. It is common for such scholars to sit on the *shariah* boards of multiple institutions; some senior scholars may sit on the boards of 15 or more institutions. The activities of individual boards are supervised by an independent body, the International Association of Islamic Bankers. This association's Supreme Religious Board examines the judgments, or *fatwas*, of individual *shariah* boards to ensure conformity to *shariah* law.

ADVANTAGES

- The board's role is well defined, in ensuring that the institution's activities are fully compliant with *shariah* law is its responsibility.
- Given the speed of change in the financial services industry, the board plays a vital role in advising the institution as to the feasibility of potential new products and services.
- *Shariah* audits can also be undertaken in conjunction with the board to give greater reassurance to customers.

DISADVANTAGES

- *Shariah* law is highly subject to interpretation, particularly in relation to its significance in the demand-driven financial services industry.
- Inconsistencies occur between different boards in their interpretations of what is and what is not permissible.
- Precedents are not binding in Islamic jurisdictions, with the result that personnel changes to a board may shift the balance of collective opinion over time.

ACTION CHECKLIST

- ✔ Some Islamic investors may seek reassurance that products and services which have been approved by *shariah* boards outside their own jurisdictions are truly compliant with their own *shariah*-compliant objectives.
- ✔ Given the complexity of some Islamic *sukuk* structures (the arrangements established to create the Islamic equivalent of a bond), it is important that *shariah* boards are given the considerable resources needed to ensure the true compliance of these instruments.

DOS AND DON'TS

DO

- Institutions must ensure that *shariah* boards have a high level of autonomy and independence, protecting them from commercial pressures.
- *Shariah* boards must be well resourced to ensure full compliance with both legal and religious requirements.

DON'T

- Don't expect every board member to be an expert on every aspect of Islamic finance. While *shariah* boards require a range of members with a diverse range of religious and financial knowledge, institutions should not expect individual board members to be experts in every aspect of their wide-ranging brief. However, board members with specialized knowledge of particular aspects can work very effectively on sub-boards related to particular initiatives or projects.
- Don't overlook the need to ensure that *shariah* board members are well informed about developments and trends in the global financial marketplace.

⏩ MORE INFO

Books:

Archer, Simon, and Rifaat Ahmed Abdel Karim. *Islamic Finance: The Regulatory Challenge*. Singapore: Wiley, 2007.

El-Gamal, Mahmoud A. *Islamic Finance*. Cambridge, UK: Cambridge University Press, 2006.

Articles:

Ahmed, El Waleed M. "A unified voice: The role of Shariah advisery boards in Islamic finance." *Business Islamica* (October 2007).

Ebrahim, M. Shahid, and A. El-Jelly. "Debt financing in Islam." *American Journal of Islamic Finance* 5:1 (1994): 11.

Websites:

Harvard Law School Islamic Legal Studies Program—Islamic Finance Project: www.hifip.harvard.edu

Islamic Financial Services Board: www.ifsb.org

"Thinking about change is a redundancy. All thinking is about change." Edgar "Bronfman, Jr."

     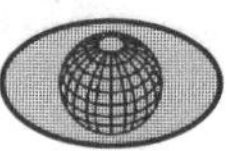   

Stress Testing to Evaluate Insurance Cover

DEFINITION

Stress testing aims to determine how well systems and procedures perform when subjected to a wide range of operational conditions. It is frequently employed to help assess performance during extreme or unexpected conditions. During stress testing, a system is subjected either to sudden extreme demands or to gradually higher loads until the point is reached when at least one element of the system stops delivering the desired level of performance. This evaluation helps companies to understand the kind of market conditions under which key elements of their businesses become vulnerable.

Although retail-focused insurance products have become more standardized in recent years, and are increasingly sold via the internet and call centres as consumers focus on price, the commercial insurance industry has retained a high level of complexity. This is largely driven by a broadening of the spectrum of risks faced by businesses in areas such as environmental protection, human resources, product safety, counterparty agreements, and technology. Given the wider range of risks that businesses face, partly as a result of tighter legislation and regulation, ensuring that the appropriate insurance is in place to provide robust protection against unexpected events has never been more important.

ADVANTAGES

- A better understanding of the risks—both systemic and non-systemic—facing a business can help in contingency planning.
- Regular stress testing can help to keep management vigilant in an environment of constantly changing business risks.
- This type of evaluation can identify multiple, seemingly minor chinks in the armor of a business that cumulatively could have a serious impact.
- What if? analysis can be useful in highlighting event risks that may not otherwise be immediately apparent.
- Robust financial protection can insulate businesses from the risk of a catastrophic event that could otherwise threaten the viability of the entity.

DISADVANTAGES

- Protracted evaluation over extended periods of time could divert key resources away from core business activities, potentially resulting in the business overlooking valuable opportunities.
- Extended periods of evaluation run the risk of "paralysis through analysis." Understanding the shortcomings of available options can be beneficial, but, taken to an extreme, it could be counterproductive.
- Under some circumstances, stress testing may even run the risk of effectively encouraging risky practices by creating a false sense of control.

ACTION CHECKLIST

- ✔ Encourage an environment of openness about the kinds of risk facing the business. Some risks are obvious, but more covert risks are sometimes known only to the managers of individual business units.
- ✔ Involve key business stakeholders in the evaluation of risks and alternative ways to protect against them.
- ✔ Consider how existing policies insure against multiple minor claims as well as more significant/catastrophic single incidents. Examine whether particular exclusion clauses could leave your business exposed to risks that you thought were covered.
- ✔ Do try to quantify in financial terms how falling foul of various risks could affect your business. Only once an actual liability figure is available can you expect an insurance provider to be able to provide a quotation to cover that risk.
- ✔ Be prepared to seek the advice of specialist insurance providers. The field of commercial insurance can be immensely more complex than its consumer equivalent, and risk consultants can help companies to understand and evaluate both risks and potential solutions. Industry-specific experts from specialist risk-management companies can help to devise custom solutions to protect against potential liabilities.

DOS AND DON'TS

DO

- Remember that emerging risks necessitate regular reviews of the way you protect your business.
- Involve key stakeholders in the evaluation of both risks and potential solutions.
- Consider seeking the help of specialist consultants.

DON'T

- Don't make the mistake of basing a decision purely on price. Commercial insurance is a highly complex field and insurance solutions are many and varied.
- Don't fall into the trap of thinking that insurance can cover absolutely every conceivable risk your business could face.
- Don't see the right insurance for your company as simply another expense. Securing the appropriate protection for your business can help you concentrate on doing what you do best.

▶▶ MORE INFO

Book:

Overbeck, Ludger, and Gerrit Jan van den Brink. *Integrated Stress Testing for Financial Institutions*. London: Palgrave Macmillan, 2009.

Article:

Hilbers, Paul, and Matthew T. Jones. "What If. . ?" *Finance & Development* 41:4 (December 2004).

Websites:

Risk consultancy and management companies: Willis: www.willis.com; Watson Wyatt: www.watsonwyatt.com

Society of Actuaries (includes downloadable pdf on `Effective Stress Testing' from presentation by Mark Chaplin, SOA Annual Meeting, Oct 2007): www.soa.org

     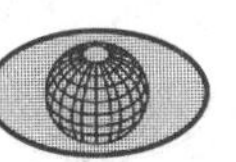   

Understanding and Calculating Probable Maximum Loss (PML)

DEFINITION

Probable maximum loss (PML) is a term chiefly used in the insurance industry. PML is the anticipated value of the biggest monetary loss affecting a business and/or a building that could result from a catastrophe, whether natural or otherwise, called for this purpose a "maximum credible event" (buildings are considered separately by insurers as the owner may be different from the owner(s) of any businesses contained therein). For example, the catastrophe could be a hurricane, floods, or other severe weather event, or other disaster that has a given probability of occurrence within a stated time period (such as the loss of a building and the value of the business contained therein as a result of fire). PML is usually expressed as a percentage of the total value, experienced by a structure or collection of structures when subjected to a maximum credible event. The PML is usually smaller than the maximum foreseeable loss (MFL), which assumes that all protective features fail, resulting in a complete write off. For example, in a fire this would include such things as failure of the sprinkler systems in the building. Underwriting decisions are typically influenced by the evaluation of the PML. The amount of reinsurance for a known risk is also normally based on the valuation of the PML. PML and MFL are both calculated as the percentage of a building or business that under normal conditions could be damaged or destroyed in a single event. The calculation takes into account variables such as construction of the building, susceptibility of the contents (including the value of any business), and protection measures. The MFL calculation also includes failures of key loss reduction systems in place (for example, sprinkler systems failing to activate in the case of a fire).

ADVANTAGES

- Consistent, accurate estimates of PML and MFL help to understand the extent of the risk involved, analyze the hazards and potential losses in order to manage them better, assess economic losses, determine the amount of reinsurance, and satisfy any reinsurance requirements.

DISADVANTAGES

- Calculating PML and paying for the resulting insurance may not be viable in geographic areas that are typically subject to natural disasters such as earthquakes or hurricanes. It may be cheaper, instead, to purchase business continuity insurance to cover for such losses caused by fire or other destruction.

ACTION CHECKLIST

✔ Carry out a risk assessment before calculating the PML, to reduce insurance costs. The information gleaned from this can be used to assist the insured to develop long-term strategies for risk reduction. Such strategies could include upgrading buildings and equipment, developing better operating procedures, transferring risk through insurance, and improving emergency response and business recovery plans.

DOS AND DON'TS

DO

- Take a practical and logical approach that covers all important aspects of a maximum credible event, such as damage to structures, equipment and inventory, business interruption costs, and the safety of staff.

DON'T

- Don't underestimate the potential amount of downtime your business may experience if hit by the kind of loss covered by PML.

▸▸ MORE INFO

Books:

Grace, Martin Francis, Robert W. Klein, Paul R. Kleindorfer, and Michael R. Murray. *Catastrophe Insurance: Consumer Demand, Markets and Regulation*. Boston, MA: Kluwer Academic, 2003.

Grossi, Patricia, Howard Kunreuther, and Chandu C. Patel. *Catastrophe Modeling: A New Approach to Managing Risk*. New York: Springer, 2005.

Messy, Flore-Anne. *Catastrophic Risks and Insurance*. Policy Issues Series. Paris: OECD Publishing, 2005.

Article:

Woo, Gordon. "Natural catastrophe: Probable maximum loss." *British Actuarial Journal* 8:5 (2002): 943–959.

See Also:

★ Building Potential Catastrophe Management into a Strategic Risk Framework (pp. 430–432)

★ Business Continuity Management: How to Prepare for the Worst (pp. 433–436)

✔ Applying Stress-Testing to Business Continuity Management (p. 969)

✔ Identifying Your Continuity Needs (p. 986)

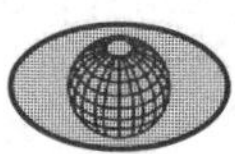

Understanding the Components of an Insurance Contract

DEFINITION

Within all the small print that comes with any new insurance contract, there are some of the most complicated legal provisions and contractual terms that you are likely to find anywhere. The insurance industry spends millions on lawyers' fees and has teams of in-house professionals constantly updating and revising the terms of their contracts to cover every possible eventuality. It is, therefore, worthwhile being familiar with some of the main components of these contracts.

Agreement (proposal and acceptance): There can be no contract without the compliance or mutual consent of the parties. The agreement reviews the major pledges of the insurance company. It explains the dangers covered, the risks assumed, and the nature of coverage.

Utmost good faith: This requires both parties to the insurance contact to deal in good faith. In particular, it imposes on the insured a duty to disclose all relevant facts that relate to the risk to be covered.

Competent Parties: For a contract to be binding, both parties must have the legal power to sign a contract.

Declarations: These identify who or what is insured, the insured's address, the insuring company, what risks or property are covered, the amount of insurance, any applicable deductibles, the policy period, and the premium amount.

Conditions: These are the provisions, rules of conduct, duties, and obligations required for coverage. If the policy conditions are not met, the insurer can deny the claim.

Exclusions: These clauses describe property, perils, hazards, or losses arising from specific causes that are not covered by the policy.

All insurance contracts basically have the same principles and processes. They assume the risk of an event that may or may not occur, and pay the cost of it if it does.

ADVANTAGES

- Businesses can cover financial risks by taking out insurance in areas such as property, public and product liability, professional indemnity, employee benefits, employers' liability, motor, and medical expenses.
- Life insurance provides a monetary benefit to a descendant's family or other designated beneficiary, and may specifically provide income for an insured person's family or cover funeral and other final expenses.
- Life-insurance policies often allow the option of having the proceeds paid to the beneficiary either as a lump sum cash payment or as an annuity.

DISADVANTAGES

- The complexity of business insurance contracts requires expert help, which is not always unbiased.
- Cover can sometimes include remote risks that could be covered out of a specific set-aside investment fund.
- This fund could be earning income for the business and used only if the risk occurs.

ACTION CHECKLIST

- ✔ Consider how existing policies insure against multiple minor events as well as more significant/ catastrophic single incidents. Examine whether particular exclusion clauses could leave your business exposed to risks you thought were covered.
- ✔ In what circumstances will the policy pay out and what risks are not covered?
- ✔ Try to quantify in financial terms how falling foul of various risks could impact on your business. Only once an actual liability figure is available can you expect an insurance provider to be able to give a quotation to cover that risk.
- ✔ Be prepared to seek the advice of specialist risk consultants. The field of commercial insurance can be far more complex than its consumer equivalent and risk consultants can help companies to understand and evaluate both risks and potential solutions.
- ✔ Consider the conditions you must meet to keep the policy valid.
- ✔ Get several quotes and at least two expert opinions.

DOS AND DON'TS

DO

- Regularly update your frameworks for assessing risks and keep your policies up to date to reflect those risks.

DON'T

- Don't make the mistake of basing a decision purely on price. Insurance is highly complex and insurance solutions are many and varied.

›› MORE INFO

Books:

Clarke, Malcolm A., Julian M. Burling, and Robert L. Purves. *The Law of Insurance Contracts*. 2nd ed. London: LLP, 2002.

Stempel, Jeffrey W. *Stempel on Insurance Contracts*. 3rd ed. New York: Aspen Publishers, 2006.

Tarr, Julie-Anne. *Disclosure and Concealment in Consumer Insurance Contracts*. London: Cavendish, 2002.

Articles:

Evening Chronicle. "Insure puzzles." May 2008.

Forde, Arnella J. "Insurance". *On Wall Street* (August 2007).

Websites:

American Insurance Association: www.aiadc.org

Association of British Insurers: www.abi.org.uk

See Also:

✔ Corporate Insurance Cover: A Primer (p. 979)

"We haven't touched—or really even bothered with white collar productivity. Until now. . .The White Collar Revolution is finally on. . .I believe that 90+ percent of White Collar Jobs will disappear or be reconfigured beyond recognition. Within 10 to 15 years." Tom Peters

  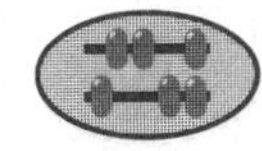 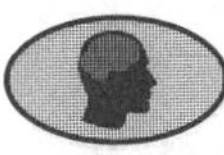  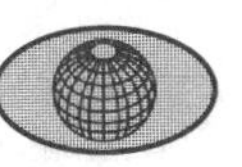   

Calculating a Company's Net Worth

DEFINITION

The net worth of a company (sometimes referred to as its net assets) is measured by subtracting the total assets of the company from its total liabilities. Thus, net worth represents the liquidation proceeds a company would fetch if its operations were to cease immediately and the firm were sold off. For example, if a company has total assets of US$80 million and total liabilities of US$40 million, its net worth would amount to US$40 million. In this example, the company might own a factory worth US$40 million, machinery valued at US$20 million, and a fleet of vans valued at a further US$20 million. Its liabilities might consist of a loan of US$40 million used to fund the purchase of the machinery and vans. The net worth of a company is also known as the shareholders' equity.

Net worth can be easily identified by referring to the company's balance sheet, which will detail its total assets and liabilities, as well as its net worth. Of course, the balance sheet does not necessarily reflect the current market value of a firm but simply expresses the value at a particular point in time, i.e. when the balance sheet was drawn up. It is also important to remember that net worth does not take any account of how profitable the company is. It may be worth more or less if sold as a going concern.

ADVANTAGES

- It is easy to find out the net worth of a company—simply refer to its latest balance sheet.
- Net worth provides a simple and straightforward way of measuring a company's breakup value if it were to cease trading.

DISADVANTAGES

- The balance sheet does not necessarily reflect the current market value of a firm but simply expresses the value at a particular point in time, i.e. when the balance sheet was drawn up.
- It is also worth remembering that a company may have a different value if it is sold as a going concern. Net worth may underestimate or overestimate the true value of a company by a considerable extent. It does not take into account intangible assets such as goodwill, copyright, patents, and intellectual property. It also ignores how much revenue and profit (or loss) a company is generating.

ACTION CHECKLIST

✔ Obtain the company's net worth from its latest balance sheet.

✔ Obtain as much other financial information as possible, including figures for revenue and profit (or loss).

✔ Look at other indicators, such as the firm's order book, and try to assess nonfinancial factors such as goodwill and the competitiveness of the company's goods and services.

DOS AND DON'TS

DO

- Obtain an estimate of the intangible assets of a company, such as intellectual property.
- Look at other measures of corporate health, such as revenues, costs, and profits (or losses), as well as forward indicators such as order books.
- Try to obtain estimates of the current value of the company's assets and liabilities, rather than rely on figures from the balance sheets, which may be considerably out of date in volatile market conditions.

DON'T

- Don't assume that net worth provides an accurate guide to the current value of a company.

▸▸ MORE INFO

Books:

Baker, H. Kent, and Gary E. Powell. *Understanding Financial Management: A Practical Guide*. Malden, MA: Blackwell Publishing, 2005.

Bandler, James. *How to Use Financial Statements: A Guide to Understanding the Numbers*. Burr Ridge, IL: Irwin, 1994.

Dickie, Robert B. *Financial Statement Analysis and Business Valuation for the Practical Lawyer*. 2nd ed. Chicago, IL: American Bar Association, 2006.

Articles:

Cummins, J. G., K. A. Hassett, and S. D. Oliner. "Investment behavior, observable expectations, and internal funds." *American Economic Review* 96:3 (2006): 796–810.

Halliwell, L. J. "ROE, utility, and the pricing of risk." *CAS Forum* (Spring 1999). Online at: www.casact.org/pubs/forum/99spforum/99spf071.pdf

Huberman, Gur. "Familiarity breeds investment." *Review of Financial Studies* 14:3 (2001): 659–680.

Website:

Venture Navigator is a free online business support service for startups, small businesses, and entrepreneurs provided by the Business Edge Consortium: www.venturenavigator.co.uk

See Also:

★ Maximizing Value when Selling a Business (pp. 412–414)

✔ Estimating Enterprise Value with the Weighted Average Cost of Capital (p. 860)

✔ Planning the Acquisition Process (p. 959)

✔ Planning the Disposal Process (p. 960)

Damodaran on Valuation: Security Analysis for Investment and Corporate Finance (p. 1245)

"It is very unusual to find a company with one asset on its balance sheet that is worth £12 billion." Phil Nolan

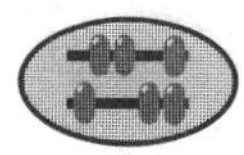
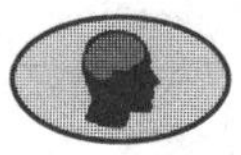

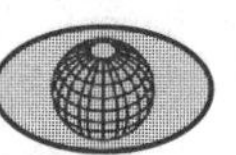

Calculating Total Shareholder Return

DEFINITION

When assessing the performance of stocks, inexperienced investors risk falling into the trap of looking purely at stock price movements, in the process ignoring the value of dividends which may be paid. Total shareholder return (TSR) over a period is defined as the net stock price change plus the dividends paid during that period. While it is possible that a stock could deliver a negative price performance over a certain period yet still generate a positive total shareholder return should the dividend paid outweigh the stock price fall, in practice this happens only rarely. In most markets, the dividend yield indicators are low, with the result that stock prices are generally the key driver of TSR. However, the importance of the dividend component of the total return calculation is typically more significant in traditionally higher-yielding areas of the stock market such as utilities, tobacco companies, and beverage producers.

Total shareholder return over a period can be calculated as follows:

$$\text{Total Shareholder Return \%} = \text{Stock price}_{\text{end of period}} - \text{Stock price}_{\text{start of period}} + \text{Dividends paid} / \text{Stock price}_{\text{start of period}}$$

Importantly, when calculating TSR, we must take account of only the dividends that our period of ownership of the stock entitles us to receive, so we need to take account of the stock ex-dividend date rather than the dividend payment date. It could be that we own the stock on the day when the dividend is actually payable, yet we would only be entitled to receive the dividend had we owned the stock on the ex-dividend day.

An alternative ways of thinking of total shareholder return is the internal rate of return of all cash flows paid to investors during a particular period. However, whichever method we choose to calculate total shareholder return, the result essentially represents an indication of the overall return generated for stockholders, expressed in percentage terms. In all cases, the "dividends paid" element of the calculation should also include any special cash payments returned to stockholders, as well as any stock buyback programs. The figure should also take account of any special one-off dividend payments, as well as regular dividend payouts.

ADVANTAGES

- TSR represents a readily understood figure of the overall financial benefits generated for stockholders.
- The figure can be interpreted as a measure of how the market evaluates the overall performance of a company over a specified period.
- Given that TSRs are expressed in percentage terms, the figures are readily comparable between companies in the same sector.

DISADVANTAGES

- TSRs can be calculated for publicly traded companies at the overall level, but not at a divisional level.
- The calculation is not "forward looking" in that it reflects the past overall return to shareholders, with no consideration of future returns.
- TSR is externally focused in that it reflects the market's perception of performance; it could, therefore, be adversely impacted should a share price of a fundamentally strong company suffer excessively in the short term.

ACTION CHECKLIST

- ✔ Calculate the share price change over the specified period plus any dividends paid to generate a simple TSR calculation.
- ✔ If necessary, be prepared to make adjustments for special events such as share buybacks and/or splits in stocks' prices.
- ✔ Investors can use TSR percentages to make comparisons against industry benchmarks.
- ✔ From a company perspective, remuneration packages can be linked to TSR.

DOS AND DON'TS

DO

- Consider how TSR calculations might be applied to mutual funds as well as company stocks, thus taking account of income paid out by yield-orientated funds when looking at their annual performance.
- However, remember that TSR reflects past performance rather than a perception or indication of future returns.

DON'T

- Don't forget that past performance shouldn't be taken as the best guide to future returns.
- Don't look to calculate TSR for privately held companies as the calculation requires stock price inputs.

›› MORE INFO

Books:

Ward, Keith. *Marketing Strategies: Turning Marketing Strategies into Shareholders Value*. Burlington, MA: Butterworth-Heinemann, 2004.

Young, David S., and Stephen F. O'Byrne. *EVA and Value Based Management*. New York: McGraw-Hill, 2000.

Articles:

Elali, Wajeeh. "Contemporaneous relationship between EVA and shareholder value." *International Journal of Business Governance and Ethics* 2 (October 2006).

Gardner, Tim, and Eric Spielgel. "Total shareholder return: Planning a perfect future." *Public Utilities Fortnightly* (January 2006).

See Also:

★ Dividend Policy: Maximizing Shareholder Value (pp. 152–155)
★ Why EVA is the Best Measurement Tool for Creating Shareholder Value (pp. 843–844)
✔ Investors and the Capital Structure (p. 911)
✔ Using Shareholder Value Analysis (p. 953)

"Only man is not content to leave things as they are but must always be changing them, and when he has done so, is seldom satisfied at the result." Elspeth Huxley

  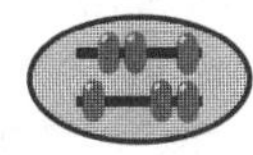 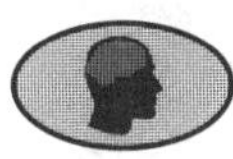  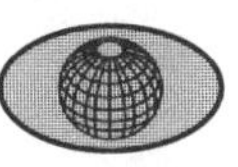   

Fund of Hedge Funds: Understanding the Risks and Returns

DEFINITION

Generally, a fund of funds is a fund that invests in other funds in order to provide investors with a lower-risk product through exposure to a larger number of vehicles, often of different types and with different regional focuses.

A hedge fund of funds is one that invests in a pool of hedge funds, instead of just investing in an individual fund. It is any fund of funds that pools capital together, while employing two or more submanagers that invest in two or more funds, and which is not dictated to by the underlying investment of such funds.

Funds of funds are set up as limited partnerships, which offer advantages to the investor. Due diligence is a primary benefit, because managers can use their time and expertise to evaluate strategies and analyze individual fund performance—a task that would be a difficult undertaking for an individual investor. The fund of funds tries to avoid untoward risk because of the different investment strategies employed by the principal fund managers. Funds of funds can be invested in, for example, a venture fund, a long/short fund, a distressed fund, and/or a private equity fund. Investors assign assets to a fund of funds mainly to limit their risk to exposure.

However, funds of funds do have some disadvantages, such as the double layer of fees and the issue of transparency. When investing in a fund of funds, a backer must pay not only the fees of the pool of funds, but also the fees of the fund of funds manager. Transparency about the fund of funds manager's background and reputation, not to mention the nature of the investments made, are issues of primary importance.

ADVANTAGES

- Funds of hedge funds normally offer a lower risk than single funds, because they are invested in a wider variety of sectors, with national and international focuses.
- Because managers can devote all of their time to evaluating strategies and analyzing individual fund performance, they are more likely to achieve a better return than an individual investor.
- Because principal fund managers are specialists in their investment areas, funds of funds benefit from the different specialist investment strategies employed.

DISADVANTAGES

- When investors buy into a fund of funds, they are charged management fees twice: First by the fund of funds manager, and then by the individual fund managers.
- Funds of hedge funds are inevitably very secretive, which makes it difficult for an investor to assess the fund manager's performance on a daily basis.
- The Securities & Exchange Commission (SEC), the Financial Services Authority (FSA), and other securities supervisory bodies generally have limited powers to check on hedge fund activities.

ACTION CHECKLIST

✔ Find out what you will be paying in total fees: after you have deducted the double fees, it might prove wiser to select less risky investments.

✔ Check the long-term track record of the fund of funds: an experienced manager, who delivers a consistent (though perhaps lower) return, is probably a better bet than a new start-up. The manager's skills, background, and reputation, and the type of investments made, are very important issues.

DOS AND DON'TS

DO

- Research the different funds and their tactics, and make sure that you have analyzed your real return on investment after fees and expenses.
- Engage your lawyers and accountants in the evaluation of the risks and possible benefits of investing in funds of hedge funds.

DON'T

- Don't take your investment in funds of hedge funds for granted; market and legislative developments can mean that the playing field changes. Just because a risk, area, market, or country has been stable in the past is no guarantee that it will be the same in the future.

➤➤ MORE INFO

Books:

Drobny, Steven. *Inside the House of Money: Top Hedge Fund Traders on Profiting in the Global Markets*. Hoboken, NJ: Wiley, 2006.

Jaeger, Robert A. *All About Hedge Funds: The Easy Way to Get Started*. New York: McGraw-Hill Professional, 2002.

Jaffer, Sohail. *Funds of Hedge Funds: For Professional Investors and Managers*. London: Euromoney Books, 2003.

Nicholas, Joseph G. *Hedge Fund of Funds Investing: An Investor's Guide*. New York: Bloomberg Press, 2004.

Articles:

Chen, Peng. "Hedge funds: Are they worth it?" *On Wall Street* (August 1, 2006).

Jones, Bernard. "Hedge funding." *Investors Chronicle* (May 25, 2007). Online at: www.investorschronicle.co.uk/Columnists/default/article/20070525/6f0caf76-21b4-11dc-85f6-00144f2af8e8/Hedge-funding.jsp

Mackintosh, James. "German bank puts hedge fund unit up for sale." *Financial Times* (March 6, 2009). Online at: www.ft.com/cms/s/0/6bc60974-09ee-11de-add8-0000779fd2ac.html

Websites:

The Financial Services Authority: www.fsa.gov.uk

Hedge fund research: www.morningstar.com

HedgeFund.net: www.hedgefund.net/

Rothschild Solomon: www.webmonopoly.net/rothschild/hedge_funds.htm

"Business re-engineering isn't about fixing anything—it's about starting again, about re-inventing our corporation from top to bottom." Michael Hammer

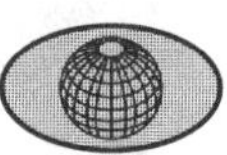

Hedge Funds: Understanding the Risks and Returns

DEFINITION

Although hedge funds seem to have hit the headlines only recently, the first of these funds was actually started in 1949.

Hedge funds are normally run by small teams of portfolio managers, traders, and analysts, investing private pools of capital with few restrictions as to the areas in which they can speculate. Hedge funds benefit from limited regulation and are not required to make periodic reports to the Securities & Exchange Commission (SEC) under the Securities and Exchange Act of 1934. In order to be exempt from direct regulation, a hedge fund must be open to a limited number of accredited investors.

Hedge funds use a wide array of strategies, and sometimes are not "hedged" against the market at all. Many, but not all, of these funds aim to produce much higher returns than other investment vehicles, and markets with high volatility are often preferred, as they sometimes yield the highest returns (but also the greatest risks).

Hedge funds have the advantage that they can employ a large number of strategies and can invest in more areas than other investments. They may use leverage, short-selling, asset-backed lending, arbitrage, or a variety of other techniques in order to gain maximum returns for investors.

Hedge fund managers normally earn both a management fee and a performance or incentive fee. Performance fees are intended to be an inducement for the investment managers to produce the greatest returns they can. Typical fees are a management fee of 2% of the fund's net asset value per annum and a performance fee of 20% of the fund's profits. Fees are payable from the fund to the investment manager, and are taken directly from the assets that the backer holds in the fund.

A hedge fund can apply a high watermark to an investor's money, where the manager will only receive performance fees, on the invested money, when its value is greater than its previous greatest value.

ADVANTAGES

- Hedge funds can make use of a larger number of strategies and can invest in many more areas than with traditional investment products.
- Performance fees, calculated as a percentage of the fund's profits, act as an incentive for managers to perform above average.

DISADVANTAGES

- To make money and not disclose strategies, hedge funds are of necessity very secretive, with few public disclosure requirements. This makes it difficult for investors to assess how well or badly their fund managers are doing.
- Some, though not all, hedge funds borrow and speculate with (leverage) sums that are many times larger than the initial investment. This is fine when the investment works, but it can mean that the fund folds if it doesn't.
- When a hedge fund uses short selling as an investment strategy, rather than as a hedging strategy, it can experience very high losses if the market turns against it.
- The SEC and other securities regulators generally have limited ability to check routinely on hedge fund activities.

ACTION CHECKLIST

- ✔ Before investing in hedge funds, you should be aware of the risks as well as the rewards: Leverage amplifies profits but also losses; short selling opens up new investment opportunities; riskier investments typically provide higher returns but, as in poker, you shouldn't sit down at the table if you can't afford to lose.
- ✔ Qualify and quantify in financial terms how the failure of the fund could impact on your life or business.
- ✔ Seek the advice of specialists and always ask for a second opinion. There are over 10,000 hedge funds in existence, with close to $3 trillion in assets under management; separating the wood from the trees can be a difficult and risky process.

DOS AND DON'TS

DO

- Seek advice, preferably from a specialist in the industry who has some years of experience and has seen both the good and the bad.
- Involve your lawyers and accountants in the evaluation of both the risks and the potential benefits of investing in a hedge fund.

DON'T

- Don't jump or be pushed into a decision. Take time to do your research before deciding.
- Don't follow tips or the sheep—sleep on it before you make your move.

▸▸ MORE INFO

Books:

Black, Keith H. *Managing a Hedge Fund: A Complete Guide to Trading, Business Strategies, Operations, and Regulations*. New York: McGraw-Hill Professional, 2004.

Lhabitant, François-Serge. *Handbook of Hedge Funds*. Chichester, UK: Wiley, 2006.

Nicholas, Joseph G. *Investing in Hedge Funds*. New York: Bloomberg Press, 2005.

Ridley, Matthew. *How to Invest in Hedge Funds: An Investment Professional's Guide*. London: Kogan Page, 2004.

Articles:

Investment Adviser. "Democratizing the hedge fund." March 2008.

Sender, Henny, and Javier Blas. "Hedge funds turn to gold." *Financial Times* (March 8, 2009). Online at: www.ft.com/cms/s/0/37fcba70-0c0a-11de-b87d-0000779fd2ac.html

Websites:

Hedge fund database: www.barclayhedge.com

Hedge fund investment: www.business.com

HedgeWorld: www.hedgeworld.com

US Securities and Exchange Commission: www.sec.gov

"One of the lessons from the Darwinian world is that the excellence of an organism's nervous system helps determine its ability to sense change and quickly respond, thereby surviving or even thriving." Bill Gates

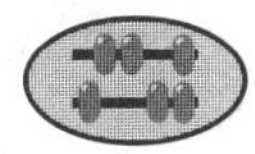
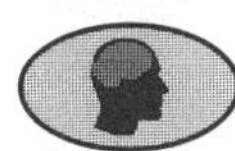

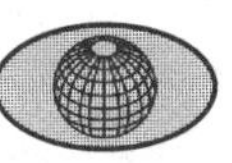

How to Use Credit Rating Agencies

DEFINITION

A credit rating agency is a company that assigns credit ratings to issuers of debt instruments and to the debt instruments themselves. A wide variety of organizations may issue debt in the primary market and thus come under the scrutiny of the credit rating agencies. These include companies, national, and local governments, and government and semi-government entities. Their debt instruments are then traded on a secondary market. Credit rating agencies assign ratings that seek to determine how creditworthy the issuer is, i.e. to gauge the level of risk that they will be unable to repay the loan.

An entity with very strong finances will be given the highest rating, often described as AAA, while the least creditworthy will receive the lowest rating, normally D, which applies to debt that is already in arrears. An entity with low credit ratings will have to pay a premium in terms of the interest on loans in order to compensate the lender for the higher risk that the loan may not be repaid. The rating agencies constantly monitor all the instruments they rate and will issue upgrades or downgrades if an issuer's creditworthiness has changed.

Ratings are an invaluable tool for investors, providing a convenient way to identify the creditworthiness of a potential investment. Issuers use credit ratings to provide an independent analysis of their own creditworthiness, thus helping to determine the value of the instruments they issue. Government regulators and other agencies also use credit ratings to gauge the health of their financial system. Thus, regulators allow banks to use credit ratings from certain approved ratings agencies when calculating their net capital reserve requirements. Regulators could, for example, allow banks to include highly rated, liquid bonds when calculating their net capital reserve requirements.

The three largest credit rating agencies are Standard & Poor's, Moody's, and Fitch. All have come under fire as a result of the global credit crunch that developed in 2007. In July 2008, a damning report from the US Securities and Exchange Commission identified "serious shortcomings" in the rating of securities related to subprime mortgages, the products that triggered the crisis. Credit rating agencies have also come under fire for problems in structured finance products that they have rated, particularly in assigning AAA ratings to structured debt, which in a large number of cases has subsequently been downgraded or defaulted. There is thus increasing pressure to introduce greater regulation of the credit rating agencies.

ADVANTAGES

- The ratings assigned by credit rating agencies allow investors to quickly, cheaply, and conveniently identify the risk involved in buying a particular debt instrument or in developing a business relationship with a particular organization.
- The use of ratings opens capital markets to entities such as new companies.
- Credit ratings give you an insight into an entity from an independent expert analyst.

DISADVANTAGES

- The rating agencies have come under criticism as a result of the credit crunch. Many AAA-rated companies were downgraded to very low levels within a very short space of time.
- Credit rating agencies have come under fire for failing to downgrade companies quickly enough, with some companies faltering despite being assigned relatively good ratings.
- Credit rating agencies have been criticized for developing too close a relationship with the management of the companies that they rate.
- Credit rating agencies have been criticized for their role in rating structured finance products, and in particular for large losses in the collateralized debt obligation (CDO) market that occurred despite being assigned top ratings by the agencies.

ACTION CHECKLIST

- ✔ Look at the ratings from as many credit rating agencies as possible.
- ✔ Gather as much other information as you can on a potential investment or business partner.

DOS AND DON'TS

DO

- Be aware that issuers pay the rating agencies a fee. Critics say that this creates a potential conflict of interest.
- Conduct your own research as well as looking at the analysis supplied by the agencies.

DON'T

- Don't forget that the ratings agencies are not infallible.
- Don't forget that entities are subject to constant monitoring by the credit rating agencies. Ratings can and do change over time.

▸▸ MORE INFO

Books:

Beder, Sharon. *Suiting Themselves: How Corporations Drive the Global Agenda*. London: Earthscan, 2005.

Brooks, Chris. *Introductory Econometrics for Finance*. 2nd ed. Cambridge, UK: Cambridge University Press, 2008.

Ganguin, Blaise, and John Bilardello. *Fundamentals of Corporate Credit Analysis*. New York: McGraw-Hill, 2005.

Articles:

Goodhart, C. A. E. "The background to the 2007 financial crisis." *International Economics and Economic Policy* 4:4 (February 2008): 331–346.

Maxwell, James. "Ratings agencies Eye ERM for all industries." *Financial Executive* (March 2008).

Wray, L. Randall. "Lessons from the subprime meltdown." *Challenge* 51:2 (March–April 2008): 40–68.

Website:

VentureNavigator: www.venturenavigator.co.uk

   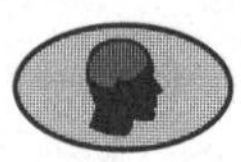  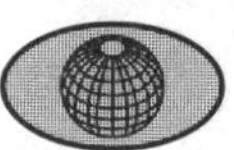   

Investing in Employee Pension Plans: Understanding the Risks and Returns

DEFINITION

As baby boomers have reached retirement age, many have found that those much anticipated leisure years have eluded them. They have had to carry on working because company pension plans that were meant to deliver a comfortable retirement have often done anything but.

There are basically two types of pension plan: a defined-contribution (DC) scheme and a defined-benefit (DB) scheme.

In a DC scheme the employee takes on the investment risk and the pension received depends on, among other things, the performance of the fund into which the employee and employer have paid. Most workers have little or no knowledge of financial schemes, and those extending over long periods of a working lifetime tend to generate apathy among those who are not well informed. To save for your retirement, you need to be able to make accurate, well-informed decisions. However, very few people have the skills, patience, or interest to sit down and work out what they will need to retire comfortably. An even larger dilemma is that the level of contributions from both employers and employees into DC schemes is not always sufficient and, if less money goes in, generally less money comes out. Added to that is that the costs of running DC schemes are, on average, higher than for a DB scheme, having expense ratios of more than 1%.

In a DB scheme, the employer takes on most of the burden by promising employees a retirement income based on their pay and length of service. When these schemes were first introduced 50 years ago, their costs were manageable and they were often used as a bargaining chip, so that employers could avoid paying higher wages. However, with rising wages and the depredations of inflation, the promises of a DB pension became more expensive and burdensome for companies to keep. The soaring costs of DB pensions have encouraged many employers to switch to DC schemes. The argument is often that DB schemes place too heavy a burden on company management and, in effect, require companies to wager money on the financial markets in order to meet their pension commitments.

ADVANTAGES

- DC schemes allow businesses to get on with business and not waste their time and skills on running pensions.
- DB schemes promise employees a retirement income based on their pay and length of service, with the employer taking the risk.

DISADVANTAGES

- DC schemes leave many employees facing a retirement income well short of their expectations.
- DB schemes tend to discourage mobility and reward those who spend their whole career at a single firm.
- In a DC scheme the employee takes on the investment risk and the pension received depends on the investment performance of the fund.

ACTION CHECKLIST

✔ What type of pension plan does your company have, and is it open to new employees?

✔ Check the pension forecasts and see, after taking into account inflation, what percentage of your final salary you will receive as a pension.

✔ Lower contributions almost inevitably mean lower pensions. Therefore, if in doubt, invest in a private pension plan to make up what you estimate will be the shortfall.

DOS AND DON'TS

DO

- Check if you can take your pension rights with you if you change companies.
- If you invest in a private pension, plan ahead, assess what income you will need, and link your yearly contributions to that target.

DON'T

- Don't take your pension plan for granted. Complacency may mean that you have to carry on working instead of retiring comfortably.

▸▸ MORE INFO

Books:

Hill, M. *Pensions*. Bristol: Policy Press, 2007.

McGill, D. M., *et al. Fundamentals of Private Pensions*. Oxford: Oxford University Press, 2005.

Munnell, A. H. *The Economics of Private Pensions*. Washington, DC: Brookings Institution Press, 1982.

Articles:

Bellers, C. "Investment spotlight—deregulation of pensions—or dilution." *Pensions Management* (December 1, 2007). Online at: www.highbeam.com/doc/1G1-172205023.html

Money Management. "Tools for pension investment." *Money Management* (March 1, 2007). Online at: www.highbeam.com/doc/1G1-160176900.html

Websites:

Allianz Knowledge—Aging populations: knowledge.allianz.com/en/special/aging_populations.html

Pension Benefit Guaranty Corporation (PBGC): www.pbgc.gov

See Also:

★ Pension Schemes: A Unique and Unintended Basket of Risks on the Balance Sheet (pp. 93–96)

✔ Preparing Financial Statements: Balance Sheets (p. 1043)

✔ Understanding Asset–Liability Management (Full Balance Sheet Approach) (p. 889)

✔ Understanding the Balance Sheet (p. 894)

✔ Understanding the Relationship between the Discount Rate and Risk (p. 896)

"Unlike other industries, our pace of change is so fast that I don't think it's right to expect the same type of concentration as in the auto industry." Michael Dell

  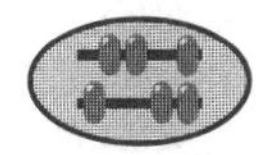   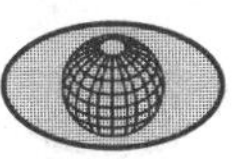  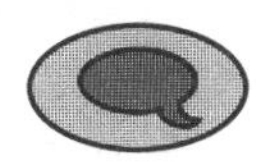 

Mean–Variance Optimization: A Primer

DEFINITION

Mean–variance optimization (MVO) is a quantitative tool used to spread investment across different assets within a portfolio by assessing the trade-off between risk and return in order to maximize the return while minimizing any risks. The concept was devised by economist Harry M. Markowitz, who developed an algorithm to calculate optimized returns over a specified period. MVO is part of Markowitz's modern portfolio theory (MPT), which assumes that investors will optimize their investment portfolios through diversifying their investments on a balanced risk–return basis. Markowitz's concept of efficiency as laid out in MVO contributed to the development of the capital asset pricing model (CAPM).

The Markowitz algorithm relies on inputting three data sets on a graph: expected return per asset, standard deviation of each asset (a metric for risk), and the correlation between the two. Together these produce what Markowitz named the "efficient frontier," or those assets expected to produce better returns than others that carry the same or fewer risks, and, conversely, a smaller risk than those expected to produce the same or a higher rate of return. Investors should ensure the three data sets, or inputs, represent their expectations of probability for the specified period, as well as include possible outcomes, each with a return per asset and probability of occurrence. The expected return, standard deviation, and correlations can then be calculated with standard statistical formulae.

ADVANTAGES

- Because MVO assumes that investors are risk-averse and will choose a less-risky investment among any assets that offer similar expected returns, it is a useful tool for identifying assets that have the most favorable risk–return profile.

DISADVANTAGES

- MVO treats return as a future expectation and uses volatility as a proxy for risk, the flaw being that volatility is a historical parameter and you cannot assume that today's prices provide an accurate forecast for the future.

ACTION CHECKLIST

- ✔ Be aware of the risks of using only historical data for your inputs—you may prefer to use your own estimates for a given asset's future performance in the specified period.
- ✔ Watch out for something called mean reversion. This occurs when an asset performs extremely well for a period and then performs spectacularly badly in the following period, or vice versa. If you have used historical data for your inputs, your outputs will indicate a strong (weak) future performance, but if mean reversion occurs, you will have results opposite to what you expected in the specified period.

DOS AND DON'TS

DO

- Make careful decisions about which data sets to use as inputs.
- Pay extra attention when calculating the expected returns, as your choices will determine the actual returns that you assign to each asset in the investment portfolio.

DON'T

- Don't assume that historical data are an accurate reflection of future performance.

▸▸ MORE INFO

Book:

Markowitz, Harry M. *Portfolio Selection*. 2nd ed. Malden, MA: Blackwell Publishers, 1991.

Article:

Markowitz, Harry. "Portfolio selection." *The Journal of Finance* 7:1 (1952): 77–91.

Website:

Full text of Markowitz book: cowles.econ.yale.edu/P/cm/m16

See Also:

★ Asset Allocation Methodologies (pp. 281–285)
✔ Trading in Commodities: Why and How (p. 945)
✔ Trading in Corporate Bonds: Why and How (p. 946)
Harry Markowitz (p. 1175)
William F. Sharpe (p. 1193)

"Paradigm Shift: A euphemism companies use when they realize the rest of their industry has expanded into Guangdong while they were investing in Orange County." Anonymous

   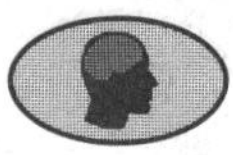  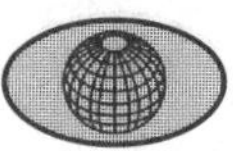   

An Overview of *Shariah*-Compliant Funds

DEFINITION

Shariah-compliant funds are investment vehicles which are fully compliant with the principles of Islam. The funds are prohibited from making investments in industries categorized as morally deficient, such as those related to gambling or alcohol. Because Islam does not permit any form of exploitation, any kind of investment in conventional banking is outlawed. With the concept of debt also contrary to the principles of Islam, investment in highly leveraged companies is also not permitted for *shariah*-compliant funds. The exclusions extend to potential investments in other funds which offer guaranteed returns. Any use of futures and options, either by the fund managers or by companies in which the funds invest, is also likely to attract close scrutiny by the funds' supervisory *shariah* boards.

Due to the rapid growth in Islamic finance over recent years, the available range of *shariah*-compliant funds has expanded as financial services providers seek to tap into the increasing demand for investment products which respect the principles of Islam. The most common forms of *shariah*-compliant funds are described below.

Ijarah

Ijarah (also transliterated *ijara*) is a leasing-type fund that acquires assets such as real estate or equipment and then leases them out to another party in return for a regular rental payment. In all cases the fund retains ownership of the asset and must ensure that usage of the asset is at all times in accordance with Islamic principles.

Murabahah

Murabahah (or *murabaha*) is a kind of development fund that acquires assets and then sells them to a client at a predetermined price which reflects the fund's cost of acquiring the asset plus a profit margin. Sometimes described as "cost-plus" funds, *murabahah* investment vehicles do not hold long-term ownership of the assets, but instead generate a financial return from the payment obligations taken on by clients for a pre-agreed period.

Equity

Equity funds invest directly in companies through the purchase of shares. Given the difficulties involved in scrutinizing every aspect of how a company operates to verify *shariah*-compliance, this new, more progressive attitude allows investment in companies that operate in permitted industries, with the proviso that a proportion of the returns generated for the fund from any interest-bearing deposits held by the company must be donated to charity.

Commodity

Commodity funds invest in physical commodities, although speculative activities such as short selling are not permitted. However, the fund manager may make use of *istisna'a* contracts, pre-agreeing the price of goods to be manufactured and delivered at a specified future date, with the manufacturer benefiting from advance receipt of the agreed sale price. Commodity fund managers can also use *bay al-salam* contracts. These can be compared to conventional forward contracts, though the key *shariah*-compliant differentiator is that the seller's position is protected because payment is passed to the seller on agreement of the contract rather than on its completion. However, in return for the effective transfer of contract risk, the buyer is compensated by the fact that the agreed delivery price is set at a discount to the physical spot price.

ADVANTAGES

- *Shariah*-compliant investment funds provide a means of investing while still honoring the high morals and principles of Islam.
- *Shariah*-compliant funds promote large-scale investment along lines similar to the niche ethical funds available to Western consumers.

DISADVANTAGES

- The funds can be more expensive to develop and administer than mainstream funds due to the need for greater verification of compliance with *shariah* principles.

ACTION CHECKLIST

- ✔ Assess the full range of available *shariah*-compliant investment products before selecting the type you wish to use.
- ✔ Consider how much risk you are prepared to assume before investing.
- ✔ Mainstream investors may also wish to consider potential investments in *shariah*-compliant funds.

DOS AND DON'TS

DO

- Pooled investment vehicles generally offer good value compared to direct investments, but you should still compare fund management charges between different providers.
- Consider using index products such as exchange-traded funds to gain exposure to Islamic investment indices.

DON'T

- Don't feel you have to verify the compliance of a fund yourself—contact a fund provider for advice.
- Don't expect guaranteed attractive returns, even from the most ethical forms of investment.

➤➤ MORE INFO

Books:

Anwar, Habiba, and Roderick Millar (eds). *Islamic Finance: A Guide for International Business and Investment*. London: GMB Publishing, 2008.

Jaffer, Sohail (ed). *Islamic Asset Management: Forming the Future for Shari'a-Compliant Investment Strategies*. London: Euromoney Books, 2004.

Vogel, Frank E., and Samuel L. Hayes, III. *Islamic Law and Finance: Religion, Risk, and Return*. The Hague: Kluwer Law International, 1998.

Articles:

Feinberg, Phyllis. "Seeking pension money: Mutual fund family follows Islamic law." *Pensions & Investments* (October 30, 2000).

Siddiqi, Moin A. "Growing appeal of Islamic investment funds." *Middle East* (July 1, 1997).

"Large companies not paying attention to change will get hurt. The web will be one more area of significant change and those who don't pay attention will get hurt, while those who see it early enough will get rewarded."
Steve Jobs

  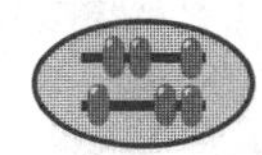 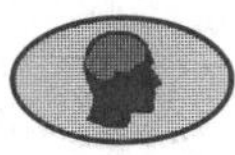  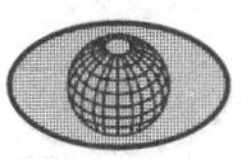   

Overview of Tax Deeds

DEFINITION

A tax deed is usually entered into upon an acquisition of the majority shares in a company. The tax deed is concerned with the tax affairs of the business and the company acquired. Under the tax deed, the seller agrees to pay to the buyer any tax liability and charge resulting from an event occurring before the buyer acquired the company. This includes any reasonable costs and expenses which were properly incurred and payable by the company or the buyer in connection with any reasonable action to avoid or settle a tax claim or liability. In any tax deed, the sellers will seek to limit their liability in such an undertaking to a maximum agreed amount. For example, the undertaking will not be given and the seller will not be liable to the extent that any provision or reserve in respect of the liability to taxation was taken into account in the accounts of the company. Also the seller will not be made to pay if the amount has already been recovered by the buyer under the sale and purchase agreement. The tax deed will also deal with the procedure to be followed by the parties in the event of a tax claim which the seller is not aware of. The deed will also cover how the payments, if any, will be made and scheduled. The undertaking by the seller will usually be valid for a period of seven years from the date of acquisition of the company but this can vary depending upon the laws of the applicable jurisdiction.

ADVANTAGES

- A tax deed sets out the terms and conditions under which the buyer of a company will be compensated for any tax liability that he/she must pay after the acquisition as a result of an event which occurred before the date of the acquisition.
- Because a tax deed is an agreement, it can be negotiated and agreed by the two parties, the buyer and the seller.
- Tax deeds protect buyers from unnecessary and unforeseen tax liabilities they may have as a result of acquiring a company. In general, they are reasonably standard and accepted as a necessary document by the parties of an acquisition of a majority of shares in a company.

DISADVANTAGES

- Negotiating a tax deed can be complex and time consuming. It involves thorough knowledge of the documentation and requires specialist legal, accounting, and tax advice and can therefore be an expensive process.

ACTION CHECKLIST

- ✔ Carefully study any tax deed which you might sign. Obtain as much information from as many sources as you can before committing to expensive liabilities. Do not sign a document that you do not understand.
- ✔ Through your advisers try and limit your exposure of liabilities to an amount you feel comfortable with. If your company has had its tax affairs in order you do not have much to worry about.

DOS AND DON'TS

DO

- Choose your advisers carefully. Make sure that you understand the undertakings you are giving. Involve your tax advisers and accountants in the negotiation process.
- Involve your solicitors in the evaluation of both the risks and potential benefits of entering into a tax deed.
- If you know of any tax liabilities that are due before the completion of your sale, disclose them and try to sort them out with the relevant authorities.

DON'T

- Don't make the mistake of ignoring the importance of the undertakings you will give in a tax deed. They can come back to haunt you.
- Don't overlook the importance of negotiating undertakings and indemnities that you could give with confidence. Make sure that if you know of anything that may go against these warranties, you disclose them to the buyer.

▸▸ MORE INFO

Books:

CCH Tax Law Editors. *US Master Sales and Use Tax Guide*. Chicago, IL: CCH, 2007.

Reuvid, Jonathan. *Mergers and Acquisitions: A Practical Guide for Private Companies and their UK and Overseas Advisers*. Philadelphia, PA: Kogan Page, 2008.

Articles:

Gustafson, Jeanne. "GenPrime signs big distribution agreement." *Journal of Business* (October 2000).

Quinn, Robert M. "Florida tax deed sales are getting risky." *Florida Bar Journal* 81:7 (July/August 2007).

Websites:

AllBusiness: www.allbusiness.com

ArticleBase: www.articlebase.com

See Also:

★ Due Diligence Requirements in Financial Transactions (pp. 398–401)

★ How Taxation Impacts on Liquidity Management (pp. 55–56)

✔ Acquiring a Company (p. 955)

✔ Planning the Acquisition Process (p. 959)

✔ Structuring M&A Deals and Tax Planning (p. 962)

"Passion for change drives great business people. It moves them restlessly from industry to industry."
Paul Corrigan

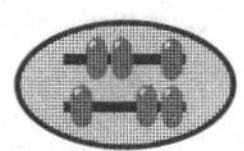

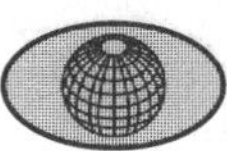

Structured Investment Vehicles

DEFINITION

A structured investment vehicle, or SIV, is a limited-purpose operating company or "virtual bank" that undertakes arbitrage activities by purchasing mostly highly rated medium- and long-term fixed-income assets. These assets are funded though the issue of short-term, highly rated commercial paper or medium-term notes, which traditionally offer a rate close to the London Interbank Offered Rate (Libor). The SIV thus makes its profits from the spread between the short-term borrowing rate and long-term returns. A SIV has an open-ended and rollover business structure whereby it buys new assets as the old ones mature.

The costs of running a SIV are balanced by the economic returns: that is, the net spread to pay subordinated note-holder returns and the generation of management fee income. Most SIVs are administered or sponsored by banks, but a number are managed independently. The number of SIVs has proliferated in recent years and they control assets worth hundreds of billions of dollars. SIVs are generally quite opaque, invest in complex securities, and often do not need to be displayed on a bank's balance sheet.

The subprime crisis has caused a widespread liquidity crunch in the commercial paper markets and, given that SIVs rely on making their profits from the spread between the short-term borrowing rate and long-term returns, many SIVs have seen their business drastically reduced. Although the Federal Reserve and the European Central Bank have injected billions of dollars and euros into the market, a number of independent SIVs have closed, while other SIVs are being supported by their sponsoring banks.

ADVANTAGES

- SIVs offer good returns in highly liquid markets.
- Most SIVs are sponsored by banks, which back them when they have liquidity problems.

DISADVANTAGES

- Most SIVs issue a mixture of commercial paper or of medium-term notes, and their weighted-average liability to maturity is normally from four to six months, but the assets in the vehicle will have significantly longer average maturities.
- SIVs suffer from the credit risks associated with assets and hedges and the market risk linked to the cost of liquidating assets and hedges. There is the potential for defaults due to a lack of liquidity in world financial markets.
- Some of the SIV's assets may entail due diligence by potential purchasers, thus increasing the sale period for these assets.
- Losses can result from unhedged changes in currencies and interest rates.

ACTION CHECKLIST

✔ In the current illiquid market conditions, make sure that the SIV has a portfolio of highly liquid assets and less liquid, higher-yielding investments.

✔ Ensure that the SIV is exposed to a range of fixed-rate and currency assets and that the portfolio is conservatively hedged.

DOS AND DON'TS

DO

- Use the rating agencies (Moody's, Standard & Poor's, and Fitch IBCA) to check on the SIV. Whatever their faults in the past, rating agencies have tightened up their criteria and will give a good guide to the viability of a particular asset.
- Check who the principal backers are.

DON'T

- Don't forget that although many SIVs are administered or sponsored by banks, a number are managed independently, which might make them more likely to have liquidity problems.

▸▸ MORE INFO

Books:

de Servigny, Arnaud, and Norbert Jobst (eds). *The Handbook of Structured Finance.* New York: McGraw-Hill, 2007.

El-Erian, Mohamed. *When Markets Collide: Investment Strategies for the Age of Global Economic Change.* New York: McGraw-Hill, 2008.

Tavakoli, Janet M. *Collateralized Debt Obligations and Structured Finance: New Developments in Cash and Synthetic Securitization.* Hoboken, NJ: Wiley, 2003.

Articles:

Dolbeck, Andrew. "SIV survival: The fate of structured investment vehicles." *Weekly Corporate Growth Report* (November 5, 2007).

Investment Adviser. "JP Morgan investors opt for new vehicle." *Investment Adviser* (March 3, 2008). Online at: goliath.ecnext.com/coms2/browse_R_I065-200803_451_525

Websites:

Use search options on these websites to look up "structured investment vehicles."

Bank of Montreal: www.bmo.com

Citigroup: www.citi.com

See Also:

★ Credit Ratings (pp. 534–536)
★ Investing in Structured Finance Products in the Debt Money Markets (pp. 337–340)
★ Viewpoint: Leigh Skene (pp. 238–241)
✔ How to Use Credit Rating Agencies (p. 939)
✔ Money Markets: Their Structure and Function (p. 1016)

"To achieve satisfactory investment results is easier than most people realize; to achieve superior results is harder than it looks." Benjamin Graham

  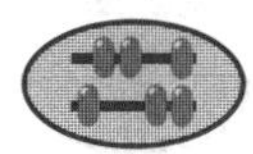   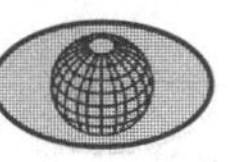   

Trading in Commodities: Why and How

DEFINITION

In contrast to other kinds of investment, such as stocks or bonds, when you trade in commodities or futures you do not in fact buy or own anything. You are speculating on the future direction of the price of the commodity. The terms "commodities" and "futures" are often used to describe commodity trading or futures trading. *Commodities* are the actual physical goods, such as corn, soybeans, gold, or crude oil. *Futures* are contracts for those commodities, which are traded at a futures exchange such as the Chicago Board of Trade.

Futures are standardized contracts among buyers and sellers of commodities, specifying the amount of a commodity, grade/quality, and delivery location. Each futures exchange has producers and consumers who want to hedge their risks of future price changes. In between them are the traders, who do not actually buy and sell the physical commodities but are there to help maintain an organized market and provide liquidity. Futures markets are generally very actively traded, so typically there is a large daily price range and trading volume.

Futures contracts have now expanded beyond just physical commodities, and there are futures contracts on financial markets such as the S&P500, treasury notes, currencies, etc.

Futures markets can be traded in both up and down. If a trader expects the market to move upwards, he will make a long trade by buying a contract and leave the trade by selling a contract. Conversely, if a trader expects the market to move downwards, he will make a short trade by selling a contract and leave the trade by buying a contract. By being able to trade in both directions, traders can make a profit or loss regardless of which direction the market is moving. In order to make decisions about when to trade commodity futures, traders tend to use price-activity charts that show futures movements and which are easily understood when tackling historical and current price movements.

ADVANTAGES

- Futures markets are available with a wide variety of underlying instruments, which in turn offer a wide range of price movements and liquidity. Some are available for day-trading 24 hours per day.
- Futures markets can be day-traded without any restrictions, which makes them preferable to stock markets that have day-trading restrictions.
- Futures markets are offered with trades in currencies such as the euro to US dollar exchange rate, stock indexes such as the Dow Jones and DAX, and commodities such as gold, silver, and oil.

DISADVANTAGES

- Unforeseen events such as floods, droughts, government currency interventions, and crop reports can cause sudden and unpredictable losses.
- Risk and reward go hand in hand. It is ridiculous to expect to be able to earn above-average profits without above-average risks.

ACTION CHECKLIST

- ✔ Learn about and specialize in a particular commodity before you begin trading. Every commodity has different trading guidelines and a profile that includes the basics of contract specifications, market reports, and charts.
- ✔ Begin trading with small amounts until you learn the ropes; trades on some exchanges are available for as little as $100.

DOS AND DON'TS

DO

- Do your homework and start by trading in small amounts until you are thoroughly familiar with your chosen commodity.
- Use price-activity charts before making decisions about when to trade in futures.

DON'T

- Don't forget that, although the risks can be managed, they can never be eliminated. Keep in mind that the high returns are available only because the trader is being paid to take risk away from others.
- Don't forget that losses are part of the process and that the best traders lose money, but over time they make even more.

⏩ MORE INFO

Books:

Buckley, John (ed). *Guide to World Commodity Markets: Physical, Futures and Options Trading.* 7th ed. London: Kogan Page, 1996.

Chicago Board of Trade. *Commodity Trading Manual.* London: Lessons Professional Publishing, 1998.

Gregoriou, Greg N., Vassilios N. Karavas, François-Serge Lhabitant, and Fabrice Rouah. *Commodity Trading Advisers: Risk, Performance Analysis, and Selection.* Hoboken, NJ: John Wiley and Sons, 2004.

Articles:

Chong, Sidney. "Commodity investment." *Australasian Business Intelligence* (July 27, 2006).

M2 PressWIRE. "Maximizing returns through fundamental analysis in commodity investing." *M2 PressWIRE* (March 10, 2008).

Websites:

UK Financial Services Authority: www.fsa.gov.uk

US Commodity Futures Trading Commission: www.cftc.gov

See Also:

★ The Role of Commodities in an Institutional Portfolio (pp. 372–375)
✔ Swaps, Options, and Futures: What They Are and Their Function (p. 882)
Portfolio Selection: Efficient Diversification of Investments (p. 1309)
Mining (pp. 1525–1527)
Oil and Gas (pp. 1527–1529)

"There are two sorts of forecasters. Those who don't know and those who don't know they don't know."
J. K. Galbraith

  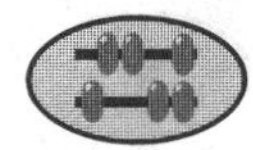   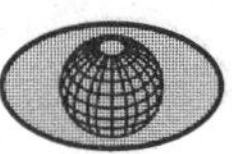   

Trading in Corporate Bonds: Why and How

DEFINITION

The term "corporate bond" is, from time to time, used to refer to all bonds except those issued by governments in their own currencies. However, it should actually be applied only to longer-term debt instruments that are issued by corporations.

Corporate bonds promise a higher return than some other investments, but the higher return comes at a cost. Most corporate bonds are debentures, which means that they are not secured by collateral. Investors in these bonds must take on not only the interest rate risk but the credit risk, which is the chance that the corporate issuer will default on its debt. It is important that investors in corporate bonds know how to weigh up credit risk and its possible payoffs. Rising interest rates can reduce the value of your bond investment, and a default can almost eliminate it. The *total yield* on a bond is all gains from coupons and price appreciation, and *current yield* is that from coupon payments.

Corporate bonds are like no other bonds in that they carry an implied risk. Takeovers, corporate restructuring, and leveraged buyouts can change a corporate bond's credit rating and price. Institutional investors use credit rating agencies such as Moody's, Standard & Poor's, and Fitch IBCA to check credit risk. However, many investors also use interest-coverage ratios and capitalization ratios. The *interest-coverage ratio* tells one how much money the company generates each year to fund the annual interest on its debt. The higher the ratio the better, but a company should at least generate enough earnings to service its annual debt. The *capitalization ratio* shows the company's degree of financial leverage. The lower the capitalization ratio, the better the company's financial leverage.

There are also other risk factors. If the bond is *callable*, the company has the right to buy it back after a period of time, while the *poison pill provision* permits shareholders to buy stock at a heavily discounted price to prevent or hinder takeovers. *Putable* bonds have a feature designed to protect against interest rate fluctuations, which allows the holder to return, or "tender," the bond to the issuer at par before the bond's maturity date. With junk bonds (i.e., those rated below S&P's BBB), the risk of losing everything is high and investors should consider the diversification of a high-yield bond fund, which can support a few defaults while still giving high returns.

ADVANTAGES

- Corporate bonds offer higher yields than their treasury equivalents. If you can spot the right investment, the compounding interest over the life of the bond can be quite astounding.
- The default risk on corporate bonds can be quantified using spread analysis, which seeks to determine the difference in yield between a given corporate bond and a risk-free treasury bond of the same maturity.

DISADVANTAGES

- Corporate bonds have an implied event risk. Takeovers, corporate restructuring, and even leveraged buyouts can penalize a bond's credit rating and price.
- Rising interest rates can reduce the value of your bond investment; a default can almost eliminate it.

ACTION CHECKLIST

- ✔ Assess the bond's credit risk rating in lists published by Standard & Poor's, Moody's, and Fitch IBCA.
- ✔ Analyze the credit risk and remember that bonds may have multiple issuances; each of these issues will receive different ratings from the credit agencies due to the fact that they have different repayment structures and conditions.

DOS AND DON'TS

DO

- Use interest-coverage ratios and capitalization ratios to back up the ratings given by Standard & Poor's, Moody's, and Fitch IBCA.
- Think about investing in a high-yield bond fund, which can support a few failures yet still provide high returns.

DON'T

- Don't take on credit risk or default from a single corporate bond issue unless you are receiving enough extra yield to cover the risk.

▸▸ MORE INFO

Books:

Crabbe, Leland E., and Frank J. Fabozzi. *Managing a Corporate Bond Portfolio*. Wiley Finance, Frank J. Fabozzi Series. New York: Wiley, 2002.

Swensen, David F. *Unconventional Success: A Fundamental Approach to Personal Investment*. New York: Simon & Schuster, 2005.

Wilson, Richard S., and Frank J. Fabozzi. *Corporate Bonds: Structures & Analysis*. New York: Wiley, 1995.

Article:

Investment Adviser. "The complete James Bond guide to investing." *Investment Adviser* (May 21, 2007).

Websites:

Fitch Ratings: www.fitchratings.com

Moody's Investors Service: www.moodys.com

Standard & Poor's: www.standardandpoors.com

Wall Street & Technology corporate bond trading systems directory: www.wallstreetandtech.com/corporatebond/directory

See Also:

★ Credit Ratings (pp. 534–536)

✔ The Bond Market: Its Structure and Function (p. 1010)

✔ How to Use Credit Rating Agencies (p. 939)

✔ Raising Capital by Issuing Bonds (p. 1020)

✔ Trading in Government Bonds: Why and How (p. 948)

"Change is inevitable, but it is in us to control its content and directions." Indira Gandhi

  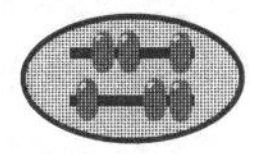 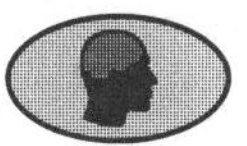  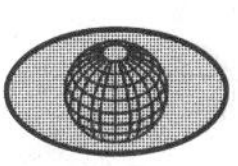   

Trading in Equities on Stock Exchanges

DEFINITION

Equity trading is the buying and selling of company stocks and shares. Stocks and shares in publicly traded companies are bought and sold through one of the major stock exchanges, which serve as managed auctions for stock. A stock exchange, share market, or bourse is a company, corporation, or mutual organization that provides facilities for stockbrokers and traders to trade stocks and other securities. Stock exchanges also provide facilities for the issue and redemption of securities, trading in other financial instruments, and the payment of income and dividends. To be traded on a stock exchange, a company has to be listed on it. Some international companies are listed on more than one exchange.

A share is one of a finite number of equal portions in the capital of a company, and a person owning shares is called a shareholder. Shares entitle the owner to a proportion of distributed, nonreinvested profits known as dividends, and to a proportion of the value of the company in the event of liquidation. Shares are classed as voting (Class A), with the right to vote on the board of directors, or nonvoting (Class B). This right can often affect the value of the share.

The value of a publicly traded company is called its market capitalization. This is calculated as the number of shares outstanding (as opposed to those authorized but not necessarily issued) times the price per share. A company's market capitalization should not be confused with the fair market value of the company, as the price per share can be influenced by factors such as the volume of shares traded.

A stockbroker is a qualified and regulated professional who buys and sells shares and other securities on his or her own behalf, or on behalf of investors. Equity trading can be performed by the owner of the shares or by a stockbroker authorized to buy and sell on behalf of the owner (in return for a commission). Most trading is carried out on electronic networks, which offer the advantages of up-to-the-second prices and information on the number of shares bought or sold, together with speed and a low transaction cost. The initial public offering (IPO) of stocks and shares to investors is done on the primary market and any subsequent trading is done in the secondary market.

ADVANTAGES

- Holding shares allows an investor to spread investment risk and participate in some of the world's premier companies.
- As a general rule, shares as an investment vehicle have, over the long run, outperformed all other types of investment.

DISADVANTAGES

- Share prices can be very volatile, and the value of shares depends on a number of external factors over which the investor has no control.
- Different shares can have different levels of liquidity, i.e., demand from buyers and sellers. Normally, blue chip stocks have greater depth and liquidity. The lower the market capitalization, the lower the liquidity, which may affect the ease with which the shares can be sold. Liquidity also affects share prices because, if the shares have low liquidity, it is sometimes more difficult to convert them into cash.

ACTION CHECKLIST

- ✔ To trade shares, you must have an account with a stockbroker or a licensed intermediary (financial planner, accountant, etc). This is to ensure that the trading environment is secure. Many new investors start using stockbrokers but others prefer to do their own research and use online brokers.
- ✔ Most brokers require you to have an account to ensure that you have the funds to cover orders. Some online brokers require you to have an account with an associated financial institution before you can begin trading.
- ✔ When placing a buy or sell order, there are two ways you can trade. Shares can be traded at *market order*, which means buying at the prevailing market price. The alternative is the *limit order*, where you set the minimum or maximum price.

DOS AND DON'TS

DO

- Research the company, and take into account any risks you feel might arise. If in doubt, use a *stop loss* to help protect your investment.

DON'T

- Don't invest on the basis of tips unless you are extremely confident of the source. More often than not, tipped shares—like tipped horses—will end up as "also-rans."

▸▸ MORE INFO

Books:

Maginn, John L., Donald L. Tuttle, Jerald E. Pinto, and Dennis W. McLeavey. *Managing Investment Portfolios: A Dynamic Process.* 3rd ed. CFA Institute Investment Series. Hoboken, NJ: Wiley, 2007.

Mobius, Mark. *Equities: An Introduction to the Core Concepts.* Singapore: Wiley, 2006.

Morris, Virginia B., and Kenneth M. Morris. *Standard & Poor's Guide to Money & Investing.* New York: Lightbulb Press, 2005.

Articles:

Investment Adviser. "Worldwide equity trading portal comes to the market." November 5, 2007. Online at: www.ftadviser.com/InvestmentAdviser/Archive/News/article/20071105/03d3b720-ea51-11dc-abcd-0015171400aa/Worldwide-equity-trading-portal-comes-to-the-market.jsp

Mehta, Nina. "TradeWeb eyes equity expansion in 2008." *Traders* (December 2007). Online at: www.tradersmagazine.com/issues/20_275/100087-1.html

Websites:

E*TRADE Financial, US online trading: www.etrade.com

Interactive Investor, a UK online share dealing provider: www.iii.co.uk/sharedealing

"No one has ever accused us of lagging behind. In fact, I am willing to turn an entire company upside down if it's time to do that. We're in perpetual evolution." Richard Branson

  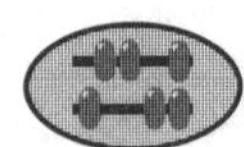 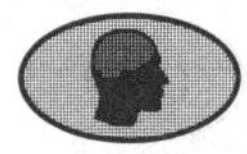  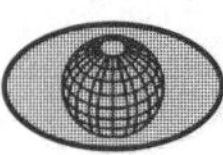   

Trading in Government Bonds: Why and How

DEFINITION

A government bond is a bond issued by a national government, denominated in the country's own currency. Sovereign bonds are those issued by foreign governments in their own currencies. Government bonds are usually thought of as risk-free, because even if a government has problems it can always raise taxes or simply print more money to redeem the bond. The maturities of sovereign bonds vary and will depend on the issuing government. The US government is the largest seller of government or treasury bonds in the world. Its bonds are auctioned in February and August, and have 30-year maturities.

In the *primary market*, bonds are sold in auctions. Bids are divided into competitive and noncompetitive bids. Competitive bids are restricted to primary government dealers, while noncompetitive bids are open to individual investors and small institutions.

Secondary market trading in bonds occurs in the over-the-counter (OTC) market. All US government securities are traded OTC, with the primary government securities dealers being the largest and most important market participants. In the secondary market a wide variety of investors use bonds for investing, hedging, and speculation. These investors include commercial and investment banks, insurance companies, pension funds, mutual funds, and retail investors.

While some electronic bond trading is available to retail investors, the entire bond market remains very much an OTC market. The bond market, unlike the equity markets (where electronic dealing and transparency have leveled the playing field for individual and institutional investors), lacks price transparency and liquidity, except in the case of government bonds. For the independent bond investor who would prefer to spread his or her risk and not pay the high fees for a managed fund, a good alternative is an *exchange-traded fund* or an *index bond fund*, which will track government bond indices and, given the high liquidity of these bonds, will present fewer problems than corporate bonds.

ADVANTAGES

- Price transparency and liquidity for government bonds are comparatively high, providing a safe platform for a wide range of investors to hedge and speculate. These investors include commercial and investment banks, insurance companies, pension funds, mutual funds, and retail investors.
- Government bonds are generally referred to as risk-free bonds, because governments can simply raise more taxes or print more money to pay for them.
- Government bonds are highly liquid and investors can recover some of their investment quickly if necessary.

DISADVANTAGES

- There is foreign-exchange risk for investors when the currency of the bonds in which they have invested declines in relation to their own.
- The risks of trading in government bonds stem, above all, from changes in interest rates, which can cause fluctuations in prices for bonds.
- Bond prices are influenced by economic data such as employment, income growth/decline, and consumer and industrial prices. Any information that implies rising inflation will weaken bond prices, as inflation reduces the income from a bond.

ACTION CHECKLIST

✔ If you are investing in sovereign funds, how safe is the government or region? Don't forget that in 1998 the Russian government defaulted on its debt.

✔ What are interest rates going to do? Investors who buy and sell bonds before maturity are exposed to many risks, most importantly changes in interest rates. When interest rates increase, new issues will pay a higher yield and the value of existing bonds will fall. When interest rates decline, the value of existing bonds will rise as new issues pay a lower yield.

DOS AND DON'TS

DO

- Before you buy, check how quickly you will be able to sell if necessary, and at what discount and dealing fee.

DON'T

- Don't unless you are completely confident, invest in only one type of bond. An exchange-traded fund or an index bond fund might be a much safer bet.

▸▸ MORE INFO

Books:

Faerber, Esmé. *All About Bonds and Bond Mutual Funds: The Easy Way to Get Started.* 2nd ed. New York: McGraw-Hill, 1999.

Rini, William A. *Mathematics of the Securities Industry.* New York: McGraw-Hill Professional, 2003.

Wong, M. Anthony, in collaboration with Robert High. *Trading and Investing in Bond Options: Risk Management, Arbitrage, and Value Investing.* Wiley Finance. New York: Wiley, 1991.

Articles:

"Comment: Investment—Getting the best from bonds." *Pensions Management* (April 2008). Online at: findarticles.com/p/articles/mi_hb6599

Lee, John P. "Bonds up on subprime speculations." Article on TradingMarkets.com (June 2008).

Rodier, Melanie. "The massive growth of electronic bond trading." *Wall Street & Technology* (April 15, 2008).

Websites:

Bloomberg.com: www.bloomberg.com/markets/rates/index.html

FTSE Global Bond Index, a series of fixed-income indices covering the principal government bond markets, global emerging, European covered, sterling- and euro-denominated corporate markets: www.ftse.com/Indices/FTSE_Global_Bond_Index_Series

Lehman Aggregate Bond Index: www.lehman.com

"I am not the one who transforms the company. . .The marketplace is what is changing France Télécom; the customers and the competition are its alpha and its omega. A company requires a leader, but individually no one can pretend to be the driving force." Michel Bon

  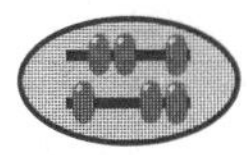   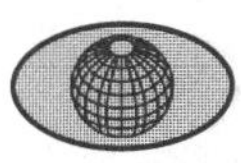   

Understanding and Using the Repos Market

DEFINITION

A repo, or repurchase agreement, is an agreement between two parties whereby one party sells the other a security at a specified price with a commitment to buy the security back at a later date. A repo is economically similar to a secured loan, with the buyer receiving securities as collateral to protect against default. Virtually any security can be used as a repo: treasury and government bills, corporate and government bonds, and stocks or shares can all be used as securities to back a repo. Although the transaction is similar to a loan, it differs in that the seller repurchases the legal ownership of the securities from the buyer at the end of the agreement. Also, while the legal title to the securities passes from the seller to the buyer, coupons that are paid while the repo buyer owns the securities are normally passed directly to the repo seller.

Repos are contracts for the sale and future repurchase of a financial asset, normally treasury securities. The annualized rate of interest paid on the loan is known as the repo rate. Repos can be of any duration, but are most commonly overnight loans, or *overnight repos*. Repos longer than this are known as *term repos*. There are also *open repos*, which can be terminated by either side on a day's notice. The lender normally receives a margin on the security, meaning that it is priced below market value, typically by 2% to 5%, depending on maturity. Repos are normally not for the smaller investor: in the primary market dealers frequently transact hundreds of millions of dollars, and in the secondary market repos of one million dollars are not uncommon.

The Federal Reserve Bank also uses repos in its open-market operations as a method of fine-tuning the money supply. To expand the supply of money temporarily, the Federal Reserve arranges to buy securities from non-bank dealers, which deposit the proceeds in their commercial bank accounts, thereby adding to reserves. The repos usually last 1 to 15 days, or whatever length of time the Federal Reserve needs to make the adjustment. When it wishes to reduce the money supply, it reverses the process using a "matched sale purchase transaction": it sells securities to dealers, who either draw on bank balances directly or take out a bank loan to make the payment, thereby withdrawing reserves.

ADVANTAGES

- Repos allow investors to keep surplus funds invested without losing liquidity or incurring price risk or credit risk because the collateral is more often than not in high-class securities.
- Repos can be used for investing surplus funds in the short term, or for short-term borrowing against collateral. Corporations can use repos to help manage their liquidity and short-term financing of their inventories.

DISADVANTAGES

- Overnight changes in interest rates or currency fluctuations can affect the value of a dealer's securities holding, and a dealer who holds a large position takes a risk.
- Repos are normally not for the smaller investor: in the primary market dealers frequently transact hundreds of millions of dollars, and in the secondary market repos of one million dollars are not uncommon.
- The seller could default on his or her obligation and fail to repurchase the securities.

ACTION CHECKLIST

- ✔ What type of repo are you buying, and in which international market? Will risk and return be affected by currency fluctuations, credit risk, the type and liquidity of the security, or third-party involvement?
- ✔ Does the securities dealer have a special repo account at a clearing bank to settle his or her trades?
- ✔ Primary dealers must be authorized by the Federal Reserve Bank to bid on newly issued treasury securities for resale on the markets.

DOS AND DON'TS

DO

- Check on any repos in equity securities. Complications can arise sometimes because of greater complexity in the tax rules on dividends.

DON'T

- Don't fail to check on the credit risk associated with the repo, i.e. type and liquidity of security, other parties involved, etc.

▸▸ MORE INFO

Books:

Fabozzi, Frank J. (ed), and Moorad Choudhry. *The Handbook of European Fixed Income Securities*. Frank J. Fabozzi Series. Hoboken, NJ: Wiley, 2004.

Levinson, Marc. *Guide to Financial Markets*. 4th ed. London: Profile, 2006.

Mathieson, Donald J., and Garry J. Schinasi. *International Capital Markets: Developments, Prospects, and Key Policy Issues*. Washington, DC: International Monetary Fund, 2001.

Articles:

de Teran, Natasha. "Euribor swap a boost for repo market." *Financial News* (September 15, 2003).

Wright, Ben. "Growth of European repo market stalls." *Financial News* (March 16, 2003).

Websites:

European Central Bank: www.ecb.int

US Federal Reserve: www.federalreserve.gov

See Also:

★ Investing in Structured Finance Products in the Debt Money Markets (pp. 337–340)

✔ Identifying Weak Points in Your Liquidity (p. 868)

✔ Measuring Liquidity (p. 875)

✔ Money Markets: Their Structure and Function (p. 1016)

"Corporate insiders. . .can seldom transform an organizationorganisation beset by inertia." John P. Kotter

  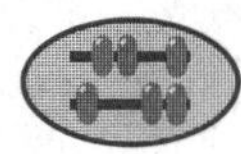   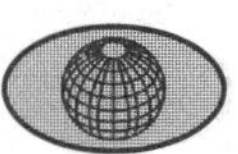   

Understanding Price Volatility

DEFINITION

In a free market, prices are effectively set by the relative levels of supply and demand for the underlying asset. Thus, prices are naturally impacted by rapid changes in the levels of confidence and conviction of market participants, both over short and long terms. Though price fluctuations are part of normal free market activity, at times unexpected major events can have a significant impact on the market's confidence. During such periods, normal price movements can give way to greater price swings, as market prices gyrate according to the participants' rapidly changing view of fair value. These price swings are exacerbated in periods of sharp market declines, partly because liquidity can also fall as fewer market participants are willing to attempt to underpin tumbling markets hit by panic selling. In contrast, rising markets typically enjoy higher levels of liquidity, but can, nevertheless, also suffer from rapid price swings, although these are frequently less dramatic in nature than in sudden market slides. Nevertheless, all kinds of market uncertainty can breed volatility.

Though the general concept of volatility is widely understood, in statistical terms volatility represents the relative rate at which the price moves up or down, as defined by the daily price movement's annualized standard deviation. Thinking in terms of the "bell curve" image associated with the mention of statistical calculations, one standard deviation represents the maximum daily movement we can expect 68% of the time, while the range of two standard deviations should cover 95% of daily net changes. However, it's important to recognize that by utilizing the input of past data, we are calculating *historical volatility*. Another way of expressing volatility is *implied volatility*, which uses the prices of market instruments, such as options, to evaluate investors' forecasts of future volatility. Though the models developed for options pricing can be highly complex, it is predictable that options prices are likely to be higher at a time of greater perceived uncertainty and elevated volatility, than at other times when investors' expectations of market conditions are more benign.

ADVANTAGES

- Volatility calculations allow comparisons of market conditions during different eras.
- The pricing of derivative instruments, such as options, relies on some form of volatility variable.
- Elevated levels of market volatility can create opportunities for longer-term investors.

DISADVANTAGES

- Volatility-related calculations can be complex, particularly when related to advanced options pricing models.
- High levels of volatility can add to existing levels of market uncertainty, creating a vicious circle for inexperienced market participants.

ACTION CHECKLIST

- ✔ Visualize the basic "bell curve" image of past price movement outcomes to help introduce the concept of volatility to inexperienced investors.
- ✔ Acknowledge that volatility in itself is not a guide to market direction, as volatility can move independently of market sentiment.
- ✔ Consider how derivative instruments, such as options, caps, and collars, could help you towards your volatility and wider risk management objectives.

DOS AND DON'TS

DO

- Recognize the difference between historical (backward-focused) and implied volatility (based on future perceptions).
- Appreciate that volatility isn't a "bad thing" or a "good thing" as such—it's part and parcel of free markets.

DON'T

- Don't waste resources crunching the numbers manually—use spreadsheets or specialized volatility/options pricing packages for calculations.
- Don't mistake calculations based on historical data as any definitive guide to the market's future movements—more stocks can be subject to movements beyond the "predicted" standard deviations than the numbers might suggest.

▸▸ MORE INFO

Books:

Knight, John, and Stephen Satchell. *Forecasting Volatility in the Financial Markets*. 3rd ed. Quantitative Finance Series. Woburn MA: Butterworth-Heinemann, 2007.

Taylor, Stephen J. *Asset Price Dynamics, Volatility and Prediction*. Princeton, NJ: Princeton University Press, 2007.

Articles:

Garman, Mark B., and Michael J. Klass. "On the estimation of security price volatility from historical data." *Journal of Business* 53:1 (1980): 67–78. Updated version online at: www.fea.com/resources/pdf/a_estimation_of_security_price.pdf

Mazzucato, M., and W. Semmler. "The determinants of stock price volatility: An industry study." *Nonlinear Dynamics, Psychology, and Life Sciences* 6:2 (2002). Online at: oro.open.ac.uk/9463/

Website:

Volatility and option price calculator: www.option-price.com

See Also:

★ The Ability of Ratings to Predict the Performance of Exchange-Traded Funds (pp. 277–280)
★ The Impact of Index Trackers on Shareholders and Stock Volatility (pp. 325–327)
Eugene Fama (p. 1164)
How the Stock Market Works (p. 1274)

"Business leaders must not cling to old ways of doing business, or allow inertia or complacency to prevent them from making the decisions that they will eventually be forced to make." Patricia Hewitt

  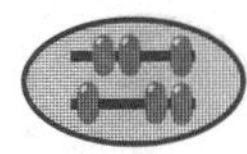   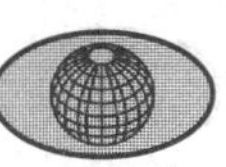   

Understanding Private Equity Strategies: An Overview

DEFINITION

Private equity firms generally want to buy companies or parts of companies for their portfolios, repair them, enhance them, and sell them on. The investment period is seldom less than a year and can be as long as 10 years, but the objective is always to sell the business on at a substantial profit. Private equity investors have three main investment strategies:

1 *Venture capital* is a broad class of private equity that normally refers to equity investments in less mature companies. Venture capital is often subdivided according to the phase of maturity of the company, ranging from capital used for the launch of start-up companies to later-stage and growth capital. It is often used to fund the expansion of an existing business that is generating revenue but may not yet be profitable or generating sufficient cash flow to fund future investment.

2 *Growth capital* refers to equity investments (most often minority investments) in more mature companies that are looking for capital to expand or restructure operations, enter new markets, or finance a major acquisition without a change in the control of the business.

3 The *leveraged buyout* (LBO) is a strategy of equity investment whereby a company, business unit, or business asset is acquired from the current shareholders, typically with the use of financial leverage. The companies involved in these buyouts are generally more mature and generate cash flows.

Occasionally, investments are made in *distressed* or *special* situations, where the equity or debt securities of a distressed company are unlocked as a result of a one-off opening, such as market turmoil or changes in financial regulations.

ADVANTAGES

- Private equity can provide high returns, with the best private equity investments significantly outperforming the public markets. The potential benefits for successful investors can be annual returns of up to 30%.
- An important perceived advantage of private equity is that the agency problem is reduced, because the owners have direct contact with the managers and can do detailed monitoring.
- Because private equity firms focus on just a few investments, their due diligence is much more solid (and costly) than that of the investor in a public company.
- Not only is a far larger share of executive pay tied to the performance of the business, but top managers may also be required to put a major chunk of their own money into the deal and have an ownership mentality rather than a corporate mentality.
- With LBOs, management can focus on getting the company right without having to worry about shareholders.

DISADVANTAGES

- Most private equity investments have significant entry requirements, stipulating a considerable initial investment (normally upwards of $1,000,000), which can be drawn upon at the manager's discretion.
- Private equity investment is for those who can afford to have their capital locked in for long periods of time and who are able to risk losing it.

ACTION CHECKLIST

- ✔ Bankers are much more wary of leveraged financing nowadays, and they should be included at the beginning of the planning, as well as during the negotiation stages.
- ✔ Carefully analyze any business you might be proposing to acquire. Does its portfolio fit the characteristics required to mount an LBO? Can you revamp it, enhance it, and sell it? What time-frame will you be looking at?
- ✔ Use specialist financial researchers and advisers. Remember that any undiscovered potential liabilities might cost more in the long run.

DOS AND DON'TS

DO

- In the primary stages, involve your lawyers and accountants in the evaluation of both the risks and the potential benefits of an acquisition.
- When the company has been acquired, use incentives to engage the onboard key business managers in helping with the turnaround process.
- Involve key stakeholders, and spell out in clear terms the risks the organization may be facing, their probability, and their potential impact, whether positive or negative.

DON'T

- Don't put the cart before the horse and make the mistake of being drawn to a business that has not been thoroughly investigated. Consider not only whether it can be turned around, but also whether you can get the financing.

▸▸ MORE INFO

Books:

Fraser-Sampson, Guy. *Private Equity as an Asset Class*. Wiley Finance Series. Chichester, UK: Wiley, 2007.

Maginn, John L., Donald L. Tuttle, Jerald E. Pinto, and Dennis W. McLeavey (eds). *Managing Investment Portfolios: A Dynamic Process*. 3rd ed. CFA Institute Investment Series. Hoboken, NJ: Wiley, 2007.

Morris, Virginia B., and Kenneth M. Morris. *Standard and Poor's Guide to Money and Investing*. New York: Lightbulb Press, 2005.

Articles:

Dewar, Sally. "Private equity." Australasian Business Intelligence (June 2007). *Journal of Applied Corporate Finance* 19:3 (Summer 2007).

McKellar, Peter. "An appetite for private equity." *Investment Adviser* (April 2008).

Website:

The British Private Equity and Venture Capital Association: www.bvca.co.uk

"You can't fight against the future. Time is on our side." William Ewart Gladstone

     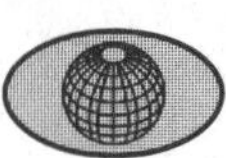   

Using Investment Funds (Unit and Investment Trusts)

DEFINITION

Unit investment trusts (UITs) are companies that are registered to make investments on behalf of their clients. They buy and hold a portfolio of stocks and bonds, which they then sell to investors. These portfolios are known as "units." The purchasers of units are known as unit holders, and they receive interest on the investment that they make in this way.

UITs have a termination date according to the investment units they offer. Long-term bonds may be held for as long as 20 to 30 years. When the termination date arrives, unit holders may choose to receive the proceeds or reinvest them in another trust.

Units are bought and sold through the fund manager. The value of the units may rise or fall according to the overall value of the fund. This value moves according to the underlying share prices in the fund.

In investment trusts, the buyer invests directly in the shares of different companies rather than indirectly through shares in a pooled fund. This is the main difference between investment trusts and unit trusts. The value of these trusts can fluctuate more often and more significantly than that of unit trusts, as share prices are more directly affected by supply and demand.

The companies offering these trusts are diverse in terms of risk, and the buyer can choose among high- and low-risk investments, as is also the case with unit trusts.

ADVANTAGES

- The main advantage of a UIT is its diversification. The UIT buys various types of stocks or bonds, which helps its investors to reduce their risk. The risk is mitigated by potential gains in some securities that offset the risk of loss in others. The idea here is that some of the purchased securities will always show gains, even if others do not.
- UITs provide the average investor with more possibilities in terms of investments than would otherwise be the case. In other words, UIT investments can be much less costly than constructing a portfolio of individual securities.
- The diversity offered by both UITs and investment trusts provides the buyer with both security and reasonable investment prices.
- A further advantage is the two different types of UIT, offering the investor even further choices. Fixed-income and equity UITs provide the buyer with almost any level of risk and investment objective desired.

DISADVANTAGES

- First-time investors might be tempted to take risks for which they are unprepared. It is therefore important to take great care to investigate all the markets involved. Diversifying investments means diversifying risks. While this may be an advantage, it can also bring certain disadvantages. There is always the risk, for example, that losses in some securities may outweigh the gains in others. However, with the necessary precautions, UITs and investment trusts offer perhaps the best opportunity for investors to enter the market.

ACTION CHECKLIST

- ✔ Ensure that you have enough funds to invest your chosen amount in a UIT or investment trust.
- ✔ Obtain the trust's prospectus, which will contain specific information about your investment.
- ✔ Make sure that you are fully informed of the level of risk you are taking and that you are comfortable with this risk level.

DOS AND DON'TS

DO

- Consult experienced financial advisers and investment brokers before investing.
- Look carefully at the variety of choices within the UIT and investment markets.
- Ensure that you are aware of the legislation relating to the company and investment you choose.
- Ensure that you receive an annual report from your UIT as it will contain valuable information about your investment.

DON'T

- Don't invest if you have not carefully considered and discussed your options with your financial advisers.
- Don't make an investment if you are not sure that you can handle the risks involved.
- Don't invest without having sufficient funds to do so; your current financial security is as important as your wealth in the future.

▸▸ MORE INFO

Books:

Burton, H., and D. C. Corner. *Investment and Unit trusts in Britain and America.* London: Elek, 1968.

Downes, John, and Jordan Elliot Goodman. *Finance and Investment Handbook.* 7th ed. Hauppauge, NY: Barron's, 2006.

Duddington, John. *Equity and Trusts.* 2nd ed. Law Express Series. Harlow, UK: Pearson Education, 2008.

Edwards, Richard, and Nigel Stockwell. *Trusts and Equity.* 8th ed. Foundation Studies in Law Series. Harlow, UK: Pearson Education, 2007.

See Also:

★ Investing Cash: Back to Basics (pp. 334–336)

✔ Appraising Investment Opportunities (p. 1058)

✔ Mean–Variance Optimization: A Primer (p. 941)

✔ Trading in Corporate Bonds: Why and How (p. 946)

Gary Brinson (p. 1156)

"Others appear frozen in the headlights—aware of the likely impact, yet paralysed by the fear of major transformations." Patricia Hewitt

     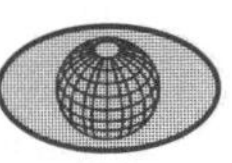   

Using Shareholder Value Analysis

DEFINITION

Shareholder value is a term that suggests that the decisive measure of a company's success is how well it enriches its shareholders. Shareholder Value Analysis (SVA) is one of a number of techniques used as substitutes for traditional business measurements. It became fashionable in the 1980s, when it was linked to Jack Welch, then CEO of General Electric.

Essentially, the idea is that shareholders' money should be used to earn a higher return than it could by investing in other assets with the same amount of risk. To calculate shareholder value, you estimate the total net worth of a company, i.e. total assets minus total liabilities, and divide this figure by the value of its shares. The result gives you the shareholder value of the company. The basic rule of SVA is that a company adds value for its shareholders only when equity returns exceed equity costs. When that value has been calculated, the company can take steps to improve its performance and also use SVA to measure the success of those actions.

Although there are some complex formulae for working out shareholder value, it can also be determined using three simpler approaches:

- Discount the expected cash flows to the present to reach an estimated economic value for the business.
- Use the appropriate cost of capital for the business to find the actual cost of investment discounted to the present.
- Work out the economic value of the business by calculating the difference between the results of the above analyses.

SVA is also known as value-based management. The principle is that the management of any company should first and foremost consider how the interests of its shareholders will be affected by any decisions it takes. This is not a new management theory; it is the legal premise upon which any publicly traded company is set up.

ADVANTAGES

- SVA holds that management should first and foremost consider the interests of shareholders in its business decisions.
- SVA takes a long-term view and is about measuring and managing cash flows over time. It provides the user with a clear understanding of value creation or degradation over time within each business unit.
- SVA offers a common approach, which is not subject to the particular accounting policies that are adopted. It is therefore globally applicable and can be used across most sectors.
- SVA forces companies to focus on the future and their customers, with specific attention to the value of future cash flows.

DISADVANTAGES

- The concentration on shareholder value does not take into account societal needs. Shareholder value financially benefits only the owners of a corporation; it does not provide a clear measure of social factors such as employment, environmental issues, or ethical business practices. Therefore, a management decision can maximize shareholder value while adversely affecting third parties, including other companies.
- It can be extremely difficult to estimate future cash flows accurately—a key component of SVA. This can lead to the use of faulty or ambiguous figures as the basis for strategic decisions.
- The development and implementation of an SVA system can be long and complex.
- Management of shareholder value requires more complete information than traditional measures and can therefore take up management time.

ACTION CHECKLIST

- ✔ Before adopting SVA, it is important to understand the implications it will have for your business.
- ✔ You should consult professional advisers, such as accountants or consultants who specialize in this area and who can inform you of what the ramifications may be.
- ✔ SVA is based on the principle that creation and maximization of shareholder value is the most important measure of a business's performance.
- ✔ All members of the organization must be committed to the principle for it to work effectively.

DOS AND DON'TS

DO

- Consult professional advisers, such as accountants or consultants who specialize in this area. The changes required to implement SVA could be costly—even more so if you find you need to reverse them.

DON'T

- Don't take on board SVA as a system unless you are positive that your overriding concern is shareholder value.

➤➤ MORE INFO

Books:

Barker, R. *Determining Value: Valuation Models and Financial Statements.* Harlow, UK: Pearson Education, 2001.

Business: The Ultimate Resource. 2nd ed. London: Bloomsbury Publishing, 2006.

Pike, R., and B. Neale. *Corporate Finance and Investment: Decisions and Strategies.* 5th ed. Harlow, UK: Pearson Education, 2006.

Articles:

Business Wire. "Discover how the report ` Shareholder value—a value creation approach' will enable your organisation to deliver superior long-term value to its shareholders." *Business Wire* Press Release (24 June, 2008). Online at: www.reuters.com/article/pressRelease/idUS111282+24-Jun-2008+BW20080624

Chartered Management Institute. "Shareholder value analysis (Checklist 160)." Checklists: Managing Information and Finance, October 1, 2005. Online at: www.accessmylibrary.com/coms2/summary_0286-12721573_ITM

Websites:

American Accounting Association (AAA): www.aaa-edu.org

Institute of Internal Auditors: www.theiia.org

"You can't permit a honeymoon of small changes over a year or two. A long series of small changes just prolongs the pain." Percy Barnevik

   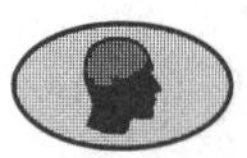  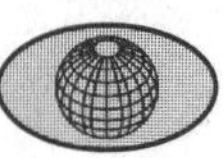   

Achieving Success in International Acquisitions

DEFINITION

All too often domestic acquisitions fail to deliver all of the shareholder value envisaged by management ahead of the deal. According to a 2003 survey by KPMG, 70% of M&A transactions failed to achieve the goals set by top management. Throw into the mix the further complications of international acquisitions, such as possible culture clashes and suspicions over the impact of foreign control, and the prospects of making a real success of an international acquisition would seem to diminish even further. However, there are several issues, such as the need to ensure effective communication and the importance of technology integration, which companies should consider ahead of an international deal as together these could significantly increase the prospects for success.

As with domestic acquisitions, potential acquirers should fully assess the extent of the strategic fit between the companies, considering whether the businesses could be combined in such a way as to unlock sufficient benefits as a single entity. In some cases, companies that have had a long period of successful strategic partnerships can find that their existing operational familiarity can work to their advantage in a merger or acquisition. From the employees' perspective, experience of working in partnership with a potential acquirer may also allay some concerns over the risk of a serious culture clash.

Effective communication is at least as important in international acquisitions as in domestic transactions. Such communication should extend beyond the boundaries of the companies involved to include clients, suppliers, local authorities, and governments, as well as employees and investors, as a failure to communicate effectively and truthfully with any party could create suspicion over the objective of the acquisition.

While cultural factors can play an important role in the success or failure of an international acquisition, conventional practicalities of day-to-day operations of the combined entities must also be given adequate consideration. For example, a survey by PricewaterhouseCoopers in 2000 found that the integration of information systems was the biggest challenge following an acquisition, with almost three in four firms reporting problems in this area.

ADVANTAGES

- International acquisitions can improve operational efficiency (for example, through economies of scale), enabling companies to compete more effectively against the backdrop of increased globalization.
- Acquisitions can also help a company to capitalize further on an existing competitive advantage.
- International acquisitions can enable the acquirer to gain access to an existing network of clients and suppliers rapidly in a new market. Establishing an effective presence in a foreign market from scratch, by means other than an acquisition, could take many years.

DISADVANTAGES

- Most acquisitions fail to deliver all the originally projected benefits.
- Poorly managed acquisitions can create a climate of suspicion among employees of the target company, affecting morale and productivity.
- Acquisitions can involve a considerable drain on management resources and can also generate high transaction costs.

ACTION CHECKLIST

- ✔ Take time to identify a target company that has some strategic fit with your own organization.
- ✔ Consider how closely the target company should be integrated following acquisition. There is some evidence that close integration can be disadvantageous in cases where the cultural fit between companies is limited.
- ✔ Learn from the successes and failures of other similar cross-border acquisitions in specific industries.

DOS AND DON'TS

DO

- Take professional advice on the regulatory environment in the target market at an early stage in the process.
- Ensure that all relevant information is effectively communicated to all stakeholders before and after the acquisition.
- Utilize the experience of managers from the acquired company in the post-merger management team.

DON'T

- Don't ignore the importance of cultural factors as well as operational requirements when planning an acquisition.
- Don't underestimate the importance of due diligence, particularly in markets where business practices may be different from those in your domestic market.
- Don't change management personnel unnecessarily as this can be highly disruptive to existing operations.

▸▸ MORE INFO

Books:

BenDaniel, David J., Arthur H. Rosenbloom, and James J. Hanks, Jr. *International M&A, Joint Ventures and Beyond: Doing the Deal, Workbook*. 2nd ed. Hoboken, NJ: Wiley, 2002.

Child, John, David Faulkner, and Robert Pitkethly. *The Management of International Acquisitions*. Oxford: Oxford University Press, 2001.

Articles:

Duncan, Catriona, and Monia Mtar. "Determinants of international acquisition success: Lessons from FirstGroup in North America." *European Management Journal* 24:6 (2006): 396–410.

Lynch, Richard. "International acquisition and other growth strategies: Some lessons from the food and drink industry." *Thunderbird International Business Review* 48:5 (2006): 605–622.

Website:

International Network of M&A Partners (IMAP): www.imap.com

"If you want to succeed you should strike out on new paths rather than travel the worn paths of accepted success." Anita Roddick

     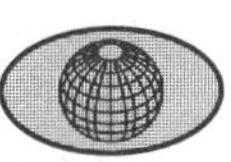   

Acquiring a Company

DEFINITION

The acquisition of a company involves buying the company's shares. The expression is also used when the business of a company is acquired. In legal terms, the consequences of an acquisition of shares or an acquisition of business assets are different. One of the key differences is that an acquisition of shares involves buying the underlying business of that company, with all of its assets but also its liabilities. By acquiring the business only, the assets are transferred but in principle the liabilities are left with the seller. There are some exceptions to this rule so it is advisable to seek specific legal, financial, and commercial advice before taking any decision.

The process starts with the identification of the business to be acquired. The commercial price of the shares is linked to the value of the business of the company. Usually, negotiations will take place between the buyer and the seller, with a purchase price agreed upon. The next stage involves the investigation of the business to be acquired, a process often called due diligence. In order to reassure the seller, a confidentiality agreement should be signed to protect the seller against any leaks of sensitive company-specific information to third parties. The process involves: a legal due diligence (undertaken by the buyer's lawyers), which investigates the legal rights and obligations affecting the business of the company; a financial due diligence (undertaken by the buyer's accountants), which looks at all the financial, accounting and tax affairs of the company; and a commercial due diligence (usually undertaken by the buyer's own team), which looks mainly at the integration and practical aspects of the business following the acquisition. These final aspects could include: the integration of key members of staff in the buyer's operations; and the revision of commercial and insurance contracts to facilitate the planning of logistical aspects of the buyer's operations and to avoid any unnecessary duplication of suppliers or insurance.

Following the due diligence process, the legal documentation is drafted, agreed upon, and ultimately signed. In practice, negotiations can break down as a result of the discovery of underlying liabilities that seriously devalue the business of the seller's company. The sale and purchase agreement will incorporate certain warranties and indemnities that the seller will be required to give to the buyer. Warranties are factual statements regarding the state of the seller's business affairs, while indemnities provide the buyer with rights to obtain a certain payment in specific circumstances. Warranties can also result in a payment by the seller to the buyer, but actual proof of a loss is required before any payment is due.

ADVANTAGES

Advantages of a business-asset acquisition, rather than a share acquisition:

- An existing business can be improved by acquiring certain assets without the difficulties and costs involved in acquiring the seller's company.
- The assets will be acquired at the current market value, which will give them a high base cost in terms of capital gains tax. The purchase will, therefore, attract maximum capital allowances. The seller can obtain certain reliefs against capital gains tax.
- Overall, a less complicated and less thorough investigation is required than in a share acquisition. The latter would involve the valuation and assessment of all the existing rights and liabilities of the seller's company, including all contractual agreements.

DISADVANTAGES

- In the United Kingdom, for example, VAT is chargeable on an asset sale but not on a share sale.
- Stamp duty for an acquisition of shares is paid by the buyer. In the United Kingdom the rate of 0.5% of the price of the shares, while for assets the rate is 4%.

ACTION CHECKLIST

- ✔ Study carefully any business you might acquire. Obtain as much information from as many sources as you can before committing to an expensive due diligence process.
- ✔ Know your market and make sure that you have analyzed the consequences for your own business of the acquisition of another business.
- ✔ Be prepared for a long and complicated due diligence process, which could prove time consuming as well as costly.
- ✔ Economize by negotiating a reasonable rate with your legal and financial advisers, but remember that it is better to incur costs by conducting a thorough investigation than to accept a level of service that may fail to reveal potentially costly liabilities.

DOS AND DON'TS

DO

- Involve your solicitors and accountants in the evaluation of both the risks and potential benefits of an acquisition, as well as the due diligence process.
- Negotiate your rates and make a contingency plan for any cost overrun.
- Plan carefully the integration of the new business within your own.

DON'T

- Don't be attracted by a business that has not been thoroughly investigated.
- Don't overlook the importance of negotiating complex warranties and indemnities that would protect you in the event that underlying liabilities are discovered.

▸▸ MORE INFO

Books:

Dewhurst, John. *Buying a Company: The Keys to Successful Acquisition*. London: Bloomsbury Publishing, 1997.

Rao, P. M. *Mergers and Acquisitions of Companies*. New Delhi, India: Deep & Deep Publications, 2002.

Smith, Ian. *Financial Techniques for Business Acquisitions and Disposals*. 2nd ed. Hawksmere Report Series. London: Throgood Publishing, 1998.

Article:

Rowan-Robinson, Jeremy, and Norman Hutchinson. "Compensation for the compulsory acquisition of business interests: Satisfaction or sacrifice." *Journal of Property Valuation and Investment* 13:1 (1995): 44–65.

"I buy when other people are selling." J. Paul Getty

  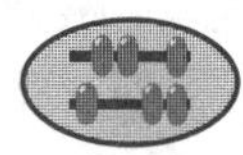   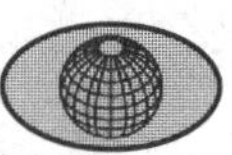   

Acquisition Accounting

DEFINITION

Acquisition accounting relates to the accounting procedure following the take-over of one company by another. The resulting entity is often known as a business combination. Exact standards may vary from one country to another so it is important to obtain professional advice on the procedures relating to acquisition accounting in the country in which the business combination will be operating. In the UK, for example, the Accounting Standards Board FRS 7 Standard sets out the principles of accounting for a business combination under the acquisition method of accounting. In the USA, the Financial Accounting Standard Board's Statement No 141 sets out what a reporting entity should provide in its financial reports in relation to a business combination and its effects. However, there is a process of convergence taking place across the globe, led by the International Accounting Standards Board (IASB). Its standards: IFRS 3 Business Combinations and of IAS 27 Consolidated and Separate Financial Statements are increasingly recognized by governments around the world.

Prior to June 2001, two accounting methods could be used when a merger or acquisition took place. They were the purchase method and the pooling of interests method. However, the purchase method is now compulsory in the USA and the EU and wherever else the IFRS standard issued by the IASB is recognized. Under the purchase method, the assets and liabilities of the merged company are presented at their market values as on the date of acquisition. The acquisition must be estimated at fair value and the difference between the purchase price and the fair value should be recognized as goodwill. Under the pooling of interests method, transactions are considered as exchange of equity securities. The assets and liabilities of the two firms are combined according to their book value on the acquisition date.

ADVANTAGES

- The increasing use of the purchase method means that it is easier to compare potential acquisition targets around the world in accountancy terms at least.
- Under the purchase method, a company cannot create a restructuring provision to provide for future losses or restructuring costs as a result of an acquisition. Such costs must be treated as post acquisition costs. Consequently, it is easier to gauge the impact of restructuring costs on profits, and prevent the use of provisions to exaggerate the immediate impact of an acquisition on profits, while boosting reported profits in subsequent years.

DISADVANTAGES

- One of the main drawbacks of the purchase method is that it may overrate depreciation charges because the book value of assets used in accounting is generally lower than the fair value if the economy is experiencing relatively high inflation.
- If the amount paid for a company is greater than fair market value - the difference is reflected as goodwill. Since goodwill must be written off against future earnings, the pooling of interests method is preferable to the purchase method.

ACTION CHECKLIST

- ✔ Check which acquisition accounting standards apply in the country in which you are undertaking an acquisition.
- ✔ If you can use either the purchase method or the pooling of interests method take professional advice on which is the most advantageous.

DOS AND DON'TS

DO

- Obtain advice from legal and accounting professionals before proceeding with any acquisition.
- Remember that, the purchase method, of accounting must identify the acquirer (the entity that obtains control over the other entity).

DON'T

- Don't forget that, under the purchase method, investors are likely to disregard the impact of goodwill.
- Don't forget that, under the purchase method, the elimination of provisions creates extra visibility and helps prevent abuses.

MORE INFO

Books:

Lajoux, Alexandra Reed. *The Art of M&A Integration: A Guide to Merging Resources, Processes, and Responsibilities.* New York: McGraw-Hill Professional, 2005.

Lewis, Richard, and David Pendrill. *Advanced Financial Accounting*. London: Pearson Education, 2004.

Siegel, Joel G., Nick Dauber, and Jae K. Shim. *The Vest Pocket CPA.*. Hoboken, NJ: Wiley, 2005.

Articles:

Dos Santos, M. B., V. R. Errunza, and D.P. Miller. "Does corporate international diversification destroy value? Evidence from cross-border mergers and acquisitions." *Journal of Banking and Finance* 32:12 (2008): 2716–2724.

James, K., J. How, and P. Verhoeven. "Did the goodwill accounting standard impose material economic consequences on Australian acquirers?" *Accounting and Finance* 48:4 (2008): 625–647.

Pasiouras, F., C. Gaganis, and C. Zopounidis. "Regulations, supervision approaches and acquisition likelihood in the Asian banking industry" *Asia Pacific Financial Markets* 15:2 (2008): 135–154.

Wesbite:

International Accounting Standards Board: www.iasb.org

See Also:

✔ Structuring M&A Deals and Tax Planning (p. 962)
✔ Using IRR for M&A Financing (p. 964)
✔ Using the Market-Value Method for Acquisitions (p. 966)

"People are no longer content to talk merely of organizational change. . .the new aspiration is for organizational transformation." S. K. Chakraborty

  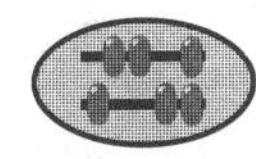 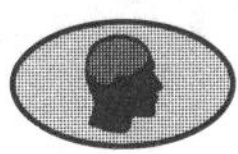  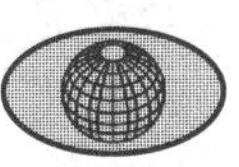 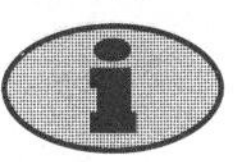  

M&A Regulations: A Global Overview

DEFINITION

Mergers and acquisitions (M&A) has become a mundane expression, used daily in the media. In order to operate successfully in a global economy, corporations have become transnational and have to perform at a multinational level. To achieve such expansion, corporations acquire other companies or merge with them. These large corporations are publicly owned, listed on stock exchanges or alternative markets around the world, and engage in M&A activities that are thoroughly regulated by governments to protect the shareholders of target companies.

The laws and regulations governing M&A are very complex and strict. High levels of expertise and specialist advice are required, and corporations use several teams of lawyers who specialize in the jurisdictions involved in M&A.

In 2003, the European Parliament published a directive that regulated the way in which securities were to be offered to the public or admitted to trading. This became known as the EU Prospective Directive. Its scope was to harmonize and homogenize capital markets within the European Union. In essence, the directive allows a company that issues shares in more than one EU member state to be governed by a single member state, rather than by each member state in which the shares are offered.

In the United States, federal securities laws and regulations are generally applicable if US investors own securities in a foreign target company. In the United States, the Securities and Exchange Commission is the body that supervises and oversees the most important participants in the securities world, such as securities exchanges, dealers, brokers, and mutual funds. Its most important role is to promote disclosure and transparency of market information by maintaining fair dealing and ensuring protection against fraud.

In Australia, the responsibility belongs to the Australian Stock Exchange and the Australian Securities and Investments Commission, while the relevant body in the United Kingdom is the London Stock Exchange.

In September 2006 the Regulations on Foreign Investors' Mergers and Acquisitions of Domestic Enterprises came into force in China, as a direct result of an increase in M&A transactions and the general opening up of the country.

Japan has recently eased regulation on foreign investment by introducing legislation that allows foreign-owned companies to invest in Japanese companies through stock-for-stock (share-for-share) exchanges with the Japanese subsidiaries of those companies.

ADVANTAGES

- M&A regulations protect shareholders and investors in the acquirer and target company.
- In general M&A regulations allow for the harmonization and homogenization of international markets and thus maintain transparency, fair dealing, and protection against fraud.

DISADVANTAGES

- M&A regulations are very complex.
- Specialist financial and legal advice is always required when participating in M&A activity.
- The cost of an acquisition is usually high, and specialist advice only adds to this cost.

ACTION CHECKLIST

- ✔ Recognise the complexity of M&A regulations.
- ✔ Seek specialist professional advice at an early stage when considering a possible M&A deal.
- ✔ Appreciate that while the costs of enlisting professional help to explore global M&A opportunities can be high, the long-term rewards from successful international deals can be considerably higher.

DOS AND DON'TS

DO

- Carefully balance the implications of a developing business against the advantages and disadvantages of acquiring an existing one before committing to any expense.
- Obtain relevant advice regarding the acquisition or merger.
- Research the market carefully before making a decision.

DON'T

- Don't underestimate the need for proper research and professional advice.
- Don't ignore the importance of integrating the new operations within the existing business; otherwise the consequences could be costly.
- Don't be afraid to decide against the acquisition if the signs are that it will not be a good investment.

▸▸ MORE INFO

Books:

Gaughan, P. *Mergers and Acquisitions*. Hoboken, NJ: Wiley, 2002.

Sherman, Andrew J. *Mergers and Acquisitions from A to Z*. 2nd ed. New York: AMACOM, 2006.

Article:

Machiz, Robert B. "The MoneySoft M&A outlook for 2008: Friction in the marketplace." *Acquisition Marketplace Review* (May 2007). Online at: www.mergerdigest.com/MAOutlookfor2008.htm

Websites:

Beyond the Deal: www.beyondthedeal.com

BizChinaUpdate: www.bizchina-update.com

MoneySoft, Inc.: www.moneysoft.com

US Securities and Exchange Commission: www.sec.gov

See Also:

✔ Achieving Success in International Acquisitions (p. 954)
✔ Acquiring a Company (p. 955)
✔ The Rationale for an Acquisition (p. 961)

"When it comes to mergers, hope triumphs over experience." Irwin Stelzer

     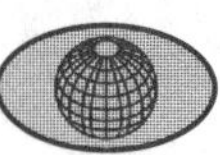   

Management Buyouts

DEFINITION

A management buyout (MBO) is the acquisition of a business by its management. The management will usually buy the target business from its parent company. The management will incorporate a new company to buy the business or shares of the target company. The transaction usually involves another party, a venture capitalist, which, together with the management, will invest in the new company. A venture capitalist is a company or fund that invests in unquoted companies. The investment usually takes the form of an equity stake.

In an MBO it is very important to establish whether the parent company, the vendor, is willing to sell. The management are usually in a very good position to buy, since they already understand the business they intend to acquire. Funding the acquisition usually requires not only the personal financial commitment of the managers but also additional funding in the shape of a loan or an equity investment.

It is essential that the management establish a coherent business plan, which will help not only in obtaining the funding required for the MBO but also in convincing the parent company that the managers are the best buyers for the business. As for investors, what they need is assurance that the business will be able to continue successfully and that it will provide them with a profitable return on their investment.

In an MBO, confidentiality while negotiations are taking place between the parent company and the management team is essential. The consequences of a leak could be damaging to the business and its staff.

ADVANTAGES

- An MBO will give the management the chance to run their business.
- The new company will have a highly motivated management team, who are not only eager to make a profit but also have a deep knowledge of the business they will be running.
- Since the management understand and have been involved in the running of the business to be acquired, the commercial due diligence that is usually undertaken when a company is acquired should be easier and less time-consuming.

DISADVANTAGES

- An MBO involves a very serious financial commitment and acceptance of risk by the management. The management will move from being employees to being owners of the business. If the business is not successful, they will feel it directly.
- Even though the commercial due diligence required could be less extensive, the legal and financial affairs of the business still need to be examined. This will involve advice and expense.
- Since acquisition by an MBO is highly leveraged (i.e. has a high proportion of debt relative to equity), this does not put the new company in the best position to compete on price.

ACTION CHECKLIST

- ✔ Think carefully about the business before you acquire it. Obtain as much information from as many sources as you can before committing to an expensive due diligence process.
- ✔ Know your market and make sure that you have analyzed the consequences of owning your own business.
- ✔ Be prepared for a long and complicated due diligence process, which could prove time-consuming as well as costly.
- ✔ Economize by negotiating a reasonable rate with your legal and financial advisers, but remember that it is better to incur costs by conducting a thorough investigation than to accept a level of service that may fail to reveal potentially costly liabilities.
- ✔ Always be aware of confidentiality while the MBO is being planned, as any leak can affect the confidence of the staff and affect the performance of the business.

DOS AND DON'TS

DO

- Involve your lawyers and accountants in the evaluation of both the risks and potential benefits of an MBO, as well as in the due diligence process.
- Negotiate your rates and make a contingency plan for any cost overrun.
- Draw up an accurate and achievable business plan.

DON'T

- Don't make the mistake of being attracted by the idea of owning a business without fully weighing up the risks you might be taking.
- Don't underestimate the importance of finance and the financial commitment that owning a business will entail. The risks to the owners of a business are high if the business does not perform.
- Don't forget that many of the banks that offer finance will be looking for collateral for the loan, and the managers could be required to provide personal guarantees that will affect their personal wealth if things do not work out.

⏩ MORE INFO

Books:

Sharp, Garry. *Buy Outs: A Guide for the Management Team*. London: Euromoney Institutional Investor, 2002.

Wright, Mike, and Hans Bruining. *Private Equity and Management Buy-outs*. Cheltenham, UK: Edward Elgar Publishing, 2008.

Articles:

Amess, Kevin, Sarah Brown, and Steve Thompson. "Management buyouts: Supervision and employee discretion." *Scottish Journal of Political Economy* 54:4 (2007): 447–474.

Baier, Richard. "Structuring an effective management team buy-out." *National Underwriter Life & Health—Financial Services Edition* (September 15, 2003).

Websites:

Business advice, resources, and forms for large and small businesses: www.allbusiness.com

Practical advice for business from Business Link (UK): www.businesslink.gov.uk

"Be careful, be cautious, do not rush into negotiations. . .be careful what you give away now, you may wish you had not done so should in future the balance of forces turn in your favour." Oliver Tambo

  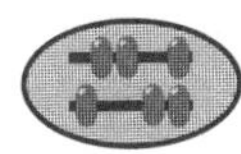 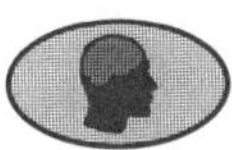  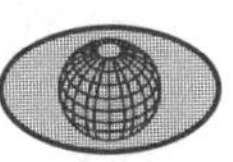   

Planning the Acquisition Process

DEFINITION

After a buyer decides to acquire a business, the process starts with the search for a suitable business. The targeted business could be known to the buyer or could be a competitor of the buyer. It could also be advertised for sale in a trade journal or newspaper, or the buyer could be approached directly by the seller or its intermediary.

After finding a business, the buyer must assess its value in order to establish the best offer price. If the business to be acquired is part of a company, it will have to file yearly accounts, which are of public record.

Every business is affected by cash flow, profit and loss, and how its finances are run. The balance sheet and accounts will give a good indication of all these elements. A buyer should also look at: the overall market within which the targeted business operates; the business's performance and reputation; its competitors; and any other interested buyers. Another element to look at is the legislation in the country where the business operates. The logistics of acquiring a national business and an international business can be very different. A buyer should obtain information on the management of the targeted business. If a business is well managed, it is usually successful and well reputed. The buyer should also consider the workforce.

The buyer should consider the advantages the acquisition will have upon its own business and should start planning how it will be integrated within its own company.

In order to consider the purchase more thoroughly, more detailed investigations should be made. During this process, the buyer may well like to involve advisers who will provide a more thorough and objective valuation. However, this assistance may be expensive.

This investigation should give a buyer an idea of the value of the business and of the offer to make to the seller. The initial information will be verified by the later due diligence process, which takes place with the permission and cooperation of the seller. The buyer will approach the seller either directly or via its advisers and make an offer for the business. Negotiations on the price will usually commence, with the buyer and seller subsequently signing a document called heads of term. This will deal with the main points of the acquisition, such as price, warranties to be given by the seller and other essential conditions. The buyer and its advisers will have to sign a confidentiality agreement, which will protect the data disclosed by the seller and will give the buyer access to more detailed information from the seller's private records. The due diligence process can last a few weeks, depending on the amount and complexity of the information to be investigated. The buyer will look in detail at all the business's contracts with clients and suppliers, insurance, employees' records, any intellectual property and IT issues, and any existent litigation. A buyer should also look at the business premises, any licences, and environmental issues. Separately, the buyer's accountants will investigate the financial details of the business. At the end of the due diligence process, the buyer will usually receive a legal due diligence report from its lawyers and a financial due diligence report from its accountants. These, together with the buyer's own commercial and business assessment, will provide a very clear picture of the business and will allow the buyer to decide whether the acquisition is worth making or not.

ADVANTAGES

A well-informed and prepared buyer:

- Will be in a better position to decide whether the target business is worth buying in the first place.
- Will be able to decide on an accurate valuation of the business and make a competitive offer price.
- Will have a thorough understanding of the business to be sold and will, therefore, be able to conduct more advantageous negotiations.
- Will be better able to help in running and integration of the business once the acquisition is made.

DISADVANTAGES

- Initial investigations and later due diligence could be costly, and may show that the business is not worth acquiring.
- An acquisition involves huge effort and a concentration of resources, which sometimes could be used to improve its own business.

ACTION CHECKLIST

- ✔ Consider carefully any business you might acquire. Obtain as much information from as many sources as you can before committing to an expensive due diligence process.
- ✔ Know your market and make sure that you have analyzed the consequences for your own business of the acquisition of another.
- ✔ Be prepared for a long and complicated due diligence process, taking time and being costly.
- ✔ Economise by negotiating a reasonable rate with your legal and financial advisers, but remember that it is better to incur costs by conducting a thorough investigation than to accept service that may fail to reveal potentially costly liabilities.

DOS AND DON'TS

DO

- Involve your solicitors and accountants in the evaluation of both the risks and potential benefits of an acquisition, as well as in the due diligence process.
- Negotiate your rates and make a contingency plan for any cost overrun.
- Plan carefully the integration of the new business within your own.

DON'T

- Don't make the mistake of being attracted by a business that has not been thoroughly investigated.
- Don't overlook the importance of negotiating complex warranties and indemnities that would protect you in the event that underlying liabilities are discovered.

⏩ MORE INFO

Book:

Williams, Sara. *The Financial Times Guide to Business Start Up 2009*. 22nd ed. Harlow, UK: FT Prentice Hall, 2008.

Article:

Jeremy Rowan-Robinson and Norman Hutchinson. "Compensation for the compulsory acquisition of business interests: Satisfaction or sacrifice." *Journal of Property Valuation and Investment* 13:1 (1995): 44–65.

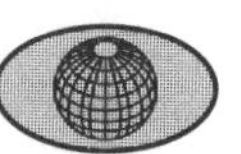

Planning the Disposal Process

DEFINITION

The preparation for the disposal process starts after the seller has decided to sell the business. There can be several reasons why someone might want to sell his business. The business could need substantial investment, and selling a percentage of shares – and, therefore, a share in the business – would bring in the necessary finance to help develop the business overall. Lifestyle factors could also be involved: a seller may want to sell the whole of his business because of a wish to retire or to do something completely different.

Whatever the reason for the sale, preparing a business for disposal requires time and effort, and it can be expensive. In certain circumstances, a buyer may only be interested in the goodwill of the business sold and certain of its assets. A seller should be aware that such a sale would leave him with the rest of the business, including its liabilities. Usually, the best time to sell a business is when it is doing well, has a good set-up and is running smoothly, bringing in high profits, and has a successful financial and management record. Then a seller can fully capitalise on its success. In some cases, the buyer of a business is its own management team. This is known as a management buy-out (MBO).

A seller should start preparing for the sale long in advance. He or she needs to make sure that all papers, legal documents and contracts, permits for the business, and its books are in good order. He or she should involve professional advisers, legal and financial, as early as possible. Their help and advice will be required during the disposal process, but they can also provide useful tips when preparing the business for sale.

Staff knowledge of the planned sale is not necessary at this stage. Usually, managers are told because his or her cooperation is required when preparing the sale, but spreading the knowledge of the potential sale through the entire workforce could have a negative influence on the running of the business, as staff could begin to worry about work security.

With the advice of accountants, a seller should consider any tax issues that will affect a disposal, so that the tax burden is minimised. Any buyer will be interested in a well-run business with a good grip on its credit and creditors. A seller should consider renegotiating inefficient contracts with clients and utility providers and should sort out any existent and potential litigation.

ADVANTAGES

- A well-prepared seller will be in a better position to negotiate a good price for the business.
- A well-prepared seller will be in a better position to assess what warranties they will be able to give to the buyer without submitting himself or herself to unexpected risk.
- An MBO could be more advantageous for a seller, as the managers know the business inside out.

DISADVANTAGES

- The initial investigations and later due diligence process could be expensive, both financially and in terms of time, if the acquisition does not go ahead.
- Preparing for a sale will involve huge effort and a concentration of resources, which sometimes could be used to improve the business itself.
- Selling is frequently emotionally difficult on a seller.
- In an MBO, less money is usually offered for a business, because managers may not have access to good finance.

ACTION CHECKLIST

✔ Consider carefully the need to sell and why you want to sell. It may well be that the timing is not ideal and that waiting could be advantageous.

✔ Be prepared for a long and complicated due diligence process, which could prove time consuming as well as costly.

DOS AND DON'TS

DO

- Involve your solicitors and accountants in the evaluation of both the risks and potential benefits of a disposal, as well as the due diligence process.
- Negotiate your rates and make a contingency plan for any cost overrun.
- Plan carefully the tax implications of the disposal.

DON'T

- Don't make the mistake of selling at the wrong time if waiting a while could bring a higher price.
- Don't overlook the importance of mitigating your liabilities under any warranties and indemnities given to the buyer, obtaining advice, and understanding your business.

▸▸ MORE INFO

Books:

Smith, Ian. *Financial Techniques for Business Acquisitions and Disposals*. 2nd ed. Hawksmere Report Series. London: Throgood Publishing, 1998.

Steingold, Fred S. *The Complete Guide to Selling a Business*. 3rd ed. Berkeley, CA: Nolo, 2007.

Williams, Sara. *The Financial Times Guide to Business Start Up 2009*. 22nd ed. Harlow, UK: FT Prentice Hall, 2008.

Articles:

Gleeson, Alan. "Why business planning is not just for start-ups". Online at: articles.bplans.co.uk/writing-a-business-plan/why-business-planning-is-not-just-for-start-ups

Gole, William J., and Paul J. Hilger. "Managing corporate divestiture transactions." *Journal of Accountancy* (August 2008): 48–51. Online at: www.journalofaccountancy.com/Issues/2008/Aug/ManagingCorporateDivestitureTransactions

Growing Business. "Selling a business." August 2007. Online at: www.growingbusiness.co.uk/06959143453634975457/selling-a-business.html

Website:

Merrill DataSite: merrilldatasite.com

"**Inequality of knowledge is the key to a sale.**" Deil O. Gustafson

  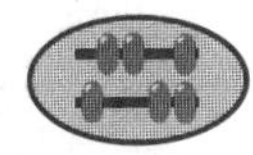 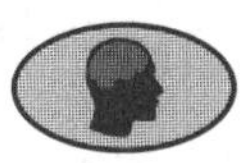  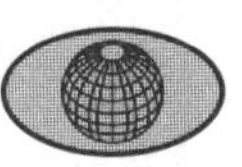   

The Rationale for an Acquisition

DEFINITION

Companies and businesses are bought and sold regularly all over the world. Acquisition is a complex and expensive process that influences both the business and financial future of the buyer. Why would a person either physical or legal decide it is time to acquire a company or business? Which factors drive its decisions and define its thought process?

A person with no experience of running a business may find it difficult to assess and scale the difficulties and risks of an acquisition. At the opposite extreme, an experienced business person may readily understand and be able to assess more clearly the reasons for an acquisition. It may be that the buyer wants to develop his existent interests and the acquired business will provide the key technology to help with the expansion of the overall operation. The business to be acquired may bring to the buyer the perfect supply chain, which otherwise will take time and expense to set up from scratch. It could well be that the workforce of the company to be acquired has such specialist skills and knowledge for these to be the main incentive for the acquisition, as an alternative to instigating a training programme for existing employees. Another reason could be that the brand and customers of the business to be purchased are of such value that they justify the acquisition rather than the time and expense of the buyer building its own.

Whatever the reasons for an acquisition, a buyer should consider the following practical suggestions.

ADVANTAGES

- Any existing, successful business will already be functioning and properly set up.
- The workforce of the business will already be in place and well organized.
- The business's marketing and contacts will be established.
- Its customer base will also be well established.
- Acquiring a well-developed business or company will make it easier to borrow money, because the company will already have a good business plan in place and will offer credibility to the lender.

DISADVANTAGES

- The acquisition of an existing company or business could have a negative effect on the business's reputation within the market if the acquisition is not done professionally, with due diligence and care.
- An acquisition can negatively influence a business's staff, who are usually excluded from any negotiations.
- The cost of an acquisition is usually high and will have to be paid all at once.
- Contracts with suppliers and contractors may have to be reassessed and renegotiated.
- Any missteps in integrating the new business can be costly.

DOS AND DON'TS

DO

- Carefully balance the implications of a developing business against the advantages and disadvantages of acquiring an existing one before committing to any expense.
- Obtain relevant advice regarding the acquisition.
- Research the market carefully before making a decision.

DON'T

- Don't rush into the unknown without a proper plan. It is easier to make a good decision in a market and area of business to which you are already accustomed.
- Don't underestimate the need for proper research and professional advice.
- Don't ignore the importance of integrating the new operations within the existent business, otherwise the consequences could be costly.
- Don't be afraid to decide against the acquisition if the signs are that it will not be a good investment. However, make sure that no commitment to buy has been made in the relevant jurisdiction.

➡ MORE INFO

Books:

Miller, Edwin *Mergers and Acquisitions: A Step-by-Step Legal and Practical Guide*. Hoboken, NJ: Wiley, 2008.

Smith, Ian. *Financial Techniques for Business Acquisitions and Disposals*. 2nd ed. Hawksmere Report Series. London: Throgood Publishing, 1998.

Williams, Sara. *The Financial Times Guide to Business Start Up 2009*. 22nd ed. Harlow, UK: FT Prentice Hall, 2008.

Article:

Rowan-Robinson, Jeremy, and Norman Hutchinson. "Compensation for the compulsory acquisition of business interests: Satisfaction or sacrifice." *Journal of Property Valuation and Investment* 13:1 (1995): 44–65.

Websites:

Business Link is a free business advice and support service, available online and through local advisers: www.businesslink.gov.uk

PricewaterhouseCoopers: www.pwc.com

See Also:

★ Acquisition Integration: How to Do It Successfully (pp. 390–391)
✔ Achieving Success in International Acquisitions (p. 954)
✔ Acquiring a Company (p. 955)
✔ Planning the Acquisition Process (p. 959)
✔ Structuring M&A Deals and Tax Planning (p. 962)

"Outworn policies may remain in force simply because of sheer inertia or lack of perception amongst policy makers." S. K. Chakraborty

     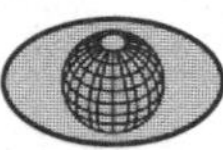   

Structuring M&A Deals and Tax Planning

DEFINITION

In planning for an acquisition, a decision needs to be made on whether the deal involves simply buying the target company's shares or actually acquiring the business itself. Though the distinction may at first glance appear to be a technicality, in practice its significance can be considerable. This is because the acquisition of shares involves buying not only the underlying business of the target company, but also its assets, both tangible and intangible, and, crucially, its liabilities. In this respect, a share-based acquisition can carry higher risk for the acquirer, potentially exposing them to the risk of unforeseen skeletons in the closet. To help compensate for the higher practical risk of the share-based acquisition, buyers can demand warranties from the seller as part of the deal.

However, in spite of the prospect of having to agree to these terms to help protect the buyer from unknown potential risks, there can be some financial advantages for the seller in a share-based transaction. Chiefly, US tax law dictates that, provided they have held the stock for a minimum of one year, selling stockholders need to pay tax only once on the deal. This is levied at personal capital gains tax rates on the difference between their original share purchase price and the agreed acquisition sale price.

Although the stock transaction route can be highly advantageous from the seller's perspective, the tax treatment of fixed assets can be disadvantageous for the buyer, who generally inherits the historically used depreciation structure. Under some specific circumstances other alternatives can apply, although the buyer nevertheless still assumes greater potential exposure to bombshells such as pension fund liabilities and product-related claims when making a share-based acquisition. However, this needs to be balanced against some of the pluses of a share-based deal from the buyer's perspective.

Structuring a deal on the basis of the transfer of the assets of a business permits a buyer to sidestep most unforeseen liabilities and also to benefit from much greater flexibility in writing off asset depreciation. The chief downside is that the seller can effectively be hit twice by tax, substantially reducing the benefit the seller enjoys after the proceeds are taxed first at the corporate level. Should the corporation then be liquidated and the proceeds shared among stockholders, these beneficiaries are then liable for tax at the personal level. Given the complexity of the issues involves, sellers should seek professional advice at an early stage when considering entering into a transaction.

ADVANTAGES

- Well-structured deals can bring many pluses for both buyer and seller, allowing both parties to adjust their market exposure to reflect changes in their business objectives or personal circumstances.
- Stock-based transactions are frequently preferred by sellers, offering attractive tax advantages to those who have held shares for longer than one year prior to the sale.
- Stock-based deals can help buyers to benefit from existing contractual arrangements.

DISADVANTAGES

- The structuring of deals and the associated negotiations are, by their very nature, complex and time-consuming, with no guarantee that a deal will ultimately result.
- An asset-based deal will typically expose the seller to two levels of taxation, corporate and personal.
- A stock-based transaction can be unattractive to a buyer given the tax treatment of fixed asset values.

ACTION CHECKLIST

- ✔ Appreciate and understand the importance of the structure of the transactions.
- ✔ Aim to find a consensus over the final structure of the deal.
- ✔ Seek up-to-date professional advice on taxation matters, as specific circumstances may alter the taxation implications for one or both sides.
- ✔ Bear in mind the importance of the after-tax numbers resulting from a proposed deal, rather than the pre-tax figure.
- ✔ Recognize that only with a comprehensive understanding of the taxation implications of the deal can realistic discussions take place to strike a deal that is acceptable to both sides.

DOS AND DON'TS

DO

- Aim to maintain cordial negotiations whenever possible.
- Seek warranties wherever appropriate when buying to guard against potentially crippling unforeseen surprises.
- Remember that sellers looking to realize the cash from the transaction at an early stage will generally be exposed to higher tax liabilities.

DON'T

- Don't skimp on the cost of professional tax advice, particularly given the substantial tax implications associated with particular deal structures.
- Don't leave involving your lawyers and accountants until the last minute, as only with informed professional advice can your options be considered objectively.
- Don't ignore the importance of effective communication with key stakeholders during the planning process.

➤➤ MORE INFO

Articles:

Ayers, Benjamin C., Craig E. Lefanowicz, and John R. Robinson. "The effect of shareholder-level capital gains taxes on acquisition structure." *The Accounting Review* 79:4 (2004): 859–887.

Erickson, Merle. "The effect of taxes on the structure of corporate acquisitions." *Journal of Accounting Research* 36:2 (1998): 279–298.

Website:

International Network of M&A Partners (IMAP): www.imap.com

"It was as true as. . .taxes. And nothing's truer than taxes." Charles Dickens

  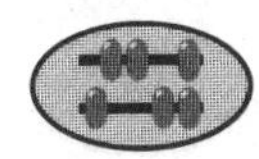   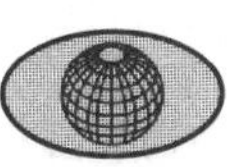   

Using Dividend Discount Models

DEFINITION

Dividend discount models are essentially tools that have been developed to value a stock on the basis of estimated future dividends, discounted to reflect their value in today's terms.

Many variations of dividend discount models exist, but their central basis is the following formula:

Estimated valuation = $D / (R - G)$

where D is present dividend per share, R is discount rate, and G is dividend growth rate.

Variations on the standard model can be used, depending on the company's stage in the growth cycle, but the common theme of dividend discount models is that the resulting estimated valuation is compared with the share's prevailing market price to determine whether the share is presently trading above or below its fair value.

ADVANTAGES

- Dividend discount models attempt to put a valuation on shares, based on forecasts of the sums to be paid out to investors. This should, in theory, provide a very solid basis to determine the share's true value in present terms.
- Dividend discount models can be of great use over the short to medium term, making use of widely available company research over timescales of up to five years.
- In stable industries, dividend discount models can still be of value over the longer term if investors are prepared to make the assumption that current dividend payout policies will remain in place.

DISADVANTAGES

- Standard dividend discount models are of no value in determining the estimated value of companies that don't pay dividends. This is typically not a problem in mature industries such as utilities and food, but the models are generally of less value in industries such as technology and mobile telecoms, where investors commonly look for share price appreciation rather than high dividend payments.
- The ability of a company to maintain a certain rate of dividend growth over the longer term can be extremely difficult to forecast accurately. Dividend discount models rely heavily on the validity of the data inputs, making them of questionable value given the challenges associated with accurately forecasting growth rates beyond five or so years.
- When used for longer-term analysis, the valuations provided by dividend discount models take no account of the possibility of a deliberate change to a company's dividend policy. This can further compromise the usefulness of dividend discount models over the longer term.

ACTION CHECKLIST

✔ Make every effort to establish the integrity and validity of the data to be input into a dividend discount model. The calculation relies on the accuracy of the source data, making the result very susceptible to inaccurate inputs.

✔ Consider using a dividend discount model as a screening tool, such that stocks that are apparently undervalued according to the model could be scrutinized more closely using alternative valuation techniques.

DOS AND DON'TS

DO

- Recognize the limitations imposed by the assumption made by standard dividend discount models that dividend growth rates will be fixed in perpetuity.
- Consider whether a multi-stage dividend discount model would be more appropriate. These models take account of the various stages in a company's development, from growth to maturity.

DON'T

- Don't attempt to use standard dividend discount models for growth-orientated companies that have yet to establish dividend payouts.
- Don't invest purely on the basis of the result of a single dividend discount model calculation in isolation. Given the total reliance on the data inputs, using a wider range of valuation tools could result in better investment decisions.

▶▶ MORE INFO

Books:

Correia, Carlos, *et al. Financial Management*. 6th ed, spiral bound. Lansdowne, South Africa: Juta, 2007.

Stowe, John D., *et al. Equity Asset Valuation*. Hoboken, NJ: Wiley, 2007.

Articles:

Beneda, Nancy L. "Estimating free cash flows and valuing a growth company." *Journal of Asset Management* 4:4 (2003): 247–257.

Foerster, Stephen R., and Stephen G. Sapp. "The dividend discount model in the long-run: A clinical study." *Journal of Applied Finance* 15:2 (2005): 55–75.

Harris, Robert S., Kenneth M. Eades, and Susan J. Chaplinsky. "The dividend discount model." Darden case no. UVA-F-1234. Online at: ssrn.com/abstract=909419

See Also:

★ Valuation and Project Selection When the Market and Face Value of Dividends Differ (pp. 382–385)

✔ Calculating a Company's Net Worth (p. 935)

✔ Estimating Enterprise Value with the Weighted Average Cost of Capital (p. 860)

✔ An Overview of Stockholders' Agreements (p. 1019)

✔ Using Shareholder Value Analysis (p. 953)

"In today's mercurial, unpredictable economy, businesses that fail to grow and change will stagnate and die. Taking care of business means having your feet firmly on the ground." Heather Robertson

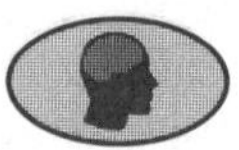

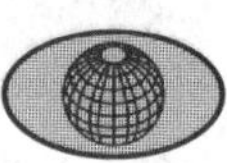

Using IRR for M&A Financing

DEFINITION

Also known as the economic rate of return, the internal rate of return (IRR) is an indication of the level of growth that can be expected from a project or acquisition. The calculation generates a percentage figure by comparing the value of the proposal's cash outflows with its cash inflows as they vary over the lifetime of the investment.

IRR is frequently used to help assess the outright viability of a project or acquisition by taking into account the cost of capital or the investor's required rate of return. The latter is sometimes referred to as the hurdle rate and is frequently adjusted to take into account the risk levels of different projects.

Acquisitions that are expected to generate returns greater than the cost of capital or the required rate of return are generally accepted, with those falling short typically rejected. IRR is also regularly employed as a means of comparing the expected returns from a number of alternative options, helping to steer investment toward the venture that offers the prospect of the highest returns. In practice, the returns from projects or acquisitions can differ substantially from the levels predicted by the IRR calculation, but the method has retained favor among many potential investors looking for a tool to help decide between alternative investment options.

ADVANTAGES

- IRR generates a relatively simple percentage figure for a project. The method provides a quick and easy way to assess the viability of a project by comparing the projected IRR with the company's risk-adjusted hurdle rate. IRRs can also help investors to select between various options.
- The practical value of the IRR calculation is further underlined by the fact that the calculation takes into account all cash flows, subject to discounting for time.

DISADVANTAGES

- The IRR method does not take into account possible changes in interest rates during the lifespan of the venture. Such changes could significantly alter a company's required hurdle rate given the potential impact on the firm's cost of capital. For short-term projects this limitation can often be overlooked, but the large scope for movements in interest rates over the lifespan of a 10-year project is considerable, compromising the value of the IRR for longer-term projects.
- IRR can sometimes be confused with return on capital employed, as both calculations express results in percentage terms. Care needs to be taken to differentiate between these cash-based and profit-based methods.
- The IRR calculation is based on a presumption that cash generated during the project is subsequently put to work to generate the same return as the average IRR over the lifetime of the project. Although this reinvestment is entirely feasible, in practice reinvested cash often generates lower subsequent returns.

ACTION CHECKLIST

- ✔ To calculate the IRR, we need to establish the various parameters at which the net present value (NPV) of a proposed M&A deal is zero (i.e. the exact level at which the proposed venture is neither a winner nor a loser in dollar terms).
- ✔ Typically, this involves guessing a projected rate of return, *r*, from the investment, and then performing the following calculation:

$$\text{NPV} = \frac{\text{initial investment} + \text{1st year's income}}{(1 + r)} + \frac{\text{2nd year's income}}{(1 + r)^2} + \frac{\text{3rd year's income}}{(1 + r)^3} + \ldots$$

- ✔ Should the resulting NPV figure be positive, the calculation is then repeated using a lower value of *r*. If the NPV is negative, a larger *r* is used. Clearly, the operation is more efficiently performed using a computer spreadsheet than by hand.
- ✔ After repeated calculations, a level of *r* that generates a NPV of zero will be established. This equates to the projected IRR of the deal.

DOS AND DON'TS

DO

- Consider the possibility that any merger or acquisition could involve risks that are difficult or impossible to foresee. To help compensate for such uncertainties, consider how much of a premium a project's IRR should have over the cost of funding.
- Remember that the IRR methodology can accommodate variations in projected annual incomes from proposed deals but does not offer the facility to model changes in funding costs throughout the lifespan of the deal. This can be a major drawback for longer-term project calculations.

DON'T

- Don't interpret IRR as the be all and end all of project financing. Recognize its uses, but at the same time understand its limitations.
- Don't ignore the costs and expenses involved in the acquisition process. Care should be taken to evaluate the costs in terms of management time and resources, as well as in purely financial terms.

▸▸ MORE INFO

Books:

Reed, Stanley F., Alexandra R. Lajoux, and H. Peter Nesvold. *The Art of M&A: A Merger Acquisition Buyout Guide*. 4th ed. New York: McGraw-Hill, 2007.

Siegel, Joel G., and Jae K. Shim. *Accounting Handbook*. 4th ed. Hauppauge, NY: Barron's Educational Series, 2006.

Articles:

Hartman, Joseph C., and Ingrid C. Schafrick. "The relevant internal rate of return." *Engineering Economist* 49:2 (2004): 139–158.

Steele, Anthony. "A Note on Estimating the Internal Rate of Return from Published Financial Statements." *Journal of Business Finance & Accounting* 13:1 (1986): 1–13.

Websites:

Alliance of Merger & Acquisition Advisers (AM&AA): www.amaaonline.org

M&A Source—organization of middle-market intermediaries: www.masource.org

"A business cannot stand still. It has to be dynamic. The world around us changes all the time and there can be no holy cows." Nicola Horlick

  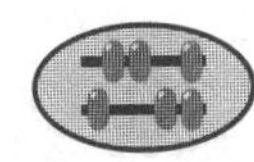   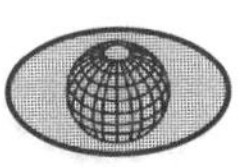   

Using the Comparable Net Worth Method in Squeeze Outs

DEFINITION

During the acquisition of a company listed on the stock exchange, a purchaser will frequently manage to acquire a large majority stake as other investors, attracted by the terms of the takeover offer, sell their shares to the acquiring company at the offered terms. However, should a sufficiently small minority of shareholders reject the terms of the acquisition, a squeeze out is a possible route for the purchaser to force a compulsory share buyback from the minority holders, ahead of the company's delisting from one or more stock markets. This only becomes an option if the minority shareholders account for only a small proportion of the company's outstanding capital.

Under such circumstances, relations between the controlling and the minority shareholders can often be strained, due to widely differing views on the true value of the shares or, occasionally, some investors' fundamental reluctance to sell their holding for a variety of reasons. In such cases, should the controlling shareholder decideto try to acquire all remaining shares, the comparable net worth method is often employed to put an appropriate value on the minority shareholders' interests through a comparison of the target company's assets minus liabilities with adjusted equivalent figures for a selection of similar companies. Though this method is only one of several options to help arrive at a valuation, it has found some favor in the United States, becoming one of the officially approved valuation methods in Pennsylvania following a long legal process.

ADVANTAGES

- The primary advantage is that this method uses information that is already public, thus respecting the typical requirements of controlling purchasers that potentially sensitive information such as sales projections are not put into the public domain.
- The method can also be advantageous to the minority shareholders, in that the resulting valuation can sometimes exceed the figure generated by other valuation methods.

DISADVANTAGES

- The method does not produce a definitive valuation, so the result is often subject to dispute. Even the choice of companies forming the comparison group can be contentious.
- The analysis of comparable companies' accounts can be very complex, particularly in terms of the adjustments made according to differing treatments of inventories and receivables across the comparison group.
- From the controlling shareholders' perspective, the valuation resulting from this method (which is often appreciably higher than the figure generated by alternative techniques) can represent a high price to be paid in return for the retention of sensitive information ahead of the squeeze out. However, this higher price can sometimes underline the fundamental value that the acquirer is seeking to unlock with the original takeover move.

ACTION CHECKLIST

- ✔ To make use of the comparable net worth method, first select between five and 10 similar listed companies to form the comparison group. To help address disputes over the choice of companies, an independent third party could be chosen to decide on the composition of the comparison group.
- ✔ Study their accounts in minute detail, making all necessary adjustments in an effort to improve comparability with the target company. In practice, most adjustments are made in areas such as cash and inventories, while other adjustments should be made to take account of cash surpluses or deficits. The adjustment process is best carried out by an independent third party to help address possible disagreements over the methods employed.
- ✔ The result of this adjustment process is a range of comparable net worth numbers that can be weighed against the companies' prevailing stock prices to help in the relative-value calculation.

DOS AND DON'TS

DO

- Remember that the comparable net worth method is one of more than a dozen widely recognized methods of valuing companies, albeit a commonly used valuation tool, when a controlling shareholder wishes to move toward a possible delisting.
- Attempt to find truly comparable companies to form the comparison group. Ideally, the selected companies will be similar to the target company in accounting terms, thereby keeping potentially contentious adjustments to a minimum. In practice, however, closely comparable companies can be very difficult to find.

DON'T

- Don't expect all interested parties to concur with the results of the comparable net worth method. As ever, the valuation is likely to be the subject of ongoing discussions.
- Don't ignore the potential value of discounted cash flow methods. A time-discounted snapshot of future earnings projections, subject to risk adjustments where appropriate, can provide a useful assessment of a company's value. Similarly, the average rate of return and payback methods can be useful starting points for discussion, although the comparable net worth method remains a key valuation tool to squeeze out unwanted minority shareholders.

➤➤ MORE INFO

Article:

Bates, Thomas W., Michael L. Lemmon, and James S. Linck "Shareholder wealth effects and bid negotiation in freeze-out deals: Are minority shareholders left out in the cold?" *Journal of Financial Economics* 81:3 (September 2006): 681–708.

Websites:

Alliance of Merger & Acquisition Advisers: www.amaaonline.org/amHome.asp

M&A Source, organization of middle-market intermediaries: www.masource.org

"I realised that if you want to change something, nine times out of ten you can change it more effectively from within." Niall Fitzgerald

  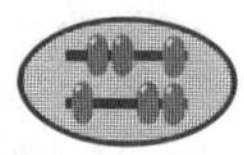   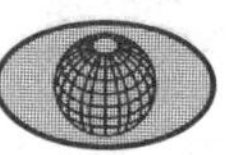   

Using the Market-Value Method for Acquisitions

DEFINITION

The capitalization of a publicly traded company is calculated simply by multiplying the market price per share by the number of shares in issue.

For the purposes of valuing a potential acquisition, however, the basic market-value method involves the study of a range of related companies, ideally at a similar stage in the growth cycle and in the same industry or sector, to determine a range of price-to-earnings (P/E) ratios for comparable companies. The resulting lowest and highest of these P/E ratios can subsequently be used to establish a base valuation band for the target company. Alternatively, an average P/E for the group could be used to calculate a central valuation.

This base valuation method assumes that the prevailing market prices across the group of comparable companies fully reflect all available information relating to their businesses and prospects, as the "efficient" market has already priced in all relevant valuation information.

In almost all acquisitions, the valuation will then need to be upwardly adjusted to reflect an appropriate acquisition premium. The level of this premium typically depends on transaction ratings, which are researched based on factors such as the P/Es that are eventually paid for comparable deals, frequently adjusted to reflect present market conditions.

ADVANTAGES

- The market-value method is widely recognized, and was adopted as the industry-standard method of valuing companies ahead of acquisitions. Although other approaches have found favor more recently, the market-value method remains a standard valuation tool for the due-diligence processes undertaken ahead of acquisitions.
- The method provides a fundamentally sound basis for company valuation as long as a number of truly comparable companies can be identified.

DISADVANTAGES

- Because of its reliance on prevailing market prices, the method is applicable only to publicly traded companies. Alternative valuation tools must be employed to establish the values of private companies.
- While P/E ratios are relatively easy to establish for actively traded large-cap stocks, smaller, less liquid stocks may attract infrequent share transactions. For example, microcap stocks traded on junior or fledgling markets may experience sparse trading activity at times, making P/E ratios more difficult to assess.
- Disputes can arise over which companies should be included in the comparables category for calculating P/Es. Because of the lack of hard and fast rules, a prospective buyer could lean towards comparables with lower P/Es, while a more optimistic seller might prefer to include related companies with more demanding P/E multiples.
- The appropriate level for an acquisition premium can be difficult to determine. Proposed acquisition valuations often need to be revised upwards to improve the chances of success of a deal.

ACTION CHECKLIST

- ✔ Before relying on the market-value method, you need to be satisfied that the underlying market is truly efficient. Be aware that some scope exists, particularly among less liquid, sparsely traded smaller companies, for unscrupulous manipulation of market prices ahead of an acquisition.
- ✔ Consider the potential benefits of using a range of P/Es across comparable companies to give a wider valuation band.
- ✔ Research the acquisition premiums paid in comparable acquisitions, making adjustments for changes to the operating environment.

DOS AND DON'TS

DO

- Make every effort to achieve a non-contentious valuation using reasonable comparisons with other companies in the industry.
- Pay close attention to the risk of potential accounting differences between comparable companies, as these could have significant impacts on the resulting average P/E ratios.
- Be prepared to revise the proposed acquisition price depending on stakeholder reaction. In many cases, an improved valuation can have a significantly higher prospect of securing the acquisition.

DON'T

- Don't blindly attempt to use P/E ratios from large-cap companies when seeking to apply the market-value method to smaller companies. Large differences in ratios frequently occur across the capitalization spectrum and can lead to major valuation errors.
- Don't overlook other means of valuing target companies. Although the market-value method was traditionally the industry standard, discounted cash flow techniques have increasingly found favor in recent years, to the extent that they have now largely displaced the market-value approach in all but due-diligence processes.

➤➤ MORE INFO

Books:

Hitchner, J. R. *Financial Valuations: Applications and Models*. Hoboken, NJ: Wiley, 2003.

Lajoux, A. R., and J. F. Weston. *The Art of M&A Financing and Refinancing*. New York: McGraw-Hill, 1999.

Articles:

Sterling, R. R. "The market value method according to Sterling: A reply." *Abacus Journal of Accounting, Finance and Business Studies* 8:1 (1972): 91–101.

Weaver, Samuel C., Robert S. Harris, Daniel W. Bielinski, and Kenneth F. MacKenzie. "Merger and acquisition valuation: Panel discussion." *Financial Management* 20:2 (1991): 85–96.

See Also:

✔ Acquiring a Company (p. 955)

"The coming world quake means more than just new machines. It promises to restructure all the human relationships and roles in the office as well." Alvin Toffler

  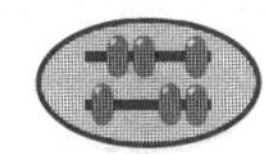 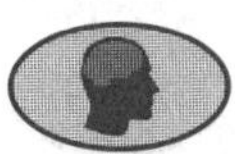  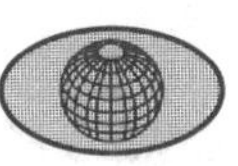   

Administering Contracts Successfully

DEFINITION

The essence of every business is contracts based. Any company or business, however simple or complex, enters into contracts with suppliers, customers and contractors. For a successful result these contracts have to be properly managed and understood. Each contract has specific terms and conditions that have to be respected and complied with. It is essential therefore, that each contract is dealt with and that procedures are put in place to supervise and control the progress of every contract.

The accounts department will deal with the payments of utilities on time and the invoicing department will send invoices to customers. Accounts should monitor the cash flow of the business and the payment and receipt of invoices. Some companies will have a debt recovery team that will chase unpaid invoices and if necessary will ask the company's solicitors to deal with any unpaid invoices.

Ordering procedures of a company for any goods, materials or services are as important as the payment procedures. Any equipment needs to be maintained and the company may need to set up equipment maintenance contracts that also need to be monitored. Running contracts successfully will involve a set up of good management reporting procedures and good communication between the teams and departments of a company.

Defaults on any contracts as a result of poor monitoring of their performance will have a negative impact on the business and reputation of a company. Any ongoing litigation will affect the performance of the business, waste resources, and will take its financial toll on the business.

In certain circumstances, a company can appoint a specialised contractor whose sole role is to administer the contracts that the company enters into. This is expensive but in certain circumstances beneficial.

Managers of a business should actively communicate with the employees in order to find out any difficulties they may have in the performance and monitoring of the contracts.

ADVANTAGES

- Will render a business successful.
- Will provide an active and good cash-flow.
- Will ensure that customers are satisfied with the performance of the contracts.
- Will increase the reputation of the business and its potential growth.

DISADVANTAGES

- In fairness, there are not many disadvantages that come as a result of a successful administration of contracts by a company except maybe cost related. In certain situations training of the staff and establishing a good procedure of administration will increase the costs of a business.

ACTION CHECKLIST

- ✔ Always check the terms of a contract you enter into in order to understand and be ready to comply with it.
- ✔ Make sure that you put in place a timetable of deadlines of all the contracts you enter into in order to allow you to follow and respect their terms.
- ✔ Consult your customers frequently to assess if they are happy with your services and contracts you offer.

DOS AND DON'TS

DO

- Set up a procedure to deal with all the contracts of the business that will include a checklist of how to supervise and monitor the performance of the contract.
- Train the employees to deal with and administer contracts.
- Understand the terms and conditions of each contract.
- If necessary invest in contract management software that will improve the administration process.
- Review invoices regularly. If any problems occur and payment might be delayed, contact the supplier and discuss any problem.

DON'T

- Don't ignore the need to properly administer contracts.
- Don't underestimate the need for proper procedures and professional advice if necessary in understanding the terms and condition of any commercial contracts.

▸▸ MORE INFO

Book:

Attree, Rebecca. *International Commercial Agreements*. Thorogood Professional Insights Series. London: Thorogood, 2002.

Article:

Cook, John A., Theresamarie Mantese, and Christine L. Pfeiffer. "Contract is signed: Now what?" *Michigan Bar Journal* (September 2005).

Websites:

Business.com: www.business.com

Management Forum: www.management-forum.co.uk

Symfact compliance solutions: www.symfact.com

"If the shoe doesn't fit, must we change the foot?" Gloria Steinem

  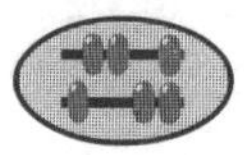   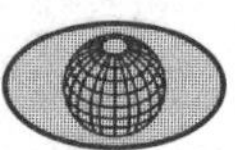   

Applying Cost–Benefit Analysis to Project Appraisal

DEFINITION

Cost–benefit analysis is a widely used, straightforward technique for deciding whether to initiate an action or implement changes. Simply put, it involves adding up the value of the benefits of a course of action and subtracting what it will cost to obtain those benefits. Costs are usually either one-off (for example, start-up costs for materials or equipment) or ongoing (such as staff), whereas benefits tend to unfold over a period of time.

When conducting your analysis, you calculate your payback period, which is the length of time it takes for the benefits to repay the costs of implementing them. It is typical to specify a set payback period of, for example, three years, even if the benefits continue to be reaped long after. The end of the payback period is also known as the breakeven point. This can sometimes be more important than any overall benefits delivered by a project, for example because the organization had to borrow funds to purchase expensive plant. Breakeven is easily calculated by plotting costs and income on a graph—it occurs at the point where the two lines cross. Determining the time span of the payback period is not always easy as many benefits don't have a monetary value or can continue long after the end of payback. The only way to account fully for the effect of time would be to discount all cash flows at the cost of capital.

At its simplest, a cost–benefit analysis assumes that there are only financial costs and financial benefits. For example, a bank needs to train its call centre staff. The analysis would subtract the cost of the training days from the economic benefit that calls will be answered more quickly and efficiently, enabling the bank to handle more calls overall and resolve customer problems more cheaply. Such a simple analysis would not measure the cost of "lost" staff time while they are not on duty, or the benefit of staff having a clearer understanding of standard procedures.

A more sophisticated approach involves trying to work out a monetary value for intangible costs and benefits. This can be highly subjective. For example, when customers praise your call centre staff, how much would it have cost to pay a PR firm to boost the bank's image of handling customer complaints? Calculating intangibles usually raises many questions that need clear answers.

Where very large sums of money are involved, such as in financial market transactions, project evaluation using cost–benefit analysis can be extremely complex, yet of vital importance to ensure that money is spent as wisely as possible.

ADVANTAGES

- The advantage of conducting a cost–benefit analysis is that you can weigh up all the positive and negative impacts of a project using their equivalent financial value to determine whether, on balance, the project is worthwhile.

DISADVANTAGES

- The chief risk in performing a cost–benefit analysis is that the results will only be as accurate as the estimated costs and benefits. Studies have shown that actual costs often turn out to be far higher than estimated, while actual benefits are often lower. This is especially true where intangibles are included in the analysis. It may be safer to perform a straightforward rate-of-return analysis.

ACTION CHECKLIST

- ✔ Work out how much it will cost to make the change, then calculate the benefit you will gain from it.
- ✔ Use mapping tools such as Gantt charts or PERT (program evaluation and review technique) to calculate timescales for implementing a project or introducing a change.
- ✔ A SWOT (strengths, weaknesses, opportunities, threats) analysis can help to keep you focused on what the project should achieve.
- ✔ Calculate the payback period. This is usually the length of the project, but it may be longer if you are aiming for long-term effects resulting from a limited-term project. Remember that you may need to discount the cash flows at the cost of capital if you want to fully take into account the effect of time.

DOS AND DON'TS

DO

- Remember that benefits are often intangible, i.e. they have no monetary value.
- Make a firm decision on whether to include intangible items within the analysis. As you must estimate a value for these, this inevitably brings an element of subjectivity into the process.

DON'T

- Don't forget to include a risk analysis as part of your overall planning.
- Don't forget to make a cash flow forecast for decisions that will have a purely financial outcome.

▸▸ MORE INFO

Books:

Brealey, Richard A., Stewart C. Myers, and Franklin Allen. *Principles of Corporate Finance*. 9th ed. McGraw-Hill/Irwin Series in Finance, Insurance, and Real Estate. Boston, MA: McGraw-Hill/Irwin, 2008.

Chakravarty, Sukhamoy. "Cost-benefit analysis." In Eatwell, John, Murray Milgate, and Peter Newman (eds). *The New Palgrave: A Dictionary of Economics*. Basingstoke, UK: Palgrave Macmillan, 1987, pp. 687–690. (Dictionary online at: www.dictionaryofeconomics.com/dictionary)

Nas, Tevfik F. *Cost-Benefit Analysis: Theory and Application*. Thousand Oaks, CA: Sage Publications, 1996.

"The thought pattern that keeps most people poor: they criticize instead of analyse." Robert Kiyosaki

  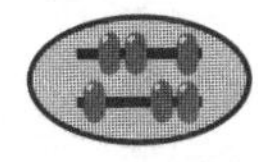   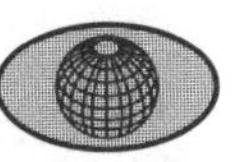   

Applying Stress-Testing to Business Continuity Management

DEFINITION

Business continuity management (BCM) is an important component of the risk management framework for regulated institutions. It increases the resilience to business disruption that may arise from internal or external events and should reduce any adverse impact on business operations, as well as profitability and reputation.

Business operations have become increasingly complex over the years, increasing their vulnerability to disruption by outside events. BCM has thus become an essential part of a company's risk management framework. A whole industry has sprung up devoted to supporting companies on BCM issues.

Although major disruptions to business are rare, few have forgotten the events of 9/11, which resulted in massive disruption to business. External threats from terrorism, computer crime, and viruses are unlikely to go away. Businesses need to put in place continuity plans that are consistent with the scale of their operations.

Stress-testing is crucial to an organization's BCM and its planning for risk management. Stress-testing and scenario analysis both provide management with the information it needs to assess and adjust risks to the organization and to mitigate them effectively. They enable firms to understand how they should deal with certain threats, pick up on any shortfalls, and implement actions to improve their processes for BCM.

Wider use of BCM, stress-testing, and scenario analysis would have a beneficial effect on the robustness of the world's financial systems. There is, however, no simple formula for a company to follow for its own stress-testing and scenario analysis.

Depending on its size and global reach, each organization must formulate its own strategies and plans for testing its BCM processes.

ADVANTAGES

Stress-testing of business continuity management should:

- reduce the impact of disruptions to business operations in the event of a problem;
- increase protection to stakeholders and beneficiaries;
- promote confidence in the organization and the whole financial system.

DISADVANTAGES

- The cost of planning and actions.
- The time spent on the whole process.

ACTION CHECKLIST

- ✔ Put a BCM strategy in place.
- ✔ Set up methods and routines for stress-testing and scenario analysis.
- ✔ Carry out regular tests.
- ✔ Determine follow-up points.
- ✔ Carry out any necessary actions to improve the BCM plan.

DOS AND DON'TS

DO

- Review your BCM plans and processes regularly.
- Identify actions to update your BCM as appropriate.
- Follow up these actions.

DON'T

- Don't leave your BCM proposals unmonitored once you have put them in place.
- Don't restrict stress-testing to specific threats.

➧ MORE INFO

Books:

Hiles, Andrew (ed). *The Definitive Handbook of Business Continuity Management*. 2nd ed. Chichester, UK: Wiley, 2007.

Osborne, Andy. *Practical Business Continuity Management: Top Tips for Effective, Real-World Business Continuity Management*. Evesham, UK: Word4Word, 2007.

Journal:

Journal of Business Continuity & Emergency Planning. Online at: www.henrystewart.com/jbcep

Websites:

Continuity Central for business continuity news, information, and resources: www.continuitycentral.com

UK Resilience, a British government news and information service for emergency practitioners, has this page on business continuity: www.ukresilience.gov.uk/preparedness/businesscontinuity.aspx

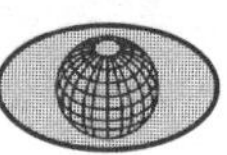

Applying Stress-Testing to Operational Risk Exposure

DEFINITION

As global financial markets have become more diversified and complex, many more "new" economies have entered the markets. With the greater number of players and the increased funds available, it has become imperative that all parties with a vested interest in markets and risk exposure —from investment banks to private investors—are properly prepared to assess exposure and able to quantify risk. Stress-testing refers to the various ways that financial and other entities estimate their vulnerability to an exceptional event of plausibility.

The use and practice of stress-testing have increased over the past decade following the occurrence of several notable events in the financial markets: the 1997 Asian crisis, the Enron scandal of 2001, and the collapse of Barings Bank in 1995. As the markets turned bearish in late 2007, it has become standard practice for an institution to acquire the ability to stress-test itself accurately.

Many major institutions stress-test their portfolios on a monthly basis to assess their risk profile and gauge the possible effects of various scenarios on their profit and loss accounts. Stress-testing requires that employees are trained to understand the mathematics and theory behind the process to ensure that the information garnered is both accurate and comprehensive.

Stress-testing can be divided into two distinct categories: simple sensitivity tests (SST), and scenario analysis.

The SST explores changes to a portfolio's value following a change in one risk factor, for example interest rates. It is a very simple yet effective way of flagging up major deficiencies and weaknesses in a portfolio. The SST is frequently used by smaller banks and institutions as well as private investors. The drawback of this technique is that it is not plausible that just one variable should change—a massive increase in US interest rates, for example, would have a massive effect on exchange rates and equities.

This is why larger and more complex organizations use scenario analysis, which takes into account a wide range of possible variables such as exchange rates, equity prices, and interest rates, and extrapolates possible outcomes and their probabilities. The process is not dissimilar to forecasting the weather—like the weather, a financial forecast is susceptible to change and must be repeated regularly.

Stress-testing is only as accurate as the information fed into it. Thus, practitioners must have a thorough understanding of economic theory and the effects on the institution's portfolio. It is an exceptionally flexible tool that can be applied to virtually any aspect of an institution's operations that have substantial exposure to risk —country risk, illiquidity exposure, etc. It is not an end-product as stress-testing treats variables separately; companies are currently trying to develop a testing procedure that is more holistic and accumulative in scope.

ADVANTAGES

A properly conducted stress-test program can help insure against otherwise unnoticed risks and flag problematic investment strategies. If the scenarios and metrics of the system are set clearly, a great deal of benefit can be gained, both for long-term strategy and for day-to-day management. Taking a risk is fine, but it must be accurately gauged, and a properly conducted stress-testing procedure can greatly reduce the potential for error in exposure calculations.

DISADVANTAGES

If conducted improperly, stress-testing can create a false sense of security. Any stress-test that scored exposure to risk too low would be exceptionally dangerous to an institution. It can be time-consuming and expensive to train employees to use stress-testing, and it must be applied in continually changing environments.

ACTION CHECKLIST

- ✔ Ensure that the users of the system and the institution's managers understand the limitations, intent, and scope of the process.
- ✔ Ensure that the results are produced in a comprehensible format.
- ✔ Ensure that the stress-test is company-wide.

DOS AND DON'TS

DO

- Introduce stress-testing; but
- Make the reports comprehensible and comprehensive.

DON'T

- Don't be deluded into believing that stress-testing is an end in itself. Like all tools, it will only be of benefit if used properly.
- Don't assume that just because a stress-test has been conducted the process is complete.

⏩ MORE INFO

Book:

Engelmann, Bernd, and Robert Rauhmeier (eds). *The Basel II Risk Parameters: Estimation, Validation, and Stress Testing*. Berlin: Springer-Verlag, 2006.

Articles:

Sorge, Marco. "Stress-testing financial systems: An overview of current methodologies." BIS working paper no. 165. Basel: Bank for International Settlements, 2004.

Sorge, Marco, and Kimmo Virolainen. "A comparative analysis of macro stress-testing methodologies with application to Finland." *Journal of Financial Stability* 2:2 (June 2006): 113–151.

Tan, Kok-Hui, and Inn-Leng Chan. "Stress testing using VaR approach—a case for Asian currencies." *Journal of International Financial Markets, Institutions and Money* 13:1 (February 2003): 39–55.

See Also:

★ A Holistic Approach to Business Risk Management (pp. 52–54)
✔ Establishing a Framework for Assessing Risk (p. 1034)

"**Economic distress will teach men, if anything can, that realities are less dangerous than fancies, that fact-finding is more effective than fault-finding.**" Carl Becker

  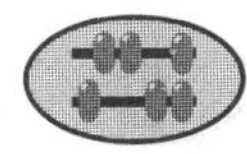   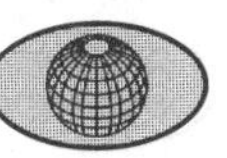   

Basic Steps for Starting a Business

DEFINITION

You think you have a winning idea that's going to make you a fortune. But before you jump in head first, you should carry out some research to see whether your idea really is feasible. That means finding out who your competitors will be and whether there is an opening in the market for your product or service. Do you have the necessary skills to run the business? Gathering and analyzing this information will help you formulate your business plan and goals.

Your initial research should focus on these key questions:

- Is your idea feasible?
- Do you have the financial capacity to carry out the project?
- Is there a market for your product or service?
- How will you protect your idea?
- Who are your competitors, and what differentiates your product from theirs?

Once you have answered these questions satisfactorily, you should draw up a business plan. Most financial institutions provide business plan templates. Alternatively, you could use an off-the-shelf computer program. Your plan should contain:

- a summary describing the elements of your business;
- a description of your business concept;
- an analysis of your business *within the market* in order to decide how and where your company or products or services fit;
- strategies and goals for the market, and for overcoming the competition you face;
- an outline of how your products or services match your strategies and goals;
- information on how you will market your products;
- an estimate of your sales forecasts;
- what type of financing you will need, who will provide it, and at what cost.

Researching and writing your business plan may seem like a colossal task, but with thorough preparation you will have all the relevant information available and evaluated before you open your doors. As you go through the planning process, you will develop your knowledge and understanding of the proposed business, improve your chances of success, and reduce your risk of failure as a start-up owner. In short, you will be ready to run your business and equipped to compete.

First impressions count, and an accurate, easy-to-read, and well-organized text will convey professionalism and credibility. Have your figures checked by an accountant and the text proofread.

Naming your business accurately is important. Word play might be clever or funny, but it could add to the difficulty customers have in remembering and finding you. It's also tempting to abbreviate your business name to make communications and correspondence easier, but an acronym doesn't say what you do. The general rule is: Keep it simple and try to describe what you do.

ADVANTAGES

- Starting a business allows you to be your own boss and lets you make the decisions that shape your success.
- You get to choose how long and how hard you work.
- The owner receives all the profits, meaning that all earnings go to the sole proprietor.
- If the business is successful, you may be able to reap a tidy sum on retirement by selling the business at a profit.

DISADVANTAGES

- All the responsibility falls on your shoulders. Good or bad, you have to take decisions that may affect the livelihood of your family and employees.
- If you incur debts of any sort, you may have to repay them out of your personal income and assets.
- You may find it difficult to go on vacation or be absent from work for long.

ACTION CHECKLIST

✔ First, do some basic research to see whether your idea really is feasible. Ask yourself whether you have the financial capacity to carry out the project. Is there a market for your product or service, and how will you protect your idea? Who are your competitors, and what distinguishes your product from theirs? If the answers are positive, start to build a detailed business plan.

✔ Second, ask yourself whether you are made of the right stuff to run your own business. Do you have the character, temperament, drive, and staying power?

DOS AND DON'TS

DO

- Take the time to draw up an effective business plan. It might take a month or two, but it will not only help you assess your business idea, it will also tell you whether you are ready and able to carry it out.

DON'T

- Don't use your savings to set up in business without researching and evaluating your ideas. Many chambers of commerce have successful retired business people who will be happy to give you advice on a volunteer basis.

▸▸ MORE INFO

Books:

Adams, Bob. *Adams Streetwise Small Business Start-up: Your Comprehensive Guide to Starting and Managing a Business*. Holbrook, MA: Adams Media, 2002.

Kennedy, Joe. *The Small Business Owner's Manual: Everything You Need to Know to Start Up and Run Your Business*. Franklin Lakes, NJ: Career Press, 2005.

The Ultimate Small Business Guide: A Resource for Startups and Growing Businesses. London: Bloomsbury Publishing, 2004.

Articles:

Freeburn, Chris. "Starting a business: Part I." *Small Business Online Community* (August 8, 2008). Online at: smallbusinessonlinecommunity.bankofamerica.com/blogs/startingABusiness/2008/08/08/starting-a-business-part-i

Pedzich, Joan. "Resources for starting a business." *The Daily Record (Rochester, NY)* (February 26, 2008).

Websites:

Canada Business—Services for Entrepreneurs: www.canadabusiness.ca

US Small Business Administration: www.sba.gov

"The newness of an idea matters less than its ease of use." Mari Matsunaga

  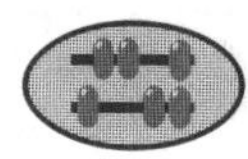 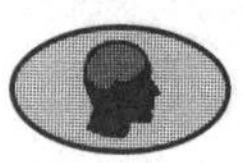  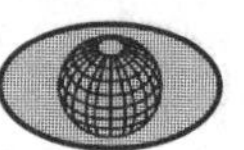   

Building an Efficient Credit and Collection Accounts System

DEFINITION

A credit account relates to credit extended by a business to a customer, which may be another business. A collection account is an account that is in default of the contractual terms (i.e. has passed the due date). It may be assigned to additional collection efforts by the creditor, or passed on to a professional collection agency.

Overdue credit accounts and nonpayment of accounts receivables have an adverse impact on a company's solvency and restrict its dealings. Legal proceedings against defaulting customers cost money and use resources. In addition, they have a detrimental effect on business relationships.

Small businesses must have proper credit and collection policies. Such policies allow a business to collect what they are owed more efficiently from their customers. Good policies help to ensure that a company's customers pay on time or in full. They also help a company to avoid bad accounts, or ditch customers when their accounts turn bad, and keep cash flowing into the business.

As consumer debts increase, competition grows, and interest rates rise, companies are looking at new ways to improve collection rates. Technology is increasingly playing a role in this. Many companies now expect customers to settle debts electronically via BACS (bankers' automated clearing service) transfer, for example, which is cheaper and faster than clearing checks. internet banking now also enables direct debits to be set up quickly. Many companies are also using dedicated software to manage their credit and collection accounts, which reduces dependence on staff or external collection agencies.

The fact is that some debtors fall behind with payments because they can't pay. In such a situation it is better for a company to try to match settlements to the debtor's ability to pay. Slow payment is better than no payment. Information from credit reports and account activity should enable collectors to make better decisions about what payments might best suit a debtor's circumstances.

ADVANTAGES

- Effective collection of debts improves cash flow and helps to grow the bottom line.
- A well-organized credit department can make informed decisions about bad accounts and offer credit only to verified customers.

DISADVANTAGES

- Implementing credit and collection policies can be expensive, at least initially.
- It can also seem like a lot of effort for something that a company hopes to receive without such measures.

DOS AND DON'TS

DO

- Chase up all bad debtors.
- Try to match payment schemes with a debtor's ability to pay.
- Consider the use of technology to improve your collection accounts.

DON'T

- Don't pretend it won't happen. Bad debtors are a fact of business life.
- Don't ignore bad debtors—keep on top of them.
- Don't become a bad debtor yourself as a result of your own bad debts.

ACTION CHECKLIST

- ✔ Analyze your good and bad debtors.
- ✔ Keep a close watch on your cash flow.
- ✔ Ask your debtors if they will be able to pay on time.
- ✔ Indicate penalties for late or nonpayment.
- ✔ Issue a reminder at the end of the payment period.
- ✔ Investigate software options.

⏩ MORE INFO

Books:

Bond, Cecil J. *Credit Management Handbook: A Complete Guide to Credit and Accounts Receivable Operations*. New York: McGraw-Hill, 1993.

Schaeffer, Mary S. *Essentials of Credit, Collections, and Accounts Receivable*. Hoboken, NJ: Wiley, 2002.

"I feel these days like a very large flamingo. No matter what way I turn, there is always a very large bill."
Joseph O'Connor

  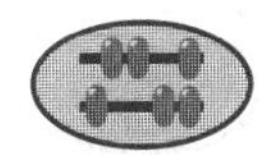 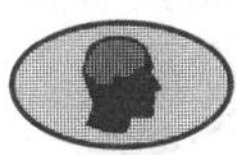  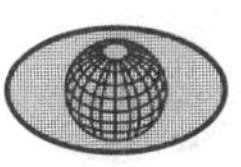   

Building an Electronic Invoicing System

DEFINITION

E-invoicing systems can provide a comprehensive solution to the problems associated with large volumes of paper invoices. Traditional paper-based billing processes are inherently vulnerable to errors, particularly when staff are deluged with high volumes of invoices, potentially leading to problems such as missed, duplicate, or unauthorized payments. Paper-based invoicing systems based on multiple staff approvals are also prone to unnecessary payment delays. For example, if one or more of the authorized sign-off managers is absent, paper invoices may be misplaced, ultimately creating payment delays, which can put severe strain on client/supplier relationships. Though increasing the headcount of accounts payable units can improve internal departmental capacity, there may be payment-related problems originating elsewhere within the organization, and also there are significant departmental running costs.

Many companies' first step towards e-invoicing is simply to scan all paper invoices received or to create supplier/client point-to-point invoicing systems. However, centralized, hub-based e-invoicing systems soon come to the fore, supported by legislative changes and the development of e-invoicing standards, typically based on XML (extensible mark-up language) computer code. The design and implementation of an e-invoicing system largely depends on the firm's unique needs, in terms of factors such as invoice volumes, currency conversion needs, approvals process, and the level of integration necessary with other existing management information systems. Another key determinant of successful development is, frequently, the adoption of an e-invoicing system partner with the experience and resources to customize e-invoicing solutions to fit companies' highly specific needs. Among other advantages, e-invoicing system specialists can help clients to overcome compatibility issues between payment system platforms, by supplying a payments hub system with an interface that can be adapted to clients' specific needs.

ADVANTAGES

- A well-implemented e-invoicing system can improve supplier and buyer relationships by making the payments process more reliable.
- E-invoicing can create significant internal cost savings for the business by streamlining the invoice payment process.
- Payment-related information can be supplied directly from the e-invoicing system into management reports as part of a wider management information system.

DISADVANTAGES

- E-invoicing systems can be expensive to introduce, with the necessary investment only recouped if a threshold volume of invoicing makes use of the system.
- There is no universal standard in e-invoicing systems; each company's precise needs are distinct.
- The supplier can sometimes have little short-term incentive to participate in e-invoicing systems, given that the potential cost savings tend to arise on the buyer side. However, in a competitive environment, suppliers can feel under pressure to comply, to retain the business.

ACTION CHECKLIST

- ✔ A company and its chosen system partners should liaise closely with clients and suppliers when designing and implementing systems—the full benefits of e-invoicing are only achievable if the system is used close to its maximum capacity.
- ✔ Ask chosen system partners to work with any suppliers holding out for paper-based invoice submission—some e-invoicing hub operators can supply software to help with the transition.
- ✔ Consult financial advisers over tax considerations ahead of implementing an e-invoicing system. Legal advice in particular jurisdictions is also advised.
- ✔ Explore how the implementation of e-invoicing systems could improve your company's competitive position, for example, new efficiencies might enable your sales team to win new business ahead of alternate suppliers.

DOS AND DON'TS

DO

- Once your basic e-invoicing system is operational, use the system initially for internal clients to help identify any outstanding post-testing problems, before exposing external clients to any possible gripes.
- When assessing the cost of introducing an e-invoicing system, consider how a well-run system could help to improve the quality of input to wider management information systems.

DON'T

- Don't use e-mail invoices as input to your e-invoicing system as this can expose the network to viruses. Invoice-related communications are best accepted via a secure, closed network.
- Don't choose an e-invoicing system based purely on initial costs. Internally developed systems may appear cheaper initially, but may prove costly in terms of reliability and compatibility issues, while general IT supplier companies may lack relevant specialist e-invoicing and payment systems experience.

▸▸ MORE INFO

Books:

Groucutt, Jonathan, and Paul Griseri. *Mastering E-Business*. London: Palgrave MacMillan, 2004.

Wille, Patrick, Marc Govers, and I. Desmeytere. *VAT Aspects of Electronic Invoicing and E-Commerce*. Brussels: Intersentia, 2000.

Article:

Corbitt, Terry. "E-invoicing: Are you up to speed?" *Credit Management* (June 2004).

Websites:

"Global e-invoicing: Hewlett-Packard case study" audio presentation: www.insight24.com/webcasts/content-92569_1

GXS—System provider's guide to e-invoicing: www.gxs.com/eBooks/eInvoicing/

"With the only certainty in our daily existence being change, and a rate of change growing always faster in a kind of technological leapfrog game, speed helps people think they are keeping up." Gail Sheehy

   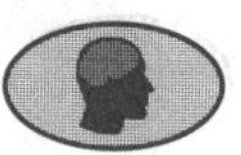  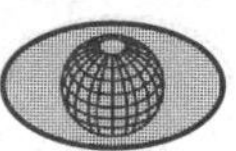   

Business Process Reengineering

DEFINITION

Business process reengineering (BPR) was developed in the early 1990s and refers to a management technique that companies can use to become more efficient. BPR was most famously espoused by management consultants Michael Hammer and James A. Champy in a best-selling book, "Reengineering the Corporation." The authors argued that companies should reinvent the way in which their work was to be accomplished. BPR requires companies to objectively review their business processes and take any necessary measures to maximize customer value and minimize the cost of delivering a product or service, usually through greater use of information technology. The reengineering focused on fundamental business processes as opposed to departments or organizational units.

Hammer and Champy argued that "It is no longer necessary or desirable for companies to organize their work around Adam Smith's division of labor" because task-oriented jobs were becoming obsolete. They recommended that post-industrial companies be "reengineered." The BPR process required a leader with vision, information technologies, close consultation with suppliers to reduce inventories, and empowerment of employees so that decision-making "becomes part of the work."

However, BPR was heavily criticized because it resulted in huge redundancies, and firms that undertook a process of BPR often reported disappointing results. Critics also argued that BPR dehumanized the workplace. Business process management, which seeks to continuously improve processes, has since replaced BPR as the major influence on managerial thinking.

ADVANTAGES

- BPR has proved successful in reinvigorating a wide range of companies, including Ford, Procter & Gamble, American Airlines, and General Motors.
- By reviewing the entire business, companies may well be able to spot areas where they can improve efficiency.

DISADVANTAGES

- BPR assumes that a company's existing processes are the main drag on its performance and the main barrier to the company reaching its full growth potential. But this may not be the case.
- BPR has come under fire for its clinical focus on efficiency and technology and for ignoring the human element of an organization that is subjected to a reengineering initiative.
- BPR has been accused of underestimating the resistance to change that is likely to exist in an organization.

ACTION CHECKLIST

- ✔ Compare the costs and benefits of BPR with those of other methods of improving your business, such as business process management.
- ✔ Try to determine whether your company needs the radical change demanded by BPR or whether there are other ways in which you could improve performance. This should involve a rigorous analysis of whether your firm is underperforming competitors, and if so, why this is the case.

DOS AND DON'TS

DO

- Consider the potential impact on morale. Implementing BPR can lead to large layoffs that leave remaining staff insecure, overworked, and demotivated. This can adversely affect the efficiency of the business and customer service.
- Talk to other companies that have implemented BPR. Find out whether they regard BPR as a success. What benefits has it delivered and what costs have been incurred?

DON'T

- Don't assume that BPR is a panacea for your company's ills.
- Don't forget that BPR dates back to the early 1990s. It may still have valid points, but new management theories have since been developed.

▸▸ MORE INFO

Books:

Butler, David. *Business Development: A Guide to Small Business Strategy*. Oxford: Butterworth-Heinemann, 2001.

Hammer, Michael, and James Champy. *Reengineering the Corporation: A Manifesto for Business Revolution*. New York: HarperCollins, 2003.

Joy-Matthews, Jennifer, David Megginson, and Mark Surtees. *Human Resource Development*. 3rd ed. London: Kogan Page, 2004.

Nakayama, Makoto, and Norma Sutcliffe. *Managing IT Skills Portfolios: Planning, Acquisition, and Performance Evaluation*. Hershey, PA: Idea Group Publishing, 2005.

Articles:

Liebowitz, Jay. "Bridging the knowledge and skills gap: Tapping federal retirees." *Public Personnel Management* 33:4 (2004): 421–447.

Lloyd, Jerry. "Skills for business: An evolving network." In "The skill factor," Special supplement, *New Statesman* 132 (March 2003): 8–9. Online at: www.newstatesman.com/pdf/skillssupp.pdf

Website:

12Manage page on business process reengineering: www.12manage.com/methods_bpr.html

"If we don't change, we don't grow. If we don't grow, we aren't really living." Gail Sheehy

  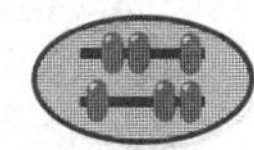 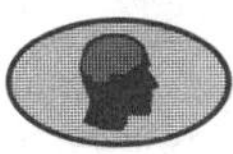  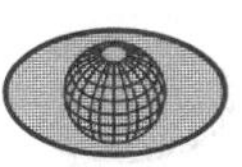   

Calculating Return on Investment in Human Resources

DEFINITION

In today's competitive labour market, the human resource (HR) department has been transformed from a stuffy old necessary evil into an active department that has risk management functions.

In general, in order to calculate a return on investment (ROI), the total profit generated must be divided by the total value of the assets used in creating that profit. However, HR is usually nonprofit generating, and from this stems the difficulty in assessing its ROI within a company. So, to assess the value that HR can bring, one must look at the role that HR plays in increasing a company's profits.

One of the most important roles of HR is the recruitment and training of a company's employees. The more sensitive and active an HR department is in promoting, training, and in general being open and listening to the needs of employees, the greater the value the company will receive from its workforce. Contented, happy employees directly influence a company's productivity. Therefore, to calculate the return on investment in HR, one should look at the relationship between the sales value derived from each training day and the total number of the training days involved, and dividing the result by the total cost of training. Basically, one is assessing the investment in human capital by considering the cost of training programs per employee, and trying to determine how much more revenue this has brought to the company.

Very few companies measure the correlation between staff training and employee turnover. There are also other elements, such as morale and job satisfaction, that are too subjective to assess with accuracy. What HR should focus on is the direct relationship between investment in the company's workforce and the success of its business, along with an assessment of the relation between the cost of staff training and development with the productivity and longevity of stay of employees within the company.

It is also important to emphasize that a relatively correct assessment of ROI can only be done after an HR department has accumulated the necessary data over a number of years.

ADVANTAGES

- Calculating the return on investment in its staff will help a company to improve its recruitment and training process, and determine how efficient its HR department is.
- Putting in place a good selection process for employees will enhance a company's performance.

DISADVANTAGES

- Calculating the ROI in human resources involves a long and tedious process of accumulating data before it can be done.
- Some subjective aspects of HR work, such as staff morale and satisfaction, are difficult to assess with certainty.

ACTION CHECKLIST

- ✔ Appoint efficient HR managers.
- ✔ Highlight the need to keep as many records as possible on the movement of staff in and out of the company.
- ✔ Assess whether training programs have any relation to staff turnover and try to determine the contribution they make to the productivity of the company.

DOS AND DON'TS

DO

- Select employees through a thorough process of interviews and evaluation.
- Obtain relevant information on the experience and skills of a potential employee before hiring them.
- As a manager, communicate at all times with your HR department to understand the movement of employees in and out of the company.
- Provided that they are cost-effective, be prepared to use specialist recruitment consultants, who will be able to help you find the right employees for your company.

DON'T

- Don't underestimate the importance of HR in providing the company with feedback on its investment in staff.
- Don't ignore the need for proper research and professional advice when selecting employees.

➧ MORE INFO

Book:

Phillips, Jack J. *Return on Investment in Training and Performance Improvement Programs*. 2nd ed. Burlington, MA: Butterworth-Heinemann, 2003.

Articles:

Harris, Kimberly J. "Calculating ROI for training in the lodging industry: Where is the bottom line?" *International Journal of Hospitality Management* 26:2 (2007): 485–498.

Wells, Susan J. "Finding wellness's return on investment: Calculating wellness programs' ROI is sometimes complex, but it can be done." *HR Magazine* (June 2008).

Websites:

Business resources: www.business.com

HR tools, info, and resources: www.hr.com

"Organizations that are change leaders are designed for change. But people need continuity. . .they do not function well if the environment is not predictable, not understandable, not known." Peter F. Drucker

     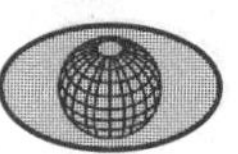   

Choosing the Right Payment Policy

DEFINITION

Choosing the right payment policy is critical to the success of any company. To generate revenue, you need to enhance the flow of customers to your business, perhaps by allowing them to pay for a good or service in installments, but at the same time you must generate sufficient cash flow for your business to prosper. You also need to ensure that your customers understand how much they need to pay and when they must settle up. They are more likely to pay you on time if these terms are clearly set out in writing at the start of any business relationship. You can also help your clients, and thus boost income, by being flexible over how you accept payment, for example, by credit card or a loan agreement. Arranging finance for clients can also open up new revenue streams.

On the cost side, negotiating credit terms with your suppliers has obvious advantages. You can, for example, bank revenues and earn interest on them before you need to pay for the goods or services that helped to generate those revenues.

If you adopt a system whereby customers are permitted to pay in installments, you must install a robust credit management system, which is a means of ensuring that your invoices are paid on time. This will minimize the time and effort spent chasing unpaid invoices and will ensure that the resources you expend on credit management are used efficiently. However, it is important to remember that you don't have to adopt the same payment policy for every customer. If you are unsure about the creditworthiness of a particular client, simply insist on cash payment before you supply goods or services.

ACTION CHECKLIST

- ✔ Simply accepting cash removes the need to install time-consuming and costly credit management systems.
- ✔ Generating immediate cash payments will boost the income you receive from interest.
- ✔ The generation of immediate cash payments may also make your business more attractive to potential purchasers.

ADVANTAGES

- Choosing the right payment policy allows you to balance the need to generate sufficient cash flow against the need to encourage sales by offering flexible payment terms.
- If you can offer finance to your clients, you can develop an additional source of income on top of the goods or services you are selling them.
- Negotiating flexible terms with suppliers can also boost your company's finances.

DISADVANTAGES

- Choosing the right payments policy can involve considerable expense and prove time-consuming. Expenses include the cost of purchasing software as well as training staff in the use of this software. You may also have to hire specialist consultants to advise you on which payment policy you should pursue.

DOS AND DON'TS

DO

- Get a lawyer to draw up a payment policy. This will protect your rights as a seller and will give you full ownership of the goods until the customer pays for them in full.
- Install a robust credit management system. Seeking to save money at this stage could prove very costly in the long run.
- Continuously monitor your existing customers' credit histories. Circumstances change, and a business with a good credit rating may not retain that status indefinitely. Increasingly delayed payment could mean that it is in financial trouble.
- Make sure that your payment terms are displayed prominently on any invoice. For example, you could include a box on the front of the document for the customer to sign in acceptance of the terms and conditions of sale.

DON'T

- Don't sell blind. Before you issue credit to new customers, you should first evaluate their ability to pay.
- Don't rule out potential clients just because they have a less than perfect credit history. You can always ask them to pay part or all of the bill immediately, or give them shorter payment terms.

▸▸ MORE INFO

Books:

Bluman, Allan G. *Business Math Demystified: A Self-teaching Guide*. New York: McGraw-Hill Professional, 2006.

Droms, William G. *Finance and Accounting for Nonfinancial Managers: All the Basics You Need to Know*. 5th ed. Cambridge, MA: Perseus, 2003.

Steingold, Fred S. *Legal Guide for Starting & Running a Small Business*. 10th ed. Berkeley, CA: Nolo, 2008.

Articles:

Abad Peiro, J. L., N. Asokan, M. Steiner, and M. Waidner. "Designing a generic payment service." *IBM Systems Journal* 37:1 (1998): 72–88. Online at: www.research.ibm.com/journal/sj/371/abadpeiro.html

Emery, G., and N. Nayar. "Product quality and payment policy." *Review of Quantitative Finance and Accounting* 10:3 (1998): 269–284.

Wilson, N., and B. Summers. "Trade credit terms offered by small firms: Survey evidence and empirical analysis." *Journal of Business Finance & Accounting* 29:3 (2002): 317–351.

Website:

Business support, information, and advice from the UK government: www.businesslink.gov.uk

"If you don't sell, it's not the product that's wrong, it's you." Estée Lauder

  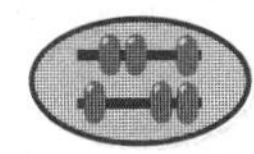   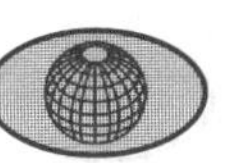   

Commercial Aspects of Licensing

DEFINITION

To license means to give permission to use a certain property in exchange for payment. Such properties can be tangible, such as manufactured products, or intangible, such as intellectual property rights (brand, copyright, trademark, design rights, etc.), or computer software. The parties to a licensing agreement are the owner of the licensed property (the licensor) and the party to whom the license is granted (the licensee).

The licensor and the licensee will usually enter into a licensing agreement which is drafted by the licensor, then negotiated and amended by the licensee.

License agreements can be difficult to understand, and it is advisable for both parties to obtain legal advice to guide them in their negotiations.

Under a licensing agreement, the licensor grants the licensee the right to manufacture certain products or use certain intellectual property rights in a well-defined territory, for a certain period of time, in exchange for a licensing fee. The license can be exclusive or nonexclusive. An exclusive license gives the licensee the sole right to manufacture or use the products in that territory, while a nonexclusive license usually means that there are other licensees using the same rights or manufacturing the same products. Exclusive licenses are, therefore, more expensive and sought after.

Before entering into a licensing agreement, a licensee should thoroughly investigate the market and territory and weigh the advantages and disadvantages of obtaining a license and operating within that market. If the license to be obtained relates to the manufacturing and sale of products, it is advisable to think of the way in which these products will be distributed and sold. A licensor of a top brand will have certain requirements as to how its products are presented and sold. Publicity and marketing will be expensive and should be included in the licensing budget. There will be a difference between the price that the licensee pays to the licensor for a product and the price at which the same product is sold to the consumer. The licensee should weigh these prices carefully in order to assess its profit margin.

For certain products, a royalty fee may be charged to the licensee in addition to the price of the license. This is usually calculated as a percentage of the net takings for the product and will be dealt with in the licensing agreement.

Intellectual property rights usually remain in the ownership of the licensor. The licensee can only use them in accordance with the terms of the license and for the duration of the agreement.

The licensor will include in the agreement certain conditions under which the licensed property can be used. If these conditions are breached, the licensor can revoke the license altogether. It is therefore important that a licensee fully understands such conditions when he enters into the license.

Certain licenses will not allow a licensee to sublicense or assign the license to anyone else without the express written consent of the licensor. This way, a licensor can remain in full control of the distribution of the products in the territory covered by the license.

A licensed product should come with certain warranties given by the licensor. These will be negotiated in depth. However, the licensee should try to obtain as many as it can.

ADVANTAGES

- Licensing allows a licensor to increase the market for its brand by giving others the right to use it under certain conditions and for a certain price.
- It also allows a licensee to operate a business and to exploit, for the licensee's own benefit and profit, a product that belongs to someone else and that would otherwise be too expensive to acquire.

DISADVANTAGES

- Negotiating a licensing agreement can be complex and time consuming. It involves thorough research of the market and territory in which the products will be sold or used.

ACTION CHECKLIST

- ✔ Study carefully any license you might acquire. Obtain as much information from as many sources as possible before committing to an expensive licensing agreement.
- ✔ Know your market and make sure that you have analyzed the consequences for your own business of entering into a licensing agreement.
- ✔ Be prepared for long and complicated negotiations, which could prove time consuming as well as costly.
- ✔ Economize by negotiating a reasonable rate with your legal advisers, but remember that it is better to incur costs by obtaining legal advice than to enter into a license under terms that you do not understand.

DOS AND DON'TS

DO

- Involve your solicitors in the evaluation of both the risks and potential benefits of entering into a license.
- Negotiate your rates and make a contingency plan for any cost overrun.
- Plan carefully how the license will operate in the territory.

DON'T

- Don't be attracted by a license that has not been thoroughly investigated.
- Don't overlook the importance of negotiating warranties and indemnities that would protect you in the event that underlying liabilities are discovered.

▸▸ MORE INFO

Books:

Nimmer, Raymond T., and Jeff C. Dodd. *Modern Licensing Law*. 2008–2009 ed. Eagan, MN: West, 2008.

Sherman, Andrew J. *Franchising and Licensing: Two Powerful Ways to Grow Your Business in Any Economy*. 3rd ed. New York: Amacom, 2004.

Articles:

Nimmer, Raymond T. "UCITA and the continuing evolution of digital licensing law." *Computer and internet Lawyer* 21:2 (2004): 10–16.

Loe, Nancy E. "Avoiding the golden fleece: Licensing agreements for archives." *The American Archivist* 67:1 (2004): 58–85.

"Owning the intellectual property is like owning land: You need to keep investing in it again and again to get a payoff; you can't simply sit back and collect rent." Esther Dyson

  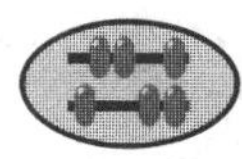 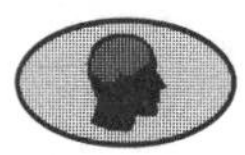  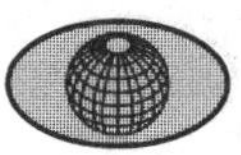   

Competition Law: Key Financial Issues

DEFINITION

Competition is one of the main driving forces of economic activity. From the consumer perspective, free and fair competition keeps prices down and helps to ensure the quality of products, while from the producer perspective effective competition boosts productivity, drives efficiency, and promotes innovation. Competition instills discipline in sellers, obliging them to provide quality at an attractive price relative to rivals.

Competition laws, known in the United States as antitrust laws, broadly aim to ensure that competition is free and fair by regulating companies' market power. However, in general terms, most countries' competition legislation aims to set limits for competitors' activities by defining circumstances in which a state or regulator may intervene in the market to ensure that an obstacle to competition is removed, or when the market has effectively ceased to function correctly. Under the major global jurisdictions, competition law permits intervention to tackle many sources of potential market aberrations, such as price manipulation by cartels, the abuse of market power by a monopoly operation, or proposed mergers which could act to the detriment of free and fair competition.

Companies should ensure that they fully understand the intricacies of competition law in all jurisdictions in which they operate, both to meet their own obligations and to help protect their market position and generally defend their rights against rivals. Companies found to be in breach of competition laws risk finding not only that any relevant contracts signed may be unenforceable, but offenders could also face a heavy fine which could, in some cases, threaten the viability of the business. In the United States, the consequences of being found in breach of the Sherman Antitrust Act (1890) can be particularly severe, involving criminal penalties of up to $100 million for a corporation and up to $1 million for an individual, who could also risk spending up to 10 years in prison.

The Organisation for Economic Co-Operation and Development (OECD) recently demonstrated that member states which have implemented reforms to promote competition have actually enjoyed higher levels of economic growth and lower levels of unemployment than those members that are more resistant to change. A 2008 report from the OECD cited the example of Australia, which implemented a series of pro-competitive reforms, both at the national and state levels, in the mid-1990s, measures which helped the country's economy to become one of the OECD's leading performers in the new millennium.

ADVANTAGES

- Competition laws define the boundaries of acceptable trading practices in an effort to create a level playing field for all market participants.
- The laws aim to protect consumers from sharp practices, such as price fixing and other market manipulation.
- Competition laws can promote efficiency and innovation by protecting the rights of companies that bring new or improved products or services to market.
- Trading blocs such as the European Union, NAFTA, Mercosur, and ASEAN have extended the benefits of free trade beyond national borders, promoting and managing trading activities free of import tariffs.

DISADVANTAGES

- Global competition law is something of a misnomer—though international bodies such as the World Trade Organization (WTO) can push initiatives aimed at preventing anticompetitive cross-border trade practices, laws set by individual jurisdictions such as the United States and the European Union apply.
- The boundaries between the passing of laws to protect domestic markets from unfair competition and the introduction of measures purely to protect national producers from overseas competition can often be blurred. Trade disputes between countries or regions can escalate rapidly, with the imposition of crippling import tariffs.
- The pace of technological innovation can create challenges for lawmakers.

ACTION CHECKLIST

✔ Seek professional advice to understand the significance of competition laws in any particular jurisdiction before commencing business activity there.

✔ Competition legislation has grown rapidly over recent years, driven in part by the deregulation of formerly state-controlled industries such as utilities, telecoms, and mail services. It is important to keep abreast of changes that could impact on your.

✔ Understand that competition laws can represent opportunities for companies driven by innovation, as well as a threat to those who attempt to restrict market choice.

DOS AND DON'TS

DO

- Appreciate the complexity of trying to get to grips with the concept of "global" competition laws; according to the Asian Development Bank there are at least 100 different systems of competition law across the world.
- Consider how competition laws could actually protect your business and help to safeguard investment in areas such as new product development.

DON'T

- Don't make assumptions about competition laws in one country based on experience elsewhere, as significant differences apply between jurisdictions.
- Don't ignore the political element in the way some countries' competition laws are structured, particularly in socially sensitive areas such as utilities.

›› MORE INFO

Book:

Taylor, Martin D. *International Competition Law: A New Dimension for the WTO?* Cambridge, UK: Cambridge University Press, 2006.

Article:

Kolasky, William. "International comity in antitrust: Advances and challenges." *Legal Backgrounder* 22:16 (May 2007). Online at: www.wilmerhale.com/services/practice/pubs.aspx?firmService=337

Website:

Asian Development Bank Competition Law Toolkit: www.adb.org/Documents/Others/OGC-Toolkits/Competition-Law

"Thou shalt not covet, but tradition approves all forms of competition." Arthur Hugh Clough

  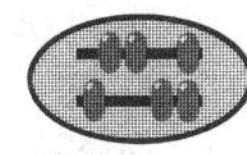 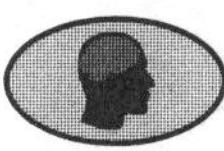  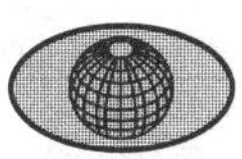   

Corporate Insurance Cover: A Primer

DEFINITION

In every country in the world companies are legally required to have a minimum level of insurance cover. It is also prudent to pay for some insurance beyond this basic level. Occasionally, forms of insurance have different names in different countries. This primer uses the British descriptions.

Perhaps the most important form of insurance is employers' liability. This offers cover against bodily injury, illness, or disease suffered in the course of employment.

Public liability ensures that a company is able to pay damages for bodily injury, illness, disease, loss, or damage to property caused by the insured. Product liability covers damages arising from the supply of a defective product. This could include anything from power tools to computer software.

Professional indemnity is mandatory for certain occupations. It protects against legal action by clients claiming damages for what they see as negligent or bad services.

Business interruption insurance is increasingly popular. This provides compensation if, for example, your property is damaged in a way that disrupts your business activities. This may be on the basis of gross profit where a company is making or selling goods. Clubs and other businesses supplying a service may be covered on the basis of gross revenue.

Property and buildings insurance is a complex area with a number of variables. Basic cover will include damage arising, for instance, from fire, lightning, and gas explosions. Additional cover can include threats such malicious damage, flood, or leakage from sprinkler systems. So-called "all-risks" insurance will protect against most eventualities, but not wear and tear or mechanical breakdown.

Contents cover for business assets and equipment is also an area where insurance companies offer a number of different types of policy. Stock is normally covered at cost price, but equipment may be insured for replacement as new or taking into account deterioration. Theft following forcible entry is normally covered, but stealing by employees is generally excluded, although there are special policies for employee dishonesty.

Specific policies insure money lost or stolen from your premises or in transit to the bank. Goods in transit insurance protects against damage to stock carried in your own vehicles, by road hauliers, or by post. A recent addition to policies available protects against damage or consequential loss arising from acts of terrorism.

Many large insurers and brokers offer single policies covering the three main areas of commercial insurance: liabilities; business assets and equipment; and property and buildings. The advantage of this approach is that it should reduce the risk of overlaps or gaps in coverage, although it may be more economical to shop around for specialist policies.

Many organizations will also require other forms of insurance for: commercial vehicles and company cars; business travel; accident and sickness; and employee health. There are also more specialist requirements, such as marine cargo and engineering inspection.

Insurance brokers who specialize in covering commercial clients will be able to offer policies for all these areas.

ADVANTAGES AND DISADVANTAGES

It's not really appropriate to talk of the advantages and disadvantages of taking out corporate insurance, as in many cases having insurance is compulsory.

ACTION CHECKLIST

- ✔ Find a suitable broker who specializes in the type of insurance you need.
- ✔ Check the terms. Not all insurers offer cover for the same thing.
- ✔ Check the laws and regulations for your industry to learn which types of insurance are compulsory for your business.

DOS AND DON'TS

DO

- Shop around to compare premiums and policies.

DON'T

- Don't cut corners. It may be a false economy, and you could end up in court if someone brings a claim you do not have cover for.

➡ MORE INFO

Books:

Blanchard, Ralph H. *Introduction to Risk and Insurance*. Frederick, MD: Beard Books, 2001.

Harrington, Scott E., and Gregory R. Niehaus. *Risk Management and Insurance*. New York: McGraw-Hill/Irwin, 2004.

  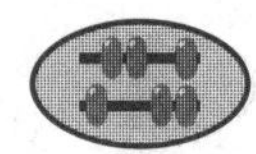 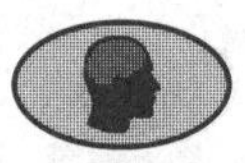  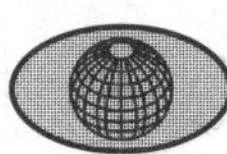   

Costing a New Project

DEFINITION

Before launching any new project, you need to determine its total cost. To ensure that all costs are covered, the first step is to break down all costs into direct and indirect costs. Direct costs include materials and labor that are directly involved in the project. Indirect costs cover operating expenses, such as administrative labor, marketing, office supplies, utilities, and rent.

It is then necessary to estimate each element of direct and indirect costs to obtain the total cost of the project. Some costs, such as labor, or products and services that are bought regularly, are easy to estimate. However, other costs may be more uncertain. You may, for example, have to include a new service or product with unusual specifications. The project budget should then include a design allowance to cover cost overruns. It is also wise to include a contingency sum to cover unexpected events such as unusual weather or problems with suppliers—always a possibility on large projects. So the budget for any new project should contain figures for the estimated cost, plus a contingency fund and design allowance, and any profit. The project manager's role is to keep the actual cost at or below the estimated cost, to use as little of the design allowance and contingency as possible, and to maximize the profit earned from the project.

ADVANTAGES

- Good information is crucial to managing a project well. Understanding the costs of a new project and how they break down is critical in determining whether the project will be profitable or not.
- Producing a detailed project costing enables the project manager to ascertain whether a project is proceeding according to schedule. He can quickly identify areas where costs are running out of control and take steps to rectify these problems.

DISADVANTAGES

- If the project is relatively small, the fees involved in costing the project may be excessive.

ACTION CHECKLIST

- ✔ Draw up a detailed list of all the elements and costs involved in the project. Make sure that you include indirect as well as direct costs.
- ✔ Find out whether project management software could assist in managing project costs.

DOS AND DON'TS

DO

- Talk to all the staff involved in the project to make sure that you have a complete breakdown of costs.
- Talk to suppliers to obtain an idea of the costs of the products and services involved in the project.
- Set aside a contingency fund and a design allowance.

DON'T

- Don't assume that the cost of a particular service or input will remain constant over the lifetime of a project.
- Don't guess the costs of certain elements of a project.

▸▸ MORE INFO

Books:

Baker, H. Kent, and Gary E. Powell. *Understanding Financial Management: A Practical Guide*. Malden, MA: Blackwell Publishing, 2005.

Bandler, James. *How to Use Financial Statements: A Guide to Understanding the Numbers*. Burr Ridge, IL: Irwin, 1994.

Dickie, Robert B. *Financial Statement Analysis and Business Valuation for the Practical Lawyer*. 2nd ed. Chicago, IL: American Bar Association, 2006.

Articles:

Akintoye, Akintola. "Analysis of factors influencing project cost estimating practice." *Construction Management & Economics* 18:1 (2000): 77–89.

Munns, A. K., and B. F. Bjeirmi. "The role of project management in achieving project success." *International Journal of Project Management* 14:2 (1996): 81–87.

Raz, T., and D. Elnathan. "Activity based costing for projects." *International Journal of Project Management* 17:1 (1999): 61–67.

Website:

UK government website providing advice for businesses: www.businesslink.gov.uk

  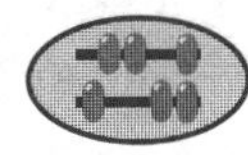 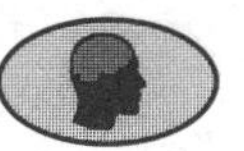  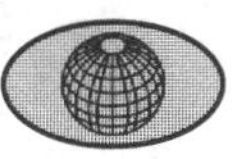  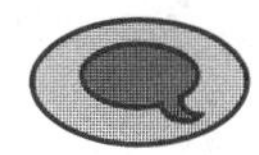 

Creating a Risk Register

DEFINITION

A risk register, also sometimes called a "risk log", is usually used when planning for the future. Future plans may include project plans, organizational plans, or financial plans. Risk registers are used in the area of risk management.

Risk management is a method of managing risks or uncertainty relating to a perceived threat. Risk management will usually involve having strategies in place to deal with risks, whether by avoiding the risk, transferring it elsewhere, reducing its effect, or dealing with the consequences. Financial risk management deals with risks that can be managed using traded financial instruments.

Risk management uses risk registers to identify, analyze, and manage risks in a clear, concise way. A risk register usually takes the form of a table—however long or wide that may end up being.

A risk is an event that, if it occurred, would have an adverse (or positive) impact on a project, investment, or similar. The risk register contains information on each risk that is identified. One of the main skills in risk management is to successfully identify all possible risks. The risk register should contain, in summarized form, the planned response in the event that a risk materializes, as well as a summary of what actions should be taken beforehand to reduce a particular risk. Much financial legislation, such as Basel II, also impels organizations to take steps to reduce risk. Risks are often ranked in order of likelihood, or of their impact. The risk register lists the analysis and evaluation of the risks that have been identified.

ADVANTAGES

- A risk register can identify and make provision for dealing with risks, enabling an organization to save millions if things go wrong.
- Should a risk materialize, there is already a set list of actions to run through immediately to start minimizing the consequences.
- An organization can have the confidence to press on with a project or investment knowing that procedures to deal with any risks arising have been put in place.

DISADVANTAGES

- Much time, effort, and money can be spent on creating risk registers to deal with events that will never occur.

ACTION CHECKLIST

- ✔ Establish a risk management team. The team should meet regularly to discuss the risks associated with each project, investment, etc., to review procedures, and to ensure that the risk register is kept up to date. Appoint a team member to keep abreast of any legislative requirements that may affect the risk register.
- ✔ Identify and list all potential risks, and decide on the likelihood of their occurrence. Determine the expected impact if they do occur. Identify any interdependencies with other risks and what knock-on effects there may be.
- ✔ Decide who will bear the risk.
- ✔ Identify countermeasures to mitigate the risk before it occurs.
- ✔ Keep track on the risk register of the current status of any risk that has occurred and what action is being taken.

DOS AND DON'TS

DO

- Create a risk register for each new project or investment.
- List each risk as a separate entry in the register's table.
- Identify an "owner" for each risk, i.e. a person who will be in charge of resolving the risk.
- Follow up on actions and status for each risk identified.
- Revisit the risk register regularly to evaluate any changes to the likelihood of a risk and its potential impact. Changes to projects and investments should also be evaluated for their effect on previously assessed risks or new risks that may arise.

DON'T

- Don't ignore the possibility of risks becoming a reality.
- Don't lose track of the risk register.

▸▸ MORE INFO

Books:

Ackermann, Fran. *Systemic Risk Assessment: A Case Study.* Management Science Theory Method and Practice Series. Glasgow, UK: Department of Management Science, University of Strathclyde, 2003.

Bateman, Mike. *Tolley's Practical Risk Assessment Handbook*. 5th ed. Boston, MA: Elsevier, 2006.

Brinded, Malcolm. *Perception vs Analysis: How to Handle Risk.* Eighth Annual Royal Academy of Engineering Lloyd's Register Lecture. London: Royal Academy of Engineering, 2000.

Journal:

Risk Management. Published quarterly by Palgrave Macmillan. Online at: www.palgrave-journals.com/rm

Website:

The Institute of Risk Management (UK): www.theirm.org

   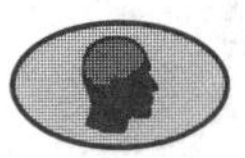  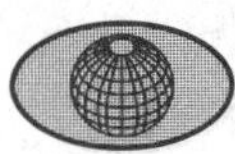   

Distribution Agreements

DEFINITION

A distributor is an individual or a legal person who has been appointed by another individual or company (the supplier) to distribute its products within a defined territory.

The supplier and distributor enter into a distribution agreement, which is drafted by the supplier, then negotiated and amended by the distributor. Certain distributors can be agents of the supplier, but this is not always the case.

The distributor can be exclusive or nonexclusive. An exclusive distribution agreement gives the distributor the sole right to distribute and sell the products in that territory—the principal will not appoint any other distributors. A nonexclusive arrangement means that there will be other distributors of the same products.

In general, a distributor will purchase the products from the supplier and agrees not to distribute or manufacture during the period that the distribution agreement is valid any goods that compete with the products of the supplier.

A distributor could be an agent of the supplier, but this is unusual as the supplier generally prefers to keep things relatively simple and not give a distributor the power to directly commit it to any contracts that an agency would imply.

Under a distribution agreement, the distributor would have certain obligations, such as: to use all reasonable endeavors to promote the distribution and sale of the products in the territory; to employ a sufficient number of suitably qualified personnel to fulfill its obligation under the agreement; to maintain appropriate levels of stock of the products; and to insure all products against all risks.

A supplier will be also be required to supply the products to the distributor on time and, in the case of exclusive distribution, not to supply the products to anyone else in the territory.

The distribution agreement will contain detailed clauses as to pricing, advertising, and promotion of the products.

In general the distributor will be expected to obtain and comply with all the appropriate import licenses or permits necessary for the entry of the products into the territory.

ADVANTAGES

- A distribution agreement allows a manufacturer or supplier to increase the market for its brand by giving others the right to sell and distribute it under certain conditions and for a certain price.
- It also allows a distributor to operate a business and to exploit, for its benefit, a product that belongs to someone else and would otherwise be too expensive to acquire.

DISADVANTAGES

- Distribution arrangements can be quite expensive for a distributor as thorough research is needed into the obtaining of licenses, permits, and insurance for the products.
- Negotiating a distribution agreement can be complex and time-consuming. It involves thorough research of the market and territory in which the products will be sold or used.
- Exclusive distribution arrangements are expensive.

ACTION CHECKLIST

✔ Study carefully any distribution agreement which you might sign. Obtain as much information from as many sources as you can before committing to an expensive agreement.

✔ Know your market and make sure that you have analyzed the consequences of entering into a distribution agreement for your own business. Plan for contingencies. Take into account any cost of import duties, storage, and insurance.

✔ Be prepared for long and complicated negotiations, which could prove time-consuming as well as costly.

DOS AND DON'TS

DO

- Choose your distributor carefully before you enter into an agreement that could potentially damage your brand.
- Involve your solicitors in the evaluation of both the risks and benefits of entering into a distribution agreement.
- Negotiate your rates and make a contingency plan for any cost overrun.
- Plan carefully how the chain of distribution will operate in the territory.

DON'T

- Don't make the mistake of being attracted by a distributor or supplier that you do not know and has not been thoroughly investigated.
- Don't overlook the importance of negotiating warranties and indemnities that would protect you in the event that the products are damaged while in the care of the distributor.

⏩ MORE INFO

Books:

Clasen, T. F. (ed). *International Agency and Distribution Agreements*. Looseleaf ed. London: Lexis Law Publishing, 1991. Also published as *International Agency and Distribution Agreements: Analysis and Forms*. Salem, NH: Butterworth Legal Publishers, 1990.

Singleton, S. *Commercial Agency Agreements: Law and Practice*. 2nd ed. London: Tottel Publishing, 2005.

Article:

Gustafson, J. "GenPrime signs big distribution agreement." *Journal of Business* (October 9, 2000). Online at: www.highbeam.com/doc/1P3-1584030011.html

Website:

All Business resources and advice for small companies: www.allbusiness.com

"**Every organization of today has to build into its very structure the management of change.**" Peter F. Drucker

  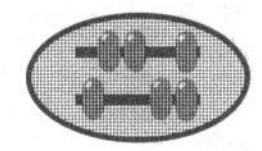 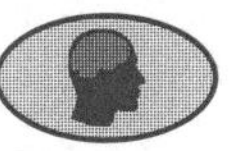 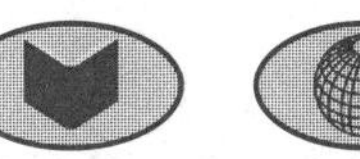 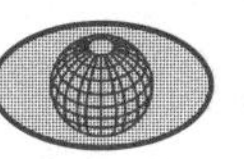   

Efficient Invoicing Procedures

DEFINITION

An invoice is a document issued by a seller to a purchaser that formally requests payment for goods or services supplied. The issuing of an invoice indicates that the buyer must now settle their account with the seller according to the agreed payment terms.

An invoice is usually printed on company stationery and contains certain standard information:

- The word "Invoice."
- A unique reference number.
- Date of the invoice.
- The seller's tax or company registration details, where required.
- The purchaser's name and contact details.
- Description of the goods or services, and date when delivered.
- A purchase order number.
- Unit price, where relevant.
- Total amount payable, including a breakdown of any taxes, if required.
- Payment terms, including method of payment, date due, and details of any applicable late payment charges.

Invoicing legislation varies globally, requiring additional information in some cases. For example, in the United States the Defense Logistics Agency requires an employer identification number; in the European Union, a VAT (value added tax) number is needed on invoices if either entity is registered for VAT.

It is vital to have good invoicing policies and procedures in place to ensure a smooth cash flow into the business. Conversely, clients generally appreciate knowing your invoicing terms. Set out clear payment terms—30 days is standard in many countries by default, but sometimes it makes sense to shorten or lengthen the payment period.

Depending on the size of the company, issuing and/or tracking invoices should be done daily, weekly, or monthly.

Figure 1. Example invoice

Invoice No: 032/08

John Smith
Purchasing Manager
Grommet Retail Ltd
15 Brown Street
London W8 9XX

ACME WIDGETS CO. LTD
Acme House
42 Sussex Road
London SE26 2PZ
Tel: 020 8123 4567
Fax: 020 8123 4568

Date: 2 September 2008

INVOICE

Order No. 987654 Delivery No. 321 Delivery date: 1 September 2008

10,000 2mm widgets @ $1.20 per widget (product code: 0042M)	$12,000.00
Sub Total	$12,000.00
VAT @ 17.5%	$ 2,100.00
TOTAL DUE	$14,100.00

Terms of payment 30 days

Please note that late payment is subject to interest charges and associated compensation payment under the UK Late Payment of Commercial Debts (Interest) Act 1998.

Please transfer payment to Acme Widgets Co. Ltd, Clark's Bank, 88 Acacia Avenue, London SE36 1XP, account number 03689043, sort code 20-31-82.

Registered office: Acme House, 42 Sussex Road, London SE26 2PZ
Registered in England number: 98705432 VAT no: 66-777-888

ADVANTAGES

- A well thought out invoicing policy not only helps keep cash flowing, it also ensures that its administration is streamlined and easy to maintain.

DISADVANTAGES

- There are no disadvantages to having a clear invoicing process.

ACTION CHECKLIST

✔ Investigate automating your invoicing with suitable software. Various packages exist that can be linked to accounting programs, and some generate invoices as soon as the accounts are updated per client.

✔ Look at the options for e-billing of clients to reduce postal and administrative costs for both parties.

✔ Ensure that clients are aware of the range of payment options. It is possible to pay by BACS (Bankers' Automated Clearing Services) transfer and other electronic payment systems such as PayPal or WorldPay, as well as by standing order, direct debit, and check.

DOS AND DON'TS

DO

- Quote any relevant legislation on late payment on the invoice to encourage clients to pay in good time.
- Consider offering discounts to clients who pay early.
- Prompt clients to pay by e-mailing a polite reminder a week before the due date. Likewise, a statement of account a week after can galvanize late payers.

DON'T

- Don't get heavy-handed as soon as an invoice is one day overdue. Better to have a clear policy that sets out incremental stages of action for late or nonpayers.

▸▸ MORE INFO

Book:

Sher, David, and Martin Sher. *How to Collect Debts (and Still Keep Your Customers)*. New York: AMACOM, 1999.

Website:

Better Payment Practice Campaign—A UK-based website with information on late payment legislation and templates for invoices and follow-up action letters: www.payontime.co.uk

"God is in the details." Ludwig Mies van der Rohe

   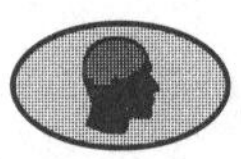  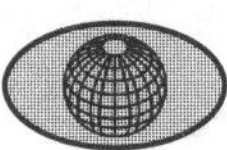  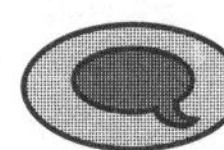 

Ensuring Effective Financial Control

DEFINITION

A number of elements must be in place for effective financial management of a company or project to take place. Effective financial control is defined as keeping costs to an agreed level, ensuring that a project is developed within budget. Critically, all managers should take responsibility for financial management and should not assume that this falls within the remit of the accounts team alone. Strategic or long-term planning is also a critical building block for effective financial control. This planning can help you to decide where your financial priorities lie and how much of your total budget can be allocated to different areas of the company or project.

Good financial and accounting systems are paramount: it is essential that management has current, accurate, and relevant financial data to ensure sound decision-making. In addition, this information must be presented in a useful form that addresses the needs of individual managers. Internal controls should be robust and should be rigorously overseen. This could apply, for example, to the handling of cash by employees. Devolving the management of budgets can bring advantages in terms of flexibility, but there must be a clear reporting structure, so that, for example, it is easy to identify who is responsible for making spending decisions.

Income-driven budgeting, whereby expected income is determined and expense levels are set within this constraint, is a key way of ensuring that there is effective financial control of a project. Some organizations estimate their expected income by increasing or reducing the previous year's income by a set percentage. However, a more prudent method is to start from zero and build the income forecast from the bottom up.

ADVANTAGES

- Effective financial management is a critical determinant of the failure or success of a project or company.
- Effective financial control ensures that the company or project is run as efficiently as possible, ensuring that its full potential is realized.

DISADVANTAGES

- There are no disadvantages.

ACTION CHECKLIST

✔ Draw up a strategic or long-term plan to enable you to determine where the financial priorities of a company or project lie.

✔ See that all managers know that they are responsible for ensuring effective financial management and that it is not simply the responsibility of the accounts team.

DOS AND DON'TS

DO

- Invest in accounting and management information systems.
- Draw up robust internal controls to cover issues such as cash handling.
- Make sure that there is a clear reporting structure and that all members of staff know who is responsible for setting a particular budget and who can authorize spending.

DON'T

- Don't ignore your accountant. Accountants have a unique understanding of the key drivers of revenues and costs in a business and can provide invaluable assistance in reviewing financial performance throughout the year. In addition, your accountant can model results for you based on different assumptions and can help you to get a much clearer picture of the risks that might need to be managed.

▸▸ MORE INFO

Books:

Besley, Scott, and Eugene F. Brigham. *Essentials of Managerial Finance*. 14th ed. Mason, OH: Cengage Learning, 2007.

Brigham, Eugene F., and Joel F. Houston. *Fundamentals of Financial Management*. Mason, OH: Cengage Learning, 2007.

Moyer, R. Charles, and James R. McGuigan. *Contemporary Financial Management*. Mason, OH: Cengage Learning, 2008.

Articles:

Kaplan, R. S., and D. P. Norton. "The balanced scorecard: Measures that drive performance." *Harvard Business Review* (January–February 1992): 71–79.

Peel, Michael J., and John Bridge. "How planning and capital budgeting improve SME performance." *Long Range Planning* 31:6 (1998): 848–856.

Report:

Richardson, John, and Thom Wham. "Business planning: Budgeting and marketing your FIRST team." StLouisFirst.org (November 6, 2004). Online at: www.stlouisfirst.org/knowledge/budgetingmarketing.pdf

Website:

UK Government website providing advice for businesses: www.businesslink.gov.uk

"To make knowledge productive. . .requires the systematic exploitation of opportunities for change."
Peter F. Drucker

     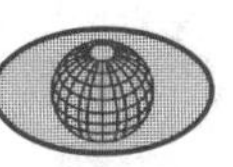   

How to Optimize Stock Control

DEFINITION

Stock control is how an organization ensures that its stocks are at levels that meet predetermined standards of service and allow funds to be released as working capital. Stock control, also known as inventory control, determines how much stock a company has at a given point in time and how it keeps track of it. It applies to every item used to produce a product or service, from raw materials to finished goods, and refers to any kind of stock at every stage of the production process, from purchase and delivery to using and reordering the stock.

Effective practice in stock control requires effort and resources to introduce a system which offers maximum advantage at a reasonable cost and takes into consideration the cost of finance, storage, insurance, handling, obsolescence, and theft. Efficient stock control ensures that a company has the right amount of stock in the right place at the right time, and that minimum capital is tied up. It also helps to protect production should any problems arise with the supply chain.

Holding too much stock can result in a company having too much cash tied up in stock, but holding too little can lose clients. Efficient stock control facilitates "just in time" stock management, with an order schedule that forecasts stock reordering requirements for a period of time ahead, based on factors such as open sales orders, open purchase orders, and the required-by date.

ADVANTAGES

- Good stock control reduces costs and improves efficiency, while ensuring that a company can meet fluctuations in customer demand.

DISADVANTAGES

- Overstocking increases costs, and there is a risk of overestimating the level of demand for products.
- Held stock may become damaged or obsolete, or perish.
- Poor stock control can lead to a potential loss of sales or missed orders, and large stocks may be subject to theft.

ACTION CHECKLIST

- ✔ Choose a suitable stock control system, from simple ledger books and card indexes to highly computerized systems, that will provide knowledge of current stocks on a regular basis and record supplies received and sales, deliveries, outputs, and usage.
- ✔ Use common sense—the cost of the system and its operation should not be greater than the cost of the problem it is intended to solve.
- ✔ Identify current stock levels, record receipts/dispatches, and identify reordering levels and quantities.
- ✔ Establish a regular pattern of auditing and stock checking.
- ✔ Analyze usage of all items in terms of volume and strategic/nonstrategic stock.
- ✔ Identify key products that must be available on demand.
- ✔ Classify products in terms of importance to overall turnover but not in big product families or in other broad product groupings.
- ✔ Focus attention on the items that produce the most revenue.
- ✔ Identify the level of stock that must be held to avoid the risk of missing core opportunities or failing to supply basic needs.

DOS AND DON'TS

DO

- Plan your storage area carefully, locating the most frequently used items in an accessible place, and choose appropriate stacking methods such as pallets, shelving, or bins. Instigate an appropriate labeling system for easy stock identification.
- Implement a stock rotation system and ensure that availability meets requirements.
- Pay attention to environmental conditions, high/low temperatures, and humidity.
- View stock as money.

DON'T

- Don't rule out the possibility of pilferage, excessive waste, or other forms of shrinkage.
- Don't view stocktaking as an annual chore, but do it regularly on a partial basis.
- Don't hold on to stock just to fill the warehouse.
- Don't store every item in the same environment.
- Don't buy speculatively.

▸▸ MORE INFO

Books:

Baily, Peter, Gerard Tavernier, and Richard Storey. *Stock Control Systems and Records.* 2nd ed. Aldershot, UK: Gower, 1984.

Emmett, Stuart, and David Granville. *Excellence in Inventory Management: How to Minimise Costs and Maximise Service.* Cambridge, UK: Cambridge Academic, 2007.

Wild, Tony. *Improving Inventory Record Accuracy: Getting Your Stock Information Right.* Oxford: Butterworth-Heinemann, 2004.

"All of our long-term suppliers are very profitable." Marcus Sieff

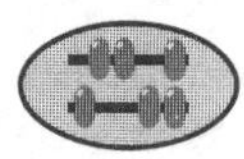
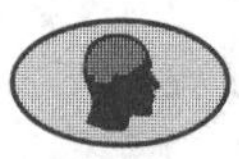

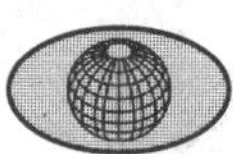

Identifying Your Continuity Needs

DEFINITION

In order for a company to be prepared to recover from the impact of a disaster such as a fire, flood, or explosion, it has to identify its key functions and the risks that are faced. Critical activities and resources can be identified through a business impact analysis (BIA), while a concurrent risk assessment will aid recognition of threats.

The aim of analysis is to create two types of plan, which may overlap. An incident management plan covers the initial impact, including procedures such as evacuation. The longer-term business continuity plan prepares an organization to keep delivering key products and services afterwards.

Plans have to be tested to ensure that they work. Staff also have to be trained in the procedures. The frequency of planning exercises depends on the speed of change within an organization and the outcome of previous drills where weaknesses have been identified.

The British Standards Institution (BSI) has developed a standard BS 25999 for business continuity management. In North America the equivalent is the National Fire Protection Association NFPA 1600: *Standard on Disaster/Emergency Management and Business Continuity Programs*. Globally, the International Organization for Standardization (ISO) has published the ISO/PAS 22399:2007 *Guideline for Incident Preparedness and Operational Continuity Management*.

ADVANTAGES

- Having a continuity plan in place gives peace of mind. You may never need it, but it's there if the worst happens.

DISADVANTAGES

- Failing to prepare for disaster could result in serious financial loss or even bankruptcy if there is a major incident.

▸▸ MORE INFO

Websites:

International Organization for Standardization (ISO). ISO/PAS 22399:2007: "Societal security—Guideline for incident preparedness and operational continuity management." Available from: www.iso.org

National Fire Protection Agency: www.nfpa.org

UK Government business continuity guidance: www.preparingforemergencies.gov.uk/business

US Federal Emergency Management Agency has a section on business recovery planning: www.fema.gov

ACTION CHECKLIST

1. Undertake a business impact analysis

- ✔ Identify the products and services that will suffer the greatest impact as a result of disruption.
- ✔ Break the results down to analyze the impact on output from disruptions lasting 24 hours, up to two days, up to a week, and up to two weeks.
- ✔ Identify the so-called "maximum period of tolerable disruption" of service and product delivery that the organization can cope with before its viability is threatened.
- ✔ Set a recovery time for each of the key products and services, allowing for unforeseen difficulties.
- ✔ Create a document listing the activities required to deliver the key products and services.
- ✔ Ensure that the necessary resources are allocated to meet the requirements.

2. Carry out a risk assessment

- ✔ Identify the risks to the organization, including loss of staff, key suppliers, utilities, access to premises, IT, and telecommunications systems.
- ✔ Establish the likelihood of each risk.
- ✔ List existing arrangements for dealing with the risks.
- ✔ List arrangements that should be put in place to deal with the risks.
- ✔ Assign a likelihood score to each risk.

3. Decide what action the organization should take for each of the identified risks; for example:

- ✔ Deal with the risk by planning to continue service and product delivery at an acceptable minimum level.
- ✔ Tolerate the risk if the cost of its reduction outweighs the potential benefits.
- ✔ Transfer the risk to a third party or take out insurance.
- ✔ Terminate the activity. In some circumstances, particularly where an item is time-sensitive, it may be appropriate to suspend delivery.

4. Develop, publish, and circulate plans

- ✔ Establish an overall plan then decide how many plans are required within that. This will depend on the size and scope of the organization.
- ✔ State the purpose and scope of each plan.
- ✔ Identify who owns each plan and is responsible for its maintenance.
- ✔ List the individuals and their roles within the plan.
- ✔ Describe the circumstances, methods, and who is responsible for invoking the overall plan and its individual components.
- ✔ List appropriate contact details.
- ✔ For the initial response to an incident, list the tasks, responsibilities, and methods by which they are to be communicated.
- ✔ For business continuity, outline critical activities, the process by which they are to be recovered, and the timescale.

5. Test, maintain, and review plans

- ✔ Parts of the plan can and should be tested, such as back-up power, contact lists, and the process of activation.
- ✔ Staff should be brought together for training to discuss plans and identify weaknesses.
- ✔ Scenario-based desktop exercises can be used to validate plans and train key staff.
- ✔ Live exercises can cover one aspect of a plan, such as evacuation, or to test a full plan.

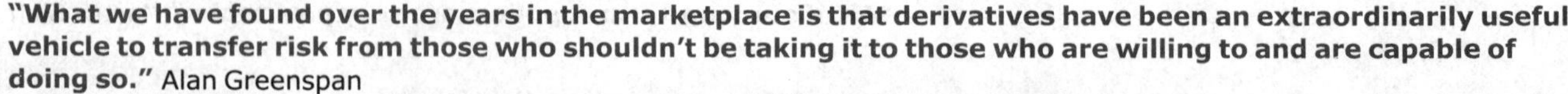
"What we have found over the years in the marketplace is that derivatives have been an extraordinarily useful vehicle to transfer risk from those who shouldn't be taking it to those who are willing to and are capable of doing so." Alan Greenspan

  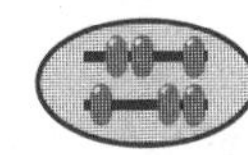 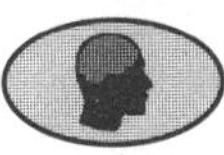  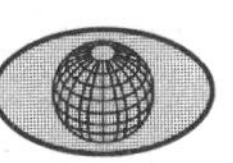   

Insuring Against Business Interruption

DEFINITION

Most companies have insurance against specific risks, but they do not always cover the indirect losses arising from an event. A buildings policy will, for instance, commonly include cover for rebuilding after a fire and replacing equipment. If the business is unable to trade and has to move to other premises, it will face considerable loss of income. It will still, however, face continuing costs such as wages, tax, and loan repayments. At the same time there may be additional charges for the rent of emergency accommodation and to pay overtime to staff.

Interruption insurance can fill the gaps in existing policies. It can cover both the continuing and emergency costs faced by the business and the loss of income arising from the enforced shutdown. It is the latter part of the policy that makes this a complex area. Estimating and proving current earnings can be problematic—especially if, for instance, a fire has triggered the payout and destroyed some of the records. In essence an insurer is being asked to pay for sales that the insured believes it would have had. An added complication is that few businesses will restart at the same level they were at before the interruption.

DOS AND DON'TS

DO

- Find a broker who specializes in insurance for business disruption.
- Obtain quotations from several insurers to compare premiums and policies.

DON'T

- Don't be tempted to opt for the cheapest policy as it may be a false economy. If a disaster does occur, you may find you are not covered for everything you need to keep the business running as smoothly as possible while you get back on track.

ACTION CHECKLIST

1. Identify all interruption costs

Ensure that all business interruption costs are covered, including the impact on all areas of the organization if one part is out of action.

2. Identify all sources of income and potential loss

Conduct a thorough review to determine the sources of income that would be lost and other costs or losses that might result from a shutdown.

- ✔ Forms of income will vary according to the type of business and can be a combination of revenue, fees, or rental.
- ✔ Penalty payments should be included as a major incident could affect a company's ability to complete a project.
- ✔ Interruption insurance will probably not cover some forms of income, such as interest on investments or sales of assets.

3. Check the supply chain

Examine the supply chain to make sure there is no over-dependency on one or two suppliers. Consider adding suppliers to the policy if reliance is unavoidable.

4. Coordinate insurance with the continuity plan

Insurance should be coordinated with the company's business continuity plan.

5. Include recovery costs

Ensure that all the costs and time that would be needed to restore the business are covered, including:

- ✔ Demolition, redesign, and rebuilding.
- ✔ Replacement of specialist machinery.
- ✔ Rehiring staff.

6. List all the company's business activities

Some of the items to include here may be less obvious than others.

- ✔ Include acquisitions, new divisions, and new ventures.
- ✔ Ensure that long-term projects are covered even if they have not yet produced income.
- ✔ Consider including key suppliers if damage to their premises could have serious repercussions on your business.
- ✔ Ensure that power suppliers are included, and check to see when coverage commences. There is a week's "deductible" in many policies.

7. Review the amount insured regularly

In conducting regular reviews of the amount covered, the following points may need consideration:

- ✔ Many large organizations with multiple profit centers include intergroup sales, which can inflate the premium through double counting.
- ✔ Make sure the projected figures for lost earnings are accurate for the whole insured period, which may be two or more years.
- ✔ Consider including a premium adjustment clause to take account of actual rather than projected earnings at the end of the year.

⏩ MORE INFO

Books:

Blanchard, Ralph H. *Introduction to Risk and Insurance*. Frederick, MD: Beard Books, 2001.

Harrington, Scott E., and Gregory R. Niehaus. *Risk Management and Insurance*. New York: McGraw-Hill/Irwin, 2004.

See Also:

✔ Corporate Insurance Cover: A Primer (p. 979)
✔ Stress Testing to Evaluate Insurance Cover (p. 932)

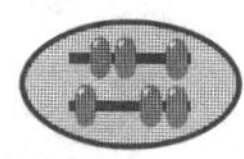

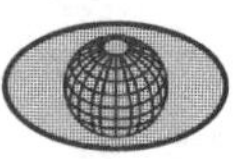

Intellectual Property—Copyright

DEFINITION

Intellectual property is a legal concept that provides for the exclusive ownership of abstract creations. It entitles the owner of such rights to charge for the use of the property or sell it.

Copyright is a concept of intellectual property that gives the author of a creative work the right to be credited for that work and to control its distribution. A copyrighted work may be reproduced only with the copyright owner's permission. There is no standard length of copyright protection, which varies according to the type of work protected and the country where protection is sought.

Copyright is applicable to most creative works, such as literature, drama, music, recordings of sound and film, and broadcasts. It comes into existence purely as a result of the work being produced; the author does not have to apply for copyright. For copyright to be recognized, the work must be original and in a fixed medium. Original ideas cannot be copyrighted unless they take the form of written or broadcasted work. Any items that are already in the public domain cannot be the subject of a copyright claim.

Copyright gives an author a monopoly over certain rights: the right of reproduction, the right to create derivative works, the right to performance, the right to display, the right to distribution, and the right to digitally transmit its performance.

People wanting to publish their work usually enter into a publication and license agreement with a publisher. In the agreement, the author grants exclusive or nonexclusive rights to publish, reproduce, distribute, and use the work in any form for a defined period of time. Nowadays, much work is self-published on websites that support user-generated content, social networks, wikis, and blogs.

Authors are usually asked to give a warranty that what they have written does not defame or invade the privacy of any person, nor infringe anyone's rights.

If copyright infringement occurs, an author may be entitled to an injunction (a court order to stop the infringement), damages, a refund of lawyers' fees relating to the infringement, and an order to confiscate and destroy any copies that infringe the copyright. On the other hand, if a written work infringes the rights of another person, that person will be entitled to damages, which the author will have to pay.

ADVANTAGES

- The author of a creative work is automatically protected by copyright.
- Copyright allows the author of a creative work to profit from it by charging for its use or by selling the copyright.
- Copyright gives the author exclusive rights to the use of the work. This will deter others from copying the work or pretending that they were the authors.
- An author may take legal action against any person who infringes their copyright and is entitled to compensation for that infringement.

DISADVANTAGES

- Copyright is recognized only for work in a fixed form; ideas, however original, are not protected.

ACTION CHECKLIST

✔ Always protect your copyright and take action in relation to any infringement.

✔ Obtain legal advice to protect your copyright if you suspect an infringement.

DOS AND DON'TS

DO

- Balance the cost of taking action against a perceived infringement of a copyright against the consequences of nonaction.
- If necessary, involve your lawyers in the evaluation of both the risks and potential benefits of taking any action.

DON'T

- Don't ignore an infringement of your copyright; take action against it.

▸▸ MORE INFO

Books:

Poltorak, Alexander I., and Paul J. Lerner. *Essentials of Intellectual Property*. New York: Wiley, 2002.

Stim, Richard W. *Intellectual Property: Patents, Trademarks and Copyrights*. 2nd ed. Florence, KY: Delmar Cengage Learning, 2000.

Articles:

Gordon, Wendy J. "Excuse and justification in the law of fair use: Transaction costs have always been only part of the story." *Journal of the Copyright Society of the USA* 50 (2003): 149.

Novos, I. E., and M. Waldman. "The effects of increased copyright protection: An analytical approach." *Journal of Political Economy* 92:2 (1984): 236.

Websites:

Copyright law of the United States: www.loc.gov/copyright/title17

Informaworld—information for academic, professional, and business communities: www.informaworld.com

Lawdit Solicitors—UK commercial solicitors specializing in intellectual property and litigation: www.lawdit.co.uk

Mandour & Associates, California Intellectual Property law firm: www.mandourlaw.com

The Publishing Law Center: www.publaw.com

"Faced with change, employees have one question: What's going to happen to me? A successful change management communication program will avoid that question." Scott Adams

Intellectual Property—Patents—An International Overview

DEFINITION

As seen previously, intellectual property is a legal concept that enables the ownership of creations as physical property. It entitles the owner of intellectual property rights to take advantage of his/her ownership and charge for the use of the property or to sell it.

A patent is an intellectual property right that is awarded to an inventor. Each country has its own laws regarding the registration of patents, so to protect a patent in more than one country it has to be registered in each of the relevant countries. A patent gives protection for an average period of 20 years.

A patent prevents others from selling, using, or making the invention in a particular country or importing the invention into that country. Unlike the other intellectual property rights, it grants only the exclusivity nature of that right and not the right itself. An inventor can sell, use, or make his or her invention without a patent.

There are three recognized forms of patent: utility patents, which cover machines and processes; design patents, which cover the design and composition of matter; and plant patents, which are related to plant.

In general, only the inventor can apply for a patent. Any person who falsely claims to be the inventor will be liable to criminal penalties. An inventor can apply for a patent him/herself, but in most cases a specialized patent agent and attorney are appointed to deal with the application. This is because the process itself is complicated and specialist knowledge is required to deal with the application.

Not every invention can be patented. To qualify for a patent, an invention has to be new—which means that it has not been patented before, or described before in any specialized publication—anywhere in the world. The invention also has to have a useful purpose from an operational point of view.

In the United States, applications for patents are made to the US Patent and Trademark Office.

ADVANTAGES

- A patent gives an inventor the right of exclusivity over an invention.
- It allows the inventor to take legal action against any person who uses the invention without permission, and to receive compensation for that use.
- Only the inventor can apply for a patent.
- A patented invention will be more valuable to an investor.

DISADVANTAGES

- Patent registration can be expensive and meticulous in terms of the detail required.
- Not all inventions are patentable.
- In general, patents need to be renewed. The average duration of protection is 20 years.
- Registration is limited to a particular territory. To protect an invention in other countries and territories, new registrations are required.

ACTION CHECKLIST

- ✔ To avoid future problems, always consider obtaining a patent for your invention.
- ✔ Obtain advice on whether your invention is patentable.
- ✔ Investigate the cost of registration and the countries in which your invention may need to be protected.
- ✔ Balance the cost of obtaining a patent against the possible cost of leaving the invention without a patent and the time spent defending your rights if they are breached.

DOS AND DON'TS

DO

- Consider obtaining a patent for your invention.
- Balance the cost of applying for a patent against the consequences of nonapplication.
- As the application process is complex, budget for instructing a patent agent to apply for you.
- Think carefully about other countries and territories in which your invention may need protection by registering the patent.

DON'T

- Don't think that by inventing something it will automatically qualify for a patent. Not all inventions are patentable.
- Don't ignore a breach or infringement of your patent. Take action.

▸▸ MORE INFO

Books:

Stim, Richard W. *Intellectual Property: Patents, Trademarks and Copyrights*. 2nd ed. Florence, KY: Delmar Cengage Learning, 2000.

US Department of Commerce. *Patents and How to Get One: A Practical Handbook*. Mineola, NY: Dover Publications, 2003.

Article:

Connor, Marco Tom. "European patents: What's new in 2008 for the applicants?" *Journal of the Patent and Trademark Office Society (JPTOS)* 90:8 (2008).

Websites:

Intellectual Property Office, UK: www.ipo.gov.uk

Journal of the Patent and Trademark Office Society: www.jptos.org

US Patent and Trademark Office: www.uspto.gov

  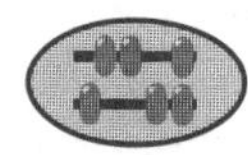   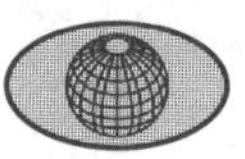   

Intellectual Property—Registered Designs and Trademarks

DEFINITION

Intellectual property is a legal concept that provides for the exclusive ownership of abstract creations. It entitles the owner of such rights to charge for the use of the property or sell it.

Design is an intellectual property right that relates to the appearance of a product. Usually, a design right arises automatically when an author creates an original design, but in certain jurisdictions a design has to be registered to guarantee its protection.

A trademark is a registered symbol or sign that is created to distinguish a product from its competitors. A trademark can be a logo, name, shape, color, sound, slogan, or domain name, or any combination of these. To be recognized as a trademark, it must be distinctive—i.e. it must not be similar or identical to other trademarks. It also must not be deceptive or contrary to law. The usual duration of a trademark's registration is 10 years, after which it must be renewed.

A trademark is protected by registering it in a specific territory or country. Each country has its own rules and regulations regarding registration. The registration process can be expensive, but it is important to consider the risks of nonregistration.

Registration of a trademark usually starts with a search to see if there are any conflicting or similar trademarks. An attorney or agent can be instructed to prepare the application. The formal application will be analyzed to determine whether the trademark meets the necessary legal criteria to be registered. Any challenges from third parties must be answered before registration is confirmed.

ADVANTAGES

- Registering a design or trademark allows the owner to control who uses it and how it is used.
- Intellectual property rights allow the author of a creative work to profit from it by charging for its use or by selling or licensing the rights.
- Registration gives the owner exclusive rights to the use of the property. This will deter others from misusing it or pretending that they are the owners.
- Registering a design or trademark allows the owner to take legal action more easily against anyone who uses the design or trademark without permission, and to be compensated for misuse.

DISADVANTAGES

- In certain circumstances registration can be expensive.
- Not all symbols or designs can be registered.
- In general, registration needs to be renewed periodically. Designs are protected for up to 25 years, but trademark registrations need to be renewed every 10 years.
- Registration is limited to a particular territory. To protect designs and trademarks in other territories additional registrations are required.

ACTION CHECKLIST

✔ Always consider protecting your design or trademark to avoid future problems.

✔ Get advice about whether your designs or trademarks can be registered. Check out the cost of registration and the countries in which you would like them to be registered. Try to balance the cost of registration against the possible cost of nonregistration and the time spent dealing with the defense of your rights if they are breached.

DOS AND DON'TS

DO

- Consider registering your designs and trademarks.
- Balance the cost of registering against the risk and complications of being unprotected.
- If necessary, involve your lawyers in the evaluation of both the risks and potential benefits of registering your designs and trademarks.
- Decide carefully in which countries you will protect your intellectual property.

DON'T

- Don't think that having a design or trademark will give you protection without registration.
- Don't assume that all designs or symbols can be registered.
- Don't ignore an infringement of your design or trademark.

▶▶ MORE INFO

Books:

Poltorak, Alexander I., and Paul J. Lerner. *Essentials of Intellectual Property*. New York: Wiley, 2002.

Stim, Richard W. *Intellectual Property: Patents, Trademarks and Copyrights*. 2nd ed. Florence, KY: Delmar Cengage Learning, 2000.

Articles:

Dinwoodie, G. "The integration of international and domestic intellectual property lawmaking." *Columbia VLA Journal of Law and the Arts* 23 (2000): 307.

Sosinsky, G. J. "Laudatory terms in trademark law: Square pegs in round holes." *Fordham Intellectual Property, Media and Entertainment Law Journal* 9:747 (1999): 725–773.

Websites:

Lawdit Solicitors—UK commercial solicitors specializing in intellectual property and litigation: www.lawdit.co.uk

Questia—online library of books and journals: www.questia.com

Source for trademark clearance searching and monitoring: www.trademark.com

United States Patent and Trademark Office: www.uspto.gov

See Also:

★ Protecting Your Intellectual Property—Registered Rightss (pp. 497–498)

★ The Value and Management of Intellectual Property, Intangible Assets, and Goodwill (pp. 109–112)

     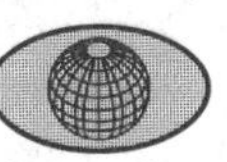   

International Comparisons of Company Law

DEFINITION

A company is a legal entity created by law that consists of one or more persons. For a company to exist, it has to be incorporated and governed by its bylaws. A company comes into existence when the relevant incorporation body issues a certificate of incorporation.

The incorporation procedures differ from jurisdiction to jurisdiction and depend on the company laws governing the country in which the company is incorporated. In general, most company laws are there to regulate the running of companies in the interest of investors and shareholders. The overall purpose is transparency and accountability.

A company is considered to be domestic in the country in which it is incorporated and foreign in every other country. In the United States, a company is also considered foreign if it is incorporated in another state of the Union. This has implications not only for the formalities of incorporation but also in relation to the financial and tax regime of the company. The company laws governing the company will be those where the company is resident.

The procedures for incorporating a company in the United States depend on the state in which the company is incorporated. There is no general corporation law or federal common law relating to corporations. The main recognized commercial jurisdictions are the states of Delaware, New York, and California.

Each country of the European Union has its own specific requirements regarding the formalities of incorporation and the types of companies that may be formed. Some countries require greater formalities than others. In the United Kingdom, for example, incorporating a company is relatively easy and not expensive.

In May 2006 a new company law came into force in Japan. The new law simplified many of the formalities of incorporation, reduced its cost, and made the governing of companies more flexible.

ADVANTAGES

- Company law provides a regulated environment for companies to operate in.
- It protects shareholders and investors in a company.
- In general, company law allows for the harmonization and homogenization of international markets, thus maintaining transparency, fair dealing, and protection against fraud.

DISADVANTAGES

- Company law is very complex and specialized.
- When dealing with more complex company law issues, it is wise to obtain legal advice.

ACTION CHECKLIST

- ✔ Check the company laws of the country in which you incorporate your company.
- ✔ Obtain specific legal and tax advice and make sure that you understand the implications and responsibilities of incorporation and ownership of a company in that particular jurisdiction.
- ✔ Be prepared to comply with the formalities of incorporation and also with the filing requirements and formalities required to be made after the incorporation.

DOS AND DON'TS

DO

- When incorporating or acquiring a company, always seek to understand the company laws of the country or region in which the company is registered.
- Obtain relevant advice regarding the acquisition or incorporation of a company.
- Research the market carefully before making a decision to incorporate a company in that country.

DON'T

- Don't underestimate the need for proper research and professional advice.
- Don't ignore the importance of understanding directors' duties and secretarial duties under company law; if you do, the consequences could be costly.

➤➤ MORE INFO

Books:

Cheffins, Brian R. *Company Law: Theory, Structure and Operation*. Oxford: Clarendon Press, 1997.

Villiers, Charlotte. *Corporate Reporting and Company Law*. Cambridge, UK: Cambridge University Press, 2006.

Article:

Pistor, K., Y. Keinan, J. Kleinheisterkamp, and M. West. "The evolution of corporate law: A cross-country comparison." *Journal of International Economic Law* 23:4 (2003): 791–871.

Websites:

Company Law Forum (UK): www.companylawforum.co.uk

German Law Journal: www.germanlawjournal.com

Mondaq—Latest thinking on legal, accounting, regulatory, and commercial issues: www.mondaq.com

See Also:

- ✔ International Comparisons of Company Law (p. 991)
- ✔ Islamic Law of Contracts (p. 995)
- ✔ Practical Techniques for Commercial Mediation (p. 1001)
- ✔ Understanding the Components of an Insurance Contract (p. 934)

  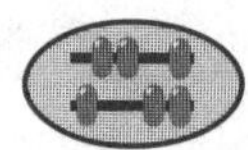   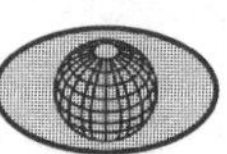   

Inventory—How to Control It Effectively

DEFINITION

Inventory control, or stock control, is concerned with how much stock you have at any one time, and how you keep track of it. Effective inventory control applies to every item you use to produce a product or service, from raw materials to finished goods. It covers stock at every stage of the production process, from purchase and delivery to using and re-ordering the stock.

There are four main types of stock:

- raw materials and components—ready to use in production;
- work in progress—stocks of unfinished goods in production;
- finished goods ready for sale;
- consumables—for example, fuel and stationery.

Effective inventory control is critical to the success of a business. By making sure that capital is not tied up unnecessarily, you can help to lower the cost of running a business and maintain customer loyalty; clients may migrate to other suppliers if you are unable to supply them with the goods they need when they need them. It can protect production if problems arise with the supply chain, and eliminate waste if you are involved in the supply of perishable goods.

Maintaining accurate order records is the first step on the path to controlling inventory. Order sheets should be established by vendor and should include all vital information, such as the name of the customer, their phone number and e-mail address, the date and time the order is placed, the name of the contact person, and other information. You can thus quickly compile a record of all the orders your company receives. From this, it will be possible to determine seasonal and yearly fluctuations in sales and decide which items to discontinue. You will know when to order and will be able to reduce shortages of stock and avoid over-ordering. Computerizing this system will enable you to manage your inventories in the most efficient manner.

Once you have all this information, you can decide which inventory-control system you wish to adopt. There are three basic systems:

- *Minimum stock level*—you identify a minimum stock level and re-order when the stock reaches that level. This is known as the "re-order level."
- *Stock review*—you regularly review your stock. At every review, you place an order to return stocks to a predetermined level.
- *Just in Time (JIT)*—this method aims to reduce costs by keeping stock to a minimum. There is a risk that you may run out of stock, so you need to be confident that your suppliers can deliver on demand.

You also need to know the lead time required when ordering some items. This will help you to maintain an optimum level of stock. Ideally, the current stock of an item should be running out just as the new shipment comes in.

ADVANTAGES

- Efficient inventory control allows you to have the right amount of stock in the right place at the right time.
- Keeping an optimum amount of stock, rather than too much, frees up capital that would otherwise be tied up in stock.
- It guards against your customers being disappointed and taking their business elsewhere.
- It prevents stock from deteriorating or simply falling out of fashion.

DISADVANTAGES

There are no disadvantages involved in efficiently managing your inventories.

ACTION CHECKLIST

- ✔ Establish accurate order records containing vital information such as the name of the customer, their phone number and e-mail address, the date and time the order was placed, and the name of the contact person.
- ✔ Decide which inventory-control system suits your business best.
- ✔ Look to computerize your inventory control. There are software packages that can control your stock for a fraction of the cost of managing it manually.

DOS AND DON'TS

DO

- Make sure that you have good security controls in place to protect your stock. For example, you should mark expensive portable equipment such as computers, and put CCTV in car parking areas and other key locations.
- Make sure that one person is in charge of stock control. Depending on the size of the business, this could either be a dedicated stock controller or an administrator who also undertakes other activities.

DON'T

- Don't forget that, for security reasons, it is good practice to have different staff responsible for finance and stock.

›› MORE INFO

Books:

Axsäter, Sven. *Inventory Control*. 2nd ed. New York: Springer, 2006.

Frazelle, Edward. *Supply Chain Strategy: The Logistics of Supply Chain Management*. New York: McGraw-Hill, 2001.

Various. *Business: The Ultimate Resource*. 2nd ed. London: A&C Black Publishers, 2006.

Articles:

Axsäter, Sven. "A framework for decentralized multi-echelon inventory control." *IIE Transactions* 33:2 (2001): 91–97.

Dooley, Frank. "Logistics, inventory control, and supply chain management." *Choices* 20:4 (2005): 287–291.

"Only recently have people begun to recognise that working with suppliers is just as important as listening to customers." Barry J. Nalebuff

  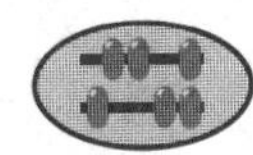   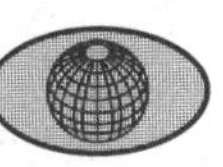   

Invoicing and Credit Control for Small and Medium-Sized Enterprises

DEFINITION

Invoicing and credit control should be priorities in all businesses. Poor management of cash flow is the main reason that SMEs go under. A good credit control system is an indispensable part of any business's accounting procedures. Maintaining dependable cash flow, avoiding bad debt, and minimizing late payments are essential for survival. Therefore, while you are planning the business, prepare an invoicing and credit control system that will bring in your money on time.

- An invoice should be easy to read, clearly showing who has sent the invoice, to whom, for what, for how much, how to respond, and when to respond by. It should always be accurate in every detail, and to the penny, when quoting amounts. Inaccuracy is an excuse to query and delay payment. Always put a retention of title on your invoice, for example, "All goods are the property of E.G. Inc. until paid for in full."
- Put in place a detailed credit control system that allows you to identify whether an invoice has been created, sent to clients, and/or paid, or needs chasing up.
- Do credit checks on customers, especially when orders are large. Try to get them to put down a deposit as a sign of good faith. This applies particularly when you have to buy in special materials. If a customer doesn't want to put down a deposit, it may be an indication that they should be avoided. With large orders allow for "stage payments" invoicing, as large orders that are payable only at the end of the project can be ruinous to your cash flow.
- Decide on your general payment terms, including a payment date. Always have a "payable by" clause on your invoice and make sure that it is unambiguously linked to a date on the invoice. Bear in mind that new customers should be given only a short time in which to pay. Print terms clearly on the invoice and go through them with customers. It is best not to offer a discount for early payment; most people will just take advantage of it and still pay late.
- Prompt invoicing is essential—aim to send out invoices the day after the goods are delivered. Start an automatic reminder system that flags overdue invoices so that you can chase them up.

Make it a priority to set up a detailed credit control system. A good system is an essential part of any SME's accounting procedures, and getting control of your invoicing is essential if you want to succeed.

ADVANTAGES

- A detailed credit control system allows you to identify whether an invoice has been created, sent to clients, and paid, or needs chasing up.
- A good credit control system will help to maintain cash flow, avoid bad debt, and minimize late payments, contributing to the smooth running of your business.
- Staged payments on large orders can help your cash flow.

DISADVANTAGES

- Not getting paid for the work that you do, or the products that you sell, is very common. You will probably always have a few debtors.

ACTION CHECKLIST

✔ Find out whether your level of credit control is better than those of other businesses in the same sector.

✔ Ask the client to sign a purchase order, agreeing what they want, and when and how they will pay. The purchase order should also contain terms and conditions that cover areas such as modification from the original requirement, quality standards, etc.

✔ Your invoice should always be accurate in every detail and to the penny when quoting amounts. Inaccuracy gives customers an excuse to query and delay payment.

✔ Invoice promptly—aim to send out your invoice the day after delivery of the goods.

DOS AND DON'TS

DO

- On the basis of a credit check, give a customer a credit limit if necessary and do not let them exceed it.
- Follow up invoices before their due date.
- Have a no-credit or cash-only list for late-paying customers.

DON'T

- Don't think you can just "wing it"; a good credit control system is essential for survival.

▸▸ MORE INFO

Books:

Bragg, Steven M. *Accounting Reference Desktop*. Hoboken, NJ: Wiley, 2002.

Shavick, Andrea. *The Cheque's in the Post: Credit Control for the Small Business*. London: Kogan Page, 1998.

Various. *Business: The Ultimate Resource*. 2nd ed. London: A&C Black Publishers, 2006.

Articles:

Credit Management. "Track those invoices." *Credit Management* (April 2008).

Hirst, Sue. "Business invoicing: Steps to avoid bad debts." FlyingSolo.com.au (October 2007). Online at: www.flyingsolo.com.au/p244391586_Business-invoicing-Steps-to-avoid-bad-debts.html

Market Business Wire "Basware Emerges as a Market Leader in Independent Report on the Electronic Invoice Presentment and Payment." (June 2008).

Websites:

American Bureau of Credit Control: www.abcollect.com

Budgeting4Business Credit Controller software: www.budgeting4business.com/credit-control-scoring/credit-controller.htm

See Also:

★ Factoring and Invoice Discounting: Working Capital Management Options (pp. 49–51)

✔ Building an Efficient Credit and Collection Accounts System (p. 972)

"Creditors have better memories than debtors." Benjamin Franklin

     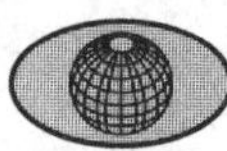   

Islamic Commercial Law

DEFINITION

Given that Islam-derived laws encompass all aspects of how Muslims should live their lives and instill a strong sense of the highest moral values, it should be no surprise that Muslims are expected to conduct commercial transactions according to the same principles of equality, justice, and general sense of fair play. Exploitation of any kind is expressly forbidden, including any attempt to capitalize on a counterparty's poor negotiating position due to unforeseen circumstances. Speculative activity of any kind is also banned, as are transactions or investments of any kind involving products or services prohibited by Islam, such as alcoholic drink, pork-derived foods, gambling, or pornography. Laws are also structured in such a way to prohibit the charging of interest of any kind, given that Islam expressly forbids any usage of money to make money. Instead, Islamic commercial law supports a partnership-based approach to business with, for example, finance providers treated as stakeholders with an interest in the success of a business rather than external lenders charging interest for the use of their money. Inspired by the Prophet Mohammed's experience as a merchant in Mecca, laws strictly govern agreements such as leasing deals, partnerships, and currency exchanges.

Though aspects of Islam-derived commercial laws bear close comparison with their Western counterparts, other features intended to defend the interest of the counterparties stand in marked contrast to the basic principles of Western commercial laws. For example, while under mainstream Western jurisdictions signed commercial agreements would be binding on both parties unless specific exit clauses are triggered, when applied in modern finance, many basic Islamic contracts can be nonbinding in nature.

Given the trend of increasing commercialism in many Muslim countries as their economies have developed, developments in Islam-inspired commercial law have sought to cater for the needs of Muslims to engage in transactions such as buying their homes, or investing for their future, yet without in any way compromising the principles and moral values enshrined by Islam. Some relatively liberal countries such as Qatar and Bahrain have sought to strike a balance between these potentially conflicting objectives, introducing commercial legal frameworks to enable transactions involving, for example, acceptably low levels of interest or permitting forms of insurance contracts to cover certain types of risk. However, these reforms are not reflected in other countries such as Iran, which retain a strict interpretation of Islamic-led commercial law.

ADVANTAGES

- Islamic commercial law provides a framework for commercial transactions while upholding the high moral values and principles of Islam.
- Laws are structured to support a longer term stakeholder approach, rather than a short-term, "quick return" attitude to business.
- Some countries have chosen to adopt a more business-friendly, progressive attitude to their interpretation of Islamic inspired law.

DISADVANTAGES

- Some elements of Islam-derived commercial law can be confusing to non-Muslims, notably the nonbinding nature of contracts under certain circumstances.
- While reflecting Islam's rejection of involvement in speculative activities, it could be argued that laws potentially expose businesses to risk, given restrictions on products such as conventional insurance.
- Adherence to traditional ways of overseeing business could mean that Muslim businesses are hampered by legal restrictions.

ACTION CHECKLIST

- ✔ Recognize how faith and business practices are intertwined in Muslim countries.
- ✔ Accept that the interpretation of some aspects of *shariah*-inspired laws may be subject to slightly different interpretations in different countries.
- ✔ Acknowledge the importance of equality, fairness, and compassion in commercial activities in Muslim jurisdictions. Businesses don't simply pay lip service to these concepts; rather, they are fundamental principles on which all transactions are based.
- ✔ Recognize that individual attitudes to financial products may differ between national jurisdictions. Products such as futures and options may be classed as speculative instruments and, therefore, prohibited in some countries, while others may permit their use as tools to hedge risk.

DOS AND DON'TS

DO

- Acknowledge that law in Muslim countries has a broader role in governing how people live their lives than in the West.
- Take qualified legal advice as to the applicable Islam-inspired law in any particular jurisdiction.

DON'T

- Don't think of Islam-inspired law as a relict of the past. In reality, the influence of *shariah*-inspired law is growing as the prosperity of the followers of Islam across the world grows.

▸▸ MORE INFO

Books:

Ballantyne, William M., and Howard L. Stovall. *Arab Commercial Law: Principles and Perspectives*. Chicago, IL: American Bar Association Publishing, 2002.

Hashim Kamali, Mohammad. *Islamic Commercial Law: An Analysis of Futures and Options*. London: Islamic Texts Society, 2000.

Articles:

Hegazy, Walid S. "Contemporary Islamic finance: From socioeconomic idealism to pure legalism." *Chicago Journal of International Law* 2 (Winter 2007).

Saleh, Samir A. "Commercial law in the Gulf states." *International & Comparative Law Quarterly* 35 (1986).

"Remember when railway companies were the reigning industrial forces? Then, airlines companies came along. . .How many railway companies became airline companies? None! How many industrial companies will become information companies? Not too many!" William (Walid) Mougayar

     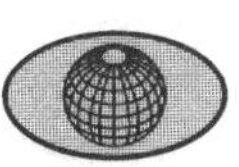   

Islamic Law of Contracts

This checklist offers a brief guide to the nature of contracts in Islam-derived law, and outlines some key differences between these contracts and their Western legal system equivalents.

DEFINITION

The basic prerequisites to establish a valid contract agreement under Islamic law relate to the legal status of the parties seeking to sign the contract, the way the contract is presented/accepted, and finally the subject and consideration of the actual contract

Parties seeking to engage in a contract may only do so if they are considered legally fit to do so—essentially, adults of sound judgment. Both written and verbal contracts can be considered acceptable, with the proviso that the offer and the acceptance must be performed at the same meeting session, without any interruption or venue change before immediate acceptance. In contrast to Western conventions, Islamic law permits acceptance by conduct; under some circumstances, even not responding to a proposal can imply acceptance. Even once an offer has been accepted during a single session, Islamic law includes the principle that parties retain the right to revoke the contract until the moment either party physically departs the venue. However, interpretation of how this principle can be best applied in practice in the modern era can vary between countries.

In terms of the contract content, Islamic-derived law stresses that the subject of the contract must not relate to prohibited items (such as alcohol, tobacco, or gambling equipment), must be legally owned by one party in the contract and in existence at the time of the contract agreement (i.e., items yet to be built may not to be the subject of a standard contract), and must be physically deliverable. As with other legal systems, the exact nature of the goods must be clearly defined in terms of quality and specifications. With the exception of money-exchange deals, the price at which goods will change hands must be agreed at the time of the contract—agreements cannot be based on either future market rates or on the opinion of any external party. While many different types of contract exist, the most common contract for the sale of goods is the *mu'awadat* contract of exchange. These can include a barter-style exchange of goods, a sale of goods in exchange for money, or a money-exchange deal. Another common form of contract is *ijara*, which is commonly used in leasing, either for equipment, real estate, or to provide access to labor.

ADVANTAGES

- Contracts in Islam-derived law fully respect the high moral principles of values expected of all Muslims.
- Islamic contract law is regarded as a product of divine intervention and has been in use for many centuries across the North Africa, the Middle East, and Asia.
- Contract law in Muslim countries supports only transactions which would be classified as "ethical" in the West.

DISADVANTAGES

- Islamic contract law can be highly complex, both in terms of its jurisprudence and in its application.
- Technological innovations such as fax and e-mail systems have created some grey areas as to what constitutes a single session of contract discussions.
- Careful consideration needs to be given to the implications of one party failing to honor the contract, given that Islam prohibits any exploitation of another party's genuine misfortunes.

ACTION CHECKLIST

- ✔ Variations in the details of contract law do occur from country to county. Therefore, acknowledge potential differences in the implementation of Islamic contract law in more liberal Muslim nations such as Qatar, compared to more conservative peers such as Yemen.
- ✔ When considering potential agreements, *shariah* committees in Islamic financial institutions may pass a judgment on the compatibility of the proposed contract with the ideals of Islam. However, given the subjectivity element, you should appreciate that variations may occur in contracts acceptable to different institutions.

DOS AND DON'TS

DO

- Understand the practicalities of "penalty" clauses you may wish to insert into a contract. *Shariah* law does not permit the charging of interest (*riba*), and any penalties due may need to be paid to charity under some circumstances.
- Seek expert advice related to Islamic contract law. Given the complexity of many elements of Islamic law of contract, particularly the definition of what constitutes acceptance of a verbal proposal, expert qualified advice should be sought before contract discussions begin, let alone any contract is signed.

DON'T

- Don't assume that the principles of Islamic law bear close comparison with those of Western laws. Contracts agreed under Muslim-derived laws can be less binding in nature than most contracts drawn up under Western legal systems. Take professional advice to determine under what circumstances the agreed contract may not apply in practice.
- Do not assume that the implementation of Islam-derived law takes the same form throughout the Muslim world. Western-leaning countries such as the United Arab Emirates may adopt a more progressive approach to contract law than nations such as Iran or Pakistan.

▸▸ MORE INFO

Books:

Rayner, Susan. *The Theory of Contracts in Islamic Law*. London: Graham and Trotman, 1991.

Vogel, Frank E., and Samuel L. Hayes. *Islamic Law and Finance: Religion, Risk and Return*. The Hague: Kluwer Law, 1998.

Articles:

Hussein, Hassan. "Contacts in Islamic law: The principles of commutative justice and liberality." *Journal of Islamic Studies* 13:3 (September 2002).

Islam, M. W. "Dissolution of contract in Islamic law" *Arab Law Quarterly* 13:4 (1998).

"You can't change anything if you don't bring people with you." Carolyn McCall

  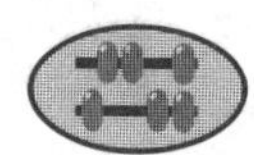   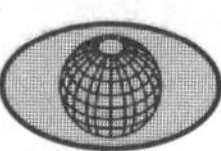   

Managing and Auditing the Risk of Business Interruption

DEFINITION

The key to managing disruptions to business processes successfully is a business continuity plan (BCP) that brings together the company's documented approach to dealing with incidents.

CONSIDER INSURANCE

Developing a continuity plan will also reveal events that will lead to business interruptions which cannot be dealt with internally. In these cases it may be necessary to consider the use of insurance to cover potential losses.

There are a vast number of policies that are designed to cover the cost of recovering from an event. It should be noted, however, that although these offer some protection, they will not restore a business to the position in its markets that it occupied prior to an interruption.

As the policies are intended to cover financial losses, the insured company needs to ensure that its documentation takes into account all income and losses that could result from an interruption. This may include items such as penalty payments for failing to complete contracts as well as lost sales.

ACTION CHECKLIST

There are five key stages in this risk management process.

1. Establish the context

The first stage for an organization that is developing a business continuity plan is to identify its business processes, the interdependencies between these processes, and their priority in relation to the organization's key objectives. These interdependencies should then be mapped.

2. Identify and assess the risks

Once the organization has identified the key processes, it can undertake a business impact analysis to assess the effect of the loss of one of those processes. It should identify the maximum acceptable outage times for those processes within the context of overall business continuity.

Risks can be rated according to their significance in terms of business interruption—for instance, by measuring their likely duration. High-rated risks will cause an interruption that is longer than the maximum acceptable outage.

Some risks may be tolerated because they are relatively minor in their impact on the whole business process and toleration is the most cost-effective approach. Other risks can be treated either by a preventive approach, which reduces the risk of the interruption happening, or by corrective controls that are intended to respond to an event and ameliorate its consequences.

3. Implement treatments

The company should then identify potential plans and controls that are designed to minimize the effect of business interruptions. The most effective mixture of preventative and reactive controls and plans should be selected on the basis of the organization's priorities and objectives. Documentation should include names of responsible parties, the plan's budget allocation, and the timetable for both the implementation of the plan and the frequency of its review.

4. Monitor and review

Sufficient documentation needs to be provided to enable periodic revision and auditing of the effectiveness of the plan and controls. Some companies integrate risk assessment into their overall annual business planning process to ensure its periodic review.

5. Test the plan

Although it might be impractical and unnecessarily disruptive to test the whole plan, recovery processes and procedures can be trialed in a variety of ways. For instance, scenarios can be created and teams can be challenged to find weaknesses in a plan. They may spot, for example, that the recovery of one process is dependent on the completed function of another, or that they do not know where to find vital sources of information.

➤➤ MORE INFO

Books:

Barnes, James C. *A Guide to Business Continuity Planning*. Chichester, UK: Wiley, 2001.

Hiles, Andrew (ed). *The Definitive Handbook of Business Continuity Management*. 2nd ed. Chichester, UK: Wiley, 2007.

Website:

BS 25999 Business continuity: www.bsi-global.com/en/Assessment-and-certification-services/management-systems/Standards-and-Schemes/BS-25999

"The recovery of profitability has been amazing following the reorganisation, leaving Barings to conclude that it was not actually very difficult to make money in the securities business." Peter Baring

  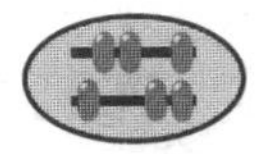 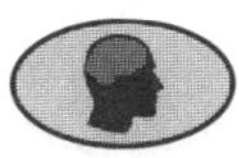  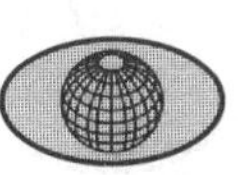   

Managing Bankruptcy and Insolvency

DEFINITION

An insolvent company is one that cannot pay its debts. Cash flow insolvency is the inability to pay debts as they fall due, while balance sheet insolvency occurs when a company has negative net assets and its liabilities exceed the assets. A company can be cash flow insolvent but balance sheet solvent if its assets are illiquid, particularly against short-term debt. Conversely, a company could have negative net assets on the balance sheet but still be cash flow solvent if income can meet debt obligations. Bankruptcy (liquidation in the United Kingdom) occurs when a court rules that a company is unable to pay its creditors. Creditors can force bankruptcy by filing a suit in court against the company in debt, but more usually a company will initiate bankruptcy proceedings itself.

Insolvency law around the world varies, but is generally aimed at protecting creditors' interests and keeping a business afloat. As companies generally want to avoid bankruptcy, the usual practice today is for an insolvent company to file for "bankruptcy protection" (in the United Kingdom, the equivalent is for the company to go into what is called "administration"). An administrator can be appointed by the company directors, or creditors can ask a court to appoint one (without petitioning for bankruptcy). The administrator's job is rescue the business and maintain it as a going concern. To this end, administrators work to restructure the business and its debts in order to pay off creditors and ensure the company emerges in good financial health for the future.

Bankruptcy may follow insolvency, but can also be initiated without going into administration. Bankruptcy laws vary enormously around the world, but all legislation has the aim of winding up the company and paying off creditors. Receivers are appointed by the court to manage this process. The largest creditors will have priority as the debts, or portions of them, are cleared. Some—particularly customers who bought goods but never received them—may never see their money again.

ADVANTAGES

- Appointing administrators is often the smartest option for an insolvent company, as it keeps the company trading and encourages managers to face up to the challenges of learning from their previous errors.
- Bankruptcy may be the best option for a smaller company if its debts are too big to be managed by administration, although there are downsides (see below).

DISADVANTAGES

- Public knowledge of financial problems can cause reputational damage to an insolvent company, possibly hampering the restructuring process and causing customers to decline to do business.
- In many jurisdictions, company directors are banned from running a business for a set period of time if they are involved in a bankruptcy. In some jurisdictions, company directors may be forced to surrender personal assets to clear company debts.
- In some jurisdictions, being made bankrupt can make it very difficult for a company owner to start a new business in the future.

ACTION CHECKLIST

✔ If you need to appoint administrators, choose a firm that has a strong track record in turning ailing businesses around.

✔ It may be worth asking a different firm of accountants to give a second opinion on the company's books to see if there is any other way forward.

DOS AND DON'TS

DO

- Weigh up all the options before embarking on any course of action.
- Take appropriate advice, including consulting your bank and other financial advisers.

DON'T

- Don't rush into making a decision to go bankrupt as other options may be better.
- Don't forget that bankruptcy fraud (concealment of assets, concealment or destruction of documents, making false statements, etc) is a crime.

⏩ MORE INFO

Books:

Marsh, David, and Roger Sproston. *Bankruptcy Insolvency and the Law: A Straightforward Guide*. 4th ed. Brighton, UK: Straightforward Publishing, 2006.

Hunter, Muir. *Going Bust?: How to Resist and Survive Bankruptcy and Winding Up*. St Albans, UK: XPL Publishing 2007.

Gilson, Stuart C. *Creating Value Through Corporate Restructuring: Case Studies in Bankruptcies, Buyouts and Breakups*. New York: Wiley, 2001.

"Change is scientific, progress is ethical; change is indubitable, whereas progress is a matter of controversy."
Bertrand Russell

   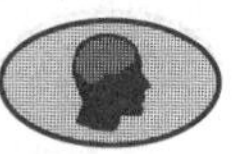  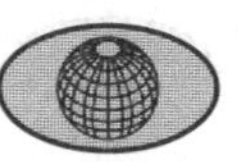   

Performing a Skills Gap Analysis

DEFINITION

A skills gap analysis is undertaken to identify the skills that an employee needs, but may not have, to carry out his or her job or to perform certain tasks effectively. The skills gap concept is used in areas such as business, educational institutes, and sport. The first step in performing an analysis is to identify all the skills required by an individual to carry out his or her work. It should then be possible to identify the critical and noncritical skills that are needed to carry out a role effectively.

A critical skill is one that is required to complete a task successfully. Noncritical skills enable a task to be completed more quickly or efficiently, or at less cost than would otherwise be the case. There is a relatively simple method for determining whether a skill is critical or noncritical. Quite simply, if an employee lacks a skill but completes a task satisfactorily, the skill is noncritical. Conversely, if a person completes a task but the outcome is unsatisfactory, the missing skill is critical.

By applying skills gap analysis across a company it is possible to find out which skill and knowledge shortfalls there are in an organization. It is then possible to target training resources on those necessary skills that require the most attention. This should result in the optimal use of resources in terms of improving the overall performance of the company.

For individuals, skills gap analysis can be used to produce personal development and training plans, support appraisals, and pay reviews. It can also be used to bolster morale by showing how they have progressed over time.

For a department, skills gap analysis can be used to identify which staff members have most knowledge of particular aspects of the business as well as those with skill gaps. Furthermore, it can aid recruitment by identifying the candidate whose skills best match those needed to function effectively in a particular role. For example, in an application of skills gap analysis to the role of a firefighter, the essential skills considered were: critical thinking, oral communication, and the ability to work with others. Analysis also allows benchmarking and encourages tutoring and mentoring within teams.

Skills gap analysis can be undertaken using paper-based assessments and supporting interviews. However, if an analysis is to be performed across a large number of employees, it can create a huge management and administrative burden. Many firms therefore use skill management software.

Analysis can be applied on a continuing basis or as a one-off exercise. Specialized software can generate a skills gap analysis report with a few clicks of the mouse. Paper-based reports take somewhat longer, depending on how many questions there are to answer.

ADVANTAGES

- A skills gap analysis can provide a critical overview of a company, allowing management to determine if staff have the necessary skills to meet corporate objectives or achieve a change in strategy.
- It provides an analysis of skill gaps in an organization, department, or role.
- Analysis helps companies to prioritize their training resources.
- Analysis can help with recruitment and training, and it gives management a basis for deciding which staff should be retained and which are expendable.

DISADVANTAGES

- Conducting a skills gap analysis can be costly in terms of the required investment in paper-based assessments or software, as well as the time required from staff to participate and for management to evaluate the results.
- It may be simpler and more cost-effective to ask line managers to identify skill gaps in their department, or simply to ask staff in which areas they need additional training.
- The assessment can be subjective and open to distortion if staff do not answer questions correctly.

ACTION CHECKLIST

- ✔ Determine whether a paper-based assessment or purchase of software is the most efficient use of resources.
- ✔ Ensure that you have identified all the critical and noncritical skills that are needed to carry out a role effectively.

DOS AND DON'TS

DO

- Consider the potential impact of a skills gap analysis on morale. Assessing an employee's capabilities can create fear and suspicion unless the reason for the analysis is understood and communicated effectively.

DON'T

- Don't assume that you need to create a bespoke (in-house) framework to perform a skills gap analysis. Off-the-shelf frameworks can be suitable when adapted to your company's needs.
- Don't focus only on training needs. Skills gap analysis can be used to plan recruitment and redundancy programs, support organizational restructures, build effective teams, and manage business change.

➧ MORE INFO

Books:

Butler, David. *Business Development: A Guide to Small Business Strategy*. Oxford: Butterworth-Heinemann, 2001.

Joy-Matthews, Jennifer, David Megginson, and Mark Surtees. *Human Resource Development*. 3rd ed. London: Kogan Page, 2004.

Nakayama, Makoto, and Norma Sutcliffe. *Managing IT Skills Portfolios: Planning, Acquisition and Performance Evaluation*. Hershey, PA: Idea Group Publishing, 2005.

Articles:

Liebowitz, Jay. "Bridging the knowledge and skills gap: Tapping federal retirees." *Public Personnel Management* 33:4 (2004): 421–447.

Stevenson, Paul. "Undertaking a skill gap analysis." Online at: www.nccmembership.co.uk/pooled/articles/BF_WEBART/view.asp?Q=BF_WEBART_297088

Wilby, Peter, and Natalie Brierley (eds). "The skills factor: A revolution in education and training." Supplement to *New Statesman* issue 10 (March 2003). Online at: www.newstatesman.com/pdf/skillssupp.pdf

"Structure will become a dynamic enabler of both change and unchange, the ultimate model of organizational chaos." Igor Ansoff

  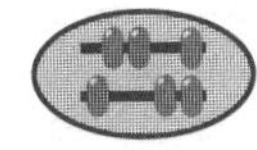   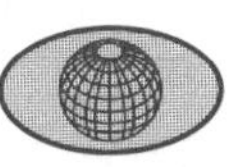 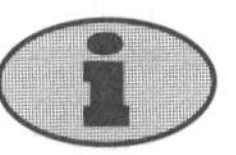  

Performing Total Cost of Ownership Analysis

DEFINITION

Originally developed by Gartner Research in 1987, total cost of ownership (TCO) analysis is a tool which aims to systematically calculate the overall costs involved in buying, running, and developing a system or asset over its full life cycle. Frequently employed as a decision-support tool in information technology environments, TCO analysis is also widely used to help to assess the likely costs involved in acquiring, installing, and operating, then finally developing a wide range of systems or assets, such as production machinery, vehicles, or even scientific equipment.

Thorough TCO analysis can help businesses to gain a deeper understanding of the true life cycle costs involved in a potential decision. For example, it can help managers to avoid rushing into a deal that at first glance appears to represent good value on the basis of a low acquisition cost, when analysis of the operational and development costs could paint a very different picture. Detailed TCO studies can help to bring operating costs that are not obvious but nevertheless substantial to light ahead of a critical decision. TCO analysis can be especially valuable in IT-related decisions, when the cost of operating a computer system for several years is usually a large multiple of the initial purchase costs.

To perform TCO analysis, a matrix is usually employed, with one axis listing the full stages of the particular case subject's life cycles. These should include (but not necessarily be limited to) the purchase/procurement phase, the operational/maintenance phase, and the development/growth phase. The other axis is typically more complex, detailing all the categories of resources that are set to be required, even to a small degree, from the beginning to the end of the product's useful life cycle. In typical applications such as IT systems, the resources axis could include basic costs related to hardware, software, internal staff expense, external consultancies, and facilities. For more advanced IT systems these broad categories could be expanded considerably. TCO analysis permits the projected costs for each stage in the life cycle to be broken down into individual years, thereby increasing the transparency of the cost patterns.

ADVANTAGES

- In its basic form, TCO analysis forms a readily understandable decision-support tool.
- TCO can grow with the complexity of the application, with scope to develop both the resources and life cycle matrices.
- The analysis can help to shed light on costs that could otherwise be simply overlooked.

Table 1. Sample matrix for TCO analysis

	Purchase	Operation	Development and growth
Staff provision			
Hardware			
Software			
External consultancies			
Facilities			

DISADVANTAGES

- TCO focuses purely on costs, with no consideration given to benefits.
- TCO's analysis on costs risks emphasizing the benefits of the cheaper option rather than a potentially more advantageous but more expensive alternative.
- Even the most thorough cost analysis process cannot guarantee to take account of every conceivable cost that could ever arise.

ACTION CHECKLIST

- ✔ Identify and understand the full spectrum of your cost base before performing TCO analysis; remember some costs may be far from obvious.
- ✔ Consider how technological change could potentially shorten or extend the possible lifespan of the asset.
- ✔ Use TCO as a means to study how standardized IT costs vary over time; this may help to decide when a product is nearing the end of its commercial life cycle.

DOS AND DON'TS

DO

- Consult as many potential stakeholders as possible when constructing the TCO matrix—some specialists can help to expose otherwise-hidden cost.
- Remember that TCO is most useful when comparing options that deliver similar perceived levels of benefit.
- Use TCO in conjunction with other management aids, such as cost/benefit analysis.

DON'T

- Don't include in the matrix costs that have no relevance to the option under consideration—adding in unnecessary costs only complicates the picture.
- Don't make the mistake of seeing any one single decision-support tool as providing the definitive answer.
- Don't ignore the initial costs associated with TCO analysis, even though TCO has proven its value over the long term in helping companies to choose options involving lower costs across the full life cycle.

▸▸ MORE INFO

Book:

Devi, Mita. *Total Cost of Ownership: An Introduction*. Hyderabad, India: ICFAI University Press, 2005.

Articles:

Baily, John Taylor, and Stephen R. Heidt. "Why is total cost of ownership important?" *Darwin Magazine* (November 2003). Online at: www.darwinmag.com/read/110103/question74.html

Ellram, L. M. "Activity based costing and total cost of ownership: A critical linkage." *Journal of Cost Management* 8:4 (1995): 22–30.

Website:

Council of Supply Chain Management Professionals—TCO Education: cscmp.org/Education/Desc/PEX408.asp

"In every difficult situation is potential value. Believe this, then begin looking for it." Norman Vincent Peale

  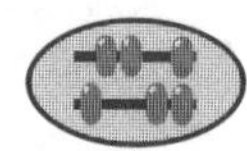   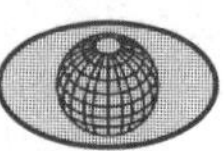  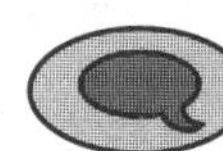 

Practical Purchasing Procedures

DEFINITION

A business or organization may buy goods or services either to resell to customers or for its own use. When choosing suppliers and merchandise, you need to consider price, quality, availability, reliability, and technical support. The goal of purchasing is to obtain the highest-quality goods and services at the lowest possible cost to your business. In order to accomplish this successfully, you need to keep abreast of changes affecting both the supply of and demand for products and materials, track market conditions and price trends, and be aware of sales and inventory levels. It is also advisable to have a working technical knowledge of the goods or services to be purchased and to make up a spec sheet for each product to include brand, model, price, service requirements, and payment terms.

ADVANTAGES

- Good purchasing practices will help you to avoid throwing away money by investing in unsuitable and expensive purchases.
- You will save time and money by using spec sheets, as you will be able to select the brand, model, price ceiling or price range, any features, and any other required options.
- By asking for quotes you can often get discounts and perhaps extra information from the supplier, which could help you get a better deal the next time.

DISADVANTAGES

- Many small businesses just don't have the expertise or time to check how much they should be paying for certain goods and services. They could be throwing away money by not getting the best deals.
- In a market such as fashion or technology, where trends can change overnight, it is often almost impossible for businesses to keep up fully with market conditions and price movements.

ACTION CHECKLIST

✔ **Vendors**: Take the time to thoroughly understand the product/service—the more research you do, the better placed you will be to make good judgments. You may want to check out vendors by getting references from other customers, reading product reviews, visiting the vendor's plants, and perhaps sampling the product or service.

✔ **Quotes**: For costly purchases, always ask to see a salesperson, as they can often get you discounts and perhaps recommend more suitable products. You should also try to get at least two or three quotes. Make sure the quotes you are comparing are "like for like". If you need further information, ask your suppliers so that you can make an informed decision. And don't just consider price—quality, service, and added value should also be taken into consideration.

✔ **Spec sheets**: You will need to create a spec sheet for each product you buy. This could specify: brand, model, price ceiling or price range, and any features and options. You should also specify delivery times, warranty or service requirements, and payment terms (for example COD or net 30/60/90 days).

✔ **Purchase orders**: Your purchase order should specify the name of the item or service being purchased and any details specified in your spec sheet, such as brand, quantity, style, type, or color. You will also need to specify packing and receiving requirements, delivery date, delivery address, shipping method, and payment.

✔ **Receiving goods**: Count the number of items delivered and check for any damage. Remember that when you sign for delivery you are generally agreeing that the quantity is correct and that the shipment has suffered no obvious damage. As soon as you can, open the shipment and examine it to check specs, quantity, and quality. If there are any problems, call the supplier immediately.

✔ **Legal aspects**: Check on any legislation affecting your purchasing decisions. Make sure that you are clued up on any legal requirements for the product or service you are buying.

✔ **Contract renewal**: Make a note of contract renewal dates and set yourself a reminder so that you have plenty of time to consider your options.

DOS AND DON'TS

DO

- Consider using a specialist—they can save you time and hassle, as well as using collective bargaining to get better deals.

DON'T

- Don't renew existing contracts out of habit or because it's easier. Check! Your requirements or the market may well have changed.

⏩ MORE INFO

Books:

Baily, Peter, David Farmer, David Jessop, and David Jones. *Purchasing, Principles and Management*. 9th ed. Harlow, UK: Pearson Education, 2005.

Harding, Michael, Warren Harding, and Mary Lu Harding. *Purchasing*. 2nd ed. Hauppauge, NY: Barron's Educational Series, 2001.

Lysons, Kenneth, and Brian Farrington. *Purchasing and Supply Chain Management*. 7th ed. Harlow, UK: Pearson Education, 2005.

Articles:

Dominick, Charles. "Negotiating successfully in inflationary times." *Next Level Purchasing* (August 2008).

Hardt, Chip W., Nicolas Reinecke, and Peter Spiller. "Inventing the 21st-century purchasing organization". *The McKinsey Quarterly* (November 2007).

Websites:

American Purchasing Society: www.american-purchasing.com

Institute for Supply Management: www.ism.ws

See Also:

✔ Building an Efficient Credit and Collection Accounts System (p. 972)

✔ Creating a Standardized Process (p. 856)

"Very often the best way to find out whether something is worth making is to make it, distribute it and then to see, after the product has been around for a few years, whether it was worth the task." Edwin Land

  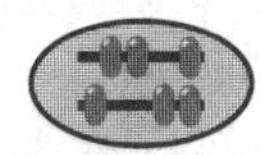 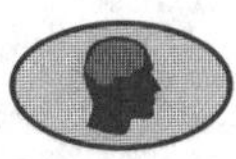  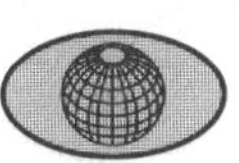   

Practical Techniques for Commercial Mediation

DEFINITION

Mediation is a negotiation process between two or more parties to a dispute, assisted by the participation of an independent third party that is assigned the objective of exploring how their differences might be settled without resorting to the law courts. However mediators are chosen, it is important that the parties to a dispute should be satisfied that they are impartial as only then can they explore ways of reaching an agreement that is acceptable to all.

For the mediation process to be most effective, the mediator should not attempt to impose preconditions on the parties before mediation commences. However, it is commonplace for mediators to ask all parties to respect the confidentiality of information presented during the mediation process. This is to remove the risk that the content of a mediation session could be interpreted as an admission of any kind (even, for example, to the extent that it was seen by one party as the basis for subsequent legal action), a risk that could severely undermine the mediation's chances of success.

The mediation process often begins with open discussions involving all parties involved in the dispute, helping the mediator to understand both the issues and the perspectives and concerns of all parties. Individual meetings between each party and the mediator are then normally held to explore the issues in more detail and to allow the mediator to discover exactly which issues are of greatest concern to each party, as well as to identify areas that offer realistic scope for compromise. For this stage of the process to operate effectively, it is important that the mediator has earned the absolute trust of both parties, given the need for each party to take the mediator into their confidence and reveal those points on which they would give ground in exchange for a similar gesture by the other side, whether on the same points or on others. The mediator should be prepared to pose direct questions to each party to help identify both the limits of their flexibility and what they would seek in return for giving ground in particular areas.

Subsequent informal meetings between all parties can frequently generate some kind of resolution of the dispute without either side giving up entirely on the issues that are most important to them. Again, it is worth stressing that *conventional* mediation does not attempt to impose any solution on the parties; agreement is entirely optional. In contrast, *binding* mediation has parallels with court or arbitration hearings, in that compliance with the settlement is binding, with neither party having any assurance that the settlement is one to which they would have agreed in conventional mediation.

ADVANTAGES

- Conventional mediation offers an informal, free exchange of ideas, aiming to come to a resolution of the dispute.
- Costs are generally appreciably lower than those associated with the legal route of dispute resolution.
- Conventional mediation offers a no-obligation route to a possible resolution without the risk of an unacceptable solution being imposed on either party.
- Mediation can often bring about an acceptable resolution in a shorter time frame than a resort to the courts.
- Mediation can bring about a noncontentious resolution, often allowing the parties to maintain a reasonable business relationship. In contrast, litigation is likely to sour relations between parties.

DISADVANTAGES

- Mediation is only possible if all parties to a dispute agree to participate.
- Some parties may be convinced of the strength of their legal position and view mediation as a process that could lead to them needlessly giving ground.
- Mediation offers no guarantee of a resolution. In contrast, litigation will bring about a definite decision.
- Even if unsuccessful, mediation results in costs to be borne by both parties.

ACTION CHECKLIST

- ✔ Select a mediator with a genuine understanding of commercial issues—for example a neutral person with a background in accountancy or law.
- ✔ The parties in dispute must have confidence in the integrity and independence of the mediator.
- ✔ Agree a framework for the discussions and clarify whether the mediation outcome is binding.
- ✔ Ensure that the mediator explores the scope for compromise in a nonjudgmental way.
- ✔ When a solution has been found, the mediator should assist legal representatives in the preparation of a formal resolution agreement.

DOS AND DON'TS

DO

- Ensure that all parties are confident that the mediator is neutral.
- Conduct discussions in a positive, nonconfrontational way.
- Ensure that all parties understand the potential costs of not finding an acceptable compromise through mediation—one of which is a settlement imposed through litigation.

DON'T

- Don't allow needless timescales to be imposed on the mediation process; discussions held in an unpressurized environment are more likely to succeed.
- Don't abandon mediation at the first difficulty—positions may not be as entrenched as they at first appear.
- Don't expect a mediator to play the role of an adviser. Although background commercial awareness is desirable in a mediator, they should not be asked for advice. It is for individual parties to decide for themselves what would be acceptable.

▸▸ MORE INFO

Books:

Chern, Cyril. *International Commercial Mediation*. London: Informa Law, 2008.

Newmark, Chris, and Anthony Monaghan (eds). *Butterworths Mediators on Mediation: Leading Mediator Perspectives on the Practice of Commercial Mediation*. Haywards Heath, UK: Tottel Publishing, 2005.

Article:

Pribetic, Antonin I. "A strategic functionalist approach to international commercial mediation." *ICFAI Journal of Alternative Dispute Resolution* 7:2 (2008): 37–58.

"Diplomacy is the art of letting someone else have your way." David Frost

  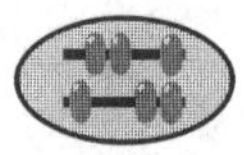   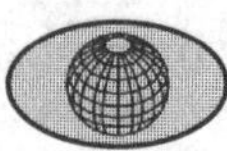   

The Principles of Litigation

DEFINITION

Disputes arising between parties can generally be resolved through a process of negotiation. This frequently involves the help of an independent third party, either in the form of a mediator seeking a mutually agreeable compromise, or of an arbitrator who can be granted the authority to impose a settlement on the parties. However, should the negotiation option fail, it may be necessary to seek the decision of a court. The legal process of determining a resolution to a dispute in a law court is known as litigation.

Before the main litigation process can begin, one party to the dispute must make a formal demand on the counterparty setting out their requirements for a resolution. This typically takes the form of an attorney's letter. In many cases this formal step will provoke a response from the counterparty, which previously may have failed to address the issue in dispute. Subsequently, the disputing parties and their lawyers will usually meet to explore possible solutions. However, should no solution be found, the formal process of litigation begins with the lodging of a complaint with the court that specifies what the counterparty did (or did not do) to give rise to the dispute. Once the other party is served with notification of the formal legal process, a response is required within a specified timescale. Should this not be forthcoming, that party is then said to be in default, and loses the action.

If a response is forthcoming but is unsatisfactory to the complainant, there follows a request to the counterparty in an effort to clarify the key issues. This response can lead to further communications to establish the specific issue in dispute. Once the parties have clearly defined the nature of the complaint, the precise issues to be resolved are formally established. Next follows a process of discovery, during which the parties attempt to generate evidence to back up their case, often using documents or the views of witnesses. An important principle of litigation that applies from this stage is that facts must be differentiated from opinions. Next, in a stage known as the motions phase, both parties attempt to define the precise issue or issues in dispute. This is a process that can sometimes result in a decision by a pretrial court or arbitrator, and it may occur when the facts of a case are undisputed, with the judgment depending solely on how the law applies in that case. Should such arbitration fail, the case proceeds to a formal court hearing at which both sides present their case and a judgment is made. Following possible efforts to appeal against the decision, the winning party can then move to claim payment of whatever sum is awarded in the judgment.

ADVANTAGES

- Litigation provides a definitive financial resolution of a dispute.
- The threat of litigation against a secretive corporation can provoke a resolution if it is keen to avoid public disclosure of information in a court.
- The result of litigation can set a legal precedent, and so is an attractive option for parties wishing to bring a test case.

DISADVANTAGES

- Trials can become complicated and expensive procedures compared to other forms of dispute resolution.
- Litigation may result in bad publicity for all parties concerned.
- The process creates ill-feeling between parties, making it difficult to continue business relationships.

ACTION CHECKLIST

- ✔ Consider whether alternative forms of dispute resolution, such as mediation or arbitration, may be more appropriate.
- ✔ Take account of the possibility that litigation could require the disclosure of sensitive information in court.
- ✔ Prolonged litigation can create lingering uncertainty over the outcome for all parties. Consider how much this might disrupt your business before choosing this route.

DOS AND DON'TS

DO

- Assess the possibility of reputational damage before embarking on litigation.
- Pursue all other forms of dispute resolution before embarking on litigation as formal legal action is likely to make an ongoing business relationship with the opposing party impossible.
- Find out whether earlier similar cases have set legal precedents that could be used as leverage in prelitigation negotiations.

DON'T

- Don't underestimate the potential costs of complex litigation proceedings, particularly should the discovery phase of the action involve expert testimony.
- Don't ignore the costs that could be awarded against you if you lose the case.

›› MORE INFO

Books:

Jeans, James W. *Litigation*. 2nd ed. Charlottesville, VA: Michie Co., 1992.

McElhaney, James W. *McElhaney's Litigation*. Chicago, IL: American Bar Association, 1995.

Articles:

Pannill, William. "Litigator's bookshelf: In the interest of justice" *Litigation Journal* 31:3 (Spring 2005).

Williams, R. Scott, and Mark M. Maloney. "Litigator's perspective: Welcome to bankruptcy court." *American Bankruptcy Institute Journal* 26: 10 (December 2007/January 2008): 28.

Website:

American Bar Association: www.abanet.org

"There are two broad ways to categorize large-scale change. The first is on the basis of scope, or the breadth of change. The second is on the basis of the timing of the industry change cycles." David A. Nadler

  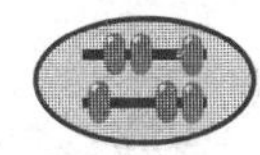   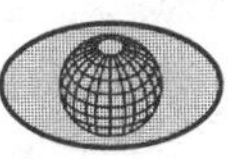   

Setting Up a Key Risk Indicator System

DEFINITION

Key risk indicators (KRI) are measurements that are used by management to show how risky an activity is—a project or an investment, for example. They are called key because they warn of the most obvious areas where problems may arise. KRI help to flag up warnings of a possible adverse impact arising from an activity in the future.

In the United States the Risk Management Association (RMA) manages an initiative that is designed for financial services companies interested in improving their risk management. Going by the name of the KRI Library and Services, its aim is to achieve a degree of consistency and standardization to enable KRI to be compared, analyzed, and reported at the corporate level. The RMA's intention is that the library initiative will lead to distinct improvements in the effective use and benchmarking of KRI with peer groups.

Most companies find the development of effective KRI to be a key challenge. In financial institutions there are plenty of credit risk and market risk indicators, many with frameworks set out within existing financial legislation. However, pulling these data together and developing operational risk indicators is not easy. Conversely, nonfinancial institutions may be in possession of a mass of business and quality information gained from balanced scorecard and quality initiatives. However, their difficulty lies in developing KRI for financial risk or technology risk.

All companies have the awkward task of developing KRI that can provide effective early warning of potential future problems.

It is in the area of forecasting losses that KRI are most likely to gain their stripes, but the majority of companies have yet to master the techniques of setting up effective KRI systems that can do this.

ADVANTAGES

- KRI can provide early warning of future losses or other problems.
- They are useful in supporting management decisions and actions.
- They can be benchmarked both internally and externally.

DISADVANTAGES

- Mastering KRI has proven difficult to date.
- The company has to believe in them, even though past history may not fully support their value.

ACTION CHECKLIST

Some of the following resources can be useful in helping create your own KRI list.

✔ Policies and regulations, particularly those that are aimed at regulating the business activities of the company. Such KRI may include risk exposures relating to compliance with regulatory requirements and standards.

✔ Strategies and objectives. Corporate and business strategies, as established by senior management, are a good source.

✔ Previous losses and incidents. Databases containing historical losses and incidents can provide useful input on what processes or events can cause losses.

DOS AND DON'TS

DO

- Make your KRI quantifiable.
- Base KRI on consistent methodologies and standards.
- Track them along a timeline against standards or limits.
- Link KRI to objectives, risk owners, and standard risk categories.
- Run regular overviews to check that your formulae are still relevant and accurate in assessing risk.

DON'T

- Don't complicate risk.
- Don't be too simplistic.
- Don't put 100% faith in your initial KRI.

▸▸ MORE INFO

Books:

Alexander, Carol. *Mastering Risk, Volume 2: Applications. Your Single-Source Guide to Becoming a Master of Risk*. Mastering Series. Upper Saddle River, NJ: FT Prentice Hall, 2001.

PricewaterhouseCoopers for Committee of the Sponsoring Organizations of the Treadway Commission (COSO). *Enterprise Risk Management—Integrated Framework*. New York: AICPA, 2004. Hard copies (two volumes) can be ordered from COSO (www.coso.org) or from the Institute of Internal Auditors (www.iia.org.uk)

Websites:

KRI Library Services (US): www.kriex.org

The Institute of Risk Management (UK): www.theirm.org

The Risk Management Association (US): www.rmahq.org/RMA

Structuring and Negotiating Joint Ventures

DEFINITION

Joint ventures are set up for many reasons: to carry out a specific project or simply to assist with the growth and continuation of a business.

The parties to a joint venture can be individuals, partnerships, companies, or other organisations or associations. In certain cases, the joint venture can be created through the incorporation of a company that becomes a party to the joint-venture agreement. In other cases, the parties can sign a collaboration agreement.

The parties must think carefully about what they are trying to achieve through the joint venture. Do the parties want to have a period of exclusive negotiation, will they require a confidentiality undertaking, and will they sign a letter of intent to solidify their intention as a preamble for negotiations?

Things to consider include whether the joint venture will have any limitations in terms of territory in which it will operate. Also, what consents, approvals, licences, and permits are necessary for the joint venture to operate? If the joint venture will operate at a cross-border level, in which jurisdictions will it be established? Consider also whether there are any laws governing foreign ownership or investment. Are they any exchange controls in force? What relevant taxes and duties are imposed?

The parties to a joint venture can provide their own funding for the joint venture or use external sources for funding. The parties' investment can be cash or payment in kind, such as expertise and resources. The parties must agree the percentage in which they will benefit from the joint venture. They must also agree working-capital requirements, any losses, and think about any expansion costs.

If the joint venture is through a company, the parties must agree the extent to which participation in the joint venture is transferable. Should the joint-venture company be wound-up if one of the parties wants to come out of it?

The joint venture will have to be thoroughly organised. The parties will agree the composition of the board and how the board will operate and vote.

Another very important consideration is whether the parties will be prohibited from competing with the joint venture at all or just in that particular territory.

Deadlock provisions are essential in a joint-venture agreement. This is when the parties cannot agree on certain voting issues and a decision cannot be taken. The joint-venture agreement must deal with this and set up a procedure to be followed in the event of a deadlock. For example, a voting deadlock at board level can be solved by giving a casting vote to the chairman or by involving an independent expert or arbitrator. The agreement must also establish the duration of the joint venture and how it can be terminated. In the event of termination, the agreement must deal with the distribution of assets, the discharge of any outstanding contracts, and the liabilities of the joint venture.

ADVANTAGES

- A joint venture allows two competitors to join forces, increase their market exposure, and compete at a higher level against other, more powerful companies in the same industry.
- It also allows two connected businesses to cooperate on a joint project in a certain market.

DISADVANTAGES

- Negotiating a joint venture can be complex and time consuming. It involves thorough research of the market and territory in which the products will be sold or the project will be organised.
- Joint ventures can be expensive to set up initially.

ACTION CHECKLIST

✔ Study any joint venture you might set up carefully. Obtain as much information from as many sources as you can before committing to an expensive joint-venture agreement. Plan it carefully and set up a realistic business plan with your business partner.

✔ Know your market and make sure that you have analysed the consequences for your own business of entering into a joint-venture agreement.

✔ Economize by negotiating a reasonable rate with your legal advisers, but remember that it is better to incur costs by obtaining legal advice than to enter into a joint venture under terms that you do not understand.

DOS AND DON'TS

DO

- Choose your partner in the joint venture carefully, as you will be legally bound for a set period of time, under obligations that will prove costly if they are not successfully performed.
- Involve your solicitors in the evaluation of both the risks and potential benefits of entering into a joint venture.
- Negotiate your rates and make a contingency plan for any cost overrun.
- Plan carefully how the joint-venture will operate, how the profits will be distributed and who will take responsibility for what.

DON'T

- Don't make the mistake of being attracted by the idea of a joint venture that has not been thoroughly planned and thought through.
- Don't overlook the importance of setting up a contingency plan in case the joint venture will not work and the relationship breaks down.

▸▸ MORE INFO

Books:

Glover, Stephen I., and Craig M. Wasserman (eds). *Partnerships, Joint Ventures & Strategic Alliances*. Business Law Corporate Series. New York: Law Journal Press, 2004.

Walmsley, John. *Handbook of International Joint Ventures*. London: Graham & Trotman, 1982.

Article:

Geringer, J. Michael, and Louis Hebert. "Measuring Performance of International Joint Ventures." *Journal of International Business Studies* 22:2 (June 1991): 249–263.

"Building trust between partners in a joint venture can be seen as the first necessary step in developing a successful alliance." Jan Selmer

  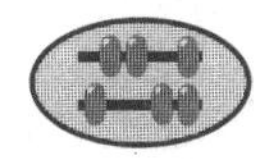 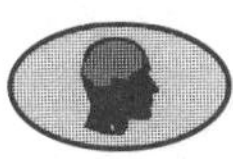  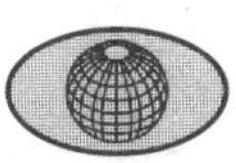   

Structuring, Negotiating, and Drafting Agency Agreements

DEFINITION

An agent is an individual or a legal person who has been appointed by another individual or company (the principal) to act on his, her, or its behalf and to create legal relations between him/her/it and other parties.

The agent and the principal usually enter into an agency agreement, which is drafted by the principal, and then negotiated and amended by the agent. Agency agreements can be oral or written and, in certain cases, can be implied by the conduct of the parties.

An agent can be appointed for many purposes, which can include the distribution, sales, and consignment of goods, or to negotiate, represent, and act on behalf of a principal who is an artist.

From a legal point of view, an agent can exercise all powers given to him or her under the agreement. The agent must carry out with skill and diligence the instructions given by the principal. He or she must promote the principal's interests and must not profit secretly from the agency.

Before entering into an agency agreement, the parties should thoroughly investigate the market and territory and weigh the advantages and disadvantages of establishing an agency and operating within that market. If the agency to be set up relates to the manufacturing and sale of products, it is advisable to think of the way in which these products will be distributed and sold. Under an agency agreement for the sale of goods manufactured by the principal, the principal gives the agent the right to sell its products in a well-defined territory, for a certain period of time, in exchange for a commission fee. The agency can be simple, sole, or exclusive. A *sole agency* means that the principal will not appoint any other agents within that territory but the principal itself is still entitled to sell the goods there. An *exclusive agency* gives the agent the sole right to sell products in that territory: the principal will not appoint any other agents or sell the products itself. A *simple agency* usually means that there are other agents in the territory, as well as the principal, all selling the same products. Exclusive agencies are, therefore, the most expensive and sought after.

The agency agreement should stipulate in detail the commission an agent will be paid. This is usually calculated as a percentage of the gross takings for the product.

An agency agreement must be clear and well structured. It should specify in detail the scope of the agency, the territory where the agency will operate, the obligations of the principal and the agent, the commission, and the payment terms. It should also specify the duration of the agency and any termination clauses. Conflict clauses should be included to deal with nonperformance and breach of contract, with provision for solutions such as mediation.

As an agent will be able to bind a principal to other parties legally, special care should be taken in making sure that the right agent is appointed. Warranties and indemnities should be sought from an agent to cover any potential liabilities a principal may have. On the other hand, an agent should be careful not to take any responsibility for the products of a principal and should seek to be compensated in this respect should it be necessary.

ADVANTAGES

- An agency allows a principal to increase the market for its brand by giving others the right to use it under certain conditions and for a certain price.
- It also allows an agent to operate a business and to exploit, for his or her benefit, a product that belongs to someone else and that would otherwise be too expensive to acquire.

DISADVANTAGES

- Negotiating an agency agreement can be complex and time-consuming. It involves thorough research of the market and territory in which the products will be sold or used.
- Exclusive and sole agencies are more expensive than simple agencies.

ACTION CHECKLIST

✔ Study any agency with which you might sign. Obtain as much information from as many sources as you can before committing to an expensive agency agreement.

✔ Know your market and make sure that you have analyzed the consequences for your own business of entering into an agency agreement.

✔ Be prepared for complicated negotiations, which could prove time-consuming and costly.

✔ Economize by negotiating a reasonable rate with your legal advisers, but remember that it is better to incur costs by obtaining legal advice than to enter into an agency agreement under terms that you do not understand.

DOS AND DON'TS

DO

- Choose your agent carefully.
- Involve your solicitors in the evaluation of both the risks and potential benefits of entering into an agency agreement.
- Negotiate your rates and make a contingency plan for any cost overrun.
- Plan carefully how the agency will operate in the territory.

DON'T

- Don't make the mistake of being attracted by an agency that has not been thoroughly investigated.
- Don't overlook the importance of negotiating warranties and indemnities that will protect you in the event that underlying liabilities are discovered.

➧ MORE INFO

Article:

Lianos, Ioannis. "Commercial agency agreements, vertical restraints, and the limits of Article 81(1) EC: Between hierarchies and networks." *Journal of Competition Law and Economics* 3:4 (2007): 625–672.

Website:

ArticleBASE web content management: www.articlebase.com

"To me the law seems like a sort of maze through which a client must be led to safety; a collection of reefs, rocks and underwater hazards through which he or she must be piloted." John Mortimer

  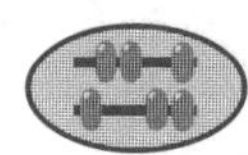   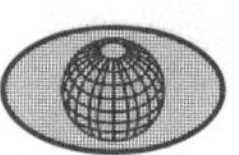   

Understanding and Calculating RORAC, RARORAC, and RARORAC

DEFINITION

RORAC is the return on risk-adjusted capital. (Risk-adjusted capital is capital that has been adjusted after balancing the five main risk metrics—alpha, beta, r-squared, standard deviation, and the Sharpe ratio—against each other so that return can be calculated on a level playing field.) It should not be confused with RAROC, which is risk-adjusted return on capital, and its close cousin, RARORAC, risk-adjusted return on risk-adjusted capital. The capital that is being invested, or risked, is usually called economic capital.

RORAC is generally used to evaluate projects or investments that have a high element of risk for the capital involved. The RORAC formula (RORAC = Net income / Allocated economic capital) allows comparison of investments that have different levels of risk or different risk profiles. Here, the economic capital is adjusted for the maximum potential loss after calculating probable returns and/or their volatility. It is a very useful method of quantifying and managing acceptable levels of exposure to risk. Note that RORAC is used when the risk may vary according to capital assets used—it is the capital itself that is adjusted for those risks, rather than the rate of return.

RAROC is a method for measuring risk-based profitability that also enables a consistent comparison of the risky financial returns of a range of projects or investments. It is usually defined as the ratio of risk-adjusted return to the economic capital. Rather than adjust the risk of the capital (as in RORAC), it is the risk of the return itself that is adjusted and measured. One of two formulae may be used: RAROC = Expected return / Economic capital, or RAROC = Expected return / Value at risk. Using capital based on risk improves the capital allocation across any scenario in which capital is risked for a return expected to be above the risk-free rate.

RARORAC is increasingly used as a measure to assess both the risk-adjusted economic capital and the risk-adjusted return on an investment. It uses the capital adequacy guidelines as defined by Basel II. It is calculated by dividing the risk-adjusted return by the economic capital after including the diversification benefits.

ADVANTAGES

- These ratios allow for the incorporation of market risk, credit risk, and operational risk within a single comprehensive framework that shows the interrelationships between different sorts of risk and scenarios where there might be a too-high concentration of risks.

DISADVANTAGES

- These ratios cannot cover systemic risks, which still need to be calculated separately.

ACTION CHECKLIST

✔ Make sure you develop a risk-conscious compensation structure. By considering RORAC, rather than conventional, accounting-based, profit-and-loss calculations, it is possible to compensate managers for minimizing risk and maximizing return. Including RORAC in a company's compensation structure gives risk management authority, encourages responsible, longer-term decision making, and discourages the short-term "quarterly profits" mentality.

DOS AND DON'TS

DO

- Use these ratios to make informed decisions on the value of investments or projects and to create long-term strategies that bear risk in mind.
- Consider their use as part of the discipline of building a comprehensive risk management strategy.

DON'T

- Don't forget that these ratios are flexible enough to apply as a metric to business models, cash flow projections, and other corporate financial conventions, as a means of integrating risk management from diverse areas.

▸▸ MORE INFO

Books:

Crockford, Neil. *An Introduction to Risk Management*. Cambridge, UK: Woodhead-Faulkner, 1986.

Lam, James. *Enterprise Risk Management: From Incentives to Controls*. Hoboken, NJ: Wiley, 2003.

Tapiero, Charles. *Risk and Financial Management: Mathematical and Computational Methods*. Hoboken, NJ: Wiley, 2004.

"Discontinuous change, because it shatters the framework of the existing organization and scrambles the internal patterns of informal relationships, presents its own very special set of issues for leaders of change."
David A. Nadler

   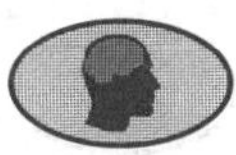  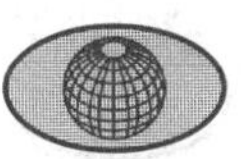   

Understanding Continuity Insurance

DEFINITION

This type of insurance provides a valuable safety net for organizations in the event of a serious disruption and is not a substitute for business continuity planning. It is not sold separately, but either as part of a general package or with buildings insurance.

If an event such as a fire damages a company's premises and prevents it from operating, business continuity insurance covers the profits that would have been earned if the disaster had not happened. The amount of compensation is determined by an examination of the company's business records.

Policies also generally cover operating expenses, such as power bills, which continue even when normal business activities come to a halt. Most policies, however, have a two-day waiting period before claims are covered.

Premiums are determined both by policy limits and the type of business covered. For instance, a restaurant would probably pay more than an office-based business. That is because the risk of a restaurant catching fire is probably greater than an office, and it would be harder to transfer the business to alternative premises.

It is very important that a business continuity or interruption policy is absolutely watertight, even if that takes a great deal of time and effort. If holes are found after a disaster, it could be too late.

ADVANTAGES

- Insurance cover is a useful, even vital, adjunct to a business continuity plan.

DISADVANTAGES

- Insurance can cover lost income following a disaster such as a fire, but it won't restore a company's competitive position in the marketplace if it ceases trading for an extended period.

ACTION CHECKLIST

1. Ensure that insurance is coordinated with the business continuity plan

In particular, indemnity periods should cover the full time it will take the organization to recover from a disaster, including:

- ✔ Time for demolition, redesign, and rebuilding;
- ✔ How long it will take to replace specialist machinery;
- ✔ Rehiring if staff have been laid off;
- ✔ Also, if there are multiple sites, decide whether the same indemnity period is applicable to all.

2. Identify all sources of income and potential loss

Identify what income would be lost as the result of a shutdown and other costs or losses that might result.

- ✔ Most forms of income can be covered; these vary according to type of business and can be a combination of revenue, fees, or rental.
- ✔ Make sure penalty payments are included if a major incident could affect the company's ability to complete a project.
- ✔ Some income will not be covered, such as interest on investments or sales of assets.

3. List all business activities

In listing business activities you should:

- ✔ Be sure to add acquisitions, new divisions, and new ventures;
- ✔ Ensure that long-term projects are covered even if they have not yet produced income;
- ✔ Consider including key suppliers if damage to their premises could have serious repercussions on your business;
- ✔ Ensure that power suppliers are included, and check to see when coverage commences. There is a week's "deductible" in many policies.

4. Review the amount insured regularly. It may be useful to consider the following points.

- ✔ Many large organizations with multiple profit centers include intergroup sales that can inflate the premium through double counting.
- ✔ Make sure the projected figures for lost earnings are accurate for the whole insured period, which may be two or more years.
- ✔ Consider including a premium adjustment clause to take account of actual rather than projected earnings at the end of the year.

5. Include other potential costs and savings. Include both the increased payroll costs and savings that would follow a disaster:

- ✔ Estimate how many seasonal and other staff could be laid off;
- ✔ Make provision for redundancy payments if necessary;
- ✔ List the key staff who would need to be kept on to enable the company to resume full working.

⏩ MORE INFO

Websites:

The Continuity Forum provides information and help for business continuity management: www.continuityforum.org

Continuity Insurance & Risk (CIR) Magazine: www.cirmagazine.com

  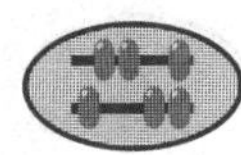 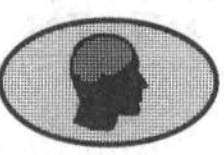  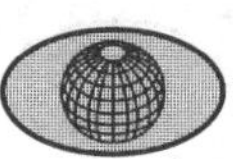  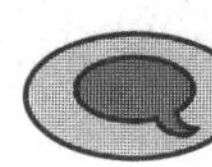 

Understanding the Financial Aspects of Employing People

DEFINITION

The financial aspects of hiring an employee go far beyond the visible cost of paying them a salary. There are many factors and hidden costs that need to be taken into account. National and international legislation also determine a company's financial obligations to an employee to a certain extent. Thus, the true cost of hiring a worker will be more than the agreed wage, and the additional costs need to be budgeted for in the accounts.

Apart from the salary, an employer pays additional up-front costs for items such as the employer's portion of the social security and pension contributions. In many countries employers also have a legal obligation to pay holiday pay and sickness benefit contributions, as well as collecting taxes for the government and paying tax credits to an employee where there is entitlement. Where women of child-bearing age are employed, there is also the cost of maternity leave to consider, the length of which depends on national laws; companies can usually claw most of this back from the government to cover the cost of hiring a temporary replacement. Other legislative issues to consider include matters such as a legal minimum wage and, in some countries, such as the United Kingdom, companies have to meet the cost of running checks to ensure they are not hiring illegal immigrants.

Particularly in the European Union, many countries have employment protection legislation in place, making it difficult for companies to fire staff with little or no notice. Companies therefore need to budget for funds to cover periods when they may need to downsize quickly to reduce costs. Garden leave, where an employee is paid to stay at home instead of working out their notice, is another expense that may need to be covered.

Other staffing costs that need to be budgeted for include items such as training (whether one-off or regular sessions), insurance relating to safety in the workplace, and pay rises. Companies seeking the best staff may wish to offer perks such as private health insurance, travel subsidies to and from the workplace, childcare allowances, and extras such as gym memberships. In very large corporations it is also becoming common practice to use a golden parachute clause in the employment contract. This ensures that an employee will receive certain major benefits if employment is terminated, typically including severance pay, cash bonuses, and share options.

On top of all these costs, there is the additional cost of administration. Whereas small firms often outsource payroll administration, large companies typically have qualified payroll accountants working in-house, as well as a human resources department to handle all the related issues.

ACTION CHECKLIST

- ✔ Have in place accountants experienced in payroll budgeting.
- ✔ Hire or outsource to qualified HR staff who are experienced in the legal and financial aspects of employing staff.
- ✔ Develop a long-term strategy for hiring staff as the business expands or, in some cases, downsizes.
- ✔ Ensure that you have considered and budgeted for all possible scenarios when calculating the salaries you will offer.

DOS AND DON'TS

DO

- Familiarize yourself with the legal requirements in your country.
- Look at tax breaks that are sometimes offered for hiring certain kinds of staff.
- Budget for unexpected costs such as several resignations happening at once, or the costs arising from a legal dispute over the terms of a contract.

DON'T

- Don't try to cut legal corners—the penalties are usually severe.
- Don't forget that even advertising for staff is a cost you need to account for.

➤➤ MORE INFO

Books:

Ashenfelter, Orley C., and Richard Layard (eds). *Handbook of Labor Economics*. Amsterdam: Elsevier/North-Holland, 1986.

Blundell, Richard, and Thomas MaCurdy. "Labour supply." In Durlauf, Steven N., and Lawrence E. Blume (eds). *The New Palgrave Dictionary of Economics*. 2nd ed. Basingstoke, UK: Palgrave Macmillan, 2008. (Dictionary online at: www.dictionaryofeconomics.com/dictionary)

Stone, Raymond J. *Human Resource Management*. 6th ed. Milton, Australia: Wiley, 2008.

Article:

Lee, Eddy. "Globalization and employment: Is anxiety justified?" *International Labour Review*, 135:5 (1996): 485–498.

"Change means avoiding the predictable and known ways of doing things which we learn to adjust to."
John Harvey-Jones

   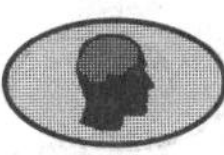  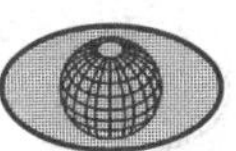   

What Is Benchmarking?

DEFINITION

Benchmarking is a tool for analyzing an organization or company's processes and activities to see if they represent best practice. The aim of benchmarking is always to raise an organization's performance to the highest standard.

ACTION CHECKLIST

1. Planning the benchmarking project

- ✔ First understand your own business before making comparisons with others.
- ✔ Look at the business units within your organization and identify their outputs.
- ✔ Decide which are the key processes to benchmark, ensuring that any improvements will be apparent to customers.

2. Select targets

- ✔ Look for processes in your own and other industries that match those of your own organization.
- ✔ Identify the organizations that are best in class for those processes by talking to customers, analysts, trade publications, and suppliers.

3. Decide methodology

- ✔ As there are so many types of process to be measured, information will come from a variety of sources, including structured interviews, surveys, and publicly available data.
- ✔ Make sure your analysis compares "apple with apples" and is as accurate as possible.

4. Collect data and analyze discrepancies

- ✔ Establish what is best practice for each benchmarked process.
- ✔ Compare the gaps between your organization's performance and those benchmarked processes.

5. Make improvements

- ✔ Modify processes to equal or raise your company's performance above that of the highest standard measured.

As the idea is to evaluate the outcome of specific activities, the comparisons do not have to be drawn from competitors. It may be possible to use generic benchmarks based on data from processes that are common across an industry, or functional benchmarks for processes that exist in many unrelated industries. Alternatively, internal benchmarking can compare common activities across the different divisions of an organization.

If it is felt that the most effective data will come from similar businesses, there are two possible approaches: collaborative benchmarking, which is when two or more companies share information on processes; and competitive benchmarking, where the performance of competitors is analyzed. The latter is frequently carried out by a third party.

It is not unusual for competing companies to share benchmarking data. It is not necessary to publish commercially sensitive information in order for a number of companies within an industry to benefit from improvements in efficiency.

The benchmarking information will come from a variety of sources, including interviews, surveys, and published data. Care has to be taken that not only is the information directly comparable, but also that it includes all the relevant areas. It is not uncommon for companies to become fixated on cost-cutting, for example, while ignoring customer care, perhaps because it is less easy to measure.

Once the results of a benchmarking exercise have been presented and agreed, the information can be used as a basis for changes that should improve the organization's processes. These can then provide a baseline for the next round.

ADVANTAGES

- Benchmarking can provide tangible and measurable improvements for an organization.
- It opens up organizations to different ways of operating.
- It provides an objective measure of the success of an organization's processes.
- It encourages focus on key areas for improvement.

DISADVANTAGES

- Benchmarking can be expensive and time-consuming.
- Comparisons may be inappropriate for some processes.
- It can give an organization the answers it wants to hear.
- Comparisons just show that one organization is different from another.
- It can just encourage a process of playing catch-up rather than innovation.

DOS AND DON'TS

DO

- Pick variables that are relatively easy to measure.
- Ensure that the processes being measured are directly comparable.
- Put sufficient human and financial resources into the project.
- Focus on variables that will respond to actions.
- Produce a succinct summary of benefits for senior management.

DON'T

- Don't spread your net too wide by selecting unmanageable areas to research.
- Don't assume your competition's success is solely due to the differences you've measured.
- Don't forget about less easily measured areas such as customer satisfaction.

➤➤ MORE INFO

Books:

McNair, Carol J., and Kathleen H. J. Leibfried. *Benchmarking: A Tool for Continuous Improvement.* New York: HarperBusiness, 1992.

Watson, Gregory H. *Strategic Benchmarking Reloaded with Six Sigma: Improving Your Company's Performance Using Global Best Practice.* Hoboken, NJ: Wiley, 2007.

Zairi, Mohamed. *Effective Management of Benchmarking Projects: Practical Guidelines & Examples of Best Practice.* Oxford: Butterworth-Heinemann, 1998.

Website:

Benchmarking Plus Australia: www.benchmarkingplus.com.au

"I relished the challenge of working on the lowest circulations in Fleet Street in one of the most competitive markets in the world." Trish Wadley

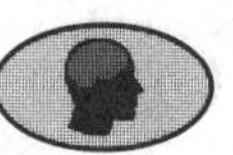

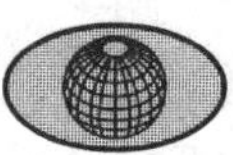

The Bond Market: Its Structure and Function

DEFINITION

The bond market is the market for debt securities in the form of bonds where buyers and sellers determine their prices and therefore their accompanying interest rates. It is also known as the fixed-income or debit or credit market.

In purchasing a bond you are effectively lending money to a government, corporation, or municipality, known as the issuer, which agrees to pay you a certain rate of interest during the lifetime of the bond and repay its principal or face value when it matures or becomes due.

The international bond market is estimated to have a size of almost US$47 trillion. The US bond market is the largest in the world, with an outstanding debt of more than US$25 trillion. In 2007, the volume of trade in the US bond market was US$923 billion.

Since 2000, the international bond market has doubled in size as a result of the activity of big multinational companies. According to the International Capital Market Association, about US$10 trillion worth of bonds were outstanding in 2007.

The individual government bond markets have a high level of liquidity and considerable size—these are included in the international bond market. They are noted for their low credit risk and are unaffected by interest rates.

Trading generally takes place over the counter (known as OTC) between broker dealers and big institutions. The stock exchanges list a small number of bonds too.

The largest centralized bond market is the New York Stock Exchange (NYSE), which mainly represents corporate bonds. In contrast to this, most governments have bond markets that lack centralization, mostly due to the fact that bond issues vary widely and there is a large choice of different securities by comparison.

Most outstanding bonds are in the hands of institutions: pension funds, mutual funds, and banks. This is because individual bond issues are so specific and a large number of smaller issues lack liquidity.

The volatility of the bond market is in direct proportion to the monetary and economic policy of the country of the participant.

The main difference between corporate and government bonds is that the latter are guaranteed and thus carry a low risk of investment, albeit at a lower rate of return. Corporate bonds generally offer a higher rate of return on investment, but carry more risk—if the company fails, the bondholder risks losing their investment.

ADVANTAGES

- It is considered a wise move to invest in bonds as part of a considered diversified investment portfolio that also consists of stocks and cash. They are considered to be a relatively safe investment for increasing capital and receiving a reliable interest income. The principal and interest are set at the time the bond is purchased. If the owner collects the coupon and holds it to maturity, the market is irrelevant to final payout. As a long-term investment, bonds may be considered a wise choice—bearing in mind the disadvantages.

DISADVANTAGES

- Bonds are not advisable for short-term savings for the individual participant in the market.
- Long-term commitment is essential as the participant who cashes in before maturity is open to the risk of fluctuations in interest rates. Whenever there is an increase in interest rates, there is a corresponding decrease in the value of existing bonds. Conversely, a decrease in interest rates will correspond to a rise in the value of existing bonds. This is due to the fact that new issues pay out a lower yield. The basic concept of bond market volatility is that the value of bonds and changes in interest rates run inversely to each other.
- When interest rates drop, investors have to reinvest their interest income and return of principal at lower rates.
- The final purchasing power of an investment in bonds is reduced by a corresponding increase in inflation, which also results in higher interest rates and correspondingly lower bond prices.
- If there is a decline in the bond market as a whole, individual securities also fall in value.
- Timing is crucial: a security may in the future unexpectedly underperform relative to the market.
- A bond may perform poorly after purchase, or it may improve after you sell it.
- Corporate bonds have relatively low liquidity compared with government bonds, which usually have a short lock-in period (i.e. they can be cashed in quickly).

ACTION CHECKLIST

✔ Make sure that you can afford to invest in long-term savings before you commit yourself to taking out bonds.

✔ Have another form of savings as an emergency fund in case you meet with an unexpected financial problem in the future.

✔ Read all the available literature and take advice from an impartial financial consultant before making a final commitment.

DOS AND DON'TS

DO

- Be sure to choose a security that is approved by a financial expert.

DON'T

- Don't rush into a transaction or pay over the odds for it.

▸▸ MORE INFO

Books:

Adams, Tom. *Savings Bond Adviser: How U.S. Savings Bonds Really Work—With Investment, Tax, and Estate Strategies*. 5th ed. New York: Alert Media, 2007.

Pederson, Daniel J. *Savings Bonds: When to Hold, When to Fold and Everything In-Between*. 4th ed. Detroit, MI: TSBI Publishing, 1999.

Website:

Investopedia introduction to bonds: www.investopedia.com/university/bonds

See Also:

✔ Trading in Corporate Bonds: Why and How (p. 946)

"If it is virtually impossible to make worthwhile predictions about the price movement of stocks, it is completely impossible to do so for bonds." Benjamin Graham

  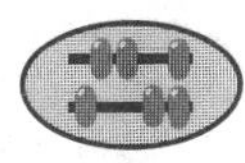   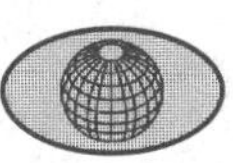   

Dealing with Venture Capital Companies

DEFINITION

Small and growing businesses seeking to finance further development, but which cannot raise the necessary funds through a bank loan or overdraft, or by an injection of further capital from the current owner, may find that venture capitalists provide the best solution to their needs. Venture capital (VC) is the term used for unsecured funding provided by specialist firms in return for a proportion of a company's shares. Venture capital investments are seen as relatively high risk for the lender because they are unsecured.

VC funds are often used in conjunction with a management buyout or buyin, in which a management team is demonstrating its commitment to a firm's success by investing their own money in the business.

Venture capital firms consider various factors before committing funds to a business. These include the track record of the business and whether the management team has a proven record of success; for this reason, VC companies generally do not consider start-ups as suitable for investment. They will seek to determine whether the management's plans for the business are credible. They will also try to determine whether a viable exit strategy can be achieved within a preferred timescale, usually within three to five years of making their investment. This could be executed via a trade sale, stock market listing, refinancing by another institution, or a repurchasing of the entire capital by management.

In return for their investment, VC firms make a number of demands, including the following:

- A high return (perhaps a compound return of 25% or more), largely generated by growth in the capital value of the business.
- Representation on the company's board.

In the past, companies have approached venture capital funds to provide seed, start-up, and expansion financing, as well as management/leveraged buyout financing. However, nowadays VC companies focus almost entirely on funding businesses that have proprietary technology or knowledge. Thus they tend to favor businesses with a product or service that offers a unique selling point or other competitive advantage.

ADVANTAGES

- VC investors put money into risky or innovative businesses and projects that might otherwise have trouble obtaining funding.
- Apart from providing funding, a VC company takes an active role in the management of a business, to which it can bring a great deal of administrative expertise and market knowledge. It may also have valuable skills and contacts, and can assist with strategy and key decision-making.
- Having invested in a project, a VC company will do all it can to ensure that it is a success.
- VC companies can also provide access to funding by other VC investors.
- Investors are often prepared to provide follow-up funding as the business grows.

DISADVANTAGES

There may be disadvantages to accepting VC investment, and the following points should be considered carefully.

- Is the VC company acting as a lead investor? If so, are there complementary or competing companies in its portfolio? Does it have experience with similar types of investment?
- Will the VC company be able to come up with extra financing if it becomes necessary?
- What type of role does it want in the management of your business?
- Can your management team live up to the conditions demanded by the VC company, and does it have complementary skills?
- If your firm reaches the deal negotiation stage with a VC investor, you will have to pay legal and accounting fees whether or not you are successful in securing funds.

DOS AND DON'TS

DO

- Seek expert legal and financial advice when negotiating any agreement with a VC company.
- Be aware of the significant time required to complete the process.
- When researching venture capitalists, go for geographic and industry specializations that complement your own.

DON'T

- Don't take on venture capital unless you are sure that you can cope mentally and physically with the provider's requirements.
- Don't forget that you will lose some of your power to make management decisions.
- Don't forget that there can be legal and regulatory issues to comply with when raising finance.

➤➤ MORE INFO

Books:

Cardis, Joel, *et al*. *Venture Capital: The Definitive Guide for Entrepreneurs, Investors, and Practitioners*. New York: Wiley, 2001.

Gladstone, David, and Laura Gladstone. *Venture Capital Handbook: An Entrepreneur's Guide to Raising Venture Capital*. Upper Saddle River, NJ: Prentice Hall, 2002.

Hill, Brian E., and Dee Power. *Inside Secrets to Venture Capital*. New York: Wiley, 2001.

Articles:

Arthur, Jeff. "Cashing in with venture capital." *SaskBusiness* (January–February 2008).

Iwata, Edward. "Venture capital spreads the wealth around the country." *USA Today* (March 11, 2008).

Websites:

British Venture Capital Association (BVCA): www.bvca.co.uk

European Private Equity & Venture Capital Association (EVCA): www.evca.com

National Venture Capital Association (NVCA, US): www.nvca.org

vFinance directory of venture capital resources and related services: www.vfinance.com

See Also:

★ Avoiding the Mistakes of the Past: Lessons from the Startup World (pp. 749–750)

★ Sources of Venture Capital (pp. 579–581)

"There are two options: adapt or die." Andrew S. Grove

     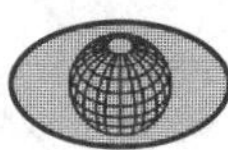   

Financial Intermediaries: Their Role and Relation to Financial Markets

DEFINITION

Generally, when a company wants to enter a financial market, it uses the services of a financial intermediary rather than entering directly. In many transactions the intermediary will be the company's commercial bank, which will broker financial deals such as loans. For more complex or specialist deals a company is likely to turn to an intermediary that specializes in transactions for financial products such as mutual funds, pension funds, bonds and shares, and insurance. In such cases, the intermediary may be a fund or insurer itself.

A financial intermediary typically facilitates the channeling of funds between lenders and borrowers indirectly, in the form of a loan or a mortgage. Sometimes the intermediary may lend money directly via the financial markets. This is known as financial disintermediation.

The intermediary's role is to seek the best possible investment opportunities on behalf of its clients. The intermediary will often have contacts within its areas of expertise that would not be accessible to private individuals using a retail bank, for example. This enables the intermediary to broker the most appropriate deals for its client, which is spared the trouble of having to seek these out itself. The intermediary charges a fee to the client for its services.

ADVANTAGES

- Lending is often less risky through an intermediary, who can, for example, diversify lending, providing the company with a variety of different loan plans. If some loans then prove themselves to be unviable, they are offset by those that are sound. Experience is an important element of this. By making many and diverse loans, financial intermediaries gain experience in identifying clients who will be able to repay their loans, as well as those who will not. This reduces risk and minimizes the number of unviable loans for the client, who is spared the burden of making expensive mistakes.
- Financial intermediaries have liquidity, which means they are in a position to convert assets to money quickly. This has obvious advantages in terms of obtaining cash when it is needed. For a company this can be of crucial importance if it experiences difficulties such as temporary cash flow problems.

DISADVANTAGES

- The main disadvantage is that, on top of their fee, financial intermediaries often take a percentage of profits as part of any transaction they broker. Direct loaning can significantly increase the potential income of such a loan for the intermediary. However, the advantages outlined above significantly mitigate any such disadvantages. That is why many companies use intermediaries rather than entering the market directly.

ACTION CHECKLIST

- ✔ Ask around for recommendations. Your bank should have knowledge of specialist intermediaries who can cater for your needs, for example. Your accountant or lawyer may also have useful contacts.
- ✔ Investigate a financial intermediary thoroughly before entering into a relationship. Check that they have any necessary certification or license.
- ✔ You should be confident that your intermediary is a responsible and experienced broker and/or lender.

DOS AND DON'TS

DO

- Approach your decision by comparing and contrasting several choices of intermediary.
- Research your options carefully to ensure that potential intermediaries are both experienced and economically sound.
- Have interview meetings with intermediaries you are considering to ensure that you will be able to work with each other before you enter into any financial relationship.

DON'T

- Don't rush hastily into a relationship with an intermediary.
- Don't use an intermediary who cannot produce evidence of the right certification or license to practice.

▸▸ MORE INFO

Books:

Harrison, Tina. *Marketing Financial Services*. 2nd ed. New York: FT Prentice Hall, 2000.

Taylor, Bernard, and Ian Morison (eds). *Driving Strategic Change in Financial Services*. Cambridge, UK: Woodhead Publishing, 1999.

"A bank is a place that will lend you money if you can prove that you don't need it." Bob Hope

  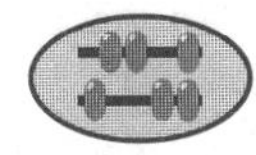 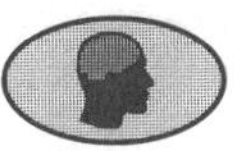  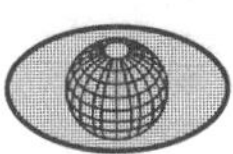   

Franchising a Business

DEFINITION

The term "franchising" can refer to a number of different business models, including licensing, distributor, and agency arrangements. Here, however, we take it to mean "business-format franchising." The British Franchise Association defines this concept as the granting of a license by a franchisor to a franchisee that "entitles the franchisee to trade under the trademark/trade name of the franchisor and to make use of an entire package, comprising all the elements necessary to establish a previously untrained person in the business and to run it with continual assistance on a predetermined basis."

Franchising can provide an excellent means of expanding a business rapidly and in a cost-effective manner. It can also generate a number of revenue streams for the franchisor. These include: the franchise fee; franchise royalties; equipment sales; supplies; material sales; sales of services; property rental; and rebates from vendors of equipment and supplies.

Each business outlet is owned and operated by the franchisee. However, the franchisor retains control over the way products and services are marketed and sold, and controls the quality and standards of the business. Not all businesses can be franchised, but most business concepts can be. Businesses that can be franchised tend to be unique and very new, with the potential to expand nationally or internationally, and profitable, with the ability to generate continuous and predictable profits. They tend to have a systemized business model, with efficient operating procedures that can be easily transferred from one location to another, and an easily understandable format, so that it is straightforward to train other people to manage the operation. They should also be affordable, so that a wide range of potential franchisees can be attracted.

ADVANTAGES

- It can be difficult to raise capital to expand a business. If you use franchising, the capital is provided by the franchisee.
- Franchisees tend to be highly motivated, since it is their capital that is at risk.
- Franchising allows you to expand a business very rapidly.
- Expanding the business leads to economies of scale, with benefits such as greater buying power.

DISADVANTAGES

- You need an effective marketing program and very good salespeople to develop the concept and drive sales forward once the franchise network has been established.
- You inevitably lose some control of the business unless you have a very strict operating model and the ability to oversee the way each franchisee is operating the business.
- It can be difficult to manage the business if it grows very rapidly (as is often the case with franchise networks).
- The threat of litigation between franchisor and franchisee can be high, particularly if the franchisee fails to make the profits they expected.

ACTION CHECKLIST

- ✔ Identify whether the business concept you are developing is suitable for a franchise arrangement.
- ✔ Register your trade name and trademarks with the relevant trademark office. You should also register your name and marks in all the countries or provinces where you do business or intend to do business.
- ✔ Open four or five business units before embarking on a national expansion. This will give you time to identify any potential pitfalls. You will also be able to gauge whether the business format can be copied from one geographic location to another.

DOS AND DON'TS

DO

- Avoid conflict and potential litigation by supporting your franchisees and ensuring that they are successful.
- Make sure you have enough staff to support the growth of your franchisees and service their needs.
- Draw up a very strict franchise agreement that allows the franchisee little latitude to vary from your system..

DON'T

- Don't ignore the importance of training. Even franchisees in a simple business model will require a very strong training program so that they are completely conversant with your systems and procedures.
- Don't think you can relax once franchisees have signed on. They will need continuous support if their business, and thus you, are to be successful.

➤➤ MORE INFO

Books:

Shook, Carrie, and Robert L. Shook. *Franchising: The Business Strategy that Changed the World*. Englewood Cliffs, NJ: Prentice Hall, 1993.

Spinelli, Stephen, Jr., Robert M. Rosenberg, and Sue Birley. *Franchising: Pathway to Wealth Creation*. Upper Saddle River, NJ: FT Prentice Hall, 2004.

Tarbutton, Lloyd T. *Franchising: The How-to Book*. Englewood Cliffs, NJ: Prentice Hall, 1986.

Articles:

Kaufmann, Patrick J., and Rajiv P. Dant. "Multi-unit franchising: Growth and management issues." *Journal of Business Venturing* 11:5 (1996): 343–358.

Mathewson, G. F., and R. A. Winter. "The economics of franchise contracts." *Journal of Law and Economics* 28:3 (1985): 503–526.

Website:

UK government website providing advice for businesses: www.businesslink.gov.uk

See Also:

✔ Assessing Economies of Scale in Business (p. 1060)

✔ The Objectives of Corporate Planning and Budgeting (p. 877)

"If we had the means to review and judge the effectiveness of operations, we could safely leave the prosecution of these operations to the men in charge of them." Alfred P. Sloan

How to Use Receivables as Collateral

DEFINITION

Receivables are money owed by customers, whether they are individuals or businesses, to another entity for goods or services that have been delivered or used, but have not yet been paid for. Receivables are usually due within a short time period, which typically ranges from a few days to a year.

Accounts receivable financing is used by companies facing short-term cash flow problems, and it can take many forms. The major source of accounts receivable financing is commercial finance companies and factoring companies, as well as banks that will consider receivables as security or collateral for a business loan. Most companies operate by allowing a portion of sales to be on credit, usually to customers that are invoiced periodically, which removes the burden of physically making payments as each transaction occurs. Credit acts as an IOU for goods or services already received or rendered and is given in good faith. Collateralizing receivables is a form of secured lending that gives companies short-term financing by selling their trade receivables or pledging receivables as collateral for a loan from a lender. Until the global financial crisis of 2008, receivables were securitized as well.

Direct sale of accounts receivable is called factoring. A loan from a bank secured or collateralized against accounts receivable is known as a discount, where the borrower draws against a line of credit that is less than the full value of the trade credits. Accounts receivable financing is a flexible way of obtaining credit, and borrowers' financing costs are related directly to their business cycle. In a general assignment, all receivables can serve as collateral, with new receivables substituted for those collected. In a specific assignment, the parties involved can specify who will receive collection, whether customers will be notified of the arrangement, and which accounts are to be collateralized.

Accounts receivable factoring is different from using accounts receivable as loan collateral because you sell the receivables to a factor at a discount; the factor then collects the debt and you don't have to worry about loan repayments. Accounts receivable factoring makes up about a third of all financing secured by American companies using accounts receivable and inventory as collateral.

When a loan is obtained from a bank with receivables as collateral, there are rather more formal guidelines. Banks and finance companies insist on weekly reports on sales, collections, and ineligibility analysis, as well as internally generated financial statements with detailed accounts receivable and accounts payable information. The amount borrowed is then repaid within a specified short-term period as the receivables are collected.

ADVANTAGES

- Collateralizing receivables can provide another source of working capital, freeing up essential funds for items such as payroll and taxes.
- This form of financing can provide relief from the responsibility of collection from nonpaying and slow-paying clients.

DISADVANTAGES

- Receivables financing is often priced at spreads above the bank prime rate and is relatively expensive compared with other forms of credit, particularly factoring.
- The older the account, the less value it has.

ACTION CHECKLIST

- ✔ When you sell an account to an accounts receivable factoring company, try to get a personal recommendation for the company and ensure that your accounts receivable factoring agreement states the exact conditions and charges for the purchase of your accounts receivable.
- ✔ Check the rates carefully and find out the amount a lender is willing to advance against the value of your collateralized receivables. The borrowing base is determined by multiplying the value of the assigned collateral by a discount factor, a process known as margining.

DOS AND DON'TS

DO

- Set up an easy-to-check accounts receivable report.
- Have a system in place to assess monies owed and monies unpaid.

DON'T

- Don't wait too long to take action on debts.
- Don't fall back on sentiment and loyalty.
- Don't forget to check bank rates, loan rates, and factoring rates.
- Don't use accounts receivable factoring as a way to get ready cash.

➡ MORE INFO

Books:

Bond, Cecil J. *Credit Management Handbook: A Complete Guide to Credit and Accounts Receivable Operations.* New York: McGraw-Hill, 1993.

Salek, John G. *Accounts Receivable Management Best Practices.* Hoboken, NJ: Wiley, 2005.

"Incremental change is not enough. The whole command and control tradition is being turned on its head."
Richard Pascale

  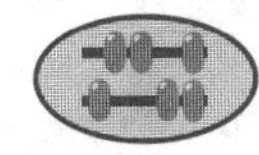 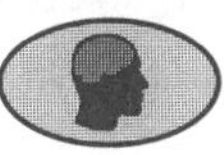  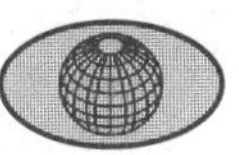   

Measuring Gearing

DEFINITION

Gearing, also known as leverage, is an indicator of a company's ability to service its debt. Gearing is usually expressed as a percentage and is calculated by dividing the company's debt by its equity. Gearing shows the degree to which a firm's activities are funded by owners' funds versus creditors' funds. The higher a company's degree of leverage, the more the company is considered risky. If a company has a large amount of debt in proportion to its equity, this could be a warning that the company may have problems paying its debts in the future. As when using most ratios, an acceptable level of risk is determined through comparison with other companies in the same industry.

The three most common examples of gearing ratios are:

- The debt/equity ratio (total debt/total equity), multiplied by interest earned (earnings before interest and taxes, divided by total interest).
- The equity ratio: total equity/total assets.
- The debt ratio: total debt/total assets.

In derivatives markets, gearing compares the amount of cash spent purchasing an option or a futures contract with the actual value of the underlying position. The more highly leveraged the trading position, the bigger the risk that a minor change in market prices will totally wipe out the investment. Equally, however, a minor change in markets in the right direction could generate large profits in relation to the size of the investment.

Negative gearing is when an investor borrows to buy an asset, but the returns on the asset do not cover the interest on the loan. A negative gearing strategy works when the asset rises in value and creates enough capital gains to cover the initial investment loss. The investor must finance the shortfall until the asset is sold.

ADVANTAGES

- Gearing ratios allow potential investors to judge the viability, liabilities and likely future performance of a company or industry.
- Gearing ratios permit analysts to read between the lines of financial statements and quantify a company's strengths and weaknesses.
- Gearing ratios provide lead indications of potential problem areas and allow corrective measures to be taken.

DISADVANTAGES

- Gearing ratios may not always reflect the true nature of a company's accounts, as managers may attempt to gloss over problems.
- Gearing ratios are only predictive, based on past performance; and cannot take into account future events.
- Using gearing ratios to make comparisons between companies and industries is not always possible, due to different worldwide accounting standards.

ACTION CHECKLIST

✔ Obtain as much information as you can, and compare a company's ratios to those of other firms in the same industry, before committing to an expensive decision.

✔ Make sure that you have analyzed the gearing ratios in detail. If in doubt, consult an expert analyst.

✔ Be sure you thoroughly understand the ratios. Economizing by taking shortcuts or skipping details may cost more in the long run.

DOS AND DON'TS

DO

- When comparing a business's gearing ratios with its competitors, allow for any material differences in accounting policies between the compared company and industry norms.

DON'T

- Don't rely solely on gearing ratios. Use market research to confirm the results. Don't fall into the trap of thinking that gearing ratios are infallible.

▸▸ MORE INFO

Books:

Chadwick, Leslie. *Essential Finance and Accounting for Managers*. Harlow, UK: Pearson Education, 2002.

Fraser-Sampson, Guy. *Private Equity as an Asset Class*. Chichester, UK: Wiley, 2007.

Myddelton, David Roderic. *Managing Business Finance*. Harlow, UK: Pearson Education, 2000.

Articles:

Calder, Stephen. "Super leverage." *Australasian Business Journal* (January 2008).

Rees, Mathew. "On leveraged buyouts." *The International Economy* (June 2008).

Websites:

American Express: www133.americanexpress.com/osbn/tool/ratios/financialratio.asp

Fool.co.uk: www.fool.co.uk/school/2005/sch050803.htm

"A company with no sense of crisis and no appetite for reform will eventually lose the battle against time and disappear." Kunio Takeda

     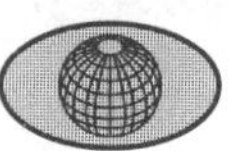   

Money Markets: Their Structure and Function

DEFINITION

Money markets are the part of the global financial market that deals with short-term lending and borrowing. They are often used as a solution to short-term cash needs by governments, large institutions, and, sometimes, individuals.

Generally, participants in the money markets are retail banks and large corporate organizations that can trade with each other using the benchmark of the London Interbank Offered Rate (Libor). This rate is generated on a daily basis through researching the interest rates at which banks are prepared to lend on unsecured assets. The money markets are considered to be quite a low-risk investment, but they do not promise particularly high gains either.

Typically, a transaction in a money market will be of very short duration and will be of a particular type of dealing called "paper." Examples of papers are treasury bills, repurchase agreements, and foreign currency swaps. The time frame of the transaction may range from one day to 13 months, and it is this short-term approach that sets money markets apart from the capital market.

Repurchase agreements, or "repos," are very short term loans, often lasting for only a day, where assets are sold to an investor with an agreement to repurchase them at a later date for a fixed price. In foreign currency swaps, currencies are swapped with an agreement to reverse the deal at a later, agreed date.

ADVANTAGES

- For an organization in need of a quick cash injection the money markets are extremely useful. They generally allow easy borrowing or lending in a low-risk environment. For example, a one-day loan where the seller can repurchase its securities for a set price at a certain time in the future is extremely safe. If we compare this transaction to those made in the unforgiving world of the stock market, where investors have no control over the future performance of their stocks, it is easy to see the appeal of money markets.

DISADVANTAGES

- Money markets are particularly low risk and therefore are not suitable for an investor looking for high returns.
- The money markets are used for short-term loans only and are not designed to achieve long-term growth of assets.
- Despite the apparent low risk of the money markets, all transactions in them must be properly assessed in the context of the global market. When the global financial markets go through one of their periodic cycles of turmoil and instability, one should always err on the side of caution with any investment.

ACTION CHECKLIST

- ✔ Consider your reasons for investing. Do you require a quick cash release or are you planning for the long term?
- ✔ What kind of investment are you looking for? Consult your financial adviser to determine what type of transaction would work best for your company.
- ✔ Check carefully on the financial status of the organization with which you are considering entering into a money market agreement.

DOS AND DON'TS

DO

- Research all the available fundraising options fully.
- Give yourself as comprehensive an understanding of the current financial market as you can before investing.
- Examine your motives for using the money markets as a long-term investment may make more sense.

DON'T

- Don't invest in the money markets if you are looking for a high return on your investments.
- Don't believe that because the money markets are low risk your assets are perfectly safe.

➤➤ MORE INFO

Books:

Choudhry, Moorad. *Bond and Money Markets: Strategy, Trading, Analysis*. Oxford: Butterworth-Heinemann, 2003.

Choudhry, Moorad. *The Money Markets Handbook: A Practitioner's Guide*. Singapore: Wiley, 2005.

Article:

Fleming, Jeff, Chris Kirby, and Barbara Ostdiek. "Information and volatility linkages in the stock, bond, and money markets." *Journal of Financial Economics* 49:1 (1998): 111–137.

Websites:

The Bank of England's framework for its operations in the sterling money markets: www.bankofengland.co.uk/markets/money

The US Federal Reserve's policy for its dollar operations: www.federalreserve.gov/monetarypolicy

"The more volatile the market, the quicker an organization's success formula becomes obsolete."
Daryl R. Conner

  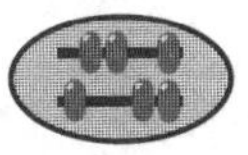 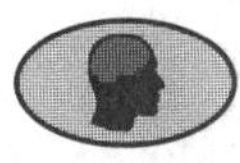  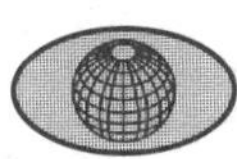   

Options for Raising Finance

DEFINITION

Funding small and medium sized enterprises is a major part of the general business finance market. When a budding company is growing rapidly and needs to invest in capital equipment or other assets, its financial capital may be insufficient. Few emerging companies are able to finance their expansion plans from cash flow alone. Therefore, entrepreneurs need to consider raising finance from external sources. Once they have decided to raise capital, they need to consider what source and type of finance will suit their needs.

Venture capital: is intended for higher risks, such as start up situations and development capital for established companies.

Joint venture: find an individual or organization to both invest in and work with a company in its business project.

Limited company: raise capital by setting up a limited company and selling shares to investors.

Banks for working capital: short term finance or the working capital necessary to fund the day to day running of the business. This can take the form of an agreed overdraft, where the interest will be calculated on your daily outstanding balance and charged on a monthly or quarterly basis.

Banks for medium term loans: a loan paid back over an agreed term (typically three to ten years), where principal and interest are paid off monthly. This type of loan is used mainly to invest in equipment, expansion, and development.

Banks for long term loans: the most common way to arrange long term borrowing. This type of loan is normally used to purchase assets such as a business, land, buildings, plant, or machinery that can be shown to directly or indirectly add to profit over a number of years.

Factoring and invoice discounting: to improve cash flow, finance can also be raised against customer debts using factoring or invoice discounting.

Leasing: provides finance for the acquisition of specific assets, such as cars, equipment, and machinery. Leasing involves a deposit and repayments over, typically, three to ten years. The financier purchases the equipment you require and then leases it to you in return for regular payments for the duration of the lease period.

Personal loans: if it is impossible to arrange a loan in your business's name, you could consider arranging a personal loan. However, check that the conditions do not jeopardize control of the business and that you are very confident of being able to repay or you may lose the assets put up as collateral.

Family and friends: To avoid any misunderstandings and/or resolve any dispute if things go wrong, it is imperative to make a written agreement, including the timescale and interest payments.

ADVANTAGES

- Finding the finance on the right terms allows small and medium sized enterprises to invest in land, new capital equipment, R&D, etc. Very few emergent companies are able to finance their expansion plans from cash flow alone.
- Raising finance helps to avoid the dilution of business control or share capital.

DISADVANTAGES

- Venture capitalists normally want preference shares or loan stock in addition to their equity stake.
- Joint ventures and the setting up of limited companies can often result in the loss of control over aspects such as policy and development.
- Banks have the power to place a business into administration or bankruptcy if it defaults on debt interest or repayments.
- Borrowing from family or friends can lead to disputes or interference in the management of the venture.

ACTION CHECKLIST

✓ Prepare a written business plan explaining in detail your business objectives, your operating plan, projected earnings, marketing strategy, and other relevant information.

✓ Use the strategy laid out in the business plan to help you assess all the alternatives and then negotiate terms with several financial providers before choosing the one that suits you best.

DOS AND DON'TS

DO

- Consider what source and type of finance suits your needs. Then match the method of funding and the term of the loan to the reason for the finance.

DON'T

- Don't forget that your financing decisions may have an impact on business cash flow and taxation obligations.

⏵⏵ MORE INFO

Books:

Burk, James E., and Richard P. Lehman. *Financing Your Small Business: From SBA Loans and Credit Cards to Common Stock and Partnership Interests*. Naperville, IL: Sourcebooks, 2006.

Lister, Kate, and Tom Harnish. *Finding Money: The Small Business Guide to Financing*. Chichester, UK: Wiley, 1995.

Timmons, Jeffry A., Stephen Spinelli, and Andrew Zacharakis. *How to Raise Capital: Techniques and Strategies for Financing and Valuing Your Small Business*. Maidenhead, UK: McGraw-Hill Professional, 2005.

Articles:

Thomas, Tony. "How to raise business finance." *NZ Business* (June 2006).

Williams, Gary. "How to balance ownership with the need to raise capital." *Deseret News* (May 2008).

Websites:

Support for small and medium-sized enterprises: www.rba.co.uk

The US Chamber of Commerce: www.uschamber.com

     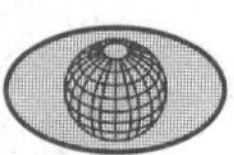   

Overview of Loan Agreements

DEFINITION

Most businesses need to borrow money, and obtaining a loan from a bank is the most usual way of financing a business. If successful in an application for a loan, an individual, partnership, or company has to enter into a loan agreement that sets out the terms on which the loan is given.

A loan agreement is entered into by the bank as lender, and by the individual, partnership, or company that borrows as borrower.

A loan agreement contains all the terms and conditions under which the lender will lend the borrower the money. It states the amount of the loan, when the amount will be lent, the tranches if the money is to be lent in amounts at different dates, the repayment schedule, the interest to be paid by the borrower, and other conditions, terms, and warranties required by the lender from the borrower.

The repayment schedule is usually very precise and will state the exact dates on which the lender expects to be paid back by the borrower. The loan agreement can contain a voluntary prepayment clause that will allow a borrower to prepay the loan in certain circumstances. It may also set out mandatory prepayment obligations that apply in certain cases—for example, if the borrower sells or lists its business, or if the business is acquired by someone else and control changes hands.

A loan agreement specifies the rate of interest, and how this will be calculated and paid by the borrower. It also deals with the consequences and penalties in the case of default on payments by the borrower.

The borrower usually has to pay the lender an arrangement fee for the loan and is also expected to pay all reasonable legal, accountancy, valuation, and due diligence costs and other fees, costs, and expenses of arranging the loan.

In general, a bank will not give a loan without obtaining security for that loan. The loan agreement will contain details of the debentures, guarantees, or charges given by the borrower as security for the loan.

The borrower will be asked to make and give certain representations and warranties in relation to its constitution and business. It will also be required to give certain covenants (promises) as to how it will conduct its business in the future.

ADVANTAGES

- A loan agreement sets out the terms and conditions upon which a bank will lend money to a borrower.
- Because it is an agreement, it can be negotiated and agreed by the two parties.
- A loan agreement protects both parties and is a legally enforceable agreement.

DISADVANTAGES

- In practice, a bank sets its own conditions for lending, and a borrower will have to comply and agree to such terms if it needs the funds.
- Negotiating a loan agreement can be complex and time-consuming. The documentation must be thoroughly understood, and if specialist legal advice is required the process may be expensive.

ACTION CHECKLIST

- ✔ Study a loan agreement carefully before you sign. Obtain as much information from as many sources as you can before committing to an expensive agreement.
- ✔ Shop around for a better deal. Go to several banks and see if there are better offers and conditions for the loan you want.
- ✔ Be prepared for long and complicated negotiations, which could prove time-consuming and costly.

DOS AND DON'TS

DO

- Choose your bank carefully.
- Make sure that you understand the conditions of your loan.
- Involve your solicitors in the evaluation of both the risks and benefits of entering into a loan agreement.
- Check if it's possible to negotiate the terms and conditions of the loan.
- If in trouble with repayments, tell your bank as they may be able to help in various ways, such as temporarily reducing your repayments.

DON'T

- Don't make the mistake of being attracted by a loan without understanding the implications of all the terms of the loan and the total cost to your business.
- Don't overlook the importance of negotiating warranties and indemnities that you will be able to give with confidence. If you know of anything that may go against these warranties, disclose it to the bank.
- Don't ignore the importance of telling the bank if you have problems with repayments. It might prove to your advantage.

▸▸ MORE INFO

Books:

Clasen, Thomas F. (ed). *International Agency and Distribution Agreements*. Looseleaf ed. Charlottesville, VA: Lexis Law Publishing, 1991.

Singleton, Susan. *Commercial Agency Agreements: Law and Practice*. 2nd ed. Haywards Heath, UK: Tottel Publishing, 2005.

Article:

Gustafson, Jeanne. "GenPrime signs big distribution agreement." *Journal of Business* (October 9, 2008).

Websites:

About.com Business Finance: bizfinance.about.com

AllBusiness: www.allbusiness.com

National Federation of Independent Business (US): www.nfib.com

Western Economic Diversification Canada: www.wd-deo.gc.ca

   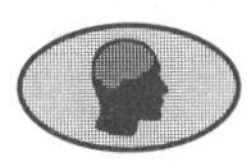  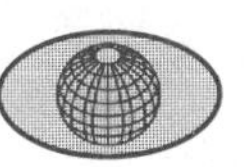   

An Overview of Stockholders' Agreements

DEFINITION

The shares (or stock) issued by most limited companies are classed as "ordinary," and each share carries one vote. Majority shareholders will therefore control voting in the company. Since minority shareholders may resent not having any say in important company decisions, conflicts can arise. To minimize these, it is advisable that the shareholders sign a stockholders' agreement—which will give small shareholders a voice in these big decisions.

Stockholders' agreements are more commonly used in certain circumstances: for example, when some shareholders are not directors and thus do not have much of a role in the decisions of the board, or in the case of equal-stake joint ventures.

A stockholders' agreement will establish the constitution of the board, the number of directors, which shareholder(s) will have the right to appoint directors (and how many), and who will be the chairman of the board and have the casting vote if needed. It will also decide who will have management control and how board meetings and voting will operate.

The agreement can also establish that certain business issues will require the approval of 100% of the shares. These are usually only very important issues, such as: the company entering into a contract with directors or shareholders; the incurring of expenditure or liability over a certain predetermined value; the company giving a guarantee or taking on an encumbrance (debt) of a certain value; the sale, transfer, lease, or licensing of any of the assets of the company other than in the ordinary course of business; or the altering of any provisions of the company bylaws.

In general, a stockholders' agreement is a contract between shareholders that can stipulate more or less anything, as long as it does not contravene the law or the bylaws of the company

ADVANTAGES

- Stockholders' agreements protect minority shareholders and allow them to participate in decisions from which they might otherwise be excluded.
- Stockholders' agreements are not regulated. Shareholders have the flexibility to decide the type of contract they want.
- The stockholders' agreement can also restrict the transfer of shares and will establish pre-emption rights (the right of existing shareholders to be the first to acquire the shares of another shareholder).

DISADVANTAGES

- Assenting to a stockholders' agreement may involve extensive negotiations and require professional advice. It could be expensive to draft and put in place.

ACTION CHECKLIST

- ✔ Study any shareholder agreement carefully before signing. Be clear what you would like to achieve from it.
- ✔ Be prepared for extensive negotiations, which could prove time-consuming as well as costly.
- ✔ Economize by negotiating a reasonable rate with your legal and financial advisers, but remember that it is better to incur costs and understand the agreement you sign than to enter into an agreement that you do not understand and may not represent your interests.

DOS AND DON'TS

DO

- Involve your lawyers in the negotiation of a stockholders' agreement.
- Think carefully what you would like to achieve from it.
- If necessary, request the right to appoint a director as your representative on the board. In this way, you can influence decisions in the company at board level.

DON'T

- Don't make the mistake of entering into a stockholders' agreement that you do not understand and does not represent your interests.

▸▸ MORE INFO

Books:

Comben, Andrew. *Joint Ventures and Shareholders' Agreements*. 2nd ed. Haywards Heath, UK: Tottel Publishing, 2005.

Stedman, Graham, Janet Jones, and John Cadman. *Shareholders' Agreements*. 4th ed. Andover, UK: Sweet & Maxwell, 2003.

Articles:

Sisca, Eileen R., and Eckert Seamans. "Protect your investment with a shareholders' agreement." *Leader's Edge* 2:9 (1999): 4.

Waldman, Glenn J. "The shareholders' agreement—don't leave your P.A. without it." *Florida Bar Journal* 71:9 (1997): 57.

Websites:

Canadian legal resources: www.canadalegal.com

Exile From the Herd: The Official Mark Jeftovic blog: www.privateworld.com

International Financial Law Review: www.iflr.com

Net Lawman legal documents (UK): www.netlawman.co.uk

"Character is a by-product; it is produced in the great manufacture of daily duty." Woodrow Wilson

     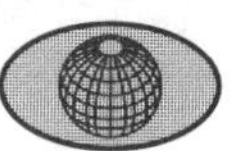   

Raising Capital by Issuing Bonds

DEFINITION

Raising capital by issuing bonds is a popular alternative to selling shares, as it allows a company to avoid relinquishing ownership of part of the business. A bond is a loan in the form of a debt security. The authorized issuer (the borrower) owes the bondholder (the lender) a debt and has an obligation to repay the principal and the coupon (interest) on the maturity of the loan. Bonds enable the issuer to finance long-term investments with external funds.

The loan collateral may be the company's land, buildings, or other physical assets that can be sold off if the issuer defaults on repayment of the principal. In today's bond markets, however, a much wider range of assets can fulfill the function of collateral, such as receivables that produce a flow of income.

ADVANTAGES

- Taking on debt by issuing bonds is usually cheaper than either a bank overdraft or the cost of raising equity through a share issue. A major advantage is that the return on debt (interest) is tax-deductible, whereas the return on equity (dividends) is paid out of a company's profits, which are taxed before dividend payments can be made to stockholders.
- Financing by raising debt is a useful way of monitoring a corporation's overall health, as the ability to repay the debt reflects the overall financial stability of the company.
- Bonds offer a more secure return for investors—dividends are paid out purely at the discretion of the company, whereas interest on debt must be paid according to the set terms of the bond.
- Debt issuance can also be advantageous from a governance point of view. In the United States and United Kingdom, for example, creditors have no influence on the board or company policy—unlike stockholders, who often have the right to vote on policies and the appointment of directors. Financing through debt can thus be very useful for companies that do not want to relinquish control to others.

DISADVANTAGES

- The risks for bondholders rise as more debt is issued.
- The debt covenants may prove too restrictive for the company. A company that is highly leveraged is more likely to face cash flow difficulties as it has to meet the coupon payments regardless of its income. The cost of servicing the debt may rise beyond the ability to pay, either because of external events, such as falling income, or because of internal problems, such as poor company management. The company may find that it runs into solvency problems if the amount of debt becomes higher than the value of its realizable assets. Thus, the cost of debt rises as its proportion rises in relation to equity. The higher the debt-to-equity ratio, the greater the risk.
- If the company is publicly listed on a stock exchange, the risk to stockholders increases when debt is issued. This is due to the increased claims of the creditors, or bondholders, on the company's capital and earnings, which must be used to service the debt before anything else. And if the company has problems servicing the debt, stockholders risk the loss of their equity in the case of bankruptcy.

ACTION CHECKLIST

✔ *Choose the right type of debt.* For large investments, you generally have a choice of borrowing the principal from a creditor, usually a bank, or issuing bonds underwritten by the bank that can be sold to investors. If the bond can be retraded, it is beneficial for the bondholders as they can exit at the right moment, but the company still has access to the funds via new purchasers.

✔ *Choose the right interest rate.* Bonds usually have either a fixed interest rate for a specified period or a floating rate linked to an agreed index. Fixed-rate debt means that the issuer knows the exact cost across the debt's lifetime and can budget for the principal and interest payments each year. Floating-rate debt usually has a mark-up over the base rate set by the central bank in charge of the currency that is being borrowed, meaning that the issuer may have to pay more if monetary policy is tightened and interest rates rise during the period of the loan.

DOS AND DON'TS

DO

- Do a full cost analysis to determine if debt will be cheaper for the company than equity.
- Take into account that unexpected market volatility and inflation will affect the coupon level.

DON'T

- Don't issue bonds if you think that meeting regular payments to the bondholders will overstretch your cash flow.

➤➤ MORE INFO

Books:

Brown, Patrick J. *An Introduction to the Bond Markets*. Hoboken. NJ: Wiley, 2006.
Choudhry, Moorad. *The Bond and Money Markets: Strategy, Trading, Analysis*. Oxford: Butterworth-Heinemann, 2003.

     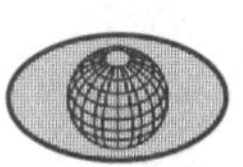   

Raising Capital by Issuing Shares

DEFINITION

A company that wants to raise capital by issuing shares has several options. If it is not yet listed on a stock exchange, the company can prepare for an initial public offering (IPO), in which it will be valued and an opening price will be set for its shares when they are released onto the market. How much finance can be raised through an IPO depends partly on the perceived value, and thus share price, of the company, and partly on how much interest there is in the shares when they are released on the market.

For a company that is already listed on an exchange, an alternative route is to launch an additional share issue (also known as a seasoned equity offering, or SEO) or a rights issue. A SEO is a new equity issue by a company following its IPO. A rights issue permits existing stockholders to purchase a designated number of new shares from a company at a specified price within a specified time. The offer may be rejected, or accepted in full or in part, by each stockholder. Rights are usually transferable, meaning that the holder can sell them on the open market. The additional shares in a rights issue are generally issued to stockholders on a pro rata basis—for example, in a two-for-five rights issue stockholders are offered two shares for every five they already hold.

Renounceable rights are rights offered by a company to existing stockholders to purchase further stock, usually at a discount. These rights have a value and can be traded. If rights are to be issued, the company has to set the price of the new shares, determine how many it will sell, and assess how the current share value will be affected as well as the effect on new and existing stockholders. Nonrenounceable rights are not transferable and cannot be bought or sold; these rights must be taken up or they will lapse.

ADVANTAGES

- For a company that has reached a certain size and has a strong reputation, an IPO can be a good route to raising a large sum of capital that will enable it to expand, or invest in assets that will enable it to grow in the future.
- The company does not need to repay this share capital, but instead agrees to distribute future profits to stockholders in return for their investment.
- Once listed, a company can periodically issue further shares via a rights issue, raising yet more capital for expansion without running up debt. Being in a position to raise capital from the stock markets, rather than privately from individual investors, is a major incentive for many companies to issue shares on an exchange.

DISADVANTAGES

- The main disadvantage of issuing shares through an IPO is that a company's owners no longer have full control of the business and become accountable to stockholders. Stockholders can block plans if they believe they pose too great a risk to their investment.
- Any issuance of further shares dilutes the holdings of existing stockholders as a proportion of the company's total shares. This can lead to dissatisfaction from minority stockholders, who have the most to lose. In some jurisdictions, such as the UK, stockholders have preemptive rights by law, which means they have the right to purchase new issuances first. In other jurisdictions, such as the US, preemptive rights must be enshrined in a company's constitution. Stockholders who do not have preemptive rights are most at risk of seeing their investment diluted.

ACTION CHECKLIST

✔ Consider whether options for raising capital other than a share issue might be more suited to your investment plans.

✔ Consult your bank and other financial advisers on the time scale for an IPO or rights issues, and on the timing of the offer.

DOS AND DON'TS

DO

- Issue a proper prospectus for your share offer.
- Keep stockholders informed about how much dividend they can expect to receive each year.

DON'T

- Don't issue shares if you are not prepared to give up a certain amount of decision-making to stockholders.

▸▸ MORE INFO

Books:

Gregoriou, Greg N. *Initial Public Offerings: An International Perspective*. Amsterdam: Butterworth-Heinemann, 2006.

Temple, Peter. *First Steps in Shares*. Harlow, UK: Pearson Education, 2001.

Articles:

Goergen, M., A. Khurshed, and R. Mudambi. "The strategy of going public: How UK firms choose their listing contracts." *Journal of Business Finance & Accounting* 33:1–2 (2006): 79–101.

Loughran, T., and J. R. Ritter, "Why don't issuers get upset about leaving money on the table in IPOs?" *Review of Financial Studies* 15:2 (2002): 413–443.

     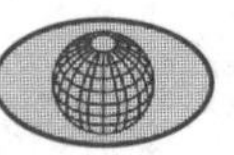   

Raising Capital through Private and Public Equity

DEFINITION

Many publicly listed companies needing to raise funds for investment choose not to offer shares or issue bonds on the open markets, but instead look for capital on the private equity markets. In the former case, funding comes from a publicly listed company looking to invest in other companies that offer synergy, as well as good financial returns. In the latter, the funds come from institutional investors who invest their wealth indirectly through private equity funds—private equity being a class of assets that are not publicly traded on the exchanges. Institutional investors provide such capital with the aim of achieving risk-adjusted returns that exceed those possible on the stock markets.

In both cases, a percentage stake in the company is surrendered in exchange for the investment, and the deal usually includes one or more seats on the board of directors as well. Companies seeking equity funding may use a financial intermediary to broker the best deal for the investment.

Companies that raise investment capital in this way can usually expect to deliver a return on investment through one of the following routes: *Recapitalization*, in which the company distributes dividends or cash to its stakeholders; a *merger* or *acquisition*, in which the company may be absorbed by or merged with its public equity investor, or sold for either cash or shares in another company by its private equity backers; a *buy-out*, in which the equity investor agrees to pull out in exchange for a cash sum from the company, which thereupon regains its independence; or an *initial public offering* (*IPO*), whereby company shares are offered to the public on a stock exchange, which offers the equity investor both an immediate partial cash return on its investment, in addition to a public market in which additional share issues can be placed at a later date.

ADVANTAGES

- Raising capital through equity can be a good choice for companies that are not ready for an IPO or are unwilling to finance expansion through debt.
- An equity deal means that the company has access to business experts through its investors, who can help to steer the business strategically as well as financially.

DISADVANTAGES

- Taking the equity route can lock a company into an agreement over a long time frame.
- The company may have to surrender a large stake in return for investment, possibly as much as 50%, and also provide seats on the board.
- Investors may interfere with the company's business plan and other areas of strategic importance.
- With either type of equity deal, there needs to be chemistry between the counterparties. Lack of chemistry can lead to board disagreements and other problems, souring the relationship.
- It can be difficult for a company to extricate itself from an equity investment arrangement, depending on the terms of the deal.

ACTION CHECKLIST

✔ Look for synergies if choosing the equity investment route, as the relationship with investors is likely to be more fruitful and less fraught if the counterparties feel they want the same things for the business, and can agree on essentials such as direction and strategy.

✔ Private equity firms are more likely to be concerned about the long-term relationship in terms of ultimate financial return, whereas a public equity investor may be concerned only with the bottom line.

DOS AND DON'TS

DO

- Hold talks with a range of potential investors to compare the deals on offer.
- Look at other possible financing options—an equity deal may not always be the right solution.

DON'T

- Don't enter into an equity deal if you feel pressured to give away a greater stake in the business than you want to. You may regret it later.
- Don't be afraid to bargain hard at the negotiating stage of the deal.

▸▸ MORE INFO

Books:

Fraser-Sampson, Guy. *Private Equity as an Asset Class*. Chichester, UK: Wiley, 2007.

Jenkinson, Tim, and Alexander Ljungqvist. *Going Public: The Theory and Evidence on How Companies Raise Equity Finance*. 2nd ed. Oxford: Oxford University Press, 2001.

Mathonet, Pierre-Yves, and Thomas Meyer. *J-Curve Exposure: Managing a Portfolio of Venture Capital and Private Equity Funds*. Chichester, UK: Wiley, 2007.

Mavrikakis, Alexis. *Public Companies and Equity Finance 2009*. Guildford, UK: College of Law Publishing, 2009.

Sovereign Wealth Funds—Investment Strategies and Objectives

DEFINITION

Sovereign Wealth Funds' (SWFs) investment decisions are typically made with one of two goals in mind: Either the funds are seeking an attractive rate of return in purely economic terms, or they are hoping to generate strategic benefits for their country. In the former case, SWFs regularly describe themselves as passive investors in that they do not seek to influence or control the companies they invest in, sometimes preferring to avoid holding voting shares at all. In contrast to typical private equity investors, SWFs are also frequently happy to put their faith in existing company management, rather than aiming to parachute their own executives onto the board. When a SWF invests in a company for strategic benefits, commonly in sectors such as financial services or leisure, the objective is usually to gain insights into the management's operational expertise with a long-term view of helping to develop or grow a related industry in the fund's own country.

While many SWFs may emphasize that their investment strategies tend to be longer term and more "hands off" than the average private equity investor, there are signs that some SWFs are prepared to work more closely with these more active investors to help achieve their investment goals. For example, Abu Dhabi-based Mubadala's 2007 purchase of a 7.5% stake in Carlyle, and news that China Investment Corporation (CIC) had raised its stake in Blackstone to around 12.5% in late 2008, raised the prospect of further cooperation between SWFs and private equity groups.

Though many SWFs have demonstrated their willingness to hold a geographically diverse spread of assets, few have historically provided much insight into the precise investment strategies they employ to achieve their stated objectives. However, Norway's GPF-G Fund (Government Pension Fund—Global), the world's second-largest SWF (after the Abu Dhabi Investment Authority), is the notable exception, providing regular updates on its holdings and demonstrating a high level of commitment to ethical investing. Nevertheless, the SWFs' general perceived lack of investment transparency and doubts over their commitment to high standards of corporate governance standards have done little to help the image of SWFs. Though political pressure is growing in some jurisdictions for greater standards of transparency and improved disclosure from SWFs with the potential to acquire assets of significant national importance or prestige, there is evidence that many SWFs would prefer to work within more loosely worded "best practice" investment frameworks. In October 2008, the International Working Group of Sovereign Wealth Funds presented a proposed set of principles guiding the operations of SWFs to the International Monetary Fund's (IMF) policy-focused International Monetary and Financial Committee. Both the IMF and the Organisation for Economic Co-operation and Development (OECD) are set to present their own proposals in reports due in 2009.

ADVANTAGES

- The long-term and "hands-off" nature of investments by SWFs can make them attractive shareholders for some companies.
- SWFs have been a particularly valuable source of immediate capital injections into financial institutions whose balance sheets have been in urgent need of strengthening.
- High levels of investable cash give SWFs the ability to capitalize on opportunities generated by market swings, with the meaning SWFs can be a stabilizing influence during times of market volatility.

DISADVANTAGES

- Doubts persist in some quarters over the motives behind some SWFs investments, particularly those made for long-term strategic reasons.
- Political concerns are frequently raised over the prospect of key national resources falling under the control of secretive overseas investors, particularly in view of most SWFs' poor disclosure standards.

ACTION CHECKLIST

✔ By moving towards the adoption of best practice guidelines to be proposed by the IMF and the OECD, it should be possible to alleviate some concerns over the lack of transparency and disclosure of most SWFs.

✔ By taking non-voting shares only, SWFs can help to overcome objections over the motivation for some of their more politically sensitive investments.

DOS AND DON'TS

DO

- Recognize the increasing scope for private equity and SWF investors to cooperate on investment projects.
- Appreciate that the generally poor level of transparency of SWFs does little to alleviate concerns over their motives when making overseas investments.

DON'T

- Don't be afraid of improved disclosure; follow the example of Norway's pension SWF.
- Don't overlook the role of SWFs, as cash-rich, long-term investors, in helping to stabilize volatile markets and recapitalize struggling companies.

▸▸ MORE INFO

Book:

Hassan, Adnan. *A Practical Guide to Sovereign Wealth Funds*. London: Euromoney Institutional Investor, 2008.

Articles:

Jen, Stephen. "Sovereign wealth funds: What they are and what's happening." *World Economics Journal* 8:4 (2007): 1–7.

Raphaeli, Nimrod, and Bianca Gersten. "Sovereign wealth funds: Investment vehicles for the Persian Gulf countries." *Middle East Quarterly* 15:2 (2008): 45–53.

Websites:

International Working Group of Sovereign Wealth Funds: www.iwg-swf.org

Opalesque Sovereign Wealth Funds Briefing: www.opalesque.com/SWF_Briefing

Sovereign Wealth Fund Institute: www.swfinstitute.org

Sovereign Wealth Fund news service: www.swfradar.com

"Consolidation is going to take place and it's better to lead than to follow. If you lead you have the best opportunity to gain the best partners." Niall Fitzgerald

     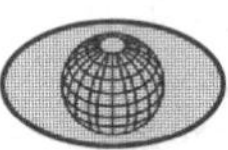   

Steps for Obtaining Bank Financing

DEFINITION

A major problem for both emerging and established companies is the cost of raising capital. Can the owners obtain bank financing instead of incurring dilution by giving up additional ownership in the company? An owner of a promising business may perceive itself as being creditworthy, however a bank will require "proof," for example in the form of a full quarter or year of sustained profitability, depending on the industry and levels of profitability. Decision makers at the bank will judge the company on a number of factors, including the following ratios:

- Leverage/gearing: to guarantee the company is sufficiently capitalized, i.e. total liabilities divided by tangible net worth.
- Liquidity: to guarantee sufficient working capital; measured by current ratio, i.e. current assets divided by current liabilities.
- Debt service coverage: to guarantee the company has sufficient operating cash flow to cover principal and interest and any capital leases.

Companies will need to present a written business plan explaining business objectives in detail, operating plans, projected earnings for the next one to five years, marketing strategy, and other relevant information. Marketing strategies must be outlined in detail to lend credence to sales projections. The first two years of projections should be detailed by month or by quarter to measure the projected performance against financial ratios. These projections should be composed of balance sheets, income statements, and cash-flow statements. The bank will also want to know:

- How much money do you need?
- How do you plan to use the money? (For example, to buy new assets, to pay off debts, or to pay operating expenses?)
- How long will it take you to repay the loan? (Use your cash flow projections to help plan the repayments.)
- What loan repayments can you afford to make without damaging the business?
- What can you offer as security for the loan? (Bankers generally require personal guarantees from the owners.)

The bank will also want to determine whether the management has the skills to run the business. Typical questions include: is the manager/owner talented enough to direct the company? Are the sales team knowledgeable about the industry and have they demonstrated successful sales growth in other companies? Does the financial officer have an in depth understanding of the financial background of the company? Do the management team get on well together and complement each other?

ADVANTAGES

- Bank financing allows the owners to keep a major interest in the company, instead of diluting interest by selling shares. Looking for bank financing will force the owners to focus on detailed projections. In order to present a written business plan, the owners must concentrate on the strategic planning that is vital to a business's survival. Building a successful relationship with the bank will help with future business expansion.

DISADVANTAGES

- Research, preparation, and presentation of the details required by the bank will take time away from the day to day functions of running the business.
- The company will be leveraged and therefore subject to detailed bank scrutiny during the period of the loan.
- An unfavorable payback period.

ACTION CHECKLIST

✔ Prepare a detailed business plan explaining objectives, operations, marketing strategy, and projected earnings for the next five years.

✔ Make sure you are not taking on too much debt. There is no sense in taking out a loan that will squeeze out your profits and bleed your business dry. Check your leverage/gearing and liquidity ratios and then capacity for debt service coverage.

✔ Prepare answers to the bank's key questions. For example, how much money do you need? How do you plan to use the money? How long will it take you to repay the loan? What will you use as security for the loan?

DOS AND DON'TS

DO

- Get expert advice when preparing your proposal. Getting a bank loan for an emerging company or even an established business is not always simple.

DON'T

- Don't go to the bank thinking that you'll get the loan just because you have a good idea. You will need to take a rigorously detailed proposal.

▸▸ MORE INFO

Books:

Burk, James E., and Richard P. Lehman. *Financing Your Small Business: From SBA Loans and Credit Cards to Common Stock and Partnership Interests*. Naperville, IL: Sourcebooks, 2006.

Sisson, Robert. *Financing the Small Business: A Complete Guide to Obtaining Bank Loans and All Other Types of Financing*. Cincinnati, OH: Adams Media Corporation, 2002.

Timmons, Jeffry A., Stephen Spinelli, and Andrew Zacharakis. *How to Raise Capital: Techniques and Strategies for Financing and Valuing Your Small Business*. Maidenhead, UK: McGraw-Hill Professional, 2005.

Articles:

Business Wire. "Bank loans are harder to get for small business." May 2008.

Iacobuzo, Theodore. "Can't get a bank loan? Try asking your online peers." *Banking Technology News* (January 2006).

Websites:

HSBC: www.hsbc.com

Wells Fargo Bank: www.wellsfargo.com

See Also:

✔ Assessing Cash Flow and Bank Lending Requirements (p. 854)

✔ Retail Banks: Their Structure and Function (p. 930)

"I recognize that I am made up of several persons and that the person that at the moment has the upper hand will inevitably give place to another. But which is the real one? All of them or none?" W. Somerset Maugham

   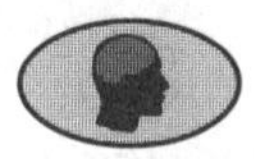  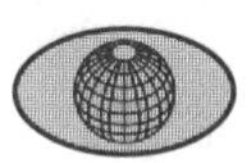   

Stock Markets: Their Structure and Function

DEFINITION

A stock market is a private or public market for the trading of stocks and shares in companies and derivatives of company stocks at an agreed price. These include securities listed on a stock exchange as well as those traded privately. A stock market is sometimes also known as an equity market.

The estimated size of the world stock market is around US$51 trillion. Even larger, it is estimated that the world derivatives market is worth about US$480 trillion face, or nominal, value; that is well over ten times the size of the whole world economy. However, the derivatives market is stated in terms of notional values and therefore cannot be directly compared to stocks, which refer to an actual value.

Stock markets specialize in bringing buyers and sellers of stocks and securities together. Famous stock exchanges include the New York Stock Exchange, the London Stock Exchange, the Deutsche Börse, and the Paris/Amsterdam Euronext.

A stock market is an important way for a company to raise money. It allows businesses to be publicly traded, or to raise extra capital for expansion by selling shares in the company in a public market. Share owners then have a share of ownership of that company. A stock market provides liquidity to give investors the chance to sell securities rapidly and easily. This makes investing in stocks attractive compared with, for example, real estate, which is less liquid.

The price of shares and other assets plays an important part in the economic activity of a country. It can influence or reflect the social mood of a country. A stock market is often taken as a primary indicator of a country's economic well-being as it enables the efficient allocation of capital. Stock prices reflect where capital is being invested, or should be. If share prices are rising, this is usually coupled with increased business investment, and vice versa. Share prices also have an influence on the wealth of households, and thus on how much they spend. Central banks watch the movement of the stock market closely and also the smooth operation of financial system functions. This was highlighted in September 2008, when stock markets plunged in response to failing financial institutions—particularly in the United States—and central banks stepped in to try to arrest the slide.

Stock exchanges act as a clearing house for each transaction made on them. This means that they guarantee payment to the seller of the security and collect and deliver the shares. In this way there is no risk to a buyer or seller of a default on the transaction.

With these activities functioning smoothly, economic growth is enhanced because lower costs and enterprise risks help to promote the production of goods and services, and employment. As such, financial systems contribute to increased prosperity.

ADVANTAGES

- Trading in stock and shares can be done rapidly and easily, making them an attractive liquid investment.
- A rising stock market helps to boost prosperity in a country and promote a confident social mood.
- Stock markets allow anyone to participate in the growth of any listed company.

DISADVANTAGES

- Share prices can change very quickly in today's electronic markets, driven by trading by very large institutions.
- A falling stock market creates an unhappy mood in a country and can lead to difficult economic times and unemployment.
- Prices of stocks and shares can fall as well as rise.

ACTION CHECKLIST

- ✔ Check the history of a stock market. How long ago was it established? How stable is it? How does its average performance rate compared with other exchanges?
- ✔ Check the risks involved in a particular stock market. Is it easy to buy and sell on your chosen stock market? What fees are involved? How well is it regulated? Some countries regulate less well than others, increasing your risk.
- ✔ Check how easy it is to find current prices on your chosen stock market.

DOS AND DON'TS

DO

- Understand the volatility and risk of a stock market before investing.
- Understand the risks involved. Some emerging markets have higher growth potential, but much higher risks too.
- Keep an eye on the progress of the stocks and shares you have purchased.

DON'T

- Don't rush into stock market investments.
- Don't buy when the price is high.
- Don't sell when the price is low.

➤➤ MORE INFO

Books:

Becket, Michael. *How the Stock Market Works: A Beginner's Guide to Investment*. 2nd ed. London: Kogan Page, 2004.

Chapman, Colin. *How the Stock Markets Work*. 9th ed. London: Random House Business Books, 2006.

Gough, Leo. *How the Stock Market Really Works: The Guerilla Investor's Secret Handbook*. 4th ed. Harlow, UK: Pearson, 2008.

Websites:

Financial Times markets page: www.ft.com/markets
London Stock Exchange: www.londonstockexchange.com
New York Stock Exchange: www.nyse.com
Wall Street Journal: online.wsj.com

See Also:

✔ Trading in Equities on Stock Exchanges (p. 947)
How the Stock Market Works (p. 1274)

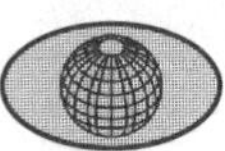

Understanding and Using Interest Coverage Ratios

DEFINITION

An interest coverage ratio is, simply, a measure of a company's ability to pay interest on its debt and is thus an indicator of its safety margin when deciding if the business is a good credit risk.

To calculate the interest coverage ratio, a company's operating income (also known as earnings before interest and taxes, or EBIT) is divided by its interest charges over a defined period, typically a quarter or half-year. Sometimes, EBITDA (where DA is depreciation and amortization) is used instead of EBIT in the calculation. The ratio shows how many times a company can cover its interest charges on a pre-tax basis. For example, a ratio of 5× would indicate that a company has the ability to cover its debt costs five times over. Paying the interest charges on the most senior debt increases the ratio as it reduces the amount of liabilities on that deal. The interest payments due also lessen as the debt is cleared.

The lower the ratio, the more a company is burdened by the cost of its debt. An interest coverage ratio of 2.5× is a warning sign of potential financial problems. A ratio of 1.5× or less should trigger serious concern about a company's overall financial health. When the ratio is less than 1×, it means the company is not earning enough revenues to pay its interest charges. It may then have to honor its debt obligations by borrowing further funds or using cash to hand. Failing to meet these obligations could force a company into bankruptcy.

Conversely, a high coverage ratio indicates that the company is financially secure enough to meet its interest payments on time. However, a high ratio may also be a sign that a company has an undesirable lack of debt or is paying off its debt too quickly, using earnings that might be better invested in projects that could yield better returns. Furthermore, it is sometimes cheaper for a company to borrow more funds at a lower cost of capital than it is currently paying for its existing debt to meet those obligations.

ADVANTAGES

- An interest coverage ratio is a very useful indicator of a company's general financial health and one that can be quickly calculated using the most up-to-date financial data available.

DISADVANTAGES

- The interest coverage ratio metric should never be used as the sole test of a company's financial soundness. Only if you have access to the current books can you know if there are otherwise unknown changes in a company's financial situation. Use other metrics in conjunction, such as the debt-to-equity ratio, to gain a fuller picture.

▸▸ MORE INFO

Books:

Duffie, Darrell, and Kenneth J. Singleton. *Credit Risk: Pricing, Measurement, and Management*. Princeton Series in Finance. Princeton, NJ: Princeton University Press, 2003.

Lando, David. *Credit Risk Modeling: Theory and Applications*. Princeton Series in Finance. Princeton, NJ: Princeton University Press, 2004.

van Deventer, Donald R., and Kenji Imai. *Credit Risk Models & the Basel Accords*. Wiley Finance Series. Singapore: Wiley, 2003.

  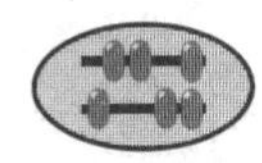   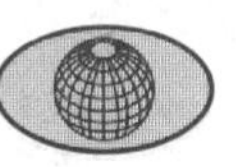   

Understanding and Using Leverage Ratios

DEFINITION

Leveraging is a way to use funds whereby most of the money is raised by borrowing rather than by stock issue (for a company) or use of capital (by an individual). At its most basic, leveraging means taking out a loan so that you can invest the money and hoping your investment makes more money than you will have to pay in interest on the loan.

The leverage ratio is used to calculate the financial leverage of a company. This information gives an insight into the company's financing methods, or it can be used to measure the company's ability to meet its financial obligations. There are a number of different ratios, but the main factors involved are debt, equity, assets, operating income, and interest expenses.

The most commonly used ratio is debt to equity (D/E, or financial leverage), which indicates how much the business relies on debt financing. In normal circumstances the typical D/E ratio is 2:1, with only one-third of the debt in the long term. A high D/E ratio might show up possible difficulty in paying interest and capital while obtaining extra funding. As an example, if a company has US$10 million of debt and US$20 million of equity, it has a D/E ratio of 0.5 (US$10 million/US$20 million).

Another leveraging ratio can be used to measure the operating cost mix. This helps to understand how any change in output may affect operating income. There are two types of operating costs: fixed and variable. The mix of these will differ depending on the company and the industry. A high operating leverage can lead to forecasting risk. For example, a tiny error made in a sales forecast could trigger far bigger errors when it comes to projecting cash flows based on those sales.

There is also interest coverage, which measures a company's margin of safety and indicates how many times the company can make its interest payments. This figure is calculated by dividing earnings prior to interest and taxes by the interest expense.

ADVANTAGES

Leveraging means borrowing money to invest. Anyone who takes out a mortgage is effectively leveraging. By paying a deposit to obtain a loan, you can buy a home that otherwise you would not be able to afford. Although property prices can and do fall periodically, over the long term property usually increases in value. If it does, you can sell the property and make a profit on your original mortgage loan.

Leveraging enables an individual or a company to gain access to larger capital sums to make investments, with the aim of making a profit by doing so.

Strategies in leveraging run from basic to highly sophisticated, and the degree of risk varies in the same way. The benefits of leveraging will depend on your financial situation, your objectives, and your attitude to risk.

DISADVANTAGES

Anything that has the potential to make money involves some risk. Gains can be better than normal; losses can be worse. A change in interest rates can have an effect on your profit too. There is a risk that your investment will not make enough profit to pay off the interest on your loan.

You can mitigate the risks by diversifying your portfolio, thereby guarding against high losses, although this will probably limit opportunities to make spectacular gains. A fixed-rate loan can protect against a rise in interest rates.

ACTION CHECKLIST

- ✔ Are you comfortable borrowing money that you might struggle to pay back?
- ✔ Are you comfortable with high risk in your finances?
- ✔ Are you confident that interest rates will not rise to add further risk to your borrowings?
- ✔ Are you confident your investment will make more than the interest you have to pay back on your loan?

DOS AND DON'TS

DO

- Look at leveraging as a way of using other people's money (by way of a loan) to make your own investments.
- Understand how your loan works and what and when you will have to pay back.
- As much research as you can. And then more research.

DON'T

- Don't get involved with leveraging if you are uncomfortable with financial risk.
- Don't choose an investment without a full understanding of what you are investing in.

▸▸ MORE INFO

Books:

Marr, Bernard. *Strategic Performance Management: Leveraging and Measuring Your Intangible Value Drivers*. Oxford: Butterworth-Heinemann 2006.

Matthäus-Maier, Ingrid, and J. D. von Pischke (eds). *Microfinance Investment Funds: Leveraging Private Capital for Economic Growth and Poverty Reduction*. Berlin: Springer-Verlag, 2006.

Militello, Frederick C., and Michael D. Schwalberg. *Leverage Competencies: What Financial Executives Need to Lead*. Upper Saddle River, NJ: FT Prentice Hall, 2002.

     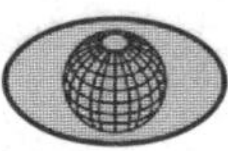   

Understanding Capital Markets, Structure and Function

DEFINITION

Capital markets provide a wide range of products and services that are related to financial investments. Capital markets include the stock market, commodities exchanges, the bond market, and just about any physical or virtual service or intermediary where debt and equity securities can be bought or sold. Their primary purpose is to raise funds and channel investors' money to areas where there is a deficit or need for investment. They play a vital role as intermediaries between governments and companies, which use them to finance a myriad of activities.

The capital markets can be broken down into the primary market, where new stocks and bonds are issued to investors, and the secondary market, where existing stocks and bonds are traded.

In the primary market, governments, companies, or public sector organizations can obtain funding through the sale of a new stock or bonds. These are normally issued through securities dealers and banks, which underwrite the offered stocks or bonds. The issuers earn a commission, which is built into the price of the security offering.

In the secondary market, stocks and shares in publicly traded companies are bought and sold through one of the major stock exchanges, which serve as managed auctions for stock. A stock exchange, share market, or bourse is a company, corporation, or mutual organization that provides facilities for stockbrokers and traders to trade stocks and other securities. Stock exchanges also provide facilities for the issue and redemption of securities, trading in other financial instruments, and the payment of income and dividends.

ADVANTAGES

- Capital markets provide the lubricant between investors and those needing to raise capital.
- Capital markets create price transparency and liquidity. They provide a safe platform for a wide range of investors—including commercial and investment banks, insurance companies, pension funds, mutual funds, and retail investors—to hedge and speculate.
- Holding different shares or bonds allows an investor to spread investment risk.
- The secondary market gives important pricing information that permits efficient use of limited capital.

DISADVANTAGES

- In capital markets, bond prices are influenced by economic data such as employment, income growth/decline, consumer prices, and industrial prices. Any information that implies rising inflation will weaken bond prices, as inflation reduces the income from a bond.
- Prices for shares in capital markets can be very volatile. Their value depends on a number of external factors over which the investor has no control.
- Different shares can have different levels of liquidity, i.e. demand from buyers and sellers.

ACTION CHECKLIST

✔ When placing a buy or sell order, there are two ways you can trade. Shares can be traded at *market order*, which means buying at the prevailing market price. The alternative is the *limit order*, in which you set the minimum or maximum price.

✔ What are interest rates going to do? Investors who buy and sell bonds before maturity are exposed to many risks, most importantly changes in interest rates. When interest rates increase, new issues will pay a higher yield and the value of existing bonds will fall. When interest rates decline, the value of existing bonds will rise as new issues pay a lower yield.

DOS AND DON'TS

DO

- Before you buy, check how quickly you will be able to sell if necessary, and at what discount and dealing fee.

DON'T

- Don't, unless you are completely confident, invest in only one type of bond or security. An exchange-traded fund or an index fund might be a much safer bet.

▸▸ MORE INFO

Books:

Fabozzi, F. J., F. Modigliani, and F. J. Jones. *Capital Markets: Institutions and Instruments*. Upper Saddle River, NJ: Prentice Hall, 2002.

Maginn, J. L., Donald L. Tuttle, Dennis W. McLeavey and Jerald E. Pinto (eds).*Managing Investment Portfolios: A Dynamic Process*. 3rd ed. Hoboken, NJ: Wiley, 2007.

McInish, T. H. *Capital Markets: A Global Perspective*. Malden, MA: Blackwell Publishing, 2000.

Articles:

Mehta, N. "TradeWeb eyes equity expansion in 2008." *Traders Magazine* (December 2007). Online at: www.tradersmagazine.com/issues/20_275/100087-1.html

Rodier, M. "The massive growth of electronic bond trading." *Wall Street Technology* (April 15, 2008). Online at: www.wallstreetandtech.com/electronic-trading/showArticle.jhtml?articleID=207200781

Websites:

FTSE Global Bond Index: markets.ft.com/markets/overview.asp

Interactive Investor: www.iii.co.uk/sharedealing

"**Courtesy is the ornament of a noble man.**" Bhartrihari

  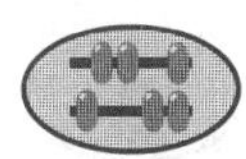   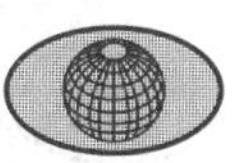   

Understanding Debt Cover

DEFINITION

Debt cover is defined as the ratio of a company's total assets to its debt. It helps to assess the amount of cash flow available to meet annual interest and principal payments on a debt, including sinking fund payments. Should a company be wound up, the ratio would indicate by how much the shareholders' redemption value and prior charges and any future capital charges would be covered by the assets. This useful metric indicates how easily a company can meet its interest and principal payments from its revenues.

Debt cover is calculated by dividing a company's operating income (either EBIT or EBITDA) by the debt expenses, i.e. the interest charges. Banks typically use debt cover as an indicator for determining economic risk when making loans. Typically, a bank looks for a ratio of between 1.15× and 1.35× (net operating income divided by annual debt service) to be satisfied that there is sufficient cash flow available on an ongoing basis to repay the loan instalments.

However, the debt cover may sometimes be less than 1× for a loan. This does not necessarily mean that the company is at risk of default, although it is certainly an indicator of potential financial problems ahead as it means there is, at the time of calculation, a negative cash flow. For example, a ratio of 0.9× indicates that there is only enough net operating income to cover 90% of annual debt payments, and the company would therefore have to repay borrowings using cash or by taking out a further loan. Usually banks are unlikely to lend where there is negative cash flow, but they may decide to take the risk if the company can clearly demonstrate that this is a temporary blip.

Over a period of time the debt cover should improve as a company pays down its debts and, generally speaking, as with other metrics that measure credit risk, the higher the ratio the better as it means a lower risk of capital loss.

ADVANTAGES

Debt cover is a useful measure of financial strength. It can indicate not only what the debt cover was at a particular point in time, but also how much it has changed since it was last evaluated. It is thus a way of assessing a company's financial quality and associated risk levels.

DISADVANTAGES

Debt cover should never be used as the sole metric test of a company's financial soundness. Only if you have access to the current books can you know if there are otherwise unknown changes in a company's financial situation. Use other metrics in conjunction, such as the interest coverage ratio, to gain a fuller picture.

▸▸ MORE INFO

Books:

Duffie, Darrell, and Kenneth J. Singleton. *Credit Risk: Pricing, Measurement, and Management*. Princeton Series in Finance. Princeton, NJ: Princeton University Press, 2003.

Lando, David. *Credit Risk Modeling: Theory and Applications*. Princeton Series in Finance. Princeton, NJ: Princeton University Press, 2004.

van Deventer, Donald R., and Kenji Imai. *Credit Risk Models & the Basel Accords*. Wiley Finance Series. Singapore: Wiley, 2003.

"There may be said to be two classes of people in the world: Those who constantly divide the people of the world into two classes and those who do not." Robert Benchley

  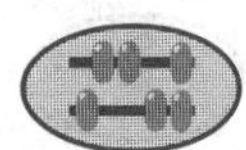 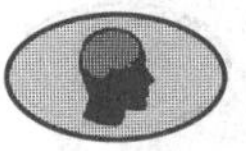  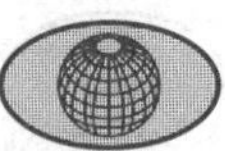   

Understanding Fixed-Charge Coverage

DEFINITION

Fixed-charge coverage is a financial ratio that is used to gauge the quality of a bond issue or the ability of a project to meet its debt repayments. It is calculated by dividing total fixed charges into the net income (or earnings before interest and tax) available for these charges. The fixed charges are gross interest, contractual payments under operating leases, and preference dividends.

Thus, a fixed-charge coverage ratio would look like this:

$$\text{Fixed-charge coverage} = \text{EBIT} + \frac{\text{Fixed charge}}{\text{Fixed charge + interest}}$$

where EBIT is earnings before interest and tax, and the fixed charge is before tax.

Generally, the greatest fixed charge a company is likely to face is the interest on its debt. However, the fixed-charge coverage ratio assumes particular importance if the company you are evaluating spends heavily on leases, such as leases on buildings and equipment. A lease payment is effectively the same thing as a debt payment, and it should be taken just as seriously. The lower a company's net income, the greater the negative impact of the lease payments on the ratio.

Overall, the lower the ratio, the worse is the financial position of the company. Bond issues can contain covenants that set limits on how low the fixed-charge coverage ratio can fall. Such a covenant is designed to provide the lender with protection, so that the borrower's financial position will remain more or less the same as it was when the loan was made. Thus, a bond may contain a covenant that prevents the fixed-charge coverage ratio from falling below 2.

ADVANTAGES

- The fixed-charge coverage ratio is readily identifiable.
- It provides a straightforward measure of the financial health of a company.

DISADVANTAGES

- There is no standardized procedure for determining either fixed charges or the net income available for these charges.
- Other ratios may provide a better indicator of a company's financial health.

ACTION CHECKLIST

- ✔ Identify the fixed-charge coverage ratio from the company's accounts.
- ✔ If it is less than 1, speak to the company's managers immediately to ascertain how they plan to meet their fixed-cost obligations.

DOS AND DON'TS

DO

- Remember that if a company has a fixed-charge coverage of less than 1, it cannot meet its fixed obligations through earnings and thus must rely on other funds, such as extra borrowings or drawing down working capital.
- Remember that this ratio often comes into play if you have a working-capital loan; the lender will insist that a specific fixed-charge coverage ratio is maintained or your loan will be recalled.
- Remember to try to gauge the attitudes of managers toward taking on more debt as the existing debt matures.

DON'T

- Don't just rely on the fixed-charge coverage ratio. Other ratios that can be used to measure a company's ability to meet its debt obligations include the interest coverage ratio and the debt service coverage ratio.
- Don't ignore the proforma coverage ratio. It has essentially the same components as the fixed-charge coverage ratio but is forward looking. It can tell you whether this year's earnings (if repeated) would be able to cover what must be paid in the coming year.

►► MORE INFO

Books:

Geddes, Ross. *Valuation and Investment Appraisal*. London: Financial World Publishing, 2002.

Holmes, Geoffrey, Alan Sugden, and Paul Gee. *Interpreting Company Reports and Accounts*. 10th ed. Harlow, UK: FT Prentice Hall, 2008.

The Ultimate Small Business Guide: A Resource for Startups and Growing Businesses. New York: Basic Books, 2004.

Articles:

Beattie, Vivien. "Logistics, inventory control, and supply chain management." *Journal of Business Finance and Accounting* 33:9.

Goodacre, Alan. "Operating lease finance in the UK retail sector." *The International Review of Retail, Distribution and Consumer Research* 13:1 (2003): 99–125.

Website:

American Bankruptcy Institute: www.abiworld.org/AM/Template.cfm?Section=Home

"Every man is as Heaven made him, and sometimes a great deal worse." Miguel de Cervantes

     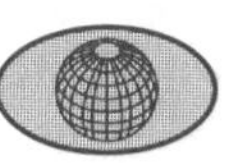   

Using Mezzanine Financing

DEFINITION

Mezzanine financing can be an ideal solution for firms looking for a quick injection of capital to grow their already successful business without giving up an interest in that business.

Mezzanine financing presents a way for publicly and privately held companies to obtain financing without ownership of the company being given up. It is a mixture of traditional debt financing and equity financing that offers the benefits of both. Mezzanine financing, like equity financing, is an unsecured debt that requires no collateral, unlike a traditional bank loan. Like debt financing, mezzanine financing is very flexible and does not necessarily involve giving up an interest in the company. Likely sources of mezzanine financing are private investors, insurance companies, mutual funds, pension funds, and banks.

Because mezzanine financing is normally provided very quickly, with little due diligence by the lender and with little or no collateral required from the borrower, this type of financing tends to be expensive, with the lender seeking a return of between 20% and 30%. Mezzanine financing also has the advantage that it is treated like equity on a company's balance sheet, which may make it easier to obtain standard bank financing.

To attract mezzanine financing, a company usually must demonstrate:

- A track record in the industry, with an established reputation and product.
- A history of profitability, or at least of breaking even.
- A viable expansion plan for the business through acquisition, broader penetration of the market, etc.
- Solid management and operations planning.
- An established business plan.

In leveraged buyouts, mezzanine capital is often used in conjunction with other securities to fund the purchase price of the company that is being acquired. Typically, mezzanine capital will be used to fill a financing gap between less expensive forms of financing (senior loans, second-lien loans, high-yield financing) and equity.

Due to the lack of valid collateral, as well as the high speed of lending, mezzanine financing is typically more difficult to obtain than a traditional bank loan or equity financing. However, the benefits are that mezzanine financiers do not normally interfere in company management and, except in the case of a default, they do not want an interest in the company. Whereas traditional equity investors may attempt to gain some level of company control, mezzanine financiers will do what they can to ensure that the debt is paid off without resorting to default.

ADVANTAGES

- Mezzanine financing often offers more flexible financing options, such as coupons and covenants that take into account the business's cash flow.
- Mezzanine financing provides business owners with the funds they may need to buy another business or to expand.
- Little or no due diligence and collateral.
- Generally no loss of ownership control.

DISADVANTAGES

- Mezzanine financing is normally aggressively priced, with lenders seeking returns of between 20% and 30%.
- Financiers can include restrictive covenants that the borrower has to endure. These can include agreements by the lender not to borrow more money or refinance senior debt from traditional loans.
- Financiers might want to have a vote on the board of directors.
- Many financial experts believe that this type of financing has aggravated the recent credit crunch.

ACTION CHECKLIST

- ✔ What other avenues of financing are available that would not load the company with so much debt?
- ✔ In return for the loan, does the company have to cede some independence to the lender?
- ✔ Does the loan restrict the company to spending money in certain areas?
- ✔ Does your company have a strong market position based on its products/technology and a market share that will allow it to repay the loan?
- ✔ Does your company have a focused business strategy and positive long-term development prospects?
- ✔ Do you have positive, stable cash flows that can be forecasted reliably?

DOS AND DON'TS

DO

- Check that the possibilities for funding from other resources have been exhausted or are insufficient.

DON'T

- Don't use mezzanine financing if there are serious underlying business problems that need to be addressed.

➤➤ MORE INFO

Books:

Fabozzi, Frank J. (ed). *The Handbook of Financial Instruments*. Hoboken, NJ: Wiley, 2002.

Longenecker, Justin G., Carlos W. Moore, J. William Petty, and Leslie E. Palich. *Small Business Management: An Entrepreneurial Emphasis*. 13th ed. Mason, OH: Thomson-Southwestern Publishing, 2005.

Vance, David E. *Raising Capital*. New York: Springer Science+Business Media, 2005.

Articles:

Chang, Ellen. "Mezzanine capital." *Oil & Gas Investor* (March 2008).

"Mezzanine." *Investors Chronicle* (December 2003).

Websites:

Bank of America—TriSail mezzanine finance: corp.bankofamerica.com/public/public.portal?_pd_page_label=trisail/index

Wells Fargo mezzanine capital: www.wellsfargo.com/com/bus_finance/mezzanine_cap

Balancing Hedging Objectives with Accounting Rules (FAS 133)

DEFINITION

FAS 133 was published in 1998 and introduced in 2001 to establish accounting and reporting standards for stand-alone derivatives and those embedded in other contracts. The aim was to provide greater transparency by requiring companies to record derivative contracts as assets or liabilities on their balance sheets.

Gains and losses on derivatives can be deferred until they mature, but only if the company proves that they are being used to manage risk rather than for market speculation. Companies have to provide evidence that the timing and the amount of the derivative matches the commodity against which it is being hedged.

The reporting requirements are extremely onerous. Hedges have to be documented before or as soon as they are implemented, and companies have to explain why the transaction is being undertaken. Every three months derivatives have to be marked to market to prove that the underlying exposure is being hedged effectively.

Although FAS 133 offers detailed direction on how derivatives can qualify for hedge accounting, critics say that the rules manage to be both overly complex and vague. Indeed, the FASB is in the process of trying to simplify the standard.

Currently, three categories of hedge are allowed by the standard:

- fair-value hedges for recognized assets;
- cash flow hedges for recognized assets or forecast transactions;
- hedges for foreign currency exposure.

If a hedge is "highly effective," it will not affect reported earnings. According to the standard, a hedge is defined as "highly effective" if changes in the fair value or cash flow of the hedged item and the hedging derivative offset each other to a significant extent.

At the moment the rules are complex, and because of the quarterly reporting requirement some derivatives will fail to meet the "highly effective" definition throughout their lifespan.

A number of companies have also had to restate their accounts because of their failure to satisfy the complex reporting documentation required by FAS 133. Hotel and casino operator Wynn had to restate its earnings for 2003, 2004, and part of 2005. Sunglasses manufacturer Oakley had to restate its reports for five years up to 2005. And at the beginning of 2007 General Electric said its restatement would reduce earnings by a total of $343 million. Earnings were to be cut for 2001 and 2002, and increased for 2003, 2004, and 2005.

ADVANTAGES

- FAS 133 introduced more transparent accounting standards following substantial hedging losses in the mid-1990s arising from the use of derivatives.

DISADVANTAGES

- FAS 133 is one of the most complex accounting standards ever introduced, running to over 200 pages. This has led to some major companies being forced to restate their earnings over a number of years.
- Initially there was concern that the non-applicability of hedge accounting in some circumstances could lead to unnecessary volatility in corporate earnings. This now seems to be less of a concern as companies have come to grips with the measures.

▸▸ MORE INFO

Book:

Green, James F., and the Accounting Research Manager Group. *2007 CCH Accounting for Derivatives And Hedging*. Chicago, IL: CCH, 2006.

Websites:

The Financial Accounting Standards Board official website: www.fasb.org

iTreasurer.com focus on FAS 133: www.fas133.com

See Also:

★ Fair Value Accounting: SFAS 157 and IAS 39 (pp. 635–637)
★ To Hedge or Not to Hedge (pp. 100–102)
✔ Key Accounting Standards and Organizations (p. 1038)
✔ The Ten Accounting Principles (p. 1050)
✔ Understanding Hedge Ratios (p. 892)

"Strategy, policies and standards are set globally...but you still need local engagement skills." Raoul Pinnell

  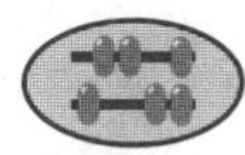   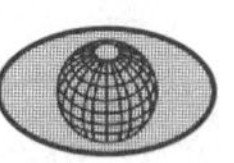   

The Chief Audit Executive's (CAE) Roles and Responsibilities

DEFINITION

The CAE has an in-depth knowledge of the business and is concerned principally with its systems for internal control and efficiency of operations, the reliability of its financial reporting, and its observance of relevant laws and regulations.

Corporate accounting scandals and the resultant outcry for transparency and honesty in reporting have led to a progressively more important role for the CAE. A CAE has two important and sometimes conflicting functions within an organization. The first is to examine and evaluate the organization's systems of internal control, as part of the requirement for stricter corporate governance. The second is to be cognizant with the risks, goals, policies, and processes of the organization fully while maintaining autonomy from management direction and control.

The CAE normally reports directly to the management and audit committee and is responsible for producing an annual assessment of the effectiveness of the organization's risk management and processes for control and governance, as set out by the board or management. Risk management deals with the way an organization sets goals, then recognizes, interprets, and reacts to risks that could affect its ability to realize those goals. Processes for control and governance deal with the effectiveness and efficiency of operations, the reliability of financial reports and conformity with appropriate rules and laws.

ADVANTAGES

- CAEs improve business organization and risk management by providing reassurance on the effectiveness and efficiency of operations, the reliability of financial reporting, and compliance with applicable laws and regulations.
- CAEs provide management with an in-depth and unbiased understanding of the risks that the organization may be facing, allowing for pre-emptive planning.
- CAEs give company officers and directors forewarning of ethical and legal issues that the organization may be facing.

DISADVANTAGES

- Although CAEs are meant to be independent and impartial, they are paid by the company and are an integral part of the company's management. This can lead to conflicts of interest.
- CAEs' judgments, estimates, and interpretations are not always objective because of their close relationships with the organizations for which they work.
- A CAE's relationship with the management of a company is generally informal and the CAE's position does not carry the power to change processes.
- Although there are international bodies such as the Institute of Internal Auditors (IIA), CAEs as a profession are unregulated.

ACTION CHECKLIST

- ✔ Has the CAE previously worked in related business fields? If so, for how long and what did they achieve?
- ✔ How good is the CAE's track record on risk assessment and planning for contingencies?
- ✔ In assessing business processes, how up-to-date is the CAE with information audit technology controls?
- ✔ To which internationally recognized standards-setting body, such as the IIA, does the CAE belong?

DOS AND DON'TS

DO

- Allow CAEs unrestricted access to information, to enable them to evaluate risks, management activities and personnel better.
- Take into account that CAEs are not responsible for carrying out company activities; their role is solely advisery.
- Consult with the CAE if there are any implications where ethical or legal issues may be involved.

DON'T

- Don't involve CAEs in decisions that might compromise their autonomy as independent internal auditors.

⏩ MORE INFO

Websites:

Institute of Internal Auditors: www.theiia.org

Knowledge Leader: www.knowledgeleader.com

"I am a risk taker but only within rules. I just like the support that an organisation gives, combined with the freedom to express myself." Guy Hands

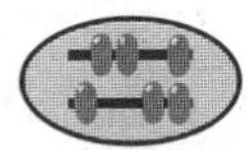

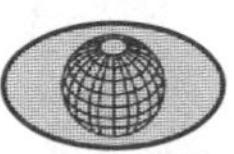

Establishing a Framework for Assessing Risk

DEFINITION

Instituting a framework for identifying risks (or opportunities), assessing their probability and impact, and determining which controls should be in place can be critical to achieving the company's business objectives. Identifying and proactively addressing risks and opportunities helps businesses to defend themselves. Debt rating agencies and regulators are also increasingly stipulating that companies institute risk-identifying frameworks.

Enterprise Risk Management (ERM) is a name given to the structures, methods, and procedures used by organizations to identify and combat risk. The setting up and monitoring of ERM is typically performed by management as part of its internal control activities, such as appraisals of analytical reports or management committee meetings with relevant experts to make sure that the risk-response strategy is working and that the objectives are being achieved.

Once the risks have been identified and assessed, management chooses a risk-response approach. This may include:

- Avoidance: Leave risky activities.
- Reduction: Lessen their probability or impact.
- Share or insure: Diminish risk by transferring or sharing.
- Accept: In response to a cost/benefits analysis, take no action.

The most widely used ERM frameworks are COSO (from an organization that prepares audit-related reports) and RIMS (The Risk and Insurance Management Society). Both use methods for identifying, analyzing, responding to, and scrutinizing risks or opportunities within the internal and external settings of the business.

ADVANTAGES

- ERM allows an enterprise to identify and prioritize the risks that might be facing the organization.
- An improved understanding of the risks—both systemic and non-systemic—facing businesses can help in contingency planning for when the unexpected happens.
- Robust identification of risks can protect businesses from events that might otherwise threaten the viability of the entity.

DISADVANTAGES

- Protracted risk-framework evaluation could be counterproductive if the fruitless pursuit of perfection leaves the company exposed to the very risks it hoped to avoid.
- Evaluating risks depends on judgments, estimates, and interpretation. Risks are often intangible issues that might be highly relevant but cannot be easily measured.

ACTION CHECKLIST

- ✔ Overcome resistance to the introduction or upgrading of risk frameworks by ensuring that the board and managers are conscious of the fact that it is in everyone's interest to be aware of business risks.
- ✔ Encourage an open environment when establishing a risk framework. Some risks are obvious, but stakeholders or managers of individual business sectors may sometimes know more about hidden risks.
- ✔ Engage key business stakeholders and managers in the evaluation of risks and when seeking the best resolutions for those risks.

DOS AND DON'TS

DO

- Regularly update risk-assessment frameworks, as these can help to keep management informed of the constantly changing business environment and its risks.
- Spell out in clear terms the risks that the organization may be facing, their probability, and their potential impact.

DON'T

- Don't take risks for granted; just because a risk has been the same in the past, there is no guarantee that it will be the same in the future. Only by fully understanding the risks and updating risk frameworks can you counteract the dangers.
- Don't get bogged down by risk frameworks. Risk is sometimes a natural and acceptable part of doing business.

▸▸ MORE INFO

Websites:

American Accounting Association: www.aaa-edu.org

The Society of Actuaries: www.soa.org

"Control and learning are deeply embedded in the specific cultural and institutional ethos of an organization."
Yanni Yan

  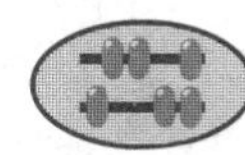   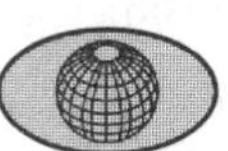   

The EU Regulatory Regime

DEFINITION

Within the EU, the approach to regulation of the markets is twofold. Member states each have their own regulatory body at national level, the role and purpose of which is to set policy, enforce applicable laws, license providers of financial services, work to prevent financial crime, and maintain confidence in the financial system. The more well-known regulatory bodies include the Financial Services Authority (United Kingdom), Autorité des Marchés Financiers (AMF) (France), Bundesanstalt für Finanzdienstleistungsaufsicht (BaFin) (Germany) and the Netherlands Authority for the Financial Markets.

There is no supranational regulatory body for the whole of the EU. Instead, markets around the EU are managed through the imposition of Directives, with which member states must comply. The European Commission launched its Financial Services Action Plan (FSAP) in 1999, which was the cornerstone of the EU's aim to create a single market for financial services, and was intended to last for six years. The FSAP consisted of 42 articles aimed at harmonizing financial services markets within the EU. The most important Directive that emerged from this action plan is the Markets in Financial Instruments Directive (MiFID), which came into effect in 2007.

During the development of the FSAP, in 2001 the EU adopted what became known as the Lamfalussy process, named after Alexandre Lamfalussy, chair of the EU advisery committee that created it. The Lamfalussy process concentrates solely on the development of financial services industry regulations for EU member states, and it has four levels, each focusing on a specific stage of the implementation of legislation.

At level one, the European Parliament and the Council of the European Union work to draft a piece of legislation, establish the core values of this law, and develop guidelines for its implementation. At level two, sector-specific committees and regulators advise on technical details for the law, which is then voted on by member state representatives. At level three, national regulators work on coordinating the new regulations with other member states. Because of the diversity of member states, laws and Directives need to be flexible as to how they are adopted in each nation, while making use of the so-called passport approach (see "Solvency II: Its Development and Aims," p. 1048) that ensures harmonization. Level four consists of compliance with, and enforcement of, the new rules and laws.

The adoption of MiFID has to date been the most significant piece of legislation introduced under the Lamfalussy process, which is intended to offer a number of benefits over the traditional legislative process, such as engendering a more consistent approach to interpretation, convergence of national supervisory practices, and an improved quality of financial services legislation.

Besides MiFID, there are three other Lamfalussy Directives—the Prospectus Directive, the Market Abuse Directive, and the Transparency Directive.

The Prospectus Directive requires anybody offering shares to the public in the EU to issue a prospectus that complies with the detailed rules issued by EU countries under the Directive. A key plank of the Prospectus Directive allows companies to issue a prospectus in one EU country that would cover subsequent offers of securities to the public or admission to trading throughout Europe, with minimal translation obligations.

The Market Abuse Directive introduces a common approach for preventing and detecting market abuse, and ensuring a proper flow of information to the market. New measures include the following requirements:

- issuers to keep "insider lists" of persons who have access to inside information;
- trading firms to disclose: information on deals where involved staff have any personal interest in an issuer's shares and any related derivatives; their research sources and methods, and any conflicts of interest that may impact on the impartiality of the research;
- reporting of any suspicious transactions.

The Transparency Directive is designed to enhance transparency on EU capital markets, by establishing mechanisms and minimum requirements for periodic financial reporting and on the disclosure of major stockholdings for issuers whose securities are traded on any regulated market in the EU. It also establishes disclosure requirements on an ongoing basis about issuers who trade securities on a regulated market situated, or operated within, the EU, for investors who invest in these securities.

▸▸ MORE INFO

Book:

Katz, Etay. *Financial Services Regulation in Europe*. 2nd ed. Oxford: Oxford University Press, 2008.

"Men's natures are alike; it is their habits that carry them apart." Confucius

  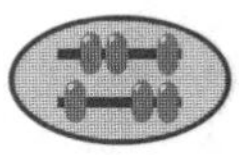   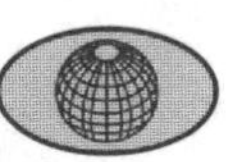   

International Financial Reporting Standards (IFRS): The Basics

DEFINITION

The increasing pace of globalization over recent years has forced the pace for the adoption of truly comparable and consistent international accounting standards. A decade ago, national versions of Generally Accepted Accounting Principles (GAAP) were commonplace. Nowadays, IFRS has gained broad acceptance and is used in over 100 countries. The United States is moving towards the convergence of US GAAP and IFRS, with the present timetable indicating that the set of standards will be applied to large public companies in 2014, though some should have the option to make the move even earlier. Since early 2008, IFRS has been allowed in the United States without reconciliation for foreign private issuers. The Securities and Exchange Commission's (SEC's) roadmap suggests that the decision over the future adoption of IFRS should be made in 2011, though the SEC has suggested that this timescale may be subject to delays.

Presently, the widespread use of US GAAP rather than IFRS can create difficulties for financial analysts, given the challenges in making financial comparisons. However, the timelines for change are far from clear. A joint initiative by the Financial Accounting Standards Board (FASB) and the International Accounting Standards Board (IASB) is aiming to converge existing standards into a single set of standards. In contrast, IFRS has been a requirement in Europe for listed companies since 2005.

In light of the increasingly international trend of IFRS, some emerging economies have been quick to adopt IFRS as their national version of GAAP.

First adopted in 2001, IFRS includes many of the International Accounting Standards (IAS) previously set by the IASB with the objective of improving the level of transparency of companies' finances. IFRS also generally includes the International Financial Reporting Interpretations Committee (IFRIC) interpretation and that of its predecessor, Standing Interpretations Committee (SIC), prior to March 2002. While the impact of the adoption of the IFRS on company accounts varies between countries, the set of standards imposes very strict disclosure requirements on companies. Intended to improve the visibility of companies' liabilities, IFRS requires the full disclosure of pension-related obligations, while executive remuneration visibility is also tackled, with IFRS dictating that stock options granted to executives must be included in the accounts. IFRS also has implications for the way companies account for their fixed assets, setting requirements over the fair value of assets. The impact of the adoption of IFRS can also have significance in areas such as merger and acquisition strategy, the provision of bank covenants, and distributions.

ADVANTAGES

- IFRS improves the level of comparability between the accounts of companies across different countries.
- The stringent disclosure requirements improve the visibility of liabilities such as future pension costs and employee stock schemes.
- The adoption of IFRS can provide greater reassurance for investors, credit rating agencies and lenders, potentially giving companies access to lower-cost capital in line with the lower risk.

DISADVANTAGES

- The adoption of IFRS can bring significant additional short-term costs to businesses, such as fees to pay specialist external accountants.
- As adjustments to comply with IFRS can make year-on-year performance comparisons difficult for investment analysts, potentially creating uncertainty and stock price volatility, companies must also devote resources to the preparation of accounts using the legacy conventions.

ACTION CHECKLIST

✔ Consider the benefits of introducing IFRS to management reporting, bringing improved quality and consistency to internal company information on which key decisions are based.

✔ Multinationals should examine the benefits of adopting IFRS throughout their organization to improve international comparability.

✔ Companies should be prepared to utilize external expertise to help with the transition to IFRS conventions.

DOS AND DON'TS

DO

- Companies adopting IFRS should budget for higher short-term costs.
- Aim to embed the principles of IFRS throughout all levels of an organization to extract maximum benefit.
- Explore the potential benefits in using XBRL (Extensible Business Reporting Language) in financial reporting.

DON'T

- Don't see IFRS as a "threat;" it can bring long-term material benefits, such as higher investor confidence and lower-cost capital.
- Don't ignore IFRS until you are obliged to adopt it by regulators. An understanding of IFRS can help companies to prepare for its adoption, and can offer firms the flexibility to adopt IFRS at a time that works to their advantage.

▸▸ MORE INFO

Articles:

Daske, Holger. "Economic benefits of adopting IFRS or US-GAAP—Have the expected cost of equity capital really decreased?" *Journal of Business Finance & Accounting* 33:3–4 (April/May 2006): 329–373.

Hail, Luzi, Holger Daske, Christian Leuz, and Rodrigo Verdi. "Mandatory IFRS reporting around the world: Early evidence on the economic consequences." *Journal of Accounting Research* 46:5 (December 2008): 1085–1142.

Websites:

The American Institute of Certified Public Accountants' IFRS website: www.ifrs.com

Details regarding Ernst & Young's *International GAAP* 2009 update: www.ey.com/global/content.nsf/International/Assurance_-_IFRS_-_Overview

Details regarding PricewaterhouseCoopers's *IFRS Manual of Accounting*: www.pwc.co.uk/eng/publications/ifrs_manual_of_accounting.html

International Accounting Standards Board: www.iasb.org

"Companies that stay ahead of change are ones in which their people see change as something they themselves accomplish and not something that is imposed on them. They see lots of opportunities to take initiative." Rosabeth Moss Kanter

  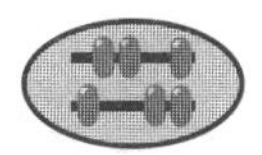   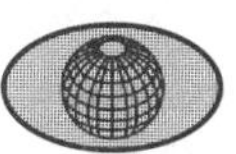   

The IIA Code of Ethics

DEFINITION

Established in 1941, the Institute of Internal Auditors aims to provide global leadership for the profession. Based in Florida, the Institute is the internal auditing industry's recognized authority across the world and is keen to promote the profession through improved education. The Institute's membership base covers 165 countries, with members spread across professions such as risk management, corporate governance, information-technology auditing and education, as well as mainstream internal auditing.

The objective of the Institute's code of ethics is to create an ethical culture throughout the profession. The Institute's members aim to help organizations to achieve their objectives through disciplined and highly systematic efforts to strengthen their governance, control, and risk-management procedures. The code of ethics not only covers the core activity of internal auditing but also extends to cover principles relevant to the profession, as well as the rules of conduct to which practitioners should adhere.

ADVANTAGES

- The code of ethics helps to ensure the objectivity of internal auditors, aiming to assist them to assess all relevant factors without being unduly influenced by others or by their own interests.
- By defining the standards expected of internal auditing professionals, the code helps to reinforce the trust that forms the main foundation of the profession. The code also aims to ensure that individual internal auditors have the required competencies to cover the particular task they are expected to perform.
- The confidentiality element of the code aims to make certain that internal auditors always appreciate the value of information. It underlines their requirement to safeguard information at all times, subject only to legal or professional obligations.
- The Institute has disciplinary procedures in place for instances where members are accused of violating the code of ethics, helping to ensure that members can be trusted to act in a consistently professional manner.

DISADVANTAGES

- Ethical standards in business can vary widely from country to country. Therefore, auditing professionals in some countries may have to work harder than those in other countries to fully achieve all the standards expected of a global code of ethics.
- Cultural differences between companies could also put more pressure on internal auditors in some organizations to adhere to the consistently high standards demanded by the code.

ACTION CHECKLIST

✔ In joining the Institute, professionals commit to the highest standards of integrity and professionalism, offering a high level of reassurance to clients.

✔ By encouraging employees to become members, companies help their internal auditors in areas such as self-development, potentially significantly increasing their long-term value to the organization.

✔ The Institute unites over 150,000 internal auditing professionals worldwide. Membership brings access to valuable resources, such as a dedicated resource library, a technical helpline and the latest published professional guidance. Access to these resources can bring significant benefits to an organization.

DOS AND DON'TS

DO

- Recognize that internal auditing is a progressive profession, the development of which is driven by clients' increasingly demanding needs.
- Take advantage of the Institute's commitment to help internal auditors to achieve their full potential through training and development. For example, the Institute offers a wide range of in-house, company-specific courses.

DON'T

- Don't interpret the code of ethics as simply a list of aspirations for internal auditors. The Institute demands the highest standards of professionalism from its members.
- Don't forget that, despite the best efforts of the Institute to ensure uniformity of standards across the profession worldwide, some individuals may benefit from extra employer support in view of the variations in business ethical standards across different countries and cultures.

▸▸ MORE INFO

Books:

Pickett, K. H. Spencer. *The Internal Auditor at Work: A Practical Guide to Everyday Challenges*. Hoboken, NJ: Wiley, 2004.

Root, Stephen J. *Beyond COSO: Internal Control to Enhance Corporate Governance*. Hoboken, NJ: Wiley, 2000.

Articles:

Colbert, Janet L. "New and expanded internal audit standards." *CPA Journal* (May 2002).

Gavin, Thomas A., Richard A. Roy, and Glenn E. Sumners. "A corporate code of conduct: The internal auditor's role." *Managerial Auditing Journal* 5:2 (1990). (Also published in *Leadership & Organization Development Journal* 11:3 (1990): 32–40.)

Website:

Institute of Internal Auditors (IIA): www.theiia.org

"If networks are to be more efficient. . .this will come about only on the basis of a high level of trust and the existence of shared norms of ethical behavior between network members." Francis Fukuyama

  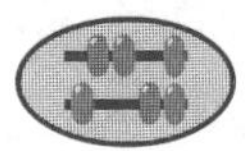 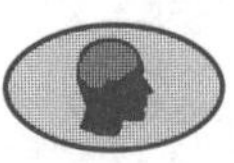  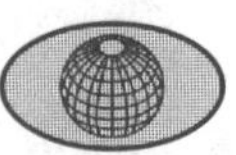   

Key Accounting Standards and Organizations

DEFINITION

Accounting standards are rules according to which accounting statements have to be prepared. They demand minimum levels of disclosure, establish fundamental principles, delineate the meanings of terms, and stipulate how numbers must be calculated. Accounting standards vary not only between countries but also between industries.

The financial situation and operations of a business are reported through accounting statements, which are generally required by law and are prepared by an enterprise to communicate its performance. The balance sheet provides information on the financial position of a business. The income statement provides information on the performance of a business. The elements of the balance sheet are assets, liabilities, and equity. The elements of the income statement are revenues, expenses, gains, losses, and other items. Collectively, the six fundamentals are referred to as the core accounts in an accounting statement.

There are no legally laid down, internationally recognized accounting standards. Generally Accepted Accounting Principles (GAAP) are sets of rules, accounting principles, and standards that are used in specific countries, regions or industries.

In March 2001, in an attempt to bring about an internationally accepted accounting standard, the International Accounting Standards Committee (IASC) Foundation was formed as a not-for-profit corporation, incorporated in the US State of Delaware. The IASC Foundation is the parent entity of the International Accounting Standards Board (IASB), an independent accounting-standards regulator based in London, United Kingdom. The IASB is responsible for developing the International Financial Reporting Standards (IFRS) and for promoting the use and application of these standards. In the global trading world, even countries that have not adopted IFRS are now attempting to converge their national standards with IFRS.

In the case of European Union (EU) members, both EU and national legislation apply and incompatible requirements may mean that reconciliations need to be made available or more than one set of accounts needs to be presented. Companies that have EU and US listings will also need to reconcile or present more than one set of accounts.

ADVANTAGES

- Financial standards protect governments, businesses and consumers alike, as they set down standardized rules of conduct, which give society financial stability and, if the rules are broken, recourse in law.
- Financial standards allow for the comparison of companies on equal terms. This gives potential investors the tools to judge and compare the viability and liabilities of companies or industries.
- Financial standards provide regulatory benchmarks for companies and individuals.
- Financial standards give governments the instruments to impose impartial taxes to pay for government services.

ACTION CHECKLIST

- ✔ Check which GAAP are used in the specific enterprise, business area or country in which you are interested.
- ✔ If in doubt, contact the authority that sets GAAP in your area of interest.
- ✔ Obtain as much information as you can and be ready to be involved in a long and tedious process.
- ✔ Seek specialist help, from different sources. Accountants, like doctors, are not infallible.
- ✔ Don't be afraid to ask what may seem naïve or awkward questions.
- ✔ Consider how different accounting standards may affect your attitude and judgment when quantifying risk.

DOS AND DON'TS

DO

- Check which accounting statements have to be prepared according to the correct GAAP norms.
- Make sure that particular accounting standards apply to the specific industry.
- When in doubt, contact the authority that sets the nationally accepted accounting principles.
- Get professional advice; "cooking the books" is not that uncommon, especially in loosely regulated countries.
- When operating in countries with unfamiliar accounting standards, get in touch with your country's consular officials, who will generally have a list of reliable local accountants.
- Carefully examine any departures from GAAP norms, as they may indicate deeper problems.

DON'T

- Don't rely on accounting standards to protect you from fraud.
- Don't be put off by the complexity of GAAP when investigating a company.
- Don't make the mistake of basing a decision purely on GAAP. Accounting standards are highly complex and require professional advice.
- Don't forget that if an enterprise is a multinational, it may have to prepare two or more reconcilements.
- Don't forget that in the case of EU members, both EU and national legislation apply.

▸▸ MORE INFO

Websites:

International Accounting Standards Board: www.iasb.org

The Financial Reporting Council: www.frc.org.uk

"Important principles may and must be inflexible." Abraham Lincoln

Key Components of a Corporate Risk Register

DEFINITION

Most large enterprises have a procedure for managing corporate risks. The procedure is intended to identify, record, and communicate risks in terms of their comparative importance to the company. The corporate risk register also forms the basis for reporting risk issues in the annual report. The information is usually stored in a central register, catalog, or inventory of risks. This should contain information suitably sorted, standardized, and merged for relevance to the appropriate level of management. Its key function is to provide management, the board, and key stakeholders with significant information on the main risks faced by the business. Every risk in the register should have the following features: opening date, title, short description, probability, and importance. A risk might also have a dedicated manager responsible for its resolution.

A risk register should help management to:

- understand the nature of the risks the business faces;
- be aware of the extent of those risks;
- identify the level of risk that they are willing to accept;
- recognize its ability to control and reduce risk.

However, a risk register is often out of date, incomplete, or inconsistent when selecting the appropriate controls and countermeasures for each risk. Many companies, therefore, use outside risk consultants. These consultants, working in conjunction with company staff, are better able to take an objective view of risks, assess their relative importance, and assign priorities.

ADVANTAGES

- A corporate risk register provides management and the board with important information on the main risks faced by the business.
- The register allows management to identify and prioritize risks, ensuring that risks with the greatest probability or the greatest potential loss are handled first.

DISADVANTAGES

- If risks are improperly assessed and prioritized, they can divert resources that could be used more profitably.
- Unless it is competently maintained and updated, the risk register may not be comprehensive or consistent, leading to unrecognized risks.
- The risk information may not be presented in a logical and unbiased form and, as such, can unintentionally mislead.

ACTION CHECKLIST

- ✔ Thoroughly check the risk register against any potential business risk you might foresee and compare similar companies' risk registers.
- ✔ Research your market and make sure that you have analyzed the consequences of any risks upon your own business.
- ✔ Encourage an atmosphere of openness about the kinds of risks facing the organization. Some risks are obvious, but managers of individual business units may sometimes know more about hidden risks. Only by fully understanding risks can you attempt to counteract them.

DOS AND DON'TS

DO

- Seek the advice of specialist strategic risk advisers. Risk management is very complex. Experts from specialist risk management companies can help devise custom risk registers to protect against potential problems.
- Keep in mind the distinction between risk and uncertainty. Risk can be measured by using the formula: Impact multiplied by Probability.
- Quantify and differentiate between risks that are merely the cost of doing business and those that might have an impact on objectives.

DON'T

- Don't make the error of failing to check the risk register thoroughly for inconsistencies.
- Don't believe that you can totally cover every risk your business could face.
- Don't rely on single controls and countermeasures for each risk.

▸▸ MORE INFO

Websites:

American Institute of Certified Public Accountants: www.aicpa.org

Knowledge Leader: www.knowledgeleader.com

"If a gentleman is frivolous, he will lose the respect of his inferiors." Confucius

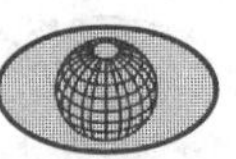

The Key Components of an Audit Report

DEFINITION

An audit is the examination and verification of an organization's financial statements and records. Audits provide independent and impartial opinion as to whether the information is presented objectively. Most organizations—privately held businesses, publicly owned corporations, and nonprofit organizations—have to prepare financial reports, which are audited. These reports assist owners and managers to make decisions, and help to show the company's financial status to stockholders, employees, regulators, and the public.

When reviewing an audit report on a company, key questions include: What is the source of its revenue? Where, and on what, does it spend its income? How much profit is it earning?

The answer lies in the company's financial statements, and, by law, all public companies have to make these statements freely available to everyone.

These financial statements can be broken down into two key components: the profit-and-loss statement (or income statement) and the balance sheet.

The profit-and-loss statement tells us whether the company is making a profit. It indicates how revenue is transformed into net income. Profit-and-loss statements cover a period of time—usually a year or part of a year.

The balance sheet is a snapshot of a business's financial health at a specific moment in time—usually the close of an accounting period. A balance sheet shows assets, liabilities, and stockholders' equity/capital. Assets and liabilities are divided into short-term and long-term obligations. The balance sheet does not show the flows into and out of the accounts during the period. A balance sheet's assets should equal liabilities plus owners' equity.

There are two kinds of audit: internal and external.

Internal audits ensure that the management of the business is meeting internal goals such as productivity, quality, compliance controls, consistency, and cost, as well as external goals such as customer satisfaction and market share.

External audits are carried out by outside auditors, who do not have any ties to the organization or its financial statements. The outside auditor checks the financial statements prepared by management for balance, and also to see whether the company is adhering to professional standards and Generally Accepted Accounting Principles (GAAP).

ADVANTAGES

- External audits improve understanding of underlying business trends and provide an objective opinion as to whether the information is presented fairly.
- Internal audits let managers know whether a business can expand or needs to adopt a more conservative approach. Can it deal with the normal ebbs and flows in revenue, or should it take immediate steps to bolster cash reserves?
- Internal audits focus on processes within the business, and can identify and help to analyze trends, particularly in the area of receivables and payables, i.e. is the receivables cycle lengthening? Can receivables be collected more aggressively? Is some debt uncollectible?

DISADVANTAGES

- Results sometimes depend on the accounting methods used. Measuring and reporting give management considerable discretion and the opportunity to influence an audit's results.
- Internal audits are not always carried out rigorously and the figures may not reflect the true financial position of the company. Salaries for internal audit staff are paid for by the organization. This can lead to questions about objectivity.

ACTION CHECKLIST

- ✔ Carefully analyze any profit-and-loss statements for differences during the reporting period. Anomalies might be due to seasonal or other variations, or may indicate deeper problems.
- ✔ When reviewing internal audits, be prepared to be involved in a long and detailed process of analysis. Some areas will need clarification by experts.
- ✔ Check which GAAP are used in the internal audit of the business in which you are interested.
- ✔ Internal audits are not infallible. If you are unsure about specific areas or numbers, don't hesitate to ask for clarification.

DOS AND DON'TS

DO

- Make sure that you take the time and effort to analyze the audit. If in doubt, consult an independent auditor.
- Use your judgment when reviewing internal audits; results do not always tell the whole story.

DON'T

- Don't assume that all audits truly reflect a company's financial position; they only reflect the auditor's opinion.

▸▸ MORE INFO

Books:

Cardwell, Harvey. *Principles of Audit Surveillance*. Philadelphia, PA: R. T. Edwards, 2005.

President's Council on Integrity and Efficiency (US), US General Accounting Office. *Financial Audit Manual*. Darby, PA: DIANE Publishing, 2000.

Wealleans, David. *The Quality Audit for ISO 9001:2000: A Practical Guide*. Burlington, VT: Gower Publishing, 2005.

Articles:

Accountancy SA. "Auditing." (October 2008).

US General Accounting Office. "Financial audits: The vast majority of executive branch entities included in the Federal Budget are statutorily required to have their financial statements audited." (September 2005).

Websites:

American Accounting Association: www.aaa-edu.org

The Institute of Internal Auditors: www.theiia.org

"Having a character that consists mainly of defects, I try to correct them one by one, but there are limits to the altitude that can be attained by hauling on one's own boot-straps." Clive James

   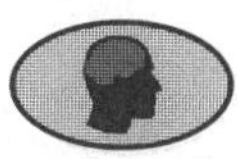  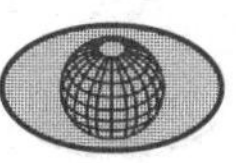   

Middle East: Regulatory Structure and Powers

DEFINITION

The Middle East region consists of Afghanistan, Bahrain, Egypt, Iran, Iraq, Israel, Jordan, Kuwait, Lebanon, Oman, Pakistan, Qatar, Saudi Arabia, Syria, United Arab Emirates (UAE), West Bank and Gaza, and Yemen. Sometimes the region is grouped with North African countries, together known as the MENA (Middle East and North Africa) region, and includes Algeria, Djibouti, Libya, Mauritania, Morocco, Somalia, Sudan, and Tunisia.

Only Saudi Arabia is part of the G20, so MENA's influence on the G20 is limited, and, critically, the influence of the G20 on MENA is also limited.

Saudi Arabia's membership of G20 means that it can carry influence in the Middle East region. King Abdullah has quietly built Saudi Arabia into a major power in the region, which gives the country the opportunity to exert power in the area, by influencing policies.

The Gulf Cooperation Council (GCC) is making progress to fit in with global frameworks, with 89% of Middle East banking assets expected to be covered by Basel II by the end of 2009. The banking sector is better developed in the Middle East than elsewhere in the MENA region.

The development of regulatory institutions in the GCC has shown marked progress, as growth in the finance sector has brought with it increased awareness of the need to keep up and, indeed, be proactive. Saudi Arabia's Capital Market Authority is one example of a new regulatory authority in the region, and Qatar is seeing the streamlining of market regulators; both are examples of the development of effective bodies. The Dubai International Financial Centre has introduced a more accessible court system, working with new regulations in English, and the Dubai Financial Services Authority issued a hedge fund code of practice at the end of 2007—the first such code to be issued by a financial market regulator.

Regulators in the region are growing in size, and strengthening their links regionally and internationally, but the picture remains mixed, with some further down the line with Basel II than others. As plans for a GCC common currency and the creation of a common GCC market seem to be making some progress, the opening of markets will mean that regulators will have to work more closely to create a common approach.

Saudi Arabia has the biggest economy in the region. In 2003 it established the Capital Market Authority, which issues rules, regulations, and instructions related to the capital markets. In Qatar, the Qatar Financial Centre Regulatory Authority was set up in 2005, and in 2004 the Central Bank of Bahrain issued its *CBB Rulebook*, with updates appearing regularly ever since. The regulatory framework for banking in the UAE stipulates that banks must have fully paid-up capital of at least AED 40 million, and must place a tenth of their net annual profits in a special reserve until the fund amounts to half the capital.

Progress has undoubtedly been made, but with freer markets and greater foreign interaction, more will be required. World Trade Organization (WTO) accession initiatives and International Monetary Fund (IMF) financial sector assessment programs will bring challenges in the future. Opening the markets to foreign capital regulators will increase risks in the sector and the region.

There is little doubt that in order to promote continuing and lasting economic growth, financial sector reform and regulation should be a high priority. Studies have shown that well-developed financial systems promote efficiency and growth owing to reduced information, transaction, and monitoring costs. A study carried out by the IMF showed that MENA countries were fairly strong in financial regulation and supervision, but there are wide variations. In those countries with the most advanced financial sectors, appropriate financial regulation and supervision was found to be an important part of development of the financial sector. In other words, better financial sector regulation promotes a more healthy financial system and economy.

MORE INFO

Books:

Middle East and Arabic Countries Banking Law Handbook. 2nd ed. Washington, DC: International Business Publications, 2006.

Ross, Tim. *Financial Services Regulation in the Middle East*. 2nd ed. Oxford: Oxford University Press, 2008.

Sabri, Nidal Rashid. *Financial Markets and Institutions in the Arab Economy*. New York: Nova Science Publishers, 2008.

Article:

Gentzoglanis, Anastassios. "Financial integration, regulation and competitiveness in Middle East and North Africa countries." *Managerial Finance* 33:7 (2007): 461–476.

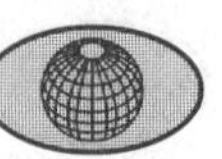
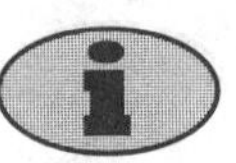

MiFID—Its Development and Aims

DEFINITION

The European Commission's Markets in Financial Instruments Directive (MiFID, EU Directive 2004/39/EC), was implemented on November 1, 2007, replacing the Investment Services Directive, and applies to all 27 EU member states plus Iceland, Norway, and Liechtenstein. Each country must incorporate MiFID either into local law or into the rules of the local regulatory handbook, depending on how financial regulation is applied in that state.

The objective of MiFID, apart from increased harmonization, is to boost innovation and competition across the financial markets within the European Union and adjoining states, improve liquidity in the markets, and reduce costs for issuers and investors.

REGULATORY APPROACH

As the key plank of the European Commission's Financial Services Action Plan, MiFID's 42 measures bring significant changes to how EU financial service markets operate. Whereas previous EU financial service legislation focused on "minimum harmonization and mutual recognition," MiFID's "maximum harmonization" principle places emphasis on home state supervision within a level playing field. The EU "passport" approach has been retained, but the old "concentration rule," which let member states require investment firms to route client orders through regulated markets, has been abolished.

MiFID's various articles cover almost all tradable financial products, with the exception of certain foreign exchange trades. This includes commodity and other derivatives such as freight, climate, and carbon derivatives, which were not covered by the Investment Services Directive. Any investment firm operating in Europe's financial markets is affected.

MiFID distinguishes between "investment services and activities" (core services) and "ancillary services" (non-core services). Details of these can be found in Annex 1 Sections A and B of the MiFID Level 1 Directive. A company providing core services is subject to MiFID in respect of both these and also ancillary services and can use the MiFID passport to provide them to other member states. However, a company engaged only in ancillary services is not subject to MiFID and cannot benefit from the MiFID passport.

GOOD PRACTICE

MiFID sets out various elements of good practice, such as how an investment firm should protect its customers or retain records. These apply to whatever is being traded. The following areas form the key aspects of the directive.

Authorization, Regulation, and Passporting

Companies are authorized and regulated in their "home state," typically the country in which they are registered. They can use the passport to provide services to customers in other member states.

Client Categorization and Order Handling

Companies must categorize clients as "eligible counterparties," professional clients, or retail clients (these have increasing levels of protection). Clear procedures must be in place to categorize clients and assess their suitability for each type of investment product. There are stringent requirements on the information to be collected when accepting client orders, to ensure that the company is acting in its clients' best interests, and on how orders from different clients may be aggregated. Appropriate investment advice or suggested financial transactions must be verified before being given.

Pre- and Post-Trade Transparency

Before trading, operators of continuous order-matching systems must aggregate their order information on liquid shares available at the five best price levels on the buy and sell side. The best bids and offers of market-makers must be made available for quote-driven markets. Post-trade, companies must publish the price, volume, and time of all trades in listed shares, even where conducted outside of a regulated market, unless certain requirements are met to allow for deferred publication.

Best Execution

Companies must take all reasonable steps to obtain the best possible result in the execution of a client order. This includes not just the execution price but also cost, speed, likelihood of execution, likelihood of settlement, and any other relevant factors.

Systematic Internalizers

A systematic internalizer is a company that executes orders from its clients against its own book or against orders from other clients. Under MiFID, systematic internalizers are treated as mini-exchanges and are thus subject to pre-trade and post-trade transparency requirements.

▸▸ MORE INFO

Book:

Skinner, Chris (ed). *The Future of Investing in Europe's Markets after MiFID*. Chichester, UK: Wiley, 2007.

Article:

Global Investment Technology "Market participants anticipate dramatic shifts as trading moves from exchanges to newer MTFs." 17:23 (September 15, 2008): 1, 10–11.

Websites:

European Commission MiFID pages: ec.europa.eu/internal_market/securities/isd/index_en.htm#isd

MiFID resources: www.mifidirective.com

"If you want truly to understand something, try to change it." Kurt Lewin

     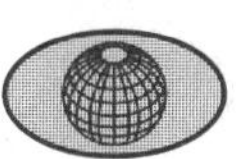   

Preparing Financial Statements: Balance Sheets

DEFINITION

A balance sheet is a snapshot of a business's financial health at a specific moment in time, usually at the close of an accounting period. A balance sheet comprises assets, liabilities, and stockholders' equity/capital. Assets and liabilities are divided into short-term and long-term obligations. On a balance sheet, assets should equal liabilities plus owners' equity.

- *Assets:* Current assets are those that can be converted to cash in one year or less. Common current assets include cash, account receivables, inventory (products manufactured or even work in progress held for sale in the normal course of business), prepaid expenses, and investment securities. Long-term assets are assets that companies retain for an extended time, such as land, plant, and machinery. Long-term assets earn income and/or are held to manage the companies in which the investment is made. Intangible assets also come under the broad category of long-term assets. Intangible assets are those that have no physical or tangible characteristics, for example patents, trademarks, copyrights, and goodwill.
- *Liabilities:* Current liabilities are debts to outsiders that should be paid within one year. Some common items that fall into this category are accounts payable and accrued liabilities, such as salaries and wages that have been incurred but not yet paid. Long-term liabilities are obligations that do not have to be met within one year. These might include long-term notes, bonds, and mortgages.
- *Stockholders' equity/capital:* The difference between the assets and the liabilities is referred to as stockholders' equity. Equity is the amount of capital that would remain once the liabilities were satisfied.

ADVANTAGES

- A balance sheet helps managers to decide if the business is in a position to expand, if it can easily handle the normal financial ebbs and flows of revenues and expenses, or if it should take immediate steps to boost cash reserves.
- Balance sheets can identify and analyze trends, particularly in the area of receivables and payables. Is the receivables cycle lengthening? Can receivables be collected more aggressively? Is some debt un-collectable? Has the business been slowing down payables to forestall a cash shortage?

DISADVANTAGES

- A balance sheet shows a snapshot of a company's assets, liabilities and stockholders' equity at the end of the reporting period. It does not show the flows into and out of the accounts during the period.
- Some numbers depend on judgments, estimates, and interpretation. Intangible assets are factors that might be highly relevant but cannot be reliably measured.
- Financial standards are not always applied to the letter, and balance sheets may not be a true reflection of the financial position of the company.

DOS AND DON'TS

DO

- Involve managers and key stakeholders in the company when evaluating balance-sheet findings.
- Determine whether ratios were calculated before or after adjustments were made to the balance sheet. In many cases, these adjustments can significantly affect the ratios.

DON'T

- Don't fall into the trap of thinking that financial ratios are infallible when analyzing balance sheets using ratios; use research to confirm results.
- Don't rely on factors that cannot be reliably measured. Some numbers, such as those for intangible assets, depend on judgments, estimates, and interpretation.

ACTION CHECKLIST

✔ Quantify in financial terms how decisions based on the balance sheet could impact on the business.

✔ Obtain as much information as possible and compare financial ratios before committing to expensive decisions.

✔ Be prepared to be involved in a long and complicated process of analysis. Some gray areas will not be resolved by financial ratios.

▸▸ MORE INFO

Websites:

HM Treasury, United Kingdom (audit policy and advice): www.hm-treasury.gov.uk
Institute of Management Accountants: www.imanet.org
US Treasury: www.ustreas.gov

"I set a rule that people weren't allowed to send good news unless they sent around an equal amount of bad news. We had to get a balanced picture. In fact, I kind of favored just hearing about the accounts we were losing because. . .bad news is generally more actionable than good news." Bill Gates

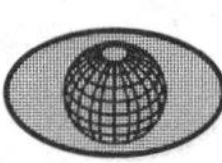

Preparing Financial Statements: Profit and Loss Accounts (P&Ls)

DEFINITION

A profit and loss account, also known as an income statement or a statement of revenue and expense, is a financial statement that indicates how revenue (money received from the sale of products and services before expenses are taken out) is transformed into net income (the result after all revenues and expenses have been accounted for). The important thing to remember about P&Ls is that they represent a period of time (usually a year or part of a year), rather than being snapshots. They should indicate to managers and investors whether a company made a profit or a loss during the period of time being reported. This contrasts with the balance sheet, which represents a single moment in time.

P&Ls can be broken into two groups: revenues and expenses. Both the revenues and expenses are recorded in the year (or other time period) that they are earned or accrued, not when the revenue is actually received or the expenses paid.

Revenues are the income the business receives in exchange for the products or services it provides. In most cases, revenues are associated with the sale of goods or services. Some of the more common sources of revenue are sales revenue, service revenue, and interest revenue.

The recorded expenses reflect the amount of resources used in earning the reported revenue. Some common examples of expenses are: salaries, research and development, bad debt, depreciation for the current year, and taxes.

For the investor, P&Ls also report earnings per share (EPS). This calculation shows how much money stockholders would receive if the company decided to distribute all of its net earnings for the period reported.

ADVANTAGES

- P&Ls should help investors and creditors to determine the past performance of the enterprise, predict future performance, and assess the enterprise's capability to generate future cash flow.
- P&Ls, along with balance sheets, are the most basic elements required by potential lenders, such as banks, investors, and vendors. Lenders will use the financial information contained in P&Ls to determine credit limits.
- P&Ls can also track dramatic increases in product returns or the cost of goods sold as a percentage of sales. They can also be used to determine income tax liability.

DISADVANTAGES

- Factors that might be highly relevant but cannot be reliably measured (for example brand recognition and customer loyalty) are not reported in P&Ls.
- Some numbers depend on the accounting methods used. The use of current costs or exit prices leaves room for manipulation. Measuring and reporting give management considerable discretion and the opportunity to influence results.
- Some numbers depend on judgments, estimates and interpretation.

ACTION CHECKLIST

- ✔ Use financial ratios on the P&Ls to evaluate the overall financial condition. Financial-ratio analysis will gauge viability, liabilities, and projected future performance.
- ✔ Carefully analyze any P&Ls for differences during the reporting period. Anomalies might be due to seasonal or other variations, or may indicate deeper problems.
- ✔ Consult and question managers and key business stakeholders in the evaluation process for P&Ls.

DOS AND DON'TS

DO

- Make sure that you have used the financial ratios when analyzing profit and loss accounts. If in doubt, consult an expert analyst.
- Consider seeking the help of specialist consultants.
- Check for any changes in accounting policies or anomalies that occurred during the period. Carefully examine any departures from industry norms.

DON'T

- Don't take shortcuts. Accounting can be a complicated process and remember that any undiscovered problems might cost more in the long run.
- Don't rely on accounting standards to protect you from fraud.
- Don't assume that P&Ls are a true reflection of a company's financial position. Measuring and reporting permit considerable discretion and the opportunity to influence results.

▸▸ MORE INFO

Websites:

American Accounting Association: www.aaa-edu.org

Business Link: www.businesslink.gov.uk

"When the facts change, I change my mind." John Maynard Keynes

  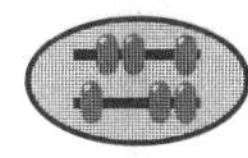   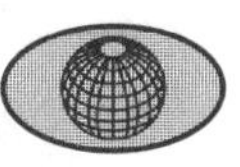   

Principles of Financial Services Regulation

DEFINITION

Financial regulations attempt to ensure that financial institutions adhere to specific requirements, restrictions, and guidelines that aim to maintain the integrity of the financial system and which may be legislated or exist as a voluntary or obligatory code of conduct.

Primarily, financial regulation should attempt to follow these three strategic principles:

1 Promote efficient, fair and orderly markets.
2 Help retail customers obtain a fair deal.
3 Improve business capability and regulatory effectiveness of the financial overseer.

A financial overseer or regulatory body usually regulates most financial services markets, exchanges, and firms in its country, setting standards that financial institutions must meet. This body can take action against companies that fail to meet those standards. For example, in the UK, the Financial Services Authority (FSA) has been the single financial services regulator since 2001. Its powers were (and are) not all encompassing, but have grown since inception. For example, mortgage business has been regulated since November 2004, and general insurance activities since January 2005.

A regulatory body typically has wide-ranging powers to make and enforce rules, and to carry out investigations in order to attain the principles of financial services regulation. The regulator will attempt to assess and monitor the risk of an activity or a firm and ascertain whether it has the potential to cause harm in one of the following areas:

- Market confidence;
- Public awareness;
- Consumers;
- Financial crime.

The regulator is charged with maintaining confidence in the financial system; maintaining and raising public understanding of the financial system; protection of consumers; preventing and/or reducing financial crime; and negating the ways in which a business could be used for financially criminal activities. A regulator's remit is broad, and as achieving one hundred percent compliance is nigh on impossible, it must prioritize its activities. Building on the three principles, a financial regulator must use its often limited resources in the most efficient and economic manner. The regulatory body typically produces regular reports on various aspects of a country's financial systems; these may result in recommendations for changes in legislation or regulations, where loopholes or faults have been shown to exist.

In terms of companies themselves, the senior management is usually responsible for the business activities and ensuring compliance with the regulations, including risk management and internal controls, such as Chinese Walls. This principle has the objective of preventing unnecessary intrusion by the regulator into the business of a firm.

Financial regulation within a country is, of course, complicated by the international overlap of financial laws and markets. Thus, each country's financial regulator must seek cooperation with those of other countries and reach joint agreement with international standards.

During the global economic turmoil of 2008, UK Prime Minister Gordon Brown appealed to world leaders to back the premise of an international supervisory body to restore order to the chaotic markets. His appeal was part of a long campaign to win support for more effective regulation of global capitalism.

Regulators must achieve all these goals while maintaining aspects of healthy competition, minimizing the cost to companies of compliance, and considering competition and innovation that can improve financial services for everyone.

▸▸ MORE INFO

Books:

Hood, Christopher, Henry Rothstein, and Robert Baldwin. *The Government of Risk: Understanding Risk Regulation Regimes*. Oxford: Oxford University Press, 2004.

Howells, Peter, and Keith Bain. *Financial Markets and Institutions*. 5th ed. New York: FT Prentice Hall, 2007.

Mills, Annie. *Essential Strategies for Financial Services Compliance*. Chichester, UK: Wiley, 2008.

Websites:

Federal Financial Institutions Examination Council: www.ffiec.gov
Financial Services Authority (UK): www.fsa.gov.uk
US Securities and Exchange Commission (SEC): www.sec.gov

"Be more concerned with your character than with your reputation. Your character is what you really are, while your reputation is what others think you are." Dale Carnegie

  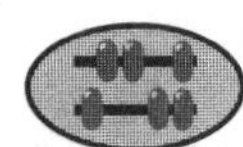   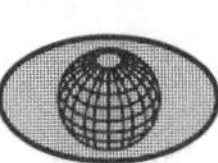   

Regulatory and Capital Issues under *Shariah* Law

DEFINITION

Following the early development of Islamic finance in the Middle East, the growth in *shariah*-compliant financial services over the last decade has been dramatic. Local and national banks in predominately Muslim countries have sought to introduce compliant products and services to their customers. International banks have also been quick to recognize the potential in adding Islamic products to their range.

The relentless advance of *shariah*-compliant finance has generated debate on how Islamic finance should respond to developments in the international financial regulatory environment. Though at first glance amended regulatory standards and governance requirements may seem unworkable in the context of Islamic finance, in many instances, the amended standards and expectations can be easily integrated. In fact, the biggest challenge towards achieving greater compatibility between international regulatory and capital standards and Islamic finance is frequently how to change providers' attitudes to greater integration.

The Dubai Financial Services Authority provides a good example of how a new regulatory framework can be developed to be compatible with both mainstream and Islamic finance companies. Dubai, a major centre for *sukuk* investment, has created a common law-based legal system and a regulatory environment which is based on existing international structures yet is supportive of the key aspects of Islamic finance. Given its leading position in the *sukuk* market, the Emirate also enforces high standards of disclosure and transparency.

Product and industry trade bodies have shown the value of international collaboration on regulatory progress. Given rising interest in Islamic derivative trading over recent years, the International Swaps and Derivatives Association (ISDA) has been working with the International Islamic Financial Market (IIFM) towards the goal of creating a guideline framework for the industry. The work under development is to be called the ISDA/IIFM *ta'hawwut* (hedging) master agreement and, as at January 2009, is on course to be the standard contract for international cross border Islamic derivatives transactions. However, despite the progress towards these standard contracts, the ISDA has stressed the need for individual Islamic jurisdictions to strengthen their own regulatory and legislative environments to ensure that the agreed transactions are legally enforceable. The ISDA also highlighted that issues related to regulatory capital, and accounting policies surrounding Islamic derivatives transactions need to be addressed by local regulators.

ADVANTAGES

- Improved regulatory and capital structures can play an important role in the ongoing success of Islamic finance.
- Increased transparency and better governance should boost the uptake of new financial products.
- Collaboration between states and organizations can result in major advances to promote the growth of Islamic finance

DISADVANTAGES

- Conventional Western risk management often views Islamic finance as carrying very specific risks related to issues such as the lack of consistent *shariah* compatibility standards. Particular concerns have been raised over the application of the Basel II accord/capital adequacy requirements which were originally created for mainstream western banks, with no regard to the very specific risks faced by Islamic institutions.
- Regulatory attitudes between Western and Islamic systems can differ greatly. For example, a Western regulator may question whether a *shariah* board's role is advisery, and if it has executive powers?
- Difficulties can arise for regulators as to how to classify some Islamic financial products. For example, *musharaka* home purchase products may not be approved as a regulated mortgage product.

ACTION CHECKLIST

✔ Recognize the compatibility between many aspects of Western and Islamic systems. In other aspects, differences may not be as stark as they first appear. For examples, Islamic corporate governance standards may appear weak by formal western standards but some could argue that in practice, these are underpinned by the Islamic emphasis on integrity and sense of fair play.

✔ Appreciate that excessively tight regulatory structures could hamper the development of innovative new products.

DOS AND DON'TS

DO

- Acknowledge that improved regulatory structures can only be achieved where a supportive political backdrop for change exists.
- Islamic product providers should consider whether their products could also appeal to non-Muslims.
- The increasing overlap of Western and Islamic finance could be demonstrated when a non-Muslim country eventually issues *sukuk*. Mooted for some years by the UK government, the form of any future issue could be worthy of close scrutiny as Western sovereign issuers look to tap into massive demand for *shariah*-compliant investment products.

DON'T

- Don't expect regulation to generate product innovation.
- Don't expect a true "single market" for Islamic products.

▸▸ MORE INFO

Article:

UK Financial Services Authority. "Islamic finance in the UK: Regulation and challenges." Online at: www.fsa.gov.uk/pubs/other/islamic_finance.pdf

Website:

Harvard Law School Islamic Finance Project: ifptest.law.harvard.edu

"The first step toward change is acceptance. Once you accept yourself, you open the door to change."
Stephen Covey

  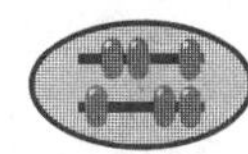   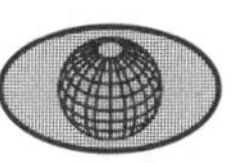 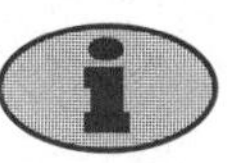  

Sarbanes–Oxley: Its Development and Aims

DEFINITION

The Sarbanes–Oxley Act is a US federal law that was enacted in response to several major corporate and accounting scandals, such as those affecting Enron and WorldCom, which involved large-scale internal fraud. These scandals damaged confidence in US financial markets. A variety of complex factors created the conditions and culture in which the fraudulent activities were able to flourish undetected for a number of years, including conflicts of interest and incentive compensation practices. The analysis of their complex and contentious root causes contributed to the passage of the bill in 2002. The Act was named after Senator Paul Sarbanes and Representative Michael G. Oxley. It is also known as the Public Company Accounting Reform and Investor Protection Act of 2002 and is often referred to as Sarbanes–Oxley, Sarbox, or SOX.

The act imposes high standards of accountability and transparency on the boards and management of all US publicly listed companies and public accounting firms. The legal framework established a new, quasi-public agency, the Public Company Accounting Oversight Board (PCAOB), which has responsibility for the overseeing, registration, regulation, inspection, and disciplining of accountancy companies that carry out audits of public companies.

Beside the PCAOB, Sarbox covers issues such as auditor independence, corporate governance, assessment of internal control, enhanced financial disclosure, analysts' conflicts of interest, corporate tax, and corporate fraud. There are 11 legislative sections for this purpose, known as titles, which enable the imposition of additional corporate board responsibilities as well as criminal penalties. The Securities and Exchange Commission (SEC) has the power to implement rulings on requirements to comply with Sarbanes–Oxley.

There remains much disagreement over whether Sarbox has been a useful piece of legislation. Although the Act has helped to restore public confidence in the US capital markets and has strengthened corporate accounting controls, there is also evidence to suggest that it has displaced business from the United States to the United Kingdom, where regulations for the financial sector are less overbearing. In the United Kingdom, the nonstatutory Combined Code of Corporate Governance, monitored by the Financial Services Authority, is similar to Sarbox but has a lighter touch.

As the capital markets are global, Sarbox has also affected non-US companies cross-listed in the United States. Companies based in countries with poor regulation have benefited from better credit ratings by complying with Sarbox, despite the cost. Companies in countries that have a strong regulatory regime already benefit from adequate transparency, so the cost of compliance with Sarbox is less. Either way, companies that choose to be cross-listed on other exchanges, such as the London Stock Exchange, benefit from better credit ratings anyway. Studies comparing new foreign listings on both the US and UK exchanges between 1995 and 2006 showed that Sarbox had no real impact on the listing preferences of large foreign companies for the main exchanges. However, since Sarbox was enacted there is evidence that small foreign companies choosing between Nasdaq and the London Stock Exchange's Alternative Investment Market are less likely to opt for the US listing. It is thought that this is due to the higher costs associated with compliance with Sarbox. Certainly, the Alternative Investment Market has enjoyed spectacular growth since Sarbox was enacted, and this cannot be put down to coincidence alone.

Legislation or regulation similar to Sarbanes–Oxley has been introduced in Canada, Japan, Australia, South Africa, France, Germany, and Italy, ensuring that tighter antifraud controls have been brought into play in most major markets.

➤➤ MORE INFO

Books:

Anand, Sanjay. *Sarbanes–Oxley Guide for Finance and Information Technology Professionals*. 2nd ed. Hoboken, NJ: Wiley, 2006.

Bainbridge, Stephen M. *The Complete Guide to Sarbanes–Oxley: Understanding How Sarbanes–Oxley Affects Your Business*. Avon, MA: Adams Media, 2007.

Marchetti, Anne M. *Sarbanes–Oxley Ongoing Compliance Guide: Key Processes and Summary Checklists*. Hoboken, NJ: Wiley, 2007.

Website:

US Government Printing Office—Go to "Catalog of Publications" and search on Sarbanes-Oxley: www.access.gpo.gov

"I have come to view strong corporate governance as indispensable to resilient and vibrant capital markets. And without financial reporting premised on sound, honest numbers, capital markets will collapse upon themselves, suffocate, and die." Arthur Levitt, Jr

Solvency II: Its Development and Aims

DEFINITION

Solvency II is the most up-to-date and comprehensive set of regulatory requirements for insurance companies operating within the member states of the European Union (EU). The original solvency regulations for insurers were introduced in the early 1970s and later updated under Solvency I. Since then, the principle of risk management has become an integral component of capital adequacy for insurers, and sophisticated risk management systems have been developed and implemented. The Solvency II Directive, to be introduced across the EU in 2012, replaces the existing 14 Directives and forms part of the European Commission's Better Regulation program, which aims to simplify the regulatory environment and reduce red tape. It has been nicknamed "Basel for insurers" as it bears a number of similarities to the Basel II banking regulations.

The EU's principle of the single market drives the rationale behind Solvency II, with the aim of introducing harmonized regulations and legislation for insurance services in the member states. Currently, insurers within the EU use the "passport" system (a single license across all member states), which is based on the concept of maximum harmonization and mutual recognition. A significant number of member states have introduced national reforms where they believe that the current minimum requirements are insufficient. This has led to a patchwork of regulatory requirements across the EU, which Solvency II aims to resolve.

Solvency II is based on economic principles for the measurement of assets and liabilities. It has a very wide scope, and consists of a comprehensive risk management framework that defines the required levels of capital adequacy, outlines procedures to identify, measure and manage levels of risk, modernizes the supervisory regime, increases the international competitiveness of European insurers, extends market integration, and improves consumer protection. Insurers will have to take account of all types of risk to which they are exposed, and manage those risks more effectively. Like Basel II, the proposed Solvency II framework consists of three main pillars.

Pillar 1 consists of the quantitative requirements for increasing financial soundness. The solvency requirements for insurers will be more sophisticated, in order to guarantee that they have sufficient capital to withstand adverse events, such as acts of God or major accidents. Current EU solvency requirements only cover insurance risks; under Solvency II, insurers will have to hold capital against market risk, credit risk, and operational risk, all of which pose material threats to insurers' solvency.

Pillar 2 sets out requirements for the governance, risk management, and effective supervision of insurers. Insurers will be obliged to focus on the active identification, measurement, and management of risks, and to take into account all future developments, such as new business plans or the possibility of catastrophic events, that might affect their financial standing. Under Solvency II, insurers must use the "Own Risk and Solvency Assessment" to assess their capital needs in light of all risks. The "Supervisory Review Process" (SRP) will shift supervisors' focus from compliance monitoring and capital to evaluating insurers' risk profiles and the quality of their risk management and governance systems.

Pillar 3 focuses on disclosure and transparency requirements. Insurers will have to disclose certain information publicly. This will enforce greater market discipline, and help to ensure the stability of insurers and reinsurers. Insurance companies will also be required to report a far greater amount of information to their supervisors. Solvency II also imposes a "group supervisor" in each country that will have specific responsibilities to be exercised in close cooperation with the relevant national supervisors. The aim is to streamline supervision and ensure that groupwide risks are not overlooked. Groups should be able to operate more efficiently, while policyholders will receive a higher level of protection. Groups that are sufficiently diversified may also be allowed to reduce their capital adequacy if they meet certain conditions.

›› MORE INFO

Books:

Doff, Rene. *Risk Management for Insurers: Risk Control, Economic Capital and Solvency II*. London: Risk Books, 2007.

Rusalovskiy, Artem. *Challenges of Solvency II Implementation*. Saarbrücken, Germany: VDM Verlag, 2008.

Websites:

EU Solvency II index page: ec.europa.eu/internal_market/insurance/solvency/index_en.htm

Solvency II Frequently Asked Questions (FAQs): europa.eu/rapid/pressReleasesAction.do?reference=MEMO/07/286&format=HTML&aged=0&language= EN&guiLanguage=en

"You can tell a lot about a fellow's character by his way of eating jelly beans." Ronald Reagan

  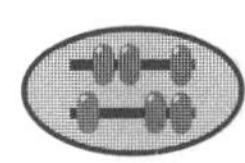   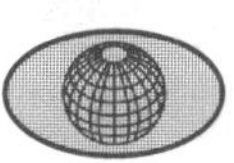   

Stress Testing and Scenario Analysis for Keeping Up with Regulation

DEFINITION

Stress testing generally refers to examining how a company's finances respond to an extreme scenario. The stress-testing process is important for prudent business management, as it looks at the "what if" scenarios companies need to explore to determine their vulnerabilities. Since the early 1990s, catastrophe modeling, which is a form of scenario analysis for providing insight into the magnitude and probabilities of potential business disasters, has become increasingly sophisticated. Regulators globally are increasingly encouraging the use of stress testing to evaluate capital adequacy. As financial products, markets, and regulations become increasingly complex, the challenges for treasurers, supervisors, bankers, and regulators become ever greater in trying to keep up with the risks. Business leaders must ensure that the risk management and control framework within their businesses can keep up with changes in markets, financial instruments, business models, and regulation in order to help protect their long-term sustainability and profitability. There have been calls—likely to be heeded—for even more strengthening of regulation in areas such as off-balance sheet risk, liquidity and funding risk, and incremental trading risk.

There have also been calls for improved stress testing and scenario analysis, particularly in the wake of the 2008 banking crisis when it became clear quickly that something had gone badly wrong with the banks' stress-testing regimes. Although financial institutions monitor and forecast for various risks—operational, market, and credit, as well as sensitivity analysis—to determine how much capital they should hold, it seems that many of them ignored the risks of overextended credit in this case.

When new regulations are brought into play, financial institutions adapt themselves, but adaptation is not the only way forward. They must learn how to best use the data that they already possess to enable them to embrace regulatory change without seeing it as a burden. Although companies seek to increase reliability and profitability, and regulation can be a drain on costs, the seamless integration of risk management processes and tools—which includes stress testing and scenario analysis—should give them a competitive advantage and enable them to become more sustainable.

Ongoing business planning is dependent on accurate forecasting. Without good stress testing and scenario analysis, big corporations cannot make accurate business forecasts. One approach is to view the business from a portfolio perspective, with capital management, liquidity management, and financial performance integrated into the process. Comprehensive stress testing and scenario analysis must take into account all risk factors, including credit, market, liquidity, operational, funding, interest, foreign exchange, and trading risks. To these must be added operational risks due to inadequate systems and controls, insurance risk (including catastrophes), business risk factors (including interest rate, securitization, and residual risks), concentration risk, high-impact low-probability events, and cyclicality and capital planning.

ADVANTAGES

- Senior management needs to be involved in the development of scenarios that could affect their business and, in some cases, the economy as a whole. Accurate analysis of business strategies is critical for compliance with regulation and improving performance. When both these goals are achieved, adapting the company for regulatory compliance can be seen as an opportunity for competitive advantage.

DISADVANTAGES

- There are no real disadvantages to performing stress testing and scenario analysis. However, it can be very expensive, which may be a deterrent to using them.

ACTION CHECKLIST

✔ Include stress testing and scenario analysis in your business planning every year, or even every quarter, or more often if the situation changes enough to justify it.

✔ Investigate software options that can help predict scenario outcomes.

DOS AND DON'TS

DO

- Employ external specialists to conduct stress testing if your company is not big enough to justify an internal department for this purpose.
- Keep asking "what if?"

DON'T

- Don't ignore the need to perform these analyses.

▸▸ MORE INFO

Book:

Halliman, Charles. *Business Intelligence Using Smart Techniques: Environmental Scanning Using Text Mining And Competitor Analysis Using Scenarios And Manual Simulation*. Houston, TX: Information Uncover, 2006.

Article:

de Bandt, O, C. Bruneau, and W. El Amri. "Stress testing and corporate finance." *Journal of Financial Stability* 4:3 (2008): 258–274.

Reports:

Brawn, David, and Alan Cathcart. "Stress testing and scenario analysis in risk management." London: Financial Services Authority. October 25, 2006. Online at: www.prmia.org/Chapter_Pages/Data/Files/778_2227_Stress%20Testing%20October_06_London_presentation.pdf

Risk Training. "Integrating stress tests and scenario analysis for strategic management of a financial institution." December 4, 2006. Online at: www.sergeandjoao.com/Presentations/AdvancedStressTestingLonDec4th_06.pdf

See Also:

★ Why Organizations Need to be Regulated—Lessons from History (pp. 736–738)

  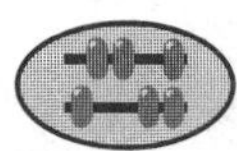   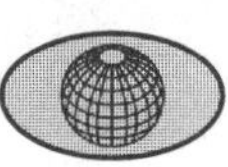   

The Ten Accounting Principles

DEFINITION

The field of accounting is governed by certain general concepts. These general concepts, referred to as basic accounting principles and guidelines, are the basis for a detailed and comprehensive set of accounting rules and standards.

We can better recognize the value of Generally Accepted Accounting Principles (GAAP) if we understand the ten principles and guidelines on which they are based:

1 *Economic Entity Assumption*: For accounting purposes, a sole proprietorship and its owner are considered to be two separate entities.
2 *Monetary Unit Assumption*: For accounting purposes, economic activity is measured in US dollars.
3 *Time Period Assumption*: There is an assumption that it is possible to report the activities of a business in distinct time intervals.
4 *Cost Principle*: Cost refers to the price of a purchase when it was originally bought and, therefore, amounts on financial statements refer to historical cost.
5 *Full Disclosure Principle*: If information is vital to a lender or investor, that information should be disclosed within the financial statement or its notes.
6 *Going Concern Principle*: It is assumed that a company will continue to exist long enough to meet its objectives and obligations and that it will not shut down in the foreseeable future.
7 *Matching Principle*: This obliges companies to use the accrual basis of accounting, which requires that expenses be matched with revenues.
8 *Revenue Recognition Principle*: Under the accrual basis of accounting, revenues are recognized when a product has been sold or a service performed, regardless of when the money is actually received.
9 *Materiality*: This basic accounting principle or guideline permits an accountant to violate another accounting principle if an amount is insignificant or immaterial.
10 *Conservatism*: Where there are two acceptable alternatives for reporting an item, conservatism directs the accountant to choose the alternative that will result in less net income and/ or a lower asset amount.

ADVANTAGES

- These general concepts direct the field of accounting and form the foundation on which more detailed, complicated and legalistic accounting rules are based.
- The Financial Accounting Standards Board (FASB) uses the basic accounting principles and guidelines as the starting place for its own set of accounting rules and standards, which are more detailed and comprehensive.
- If we understand the ten principles and guidelines, it is easier to comprehend GAAP.

DISADVANTAGES

- Although the basic accounting principles and guidelines form the basis for GAAP, the latter have become more complex over the years because financial transactions have become more complex and variations in reporting exist from industry to industry and from country to country.

ACTION CHECKLIST

✔ Use the ten principles and guidelines as a way to help understand the more complex GAAPs that are used in the specific enterprise, business area or country in which you are interested.

›› MORE INFO

Websites:

Financial Accounting Standards Board: www.fasb.org

General Accounting Office: www.gao.gov

"We made a professional judgement about the appropriate accounting treatment that turned out to be wrong."
Joseph Berardino

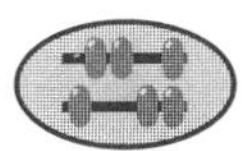
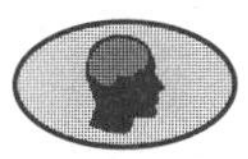

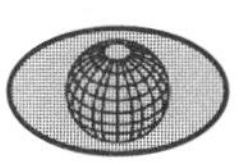

Understanding Internal Capital Adequacy Assessment Process (ICAAP)

DEFINITION

Under Basel II, ICAAP is a new requirement for financial institutions, requiring the following assessments:

- Pillar I minimum capital requirements;
- the extent of total stockholder funds required to meet a firm's strategy and maintain minimum capital requirements;
- ensuring that material risks of the firm are understood by its board, and that there is sufficient and appropriate risk management.

Four crucial elements in any ICAAP are:

1 assessment (identification and measurement) of the risks a bank is, or may be, exposed to;
2 application of mitigation techniques that may help to lower capital requirements;
3 stress-testing techniques;
4 role of the board of directors and management.

Pillar II requires that risks are presented to, and discussed by, the board to ensure its acceptance and understanding. Pillar II also requires a bank to maintain capital ratios and convince the regulator. Risk models and capital are only part of this. A financial institution must also consider any other internal risks that the firm may face which may result in losses such as fraud, rogue trading, or strategy failure.

The preparation of a capital plan should incorporate all risks, and requires the cooperation of, and collaboration with, the finance, treasury, business, and risk departments. Capital plans are usually based on a firm's forecasts for growth, given the maintenance of a capital ratio.

The ICAAP should be customized for each firm, taking into account the particular risks and information available. The process usually consists of the following stages:

1 Identifying risks—List all material risks, interview staff in relevant departments, and assess the probability of risks occurring.
2 Assessing capital—How much capital would a risk require?
3 Forward capital planning—Assess how the capital calculated from the capital assessment might be altered by its business plan, i.e. perform stress and scenario analyses.
4 Conclusion—What are the ranges of capital identified, and how much internal capital should a firm hold?

Managers should also consider the following risks:

- credit risk;
- market risk;
- operational risk;
- liquidity risk;
- insurance risk;
- concentration risk;
- residual risk;
- securitization risk;
- business risk;
- interest rate risk;
- pension obligation risk;
- any other risks identified.

The ICAAP typically has the following structure:

1 executive summary;
2 background of the ICAAP process;
3 statement of firm's attitude to risk;
4 business strategy;
5 risk assessment;
6 capital planning;
7 stress and scenario testing;
8 adoption of the ICAAP.

Banks tend to calculate the capital buffer they hold by simply extrapolating figures from previous events, instead of using a forecast risk profile. The ICAAP should clearly distinguish between a company's regulatory capital, its actual capital, and the capital it needs to hold for business purposes. Using a newly developed ICAAP should provide firms with the best capital buffer required, and the best level of funds from stockholders. Risks are often considered by a bank, yet are not always reflected in strategic options and capital planning. ICAAP requires stress and scenario analysis to demonstrate risks at an enterprise level.

Firm managers must show that ICAAP is an integral part of its processes and demonstrate that senior management both supports and is engaged in the ICAAP. In addition, companies need to explain in detail how they will use the ICAAP as they move forward and how key risk indicators and economic capital indicators/assumptions can be updated and presented to the board of directors when required. ICAAP is still in its early stages—companies are being encouraged to embrace the process for the sake of their business rather than for purposes of regulation. Management should understand the positive benefits and strive, through ICAAP, to make the business more efficient and less risky.

MORE INFO

Report:

Financial Services Authority. "ICAAP submission—suggested format." November 22, 2007. Online at: www.fsa.gov.uk/pages/About/What/International/pdf/ICAAP_sub.pdf.

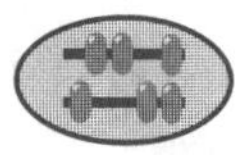
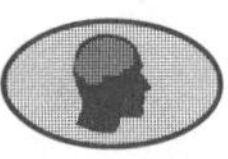

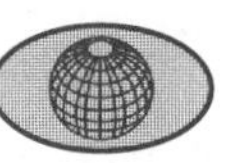

Understanding Impairment Accounting: What It Is and When It Is Used

DEFINITION

Impairment of assets is the diminishing in quality, strength, amount, or value of an asset. The term "long-lived asset" refers to such properties as a business organization's buildings, land, machinery, and equipment. These assets may be susceptible to an impairment (decline) of their value, which may be caused by factors such as poor management, new competition, and technological innovations. Impairment losses are stated in the profit-and-loss account. The impairment value is measured by comparing the value of the fixed asset or income-generating unit with its recoverable amount. The recoverable amount is the highest value that can be obtained from selling the fixed asset or income-generating unit.

As with most generally accepted accounting principles (GAAP), the definition of impairment is often in the eye of the beholder. Determining fair value has always been problematic, with different professionals arriving at different valuations. There is limited guidance as to how or when to recognize impairments, how impairments should be measured, and how impairments should be disclosed.

The impairment of assets provides investors with a way to evaluate corporate management and its decision-making track record. Investors, creditors, and financial analysts who have not kept their eye on the ball are often surprised when asset write-downs are reported.

ADVANTAGES

- Impairment charges, if applied correctly, provide investors and analysts with ways to assess company management and its decision-making track record. Managers that must write down or write off assets due to impairment have not made first-class investment choices.
- Many business failures are preceded by a decline in the impairment value of assets. Such revelations could serve as early warning signals to investors and creditors.

DISADVANTAGES

- It can be difficult to determine which measure of value should be used when assessing impairment. Options include current cost (replacement cost), current market value (selling price), net realizable value (selling price minus disposal costs), or the sum of the future net cash flows from the income-generating unit.
- There is little detailed guidance on accounting for asset impairments, when to recognize impairments, how impairments should be measured, and how impairments should be disclosed. The definition of impairment is often, therefore, just a matter of individual judgment.

ACTION CHECKLIST

- ✔ Study carefully the impairment of assets of any business in which you have an interest. Obtain as much information from as many different sources as possible to confirm the findings before making decisions.
- ✔ Check which measure of value was used when assessing impairment: Current cost (replacement cost), current market value (selling price), net realizable value (selling price minus disposal costs), or the sum of the future net cash flows from the income-generating unit.
- ✔ Don't take shortcuts because hidden potential write-downs may cost more in the long run.
- ✔ Check which GAAP are used in the specific enterprise, business area, or country in which you are interested.

DOS AND DON'TS

DO

- Make sure that you have checked the financial ratios used in the impairment analysis in detail. If in doubt, consult an expert analyst.
- Involve accountants and industry experts in your evaluation of the financial impairment of a company.
- When comparing a business's impairment valuations with other firms in an industry, allow for any material differences in accounting policies between the compared company and industry norms.

DON'T

- Don't take for granted goodwill valuations that have sometimes come from acquisitions during the "bubble" years, when companies overpaid for assets by using overpriced stock.
- Don't rely solely on ratios when making decisions. Use market research to confirm the results.
- Don't fall into the trap of thinking that financial ratios are infallible.

▸▸ MORE INFO

Books:

Horngren, Charles T., Gary L. Sundem, John A. Elliott, and Donna Philbrick. *Introduction to Financial Accounting*. 9th ed. Upper Saddle River, NJ: Prentice Hall, 2006.

Nikolai, Loren A., and John D. Bazley. *Intermediate Accounting*. 9th ed. Mason, OH: South-Western, 1999.

Rolfe, Tom. *Financial Accounting and Tax Principles: Managerial Level*. Oxford: Butterworth-Heinemann, 2007.

Articles:

Gula, Michelle. "Weathering the credit market storms: A down credit cycle combined with new credit impairment accounting rules bring both challenges and opportunities." *ABA Banking Journal* (October 2007).

"Impairment of assets." *Australasian Business Intelligence* (March 2007).

Websites:

American Accounting Association: aaahq.org

Financial Accounting Standards Board: www.fasb.org

International Federation of Accountants: www.ifac.org

"The depths and strength of a human character are defined by its moral reserves. People reveal themselves completely only when they are thrown out of the customary conditions of their life, for only then do they have to fall back on their reserves." Leon Trotsky

     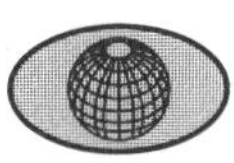   

Understanding Internal Audits

DEFINITION

The Institute for Internal Auditors (IIA) defines internal auditing as "an independent, objective assurance and consulting activity designed to add value and improve an organization's operations." An internal audit "helps an organization accomplish its objectives by bringing a systematic, disciplined approach to evaluate and improve the effectiveness of risk management, control and governance processes."

The following comprise a set of guidelines for initiating an internal audit:

- Clarify guidelines and expectations with management (for example, purpose, timing, scope).
- Set up an audit committee and, with its help, develop an audit charter.
- Consider an appropriate budget and staffing model.
- Formulate reporting responsibilities for the internal audit function.
- Initiate a risk assessment, with management and audit committee involvement.
- Develop an internal audit plan in response to the risk assessment.
- Determine staffing requirements.
- Carry out the audit plan, including a monitoring and follow-up system.
- Update the risk assessment plan as circumstances change.
- Enhance and modify the audit function to meet the organization's changing needs.

If an evaluation of internal controls is to be effective, the audit function should be properly financed. When making staffing decisions, companies should look at their risk profiles. A business facing a significant number of risks or particularly complex risks will require various types of specialist expertize. A chief audit executive heads most internal audit departments, with specialist support staff.

ADVANTAGES

- Internal audits improve understanding of underlying business trends by giving independent objective financial information.
- Internal audits let managers know if a business can expand or needs to pull back, if it can deal with the normal revenue ebbs and flows, or if it should take immediate steps to boost cash reserves.
- Internal audits can identify and help to analyze trends, particularly in the areas of receivables and payables. For example, is the receivables cycle lengthening? Can receivables be collected more aggressively? Is some debt un-collectable?

DISADVANTAGES

- Results sometimes depend on the accounting methods used. Measuring and reporting give management considerable discretion and opportunity to influence results.
- Internal audits are not always rigorously carried out, and figures may not be a true reflection of the financial position of the company.
- Salaries for internal audit staff are paid for by the organization; this can lead to bias.

ACTION CHECKLIST

- ✔ When reviewing internal audits be prepared to be involved in a long and detailed process of analysis where some areas will need clarification by experts.
- ✔ Check which Generally Accepted Accounting Principles (GAAP) are used in the internal audit of the business area or country in which you have an interest.
- ✔ Internal audits are not infallible. If you are unsure about specific areas or numbers, don't hesitate to ask for clarification

DOS AND DON'TS

DO

- Make sure that you take the time and effort to analyze the internal audit and, if in doubt, consult an external expert.
- Use your judgment when reviewing internal audits; numbers do not always tell the whole story.

DON'T

- Don't leave out the boring bits; number crunching is not always effortless or interesting, and often it is tempting to skip parts. Sometimes, however, the truth lies in the detail.

▸▸ MORE INFO

Websites:

HM Treasury, United Kingdom (Audit policy and advice): www.hm-treasury.gov.uk
Institute of Internal Auditors: www.theiia.org
US Treasury: www.ustreas.gov

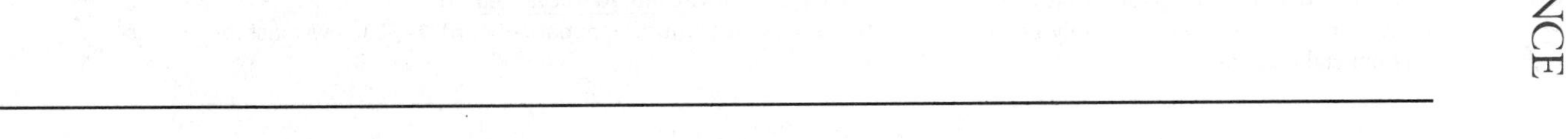

"He is a man of brick. As if he was born as a baby literally of clay and decades of exposure have baked him to the color and hardness of brick." John Updike

  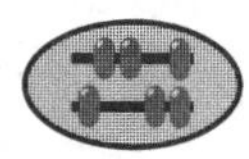   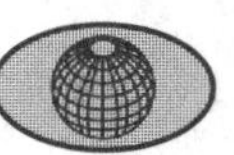   

Understanding the Key Components of GAAP: The Continuing Concern Concept

DEFINITION

Generally Accepted Accounting Principles (GAAP) are not a fixed set of rules. They are guidelines or a group of objectives and concepts that have evolved on the best way to govern how financial statements are prepared and presented.

The guidelines are as follows:

- The *business entity concept* provides that the balance sheet of the business must reflect the financial position of the business alone.
- The *continuing concern concept* assumes that a business will continue to operate, unless it is known otherwise.
- The *principle of conservatism* provides that accounting for a business should be fair and that evaluations and estimates should be reasonable.
- The *objectivity principle* states that accounting will be recorded on the basis of objective evidence—that accounting entries will be based on fact and not on personal opinion or feelings.
- The *time period concept* provides that accounting takes place over specific fiscal periods of equal length.
- The *revenue recognition convention* provides that revenues are recognized at the time the transaction is completed.
- The *matching principle* states that each expense item related to revenue earned must be recorded in the same accounting period as the revenue it helped to earn.
- The *cost principle* states that accounting for purchases must be at their cost price.
- The *consistency principle* requires accountants to apply the same methods and procedures from period to period, because the readers of financial statements have the right to assume that consistency has been applied if there is no statement to the contrary.
- The *materiality principle* requires accountants to use GAAP except when to do so would be expensive or difficult, and where it makes no real difference if the rules are ignored.
- The *full disclosure principle* states that any and all information that affects the full understanding of a company's financial statements must be included with the financial statements.

GAAP compliance is vital. It helps businesses to maintain their creditability with creditors and shareholders because the principles reassure the public that a company's financial reports accurately portray its financial position.

Note that Generally Accepted Accounting Principles are known in the United Kingdom as Generally Accepted Accounting Practice.

ADVANTAGES

- These are general rules and concepts that direct the field of accounting and form the foundation on which more detailed, complicated, and legalistic accounting rules are based.
- The Financial Accounting Standards Board (FASB) uses the basic GAAP accounting principles and guidelines as the starting place for its own, more detailed and comprehensive set of accounting rules and standards.

DISADVANTAGES

- GAAP compliance poses challenges to small businesses with limited resources.
- GAAP are not strict rules. They are only guidelines or a group of objectives and concepts that have evolved on the best way to govern how financial statements are prepared and presented.
- Measuring and reporting give management considerable discretion and the opportunity to influence results. Those results sometimes depend on the accounting methods used.

ACTION CHECKLIST

- ✔ When reviewing audits based on GAAP, be prepared to be involved in a long and detailed analysis. Some areas will need clarification by experts.
- ✔ Check which GAAP are used in the internal audit of the business in which you are interested.
- ✔ GAAP is not infallible. If you are unsure about specific areas or numbers, ask for clarification.
- ✔ Don't be frightened to ask what may seem naïve or uncomfortable questions.
- ✔ Use the GAAP concepts and guidelines as a basis to help you understand the more complex accounting practices that are used in the specific enterprise, business area, or country in which you are interested.

DOS AND DON'TS

DO

- Make sure that you take the time and make the effort to analyze the accounts. If in doubt, consult an independent expert.

DON'T

- Don't skip the boring bits; accounting is not always simple or interesting, and often it is easier to skip parts. However, sometimes the truth lies in the detail.

⏩ MORE INFO

Books:

Bragg, Steven M. *GAAP Implementation Guide*. Hoboken, NJ: Wiley, 2004.

Epstein, Barry J., Ralph Nach, and Steven M. Bragg. *Wiley GAAP 2007: Interpretation and Application of Generally Accepted Accounting Principles*. Hoboken, NJ: Wiley, 2006.

Articles:

Cangemi, Michael P. "Warning: U.S. GAAP likely headed for extinction." *Financial Executive* (March 1, 2008). Online at: www.highbeam.com/doc/1G1-176981496.html

Sayther, Colleen. "Widening the gap: Big GAAP vs. little GAAP." *Financial Executive* (September 1, 2004). Online at: www.allbusiness.com/finance-insurance/222110-1.html

Websites:

Federal Accounting Standards Advisery Board (FASAB) Generally Accepted Accounting Principles: www.fasab.gov/accepted.html

International Accounting Standards Board (IASB): www.iasb.org/Home

"And so, my fellow Americans: ask not what your country can do for you. Ask what you can do for your country." John F. Kennedy

   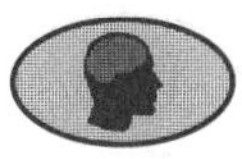  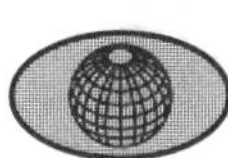   

United Kingdom: Regulatory Structure and Powers

DEFINITION

All financial services and markets within the jurisdiction of the United Kingdom are regulated by the Financial Services Authority (FSA), an independent, nongovernmental, quasi-judicial body. In its role as the competent authority for the listing of stocks on a stock exchange, it is known as the UK Listing Authority (UKLA), and maintains the Official List of securities traded on UK regulated markets as defined in the Investment Services Directive.

The UK financial services industry was entirely self-regulating, and regulatory powers were spread across a large number of bodies, until 1985, when the Securities and Investments Board Ltd (SIB) was incorporated and given certain statutory regulatory powers under the Financial Services Act 1986. Following the collapse of Barings Bank, self-regulation was ended and regulatory responsibilities were consolidated within the SIB. The SIB became the FSA in 1997, and now exercises statutory powers legislated in the Financial Services and Markets Act 2000.

The FSA currently has responsibility for regulating banks, insurance companies and financial advisers, and mortgage business and general insurance brokers. The FSA has four statutory objectives as defined by the Financial Services and Markets Act:

1. market confidence: to maintain confidence in the financial system;
2. public awareness: to promote public understanding of the financial system;
3. consumer protection: to secure the appropriate degree of protection for consumers;
4. reduction of financial crime: to limit the possibilities to commit financial crime by regulated persons.

The FSA's statutory objectives are backed up by a number of regulatory principles, which it must follow when carrying out its duties. These are:

- efficiency and economy: using its resources in the most efficient and economic manner;
- role of management: this principle aims to prevent the FSA intruding unnecessarily into a company's business. The FSA holds a company's senior management responsible for its activities, and for ensuring that it complies with regulatory requirements. A company must, therefore, have sufficient risk management controls in place, have designated lines of responsibility, and ensure its business can be adequately monitored and controlled;
- proportionality: any restrictions the FSA imposes on the industry must be in proportion to the benefits that are expected to result, and the FSA must consider the costs to companies and consumers. This applies to the different regulatory requirements for both the wholesale and the retail markets;
- innovation: the FSA aims to facilitate innovation in regulated activities, such as permitting different ways of compliance so that market participants do not face too many restrictions when launching new financial products and services.
- international character: the FSA aims to maintain the United Kingdom's competitive position by monitoring the international financial services industry and cooperating with overseas regulators, for the purpose of agreeing international standards.
- competition: the FSA strives to minimize any adverse effects on competition arising from its activities and to facilitate competition within the United Kingdom's financial sector. This includes reducing regulatory barriers to entry or business expansion. The FSA's rules and practices on competition are monitored by HM Treasury, the Office of Fair Trading, and the Competition Commission within the framework of the Financial Services and Markets Act.

The FSA is accountable to Treasury ministers, and thence to Parliament. It is funded entirely by the companies it regulates through a mix of fines, fees, and compulsory levies. The Treasury appoints all the FSA's board members, and sets out the scope of activities that should be regulated. The board decides on the shape of the regulatory regime and determines overall policy. Day-to-day decisions are the responsibility of the executive, which is divided into three sections—retail markets, wholesale and institutional markets, and regulatory services—each headed by a managing director.

The Financial Services and Markets Tribunal is an independent judicial body that has responsibility for handling appeals against the FSA's regulatory decisions.

▸▸ MORE INFO

Books:

Bazley, Stuart and Andrew Haynes. *Financial Services Authority Regulation and Risk-based Compliance*. 2nd ed. Haywards Heath, UK: Tottel Publishing, 2006.

Financial Services Authority. *FSA Handbook: Regulatory Processes Decision Procedure and Penalties*. London: Butterworths Law, 2007.

Websites:

The Compliance Exchange: www.compliance-exchange.com/

Financial Services Authority: www.fsa.gov.uk/

UKLA Official List: www.fsa.gov.uk/ukla/officialList.do

UK Listing Authority: www.fsa.gov.uk/Pages/Doing/UKLA/index.shtml

  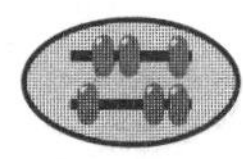   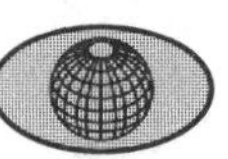 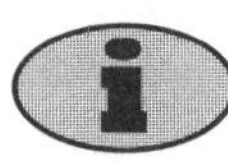  

Using and Understanding Financial Ratios for Analysis

DEFINITION

Ratio analysis uses an amalgamation of financial or operating data from a company or industry to provide a basis for comparison. Every ratio measures a unique association that may have an impact on other ratios. In accounts, a financial ratio or accounting ratio is used to evaluate the overall financial condition of a company or other organization. Company owners, stockholders, or potential investors use ratio analysis to gauge viability, liabilities, and future performance.

A company owner should continuously evaluate the performance of the company by comparing its historical figures with those for industry competitors and even with those for successful businesses in other industries. To complete a thorough examination of a company's proficiency, however, an owner needs to look at more than easily attainable numbers such as sales, profits, and total assets. Ratio analysis needs to be used to read between the lines of financial statements and make sense of the numbers. This will allow the owner to identify and quantify the company's strengths and weaknesses, evaluate its financial position, and understand the risks it may be facing.

For private and institutional investors, ratios are important profit tools in financial analysis. Although ratios report mostly on past performance, they can be predictive too, and can provide indications of potential problem areas. Ratio analysis is used primarily to compare a company's financial results over a period of time–a method sometimes called trend analysis. Trend analysis can also show how a company's ratios stack up against those of other businesses, both within and outside the industry. Ratios allow for comparisons between companies, between industries, between time periods for a single company, and between a single company and its industry.

A multitude of financial ratios is available. The following are generally considered the most important:

- *Liquidity Ratios* measure how readily a company can meet its obligations.
- *Profitability Ratios* give an indication of the earnings and profitability potential of a company.
- *Asset Management Ratios* gauge how efficiently a company can change assets into sales.
- *Debt Management Ratios* indicate how debt-leveraged a company is, and how it can manage the debt in terms of assets and operating income.
- *Dividend/Market Value Ratios* measure how well a company uses its assets to generate earnings.
- *Profitability Ratios* indicate earnings and potential profitability.

ADVANTAGES

- Financial ratios use a combination of financial and/or operating data to allow potential investors to judge the viability, liabilities, and probable future performance of a company or industry.
- Ratio analysis permits analysts to read between the lines of financial statements and make sense of the numbers, thereby identifying and quantifying a company's strengths and weaknesses.
- Financial ratios can provide indications of potential problem areas and allow corrective measures to be taken.

DISADVANTAGES

- Due to different worldwide accounting standards, comparisons between companies and industries are not always possible.
- Financial ratios may not always reflect the true nature of a company's accounts, as managers may attempt to gloss over problems.
- Financial ratios are based only on past performance; they cannot take into account future events.

ACTION CHECKLIST

- ✔ Obtain as much information and compare as many ratios as possible before committing to an expensive decision.
- ✔ Make sure that you have analyzed the financial ratios in detail. If in doubt, consult an expert analyst.
- ✔ Be prepared to be involved in a long and complicated process of analysis. Some gray areas will not be resolved by financial ratios.
- ✔ Do not economize by taking shortcuts, because hidden problems may cost more in the long run.

DOS AND DON'TS

DO

- In a comparative analysis of a company's financial statements over a period of time, make allowances for any changes in accounting policies that occurred during the period.
- When comparing a business with others in an industry, allow for any material differences in accounting policies between the compared company and industry norms.
- Determine whether ratios were calculated before or after adjustments were made to the balance sheet or income statement, such as non-recurring items and inventory or pro forma adjustments. In many cases, these adjustments can significantly affect the ratios.
- Carefully examine any departures from industry norms.

DON'T

- Don't rely only on ratios when making decisions. Use market research to confirm the results.
- Don't fall into the trap of thinking that financial ratios are infallible.

▸▸ MORE INFO

Website:

American Express: www133.americanexpress.com/osbn/tool/ratios/financialratio.asp

See Also:

✔ Understanding and Using Interest Coverage Ratios (p. 1026)
✔ Understanding Fixed-Charge Coverage (p. 1030)

"For every five well-adjusted and smoothly functioning Americans, there are two who never had the chance to discover themselves. It may well be because they have never been alone with themselves." Marya Mannes

     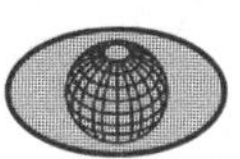   

What Is Forensic Auditing?

DEFINITION

Forensic auditing is a blend of traditional accounting, auditing, and financial detective work. Technology has an increasingly important role to play, with complex data analysis techniques employed to help flag areas that warrant further investigation.

Forensic auditing offers a toolset that company managers can use to help detect and investigate various forms of white-collar financial impropriety and inappropriate or inefficient use of resources. As company structures and controls become ever more complex, so too does the scope for employees with specialized knowledge of the way control systems work to bypass them. In the past, various forms of auditing have been employed after a major control breach has come to light, but executives are now increasingly looking at forensic auditing to help identify vulnerabilities in financial control.

ADVANTAGES

- Forensic auditing strengthens control mechanisms, with the objective of protecting the business against financial crimes, be they potentially catastrophic one-off events that could threaten the viability of the business, or smaller-scale but repetitive misappropriations of company assets over a number of years.
- Forensic auditing can play an important role for companies under review by regulatory authorities and can also be invaluable to ensure regulatory compliance. For example, forensic auditing can be useful in helping companies to ensure that their anti-money laundering procedures are both effective and robust.
- Forensic auditing can help protect organizations from the long-term damage to reputation caused by the publicity associated with insider crimes. A forensic audit also provides a sound base of factual information that can be used to help resolve disputes, and can be used in court should the victim seek legal redress.
- Forensic auditing can improve efficiency by identifying areas of waste.
- Forensic auditing can help with the detection and recording of potential conflicts of interest for executives by improving transparency and probity in the way resources are used, in both private and public entities.

DISADVANTAGES

- A poorly managed forensic audit could consume excessive amounts of management time and could become an unwelcome distraction for the business.
- Forensic audits can have wide-ranging scope across the business. Under certain circumstances, the scope of the audit may need to be extended, with a corresponding increase in the budget.
- Some employees can interpret a proactive forensic audit as a slight on their integrity, rather than as a means to improve control procedures for the benefit of the business.

ACTION CHECKLIST

- ✔ Understand your risks, routes to their potential exploitation, and the tools available to detect abuses, fraud, or wastage.
- ✔ Analyze numerical data, comparing actual costs against expected costs.
- ✔ Investigate possible reasons for inconsistencies.
- ✔ Consider whether covert detection techniques might be more appropriate when investigating cases of possible fraud. Higher-profile full forensic audits can deter future fraud but could also reduce the likelihood of witnessing the culprit carrying out a fraudulent act.
- ✔ External auditing specialists with extensive experience of complex forensic audits can offer industry-specific experience, auditing management expertise, and advanced interviewing techniques. A combination of these external specialists and companies' internal accountants/auditors can achieve shorter audit timescales and lower levels of disruption to the business.

DOS AND DON'TS

DO

- Remember that well-resourced forensic auditing processes can help to identify misreporting at many levels of an organization.
- Bear in mind that regular proactive forensic audits can help businesses to ensure that their processes stay robust.
- Be prepared to widen the scope of a forensic audit to ensure maximum effectiveness.
- See forensic auditing as a continuous process, rather than a one-off event. On completing one audit, restarting the process could uncover something relevant that was previously overlooked.
- Be prepared to share the findings of the forensic audit with other areas of your company, and take into account industry best practice to improve efficiency and combat fraud.

DON'T

- Don't lose sight of the objective of a forensic audit. The cost of a forensic audit can be high, but the potential cost of not undertaking an audit and implementing its findings can be even higher.
- Don't fall into the trap of overlooking the importance of the "forensic" element of the audit. With the results of such a process deemed suitable for inclusion in legal proceedings, the high potential costs of the forensic audit process could easily be recovered from dispute resolution or higher levels of loss recovery.

▸▸ MORE INFO

Book:

Cardwell, Harvey. *Principles of Audit Surveillance*. Reprise Edition. Philadelphia, PA: R.T. Edwards, 2005.

Articles:

Brannen, Laurie. "Is a forensic audit in your future?" *Business Finance* (June 2007).

Roberts, Marta. "Fraud fight in the Wild West." *Security Management* 48:11 (2004).

Websites:

American Institute of Certified Public Accountants: www.aicpa.org

Institute of Chartered Accountants in England and Wales: www.icaew.com

Institute of Forensic Accounting & Investigative Audit: www.ifaia.org

"But change and the willingness to change, to try anything, try anyone's idea, it might not work. But it won't break the company when it doesn't." Sam M. Walton

     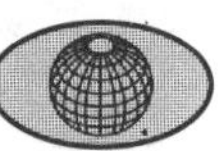   

Appraising Investment Opportunities

DEFINITION

As a rule, one of the most critical decisions for any business is long-term investment. This investment can be the purchase of land, buildings, machinery, or other assets in the expectation of earning an income over and above the funds committed. Appraisals are performed to find out whether such investments will yield returns to an organization over a period of time. The appraisals look at the outflows and inflows of funds, the duration of the investment, the scale of risk attached, and the cost of acquiring the funds.

The critical questions in an investment appraisal are:

- What is the extent of the investment, and can the business meet the expense?
- How long will it take to pay back the investment?
- When will the investment start to yield returns?
- What is the return on the investment?
- Would the money be better employed elsewhere?

The methods used when conducting an investment appraisal are:

- *Payback*: The amount of time needed to repay the initial investment.
- *Average rate of return*: The profits from an investment as a percentage of the initial capital cost.
- *Net present value*: Uses opportunity cost (i.e. the cost of an alternative choice when making a decision that must be given up in order to follow a certain action) to put a value on cash inflows from the capital invested.
- *Internal rate of return*: The annual percentage return on an investment when the sum of the discounted cash inflows over the life of the investment is equal to the sum of the capital invested.

ADVANTAGES

- Investment appraisals allow managers to make long-term plans on the projects that will yield the best returns for the business.
- *Payback* is easily understood and calculated.
- *Average rate of return* is easily understood and employs commonly used accounting rules.
- *Net present value* recognizes that a business incurs costs, such as interest on borrowing.
- *Internal rate of return* shows how well an investment will perform under different interest rates.

DISADVANTAGES

- The feasibility of the investment appraisal depends on many unknowns, for example the viability of information, financial analysis, and the management skills on which the project is based.
- *Payback* does not take into account optimal payback time or the effect on profitability.
- *Average rate of return* does not take into account the duration of the investment or the timing of cash flows.
- *Net present value* is sensitive to the discount rate applied.
- Management may focus on maximizing the internal rate of return and not net present value.

ACTION CHECKLIST

- ✔ Identify the key investment objectives for the organization and plan around those objectives.
- ✔ Have realistic in-depth budgets been calculated?
- ✔ Will rapid technological change make plant and machinery obsolete sooner and, therefore, will the payback period need to be shortened?
- ✔ Are resources invested in the most profitable objectives, and what alternatives are available?
- ✔ Has a risk analysis been carried out on the project to take into account risks and their impact?

DOS AND DON'TS

DO

- Take into account the duration and timing of cash flows.
- Consider how emerging risks necessitate regular reviews, and how risks such as new technology might affect the long-term viability of the project.
- Involve key stakeholders in an investment appraisal.
- Consider seeking the help of specialist consultants.

DON'T

- Don't make the mistake of being attracted to a project that has not been thoroughly investigated and appraised.
- Don't take risks for granted; although a risk may have been the same in the past, there is no guarantee that it will be the same in the future.

▸▸ MORE INFO

Books:

Langdon, K. *Investment Appraisal*. Oxford: Capstone, 2002.

McLaney, E. *Business Finance: Theory and Practice*. 7th ed. Harlow, UK: Pearson Education, 2006.

Pettinger, R. *Investment Appraisal: A Managerial Approach*. Basingstoke, UK: Palgrave Macmillan, 2000.

Articles:

Chartered Management Institute. "Investment appraisal (Checklist 181)." *Chartered Management Institute: Checklists: Small Business* (October 1, 2005). Online at: www.thefreelibrary.com/Investment+appraisal-a0141751344

Steven, G. "Management accounting-decision management: The internal rate of return may be a flawed investment appraisal method, writes Grahame Steven, but there is a small modification that can help." *Financial Management* (March 2008). Online at: http://findarticles.com/p/articles/mi_m0JQT/is_/ai_n25020555

Websites:

International Federation of Accountants (IFAC): www.ifac.org

Institute of Internal Auditors (IIA): www.theiia.org

See Also:

★ Capital Budgeting: The Dominance of Net Present Value (pp. 23–26)

✔ Understanding the Relationship between the Discount Rate and Risk (p. 896)

"While we stop to think, we often miss an opportunity." Publilius Syrus

  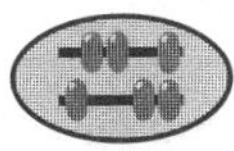   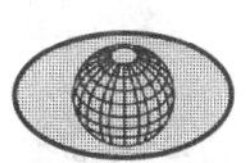   

Assessing Business Performance

DEFINITION

Regular assessments of business performance are vital. It is easy to lose direction and focus only on the day-to-day development of your business. Longer-term and more strategic planning is necessary to get the most out of your business and market opportunities.

Companies need to:

- Review their activities and reevaluate the products that they make or the services they provide. Why are these products or services successful? Are they priced correctly? What could be improved? Is there a market for new or complementary products or services?
- Assess business efficiency. How do you compare with the competition? Are your IT systems adequate? How flexible are your structures? How well do you address customers' needs? Do you have in place an appraisal system for investment opportunities?
- Assess staff. Do you have a high turnover of staff? Are they motivated? Are their skills adequate, or do they need retraining?
- Redefine goals. Where is the business now, where is it going, and how is it going to get there?
- Companies should review their financial statements to help assess their performance:
- The profit and loss statement tells the company whether it is making a profit, as it indicates how revenue is transformed into net income.
- The balance sheet shows assets, liabilities, and shareholders' equity/capital.
- The cash flow forecast or statement identifies the sources and amounts of cash coming into and going out of a business over a given period.

Another way to assess a company's performance is to employ ratio analysis, which uses a combination of financial and/or operating data as a basis for making comparisons with other companies:

- Liquidity ratios give a measure of how readily a company can meet its obligations.
- Profitability ratios give an indication of the earnings and profitability potential of a company.
- Asset management ratios gauge how efficiently a company can change assets into sales.
- Debt management ratios indicate how debt-leveraged a company is, and how it can manage the debt in terms of assets and operating income.
- Dividend/market value ratios measure how well a company uses its assets to generate earnings.
- Profitability ratios indicate earnings and potential profitability.

ADVANTAGES

- Regularly assessing business performance allows for longer-term and more strategic planning, which is necessary to optimize business and market opportunities.
- Ratio analysis permits analysts to read between the lines of financial statements and identify a company's strengths and weaknesses.
- Financial ratios provide lead indications of potential problem areas and allow corrective measures to be taken.

DISADVANTAGES

- Profit and loss statements do not report factors that might be highly relevant but cannot be reliably measured (for example, brand recognition and customer loyalty).
- A balance sheet shows a snapshot of a company's assets, liabilities, and shareholders' equity. It does not show the flows into and out of the accounts during the period.
- Financial ratios are based on past performance; they cannot take into account future events.

ACTION CHECKLIST

- ✔ What direction should the company take over the next three to five years?
- ✔ What are the company's markets, and how should it compete?
- ✔ How can the company gain market advantage and compete better in the future?
- ✔ What resources will be needed in assets, finance, staff, etc.?
- ✔ Obtain as much information and compare as many ratios as you can when assessing a business's performance.

DOS AND DON'TS

DO

- Determine whether ratios were calculated before or after adjustments were made to the balance sheet or income statement, such as nonrecurring items and inventory or pro-forma adjustments. In many cases, these adjustments can significantly affect the ratios.

DON'T

- Don't rely solely on ratios when taking decisions. Use market research to confirm the results.
- Don't fall into the trap of thinking that financial ratios are infallible.

▸▸ MORE INFO

Books:

Business: The Ultimate Resource. 2nd ed. London: A&C Black Publishers, 2006.

Porter, L. J., S. J. Tanner, and European Centre for Business Excellence. *Assessing Business Excellence: A Guide to Business Excellence and Self-Assessment.* Oxford: Butterworth-Heinemann, 2004.

Young, P. C., and S. C. Tippins. *Managing Business Risk: An Organization-wide Approach to Risk Management.* New York: AMACOM, 2000.

Articles:

Donley, S. "Business performance: The management grill—how to assess strategic tools." *New Zealand Management* 52:2 (March 2005: 43).

Marketwire. "IBM unveils new financial management tool to help companies analyze and improve finance effectiveness." Marketwire press release (July 25, 2008). Online at: www.marketwire.com/press-release/Ibm-NYSE-IBM-882787.html

Websites:

JIT Software: www.jit-software.com

Value Based Management.net—Management methods, models, and theories: www.valuebasedmanagement.net

"Our fixation with financial measures leads us to downplay or ignore less tangible non-financial measures."
Tom Peters

  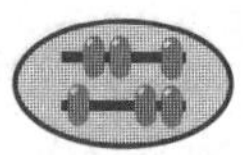   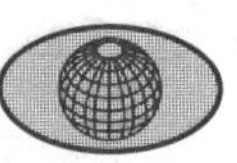   

Assessing Economies of Scale in Business

DEFINITION

Economies of scale arise when the cost per unit falls as output increases due to efficiencies gained in the production process. Normally, this is because fixed costs are shared across a larger number of goods. Adam Smith believed that the two major steps required to achieve economies of scale were specialization and the division of labor. Diseconomies of scale happen when a firm produces goods or services at an increased cost per unit.

For example, a computer manufacturer producing 1,000 computers at $250 each could expand to produce 2,000 computers at $200 each. The manufacturer's total production costs have risen from $250,000 to $400,000, but the cost of each computer has fallen from $250 to $200. If the manufacturer sells the computers for $350 each, the profit margin per computer rises from $100 to $150.

Economies of Scale

- *Management*: In larger businesses, managers are specialists in particular fields and are likely to be more efficient, as they possess high levels of skills and experience.
- *Purchasing*: As businesses develop, they require larger quantities of production inputs. Larger orders of raw materials will enable them to obtain lower prices from suppliers.
- *Technology*: The use of advanced machinery allows more efficient mass production. Larger companies also have the capacity to invest more heavily in research and development.
- *Funding*: Larger firms, which generally have longer and more stable track records, find it easier to find lenders and to raise money at lower interest rates.
- *Marketing*: Many marketing costs, such as advertising and managing a sales force, are fixed. As a business gains market share, it can reduce the average marketing cost per unit.

Diseconomies of Scale

- *Communication*: As firms grow larger, channels of communication slow. This can lead to increased costs and duplication of effort.
- *Bureaucracy*: The bigger the business, the larger is the proportion of the workforce that is employed in management.
- *Competition*: Larger businesses with multiple brands often find that their own products are competing with each other.
- *Industrial relations*: Confrontations can occur between management and labor as goals and interests diverge.

ADVANTAGES

- The cost per unit falls as output increases, due to efficiencies gained in the production process.
- The sharing of fixed costs over a larger number of goods leads to lower prices.
- Managers in large companies are specialists in particular fields and should be more efficient.
- As their purchasing power increases, businesses are able to obtain lower prices for raw materials.
- Large-scale production normally takes advantage of more technically advanced and more cost-effective machinery.
- Larger firms generally find it easier to raise money at lower interest rates.
- Many marketing and sales costs are fixed, so a larger business can reduce the average marketing cost per unit.

DISADVANTAGES

- A large business is able to pass on lower costs to customers through lower prices and thus increase its market share. This could be a threat to smaller businesses, which might close because of the competition.
- Clogged channels of communication in large businesses can lead to increased costs and duplication of effort.
- Large companies may have a top-heavy workforce, with too many bosses and not enough workers.
- Companies with multiple brands can find that these brands compete with each other.

ACTION CHECKLIST

- ✔ How efficient is your production process, and how do your unit costs compare with the competition?
- ✔ Could you use just-in-time (JIT) ordering to make your purchasing process more effective and, at the same time, obtain lower prices for your raw materials?
- ✔ Conduct an investment appraisal to find out whether the company is using the most cost-effective and technically advanced machinery.

DOS AND DON'TS

DO

- Consider conducting regular reviews of the various aspects of economies of scale to fine tune your production.

DON'T

- Don't forget how diseconomies of scale can upset the best-laid plans.

▸▸ MORE INFO

Books:

Jeston, J., and J. Nelis. *Business Process Management: Practical Guidelines to Successful Implementations*. Oxford: Butterworth-Heinemann, 2006.

Longenecker, Justin G., *et al. Small Business Management: An Entrepreneurial Emphasis*. 13th ed. Mason, OH: South-Western College Publishing, 2005.

McClave, J. T., P. G. Benson, and T. Sincich. *Statistics for Business and Economics*. Upper Saddle River, NJ: Pearson Prentice Hall, 2007.

Articles:

Fielding, Roy T. "Economies of scale." Blog, September 22, 2008. Online at: roy.gbiv.com/untangled/2008/economies-of-scale

Hirsch, A. "Adam Smith's legacy: His place in the development of modern economics." Book review, *Southern Economic Journal* (January 1, 1995).

Linux Information Project. "Economies of scale definition." *Linux Information Project* (2006). Online at: www.bellevuelinux.org/economies_of_scale.html

UXL Newsmakers. "Adam Smith." *UXL Newsmakers* (2005). Online at: findarticles.com/p/articles/mi_gx5221/is_2005/ai_n19140352

See Also:

★ Asset and Liability Management (pp. 1559–1560)

✔ Key Components of an Optimal Enterprise Resource Planning System (p. 870)

"There are as many foolhardy ways to grow as there are to downsize." Gary Hamel

  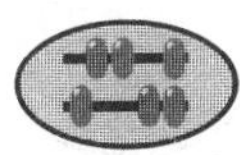   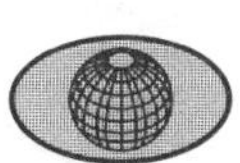   

Understanding Decision-Tree Analysis

DEFINITION

In operational areas, a decision tree—also known as a tree diagram—is a tool for reaching decisions. It uses a diagram or model of decisions and their possible outcomes, including chance events, resource costs, and utility. A decision tree can be used to select the strategy most likely to attain a specific goal. Decision trees are also used as predictive models in data mining (the science of uncovering hidden patterns in data) and machine learning (the development of algorithms and other techniques that enable computers to "learn").

Decision trees have three types of node:

1 *Decision nodes*: In the diagram these are usually represented by squares;
2 *Chance nodes*: Represented by circles;
3 *End nodes*: Represented by triangles.

A tree is usually drawn from left to right, with splitting paths (burst nodes) but no converging paths (sink nodes). Thus, when drawn by hand, the diagram tends to get very big to the right.

Decision trees can be a very effective structure for exploring options and investigating the consequences of choices of action. They can also help to form a picture of the risks and rewards for each possible course of action. In a financial context, decision trees can help to determine the best strategies for investment.

Drawing a decision tree begins with the decision that needs to be made, usually represented by a small square on the left-hand side of a large sheet of paper. For each possible choice a line is drawn out to the right, with a short description written along each line. At the end of each line the result, or outcome, should be stated; this may be an uncertain outcome (circle) or another decision (square), and the result should be written above the symbol. The process is repeated as required from each new decision square, always annotated with descriptions. Once drawn, the tree should be reviewed, as it is unlikely that all possibilities will emerge during the first round.

To work out which option has the greatest value, the decision tree is evaluated by assigning a cash value to each possible outcome. For each circle (an uncertain outcome), the probability of each outcome is estimated as a percentage, with the total of all possible outcomes for each course of action equaling 100%. Obviously, best guesses are often required.

To calculate a tree value, starting on the right-hand side of the tree, each calculation is completed on reaching a node (square or circle) and then recording the result. To calculate the vale of an uncertain outcome (circle), the value of the outcomes is multiplied by the probability as previously estimated.

ADVANTAGES

- Decision trees are simple to understand and interpret.
- They are worth doing even with quite uncertain data. Intuitive insights can be gained based on descriptions of a situation by experts.
- Decision trees lay out a problem clearly so that all options can be explored, and they allow a full analysis of the possible consequences of a decision.
- They provide a method for quantifying the values of outcomes and their probabilities.
- Decision trees assist in making decisions with existing information and best guesses.
- Decision trees can be used to optimize an investment portfolio.

DISADVANTAGES

- Diagrams can become very large when drawn by hand.
- Trees created from numeric datasets can be complex.

ACTION CHECKLIST

✔ Identify the decision you need to make.

✔ Draw a line to the right for each solution with a description.

✔ Consider the outcome at the end of each line.

✔ Repeat the process for each new decision.

✔ When complete, review the tree, evaluate it, and calculate the values.

DOS AND DON'TS

DO

- Review a decision tree often.
- Review the evaluation values regularly.

DON'T

- Don't consider your first effort as final but continually review and revise it.

▸▸ MORE INFO

Books:

Cai, Jingfeng. *Decision Tree Pruning Using Expert Knowledge: Cost-sensitive Pruning*. Saarbrücken, Germany: VDM Verlag, 2008.

de Ville, Barry. *Decision Trees for Business Intelligence and Data Mining Using SAS Enterprise Miner*. Cary, NC: SAS Institute, 2006.

Rokach, Lior, and Oded Maimon. *Data Mining with Decision Trees: Theory and Applications*. Singapore: World Scientific Publishing, 2008.

Article:

Yuan, Yufei, and Michael J. Shaw. "Induction of fuzzy decision trees." *Fuzzy Sets and Systems* 69:2 (1995): 125–139.

Websites:

The Times 100—Decision tree analysis: www.thetimes100.co.uk/theory/theory--decision-tree-analysis--323.php

Time-Management-Guide.com: www.time-management-guide.com/decision-tree.html

Wikipedia—Example of an investment decision tree: en.wikipedia.org/wiki/File:Investment_decision_Insight.png

See Also:

★ Using Decision Analysis to Value R&D Projects (pp. 828–831)

✔ Applying Cost–Benefit Analysis to Project Appraisal (p. 968)

     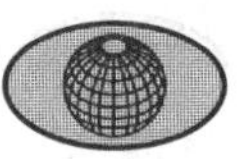   

Understanding Key Performance Indicators

DEFINITION

A key performance indicator (KPI) is a way for an organization to measure its success or otherwise in reaching its defined goals or objectives. KPIs can be very useful as a means of assessing an organization's current position and deciding on new strategies if necessary. While KPIs are sometimes used to measure progress toward meeting financial goals, such as increasing turnover by 25% within six months, KPIs are more likely to be used to evaluate activities that are normally difficult to measure—for example, levels of customer satisfaction or employee participation. KPIs are probably most effective when used to monitor knowledge-based processes.

Whatever the set goal, KPIs must be measurable. Thus, a general goal of increasing the number of returning customers would be hard to measure using KPIs, but a defined goal of increasing the number of returning customers by 25% within one year would be measurable, as the parameters are clearly set. A KPI metric generally consists of a timeframe, a target, and a benchmark, which together measure the achievability of the goal.

The KPIs used by an organization will vary depending on the nature of its business. A call center operation uses a different set of KPIs from those used by a manufacturing firm.

KPIs are usually measured in real time, but the results are usually stored so that progress can be measured on a daily, weekly, yearly, or otherwise basis—such as hourly. KPIs are often derived from raw data. There are four basic subtypes of KPI:

- *Quantitative indicators* are numerical terms, such as the percentage of customers who buy widgets every year;
- *Practical indicators* interface with existing processes, such as lists of employee capabilities;
- *Directional indicators* demonstrate improvement or progress (or not), such as comparing last month's sales to this month's;
- *Actionable indicators* reflect an organization's ability to effect change, such as KPIs showing that the company would do better by outsourcing some processes.

ADVANTAGES

- KPIs show an organization where it is going wrong, enabling management to make the necessary changes to turn things around.
- KPIs give an organization an edge over its competitors.

DISADVANTAGES

- KPIs can be expensive to use, or even impossible (you cannot quantify staff morale, for example).
- KPIs have limitations to the exactness of results, which often may only be a rough guide rather than a concrete measurement.
- Once designed, KPIs can be difficult to change unless you are prepared to disregard carefully built-up comparison yardsticks, such as year-on-year customer satisfaction levels.
- KPIs may be difficult to compare among peers—competitive analysis may be best left to an external specialist.

ACTION CHECKLIST

✔ Make sure you design each KPI carefully and include all necessary factors to achieve measurable results.

✔ Only use KPIs that focus on whether an organization is achieving its goals or living up to its mission.

DOS AND DON'TS

DO

- Ensure that everyone in the organization is aware that KPIs are in use.
- Focus on meeting the outcomes.
- Use KPI results as a carrot to motivate staff, where you can be reasonably sure they can actually carry out change.

DON'T

- Don't use too many KPIs at the risk of staff spreading their focus too thinly.
- Don't attempt to use a KPI to measure something that cannot be measured at all.

▸▸ MORE INFO

Books:

Franceschini, Fiorenzo, Maurizio Galetto, and Domenico Maisano. *Management by Measurement: Designing Key Indicators and Performance Measurement Systems*. Berlin: Springer 2007.

Parmenter, David. *Key Performance Indicators: Developing, Implementing, and Using Winning KPIs*. Hoboken, NJ: Wiley, 2007.

Websites:

EPM Review for KPI resources: www.epmreview.com

KPI Portal: www.kpi-portal.com

See Also:

★ Enhance Competitive Performance via Critical Key Performance Indicators (KPIs) (pp. 759–762)
★ Managing Interest Rate Risk (pp. 78–80)
★ Navigating a Liquidity Crisis Effectively (pp. 86–88)
✔ Assessing Business Performance (p. 1059)
✔ Measuring Financial Health (p. 874)

"Nurture your mind with great thoughts. To believe in the heroic makes heroes." Benjamin Disraeli

  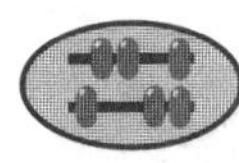   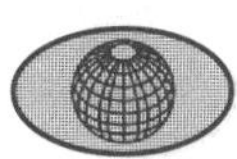   

Understanding Pareto's Law

DEFINITION

Pareto's Law is an inexact rule that, in a given situation, 80% of the effects come from 20% of the causes. Italian economist Vilfredo Pareto noted that 80% of Italian income went to 20% of the population. Pareto's Law was named after him by business management specialist Joseph M. Juran, who spotted that the 80–20 rule was common across many areas of business. For example, 80% of sales generally come from 20% of one's clients.

Pareto's Law has many useful applications in business. A Pareto chart is a type of bar chart, used to illustrate the 80–20 assumption, in which the values plotted are in descending order with a line graph showing the cumulative totals of each category from left to right. Such charts are used to monitor, for example, logistics, procurement, stock control, or quality control.

Where there is a large enough data set, Pareto's Law can be expressed as a mathematical formula. Here, k is a number between 50 and 100 and $k\%$ is $(100 - k)\%$ of the data set. The number k can be any value between 50 (where 50% of sales comes from 50% of a company's customers) to almost 100 (where, for example, $k = 98$, or 98% of sales are to just 2% of clients). Most of the time, in most data sets, k seems to hover around the 80 mark.

Sometimes when logistics are examined, a Pareto calculation may show up a ratio of 80–15 or 80–25. There is no need to panic about this as there is no requirement for the figures to add up to 100. The two figures measure different data sets, such as amount of sales versus number of clients. So, for example, 80–15 would mean 80% of sales coming from 15% of your customers, the remaining 20% of sales being made to 85% of clients.

ADVANTAGES

- The 80–20 rule is a handy tool for making a quick assessment of almost any measurable logistic before going on to make a more in-depth calculation and assessment of the facts.

DISADVANTAGES

- Pareto's Law is only a rule of thumb application and therefore must never be used as a stand-alone means of calculation. The principle is often misused. For example, it would be inaccurate to assume that if a solution to a problem fits 80% of cases it must be the right solution. There is a clear implication, instead, that the solution should need just 20% of available resources to solve all cases.

DOS AND DON'TS

DO

- Remember that Pareto's Law is only a guide and rarely 100% accurate.
- Carry out proper in-depth research to back up any findings produced by Pareto's Law.

DON'T

- Don't make assumptions with Pareto's Law and base important strategies or policies on basic findings.

➤➤ MORE INFO

Books:

Gen, Mitsuo, and Runwei Cheng. *Genetic Algorithms & Engineering Optimization*. Wiley Series in Engineering Design and Automation. New York: Wiley, 2000.

Rushton, A., J. Oxley, and P. Croucher. *The Handbook of Logistics and Distribution Management*. 2nd ed. London: Kogan Page, 2000.

Articles:

Bookstein, Abraham. "Informetric distributions, Part I: Unified overview." *Journal of the American Society for Information Science* 41 (1990): 368–375.

Klass, Oren S., Ofer Biham, Moshe Levy, Ofer Malcai and Sorin Solomon. "The Forbes 400 and the Pareto wealth distribution." *Economics Letters* 90:2 (2006): 290–295.

Reed, William J. "The Pareto, Zipf and other power laws." *Economics Letters* 74:1 (2001): 15–19.

Rosen, Kenneth T., and Mitchel Resnick. "The size distribution of cities: An examination of the Pareto law and primacy." *Journal of Urban Economics* 8:2 (1980): 165–186.

See Also:

★ Countering Supply Chain Risk (pp. 437–439)

★ Reducing Costs through Production and Supply Chain Management (pp. 505–507)

     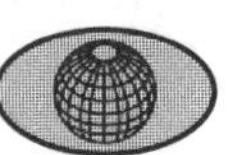  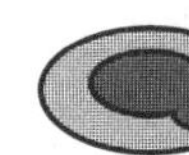 

Understanding Real Options

DEFINITION

Real options, sometimes also referred to as strategic options, are a tool that can be employed in capital budgeting analysis to help companies make better critical strategic decisions. As with financial market traded options, real options can be valued using pricing models. Real options give the holder the right but, importantly, not the obligation, to take a particular course of action. Real options are a mechanism by which a business can attempt to place an actual value on the choice of taking a particular option, and can play a valuable role in helping a company assess the financial implications of various strategic options. Real options are commonly used when dealing with the decision to initiate a new project or to abandon an existing project, depending on how, over time, actual events have differed from the original forecast. Used in conjunction with discounted cash flow techniques, real options provide businesses with a model as to how a certain course of action is likely to impact the business. Without the inclusion of real options, conventional discounted cash flow techniques can provide an incomplete assessment of the viability of a project, as they ignore the option to change course during the life of the project, perhaps taking a charge to abandon, delay, downscale, or even upscale the project.

Potential applications for real options as a decision-support model are many and varied. For example, an energy company may decide to proceed with a production operation if—and only if—the price of crude oil exceeds a level that makes the project commercially worthwhile. While standard discounted cash flow calculations may make the project appear risky and unattractive, the use of real options adds the ability to study the effects of changing course in return for a charge. This course could substantially increase the attractiveness of the venture, by factoring in the cost of the option of an effective escape from a completely negative outcome. Real options effectively make the project less risky by eliminating the "black or white" choice of one or the other. In this energy company example, real options might remove the risk of being stuck with the production costs for the life of the project, even if oil prices slipped to an unfavorable level. By attaching probability and costings on particular strategic options, the inclusion of real options can have significant impacts on expected net present value (NPV) calculations.

In addition to project viability analysis, real options can play an important role in applications such as process input options (for example, to help decide between various options in raw material sourcing), output mix options (for example, switching production from one product to another), production shutdown analysis, and output expansion options, as well project timing decision-making. The study of real options is an exciting, growing field of academic and business research, and the use of real options looks set to become a feature of mainstream business decision-making during the years ahead.

ADVANTAGES

- Real options are a powerful, flexible methodology, bringing together strategic planning with capital budgeting.
- The use of real options can give a business a significant strategic advantage, given their role in helping to identify the optimal timing for a project.
- The use of real options brings a dynamic element to the decision-making process, and can simulate this decision-making process throughout the project life cycle.
- Real options can help companies to avoid the potential pitfalls of pushing ahead with a new venture too early.

DISADVANTAGES

- Given that real options can be more conceptual than discounted cash flow techniques, real options can be more difficult to value with certainty.
- There is a view in some quarters that reliance on the use of real options exposes decision-making to managers' existing personal strategic biases.
- As with any methodology, calculations using real options rely on the quality and reliability of the input data.

ACTION CHECKLIST

- ✔ Maximize the full potential of the real options methodology by putting all possible strategic options into the mix, not just the obvious ones.
- ✔ Qualify the list to ensure that all strategic options are actually viable.
- ✔ Make use of conventional discounted cash flow techniques.
- ✔ Assign initial inputs for real options.
- ✔ Make use of options modeling software to derive pricing information.

DOS AND DON'TS

DO

- Utilize real options analysis alongside conventional techniques to demonstrate the full value of the model.
- As a project progresses, be prepared to refine/amend earlier numerical assumptions.
- Utilize NPV calculations to help verify your strategic analysis.

DON'T

- Don't ignore the value of educating managers and staff about the basic concepts behind real options analysis.
- Don't interpret the results of calculations as "gospel" on which the entire future of a business should be staked.

▸▸ MORE INFO

Book:

Mun, Johnathan. *Real Options Analysis: Tools and Techniques for Valuing Strategic Investments and Decisions*. 2nd ed. Hoboken, NJ: Wiley, 2006.

Articles:

Boyarchenko, Svetlana, and Sergei Levendorski. "Practical guide to real options in discrete time." *International Economic Review* 48:1 (February 2007).

Tong, Tony W., and Jeffrey J. Reuer. "Real options in multinational corporations: Organizational challenges and risk implications." *Journal of International Business Studies* 38:2 (March 2007): 215–230.

Website:

Real options software provider: www.realoptionsevaluation.com

"We set sail within a vast sphere, ever drifting in uncertainty, driven from end to end." Blaise Pascal

     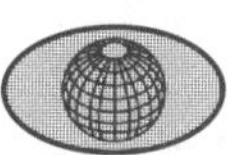   

Understanding Strategy Maps

DEFINITION

A strategy map, devised by Professors Robert S. Kaplan and David P. Norton, is a business management tool aimed at forging a strong link between a company's long-term strategies and its shorter-term operational activities. The concept of strategy mapping was originally developed by Kaplan and Norton in the "balanced scorecard," a means of assessing how successful a company is in terms of delivering on stated goals. While the basic notion of the balanced scorecard is "what you can't measure, you can't manage," further work aimed to help companies reassess their strategic goals. Kaplan and Norton subsequently shifted their focus to the principle of "what you can't measure, you can't describe" as a means to better utilize companies' intangible assets to help them achieve their objectives. The principle of strategic mapping of long-term strategy with shorter-term operational activities, previously merely one element of the balanced scorecard, was elevated to become a central strategy management tool.

Strategy maps aim to illustrate how a company links its macro strategy objectives with its key day-to-day operational elements from the four different perspectives: financial, customer, internal processes, and learning and growth. The financial element focuses primarily on enhancing the cost structure and utilizing assets towards greater productivity, while the customer element encourages companies to understand what sets them apart from their competitors. Though all elements of the strategy framework aim to improve areas such as attitudes to quality, service, partnerships, and company branding, the internal processes element aims to develop better product and service characteristics. Finally, the learning and growth element aims for companies to consider the skills and technologies that are needed to support the company's strategy. In all cases, the strategic mapping process seeks to engrain the appreciation of cause and effect. What can be improved on a "day-to-day level" is significant as, cumulatively, improvements can help improve a company's daily operational activities, helping it to achieve its longer-term strategic objectives. To better demonstrate the connections, the strategy map features a series of arrows linking objectives with individual operational activities.

ADVANTAGES

- Strategy mapping demonstrates to employees how seemingly minute improvements to operational activities can, cumulatively, contribute towards major efficiency and strategic objectives.
- Strategy mapping provides a clear, visual demonstration as to how short-term operational and medium- to long-term strategic objectives are closely aligned, helping to ensure greater "buy-in" from employees at all levels.
- Strategy mapping helps to demonstrate how a company's intangible assets can improve stockholder value.
- Strategy mapping provides a potential solution for managers unable to identify why certain strategies are not delivering tangible performance improvements.

DISADVANTAGES

- Strategy mapping requires "buy in" from individuals across all levels of the organization. If management fails to convince the workforce of the potential benefits of a successful medium- to long-term outcome, employees may feel disenfranchised from the potential benefits of improved corporate performance.
- Though strategic in its macro focus, strategy mapping is unlikely to deliver a single, massive leap forward in any single aspect. Rather, the considerable ultimate benefits of strategic mapping are often comprised of many, seemingly minor, single aspects.

ACTION CHECKLIST

- ✔ Ensure that everyone within the organization appreciates that strategy mapping is a technique which aims to align individuals' actions with the strategic objective.
- ✔ As improvements are likely to be incremental, ensure that the benefits are recognized and built on through an emphasis on the feedback/learning input.

DOS AND DON'TS

DO

- Aim to align personal performance improvement goals with those of the company.
- Base remuneration on goals related to improvements in the performance of the overall business. Setting individual performance objectives with related incentive payouts could be counterproductive if individuals shift their focus from delivering collective benefits to the pursuit of personal objectives.

DON'T

- Don't expect giant and immediate leaps forward in terms of operational efficiency, finances or customer experiences. Strategic mapping is more likely to generate numerous, gradual, incremental improvements across the organization.
- Don't set remuneration based on individual targets. Agree only on personal performance goals when you are confident that achieving them will contribute to overall performance improvement across the business.

➤➤ MORE INFO

Books:

Kaplan, Robert S., and David P. Norton. *Balanced Scorecard: Translating Strategy into Action*. Boston, MA: Harvard Business School Press, 1996.

Kaplan, Robert S., and David P. Norton. *Strategy Maps: Converting Intangible Assets into Tangible Outcomes*. Boston, MA: Harvard Business School Press, 2004.

Articles:

Irwin, D. "Strategy mapping in the public sector." *Long Range Planning* 35:6 (December 2002): 637–647.

Kaplan, Robert S., and David P. Norton "Having trouble with your strategy? Then map it." *Harvard Business Review* (September–October 2000).

Kaplan, Robert S., and David P. Norton. "The strategy map: Guide to aligning intangible assets." *Strategy & Leadership* 32:5 (2004): 10–17.

Scholey, Cam. "Strategy maps: A step-by-step guide to measuring, managing and communicating the plan." *Journal of Business Strategy* 26:3 (2005): 12–19.

Website:

The Balanced Scorecard Institute: www.balancedscorecard.org

CALCULATIONS AND RATIOS

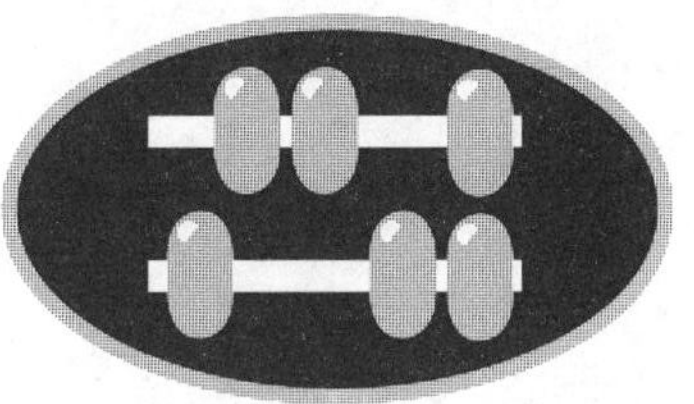

Calculations and Ratios

A Calculations and Ratios concept explains what is being measured, its importance and practical application, and tricks of the trade, which provides the reader with pointers on interpreting the results.

The Calculations and Ratios, written by specialists, provide essential mathematical calculations for target setting and maintaining standards within an enterprise. They not only address key management questions on the day-to-day financial welfare of a business, but also provide indicators that can impact on strategic decision making.

But reader beware, numbers are only a reflection of firm's financial health at any given moment in time, so it is essential to understand the dynamics that sit behind the figures—and which way they are moving.

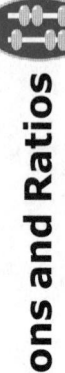

  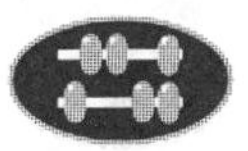   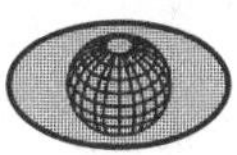   

Contents

     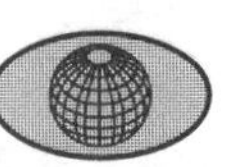   

Accounts Payable Turnover Ratio

WHAT IT MEASURES

The rate at which a company pays off its suppliers. The accounts payable turnover ratio is a short-term liquidity measure that quantifies how well a company pays its average payable amount over a single accounting period.

WHY IT IS IMPORTANT

Investors want to know how quickly your company pays its bills, which is why the accounts payable turnover ratio is important. This ratio measures your company's short-term liquidity. Investors consider a falling ratio a sign that the company is taking longer to pay suppliers than before, which might suggest cash flow problems. However, a rising ratio would suggest a relatively short time between purchase of goods and services and payment.

HOW IT WORKS IN PRACTICE

The accounts payable turnover ratio is based on the total purchases made from suppliers, divided by the average accounts payable amount over the same period, as below:

$$\text{APTR} = \frac{\text{Total supplier purchases}}{\text{Average accounts payable}}$$

For example, if a company makes $10 million in purchases from suppliers during a year, and at any given point is owed an average $1 million in accounts payable, then the accounts payable turnover ratio for the period would be 5.

TRICKS OF THE TRADE

- Most companies are required to settle accounts within 30 days to avoid damaging credit relationships, meaning there are 12 risk-free cycles in any year. A ratio of 6 suggests a company is paying its bills less often than is possible, while a ratio above 12 suggests the opposite.
- On its own, the ratio does not tell investors a great deal. The accounts payable turnover ratio must be compared against the industry average to see if the business is competitive. In addition, the ratio should be tracked over successive accounting periods to provide insight into cash flow.
- A falling accounts payable turnover ratio may suggest one of two scenarios. First, the business might be experiencing cash flow problems or disputed invoices with suppliers, which leads to slower payment. However, a successful business may extend payments to make the best possible use of cash and might have negotiated more favorable payment terms with suppliers. Additional analysis is therefore advised when faced with a changing accounts payable turnover ratio.
- An alternative approach that some experts believe is more intuitive than accounts payable turnover ratio is "days payable outstanding." This expresses turnover as the average length of time in days between purchase of goods and services, and payment. To calculate days payable outstanding, simply divide the accounts payable turnover ratio by 365.

▸▸ MORE INFO

Book:

White, Gerald I., Ashwinpaul C. Sondhi, and Dov Fried. *The Analysis and Use of Financial Statements*. Chichester, UK: Wiley, 2003.

Article:

Cars, Andreas. "The dynamic current ratio." *Investopedia*. Online at: www.investopedia.com/articles/02/090302.asp

Accounts Receivable Turnover

One of several measures used to assess operating performance, accounts receivable turnover also helps in appraising a company's credit policy and its cash flow.

WHAT IT MEASURES

The number of times in each accounting period, typically a year, that a company converts credit sales into cash.

WHY IT IS IMPORTANT

A high turnover figure is desirable because it indicates that a company collects revenues effectively, and that its customers pay bills promptly. A high figure also suggests that a company's credit and collection policies are sound.

In addition, the measurement is a reasonably good indicator of cash flow, and of overall operating efficiency.

HOW IT WORKS IN PRACTICE

The formula for accounts receivable turnover is straightforward. Simply divide the average amount of receivables into annual credit sales:

$$\text{Receivables turnover} = \frac{\text{Sales}}{\text{Receivables}}$$

If, for example, a company's sales are $4.5 million and its average receivables are $375,000, its receivables turnover is:

$$\frac{4{,}500{,}000}{375{,}000} = 12$$

TRICKS OF THE TRADE

- It is important to use the average amount of receivables over the period considered. Otherwise, receivables could be misleading for a company whose products are seasonal or are sold at irregular intervals.
- The measurement is also helpful to a company that is designing or revising credit terms.
- Accounts receivable turnover is among the measures that comprise asset utilization ratios, also called activity ratios.

▸▸ MORE INFO

Book:

Salek, John G. *Accounts Receivable Management: Best Practices*. Hobohen, NJ: Wiley, 2005

     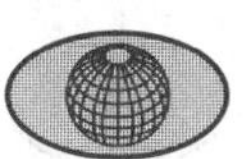   

Accrual Rate

WHAT IT MEASURES

In the pensions world, accrual rate is the rate at which an individual's entitlement to pension benefit builds up related to his or her salary, often in an employer's pension scheme.

WHY IT IS IMPORTANT

It enables an individual to receive a pension benefit that is predictable and fair, while also providing employers with a simple way to predict the potential liabilities of a pension scheme. If your organization's pension is based on an accrual rate, employees earn (or "accrue") a monthly pension amount each year they work. If the employee earns a full pension, they will receive the sum of all those annual accruals as the total pension amount. The higher the accrual, the higher the eventual pension pay-out.

HOW IT WORKS IN PRACTICE

Accrual rates are usually expressed as a fraction of final pay. They vary between different countries and industry sectors, but are generally between 1/50 and 1/80. In the case of an accrual rate of 1/60, this means the employee receives 1/60th of their pensionable earnings for each year of eligible service. To calculate the pension of an employee who retires at the age of 58 after 30 years service on a final salary of $70,000, apply this formula including the accrual rate:

$$\text{Pension liability} = \text{Accrual rate} \times \text{Final salary} \times \text{Years of service}$$

So, in this case the pension liability is:

$$\frac{1}{60} \times \$70{,}000 \times 30 = \$35{,}000$$

The lower the denominator in an accrual rate, the higher the accrued benefits for each year of eligible service. So an accrual rate of 1/50 would create a different result:

$$\frac{1}{50} \times \$70{,}000 \times 30 = \$42{,}000$$

TRICKS OF THE TRADE

- Accrual rate can be applied to an employee's "final" salary, or may sometimes be applied to what is known as the "best five"—the average of the five highest salaries an employee earns over their entire eligible years of service.
- An accelerated accrual is one that is higher than the typical 1/60 and 1/80 found in occupational pension schemes. They are most frequently used in the public sector.
- An accrual rate can sometimes be expressed as a percentage, such as 1.25% (which is equivalent to 1/80).
- Accrual rates can also be expressed as dollar amounts rather than percentages or fractions. These schemes tend to be less advantageous for employees, since the employer's contribution is not tied to the employee's salary and will not necessarily increase at the same pace.
- Accrual rates can be applied to other employee benefits (commonly holiday and sick pay), but may also be used to refer to the interest added to certain sorts of mortgage loans.

Acid-Test Ratio

A second liquidity ratio that evaluates creditworthiness, the acid-test ratio stands as a more stringent test than the current ratio, hence its name.

WHAT IT MEASURES

How quickly a company's assets can be turned into cash, which is why assessment of a company's liquidity is also known as the quick ratio, or simply the acid ratio.

WHY IT IS IMPORTANT

Regardless of how this ratio is labeled, it is considered a highly reliable indicator of a company's financial strength and its ability to meet its short-term obligations. Because inventory can sometimes be difficult to liquidate, the acid-test ratio deducts inventory from current assets before they are compared with current liabilities—which is what distinguishes it from the current ratio.

Potential creditors like to use the acid-test ratio because it reveals how a company would fare if it had to pay off its bills under the worst possible conditions. Indeed, the assumption behind the acid-test ratio is that creditors are howling at the door demanding immediate payment, and that an enterprise has no time to sell off its inventory, or any of its stock.

HOW IT WORKS IN PRACTICE

The acid-test ratio's formula can be expressed in two ways, but both essentially reach the same conclusion. The more common expression is:

$$\text{Acid-test ratio} = \frac{\text{Current assets} - \text{Inventory}}{\text{Current liabilities}}$$

If, for example, current assets total $7,700, inventory amounts to $1,200, and current liabilities total $4,500, then:

$$\frac{7{,}700 - 1{,}200}{4{,}500} = 1.44$$

A variation of this formula ignores inventory altogether, distinguishes assets as cash, receivables, and short-term investments, and then divides the sum of the three by the total current liabilities:

$$\text{Acid-test ratio} = \frac{\text{Cash} + \text{Accounts receivable} + \text{Short-term investments}}{\text{Current liabilities}}$$

If, for example, cash totals $2,000, receivables total $3,000, short-term investments total $1,000, and liabilities total $4,800, then:

$$\frac{2{,}000 + 3{,}000 + 1{,}000}{4{,}800} = 1.25$$

There are two other ways to appraise liquidity, although neither is as commonly used: the cash ratio is the sum of cash and marketable securities divided by current liabilities; net quick assets is determined by adding cash, accounts receivable, and marketable securities, then subtracting current liabilities from that sum.

     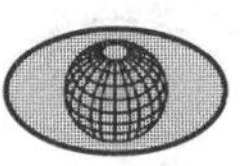   

TRICKS OF THE TRADE

- In general, the quick ratio should be 1:1 or better. This means that a company has at least a unit's worth of easily convertible assets for each unit of its current liabilities. A high quick ratio usually reflects a sound, well-managed organization in no danger of imminent collapse, even in the extreme and unlikely event that its sales ceased immediately. On the other hand, companies with ratios of less than 1 could not pay their current liabilities, and should be looked at with extreme care.
- While a ratio of 1:1 is generally acceptable to most creditors, acceptable quick ratios vary by industry, as do almost all financial ratios. No ratio, in fact, is especially meaningful without knowledge of the business from which it originates. For example, a declining quick ratio with a stable current ratio may indicate that a company has built up too much inventory; but it could also suggest that the company has greatly improved its collection system.
- Some experts regard the acid-test ratio as an extreme version of the working capital ratio because it uses only cash and equivalents, and excludes inventory. An acid-test ratio that is notably lower than the working capital ratio often means that inventory makes up a large proportion of current assets. An example would be retail stores.
- Comparing quick ratios over an extended period of time can be used to signal developing trends in a company. While modest declines in the quick ratio do not automatically spell trouble, uncovering the reasons for changes can help to find ways to nip potential problems in the bud.
- Like the current ratio, the quick ratio is a snapshot, and a company can manipulate its figures to make it look robust at a given point in time.
- Investors who suddenly become keenly interested in a company's quick ratio may signal their anticipation of a downturn in the company's business or in the general economy.

Activity-Based Costing

GETTING STARTED

Activity-based costing (ABC) attempts to create the big picture—crystal-clear, full, and accurate—by painting assorted little pictures.

- ABC identifies the relationship between a business activity and all the resources needed to conduct it by assigning costs to each of those resources, thus presenting the true total expense of the entire activity.
- ABC can account for so-called "soft," or indirect, operating costs, and thus produce a more revealing, and perhaps startlingly different, financial picture than other accounting methodologies such as standard costing might offer.
- Used properly, ABC helps management to better distinguish operations that add value from those that do not, permitting more informed decisions about such matters as pricing, product mix, capital investments, and organizational change.
- In turn, ABC's advocates praise it as a more effective tool to identify and control costs, improve productivity, and increase profits.

FAQS

When did ABC start?

ABC came of age in the 1980s amid manufacturers' furious efforts to raise the quality of their products while simultaneously eliminating every unnecessary cost from their operations. The dramatic improvements realized by manufacturers have led to ABC becoming a widely used tool, especially in the manufacturing industry.

What are the basic steps of ABC?

There are five:

1 identify the product or service to be studied;
2 determine all the resources and processes that are required to create the product or deliver the service, and their respective costs;
3 determine the "cost drivers" for each resource: the cost of labor as well as raw materials;
4 collect costs and other data, such as time taken, for each process and resource;
5 use the data to calculate the overall cost of the product or service.

What are ABC's principal advantages?

First, ABC can gauge virtually any activity, be it a manufacturing process, a business process, the performance of a service, or an administrative operation. Second, it considers a much wider variety of resources and materials than more traditional accounting methodologies, and can thus present a more complete picture.

What are ABC's primary weaknesses?

It can be a very time-consuming exercise because of the volume of data it demands. Also, if not managed properly, ABC can transform every manager into an accountant whose energies become fixed on tracking the costs of the activity, rather than on tracking and perfecting the activity itself.

What kind of business sectors use ABC?

The list ranges from accountants to zoologists. It may be especially helpful for knowledge-based businesses that rely primarily on human services and related resources, whose total costs may be difficult to measure with more traditional accounting yardsticks.

What is critical to ABC's success?

Without gaining and maintaining the enduring commitment of all individuals, even a modestly detailed initiative will probably fail. It's also best to start with pilot projects to demonstrate success.

What preliminary steps are needed?

First, an organization must understand its activities and the resources that these require. Second, it must understand thoroughly the amount of information required, and the expense of generating that information. It must also determine what level of accuracy will be acceptable.

MAKING IT HAPPEN

Creating an ABC cost accounting system requires three preliminary steps:

1 converting to an accrual basis of accounting;
2 defining cost centers and cost allocation;
3 determining process and procedure costs.

Businesses have traditionally relied on the cash basis of accounting, which recognizes income when received and expenses when paid. ABC's foundation is the accrual basis. The numbers this statement presents are assigned to the various procedures performed during a given period. Cost centers are a company's identifiable products and services, but also include specific and detailed tasks within these broader activities. Defining cost centers will of course vary by business and method of operation. What is critical to ABC is the inclusion of all activities and all resources. Once these steps have been taken, the results are often more than satisfying.

Banks and financial services firms, for example, have long used ABC-like methods to confirm that investments in automated teller machines would be both cheaper than continuing to rely on tellers and clerks and in their customers' best interests.

Railroad companies have used the methodology to determine the cost of processing bills of lading by hand, fax, and the internet. Studying such costs confirmed the wisdom of using e-commerce, generating annual savings of up to $1 million.

Publishers launching "new media" services can more accurately calculate the true costs of creating material for them, then compare such costs to those required to produce traditional publications, and draw more accurate conclusions about what best serves their long- and short-term interests.

Law firms are better positioned to confirm that the hourly fees they charge—no matter how princely they may at first appear—do, in fact, enable them to provide their services profitably.

Finally, healthcare providers use ABC to measure profitability, eliminate unnecessary costs, and plan for change. A medical practice that knows the actual cost of providing a specific service, for example, can make far better decisions about the price of managed health care.

For instance, let's say the Apple-a-Day Medical Clinic includes three physicians, Drs Peel, Core, and Stem. Their clinic has an in-house laboratory and a radiology department. All direct revenues and expenses are allocated to the physician who performs the service and incurs the expense. Indirect variable overhead costs are allocated to each physician based on the proportion of total revenues that each generates in a given period. Fixed overhead costs are divided equally among physicians. Because of their respective incomes and expense allocations, each physician would represent a separate cost center.

Additional cost centers for this medical practice could be laboratory, radiology, and administration. As cost centers are defined, they could further be classified as, say, "patient service centers" or "support centers." In this example, laboratory, radiology, and each individual physician's activity would be patient service centers, while administration would be a support center.

Once cost centers are identified, management teams can begin studying the activities each one engages in and allocating the expenses each one incurs, including the cost of employee services. In this healthcare scenario, activities would range from actual treatment by physicians and nurses, X-rays, medical tests and assessments of their results, plus such administrative support services as personnel, bookkeeping, rent, utilities, property insurance, office supplies, advertising, telecommunications expenses, and equipment costs related to the administrative function. Rent, utilities, and property insurance are usually allocated on the basis of the square footage that the particular activity covers.

Tracking and allocating the detailed costs of individual activities and procedures can be accomplished by different methods, with various degrees of accuracy. The more detailed the cost analysis, of course, the greater the accuracy of the data. Then again, as the detail increases, so does the time and expense.

The most appropriate method is developed from time studies and direct expense allocation. Management teams that choose this method will need to devote several months to data collection in order to generate sufficient information to establish the personnel components of each activity's total cost. The cost of this exercise itself can be significant, but also worthwhile. Proponents say ABC has resulted in cost savings worth as much as 14 times the cost of the exercise. More importantly, the exercise has provided solid documentation for decisions that "seemed correct," as a Chrysler Corporation team once reported, "but could not be supported with hard evidence."

Time studies establish the average amount of time required to complete each task, plus best- and worst-case performances. Only those resources actually used are factored into the cost computation; unused resources are reported separately. These studies can also advise management how best to monitor and allocate expenses which might otherwise be expressed as part of general overhead, or go undetected altogether.

Notably, determining how much of an operation's personnel is underused or unused can significantly help management planning, specifically by exposing activities that are overstaffed or understaffed. This can be especially helpful to any knowledge-based business, since payroll is almost always its highest cost. Moreover, in any business, the more efficiently an enterprise deploys its personnel, the more profitable it will be.

In addition, this type of analysis can also establish useful performance benchmarks within an operation, and might even allow for a comparison of procedure costs with industry averages.

COMMON MISTAKES

Getting Caught Up in the Details

Notwithstanding its successes, ABC remains a tool, not an end in itself. Organizations can lose sight of that fact if they are not careful, and end up allowing it to dominate their working lives.

The enormity and complexity of such a project should never be underestimated. The data requirements alone are daunting. It is all too easy to get caught up in ABC's details and mechanics. In turn, estimating some costs is often recommended, to minimize the level of detail.

At the same time, however, some details are important prerequisites of objectivity and success. For example, if time studies are not used, some other measure must be used to allocate personnel and related costs, as well as indirect costs such as percentage of revenues or income, or the number of customer calls. These methods require far less time for compiling data and are less costly,

⏩ MORE INFO

Books:

Burk, Karen B., and Douglas W. Webster. *Activity Based Costing and Performance*. Fairfax, VA: American Management Systems, 1994.

Grossman, Theodore, and John Leslie Livingstone. *The Portable MBA in Finance and Accounting*. 4th ed. Hoboken, NJ: Wiley, 2009.

Article:

Ness, Joseph A., and Thomas G. Cucuzza. "Tapping the full potential of ABC." *Harvard Business Review* (July/August 1995).

Website:

Activity Based Costing Benchmarking Association (ABCBA™): www.abcbenchmarking.com

     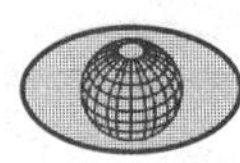   

but drawbacks abound. For one thing, accuracy suffers, and they are almost always subjective, potentially to the point of compromising the entire initiative. Being far less precise, these alternative methods also do not differentiate between used and unused personnel resources, and will not provide information on unused capacity or trends in procedure costs.

Without the aid of computer software that has been developed to automate the process, ABC can be hopelessly time-consuming. Indeed, unaided by technology, ABC might well be hoist with its own petard and exposed as an outrageous waste of time.

Like any cost accounting system, activity-based costing is not static. Once established, it needs to be maintained and updated as business conditions and organizations change.

Finally, in delivering its crystal-clear pictures, activity-based costing also has the potential to make individual champions of particular products or services squirm, because it may reveal them to be far more expensive than they might otherwise appear. All the more reason for advocating caution: "Watch out what you wish for!" If a management team is to reduce and eliminate costs, it must first identify them and grasp their impact on specific processes or products. Because activity-based costing can paint a single picture that reveals all the individual direct and indirect costs a business incurs in a given operation, it can be a powerful tool for both assessing current operations and guiding prompt and intelligent reactions as circumstances change. In fact, it's also known as activity-based management (ABM).

Alpha and Beta Values of a Security

Both alpha and beta are investment measures used to quantify risk and reward.

WHAT THEY MEASURE

A security's performance, adjusted for risk, compared to overall market behavior.

WHY THEY ARE IMPORTANT

Just as coaches would expect their most accomplished athletes to perform at a higher level than others, investors expect more from higher-risk investments. Alpha and beta give investors a quick indication of just how risky a stock or fund is.

Alpha is defined as "the return a security or a portfolio would be expected to earn if the market's rate of return were zero."

Beta is a means of measuring the volatility (or risk) of a stock or fund in comparison with the market as a whole. The beta of a stock or fund can be any value, positive or negative, but usually is between +0.25 and +1.75.

Alpha expresses the difference between the return expected from a stock or mutual fund, given its beta rating, and the return actually produced. A stock or fund that returns more than its beta would predict has a positive alpha, while one that returns less than the amount predicted by beta has a negative alpha. A large positive alpha indicates a strong performance, while a large negative alpha indicates a dismal performance.

HOW THEY WORK IN PRACTICE

To begin with, the market itself is assigned a beta of 1.0. If a stock or fund has a beta of 1.2, this means its price is likely to rise or fall by 12% when the overall market rises or falls by 10%; a beta of 0.7 means the stock or fund price is likely to move up or down at 70% of the level of the market change.

In practice, an alpha of 0.4% means the stock or fund in question outperformed the market-based return estimate by 0.4%. An alpha of −0.6% means the return was 0.6% less than would have been predicted from the change in the market alone.

Both alpha and beta should be readily available on request from investment firms, because the figures appear in standard performance reports. It is always best to ask for them, because calculating a stock's alpha rating requires first knowing a stock's beta rating, and calculating beta is a challenge! It is based on linear regression analysis, the week-to-week percentage changes in the given stock's price and the corresponding week-to-week percentage price change in a market index, over a given period of time, often 24 to 36 months. In short, beta calculations can involve mathematical complexities.

If it's any consolation, calculating alpha is far less taxing, provided the requisite data are available. The formula is:

$$\text{Alpha} = \text{Actual return} - \text{Risk-free return} - \text{Beta} \times (\text{Index return} - \text{Risk-free return})$$

If a mutual fund with a beta rating of 1.1 returned 35%, while its benchmark index returned 30%, and a US Treasury bill returned 4% (T-bill returns are usually used as the "risk-free investment"), then the fund's alpha would equal 2.4%, based on the formula:

$$\begin{aligned} 35\% - 4\% - 1.1 \times (30\% - 4\%) &= 31\% - 1.1 \times 26\% \\ &= 31\% - 28.6\% \\ &= 2.4\% \end{aligned}$$

TRICKS OF THE TRADE

- The underlying rationale for both alpha and beta is that the return of a stock or mutual fund should at least exceed that of a "risk-free" investment such as a US Treasury bill.
- Stocks of many utilities have a beta of less than 1. Conversely, most high-tech, NASDAQ-based stocks have a beta greater than 1; they offer a higher rate of return but are also risky.
- Alpha is often used to assess the performance of a portfolio manager. However, a low alpha score doesn't necessarily reflect poor performance by a fund manager, any more than a high alpha score means that a manager's performance is outstanding. At times, factors beyond a manager's control affect alpha values.

▸▸ MORE INFO

Reports:

Schwab Performance Technologies. "Troubleshooting an Incorrect Alpha." September 24, 2007. Online at: schwabpt.com/downloads/docs/pdflibrary/spt010543.pdf

Schwab Performance Technologies. "Troubleshooting an Incorrect Beta." September 24, 2007. Online at: schwabpt.com/downloads/docs/pdflibrary/spt010480.pdf

  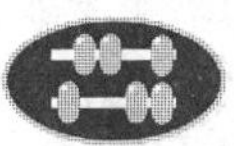 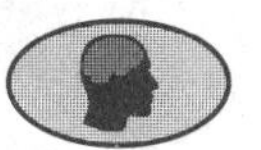  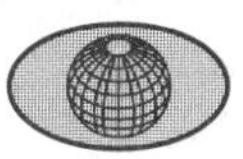   

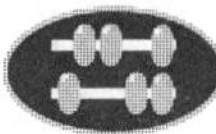

Amortization

Amortization is often regarded as being the same as depreciation, but although the two accounting practices can be difficult to distinguish, there are differences between them. Amortization is also used in connection with loans, although that is not the primary focus here.

WHAT IT MEASURES

Amortization is a method of recovering (deducting or writing off) the capital costs of intangible assets over a fixed period of time. Its calculation is virtually identical to the straight-line method of depreciation.

Amortization also refers to the establishment of a schedule for repaying the principal and interest on a loan in equal amounts over a period of time. Because computers have made this a simple calculation, business references to amortization tend to focus more on the term's first definition.

WHY IT IS IMPORTANT

Amortization enables a company to identify its true costs, and thus its net income, more precisely. In the course of their business, most enterprises acquire intangible assets such as a patent for an invention, or a well-known brand or trademark. Since these assets can contribute to the revenue growth of the business, they can be—and are allowed to be—deducted against those future revenues over a period of years, provided the procedure conforms to accepted accounting practices.

For tax purposes, the distinction is not always made between amortization and depreciation, yet amortization remains a viable financial accounting concept in its own right.

HOW IT WORKS IN PRACTICE

Amortization is computed using the straight-line method of depreciation: divide the initial cost of the intangible asset by the estimated useful life of that asset. For example, if it costs $10,000 to acquire a patent and it has an estimated useful life of 10 years, the amortized amount per year is $1,000.

$$\frac{10{,}000}{10} = \$1{,}000 \text{ per year}$$

The amount of amortization accumulated since the asset was acquired appears on the organization's balance sheet as a deduction under the amortized asset.

While that formula is straightforward, amortization can also incorporate a variety of noncash charges to net earnings and/or asset values, such as depletion, write-offs, prepaid expenses, and deferred charges. Accordingly, there are many rules to regulate how these charges appear on financial statements. The rules are different in each country, and are occasionally changed, so it is necessary to stay abreast of them and rely on expert advice.

For financial reporting purposes, an intangible asset is amortized over a period of years. The amortizable life—"useful life"—of an intangible asset is the period over which it gives economic benefit. Several factors are considered when determining this useful life; for example, demand and competition, effects of obsolescence, legal or contractual limitations, renewal provisions, and service life expectations.

Intangibles that can be amortized include:

- **Copyrights**, based on the amount paid either to purchase them or to develop them internally, plus the costs incurred in producing the work (wages or materials, for example). At present, a copyright is granted for the life of the author plus 70 years. However, the estimated useful life of a copyright is usually far shorter than its legal life, and it is generally amortized over a fairly short period.
- **Cost of a franchise**, including any fees paid to the franchiser, as well legal costs or expenses incurred in the acquisition. A franchise granted for a limited period should be amortized over its life. If the franchise has an indefinite life, it should be amortized over a reasonable period, not to exceed 40 years.
- **Covenants not to compete:** an agreement by the seller of a business not to engage in a competing business in a certain area for a specific period of time. The cost of the not-to-compete covenant should be amortized over the period covered by the covenant unless its estimated economic life is expected to be shorter.
- **Easement costs** that grant a right of way may be amortized if there is a limited and specified life.
- **Organization costs** incurred when forming a corporation or a partnership, including legal fees, accounting services, incorporation fees, and other related services. Organization costs are usually amortized over 60 months.
- **Patents**, both those developed internally and those purchased. If developed internally, a patent's "amortizable basis" includes legal fees incurred during the application process. Normally, a patent is amortized over its legal life, or over its remaining life if purchased. However, it should be amortized over its legal life or its economic life, whichever is the shorter.
- **Trademarks, brands, and trade names**, which should be written off over a period not to exceed 40 years. However, since the value of these assets depends on the changing tastes of consumers, they are frequently amortized over a shorter period.
- Other types of property that may be amortized include certain intangible drilling costs, circulation costs, mine development costs, pollution control facilities, and reforestation expenditures. They can even include intangibles such as the value of a market share or a market's composition: an example is the portion of an acquired business that is attributable to the existence of a given customer base.

TRICKS OF THE TRADE

- Certain intangibles cannot be amortized, but may be depreciated using a straight-line approach if they have a "determinable" useful life. Because the rules are different in each country and are subject to change, it is essential to rely on specialist advice.
- Computer software may be amortized under certain conditions, depending on its purpose. Software that is amortized is generally given a 60-month life, but it may be amortized over a shorter period if it can clearly be established that it will be obsolete or no longer used within a shorter time.
- Under certain conditions, customer lists that were purchased may be amortized if it can be demonstrated that the list has a finite useful life, in that customers on the list are likely to be lost over a period of time.
- While leasehold improvements are depreciated for income tax purposes, they are amortized when it comes to financial report-

  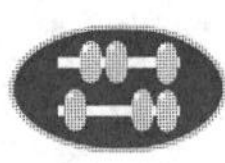   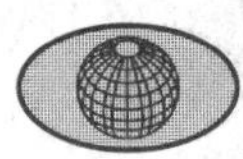   

ing—either over the remaining term of the lease or their expected useful life, whichever is the shorter.

- Annual payments incurred under a franchise agreement should be expensed when incurred.
- The internet has many amortization loan calculators that can automatically determine monthly payment figures and the total cost of a loan.

MORE INFO

Websites:

Financial Accounting Standards Board: www.fasb.org

US Copyright Office: www.copyright.gov

US Patent and Trademark Office: www.uspto.gov

Annual Percentage Rate

Different investments typically offer different compounding periods, usually quarterly or monthly. The annual percentage rate, or APR, allows them to be compared over a common period of time, namely one year.

WHAT IT MEASURES

The APR measures either the rate of interest that invested money earns in one year, or the cost of credit expressed as a yearly rate.

WHY IT IS IMPORTANT

It enables an investor or borrower to compare like with like. When evaluating investment alternatives, naturally it's important to know which one will pay the greatest return. By the same token, borrowers want to know which loan alternative offers the best terms. Determining the annual percentage rate provides a direct comparison.

HOW IT WORKS IN PRACTICE

To calculate the APR, apply this formula:

$$APR = \left(1 + \frac{i}{m}\right)^m - 1.0$$

where *i* is the interest rate quoted, expressed as a decimal, and *m* is the number of compounding periods per year. For example, if a bank offers a 6% interest rate, paid quarterly, the APR would be calculated this way:

$$\left(1 + \frac{0.06}{4}\right)^4 - 1 = (1 + 0.015)^4 - 1$$

$$= 1.015^4 - 1$$

$$= 1.0614 - 1$$

$$= 0.0614$$

$$= 6.14\%$$

TRICKS OF THE TRADE

- As a rule of thumb, the annual percentage rate is slightly higher than the quoted rate.
- When using the formula, be sure to express the rate as a decimal (that is, 6% becomes 0.06).
- When expressed as the cost of credit, remember to include other costs of obtaining the credit in addition to interest, such as loan closing costs and financial fees.
- APR provides an excellent basis for comparing mortgage or other loan rates; lenders are required to disclose it.
- When used in the context of investment, APR can also be called the "annual percentage yield," or APY.

Asset Turnover

Another of the asset utilization ratios, asset turnover measures the productivity of assets. In some circles it is also referred to as the earning power of assets.

WHAT IT MEASURES

The amount of sales generated for every dollar's worth of assets over a given period.

WHY IT IS IMPORTANT

Asset turnover measures how well a company is leveraging its assets to produce revenue. A well-managed manufacturer, for example, will make its plant and equipment work hard for the business by minimizing idle time for machines.

The higher the number the better—within reason. As a rule of thumb, companies with low profit margins tend to have high asset turnover; those with high profit margins have low asset turnover.

This ratio can also show how capital intensive a business is. Some businesses, such as software developers, can generate tremendous sales per dollar of assets because their assets are modest. At the other end of the scale, electric utilities, heavy industry manufacturers, and even cable TV companies need a huge asset base to generate sales.

Finally, asset turnover serves as a tool to keep managers mindful of the company's balance sheet along with its profit and loss account.

HOW IT WORKS IN PRACTICE

Asset turnover's basic formula is simply sales divided by assets:

$$\frac{\text{Sales revenue}}{\text{Total assets}}$$

Most experts recommend using average total assets in the formula. To determine this figure, add total assets at the beginning of the year to total assets at the end of the year and divide by two.

If, for instance, annual sales totaled \$4.5 million, and total assets were \$1.84 million at the beginning of the year and \$1.78 million at the year end, the average total assets would be \$1.81 million, and the asset turnover ratio would be:

$$\frac{4{,}500{,}000}{1{,}810{,}000} = 2.49$$

A variation of the formula is:

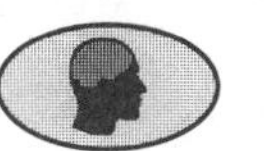

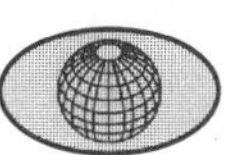

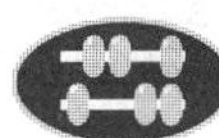

$$\frac{\text{Sales revenue}}{\text{Fixed assets}}$$

If average fixed assets were $900,000, then asset turnover would be:

$$\frac{4{,}500{,}000}{900{,}000} = 5$$

TRICKS OF THE TRADE

- This ratio is especially useful for growth companies to gauge whether or not they are growing revenue (for example) turnover, in healthy proportion to assets.
- Asset turnover numbers are useful for comparing competitors within industries. Like most ratios, they vary from industry to industry. As with most numbers, the most meaningful comparisons are made over extended periods of time.
- Too high a ratio may suggest overtrading: too much sales revenue with too little investment. Conversely, too low a ratio may suggest undertrading and an inefficient management of resources.
- A declining ratio may be indicative of a company that overinvested in plant, equipment, or other fixed assets, or is not using existing assets effectively.

Asset Utilization

Appraising asset utilization is a multi-task exercise conceived and performed in the spirit of "one manages what one measures." There is plenty to measure.

WHAT IT MEASURES

How efficiently an organization uses its resources and, in turn, the effectiveness of the organization's managers.

WHY IT IS IMPORTANT

The success of any enterprise is tied to its ability to manage and leverage its assets. Hefty sales and profits can hide any number of inefficiencies. By examining several relationships between sales and assets, asset utilization delivers a reasonably detailed picture of how well a company is being managed and led—certainly enough to call attention both to sources of trouble and to role-model operations.

Moreover, since all the figures used in this analysis are taken from a company's balance sheet or profit and loss statement, the ratios that result can be used to compare a company's performance with individual competitors and with industries as a whole.

Many companies use this measure not only to evaluate their aggregate success but also to determine compensation for managers.

HOW IT WORKS IN PRACTICE

Asset utilization relies on a family of asset utilization ratios, also called activity ratios. The individual ratios in the family can vary, depending on the practitioner. They include measures that also stand alone, such as accounts receivable turnover and asset turnover. The most commonly used sets of asset utilization ratios include these and the following measures.

Average collection period is also known as days sales outstanding. It links accounts receivable with daily sales and is expressed in number of days; the lower the number, the better the performance. Its formula is:

$$\text{Average collection period} = \frac{\text{Accounts receivable}}{\text{Average daily sales}}$$

For example, if accounts receivable are $280,000 and average daily sales are $7,000, then:

$$\frac{280{,}000}{7{,}000} = 40 \text{ days}$$

Inventory turnover compares the cost of goods sold (COGS) with inventory; for this measure, expressed in "turns," the higher the number the better. Its formula is:

$$\frac{\text{Cost of goods sold}}{\text{Inventory}}$$

For example, if COGS is $2 million and inventory at the end of the period is $500,000, then:

$$\frac{2{,}000{,}000}{500{,}000} = 4$$

Some asset utilization repertoires include ratios like debtor days, while others study the relationships listed below.

Depreciation / Assets measures the percentage of assets being depreciated to gauge how quickly product plants are aging and assets are being consumed.

Depreciation / Sales measures the percentage of sales that is tied up covering the wear and tear of the physical plant.

In either instance, a high percentage could be cause for concern.

Income / Assets measures how well management uses its assets to generate net income. It is the same formula as return on assets.

Income / Plant measures how effectively a company uses its investment in fixed assets to generate net income.

In these two instances, high numbers are desirable.

Plant / Assets expresses the percentage of total assets that is tied up in land, buildings, and equipment.

By themselves, of course, the individual numbers are meaningless. Their value lies in how they compare with the corresponding numbers of competitors and with industry averages. A company with an inventory turnover of 4 in an industry whose average is 7, for example, surely has room for improvement, because the comparison indicates that it is generating fewer sales per unit of inventory and is therefore less efficient than its competitors.

TRICKS OF THE TRADE

- Asset utilization is particularly useful to companies considering expansion or capital investment: if production can be increased by improving the efficiency of existing resources, there is no need to spend the sums expansion would cost.
- Like all families of ratios, no single number or comparison is necessarily cause for alarm or rejoicing. Asset utilization proves most beneficial over an extended period of time.
- Studying all measures at once can devour a lot of time, although computers have trimmed hours into seconds. Managements in smaller organizations may conduct asset utilization on a continuing basis, tracking particular measures monthly to stay abreast of operating trends.

  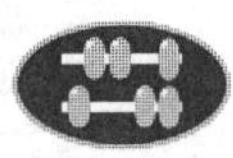   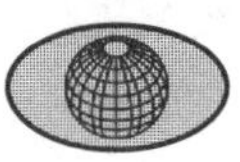   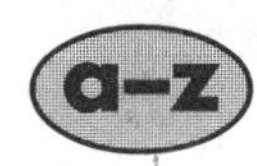

Basis Point Value

WHAT IT MEASURES

The basis point value (BPV) expresses the change in value of an asset or financial instrument that results from a 0.01 percentage change in yield. BPV is commonly used to measure interest rate risk, and may be referred to as a delta or DV01.

WHY IT IS IMPORTANT

Basis point value is extremely important in assessing the impact of changes to the value or rate of a financial instrument such as an asset or portfolio. Simply stating an absolute percentage can be unclear—a 1% increase to a 10% rate might refer to an increase to 10.1% or 11%, for example.

Basis points can be used to measure changes and differentials in interest rates and margins. For example, a floating interest rate might be set at 25 BPV above Libor. If Libor is 3.5%, this means the floating rate will be 3.75%. Basis points are also useful in describing margins, because percentage changes may be very small or unclear—even while they might have a considerable impact on the bottom line.

BPV is commonly used in financial markets to measure interest rates, and specifically the risk associated with a particular rate. It is popular because it is relatively simple to calculate and can be applied in any scenario where you have a known cash flow.

HOW IT WORKS IN PRACTICE

At its most basic, BPV is 1/100th of 1%. Therefore, there are 30 basis points between a bond with a yield of 10.3% and 10.6%. To calculate simple BPV, therefore, use this formula:

BPV = Yield × 0.0001, or 1% of 1%

It is often useful to take the calculation a step further to define the price value of a basis point (PVBP), which is the change in value of a bond or other financial instrument given a change of one basis point value. Sometimes this is also known as "dollar valuation of 01" or DV01.

To calculate PVBP, apply the following calculation:

PVBP = Initial price − Price if yield changes by 1 BPV

In the financial market, a basis point is used to refer to the yield that a bond or investment pays to the investor. For example, if a bond yield moves from 7.45% to 7.65%, it is said to have risen 20 basis points.

For example, if a bank raises interest rates from 2.5% to 2.75%, you would calculate PVBP as follows:

$0.25 \times 0.0001 \times 100 = 0.025\%$ change

(This is the difference in yield from the account created by a movement of 1 basis point.)

TRICKS OF THE TRADE

- Large financial institutions use highly specialized and sophisticated computer systems to calculate the impact of basis point changes (the DV01 figure) in real-time. These figures can be calculated in spreadsheets, but they are difficult to produce accurately, particularly for complex bonds.
- In the bond market, a basis point is used to refer to the yield that a bond pays to the investor. For example, if a bond yield moves from 1.45% to 1.65%, it has risen 20 basis points. Investors will commonly compare bond yields by weighting them according to the BPV.

▶▶ MORE INFO

Website:

Barbican Consulting guide to BPV:
www.barbicanconsulting.co.uk/quickguides/bpv

Binomial Distribution

WHAT IT MEASURES

This refers to the number of incidences of a specific outcome in a series of events or trials. For example, how many times you throw the number three when rolling a die 10 times.

WHY IT IS IMPORTANT

The binomial distribution is widely used to test statistical probabilities and significance, and is a good way of visually detecting unexpected values. It is a useful tool in determining permutations, combinations, and probabilities, where the outcomes can be broken down into two probabilities (p and q), where p and q are complementary (i.e., $p + q = 1$).

For example, tossing a coin has only two possible outcomes, heads or tails. Each of these outcomes has a theoretical probability of 0.5. Using the binomial expansion, showing all possible outcomes and combinations, the probability is represented as follows:

$(p + q)^2 = p^2 + 2pq + q^2$, or more simply, $pp + 2pq + qq$

If p is heads and q is tails, the theory shows there is only one way to get two heads (pp), two ways to get a head and a tail ($2pq$), and one way to get two tails (qq).

Common uses of binomial distributions in business include quality control, public opinion surveys, medical research, and insurance problems. It can be applied to complex processes such as sampling items in factory production lines or to estimate percentage failure rates of products and components.

HOW IT WORKS IN PRACTICE

If I toss a coin 100 times and there are 60 instances of heads and 40 of tails:

$n = 100$ (the number of opportunities where heads could occur)
$k = 60$ (the stipulated number of heads that did occur)
$p = 0.5$ (the statistical probability that heads would occur each time)
$q = 0.5$ (the complementary probability that tails would occur)

At this point, there are three ways to demonstrate probability using a binomial equation. In all three cases, k represents the number of times a specific outcome is observed, p is the probability of heads, and q is the complementary probability of tails.

  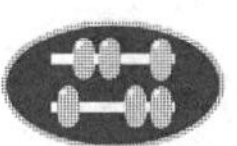 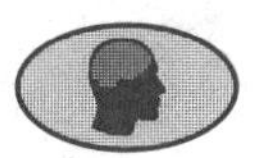  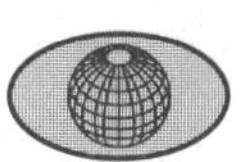   

Method 1

If n = 100, exact binomial probabilities can be calculated using repeated applications of the standard binomial formula, as below. This works out the probability of exactly *k* heads:

$$P(k) = \left[\frac{n!}{k!(n-k!)}\right] p^k q^{n-k)}$$

This is considered to be the most accurate calculation of binomial probabilities, since it involves precise calculation. However, it is best used where n is less than 1,000, or where you are using a computer program to perform more complex calculations on larger sample sizes.

Method 2

If both np and nq are greater than 5, then binomial probabilities can be estimated using an approximation to the Normal distribution. This relies on the following formula:

$$Z = \frac{(k-m) \pm 0.5}{\text{sqrt}}$$

where:
m = np, or the mean of the binomial sampling distribution
sqrt = the standard deviation of the binomial sampling distribution

Method 3

The final method of binomial distribution is the Poisson probability function, which is used where the number of occurrences (n) is less than 150, and the mean (np) and variance (npq) are within 10% of one another. In this case, you can repeatedly apply the Poisson formula to estimate binomial distribution, as below:

$$P(k \text{ out of } n) = \frac{(e-m)(mk)}{k!}$$

Do keep in mind that the results of the Poisson procedure are only approximations of the true binomial probabilities, valid only in the degree that the binomial mean and variance are very close.

TRICKS OF THE TRADE

- To satisfy the requirements of binomial distribution, the event being studied must display certain characteristics:
  - the number of trials or occurrences are fixed
  - there are only two possible outcomes (heads/tails or win/lose, for example)
  - all occurrences are independent of each other (tossing a head does not make it more or less likely you will get the same result next time)
  - all outcomes have the same probability of success
- Binomial distribution is best applied in cases where the population size is at least 10 times the sample size, and not to simple random samples.
- To find probabilities from a binomial distribution, you can perform a manual calculation, but there are online calculators available, or you can use a binomial table or computer spreadsheet.
- The binomial distribution is sometimes called a Bernoulli experiment or trial.
- The binomial *probability* refers to the probability that a binomial experiment results in exactly *x* successes. In example above, we see that the binomial probability of getting exactly one head in two coin flips is 0.5.
- A cumulative binomial probability refers to the probability that the binomial random variable falls within a specified range (for example, is greater than or equal to a stated lower limit and less than or equal to a stated upper limit).

▸▸ MORE INFO

Websites:

Penn State University on binomial distribution: www.stat.psu.edu/online/development/stat500/lesson04/lesson04_02.html

Stat Trek binomial calculator: stattrek.com/Tables/Binomial.aspx

Texas University binomial calculator: www.stat.tamu.edu/~west/applets/binomialdemo.html

Yale University on binomial distribution: www.stat.yale.edu/Courses/1997-98/101/binom.htm

Bond Yield

A bond is a certificate that promises to repay a sum of money borrowed, plus interest, on a specified date, usually years into the future. National, state, and local governments issue bonds, as do corporations and many institutions.

Short-term bonds generally mature in up to 3 years, intermediate-term bonds in 3 to 10 years, and long-term bonds in more than 10 years, with 30 years generally being the upper limit. Longer-term bonds are considered a higher risk because interest rates are certain to change during their lifetime, but they tend to pay higher interest rates to attract investors and reward them for the additional risk.

Bonds are traded on the open market, just like stocks. They are reliable economic indicators, but perform in the reverse direction to interest rates: if bond prices are rising, interest rates and stock markets are likely to be falling, while if interest rates have gone up since a bond was first issued, prices of new bonds will fall.

WHAT IT MEASURES

The annual return on this certificate (the rate of interest) expressed as a percentage of the current market price of the bond.

WHY IT IS IMPORTANT

Bonds can tie up investors' money for periods of up to 30 years, so knowing their yield is a critical investment consideration. Similarly, bond issuers need to know the price they will pay to incur their debt, so that they can compare it with the cost of other means of raising capital.

HOW IT WORKS IN PRACTICE

Bonds are issued in increments of $1,000. To calculate the yield amount, multiply the face value of the bond by the stated rate, expressed as a decimal. For example, buying a new 10-year $1,000 bond that pays 6% interest will produce an annual yield amount of $60:

1,000 × 0.06 = $60

The $60 will be paid as $30 every six months. At the end of 10

years, the purchaser will have earned $600, and will also be repaid the original $1,000. Because the bond was purchased when it was first issued, the 6% is also called the "yield to maturity."

This basic formula is complicated by other factors. First is the "time-value of money" theory: money paid in the future is worth less than money paid today. A more detailed computation of total bond yield requires the calculation of the present value of the interest earned each year. Second, changing interest rates have a marked impact on bond trading and, ultimately, on yield. Changes in interest rates cannot affect the interest paid by bonds already issued, but they do affect the prices of new bonds.

TRICKS OF THE TRADE

- **Yield to call.** Bond issuers reserve the right to "call," or redeem, the bond before the maturity date, at certain times and at a certain price. Issuers often do this if interest rates fall and they can issue new bonds at a lower rate. Bond buyers should obtain the yield-to-call rate, which may, in fact, be a more realistic indicator of the return expected.
- **Different types of bond.** Some bonds are backed by assets, while others are issued on the strength of the issue's good standing. Investors should know the difference.
- **Zero-coupon bonds.** These pay no interest at all, but are sold at a deep discount and increase in value until maturity. A buyer might pay $3,000 for a 25-year zero bond with a face value of $10,000. This bond will simply accrue value each year, and at maturity will be worth $10,000, thus earning $7,000. These are high-risk investments, however, especially if they must be sold on the open market amid rising interest rates.
- **Interest rates.** Bond values fall when interest rates rise, and rise when interest rates fall, because when interest rates rise existing bonds become less valuable and less attractive.

Book Value

No-nonsense number-crunchers adore this measure because it presents the value of common stock equity based on historical values and thus helps separate fact from fiction and fancy.

WHAT IT MEASURES

A company's common stock equity as it appears on a balance sheet.

WHY IT IS IMPORTANT

Book value represents a company's net worth to its stockholders, based on the difference between assets and liabilities plus debt. Typically, book value is substantially different from market value, especially in high-tech and knowledge-based industries whose primary assets are intangible and therefore do not appear on the balance sheet.

When compared with its market value, a company's book value helps to reveal how it is regarded by the investment community. A market value that is notably higher than book value indicates that investors have a high regard for the company. A market value that is, for example, a multiple of book value suggests that investors' regard may be unreasonably high—as was shown in the painful plunge of dot-com companies in 2000 and 2001.

The reverse is also true, of course; indeed, it may suggest that a company's stock is a bargain.

A companion measure is book value per stock. It shows the value of the company's assets that each stockholder theoretically would receive if a company were liquidated.

HOW IT WORKS IN PRACTICE

To calculate book value, subtract a company's liabilities and the value of its debt and preferred stock from its total assets. All of these figures appear on a company's balance sheet. For example:

	$
Total assets	1,300
Current liabilities	–400
Long-term liabilities, preferred stock	–250
Book value	650

Book value per stock is calculated by dividing the book value by the number of stocks issued:

$$\text{Book value per stock} = \frac{\text{Book value}}{\text{Number of stocks issued}}$$

If our example is expressed in millions of dollars and the company has 35 million stocks outstanding, the book value per stock would be $650 million divided by 35 million:

$$\frac{650}{35} = \$18.57$$

TRICKS OF THE TRADE

- Related terms include:
  - **adjusted book value** or **modified book value**, which is book value after assets and liabilities are adjusted to market value
  - **tangible book value**, which also subtracts intangible assets, patents, trademarks, and the value of research and development
  - The rationale is that these items cannot be sold outright
- Book value can also mean the value of an individual asset as it appears on a balance sheet, in which case it is equal to the cost of the asset minus any accumulated depreciation.
- Though often considered a realistic appraisal, book value can still contain unrealistic figures. For example, a building might be fully depreciated and have no official asset value but could still be sold for millions, or four-year-old computer equipment that is not fully depreciated might have asset value but no market value, given its age and advances in technology.

 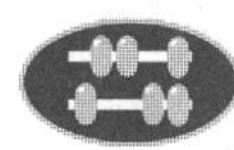 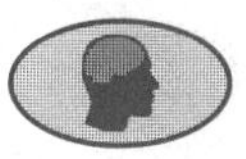  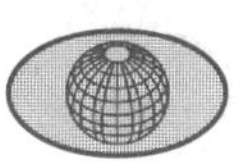  

Borrowing Costs and Capitalization

Borrowing costs are the tangible costs of incurring debt, typically expressed in terms of annual interest paid on outstanding debt or as a stated, annual coupon rate. A firm's borrowing costs are a function of its credit quality. Credit quality is determined on the type of debt security issued, capital structure, and capital-intensiveness of the business. Understanding each of the components of credit quality provides a clear picture of the determinants of a company's cost of debt financing. Borrowing costs also include the expenses incurred to issue debt securities.

GETTING STARTED

The costs of borrowing are primarily made up of interest and issuance expenses. The interest rate assigned to a particular debt instrument is based on the level of default risk assumed by the investor. Several rating agencies assess the default risk of public debt issuances and provide a rating that is indicative of credit quality. The credit quality is greater for secured/collateralized senior debt than for unsecured subordinated debt issued by the same company, and hence the former typically carries a lower rate of interest. Companies that have higher levels of debt must typically pay higher interest rates to investors to compensate them for the increased risk of default. Capital-intensive businesses can usually maintain greater debt-to-capital ratios for the same level of borrowing costs than businesses that are less capital intensive.

FAQS

What are debt issuance costs and are they always incurred when borrowing money?

Debt issuance costs are the underwriting, legal, and administrative fees required to issue the debt. These fees are significant when issuing debt in the public markets, such as bonds. However, other types of debt, such as private placements or bank loans, are cheaper to issue because they require less underwriting, legal, and administrative support. Consequently, the public issuers of debt are typically *Fortune* 500 companies, while middle-market companies tend to issue debt through private placements.

Do borrowing costs increase or decrease for callable bonds or bonds with detachable stock warrants?

When debt securities are issued with a call feature, the debt can be retired at the discretion of the company until some specified future date. The call feature represents value to the issuing company, much like a call option on equity. The issuer must compensate investors for providing this option. Therefore, the interest rate on callable bonds is typically higher than those on noncallable bonds of the same credit quality. That is, the borrowing costs increase on bonds with a call feature.

The opposite is true of bonds with detachable stock warrants. A stock warrant provides the bondholder with the right to purchase shares of common stock in the issuing company at a specified price during a defined period of time. The warrant's strike price is typically at, or higher than, the current market price of the company's stock. Nonetheless, the warrant provides value to the bondholder in the form of a call option on the company's equity. Because these warrants add to the potential total return on the debt, the stated interest rate is usually lower than that on debt issued without warrants of similar credit quality. Borrowing costs are typically lower on bonds with detachable stock warrants.

MAKING IT HAPPEN

When companies borrow money, they enter a formal obligation to make periodic payments of interest and to repay the principal balance outstanding according to an agreed schedule. The interest payments are typically based on a stated, annual percentage of the original amount borrowed. The interest paid on such obligations represents the cost of borrowing, along with the costs to issue the debt.

The Difference between Funded and Unfunded Debt

The debt can be classified as funded or unfunded. Funded debt is long-term debt or debt that has a maturity date in excess of one year. Unfunded debt is short-term debt requiring repayment within a year from issuance. Funded debt is usually issued in the public markets or in the form of a private placement to qualified institutional investors. Most unfunded debt is commercial paper or bank lines of credit.

Senior and Subordinated Debt

Debt can also be classified as senior or subordinated, based on its preference to assets in the event of default by the lender. Subordinated lenders have a junior claim to assets in the event of bankruptcy and are paid only after senior creditors' claims have been satisfied.

Senior credit can be secured or unsecured. Much of the corporate debt outstanding is referred to as a bond. However, a true bond is secured by claims against the company's property, plant, and equipment. For example, many airlines secure their public debt by mortgaging their airplanes. In this example, an airline could be forced to sell its airplanes to pay its public debt if it defaulted on the bonds. Most public debt is secured by the good faith and credit of the issuing company, and is more accurately called a debenture. A company can also pledge certain assets, like accounts receivable, inventory, or property, as collateral for a loan or debt.

Differing Levels of Risk

Even when debt is secured or collateralized, it still does not guarantee repayment by the issuer. A company's underlying asset value and its earnings may be very volatile, increasing the risk of default in a down business cycle. Because this risk can be different from one business to another, there are several national rating agencies that rate public debt based on the creditworthiness of the borrower. Investment-grade debt securities are securities that are rated in the top four categories of creditworthiness by Standard & Poor's or Moody's rating agencies. All debt securities rated below investment-grade are considered to be junk bonds.

Different Types of Interest Rate

Debt can have a fixed or floating rate of interest. Fixed-rate debt pays the same interest rate over its term. Most long-term debt is issued with a fixed rate. Many short-term loans are floating-rate instruments based on the prime lending rate, Libor (London Interbank Offered Rate), or some US Treasury security. When the rates on these securities change, the loan rate changes. For example, a line of credit whose current interest rate is 6%, based on one percentage point above the three-year Libor rate, will change to 6.25% if Libor increases by a quarter of a point. Floating-rate debt is typically used to support a business's working capital requirements.

 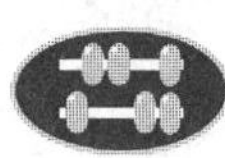   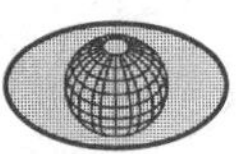   

The Determinants of Credit Quality

The interest rate and, consequently, the borrowing cost is determined by credit quality. Credit quality depends on the type of debt security, the amount of debt relative to total capital, and the capital-intensiveness of a company's business. All other things being equal, a secured or collateralized debt security is less risky than an unsecured obligation. Therefore, investors require a greater return for the additional risk assumed by investing in unsecured debt. Likewise, an investor will require a greater return for subordinated debt than for senior credit.

Credit quality also deteriorates as the level of debt grows on the balance sheet of a company. Intuitively, the greater the debt-to-capital ratio, the greater the risk of default. By continuing to add financial leverage to its business operations, a company increases the risks that in a bad year it may not be able to cover its debt service. In studies on cost of capital, it was determined that companies experiencing debt-to-capital ratios between 25% and 45% saw their cost of capital increase exponentially, indicating greater risk of financial distress.

Debt-to-Capital Ratios

Finally, companies that are more capital-intensive tend to have greater debt-to-capital ratios. For example, automobile and airline manufacturers typically maintain greater leverage than professional services and software companies. The academic explanation given for this circumstance is the degree of industry maturity, lower earnings volatility, and the ability to secure more debt with tangible assets. Consequently, companies in more capital-intensive industries tend to have lower borrowing costs at a given debt-to-capital ratio than those in less capital-intensive industries.

TRICKS OF THE TRADE

- The costs of borrowing are composed of interest payments and issuance costs. Interest paid on outstanding debt is a function of the creditworthiness of the borrower. The greater the interest rate on a debt security relative to other, similar securities, the lower the credit quality of the issuer. As credit quality falls below investment-grade, the risk of default becomes ominously greater and the costs of borrowing become more exorbitant.
- A company's capital structure is another major determinant of credit quality. There is a direct relationship between debt level and default risk. At a given debt to capital ratio, incremental borrowing costs increase dramatically as the company's risk of financial distress reaches its peak.

▸▸ MORE INFO

Book:

Brealey, Richard A., Stewart C. Myers, and Franklin Allen. *Principles of Corporate Finance*. 9th ed. Boston, MA: McGraw-Hill, 2008.

Break-Even Analysis

WHAT IT MEASURES

Break-even is the point at which a product or service stops costing money to produce and sell, and starts generating a profit for your business. This means sales have reached sufficient volume to cover the variable and fixed costs of producing and distributing your product.

WHY IT IS IMPORTANT

The ultimate goal of any business is to make money, but break-even analysis can also provide valuable information for profitable businesses in terms of setting price levels, targeting optimal variable/fixed price combinations and determining the financial attractiveness of various strategies for a business.

Break-even analysis allows a business to understand what the minimum level of sales needed is to ensure that it does not make a loss, and how sensitive the break-even point is to changes in fixed or variable expenses. It can help you to understand and examine the profit drivers of your business.

HOW IT WORKS IN PRACTICE

Say you are an entrepreneur looking to sell t-shirts across Europe. You will want to know how many t-shirts you need to sell before your venture generates a profit. This figure can then be compared to your sales forecasts to judge the likely success of your venture. There are two ways of calculating break-even points, as shown below.

The variable cost of producing a single t-shirt is $1. The fixed costs of the business over a year (those costs that won't vary month to month) include items such as telecommunications, rent, and insurance, and total $25,000 in year one. The unit price you are expecting for each t-shirt is $5 and your projected sales in year one are 50,000 units.

To calculate break-even, EITHER:

Draw a chart showing:

- sales revenue at different levels of output;
- fixed costs at different levels of output;
- total costs at different levels of output;

The point where total cost equals total sales revenue is the break-even point.

OR:

Use the data available to calculate the contribution of each unit sold or made. This is the difference between the sales revenue and the variable cost of each unit. Using the example of the t-shirts, each t-shirt brings in $5 of revenue against $1 in variable costs. The contribution of each unit is said to be $4, because the unit makes a $4 contribution towards fixed costs.

The number of units needed to be sold to break even is therefore the total fixed cost divided by the contribution per unit. The t-shirt venture would need to sell enough t-shirts to cover fixed costs ($25,000) divided by the unit contribution ($4)—in other words, 6,250 shirts.

Break-even analysis is particularly useful in comparing alternative scenarios. For example, you might consider what happens if labor costs rise and the variable cost of producing a t-shirt doubles to $2? In this scenario, the contribution per shirt falls to $3 but fixed costs remain $25,000—meaning the business needs to now sell 25,000/3 t-shirts to reach break-even (8,334 shirts).

The simple formula for this method is:

$$\text{Break-even sales (\$)} = \frac{\text{Fixed costs}}{\left(\dfrac{\text{Contribution margin}}{\text{Total sales}}\right)}$$

TRICKS OF THE TRADE

- Fundamentally, there are only three ways to reduce break-even: lower direct costs to increase the gross margin; reduce fixed expenses and lower necessary total costs; or raise prices to increase revenues.
- Categorizing costs as fixed or variable is essential for break-even analysis. Fixed costs are those not related to the volume of production, often referred to as "overheads." These costs will remain static even if you do not produce any goods, and include items such as staff salaries, insurance, property taxes, and interest. Variable costs are those related to production output or sales, and might include raw materials, commission, packaging, and shipping costs. Without a good understanding of your costs, break-even analysis will be meaningless.
- Remember that the break-even point is not a static figure. You should compare projections to real-life results every three to six months, and make adjustments if necessary. In particular, expenses tend to increase over time and you may fall below break-even point because you think it is lower than it has become.
- When conducting break-even analysis, you might want to add in a margin for profit. For example, you might want to target a specific profit margin goal and this can be incorporated into break-even analysis as follows:

$$\text{Break-even (\$)} = \frac{\text{Fixed costs} + \text{Profit goal}}{\left(\frac{\text{Contribution margin}}{\text{Total sales}}\right)}$$

- Another refinement of the break-even analysis is the "sensitivity analysis." This refers to using the break-even point to evaluate different scenarios. For example, what happens if you increase prices by 25%? What happens if unit sales fall by 20%? Using a spreadsheet, it is very simple to perform such calculations quickly, allowing you to look at different situations.

▸▸ MORE INFO

Articles:

"Fixed, variable costs and break-even." *The Times 100*. Online at: www.thetimes100.co.uk/theory/theory-fixed-variable-costs-break-even-122.php

"Mind Your Business—Break-even analysis: Debts, revenues and costs." *Biz/ed* (November 18, 2008). Online at: www.bized.co.uk/current/mind/2008_9/181108.htm

Capital Asset Pricing Model

Although at first glance it looks likes a simple formula, the capital asset pricing model (CAPM) represents an historic effort to understand and quantify something that's not at all simple: risk. Conceived by Nobel economist William Sharpe in 1964, CAPM has been praised, appraised, and assailed by economists ever since.

WHAT IT MEASURES

The relationship between the risk and expected return of a security or stock portfolio.

WHY IT IS IMPORTANT

The capital asset pricing model's importance is twofold.

First, it serves as a model for pricing the risk in all securities, and thus helps investors evaluate and measure portfolio risk and the returns they can anticipate for taking such risks.

Second, the theory behind the formula also has fueled—some might say provoked—spirited debate among economists about the nature of investment risk itself. The CAPM attempts to describe how the market values investments with expected returns.

The CAPM theory classifies risk as being either diversifiable, which can be avoided by sound investing, or systematic, that is, not diversified and unavoidable due to the nature of the market itself. The theory contends that investors are rewarded only for assuming systematic risk, because they can mitigate diversifiable risk by building a portfolio of both risky stocks and sound ones.

One analysis has characterized the CAPM as "a theory of equilibrium" that links higher expected returns in strong markets with the greater risk of suffering heavy losses in weak markets. Otherwise, no one would invest in high-risk stocks.

HOW IT WORKS IN PRACTICE

CAPM holds that the expected return of a security or a portfolio equals the rate on a risk-free security plus a risk premium. If this expected return does not meet or beat a theoretical required return, the investment should not be undertaken. The formula used to create CAPM is:

$$\text{Expected return} = \text{Risk-free rate} + (\text{Market return} - \text{Risk-free rate}) \times \text{Beta value}$$

The risk-free rate is the quoted rate on an asset that has virtually no risk. In practice, it is the rate quoted for 90-day US Treasury bills. The market return is the percentage return expected of the overall market, typically a published index such as Standard & Poor's. The beta value is a figure that measures the volatility of a security or portfolio of securities compared with the market as a whole. A beta of 1, for example, indicates that a security's price will move with the market. A beta greater than 1 indicates higher volatility, while a beta less than 1 indicates less volatility.

Say, for instance, that the current risk-free rate is 4%, and the S&P 500 index is expected to return 11% next year. An investment club is interested in determining next year's return for XYZ Software, Inc, a prospective investment. The club has determined that the company's beta value is 1.8. The overall stock market always has a beta of 1, so XYZ Software's beta of 1.8 signals that it is a more risky investment than the overall market represents. This added risk means that the club should expect a higher rate of return than the 11% for the S&P 500. The CAPM calculation, then, would be:

$$4\% + (11\% - 4\%) \times 1.8 = 16.6\%$$

What the results tell the club is that given the risk, XYZ Software, Inc, has a required rate of return of 16.6%, or the minimum return that an investment in XYZ should generate. If the investment club doesn't think that XYZ will produce that kind of return, it should probably consider investing in a different company.

TRICKS OF THE TRADE

- As experts warn, CAPM is only a simple calculation built on historical data of market and stock prices. It does not express anything about the company whose stock is being analyzed. For example, renowned investor Warren Buffett has pointed out that if a company making Barbie™ dolls has the same beta as one

     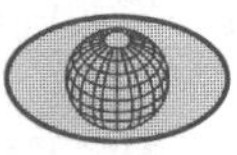   

making pet rocks, CAPM holds that one investment is as good as the other. Clearly, this is a risky tenet.

- While high returns might be received from stocks with high beta shares, there is no guarantee that their respective CAPM return will be realized (a reason why beta is defined as a "measure of risk" rather than an "indication of high return").
- The beta parameter itself is historical data and may not reflect future results. The data for beta values are typically gathered over several years, and experts recommend that only long-term investors should rely on the CAPM formula.
- Over longer periods of time, high-beta shares tend to be the worst performers during market declines.

▸▸ MORE INFO

Article:

Burton, Jonathan. "Revisiting the capital asset pricing model." *Dow Jones Asset Manager* (May/June 1998): 20–28. Online at: www.stanford.edu/~wfsharpe/art/djam/djam.htm

Website:

Contingency Analysis resource for trading, financial engineering, and financial risk management: www.contingencyanalysis.com

Capital Expenditure

WHAT IT MEASURES

Capital expenditure (capex) refers to the money a business spends purchasing or upgrading fixed assets for future business benefit. Capital expenditure can include money spent for new property that will be resold, or which might be kept for one or more years. Capital expenditure also includes money spent to improve property (or inventory) that you already own. Under international reporting standards, property is considered to be improved only if the money you spend increases or restores an item's value, prolongs its useful life, or enables the item to be used for a new purpose.

WHY IT IS IMPORTANT

Understanding capital expenditure is a vital part of assessing a company's free cash flow. Basically, if a company spends a lot on capital expenditure but doesn't show a corresponding rate of growth, it is considered a less attractive investment. Ideally, healthy companies should generate enough positive cash flow to fund dividends/growth as well as capital expenditure.

HOW IT WORKS IN PRACTICE

To enable cash flow to be properly assessed it is important to accurately calculate the amount of funds necessary to support capital expenditure—and for the business to continue to operate. This is known as capex per share.

First, you should discount any capital expenditure that is discretionary—such as real estate, which might otherwise be leased.

Then use the following formulas to calculate capex per share based on net cash outflow attributable to property, divided by the weighted average number of ordinary shares in issue during the year:

$$\text{Capital expenditure} = \text{Total asset purchases} - \text{Property asset purchases} - \text{Nonproperty asset sales}$$

and

$$\text{Capex per share} = \frac{\text{Capex}}{\text{Weighted average of shares in issue}}$$

TRICKS OF THE TRADE

- Remember that few companies have smooth capex investment over time. Most companies will have a lean capex year, followed by a year or two of heavy investment. Wherever possible, use an average capex calculation—a single figure can be extremely misleading.
- Capital expenditure is only used to refer to one-off purchases of new items or improvements to existing assets which are kept and used by the business. So the cost of buying a truck for your business is a capital expenditure, but the cost of hiring a truck is not.
- It is possible to claim tax relief on a percentage of most capital expenditure, using allowances such as "first year allowance" or "writing down allowance."
- One classic example of capital expenditure is the start-up expenses incurred when you buy or create a new business venture. These expenses are considered capital expenditure because the owner incurs them to acquire property that will be kept. These expenses may be fully deducted in year one, or may be amortized over several years.

▸▸ MORE INFO

Website:

HMRC (UK) Business Income Manual section on capex: www.hmrc.gov.uk/manuals/bimmanual/BIM35000.htm

Capitalization Ratios

Capitalization ratios, also widely known as financial leverage ratios, provide a glimpse of a company's long-term stability and ability to withstand losses and business downturns.

WHAT THEY MEASURE

By comparing debt to total capitalization, these ratios reflect the extent to which a corporation is trading on its equity, and the degree to which it finances operations with debt.

While not the focus here, capitalization ratio also refers to the percentage of a company's total capitalization contributed by debt, preferred stock, common stock, and other equity.

WHY THEY ARE IMPORTANT

By itself, any financial ratio is a rather useless piece of information. Collectively, and in context, though, financial leverage ratios present analysts and investors with an excellent picture of a company's

  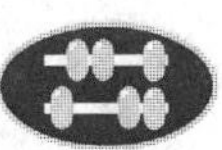   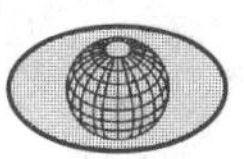   

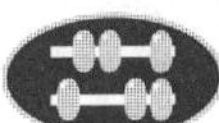

situation, how much financial risk it has taken on, its dependence on debt, and developing trends. Knowing who controls a company's capital tells one who truly controls the enterprise!

HOW THEY WORK IN PRACTICE

A business finances its assets with either equity or debt. Financing with debt involves risk, since debt legally obligates a company to pay off the debt, plus the interest the debt incurs. Equity financing, on the other hand, does not obligate the company to pay anything. It pays investors dividends—but this is at the discretion of the board of directors. To be sure, business risk accompanies the operation of any enterprise. But how that enterprise opts to finance its operations—how it blends debt with equity—may heighten this risk.

Various experts include numerous formulas among capitalization financial leverage ratios. Three are discussed separately: debt-to-capital ratio, debt-to-equity ratio, and interest coverage ratios. What's known as the capitalization ratio *per se* can be expressed in two ways:

$$\frac{\text{Long-term debt}}{\text{Long-term debt + Owners' equity}}$$

and

$$\frac{\text{Total debt}}{\text{Total debt + Preferred and common equity}}$$

For example, a company whose long-term debt totals \$5,000 and whose owners hold equity worth \$3,000 would have a capitalization ratio of:

$$\frac{5{,}000}{5{,}000 + 3{,}000} = \frac{5{,}000}{8{,}000} = 0.625$$

Both expressions of the capitalization ratio are also referred to "component percentages," since they compare a company's debt with either its total capital (debt plus equity) or its equity capital. They readily indicate how reliant a company is on debt financing.

TRICKS OF THE TRADE

- Capitalization ratios need to be evaluated over time, and compared with other data and standards. A gross profit margin of 20%, for instance, is meaningless—until one knows that the average profit margin for an industry is 10%; at that point, 20% looks quite attractive. Moreover, if the historical trend of that margin has been climbing for the last three years, it strongly suggests that a company's management has sound and effective policies and strategies in place.
- Also, all capitalization ratios should be interpreted in the context of a company's earnings and cash flow, and those of its competitors.
- Take care in comparing companies in different industries or sectors. The same figures that appear to be low in one industry can be very high in another.
- Some less frequently used capitalization ratios are based on formulas that use the book value of equity (the stock). When compared with other ratios, they can be misleading, because there usually is little relation between a company's book value and its market value—which is apt to be many times higher, since market value reflects what the investment community thinks the company is worth.

▸▸ MORE INFO

Book:

Walsh, Ciaran. *Key Management Ratios*. 4th ed. London: FT Prentice Hall, 2008.

Central Limit Theorem

WHAT IT MEASURES

The central limit theorem (CLT) is a statistical theory which holds that, given a sufficiently large sample size from a sufficiently varied population, the mean of all results will be approximately equal to the mean of the population. In addition, samples will roughly follow a normal distribution pattern (i.e., a bell-shaped curve), with variances reflecting the variance of the source population, divided by the sample size. As a rule of thumb, a population sample of 50 is required for CLT to be applied.

WHY IT IS IMPORTANT

CLT is a relatively simple analysis tool that is very important in examining returns from a particular investment. CLT is the foundation for many statistical procedures, including quality control charts, because the distribution of the phenomenon under study does not have to be normal, because the average will be.

HOW IT WORKS IN PRACTICE

CLT states that the average of the sum of a large number of independent, identically distributed random variables with finite means and variances converges to a normal random variable.

For example, if you tossed an ordinary coin 100 times, you would expect sometimes the coin to land on heads, sometimes on tails. If you score one point for each time it lands heads, the result would be the sum of 100 independent, identically distributed random variables.

The central limit theorem states that the distribution of heads will be close to a normal distribution curve. Repeating the experiment more times would create a result that, when plotted on a graph, would closely resemble the normal curve. CLT theory is based on the idea that a large population of independent variables (like the toss of a coin) is subject to independent random effects, which result in a normal distribution.

Expressed as a mathematical formula, CLT is as follows:

Let $X_1, X_2, \ldots, X_n$ be a random sample (iid) from a distribution with well-defined and finite mean (μX) and variance (SIGMA 2/x).

As n increases, the sampling distribution of the sample average and the total sum approach Normal distributions with corresponding means and variances.

TRICKS OF THE TRADE

- A very loose form of CLT says that if you add up a large number n of different random variables, and if none of those variables dominate the resultant distribution spread, the sum will eventually look Normal as n gets bigger.

     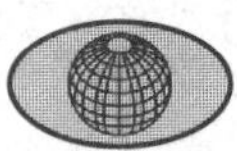   

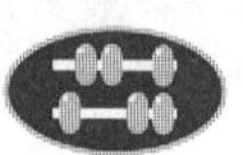

- The CLT almost always holds, but you must be cautious when using it. If the population mean doesn't exist, then CLT is not applicable. Moreover, even if the mean does exist, the CLT convergence to a normal density might be slow, requiring hundreds or even thousands of observations, rather than the few dozen in these examples.

MORE INFO

Websites:

iSixSigma on CLT: finance.isixsigma.com/dictionary/Central_Limit_Theorem-177.htm

Richard Lowry on CLT: faculty.vassar.edu/lowry/central.html

Contribution Margin

Finding the contribution margin unearths an important comparison that otherwise would lie hidden in an income statement.

WHAT IT MEASURES

The amounts that individual products or services ultimately contribute to net profit.

WHY IT IS IMPORTANT

Contribution margin helps a business to decide how it should direct or redirect its resources.

When managers know the contribution margin—or margins, as is more often the case—they can make better decisions about adding or subtracting product lines, investing in existing products, pricing products or services (particularly in response to competitors' actions), structuring sales commissions and bonuses, where to direct marketing and advertising expenditures, and where to apply individual talents and expertise.

In short, contribution margin is a valuable decision-support tool.

HOW IT WORKS IN PRACTICE

Its calculation is straightforward:

Contribution margin = Sales price – Variable cost

Or, for providers of services:

Contribution margin = Total revenue – Total variable cost

For example, if the sales price of a good is $500 and the variable cost is $350, the contribution margin is $150, or 30% of the sales price.

This means that 30 cents of every sales dollar remains to contribute to fixed costs and to profit after the costs directly related to the sales are subtracted.

Contribution margin is especially useful to a company comparing different products or services (see the example below).

	Product A	Product B	Product C
Sales price ($)	260	220	140
Variable costs ($)	178	148	65
Contribution margin ($)	82	72	75
Contribution margin (%)	31.5	32.7	53.6

Obviously, Product C has the highest contribution percentage, even though Product A generates more total profit. The analysis suggests that the company might do well to aim to achieve a sales mix with a higher proportion of Product C. It further suggests that prices for Products A and B may be too low, or that their cost structures need attention. Notably, none of this information appears on a standard income statement.

Contribution margin can also be tracked over a long period of time using data from several years of income statements. It can also be invaluable in calculating volume discounts for preferred customers, and break-even sales or volume levels.

TRICKS OF THE TRADE

Contribution margin depends on accurately accounting for all variable costs, including shipping and delivery, or the indirect costs of services. Activity-based cost accounting systems aid this kind of analysis. Variable costs include all direct costs (usually labor and materials). Contribution margin analysis is only one tool to use. It will not show so-called loss leaders, for example. And it doesn't consider marketing factors like existing penetration levels, opportunities, or mature markets being eroded by emerging markets.

Conversion Price

As often as not, when you need to calculate conversion price, it is not so much the calculation that is at issue, but observation.

WHAT IT MEASURES

The price per share at which the holder of convertible bonds, or debentures, or preferred stock, can convert them into shares of common stock.

Depending on specific terms, the conversion price may be set when the convertible asset is issued.

WHY IT IS IMPORTANT

The conversion price is a key factor in an investment strategy. Knowing it helps investors to determine whether or not it is to their advantage to convert their holdings into shares of stock, sell them on the open market, or retain them until they mature or are called by the issuing company.

At the same time, existing stockholders of the issuing company need to know the point at which the value of their shares could be diluted by the creation of additional shares without the concurrent creation of additional capital.

     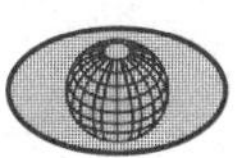   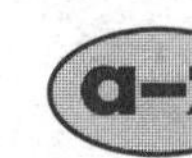

For companies themselves, a conversion price represents an additional financing option: an opportunity to convert debt into equity, an action that itself has advantages and drawbacks.

HOW IT WORKS IN PRACTICE

If the conversion price is set, it will appear in the indenture, a legal agreement between the issuer of a convertible asset and the holder that states specific terms. If the conversion price does not appear in the agreement, a conversion ratio is used to calculate the conversion price.

A conversion ratio of 25:1, for example, means that 25 shares of stock can be obtained in exchange for each $1,000 of convertible asset held. In turn, the conversion price can be determined simply by dividing $1,000 by 25:

$$\frac{1,000}{25} = \$40 \text{ per share}$$

Comparison of a stock's conversion price to its prevailing market price can help to decide the best course of action. If the stock of the company in question is trading at $52 per share, converting makes sense because it increases the value of $1,000 convertible to $1,300 ($52 × 25 shares). But if the stock is trading at $32 per share, then the conversion value is only $800 ($32 × 25), and it is clearly better to defer conversion.

TRICKS OF THE TRADE

- Conversion ratios may change over time according to the terms of the agreement. This is to ensure that a convertible asset holder is not unduly advantaged and that the value of existing stock is not diluted—which, of course, would anger existing stockholders.
- Stockholders, in turn, need to monitor closely a company that decides to issue a large number of convertible assets, since the value of their shares could ultimately be undermined.
- Convertible bonds closely follow the price of the issuing company's underlying stock. Often, in fact, the respective prices of the bond and the shares to be exchanged are almost equal.

Conversion Ratio

Conversion ratio and conversion price work in tandem and should be considered together.

WHAT IT MEASURES

The number of shares of common stock an investor will receive on converting a convertible security—a bond, debenture, or preferred stock.

The conversion price may be set when the convertible security is issued, depending on its terms.

WHY IT IS IMPORTANT

Like conversion price, the conversion ratio is an investment strategy tool which is used to determine what the value of a convertible security would be if it were converted immediately. By knowing a convertible's value, an investor can compare it with the prevailing price of the issuing company's common stock and decide whether it is best to convert or to continue holding the convertible.

By the same token, holders of common stock in the company issuing the convertible can use the conversion ratio to help to monitor the value of their stock. For example, a relatively high ratio could mean that the value of their shares would be diluted if large numbers of convertible holders were to exercise their options.

HOW IT WORKS IN PRACTICE

In the same way as conversion price, the conversion ratio may be established when the convertible is issued. If that is the case, the ratio will appear in the indenture, the binding agreement that details the convertible's terms.

If the conversion ratio is not set, it can be calculated quickly: divide the par value of the convertible security (typically $1,000) by its conversion price:

$$\frac{\$1,000}{\$40 \text{ per share}} = 25 \text{ shares}$$

In this example, the conversion ratio is 25:1, which means that every bond held with a $1,000 par value can be exchanged for 25 shares of common stock.

Knowing the conversion ratio enables an investor to decide quickly whether his convertibles (or group of them) are more valuable than the shares of common stock they represent. If the stock is currently trading at $30, the conversion value is $750, or $250 less than the par value of the convertible. It would therefore be unwise to convert.

TRICKS OF THE TRADE

- Although it is rare, a convertible's indenture can sometimes contain a provision stating that the conversion ratio will change over the years.
- A conversion ratio that is set when a convertible is issued usually protects against any dilution from stock splits. However, it does not protect against a company issuing secondary offerings of common stock.
- "Forced conversion" means that the company can make holders convert into stock at virtually any time. Convertible holders should also pay close attention to the price at which the bonds are callable.
- Conversion ratio also describes the number of shares of one common stock to be issued for each outstanding share of another common stock when a merger takes place.

  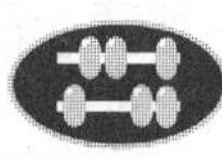 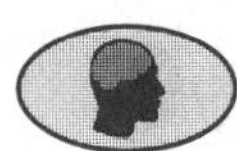  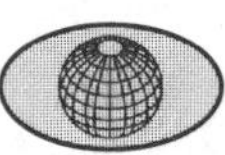   

Convertible Preferred Stock

Convertible preferred stock (known as preference shares in the United Kingdom) gives the holder the right to exchange it at a fixed price for another security, usually common stock. The trick is knowing if, and when, to exercise that right.

GETTING STARTED

- Evaluating convertible preferred stock is principally an analysis of risk rather than of a company.
- Preferred stocks are listed as equity on a balance sheet, but they perform more like bonds than common stock since most of these issues pay a fixed dividend set at the time of issue.
- While holders of preferred stock are entitled to a fixed dividend, they do not usually have voting rights.
- Preferred stocks are usually repayable at par value, and rank above the claims of ordinary stockholders but behind bank and trade creditors.
- An expensive form of capitalization, preferred stock is typically used to finance growth opportunities and capital expenditures, and to repay bank debt and nonbank short-term debt.
- Preferred stocks are often preferred by venture capitalists because they protect their investments better, and offer them greater leverage and growth opportunities.
- US income tax considerations severely limit the appeal of preferred stock among individual investors, but enhance it among corporations.

FAQS

Officially, what is convertible preferred stock?

It is a share of corporation ownership that gives holders a claim prior to the claim of common stockholders on earnings and, generally, on assets in the event of liquidation. It may also be exchanged for a fixed number of shares of common stock. Because no maturity date is stipulated, preferred stock is priced based on a stated dividend yield—in, for example, dollars, pounds, or euros—or as a percentage of par value.

How does preferred stock compare to common stock?

The dividend on common stock is uncertain and variable: high when a company performs well, low or nonexistent when it fares poorly. Holders of preferred stock, however, get a fixed dividend—and one which, if not paid, accrues until it can be. On the other hand, preferred stockholders are not usually able to vote on pertinent resolutions unless dividends fall into arrears, while holders of common stock have voting rights based on the number of shares owned.

Are there different kinds of preferred stock?

Yes. For example, callable preferred stock may be repurchased by the issuing company, typically at par value or slightly higher, while an indirect convertible may be exchanged for another convertible security, such as a bond that can be exchanged for convertible preferred stock. There are also participating preferred stocks, which entitle holders both to receive specified dividends and to participate along with holders of common stock in receiving additional dividends.

Any there other important distinguishing features of preferred stock?

First, there may be an option to receive cash for those who decline to exercise their conversion rights. Most preferred stocks also carry lower interest rates than similar fixed-interest securities, since the investor has the opportunity to convert his holdings to common stock and, in turn, to realize a capital gain if its price rises above its conversion price. Some preferred stocks also permit the investor to require the issuing company to redeem the stock after a predetermined time for an amount that gives the investor a modest profit.

Venture capitalists are known to prefer preferred stock. Why?

It gives them preference in the event of a company's liquidation or sale, which enables venture capitalists to get back their investment before other investors receive any proceeds from such events. A typical convertible preferred stock also enables venture capitalist investors to convert their shares into common stock according to a predetermined formula and to vote on major stockholder issues such as the election of directors and a change of the company's core business activity.

How are repeated conversions of preferred stock prevented from diluting the value of common stock?

The formula used to convert the convertible preferred stock into shares of common stock typically includes an adjustment mechanism—an "anti-dilution provision"—that protects the investor against any dilution in his percentage ownership caused by sale of cheaper stock to later investors. The nature and extent of the protection afforded can be very important also to the holders of the company's common stock: the greater the protection against dilution given to the holder of convertible preferred stock, the more dilution common stockholders are likely to suffer

MAKING IT HAPPEN

Like almost any stock consideration, evaluating convertible preferred stock opportunities and transactions is based on research, market knowledge, and past experience.

It is essential first to understand what a company does and how it generates cash. The next question is determining the likelihood of the company being able to pay its preferred dividends. The tools of choice are, first, a common "coverage ratio" like EBIT or EBITDA, and, second, preferred stock ratings.

EBITDA is the acronym for "earnings before interest, taxes, depreciation, and amortization." It usually measures a company's ability to handle debt service (interest payments), but can easily be adapted to include preferred stock dividends. The ratio is:

$$\frac{\text{EBITDA}}{\text{Interest expense + Preferred dividends}}$$

The higher the coverage ratio, the better.

Like corporate bonds, most preferred stocks are rated by such services as Standard & Poor's and Moody's. Each rating service uses a slightly different rating system, but they have a similar basis: "A" is good, "AAA" is better, and so on. A "B" or above is considered investment grade, but anything below that is regarded as very high risk.

Another warning point is that, if a preferred stock is rated only by one of the second-tier rating agencies, the likelihood is that the company's management was unable to get a favorable rating from Standard & Poor's or Moody's. The investor relations offices and websites of most corporations will provide the ratings. If they do not, beware—although the websites of the rating services themselves will probably list them.

There are also some guidelines to follow. For instance, preferred stocks should have a higher yield than the issuing company's comparable debt (yield is the annual dividend divided by the price). This must be gauged on a case-by-case basis.

There is another long-held contention that higher-quality companies issue standard convertible preferred stock, while lower-quality companies issue convertible exchangeable preferred stock. Similarly, it is maintained that only the "best" companies are consistently able to issue straight debt cost-effectively, while medium-quality companies issue convertible securities, and lower-quality companies or high-risk companies tend to issue additional common stock.

Conversion ratios and prices are other key facts to know about preferred stock. This information is found on the indenture statement that accompanies all issues. Occasionally the indenture will state that the conversion ratio will change over time. For example, the conversion price might be $50 for the first five years, $55 for the next five years, and so forth. Stock splits can affect conversion considerations.

In theory, convertible preferred stocks (and convertible exchangeable preferred stocks) are usually perpetual in time. However, issuers tend to force conversion or induce voluntary conversion for convertible preferred stock within 10 years. Steadily increasing common stock dividends is one inducement tactic used. As a result, the conversion feature for preferred stocks often resembles that of debt securities. Call protection for the investor is usually about three years, and a 30- to 60-day call notice is typical.

About 50% of convertible equity issues also have a "soft call provision." If the common stock price reaches a specified ratio, the issuer is permitted to force conversion before the end of the normal protection period. Converting preferred stock risks diluting common stock, of course, and among mature companies that is a valid concern. Where a company has a good track record and aggressive growth plans, however, it may benefit both investors and the company, especially if the management can maintain (or increase) profit margin.

TRICKS OF THE TRADE

- In any country, tax considerations invariably accompany the exercise of convertible preferred stock transactions. Here are considerations based on US laws:
- Like common stock, preferred stock comes with a prospectus that should answer such basic questions as: Are the dividends cumulative? Are the shares redeemable; if so, when? What is the likelihood of redemption? Has the board of directors ever suspended dividends? (If it has, this is a bad sign indicating cash flow problems).
- At least in the United States, many companies dislike issuing preferred stock because it is an expensive form of capitalization. Preferred stock pays dividends from after-tax profits, while bonds pay interest from pre-tax dollars, thus delivering a tax break that preferred stock cannot match.
- Owning preferred stocks of other companies is another matter, however: corporations are exempt from taxes on up to 80% of preferred dividend income.
- Missing preferred stock dividends is not legally a default, but a company that omits a preferred stock dividend may not pay common stock dividends. Moreover, if subsequent preferred stock dividends are missed, preferred stock shareholders may gain board seats (or more of them), and in some cases also accrue special voting rights.
- Most preferred issues are cumulative, so dividends accrue even if they are not actually paid in a given quarter. Once the dividends are resumed, and before common dividends can be paid, cumulative preferred shareholders must be paid their accrued dividends.
- If a company is liquidated, holders of preferred stock are entitled to receive their investment back before the holders of any common stock receive anything. In other words, "investment" means the amount paid for the preferred stock plus any accrued and unpaid dividends—an important consideration.
- Preferred stocks and other convertible securities offer investors a hedge: fixed-interest income without sacrificing the chance to participate in a company's capital appreciation.
- When a company does well, investors can convert their holdings into common stock that is more valuable. When a company is less successful, they can still receive interest and principal payments, and also recover their investment and preserve their capital if a more favorable investment appears.

▸▸ MORE INFO

Book:

Jenks, Philip, and Stephen Eckett. *The Global Investor Book of Investing Rules*. London: Harriman House, 2001.

Cost of Goods Sold

WHAT IT MEASURES

For a retailer, cost of goods sold (COGS) is the cost of buying and acquiring the goods that it sells to its customers. For a service company, COGS is the cost of the employee services it supplies. For a manufacturer, COGS is the cost of buying the raw materials and manufacturing its finished products.

WHY IT IS IMPORTANT

Cost of goods sold may help a company to determine the prices to charge for its products and services, and the volume of business that it needs to maintain in order to operate profitably.

For retailers especially, the cost of the merchandise sold is typically the largest expense, and thus is an absolutely critical business factor. However, understanding COGS is an important success factor for any business because it can reveal opportunities to reduce costs and improve operations.

COGS is also a key figure on an income statement, and an important consideration in computing income taxes because of its close relationship to inventory, which tax authorities treat as future income.

HOW IT WORKS IN PRACTICE

Essentially, COGS is equal to a company's opening inventory of goods and services, plus the cost of goods bought and direct costs incurred during a particular period, minus the closing inventory of goods and services.

     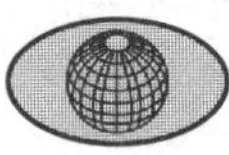   

A critical consideration is the accounting policy that a company adopts to calculate inventory values, especially if raw materials prices change during the year. This may happen often, particularly when inflation is high. Inventory values under a first in first out (FIFO) policy reflect original or older prices of materials, while a last in first out (LIFO) policy reflects current (and often more expensive) prices. Somebody computing COGS first needs to know which policy is being used, because this will affect inventory values.

COGS for a manufacturer will include a variety of items, such as raw materials and energy used in production, labor, benefits for production workers, the cost of raw materials in inventory, shipping fees, the cost of storing finished products, depreciation on production machinery used, and factory overhead expenses.

For a retail company such as Wal-Mart, COGS is generally less complex: the total amount paid to suppliers for the products being sold on its shelves.

COGS is calculated as follows:

Inventory at beginning of period	$20,000
Purchases during period	+ $60,000
Cost of goods available for sale	= $80,000
Less inventory at period end	− $15,000
Cost of goods sold (COGS)	= $65,000

Because the counting of inventory is an exhaustive undertaking for retailers, doing it quarterly or monthly would be open to error. Accordingly, tax authorities allow them to estimate cost of goods sold during the year.

Determining these estimates requires details of the gross profit margin (retailers typically use the preceding year's figure). This figure is then used to calculate the cost ratio.

Begin by assuming that net sales are 100%, then subtract the gross profit margin, say 40%, to produce a cost ratio of 60%: 100% − 40% = 60%. A monthly COGS calculation then looks like this:

Inventory at beginning of month	$10,000
Purchases during month	+ $25,000
Cost of goods available for sale	= $35,000
Less net sales during month	− $28,000
Cost ratio 100% − 40%	= 60%
Estimated cost of goods sold	= $16,800 ($28,000 × 60%)

There is one example to review, because calculating COGS for manufacturers requires additional factors:

Inventory at beginning of year	$20,000
Purchases during year	+ $50,000
Cost of direct labor	+ $15,000
Materials and supplies	+ $12,000
Misc. costs	+ $3,000
Total product expenses	= $100,000
Less inventory at year end	− $15,000
Cost of goods sold (COGS)	= $85,000

TRICKS OF THE TRADE

- Anyone who wants to determine COGS must maintain inventory and know its value!
- Because goods returned affect inventory values and, in turn, cost of goods sold, returns of goods must be reflected in COGS calculations.
- Merchandising companies may use different inventory accounting systems, but the choice has no bearing on the actual costs incurred; it only affects allocation of costs.
- COGS should not include indirect costs like administration and marketing costs, or other activities that cannot be directly attributed to producing or acquiring the product.

Covariance

WHAT IT MEASURES

Covariance measures the relationship between two random variables. For example, we might measure whether a sample population liked drinking wine, and whether they liked eating cheese. Covariance is a form of probability theory that allows us to measure the extent to which those two random variables change together. It's important to remember this does not imply causality—simply because one variable increases along with another does not mean there is necessarily a link between the two variables.

If the two variables tend to change together—showing that people who particularly enjoy drinking wine tend to particularly enjoy eating cheese—there is said to be positive covariance. If the two variables move in opposite directions—people who drink wine tend to be less keen on cheese—the covariance is said to be negative. Random variables that do not relate in either way are said to be uncorrelated.

WHY IT IS IMPORTANT

For investors, covariance is an important way of seeing how one variable is related to another, particularly when analyzing the performance of stocks or investments within a portfolio.

For example, an investor might want to see the impact that multiple changes on a portfolio affect overall returns, or the relationship between a company's debt/equity ratio and working capital cycle. Covariance is often used in measuring the performance of securities.

As a rule of thumb, a high rate of covariance suggests a portfolio that is not diversified, and which presents a high level of risk. For example, if two stock prices tend to rise and fall at the same time, these stocks would not deliver the best diversified earnings.

HOW IT WORKS IN PRACTICE

Covariance provides a way of measuring the strength of correlation between two random variables. The covariance for two random variables x and y, with a sample size of n, is as follows:

$$\text{Covariance } xy = \frac{\Sigma xx}{n}$$

As an example, imagine we asked four men to rate their liking for both cheese and wine, on a scale of 1 to 10. The results were as follows:

	Cheese (x)	*Wine (y)*	*x*	*y*	*xy*
A	3	4	−1	−2	2
B	1	4	−3	−2	6
C	3	8	−1	2	−2
D	9	8	5	2	10
Sum	16	24	0	0	16
Mean	4	6	0	0	4

To calculate the covariance, we calculate a mean for both variables. Next, both variables are transformed into deviation scores by subtracting the mean from the relevant score. The products of these deviation scores can then be calculated, summed, and averaged. The result is known as the coefficient of covariance, in this case 4.

Expressed in simpler terms: the sum of the product of variables x and y is 112, and the mean is 28. Subtracting the product of the separate means (28 − 4 × 6 yields the coefficient of covariance equal to 4).

TRICKS OF THE TRADE

- In probability theory, covariance is closely related to the concept of correlation—both of these tools are ways of measuring the similarity of two random variables.
- The coefficient of covariance has no upper or lower limits. Some statisticians point out this indeterminacy is its main disadvantage as compared with the coefficient of correlation.
- In our example, we have calculated covariance by multiplying the correlation of two random variables by the standard deviation. However, you can also calculate covariance by looking at "return surprises" (deviations from an expected return), which can be useful when analyzing securities.

Creating a Balance Sheet

WHAT IT MEASURES

The financial standing, or even the net worth or owners' equity, of a company at a given point in time, typically at the end of a calendar or fiscal year.

WHY IT IS IMPORTANT

The balance sheet shows what is owned (assets), what is owed (liabilities), and what is left (owners' equity). It provides a concise snapshot of a company's financial position.

HOW IT WORKS IN PRACTICE

However they are presented, assets must be in balance with liabilities and stockholders' equity. In other words, assets must equal liabilities plus owners' equity.

Assets include cash in hand and cash anticipated (receivables), inventory of supplies and materials, properties, facilities, equipment, and whatever else the company uses to conduct its business. Assets also need to reflect depreciation in the value of equipment, such as machinery, that has a limited expected useful life.

Liabilities include pending payments to suppliers and creditors, outstanding current and long-term debts, taxes, interest payments, and other unpaid expenses that the company has incurred.

Subtracting the value of aggregate liabilities from the value of aggregate assets reveals the value of owners' equity. Ideally, this should be positive. Owners' equity consists of capital invested by owners over the years and profits (net income) or internally generated capital, which is referred to as "retained earnings;" these are funds to be used in future operations. An example is given opposite.

ASSETS	**$**
Current:	
Cash	8,200
Securities	5,000
Receivables	4,500
Inventory & supplies	6,300
Fixed:	
Land	10,000
Structures	90,000
Equipment (less depreciation)	5,000
Intangibles/other	
Total assets	129,000

LIABILITIES	**$**
Payables	7,000
Taxes	4,000
Miscellaneous	3,000
Bonds and notes	25,000
Total liabilities	39,000
Stockholders' equity (stock, par value × shares outstanding)	80,000
Retained earnings	10,000
Total liabilities and stockholders' equity	129,000

TRICKS OF THE TRADE

- The balance sheet does not show a company's market worth, nor important intangibles such as the knowledge and talents of individual people, nor other vital business factors such as customers or market share.
- The balance sheet does not express the true value of some fixed assets. A six-year-old manufacturing plant, for example, is listed at its original cost, even though the price of replacing it could be much higher or substantially lower (because of new technology that might be less expensive or vastly more efficient).
- The balance sheet is not an indicator of past or future performance or trends that affect performance. It needs to be studied along with two other key reports: the income tax return and the cash flow statement. A published balance sheet needs to include prior period comparatives.

▸▸ MORE INFO

Website:

Conetic Software Systems, Inc: www.conetic.com

     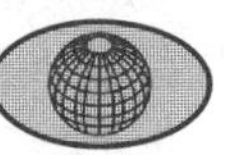 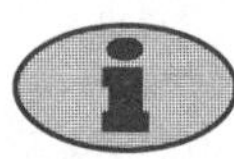  

Creating a Cash Flow Statement

WHAT IT MEASURES

Cash inflows and cash outflows over a specific period of time, typically a year.

WHY IT IS IMPORTANT

Cash flow is a key indicator of financial health, and it demonstrates to investors, creditors, and other core constituencies a company's ability to meet obligations, finance opportunities, and generally "come up with the cash" as needs arise. Cash flow that is wildly inconsistent with, say, net income, often indicates operating or managerial problems.

HOW IT WORKS IN PRACTICE

In its basic form, a cash flow statement will probably be familiar to anyone who has been a member of a club that collects and spends money. It reports funds on hand at the beginning of a given period, funds received, funds spent, and funds remaining at the end of the period.

That formula still applies to a business today, even if creating a cash flow document is significantly more complex. Cash flows are divided into three categories: cash from operations; cash investment activities; and cash financing activities. Companies with holdings in foreign currencies use a fourth category: effects of changes in exchange rates on cash.

A standard direct cash flow statement is shown opposite.

TRICKS OF THE TRADE

- A cash flow statement does *not* measure net income, nor does it measure working capital.
- A cash flow statement does not include outstanding accounts receivable, but it does include the preceding year's accounts receivable (assuming these were collected during the year for which the statement is prepared).
- Add to a cash inflow any amounts charged off for depreciation, depletion, and amortization, because cash was actually spent.
- Cash equivalents are short-term, highly liquid investments, although precise definitions may vary slightly by country. These should be included when recalculating the movement of cash in the period.
- There are alternative ways to present cash flow from operations. Some texts, for example, omit earnings and adjustments, and list instead cash and interest received, cash and interest paid, and taxes received.

CRD, Inc, statement of cash flows for year ended December 31, 20__

CASH FLOWS FROM OPERATIONS	**$**
Operating profit	82,000
Adjustments to net earnings	
Depreciation	17,000
Accounts receivable	(20,000)
Accounts payable	12,000
Inventory	(8,000)
Other adjustments to earnings	4,000
Net cash flow from operations	**87,000**

CASH FLOWS FROM INVESTMENT ACTIVITIES	**$**
Purchases of marketable securities	(58,000)
Receipts from sales of marketable securities	45,000
Loans made to borrowers	(16,000)
Collections on loans	11,000
Purchases of plant and real estate assets	(150,000)
Receipts from sales of plant and real estate assets	47,000
Net cash flow from investment activities	**(–121,000)**

CASH FLOWS FROM FINANCING ACTIVITIES ($)	**$**
Proceeds from short-term borrowings	51,000
Payments to settle short-term debts	(61,000)
Proceeds from issuing bonds payable	100,000
Proceeds from issuing capital stock	80,000
Dividends paid	(64,000)
Net cash flow from financing activities	**106,000**
Net change in cash during period	**72,000**
Cash and cash equivalents, beginning of year	27,000
Cash and cash equivalents, end of year	**99,000**

MORE INFO

Website:

International Accounting Standards Consultancy (IASC): www.iasc.co.uk

Creating a Profit and Loss (P&L) Account

WHAT IT MEASURES

A company's sales revenues and expenses over a period, providing a calculation of profits or losses during that time.

WHY IT IS IMPORTANT

Reading a P&L is the easiest way to tell if a business has made a profit or a loss during a given month or year. The most important figure it contains is net profit: what is left over after revenues are used to pay expenses and taxes.

Companies typically issue P&L reports monthly. It is customary for the reports to include year-to-date figures, as well as corresponding year-earlier figures to allow for comparisons and analysis.

HOW IT WORKS IN PRACTICE

A P&L adheres to a simple rule of thumb: "Revenue minus cost equals profit."

There are two P&L formats, multiple-step and single-step. Both follow a standard set of rules known as "generally accepted accounting principles" (GAAP). These rules generally adhere to requirements established by governments to track receipts, expenses, and profits for tax purposes. They also allow the financial reports of

   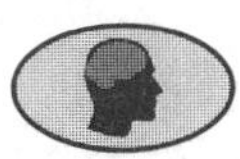  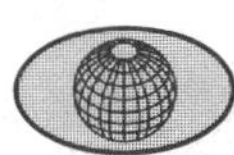   

two different companies to be compared. Note that in the United Kingdom and several other nations, sales, revenues, and receipts may all be designated as turnover.

The multiple-step format is much more common, because it includes a larger number of details and is thus more useful. It deducts costs from revenues in a series of steps, allowing for closer analysis. Revenues appear first, then expenses, each in as much detail as management desires. Sales may be broken down by product line or location, while expenses such as salaries may be broken down into base salaries and commissions.

Expenses are then subtracted from revenues to show profit (or loss). A basic multiple-step P&L is shown below.

TRICKS OF THE TRADE

- A P&L does not show how a business has earned or spent its money.
- One month's P&L can be misleading, especially if a business generates most of its receipts in particular months. A retail establishment, for example, usually generates a large percentage of its sales in the final three months of the year, while a consulting service might generate the lion's share of its revenues in as few as two months, and no revenues at all in some other months.
- Invariably, figures for both revenues and expenses reflect the judgments of the companies reporting them. Accounting methods can be quite arbitrary when it comes to such factors as depreciation expenses.

Multiple-step profit & loss accounts ($)

NET SALES			750,000
Less: cost of goods sold			450,000
Gross profit			300,000
LESS: OPERATING EXPENSES			
Selling expenses			
Salaries & commissions	54,000		
Advertising	37,500		
Delivery/transportation	12,000		
Depreciation/store equipment	7,500		
Other selling expenses	5,000		
Total selling expenses		116,000	
General & administrative expenses			
Administrative/office salaries	74,000		
Utilities	2,500		
Depreciation/structure	2,400		
Misc. other expenses	3,100		
Total general & admin expenses		82,000	
Total operating expenses			198,000
OPERATING INCOME			102,000
LESS (ADD): NONOPERATING ITEMS			
Interest expenses	11,000		
Interest income earned	(2,800)		8,200
Income before taxes			93,800
Income taxes			32,360
Net income			**61,440**

Creditor and Debtor Days

These financial measures are two sides of the same coin, since they respectively measure the flow of money out of and into a business. As such, they are reliable indicators of both efficiency and problems.

WHAT THEY MEASURE

Creditor days is a measure of the number of days on average that a company requires to pay its creditors, while debtor days is a measure of the number of days on average that it takes a company to receive payment for what it sells. It is also called accounts receivable days.

WHY THEY ARE IMPORTANT

Creditor days is an indication of a company's creditworthiness in the eyes of its suppliers and creditors, since it shows how long they are willing to wait for payment. Within reason, the higher the number the better because all companies want to conserve cash. At the same time, a company that is especially slow to pay its bills (100 or more days, for example) may be a company having trouble generating cash, or one trying to finance its operations with its suppliers' funds. Ultimately, companies whose creditor days soar have trouble obtaining supplies.

Debtor days is an indication of a company's efficiency in collecting monies owed. In this case, obviously, the lower the number the better. An especially high number is a telltale sign of inefficiency or worse. It may indicate bad debts, dubious sales figures, or a company being bullied by large customers out to improve their own cash position at another company's expense. Customers whose credit terms are abused also risk higher borrowing costs and related charges.

Changes in both measures are easy to spot, and easy to understand.

HOW THEY WORK IN PRACTICE

To determine creditor days, divide the cumulative amount of unpaid suppliers' bills (also called trade creditors) by sales, then multiply by 365. So the formula is:

$$\text{Creditor days} = \frac{\text{Trade creditors}}{\text{Sales}} \times 365$$

For example, if suppliers' bills total $800,000 and sales are $9,000,000, the calculation is:

$$\frac{800{,}000}{9{,}000{,}000} \times 365 = 32.44 \text{ days}$$

The company takes 32.44 days on average to pay its bills.

To determine debtor days, divide the cumulative amount of accounts receivable by sales, then multiply by 365. For example, if accounts receivable total $600,000 and sales are $9,000,000, the calculation is:

$$\frac{600{,}000}{9{,}000{,}000} \times 365 = 24.33 \text{ days}$$

The company takes 24.33 days on average to collect its debts.

     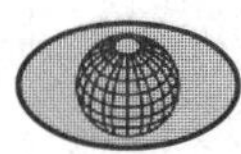   

TRICKS OF THE TRADE

- Cash businesses, including most retailers, should have a much lower debtor days figure than noncash businesses, since they receive payment when they sell the goods. A typical target for noncash businesses is 40–50 days.
- An abnormally high creditor days figure may not only suggest a cash crisis, but also the management's difficulty in maintaining revolving credit agreements.
- An increasing number of debtor days also suggests overly generous credit terms (to bolster sales) or problems with product quality.

Current Price of a Bond

WHAT IT MEASURES

The narrow range within which a given bond price falls, based on that bond's current asking price and bid price.

WHY IT IS IMPORTANT

Current prices of comparable bonds are strong indicators of a bond's buying or selling price. Changes in bond prices are also indicators of economic strength and direction.

HOW IT WORKS IN PRACTICE

The price of a bond depends on several factors.

- Interest rates: As rates rise, a bond's price falls, because it pays less interest than current offerings and is thus less attractive. Conversely, a bond becomes more attractive as interest rates fall.
- The risk perceived for the issuing entity, reflected in its credit rating from one of the major rating agencies. The price of a bond of a company in bankruptcy, for instance, will be low because the company may never be able to redeem it. The price of a bond from a strong company may include a premium over its face or "par" value because it is considered a reliable investment: a bond with a face value of $1,000 might sell for $1,050, indicating a $50 premium.
- The issuing of new bonds by corporations or other bodies (and the ratings they receive) affects the prices of existing bonds.

Daily bond tables vary in format, but list the basic information necessary for comparing prices. Only a small fraction of the outstanding bonds trade on any given day, but these representative prices provide sufficient information to estimate what a fair price would be for the bonds being considered.

When considering bonds, several pieces of information are essential:

- the bond's coupon rate—what it will pay in interest;
- how long before the principal amount of the bond matures, or if there is a call date;
- its recent price and current yield.

Essentially, all the tables provide this basic information. The US Treasury table, for example, would be listed as follows:

Rate	Maturity	Bid	Ask	Yield
7¾	Feb 2009	105:12	105:14	5.50
5⅜	Feb 2009	99:26	99:27	5.44

In the first row, the security is paying its bondholders 7¾% interest and is due to mature in February 2009. Prices in the bid and ask columns are percentages of the bond's face value of $1,000. A bid of 105:12 means that a buyer was willing to pay $1053.75, compared to the seller's lowest asking price, 105:14, or $1054.38, a difference of 63 cents per thousand.

Bond quotes follow certain conventions. Prices are given as percentages of face value, but the digits appearing after the colons are not decimals, being expressed in terms of 1/32. So 12/32nds, for example, would equal $3.75, which is appended to the 105 before the colon: $1053.75.

The bid and ask prices indicate that an investor who bought the bond at par when it was first issued can make a profit of more than 5% if it were sold now. The last column gives the yield to maturity, an interest rate summarizing the bond's overall investment value.

COMMON MISTAKES

- A bond's yield and its price are not the same. Price is what is paid for a bond; yield expresses the percentage return on the investment. Yield is most useful for comparing fixed-income investments for planning purposes, rather than as an exact measure of the return expected from an investment.
- The number of bond issues outstanding at any given time is far greater than stocks, and most bondholders buy with the intent of holding them until maturity, so the amount of trading is limited.
- There are several bond-rating agencies. A bond's rating indicates its level of risk.
- Listing tables also show the volume traded along with the current yield.
- The internet offers many calculators for quickly determining bond prices and yields.

▸▸ MORE INFO

Websites:

Bonds at The Investment FAQ: www.invest-faq.com/articles/bonds-a-basics.html

InvestingInBonds.com from the Securities Industry and Financial Markets Association: www.investinginbonds.com

     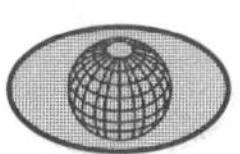   

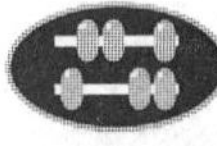

Current Ratio

The current ratio is a key liquidity ratio and a staple for anyone who borrows or lends money.

WHAT IT MEASURES

A company's liquidity and its ability to meet its short-term debt obligations.

WHY IT IS IMPORTANT

By comparing a company's current assets with its current liabilities, the current ratio reflects its ability to pay its upcoming bills in the unlikely event of all creditors demanding payment at once. It has long been the measurement of choice among financial institutions and lenders.

HOW IT WORKS IN PRACTICE

The current ratio formula is simply:

$$\text{Current ratio} = \frac{\text{Current assets}}{\text{Current liabilities}}$$

Current assets are the ones that a company can turn into cash within 12 months during the ordinary course of business. Current liabilities are bills due to be paid within the coming 12 months.

For example, if a company's current assets are $300,000 and its current liabilities are $200,000, its current ratio would be:

$$\frac{300{,}000}{200{,}000} = 1.5$$

As a rule of thumb, the 1.5 figure means that a company should be able to get hold of $1.50 for every $1.00 it owes.

TRICKS OF THE TRADE

- The higher the ratio, the more liquid the company. Prospective lenders expect a positive current ratio, often of at least 1.5. However, too high a ratio is also cause for alarm, because it indicates declining receivables and/or inventory—signs that portend declining liquidity.
- A current ratio of less than 1 suggests pressing liquidity problems, specifically an inability to generate sufficient cash to meet upcoming demands.
- Managements use current ratio as well as lenders; a low ratio, for example, may indicate the need to refinance a portion of short-term debt with long-term debt to improve a company's liquidity.
- Ratios vary by industry, however, and should be used accordingly. Some sectors, such as supermarket chains and restaurants, perform nicely with low ratios that would keep others awake at night.
- One shortcoming of the current ratio is that it does not differentiate assets, some of which may not be easily converted to cash. As a result, lenders also refer to the quick ratio.
- Another shortcoming of the current ratio is that it reflects conditions at a single point in time, such as when the balance sheet is prepared. It is possible to make this figure look good just for this occasion: lenders should not, therefore, appraise these conditions by the ratio alone.
- A constant current ratio and falling quick ratio signal trouble ahead, because this suggests that a company is amassing assets at the expense of receivables and cash.

Days Sales Outstanding

Days sales outstanding (DSO) can be considered as a tool for financial troubleshooters.

WHAT IT MEASURES

A company's average collection period, or the average number of days it takes a company to convert its accounts receivable into cash. Commonly referred to as DSO, it is also called the collection ratio.

WHY IT IS IMPORTANT

Knowing how long it takes a company to turn accounts receivable into cash is an important financial indicator. It indicates the efficiency of the company's internal collection, suggests how well a company's customers are accepting its credit terms (net 30 days, for example), and is a figure that is routinely compared with industry averages.

Ideally, DSOs should be decreasing or constant. A low figure means the company collects its outstanding receivables quickly. Typically, DSO is reviewed quarterly or yearly (91 or 365 days).

DSO also helps to expose companies that try to disguise weak sales. Large increases in DSO suggest that a company is trying to force sales either by accepting poor receivable terms or selling products at discount to book more sales for a particular period. An improving DSO suggests that a company is striving to make its operations more efficient.

Any company with a significant change in its DSO merits examination in greater detail.

HOW IT WORKS IN PRACTICE

Regular DSO requires three figures: total accounts receivable, total credit sales for the period analyzed, and the number of days in the period (annual, 365; six months, 182; quarter, 91). The formula is:

$$\text{Days sales outstanding} = \frac{\text{Accounts receivable}}{\text{Total credit sales for the period}} \times \text{Number of days in the period}$$

For example: if total receivables are $4,500,000, total credit sales in a quarter are $9,000,000, and number of days is 91, then:

$$\frac{4{,}500{,}000}{9{,}000{,}000} \times 91 = 45.5 \text{ days}$$

Thus, it takes an average of 45.5 days to collect receivables.

TRICKS OF THE TRADE

- Companies use DSO information with an accounts receivable

  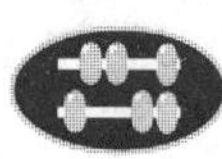   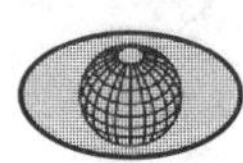   

aging report. This lists four categories of receivables: 0–30 days, 30–60 days, 60–90 days, and over 90 days. The report also shows the percentage of total accounts receivable that each group represents, allowing for an analysis of delinquencies and potential bad debts—a figure that appears on a profit and loss account.

- A rarely used related calculation, best possible DSO, shows how long it takes a company to collect current receivables. Its formula is:

$$\text{Best possible DSO} = \frac{\text{Current receivables}}{\text{Total credit sales for the period}} \times \text{Number of days in the period}$$

So, current receivables of $3,000,000 and total credit sales of $9,000,000 in a 91-day period would result in a best possible DSO of 30.3 days (3,000,000 ÷ 9,000,000 × 91).

- Only credit sales of merchandise should be used in calculating DSO; cash sales are excluded, as are sales of such items as fixtures, equipment, or real estate.
- Properly evaluating an acceptable DSO requires a standard for comparison. A traditional rule of thumb is that DSO should not exceed one-third to one-half of selling terms. For instance, if terms are 30 days, acceptable DSO would be 40 to 45 days.
- A single DSO is only a snapshot. A fuller picture would require at least quarterly calculations, and some companies review DSO monthly.
- DSO can vary widely by industry as well as company. For example, clothing wholesalers have to have the goods on retailers' shelves for months before they will be sold and the retailer is able to cover invoices. However, a computer wholesaler with a lengthy DSO suggests trouble, since computers become obsolete quickly.

Debt/Capital Ratio

Whether called debt/capital ratio, debt-to-capital ratio, or simply debt ratio, this is a fundamental tool in analyzing how a company is funded. It is also known as the gearing ratio.

WHAT IT MEASURES

The percentage of total funding represented by debt.

WHY IT IS IMPORTANT

By comparing a company's long-term liabilities to its total capital, the debt/capital ratio provides a review of the extent to which a company relies on external debt financing for its funding and is a measure of the risk to its stockholders.

The debt/capital ratio is also a measure of a company's borrowing capacity, and of its ability to pay scheduled financial payments on term debts and capital leases. Bond-rating agencies and analysts use it routinely to assess creditworthiness. The greater the debt, the higher the risk.

However, it can be misleading to assume that the lowest ratio is automatically the best ratio. A company may assume large amounts of debt in order to expand the business. Utilities, for instance, have high capital requirements, so their debt/capital ratios will be high as a matter of course. So are those of manufacturing companies, especially those developing a new technology or new product.

At the same time, the higher the level of debt, the more important it is for a company to have positive earnings and steady cash flow.

HOW IT WORKS IN PRACTICE

Although there are variations on exactly what goes into this ratio, the most common method is to divide total long-term debt by total assets (total long-term debt plus stockholders' funds), or:

$$\text{Debt/capital ratio} = \frac{\text{Total liabilities}}{\text{Total assets}}$$

For example, if the balance sheet of a corporate annual report lists total liabilities of $9,800,000 and total stockholders' equity of $12,800,000, the debt/capital ratio is (calculating in thousands):

$$\frac{9{,}800}{9{,}800 + 12{,}800} = \frac{9{,}800}{22{,}600} = 0.434 = 43.4\%$$

Some formulas distinguish different portions of long-term debt. However, that complicates calculations and many experts regard it as unnecessary. It is also common to express the formula as total debt divided by total funds, which produces the same outcome.

TRICKS OF THE TRADE

- If a company has minority interests in subsidiaries that are consolidated in the balance sheet, they must be added to stockholders' equity.
- Debt calculations should include capital leases.
- One rule of thumb holds that a debt/capital ratio of 60% or less is acceptable, but another holds that 40% is the most desirable.
- A high debt/capital ratio means less security for stockholders, because debt holders are paid first in bankruptcies. It still can be tolerable, however, if a company's return on assets exceeds the rate of interest paid to creditors.
- Do not confuse the debt/capital ratio with debt/capitalization, which compares debt with total market capitalization and fluctuates as the company's stock price changes.

Debt/Equity Ratio

Debt/equity is the most commonly used method of assessing corporate debt, but in fact there is more than one way of expressing essentially the same thing.

WHAT IT MEASURES

How much money a company owes compared with how much money it has invested in it by principal owners and stockholders.

WHY IT IS IMPORTANT

The debt/equity ratio reveals the proportion of debt and equity a company is using to finance its business. It also measures a com-

  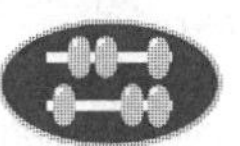 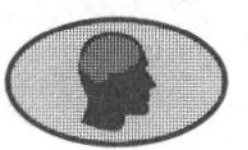  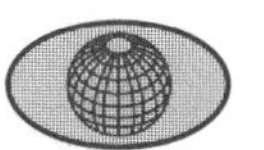   

pany's borrowing capacity. The higher the ratio, the greater the proportion of debt—but also the greater the risk.

Some even describe the debt/equity ratio as "a great financial test" of long-term corporate health, because debt establishes a commitment to repay money throughout a period of time, even though there is no assurance that sufficient cash will be generated to meet that commitment.

Creditors and lenders, understandably, rely heavily on the ratio to evaluate borrowers.

HOW IT WORKS IN PRACTICE

The debt/equity ratio is calculated by dividing debt by owners' equity, where equity is, typically, the figure stated for the preceding calendar or fiscal year. Debt, however, can be defined either as long-term debt only, or as total liabilities, which include both long- and short-term debt.

The most common formula for the ratio is:

$$\text{Debt/equity ratio} = \frac{\text{Total liabilities}}{\text{Owners' equity}}$$

In our example, a company's long-term debt is $8,000,000, its short-term debt is $4,000,000, and owners' equity totals $9,000,000. The debt/equity ratio would therefore be (calculating in thousands):

$$\frac{8{,}000 + 4{,}000}{9{,}000} = 12{,}000 \div 9{,}000$$

$$= 1.33$$

An alternative debt/equity formula considers only long-term liabilities in the equation. Accordingly:

$$\frac{8{,}000}{9{,}000} = 0.889$$

There is also a third method, which is the reciprocal of the debt-to-capital ratio; its formula is:

$$\text{Debt/equity ratio} = \frac{\text{Owners' equity}}{\text{Total funds}}$$

However, this would be more accurately defined as "equity/debt ratio."

TRICKS OF THE TRADE

- It is important to understand exactly how debt is defined in the ratio presented.
- When calculating the ratio, some prefer to use the market value of debt and equity rather than the book value, since book value often understates current value.
- For this ratio, a low number indicates better financial stability than a high one; if the ratio is high, a company could be at risk, especially if interest rates are rising.
- A ratio greater than one means assets are mainly financed with debt; less than one means equity provides most of the financing. Since a higher ratio generally means that a company has been aggressive in financing its growth with debt, volatile earnings can result owing to the additional cost of interest.
- Debt/equity ratio is somewhat industry-specific, and often depends on the amount of capital investment required.

Defining Assets

WHAT THEY MEASURE

Collectively, the value of all the resources a company uses to conduct business and generate profits. Examples of assets are cash, marketable securities, accounts and notes receivable, inventory of merchandise, real estate, machinery and office equipment, natural resources, and intangibles such as patents, legal claims and agreements, and negotiated rights.

WHY THEY ARE IMPORTANT

No business can continue for very long without knowing what assets it has at its disposal, and using them efficiently. Assets are a reflection of organizational strength, and are invariably evaluated by potential investors, banks, and creditors, and other stakeholders. Moreover, the value of assets is also a key figure that is used to calculate several financial ratios.

HOW THEY WORK IN PRACTICE

Assets are typically broken down into five different categories:

1. **Current assets**. These include cash, cash equivalents, marketable securities, inventory, and prepaid expenses that are expected to be used within one year or a normal operating cycle. All cash items and inventory are reported at historical value. Securities are reported at market value.
2. **Noncurrent assets**, or long-term investments. These are resources that are expected to be held for more than one year. They are reported at the lower of cost and current market value, which means that their values will vary.
3. **Fixed assets**. These include property, plant and facilities, and equipment used to conduct business. These items are reported at their original value, even though current values might well be much higher.
4. **Intangible assets**. These include legal claims, patents, franchise rights, and accounts receivable. These values can be more difficult to determine. Accounts receivable, for example, reflect the amount a business expects to collect, such as $9,000 of the $10,000 owed by customers.
5. **Deferred charges**. These include prepaid costs and other expenditures that will produce future revenue or benefits.

TRICKS OF THE TRADE

- Assets do not necessarily include everything of value, such as the talents of individuals, an organization's collective expertise, or the value of a customer base.
- Classic definitions of assets also often exclude or undervalue trademarks, even though there is universal agreement that these—for example, the three-point star of Mercedes-Benz or Coca-Cola's red logo—can have enormous value.
- Fixed assets are valued at their original cost, because of the prevailing opinion that they are used for business and are not for sale. Moreover, current market value is essentially a matter of opinion.
- Determining the value of patents can be challenging, because a patent has a finite life span, its value declines each year, and its useful life may be even shorter.

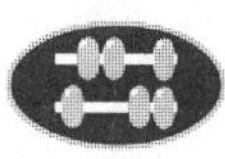

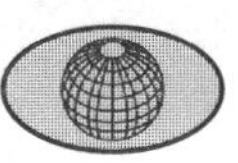

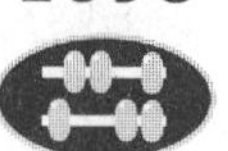

- Some experts contend that the principal assets of "knowledge-based" businesses such as consulting firms or real estate development companies are, in fact, its people. In turn, their aggregate value should be calculated by subtracting the net value of assets from market value.

Depreciation

GETTING STARTED

Depreciation is a basic expense of doing business, reducing a company's earnings while increasing its cash flow. It affects three key financial statements: balance sheet; cash flow; and income (or profit and loss). It is based on two key facts: the purchase price of the items or property in question, and their "useful life."

Depreciation values and practices are governed by the tax laws of both national governments, and state or provincial governments, which must be monitored continuously for any changes that are made. Accounting bodies, too, have developed standard practices and procedures for conducting depreciation.

Depreciating a single asset is not difficult: The challenge lies in depreciating the many assets possessed by even small companies, and it is intensified by the impact that depreciation has on income and cash flow statements, and on income statements. It is essential to depreciate with care and to rely on experts, ensuring that they fully understand the current government rules and regulations.

FAQS

What is depreciation?

It is an allocation of the cost of an asset over a period of time for accounting and tax purposes. Depreciation is charged against earnings, on the basis that the use of capital assets is a legitimate cost of doing business. Depreciation is also a noncash expense that is added into net income to determine cash flow in a given accounting period.

What is straight-line depreciation?

One of the two principal depreciation methods, it is based on the assumption that an asset loses an equal amount of its value each year of its useful life. Straight-line depreciation deducts an equal amount from a company's earnings each year throughout the life of the asset.

What is accelerated depreciation?

The other principal method of depreciation is based on the assumption that an asset loses a larger amount of its value in the early years of its useful life. Also known as the "declining-balance" method, it is used by accountants to reduce a company's tax bills as soon as possible, and is calculated on the basis of the same percentage rate each year of an asset's useful life. Accelerated depreciation also better reflects the economic value of the asset being depreciated, which tends to become increasingly less efficient and more costly to maintain as it grows older.

What can be depreciated?

To qualify for depreciation, assets must:

- be used in the business;
- be items that wear out, become obsolete, or lose value over time from natural causes or circumstances;
- have a useful life beyond a single tax year.

Examples include vehicles, machines and equipment, computers and office furnishings, and buildings, plus major additions or improvements to such assets. Some intangible assets can also be included under certain conditions.

What cannot be depreciated?

Land, personal assets, inventory, leased or rented property, and a company's employees.

MAKING IT HAPPEN

In order to determine the annual depreciation cost of assets, it is necessary first to know the initial cost of those assets, how many years they will retain some value for the business, and what value, if any, they will have at the end of their useful life.

For example, a company buys a truck to carry materials and finished goods. The vehicle loses value as soon as it is purchased, and then loses more with each year it is in service, until the cost of repairs exceeds its overall value. Measuring the loss in the value of the truck is depreciation.

Straight-line depreciation is the most straightforward method, and is still quite common. It assumes that the net cost of an asset should be written off in equal amounts over its life. The formula used is:

$$\frac{\text{Original cost} - \text{Scrap value}}{\text{Useful life}}$$

For example, if the truck cost $30,000 and can be expected to serve the business for 7 years, its original cost less its scrap value would be divided by its useful life:

$$\frac{30{,}000 - 2{,}000}{7} = \$4{,}000 \text{ per year}$$

The $4,000 becomes a depreciation expense that is reported on the company's year-end income statement under "operation expenses."

In theory, an asset should be depreciated over the actual number of years that it will be used, according to its actual drop in value each year. At the end of each year, all the depreciation claimed to date is subtracted from its cost in order to arrive at its "book value," which would equal its market value. At the end of its useful business life, any undepreciated portion would represent the salvage value for which it could be sold or scrapped.

For tax purposes, some accountants prefer to use accelerated depreciation to record larger amounts of depreciation in the asset's early years in order to reduce tax bills as soon as possible. In contrast to the straight-line method, the accelerated or declining balance method assumes that the asset depreciates more in its earlier years of use. The table overleaf compares the depreciation amounts that would be available, under these two methods, for a $1,000 asset that is expected to be used for five years and then sold for $100 in scrap.

While the straight-line method results in the same deduction each year, the declining-balance method produces larger deductions in the first years and far smaller deductions in the later years. One result of this system is that, if the equipment is expected to be sold for a higher value at some point in the middle of its life, the declining-balance method can produce a greater taxable gain in that year because the book value of the asset will be relatively lower.

  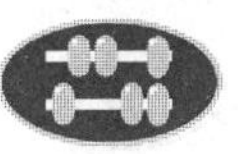   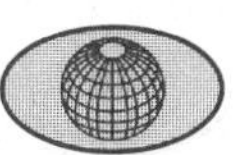   

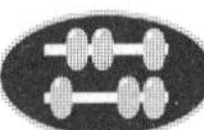

	Straight-line method		Declining-balance method	
Year	**Annual depreciation**	**Year-end book value**	**Annual depreciation**	**Year-end book value**
1	$900 x 20% = $180	$1,000 – $180 = $820	$1,000 x 40% = $400	$1,000 – $400 = $600
2	$900 x 20% = $180	$820 – $180 = $640	$600 x 40% = $240	$600 – $240 = $360
3	$900 x 20% = $180	$640 – $180 = $460	$360 x 40% = $144	$360 – $144 = $216
4	$900 x 20% = $180	$460 – $180 = $280	$216 x 40% = $86.40	$216 – $86.40 = $129.60
5	$900 x 20% = $180	$280 – $180 = $100	$129.60 x 40% = $51.84	$129.60 – $51.84 = $77.76

The depreciation method to be used for a particular asset is fixed at the time that the asset is first placed in service. Whatever rules or tables are in effect for that year must be followed as long as the asset is owned.

Depreciation laws and regulations change frequently over the years as a result of government policy changes, so a company owning property over a long period may have to use several different depreciation methods.

TRICKS OF THE TRADE

- With very specific exceptions, it is not possible to deduct in one year the entire cost of an asset if that asset has a useful life substantially beyond the tax year.
- To qualify for depreciation, an asset must be put into service. Simply purchasing it is not enough. There are rules that govern how much depreciation can be claimed on items put into service after a year has begun.
- It is common knowledge that if a company claims more depreciation than it is entitled to, it is liable for stiff penalties in a tax audit, just as failure to allow for depreciation causes an overestimation of income. What is not commonly known is that if a company does not claim all the depreciation deductions it is entitled to, it will be considered as having claimed them when taxable gains or losses are eventually calculated on the sale or disposal of the asset in question.
- While leased property cannot be depreciated, the cost of making permanent improvements to leased property can be (remodeling a leased office, for example). There are many rules governing leased assets; they should be depreciated with care.
- Another common mistake is to continue depreciating property beyond the end of its recovery period. Cars are common examples of this.
- Conservative companies depreciate many assets as quickly as possible, despite the fact that this practice reduces reported net income. Knowledgeable investors watch carefully for such practices.

▸▸ MORE INFO

Book:

Wolf, Frank K., and W. Chester Finch. *Depreciation Systems*. Ames, IA: Iowa State University Press, 1994.

Websites:

Bankrate.com on Section 179 of the United States Internal Revenue Code: www.bankrate.com/brm/itax/Edit/tips/Stories/sec179_deduction.asp

Business Owner's Toolkit: www.toolkit.com

Encyclopedia.com: www.encyclopedia.com

Discounted Cash Flow

WHAT IT MEASURES

Discounted cash flow (DCF) is a way of measuring the net present value (NPV) of future cash flow. This allows companies to express the value of an investment today based on predicted future returns. The idea behind discounted cash flow is that $1 today is worth more than $1 you might receive in the future. The money you have now can be invested and might generate interest whereas money you haven't yet received can't be used in this way, and there is a risk it might not be received. Therefore, discounted cash flow is a way of adjusting the value of future money over time to reflect its "real" value today.

WHY IT IS IMPORTANT

Discounted cash flow is most useful when future operating conditions and cash flow are variable, or where trading conditions are expected to change significantly over time. It is a good way of assessing the likely value of money the business will receive in future, and therefore DCF is considered one of the best ways of valuing an investment.

HOW IT WORKS IN PRACTICE

To calculate discounted cash flow, you must first determine the forecasted cash flow of a company, and choose a discount rate based on the expected or desired rate of return. The discount rate chosen should reflect the risk that the return will not be achieved—a higher risk should result in a higher discount rate.

Next, use the discount rate for each year to discount cash flow to the "correct" adjusted present value, as shown in the example below. Remember, cash flow will lose value over time because it is discounted for a longer period.

For example:

$$NPV = \frac{CF1}{(1+r)} + \frac{CF2}{(1+r)^2} + \frac{CF3}{(1+r)^3}$$

where NPV is the net present value of cash flows, CF1, CF2, and CF3 are predicted cash flows in years 1, 2, and 3, respectively, and r is the discount rate. It's worth remembering that, unless the series of cash flows has a known finite endpoint, a terminal value will need to be assumed.

TRICKS OF THE TRADE

- Cash flows may represent interest payments or repayments, or in the case of stocks can relate to dividends.
- There are many variations to the calculation illustrated above, and different ways to measure cash flow and discount rates in a

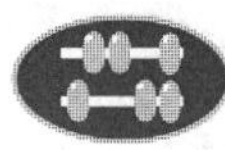

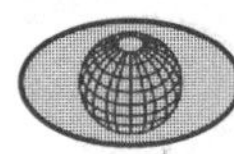

DCF calculation. All the different approaches are basically ways of estimating the return from an investment, adjusted for the time value of money.

- Like many calculations, a DCF figure is only as good as the figures used for cash flow and discount rates. Small changes in these figures can result in enormous variation in NPV figures, so it's often wiser to use DCF over a relatively short period of time and to adopt a terminal value approach, rather than discounting to infinity.
- DCF analysis of cash flow should be used when a business case deals with two potential uses of money, and wherever cash flow timing is different.

▸▸ MORE INFO:

Websites:

Investopedia tutorial on DCF analysis: www.investopedia.com/university/dcf/

Solution Matrix on DCF: www.solutionmatrix.com/discounted-cash-flow

Distinguishing Between a Capital and an Operating Lease

GETTING STARTED

Determining whether a lease obligation is an operating or capital lease, for financial reporting purposes, requires that it be evaluated on the basis of four criteria established by the FASB (Financial Accounting Standards Board). The criteria are objective rules for making a judgment about who, the lessor or the lessee, bears the risks and benefits of ownership of the leased property.

If a lease is determined to be a capital lease, an asset and corresponding liability are recorded at the present value of the minimum lease payments. The capital asset is depreciated over time, while the liability is amortized as lease payments are made. Rental payments under operating leases are simply expensed as incurred. Due to the complexity of lease agreements, management judgment still plays a large role in distinguishing between operating and capital leases.

FAQS

What are minimum lease payments?

The minimum lease payments are the rental payments to be made during the lease term, plus the amount of the bargain price, guaranteed residual value, or penalty for failure to renew the lease at the end of its original term.

In determining whether a lease should be classified as an operating or capital lease, what interest rate should be used?

The interest rate used to discount the minimum lease payments to their present value is the incremental borrowing rate of the lessee, this being the interest rate that the lessee would have been charged if the assets had been acquired by borrowing the purchase price. If the lessor's implied interest rate for the lease is known and is lower than the lessee's estimated incremental borrowing rate, then the lessee uses the implied rate to discount.

MAKING IT HAPPEN

The Four FASB Criteria

Until the 1970s, many companies used leasing as a means to purchase tangible assets without recognizing their ownership or the lease obligation on the balance sheet. In substance, leases were off-balance-sheet financing. Although all leases were required to be disclosed in the footnotes to the financial statements, even long-term finance leases did not appear as a liability. Because the basic measures of leverage do not consider off-balance-sheet obligations, the accounting profession and the investment community believed that there needed to be more stringent guidelines for classifying leases as operating or financing, and in 1976 the FASB issued Statement no. 13, "Accounting for leases." The statement sets out four criteria to distinguish between an operating and a capital (finance) lease:

- The lease agreement transfers ownership of the assets to the lessee during the term of lease.
- The lessee can purchase the assets leased at a bargain price, such as $1, at the end of the lease term.
- The lease term is at least 75% of the economic life of the leased asset.
- The present value of the minimum lease payments is 90% or greater of the asset's value.

If a lease agreement does not meet any of these criteria, the lessee treats it as an operating lease for accounting purposes. If, however, the agreement meets one of the above criteria, it is treated as a capital lease.

Accounting for a Capital Lease

Capital leases are reported by the lessee as if the assets being leased were acquired and the monthly rental payments as if they were payments of principal and interest on a debt obligation. Specifically, the lessee capitalizes the lease by recognizing an asset and a liability at the lower of the present value of the minimum lease payments or the value of the assets under lease. As the monthly rental payments are made, the corresponding liability decreases. At the same time, the leased asset is depreciated in a manner that is consistent with other owned assets having the same use and economic life.

Accounting for an Operating Lease

If the lease is classified as an operating lease, the monthly lease payments are simply treated as rental expenses and recognized on the income tax return as they are incurred. There is no recognition of a leased asset or liability.

Clearing Up Remaining Confusion

The FASB's attempt to establish objective criteria for distinguishing between operating and capital leases was a good first step. This has enabled companies to make prudent financial decisions in lease versus buy situations, based on the accounting treatment afforded a specific lease structure. Furthermore, financial professionals now have a framework within which to determine what lease terms create a capital lease. However, the use of financial engineering still occurs. Consequently, many leases that are truly financing leases are recorded as operating leases, because their provisions have been altered to avoid qualification as capital leases.

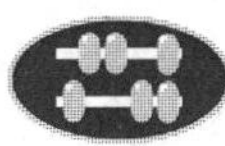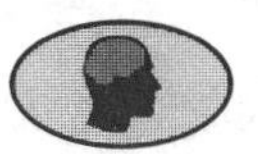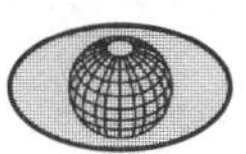

When in doubt, a manager should always ask whether the risks and benefits of ownership have truly been passed from the lessor to the lessee. Facts indicating that the transfer has occurred are when maintenance, insurance, and property tax expenses are born by the lessee, or when the lessee guarantees a specific residual value on the leased property.

▸▸ MORE INFO

Websites:

Institute of Chartered Accountants in England and Wales: www.icaew.co.uk

US Securities and Exchange Commission: www.sec.gov

Dividend Yield

WHAT IT MEASURES

An investment's dividend yield is a measure of the dividend paid on stock, expressed as a percentage over one year. This measure is frequently used in stock quotes and financial reports, and is based upon the company's annual cash dividend per share and the current stock price.

WHY IT IS IMPORTANT

A stock's dividend yield is a crucial measure for potential investors in any company since it illustrates how much cash flow is generated for each dollar invested in equity, on top of any capital gains made from a rising stock price. A relatively high-paying, stable stock will attract income investors, and the higher the dividend yield, the greater expected return for income investors. Historical data also shows that stocks which pay a dividend have generally outperformed non-dividend-paying stocks in the long term.

HOW IT WORKS IN PRACTICE

To calculate a dividend yield, you will need to use the following formula:

$$\text{Dividend yield} = \frac{\text{Annual dividend per share}}{\text{Stock price per share}}$$

For example, Company A has an annual dividend per share of $10, and the average quarterly value of its stock per share is $75. To assess the company's dividend yield, we would divide the dividend by the stock price, as follows:

$$\frac{10}{75} = 0.1333 = 13.33\%$$

On this basis, the stock has a dividend yield of 13.33%.

Company B might also pay an annual dividend per share of $10, but if its stock is trading at $20 per share, then its dividend yield will be 50%—considerably higher than Company A's dividend yield. Assuming other factors are equal, income investors would find Company B a more attractive investment opportunity.

TRICKS OF THE TRADE

- Dividend yield is often simply referred to as a "yield" in financial markets.
- The dividend yield helps to explain a company's value to investors but can vary widely depending on a company's market position, industry, earnings, cash flow, and dividend policy. Therefore, this measure is not always important for long-term investors who are concerned with a company's long-term growth.
- It isn't a guarantee, but many studies show a strong correlation between yield and returns over five years—companies with higher yields tend to offer higher returns, while lower yields lead to lower returns.
- It is common for newspapers to include yield figures in tables showing stock performance and share prices. In general, a yield of around 2–4% is considered average, and most attractive to longer-term growth investors.
- High yields are generally offered by mature, well-established companies while younger companies tend to pay lower yields because they are focused on growth. Many young companies will not pay any dividend at all.
- If a company has a low yield compared to others in the same industry, this could mean the company's stock is over-valued because investors are confident of future growth. Alternatively, it can suggest that the company can't afford to pay the expected dividends.
- If a company has a high yield in comparison to others in the same sector, it could suggest imminent dividend cuts.

▸▸ MORE INFO

Websites:

Biz/ed on dividend yield: www.bized.co.uk/compfact/ratios/investor8.htm

Investopedia dividend yield calculator: www.investopedia.com/calculator/DivCYield.aspx

Earnings at Risk

WHAT IT MEASURES

Earnings at risk (EAR) measures the quantity by which net income might change in the event of an adverse change in interest rates. It is a risk measurement which is closely linked with value at risk (VAR) calculations. The difference is that while VAR looks at the change in the entire value over the forecast horizon, EAR looks at potential changes in cash flows or earnings.

WHY IT IS IMPORTANT

Companies engaged in international business face many risks from changing currency levels to fluctuating interest rates. The challenge for investors and financial professionals is understanding and quantifying how these risks affect the profitability of the business.

Calculating EAR helps you to understand the impact of interest rate changes on your company's financial position, but it can be a

   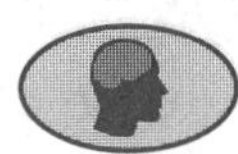  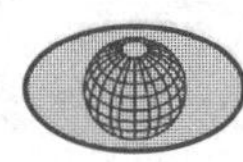   

challenge to calculate as transaction volumes grow or portfolio complexity increases. For this reason, banks and large corporations will rely on specialist computer applications using the Monte Carlo method to calculate EAR.

HOW IT WORKS IN PRACTICE

There are various models available to calculate EAR, but at heart most will calculate EAR by using a variation of:

Principal amount × Interest × Time period = Interest income and interest expense

However, EAR is not this simple in reality! Most EAR models will allow you to add in numerous factors that affect interest income and expense, such as time periods for various rates received, outstanding balances, or interest rates received and paid.

In addition, the model will simulate various possible interest rate scenarios over a period of several quarters or years, to determine their potential effect on earnings. There might be dozens of projections covering short-term rates, long-term rates, risk spreads, etc, over the specified time period. For each quarter, the model will calculate income and expense based on assumed interest rates, and can be adapted to reflect hypothetical rate changes, illustrating different strategies and customer behaviors.

If most of the likely scenarios do not seriously reduce earnings, then the organization's interest rate exposure is low. If the scenarios result in unacceptable changes, the organization might consider looking at changes to its strategy.

TRICKS OF THE TRADE

- Because of the number of variables that can be applied to EAR modeling, no two models will look the same, even if applied to the same organization. It is therefore essential to ask for specific details when analyzing any EAR summary.
- A typical EAR model will show analysis for up to a 300 basis point increase or fall in interest rates. These may be shown as a single rise/fall, or gradual change in rates. The EAR will also show a "confidence interval" showing impact according to, for example, a 90% confidence interval.
- Very few organizations devise EAR models from scratch, but will rely on summary results generated by computer. However, managers may well need to analyze EAR reports generated by specialized modeling tools and applications.

▸▸ MORE INFO

Book:

Lam, James. *Enterprise Risk Management: From Incentives to Controls*. Hoboken, NJ: Wiley, 2003.

Websites:

Approximity.com on EAR: www.approximity.com/risk/Products/cfar.html

Financial Risk Manager on EAR: www.financial-risk-manager.com/risks/market/relativevar.html

Earnings per Share

Earnings per share (EPS) is perhaps the most widely used ratio there is in the investing realm.

WHAT IT MEASURES

The portion of a company's profit allocated to each outstanding share of a company's common stock.

WHY IT IS IMPORTANT

Earnings per share is simply a fundamental measure of profitability that shows how much profit has been generated on a per-share-of-stock basis. Were the term worded as profit per share, the meaning certainly would be much clearer, if not self-evident.

By itself, EPS doesn't reveal a great deal. Its true value lies in comparing EPS figures across several quarters, or years, to judge the growth of a company's earnings on a per-share basis.

HOW IT WORKS IN PRACTICE

Essentially, the figure is calculated after paying taxes and dividends to preferred stockholders and bondholders. Barring extraordinary circumstances, EPS data are reported quarterly, semiannually, and annually.

To calculate EPS, start with net income (earnings) for the period in question, subtract the total value of any preferred stock dividends, then divide the resulting figure by the number of shares outstanding during that period:

$$\text{Earnings per share} = \frac{\text{Net income} - \text{Dividends on preferred stock}}{\text{Average number of shares outstanding}}$$

By itself, this formula is simple enough. Alas, defining the factors used in the formula invariably introduces complexities and—as some allege on occasion—possible subterfuge.

For instance, while companies usually use a weighted average number of shares outstanding over the reporting period, shares outstanding still can be either "primary" or "fully diluted." Primary EPS is calculated using the number of shares that are currently held by investors in the market and able to be traded. Diluted EPS is the result of a complex calculation that determines how many shares would be outstanding if all exercisable warrants and options were converted into common shares at the end of a quarter. Suppose, for example, that a company has granted a large number of share options to employees. If these options are capable of being exercised in the near future, that could alter significantly the number of shares in issue and, thus, the EPS—even though the E part (the earnings) is the same. Often in such cases, the company might quote the EPS both on the existing shares and on the fully diluted version. Which one a person considers depends on their view of the company and how they wish to use the EPS figure. In addition, companies can report extraordinary EPS, a figure which excludes the financial impact of unusual occurrences, such as discontinued operations or the sale of a business unit.

Net income or earnings, meanwhile, can be defined in a number of ways, based on respective nations' generally accepted accounting principles.

For example, "pro-forma earnings" tend to exclude more expenses and income used to calculate "reported earnings." Pro-forma advocates insist that these earnings eliminate all distortions and present "true" earnings that allow pure apples-with-apples comparisons with preceding periods. However, "nonrecurring expenses" seem to occur with such increasing regularity that one may wonder if a company is deliberately trying to manipulate its earnings figures and present them in the best possible light, rather than in the most accurate light.

"Cash" earnings are earnings from operating cash flow—notably,

  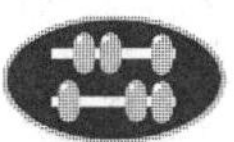   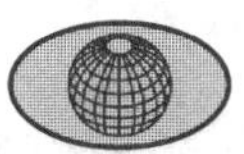   

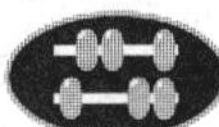

not EBITDA. In turn, cash EPS is usually these earnings divided by diluted shares outstanding. This figure is very reliable because operating cash flow is not subject to as much judgment as net earnings or pro-forma earnings.

TRICKS OF THE TRADE

- Given the varieties of earnings and shares reported today, investors need to first determine what the respective figures represent before making investment decisions. There are cases of a company announcing a pro-forma EPS that differs significantly from what is reported in its financial statements. Such discrepancies, in turn, can affect how the market values a given stock.
- Investors should check to see if a company has issued more shares during a given period, since that action, too, can affect EPS. A similar problem occurs where there have been a number of shares issued during the accounting period being considered. Which number of issued shares do you use, the opening figure, the closing figure, or the mean? In practice the usual method is to use the weighted mean number of shares in issue during the year (weighted, that is, for the amount of time in the year that they were in issue).
- "Trailing" earnings per share is the sum of EPS from the last four quarters and is the figure used to compute most price-to-earnings ratios.
- Diluted and primary shares outstanding can be the same if a company has no warrants or convertible bonds outstanding, but investors should not assume anything, and need to be sure how "shares outstanding" is being defined.

▸▸ MORE INFO

Article:

Wayman, Rick. "Types of EPS." *Investopedia*. Online at: www.investopedia.com/articles/analyst/091901.asp

EBITDA

EBITDA—an acronym that stands for "earnings before interest, taxes, depreciation, and amortization"—is slightly less inclusive than "EBIT"—earnings before interest and taxes. Both focus on profitability, and have gained popularity in the past decade as measures of operating success. But as this popularity has grown, so has the number of the measure's critics.

WHAT IT MEASURES

A company's earnings from ongoing operations, before net income is calculated.

WHY IT IS IMPORTANT

EBITDA's champions contend it gives investors a sense of how much money a young or fast-growing company is generating before it pays interest on debt, taxes, and accounts for noncash changes. If EBITDA grows over time, champions argue, investors gain at least a sense of long-term profitability and, in turn, the wisdom of their investment.

Business appraisers and investors also may study EBITDA to help to gauge a company's fair market value, often as a prelude to its acquisition by another company. It is also frequently applied to companies that have been subject to leveraged buyouts—the strategy being that EBITDA will help to cover loan payments needed to finance the transaction.

EBITDA, and EBIT, too, are claimed to be good indicators of cash flow from business operations, since they report earnings before debt payments, taxes, depreciation, and amortization charges are considered. However, that claim is challenged by many—often rather vigorously.

HOW IT WORKS IN PRACTICE

EBITDA first appeared as leveraged buyouts soared in popularity during the 1980s. It has since become well established as a financial analysis measure of telecommunications, cable, and major media companies.

Its formula is quite simple. Revenues less the cost of goods sold, general and administrative expenses, and the deductions of items expressed by the acronym EBITDA:

EBITDA =
Revenue − Expenses (excluding interest, taxes, depreciation, and amortization)

or

EBIT = Revenue − Expenses (excluding taxes and interest)

This formula does not measure true cash flow. A communications company, for example, once reported $698 million in EBIT but just $324 million in cash from operations.

TRICKS OF THE TRADE

- As yet no definition of EBITDA is enforced by standards-making bodies, so companies can all but create their own. As a result, EBITDA can easily be manipulated by aggressive accounting policies, which may erode its reliability.
- Ignoring capital expenditures could be unrealistic and horribly misleading, because companies in capital-intensive sectors such as manufacturing and transportation must continually make major capital investments to remain competitive. High-technology is another sector that may be capital-intensive, at least initially.
- Critics warn that using EBITDA as a cash flow indicator is a huge mistake, because EBITDA ignores too many factors that have an impact on true cash flow, such as working capital, debt payments, and other fixed expenses. Interest and taxes can, and do, cost a company cash, they point out, while debt holders have higher claims on a company's liquid assets than investors do.
- Critics further assail EBITDA as the barometer of choice of unprofitable firms because it can present a more optimistic view of a company's future than it has a right to claim. *Forbes* magazine, for instance, once referred to EBIDTA as "the device of choice to pep up earnings announcements."
- Even so, EBITDA may be useful in terms of evaluating firms in the same industry with widely different capital structures, tax rates, and depreciation policies.

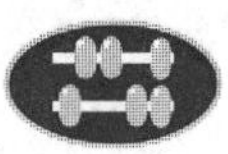

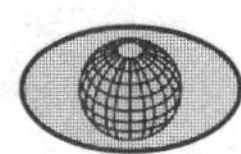

Economic Value Added

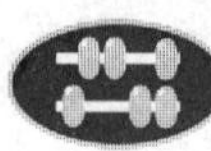

WHAT IT MEASURES

A company's financial performance—specifically, whether it is earning more or less than the total cost of the capital supporting it.

WHY IT IS IMPORTANT

Economic value added measures true economic profit, or the amount by which the earnings of a project, an operation, or a corporation exceed (or fall short of) the total amount of capital that was originally invested by the company's owners.

If a company is earning more, it is adding value, and that is good. If it is earning less, the company is in fact devouring value, and that is bad, because the company's owners (stockholders, for example) would be better off investing their capital elsewhere.

The concept's champions declare that EVA forces managers to focus on true wealth creation and maximizing stockholder investment. By definition, then, increasing EVA will increase a company's market value.

HOW IT WORKS IN PRACTICE

EVA is conceptually simple and easy to explain: From net operating profit, subtract an appropriate charge for the opportunity cost of all capital invested in an enterprise—the amount that could have been invested elsewhere. It is calculated using this formula:

EVA = Net operating profit less applicable taxes – Cost of capital

A company is considering building a new plant whose total weighted cost over 10 years is $80 million. If the expected annual incremental return on the new operation is $10 million, or $100 million over 10 years, then the plant's EVA would be positive, in this case $20 million:

100,000,000 – 80,000,000 = $20,000,000

An alternative but more complex formula for EVA is:

EVA = (Return on invested capital (%) – Cost of capital (%)) × Original capital invested

TRICKS OF THE TRADE

- EVA is a measure of dollar surplus value, not the percentage difference in returns.
- Purists describe EVA as "profit the way stockholders define it." They further contend that if stockholders expect a 10% return on their investment, they "make money" only when their share of after-tax operating profits exceeds 10% of equity capital.
- An objective of EVA is to determine which business units best utilize their assets to generate returns and maximize stockholder value; it can be used to assess a company, a business unit, a single plant, an office, or even an assembly line. This same technique is equally helpful in evaluating new business opportunities.

▸▸ MORE INFO

Website:

EVA at Stern Stewart & Co: seminars.sternstewart.com/whatiseva.html

Efficiency and Operating Ratios

For this calculation and related ratios, the lower the numbers the better.

WHAT THEY MEASURE

The portion of operating revenues or fee income spent on overhead expenses.

WHY THEY ARE IMPORTANT

Often identified with banking and financial sectors, the efficiency ratio indicates a management's ability to keep overhead costs low. This measurement is also used by mature industries, such as steel manufacture, chemicals, or auto production, that must focus on tight cost controls to boost profitability because growth prospects are generally modest.

In some industries, the efficiency ratio is called the overhead burden, which is overheads as a percentage of sales.

A different method measures efficiency simply by tracking three other measures: accounts payable to sales, days sales outstanding, and inventory turnover, which indicates how fast a company is able to move its merchandise. A general guide is that if the first two of these measures are low and third is high, efficiency is probably high; the reverse is likewise true.

HOW THEY WORK IN PRACTICE

The efficiency ratio is defined as operating overhead expenses divided by fee income plus tax equivalent net interest income. If operating expenses are $100,000, and revenues (as defined) are $230,000, then:

$$\text{Efficiency ratio} = \frac{100{,}000}{230{,}000} = 0.43$$

However, not everyone calculates the ratio in the same way. Some institutions include all noninterest expenses, while others exclude certain charges and intangible asset amortization.

To find the inventory turnover ratio, divide total sales by total inventory. If net sales are $300,000 and inventory is $100,000, then:

$$\text{Inventory turnover ratio} = \frac{300{,}000}{140{,}000} = 2.14$$

To find the accounts payable to sales ratio, divide a company's accounts payable by its annual net sales. A high ratio suggests that a company is using its suppliers' funds as a source of cheap financing

  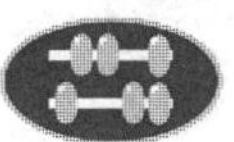 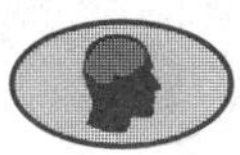  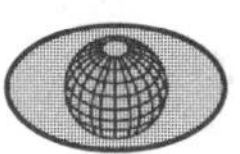   

because it is not operating efficiently enough to generate its own funds. If accounts payable are $42,000 and total sales are $300,000, then:

$$\text{Accounts payable to sales ratio} = \frac{42{,}000}{300{,}000} = 0.14 = 14\%$$

TRICKS OF THE TRADE

- Identifying "overheads" to calculate the efficiency ratio can itself contribute to overall inefficiency. Some financial experts contend that efficiency can be measured equally well by reviewing earnings per share growth and return on equity.
- Some banks identify amortization of goodwill expense, and pull it out of their noninterest expense in order to calculate what is called the cash efficiency ratio: noninterest expense minus goodwill amortization expense divided into revenue.
- In banking, an acceptable efficiency ratio was once in the low 60s. Now the goal is 50, while better-performing banks boast ratios in the mid 40s. Low ratings usually indicate a higher return on equity and earnings.

Elasticity

Elasticity measures responsiveness, and is very useful when studying the impact of pricing on supply and demand.

WHAT IT MEASURES

The percentage change of one variable caused by a percentage change in another variable.

WHY IT IS IMPORTANT

Elasticity is defined as "the measure of the sensitivity of one variable to another." In practical terms, elasticity indicates the degree to which consumers respond to changes in price. It is obviously important for companies to consider such relationships when contemplating changes in price, demand, and supply.

Demand elasticity measures how much the quantity demanded changes when the price of a product or service is increased or lowered. Will demand remain constant? If not, how much will demand change?

Supply elasticity measures the impact on supply when a price is changed. It is assumed that lowering prices will reduce supply, because demand will increase—but by how much?

HOW IT WORKS IN PRACTICE

The general formula for elasticity is:

$$\text{Elasticity} = \frac{\text{Change in } x\ (\%)}{\text{Change in } y\ (\%)}$$

In theory, x and y can be any variables. However, the most common application measures price and demand. If the price of a product is increased from $20 to $25, or 25%, and demand in turn falls from 6,000 to 3,000 (−50%), elasticity would be calculated as:

$$\frac{-50}{25} = -2$$

A value greater in magnitude than ±1 means that demand is strongly sensitive to price, while a lesser value means that demand is not price-sensitive.

TRICKS OF THE TRADE

- There are five cases of elasticity:
  - E = 1, or unit elasticity. The proportional change in one variable is equal to the proportional change in another variable: if price rises by 5%, demand falls by 5%.
  - E is greater than 1, or *just elastic*. The proportional change in x is greater than the proportional change in y: if price rises by 5%, demand falls by 3%.
  - E = infinity, or perfectly elastic. This is a special case of elasticity: any change in y will effect no change in x. An example would be prices charged by a hospital's emergency room, where increases in price are unlikely to curb demand.
  - E is less than 1, or *just inelastic*. The proportional change in x is less than the proportional change in y: if prices are increased by 3%, demand will fall by 30%.
  - E = 0, or perfectly inelastic. This is another special case of elasticity: any change in y will have an infinite effect on x.
- There are more complex formulae for determining a range of variables, or "arc elasticity."
- Elasticity can be used to affirm two rules of thumb:
  - demand becomes elastic if consumers have an alternative or adequate substitute for the product or service;
  - demand is more elastic if consumers have an incentive to save money.

Enterprise Value

In the financial world, enterprise value has a precise meaning and calculation. It is important to remember this, as many conference planners and consultants routinely rely on "enterprise value" to promote whatever concept they happen to be selling.

WHAT IT MEASURES

It measures what financial markets believe a company's ongoing operations are worth.

Some people also define enterprise value as what it would actually cost to purchase an entire company at a given moment.

WHY IT IS IMPORTANT

Enterprise value is not a theoretical valuation but a firm and finite value, logically determined. It tells an individual investor the underlying value of his stake in an enterprise. For potential acquirers considering a takeover of a company, enterprise value helps them to determine a reasonable price for their desired acquisition.

  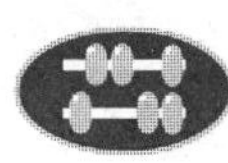   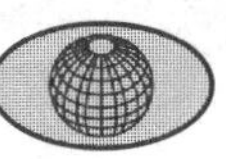   

HOW IT WORKS IN PRACTICE

Although it is a finite figure, enterprise value can be calculated in two ways. One method is quicker, but the other is more thorough and thus more reliable.

The quick way is simply to multiply the number of a company's shares outstanding by the current price per share. Using this approach, the enterprise value of a company with 2 million shares outstanding, and a share price of $25, would be:

Enterprise value = 2,000,000 × 25 = $50,000,000

However, this value is based on the market's perception of the value of its shares of stock; it also ignores some important factors about a company's fiscal health. The second, more complete, method is therefore preferred by many experts. This method calculates enterprise value as the sum of market capitalization, plus debt and preferred stock, minus cash and cash equivalents:

Enterprise value =
Market capitalization + Long-term debt + Preferred stock – Cash and equivalents

If market capitalization is $6.5 million, debt totals $1 million, the value of preferred stock is $1.5 million, and cash and equivalents total $2 million, enterprise value would be:

6.5 + 1 + 1.5 – 2 = $7 million

This more thorough calculation recognizes the existence of both a company's debt and of the amount of cash and liquid assets on hand. No matter how a stock may fluctuate, these sums are relatively constant, and the amount of debt can be very significant. Debt—and cash, too—can be just as important during a company's sale, since new owners both assume existing debt and receive any cash on hand. Indeed, more than a few acquisitions are financed in part with funds of the acquired company.

TRICKS OF THE TRADE

- Financial markets often use the market capitalization figure for enterprise value, but they really are not the same thing.
- Experts will occasionally refer to "total enterprise value," but its definition and formula are virtually identical to this second formula enterprise value. Total enterprise value is only meaningful to those who use the quick method to compute enterprise value.
- A company's value is sometimes expressed as "the total funds being used to finance it." This is increasingly used in place of the price/earnings ratio, and indicates the economic rather than the accounting return that the company is generating on the total value of the capital supporting it. Companies that have borrowed heavily to finance growth, or that have paid large premiums for acquisitions or assets, are more frequently evaluated by this method.

Exchange Rate Risk

Because formulae exist to quantify, at least to a degree, the risks that accompany any investment decision, it is logical to assume that a similar formula exists to quantify what is called both exchange rate risk and currency risk. Such logic is flawed, for no such formula exists.

WHAT IT MEASURES

The risk of a gain or loss in the value of a business activity or investment that results from changes in the exchange rates of world currencies.

WHY IT IS IMPORTANT

Each business day seems to bring more international business transactions, generated by an ever-growing number of enterprises from an ever-increasing number of countries. Enterprises in developing nations, especially, are vying for their share of world commerce.

However, the economies of these developing nations can be especially fragile, while economies of mature nations periodically sputter and suffer recessions. Asia, Latin America, and Eastern Europe have all endured economic turmoil in the past decade, while such regions as the Middle East have been volatile for several decades, principally because of the wide swings in oil prices.

Currency exchange rates can be just as volatile, and this clearly poses risks to any enterprise conducting business in foreign markets and any investor holding either stock in a foreign-based company or an interest in a mutual fund that invests in foreign companies. The effects on a company's earnings, cash flow, and balance sheet can be significant.

The main exchange rate risk to an operation or investment is that any profits realized will be partially reduced—or wiped out altogether—when they are exchanged for the domestic currency, be it US dollars, pounds sterling, the euro, or Japanese yen.

More often, exchange rate risk will affect a company's price competitiveness in a product or service also offered by a competitor whose costs are incurred in a foreign currency. If the competitor's currency weakens, its relative competitive position improves because its costs decline, enabling the competitor to reduce its price and attract a larger share of a market.

HOW IT WORKS IN PRACTICE

There is a simple way to avoid the risk posed by exchange rates: don't do business abroad! For large companies, as well as an increasing number of small and medium-sized companies, that would be like sticking one's head in the sand.

A second defense against exchange rate risks is almost as unrealistic: conduct all business in your home currency. Requiring foreign customers to pay up only in, say, dollars, puts the burden of currency fluctuations squarely on the customer's shoulders and completely insulates the selling company from any shrinkage of profits from exchange rate differences. The price of such insulation, however, is likely to be a steady loss of customers.

The practical course of action, then, is to gain a basic understanding of exchange rate risks, if only enough to sort out the reams of opinions on the subject, and to select knowledgeable advisers and use their counsel wisely. This is a sophisticated, complex realm that has been examined for over a century. It is certainly no place for amateurs.

At the same time, however, exchange rates, interest rates, and inflation rates have been linked to one another via a classic set of relationships that can serve as leading indicators of changes in risk. These relationships are:

- The **Purchasing Power Parity Theory**. While it can be expressed differently, the most common expression links the changes in exchange rates to those in relative price indices in two countries:

Rate of change of exchange rate = Difference in inflation rates

- The **International Fisher Effect** (IFE). This holds that an interest rate differential will exist only if the exchange rate is expected to change in such a way that the advantage of the higher interest rate is offset by the loss on the foreign exchange transactions. Practically speaking, the IFE implies that while an investor in a low-interest country can convert funds into the currency of a high-interest country and earn a higher rate, the gain (the interest rate differential) will be offset by the expected loss due to foreign exchange rate changes. The relationship is stated as:

Expected rate of change of the exchange rate = Interest rate differential

- The **Unbiased Forward Rate Theory**. This holds that the forward exchange rate is the best and unbiased estimate of the expected future spot exchange rate:

Expected exchange rate = Forward exchange rate

Other than these yardsticks, defending against exchange rate risk is largely a matter of observation. In the floating exchange rate environment that has existed for almost the past 30 years, currency exchange rates respond to a host of factors: political climates, the flow of imports and exports, the flow of capital, inflation rates in various countries, consumer expectations, and confidence levels, to name a few. Frequently, limits are placed on exchange rate fluctuations by government policies—actions that themselves can arouse controversy or debate.

Even so, the exchange rate risks these factors create can be arranged into three primary categories:

- **Economic exposure.** Due to changes in rates, operating costs will rise and make a product uncompetitive in the world market, thus eroding profitability. There's little that can be done about economic risk; it's simply a routine business risk that every enterprise must endure.
- **Translation exposure**. The impact of currency exchange rates will reduce a company's earnings and weaken its balance sheet. In turn, the denominations of assets and liabilities are important, although many experts contend that currency fluctuations have no significant impact on real assets.
- **Transaction exposure**. Caused by an unfavorable move in a specific currency between the time when a contract is agreed and the time it is completed, or between the time when a lending or borrowing is initiated and the time the funds are repaid. This is the most common problem that confronts most companies. Requiring payment in advance is rarely practical, and impossible, of course, for borrowing and lending.

To reduce translation exposure, experienced corporate fund managers use a variety of techniques known as currency hedging, which amounts to diversifying currency holdings, monitoring exchange rates, and acting accordingly, depending on specific conditions. Its advocates contend that taking appropriate action can greatly reduce translation risks, if not avoid them altogether. Currency hedging, however, is also technical and sophisticated.

Transaction exposure can be eased by a process known as factoring. Major exporters, in particular, transfer title to their foreign accounts receivable to a third-party factoring house that assumes responsibility for collections, administrative services, and any other services requested. The fee for this service is a percentage of the value of the receivables, anywhere from 5% to 10% or higher, depending on the currencies involved. Companies often include this percentage in selling prices to recoup the cost.

Commercial and country risks can affect exchange rates, too. Commercial risks include the default or bankruptcy of major foreign customers. While this risk mirrors what can also occur at home, foreign-based companies operate under different laws and relationships with their governments. More worrisome are country risks: political or military interventions and currency restrictions that less stable nations might impose. Insurance is available to address such risks, but it can be costly.

TRICKS OF THE TRADE

- Any number of models have been created to explain and forecast exchange rates. None has proved definitive, largely because the world's economies and financial markets are evolving so rapidly.
- A forward transaction is an agreement to buy one currency and sell another on a date some time beyond two business days. It allows an exchange rate on a given day to be locked in for a future payment or receipt, thereby eliminating exchange rate risk.
- Foreign exchange options are contracts which, for a fee, guarantee a worst-case exchange rate for the future purchase of one currency for another. Unlike a forward transaction, the option does not obligate the buyer to deliver a currency on the settlement date unless the buyer chooses to. These options protect against unfavorable currency movements while allowing retention of the ability to participate in favorable movements.
- A producer facing pricing competition caused by fluctuations in exchange rates can also use currency contracts to try to match competitors' cost structures and reduce costs.
- Companies doing larger volumes of business in a foreign country often establish a local office there to pay expenses and collect revenues in local currencies to reduce the impact of sudden and pronounced exchange rate fluctuations.
- Private sector subscription services monitor currencies and publish alerts. One US-based service has established numerical ranges that indicate risk, from 100 (no risk) to 200 (extreme risk or an outright currency crisis).
- Exchange rate risks cannot be insured against *per se*.
- The US Export-Import Bank (Eximbank) may be a source of advice for companies, especially smaller and medium-sized companies, seeking assistance.

▸▸ MORE INFO

Book:

Giddy, Ian H., and Gunter Dufey. "The management of foreign exchange risk." In Frederick D. S. Choi (ed). *Handbook of International Accounting*. New York: Wiley, 1991. Also online at: www.stern.nyu.edu/~igiddy/fxrisk.htm

Article:

Magos, Alice. "Ask Alice about foreign exchange risk." *Business Owner's Toolkit*. Online at: www.toolkit.com/news/newsDetail.aspx?aa=1&nid=248askalice

     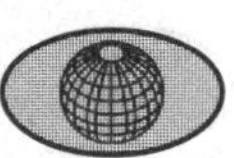   

Expected Rate of Return

Expected rate of return (ERR) is a measure conceived and crafted in the spirit of "forewarned is forearmed."

WHAT IT MEASURES

The projected percentage return on an investment, based on the weighted probability of all possible rates of return.

WHY IT IS IMPORTANT

No self-respecting businessperson or organization should make an investment without first having some understanding of how successful that investment is likely to be. Expected rate of return provides such an understanding, within certain limits.

HOW IT WORKS IN PRACTICE

The formula for expected rate of return is:

$$\text{Expected rate of return} = \sum_{i=1}^{n} [P(i) \times r_i]$$

where P(*i*) is the probability that the return r_i is achieved, i.e., the sum of the products of all possible returns and their probabilities.

A simple example, as given below, is far easier to grasp, and adequately illustrates the principle which the formula expresses. It will also probably be of more practical use to most of those who need to calculate ERR.

The current price of ABC, Inc, stock is $10. At the end of the year, ABC shares of stock are projected to be traded:

- 25% higher if economic growth exceeds expectations—a probability of 30%;
- 12% higher if economic growth equals expectations—a probability of 50%;
- 5% lower if economic growth falls short of expectations—a probability of 20%.

To find the expected rate of return, simply multiply the percentages by their respective probabilities and add the results:

$$(30\% \times 25\%) + (50\% \times 12\%) + (20\% \times -5\%) = 7.5 + 6 - 1 = 12.5\%$$

A second example:

- if economic growth remains robust (a 20% probability), investments will return 25%;
- if economic growth ebbs, but still performs adequately (a 40% probability), investments will return 15%;
- if economic growth slows significantly (a 30% probability), investments will return 5%;
- if the economy declines outright (a 10% probability), investments will return 0%.

Therefore the ERR can be calculated:

$$(20\% \times 25\%) + (40\% \times 15\%) + (30\% \times 5\%) + (10\% \times 0\%) = 5 + 6 + 1.5 + 0 = 12.5\%$$

Another method that can be used to project expected return is the capital asset pricing model (CAPM), which is explained separately.

TRICKS OF THE TRADE

- The probability totals must always equal 100% for the calculation to be valid.
- Be sure not to overlook any negative numbers in the calculations, or the results produced will be incorrect.
- An ERR calculation is only as good as the scenarios considered. Wildly unrealistic scenarios will produce an equally unreliable expected rate of return.

Fair Value Calculations

WHAT IT MEASURES

Fair value is the value of an asset or liability in a transaction between two parties. It can be used to refer to the complete assets and liabilities of a company that is being acquired by another company, or to calculate the fair value of stock market securities. However, fair value can be applied to almost any assessment of something's value.

WHY IT IS IMPORTANT

In the securities market, fair value explains the relationship between the futures contract on a market and the actual value of the index. In other words, if futures are trading above fair value, investors believe the index will rise. The opposite is true if futures are trading below fair value. If your business invests in futures, this can be crucial in your ability to raise finance. There will always be some variation around fair value because of short-term issues of supply and demand, but futures should generally be close to fair value.

HOW IT WORKS IN PRACTICE

The calculation of fair value is relatively simple as long as you have access to the necessary underlying data. The formula most often used is:

$$\text{Fair value} = \text{Cash} \times \frac{1 + r \times x}{360} - \text{Dividends}$$

where Cash is the closing index value, *r* is the current interest rate, and *x* is the time remaining until the contract expires, in days.

For example, the fair value calculation for the FTSE 100 where the closing price is 1157 points with a cash index of 1146, the interest rate is 0.57%, with 78 days before expiry of the contract, and a dividend value of 3.47 points, would be calculated as follows:

$$\text{Fair value} = 1146 \times \frac{1 + 0.0057 \times 78}{360} - 3.47$$

This calculation gives a fair value of 1156.68 points. If the FTSE is trading at 1157 then the difference between the two figures is 0.32. At this time, the stock is trading below fair value.

TRICKS OF THE TRADE

- Remember that fair value will change on a daily basis depending on the money markets.
- The key purpose of a fair value figure is to give investors a feel for the initial move of the markets "on the open." Futures trading above the fair value number indicate a positive open for the

  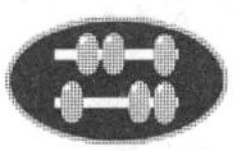   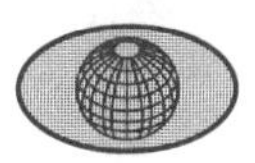   

grouping discussed, while numbers below fair value are indicative of negative openings.

- Fair value can also be used to refer more generally to a stock trading at a reasonable level considering price/earning ratios.
- Many financial news websites publish fair value data daily for key global markets, which means that you may not need to do all the calculations manually.

» MORE INFO

Website:

Mark Hanes on fair value: www.allstocks.com/html/fair_value_s_p_futures_or_prem.html

Fixed-Deposit Compound Interest

WHAT IT MEASURES

The compound interest paid on fixed deposits, which is usually paid more frequently (monthly or quarterly) than a traditional annual interest rate. As the frequency of compounding increases, so does the effective rate of interest.

WHY IT IS IMPORTANT

The structure of fixed deposits means that a fixed-deposit investment offering a headline interest rate of, perhaps 8%, will in effect pay a rate higher than this. This must be taken into account, along with the frequency of compounding, when calculating the "effective" interest rate paid.

HOW IT WORKS IN PRACTICE

If your company invests $1 million at a rate of 8% for one year, at the end of the year the investment would be worth $1,080,000 based on annual compounding.

However, with fixed-deposit compound rates, interest may be paid more frequently, in which case the value of an investment changes. After one year, an investment of $1 million compounded quarterly would be worth £1,082,432 based on quarterly compounding, for example. This translates into an effective interest rate of 8.24%, rather than 8%.

The formula for calculating fixed deposit compound interest is as follows:

$$\text{FDCI} = p\left(1 + \frac{i}{m}\right)^{mt}$$

where:

p = investment
i = interest rate
m = number of times compounded per year
t = number of years

TRICKS OF THE TRADE

- With fixed-deposit investments, investors deposit a sum of money for a fixed period ranging from a few weeks to several years, which attracts a predetermined rate of interest. Fixed deposits are offered by banks and companies, although corporate fixed deposits are considered riskier.
- Fixed deposits offer regular income through interest payments, but won't offer the same returns as a stock portfolio—a typical fixed deposit compound interest rate is between 7% and 10%.

» MORE INFO

Websites:

All Banking Solutions fixed deposit calculator: allbankingsolutions.com/fdcal.htm

MoneyChimp on compound interest: www.moneychimp.com/articles/finworks/fmfutval.htm

Yahoo compound interest calculator: au.pfinance.yahoo.com/calculators/compound-interest.html

Forward Interest Rates

WHAT THEY MEASURE

Forward interest rates are interest rates which are specified now for a loan or transaction that will occur at a specified future date. As with current interest rates, forward interest rates include a term structure which shows the different forward rates offered on transactions of different maturities. Forward rates are also known as implied forward rates.

WHY THEY ARE IMPORTANT

Forward interest rates are a vital part of forward rate agreements (FRAs), and are important in making any investment decision that is sensitive to interest rates. For corporations, this might include investments or loans, while investors will commonly use forward interest rates to compare forwards and futures for investment potential. Forward rates are also needed when you want to calculate the interest earned between two periods.

Forward rates are extrapolated from a risk-free theoretical spot rate, and should be monitored because they provide an insight into how the market is feeling about future movement of interest rates.

HOW THEY WORK IN PRACTICE

A conventional investment might offer an interest rate of 6.6% per annum, compounded annually. After two years, a $1 investment would return $1.14.

In a forward interest rate agreement, however, an investment and rate is agreed for a future date. For example, you might agree to invest $1 in one year's time, for a period of two years. The interest rate paid is a forward interest rate.

The payments on a forward interest rate agreement can be calculated using the following formula:

$$\text{Payment} = \text{Notional amount} \times \frac{\text{Reference rate} - \text{Fixed rate} \times \alpha}{1 + \text{Reference rate} \times \alpha}$$

     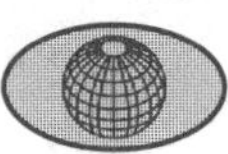   

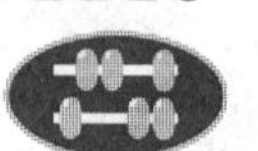

where the reference rate is the base rate, usually taken from Libor, the fixed rate is the interest rate at which the loan is agreed, and α is the time/days involved, using dating conventions.

TRICKS OF THE TRADE

- Future interest rates can be calculated more accurately by incorporating discounted cash flow over the lifetime of the loan/investment. Given a discount function, it is possible to arrange today to borrow $1 at the end of year 1 and pay 1/df(2) at the end of year 2 for a zero net investment, since each sum has a present value of $1.
- Forward rates can cover periods that only last one period, with rates denoted by the starting date. For example, a year one forward rate covers the period from the end of year 1 to the end of year 2, but on terms negotiated today.
- Forward rates are also widely used in foreign currency exchange, where investors predict likely movements in rates over time. They can also be used to price bonds, using forward rates instead of discount rates to value the bond.

MORE INFO

Article:

Finance Trainer. "Forward Rate Agreement (FRA)." Online at: www.financetrainer.com/Portals/2/Formel-Service/tcs0203_e.pdf

Websites:

Forward rate agreement calculator: ciberconta.unizar.es/bolsa/derivados2/fra.htm

Investopedia on forward rates: www.investopedia.com/exam-guide/cfa-level-1/fixed-income-investments/forward-rates.asp

Quant Notes on forward rate of agreement: www.quantnotes.com/fundamentals/basics/forwardrateofagreement.htm

Future Value

Future value is simply the estimated value of a sum of money at a given point in the future, as in, "What will the $1,000 we have today be worth in two years' time?"

WHAT IT MEASURES

Any amount of any currency.

WHY IT IS IMPORTANT

Future value is a fundamental of investment. Understanding it helps any organization or individual to determine how a sum will be affected by changes in inflation, interest rates, or currency values. Inflation, for instance, will always reduce a sum's value. Interest rates will always increase it. Exchanging the sum for an identical amount in another currency will increase or decrease it, depending on how the respective currencies perform on the world market.

Armed with this knowledge, an organization can make more informed decisions about how to generate the maximum value from its funds in a given period of time: Would it be best to deposit them in simple interest-bearing accounts, exchange them for funds in another currency, use them to expand operations, or use them to acquire another company?

HOW IT WORKS IN PRACTICE

Start with three figures: the sum in question, the percentage by which it will increase or decrease, and the period of time. In this case: $1,000, 11%, and two years.

At an interest rate of 11%, our $1,000 will grow to $1,232 in two years:

$1,000 × 1.11 = $1,110 (first year) × 1.11 = $1,232 (second year)

Note that the interest earned in the first year generates additional interest in the second year, a practice known as compounding. When large sums are involved, the effect of compounding can be significant.

At an inflation rate of 11%, by contrast, our $1,000 will shrink to $812 in two years:

$$\frac{\$1{,}000}{1.11} = \frac{\$901 \text{ (first year)}}{1.11} = \$812 \text{ (second year)}$$

TRICKS OF THE TRADE

- Express the percentage as 1.11 and multiply and divide by that figure, instead of using 11%. Otherwise, errors will occur.
- Calculate each year, quarter, or month separately, as in our examples.
- It is important always to use the **annual** rates of interest and inflation.
- A more useful tool is "present value," which estimates what value future cash flows would have if they occurred today.

MORE INFO

Website:

Future value calculator: www.calculator.net/future-value-calculator.html

Future Value of an Annuity

Calculating the future value of an annuity is another example of the principle that money invested today will be worth more in the future.

WHAT IT MEASURES

The value to which a series of fixed-amount payments made at regular intervals will grow over the specified period of time.

WHY IT IS IMPORTANT

The calculation enables companies to determine the future value of a fund receiving regular payments, such as a pension fund to which contributions are made. Individuals in companies may find the calculation equally useful if they want to establish a fund to pay the cost of future college education: they will know what their annual payments will grow to in a given number of years.

  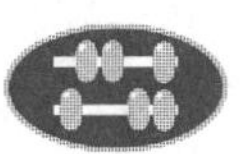 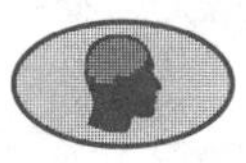  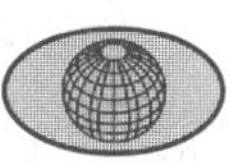 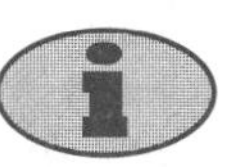  

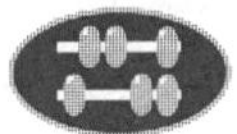

HOW IT WORKS IN PRACTICE

There are several types of annuity. They vary both in the ways they accumulate funds and in the ways they dispense earnings. The following are some examples:

- A **fixed annuity** guarantees fixed payments to the individual receiving it for the term of the contract, usually until death.
- A **variable annuity** offers no guarantee but has potential for a greater return, usually based on the performance of a stock or mutual fund.
- A **deferred annuity** delays payments until the individual chooses to receive them.
- A **hybrid annuity**, also called a combination annuity, combines features of both the fixed and variable annuity.

Financial calculators and spreadsheet programs will compute annuity calculations automatically. Manual calculations require a future-value-of-annuity table that contains figures based on the interest rate and period in question. The basic formula is:

Future value = Amount invested × Table value [interest, period]

If, for example, a pension manager puts $1,000,000 at the end of every year into his company's pension fund, the fund earns 8% interest, and there are no withdrawals, at the end of five years it will be worth:

$1,000,000 × 5.867 [table value] = $5,867,000

TRICKS OF THE TRADE

- The formula assumes that payments are made at the end of a given period.
- If a stated interest rate is not an annual rate, it must be adjusted to reflect an annual rate.
- Although their yields are low, annuities are relatively safe investments that provide level streams of cash flow for fixed periods of time.
- In the United States, annuities are tax-deferred, but also often carry an early withdrawal penalty.
- If you are calculating manually, be sure to use the designated future value of an annuity table, and not the future value table; there is a significant difference.
- The mathematical expression for the numbers appearing on a future value of an annuity table is $[(1 + i)n - 1] \div i$; i is the interest rate, and n is the number of years in question.

▸▸ MORE INFO

Book:

Walsh, Ciaran. *Key Management Ratios*. 4th ed. London: FT Prentice Hall, 2008.

Website:

Get Objects on future value of annuities: www.getobjects.com/Components/Finance/TVM/fva.html

Goodwill and Patents

One could define both goodwill and patents as figments of the imagination, the former a financier's and the latter an inventor's. The accounting realm assigns real value to both, based on the theory that both will deliver real benefits in the future.

WHAT IT MEASURES

The value of two intangible assets.

WHY IT IS IMPORTANT

Since both goodwill and patents are intangible assets, their values will be whatever negotiators conclude. Still, their values need to be reflected in financial statements. Goodwill is created in the aftermath of an acquisition, and must appear on a balance sheet. The acquisition of a patent has a cost of its own, be it the price of internal development costs, or the purchase price paid to an inventor.

HOW IT WORKS IN PRACTICE

Ultimately, the assigned values of both assets are matters of opinion, however learned the opinions may be. Each must be considered separately.

Ordinarily, goodwill is completely ignored by accountants. Only when a company has been acquired by another does goodwill become an intangible asset. It then appears on a balance sheet in the amount by which the price paid by the acquiring company exceeds the net tangible assets of the acquired company. In other words:

Goodwill = Purchase price − Net assets

If, for example, an airline is bought for $12 billion and its net assets are valued at $9 billion, $3 billion of the purchase would be allocated to goodwill on the balance sheet.

The buyer will attribute the difference to any number of reasons that give a competitive advantage, such as a loyal and long-standing customer base, a strong brand, strategic location, or productive employees.

A patent's value, meanwhile, will probably be the sum of its development costs, or its purchase price if acquired from someone else. It is usually to a company's advantage to spread the patent's value over several years. If so, the critical time period to consider is not the full life of the patent (17 years in the United States), but its estimated useful life.

For example, let's say that in January 2000 a company acquired a patent issued in January 1995 at a cost of $100,000. It concludes that the patent's useful commercial life is 10 years, not the 12 remaining before the patent expires. In turn, patent value would be $100,000, and it would be spread (or amortized in accounting terms) over 10 years, or $10,000 each year.

TRICKS OF THE TRADE

- Accounting for goodwill can vary by country, an issue that needs to be considered when evaluating or negotiating acquisitions of foreign-based companies. Moreover, the rules may change from time to time. In the United States, for example, goodwill no longer has to be amortized over 40 years.
- The total value of a patent's development costs may stretch over several years.
- The cost of a patent ultimately may have little bearing on the future revenues and profits it brings.

▸▸ MORE INFO

Website:

Patent Cafe: www.patentcafe.com

  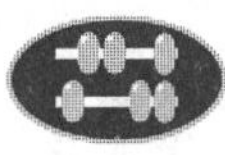   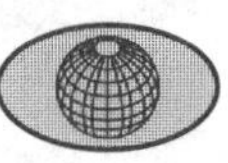   

Gross Profit Margin Ratio

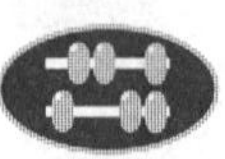

WHAT IT MEASURES

The gross profit margin ratio measures how efficiently a company uses its resources, materials, and labor in the production process by showing the percentage of net sales remaining after subtracting the cost of making and selling a product or service. It is usually expressed as a percentage, and indicates the profitability of a business before overhead costs.

WHY IT IS IMPORTANT

A high gross profit margin ratio indicates that a business can make a reasonable profit on sales, as long as overheads do not increase. Investors pay attention to the gross profit margin ratio because it tells them how efficient your business is compared to competitors. It is sensible to track gross profit margin ratios over a number of years to see if company earnings are consistent, growing, or declining.

For businesses, knowing your gross profit margin ratio is important because it tells you whether your business is pricing goods and services effectively. A low margin compared to your competitors would suggest you are under-pricing, while a high margin might indicate over-pricing. Low profit margin ratios can also suggest the business is unable to control production costs, or that a low amount of earnings are generated from revenues.

HOW IT WORKS IN PRACTICE

To calculate gross profit margin ratio, use the following formula:

$$\text{Gross profit margin ratio} = \frac{\text{Gross profit margin}}{\text{Net sales}}$$

First, determine the gross profit for the business during a specific period of time, such as a financial quarter. This is total revenue minus the cost of sales. The cost of sales includes variable costs associated with manufacturing, packaging, and freight, and should not include fixed overheads such as rent or utilities.

For example, if Company A has net sales of $10 million, while costs for inventory or production total $7 million, then the gross profit margin is $3 million. Next, divide this by net sales. In our example:

$$\frac{3{,}000{,}000}{10{,}000{,}000} = 0.3 = 30\%$$

(Simply multiply the result by 100 to see it expressed as a percentage, here a gross profit margin ratio of 30%.) Tracking several subsequent quarters will allow you to create a more accurate profit margin ratio. A more detailed version of the formula is:

$$\text{Gross profit margin ratio} = \frac{\text{Total revenue} - \text{Cost of sales}}{\text{Total sales}}$$

TRICKS OF THE TRADE

- Gross profit margins tend to remain stable over time. Significant irregularities or sudden variations might be a potential sign of financial fraud, accounting irregularities, or problems in the business.
- Gross profit margin ratios can be calculated alongside net profit margin ratios (net profit after tax ÷ sales), pre-tax profit margins (net profit before tax ÷ sales), and operating profit margins (net income before interest and taxes ÷ sales) to provide a more comprehensive insight into margins. Net profit margins and gross profit margins can be significantly different because of the impact of interest and tax expenses.
- Profit margin ratios are a popular way to benchmark against competitors. Industries will generally have standard gross profit margin ratios, which are easily discovered.
- If you use an accounting program such as QuickBooks, the software can calculate gross profit margin ratios for you, making it easier to track margin ratios over several years. If you discover fluctuations regularly occur at a particular time of year, you might try to adjust pricing to encourage greater sales at that period.

▸▸ MORE INFO

Websites:

About.com on gross profit margin: beginnersinvest.about.com/cs/investinglessons/l/blgrossmargin.htm

BizWiz.com on profit margin ratios: www.bizwiz.ca/profitability_ratio_calculation_formulas/profit_margin_ratio.html

Interest Coverage

Interest coverage, or interest cover, describes several ratios used to assess a company's financial strength and capital structure.

WHAT IT MEASURES

The amount of earnings available to make interest payments after all operating and nonoperating income and expenses—except interest and income taxes—have been accounted for.

WHY IT IS IMPORTANT

Interest coverage is regarded as a measure of a company's creditworthiness because it shows how much income there is to cover interest payments on outstanding debt. Banks and financial analysts also rely on this ratio as a rule of thumb to gauge the fundamental strength of a business.

HOW IT WORKS IN PRACTICE

Interest coverage is expressed as a ratio, and reflects a company's ability to pay the interest obligations on its debt. It compares the funds available to pay interest—earnings before interest and taxes, or EBIT—with the interest expense. The basic formula is:

$$\text{Interest coverage ratio} = \frac{\text{EBIT}}{\text{Interest expense}}$$

If interest expense for a year is $9 million, and the company's EBIT is $45 million, the interest coverage would be:

$$\frac{45\text{ million}}{9\text{ million}} = 5$$

   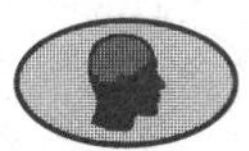  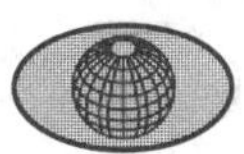   

The higher the number, the stronger a company is likely to be. Conversely, a low number suggests that a company's fortunes are looking ominous. Variations of this basic formula also exist. For example, there is:

$$\text{Cash flow interest coverage ratio} = \frac{\text{Operating cash flow} + \text{Interest} + \text{Taxes}}{\text{Interest}}$$

This ratio indicates the company's ability to use its cash flow to satisfy its fixed financing obligations. Finally, there is the fixed-charge coverage ratio, which compares EBIT with fixed charges:

$$\text{Fixed-charge coverage ratio} = \frac{\text{EBIT} + \text{Lease expenses}}{\text{Interest} + \text{Lease expense}}$$

"Fixed charges" can be interpreted in many ways, however. It could mean, for example, the funds that a company is obliged to set aside to retire debt, or dividends on preferred stock.

TRICKS OF THE TRADE

- A ratio of less than 1 indicates that a company is having problems generating enough cash flow to pay its interest expenses, and that either a modest decline in operating profits or a sudden rise in borrowing costs could eliminate profitability entirely.
- Ideally, interest coverage should at least exceed 1.5; in some sectors, 2.0 or higher is desirable.
- Interest coverage is widely considered to be more meaningful than looking at total debt, because what really matters is what an enterprise must pay in a given period, not how much debt it has.
- As is often the case, it may be more meaningful to watch interest coverage over several periods in order to detect long-term trends.
- Cash flow will sometimes be substituted for EBIT in the ratio, because EBIT includes not only cash but also accrued sales and other unrealized income.
- Interest coverage also is called "times interest earned."

Internal Rate of Return

Internal rate of return (IRR) is another analytical tool based on the time value of money principle. Some regard it as the companion to net present value.

WHAT IT MEASURES

Technically, the interest rate that makes the present value of an investment's projected cash flows equal to the cost of the project; practically speaking, the rate that indicates whether or not an investment is worth pursuing.

WHY IT IS IMPORTANT

The calculation of internal rate of return (IRR) is used to appraise the prospective viability of investments and capital projects. It is also called dollar-weighted rate of return.

Essentially, IRR allows an investor to find the interest rate that is equivalent to the monetary returns expected from the project. Once that rate is determined, it can be compared to the rates that could be earned by investing the money elsewhere, or to the weighted cost of capital. IRR also accounts for the time value of money.

HOW IT WORKS IN PRACTICE

How is IRR applied? Assume, for example, that a project under consideration costs $7,500 and is expected to return $2,000 per year for five years, or $10,000. The IRR calculated for the project would be about 10%. If the cost of borrowing money for the project, or the return on investing the funds elsewhere, is less than 10%, the project is probably worthwhile. If the alternate use of the money will return 10% or more, the project should be rejected, since from a financial perspective it will break even at best.

Typically, management requires an IRR equal to or higher than the cost of capital, depending on relative risk and other factors.

The best way to compute an IRR is by using a spreadsheet (such as Excel) or financial calculator, which do it automatically, although it is crucial to understand how the calculation should be structured. Calculating IRR by hand is tedious and time-consuming, and requires the process to be repeated to run sensitivities.

If using Excel, for example, select the IRR function. This requires the annual cash flows to be set out in columns, and the first part of the IRR formula requires the cell reference range of these cash flows to be entered. Then a guess of the IRR is required. The default is 10%, written 0.1.

If a project has the following expected cash flows, then guessing IRR at 30% returns an accurate IRR of 27%, indicating that if the next best way of investing the money gives a return of –20%, the project should go ahead.

Now	–2,500
Year 1	1,200
Year 2	1,300
Year 3	1,500

TRICKS OF THE TRADE

- IRR analysis is generally used to evaluate a project's cash flows rather than income because, unlike income, cash flows do not reflect depreciation and therefore are usually more instructive to appraise.
- Most basic spreadsheet functions apply to cash flows only.
- As well as advocates, IRR has critics who dismiss it as mislead-

▸▸ MORE INFO

Book:

Walsh, Ciaran. *Key Management Ratios*. 4th ed. London: FT Prentice Hall, 2008.

Article:

Baker, Samuel L. "The internal rate of return." March 28, 2006. Online at: hadm.sph.sc.edu/COURSES/ECON/irr/irr.html

ing, especially as significant costs will occur late in the project. The rule of thumb that "the higher the IRR the better" does not always apply.

- For the most thorough analysis of a project's investment potential, some experts urge using both IRR and net present value calculations, and comparing their results.

Liquidity Ratio Analysis

WHAT IT MEASURES

Liquidity ratios are a set of ratios or figures that measure a company's ability to pay off its short-term debt obligations. This is done by measuring a company's liquid assets (including those that might easily be converted into cash) against its short-term liabilities.

There are a number of different liquidity ratios, which each measure slightly different types of assets when calculating the ratio. More conservative measures will exclude assets that need to be converted into cash.

WHY IT IS IMPORTANT

In general, the greater the coverage of liquid assets to short-term liabilities, the more likely it is that a business will be able to pay debts as they become due while still funding ongoing operations. On the other hand, a company with a low liquidity ratio might have difficulty meeting obligations while funding vital ongoing business operations.

Liquidity ratios are sometimes requested by banks when they are evaluating a loan application. If you take out a loan, the lender may require you to maintain a certain minimum liquidity ratio, as part of the loan agreement. For that reason, steps to improve your liquidity ratios are sometimes necessary.

HOW IT WORKS IN PRACTICE

There are three fundamental liquidity ratios that can provide insight into short-term liquidity: current, quick, and cash ratios. These work as follows:

Current Ratio

This is a way of testing liquidity by deriving the proportion of assets available to cover current liabilities, as follows:

$$\text{Current ratio} = \frac{\text{Current assets}}{\text{Current liabilities}}$$

Current ratio is widely discussed in the financial world, and it is easy to understand. However, it can be misleading because the chances of a company ever needing to liquidate all its assets to meet liabilities are very slim indeed. It is often more useful to consider a company as a going concern, in which case you need to understand the time it takes to convert assets into cash, as well as the current ratio.

The current ratio should be at least between 1.5 and 2, although some investors would argue that the figure should be above 2, particularly if a high proportion of assets are stock. A ratio of less than 1 (that is, where the current liabilities exceed the current assets) could mean that you are unable to meet debts as they fall due, in which case you are insolvent. A high current ratio could indicate that too much money is tied up in current assets—for example, giving customers too much credit.

Cash Ratio

This indicates liquidity by measuring the amount of cash, cash equivalents, and invested funds that are available to meet current short-term liabilities. It is calculated by using the following formula:

$$\text{Cash ratio} = \frac{\text{Cash + Cash equivalents + Invested funds}}{\text{Current liabilities}}$$

The cash ratio is a more conservative measure of liquidity than the current ratio, because it only looks at assets that are already liquid, ignoring assets such as receivables or inventory.

Quick Ratio

The third liquidity ratio is a more sophisticated alternative to the current ratio, which measures the most liquid current assets—excluding inventory but including accounts receivable and certain investments.

$$\text{Quick ratio} = \frac{\text{Cash equivalents + Short-term investments + Accounts receivable}}{\text{Current liabilities}}$$

The quick ratio should be around 0.7–1, with very few companies having a cash ratio of over 1. To be absolutely safe, the quick ratio should be at least 1, which indicates that quick assets exceed current liabilities. If the current ratio is rising and the quick ratio is static, this suggests a potential stockholding problem.

TRICKS OF THE TRADE

- All of these ratios have advantages and disadvantages. It is important to remember that any ratio that includes accounts receivable assumes a liquidation of accounts receivable—this may not be possible, practical, or desirable in many situations.
- Liquidity ratios should therefore be considered alongside ratios demonstrating the time it would take to convert assets to cash—a conversion time of several months compared to a few days would seriously affect liquidity.
- Some analysts use a fourth liquidity ratio to measure business performance, known as the "defensive interval." This measures how long a business can survive without cash coming in—and ideally should be between 30 and 90 days.

▸▸ MORE INFO

Book:

Berman, Karen, and Joe Knight, with John Case. "Liquidity ratios: Can we pay our bills?" In *Financial Intelligence: A Manager's Guide to Knowing What the Numbers Really Mean*. Boston, MA: Harvard Business School Press, 2005. Also available separately.

Website:

Business Link on using accounting ratios to assess business performance: www.businesslink.gov.uk/bdotg/action/detail?type=RESOURCES&itemId=1074500081

   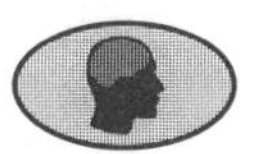  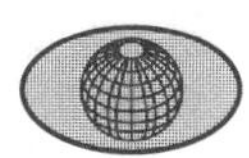 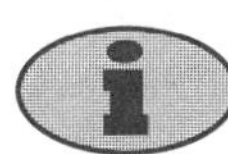  

Management Accounts

WHAT THEY MEASURE

Company accounts fall into two categories: financial and management. While financial accounts are regulated and audited reports of financial transactions and processes, the management accounts are designed to help key business executives understand the overall performance of the business. Most companies produce these reports monthly or quarterly.

WHY THEY ARE IMPORTANT

Rather than focusing on financial metrics, management accounting focuses on operations and the value chain, as opposed to the historical activities of external financial reporting and auditing. They tend to be forward-looking and focused on identifying new revenue, cash flow, profit forecasts, and growth opportunities. Management accounts help executives carry out planning, control, and administration duties effectively. They mean you can see whether profitable parts of the business are subsidizing less successful activities, you can compare performance with forecasts, can identify trends, and manage resources better.

HOW THEY WORK IN PRACTICE

At their most basic, management accounts are reports that provide analysis of business performance and strategy broken down into different business activities or products. Each section of the report should provide an overview of cash flow, profit margins, liabilities, and forecasts for key business metrics.

In practice, management accounts are usually more complex than this. Management accountants may follow any of a number of management accounting methodologies, which will dictate what information is collected, and how it might be presented. Popular approaches to management accounting include:

Lifecycle costing: A form of management accounting that analyses the cost of manufacturing an individual product or service, and looks for how this might be improved.

Activity-based costing: Considers the costs involved in key manufacturing and business processes, such as running a single payroll, or a single product manufacturing cycle.

GPK: A German methodology for management accounting, sometimes known as marginal planned cost accounting. This system was created to provide a consistent, accurate view of how managerial costs are calculated and assigned to a company's products and services.

Lean accounting: A management accounting methodology that was designed in the 1990s for use in just-in-time manufacturing environments and service businesses.

Resource consumption accounting: Focuses on identifying areas with potential for business optimization. Governed by the RCA Institute, this approach to accounting promotes consistency and professionalism in management accounts.

Throughput accounting: Recognizes the relationships between the various elements of the modern manufacturing process, and uses calculations to measure the contribution each part makes per unit of resource.

Management accounting can be applied to virtually any business, and each methodology can be tailored to meet the needs of different industries and sizes of company. However, any management accounting program should incorporate most of the following elements:

- variance analysis
- rate and volume analysis
- price modeling and profit margin analysis
- cost analysis
- cost/benefit analysis
- lifecycle cost analysis
- capital budgeting
- strategic analysis
- annual budgeting
- sales and financial forecasting
- cost allocation

TRICKS OF THE TRADE

- Management accounting is easier if you build in regular systems to capture key information on a daily or weekly basis. Day to day, business managers should record information into a management accounts spreadsheet or application, including details of transactions made, results of financial changes, and projections of future trade.
- There are many off-the-shelf software packages that can be used for this purpose. The key is to select something easy to use—it's not an effective use of resources to spend weeks learning the intricacies of a financial reporting tool if your job is not financial.
- There is no pre-determined format for management accounts, nor any legal requirement to prepare them—but few businesses can survive without them.

▸▸ MORE INFO

Website:

Business Link on management accounts:
www.businesslink.gov.uk/bdotg/action/detail?r.l1=1073858790&r.l3=1073933591&r.lc=en&type=RESOURCES&itemId=1073791255&r.l2=1073858944&r.s=sc

Marginal Cost

Marginal cost is based on the economic theory that the more goods are produced, the lower will be the per-unit cost.

WHAT IT MEASURES

The additional cost of producing one more unit of product, or providing service to one more customer.

WHY IT IS IMPORTANT

Sometimes called incremental cost, marginal cost shows how much costs increase from making or serving one more, an essential factor when contemplating a production increase, or seeking to serve more customers.

If the price charged is greater than the marginal cost, then the revenue gain will be greater than the added cost. That, in turn, will increase profit, so the expansion in production or service makes economic sense and should proceed. Of course, the reverse is also true: If the price charged is less than the marginal cost, expansion should not go ahead.

     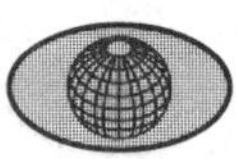   

HOW IT WORKS IN PRACTICE

The formula for marginal cost is:

$$\text{Marginal cost} = \frac{\text{Change in cost}}{\text{Change in quantity}}$$

If it costs a company $260,000 to produce 3,000 items, and $325,000 to produce 3,800 items, the change in cost would be:

325,000 – 260,000 = $65,000

The change in quantity would be:

3,800 – 3,000 = 800

When the formula to calculate marginal cost is applied, the result is:

$$\frac{65{,}000}{800} = \$81.25$$

If the price of the item in question were, say, $99.95, expansion should proceed.

TRICKS OF THE TRADE

- A marginal cost that is lower than the price shows that it is not always necessary to cut prices to sell more goods and boost profits.
- Using idle capacity to produce lower-margin items can still be beneficial, because these generate revenues that help cover fixed costs.
- Marginal cost studies can become quite complicated, because the basic formula does not always take into account variables that can affect cost and quantity. Software programs are available, many of which are industry-specific.
- At some point, marginal cost invariably begins to rise; typically, labor becomes less productive as a production run increases, while the time required also increases.
- Marginal cost alone may not justify expansion. It is best to determine also average costs, then chart the respective series of figures to find where marginal cost meets average cost, and thus determine optimum cost.
- Relying on marginal cost is not fail-safe; putting more product on a market can drive down prices and thus cut margins. Moreover, committing idle capacity to long-term production may tie up resources that could be directed to a new and more profitable opportunity.
- An important related principle is contribution: the cash gained (or lost) from selling an additional unit.

Marginal Rate of Substitution

WHAT IT MEASURES

Sometimes referred to as MRS, the marginal rate of substitution measures the rate at which an individual must give up one asset to obtain a single additional unit of a second asset, while keeping overall utility constant. MRS can measure physical goods, but also assets such as labor or time. The result is generally plotted on an "indifference curve," which shows the utility value for each combination of assets. MRS is also often used to show the rate at which a consumer will substitute one product or service with an alternative.

WHY IT IS IMPORTANT

MRS enables businesses to analyze how a rational user/consumer/organization chooses between two goods. For example, how will a change in the wage rate affect the choice between leisure time and work time? How far will price increases affect a consumer's choice of drinking water?

HOW IT WORKS IN PRACTICE

To calculate MRS, we begin by creating an indifference curve, a line showing all the possible combinations of two goods/assets. The line plots the combinations that result in the same utility or value to the consumer.

In Figure 1, the graph shows a person receives the same utility from 4 hours of work and 6 hours of leisure as from 7 hours of work and 3 hours of leisure.

MRS is the amount of one asset (leisure) that needs to be sacrificed to obtain one unit of the second asset (work) while achieving the same utility (satisfaction).

The simple equation to calculate MRS is as follows:

Figure 1. An example indifference curve

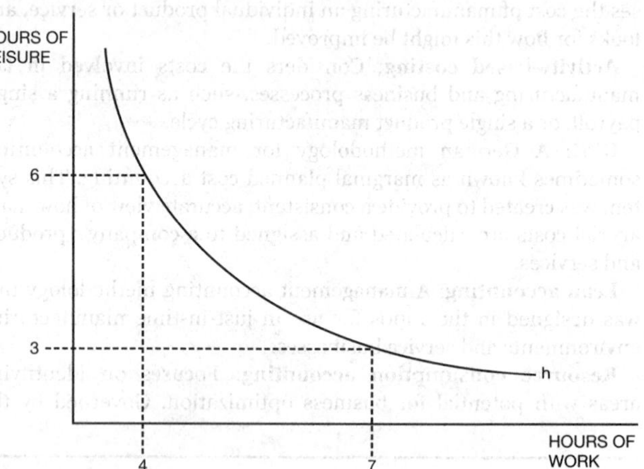

$$\text{MRS} = -dy/dx$$

where d = change in good, and x and y represent different goods, products, or services. This calculation assumes utility remains constant.

For example, if the MRS is 2 then the consumer will give up 2 units of y to obtain one additional unit of x.

Using the example above, the marginal rate of substitution between the two selected variables is:

  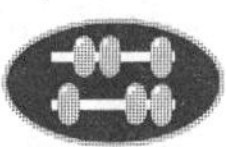   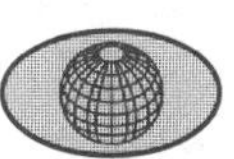   

$$MRS = \frac{-(6-3)}{(4-7)} = \frac{-3}{-3} = 1$$

TRICKS OF THE TRADE

- Marginal rate of substitution diminishes over time because there is a principle of diminishing marginal utility—so the more units are consumed, the less additional satisfaction each addition creates (in other words, the more we consume something, the more willing we are to substitute it away).
- It is possible to create graphs showing more than one indifference curve—in this case, the resulting graph is called an "indifference curve map."
- A key limitation of MRS is that the relationship between two goods remains constant. In reality, it may be that as a worker increases their salary, they desire more leisure time because they have more disposable income. An increase in tea consumption may decrease the marginal utility of coffee.
- It is common to add a budget line to MRS graphs, to separate affordable and unaffordable consumption possibilities.

MORE INFO

Book:

Pindyck, Robert S., and Daniel L. Rubinfeld. *Microeconomics*. 7th ed. Upper Saddle River, NJ: Pearson/Prentice Hall, 2008.

Website:

Answers.com on MRS: www.answers.com/topic/marginal-rate-of-substitution

Market/Book Ratio

WHAT IT MEASURES

Market/book ratio, sometimes called price-to-book ratio, is a way of measuring the relative value of a company compared to its stock price or market value.

WHY IT IS IMPORTANT

Market/book ratio is a useful way of measuring your company's performance and making quick comparisons with competitors. It is an essential figure to potential investors and analysts because it provides a simple way of judging whether a company is under or overvalued. If your business has a low market/book ratio, it's considered a good investment opportunity.

HOW IT WORKS IN PRACTICE

At its most simple, market/book ratio measures the market capitalization (expressed as price per stock) of a business divided by its book value (the value of assets minus liabilities). The book value of a company refers to what would be left if the business paid its liabilities and shut its doors, although, of course, a growing business will always be worth more than its book value because it has the ability to generate new sales.

To calculate market/book ratio, take the current price per stock and divide by the book value per stock:

$$\text{Market/book ratio} = \frac{\text{Market price per stock}}{\text{Book value per stock}}$$

For example, Company A might be trading at $2.20 per stock. However, the book value per stock is actually $3.00. This results in a market/book ratio of 0.73, suggesting the company's assets may in fact be undervalued by 27%.

Market-to-book value can alternatively be calculated as follows:

$$\text{Market/book ratio} = \frac{\text{Market price per stock}}{\text{Net asset value per stock}}$$

TRICKS OF THE TRADE

- Like the price-to-earnings ratio, the lower the price-to-book ratio or market/book ratio, the better the value. Investors would use a low price-to-book ratio on stock screens, for instance, to identify potential candidates for new investment. As a rule of thumb, a market/book ratio above one suggests the company is undervalued, while a ratio over one suggests the company might be overvalued.
- A low market/book ratio could suggest a company's assets are undervalued, or that the company's prospects are good and earnings/value should grow.
- Market/book ratios are most useful when valuing knowledge-intensive companies, where physical assets may not accurately or fully reflect the value of the business. Technology companies and other businesses that don't have a lot of physical assets tend to have low book-to-market ratios.

Net Added Value (NAV) and Adjusted NAV

WHAT IT MEASURES

Net added value, or net asset value, is the value of a corporate asset or business based on its assets minus its liabilities. Adjusted NAV refers to the value once it has been adjusted for any known or suspected differences between market value and book value. In share dealing, NAV refers to the value of a portfolio minus its liabilities.

WHY IT IS IMPORTANT

For investors, the NAV gives an idea of appropriate share prices. For example, if a fund's NAV is $10, you should expect that you can buy the fund's shares for $10 each, although there are exceptions to this rule, such as a newly launched fund. NAV is particularly important when valuing shares in companies where much of the value comes from assets rather than the profit stream—such as investment trusts, but also property companies.

HOW IT WORKS IN PRACTICE

To calculate NAV for an investment portfolio, you should use the following formula:

 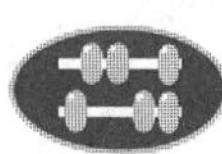   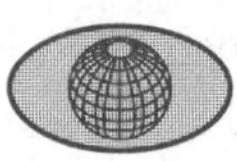 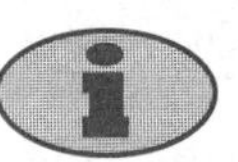  

$$NAV = \frac{\text{Market value of all securities + Cash + Equivalent holdings – Liabilities}}{\text{Total shares outstanding}}$$

For example, if a mutual fund holds $10.5 million in securities, $2 million in cash, and has liabilities totaling $0.5 million, with one million shares outstanding, then the NAV calculation would be as follows:

$$NAV = \frac{10.5 + 2 - 0.5}{1} = \$12$$

TRICKS OF THE TRADE

- When calculating NAV for collective investments such as mutual funds, NAV is the total value of the portfolio less liabilities, calculated on a daily basis. Another alternative measurement for NAV is to add together unit capital and reserves held by a fund.
- In corporate valuations, NAV is the value of assets less liabilities. Assets include anything owned, whether in possession or not, while a liability is anything that is a potential cost to the business. Obviously this means calculating NAV for corporate entities is more difficult, and might be based on book value, carrying value, historical costs, amortized cost, or market value.
- NAV is a good way to keep track of price changes and asset valuations. However, you should keep in mind that the NAV calculation will change from day to day, and does not necessarily reflect the performance of the fund. In the early days of a fund, NAV will rise and fall as the fund's managers take their fees, and each time the fund makes a payout to shareholders. When a fund opens, it often trades at a premium to NAV, later falling to a discount.
- In general, a low NAV is considered a better investment opportunity than a high NAV. However, because NAV values on investment portfolios are calculated daily, critics argue that they are not a good performance indicator.
- In mutual funds, NAV per share is calculated at the close of trading each day based on closing share prices of securities held in the fund's portfolio. Any buy and sell orders are processed based on the day's NAV.
- The price that investors pay to purchase unit trust units is based on the approximate NAV per unit, plus fees that will be imposed by the unit's managers such as purchase fees.
- While you can calculate NAV for almost any business or fund, it is not of any real use when applied to service companies where there are few assets of value, such as plants, property, or equipment.

▸▸ MORE INFO

Websites:

CalcEnstein NAV calculator: www.calcenstein.com/calc/business/1015.php

Money Terms on NAV: moneyterms.co.uk/nav/

US SEC on NAV: www.sec.gov/answers/nav.htm

Net Present Value

Net present value (NPV) expresses the sum total of an investment's future net cash flows (receipts less payments) minus the investment's initial costs. It is an investment appraisal tool.

WHAT IT MEASURES

The projected profitability of an investment, based on anticipated cash flows and discounted at a stated rate of interest.

WHY IT IS IMPORTANT

Net present value helps management or potential investors weigh the wisdom of an investment—in new equipment, a new facility, or other type of asset—by enabling them to quantify the expected benefits. Those evaluating more than one potential investment can compare the respective projected returns to find the most attractive project.

A positive NPV indicates that the project should be profitable, assuming that the estimated cash flows are reasonably accurate. A negative NPV, of course, indicates that the project will probably be unprofitable and therefore should be adjusted, if not abandoned altogether.

Equally significantly, NPV enables a management to consider the time value of money it will invest. This concept holds that the value of money increases with time because it can always earn interest in a savings account. Therefore, any other investment of that money must be weighed against how the funds would perform if simply deposited and saved.

When the time value of money concept is incorporated in the calculation of NPV, the value of a project's future net cash receipts in "today's money" can be determined. This enables proper comparisons between different projects.

HOW IT WORKS IN PRACTICE

Let's say that Global Manufacturing, Inc., is considering the acquisition of a new machine. First, its management would consider all the factors: Initial purchase and installation costs; additional revenues generated by sales of the new machine's products; and the taxes on these new revenues. Having accounted for these factors in its calculations, the cash flows that Global Manufacturing projects will generate from the new machine are:

Year 1	–$100,000 (initial cost of investment)
Year 2	$30,000
Year 3	$40,000
Year 4	$40,000
Year 5	$35,000
Net total	$145,000

At first glance, it appears that cash flows total a whopping 45% more than the $100,000 initial cost, a strikingly sound investment indeed.

Alas, it's not that simple. Time value of money shrinks return on the project considerably, since future dollars are worth less than present dollars in hand. NPV accounts for these differences with the help of present value tables. These user-friendly tables, readily available on the internet and in references, list the ratios that express the present value of expected cash flow dollars, based on the applicable interest rate and the number of years in question.

In our example, Global Manufacturing's cost of capital is 9%. Using this figure to find the corresponding ratios in the present value table, the $100,000 investment cost, and expected annual revenues during the five years in question, the NPV calculation looks like this:

  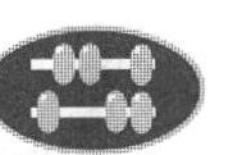 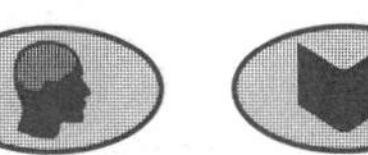 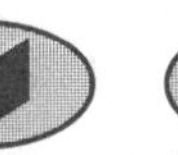 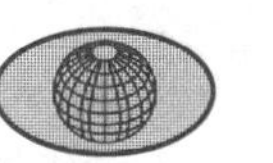   

Year	Cash flow	Table factor (at 9%)	Present value
1	($100,000)	× 1.000000	= ($100,000)
2	$30,000	× 0.917431	= $27,522.93
3	$40,000	× 0.841680	= $33,667.20
4	$40,000	× 0.772183	= $30,887.32
5	$35,000	× 0.708425	= $24,794.88
NPV			$16,873.33

Summing the present values of the cash flows and subtracting the investment cost from the total, the NPV is still positive. So, on this basis at least, the investment should proceed.

TRICKS OF THE TRADE

- Beware of assumptions. Interest rates change, of course, which can affect NPV dramatically. Moreover, fresh revenues (as well as new markets) may not grow as projected. If the cash flows in years 2–5 of our example fall by $5,000 a year, for instance, NPV shrinks to $5,260.89, which is still positive but less attractive.
- NPV calculations are performed only with cash receipts payments and discounting factors. In turn, NPV is a tool, not *the* tool. It ignores other accounting data, intangibles, sheer faith in a new idea, and other factors that may make an investment worth pursuing despite a negative NPV.
- It is important to determine a company's cost of capital accurately.

▸▸ MORE INFO

Book:

Walsh, Ciaran. *Key Management Ratios*. 4th ed. London: FT Prentice Hall, 2008.

Nominal and Real Interest Rates

WHAT THEY MEASURE

When calculating interest rates, the nominal rate of interest refers to an interest rate calculated without any adjustment for inflation or for the full effect of compounding. The real interest rate includes compensation for value lost through inflation, whereas the nominal rate excludes this. Finally, the effective interest rate (sometimes known as the annual equivalent rate, or AER) is a rate that takes account of the impact of compounding.

If you purchase a bond for one year that pays 6% interest at the end of the 12 months, a $100 investment would return $106. The 6% interest is a nominal interest rate—it does not account for inflation during that year.

Imagine investing in the same bond and accounting for a 3% inflation rate for the year. If you buy an item for $100 at the start of the year, the same item would cost $103 at the end of the year. If we then invest the $100 into the 6% bond for one year, we lose $3 to inflation—meaning the real interest rate of the bond is actually 3%.

Alternatively, imagine investing the same $100 into the bond over 12 months. At 6%, your money would return $106 after one year. However, if interest is compounded every six months, you will actually earn slightly more. After six months, you would earn $3 interest. At the end of the year, the bond will pay 3% of your new investment total of $103, or $3.09. Your investment would then return $106.09 over a year, making the effective annual rate 6.09%, slightly higher than the nominal interest rate of 6%.

WHY THEY ARE IMPORTANT

When calculating interest rates, most calculations ignore the cost to the lender of not having funds available for a period of time—by the time a loan is repaid, the cost of items may have increased so that the money is now worth less. If you know what inflation is going to be, real interest rates are a powerful tool in analyzing the value of potential investments, because they take account of the erosion of spending power over the lifetime of an investment.

Calculating the effective rate is important because interest on different investments might be paid weekly, monthly, or annually. The effective annual interest rate can compare the returns or costs of different loans more accurately than a nominal interest rate.

HOW THEY WORK IN PRACTICE

The difference between real and nominal interest rates is simply expressed as: Real interest rate = Nominal rate − Inflation. More formally, it can also be described in the equation:

$$(1 + N) = (1 + r) - (1 + i)$$

where:

N is the nominal interest rate
r is the real interest rate
i is the rate of inflation

This calculation is sometimes referred to as the Fisher equation. If you do not know the rate of inflation, it can be predicted using the following formula:

$$i = \frac{\text{CPI this year} - \text{CPI last year}}{\text{CPI last year}}$$

If you know the nominal interest rate and the number of compounding periods, it is possible to calculate the effective annual rate using the following formula:

$$\text{EAR} = (1 + N/P)^{P-1}$$

where:

N is the nominal rate
P is the number of compounding periods

TRICKS OF THE TRADE

- If inflation is positive then the real interest rate will be lower than the nominal interest rate. If the economy is experiencing deflation and the inflation rate is negative, then real interest is higher than nominal interest rates.
- When calculating effective interest rates, remember they will generally not include one-off charges such as set-up fees. In addition, while financial regulators closely control how the APR is expressed, there are fewer controls on the AER.
- The Fisher hypothesis states that, over time, inflation and nominal interest rates move together, so real interest rates are stable

  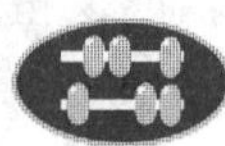   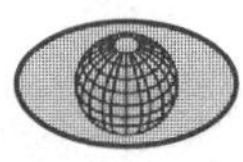   

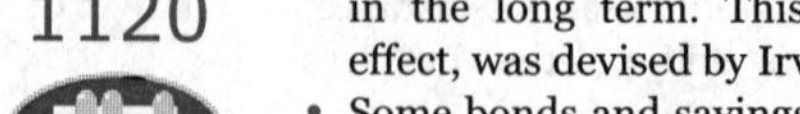

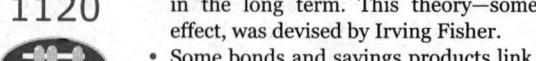

in the long term. This theory—sometimes called the Fisher effect, was devised by Irving Fisher.

- Some bonds and savings products link payments to an inflation index, so in effect pay a real interest rate. An example would be government-issued gilt.
- Sometimes it can be beneficial to value investments without taking inflation into account. This can be done by discounting using real interest rates.

▸▸ MORE INFO

Article:

Moffatt, Mike. "What's the difference between nominal and real? Real variables and nominal variables explained." *About.com*. Online at: economics.about.com/cs/macrohelp/a/nominal_vs_real.htm

Option Pricing

WHAT IT MEASURES

There are two sorts of options in stock market trading: call and put. Option pricing uses mathematical models to calculate the value of a stock option and how it changes in response to changing conditions.

There are two key components to option pricing: the intrinsic value, which measures the amount by which an option is "in the money;" and the time value, which measures the amount paid for the time the option has before it expires.

WHY IT IS IMPORTANT

Stock traders use option pricing models to predict which options can be used to capture a potential move in a stock, and gain advantage in a trade. Option pricing is also important in risk management, because it can be used to quantify the risk associated with buying, selling, owning, and trading specific options with a high level of accuracy.

HOW IT WORKS IN PRACTICE

To understand option pricing, you must understand the four basic drivers of option prices: current stock price, intrinsic value, time to expiration, and volatility.

Stock price is important because if the price of a stock rises, the cost of a call option will also rise (though not necessarily at the same rate).

Intrinsic value is important because it measures how far an option is "in the money" (ITM), or what proportion of the option's value isn't lost over time. The intrinsic value of the call option is the stock price minus the call strike price.

Time value is the difference between the option's price and its intrinsic value. The more time an option has until it expires, the greater chance it will become "in the money"—and therefore the option becomes more valuable.

Option pricing is related to volatility expected in the market up to the time of expiration. If the market expects little movement in a stock's value, volatility is low, which results in a lower time value.

The most well-known method of modeling option pricing was developed by Fischer Black and Myron Scholes in 1973. The Black–Scholes model works as follows:

$$C = SN(d_1) - Ke^{(-rt)} N(d_2)$$

where:
C = call premium
S = current stock price
t = time to expiration
k = option price
r = risk-free interest rate
N = normal distribution
e = exponential term

The first part of the calculation, $SN(d_1)$, shows the expected benefit of buying the stock outright. This is calculated by multiplying together the stock price and the change in call premium caused by a change in the underlying stock price.

The second part of the equation shows the present value of paying the exit price on the day the option expires. The fair value of the option price is then calculated by looking at the difference between the option's current value and value at expiration.

The Black–Scholes model of option pricing relies on several assumptions, which should be taken into account. These are:

- the stock pays no dividends during the option's life
- the stock can only be exercised on the expiration date
- markets are efficient
- no commissions are charged
- interest rates are consistent, predictable, and known
- returns are normally distributed

TRICKS OF THE TRADE

- A major potential limitation of the Black–Scholes model is the assumption that no dividends are paid on stock during the lifetime of the option—because most stocks do pay dividends. One way to resolve this is to subtract the discounted value of a future dividend from the stock price.
- In Europe, it is common that options can only be exercised on the expiration date, whereas in the United States they might be exercised at any time. This makes American options more flexible and therefore more valuable.
- The Black–Scholes model has been refined over time by a number of financial scholars, including Merton (who devised a model to take account of dividends) and Ingerson (who devised a model that did not require constant interest rates).

▸▸ MORE INFO

Article:

Wagner, Hans. "Understanding option pricing." *Investopedia*. Online at: www.investopedia.com/articles/optioninvestor/07/options_beat_market.asp

Website:

Risk Glossary on option pricing theory: www.riskglossary.com/articles/option_pricing_theory.htm

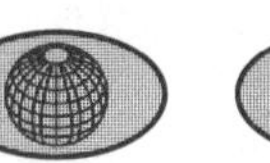

Payback Period

At first glance, payback is a simple investment appraisal technique, but it can quickly become complex.

WHAT IT MEASURES

How long it will take to earn back the money invested in a project.

WHY IT IS IMPORTANT

The straight payback period method is the simplest way of determining the investment potential of a major project. Expressed in time, it tells a management how many months or years it will take to recover the original cash cost of the project—always a vital consideration, and especially so for managements evaluating several projects at once.

This evaluation becomes even more important if it includes an examination of what the present value of future revenues will be.

HOW IT WORKS IN PRACTICE

The straight payback period formula is:

$$\text{Payback period} = \frac{\text{Cost of project}}{\text{Annual cash revenues}}$$

Thus, if a project costs $100,000 and is expected to generate $28,000 annually, the payback period would be:

$$\frac{100{,}000}{28{,}000} = 3.57 \text{ years}$$

If the revenues generated by the project are expected to vary from year to year, add the revenues expected for each succeeding year until you arrive at the total cost of the project.

For example, say the revenues expected to be generated by the $100,000 project are:

Year	Revenue	Total
Year 1	$19,000	$19,000
Year 2	$25,000	$44,000
Year 3	$30,000	$74,000
Year 4	$30,000	$104,000
Year 5	$30,000	$134,000

Thus, the project would be fully paid for in Year 4, since it is in that year that the total revenue reaches the initial cost of $100,000.

The picture becomes complex when the time value of money principle is introduced into the calculations. Some experts insist this is essential to determine the most accurate payback period. Accordingly, present value tables or computers (now the norm) must be used, and the annual revenues have to be discounted by the applicable interest rate, 10% in this example. Doing so produces significantly different results:

Year	Revenue	Present value	Total
Year 1	$19,000	$17,271	$17,271
Year 2	$25,000	$20,650	$37,921
Year 3	$30,000	$22,530	$60,451
Year 4	$30,000	$20,490	$80,941
Year 5	$30,000	$18,630	$99,571

This method shows that payback would not occur even after five years.

TRICKS OF THE TRADE

- Clearly, a main defect of the straight payback period method is that it ignores the time value of money principle, which, in turn, can produce unrealistic expectations.
- A second drawback is that it ignores any benefits generated after the payback period, and thus a project that would return $1 million after, say, six years might be ranked lower than a project with a three-year payback that returns only $100,000 thereafter.
- Another alternative to calculating by payback period is to develop an internal rate of return.
- Under most analyses, projects with shorter payback periods rank higher than those with longer paybacks, even if the latter promise higher returns. Longer paybacks can be affected by such factors as market changes, changes in interest rates, and economic shifts. Shorter cash paybacks also enable companies to recoup an investment sooner and put it to work elsewhere.
- Generally, a payback period of three years or less is desirable; if a project's payback period is less than a year, some contend it should be judged essential.

Payout Ratio

Dividend cover, and its US equivalent, payout ratio, is a quick reflection of profitability, which is used to evaluate and select investments.

WHAT IT MEASURES

Dividend cover expresses the number of times a company's dividends to common stockholders could be paid out of its net after-tax profits.

Payout ratio expresses the total dividends paid to stockholders as a percentage of a company's net profit in a given period of time.

WHY IT IS IMPORTANT

Whether defined as dividend cover or payout ratio, it measures the likelihood of dividend payments being sustained, and thus is a useful indication of sustained profitability. However, each ratio must be interpreted independently.

A low dividend cover suggests it might be difficult to pay the same level of dividends in a downturn, and that a company is not reinvesting enough in its future. High cover, therefore, implies just the opposite. Negative dividend cover is unusual, and a clear sign of trouble.

The payout ratio, expressed as a percentage or fraction, is an inverse measure: A high ratio indicates a lack of reinvestment in the business, and that current earnings cannot sustain the current dividend payments. In other words, the lower the ratio, the more secure the dividend—and the company's future.

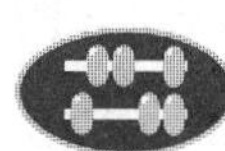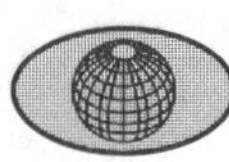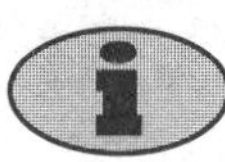

HOW IT WORKS IN PRACTICE

Dividend cover is so named because it shows how many times over the profits could have paid the dividend. If the figure is 3, for example, a firm's profits are three times the level of the dividend paid to shareholders. To calculate dividend cover, divide earnings per share by the dividend per share:

$$\text{Dividend cover} = \frac{\text{Earnings per share}}{\text{Dividend per share}}$$

If a company has earnings per share of $8, and it pays out a dividend of $2.10, dividend cover is:

$$\frac{\$8}{\$2.10} = 3.80$$

An alternative formula divides a company's net profit by the total amount allocated for dividends. So a company that earns $10 million in net profit and allocates $1 million for dividends has a dividend cover of 10, while a company that earns $25 million and pays out $10 million in dividends has a dividend cover of 2.5:

$$\frac{\$10{,}000{,}000}{\$1{,}000{,}000} = 10$$

$$\frac{\$25{,}000{,}000}{\$10{,}000{,}000} = 2.5$$

The payout ratio is calculated by dividing annual dividends paid on common stock by earnings per share:

$$\text{Payout ratio} = \frac{\text{Annual dividend}}{\text{Earnings per share}}$$

Take the company whose earnings per share is $8 and dividend payout is $2.10. Its payout ratio would be:

$$\frac{2.10}{8 = 0.263} = 26.3\%$$

TRICKS OF THE TRADE

- A dividend cover ratio of 2 or higher is usually adequate, and indicates that the dividend is affordable. By the same token, the payout ratio should not exceed two-thirds of earnings. Like most ratios, however, both vary by industry. US real estate investment trusts, for example, pay out almost all their earnings in dividends because US tax laws exempt them from taxes if they do so. American utilities also offer high payout rates.
- A dividend cover ratio below 1.5 is risky, and a ratio below 1 indicates that a company is paying the current year's dividend with retained earnings from a previous year—a practice that cannot continue indefinitely.
- The higher the dividend cover figure, the less likely the dividend will be reduced or eliminated in the future, should profits fall. Companies that suffer sharp declines or outright losses will often continue paying dividends to indicate that their substandard performance is an anomaly.
- On the other hand, a high dividend cover figure may disappoint an investor looking for income, since the figure suggests directors could have declared a larger dividend.
- A high payout ratio clearly appeals to conservative investors seeking income. However, when coupled with weak or falling earnings it could suggest an imminent dividend cut, or that the company is short-changing reinvestment to maintain its payout.
- A payout ratio above 75% is a warning. It suggests the company is failing to reinvest sufficient profits in its business, that the company's earnings are faltering, or that it is trying to attract investors who otherwise would not be interested.
- Newer and faster-growing companies often pay no dividends at all in order to reinvest earnings in the company's development.
- Historically, dividends have provided more than 40% of a stock investor's total portfolio return. However, the figure has been about half that over the last 20 years.

Portfolio Analysis: Duration, Convexity, and Immunization

WHAT THEY MEASURE

Duration is a measure of how sensitive the price of bonds are to changes in interest rates (otherwise known as interest rate risk). For example, if interest rates rise 1%, a bond with a two-year duration will fall about 2% in value. Convexity is a measure of how prices rise when yields fall, and can also be used to measure interest rate risk.

WHY THEY ARE IMPORTANT

Using a combination of duration and convexity allows traders to hedge investments to minimize or offset the impact of changes in interest rates—a process known as immunization.

HOW THEY WORK IN PRACTICE

Duration is a weighted average of the present value of a bond's payments. It provides an insight into how sensitive a bond or portfolio is to changes in interest rates. The longer the duration, the longer the average maturity and, therefore, the bond's sensitivity to interest rate changes. Securities with the same duration have the same interest rate risk exposure. Duration can be expressed in years (to average maturity) or as a percentage (the percentage change in price for a 1% change in its yield to maturity).

$$\text{Duration} = \frac{P_- - P_+}{2 \times P_0 \times \Delta y}$$

where:
P_o = bond price
P_- = bond price when interest rates are incremented
P+ = bond price when rates are decremented
Δy = change in interest rates (decimal form)

Convexity is a measure of the rate at which duration changes as yields fall, and is expressed in squared time (t + 1). To estimate

   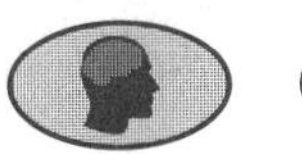  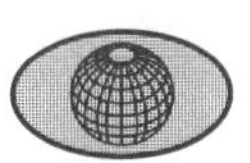   

the convexity of a bond or portfolio, we can use the following formula:

$$\text{Convexity approximation} = \frac{P_+ + P_- - 2P_0}{2P_0(\Delta y)^2}$$

Immunization: To immunize a portfolio, you need to know the duration of the bonds and adjust the portfolio so the duration is equal to the investment time horizon. For example, you might select bonds that you know will return $10,000 in five years' time regardless of interest rate changes.

Normally, when interest rates go up, bond prices go down. But if a portfolio is immunized, the investor receives a specific rate of return over time regardless of what happens to interest rates, because the portfolio's duration is equal to the investor's time horizon. This means any changes to interest rates will affect the bond's price and reinvestment at the same rate, keeping the rate of return steady. Maintaining an immunized portfolio means rebalancing the portfolio's average duration every time interest rates change, so that the average duration continues to equal the investor's time horizon.

TRICKS OF THE TRADE

- The concept of duration was first developed by Frederick Macaulay in 1938, as a tool for measuring bond price volatility in relation to the length of a bond. However, there are other formulae for calculating duration, including "effective duration" and "modified duration."
- Convexity is usually a positive term, but sometimes the term is negative, such as occurs when a callable bond is nearing its call price. In this case, traders use modified convexity, which is the measured convexity when there is no expected change in future cash flows, or effective convexity, which is the convexity measure for a bond for which future cash flows are expected to change.
- The notion of bond convexity should not be confused with the convexity of the yield curve (see: Term Structure of Interest Rates). The latter can assume an arbitrary shape (although a normal yield curve has negative convexity), and complex stochastic models have been proposed for its evolution.

▸▸ MORE INFO

Article:

Radcliffe, Brent. "Immunization inoculates against interest rate risk." *Investopedia*. Online at: www.investopedia.com/articles/financial-theory/09/bond-interest-rate-immunization.asp

Website:

This Matter on duration and convexity: thismatter.com/money/bonds/duration-convexity.htm

Price/Earnings Ratio

WHAT IT MEASURES

The price/earnings (P/E) ratio is simply the stock price divided by earnings per share (EPS). While EPS is an actual amount of money, usually expressed in cents per share, the P/E ratio has no units—it is just a number. Thus if a quoted company has a stock price of $100 and EPS of $12 for the last published year, then it has a historical P/E of 8.3. If analysts are forecasting for the next year an EPS of, say, $14 then the forecast P/E is 7.1.

WHY IT IS IMPORTANT

Since EPS is the annual earnings per share of a company, it follows that dividing the stock price by EPS tells us how many years of current EPS are represented by the stock price. In the above example, then, the P/E of 8.3 tells us that investors at the current price are prepared to pay 8.3 years of historical EPS for the stock, or 7.1 years of the forecast next year's EPS. Theoretically, the faster a company is expected to grow, the higher the P/E ratio that investors would award it. It is one measure of how cheap or expensive a stock appears to be.

HOW IT WORKS IN PRACTICE

Forecasts can go wrong, of course, resulting in the infamous profit warnings that are issued by some companies. In these they warn that expected profit targets, for various reasons, will not be met. Understandably, a slump in the stock price is the normal reaction, and analysts would then downgrade their existing forecast EPS. If, in the above example, our forecast of $14 for next year was halved to $7 following a profit warning, the forecast P/E on the same price of $100 would immediately double to 14.3—but in practice the price would usually fall substantially, thus cutting back the forecast P/E.

The P/E ratio is mainly useful in comparisons with other stocks rather than in isolation. For example, if the average P/E in the market is 20, there will be many stocks with P/Es well above and well below this, for a variety of reasons. Similarly, in a particular sector, the P/Es will frequently vary quite widely from the sector average, even though the constituent companies may all be engaged in broadly similar businesses. The reason is that even two businesses doing the same thing will not always be doing it as profitably as each other. One may be far more efficient, as demonstrated by a history of rising EPS compared with the flat EPS picture of the other over a series of years, and the market might recognize this by awarding the more profitable stock a higher P/E.

TRICKS OF THE TRADE

- Take care. The market frequently gets it wrong and many high-P/E stocks have in the past been the most awful long-term investments, losing investors huge amounts of money when the promise of future rapid growth proved to be a chimera. In contrast, many low-P/E companies, often in what are perceived as dull industries, have proved over time to be outstanding investments.
- The P/E is an investment tool that is both invaluable and yet requires extreme caution in its application when comparing and selecting investments. It remains, however, by far the most commonly utilized ratio in investment analysis.

▸▸ MORE INFO

Book:

Walsh, Ciaran. *Key Management Ratios*. 4th ed. London: FT Prentice Hall, 2008.

 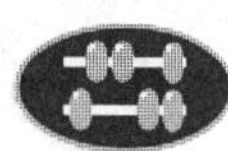   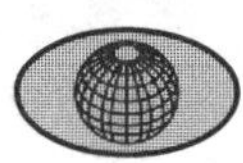   

Price Elasticity

WHAT IT MEASURES

Price elasticity (sometimes known as price elasticity of demand, or PED) measures how demand for a product or service changes when the price charged is changed.

WHY IT IS IMPORTANT

Price elasticity enables you to predict how sales will be impacted if the price of a product or service is raised. Elasticity measures the responsiveness of consumers to changes in price, and gives businesses a curve to help analyze demand as it relates to price. Businesses can use elasticity to make effective pricing strategies. For example, if demand is inelastic, it may be possible to increase revenues by increasing the price of a product. If demand is elastic, however, businesses would be more likely to invest in advertising to try and build brand loyalty and create inelastic demand.

HOW IT WORKS IN PRACTICE

The basic formula to calculate price elasticity is as follows:

$$\text{Price elasticity} = \frac{\text{Percentage change in quantity demanded}}{\text{Percentage change in price}}$$

To calculate price elasticity on a product that has changed in price from $10 to $12, we need to know the quantity of goods sold at each price. Imagine that at $10, your company sold 150,000 items but at $12, the company sold 110,000 items.

Next, you need to calculate the percentage change in quantity and the percentage change in price. To calculate the percentage change in quantity demanded, use the following calculation:

$$\frac{\text{New quantity} - \text{Old quantity}}{\text{Old quantity}}$$

So:

$$\frac{110{,}000 - 150{,}000}{150{,}000} = \frac{-40}{150} = -0.2667 = -26.67\%$$

While the percentage change in price is calculated as follows:

$$\frac{\text{New price} - \text{Old price}}{\text{Old price}}$$

So:

$$\frac{12 - 10}{12} = \frac{2}{12} = 0.1667 = 16.67\%$$

Using these two figures we calculate the price elasticity as follows:

$$\frac{-26.67\%}{16.67\%} = -1.6$$

We can therefore conclude, ignoring the minus sign as is conventional, the price elasticity of this product, when the price increases from $10 to $12, is 1.6.

TRICKS OF THE TRADE

- When interpreting elasticity figures, the higher the number, the more sensitive consumers are to price changes. A very high figure suggests that if the price goes up, demand for the product or service will fall steeply. A lower figure suggests demand will not be substantially affected by price increases. This type of product is known as "inelastic."
- As a rule of thumb, an inelastic product will have a price elasticity score of one or less. If the elasticity of demand is exactly one, then a small increase or fall in price would result in value of sales remaining steady—the change in volume will exactly balance.
- Sometimes you will find negative elasticity scores (as in the example above)—when prices increase by 10% and sales fall by 20%, the elasticity score would be −2, for example. However, when using elasticity scores, the negative is ignored and expressed simply as the absolute figure "2."
- Elasticity scores change more dramatically over longer periods. This is because people have time to change buying habits over a period of time. Sales might therefore not be affected much by a price increase in year 1, but be significantly impacted by year 3.
- Goods that are elastic tend to be luxury or expensive purchases (cars, holidays, etc) while inelastic goods are those where there are many alternatives available, and which are bought frequently (bread or milk, for example).
- Elasticity is unlikely to be the same across an entire market. Certain firms will always be able to charge above market rates, while others will tend to under-cut the market price to maintain revenues.

▸▸ MORE INFO

Websites:

Money Terms on price elasticity: moneyterms.co.uk/price-elasticity/

Quick MBA on price elasticity of demand: www.quickmba.com/econ/micro/elas/ped.shtml

Robert Schenk on price elasticity: ingrimayne.com/econ/elasticity/Elastic1.html

Price/Sales Ratio

WHAT IT MEASURES

The price/sales (P/S) ratio is another measure, like the price/earnings (P/E) ratio, of the relative value of a stock when compared with others.

WHY IT IS IMPORTANT

Like many such price-based ratios, it does not mean too much in isolation but acquires worth when making comparisons. So a figure of 0.33 does not say a lot on its own, until you start to look at how this matches up to the market average or the sector average, for example.

HOW IT WORKS IN PRACTICE

The P/S ratio is obtained by dividing the market capitalization by

     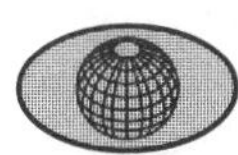   

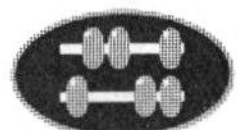

the latest published annual sales figure. So a company with a capitalization of $1 billion and sales of $3 billion would have a P/S ratio of 0.33.

P/S will vary with the type of industry. You would expect, for example, that many retailers and other large-scale distributors of goods would have very high sales in relation to their market capitalizations—in other words, a very low P/S. Equally, manufacturers of high-value items would generally have much lower sales figures and thus higher P/S ratios. Like anything to do with share analysis (this being more of an art than a science), it is not always that clear cut. . .but that would be the general trend. If you rank companies by ascending P/S, you will usually find that supermarket chains figure among the lowest.

A company with a lower P/S is cheaper than one with a higher ratio, particularly if they are in the same sector so that a direct comparison is appropriate. The lower P/S means that each share of the company is buying you more of its sales than those of the higher P/S company.

Note, though, that it is cheaper only on P/S grounds; that does not mean it is necessarily the more attractive share. There will often be reasons why it has a lower ratio than another, ostensibly similar, company, most commonly because it is less profitable. As far as corporate efficiency goes, this ratio considers only sales, the top line of the profit and loss account. It is a long way from there to the bottom line, the bit that really counts (that is, how much profit the company has made).

TRICKS OF THE TRADE

- A company with a loss would thus still have a P/S ratio, even though it would have no P/E ratio. In consequence, like all investment analysis tools, P/S has to be used with care—but it can be of use for investors. P/S was cited in an extensive study of the New York Stock Exchange as one leading indicator for selecting very long-term shares that perform well.

▸▸ MORE INFO

Book:

O'Shaughnessy, James. *What Works on Wall Street: A Guide to the Best-Performing Investment Strategies of All Time*. 3rd ed. New York: McGraw-Hill, 2005.

Quantitative Methods

WHAT THEY ARE

Quantitative methods are a number of statistical and mathematical tools that can be used to capture and analyze information on quantitative data—anything that can be measured or counted.

What differentiates quantitative from qualitative methods is that quantitative methods usually rely on a variation of the scientific method to generate measurable results. Quantitative methods are therefore formulae and models used to generate hypotheses, capture and measure data, or evaluate the results.

WHY THEY ARE IMPORTANT

Imagine you wanted to know whether a particular action would increase the yield of a bond portfolio. If you perform the action once and the yield increases, would you be convinced? If it happened three times consecutively, would you be convinced?

Quantitative methods are used to measure and model outcomes, eliminating rogue results and other influences. Formulating a financial problem or hypothesis into a quantitative model allows us to apply statistical analysis to the problem and calculate the probability of certain outcomes—such as how likely a yield is to increase when a specific action is taken.

For investment managers, quantitative methods are most commonly used to value different classes of securities, analyze criteria for guiding investment decisions, measure risk and asset return, and use statistical techniques for forecasting. They can also be used for calculating yields and prices, frequency distributions, risk and probability, correlation, and regression analysis.

HOW THEY WORK IN PRACTICE

As previously discussed, in finance, quantitative methods are used to perform statistical analysis on a range of financial hypotheses and problems. The first stage in any quantitative method is the development of a theory or hypothesis, against which data can be measured or compared, followed by the application of either descriptive or inferential statistical methods.

Descriptive statistical methods describe properties of the data in front of us, while inferential methods allow us to draw conclusions from data in front of us. For example:

"The average income of the portfolio was $2.8 million per annum over the five-year period" is a descriptive statistic, while "The sample of 50 annual yields from the total portfolio indicates the average income of the portfolio was between $2.6 and $2.9 million per annum," is an inferential statistic.

To test your hypothesis, you might use any of a number of statistical tools, the most common including linear regression. The classical linear regression model (CLRM) is used in finance to estimate unknown parameters using statistical methods. Once you have created regression boundaries you can compute confidence intervals and perform hypothesis testing. An alternative approach is the multiple linear regression model (MLRM), which is used for hypothesis testing in scenarios where there is more than one unknown variable.

Other statistical methods used in quantitative analysis include forecasting tools such as correlation analysis, co-efficiency of correlations, and determination and learning curves.

TRICKS OF THE TRADE

- Although quantitative methods have existed since people first recorded numerical data, the modern idea of quantitative methods has its roots in Auguste Comte's positivist framework.
- Quantitative methods also incorporate the basic principles of statistical interference—the process of making inferences from a small sample about the behavior of a larger population. Two main approaches are estimation and hypothesis testing.

▸▸ MORE INFO

Books:

Brealey, Richard A., Stewart C. Myers, and Franklin Allen. *Principles of Corporate Finance*. 9th ed. Boston, MA: McGraw-Hill, 2008.

Gujarati, Damodar N. *Essentials of Econometrics*. 3rd ed. Boston, MA: McGraw-Hill, 2006.

Oakshott, Les. *Essential Quantitative Methods for Business, Management and Finance*. 3rd ed. Basingstoke, UK: Palgrave Macmillan, 2006.

   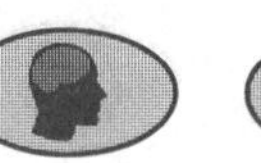 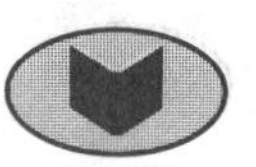 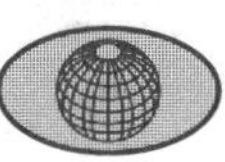   

Rate of Return

This may well be as basic and important a computation as there is in finance.

WHAT IT MEASURES

The annual return on an investment, expressed as a percentage of the total amount invested. It also measures the yield of a fixed-income security.

WHY IT IS IMPORTANT

Rate of return is a simple and straightforward way to determine how much investors are being paid for the use of their money, so that they can then compare various investments and select the best—based, of course, on individual goals and acceptable levels of risk.

Rate of return has a second and equally vital purpose: As a common denominator that measures a company's financial performance, for example, in terms of rate of return on assets, equity, or sales.

HOW IT WORKS IN PRACTICE

There is a basic formula that will serve most needs, at least initially:

$$\text{Rate of return} = \frac{\text{Current value of amount invested} - \text{Original value of amount invested}}{\text{Original value of amount invested}}$$

If $1,000 in capital is invested in stock, and one year later the investment yields $1,100, the rate of return of the investment is calculated like this:

$$\frac{1100 - 1000}{1000} = 0.1 = 10\%$$

Now, assume $1,000 is invested again. One year later, the investment grows to $2,000 in value, but after another year the value of the investment falls to $1,200. The rate of return after the first year is:

$$\frac{2000 - 1000}{1000} = 1 = 100\%$$

The rate of return after the second year is:

$$\frac{1200 - 2000}{2000} = -0.4 = -40\%$$

The average annual return for the two years (also known as average annual arithmetic return) can be calculated using this formula:

$$\text{Average annual return} = \frac{\text{Rate of return for year 1} + \text{Rate of return for year 2}}{2}$$

Accordingly:

$$\frac{100\% + -40\%}{2} = 30\%$$

Be careful, however! The average annual rate of return is a percentage, but one that is accurate over only a short period, so this method should be used accordingly.

The geometric or compound rate of return is a better yardstick for measuring investments over the long run, and takes into account the effects of compounding. As one might expect, this formula is more complex and technical, and beyond the scope of this article.

TRICKS OF THE TRADE

- The real rate of return is the annual return realized on an investment, adjusted for changes in the price due to inflation. If 10% is earned on an investment but inflation is 2%, then the real rate of return is actually 8%.
- Do not confuse rate of return with internal rate of return, which is a more complex calculation.
- Some mutual fund managers have been known to report the average annual rate of return on the investments they manage. In the second example, that figure is 30%, yet the value of the investment is only $200 higher than it was two years ago, or 20%. So, read such reports carefully.

▸▸ MORE INFO

Book:

Walsh, Ciaran. *Key Management Ratios*. 4th ed. London: FT Prentice Hall, 2008.

Reading an Annual Report

GETTING STARTED

Many companies must publish an annual report to its stockholders as a matter of corporate law. The primary purpose of this report is to inform stockholders of the company's performance. As a legal requirement, the report usually contains a profit and loss account, a balance sheet, a cash flow statement, a directors' report, and an auditors' report. The different elements tell you about different aspects of the company's performance and can be read in a particular order to build up a true picture of how it is doing.

Many companies also provide a lot of other nonstatutory information on their affairs, in the interests of general communication. In some cases, this may be little more than gloss, contrived to illustrate the company's wonderful achievements while remaining strangely silent on negative features.

FAQS

Is there any difference between annual reports from private and public companies?

The main difference is usually length. The reports of privately held companies are far shorter because their mandatory reporting requirements are much reduced. Additionally, they are less concerned with image, and consequently will tend to omit the noncompulsory public relations features that are present in public company reports.

What guarantee is there that an annual report is a true picture of a company's performance and not just propaganda put out by directors?

All annual reports have to include a report from the auditors, who are independent accountants charged with investigating a company's financial affairs to ensure that the published figures give a true and fair view of performance. Their investigation cannot extend to examining every single transaction (impossible in a company of any size), so they use statistical sampling and other risk-based testing procedures to assess the quality of the company's systems as a basis for producing the annual report. They are not infallible, but they stand between the stockholders and the directors as a way of trying to ensure probity in the running of a company.

MAKING IT HAPPEN

Understanding the Main Contents of an Annual Report

The best way to look at this is to take an example. Standard sections in annual reports can vary from country to country, but the following is the contents list of the annual report of a medium-sized US public company—let's call it X, Inc.

- X World;
- Chairman's Statement;
- Chief Executive's Review;
- Financial Review;
- Board of Directors;
- Board Report on Remuneration;
- Directors' Responsibilities;
- Report of the Auditors;
- Financial Statements;
- Five-Year Record;
- Stockholder Information.

Here's what each of these sections is about:

X World: Belongs in the PR area. It tells you about the company, its products and markets.

Chairman's Statement: Comments on the group results for the year and on future developments. It also provides detail on earnings per share and dividends.

Chief Executive's Review: Goes into more detail about individual divisions, breaking down the operating results from areas around the world. It tells us a bit about discontinued businesses and new ones acquired.

Financial Review: Expands on the two previous sections in a more quantitative way, looking at things like cash flow and how it affected group debt; interest charges; the effect of exchange rate fluctuations on profits, assets and liabilities; exceptional items that affect the profits (such as the disposal of a subsidiary company), and so on.

Board of Directors: Lists the directors, with a brief description and photo of each.

Board Report on Remuneration: Describes the work of a committee of nonexecutive directors, who decide the directors' income and that of other senior employees. Their remit includes looking at service contracts, bonus and stock option plans, plus pension plans. It includes an analysis of the pay of each director, with comparable figures for the previous year, plus details of stock options, and so on.

Directors' Responsibilities: A mandatory statement showing exactly what the directors are obliged to discharge with regard to the annual report, maintaining accurate accounting records, and so on.

Report of the Auditors: This is simply what it says. Their findings are published using standard language.

Financial Statements: These are the main purpose of the annual report. In the example of X, Inc., they consist of:

- *Consolidated Profit and Loss Account.* The profit and loss account of all the group as one consolidated account.
- *Consolidated and Company Balance Sheets.* The former is the group balance sheet and the latter is for the parent company alone.
- *Consolidated Cash Flow Statement.* A guide to how the money flowing in and out of the company was utilized.
- *Management's Responsibility for Financial Reporting.*
- *Management's Discussion and Analysis.*
- *Notes to the Financial Statements.* These amplify numerous points contained in the figures and are usually critical for anyone wishing to study the financial statements in detail.

Five-Year Record: Shows a very abbreviated set of profit and loss and balance sheet figures for the current and previous four years. Some companies provide a 10-year record.

Stockholder Information: Deals with matters such as the registered office, stockholder registrars, brokers, lawyers, dates for meetings and dividend payments, and other points.

Choosing the Right Order in which to Read the Report

One way is simply to read the report from cover to cover, like a book. However, if you are not experienced with these things, that may lead you to giving equal weight to all the contents and, perhaps, overvaluing the glossy PR bits at the expense of the hard facts shown by the figures.

Start with the Auditors' Report

Remember that this thin gray line of accountants is all that stands between the outside stockholder and the directors. To speed up matters, look at the final paragraph—their opinion. Does that statement give a true and fair view? If so, fine. If not, then it is said to be "qualified." Qualifications vary in depth from the disastrous, meaning that the company has gotten something seriously wrong, to perhaps a difference of opinion between the auditors and the board over some accounting matter. Most auditors' reports are unqualified, but, if there is a qualification present, you will have to judge how much the financial statements can be relied upon as a measure of the company's performance.

Next, Turn to the Five/Ten-Year Review

This is where you build up a mental picture of the company's financial history. Look at earnings per share (EPS)—is it increasing, decreasing, fluctuating wildly? This gives you an idea of how it has been doing over the period. Look at dividends, if any, and consider their pattern. Do they follow EPS or, as is likely, are they showing a smoother picture? Look at company debt, if the information is there, and compare it with stockholders' funds. How is it changing over the years?

Generally, try to build up a view as to whether the company is doing better, worse, or perhaps has no particular pattern over the period. Depending on your reasons for reading the report, a set of prejudices will have begun to develop from this historical picture. If it shows a declining financial situation, this could be a good thing from some points of view—if you wish to acquire the company, for example. If you are an employee though, it would not be very encouraging. So reading reports depends to some extent on which angle you are coming from.

Now Read the Chairman's and Directors' Comments

These will give a deeper feel for the company's business, over and above the raw numerical data. Try to exercise a degree of skepticism

  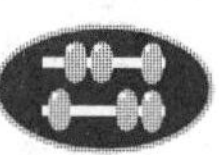   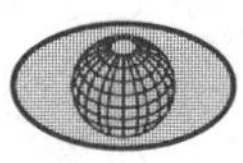 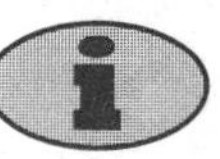  

in some areas, because it is natural for directors to attempt to play up the good points and play down the less good ones.

Get to the Heart of the Matter

The kernel of the report is the Financial Statements and the huge number of notes that accompany them. A lot of it is in highly technical accounting terminology, but it gives you the intimate financial detail on the year. Never ignore the notes—they are critical. In fact some investment analysts read the report from the back, because the notes are so important.

Notes have increased dramatically over the years as new legal and accounting standards have been introduced, primarily to enforce standardization so that financial reports are more comparable, but also to avoid "creative accounting," whereby some companies have tried to conceal (legitimately) financially undesirable situations.

Relax with the Glossy Stuff

Having absorbed all that really matters, settle back and read the glossy parts that tell you how wonderful the company is. Just remember to exercise a mild degree of cynicism here—this is the least important, though no doubt the most visually attractive, part of the annual report. The real picture of the company is the numbers, not the photo of the guy in the hard hat standing on an oil rig!

A Common Mistake

Don't pay too much attention to pretty pictures and directors' comments and too little to the accounting data.

This can give a false view of how well, or badly, the company is doing. Understandably, many people have difficulty in comprehending the figures. But if you want to appreciate annual reports properly, then learning to read financial reports is essential.

Some cynics among investment analysts have even expressed the view that there is an inverse relationship between the number of glossy pages in an annual report and the company's actual performance. Maybe that's a little harsh. . .but there might be something in it.

» MORE INFO

Websites:

The Accounting Standards Board (UK): www.frc.org.uk/asb
Securities and Exchange Commission (US): www.sec.gov

Reserve Ratio

Also called the "reserve requirement," the reserve ratio is a device used both to facilitate financial stability and to influence credit conditions.

WHAT IT MEASURES

In the United Kingdom and in certain European countries there is no compulsory ratio, although banks will have their own internal measures and targets to be able to repay customer deposits as they forecast they will be required. In the United States the policy is more prescriptive, and specified percentages of deposits—specified by the Federal Reserve Board—must be kept by banks in a noninterest-bearing account at one of the 12 Federal Reserve Banks located throughout the country.

WHY IT IS IMPORTANT

To provide stability. In view of the volume and unpredictability of transactions that clear through their accounts every day, banks and financial depositories must maintain a cushion of funds to protect themselves against debits that could leave their accounts overdrawn at the end of the day, and thus subject to penalty.

As a result of the creation of reserve ratios, periods of financial stress are no longer characterized by runs on banks by depositors.

HOW IT WORKS IN PRACTICE

In Europe, the reserve requirement of an institution is calculated by multiplying the reserve ratio for each category of items in the reserve base, set by the European Central Bank, with the amount of those items in the institution's balance sheets. These figures vary according to the institution.

The required reserve ratio in the United States is set by federal law, and depends on the amount of checkable deposits a bank holds. The first $44.3 million of deposits are subject to a 3% reserve requirement. Deposits in excess of $44.3 million are subject to a 10% reserve requirement. These breakpoints are reviewed annually in accordance with money supply growth. No reserves are required against certificates of deposit or savings accounts.

The reserve ratio requirement limits a bank's lending to a certain fraction of its demand deposits. The current rule allows a bank to issue loans to an amount equal to 90% of such deposits, holding 10% in reserve. The reserves can be held in any combination of vault cash and deposit at a Federal Reserve Bank.

A bank facing a reserve deficiency has several options. It can try to borrow reserves for one or more days from another bank, sell marketable assets such as government securities, or bid for funds in the money market, such as large certificates of deposit (CDs) or eurodollars. As a last resort, it can pledge collateral and borrow at the Federal Reserve's discount window.

In order to meet deposit withdrawal contingencies, many banks maintain a margin of excess reserves above the required reserve ratio, since the required reserves are really not available to meet withdrawal liquidity needs. Excess reserves are higher than those needed to meet reserve and clearing requirements, and provide extra protection against overdrafts and deficiencies in required reserves.

TRICKS OF THE TRADE

- Because reserves earn no interest, they have an adverse effect on bank earnings.
- In practice, the required reserve ratio has been adjusted only infrequently by the US Federal Reserve Board.
- US depository institutions hold required reserves in one of two forms: vault cash on hand at the bank or—more significant for monetary policy—required reserve balances in accounts with the Reserve Bank for their respective Federal Reserve District.

   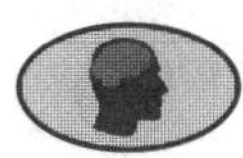  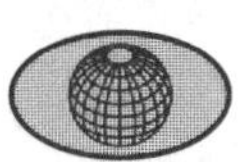   

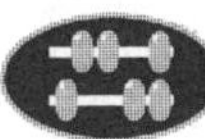

Residual Value

WHAT IT MEASURES

Residual value is the value an asset will have after it has been depreciated, or amortized. Residual value is sometimes referred to as "salvage" value.

WHY IT IS IMPORTANT

According to international financial reporting standards, residual value is the value an asset should have if it is in the expected condition at the end of its useful life, after the cost of selling it.

HOW IT WORKS IN PRACTICE

When calculating the residual value of a business asset, the salvage value is used in conjunction with the purchase price and accounting methods to determine the amount by which the asset depreciates each period. For example, with a straight-line basis, an asset that cost $5,000 and has a salvage value of $1,000 and a useful life of five years would be depreciated at $800 ([5,000 – 1,000] ÷ 5) each year.

This straight-line method uses the following formula to calculate residual value:

$$\text{Depreciation expense} = \frac{\text{Cost of fixed asset} - \text{Scrap value}}{\text{Lifespan}}$$

An alternative approach is to use the declining-balance method, which assumes that an asset loses value more rapidly in the early part of its useful lifetime. In the case of machinery, this is often a more realistic approach. To calculate residual value using this methodology, each period of depreciation is based on the previous year's net book value, estimated lifespan, and a factor of 2 (known as the double-declining balance). For example:

$$\text{Depreciation expense} = \text{Previous period NBV} \times \frac{\text{Factor}}{\text{N}}$$

For the double-declining balance method, using the vehicle example from above, we compute the depreciation after the first year:

$$17000 \times \frac{2}{5} = \$6800$$

In business accounting there are three common methods of calculating the residual value of a business:

1 **Perpetuity business valuation**: Using this methodology, the business assumes the company's future cash flow will continue indefinitely, and the residual value of the asset is calculated according to the following formula:

$$\text{Residual value} = \frac{\text{Free cash flow in year } n}{r}$$

where r is the discount rate and n is the last year of the analysis period.

2 **Liquidation business valuation**: Using this methodology assumes the most conservative way to calculate residual value is to assume the asset will be liquidated at the end of the forecasting period. So, residual value is calculated as being the net liquidation value—the asset's value (including cash, inventory, plant) less liabilities. This value is discounted for the beginning of the period, before adding it to the discounted cash flow, to calculate the company's value.

3 **Price earnings valuation**: Assumes the best way to determine a venture's residual value is to calculate its market price using the relevant price earning factor as follows:

$$\text{Residual value} = \frac{\text{Net profit in year } n \times \text{Comparative PE}}{r}$$

where r is the discount rate and n is the selected year. Comparative PE refers to the PE of any similar company, or the industry average. The result is then discounted to the beginning of the plan period and added to discounted cash flow.

TRICKS OF THE TRADE

- Residual values should be reviewed annually alongside the useful life of assets, and depreciation adjusted if the residual value of an asset has changed.
- Intangible assets have a zero residual value. Some tangible assets may also have a zero residual value if they cannot be resold, or if there are costs associated with their disposal that outstrip the residual value.
- Residual values used for calculating depreciation should be calculated per asset, but most companies would simplify the calculations by grouping together items into categories.
- Residual value can be built into leases. The residual value of leased assets is the cost of the asset minus less repayments of capital made over the lifetime of the lease.

▸▸ MORE INFO

Article:

White, Diane. "Depreciation of fixed assets: Straight line, units-of-production, and double declining method." Suite101.com (September 15, 2008). Online at: accounting.suite101.com/article.cfm/depreciating_tangible_fixed_assets

Website:

Money Terms on residual value: moneyterms.co.uk/residual-value/

Return on Assets

Return on assets—or simply ROA—may also be termed return on total assets (ROTA) or return on net assets (RONA). Whatever its designation, it is often referred to as the No. 1 ratio in finance.

WHAT IT MEASURES

A company's profitability, expressed as a percentage of its total assets.

WHY IT IS IMPORTANT

Return on assets measures how effectively a company has used the total assets at its disposal to generate earnings. Because the ROA formula reflects total revenue, total cost, and assets deployed, the ratio itself reflects a management's ability to generate income during the course of a given period, usually a year.

Naturally, the higher the return, the better the profit perform-

     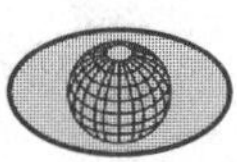   

ance. ROA is a convenient way of comparing a company's performance with that of its competitors, although the items on which the comparison is based may not always be identical.

HOW IT WORKS IN PRACTICE

To calculate ROA, divide a company's net income by its total assets, then multiply by 100 to express the figure as a percentage:

$$\text{Return on assets} = \frac{\text{Net income}}{\text{Total assets}}$$

If net income is $30, and total assets are $420, the ROA is:

$$\frac{30}{420} = 0.0714 = 7.14\%$$

A variation of this formula can be used to calculate return on net assets (RONA):

$$\text{Return on net assets} = \frac{\text{Net income}}{\text{Fixed assets + Working capital}}$$

And, on occasion, the formula will separate after-tax interest expense from net income:

$$\text{Return on assets} = \frac{\text{Net income + Interest expense}}{\text{Total assets}}$$

It is therefore important to understand what each component of the formula actually represents.

TRICKS OF THE TRADE

- Some experts recommend using the net income value at the end of the given period, and the assets' value from the beginning of the period, or an average value taken over the complete period, rather than an end-of-the-period value; otherwise, the calculation will include assets that have accumulated during the year, which can be misleading.
- While a high ratio indicates a greater return, it must still be balanced against such factors as risk, sustainability, and reinvestment in the business through development costs. Some managements will sacrifice the long-term interests of investors in order to achieve an impressive ROA in the short term.
- A climbing return on assets usually indicates a climbing stock price, because it tells investors that a management is skilled at generating profits from the resources that a business owns.
- Acceptable ROAs vary by sector. In banking, for example, a ROA of 1% or better is a considered to be the standard benchmark of superior performance.
- ROA is an effective way of measuring the efficiency of manufacturers, but can be suspect when measuring service companies, or companies whose primary assets are people.
- Other variations of the ROA formula do exist.

Return on Investment

Return on investment (ROI) is a ratio that is used frequently—perhaps too frequently. Its definition can vary widely. Indeed, ROI today is not only a family of measurements of the performance of invested capital but also a concept, one used to justify expenditure on almost everything.

WHAT IT MEASURES

In the financial realm, the overall profit or loss on an investment expressed as a percentage of the total amount invested or total funds appearing on a company's balance sheet.

WHY IT IS IMPORTANT

Like return on assets or return on equity, return on investment measures a company's profitability and its management's ability to generate profits from the funds investors have placed at its disposal.

One opinion holds that if a company's operations cannot generate net earnings at a rate that exceeds the cost of borrowing funds from financial markets, the future of that company is grim.

HOW IT WORKS IN PRACTICE

The most basic expression of ROI can be found by dividing a company's net profit (also called net earnings) by the total investment (total debt plus total equity), then multiplying by 100 to arrive at a percentage:

$$\text{Return on investment} = \frac{\text{Net profit}}{\text{Total investment}}$$

If, say, net profit is $30 and total investment is $250, the ROI is:

$$\frac{30}{250} = 0.12 = 12\%$$

A more complex variation of ROI is an equation known as the Du Pont formula:

$$\text{ROI} = \frac{\text{Net profit after taxes}}{\text{Total assets}} = \frac{\text{Net profit after taxes}}{\text{Sales}} \times \frac{\text{Sales}}{\text{Total assets}}$$

If, for example, net profit after taxes is $30, total assets are $250, and sales are $500, then:

$$\frac{30}{250} = \frac{30}{500} \times \frac{500}{250} = 12\% = 6\% \times 2 = 12\%$$

Champions of this formula, which was developed by the Du Pont Company in the 1920s, say that it helps to reveal how a company has both deployed its assets and controlled its costs, and how it can achieve the same percentage return in different ways.

For stockholders, the variation of the basic ROI formula used by investors is:

$$\text{ROI} = \frac{\text{Net income + Current value − Original value}}{\text{Original value}}$$

If, for example, somebody invests $5,000 in a company and a year later has earned $100 in dividends, while the value of the stock is $5,200, the return on investment would be:

$$\frac{100 + 5{,}200 - 5{,}000}{5{,}000} = \frac{300}{5{,}000} = 0.06 = 6\%$$

TRICKS OF THE TRADE

- Securities investors can use yet another ROI formula: net income divided by common stock and preferred stock equity plus long-term debt.
- It is vital to understand exactly what a return on investment measures—for example, assets, equity, or sales. Without this understanding, comparisons may be misleading or suspect. A search for "return on investment" on the internet, for example, harvests everything from staff training to e-commerce to advertising and promotions!
- Be sure to establish whether the net profit figure used is before or after provision for taxes. This is important for making ROI comparisons accurate.

Return on Sales

Although return on sales (ROS) is another tool used to analyze profitability, it is perhaps a better indication of efficiency. In some business environments, it is also called margin on sales percentage, or net margin.

WHAT IT MEASURES

A company's operating profit or loss as a percentage of total sales for a given period, typically a year.

WHY IT IS IMPORTANT

Return on sales (ROS) shows how efficiently management uses the sales dollar, thus reflecting its ability to manage costs and overheads and operate efficiently. It also indicates a company's ability to withstand adverse conditions such as falling prices, rising costs, or declining sales. The higher the figure, the better a company is able to endure price wars and falling prices.

Return on sales can be useful in assessing the annual performances of cyclical companies that may have no earnings during particular months, and of companies whose business requires a huge capital investment and thus incurs substantial amounts of depreciation.

HOW IT WORKS IN PRACTICE

The calculation is very basic:

$$\text{Return on sales} = \frac{\text{Operating profit}}{\text{Total sales}}$$

So, if a company earns \$30 on sales of \$400, its return on sales is:

$$\frac{30}{400} = 0.075 = 7.5\%$$

TRICKS OF THE TRADE

- While easy to grasp, return on sales has its limits, since it sheds no light on the overall cost of sales or the four factors that contribute to it: Materials, labor, production overheads, and administrative and selling overheads.
- Some calculations use operating profit before subtracting interest and taxes; others use after-tax income. Either figure is acceptable as long as ROS comparisons are consistent. Obviously, using income before interest and taxes will produce a higher ratio.
- The ratio's operating profit figure may also include special allowances and extraordinary nonrecurring items, which, in turn, can inflate the percentage and be misleading.
- The ratio varies widely by industry. The supermarket business, for example, is heavily dependent on volume and usually has a low return on sales.
- Return on sales remains of special importance to retail sales organizations, which can compare their respective ratios with those of competitors and industry norms.

Return on Stockholders' Equity

Return on equity (ROE) is probably the most widely used measure of how well a company is performing for its stockholders.

WHAT IT MEASURES

Profitability, specifically the percentage return that was delivered to a company's owners.

WHY IT IS IMPORTANT

ROE is a fundamental indication of a company's ability to increase its earnings per share and thus the quality of its stock, because it reveals how well a company is using its money to generate additional earnings.

It is a relatively straightforward benchmark, easy to calculate, and is applicable to a majority of industries. ROE allows investors to compare a company's use of their equity with other investments, and to compare the performance of companies in the same industry. ROE can also help to evaluate trends in a business.

Businesses that generate high returns on equity are businesses that pay off their stockholders handsomely and create substantial assets for each dollar invested.

HOW IT WORKS IN PRACTICE

To calculate ROE, divide the net income shown on the income statement (usually of the past year) by stockholders' equity, which appears on the balance sheet:

$$\text{Return on equity} = \frac{\text{Net income}}{\text{Owners' equity}}$$

  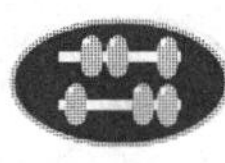   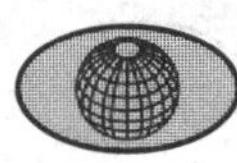   

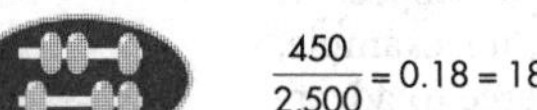

For example, if net income is $450 and equity is $2,500, then:

$$\frac{450}{2{,}500} = 0.18 = 18\%$$

TRICKS OF THE TRADE

- Because new variations of the ROE ratio do appear, it is important to know how the figure is calculated.
- Return on equity for most companies certainly should be in the double digits; investors often look for 15% or higher, while a return of 20% or more is considered excellent.
- Seasoned investors also review five-year average ROE, to gauge consistency.
- A word of caution: Financial statements usually report assets at book value, which is the purchase price minus depreciation; they do not show replacement costs. A business with older assets should show higher rates of ROE than a business with newer assets.
- Examining ROE with return on assets can indicate if a company is debt-heavy. If a company has very little debt, it is reasonable to assume that its management is earning high profits and/or using assets effectively.
- A high ROE also could be due to leverage (a method of corporate funding in which a higher proportion of funds is raised through borrowing than issuing stock). If liabilities are high the balance sheet will reveal it, hence the need to review it.

▸▸ MORE INFO

Book:

Walsh, Ciaran. *Key Management Ratios*. 4th ed. London: FT Prentice Hall, 2008.

Risk-Adjusted Rate of Return

Knowing an investment's risk-adjusted return goes a long way toward determining just how much "bang for the buck" is really being generated.

WHAT IT MEASURES

How much an investment returned in relation to the risk that was assumed to attain it.

WHY IT IS IMPORTANT

Being able to compare a high-risk, potentially high-return investment with a low-risk, lower-return investment helps to answer a key question that confronts every investor: Is it worth the risk?

By itself, the historical average return of an investment, asset, or portfolio can be quite misleading and a faulty indicator of future performance. Risk-adjusted return is a much better barometer.

The calculation also helps to reveal whether the returns of the portfolio reflect smart investment decisions, or the taking on of excess risk that may or may not have been worth what was gained. This is particularly helpful in appraising the performance of money managers.

HOW IT WORKS IN PRACTICE

There are several ways to calculate risk-adjusted return. Each has its strengths and shortcomings. All require particular data, such as an investment's rate of return, the risk-free return rate for a given period (usually the performance of a 90-day US Treasury bill over 36 months), and a market's performance and its standard deviation.

Which one to use? It often depends on an investor's focus, principally whether the focus is on upside gains or downside losses.

Perhaps the most widely used is the **Sharpe ratio**. This measures the potential impact of return volatility on expected return and the amount of return earned per unit of risk. The higher a fund's Sharpe ratio, the better its historical risk-adjusted performance, and the higher the number the greater the return per unit of risk. The formula is:

$$\text{Sharpe ratio} = \frac{\text{Portfolio return} - \text{Risk-free return}}{\text{Std deviation of portfolio return}}$$

Take, for example, two investments, one returning 54%, the other 26%. At first glance, the higher figure clearly looks the better choice, but because of its high volatility it has a Sharpe ratio of 0.279, while the investment with a lower return has a ratio of 0.910. On a risk-adjusted basis the latter would be the wiser choice.

The **Treynor ratio** also measures the excess of return per unit of risk. Its formula is:

$$\text{Treynor ratio} = \frac{\text{Portfolio return} - \text{Risk-free return}}{\text{Portfolio's beta}}$$

In this formula (and others that follow), beta is a separately calculated figure that describes the tendency of an investment to respond to marketplace swings. The higher the beta, the greater the volatility, and vice versa.

A third formula, **Jensen's measure**, is often used to rate a money manager's performance against a market index, and whether or not an investment's risk was worth its reward. The formula is:

$$\text{Jensen's measure} = \text{Portfolio return} - \text{Risk-free return} - \text{Portfolio beta} \times (\text{Benchmark return} - \text{Risk-free return})$$

TRICKS OF THE TRADE

- A fourth formula, the **Sortino ratio**, also exists. Its focus is more on downside risk than potential opportunity, and its calculation is more complex.
- There are no benchmarks for these values. In order to be useful the numbers should be compared with the ratios of other investments.
- No single measure is perfect, so experts recommend using them broadly. For instance, if a particular investment class is on a roll

▸▸ MORE INFO

Websites:

FinPortfolio tutorial on risk-adjusted return: www.finportfolio.com/education/tutorial/tutorial_risk-adjusted_return.html

Pension Research Institute on Sortino ratio: www.sortino.com/htm/Sortino%20Ratio.htm

and does not experience a great deal of volatility, a good return per unit of risk does not necessarily reflect management genius. When the overall momentum of technology stocks drove returns straight up in 1999, Sharpe ratios climbed with them, and did not reflect any of the sector's volatility that was to erupt in late 2000.

- Most of these measures can be used to rank the risk-adjusted performance of individual stocks, various portfolios over the same time, and mutual funds with similar objectives.

Scenario Analysis

WHAT IT MEASURES

Businesses have always planned for "what if" scenarios—and based their decision-making on likely future events. Scenario analysis is simply a formal tool to model the likelihood of various scenarios and their outcomes. Scenario analysis has been widely used in asset management and risk management since the 1970s, to analyze interest rate risks. However, it can be applied to a wide set of corporate and financial activities, including equity prices, exchange rates, commodity prices, and volatility of prices.

WHY IT IS IMPORTANT

Scenario analysis helps companies and investors to measure the expected value of an investment. By combining this information with probability, analysts can make highly accurate predictions about the likelihood of realizing the expected value. Comparing the probability distribution of an event is equivalent to calculating the risk of an investment and important for the same reason—it allows you to make better decisions about business and financial investments.

There are many different approaches to scenario analysis, but one common method is to determine the high/low spread and standard deviation from daily or monthly returns, then compute the value of the portfolio if each security generated returns two or three basis points above and below this average.

This method means the investor or company can have reasonable certainty that the value of a portfolio will remain within expected parameters over a given period of time.

HOW IT WORKS IN PRACTICE

A typical use of scenario analysis would be to consider what happens to the value of a security if interest rates fell, remained static, or increased.

The first step is to consider all the possible outcomes, or paths, that will be taken by relevant risk factors (in this case, interest rates). Each potential outcome is considered over the same time period. In the simple example below, we can see all the relevant outcomes that might be affected by a 100 basis point fall in interest rates, followed by 24 months of static rates:

Time (months)	1-month Libor	3-month Libor	6-month Libor	12-month Libor	COFI
0	3.11	3.79	3.84	4.00	3.54
6	2.11	2.79	3.84	4.00	3.54
12	2.11	2.79	3.84	4.00	3.54
18	2.11	2.79	3.84	4.00	3.54
24	2.11	2.79	3.84	4.00	3.54

Once you have identified the scenario, the next step is to project what happens for each of these rates at the given point in time. This extrapolation may be relatively simple, showing the cost of debt in each scenario, or might be more complex—for example, by incorporating other financial data to produce a cash flow forecast, or value at risk metric.

TRICKS OF THE TRADE

- Scenario analysis allows analysts to plan for their "worst-case scenario." Being able to quantify the potential costs of a possible outcome is vital in risk management and forming business strategy. Scenario planning can be highly detailed, and customized to accommodate any number of variables, such as the flattening of the yield curve or narrowing spreads.
- One advantage of scenario analysis is that it is simple to use and very flexible. It can address almost any present or future risk, and can anticipate the impact of future business decisions. However, its major drawback is that it can only consider the impact of risks that are anticipated—outputs are entirely limited to paths suggested by the user, and so if you overlook a risk, it will not be calculated.
- It is also important to remember that if scenario analysis is based on probability, there is still a potential that the low and high extreme values could occur. This is why scenario analysis is often run alongside risk analysis to determine whether these potential risks are within acceptable tolerance levels.
- When dealing with complex scenarios over multiple time periods and involving many possible outcomes (such as the impact on 1,000 clients of 100 different interest rate permutations) scenario analysis can be extremely cumbersome, generating large and complex tables. In such instances, duration analysis can provide more user-friendly analysis.
- Another alternative is to use scenario analysis and the Monte Carlo method, to calculate results based on a large number of random scenarios. This approach is sometimes also referred to as "simulation analysis."

➤➤ MORE INFO

Websites:

Mind Tools on scenario analysis: www.mindtools.com/pages/article/newSTR_98.htm

MS Excel scenario analysis: office.microsoft.com/en-us/excel/HA011996481033.aspx

  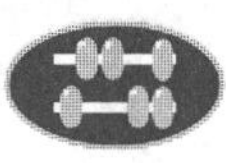   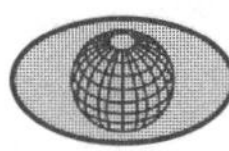   

Sharpe Ratio

WHAT IT MEASURES

The Sharpe ratio, devised in 1966 by economist William F. Sharpe, measures the ratio of return from a portfolio to volatility. It is used to compare and select investment options, and identify which portfolio offers the most risk-efficient investment.

WHY IT IS IMPORTANT

The Sharpe ratio provides a simple way compare two assets with the same expected return—showing which will give the greatest return given an equal level of risk. The key advantage of the Sharpe ratio is that it can be easily calculated without needing any additional data regarding the asset's profitability.

HOW IT WORKS IN PRACTICE

The Sharpe ratio is calculated by subtracting the risk-free rate from the return of the portfolio, then dividing by the standard deviation of the portfolio. To use the Sharpe ratio, apply the following formula:

$$\text{Sharpe ratio} = \frac{\text{Expected rate of return} - \text{Risk-free rate}}{\text{Standard deviation of the portfolio}}$$

The higher the Sharpe ratio, the better the return for each unit of risk. How does this work in practice?

Imagine that portfolio A generates a return of 15%, while portfolio B generates a return of just 12%. It would seem at first glance that portfolio A has performed better. However, if portfolio A was much riskier then it may be the case that B has a better risk-adjusted rate of return.

If we imagine the risk-free rate in this scenario is 5% and the portfolios have standard deviations of 8% and 5% respectively, then we can see that portfolio A would have a Sharpe ratio of 1.25, while portfolio B would have a Sharpe ratio of 1.4. This suggests that, adjusted for risk, portfolio B presents the better investment.

TRICKS OF THE TRADE

- When using the Sharpe ratio, a score of 1 or better is considered good. A ratio above 2 is considered very good, and 3 would be considered excellent.
- Using the Sharpe ratio doesn't always provide an accurate analysis of return on risk or volatility. This is because portfolio standard deviation can reflect upside or downside returns—and the ratio does not differentiate between these outcomes. Some analysts argue that using standard deviation to measure volatility is not strictly effective, since standard deviation is not a measure of volatility. Instead, standard deviation is really a rough proxy for concepts such as "risk."
- When using the Sharpe ratio, it is wise to adjust the ratio for portfolio analysis. If you are comparing two potential investments for portfolios, then the ratio may not be accurate if one investment is highly correlated with other investments in the portfolio. The solution is therefore to use different Sharpe ratios for different portfolios.
- The Sharpe ratio is unusual in that it can be applied to both ex-ante (expected) returns and ex-poste (historical) returns.

▸▸ MORE INFO

Article:

Sharpe, William F. "The Sharpe ratio." *Journal of Portfolio Management* (Fall 1994). Online at: www.stanford.edu/~wfsharpe/art/sr/sr.htm

Website:

Hedge Funds Consistency Index on Sharpe ratio: www.hedgefund-index.com/d_sharpe.asp

Statistical Process Control Methods

WHAT IT MEASURES

Statistical Process Control (SPC) is a tool for monitoring and controlling variation in processes such as manufacturing of goods, testing, or statistical results. It was created in the 1920s by Dr W. Edwards Deming, who claimed the majority of variation was due to operator over-adjustment. SPC requires an organization to:

- determine the process parameters that need to be monitored;
- create a control chart to confirm the process is under control;
- collect data to compare with the control chart to identify process variation.

WHY IT IS IMPORTANT

SPC itself doesn't improve your processes—it can only tell you if variation has increased beyond normal levels. However, this information enables businesses to incorporate or eliminate the changes causing an abnormal variation. This is important because it provides an understanding of business baselines, gives insights into possible process improvements, and shows the value and results of existing processes. SPC can also provide real-time analysis to establish where business processes can be improved, improving decision-making.

HOW IT WORKS IN PRACTICE

The key tool in applying SPC is the control chart that illustrates what a process looks like (statistically) when it is in-control. Control charts typically measure variable data and monitor the process target (mean result) and process range. There are a number of different sorts of control chart but among the most common are the X⁻ chart (pronounced "x bar" but also known as the averages or means chart), and the R chart (also known as the range chart).

This type of control chart has three key elements: a center line, an upper control limit, and a lower control limit. The center line on an X⁻ control chart is the process mean, while the center line on an R chart is the mean range.

The upper and lower control limits (UCL and LCL) are set to represent deviation from the mean that includes 99.7% of all data points (i.e., plus and minus 3 standard deviations from the mean). Data is then collected from the process and the mean plotted on the

$\bar{X}$ and R charts—which can be interpreted to determine if the process is staying in-control or is out-of-control.

In the example below, a company is manufacturing pencils that are 16mm in diameter (mean), and they want to know if the process is in-control, and the level of variation in the pencils created.

The company begins by collecting a series of sample measurements, which are placed in subgroups. Next, the mean of each subgroup is calculated by adding all the measurements together and dividing by the number of measurements in the subgroup.

Next, the company calculates the mean of all of the means—this gives an overall mean for the data. This overall mean is the centre line in the control chart—in our example this is 13.75.

Next, the company must calculate S, the standard deviation of the data points. This can be easily calculated in Excel using the formula =STDEV (data points).

Next, calculate the UCL and LCL as follows:

$$UCL = CL + 3 \times S$$
$$LCL = CL - 3 \times S$$

where CL is the center line or overall mean value. Draw a line on the control chart to represent the UCL and LCL.

On your $\bar{X}$ chart, the x-axis shows the subgroup means from your original calculation. The y-axis represents actual measurements from the process over time. As a rule of thumb, the process is considered out-of-control if any point falls beyond the UCL or LCL lines (i.e., more than 3 standard deviations from the mean).

Control charts may also indicate a process is out-of-control if eight consecutive points fall on the same side of the center line, or if more than two consecutive points are more than one standard deviation point from the mean.

TRICKS OF THE TRADE

- Using a spreadsheet application, it is possible to calculate standard deviation and mean for a set of data. In Excel this is done using the STDEV and AVERAGE functions.
- The benefits of SPC won't be immediately realized in every organization. SPC is best applied where there are clearly defined and consistent processes, and where the organization's leadership is willing to identify and address new problems that might be identified by SPC.

▸▸ MORE INFO

Books:

Oakland, John. *Statistical Process Control*. 6th ed. Amsterdam: Elsevier Butterworth-Heinemann, 2008.

Stapenhurst, Tim. *Mastering Statistical Process Control: A Handbook for Performance Improvement Using SPC Cases*. Amsterdam: Elsevier Butterworth-Heinemann, 2005.

Websites:

iSixSigma links on control charts: www.isixsigma.com/st/control_charts/

MiC Quality SPC course: www.margaret.net/spc/

Stochastic Modeling

WHAT IT MEASURES

Stochastic modeling uses thousands of simulations to produce probability distributions for various outcomes. It is widely used to predict how stock markets, bonds, and gilts will perform in the future.

WHY IT IS IMPORTANT

Advocates of stochastic modeling argue that randomness is a fundamental characteristic of financial markets. While some agents may be more successful at predicting future trends than others, modeling the likely outcome of investment activities must take account of probability, and particularly the risk of random events negatively impacting investments.

Many investment tools are "deterministic" in that they are clockwork systems which, given the same starting conditions, will generate exactly the same answer. This approach is not perfect when applied to financial markets, where there is an important element of chance, specifically relating to volatility and distribution.

Stochastic modeling provides a structured way of looking at a portfolio, taking into account random factors such as inflation or risk tolerance. If modeling shows a low probability of reaching investment goals, the fund can be diversified or contribution levels altered.

HOW IT WORKS IN PRACTICE

Stochastic modeling relies upon Monte Carlo simulation to generate random numbers upon which a stochastic formula is applied. This shows what impact specific random events will have on the distribution of probable outcomes.

For example, imagine you wanted to calculate the probability that a million door handles manufactured using four key parts would be too short or long to be used. You would have a million of each of the four different parts, and randomly select the parts to assemble each handle.

To calculate the probability, you would define a range of measurements for each part, and simulate what happens when randomly selected parts are put together. Of course, this is not something that could be calculated manually. Instead, a stochastic model would calculate thousands of probable outcomes based on a large number of random simulations, reflecting the random variation of combinations.

The Monte Carlo method has four key stages:

1. Define a range of possible inputs
2. Generate input randomly from the domain
3. Perform deterministic computation using these inputs
4. Aggregate the results of the individual computations

▸▸ MORE INFO

Book:

Morgan, Bryon J. T. *Applied Stochastic Modelling*. 2nd ed. Boca Raton, FL: Chapman & Hall/CRC, 2009.

Report:

du Toit, Barry. "Risk, theory, reflection: Limitations of the stochastic model of uncertainty in financial risk analysis." RiskWorX, June 2004. Online at: www.riskworx.com/insights/theory/theory.pdf

  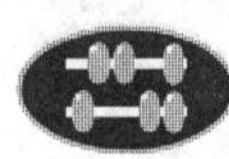   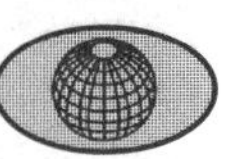   

TRICKS OF THE TRADE

- Stochastic modeling used to be known as "statistical sampling." Prior to the emergence of computers, it was rarely used because of the number of calculations involved in modeling, but there are now many off-the-shelf computer applications that can handle stochastic modeling quite easily.
- The Monte Carlo model was popularized by von Neumann, Ulam, and Fermi, among others, in the 1930s. The roots of the model actually lie in physics, and the model is still widely used by scientists as well as economists.
- The Monte Carlo simulation model is often used when the model is complex, nonlinear, or involves more than just a couple of uncertain parameters. A simulation can typically involve over 10,000 evaluations of the model, a task which in the past was only practical using super computers.

Stress Testing

WHAT IT MEASURES

Stress testing is a risk management tool that helps to identify how vulnerable a business, portfolio, or venture might be to unusual, negative circumstances. It may involve scenario analysis or simulation, based on hypothetical or historical data.

WHY IT IS IMPORTANT

Stress testing is extremely useful to financial analysts because it provides them with additional information on potential portfolio losses in the event of extreme, but unlikely events. Crucially, stress testing enables risk managers to test how robust a particular investment or instrument will be in the event of a serious change in circumstances.

The current "credit crunch" is a perfect example of the importance of stress testing. Institutions that conducted thorough stress tests based on a simultaneous lack of credit coupled with increased exposure to collateral debt obligations have been less seriously affected, according to financial regulators.

HOW IT WORKS IN PRACTICE

Stress testing is used to test instruments against scenarios such as: What happens if the market collapses by 60%? What happens if interest rates on our loans double? What if our lease costs increase by 75%?

The most common approach to stress testing is to use Monte Carlo simulation. This involves taking a number of randomized scenarios, ranging from modest to extreme outcomes (say a 90% drop in sales, versus a 90% increase in sales), and modeling the results on a probability distribution curve.

Most stress testing exercises involve multiple stressors. There is usually also the ability to test the current ability to cope with a known historical scenario. In recent years, many companies have tested their ability to cope with the kind of recession seen in Europe during the 1990s, for example.

There are three basic kinds of event a stress test can be applied to: Extreme event (current positions combined with historical event); risk factor shock; and external factor shock (shock of any external index factor, such as oil prices or exchange rates).

There are two basic sorts of stress test—sensitivity tests and scenario tests. A sensitivity test assesses the impact of large movement in financial variables on portfolio values without needing a specific reason. For example, you might test what happens if interest rates fall by 20%, or the cost of equity rises by 15%. Sensitivity tests can be run quickly and easily, but lack historical perspective.

Scenario tests are more costly and complex, but provide a better insight into long-term risk. They are constructed either within the context of a specific portfolio or based on a specific set of historical circumstances. Risk managers identify a portfolio's key drivers and test what happens if those drivers are stressed beyond value at risk (VAR) levels. Many risk managers use a hybrid approach of scenario and sensitivity testing.

TRICKS OF THE TRADE

- In many countries, stress testing is a regulatory requirement. In the United Kingdom, for example, the Financial Services Authority (FSA) requires certain financial institutions to conduct stress tests and ensure they have sufficient capital reserves available to handle extreme events.
- Stress testing is mostly used to analyze market risk, and the impact of market changes on portfolios such as interest rates, equity, exchange rates, and commodity instruments. These portfolios are suitable for stress testing because their market prices are regularly updated, giving sufficient data to analyze.
- VAR analysis is a very useful risk management tool, but it is not able to incorporate all possible risk outcomes, particularly sudden, dramatic changes in market circumstances.
- Stress testing is often used as a tool to communicate risk to business leaders. Rather than the hypothetical probabilities of VAR, stress testing provides a response to a very specific set of circumstances.
- Regulators commonly use stress testing to consider the vulnerability of entire financial systems. Stress tests were recently used by the Bank of England as part of a Financial Sector Assessment Program (FSAP), which considered how 10 large domestic banks would deal with a 35% decline in global stock prices, and a 12% decline in domestic property prices.

▸▸ MORE INFO

Book:

Rösch, Daniel, and Harald Scheule (eds). *Stress-Testing for Financial Institutions: Applications, Regulations and Techniques*. London: Risk Books, 2009.

Article:

Bunn, Philip, Alastair Cunningham, and Mathias Drehmann. "Stress testing as a tool for assessing systemic risks." *Financial Stability Review* (June 2005). Online at: www.bankofengland.co.uk/publications/fsr/2005/fsr18art8.pdf

   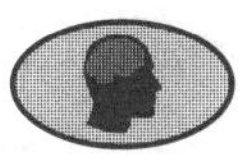  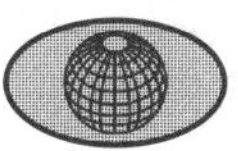  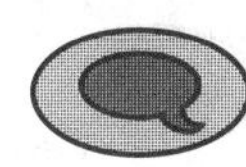 

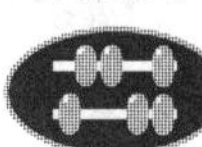

Swap Valuation

WHAT IT MEASURES

In finance, a swap is a derivative in which two parties agree to exchange one stream of cash flow against another. The swap buyer makes a stream of interest payments on a principal sum to the seller, based on the present value of the asset, for a fixed period of time. The seller then receives payments from the seller, which are usually based on a fixed rate, such as Libor. The swap valuation is the price that each party assigns to the components of the swap, and dictates the level of payments made by the buyer of the swap.

WHY IT IS IMPORTANT

Interest rate swaps were originally created to allow large corporations to avoid the cost of exchange controls. Today, they are one of the most popular and flexible financial instruments. They can be used by hedge funds to managed fixed or floating assets and liabilities, while speculators often use swaps to profit from changes in interest rates.

HOW IT WORKS IN PRACTICE

Interest rate swaps do not generate revenue themselves, they merely convert one interest rate basis to another. This type of swap is known as a "plain vanilla" swap, and is by far the most common form of swap.

Because the interest rate swap is simply a series of cash flows occurring at known future dates, it is possible to calculate its value by using a series of estimated discount cash flows.

To calculate a theoretical swap rate (TSR) for the fixed component of a swap contract, use the following formula:

$$\text{TSR} = \frac{\text{Present value of the floating rate payments}}{\text{Notional principal}_i \times \text{days} \div 360 \times \text{df}_i}$$

For example, company A and company B agree to a $100 million vanilla swap over three years with company A paying the swap rate, and company B paying six-month Libor floating rate.

Using the formula, it is possible to calculate a swap rate value by using the six-month Libor rate to estimate the present value of the floating rate payments.

First, calculate the present value (PV) of the payment, using Libor forward rates for three years.

As with the floating rate payments, Libor forward rates are used to discount the notional principal for the three-year period. The PV of the notional principal is calculated by multiplying the days in the period and the floating rate forward discount factor.

In our example above, the present value of the notional principal over six bi-annual payments would be calculated at $278,145,000 using the Libor forward rate to discount the cash flow.

To calculate the theoretical swap rate, we would use the following calculation:

$$\text{TSR} = \frac{12{,}816{,}663}{278{,}145{,}000} = 0.046 = 4.6\%$$

In this scenario, the buyer would therefore pay a fixed rate of 4.61% to the seller of the swap, in exchange for receiving six-month Libor interest payments.

TRICKS OF THE TRADE

- Remember, that in an interest rate swap, the principal amount is not exchanged between the counterparties. Rather, interest payments are based on a "notional amount."
- In addition, because the fixed rate component of the swap is based on the rate that values the fixed rate payments at the same present value as the variable rates, there is no advantage to either party at the time of entering a swap and no upfront payment is made. During the life of the swap, the same valuation is used, but since interest rates change, the PV of the variable rate will also change—creating an advantage for one party.
- A swap will typically last for between one and 15 years. The period of the contract is known as the swap's tenor or maturity. The counterparty paying the fixed rate is known as the buyer of the swap, while the floating-rate payer is known as the seller.
- While it is important to understand the theoretical basis of swap valuation, there are a number of computer programs that will perform complex calculations to provide highly accurate valuations.
- You may sometimes see the floating and fixed components of a swap referred to as the "legs" of the swap.

MORE INFO

Books:

Buetow, Gerald W., and Frank J. Fabozzi. *Valuation of Interest Rate Swaps and Swaptions*. New Hope, PA: Frank J. Fabozzi, 2001.

Rogers, Simon. *Swaps in Practice: The Products, Pricing and Applications*. London: Euromoney Books, 2004.

Article:

Duffie, Darrell. "Credit swap valuation." *Financial Analysts Journal* 55:1 (January/February 1999): 73–87. Preprint online at: www.defaultrisk.com/pp_crdrv_57.htm

Term Structure of Interest Rates

WHAT IT MEASURES

A mathematical description of the relationship between interest rates (or the cost of borrowing) and the time to maturity of a debt in a given currency, often used in relation to fixed securities. The resulting relationship is plotted on a graph that is known as a "yield curve." This curve can then be analyzed to measure the expected yield of securities over time.

WHY IT IS IMPORTANT

The term structure or yield curve graph shows investors how returns compare to government-issued Treasury bonds (which are considered risk-free), and how an investment compares with other fixed-income securities with the same maturity.

By observing the shape of the graph, investors can gain insight into the likely future direction of the economy and identify trading

 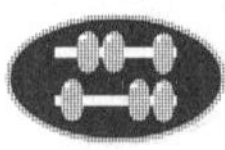   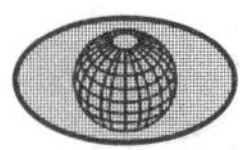   

opportunities. This is important to investors but also to businesses, since most strategic business decisions depend on the availability and cost of capital—which is determined by interest rates.

HOW IT WORKS IN PRACTICE

The yield curve plots the annualized percentage increase in the yield of a specific investment. For example, if a bank account returns an interest rate of 4%, the yield is said to be 4%. However, most investments offer different returns over time. A bank may offer a higher interest rate for deposits that are invested over five years, for example.

The yield is therefore expressed as a function P(t), where t is the period of time invested over. This means that P(t) represents the value today of receiving one unit of currency t years in the future. P is usually an increasing function of t. The formula for calculating the yield (or interest term structure) for borrowing money of a period of time is as follows:

$$Y_t = (1/P(t)) - 1$$

The yield curve function P is actually only known with certainty for a few specific maturity dates, the other maturities are calculated by interpolation.

The simplest method of calculating the function P, and therefore the term structure of interest rates, is using the market expectations hypothesis. This states that if investors have an expectation of what one-year interest rates will be, then year-two interest rates will be calculated by compounding the first year's interest rate with the current year's. Over a longer term, rates are calculated as equal to the geometric mean of the yield on short-term rates. This information can be used to construct a simple yield curve.

TRICKS OF THE TRADE

- Critics point out this approach neglects the risk involved in bonds, while other analysts use the liquidity preference model, which includes a premium in the calculation to reflect the benefit of holding long-term bonds (the term premium). This explains the upward curve of most long-term yields.
- There are three basic patterns revealed by term structure graphs:
  1. The normal yield curve: The line illustrating normal market conditions, where there are no significant changes expected to the economy and growth is fixed and predictable. In this market, fixed-income securities will likely generate higher yields the further away the maturity date.
  2. The flat yield curve illustrates a market that is transitioning and where future movement is unclear, creating a flatter curve than the normal yield curve.
  3. The inverted yield curve is rare and seen only during abnormal markets, where investors expect interest rates to decline over time, which will lead to lower yields further into the future.

▸▸ MORE INFO

Website:

Answers.com on yield curve: www.answers.com/topic/yield-curve

Tick Value

WHAT IT MEASURES

There are in fact two different uses of the term "tick value."

1. Tick value can refer to the value of the minimum price movement of a traded stock allowed by an exchange. For example, many US stock markets have a tick *size* of 0.01, which translates into a tick *value* of one cent for the NYSE. In contrast, the EUR futures market has a tick value of 0.0001.
2. Tick value can also refer to the number of buyers and sellers of a stock who are bidding above or below the current market value of a stock.

WHY IT IS IMPORTANT

For traded companies, tick value is part of the contractual requirement to be listed on a stock market. Understanding tick value can also help when assessing the risk associated with investment opportunities: Markets with smaller tick values will generate smaller gains and losses with each price movement of a stock.

For investors, tick value also gives a good indication of how many investors are buying a stock on upticks versus downticks, which can be tracked over time to see whether market sentiment is broadly rising or falling.

HOW IT WORKS IN PRACTICE

Stock value relating to market sentiment is calculated according to the number of people placing orders to buy and sell a stock at any given time.

For example, at 9am Company A's stock will have a spread value, based on the difference between highest price buyers will pay, and the lowest bid sellers will accept. For frequently traded stocks, the spread will tend to be relatively small.

A buyer might believe the value of Company A's stock is increasing, and wants to buy stock now. They will therefore place an order for stock, and accept the best offer available from a seller. This sort of transaction is said to have happened on an "up tick" where the market is expected to rise. The opposite, where the seller accepts the best price offered by a buyer, is said to happen on a "down tick."

Stock exchanges calculate tick value by measuring precisely how many trades happen on each of these trajectories every few seconds. For example, on the NYSE, the tick value is taken every six seconds. A tick value of +100 means that 100 more issues traded on down ticks rather than up ticks. Tracking the tick value over time allows you to gain insight into market sentiment.

▸▸ MORE INFO

Articles:

Porter, David C., and Daniel G. Weaver. "Tick size and market quality." *Financial Management* 26:4 (Winter 1997): 5–26.

Small Investors Software Co. "NYSE tick—Statistical analysis." July 3, 2003. Online at: www.smallinvestors.com/SP500/TickNyse.htm

Steenbarger, Brett. "A NYSE TICK primer: How to assess intraday sentiment." TraderFeed (December 16, 2008). Online at: traderfeed.blogspot.com/2008/12/nyse-tick-primer-how-to-assess-intraday.html

TRICKS OF THE TRADE

- Among European currency exchanges, the euro futures market has a tick value of $12.50, compared to $6.25 for the British pound futures market. Tick values in stock indexes vary widely, from $5 for the Dow Jones futures market up to $12.50 for the S&P 500.
- Some statisticians have attempted to use tick data to analyze market performance and make predictions based on average ticks over 20 days. Generally speaking, ticks of more than +1000 or less than −800 would suggest excessive market optimism or pessimism.

Time Value of Money

WHAT IT MEASURES

Time Value of Money (TVM) is one of the most important concepts in the financial world. If a business is paid $1 million for something today, that money is worth more than if the same $1 million was paid at some point in the future. The reason money given today is worth more is straightforward: If I have money today, I have the potential to earn interest on the capital.

TVM values how much more a given sum of money is worth now (or at a specific future date) compared to in the future (or, in the case of a future payment, a date that is even further in the future). TVM calculations take into account likely interest gains, discounted cash flow, and potential risk, to create a value figure for a specific amount of money or investment opportunity.

There are several calculations commonly used to express the time value of money, but the most important are present value and future value.

WHY IT IS IMPORTANT

If company A has the opportunity to realize $10,000 from an asset today, or two years in the future, TVM allows the company to calculate exactly how much more that $10,000 is worth if it's received today, as opposed to in the future. It is important to know how to calculate the time value of money because it means you can distinguish between the value of investment opportunities that offer returns at different times.

HOW IT WORKS IN PRACTICE

If a business has the option of receiving a $1 million investment today or a guaranteed payment of the same amount in two years' time, you can use TVM calculations to show the relative value of the two sums of money.

Option A, take the money now: The business might accept the $1,000,000 investment immediately and put the capital into an account paying a 4.5% annual return. In this account, the $1,000,000 would earn $92,025 interest over two years (annually compounded), making the future value of the investment $1,092,025. This can be expressed using the following formula:

$$\text{Future value} = 1{,}000{,}000 \times (1 + 0.045)^2$$

which might be expressed as:

$$\text{Future value} = \text{Original sum} \times (1 + \text{Interest rate per period})^{\text{No of periods}}$$

Obviously, the present value of the $1 million if it is received today would be $1 million. But if the money isn't received for another two years, we can still calculate its present and future values.

The present value of a future $1 million investment is based on how much you would need to receive today to receive $1 million in two years' time. This is done by discounting the $1,000,000 by the interest rate for the period. Assuming an annual interest rate of 4.5%, we can calculate the present value using the following formula:

$$\text{Present value} = \frac{\text{Future value}}{(1 + \text{Interest rate per period})^{\text{No of periods}}}$$

Using this formula, we can see that the present value of a future payment of $1 million in two years' time is:

$$\frac{1{,}000{,}000}{(1 + 0.045)^2} = \$915{,}730$$

In other words, the investment in two years time is the equivalent of receiving $915,730 today, and investing it at 4.5% for two years.

TRICKS OF THE TRADE

- There are five key components in TVM calculations. These are: present value, future value, the number of periods, the interest rate, and a payment principal sum. Providing you know four of these values, you can rearrange the TVM formulae to calculate the fifth.
- When calculating TVM, you may sometimes need to supplement the calculation to discount future payments to take account of risk as well as time value. Discount rates can be adjusted to take account of risks like the other party not paying you back (default risk) or the fact that the item you intended to purchase has become more expensive, reducing the buying power of the money. In this case, the company lending the principal sum might insist on a higher interest rate to compensate for the risk.
- If a future payment is not certain, you can use the capital asset pricing model to calculate the risk involved.

▸▸ MORE INFO

Websites:

Money-zine TVM calculator: www.money-zine.com/Calculators/Investment-Calculators/Time-Value-of-Money-Calculator/

TVMCalcs.com guide: www.tvmcalcs.com/tvm/tvm_intro

     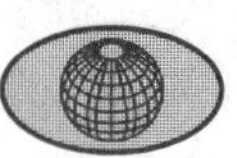   

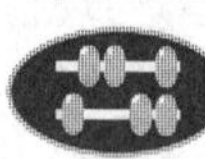

Total Return

Total return is one more way to evaluate investment decisions, and because it totals all factors it is perhaps a calculation that investors value most—or should.

WHAT IT MEASURES

The total percentage change in the value of an investment over a specified time period, including capital gains, dividends, and the investment's appreciation or depreciation.

WHY IT IS IMPORTANT

Total return furnishes fundamental information that every investor seeks sooner or later: All things considered, just how much did my investment return?

That in itself makes total return rather important. In addition, there are several sound reasons for paying close attention to each of its components. For those who invest to maximize income, dividends will be very important. For those who invest for long-term growth, capital appreciation will be equally important.

Knowing how much of an investment's total return is attributable to each of the components can help in assessing how volatile the fund is likely to be, how tax-efficient it is, and how much steady income it can be expected to produce.

HOW IT WORKS IN PRACTICE

The total return formula reflects all the ways in which an investment may earn or lose money: dividends as income, capital gains distributions, and capital appreciation—the increase or decrease in the investment's net asset value (NAV):

$$\text{Total return} = \frac{\text{Dividends} + \text{Capital gains distributions} \pm \text{Change in NAV}}{\text{Initial NAV}}$$

If, for instance, you buy a stock with an initial NAV of $40, and after one year it pays an income dividend of $2 per share and a capital gains distribution of $1, and its NAV has increased to $42, then the stock's total return would be:

$$\frac{2+1+2}{40} = \frac{5}{40} = 0.125 = 12.5\%$$

TRICKS OF THE TRADE

- The total return time-frame is usually one year, and it assumes that dividends have been reinvested.
- If a fund's capital gains exceed its capital losses for the year, most of the net gain must be distributed to stockholders as a capital gains distribution.
- Total return measures past performance only; it cannot predict future results.
- Total return generally does not take into account any sales charges that an investor paid to invest in a fund, or taxes he or she might owe on the income dividends and capital gains distributions received.
- Rules of the US Securities & Exchange Commission require a company to show a comparison of the total return on its common stock for the last five fiscal years with the total returns of a broad market index and a more narrowly focused industry or group index.
- Total return can be a key yardstick in selecting funds once an investor has set objectives and a time horizon, and made decisions about risk and reward.

Treynor Ratio

WHAT IT MEASURES

The Treynor ratio, as devised by Jack Treynor, is a measurement of a portfolio's return earned in excess of what would be earned on a risk-free investment. The higher the Treynor ratio, the better the performance of the portfolio or stock being analyzed.

WHY IT IS IMPORTANT

The Treynor ratio is used to calculate returns over and above what would be generated by a risk-free investment. Whenever the Treynor ratio is high, it denotes that the investor received high yields for each unit of market risk. One of the key advantages of Treynor is that it shows how a fund will perform not in relation to its own volatility but the volatility it brings to an overall portfolio.

HOW IT WORKS IN PRACTICE

The Treynor Ratio divides a portfolio's excess return by its "beta." This is the widely used measure of market-related risk in a stock or collection of stocks. If a stock has a beta of 0.5, it tends to move up or down with the market, but only half as far as the overall market. If a stock has a beta of 1.25 and the market moves up by 10%, that stock would move up by 12.5%.

The formula for the Treynor Ratio is as follows:

$$\text{Treynor ratio} = \frac{\text{Average portfolio return} - \text{Average risk return of risk-free investment}}{\text{Beta of portfolio}}$$

The formula can be applied to any fund or portfolio where you can find a beta value—the beta is a measurement of market-related risk.

An investor might use the Treynor ratio to calculate the return generated by a fund over the return of short-term Treasury bills. If the fund returns 12% over three years, while the Treasury bill rate is 1.5% and the fund's beta is 0.5, then we can see the Treynor ratio is 21 (= [12 − 1.5] ÷ 0.5).

TRICKS OF THE TRADE

- Like the Sharpe ratio, the Treynor ratio doesn't quantify the value added—it is simply a ranking mechanism. Where the two mechanisms differ is that the Sharpe ratio considers total risk (the standard deviation of the portfolio) while the Treynor ratio considers systematic risk (the beta of a portfolio versus the benchmark).
- In practice, it's possible to simply look up Treynor ratios for many listed equity funds. For example, many newspapers and

financial websites will list Treynor figures under "performance" data, usually over three, five, and 10 years.

- It is worth considering how Treynor Ratios change over time and in relation to similar funds—a three-year ratio may be negative while five-year and 10-year figures are positive. This could be because the fund is mismanaged but also could reflect a market downturn or a short-term problem.

Value at Risk

WHAT IT MEASURES

Value at risk (VAR) is a useful tool for anyone looking to quantify the risk of a particular project or investment opportunity by measuring the potential loss that might be incurred over a certain period of time. VAR measures what is the most that an investor might lose, based on a specific level of confidence, over a specific period of time. For example, "What's the most I can—with a 95% level of confidence—expect to lose over the next 12 months?"

WHY IT IS IMPORTANT

Most risk measurements focus on volatility whereas VAR focuses specifically on losses. It is commonly used to evaluate risk across a portfolio, but can also be applied to single indexes or anything that trades like a stock. VAR is important because it provides financial executives with a method of quantifying risk that is rigorous but also easily understood by nonfinancial executives.

HOW IT WORKS IN PRACTICE

The most common method of calculating VAR is the variance-covariance approach, sometimes referred to as "parametric VAR." Parametric VAR is a percentile-based risk measure that measures the expected loss of a portfolio over a specific period of time, depending on the confidence. To calculate parametric VAR, use the following formula:

Mean × HPR + (Z score × Std Dev × SQRT (HPR)

where Mean is the average expected (or actual) rate of return, HPR is the holding period, Z score is the probability, Std Dev is the standard deviation, and SQRT is the square root (of time).

To calculate the VAR of a portfolio worth $1 million with an expected average annual return of 13%, a standard annual deviation of 20% (equal to a daily deviation of 1.26%), and a 95% confidence score, therefore, you would perform the following calculation:

13 × 1 + (95 × 1.26 × SQRT) = 6.037%

This results in a 10-day VAR of $60,370. This means that your biggest potential loss over any 10-day period should not exceed $60,370 more than 5% of the time, or approximately once a year.

TRICKS OF THE TRADE

- VAR is now increasingly accepted as the *de facto* standard for risk measurement. In 1993, when the Bank of International Settlements members met in Basel, they amended the Basel Accord to require banks to hold in reserve enough capital to cover 10 days of losses based on a 95% 10-day VAR.
- A simpler alternative approach to calculating VAR is using the historical method—this simply takes all empirical profit and loss history and puts the returns in order of size. If we had 100 historical returns, the VAR for a 99% confidence score would simply be the second largest loss. Critics argue that very few portfolios have enough historical data to make this approach reliable, however.
- A third approach to calculating VAR is the simulation or Monte Carlo method, which uses computerized simulation to generate thousands of possible returns from a parametric assumption, then ordering them in the same way as with an historical calculation.
- Although VAR is often described as the "maximum possible" loss, this only applies at a single percentage confidence score. It is always possible to lose more by applying a higher confidence level—this is known as the conditional value at risk (CVAR), expected shortfall, or extreme tail loss.

▸▸ MORE INFO

Books:

Butler, Cormac. *Mastering Value at Risk: A Step-by-Step Guide to Understanding and Applying VAR*. London: FT Prentice Hall, 1999.

Choudhry, Moorad. *An Introduction to Value-at-Risk*. 4th ed. Chichester, UK: Wiley, 2006.

Websites:

Investopedia on VAR: www.investopedia.com/articles/04/092904.asp

Risk Glossary on VAR: www.riskglossary.com/link/value_at_risk.htm

Weighted Average Cost of Capital

WHAT IT MEASURES

The weighted average cost of capital (WACC) is the rate of return that the providers of a company's capital require, weighted according to the proportion each element bears to the total pool of capital.

WHY IT IS IMPORTANT

WACC is one of the most important figures in assessing a company's financial health, both for internal use (in capital budgeting) and external use (valuing companies on investment markets). It gives companies an insight into the cost of their financing, can be used as a hurdle rate for investment decisions, and acts as a measure to be minimized to find the best possible capital structure for the company. WACC is a rough guide to the rate of interest per monetary unit of capital. As such, it can be used to provide a discount rate for cash flows with similar risk to that of the overall business.

     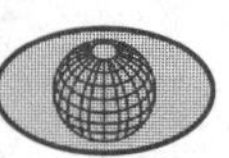   

HOW IT WORKS IN PRACTICE

To calculate the weighted average cost of capital, companies must multiply the cost of each element of capital for a project—which may include loans, bonds, equity, and preferred stock—by its percentage of the total capital, and then add them together.

For example, a business might consider investing $40 million in an expansion program. The financing is raised through a combination of equity (such as $10m of stock with an expected 10% return) and debt (for example, $30m bond issue, with 5% coupon).

In this simple scenario, WACC would be calculated as follows:

Equity ($10m) divided by total capital ($40m) = 25%,
multiplied by cost of equity (10%) = 2.5%

Debt ($30m) divided by total capital ($40m) = 75%,
multiplied by cost of debt (5%) = 3.75%

The two results added together give a weighted cost of capital of 6.25%.

In reality, interest payments are tax deductible, so a more accurate formula for WACC is:

$$WACC = DP \times DC - T + EP \times EC$$

where DP is the proportion of debt financing, DC is the cost of debt financing, T is the company's tax rate, EP is the proportion of equity finance, and EC is the cost of equity finance.

TRICKS OF THE TRADE

- To accurately calculate WACC, you need to know the specific rates of return required for each source of capital. For example, different sources of finance may attract different levels of taxation, or interest, which should be accounted for. A true WACC calculation could therefore be much more complex than the example provided here.
- Critics of WACC argue that financial analysts rely on it too heavily, and that the algorithm should not be used to assess risky projects, where the cost of capital will necessarily be higher to reflect the higher risk.
- Investors use WACC to help decide whether a company represents a good investment opportunity. To some extent, WACC represents the rate at which a company produces value for investors—if a company produces a return of 20% and has a WACC of 11%, then the company creates 9% additional value for investors. If the return is lower than the WACC, the business is unlikely to secure investment.
- Although the WACC formula seems simple, different analysts will often come up with different WACC calculations for the same company depending on how they interpret the company's debt, market value, and interest rates.

›› MORE INFO

Book:

Pratt, Shannon P., and Roger J. Grabowski. *Cost of Capital: Applications and Examples*. Hoboken, NJ: Wiley, 2008.

Websites:

Money Terms on WACC: moneyterms.co.uk/wacc/

12 Manage on WACC: www.12manage.com/methods_wacc.html

Working Capital

Working capital is concrete proof of the business axiom "It takes money to make money."

WHAT IT MEASURES

The funds that are readily available to operate a business. Working capital comprises the total net current assets of a business, which are its inventory, debtors, and cash—minus its creditors.

WHY IT IS IMPORTANT

Obviously, it is vital for a company to have sufficient working capital to meet all of its requirements. The faster a business expands, the greater will be its working capital needs.

If current assets do not exceed current liabilities, a company may well run into trouble paying creditors who want their money quickly. Indeed, the leading cause of business failure is not lack of profitability, but rather lack of working capital, which helps to explain why some experts advise: "Use someone else's money every chance you get, and don't let anyone else use yours."

HOW IT WORKS IN PRACTICE

Working capital is also called net current assets or current capital, and is expressed as:

Working capital = Current assets – Current liabilities

Current assets are cash and assets that can be converted to cash within one year or a normal operating cycle; current liabilities are monies owed that are due within one year.

If a company's current assets total $300,000 and its current liabilities total $160,000, its working capital is:

300,000 – 160,000 = $140,000

The working capital cycle describes capital (usually cash) as it moves through a company: It first flows from a company to pay for supplies, materials, finished goods inventory, and wages to workers who produce goods and services. It then flows into a company as goods and services are sold and as new investment equity and loans are received. Each stage of this cycle consumes time. The more time the stages consume, the greater the demands on working capital.

TRICKS OF THE TRADE

- Good management of working capital includes actions like collecting receivables faster and moving inventory more quickly; generating more cash increases working capital.
- While it can be tempting to use cash to pay for fixed assets like computers or vehicles, doing so reduces the amount of cash available for working capital.

›› MORE INFO

Websites:

PlanWare on the working capital: www.planware.org/workcap.htm

Study Finance (University of Arizona) on working capital management: www.studyfinance.com

- If working capital is tight, consider other ways of financing capital investment, such as loans, fresh equity, or leasing.
- Early warning signs of insufficient working capital include pressure on existing cash; exceptional cash-generating activities such as offering high discounts for early payment; increasing lines of credit; partial payments to suppliers and creditors; a preoccupation with surviving rather than managing; frequent short-term emergency requests to the bank, for example, to help pay wages, pending receipt of a check.
- Several ratios measure how effectively and efficiently working capital is being used. These ratios are explained separately.

Working Capital Cycle

WHAT IT MEASURES

The working capital cycle measures the amount of time that elapses between the moment when your business begins investing money in a product or service, and the moment the business receives payment for that product or service. This doesn't necessarily begin when you manufacture a product—businesses often invest money in products when they hire people to produce goods, or when they buy raw materials.

WHY IT IS IMPORTANT

A good working capital cycle balances incoming and outgoing payments to maximize working capital. Simply put, you need to know you can afford to research, produce, and sell your product.

A short working capital cycle suggests a business has good cash flow. For example, a company that pays contractors in 7 days but takes 30 days to collect payments has 23 days of working capital to fund—also known as having a working capital cycle of 23 days. Amazon.com, in contrast, collects money before it pays for goods. This means the company has a negative working capital cycle and has more capital available to fund growth. For a business to grow, it needs access to cash—and being able to free up cash from the working capital cycle is cheaper than other sources of finance, such as loans.

HOW IT WORKS IN PRACTICE

The key to understanding a company's working capital cycle is to know where payments are collected and made, and to identify areas where the cycle is stretched—and can potentially be reduced.

The working capital cycle is a diagram rather than a mathematical calculation. The cycle shows all the cash coming in to the business, what it is used for, and how it leaves the business (i.e., what it is spent on).

A simple working capital cycle diagram is shown opposite. The arrows in the diagram show the movement of assets through the business—including cash, but also other assets such as raw materials and finished goods. Each item represents a reservoir of assets—for example, cash into the business is converted into labor. The working capital cycle will break down if there is not a supply of assets moving continually through the cycle (known as a liquidity crisis).

The working capital diagram should be customized to show the way capital moves around your business. More complex diagrams might include incoming assets such as cash payments, interest payments, loans, and equity. Items that commonly absorb cash would be labor, inventory, and suppliers.

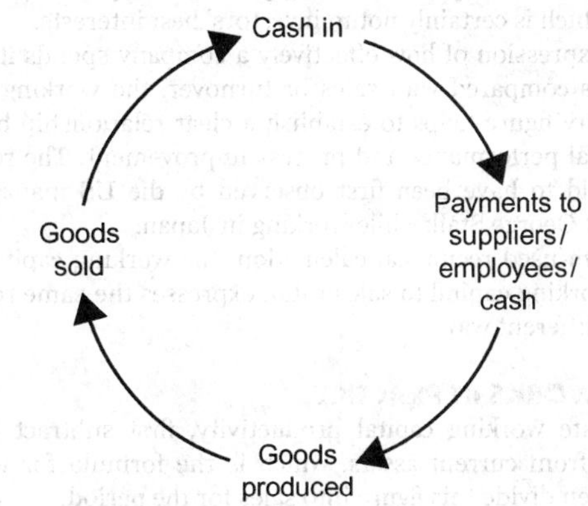

The key thing to model is the time lag between each item on the diagram. For some businesses, there may be a very long delay between making the product and receiving cash from sales. Others may need to purchase raw materials a long time before the product can be manufactured. Once you have this information, it is possible to calculate your total working capital cycle, and potentially identify where time lags within the cycle can be reduced or eliminated.

TRICKS OF THE TRADE

- For investors, the working capital cycle is most relevant when analyzing capital-intensive businesses where cash flow is used to buy inventory. Typically, the working capital cycle of retailers, consumer goods, and consumer goods manufacturers is critical to their success.
- The working capital cycle should be considered alongside the cash conversion cycle—a measure of working capital efficiency that gives clues about the average number of days that working capital is invested in the operating cycle.

▸▸ MORE INFO

Articles:

Harper, David. "Financial statements: Working capital." *Investopedia*. Online at: www.investopedia.com/university/financialstatements/financialstatements6.asp

Johnson, Millard. "Revving up the working capital cycle." *Corporate Report Wisconsin* (July 1, 2004). Online at: www.allbusiness.com/accounting/959776-1.html

     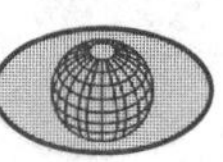   

Working Capital Productivity

However expressed or calculated, working capital productivity is a measurement that offers a snapshot of a company's efficiency by comparing working capital with sales or turnover.

WHAT IT MEASURES

How effectively a company's management is using its working capital.

WHY IT IS IMPORTANT

It is obvious that capital not being put to work properly is being wasted, which is certainly not in investors' best interests.

As an expression of how effectively a company spends its available funds compared with sales or turnover, the working capital productivity figure helps to establish a clear relationship between its financial performance and process improvement. The relationship is said to have been first observed by the US management consultant George Stalk while working in Japan.

A seldom-used reciprocal calculation, the working capital turnover or working capital to sales ratio, expresses the same relationship in a different way.

HOW IT WORKS IN PRACTICE

To calculate working capital productivity, first subtract current liabilities from current assets, which is the formula for working capital, then divide this figure into sales for the period.

$$\text{Working capital productivity} = \frac{\text{Sales}}{\text{Current assets} - \text{Current liabilities}}$$

If sales are $3,250, current assets are $900, and current liabilities are $650, then:

$$\frac{3250}{900-650} = \frac{3250}{250} = 13$$

In this case, the higher the number the better. Sales growing faster than the resources required to generate them is a clear sign of efficiency and, by definition, productivity.

The working capital to sales ratio uses the same figures, but in reverse:

$$\text{Working capital/sales ratio} = \frac{\text{Working capital}}{\text{Sales}}$$

Using the same figures in the example above, this ratio would be calculated:

$$\frac{250}{3250} = 0.077 = 7.7\%$$

For this ratio, obviously, the lower the number the better.

TRICKS OF THE TRADE

- By itself, a single ratio means little; a series of them—several quarters' worth, for example—indicates a trend, and means a great deal.
- Some experts recommend doing quarterly calculations and averaging them for a given year to arrive at the most reliable number.
- Either ratio also helps a management compare its performance with that of competitors.
- These ratios should also help to motivate companies to improve processes, such as eliminating steps in the handling of materials and bill collection, and shortening product design times. Such improvements reduce costs and make working capital available for other tasks.

Yield

WHAT IT MEASURES

Stocks that pay dividends (note that not all do) will produce an annual cash return to the investor. Simply dividing this cash return by the current stock price and expressing that as a percentage is known as the "yield"—that is, the annual percentage income at the current price. As far as newspapers are concerned, the yield figure they publish is usually the historical one.

Analysts will often provide forecasts for dividends in terms of earnings per share (EPS), and thus the forecast yield can then be calculated. Forecasts can, of course, go wrong, and consequently there is some risk in relying on them.

WHY IT IS IMPORTANT

Yield, after the price/earnings ratio, is one of the most common methods of comparing the relative value of stocks, and that is why it is so widely quoted in the press. The majority of investors like to see a cash income from their stocks, although to some extent this is a cultural thing. There are more companies in the United States, for example, that pay no dividends than in the United Kingdom.

HOW IT WORKS IN PRACTICE

You can compare yields against the market average or against a sector average, which in turn gives you some idea of the relative value of the stock against its peers, much like other ratios. Other things being equal, a higher-yield stock is preferable to that of an identical company with a lower yield. The higher-yield stock is cheaper. In practice, of course, there may well be good reasons why the market has decided that the higher yielder should be so—possibly it has worse prospects, is less profitable, and so on. This is not always the case; the market is far from being a perfectly rational place.

An additional feature of the yield (unlike many of the other stock analysis ratios) is that it enables comparison with cash. When you put cash into an interest-bearing source like a bank account or a government stock, you get a yield—the annual interest payable. This is usually a pretty safe investment. You can compare the yield from this cash investment with the yield on stocks, which are far riskier. This produces a valuable basis for stock evaluation. If, for example, you can get 4% in a bank without capital risk, you can

  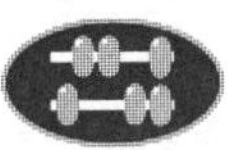   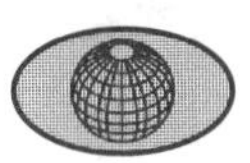   

then look at stocks and ask yourself how this yield compares—given that, as well as the opportunity for long-term growth of both the stock price and the dividends, there is plenty of capital risk.

TRICKS OF THE TRADE

- Care is necessary, however, because unlike banks paying interest, companies are under no obligation to pay dividends at all. Frequently, if they go through a bad patch, even the largest and best-known household name companies will cut dividends or even abandon paying them altogether. So, stock yield is much less reliable than bank interest or government stock interest yield.
- Despite this, yield is an immensely useful feature of stock appraisal. It is the only ratio that tells you about the cash return to the investor, and you cannot argue with cash. EPS, for example, is subject to accountants' opinions, but a dividend once paid is an unarguable fact.

▸▸ MORE INFO

Websites:

Accounting Standards Board (UK): www.frc.org.uk/asb

Securities and Exchange Commission (US): www.sec.gov

Z-Score

WHAT IT MEASURES

The z-score is a measure of the financial health of a company. Devised in the 1960s by Edward Altman, the score uses statistical techniques to predict the likelihood that a company will fail because of bankruptcy within two years.

The z-score was originally created based on Altman's analysis of 33 bankrupt manufacturing companies with assets averaging $6.4 million and a further 33 nonbankrupt companies with assets between $1 million and $25 million. Altman's analysis showed that 95% of the bankrupt companies had a z-score that suggested financial problems.

WHY IT IS IMPORTANT

Since the 1980s, auditors have used the z-score to help identify companies with serious cash problems. The measure is also used to help score applicants for loans. Stockbrokers commonly use the z-score to determine if a company is a good investment.

HOW IT WORKS IN PRACTICE

The z-score combines five common business ratios and uses a weighting system devised by Altman to produce a score somewhere between −4 and +8. Each of the components that make up the final z-score are rated independently, and each component has a different weight in the calculation of the overall z-score. The exact emphasis on each factor can vary slightly from one industry to another, using more specific z-score calculators.

All the information needed to calculate a z-score is available in company financial reports. The original formula to calculate a z-score is as follows:

$$z = 1.2T1 + 1.4T2 + 3.3T3 + 0.6T4 + 0.999T5$$

where:
T1 = working capital/total assets
T2 = retained earnings/total assets
T3 = earnings before interest and tax/total assets
T4 = market value of equity/book value of total liabilities
T5 = sales/total assets

A score can be analyzed as follows:
>2.99: the company is considered "safe"
1.8–2.99: there is some risk of financial distress
<1.8: there is serious risk of financial distress

TRICKS OF THE TRADE

- Although the numbers that go into the z-score can be influenced by external events, it is a useful tool to provide a quick analysis of where a company stands compared to competitors, and for tracking the risk of insolvency over time.
- Studies have shown the z-score is an accurate prediction of company failure rates in between seven and eight out of 10 cases.
- The formula was originally devised to be used for public companies, but amendments have since been made to allow z-scores to be calculated for privately held companies. In this case, the calculation that should be used is as follows:

$$0.717T1 + 0.87T2 + 0.420T4 + 0.998T5$$

For private companies, a score of 2.9 is "safe," while a score below 1.23 is considered a serious risk of financial distress.

▸▸ MORE INFO

Book:

Altman, Edward I. "The z-score bankruptcy model: Past, present, and future." In Edward I. Altman and Arnold W. Sametz (eds). *Financial Crises: Institutions and Markets in a Fragile Environment*. New York: Wiley, 1977.

Website:

UK Insolvency Helpline z-score business health calculator: www.insolvencyhelpline.co.uk/interactive-tools/z-calc.php

FINANCE THINKERS AND LEADERS

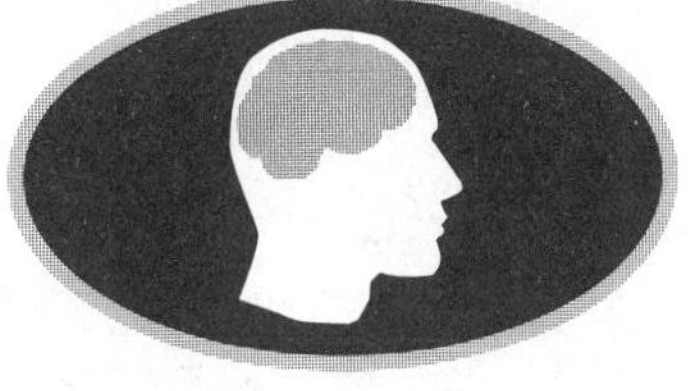

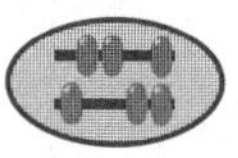

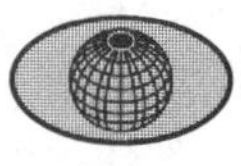
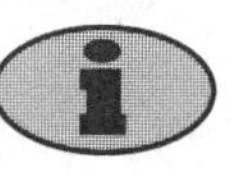

Finance Thinkers and Leaders

Profiling the top finance thinkers and pioneers

This section provides over fifty concise summaries of the some of the most influential finance theorists, practitioners, and thought leaders. The Finance Thinkers and Leaders range from originators of financial theory through to those who created practical applications in real-life situations. One factor links them all—they have all had an impact on current business practice.

The profiles include summaries of the career and thinking of the most important and influential thought leaders and practitioners in the field, as well as an assessment of their contribution to the world of modern finance. We also provide a list of key works and sources if you need to read further.

Our aim has been to identify the key figures who have laid down the foundations of finance and provide the reader with insights behind their practical application.

   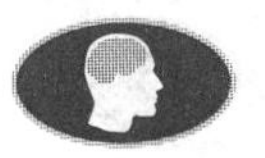  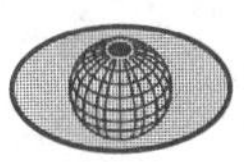   

Contents

  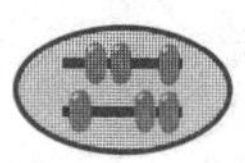   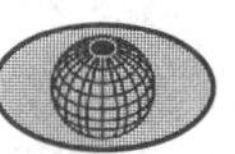   

Prince Al-Walid bin Talal • Billionaire member of Saudi royal family and international investor

1955 Born in Riyadh, Saudi Arabia.
1979 Received BS in Business Administration from Menlo College.
1980 Founded Kingdom Holding Company.
1985 Received Master of Social Science degree at the Maxwell School of Citizenship and Public Affairs of Syracuse University.

LIFE AND CAREER

Prince Al-Walid bin Talal bin Abdul Aziz Al Saud, commonly known as Prince Al-Walid, is a member of the Saudi royal family, his grandfather being Abdul Aziz al Saud, the founding king of Saudi Arabia. He is an entrepreneur, businessman, and international investor who began his business career after graduating from Menlo College, funded by a US$30,000 loan from his father and a US$300,000 mortgage on his house. He initially brokered deals with foreign firms wishing to do business in Saudi Arabia, before negotiating land deals in the 1980s, and some major investments in the Saudi banking industry. He continued to amass his fortune through investments in real estate, and the stock market. He is a Lebanese citizen, after his mother, and has been a special envoy for UNICEF. He has received many honorary degrees and academic awards, and is heavily involved in charitable activities across the Middle East, Asia, and Africa. It is estimated that he donates more than US$100 million annually to charity.

KEY THINKING

- Al-Walid is said to be the world's most influential Arab businessman, and one of the richest people in the world, with an estimated net worth of US$30 billion.
- He started his investment career in Saudi Arabia, through joint ventures with foreign companies, reinvesting the profits in real estate in Riyadh that greatly appreciated in value.
- He then focused on the country's banking sector, taking a controlling stake in the unprofitable United Saudi Commercial Bank (USCB) in 1986, returning it to profit within two years.
- In the late 1980s, he extended his investment portfolio out of the Middle East, buying shares in a number of US banks, before focusing all his bank investments in Citicorp.
- After many further strategic investments, the bulk of his fortune is now invested in a variety of high-profile US corporations—he is the largest single foreign investor in the country.
- He donated US$10 million to a relief fund after the attack on the World Trade Center, but became a controversial figure after asking the US to re-examine its policies in the Middle East; Mayor Giuliani returned the donation.
- In the Middle East, however, the confrontation turned him into one of the most respected public figures in the Arab world.
- He has also contributed a considerable amount to educational initiatives focused on uniting the gap between Western and Islamic communities; in 2005, he donated US$20 million each to Harvard and Georgetown universities to fund Islamic studies.
- In 2005, he purchased the Savoy hotel in London for £250 million, and donated US$20 million to the Louvre Museum in Paris, to help fund the construction of a wing for its collection of Islamic art.
- He donated US$500,000 towards a fund to honor former US president, George HW Bush in 2002.
- His latest project is the Mile High Tower, to be located in Jeddah; planned to be twice the height of the world's current tallest building, it is expected to cost US$10 billion.

IN PERSPECTIVE

- Al-Walid founded the private investment firm, Kingdom Holding Company, his base for investments in the banking, hotel, and real-estate sectors.
- After his major investments in Citicorp, he made a number of key acquisitions in other faltering blue-chip international businesses, including Eurodisney, New York's Plaza Hotel, London's Canary Wharf, and Apple Computers.
- In 2000, he moved his investments into high-tech companies, such as Compaq, Kodak, eBay, and Amazon.com.
- He is now considered to be the strongest political contender among the third-generation Saudi royals who will one day inherit power.
- He has called for the introduction of elections to Saudi Arabia's 120-member advisory council, to help reduce domestic problems in the country.
- His donations to religious institutions in the Middle East and the building of many new mosques in Saudi Arabia have made him a popular figure in the region.
- He is vocal advocate on women's rights, and hired the first female airline pilot in Saudi Arabia.

▸▸ MORE INFO

Book:

Khan, Riz. *Alwaleed: Businessman, Billionaire, Prince*. London: HarperCollins, 2005.
The only biography of Al-Walid, it delves into his rise from a modest bank loan into a businessman and investor, with a portfolio containing Citigroup, Disney, Apple, and the Four Seasons Hotels.

"Banks are the eyes of an economy." Prince Al-Walid bin Talal

  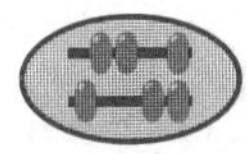 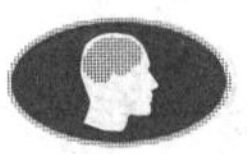  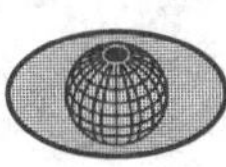   

Igor Ansoff · The father of modern strategic management

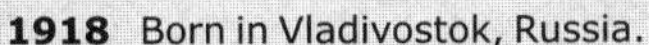

1918 Born in Vladivostok, Russia.
1937 Emigrated to the US.
1950 Joined the Rand Corporation.
1956 Worked at Lockheed Aircraft Corporation.
1957 Published article on "Strategies for Diversification".
1963 Appointed Professor of Industrial Administration at the Carnegie Institute of Technology.
1965 Publication of *Corporate Strategy*.
1968 Appointed Founding Dean and Professor of Management at Vanderbilt University.
1973 Appointed Professor at the European Institute for Advanced Studies in Management.
1976 Appointed Professor at the Stockholm School of Economics.
1979 Publication of *Strategic Management*.
1984 Appointed Professor at the United States International University (USIU).
1984 Publication of *Implementing Strategic Management*.
2000 Retired from academic life.
2000 Named Distinguished Professor Emeritus at the USIU.
2002 Died in San Diego, California.

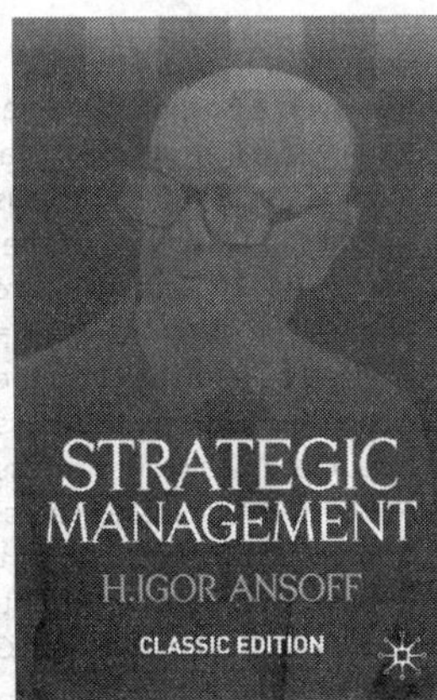

LIFE AND CAREER

Igor Ansoff was a mathematician, university professor, and business consultant. After studying general engineering at the Stevens Institute of Technology, and receiving a PhD in Applied Mathematics from Brown University, he joined the UCLA Senior Executive Program. During World War II he was a member of the US Naval Reserve, serving as liaison with the Russian navy and as an Instructor in Physics at the US Naval Academy. After the war, he worked at the Rand Corporation before moving to Lockheed, where he went on to become Vice-President of Plans and Programs, and then Vice-President and General Manager of the Industrial Technology division. He was a professor at the United States International University and acted as consultant for many multinational corporations, such as Philips, General Electric, and IBM.

KEY THINKING

- Igor Ansoff helped define corporate strategy and planning as a management activity in its own right; before him, strategic analysis was based purely around budget projections.
- He explored how an organization needed to anticipate future challenges in developing strategy, and put in place a strategic response to counter these challenges.
- He also researched how an organization should focus on core capability, as this ensures a link between its past and future activities.
- This led to the identification of four key strategy components: product-market scope, growth vector, competitive advantage, and synergy.
- He originated the phrase "paralysis by analysis" to describe how excessive planning can impede practical action.

IN PERSPECTIVE

- He argued that a company should not just be self-serving, as this will lead to stagnation; he proposed that long-term profitability results from an understanding of the context in which it operates.
- He developed the Ansoff Matrix, or "product-mission matrix", to analyse the risk component in different growth strategies.
- There are four strategies in the Matrix: market penetration, market expansion, product expansion, and diversification –these help track strategies for growth through existing or new products, in existing or new markets.
- He focuses on diversification–he saw it as transforming previous processes and traditions, and necessitating careful planning and analysis, and the development of new skills, techniques, and resources.
- In *Strategic Management* he discussed strategic planning as a multidisciplinary system, which should integrate individual and group dynamics, as well as political processes and organizational culture.
- The issue of turbulence is central to Ansoff's thinking on strategy–in *Strategic Management* he developed a framework for strategy formulation to assist planning in the post-war economy of the US.
- He also discussed what he saw as the five "turbulence levels" in a business environment: repetitive, expanding, changing, discontinuous, and surprising– as well as the standard types of organizational decision: strategy, policy, programs, and standard operating procedures.
- He developed a new classification of decision-making which became known as Strategy-Structure-Systems, or the 3S model.

▸▸ MORE INFO

Books:

Ansoff, H. Igor. *Corporate Strategy: An Analytic Approach to Business Policy for Growth and Expansion*. New York: McGraw-Hill, 1965.
Ansoff, H. Igor. *Strategic Management*. New York: Wiley, 1979.
Antoniou, Peter H., and Patrick E. Sullivan. *The Igor Ansoff Anthology*. Charleston, SC: BookSurge Publishing, 2006.

See Also:

Corporate Strategy: An Analytic Approach to Business Policy for Growth and Expansion (p. 1243)

"Structure will become a dynamic enabler of both change and unchanged, the ultimate model of organizational chaos." Igor Ansoff

Louis Bachelier · The father of financial mathematics

1870 Born in Le Havre, France.
1895 Received a Bachelor in Sciences from the Sorbonne.
1897 Received a Certificate in Mathematical Physics.
1900 Publication of his PhD thesis, *The Theory of Speculation.*
1909 Appointed a Lecturer at the Sorbonne.
1912 Publication of *Calcul des Probabilités.*
1914 Publication of *Le Jeu, la Chance et le Hasard.*
1914 Drafted as a private into the French army.
1919 Appointed Assistant Professor at University of Besançon.
1922 Appointed Assistant Professor at University of Dijon.
1925 Appointed Associate Professor at University of Rennes.
1927 Appointed full Professor at University of Besançon.
1937 Appointed Professor Emeritus at University of Besançon.
1937 Publication of *Les Lois des Grands Nombres du Calcul des Probabilités.*
1937 Retires from academic life.
1938 Publication of *La Spéculation et le Calcul des Probabilités.*
1939 Publication of *Les Nouvelles Méthodes du Calcul des Probabilités.*
1946 Dies in Saint-Servan-sur-Mer, France.

LIFE AND CAREER

Louis Bachelier pioneered the study of financial mathematics well before it became central to financial practice. As a young man, he moved to Paris to study at the Sorbonne, where his doctoral thesis, *The Theory of Speculation*, helped originate the mathematics and modeling of finance, and the theory of Brownian motion. He was later offered a permanent professorship at the Sorbonne, with support from the Council of Paris University. However, he was unable to take up the position because World War I intervened and he was drafted into the French army. After the war he returned to academic life, and continued to research and write on financial mathematics, risk and probability. Public acknowledgement of his work, richly deserved for the innovations he brought to financial theory, did not really arrive until after his death, when he was rediscovered by those founding modern financial theory in the 1950s.

KEY THINKING

- Bachelier is credited as the first person to model Brownian motion, as part of his thesis on *The Theory of Speculation,* to show that advanced mathematics could be used in the study of finance to evaluate stock options.
- In mathematics, the Brownian motion is often referred to as the Wiener process, and Bachelier applied its simple stochastic process to modeling random fluctuations in stock prices.
- His work on chance, probability and risk anticipated the random movements of financial market prices and has become an integral part of modern financial theory.
- When he initially applied to join the University of Dijon he was rejected due to a misinterpretation of one of his papers by Paul Lévy, who appeared not to know of Bachelier or his work. Lévy later realized his error, and apologized to Bachelier.

IN PERSPECTIVE

- Bachelier's successful defense of his thesis in 1900 marked the birth of mathematical finance, and it was later published in the influential French journal, *Annales Scientifiques de l'Ecole Normale Supérieure.*
- His analysis of Brownian motion so that it could be applied to the mathematical modeling of price movements, and the evaluation of contingent claims in financial markets, is often thought of as one of the most important mathematical discoveries of the twentieth century.
- His groundbreaking analysis of the stock and option markets included several key ideas for the development of both finance and probability.
- Between 1900 and 1914, he developed the mathematical theory of diffusion processes in a series of papers published in reputed French journals.
- In his book *Le Jeu, la Chance et le Hasard,* Bachelier considered the systematic use of the concept of continuity in probabilistic modeling.
- He introduced many of the concepts of what later became stochastic analysis, in his attempt to find a theory for the valuation of financial options. His findings were similar to the work of Fischer Black, Myron Scholes, and Robert Merton in their seminal paper of 1973.

▸▸ MORE INFO

Books:

Bachelier, Louis. *Louis Bachelier's Theory of Speculation: The Origins of Modern Finance.* Princeton, NJ: Princeton University Press, 2006. This new translation of Bachelier's seminal work also contains a commentary on the development of stochastic analysis and financial economics.

Cootner, Paul H. (ed). *The Random Character of Stock Market Prices.* Cambridge, MA: MIT Press, 1964. A collection of research reprints on the randomness of the market up to 1964. It includes the first full English translation of Bachelier's thesis, *The Theory of Speculation.*

Website:

Bachelier Finance Society, founded in 1996 by researchers in mathematical finance as a forum where academics and practitioners could exchange ideas and discuss their work: www.stochastik.uni-freiburg.de/bfsweb

"The mathematical expectation of the speculator is zero." Louis Bachelier

  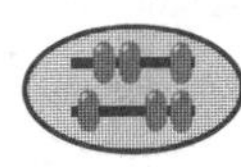   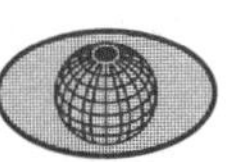   

Gary Becker · Nobel Prize-winning economist

1930 Born in Pottsville, Pennsylvania.
1951 Received BA from Princeton University.
1953 Received MA from the University of Chicago.
1954 Appointed Assistant Professor at the University of Chicago.
1955 Received PhD from the University of Chicago.
1957 Appointed Assistant and Associate Professor of Economics at Columbia University.
1957 Appointed Member, Senior Research Associate and Research Policy Advisor, National Bureau of Economic Research.
1957 Publication of *The Economics of Discrimination*.
1960 Appointed Professor of Economics at Columbia University.
1964 Publication of *Human Capital*.
1967 Received John Bates Clark Medal of the American Economic Association.
1983 Appointed University Professor of Economics and Sociology at the University of Chicago.
1987 Appointed President of the American Economic Association.
1991 Publication of *A Treatise on the Family*.
1992 Received Nobel Memorial Prize in Economic Sciences.
1996 Publication of *Accounting for Tastes*.
2000 Received National Medal of Science.
2007 Received Presidential Medal of Freedom.

LIFE AND CAREER

Gary Becker is an internationally renowned economist, Nobel Prize winner, business writer, and specialist on the sociological aspects of economic theory and analysis. He is regarded as one of the most influential economists of the 20th century, and has inspired much empirical research, due to his innovative work in different areas. He has taught economics at Columbia University for nearly 50 years, written a monthly column for *Business Week* for 20 years, and now coproduces an economics internet blog with Richard Posner. He has previously been on the board of directors at the Manhattan Institute, a member of the Advisory Committee to the Secretary of Defense, a member of the Accenture Energy Advisory Board, and is currently on the board of directors for the New Center for Accelerating Medical Innovations, the Merc Advisory Board on Innovation, and the Hoover Energy Task Force.

KEY THINKING

- Becker focused much of his research on how individuals make choices when investing in human capital based on benefits and cost, and the potential rate of return, in terms of marriage, divorce, fertility, and social welfare.
- He received the Nobel Prize for his work in extending economic theory to new areas of human behavior, including sociology, demography and criminology.
- His economic research also examines the impact of positive and negative habits––such as punctuality and alcoholism––on human capital, the different rates of return, and the resulting macroeconomic implications.
- In his study of discrimination in the workplace, he found it was less prevalent in highly competitive industries that focused on market success, but was greater in regulated industries that were less competitive.
- He also proposed that when minorities are a very small percentage of the population, the cost of discrimination mainly falls on minorities, but when their representation is higher, the cost of discrimination falls on both the minorities and the majority.

IN PERSPECTIVE

- His research considered the overlap between economics and areas of sociology, such as racial discrimination, crime, family organization, and drug addiction.
- He analyzed criminal behavior based on rational decision-making, and how criminals weigh the benefits of their crimes against risks of apprehension, conviction, and punishment.
- This led him to propose the best way to reduce crime was by increasing either the probability or the severity of punishment.
- In *A Treatise on the Family,* he examined social interaction and how time is allocated within the family, using economic theory to explain the reasoning behind decisions to have children and to educate them, and the decisions to marry and to divorce.
- This helped him originate the "rotten kid theorem", which states that children in a family, even if they normally act selfishly, will help one another if sufficiently incentivized.
- He also analyzed the workings of democracy, especially with regard to interest groups exploiting other groups, based on the concept of deadweight loss.

▸▸ MORE INFO

Books:

Becker, Gary S. *Accounting for Tastes.* Cambridge, MA: Harvard University Press, 1996. A collection of articles that examine issues surrounding the reasoning and impact of preferences and values.

Becker, Gary S. *The Economics of Life: From Baseball to Affirmative Action to Immigration, How Real-World Issues Affect Our Everyday Life.* New York: McGraw-Hill, 1997. Essays from *Business Week* that look at the ways market incentives can influence human behavior.

Becker, Gary S. *A Treatise on the Family.* Cambridge, MA: Harvard University Press, 1981. His seminal work on the family, in which Becker applies economic theory and assumptions to personal and family decision-making.

"Fines are preferable to imprisonment and other types of punishment because they are more efficient."
Gary Becker

     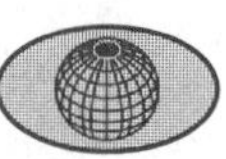   

Peter L. Bernstein • The foremost chronicler of risk

1919 Born on January 22.
1941 Graduated from Harvard College with a degree in Economics.
1941 Joined the Federal Reserve Board as a Researcher.
1951 Appointed Chief Executive of an investment counsel firm.
1970 Publication of *Economist on Wall Street.*
1973 Founded Peter L. Bernstein, Inc.
1974 Became the first Editor of *The Journal of Portfolio Management.*
1977 Publication of *Streetwise: The Best of the Journal of Portfolio Management.*
1992 Publication of *Capital Ideas: The Improbable Origins of Modern Wall Street.*
1995 Publication of *Portable MBA in Investment.*
1996 Publication of *Against the Gods: The Remarkable Story of Risk.*
1998 Publication of *Investment Management.*
2004 Publication of *The Power of Gold: The History of an Obsession.*
2007 Publication of *Capital Ideas Evolving.*
2007 Publication of *Wedding of the Waters.*

LIFE AND CAREER

Peter L. Bernstein is a prolific and award-winning author on finance and risk, and founder and president of Peter L. Bernstein, Inc., an international consultancy for institutional investors and corporations. After serving as an intelligence officer in Europe during World War II, he became a member of the research staff at the Federal Reserve Bank of New York. He then taught economics at Williams College and the New School for Social Research in New York City, before moving into commercial banking. He was the first editor of *The Journal of Portfolio Management*, and remains consulting editor. He produces a newsletter on the capital markets, and writes regularly for journals and the popular press. He also lectures widely on risk management, asset allocation, portfolio strategy, and market history, and has received major awards for his books.

KEY THINKING

- Bernstein's books are popular and insightful; he has taken difficult concepts in finance, mathematics, philosophy, history, and psychology, and made them accessible for a wide audience.
- In his book, *Capital Ideas,* he traces the origins of Wall Street, and profiles some of the pioneers of modern investment theory over the years, including Louis Bachelier, Harry Markowitz, William Sharpe, Fischer Black, Myron Scholes, Robert Merton, and Franco Modigliani.
- In *Against the Gods*, Bernstein analyzes probability and its applications, using a readable blend of biography, history, and science to examine the role played by famous thinkers in helping the evolution from a superstitious outlook to modern risk management.
- *Against the Gods* also reviews the history of numerical measurement, probability theory, and the history of financial risk instruments.
- The book explains probability, uncertainty, the difference between luck and skill, the interactions between gambling and investing, and rational versus irrational decision-making.

IN PERSPECTIVE

- Bernstein has the ability to combine historical ideas with economics, and the theory and practice of investment management.
- *Capital Ideas* explores the development of new theories in risk, valuation, and investment returns, and focuses on the implementation of these theories in the world of investment management. It shows how these theories explain the link between risk and reward, and the advantages of diversification, and provides a clear framework for valuing financial options.
- Bernstein recently produced a sequel to *Capital Ideas*, called *Capital Ideas Evolving*, which defended the theories of the first book, and extended his examination of the key ideas that drive modern financial practice.
- *Against the Gods* also shows how the concept of risk originated and traces its progression through history, up to our modern understanding of how it affects us all.
- It examined Pascal's Wager in detail, a concept that was ahead of its time in terms of both probability theory and decision theory; it is based on consequences being more important than probabilities.

▸▸ MORE INFO

Books:

Bernstein, Peter L. *Against the Gods: The Remarkable Story of Risk.* New York: Wiley, 1996.

Bernstein, Peter L. *Capital Ideas: The Improbable Origins of Modern Wall Street.* New York: Free Press, 1992.

Bernstein, Peter L. *Capital Ideas Evolving: The Improbable Origins of Modern Wall Street.* Hoboken, NJ: Wiley, 2007.

Website:

Author's company website: www.peterlbernsteininc.com

See Also:

Against the Gods: The Remarkable Story of Risk (p. 1215)

"The long run ain't what it used to be. Stocks don't have to do well in the future because they did well in the past. In fact, the opposite may be more likely." Peter L. Bernstein

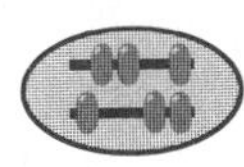
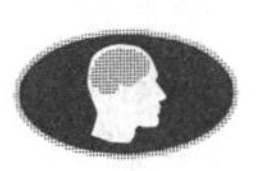

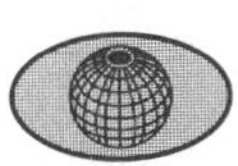

Fischer Black · The high priest of modern finance

1938 Born in Georgetown, USA.
1959 Received BA in Physics.
1964 Received PhD in Applied Mathematics from Harvard.
1965 Joined the consulting firm Arthur D. Little.
1969 Founded his own consulting firm, Associates in Finance.
1972 Appointed Visiting Professor and then full Professor at the Graduate School of Business, University of Chicago.
1975 Appointed to MIT Sloan School of Management.
1973 Published seminal paper, "The Pricing of Options and Corporate Liabilities", with Myron Scholes.
1984 Joined Goldman Sachs as Partner.
1994 Received the Financial Engineer of the Year award from the International Association of Financial Engineers.
1995 Died in New York.
2002 The American Finance Association established the Fischer Black Prize.

LIFE AND CAREER

Fischer Black was an economist who applied his analysis of Keynesian and monetarist theories to finance and investment, thereby helping to revolutionize the industry. He was originally an academic at the Graduate School of Business, University of Chicago, where he was Director of the Center for Research in Security Prices, and MIT, before moving to Wall Street and a position at Goldman Sachs. He made the transition at a decisive time, as financial engineering was just emerging, and he played a critical part in applying quantitative strategies to investment practices for the first time. He was the co-author of the famous Black–Scholes equation, which developed an option pricing model that is still used widely today. He would have won the Nobel Prize for Economics but for his untimely death, aged 57, due to cancer.

KEY THINKING

- Black is best known for his work on the problem of how best to price a call option, which had been worked on for many years by researchers taking both a theoretical, and an empirical point of view.
- This research produced the celebrated Black–Scholes formula, based on his 1973 paper with Myron Scholes, "The Pricing of Options and Corporate Liabilities".
- The Black–Scholes equation derived the Black–Scholes–Merton differential equation, thereby solving the stock option pricing problem.
- In the announcement of the 1997 Nobel Prize for Economics, awarded to Myron Scholes and Robert Merton, the Nobel committee pointed out Black's key role in their work.

IN PERSPECTIVE

- Black's work on option valuation marked the emergence of continuous time finance, which is now used to value derivative instruments across the industry. Derivatives, now traded in their trillions of dollars each year, are mostly valued using the mathematical methods Black helped develop in the early 1970s.
- In addition to his work with Scholes and Merton, he also made other important contributions, including his work on portfolio insurance, commodity futures pricing, bond swaps and interest rate futures, global asset allocation models, dividend policy, international trade, business cycles, and labor economics.
- He was also the co-developer of the Black–Derman–Toy interest-rate derivatives model, originally created for in-house use by Goldman Sachs in the 1980s.
- He analyzed the capital asset pricing model (CAPM) in terms of monetary policy and Keynesian economics, and discussed the most effective ways it could be used.
- He was a forerunner in the use of computer technology and efficient trading systems.
- He thought that trying to model reality was more important than attempting closed-form analytical solutions.

⏩ MORE INFO

Books:

Black, Fischer. *Business Cycles and Equilibrium*. New York: Blackwell, 1987. A collection of essays in which Black examines the role of equilibrium in a developed economy, arguing that mathematical models actually restrain creativity.

Black, Fischer. *Exploring General Equilibrium*. Cambridge, MA: MIT Press, 1995. Here Black assesses general equilibrium theory, and discusses what it reveals about business cycles, growth, and labor economics.

Mehrling, Perry. *Fischer Black and the Revolutionary Idea of Finance*. Hoboken, NJ: Wiley, 2005. A full biography, and an examination of Black's place in the development of modern quantitative finance.

"Most so-called anomalies don't seem anomalous to me at all. They seem like nuggets from a gold mine, found by one of the thousands of miners all over the world." Fischer Black

  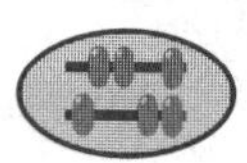   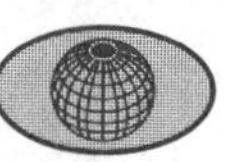   

Gary Brinson • One of the world's most influential investment managers

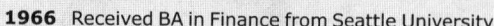

1966 Received BA in Finance from Seattle University.
1969 Received MBA from Washington State University.
1969 Appointed as an analyst at Travelers Insurance Co.
1979 Appointed Chief Investment Officer for the First National Bank of Chicago.
1989 Co-founded Brinson Partners.
1991 Named Outstanding Financial Executive by the Financial Management Association.
1994 Sold Brinson Partners to Swiss Bank Corp.
1994 Co-founded GP Brinson Investments.
1999 Received the Award for Professional Excellence from the Association for Investment Management Research.
2000 Co-founded the Brinson Foundation.

LIFE AND CAREER

Gary Brinson is a global investment expert, writer, and founder and retired chair of Brinson Partners, and private investment firm, GP Brinson Investments. He started his career at Travelers Insurance and went on to become Chief Investment Officer for the First National Bank of Chicago, where he set up its asset-management unit. He orchestrated a management buyout of the division to create Brinson Partners, Chicago, which he later sold to Swiss Bank Corp. His next step was to launch GP Brinson Investments, LLC, which he ran until his retirement in 2000. Since then, he and his family have run the philanthropic Brinson Foundation, which gives grants in education, science and public health. He is a former executive committee member and past chairman of the Institute of Chartered Financial Analysts, and is a trustee of the Research Foundation of the Institute of Chartered Financial Analysts. He has also lectured and written on professional investment for many years.

KEY THINKING

- The management buyout of the asset management unit he set up at First National Bank of Chicago, and its subsequent purchase by Swiss Bank Corp and merger with the Union Bank of Switzerland, created one of the world's largest money managers, in control of the combined banks' institutional assets.
- His asset allocation theory is based on four key principles: thinking globally, realizing that the value of asset classes should not rise and fall together, focusing on the long term, and monitoring and adjusting allocations to accommodate changed investment climates.
- He has promoted the professionalism of investment management by taking an active part in its industry association, the Association of Investment Management & Research (AIMR) and its Research Foundation.
- The January 2003 issue of *CFA Magazine* named Brinson as one of seven living legends in the investment profession.

IN PERSPECTIVE

- He was one of the first financial gurus to spot the value in investing overseas during his time at Brinson Partners, and was a pioneer of asset allocation techniques.
- Argued that investment decisions should prioritize markets or asset classes, and that the focus should be on overall portfolio risk rather than the risk of individual assets.
- Believed that asset allocation should combine different asset classes in ways that increase returns without an equal increase in risk, or that can reduce risk without sacrificing returns.
- Considered that with an international portfolio, it is possible to get equity-like returns with the low volatility you would expect from a mixture of stocks and bonds.
- He co-authored a paper in 1986, pointing out that asset allocation, not stock picking, drives portfolio performance, and that differences in stock selection explain very little of the variation in results for investors over the long run.

MORE INFO

Books:

Ibbotson, Roger G., and Gary P. Brinson. *Global Investing: The Professional's Guide to the World Capital Markets.* New York: McGraw-Hill, 1993. Examines asset classes, investment theory, and international investing in a practical way.

Mintz, Steven L., Dana Dakin, and Thomas Willison. *Beyond Wall Street: The Art of Investing.* New York: Wiley, 1998. An overview of investing that features eight well-known figures of the investment world, including a profile of Brinson.

"Extreme dislocations in markets inevitably occur." Gary Brinson

  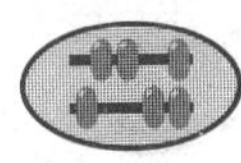 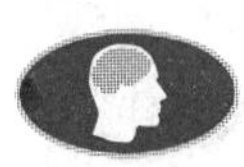  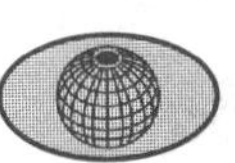   

Warren Buffett • The sage of Omaha

1930 Born in Omaha, Nebraska.
1950 Received BS from the University of Nebraska.
1951 Received MS in Economics from Columbia Business School.
1951 Co-founded Buffett-Falk & Co.
1954 Appointed as a security analyst at Graham-Newman Corp.
1956 Founds Buffett Partnership Ltd.
1962 Became dollar millionaire.
1965 Acquired Berkshire Hathaway.
1967 Berkshire Hathaway bought National Indemnity Company and National Fire & Marine Insurance Company.
1970 Appointed Chairman and Chief Executive Officer of Berkshire Hathaway.
1995 Acquired major stake in McDonald's.
1996 Acquired GEICO.
1998 Bought Executive Jet Corporation.
2001 Became the second-richest man in the US.
2001 Announced new investment strategy.
2003 Acquired Burlington Industries.
2003 Named by *Forbes* as the second-richest man in the world.
2004 Appointed an economic advisor by John Kerry during US presidential elections.
2008 Named by *Forbes* as the richest man in the world, worth US$62 billion.

LIFE AND CAREER

Warren Buffett is a multibillionaire investor, businessman and philanthropist, and one of the most influential people in the financial world. As a child, he quickly started making business deals, before studying at Columbia Business School under investment guru, Benjamin Graham, the first proponent of value investing. He formed the investment firm, Buffett-Falk & Co., and worked as an investment salesman, before Graham offered him a job at the Graham-Newman Corporation. Buffett soon realized he preferred to work independently, so he launched his own family investment partnership at the age of 25, with starting capital of US$100,000. He later decided to turn around one of his acquisitions, the unprofitable Berkshire Hathaway textile company. During the market collapse of 1973, he purchased a series of companies at bargain prices. Berkshire Hathaway is today a massive holdings company for a variety of businesses, with assets and sales totaling many billions of dollars. In 2006, it gave away US$30.7 billion in shares to the Gates Foundation, the largest charitable donation in history.

KEY THINKING

- Buffett was named as the richest man in the world, with a fortune of US$62.3 billion, in early 2008, by *Forbes* magazine.
- His investing career started with his own personal investment strategy of looking for stocks that offered outstanding value–those that were relatively cheap given their asset value–and then holding those shares for the long term.
- When he took over Berkshire Hathaway, Buffett focused on restructuring the company's financial framework, and using it as a holding company for other investments.
- He grew Berkshire Hathaway into the 12th largest corporation in the US, through the implementation of his investing principles; this strategy proved extremely successful–shareholders who invested US$10,000 in the company in 1965 have made more than US$50 million.
- He avoids stock bubbles that are generated by media coverage, such as the internet boom of the late 1990s; since 2000, he has ignored the technology sector, and focused on bricks, carpets, insulation, and paint.
- He is a Democratic supporter, and acted as an economic advisor to John Kerry, the Democratic candidate for the US presidential elections in 2004.

IN PERSPECTIVE

- Buffett was influenced by investment pioneer Benjamin Graham, in particular his work on value investing. Buffett further developed these theories by researching companies whose shares seemed cheap given their growth prospects.
- This approach was groundbreaking for its time, as it meant also examining a company's intangible assets, such as brand value.
- He invests by sticking rigidly to his own investment principles and avoiding bandwagons–he will not invest in a business he does not understand–but has successfully picked some key stocks at a cheap price, such as Coca-Cola and American Express, when they were at a low point in their business cycle.

▸▸ MORE INFO

Books:

Hagstrom, Robert G. *The Warren Buffett Way: Investment Strategies of the World's Greatest Investor*. New York: Wiley, 1994. Details Buffett's life and business career and gives a clear overview of his investment techniques and strategies.

Lowenstein, Roger. *Buffett: The Making of an American Capitalist*. New York: Random House, 1996. Looks at his personal life, as well as focusing on his early investments and the long-term growth strategies that made his fortune.

Schroeder, Alice. *The Snowball: Warren Buffett and the Business of Life*. London: Bloomsbury Publishing, 2008. Written with Buffett's full cooperation and collaboration, it combines his business expertise, life story and philosophy, and is useful for those wanting pointers for investment success.

See Also:

The Snowball: Warren Buffett and the Business of Life (p. 1319)
The Warren Buffett Way (p. 1332)

"Shares are not mere pieces of paper. They represent part-ownership of a business. So, when contemplating an investment, think like a prospective owner." Warren Buffett

     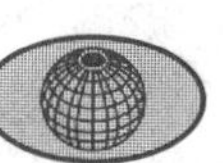   

Andrew Carnegie · The original wealthy philanthropist

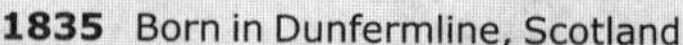

1835 Born in Dunfermline, Scotland.
1848 Carnegie family left Scotland for America.
1853 Joined the Pennsylvania Railroad.
1856 Took out a loan and made first investment.
1859 Promoted to superintendent at Pennsylvania Railroad.
1861 Invested in an oil company in Pennsylvania.
1865 Founded Keystone Bridge Co.
1875 Opened his first steel plant, the Edgar Thomson Works.
1878 Supplied steel for the Brooklyn Bridge.
1883 Acquired the Homestead Works.
1886 Publication of *Triumphant Democracy*.
1889 Publication of *The Gospel of Wealth*.
1892 Formed Carnegie Steel.
1901 Bought out by JP Morgan for US$480 million,.
1905 Established Carnegie Teachers' Pension Fund.
1910 Established the Carnegie Endowment for International Peace.
1911 Established the Carnegie Corporation, which gave away 90% of his fortune.
1919 Died in Lenox, Massachusetts.

LIFE AND CAREER

Andrew Carnegie was born into poverty in Scotland and moved to the United States with his family when he was 12. After a succession of jobs he joined the Pennsylvania Railroad, as a telegraph operator and was quickly promoted. He started investing when only 21, and continued to invest wisely, especially in the burgeoning oil industry. By the time he was 30, he was the principal shareholder in several successful companies, a partner in others, and a respected and powerful businessman and industrialist. After building up the steel industry in Pittsburgh, he sold it to JP Morgan, and devoted the rest of his life to his philanthropic activities and writing.

KEY THINKING

- Carnegie epitomizes the rags to riches story, a poor immigrant who started his career in a cotton mill when he was 13, working long hours for just US$1.20 a week.
- During the American Civil War, he developed production to aid the provision of munitions to the Union, and later became the first mass producer of railroad lines.
- He established and then dominated the American steel industry.
- He became friends with poets, philosophers, business leaders, and statesmen, and himself became a major player on the political scene.
- Carnegie made US$225,639,000 from selling his business to JP Morgan, making him one of the wealthiest men in the world.
- Even before he made his fortune, Carnegie had resolved to give away money if he became rich, as he thought that the rich had a moral obligation to be benevolent.

IN PERSPECTIVE

- He started investing at a young age with the help of his employer at Pennsylvania Railroad Company.
- Bought the Homestead Steel Works in 1888, which helped form part of Carnegie Steel Company, and acquired other specialized companies that eventually became the United States Steel Corporation.
- Carnegie's reputation was affected by accusations of strikebreaking at the Homestead Works in 1892, when the unions fought a pay cut, which resulted in an extended lock-out. Non-unionized workers and detectives were brought in.
- He was bought out by the banker, John Pierpont Morgan, who envisioned a single US-wide, steel-producing organization that could ensure lower prices and better wages.
- Carnegie started writing and contributing to magazines and periodicals, and wrote *Triumphant Democracy*, which examined the progress America had made in society and industry.
- In *The Gospel of Wealth*, he considered the role of the wealthy businessmen in society. He felt that all personal monies above what was needed to live should be used for the benefit of the community.
- During his lifetime, he reportedly gave away more than US$350 million.
- In 1908, he commissioned Napoleon Hill to research a book on how the wealthy had made their fortune, which was successfully published after Carnegie's death as *The Law of Success*, and *Think and Grow Rich*, which are regularly reissued.
- His name lives on in the institutions and awards he founded, such as the Carnegie Corporation of New York, Carnegie Hall in New York City, the Carnegie Endowment for International Peace, Carnegie Mellon University, the Carnegie Museum of Art in Pittsburgh (which awards the Carnegie Prize), the Carnegie Museum of Natural History, the Carnegie Medal for literature, and the Carnegie Hero Fund.

›› MORE INFO

Books:

Carnegie, Andrew, and Gordon Hutner. *The Autobiography of Andrew Carnegie and the Gospel of Wealth*. New York: Signet Classics, 2006.
Krass, Peter. *Carnegie*. New York: Wiley, 2002.
Nasaw, David. *Andrew Carnegie*. New York: Penguin Press, 2006.

"No man can become rich without himself enriching others." Andrew Carnegie

  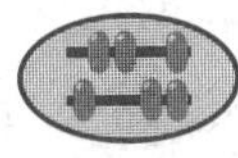 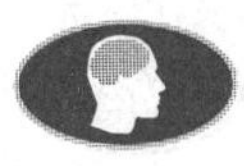  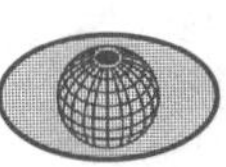 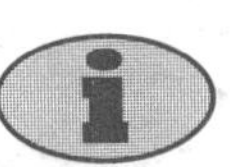  

Ronald Harry Coase • Influential economist and social policy innovator

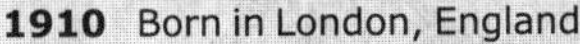

1910 Born in London, England.
1931 Received BSc in Economics from the London School of Economics.
1932 Taught at Dundee School of Economics & Commerce.
1937 Published seminal paper on "The nature of the firm."
1938 Appointed Lecturer at the London School of Economics.
1947 Appointed Reader at the London School of Economics.
1950 Publication of *British Broadcasting: A Study in Monopoly*.
1951 Received PhD in Economics from the University of London.
1951 Moved to the United States.
1951 Taught at the University of Buffalo.
1958 Worked at the Center for Advanced Study in the Behavioral Sciences at Stanford University.
1959 Started teaching at the University of Virginia.
1961 Published key paper on "The problem of social cost."
1964 Appointed to the faculty of the law school at the University of Chicago.
1964 Appointed editor of the *Journal of Law & Economics*.
1977 Appointed Senior Research Fellow at the Hoover Institution, Stanford University.
1991 Appointed Visiting Distinguished Professor at the University of Kansas.
1991 Awarded the Alfred Nobel Memorial Prize in Economic Sciences.
1996 Became Founding President of the International Society for New Institutional Economics.

LIFE AND CAREER

Ronald Coase is an economist and author, and is the Professor Emeritus of Economics at the University of Chicago Law School. In the early 1940s, he entered government service before becoming an academic in England and then the United States. He has written several crucial papers that have helped the development of economic theory and practice. He won the Nobel Prize in Economics for discovering and explaining the significance of transaction costs and property rights for the institutional structure and functioning of the economy. He is Research Advisor to the Ronald Coase Institute, and his current work focuses on the nature of the firm, producers' expectations, and natural monopolies. He has received many honorary degrees, and is a Fellow of the British Academy, the European Academy, and the American Academy of Arts and Sciences.

KEY THINKING

- Coase is best known for two articles: "The nature of the firm," which introduces the concept of transaction costs to explain the size of firms, and "The problem of social cost," which discusses where to apportion the blame for externalities.
- He takes an approach to economic problems which starts with observation and attempts to understand why things operate as they do, before putting together a working theory.
- His transaction costs approach is influential in modern organizational theory.

IN PERSPECTIVE

- Coase's paper on "The nature of the firm" was to establish the field of transaction cost economics. It explains why the economy is populated by a number of business firms, instead of being only made up of many independent, self-employed people who contract with one another.
- He considers that firms are similar to centrally planned economies, but that firms are formed voluntarily, through people making choices based on "transaction costs."
- The paper on "The problem of social cost" set out what became the *Coase Theorem* and a new field in economic research, law and economics; it is one of the most cited papers in economics.
- He wrote the paper after criticism from a number of senior economists about his theories on the rationale of a property rights system; he met up with them, persuaded them he was right, and they asked him to write up his views for publication.
- He made a crucial contribution to economic debate with the *Coase Conjecture*, which argues that a monopoly in durable goods does not have market power because the monopolist is unable to commit to not lowering its prices in future periods.
- He played a key role in reform of the policy for allocation of the electromagnetic spectrum, due to his paper on "The Federal Communications Commission."

▸▸ MORE INFO

Books:

Coase, R. H. *Essays on Economics and Economists.* Chicago, IL: University Of Chicago Press, 1994.

Coase, R. H. *The Firm, the Market, and the Law.* Chicago, IL: University of Chicago Press, 1988.

Medema, Steven G. (ed). *The Legacy of Ronald Coase in Economic Analysis.* Aldershot, UK: Edward Elgar, 1995.

Website:

Author's website: www.ronaldcoase.org

"If you torture the data long enough, it will confess." Ronald Harry Coase

John C. Cox • One of the vanguards of options modeling

1975 Received PhD from the Wharton School at the University of Pennsylvania.
1976 Developed the Cox–Ross–Rubinstein binomial model for options pricing.
1985 Published the Cox–Ingersoll–Ross term-structure model.
1998 Received the IAFE/Infinity Financial Engineer of the Year award.

LIFE AND CAREER

John Cox is an academic and leading theorist on the pricing of derivatives. He was at the forefront of the revolution in options modeling in the 1970s. He is the Nomura Professor of Finance at the Sloan School of Management at MIT, and has been a consultant for a number of securities firms. He has also served as an adviser to government agencies in several countries.

KEY THINKING

- Cox has made a significant contribution to the development of financial engineering technology.
- His work with Stephen Ross explored the foundations of option valuation and established the principle of risk-neutral valuation.
- He is known as one of the developers of the influential Cox–Ross–Rubinstein binomial model for the pricing of options.
- In the mid-1970s, Cox, Stephen Ross of MIT, and Jon Ingersoll of Yale University published a number of papers that led to the Cox–Ingersoll–Ross term-structure model, which provided a consistent approach to the valuation of interest-rate derivatives.
- In a paper co-authored with Fischer Black in 1976, he examined how bond provisions can bring about a firm's bankruptcy or reorganization, one of the first to deal with default premiums and credit spreads.
- In a 1981 article, Cox argued that forward and futures prices will not necessarily be identical.
- In the late 1980s, Cox solved a long-standing problem in portfolio theory with Chi-fu Huang.
- He has studied the use of option technology to analyze corporate securities and intertemporal portfolio policies.

IN PERSPECTIVE

- The Cox–Ross–Rubinstein model became popular due to its relative simplicity and flexibility in that it uses a "discrete-time" model of the varying price over time of the underlying financial instrument, and can be applied to the pricing of American as well as European options.
- The model was built on earlier work on Poisson models by Cox and Ross, and the Cox–Ingersoll–Ross model for the term structure of interest rates.
- The model allowed a better understanding of how derivative securities are priced, as it is based on the fact that investor risk preferences played no part in the pricing of derivatives—the concept of risk-neutral pricing.
- Although there are now computational alternatives to the Cox–Ross–Rubinstein model, the model is still popular due to its value as a teaching tool.
- Cox has also developed a simple numerical scheme for valuing American options that is used by most firms dealing in equity derivatives.
- For dynamic investment strategies, he has examined how best to manage a portfolio over time to meet specific objectives.
- His later research in asset pricing led to a widely used model of the term structure of interest rates.

▸▸ MORE INFO

Book:

Cox, John C., and Mark Rubinstein. *Options Markets.* Englewood Cliffs, NJ: Prentice Hall, 1985. One of the first popular derivatives textbooks, it examines the options markets in terms of theoretical research and actual trading strategies for puts and calls.

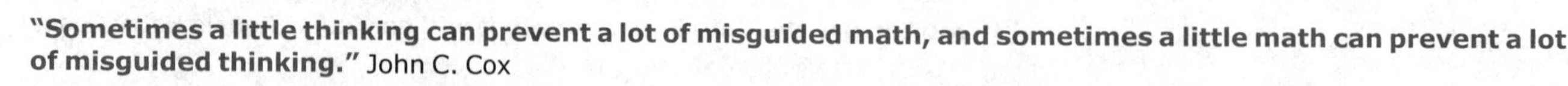

"Sometimes a little thinking can prevent a lot of misguided math, and sometimes a little math can prevent a lot of misguided thinking." John C. Cox

  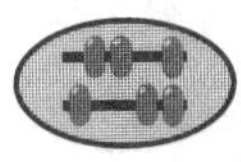   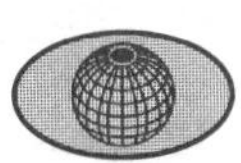   

Gottlieb Daimler · Pioneer of internal combustion engines and automobiles

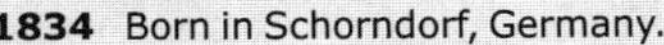

1834 Born in Schorndorf, Germany.
1872 Appointed as technical director at Deutz-AG-Gasmotorenfabrik.
1885 With colleague Wilhelm Maybach, developed and patented the first of their petrol engines.
1885 Created the world's first motorcycle.
1886 Built the first motor vehicle to reach 10mph.
1887 Sold the first foreign licenses for engines.
1890 Founded Daimler Engines Company (DMG).
1892 DMG sold its first automobile.
1893 Resigned from DMG.
1894 Returned to DMG.
1894 Co-designed the Phoenix engine.
1900 Died in Canstatt, Germany.

LIFE AND CAREER

Gottlieb Daimler was a mechanical engineer, designer, and industrialist, who pioneered internal-combustion engines and automobile development in the early years of the industry. He started in engineering at the age of 18, working at various firms, before he and colleague Wilhelm Maybach joined the world's largest manufacturer of stationary engines, Deutz-AG-Gasmotorenfabrik, to take responsibility for the development of gas engines. In 1882, they left Deutz-AG-Gasmotorenfabrik, and started independently to design engines that could use petroleum as a fuel. For the next few years they developed different engines, beginning with their revolutionary Grandfather Clock engine, which they installed in a number of forms of transport. In 1889, they made their first purpose-built automobile and founded Daimler Motoren Gesellschaft (DMG).

KEY THINKING

- In the 1870s, Daimler worked at Deutz Gasmotorenfabrik, where one of the partners was Nikolaus Otto, a pioneer of the four-stroke engine. Daimler assembled a team of the best engineers, including Wilhelm Maybach, from the different companies he had worked at.
- Daimler and Maybach became central figures in the evolution of automation when they designed the Grandfather Clock engine, the first of their engines that used petrol as fuel.
- In 1885, they fitted the Grandfather Clock engine onto a two-wheeler, the first rudimentary motorcycle.
- The following year, they installed a larger version of the engine onto a stagecoach, to become the first four-wheeled vehicle to reach 16 kilometers per hour.
- They tried to use the new engine in as many ways as possible, by installing it in boats, streetcars and trolleys, and airships, although boat engines would be the main focus for several years.
- The Grandfather Clock engine was also used in the first airship, which made its inaugural flight in 1888.
- In 1924, the DMG management signed a long-term cooperation agreement with Karl Benz's Benz & Cie, and, in 1926, the two companies merged to become Daimler-Benz, now part of Daimler AG.
- Daimler was accepted into the Automotive Hall of Fame in 1978, and has also had a stadium named after him in Stuttgart.

IN PERSPECTIVE

- Daimler and business partner, Wilhelm Maybach, made great innovations in the development of small, fast engines that could be mounted on any kind of locomotion device.
- The building of small, light, high-speed engines for use on land, water, and air, was the basis for the Daimler logo of a three-pointed star.
- They later designed the Phoenix engine, which was manufactured by DMG–it was fitted to an automobile, and won the petrol engine category of the first car race in history, the Paris to Rouen in 1894.

▸▸ MORE INFO

Books:

Adler, Dennis. *Daimler and Benz, the Complete History: The Birth and Evolution of the Mercedes-Benz*. New York: Collins, 2006. The official history of both Daimler and Benz.

Burgess-Wise, David, and Edward Douglas-Scott Montagu of Beaulieu. *A Daimler Century: The Full History of Britain's Oldest Car Maker*. Sparkford, UK: Patrick Stephens, 1995. Examines the history of Daimler in the UK, from its leading role in land and aircraft weaponry, to automotive transmissions, and the use of Daimler cars by royalty and the police.

"Nothing but the best." Gottlieb Daimler

  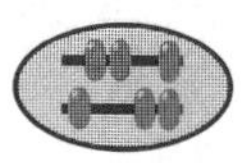   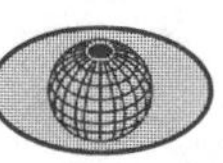   

Joseph de la Vega • Author of *Confusion of Confusions*, the oldest book on the stock exchange business

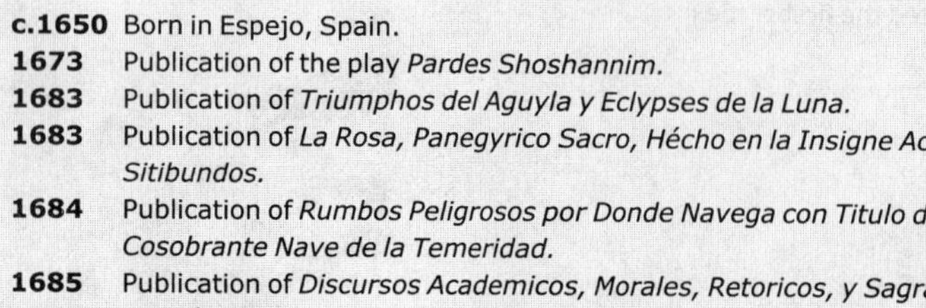

c.1650 Born in Espejo, Spain.
1673 Publication of the play *Pardes Shoshannim.*
1683 Publication of *Triumphos del Aguyla y Eclypses de la Luna.*
1683 Publication of *La Rosa, Panegyrico Sacro, Hécho en la Insigne Academia de los Sitibundos.*
1684 Publication of *Rumbos Peligrosos por Donde Navega con Titulo de Novelas la Cosobrante Nave de la Temeridad.*
1685 Publication of *Discursos Academicos, Morales, Retoricos, y Sagrados Que Recitó en la Florida Academia de los Floridos.*
1688 Publication of *Confusion of Confusions.*
1690 Publication of *Retrato de la Prudencia, y Simulacro del Valor, al Augusto Monarca Guilielmo Tercero, Rey do la Gran Bretaña.*
1692 Died in Amsterdam.

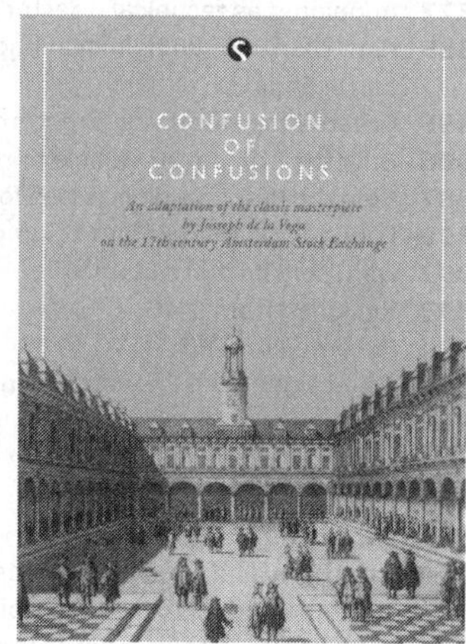

LIFE AND CAREER

Joseph de la Vega (also known as Joseph Penso) was a businessman, writer, and philanthropist who lived in 17th century Amsterdam in a community of Portuguese Jews whose ancestors had fled the Spanish Inquisition. He wrote his first play, *Pardes Shoshannim*, when only 18 and went on to become a respected merchant, and a Spanish poet. He became famous for his masterpiece, *Confusion of Confusions*, the oldest book ever written about stock exchanges. He was elected to several posts in the Jewish, and in the financial communities, including the honorary offices of President of the Academia de los Sitibundos, and Secretary of the Academia de los Floridos. He maintained an extensive correspondence with a number of sovereigns, and other prominent contemporaries.

KEY THINKING

- De la Vega's best-known work, *Confusion of Confusions*, consists of a series of dialogues between a philosopher, a merchant, and a shareholder, describing the workings of the Amsterdam Stock Exchange, the world's first stock exchange.
- It provides a context and understanding of the market participants, the intricacies of speculation and trading, and the financial instruments used at the time, while displaying an affection for the market and its greedy speculators.
- He presents four rules of speculation that are still relevant today: never advise anyone to buy or sell shares; accept both your profits and losses; profits from share dealing never last; you need both money and patience.

IN PERSPECTIVE

- *Confusion of Confusions* was one of the first analytical attempts to describe the different kinds of financial operations taking place at the time. It explores the impact of crowd behavior, and trading trickery on the financial markets.
- Describes the diverse tactics and schemes used by investors playing the Amsterdam market, even though there were only two stocks being traded—the Dutch East India Company and the Dutch West India Company—businesses that depended on risk-laden expeditions around the world.
- He shows that, even then, there were bulls, bears, panics, bubbles, short selling, margin trading, and most of the other features of modern exchanges.
- Discusses trading operations that were complex, involving both options and forward trades; such trading was used both to hedge, and to speculate.
- Shows how many facets of investing are timeless, as he recognizes the value of information and analysis, and how speculators tend to be either optimists or pessimists; de la Vega's advice is to maintain a balance between the two.
- Explains how government regulation banned short selling, but that this was ignored as short sellers were often needed to make markets.

▸▸ MORE INFO

Book:

Mackay, Charles, and Joseph de la Vega. *Extraordinary Popular Delusions and the Madness of Crowds* and *Confusión de Confusiones*. New York: Wiley, 1996. The two classics combined in one volume, with a translation of De la Vega's first-hand account of the market manipulations of the Amsterdam stock exchange.

See Also:

Confusión de Confusiones (p. 1239)

"What really matters is an awareness of how greed and fear can drive rational people to behave in strange ways when they gather in the marketplace." Joseph de la Vega

     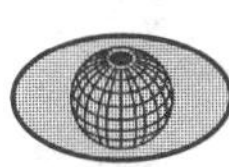   

Marc Faber • Contrarian investor and market predictor

1946 Born in Zurich, Switzerland.
1970 Received PhD in Economics from the University of Zurich (at the age of 24).
1970 Started work for White Weld & Co. Ltd in New York City, Zurich, and Hong Kong.
1973 Moved to Hong Kong.
1978 Appointed Managing Director at Drexel Burnham Lambert (HK) Ltd.
1990 Founded Marc Faber Ltd.
2002 Publication of *Tomorrow's Gold: Asia's Age of Discovery*.

LIFE AND CAREER

Marc Faber is an economic historian, investment analyst, entrepreneur, and writer. He went to school in Geneva and Zurich, and studied Economics at the University of Zurich. He went on to be a trader and managing director of Drexel Burnham Lambert when the firm was the junk-bond king of Wall Street. He later set up his own business to act as an investment advisor, and fund manager. He is board director of numerous companies, including Ivanhoe Mines. He is also a regular speaker at various investment seminars, and a regular contributor to several leading financial publications around the world. He is now based in Thailand, and publishes a monthly investment newsletter, *The Gloom, Boom & Doom Report*, under the name Dr Doom. He became well known for advising his clients to get out of the stock market one week before the October 1987 crash.

KEY THINKING

- Marc Faber is known for his contrarian investment approach, and he runs his own company based on the same philosophy.
- A regular speaker on the investment circuit, often in the financial press for his non-conformist viewpoint and alternative investment philosophy, he specializes in the Asian markets, and focuses on advising clients on investments that have great potential.
- He is a regular contributor to several leading publications, including *Herald Tribune*, *Wall Street Journal*, *Forbes*, and *International Wealth*, as well as several websites.
- His market predictions have been timely: in 1987, he warned his clients to cash out a week before Black Monday on Wall Street; in 1990, he forecast the bursting of the Japanese Bubble; in 1993, he correctly predicted the collapse in US gaming stocks; and in 1997, he foresaw the Asia–Pacific financial crisis.

IN PERSPECTIVE

- He invests and acts as a fund manager to private wealthy clients, and publishes a monthly investment newsletter, *The Gloom, Boom & Doom Report*, which highlights unusual investment opportunities.
- He has given many interviews that reflect his bearish views on a wide variety of investments, including stocks, real estate, and commodities.
- He takes a bearish approach to the long-term outlook for the US dollar, as he believes that the Fed is oversupplying money, which has a negative impact on inflation, and is bad for the value of the currency.
- Since 2000, he has accurately predicted the rise of oil, precious metals, and other commodities, as well as the slide of US dollar from 2002, and various mini-corrections since then.
- He predicted the peak of the US housing bubble earlier than most, and now foresees a new wave of credit collapses across the world.
- In his book, *Tomorrow's Gold: Asia's Age of Discovery*, he predicted the rise of the Chinese market and economy.
- He has been successful in forecasting the performance of US equities over the past few years, and he remains pessimistic about the prospects for the American economy and stock market.
- Believes that there are few value investments still around, except for farmland, and real estate in some emerging markets, such as Argentina and Vietnam.

▸▸ MORE INFO

Books:

Faber, Marc. *Tomorrow's Gold: Asia's Age of Discovery.* Hong Kong: CLSA, 2003. A bestselling account of Faber's search for the outperforming asset classes of the future, based on historical analysis, and charting how old investor trends developed. Also assesses how new patterns might emerge.

Vittachi, Nury. *Riding the Millennial Storm: Marc Faber's Path to Profit in the Financial Markets.* Singapore: Wiley, 1998. Discusses Faber's life, investment techniques, and financial predictions.

Website:

Marc Faber's website: www.gloomboomdoom.com

"A mania is a mania, and the experts are caught in it just as the public is." Marc Faber

Eugene Fama · Author of the efficient markets hypothesis

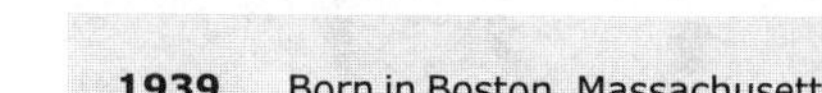

1939 Born in Boston, Massachusetts.
1960 Receives a BA from Tufts University.
1963 Appointed Assistant Professor of Finance, University of Chicago, Graduate School of Business.
1963 Received MBA from University of Chicago, Graduate School of Business.
1964 Received PhD from University of Chicago, Graduate School of Business.
1966 Appointed Associate Professor of Finance, University of Chicago, Graduate School of Business.
1968 Appointed Professor of Finance, University of Chicago, Graduate School of Business.
1972 Publication of *The Theory of Finance*.
1973 Appointed Professor of Finance, University of Chicago, Graduate School of Business.
1975 Appointed Visiting Professor, Catholic University of Leuven and European Institute for Advanced Studies in Management, Belgium.
1982 Appointed Visiting Professor, Anderson Graduate School of Management, University of California.
1982 Joined Board of Directors, Dimensional Fund Advisors.
1984 Appointed Distinguished Service Professor of Finance Graduate School of Business, University of Chicago.
2001 Became the first elected Fellow of the American Finance Association.

LIFE AND CAREER

Eugene Fama was a tenured professor at the University of Chicago before he was 30, where he taught portfolio theory before modern finance became established. He has spent his career at the Graduate School of Business, University of Chicago, where he revolutionized thinking on the efficient markets hypothesis, and where he is now Chairman of its Center for Research in Security Prices. He is also Director of Research at Dimensional Fund Advisors, and is an advisory editor of the *Journal of Financial Economics*. He was the first elected Fellow of the American Finance Association, and is also a Fellow of the Econometric Society and the American Academy of Arts and Sciences. He has received numerous honorary degrees, and was the co-winner of the Smith Breeden Prize for the best paper in the *Journal of Finance* in 1992, and received the first Deutsche Bank Prize in Financial Economics in 2005.

KEY THINKING

- Eugene Fama is a prolific author and researcher, having written two books, and published more than 100 articles in academic journals. He is among the most cited of America's financial researchers.
- He is identified with research on markets, particularly with regard to developments in the efficient market hypothesis, and the random walk theory, as well as his work on portfolio theory and asset pricing, both theoretical and empirical.
- Coined the term "efficient markets theory" in a 1970 paper on efficient capital markets, arguing that it is practically impossible for someone to consistently beat the stock market because of the wide availability of information.
- He was the first of many to study how stock prices respond to an event, using price data from a newly available database.
- Focuses much of his study on the relation between risk and return, and the implications for portfolio management.
- Has also made innovations in how we understand the functioning of markets, asset pricing theory, and corporate finance.

IN PERSPECTIVE

- He helped popularize the efficient market hypothesis, and the random walk theory.
- The efficient market hypothesis evolved from his PhD thesis, and suggested that stock markets are efficient because securities will be appropriately priced, and reflect all available information in a market with well-informed investors.
- The random walk theory was discussed in one of his papers, concluding that stock price movements are unpredictable, and follow a random walk.
- His work on efficient markets proposed two key improvements, by classifying three types of efficiency--strong form, semi-strong form, and weak efficiency--and by identifying the notion of market efficiency with the model of market equilibrium.
- His work on the efficiency of markets has helped create many new finance products, and aided the development of new futures contracts for hedging risks.
- He has written a series of papers with Kenneth French that question the validity of the capital asset pricing model (CAPM), as not taking into account market capitalization and book value to market value.
- In portfolio management, Fama and French also developed a successful three-factor model to describe market behavior.

▸▸ MORE INFO

Books:

Fama, Eugene F. *Foundations of Finance: Portfolio Decisions and Securities Prices.* New York: Basic Books, 1976. A readable introduction to financial theory that examines stocks and portfolios in great detail.

Fama, Eugene F., and Merton H. Miller. *The Theory of Finance.* New York: Holt, Rinehart and Winston, 1972. Provides a systematic grounding in basic financial theory.

See Also:

The Theory of Finance (p. 1325)

"In an efficient market at any point in time the actual price of a security will be a good estimate of its intrinsic value." Eugene Fama

  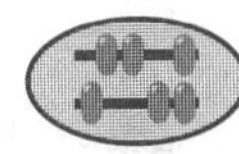   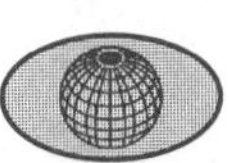   

Irving Fisher · Renowned neoclassical economist of the early 20th Century

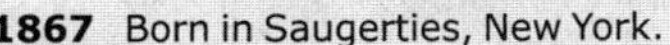

1867 Born in Saugerties, New York.
1888 Received BA from Yale University.
1891 Received PhD in Economics from Yale University.
1892 Appointed Professor of Mathematics at Yale University.
1895 Appointed Professor of Political Economy at Yale University.
1906 Publication of *The Nature of Capital and Income.*
1907 Publication of *The Rate of Interest.*
1910 Publication of *Introduction to Economic Science.*
1912 Became a scientific advisor to the Eugenics Record Office.
1928 Publication of *Money Illusion.*
1929 Appointed Professor of Economics at Yale University.
1930 Publication of *The Stock Market Crash and After.*
1930 Publication of *The Theory of Interest.*
1895 Appointed Professor Emeritus at Yale University.
1947 Died in New York City.

LIFE AND CAREER

Irving Fisher was a mathematical economist, and a pioneer of neoclassical economics and modern behavioral economics, who contributed to the fields of economics, mathematics, statistics, demography, public health and sanitation, and public affairs. He was the first to earn a PhD in Economics from Yale University, where he taught for his entire academic life. He was also a prolific writer covering a wide array of topics. He was best known for his research on the theory of interest, and capital theory. He lost much of his personal wealth and damaged his reputation in the 1929 Wall Street Crash, after reassuring investors that stock prices were not overinflated, but were on a new, permanent plateau. He was also a health campaigner, and eugenicist.

KEY THINKING

- He had several concepts named after him, including the Fisher equation, the Fisher hypothesis, and the Fisher separation theorem.
- The Fisher equation estimates the relationship between nominal and real interest rates under inflation, and is used to predict nominal and real interest-rate behavior.
- The Fisher hypothesis proposes that the real interest rate is independent of monetary measures, especially the nominal interest rate.
- The Fisher separation theorem asserts that the firm's investment decisions are independent of the owner's preferences, investment decisions are independent of the financing decision, and that the value of a capital project is independent from methods used to finance the project.
- The International Fisher Effect, which predicts international exchange-rate drift independent of inflation, was also named after him.
- His theories of capital and investment were first presented in *Nature of Capital and Income* and *The Rate of Interest*, and more fully analyzed in his groundbreaking *The Theory of Interest.*
- *The Theory of Interest* examined capital, capital budgeting, credit markets, and the determinants of interest rates, including the rate of inflation, and developed his concept of intertemporal choice.
- His treatment of the *Money Illusion* anticipated later research on the psychology of decision-making by Daniel Kahneman and Amos Tversky; discuss the impact on investors and savers of the tendency to think of currency in nominal, rather than real terms.
- In *The Making of Index Numbers,* he looks at the critical role of index numbers in monetary theory, statistical theory, econometrics, and index number theory.

IN PERSPECTIVE

- Fisher was a central figure of American economics in the first half of the 20th Century, through his analysis of equilibrium price, his theory of capital and investment, his resurrection of the quantity theory of money, the theory of index numbers, the Phillips Curve, and his work on debt deflation.
- He was also one of the first to subject macroeconomic data, including the money stock, interest rates, and price levels, to statistical analysis; in the 1920s, he introduced the technique later called distributed lags.
- He initially made his fortune from inventing an index card system, later known as the Rolodex, but lost it all in the Great Crash.
- Strongly advocated the establishment of a 100% reserve requirement banking system.
- Gained mainstream recognition through his work as a health campaigner and eugenicist, and his bestseller, *How to Live: Rules for Healthful Living Based on Modern Science.*

▸▸ MORE INFO

Books:

Allen, Robert Loring. *Irving Fisher: A Biography.* Cambridge, MA: Blackwell Publishers, 1993.

Dimand, Roger W., and John Geanakoplos (eds). *Celebrating Irving Fisher: The Legacy of a Great Economist.* Malden, MA: Blackwell, 2005.

Fisher, Irving Norton. *My Father, Irving Fisher.* New York: Comet Press Books, 1956.

"The rate of interest acts as a link between income-value and capital-value." Irving Fisher

     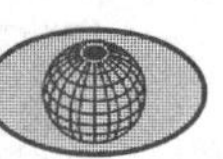   

John Kenneth Galbraith • Leading 20th-century economist and institutionalist

1908 Born in Iona Station, Ontario, Canada.
1931 Received BSc from the Ontario Agricultural College.
1933 Received MSc from the University of California, Berkeley.
1934 Received PhD in Agricultural Economics from the University of California, Berkeley.
1934 Appointed as tutor at Harvard University.
1939 Taught at Princeton University.
1943 Appointed as editor of *Fortune* magazine.
1947 Co-founded Americans for Democratic Action.
1949 Appointed as Professor of Economics at Harvard University.
1952 Publication of *American Capitalism: The Concept of Countervailing Power.*
1954 Publication of *The Great Crash, 1929*.
1958 Publication of *The Affluent Society*.
1961 Appointed as US Ambassador to India.
1967 Publication of *The New Industrial State*.
1977 Presented *The Age of Uncertainty* for the BBC in the United Kingdom.
1972 Appointed President of the American Economic Association.
1975 Became Professor Emeritus at Harvard University.
1990 Publication of *A Short History of Financial Euphoria*.
2006 Died in Cambridge, Massachusetts.

LIFE AND CAREER

J. K. Galbraith was one of the most influential and best-known economists and writers of the 20th century. He taught at Harvard and Princeton, before serving as deputy head of the Office of Price Administration during WWII. He was also a leader of the Strategic Bombing Surveys of Europe and Japan, an advisor to post-war administrations in Germany and Japan, and later became US Ambassador to India. During the 1950s and 1960s, his economics books, based on his ideas of liberalism and progressivism, became international bestsellers. As well as teaching at Harvard for many years, he served in the administrations of Franklin D. Roosevelt, Harry Truman, John F. Kennedy, and Lyndon B. Johnson, and was a two-time recipient of the Presidential Medal of Freedom.

KEY THINKING

- Galbraith was a Keynesian economist and liberal, and seen as the rebel of modern economics, due to his advocacy of government spending to combat unemployment, and warnings over the dangers inherent in deregulated markets, corporate greed, and overspending on the military.
- He rejected the technical and mathematical views of neoclassical economics, as being divorced from reality, and argued that most economists were ignoring key areas, such as advertising, corporate ownership, and the influence of government spending.
- In examining the priorities of modern economics, he supported the use of national wealth for public services and not private consumption, the curbing of demand through consumption taxation, and publicly funding education programs aimed at ordinary people.
- He propounded the advantages of countervailing forces in the economy, where groups such as labor unions helped maintain a political and social balance.
- Was also described as the first post-materialist, due to his contention that continually increasing material production was not a sign of economic well-being.

IN PERSPECTIVE

- *The Affluent Society* turned him into a celebrity—it proposed that classical economic theory may have worked for previous eras, but that the rising affluence of the US in the 1950s needed completely new economic theories.
- *American Capitalism* was also a popular success for its critique of the excesses of consumerism, and predictions about the economy becoming dominated by big business, labor, and government.
- In *Economics and the Public Purpose*, he examined the issue of "political capture" by firms, and discussed issues surrounding political processes, public education, and the provision of public goods.
- Followed the views of Thorstein Veblen, that economic activity was not bound by inviolable laws, but was a complicated mix of the cultural and political.
- In *New Industrial State*, he expanded his theory of the firm, arguing that current concepts of the perfectly competitive firm were unsuccessful, but that they were oligopolistic, autonomous institutions vying for market share.
- He was involved in the presidential campaigns of Eugene McCarthy, and George McGovern.
- During the 1980s, he criticized President Reagan and President Bush's policies of trickle-down economics.

⏩ MORE INFO

Books:

Galbraith, John Kenneth. *The Affluent Society*. Boston, MA: Houghton Mifflin, 1958.
Parker, Richard. *John Kenneth Galbraith: His Life, His Politics, His Economics*. New York: Farrar, Straus, and Giroux, 2004.
Stanfield, James Ronald, and Jacqueline Bloom Stanfield (eds). *Interviews with John Kenneth Galbraith*. Jackson, MS: University Press of Mississippi, 2004.

See Also:

The Great Crash, 1929 (p. 1272)

"Trickle-down theory—the less than elegant metaphor that if one feeds the horse enough oats, some will pass through to the road for the sparrows." John Kenneth Galbraith

   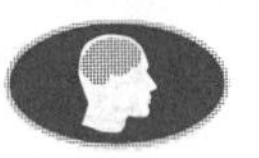  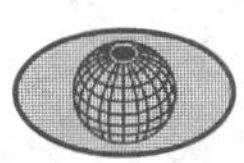   

Louis Gerstner • Breathed new life into IBM

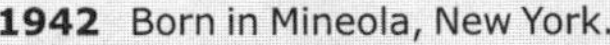

1942 Born in Mineola, New York.
1963 Received BA in Engineering from Dartmouth College.
1965 Received MBA from Harvard Business School.
1965 Appointed director of McKinsey & Co., Inc.
1978 Appointed Executive Vice-President and Head of the Charge Card Division at American Express.
1979 Appointed President of the Travel Related Services Group at American Express.
1982 Appointed Chairman and Chief Executive Officer of Travel Related Services at American Express.
1985 Appointed President of American Express.
1989 Appointed Chief Executive Officer and Chairman of RJR Nabisco, Inc.
1993 Appointed Chairman and Chief Executive Officer of IBM Corporation.
2001 Became an honorary Knight of the British Empire.
2002 Retired from IBM.
2003 Founded the Teaching Commission.
2003 Appointed Chairman of The Carlyle Group.

LIFE AND CAREER

Louis Gerstner is a leading business executive, and educationalist. He saved IBM from closure in the 1990s, and transformed it into a global leader in the field of information technology. Prior to joining IBM, he was President of American Express, and Chairman and Chief Executive Officer of RJR Nabisco, Inc. He is also a director of Bristol-Myers Squibb Co., a member of the advisory boards of DaimlerChrysler and Sony Corporation, a member of the board of the Council on Foreign Relations, a member of the Business Council, and a Fellow of the America-China Forum. He has served on the boards of many international companies, and is a member of the National Academy of Engineering, a Fellow of the American Academy of Arts and Sciences, and has been awarded honorary doctorates from a number of US universities.

KEY THINKING

- While President of American Express, the financial services group faced tough competition from both Visa and MasterCard, which meant that he had to innovate to retain and build market share.
- He introduced new uses for the Amex card to help grow its market; and persuaded large stores to accept American Express cards, making it one of the most popular credit cards in the world.
- He also marketed the card to new customers, and sold the benefits of the card to international companies to address problems over business expenses.
- He created new business lines, such as the Gold Card, to appeal to high-end clients, which helped increase membership from 8.6 million to 30.7 million during his tenure.
- Gerstner prevented the collapse of IBM in the early 1990s, and resolved a number of issues around its operational strategy.
- He reversed the trend of divisional rebranding and self-management, as well as lack of international focus, and recognized the need for a broad-based information technology integrator, to ensure it developed as a single, coherent business.
- He focused on the IT services part of the business, and embraced the information age and the internet, which allowed this division to become the most successful part of the corporation.

IN PERSPECTIVE

- Gerstner's reinvention of IBM has been hailed as the great American business story of our time. The company was being broken up, its value was plummeting, sales were poor, and it needed direction. He turned it into the most reputable information services business of the modern computer era.
- He imposed a new management style and corporate culture on IBM, one that was ruthless about staff numbers, operated new cost controls, reduced its non-essential asset base, and built it into a successful business. He also injected flexibility, enabling IBM to deal with the fast-evolving technology market.
- He was also a powerful advocate for quality education. At IBM, he established Reinventing Education, an educational partnership with a number of states and school districts, enabling them to benefit from IBM technology, and technical assistance.
- He founded the Teaching Commission, to help develop policy recommendations to solve the problems of the teaching crisis, and co-chaired Achieve, an organization focused on improving academic standards for public schools in the US.
- He is co-author of the book, *Reinventing Education: Entrepreneurship in America's Public Schools*, and received many awards for his work in education.
- For his work in public education and business, he was awarded an honorary knighthood by Queen Elizabeth II in 2001.

▸▸ MORE INFO

Books:

Garr, Doug. *IBM Redux: Lou Gerstner and the Business Turnaround of the Decade.* New York: HarperBusiness, 1999.

Gerstner, Louis V. *Who Says Elephants Can't Dance? How I Turned Around IBM.* New York: HarperBusiness, 2002.

Slater, Robert. *Saving Big Blue: Leadership Lessons and Turnaround Tactics of IBM's Lou Gerstner.* New York: McGraw-Hill, 1999.

"Watch the turtle. He only moves forward by sticking his neck out." Louis Gerstner

   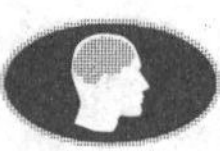  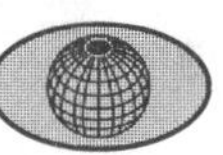   

Benjamin Graham • The father of modern security analysis

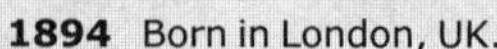

1894 Born in London, UK.
1895 Moved to New York with his family.
1914 Graduated from Columbia University.
1926 Formed an investment partnership with Jerome Newman.
1926 Started lecturing on finance at Columbia University Business School.
1934 Publication of *Security Analysis.*
1937 Publication of *The Interpretation of Financial Statements.*
1937 Publication of *Storage and Stability: A Modern Ever-normal Granary.*
1944 Publication of *World Commodities and World Currency.*
1949 Publication of *The Intelligent Investor.*
1956 Retired from the faculty of Columbia University Business School.
1976 Died.

LIFE AND CAREER

Benjamin Graham was an economist and investor who defended rigorous security analysis throughout his career. He studied at Columbia University, but declined a teaching position to be a chalker on Wall Street with Newburger, Henderson and Loeb. Bright and ambitious, he was soon undertaking financial research for the firm, and was eventually made a partner. Although the market crash of 1929 almost wiped him out, Graham continued to make useful returns for the firm, while also writing investment books, and lecturing at Columbia. He was a strong advocate of financial analysis training, and helped found the Chartered Financial Analyst (CFA) program. Warren Buffett studied under him at Columbia, and asked him for an investing job, which Graham eventually gave him, starting Buffett on his career.

KEY THINKING

- Graham revolutionized investment thinking by introducing the concepts of security analysis, fundamental analysis, and value investing.
- His books expanded on the definition of a cheap company, based on a principle of *margin of safety*. His preference for value investing was based on investors seeking out bargains among undervalued companies, buying into them, and then waiting for their fair value to be realized.
- Two of his books, *Security Analysis* and *The Intelligent Investor*, are considered the bibles for both individual investors, and financial professionals.
- Created an imaginary investor called Mr Market to demonstrate his views about wise investing, and choosing stocks based on their fundamental value rather than because of advice or market direction.

IN PERSPECTIVE

- In *Security Analysis*, he presented his principles of value-oriented investment, using fundamentals in guiding the valuation of securities; he extended this approach in his books, *Interpretation of Financial Statements* and the *Intelligent Investor*.
- Distinguished between the passive and the active investor. The former invests cautiously, looks for value stocks and buys for the long term, while the active investor takes more time getting to know companies to find the best buys in the market.
- Recommended that investors spend time and effort to analyze the financial state of companies.
- Criticized corporations that produced unhelpful financial reports, which hid the real state of their finances from potential investors.
- Advocated dividend payments for shareholders, instead of firms keeping all of their profits as retained earnings. Dividends, he argued, indicated that a company was profitable, and could offer a return even if its stock was performing poorly.
- Popularized the examination of price-to-earnings ratios, debt-to-equity ratios, dividend records, net current assets, book values, and earnings growth.
- In *Storage and Stability*, he examined wider economic issues, such as the effect of deflation on farmers, workers, and producers, and proposed the creation of pools of commodities to act as buffer stocks against general price deflation.
- In *World Commodities and World Currency*, he proposed an international "commodity standard", where macroeconomic policies would focus on a general basket of commodities, a concept supported by Keynes, Hayek, and Friedman.

▸▸ MORE INFO

Books:

Au, Thomas P. *A Modern Approach to Graham and Dodd Investing*. Hoboken, NJ: Wiley, 2004.

Graham, Benjamin. *Benjamin Graham, the Memoirs of the Dean of Wall Street*. New York: McGraw-Hill, 1996.

Graham, Benjamin. *The Intelligent Investor: A Book of Practical Counsel.* New York: Harper, 1949.

Lowe, Janet. *The Rediscovered Benjamin Graham: Selected Writings of the Wall Street Legend*. New York: Wiley, 1999.

Website:

Website providing advice and information on investing using Graham's techniques: www.grahaminvestor.com

See Also:

The Intelligent Investor (p. 1280)

"Wall Street people learn nothing and forget everything." Benjamin Graham

   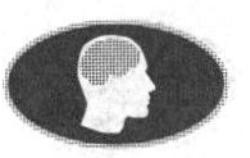  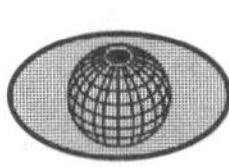   

Alan Greenspan · The longest-serving Chairman of the US Federal Reserve

1926 Born in New York City.
1948 Received BS in Economics from New York University.
1948 Appointed as an economic analyst at the Conference Board.
1950 Received MA in Economics from New York University.
1955 Appointed Chairman and President of Townsend-Greenspan & Co., Inc.
1968 Appointed Coordinator of Domestic Policy for Richard Nixon's nomination campaign.
1974 Appointed Chairman of the Council of Economic Advisers.
1977 Received PhD from New York University.
1982 Appointed Director of the Council on Foreign Relations.
1987 Appointed Chairman of the Board of Governors of the Federal Reserve Board.
2002 Awarded the Knight Commander of the British Empire.
2005 Awarded the Presidential Medal of Freedom.
2005 Awarded an honorary Doctorate in Commercial Science by New York University.
2006 Left the Federal Reserve Board.
2007 Appointed as a special consultant by PIMCO.
2007 Appointed as a special advisor at Deutsche Bank.
2008 Appointed as an advisor at Paulson & Co.

LIFE AND CAREER

Alan Greenspan is an economist who dominated the financial world for nearly 20 years as Chairman of the Federal Reserve. He was a respected economic advisor, and long-running President of Townsend-Greenspan & Co, when he took over at the Federal Reserve in 1987, just before the stock market crisis of that year. He was reappointed at successive four-year intervals until retiring in 2006, after an unprecedented tenure as chairman. Following his retirement, Greenspan took up an honorary position at the UK Treasury, and now works as a private advisor and consultant through his company, Greenspan Associates LLC. He has also served as a member of the Group of Thirty, the Washington-based financial advisory body, and as a corporate director for many multinational businesses such as Alcoa, Automatic Data Processing, Inc., JP Morgan, and the Mobil Corporation.

KEY THINKING

- Greenspan has been praised as the greatest central banker in memory, running the Federal Reserve during many of the economic events of recent years, and is considered to be the leading authority on American domestic economic and monetary policy.
- His handling of the stock market crash of 1987 just after he took office was the first success of his tenure. His statement that the Fed was ready to provide the necessary liquidity helped minimize the impact of the crash.
- He was also lauded for his handling of the dotcom economic boom of the 1990s, and the transformation of global business that resulted.
- Although he was known for the complexity of his utterances, this was thought to be a useful technique for gaining flexibility in meaning, and avoiding extreme market reaction.

IN PERSPECTIVE

- He became known for the "Greenspan put", the monetary policy that lowered the Fed Funds rate, to improve liquidity and avoid further economic downturn–– used to resolved economic problems brought about by the Gulf war, the Mexican crisis, the Asian crisis, the LTCM debacle, Y2K, and the bursting of the dotcom bubble.
- He made a now-famous comment about irrational exuberance and escalating stock prices in 1996—and, as there was an immediate downturn in the international stock markets, the phrase became part of common parlance about economic excess.
- He has come under some criticism for monetary policies that encouraged excessive speculation, and for supporting former US president George W Bush's demolition of the budget surpluses built up in the Clinton years.
- Considers the current subprime crisis as being a product of the housing bubble, low interest rates, and rising house prices across the world.
- He views the subprime market as being beneficial in allowing people on low incomes to own homes, and believes focus should be on the financial securitization of so-called toxic debt, which has caused the problems.

›› MORE INFO

Books:

Greenspan, Alan. *The Age of Turbulence: Adventures in a New World.* New York: Penguin Press, 2007.
Martin, Justin. *Greenspan: The Man Behind Money*. Cambridge, MA: Perseus Publishing, 2000.
Woodward, Bob. *Maestro: Greenspan's Fed and the American Boom.* New York: Simon & Schuster, 2000.

See Also:

The Age of Turbulence: Adventures in a New World (p. 1217)

"Since becoming a central banker, I have learned to mumble with great incoherence. If I seem unduly clear to you, you must have misunderstood what I said." Alan Greenspan

     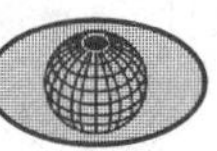   

Friedrich Hayek · Influential social theorist and advocate of free markets

1899 Born in Vienna.
1914 Joined the Austro-Hungarian army in World War I.
1921 Received doctorate in Law from the University of Vienna.
1923 Received doctorate in Political Science from the University of Vienna.
1923 Appointed as research assistant at New York University.
1931 Appointed to the faculty of the London School of Economics.
1938 Emigrated to the United Kingdom to avoid the Nazi control of Austria.
1944 Publication of *The Road to Serfdom.*
1950 Appointed Professor at the University of Chicago.
1960 Publication of *The Constitution of Liberty.*
1962 Appointed Professor at the University of Frieburg.
1974 Received the Nobel Memorial Prize in Economics, shared with Gunnar Myrdal.
1984 Appointed a Member of the Order of the Companions of Honour in the UK.
1988 Publication of *The Fatal Conceit.*
1991 Receives the US Presidential Medal of Freedom.
1992 Died in Freiburg, Germany.

LIFE AND CAREER

Friedrich Hayek was an influential Austrian economist, and political philosopher, known for his defense of classical liberalism and free-market capitalism in the mid-20th century. After being decorated for bravery in World War I, and aiding the Austrian government at the Treaty of Versailles, he founded and served as director of the Austrian Institute for Business Cycle Research, before joining the faculty of the London School of Economics. In 1947, he was an organizer of the Mont Pelerin Society, a group of classical liberals who opposed socialism in various areas. Hayek received the Nobel Prize, along with Gunnar Myrdal, for his work on the theory of money and economic fluctuations, and the interdependence of economic, social, and institutional phenomena. Hayek was a prolific researcher and writer over nearly seven decades, and was seen as a central figure in the move from interventionism and Keynesian policies towards classical liberalism. He was also instrumental in the founding of the Institute of Economic Affairs, the free-market think-tank that inspired Reaganomics and Thatcherism.

KEY THINKING

- Hayek propounded free-market economics, and applied his thinking to issues of political organization, the impact of capital, and the business cycle.
- He opposed government intervention in the marketplace, and was a fierce critic of Keynesian welfare economics.
- His writings also strongly criticized collectivism, as being dependent on a central authority; he argued that the central role of the state should be to maintain the rule of law, and avoid arbitrary intervention as much as possible.
- In *The Road to Serfdom,* his classic work on liberalism, political philosophy, cultural history, and economics, he warned against the dangers of state control, and collectivist principles that can lead to tyranny.
- Using the Soviet Union and Nazi Germany as examples, he explained that in a centrally planned economy, the distribution of resources would always devolve onto a small group, which would not be able to process the necessary information to distribute the resources effectively.
- In *Prices and Production* and *The Pure Theory of Capital,* he explained the origin of the business cycle in terms of central bank credit expansion, and its transmission over time.
- *Prices and Production* introduced the concept of Hayekian triangles, to depict the relationship between the value of capital goods and their place in the temporal sequence of production.
- In *The Pure Theory of Capital,* he described how the economy's structure of production depends on the characteristics of capital goods.

IN PERSPECTIVE

- One of the foremost members of the Austrian school of economics, he advocated individualism, and economic theories based on the basic principles of human action.
- His research on social and political philosophy was based on an understanding of the limits of human knowledge and the concept of *spontaneous order* in social institutions–arguing in favor of organizing society around a market order, where the state is focused on enforcing a free market based around the individual.
- His early works on industrial fluctuations, and prices as signals, were influential, as were his contributions to jurisprudence and cognitive science.

▸▸ MORE INFO

Books:

Caldwell, Bruce. *Hayek's Challenge: An Intellectual Biography of FA Hayek.* Chicago, IL: University of Chicago Press, 2004. A full biography of Hayek, examining the background to his writings, and discussing his ideas in the context of economic theory.

Ebenstein, Alan. *Friedrich Hayek: A Biography.* New York: Palgrave, 2001. Considers Hayek's life and thinking, and provides a chronological overview of his writings.

Hayek, Friedrich. *The Road to Serfdom.* London: G. Routledge & Sons, 1944. The book which influenced the political ideologies of Thatcher and Reagan, and led to the revival of neoclassical economics in the West, and the lessening of Keynesian influence.

"A claim for equality of material position can be met only by a government with totalitarian powers."
Friedrich Hayek

  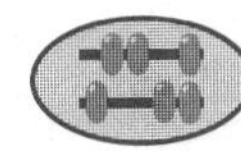   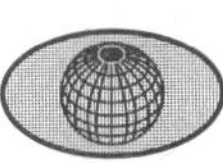   

Daniel Kahneman · Nobel laureate who helped develop prospect theory

1934 Born in Tel Aviv, Israel.
1954 Received BA in Psychology and Mathematics from Hebrew University, Jerusalem.
1961 Received PhD in Psychology from the University of California, Berkeley.
1961 Appointed Lecturer in Psychology, Hebrew University.
1966 Appointed Senior Lecturer in Psychology, Hebrew University.
1966 Appointed Fellow, Center for Cognitive Studies and Lecturer in Psychology, Harvard University.
1970 Appointed Associate Professor, Hebrew University, Jerusalem.
1973 Appointed Professor, Hebrew University, Jerusalem.
1977 Appointed Fellow, Center for Advanced Studies in the Behavioral Sciences.
1978 Appointed Professor of Psychology, the University of British Columbia.
1982 Received the Distinguished Scientific Contribution Award of the American Psychological Society, with Amos Tversky.
1984 Appointed Associate Fellow, Canadian Institute for Advanced Research.
1986 Appointed Professor of Psychology, University of California, Berkeley.
1993 Appointed Professor of Psychology and Public Affairs, Woodrow Wilson School, Princeton University.
2000 Appointed Fellow, Center for Rationality, Hebrew University, Jerusalem.
2002 Received the Nobel Memorial Prize in Economics.
2007 Appointed Professor of Psychology and Public Affairs, Emeritus, and Senior Scholar, Woodrow Wilson School, Princeton University.
2007 Received the Distinguished Lifetime Contribution Award, American Psychological Association.

LIFE AND CAREER

Daniel Kahneman is a psychologist and Nobel laureate, notable for his work on behavioral finance, and hedonic psychology. He spent his childhood years in Paris, before moving to Palestine after World War II. After obtaining his undergraduate degree in Jerusalem, he served in the psychology department of the Israeli Defense Forces. In 1958, he went to the US to study at the University of California, Berkeley. He was also a visiting scientist at the University of Michigan and the Applied Psychological Research Unit in Cambridge. He is now a Senior Scholar at the Woodrow Wilson School of Public and International Affairs, and Professor of Psychology and Public Affairs Emeritus at the Woodrow Wilson School, the Professor of Psychology Emeritus at Princeton University, and a Fellow of the Center for Rationality at Hebrew University, Jerusalem.

KEY THINKING

- Kahneman's early work focused on visual perception and attention, before he went on to research with Amos Tversky and others, establishing a cognitive basis for common human errors using heuristics and biases, and developing prospect theory, which describes decision-making processes in situations that involve risk.
- He and Tversky published a series of important articles on judgment and decision-making, which culminated in the publication of their seminal work on prospect theory in 1979.
- In 2002, he received the Nobel Memorial Prize in Economicsalongside Amos Tversky for their work on decision-making under uncertainty, and for demonstrating how human decisions may systematically depart from those predicted by standard economic theory.

IN PERSPECTIVE

- Kahneman and Amos Tversky started collaborating in 1968, with their first paper together being "Belief in the Law of Small Numbers", published in 1971.
- They published many more articles in peer-reviewed journals over the next few years; apart from "Prospect Theory", the most important was "Judgment Under Uncertainty: Heuristics and Biases", published in the journal, *Science*.
- Thaler's paper, "Toward a Positive Theory of Human Choice", in 1980, a key text in the development of behavioral economics, built on Kahneman and Tversky's work on prospect theory.
- During the 1990s, Kahneman began to focus his research more on the field of hedonic psychology, which was becoming more mainstream as part of the positive psychology movement.
- In 1992, he worked with Carol Varey to introduce a method of evaluating moments and episodes, to capture "experiences extended across time".

▸▸ MORE INFO

Books:

Kahneman, D., E. Diener, and N. Schwarz (eds). *Well-being: The Foundations of Hedonic Psychology.* New York: Russell Sage Foundation, 1999.

Kahneman, D., P. Slovic, and A. Tversky. *Judgment Under Uncertainty: Heuristics and Biases.* New York: Cambridge University Press, 1982.

Kahneman, D, and A. Tversky. (eds). *Choices, Values and Frames.* New York: Cambridge University Press, 2000.

"The brain scientists are the wave of the future in the financial world. If you seek to maximize understanding, whether you're in academia or in the investment community, you'd better pay serious attention to them."
Daniel Kahneman

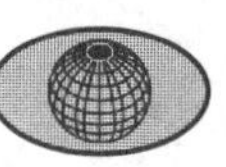

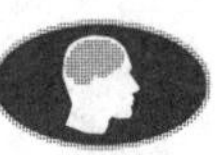

John Maynard Keynes · Key economic thinker of the 20th century

1883 Born in Cambridge, UK.
1897 Received scholarship to Eton.
1902 Attended Cambridge University.
1906 Joined the Civil Service.
1909 Elected Fellow of King's College, Cambridge University.
1911 Appointed editor of the *Economic Journal.*
1919 Appointed Chief Treasury representative at the Paris Peace Conference.
1919 Published *Economic Consequences of the Peace.*
1921 Appointed chairman of the National Mutual Life Insurance Company.
1921 Published *Treatise on Probability*.
1923 Published *Tract on Monetary Reform*.
1923 Began contributing monthly columns to *The Nation.*
1929 Appointed Fellow of the British Academy.
1929 Appointed to the UK government's Macmillan Committee of Enquiry into Finance and Industry.
1930 Published *Treatise on Money*.
1936 Published *The General Theory of Employment, Interest and Money.*
1940 Published *How to Pay for the War.*
1940 Appointed as a government economic adviser.
1941 Elected to the Court of the Bank of England.
1942 Awarded a peerage.
1944 Represented Britain at the Bretton Woods conference.
1946 Died in Tilton, East Sussex, UK.

LIFE AND CAREER

J.M.Keynes was an internationally renowned economist, who had a major impact on 20th century economic practice and fiscal policy. He was educated at Eton and Cambridge University, before entering the India Office of the Civil Service. He later returned to Cambridge to teach economics, while he developed his economic theories, and wrote some of the major economic texts of his time. He was also involved in the war effort for the Treasury Office, and advised various chancellors between 1940 and 1946. He was particularly central to the creation of the International Monetary Fund and the World Bank, in the aftermath of World War II.

KEY THINKING

- The effect of Keynesian economics and theory still reverberates; his work on economic policy, and social progress was hugely influential in forming modern economic thinking.
- He strongly advocated interventionist policies, and governmental use of fiscal and monetary measures to mitigate the adverse effects of recessions and booms.
- He believed that government borrowing was necessary for undertaking large-scale public works that would stimulate the economy during a recession.
- The promotion of deficit spending to help employment became the basis of government economic policy.
- During World War II, Keynes was actively involved in discussions on the post-war economic landscape, particularly the creation of the International Monetary Fund, the World Bank, and the Bretton Woods system for international currency management.
- At that time, he also met with Roosevelt's economic advisors to counter prevalent laissez-faire policies, and supported the President's New Deal, and the promotion of high employment, production, and purchasing power.
- He was a pivotal figure in the request for American assistance for the UK economy after the war.

IN PERSPECTIVE

- His *Treatise on Probability* explored the foundations of knowledge regarding the meaning and measurement of probability, depicting probability as a logical relation, and therefore objective.
- In *Economic Consequences of the Peace,* he criticized the allies for the harshness of the reparations they imposed on Germany at the end of the World War I. The later rise of Hitler was thought by many to justify this condemnation.
- In *A Tract on Monetary Reform* he called for an end to the Gold Standard, on the basis that devaluation was preferable to deflation, and that sterling was overvalued. The British government later abandoned the Standard, and was forced to devalue sterling by 20%.
- In *A Treatise on Money* he distinguished between investments and saving, proposing that if investments exceeded saving, it led to inflation, but if saving exceeded investment, there would be recession.
- In *The General Theory of Employment, Interest and Money,* he argued, that unemployment occurs if people don't spend enough money.
- In *How to Pay for the War*, he supported low interest rates, and compulsory saving to prevent the type of inflation that happened after World War I.

›› MORE INFO

Books:

Davidson, John. *John Maynard Keynes.* Basingstoke, UK: Palgrave Macmillan, 2007.
Keynes, John Maynard. *The General Theory of Employment, Interest and Money.* Basingstoke, UK: Palgrave Macmillan, 2007.
Minsky, Hyman. *John Maynard Keynes.* New York: McGraw-Hill, 2008.

"In the long run, we're all dead." John Maynard Keynes

  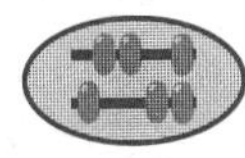   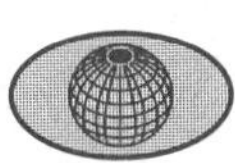 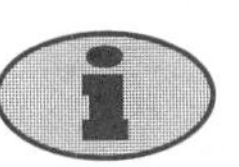  

Edwin Lefèvre · American writer and statesman, best known for his writings on Wall Street

1871 Born in Colon, Colombia.
1901 Publication of *Wall Street Stories*.
1905 Publication of *Golden Flood*.
1907 Publication of *Sampson Rock of Wall Street*.
1909 Appointed an Ambassador of the United States.
1916 Publication of *Plunderers*.
1917 Publication of *To the Last Penny*.
1919 Publication of *Simonetta*.
1923 Publication of *Reminiscences of a Stock Operator*.
1943 Died in Dorset, Vermont.

LIFE AND CAREER

Edwin Lefèvre was a journalist, writer, and statesman, and is best known for his writings on Wall Street, which were successful in the 1920s and early 1930s. He was born to American parents, and educated at Michigan Military Academy and Lehigh University. He was an independently wealthy investor, who turned to writing short stories about what he observed on Wall Street. He followed this with several novels about money and finance. During the presidency of William Howard Taft, Lefèvre was appointed an Ambassador of the United States, serving in a number of European countries. After that, he returned to his home in Vermont to continue his writing, publishing short stories in magazines such as *Harper's*, newspapers such as the *Saturday Evening Post*, and writing novels. He retired in the 1930s, at the time of the Great Depression, when interest in the stock market waned.

KEY THINKING

- After operating successfully as a investor, and then writing a number of articles and fictional books about Wall Street, Lefèvre turned to fact for his classic on stock-market trading, *Reminiscences of a Stock Operator*.
- After signing up to work exclusively for the *Saturday Evening Post,* he wrote a series of 12 articles that told the story of a professional stock trader on Wall Street.
- Presented as fiction, the series was generally accepted to be a biography of star trader, Jesse Livermore; the articles subsequently became the book, *Reminiscences of a Stock Operator*.
- The book has been a success ever since it was first published, being continually reprinted, as well as being translated into many languages.
- His writing was insightful and popular, and contained many aphorisms about the financial world.

IN PERSPECTIVE

- Lefèvre offered a perspective of the mindset of a high-stakes speculator in *Reminiscences of a Stock Operator*, explaining the motivation behind their successes as being due to a need to express their own ingenuity.
- Jesse Livermore, dubbed "Larry Livingston" in the book, was an infamous trader who amassed and lost several fortunes, before finally committing suicide with a revolver.
- In *Reminiscences of a Stock Operator*, Lefèvre describes in great detail the bucket shops that operated in the late 19th and early 20th centuries. They were essentially betting parlors where people could wager on stocks.
- They used many tricks to fool their customers, such as falsely reporting stock trades, and arranging "wash sales".
- Lefèvre recognized the role of psychology in investing. He felt that traders should factor in market precedents, the psychology of the public, the limitations of brokers, as well as their own psychological traits and weaknesses.

▸▸ MORE INFO

Books:

Lefèvre, Edwin. *Making of a Stockbroker.* New York: George H Doran Co., 1925. A follow-up to *Reminiscences of a Stock Operator,* but this time the stock trader was a real person, John K Wing, a senior partner of Bronson and Barnes, a major Boston stock brokerage. Written as a factual biography, Wing's more honest approach to the markets contrasts with that of Livermore.

Lefèvre, Edwin. *Reminiscences of a Stock Operator.* New York: George H Doran Co., 1923. The classic fictionalized biography of the famous speculator, Jesse Livermore. It is a readable and insightful account of making and losing a fortune a few times over.

Lefèvre, Edwin. *Wall Street Stories*. New York: McClure, Phillips & Co., 1901. A collection of stories based on well-known investing personalities of the time, this is the book that launched Lefèvre's literary career.

See Also:

Reminiscences of a Stock Operator (p. 1315)

"After spending many years in Wall Street, and after making and losing millions of dollars I want to tell you this: it never was my thinking that made the big money for me. It always was my sitting. Got that? My sitting tight!" Edwin Lefèvre

     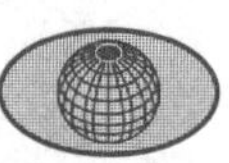   

Burton Malkiel • American economist, and author of classic finance book, *A Random Walk Down Wall Street*

1932 Born in Boston, Massachusetts.
1953 Received BA from Harvard College.
1955 Received MBA from Harvard Graduate School of Business Administration.
1955 Served as a First Lieutenant in the Finance Corps of the US Army.
1958 Appointed an associate with Smith Barney & Co.
1964 Received PhD from Princeton University.
1964 Appointed Assistant Professor at Princeton University.
1966 Appointed Associate Professor, and Director of the Financial Research Center, Princeton University.
1966 Publication of *The Term Structure of Interest Rates.*
1968 Appointed as Professor of Economics at Princeton University.
1973 Publication of *A Random Walk Down Wall Street.*
1975 Appointed Member of the Council of Economic Advisors.
1978 Appointed President of the American Finance Association.
1980 Publication of *The Inflation Beater's Investment Guide.*
1981 Appointed Professor of Management Studies and Dean of Yale School of Management.
1982 Publication of *Winning Investment Strategies.*
2003 Publication of *The Random Walk Guide to Investing.*
2007 Publication of *From Wall Street to the Great Wall.*

LIFE AND CAREER

Burton Malkiel is an economist and author of the seminal investment book, *A Random Walk Down Wall Street*. He began his career in investment banking for Smith Barney & Co., before teaching at Princeton, where he became Professor of Economics at Princeton University, and Chairman of the Economics Department. He is a past appointee to the President's Council of Economic Advisors, and has served on the boards of several financial corporations, including Prudential Financial, and the Vanguard Group. He has also served on several investment management boards, the advisory panel of the investment management firm, Research Affiliates, and the Investment Committee for the American Philosophical Association.

KEY THINKING

- Malkiel is a leading proponent of the efficient market hypothesis, which contends that prices of publicly traded assets reflect all publicly available information.
- He argues that stocks are priced so efficiently that no professional can exploit differences in pricing with any consistency. For the personal investor, it is even more difficult to beat the market, as they have to pay management fees, trading costs, and taxes.
- Also considers how difficult it is to predict which companies are worth investing in, and contends that chance can predict just as successfully as the experts.
- His solution is to use a widely diversified, low-fee, low-turnover investment strategy such as index funds, or exchange-traded funds.
- Shows how the benefits of broad diversification in a stock portfolio have been proved over the years, and for investors diversifying into other asset categories, such as bonds, real estate, and cash.
- Proposes that it is best to index most of a portfolio, and only undertake some stock speculation around the edges, which reduces the risk involved.
- Describes why investors should place their money in a fund with a level of risk they are comfortable with, and then leave it until retirement.

IN PERSPECTIVE

- In *A Random Walk Down Wall Street,* an investment classic that is now in its ninth edition, Malkiel explains why diversification is critical in a portfolio, and argues that asset allocation should always be done appropriately.
- He has revised the book over the years, re-examining his views on market manias in terms of the internet bubble, and strongly defends efficient markets, and index fund investing.
- His influential article, *The Valuation of Closed-End Investment Company Shares*, in the *Journal of Finance*, discussed why closed-end fund companies trade at market valuations lower than the net value of their assets.
- Compares the different types of mutual funds and hedge funds in terms of investment opportunities.

▸▸ MORE INFO

Books:

Malkiel, Burton G. *A Random Walk Down Wall Street.* New York: Norton, 1973. The groundbreaking book that made Malkiel famous, it offers guidance on successful long-term investing, arguing that it is better to buy and hold an index fund than trade in individual stocks, and actively managed funds.

Malkiel, Burton G. *The Random Walk Guide To Investing: Ten Rules for Financial Success.* New York: WW Norton, 2003. The follow-up to his bestseller, this book outlines Malkiel's 10-point plan for investing, and provides practical advice for the beginner.

See Also:

A Random Walk Down Wall Street: The Time-Tested Strategy for Successful Investing (p. 1313)

"A blindfolded monkey throwing darts at a newspaper's financial pages could select a portfolio that would do just as well as one carefully selected by the experts." Burton Malkiel

  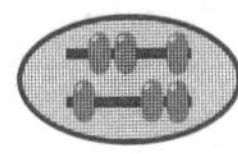 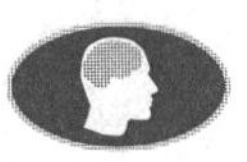  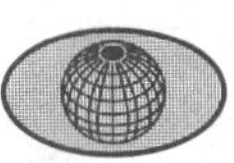   

Harry Markowitz · The grandfather of modern portfolio theory

1927 Born in Chicago.
1950 Received MA from the University of Chicago.
1952 Appointed as researcher at the RAND Corporation.
1954 Received PhD from the University of Chicago.
1955 Invited to be a student member of the Cowles Foundation for Research in Economics.
1959 Publication of *Portfolio Selection.*
1962 Co-founded CACI International.
1962 Publication of *SIMSCRIPT: A Simulation Programming Language.*
1963 Worked at the Consolidated Analysis Centers, Inc.
1968 Taught at the University of California, Los Angeles.
1969 Worked at the Arbitrage Management Co.
1974 Worked at IBM's TJ Watson Research Center.
1983 Appointed Professor of Finance at Baruch College, City University of New York.
1990 Received the Nobel Memorial Prize in Economics.
1994 Appointed Professor of Economics at the Rady School of Management, University of California, San Diego.

LIFE AND CAREER

Harry Markowitz is an influential economist, best known for his groundbreaking work on modern portfolio theory. He studied at the University of Chicago, and worked at the Cowles Foundation, based at Yale, before joining the RAND Corporation, where he helped develop SIMSCRIPT, the first simulation programming language. He went on to co-found CACI International, and to provide support and training for the program after it was released to the public. He was awarded the Von Neumann Prize in Operations Research Theory in 1989, before receiving the Nobel Memorial Prize in Economics for his work on portfolio theory, sparse matrix techniques, and SIMSCRIPT, the following year.

KEY THINKING

- Harry Markowitz started specializing in the application of mathematics techniques to the analysis of the stock market while studying at the University of Chicago.
- His work on stock prices and portfolio selection introduced the concept of risk into valuation for the first time, and led to the development of his theory of portfolio allocation under uncertainty, published in 1952 by the *Journal of Finance*.
- His research emphasized the importance of measuring the risk of an entire portfolio, rather than the risk on an individual security level.
- He built his basic concept of portfolio theory on John Burr Williams's *Theory of Investment Value.*

IN PERSPECTIVE

- Harry Markowitz's research focuses on the effects of asset risk, correlation, and diversification on expected investment portfolio returns.
- His work put risk at the center of investing, and attempted to measure the appropriate amount of risk to undertake, as higher returns are dependent on greater risk, and the greater the risk, the greater the possibility of loss.
- Markowitz showed how an investor's portfolio choice can be reduced to balancing just two dimensions: the expected return on the portfolio, and its variance or standard deviation, depending on the circumstances.
- At the RAND Corporation, he researched optimization techniques, developing the critical line algorithm for the identifications of the optimal mean-variance portfolios. This was found to be lying on what was later named the Markowitz Frontier.
- A Markowitz Efficient Portfolio is one where no added diversification can lower the portfolio's risk for a given return expectation, while the Markowitz Efficient Frontier is the set of all portfolios that will give the highest expected return for each given level of risk. These concepts of efficiency were essential to the development of the capital asset pricing model.
- In *Portfolio Selection*, he produced a theory for optimal investment in stocks that differ in their expected return and risk.
- He was the first to place a number on risk relative to investing, defying the traditional view that risk should only be assessed in general terms; he quantified what an investor wants to avoid by using a range of possible return outcomes, based on the past variability of returns.

▸▸ MORE INFO

Books:

Bernstein, Peter L. *Capital Ideas: The Improbable Origins of Modern Wall Street.* New York: Free Press, 1992.
Markowitz, Harry M. *Portfolio Selection: Efficient Diversification of Investments.* New York: Wiley, 1959.
Williams, John Burr. *Theory of Investment Value.* Cambridge, MA: Harvard University Press, 1938.

See Also:

Portfolio Selection: Efficient Diversification of Investments (p. 1309)

"It's like a crapshoot in Las Vegas, except in Las Vegas the odds are with the house. As for the market, the odds are with you, because on average over the long run, the market has paid off." Harry Markowitz

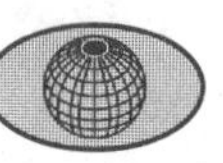

Robert Merton · Nobel Prize-winning economist and financial innovator

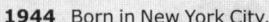

1944 Born in New York City.
1966 Received BS in Engineering Mathematics from Columbia University.
1967 Received MS in Applied Mathematics from Caltech.
1970 Received PhD in Economics from Massachusetts Institute of Technology (MIT).
1970 Appointed Assistant Professor at Sloan School of Management, MIT.
1974 Appointed Professor at Sloan School of Management, MIT.
1979 Appointed Research Associate, National Bureau of Economic Research.
1986 Appointed President of the American Finance Association.
1987 Appointed Visiting Professor of Finance, Graduate School of Business Administration, Harvard University.
1988 Appointed University Professor at Graduate School of Business Administration, Harvard University.
1993 Became co-founder of Long-Term Capital Management.
1997 Received the Alfred Nobel Memorial Prize in the Economic Sciences, with Myron Scholes.
1999 Received the Lifetime Achievement in Mathematical Finance award.
2001 Appointed Managing Director, JP Morgan Chase.
2002 Became co-founder and Chief Science Officer, Integrated Finance Ltd.

LIFE AND CAREER

Robert Merton is an internationally renowned economist, financial innovator, and recipient of the Noble Memorial Prize in Economic Sciences for his work on stock options. He is best known for his seminal work on the development of the Black–Scholes model, the intertemporal capital asset pricing model, Merton's Portfolio Problem, and the Merton Model, and has been a key figure in the shaping of the global financial system. He was a founder of Long-Term Capital Management, and was recently appointed Chief Science Officer of Trinsum Group, and chairman of the board of directors of Daedalus Software.

KEY THINKING

- Robert Merton was a pioneer in producing models that dealt with risk, and helped revolutionize modern financial theory and practice.
- In particular, he had a great influence on the Black–Scholes formula for pricing stock options which, for the first time, enabled option contracts to be effectively evaluated and priced in an open market.
- He supplied the crucial arbitrage that underpins the logic of the Black–Scholes formula, being the first to publish the differential equation that became known as the Black–Scholes equation, in a paper on continuous-time speculative processes.
- In studying the work done by Black and Scholes on option pricing, he found that the limit of continuous trading was the only circumstance that would provide a risk-free, zero-arbitrage position on the option or stock.
- Merton then produced a more general derivation of the formula, which was acknowledged in a footnote in the celebrated Black and Scholes' paper of 1973.
- He later generalized it further, and it is now applied to many different types of option contracts, and other contingent claim contracts, helping the options markets to become one of the biggest and most active security markets.
- His application of continuous-time financial mathematics to the problem of option pricing earned him the Nobel Prize, shared with Myron Scholes, and which acknowledged the late Fischer Black.

IN PERSPECTIVE

- In 1969, he published Merton's Portfolio Problem, which proposed a formula to help people decide how much of their income they should spend and how much should be used for investing.
- The Merton Model, which he presented in 1970, was a method of valuing a corporate bond based on default probability using a form of the Black–Scholes equation; it was extended by Robert Jarrow and Stuart Turnbull for the Jarrow–Turnbull Model.
- High-profile defaults such as Enron and WorldCom, and the rise of credit derivatives have made the Merton Model more popular among credit analysts.
- In 1973, he introduced the intertemporal capital asset pricing model (ICAPM), which incorporates hedges that investors make to protect themselves from shortfalls in savings.
- In 2002, he was a key figure in the advocacy of expensing the stock options awarded as part of a compensation package.

▸▸ MORE INFO

Books:

Bodie, Zvi, and Robert C. Merton. *Finance*. Upper Saddle River, NJ: Prentice Hall, 1998.
Merton, Robert C. *Continuous-time Finance*. Cambridge, MA: Blackwell Publishing, 1990.

Article:

Black, Fisher, and Myron Scholes. "The pricing of options and corporate liabilities". *Journal of Political Economy* 81:3 (May–June 1973): 637–654.

See Also:

Finance (p. 1254)

"[Continuous-time finance] is the study of how best to allocate and deploy resources across time in an uncertain environment and of the role of economic organizations in facilitating these allocations."
Robert Merton

  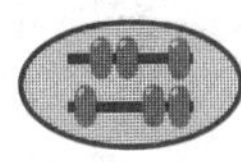 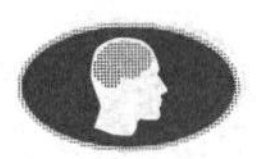  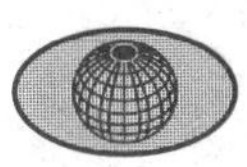   

Merton Miller • Nobel Prize-winning economist, and activist supporter of free-market solutions

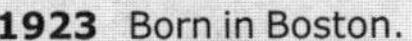

1923 Born in Boston.
1943 Received BA from Harvard University.
1944 Worked at the US Treasury Department.
1952 Received PhD in Economics from Johns Hopkins University.
1952 Taught Economics at London School of Economics.
1953 Taught Economics at Carnegie Mellon University.
1958 Publication of *The Cost of Capital, Corporate Finance and the Theory of Investment.*
1961 Appointed Professor of Economics at the University of Chicago.
1972 Publication of *The Theory of Finance.*
1975 Appointed Fellow of the Econometric Society.
1976 Appointed President of the American Finance Association.
1985 Appointed Member of the Chicago Board of Trade.
1990 Appointed Member of the Chicago Mercantile Exchange.
1990 Received the Nobel Memorial Prize in Economic Sciences, with Harry Markowitz and William Sharpe.
1991 Publication of *Financial Innovations and Market Volatility.*
1997 Publication of *Merton Miller on Derivatives.*
2000 Died in Chicago.

LIFE AND CAREER

Merton Miller was a Professor of Economics, a financial innovator, economist, and renowned financial author. He worked during World War II as an economist in the Division of Tax Research of the US Treasury Department, and subsequently in the Division of Research and Statistics of the Board of Governors of the Federal Reserve System. He then received his doctorate, and was appointed Visiting Assistant Lecturer at the London School of Economics, before being appointed a professor at the University of Chicago. He also served as a public director of the Chicago Mercantile Exchange, and was chairman of its special academic panel considering the 1987 financial market crash.

KEY THINKING

- Merton Miller made pioneering contributions to financial economics through his theory of corporate finance, and the evaluation of firms on markets. He was an influential supporter of a free-market response to economic issues.
- He built on the work of Harry Markowitz on portfolio theory and William Sharpe in the development of the capital asset pricing model, and received the Nobel Prize for his research.
- He built a reputation as one of the most important developers of theoretical and empirical analysis in corporate finance, and collaborated with Franco Modigliani in a seminal article on the cost of capital, and investment theory.
- The Miller–Modigliani Theorem ran against the traditional view that a company should reduce its cost of capital by finding the right debt-to-equity ratio, but argued that there is no right ratio, but that corporate managers are better off reducing their tax liability, and increasing corporate wealth.
- The theorem changed the focus from how investors choose which securities to buy, to how companies decide what securities they should sell.
- In his book, *Financial Innovations and Market Volatility,* he attacked the view that financial innovations have created increasing market volatility, which has a detrimental effect on saving, and business investors.
- He argued that regulators should not use the power of the state to control financial innovation, as this would increase the cost of trading in the domestic markets, while decreasing their international competitiveness.

IN PERSPECTIVE

- Merton Miller helped to interpret the complexities of the futures markets to academia, business, and regulators.
- His analysis of capital structure was critical to resolving the relationship between the capital asset structure of a company, and its dividend policy, market value, and cost of capital.
- As a public director of the Chicago Board of Trade, his work focused on the economic and regulatory problems of the financial services industry, and especially of the securities and options exchanges.
- At a time when the Chicago markets were being blamed for the 1987 stock market crash, he defended them, helping to dissuade regulators from bringing in rules to contain them.
- He argued that the problems between the securities and futures markets centered on Wall Street being unhappy that the Chicago exchanges were taking business from them.
- He opposed government regulation of the exchanges, explaining that futures contracts are similar to other financial products, and have value to those who buy them.

▸▸ MORE INFO

Books:

- Fama, Eugene F and Merton H Miller. *The Theory of Finance*. New York: Holt, Rinehart and Winston, 1972.
- Miller, Merton H. *Financial Innovations and Market Volatility*. Cambridge, MA: Blackwell, 1991.
- Miller, Merton H. *Merton Miller on Derivatives*. New York: Wiley, 1997.

See Also:

The Theory of Finance (p. 1325)

"What counts is what you do with your money, not where it came from." Merton Miller

     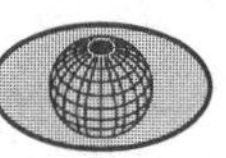   

Franco Modigliani · Nobel Prize-winning macroeconomist

1918 Born in Rome, Italy.
1939 Received the degree of Doctor Juris from the University of Rome.
1939 Moved to the United States.
1942 Taught Economics and Statistics at Columbia University, and Bard College.
1944 Received D.Soc.Sci. from the New School for Social Research.
1944 Appointed Lecturer and Research Associate at the Institute of World Affairs.
1948 Joined the faculty at University of Illinois at Urbana-Champaign.
1948 Received the Political Economy Fellowship of the University of Chicago.
1948 Appointed as research consultant at the Cowles Commission for Research in Economics.
1952 Appointed Professor at the Graduate School of Industrial Administration at Carnegie Mellon University.
1962 Appointed Professor of Economics at MIT.
1962 Appointed President of the Econometric Society.
1970 Named as an Institute Professor at MIT.
1976 Appointed President of the American Economic Association.
1980 Publication of *The Collected Papers of Franco Modigliani.*
1985 Received the Nobel Memorial Prize in Economics.
1988 Appointed as Professor Emeritus at MIT.
1994 Publication of *Foundations of Financial Markets and Institutions.*
2001 Publication of *Adventures of an Economist.*
2003 Died in Cambridge, Massachusetts.

LIFE AND CAREER

Franco Modigliani was an Italian-American economist, and professor at the MIT Sloan School of Management. He emigrated to the United States a few days before the start of World War II. He was then awarded a fellowship by the Graduate Faculty of Political and Social Science of the New School for Social Research. While there, he studied under Jacob Marschak, who helped him develop solid foundations in economics and econometrics. He went on to develop pioneering macroeconomic and econometric theories that changed the way we look at company behavior, and individual savings. He received the Nobel Prize for Economics in 1985 for his work on household savings, and the dynamics of financial markets. He also worked as a consultant to the US Treasury, the Federal Reserve System, and a number of European banks.

KEY THINKING

- Modigliani was at the forefront of postwar macroeconomics, and had a great influence on the development of Keynesian economics.
- While at the Cowles Commission, he was involved in two pieces of critical research, on the theory of choice under uncertainty, and statistical inference from non experimental observations.
- His first article in English, "Liquidity preference and the theory of interest and money," was a major contribution to the debate between Keynesian and classical economics.
- In the 1950s and early 1960s, he made two critical contributions to economics: formulating the Modigliani–Miller Theorem, with Merton Miller, and originating the lifecycle hypothesis.
- His research with Miller on financial markets focused on the effects that a company's financial structure, and its future earning potential have on the market value of its stock.
- They concluded that the market value of a company had no real relationship to the size and structure of its debt. Instead, they concluded that stock-market values are determined mainly by what organizations are expected to earn in the future.
- He received the Nobel Memorial Prize in Economics for his research on the lifecycle theory, an analysis of personal savings that had practical applications.

IN PERSPECTIVE

- The Modigliani–Miller Theorem demonstrates that, under certain assumptions, the value of a firm is not affected by whether it is financed by selling shares or borrowing money, and that the market value of a company's stock depends primarily on investors' expectations of what that company will earn in the future.
- His research on the lifecycle hypothesis analyzed individual behavior and aggregate saving, and proposed that consumers would aim for a stable level of income throughout their life, such as by saving during their working years, and spending during their retirement.
- Co-authored a paper on the predictability of social events, when the agent reacts to prediction, which became one of the tenets of the "theory of rational expectations."
- Explored new areas of research, including international finance and the international payment system, inflation, credit rationing, the term structure of interest rates, and the valuation of speculative assets.

▸▸ MORE INFO

Books:

Fabozzi, Frank J., and Franco Modigliani. *Capital Markets: Institutions and Instruments.* Englewood Cliffs, NJ: Prentice Hall, 1992.
Modigliani, Franco. *Adventures of an Economist.* Rome: Laterza, 1999.
Szenberg, Michael, and Lall Ramrattan. *Franco Modigliani: An Intellectual Biography.* New York: Palgrave Macmillan, 2008.

". . . challenging the self-evident orthodoxies of the moment, be it that the classics are altogether outdated, or that the rich must save a larger fraction of their income than the poor, or that debt financing is cheaper because the interest rate on high-quality debt is lower than the return on equity." Franco Modigliani

  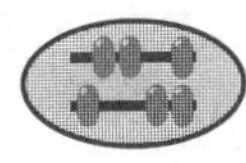 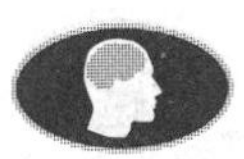  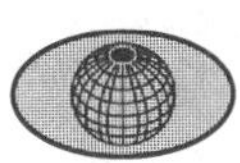 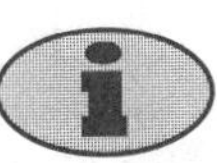  

J. P. Morgan · Legendary American banker

1837 John Pierpont Morgan born in Hartford, Connecticut.
1857 Joined Duncan, Sherman, and Co.
1862 Founded Dabrey, Morgan, and Co.
1871 Teamed up with the firm of Drexel to form Drexel, Morgan, and Co.
1879 Put together stock offering of US$18 million for the New York Central Railroad.
1887 US government passed the Interstate Commerce Act.
1895 Helped avert US financial crisis.
1907 Bailed out US government again.
1912 Appeared before Pujo Committee.
1913 Died in Rome.

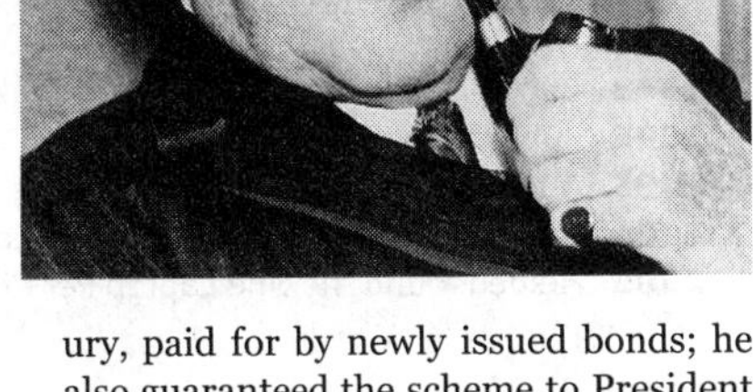

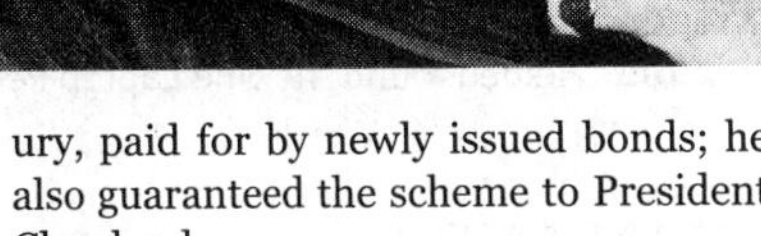

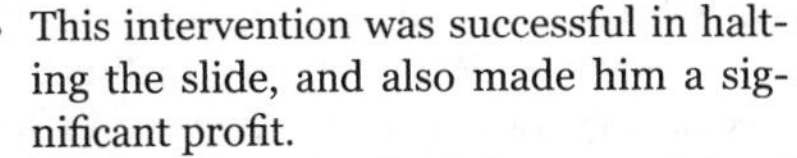

LIFE AND CAREER

JP Morgan was a renowned banker and businessman. He took an early interest in business, spending time checking receipts, and the expenditure of his allowance rather than playing games. After studying at the University of Göttingen in Germany, he was asked to become an assistant to one of the professors, but he preferred to start out in business, joining Duncan, Sherman, and Co, a firm with which his father had an association. He made money out of the American Civil War, and founded his own company, Dabrey, Morgan, and Co. By 1871, he had teamed up with the firm Drexel, to form Drexel, Morgan, and Co, and quickly established himself as one of the leading financiers in New York. After the war, he continued to build up his banking and business empire. He came to the rescue of the US financial system on a couple of occasions, and also served as president of the Metropolitan Museum of Art.

KEY THINKING

- JP Morgan built a portfolio of business interests in the key industries of the day—railways, shipping, and electricity.
- He helped consolidate much of the railroads in the US, create US Steel, and was involved in the creation of General Electric, AT&T, and International Harvester.
- As an industry magnate and a powerful industry figure, he came to be seen as a de facto US central banker, being called upon to assist the financial world in times of trouble, and he helped avert a US financial crisis in 1895.

IN PERSPECTIVE

- Morgan established a reputation as a leading financier, with a considerable salary, and industrialists and governments regularly asked him for advice.
- During the 1870s, he focused on the railway industry, resolving disputes, and organizing private investment from the US and Europe to upgrade the system, and generate operating efficiencies.
- However, he failed in an attempt to unite the railways against the government after the passing of the Interstate Commerce Act in 1887, which banned price-fixing in the industry.
- The financial crisis of 1895 originated from the withdrawal of funds from the US by British investors–as the banks were failing, and the stock market collapsing. So the US government used gold reserves to strengthen the financial system, and asked Morgan for help.
- He suggested an economic and a political answer to the crisis–a syndicate of investors would sell gold coin to the US Treasury, paid for by newly issued bonds; he also guaranteed the scheme to President Cleveland.
- This intervention was successful in halting the slide, and also made him a significant profit.
- He was then involved in a number of high-profile deals, including the financing of US Steel, the largest steel corporation in the world.
- He was also an important figure in the creation of industry trusts, but these were seen as collusive business practices by President Theodore Roosevelt, who started cracking down on this practice, making an example of Morgan in the process.
- By the 1890s, these government attacks had turned him into an unpopular figure in the US, and he spent his later years amassing an art collection, and travelling.

▸▸ MORE INFO

Books:

Chernow, Ron. *The House of Morgan: An American Banking Dynasty and the Rise of Modern Finance.* New York: Atlantic Monthly Press, 1990. Details the influence and operations of Morgan's banks on economic development since the late 18th century, based on research into the family archives.

Strouse, Jean. *Morgan: American Financier.* New York: Random House, 1999. Examines both Morgan's activities as America's leading banker, and his frenetic social life during the Gilded Age.

Wheeler, George. *Pierpont Morgan and Friends: The Anatomy of a Myth.* Englewood Cliffs, NJ: Prentice Hall, 1973. Examines his career and business partnerships.

"A man always has two reasons for doing anything: a good reason and the real reason." J. P. Morgan

  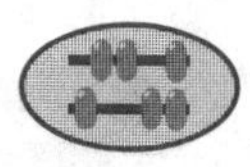   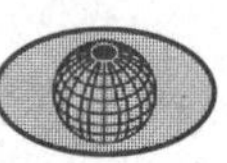   

Nicholas Negroponte · Greek-American digital innovator, and computer scientist

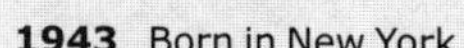

1943 Born in New York.
1961 Graduated from Choate Rosemary Hall.
1966 Received Masters in Architecture from Massachusetts Institute of Technology (MIT).
1966 Joined the faculty of MIT.
1967 Founded the Architecture Machine Group at MIT.
1985 Co-founded the MIT Media Lab.
1992 Helped create *Wired* magazine.
1993 Began regular column in *Wired.*
1995 Publication of *Being Digital.*
1995 Appointed to the board of directors of Motorola Inc.
2000 Resigned as director of the Media Lab.
2005 Helped found the One Laptop Per Child organization.

LIFE AND CAREER

Nicholas Negroponte is Professor of Media Technology at Massachusetts Institute of Technology (MIT), and a pioneer in the field of computer-aided design, and is best known as the founder of MIT's Media Lab. He taught at MIT, Yale, Michigan, and the University of California at Berkeley. He has provided start-up funds for more than 40 companies, including *Wired* magazine, and was the founder of The One Laptop Per Child organization. He is also founder and chairman of the 2B1 Foundation, the founding chairman of the International Federation of Information Processing Societies, and the first executive director of the World Center for Personal Computation and Human Development. He is currently involved in a number of venture capital funds, and has acted as an advisor to the European Commission.

KEY THINKING

- He founded MIT's Architecture Machine Group, to explore new approaches to human–computer interaction.
- As co-founder and director of the MIT Media Lab, he helped build it into one of the foremost research units exploring new media and digital innovation.
- His monthly columns for *Wired* magazine focused on the basic theme: "move bits, not atoms", and were integral to his bestseller *Being Digital*.
- As founder and chairman of One Laptop Per Child (OLPC), he pioneered the movement for affordable educational computers for poor children in the developing world.

IN PERSPECTIVE

- *Being Digital* provides an overview of the development of media technology, and offers new ways of looking at the implications of technology and mass media. It also describes Negroponte's own involvement in the development of digital innovations such as multimedia, personal computing, virtual reality, and the internet.
- It was seen as influential in the evolution of the digital economy, as based around his forecasts on how the interactive world, the entertainment industry, and information would eventually merge.
- The aim of his work with OLPC is to provide educational resources so children can be more active in their own learning. The idea is to distribute millions of cheap, wireless-internet-enabled, pedal-powered laptop computers by 2010.
- With the backing of multinational companies such as News Corporation and Google, OLPC is discussing potential orders for millions of these specialized computers with countries including Brazil, Thailand, Egypt, China, and South Africa.
- In 2007, Negroponte was appointed to a committee aimed at assuring the continued journalistic and editorial integrity, and independence of the *Wall Street Journal*, and other Dow Jones publications, after its merger with News Corporation.

▸▸ MORE INFO

Books:

Negroponte, Nicholas. *Being Digital*. New York: Knopf, 1995. His groundbreaking and influential book on the transformation in technology and society.

Palfrey, James, and Urs Gasser. *Born Digital: Connecting with a Global Generation of Digital Natives.* New York: Basic Books, 2008. A similar treatment of the digital revolution, exploring the emerging global culture of connectivity, communication, and content.

See Also:

Being Digital (p. 1226)

"The change from atoms to bits is irrevocable and unstoppable."**"The change from atoms to bits is irrevocable and unstoppable."** Nicholas Negroponte

  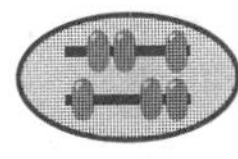   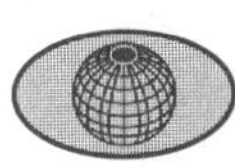   

Paul H. O'Neill · Former Secretary to the US Treasury

1935 Born in St. Louis, Missouri.
1961 Received degree in Economics from Claremont Graduate University.
1961 Appointed as a computer systems analyst with the Veterans Administration.
19?? Received Master of Public Administration from Indiana University.
1967 Appointed to the US Office of Management and Budget.
1974 Appointed as Deputy Director of the US Office of Management and Budget.
1977 Appointed Vice-President of International Paper.
1985 Appointed President of International Paper.
1987 Appointed Chairman and Chief Executive Officer of Alcoa.
1995 Appointed Chairman of the Rand Corporation.
1997 Co-founded the Pittsburgh Regional Healthcare Initiative.
2001 Appointed US Secretary of the Treasury.

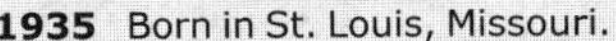

LIFE AND CAREER

Paul H. O'Neill is an influential economist, who served under the administrations of Richard Nixon and Gerald Ford, and was the US Secretary of the Treasury under George W. Bush, before resigning, and becoming a harsh critic of the Bush regime. After receiving a bachelor's degree in Economics from California State University, Fresno, he went on to gain further degrees at Claremont Graduate University and Indiana University. He worked at the Veterans' Administration, and the US Office of Management and Budget, was appointed President of International Paper, and then Chairman and Chief Executive Officer of Alcoa. His management of Alcoa was a successful one, with the company increasing its revenues from US$1.5 billion in 1987 to Us$23 billion in 2000. He later returned to the public sector under President George W Bush, where he was noted for taking a different approach, such as touring Africa with singer, Bono, before resigning after disputes with the Bush team over tax issues.

KEY THINKING

- Paul H. O'Neill was US Secretary of the Treasury during part of the first administration of George W Bush, before resigning in 2002 due to differences in opinion over governmental and tax policies; he has since become a vocal critic of the Bush administration.
- As US Secretary of the Treasury, he was an outspoken member of the administration, often offering opinions that ran counter to the administration's party line.
- He argued against the invasion of Iraq as part of the war on terror, setting himself in opposition to the neo-conservatives in Bush's team.
- He worked hard to push through serious financial and diplomatic engagement in the battle against AIDS in Africa.

IN PERSPECTIVE

- He was asked to be Secretary of Defense by President George H. W. Bush in 1988, but he declined, instead recommending Dick Cheney for the position.
- O'Neill was then appointed to chair an advisory group on education by the president; under his leadership, the advisory group made important recommendations concerning national standards, and unified testing standards.
- While working at the Pittsburgh Regional Healthcare Initiative, he was instrumental in improvements in patient safety and the quality of healthcare; it created a coalition that addressed the existing problems as a region, adopting the scheme of "Perfecting Patient Care".
- A report he commissioned as Treasury Secretary showed that there were potential federal budget deficits of more than US$500 billion, and that massive tax increases or spending cuts would be necessary to meet benefit promises. O'Neill was unhappy that the report's findings were omitted from the 2004 annual budget report.
- As Secretary of the Treasury, his style was often at odds with the financial markets, as well as some of the policy decisions that originated from political advisors who disagreed with the views of leading cabinet officials.
- He questioned President Bush's plans for tax cuts, and his desire to investigate alleged Al-Qaeda funding from some US-allied countries, which led to him being sacked in December 2002.

▸▸ MORE INFO

Book:

Suskind, Ron. *The Price of Loyalty: George W Bush, the White House, and the Education of Paul O'Neill.* New York: Simon & Schuster Paperbacks, 2004. An examination of the Bush administration during O'Neill's tenure; it presents Bush's economic policies as irresponsible, claims that he was not greatly involved in meetings, and argues that the war against Iraq was planned in advance.

"Our intention is to give people, however you might stylize it, a tax cut or a pay raise." Paul H. O'Neill

     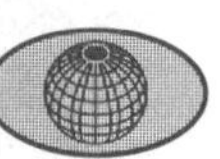   

Michael Eugene Porter • Leading authority on competitive strategy

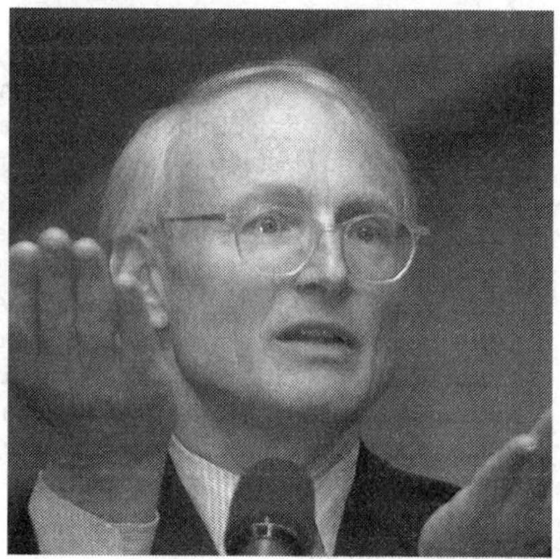

1947 Born in Ann Arbor, Michigan.
1969 Received BSE in Aeronautical Engineering from Princeton University.
1971 Received MBA from Harvard Business School.
1973 Received PhD in Business Economics from Harvard University.
1973 Joined the faculty of Harvard Business School.
1980 Publication of *Competitive Strategy.*
1980 Publication of *Competitive Advantage.*
1983 Publication of *Cases in Competitive Strategy.*
1985 Elected a Fellow of the International Academy of Management.
1988 Elected a Fellow of the Academy of Management.
1994 Founded and appointed Chairman and Chief Executive Officer of The Initiative for a Competitive Inner City.
2006 Publication of *Redefining Health Care.*
2008 Received the Lifetime Achievement Award from the US Department of Commerce.
2008 Publication of *On Competition.*

LIFE AND CAREER

Michael Porter is a university professor at Harvard Business School, and an influential thinker on management strategy and economics. His ideas on strategy have become the basis for the required strategy course at the Harvard Business School, and his work is taught in virtually every business school around the world. He also created and chairs Harvard's program for newly appointed CEOs, and he is a leading authority on the competitiveness and economic development of nations, states, and regions. He is the cofounder of the Monitor Group, and has acted as a consultant to businesses, and governments. He is a Fellow Member of the Strategic Management Society. He has played an active role in US economic policy with the Executive Branch, Congress, and international organizations, and is a founding member of the Executive Committee of the Council on Competitiveness. He also chairs the selection committee for the annual Corporate Stewardship Award of the US Secretary of Commerce, and the Global Competitiveness Report.

KEY THINKING

- Michael Porter is at the forefront of advances in research on competitive advantage, by focusing on how a company, region, or country can successfully develop a winning competitive strategy.
- He has shown how this can be achieved through an improvement in organizational innovation, and through factor conditions, demand conditions, related and supporting industries, and company strategy, structure, and rivalry.
- He originated and popularized the concept of the value chain, where products pass through all activities of the chain in order, and increase in value at each activity.
- In *The Competitive Advantage of Nations*, he identifies the fundamental determinants of national competitive advantage in an industry, shows how they work together as a system, and examines "clustering", in which groups of successful firms and industries emerge in one country to gain leading positions in the world market.
- He originated the "Porter Hypothesis", which argues that environmental progress and economic competitiveness are more complementary than previously thought.

IN PERSPECTIVE

- Porter's theories on business clusters, and their impact on economic development, have resulted in many cluster initiatives around the world.
- He has explained how, to ensure competitiveness, an organization must choose between three generic strategies: cost leadership, differentiation, and focus.
- These strategies are driven by five competitive forces: the bargaining power of customers, the bargaining power of suppliers, the threat of similar products being brought to market, the threat of new market entrants, and the level of existing competition.
- He focuses on both primary and secondary business activity, with the former being concerned with turning raw materials into products, and the latter relating to activities that support the primary, such as procurement, technology development, human resources, and company infrastructure.
- He produced three critical tests for success: attractiveness, cost-of-entry, and the better-off test, and has introduced seven steps to tackle these questions.
- In a number of articles, he has introduced a new framework for developing strategy in foundations and other philanthropic organizations, and examined how corporations should think strategically about their social responsibility.
- In his latest book, *Redefining Health Care*, he examines competition in the health care system, and looks at ways of improving health care delivery.

▸▸ MORE INFO

Books:

Porter, Michael. *Cases in Competitive Strategy.* New York: Free Press, 1983.
Porter, Michael. *Competitive Advantage: Creating and Sustaining Superior Performance.* New York: Free Press, 1985.
Porter, Michael. *Competitive Strategy: Techniques for Analyzing Industries and Competitors.* New York: Free Press, 1980.

See Also:

The Competitive Advantage of Nations (p. 1237)
Competitive Strategy: Techniques for Analyzing Industries and Competitors (p. 1238)

"National and economic prosperity is created, not inherited." Michael Eugene Porter

  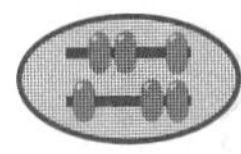 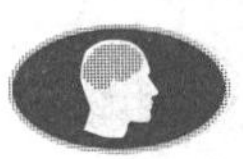  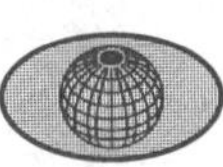   

C. K. Prahalad · Influential thinker on competition and innovation

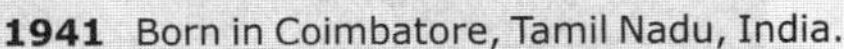

1941 Born in Coimbatore, Tamil Nadu, India.
1960 Received BSc from Loyola College, the University of Madras.
1960 Worked as an industrial engineer for Union Carbide.
1966 Received MBA from the Indian Institute of Management.
1975 Received DBA from Harvard Business School.
1975 Appointed Visiting Research Fellow at Harvard Business School.
1975 Appointed Professor and Chairman of the Management Education Program, Indian Institute of Management.
1977 Appointed Associate Professor of Business Administration, University of Michigan Business School.
1981 Appointed Visiting Professor at INSEAD, France.
1987 Appointed Professor of Corporate Strategy and International Business at the Graduate School of Business Administration, University of Michigan.
1994 Publication of *Competing for the Future.*
2000 Received the Lal Bahadur Shastri Award for contributions to Management and Public Administration.
2004 Publication of *The Fortune at the Bottom of the Pyramid.*
2004 Publication of *The Future of Competition.*
2008 Publication of *The New Age of Innovation.*

LIFE AND CAREER

C. K. Prahalad is an important figure in the development of management strategy, as well as a professor of corporate strategy, writer, and consultant. He studied at the Indian Institute of Management, before completing his MBA, and then his DBA at Harvard. He was co-founder and CEO of Praja Inc, a software company sold to TIBCO, in the US, in 2002. He is also a member of the blue ribbon commission of the United Nations on Private Sector and Development, and serves on the board of directors of NCR Corporation, Hindustan Lever Limited, and the World Resources Institute. He is also the chairman and founder of The Next Practice.

KEY THINKING

- Prahalad's research has concentrated on the ability of large organizations to maintain their competitiveness when faced with international competition, and a changing business environment.
- He has analyzed strategic intent, and how the corporate imagination has to be able to access the potential of core competencies, arguing that organizations must have the imagination to visualize new markets, and the ability to move into them ahead of the competition.
- The four elements that help this imaginative effort are the ability to look beyond existing markets, the search for innovative products, the overturning of assumptions over price and performance, and being able to lead (rather than follow) customers.

IN PERSPECTIVE

- In his work with Gary Hamel on *Competing for the Future,* he presents a new view of competitiveness, strategy, and organizations, taking the ideas of strategic intent, core competence, and strategy as stretch and leverage, and develops them into a new strategy model.
- His concept of strategic intent is about being successful at all levels and functions of an organization; it uses stretch targets to create competitive advantage, and is based on senior management developing the organization in a strategic way.
- This far-reaching work shows how a core competency (a term he helped originate) is based on an ability to transcend products and markets, and should result when an organization is able to combine different technologies, learning, and relationships.
- In *The Fortune at the Bottom of the Pyramid,* he shows how multinational companies can seize the opportunity presented by the world's poor—as both a growth market for the right business model, and as a pool of potential innovators.
- It also presents a strategic framework for leveraging corporate resources towards strategic intent, by presenting an overview of how an industry can evolve.
- In *The New Age of Innovation,* he shows how value creation needs business managers to transform their processes, technical systems and supply chain management to implement social and technological infrastructure changes capable of improving the chances of successful corporate and product innovation.

▸▸ MORE INFO

Books:

Hamel, Gary, and C. K. Prahalad. *Competing for the Future.* Boston, MA: Harvard Business School Press, 1994.
Prahalad, C. K., and M. S. Krishnan. *The New Age of Innovation: Driving Co-created Value Through Global Networks.* New York: McGraw-Hill, 2008.
Prahalad, C. K., and Venkat Ramaswamy. *The Future of Competition: Co-creating Unique Value with Customers.* Boston, MA: Harvard Business School Press, 2004.

See Also:

Competing for the Future (p. 1236)

"Strategy is about stretching limited resources to fit ambitious aspirations." C. K. Prahalad

David Ricardo · Founder of the classical school of economics

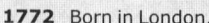

1772 Born in London.
1786 Started work at the London Stock Exchange.
1810 Publication of *The High Price of Bullion, a Proof of the Depreciation of Bank Notes.*
1814 Retired from business.
1815 Publication of *Essay on Profits.*
1815 Publication of *An Essay on the Influence of a Low Price of Corn on the Profits of Stock.*
1817 Publication of *On the Principles of Political Economy and Taxation.*
1819 Became Member of Parliament for Portarlington.
1821 Became a founding member of the Political Economy Club.
1823 Died at Gatcombe Park, Gloucestershire, UK.

LIFE AND CAREER

David Ricardo was a political economist and writer, and one of the most important figures in the development of economic theory, introducing the theory of rent, and the concept of comparative advantage to the classical system of political economy. After a brief schooling in Holland, he joined his father at the London Stock Exchange, where he learnt about the financial system, which provided an education on the stock market, and real estate that would prove invaluable to his later work. As a businessman, financier, and speculator, he amassed a considerable fortune, which enabled him to retire from business at the age of 42, to pursue a career in politics, and economic research. He was also a Member of Parliament, and one of the original members of the Geological Society.

KEY THINKING

- Ricardo was one of the most influential economists to develop the classical system of political economy, along with Thomas Malthus, and Adam Smith, and is credited with systematizing economic thought.
- He first gained recognition during the "bullion controversy" of 1809, when he argued that inflation had resulted from the Bank of England's propensity to over-issue bank notes.
- In his famous treatise, *Principles of Political Economy and Taxation,* Ricardo laid out the foundations for the principles of a market economy. He also described the guiding concepts behind economic theories such as the law of diminishing returns, and economic rent.
- In *Principles of Political Economy and Taxation*, he integrated his theory of value with his theory of distribution.
- The law of comparative advantage that Ricardo formulated made a significant contribution to political economics. It was developed from Adam Smith's theory of the division of labor, discussed in his seminal work, *An Inquiry into the Nature and Causes of the Wealth of Nations,* and has since become a central tenet of free trade, open markets, and anti-protectionism.
- In *An Essay on the Influence of a Low Price of Corn on the Profits of Stock*, he presented the law of diminishing returns, which states that as more and more resources are combined in production with a fixed resource, the additions to output will diminish.
- In his *Essay on Profits*, he contended that profits depend on high or low wages; wages on the price of necessaries; and the price of necessaries chiefly on the price of food.
- His views have been influential in the work of many more recent economists, including Friedrich Hayek, who discussed the Ricardo Effect based on his theories on the interrelationships between capital, labor, output, and investment.

IN PERSPECTIVE

- Ricardo's law of comparative advantage argues that a nation, which trades in products purchased at a lower cost from another country, is likely to be more prosperous than if it had made the products at home.
- This concept ensures international trade will bring benefits for all countries, but that each country should specialize in making the products in which it possesses a comparative advantage.
- He developed theories of rent, wages, and profits, to explain that as more land was cultivated, farmers would have to start using less-productive land, so that landowners are the ones who gain from productive land.
- He argued that, in the long run, prices reflect the cost of production, calling this long-run price a natural price. The natural price of labor was the cost of its production, the cost of maintaining the laborer.
- His concept of Ricardian equivalence contends that in some circumstances a government's choice of how to pay for its spending might have no effect on the economy.
- Ricardo was admired for his ability to arrive at complex conclusions without the use of mathematics.

▸▸ MORE INFO

Books:

Henderson, John P., and John B. Davis. *The Life and Economics of David Ricardo*. Boston: Kluwer Academic, 1997. A full examination of Ricardo's life and career, including his later work on money and banking, and international trade.

Ricardo, David. *On the Principles of Political Economy and Taxation*. London: J. Murray, 1817. The groundbreaking book that presents his theory of comparative advantage for the first time, as well as discussing the labor theory of value.

Ricardo, David, and J. R. McCulloch. *The Works of David Ricardo*. London: J. Murray, 1846. An authoritative look at Ricardo's life and work that has been reissued many times.

"There can be no rise in the value of labor without a fall of profits." David Ricardo

  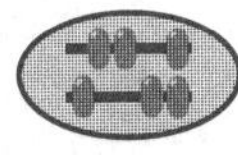 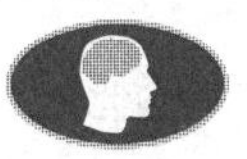  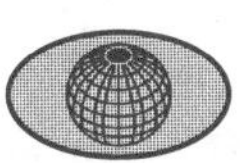   

John D. Rockefeller · American industrialist, and the world's first dollar billionaire

1839 Born in Richford, New York.
1855 Started work at Hewitt & Tuttle.
1859 Founded Rockefeller, Andrews, & Flagler.
1862 Entered oil-refining business.
1869 Rockefeller, Andrews, & Flagler became the Standard Oil Company of Ohio.
1882 The Standard Oil businesses brought under the control of the Standard Oil Company.
1890 Nationwide distribution system reached most towns in the US.
1892 The Trust was dissolved by Ohio government, and reconstituted as Standard Oil Trust.
1900 Standard Oil controlled more than three-quarters of the US petroleum industry.
1904 Standard Oil delivery carts served 80% of US towns.
1911 Resigned as president and Standard Oil Trust was dissolved.
1913 Established Rockefeller Foundation.
1937 Died in Ormond Beach, Florida.

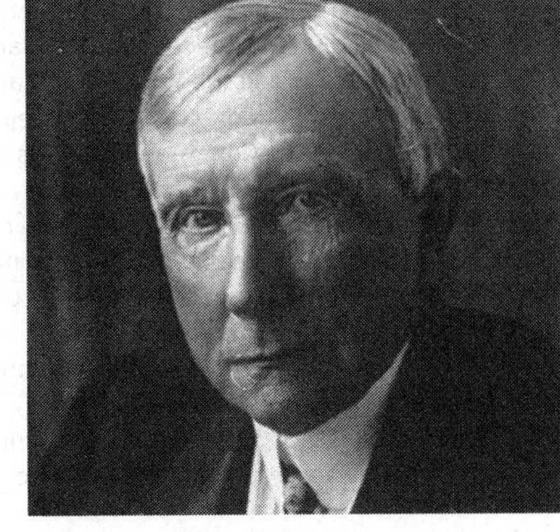

LIFE AND CAREER

John D. Rockefeller was an industrialist, the patriarch of America's best-known family, and the world's richest man of his time. After only a year at high school, and a short time at Folsom Mercantile College, he became an office boy and assistant bookkeeper at the firm of Hewitt & Tuttle. He stayed there for three years, before starting his own business. After this proved successful, he moved into the oil business, buying out most of the local competition, and setting his sights on building a national oil company with a national delivery network. He withdrew from active management of the company in 1897, remaining president until 1911, when the Standard Oil Trust was dissolved by the US government. His final years were devoted to philanthropy, giving away the bulk of his huge fortune through the Rockefeller Foundation.

KEY THINKING

- John D. Rockefeller, the founder of the famously wealthy family dynasty, built up the most powerful oil business in the US, Standard Oil, which refined and marketed nearly 90% of the oil produced in the country.
- His development of Standard Oil to a near-monopolistic position in the US oil industry was part of the larger shift from small business operations to the rise of giant corporations.
- He was extremely successful in creating an empire, and becoming massively wealthy through buying up the competition, and focusing the company on business development and growth.
- His approach received much criticism. There were accusations about the use of unscrupulous tactics, collusion with the railroads, use of predatory pricing, monopolistic practices, and the bribery of political officials.
- The trust that he formed to run Standard Oil was attacked by President Roosevelt, who fought a personal battle against industry trusts in general, and Standard Oil in particular.

IN PERSPECTIVE

- John D. Rockefeller entered the oil industry just as oil was becoming central to the US economy and many refineries were being opened, and he was able to take advantage of the boom.
- Although there was were a large number of companies competing against each other, which forced down prices and made many of them bankrupt, Rockefeller merged his company with the Standard Oil Company of Ohio with US$1 million of capital, and became its president.
- He applied the "combination" strategy to the oil industry that legendary US banker J. P. Morgan had successfully applied to the steel industry––buying up competitors across the country, and spreading the risk inherent in the industry.
- By 1882, his success had enabled him to unite all the businesses of Standard Oil into the single organization of the Standard Oil Trust, which controlled the majority of the oil industry in the US.
- The predominance of the Trust brought criticism, and the Attorney General of Ohio successfully managed to dissolve it. However, it soon reformed as the Standard Oil Company (New Jersey), to take advantage of New Jersey's less-stringent laws.
- In 1911, the US Supreme Court ordered the dissolution of the Standard Oil Company (New Jersey), asserting that it contravened the country's antitrust laws, and all the parts of the business were split into separate entities.
- After his retirement, Rockefeller spent his time on philanthropic work. He donated more than US$35 million to the University of Chicago, founded the Rockefeller Institute for Medical Research, the Rockefeller Foundation, and the Rockefeller Sanitary Commission.
- At its height, Rockefeller's wealth reached US$900 million, but he had given all but US$26,410,837 of it away by the time he died.

▸▸ MORE INFO

Books:

Chernow, Ron. *Titan: The Life of John D. Rockefeller, Sr.* New York: Random House, 1998.

Morris, Charles R. *The Tycoons: How Andrew Carnegie, John D. Rockefeller, Jay Gould, and J. P. Morgan Invented the American Supereconomy.* New York: H. Holt and Co., 2005.

"The way to make money is to buy when blood is running in the streets." John D. Rockefeller

  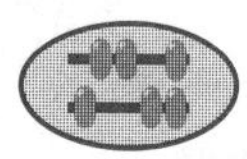  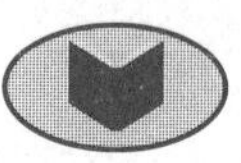 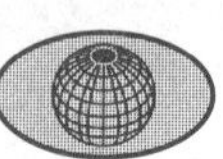   

Stephen A. Ross · Creator of the arbitrage pricing theory

1965 Received BS in Physics from CalTech.
1970 Received PhD in Economics from Harvard University.
1976 Appointed Professor of Economics and Finance at Yale School of Management.
1979 Developed the Cox–Ross–Rubinstein model.
1985 Developed the Cox–Ingersoll–Ross model.
1988 Publication of *Corporate Finance.*
1988 Appointed President of the American Finance Association.
1991 Publication of *Fundamentals of Corporate Finance.*
1996 Received the Financial Engineer of the Year award from the International Association of Financial Engineers.
1996 Publication of *Essentials of Corporate Finance.*
2005 Publication of *Neoclassical Finance*.
2006 Received the CME-MSRI Prize in Innovative Quantitative Application.
2007 Won the Jean-Jacques Laffont Prize from the Toulouse School of Economics.

LIFE AND CAREER

Stephen Ross is Professor of Financial Economics at the MIT Sloan School of Management, and Chairman of the Investment Advisory Board of IVC International Compensation Valuation, Inc. He is also Principal and CIO of Ross Institutional Investors, LLC. After gaining a PhD in Economics from Harvard, he went on teach at the Wharton School and Yale School of Management, before joining MIT. He has founded several investment services firms, acted as a consultant to a number of investment banks and corporations, and served as an advisor to government departments such as the US Treasury, the Commerce Department, and the Internal Revenue Service. He is a former director of Freddie Mac, a Fellow of the Econometric Society, and is a past president of the American Finance Association. He has been the recipient of numerous prizes and awards, including the IAFE Financial Engineer of the Year Award.

KEY THINKING

- Stephen Ross has initiated several important theories, and models in financial economics. He has published more than 100 articles, and one of the classic textbooks on corporate finance.
- He is best known for creating the arbitrage pricing theory, a general theory of asset pricing which argues that the expected return of a financial asset can be modeled as a linear function of various factors, and market indices.
- He was an initiator of the concept of risk-neutral pricing, and the binomial model for pricing derivatives.

IN PERSPECTIVE

- Stephen Ross developed the influential arbitrage pricing theory, an alternative pricing model to the capital asset pricing model (CAPM).
- Unlike CAPM, the arbitrage pricing theory may specify returns as a linear function of more than a single factor.
- He also helped develop the influential Cox–Ross–Rubinstein model, a binomial options pricing model he worked on with John Cox and Mark Rubinstein.
- This model provides a numerical method for the valuation of options, which incorporates a discrete-time model, and a risk-neutrality assumption.
- The financial models he has worked on, including term-structure models and option pricing models, have become standard practice for pricing on the financial markets.
- In 1985, he contributed to the creation of the Cox–Ingersoll–Ross model for interest-rate dynamics, now a central tenet of neoclassical finance.
- This model is a one-factor model that describes the evolution of interest rates, as ascribing movements to market risk alone.
- He gave the inaugural lecture of the Princeton Lectures in Finance in 2001, defending neoclassical finance, including the concepts of efficiency and rationality in the markets.

▸▸ MORE INFO

Books:

Ross, Stephen A., and Randolph W. Westerfield. *Corporate Finance*. St. Louis, MO: Times Mirror/Mosby College Pub, 1988. A textbook presenting corporate finance that integrates the key features of the subject, and develops the main concepts of modern finance for students.

Ross, Stephen A., Randolph W. Westerfield, and Bradford D. Jordan. *Essentials of Corporate Finance.* Chicago, IL: Irwin, 1996. Distils corporate finance down to its essential features, examining the main concepts and principles for a wide audience.

Ross, Stephen A., Randolph W. Westerfield, and Bradford D. Jordan. *Fundamentals of Corporate Finance.* Homewood, IL: Irwin, 1991. Classic textbook that provides a concise overview of all the basic financial topics in a highly accessible manner.

"You can't operate a company by fear, because the way to eliminate fear is to avoid criticism. And the way to avoid criticism is to do nothing." Stephen A. Ross

  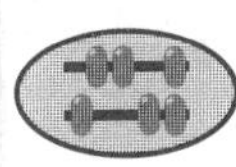   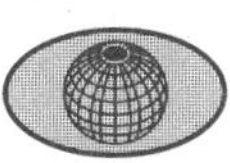   

Nouriel Roubini • Leading economic policy advisor

1959 Born in Istanbul, Turkey.
1976 Attended Hebrew University, Jerusalem.
1982 Received BA in Economics from Bocconi University, Milan.
1988 Received PhD from Harvard University.
1988 Became a Faculty Research Fellow, National Bureau of Economic Research.
1988 Appointed as Visiting Economist and Consultant, International Monetary Fund, Washington DC.
1991 Became a Research Fellow at the Centre for Economic Policy Research, London.
1993 Appointed Associate Professor at the Department of Economics, Yale University.
1995 Appointed Associate Professor at Stern School of Business, New York University.
1995 Became a Consultant for the World Bank, Washington DC.
1997 Founded RGE Monitor.
1998 Appointed Senior Economist for International Affairs, White House Council of Economic Advisors.
1999 Appointed Director of the Office of Policy Development and Review at the US Treasury Department.
2000 Appointed Advisor to the US Treasury Department.
2000 Appointed Senior Advisor to the Under Secretary for International Affairs.
2004 Publication of *Bailouts or Bail-ins? Responding to Financial Crises in Emerging Economies.*
2006 Publication of *New International Financial Architecture.*

LIFE AND CAREER

Nouriel Roubini is Professor of Economics and International Business, Stern School of Business, New York University, and founder and chairman of Roubini Global Economics. After gaining his PhD from Harvard, and joining the faculty of NBER, he worked for the IMF, before returning to academia at Yale, and then Stern School of Business. He has been a Senior Economist for International Affairs on the staff of the President's Council of Economic Advisors, and has served in various roles at the Treasury Department. He is a Member of the Bretton Woods Committee, the Council on Foreign Relations Roundtable on the International Economy, the Academic Advisory Committee, Fiscal Affairs Department, International Monetary Fund, and the Council on Foreign Relation's Roundtable on the International Economy. He also founded the RGE website, a respected economic information resource.

KEY THINKING

- Nouriel Roubini is an internationally known expert in international macroeconomics, and a long-time consultant to the International Monetary Fund, and a number of other public and private institutions, including the US government.
- He has published numerous policy papers and books on key international macroeconomic issues, and is regularly cited as an authority in the media for his views on the future course of the economy.
- He has been a participant and speaker at G-20 meetings of deputy finance ministers, and Central Bank governors' meetings, where he worked on the Asian and global financial crises of 1997–1998, and the subsequent reform of the international financial architecture.
- As Chairman of RGE Monitor, an economic consultancy for financial analysis, he provides strategic financial guidance to businesses.

IN PERSPECTIVE

- Nouriel Roubini's research focuses on international macroeconomics and finance, fiscal policy, political economy, growth theory, and European monetary issues.
- He is known for his bearish views, and was one of the first to forecast a recession in 2006.
- In the book, *Bailouts or Bail-ins?*, he argued that economic policy for troubled emerging markets needed to recognize that each crisis is different and needs to be handled within a framework that provides consistency and predictability to borrowing countries, as well as those who invest in their debt.
- In *Political Cycles and the Macroeconomy*, he explains that the dynamics of political cycles are not short-termist, but more complex, underpinned by an analysis of the relationship between macroeconomic and political policies.

▸▸ MORE INFO

Books:

Alesina, Alberto, and Nouriel Roubini. *Political Cycles and the Macroeconomy.* Cambridge, MA: MIT Press, 1997. Examines the relationship between political and economic cycles, the timing of elections, government ideology, and how the nature of competition among political parties can influence economic matters.

Roubini, Nouriel, and Brad Setser. *Bailouts or Bail-ins? Responding to Financial Crises in Emerging Economies.* Washington DC: Institute for International Economics, 2004. Discusses emerging markets, international capital markets, rescue loans, currency devaluations, debt default, and what options are available to resolve the critical issues.

Roubini, Nouriel, and Marc Uzan (eds). *New International Financial Architecture.* Cheltenham, UK: Edward Elgar, 2006. A collection of articles that consider the evolution of international finance during the 1990s.

Website:

Roubini's Global EconoMonitor: www.rgemonitor.com/blog/roubini

"Global imbalances are growing, cross-border financing needs are increasing, and a smooth-functioning financial system is now essential for this." Nouriel Roubini

   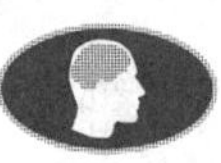  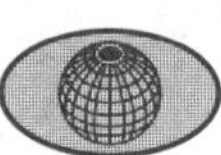   

Paul Samuelson · One of the founders of modern neoclassical economics

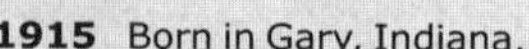

1915 Born in Gary, Indiana.
1935 Received BA from the University of Chicago.
1936 Received MA from Harvard University.
1940 Appointed Assistant Professor of Economics at MIT.
1941 Received PhD from Harvard University.
1944 Appointed Associate Professor of Economics at MIT.
1944 Became staff member of the Radiation Laboratory.
1945 Became a part-time Professor of International Economic Relations at Fletcher School of Law and Diplomacy.
1947 Appointed Professor of Economics at MIT.
1947 Publication of *Foundations of Economic Analysis.*
1947 Awarded the John Bates Clark Medal.
1948 Received Guggenheim Fellowship.
1951 Appointed President of the Econometric Association.
1961 Appointed President of the American Economic Association.
1965 Elected President of the International Economic Association.
1966 Publication of his collected scientific papers begins.
1970 Awarded the Nobel Memorial Prize in Economics.

LIFE AND CAREER

Paul Samuelson is an influential economist, academic, and consultant who changed the face of economic theory and practice, through his innovations in many areas of economic research. He has worked for the National Resources Planning Board, the War Production Board, and Office of War Mobilization and Reconstruction, the Bureau of the Budget, the Research Advisory Panel to the President's National Goals Commission, the Research Advisory Board Committee for Economic Development, and was a member of the National Task Force on Economic Education. He is an informal consultant for the United States Treasury, and the Council of Economic Advisors. He is also a consultant to the Federal Reserve Bank, and was Economic Advisor to Senator, candidate, and President-elect Kennedy. He was awarded the Nobel Memorial Prize in Economics for his contribution to neoclassical economic theory.

KEY THINKING

- Paul Samuelson was a leading light of the Harvard generation of 1930s, where he studied under Schumpeter and Leontief, before becoming Professor of Economics at MIT, and creating a powerful economics department.
- He was one of the first economists to generalize and apply mathematical methods developed for the study of thermodynamics to a diverse range of economic issues.
- He helped create the neoclassical synthesis, incorporating Keynesian and neoclassical principles, which now dominates mainstream economics.
- He was one of the progenitors of the Paretian revival in microeconomics, and the neo-Keynesian Synthesis in macroeconomics during the post-war period.

IN PERSPECTIVE

- He takes a neoclassical approach to economic theory, focusing on reducing the number of variables, and keeping only a minimum set of simple economic relations and, if possible, rewriting it as a constrained optimization problem.
- His *Foundations of Economic Analysis* is typical of his perspective, as it considers the universal nature of consumer behavior as the key to economic theory, underpinned by mathematical rigor.
- *Foundations of Economic Analysis* helped revive neoclassical economics, and launched the era of mathematization of economics.
- He was one of the first economists to generalize and apply mathematical methods developed from the study of thermodynamics–optimizing behavior of agents, and stability of equilibrium as to economic systems, which was based on classical thermodynamics.
- This innovation established comparative statics in economics, the method for calculating how a change in any parameter affects an economic system.
- Both the multiplier-accelerator macrodynamic model, and his presentation of the Phillips Curve helped make his name.
- In microeconomics, he is responsible for the theory of revealed preference, and also developed the Bergson–Samuelson social welfare functions.
- His work on speculative prices anticipated the efficient markets hypothesis in finance theory, while his research on diversification, and the concept of a "lifetime portfolio" are also respected innovations.
- In international trade theory, he is responsible for the Stolper–Samuelson theorem, and the Factor Price Equalization theorem.

▸▸ MORE INFO

Books:

Samuelson, Paul A. *Economics.* New York: McGraw-Hill, 1948. Described as the best-selling economics textbook of all time, this classic book gave birth to modern economics.

Samuelson, Paul A. *Foundations of Economic Analysis.* Cambridge, MA: Harvard University Press, 1947. His magnum opus, a seminal textbook that became a benchmark of neoclassical economics, and helped instigate the mathematization of economics.

Szenberg, Michael, Aron A. Gottesman, and Lall Ramrattan. *Paul A. Samuelson: On Being an Economist.* New York: Jorge Pinto Books, 2005. A timely re-examination of Samuelson's career, writings, and research.

"I tell people [investing] should be dull. It shouldn't be exciting. Investing should be more like watching paint dry or watching grass grow. If you want excitement, take US$800 and go to Las Vegas." Paul Samuelson

Jean-Baptiste Say • Early classical political economist

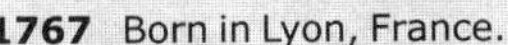

1767 Born in Lyon, France.
1792 Fights as a volunteer in the campaign of Champagne.
1793 Appointed secretary to the Minister of Finance in the French government.
1794 Edited the periodical, *La Decade Philosophique, Litteraire, et Politique.*
1799 Appointed a member of the French Tribunate.
1800 Publication of *Olbie, ou Essai sur les Moyens de Reformer les Moeurs d'une Nation.*
1803 Publication of *A Treatise on Political Economy.*
1819 Appointed to the Chair of Industrial Economy at the Conservatoire des Arts et Métiers.
1820 Publication of *Lettres Malthus.*
1828 Publication of *Cours Complet D'economie Politique Pratique.*
1830 Appointed a member of the Council-General of the Department of the Seine.
1831 Appointed Professor of Political Economy at the Collège de France.
1832 Died in Paris.

LIFE AND CAREER

Jean-Baptiste Say was an economist and businessman, writer, social philosopher, and a successful entrepreneur, and businessman. He initially worked as clerk to a merchant in England before returning to France, where he was employed at a life assurance company. His first published work was a pamphlet on the liberty of the press, published in 1789. He taught at the Conservatoire des Arts and Métiers, and Collège de France and, after being removed from the Tribunate by Napoleon in 1804, he founded a large spinning mill. The restoration of the Bourbon government brought him many honors, and he was subsequently invited to deliver a course of lectures on economics. He is best known as the author of the law of markets, known as Say's Law of Markets (or Say's Law), and as the first to coin the term "entrepreneur".

KEY THINKING

- Say was a central figure in classical economics; he led the revival in the study of political economy, and supported it during a time of opposition to liberal views.
- His most celebrated work was *A Treatise on Political Economy,* which expounded laissez-faire economic principles, and a combination of the utility theory of demand, and Adam Smith's cost theory of supply.
- *A Treatise on Political Economy* was not popular with Napoleon Bonaparte, who demanded he rewrite parts of it to support his move towards protectionism and regulation. When Say refused, Napoleon banned the book and threw him out of the Tribunate.

IN PERSPECTIVE

- Say championed classically liberal principles and argued in favor of competition and free trade, and the lifting of restraints on business.
- He believed that society benefits if the precepts of political economy are widely known, and understood by the people.
- Say's Law of Markets, as outlined in *A Treatise on Political Economy,* states that total demand in an economy cannot exceed or fall below total supply in that economy, so that there can be no demand without supply, and that recession does not occur because of failure in demand, or lack of money.
- Rather, he argued, the more goods that are produced, the more those goods can constitute a demand for other goods, so that prosperity can be increased by stimulating production, not consumption.
- He also proposed that the creation of more money results in inflation. This, he suggested, was because a greater amount of money demanding the same quantity of goods does not represent an increase in real demand.
- Studied the role of entrepreneurs, and their unique importance to the economy as risk-takers and contributors to production, as compared with the manager or the capitalist.

▸▸ MORE INFO

Books:

Hollander, Samuel. *Jean-Baptiste Say and the Classical Canon in Economics: The British Connection in French Classicism.* London: Routledge, 2005. Examines the similarities and differences between Say's views on economics and the Ricardo School, supported by extensive analysis of Say's writings.

Say, Jean-Baptiste. *A Treatise on Political Economy.* Paris: Déterville, 1803. His most famous book, which helped Say spread his liberal economic ideas, and views on laissez-faire and free trade in many parts of the world.

Whatmore, Richard. *Republicanism and the French Revolution: An Intellectual History of Jean-Baptiste Say's Political Economy.* Oxford: Oxford University Press, 2001. Provides context on the conflict between modern republicanism and other theories of governing societies through Say's writing.

"No set of men are more bigoted to system, than those who boast that they go upon none." Jean-Baptiste Say

     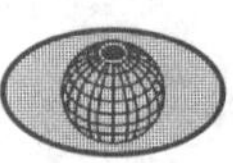 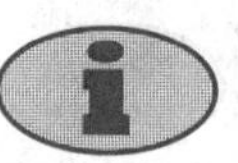  

Myron Scholes · Leading economist, and co-author of the Black–Scholes equation

1941 Born in Timmins, Ontario, Canada.
1961 Received BA in Economics from McMaster University, Ontario.
1964 Received MBA.
1968 Appointed Associate Professor at Sloan School of Management, MIT.
1969 Received PhD from the University of Chicago.
1973 Appointed Associate Professor at the University of Chicago.
1973 Published seminal paper, "The Pricing of Options and Corporate Liabilities", with Fischer Black.
1983 Joined Stanford University.
1990 Joined Salomon Brothers as a Special Consultant.
1992 Publication of *Taxes and Business Strategy: A Planning Approach*.
1994 Co-founded Long-Term Capital Management (LTCM) hedge fund.
1996 Became Professor of Finance Emeritus at Stanford University.
1997 Awarded the Nobel Memorial Prize in Economic Science.

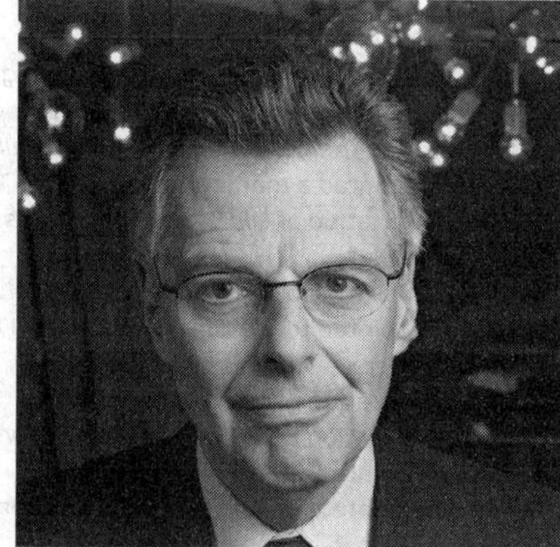

LIFE AND CAREER

Myron Scholes is Emeritus Professor of Finance at Stanford, the chairman of Platinum Grove Asset Management, and serves on the boards of various organizations, such as the Chicago Mercantile Exchange, and Dimensional Fund Advisors. In 1973, he published a paper with Fischer Black that presented the Black–Scholes equation, an option-pricing model still widely used in today's markets. In 1990, he joined Salomon Brothers as a managing director, and co-head of its fixed-income derivative sales and trading group, while still conducting research and teaching at Stanford University. He is also a director of the Capital Preservation Fund, a research associate of the National Bureau of Economic Research, and a member of the American Economic Association, and the American Finance Association.

KEY THINKING

- Received the Nobel Prize for developing the Black–Scholes model, a new method for determining the value of derivatives, which provides the framework for options valuation, which has become standard in financial markets.
- The Black–Scholes model is used for a vast number of options trades executed every year, and is the basis for all other binomial option models.
- Wrote several papers on investment banking and incentives with Mark Wolfson, and developed a new theory of tax planning under uncertainty and information asymmetry.
- He has recently focused on the interaction and evolution of markets, and financial institutions.

IN PERSPECTIVE

- Myron Scholes has studied and worked with some of the leading figures in finance and financial economics, including Fischer Black, Robert Merton, Eugene Fama, Merton Miller, Paul Cootner, and Franco Modigliani.
- While he was at MIT Sloan School of Management, he started working with Black, and Merton, who was also at MIT. They undertook groundbreaking research in asset pricing and derivative pricing models, including the work on their famous option-pricing model.
- They also developed and extended the field of contingent-claims pricing, and examined continuous-time stochastic processes to the problem of devising hedging strategies.
- Scholes worked on testing the capital asset pricing model (CAPM) with Fischer Black and Michael Jensen, and developed option-pricing technology with Black.
- At the Graduate School of Business at the University of Chicago, he worked on the effects of taxation on asset prices and incentives, and studied the effects of the taxation of dividends on the prices of securities with Fischer Black and Merton Miller.
- Also while at Chicago, he started working with the Center for Research in Security Prices, developing and analyzing high-frequency market data, and helped develop large research data files of daily security prices.
- He examined the efficiency frontier of portfolios--how to construct baskets of assets with optimal trade-offs between risk and return, and focused on the limit of risk-free portfolios.
- In 1994, he joined several colleagues, including John Meriwether and Robert Merton, in founding Long-Term Capital Management (LTCM).
- LTCM was initially extremely successful, with annualized returns of more than 40%; however, in 1998, following crises in the markets in East Asia and Russia, it became the biggest hedge-fund collapse ever seen, losing US$4.6 billion in less than four months.

▸▸ MORE INFO

Books:

Lin, Terence and Andrew W. Lo (eds). *The Derivatives Sourcebook*. Boston, MA: Now Publishers, 2006. A complete bibliography of derivatives literature and research, which cites the pioneering work of Scholes, Black, and Merton.

Marlow, Jerry. *Option Pricing: Black–Scholes Made Easy*. New York: Wiley, 2001. A detailed guide to understanding and applying one of the most important options trading tools.

Scholes, Myron. *Taxes and Business Strategy: A Planning Approach*. Englewood Cliffs, NJ: Prentice Hall, 1992. Analyzes the critical issues in tax accounting, economics, and corporate strategy in a readable and practical way.

See Also:

Taxes and Business Strategy: A Planning Approach (p. 1322)

"The world is our laboratory." Myron Scholes

  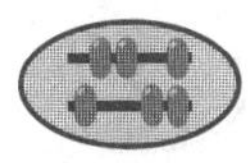   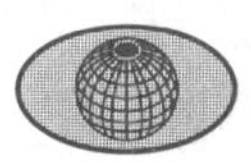   

Ernst Friedrich Schumacher • Internationally renowned economist, and environmentalist

1911 Born in Bonn, Germany.
1930 Rhodes Scholar, New College, Oxford.
1932 Earned Diploma in Economics, Columbia University, New York.
1933 Appointed Assistant Lecturer at the School of Banking, Columbia University.
1950 Appointed Chief Economic Advisor to the British Coal Board.
1966 Co-founded the Intermediate Technology Development Group.
1970 Appointed President of the Soil Association.
1973 Publication of *Small Is Beautiful.*
1977 Publication of *A Guide for the Perplexed.*
1977 Died in Switzerland.
1979 Publication of *Good Work.*

LIFE AND CAREER

Ernst Schumacher was a celebrated economic thinker, with a professional background as a statistician and economist in Britain. He was a Rhodes Scholar at Oxford and continued his studies at Columbia University, before returning to England before the World War II. Although he was interned during the war, his abilities caught the attention of John Maynard Keynes, who organized his release from internment. He was then able to help the British government mobilize both economically and financially during World War II. Keynes also found him a position at Oxford University. After the war, he worked as an economic advisor and then Chief Statistician for the British Control Commission, rebuilding the German economy. He then worked as Chief Economic Advisor to the British Coal Board for many years, as well as starting his own business producing battery-operated vehicles. He was an author, and one of the chief editorial writers at *The Times* in London, as well as publishing articles in *The Economist* and *Resurgence.*

KEY THINKING

- Ernst Schumacher is best known for his views on the unsustainability of current economic practices, his proposals for human-scale, decentralized, and appropriate technologies, and his economic planning during Britain's post-war economic recovery.
- He proposed the idea of "smallness within bigness", a form of decentralization where large organizations behave like related groups of small organizations to become economically successful.
- His work coincided with the development of mainstream ecology, and he became a renowned figure in the environmental movement.
- His famous essay on Buddhist economics was based on his experiences as advisor to the India Planning Commission, as well as to the governments of Zambia and Burma.
- In *Small Is Beautiful*, he proposed a system of regional economies based on social and ecological principles, and predicted the impending global fuel crisis.
- This book was influential in the development of economics based on humanist principles, reflecting his views on sustainability, and his critique of society as being founded on materialism, greed, and envy.
- While at the National Coal Board, he argued that coal should be preferable to petrol as the main energy source for the world's population. This view was based on his analysis of oil as a finite resource.

IN PERSPECTIVE

- Schumacher's development theories were based around the concepts of intermediate size, and intermediate technology.
- He argued that there should be a shift towards intermediate technologies based on the needs and skills of the people of developing countries, rather than the prevailing ideas of growth, and mass production for its own sake.
- He felt the principles of Buddhist economics focus on the economic rationality of good work as essential to human development, and that production should use local resources, and revolve around local needs.
- He proposed an economic, village-based framework, where human needs and limitations were understood, as was the appropriate use of technology.
- He traveled throughout many developing countries, encouraging local governments to form self-reliant economies, through his development charity, Intermediate Technology Development Group.
- He thought that all major corporations should have a fund for research into, and development of innovative technology.
- He argued against deforestation, and researched the future potential of trees, work that was taken up by the Soil Association after his death.

➤➤ MORE INFO

Books:

Schumacher, E. F. *A Guide for the Perplexed.* New York: Harper & Row, 1977.
Schumacher, E. F. *Small Is Beautiful: A Study of Economics as if People Mattered.* London: Blond and Bruggs, 1973.
Wood, Barbara. *E. F. Schumacher: His Life and Thought.* London: Jonathan Cape, 1984.

"Man is small, and, therefore, small is beautiful." Ernst Friedrich Schumacher

  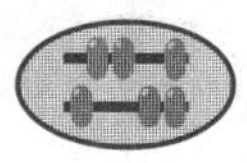   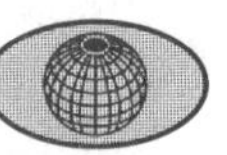   

Joseph Schumpeter · Economist, and political scientist

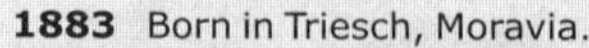

1883 Born in Triesch, Moravia.
1906 Received PhD in Law from the University of Vienna.
1909 Appointed Professor of Economics and Government at the University of Czernowitz.
1911 Appointed Professor of Economics at the University of Graz.
1919 Appointed Austrian Minister of Finance.
1920 Appointed President of the Biederman Bank.
1925 Appointed to a Professorship at the University of Bonn.
1932 Lectured at Harvard University.
1934 Publication of *Theory of Economic Development.*
1939 Publication of *Business Cycles.*
1940 Appointed President of the Econometric Society.
1942 Publication of *Capitalism, Socialism and Democracy.*
1948 Appointed President of the American Economic Association.
1950 Died in Taconic, Connecticut.

LIFE AND CAREER

Joseph Schumpeter was an influential economist, classical liberalist, and political scientist, whose research on economic analysis, capitalism, business cycles, and entrepreneurship were central to the development of economic theory in the first half of the 20th century. He was Austrian minister of finance during a period of hyperinflation–which caused his dismissal–before turning to banking. As president of Biederman Bank, he made and lost a fortune, which prompted him to pursue a career in academia. He taught at the University of Bonn, before teaching economics for many years at Harvard, where his pupils included Alan Greenspan and Robert Solow. He was one of the first to study and theorize on the concept of entrepreneurship, and based his research on an attempt to integrate and unite the different social sciences.

KEY THINKING

- Schumpeter was one of the first to analyze the role of entrepreneurs, in *Theory of Economic Development*, arguing that they created innovation and technological change, in the face of competition and falling profits.
- He proposed that the wider economy also benefits from large corporations that have the resources to invest in research and development.
- In *History of Economic Analysis,* he expanded his theory of entrepreneurship and theory of growth into a wider theory of the development of capitalism, also integrating it into theories of the business cycle, and socioeconomic evolution.
- In *Capitalism, Socialism, and Democracy* he defended capitalism as helping to create entrepreneurship, and distinguished inventions from innovations.
- He also discussed how capitalism might evolve, applying the phrase "creative destruction" to describe how traditional ways of doing things are replaced by the new.
- In *Business Cycles,* he develops his arguments against government intervention in industry, first presented in *Theory of Economic Development.*

IN PERSPECTIVE

- Schumpeter believed continual change in the economy meant most businesses fail, becoming victims of innovation by their competitors.
- Argued that entrepreneurs innovate, not just by figuring out how to use inventions, but also by introducing new means of production, new products, and new forms of organization.
- He discounted perfect competition as being the most efficient way to maximize economic wellbeing, viewing some type of monopoly as preferable to holding back competition from innovation.
- He challenged the classical view that democracy is a process by which the electorate choose the politicians who would best carry out the common good, arguing that this was unrealistic, and that politicians set the agenda and manipulate the people.
- He integrated a sociological understanding into his work, as he preferred to use sociology to explain economic principles, rather than the abstract models of his predecessors.
- Helped found the concept of "evolutionary economics", as based on economic change brought about by the interaction between individuals, and the economy as a whole.

▸▸ MORE INFO

Books:

Backhaus, Jürgen (ed). *Joseph Alois Schumpeter: Entrepreneurship, Style, and Vision.* Boston, MA: Kluwer Academic Publishers, 2003. Examines Schumpeter's theories of entrepreneurship and economic development, and contains some of his less well-known, but important works published before he left Europe.

McCraw, Thomas K. *Prophet of Innovation: Joseph Schumpeter and Creative Destruction.* Cambridge, MA: Belknap Press of Harvard University Press, 2007. Examines the destruction of businesses and careers in the struggle for a better material life.

Schumpeter, Joseph. *Capitalism, Socialism and Democracy.* New York and London: Harper & Brothers, 1942. Predicts the downfall of capitalism, as it progresses towards a form of hostile corporatism, led by intellectuals amid "creative destruction".

"The ballot is stronger than bullets." Joseph Schumpeter

     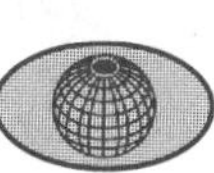   

William F. Sharpe · Nobel Prize-winning financial economist

1934 Born in Boston, Massachusetts.
1955 Received BA in Economics from the University of California, Los Angeles.
1956 Received MA in Economics from the University of California.
1956 Appointed as an economist at the Rand Corporation.
1961 Received PhD in Economics from the University of California.
1961 Appointed Associate Professor at the University of Washington.
1968 Appointed Professor at the University of California at Irvine.
1970 Appointed Professor at Stanford University.
1970 Publication of *Portfolio Theory and Capital Markets.*
1971 Appointed Professor of Finance at Stanford University.
1978 Publication of *Investments.*
1980 Appointed President of the American Finance Association.
1986 Co-founded and became President of Sharpe-Russell Research.
1987 Publication of *Asset Allocation Tools.*
1989 Became Professor Emeritus of Finance at Stanford University.
1990 Received the Nobel Memorial Prize in Economic Sciences.
1990 Became Chairman of William F Sharpe Associates.
1993 Appointed Professor of Finance at Stanford University.
1996 Co-founded Financial Engines.
2007 Publication of *Investors and Markets.*

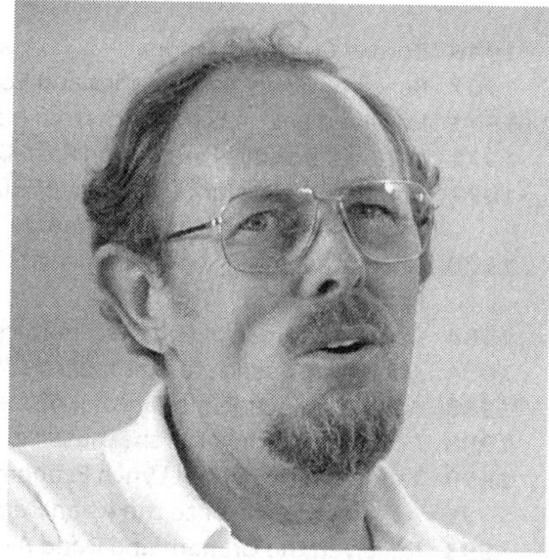

LIFE AND CAREER

William Sharpe is Professor of Finance, Emeritus at Stanford University's Graduate School of Business, a Nobel Prize-winning economist, and a key figure in the development of investment theory. He joined the Stanford faculty in 1970, having previously taught at the University of Washington and the University of California at Irvine. He has worked at the National Bureau of Economic Research, studying issues of bank capital adequacy, and has published renowned research articles in a number of professional journals. He has also been a consultant to Merrill Lynch and Wells Fargo, and co-founded Financial Engines in 1996, to provide investment management advice, especially for those in employer-sponsored retirement plans.

KEY THINKING

- Sharpe received the Nobel Prize for his research on the capital asset pricing model (CAPM), where he structured a portfolio's risk into systematic or non-specific risk, and non-systematic or specific risk.
- The research was based on his search for an equilibrium theory of asset pricing and Harry Markowitz's portfolio theory, and is now a foundation for financial economics.
- His research into equilibrium in capital markets focused on its implications for investment portfolio decision-making.
- The model shows how every investment carries two distinct risks––the risk of being in the market, or systematic risk, which cannot be diversified away, and unsystematic risk, which is specific to a company's fortunes.
- One implication of Sharpe's work is that the expected return on a portfolio in excess of a riskless return should be beta times the excess return of the market.

IN PERSPECTIVE

- Sharpe, Harry Markowitz and Merton Miller all shared the Nobel Prize for their contributions to financial economics, which helped establish it as a separate field of study.
- Sharpe showed how CAPM implies a single mix of risky assets fits in every investor's portfolio––those who want a high return should hold a portfolio heavily weighted with the risky asset, while those who want a low return hold a portfolio heavily weighted with a riskless asset.
- He produced a number of innovations in investment analysis, including the Sharpe Ratio for risk-adjusted investment performance analysis––the ratio evaluates the level of risk a fund accepts against the return it delivers.
- He also contributed to the development of the binomial method for the valuation of options, as well as the gradient method for optimizing asset allocation, and returns-based analysis for evaluating the style and performance of investment funds.
- He developed a method for finding approximate solutions to a class of portfolio analysis problems, which has been widely implemented.

▸▸ MORE INFO

Books:

Sharpe, William F. *Investments.* Englewood Cliffs, NJ: Prentice-Hall, 1978. His successful textbook, which has been updated and revised over the years, provides the theoretical framework for understanding securities, and the securities markets.

Sharpe, William F. *Investors and Markets: Portfolio Choices, Asset Prices, and Investment Advice.* Princeton, NJ: Princeton University Press, 2007. His most recent book, which is a technical overview of investment theory, and explains his approach to asset pricing in an accessible style. It also summarizes much of Sharpe's seminal work over the years.

Sharpe, William F. *Portfolio Theory and Capital Markets.* New York: McGraw-Hill, 1970. His classic book on investment and portfolio theory. It presents his groundbreaking work on the capital asset pricing model, and examines the behavior of the financial markets under different conditions.

See Also:

Portfolio Theory and Capital Markets (p. 1310)

"Some investments do have higher expected returns than others. Which ones? Well, by and large they're the ones that will do the worst in bad times." William F. Sharpe

   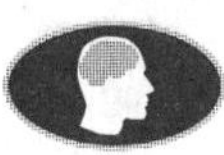  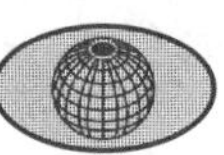   

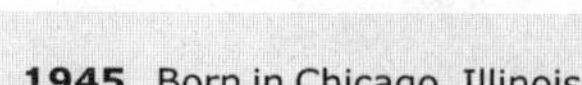

Jeremy Siegel · Renowned finance academic, and writer

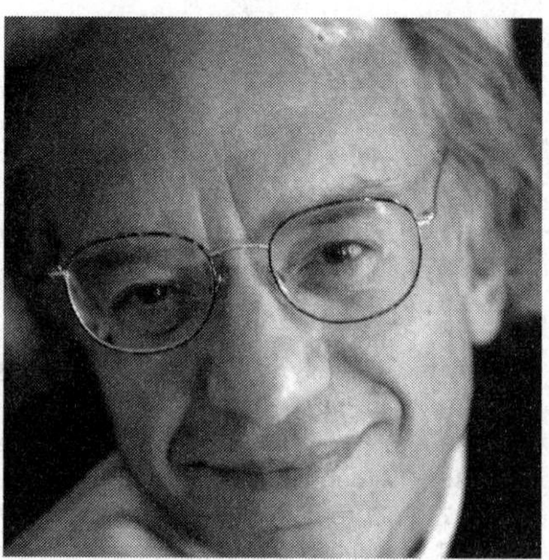

1945 Born in Chicago, Illinois.
1967 Received BA in Mathematics and Economics from Columbia University.
1971 Received PhD in Economics from Massachusetts Institute of Technology.
1971 National Science Foundation Post-Doctoral Fellowship at Harvard University.
1972 Appointed Assistant Professor of Business Economics, Graduate School of Business, University of Chicago.
1976 Appointed Professor of Finance at the Wharton School of the University of Pennsylvania.
1984 Appointed Head of Macroeconomics Training for JP Morgan.
1984 Appointed Associate Editor of the *Journal of Money, Credit and Banking.*
1988 Appointed Academic Director of the US Securities Institute.
1988 Appointed Director in the Trust Department at the Continental Bank.
1990 Taught on the Merrill Lynch Economics and Finance Program.
1991 Appointed Advisor to the Asian Securities Industry Association.
1993 Received the Graham and Dodd Award from the Association for Investment Management and Research.
1994 Publication of *Stocks for the Long Run.*
1998 Received the American Library Association Outstanding Academic Book Award for *Stocks for the Long Run*.
2001 Appointed a Fellow of the World Economic Forum, Davos, Switzerland.
2005 Publication of *The Future for Investors.*
2005 Received the Nicholas Molodovsky Award from the Chartered Financial Analysts Institute.

LIFE AND CAREER

Jeremy Siegel is Professor of Finance at the Wharton School of the University of Pennsylvania, and provides analysis of the economy and financial markets in the press, on television networks, and at conferences, and international programs. He writes regular columns for *Kiplinger's Personal Finance* and *Yahoo! Finance,* and is an advisor to Wisdom Tree Investments. He has also contributed articles to *The Wall Street Journal, Barron's, Financial Times,* and other national and international news media. He is currently the academic director of the US Securities Industry Institute.

KEY THINKING

- Jeremy Siegel is a staunch proponent of long-term investing, and is a respected teacher, having received the highest teaching rating in a worldwide ranking of business school professors conducted by *Business Week* magazine.
- He has long argued that a diversified basket of inherently risk-laden equities, if retained over a long period, will produce better returns, and be safer than traditional secure investments such as bonds, and bank savings accounts.
- He and Robert Shiller, a professor at Yale School of Management, have frequently debated with each other on TV about the stock market, and its future returns, and have become financial media celebrities.
- In *Revolution on Wall Street,* he analyzes how the market dominance of Wall Street has been overturned by new alternative markets with cheaper transaction systems, government regulation, and bureaucratic problems.
- In *Stocks for the Long Run,* he shows the amateur how to understand market forces, and the best way to put together a successful portfolio, based on an awareness of stock behavior, past trends, and future movements.
- In *The Future for Investors*, he argues that more traditional companies perform better over time than growth stocks, especially those in the technology sector.

IN PERSPECTIVE

- Jeremy Siegel describes stocks as being undervalued for the last 200 years, and that stock markets in the digital age are now more efficient, and safer over the long term.
- He conducted an in-depth study for the New York Stock Exchange in the 1980s, the data for which proved that the compound annual real return on US stocks has been nearly 7% over the past 200 years.
- He has predicted that an unprecedented wave of innovation will create economic growth in the US, which will provide strong returns for those investors who show patience. The prediction is based on his analysis of global trends, such as demographics and shifts in labor, manufacturing capacity, and capital movement.

►► MORE INFO

Books:

Blume, Marshall E., Jeremy J. Siegel, and Dan Rottenberg. *Revolution on Wall Street: The Rise and Decline of the New York Stock Exchange.* New York: W. W. Norton, 1993.
Siegel, Jeremy J. *The Future for Investors: Why the Tried and the True Triumph Over the Bold and the New.* New York: Crown Business, 2005.
Siegel, Jeremy J. *Stocks for the Long Run: A Guide for Selecting Markets for Long-Term Growth.* Burr Ridge, IL: Irwin, 1994.

Website:

Siegel's own website: www.jeremysiegel.com

See Also:

Stocks for the Long Run: The Definitive Guide to Financial Market Returns and Long-Term Investment Strategies (p. 1320)

"The economy will start screaming uncle eventually." Jeremy Siegel

     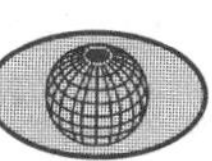   

Ernst Werner von Siemens • Founding father of electrical engineering

1816 Born in Lenthe, Germany.
1841 Co-invented an electroplating process.
1842 Awarded his first patent, for a gold electroplating process.
1844 Worked in the artillery workshops in Berlin.
1845 Became a founding member of the Physical Society in Berlin.
1845 Patented a dial and printing telegraph.
1847 Co-founded the Siemens & Halske Telegraph and Construction Enterprise.
1849 Constructed the first electrical, long-distance telegraph line in Europe.
1851 Siemens & Halske built the first electric fire-alarm system for Berlin.
1861 Co-founded the German Progressive Party.
1862 Became a member of the Prussian Parliament.
1866 Constructed the first dynamo.
1875 Completed the laying of a transatlantic telegraph cable.
1877 Became a member of the State Patent Office.
1879 Demonstrated the first electric railway at the Berlin Industrial Exhibition.
1879 Co-founded the Electrotechnical Society in Berlin.
1880 Built the world's first electric elevator.
1881 Built the first trolley bus system in Berlin.
1888 Awarded Prussian hereditary peerage.
1890 Retired.
1892 Died in Berlin, Germany.

LIFE AND CAREER

Ernst Werner von Siemens was a German electrical engineer, industrialist, and inventor, who played a crucial role in the development of telegraphy, and created a number of major inventions in the industry. After leaving school, he joined the army to train in engineering, and attended an engineering college in Berlin, augmenting his earnings through his inventions. While serving a short prison sentence at Magdeburg, for acting as second in a duel between fellow officers, he carried out chemistry experiments in his cell, and invented a gold and silver electroplating process, for which he was granted his first patent in 1842. At that time, he met the mechanical engineer, Johan Georg Halske, who became a close associate. Together, they founded the Siemens & Halske Telegraph Construction Company. They originally intended to make electrical apparatus, but followed this with many innovations that transformed the industry. By 1870, the company was employing more than 1,000 people in Germany and abroad.

KEY THINKING

- Ernst Werner von Siemens was a leading pioneer of electrical telegraphy, inventing a number of devices, including the first electric dynamo.
- The discovery of the dynamo electric principle enabled Siemens & Halske to develop and manufacture electrical lighting, and power-generating equipment.
- He was a member of a commission in Berlin looking at the introduction of electric telegraphs to replace the optical ones previously used in Prussia; he also persuaded the commission to adopt underground telegraph lines.
- He also laid the first telegraph line, built the first electric railway in Germany, and proposed the Siemens unit of electrical conductance.
- Siemens also helped lay the first submarine mines, fired by electricity, in Kiel in 1848.
- He received a German patent for an electromechanical moving-coil transducer, later adapted for the Bell System for use as a loudspeaker.
- With his brother, Sir William Siemens, he originated and developed a widely used steelmaking process.

IN PERSPECTIVE

- The creation of the dynamo helped establish electricity as a driving force of industrial and economic change.
- He investigated the electrostatic charges of telegraph conductors and their laws, which enabled him to test underground and submarine cables, and discover any faults in their insulation.
- The construction and application of the first dynamometer was also essential to underwater cable laying, and he designed a press for covering wire with gutta-percha, a crucial development in the insulation of underground cables.
- Under his direction, the firm of Siemens & Halske went on to lay cables across the Mediterranean, and from Europe to India; he also designed the first specialist cable-laying ship, which went on to lay five Atlantic cables in 10 years.
- His discovery of the dynamo-electric principle solved the problem of DC batteries being necessary for the generation of continuous current and high voltage.
- He won the first government contract to set up a telegraph line between Berlin and the National Assembly at Frankfurt, before supervising the laying of lines around Germany.

▸▸ MORE INFO

Books:

Feldenkirchen, Wilfried. *Werner von Siemens: Inventor and International Entrepreneur.* Columbus, OH: Ohio State University Press, 1994.
Siemens, Werner von and W. C. Coupland. *Personal Recollections of Werner von Siemens.* New York: D. Appleton and Company, 1893.
Weiher, Sigfrid von. *Werner von Siemens, A Life in the Service of Science, Technology and Industry.* München, Germany: Oldenbourg, 1966.

"Technology has acquired the means to generate electric currents of unlimited strength in an inexpensive and convenient way at any place where mechanical power is available. This fact will be of utmost importance in several of its branches." Ernst Werner von Siemens

Adam Smith • The father of modern economics

1723 Born in Kirkcaldy, Scotland.
1748 Appointed Lecturer in Literature at Edinburgh University.
1751 Appointed Professor of Literature at Glasgow University.
1752 Appointed Professor of Moral Philosophy at Glasgow University.
1762 Received the title of Doctor of Laws from Glasgow University.
1763 Publication of *The Theory of Moral Sentiments.*
1763 Publication of *Lectures on Justice, Police, Revenue, and Arms.*
1763 Appointed tutor to the Duke of Buccleuch.
1764 Publication of *A Treatise on Public Opulence.*
1773 Elected as a Fellow of the Royal Society of London.
1775 Elected as a Member of the Literary Club.
1776 Publication of *The Wealth of Nations.*
1778 Appointed Commissioner of Customs in Scotland.
1783 Co-founded the Royal Society of Edinburgh.
1787 Elected Lord Rector of the Glasgow University.
1790 Died in Edinburgh.

LIFE AND CAREER

Adam Smith was a moral philosopher, a pioneer of political economy, and one of the key figures of the Scottish enlightenment in the 18th century. At 14, he won a scholarship to study mathematics and moral philosophy at Glasgow University, before studying at Balliol College, Oxford. He returned to Glasgow University in 1751, to teach literature, before being appointed Professor of Moral Philosophy at the university. He was then appointed tutor to the Duke of Buccleuch, during his grand tour of Europe, when he met Benjamin Franklin, Francois Quesnay, Voltaire, and Rousseau, among others. He spent much of his later life writing on economics, social issues, and philosophy, which brought him great popularity.

KEY THINKING

- Adam Smith was an anti-establishment figure, and a social radical who believed in liberty and equality. His writing focused on the transformation of industry and commerce in Europe.
- His magnum opus and most influential work, *The Wealth of Nations,* was an immediate success, selling out the first edition in only six months, and was the first modern work on economics.
- It helped popularize his laissez-faire arguments for government non-intervention, and provided a rationale for free trade, and capitalism. It hastened the end of the mercantilist era, and ignited a new economic approach based on individualism, and the "natural laws" he espoused.
- The three main concepts he proposed are now the foundation of free market economics: division of labor, the pursuit of self-interest, and the freedom to trade.
- In *The Theory of Moral Sentiments,* he also explores moral judgments within the context of people being motivated by self-interest, while acknowledging that individuals have "social propensities" for sympathy, justice and benevolence.
- This theory of sympathy is based on the argument that, in observing others, we are made aware of our own actions, and the moral context for our behavior.

IN PERSPECTIVE

- In *The Wealth of Nations,* he argued that all human powers are subject to natural, moral, and physical laws, and proposed that government should leave economic matters alone, to work naturally, which he argued would benefit individuals and the state.
- His book expounds the value of individual liberty, and the pursuit of self-interest as being of value for society as a whole. His natural law involves a "law of labor", where the environment provides the products necessary for subsistence, in return for their labor, and that everyone should therefore have the right to do what they need to preserve their existence.
- He found the free market ensured the best balance in goods and services through a so-called "invisible hand"—that society and commerce benefits from people behaving in their own interests.
- He believed that while human motives were often driven by selfishness and greed, the competition in the free market would tend to benefit society as a whole by keeping prices low, while still building in an incentive for the production of a wide variety of goods and services.

►► MORE INFO

Books:

Buchan, James. *The Authentic Adam Smith: His Life and Ideas.* London: Profile, 2006. This comprehensive study of Smith goes beyond his role as founder of the laissez-faire approach to free markets, to also consider his writings on philosophy, and aesthetics.

Smith, Adam. *An Inquiry into the Nature and Causes of the Wealth of Nations.* London: W. Strahan and T. Cadell, 1776. Ten years in the writing, his most famous work presents a range of ideas that challenged the contemporary mercantilist government, and its protectionist laws.

Smith, Adam. *The Theory of Moral Sentiments.* London: A. Millar, 1759. Presents a framework for a new system of morals, making it a seminal text in the development of moral and political thought.

See Also:

The Money Game (p. 1299)
The Wealth of Nations (p. 1333)

"There is no art which one government sooner learns of another than that of draining money from the pockets of the people." Adam Smith

  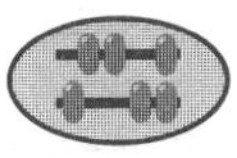   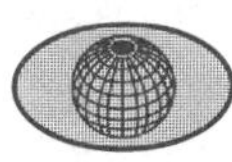   

George Soros • Billionaire philanthropist who "broke" the Bank of England

1930 Born in Budapest, Hungary.
1947 Emigrated to England.
1952 Graduated from the London School of Economics.
1956 Moved to the United States.
1956 Appointed as an arbitrage trader at FM Mayer.
1959 Joined Wertheim and Co as an analyst.
1963 Joined Arnhold and S Bleichroeder Advisers.
1967 Ran the offshore investment fund, First Eagle, for Arnhold and S Bleichroeder.
1969 Appointed head of a second fund for Arnhold and S Bleichroeder, Double Eagle.
1970 Co-founded the Quantum Fund.
1987 Publication of *The Alchemy of Finance*.
2006 Publication of *The Age of Fallibility: Consequences of The War on Terror*.

LIFE AND CAREER

George Soros is a financial speculator, stock investor, billionaire, philanthropist, and political activist, and is known for "breaking the Bank of England" on Black Wednesday in 1992. He was 13 when Nazi Germany invaded Hungary. To avoid being apprehended by the Nazis, his father sent him to live with a non-Jewish employee, posing as his godson. His first experience of finance was trading currencies during the Hungarian hyperinflation period of 1945–1946. In 1946, he escaped the Soviet occupation and moved to England to study. After graduating from LSE, he secured a position with London merchant bank, Singer & Friedlander, before becoming a trader and analyst, and then managing increasingly successful investment funds. After making his fortune, he turned to philanthropy, and politics. He is the founder and chairman of Soros Fund Management and the Open Society Institute, and is also a former member of the board of directors of the Council on Foreign Relations, and of the Carlyle Group.

KEY THINKING

- George Soros is probably the most successful speculator of all time; he ascribes his success to being able to recognize when his predictions are wrong.
- The Quantum Fund, which he founded with Jim Rogers, returned 42.6% per year in its first 10 years and helped make Soros' fortune. In 2007, the fund returned almost 32%, netting him US$2.9 billion.
- On Black Wednesday in 1992, he gained celebrity (and money) by selling short more than US$10 billion worth of pounds, earning an estimated US$1.1 billion in the process, when the Bank of England was forced to withdraw the currency from the European exchange rate mechanism (ERM), and to devalue the pound.
- He now spends most of his time writing, focusing on his philanthropic activities, and using his wealth in emerging markets in a bid to encourage them towards democracy.

IN PERSPECTIVE

- He is reported to use the investing technique of buying during the upturns and taking the profit, waiting patiently, and then selling short during the downward cycle.
- Reputed to have given away more than US$6 billion, he has been active as a philanthropist since the 1970s, when he began providing funds to help black students attend the University of Cape Town, South Africa, during apartheid.
- He has increasingly funded projects opposing totalitarian regimes in emerging countries; promoting non-violent democratization in the post-Soviet states, supporting the Solidarity movement in Poland, and the Czechoslovak human rights organization, Charter 77. His funding and organization of Georgia's Rose Revolution was considered critical to its success.
- He has developed a philosophy of "reflexivity", largely influenced by Karl Popper, under whom he studied at the London School of Economics.
- Under reflexivity, events create expectations that influence the financial markets–the markets, in turn, then influence these events, creating a cycle (which can be either "virtuous or vicious").
- He argues that reflexivity, and the biases affecting market transactions, can change the fundamentals of the economy, which are typically marked by disequilibrium rather than equilibrium, and that the efficient market hypothesis does not apply in these situations.
- In 1988, he was accused of insider dealing regarding a takeover attempt of Société Générale, and fined US$2 million by a French court, although he denied any wrongdoing and said news of the takeover was public knowledge.

▸▸ MORE INFO

Books:

Kaufman. Michael T. *Soros: The Life and Times of a Messianic Billionaire.* New York: Knopf, 2002. The authorized biography of Soros, which looks at how he made his fortune.

Soros, George. *The Alchemy of Finance: Reading the Mind of the Market.* New York: Simon & Schuster, 1987.

Soros, George. *The New Paradigm for Financial Markets: The Credit Crisis of 2008 and What It Means.* New York: PublicAffairs, 2008.

Website:

Soros' website: www.georgesoros.com

See Also:

The Alchemy of Finance: Reading the Mind of the Market (p. 1218)

"My peculiarity is that I don't have a particular style of investing or, more exactly, I try to change my style to fit the conditions." George Soros

     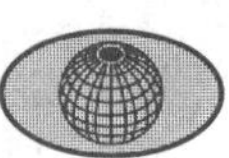   

Joseph Stiglitz · American economist renowned for his critical view on globalization

1943 Born in Gary, Indiana.
1965 Researcher at University of Chicago.
1966 Appointed Assistant Professor at Massachusetts Institute of Technology.
1967 Received PhD from Massachusetts Institute of Technology.
1969 Fulbright Research Fellow at the University of Cambridge.
1979 Received the John Bates Clark Medal.
1995 Appointed Chairman of the Council of Economic Advisers.
1997 Appointed Chief Economist of the World Bank.
2000 Founded the Initiative for Policy Dialogue.
2001 Appointed a Professor at Columbia University.
2001 Received the Nobel Memorial Prize in Economic Sciences.
2002 Publication of *Globalization and Its Discontents.*
2003 Appointed University Professor at Columbia University.
2003 Publication of *The Roaring Nineties.*
2006 Publication of *Making Globalization Work.*
2008 Publication of *The Three Trillion Dollar War.*

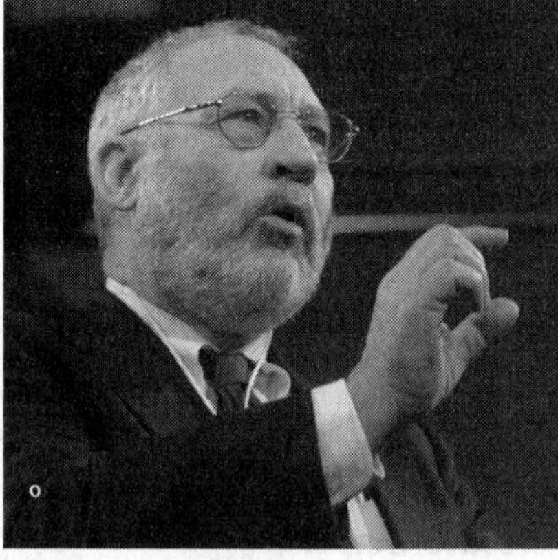

LIFE AND CAREER

Joseph Stiglitz is an economist, a writer on globalization and its effects, and a former senior vice-president and chief economist of the World Bank. He has held professorships at Yale, Duke, Stanford, Oxford, and Princeton universities, and currently teaches at Columbia. He chairs the University of Manchester's Brooks World Poverty Institute, Columbia's Committee on Global Thought, and is President Elect of the International Economic Association. He is the most cited economist in the world, and has served in the Clinton Administration, as chair of the President's Council of Economic Advisors, in which capacity he also served as a member of the cabinet. He has been a member of the Intergovernmental Panel on Climate Change, and was recently appointed to chair a Commission on the Measurement of Economic Performance and Economic Progress.

KEY THINKING

- Stiglitz helped develop a new branch of economics, "the economics of information", which explores information asymmetries; it was based on his research on screening, for which he was awarded the Nobel Memorial Prize.
- He has been a critic of the management of globalization, free-market economists, and international institutions such as the International Monetary Fund, and the World Bank.
- His tenure at the World Bank was during protests against globalization, and he was fired as Chief Economist for expressing dissent with its policies.
- In his book, *Stability with Growth,* he focused on macroeconomic policy and capital market liberalization, and developed a new framework for assessing alternative policies, based on real stability and long-term, sustainable, and equitable growth.
- *Making Globalization Work* considers the global economy, and the mechanisms by which developed countries exert an excessive influence over developing nations.
- He argues that through tariffs, subsidies, a complicated patent system, and pollution, economies are being economically and politically destabilized, and that strong, transparent institutions are needed to redress the balance.
- In *Globalization and Its Discontents,* he argues that developing economies are not really developing at all, and blames the IMF for stifling growth and information.
- In *Whither Socialism?,* he analyzes information economics and the theory of markets with imperfect information and imperfect competition, and offers a critique of both free-market and socialist approaches.
- This research counters prevailing neoclassical economics, arguing that markets are only efficient under exceptional circumstances.

IN PERSPECTIVE

- Stiglitz has made major contributions to macroeconomics and monetary theory, to development economics and trade theory, to public and corporate finance, to the theories of industrial organization and rural organization, and to the theories of welfare economics, and of income and wealth distribution.
- He also pioneered such concepts as adverse selection and moral hazard, which have now become standard tools of researchers and policy analysts.
- The Shapiro–Stiglitz model of efficiency wages, which he developed with the economist Carl Shapiro, examines unemployment, and why wages are not bid down to enable full employment.
- The model states that unemployment is driven by the information structure of employment, and dependent on the cost to firms in knowing how much effort their workers are putting in.

▸▸ MORE INFO

Books:

Chang, Ha-Joon. *The Rebel Within: Joseph Stiglitz and the World Bank.* London: Anthem Press, 2001.
Stiglitz, Joseph. *Globalization and Its Discontents.* New York: W.W. Norton, 2002.
Stiglitz, Joseph, and Linda J. Bilmes. *The Three Trillion Dollar War: The True Cost of the Iraq Conflict.* New York: W. W. Norton, 2008.

See Also:

Globalization and Its Discontents (p. 1270)

"Economists often like startling theorems, results which seem to run counter to conventional wisdom."
Joseph Stiglitz

  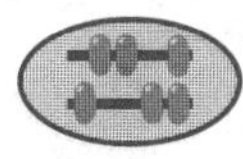   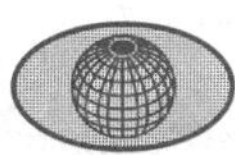   

Sun Tzu · Author of *The Art of War*

c.544 BC Lived and wrote.
c.496 BC Died.
1780 First European translation of *The Art of War*.
1910 First English translation of *The Art of War*.

LIFE AND CAREER

Sun Tzu was a military general, thought to be a contemporary of Confucius. He was a member of the Chinese aristocratic class of *shi*, and came from a family of army officers, which gave him a familiarity with military matters. He became a mercenary, and was later appointed as a general, leading a number of successful campaigns. It is believed that Wu, now Anhui Province, under whose sovereign he served, became a dominant power at the time. *The Art of War* is said to have been based on Sun Tzu's direct experience in military campaigns. It became standard practice for Chinese military leaders to familiarize themselves with his writings, and in modern times *The Art of War* has been a source of maxims, and strategic guidance for military, as well as business leaders.

KEY THINKING

- Although there is some doubt about its historical accuracy and authenticity, Sun Tzu's *The Art of War* is a recognized classic of military strategy that has a continuing relevance for decision-makers in all areas.
- It has been greatly influential, with adherents including the first emperor of unified China, Japanese leaders during its unification period, and among the teachings of the samurai. Napoleon even referred to it during his war on Europe.
- It not only contains the original writing of the author, but also commentary and notes from later military philosophers that reinforce the teachings.
- Modern Chinese scholars also base their theories on the strategic guidance it offers, relating their struggles to those of the China of Sun Tzu's time.
- The anecdotes and ideas are divided into a number of key sections, including strategic assessment, offensive strategy, formation, adaptations, maneuvering armies, terrain, and the use of spies.
- The book discusses five factors that impact on the result of war: politics, weather, terrain, leadership, and discipline.
- The ancient tome also examines seven factors critical to strategic success: whose moral influence is greatest, who has the better leader, who has the advantage of nature and terrain, who has the most effective laws, which troops are stronger and better trained, and whose system of rewards and punishments is clearer.

IN PERSPECTIVE

- *The Art of War,* one of the oldest books on martial strategy, presents a complete philosophy for managing conflicts and winning strategic battles, and has played an important role in the development of management thinking.
- It has become popular among political leaders, and those in business management, as well as for military theorists, as it considers strategy in a generic way, which gives it a relevance for public administration and planning.
- Provides advice on timeless concepts such as information and intelligence, tactics, on competition, planning, attention to detail, cunning, leadership, and communication.
- Recommends innovative tactics such as using the momentum of your enemy's own moves to defeat him.
- Although some of the writing is confusing to today's reader, many of the aphorisms presented should be interpreted in the context of Taoist thought and practice, a spiritual dimension that has given the book added resonance through the ages.

▸▸ MORE INFO

Books:

Krause, Donald G. *"Art of War" for Executives.* New York: Berkeley Publishing Group, 1995. A version aimed at management executives, giving an understanding of how to deal with the strategic and competitive challenges they face.

Sun Tzu. *The Art of War.* Berkeley, CA: Ulysses Press, 2007. The most recent version, looking at how Taoist strategy is still influential in both Asian and Western culture and politics.

Wing, RL. *The Art of Strategy: A New Translation of Sun Tzu's "The Art of War".* New York: Doubleday, 1998. An innovative version, combining author commentary and insights with Chinese calligraphy.

See Also:

The Art of War (p. 1220)

"Opportunities multiply as they are seized." Sun Tzu

     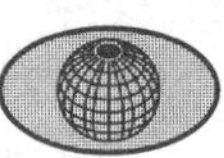   

Richard Thaler · Influential thinker on behavioral finance

1945 Born in East Orange, New Jersey.
1967 Received BA from Case Western Reserve University.
1970 Received MS from the University of Rochester.
1974 Received PhD in Economics from the University of Rochester.
1978 Appointed Assistant Professor of Economics and Public Administration, Graduate School of Business and Public Administration, Cornell University.
1980 Appointed Associate Professor, Johnson Graduate School of Management, Cornell University.
1986 Appointed Professor of Economics, Johnson Graduate School of Management, Cornell University.
1991 Appointed Visiting Scholar, Russell Sage Foundation, New York.
1991 Publication of *Quasi-Rational Economics*.
1993 Publication of *The Winner's Curse*.
1993 Publication of *Advances in Behavioral Finance*.
1995 Appointed Professor of Behavioral Science, Economics and Finance at the Graduate School of Business, the University of Chicago.
1995 Appointed Director of the Center for Decision Research, University of Chicago.
2005 Received the Paul A. Samuelson Award.
2008 Publication of *Nudge*.

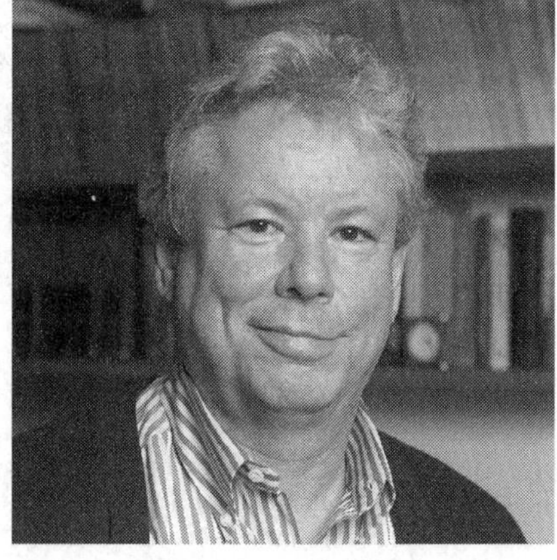

LIFE AND CAREER

Richard Thaler taught at Cornell University and Massachusetts Institute of Technology Sloan School of Management, and is now Professor of Behavioral Science, Economics and Finance at the Graduate School of Business, the University of Chicago, and Director of its Center for Decision Research. He regularly consulted with Barack Obama's economic advisor for the 2008 presidential campaign. Thaler has also organized a series of behavioral finance seminars along with Robert Shiller, another behavioral finance expert, at the Yale School of Management. He is an associate at the National Bureau of Economic Research, co-head of its Behavioral Finance Project, and is the founder of Fuller & Thaler Asset Management, Inc.

KEY THINKING

- Richard Thaler is a pioneer in behavioral economics and finance, as well as the psychology of decision-making, helping transform the study of economics by trying to understand how people behave financially.
- He gained attention for a regular column in the *Journal of Economic Perspectives on Anomalies*, where he examined economic behavior that ran counter to traditional microeconomic theory.
- He has written on a wide variety of subjects, from savings and investing, to marketing, decision-making, and financial markets. Recent papers have included an examination of behavior on the television game show, *Deal or No Deal*, and an analysis of the National Football League Draft.
- He has continued to demonstrate the irrationalities inherent in the financial markets, arguing against the neoclassical view that rationality underpins the financial system.
- In *Nudge*, Thaler and co-author Sunstein examine everyday factors that can influence our decisions.
- They argue that institutions, including the government, should use the science of choice and decision-making to impel people to improve their lives, based on the insights of behavioral economics.

IN PERSPECTIVE

- Thaler is considered to have originated the field of behavioral economics, an area of study that integrates psychological research with economic theory.
- He developed the work of Nobel Prize-winning psychologists Daniel Kahneman and Amos Tversky, and their analysis of why people are more concerned with changes in wealth than with their absolute level.
- This research helped explain Thaler's work on anomalies; Kahneman cited his joint work with Thaler as a major factor in his receiving the Nobel Prize in Economics.
- Thaler also focused on "mental accounting", which is based on Kahneman and Tversky's "framing" principle, which examines how the positioning of choices prejudices the outcome.
- He proposed that most people are prone to error, irrationality, and emotion, and that they behave in ways not always consistent with maximizing their own financial wellbeing.
- He received the Paul A Samuelson Award for his work on the "Save More Tomorrow" project, a plan that allows employees to commit some of their future salary increases toward retirement accounts.

▸▸ MORE INFO

Books:

Thaler, Richard H. (ed). *Advances in Behavioral Finance*. New York: Russell Sage Foundation, 1993.

Thaler, Richard H. *The Winner's Curse: Paradoxes and Anomalies of Economic Life*. New York: Free Press, 1992.

Thaler, Richard H., and Cass R. Sunstein. *Nudge: Improving Decisions About Health, Wealth, and Happiness*. New Haven, CT: Yale University Press, 2008.

See Also:

Advances in Behavioral Finance (p. 1214)

"We can understand much more about the behavior of markets, even financial markets, if we learn more about the behavior of the people who operate in these markets." Richard Thaler

  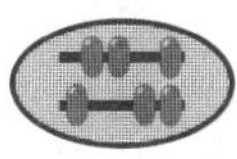   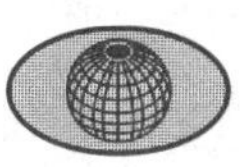   

James Tobin · American economist proponent of Keynesian economics

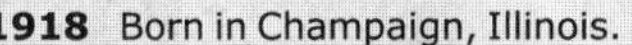

1918 Born in Champaign, Illinois.
1940 Received BA from Harvard University.
1941 Worked as an economist in the Office of Price Administration and Civilian Supply and the War Production Board in Washington DC.
1947 Received PhD from Harvard University.
1947 Elected as a Junior Fellow of Harvard University's Society of Fellows.
1950 Appointed Associate Professor of Economics at Yale University.
1955 Appointed President of the Cowles Foundation.
1957 Appointed Sterling Professor at Yale University.
1958 Appointed President of the American Econometric Association.
1955 Received the John Bates Clark medal.
1961 Served as a member of John F Kennedy's Council of Economic Advisors.
1962 Started work as a consultant.
1971 Appointed President of the American Economic Association.
1971 Publication of *Essays in Economics.*
1972 Publication of *Is Growth Obsolete?*
1977 Appointed President of the Eastern Economics Association.
1981 Received the Nobel Memorial Prize in Economic Sciences.
2002 Died in New Haven, Connecticut.

LIFE AND CAREER

James Tobin was a renowned economist, writer, and Nobel Prize winner, known for his work on portfolio theory, Keynesian economics, Tobin's q, and the Tobit Model. He taught at Yale for many years, and researched and wrote primarily on macroeconomic issues, as well as working as an economics expert, and policy consultant. He was a member of President Kennedy's Council of Economic Advisors, served two terms as president of the Cowles Foundation, and several terms as a member of the board of governors of the Federal Reserve System Academic Consultants. He was also a consultant of the US Treasury Department, and an advisor to 1972 presidential candidate, George McGovern. He received the Nobel Memorial Prize in Economic Sciences in 1981, for his analysis of the financial markets, and their relations to expenditure decisions, employment, production, and prices.

KEY THINKING

- James Tobin was a central figure in the development of economics research and monetary policy in the 20th century.
- He made pioneering contributions to the field of macroeconomics, the study of investment, monetary theory and policy, fiscal policy, and public finance. He was also interested in consumption and saving, unemployment and inflation, portfolio theory, and asset market econometrics.
- His work as a consultant helped design the Keynesian economic policy implemented by the Kennedy administration.
- In 1972, he submitted a proposal for a levy, known as the Tobin Tax, on international currency transactions, as part of an attempt to reduce short-term currency speculation. The tax has recently been at the forefront of discussions about various economic crises.

IN PERSPECTIVE

- His research extended Keynesian economic theory by clarifying issues such as risk, portfolio management, and the role of financial markets in communicating information about underlying economic conditions.
- Tobin's work advanced portfolio theory, and led to the modern theory of portfolio choice asset pricing—that diversification of interests offers the best possibility of security for investors, and that investments should not always be based on highest rates of return.
- He developed Tobin's q, which is a ratio comparing the value of a company given by financial markets with the value of a company's assets, and is calculated by dividing the market value of a company by the replacement value of its assets.
- He introduced the Tobit Model, a frequently used tool for modeling censored variables in econometrics research, and which focuses on the relationship between a non-negative dependent variable and an independent variable.
- Other research included an examination of the inherent pitfalls in financial model building, portfolio balance, and flow-of-funds models, the lifecycle model and social security, and econometric methodology, including the Tobit estimator.
- He also made contributions to mean-variance portfolio demand and asset pricing theory, especially the portfolio separation theorem.

⏩ MORE INFO

Books:

Brainard, William C., William D. Nordhaus, and Harold W. Watts (eds). *Money, Macroeconomics, and Economic Policy: Essays in Honor of James Tobin.* Cambridge, MA: MIT Press, 1991.

Tobin, James. *Essays in Economics.* Chicago, IL: Markham Pub. Co., 1971. Presents his macroeconomic writings from the 1940s to 1970.

ul Haq, Mahbub, Inge Kaul, and Isabelle Grunberg (eds). *The Tobin Tax: Coping with Financial Volatility.* New York: Oxford University Press, 1996.

"The miserable failures of capitalist economies in the Great Depression were root causes of worldwide social and political disasters." James Tobin

  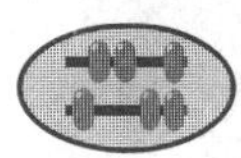 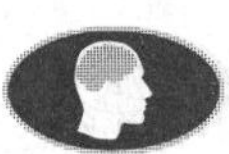  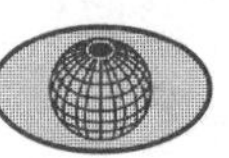   

Amos Tversky • Pioneer of cognitive science

1937 Born in Haifa, Israel.
1961 Received BA from Hebrew University.
1965 Received PhD from the University of Michigan.
1966 Taught at Hebrew University in Jerusalem.
1970 Became a Fellow at the Center for Advanced Study in the Behavioral Sciences, Stanford University.
1978 Joined the faculty at Stanford University.
1980 Elected to the American Academy of Arts and Sciences.
1982 Received the American Psychological Association's award for distinguished scientific contribution, with Daniel Kahneman.
1984 Received the MacArthur Fellowship.
1984 Received the Guggenheim Fellowship.
1985 Elected to the National Academy of Sciences.
1991 Became a member of the faculty senate at Stanford University.
1992 Appointed as Professor of Behavioral Sciences at Stanford University.
1996 Died in Stanford.

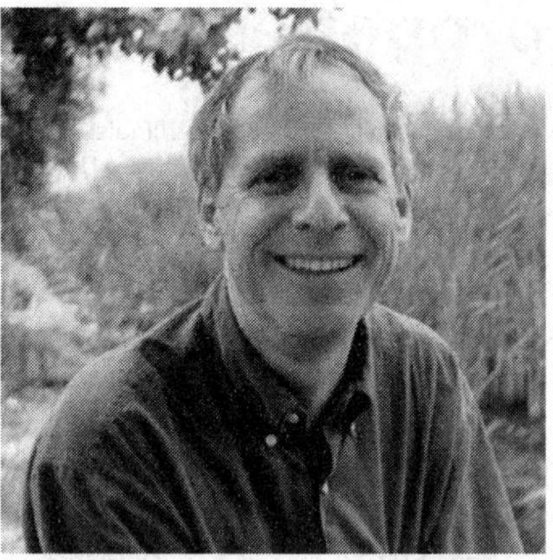

LIFE AND CAREER

Amos Tversky became a war hero at the tender age of 19. He was an officer in an elite paratrooper unit, which fought in three wars, when he earned Israel's highest military decoration by saving the life of a fellow soldier. He went on to become one of the world's most respected and influential psychologists, and a pioneer of cognitive science. He was a professor at Stanford, contributing to a number of interdisciplinary programs, and was a co-founder with Kenneth Arrow of the Stanford Center of Conflict and Negotiation. He was also a member of the Academic Council's advisory board to the president and provost. His accomplishments were recognized with many academic honors, and he would also have received the Nobel Memorial Prize in Economics, but for his untimely death.

KEY THINKING

- Amos Tversky helped create the field of cognitive science with longtime collaborator, Daniel Kahneman, and was a key figure in the discovery of systematic human cognitive bias, and the handling of risk.
- With Kahneman, he originated Prospect Theory to explain irrational human economic choices.
- His work in behavioral economics applied to financial markets, and challenged the efficient market hypothesis.
- His work on the limits of human rationality and decision-making had a major impact on philosophy, social sciences, statistics, political science, law, and medicine.

IN PERSPECTIVE

- His approach was based on counterintuitive results, using practical experiments and formalizations, and drawing on everyday experience to assess the processes and failures of human judgment and decision-making.
- His early work with Kahneman focused on the psychology of prediction, probability judgment, and cognitive illusion, arguing that people repeatedly make errors in judgment, and economic choices that can be predicted and categorized.
- They demonstrated that very small risks are given disproportionate weight, that prospective losses and gains are not treated symmetrically, that the presence or absence of non-selected alternatives can reverse preference orderings, and that the manner in which options are framed can exert an influence on decision-makers.
- They also devised a series of ingenious experiments to expose the illogical ways in which people make decisions that involve probability—including playing roulette, or guessing what someone does for a living.
- Kahneman received the Nobel Prize for the work he did in collaboration with Tversky, and it is assumed that Tversky would have shared the prize but Nobel prizes are not awarded posthumously.
- In his decision-making analysis, he pointed out the misconception in basketball that players tend to get "hot"-- that they sometimes score many more consecutive shots than would normally be expected-- arguing that this was nothing more than the standard laws of chance, and a problem of human cognition.
- Produced many classic papers focusing on the gap between actual human intellectual performance and the normative standards that should seemingly govern such performance.

▸▸ MORE INFO

Books:

Kahneman, Daniel, Paul Slovic, and Amos Tversky (eds). *Judgment under Uncertainty: Heuristics and Biases.* Cambridge, UK: Cambridge University Press, 1982. Describes various judgmental heuristics and the biases they produce, not only in laboratory experiments, but also in important social, medical, and political situations.

Kahneman, Daniel and Amos Tversky (eds). *Choices, Values, and Frames.* New York: Russell Sage Foundation, 2000. Presents an empirical and theoretical challenge to classical utility theory, offering Prospect Theory as a realistic alternative.

Krantz, David H., R. Duncan Luce, Patrick Suppes, and Amos Tversky. *Foundations of Measurement* (3 vols). New York: Academic Press, 1971. A classic series in quantitative measurement.

"People use mental approximations to understand an uncertain world. As a result, we make certain types of errors in judgment." Amos Tversky

Arnold, Lord Weinstock · One of Britain's most revered industrialists

1924 Born in Stoke Newington, London.
1944 Graduated from the London School of Economics.
1944 Appointed a Junior Administrative Officer in the Admiralty.
1954 Appointed Managing Director of Radio & Allied Industries.
1963 Appointed Managing Director of General Electric Company.
1970 Knighted.
1971 Appointed Director of Rolls-Royce.
1980 Made a life peer, as Baron Weinstock of Bowden.
1996 Appointed Chairman Emeritus of General Electric Company.
2002 Died in Bowden Hill, Wiltshire, UK.

LIFE AND CAREER

Lord Weinstock was an industrialist and business leader during the post-war period. After spending his military service in the Admiralty, working on government procurement in the Production and Priority Branch, he became a civil servant, before going into finance and property development in London. He later joined his father-in law's electronics company, Radio & Allied Industries Ltd, which he helped merge with General Electric Company, becoming its largest shareholder. He then built GEC into one of the Britain's largest companies, with wide interests in everything from military equipment to trains and telephones. He was an advisor to four British prime ministers, including Margaret Thatcher. He was a trustee of the British Museum, the Royal Philharmonic Orchestra Foundation Fund, and a senior trustee of the Next Century Foundation, a peace process organization he helped establish. He also established the Weinstock Fund, a charitable foundation.

KEY THINKING

- Weinstock led General Electric Company (GEC) for more than three decades, building it into one of the biggest and most successful industrial conglomerates in the UK, during a period of steady decline in manufacturing.
- In the 1960s, he was a pioneer of the hostile takeover and used aggressive tactics to create a monopoly position for GEC in the electrical engineering and defense electronics industries.
- His takeovers were encouraged by Harold Wilson's government, which was keen to make British manufacturing more competitive.
- In the 1970s and 1980s, he continued to grow the business—both organically, and by acquiring rivals.
- During the economic recession of the early 1990s, GEC retained its market leading position by slashing costs, closing inefficient factories, and confronting the unions.
- Weinstock's unbending management style helped the group generate profits of £1 billion a year during the downturn. However, while the company also amassed cash reserves of more than £3 billion, City investors felt that a change was long overdue.
- Weinstock eventually stepped down in 1996 after 33 years as managing director to become honorary "chairman emeritus", and to make way for Lord Simpson of Dunkeld as his chosen successor. Simpson renamed the company Marconi to underline the end of the Weinstock era, and pursued bold new strategies which would ultimately bring it to disaster.

IN PERSPECTIVE

- Weinstock was a central figure in the business world of the 1960s, when he pioneered a wave of mergers, mostly hostile, which changed the face of British industry.
- The largest of these was GEC's takeover of the larger Amalgamated Electrical Industries, backed and financially supported by the government's Industrial Reorganisation Commission.
- His program of rationalization at GEC transformed the UK's electronics industry, as he introduced efficiency measures, stringent cost-cutting, staff reductions, and implemented mergers to inject new growth into the company.
- This returned GEC to profit, and restored the City's confidence in its plans for development.
- Weinstock was known for his uncompromising management style: during his tenure at GEC, he cut the number of employees from 250,000 down to just 57,000.
- His managerial approach in the 1990s set the tone for lean management, and flat organizational structures.
- As GEC's profits and growth started to decrease, it became increasingly unpopular with Prime Minister Margaret Thatcher and the City.
- In an effort to protect GEC from takeover bids, Weinstock formed alliances with Alsthom in France, Siemens in Germany and General Electric in the US. But his actions could not stop the company's decline and, by the time he left GEC, much of the group had been broken up into smaller partnerships.

▸▸ MORE INFO

Books:

Aris, Stephen. *Arnold Weinstock and the Making of GEC.* London: Aurum Press, 1998.
Gives a detailed history of the UK's electronics industry, putting in context the meteoric rise of GEC, as well as the effects of technological change, and the evolution of the consumer market.

Brummer, Alex, and Roger Cowe. *Weinstock: The Life and Times of Britain's Premier Industrialist.* London: HarperCollins Business, 1998. An empathetic biography of Weinstock's career, detailing the business and political issues faced during his years in charge of GEC.

"You must live as if you are immortal." Arnold, Lord Weinstock

     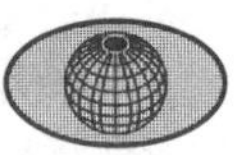   

Jack Welch • Innovative and revered business leader

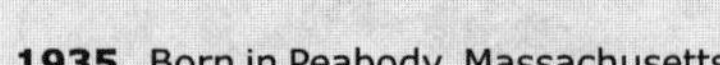

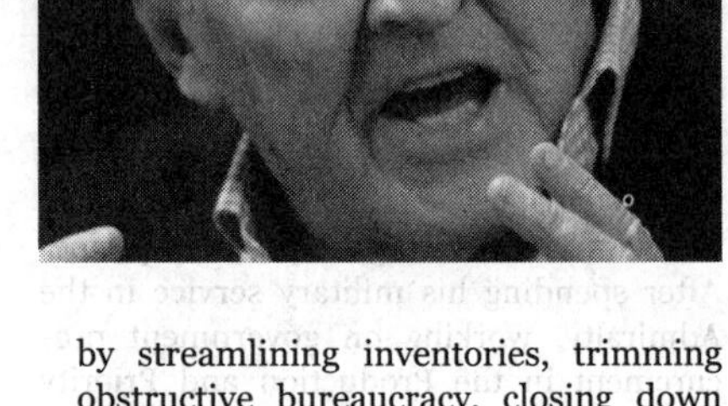

1935 Born in Peabody, Massachusetts.
1957 Received BS in Chemical Engineering from the University of Massachusetts Amherst.
1960 Received MS and PhD from the University of Illinois at Urbana-Champaign.
1960 Appointed as a junior engineer at General Electric.
1963 Put in charge of chemical development at General Electric.
1968 Became General Electric's youngest ever general manager.
1972 Appointed Vice-President of General Electric.
1977 Appointed Senior Vice-President of General Electric.
1979 Appointed Vice-Chairman of General Electric.
1981 Appointed Chief Executive Officer of General Electric.
1986 Bought RCA.
1995 Introduced Six Sigma at General Electric.
1999 Named as *Fortune's* Manager of the Century.
2001 Retired as Chief Executive Officer of General Electric.
2001 Publication of *Straight from the Gut.*
2005 Publication of *Winning.*
2006 Began teaching at the MIT Sloan School of Management.

LIFE AND CAREER

Jack Welch was a business leader, and the youngest and most successful Chief Executive Officer of General Electric. After receiving a PhD in Chemical Engineering from the University of Illinois, he joined General Electric in 1960. Over the next few years, he rose through the organization, becoming its head in 1981. With the intention of building it into the world's most valuable company, he transformed its organizational structure during the 1980s, paring down its hierarchy and bureaucracy, and devolving power to individual business units in a move towards decentralization. By 1999, it was the second-most-profitable company in the world, and Welch had become a role model for his generation. Since resigning in 2001, he has been writing as well as teaching at MIT.

KEY THINKING

- Jack Welch built a reputation as one of the world's top executives during his 20-year reign as CEO of General Electric. He helped modernize the company and completely reorganized its structure by introducing Six Sigma—a business management system originally developed by Motorola—in a bid to make it more agile and efficient.
- The result of his leadership and organizational overhaul was a 600% increase in profits and 100 consecutive quarters of increased earnings, turning General Electric into one of the most profitable companies in the world.
- The year before Welch was appointed CEO, General Electric made revenues of around US$26.8 billion. By 2000, this figure had increased to nearly US$130 billion. The company's market value rose from US$14 billion to more than US$410 billion by the end of 2004.
- In the 1980s, he streamlined the company to make it more competitive and, in the 1990s, modernized it by changing its base from manufacturing to financial services, through numerous acquisitions.
- His philosophy was that a company should be one of the top two in a particular industry, or leave it completely.

IN PERSPECTIVE

- Welch's leadership style involved impelling managers to improve performance, rewarding the top 20% with bonuses and stock options, and firing the bottom 10% each year.
- He also strove to eradicate inefficiency by streamlining inventories, trimming obstructive bureaucracy, closing down underperforming business units, and reducing payrolls.
- During the 1980s, he made slashed the workforce, reducing General Electric from 411,000 employees at the end of 1980, to 299,000 by the end of 1985, helping to greatly increase its market capital.
- His attack on stifling bureaucracy was an attempt to develop a company without boundaries; one that was able continually to change and evolve, according to fluctuations in external circumstances. He hoped this would encourage innovation, and the communication of ideas at all levels across the organization.
- He adopted the Six Sigma quality program in the 1990s, in a bid to create products which were close to perfection, based on a rigorous measurement, testing, and implementation process. This led to greatly increased revenues for General Electric.
- Welch resigned from GE in 2001, and was succeeded by Jeffrey Immelt in a highly public succession battle,

⏩ MORE INFO

Books:

Slater, Robert. *Jack Welch and the GE Way: Management Insights and Leadership Secrets of the Legendary CEO.* New York: McGraw-Hill, 1999.
Welch, Jack, and John A. Byrne. *Jack: Straight from the Gut.* New York: Warner Books, 2001.
Welch, Jack, and Suzy Welch. *Winning: The Ultimate Business How-to Book.* New York: HarperBusiness, 2005.

"For a large organization to be effective, it must be simple." Jack Welch

  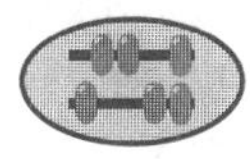   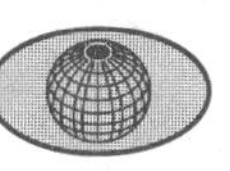   

Mohammad Yunus • Banker to the poor

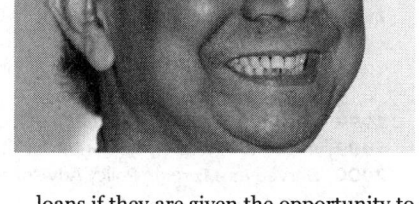

1940 Born in Chittagong, British India (now Bangladesh).
1960 Received BA in Economics from Dhaka University.
1961 Received MA in Economics from Dhaka University.
1961 Appointed as Lecturer in Economics at Chittagong College.
1965 Received Fulbright Scholarship to study in the US.
1969 Appointed as Assistant Professor of Economics at the Middle Tennessee State University.
1971 Received PhD in Economics from Vanderbilt University.
1999 Publication of *Banker to the Poor.*
1999 Awarded the Indira Gandhi Prize for Peace, Disarmament and Development.
2006 Received the Nobel Peace Prize, jointly awarded to the Grameen Bank.
2007 Publication of *Creating a World Without Poverty.*

LIFE AND CAREER

Mohammad Yunus is a banker and economist, best known for his work in developing the concept of microcredit, and extending it to the poor in Bangladesh. After receiving his PhD and teaching in the US, he worked at the Bureau of Economics as a research assistant, and ran the Bangladesh Information Center during the Liberation War of Bangladesh. After the war, he returned to Bangladesh, was appointed to the government's Planning Commission, and later became Professor of Economics at Chittagong University, where he first started to apply microcredit, the extension of small loans, to workers and entrepreneurs too poor to qualify for a bank loan. He founded the Grameen Bank and Grameen Foundation to further this concept, and was later awarded the Nobel Peace Prize for his work in alleviating poverty in small Bangladeshi villages. He has also served on the board of directors of the United Nations Foundation, is a founding member of Global Elders, and is a member of the Africa Progress Panel.

KEY THINKING

- Yunus first became involved with poverty reduction after observing the famine of 1974, and established a rural economic program as a research project, a scheme that was adopted by the government.
- In 1976, during visits to the poorest areas near Chittagong University, he realized that very small loans could make a disproportionate difference to alleviating poverty.
- He started making micro-loans to women in a nearby village who were making bamboo furniture, but had to take out expensive loans to buy the bamboo, and then pay the profit back to the moneylenders.
- His first loan was US$27 to 42 women in the village. He soon realized it would be necessary to create an institution which specialized in giving credit to poor people if the project was to develop.
- In 1976, he secured a loan from the government's Janata Bank, specifically for offering loans to the poor. By 1983, the bank had 28,000 customers, and the pilot project grew into a fully-fledged bank, renamed the Grameen Bank.
- The microcredit revolution continued to develop and, by 2007, the Grameen Bank had issued over US$6 billion to 7.4 million borrowers.

IN PERSPECTIVE

- Yunus encountered resistance to his scheme, from politicians, clergy, and some of the men in the villages.
- The conventional banking system had been reluctant to give credit to people with no collateral to guarantee a loan.
- His concept of microcredit was based on the belief that poor people will repay loans if they are given the opportunity to commercialize their ideas, making microcredit a viable business model.
- To ensure repayment, the bank uses a system of small informal groups which apply together for loans, and its members act as co-guarantors of repayment and support one another's efforts.
- Many microcredit projects lend specifically to women––more than 94% of Grameen loans have gone to women, who suffer disproportionately from poverty, and who are more likely than men to give their earnings to their families.
- The concept has also been applied in industrialized nations, including the US, where Yunus has helped introduce microcredit schemes to some of the poorer communities in Arkansas, working with Bill and Hillary Clinton.

▸▸ MORE INFO

Books:

Bornstein, David. *The Price of a Dream: The Story of the Grameen Bank and the Idea That Is Helping the Poor to Change Their Lives.* New York: Simon & Schuster; 1996. Tells the story behind the bank and the microcredit revolution.

Yunus, Mohammad. *Creating a World Without Poverty: How Social Business Can Transform Our Lives.* New York: Public Affairs, 2007. His new book, which shows how social business can be achieved by using the free market to help the poor. It outlines Yunus' vision for this new business model, and tells how some companies are already successfully implementing it.

Yunus, Mohammad, and Alan Jolis. *Banker to the Poor: The Story of the Grameen Bank.* New York: Public Affairs, 1999. The groundbreaking book that first showed how the concept of microcredit can help those trapped in a cycle of poverty, and without access to conventional banking.

Website:

Yunus' website: www.muhammadyunus.org

See Also:

★ Viewpoint: Muhammad Yunus (p. 274–276)
Banker to the Poor: The Story of the Grameen Bank (p. 1222)
Bangladesh (p. 1355–1356)

"Poor people are not asking for charity. Charity is not a solution for poverty." Mohammad Yunus

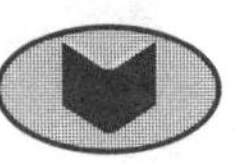
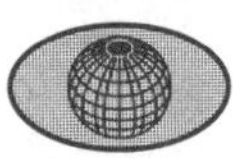

Robert Zoellick · President of the World Bank

1953 Born in Naperville, Illinois.
1975 Graduated from Swarthmore College.
1981 Received JD from Harvard Law School.
1981 Received Master of Public Policy from Harvard University School of Government.
1982 Served as a law clerk in the United States Court of Appeals for the District of Columbia.
1985 Worked at the US Treasury.
1991 Appointed Personal Assistant to President Bush for the G7 Summits.
1992 Appointed White House Deputy Chief of Staff.
1992 Received the Knight Commander's Cross of the Order of Merit of the Federal Republic of Germany.
1993 Appointed Executive Vice-President at the Federal National Mortgage Association.
1997 Appointed Professor of National Security at the US Naval Academy.
1999 Appointed Head of the Center for Strategic and International Studies.
2000 Served as a Foreign Policy Advisor to President Bush during the presidential election.
2001 Appointed US Trade Representative by President Bush.
2005 Appointed Deputy Secretary of State.
2007 Appointed President of the World Bank.

LIFE AND CAREER

Robert Zoellick is currently President of the World Bank, having previously been US Deputy Secretary of State. After studying at Harvard Law School and Harvard University, he worked at the US Court of Appeals, before moving to the Treasury department. He has also been a managing director at Goldman Sachs, and managing director and chairman of Goldman Sachs' Board of International Advisors. He was appointed President George H. W. Bush's personal representative for the G7 Economic Summits in 1991 and 1992, before being appointed White House Deputy Chief of Staff and Assistant to the President. During the 1990s, he also served on many non-profit boards, including the Council on Foreign Relations, the European Institute, and the Institute of International Economics. He served in the Executive Office and on the firm's Risk and Business Practices Committees, and was a US Trade Representative between 2001 and 2005.

- In 2000, he aided the new foreign policy directions that would come with a Bush Jr administration; he supported the use of military superiority that would allow the US to manage international order.
- In 2001, he worked on the Doha Development Agenda, and three years later spearheaded the international effort to revitalize the Doha negotiations, by putting together a new framework for the next stage of commitments.
- He also devised the plans to launch a Middle East Free Trade Area, the Enterprise for ASEAN Initiative, and other ventures to increase trade and development.
- At Fannie Mae, he supervised the restructuring of its affordable housing business, as well as the legal, regulatory, government and industry relations, and international services.
- He has been instrumental in making new free-trade agreements with a number of countries, and led the State Department in the NAFTA and Uruguay Round (GATT) negotiations.

IN PERSPECTIVE

- As head of the Office of Oceans, Environment, and Science at the State Department, he guided the US negotiations in achieving the Global Climate Change Framework Agreement of 1992.
- As a counselor at the State Department, and Under Secretary of State for Economics, he was central to the creation of the Asia Pacific Economic Cooperation forum, for which he received the Distinguished Service Award.
- While a US Trade Representative, he was involved in negotiations to bring China and Taiwan into the World Trade Organization.
- He played an important role in the discussions which took place at the end of the Cold War, persuading the US government to support the reunification of West and East Germany, and representing them at the multiparty negotiation over the future of Germany.

KEY THINKING

- Robert Zoellick has been stalwart promoter of US economic interests, and political security issues for many years.
- He has also played leading roles in a number of high-profile administration decisions, including the effort to mediate the crisis in Sudan, where he helped persuade Darfur's rebel leaders to sign a peace accord.

▸▸ MORE INFO

Books:

Guide to the World Bank. Washington, DC: World Bank, 2003. A useful introduction to how the World Bank operates, its governance, structure, organizing principles, and areas of international interest.

Woods, Ngaire. *The Globalizers: The IMF, the World Bank, and Their Borrowers.* Ithaca, NY: Cornell University Press, 2006. Focuses on the political side of how the IMF and World Bank operate, and the relationships between them and their clients.

"A modern Republican foreign policy recognizes that there is still evil in the world—people who hate America and the ideas for which it stands. . . The United States must remain vigilant and have the strength to defeat its enemies." Robert Zoellick

FINANCE LIBRARY

Finance Library

Summarizing the most influential finance books of all time

There is a vast amount of literature covering the world of finance, and thousands more new publications emerge every year. Finance professionals are time-poor, so we have narrowed the array of titles down to the ground-breaking and most popular works.

The Finance Library extracts the main lessons from the cornerstone titles and the most influential. They include both well-regarded new titles such as Nassim Nicholas Taleb's *The Black Swan*, as well as time-honored classics such as J. K. Galbraith's *The Great Crash* and *Portfolio Theory and Capital Markets* by William F. Sharpe.

Each summary includes a quick analysis of the book's contribution to finance thinking and practice, as well as a list of the key points emerging from the work.

   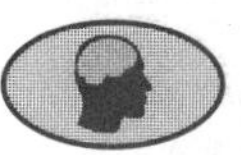  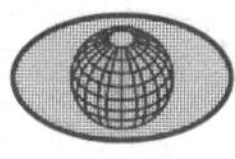   

Contents

   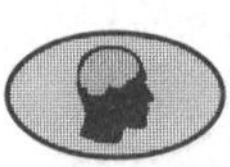  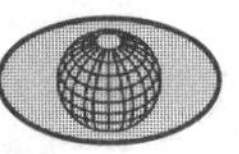   

  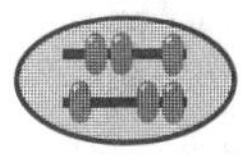 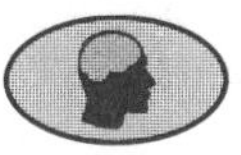  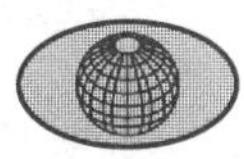   

  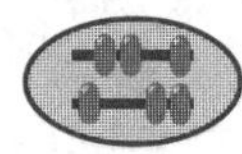   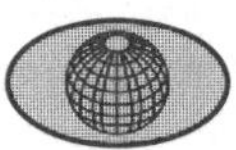   

Absolute Returns: The Risk and Opportunities of Hedge Fund Investing

ALEXANDER M. INEICHEN (2003)

WHY READ IT?

- A non-technical, yet sophisticated examination that shows investors how to make educated decisions about hedge fund investment.
- Presents a wide-ranging and detailed examination of hedge funds, which have been much in the headlines, especially due to large failures such as with Long-Term Capital Management.
- Considers the astonishing success of some hedge fund managers, but also points out the common misconceptions, and the risks as well as the rewards.

GETTING STARTED

Absolute Returns is a practical guide to strategies of hedge funds and alternative investments, which examines the complex risks of hedge funds. It reveals how hedge funds really operate, and is written by someone who has worked with them for many years.

AUTHOR

Alexander Ineichen is Managing Director and Senior Investment Officer in the Alternative Investment Solutions Team at UBS Global Asset Management. He was previously at Swiss Bank Corporation, and is a member of the Chartered Financial Analyst Institute and the Board of Directors of the Chartered Alternative Investment Analyst Association.

CONTEXT

- Details the history, folklore, scandals, personalities, and performance data, of the hedge fund industry.
- Looks at how hedge funds were once limited to an elite group of investors, but are now opening up to less sophisticated, less wealthy speculators.
- Classifies hedge funds according to the strategies they employ, such as relative value, event-driven, and macro, and analyzes the historical performance of the various strategies.
- Looks at how the hedge funds perform better in bear markets, when traditional investment strategies do not.
- Suggests there are two types of investors: pioneers and lemmings (leaders and followers).

IMPACT

- Provides an informed, insider's view of the workings of hedge funds, and the strategies that hedge fund managers use to achieve superior investment performance.
- Argues for hedge funds as a place to invest, and that hedge fund fees aren't excessive on a risk-adjusted return basis. A recurring theme is that hedge funds have outperformed equity indexes, and don't have the same risk.
- Distinguishes between absolute and relative returns, with traditional money managers pursuing returns relative to some benchmark, and hedge fund managers preferring absolute returns.
- Points out the diversification benefits of hedge funds—which are more important to many institutional investors than the purported alpha of hedge funds.

QUOTATIONS

"There are no rules about the game except that it will change. But, most importantly, one should avoid becoming the game."

"The pioneers who were buying into hedge funds during the 1990s were primarily uncomfortable with where equity valuations were heading."

"Managing hedge funds has at least as much to do with risk management as with picking stocks or following a market."

▸▸ MORE INFO

Books:

Drobny, Steven. *Inside the House of Money: Top Hedge Fund Traders on Profiting in the Global Markets.* Hoboken, NJ: Wiley, 2006. Examines the hidden world of hedge funds and how their star traders operate.

Ineichen, Alexander M. *Asymmetric Returns: The Future of Active Asset Management.* Hoboken, NJ: Wiley, 2007. Ineichen's latest book is a guide for active asset management and achieving an asymmetric return profile.

See Also:

A Demon of Our Own Design. Another insider's guide to markets, hedge funds, and the perils of financial innovation. (p. 1247)

Hedge Funds, Fund Management, and Alternative Investments (pp. 1641–1643)

"There are no rules about the game except that it will change. But, most importantly, one should avoid becoming the game."

  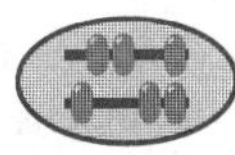   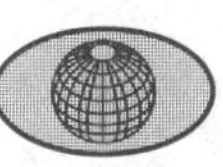   

Accounting and Finance for Non-Specialists

PETER ATRILL and EDDIE MCLANEY (1995)

WHY READ IT?

- Teaches the basics of accounting and finance, with each chapter including a summary, glossary, and exercises (with answers at the end of the book).
- Taking a practical and non-technical approach, it uses tables, graphs, and source material to illustrate key points.
- All essential terms are explained to ensure the reader can use the book as an introduction and quick reference guide.

GETTING STARTED

This is a textbook primarily aimed at those studying introductory level accounting and finance as part of a course, and, for those with a little knowledge, looking for a reference. It may also be used by employees wanting to gain a better understanding of the role accounting and finance plays in the business world. The book shows the reader how to compile cash flows, profit and loss accounts, and vertical balance sheets.

AUTHORS

Peter Atrill is a freelance academic and author working with leading institutions in the United Kingdom, Europe, and South East Asia. He was previously Head of Business and Management at the University of Plymouth Business School.

Eddie McLaney is a Visiting Fellow in Accounting and Finance at the University of Plymouth Business School.

CONTEXT

- Places the concept of accounting and finance in a business context, allowing the reader to see practical reasons for learning the subject.
- Provides a thorough guide for those with no prior knowledge or understanding of the subject.
- Prepares the ground for increased learning and more in-depth study.
- There is a companion website for the book that contains further learning material, as well as the answers to the Review Questions from each chapter.

IMPACT

- This is a teaching text aimed at introducing beginners to the wider world of accounting and finance.
- Explains the importance of accounting and finance within a company, and the information they bring to decision-making at all levels.
- Includes self-assessment sections and activities within each chapter to allow practical learning.
- Can be used as a reference text for non-accounting and finance people as a means of understanding how a company works, and how budgets and reports are used.

QUOTATIONS

"When you become a manager, even a junior one, it is almost certain that you will have to use financial reports to help you carry out your management tasks."

". . .you need a bit of 'street wisdom' in accounting and finance in order to succeed. This accounting and finance book is aimed at giving you just that."

"Another way of viewing accounting is as part of the total information system within a business."

▸▸ MORE INFO

Books:

Black, Geoff. *Introduction to Accounting and Finance.* 2nd ed. Harlow, UK: FT Prentice Hall, 2005. Aimed at beginners and those with some previous experience, it uses self-assessment techniques, and is often used as a set text in business management courses.

Wood, Frank, and Alan Sangster. *Business Accounting: v.1.* 9th ed. Harlow, UK: FT Prentice Hall, 2002, and Wood, Frank, and Alan Sangster. *Business Accounting: v.2.* 10th ed. Harlow, UK: FT Prentice Hall, 2005. Bestselling textbooks aimed at new students, the second version building on the content of the first, explaining the basics of financial accounting.

See Also:

Accounting (pp. 1550–1553)

"When you become a manager, even a junior one, it is almost certain that you will have to use financial reports to help you carry out your management tasks."

  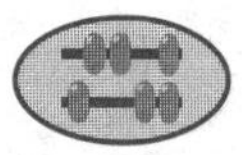   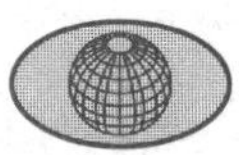   

Advances in Behavioral Finance

RICHARD H. THALER (ED) (1993)

WHY READ IT?

- A team of experts from leading business schools present key papers on this increasingly important topic in finance.
- Considered a major text in the development of theory, containing the latest research on how behavior and psychology affect the financial markets.
- Assesses how individual behavior affects a number of areas, including speculative prices, and when it is best to sell both successful and unsuccessful stocks.

GETTING STARTED

Advances in Behavioral Finance is a collection of seminal research papers from this emerging field of science. It examines discrepancies in the markets, and develops a theoretical basis for explaining each discrepancy based on recent advances in behavioral finance, laying the groundwork for an advanced understanding of the impact of behavior. It also takes an international perspective to examine how behavior affects the international equity markets and exchange risk.

EDITOR

Richard H. Thaler (b. 1945) is Professor of Behavioral Science and Economics at Chicago University's Graduate School of Business. He previously taught at Cornell, the University of British Columbia, the Sloan School of Management, and the Center for Advanced Study in Behavioral Sciences, and has received the Paul A. Samuelson Award.

CONTEXT

- Shows how behavioral finance, as one of the most controversial areas of the financial world, argues that not all economic decisions can be described by the equilibrium conditions in the economy and markets.
- Looks at why overreactions occur in the stock market, particularly with regard to the measurement of abnormal performance, and reactions to earnings announcements.
- Discusses aspects of corporate finance, focusing on the behavioral impact of a preference for cash dividends, corporate takeovers, and initial public offerings.

IMPACT

- Examines volatility and movements in stock prices in relation to behavioral characteristics.
- Discusses the effect of noise and information on the markets, such as through trader risk and investor sentiment.
- Considers which types of economic outcome are affected by biased expectations.
- Assesses how economic agents really act in a less that rational way, and the extent and impact of biased expectations.
- Analyzes the failure of competition and high interest rates in the credit card market.

QUOTATIONS

"We can understand much more about the behavior of markets, even financial markets, if we learn more about the behavior of the people who operate in these markets."

"A person with information or insights about individual firms will want to trade, but will realize that only another person with information or insights will take the other side of the trade."

"Noise creates the opportunity to trade profitably, but at the same time makes it difficult to trade profitably."

▸▸ MORE INFO

Books:

Shefrin, Hersh. *Beyond Greed and Fear: Understanding Behavioral Finance and the Psychology of Investing.* Boston, MA: Harvard Business School Press, 1999. Shows how investors are motivated by fear, hope, overconfidence, and the need for short-term gratification, to help behavioral finance be seen as being just as important as market fundamentals.

Thaler, Richard (ed). *Advances in Behavioral Finance, Vol II.* Princeton, NJ: Princeton University Press, 2005. Gives an overview of the development of behavioral finance from a variety of experts, and examines the importance of behavioral approaches to other areas of economic life.

See Also:

Richard Thaler (p. 1200)

Inefficient Markets: An Introduction to Behavioral Finance. Describes how the principles of behavioral finance conflict with investor rationality and perfect arbitrage. (p. 1276)

Behavioral Finance (pp. 1566–1567)

"We can understand much more about the behavior of markets, even financial markets, if we learn more about the behavior of the people who operate in these markets."

  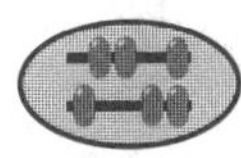   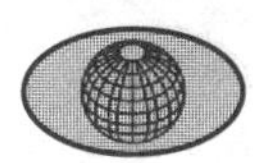   

Against the Gods: The Remarkable Story of Risk

PETER L. BERNSTEIN (1996)

WHY READ IT?

- Provides a fascinating analysis of risk and probability that draws upon history and biography to trace their development and use.
- Without dumbing down, tells the story of a series of scientists and amateurs who discovered the notion of risk, and scientifically linked the present to the future.
- Looks at the basis and context on which people constantly make choices, arrive at decisions, and take risks.

GETTING STARTED

Against the Gods, the international best-seller and winner of the Booz Allen Business Book Award, is a readable analysis of probability and its applications, blending biography with history and science to show how famous thinkers such as Pascal, Bernoulli, Keynes, and Markowitz helped us evolve from superstition to the super computer. The origins, historical progression, and modern understanding of risk are presented in an anecdotal style free of heavy math.

AUTHOR

Peter L. Bernstein (b. 1919) is an author and President of Peter L. Bernstein, Inc. He produces a popular semi-monthly analysis of the capital markets and the real economy, and previously taught economics at the Graduate Faculty of the New School for Social Research in New York City.

CONTEXT

- Tells the story of risk, from it not existing in the ancient world, through its emergence in Renaissance times, to the evolution of our modern theories of risk management in finance.
- Provides mini biographies of mathematicians, gamblers, and others who made significant contributions to our understanding of probability and risk, making this story one of human endeavor.
- Argues that people had to make an intellectual leap, to believe that outcomes could be influenced by their actions and were not merely in the "hands of the Gods" or a matter of fate. This capacity sets modern civilization apart from all that came before it.
- Reviews the history of numerical measurement, probability theory, and the history of financial risk instruments.

IMPACT

- Looks at how we mistakenly define risk as the "chance of loss," and uncertainty as "not understood," so that we often behave as if the past is the best indication of the future course of events.
- Considers that the understanding of probability that we now have allows us to take informed risks and make the sort of sophisticated decisions critical to progress.
- Brings to life such ideas as probability, uncertainty, the difference between luck and skill, the interactions between gambling and investing, and rational versus irrational decision-making.

QUOTATIONS

"The revolutionary idea that defines the boundary between modern times and the past is the mastery of risk."

"The goal of wresting society from the mercy of the laws of chance continues to elude us."

"Reality is a series of connected events, each dependent on another, radically different from games of chance in which the outcome of any single throw has zero influence on the outcome of the next throw."

▸▸ MORE INFO

Books:

Bernstein, Peter L. *Capital Ideas: The Improbable Origins of Modern Wall Street*. New York: Free Press, 1992. Shows how a group of academics and economists changed the way that Wall Street ran the world's investments.

Website:

Author's website: www.peterlbernsteininc.com

See Also:

Peter L. Bernstein (p. 1154)

Fooled By Randomness: The Hidden Role of Chance in Life and the Markets. A readable account of the tendency to explain random events as due to cause and effect rather than chance. (p. 1263)

Risk Management (pp. 1721–1724)

"The revolutionary idea that defines the boundary between modern times and the past is the mastery of risk."

  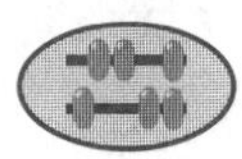   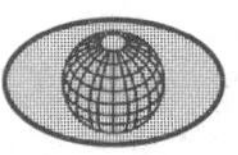   

The Age of Discontinuity: Guidelines to Our Changing Society

PETER F. DRUCKER (1969)

WHY READ IT?

- One of the key books in the development of modern management thinking, it gives a valuable insight into the changing nature of management, innovation, and entrepreneurship in the knowledge economy.
- Explains and analyzes the new challenges, opportunities, roles, and responsibilities in the workplace of an evolving entrepreneurial economy.
- Informs that knowledge, rather than labor, is the new measure of economic society—and predicts the rise of the knowledge worker long before the term came into common usage.

GETTING STARTED

The Age of Discontinuity shows how the manager as knowledge worker is a new breed of thoughtful, intelligent executive, who is paid for applying knowledge, exercising judgment, and taking responsible leadership within the organization.

The knowledge worker thinks of themself as another professional. While dependent on the organization for access to income and opportunity, the organization equally depends on him or her.

AUTHOR

Peter F. Drucker (1909–2005) was a popular business and management thinker, and prolific writer on business management, entrepreneurship and economics. He was a Professor at the Graduate School of Management, Claremont Graduate University, and was a consultant. He was also awarded the Presidential Medal of Freedom.

CONTEXT

- Argued that the knowledge worker sees him or herself as just another professional, no different from the lawyer, the teacher, the preacher, the doctor, or the government servant of yesterday. They have the same education, but more income—and probably greater opportunities as well.
- Discusses the knowledge worker as a new breed of executive—a highly trained, intelligent managerial professional who realized their own worth and contribution to the organization.
- Sees the manager as a responsible individual rather than a paper shuffler.
- Examines how the knowledge workers now own the means of production through such financial factors as pension funds and investment trusts.

IMPACT

- Suggests that our advanced economies must shift to depend on knowledge work rather than industrial strength.
- Presents the rise of the knowledge worker as part of the evolution of business management into a respectable and influential discipline.
- Mapped out the demise of the age of mass, labor-based production, and the advent of the knowledge-based, information age.
- If knowledge, rather than labor, was the new measure of economic society then the fabric of capitalist society had to change.
- Considers that the knowledge worker and the organization are interdependent.
- Knowledge was not only power, but it was also ownership.
- Contains startlingly correct predictions about what would happen in the new economy and marketplace.

QUOTATIONS

"If knowledge, rather than labor, is the new measure of economic society then the fabric of capitalist society must change."

▸▸ MORE INFO

Books:

Drucker, Peter. *Managing for the Future: The 1990s and Beyond.* New York: Tuman Talley Books, 1992. Attempts to explain to executives the rapidly changing world in which they are working.

Drucker, Peter. *The Practice of Management.* New York: Harper, 1954. A classic of management thinking, it was way ahead of its time in examining how the role of the manager was developing during the 20th century, and laid the foundations for the idea of the knowledge worker.

"If knowledge, rather than labor, is the new measure of economic society then the fabric of capitalist society must change."

     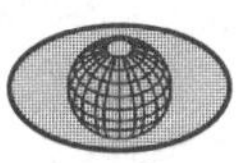   

The Age of Turbulence: Adventures in a New World

ALAN GREENSPAN (2007)

WHY READ IT?

- Tells the story of Greenspan's early life, his professional career and his chairmanship of the Federal Reserve Board.
- Details why he thinks the global economy has evolved into a new and turbulent system over the last few years.
- Explains the dynamics behind recent world events through the perspective of his career and experiences.

GETTING STARTED

The Age of Turbulence comprises autobiography and reflections on America's economic history since the 1950s through his experience in business, in government, and as Chairman of the Federal Reserve Board.

It also examines the author's views on global growth, the extent of competition and openness to trade, international institutions, the development of economic policies, and how he expects these to develop over the next few years.

AUTHOR

Alan Greenspan (b. 1926) served as Chair of the Council of Economic Advisers between 1974 and 1977, and in 1987 was appointed Chairman of the Federal Reserve Board, a position he held until his retirement in 2006.

CONTEXT

- Greenspan chaired the Federal Reserve Board during some of the biggest recent events, including the 1987 stock market crash and 9/11.
- As the dominant force in American economic policy, he became such a key figure that people continually tried to interpret what he said and guess what he would do.
- Comments on a range of key economic issues such as the debt markets, globalization and regulation, equality, pensions, corporate governance, and energy.
- Offers his insider views on a succession of American presidents and British prime ministers.
- Covers the new economy from the standpoint of a neo-classical market economy.

IMPACT

- Examines how he kept the economy steady and growing during economic, financial, and political upheavals.
- Discusses the economic growth of other countries and what they must do to ensure increasing prosperity.
- Talks about President Bush and public spending, the need to raise taxes on energy to encourage conservation, the risk of increased inflation, and whether the Iraq war was about oil.
- Defends his unpopular decision to raise interest rates, and discusses the effect this had on the stock market and real estate.

QUOTATIONS

"Markets have become too huge, complex, and fast-moving to be subject to twentieth-century supervision and regulation."

"Almost all of the developed world is at the edge of a demographic abyss for which there is no precedent."

"Capitalism expands wealth primarily through creative destruction—the process by which the cash flow from obsolescent, low-return capital coupled with new savings is invested in high-return, cutting-edge technologies."

►► MORE INFO

Book:

Yergin, Daniel, and Joseph Stanislaw. *The Commanding Heights: The New Reality of Economic Power.* New York: Simon & Schuster, 1998. An analysis of the shift of assets from central governments to private enterprise and how deregulation and privatization affect economic power in the world.

See Also:

Alan Greenspan (p. 1169)

"Markets have become too huge, complex, and fast-moving to be subject to twentieth-century supervision and regulation."

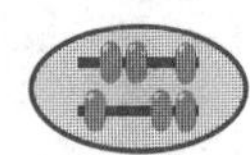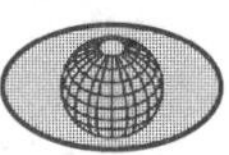

The Alchemy of Finance: Reading the Mind of the Market

GEORGE SOROS (1987)

WHY READ IT?

- Gives insight into Soros's investment strategies, and the decision-making processes of the most successful money manager of our time.
- Depicts how he ran the hugely successful Quantum Fund in the mid-1980s, giving examples of his approach and lessons in how to make money in times of uncertainty.
- He recommends his technique of being adaptive and flexible, as there is no way of knowing how any market situation will turn out.

GETTING STARTED

The Alchemy of Finance analyzes current financial trends, and presents a new paradigm by which to understand the financial market today. It details Soros's innovative investment practices that have made him into a billionaire, along with his views of international finance and the global economy. It is quite philosophical in outlook, and technical in his examination of the connection between thought and reality, and how they apply to the financial markets.

AUTHOR

George Soros (b. 1930) is President of Soros Fund Management and Co-Founder and Chief Investment Advisor to the Quantum Fund. A billionaire investor, philanthropist, and author, he is also active in education, culture, and economic aid and development through his Open Society Fund and the Soros Foundation.

CONTEXT

- Provides an in-depth discussion of Soros's "theory of reflexivity," explaining its key analytical principles in the context of boom–bust cycles in financial markets and economies, and its applications in his successful trading system.
- The basic premise of reflexivity is events create expectations that influence the financial markets; the markets, in turn, then influence these events, creating a cycle.
- Offers a unique contrarian insight into our understanding of supposedly obvious economic and financial ideas, such as his denial of the efficient markets hypothesis and financial markets equilibria.
- Argues that the market is a useful early warning system for potential economic catastrophes, as they reflect the fears of investors.
- Proposes a human uncertainty principle that suggests our understanding is often incoherent and always incomplete, inspired by Heisenberg's rule about quantum particles.

IMPACT

- He became famous for making a billion dollars in one day by shorting the British pound against the US dollar and other currencies, and this book provides important business and investing lessons.
- Examines his technique of buying during the upturns and taking the profit, waiting for a while, then sell shorts during the downward cycle.
- Discusses how Soros trades in the currencies and commodities markets, simplifying his model into eight variables.

QUOTATIONS

"I seek to lay the groundwork for a new paradigm that is applicable not only to financial markets but to all social phenomena."

"Financial markets are always wrong in the sense that they operate with a prevailing bias."

"Equilibrium itself has rarely been observed in real life—market prices have a notorious habit of fluctuating."

▸▸ MORE INFO

Books:

Cunningham, L. A. (ed). *The Essays of Warren Buffett: Lessons for Investors and Managers*. New York: Cardozo Law Review, 1997. A compilation of the writing and thinking of the great investor.

Soros, George. *Soros on Soros: Staying Ahead of the Curve*. New York: Wiley, 1995. Produced in an interview format, revealing his views on investing, global finance, and world affairs.

See Also:

George Soros (p. 1197)

The Intelligent Investor: A Book of Practical Counsel. The classic bestseller of value investing, which shows how to best develop long-term strategies. (p. 1280)

Investment (pp. 1653–1658)

"I seek to lay the groundwork for a new paradigm that is applicable not only to financial markets but to all social phenomena."

  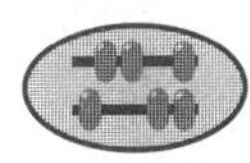   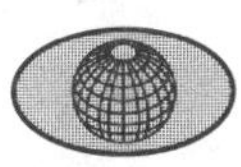   

The Art of Japanese Management

RICHARD TANNER PASCALE and ANTHONY J. ATHOS (1981)

WHY READ IT?

- Played a crucial role in the discovery of Japanese management techniques.
- Examines Japanese management styles and methods, and advises how US companies can learn from them.
- Provides a systematic framework for comparing Japanese and American approaches to management.

GETTING STARTED

The Art of Japanese Management, one of the first business bestsellers, was based on research of 34 Japanese companies, and successfully challenged the long-held assumption that the United States was the font of all managerial wisdom.

By the late 1990s, growing Japanese superiority threatened the United States' dominant position in world markets. In the authors' view, a major reason for the superiority of the Japanese is their managerial skill. Japanese managers have vision, something notably lacking in the West.

AUTHORS

Richard Tanner Pascale is an Associate Fellow of Oxford University, and a business consultant. He also served as an advisor in Iraq, and was also a White House Fellow, Special Assistant to the Secretary of Labor and Senior Staff of a White House Task Force.

Anthony J. Athos (1934–2002) was Chair of Business Administration at Harvard Business School, and previously an Associate Professor at the University of Southern California. In later years he focused on coaching CEOs and management in implementing changes.

CONTEXT

- Presents the seven S concept, which introduced a framework for comparing the different approaches of Japanese and US management.
- The framework lists the seven important categories that managers should take into account—strategy, structure, skills, staff, shared values, systems, and style.
- Argues that a major reason for the superiority of the Japanese is their managerial skills, largely due to their vision, something found to be lacking in the West, where the tools are there but vision is limited.
- Shows how beliefs, assumptions, and perceptions about management frequently constrain US managers.
- Describes how Japanese managers enhance their modus operandi through dynamic visions, rather than superficial or generic statements of corporate intent.

IMPACT

- Provides insights into the mythology of Japanese management and the inadequacy of much Western management practice.
- Details how the Japanese organizations succeeded largely because of the attention they gave to the soft Ss—style, shared values, skills, and staff, while the West remained preoccupied with the hard Ss of strategy, structure, and systems.
- Champions a management vision that proved highly influential, and helped create an industry of books about corporate strategy.

QUOTATION

"The Western vision of management circumscribes our effectiveness."

▸▸ MORE INFO

Books:

Collins, James C. *Good to Great: Why Some Companies Make the Leap and Others Don't.* New York: Harper Business, 2001. Analyzes companies that were able to make substantial improvements in their performance over time.

Peters, Thomas J. *In Search of Excellence: Lessons from America's Best-Run Companies.* New York: Harper & Row, 1982. One of the most influential business books ever published, it presented many key concepts of organizational behavior and managerial theory.

Porter, Michael E. *Competitive Advantage: Creating and Sustaining Superior Performance.* New York: Free Press, 1985. Introduced a new way of understanding what a firm does, and the concept of the value chain.

See Also:

● Japan (pp. 1417–1418)

  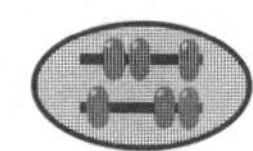   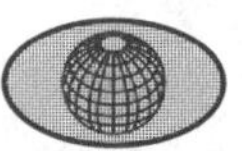   

The Art of War

SUN TZU (revised ed 1971, originally 6th Century BC)

WHY READ IT?

- A compilation of the legendary military strategies and writings of a Chinese general from the 6th Century BC that are thought to encapsulate basic and eternal truths.
- As one of the oldest books on martial strategy in the world, it has had a great influence on Eastern and Western thinking, business tactics, and beyond.
- Sun Tzu has long been revered in the East. He is said to be required reading not only for Eastern military tacticians but also for Eastern businesspeople.

GETTING STARTED

The Art of War is believed to have resulted from the author's own successful military campaigns in present-day Anhui Province, which helped it become a dominant power of that time. This resulted in it becoming standard practice for Chinese military chiefs to familiarize themselves with his writings. The book is also a source of maxims for business leaders.

AUTHOR

Sun Tzu (c. 544 BC–c. 496 BC) was a General and a contemporary of Confucius, according to sources. He was a member of the *shi*, who were landless Chinese aristocrats, worked as a mercenary, and was later hired as a General after finishing his famous military treatise.

CONTEXT

- Oft-quoted, the military language and imagery have played an important role in the development of management thinking.
- Provides timeless insight into strategy, leadership, and survival in a hostile, competitive environment.
- Recommends innovative tactics such as using the momentum of your enemy's own moves to defeat him.
- Gives sound advice on knowing your markets that still has resonance in today's business environment.
- Emphasizes getting the strategy right as the most important element of success.

IMPACT

- Benefits from the attraction of military analogy as comparative to business competitiveness.
- Influential as heroic ideas appeal just as much to a managing director as a military general, and can be used to gain advantage in the boardroom and battlefield alike.
- Argues that strategy is as old as human conflict; anyone who has to devise a plan or manage a campaign, can do with all the help they can get.
- Strategies are still appreciated as the views expressed leave no room for sentiment or distraction.

QUOTATIONS

"Water flows in accordance with the ground; an army achieves victory in accordance with the enemy."

"The best approach is to attack the other side's strategy; next best is to attack his alliances; next best is to attack his soldiers; the worst is to attack cities."

"Why destroy when you can win by stealth and cunning? To subdue the enemy's forces without fighting is the summit of skill."

▸▸ MORE INFO

Books:

Krause, Donald G. *"Art of War" for Executives.* New York: Berkeley Publishing Group, 1995. An interpretation of the book that incorporates modern business lessons on the strategic and competitive challenges facing executives.

Michaelson, Gerald A. *Sun Tzu: The Art of War for Managers—50 Strategic Rules.* Alcoa, TN: Pressmark International, 1998. Provides a new translation, along with comparisons, and examples of how others have applied the key strategic principles.

Wing, R. L. *The Art of Strategy: A New Translation of Sun Tzu's "The Art of War."* New York: Doubleday, 1998. An innovative version, combining author commentary and insights with Chinese calligraphy.

See Also:

Sun Tzu (p. 1199)

"Water flows in accordance with the ground; an army achieves victory in accordance with the enemy."

  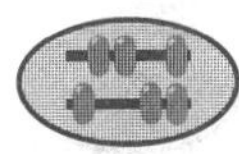 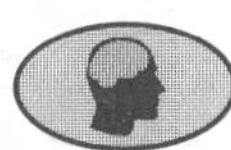  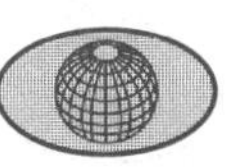   

Balanced Scorecard: Translating Strategy into Action

ROBERT S. KAPLAN and DAVID P. NORTON (1996)

WHY READ IT?

- The originators of the Balanced Scorecard present this innovative methodology, and show how managers can use it to maximize the potential of their companies.
- Details how to build a Balanced Scorecard specifically tailored to an organization, and provides the practical tools needed for implementation.
- Describes the impact of using a Balanced Scorecard as a strategic management system, and how it helps clarify both vision and strategy and translate them into action.

GETTING STARTED

Balanced Scorecard focuses on how to successfully execute business strategy using this management model, and provides a guide to building a Balanced Scorecard. It puts in place a new management system for companies to re-focus on the long term for customers, employees, new product development, and systems, rather than concentrating just on short-term profit. It bridges the gap between strategic goals and performance monitoring, and has been implemented by over 300 major organizations.

AUTHORS

Robert S. Kaplan (b. 1940) is Professor of Leadership Development at Harvard Business School, and Chairman of the Balanced Scorecard Collaborative. He has previously been on the faculty and Dean of the business school at Carnegie Mellon University, and has received numerous awards.

David P. Norton is co-founder and President of Palladium Group. He has also been President of Renaissance Solutions, co-founded and served as President and CEO of the Balanced Scorecard Collaborative, and co-founded and was President of Nolan, Norton & Co.

CONTEXT

- Shows how the Balanced Scorecard works as a measurement and management system for channeling the potential, skills, and knowledge of people towards realizable long-term goals.
- Emphasizes financial results and the human issues that drive them, by integrating a customer perspective, an internal perspective, and a learning and growth perspective.
- Examines the importance of employee learning and growth, internal business processes, and customer knowledge, rather than just short-term financial gain.
- Considers how the scorecard facilitates management processes such as individual and team goal setting, compensation, resource allocation, budgeting and planning, and strategic feedback and learning.
- Analyzes how the scorecard has innovated some of the concepts of previous management models such as Total Quality Management.

IMPACT

- Demonstrates how senior executives are using the Balanced Scorecard to guide current business performance and putting in place targets for future performance.
- Focuses on the vision and strategy of a business, and provides managers with a comprehensive overview of financial performance.
- Shows how to use measures for financial performance, customer knowledge, internal business processes, and learning and growth.
- Considers how the Balanced Scorecard evolves with the organization, unlike many other business models.

QUOTATIONS

"The Balanced Scorecard. . .provides managers with the instrumentation they need to navigate to future competitive success."

"The Balanced Scorecard complements financial measures of past performance with measures of the drivers of future performance."

"The Balanced Scorecard fills the void that exists in most management systems—the lack of a systematic process to implement and obtain feedback about strategy."

▸▸ MORE INFO

Books:

Kaplan, Robert S., and David P. Norton. *The Strategy-Focused Organization: How Balanced Scorecard Companies Thrive in the New Business Environment.* Boston, MA: Harvard Business School Press, 2001. Explains how companies have used the Balanced Scorecard approach over nearly 10 years, and shows how others can implement it successfully.

Niven, Paul R. *Balanced Scorecard Step-by-Step: Maximizing Performance and Maintaining Results.* New York: Wiley, 2002. Provides practical insight on how best to implement the Balanced Scorecard, based on the author's experience in many organizations.

Olve, Nils-Göran, Jan Roy, and Magnus Wetter. *Performance Drivers: A Practical Guide to Using the Balanced Scorecard.* Chichester, UK: Wiley, 1999. An overview of Balanced Scorecard practice.

"The Balanced Scorecard. . .provides managers with the instrumentation they need to navigate to future competitive success."

     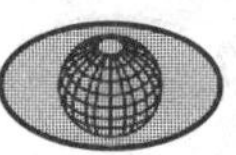   

Banker to the Poor: The Story of the Grameen Bank

MUHAMMAD YUNUS and ALAN JOLIS (1998)

WHY READ IT?

- Tells the story of how Muhammad Yunus began to assist the poor in Bangladesh with a $27 loan and ended with the Nobel Peace Prize.
- Shows how the concept of microcredit can help the most needy, those trapped in a cycle of poverty, and without access to traditional banking.
- Explains how the Grameen Bank has grown into a $2.5 billion enterprise, and microfinancing has spread to over 50 countries, based on the principle of lending to the poorest people in developing countries.

GETTING STARTED

Banker to the Poor recounts the author's early life, and how he first applied the concept of microfinance to alleviating poverty in Bangladesh. He began by helping poor villagers to break the cycle of selling their produce to money lenders for a minimal price, by providing them with a small loan, which they were soon able to repay. Yunus went on to found the Grameen Bank to put microcredit into practice on a larger scale. This has been so successful, it has been copied around the world.

AUTHORS

Muhammad Yunus (b. 1940) was awarded a Fulbright Scholarship and then a PhD from Vanderbilt University. After becoming a Professor of Economics in Bangladesh, he successfully applied microcredit to the poor, became Founder of Grameen Bank, and in 2006, he and the bank were jointly awarded the Nobel Peace Prize.

Alan Jolis is a journalist and writer, and has also produced several novels for children.

CONTEXT

- Yunus's work in providing microfinance to the poor was acknowledged by world leaders and the World Bank as a fundamental weapon in the fight against poverty.
- Discusses how microcredit schemes have worked in different countries, and how they have solved many social and economic problems.
- Shows how extending credit to poor people gives them the initiative and self-reliance to help themselves.
- Most of the Grameen Bank's loans are to women, and since its inception, there has been an astonishing loan repayment rate of over 98%.
- Shows how microfinance creates a sense of pride and responsibility, and generates incremental improvements as opposed to charity or donations.

IMPACT

- Details his refusal of assistance from other agencies, the World Bank, and the Bangladeshi government, preferring to stick to independent assets.
- Shows how banks can lend to those unable to raise any collateral and still operate as a profitable business.
- Expounds the belief that poverty is not created by the poor; it is created by the institutions and policies that surround them.
- Details how Grameen has now expanded from loans for income to now include housing and education loans.
- Shows the value of creating self-employment for income-generating activities and housing.
- Encourages women to take loans and work, something of a taboo to Muslim women living in Bangladesh.

QUOTATIONS

"What good were all these elegant [economic] theories when people died of starvation on pavements and on doorsteps?"

"Unless the poor can be liberated from the bondage of the money-lender, no economic programme can arrest the steady process of alienation of the poor."

"I have always believed that the elimination of poverty from the world is a matter of will."

▸▸ MORE INFO

Books:

Armendairiz, B., and Jonathan Morduch. *The Economics of Microfinance.* Cambridge, MA: MIT Press, 2005. Draws on lessons from academia and international practice to challenge conventional assumptions.

Bornstein, David. *The Price of a Dream: The Story of the Grameen Bank and the Idea That Is Helping the Poor to Change Their Lives.* New York: Simon & Schuster, 1996. Tells the story behind the bank.

Website:

Author's Website: www.muhammadyunus.org

See Also:

- Mohammad Yunus (p. 1205)
- Bangladesh (pp. 1355–1356)
- Business Ethics and Codes of Practice (pp. 1580–1583)
- Social Responsibility of Management (pp. 1735–1737)

"What good were all these elegant [economic] theories when people died of starvation on pavements and on doorsteps?"

     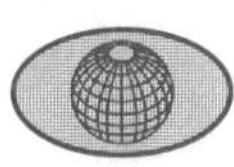   

Barbarians at the Gate: The Fall of RJR Nabisco

BRYAN BURROUGH and JOHN HELYAR (1990)

WHY READ IT?

- An engrossing story, revealing the financial frenzy and power struggle around the RJR Nabisco takeover in the 1980s.
- Puts into context the investment boom of LBOs at the time, and captures the culture of competition in the 1980s.
- Shows how large-scale financial events are dominated by the characters involved, and their struggle for power.
- Shows how the LBO wave of the 1980s was defined by making quick gains, which has now evolved into a greater focus on building sustainable increases in value.

GETTING STARTED

Barbarians at the Gate is a financial bestseller (also made into a movie) that explores the takeover battle for RJR Nabisco in 1988, which was one of the largest ever leveraged buyouts (LBOs). It combines a biography of CEO Ross Johnson with a detailed examination of how and why the planned LBO went wrong.

AUTHORS

Bryan Burrough (b. 1961) is an author and journalist, special correspondent at *Vanity Fair* magazine, a former *Wall Street Journal* reporter, and three-time winner of the Gerald Loeb Award for Distinguished Business and Financial Journalism.

John Helyar is an enterprise reporter for Bloomberg News. He previously worked as a reporter for the *Wall Street Journal*, as a senior writer for *Fortune*, and as a senior writer for ESPN.

CONTEXT

- Describes the mechanics of LBOs in taking a public corporation private, using vast sums of capital to buy out shareholders.
- Shows how Johnson's key mistake was to rely on Shearson Lehman Hutton and Salomon Bros to support the bid. Both firms were hurt by the 1987 stock market crash and had little LBO experience. Johnson's rivals were KKR and Drexel, the biggest players in LBOs and junk bonds respectively.
- Details the fight for control of the multinational between these groups and others over several hectic weeks.
- Examines how Johnson allowed the deal to become public knowledge too early, which undermined his strategy for control.
- Discusses the Nabisco LBO in terms of wider economic trends of the time.

IMPACT

- Considers LBOs as one of the most lucrative investments at the time, which meant that corporations faced numerous takeover battles, often undermining corporate performance.
- Shows how the personality of top management can bring about organizational and financial problems.
- Looks at financial issues, as well as the human story behind deal negotiations.
- Managers learnt from the Wall Street ructions that ensued, and became more adept at handling the media.

QUOTATION

"We've got our fee, let's go on with the next deal."

MORE INFO

Book:

Stewart, James B. *Den of Thieves*. New York: Simon & Schuster, 1991. Tells the story behind the biggest insider trading ring in Wall Street history during the 1980s.

Movie:

Jordan, Glen (dir). *Barbarians at the Gate*. HBO, 1993. Emmy-nominated TV film of the book, starring James Garner.

See Also:

- *Liar's Poker.* Describes the author's time working on Wall Street in the 1980s. (p. 1288)
- *When Genius Failed: The Rise and Fall of Long-Term Capital Management.* Examines the collapse of LTCM in a readable style. (p. 1335)

  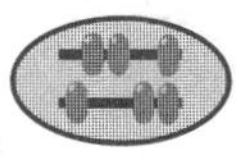   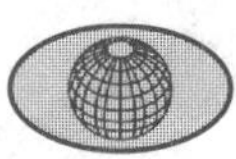   

The Basel Handbook: A Guide for Financial Practitioners

MICHAEL K. ONG (ED) (2004)

WHY READ IT?

- Edited by a respected risk manager who has held senior positions in academia and banking.
- Provides a comprehensive overview and analysis of the changes to the Basel Accord, with each part examined separately to aid understanding.
- Written by a team of expert practitioners and researchers to give a practical and focused look at the three main pillars of the Accord.

GETTING STARTED

The Basel Handbook advises financial practitioners of the consequences of the latest Basel Accord (Basel II), focusing on the challenges banks face in complying with the new requirements. The three pillars of Basel II are a milestone in financial regulation, and part of the on-going development of banking models to manage risk, control capital adequacy, and standardize public disclosure.

EDITOR

Michael K. Ong is Professor of Finance and Director of the Finance program at the Stuart Graduate School of Business, Illinois Institute of Technology. He was previously Executive Vice President and Chief Risk Officer for Credit Agricole Indosuez.

CONTEXT

- Includes contributions from those involved in putting in place the regulations for financial institutions, as well as practitioners in the credit and operational risk industry.
- Highlights the major changes to the Accord, and offers guidance on the three component pillars: minimum capital requirement, supervisory review process, and market discipline.
- Lays out practical guidelines for implementing all the systems affected required by the Accord's various regulations.
- Assesses the possible constraints that may be imposed, and looks at the implications of Basel II on ratings agencies, the financial industry, global and local competition, and costs and capital.

IMPACT

- Features a detailed overview that assesses the impact of the Accord's various regulations on the financial industry.
- Focuses on practical implementation of standards for regulating on the capital banks must put aside to guard against the financial and operational risks.
- Shows how the standards can help protect the international financial system from problems of capital loss and potential collapse.
- Examines the risk and capital management requirements designed to ensure that a bank holds capital reserves appropriate to the risk it is exposed to through lending.
- Covers all the main related issues, such as the treatment of credit risk, securitization, and the need for an operational risk framework.

QUOTATIONS

"[Basel II] strives to incorporate a more enhanced supervisory review process and then overlays it with greater transparency by requiring public disclosure as part of market discipline."

"Basel II should not be simply about capital adequacy. It is more about improving risk management within the financial industry."

"Basel II acknowledges that credit risk management techniques have improved greatly since the first Accord in 1988 and incentivises banks to manage risks better by rewarding them with lower capital charges."

⏩ MORE INFO

Books:

Akkizidis, Ioannis S., and Vivianne Bouchereau. *Guide to Optimal Operational Risk and Basel II.* Boca Raton, FL: Auerbach Publications, 2005. Presents the key elements of operational risk management that are also aligned with Basel II, and shows how to design and implement an operational risk management system.

Lambrecht, Marc B. *The Basel II Rating: Ensuring Access to Finance for Your Business.* Aldershot, UK: Gower, 2005. Examines how to acquire a Basel II rating, especially for those who are seeking access to equity or finance from a bank, showing what information you need and how to maximize your rating results.

Ong, Michael K. *The Basel Handbook: A Guide for Financial Practitioners.* 2nd ed. London: Risk Books, 2007. A fully updated and expanded edition, which reflects changes to the new Basel II Accord.

"[Basel II] strives to incorporate a more enhanced supervisory review process and then overlays it with greater transparency by requiring public disclosure as part of market discipline."

     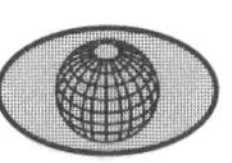   

A Behavioral Theory of the Firm

RICHARD CYERT and JAMES G. MARCH (1963)

WHY READ IT?

- A classic work on organizational theory and behavior by two highly respected academics.
- Provides a useful introduction to the complex world of decision-making, and evaluates traditional approaches and real-world alternatives.
- Describes the series of steps that the rational model of decision-making is based on.

GETTING STARTED

A Behavioral Theory of the Firm examines the academic discipline of decision sciences, which is devoted to analyzing and understanding management decision making. It discusses how decision-making is becoming ever more demanding due to the growth in complexity, and observes that difficult decisions are now not solely the preserve of senior managers.

AUTHORS

Richard Cyert (1921–1998) was an economist and statistician. He taught at the Carnegie Institute of Technology, before becoming Dean at the Graduate School of Industrial Administration, and then President of Carnegie Mellon University in Pittsburgh.

James G. March is Professor Emeritus at Stanford University, which he joined after serving on the faculties of Carnegie Institute of Technology and the University of California, Irvine.

CONTEXT

- Asserts that the five principle goals of the modern organization are production, inventory, sales, market share, and profit.
- Also proposes nine steps in the decision process: forecasting competitors' behavior; forecasting demand; estimating costs; specifying objectives; evaluating plans; re-examining costs; re-examining demand; re-examining objectives; and selecting alternatives.
- Looks at why goals can be inconsistent, focusing on decentralization, short-termism, and the resources available to the organization being insufficient to maintain unity.
- Examines how models emerged to explain the workings of commerce, and how these were extended to explain the way in which decisions were made.
- Argues that decision theory and the use of models is reassuring, as they lend legitimacy to decisions that may otherwise be based on prejudices or hunches.
- Posits that identifying what you need to make a decision about is often more important than the actual decision itself.

IMPACT

- Shows how, to work successfully, decision-making models need standard operating procedures. These procedures may focus on avoiding uncertainty, maintaining the rules, or using simple rules.
- Points out that there are also task performance rules, continuing records and reports, information-handling rules, and plans, which provide a link between the individual and the organization.
- Discusses how a major problem for business decision-making theory is that individuals have goals, while collective groups do not. This creates a need for useful organizational goals, although there is such a thing as an organizational mind.
- The belief in decision theory persists, and most management books and ideas are inextricably linked to helping managers make better decisions.

QUOTATION

"Managers make decisions based on a combination of intuition, experience, and analysis."

▸▸ MORE INFO

Books:

March, James G., and Herbert A. Simon. *Organizations.* New York: Wiley, 1958. Provides an original and definitive treatment of such fundamental concepts as bounded rationality, attention focus, and problem solving.

Nelson, Richard R., and Sidney G. Winter. *An Evolutionary Theory of Economic Change.* Cambridge, MA: Belknap Press, 1982. Attacks mainstream, neoclassical economics, focusing instead on the basic question of how firms and industries change over time.

Simon, Herbert A. *Administrative Behavior.* New York: Macmillan, 1947. Written for managers and other professionals who wish to understand the decision-making processes at the heart of organizations and management.

"Managers make decisions based on a combination of intuition, experience, and analysis."

  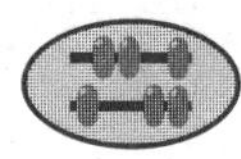   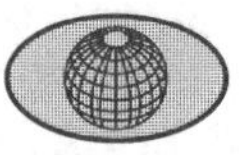   

Being Digital

NICHOLAS NEGROPONTE (1995)

WHY READ IT?

- Provides an overview of the development of media technology, and new ways of looking at the implications of technology and mass media.
- Describes Negroponte's involvement in the development of digital innovations such as multimedia, personal computing, virtual reality, and the internet.
- Before the main revolution in digital technology, he made some key predictions about what would happen.

GETTING STARTED

Being Digital was influential in the evolution to the digital economy, and acts as a guide to the huge changes in new technology and how they will impact on our lives.

It provides an informative history of the rise of technology and some interesting predictions for its future (many of which have already come true), such as how the interactive world, the entertainment world and the information world would eventually merge.

AUTHOR

Nicholas Negroponte (b. 1943) graduated from MIT, before joining the faculty in 1966. He went on to co-found the MIT Media Laboratory and become Professor of Media Technology. He is also the founder of the One Laptop per Child association, and has provided start-up funding for new companies.

CONTEXT

- Analyzes the advantages and disadvantages of the different technologies, and predicts how the technologies will evolve, through the belief that everything will be digitalized, especially information.
- Questions how we can shape technologies, infrastructures, and policies to provide maximum benefit.
- He foresaw that people would spend more hours on the internet than watching network television.
- Examines information technology and how it improves business and home life through such developments as error correction and data compression.
- Predicts that computers will be able to sense human presence and imitate face-to-face communication.

IMPACT

- Explains how in the new digital age we will be less restricted by space and time, as technology reduces the need to be in a specific place at a specific time.
- Takes the view that television and radio will be available on-demand and asynchronously, and that increased use of the internet will aid global networking; digital innovation will also change the way in which we learn.
- Offers his ideas on how the information infrastructure should be shaped, where the effort should be placed, and the impact on all of us.

QUOTATIONS

"Being digital will change the nature of mass media from a process of pushing bits at people to one of allowing people (or their computers) to pull at them."

"We think today solely from the perspective of what would make it easier for a person to use a computer. It may be time to ask what will make it easier for computers to deal with humans."

▸▸ MORE INFO

Book:

Palfrey, James, and Urs Gasser. *Born Digital: Connecting with a Global Generation of Digital Natives.* New York: Basic Books, 2008. Explores the emerging global culture of connectivity, communication and content.

See Also:

Nicholas Negroponte (p. 1180)
Information Rules: A Strategic Guide to the Network Economy. Focuses on information and networks, and practical business benefits. (p. 1277)
E-Commerce (pp. 1508–1510)

"being digital will change the nature of mass media from a process of pushing bits at people to one of allowing people (or their computers) to pull at them."

  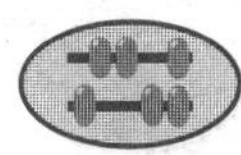   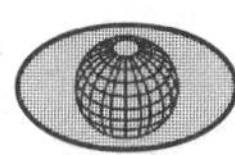   

The Black Swan: The Impact of the Highly Improbable

NASSIM NICHOLAS TALEB (2007)

WHY READ IT?

- Discusses how Black Swans—large-scale random occurrences—and chance and luck affect everyday life, and how you cannot predict the future from what happened in the past.
- Explains why we cannot predict large events in life and argues that we should stop trying to forecast them and start taking advantage of the uncertainty.
- Combines an examination of financial theory with Taleb's own philosophy, and provides an account of growing up in war-torn Lebanon.

GETTING STARTED

The book argues that high-impact rare events, Black Swans, are not nearly as rare as people think, and that their impact is so disproportionately large that they affect much of what happens in the world. It argues that we are exposed to randomness all the time, and that Black Swans are unpredictable regardless of the amount of analysis of previous events. It expands on many of the ideas Taleb explored in his previous book, *Fooled by Randomness*, particularly why life doesn't behave as we expect, and how it is important to remember this to avoid mishap.

AUTHOR

Nassim Nicholas Taleb (b. 1960) is Professor of Marketing at London Business School, Adjunct Professor of Mathematics at the Courant Institute of Mathematical Sciences, New York University, and on the affiliated faculty of Wharton School Financial Institutions Center. He previously held senior positions at major investment banks.

CONTEXT

- Considers the narrative that we impose on our lives to be an illusion that protects us from realizing our life is more random and fragile than we imagine.
- Argues that you cannot eliminate risk, you can only prepare for it, so we should organize our lives to minimize the effect of the negative Black Swans and maximize the impact of the positive ones.
- Taleb calls himself a "skeptical empiricist," as he believes that experience tells us that surprising things will always happen, for which there is supporting evidence all around.
- Disparages a variety of professions that rely on forecasting future trends, such as traders, hedge fund managers, Wall Street bankers, financial risk managers, and economists (even Nobel-winning economists), as unable to predict Black Swans.
- Argues against the use of the Bell Curve of traditional investment theory, which does not tally with his concept of unlikely and extreme events.
- Supports the work of Benoit Mandelbrot, who also thought that Gaussian distributions are not helpful for modeling market behavior.

IMPACT

- Argues that we are permanently exposed to large unexpected events that can wreck all our plans in an instant, and which we can do nothing about.
- Takes a reductivist viewpoint about the uniqueness of experience, and points out that all true learning is based on a few logical truths.
- Finds most specific forecasting to be pointless, as large, rare, and unexpected events will always render forecasts useless.
- Points out the worryingly common flaws in our perceptions with anecdotes and examples, using a range of characters to bring out the essence of his arguments.

QUOTATIONS

"Memory is. . .a self-serving dynamic revision machine: you remember the last time you remembered the event and, without realizing it, change the story at every subsequent remembrance."

"We have far too many possible ways to interpret past events for our own good."

"Black Swan logic makes what you don't know far more relevant than what you do know."

⏩ MORE INFO

Book:

Ball, Philip. *Critical Mass: How One Thing Leads to Another.* New York: Farrar, Straus, and Giroux, 2004. Explains social behavior by applying formulas borrowed from physics.

See Also:

- *Fooled by Randomness: The Hidden Role of Chance in the Markets and in Life.* Taleb's earlier book on risk, probability, and random events, from which he elaborated his theories. (p. 1263)
- *The (Mis)behaviour of Markets: A Fractal View of Risk, Ruin and Reward.* Examines how financial markets really work, by looking at price movement and models. (p. 1298)

"Memory is. . .a self-serving dynamic revision machine: you remember the last time you remembered the event and, without realizing it, change the story at every subsequent remembrance."

  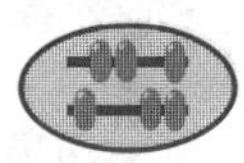   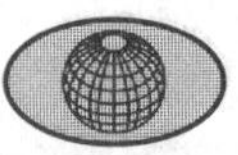   

Blink: The Power of Thinking without Thinking

MALCOLM GLADWELL (2005)

WHY READ IT?

- Analyzes the power of first impressions, how we can know things in an instant, and then make successful decisions based on little or no information.
- Considers how we rapidly and accurately process information in our subconscious and examines the hunches, suspicions, and initial impressions we form without being sure of how or why we make them.
- Argues that we can make better snap judgments if we train our mind and senses to focus only on the most relevant information.

GETTING STARTED

Blink examines how we are continually making quick judgments and how successful these can actually be. Based on research and told in an evocative and anecdotal style, it looks at the many ways that the subconscious makes accurate decisions very quickly, but shows that choices made "in the blink of an eye" will be more accurate if based on experience or preparation. It argues that we should concentrate on the small picture and focus on the meaning of "thin slices" of behavior, rather than overanalyzing matters, as long as we are aware of the potential pitfalls of following our instincts.

AUTHOR

Malcolm Gladwell (b. 1963) was a reporter and then New York bureau chief for the *Washington Post* before becoming a staff writer for the *New Yorker* magazine in 1996. His first book, *The Tipping Point*, is an international bestseller.

CONTEXT

- Discusses how people make instant but successful decisions in a wide range of fields such as psychology and police work.
- Examines the concept of "thin slicing," of how initial judgments are made, and how taking longer to make decisions often reduces their efficacy.
- Considers thin slicing to be about simplifying complexity in our lives and finding patterns in chaos.
- Assesses studies on autism, facial reading, and cardio uptick to argue that training can greatly enhance decision-making.
- Proposes that how we behave is due to a combination of instinct, reaction, and more deliberate analysis, but that we must avoid preconceptions and stereotyping.

IMPACT

- Shows how the "blink factor" occurs when our subconscious makes a decision instantly and in an unemotional way, which it is well suited to.
- Addresses how difficult it is to make decisions in stressful conditions, such as when police and soldiers are expected to make rational choices at times of cognitive overload.
- Examines the problems of snap judgments, which can consistently treat people differently due to their gender, race, age, and clothes, regardless of income, residence, and education.
- Discusses a number of occasions when snap judgments have been failures of judgment, such as the Diallo shooting, the election of Warren G. Harding as US President, and the introduction of New Coke.

QUOTATIONS

"We live in a world that assumes that the quality of a decision is directly related to the time and effort that went into making it."

". . .there are moments, particularly in times of stress,. . .when our snap judgments and first impressions can offer a much better means of making sense of the world."

"Every moment—every blink—is comprised of a series of distinct moving parts, and every one of these parts offers an opportunity for interventions, for reforms, and for correction."

⏩ MORE INFO

Books:

Linden, David J. *The Accidental Mind: How Brain Evolution Has Given Us Love, Memory, Dreams, and God*. Cambridge, MA: Belknap Press, 2007. Argues against the usual assumption that the brain is well designed, maintaining that it has actually evolved to give us our foibles and fallible humanity.

Tavris, Carol, and Elliot Aronson. *Mistakes Were Made (But Not by Me): Why We Justify Foolish Beliefs, Bad Decisions, and Hurtful Acts*. Orlando, FL: Harcourt, 2007. Discusses how our brains are programmed for self-justification, and offers an explanation of how we often deceive ourselves about our decisions.

See Also:

The Tipping Point: How Little Things Can Make a Big Difference. Looks at why social epidemics and trends reach a tipping point where there is suddenly a huge interest and take up for an idea, product, or message. (p. 1327)

"We live in a world that assumes that the quality of a decision is directly related to the time and effort that went into making it."

  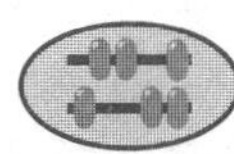   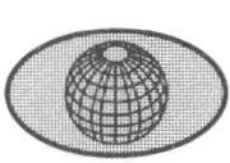 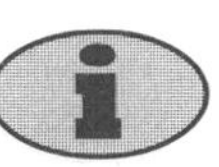  

Blue Ocean Strategy: How to Create Uncontested Market Space and Make the Competition Irrelevant

W. CHAN KIM and RENÉE MAUBORGNE (2005)

WHY READ IT?

- Describes new ways of doing business, by spending less money trying to carve out small profits doing the same thing as ever, and moving into new sectors where there is more opportunity to grow.
- *Blue Ocean Strategy* offers a set of tools and techniques to help you develop a successful business strategy, make the competition irrelevant, and create strong profit growth.
- Covers both strategy formulation and strategy execution, and discusses the BOS principles of value innovation.

GETTING STARTED

Blue Ocean Strategy argues that organizations should pursue new market space where they can develop, rather than being caught up in traditional competition. Based upon a large-scale study that found that differentiation and low cost could make the competition irrelevant and provide new profit areas.

Research in a number of industries brings insight into how success has been achieved through opportunity found in previously neglected markets.

AUTHORS

W. Chan Kim is co-founder and Co-Director of the INSEAD Blue Ocean Strategy Institute and The Boston Consulting Group, and Professor of Strategy and International Management at INSEAD. He is an advisory member for the European Union, a Fellow of the World Economic Forum, and a winner of the Eldridge Haynes Prize.

Renée Mauborgne is co-founder and Co-Director of the INSEAD Blue Ocean Strategy Institute and Distinguished Fellow and a Professor of Strategy at INSEAD. She is a Fellow of the World Economic Forum and a winner of the Eldridge Haynes Prize. She won the 2007 Asia Brand Leadership Award.

CONTEXT

- Puts the emphasis on quality of experience rather than the benefits of a new technology.
- Sets out three key concepts: value innovation, tipping point leadership, and fair process.
- Offers powerful tools to conceptualize the new market space, define it in detail, craft a profit strategy, and actualize its implementation.
- Focuses on creating uncontested market space, creating and capturing new demand, and framing the whole of a company's activities in pursuit of differentiation and low cost.
- Shows how to pursue a strategy that enables a company to free itself from industry boundaries.

IMPACT

- A blue ocean is created where a company's actions favorably affect both its costs and its value for buyers.
- Based primarily on value innovation, when utility, price, and cost are aligned with innovation.
- Identifies key qualities or consumer needs in a market, and then reduces, eliminates, increases, or creates qualities, until new market space is found.

QUOTATIONS

"Our aim is to make the formulation and execution of blue ocean strategy as systematic and actionable as competing in the red waters of known market space."

"The only way to beat the competition is to stop trying to beat the competition."

"Tipping point leadership builds on the rarely exploited corporate reality that in every organization, there are people, acts, and activities that exercise a *disproportionate influence* on performance."

▸▸ MORE INFO

Books:

Collins, James C., and Jerry I. Porras. *Built to Last: Successful Habits of Visionary Companies*. New York: HarperBusiness, 1994. A visionary book on what makes the difference between a good company and a great one.

Peters, Thomas J., and Robert H. Waterman. *In Search of Excellence: Lessons from America's Best-Run Companies.* New York: Harper & Row, 1982. Ground-breaking analysis of management success.

Porter, Michael E. *Competitive Advantage: Creating and Sustaining Superior Performance*. New York: The Free Press, 1985. Presents a more traditional view of strategic thinking.

Website:

See the Blue Ocean Strategy Website for further information on the book: blueoceanstrategy.org/consultancy

"Our aim is to make the formulation and execution of blue ocean strategy as systematic and actionable as competing in the red waters of known market space."

     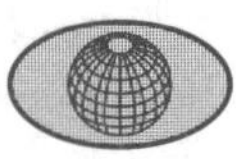   

The Bottom Billion: Why the Poorest Countries Are Failing and What Can Be Done About It

PAUL COLLIER (2007)

WHY READ IT?

- A number of the poorest countries have problems that defy traditional approaches to alleviating poverty.
- Describes the failure of current policies to help these countries and proposes new solutions to unlock the poverty trap.
- Looks at how some countries have developed well, and what policies can get the poorest to replicate their success.

GETTING STARTED

The Bottom Billion argues that the economies of the poorest countries in the world have not grown in the last 30 years because they are stuck in one or more of the following traps: the conflict trap, the natural resource trap, the "landlocked with bad neighbours" trap, and the bad governance trap.

It makes three suggestions to help: military intervention; laws, statutes, and charters for improved governance; and trade preferences. Then it explains the strengths and weaknesses of each approach.

AUTHOR

Paul Collier is Professor of Economics and Director of the Centre for the Study of African Economics at Oxford University. Formerly Director of Development Research at the World Bank and Advisor to the British government's Commission on Africa, he is one of the world's leading experts on African economies.

CONTEXT

- Recommends focusing only on the very poorest countries, and concentrating not just on aid but a broader range of policy instruments.
- Proposes better delivery of aid, occasional military intervention, international charters, and smarter trade policy as solutions.
- Approach not founded on emotion or guilt, but cost–benefit analysis (for instance, puts a price tag on the cost of a civil war) to help decision makers.
- Aid that is provided must be committed, targeted, and given for over a decade to post-conflict societies.
- Looks at how the WTO could play a more useful role, and how to increase private investment.

IMPACT

- Considers that throwing money at the problem doesn't work after a certain point, but that a combination of different policy instruments can be used to play a key role in helping the poor attain growth.
- Discusses what kinds of aid are most likely to help post-conflict and corrupt countries.
- Criticizes the entrenched elite of certain countries and aid policy that has not worked due to misadministration.
- Argues that anti-globalization is wrong but, with intervention from other nations, reform-minded citizens of problem states can find help to improve their situation.

QUOTATIONS

"The left will find that approaches it has discounted, such as military interventions, trade, and encouraging growth, are critical means to the end it has long embraced. The right will find that, unlike the challenge of global poverty reduction, the problem of the bottom billion will not be fixed automatically by global growth, and that neglect now will become a security nightmare for the world of our children."

"A world with a vast running sore—a billion people stuck in desperate conditions alongside unprecedented prosperity."

"An impoverished ghetto of 1bn people will be increasingly impossible for a comfortable world to tolerate."

▸▸ MORE INFO

Books:

Calderisi, Robert. *The Trouble with Africa: Why Foreign Aid Isn't Working.* New York: Palgrave Macmillan, 2006. Examines the corruption, greed, and incompetence that undermine the aid effort.

Easterly, William. *The White Man's Burden: Why the West's Efforts to Aid the Rest Have Done So Much Ill and So Little Good.* New York: Penguin Press, 2006. Sees aid as a disaster and emphasizes the need for local solutions to poverty rather than Collier's belief that collective action can benefit the poorest countries.

Sachs, Jeffrey. *The End of Poverty: How We Can Make it Happen in Our Lifetime.* New York: Penguin Press, 2005. Argues that poverty can be eradicated with a few simple steps, and approaches global poverty as a problem to be solved through increased Western aid.

"An impoverished ghetto of 1bn people will be increasingly impossible for a comfortable world to tolerate."

     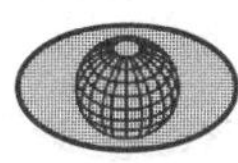   

The Box: How the Shipping Container Made the World Smaller and the World Economy Bigger

MARC LEVINSON (2006)

WHY READ IT?

- A compelling account of how container shipping developed from modest beginnings into a huge industry that made the boom in global trade possible.
- Shows how container shipping transformed global economic geography.
- Explains how the arrival of the shipping container changed the traditional working practices of the large ports, related industries, and cities, along with its impact on longshoremen, labor unions, and governments.

GETTING STARTED

The Box tells the absorbing story of the shipping container: the world worked one way before it came along and in a completely different way in its wake. Levinson shows how a simple idea played a pivotal role in the development of today's global economy. He details the success of the standardized container and its use in international shipping, helping the industry to evolve from old, labor-intensive, manual loading of ships to the mostly automated industry of enormous container ships and specialized ports around the world. Levinson also weaves in tales of the history and politics involved, and shows how the greater efficiency of cargo transferral has dramatically altered global trading.

AUTHOR

Marc Levinson is an economist and author of three previous books. He was formerly finance and economics editor of the *Economist*, a writer at *Newsweek*, and editorial director of the *Journal of Commerce*.

CONTEXT

- Argues that the shipping container was a critical factor in the development of globalization, through cost reduction and increased efficiency.
- Discusses how the dramatic increase in trade brought about by containerization transformed global supply chains, logistics, and outsourcing.
- Provides insight into Malcom McLean, whose drive and entrepreneurism led him to introduce modern containerization methods in 1956 by moving 58 truck trailers on a refitted tanker between Newark and Houston.
- Tells of McLean's struggle to turn containerization into a global industry, the years of high-stakes bargaining needed to win support from two of the titans of organized labor—Harry Bridges and Teddy Gleason—and the sensitivities about standards that would make it possible for a container to travel on any truck, train, or ship.
- Tells how McLean's success in supplying the US forces in Vietnam was pivotal in persuading the world of the container's potential. Details how containerization made possible "just-in-time" manufacturing on a global basis, which meant lower costs and improved productivity.

IMPACT

- Explains why ports such as New York and London were gradually replaced by new deepwater ports designed to facilitate the loading and unloading of containers.
- Discusses the impact of container shipping on the location of manufacturing and industry to make the most of transport infrastructure and cost savings.
- Examines how government regulators tried to obstruct the expansion of containerization to protect commercial interests and limit competition.
- Looks at the shift in economic power that containerization produced, such as the rise of Asia through the provision of inexpensive consumer goods that could be distributed much more cheaply.
- Discusses new uses for shipping containers, such as their potential to be used as designer homes, or even to hide atomic weapons.

QUOTATIONS

"The container is at the core of a highly automated system for moving goods from anywhere, to anywhere, with a minimum of cost and complication on the way."

"An enormous containership can be loaded with a minute fraction of the labor and time required to handle a small conventional ship half a century ago."

"Container shipping. . .has helped some cities and countries become part of the new global supply chains, while leaving others to the side."

▸▸ MORE INFO

Books:

Cudahy, Brian J. *Box Boats: How Container Ships Changed the World*. New York: Fordham University Press, 2006. An account of the revolution in container ships that covers some of the same ground but focuses more on the transformation of the shipping industry.

Stopford, Martin. *Maritime Economics*. 3rd ed. London: Routledge, 2008. Provides a useful introduction to how global shipping operates, and it examines the economic theory that underpins the industry.

See Also:

Shipping (pp. 1534–1536)

"The container is at the core of a highly automated system for moving goods from anywhere, to anywhere, with a minimum of cost and complication on the way."

  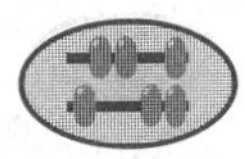   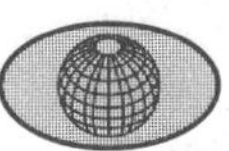   

Business @ the Speed of Thought: Succeeding in the Digital Economy

BILL GATES (1999)

WHY READ IT?

- One of the leaders of the digital revolution discusses the benefits of improved business technology.
- Shows why it is necessary to adapt to the challenge of digital innovation.
- Through a 12-step program, it offers real-world, practical advice for managers to update their businesses technologically.

GETTING STARTED

Business @ the Speed of Thought looks at the fundamental issues for an organization wanting to become more efficient, regardless of the size of its assets, the nature of the industry, and the degree of competition.

Through examples of companies that have already successfully engineered information networks to encourage growth, it advocates digitalization of all aspects of business life, and propounds the theory of the digital nervous system, which envisages paperless offices in a networked environment.

AUTHOR

Bill Gates (b. 1955) is Chairman of Microsoft Corporation, which he co-founded in 1975, and helped build into a multinational technology company. In July 2008 he transitioned out of a day-to-day role in the company to spend more time on his global health and education work at the Bill & Melinda Gates Foundation.

CONTEXT

- Shows how and why a business needs to adapt its internal business systems to survive and embrace the latest technology.
- Introduces the concept of the digital nervous system, which allows companies to improve efficiency, growth, and profit, by developing an infrastructure that allows for the free movement of information. This information flow means news travels quickly and improves strategic decision-making.
- Allows the business to manage inventory, sales, and customer relationships better.
- Examples are provided of applied digitalization in various companies, government organizations, schools, and institutions.
- Emphasizes that what limits is not the technology itself but the ability to exploit it.

IMPACT

- Demonstrates how integrated technology can transform business by energizing customer/partner relationships, employees, and processes, and offers practical advice on how this can be achieved.
- Focuses on the sharing of information and a global outlook as essential for success.
- Explains how the impact and consequences of digital working changes the economy and society.
- Shows that networking for teams and relationships has become more visible and relevant.
- Claims that good information flow for even the smallest of organizations can benefit repeat custom.

QUOTATIONS

"Business is going to change more in the next ten years than it has in the last fifty."

"The most meaningful way to differentiate your company from your competition...is to do an outstanding job with information. How you gather, manage and use information will determine whether you win or lose."

"Business leaders who succeed will take advantage of a new way of doing business, a way based on the increasing velocity of information. The new way is not to apply technology for its own sake, but to use it to reshape how companies act."

MORE INFO

Book:

Seybold, Patricia B., and Ronni T. Marshak. *Customers.com: How to Create a Profitable Business Strategy for the Internet and Beyond.* London: Century Business, 1998. How to compete in a digital business environment.

Website:

Book website: www.speed-of-thought.com includes further details on some of the topics covered.

See Also:

Information Rules: A Strategic Guide to the Network Economy. How to use information and networks to create business success. (p. 1277)

E-Commerce (pp. 1508–1510)

"Business is going to change more in the next ten years than it has in the last fifty."

  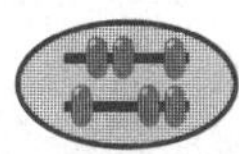   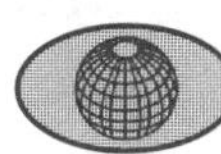   

The Caring Economy: Business Principles for the New Digital Age

GERRY MCGOVERN (1999)

WHY READ IT?

- One of the first books to outline how both businesses and individuals should wholeheartedly embrace the internet.
- Explains how new attitudes, rules, and business principles are needed to ensure success in the digital age.
- Stresses the importance of people, connectedness, community, trust, and interaction in the new economy, to ensure value and vision.

GETTING STARTED

The Caring Economy examines the author's digital philosophy and its application to business, seeing empowerment and people-focused strategies as vital for success, rather than technological change. It considers that the digital age demands new thinking and a whole new set of business principles, and offers advice on making the best use of the internet, including how to build brands online.

AUTHOR

Gerry McGovern is founder and Chief Executive Officer of Nua, and writes a popular weekly e-mail newsletter. He is a founding member of the Irish Internet Association and the Content Management Professionals Association.

CONTEXT

- Discusses the history of the internet, the truths and myths of the information society, globalization, and the strengths and limitations of computer-based business.
- Shows how people are impacted by, and impact on, new technologies and digital business issues, and claims that to succeed business should care for people—staff, customers, locals, and the people who visit their websites.
- Demonstrates how effective communication and customer interaction will be even more important in the new millennium, and how these need to be kept as simple as possible.
- Proposes that the business ambition of always becoming bigger through mergers and acquisitions sacrifices too much of value.

IMPACT

- Presents a number of people-centered rules for success, including empowerment, focusing on niches, focusing on value rather than costs, using information quickly to gain value from momentum, keeping communication simple, protecting and building your brand and good name, and having a long-term vision.
- Focuses on niches and communities of interest, delivering unique products and services; in the digital age, it pays to specialize.
- Analyzes the three properties of information: content, structure, and publication.
- Provides 10 points that are intended to help guide thinking and actions in the new economy.

QUOTATIONS

"What drives the internet is not technology, it's the human touch."

"A society that stops caring is in for trouble in the long term."

▸▸ MORE INFO

Book:

Tapscott, Don. *The Digital Economy: Promise and Peril in the Age of Networked Intelligence*. New York: McGraw-Hill, 1996. Examines the coming of the digital age, and how technology has changed the way individuals and society interact.

See Also:

Being Digital. An introduction to the information revolution from another of its early visionaries. (p. 1226)

Information Rules: A Strategic Guide to the Network Economy. Focuses on information and networks, and practical business benefits. (p. 1277)

E-Commerce (pp. 1508–1510)

"What drives the internet is not technology, it's the human touch."

  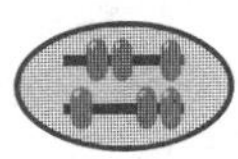   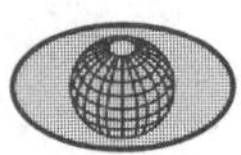   

Cashflow Reengineering: How to Optimize the Cashflow Timeline and Improve Financial Efficiency

JAMES SAGNER (1997)

WHY READ IT?

- Provides focused advice on how a company can better manage its money and improve organizational decision-making.
- Applies principles of reengineering to the everyday problems of cashflow management.
- Guides you through practical techniques for assessing a cashflow system, including the time-value of money, gross margin analysis, scenario impact analysis, and the payment stream matrix.

GETTING STARTED

Shows how to improve business efficiency through cashflow reengineering, a process that has become increasingly important for companies rethinking and restructuring the way they operate. The reengineering puts them in a much better financial position, increases the available cash, and improves internal processing systems.

Explains how to accurately diagnose a company's cashflow problems and successful treat them through effective management. This means changing the system rather than just patching things up.

AUTHOR

James Sagner is a Principal of Sagner/Marks, a treasury consulting firm, and an expert in treasury management. He was previously a consultant at A. T. Kearney and Chief Economist for the Maryland Department of Transportation, and has managed over 250 large-scale company studies.

CONTEXT

- Details 10 management principles and procedures that have helped companies save millions.
- Provides the tools you need to gain the competitive advantages that result from effective cashflow management.
- Shows how people throughout an organization have a significant impact on cash, and offers techniques for working cross-functionally to cut costs without cutting people.
- Complements *Reengineering the Corporation* (see p. 1314) to help businesses rebuild their internal systems, in this case to manage cash in a more profitable manner.
- Focuses on numerous corporate activities that affect cashflow as well as on the negative side of more traditional methodologies.

IMPACT

- Takes a practical approach to helping you analyze specific situations and create solutions that are useful to your company.
- Implement an efficient cashflow timeline that tracks cash in, through, and out the system.
- Offers specific advice, such as cutting the corporate float, so that money works for you rather than being caught up in the system.
- Helps you determine where outsourcing would be an efficient alternative to in-house systems.
- Provides a useful working model for treasurers.

QUOTATIONS

"Reengineering: the concept of redesigning an organization to save costs and time and to improve service, attempts to determine and implement more efficient business processes."

"The principal areas to benefit from reengineering are those portions of the cashflow timeline that fall outside of traditional financial management."

"At the heart of profitability analysis is the concept of opportunity cost."

▸▸ MORE INFO

Books:

Graham, Alastair. *Cashflow Control*. New York: AMACOM, 2000. Analyzes cashflow and its management.

Hammer, Michael. *Beyond Reengineering: How the Process-Centered Organization is Changing Our Work and Our Lives*. New York: HarperBusiness, 1996. Describes the large-scale shift from procedure to process.

See Also:

Reengineering the Corporation: A Manifesto for Business Revolution. Pioneering work in this field. (p. 1314)

"Reengineering: the concept of redesigning an organization to save costs and time and to improve service, attempts to determine and implement more efficient business processes."

     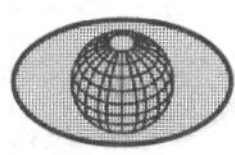   

Common Stocks and Uncommon Profits

PHILIP A. FISHER (1958)

WHY READ IT?

- Known as the father of qualitative analysis, Fisher is one of the most influential investors; his philosophies are considered timeless, and are still being applied by today's financiers and investors such as Warren Buffett.
- Expounds the importance and success of value investing, which laid the foundation for many of today's investment principles.
- Considers that the investor should always think in the long term, buy what they understand, and own only a few stocks.

GETTING STARTED

Common Stocks and Uncommon Profits is a classic that presents the principles of growth investment and recommends rigorous research for stock investing. It provides guidance and a proven strategy for choosing which companies to put money into, through 15 rules that act as a template for investing, based on their true value rather than current trends or tips from finance professionals. As a long-term investor himself, Fisher bought into a number of growth companies that are still very profitable today.

AUTHOR

Philip A. Fisher (1907–2004) began his career as a securities analyst, before founding Fisher & Company, an investment counseling business. He also taught investment at Stanford's Graduate School of Business.

CONTEXT

- Discusses the "scuttlebutt" method that Fisher made famous, which is based on research and understanding a company by talking to everyone that company interacts with.
- Bases his approach on traditional company variables, and more recent innovations such as organizational adaptability and leadership ability.
- Provides guidelines for developing a personal investment philosophy, as there is no real one-size-fits-all strategy in the investing world.
- Points out that investors have had the greatest success when buying stocks during a market downturn and holding them until an upswing, or by investing in a small portfolio that grows over the years.
- Considers that long-term investors shouldn't sell stocks without a good reason, such as a major problem with the company.
- Argues against the efficient market hypothesis, as the future performance of stocks is not reflected in the current price.

IMPACT

- Presents a list of 15 points to help identify the types of companies to invest in, and the ones to avoid.
- Argues that it is better to pay more for a strong business than a discount for a poor business, and shows how to research such businesses in the securities market.
- Consider a stock's worth in terms of potential growth, not just price trends and absolute value.
- Emphasizes prospective growth in earnings and quality of management.

QUOTATIONS

"The typical investor has usually gathered a good deal of half-truths, misconceptions, and just plain bunk. . .about successful investing."

"The young growth stock offers by far the greatest possibility of gain."

"When companies deteriorate, they usually do so for one of two reasons: either there has been a deterioration of management, or the company no longer has the prospect of increasing the markets for its product in the way it formerly did."

►► MORE INFO

See Also:

- *The Intelligent Investor: A Book of Practical Counsel.* The classic bestseller that focuses on value investing, while Fisher's preference is for investing for growth. (p. 1280)
- *One Up on Wall Street: How to Use What You Know to Make Money in the Market.* Shows how small investors can invest better than most professionals, if they focus on quality companies they can understand, and use commonsense to identify growth stocks. (p. 1305)
- *A Random Walk Down Wall Street: The Time-Tested Strategy for Successful Investing.* Evaluates the investment opportunities from a variety of financial products. (p. 1313)

"The typical investor has usually gathered a good deal of half-truths, misconceptions, and just plain bunk. . .about successful investing."

  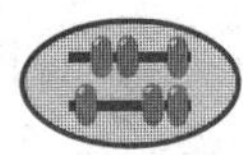 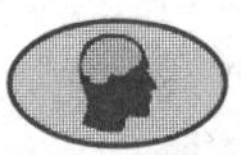  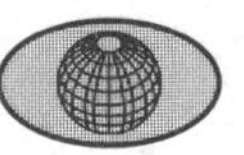   

Competing for the Future

GARY HAMEL and C. K. PRAHALAD (1994)

WHY READ IT?

- Regarded as the definitive book on strategy for contemporary business, which created a blueprint for new industry structures.
- Presents a new approach for developing complex, robust strategies that focus on consistent strategic intent and core competencies.
- Argues that few managers spend enough time looking to the future, and outlines a number of rules for success.

GETTING STARTED

Competing for the Future criticizes the narrow, traditional, mechanistic view of strategy and calls for a broader approach that recognizes a company's core competencies. It proposes instead that far from being a simple annual exercise, strategy should be multi-faceted, emotional as well as analytical, and concerned with meaning, purpose, and passion.

AUTHORS

Gary Hamel (b. 1954) was a founder of Strategos, a management consulting firm, and is a visiting Professor of Strategic Management at London Business School. He is also director of the Woodside Institute, a non-profit research foundation.

C. K. Prahalad is Professor of Corporate Strategy at Ross School of Business, the University of Michigan, and a cofounder of Praja Inc. He is on the commission of the United Nations on Private Sector and Development, and was the first recipient of the Lal Bahadur Shastri Award.

CONTEXT

- Examines how the debate on the meaning and application of strategy is long-running. They contend that strategy should be looked on as a learning process, and that currently it is bound up in a straitjacket of narrow, and narrowing, perspectives.
- Helped develop strategic thinking to the current focus on transforming not just individual organizations, but entire industries.
- Argues that the true challenge is to create revolutions when you are large and dominant, and that small entrepreneurial offshoots are not the route to organizational regeneration.
- Shows that downsizing is an easy option, growth comes from creating a difference, and vitality comes from within the organization.

IMPACT

- Proposes that companies should concentrate on strategizing rather than strategy or planning, and look at the fundamental preconditions for developing complex, variegated, robust strategies.
- Looks at why organizations should see themselves as a portfolio of core competencies, which would help to grow opportunity share, as opposed to market share.
- Argues that a huge proportion of strategists are economists and engineers who share a mechanistic view of strategy.
- The strategic prognosis falls between two extremes: the arch-rationalists, insisting on a constant stream of data to support any strategy, and the thriving-on-chaos school, with its belief in freewheeling organizations where strategy is a moveable feast.

QUOTATION

"A company surrenders tomorrow's businesses when it gets better without getting different."

▸▸ MORE INFO

Books:

Hamel, Gary. *Leading the Revolution: How to Thrive in Turbulent Times by Making Innovation a Way of Life.* Boston, MA: Harvard Business School Press, 2000. Examines how industrial society is being replaced by the rise of the new economy.

Porter, Michael E. *Competitive Advantage: Creating and Sustaining Superior Performance.* New York: Free Press, 1985. Groundbreaking book that introduced the concept of the value chain and a whole new way of rationally understanding what a firm does.

See Also:

C. K. Prahalad (p. 1183)

Blue Ocean Strategy: How to Create Uncontested Market Space and Make the Competition Irrelevant. Details how companies should be tapping into new market spaces. (p. 1229)

"A company surrenders tomorrow's businesses when it gets better without getting different."

 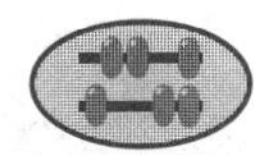 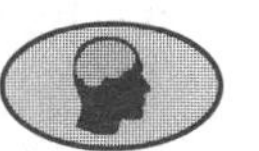  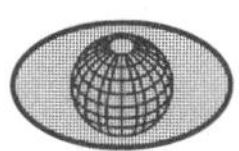   

The Competitive Advantage of Nations

MICHAEL E. PORTER (1990)

WHY READ IT?

- Builds on Porter's earlier books on competition among companies, to introduce a theory on how nations compete against each other and how skills and success can become clustered in different areas.
- Re-examines the nation state, suggesting that its basic role is now an economic one, and that it has a key role to play in ensuring the competitive success of the companies operating within its borders.
- Gives useful examples from 10 countries to support his arguments about global competitive advantage and success.

GETTING STARTED

The Competitive Advantage of Nations offers a radical new perspective on the role of nations: from being military powerhouses they are now economic units whose competitiveness is their key to power. It emerged from Porter's work on US President Ronald Reagan's Commission on Industrial Competitiveness.

AUTHOR

Michael E. Porter (b. 1947) is a Professor at Harvard Business School, and has won many fellowships and awards for his work on competitive strategy. He was appointed to the President's Commission on Industrial Competitiveness by President Reagan, and is a four-time recipient of the McKinsey Award.

CONTEXT

- Enquires into what makes national economies successful, and how they can affect company success to improve the well-being of the nation.
- Develops the concept of the national diamond made up of four forces: factor conditions; demand conditions; related and supporting industries; and company strategy, structure, and rivalry; which together determine whether a nation has competitive advantage or not.
- Offers a series of prescriptions about what governments should do to improve their country's competitiveness.
- Argues that companies and industries have become globalized, and more international in their scope and aspirations than ever before.
- Provides an account of why particular industry clusters emerged in some countries and not others, and why they are able to create and sustain competitive advantage against the world's best competitors in a particular field.

IMPACT

- Asks what makes a nation's businesses and industries competitive in global markets and what propels a whole nation's economy to advance.
- Shows that when governments deliberately set out to help companies compete their efforts are often counterproductive.
- Proposes a theory on the relationship between the nation state and the globalized economy that many have disagreed with in terms of market access.

QUOTATIONS

"Productivity is the prime determinant in the long run of a nation's standard of living."

"Nations don't compete. Companies compete. Nations can make it hard or easy for them to do so."

"Nations succeed not in isolated industries, but in clusters of industries connected through vertical and horizontal relationships."

▸▸ MORE INFO

Book:

Porter, Michael E. *Competitive Advantage: Creating and Sustaining Superior Performance*. New York: The Free Press, 1985. Presents a traditional view of strategic thinking.

See Also:

Michael Eugene Porter (p. 1182)

Competing for the Future. Presents a new approach for developing strategy that focuses on strategic intent and core competencies. (p. 1236)

     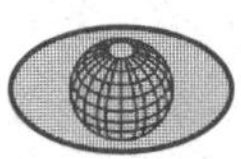   

Competitive Strategy: Techniques for Analyzing Industries and Competitors

MICHAEL E. PORTER (1980)

WHY READ IT?

- A hugely popular book that is taught in most business schools, and read by those interested in business success.
- It put strategic innovation at the forefront of management thinking, and proposes a solution to the eternal strategy dilemma.
- Shows how companies with a clear strategy outperform those whose strategies are unclear, or those that attempt to achieve both differentiation and cost leadership.

GETTING STARTED

Competitive Strategy, a modern classic of business thinking, provides a strong conceptual foundation for developing corporate strategy. It offers a rational and straightforward method for companies to extricate themselves from strategic confusion—and three generic strategies for dealing with competitive forces: differentiation, overall cost leadership, and focus, which for many have become the rules of the game.

AUTHOR

Michael E. Porter (b. 1947) is a Professor at Harvard Business School, and has won many fellowships and awards for his work on competitive strategy. He was appointed to the President's Commission on Industrial Competitiveness by President Reagan, and is a four-time recipient of the McKinsey Award.

CONTEXT

- The rules of competition are embodied in competitive forces such as the entry of new competitors, the threat of substitutes, the bargaining power of buyers, and the rivalry among existing competitors.
- Bases its argument around three generic strategies which help avoid losing out to competitors, and five competitive forces, that determine what a company must do to remain competitive.
- Shows how differentiation entails competing on the basis of value added to customers, so that customers will pay a premium to cover higher costs.
- Explains how the strength of the competitive forces determines the ability of companies to earn rates of return on investment in excess of the cost of capital.
- Offers a guide as to whether some particular strategy, once implemented, can produce worthwhile profits.

IMPACT

- Explains how effectively implementing any of these generic strategies usually requires total commitment, which is diluted if there is more than one primary target.
- Argues that if a company fails to focus on any of the three generic strategies it is liable to encounter problems.
- Synthesizes all that economists know about what determines industry and company profitability.
- Presents a rationalist's solution to the long-running strategic dilemma between pragmatism, where companies have to respond to their own specific situations, and responsiveness, which opens up competitive advantage.
- The current consensus contends that the competitive forces are truer to reality than the generic strategies.

QUOTATION

"Strategy is a choice on how to compete."

▸▸ MORE INFO

Book:

Porter, Michael E. *Competitive Advantage: Creating and Sustaining Superior Performance*. New York: The Free Press, 1985. Presents a traditional view of strategic thinking.

See Also:

Michael Eugene Porter (p. 1182)

Competing for the Future. Presents a new approach for developing strategy that focuses on strategic intent and core competencies. (p. 1236)

The Competitive Advantage of Nations. Discusses how nations compete against each other and how skills and success can become clustered in different areas. (p. 1237)

"Strategy is a choice on how to compete."

     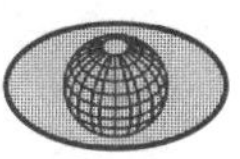   

Confusión de Confusiones

JOSEPH DE LA VEGA (1688)

WHY READ IT?

- This is the oldest book ever written about the stock exchange business, and it made de la Vega famous for his insights and stories about speculation in the 17th century.
- Considered a classic, as the type of trading intricacies and market manipulations of the time are still with us today.
- Presents four rules of speculation that are still relevant: never advise anyone to buy or sell shares; accept both profits and losses; profits do not last; you need both money and patience.

GETTING STARTED

Confusión de Confusiones consists of a series of dialogs between a philosopher, a merchant, and a shareholder describing the workings of the Amsterdam Stock Exchange, the first in the world. The dialog gives the perspectives of the various market participants and the particulars of speculation and trading at the time. Although it discusses tactics and schemes used by traders and brokers trying to influence prices and play the market, it also takes an affectionate look at the market and its members.

AUTHOR

Joseph de la Vega (also known as Joseph Penso de la Vega; c.1650–1692) was a businessman, writer, and philanthropist who lived in Amsterdam in a community of Portuguese Jews whose ancestors had fled the Spanish Inquisition. He was elected to several posts in the Jewish and financial communities, including the honorary office of President of the Academia de los Sitibundos.

CONTEXT

- Only two stocks were traded on the Amsterdam Stock Exchange at the time, the Dutch East India Company and the Dutch West India Company, both businesses dependent on risky operations around the world.
- The trading operations on the exchange were complex, involving options and forward trades to both hedge and speculate.
- There were also a number of other features of modern exchanges, such as bulls, bears, panics, bubbles, short selling, and margin trading.
- Argues that the most successful speculators maintain a balance between optimism and pessimism.
- Describes how the Dutch government banned short selling, but that this was ignored as short sellers were often needed to make markets.

IMPACT

- Gives an overview of who was trading on the Amsterdam Stock Exchange at the time, the types of speculation and trading going on, and the financial instruments used.
- Examines how bull and bear markets can be manipulated and the consequences, teaching how crucial it is to know the rules and think about how they could be used against you.
- Explores the impact of crowd behavior and trading scams on the financial markets.
- Stresses the importance of information and analysis in successful stock trading.

QUOTATIONS

"What really matters is an awareness of how greed and fear can drive rational people to behave in strange ways when they gather in the marketplace."

"[At the stock exchange] concealment of facts, quarrels, provocations, mockery, idle talk, violent desires, collusion, artful deceptions, betrayals, cheatings and even the tragic end are to be found."

"Some gamble for the fun of it, some for vanity, many are spendthrifts, many find satisfaction in their occupation, and quite a few [just] make a living [at the stock exchange."

MORE INFO

Book:

Chancellor, Edward. *Devil Take the Hindmost: A History of Financial Speculation.* New York: Farrar, Straus, Giroux, 1999. Examines the development of stock exchanges and speculative manias through history.

See Also:

Joseph de la Vega (p. 1162)

Extraordinary Popular Delusions and the Madness of Crowds and *Confusión de Confusiones*. This important volume combines the two classics in a new edition. Mackay's seminal work on the impact of crowd behavior and trading trickery on the financial markets takes in the tulip mania and the South Sea bubble; it also tells of popular delusions and mass panics, and examines crowd psychology. (p. 1251)

Reminiscences of a Stock Operator. The classic trading biography of Jesse Livermore, a hugely successful American speculator of the early 1900s who won and lost millions of dollars playing the stock and commodities markets. (p. 1315)

Capital Markets and Stock Markets (pp. 1588–1590)

"What really matters is an awareness of how greed and fear can drive rational people to behave in strange ways when they gather in the marketplace."

  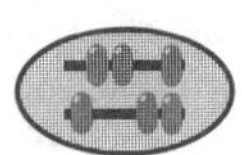   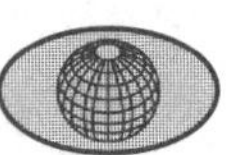   

Conquer the Crash: You Can Survive and Prosper in a Deflationary Depression

ROBERT R. PRECHTER (2003)

WHY READ IT?

- Aimed more at the financial amateur than expert, it explains why the boom times are now behind us, and what we can do to face the economic problems that lie ahead.
- Contains practical tips and guidance on how to deal with the stock market, and other financial areas such as real estate, bonds, insurance, banking, annuities, and precious metals.
- Compares the socio-economic mindset of previous boom–bust cycles to that of today to explain why we are repeating history.

GETTING STARTED

Conquer the Crash argues that deflation and depression are now inevitable. Premised on the author's interpretation of the Elliott Wave Principle, and the idea that mass investor psychology drives markets, it explains why the economy is about to enter a depression that few investors are prepared to deal with. Using technical analysis of the nature of the markets, it offers a guide to understanding and avoiding the losses that normally occur in a bear market.

AUTHOR

Robert R. Prechter (b. 1949) is President of Elliott Wave International, Executive Director of the Socionomic Institute, and has published *The Elliott Wave Theorist*, a monthly forecasting publication for many years. He previously worked at Merrill Lynch, and has served as President of the Market Technicians Association.

CONTEXT

- Introduces the Elliott Wave Principle, which argues that stock market prices rise and fall in discernible patterns and that those patterns can be linked together into waves.
- Some argue that the successful practice of the Elliott Wave Principle relies too heavily on judgement and sentiment, although it appears to be an exact science.
- Explains that there have always been economic cycles, and this will continue due to human activity and nature always adhering to the same fractaled pattern.
- Prechter bases his views on behavioral economics and inefficient market theory that irrational bubbles will form in the markets.
- Relates the current situation to the United States in the early 1930s and Japan over the last 12 years.

IMPACT

- Assembles an array of data to explain how the boom years and market excess of the last decade are now giving way to an extensive bear market.
- Also explores market history, social psychology, and the prevailing money myths to back up this case.
- Advises that we should pay off our bills, pay off our mortgages, buy some precious metals or put our money in a safe bank, not invest in stocks, not rely on the government to protect us, and get ready to profit once we are at the bottom to take advantage of the next uprise.

QUOTATIONS

"It is better to be safe and wrong than exposed and wrong."

"In essence, bull and bear markets are social mood trends."

▸▸ MORE INFO

Books:

Brussee, Warren. *The Second Great Depression.* Bangor, ME: Booklocker.com, 2005. Highlights the growing problems from huge consumer debt that are starting to beset the global marketplace.

Frost, A.J., and Robert R. Prechter. *The Elliott Wave Principle: Key to Market Behavior.* Chappaqua, NY: New Classics Library, 1978. A classic text that examines the Elliott Wave Principle for forecasting stock market behavior.

Schiff, Peter D. *Crash-proof: How to Profit from the Coming Economic Collapse.* Hoboken, NJ: Wiley, 2007. Similar in approach, as it offers useful tips on how to depression-proof your finances, and assesses the financial problems we face.

"It is better to be safe and wrong than exposed and wrong."

   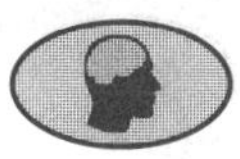  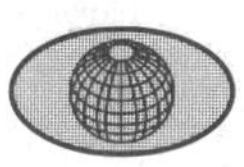   

Corporate Financial Management

GLEN ARNOLD (1998)

WHY READ IT?

- A comprehensive introductory text on corporate finance that helps the beginner move up to an intermediate level of knowledge.
- Sets out the basic principles of finance in a clear style, while working through the main elements of business management.
- Examines financial decision-making, and how the financial markets operate, while integrating it into a practical analysis of how companies operate.

GETTING STARTED

Corporate Financial Management is a comprehensive introduction to corporate finance that covers all the relevant topics, as well as emerging issues such as risk management using derivatives and shareholder value analysis. It is a practical and focused textbook that is used on many undergraduate and business courses.

AUTHOR

Glen Arnold is Professor of Finance at Salford Business School, Manchester, and the Director of the Finance, Accounting and Banking Research Interest Group, as well as being a bestselling finance textbook author.

CONTEXT

- Aimed primarily at second/third-year undergraduates of accounting and finance, economics, business studies/management.
- Provides an overview of the financial world, from an extensive treatment of the investment decision, risk and return, and sources of finance, to a comprehensive analysis of corporate value, including mergers, risk management using derivatives, and managing exchange rate risk.
- Explores the theory behind corporate finance, and looks at where it impacts on real-world practice. The emphasis is on connecting finance theory to practical management, and examining current theoretical re-evaluations.
- Uses extensive case studies and examples to explain financial theory, and worked examples and questions in each chapter to aid learning.

IMPACT

- The core principles of corporate financial management are explained with the beginner in mind.
- Uses a learning format, and includes *Financial Times* articles, and key concepts summarized at the end of each chapter.
- Has been internationally developed to the quality of a typical US finance textbook.
- Non-technical treatment, as equations and math are kept to a minimum.
- Contains useful references to other materials for further learning.

QUOTATIONS

"Without a vibrant and adaptable finance sector all parts of the economy would be starved of investment and society would be poorer."

"It is vital for the health of the firm and the economic welfare of the finance providers that management employ the best techniques available when analysing which of all the possible investment opportunities will give the best return."

"Defining and measuring future receipts and outlays accurately is central to successful project appraisal."

⏩ MORE INFO

Books:

Arnold, Glen. *Essentials of Corporate Financial Management.* Harlow, UK: FT Prentice Hall, 2007. Textbook aimed at courses on the core topics of finance.

Emery, Douglas R., and John D. Finnerty. *Corporate Financial Management.* London: Prentice Hall International, 1997. Connects theory and practice, with many useful examples from the corporate world.

Weaver, Samuel C., and Fred Weston. *Strategic Financial Management: Application of Corporate Finance.* Mason, OH: Thomson/South-Western, 2008. Works through the tools, techniques, and concepts for understanding financial management.

"Without a vibrant and adaptable finance sector all parts of the economy would be starved of investment and society would be poorer."

  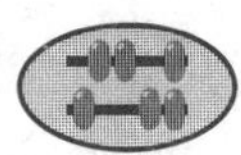   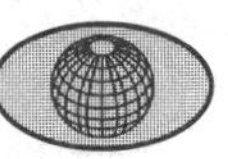   

Corporate-Level Strategy: Creating Value in the Multibusiness Company

MICHAEL GOOLD, ANDREW CAMPBELL, and MARCUS ALEXANDER (1994)

WHY READ IT?

- Argues that because most large companies are now multibusiness organizations, there is a great need to change how they are structured to help them add value.
- Recommends that multibusiness organizations should aim for a tighter fit between individual company strategies and the overall corporate strategy.
- Suggests that although large conglomerates claim to add value through synergy and economies of scale, this is not really the case.

GETTING STARTED

Corporate-Level Strategy puts the case for a tight fit between the main parent company's strategy and its businesses' strategies, arguing that this will promote success. This needs to be thought through properly, to ensure that the most is made from company structure and interactions.

AUTHORS

Michael Goold is founding Director of the Ashridge Strategic Management Centre. Before joining Ashridge, he was a Senior Fellow at the London Business School. He was also a Vice President and Director of the Boston Consulting Group.

Andrew Campbell is a Director of Ashridge Strategic Management Centre. Before joining Ashridge, he was a Fellow of the Centre for Business Strategy at London Business School. He has also worked at McKinsey & Co.

Marcus Alexander is a Director of the Ashridge Strategic Management Centre, and a Professor at the London Business School. He has previously worked in investment banking, at the Boston Consulting Group, and in business.

CONTEXT

- Notes that while individual businesses within the organization often have strategies, the corporation as a whole may not.
- Introduces the concept of heartland businesses and shows how it can help corporations improve their overall performance, as this type of business is more broad-ranging and can cover different industry sectors, markets, and technologies.
- Discusses successful corporate strategies for multibusiness organizations, exploring the role of the parent, its distinctive characteristics, and how each parent will only be effective with certain sorts of businesses.
- Argues that corporate strategy should be driven by parenting advantage to create more value in the portfolio of businesses than would be achieved by any rival. To do so requires a fundamental change in perspective on the role of the parent and the approach of the organization.

IMPACT

- Discusses how there must be a clear vision regarding the role of the parent organization, that the parent must concentrate on "heartland businesses" that it understands.
- Separates the concept of heartland businesses from core businesses, with the former being a better fit with the parent organization.
- Calculates that in most multibusiness companies the whole is worth less than the sum of its parts.
- The research runs counter to the findings of authors such as Alfred Chandler in *Strategy and Structure* and Peter Drucker in *The Practice of Management*, in that it is possible for the corporate level to add value.

QUOTATIONS

"The parent has an innate feel for its heartland that enables it to make difficult judgments and decisions with a high degree of success."

"Heartland businesses are well understood by the parent; they do not suffer from inappropriate influence and meddling that can damage less familiar businesses."

⏩ MORE INFO

Books:

Goold, Michael, and Andrew Campbell. *Designing Effective Organizations: How to Create Structured Networks.* San Francisco, CA.: Jossey-Bass, 2002. Winner of the Igor Ansoff Strategic Management Award, it takes on corporate-level organizational design.

Porter, Michael E. *Competitive Advantage: Creating and Sustaining Superior Performance*. New York: The Free Press, 1985. Presents a traditional view of strategic thinking.

See Also:

Blue Ocean Strategy: How to Create Uncontested Market Space and Make the Competition Irrelevant. Offers a set of tools and techniques to help you develop a successful strategy in new marketplaces. (p. 1229)

Corporate Strategy (pp. 1606–1609)

"The parent has an innate feel for its heartland that enables it to make difficult judgments and decisions with a high degree of success."

  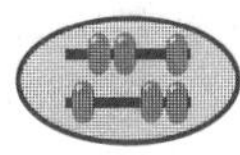   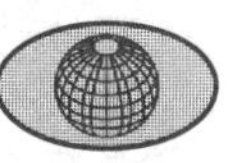   

Corporate Strategy: An Analytic Approach to Business Policy for Growth and Expansion

H. IGOR ANSOFF (1965)

WHY READ IT?

- Was the first book to concentrate entirely on strategy, and remains one of the classics of management literature.
- Provides a powerful, rational model by which strategic and planning decisions can be made.
- Ansoff was the originator of the strategic management concept, and responsible for establishing strategic planning as a management activity in its own right.

GETTING STARTED

Corporate Strategy develops a series of concepts and procedures that managers can use to promote strategic decision-making within an organization. The book is based on the author's experiences as a strategist at Lockheed, and argues that, in developing strategy, it is essential to systematically anticipate future environmental challenges to an organization, and draw up appropriate strategic plans for responding to them.

AUTHOR

H. Igor Ansoff (1918–2002) was Vice President at Lockheed Aircraft Corporations, and Professor of Industrial Administration at the Carnegie Institute of Technology. He also taught at a number of other universities, and was named as Distinguished Professor Emeritus at the United States International University on his retirement.

CONTEXT

- Saw strategic planning as a complex sequence, or cascade, of decisions and defined two main concepts essential to understanding its nature, and, therefore, to implementing it successfully.
- Examines how decision planning is central to the concept of gap analysis: see where you are, identify where you wish to be, and identify the tasks that will take you there.
- Introduces the word "synergy" to the management vocabulary. Although the term has become overused, Ansoff's explanation (2 + 2 = 5) remains memorably simple.
- Presents the strategy tool known as the Ansoff matrix, which depicts the product and market choices available to an organization.
- Provides a rational model for decision-making that concentrates on corporate expansion and diversification, rather than on strategic planning as a whole.

IMPACT

- Discusses several new theoretical concepts such as partial ignorance, business strategy, capability and competence profiles, and synergy.
- Sees strategic management as a powerful applied theory, offering a degree of coherence and universality lacking in the more traditional, functionally dominated management theories.
- While it was a remarkable book for its time, its flaws have been widely acknowledged, most honestly by Ansoff himself. It is highly prescriptive and advocates heavy reliance on analysis.
- Attempts to prove that strategic management can be a dynamic tool able to cope with the unexpected twists of turbulent markets.
- Helped to create the language and processes that allowed modern industrial companies to address the deep questions of corporate strategy for the first time.
- Examined corporate advantage long before its more modern analysis in the 1980s.

QUOTATION

"Paralysis by analysis."

▸▸ MORE INFO

Book:

Porter, Michael E. *Competitive Advantage: Creating and Sustaining Superior Performance*. New York: The Free Press, 1985. Presents a traditional view of strategic thinking.

See Also:

Igor Ansoff (p. 1151)

Competing for the Future. Presents a new approach for developing strategy that focuses on strategic intent and core competencies. (p. 1236)

Corporate Strategy (pp. 1606–1609)

  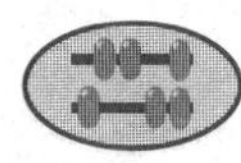   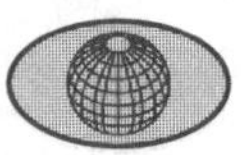 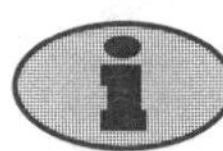  

Cost and Effect: Using Integrated Cost Systems to Drive Profitability and Performance

ROBERT S. KAPLAN and ROBIN COOPER (1997)

WHY READ IT?

- Two highly respected academics present a resource for understanding and implementing activity-based cost management, and show how to improve company profits and performance.
- Provides a detailed blueprint to enable managers to make better decisions and to promote organizational learning.
- Explains why activity-based costing has great benefits, not only for accounting but also management and business strategy.

GETTING STARTED

Cost and Effect demonstrates how the principles of activity-based costing and other advanced cost management techniques, such as target and kaizen costing, can drive business performance. It can be seen as a guidebook for managers to gain benefits from these techniques. Thought of as a classic in managerial accounting literature, the book helps the business and finance communities rethink how a company should handle cost.

AUTHORS

Robert S. Kaplan (b. 1940) is Professor of Leadership Development at Harvard Business School, and Chairman of the Balanced Scorecard Collaborative. He has previously been on the faculty and Dean of the business school at Carnegie Mellon University, and has received numerous awards.

Robin Cooper is a Professor at Goizueta Business School, Emory University, and was formerly Professor of Management at Claremont University. He was previously on the faculty of the Harvard Business School, and is a Fellow of the Institute of Chartered Accountants in England and Wales.

CONTEXT

- Focuses on the need for accurate financial reporting and cost management, by integrating financial reporting processes built around activity-based costing.
- Assists in determining where improvements in quality, efficiency, and productivity will have the highest payoffs.
- Offers practical guidance on negotiating more effectively on price, product features, quality, delivery, and service.
- Uses examples from leading companies to show how to create integrated, knowledge-based systems that provide meaningful information on performance.
- Examines how to design products and services that meet customers' expectations, and that can be produced and delivered at a profit.
- Explains how cost and performance measurement systems can enhance organizational profitability and performance.

IMPACT

- Reveals that most managers don't know how to measure accurately, influence, or understand the fundamental cost drivers in their businesses.
- Analyzes the different systems in managerial cost accounting, and presents quality and productivity improvement systems such as TQM and Six Sigma that could contribute to company performance.
- Shows how to integrate activity-based cost systems into reporting and budgeting processes.
- Links the advantages of activity-based costing to economic value added and enterprise systems.

QUOTATIONS

"We use two powerful concepts. . .that enable the finance function to shift from being the passive reporter of the past to a proactive influencer of the future."

"In today's highly competitive environments, it is not enough to be the most efficient player; it is also necessary to be part of the most efficient supply chain."

"[We provide a] guided tour for how companies can migrate from inadequate, traditional cost systems to a destination where cost and performance measurement systems are explicitly designed to produce the right information at the right time for essential managerial learning, decisions, and control."

MORE INFO

Books:

Cokins, Gary. *Activity-Based Cost Management Making it Work: A Manager's Guide to Implementing and Sustaining an Effective ABC System.* Chicago, IL: Irwin Professional Publishing, 1996. Explains how and why you should implement an effective ABC management system.

Kaplan, Robert S., and Steven R. Anderson. *Time-Driven Activity-Based Costing: A Simpler and More Powerful Path to Higher Profits.* Boston, MA: Harvard Business School Press, 2007. Provides a model for managers wanting to estimate the resource demands imposed by each transaction, product, or customer.

"We use two powerful concepts. . .that enable the finance function to shift from being the passive reporter of the past to a proactive influencer of the future."

  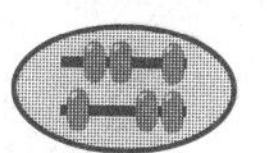   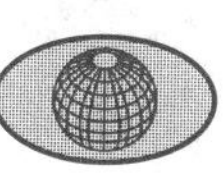   

Damodaran on Valuation: Security Analysis for Investment and Corporate Finance

ASWATH DAMODARAN (1994)

WHY READ IT?

- Combining analysis of both the theory and practice of business valuation, this is a highly regarded text on how to best measure the value of a particular asset.
- Damodaran has a great reputation as a teacher and authority, and he here critically evaluates the leading valuation models to help pick the right model for any scenario.
- Provides practical frameworks for addressing the key issues of company valuation.

GETTING STARTED

Damodaran on Valuation provides focused guidance on asset valuation for practitioners involved in securities analysis, portfolio management, M&A, and corporate finance. It offers a systematic examination of the three basic approaches to valuation—discounted cash flow valuation, relative valuation, and contingent claim valuation—and explains the concepts and techniques of valuation in an understandable manner.

AUTHOR

Aswath Damodaran is Professor of Finance at the Stern School of Business, and has also taught at the University of California, Berkeley. He was the youngest winner of the University-wide Distinguished Teaching Award, and profiled in *Business Week* as one of the top 12 business school professors.

CONTEXT

- Examines a variety of real-life firms where the direct application of valuation models has failed, identifies the problems, and offers solutions.
- Explains the value and limitations of models in order to illustrate key techniques.
- Assists the development of the skills needed to select the right model for any valuation scenario.
- Presents how to implement the right model, and the kinds of firms to which it is best applied.
- Discusses many of the common myths of valuation, regarding objectivity, supposed timelessness, precision, quantitativeness, and process.
- Focuses throughout on application, including how to develop an understanding of stock fundamentals.

IMPACT

- Emphasizes the usefulness and benefits of the variety of valuation models available to businesses.
- Presents tools designed for a variety of demands, such as estimating the cost of equity, estimating growth rates, measuring free cash flow to equity, valuing firms, estimating the value of assets by looking at the pricing of comparable assets, and measuring the value of assets that share option characteristics.
- Provides spreadsheets that have been prepared to allow readers to apply what they are learning immediately.

QUOTATIONS

"Reasonable estimates of value can be made for most assets and that the same fundamental principles determine the value of all types of assets, real as well as financial."

"Valuation is not an objective exercise, and any preconceptions and biases that an analyst brings to the process will find its way into the value."

"Matching the valuation model to the asset or firm being valued is as important a part of valuation as understanding the models and having the right inputs."

⏩ MORE INFO

Books:

Damodaran, Aswath. *The Dark Side of Valuation: Valuing Old Tech, New Tech, and New Economy Companies.* Upper Saddle River, NJ: FT Prentice Hall, 2001. Details various ways to adapt conventional valuation methods for companies.

Damodaran, Aswath. *Study Guide for Damodaran on Valuation: Security Analysis for Investment and Corporate Finance.* New York: Wiley, 1994. A supporting learning resource for the main book.

See Also:

Valuation: Measuring and Managing the Value of Companies. Provides insight into how to measure, manage, and maximize a company's value, from a more technical perspective. (p. 1330)

Corporate Valuation (pp. 1610–1613)

"Reasonable estimates of value can be made for most assets and that the same fundamental principles determine the value of all types of assets, real as well as financial."

  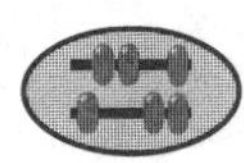   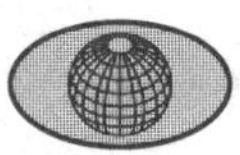   

The Death of Distance: How the Communications Revolution Is Changing Our Lives and Our Work

FRANCES CAIRNCROSS (1997)

WHY READ IT?

- An ideas book on how the internet connects people to information, services, and entertainment, and how new technology is changing our lives to make distance irrelevant.
- Outlines 30 specific developments that the author believes will impact on business and society in the near future.
- Focuses on future trends, and the belief that as countries become more economically interdependent, people will communicate more freely, which will increase understanding and tolerance, and promote peace.

GETTING STARTED

The Death of Distance examines how converging communications technology is reshaping business, politics, economics, and our daily lives. It examines why and how distance is becoming less relevant due to digital technology and the internet, and the cost of doing business is being dramatically reduced. Some of the predictions have already come true, such as some developing countries now providing online services for the rest of the world, while others have not.

AUTHOR

Frances Cairncross (b. 1944) is an economist, journalist, and academic, who worked at *The Economist* for 20 years, most recently as Management Editor. She became Rector of Exeter College, Oxford, in 2004, and has chaired the Economic and Social Research Council.

CONTEXT

- Considers the practical impact of technological advancement on how we work and live, and the changing nature of organizations, communities, government authority, culture, and languages.
- Argues that open communication is obliterating distance as a relevant factor in how we conduct our business and personal lives.
- Discusses the changes likely to result, including greater self-policing of businesses, loss of personal privacy, and a lesser need for countries to seek immigration.
- Analyzes how the rise of new technology has created a digital divide, as well as the democratizing effects of digital communications on different sectors.
- Looks at how the increased movement of information across boundaries affects national laws involving libel, copyright, child pornography, and other criminal acts.
- Foresees that common interests, experiences, and pursuits will bind communities together rather than proximity.

IMPACT

- Examines the impact of new ideas and information travelling faster around the world than ever before.
- Argues that the value of strong brands will increase greatly as global markets evolve.
- Describes how international companies will organize workloads according to the world's three main time zones.
- Considers that size will no longer be essential to business success, as small companies offer services that previously only multinationals provided.
- The cost of starting new businesses will decline, and companies will more easily buy in services from new start-ups.
- Discusses the implications of workers able to earn a living from anywhere.

QUOTATIONS

"The death of distance loosens the grip of geography."

"The death of distance as a determinant of the cost of communications will probably be the single most important economic force shaping society in the first half of the next century."

"The main impact of the death of distance will be to make communication and access to information in all its forms more convenient."

▸▸ MORE INFO

Book:

Palfrey, James, and Urs Gasser. *Born Digital: Connecting with a Global Generation of Digital Natives.* New York: Basic Books, 2008. Explores the emerging global culture of connectivity, communication, and content.

See Also:

- *Being Digital.* An introduction to the information revolution from one of its early visionaries. (p. 1226)
- *Information Rules: A Strategic Guide to the Network Economy.* Focuses on information and networks, and practical business benefits. (p. 1277)

"The death of distance loosens the grip of geography."

  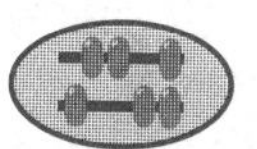 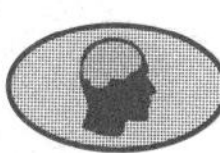  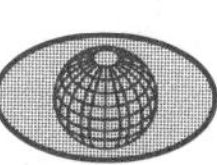   

A Demon of Our Own Design

RICHARD BOOKSTABER (2007)

WHY READ IT?

- A timely book on the risks underpinning the hedge fund industry, and the markets in general.
- Bookstaber was involved in the design of some of the complex options and derivatives described in the book, which are contributing to the market downturn.
- Discusses why, although there is greater market sophistication, improved technology, and improved oversight and regulation, the markets are becoming more risky all the time.

GETTING STARTED

A Demon of Our Own Design provides an entertaining guide to how the markets work, the dynamics of the hedge fund industry, and the risks inherent in financial innovation. It examines some of the financial disasters of the last 25 years in a readable style, and worries us with the premise that the financial products developed over the past few decades have become too complicated for our own good.

AUTHOR

Richard Bookstaber (b. 1950) is a finance writer and runs an equity hedge fund, having also been at Ziff Brothers Investments and Moore Capital Management. He was previously a Managing Director at Salomon Brothers and on their Risk Management Committee.

CONTEXT

- Shows how the very things done to make markets safer have actually created a world that is far more dangerous, and examines the dynamics behind such financial calamities as the 1987 crash and the demise of Long-Term Capital Management.
- Takes an insider's perspective on the management decisions made by some of the world's most powerful financial operators, including Warren Buffett, Sandy Weill, and John Meriwether.
- Recounts the author's own contribution to market calamities, and the market complexity due to derivatives and structured products.

IMPACT

- Argues that the increasing specialization of financial instruments means that there will be greater uncertainty, and we will be more vulnerable to larger problems.
- Discusses the crises occurring from tight coupling, where the close interlinking of factors is causing problems in different industries.
- Considers much that is currently relevant in risk management, the capital markets, and the liquidity crisis.
- Calls for a slower rate of market innovation and trading, which originates from his economist background and distaste for risk.
- Explains the many complex relationships between securities in an understandable style.
- Thinks of financial markets as inherently unstable, and says this should limit how far we should go in pursuit of profit.

QUOTATIONS

"The financial markets that we have constructed are now so complex, and the speed of transactions so fast, that apparently isolated actions and even minor events can have catastrophic consequences."

"Virtually all mishaps over the past decades had their roots in the complex structure of the financial markets themselves."

"The danger to the system is the system."

▸▸ MORE INFO

Book:

Knee, Jonathan A. *The Accidental Investment Banker: Inside the Decade That Transformed Wall Street.* Oxford: Oxford University Press, 2006. A look at the role of the investment banker and the deal culture, from one who has been there.

See Also:

- *Liar's Poker: Rising Through the Wreckage on Wall Street.* An entertaining and revealing account of the author's time at one of the big investment banks. (p. 1288)
- *Traders, Guns & Money: Knowns and Unknowns in the Dazzling World of Derivatives.* An entertaining introduction to derivatives trading and its impact on the financial markets by a veteran of the industry. (p. 1328)
- Hedge Funds, Fund Management, and Alternative Investments (pp. 1641–1643)

"The financial markets that we have constructed are now so complex, and the speed of transactions so fast, that apparently isolated actions and even minor events can have catastrophic consequences."

     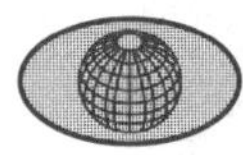   

Digital Capital: Harnessing the Power of Business Webs

DON TAPSCOTT, DAVID TICOLL, and ALEX LOWY (2000)

WHY READ IT?

- Provides insight into the growing importance of new electronic marketplaces.
- Explores how the internet and digital media open up new avenues to wealth creation, using real-world examples.
- Guides companies wanting to successfully develop business-to-business exchanges or other electronic alliances and accumulate digital capital.

GETTING STARTED

Digital Capital examines how companies are reinventing their business models around the way the internet is now being used, and is aimed at those who don't know how to create an internet-based business model or want to improve the one they already have. Introduces key concepts of e-commerce, business webs, and models, discusses the changes that are occurring in the global economy, and outlines eight strategic stages in creating a successful business web.

AUTHORS

Don Tapscott (b. 1947) is Chief Executive and Founder of New Paradigm, a think-tank and strategy consulting company. He teaches at the Rotman School of Management at the University of Toronto, and is the author of a number of books on business strategy and the digital economy.

David Ticoll is a Research Fellow at the University of Toronto Knowledge Media Design Institute. He writes on business strategy and technology, and is a director of the Information Technology Association of Canada. He is presently the CEO of Convergent Strategies.

Alex Lowy is a business writer and was previously Director of Training & Development for the City of Toronto. He went on to co-found The Alliance for Converging Technologies, and is an adjunct faculty member at two business schools; in 2003 he formed the Transcend Strategy Group.

CONTEXT

- Advises on how to establish competitive business models based around digital media.
- Explains the different business frameworks and their characteristics: agoras, aggregations, value chains, alliances, and distributive networks.
- Discusses how business webs manage to cut through traditional barriers to enable buyers and sellers to meet, negotiate, and assign value to goods freely.
- Examines different types of industry and how they can benefit from business webs, from retailers who can aggregate, to banks that use distributive networks.
- Features companies that have transformed their industries through innovative changes in the way they talk to their customers.
- Discusses the economic impact of the internet on existing business models.

IMPACT

- Works through the systems of suppliers, distributors, services providers, infrastructure providers, and customers that use the internet for business communications and transactions.
- Considers how to build on the business models that use the internet to best advantage, to help create effective business networks.
- Describes new digital marketing innovations such as immediate shopping, improved customer relationships, better communication, price discovery, and experience rather than product.
- Shows how different companies can add knowledge and value to a product or service through innovation, enhancement, cost reduction, or customization.

QUOTATIONS

"Think of customers as part of your b-web and prospects as candidates for relationships, not as markets for your products."

"B-webs are the mechanisms for the accumulation of digital capital, the knowledge- and relationship-based currency of the new economy."

"If the corporation embodied capital in the industrial age, then the b-web does the same for the digital economy."

▸▸ MORE INFO

See Also:

- *Being Digital.* An introduction to the information revolution from one of its early visionaries. (p. 1226)
- *Information Rules: A Strategic Guide to the Network Economy.* An accessible guide to marketing and distributing in the network economy (p. 1277)
- E-Commerce (pp. 1508–1510)

"Think of customers as part of your b-web and prospects as candidates for relationships, not as markets for your products."

     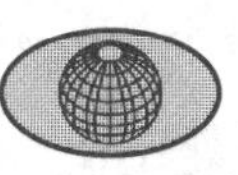   

The Essence of Financial Management

DAVID R. MYDDELTON (1995)

WHY READ IT?

- Useful as a reference for managers wanting to improve their knowledge and skills in financial management.
- Examines the current issues and topics of financial management and corporate finance.
- Takes a practical approach to the subject, showing how to implement the concepts and techniques discussed.

GETTING STARTED

The Essence of Financial Management provides a comprehensive overview of the theory and main techniques of financial management. It assists managers new to financial matters, and gives them a full understanding of the financial objectives of a business, the environment in which the business operates, and fundamental accounting concepts such as the balance sheet, P&L statement, and return on investment.

AUTHOR

David R. Myddelton taught at the School of Management, Cranfield University, for 40 years until retirement in 2005, having been Professor of Finance and Accounting since 1972. He is now the Emeritus Professor of Finance and Accounting at the School.

CONTEXT

- Aimed at those new to finance who are looking for a sound and useful primer on the topic.
- Defines the basic concepts and themes involved in financial management.
- Explores the problems financial managers face on a daily basis: time, uncertainty, liquidity, inflation, tax planning, and other critical issues.
- Includes a useful glossary.

IMPACT

- Presents all the financial management techniques a non-financial manager needs to know.
- Presents the four basic accounting concepts: going concern, accruals, consistency, and prudence.
- Advises on how to treat the components of interest rates, from term structure to short-termism.
- Details the uses of cash, working capital, and capital project appraisal.
- Examines borrowing and the cost of debt, and the main impact areas.
- Gives an overview on shares, the markets, and modern portfolio theory.
- Discusses corporate finance, including cost of capital, gearing, and mergers.

QUOTATIONS

"Both cash and profit matter, but people sometimes wonder whether one matters more than the other."

"Equity investors cannot avoid market risk, which stems from the uncertainties of the whole economy."

"Any change in the future prospects of a business—especially its future earnings or the risks involved—may affect a share's present market value."

▸▸ MORE INFO

Book:

Brigham, Eugene F., and Joel F. Houston. *Fundamentals of Financial Management.* Hinsdale, IL: Dryden Press, 1978. Focused guidance for teaching undergraduate corporate finance, with an online student assessment and tutorial resource.

See Also:

- *The Finance Manual for Non-Financial Managers.* Gives a good grounding in corporate finance for the beginner. (p. 1255)
- *Financial Control for Non-Financial Managers.* A practical and easy guide to financial control. (p. 1257)

"Both cash and profit matter, but people sometimes wonder whether one matters more than the other."

  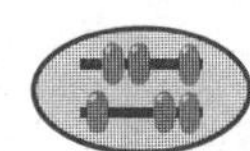   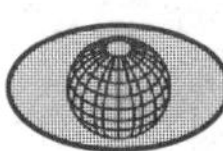   

The EVA Challenge: Implementing Value-Added Change in an Organization

JOEL M. STERN and JOHN S. SHIELY (2001)

WHY READ IT?

- The co-founder of the EVA concept explains how it can be used for measuring a company's true profitability and providing a strategy for enhancing corporate and shareholder wealth.
- Shows how to customize EVA initiatives for different types of organization, to improve corporate economic value by focusing on corporate, financial, and market performance.
- Compares EVA with other performance measures and financial management systems, and presents the benefits of knowing how value can be best created and maintained

GETTING STARTED

The EVA Challenge is an introductory overview on the benefits of using Economic Value Added to measure corporate performance, and increase shareholder value. It is a means to alter organizational priorities and behavior, and acts as a basis for incentive compensation, and unity between management actions and shareholder needs. It was created as an alternative to the Generally Accepted Accounting Procedures (GAAP), and has been utilized by many large companies to improve shareholder value.

AUTHORS

Joel M. Stern is Managing Partner of Stern Stewart & Co., and currently serves on the faculties of five graduate business schools. He is a writer, and a columnist for the *Sunday Times* of London.

John S. Shiely is President of Briggs & Stratton. He began his career as a tax accountant at Arthur Andersen & Co., before working as a lawyer with Hughes Hubbard & Reed and Allen-Bradley/ Rockwell Automation.

CONTEXT

- Presents a completely new way for companies to value and measure their performance, drawing on strategy, management, accounting, finance, and economics, to attain a tailored model of EVA implementation.
- Analyzes how GAAP-based corporate reporting rules were designed to protect lenders by depicting a company's liquidation value, making it a conservative and inaccurate picture of financial strength.
- Argues that EVA is ideal for knowledge-based companies making heavy infrastructure investments today for any anticipated return later.
- Proposes that an EVA program must have the full backing of the management board.

IMPACT

- Covers all stages of EVA, including strategy development, organizational design, training, and incentive compensation.
- Shows that to get the most out of EVA, companies should install all of its systems—measurement, management, and incentive.
- Explains why the opportunity cost of capital has been miscalculated, due to the split between ownership and control, and traditional accounting measurements being mis-applied.
- Discusses how EVA can improve the accuracy of corporate reporting by more accurately reflecting the value of intangible assets.

QUOTATIONS

"EVA is the profit that remains after deducting the cost of the capital invested to generate that profit."

"EVA is simple and easy enough for non-financial types to grasp and to apply."

"EVA is the prime mover of shareholder value."

▸▸ MORE INFO

Books:

Ehrbar, Al. *EVA: The Real Key to Creating Wealth.* New York: Wiley, 1998. A senior VP of Stern Stewart outlines the applications and benefits that can be gained by employing EVA.

Grant, James L. *Foundations of Economic Value Added.* New Hope, PA: Frank J. Fabozzi Associates, 1997. Examines the role of economic profit analysis in the process of wealth creation.

Young, S. David. *EVA and Value-Based Management: A Practical Guide to Implementation.* New York: McGraw-Hill, 2001. Looks at how to implement both EVA and VBM successfully.

"EVA is the profit that remains after deducting the cost of the capital invested to generate that profit."

  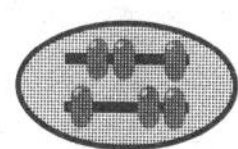   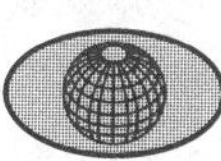 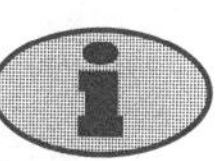 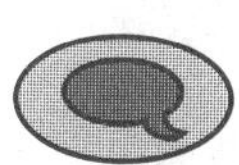 

Extraordinary Popular Delusions and the Madness of Crowds

CHARLES MACKAY (1841)

WHY READ IT?

- Examines the psychology of crowds and mass mania throughout history, including many of the classic scams, financial bubbles, mass hysteria, and deceptions that have characterized the business world and beyond.
- At once a gripping thriller and fascinating historical document, the book discusses the underlying processes that lead markets into boom-and-bust cycles that still occur today.
- Considers why people form into irrational groups when they engage in collective action.

GETTING STARTED

Extraordinary Popular Delusions and the Madness of Crowds is a seminal work in the development of understanding crowd psychology. It provides an overview of the great financial manias and irrational behavior in other areas of life, focusing on the fads, delusions, crazes, panics, and buying binges that originally arise from seemingly rational ideas. It is often cited as the best book ever written about market psychology.

AUTHOR

Charles Mackay (1814–1889) was a Scottish journalist, poet, author, and songwriter. He worked on *The Morning Chronicle*, and then was editor of *The Glasgow Argus*. He moved to London to work on *The Illustrated London News*, becoming its editor in 1852. He was also a correspondent for *The Times* during the American Civil War.

CONTEXT

- Describes in detail what drove a range of infamous financial manias, focusing on John Law's Mississippi Scheme, the South Sea Bubble, and the tulip mania of the 17th century.
- Shows how the Mississippi Company bubble was created by issuing new shares in the company and printing private banknotes as part of a plan to restructure France's national debt. But with nothing solid to support the price, the shares eventually collapsed.
- Discusses how speculation around the South Sea Bubble was encouraged by the early success of investors in the Mississippi scheme.
- Was the first book to analyze the famous case of tulip mania in The Netherlands, recounting the astounding prices fetched by tulip bulbs due to speculative hysteria.
- Examines other instances of mass hysteria and delusion, including the witch mania in New England, the Crusades, alchemy, the philosopher's stone, the prophecies of Nostradamus, the Rosicrucians, and millennialism.

IMPACT

- Lays bare crowd psychology and motivation, and how the cycle of boom and bust is helped by the provision of easy credit with the intention of maintaining a boom.
- Shows how history repeats itself, with destructive consequences, but that busts can be avoided by understanding the patterns involved and the greed that promotes mass panics in business and finance, politics, and superstitions.
- Discusses the nature of bubbles and the conditions needed to bring them about, and how they act as a method for transferring wealth from the many to the few.

QUOTATIONS

"Men, it has been well said, think in herds; it will be seen that they go mad in herds, while they only recover their senses slowly, and one by one."

"Money, again, has often been a cause of the delusion of the multitudes. Sober nations have all at once become desperate gamblers, and risked almost their existence upon the turn of a piece of paper."

"Of all the offspring of Time, Error is the most ancient, and is so old and familiar an acquaintance, that Truth, when discovered, comes upon most of us like an intruder, and meets the intruder's welcome."

▸▸ MORE INFO

Books:

Chancellor, Edward. *Devil Take the Hindmost: A History of Financial Speculation.* New York: Farrar, Straus, Giroux, 1999. Examines the development of stock exchanges and speculative manias through history; it also coves some of the same topics, such as tulip mania and the Mississippi and South Sea bubbles.

Le Bon, Gustave. *The Crowd: A Study of the Popular Mind.* London: Ernest Benn, 1896. Le Bon's classic book on mass psychology. Written in an entertaining style, it was an influence on Freud's work on group behavior.

"Men, it has been well said, think in herds; it will be seen that they go mad in herds, while they only recover their senses slowly, and one by one."

  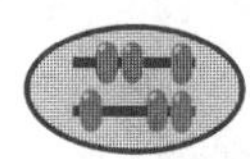   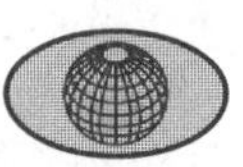   

A Farewell to Alms: A Brief Economic History of the World

GREGORY CLARK (2007)

WHY READ IT?

- Attempts to answer why some countries have become developed and comparatively rich while others have not and remain poor.
- Finds that income inequality between societies has increased in recent years.
- Proposes the theory that social evolution explains economic growth, and that stability and security were essential to the development of a thriving economy.

GETTING STARTED

A Farewell to Alms aims to uncover the laws underlying human history through quantitative research, and explain the unbalanced nature of economic development.

It looks at why some parts of the world are rich and others poor, and why the industrial revolution occurred in 18th century England. Clark suggests that culture and a gradual improvement in economic rigor explains the differences.

AUTHOR

Gregory Clark (b. 1957) is Professor of Economics and Chair of the economics department at the University of California, Davis. His main research is on long-run economic growth and the wealth of nations; he teaches undergraduate and graduate world economic history, and helps organize the economic history seminar.

CONTEXT

- Argues that, throughout history, population was at equilibrium—whenever technological improvements increased productivity, the result was not better living conditions, but higher population.
- Explains that the rich had twice as many offspring as the poor, which meant that the skills and behaviors of the rich seeped down to eventually trigger the industrial revolution.
- In the past, he notes that markets were much less regulated; property rights were more secure, and there was more balance on the return on human capital.
- Finds that cultural differences were shaped by selective pressures that people experience differently from each other.

IMPACT

- Argues against current thinking that industrialization happened because of improved institutional stability.
- Finds that the average person in 1800 was no better off in terms of life expectancy and stature than the average person in 100,000 BC.
- Challenges the belief in the superiority of free markets and the faith in the equality of mankind.
- Considers that the poor can be helped by outside assistance only through a radical change in the way that things are structured.

QUOTATIONS

"Though the book is about economics, we shall see that in the long run economic institutions, psychology, culture, politics, and sociology are deeply interwoven."

"The gap in incomes between countries is of the order of 50:1. There walk the earth now both the richest people who ever lived and the poorest."

"Money will buy happiness, but that happiness is transferred from someone else, not added to the common pool."

➤➤ MORE INFO

Books:

Landes, David S. *The Wealth and Poverty of Nations: Why Some Are So Rich and Some So Poor*. New York: W. W. Norton, 1998. Considers the growing gulf between rich and poor.

Pomeranz, Kenneth. *The Great Divergence: China, Europe, and the Making of the Modern World Economy*. Princeton, NJ: Princeton University Press, 2000. A similar treatment examining the divergence in economies.

See Also:

The Wealth of Nations. One of the founders of modern economics examines growth and early market capitalism. (p. 1333)

"Though the book is about economics, we shall see that in the long run economic institutions, psychology, culture, politics, and sociology are deeply interwoven."

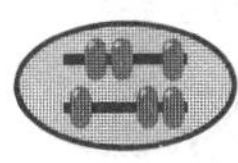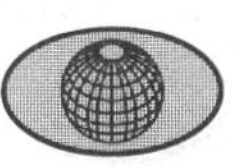

FIASCO: The Inside Story of a Wall Street Trader

FRANK PARTNOY (1997)

WHY READ IT?

- This is an insider's account of working as a derivatives salesman at Morgan Stanley in the 1990s.
- It was the first book to examine the derivatives trading industry in detail, and it warned of the dangers of buying and selling products so complex that many of the traders did not understand them.
- Tells the story behind many of the best-known derivatives fiascos, including Orange County, Barings, and Procter & Gamble, where collectively billions of dollars were lost.

GETTING STARTED

FIASCO tells the story of the author's time in the financial jungle of Wall Street and of his experience at Morgan Stanley as a young derivatives salesman. He was taught how to buy and sell billions of dollars worth of derivative securities, many of which were so complex that even the traders didn't understand them properly. The book acts as an introduction to derivatives on a practical level, examines some of the most infamous fiascos and the largely unregulated market in derivatives products, and criticizes the whole field of financial investments.

AUTHOR

Frank Partnoy is Professor of Law at the University of San Diego. Prior to that, he worked as an investment banker at Credit Suisse First Boston and Morgan Stanley in New York, and as an attorney at Covington & Burling in Washington, DC.

CONTEXT

- Takes the reader through the author's time on Wall Street, most of which was spent in Morgan Stanley's high-profile derivatives group.
- Discusses the little-known world of structuring, marketing, and selling derivatives, and the macho attitudes and fierce competition within the investment banks.
- Exposes the contempt that the salesmen had for their clients, and the lack of ethics in an industry that was awash with money.
- Provides insights into the types of exotic products being structured by the investment banks, and the reasons for doing so, making them understandable for a nonspecialist reader.

IMPACT

- Provides an insider's record of the financial world in New York and Tokyo during the 1990s, and analyzes the losses suffered as a result of misguided betting in the derivatives market.
- Tells the story through the characters he worked with, accompanied by vivid descriptions of the derivatives transactions his firm once thrived on.
- Discusses the trader mentality, working terminology, and aggressive approach to selling that was integral to how the salesmen operated and how the investment banks drive their performance.
- Provides real-life examples of biased and self-aggrandizing behavior in the major investment banks.
- Examines the thriving practice of "off-balance-sheet" derivative speculation.

QUOTATIONS

"What lessons did I draw from my experience selling derivatives? I believe derivatives are the most recent example in the history of finance: Wall Street bilks Main St."

"Wall Street has made, and continues to make, a huge amount of money on derivatives by trickery or deceit."

"Derivatives remain unseen, yet ubiquitous. Time bombs are ticking away, concealed in the underbelly of our investment portfolios."

▸▸ MORE INFO

Books:

Partnoy, Frank. *Infectious Greed: How Deceit and Risk Corrupted the Financial Markets*. New York: Times Books, 2003. The sequel to *FIASCO*, it demonstrates how companies have hidden their exposure to risk from shareholders and manipulated the markets.

Stewart, James B. *Den of Thieves*. New York: Simon & Schuster, 1991. Tells the story behind the biggest insider-trading ring in Wall Street history during the 1980s.

See Also:

Liar's Poker: Rising Through the Wreckage on Wall Street. An entertaining and revealing book that is also an insider's view of finance but discusses the technical side of trading in less detail. (p. 1288)

"What lessons did I draw from my experience selling derivatives? I believe derivatives are the most recent example in the history of finance: Wall Street bilks Main St."

   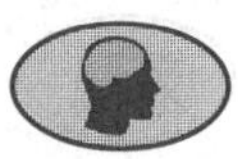  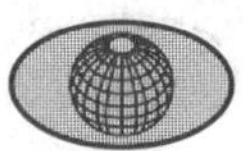   

Finance

ZVI BODIE and ROBERT C. MERTON (2000)

WHY READ IT?

- Works through all the main topics of corporate finance, as well as ranging into other topics, giving the book a broader scope than usual for such textbooks.
- Focuses on practical financial decision-making and applied finance.
- Aimed at MBA and undergraduate students and business professionals, using an integrated approach to teach the basics of finance.

GETTING STARTED

Two leading finance academics provide an overarching and focused approach to the teaching of finance that will be of use to students on different levels, and teachers needing a practical guide that covers all the specifics of the subject.

Finance encompasses all the main subfields of finance—corporate finance, investments, financial institutions and markets—within a single unifying conceptual framework, to provide a book that works as a self-study guide or a textbook that instructs on all the main concepts of finance.

AUTHORS

Zvi Bodie (b. 1943) is Professor of Finance and Economics at Boston University School of Management. He has served on the finance faculties at Harvard Business School and Sloan School of Management, and is a member of the Pension Research Council at the Wharton School.

Robert C. Merton (b. 1944) is a Professor at the Harvard Business School. He previously served on the finance faculty of Sloan School of Management, and is a Senior Fellow of the International Association of Financial Engineers. He is a past president of the American Finance Association, and a member of the National Academy of Sciences. Dr Merton received the Nobel Prize in Economic Sciences in 1997.

CONTEXT

- Published after rigorous development, input, and review from hundreds of colleagues teaching introductory finance courses.
- As a teaching resource, the text organizes the key principles of finance into three analytical silos: optimization over time, asset valuation, and risk management.
- Using a full array of learning features, including examples, concept questions, special-interest boxes, end of chapter problems, an instructor's manual, a set of spreadsheet templates, and an accompanying CD that includes a spreadsheet modeling handbook.
- Provides a useful overview of resource allocation over time under conditions of uncertainty.

IMPACT

- Encompasses all the subfields of finance within a single unifying framework and incorporates international material.
- Tries to change the way finance is taught in business schools, to incorporate other key topics not normally covered.
- Sets out the basic principles of the discipline, from defining what finance is to complex portfolio theory, then applies them to a wide variety of situations.
- Integrates all the main concepts throughout.
- Useful for non-finance specialists, as well as those interested in business and personal finance.

QUOTATIONS

"Finance as a scientific discipline is the study of how to allocate scarce resources over time under conditions of uncertainty."

"A basic tenet of finance is that the ultimate function of the system is to satisfy people's consumption preferences."

"Asset prices and interest rates provide critical signals to managers of firms in their selection of investment projects and financing arrangements."

▸▸ MORE INFO

Book:

Ross, Stephen A., Randolph W. Westerfield, and Jeffrey Jaffe. *Corporate Finance*. St. Louis: Times/Mirror/Mosby College Publishing, 1988. Examines the fundamentals of the subject in an integrated manner.

See Also:

Robert Merton (p. 1176)

Corporate Financial Management. A comprehensive introductory-level text. (p. 1241)

Principles of Corporate Finance. The main textbook on corporate finance. (p. 1312)

"Finance as a scientific discipline is the study of how to allocate scarce resources over time under conditions of uncertainty."

  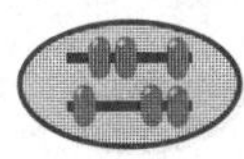   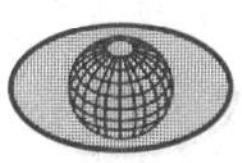   

The Finance Manual for Non-Financial Managers: The Power to Make Confident Financial Decisions

PAUL MCKOEN and LEO GOUGH (1996)

WHY READ IT?

- Information and advice on both core and new financial skills for the non-financial manager.
- Gives a full explanation of the financial tools, terms, techniques, and strategies necessary for successful management.
- Experienced finance experts bring their expertise to explaining the inner mysteries of the corporate finance world.

GETTING STARTED

The Finance Manual for Non-Financial Managers educates non-financial managers and business people of any ability in business finance. Discusses the full range of financial terms, including pricing, costing analysis, corporate taxation, and organizational control.

AUTHORS

Paul McKoen is Finance Director for Vertex and a Fellow of the Chartered Institute of Management Accountants. He was previously with Ford Motor Company in a range of management positions.

Leo Gough is an experienced financial journalist who has written many books on finance and investment, and edits a number of investment newsletters on emerging markets and technology stocks.

CONTEXT

- Written for non-financial managers who need to be able to successfully use and control financial information and processes.
- Provides the beginner with the necessary information to get them started, and the more experienced with some of the technical skills to complete their management toolkit.
- Works step-by-step through the complexities of the profit and loss account and the balance sheet.
- Enables the non-financial professional to use the same tools as an accountant.

IMPACT

- Helps the manager to fully understand the financial implications of their decisions.
- Combines well-presented ideas and information with examples, case studies, fast-track tips, and checklists.
- Examines risk analysis and strategic company acquisitions from a financial framework.
- Integrates with the Management Charter Initiative standards.

QUOTATIONS

"For budgets to be fully effective, managers at all levels need to understand and agree with them."

"Pricing requires a good knowledge of financial analysis techniques as well as a thorough knowledge of the market place."

"Strategic and market risks must be understood fully in order that plans can be developed to keep the company moving forward."

▸▸ MORE INFO

Books:

Fitzgerald, Ray. *Business Finance for Managers: An Essential Guide to Planning, Control and Decision Making.* 3rd ed. London: Kogan Page, 2002. Practical advice for managers with little financial experience.

Ryan, Bob. *Finance and Accounting for Business.* London: Thomson Learning, 2004. Introduces financial accounting, management accounting and financial management for non-specialists.

See Also:

Financial Control for Non-Financial Managers. A practical and easy guide to financial control. (p. 1257)

"For budgets to be fully effective, managers at all levels need to understand and agree with them."

  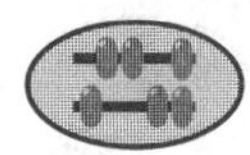   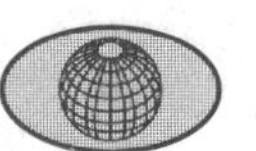 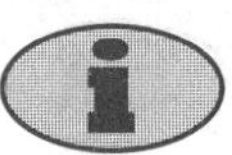  

Financial Accounting and Reporting

BARRY ELLIOTT and JAMIE ELLIOTT (12th ed 2008, originally 1993)

WHY READ IT?

- Offers clear and well-structured analysis of the main issues in financial accounting and reporting.
- Includes extensive coverage of International Accounting Standards (IASs) and International Financial Reporting Standards (IFRSs), and uses the latest International Accounting Standards as a framework.
- Examines the underlying tension between theory and practice, and analyzes the use of company accounts.

GETTING STARTED

Financial Accounting and Reporting provides you with the necessary knowledge and skills to understand and apply current financial reporting methods, as well as the relevant financial accounting standards. It is a comprehensive text for university students studying the subject, as well as the industry professional, and includes numerous exercises, varying in level of difficulty.

AUTHORS

Barry Elliott is a training consultant; he has extensive teaching experience and as an external examiner at all levels of professional education.

Jamie Elliott is a Director with Deloitte & Touche. Prior to this he was a University Lecturer, and then an Assistant Professor on MBA and executive programs at the London Business School.

CONTEXT

- Discusses, in detail, income and asset value measurement systems, the regulatory framework, balance sheets, consolidated accounts, how to interpret financial accounts, and the issue of accountability.
- Gives you the tools to critically appraise the underlying accounting concepts and financial reporting methods.
- Focuses on financial accounting, reporting, and analysis modules for second and final-year undergraduate courses in accounting, business studies, MBAs, specialist MSc courses, and professional courses that prepare for professional accountancy examinations.
- Outlines recent developments in corporate governance by regulators prompted by accounting scandals and stakeholder activism.

IMPACT

- Provides an overview of UK accounting standards, as well as covering International Financial Reporting Standards, and International Accounting Standards.
- Uses practical applications and illustrations taken from real-world international company reports and accounts.
- Discusses the dynamics between those who prepare financial reports, stakeholders, auditors, academic accountants, and standard setters.

QUOTATIONS

"The accountant needs to be skilled in identifying the information that is needed and conveying its implication and meaning to the user."

"To be useful, the financial information. . .needs to be ***comparable*** *over time and between companies and* ***understandable****."*

"Corporate governance guidelines are developed so that it can be seen whether the directors are maximising returns to shareholders, the business risk is set at a reasonable level, that a director or a board of directors do not become dominant to the detriment of the shareholders, and that the remuneration of the directors is reasonable."

▸▸ MORE INFO

Books:

Alexander, David, and Anne Britton. *Financial Reporting: The Theoretical and Regulatory Framework*. London: Chapman and Hall, 1993. Combines financial accounting theory with a detailed examination of the legal and regulatory framework of accounting.

Moscove, Stephen A., Mark G. Simkin, and Nancy A. Bagranoff. *Core Concepts of Accounting Information Systems.* New York: Wiley, 1997. Offers concise and user-friendly coverage of the key topics.

Stolowy, Hervé, and Michel J. Lebas. *Corporate Financial Reporting: A Global Perspective.* London: Thomson Learning, 2002. Introduces financial accounting for business students.

"The accountant needs to be skilled in identifying the information that is needed and conveying its implication and meaning to the user."

   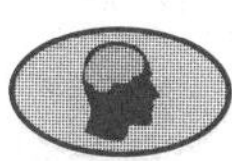  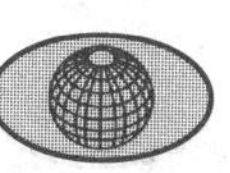 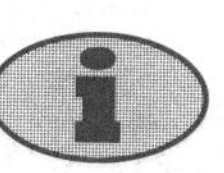  

Financial Control for Non-Financial Managers

DAVID IRWIN (1995)

WHY READ IT?

- Aimed at managers new to financial responsibility, guiding them on how to understand and use the figures at their disposal to control their businesses.
- Explains the inner workings of financial planning, and how to develop effective budgets and forecasts.
- Demonstrates how effective financial control helps the management of the whole business.

GETTING STARTED

Financial Control for Non-Financial Managers provides practical guidelines for building a successful financial strategy and solving any major financial problems that your business may face. It explains in understandable language the main financial concepts and provides tools for enhancing your effectiveness as a business manager. The book is focused on helping business managers who have financial responsibility but little experience of accounting.

AUTHOR

David Irwin (b. 1955) is a consultant and a non-executive Chairman of Cobweb Information. He is also a member of the Investment Committee and a non-executive member of the Board of Oxfam's Enterprise Development Programme, and was previously founder and Chief Executive of the Small Business Service.

CONTEXT

- Covers creating and analyzing income statements, balance sheets, and cash flow statements; establishing and managing realistic operating budgets; selecting profitable projects or activities; calculating budgets to achieve stated financial goals; and applying financial principles to real-world situations.
- Examines the need for financial control, how to understand the figures, how to best plan for profit, and how to exercise financial control over your business.
- Describes how to integrate financial concepts and policies into management decisions and the budgeting process.
- Shows how to apply effective analytical tools and techniques to potential strengths and weakness in the financial report.
- Suggests appropriate financial indicators for inclusion in a company's strategic objectives and planning.

IMPACT

- Shows how to provide a product or service efficiently and with quality, at an acceptable cost, and at the right time.
- Evaluates the financial viability of projects and activities through sound financial control, for managers who previously did not have the knowledge to do so.
- Explains the business cycle of plan, do, check, and act, in terms of tight financial control.
- Focuses on how good financial management allows you to successfully use the tactics, tools, and techniques that will enhance your projects and the overall business.
- Shows how a properly thought-out operating budget can improve business performance.

QUOTATIONS

"Good financial results will not arise by happy accident. They will arrive by realistic planning and tight control over expenses."

"It is essential for any business to set both long-term and short-terms objectives."

"It is important to identify what [data] is likely to be helpful for your particular circumstances, and then to use the information derived to provide effective control."

›› MORE INFO

Books:

Fitzgerald, Ray. *Business Finance for Managers: An Essential Guide to Planning, Control and Decision Making.* 3rd ed. London: Kogan Page, 2002. Practical advice for managers with little financial experience.

Pendlebury, Maurice, and Roger Groves. *Company Accounts: Analysis, Interpretation, Understanding.* London: Unwin Hyman, 1990. Provides an overview of annual reports and company accounts, and an introduction to analyzing and interpreting financial statements.

Ryan, Bob. *Finance and Accounting for Business.* London: Thomson Learning, 2004. Introduces financial accounting, management accounting, and financial management for non-specialists.

"Good financial results will not arise by happy accident. They will arrive by realistic planning and tight control over expenses."

  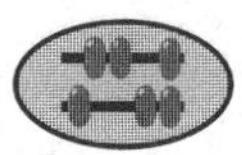   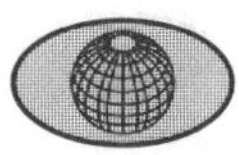   

Financial Management

JAE K. SHIM and JOEL G. SIEGEL (2nd ed 1998, originally 1986)

WHY READ IT?

- Is a comprehensive primer that provides a good depth of discussion without being too theoretical.
- Emphasizes the practical application of principles, concepts, and tools of financial management.
- Offers a complete overview of the subject using easy learning features, and can be used to reinforce course material for students.

GETTING STARTED

Financial Management, part of the popular Schaum's Outlines series of textbooks, is a basic run through of all the main aspects of current financial practice. It is used for quick learning or exam preparation, and has been fully updated to reflect changes in the rules and regulations governing corporate finance, including the Sarbanes–Oxley Act, passed in 2002.

AUTHORS

Jae K. Shim is Professor of Business Administration at California State University at Long Beach. He has written extensively, and is a recipient of the 1982 Credit Research Foundation Award for an article on financial management.

Joel G. Siegel was Professor of Finance and Accounting at Queens College of the City University of New York. He received the Outstanding Educator of America Award in 1972.

CONTEXT

- Examines the essentials of financial analysis, financial forecasting, planning, budgeting, and the management of working capital.
- Also gives a useful perspective on such critical aspects of financial management as short-term financing, risk, return, valuation, capital budgeting, cost of capital, leverage and capital structure, options, futures, mergers and acquisitions, and multinational finance.
- Discusses the Sarbanes–Oxley Act and its implications in detail, and features new sections on risk management, corporate governance, real options, and behavioral finance.

IMPACT

- Offers step-by-step solutions, additional practice problems, with answers supplied, clear explanations of financial management concepts and practices, and a comprehensive exam to test your mastery of the material.
- Helps you refresh knowledge, prepare for tests, and study quickly and effectively, without having to take the time to read lengthy textbooks.
- Presents the material in a straightforward and easy-to-understand manner, and is suited to real-world application.
- Designed for both undergraduate and graduate students, and offers a short cut to a faster understanding of key topics.
- Can be used as preparation for Certified Management Accountant and Chartered Financial Analyst exams, or for independent study.

QUOTATIONS

"The focus on wealth maximization continues in the new millennium."

"Financial statement analysis involves the calculation of various ratios."

"Financial forecasting, an essential element of planning, is the basis for budgeting activities and estimating future financing needs."

▸▸ MORE INFO

Books:

Brigham, Eugene, F., and Michael C. Erhardt. *Financial Management: Theory and Practice.* Hinsdale, IL: Dryden Press, 1977. Covers all the main financial management topics in a practical way.

Damodaran, Aswath. *Corporate Finance: Theory and Practice*. New York: Wiley, 1997. Takes a more applied approach to corporate finance than is usual, using real companies and real data throughout.

See Also:

Corporate Financial Management. A comprehensive introductory-level text. (p. 1241)

"The focus on wealth maximization continues in the new millennium."

  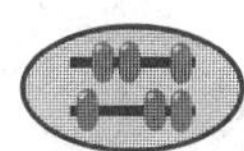   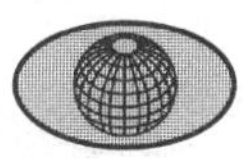   

Financial Management: An Introduction

JIM MCMENAMIN (1999)

WHY READ IT?

- Teaches the basics of accounting and finance from a UK perspective.
- Useful when integrated into a course by tutors and academics as a stand-alone module.
- Each chapter includes a content overview, an outline of the learning objectives, and review questions and exercises (with answers at the end of the book), allowing for practical learning.

GETTING STARTED

Financial Management is primarily aimed at undergraduates and postgraduates studying the topic as part of a wider course. However, it may also be used by professionals and managers to gain a better understanding and appreciation of the role financial management plays within the business world. This book focuses on strategic and tactical elements, as well as operational, and is split into seven parts dealing with the core concepts and scope of financial management, strategic decision-making, and financial planning.

AUTHOR

Jim McMenamin was a Lecturer in Financial Management at the University of Ulster, and is the author of several financial books.

CONTEXT

- Aims to provide practical information for use in a general business or management career.
- Includes key contemporary features such as corporate governance, ethics, and stakeholder theory.
- Offers a modular structure that follows a model of the financial process allowing the reader to relate and understand concepts, techniques, and theories.
- Appropriate for use as a teaching text by tutors of undergraduate and postgraduate courses.
- Focused on financial management within the United Kingdom.

IMPACT

- This is a teaching text aimed at providing students with an understanding of the role of financial management and the impact it has on business.
- Emphasizes the need for accurate financial information to allow for sound and practical decision-making.
- Shows the different aspects of financial management and how the process is put into practice.
- Includes self-assessment sections and activities within each chapter to allow practical learning.

QUOTATIONS

"...financial management does not exist in isolation but is an integral part of the general management of any organisation."

"Virtually all individuals and organisations...are in some way involved in financial management."

"The critical activity of the financial management process is that of financial decision-making, specifically decisions aimed at creating maximum value for the owners of the business."

▶▶ MORE INFO

Book:

Atrill, Peter, and Eddie McLaney. *Financial Management for Non-Specialists.* London: Prentice Hall, 1997. Introduces the basic principles and underlying concepts of accounting and finance.

See Also:

Financial Accounting and Reporting. Now in its 12th edition, this market-leading book is suitable for both students and professionals, and examines International Accounting Standards and International Financial Reporting Standards. (p. 1256)

"...financial management does not exist in isolation but is an integral part of the general management of any organisation."

  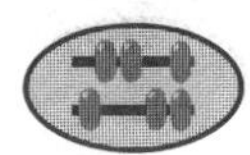   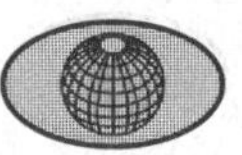   

Financial Management for the Small Business

COLIN BARROW (1984)

WHY READ IT?

- Designed to assist with the basics of business finance for the managers of small businesses.
- Focuses on key areas, informing on financial statements, financial analysis, business plans, and budgets.
- Gives advice on successful financial planning and control, and how to operate a small business from a solid financial platform.

GETTING STARTED

Financial Management for the Small Business provides an introduction to financial management, aimed primarily at those who have little experience with business accounts. As the most common cause of business failure is poor financial control due to an ignorance of business finance, it is essential to have a sound knowledge of the basics of financial management; this book gives that grounding in a practical and focused way.

AUTHOR

Colin Barrow was Head of the Enterprise Group at Cranfield School of Management for many years. He is the author of many business books, and was previously in industry before teaching at Stirling University, and being a Visiting Professor at Suffolk University, Boston.

CONTEXT

- Provides advice on proper financial planning and control, making it an important resource for both existing small businesses and entrepreneurs considering launching one.
- Helps the beginner become financially literate, and have the tools to undertake all the standard financial operations of a business.
- Covers the essentials of financial management such as balance sheets, P&L accounts, cash flow, control of working capital and fixed assets, costs, pricing and profit decisions, budgeting and bookkeeping, improving performance, and writing and presenting business plans.

IMPACT

- Focuses on business planning and budgeting, a vital area of finance for businesses looking to launch or those wanting to expand.
- Helps to clarify difficult terms and concepts for those who find business finance confusing.
- Reinforces essential points through the use of questions within each section, and includes a glossary of key accounting terms.

QUOTATIONS

"The first steps towards an understanding of finance are the most difficult."

"All methods of financing have important implications for your tax and financial position."

"While bad luck plays a part in some failures, a lack of reliable financial information plays a part in most."

▸▸ MORE INFO

Books:

Barrow, Colin. *The Business Plan Workbook.* London: Kogan Page, 2005. A guide to the processes and procedures required to put together a successful business plan.

Wilson, Peter. *The Barclays Guide to Financial Management for the Small Business.* Oxford: Blackwell, 1990. Advice for small businesses wanting to improve their understanding of financial and management accounts.

See Also:

i Small and Growing Businesses (pp. 1729–1734)

"The first steps towards an understanding of finance are the most difficult."

  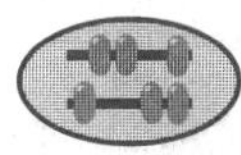   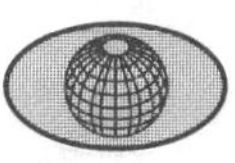  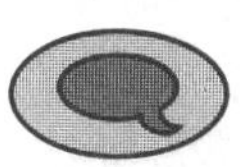 

Financial Strategy: Adding Stakeholder Value

JANETTE RUTTERFORD (ED) (1998)

WHY READ IT?

- An edited collection of writing from key figures in the business strategy and financial planning community.
- Outlines the major ways in which financial strategy can add value to a business, especially in the areas of investment, performance, value, risk management, and governance.
- Can be used as course material for MBA and advanced undergraduate students of financial strategy and financial management, but also of benefit for finance professionals.

GETTING STARTED

Financial Strategy is a collection of writing from some of the leading thinkers in financial strategy; with an emphasis on added value for organizations, each chapter looks at different ways to ensure this, particularly through investment, financing, and risk management. It also covers the debate on corporate governance and performance measurement, and focuses on the place of financial strategy in the modern business.

EDITOR

Janette Rutterford is Professor of Financial Management at the Open University Business School, having previously worked in corporate finance and investment.

CONTEXT

- Reflects the recent developments in financial strategy, which have added value to organizations, and gives a useful overview of best practice.
- Discusses innovations such as financial restructuring, the role of real options, financial engineering, and economic value added, and their impact on business strategy.
- Examines how derivatives can be used to alter the risk-return profile for risks such as currency, interest rate, or credit, to suit organizational preferences.

IMPACT

- Focuses on decision-making as a pivotal factor in business success—investment, financing, and risk management decisions.
- Shows how performance measurement is critical to successful strategic planning—cash flows, regulatory standardization to ensure compatibility of financial reporting, and financial performance measures.
- Examines the changed relationship between accounting and finance within the organizational structure.
- Discusses the application of financial strategy to organizations in the public and private sectors internationally.
- Looks at how choosing the right capital structure can add value, regardless of production or marketing decisions.
- Addresses issues relevant to UK and US-listed companies, as well as an international audience.

QUOTATIONS

"It has become clear that financial strategy on its own can have a major impact on organisations."

"Future changes to [risk management] practices seem inevitable if only because it is naïve to believe that current systems have eradicated the potential for any future financial calamities."

"The more emphasis that the financial markets place on earnings. . .the more pressure there is on managers to deliver the expected performance."

▸▸ MORE INFO

Books:

Pike, Richard, and Bill Neale. *Corporate Finance and Investment: Decisions and Strategies.* London: Prentice Hall, 1993. Takes a practical approach to key concepts and techniques on a broad range of contemporary issues in corporate finance.

Stern, Joel N., and Donald H. Chew, Jr (eds). *The Revolution in Corporate Finance.* Oxford: Blackwell, 1986. Although this textbook of collected writings has a similar structure, it is focused less on shareholder value than the practical implications of recent theoretical advances.

See Also:

Corporate Financial Management. A comprehensive introductory-level text with a practical focus. (p. 1241)

"It has become clear that financial strategy on its own can have a major impact on organisations."

  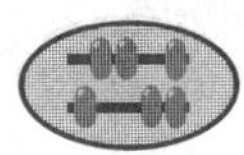   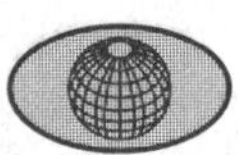   

The Financial Times Handbook of Financial Management

STEVE ROBINSON (1995)

WHY READ IT?

- For the business professional who is lacking a basic knowledge of financial concepts and tools.
- Provides essential guidance for the manager's toolkit, to help them achieve financial objectives in their work.
- Summarizes the role of finance in key international business issues, enabling the manager to make the right business decisions.

GETTING STARTED

The Financial Times Handbook of Financial Management helps you understand financial ideas and terms used by financial professionals and bankers. It brings a greater understanding of the dynamics of business and how companies measure and report, and gives insight into enhancing shareholder value through sound financial principles.

AUTHOR

Steve Robinson (b. 1943) is Head of Open Executive Programmes, School of Growth, Innovation and Enterprise, Henley Management College. He joined Henley in 2002 after 14 years at Ashridge Management College, the last seven as MBA Director. He is also a business consultant.

CONTEXT

- Examines the key financial elements of the business world, from starting a company, to undertaking a business valuation or financial appraisal of a forthcoming project.
- Uses clear language to explain complex terms, and illustrate the main issues through recent case examples of how companies have handled key areas of financial management.
- Looks at other critical elements of business financing, funding, and borrowing, offering practical guidance.
- Gives a framework for decision-making based on sound financial principles, such as completing financial analyses, and carrying out project appraisals and valuations.
- Shows how to measure business performance and examines the use of key financial data.
- Provides insight into accounting and market measures, as well as how to best manage assets and liabilities.

IMPACT

- Presents a synopsis of finance as a refresher or thorough grounding for non-specialists
- Shows how to manage operational financial decisions, such as pricing, outsourcing, and profitability analysis.
- Details how to manage money internationally, and covers currency risk.
- Contains useful case studies that highlight the impact of financial decisions on a company's operations.
- Examines the multi-disciplinary role of finance within a corporate framework.
- Helps with an appreciation of the relationship between financial markets and other markets.

QUOTATIONS

"Comprehensive analysis of business performance must include both absolute and relationship numbers to enable comparison with competition and industry standards."

"Strategy defines the broad direction of the business, operational tactics determine the precise route and pace."

"Much of the financial information available to investors concentrates on the past, yet returns will only come in the future."

▸▸ MORE INFO

Books:

Brigham, Eugene F., and Joel F. Houston. *Fundamentals of Financial Management.* Hinsdale, IL: Dryden Press, 1978. An introductory guide to corporate finance and financial management.

Emery, Douglas R., and John D. Finnerty. *Corporate Financial Management.* London: Prentice Hall International, 1997. Connects theory and practice, with many useful examples from the corporate world.

See Also:

Corporate Financial Management. A comprehensive introductory-level text. (p. 1241)

"Comprehensive analysis of business performance must include both absolute and relationship numbers to enable comparison with competition and industry standards."

   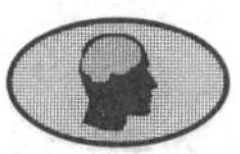  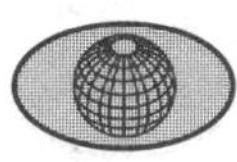   

Fooled by Randomness: The Hidden Role of Chance in Life and in the Markets

NASSIM NICHOLAS TALEB (2004)

WHY READ IT?

- The author is a professional trader and mathematics professor who wants to change how we think about risk, probability, and random events.
- A readable account of the tendency to explain random events as due to cause and effect rather than chance.
- Considers the real nature of success and failure among traders, and compares this to other professions, where skill and practice bring improvement and success.

GETTING STARTED

Fooled by Randomness examines what randomness means in practical terms and why human beings are so prone to mistake luck for skill. It argues that we shouldn't attribute success to skill alone, and that it is also wrong to assume intelligence is a necessary condition for wealth. We get an excellent insight into the role of probability in the markets as well as in daily life, and the role that randomness plays in practically everything we do.

AUTHOR

Nassim Nicholas Taleb (b. 1960) is Professor of Marketing at London Business School, Adjunct Professor of Mathematics at the Courant Institute of Mathematical Sciences, New York University, and on the affiliated faculty of Wharton School Financial Institutions Center. He previously held senior positions at major investment banks.

CONTEXT

- Distils all Taleb's empirical thoughts on the nature of chance, through statistics, probability, philosophy, trading, economics, pop culture, classical literature, and psychology.
- Considers that traders are successful due to statistics and good fortune, rather than skill, and compares this unfavorably with other professions. Examines why attributing causes to explain events is a basic human instinct, driven by the need for control and not being at the mercy of chance. Argues against the prevalent feeling that if something has happened before, then it will necessarily happen again.
- Claims that we should ignore much of the information we are normally exposed to, and that investment advice from any source has no value.
- Gives advice on successful investing, based on not chasing fads, or looking at your investments too often, and being open to both sides of any argument.

IMPACT

- Considers how we have lost the distinction between noise and signal: noise (market volatility) is mistaken for signal (predictable responses), so that luck is mistaken for skill.
- Shows disdain and frustration at the abuse of statistics and logic by experts.
- Proposes that the human mind is just not made to understand randomness. Provides insights into the world of quantitative finance that also hold true for the wider world.
- Presents a framework for what to expect when speculating, and avoiding self-delusion and common mistakes.
- Examines the concept of alternate outcomes and alternate histories, especially for extreme events.

QUOTATIONS

"We underestimate the share of randomness in just about everything."

"Mild success can be explainable by skills and labor. Wild success is attributable to variance."

"Mixing forecast and prophecy is symptomatic of randomness-foolishness."

MORE INFO

Website:

There is a concise summary of the book at the author's website: www.fooledbyrandomness.com

See Also:

- *Against the Gods: The Remarkable Story of Risk.* An excellent and readable summary of the development of risk management through the 20th Century. (p. 1215)
- *The Black Swan: The Impact of the Highly Improbable.* His latest book on extreme events, which has become a bestseller. (p. 1227)
- *The (Mis)behaviour of Markets: A Fractal View of Risk, Ruin and Reward.* Examines how financial markets really work, by looking at price movement and models. (p. 1298)

"We underestimate the share of randomness in just about everything."

     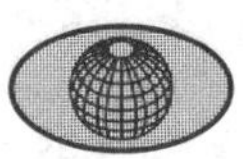 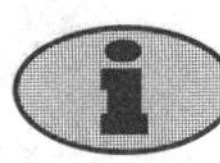  

Foundations of Multinational Financial Management

ALAN C. SHAPIRO and ATULYA SARIN (6th ed 2008, originally 1991)

WHY READ IT?

- A focused and practically oriented textbook that examines real-life financial management decision-making in an international context.
- Provide a clear strategy for understanding the impact of financial management processes on business operations.
- Demystifies and simplifies the subject in a clear conceptual framework that helps learning.

GETTING STARTED

Foundations of Multinational Financial Management explores all the main traditional areas of corporate finance, including working capital management, capital budgeting, cost of capital, and financial structure, from the perspective of a multinational corporation. It lays out the key concepts and processes in an understandable style, which has made it a core text for dedicated courses on financial management in business schools.

AUTHORS

Alan C. Shapiro is Professor of Banking and Finance at Marshall School of Business, University of Southern California. He was previously an Assistant Professor at Wharton, and has been a Visiting Professor at Yale and a number of business schools.

Atulya Sarin is Professor of Finance in the Leavey School of Business at Santa Clara University. He publishes in leading finance, economics, and management journals and served on the editorial board of the *Journal of Financial Research.*

CONTEXT

- Examines international financial management as a logical extension of the principles and valuation framework provided by domestic corporate financial management.
- Treats international financial management as part of a natural development of the principles learned on foundational courses in financial management.
- Focuses on the macroeconomic issues of how a multinational firm operates.
- This is a concise version of the author's bestselling textbook, *Multinational Financial Management.*

IMPACT

- Provides insight on how being a multinational firm creates business difference, and how to take advantage of this in practical terms.
- Offers a variety of real-life examples, both numerical and institutional, that demonstrate the use of financial analysis and reasoning in solving international financial problems.
- Provides a clear conceptual framework for analyzing key financial decisions and the particular characteristics of multinational firms.
- Emphasizes broad concepts and practices rather than providing extensive theoretical or quantitative material.
- Discusses how the United States is gaining competitive advantage from the new era of price and service competition, deregulation, increased technology, wider corporate control, mergers and leveraged buy-outs, and global standardization.

QUOTATIONS

"Companies today operate within a global marketplace and can ignore this fact only at their peril."

"The true multinational corporation is characterized more by its state of mind than by the size and worldwide dispersion of its assets."

"In a world in which change is the rule and not the exception, the key to international competitiveness is the ability of management to adjust to change and volatility at an ever faster rate."

▸▸ MORE INFO

Books:

Desai, Mihir A. *International Finance: A Casebook.* Hoboken, NJ: Wiley, 2007. Offers a unique perspective on making financial decisions in a globalizing world, based on how firm financing and investment decisions must adapt to circumstances in the international marketplace.

Shapiro, Alan C. *Multinational Financial Management.* 8th ed. Hoboken, NJ: Wiley, 2006. Shapiro's full textbook, which gives an overview of how to make sound financial decisions in the multinational firm.

See Also:

Multinational Business Finance. Examines the complexities and specific issues of international finance, with a focus on managerial responsibilities. (p. 1301)

International Management (pp. 1650–1652)

"Companies today operate within a global marketplace and can ignore this fact only at their peril."

     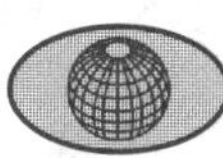   

Frank Wood's Business Accounting, Volumes 1 and 2

FRANK WOOD and ALAN SANGSTER (11th ed 2008, originally 1967)

WHY READ IT?

- Provides a clear and straightforward introduction to the core techniques and skills required to fully understand the foundations of financial and business accounting.
- Each key topic is reinforced through worked examples and self-assessment material to help monitor progress and learning.
- Useful for anyone new to accountancy and bookkeeping, or those who wish to update their bookkeeping skills.

GETTING STARTED

Frank Wood's Business Accounting is one of the most popular textbooks on accounting and bookkeeping in business, and is used on a wide variety of courses, both at secondary and tertiary level, and for those studying for professional qualifications. Now in its 11th edition, it is a good primer to all the key principles and processes of the discipline.

AUTHORS

Frank Wood (1926–2000) was a best-selling author of books on accountancy and bookkeeping. As well as being a highly successful author, publisher, and teacher, he used his influence to raise money for charity.

Alan Sangster is Professor of Accounting at the Open University Business School, and was previously at Queen's University of Belfast, the University of Aberdeen, and the University of Strathclyde.

CONTEXT

- Comprehensive analysis of how to prepare accounts for sole traders, partnerships, companies, and groups, with a detailed examination of the key differences.
- Provides a primer to accounting—clear and well laid out, with plenty of useful examples.
- Takes a universal approach that is useful to students from a broad range of educational backgrounds.
- Bases its teaching around the information needed to accord with the criteria and requirements established by various prominent examination boards.
- Contains real exam questions at the end of every chapter, with exam guidance to help students prepare better and improve their results.

IMPACT

- Intensive coverage of the underlying techniques and skills of accounting.
- Provides a full understanding of double-entry bookkeeping and the preparation of accounting information.
- Features hundreds of review questions, activities and multiple-choice questions, so that students can judge how well they understand, and can apply what they are learning.
- Follows a logical progression and focused activities designed to reinforce an understanding of key concepts.

QUOTATIONS

"Accounting involves deciding what amounts of money are, were, or will be involved in transactions (often buying and selling transactions) and then organising the information obtained and presenting it in a way that is useful for decision making."

"The primary objective of accounting is to provide information for decision making."

"Management accounting produces the financial forecasts that guide planning."

▸▸ MORE INFO

Books:

Drury, Colin. *Management Accounting for Business Decisions*. London: International Thomson Business Press, 1997. Comprehensive and detailed text that uses real-world examples to good effect.

Kimmel, Paul D., Jerry J. Weygandt, and Donald E. Kieso. *Financial Accounting: Tools for Business Decision Making*. New York: Wiley, 1998. Teaches fundamental accounting procedures with an emphasis on the relationship between the procedure and fundamental accounting.

Website:

There is a regularly updated companion website at www.pearsoned.co.uk/wood, which includes further self-test questions and accounting standards updates.

See Also:

Financial Accounting and Reporting. Well-structured and comprehensive treatment, that provides a strong balance between theory and practice. (p. 1256)

Accounting (pp. 1550–1553)

"Accounting involves deciding what amounts of money are, were, or will be involved in transactions (often buying and selling transactions) and then organising the information obtained and presenting it in a way that is useful for decision making."

  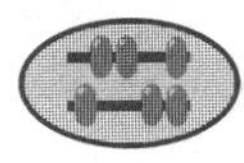   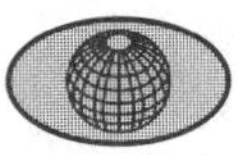   

Freakonomics: A Rogue Economist Explores the Hidden Side of Everything

STEVEN D. LEVITT and STEPHEN J. DUBNER (2005)

WHY READ IT?

- Urges the reader to look deeper into the underlying causes of everyday events.
- Examines the use of incentives and how they drive human behavior.
- Provides insight into a range of issues such as why crack dealers live with their parents, and trends in baby names.

GETTING STARTED

Freakonomics examines a number of everyday events, and challenges the received wisdom and myths of each through detailed analysis of underlying data. It brings economics (and statistics) into the mainstream through an accessible look at a wide range of behaviors and social issues. Combining economics lite and unorthodoxy to uncover new truths, and show that nothing is what it seems and that assumptions can be dangerous.

AUTHORS

Steven D. Levitt teaches economics at the University of Chicago. His economic research areas include themes such as guns and game shows and have triggered debate in media and academic circles. He recently received the American Economic Association's John Bates Clark Medal.

Stephen J. Dubner writes for the *New York Times* and the *New Yorker*, and is the author of *Turbulent Souls* and *Confessions of a Hero-Worshipper*.

CONTEXT

- Avoids being academic in style, but is based on stringent research and data analysis.
- Proposes that we should challenge orthodoxy through questioning the underlying causes of typical aspects of social events.
- It goes beyond correlations to seek causation, for instance attributing the dramatic fall of US crime rates in the 1990s to greater access to abortion 20 years earlier, rather than traditional explanations like improved policing methods.
- Examines other off-beat questions such as why the Ku Klux Klan are like a group of real estate agents, what makes a perfect parent, where have all the criminals gone, and what is the link between schoolteachers and sumo wrestlers.

IMPACT

- Brings economic analysis and what economists actually do to a wider audience.
- Explains that the main interest of economists is the study of incentives, causes, and behavior, illustrating this with many reader-friendly examples.

QUOTATIONS

"If morality represents an ideal world, then economics represents the actual world."

"It wasn't gun control or a strong economy or new police strategies that finally blunted the American crime wave. It was, among other factors, the reality that the pool of potential criminals had dramatically shrunk."

"The gulf between the information that we publicly proclaim and the information that we know to be true is often vast. (Or, put a more familiar way: we say one thing and do another)."

▸▸ MORE INFO

Book:

Landsburg, Steven E. *The Armchair Economist: Economics and Everyday Life.* New York: Free Press, 1993. Key issues in economics explained in a humorous way.

Website:

Book website, including reviews, articles and a blog: freakonomicsbooks.com

See Also:

- *The Tipping Point: How Little Things Can Make a Big Difference.* Groundbreaking book on the phenomenon of social epidemics, the underlying reasons that make things change. (p. 1327)
- *The Undercover Economist.* Looks at how economic principles can explain everyday situations. (p. 1329)

"If morality represents an ideal world, then economics represents the actual world."

  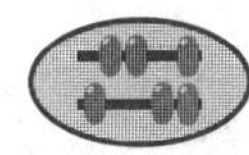 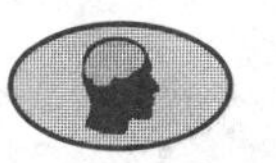  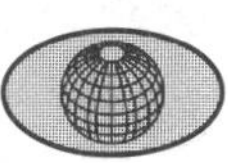   

The Functions of the Executive

CHESTER I. BARNARD (1938)

WHY READ IT?

- Creates a complete (and moral) management theory that still has a great deal of relevance to modern management principles.
- Highlights the importance of communication, and argues that everyone in the organization needs to know what and where the communications channels are.
- Defines a business as a cooperative system where all groups in the system have to be satisfied.

GETTING STARTED

The Functions of the Executive collects together Barnard's lectures on management, which strike a chord with contemporary management thinking. His ideas on communication and the importance of short lines of communication remain relevant. In arguing that there was a morality to management, Barnard played an important part in broadening the managerial role from one simply of measurement, control, and supervision, to one also concerned with more abstract notions, such as values.

AUTHOR

Chester I. Barnard (1886–1961) was Head of the Pennsylvania and then New Jersey Bell companies. During World War II he was President of the United Service Organizations for National Defense and Director of the National War Fund. He later became a US representative on the Atomic Energy Committee.

CONTEXT

- Asserts that an organization allows people to achieve what they could not achieve as individuals, as they and their actions are interconnected.
- Discusses how successful organizations need short and direct lines of communication to enable everyone to be tied into the organizations' objectives.
- Argues that it is vital that chief executives nurture the goals and values of the organization, and translate them into action, rather than just use meaningless jargon.
- Sees the distinguishing mark of executive responsibility as being able to cope with moral dilemmas, and suppress their personal desires for immediate praise and material gratification.

IMPACT

- Rejects the concept of an organization as comprising a definite group of people whose behavior is coordinated only because they are linked together by some explicit goal or goals.
- Proposes that only when the employees have faith in the purpose of the organization and the competence of the leadership will they be able to act effectively.
- Shows how management is about defining the best purpose of a business, and adapting this purpose to the opportunities and threats it faces.

QUOTATIONS

"In a community, all acts of individuals and of organizations are directly or indirectly interconnected and interdependent."

"The essential functions are, first, to provide the system of communications; second, to promote the securing of essential efforts; and third, to formulate and define purpose."

▸▸ MORE INFO

Books:

Drucker, Peter. *The Practice of Management*. New York: Harper, 1954. A classic of management thinking, it was way ahead of its time in examining how the role of the manager was developing during the 20th Century, and laying the foundations for the idea of the knowledge worker.

Peters, Thomas J. *In Search of Excellence: Lessons from America's Best-Run Companies*. New York: Harper & Row, 1982. One of the most influential business books ever published, it presented many key concepts of organizational behavior and managerial theory.

"In a community, all acts of individuals and of organizations are directly or indirectly interconnected and interdependent."

  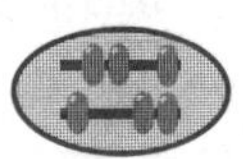   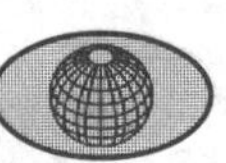   

Futures, Options, and Swaps

ROBERT W. KOLB (1994)

WHY READ IT?

- A comprehensive educational tool for those wanting a detailed grounding in these complex derivatives.
- Explains difficult concepts that the student needs to understand in this very technical subject area.
- Useful for non-quantitative capital market professionals who are looking for a broad introduction to derivative instruments.

GETTING STARTED

Futures, Options, and Swaps is a widely used textbook that provides a practical introduction to derivatives and their use in the capital markets. It analyzes basic theory to aid understanding of the role that financial engineering plays in pricing and hedging these instruments, and also examines the basic principles of finance engineering.

AUTHOR

Robert W. Kolb (b. 1949) is Professor of Finance and Chair of Applied Ethics at the business school, Loyola University. He has held appointments at the University of Florida, Emory University, University of Miami, and was Professor of Finance and Assistant Dean for Business and Society at the University of Colorado at Boulder.

CONTEXT

- Provides a practical orientation, covering futures, options, and swaps from the perspective of implementation.
- A clear and readable account of all the key topics, providing learning material in a concise style that doesn't miss any of the main steps.
- Balances introductory analysis with more advanced treatment, and offers coverage of several major types of financial derivatives and their use.
- Makes no assumption about the knowledge level of the reader.

IMPACT

- Offers commentary throughout as to why one might use a certain financial instrument for a given reason or problem, making it a thorough, practical resource.
- Is the only non-AIMR text that is required reading for all three CFA exams.
- Preferred by many over Hull (see p. 1307), for those whose background is not mathematics, engineering, or hard sciences. Although technical, it avoids complex terminology.
- Includes advanced formulas in the latter part of the book if you want to get deeper.

QUOTATIONS

"While financial derivatives are undeniably risky in some applications, they also provide a powerful tool for limiting risks that individuals and firms face in the ordinary conduct of their business."

"Large pension funds and investment banking firms trade options in conjunction with stock and bond portfolios to control risk and capture additional profits."

"In the short time since they started trading. . ., options have helped to revolutionize finance."

▸▸ MORE INFO

Books:

Chisholm, Andrew. *Derivatives Demystified: A Step-by-Step Guide to Forwards, Futures, Swaps and Options.* Chichester, UK: Wiley, 2004. Explains derivative products in a straightforward way, focusing on applications and intuitive explanations.

Wilmott, Paul. *Paul Wilmott on Quantitative Finance.* Chichester, UK: Wiley, 2000. Introduces fundamental mathematical tools and financial concepts to help understand quantitative finance, portfolio management, and derivatives.

See Also:

Options, Futures, and Other Derivatives. The renowned "bible" on the subject, which is in-depth and technical. (p. 1307)

Derivatives and Quantitative Finance (pp. 1618–1621)

"While financial derivatives are undeniably risky in some applications, they also provide a powerful tool for limiting risks that individuals and firms face in the ordinary conduct of their business."

     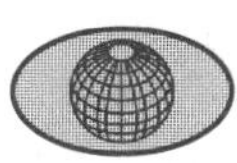   

The Global Financial System: A Functional Perspective

DWIGHT B. CRANE, KENNETH A. FROOT, SCOTT P. MASON, ANDRÉ F. PEROLD, ROBERT C. MERTON, ZVI BODIE, ERIK R. SIRRI, and PETER TUFANO (1995)

WHY READ IT?

- A collection of eight essays written by top finance academics and thinkers at Harvard Business School.
- Places a focus on how the performance of the financial system is evolving, and the implications this has for the future.
- Examines how each of the main functions of the financial system meets a basic organizational need.

GETTING STARTED

In *The Global Financial System* leading financial scholars present essays examining the performance of the global financial systems, and how a focus on functional and strategic perspectives can inform on the changes underway in the financial system. Covering such critical functions as the financial environment, payment systems, pooling, resource transfer, and the allocation of risk, it takes a critical but analytical overview of how to impose best practice on the financial system.

AUTHORS

Dwight B. Crane was a member of the Finance Faculty at Harvard Business School, and was also previously Senior Associate Dean, and the Chair of the School's European Research Initiative. Prior to joining the faculty, he was an economist and a Director at Mellon Bank.

Kenneth A. Froot is Professor of Business Administration at Harvard University's Graduate School of Business Administration. He is a founding Partner of FDO Partners and State Street Associates, and was a consultant to the IMF, the World Bank, and the Federal Reserve.

Scott P. Mason (1948–1998) was Professor of Finance and Banking at Harvard Business School, and was the Chair of the finance department. He was previously with Goldman Sachs, and went on to become President and Chief Executive Officer of Investment Technology Group.

André F. Perold is Professor of Finance and Banking at the Harvard Business School, and served as Senior Associate Dean. He is also a founder and Chair of the Investment Committee of HighVista Strategies.

Robert C. Merton (b. 1944) is a Professor at Harvard Business School, a Senior Fellow of the International Association of Financial Engineers, a past President of the American Finance Association, and a member of the National Academy of Sciences; he was awarded the Nobel Memorial Prize in Economic Sciences in 1997.

Zvi Bodie is Professor of Management at Boston University, and has served on the finance faculty at the Harvard Business School and MIT Sloan School of Management. He has published widely on pensions and investment strategy.

Erik R. Sirri is the Director of Market Regulation at the Securities and Exchange Commission. He is currently on leave as Professor of Finance at Babson College, and was previously at Harvard Business School, worked at NASA, and was a Governor of the Boston Stock Exchange.

Peter Tufano is Professor of Financial Management at Harvard Business School, and has served as a Senior Associate Dean at the school. He was previously Director of Faculty Development and Head of the Finance Unit at HBS.

CONTEXT

- Provides a collection of cutting-edge essays that examine the performance of the basic financial functions underlying global financial systems.
- Discusses the impact of key elements such as payments, lending and investing, pooling funds, allocating risk, providing information, and dealing with incentive issues, to evaluate the new financial environment.
- Looks at the challenges facing managers of financial institutions and public policy officials.
- Examines the needs of government as user, producer, and overseer of the financial system.
- Looks at why corporations hedge by themselves, and also how asymmetric information affects financial instruments.

IMPACT

- Identifies the fundamental changes occurring in the basic functions of financial systems, and presents insights about the future development of the financial institutions and markets.
- Considers the dynamics of financial change and the design of financial products and services.
- Discusses how the rapidly changing geopolitical, regulatory, and technological boundaries have rendered strategic and public policy decision-making increasingly difficult and complex.
- Includes recommendations on issues of public policy and regulation.

QUOTATIONS

"Institutional form follows function."

"Even when the outward identities are the same, the functions financial institutions perform often differ dramatically."

"The basics functions performed by the financial system are stable across time and place, but the institutional ways that they are performed are not."

▸▸ MORE INFO

Books:

Abdelal, Rawi. *Capital Rules: The Construction of Global Finance.* Cambridge, MA: Harvard University Press, 2007. Focuses on the lowering of national borders to movement of capital, and its impact on the international economy.

Allen, Larry. *The Global Financial System: 1750–2000.* London: Reaktion Books, 2001. Traces the history and development of global finance.

Valdez, Stephen. *An Introduction to Global Financial Markets.* Basingstoke, UK: Macmillan Business, 1997. Provides a broad introduction to the financial markets.

"Institutional form follows function."

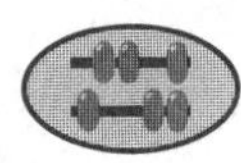

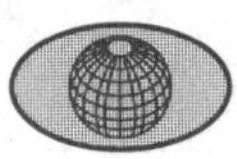

Globalization and Its Discontents

JOSEPH STIGLITZ (2002)

WHY READ IT?

- One of the main authorities on the global economy and international finance examines the impact of economic policies and development in an easy-to-understand manner.
- Focuses on the real impact that economic theory has on people's lives.
- Offers solutions as well as criticisms, rather than just being an attack on the effects of globalization.

GETTING STARTED

Globalization and Its Discontents considers the functions and powers of the main institutions that govern globalization—the IMF, the World Bank, and the World Trade Organization—along with the ramifications of their policies. Examines the effect of global economics on the lives of people in developing countries, concluding that pursuit of free trade in these countries has been disastrous, and explaining why.

AUTHOR

Joseph Stiglitz (b. 1943) is a Professor at Columbia University, and has taught at Yale, Princeton, Stanford, MIT, and Oxford. He has been Chairman of the Council of Economic Advisers, and Chief Economist and Senior Vice-President of the World Bank. He was awarded the Nobel Prize in Economics in 1971.

CONTEXT

- Informs on Stiglitz's tenure as an economic adviser to the White House and the Chief Economist at the World Bank.
- Analyzes the original roles of the IMF, the World Bank, and the WTO, and how they do not live up to their mandates.
- Examines how the critical transition of a country to a market economy is being carried out, and demands more focus on improving the infrastructure before it happens.

IMPACT

- Believes that globalization can be a positive force against poverty, but only if the IMF, World Bank, and WTO become more transparent and improve how they operate.
- Argues that standard IMF policy has tended to approach countries in financial crises with the same rather crude economics as that used on Wall Street.
- Regards the IMF as being unhelpful to poorer countries, making them rein in during recessions, and assisting international lenders to get their money when there is the chance a developing country might go bankrupt.
- Explains that the removal of barriers to free trade and the closer integration of national economics has the potential to enrich everyone in the world, if only it is managed better.
- Examines the interactions between exchange rates, exchange rate support, inflation, liquidity, government deficits, and monetary and structural reform.

QUOTATIONS

"[At the World Bank] decisions were made on the basis of what seemed a curious blend of ideology and bad economics, dogma that sometimes seemed to be thinly veiling special interests."

"Those who vilify globalization too often overlook its benefits."

"[The IMF has changed] from serving global economic interests to serving the interests of global finance."

▸▸ MORE INFO

Books:

Kuttner, Robert. *Economic Illusion: False Choices between Prosperity and Social Justice.* Boston, MA: Houghton Mifflin, 1984. An examination of the fit between capitalism and political democracy.

McMillan, John. *Reinventing the Bazaar: A Natural History of Markets.* New York: Norton, 2002. An accessible description of markets, as well as an explanation of their underlying mechanisms.

Monbiot, George. *Manifesto for a New World Order.* New York: New Press, 2004. Examines the flaws on the left and right, and offers instead a radical vision of a new global democratic order that transcends the traditional nation-state.

See Also:

Joseph Stiglitz (p. 1198)
International Finance (pp. 1647–1649)

"[At the World Bank] decisions were made on the basis of what seemed a curious blend of ideology and bad economics, dogma that sometimes seemed to be thinly veiling special interests."

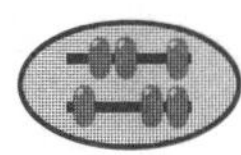

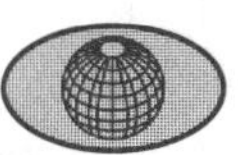

Governance and Risk: An Analytical Handbook for Investors, Managers, Directors, and Stakeholders

GEORGE DALLAS (ED) (2004)

WHY READ IT?

- A team of expert authors offer a global overview on corporate governance trends, and how integral risk has become for any organization.
- Shows how to assess the complex issues of governance and risk management that have been highlighted by scandals and corporate collapses, and the increasing need for a rigorous governance system.
- Examines the key aspects of corporate governance and risk practices, and links them to practical performance steps that companies should follow.

GETTING STARTED

Governance and Risk has been written by a group of experts, mostly affiliated with Standard & Poor's, including senior members from their Governance Services group, to offer a comprehensive state-of-play report. Aimed at analysts and business professionals, it provides a clear analytical framework for examining and benchmarking governance standards in all companies, using a balanced and rational approach.

EDITOR

George Dallas is Managing Director and Global Practice Leader for Corporate Governance at Standard & Poor's, where he has also served as head of Global Emerging Markets and regional head for S&P's Ratings Services in Europe. He previously worked at Wells Fargo Bank.

CONTEXT

- Presents the analytical framework used by Standard & Poor's in its governance scoring and evaluation process for individual companies.
- Details corporate governance practices around the world, and examines the diversity of governance practices that global investors need to understand through a common analytical framework.
- Analyzes the impact of governance and risk issues from a variety of perspectives, including the economic, legal, and social.

IMPACT

- Covers all the main topics of governance and an increasingly critical set of wider themes, such as social and environmental reporting, directors' liability, and managed fund governance.
- Discusses how realistic it is to expect market participants to practice self-governance in the current financial climate, and the inherently conflicting interests within the modern corporation.
- Explores ownership structures and external influences, shareholder rights and stakeholder relations, transparency, disclosure and audit, and board structure and effectiveness.
- Argues for thinking of corporate governance as a risk factor, and provides a practical scoring methodology that helps rate a company.
- Takes a cross-disciplinary approach, setting out a framework for examining the different facets of corporate governance.

QUOTATIONS

"The development and institutionalization of corporate governance analysis is a long-term journey."

"Good governance should be rewarded, and bad governance should be punished."

"The market needs strong analytical tools and reliable benchmarks to assess governance risk."

MORE INFO

Books:

Coyle, Brian. *Risk Awareness and Corporate Governance.* Canterbury, UK: Financial World, 2002. A guide to the principles of risk awareness and management, and the requirements of corporate law and directors' responsibilities.

Monks, Robert A. G., and Nell Minow. *Corporate Governance.* 4th ed. Oxford: Blackwell, 2008. Explains the key concepts of corporate governance in a textbook format.

Shaw, John C. *Corporate Governance and Risk: A Systems Approach.* Hoboken, NJ: Wiley, 2003. Provides a framework for redesigning decision-making, risk, and governance processes.

"The development and institutionalization of corporate governance analysis is a long-term journey."

   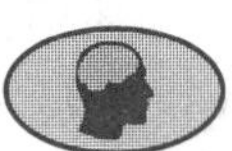  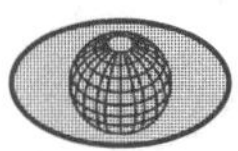   

The Great Crash, 1929

JOHN KENNETH GALBRAITH (1955)

WHY READ IT?

- Entertaining account of the market mania and resulting historic crash of 1929.
- Tells a relevant and timely story of over-investment and market frenzy, and why financial bubbles since then have always been compared to the Great Crash.
- Traces the market fluctuations of the time, showing how the crash evolved and helped ignite a full economic depression.

GETTING STARTED

The Great Crash, 1929 depicts a time of rampant speculation, record trading volumes, and assets bought not because of their value but because of a gold-rush mentality. An enjoyable read, it offers an explanation of the market dynamics during the late 1920s, and how people got caught up in the stock market frenzy that led to the 1929 crash, and how the aftermath affected the economy.

AUTHOR

John Kenneth Galbraith (1908–2006) was an influential economist and author. He was an Economics Professor at Harvard, and later became an adviser to President Kennedy, President of Americans for Democratic Action, President of the American Economic Association, and was awarded the Presidential Medal of Freedom on two occasions.

CONTEXT

- Shows the sustained mania for investment of the time in terms of crowd psychology—the investors wanted to believe that speculation would lead to great wealth.
- Shows in detail the impact of speculative enthusiasm and how it caused the market to become extremely overvalued, and that despite the losses, people kept buying for the rise.
- Details how government inaction enabled financial firms to operate in too risky and unethical a fashion.
- Explodes a few myths about the crash, such as that it was caused by a lack of available securities, and that it hugely increased the suicide rate.

IMPACT

- Explains the increase in embezzlement of the time, euphemistically called "informal financial arrangements," and how the crash impacted on some of the big names of the time.
- Details the cause of the crash as also being due to a mixture of bad income distribution, bad corporate structure, bad banking structures, and lack of economic intelligence.
- The similarities to more recent market downturns are unmistakable, from the trends toward corporate mergers and industry consolidations to the bubbles around certain sectors—investment trusts in the late 1920s and tech stocks in the late 1990s, and the current subprime and housing market problems.
- Uses the story to show why economies are not self-sustaining after all, but susceptible to supply and demand shifts.

QUOTATIONS

"As a protection against financial illusion or insanity, memory is far better than law."

"A roaring boom was in progress in the stock market and, like all booms, it had to end."

"But now, as throughout history, financial capacity and political perspicacity are inversely correlated."

▸▸ MORE INFO

Books:

Gow, Mary. *The Stock Market Crash of 1929: Dawn of the Great Depression.* Berkeley Heights, NJ: Enslow, 2003. Captures this key part of American history through firsthand accounts and quotes, and examines subsequent economic crises.

Sobel, Robert. *The Great Bull Market: Wall Street in the 1920s.* New York: Norton, 1968. An informative and enjoyable account of the times.

Williams, Andrea D. (ed). *The Essential Galbraith.* Boston, MA: Houghton Mifflin, 2001. A selection of Galbraith's writings that show how relevant he still is.

See Also:

John Kenneth Galbraith (p. 1166)

"As a protection against financial illusion or insanity, memory is far better than law."

     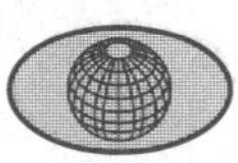   

The Gridlock Economy: How Too Much Ownership Wrecks Markets, Stops Innovation, and Costs Lives

MICHAEL HELLER (2008)

WHY READ IT?

- Analyzes how too much ownership, especially of property, is blocking economic development and innovation.
- Shows why property, whether physical or intellectual, is now broken down into such small units that it lacks full value or usefulness.
- Examines the obstructions to an efficiently working economy, and offers means to identify and resolve the difficulties brought about by gridlock.

GETTING STARTED

The Gridlock Economy considers many important social and economic problems, and shows how they are created and exacerbated by the structure of ownership and property rights. Gridlock occurs when ownership, competition, and usage are not working properly, and affects many different areas of our lives. It examines the impact of excessive property rights that create underused resources, and looks at issues such as patent rights, copyright laws, airport delays, robber barons, and rap music, and how real estate laws lead to a loss of family estates. Heller argues that all the examples he provides are part of the same problem of gridlock stifling efficiency, productivity, and innovation.

AUTHOR

Michael Heller (b. 1962) is Professor of Real Estate Law at Columbia Law School. He was previously a Fellow at the Center for Advanced Study in the Behavioral Sciences, taught at the University of Michigan Law School, UCLA, and NYU. He also worked at the World Bank.

CONTEXT

- Examines private ownership and the effect it has on the economy; it generates wealth, but it can also create gridlock if there is too much ownership in the wrong place.
- Considers the social impact of having too many competing owners, and the risks and costs of gridlock.
- Argues that when too many people own a part of a resource, cooperation can be replaced by discord, which can contribute to a loss of wealth, and problems over usage.
- Explains why gridlock doesn't have to happen, that it is a result of choices we make about our resources.
- Offers insights into how to identify gridlock, and how it can be overcome to improve the economy, identifying entrepreneurship as critical to resolving some of the problems.

IMPACT

- Describes what Heller calls the "tragedy of the anti-commons," the lack of individual property rights, that means traditional methods of ownership are blocking wealth creation in the modern economy.
- Considers the complexity of property ownership in modern economies is increasing the amount of gatekeepers, those who have to give permission for things to be done.
- Shows how this complexity is escalating the likelihood of gridlock, describing ownership conflict as similar to traffic congestion, blocking innovation.
- Provides examples of gridlock in different industries, such as why new runways aren't built to ease air travel delays, the problems of patent owners blocking pharmaceutical companies from developing a cancer cure, and why most of the cell phone broadcast spectrum isn't being used.
- Analyzes the current mortgage crisis, and how it is affected by the gridlock of loans being repackaged and sold to investors many times over, distorting ownership and making it very difficult to restructure the loans.

QUOTATIONS

"We can unlock the grid once we know where to start."

"Gridlock is a paradox. Private ownership usually increases wealth, but too much ownership has the opposite effect: it wrecks markets, stops innovation, and costs lives."

"Underuse results from mistakes and gaps in economic, legal, and social organization. It is an artifact of ownership gone awry."

▸▸ MORE INFO

Book:

Fox, Merritt B., and Michael A. Heller (eds). *Corporate Governance Lessons from Transition Economy Reforms*. Princeton, NJ: Princeton University Press, 2006. A collection of essays that highlight how corporate governance has developed in post-socialist economies.

Website:

The book's official website: www.gridlockeconomy.com

See Also:

- *Freakonomics: A Rogue Economist Explores the Hidden Side of Everything*. As in *The Gridlock Economy* and *Tipping Point*, this book examines mainstream behaviors and social issues, challenging received wisdom and myths. (p. 1266)
- *Tipping Point: How Little Things Can Make a Big Difference*. Looks at how social epidemics and trends are created in different industries, before reaching a tipping point, and have a widespread impact. Similar in that it looks at everyday problems. (p. 1327)

"We can unlock the grid once we know where to start."

   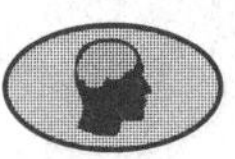  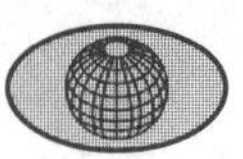   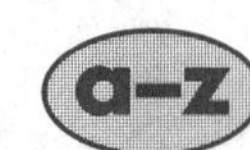

How the Stock Market Works

MICHAEL BECKET (2002)

WHY READ IT?

- Introduces the stock market, from defining shares, to all the major financial products, trading, investing, share picking, understanding company accounts, and the markets.
- Provides all the information and advice necessary to start investing in the markets, explained in simple language.
- With the current problems in the stock exchanges, it is even more important to have the correct information for trading.

GETTING STARTED

A comprehensive guide to the main aspects of the stock market, aimed at beginners. A starting point for anyone thinking about investing in shares and needing a strong overview about what is involved.

Helps the reader understand the variety of different exchanges and how to invest in them. With the ever-increasing amount of markets and products, it has become easier and cheaper to trade, but less easy to trade successfully.

AUTHOR

Michael Becket is a financial journalist who was the Daily Telegraph's small business editor for 10 years. He is currently freelancing for a number of journals and is the author of several successful books, including *An A to Z of Finance.*

CONTEXT

- This book is not just for investors, but for anyone who wishes to understand our financial system—how it works, and how we all fit into it.
- Sets out the fundamental rules and the ways that systems operate—what is being traded, how it is traded, and who does the trading.
- Explains the wide variety of different products on offer, such as shares, gilts, futures, and options.
- Cuts through the mystique with useful information for the amateur.

IMPACT

- There is still money to be made in the market, but you need essential guidance of the type provided by this book, as well as caution, common sense, and luck.
- Gives you the knowledge to ask the right questions, make better choices, and not to be fooled by the wrong guidance.
- Answers key questions on share ownership, costs, where and when to buy and sell, and how to understand financial information.

QUOTATIONS

"The money that can be released for shares depends on personal risk/reward calculations."

"The odds are way ahead of other forms of gambling, and the return is better than other forms of investment, and careful research, monitoring and evaluation can certainly reduce risks on the stock market."

"Competition among stockbrokers is. . .increasing with the number of sites on the internet rising daily, so the cost could start coming down, and with it the minimum economic investment."

▸▸ MORE INFO

Books:

Gough, Leo. *How the Stock Market Really Works: The Guerrilla Investor's Secret Handbook.* London: FT Prentice Hall, 2001. A guide to intelligent private investing.

Wyss, B. O'Neill. *Fundamentals of the Stock Market.* New York: McGraw-Hill, 2001. A practical guide to understanding the stock markets.

See Also:

Capital Markets and Stock Markets (pp. 1588–1590)

"The money that can be released for shares depends on personal risk/reward calculations."

  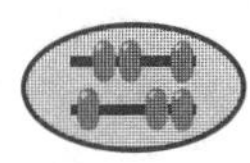 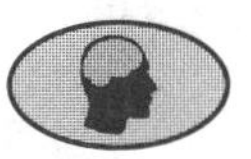  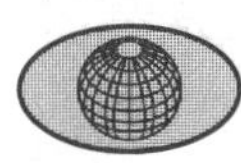   

How to Be Rich

J. PAUL GETTY (1965)

WHY READ IT?

- One of the richest men in the world gives advice on how to live with a lot of money, especially why richness is more about how you act and what your goals are.
- Recounts how Getty made his fortune, as well as providing lessons from his business life.
- Outlines his basic business principles, with practical tips on types of investments.

GETTING STARTED

How to Be Rich is a book about how to be rich, not how to get rich. It looks at the development of a particular state of mind rather than detailing a sure-fire formula for monetary acquisition. Getty felt that the whole point of becoming rich was to enhance your own life, as well as the lives of those around you.

Details Getty's hands-on and committed approach to his working life, and how he preferred to operate beside his workers and deal with problems personally.

AUTHOR

J. Paul Getty (1892–1976) was an American industrialist and Founder of the Getty Oil Company. He graduated from Oxford University with degrees in economics and political science, before working on his father's oil fields. Running his own oil company, he became a millionaire in 1916. He founded the J. Paul Getty Museum in California in 1974.

CONTEXT

- Discusses business operations and management from the viewpoint of someone who has been extremely successful.
- Useful for anybody planning to go into business, and executives rising through the ranks and those who would like to.
- Presents useful tips on how to manage and get the best out of your people and your business.
- Provides the intellectual tools for ending bad business and personal habits, and developing productive and beneficial new ones.
- Covers his thoughts on health, charity, personality, falling standards in morality and kindness, and the disappearance of art and classical music from the mainstream.

IMPACT

- Describes the characteristics of a true entrepreneur.
- Believed that there is no magic to becoming rich—you have to work hard and for yourself.
- Believed in treating employees well and encouraging them to think and act as if they were running their own company, in order to get the best out of them.
- Readily admits his failings and tries to appreciate the characteristics that promote success.

QUOTATIONS

"*'Richness' is at least as much a matter of character, of philosophy, outlook and attitude, as it is of money.*"

"*Wealth is something with which one has to learn to live—and the task is not always as simple as might be imagined.*"

"*[Those] who will make their marks in commerce, industry and finance are the ones with freewheeling imaginations and strong, highly individualistic personalities.*"

▸▸ MORE INFO

Books:

Getty, J. Paul. *As I See It: The Autobiography of J. Paul Getty*. London: W. H. Allen, 1976.

Hill, Napoleon. *Think and Grow Rich*. Meriden, CN: The Ralston Society, 1937.
A classic motivational book based on the work and lives of some of the most successful people of the industrial era, underpinned by 13 universal principles.

Kiyosaki, Robert T. *Rich Dad, Poor Dad*. Paradise Valley, AZ: TechPress, 1998. It explains how to acquire income-generating assets so that the traditional job route to wealth can be discarded.

   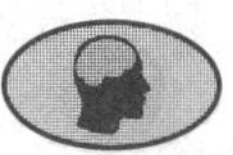  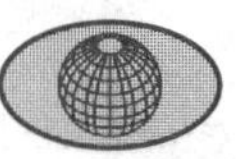   

Inefficient Markets: An Introduction to Behavioral Finance

ANDREI SHLEIFER (2000)

WHY READ IT?

- Provides a broad introduction to the current opportunities and challenges in behavioral finance, the study of how people make decisions under financial uncertainty.
- Useful for those responsible for managing money or involved in trading in the financial markets.
- Presents a model of investor sentiment regarding individual decision-making under conditions of uncertainty.

GETTING STARTED

Inefficient Markets provides the theoretical framework of modern finance theory and the efficient markets hypothesis, a key tenet in the financial markets for the last few years. Taking a new approach, it builds on the economic analysis of real-world markets, focusing on investor sentiment and limits to arbitrage.

AUTHOR

Andrei Shleifer (b. 1961) is Professor of Economics at Harvard University. After obtaining his AB and PhD, he has held a post in the Department of Economics at Harvard since 1991. In 1999, he received the John Bates Clark Medal; he is ranked among the 10 top economists in the world by IDEAS/RePEc.

CONTEXT

- Examines the three main forms of efficient markets hypothesis: technical analysis, fundamental analysis, and insider trading.
- Discusses investor sentiment, the limits of arbitrage, the closed-end fund puzzle, positive feedback investment, and both market overreaction and underreaction to news.
- Presents and evaluates models of inefficient markets that both explain the available financial data better than does the efficient markets hypothesis and generates new empirical predictions.
- Shows how investor sentiment can form a positive trading environment in which arbitrage can actually destabilize the market.
- Stresses that risky arbitrage means that it is difficult to take advantage of pervasive irrationality.

IMPACT

- Explains that arbitrage is of limited usefulness in relatively competitive markets, much less in more complicated environments.
- Observes that the assumptions of investor rationality and perfect arbitrage are contradicted by psychological and institutional evidence.
- Demonstrates the limits of arbitrage in maintaining efficient markets through a model for predicting the returns of arbitrageurs and noise traders.
- Develops a model of investor sentiment based on investors' patterns of psychological reaction.
- Admits that it is hard to prove with certainty that financial markets are or are not efficient.

QUOTATIONS

"Remarkably, the EMH does not live or die by investor rationality."

"The field of behavioral finance. . .has presented financial economics with a new body of theory, a new set of explanations of empirical regularities, as well as a new set of predictions."

"Behavioral finance has provided both theory and evidence which suggest what the deviations of security prices from fundamental values are likely to be, and why they persist over time without being eliminated by arbitrage."

➤➤ MORE INFO

Books:

Shefrin, Hersh. *Beyond Greed and Fear: Understanding Behavioral Finance and the Psychology of Investing*. Boston, MA: Harvard Business School Press, 2000. A general treatment of the subject that helps us understand the behavior behind stock selection, financial services, and corporate financial strategy.

Thaler, Richard H. *The Winner's Curse: Paradoxes and Anomalies of Economic Life.* New York: Free Press, 1992. A good introduction to behavioral finance, which challenges received wisdoms in many financial transactions.

See Also:

Advances in Behavioral Finance. Offers a wide-ranging overview of behavioral finance over the past 10 years. (p. 1214)

Behavioral Finance (pp. 1566–1567)

"Remarkably, the EMH does not live or die by investor rationality."

  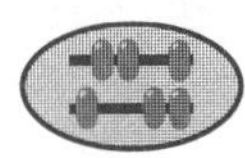   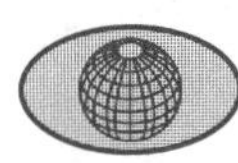   

Information Rules: A Strategic Guide to the Network Economy

CARL SHAPIRO and HAL R. VARIAN (1999)

WHY READ IT?

- An excellent primer for those entering the IT industry, business leaders wanting guidance, and those interested in the network economy.
- Get a better understanding of the information business landscape—presents techniques for competing strategically and successfully.
- Discusses the importance of economics in the new digital age, despite information not being a traditional commodity.

GETTING STARTED

Information Rules analyzes how economic systems work in conjunction with today's network economy, and offers guidelines for practical business strategies based on sound economic principles.

AUTHORS

Carl Shapiro is Professor of Business Strategy, Haas School of Business, and Department of Economics, University of California at Berkeley. From 1995 to 1996, he served as Deputy Assistant Attorney General for Economics, Antitrust Division, US Department of Justice.

Hal R. Varian is a Professor and Dean of the School of Information Management and Systems, with joint appointments at the Haas School of Business and the Department of Economics, University of California at Berkeley.

CONTEXT

- Although information has replaced industrial goods as the key driver of world markets, the economic principles that drove the old economy still apply.
- Focuses more on the underlying economic forces that determine success and failure than actual technological change.
- Considers how to market and distribute goods in the network economy, citing important examples from different industries.
- Discusses how best to deal with such issues as pricing, versioning, rights management, lock-in approaches, and information policy in the network economy.
- Describes how the new style of economy makes it possible for inventors and entrepreneurs to build a large-scale business from scratch comparatively quickly.

IMPACT

- Helps business managers develop effective strategies around information technology.
- Explains how to evaluate the consequences of pricing, protecting new versions of information products, services, and systems.
- Companies need to be able to embrace change, based on certain fundamental principles that define the exchange of goods in a free-market economy.
- Shows how to plan product lines of information goods and manage intellectual property rights.

QUOTATIONS

"Technology changes, economics laws do not."

"It is not enough to have the best product, you have to convince customers that you will win."

"You must price your information goods according to customer value, not according to your production cost."

▸▸ MORE INFO

Books:

Arthur, W. Brian. *Increasing Returns and Path Dependence in the Economy.* Ann Arbor, MI: University of Michigan Press, 1994. Discusses some key ideas such as positive feedback and increasing returns.

Kelly, Kevin. *New Rules for the New Economy: 10 Ways the Network Economy is Changing Everything.* London: Fourth Estate, 1998. Guidelines for operating in the new business environment.

Shwartz, Evan I. *Webonomics: Nine Essential Principles for Growing Your Business on the World Wide Web.* New York: Bantam Books, 1997. Quite old now, but still offers useful advice for marketing on the Internet.

Shy, Oz. *The Economics of Networked Industries.* Cambridge, UK: Cambridge University Press, 2001. Examines the latest developments in network economics.

See Also:

Information Technology (pp. 1522–1523)

     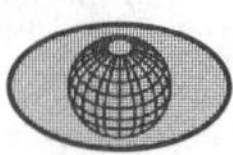   

Innovation Corrupted: The Origins and Legacy of Enron's Collapse

MALCOLM S. SALTER (2008)

WHY READ IT?

- Analyzes the collapse of Enron, and the management behavior and practices that took the company from the most lauded of its generation to bankruptcy.
- Examines how Enron's risk analysis and control system failed to counteract its management style, and why success built without ethical foundation can lead to disaster.
- Recommends actions that can be taken to prevent similar corporate breakdowns in the future, including changes to regulatory oversight, executive compensation, and performance measurement.

GETTING STARTED

Innovation Corrupted is a well-researched and analytically rigorous examination of the causes of the collapse of Enron in 2001, the largest bankruptcy in American economic history. Salter examined the technical analysis and sworn testimonies in court documents, obtained internal Enron documents, and interviewed former Enron executives and staff. He shows how Enron executives maximized opportunities for enormous personal gain, distracting them from the responsibilities of institutional integrity, sound corporate governance, and ethical working practices.

AUTHOR

Malcolm S. Salter is Professor of Business Administration, Emeritus, at the Harvard Business School, where he has been a member of the faculty since 1967. He has previously taught at the Harvard Law School and the Kennedy School of Government. He was President of Mars & Co from 1986 to 2006.

CONTEXT

- Presents a historical overview of Enron's rise, strategic successes and failures, its business model, and how its top executives managed the business.
- Discusses how warning flags were ignored both within the business and by others, who instead focused on the capital markets and profit-making.
- Analyzes why external watchdogs, such as security analysts, credit rating agencies, and regulatory authorities, failed to publicize Enron's problems.
- Looks at how Enron sold overvalued and underperforming assets off-balance-sheet, and how these complex entities managed reported earnings and minimized reported debt to support the company's credit rating and stock price.
- Recommends a private-equity model of corporate governance to help solve possible governance breakdowns in public companies, proposing that directors should adopt such a model to ensure proper oversight.

IMPACT

- Shows the impact of declining corporate ethical standards, failings at board level, and the collusion of external intermediaries in the collapse of Enron.
- Proposes practical recommendations for preventing future Enron-type disasters, including board members having a sound knowledge of the business, improved executive incentivization, and ethical discipline being instilled throughout the organization.
- Considers the collapse in terms of managerial arrogance, which led to ill-advised diversification and badly implemented administrative processes.
- Discusses why Enron's board failed to detect and prevent violations of accounting principles and rules.
- Examines the collusion of investment banks in misrepresenting the financial conditions at Enron.

QUOTATIONS

"Enron's collapse involved the corruption of a remarkable strategy of innovation."

"Before fraud at Enron there was fatal thoughtlessness and incompetence among its executives."

"Overwhelmed regulatory systems were vulnerable to manipulation and evasion—particularly at Enron's creative hands."

▸▸ MORE INFO

Book:

Swartz, Mimi, and Sherron Watkins. *Power Failure: The Inside Story of the Collapse of Enron.* New York: Doubleday, 2003. The story of the Enron accountant who first tried to alert management to the accounting fraud.

See Also:

- *The Smartest Guys in the Room: The Amazing Rise and Scandalous Fall of Enron.* A detailed exposé of Enron from two journalists; McLean was one of the first to identify problems with the market innovator. (p. 1318)
- *What Went Wrong at Enron: Everyone's Guide to the Largest Bankruptcy in US History.* Discusses the collapse of Enron in an interesting and understandable way; published not long after its bankruptcy. (p. 1334)

"Enron's collapse involved the corruption of a remarkable strategy of innovation."

  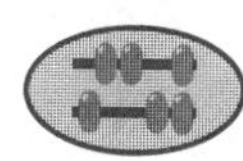   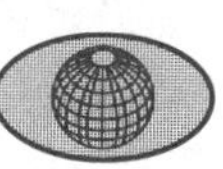   

Intellectual Capital: The New Wealth of Organizations

THOMAS A. STEWART (1997)

WHY READ IT?

- The definitive guide to understanding and managing intangible assets, from the pioneer of knowledge management.
- Shows how theories on knowledge management are valuable to any organization that wants to improve the return on its intellectual capital.
- Argues that knowledge working will change the pattern of careers in the 21st century.

GETTING STARTED

Intellectual Capital is a guide to the strategic and practical issues of identifying, capturing, and using knowledge to improve a company's competitive advantage. It explains not only why intellectual capital will be the foundation of corporate success in the future, but also offers practical guidance to companies about how to make best use of their intangible assets.

AUTHOR

Thomas A. Stewart (b. 1948) is the Editor and Managing Director of the *Harvard Business Review*. Prior to this, he was the Editorial Director of *Business 2.0*, and a member of the Board of Editors of *Fortune*. He is also a Fellow of the World Economic Forum.

CONTEXT

- Details how the emphasis has shifted from traditional capital, with financial or physical characteristics, to intangible assets and intellectual capital.
- Breaks intellectual capital down into three areas—human capital, customer capital, and structural capital—and examines the impact of each type on how a business operates.
- Argues that real value comes from capturing and deploying intellectual capital to best advantage, but that you cannot define and manage intellectual assets unless you know what you want to do with them.
- Discusses 10 key principles for managing intellectual capital: who owns it, how to manage it, how to create usable human capital, its scarcity, the place of information and knowledge, and how human, structural, and customer capital can work together.
- Shows why knowledge has become the pre-eminent economic resource and why managing it properly is an essential economic task.

IMPACT

- Discusses knowledge working and individual career paths, and how careers have become a series of gigs rather than steps.
- Looks at why project management is now important for career building, and observes that expertise is more relevant than power.
- Argues that either insiders or outsiders can perform most roles, which has an impact on how businesses are structured.
- Proposes that the fundamental career choice is not between one company and another, but between specializing and generalizing.

QUOTATIONS

"Intellectual capital is intellectual material—knowledge, information, intellectual property, experience—that can be put to use to create wealth. It is collective brainpower. It's hard to identify and harder still to deploy effectively. But once you find it and exploit it, you win."

"You cannot define and manage intellectual assets unless you know what you want to do with them."

›› MORE INFO

Books:

Davenport, Thomas H., and Laurence Prusak. *Working Knowledge. How Organizations Manage What They Know.* Boston, MA: Harvard Business School Press, 1998. Asserts that learning how to identify, manage, and foster knowledge is vital for companies who hope to compete in the global economy.

Stewart, Thomas A. *The Wealth of Knowledge: Intellectual Capital and the Twenty-First Century Organization.* New York: Currency, 2001. Emphasizes the importance of intellectual, as well as bricks and mortar and other forms of capital, in accounting for the worth of corporations.

See Also:

Knowledge Management (pp. 1664–1668)

"Intellectual capital is intellectual material—knowledge, information, intellectual property, experience—that can be put to use to create wealth. It is collective brainpower. It's hard to identify and harder still to deploy effectively. But once you find it and exploit it, you win."

  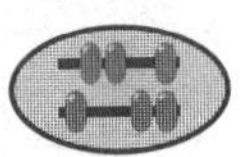   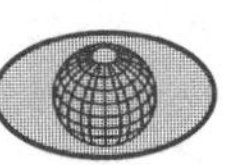  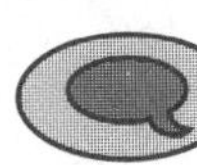 

The Intelligent Investor

BENJAMIN GRAHAM (1949)

WHY READ IT?

- Presents many of the principles of investing that the author created and taught, and which investors still use today.
- Graham was a mentor to Warren Buffett, who developed many of the methods covered in this book to make his fortune.
- Shows how to excel at making money in the stock market without taking big risks, centered round his concept of margin of safety.

GETTING STARTED

The Intelligent Investor, often described as the bible of value investing, gives a strong grounding in how to approach the stock market. Value investing helps shield investors from substantial error and teaches them to develop long-term strategies. It considers everything you need to know about investing, not only in stocks, but in business generally.

- Invest for the long-term in large, steady, straightforward businesses that adhere to certain financial criteria, but only when the market price is a bargain.
- Discusses different approaches to investing and compares defensive investing, investing using analysis, and speculating.

AUTHOR

Benjamin Graham (1894–1976) was widely recognized as the father of value investing, and his "margin of safety" concept changing the landscape of investing. He taught for nearly 30 years at Columbia University's business school, and his advocacy for financial analysis training was a catalyst for the Chartered Financial Analyst (CFA) program.

CONTEXT

- Examines the philosophy of value investing.
- Discusses the concept of margin of safety, where investments should be based on the fundamentals and be below the intrinsic value.
- Covers useful metrics for valuing a company, and states that avoiding losses is more important than making gains.

IMPACT

- Proposes that an investor should look at the market as if it were a business partner who is offering to buy you out, or sell you his interest daily.
- Introduces the idea of examining a company's stock as though you might buy the whole company.
- Advocates the use of market psychology, that by using the fear and greed of the market, you can find advantage.
- Argues strongly about looking at the returns one can expect from the market compared with a company one actively manages.
- Considers that shareholders should act more like owners and not simply submit to management practices.

QUOTATIONS

"The stock market often goes far wrong, and sometimes an alert and courageous investor can take advantage of its patent errors."

". . .to have a true investment there must be present a true margin of safety [which] can be demonstrated by figures, by persuasive reasoning, and by reference to a body of actual experience."

". . .the chief losses to investors come from the purchase of low-quality securities at times of favorable business conditions."

▸▸ MORE INFO

Books:

Arnold, Glen. *The Financial Times Guide to Investing.* London: FT Prentice Hall, 2004. An introduction to investing, and how to invest successfully.

Buffett, Warren. *The Essays of Warren Buffett: Lessons for Corporate Investors.* New York: L. Cunningham, 2001. Financial acumen from the successful protégé.

See Also:

Benjamin Graham (p. 1168)
Common Stocks and Uncommon Profits. A classic on the art of investment. (p. 1235)

"The stock market often goes far wrong, and sometimes an alert and courageous investor can take advantage of its patent errors."

  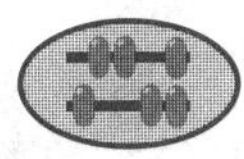 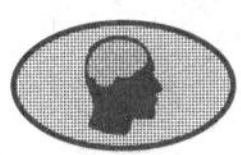  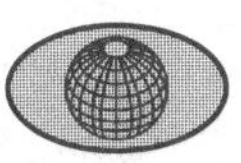   

International Financial Management

CHEOL S. EUN and BRUCE G. RESNICK (4th ed 2006, originally 1998)

WHY READ IT?

- Combines an analysis of the essential financial concepts with a practical approach to implementation.
- Offers a conceptually solid treatment of international financial topics, teaching what is necessary to become an effective global financial manager.
- Used as course material by many of the top business schools, including Wharton, Stanford, Northwestern, and INSEAD.

GETTING STARTED

International Financial Management examines the fundamentals of the macroeconomic environment. Now in its fourth edition, this textbook provides a comprehensive overview of the tools and techniques of international financial management.

AUTHOR

Cheol S. Eun is a Professor of Finance and Chair in International Finance at Georgia Institute of Technology. Before that he taught at a number of universities, received the Krowe Teaching Excellence Award at the University of Maryland, and worked as a consultant.

Bruce G. Resnick is a Professor of Management at the Babcock Graduate School of Management, Wake Forest University. He has also taught at a number of other universities, and worked as a consultant.

CONTEXT

- Provides a comprehensive overview of the financial environment in which the multinational firm and its managers functions.
- Analyzes foreign exchange management and financial management in a multinational firm.
- Looks at how to deal with exchange risk and market imperfections, using the various instruments and tools available.
- Emphasizes financial theory, rather than the usual textbook focus on business processes.

IMPACT

- Teaches how to be an effective global financial manager.
- Helps the reader have a practical understanding of the techniques necessary to work in the foreign exchange markets.
- Provides you with the requisite knowledge, and illustrative examples, rather than showing how to implement key concepts.
- Useful as a textbook that can be used as a companion to course notes, it often presents material in the form of a tutorial.
- Can be used as preparation for the CFA charter examinations, or for senior-level finance undergraduates and MBA students, as well as finance professionals needing a reference on investments.

QUOTATIONS

"We are now living in a world where all the major economic functions—consumption, production, and investment—are highly globalized. It is thus essential for financial managers to fully understand vital international dimensions of financial management."

"There is a growing consensus around the world that it is vitally important to strengthen corporate governance to protect shareholder rights, curb managerial excesses, and restore confidence in capital markets."

"The market for foreign exchange is the largest financial market in the world by virtually any standard."

▸▸ MORE INFO

Books:

Hill, Charles W. L. *International Business: Competing in the Global Marketplace.* Burr Ridge, IL: Irwin, 1994. Discusses the internationalization process, why businesses choose to go global, and the managerial implications of doing so.

Madura, Jeff. *International Finance Management.* 9th ed. Mason, OH: Thomson/South-Western, 2008. Provides a background to international finance, and focuses on the managerial aspects from a corporate perspective.

Shapiro, Alan C. *Multinational Financial Management.* 8th ed. Hoboken, NJ: Wiley, 2006. Focuses on decision-making in an international context.

See Also:

International Management (pp. 1650–1652)

"We are now living in a world where all the major economic functions—consumption, production, and investment—are highly globalized. It is thus essential for financial managers to fully understand vital international dimensions of financial management."

 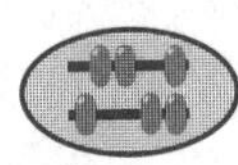   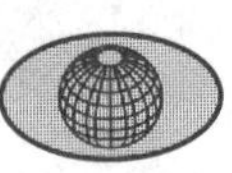   

Introduction to Accounting

PRU MARRIOTT, J. R. EDWARDS, and H. J. MELLETT (3rd ed 2002, originally 1989)

WHY READ IT?

- Provides an accessible introduction to accounting for students.
- Analyzes the basic accounting techniques and concepts and shows how to apply them in a practical way.
- Flexible learning resource that can be easily used for working on your own or in a classroom.

GETTING STARTED

Introduction to Accounting is a practical textbook for those studying accounting who need a rigorous overview and practical focus on the main aspects and standards in the accounting profession. It covers the key concepts, processes, and features for those wanting extensive analysis and a reference resource, and the guidance necessary for successful specialization on this topic.

AUTHORS

Pru Marriott is Head of the Department of Accounting, Economics and Finance at Winchester Business School. She has over 20 years experience of teaching and managing undergraduate and postgraduate accounting programmes, and is a member of the editorial board of the *Journal of Accounting Education.*

John Richard Edwards is Professor and Head of Accounting and Finance Section at the University of Cardiff, a Fellow of the Institute of Chartered Accountants in England and Wales, and an Associate of the Chartered Institute of Taxation.

Howard Mellett is Professor of Accounting at the University of Cardiff, Head of Section, and Joint Co-ordinator of the Financial Reporting and Business Communication Research Unit at the University.

CONTEXT

- Examines key topics such as accounting frameworks, balance sheets, calculating profit, the double entry system, asset valuation, partnerships, company accounts and how to understand them, decision making, and costing and budgetary control.
- Uses detailed questions, many of which have been taken from major accounting examination bodies.
- Includes recent developments in reporting financial performance and the treatment of goodwill and intangible fixed assets, and discusses issues of research and development, and regulatory updates.
- Provides fully illustrated and worked examples to help learning.

IMPACT

- Aimed at the non-specialist and those intending to specialize in accounting at undergraduate or postgraduate level.
- One of the best primers on accounting, which has been used extensively on courses as a key educational tool.
- Examines the various stages in the accounting and decision-making processes to show the reader how to successfully integrate accounting techniques into corporate performance and strategic development.

QUOTATIONS

"The financial aspects of human enterprise cannot be ignored; the activities of almost any undertaking have financial consequences that should be measured and controlled."

"Accounting statements should contain only those financial facts that are material, or relevant, to the decision being taken by the recipient of the report."

MORE INFO

Books:

Ainsworth, Penne, and Dan Deines. *Introduction to Accounting: An Integrated Approach.* Chicago, IL: Irwin, 1997. Takes an unusual approach by integrating financial and managerial accounting, and focusing on the business process.

Black, Geoff. *Introduction to Accounting and Finance.* Harlow, UK: FT Prentice Hall, 2005. A student textbook that is applied, and includes interactivity for learning.

Horngren, Charles T. *Introduction to Financial Accounting.* Englewood Cliffs, NJ: Prentice Hall, 1981. Combines financial statement analysis with coverage of cash flows for MBA introductory courses or higher-level undergraduate courses.

Website:

Solutions website: www.sagepub.co.uk/resources/marriott

See Also:

Accounting (pp. 1550–1553)

"The financial aspects of human enterprise cannot be ignored; the activities of almost any undertaking have financial consequences that should be measured and controlled."

  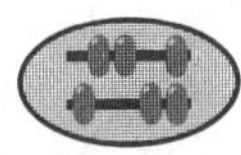   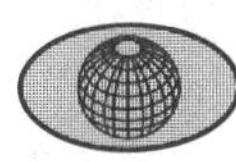   

An Introduction to Islamic Finance Theory and Practice

ZAMIR IQBAL and ABBAS MIRAKHOR (2007)

WHY READ IT?

- Two of the best-known authorities in Islamic economics, finance, and banking provide an insightful and comprehensive introduction to Islamic financial principles and practice.
- Offers a concise background on the development of Islamic finance, and a practical overview of the main products and processes.
- Reflects on the progress that Islamic financial markets have made over the last few years, which has helped create an appetite for the Western finance and banking industry to expand into this emerging market.

GETTING STARTED

An Introduction to Islamic Finance Theory and Practice explains the fundamental principles of an economic and financial system governed by Sharia law (Islamic law), and introduces all of the key elements and concepts of Islamic finance. It shows how the surge of interest in Islamic finance practices is based on a demand for more ethical investing, and a greater appreciation of the principles of, and potential under, Islamic law.

AUTHORS

Zamir Iqbal is a Principal Financial Officer in the Risk and Analytics department in the Treasury of the World Bank. He has previously been a member of the adjunct faculty of international finance at the George Washington University.

Abbas Mirakhor is an Executive Director of the IMF, and has taught at various universities in the United States and Iran. He has received several awards, including the Order of Companion of Volta for service to Ghana, and the Quaid-e Azam star for service to Pakistan.

CONTEXT

- Places Islamic finance and banking within the context of Islamic teachings and principles, as well as modern Western finance and banking practices.
- Explains the fundamental principles and functions of an economic, banking, and financial system operating under Sharia law.
- Offers an overview of the principal concepts, focusing on financial contracting, instruments and intermediation, capital markets, regulation and governance, and how risk relates to Islamic finance.
- Examines the numerous tenets of Islam and how they impact on finance and banking, such as social justice, equality, preservation of property rights, sanctity of contracts, and the prohibition of *riba*.

IMPACT

- Useful as a resource for those seeking to invest in the Islamic finance markets, and also Islamic banks and financial institutions who are redesigning their risk management and diversifying their portfolios.
- Assesses the historical systems and financial instruments used by Muslim societies, and discusses the key tenets of Islam in relation to the economic behavior of individuals, society, and state.
- Examines the challenges of globalization, and how Islamic finance is developing to meet them.
- Provides insights into the fast-growing Islamic financial services industry, and incorporates examples and practical discussions which help give an understanding of this evolving market.

QUOTATIONS

"Islam propounds the guiding principles, and prescribes a set of rules, for all aspects of human life, including the economic aspect."

". . .the foremost priority of Islam and its teachings on economics is about 'Justice and Equity'."

"Islam's unconditional prohibition of Riba *(interest). . .changes the landscape of the Islamic financial system."*

▸▸ MORE INFO

Books:

Ayub, Muhammad. *Understanding Islamic Finance*. Hoboken, NJ: Wiley, 2007. Introduces this growing market, with a detailed overview and descriptions of all the major products and processes.

Iqbal, Munawar. *A Guide to Islamic Finance*. London: Risk Books, 2007. A focused report that explains the precepts of Islamic finance and how to develop products that would comply with Islamic principles.

Saiful, AzharRosly. *Critical Issues on Islamic Banking and Financial Markets: Islamic Economics, Banking and Finance, Investments, Takaful and Financial Planning*. Bloomington, IN: AuthorHouse, 2005. A primer on modern Islamic financial transactions and the principles of Sharia financial instruments.

See Also:

Islamic Finance (pp. 1659–1663)

"Islam propounds the guiding principles, and prescribes a set of rules, for all aspects of human life, including the economic aspect."

  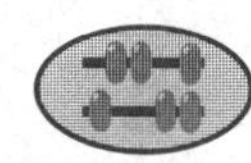   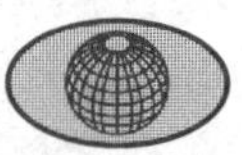   

Inventing Money: The Story of Long-Term Capital Management and the Legends Behind It

NICHOLAS DUNBAR (2000)

WHY READ IT?

- Tells the story of the unfolding drama and high-profile collapse of one of the biggest hedge funds in the world.
- Gives insight into the arcane workings of the hedge fund industry and its biggest players, including Nobel Prize winners.
- Looks at the opportunities and risks of derivatives, and their use by LTCM.

GETTING STARTED

Inventing Money leads the reader through the beginnings of the financial revolution partly initiated by Robert Merton and Myron Scholes, on through John Meriwether's infamous bond arbitrage group, to their formation of LTCM, probably the most famous hedge fund in history.

The book explains the background to how the collapse happened: the involvement of losses around Russian government debt, credit spreads in the world markets, stampeding investors, and borrowings that took LTCM's total exposure over US$100 billion.

AUTHOR

Nicholas Dunbar (b. 1965) studied physics at Manchester, Cambridge, and Harvard. After working in feature films and television, he turned to finance and science writing, focusing on the derivatives industry, joining *Risk* magazine in 1998 as Technical Editor, and is now also Editor of *Life & Pensions* magazine.

CONTEXT

- Provides an overview of modern portfolio theory for a non-technical reader.
- LTCM was founded by some of those who revolutionized the finance markets in recent years.
- One of the founders of LTCM was John Meriwether, who was also featured in Michael Lewis' *Liar's Poker*.
- Also covers the same ground as *When Genius Failed*, but looks more at derivatives use and the arbitrage theories upon which the fund was based.
- Explains clearly what went wrong and how such intelligent people could fail in such a big way.
- Although it was the failure of lauded financial theories that brought down the fund, central to it all was also the fact that key risk management systems proved unsuccessful.

IMPACT

- Exposes the truths behind the LTCM collapse by focusing on the individuals and institutions involved.
- Provides a telling account of the world of derivatives and markets not easily accessible for those not in them.
- The reader can understand the financial positions taken by LTCM, and understand how artificially engineered financial instruments can generate such an enormous impact on the markets and international economics.
- It succeeds in explaining how these supposedly "risk-free" trades manage to make profit and be perfectly hedged.

QUOTATIONS

"Just as the engineering of digital bits would eventually lead to the internet, the mathematically driven engineering of stocks, bonds and other securities would create the modern trillion-dollar financial system."

"At $4 billion, LTCM experienced the greatest derivatives loss in the history of finance."

". . .economic analysts paid by investment banks to produce daily reports for clients were lost for words, as the market appeared to go insane."

➤➤ MORE INFO

See Also:

- *Liar's Poker: Rising Through the Wreckage on Wall Street.* An entertaining and revealing account of the author's time at one of the big investment banks. (p. 1288)
- *When Genius Failed: The Rise and Fall of Long-Term Capital Management.* Also covers the collapse of LTCM, but provides less financial context, focusing more closely on the players, and telling the story in a readable style. (p. 1335)

"Just as the engineering of digital bits would eventually lead to the internet, the mathematically driven engineering of stocks, bonds and other securities would create the modern trillion-dollar financial system."

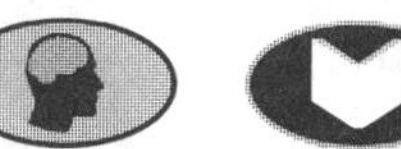
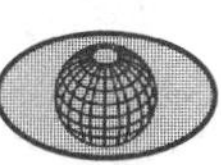

Investments

ZVI BODIE, ALEX KANE, and ALAN J. MARCUS (8th ed 2008, originally 1989)

WHY READ IT?

- Introduces financial concepts, markets, and instruments; shows how to develop a basic finance toolbox, and how to apply it in a portfolio setting.
- Analyzes all the core concepts in investment, and explains market structure and environment.
- Blends practical and theoretical coverage, and is useful for those wanting to develop a greater knowledge of portfolio theory.

GETTING STARTED

Investments, now in its eighth edition, is an introductory textbook that focuses on the practical aspects of investing and investment strategy. It is the leading textbook for the graduate/MBA investments market, as it gives a good overview of investment techniques and opportunities, and offers a comprehensive analysis of investment theory and the concepts involved.

AUTHORS

Zvi Bodie is Professor of Management at Boston University, and has served on the finance faculty at the Harvard Business School and MIT Sloan School of Management. He has published widely on pension finance and investment strategy.

Alex Kane is Professor of Finance and Economics at the School of International Relations and Pacific Studies, University of California, San Diego. He is a member of the American Economic Association and the American Finance Association, and has held academic appointments at UCLA and Harvard.

Alan J. Marcus is Professor of Finance at the School of Management, Boston College. He also currently serves on the Research Foundation Advisory Board of the CFA Institute.

CONTEXT

- Communicates complex investment concepts to those with little or no background in finance.
- Helps you understand, analyze, and utilize all the major investment tools.
- Discusses concepts such as derivatives, which can alter the characteristics of portfolios.
- Examines why the security markets are nearly efficient, and how this ensures that securities are priced appropriately, given their risk and return attributes.
- Balances theory and application of both the basics and advanced topics, and explains the pros and cons of various financial models.
- Although not overly technical, does assume some basic mathematical knowledge.

IMPACT

- Introduces the most basic financial concepts that are used in portfolio construction and management.
- Emphasizes asset allocation, and provides a broader assessment of futures, options, and other derivative security markets than most investment texts.
- Not for those wanting a deep understanding of the background research that developed the theories.
- Provides a variety of real-life examples to supplement their explanations, which provides context for some of the abstract concepts.
- Contains helpful guidance for the Professional Risk Manager Certification, and is used in the certification programs of the Financial Planning Association and the Society of Actuaries.

QUOTATIONS

"When complex derivatives are misunderstood, firms that believe they are hedging might in fact be increasing their exposure to various sources of risk."

"Securities in the capital market are much more diverse than those found within the money market."

"For some firms, macroeconomic and industry circumstances might have a greater influence on profits than the firm's relative performance within its industry."

▸▸ MORE INFO

Books:

Bodie, Zvi, Alex Kane, and Alan J. Marcus. *Student Solutions Manual to Accompany Investments.* New York: Irwin/McGraw-Hill, 2006.

Brown, Keith, and Frank K. Reilly. *Investment Analysis and Portfolio Management.* Hinsdale, IL: Dryden Press, 1979. Takes a more quantitative approach to the valuation of various assets and is more comprehensive.

Sharpe, William, Gordon J. Alexander, and Jeffrey W. Bailey. *Investments.* Englewood Cliffs, NJ: Prentice Hall, 1978. More of a technical and detailed coverage of the same topics.

Website:

The website for the book includes materials such as spreadsheets directly related to the content: www.mhhe.com/bkm

See Also:

Investment (pp. 1653–1658)

"When complex derivatives are misunderstood, firms that believe they are hedging might in fact be increasing their exposure to various sources of risk."

  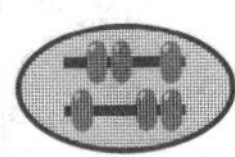   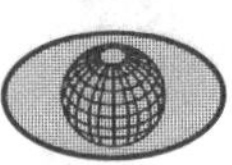  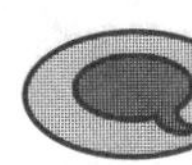 

Irrational Exuberance

ROBERT J. SHILLER (2000)

WHY READ IT?

- Uses a combination of economics, econometrics, sociology, and psychology to analyze stock market movements, and explain how speculative bubbles come about.
- Cautions that the market in 2000 was overvalued by historical standards, which made it inherently unstable, and therefore liable to crash.
- Analyzes why the current housing market crisis is part of a speculative bubble, which may trigger declining home prices for many years.

GETTING STARTED

Irrational Exuberance looks at how unstable the financial markets can be under a free-market economy. It explains how Alan Greenspan's phrase "irrational exuberance," which he used to describe the behaviour of investors who had driven the value of shares on the New York Stock Exchange to record levels, is a valid one to describe the mood of bull markets and psychology of investing. Originally published just before the market downturn, it made Shiller famous as a guru of speculative bubbles, and has been recently republished to cover other volatile markets in the same context.

AUTHOR

Robert J. Shiller is Professor of Economics at Yale University, and Professor of Finance and Fellow at the International Center for Finance, Yale School of Management. He received the Paul A. Samuelson Award, and has served as Vice President of the American Economic Association, and President of the Eastern Economic Association.

CONTEXT

- Discusses factors that were driving stocks up when the book was published, including increased internet usage, greater coverage of financial news, optimistic punditry, low inflation, and the rise of the mutual fund industry.
- Assesses different stock market booms over the years, which betrayed all the signs of a speculative bubble; during each, there was much talk of it being a "new era."
- Looks at how people make decisions in uncertain situations by preferring familiar patterns, especially when determining their stock picking and timing.
- Demonstrates that financial markets occasionally get out of sync with economic fundamentals, and that trends or herd influences pull markets around in an exaggerated way.

IMPACT

- Warns that there is too great a reliance on stocks as the only investment vehicle worth using, and recommends that investors consider looking beyond stocks as a way to diversify and hedge against the inevitable downturn.
- Lays out an intuitive case for how to avoid investing in major market excesses when they occasionally occur.
- Attempts to disprove that stocks or real estate are necessarily the best thing to invest in on a long-term basis.
- Argues that private pension plans that depend on the stock market should be modified, and offers a solution that includes improved public institutions and a broader array of investment options.

QUOTATIONS

"Emotions and heightened attention to the market create a desire to get into the game. Such is irrational exuberance today in the United States."

"The emotional state of investors when they decide on their investments is no doubt one of the most important factors causing the bull market."

"Stock market expansions have often been associated with popular perceptions that the future is brighter or less uncertain than it was in the past."

▸▸ MORE INFO

Books:

Kindleberger, Charles P., Robert Aliber, and Robert Solow. *Manias, Panics, and Crashes: A History of Financial Crises.* 5th ed. Hoboken, NJ: Wiley, 2005. An account of how the mismanagement of money and credit has led to financial disasters over the years.

Shiller, Robert J. *The New Financial Order: Risk in the 21st Century.* Princeton, NJ: Princeton University Press, 2003. Describes a number of fundamental ideas that use information technology and financial theory to manage some of the risks that are generally ignored by risk management institutions.

See Also:

Fooled by Randomness: The Hidden Role of Chance in the Markets and in Life. Taleb's earlier book on risk, probability, and random events, from which he elaborated his theories. (p. 1263)

"Emotions and heightened attention to the market create a desire to get into the game. Such is irrational exuberance today in the United States."

  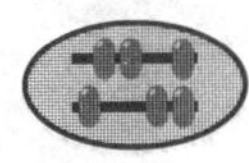   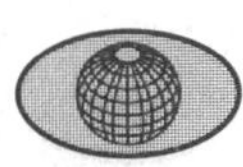   

Juran on Planning for Quality

JOSEPH M. JURAN (1988)

WHY READ IT?

- Juran was a key figure in the quality revolution, developing all-embracing theories of what quality meant for business.
- Argues that quality has to be the goal of each employee, individually and in teams, and was an early exponent of what has become known as empowerment.
- Juran was the first to incorporate the human aspect of what is referred to as Total Quality Management.

GETTING STARTED

The message of *Planning for Quality* is that quality is nothing new. Juran was a great believer in allowing staff greater freedom, and felt that quality should be the goal of each employee. He defined the key elements in a quality philosophy as quality planning, quality management, and quality implementation, and was known as the man who taught Japan how to manage for quality, through a series of lectures that were well received there by senior managers.

AUTHOR

Joseph M. Juran (1904–2008) was the Founder of the Juran Institute, Inc. He was previously Head of Industrial Engineering at Western Electric, played a part in setting up the Malcolm Baldrige National Quality Award, and was Head of the Department of Industrial Engineering at New York University.

CONTEXT

- Proposes that quality planning should ideally consist of identifying who the customers are, determining their needs, translating those needs into the right language, and optimizing the product features so as to meet both the company's needs and the customer needs.
- Considers there is more to quality than specification and rigorous testing: it cannot be delegated and has to be the goal of each employee, individually and in teams.
- Argues that quality philosophy should be built around a company-wide quality management, which aims to disseminate quality to all, rather than delegating it.
- Shows how quality should be seen as an invariable sequence of steps.

IMPACT

- After talking to Japanese senior managers in the 1950s, Juran's message was enthusiastically absorbed, and helped ensure that quality became a priority for them. Quality has been less important in the West, where it is treated more as an operational issue than a managerial one.
- Shows how, in the post-war years, businesses wrongly assumed their Asian adversaries were copycats rather than innovators.
- Compares modern manufacturing products to design specifications, and then inspecting them for defects to protect the buyer was something the Egyptians had mastered 5,000 years previously when building the pyramids.
- Criticizes Deming's *Out of the Crisis* as being over-reliant on statistics, as his approach is less mechanistic and places greater emphasis on human relations.

QUOTATION

"Quality planning consists of developing the products and processes required to meet the customers' needs."

▸▸ MORE INFO

Books:

Juran, J. M. *Juran on Leadership for Quality: An Executive Handbook.* New York: Free Press, 1989. A companion volume to his book on planning for quality, that focuses on the leadership role of upper management.

Juran, J. M. *Juran on Quality by Design: The New Steps for Planning Quality into Goods and Services.* New York: Free Press, 1992. Building on the experiences of companies and managers, presents a new, comprehensive approach to planning, setting, and reaching quality goals.

Juran, J. M. *Juran's Quality Handbook.* New York: McGraw-Hill, 1951. A regularly updated reference on quality management and engineering that argues for new standards in tools for quality.

Website:

Author website: www.jmjuran.com

"Quality planning consists of developing the products and processes required to meet the customers' needs."

Liar's Poker: Rising Through the Wreckage on Wall Street

MICHAEL LEWIS (1989)

WHY READ IT?

- Shows the reality behind bond trading in the 1980s—the deals, the salaries, the greed, and the ambition.
- A funny and absorbing insight into human nature, it explores the drivers of success and failure in a complex, dynamic financial environment.
- Examines how a culture of excessive competition contributed to Salomon's financial collapse.

GETTING STARTED

Liar's Poker explores the characters and forces behind Salomon Brothers' bond-trading empire in the 1980s. It gives an entertaining autobiographical account of the author's time there, and analyzes the benefits and costs of competition between individuals and between firms. It also provides a behind-the-scenes exposé of a successful dealing house during its heyday, and how Salomon failed to use information to understand its competitors—just as in poker, this is essential to success.

AUTHOR

Michael Lewis (b. 1960) is a bestselling author, and a journalist with the *New York Times* and Bloomberg. Prior to this, he was a bond salesman at Salomon Brothers both on Wall Street and in London. He is also a Visiting Fellow at the University of California, Berkeley.

CONTEXT

- The title of the book is based on the game that is occasionally played on Wall Street, involving gambling on the serial number of a dollar bill.
- Depicts how an organization's culture is critical to its success by examining how Salomon's culture of bond trading became increasingly competitive and ambitious.
- Shows how actively competing with others is often key to success in a business environment, but competition at the expense of teamwork can be disastrous.
- Attributes Salomon's difficulties after 1987 to its management's lack of focus and their behaving more like traders than managers—seeking to "manage by numbers."
- Highlights the character traits of a successful trader as fast, ambitious, and addicted to gambling.

IMPACT

- Provides a lesson in market failure, where Salomon operated a near monopoly in such areas as mortgage bonds and made enormous, but unsustainable, profits.
- Examines how remuneration of traders became an issue, and notes that the unwillingness to pay substantial bonuses to successful young traders caused discontent.
- Details how the collapse of Salomon's mortgage department was the result of poor communication between business units, a lack of market awareness, and dwindling employee loyalty.
- Looks at how Salomon failed to maintain customer loyalty, as their traders focused exclusively on commission-based bonuses, and appeared neither to value customers nor to show loyalty to their firm.

QUOTATION

"In any market, as in any poker game, there is a fool."

▸▸ MORE INFO

See Also:

- *Barbarians at the Gate: The Fall of RJR Nabisco.* The story behind the financial frenzy and power struggle of the Nabisco takeover in the 1980s. (p. 1223)
- *Inventing Money: The Story of Long-Term Capital Management and the Legends Behind It.* Examines the LTCM debacle, detailing the financial deals and the hedge fund industry. (p. 1284)
- *When Genius Failed: The Rise and Fall of Long-Term Capital Management.* Also covers the collapse of LTCM, but provides less financial context, focusing more closely on the players, and telling the story in a readable style. (p. 1335)

"In any market, as in any poker game, there is a fool."

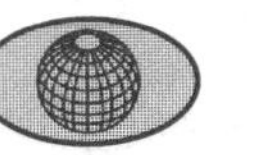
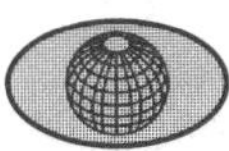

The Living Company: Habits for Survival in a Turbulent Business Environment

ARIE DE GEUS (1997)

WHY READ IT?

- Provides the testimony of someone who was a professional businessman, but who believes that companies must be fundamentally humane to prosper.
- Explains why so many companies don't last, and teaches about corporate longevity and how to survive the upheavals of change and competition over the years.
- Puts its faith in company learning, and represents a careful and powerful riposte to corporate nihilism.

GETTING STARTED

The Living Company looks at the problem of corporate failure, presenting alarming statistics on the relatively short life of European and Japanese enterprises. It argues that short-term focus on profits, rather than nurturing people, is a key factor in failure. As a winner of the *Financial Times*/Booz-Allen & Hamilton Global Business Book Award, it is a classic text on how businesses can be run effectively.

AUTHOR

Arie de Geus (b. 1930) was the Head of Shell Oil Company's Strategic Planning Group, and is a public speaker. Since his retirement he has advised many government and private institutions, worked for MIT's Center for Organizational Learning, and as a visiting fellow at London Business School.

CONTEXT

- Considers all corporate activities to be grounded in two hypotheses: the company is a living being, and decisions result from a learning process.
- Argues that corporations should last as long as two or three centuries, but the reality is that companies usually die young, as they focus on profits rather than on human issues.
- Sees a successful company as one that can learn effectively, and dedicate a great deal of time to nurturing its people.
- Shows that learning means being prepared to accept continuous change, and a company can only change if its community of people changes with it.
- Identifies four key characteristics of long-lived companies: being sensitive to their environment, being cohesive, having a strong sense of identity and tolerance, and being conservative in financing.
- Proposes that the wisdom of the past be appreciated and used, rather than cast out in the manner of a cultural revolution.

IMPACT

- Based on thorough research while at Shell to identify the characteristics of corporate longevity, it was found that the onus should be on keeping excitement to a minimum; the average human centenarian advocates a life of abstinence, caution, and moderation; and so it is with companies.
- Sees the living company as an organism, existing primarily for its own survival and improvement.
- There is more to a company and to its longevity than mere money making. The skills, capabilities, and knowledge of people are paramount; capital is no longer king.
- As compared with the movement in corporate reengineering, de Geus thinks that businesses should evolve rather than start completely afresh.

QUOTATION

"Learning is tomorrow's capital."

▸▸ MORE INFO

Books:

Schwartz, Peter. *The Art of the Long View: Planning for the Future in an Uncertain World.* New York: Doubleday/Currency, 1991. A related, helpful exploration of how to go beyond trying to forecast the future to actually preparing for it.

Senge, Peter M. *The Fifth Discipline: The Art and Practice of the Learning Organization.* New York: Doubleday/Currency, 1990. Senge, a colleague at the Society for Organizational Learning, explains the concept of the learning organization and how successful organizations must continually adapt and learn.

Website:

Author's website: www.ariedegeus.com

     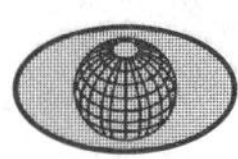   

Macroeconomics

N. GREGORY MANKIW (6th ed 2006, originally 1992)

WHY READ IT?

- It explains concepts clearly and uses relevant examples to convey meaning.
- Covers all the main macroeconomic topics, including science, data, money, inflation, unemployment, short-run and long-run factors, and the business cycle.
- Incorporates real-world issues and data throughout, rather than being overly academic.

GETTING STARTED

Macroeconomics is a widely adopted intermediate-level textbook that communicates the principles of macroeconomics in a comprehensible style.

It integrates many learning tools such as case studies, information boxes, graphs, mathematical notes, chapter summaries, key concepts, questions for review, problems, and applications, to ensure it can be used by students and teachers, as well as those needing a refresher on the topic.

AUTHOR

N. Gregory Mankiw (b. 1958) is Professor of Economics at Harvard University. He has been a Research Associate of the National Bureau of Economic Research, and an Adviser to the Federal Reserve Bank of Boston and the Congressional Budget Office. From 2003 to 2005 he served as Chairman of the President's Council of Economic Advisers.

CONTEXT

- A focused and practical textbook that balances its coverage between short- and the long-run macroeconomic issues.
- Integrates Keynesian and classical ideas to give a pedagogical overview of the issues.
- Uses a variety of simple models to put its points across.
- Examines the economic behavior of human beings as well as nations and the economic interactions between nations, including aspects of the economy such as money, savings, growth, stocks and flows, inflation, unemployment, taxation, and national budgets.
- Ensures that the math is understandable and applicable.

IMPACT

- Examines the long run when prices are flexible before moving on to the short run when prices are sticky.
- Emphasizes the empirical and experiential throughout, to ensure relevancy.
- Is clear about the limits regarding what economists really know about the economy.
- Analyzes how changes in policies and variables affect aggregate functions.
- Discusses key concepts such as the IS-LM model, Solow steady state, and the Keynesian consumption function.
- Presents the economic ideas of one of the key figures in the Bush White House.

QUOTATIONS

"I incorporate many of the contributions of the classical economists before Keynes and the new classical economists of the past three decades."

"Instead of pretending that there is one model that is complete enough to explain all facets of the economy, I encourage students to learn how to use and compare a set of prominent models."

"The basic principles of macroeconomics do not change from decade to decade, but the macroeconomist must apply these principles with flexibility and creativity to meet changing circumstances."

▸▸ MORE INFO

Books:

Blanchard, Olivier. *Macroeconomics*. Upper Saddle River, NJ: Prentice Hall, 1997. Presents a unified view of macroeconomics, connecting the short run, medium run, and long run.

Chamberlin, Graeme, and Linda Yueh. *Macroeconomics*. London: Thomson Learning, 2006. A general textbook that takes an international perspective.

Website:

Author blog: gregmankiw.blogspot.com

"I incorporate many of the contributions of the classical economists before Keynes and the new classical economists of the past three decades."

  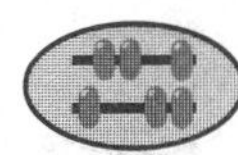   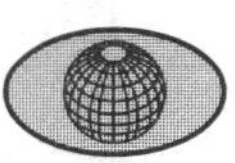   

Management Accounts: How to Use Them to Control Your Business

TONY SKONE (1995)

WHY READ IT?

- Explains management accounts in an easily understandable style, especially for managers needing to make strategic decisions regarding their business.
- The emphasis throughout the book is on applying the information.
- Explains the jargon, identifies both what is important and what is irrelevant, and advises on what accounts information you should be receiving.

GETTING STARTED

To run a business successfully it is essential that you be able to analyze the well-being of your business, and make informed decisions about future operations. *Management Accounts* gives you the tools to do this, and shows how individual decisions affect the profitability, cashflow and risk profile of a business. It helps you improve your contribution to the planning and financial control of an organization.

AUTHOR

Tony Skone (b. 1939) is a financial, tax, and cost consultant, Principal of Management and Training Consultants, and has lectured at business schools as well as holding a post as Senior Lecturer at the University of Westminster. He is author and co-author of several business finance books.

CONTEXT

- Use your management accounts to get the full picture of how your business has been performing in many different areas. The accuracy and relevancy of the financial information should underpin future decision making.
- Provides a guide to management accounts written from the perspective of the user.
- Use your management accounts to examine sales revenue and expected cashflow.
- Includes guidance on how to analyze data on sales, purchasing, and fixed assets.
- Helps an understanding of the differences between expected and actual achievements.
- Illustrates the control mechanisms available, including the control of budgets and working capital.

IMPACT

- Suggests a variety of spreadsheet applications using numbers and graphs, and provides two formulas for calculating break-even and profit.
- Demonstrates how to develop your ratio analysis, and the use of spreadsheets and the financial scorecard.
- Helps you spot worrying trends, such as stock levels increasing against flat sales.

QUOTATIONS

"What accountants have to do is to become better communicators while managers have to become financially literate, that is, they have to learn to speak the language of business—money."

"It is people who make things happen, not money."

"The selection of appropriate ratios and the keeping of some form of financial scorecard will provide the basis for more effective control of the business."

⏩ MORE INFO

Books:

Mott, Graham. *Accounting for Managers.* London: Kogan Page, 1994. Part of a fast-track MBA series.

Terry, Leslie Alfred. *Business Accounts.* London: Pitman & Sons, 1935. An introduction to business accounting.

"What accountants have to do is to become better communicators while managers have to become financially literate, that is, they have to learn to speak the language of business—money."

  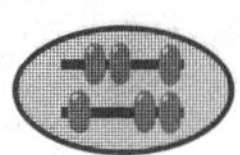   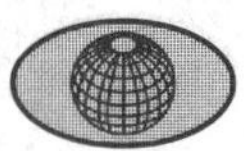   

Managing

HAROLD GENEEN and ALVIN MOSCOW (1984)

WHY READ IT?

- Explains Geneen's approach to management, which he successfully used at ITT to ensure huge growth and help it become the world's greatest conglomerate.
- Shows how his success was based on amassing all the facts so that decisions became self-evident—Geneen wanted no surprises, and worked hard to ensure this.
- Examines his obsessive belief that the conglomerate could be made to work as a business structure. He believed that ITT could manage any business in any industry if it knew the figures.

GETTING STARTED

Managing relates the management style and culture that Geneen used at ITT to turn it into a successful global conglomerate. It highlights the importance of knowing the numbers in minute detail, and applying traditional methods to business operations. It examines how he applied rigorous detail to managing, in order to make people as predictable and controllable as the capital resources they managed.

AUTHORS

Harold Geneen (1910–1997) was CEO of Raytheon, and then President and CEO of International Telephone and Telegraph Corporation (ITT), where he grew the company into a multinational conglomerate, primarily through the biggest series of acquisitions and mergers that has ever been seen.

Alvin Moscow (b. 1925) was a news reporter for Associated Press, before helping Richard Nixon in writing *Six Crises*. He went on to be a speechwriter, general spokesman, and political analyst for Nixon, a writing consultant for William Paley, and write many of his own books.

CONTEXT

- Geneen's success was based on hard work, a fanatical attention to detail and knowing every single figure possible, and an obsessive belief that the conglomerate could be made to work.
- Examines the author's rigorous management style, which was unforgiving, built on a degree of intellectual rigor that bordered on ruthlessness.
- Describes his career with ITT, and the huge international acquisitions and diversifications he oversaw.
- Details how he micro-managed the business, holding management meetings throughout the world for over 200 days a year.

IMPACT

- Shows how Geneen inculcated a remarkable culture within ITT, his success in growing the business meaning that people followed his methods with unquestioning faith.
- His fundamentalist style of management by numbers rather than through people remains popular—management consultants, for example, continue to use rational models based on pouring over the figures.
- Can be said to have elevated management to a new level. His system required a team of highly numerate, professional managers who had to take responsibility.
- The Geneen legacy is most notably evident in the conglomerates that continue to survive; General Electric, for example, is a company with interests in everything.

QUOTATIONS

"Putting deals together beats spending every day playing golf."

"Managers should have the temerity, intellectual curiosity, guts and/or plain impoliteness, if necessary, to be sure that what they do have is indeed what we will call an unshakeable fact."

⏩ MORE INFO

Books:

Drucker, Peter F. *The Essential Drucker.* Oxford: Butterworth-Heinemann, 2001. A compilation of the management guru's key thinking and principles of business management.

Geneen, Harold, and Brent Bowers. *The Synergy Myth and Other Ailments of Business Today.* New York: St. Martin's Press, 1997. Geneen here shares his ideas about business success, and attacks management philosophies that he sees as supplanting the old-fashioned values such as hard work and risk-taking that he prefers.

"Putting deals together beats spending every day playing golf."

     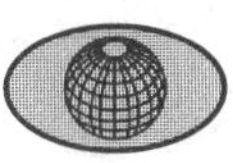   

Managing Across Borders: The Transnational Solution

CHRISTOPHER A. BARTLETT and SUMANTRA GHOSHAL (1989)

WHY READ IT?

- Regarded as a classic of international business processes, *Managing Across Borders* has helped the focus on how organizations should be structured for success in the global economy.
- Maps out the new business reality of globalization and the kinds of organizations a borderless business world requires.
- Identifies and assesses the variety of organizational forms prevalent among global companies.

GETTING STARTED

Managing Across Borders argues that changing patterns of international management have led to a new global model, in which enabling innovation and disseminating knowledge in globally dispersed organizations is an increasingly important challenge. It emphasizes networking across global organizations and the transferral of learning and knowledge as key to growth and development.

AUTHORS

Christopher A. Bartlett (b. 1943) is Professor of Business Administration at Harvard Graduate School of Business Administration. Prior to that, he was a Marketing Manager with Alcoa, and a management consultant with McKinsey. He is a Fellow of the Academy of Management, and the Academy of International Business.

Sumantra Ghoshal (1948–2004) was Professor of Strategic and International Management at the London Business School, a member of the Committee of Overseers of the Harvard Business School, and was the founding Dean of the Indian School of Business in Hyderabad.

CONTEXT

- Shows that competition is forcing many businesses to adopt a new global model—the transnational—that combines local responsiveness with global efficiency and the ability to transfer know-how better, cheaper, and faster.
- The transnational company is made up of a network of specialized or differentiated units, which focus on managing integrative linkages between local businesses as well as with the center.
- Sees integration and the creation of coherent systems for value delivery as the new drivers of organizational structure.
- Considers how global organizations offer scale efficiencies and cost advantages through standardized products.
- Shows how international companies also have the ability to transfer knowledge and expertise to overseas environments that are less advanced.

IMPACT

- Observes that what binds the companies together is a set of shared values and beliefs that should be developed and managed effectively.
- Discusses three techniques crucial to an organization's psychology: a shared understanding of the company's mission and objectives, the actions and behavior of senior managers set a good example, and that personnel policies must develop flexible organization processes.
- Signals the demise of the independence of divisional organization structures of the kind first developed by General Motors.

QUOTATION

"Integration and the creation of a coherent system for value delivery are the new drivers of organizational structure."

▸▸ MORE INFO

Books:

Bartlett, Christopher A., Sumantra Ghoshal, and Paul W. Beamish. *Transnational Management: Text, Cases & Readings in Cross-Border Management.* 5th ed. Boston, MA: McGraw-Hill/Irwin, 2008. Combines text material, Harvard and London Business School cases, and readings to present the best of current research and thought on the global business environment.

Ghoshal, Sumantra, and Christopher A. Bartlett. *The Individualized Corporation: A Fundamentally New Approach to Management.* New York: HarperBusiness, 1997. Presents a new approach to business strategy that centers on corporate purpose and culture, not the industrial machine.

See Also:

i International Management (pp. 1650–1652)

"Integration and the creation of a coherent system for value delivery are the new drivers of organizational structure."

   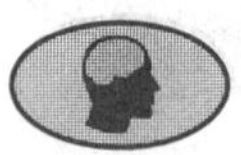  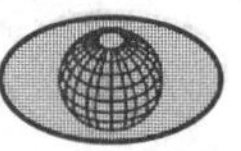   

Managing Financial Resources

MICK BROADBENT and JOHN CULLEN (1993)

WHY READ IT?

- Addresses the complexities of financial planning and control, and explains key concepts.
- Focuses on finance for the non-financial manager, helping them understand the principles involved in managing financial resources.
- Makes it easier for educators to prepare materials, and structure courses for students at different levels.

GETTING STARTED

Managing Financial Resources examines relevant issues such as performance measures and cost analysis, methods of improving profitability, and techniques of financial monitoring and control, concentrating on how to apply accountancy to managerial issues. It also provides a full range of tutorials on managing resources, and assists in teaching management courses at certificate and diploma level.

AUTHORS

Mick Broadbent is Head of Department, Accounting, Finance and Economics, and Professor of Accounting, Acting Head of the Business School, University of Hertfordshire. He is a Quality Assurance Agency Collaborative Provision Auditor and a member of the Chartered Institute of Management Accountants Expert Assessment Panel.

John Cullen is Professor of Management Accounting at the Management School, Sheffield University. He is Vice-Chairman of the Committee of Heads of Accounting, is also a member of the Freight Logistics Research Group at the Department for Transport, and undertakes supply chain consultancy projects.

CONTEXT

- Analyzes relevant topics such as public sector management issues, audit commission, and capital investment decisions.
- Discusses essential finance resource topics such as stakeholder analysis for published reports and accounts, intellectual property, performance measurement, outsourcing, and new developments in the public sector.
- Helps the reader to develop essential and relevant management skills.
- Real examples and case studies are used throughout to illustrate the main points in a practical way.
- Includes 20 self-contained tutorial sessions, each containing activities, session plans and outcomes.

IMPACT

- Suitable for managers on the Diploma in Management or part one of the Postgraduate Diploma, especially those accredited by the Chartered Management Institute and Edexcel.
- Can also be used as a practical resource by managers and MBA students.
- Easy to use and able to be customized for different courses.
- Examines key issues, including break-even analysis and how to assess financial performance.
- Based on the Management Charter Initiative's Occupational Standards for Management NVQs and SVQs at level 4.

QUOTATIONS

"The recording of financial information within an enterprise is a natural part of good business practice."

"The key to understanding management accounting is to recognize that costs are classified in many different ways depending upon the purpose for which the information is to be used."

"An understanding of cost behaviour is crucial for both short and long-term decision making."

▸▸ MORE INFO

Book:

Ryan, Bob. *Finance and Accounting for Business.* London: Thomson Learning, 2004. An introductory overview of financial accounting, management accounting, and financial management for non-specialist students.

See Also:

Accounting and Finance for Non-Specialists. Examines the basic principles and underlying concepts of accounting and finance in a practical and non-technical style. (p. 1213)

"The recording of financial information within an enterprise is a natural part of good business practice."

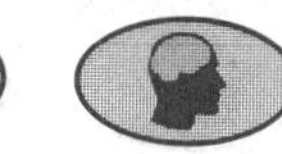

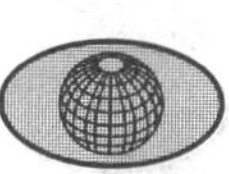

Market Wizards: Interviews with Top Traders

JACK D. SCHWAGER (1989)

WHY READ IT?

- Shows how successful traders have beaten the markets and made millions, through detailed interviews that discuss their strategies and trading techniques.
- Provides a number of themes that offer useful advice for all levels of investors wanting to improve their trading approach and methodologies.
- Discusses traders from a variety of areas, such as the futures and currency markets, equity trading, and floor trading, and examines the psychology of trading.

GETTING STARTED

Market Wizards was the first in a trilogy of interview-based, bestselling books that Schwager published, which provide insight into the backgrounds, personalities, experiences, and techniques of top traders. It offers advice on how to be a successful market speculator, how to implement a sound trading philosophy, and how to use effective techniques and disciplines to beat the market. Each interview has an introduction to the trader, an edited transcript of the interview, and a brief summary of their trading strategies.

AUTHOR

Jack D. Schwager (b. 1948) is a managing director and principal of The Fortune Group, and a finance author. He worked for many years on Wall Street as a director of futures research and the co-principal of a commodity trading advisory firm. He is also a regular seminar speaker.

CONTEXT

- Gives a useful overview of trading and investing techniques in different types of markets over the last 30 years, as most interviewees started trading in the 1970s and are still operating successfully now.
- Examines the human side of trading, as the interviews discuss the investors' experiences, how they honed their skills and developed personal philosophies and styles, and examine aspects of their daily trading operations.
- Common characteristics of the traders include a strong desire for success, confidence about their abilities over the long run, a winning strategy that they stuck with, risk awareness, being patient until the right trade came along, acting independently, and understanding that losing is part of the game.
- Provides the opportunity to understand and apply well-established trading rules to your own investing.
- Learn the importance of creating your own individual trading system that plays to personal strengths.

IMPACT

- Reveals the money and risk management tips and philosophies of professional traders.
- Outlines a number of key trading principles, such as "cut your losses, let your winners run," "have patience to wait for the right trade to come along," and "getting your ego out of trading decisions."
- Demonstrates the success of a wide variety of trading and investing styles.
- Examines the mistakes that most traders make during their careers, and compares the characteristics of losing traders with those of successful ones.
- Discusses key trading concepts such as discipline, capital preservation, risk management, individual responsibility, flexibility, intellectual honesty, and consistency.
- Emphasizes the importance of planning your trades, and the best time to buy and sell.
- Explains program trading, portfolio insurance, and options, in appendixes.

QUOTATIONS

"Diversification is a hedge for ignorance. I think you are much better off owning a few stocks and knowing a great deal about them."

"One of the jobs of a good trader is to imagine alternative scenarios. I try to form many different mental pictures of what the world should be like and wait for one of them to be confirmed."

"You don't need any education at all to [trade]. The smarter you are, the dumber you are. The more you know, the worse it is for you."

▸▸ MORE INFO

Books:

Schwager, Jack. *A Complete Guide to the Futures Markets: Fundamental Analysis, Technical Analysis, Trading, Spreads, and Options.* New York: Wiley, 1984. The seminal reference book on the futures markets, which examines price forecasting in the commodity futures market.

Schwager, Jack. *Stock Market Wizards: Interviews with America's Top Stock Traders.* New York: Harper Business, 2001. The third volume in this series, providing more insights into the trading styles of top traders.

See Also:

Reminiscences of a Stock Operator. The trading biography of trader Jesse Livermore, a hugely successful American speculator of the early 1900s who won and lost many fortunes on the stock and commodities markets. (p. 1315)

"Diversification is a hedge for ignorance. I think you are much better off owning a few stocks and knowing a great deal about them."

 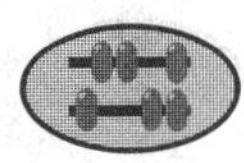 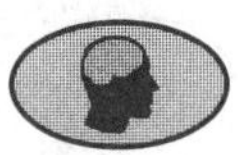  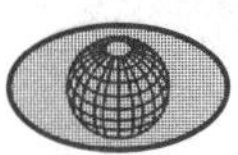   

Mastering Financial Management: Demystify Finance and Transform Your Financial Skills of Management

STEPHEN BROOKSON (1998)

WHY READ IT?

- Enables business managers and executives to master the essentials of financial management, and to learn techniques of immediate use.
- Explains commercially vital concepts, processes, practices, and terminology, and shows how they should best be adopted and implemented.
- Covers finance and accounting in a way that brings competitive advantage to those previously with little knowledge of the subject.

GETTING STARTED

Mastering Financial Management provides practical coaching in financial accounting, management accounting and financial management. With guidance on financial statements and financial information, it helps you understand and use financial techniques and improve individual and organizational performance.

AUTHOR

Stephen Brookson is a Chartered Accountant, and was a consultant with Ernst & Young, before leaving to set up his own training consultancy business. He presents seminars and training events in both the public and private sectors.

CONTEXT

- Provides a practical guide to financial accounting, budgetary control, and management accounting.
- Offers a framework for understanding the relationship between the company and its providers of capital.
- Examines the principles and structure of financial management and details the main techniques for strategic, tactical, and operational decision-making based on sound budgeting and financial planning.
- Helps you respond to current business challenges through relevant knowledge of management finance.
- Covers the finance basics on accounts, balance sheets, assets and liabilities, and ratios.
- Advises on corporate financial health and how to analyze business performance.
- Discusses the rules governing accounting, and looks at the fundamentals of taxation and its commercial implications.

IMPACT

- Gives you the essentials of managing company finances, either for a department or the whole business, and the confidence to develop the full range of key attributes.
- Aimed just as much at personal development as job skills, it helps those needing a financial grounding as a critical business expertise.
- In line with others in the Masters in Management series, it is aimed at decision-makers, general managers, team leaders and implementers, and senior-level executives.
- Enables effective decision-making and investment appraisal.
- Offers a variety of practical learning features throughout, such as key questions, action checklists, activities, guides to best practice, key learning points, and key management concepts.

QUOTATIONS

"Finance is the critical business skill to possess before you can set course for a successful business career."

"It is a common fault that most people preen their profit and loss accounts incessantly, whilst paying only lip service to their balance sheets and cash flow."

"Those managers who may have an inkling that all is not well with the costs are excluded by jargon and witchcraft, and so the errors continue."

▸▸ MORE INFO

Books:

Brigham, Eugene F., and Joel F. Houston. *Fundamentals of Financial Management.* Hinsdale, IL: Dryden Press, 1978. An introductory guide to corporate finance and financial management.

Whiteley, John. *Mastering Financial Management.* Basingstoke, UK: Palgrave Macmillan, 2004. Introduces financial management in a practical way, and usefully examines company accounts, with guidance on how to make your financial reports interesting and influential.

See Also:

The Financial Times Handbook of Financial Management. Explores financial management, with useful analysis of business dynamics, and how they are measured and reported. (p. 1262)

"Finance is the critical business skill to possess before you can set course for a successful business career."

  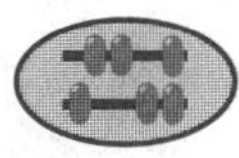   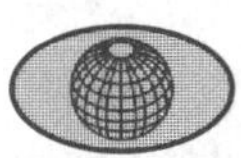   

Mastering Risk, Volume 1: Concepts

JAMES PICKFORD (ED) (2000)

WHY READ IT?

- An impressive cast of contributors bring the latest ideas on the management of financial risk and offer a guide to best practice.
- Provides a comprehensive overview of the key concepts of risk management.
- The practical relevance of these concepts is highlighted throughout with recent examples and short case studies.

GETTING STARTED

Mastering Risk is a collection of all 10 issues of the respected Mastering Risk supplement to the *Financial Times*. It contains 50 articles from contributors working in top business schools and the business community, to take the reader through a broad range of risk issues, from the traditional insurance type risks to more high-level financial risk management, and covers both core areas and emerging fields of importance.

EDITOR

James Pickford is the Business Life Editor of the *Financial Times*.

CONTEXT

- Brings you the current thinking from some of the leading authorities on risk, to examine the concept of risk control in all aspects of business and finance management.
- The variety of backgrounds of the risk experts featured ensures this a balanced perspective on risk.
- Traces the development of attitudes, and introduces the latest ideas and approaches from the US and Europe.
- Contains definitive explanations of the types of risk, and helps an understanding of the nature of these risks.
- Approaches risk measurement, risk categorization, and risk perception in a variety of ways to give a perceptive overview of how they can be tackled.

IMPACT

- Covers the essentials of risk measurement, risk strategy, financial risk, operational risk, regulation and political risk, insurance and systemic risk, and extreme events.
- Analyzes the techniques used to identify and measure risk, the methods of managing financial and non-financial risk, and investigates emerging areas of risk such as e-commerce and reputation management.
- Explains the methods of assessing and controlling risks, and the role that different parts of the organization should play in risk management.
- Avoids the mathematics of risk, to focus on accessible definitions and explanations of the subject.
- In examining risk, it also delves into other disciplines, such as psychology, investment, law, statistics, and marketing.

QUOTATIONS

"Companies that implement a well-designed risk management strategy increase their shareholders' wealth."

"The perception of risk is a complex and subjective process."

"The enormous growth and development in both financial and electronic technologies have created a richer palette of risk management techniques."

▸▸ MORE INFO

Books:

Alexander, Carol (ed). *Mastering Risk, Volume 2: Application*. Harlow, UK: FT Prentice Hall, 2001. The second part, consisting of specially commissioned chapters that cover the application side of risk management.

Borge, Dan. *The Book of Risk*. New York: Wiley, 2001. Examines the process of decision-making in an uncertain world, and the role of risk management.

See Also:

Against the Gods: The Remarkable Story of Risk. A history of the effort to understand risk and probability. (p. 1215)

Risk Management (pp. 1721–1724)

"Companies that implement a well-designed risk management strategy increase their shareholders' wealth."

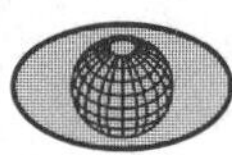

The (Mis)behavior of Markets

BENOIT MANDELBROT and RICHARD L. HUDSON (2004)

WHY READ IT?

- The founder of fractal geometry re-evaluates the standard tools and models of modern financial theory.
- Examines how the traditional finance models originated, arguing that, since financial markets are unpredictable and far riskier than first thought, it is necessary to find alternatives.
- Presents a different method of predicting stock price movements, founded on his fractal theories.

GETTING STARTED

The (Mis)behavior of Markets explains what a fractal view of the world of finance would look like, based on applying Mandelbrot's theory of fractal geometry to equity prices and their movements. Also integrating economics and chaos theory, it considers the failings of modern financial theory, and shows how his mathematical model based on fractals can improve on the existing financial models, such as the Black–Scholes formula for option pricing and the capital asset pricing model.

AUTHORS

Benoit Mandelbrot (b. 1924) is Professor of Mathematical Sciences at Yale University and a Fellow Emeritus at IBM's Thomas J. Watson Laboratory. As the originator of fractal geometry, he received the Wolf Prize in Physics, the Japan Prize in science and technology, and an award from the US National Academy of Sciences.

Richard L. Hudson was a reporter and editor for the *Wall Street Journal* for 25 years, before being appointed the managing editor of its European edition. He graduated from Harvard University and was a Knight Fellow of MIT in 1991.

CONTEXT

- Argues that current models of financial theory are flawed, as they do not properly explain real market prices and their fluctuations, and are inadequate to control actual levels of investment risk.
- Considers that these models, such as modern portfolio theory, the capital asset pricing model, and Black–Scholes, depend on the mistaken belief that investments conform to the simple distribution of the bell curve.
- Demonstrates that the Gaussian Normal distribution is an oversimplification of financial prices due to "fat tails," concentration, and extreme events.
- Presents empirical evidence showing that the commodity, futures, money, stock, and other market price movements are not generally Normally distributed.
- Proposes instead the use of predictive ideas based on fractal geometry, which better reflect the inherent turbulence and volatility of the market.
- Describes 10 heresies of finance, including market turbulence and riskiness, timing, market similarities and uncertainties, and the inevitability of bubbles.

IMPACT

- Criticizes how economic and modern financial theory has developed, in terms of theories of price movements.
- Analyzes how the markets really behave, suggesting that a "multifractal" approach is preferable to the random walk and efficient market theories, which assume that prices changes conform to the bell curve.
- Argues that returns follow a multifractal—a fractal both in value and in time; this model can create pictures of financial returns that are similar to real financial returns.
- Admits that multifractals should be researched further and are not presently able to build a successful model for a particular market.
- Discusses the observation that prices are not random but have inherent patterns, which substantiates a new way of looking at markets: "econophysics."

QUOTATIONS

"Patterns are the fool's gold of financial markets."

"Continuity is a fundamental assumption of conventional finance."

"What passes for orthodoxy in economics and finance, proves on closer examination to be shaky business."

▸▸ MORE INFO

Books:

Mandelbrot, Benoit. *Fractals and Scaling in Finance: Discontinuity, Concentration, Risk.* New York: Springer, 1997. Combines new material with reprints of Mandelbrot's classic papers, which helped an analysis of evaluating the risks involved in trading strategies.

Peters, Edgar E. *Fractal Market Analysis: Applying Chaos Theory to Investment and Economics.* New York: Wiley, 1994. An accessible study of how to use fractals to explain behavior and understand price movements.

See Also:

Fooled by Randomness: The Hidden Role of Chance in the Markets and in Life. Taleb's influential examination of risk, probability, and random events. (p. 1263)

"Patterns are the fool's gold of financial markets."

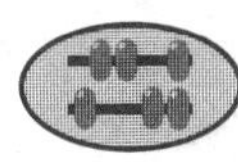

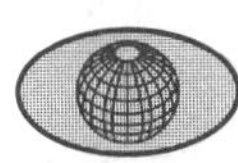

The Money Game

ADAM SMITH (1976)

WHY READ IT?

- An influential and thought-provoking book about money and how to make it, based on the experiences of a Wall Street insider.
- A classic book, oft-quoted by investors, that foreshadows almost every major investment paradox or problem that is faced today.
- Can be thought of as one of the first books about behavior finance, in its descriptions of trading, crowd psychology, and the stock markets.

GETTING STARTED

The Money Game describes the psychological factors influencing the stock market of the 1960s. Based on a set of essays submitted by the fictitious Mr Smith to a variety of financial publications between the mid-1960s and the early 1970s, it is a well-written, humorous, and intelligent examination of the money machine. It describes the style of the boardrooms and trade pits of Wall Street in the 1960s, and a new generation of Wall Street money managers, referred to as "the gunslingers," who approach the management of other people's money with a distinct lack of care.

AUTHOR

Adam Smith is a pseudonym for George J. W. Goodman (b. 1930), a business journalist who also wrote novels, investment books, and a television show. He also presented lectures on the media at Princeton for several years, and was Editor of *The Institutional Investor*.

CONTEXT

- Depicts a trading culture where money is how you keep score—if you make lots of money, you are winning the game. The game is there to be played—win, lose, or draw—and the money managers cannot help but play.
- Offers timeless insights into how and why players, amateur and professional, really play the money game, all within the context of the excesses of the 1960s.
- Discusses such diverse subjects as crowd psychology, inkblots, and random walks, and their application to the markets from an original point of view.
- Looks at the fundamental principles of fear and greed in the context of investment strategy.
- Examines the success of technical analysis, fundamental analysis, efficient market theory, the random walk, and Dow theory, and finds them all lacking.

IMPACT

- Discusses the fallibility of numbers, trends, and data analysis as systems dependent on the reading of the past to determine the future.
- Shows how professional money managers operate, and notes that even though they have more money and information than the amateur, they still are unable to accurately predict the markets.
- Advises that people thinking about getting involved in investing would do well to look inward to find their own trading style before making any outward financial moves.

QUOTATIONS

"If I really had a system for making money in the market and it worked all the time, first of all, I wouldn't tell anybody and second of all, I would soon have just about all the money there is."

"The real object of the Game is not money, it is the playing of the Game itself."

"If you are going to operate with intuition—or judgment—then it follows that the first thing you have to know is yourself."

▸▸ MORE INFO

Book:

Smith, Adam. *Supermoney*. New York: Random House, 1972. The follow-up to *The Money Game,* which has recently been re-issued with a new foreword and preface.

See Also:

Adam Smith (p. 1196)

One Up on Wall Street: How to Use What You Already Know to Make Money in the Market. Analyzes the best way to make money in the stock market. (p. 1305)

Reminiscences of a Stock Operator. The classic book, does for traders what *The Money Game* does for investors. (p. 1315)

"If I really had a system for making money in the market and it worked all the time, first of all, I wouldn't tell anybody and second of all, I would soon have just about all the money there is."

     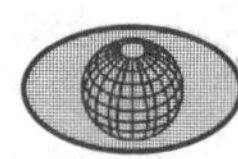   

Monkey Business: Swinging Through the Wall Street Jungle

JOHN ROLFE and PETER TROOB (2000)

WHY READ IT?

- Gives a searing expose of the life of investment bankers in a mergers and acquisitions department at a leading Wall Street bank.
- Through personal stories and anecdotes, we learn about the processes and practices of young investment bankers, as well as the boredom and drudgery of their daily lives—which is far from the glamour that led them to apply in the first place.
- Reveals the macho mentality of their workplace, the invective, belittling of others, lack of sleep, and visits to less than glamorous nightspots.

GETTING STARTED

Monkey Business tells of two young business school graduates who were lured to Wall Street with high hopes of making their fortunes and leading life in the fast lane. Rolfe and Troob give an insider's account of how the business is run, through an entertaining, sarcastic, and somewhat pessimistic view of the life of an investment banker. The combination of a lack of values, the vulgar and patriarchal approach of their colleagues, and the extreme hours and endless work, which are related in amusing detail, finally convinces the young men that investment banking is not for them.

AUTHORS

John Rolfe taught at Virginia Tech and the University of Florida, before doing broadcast research in New York. In 1993 he was at the Wharton School of Business. He then joined Donaldson, Lufkin & Jenrette, before becoming a principal with a private investment organization. He is now a freelancer.

Peter Troob worked for Kidder Peabody in New York, and in 1993 entered the graduate program at the Harvard Business School. He later joined Donaldson, Lufkin & Jenrette, and is currently a partner with a private investment organization.

CONTEXT

- The story of a journey from MBA to Wall Street that shows how many young people enter investment banking dreaming of big bonuses and a glamorous lifestyle, but without an awareness of what life is really like as a trainee in this world.
- Through a range of personal stories, the authors give an insight into what to expect as a junior investment banker at a major firm.
- Shows the business processes and how money is made in the M&A departments of investment banks, covering deal origination, preparing a pitch book, how a company's valuation is reached, and how to read a prospectus that has been through countless drafts.
- Provides a useful understanding of the valuation process and the methods involved in valuing a company for an acquisition or a stock offering.
- Gives an account of due diligence, with stories about traveling to many different countries in a short period of time, making the authors too exhausted to remain awake during presentations.

IMPACT

- Details the authors' appointment as junior associates at the elite Wall Street investment bank Donaldson, Lufkin & Jenrette, tempted by visions of money and glamour.
- Explains that what they actually found was relentless hard work, boredom, bureaucracy, and incompetence, which they depict as representative of the whole banking sector.
- The continuous tensions between work and leisure, money and time, provide an understanding of how banks operate and use junior staff to build business.
- Discusses the working lifestyle of young investment bankers, what happens behind the scenes of the deal making, and what they will do to generate fees.
- Provides a guide on what to avoid, and how not burn out in the investment banking jungle.

QUOTATIONS

"We realized that the compensation levels and the perks weren't in place because being an associate in investment banking was a great job. They were in place because the job sucked."

"The investment banking community has long been an oligopoly, with only a handful of real players with the size and scale to drive through the big deals."

"Investment banking is a profession characterized by extremes. Whether it's money, booze, food, sex, or work hours, the typical banker believes that more is better."

▸▸ MORE INFO

See Also:

- *Barbarians at the Gate: The Fall of RJR Nabisco.* An absorbing tale of a 1980s corporate takeover. (p. 1223)
- *Liar's Poker: Rising Through the Wreckage on Wall Street.* This is also an insightful account of young MBAs and their experiences at a major investment bank. However, where *Monkey Business* is set in the 1990s and focuses on M&A, *Liar's Poker* is about life as a bond trader in the 1980s. (p. 1288)
- *Traders, Guns and Money: Knowns and Unknowns in the Dazzling World of Derivatives.* An entertaining introduction to derivatives trading and its impact on the financial markets by a veteran of the industry. (p. 1328)

"We realized that the compensation levels and the perks weren't in place because being an associate in investment banking was a great job. They were in place because the job sucked."

  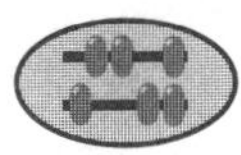   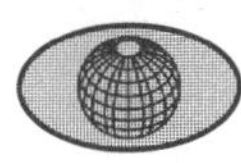   

Multinational Business Finance

DAVID K. EITEMAN, ARTHUR I. STONEHILL, and MICHAEL H. MOFFETT
(11th ed 2007, originally 1973)

WHY READ IT?

- Helps managers of multinational enterprises recognize and capitalize on the unique characteristics of the global markets.
- Communicates the background and complexities of international finance, maintaining a managerial focus.
- Examines the environment that the multinational business operates in, and offers guidance on the specific financial and business measures that need to be taken into account for varying circumstances.

GETTING STARTED

Multinational Business Finance is a textbook that provides practical insights into current financial management practices, and is a learning resource for students of international finance, as well as being useful as focused training for professionals. Now in its 11th edition, it can also be seen as a reference resource on the tools and techniques of business finance, as it works through the complexities of international finance in an authoritative manner.

AUTHORS

David K. Eiteman is Professor Emeritus at Anderson School of Management, UCLA, and has held appointments at a number of academic institutions. He is a former President of the International Trade and Finance Association, the Society for Economic and Management in China, and the Western Finance Association.

Arthur I. Stonehill is a Professor of Finance and International Business, Emeritus, at Oregon State University, and has held appointments at a number of academic institutions. He is a former President of the Academy of International Business, and a Western Director of the Financial Management Association.

Michael H. Moffett is Associate Professor of Finance at Thunderbird, The American Graduate School of International Management. He was formerly Associate Professor of Finance at Oregon State University, and has held a number of other teaching appointments.

CONTEXT

- Provides a number of real-world case studies that apply key concepts to the types of situations an international manager would face, in order to help them make financial decisions that increase firms' values.
- Does not go extensively into all the mathematical theory, but covers the requisite practical information of international business finance.
- Analyzes accounting exposures, and the impact of foreign affiliates on financial statements, and what this means for the operations of multinational business.
- Considers the essential and developing financing issues underpinning the global firm, such as cost of capital, financial structures, sourcing equity, and sourcing debt on a global basis.
- Covers issues of foreign investment decisions, particularly as they affect corporate strategy, capital budgeting, international acquisitions and valuation, and the necessary risk adjustments.

IMPACT

- Updated to provide insights into current financial management practices, and features a streamlined presentation, expanded attention to emerging markets, several new chapters, and four new decision cases with an emerging markets focus.
- Examines the changing attitudes towards the impact multinational corporations have on local businesses.
- Offers a number of tests, guidelines, and key issues, with teaching cases and internet coverage, to aid learning.

QUOTATIONS

"[Multinational enterprises] face unique risks that do not hamper domestic firms as much. These risks are related to foreign exchange risks and political risks."

"An important task of the financial manager is to measure foreign exchange exposure and to manage it so as to maximize the profitability, net cash flow, and market value of the firm."

"The ability of a firm to achieve a globally competitive cost and availability of capital depends on its success at attracting international portfolio investors."

▸▸ MORE INFO

Books:

Butler, Kirt C. *Multinational Finance.* Cincinnati: South-Western, 1997. Provides a concise treatment of the investment and financial decisions facing the multinational corporation.

Moffett, Michael H. *Cases in International Finance.* Boston, MA: Addison-Wesley, 2001. Further decision cases that complement the textbook.

Shapiro, Alan C. *Multinational Financial Management.* 8th ed. Hoboken, NJ: Wiley, 2006. Treats international financial management as a natural extension of financial management principles.

Website:

The book's website contains resources for students and instructors: wps.aw.com/aw_eiteman_mbf_11

See Also:

International Finance (pp. 1647–1649)

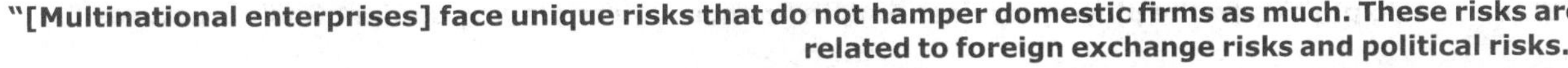
"[Multinational enterprises] face unique risks that do not hamper domestic firms as much. These risks are related to foreign exchange risks and political risks."

     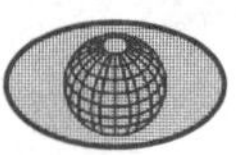   

My Life as a Quant

EMANUEL DERMAN (2004)

WHY READ IT?

- An honest and engaging account of the author's life, career, and experiences as a physicist and in quantitative finance.
- Shows how and why Derman made the transition from academia to Wall Street, and details the differences between the two worlds.
- Analyzes how the quantitative finance industry evolved, and its place in the investment community.
- Analyzes the varying styles and approaches of quants and traders and their incompatibility.
- Provides insights into how investment banks work, and the role that quants play in developing new products and trading strategies.
- Examines the nature of discovery in physics and how this compares with computational and theoretical finance.
- Derman comes across as humble, self-critical, philosophical, and intelligent as he reflects on his life and career; he feels that he wasn't able to be a success in his physics career, and that there was a wide disparity between youthful ideals and mature compromises.

GETTING STARTED

Derman was one of the first physicists to move into finance and use his skills in quantitative modeling and trading during the emergence of financial engineering and exotic derivatives in the 1980s and 1990s. In *My Life as a Quant,* he describes coming to terms with such a complete mindshift, and how he was able to apply his scientific skills to a burgeoning new area of research.

AUTHOR

Emanuel Derman is a Professor and Director of the Financial Engineering program at Columbia University. He was previously a Managing Director at Goldman Sachs, and has been named the SunGard/IAFE Financial Engineer of the Year, and appointed to the Risk Hall of Fame.

CONTEXT

- Describes Derman's interactions with famous scientists and big players on Wall Street, including Fischer Black, with whom he collaborated on the widely used Black–Derman–Toy model.
- Analyzes the development of quantitative finance as a practical discipline and its place in the hierarchy of finance, where traits like salesmanship, practical trading skills, and internal politicking are more of a dominant culture.
- Explains how the best financial quants combine mathematics, intuition, financial insight, business knowledge, and technology.

IMPACT

- Follows Derman's transformation from young scientist to Managing Director and head of the renowned quantitative strategies group at Goldman Sachs.

QUOTATIONS

"When you do physics you're playing against God; in finance, you're playing against God's creatures."

"Traders and quants are genuinely different species."

"Personality plays a larger part in economic writing because truth's part is smaller."

▸▸ MORE INFO

Books:

Bernstein, Peter L. *Capital Ideas: The Improbable Origins of Modern Wall Street.* New York: Free Press, 1992. Shows how a group of academics and economists changed the way that Wall Street ran the world's investments.

Mehrling, Perry. *Fischer Black and the Revolutionary Idea of Finance.* Hoboken, NJ: Wiley, 2005. Describes Black's life, and examines the history, players, and ideas of the evolving risk management industry.

See Also:

Fooled By Randomness: The Hidden Role of Chance in Life and the Markets. A readable account of the tendency to explain random events as due to cause and effect rather than chance. (p. 1263)

"When you do physics you're playing against God; in finance, you're playing against God's creatures."

  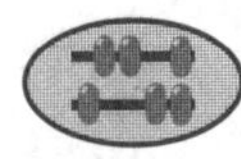   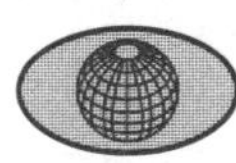   

A Non-Random Walk Down Wall Street

ANDREW W. LO and A. CRAIG MACKINLAY (1999)

WHY READ IT?

- Two distinguished researchers and authors offer an in-depth and technical exposition of the movements of markets.
- Examines and challenges in detail the random walk hypothesis, which is considered one of the foundations of financial theory and modeling.
- Finds that markets are not completely random, and that predictable components do exist in recent stock and bond returns, confronting a precept of financial economics and many investment strategies.

GETTING STARTED

A Non-Random Walk Down Wall Street puts the random walk hypothesis to the test. As a compilation of key research and writing from two reputed academics, it analyzes the markets and their non-randomness in detail, using a mathematically rigorous approach to reinforce their arguments.

AUTHORS

Andrew W. Lo is Professor of Finance at the MIT Sloan School of Management and the Director of MIT's Laboratory for Financial Engineering. He is also a Governor of the Boston Stock Exchange, and Founder and Chief Scientific Officer of AlphaSimplex Group.

A. Craig MacKinlay is Professor of Finance at Wharton. He has received the Paul A. Samuelson Award, and is a Research Associate of the National Bureau of Economic Research.

CONTEXT

- Focuses on financial economics, and the techniques used in advanced econometric analysis, to clarify common myths about efficient market theory and the random walk hypothesis.
- Examines the techniques for detecting predictabilities, and evaluates their statistical and economic significance.
- Concludes that the random walk model is not consistent with the behavior of weekly returns.
- Argues that day traders tend to overreact to news, making it possible to profit by taking the opposite side of their trades.

IMPACT

- Argues that the random walk hypothesis is false, that the financial markets are not inherently random, and that day-to-day movements in stock prices are not what many models predict.
- Tracks the course of the authors' research on the predictability of stock prices, from early work on rejecting random walks in short-horizon returns to their analysis of long-term memory in stock market prices.
- Attempts to show that the financial markets do contain a certain degree of predictability, and illustrate this by analyzing empirical data and through mathematical proof.
- Presents an enquiry into the pitfalls of "data-snooping biases" that have arisen from the use of the same historical databases for discovering anomalies and developing seemingly profitable investment strategies.

QUOTATIONS

"The Random Walk Hypothesis and. . .the Efficient Market Hypothesis have become icons of modern financial economics that continue to fire the imagination of academics and investment professionals alike."

"Unforecastable prices need not imply a well functioning financial market with rational investors, and forecastable prices need not imply the opposite."

"The apparent inconsistency between the broad support for the Random Walk Hypothesis and our empirical findings is largely due to the common misconception that the Random Walk Hypothesis is equivalent to the Efficient Market Hypothesis."

▸▸ MORE INFO

Books:

Campbell, John Y., Andrew W. Lo, and A. Craig MacKinlay. *The Econometrics of Financial Markets.* Princeton, NJ: Princeton University Press, 1997. Covering a broad sweep of empirical finance, it combines theory and practice to examine statistical techniques and their application to finance.

See Also:

The Intelligent Investor: A Book of Practical Counsel. The classic bestseller of value investing, which shows how to best develop long-term strategies. (p. 1280)

A Random Walk Down Wall Street: The Time-Tested Strategy for Successful Investing. Evaluates the investment opportunities from a variety of financial products in a more accessible manner. (p. 1303)

"The Random Walk Hypothesis and. . .the Efficient Market Hypothesis have become icons of modern financial economics that continue to fire the imagination of academics and investment professionals alike."

  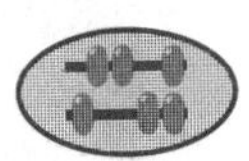   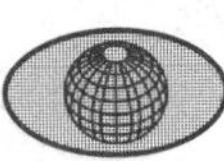   

On the Economy of Machinery and Manufactures

CHARLES BABBAGE (1832)

WHY READ IT?

- Babbage was one of the great minds of the first industrial revolution, credited with the first attempts at constructing a programmable computer.
- Offers a fascinating insight into the early development of manufacturing techniques and factory operations.
- Examines in detail two key areas: economies of scale and the division of labor, and their impact on industrialization.

GETTING STARTED

A bestseller of its day, *On the Economy of Machinery and Manufactures* is one of the first studies to recognize the importance of factories, both economically and socially. Babbage's fundamental approach was highly scientific, and he held that mechanical principles regulate the application of machinery to manufacturing.

AUTHOR

Charles Babbage (1791–1871) was a mathematician, philosopher, and mechanical engineer, who originated the first prototype computer. He co-founded the Analytical Society, was appointed to Chair of Mathematics at Cambridge, and founded the British Association for the Advancement of Science and the Statistical Society of London.

CONTEXT

- Emphasizes the practical elements of factory management in the early industrial era, and also the formation of interpretive theory.
- Details how mechanical principles govern manufacturing, and that merchants and manufacturers are the best people to supply the data for economists to use in their assessment of society.
- Argues that good factory organization is essential, and factories require an entire system of operation.
- Shows how it is vital to calculate the life expectancy of capital equipment for the smooth running of factories.
- Considers that the gathering of evidence is essential, which Babbage did through touring factories; also provides helpful hints and a checklist of questions on how to acquire the right information when touring a factory.

IMPACT

- Encourages managers to follow his example and gather their own data, as it is a pre-requisite for knowing how to gain more business.
- Establishes that machinery for producing any commodity in great demand seldom actually wears out due to continuous new improvements needed.
- Babbage was a pioneer of modern management, whose approach is similar to that later adopted by the champion of scientific management, Frederick Taylor. He beckoned in the industrial era and, in doing so, laid the intellectual groundwork for Marx, Engels, and John Stuart Mill.

QUOTATIONS

"Political economists have been reproached with too small a use of facts, and too large an employment of theory."

"The merchant and manufacturer are the best people to supply readily, and with so little sacrifice of time, the data on which all the reasoning of political economists are founded."

▸▸ MORE INFO

Books:

Hyman, Anthony. *Charles Babbage: Pioneer of the Computer.* Princeton, NJ: Princeton University Press, 1982. Looks at the career of Babbage, and the engines that were the forerunners of the modern computer.

Sherman, Josepha. *Charles Babbage and the Story of the First Computer.* Newark, DE: Mitchell Lane Publishers, 2006. An account of Babbage's life and work.

Swade, Doron. *The Difference Engine: Charles Babbage and the Quest to Build the First Computer.* New York: Viking, 2001. The author grappled with the technical difficulties of the time, as he led a team that built a working model of a Difference Engine.

"Political economists have been reproached with too small a use of facts, and too large an employment of theory."

  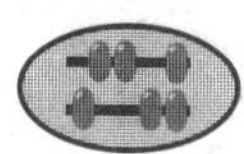   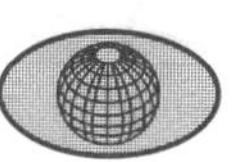   

One Up on Wall Street: How to Use What You Already Know to Make Money in the Market

PETER LYNCH (1989)

WHY READ IT?

- An introduction to the stock market, and what to look for when investing your money, without relying on what the experts tell you.
- Presents the author's proven strategies and principles on stock investing in a readable manner.
- Argues that small investors can research stocks better than most professionals, and that they should focus on quality, undervalued companies they can understand, and use common sense to identify those that will grow.

GETTING STARTED

One Up on Wall Street considers stock market investing from the standpoint of the amateur, arguing that the most successful type of investor does their homework, studies the fundamentals of a company, and then invests for the long term only in what they can understand. A bestseller, it provides an easy to understand and entertaining approach, and a set of fundamental rules that are easy to put into practice.

AUTHOR

Peter Lynch (b. 1944) is a successful fund manager and stockpicker. He previously managed the Fidelity Magellan Fund, the top-ranked general equity mutual fund in America, and has written several bestselling stock investing books. He was previously an analyst, and also writes a column for *Worth* magazine.

CONTEXT

- Lynch is a proponent of stock analysis and value investing, and focuses on analyzing company fundamentals such as sales, earnings, and growth rates.
- Categorizes different types of companies—stalwarts, fast growers, slow growers, cyclicals, asset plays, and turnarounds—in terms of their investment opportunity.
- Asserts that amateurs can be as good or even better than investment professionals as long as they are alert for opportunity, and invest in what they know, using local knowledge as much as possible.
- Shows how difficult it is to time the market, so you should ignore the experts and think for yourself, focusing on quality stocks at reasonable prices.
- Discusses the qualitative aspects of investing, including portfolio balance, picking winners, and when best to buy and sell.

IMPACT

- Advises that it is better to understand what kind of company to invest in and set specific investment objectives before purchase of a stock.
- Shows how to categorize the companies, and what strategy to use when investing in each of them.
- Informs on how to identify companies, how to analyze their prospects for growth, and how to continue monitoring potential growth.
- Argues that to beat the market you should choose a small portfolio of stocks that grow at a higher rate than the market average.

QUOTATIONS

"I continue to think like an amateur as frequently as possible."

"Stocks are most likely to be accepted as prudent at the moment they're not."

"Only invest what you could afford to lose."

▸▸ MORE INFO

Book:

Lynch, Peter. *Beating the Street.* New York: Simon & Schuster. 1993. A book aimed at all levels of investors, shows how to spot companies that will outperform.

See Also:

- *The Intelligent Investor: A Book of Practical Counsel.* The classic bestseller of value investing, which shows how to best develop long-term strategies. (p. 1280)
- *Stocks for the Long Run: A Guide to Selecting Markets for Long-term Growth.* Examines the workings of the stock market, and the strategies, tools, and techniques investors can use to make meaningful stock returns over time. (p. 1320)

"I continue to think like an amateur as frequently as possible."

  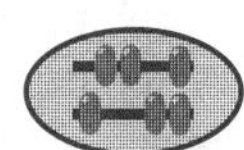 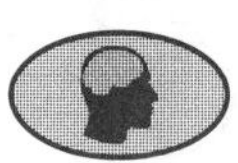  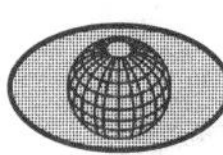   

1306 Option Volatility and Pricing: Advanced Trading Strategies and Techniques

SHELDON NATENBERG (1994)

WHY READ IT?

- One of the most widely read books among active option traders around the world.
- Although geared primarily towards professionals and traders, it will also be useful for amateurs interested in how to trade options.
- Points out the key concepts essential to successful trading, including option pricing, and strategies for training up to a desired level.

GETTING STARTED

Option Volatility and Pricing presents the fundamentals of option theory, and shows how it can be used to identify and exploit trading opportunities. It works through many of the classic trading strategies, so that the trader can select the best strategy for themself in terms of market conditions and personal risk tolerance. It considers the technicalities of how traded options work without being too mathematical.

AUTHOR

Sheldon Natenberg a recipient of the Traders' Hall of Fame Lifetime Achievement, began his trading career in 1982 at the Chicago Board Options Exchange. Since 1985 he has been trading commodity options at the Chicago Board of Trade, and conducting seminars at many of the world's exchanges.

CONTEXT

- Discusses the most current developments and trends in option products and trading strategies, such as pricing models, volatility considerations, basic and advanced trading strategies, and risk management techniques.
- Explains the underlying fundamentals in an understandable way.
- Looks at option strategies and definitions of different popular pricing models, as well as what goes into developing a theoretical option-pricing model.
- Describes how to determine if an option is over or undervalued.

IMPACT

- Examining both the theory and reality of option trading, it shows that option pricing and modeling cannot be an exact science due to volatility.
- Explains the essentials of volatility in great detail, and how to apply it to different option positions.
- Reveals the mechanics of how to price an option.
- Discusses the Normal distribution and how it relates to volatility and investing in options.

QUOTATIONS

"The direction in which the underlying market moves can have a significant effect on the profitability of an option strategy."

"Every trader who enters the marketplace must balance two opposing considerations, reward and risk."

"Only a trader who fully understands what a model can and cannot do will be able to make the model his servant rather than his master."

▸▸ MORE INFO

Book:

Cohen, Guy. *The Bible of Options Strategies: The Definitive Guide for Practical Trading Strategies*. London: FT Prentice Hall, 2005. A reference of the world's 60 best options trading strategies.

See Also:

Futures, Options and Swaps. (p. 1268)

Options, Futures, and Other Derivatives. The renowned title on the subject, which is more in-depth and technical than Natenberg. (p. 1307)

Derivatives and Quantitative Finance (pp. 1618–1621)

"The direction in which the underlying market moves can have a significant effect on the profitability of an option strategy."

  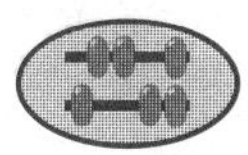   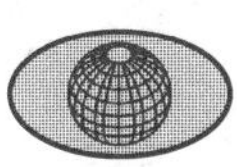   

Options, Futures, and Other Derivatives

JOHN C. HULL (7th ed 2008, originally 1989)

WHY READ IT?

- Introduces the world of derivatives, pricing, and risk management in clear and understandable terms.
- Provides a practitioner-focused overview of market dynamics and a feel of real market conditions.
- Offers a comprehensive overview of all the most relevant materials on the range of derivatives, together with derivations of all the formulas.

GETTING STARTED

Options, Futures, and Other Derivatives has long been the standard text for learning about financial engineering and derivatives; now in its seventh edition, it is a comprehensive treatment of all the main topics in mathematical finance. Widely used by academics and practitioners, especially traders, it is one of the most cited books on derivatives, teaching you how to analyze and trade these products.

AUTHOR

John C. Hull (b. 1946) is Professor of Derivatives and Risk Management at the Rotman School of Management, University of Toronto. He has acted as consultant to several financial institutions, won many teaching awards, and was voted Financial Engineer of the Year by the International Association of Financial Engineers in 1999.

CONTEXT

- Bridges the gap between the theory and practice of derivatives, and helps develop a working knowledge of how derivatives can be analyzed.
- Examines in detail the valuation of derivatives, presenting a unifying framework for derivative valuation.
- Provides a good grounding in pricing derivatives and explains clearly all the techniques you need for numerical valuation.
- Describes the basic principles of derivatives theory, and presents them in an intuitive way.

IMPACT

- The mathematics is stripped down to essentials, allowing you to quickly grasp the key assumptions underlying various models.
- Suitable for practitioners who want to acquire a working knowledge of how to analyze derivatives, and by MBAs who need a solid grounding in derivatives but want to avoid too much math.
- Updated to include new material on using futures for hedging, numerical procedures, swaps, credit risk, real options, insurance, and derivative crises.
- Includes MS Excel-based software that allows users to calculate options prices, imply volatilities, and calculate Greeks for European options, American options, exotic options, and interest rate derivatives.

QUOTATIONS

"We have now reached the stage where anyone who works in finance needs to understand how derivatives work, how they are used, and how they are priced."

"To avoid the sort of problems Barings encountered, it is very important for both financial and nonfinancial corporations to set up controls to ensure that derivatives are being used for their intended purpose."

"It is essential that all companies define in a clear and unambiguous way limits to the financial risks that can be taken."

▸▸ MORE INFO

Books:

Baxter, Martin, and Andrew Rennie. *Financial Calculus: An Introduction to Derivative Pricing*. Cambridge, UK: Cambridge University Press, 1996. Follows a pure math approach, focusing theory around mathematical theorems.

Hull, John C. *Options, Futures, and Other Derivatives: Student Solutions Manual.* Upper Saddle River, NJ: Pearson Education, 2008. Full manual for the seventh edition.

Wilmott, Paul. *Derivatives: The Theory and Practice of Financial Engineering.* Chichester, UK: Wiley, 1998. Takes a more applied math approach.

Website:

PowerPoint slides and updates to the software provided can be downloaded from the author's website: www.rotman.utoronto.ca/~hull

See Also:

Futures, Options and Swaps. Explains difficult concepts that the student needs to understand in this very technical subject area. (p. 1268)

Derivatives and Quantitative Finance (pp. 1618–1621)

"We have now reached the stage where anyone who works in finance needs to understand how derivatives work, how they are used, and how they are priced."

   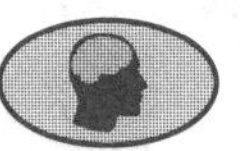  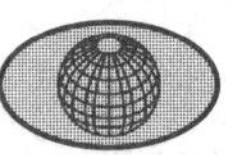  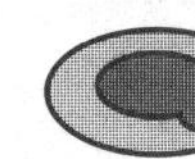 

1308 The Portable MBA in Finance and Accounting

THEODORE GROSSMAN and JOHN LESLIE LIVINGSTONE (EDS)
(4th ed 2009, originally 1992)

WHY READ IT?

- Provides a simplified learning resource for understanding finance and accounting as an organizational tool, especially for those who do not have time to do an MBA.
- Helps explain how the numbers work, how they can be used for competitive advantage, and how to use them for managing a business more effectively.
- Written by a team of professors from top business schools, it offers an overview of all the key concepts, topics, and terms.

GETTING STARTED

The Portable MBA in Finance and Accounting, now in its fourth edition, is a practical handbook on all the main aspects of the subject. It covers the basics for the financial management of companies of any size, including start-ups, and non-profit organizations. It offers a thorough grounding in applying finance and accounting to business needs, and the skills in budgeting and financial planning that are critical to running a business.

- Explains the main elements of pricing products and making profitable bids, business valuations, and managing financial risks with options, hedges, and derivatives.
- Also focuses on a range of practical topics, such as the responsibilities of governors and directors, bankruptcy, M&A, income tax, managing foreign exchange risk, activity-based costing, and creating a successful business plan.

IMPACT

- Provides practical and accessible definitions of key finance and accounting topics.
- Discusses strategies used in leading companies and business units on a daily basis.
- Illustrates how a manager can use spreadsheets to monitor how prices and costs affect business performance, and how financials can be used to build an effective strategy.
- Details how day-to-day business activities translate into the standard accounting reports.
- Assumes no prior financial and accounting knowledge or experience, and avoids excessive mathematics.
- Each chapter has useful internet links and further reading.

EDITORS

Theodore Grossman is a senior member of the faculty of Babson College, and was Founder of TRG Systems, Inc. He consults nationally for retailers and suppliers of retail technology.

John Leslie Livingstone directs his own consulting company. He was previously a Professor at Ohio State University, Chair at Georgia Institute of Technology, Chairman of the Department of Accounting at Babson College, and a Senior Partner at Coopers & Lybrand.

CONTEXT

- A useful reference for business managers needing an update on finance and accounting tools, techniques, and processes.
- Shows how to quickly grasp financial statements, analyze profitability, develop and use sophisticated cost-analysis tools, and perform financial forecasting and strategic budgeting.

QUOTATIONS

"All successful businesspeople should have a good basic understanding of financial statements and of the main financial ratios."

"An estimation of the sustainable portion of earnings should be the centerpiece of analyzing business earnings."

"Businesses cannot operate effectively without estimating the financial implications of their strategic plans and monitoring their progress throughout the year."

▸▸ MORE INFO

Books:

Bruner, Robert F., Mark R. Eaker, R. Edward Freeman, Robert E. Spekman, Elizabeth Olmsted Teisberg, and S. Venkataraman. *The Portable MBA*. 4th ed. Hoboken, NJ: Wiley, 2003. Based on the first year of an MBA program, this is a comprehensive overview on marketing, economics, ethics, technology, and strategy.

Siciliano, Gene. *Finance for Non-Financial Managers*. New York: McGraw-Hill, 2003. Guide to understanding financial reports, and how to use them to make informed decisions.

Silbiger, Steven. *The Ten-Day MBA: A Step-by-Step Guide to Mastering the Skills Taught in America's Top Business Schools*. New York: W. Morrow, 1993. A reference for MBAs and those in business, providing a basic framework for business courses.

"All successful businesspeople should have a good basic understanding of financial statements and of the main financial ratios."

  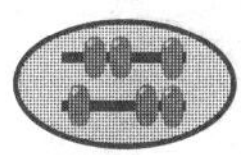   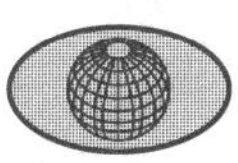  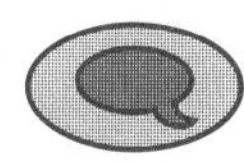 

Portfolio Selection: Efficient Diversification of Investments

HARRY MARKOWITZ (1959)

WHY READ IT?

- An acknowledged classic in the evolution of modern finance by a Nobel Prize-winning academic.
- A practical starting point for anyone interested in the efficient management and diversification of financial portfolios.
- Introduces the concepts around portfolio management and explains them in an easily understandable way.

GETTING STARTED

Portfolio Selection is based on the theory that investors should focus on selecting optimal portfolios as opposed to optimal assets, the first major breakthrough in the field of modern financial theory. This seminal work provides an insight into the early thinking and development of portfolio theory, and is a strong reference for individuals and financial institutions selecting optimal portfolios.

AUTHOR

Harry Markowitz (b. 1927) is Adjunct Professor of Finance at Rady School of Management. He developed his seminal theory of portfolio allocation under uncertainty in 1952, and went on to receive a PhD from the University of Chicago. He won the Nobel Prize in Economics in 1990, while a Professor of Finance at Baruch College.

CONTEXT

- Explains the theory upon which modern portfolio theory is based in an accessible manner without recourse to unnecessary mathematical terminology, and combines finance, economics, research, and computers to do so.
- Was the first book to consider risk along with return in portfolio management.
- The concepts are still used today by some of the world's biggest financial institutions to help them optimize returns.
- It created the mathematics of portfolio selection in a model that has turned out to be the indispensable building block from which the theory of the demand for risky securities is constructed.
- Shows the investor how to protect their portfolio and maximize returns.

IMPACT

- Argues that risk is what drives return, rather than being a by-product of the search for higher returns.
- Describes how the portfolio should dominate its constituent assets.
- Shows that the way to minimize risk for a given level of expected return is to minimize the covariance of returns of the assets within that portfolio.
- Provided the foundation for financial economics and computational economics, and the basis for concepts such as the Capital Asset Pricing Model, Efficient Markets Hypothesis, and behavioral finance.

QUOTATIONS

"To reduce risk, it is necessary to avoid a portfolio whose securities are all highly correlated with each other."

"To understand the general properties of large portfolios we must consider the averaging together of large numbers of highly correlated outcomes."

"The results of a portfolio analysis are no more than the logical consequences of its information *concerning securities."*

▸▸ MORE INFO

Books:

Elton, Edwin J., and Martin J. Gruber. *Modern Portfolio Theory and Investment Analysis.* New York: Wiley, 1981. Examines the characteristics and analysis of individual securities, as well as the theory and practice of optimally combining securities into portfolios.

Sharpe, William. *Investors and Markets: Portfolio Choices, Asset Prices, and Investment Advice.* Princeton, NJ: Princeton University Press, 2007. Another Nobel Prize winner, this time focusing more on helping investment professionals make better portfolio choices by improving on their asset pricing.

See Also:

Harry Markowitz (p. 1175)
Investment (pp. 1653–1658)

"To reduce risk, it is necessary to avoid a portfolio whose securities are all highly correlated with each other."

  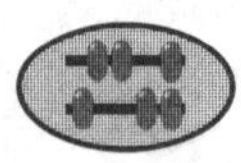   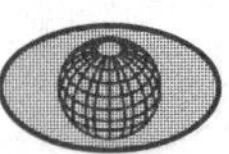   

Portfolio Theory and Capital Markets

WILLIAM SHARPE (1970)

WHY READ IT?

- A classic text on investment and portfolio theory, it presents Sharpe's groundbreaking work on the Capital Asset Pricing Model (CAPM).
- It examines how the financial markets operate and how investors can best deal with the uncertainties of pricing and risk.
- Still relevant today for investors and portfolio managers choosing investment portfolios.

GETTING STARTED

Portfolio Theory and Capital Markets introduces the Capital Asset Pricing Model, which has had a profound impact on modern finance and investment. The CAPM details why every investment contains two distinct risks, the systematic risk due to being in the market, and the unsystematic risk of a company's operations, and how they should be assessed in terms of individual securities and portfolios.

AUTHOR

William Sharpe (b. 1934) is Professor of Finance, Emeritus, at Stanford University's Graduate School of Business. He has served as President of the American Finance Association, been a consultant to Merrill Lynch, and co-founded William F. Sharpe Associates. He was the winner of the 1990 Nobel Memorial Prize in Economics.

CONTEXT

- The book that introduced CAPM to the investment community, and helped make Sharpe a recognized leader in financial research.
- Discusses the impact of the CAPM on investment theory and practice, and describes its use as a model for measuring portfolio risk along with the return an investor can expect for taking that risk.
- Explains how pricing and risk inform all investments, and the uncertainties and relationship between them impact on market knowledge.
- Discusses the implications of capital market theory, and the measures that can be used to understand the data, including the now widely used Sharpe ratio.

IMPACT

- Provides the theoretical underpinning of and groundwork for such investment standards as modern portfolio theory, derivatives pricing and investment, and equity index funds.
- Synthesizes many related areas of portfolio theory and the capital markets into a practical treatment that takes into account market volatility and uncertainty.
- Integrates historical research and analysis to improve portfolio construction and evaluation.
- Gives a useful overview of applying the economic model to a variety of securities, and how to calculate the payoff of the portfolio.
- Explains how to turn the theories into successful investment practice, and examines the impact this has.

QUOTATIONS

"Almost all empirical research deals with ex post manifestations of investor's expectations and their predictions of risk and correlations, and that such measures are subject to considerable error."

"The theoretical superiority of the market portfolio led directly to the concept of the index fund."

"[Portfolio theory] extends the classical economic model of investment under conditions of complete certainty."

▸▸ MORE INFO

Books:

Elton, Edwin J., Martin J. Gruber, Stephen J. Brown, and William N. Goetzmann. *Modern Portfolio Theory and Investment Analysis.* New York: Wiley, 1981. Examines the characteristics and analysis of individual securities, as well as the theory and practice of optimally combining securities into portfolios.

Sharpe, William. *Investors and Markets: Portfolio Choices, Asset Prices, and Investment Advice.* Princeton, NJ: Princeton University Press, 2007. Sharpe's most recent work, showing why investment professionals fail to make good portfolio choices unless they properly understand the determinants of asset prices.

See Also:

William F. Sharpe (p. 1193)

Portfolio Selection: Efficient Diversification of Investments. The classic of modern financial theory, which helped create the mathematics of portfolio selection. (p. 1309)

Capital Markets and Stock Markets (pp. 1588–1590)

"Almost all empirical research deals with ex post manifestations of investor's expectations and their predictions of risk and correlations, and that such measures are subject to considerable error."

  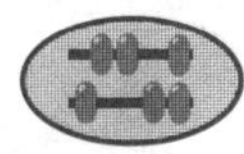   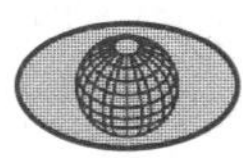   

The Practice of Management

PETER DRUCKER (1954)

WHY READ IT?

- Drucker was a major business thinker, who practically invented management as a discipline in the 1950s, and whose views are still relevant today.
- Asserts that management will remain a basic and dominant institution, with managers being at the epicenter of economic activity.
- Coined phrases such as "privatization" and "knowledge worker," and championed concepts such as "management by objectives." Many of his innovations have become accepted facts of managerial life.

GETTING STARTED

The Practice of Management is a book of huge range in its scope and historical perspectives. It laid the groundwork for many of today's accepted management practices and is an excellent primer in management thinking. It lays down five basics of the managerial role—to set objectives, organize, motivate and communicate, measure, and develop people.

AUTHOR

Peter F. Drucker (1909–2005) was a popular business and management thinker, and prolific writer on business management, entrepreneurship, and economics. He was a Professor at the Graduate School of Management, Claremont Graduate University, and was a consultant. He was also awarded the Presidential Medal of Freedom.

CONTEXT

- Details how the purpose of business is to create a customer and therefore a market, and the two essential functions of business are marketing and innovation.
- Assesses that the organization is a means to achieving business performance and results.
- Considers marketing as being not an isolated function, as it is the whole business seen from the customer's point of view.
- Argues that management has a moral responsibility, and must also be driven by objectives.
- Sees that the unique contribution of the manager as giving others vision and the ability to perform.
- Believes that each management job must be rewarding in itself, there must be a rational and just promotion system, management needs clear rules on who has the power over them, and there should be some way to appeal to a higher court.

IMPACT

- Identifies key tasks for the manager of the future: manage by objectives, take more risks for longer, be able to make strategic decisions, be able to build an integrated team, be able to communicate information, be able to see the business, and the industry as a whole, and be capable of integrating their function within it.
- In its appointments, management must realize that integrity is the one quality that a manager has to bring to the job and cannot be expected to acquire later on.

QUOTATIONS

"Management will remain a basic and dominant institution perhaps as long as Western civilization itself survives."

▸▸ MORE INFO

Books:

Drucker, Peter F. *The Daily Drucker: 366 Days of Insight and Motivation for Getting the Right Things Done.* New York: HarperBusiness, 2004. A ready source of condensed reading on Drucker's ideas, wisdom, and practical action points.

Drucker, Peter F. *Management Challenges for the 21st Century.* New York: HarperBusiness, 1999. Looks at recent social and economic change and considers how management should orientate itself to address these new realities.

Drucker, Peter F. *Managing For Results: Economic Tasks and Risk-Taking Decisions.* New York: Harper & Row, 1964. Presents Drucker's views on how organizations should perform, prosper and grow.

"Management will remain a basic and dominant institution perhaps as long as Western civilization itself survives."

  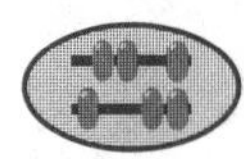   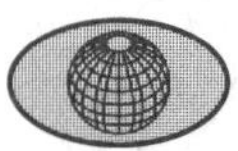   

Principles of Corporate Finance

RICHARD A. BREALEY, STEWART C. MYERS, and FRANKLIN ALLEN
(9th ed 2008, originally 1983)

WHY READ IT?

- Provides a comprehensive and practical introduction to the basic concepts and techniques of corporate finance.
- Can be beneficial throughout your career, from learning the basics as a student, to job training, to further learning such as an MBA, or as a reference for practicing financial managers.
- No previous knowledge is needed as the book takes you through all the basic information for implementing financial techniques.

GETTING STARTED

Principles of Corporate Finance is considered the bible of corporate finance, and is a teaching resource in many of the top business schools; now in its ninth edition, it teaches managers how to use financial theory to solve practical problems and to respond to change by implementing financial solutions.

AUTHORS

Richard A. Brealey is Visiting Professor of Finance at the London Business School, and a Special Adviser to the Governor of the Bank of England. He was previously a faculty member at LBS, the former President of the European Finance Association, and Director of the American Finance Association.

Stewart C. Myers is Professor of Financial Economics at MIT Sloan School of Management, and a past President of the American Finance Association. He is also a Research Associate at NBER, and a Director of the Cambridge Endowment for Research in Finance.

Franklin Allen is Co-Director of the Wharton Financial Institutions Center and the Nippon Life Professor of Finance and Economics at The Wharton School, University of Pennsylvania. His is Director of the Glenmede Fund and the Glenmede Portfolios, and is Scientific Adviser to the Central Bank of Sweden.

CONTEXT

- Enables a beginner to gain an in-depth and clear understanding of finance, investment, and the capital markets, demystifying many of the more complex topics.
- Acts as both a practical resource and learning tool on all the main tenets of financial performance and management, from the basic ideas on discounting to option pricing and innovative finance concepts.
- Explores both the theory and practice of corporate finance, as well as the essentials of economic value, the function and structure of the firm, the opportunity cost of capital, the capital asset pricing model, measures of return, risk return payoffs, financing decisions, and modern portfolio theory.

IMPACT

- Useful not only for theoretical study but also for practical work in financial positions, and preparing for examinations.
- Can be used for reviewing first principles, as well as integrating current research.
- Discusses in detail net present value and the best way to value a business.
- Incorporates lesson objectives at the start of each chapter, key points, and summary sections, to facilitate learning.
- Provides straightforward explanations, diagrams, formulas, and examples, and explains the math used in the examples.

QUOTATIONS

"Most investors are not adrenaline junkies; they don't enjoy taking risks. Therefore they require a higher expected return from risky investments."

"Long before the development of modern theories linking risk and expected return, smart financial managers adjusted for risk in capital budgeting."

"Smart managers know that it is often worth paying today for the option to buy or sell an asset tomorrow."

▸▸ MORE INFO

Books:

Damodaran, Aswath. *Corporate Finance: Theory and Practice.* New York: Wiley, 2000. Extremely applied and practical.

Ross, Stephen A., and Randolph Westerfield. *Fundamentals of Corporate Finance.* Chicago, IL: Irwin, 1995. Presents a unified valuation approach, with a management focus.

Watson, Denzil, and Antony Head. *Corporate Finance: Principles and Practice.* London: Pitman, 1998. Accessible and concise introduction to the key topic areas, incorporating a range of real-world examples.

See Also:

Corporate Financial Management. Full coverage of financial decision-making within the firm, as well as guidance on the financial markets. (p. 1241)

"Most investors are not adrenaline junkies; they don't enjoy taking risks. Therefore they require a higher expected return from risky investments."

  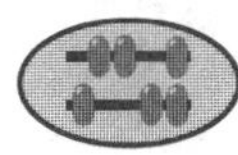   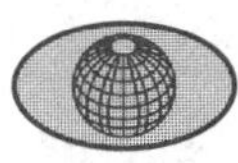   

A Random Walk Down Wall Street: The Time-Tested Strategy for Successful Investing

BURTON G. MALKIEL (9th ed 2007, originally 1973)

WHY READ IT?

- An investing classic that is also an entertaining read, this is a concise guide for the novice that challenges all preconceptions about investing.
- Shows how to manage money effectively regardless of personal income, savings, and age, and that diversification is critical to investment success.
- Also of interest to professionals, as it discusses aspects of investment such as the random walk hypothesis, the efficient market hypothesis, and portfolio theory with great insight.

GETTING STARTED

A Random Walk Down Wall Street has been a recognized classic of personal investment since it was published. Now updated and expanded for its ninth edition, it contains new analysis of behavioral finance and strategies for rearranging a retirement portfolio. It provides a history of investing, insights into how professionals invest, and the development of modern portfolio theory, and discusses how this can all be applied to managing an investment portfolio effectively. While warning against get-rich-quick schemes, it advocates asset allocation that is appropriate to both the age and the risk tolerance of the investor.

AUTHOR

Burton G. Malkiel (b. 1932) is Professor of Economics at Princeton University. He was previously Professor of Management Studies, and Dean, at Yale School of Management. He is a past appointee to the President's Council of Economic Advisors, and is a past President of the American Finance Association.

CONTEXT

- Describes a variety of investment types and styles, and recommends which investors should use, depending on personal circumstance.
- Examines market speculations that have spiraled out of control, from the tulip craze and the South Sea bubble, right up to the recent growth and the tech stocks bubbles.
- Believes in a diluted version of the efficient market hypothesis that has occasional inefficiencies, which even good money managers find it difficult to take advantage of, never mind amateur investors.
- Argues against trying to make a profit from either technical or fundamental analysis, but offers some simple rules for stock picking for those determined to invest.
- Considers some of the more complex investment topics such as modern portfolio theory and the capital asset pricing model.

IMPACT

- Provides a guide to investing that is of use to investors of any age, looks at the pitfalls and opportunities of investing, how investors often repeat their mistakes, and how they can be avoided.
- Evaluates the full range of investment opportunities, from stocks, bonds and money markets, to insurance, home ownership, gold, and collectibles.
- Explains the impact of financial risk and the riskiness of practically anything that can be invested in.
- Discusses the difference between having an attitude toward risk and a capacity to deal with it.
- Recommends ignoring the advice of all financial publications and newsletters.

QUOTATIONS

"Greed run amok has been an essential feature of every spectacular boom in history."

"The psychology of speculation is a veritable theatre of the absurd."

"The extent to which the stock market is usefully predictable has been vastly overstated."

▸▸ MORE INFO

Books:

Bernstein, William J. *Four Pillars of Investing: Lessons for Building a Winning Portfolio.* New York: McGraw-Hill, 2002. With a blend of market history, investing theory, and behavioral finance, this book enables investors to be self-sufficient, and provides the necessary tools to construct successful portfolios.

Malkiel, Burton G. *The Random Walk Guide to Investing: Ten Rules for Financial Success.* New York: W. W. Norton, 2003. A cut-down version of his classic, which condenses his thoughts into three basic points and 10 rules.

See Also:

Burton Malkiel (p. 1174)

  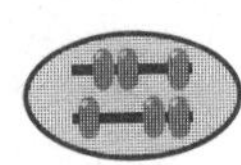   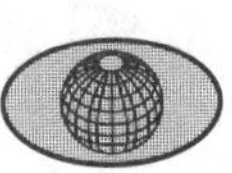   

Reengineering the Corporation: A Manifesto for Business Revolution

MICHAEL HAMMER and JAMES CHAMPY (1993)

WHY READ IT?

- This is the book that started the reengineering and process enterprise revolution, managerial innovations that have now become part of standard business practice.
- Focuses on how to improve three key areas of management—roles, styles and systems.
- Encourages organizations to take a fresh look at inefficient and outdated processes in the context of a competitive environment.

GETTING STARTED

Reengineering the Corporation is seen as the key book in the movement to corporate reengineering. It encourages organizations to take a fresh look at inefficient and outdated processes, and to focus on dramatic improvements in cost, quality, service, and speed. Although the message has been misinterpreted, reengineering remains a powerful tool for change.

AUTHORS

Michael Hammer (b. 1948) is a Senior Lecturer at the MIT Sloan School, and is a founder of several high-technology companies. He was previously a Professor of Computer Science at MIT, and was named by *Time* as one of America's 25 most influential individuals.

James Champy (b. 1942) is Chairman of Perot Systems consulting practice. He was previously Chairman and CEO of CSC Index, the management consulting arm of Computer Science Corporation.

CONTEXT

- Analyzes reengineering as a fundamental rethinking and radical redesign of business processes, to make key processes as lean and profitable as possible, discarding peripheral processes and people if necessary.
- Argues that reengineering puts a premium on the skills and potential of the people at the center of the organization, and should also tackle three key areas of management—managerial roles, styles, and systems.
- Proposes that reengineering should go far beyond just altering and refining processes: the objective should be to reverse the Industrial Revolution.

IMPACT

- Suggests that organizations should start with a blank piece of paper and map out new processes to identify how their business should operate more successfully, before attempting to translate this into concrete reality.
- Part of the problem is seen to be that managers fail to impose change on themselves—they concentrate on tearing down processes, but they leave their own jobs and management styles intact. However, the old ways of management could eventually undermine the very structure of their rebuilt enterprises.
- Reengineering is seen by some as an old concept with a new label. Frederick W. Taylor's *Principles of Scientific Management* advocated similar change, but at an individual rather than an organizational level.
- The message of the book has sometimes been taken too literally, with reengineering a synonym for downsizing or redundancy.

QUOTATION

"I tell them what I really do is I'm reversing the Industrial Revolution."

▸▸ MORE INFO

Books:

Champy, James. *Outsmart! How to Do What Your Competitors Can't.* Upper Saddle River, NJ: Financial Times Press, 2008. Shows how you can achieve breakthrough growth by consistently outsmarting your competition.

Champy, James. *Reengineering Management: The Mandate for New Leadership.* New York: HarperBusiness, 1995. Discusses the challenges managers face in trying to function in the re-engineered workplace.

Hammer, Michael. *Beyond Re-engineering: How the Process-Centered Organization is Changing our Lives.* New York: HarperBusiness, 1996. Explains how a shift to process, as a means of reengineering, is profoundly transforming the organization.

"I tell them what I really do is I'm reversing the Industrial Revolution."

  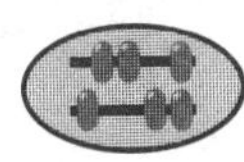   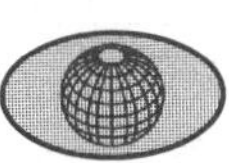   

Reminiscences of a Stock Operator

EDWIN LEFÈVRE (1923)

WHY READ IT?

- Remains the most widely read, highly recommended investment book ever written.
- Provides a highly entertaining account of a famous and successful speculator's career in the markets of the early 1900s.
- Offers insights into the workings of "bucket shops" from the turn of the century until the 1920s.

GETTING STARTED

Reminiscences of a Stock Operator is widely agreed to be a fictionalized biography of Jesse Livermore, a hugely successful American speculator of the early 1900s, who won and lost millions of dollars playing the stock and commodities markets. First published as a series of articles and illustrations in *The Saturday Evening Post*, the entire collection has been revised and published each year since its first publication, with the most recent edition including the original illustrations as they appeared in *The Saturday Evening Post*.

AUTHOR

Edwin Lefèvre (1871–1943) originally trained as a Mining Engineer, before becoming a Reporter for the *New York Sun*. He was then appointed as US Ambassador to various countries, but returned to writing both books, and short stories for such magazines as *The Saturday Evening Post*.

CONTEXT

- Written in the 1920s as a series of articles for *The Saturday Evening Post*, and considered to be the fictionalized biography of Jesse Livermore, a famous trader who operated during the early 20th Century.
- Shows how Livermore was eventually banned from the bucket shops because of how successful he was.
- Tells the story of how Livermore went on to speculate on Wall Street, where he made and lost his fortune several times over.
- Provides an accessible insight into the stock markets of the time, and how other big traders played the markets.
- Contains analysis by financial historian Charles Geisst that gives the readers an understanding of both the financial and cultural contexts.
- Observes the investing, speculating, and market of the time in acute detail.

IMPACT

- Offers a rare view of an emerging industry before the introduction of modern day technology and legislation.
- Assesses crowd psychology and market timing in a way that is still relevant today.
- Provides a study of a successful, lucrative career begun on a small budget.
- Examines both good and bad practice of the time in an historical context, based on actual events and real people.

QUOTATIONS

"Without faith in his own judgment no man can go very far in this game."

"And still the public loses money as easily as ever, because, though methods change and laws multiply and predatory wealth is curbed, the sucker is still the sucker."

"I always made money when I was sure I was right before I began. What beat me was not having brains enough to stick to my own game."

▸▸ MORE INFO

Book:

Livermore, Jesse. *How to Trade In Stocks: The Livermore Formula for Combining Time, Element and Price.* New York: Duel, Sloan & Pearce, 1940. The most successful stock trader who ever lived offers traders their first account of his trading system.

See Also:

Edwin Lefèvre (p. 1173)

Common Stocks and Uncommon Profits and Other Writings. An intuitive and accessible look at what variables should be looked at when assessing whether to invest in a company. (p. 1235)

The Money Game. Influential and thought-provoking book about money, based on actual experiences of a Wall St Insider during the '60s. (p. 1299)

  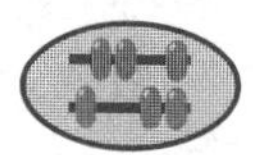   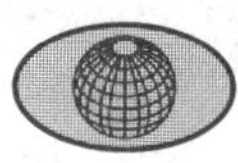   

The Rise and Fall of Strategic Planning

HENRY MINTZBERG (1994)

WHY READ IT?

- Analyzes the history of corporate strategy and its rise to prominence in business thinking, and the current dissatisfaction with strategic planning as being far from effective.
- Thinks that strategic planning is a contradictory concept, as planning encourages stability, while strategy is a more flexible idea, the direction of which can change more easily.
- Shows how over-emphasizing analysis and hard facts limits strategic planning; rather, planning should be visionary and creative.

GETTING STARTED

The Rise and Fall of Strategic Planning argues that strategy cannot be planned as business planning is concerned with analysis, while strategy making is primarily concerned with synthesis. Due to this dichotomy, strategic planning is not working, and can neither provide creativity, nor deal with it when it emerges.

AUTHOR

Henry Mintzberg is Professor of Management Studies at McGill University, Canada, and a visiting scholar at INSEAD, France. He has also been elected as an Officer of the Order of Canada, and as a Distinguished Scholar by the Academy of Management.

CONTEXT

- Describes strategic planners as tending to be detached from the reality of the organization, making false assumptions that discontinuities can be predicted, that the future will resemble the past, and that strategy making can be formalized.
- Examines why planners have typically gathered hard data on their industry, markets, and competitors. Soft data—such as networks of contacts, talking with customers, suppliers, and employees—have been ignored.
- Argues that to gain useful understanding of an organization's competitive situation, soft data need to be dynamically integrated into the planning process as the key to strategy making.
- Sees strategy formulation as having been dominated by logic and analysis, which narrow options, and promotes intuition and creativity as important to the process.
- Describes planners as having value, but only as strategy finders, analysts, and catalysts for change. They need to do more.

IMPACT

- Considers the three main pitfalls of planning practice as the assumptions that discontinuities can be predicted, that planners are in touch with the reality of the organization, and that strategy making can be formalized.
- Points out that if the system does the thinking, then strategy must be separated from business operations—and the thinkers from the doers—something the author thinks lies at the root of the problem with strategic planning.
- Challenges strategists such as Michael Porter about the alternatives for business change.

QUOTATION

"Strategy cannot be planned."

▸▸ MORE INFO

Books:

Mintzberg, Henry, Bruce Ahlstrand, and Joseph B. Lampel. *Strategy Bites Back*. Harlow, UK: FT Prentice Hall, 2005. Shows how the most interesting and most successful companies have creative, inspiring, and even playful, strategies.

Mintzberg, Henry, Bruce Ahlstrand, and Joseph B. Lampel. *Strategy Safari: A Guided Tour Through the Wilds of Strategic Management*. New York: Free Press, 1998. Defines what strategy really means for management decision-making, and draws together the various strands of strategic thought.

Porter, Michael E. *Competitive Strategy: Techniques for Analyzing Industries and Competitors*. New York: Free Press, 1980. Shows how companies with a clear strategy outperform those whose strategy is unclear.

"Strategy cannot be planned."

     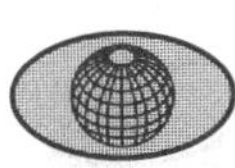   

The Six Sigma Way: How GE, Motorola and Other Top Companies are Honing Their Performance

PETER S. PANDE, ROBERT NEUMAN, and ROLAND R. CAVANAGH (2000)

WHY READ IT?

- The authors are Six Sigma experts who have taught major firms how to effectively implement this business management strategy.
- Explains how Six Sigma operates as a useful and straightforward tool that integrates a quest for perfection into organizational planning.
- Shows you how to launch a Six Sigma initiative, with examples from companies that have introduced the program.

GETTING STARTED

Shows how the Six Sigma strategy can be used to identify problems in manufacturing and business processes, and how these can then be resolved. It explains how the principles of Six Sigma can be applied to reduce costs, improve productivity, increase market share, and have a generally beneficial effect on any type of organization. This is a comprehensive guide for adapting and implementing this established quality management system, originally popularized by Jack Welch when he ran General Electric.

AUTHORS

Peter S. Pande is founder and President of Pivotal Resources, an international consulting firm that has helped companies such as Citicorp and Chevron implement Six Sigma systems.

Robert Neuman is a senior consultant with Pivotal Resources, and speaker on business improvement methods and Six Sigma.

Roland R. Cavanagh is a professional engineer and consultant with Pivotal Resources, who has worked with companies such as America West Airlines, Commonwealth Edison, and Tencor Instruments.

CONTEXT

- Examines how Six Sigma operates as a data-driven management system, with performance objectives that are based on perfect attainment.
- Shows how Six Sigma generates sustained success, introduces performance goals, improves value to customers, promotes learning, and executes strategic change.
- Focuses on the practical implementation and fundamentals, key stages, and quality improvement tools in the Six Sigma system.
- Debunks certain myths around the system, such as the view that it's only of benefit to manufacturing companies, and that it uses a plethora of high-level statistics.
- Examines the differences between Six Sigma and other business strategies such as Total Quality Management.
- Incorporates examples from business leaders and managers that have used Six Sigma in their companies.

IMPACT

- Identifies key elements that can be applied to different business activities and challenges, to help maximize performance.
- Looks at how the benefits of Six Sigma can be achieved by a whole enterprise, or even just a single department within it.
- Presents a roadmap for introducing a Six Sigma program, focusing on basic measurement and analysis techniques, and showing how to achieve support from management and staff.

QUOTATIONS

"Six Sigma can inspire and motivate better ideas and performance from people—and create synergy between individual talents and technical prowess."

"Any level of Six Sigma effort takes an investment in time, energy, and money."

"Results come much faster when an organizations is willing to admit to its shortcomings, learn from them, and start setting priorities to correct them."

▸▸ MORE INFO

Books:

Breyfogle, Forrest W. *Implementing Six Sigma: Smarter Solutions Using Statistical Methods.* New York: Wiley, 1999. A useful reference on the key tools and how a Six Sigma program is typically implemented.

Pande, Peter S., Robert Neuman, and Roland R. Cavanagh. *The Six Sigma Way Team Fieldbook: An Implementation Guide for Process Improvement Teams.* New York: McGraw-Hill, 2002. A companion guide that focuses on the work of the project management teams.

Pyzdek, Thomas. *The Six Sigma Handbook: The Complete Guide for Greenbelts, Blackbelts, and Managers at All Levels.* New York: McGraw-Hill, 2001. Analyzes the systems and statistical tools that underpin this approach to management.

See Also:

i Business Appraisal and Performance Measurement (pp. 1576–1579)

"Six Sigma can inspire and motivate better ideas and performance from people—and create synergy between individual talents and technical prowess."

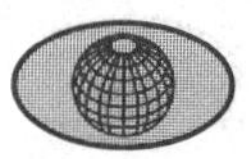

The Smartest Guys in the Room: The Amazing Rise and Scandalous Fall of Enron

BETHANY MCLEAN and PETER ELKIND (2003)

WHY READ IT?

- Tells of Enron's rise and dramatic fall from a US$70 billion company to bankruptcy.
- Hailed as one of the biggest success stories in corporate America for a generation, the success was shown to be illusory and based on deception. This book details the full story of its downfall and the greed that led to it.
- Examines the corporate culture, where the behavior of senior executives allowed things to escalate.

GETTING STARTED

The Smartest Guys in the Room covers the history of the celebrated and then notorious energy company Enron from its inception to spectacular collapse, the first of a series of major corporate scandals. It details the combination of intelligence and arrogance that helped create an environment that was hailed as visionary but where financial maneuvering for profit overstepped into the illegal.

AUTHORS

Bethany McLean (b. 1970) is Editor-at-Large for *Fortune*. In 2001 she was one of the first reporters to raise questions about Enron. She was previously an Analyst at Goldman Sachs, and has a BA in English and mathematics from Williams College.

Peter Elkind is Editor-at-Large for *Fortune*. He has twice won the World Leadership Forum's Journalist of the Year award, and has been a guest on numerous radio and television programs. He graduated with honors from Princeton University.

CONTEXT

- Bethany McLean was the first journalist to question the accounting validity of the profits that Enron was making—within a year of her original article, Enron was facing the largest bankruptcy in US history.
- Tells of the top executives: CEO Kenneth Lay, Jeff Skilling, and CFO Andrew Fastow, the huge salaries and bonuses, and the complicity of the lawyers and accountants.
- Details the stories of employees who lost their jobs, disappointed shareholders, executives receiving prison sentences, and even suicide.
- Describes the culture of landing big deals, particularly in new industries and markets, and the subsequent failure to follow through and financially contribute to the company.

IMPACT

- Exposes the complicity of the investment banks, the accountants, and the lawyers that directly benefited without looking into the details behind their profit-making.
- Questions key aspects of corporate governance, such as business performance being pegged to the stock price, so that executives ensured strong financial statements to obscure the fact that the profits were not real.
- Examines Enron's use of "mark to market" accounting, which was largely responsible for obscuring the losses that had been made.
- Depicts the creative accounting methods such as hiding massive debt in off-balance-sheet schemes so that Enron could present itself as fantastically profitable.

QUOTATIONS

"The Enron scandal grew out of a steady accumulation of habits and values and actions that began years before and finally spiraled out of control."

"The tale of Enron is a story of human weakness, of hubris and greed and rampant self-delusion; of ambition run amok; of a grand experiment in the deregulated world; of a business model that didn't work; and of smart people who believed their next gamble would cover their last disaster—and who couldn't admit they were wrong."

"The government [indictment] portrayed Enron as a company that was operated to create the illusion of prosperity, not the reality. In other words: a fraud."

⏩ MORE INFO

Books:

Eichenwald, Kurt. *Conspiracy of Fools: A True Story.* New York: Broadway Books, 2005. Also on the Enron story, but portrayed in more of a novelistic style.

Swartz, Mimi, and Sherron Watkins. *Power Failure: The Inside Story of the Collapse of Enron.* New York: Doubleday, 2003. The personal story from Watkins, who was the Enron accountant who tried to alert Kenneth Lay about the accounting improprieties.

Movie:

Gibney, Alex (dir). *Enron: The Smartest Guys in the Room*, 2005. DVD documentary based on the book.

"The Enron scandal grew out of a steady accumulation of habits and values and actions that began years before and finally spiraled out of control."

  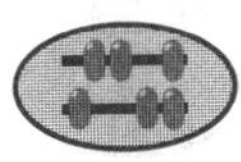   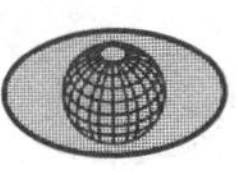   

The Snowball: Warren Buffett and the Business of Life

ALICE SCHROEDER (2008)

WHY READ IT?

- The first full biography of Warren Buffett, the most famous investor of all time, written with his full cooperation and collaboration.
- Gives a lucid account of his life and career, from his first financial forays to becoming a revered investment guru.
- Analyses his business deals and strategies, as well as mistakes, by looking at the development of his investing style, his many investment partnerships, and how he built up his fortune.

GETTING STARTED

The Snowball is a comprehensive and revealing biography, based on interviews with Buffett, his wife, children, friends, and business associates—with the help of unprecedented access to his files. It covers the narrative of his upbringing in a middle-American family, his early pursuit of profitable business ideas, how he became a millionaire by the time he was 30, and the deals that helped grow Berkshire Hathaway into a multibillion dollar company. Through this fascinating financial success story, we learn about his personality, intellect, and humanity, as well as about the investment philosophy and worldview that has helped him to great wealth.

AUTHOR

Alice Schroeder is an insurance analyst and a managing director at Morgan Stanley. She received an MBA from the University of Texas at Austin, before becoming a certified public accountant, working for Ernst & Young.

CONTEXT

- *Snowball* is a thorough and inclusive biography of the world's greatest investor, examining his family history, his youthful adventures, and how he developed his investment acumen.
- It shows how Buffett came from a line of small business owners, and how his parents toiled through the Great Depression, and how his somewhat unbalanced mother shaped his outlook on life.
- Reveals that his investment career took off with the purchase of textile firm Berkshire Hathaway, and explains how he grew it into the 12th largest corporation in the United States.
- It combines biographical detail with an examination of his business deals, focusing on the development of his expertise, strategy, and investment philosophy.
- Lays bare the real Buffett—his moral viewpoint, honesty, and integrity, as well as his many contradictions, such as his frugality, eccentric eating habits, and choice of clothing.
- Details how he built up his business expertise, and the success of his many investment partnerships.

IMPACT

- Gives a detailed account of his investments over the years, how he selected companies in which to invest, his definition of risk, and how he decided how much to actually invest in each company.
- Shows his successful preference for long-term investing in sound businesses that he can understand, as well as belief in stewardship and integrity towards these companies.
- Examines how he has evolved into the figurehead of value investing after his guru Benjamin Graham, rather than as someone who follows market bubbles, such as the tech boom of the late 1990s.
- Looks at his dependence on friends and a network of business associates, and how his collaboration with other investment managers proved essential to his success.
- Provides insight into Buffett's focus on customer loyalty, the quality of management, choosing allies carefully, and avoiding unnecessary diversity.
- Shows how he was one of the first to point out the inherent danger in derivative products, and how they could affect the financial system.
- Argues that he prefers being involved in new ventures to personal leadership of his investments.

QUOTATIONS

"Warren may have said he wanted to become a millionaire, but he never said that he would stop there."

"Berkshire's best opportunities always came at times of uncertainty, when others lacked the insight, resources, and fortitude to make the right judgments and commit."

"Cash combined with courage in a crisis is priceless."

▸▸ MORE INFO

Books:

Buffett, Warren. *The Essays of Warren Buffett: Lessons for Corporate America.* New York: Cardozo Law Review, 1997. A valuable overview of his thinking and strategy, with much financial wisdom from the annual reports he writes for Berkshire Hathaway.

Lowenstein, Roger. *Buffett: The Making of an American Capitalist.* New York: Random House, 1995. An entertaining biography of the man, which delves into his personality as well as investing career. Provides useful detail on the Buffett strategy of betting on the long-term growth of only a few companies.

See Also:

Warren Buffett (p. 1157)

The Warren Buffett Way: Investment Strategies of the World's Greatest Investor. The bestseller that examines Buffett's life and the development of his business and investment portfolio. (p. 1332)

"Warren may have said he wanted to become a millionaire, but he never said that he would stop there."

  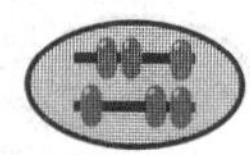   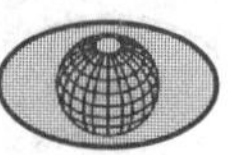   

Stocks for the Long Run: The Definitive Guide to Financial Market Returns and Long-Term Investment Strategies

JEREMY J. SIEGEL (4th ed 2008, originally 1994)

WHY READ IT?

- Siegel is one of the most respected investment strategists, and he here updates his most famous book to cover today's financial world and markets.
- Is of benefit to professional investors, as well as those new to investing and wanting to know how the market works.
- Takes a long-term approach to value investing, arguing that you have to be in it for the long haul to be successful.

GETTING STARTED

Stocks for the Long Run, now in its fourth edition, examines today's turbulent stock market with the strategies, tools, and techniques investors need to achieve meaningful stock returns over time. It provides an understanding of how to implement a reliable investment strategy, and draws upon historical market data to make a compelling case for stocks as the most dependable investment strategy.

AUTHOR

Jeremy J. Siegel (b. 1945) is Professor of Finance at Wharton, and has also taught at the Graduate School of Business of the University of Chicago. He has worked at J. P. Morgan, is currently the Academic Director of the US Securities Industry Institute, and appears frequently in the media.

CONTEXT

- Provides a powerful summary of the historical data available on investing and market returns, to support Siegel's preference for empiricism and a scientific method to choosing stocks.
- Examines the various investment theories and styles that can be used, as well as the economic influences that impact on investing, and the newer products available, such as exchange-traded funds.
- Discusses the value of patience and understanding your timescales before fixing on a particular investment mix.
- Considers how behavior influences investment decisions and potential success.

IMPACT

- Argues for a long-term and patient approach to stock investing and maintaining a long-term portfolio, especially given the regular fluctuations of the stock market.
- Analyzes the merits of short and long-term stock investing, and shows why the latter yields superior performance and lower risk.
- Covers the entire spectrum of opportunities that exist for investors, from international markets to the debate over growth versus value stocks.
- Shows what the long-term investor must address in organizing their portfolio, from diversification to tax advantages.
- Explains how to calculate stock returns and more technical aspects of analyzing stocks.

QUOTATIONS

"Investing in international equities [is] not only important but critical to developing a comprehensive investment strategy."

"The worst course an investor can take is to follow the prevailing sentiment about economic activity."

"Which stocks you own is secondary to whether you own stocks, especially if you maintain a balanced portfolio."

▸▸ MORE INFO

Book:

Ellis, Charles D. *Winning the Loser's Game: Timeless Strategies for Successful Investing*. New York: McGraw-Hill, 3rd ed., 1998. Offers strategies for controlling your investments, by working with the markets instead of against them.

Website:

Author website at: www.jeremysiegel.com.

See Also:

Jeremy Siegel (p. 1194)

The Intelligent Investor: A Book of Practical Counsel. The classic bestseller of value investing, which shows how to best develop long-term strategies. (p. 1280)

A Random Walk Down Wall Street: The Time-Tested Strategy for Successful Investing. Evaluates the investment opportunities from a variety of financial products. (p. 1303)

"Investing in international equities [is] not only important but critical to developing a comprehensive investment strategy."

  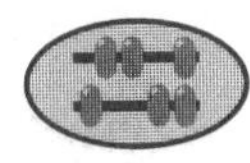   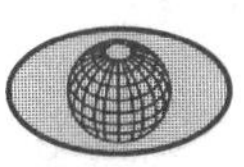   

Take On the Street: What Wall Street and Corporate America Don't Want You to Know

ARTHUR LEVITT (2002)

WHY READ IT?

- Describes how the US securities markets work, their differences, the relationships within them, and why they act as they do.
- Explains the relationship between brokers, analysts, corporations, and politicians.
- A guide to what is happening with an investor's money and how it is possible to maintain control of it.

GETTING STARTED

Take On The Street examines the US stock markets, the dangers faced by individual investors when they invest money in them, and how these dangers can be avoided. It takes the reader through many real examples of malpractice, and uses them to examine how the industry works. The main message is that investors need to research all aspects of the market before investing.

AUTHOR

Arthur Levitt (b. 1931) was the longest-serving chairman of the US Securities and Exchange Commission, which he ran between 1993 and 2001. After working on Wall Street as a broker, and later chairing the American Stock Exchange, he became Chairman of the NYC Economic Development Corporation. He has been a Senior Advisor to the Carlyle Group since leaving the SEC.

CONTEXT

- Provides a personal account of the author's time as the Chairman of the SEC.
- Shows the influence of political parties and individuals on the US stock markets.
- Explains how the brokerage system works, what commissions, bonuses, and fees to expect, and how and when these are paid.
- Offers advice on how to make the most of investments, and how to influence the workings of the markets.
- Examines the Enron collapse to show how the policy changes he championed could help remove corruption within the industry.
- Shows the bigger picture when it comes to trading on the US markets.

IMPACT

- Controversially analyzes the workings of an industry commonly regarded as complex and difficult for outsiders to understand.
- Examines the nature of political influence on those that work within the US markets and how this helped to shape an industry the author believes to be fundamentally corrupt.
- Includes correspondence between the author and key players such as senators and the chief executive of Enron.
- Intended as a warning to market investors, but also as a guide to how to be successful and use the system to advantage.

QUOTATIONS

"By learning about conflicts, motivations, and political favoritism, investors can become more discerning in how they use the power of their money and the power of their shareholder vote."

"America's markets operate by a set of rules that are half written and half custom. That makes the individual's responsibility to discern hidden motivations and conflicts of interest as important as any law or regulation."

"If you understand the basic mechanics of how stocks trade, you'll be better equipped to watch out for your own interests."

▸▸ MORE INFO

Books:

Casparino, Charles. *Blood on the Street: The Sensational Inside Story of How Wall Street Analysts Duped a Generation of Investors.* New York: Free Press, 2005. A detailed account of the US stock markets in the late 1990s, the Internet bubble, and how doctored research on Internet companies was created by large investment banks at the expense of smaller investors.

Schwager, Jack D. *New Market Wizards: Conversations with America's Top Traders.* New York: HarperBusiness, 1992. A series of interviews with traders focused on the trading psychology, and information and advice on how to be a successful trader.

"By learning about conflicts, motivations, and political favoritism, investors can become more discerning in how they use the power of their money and the power of their shareholder vote."

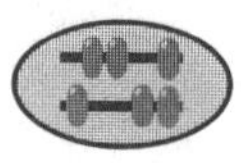

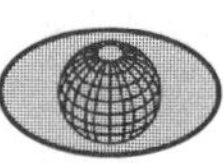

Taxes and Business Strategy: A Planning Approach

MYRON S. SCHOLES, MARK A. WOLFSON, MERLE M. ERICKSON, EDWARD L. MAYDEW, and TERRENCE J. SHEVLIN (4th ed 2008, originally 1992)

WHY READ IT?

- Focuses on the importance of effective tax planning in the business and investment decision-making process.
- Presents the implications of certain taxation issues in a straightforward and understandable fashion.
- Analyzes the main tax issues faced by investment bankers, making it an essential resource for planning tax and business strategy.
- Uses an abundance of examples that can be applied directly to situations that arise in the real world.

GETTING STARTED

Taxes and Business Strategy, now in its fourth edition, addresses contemporary tax issues and provides a clear framework for understanding how taxation influences asset prices, equilibrium returns, and the form and content of contractual agreements. It analyzes the critical issues in tax accounting, economics, and corporate strategy in a readable and practical way.

AUTHORS

Myron S. Scholes (b. 1941) is Professor of Finance Emeritus at the Stanford University Graduate School of Business, and Chairman of Platinum Grove Asset Management. He has previously been President of the American Finance Association, and was awarded the Alfred Nobel Memorial Prize in Economic Sciences in 1997.

Mark A. Wolfson is Consulting Professor at the Stanford Graduate School of Business. He is a Managing Partner of Oak Hill Capital Management.

Merle M. Erickson is Professor of Accounting at the University of Chicago Booth School of Business, and is a co-editor of the *Journal of Accounting Research*. He has received several awards from the American Taxation Association

Edward L. Maydew is the David E. Hoffman Distinguished Professor of Accounting at the Kenan-Flagler Business School, University of North Carolina. He also serves as Director of Research for the UNC Tax Center.

Terrence J. Shevlin is Professor of Accounting, the Paul Pigott-PACCAR Professor of Business Administration, and Chair, Department of Accounting, at the Foster School of Business, University of Washington.

CONTEXT

- Provides extensive analysis of technical tax rules applied to corporate mergers and acquisitions, an explanation of accounting for income taxes, a discussion on college savings plans, and a practical evaluation of the new tax rates on dividends and capital gains.
- Examines the pervasive impact of tax rules on the investment and financial decisions of businesses.
- Highlights important economic issues found in a multitude of tax-related transactions.
- Focuses more clearly on the economic consequences of alternative contractual arrangements than on the precise tax laws governing the arrangements.

IMPACT

- Relevant for those in investment banking, law, private equity, and other fields where tax plays a large role in determining the outcome and structure of deals and compensation.
- Provides a multi-perspective framework for thinking about tax issues and how taxes can impact the value of a transaction.
- Serves as a guide for any investment banker or experienced professional wanting to develop more efficient structuring alternatives for clients.
- Integrates an understanding of the tax laws with fundamentals of corporate finance and microeconomics.
- Shows how accountants and economists can unify the way they think about taxation.
- Useful as course material for studying tax strategy, investment banking, corporate finance, strategy consulting, money management, and venture capital.

QUOTATIONS

"Traditional approaches to tax planning fail to recognize that effective tax planning and tax minimization are very different things."

"We view efficient tax planning as part of the larger problem of the efficient design of organizations."

"From a social policy standpoint, tax rules are most controversial when they are designed to discriminate among different economic activities."

MORE INFO

Books:

Block, Cheryl D. *Corporate Taxation: Examples And Explanations.* New York: Aspen Law & Business, 1998. Builds your understanding through application of hypothetical examples.

Karayan, John E., Charles W. Stenson, and Joseph W. Neff. *Strategic Corporate Tax Planning.* Hoboken, NJ: Wiley, 2002. A corporate guide to understanding the basic tax implications of everyday business.

See Also:

Myron Scholes (p. 1190)

"Traditional approaches to tax planning fail to recognize that *effective tax planning* and *tax minimization* are very different things."

  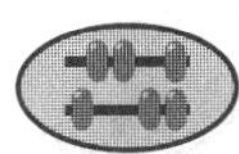   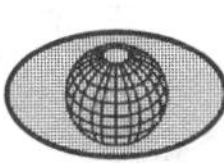   

Technical Analysis of the Financial Markets: A Comprehensive Guide to Trading Methods and Applications

JOHN J. MURPHY (1999)

WHY READ IT?

- Offers a clear and concise explanation of the underlying concepts and practical uses of technical analysis in a way that anyone approaching the markets can understand.
- Provides a guide to understanding and interpreting stock and commodity charts, and stock market movements.
- Covers all the essentials for learning how to use technical analysis, before tackling the more advanced principles and the linkages between them.

GETTING STARTED

Technical Analysis of the Financial Markets is known as the "bible" on TA; it is useful both for beginners and experienced traders, as it describes all the main tools, techniques, and applications for market trading and investment based on charting and historic data. Murphy interprets the role of the technical forecasters in today's financial climate, and explains how they apply their techniques to the financial markets.

AUTHOR

John J. Murphy (b. 1952) is founder and President of MurphyMorris, Inc. He was previously a Director of Technical Analysis for Merrill Lynch, and was the Technical Analyst for CNBC-TV for many years.

CONTEXT

- Shows how TA uses historic trading data, especially prices, volume, and open interest, in order to predict future prices of securities, currencies, and commodities.
- Examines all the key techniques, such as chart construction, fundamental vs technical analysis, trends, major technical pattern recognition, moving averages, oscillators, times cycles, and computer trading systems.
- Covers different methods of charting, including bar, point, figure, and candlestick, and how patterns and indicators are used.
- Considers all that is needed to understand the underlying structure and psychology of the financial markets.
- Reviews quantitative techniques, such as moving averages, oscillators, and Boillinger Bands.

IMPACT

- Examines the basic structure of all major TA techniques, to help choose the best method for specific trading and investment decisions.
- Details how to apply basic and sophisticated TA methods, emphasizing charting techniques, numerical indicators, and the importance of trend in the financial markets.
- Many believe that technical analysis of stock charts helps you make better trades and more consistent profits; some prefer fundamental analysis, or a combination of the two.
- Provides examples and analysis of market moves and quotes from the author's newsletter.
- Recognized by the main industry associations, and is required reading for both the Chartered Market Technicians designation and the Diploma of International Technical Analysis.

QUOTATIONS

"The statement 'market action discounts everything' forms what is probably the cornerstone of technical analysis."

"The fundamentalist studies the cause of market movement, while the technician studies the effect."

"By following all the markets [the technician] gets an excellent feel for what markets are doing in general, and avoids the 'tunnel vision' that can result from following only one group of markets."

▸▸ MORE INFO

Books:

Edwards, Robert D., John Magee, and W. H. Charles Bassetti. *Technical Analysis of Stock Trends.* 9th ed. Boca Raton, FL: CRC Press, 2007. Was the first to produce a methodology for interpreting the predictable behavior of investors and markets.

Murphy, John J. *Study Guide for Technical Analysis of the Financial Markets: A Comprehensive Guide to Trading Methods and Applications.* New York: New York Institute of Finance, 1999. Study guide that enables the reader to monitor and review their progress.

Pring, Martin J. *Technical Analysis Explained: The Successful Investor's Guide to Spotting Investment Trends and Turning Points.* New York: McGraw-Hill, 1985. Provides a practical introduction, explaining how to understand, interpret, and predict major market moves.

"The statement 'market action discounts everything' forms what is probably the cornerstone of technical analysis."

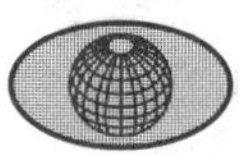

Test Your Financial Awareness

JOHN HODGSON (2000)

WHY READ IT?

- Gives an introduction to the basics of finance and what you need to know to successfully operate as a financial manager.
- Uses a question and answer format to help you hone financial skills and knowledge.
- Helps provide an understanding of the "black art" that is finance.

GETTING STARTED

Test Your Financial Awareness introduces basic financial awareness, tests understanding, and enables you to calculate key financial measures as well as make better business decisions. It is useful for those responsible for utilizing assets, and analyzing sales revenues, costs, and expenses; there are financial awareness quizzes throughout to explain all the concepts.

AUTHOR

John Hodgson is a founder of R. H. International & Associates and CEO of R. H. America. He also operates as an External Tutor on behalf of the Institute of Management and the Institute of Directors, and is on the board of several multinational manufacturing organizations.

CONTEXT

- Provides a basic financial awareness, and assesses financial knowledge and capability with a before-and-after test.
- Explains how to calculate relevant financial measures, and how to improve business decisions based on financial data and analysis.
- Describes a framework for financial management and commercial business processes as part of the core competencies for managers.
- Presents all the key terms in an accessible manner, using diagrams and examples to increase insight and aid retention.
- Helps to clarify confusing financial concepts by highlighting different descriptions used in business, the professional services, and in other countries.

IMPACT

- Addresses the more difficult areas of finance, such as the relationship between the P&L account and the balance sheet.
- Helps you understand how to measure the productivity of a company, and how to improve it.
- Explains the significance of financial accounts in analyzing and improving business performance.
- Assesses the organizational reality behind financial data to provide an understanding of the real health of the company.

QUOTATIONS

"More and more people. . .are expected to make decisions based on financial input."

"To improve return on investment a company aims to maximise the return and minimise the investment parts of the equation."

"The productivity equation can be used by everybody in every organisation to improve company results."

▸▸ MORE INFO

Books:

Fitzgerald, Ray. *Business Finance for Managers: An Essential Guide to Planning, Control and Decision Making.* 3rd ed. London: Kogan Page, 2002. Practical advice for managers with little financial experience.

Ryan, Bob. *Finance and Accounting for Business.* London: Thomson Learning, 2004. Introduces financial accounting, management accounting and financial management for non-specialists.

See Also:

The Finance Manual for Non-Financial Managers. Gives a good grounding in corporate finance for the beginner. (p. 1255)

"More and more people. . .are expected to make decisions based on financial input."

  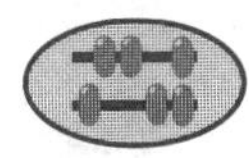   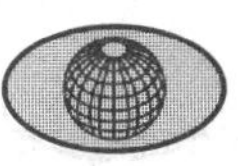   

The Theory of Finance

EUGENE F. FAMA and MERTON H. MILLER (1972)

WHY READ IT?

- Helped shape the field of finance as a separate discipline, and became a landmark book across business schools worldwide.
- Examines the essential theoretical frameworks of finance, and also provides a resource to understanding how the building blocks of finance are organized.
- Uses a framework for learning that combines a variety of approaches to give a full perspective on key concepts.

GETTING STARTED

The Theory of Finance provides a systematic and rigorous grounding in the basic theory of finance by two of the most reputable names in the history of finance. Acting as a textbook rather than an exposition of a single view, it is a groundbreaking treatment of all the developing concepts of finance as we now know them.

AUTHORS

Eugene F. Fama (b. 1939) is Professor of Finance at the University of Chicago Graduate School of Business. He was the first elected Fellow of the American Finance Association, and has received numerous honors. He is a Fellow of the Econometric Society and the American Academy of Arts and Sciences.

Merton H. Miller (1923–2000) was a Professor at the University of Chicago Graduate School of Business, and a Fellow of the Econometric Society, the American Academy of Arts and Sciences, and the American Economic Association. He was awarded the Nobel Memorial Prize in Economic Sciences in 1990.

CONTEXT

- Analyzes certainty models in terms of models of the accumulation and allocation of wealth, durable commodities and investment, market value, dividends, and criteria for optimal investment decisions.
- For uncertainty models, focuses on financing and investment decisions, cost of capital, the expected utility approach to the problem of choice under uncertainty, two-period consumption-investment models, risk, return and market equilibrium, and multi-period models.
- Ensures that all the main points are covered in a variety of ways: mathematically, verbally, graphically, and, in a few cases, by numerical examples.

IMPACT

- Assumes that all securities are traded in perfect markets, but avoids the danger of focusing only on models based on perfect market assumptions by discussing the pitfalls of applying these models to real-world problems without thinking.
- Relies much more on the standard apparatus of economic theory than is typically the case in finance books.
- Its emphasis on essential theory means there's little analysis on practical management or business.
- Does not provide examples about how to apply the theory in quantitative terms, or empirically, to real-world decision problems.
- Presents the material in order of difficulty and logical priority, and keeps mathematical requirements to a minimum.

QUOTATIONS

"The theory of finance is concerned with how individuals and firms allocate resources through time."

"The financing decisions of firms are a matter of indifference to their security holders—it follows that operating and financing decisions are separable."

"There is much evidence in support of the position that perfect market models. . .have substantial value in describing real-world economic phenomena."

▸▸ MORE INFO

Books:

Copeland, Thomas E., and J. Fred Weston. *Financial Theory and Corporate Policy.* Reading, MA: Addison-Wesley, 1983. A useful textbook that presents a unified treatment of finance, combining theory, empirical evidence and applications.

Tirole, Jean. *The Theory of Corporate Finance.* Princeton, NJ: Princeton University Press, 2006. An empirical study structured around the basic finance models.

See Also:

Eugene Fama (p. 1164)
Merton Miller (p. 1177)

"The theory of finance is concerned with how individuals and firms allocate resources through time."

     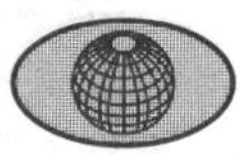   

The Theory of Social and Economic Organization

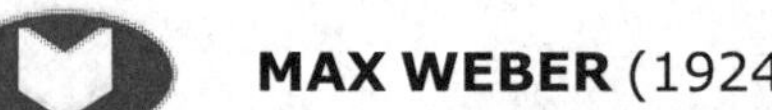

MAX WEBER (1924)

WHY READ IT?

- Weber was a key theorist in the history of social and economic development.
- This is a crucial study for understanding how modern organizations work.
- Argues that bureaucracy is the most efficient way of implementing the rule of law if undertaken properly.

GETTING STARTED

The Theory of Social and Economic Organization grew out of Weber's philosophical inquiries into the nature of authority and how it is transmitted. He identified three types of authority: the charismatic, based on the individual qualities of a leader and reverence for them among his or her followers; the traditional, based on custom and usage; and the rational-legal, based on the rule of objective law.

AUTHOR

Max Weber (1864–1920) was a sociologist and economist, and Professor of Political Economy at the universities of Freiburg and Heidelberg in Germany. He is best known today as one of the founding fathers of modern sociology, and for his scholarly writings.

CONTEXT

- Describes bureaucracy as the most efficient and rational means of organization, and without a realistic substitute.
- Shows how the purely bureaucratic type of administrative organization is, from a purely technical point of view, capable of attaining the highest degree of efficiency. It is, in this sense, the most rational known means of carrying out imperative control over human beings.
- Considers that aspects of the bureaucratic model remain alive and well in a great many organizations where hierarchies, demarcations, and exhaustive rules dominate.
- Found that the most important feature of bureaucracy—its main strength as well as its main weakness—is its impersonality. Discusses how this impersonality is a strength, in that it minimizes the potential abuse of power by leaders, but is a weakness as delays in information movement make bureaucracies slow to react.
- Analyzes the main principles identified as rational-legal bureaucracy, concerning how organizations are structured, specific areas of competence, the structuring of functions, the separation of administration from the means of production, and the recording of the rules and decisions.

IMPACT

- Bureaucratic organization as expounded by Max Weber became the model for the 20th-century organization, and was encapsulated in Alfred Sloan's General Motors and Harold Geneen's ITT.
- Strictly implemented, and in combination with regimented mass-production as practiced by Henry Ford, who echoed some of Weber's thoughts on strict demarcations and a mechanistic approach, it could produce a nightmare scenario for the world of work in the future.
- Today's organizations are imagined as more elusive and ever changing, rather than efficient and static. The regularity of the machine age has given way to the complexity of the information age.

QUOTATION

"Large organizations require that the people involved put the cause of the organization before their own aspirations."

▸▸ MORE INFO

Books:

Allen, Kieran. *Max Weber: A Critical Introduction.* London: Pluto Press, 2004. Summarizes Weber's ideas and writing.

Giddens, Anthony. *Capitalism and Modern Social Theory: An Analysis of the Writings of Marx, Durkheim and Max Weber.* London: Cambridge University Press, 1971. Provides a basic framework and context for these major writers.

Weber, Max. *The Protestant Ethic and the Spirit of Capitalism.* 1904, London: Unwin Books, 1965 (ed). Weber's best-known and most controversial work, it contends that the Protestant ethic made possible and encouraged the development of capitalism in the West.

"Large organizations require that the people involved put the cause of the organization before their own aspirations."

     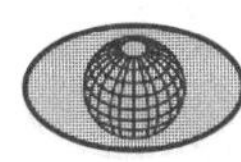   

The Tipping Point: How Little Things Can Make a Big Difference

MALCOLM GLADWELL (2000)

WHY READ IT?

- The "tipping point:" who does not now know this phrase, first coined in Gladwell's entertaining and instructive bestseller to describe how the culmination of a buildup of small changes can effect a big change?
- Gladwell suggests that ideas, products, messages, and behaviors spread like viruses so that we infect one another with preferences and recommendations, until we reach a tipping point, after which a social epidemic becomes contagious and crosses a threshold to reach saturation point.
- Events such as crime waves and fashion trends are used to explore how ideas spread rapidly, and how once the tipping point is reached, things accelerate and take on a life of their own.

GETTING STARTED

The Tipping Point examines how social epidemics and trends in different areas, such as fashion, education, business, and crime, reach a "tipping point," where interest moves from being small-scale and contained to having a widespread impact. Using an intriguing metaphor, it suggests this is similar to a viral epidemic, as contagious behavior is caused by only a few people but can spread rapidly once it reaches a certain level. *The Tipping Point* also discusses the types of people that originate major new trends, and the various contexts within which they occur.

AUTHOR

Malcolm Gladwell (b. 1963) was a reporter and then New York bureau chief for the *Washington Post* before becoming a staff writer for the *New Yorker* magazine in 1996. His second book, *Blink*, is an international bestseller. His latest book, *Outliers: The Story of Success*, was published in November 2008.

CONTEXT

- Examines what factors must converge to bring about dramatic transformations in society.
- Analyzes trends and looks at recent behavioral research to explain why we are so affected by them.
- Discusses how important context is to creating moments of critical mass and changes to group and societal behavior.
- Looks at how the "broken windows" theory—which argues that leaving things unrepaired leads to further disrepair—was used to reduce crime in New York.
- Presents other examples such as the resurgence in popularity of Hush Puppies, how suicides escalated in Micronesia, and the techniques used to develop *Sesame Street* into a groundbreaking and popular program.
- *The Tipping Point* is itself an example of viral marketing, representing the actual theories discussed in the book.

IMPACT

- Looks at why epidemics of viruses, ideas, and behavior do not always originate or spread as you would expect.
- Considers tipping points to be due to three main factors: the power of the messenger, the strength of the message, and the context in which the message is communicated.
- Discusses how the messenger must be highly connected, an expert in a specific area, or a salesman who is persuasive and can spread information.
- Shows how the message is affected by its "stickiness," so that it has an impact and is memorable, and looks at how best to create a sticky message.
- Explains why the power of context and environment is critical to reaching a tipping point and to a trend becoming widespread.

QUOTATIONS

"In a given process or system some people matter more than others."

". . .that one dramatic moment in an epidemic when everything can change all at once is the Tipping Point."

". . .the world of the Tipping Point is a place where the unexpected becomes expected, where radical change is more than a possibility. It is—contrary to all our expectations—a certainty."

MORE INFO

Books:

Cialdini, Robert. *Influence: How and Why People Agree to Things.* New York: Morrow, 1984. A classic book on persuasion that was an influence on *The Tipping Point*, it attempts to explain why people agree to things, and shows how to become a skilled persuader.

Goleman, Daniel. *Emotional Intelligence.* New York: Bantam Books, 1995. Argues that the traditional IQ is too narrow a measure, and makes the case for "emotional intelligence" being the strongest indicator of human success.

See Also:

Blink: The Power of Thinking Without Thinking. Examines how we are continually making quick judgments and how successful these can be. It looks at the many ways we do this, and argues that snap decisions will be more successful if based on experience or preparation. (p. 1228)

"In a given process or system some people matter more than others."

  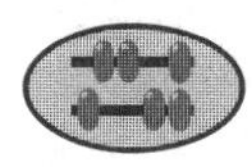   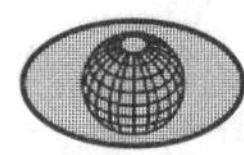   

Traders, Guns, and Money: Knowns and Unknowns in the Dazzling World of Derivatives

SATYAJIT DAS (2006)

WHY READ IT?

- An entertaining introduction to derivatives trading and its impact on the financial markets by a veteran of the industry.
- Tells the inside story of how derivatives began, how they are used, their benefits, and their dangers.
- Describes the mechanics of the financial markets and difficult concepts in a clear, amusing, and somewhat cynical style.

GETTING STARTED

Traders, Guns, and Money is written like a series of vignettes, telling of the author's professional life in finance, and how he got involved with financial derivatives. It describes the complex workings of the industry in an engaging and informative style to provide a behind-the-scenes, warts-and-all examination of the markets.

AUTHOR

Satyajit Das is an expert on derivatives, having worked for the Commonwealth Bank of Australia, Citicorp Investment Bank, and Merrill Lynch, as well as Treasurer of the TNT Group. He now acts as a consultant, advising banks and corporations, and presenting seminars on derivatives.

CONTEXT

- Details the market personalities, their motivations, weaknesses, and ability to resort to questionable tactics to make money.
- Analyzes several well-known examples of the use of derivatives as speculative bets or hedges, and explains their complex nature and significant risks.
- Gives an insightful account of how trading transactions are structured and can easily go wrong.
- Describes how the banks mistakenly believe they understand and properly hedge their own exposure.
- Helps to make sense of some of the more complex derivatives such as CDOs, CCOs, currency swaps, interest rate swaps, and inverse floaters.

IMPACT

- Shows how many of the transactions in the markets are based on misrepresentation and deception, due to the trading culture that drives the business.
- Explains the frustrations involved in working at every level of a bank, as well as the tensions and dynamics between the different functions.
- Outlines why the trading floors of the major financial centers resemble casinos.
- Shows how products are created that have integrated profit for the banks, but although they are marketed as a panacea for investors, this ignores their inherent risk and that they are little understood.
- Provides a useful critique of the run-up to the recent credit crisis.

QUOTATIONS

"The entire investment process is flawed—projected returns are too high and actual returns are measured with tools that the fund managers and asset consultants choose. It is like getting a student to mark their own exams."

"Banks make a lot of money trading, but no money is really ever made in financial markets. They merely transfer wealth: the trick is to tap into the money that flows through the markets."

"Mathematical finance lends credibility and false precision to the dismal reality of risk management."

▸▸ MORE INFO

See Also:

- *A Demon of Our Own Design: Markets, Hedge Funds, and the Perils of Financial Innovation.* A topical examination of the capital markets and risk management. (p. 1247)
- *FIASCO: Blood in the Water on Wall Street.* A dramatic account of the derivatives industry and instruments being traded. (p. 1253)
- *Liar's Poker: Rising Through the Wreckage on Wall Street.* An entertaining and revealing account of the author's time at one of the big investment banks. (p. 1288)
- Derivatives and Quantitative Finance (pp. 1618–1621)

"The entire investment process is flawed—projected returns are too high and actual returns are measured with tools that the fund managers and asset consultants choose. It is like getting a student to mark their own exams."

     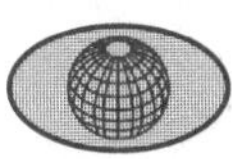   

The Undercover Economist

TIM HARFORD (2006)

WHY READ IT?

- Makes economics easier to understand by showing why it is central to how we live.
- Unlocks many of the economic mysteries of daily life in an interesting way.
- Considers how economic policy can influence how we make decisions and allocate resources more efficiently without us realizing it.

GETTING STARTED

The Undercover Economist explores the economic world in an accessible way. While providing an introduction to a variety of economic situations and anomalies, it looks at familiar situations in unfamiliar ways, and gives fresh explanations for the way fundamental principles of the modern economy work. From why there is a Starbucks on every corner to why good and cheap healthcare is so difficult to achieve, Harford brings to life the underlying reasons why things are as they are.

AUTHOR

Tim Harford (b. 1973) writes editorials and two columns for the *Financial Times*, one inspired by this book, and has presented a TV series, *Trust Me, I'm an Economist*. He has worked at the World Bank, Shell, and as an economics tutor at Oxford University.

CONTEXT

- Offers a new take on economics, explaining unusual aspects of the economy, mainly through the author walking around and observing what he sees, and explaining the underlying economic ideas.
- Examines some key principles of economics such as demand–supply interaction, market failure, perfect markets, globalization, international trade, and comparative advantage, in an interesting way and in non-technical terms.
- Illuminates his concepts with examples from around the world to reveal the intricate pressures that drive not only the economy at large but the everyday choices we make.

IMPACT

- Concentrates on the economics of a situation rather than pushing particular political viewpoints.
- Explores how choices and pricing are used to create the appearance of competitiveness while encouraging those who are price-insensitive to pay as much as possible.
- Discusses the irrationality of everyday economic decisions.
- Defends free markets and sweatshops as a necessary step for progress, contending that the market will dictate standards.
- Leaves the reader to make their own decision about whether a particular practice or action is good or bad.

QUOTATIONS

"*Economics is partly about modelling, about articulating basic principles and patterns that operate behind seemingly complex subjects like the rent on farms or coffee bars.*"

"*When economists see the world, they see hidden social patterns, patterns that become evident only when one focuses on the essential underlying processes.*"

"*In the end, economics is about people—something that economists have done a very bad job at explaining.*"

▸▸ MORE INFO

Books:

Kay, John. *Everlasting Lightbulbs: How Economics Illuminates the World*. London: Erasmus Press, 2004. Tries to make economics fun and relevant.

Landsburg, Steven E. *The Armchair Economist: Economics and Everyday Life*. New York: Free Press, 1993. Offers an economist's view of human behavior, examining everyday situations.

See Also:

Freakonomics: A Rogue Economist Explores the Hidden Side of Everything. Taking a different slant on popular economics, this book provides new perspectives on old problems. (p. 1266)

"Economics is partly about modelling, about articulating basic principles and patterns that operate behind seemingly complex subjects like the rent on farms or coffee bars."

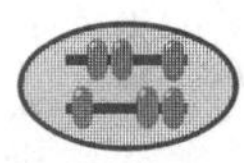

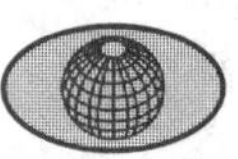

Valuation: Measuring and Managing the Value of Companies

TOM COPELAND, TIM KOLLER, and JACK MURRIN (1990)

WHY READ IT?

- Describes how to value companies, and the impact of various business decisions on corporate value.
- Advocates a systematic approach to company valuation, especially when estimating the value of alternative corporate and business strategies.
- Shows how to assess the financial impact of key business transactions such as mergers and acquisitions.

GETTING STARTED

Valuation shows how companies can create shareholder value through effective planning and implementing sound management techniques, based on the measuring and managing the value of a company. The book incorporates the practical experience and valuation knowledge of the consultants McKinsey, where the authors worked.

AUTHORS

Tom Copeland (b. 1946) was previously a Partner and Co-Leader of the corporate finance practice at McKinsey & Co, and a Professor of Finance at UCLA's Anderson School of Management.

Tim Koller is a Partner at McKinsey & Co, and Co-Leader of its corporate finance and corporate strategy practice.

Jack Murrin was previously a Partner and Co-Leader of the corporate finance practice at McKinsey & Co, and has subsequently held senior executive positions at leading financial institutions.

CONTEXT

- Encourages business leaders, corporate finance professionals, and bankers to be more disciplined on corporate valuation, describing a framework for best practice, particularly if undertaking or funding a corporate acquisition.
- Examines existing corporate valuation techniques in relation to company strategies.
- Provides detailed analysis of the discounted cash flow valuation process—how it should be developed, where particular data goes.
- Offers different perspectives, such as value-based management, on how to manage companies in order to create wealth.

IMPACT

- Provides practical guidance for investors who want to use valuation techniques to make passive investments in public companies, and managers who buy or sell business assets for their firms.
- Relies on practice, rather than academic theory, and is useful for those who have no idea how to start the valuation process.
- Real-life examples and detailed explanations of models help an understanding of the key concepts and terms.
- Ensures that all models and formulas suggested in the book can be applied using MS Excel.

QUOTATIONS

"The business environment has become extremely unstable. . .[which] demands that companies rethink their overall corporate and business-unit strategies almost continuously."

"Businesses are facing a stream of unprecedented challenges—challenges that will have a major impact on shareholder value."

"The essence of corporate strategy is to figure out how the corporation, as intermediary, can add value to the businesses it oversees."

▸▸ MORE INFO

Books:

Damodaran, Aswath. *Investment Valuation: Tools and Techniques for Determining the Value of Any Asset.*New York: Wiley, 1996. Shows how to value most types of asset, and examines the theory and application of valuation models, highlighting their strengths and weaknesses.

Rappaport, Alfred. *Creating Shareholder Value: The New Standard for Business Performance.* New York: Free Press, 1986. Describes the value-based management concept that Rappaport helped create.

Stewart, G. Bennett. *The Quest for Value*. New York: HarperBusiness, 1991. Looks at the processes that influence and control share prices, and provides a framework for corporate decision-making.

See Also:

Corporate Valuation (pp. 1610–1613)

"The business environment has become extremely unstable. . .[which] demands that companies rethink their overall corporate and business-unit strategies almost continuously."

     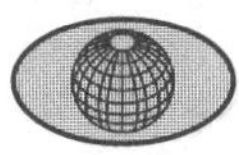   

Value at Risk

PHILIPPE JORION (1997)

WHY READ IT?

- Jorion is an acknowledged VAR expert, as well as a respected author and speaker.
- Offers a good introduction and overview of financial risk management and the Value at Risk approach.
- A key text on risk management that has been regularly updated, it examines critical developments for managing a variety of financial risk types.

GETTING STARTED

Value at Risk covers a technical subject in an accessible way, providing insight into risk management, as well as the potential downside of complex derivatives. It details how VAR has evolved over the past two decades, and examines how different risks have been assumed, new risk management techniques have been developed, new regulation has come into being, and how the approach has expanded beyond finance.

AUTHOR

Philippe Jorion (b. 1955) is a Professor of Finance at the Paul Merage School of Business, University of California at Irvine, where he is also Chancellor's Professor. He has previously taught at the universities of Columbia, Northwestern, Chicago, and British Columbia.

CONTEXT

- Explains how important it is to use sophisticated risk assessment tools, as proven by the high-profile failures at Barings Bank and Orange County.
- Offers an understandable overview of VAR, explaining that it is a single number that shows how much an investment portfolio may lose, although the actual calculation is a complex operation.
- Provides the most current information available on how to understand and implement VAR, as well as manage more recent dimensions of financial risk.
- Used by the Global Association of Risk Professionals as their main text for the Financial Risk Manager examination.

IMPACT

- Covers the different risk aspects, and discusses how risk management is achieved in banking, investment management, pension funds, and in the corporate world.
- Discusses new developments in risk management, such as extreme value theory, principal components, and copulas.
- Examines how VAR is used for measuring and controlling risk, and creating backtesting models to forecast risk and correlations.
- Details how VAR is also widely used in investment management, as it offers a conceptual framework for risk budgeting and monitoring.
- Analyzes the Basel II capital adequacy rules for commercial banks.
- Includes short questions and exercises at the end of each chapter to help monitor progress.

QUOTATIONS

"Initially confined to measuring market risk, VAR is now being used to control and manage risk actively, well beyond derivatives."

"Corporations are in the business of managing risks."

"The common denominator for any risk management activity is efficient use of capital."

▸▸ MORE INFO

Books:

Allen, Linda, Jacob Bodoukh, and Anthony Saunders. *Understanding Market, Credit, and Operational Risk: The Value at Risk Approach.* Malden, MA: Blackwell, 2004. A practical guide to using VAR models, and applying the VAR approach to the measurement of market risk, credit risk and operational risk.

Holton, Glyn A. *Value-at-Risk: Theory and Practice.* Boston, MA: Academic Press, 2003. Authoritative guide to implementing real-world VAR measures.

Website:

Detailed answers and other materials are posted on the companion website: www.pjorion.com/var

"Initially confined to measuring market risk, VAR is now being used to control and manage risk actively, well beyond derivatives."

   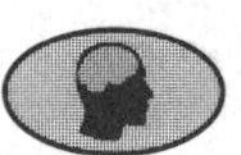  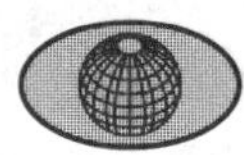   

The Warren Buffett Way

ROBERT G. HAGSTROM (1994)

WHY READ IT?

- Shows how Buffett made his name as the most successful investor of our time, and how his investment strategies made his fortune.
- Examines his numerous investments and deals, and the investment strategies and techniques he has used to beat the market over the years, regardless of market fluctuation.
- The author has himself successfully implemented many of Buffett's investment methods, and shows how the individual investor can apply them to their stock market investments.

GETTING STARTED

The Warren Buffett Way is an international bestseller that details Warren Buffett's life, experiences in business and investing in the early days—what companies he invested in and why, and how he made his huge wealth. It explains Buffett's investing strategies in an understandable way, showing how he took up a value investing approach, and underpinned all his work with rigorous research and pragmatism.

- Other core principles include not worrying about the economy, focusing on the business rather than the stock, and managing a portfolio of businesses.
- Reviews the main influences on Buffett and his career, including Benjamin Graham, Philip Fisher, and Charlie Munger, and illustrates how he integrated their investment philosophies.

IMPACT

- Examines which companies Buffett has invested in over the years, explaining why he decided to buy into them based on his investing principles.
- Discusses the value investing approach, decision-making based on real business value, and the impact of price and value on stock picking.
- Advocates focusing on the return on equity rather than earnings per share, calculating owner earnings to get a true reflection of value, and looking for companies with high profit margins.
- Examines in detail the shareholder reports from Berkshire Hathaway, which can usually only be seen if you are a shareholder.
- Shows how Buffett spends a great deal of time reading annual reports to learn about a company, and offers some of his tips for spotting accounting problems and irregularities in financial documents.

AUTHOR

Robert G. Hagstrom (b. 1956) is a business writer, Senior Vice President and Director of Legg Mason Focus Capital, and Portfolio Manager of the Legg Mason Focus Trust.

CONTEXT

- Provides an insightful summary and overview of the key principles and practices that led to Buffett becoming one of the world's richest men.
- Under the headings of business, management, financial, and value, it discusses the tenets that have guided Buffett's investing.
- Shows how Buffett's philosophy is straightforward, as it depends on buying into companies with business potential, which have a responsible management team, and show continuous growth.
- Argues that the most effective investment methods are based on taking a long-term view, usually picking businesses that are traditional and understandable.

QUOTATIONS

"Warren Buffett is idiosyncratic—it is a source of his success—but his methodology, once understood, is applicable to individuals and institutions alike."

"Warren Buffett's approach to investing is uniquely his own, yet it rests on the bedrock of philosophies absorbed from four powerful figures: Benjamin Graham, Philip Fisher, John Burr Williams, and Charles Munger."

"Buffett believes that a business should achieve good returns on equity while employing little or no debt."

▸▸ MORE INFO

Book:

Lowenstein, Roger. *Buffett: The Making of an American Capitalist.* New York: Random House, 1995. An entertaining biography of the great man—his life and investments.

See Also:

- Warren Buffett (p. 1157)
- *Common Stocks and Uncommon Profits.* The classic on the principles of growth investment and research. (p. 1235)
- *The Intelligent Investor: A Book of Practical Counsel.* The classic bestseller of value investing, which gives a more detailed overview of the concepts of margin of safety, intrinsic value, and the benefits associated with ignoring market noise. (p. 1280)

"Warren Buffett is idiosyncratic—it is a source of his success—but his methodology, once understood, is applicable to individuals and institutions alike."

  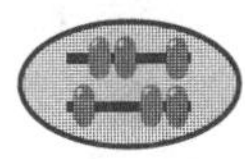   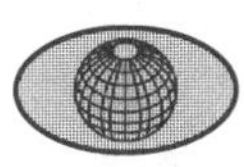   

The Wealth of Nations

ADAM SMITH (1776)

WHY READ IT?

- A classic and seminal work, it is a broad-ranging exploration of commercial and economic first principles that has influenced Western economics ever since it was written.
- Was the first comprehensive exploration of the foundations, workings, and machinations of a free market economy, concepts that are still relevant today.
- Proposes that the invisible hand of free-market competition ensures both the vitality of commercial activity and the ultimate good of all a nation's citizens.

GETTING STARTED

The Wealth of Nations, published in the same year as the signing of the American Declaration of Independence, is a keystone in the philosophical foundations of modern capitalism and the modern market economy. There are few economists over the last 200 years—and fewer politicians of a free-market persuasion—who have not been influenced by it. Smith helped shape the economic policies of British prime ministers and chancellors of the exchequer from the time of Lord North (1770–1782) to the current day.

AUTHOR

Adam Smith (1723–1790) was a political economist and philosopher, Professor of Logic, and later the Chair of Moral Philosophy, at Glasgow University. He also became a tutor to the Duke of Buccleuch, and was appointed Commissioner of Customs in Scotland.

CONTEXT

- The central thesis is that capital can best be used for the creation of both individual and national wealth in conditions of minimal interference by government.
- Propounds the concept of the invisible hand; as attempts to better the lot of a nation and its population are generally doomed to failure, and the unintended cumulative effects of self-interested striving are far more effective.
- Argues that the value of a particular good or service is determined by the costs of production. If something is expensive to produce, then its value is similarly high.

IMPACT

- Written without knowledge of the power and scope of modern corporations, let alone the power of brand names and customer loyalty, yet has a powerful relevance for the place of these in the way that Western economies are now run.
- Continues to be thought of as a right-wing manifesto, a logical exposition of the power of market forces.
- The appeal is not only to the right wing in politics, as the system of demarcation and functional separation that Smith expounded also provided the basis for the management theorists of the early 20th century, such as Frederick Winslow Taylor, and practitioners such as Henry Ford.
- The book's legacy to scientific management was the concept of the division of labor.

QUOTATIONS

"The real and effectual discipline which is exercised over a workman is not that of his corporation, but that of his customers."

"[Every individual] intends only his own gain, and he is in this, as in many other cases, led by an invisible hand to promote an end which was no part of his intention."

▸▸ MORE INFO

Books:

Buchan, James. *The Authentic Adam Smith: His Life and Ideas.* London: W. W. Norton, 2006. A portrait of the man and his work.

O'Rourke, P. J. *On the Wealth of Nations.* New York: Atlantic Monthly Press, 2007. Entertaining and accessible introduction to the great work.

Smith, Adam. *The Theory of Moral Sentiments.* London: A. Millar, 1759. More of a philosophical work, focusing on the nature of morality.

See Also:

Adam Smith (p. 1196)

"The real and effectual discipline which is exercised over a workman is not that of his corporation, but that of his customers."

  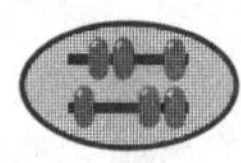   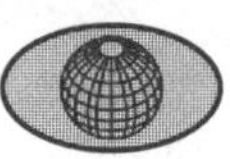   

What Went Wrong at Enron: Everyone's Guide to the Largest Bankruptcy in US History

PETER C. FUSARO and ROSS M. MILLER (2002)

WHY READ IT?

- Explains how the biggest collapse in US corporate history occurred, in an interesting and understandable style.
- Discusses how a hugely successful energy company moved away from its core competency to become a major player in many new markets.
- Shows how chasing profits at all costs, and not admitting mistakes, created a corporate culture that was deeply flawed.

GETTING STARTED

In a non-technical manner, *What Went Wrong at Enron* depicts the increasing breakdown in trust and the range of factors that contributed to such a spectacular corporate implosion. It examines the management personalities, company culture, use of special purpose entities, and the executive deception that led to Enron's collapse. Enron is shown to be a corporate product of both a willingness to bend the rules and also the opportunity to do so.

AUTHORS

Peter C. Fusaro is Chairman of Global Change Associates, co-founded the Energy Hedge Fund Center, and is an energy industry expert.

Ross M. Miller has served as a consultant to several financial institutions, authored many articles, and appeared on TV as an industry expert.

CONTEXT

- Explains how Enron first flourished in the deregulated energy and utility markets, and became a huge corporate success story.
- Shows how Enron became innovative as a key market maker in expanding areas such as water supply, pollution credits, and weather-related risks.
- Discusses the controversial use of special-purpose vehicles.
- Provides insight into the problems of mark-to-market accounting principles, the lack of full disclosure, how being the counterparty to every arbitrage trade, and the deals financed by its high stock price, brought about Enron's troubles.
- Looks at what lessons can be learned from Enron's downfall, including the need for improvements in corporate ethics and truthfulness, honesty, and transparency and disclosure in accounting and corporate structures.

IMPACT

- Exposes the lack of strategic knowledge brought about by the separation of senior management and those on an operational level.
- Discusses the problems associated with competing goals within Enron.
- Shows the damage caused by the constant positive spin that was put on performance and style, and how this led to even more exaggeration and fraudulent reporting.
- Looks at how other factors such as debt, competition, inadequate planning, and the loss of investor confidence contributed to the bankruptcy.
- Examines the failings due to self-interest and an intimidatory corporate culture.

QUOTATIONS

"The idea that drove Ken Lay and fueled Enron was that of the power of the free market system."

"A series of missteps (both accidental and calculated) and just plain bad luck brought Enron's more nefarious dealings to light, precipitating its ultimate collapse."

"For Enron, everything was beginning to go wrong at once."

⏩ MORE INFO

Books:

Cruver, Brian. *Anatomy of Greed: The Unshredded Truth from an Enron Insider.* New York: Carroll & Graf, 2002. An account of Enron's fall, told by a young MBA who joined the company shortly before the scandal broke.

Swartz, Mimi, and Sherron Watkins. *Power Failure: The Inside Story of the Collapse of Enron.* New York: Doubleday, 2003. As told by the Enron accountant who first tried to alert management to the accounting fraud.

See Also:

The Smartest Guys in the Room: The Amazing Rise and Scandalous Fall of Enron. A detailed exposé on the collapse of Enron. (p. 1318)

"The idea that drove Ken Lay and fueled Enron was that of the power of the free market system."

  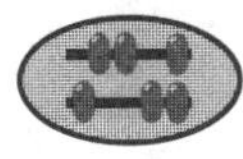 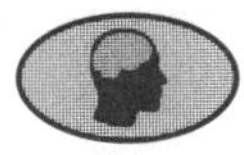  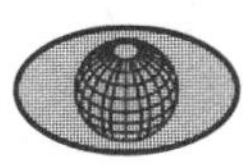   

When Genius Failed: The Rise and Fall of Long-Term Capital Management

ROGER LOWENSTEIN (2001)

WHY READ IT?

- Tells the story behind the biggest hedge fund collapse ever seen, that sent shock waves through the whole banking system.
- Provides perceptive detail into all the main characters involved, including two Nobel Prize winners.
- Gives an absorbing account of the Federal Reserve Board's unprecedented move to bail out the fund after thousands of its derivatives contracts started failing.

GETTING STARTED

When Genius Failed uncovers and examines the personalities, academic expertise, professional relationships, and finances behind LTCM's collapse. It details John Meriwether's move from Salomon Brothers, where he formed its renowned arbitrage group by hiring academia's top financial economists, through his founding of LTCM and hiring of former colleagues and future Nobel Prize laureates Robert Merton and Myron Scholes, to create the most successful hedge fund in the world. It was a fund that was based on betting big, so when things turned bad, they had a lot to lose.

AUTHOR

Roger Lowenstein reported for the *Wall Street Journal* for over a decade. His first book was *Buffett: The Making of an American Capitalist*. His work has also appeared in the *New York Times* and the *New Republic*, and he writes a column for *SmartMoney Magazine*.

CONTEXT

- Explains how the huge wealth and success of LTCM was based on investing through finding small mispricings of one security versus another, "as if it were vacuuming nickels that others couldn't see," as Myron Scholes put it.
- Shows how the trade modelers failed to give enough importance to freak events in their trading strategy, leading to its downfall.
- When the problems arose, billions disappeared quickly in these arbitrage trades. LTCM assumed that things would swing back and moved too slowly to unwind the trades.

IMPACT

- Explains how the company managed to leverage up so many times on its trades, allowing it to have an exposure to the market over a 100 times its capitalization.
- Shows how the lack of supervision and due diligence contributed to the collapse.
- Details how LTCM was built around consensus in the financial markets, so that the reputation of such famous names overcame concerns about the trades.
- Lines of credit from every major financial institution in these markets entangled the banking system in the problems.
- Exposes major weaknesses in the financial system.

QUOTATIONS

"This one obscure arbitrage fund had amassed an amazing $100 billion in assets, virtually all of it borrowed."

"Every bet was losing simultaneously. The dice were not being thrown at random, or at least they seemed as if tossed by the same malevolent hand."

"Unlike at banks, where independent risk managers watch over traders, Long-Term's partners monitored themselves. Though this enabled them to sidestep the rigidities of a big organization, there was no one to call the partners to account. . .The traders were their own watchdogs"

►► MORE INFO

See Also:

- *Inventing Money: The Story of Long-Term Capital Management and the Legends Behind It.* Also on the LTCM debacle, but with more detail on the financial deals and hedge fund industry. (p. 1284)
- *Liar's Poker.* Also discusses John Meriwether, who challenged John Gutfreund, CEO of Salomon Brothers, to one hand of liar's poker for $10 million. (p. 1288)

"This one obscure arbitrage fund had amassed an amazing $100 billion in assets, virtually all of it borrowed."

  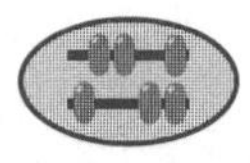   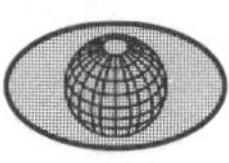   

When Markets Collide: Investment Strategies for the Age of Global Economic Change

MOHAMED A. EL-ERIAN (2008)

WHY READ IT?

- Analyzes the origins of the current financial crisis, and how to identify investment opportunities that take advantage of the financial turmoil.
- Examines the recent transformation of the global economy and the capital markets, and presents practical strategies for both investors and policy makers.
- Provides a means for investors to differentiate between the random noise generated by the financial system and key investment signals that should be understood and exploited.

GETTING STARTED

When Markets Collide argues that the current financial market upheaval is a collision between the markets of the past and those in the future. It offers an overview of the rapidly changing international financial system, and describes strategies that capitalize on the opportunities available in the new investment landscape. It also describes how to identify and manage the new types of risks that have emerged, while providing guidance on how best to allocate assets on a long-term basis.

AUTHOR

Mohamed El-Erian (b. 1958) is Chief Executive Officer of PIMCO, one of the largest investment management companies in the world. He was formerly President and Chief Executive Officer of Harvard Management Company, and spent 15 years at the International Money Fund, working on policy, capital market, and multilateral economic issues.

CONTEXT

- Examines the impact of the evolving markets on investment approaches, business strategy, and policy making.
- Provides a range of tools and techniques that aid improved investment, focusing on the mortgage markets, the emerging markets, sovereign wealth funds, and monetary policy.
- Offers insights on the credit crisis from the perspectives of academic economists, policy officials, investment bankers, and fund managers.

IMPACT

- Proposes an action plan for long-term investment success, based on the opportunities offered by this global market shift.
- Discusses the concept of "noise" in the financial system, arguing that it signals important structural changes and realignments affecting the whole investment world.
- Examines the increasing influence of sovereign wealth funds as permanent sources of investment capital with long-term investment objectives.
- Details the reasons why the emerging markets will have a much greater influence on the world economy and capital flows in the future, as developing countries increasingly hold significant and sustainable sources of global growth.
- Shows why China in particular will become a major player in the global markets, driven by an increased focus on consumer demand, and a greater resistance to Western economic downturns.

QUOTATIONS

"The forces behind the recent financial crises have not gone away. Instead, underlying global transformations will play a major role in defining and influencing the investment and policy landscape for years to come."

"Market participants need to adjust if they wish to remain successful in this new age."

"The outcome will be nothing less than a regime change in which the next stage in globalization and integration."

⏩ MORE INFO

Books:

Ferguson, Niall. *The Ascent of Money: A Financial History of the World.* New York: Penguin, 2008. An accessible and entertaining examination the history of finance and the money markets, that argues that only by looking back can we work out what to do next to avoid recurrent bubbles and crashes.

Schiff, Peter, with John Downes. *Crash Proof: How to Profit from the Coming Economic Collapse.* Hoboken, NJ: Wiley, 2007. Discusses the economic forces and structural weaknesses underlying the current financial downturn, and the measures that can be taken to protect investments and savings while it lasts.

Soros, George. *The New Paradigm for Financial Markets: The Credit Crisis of 2008 and What It Means.* New York: PublicAffairs, 2008. The investment guru examines the credit crunch, why financial experts and economists need to understand financial bubbles better, and explores why free markets behave as they do.

See Also:

Investment (pp. 1653–1658)

"The forces behind the recent financial crises have not gone away. Instead, underlying global transformations will play a major role in defining and influencing the investment and policy landscape for years to come."

  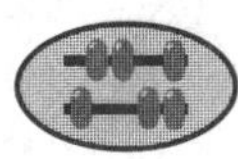   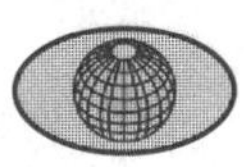   

Why Smart People Make Big Money Mistakes and How to Correct Them

GARY BELSKY and THOMAS GILOVICH (1999)

WHY READ IT?

- Examines the most common mistakes we make when spending, investing, or saving money.
- Uses behavioral economics to explain these mistakes and problems, using everyday examples and scenarios.
- Provides the reader with an alternative view of financial problems, and offers practical solutions and advice, with exercises in each chapter.

GETTING STARTED

Why Smart People Make Big Money Mistakes and How to Correct Them explores how we spend, save or invest money, to expose the common mistakes made and how they can be avoided. Using anecdotal information, the reader is invited to assess themselves and their own actions, and offered advice and practical solutions about how to change bad habits.

AUTHORS

Gary Belsky is a journalist for various magazines and has contributed to programs on CNN and ABC. He received the Gerald Loeb Award for Distinguished Business and Financial Journalism in 1990.

Thomas Gilovich is a Professor of Psychology at Cornell University and lectures internationally on everyday reasoning and decision-making and on the fallibility of human judgement. He has been published in various journals and magazines.

CONTEXT

- Offers practical advice for correcting money mistakes and gives the reader the information required to then decide how to act.
- A self-help book for the ordinary investor, it focuses on everyday money matters such as credit card use and consumer buying patterns.
- Requires no prior knowledge of financial matters, but is intended to benefit those who find dealing with money difficult.
- Uses an easy-to-understand psychological approach to understand and explain a range of different financial situations.
- Written as a personal view using the work of recognised psychologists as support material.

IMPACT

- Introduces the work of other economists and psychologists, such as Amos Tversky and Daniel Kahneman, to a wider, non-specialist audience.
- Focuses more on human behavior than the specifics of money management, and helps get the balance right in how we control our finances.
- Provides practical advice for consumers, rather than theory for academics.

QUOTATIONS

"By examining how economics came to be linked with psychology. . .you'll be much better prepared to grasp how behavioral economics can help improve your finances."

". . .there's one realm where behavioral economics has yet to achieve prominence and it may be the most important; in the minds of typical consumers, borrowers, savers, spenders and investors."

"Don't expect miracles or overnight transformations. Expect instead to learn some things about yourself, some things about the ways in which you make decisions in general and about money in particular."

▸▸ MORE INFO

Book:

Pompian, Michael M. *Behavioral Finance and Wealth Management: How to Build Optimal Portfolios that Account for Investor Biases.* Hoboken, NJ: Wiley, 2006. Explains how to use behavioral finance for investing, outlines the 20 most common biases, and shows how they can be overcome.

See Also:

Advances in Behavioral Finance. A collection of papers that explores different aspects of the subject. Quite academic in approach. (p. 1214)

"By examining how economics came to be linked with psychology. . .you'll be much better prepared to grasp how behavioral economics can help improve your finances."

  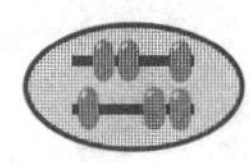   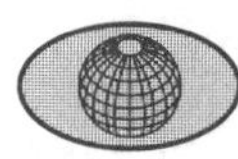   

Wikinomics: How Mass Collaboration Changes Everything

DON TAPSCOTT and ANTHONY D. WILLIAMS (2006)

WHY READ IT?

- Examines the emergence of online mass collaboration, ideas sharing, and peer production, and discusses the future potential.
- Collaboration is changing the way traditional business operates and transforming the economy in unpredictable ways.
- Looks at how companies can access more expert knowledge through idea markets, and develop new capabilities.

GETTING STARTED

Wikinomics argues for a new way of working that is collaborative and ideas driven. A wiki is software that allows anyone with access to a computer to create, edit, and link webpages, and is part of the development in which users of the web generate content.

The book discusses current collaborations to produce collective results and examines the possibilities of mass collaboration, open-source software, and new innovative working practices.

AUTHORS

Don Tapscott (b. 1947) is Chief Executive and founder of New Paradigm, a think-tank and strategy consulting company. He teaches at the Rotman School of Management at the University of Toronto, and is the author of a number of books on business strategy and the digital economy.

Anthony D. Williams has been writing about trends in technology and society for over a decade. He advises Fortune 500 firms and international institutions, including the World Bank. He holds a Masters in Research from the London School of Economics and is Vice President and Executive Editor at New Paradigm.

CONTEXT

- Discusses the new web approach, where sites such as MySpace, YouTube, and Flickr allow mass collaboration from participants in the online community.
- Examines the success of Wikipedia, the user-edited online encyclopedia that is the main example of online collaborative efforts.
- Provides ideas on how to apply wiki frameworks in your daily business.
- Shows how you can expand your business capabilities and deliver value using collective intelligence.
- Analyzes why it isn't possible to apply traditional business techniques to the internet, but that new strategies are needed to accommodate change to the way organizations are run.

IMPACT

- Proposes that sharing your company's dealings with the online community is good for its health and future progress.
- Provides detail on how communities are being formed, and how individuals share ideas and intelligence, accelerate new product development, and efficiently create new revenue streams.
- Discusses business benefits such as the reduced transaction costs possible with mass collaboration, and the new business models benefiting from openness, peering, sharing, and acting globally.

QUOTATIONS

"As a growing number of firms come see the benefits of mass collaboration, this new way of organizing will eventually displace the traditional corporate structures as the economy's primary engine of wealth creation."

"The web is now the foundation for new dynamic forms of community and creative expression."

"[Mass collaboration is] a new way for people to socialize, entertain, innovate, and transact in self-organizing peer-to-peer communities of their choosing."

▸▸ MORE INFO

Books:

Locke, Christopher, Rick Levine, and Doc Searls. *The Cluetrain Manifesto: The End of Business as Usual.* Cambridge, MA: Perseus Books, 2000. How businesses should embrace new collaborative methods of communication.

Sunstein, Cass R. *Infotopia: How Many Minds Produce Knowledge.* Oxford: Oxford University Press, 2006. How to share information and improve our lives.

Tapscott, Don. *Digital Economy: Promise and Peril in the Age of Networked Intelligence.* New York: McGraw-Hill, 1996. A review of the state of technology innovation at the time.

"As a growing number of firms come see the benefits of mass collaboration, this new way of organizing will eventually displace the traditional corporate structures as the economy's primary engine of wealth creation."

COUNTRY AND SECTOR PROFILES

  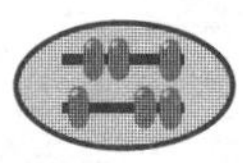      

Country and Sector Profiles

This section provides users with an up-to-date world finance almanac in two parts. The first focuses on countries and the second on industries. The information on the countries and industries will be updated online at qfinance.com, so that potential investors, or those interested in conducting business with these countries or within the industries, can quickly ascertain the current state of a particular economy or the latest developments in an industry.

Just over 100 countries are analyzed by our experienced writers, using data from official government sources as well as from respected organizations such as the World Bank, the OECD, and the IMF. Each country profile includes a description and analysis of:

- The economy and its trade profile
- Economic policy over the previous 12 months
- Economic performance over the previous 12 months
- Official support for inward investment and imports
- The tax regime and corporate tax exemptions
- Trade resources and useful web links

The countries profiled include EU, OECD, and OPEC members, plus composites of MSCI, emerging markets, and MENA indices. We have also included offshore banking centers and the major global financial centers.

The second part of this section provides profiles of 26 of the world's leading industries. These are analyzed on a global basis. Each profile contains the following components:

- Major industry developments—we provide an overview of the main commercial developments affecting the industry in the previous 12 months.
- Market analysis—our writers analyze the key developments in each industry, covering areas such as changes in the regulatory environment, in market share, and in the corporate arena.

Anthony Beachey
Section editor

  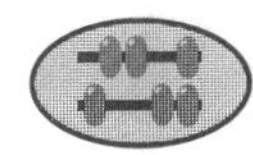      

Contents

Country Profiles

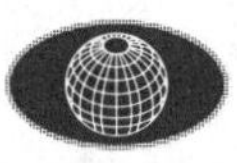

Sector Profiles

Algeria

ECONOMY AND TRADE

Algeria's economy is heavily reliant on the hydrocarbons sector, which accounts for 60% of the country's revenues and some 30% of GDP. It also accounts for a massive 95% of Algeria's exports, by value. The Algerian government is committed to opening up trade, and to encouraging inward investment, particularly by Western companies interested in using Algeria as a manufacturing base, or in doing joint ventures with local companies to help them boost export activities

When he came to power in 1999, on the promise of implementing a range of political, economic and social reforms, President Bouteflika boosted the country's ailing economy with a US$18 billion public-sector spending program. This generated four years of steady growth and won Bouteflika a second term of office. It also reduced the country's massive unemployment, bringing it down to 23%. It currently stands at around 13%.

STATISTICS

GDP growth: 3.4% (2008)
GDP per capita: US$7,100 (PPP)
CPI: 3.6%
Key interest rate: 8% (commercial bank prime rate, December 31, 2007)
Exchange rate versus dollar: Algerian dinars per US dollar—63.25 (2008)
Unemployment: 12.9% (2008)
FDI: US$14.11 billion (2008)
Current account deficit/ surplus: under 5% (US$2.913 billion)
Population: 33,769,668 (July 2008)
Source: CIA Factbook except where stated

ECONOMIC POLICY OVER 12 MONTHS

The IMF and the World Bank want to see Algeria spending more money on education, and on the creation of jobs for those entering the economy. Success on both these fronts, but particularly on the former, is seen as crucial to the country's ability to sustain its growth, and its efforts to diversify its economy beyond the oil and gas sector. Considerable progress has already been made, with education being free to all, and school attendances more than doubling to in excess of 5 million students. However, Algeria still needs to spend more on teacher training if it wants a skilled workforce capable of attracting sustained inward investment.

In early 2009, the President was seeking to amend the constitution to allow him to run for a third term of office, and seemed likely to achieve this. There is a high degree of consensus among political parties that Algeria needs a liberal market economy and a prudent fiscal and monetary policy. However, there has been speculation about the extent to which President Bouteflika is influenced by hardliners who want more state intervention, and who are seen as blocking privatization of the remaining state monopolies and industries.

In 2006, for example, President Bouteflika overturned a law, introduced the previous year, which would have allowed foreign firms to take majority stake holdings in Algerian oil and gas companies. In June 2008, he announced that foreign company investments were not benefiting the country as much as had been hoped, and said that in future they would be limited to minority shareholdings in local concerns. Nevertheless, there are those in the Algerian government determined to push ahead with liberalizing reforms.

The government has succeeded in privatizing certain sectors of the Algerian economy, and has encouraged industry to form joint ventures with some state-owned and operated organizations. Algeria wants to become a member of the World Trade Organization, a step that is seen as very positive in its implications both for domestic business and for inward investment.

The vast majority of the population lives along the Mediterranean coast, which occupies some 12% of the country's land mass. This of itself creates a large urban population, with some 45% of the country's population living in cities such as Algiers. The government's economic policy has some challenges trying to stem the mass migration of people from the poor rural areas to the more affluent cities. In part, support for Algeria's agricultural sector is designed both to accomplish this, and to generate greater wealth in a potentially lucrative sector.

The banking sector has been liberalized since 1990, and there are some 22 public and private-sector banks, 12 of which are foreign-owned. Reforms at the end of 2003 paved the way for investment banks and leasing companies. Similarly, a massive reform of the telecoms and postal sector since 2000, and a new legal and regulatory framework for a multi-operator telecommunications infrastructure are now in place. The World Bank currently rates Algeria's telecommunications market as the most liberalized in the MENA region.

ECONOMIC PERFORMANCE OVER 12 MONTHS

Thanks to its oil and gas exports, Algeria currently runs a trade surplus. This rose to US$39.07 billion at the end of 2008, up by more than 20% on the prior year's figure of US$32.53 billion. Imports, which range from consumer goods to medical and technical supplies, were worth US$39.15 billion in 2008, up 42.7% on the previous year. The country's GDP, in terms of purchasing power parity, amounted to in excess of US$240 billion in 2008, and Algeria continues to build up its foreign reserves, despite the downturn.

According to comments from Abdelkrim Mansouri, the general manager of the Algerian National Agency for the Development of Investment (ANDI), made to the official news agency APS in January 2009, foreign inward investment into Algeria is expected to continue in 2009, on the back of "good economic

 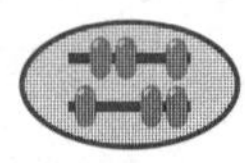      

indicators." The economy grew by over 3% in 2008 and is expected to maintain positive growth in 2009, despite the global recession.

France currently provides more than 30% of Algeria's imports, and some 60% of Algeria's trade last year was with the European Union. An agreement between Algeria and the European Union envisages the creation of a free-market area, with the phasing out of tariff barriers over the next decade. The Algerian government has also said that it intends to dismantle all monopolies in the country by 2010—a necessary condition of its joining the WTO.

Much of Algeria's current domestic economic performance outside the oil and gas sector comes from the success of its liberalization program, with a number of wealthy Algerian families launching banking and commercial ventures. According to one of President Bouteflika's close colleagues, Hamid Temmar, who has held the posts of both Commerce Minister and Minister for Participation and Investment Promotion, and who has overseen much of the reform program, Algeria is in the process "of reviewing all regulatory matters and installing a (modern) legislative framework to give (the country) a wholly liberal economy."

Algeria's bid to be accepted into the WTO hinges in part on the country's ability to introduce robust intellectual property (IP) protection laws. As a current hotbed for the illegal copying of software and music CDs—dubbed Algeria's "parallel economy" by Temmar—the country has its work cut out in this area.

Apart from hydrocarbons, areas that could be attractive to investors, and to companies looking for joint venture deals in Algeria include housing, agriculture, and some mining of local ores. Algeria is also cited by the World Bank as having considerable potential as a manufacturing base, given its proximity to Europe.

SUPPORT FOR INWARD INVESTMENT AND IMPORTS

Algeria's Supplementary Finance Law, August 1990 introduced a system of concessionaries and wholesalers who were entitled to represent foreign companies, as part of a process to liberalize imports. Importers also gained the right to hold foreign currency accounts to carry out their legitimate business. Today, the entity responsible for foreign direct investment in Algeria is the National Investment Development Agency (ANDI), created in 2001.

TAX EXEMPTIONS

All discussions on tax breaks should be taken up with ANDI. The country has five free trade zones where investments are exempt from all customs, taxes, and other fees.

▸▸ MORE INFO

Websites:

National Investment Development Agency (ANDI): www.andi.dz

Trade advice on a range of countries, including Algeria: www.alibaba.com

Trade website for MENA region: www.animaweb.org

Angola

ECONOMY AND TRADE

Angola is rich in oil, minerals, gold, and diamonds, and enjoyed an astonishing 23% growth rate in 2007 and double-digit growth in 2008, which is likely to be cut back to around 10% for 2009 if the oil price averages around US$45. Growth is almost entirely driven by the oil sector, but the government is determined to diversify, and to grow other sectors of the economy.

The 27-year-long civil war, which ended with the death of rebel leader Jonas Savimbi in February 2002, transformed Angola from being a strong exporter of food before the war, to being reliant on food imports. Before independence in 1975, Angola exported coffee, sisal, and cotton on European-dominated commercial farms. Today, as a result of the war, the countryside has been seeded with land mines, and will take many years to reclaim. However, the country has a US$7 billion line of credit from China, and strong credit from Brazil, Portugal, Germany, Spain, and the European Union, and is engaged in a massive infrastructure rebuilding program.

ECONOMIC POLICY OVER 12 MONTHS

The Angolan Central Bank has been largely successful in bringing runaway inflation under control. Consumer inflation has declined from 325% in 2000 to under 13% in 2008. A central bank policy of using oil-derived foreign exchange to buy up the country's currency, the kwanza, has stabilized the exchange rate and reined in inflation. One of the challenges, however, is the extensive use of the US dollar by the population as an alternative to the national currency.

Angola joined the OPEC group towards the end of 2006, and a year later was given a production quota of 1.9 million barrels a day (below the 2.3 million barrels it is capable of producing).

The government is committed to encouraging inward investment, and there are opportunities for foreign companies both to set up operations, and to engage in joint ventures with Angolan companies. However, Angola ranks low on the literacy and productivity league tables as the war disrupted public education.

STATISTICS

GDP growth: 15.1% (2008)

GDP per capita: US$9,100

CPI: 12.5% (2008)

Key interest rate: 17.7% (commercial bank prime rate)

Exchange rate versus dollar: kwanza per US dollar—75.023 (2008)

Unemployment: Extensive—more than half the population

FDI: US$227 million (2006, est.)

Current account deficit/surplus: 11.3% of GDP (2007)

Population: 12,531,357 (July 2008)

Source: CIA Factbook except where stated

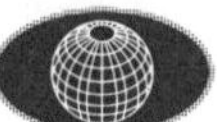

The country has great potential given its natural resources, which include not only its gold and diamond reserves, but extensive forests that constitute a great sustainable resource for both Angolan construction programs, and for export.

An IMF team that reported on Angola following an in-country inspection visit in 2007 gave the country full credit for its macroeconomic policies. The programs the government has put in place to address the ravages of nearly three decades of a vicious internal war are gaining traction. The government remains committed to continuing a high level of spending on infrastructure and the social sector, believing that this will enhance the efficiency and competitiveness of the overall economy.

Angola has been building up its internal reserves, and these will help it to weather the current volatility in the price of oil. External and domestic debt levels are relatively low. The IMF has been urging the Angolan government to design and implement fiscal policies that focus on the medium term and have an eye to a potential longer-term fall in the price of oil, and to "vigorously pursue appropriate structural reforms to support the development of the non-oil and non-oil extractive sectors of the economy (all areas where the country welcomes inward investment)."

Angola recently repaid a tranche of its Paris Club debt (some US$2.3 billion), settling principal and interest arrears, and bringing it into a better standing with the Club. The IMF also urged the Angolan government to work at bringing down the cost of doing business in the non-oil and gas sectors, including streamlining the existing costly and time-consuming registration requirements. The Angolan prime minister, Antonio Paulo Kassoma, announced in August 2008 that it was committed, in 2009, to making Angola a more attractive place in which foreign companies can invest. It also announced an ambitious job-creation program, saying it expects to create 320,000 new jobs in 2009 outside the oil and gas sector. Sector priorities for the year ahead include agriculture, geology and mining, industry, commerce, hotels, and tourism.

ECONOMIC PERFORMANCE OVER 12 MONTHS

Despite being the fastest-growing economy in Africa, Angola is still grappling with a per capita output that, at the end of the war, was among the lowest in the world, and is only gradually improving. In 1975, Angola was self-sufficient in all major food crops, and was the world's fourth-largest coffee grower. Today, the government is working hard to return to a fully diversified economy after the ravages of the civil war.

According to the World Bank, the country's economic performance over the last six years has been strong, with both the oil and non-oil sides of the economy performing well. GDP has doubled every third year, from US$19.8 billion in 2004 to US$30.6 billion in 2005, rising to US$41 billion in 2006 and US$60.4 billion in 2007.

The real growth rate of 22.3% of GDP in 2007 reflected a real growth of 20.4% in the oil sector, and a pleasing 25.7% growth in the nonoil sectors, including growth of 37% in construction, 32.6% in manufacturing, and 27.4% in agriculture.

The country runs a fiscal surplus, thanks to its oil revenues, and these surpluses have increased in the last few years, from 7.1% of GDP in 2005 to 9.9% in 2006, and 11.3% in 2007. Between 2003 and 2007, revenues grew at an annual average rate of 53%. The fact that revenues have grown faster than public expenditure explains the continued increase in surpluses. The non-oil fiscal balance, which had been running large deficits, has improved, and deficits have declined from 75% of GDP in 2003 to 55% in 2007. Excluding interest payments and grants, the non-oil deficit declined from 72.5% of non-oil GDP in 2003 to 52.6% in 2007.

The overall fiscal surplus in 2008 will be very close to the 2007 levels, at around 11% of GDP. Additionally, diamond exports are expected to grow even faster than in previous years. Net international reserves reached US$16.5 billion in July 2008, an increase of 47% compared to December 2007.

The World Bank rates the medium-term outlook for the country's economy as positive. The decline in the oil price will knock GDP back from a predicted year-on-year growth rate, prior to the current downturn, of 15% for 2009, to something like 8–10%, which the Bank sees as sustainable until 2011. The determination of the Angolan government to diversify away from oil by boosting job creation in non-oil sectors such as agriculture, construction, and services is seen as very positive, as the oil and gas sector employs only around 1% of the country's workforce.

SUPPORT FOR INWARD INVESTMENT AND IMPORTS

The National Private Investment Agency (ANIP) is the body tasked with attracting foreign investment to facilitate the reconstruction, and the economic and social development of Angola. It is responsible for the complete administrative side of investing in Angola by foreign companies, and handles all applications, including those for tax and financial incentives, licensing and company formation.

The government has announced that it intends to minimize bureaucratic impediments to inward investment, and to bring in measures to guarantee the protection of investments, while giving foreign companies the ability to transfer dividends abroad.

➤➤ MORE INFO

Websites:

Middle East and Africa Monitor (monitors trade stories for the Middle East and Africa): www.meamonitor.com

Angolan US embassy website: www.angola.org

World Bank: www.worldbank.org/angola

IMF: www.imf.org/external/country/AGO

  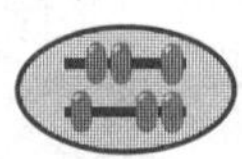      

TAX EXEMPTIONS
The government is committed to introducing further "special incentives on fiscal and customs duties," according to a recent speech by Angolan president, Jose Eduardo dos Santos.

Antigua and Barbuda

ECONOMY AND TRADE

Having achieved an average growth rate of 6.5% for a 20-year stretch during the 1970s and 1980s, fuelled by a tourism boom and strong inward investment, the two island nations of Antigua and Barbuda were crippled by a series of hurricanes in the 1990s. This was further exacerbated by a fall in tourism following the 9/11 terrorist attacks in the United States. In 2004, a new administration came to power with a fresh sense of purpose, and Antigua has experienced solid growth since 2003. Growth peaked at 12% in 2006 on the back of the Cricket World Cup. However, as the two islands are highly dependent on tourism, with US tourists constituting one-third of all visitors, the global downturn promises to create difficult times for Antigua through 2009. Agricultural production, which is almost entirely for local consumption, has to battle both a limited supply of local water, and the fact that agricultural wages are below the rates for both tourism and construction. Literacy and secondary education are around 85%, and there is some manufacturing for export. The islands have a thriving tax-haven business due to the favorable regulations for offshore banking.

STATISTICS

GDP growth: 2.1% (2008, est.)
GDP per capita: US$19,100 (2008, est.)
CPI: 1.5% (2007)
Key interest rate: 10.44% (commercial bank prime rate)
Exchange rate versus dollar: East Caribbean dollar per US dollar—2.7(fixed)
Unemployment: 11%
FDI: N/A
Current account deficit/ surplus: −US$211 million (2007, est.)
Population: 84,522
Source: CIA Factbook except where stated

ECONOMIC POLICY OVER 12 MONTHS

The Antigua and Barbuda Budget Statements set the year's policy agenda. They demonstrate, in fine detail, just how conscious the dual-island nation's present government is of the fact that Antigua and Barbuda's economic fortunes are inextricably tied to the fortunes of the developed nations. Anything that has an impact on the tourist trade, from higher oil prices which drive up aviation fuel costs and make travel more expensive, to the 2008–2009 global economic downturn, which predisposes consumers to forego expensive, exotic holidays on Caribbean islands, hits the country's economy hard.

The government has been working closely with the regional central bank, the Eastern Caribbean Central Bank (ECCB), and with the European Union and the United States to try to both manage a legacy foreign debt that exceeds 100% of GDP, and to develop the economy beyond its single mainstay of tourism. One of the positives achieved in the Eastern Caribbean Currency Union (ECCU) in 2008 was the establishment of a "Free Movement of Skills" regime across the region, which came into force on 13 June 2008. Caribbean nationals who have obtained Caribbean Vocational Qualifications (CVQ) are free to move about the region.

In the 2009 Budget Statement, the plight of those islanders in the lower economic categories in the face of these twin price surges, was noted, and some promise of additional help for the poorest was sketched out. Again, falling tourism revenues will not make that kind of promise easy to meet. The government has signed an Economic Partnership Agreement with the European Union, and has pushed particularly for technical and financial assistance for the nation's priority programs of housing, education, and manufacture. Antigua and Barbuda receive support from the European Union's 9th Economic Development Fund, amounting to some €6.3 million in 2007–2008.

The country's tax-exempt offshore banking laws and good legislative framework have created a thriving, offshore tax-haven industry. Offshore banks require a minimum paid-up capital of US$5 million, and are not subject to the reserve requirements imposed on local banks by the Antigua Banking Act.

Antigua and Barbadu have a "Digital Agenda," recognizing that computer and Internet access is a cornerstone of economic growth in the modern era. As the government said in its 2009 Budget, "The world markets increasingly demand a highly skilled, digitally minded workforce and the government has spent US$26 million over the last four years implementing increased access to computer technology in schools and communities."

ECONOMIC PERFORMANCE OVER 12 MONTHS

Economic growth in the Caribbean region slowed in 2007, following an outstanding period of growth in 2006, which achieved 8.4% year-on-year growth. This fell to 6% for the region as a whole in 2007 and to around 4% for 2008. With the ECCU economies cooling at the tail end of 2007 and throughout 2008, most sectors of the Antigua and Barbuda economy felt the chill. While the country still expects to see some growth, rather than the contraction experienced in many Western economies, that growth will be around

1–2% in 2009. The government expects the construction sector to provide much of the impetus for this growth, with some support from other sectors. Tourism, however, is expected to contract.

The country went into 2008 expecting a global trend growth of around 4.8%, or just marginally less than the 5.5% global growth average of 2006. In point of fact, by the end of 2008 it found itself staring at recession in a number of the countries that constitute its primary sources of tourist revenue. Even worse, the islands were hit very hard by extreme volatility in both the price of oil, and the price of many basic foods.

The islands' construction sector expanded its output in 2008 by 5.5%, with reasonable demand in both the private and public sectors. Tourism grew by 4.0% in 2008, and by 4.9% in 2007. However, a marked downturn in the last three months of 2008, particularly from the European Union, bodes ill for any prospect of growth in 2009. The industry was also hit by a downturn in the number of cruise ships calling at the islands (46 fewer in 2008 than in 2007), with the fall-off coming from cruise lines paring their destination portfolios in response to the high cost of oil. With oil prices back to a potential average of US$45 per barrel for 2009, that reason at least might vanish, though diminished household surpluses in the major Western economies and in Asia are expected to have an adverse impact on the number of visitors seeking Caribbean holidays.

Online gaming, which already has a presence on the island targeting the US consumer base, received a boost with the United Kingdom including the island-nation on its whitelist of online gaming countries, in accordance with Section 331 of the United Kingdom Gambling Act 2005. The effective date of the whitelisting was 21 November 2008. To make the whitelist, Antigua had to be able to show that it had the appropriate regulatory framework in place with regard to the exclusion of criminal involvement (including money laundering and the financing of terrorism). The move is seen as significant because it allows the country's existing gaming and interactive wagering companies to expand their base from the United States to the United Kingdom, and ultimately to Europe.

SUPPORT FOR INWARD INVESTMENT AND IMPORTS

Importers have to comply with the recently introduced Antigua and Barbuda Sales Tax regime (ABST), a major overhaul of the country's sales tax structure. Further details are available on the government website.

TAX EXEMPTIONS

There are various levels of tax exemptions from property tax for properties used for agriculture, and in the hotel and manufacturing sectors. Offshore banking in Antigua is protected by strict privacy laws and an offshore IBC established in Antigua and Barbuda can enjoy a tax-exemption period of 50 years, creating a secure, well-legislated offshore jurisdiction.

▸▸ MORE INFO

Websites:

Official government website: www.ab.gov.ag

Antigua and Barbuda Budget Statements: www.ab.gov.ag/gov_v2/government/speeches/2009/index_2009.html

Antigua guide: www.antigua-guide.info/past.and.present/economy

Argentina

ECONOMY AND TRADE

In the four years prior to 2008, the Argentinean economy enjoyed strong growth. However, 2008 saw the economy falter, although the country still managed a fiscal surplus of more than 3%. The country has rich resources and a highly literate population. It is famous for its agricultural exports and enjoys a diversified industrial base. The twenty-first century did not begin well for the country, with a severe depression and a run on the banks in 2001 culminating in savers not being allowed to withdraw their own money, while the government was forced to default on its foreign debt. However, abandoning the country's policy of pegging the peso to the US dollar on a one-to-one basis was the start of a climb-back by the economy. Real GDP was 18% lower in 2002 than in 1998 and more than half the country was rated as below the poverty line. The next five years saw the economy picking up sustained momentum with growth averaging 9% per annum. Mounting inflation gave cause for concern and the government responded by manufacturing more "reasonable" inflation figures, damaging its own credibility hugely in the process.

ECONOMIC POLICY OVER 12 MONTHS

Argentina's economic policy over the last 12 months can be characterized as being dominated, above all, by an increasingly desperate search by the government for funds to meet its external debt payments. This search has included Argentina's president, Cristina Fernandez de Kirchner, taking the extraordinary step of nationalizing the country's private pensions industry, which netted the government some US$29 billion, and provoked outrage among the populace. In January 2009 Kirchner had a public approval rating of just

STATISTICS

GDP growth: 6.6% (2008)
GDP per capita: US$14,500
CPI: 22% (est., not the official rate which lacks credibility)
Key interest rate: N/A
Exchange rate versus dollar: pesos per US dollar—3.1636
Unemployment: 7.8%
FDI: US$69.1 billion
Current account deficit/surplus: US$4.8 billion (first 9 months of 2007, source: Reuters)
Population: 40.482 million
Source: CIA Factbook except where stated

 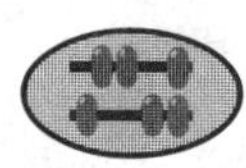      

20%, one of the lowest ever for a serving president. The stock exchange in Buenos Aires fell to a five-year low as a reaction to the move. Argentina has been frozen out of all lines of international credit since it initiated the largest sovereign default in history, defaulting on US$95 billion of debt and interest payments in 2001. The country has some US$12 billion of bonds maturing in 2009, which many thought would be impossible for it to meet. However, the country has made strenuous efforts to reassure creditors that it is willing and able to repay its debts and in its 2009 Budget announced a fiscal surplus equal to 3.3% of GDP, following a surplus of 3.15% during the previous year. The government also announced that it would be using foreign currency reserves to repay US$6.7 billion of debt to the Paris Club of lending nations, putting relations with the Paris Club on a much better footing.

The 2009 budget assumes an inflation rate of 8%, around a third of what most commentators believe the real figure to be. The country desperately needs some macroeconomic stability. One Argentinean entrepreneur famously summed up the situation over the last five years as consisting of "at least five or six different economic plans, with completely different politics, a closed economy, an open economy, privatization, non-privatization, a fixed dollar, a floating dollar, a controlled dollar, an uncontrolled dollar, brutal devaluations, increases in tariffs and frozen tariffs. You go mad or it turns you into a survivor."

Fortunately for Argentina, its entrepreneurial sector continues to demonstrate a great ability to innovate and succeed. Google made Buenos Aires its Latin American headquarters precisely because of the strength and innovation of Argentina's software industry. The country is attempting a fiscal stimulus through a massive program of pubic works, but is struggling to fund projects, since external credit is not an option.

ECONOMIC PERFORMANCE OVER 12 MONTHS

At the end of 2008 and in early 2009 the country was in the grip of one of the worst droughts in its history, turning large swathes of arable land into dust bowls. The drought is damaging the country's livestock industry, one of its prime export commodities, as well as food crops, and is adding considerably to the damage caused by the international financial crisis and plummeting commodity prices.

One of the government's plans for funding the stimulus package involves tackling the notorious under-reporting of foreign-held capital by Argentinean nationals involved in exports. The unreported capital held abroad is said to amount to in excess of US$120 billion, with a further US$50 billion of unreported capital within the country. If President Kirchner is successful in this bid, the government will generate a substantial tax windfall in 2009. However, repatriated funds will only be charged tax of 8%, and could be charged as little as 1% if the funds are reinvested locally.

Argentina is in the throes of implementing its own "New Deal" program, which began on 15 December 2008 and is estimated to be worth US$21 billion. The aim is to stimulate growth of up to 4% in 2009. According to government estimates, the program will double the number of public sector jobs to 770,000 in 2009.

The program is also designed to be a stimulus to businesses across the country as it pardons "off the books" labor practices, provided workers are registered and paid properly, generating more taxes for the government. There is a 50% tax holiday for employers who take advantage of the scheme in 2009 and a 25% holiday in 2010. The construction sector has been one of the biggest offenders with "off the books" labor, and was also one of the mainstays of Argentina's outstanding economic performance from 2003 to 2007. It is set to benefit from both the New Deal and the amnesty program, which should stimulate growth again during 2009. The expectation is that growth will surge again in 2011 and 2012, provided the government's highly interventionist economic policy does not go off the rails.

Argentina, Brazil, Paraguay, and Uruguay are all members of the Southern Common Market (MERCOSUR). Chile and Bolivia are partners. MERCOSUR represents a potential market of 200 million people and has a combined GDP in excess of US$1 trillion. Another trade grouping is the Latin American Integration Association (LAIA), which aspires to set up a Latin-American-wide common market. Argentina is also a member of the Cairns Group, which includes Australia, a group of national agricultural exporters that do not subsidize their agricultural sectors.

SUPPORT FOR INWARD INVESTMENTS AND IMPORTS

Camara Argentina de Comercio is the Argentinean department of commerce, responsible for providing consulting services to Argentine businesses interested in importing or exporting, and is also a good place for prospective importers to begin. The Bureau of Customs has responsibility for the enforcement of tariff and customs laws, and regulations. There are a host of import regulations, which the importer needs to get to grips with, including anti-dumping provisions. According to a study by the US Embassy in Argentina, the country's import tariffs range from 0% to 35%, with an average applied tariff rate in 2007 of 14%, while the MERCOSUR tariff averages around 13.6%. There are complexities in exporting to Argentina associated with the government's desire to clamp down on under-invoicing and fraudulent underpayment of customs duties. Contact the Argentinean Economic Ministry for specific advice.

▸▸ MORE INFO

Websites:

- Argentina's Economic Ministry: www.mecon.gov.ar
- Camara Argentina de Comercio: www.cac.com.ar
- Federal Express, has a long history of expediting documentation and carriage related to importing to Argentina: www.fedex.com
- Fundacion Invertir, the official "doing business in Argentina" website: www.invertir.com/argentina
- Learn about Argentina: www.argentinaturistica.com
- US embassy website, a great source: www.argentina.usembassy.gov

  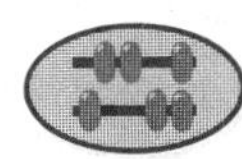      

TAX EXEMPTIONS

There are no tax-haven-type tax exemptions available. Certain civil associations and foundations can apply for tax-exempt status, but these are not-for-profit organizations, and tax-exempt status is not automatic.

Australia

ECONOMY AND TRADE

Australia has a strong economy with a per capita GDP that is comparable to that of the United Kingdom, France and Germany. Low inflation, a housing market boom, and an active program of developing export ties with Asia, and particularly with Japan and China, have been key factors in promoting 17 years of continuous growth for the country's economy. Robust business and consumer confidence and high export prices for raw materials and agricultural products fueled the economy in recent years, particularly in mining states. The country's big challenge recently—apart from the global downturn starting in late 2008—has been dealing with a growing trade deficit caused by a combination of droughts, which weakened agricultural exports, strong demand for imports from Australian consumers, and a strong currency which, again, attracted imports. The unprecedented global demand for commodities exposed infrastructure bottlenecks, and a tight labor market constrained growth in export volumes and caused inflation to rise during mid-2008. Tight global liquidity has had an impact on Australia's banking sector, which relies heavily on international wholesale markets for funding. The economy remains relatively healthy despite falling export commodity prices. The government plans to counter slowing growth in 2009 through a fiscal stimulus package.

STATISTICS

GDP growth: 1% (2008–2009, government est.)
GDP per capita: AU$39,300
CPI: 4.7% (2008 est.)
Key interest rate: 10.02% (December 31, 2007)
Exchange rate versus dollar: 1.2059 AU$ to the dollar (2008)
Unemployment: 4.5% (government, estimated to rise to 7% by 2010)
FDI: AU$333.1 billion
Current account deficit/surplus: 22% of GDP (government)
Population: 21,007,319 (July 2008)
Source: CIA Factbook except where stated

ECONOMIC POLICY OVER 12 MONTHS

While Australia has enjoyed a long, sustained period of growth thanks to sound macroeconomic policies, the surge in commodities prices during 2007 and much of 2008 rekindled broad-based inflation pressures, with the CPI index rising to 4.5%, according to the IMF. At the same time, the country's growing current account deficit increased net foreign liabilities to 60% of GDP. In response, the Reserve Bank of Australia tightened monetary policy, raising the rate by 1% between August 2007 and March 2008. The unwinding of the yen/Australian dollar carry trade contributed sharply to the sudden weakening of the Australian dollar in August 2007 and to its continued depreciation during the second half of 2008. The carry trade involves investors borrowing yen to finance rolling 90-day investments in Australian dollars (as well as in New Zealand and US dollars). This generated substantial profits and fueled strong demand for the Australian dollar, already strengthening as a result of the commodity price boom. As the Australian dollar further appreciated against the yen, the carry trade generated further profits for investors. In 2007 these positions began to unwind through a combination of market volatility, the liquidity crunch, and sharp exchange-rate movements. Investors sold out of the dollar and repaid their yen debts because the accelerating depreciation of the Australian dollar either rendered the trade unprofitable or generated a momentum that would have led to losses if the position was maintained, according to Chris Ryan, head of the international department at the Reserve Bank of Australia.

The last quarter of 2008 was also remarkable for seeing a very sharp downward shift to below-trend growth in the forecasts for Australia's trading partners. Japan is Australia's major trading partner and it saw a 20% decline in manufacturing output in the last quarter of 2008, along with weak performances from Australia's other major trading partners.

Against this backdrop, the Australian government's budget for 2008–2009, set at a time when robust growth was still being predicted for the emerging markets of China and India (both of which have since seen a substantial slowdown), anticipated nominal economic growth of 9.25%. The budget set a target for a surplus of AU$21.7 billion, or 1.8% of GDP, the largest budget surplus for over a decade, to be achieved by "disciplined" spending and the lowest real increase in government spending in a decade. The anticipated surplus has since been revised in the light of the steep global downturn, and in its update to its Mid-year Economic and Fiscal Outlook, the Australian government said it now expects to run a deficit of AU$22.5 billion for the year, as it increases spending to support growth and jobs.

The government remains committed to reducing personal income tax by AU$47 billion over four years, with the cuts being targeted at low and middle-income families. The country's medium-term fiscal objectives remain to achieve budget surpluses, on average over the economic cycle (even allowing for budget deficits to pay for stimulus packages during the downturn); to keep taxation as a share of GDP below the level for 2007–08, and to improve the government's net worth over the medium term.

  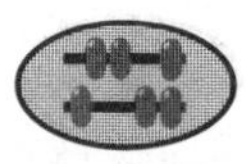      

ECONOMIC PERFORMANCE OVER 12 MONTHS

In the second half of 2008, the Australian government responded to the threat of zero growth or an actual contraction of the economy by announcing a AU$42 billion "Nation Building and Jobs Plan" to stimulate the creation of 90,000 jobs and to ensure positive growth. It expects the plan to enable the economy to achieve 1% year-on-year growth during 2008–2009, and 0.75% growth for 2009–2010. Unemployment is forecast to rise to 7% by June 2010. Australia still expects to be in a much better position than the advanced economies of the members of the G7, with its anticipated budget deficits for 2009 and 2010 being under 3% of GDP, as against the G7 average of 7%, as forecast by the IMF (assuming the global downturn does not worsen). Weak demand from China and Japan has already had an impact on Australia's exports, and, by February 2009, the Australian dollar had lost between 30% and 40% of its value against the US dollar. Slumping equity values have lowered the market capitalization of many major Australian companies by as much as 80% (source: The Australian Business), and sparked a buying spree of Australian assets by Chinese companies in particular.

The government has followed the example of other countries by guaranteeing bank deposits, and has looked to shore up the Australian construction and commercial property sector—one of the key drivers of Australia's growth strategy over the last decade—by providing liquidity support to "viable major commercial property projects." This is being done through a new body, the Australian Business Investment Partnership, capitalized at AU$4 billion (in equal measures by the government and participating banks). It will support projects such as shopping malls, commercial offices, and factories under construction. The package aims to safeguard around 50,000 jobs in the construction sector, which analysts argue were under threat, out of a total construction sector workforce of 150,000.

In February 2009, the Australian Reserve Bank cut its rate by 1%, and the cut was passed on to businesses as a reduction in the cost of debt funding. This comes on top of a AU$2.7 billion business tax break targeted at small to medium-sized businesses (part of the AU$42 billion "Nation Building and Jobs Plan." The Australian government has recognized that transport infrastructure problems across the country are having an impact on Australia's ability to respond to surges in demand for commodity exports, and has set up a national infrastructure fund to address these issues. Australia's largest source of imports is the United States, which accounts for some 15% of total imports (AU$33 billion in 2006, according to the Australian government), followed by China (13%) and Japan (9%). Australia is actively pursuing free trade agreements and has finalized comprehensive agreements with four of its ten largest trading partners, New Zealand, Singapore, the United States and Thailand and negotiations are underway with the Association of Southeast Asian Nations, China, the Gulf Cooperation Council, Malaysia and Japan.

SUPPORT FOR INWARD INVESTMENT AND IMPORTS

The first port of call for potential investors in Australia is Austrade, the Australian Trade Commission. As an open economy and a global trader, Australia is committed to liberalizing international trade and breaking down trade barriers. All goods entering Australia must be cleared by the Australian Customs Service, and the requirements are listed on its website: www.customs.gov.au. Further information is available from the Customs Information and Support Centre (tel: 1300 363 263), from the Australian Trade Commission, or the Department of Foreign Affairs and Trade.

TAX EXEMPTIONS

The Australian government agency AusIndustry operates a range of incentives to encourage inward investment that results in job creation in Australia. It is part of the Department of Innovation, Industry, Science and Research (www.ausindustry.gov.au).

▸▸ MORE INFO

Websites:

A full account of the Australian budget and economic outlook: www.budget.gov.au

The Australian Trade Commission: www.austrade.gov.au

Ausindustry, the Australian government's business program delivery division: www.ausindustry.gov.au

Austria

ECONOMY AND TRADE

Austria's economy is closely tied to the other European Union nations, and especially to the German economy. It comprises a large services sector, a sound industrial sector, and a small, but highly developed agricultural sector. The country, which has been a member of the EU's Economic and Monetary Union since 1999, has not escaped the global economic downturn and entered a recession in 2008 that is expected to persist through most, if not all, of 2009. Prior to this, the country had enjoyed several years of solid demand for its exports and benefited from record employment growth in the first half of 2008. The Austrian economy has benefited greatly in the last decade from strong commercial relations, with central, eastern, and south-eastern Europe, especially in the banking and insurance sectors. However, the Austrian

banking sector was hard hit by the recent international financial instabilities, and some of Austria's largest banks have required government support. The country faces a severe challenge in the future, even after the recession eases, as its ageing population and very low birth rate threaten to exacerbate labor and skills shortages in key sectors of the economy, such as manufacturing and services.

ECONOMIC POLICY OVER 12 MONTHS

By February 2009, the growing recession in the eurozone had forced the Austrian government, under the leadership of Chancellor Werner Faymann, to introduce not one but three stimulus packages. The coalition government, consisting of the Social Democratic Party and the Austrian People's Party, are more or less united on both the need for positive action and on the measures chosen. They have agreed, for example, to bring forward income tax reform, from 2010 to 2009, and the three stimulus packages have been pushed through swiftly, all aimed at shoring up liquidity in Austria's financial industry.

However, Austria's banks are heavily exposed to counterparty risk from banks in central and eastern Europe, where Austrian banks have loans outstanding which amount to some 70% of the country's GDP. Austria is working with other European countries, including Italy, Germany, France and Belgium, and with the European Investment Bank, the European Central Bank, the European Bank for Reconstruction and Development, the EU Cohesion Fund and the IMF to create a sufficient rescue package for the banking sectors in central and eastern Europe, according to both *The Economist* and the IMF.

Austria is committed to a prudent fiscal policy and has a target of running a balanced, sustainable budget. However, the cost of the various stimulus packages it is funding, both within and without its borders, is already creating a budget deficit that the country will find challenging in the immediate future. However, Austria has benefited, and will continue to benefit, from having introduced measures to deal with the costs associated with an ageing population, including pension, health, and long-term care costs.

In its most recent country review (June 2008), the IMF urged Austria to "re-balance and broaden" its tax base by shifting the burden of taxation away from work and entrepreneurship to fixed assets such as real estate. It has also suggested Austria can do more to implement environmental taxes and to add or raise excise duties on some, potentially harmful, consumer items such as tobacco and alcohol.

As a small, open economy, Austria needs to ensure that it is constantly reforming its processes and structures to encourage business to flourish, according to the IMF. The fact that the country's demographics are heavily weighted towards older people means that there is a chronic shortage of skills and available manpower across many Austrian industrial sectors. Yet the country is becoming considerably less open to foreign workers than it was several years earlier.

ECONOMIC PERFORMANCE OVER 12 MONTHS

Much of Austria's effort in recent months has gone on trying to soften the impact of the global downturn on the country's economy. Austrian enterprises, in particular Austria's banks, are among the largest investors in eastern and south-eastern Europe, with some Austrian banks being market-leading in these areas.

According to the IMF, Austria's 2008 budget deficit was lower than expected, at around 0.3% of GDP, instead of the anticipated deficit of 0.7%. The country's external debt, however, stood at 62.5% after the Austrian government's eastern European banking bail-out package. This is 2.5% above the limits set by the Maastricht Treaty.

Not surprisingly, the downturn, though it was slow in coming, has begun to take its toll on jobs, and unemployment increased significantly in the last quarter of 2008 and in January 2009. This reversed a trend in 2008 where employment had been growing at a rate of 1.6%. Currently, the automotive sector is the worst hit, but job-cutting is starting to spread to other sectors too.

By the end of January 2009, the country's jobless total had risen to 301,529, some 12.2% more than in December. The jobless total contained a disproportionate number of young workers, with a 22.9% rise in this category. Austria has also continued to implement measures to increase the employment of older workers and to tackle what the European Union calls "gender segregation" within the labor market.

On the positive side, Austria has moved up the European Union's "innovation rankings," a useful guide to an economy's ability to create new jobs and to achieve significant market share in emerging industries. It has climbed from eighth place and now ranks sixth in the European Union, according to the European Innovation Scoreboard 2008. Austria is also second behind Ireland as the country with the fastest improvement rate in the innovation stakes.

Headline inflation was touching 4% by mid-2008, but the deflationary impact of the recession, falling global commodity prices, and lower real interest rates have caused inflation to ease back.

The IMF argues that the Austrian government's key mid-term challenge will be to find ways of transforming the country into a more knowledge-intensive one, better suited to an ageing but highly literate population. Despite increased spending by Austrian businesses on R&D and innovation, the country is still some distance away from achieving this goal.

STATISTICS
GDP growth: 2.1% (2008), 0.3% (2009 IMF est.)
GDP per capita: $39,600
CPI: 3.7 % (2008)
Key interest rate: 6.3 %
Exchange rate versus dollar: euro/dollar rate
FDI: US$276.9 billion
Current account deficit/surplus: 0.3% (2008, IMF)
Population: 8,205,533
Source: CIA Factbook except where stated

  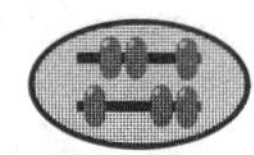      

SUPPORT FOR INWARD INVESTMENT AND IMPORTS

ABA-Invest in Austria is a government-operated consulting firm which aims to be the international investor's first business address in Austria. The ABA provides advice and services ranging from issues on incentives, to market opportunities and tax concerns.

TAX EXEMPTIONS

The country has a moderate corporate tax rate of 25% and offers attractive research incentives (contact ABA-Invest for details). Tax incentives are linked to training, research, and "invention" (innovation).

MORE INFO

Website:

Website of ABA-Invest: www.aba.gv.at

The Bahamas

ECONOMY AND TRADE

As one of the wealthiest Caribbean countries, with an economy heavily dependent on tourism and offshore banking, the Bahamas' prospects for growth are being adversely affected from two different directions. First, the global downturn has significantly affected tourism, and second, a proposed review by the US Administration, under President Obama, of offshore banking could create significant difficulties for this sector.

Tourism, together with tourism-driven construction and manufacturing, accounts for approximately 60% of GDP, and employs half of the archipelago's labor force directly or indirectly. Tourism is heavily dependent on prosperity in the United States, the source of more than 80% of visitors. To help offset the effects of the global economic downturn, particularly on employment, the Bahamas administration, headed by Hubert Ingraham, is boosting public spending on infrastructure projects. Financial services constitute the second-most important sector of the Bahamian economy and, when combined with business services, account for about 36% of GDP.

STATISTICS

GDP growth: 2.8 %
GDP per capita: US$29,900
CPI: 2.4 %
Key interest rate: 5.5 %
Exchange rate versus dollar: Bahamian dollars per US dollar: 1.0 (fixed)
Unemployment: 7.6%
FDI: Not listed
Current account deficit/ surplus: –US$1.442 billion
Population: 307,451
Source: CIA Factbook except where stated

ECONOMIC POLICY OVER 12 MONTHS

The key policy issues for the Bahamas in 2008–2009 all focus on four major themes—the impact of high food prices on the poor, how to react to a severe downturn in the tourist trade, the future of offshore banking and, last but by no means least, the challenge posed by climate change. As Prime Minister Hubert Ingraham said at a meeting in October 2008 with the IMF, much of the land mass of small island nations lies 1.5 meters above sea level. Moreover, the most significant economic development in these islands has taken place in susceptible low-lying coastal zones, all of which are at risk from the predicted rises in sea levels attendant on global warming.

Yet another policy issue to be grappled with is the debt-servicing burden across the region. Ingraham told the IMF that many island nations struggled to address social issues because of the heavy debt-servicing burden (Jamaica, he noted, spends 54 cents of every revenue dollar on debt-servicing). One of the government's fears was that rising debt caused by the downturn could increase this burden and exacerbate social challenges.

In the country's 2008 budget in May, the Bahamas introduced a moderate fiscal stimulus designed to provide financial relief to low wage earners, who were struggling to cope with high food and energy prices. However, the government also emphasized its commitment to fiscal prudence in the medium term.

New regulations for the financial sector put in place by the government in December 2000 caused many international businesses to leave the Bahamas. The laws were a response to the Bahamas being blacklisted by the Financial Action Task Force, which targets countries that have lax laws on money laundering and the funding of terrorism. The government has since acknowledged, however, that the regime put in place to ensure that the "know your customer" provisions of the Financial Transactions Reporting Act, has frustrated both locals and international clients, and contributed to driving offshore business away from the Bahamas. In the face of criticism that the Bahamas' new regime was now more stringent than that which applied in Europe and the United States, the government has sought to soften the reforms rather than to render the country's offshore industry uncompetitive.

In January 2009, the Attorney General and Minister of Legal Affairs, Michael Barnett, announced a wide-ranging program of law reform for the country for the year ahead, to modernize the country's legal system.

ECONOMIC PERFORMANCE OVER 12 MONTHS

Information from the Central Bank of the Bahamas shows that by the end of 2008, the country's tourism

  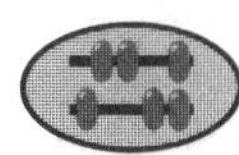   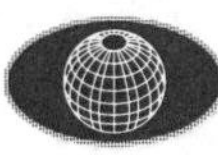   

industry was being severely affected by the global downturn. Layoffs in the hotel industry continued through December 2008 into 2009, pointing to significantly reduced seasonal activity and weaknesses in the short-term outlook for tourism. Private spending in the general economy was also characterized as "weak," being affected by both consumer uncertainty and the accumulated slowdown in credit expansion. The Bank said that both liquidity and external reserves continued to contract and there was some cause for concern in a further erosion in credit quality indicators in the banking sector, with consumer and business defaults threatening to rise.

In all, tourism, the main revenue generator for the country, fell by a further 6.1% over the first nine months of 2008, having slumped by 4.2% in 2007. The short-term signs were for matters worsening, as arrivals on the islands fell by 15.2% in the second half of 2008, according to port-of-entry data.

The average annual inflation rate firmed up during 2008 to 4.5%, from 2.5% in 2007. Cost increases on imports underlined price increases on food and drink of around 6.7%.

The islands' offshore banking sector is currently threatened in some degree by the crackdown on offshore tax havens proposed by President Obama in his presidential campaign. The US Stop Tax Haven Abuse Bill, even with the new regulatory regime in place, could have an adverse impact on both existing capital flows to the Bahamas and the formation of new offshore ventures.

The package of new laws introduced by the Bahamas in 2000 included the Financial Transactions Reporting Act and much stricter "know your customer" rules. The FTRA set a deadline of mid-2002 for the identification of the owners of all accounts in the Bahamas offshore industry established before 1 January 2001. Of itself, this caused many international businesses to leave, though the deadline was extended to 31 December 2002.

In December 2006, however, the government introduced new legislation for private trust companies, which set out that Bahamian PTCs, in common with other structures such as foundations, will not require regulatory approval. A PTC is only required to arrange its affairs with a regulated Bahamian service provider or registered representative. Bahamian trust law provides exemption from the Bahamas Exchange Control Regulations for non-resident beneficiaries, as well as exemption from all taxes and from stamp duty. The offshore banking and trust sector employs more than 10% of the country's workforce and contributes 12% of GDP, according to the Bahamas Investment Authority.

SUPPORT FOR INWARD INVESTMENT AND IMPORTS

The key agency for investors is the Bahamas Investment Authority, which operates from the Office of the Prime Minister. It is designed to be a "one-stop shop" to simplify investing in the Bahamas. Its mandate is to develop investment policies, promote investment, evaluate project proposals, monitor projects, and provide support. (Further information can be obtained from: BIA, Office of the Prime Minister, PO Box CB 10980, Nassau, NP, the Bahamas. Tel: +1 242 372-5970-4).

TAX EXEMPTIONS

Under the Hawksbill Creek Agreement, businesses established in the Freeport Free Trade Zone, a 230-square mile zone on Grand Bahamas Island, pay no taxes on profits, capital gains, etc. For investments generally into the Bahamas, contact the Bahamas Investment Authority, which has the power to negotiate on customs duty exemption.

▸▸ MORE INFO

Websites:

Tourist site with information on culture, travel, etc: www.bahamas.com

The US State Department, which has excellent country intelligence on the Bahamas: www.state.gov

Official website of the Commonwealth of the Bahamas: www.bahamas.gov.bs

Bahrain

ECONOMY AND TRADE

An archipelago of 36 islands, the Kingdom of Bahrain was the first Gulf state to discover oil, but its reserves are due to run out within the next 10–15 years. With its highly developed communication and transport facilities, Bahrain is home to numerous multinational firms with business in the Gulf. Today, petroleum production and refining account for more than 60% of Bahrain's export receipts, more than 70% of government revenues, and 11% of GDP (exclusive of allied industries).

The production and refining sector has underpinned Bahrain's strong economic growth in recent years. Aluminium is Bahrain's second major export after oil. Other major segments of Bahrain's economy are the financial and construction sectors. Bahrain is focused on Islamic banking and competes on an international scale with Malaysia as a worldwide banking centre. Continued strong growth hinges on Bahrain's ability to acquire new natural gas supplies as feedstock to support its expanding petrochemical and aluminium industries. Unemployment, especially among the young, and the depletion of oil and underground water resources are long-term economic problems.

 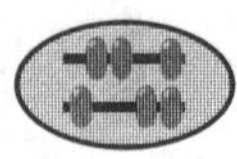 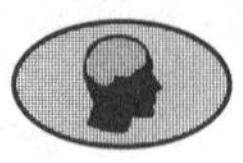  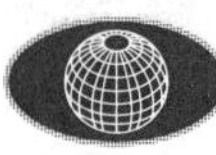   

ECONOMIC POLICY OVER 12 MONTHS

Facing the near-term exhaustion of its oil reserves (gas reserves should last another 50 years), Bahrain is actively working to diversify and privatize its economy in an attempt to reduce the country's dependence on oil. As part of this effort, in August 2006 Bahrain and the United States implemented a Free Trade Agreement (FTA), the first between the United States and a Gulf state.

The biggest element in Bahrain's diversification program, however, without doubt, has been its emergence as a major financial centre. International financial institutions operate in Bahrain, both offshore and onshore, with considerable freedom. The sector contributes 27.6% of GDP and is host to both Western finance houses and one of the Middle East's most developed Islamic banking centres, having played a major part in standardizing the regulatory elements of the Islamic banking industry.

In addition to banking, the country is putting substantial resources into developing service industries such as IT, healthcare and education. It has made use of oil revenues to build an advanced infrastructure in transportation and telecommunications, according to the US State Department.

The privatization effort has focused particularly on water and electricity utilities. In 2006, the government licensed Al Ezzal to construct an independent power plant at a cost of US$500 million. Earlier that year, it sold the Al Hidd Power Plant to a consortium of British, Japanese and Belgium companies for US$753 million.

Bahrain's current account balance is characterized by surpluses in merchandise trade and international services, and a large deficit in unilateral transfers, which is accounted for by the country's large expatriate workforce sending home a portion of its earnings. In 2003 and 2004, the balance of payments performance improved due to rising oil prices and increased receipts from the services sector. As a result, the current account balance registered a surplus of US$219 million in 2003 and a surplus of US$442 million in 2004, compared with a deficit of US$35 million in 2002. Bahrain's gross international reserves increased substantially in 2004 to US$1.6 billion, compared with US$1.4 billion in the previous three years (2001–2003).

However, the global financial crisis is likely to result in slower economic growth for Bahrain during 2009, as tight international credit and a slowing global economy combine to cause funding for many non-oil projects to dry up. Lower oil prices may also cause Bahrain's budget to slip back into deficit.

ECONOMIC PERFORMANCE OVER 12 MONTHS

The state-owned Bahrain Petroleum Company refinery dates back to 1935, and was the first refinery in the Gulf. It has a capacity of 260,000 barrels per day (b/d), and most of the oil it refines comes from Saudi Arabia. An agreement with Saudi Arabia gives Bahrain half of the net output and revenues from Saudi Arabia's Abu Saafa offshore oilfield. Liquefaction of natural gas is also a key contributor to the country's revenues. The Bahrain National Gas Company operates a gas liquefaction plant utilizing gas piped directly from Bahrain's oilfields. In contrast to the position with oil reserves, there is no immediate shortage of gas on the horizon. However, domestic demand is on the increase, a fact that was underlined during the recent economic boom, and the country is pushing ahead with exploration enthusiastically. Exploration rights have been awarded to Malaysia's Petronas and Chevron Texaco in the United States, although no significant additional discoveries had been made by February 2009.

Bahrain also owns the biggest aluminium smelting plant outside eastern Europe. The majority state-owned company, Aluminum Bahrain (Alba), has an annual production of 843,000 metric tonnes (2005 figures). It also has extrusion facilities and a rolling mill. Bahrain is also home to the Arab Iron and Steel Company iron-ore pelletizing plant (4 million tonnes annually) and a shipbuilding and repair yard.

The success of ventures such as the Bahrain Grand Prix has raised the Kingdom's international profile, and, combined with the boom in Islamic banking, has encouraged major airlines to resume services to the country. More than 370 offshore banking units and representative offices are located in Bahrain, including a large number of US firms and 32 Islamic commercial, investment, and leasing banks.

Bahrain's international airport is one of busiest in the Persian Gulf, serving 22 carriers. A modern, busy port offers direct and frequent cargo shipping connections to the United States, Europe, and the Far East. Internationally recognized Bahraini companies include Investcorp, the venture-capital firm credited with turning around the fortunes of Gucci.

In mid-2008 the tensions that occur throughout the Gulf states between migrant workers and Gulf governments came to the surface after a Bangladeshi worker murdered his Bahraini supervisor. The Bahrain Ministry of the Interior announced it would not be renewing the visas of thousands of immigrant Bangladeshi workers. However, the broad policy of the Bahrain Economic Development Board, chaired by Crown Prince Sheikh Salman bin Hamad al-Khalifa, is to make the labor market more flexible in an effort to help the Kingdom's economic diversification efforts. Some estimates put the number of nationals, in the total figure of 1,000,000 for the Kingdom's population, at barely 50%—a factor that fuels anger against migrants from Bahrain's unemployed, who make up some 15% of the population.

STATISTICS

GDP growth: 7% (2008)
GDP per capita: US$37,200
CPI: 7% cent
Key interest rate: 8.35% (31 December 2008)
Exchange rate versus dollar: Bahraini dinars per US$: 0.376 (fixed)
unemployment: 15%
FDI: US$15.2 billion
Current account deficit/surplus: US$2.269 billion
Population: 718,306
Source: CIA Factbook except where stated

MORE INFO

Websites:

The official website of Bahrain: www.bahraingovernment.com

Website of Bahrain Customs: www.bahraincustoms.gov.bh

Website of the Bahrain Economic Development Board: www.bahrainedb.com

Website of the Ministry of Industry and Commerce: www.moic.gov.by

See Also:

✔ Middle East: Regulatory Structure and Powers (p. 1041)

  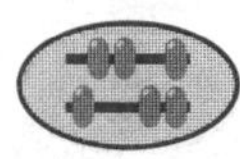      

SUPPORT FOR INWARD INVESTMENT AND IMPORTS

The Bahrain Economic Development Board (EDB) is the public agency responsible for formulating and overseeing economic development strategy in Bahrain and has responsibility for attracting direct investment into the Kingdom. It offers an investor facilitating service to first-time investors.

TAX EXEMPTIONS

The Kingdom operates a policy of zero corporate taxes. More information can be obtained from the Bahrain EDB.

Bangladesh

ECONOMY AND TRADE

Bangladesh, one of the world's poorest and most densely populated countries, faces some difficult challenges. With much of the country situated on low-lying land on the delta of the confluence of three rivers, the Ganges, Bramaputra, and Meghna, around one-third of the country is subject to annual flooding. Nevertheless, the economy has grown by between 5% and 6 % per year since 1996, despite inefficient state-owned enterprises, delays in exploiting natural gas resources, insufficient power supplies, slow implementation of economic reforms, and a turbulent political scene that saw the army taking a caretaker role prior to fresh elections on December 29, 2008. Although more than half of GDP is generated through the service sector, nearly two-thirds of Bangladeshis are employed in the agriculture sector, with rice as the single most important product. Garment exports and remittances from Bangladeshis working overseas, mainly in the Middle East and East Asia, have been the main source of economic growth. In 2008, Bangladesh pursued a monetary policy aimed at maintaining high employment, but created higher inflation in the process.

STATISTICS

GDP growth: 5.9 %
GDP per capita: US$1,500
CPI: 9.4 %
Key interest rate: 16 %
Exchange rate versus dollar: taka per US dollar—68.554
Unemployment: 2.5 %
FDI: US$104 million
Current account deficit/surplus: −US$55 million (2008)
Population: 153,546,896
Source: CIA Factbook except where stated

ECONOMIC POLICY OVER 12 MONTHS

Historically, Bangladesh has run a large trade deficit. This has been financed mostly through the remittances sent home by Bangladeshis working abroad, and through grant aid. The country has received some US$15 billion in grant aid, with a further US$15 billion promised but still to be disbursed, from donors that include the Asian Development Bank, the World Bank, the European Commission, and the UN Development Program. The newly elected government (December 29, 2008) has some serious issues of past corruption and mismanagement in government circles to deal with, and root out. It is also under pressure from numerous sources, including the IMF and foreign donors and investors, to accelerate the pace of reform and privatization, and the deregulation of the public sector. The country's infrastructure, which is periodically massively damaged by floods and other natural catastrophes, requires major investment.

Bangladesh benefits from plentiful water and rich, fertile soils, which make agriculture the major source of employment. The abnormal conditions pertaining in the country's politics prior to the elections of December 29, 2008, meant that Bangladesh's 2008–09 Budget was set by a caretaker government that could only anticipate having responsibility for implementing that Budget for half a year (the Budget is set in June and the country's fiscal year runs June to June). One of the challenges the budget set out to tackle was high and rising inflation. However, the international pricing environment at the time of the budget made matters extremely difficult. The surge in global commodity prices in the middle of 2008 meant that international market prices for food, fertilizer, fuel, vegetable oil, and a range of other essential items, including industrial raw materials, saw price increases of 50–120 % in many commodities (source: Bangladesh Centre for Policy Dialogue).

The caretaker government's main priorities for the remainder of 2008 were focused on eight objectives, as set out in the 2008 Budget Speech. These included maintaining macroeconomic stability, accelerating economic growth, containing inflation, reducing poverty, ensuring food security, ensuring regional and income equity, and removing the constraints to private-sector-led growth.

The new incoming government, for its part, has announced that it is continuing with the previous regime's Poverty Reduction Strategy (PRS), and has implemented a three-year program, beginning in 2009. The 2009 Budget has eight priority areas, maintaining the price of essential items within reach of the country's poor, generating employment, widening and deepening the social safety net, reducing regional disparity, increasing agricultural production, ensuring food security, increasing power generation, and boosting the development of the country's communications network and IT infrastructure.

   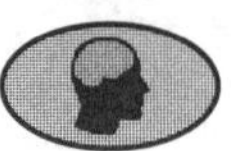  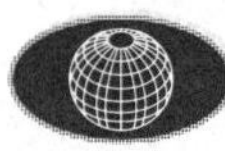  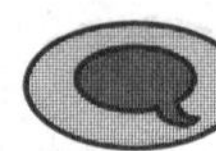 

ECONOMIC PERFORMANCE OVER 12 MONTHS

Bangladesh's agricultural sector is largely focused on rice and jute production, with the country just about keeping pace with the food requirements of its population. Yields of rice and vegetables, together with the cash crop of jute for fiber production, have gone up in recent years, thanks to better flood control and irrigation, and the more efficient use of fertilizers. During 2008, however, floods caused crop losses of rice estimated at 1.8 million tonnes. At the same time, cyclone Sidr, which hit the region, caused further losses on the same scale.

According to the Bangladesh Centre for Policy Dialogue (CPD), the year also saw improvements, however, in higher industrial growth and higher exports, as well as improvements in the remittance flows to the country from expatriate workers. The government also saw increased tax revenues, largely through more efficient tax collection, and its performance in providing food security in the aftermath of the floods and cyclone Sidr was considered reasonable.

Moves to develop the country's transport infrastructure continued through the year, although flood damage repair and the clean-up after cyclone Sidr limited what could be done. Attempts to push forward privatization have been slower than the government would wish, largely due to resistance from workers. Bangladesh has a history of not being able to resist worker wage demands in state-run industries, which exacerbates the government's attempts to keep a lid on inflation. According to both the World Bank and the IMF, the country's GDP growth is expected to be around 6.0% over the next five years. This sounds high by, say, the standards of Eurozone economies, but Bangladesh needs growth of around 8–9 % to enable its poverty reduction programs to have a real impact, according to the IMF.

One of the better-performing sectors of the Bangladesh economy has been the readymade garment sector, which is growing at around 20% a year. This industry gained from the ending of quotas under the Multi-Fiber Arrangement. However, the whole sector is under enormous cost-cutting pressure globally, and Bangladesh has to keep driving down costs if it wants this sector to stay competitive internationally.

Rising income inequality, as shown by a series of household income and expenditure surveys, is becoming a real problem for the government, and is frustrating its poverty reduction programs. Although the country achieved 2% poverty reduction per year from 2000 to 2005, for example, income inequality continued to rise. The situation worsened in the years from 2006 to end-2008. The Centre for Policy Discussion estimates that some 8.5 % of Bangladeshi homes have experienced a high enough degree of income erosion over the period (mainly through rising food prices) to push them below the poverty line.

SUPPORT FOR INWARD INVESTMENT AND IMPORTS

The body set up to promote and facilitate both domestic and foreign investment in the private sector is the Board of Investment Bangladesh (BOI), founded in 1989. It is headed by the prime minister and is part of the Prime Minister's Office.

TAX EXEMPTIONS

There is a range of tax exemptions, with exemptions from tax for the first five to seven years being possible by arrangement. Power-generation ventures can obtain 15 years' general exemption from taxation. Contact the BoI for further details.

⏩ MORE INFO

Websites:

Board of Investment, Bangladesh: www.boi.gov.bd

Centre for Policy Dialogue: www.cpd.org.bd

National web portal of Bangladesh: www.bangladesh.gov.bd

See Also:

★ Viewpoint: Muhammad Yunus (pp. 274–276)

Banker to the Poor: The Story of the Grameen Bank (p. 1222)

Barbados

ECONOMY AND TRADE

The island of Barbados has been independent of the United Kingdom since 1966. Settled initially by the British in 1627, the island was seen as an ideal location for sugar cane production, with plantations being worked by slaves until the abolition of slavery in 1834. Post-independence, tourism and light manufacturing became more important than sugar cane, and, by the 1990s, their combined contribution to GDP outstripped that of sugar production. In recent years, some three-quarters of GDP and 80% of exports have come from services. The country enjoys one of the highest per capita incomes in the region. Offshore finance and information services are important foreign-exchange earners, and thrive from having the same time zone as eastern US financial centers, and a relatively highly educated workforce. The government has made sustained efforts to reduce unemployment, to encourage direct foreign investment, and to privatize remaining state-owned enterprises. The public debt-to-GDP ratio of about 80% is likely to widen as the government undertakes a more expansionary fiscal policy to combat the impact of the global downturn.

  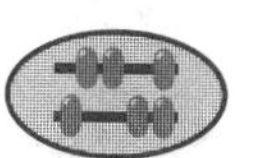   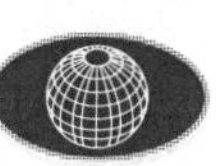   

ECONOMIC POLICY OVER 12 MONTHS

In July 2008, the Prime Minister of Barbados, David Thompson, who came to power in elections in January 2008, delivered his administration's first budget speech. At that time, the price of oil had not yet collapsed under the impact of the global slowdown, and commodity prices were still at or near record levels. The slowdown had, however, already affected growth in the Barbadian economy, which slowed to 1.8% (estimated) during the first six months of 2008, according to the prime minister's budget speech. This is in comparison to an average of 4.2% annual growth for the years 2004 to 2007. The major policy thrust of the incoming government was a pledge to end the alleged waste of the prior regime, which, after 16 years in power, had become embroiled in projects such as the notorious ABC highway "flyover" road-widening project, which overran its budget by many tens of millions of pounds before the new administration terminated the contract with the overseas construction company. Faced with price pressure on essential commodities and lower growth, the Thompson government, which had pledged to focus on domestic issues such as the cost of living, healthcare, and crime, committed to a stimulus package aimed at alleviating the impact of the downturn on the lower paid.

Despite the pressure of higher imported fuel costs, the island managed to achieve a capital account surplus for the first half of 2008 sufficient to offset import costs. Barbados's net international reserves rose by US$115.9 million to US$1,663.9 million in June 2008. However, capital outflows increased through the second half of the year, shrinking the capital and financial account surplus to the point where it could no longer offset the external current-account deficit, leaving the island with a contraction of US$202 million in its international reserves.

The Central Bank of Barbados cut the minimum deposit rate by 25 basis points in April 2008, to 4.5% (down 75 basis points from November 2007). The rate was cut again during the year to 4.0%. The cut, and subsequent rate cuts, was partially forced by the need to maintain a positive differential with interest rates abroad, particularly in the United States, in order to provide some safeguards against the outward movement of capital.

The government and the private sector in Barbados are working to prepare the country for the Caribbean Community (CARICOM) Single Market and Economy (CSME), a European-style single market.

ECONOMIC PERFORMANCE OVER 12 MONTHS

Activity in the island's construction sector, one of the main engines of growth, fell by 3.1% once the stimulus of building for the Cricket World Cup 2007 had passed. Manufacturing output and sugar production also saw growth falling back to just 1.1%. The island's chemical production also declined, following a major fire at a chemical plant in 2007. At the same time, as growth declined commodity-price increases fueled inflation, pushing the rate to 5.0% by March 2008, as against 2.7% in September 2007. By January 2009, according to a review of the year by the Central Bank of Barbados, real output growth in the Barbadian economy had shrunk to just 0.7%, substantially lower than the 3.3% expansion in output achieved in both 2006 and 2007. This made 2008 the first year since 2002 that the island's GDP grew by less than 1%. Higher expenditure by the government created a fiscal deficit estimated at 4.5% of GDP for 2008, as against a deficit of 1.9% of GDP for 2007.

In common with other island economies with a strong tourism component, Barbados has seen tourist numbers fall, in both the long-stay tourist category and the cruise segments. The picture was mixed, however, with an increase of 15.4 % in total passenger arrivals in the cruise sector for the first half of 2008, being offset by contractions in the market in the second half of the year. Overall, the tourism sector declined by a fraction of 1% for the year as a whole, following an expansion of 14.3% in 2007.

The contraction in manufacturing was also marginal, at 0.4%, following a decrease of 2.9% in 2007. According to the Central Bank, a reduction of 1.3% in miscellaneous manufacturers coupled with downturns in chemicals (5.2%), non-metallic mineral products (1.1%), and furniture production (4.3%) outweighed improvements in other key subsectors.

In the international business and financial-services sector, preliminary data as at the end of September 2008 indicated that 371 new licenses were issued for international business companies, approximately 37 more than in the same period of 2007. Seventy-five new societies with restricted liability were licensed, compared to 126 a year earlier. One new offshore banking license was granted during the period, compared to five new licenses in the same period of 2007. The unemployment rate at the end of the third quarter was 8.4%, compared with 7.4% reported at the end of September 2007. The female unemployment rate was unchanged at 8.9%, while the rate of unemployment for males increased by 1.2 percentage points to 6.6%. The reduction in employment was mainly attributed to scaled-down labor demand in the utilities, construction, and distribution sectors (source: Barbados Central Bank). The BCB expects the Barbadian economy to contract by between zero and 2% in 2009, as a consequence of the global downturn.

STATISTICS

GDP growth: 2.8% (2008)
GDP per capita: US$20,200
CPI: 5.5%
Key interest rate: 12.0%
Exchange rate versus dollar: Barbadian dollar pegged to the US dollar at a rate of BBD2:US$1
Unemployment: 10.7%
FDI: 362.2 (2003, BCB)
Current account deficit/surplus: −US$254 million (2007)
Population: 281,968
Source: CIA Factbook except where stated

▸▸ MORE INFO

Websites:

Barbados Central Bank: www.centralbank.org.bb

The Barbados Parliament official site: www.barbadosparliament.com

Invest Barbados, the government's inward investment agency: www.investbarbados.org

SUPPORT FOR INWARD INVESTMENT AND IMPORTS

Invest Barbados is the body charged with encouraging and stimulating inward investment to the country, as well as managing the Barbados brand. There is no restriction on foreign ownership of businesses.

TAX EXEMPTIONS

Barbados offers a range of tax-efficient vehicles through which investors can conduct international business. Contact Invest Barbados for details.

Belgium

ECONOMY AND TRADE

After two millennia of being invaded by various outsiders, from the Romans in the first century BC to the German Reich in 1940, Belgium is very much at the heart of European efforts to ensure a stable, prosperous, and secure European Community (EC). The country has one of the world's highest per capita GDP (ranked consistently in the top 30), and borders the Netherlands, Germany, Luxembourg, and France. Capitalizing on its central geographic location, Belgium has built a highly developed transport network, and established a well-diversified industrial and commercial base. With few natural resources, Belgium must import substantial quantities of raw materials and export a large volume of manufactures, making its economy unusually dependent on the state of world markets. Roughly three-quarters of its trade is with other EU countries. Belgium regularly outperforms the Eurozone average in terms of growth and economic indicators. The fact that Brussels, the capital of Belgium, is also home to the headquarters of the European Union has attracted a large number of multinationals to establish their European headquarters in Belgium.

STATISTICS

GDP growth: 1.5 %
GDP per capita: US$38,300
CPI: 4.6 % (2008)
key interest rate: 6.98%
exchange rate versus dollar:
euro per US dollar: 1.325 (April 8, 2009)
unemployment: 7%
FDI: US$733.9 billion (2008)
Current account deficit/surplus: 80.8% of GDP
Population: 10,403,951
Source: CIA Factbook except where stated

ECONOMIC POLICY OVER 12 MONTHS

Belgium is fully committed to the Lisbon strategy of focusing on growth and employment, and seeking to make the European Union the world's most competitive, knowledge-based economy. However, as a December 2008 report by an IMF Mission to Belgium makes clear, the country has been particularly hard hit by the global recession, and the government has had to adopt an interventionist stance, bailing out several major financial institutions, including Fortis and Dexia in late 2008. The political fallout over the problems in Belgium's financial sector ultimately caused the then prime minister, Yves Leterme, to resign, prompting new elections.

The effects of the deep recession, which took hold in Europe and the United States in the fourth quarter of 2008 particularly, will be felt especially severely in Belgium in 2009, and, in all probability, into 2010, according to the IMF. The boom in energy and commodity prices in early 2008 fueled inflation in Belgium, which peaked some way above the Eurozone average. The government of Belgium foresaw the potential this rise in inflation had to inflict severe damage on the country's competitive position, yet, at the same time, there was a clear need for a fiscal stimulus package, the effects of which could also be inflationary in the medium term.

Even before the downturn, Belgium faced difficult long-term challenges to solve, including meeting the future costs associated with an ageing population. The country's dilemma in the existing downturn is to fine-tune policy in such a way as both to stimulate the economy, and to create the minimum possible deficit while so doing. The bigger the deficit, the less scope the country will have to put money aside to pay pensions and healthcare for its ageing population.

The country's existing fiscal federalism arrangements have been exacerbating imbalances internally. Divided on linguistic lines, the country has had a devolved structure since August 1980, with Flanders managing its affairs, and the Walloon Regional Parliament managing affairs in Wallonia. Further constitutional reform established a separate parliament and government for the German-speaking cantons in 1983, with yet another regional parliament and government for the Brussels Capital Region in 1989. Structural rigidities in the economy, including mandatory wage indexation, are dampening growth and impeding job creation. The recent inflation dynamic in 2008 reawakened debate in Belgium about structural concerns, and that debate continues, although inflation began to fall by the end of 2008, as global commodity prices dropped back.

ECONOMIC PERFORMANCE OVER 12 MONTHS

Economic growth and foreign direct investment declined in 2008. In 2009, Belgium is likely to encounter negative growth of around −0.75%, increasing unemployment, and a 3% budget deficit, stemming from the world wide banking crisis. The IMF has welcomed a relatively restrained fiscal stimulus package for

     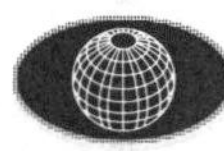   

2009 proposed by Belgium, calling it "broadly appropriate." Both regional governments and the national government in Belgium are committed to bringing forward existing investment programs. However, there will be challenges in actually deploying those programs in a timely fashion when they are most needed to stimulate the economy and cushion the downturn. The government hopes that many of its fiscal stimulus initiatives will be temporary, but there are concerns that around four-fifths of the measures it is proposing could widen the deficit in the longer term. Yet as the Belgian government made clear in its own Stability Program proposals in 2008, the country has to bring down its public debt ratio if it is to have any chance of meeting its longer-term commitments to deal with ageing-related expenditure in a sustainable manner. In 2007, the government's overall debt ratio stood at 84.9% of GDP. The idea was to shrink that deficit to 71.1% of GDP by 2011, but that goal is now looking difficult to achieve.

With exports equivalent to over two-thirds of GDP, Belgium is highly sensitive to fluctuations in international trade. The fall off in demand, caused by a deepening recession in the economies of many of the country's major trading partners, including the Eurozone, Britain, and the United States, is hitting manufacturing and related service industries hard.

The government remains strongly committed to supporting a diversified economy. Belgium's industrial and service sectors have to work particularly hard to overcome the disadvantages associated with the country having almost no natural resources. The country's industrial base includes engineering and metal products, motor vehicle assembly, transportation equipment, scientific instruments, processed food and beverages, chemicals, basic metals, textiles, glass, and petroleum. Industry is concentrated mainly in the populous Flemish area in the north. The services sector is even more important to the country, accounting for some 74.6% of GDP (source: US Department of State). About 78% of Belgium's trade is with fellow EU member states. Given this high percentage, Belgium continues to seek to diversify, and expand trade opportunities with non-EC countries.

SUPPORT FOR INWARD INVESTMENT AND IMPORTS

Invest in Belgium is the first port of call for potential investors in the country. The Fiscal Department for Foreign Investments (FDFI) provides free, confidential advice.

TAX EXEMPTIONS

There is a Tax Shelter program offering fiscal incentives for investors in Belgian or European audiovisual and film works. There are other pro-business tax incentives. Details can be obtained from the FDFI (telephone: +32 (0)257.938.66).

MORE INFO

Websites:

Official portal for information on Belgium: www.belgium.be

Invest in Belgium: www.invest.belgium.be

Bermuda

ECONOMY AND TRADE

Consisting of an archipelago of 138 coral islands, Bermuda has progressed from being a tourist haven to being one of the world's most successful offshore banking centers. As a consequence, it enjoys the third-highest per capita income in the world, some 50% higher than that of the United States, with much of the economy centered on providing financial services for international business and luxury facilities for tourists. A number of reinsurance companies relocated to the island following the September 11, 2001 attacks, and again after Hurricane Katrina in August 2005, contributing to the expansion of an already robust international business sector. Bermuda's tourism industry—which derives more than 80% of its visitors from the United States—continues to struggle, but remains the island's no. 2 industry. With only 20% of the land being arable, most capital equipment and food must be imported. Bermuda's industrial sector is small, although construction continues to be important.

ECONOMIC POLICY OVER 12 MONTHS

Bermuda, in common with other offshore and tourist-based island economies, has had to face up to the bruising impact of the global recession, which really began to have an impact on the island in mid-2008. Accordingly, in its latest budget, announced on February 20, 2009, the government has put together a medium-term stimulus plan "to bolster Bermuda's people and businesses through the economic downturn."

With the emphasis on stimulus, the government has ruled out any personal or business tax increases for the foreseeable future, and instead intends to use both reserves and balances in its Confiscated Assets Fund to cover a good part of the required expenditure in 2009–2010. The government intends to limit its borrowing to investments in hard assets, such as infrastructure building, and it is bringing forward some of its multi-year, phased capital expenditure program, and pushing hard on public–private partnership ini-

STATISTICS

GDP growth: 9.4% (December 2007, National Economic Report of Bermuda 2008)

GDP per capita: US$76,403 (US State Dept.)

CPI: 4.0% (2007, US State Dept.)

Key interest rate: 3.75% (3Q08, Bermuda 2008 Economic Report)

exchange rate versus dollar: Bermuda dollar pegged to the US dollar

Unemployment: 2.1% (2004)

FDI: N/A

Current account deficit/surplus: US$1,163 (3Q08)

Population: 66,536

Source: CIA Factbook except where stated

    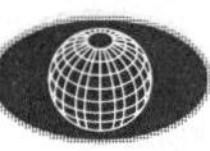   

tiatives backed by government guarantees. All Bermudian ministries were ordered to implement a 10.5% expenditure cut, to enable the government to put its stimulus package together without the need for tax increases. The general expectation is that the slowdown will have a negative impact on the government's total tax yield in the coming year (2009–2010), and the total revenue budget is projected to be US$16 million below the original estimate of US$985 million. Bermuda has also set aside an extraordinary additional sum of some US$250 million as a fallback if it needs to mount a systemic rescue of the Bermudian financial system during the crisis.

The government is committed to sustaining Bermuda's reputation as a well-regulated offshore market. Bermuda has a well-established global international insurance market, which has a substantial capital and surplus base, estimated at US$167 billion as at December 31, 2007. Aggregate total assets were US$440 billion, roughly constant with 2006. Gross premiums written for the year totaled US$124 billion. Some 40 new reinsurers established businesses in Bermuda in 2008. The government estimates that the overall downturn in the global markets in 2008 had about the same impact on financial firms in Bermuda, in terms of insurance sector losses, as a major hurricane event. Overall, though, underwriting results for the Bermuda market remain strong, indicating continuing confidence in Bermuda's leadership position as an insurance center globally, as well as in the jurisdiction's effective and practical regulatory framework.

At the end of the third quarter of 2008, the total net asset value of collective investment schemes was US$196.30 million, down some 14.9% year on year, and the island also lost some 24 mutual funds and unit trusts through the course of the year.

ECONOMIC PERFORMANCE OVER 12 MONTHS

In 2007, the most recent year for which GDP data have been compiled for Bermuda, the economy expanded by 9.4% and real GDP increased by 4.6%, exceeding the Bermudian Ministry of Finance's forecast of real growth in the range of 2.5–3.0%. Much of the outperformance came from an additional 1,700 newly registered international businesses during the year. The sector provided some US$1,593.0 million, or 27.2% of total GDP, up 22.4% on the prior year. More significantly, value-added from the financial sector contributed to more than half the growth in Bermuda, accounting for 58% of the total increase in GDP for 2007. The contribution made by international businesses to the Bermudian GDP has grown from 19.5% in 2003 to 27.2% in 2008.

Financial intermediation and services was the second-largest contributor to GDP, supported by increased licensing, supervisory, and incorporation fees collected from international business entities, and further aided by a raised demand for credit. Construction and quarrying increased by 4.7%, accounting for some US$322.5 million in output for 2007. The Bermudian Office of the Tax Commissioner estimates that employment income rose by 10.0% for the first three quarters of 2008, compared with the same period in 2007. This boosted total employment income by 11% to US$3.04 billion over the 12-month period ending September 2007. Annual inflation for 2007 was 3.8%, but concerns over the downturn affected consumer spending in 2008, and Bermuda's Retail Sales Index showed some softening during the year. Sales volumes fell for nine out of 11 months in 2008, according to the government's 2008 Economic Report. Inflation is expected to be substantially lower for 2008, once the data are available.

Despite the global downturn, the construction industry remained very active for the first three quarters of 2008, with an increase, year on year, of 7.1% of work placed. The value of new project starts rose by 3.9% to US$169.7 million, with the construction of new hotels and guest houses accounting for most of the construction work completed in 2008.

During 2008, the international business sector's contribution to overall employment on the islands remained virtually constant (a 0.3% improvement year on year). There were 15,201 international companies registered in Bermuda at the end of 2008, a decline of 177 companies, or 1.2%, over the total in 2007. Foreign-exchange earnings increased by US$427 million to US$1.5 billion, up 38.7%, over the first nine months of 2008.

SUPPORT FOR INWARD INVESTMENT AND IMPORTS

Bermuda's tax regime remains one of the world's lightest, with no withholding, capital gains, transfer, wealth, gift, or income taxes for non-resident entities. The island came out very well of both the OECD review of tax havens, and accountant KPMG's review of offshore financial centers. There are many avenues open for potential investors to seek advice, including the big four international accounting firms, and local banks such as the Bank of Bermuda.

TAX EXEMPTIONS

As above, the island is regarded as well, if lightly, regulated and unlike many offshore centers, is not blacklisted by the OECD. Bermuda has agreed to provide tax-avoidance information to other countries seeking to prosecute their nationals for tax avoidance.

▸▸ MORE INFO

Websites:

Bermuda Chamber of Commerce, good source of links to other useful sites: www.bermudachamber.bm

Official site of the Bermuda Government: www.gov.bm

Bolivia

ECONOMY AND TRADE

Landlocked Bolivia is one of the poorest and least-developed countries in Latin America, with almost two-thirds of the population living below the poverty line, and literacy levels low in many rural areas. Following a disastrous economic crisis during the early 1980s, reforms spurred private investment, stimulated economic growth, and cut poverty rates in the 1990s. The period 2003–2005 was characterized by political instability, racial tensions, and violent protests against plans—subsequently abandoned—to export Bolivia's newly discovered natural gas reserves to large, northern hemisphere markets. In 2005, the government passed a controversial hydrocarbons law that imposed significantly higher royalties, and required foreign firms then operating under risk-sharing contracts to surrender all production to the state energy company. The decline in commodity prices in late 2008, the lack of foreign investment in the mining and hydrocarbon sectors, and the suspension of trade benefits with the United States will pose challenges for the Bolivian economy in 2009.

ECONOMIC POLICY OVER 12 MONTHS

The government of Bolivia's present policies requires some knowledge of Bolivia's political history to give them their appropriate context. Bolivia's political past until the mid-1980s was tumultuous, with civilian rule alternating with military coups. When former president, Paz Estenssoro, took office in 1985 for the fourth time, the country faced hyperinflation, with prices growing at 24,000%. Social unrest, chronic strikes, and drug trafficking seemed endemic to the country. His rule marked something of a turning point, and the country's economy underwent a series of reforms that were continued by the new administration of Paz Zamora in 1989, and that of President Gonzalo Sanches de Lozada in 1993.

Relatively robust growth continued through to the mid-1990s, when the economy lost its way again under General Hugo Banzer. Sanches de Lozada returned to power, following a four-year economic recession, in the 2002 elections. Popular unrest over a decision to export Bolivia's new-found gas reserves forced his resignation, and, in 2005, Juan Evo Morales Ayma came to power on a platform pledging to nationalize the country's hydrocarbons, and alleviate poverty and discrimination towards indigenous people. On 1 May 2006, Morales nationalized the hydrocarbons sector, and tightened the state's grip on the country's natural resources.

Bolivia is rich in metals, including tin, zinc, tungsten, antimony, silver, iron, lead, and gold, and has the second-largest natural gas reserves in South America. However, the nationalization program has starved the mining and hydrocarbons sectors of much-needed foreign investment, and gas production has stagnated. Bolivia is now caught in a position where it has commitments to ramp up gas exports to both Brazil and Argentina, to levels that will make it impossible, at current production rates, for it to meet domestic demand (source: US State Department).

Bolivia's trade with neighboring countries is growing, in part because of several regional preferential trade agreements. The Bolivian government is also strongly focused on developing markets through the Bolivarian Alternative for the Americas (ALBA), whose members include Venezuela, Cuba and Nicaragua.

A bilateral investment treaty (BIT) between the United States and Bolivia came into effect in 2001. Although the Morales government has stated that it will respect all current BITs, officials have also publicly announced that they will re-open discussions now that the country's much disputed new constitution was passed on January 25, 2009.

ECONOMIC PERFORMANCE OVER 12 MONTHS

The latest IMF Report on Bolivia, dated January 29, 2009, paints a relatively favorable picture of its recent economic performance. The last few years have seen the country experiencing an export boom, led by the hydrocarbons and mining sectors. This supported an improvement in GDP growth, and a strengthening of the external and fiscal surplus positions. On the downside, inflation accelerated to 17% by mid-2008 (source: IMF), declining to 12% by the year-end on the back of falling commodity prices, and foreign investment remains low in the context of persistent political tensions.

High hydrocarbons export prices and changes in the hydrocarbons taxation regime in 2005–2006 boosted Bolivia's current account to record surpluses. It also boosted fiscal revenue, shifting the public-sector accounts from deficits into substantial surpluses. In response, the Bolivian central bank gradually allowed the Boliviano to appreciate, which contributed to a significant reduction in deposit dollarization.

Real GDP growth picked up in 2008 to an estimated 5.9% (from an average of 4.7% in 2006–2007), boosted in part by the start of production at a large mining project. The external current account has recorded a surplus of 11% of GDP, and central bank reserves have risen to historical highs.

In 2007, the United States exported $277 million of merchandise to Bolivia and imported $362 million. Bolivia's major exports to the United States are tin, gold, jewelry, and wood products, with textiles playing

STATISTICS

GDP growth: 4.8% (2008)
GDP per capita: US$4,084 (IMF estimate, source USSD)
CPI: 11.5%
Key interest rate: 12.86% (December 31, 2007)
Exchange rate versus dollar: boliviano per US dollar: 7.253 (2008)
Unemployment: 7.5% (excluding rural unemployment)
FDI: US$6.88 billion
Current account deficit/surplus: Surplus: 11% of GDP (2008, US State Department)
Population: 9,247,816
Source: CIA Factbook except where stated

     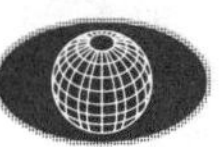   

an increasingly important role. Its major imports from the United States are electronic equipment, chemicals, vehicles, wheat, and machinery.

Agriculture accounts for roughly 14.5% of Bolivia's GDP. The amount of land cultivated by modern farming techniques is increasing rapidly in the Santa Cruz area, where climate permits two crops a year. Soybeans are the major cash crop. The extraction of minerals and hydrocarbons accounts for another 11% of GDP, and manufacturing around 17%.

According to the IMF, Bolivia's very limited integration with international capital markets means that the current global crisis has mainly affected Bolivia through declines in commodity prices, and remittances. Capital inflows have been negligible for many years, except for foreign direct investment (FDI) in hydrocarbons and mining, thereby largely insulating Bolivia's financial system from the external turmoil. However, current trends in commodity prices are certain to have a major impact on export receipts and related fiscal revenue, beginning in 2009, because of the delayed response of contractual gas export prices.

The government of Bolivia remains heavily dependent on foreign assistance to finance development projects.

SUPPORT FOR INWARD INVESTMENT AND IMPORTS

Bolivia sits at the heart of Central America, making it a strategic geographic location for foreign investors, who have the same rights, guarantees, and legal framework as local investors. However, investing in Bolivia is difficult, and potential investors will need to engage local legal, market, and financial experts to assist them.

TAX EXEMPTIONS

Bolivia has a populist government with wealth redistribution on its agenda. The tax regime is not particularly favorable to inward investment, and the country's recent nationalization of its oil and gas fields will be a worry to future investors.

▸▸ MORE INFO

Websites:

English-language site praising the East of Bolivia (Santa Cruz region, some coverage of doing business and investing in Bolivia): www.boliviabella.com

Official Bolivian government portal (in Spanish): www.bolivia.gov.bo

Country reports on Bolivia: www.imf.org

Botswana

ECONOMY AND TRADE

Formerly the British protectorate of Bechuanaland, Botswana became independent in 1966. Four decades of uninterrupted civilian leadership, progressive social policies, and significant capital investment have created one of the most dynamic economies in Africa. Mineral extraction, principally diamond mining, dominates economic activity, although tourism is a growing sector due to the country's conservation practices and extensive nature preserves.

Botswana has maintained one of the world's highest economic growth rates since independence, although growth slowed to about 5% annually in 2006–2008. Through fiscal discipline and sound management, Botswana has transformed itself from one of the poorest countries in the world to a middle-income country with a per capita GDP of nearly US$15,800 in 2008. Diamond mining has fueled much of the expansion and currently accounts for more than one-third of GDP and for 70–80% of export earnings. Tourism, financial services, subsistence farming, and cattle-raising are other key sectors. On the downside, the government must deal with high rates of unemployment and poverty. An expected leveling off in diamond mining production overshadows long-term prospects.

STATISTICS

GDP growth: 5.2% (2008)
GDP per capita: US$15,800
CPI: 12.5%
Key interest rate: 16.22%
Exchange rate versus dollar: pulas (BWP) per US dollar—6.7907 (2008)
Unemployment: 7.5%
FDI: N/A
Current account deficit/surplus: US$1.611 billion (2008)
Population: 1,842,323
Source: CIA Factbook except where stated

ECONOMIC POLICY OVER 12 MONTHS

Botswana has enjoyed one of the fastest growth rates in per capita income in the world since independence. Economic growth averaged 9% per year from 1967 to 2006. The government has maintained a sound fiscal policy, despite three consecutive budget deficits in 2002–2004, and a negligible level of foreign debt. Foreign exchange reserves were US$10.2 billion at the end of November 2007, equivalent to 28 months' cover of 2007 imports of goods and services. Botswana's impressive economic record has been built on the foundation of using revenue generated from diamond mining to fuel economic development through prudent fiscal policies and a cautious foreign policy. However, economic development spending was cut by 10% in 2004/05 as a result of recurring budget deficits and rising expenditure on healthcare services. Development spending began to increase again in 2006/07 and was budgeted to increase by 27% in the 2007/08 fiscal year.

The government is in the tenth year of a long-term development plan called Vision 2016, the full title of which is: "Long term vision for Botswana, towards prosperity for all." The "Vision" is seen as complementary to the United Nations Millennium Development Goals, to which Botswana also subscribes, and

  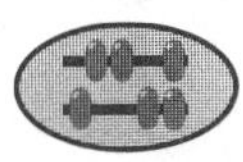   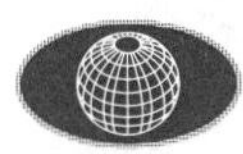   

the country's 2008 budget took for its theme the need to accelerate the achievement of Vision 2016. In practice, this meant setting policies for the reduction of poverty and job creation, as well as stimulating economic diversification. A report by the IMF into the long-term sustainability of Botswana relying on diamond mining for its fiscal stability pointed out that, at present rates of mining, the country's diamond resource could run out by 2029. This sets serious long-term challenges, to which the government is now responding.

Commenting on Botswana's economy, the World Bank calls the country "an example of prudent economic policy and growth," with the one exception being its record on HIV infection. It points out that the country's record of three decades of rapid economic growth has few parallels in modern economic history. What makes the country's example even rarer is that regimes blessed by great mineral wealth usually succumb to "the resource curse," where corruption and stagnation follow ready access to mineral riches. "Although relative income inequality has not been reduced, it has not worsened either, and with real per capita GDP growth averaging nearly 8% over the three decades, the poor are better off than before as well," the World Bank says.

ECONOMIC PERFORMANCE OVER 12 MONTHS

The government's budget for 2009 laid out its 10th National Development Plan (NDP10), taking the country through to March 2016. For the eighth successive year, Botswana's sovereign debt was rated by both Moody's Investor Services and Standard and Poor's at investment grade A, although both ratings organizations emphasized the need for diversification away from a reliance on diamond wealth to continue. The regional backdrop for the year ahead for Botswana was sketched out in a recent IMF report on Africa which estimates that African economies expanded by 5% on average in 2008, but which forecasts growth declining to 3.4% during 2009.

In fact, the Southern African Development Community (SADC) region had set a target growth rate for 2008 of 7.0% (excluding Zimbabwe). The actual growth rates for SADC in 2006 and 2007 were 6.4% and 6.8%, respectively. The average inflation rate for the region fell from 9.7% in 2006 to 8.3% in 2007. However, sharp rises in food prices and commodity costs in the first half of 2008 pushed inflation into double digits for these economies. Botswana joined the newly formed SADC Free Trade Area (launched in August 2008), and some 85% of tariffs were removed on imports from SADC member countries. This development is expected to have a beneficial impact on stimulating trade among all members of the SADC.

Botswana's own economy saw GDP growth of 12.5% from BWP71.8 billion in 2006/2007 to BWP80.1 billion in 2008/2009. However, growth measured in terms of constant prices, with 1993/94 as the benchmark, amounted to just 3.3% in 2008/09, down from growth in constant price terms of 5.3% for the previous year.

This was largely caused, according to the Botswana Budget, delivered by the minister of finance and development planning, Baladzi Gaolathe, by poor performance in the mining sector. Real growth in the non-mining sector accelerated from 5.7% in 2006/07 to 8.0% in 2008/09. This was seen as a sign that the country's drive towards a more diversified economy is gaining traction. The agricultural sector, however, contracted by 4.4% in 2007/08, by comparison with a growth rate of 11.8% in the previous year (2006/07).

Botswana's services sector turned in a strong performance, with transport and communications growing in real terms by 12.7% in 2008/09.

Unemployment was officially 23.8% in 2004, but unofficial estimates place it closer to 40%. HIV/AIDS infection rates are the second-highest in the world and threaten Botswana's impressive economic gains.

SUPPORT FOR INWARD INVESTMENT AND IMPORTS

The Botswana Development Corporation (BDC) is the state-owned investment agency, charged with encouraging investor participation by providing loans and equity capital. The Botswana Export Development and Investment Agency (BEDIA) offers a one-stop shop for foreign investors.

TAX EXEMPTIONS

Botswana runs a low-taxation environment, with corporate income tax at 25% and a special 15% tax rate is available for certain categories of manufacturing. Further information from the BEDIA.

»» MORE INFO

Websites:

Official government site for Botswana: www.gov.bw

Botswana Export Development and Investment Agency: www.bedia.bw

  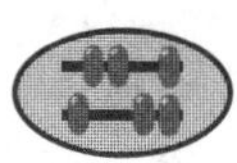   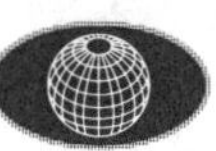   

Brazil

ECONOMY AND TRADE

After three centuries under Portuguese rule, Brazil made a peaceful transition to independence in 1822. By far the largest and most populous country in South America, Brazil has vast natural resources and continues to push for industrial and agricultural growth. It is the leading economic power in South America. The economy is characterized by large and well-developed agricultural, mining, manufacturing, and service sectors, and Brazil continues to expand its presence actively in world markets. Since 2004, Brazil's growth has yielded year-on-year increases in employment and real wages, although highly unequal income distribution is still a major problem. The economy enjoyed commodity-driven current account surpluses combined with sound macroeconomic policies that bolstered international reserves to historically high levels. The government reduced public debt year-on-year from 2004, and allowed a significant decline in real interest rates, which nevertheless remained high by world standards.

STATISTICS

GDP growth: 5.2% (2008)
GDP per capita: US$10,300
CPI: 5.8%
Key interest rate: 43.72%
Exchange rate versus dollar: real per US dollar—1.8644 (2008)
Unemployment: 8% (2008)
FDI: US$280.9 billion
Current account deficit/surplus: −US$27.33 billion
Population: 196,342,592
Source: CIA Factbook except where stated

ECONOMIC POLICY OVER 12 MONTHS

A floating exchange rate, an inflation-targeting regime, and a tight fiscal policy are the three pillars of Brazil's economic program. From 2003 to 2007, Brazil ran record trade surpluses and recorded its first current account surpluses since 1992. Brazil improved its debt profile in 2006 by shifting its debt burden toward real-denominated (the national currency) and domestically held instruments. In its July 2008 report on Brazil, the IMF praised the country for achieving years of strong growth combined with low inflation and sound macroeconomic policies. The government's achievements in lowering the public net debt-to-GDP ratios and moving significant amounts of public debt to longer maturity notes was singled out, as was the fact that the country has built up a comfortable cushion of international reserves. All these factors have significantly improved the country's ability to cope with external shocks, a fact reflected in the decision of the ratings agencies to upgrade Brazil's debt to investment grade early in 2008.

The country's president, Luiz Inacio "Lula" Da Silva, restated his commitment to fiscal responsibility by maintaining the country's primary surplus during the 2006 election. Following his second inauguration in October of that year, Da Silva announced a package of further economic reforms to reduce taxes and increase investment in infrastructure.

By 2008, the government's attempt to achieve strong growth while reducing the debt burden had created inflationary pressures. For most of 2008, the Central Bank embarked on a restrictive monetary policy to stem these pressures. Where the Central Bank had reduced interest rates by 850 basis points in the two-year period ending in October 2007, it raised the policy interest rate by 50 basis points in April and June 2008, and by a further 75 basis points in July, to a total interest rate of 13%. The idea was to contain any inflationary momentum and to anchor inflation expectations. At the same time, the onset of the global financial crisis in September 2008, combined with a collapse in the commodity price bubble and rapidly falling orders for commodities from Brazil's major trading partners rapidly had an impact on Brazil's currency and its stock market, Bovespa. The stock market had lost 41% of its value by the end of December 2008 and the country's current account ran up a deficit of more than US$27 billion, the first deficit since 2002. The Brazilian government has said that it will be monitoring both domestic demand for foreign goods (a major driver of inflation) and the impact of the global slowdown carefully, with a view to maintaining macroeconomic stability.

ECONOMIC PERFORMANCE OVER 12 MONTHS.

According to the Brazilian embassy in London, Brazil's GDP growth for 2008 is likely to be 6.3%, despite zero or near-zero growth for the final quarter of 2008. Brazil attracted record foreign direct investment in 2006 and 2007, with net capital inflows reaching nearly 7% of GDP in 2007, according to the IMF. FDI flows accounted for US$35 billion of this, or 3% of GDP. Brazil trades regularly with more than 100 nations, with 74% of exports represented by manufactured or semi-manufactured goods. Its main partners are the EEC (26%), the United States (24%), Mercosur and Latin America (21%) and Asia (12%).

The country's agrobusiness sector plays a vital role in its export performance, and for two decades has kept Brazil among the most highly productive countries as far as agricultural production is concerned. Main products include coffee, soybeans, wheat, rice, corn, cocoa, and sugar cane as well as beef. Some 15% of the country's workforce is employed in agriculture, a sector that accounts for 3.5% of total GDP.

Brazil's primary budget surplus narrowed sharply in January 2009, according to Reuters, due to a sharp rise in spending and decreases in tax revenues for the third consecutive month, on the back of slowing industrial production. The primary budget fell to US$1.87 billion, or BRL4.25 billion, from a figure that was almost four times larger (BRL15.36 billion) during the same month in 2008. The primary budget surplus includes spending by the Treasury, the Brazilian central bank and the social security system, but excludes interest payments on debt, and transfers to state and local governments. Reuters points out that

  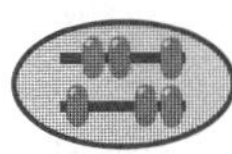      

the primary budget surplus feeds into the consolidated public-sector primary surplus, which is very closely watched by analysts who see it as a measure of Brazil's ability to pay its debts.

The global slowdown had a major impact on tax revenues, which fell by 7.26%, after adjustments for inflation, to US$25.7 billion, by comparison with 2007 tax revenues. In January 2009, corporate income tax fell by 17.5% on the 2008 figure. The government introduced tax breaks on new car sales during the second half of 2008 in order to boost demand in the economy. The Brazilian Central Bank argued, in its most recent half yearly Financial Stability Report (May 2008), that Brazil had performed better than many other emerging market economies during the global slowdown. Unlike the credit bubble in economies in the developed nations, credit growth in Brazil had not reached the point where it constituted any threat to the solidity of the country's financial system, the bank said. It noted, however, that the downturn had sharply increased volatility in share prices on the country's stock markets.

SUPPORT FOR INWARD INVESTMENT AND IMPORTS

Investe Brazil is a publicly and privately run agency whose mission is to attract investment into the country. It is assisted by Brazil Trade Net, a Foreign Affairs Ministry agency which is responsible for promoting Brazil to potential investors. The Brazilian Ministry of Labor and Employment is also charged with facilitating matters for foreign investors.

TAX EXEMPTIONS

The basic rate of tax on corporate profits is 15%, with an additional surtax of 10% on all profits in excess of US$80,000 per year (2003). There is also a "social contribution" of a further 9%.

▸▸ MORE INFO

Websites:

Official Government web site: www.brazil.gov.br

Brazil Trade Net, the trade promotion portal of Brazil's Ministry of External Relations: www.braziltradenet.gov.br

Central Bank of Brazil and Ministry of Finance: www.bcb.gov.br

See Also:

★ Viewpoint: Hamish McRae (pp. 789–790)

British Virgin Islands

ECONOMY AND TRADE

Located some 60 miles east of Puerto Rico, between the Caribbean Sea and the North Atlantic Ocean, the British Virgin Islands (BVI) were settled by the Dutch in 1648, and then annexed by the English in 1672. There are about 50 islands in the archipelago, with Tortola being the main island. The BVI were part of the British colony of the Leeward Islands from 1872 to 1960, and were granted autonomy in 1967. The BVI have the status of a British Overseas Territory. The economy is closely tied to the larger and more populous US Virgin Islands to the west. The BVI have one of the most stable and prosperous economies in the Caribbean, based on a sophisticated, well-developed offshore financial centre and a strong tourist industry. Some 820,000 tourists, mainly from the United Stateas, visited the islands in 2005. Because of traditionally close links with the US Virgin Islands, the British Virgin Islands have used the US dollar as its currency since 1959. Livestock raising is the most important agricultural activity; poor soils limit the islands' ability to meet domestic food requirements, which underlines the importance of the tourism and financial services sectors.

ECONOMIC POLICY OVER 12 MONTHS

With financial services and tourism being the twin pillars of the islands' prosperity, the BVI government of Premier Ralph O'Neal is highly interested in ensuring the continued prosperity of both these sectors. As such, the government is very keen to see that the BVI's financial offshore sector complies with international best practice and is not a haven for money-laundering. This is a particularly pressing issue as the many uninhabited islands in the BVI, together with the archipelago's proximity to Puerto Rico, which is seen as a gateway for illegal drugs entering mainland United States, have made the region a "natural" staging point for the drugs trade.

With this backdrop, the government has been eager to assure international regulators, and the international anti-money laundering body, the Financial Action Task Force (FATF) that the BVI operate a transparent regime, with formal "corridors" or gateways by which national anti-money-laundering and tax-evasion authorities can call for information from BVI-registered banks and institutions.

In July 2008, the BVI government joined the flow of offshore financial centers submitting evidence to the United Kingdom parliamentary committee's offshore inquiry. Government spokepersons took advantage of their appearance before the committee to drive home the message that the BVI operates a "robust regulatory and supervisory regime" in financial services, with a well-proven track record of international cooperation. The BVI already have tax information exchange agreements (TIEAs) in place with the United States, the United Kingdom and Australia. The OECD welcomed the BVI's initiatives in this area.

Premier Ralph O'Neal said in his 2009 Budget speech (in February 2009) that tourism to the islands had

STATISTICS

GDP growth: 6% (www.caribbean-netnews.com)
GDP per capita: US$41,000 (www.businessbvi.com)
CPI: 2% (2005–2007)
Key interest rate: N/A
Exchange rate versus dollar: N/A
Unemployment: 3.6% (1997)
FDI: N/A
Current account deficit/surplus: N/A
Population: 24,041 (July 2008)
Source: CIA Factbook except where stated

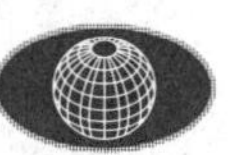

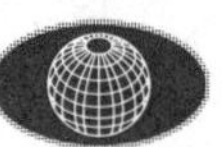

experienced a slowdown in the latter part of 2008 as a consequence of the global slowdown. This had caused layoffs and cutbacks in the sector but the government is committed to sustaining tourism through initiatives such as maintaining a subsidized transport service to Puerto Rico. Infrastructure projects such as renovation work on the Cruise Ship Pier and the tender dock for cruise ships would also go forward in 2009, Premier Ralph O'Neal has said.

The BVI's offshore sector was launched in the mid-1980s, when the government began offering offshore registration to companies wishing to incorporate in the islands. Today, incorporation fees generate substantial revenues for the islands. Roughly 400,000 companies were on the offshore registry in 2000. The adoption of a comprehensive insurance law in late 1994, which provides a blanket of confidentiality with regulated statutory gateways for investigation of criminal offences, made the British Virgin Islands even more attractive to international business.

A United Kingdom National Audit Office report on the BVI noted that it is better equipped through its Financial Investigation Agency, which dates back to 2004, to investigate financial crime, than many other offshore centers.

ECONOMIC PERFORMANCE OVER 12 MONTHS.

The BVI economy has been characterized over the last six years by low inflation, and low unemployment, with an average growth rate of 6%. Growth for 2009 is expected to fall, with the extent of the decline depending on the impact of the global slowdown on the BVI's financial services sector, and on tourism. GDP in 2007 was US$1 billion with the contribution from tourism and financial services accounting for more than 48%, and real estate, renting and business services accounting for 19%. GDP per capita is above US$41,000, giving the BVI one of the highest per capita incomes in the Caribbean. Financial services levies are the major contributor to government revenues, along with payroll taxes and import duties.

In announcing the government's budget for 2009 (27 February 2009) Premier O'Neal said that the BVI expect revenues to amount to US$279.8 million in 2009 against operational expenditure of US$252.48 million. This decline of 1.7% over the previous year estimates is directly attributable to the global slowdown, he said. O'Neal admitted that the slowdown creates "significant challenges" for the BVI economy, but at the same time also presents opportunities.

The government is looking to stimulate the economy through a variety of policies and program initiatives. O'Neal also recently announced in the BVI House of Assembly that company incorporations in the BVI had also fallen back, due to the global slowdown. The number of companies incorporating in 2008 was down by 20% on the 2007 figures. In particular, the captive insurance and mutual fund sectors of the BVI's financial services industry were hard hit by global events. As a result, the BVI administration expects to see minimal growth in incorporations in at least the first half of 2009, though the expectation is that new incorporations will pick up in the third and fourth quarters.

The managing director and chief executive officer of the BVI Financial Services Commission, Robert Mathavious, warned at the end of January 2009 that the territory's offshore centre faced challenging conditions, and not just from the global slowdown. The fact that the incoming regime of US President Obama is committed to much tighter regulation of offshore tax havens is itself a challenge, he said. The coming initiatives against offshore jurisdictions would draw a distinction between offshore jurisdictions that have implemented effective standards and are committed to transparency and the exchange of information on tax matters, and those offshore centers that seek to offer complete secrecy and privacy to those using their jurisdiction.

SUPPORT FOR INWARD INVESTMENT AND IMPORTS

The BVI are one of the premier jurisdictions for fund domiciliation, with more than 420 funds registered at the end of 2007. Key advantages to registering or recognizing a fund in the BVI include zero taxation on profits and capital gains and no minimum capital requirements.

TAX EXEMPTIONS

See above.

▸▸ MORE INFO

Websites:

Official BVI Government site: www.gis.gov.vg

Media site for Caribbean news: www.caribbeannetnews.com

Resource site for business in BVI: www.businessbvi.com

Brunei

ECONOMY AND TRADE

Bordering the South China Sea and Malaysia, the Sultanate of Brunei became a British protectorate in 1888, and achieved independence in 1984. The same family has ruled the country for more than six

centuries, and now presides over an economy that boasts one of the highest per capita GDPs in Asia. Brunei last held elections in March 1962. It is a constitutional sultanate, with the Legislative Council consisting of members appointed by the sultan. The economy encompasses a mixture of foreign and domestic entrepreneurship, government regulation, welfare measures, and village tradition. Crude oil and natural gas production account for just over half of GDP and more than 90% of exports. Substantial income from overseas investment supplements income from domestic production. The government provides all medical services, together with free education through to university, and also subsidizes rice and housing. Brunei's leaders are concerned that steadily increasing integration into the world economy will undermine internal social cohesion.

STATISTICS

GDP growth: –0.5% (2008, IMF)

GDP per capita: US$54,100 (2008)

CPI: 0.8% (IMF)

Key interest rate: 5.5%

Exchange rate versus dollar: BND per US dollar—1.5886 (2006) (the Brunei dollar is now pegged to the Singapore dollar 1:1)

Unemployment: 3.7%

FDI: N/A

Current account deficit/surplus: U$7.939 billion (2008, IMF)

Population: 381,371

Source: CIA Factbook except where stated

ECONOMIC POLICY OVER 12 MONTHS

The country is rich in natural resources and has a strategic location within the region. The majority of the country is covered in tropical rainforests, and ecotourism is gaining importance in Brunei's economic activities. The government recognizes that its future wealth, beyond oil and gas, lies in the knowledge and skills of its people, which is one of the main reasons why university education is free. Having a highly skilled workforce has been central to the government's desire to transform Brunei into a diversified, industrialized economy, and skilled workers remain in short supply.

Plans for the future include upgrading the labor force, reducing unemployment, strengthening the banking and tourism sectors, increasing agricultural production, and, in general, further widening the economic base beyond oil and gas. The main focus of attention on the development of human resources has been a focus on managerial and industrial skills, with particular emphasis on entrepreneurial skills (source: official government website).

Brunei's main exports consist of three major commodities, crude oil, petroleum products, and liquefied natural gas, which are sold largely to Japan, the United States, and ASEAN countries. The government's move to promote non-oil and gas activities gathered momentum in the 1990s, and has continued ever since. The success of its early initiatives can be seen from the fact that, in 1996, non-oil and gas activities were already contributing 64% of GDP, compared to just 24.3% in 1991.

The Sultanate also sees encouraging more foreign direct investment (FDI) as a way of strengthening the country's underdeveloped private sector. Boosting the activities of this sector will greatly assist in the movement away from a reliance on non-renewable resources. As a member of the Asia-Pacific Economic Council (APEC), which includes a number of countries in the region, Brunei is benefiting from the overall efforts being made by APEC to understand and encourage FDI flows right across the region. The Sultanate has a strong legal infrastructure backed by a competitive market environment, both of which will be attractive to foreign investors. The Brunei Investment Incentive Act (1975) provides tax advantages for start-up businesses, and ongoing incentives throughout a company's growth and expansion. These tax advantages are rated by APEC as "comparable, if not better, than those already offered by other countries in the region." Foreign investors are allowed to own and operate companies, and there are flexible forms of joint venture and minority participation available as well. No foreign ownership of land is allowed. Instead, foreign companies can apply to lease land for industrial development. Importantly, the Brunei dollar is a convertible currency, and the government does not maintain any currency controls. Nor does it limit remittances, loans, or lease payments, according to APEC.

ECONOMIC PERFORMANCE OVER 12 MONTHS

An International Monetary Fund (IMF) country report on Brunei (published in January 2008) pointed out that the country's economy contracted during the first half of 2007, following a decision by the government to cut back on energy production to both facilitate maintenance of oil and gas installations, and to optimize and conserve oil reserves. However, the IMF said that the government and the private non-energy sector provided what it termed "a positive impetus to growth" through 2007.

Inflation remained low at 0.1%, thanks in part to the Sultanate's ability to impose price controls. Credit growth rose to 5% in the first half of 2007, following a contraction in 2006. The country's banking system still has some legacy debt issues, harking back to financial problems in the country's corporate sector during the 1990s. Local bank capital adequacy ratios were high, at close to 20%, the IMF said.

Until the sudden fall in oil prices as the global slowdown took hold in late 2008, high oil and gas prices had driven large fiscal and current account surpluses. The IMF noted that the Sultanate was pursuing a sensible policy of saving a significant percentage of energy-related revenue windfalls, and investing those sums abroad. The primary fiscal surplus reached 21.5% of GDP in the financial year 2006/07. The current-account surplus reached 56% of GDP in 2006, reflecting high energy exports.

The IMF expects growth to remain weak for the near term, but to recover as the global recession eases. Brunei was due to extend the 2007 maintenance work on its oil field installations during 2008, which the IMF expected to depress export earnings and GDP growth. Over the medium term, growth of 3% per year should be achievable, it said.

The country's main medium-term challenge, apart from the global downturn, is finding ways of deepen-

 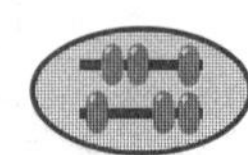      

ing and strengthening the diversification of the economy. Key reforms will include developing domestic capital markets, introducing education and training programs to achieve a more appropriate labor skills mix, and improving the business environment. Brunei has also put in place a strong financial supervisory and regulatory framework, including an anti-money-laundering regime. It has worked to harmonize Islamic banking and insurance law and regulations with conventional regulation, to create a level playing field for all the country's banks.

SUPPORT FOR INWARD INVESTMENT AND IMPORTS

In November 2001, the Brunei Economic Development Board was formed, with the primary responsibility of attracting and retaining local and foreign direct investment to further diversify the economy. Its primary focus is in attracting investment in advanced technology industries, and skill-intensive services with good export market prospects.

TAX EXEMPTIONS

Further information on these can be obtained from the Brunei Economic Development Board

MORE INFO

Websites:

Brunei Economic Development Board: www.bedb.com.bn

Ministry of Industry and Primary Resources: www.industry.gov.bn

Official government site: www.brunei.gov.bn

See Also:

✔Middle East: Regulatory Structure and Powers (p. 1041)

Canada

ECONOMY AND TRADE

A land of vast distances and rich natural resources, Canada became a self-governing dominion in 1867 while retaining ties to the British crown. Economically and technologically, the nation has developed in parallel with the United States, its neighbor to the south across an unfortified border. As an affluent, high-tech, industrial society in the trillion-dollar class, Canada resembles the United States in its market-oriented economic system, pattern of production, and affluent living standards. Since World War II, the impressive growth of the manufacturing, mining, and service sectors has transformed the nation from a largely rural economy into a primarily industrial and urban country. The 1989 US–Canada Free Trade Agreement (FTA) and the 1994 North American Free Trade Agreement (NAFTA) (which includes Mexico) ignited a dramatic increase in trade and economic integration with the United States, its principle trading partner. Canada enjoys a substantial trade surplus with the United States, which absorbs nearly 80% of Canadian exports each year.

ECONOMIC POLICY OVER 12 MONTHS

Given its great natural resources, skilled labor force, and modern capital plant, Canada has enjoyed solid economic growth, and its prudent fiscal management produced consecutive balanced budgets from 1997 to 2007. In 2008, growth slowed sharply, down from 2.5% in 2007 to 1.8%, and the economy contracted in the fourth quarter as a result of the global economic downturn. Public finances, too, are set to deteriorate for the first time in a decade. Tight global credit conditions have further restrained business and housing investment, despite the conservative lending practices and strong capitalization that made Canada's major banks among the strongest in the world.

In the budget for 2009, Canada's Minister of Finance, James Flaherty, announced a stimulus package in line with the IMF's recommendation that developed economies inject a minimum of 2% of GDP to counter the effects of the slowdown. The measures include infrastructure spending and efforts to ensure continued lending to businesses. To achieve this, the government is prepared to run a temporary budget deficit, and will, in effect, be speeding up planned infrastructure spending. As a result of the global slowdown, the Canadian economy is likely to contract by 0.8% in 2009, and it will incur a budget deficit of C$34 billion in this fiscal year, and a deficit of C$30 billion in fiscal 2010. However, the government does not foresee the deficit being long-running, as it will be in the United States, the United Kingdom, and elsewhere. Future surpluses will be used to pay down the debt incurred during the present recession, Flaherty said. By 2011, the government expects the deficit to fall to C$13 billion and to half again by 2012, with a return to a C$700 million surplus predicted for 2013. One of the initiatives planned is a C$2 billion fund to support economic diversification in communities affected by distress or decline in specific local industries, such as auto manufacture.

The Canadian remote regions—Atlantic Canada, Quebec and Western Canada—are traditionally affected first in any downturn, and the government has announced that it will provide support for regional economic development for these areas.

Some $C200 billion, part of an "Extraordinary Financing Framework," will be made available to businesses to keep the economy moving. The present downturn should not obscure the fact that Canada's

STATISTICS

GDP growth: 0.5% (2008, Statistics Canada)

GDP per capita: US$40,200 (2008)

CPI: 3% (2008)

Key interest rate: 6.1% (December 31, 2007)

Exchange rate versus dollar: C$ per US dollar—1.0364 (2008)

unemployment: 6.1% (2008)

FDI: C$586.6 billion

Current account deficit/surplus: –C$34 billion (2009, Canadian budget)

Population: 33,212,696 (July 2008)

Source: CIA Factbook except where stated

handling of economic policy up to mid-2008 was defter and produced better results than any other G7 member. It was the only G7 country to record a fiscal surplus in 2006, and was in the strongest fiscal position of all G7 countries in 2007. By the end of 2006, the country's real income per capita had risen by more than 20% compared to 2001, increasing by more than double the per capita GDP growth achieved by the United States.

ECONOMIC PERFORMANCE OVER 12 MONTHS

According to the IMF, the real GDP growth of 2.5% achieved by Canada in 2007 was driven largely by robust growth in Canada's domestic demand, particularly in private consumption and residential investment, which saw a combined growth of close to 4%. The unemployment level fell below 6%. However, the global economic slowdown took its toll on growth through 2008. According to the Canadian office of statistics, Statistics Canada, the economy shrank by 3.4% in the fourth quarter of 2008, pulling the country into its deepest recession since the 1990s. Gross domestic product fell by 1% in December 2008, compared with November 2008. The contraction over the period October–December 2008 was the first time Canada's economy had experienced a quarterly decline since the country's last recession, in 1991–1992. At the same time, the agency also revised down its figures for GDP growth in the third quarter of 2008. Instead of 1.3%, as reported, the economy actually grew by only 0.9%, it said. Taking these corrections into account, the total growth for 2008 amounted to just 0.5%.

On the positive side, core inflation, which had been on the rise in the first half of 2007, began to show signs of declining in the second half of that year, despite the impact of rising fuel prices, and is predicted to continue to fall through 2009.

Canada's current account surplus for 2006, and its track record of running surpluses came under pressure in 2007, with the external current-account surplus narrowing to just 1% of GDP as real net exports declined sharply. In part, this was due to volatility in the foreign-exchange markets, where the Canadian dollar appreciated rapidly, making Canada's exports expensive. The Canadian dollar appreciated by 45%, in real, effective terms, over the period from 2002 to 2007. In response, the Bank of Canada reduced its policy rate to 4% in two consecutive cuts of 25 basis points in December 2007 and January 2008. As outlined under "Policy" above, the government now expects to run a deficit at least until 2013.

According to Statistics Canada, the country's exports dropped by 4.7% in the fourth quarter of 2008, the deepest quarterly fall since export records began 60 years ago. As far as the balance of trade is concerned, this decline was more than offset by a fall in imports of 6.4%, as domestic demand weakened rapidly. Personal spending by Canadians also fell by 0.8%, the first time this had happened since the fourth quarter of 1995. Given these figures, both the federal government and the Bank of Canada officially declared that Canada went into recession during the fourth quarter of 2008. The prediction from the IMF is that the Canadian economy will continue to shrink in 2009, contracting by 1.2% over the year—a deeper recession than that predicted in Canada's Budget for 2009. By comparison, Canada's neighbor, the United States, saw its economy decline by 6.2% over the fourth quarter of 2008.

SUPPORT FOR INWARD INVESTMENT AND IMPORTS

Invest in Canada was created by the federal government to promote, attract and retain foreign direct investment in Canada. It is a bureau of the Department of Foreign Affairs and International Trade and provides a range of services, including guidance on incentives, regulations and taxation.

TAX EXEMPTIONS

The Invest in Canada website has a guide to incentives and taxation for foreign investors.

▸▸ MORE INFO

Websites:

Website of the Department of Finance: www.budget.gc.ca

Canada's Central Bank: www.bankofcanada.ca

Canadian government website: www.canada.gc.ca

Invest in Canada: investincanada.gc.ca

Cayman Islands

ECONOMY AND TRADE

The three-island group of the Cayman Islands (Grand Cayman, Cayman Brac and Little Cayman) are a British Overseas Territory. They were colonized by the British during the 18th and 19th centuries, and were administered by Jamaica (a former British colony) after 1863. The islands lie 268 kilometers north-west of Jamaica. In 1959, the islands became a territory within the Federation of the West Indies, but when the Federation dissolved in 1962, the Cayman Islands chose to remain a British dependency. With no direct taxation, the islands have developed into a thriving offshore financial centre. Tourism is also a mainstay and the two, together, account for around 80% of the country's GDP. The tourist industry is aimed at the luxury market and caters mainly to visitors from North America. Total tourist arrivals exceeded 2.1 million

in 2003, with about half from the United States. The Caymanians enjoy one of the highest outputs per capita and one of the highest standards of living in the world.

ECONOMIC POLICY OVER 12 MONTHS

The Cayman Islands are at risk of hurricane damage, the most recent instance being Hurricane Ivan in 2004, and one of the main policy objectives in the 2009 Budget was a commitment, backed by a US$2.3 million fund, to ensure that the country is better able to deal with and recover from natural disasters. The government also committed a US$8.5 million equity injection to expand and upgrade the Islands' Emergency Operations Centre. A further US$19.5 million went to fund a new hurricane-resistant office building to house the majority of government departments, with additional funds for sea-wall protection.

Some 25%, or US$162.7 million of the government's total planned expenditure for 2008–2009, is being targeted at education, in a bid to improve the Islands' educational infrastructure and capability. Tourism and financial services both did well out of the budget, with tourism getting US$23.6 million to enhance marketing of the Islands to potential tourists and to support local providers. The Islands' regulation, monitoring and reporting functions for the financial markets received US$23.5 million. The government's commitment to sound fiscal management continued in 2008/09, with the Islands' operating revenue forecast to be US$528.2 million. With operating expenses deducted, the government expects an operating surplus of US$13.4 million.

Public debt is expected to amount to US$412.8 million at the end of 2008–2009, including US$154.0 million of new borrowings to finance planned investment activities, including significant capital projects on the Islands. As these investments all have long-term benefits that will be enjoyed by both current and future generations, the government reasons that it is appropriate for their costs to be spread in a manner that reflects this.

The advent of modern transportation and telecommunications in the 1950s led to the emergence of what are now considered the Cayman Islands' "twin pillars" of economic development: international finance and tourism, each contributing around 40% to GDP. In 2004, there were more than 70,000 companies registered in the Cayman Islands, including 446 banks and trust companies. Forty of the world's largest banks are present in the Cayman Islands.

Tourism profits from the islands' unspoiled beaches, duty-free shopping, scuba diving, and deep-sea fishing, which draw almost a million visitors to the islands each year.

Education is compulsory to the age of 16, and is free to all Caymanian children. Schools follow the British educational system. The government operates 10 primary, one special education, and two high schools. In addition, there is a university and a law school.

ECONOMIC PERFORMANCE OVER 12 MONTHS.

The Caymans' reputation as a global offshore center continued to attract business through 2008. The "dark days" of the Cayman Islands' financial services and banking center, when the Islands were a haven for money-laundering, are now well and truly over. Financial institutions in the Caymans are now closely regulated by the Cayman Islands Monetary Authority (CIMA), which operates a stricter regime than many on-shore financial jurisdictions. From 1986, when the Caymans entered into a Mutual Legal Assistance Treaty with the United States, the territory has worked to eliminate money-laundering, and to create a model modern regulatory environment. The "know your client" regime, where banks and financial institutions are obliged to know their clients in depth and detail, has helped achieve this goal and has enhanced the Caymans' reputation as an offshore financial centre.

Several different types of licenses are offered in the Cayman Islands to the various banking institutions, included restricted and trust licenses, but the main two are either Class A or Class B. The rules governing the two categories are relatively complex and detailed. However, in essence, Class B banks are concerned mostly with offshore banking and non-resident customers with some exceptions, while Class A banks can carry on with the full gambit of banking services, both on and offshore. Of the 280-plus banks currently registered in the Cayman Islands, only six banks—Cayman National, RBC, Butterfield, Scotia, First Caribbean, and Fidelity—offered retail services at the start of 2008.

Although offshore accounts are most frequently held in the Caymans by non-residents, many people who visit regularly, live in the territory on a temporary basis, or reside permanently also hold offshore accounts. Aside from the obvious tax benefits, offshore accounts often yield higher interest rates over onshore retail banks, and make international transactions easier for those who travel frequently or who have business interests abroad.

For numerous reasons, the vast majority of offshore accounts are held by people who reside overseas. As international borders crumble in the face of global trade, more and more high-net-worth individuals, rich people, and corporations are seeking to avoid the restrictions or political instabilities of the countries in which they hold nationality, do business, or live.

As the Caymans are a tax-free jurisdiction there are no capital gains, corporation, property, or income taxes to pay—an obvious benefit to the wealthy and to multi-national companies. With no exchange

STATISTICS

GDP growth: 2.2%
GDP per capita: US$48,290
CPI: 4.4% (2004)
Key interest rate: N/A
Exchange rate versus dollar: CI per US dollar—0.80 (fixed)
Unemployment: 4.4%
FDI: N/A
Current account deficit/surplus: N/A
Population: 47,862
Source: CIA Factbook except where stated

  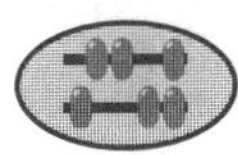   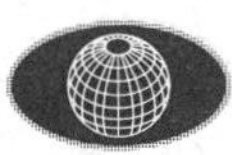   

controls, businesses can move funds in and out of the Caymans in any currency, a factor facilitating complex international trades and transactions. This, combined with confidentiality (limited to legal activity), competitive rates, a compliant regime and a stable government which supports and encourages the offshore sector, makes banking in Cayman extremely attractive to a cross-section of the international community.

SUPPORT FOR INWARD INVESTMENT AND IMPORTS

Invest Cayman is the official website of the Cayman Islands Investment Bureau. The bureau provides a single source of customized information, investment marketing materials, and services to Cayman businesses, as well as to potential foreign investors. Establishing a business in the Cayman Islands involves gaining approval from several government agencies, depending on the industry sector involved.

TAX EXEMPTIONS

The Cayman Islands is a tax-free country, with free movement of capital.

▸▸ MORE INFO

Websites:

Government site and portal: www.gov.ky

Cayman Islands Investment Bureau: www.investcayman.ky

Cayman Islands Monetary Authority: www.cimoney.com.ky

Channel Islands

ECONOMY AND TRADE

Jersey is a British Crown dependency situated off the coast of Normandy. As well as the island of Jersey itself, the dependency includes nearby islands such as the Minquiers, Écréhous, the Pierres de Lecq, and others that are no more than rocks and reefs. Together with the bailiwick of Guernsey, it forms the grouping known as the Channel Islands. Jersey's economy is based on international financial services, agriculture, and tourism. Light taxes and death duties make the island a popular tax haven.

On Guernsey, financial services, including banking, fund management, and insurance, account for about 23% of employment, and about 55% of total income in this tiny, prosperous Channel Island economy. Tourism, manufacturing, and horticulture, mainly tomatoes and cut flowers, have been declining. Financial services, construction, retailing, and the public sector have been growing. As with Jersey, light tax and death duties make Guernsey a popular tax haven.

ECONOMIC POLICY OVER 12 MONTHS

With such a significant percentage of its revenue coming from financial services, Guernsey actively promotes itself as an offshore financial center. From 1960 to 2008, companies and individuals paid income tax at the rate of 20% and there was no separate corporation tax. Guernsey levies no capital gains, inheritance, capital transfer, value-added (VAT/TVA), or general withholding taxes. However, the island has gone to some trouble to change the way its tax system works, in order to remain OECD and EU-compliant. From January 1, 2008, it changed to a "Zero 10" corporate tax system, whereby most companies pay 0% corporate tax, and a limited number of specific banking activities are taxed at 10%.

Guernsey also has a thriving non-finance industry. It is home to Specsavers Optical Group, which manages the largest optical chain in the United Kingdom and Ireland, and also operates in Scandinavia, the Netherlands, Australia, and Spain. Guernsey issues its own sterling coinage and banknotes. United Kingdom banknotes also circulate freely and interchangeably.

The island of Jersey has a special relationship with the European Union as part of the United Kingdom's Treaty of Accession in 1973. This relationship cannot be changed without the unanimous agreement of all member states and island authorities. Under it, the island is part of the customs territory of the European Community. The common customs tariff, levies, and other agricultural import measures therefore apply to trade between the island and non-member states, and there is free movement of goods and trade between the island and member states.

Jersey is not, however, part of the single market in financial services, and, as a result, is not required to implement EU Directives on such matters as movement of capital, company law, or money-laundering. However, Jersey has said that it will emulate such measures where appropriate, and is committed to enforcing international standards of financial regulation, and countering money-laundering and terrorist financing.

By March 2009, the island's financial services sector, like that of Guernsey, and, indeed, other offshore finance centers such as the Bahamas, the Cayman Islands, and the British Virgin Islands, remained under threat from planned or threatened anti-tax avoidance measures in the United States, and from the European Union. However, many Jersey and Guernsey-based financial institutions argue that the enduring appeal of both islands' offshore centers is the real value that they bring to tax planning. Opening up

STATISTICS

Guernsey

GDP growth: 3% (2005)
GDP per capita: $44,600
CPI: 3.4% (June 2006)
Key interest rate: NA
Exchange rate versus dollar: Guernsey Pound vs. $: 0.5302 (2008)
Unemployment: 0.9% (March 2006)
FDI: NA
Current account deficit/surplus: NA
Population: 65,870

Jersey

GDP growth: NA
GDP per capita: $57,000 (2005 est)
CPI: 3.7% (December 2006)
Key interest rate: NA
Exchange rate versus dollar: Jersey Pound vs. $: 0.5302 (2008)
Unemployment: 2.2% (2006)
FDI: NA
Current account deficit/surplus: NA
Population: 91,626

  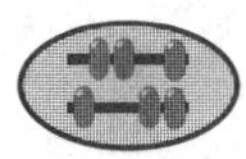   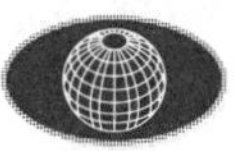   

avenues for national tax authorities to pursue tax dodgers while still retaining low or no local taxes at this time still looks a viable way forward for offshore centers.

ECONOMIC PERFORMANCE OVER 12 MONTHS

In 2005 the finance sector on Jersey accounted for about 50% of the island's output. Tourism accounts for one-quarter of GDP. Potatoes, cauliflower, tomatoes, and, especially, flowers are important export crops, shipped mostly to the United Kingdom. The Jersey breed of dairy cattle is known worldwide, and represents an important export income earner. Milk products go to the United Kingdom and other European Union countries. In recent years, the government has encouraged light industry to locate in Jersey, with the result that an electronics industry has developed, displacing more traditional industries. All raw material and energy requirements are imported, as well as a large share of Jersey's food needs.

As part of an effort to legitimate the island's offshore finance activities, Jersey has signed a number of tax information exchange agreements with foreign countries since 2002. The first such agreement was with the United States in 2002. There followed agreements with the Netherlands (2007), Germany (July 4, 2008), and with Denmark, the Faroes, Finland, Greenland, Iceland, Sweden and Norway on October 28, 2008.

On Guernsey, the evolving economic integration of the EU nations is changing the environment under which Guernsey operates. The island has come under intense criticism, led by the OECD and the Financial Action Task Force (FATF), which seeks to close loopholes—particularly offshore loopholes—that encourage money-laundering operations, and impede transparent regulation. As a result, Guernsey is reforming its practices. The island has enjoyed a great deal of success in the last two decades in attracting some of the world's best known financial institutions in banking, insurance, and reinsurance.

According to the Guernsey Financial Services Commission, the island's financial regulator, the jurisdiction holds some £61 billion in total deposits (June 30, 2008), up £3 billion from 2008. In 2008, financial services accounted for 70–80% of the island's revenues. However, Guernsey now has to negotiate efforts by the United States, the United Kingdom, and Europe, and the OECD, to "wind up" tax havens, and to prevent money going offshore, and diminishing national tax takes. The FATF conducted an evaluation of Guernsey's compliance on November 2, 2008, and issued some 40 recommendations (source: Investment International, www.investmentinternational.com).

Low tax regimes for overseas corporates setting up in Guernsey are based around corporate non-residence and avoiding local ownership. To this end, the main legal vehicles used are Exempt and International Body, limited partnerships, and trusts. In most instances, income arising abroad is lightly taxed, and income arising on Guernsey is more highly taxed. From 2008, the island's Future Tax Strategy legislation came into play, the so-called "Zero 10" system, which sees businesses and corporate entities paying zero income tax, while financial businesses subject to regulation by the Guernsey FSC are taxed at 10%.

SUPPORT FOR INWARD INVESTMENT AND IMPORTS

Jersey Enterprise provides a one-stop shop for anyone looking to grow a business on Jersey. It also assists international companies to establish and grow their businesses in Jersey. The Guernsey Enterprise Agency does much the same on Guernsey.

TAX EXEMPTIONS

Both Jersey and Guernsey have favorable tax regimes. Further information can be obtained from Jersey Enterprise and Guernsey Business.

▸▸ MORE INFO

Websites:

Official States of Guernsey website: www.gov.gg

Jersey Enterprise: www.enterprise.jersey.com

Guernsey Enterprise Agency and Guernsey Business: www.guernseybusiness.net

Chile

ECONOMY AND TRADE

After the fall of the Marxist government of Salvador Allende in 1973, through a military coup led by Augusto Pinochet, Chile endured 17 years of dictatorship before a freely elected president replaced Pinochet in 1990. Under Pinochet's regime in the 1980s, the country implemented sound economic policies, which have continued to the present, contributing to steady growth, and more than halving the rates of poverty in the country. One of the positive steps taken by the regime was to privatize many state-owned companies, and successive democratic governments since the 1990s have continued the privatization process. Chile's commitment to democratic, representative government, and its growing economic strength have made it a leader in the region. Chile has a market-oriented economy, characterized by a high level of foreign trade, and a reputation for strong financial institutions, and sound policy. As a result, it

  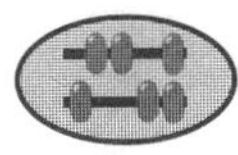 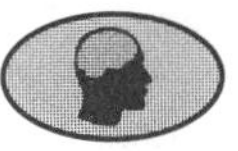  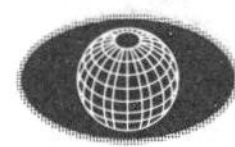   

enjoys the strongest sovereign bond rating in South America. Exports account for 40% of GDP, with commodities making up some three-quarters of total exports. Copper alone provides one-third of government revenue.

STATISTICS
GDP growth: 4%
GDP per capita: US$15,400
CPI: 8.8%
Key interest rate: 8.67%
Exchange rate versus dollar: pesos per US dollar—509.02 (2008)
Unemployment: 7.5%
FDI: US$108.9 billion
Current account deficit: −US$1.574 billion
Population: 16,601,7070
Source: CIA Factbook except where stated

ECONOMIC POLICY OVER 12 MONTHS

During the early 1990s, Chile's reputation as a role model for economic reform was strengthened when the democratic government of Patricio Aylwin took over from the military in 1990. Growth in real GDP averaged 8% during 1991–1997, but fell to half that level in 1998 when the government implemented tight monetary policies to reign in a growing current account deficit fueled by lower export earnings—the latter a product of the global financial crisis. In 1999, Chile experienced negative economic growth for the first time in more than 15 years. In the years since then, growth has averaged 4% per year. Chile deepened its longstanding commitment to trade liberalization with the signing of a free trade agreement with the United States, which took effect on January 1, 2004. Chile claims to have more bilateral or regional trade agreements than any other country. It has 57 such agreements (not all of them full free trade agreements), including with the European Union, Mercosur, China, India, South Korea, and Mexico. A new FTA with Australia comes into effect in 2009. Negotiations with Malaysia and Turkey continued in 2008. Chile is also a member of the Trans-Pacific Strategic Economic Partnership Agreement, or P4, which includes Singapore, New Zealand, and Brunei. As such, it was very much in support of a statement by the US Trade Department in 2008 that the United States will explore joining the P4 in 2009.

Chile has enjoyed strong productivity growth in the period 2000–2007, with wages rising faster than inflation. The poverty line in Chile is defined as twice the cost of satisfying the nutritional requirements of a family of four. The government's role in the economy is mostly limited to regulation, although the state continues to operate copper giant CODELCO, and a few other enterprises (there is one state-run bank).

Over the past five years, foreign direct investment inflows have quadrupled to some US$17 billion in 2008. The Chilean government conducts a rule-based, countercyclical fiscal policy, accumulating surpluses in sovereign wealth funds during periods of high copper prices and economic growth, and allowing deficit spending only during periods of low copper prices and low growth. As of September 2008, those sovereign wealth funds—kept mostly outside the country and separate from Central Bank reserves—amounted to more than US$20 billion.

ECONOMIC PERFORMANCE OVER 12 MONTHS

As a major exporter, Chile expects to feel a significant impact from the global downturn. Economic growth is expected to slow in 2009, and higher unemployment is likely. The Chilean banking system has experienced its own liquidity crisis, and, in late 2008 and early 2009, some Chilean businesses experienced difficulties financing their operations. Moreover, on November 1, 2008, the world price of copper hit its lowest point for three years. With copper accounting for more than half of all exports, the economy felt the impact sharply.

Chile has struggled to reduce the high unemployment rates of the last 15–18 years (unemployment, which averaged 5–6% in the 1990s, rose to around 10% in 1999). At the end of 2007, unemployment had been reduced to 7.1%, but it started to climb again in 2008, and is still on the rise as company layoffs continue. These factors caused many companies to reduce investment plans, cut costs, and begin layoffs towards the end of 2008. Many experts are predicting a significant increase in unemployment in 2009, largely as a result of the global economic downturn. Most international observers place some of the blame for Chile's consistently high unemployment rate on complicated and restrictive labor laws.

Chile's independent Central Bank currently pursues an inflation target of 3%. However, in 2007, inflation inched towards 8%—the first time inflation had exceeded 5% since 1998. In 2008, inflation increased further, hitting a high of 9.9% in October 2008, before moving lower again at the end of the year. In recent years, the Chilean peso's rapid appreciation against the US dollar had helped dampen inflation. However, as the global financial crisis accelerated toward the end of 2008, the Chilean peso depreciated significantly against the US dollar. Most wage settlements and loans are indexed, reducing inflation's volatility. Under the compulsory private pension system, most formal sector employees pay 10% of their salaries into privately managed funds.

Total foreign direct investment (FDI) was only US$3.4 billion in 2006, up 52% from a poor performance in 2005. However, 80% of FDI continues to go to only four sectors: electricity, gas, water, and mining. Much of the jump in FDI in 2006 was also the result of acquisitions and mergers, and has done little to create new employment in Chile. The Chilean government has formed a Council on Innovation and Competition, which is tasked with identifying new sectors and industries to promote. It is hoped that this, combined with some tax reforms to encourage domestic and foreign investment in research and development, will bring in additional FDI to new parts of the economy. In 2007, the OECD approved a "roadmap to accession" for Chile, which is still in process. The government of Chile has indicated its willingness to revisit bank secrecy laws.

  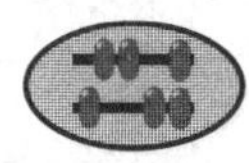   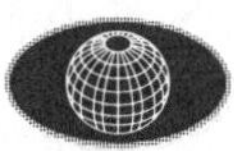   

SUPPORT FOR INWARD INVESTMENT AND IMPORTS

CORFO, the Chilean Economic Development Agency, was founded in 1939 to encourage economic growth in Chile by promoting investment, innovation, and business cluster development. The InvestChile program was created by CORFO in 2000 specifically to encourage foreign investment, with a specific focus on technological companies, and companies looking to relocate to Chile. There are incentives and services available for investors. Contact CORFO and InvestChile for information.

TAX EXEMPTIONS

There is a range of incentives available; further information is available from InvestChile.

➤➤ MORE INFO

Websites:

Chilean Government website: www.chileangovernment.cl

Chilean Investment Agency: www.investchile.com

China

ECONOMY AND TRADE

China is the world's second-largest economy after the United States, although in per capita terms it remains low-to-middle income. Until 1978, China had a centrally planned economy and was largely closed to the outside world. In the 1990s, the government restructured China's state-owned enterprises, and encouraged foreign investment. Following WTO membership in December 2001, the process of "lifting the bamboo curtain" accelerated, and China is now the leading exporter of electronics, textiles, and other manufactured goods. It has a massive current-account surplus. After pegging its currency to the US dollar, China revalued the yuan in July 2005. The currency has since appreciated by some 20% against a basket of currencies. China is struggling to maintain growth at above 8%, in the face of reduced demand for its exports. Agriculture contributes 12% of GDP, but employs 45% of the workforce. Industry contributes 48%, and services 40%. The main trading partners are the United States, Japan, South Korea, Germany, and Taiwan.

ECONOMIC POLICY OVER 12 MONTHS

2008 was a turning point for China. The government was previously confident that it would continue to be able to grow GDP by in excess of 10% a year through the "pillar" of export-led growth. However, by October 2008, the country's leadership acknowledged this goal would be impossible, owing to reduced global demand for Chinese exports.

The government of Prime Minister Wen Jiabao has since sought to rebalance the economy, away from exports and towards domestic consumer demand. David Dollar, the World Bank's country director, said, in March 2009: "We're encouraging China to look to a new growth model that depends more on domestic demand and domestic needs."

Between September and November 2008, China took various initiatives designed to keep economic growth above the psychologically important figure of 8%. These included interest-rate cuts, reduced bank reserve ratio requirements, export tax rebates, and the abolition of stamp duty on stock purchases.

The government unveiled a massive US$586bn economic stimulus package in November 2008. The stimulus funds, which are to be used from 2008 to 2010, represent about 15% of China's annual GDP.

Several measures are aimed at sections of the population who are suffering hardship as a result of the economic downturn, including rural dwellers. Citizens are being offered rebates on the purchase of refrigerators, air conditioners, televisions, and washing machines.

The stimulus package also included an easing of credit restrictions, an expansion of social welfare services, and massive spending on infrastructure. The government also intends to accelerate the phasing-out of backward and pollution-causing production processes in industries, including cars, iron, and steel.

The People's Bank of China cut rates five times between September 2008 and March 2009, by which time the benchmark interest rate had fallen to 5.31%. The central bank signaled there was scope for further cuts.

The government is sticking with its target of 8% growth in 2009. The Communist Party believes that, if growth falls below this level, it would cause mass unemployment, and spark social unrest. However, external forecasters believe that 8% is an unrealistic target. In March 2009, the World Bank reduced its forecast for 2009 growth from 7.5% to 6.5%, saying China could not "escape the impact of global weakness."

The country's latest five-year plan, approved in March 2006, made environmental protection a top priority, and channels investment into all forms of renewable energy—including wind, solar, and hydroelectric power.

STATISTICS

GDP growth: 9.8% (2008, est.)

GDP per capita: US$6,100

CPI: 6% (2008, est.)

Key interest rate: 5.31% (March 2009, Xinhua news agency)

Exchange rate: RMB per US dollar—6.82 (March 2009, xe.com)

Unemployment: 4.2% in urban areas (Beijing government, figure could be 9% if rural areas are included)

FDI: US$758.9 billion

Current account surplus US$368.2bn (2008, est.)

Population: 1.338 billion (July 2009, est.)

Source: CIA Factbook except where stated

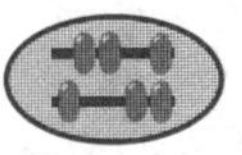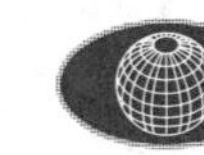

ECONOMIC PERFORMANCE OVER 12 MONTHS

China has ridden out the economic downturn far better than Europe or the United States, although the slump in the United States and Europe has hurt its export sector, causing factory closures and job losses. By March 2009, the Beijing government estimated that 20 million rural migrant workers had lost their jobs and returned home.

Economic growth fell from 13% in 2007 to 9% in 2008. By the fourth quarter of 2008, it had fallen again, this time to 6.8%. Organizations including the World Bank and the OECD predict that growth will range between 6.5% and 7.5% in 2009, the slowest rate for more than seven years. The slowdown was also, paradoxically, partly brought on by earlier government measures intended to prevent the economy from overheating.

Inflation has been falling as a result of the slowdown, and the official figures in early 2009 pointed to deflation not inflation. The rate soared to a 12-year high of 8.7% in February 2008, largely due to shortages of grain and pork. However, it had entered negative territory (–1.7%) by February 2009. A World Bank report published in December 2008 said: "After absorbing higher food and energy prices, headline inflation has receded and, with sharply lower raw commodity prices, inflation is not a concern at this point."

There are also signs in early 2009 that China's economy is stabilizing. "The nation is weathering the global slowdown better than many countries, because its banks were largely unscathed by the financial crisis, and the government quickly implemented the stimulus," the World Bank said, in a quarterly report published in March 2009.

However, the World Bank warned that falling exports are likely to slow both investment and job creation in China. The bank said it expected 16–17 million non-farm jobs to disappear during 2009, and argued that the best way to avoid social unrest would be to introduce a more effective welfare system.

The World Bank also indicated that, even though China's leadership regards maintaining growth at or above 8% as critical to maintaining social stability and securing its own legitimacy, the country will not suffer in the event of growth falling below this level. However the Washington-based institution told Beijing that introducing "a social safety net" would ease the transition to slower growth.

As a result of its strong exports and modest imports, China holds about US$2 trillion in foreign-exchange reserves, mainly in the US dollar. Its current account surplus stood at US$440 billion, as of end of 2008, up 20% over the previous year, according to government statistics.

SUPPORT FOR INWARD INVESTMENT AND IMPORTS

There are several inward investment agencies, which are able to offer assistance as part of a one-stop shop approach. The Beijing government said, in March 2009, that it would accelerate reforms of the administrative procedures for the examination and approval of foreign direct investment projects. In particular, the government said it would give greater autonomy to local authorities, and to economic and technological development zones in weighing up individuals proposals.

TAX EXEMPTIONS

The central government will consider allocating additional incentives to inward investors' fields including high technology, biotechnology, and renewable energy. Local government authorities are already competing vigorously with each other to attract investment, and foreign investors tend to be offered a range of incentives to encourage them to locate in a particular province.

›› MORE INFO

Websites:

Invest in China: www.fdi.gov.cn

Invest in Yantai, China: www.yantaifdi.gov.cn

China Business Guide: www.cbg.net.cn

China Council for the Promotion of International Trade: www.ccpit.org

State Administration of Taxation: www.chinatax.gov.cn

Ministry of Finance: www.mof.gov.cn

See Also:

★ Viewpoint: Frank Feather (pp. 763–764)
★ Viewpoint: Fred Hu (pp. 195–197)
★ Viewpoint: Hamish McRae (pp. 789–790)
★ Viewpoint: Jim Rogers (pp. 232–234)
★ Viewpoint: Linda Yueh (pp. 270–271)
★ Managing Liquidity in China—Challenging Times (pp. 81–84)

Colombia

ECONOMY AND TRADE

Colombia, along with Ecuador and Venezuela, emerged from the collapse of Gran Colombia in 1830. The country went through an extremely turbulent period in the last four decades of the 20th century, with government forces battling anti-government insurgency groups, with FARC (the Revolutionary Armed Forces of Colombia) being the main grouping. Although domestic security has greatly improved, insurgent attacks continue, and large areas of the countryside are not under government control. There is also crossover between paramilitary groups and out-and-out criminal groups aligned with Colombia's drug trafficking. Nevertheless, strong fiscal reforms and a business-friendly, pro-market economic environment have helped Colombia to generate sustained growth in the period from 2002 to 2007, before the current global downturn took hold. As a result, Colombia has managed to reduce poverty by 20% and cut unemployment by 25% since 2002. The US–Colombia Trade Promotion Agreement (CTPA) negotiations have also helped to attract record levels of foreign investment. Inequality, underemployment, and narcotics trafficking remain significant challenges.

  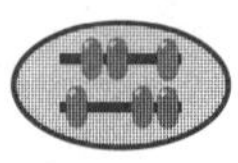   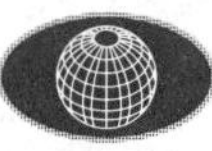   

ECONOMIC POLICY OVER 12 MONTHS

In its latest country report on Colombia, the International Monetary Fund (IMF) praised the country for its sound economic policies, and wide-ranging structural reforms. Colombia's growth since 2003 has outstripped the regional average by a substantial margin, particularly from 2005 to 2007. Underpinning this growth has been a sharp increase in private investment, itself a testimony to a more stable domestic environment, and the government's business-friendly policies. Substantial foreign direct investments led the Colombian currency to appreciate strongly over this period, although the peso is now depreciating rapidly.

Export growth was solid and broad-based, prior to Colombia's main export markets being driven into recession by the global downturn. The government has also worked hard to impose fiscal discipline, forcing down what was a hugely excessive public debt ratio, which is now much closer to the average for emerging market economies with investment-grade debt status. According to the IMF, the composition of the public debt has also improved, thanks to a significant reduction in exposure to exchange-rate fluctuations and rollover risks. External debt has fallen sharply, too, and the country is now much less reliant on raising foreign debt. At the same time, international reserves have increased significantly.

Moving to a flexible exchange-rate regime has enhanced the Colombian economy's ability to withstand shocks. Because foreign participation in Colombian financial markets is limited, and the markets have accumulated significant liquidity buffers, the country is generally in a strong position to confront the challenges posed by the current state of the global economy, the IMF judges.

Inflation is a problem throughout the region. In November 2008, inflation stood at 7.73%, down from 7.94% a month earlier but still a good deal above the Colombian Central Bank's (Banco de la Republica Colombia, BRD) target of between 3% and 4%. Commenting on its decision to lower its intervention interest rate by 50 basis points in December 2008, the BRD argued that inflation was now the lesser problem, and that world inflation in general can be expected to decrease through 2009 as a result of the global slowdown, which will hit commodity prices. Therefore, the BDR reasons, as long as the Colombian exchange rate holds up, and the government implements appropriate commercial policies, particularly with respect to food imports, the reduction in global inflation should feed through "relatively quickly" to consumer prices in Colombia. Thus, the BRD no longer felt it necessary to keep interest rates high, particularly in the face of weakening production activity figures from industry and commerce. "Weaker growth in demand and output means less inflationary pressure," it announced in a press release in December 2008.

STATISTICS

GDP growth: 3.5%
GDP per capita: US$9,000
CPI: 7.7%
Key interest rate: 15.6%
Exchange rate versus dollar: peso per US dollar—2.243
Unemployment: 11.8 per cent
FDI: US$65.69 billion
Current account deficit: −U$5.592 billion
Population: 45,644,023
Source: CIA Factbook except where stated

ECONOMIC PERFORMANCE OVER 12 MONTHS

Economic growth slipped in 2008 as a result of the global financial crisis, and weakening demand for Colombia's exports. It declined from 7.25% in the second half of 2007 to 4% in the first half of 2008, and finished the year on 4.1%, according to Colombian government statistics. In response, the administration has cut capital controls, arranged for emergency credit lines from multilateral institutions, and promoted investment incentives, such as Colombia's modernized free trade zone mechanism, legal stability contracts, and new bilateral investment treaties and trade agreements. The government has also encouraged exporters to diversify their customer base away from the United States and Venezuela, Colombia's largest trading partners.

Nevertheless, the business sector continues to be concerned about the impact of a global recession on Colombia's exports, as well as the approval of the CTPA, which is stalled in the US Congress. The BDR has issued long-term guidance on its interest-rate policy for 2009 to 2011. The broad target figure for inflation for 2009, the BDR says, is now 4–5%. The rate for 2010 is being tentatively set at 4%, with the following year's target being 3%, plus or minus 1%.

Colombia's exchange rate has been highly volatile. The peso appreciated by about 15% in real terms between the end of 2007 and mid-June 2008, according to the IMF. Then the BDR stepped up its foreign-exchange auctions, which it introduced in March 2008. Instead of monthly US$150 million purchases, it began doing US$20 million daily purchases in the spot market, and, at the same time, it raised reserve requirements on deposits. A steady weakening of the peso forced it to abandon daily purchases in early October. During the second half of 2008, the peso's real rate weakened by an estimated 20%.

In the view of the IMF, the Colombian government has done better than most, in that it has managed to ensure, through funding obtained from external sources for 2009, that the public sector will be able to meet its external financing requirements without having to tap the markets. The state-owned foreign trade bank, Bancoldex, has been funded externally, as well, and is able to provide loans to banks and corporates if there is disruption to external credit lines. Although asset values have dropped, as is normal in a sharp downturn, the IMF reckons that all the key financial soundness indicators in the economy remain solid. Non-performing loan ratios (NPLs) have risen, particularly for consumer credit, but banks are well provisioned, it says.

SUPPORT FOR INWARD INVESTMENT AND IMPORTS

There are only a few sectors of the economy that are prohibited to foreign investors (defense, and investment in real estate, other than to build premises for the investing company). In all other sectors, according to accountants, KPMG, it is sufficient to register the investment with the BDR. According to the World Competitiveness Yearbook, Colombia ranks no. 1 among the leading economies in Latin America in terms of the availability of skilled labor, and is second as far as qualified managers is concerned.

TAX EXEMPTIONS

The country has 10 duty-free zones that provide customs, exchange, and fiscal benefits (source: www.proexport.com.co).

▸▸ MORE INFO

Websites:

Banco de la Republica Colombia: www.banrep.gov.co

President's Office, Colombia: web.presidencia.gov.co/English/index.html

Cook Islands

ECONOMY AND TRADE

Named after Captain Cook, who sighted them in 1770, the islands became a British protectorate in 1888. By 1900, administrative control was transferred to New Zealand; in 1965, residents chose self-government in free association with New Zealand. The emigration of skilled workers to New Zealand, and government deficits are continuing problems. Like many other South Pacific island nations, the Cook Islands' economic development is hindered by the isolation of the country from foreign markets, the limited size of domestic markets, lack of natural resources, periodic devastation from natural disasters, and inadequate infrastructure. Agriculture, employing about one-third of the working population, provides the economic base, with major exports made up of copra and citrus fruit. Black pearls are the Cook Islands' leading export. Manufacturing activities are limited to fruit processing, clothing, and handicrafts. Trade deficits are offset by remittances from emigrants, and by foreign aid, overwhelmingly from New Zealand.

ECONOMIC POLICY OVER 12 MONTHS

In the 1980s and 1990s, the country lived beyond its means, maintaining a bloated public service, and accumulating a large foreign debt. Subsequent reforms, including the sale of state assets, the strengthening of economic management, the encouragement of tourism, and a debt-restructuring agreement, have rekindled investment and growth. In the 2008–2009 Budget, Finance Minister, Sir Terepai Maoate, said that the country's Standard and Poor's rating had improved from BB– to BB, with a positive outlook over the year as a result of prudent fiscal management. The government's goal is to provide a stable fiscal platform to enable the private sector to grow. The long-term principles guiding the Islands' fiscal policy were set out in the Ministry of Finance & Economic Management Act 1995–1996, the Act that started the move back to fiscal prudence. The goals include ensuring that unless Crown debt is at prudent levels, operating expenses will always be less than operating revenues, which means that the Act mandates an operating surplus. The Act also makes the government responsible for achieving and maintaining levels of Crown net worth that provide a buffer against future shocks. It also constrains government to ensure "a reasonable degree of predictability" about the level and stability of tax rates. While the current budget does look to external financing to build long-term infrastructure, it aims to keep such borrowing within prudent limits.

In July 2008, a Cook Islands delegation and the European Investment Bank (EIB) met to explore infrastructure funding loans. That meeting, led by Sir Terepai Maoate, went well for the Islands, and the EIB agreed to provide funding for water and sanitation developments, with the Rarotonga Apopo and Aitutaki Apopo infrastructure plans being uppermost there. The EIB also indicated that it would support alternative energy prospects to minimize the impact of climate change, and that loans for this purpose would attract very low interest rates. Loans would be in New Zealand dollars rather than euros, so the Islands will not be exposed to foreign-currency risks. The EIB also approved a NZ$5 million facility for the Bank of the Cook Islands (BCI) for private-sector initiatives, with repayments to be spread over the next 15 years. This was the first facility the BCI had obtained from the EIB.

STATISTICS

GDP growth: 0.1%
GDP per capita: US$9,100
CPI: 2.1% (2005)
Key interest rate: N/A
Exchange rate versus dollar: NZ dollars per US dollar—1.4151
Unemployment: 13.1%
FDI: N/A
Current account deficit/surplus: US$26.6 million (2005)
Population: 11,870
Source: CIA Factbook except where stated

ECONOMIC PERFORMANCE OVER 12 MONTHS

Recognizing that developing the skills of its people is crucial to building the nation, stimulating future exports, and attracting foreign inward investment, the government has committed to providing New Zealand and other internationally recognized tertiary qualifications through trades training institutions. Although there are already incentives in place to encourage Cook Islanders to return and contribute to

sustainable economic growth—the brain and skills drain to New Zealand, in particular, is seen as tremendously damaging—the government is committed to reviewing existing incentives. It also plans to put resources into a communications strategy to publicize this campaign to bring Cook Islanders home. Because the private sector is recognized to be a key growth driver, the government is bringing out a new Economic Sector Plan, which will look at where government intervention in the economy can be made successfully. With agriculture, fisheries, and pearls key to the Islands' export capabilities, there are plans for the government to help with promotional activities for commercial fisheries. The island has discovered reserves of manganese nodules in sufficient quantities to provide real economic value to the Islands. However, the government plans to ensure that extraction will not involve any detriment to the marine ecosystem, which is being managed in a long-term sustainable fashion.

Ensuring economic growth for the Outer Islands is a perennial problem for government. In 2009, it plans to work on ensuring reliable and effective access to markets for the Outer Islands, where there are challenges to be faced in regard to both sea and air transportation. One option being explored is for the government to provide storage for exports. With tourism being the main driver for the Islands' economy, the fact that the Cook Islands will be hosting the 2009 Pacific Mini Games is seen as highly important. A review of the Islands' telecommunications infrastructure is also planned.

The two main indicators of short-term economic performance on the Islands are VAT receipts, and visitor numbers. The government says that exceptional growth was recorded in VAT receipts through to the end of the 2007–2008 fiscal year, when it reported 7.9% growth, up 20% on the figure for 2006. Visitor numbers also increased, but at a much slower rate—by 5.1% between 2006 and 2007, and by just 3.0% between 2007 and 2008. The global slowdown is expected to keep growth in visitor numbers depressed through 2009. The Consumer Price Index (CPI) increased by 4.1% between December 2006 and December 2007, and the final CPI for 2007–2008 is expected to be around 4.3%, with the price of oil being the major cause of rising price inflation. However, that is expected to fall back in 2009.

SUPPORT FOR INWARD INVESTMENT AND IMPORTS

Non-Cook Islanders seeking permission to reside or do business in the Cook Islands are regulated by the Development Investment Act 1995–1996, which means that they have to get prior approval, and register their planned activities. Applications must be made to the Cook Islands Development Investment Board. The Board's investment code states that, generally, provision should be made in the case of a new foreign investment for the acquisition of equity by or on behalf of Cook Islanders, or for joint ventures with enterprises owned or controlled by Cook Islanders. In broad terms, the more equity in any joint venture Cook Islanders will have, the greater the chances of success for the application.

TAX EXEMPTIONS

There are some exemptions. The Cook Islands Development Investment Board can provide details.

MORE INFO

Websites:

Cook Islands Government: www.cook-islands.gov.ck

Ministry of Finance and Economic Management: www.mfem.gov.ck

Croatia

ECONOMY AND TRADE

The lands that today comprise Croatia were part of the Austro-Hungarian Empire until the close of World War I. In 1918, the Croats, Serbs, and Slovenes formed a kingdom known after 1929 as Yugoslavia. Following World War II, Yugoslavia became a federal, independent, communist state under the rule of Marshal Tito. Although Croatia declared its independence from Yugoslavia in 1991, it took four years of sporadic, but often bitter, fighting before occupying Serb armies were mostly cleared from Croatian lands. Under UN supervision, the last Serb-held enclave in eastern Slavonia was returned to Croatia in 1998. Once one of the wealthiest of the Yugoslav republics, Croatia's economy suffered badly during the 1991–1995 war, as output collapsed, and the country missed the early waves of investment in Central and Eastern Europe that followed the fall of the Berlin Wall. Since 2000, however, Croatia's economic fortunes have begun to improve. A rebound in tourism, and credit-driven consumer spending helped the country's economy to generate growth, although unemployment remains high.

ECONOMIC POLICY OVER 12 MONTHS

The government faces some severe challenges, all of which are being made more difficult by the global downturn. Unemployment remains high, the country faces a growing trade deficit, and the regions are developing at different speeds, with some lagging behind badly. The role of the state in the economy, a legacy of Croatia's socialist past, is generally regarded as too high, but there is considerable public resist-

STATISTICS

GDP growth: 4.8%
GDP per capita: US$16,900
CPI: 6.3%
Key interest rate: 9.33%
Exchange rate versus dollar: Kuna per US dollar—4.98 (2008)
Unemployment: 14.8% (2008)
FDI: US$19.5
Current account deficit: –U$6.156 billion
Population: 4,489,409 (July 2008)
Source: CIA Factbook except where stated

  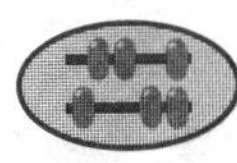      

ance to moves to privatize state assets. Similarly, public opposition makes it extremely difficult for the government to move forward on structural reforms.

However, at the time of writing, Croatia was due to become a full member of NATO at the next NATO summit in April 2009 (along with Albania). Croatia received an invitation to join NATO at the April 2008 NATO summit in Bucharest.

Perhaps more importantly for the immediate economic prospects of the country, Croatia is also bidding to join the European Union. However, its accession to EU membership is being blocked by its neighbor, Slovenia, with whom it has a long-running border dispute (Croatia first opened EU accession negotiations in 2005).

In its 2009 Budget, issued in October 2008, the Croat government said that it planned to reduce its budget deficit to close to zero through 2009, while maintaining economic growth at around 4%. In the budget, Croat finance minister, Ivan Suker, said the country was moving towards a balanced budget, while ensuring the refinancing of its maturing debt. He also announced that Croatia plans to draw all US$1.8 billion of available loans from a four-year partnership framework agreement with the World Bank. The Bank regards Croatia as an upper-middle-income country and a fully fledged market economy. It welcomes the fact that Croatia has opened its economy to global markets, through membership of both the World Trade Organization and the Central European Free Trade Agreement (CEFTA). According to the World Bank, Croatia's main development objective is to reach 75% of the EU's average per capita income by 2013. Today, with the per capita income of Croatian citizens being around US$11,500, it has only reached around 56% of the European Uniomn average. To join the European Union, the country will have to make further progress on judicial and public administration reforms, competition, anti-corruption policies, and environmental issues and agriculture. However, the EU Commission announced early in 2009 that Croatia is well placed to conclude its accession negotiations by November 2009.

ECONOMIC PERFORMANCE OVER 12 MONTHS.

In the first decade after independence in 1991, the country built the structures of a new state, created a new currency, and repaired large-scale war damages. It initiated reforms for the transition to a market economy so successfully that, by 1997, the country was awarded an investment-grade rating. The economy has been growing moderately since the 1990s: at a rate of 4–5% on average, with investments and private consumption being the main growth contributors. Output has now recovered to the pre-war level, but state aid to industry in 2008 remains almost triple the EU15 level.

With a high level of public spending, at about 49% of GDP, which is 9 percentage points of GDP above the public spending levels in new EU member states, Croatia has one of the largest public sectors in Europe. The high level of public spending contributed significantly to the progressive increase in the country's overall indebtedness. The external debt-to-GDP ratio, in US dollar terms, stood at 95.2% at the end of 2007. In this context, the country's 2009 Budget announcement is being widely welcomed as a sign that the debt issue is at last being addressed seriously (source: World Bank country report). On another positive note, more than 90% of Croatian bank assets are now held by the private sector, and public confidence in the banking system has been restored, following the country's banking crisis of 1998. The telecommunications, transport, and energy sectors have all benefited from market liberalization, and there is now a high level of competition, in particular in the mobile phone market. More than one-third of the population are Internet users, and "e-government" has become a priority of the current government. Railway restructuring is gaining pace, with full market liberalization scheduled for early 2010. Since 2008, all energy consumers are free to choose their energy provider, either within the country or from abroad.

Interest has been strengthened in long-term foreign direct investment in Croatia since EU talks started in 2005. FDI amounted to around US$4.6 billion in 2007, an increase of 45% compared to 2006. However, additional efforts are needed to boost the investment climate so that the private sector can prosper. Croatia's private-sector share of GDP increased from 60% to 70% in the period from 2003 to 2007 (source: World Bank). A tightening of monetary policy helped to stabilize a worrying growth of domestic credit expansion. Croatia's current-account deficit is still widening, but falling oil and commodity prices should have a positive impact. The deficit reached 8.6% of GDP in 2007, and is expected to pass 9% in 2008, before narrowing again in 2009.

SUPPORT FOR INWARD INVESTMENT AND IMPORTS

While Croatia has a good macroeconomic framework, and sufficient infrastructure, there are continuing weaknesses in the judiciary. The World Bank has been urging Croatia to improve the investment climate.

TAX EXEMPTIONS

Croatia operates a number of business zones, which offer direct and indirect state incentives. See www.apiu.hr for details, or contact the Ministry of Economy, Labor, and Entrepreneurship.

›› MORE INFO

Websites:

Government of Croatia (in English): www.vlada.hr/en

World Bank country briefing report on Croatia: www.worldbank.hr

  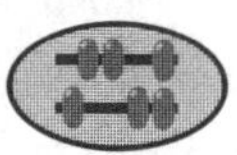   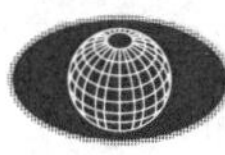   

Cyprus

ECONOMY AND TRADE

A former British colony, the island of Cyprus became independent in 1960 following years of resistance to British rule. Tensions between the Greek Cypriot majority and Turkish Cypriot minority ultimately culminated in an armed clash between Greece and Turkey, in 1974, which left more than one-third of northern Cyprus under Turkish control (Turkish Republic of Northern Cyprus, TRNC). In September 2008, the Turkish and Cypriot governments reopened unification negotiations under the auspices of the United Nations. The entire island joined the European Union in 2004, but the EU's writ is suspended for the area under Turkish control. The economic performances of the two sides of the island tend to be evaluated separately, as they are under the de facto control of two different governments. The Turkish side has roughly 40% of the per capita GDP of the southern, Greek Cypriot side, and one-third of its budget is financed directly by Turkey.

ECONOMIC POLICY OVER 12 MONTHS

On the Turkish side of the divide, agriculture and services employ around 50% of the population, with the state employing most of the remaining workforce. The Turkish enclave's fortunes are highly dependent on mainland Turkey, which has been heavily hit by the global slowdown. The Turkish Cypriot economy grew by around 10.6% in 2006, fueled by growth in the construction and education sectors, as well as increased employment of Turkish Cypriots in the area under Greek Cypriot government control. However, the Turkish side proved highly susceptible to the first signs of the global downturn, and GDP declined by about 2.0% in 2007. Turkish Cypriots are heavily dependent on transfers from the Turkish government. Ankara directly finances around one-third of the TRNC's budget. Aid from Turkey has exceeded US$400 million annually in recent years. The Turkish Cypriot economy looks certain to experience a sharp slowdown in 2008–2009, as a result of the global financial crisis. The Turkish Cypriot financial sector is dominated by mainland Turkish banks, and relies heavily on the hard-hit British and Turkish markets for tourism.

On the Cypriot side, the economy is market-based and dominated by the service sector, which accounts for 78% of GDP. Tourism, financial services, and real estate are the most important sectors. Erratic growth rates over the past decade reflect the economy's reliance on tourism, which often fluctuates with political instability in the region, and economic conditions in Western Europe. Nevertheless, the Greek Cypriot economy has grown at a rate well above the EU average since 2000. Cyprus joined the European Exchange Rate Mechanism (ERM2) in May 2005, and adopted the euro as its national currency on January 1, 2008. An aggressive austerity program in the preceding years, aimed at paving the way for the euro, helped turn a soaring fiscal deficit (6.3% in 2003) into a surplus of 1.2% in 2008. This prosperity will come under pressure in 2009, as construction and tourism slow in the face of reduced foreign demand, triggered by the ongoing global financial crisis. Growth is expected by many outside observers, including the International Monetary Fund (IMF), to slow to less than 2%, which would be its lowest level since 2003. As in the area administered by Turkish Cypriots, water shortages are a perennial problem; a few desalination plants have been added to existing plants over the last year, and are now on line. After 10 years of drought, the country received substantial rainfall over 2001–2004. Since then, rainfall has been well below average, making water rationing a necessity.

ECONOMIC PERFORMANCE OVER 12 MONTHS

In the first half of 2007, the Cypriot economy grew at a rate of 4%, a strong enough growth for Cyprus to feel confident about adopting the euro with effect from January 1, 2008. On December 5, 2008, Cypriot Finance Minister, Charilaos Stavrakis, presented the 2009 state budget, which underlined the fact that 2009 is expected to be a very difficult year because of the international economic slowdown. Despite this, the budget anticipated growth of 3%, which is at least 1 percentage point higher than most external analysts are anticipating. However, Stavrakis said that while it was possible that the government is being overoptimistic, a slightly lower growth rate would not affect implementation of the budget. The European Commission's expectation for GDP growth in Cyprus for 2009 is just 1.1%.

Even with the downturn, Cyprus managed to retain near-full employment in 2008, and this is expected to continue into 2009. If the government is successful in its prediction of a borderline fiscal surplus for 2009, then public debt is expected to be reduced to below 48% of GDP. Inflation is expected to decline during 2009 to 2.5%. Growth for 2008 looks to have been of the order of 3.7–3.8%, well above the EU-wide growth rate of 1.4%. Cypriot banks had minimal exposure to the toxic investment projects which destroyed much of the United States, United Kingdom, and European banking systems.

Despite the downturn, the Cypriot government has increased budget spending by 11%, by comparison with 2008, with €7.37 billion in expenditure, and initial estimated revenues of €6.41 billion. Dramatically

STATISTICS (not incl. TRNC)

GDP growth: 3.6% (2008)
GDP per capita: US$29,200
CPI: 5.1% (2008)
Key interest rate: 6.74% (December 2007)
Exchange rate versus dollar: euro per US dollar: 1.325 (April 2009)
Unemployment: 3.8%
FDI: U$15.04 billion
Current account deficit/surplus: −US$2.609 billion
Population: 792,604
Source: CIA Factbook except where stated

  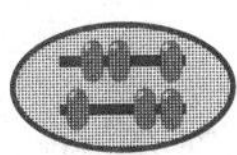      

reduced capital gains tax receipts resulting from companies on the island making less profit because of the downturn, have reduced government revenue expectations by €165 million, Stavrakis said.

The government promised no new taxes for 2009, but anticipates putting in place the biggest social spending round for 10 years, with the budget for social spending increasing by 26%. Development spending will increase by 15.5%. The main challenges faced by the Cyprus economy, the minister said, was an ageing population, which weighs heavily on the island's social security fund, and the need to bear down on consumer goods' pricing now that oil and gas prices have slumped.

For the Turkish Cypriot side, tourism remains the major growth industry, with some agriculture, with the main products being citrus fruits, grapes, and vine production. High freight costs and the shortage of skilled labor are perennial difficulties, as is the isolation of the northern part of the island. Some flexibility and movement of trade between the north and south sides of the island have helped the economy. In August 2004, new EU rules paved the way for north Cypriot goods to be sold in the south, and, a year later the Turkish Cypriot authorities responded by allowing some goods from Cyprus to be sold in northern Cyprus, although trade between the two sides remains limited.

SUPPORT FOR INWARD INVESTMENT AND IMPORTS

The Cyprus Investment Promotion Agency (CIPA) is the body that promotes foreign direct investment (FDI). The Cyprus government has removed all distinctions between foreign and local companies. State grants of up to €200,000 are available for new high-tech start-ups in special business incubators.

TAX EXEMPTIONS

Cyprus has the lowest corporate tax rate in the European Union at 10%, with a top rate of personal tax of 30%. CIPA can supply further information.

▸▸ MORE INFO

Websites:

Ministry of Finance, Cyprus: www.mof.gov.cy

Central Bank of Cyprus (those interested should see in particular speeches by the Governor of the Bank): www.centralbank.gov.cy

Czech Republic

ECONOMY AND TRADE

Following the First World War, the closely related Czechs and Slovaks of the former Austro-Hungarian Empire merged to form Czechoslovakia. With the collapse of Soviet authority in 1989, Czechoslovakia regained its freedom, and, on January 1, 1993, the country underwent a "velvet divorce" into its two national components, the Czech Republic and Slovakia. The Czech Republic joined NATO in 1999, and the European Union in 2004. The country has one of the most stable and prosperous economies in Central and Eastern Europe. Maintaining an open investment climate has been a key element of the Czech Republic's transition from a Communist, centrally planned economy to a functioning market economy. Its strong industrial tradition dates to the 19th century, when Bohemia and Moravia were the industrial heartland of the Austro-Hungarian Empire. Strong foreign direct investment (FDI) inflows are rapidly modernizing the country's industrial base and increasing productivity.

The principal industries are motor vehicles, machine-building, iron and steel production, metalworking, chemicals, electronics, transportation equipment, textiles, glass, brewing, china, ceramics, and pharmaceuticals. The main agricultural products are sugar beet, fodder roots, potatoes, wheat, and hops.

ECONOMIC POLICY OVER 12 MONTHS

As a member of the European Union, with an advantageous location in the center of Europe, a relatively low cost structure, and a well-qualified labor force, the Czech Republic is an attractive destination for foreign investment. Prior to its EU accession in 2004, the Czech government harmonized its laws and regulations with those of the European Union. The government plans to meet the criteria for joining the Eurozone around 2012.

The small, open, export-driven Czech economy grew by more than 6% annually in the period 2005–2007, and the strong growth continued throughout the first three quarters of 2008. Despite the global financial crisis, the conservative Czech financial system has remained relatively healthy. The rate of Czech economic growth, however, began to fall in the fourth quarter of 2008, mainly due to a significant drop in demand for Czech exports in Western Europe. This trend is expected to continue, with many analysts predicting that the Czech economy will contract slightly in 2009. An International Monetary Fund (IMF) country mission to the Czech Republic in November 2008 concluded that robust productivity growth, improved fiscal performances, and strong FDI inflows had put the Czech economy in a relatively comfortable position to see out the global downturn. The strong currency, the koruna, has helped to contain inflation despite sharp rises in food, fuel, and utility costs.

STATISTICS

GDP growth: 1.5% (2009, IMF)
GDP per capita: US$26,800
CPI: 3.6% (2008)
Key interest rate: 5.79% (December 31, 2008)
Exchange rate versus dollar: koruna per US dollar—17.064 (2008)
Unemployment: 6% (2008)
FDI: US$107.6 billion
Current account deficit/surplus: –US$6.46 billion (2008)
Population: 10,220,911 (July 2008)
Source: CIA Factbook except where stated

However, the IMF warned that the Czech economy would not escape unscathed from the global downturn, and the Czech authorities would have to be ready to stimulate the economy as required. Economic growth fell to 8% in 2008, and would slow sharply through 2009 to around 1.5%, the IMF said. The shrinking demand from the Eurozone, and from Germany in particular, would severely curtail both Czech exports and FDI flows into the country. At the same time, tightening credit conditions at home would affect consumer spending and corporate investment.

The country benefited from the fact that the Czech Central Bank was the first central bank in Europe to switch from a monetary tightening policy to combat inflation, to a stimulus-based approach aimed at keeping the economy moving. The bank's 75 basis-point cut in November 2008 was sharper than most commentators had expected. At the same time, falling inflation and falling commodity prices (as a result of the downturn) are projected to reduce both core and headline inflation through 2009, with headline inflation projected to fall as low as 2.5% in 2009.

ECONOMIC PERFORMANCE OVER 12 MONTHS

The higher economic growth in the Czech Republic in 2007, of 6.5%, as against the EU average of 2.9%, boosted the country's per capita GDP to 82% of the EU-27 average. The GDP figure of CZK3,558 billion was more than twice as high as the GDP achieved in the mid-1990s. FDI amounted to some €7.4 billion in 2007, with most investment going into areas of industry with a high-value-added content. Around 90% of all the inward FDI received by the Czech Republic comes from the EU-25.

Although FDI inflows will fall back in 2009, the IMF expects a sufficient inward flow to largely offset the country's modest current-account deficit. The koruna appreciated in the first half of 2008, which started to threaten Czech exports into the Eurozone, but it weakened sufficiently in the first months of 2009 to prevent too much damage. The main barrier to exports now is weak demand in the economies of the Czech Republic's main trading partners. In the IMF's view, at the exchange rates prevailing in November 2008 the koruna was broadly in line with market fundamentals, and consistent with external stability.

The Czech structural fiscal balance improved significantly in 2007, with the government's commitment to running a budget deficit of no more than 1% of GDP by 2012. As the global downturn constrains growth across Europe, the Czech Republic looks to be in a good position to stay within the Stability and Growth Pact threshold deficit of no more than 3% of GDP (although some major European countries are breaching this limit substantially as part of their economic stimulus packages). Because the government streamlined social spending very substantially in 2007, the target of a budget deficit of just 1.6% in 2009, along with cuts in corporate income tax and social security contribution rates looks achievable, the IMF says. However, it anticipates the deficit rising to 2.5% by the end of 2009. While the Czech Republic gains some benefits from having its own currency, which can devalue and, therefore, improve its export position, a considerable body of opinion is building up which favors expediting a rapid entry into the euro by the Czech Republic, Hungary, and Romania. In March 2009, World Bank President, Robert Zoellick, called for an EU-led and coordinated global support program for the economies of Central and Eastern Europe. Discussing conditions for shortening the two-year entry requirement to join the euro is one option on the table.

If the Czech government wants to stimulate the economy, its best course of action would be to bring forward planned infrastructure projects, and to work with the European Union to bring forward EU-funded projects that could help boost demand, while safeguarding the long-term fiscal position.

SUPPORT FOR INWARD INVESTMENT AND IMPORTS

CzechInvest is the investment and business development agency that aims to help potential foreign investors understand both the scope of investment opportunities in the country, and what is required. There are more than 70 municipal industrial zones, and investors locating in one of these gain access to fully serviced land at favorable prices. Tax breaks, job-creation grants, and other incentives can be applied for where greenfield projects are being initiated.

TAX EXEMPTIONS

There is a range of incentives for investors, depending on the nature of the business being set up. Further information is available from CzechInvest and the Ministry of Industry and Trade.

►► MORE INFO

Websites:

Czech site with detailed information on a range of issues, from travel to the economy: www.czech.cz

Business information on the Czech economy: www.businessinfo.cz

CzechInvest, the Investment Agency of the Czech Government: www.czechinvest.org

Denmark

ECONOMY AND TRADE

Denmark has responsibility for both Greenland and the Faroe Islands, both of which enjoy home rule, with Denmark being responsible for foreign relations, monetary affairs, and defense. The country went through two referenda (June 2, 1992 and May 18, 1993) on the Maastricht Treaty on the European Union, and secured four exemptions. It is not part of the EU common defense policy, or the euro. Its citizens are not EU citizens, and it has opted out of some legal provisions. There is considerable public determination not to lose Danish national identity in an integrated Europe.

Denmark's industrialized market economy depends on imported raw materials and foreign trade. Within the European Union, Denmark advocates a liberal trade policy. Its standard of living is among the highest in the world, and the Danes devote about 0.8% of gross national product (GNP) to foreign aid to less-developed countries. Denmark is a net exporter of food and energy. Its principal exports are machinery, instruments, and food products.

STATISTICS

GDP growth: 0.3% (2008)
GDP per capita: US$38,900 (2008)
CPI: 3.5%
Key interest rate: 4%
Exchange rate versus dollar: Danish krone to US dollar—5.0236
Unemployment: 2%
FDI: US$133.6 billion
Current account surplus: US$4.333 billion
Population: 5,484,723
Source: CIA Factbook except where stated

ECONOMIC POLICY OVER 12 MONTHS

The global financial crisis has exacerbated a slowdown in the Danish economy that began early in 2007, following a long period of steady growth. The slowdown started in the Danish housing market, and gained momentum when the financial crisis raised borrowing costs and depressed export growth, consumer confidence, and investment. However, according to an IMF country report on Denmark, published in early December 2008, most Danish banks entered the crisis with healthy capital buffers, and have coped well. The Danish practice of tightly restricting the intra-group exposures of Danish subsidiaries of foreign banks also helped considerably to avoid the "toxic asset" syndrome that has destroyed so much value in banks in other countries.

The United States is Denmark's largest non-European trading partner, accounting for about 5% of total Danish merchandise trade. Aircraft, computers, machinery, and instruments are among the major US exports to Denmark. Among major Danish exports to the United States are industrial machinery, chemical products, furniture, pharmaceuticals, canned ham and pork, windmills, and plastic toy blocks (Lego). In addition, Denmark has a significant services trade with the United States, a major share of it stemming from Danish-controlled ships engaged in container traffic to and from the United States (notably by Maersk-SeaLand). There are some 375 US-owned companies in Denmark.

The Danish economy is fundamentally strong. Since the mid-1990s, economic growth rates have averaged close to 3%, the formerly high official unemployment rate stands at around 2%, and public finances are in surplus. Except for a single year in 1998, Denmark has had comfortable balance-of-payments current-account surpluses since 1989. The surplus in 2007 was 1.1% of GDP. Denmark has maintained a stable currency policy since the early 1980s. On January 1, 1999, the krone switched from being linked to the Deutschmark, and became linked to the euro. Denmark meets, and even exceeds, the economic convergence criteria for participating in the European Monetary Union (EMU). Since the "no" referendum on the euro on September 28, 2000, there has been a change of mood, and the majority of the country now appears to favor entry into the EMU.

Danes are generally proud of their welfare safety net, which ensures that all Danes receive basic healthcare, and need not fear real poverty. However, at present, the number of working-age Danes living mostly on government transfer payments amounts to more than 680,000 persons (roughly 20% of the working-age population). This constitutes a burden on other parts of the Danish system, and remains a challenge for the government. High welfare payments certainly have an impact upon areas of government spending. Healthcare, other than for acute problems, and care for the elderly and children have particularly suffered, while taxes remain painfully high. More than one-fourth of the labor force is employed in the public sector.

ECONOMIC PERFORMANCE OVER 12 MONTHS

Although unemployment began to pick up in Denmark again after October 2008, as a result of the economic slowdown, the rate is still close to an historic low. Wage growth is more of a problem; having begun rising in mid-2007, wages are still increasing, reflecting a continuing imbalance between supply and demand, with a shortage of skilled workers despite the recession in Europe. Inflation reached just under 5% in mid-2008, according to the IMF, but ameliorated in the opening months of 2009 under the influence of falling fuel, food, and other commodity prices. The IMF warned that it is not sustainable in the medium term for Denmark to continue with poorer productivity and faster wage growth than its European counterparts.

Denmark enjoys an excellent fiscal position, with the economic boom up to 2007 generating substantial surpluses, and allowing the government to reduce its overall debt burden. The IMF expects weak growth up

to 2010, but it warns that if global growth fails to lift the world out of the downturn, a recession in Denmark will become more likely.

Pegging the krone to the euro has worked well for Denmark, holding down inflationary expectations, and keeping interest rates close to those of the Eurozone. The 2009 Danish budget strikes a good balance between allowing growth to slow in the face of record low unemployment and rapid wage growth, and the need to cushion the economy from the possibility of a slide into recession.

In March 2009, following the lead of the European Central Bank (ECB), the Danish central bank, Nationalbanken, lowered lending rates by 75 basis points, which was 25 basis points more than the ECB's rate cut, to a new low of 2.25% (as against the ECB rate of 1.5%). The Nationalbanken move reflects attempts to mitigate the strengthening of the krone against foreign currencies. The rate cut followed a similar cut of 75 basis points by the Danish central bank in January. The rate cut is expected to mean that Danish mortgage holders with a DKK1 million mortgage will save almost DKK5,000 a year, a move which the Danish government hopes will help to stimulate private spending, and boost the Danish economy. The expectation is that the Danish rate will match the ECB rate by spring 2009.

The country has topped the rankings in the World Economic Forum's Global Information Technology Report (2007–2008) for the last two years, for "outstanding levels of network readiness," and its ICT infrastructure, which has created a great environment for e-business and e-government, the report says.

SUPPORT FOR INWARD INVESTMENT AND IMPORTS

Invest in Denmark, a department of the Ministry of Foreign Affairs, argues that Denmark is a natural gateway to the Scandinavian countries and the Baltic area, with Copenhagen Airport being the main hub in Northern Europe.

TAX EXEMPTIONS

The local company tax rate is 25%, and expatriates can benefit from a special tax regime. Further information can be obtained from the Danish Ministry of Foreign Affairs. Flexible labor rules allow companies to "right-size" their work force more easily than anywhere else in Europe.

▸▸ MORE INFO

Websites:

Danish Government: www.denmark.dk/en

Invest in Denmark: www.investindk.com

Dominica

ECONOMY AND TRADE

Located about halfway between Puerto Rico and Trinidad and Tobago, Dominica was the last of the Caribbean islands to be colonized by Europeans. France ceded possession to Great Britain in 1763, which made the island a colony in 1805. In 1980, two years after independence, Dominica's fortunes improved when a corrupt and tyrannical administration was replaced by that of Mary Eugenia Charles, the first female prime minister in the Caribbean, who remained in office for 15 years. Some 3,000 Carib Indians still living on Dominica are the only pre-Columbian population remaining in the eastern Caribbean.

The Dominican economy depends on agriculture, primarily bananas, and remains highly vulnerable to climatic conditions and international economic developments. Tourism has increased as the government seeks to promote Dominica as an ecotourism destination. The government has developed a new tourism development plan, with assistance from the European Union, but the impact of this will largely have to await the ending of the current global slowdown.

ECONOMIC POLICY OVER 12 MONTHS

Hurricane Dean struck the island in August 2007 causing damage equivalent to 20% of GDP. Before this happened, the economy was rallying well, following a comprehensive restructuring of the economy, which began in 2003. This restructuring included the elimination of price controls, privatization of the state banana company, and tax increases, all of which were designed to address a severe economic crisis in 2001–2002, and which the government put in place as part of an agreement with the International Monetary Fund (IMF). The restructuring worked, and the island nation enjoyed real growth in subsequent years, with growth in 2006 reaching a two-decade high. This helped Dominica to lower its debt burden, which nevertheless remains at about 100% of GDP.

In order to diversify the island's production base, the government is attempting to develop an offshore financial sector, and has signed an agreement with the European Union to develop geothermal energy resources.

STATISTICS

GDP growth: 2.5% (2008, IMF)
GDP per capita: US$9,500
CPI: 2.4% (2006, US State Dept.)
Key interest rate: 9.17%
Exchange rate versus dollar: East Caribbean dollars to US dollar—2.7
Unemployment: 13.1% (2005, US State Dept.)
FDI: N/A
Current account deficit: –US$72 million
Population: 72,514
Source: CIA Factbook except where stated

  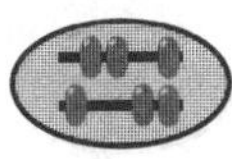   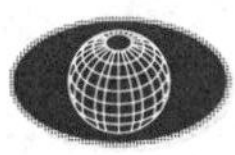   

In a report on the region in March 2009, the IMF estimated that real growth had decelerated to about 2.5% in 2008, reflecting sluggish activity in tourism and construction. Inflation accelerated during the first three quarters of 2008, but eased toward end-2008 with the retreat of world commodity prices, and slowing economic activity.

Limited fiscal consolidation achieved in 2007—reflecting higher tax revenues, and lower capital expenditure—is estimated to have unwound in 2008, due to a decline in revenues and an increase in current expenditure, with public debt standing at about 93% of regional GDP at year-end.

Real GDP right across the Eastern Caribbean region is expected to contract by about 1% in 2009, with risks tilted to the downside. According to the IMF, Dominica will have to manage risks arising from the global financial crisis and economic downturn carefully, while continuing to address fundamental issues, particularly fiscal and debt sustainability. Sharp falls of capital flows to the region (particularly foreign direct investment) will further dampen economic activity, the IMF warned.

Dominica shares the Eastern Caribbean Currency Union's (ECCU) high vulnerability to shocks, exacerbated by its elevated public debt level, all of which highlights the importance of further enhancing crisis preparedness. Additional and sustained efforts to push through structural reforms, such as tax reform, improving the business climate, and deepening regional integration, are key to enhancing competitiveness and underpinning the currency union.

ECONOMIC PERFORMANCE OVER 12 MONTHS

Agriculture dominates Dominica's economy, and nearly one-third of the labor force works in agriculture. This sector, however, is highly vulnerable to weather conditions, and to external events affecting commodity prices. In response to reduced EU banana trade preferences, the government has diversified the agricultural sector by introducing coffee, patchouli, aloe vera, cut flowers, and exotic fruits such as mangoes, guavas, and papayas. Dominica has also had some success in increasing its manufactured exports, primarily soap.

Dominica is mostly volcanic and has few beaches; therefore, tourism has developed more slowly than on neighboring islands. Nevertheless, the island's high, rugged mountains, rainforests, freshwater lakes, hot springs, waterfalls, and diving spots make it an attractive ecotourism destination. Cruise ship stopovers have increased, following the development of modern docking and waterfront facilities in the capital.

The IMF warned that recent shocks to the banking system across the Eastern Caribbean, including the saga of CL Financial Holdings in Trinidad and Tobago, and the Stanford Group in Antigua and Barbuda, underline the urgency of bringing the non-bank financial sector (including offshore financial institutions) under effective regulation. With Dominica engaged in trying to grow its offshore services, this will prove a challenge, as it will not be possible to add to the island's attractiveness as an offshore location by offering "light touch" regulation and privacy.

At the same time, 2008 saw the introduction of some major risks to the stability of the private banking system across the region, as a period of rapid private credit expansion has left the banks with deteriorating loan-books in an economic downturn. "The significance of foreign financial institutions in the ECCU also calls for strengthened cross-border regulatory cooperation and information sharing, which the Eastern Caribbean Central Bank has been pursuing," the IMF says.

"With very high public debt levels, there is little, if any, room for countercyclical fiscal policy in the ECCU. Minimizing fiscal slippages would require following through on revenue reforms (including the introduction and successful implementation of value-added taxes), containing expenditures, and enhancing efficiency (particularly public investment and civil service wage bills), and strengthening debt management. Within this framework, a well-targeted social safety net is crucial for mitigating the disproportionate impact of economic hardships on the poor," the IMF says. The region's central bank is trying to get all the island economies in the region to achieve a public-debt-to-GDP target of 60% by 2020, and Dominica still has a long way to go on that front.

After reaching a decade-high 4% growth in 2006, real output growth slowed to an average of 2% during 2007–2008, following the passage of two successive hurricanes. Fiscal performance has remained strong, posting primary surpluses averaging above 4% of GDP since 2004, despite the effects of hurricanes, and food and fuel price shocks. Looking ahead, the main challenge is to maintain this creditable fiscal performance in a hostile global environment, by prioritizing capital spending, and broadening the tax base. The Dominica administration is committed to a primary fiscal surplus target of 3% of GDP over the medium term, while reforming income taxes and strengthening safety nets to protect the most vulnerable.

SUPPORT FOR INWARD INVESTMENT AND IMPORTS

The Invest Dominica Authority provides a one-stop shop service to investors, to guide them through the various stages of investing in the country. Dominica offers free movement of capital, dividends, and profits, and an offshore legislative infrastructure. There is a range of fiscal incentives. Contact Invest Dominica for further details.

▸▸ MORE INFO

Websites:

Government of the Commonwealth of Dominica: www.dominica.gov.dm

Invest in Dominica, the agency responsible for FDI: www.investdominica.dm

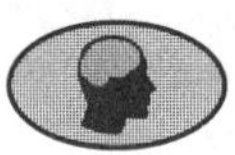

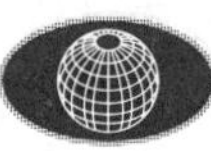

TAX EXEMPTIONS

There are various tax exemptions, including a tax holiday of up to 20 years for approved hotel and resort developments, and exemption of import duties on building materials, furniture, and fittings. The Ministry of Finance is responsible for all international business companies.

Ecuador

ECONOMY AND TRADE

What is now Ecuador formed part of the northern Inca Empire until the Spanish conquest in 1533. Quito became a seat of Spanish colonial government in 1563, and part of the Viceroyalty of New Granada in 1717. The territories of the Viceroyalty—New Granada (Colombia), Venezuela, and Quito—gained their independence between 1819 and 1822, and formed a federation known as Gran Colombia. When Quito withdrew in 1830, the traditional name was changed in favor of the Republic of the Equator. Although Ecuador marked 25 years of civilian governance in 2004, the period has been marred by political instability. Protests in Quito have contributed to the mid-term ousting of Ecuador's last three democratically elected Presidents. In 2007, a constituent assembly was elected to draft a new constitution; Ecuador's twentieth since gaining independence. The country is substantially dependent on its petroleum resources, and manufacturing is primarily for the domestic market.

STATISTICS

GDP growth: 3.4% (2008)
GDP per capita: US$7,700
CPI: 8.6% (2008)
Key interest rate: 12.5%
Exchange rate versus dollar: N/A
Unemployment: 8.7%
FDI: US$16.81 billion
Current account surplus: US$2.008 billion (2008)
Population: 14,573,101
Source: CIA Factbook except where stated

ECONOMIC POLICY OVER 12 MONTHS

The Ecuadorian economy is based on petroleum production, manufacturing (primarily for the domestic market), and agricultural production for domestic consumption and export. Principal exports are petroleum, bananas, shrimp, flowers, and other primary agricultural products.

Ecuador adopted the US dollar as its national currency in 2000, following a major banking crisis and recession in 1999. Dollarization led to stability, which helped Ecuador achieve solid economic performance up to 2006, with growth averaging 4.6% per year, supported by high oil prices, strong domestic consumer demand, increased non-traditional exports, and growing remittances (US$3 billion a year) from Ecuadorians living abroad.

President Correa's economic policies include higher social spending, increased government control over strategic sectors, and a greater share of natural resource revenues for the state. After two years in office, the overall direction of economic policy is unclear, creating uncertainty for the business community. One example of uncertain direction is debt policy, where the government initially suggested it might default, then honored the debt for almost two years, and then defaulted on some debt issuances but not others (source: US Department of State). Other examples are the fact that the government's policies for the petroleum and mining sectors were still undefined in March 2009.

An additional source of uncertainty is the new economic provisions in the 2008 constitution, which still await the issuance of implementing laws and regulations. In addition, the government is taking a number of new measures to adjust to falling petroleum revenues, and the full scope and effectiveness of those measures were unknown as of early 2009.

Ecuador is rich in natural resources, with significant oil and mineral reserves, although its mineral sector is largely undeveloped. Oil production is by both government and private companies. The state oil company, which is viewed as inefficient, operates mature oil fields that were developed by private companies in the 1970s. It has also assumed the operation of an oil field that was seized from a US oil company when that company's contract was cancelled in 2006 for alleged contract violations, an action that is being challenged in international arbitration.

Starting in 2006, the government, through laws and decrees, has changed the terms of private-sector oil contracts, and has attempted to renegotiate new contracts with those companies, although as of early 2009 it had not renegotiated any new long-term contracts. The contractual uncertainty has led to a drop in private-sector investment in the oil sector. In 2008 (until November), overall oil production had fallen slightly since 2007, and significantly since 2006. State oil-company production rose slightly, but private production fell. Ecuador is a member of OPEC.

ECONOMIC PERFORMANCE OVER 12 MONTHS

In 2007, crude and refined petroleum products accounted for 58% of total export earnings. Ecuador is the world's largest exporter of bananas and plantains (about US$1.3 billion), and a major exporter of shrimp (US$613 million). Exports of non-traditional products such as flowers (US$469 million), canned fish (US$671 million), and automobiles (US$383 million) have grown in recent years (all trade data from 2007).

   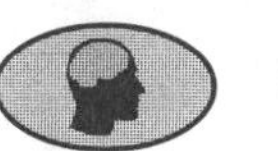     

Per capita income increased from US$1,296 in 2000 to an estimated US$3,670 in 2008, while the poverty rate fell from 51% in 2000 to 38% in 2006. In 2007, economic growth slowed, constrained by declining petroleum production and reduced private-sector investment, but appeared to recover somewhat in 2008, due to increased government spending and strong domestic demand.

By the end of 2008, it was clear that the global financial crisis and economic downturn were resulting in falling remittances sent home from Ecuadorians abroad, and falling oil prices. In January 2009, the government invoked the World Trade Organization (WTO) balance of payments safeguard provision to increase tariffs, and impose quotas on consumer goods that exceed its WTO bindings. These provisions will be evaluated by the WTO. The government also announced that it is cutting or restricting public-sector spending, although it did not provide many specifics on how it would do so.

In early 2008, an International Monetary Fund (IMF) country visit to Ecuador found some positives, including the healthy performance of non-oil exports, which led it to conclude that Ecuador's dollarized system had not generated competitiveness issues. That said, the IMF noted that Ecuador's investment and production trends lag behind other economies in the region. Among the clearest examples of this was the state oil company and the state-owned electricity company, both of which have a history of underinvestment.

The current president of Ecuador, Rafael Correa, is both left-wing and an admirer of Venezuela's president, Hugo Chavez. Opposed to increasing economic ties to the United States, President Correa is keen to address the corruption in Ecuadorian society, which is said to be far-reaching. A former university professor, Correa has a graduate degree in economics, but has yet to demonstrate that he can give clear direction to the country. The government has passed some far-reaching tax reforms, which exempt low-income earners, and progressively tax higher-income earners up to a maximum of 35%.

On the plus side, the region is one of the fastest-growing Internet markets in the world, and the entrepreneurial spirit of Ecuador's businesses has been well demonstrated by the growth of export-oriented business using the Internet to enable Ecuador's flower growers to trade around the world. Access to open-source technology, such as the Linux operating system and Java, has enabled Ecuadorian entrepreneurs to develop a flourishing software industry.

SUPPORT FOR INWARD INVESTMENT AND IMPORTS

Ecuador's legal framework is favorable to foreign investment. The government has removed barriers to the remittance of profits, and is promoting investment in sectors that had previously been barred to foreign investment. Twelve of the 20 largest mining companies in the world are now investing in Ecuador's mining sector. Further information can be obtained from the Ministry of Finance.

TAX EXEMPTIONS

Information can be obtained from the Ministry of Finance.

▸▸ MORE INFO

Websites:

Government of Ecuador (in Spanish): www.presidencia.gov.ec

Ministry of Finance (in Spanish): www.mef.gov.ec

Egypt

ECONOMY AND TRADE

Egypt has endured as a unified state for more than 5,000 years, and archeological evidence indicates that a developed Egyptian society has existed for much longer. Egypt acquired full sovereignty with the overthrow of the British-backed monarchy in 1952. The completion of the Aswan High Dam in 1971 and the resultant Lake Nasser have altered the time-honored place of the Nile River in the agriculture and ecology of Egypt. A rapidly growing population (the largest in the Arab world), limited arable land, and dependence on the Nile all continue to overtax resources. With the installation of the 2004 parliament, the government of Egypt began a new reform movement, following a stalled economic reform program begun in 1991, but moribund since the mid-1990s.

Over the last few years, the government has improved the transparency of the national budget, revived stalled privatizations of public enterprises, and implemented economic legislation designed to foster private-sector-driven economic growth and improve Egypt's competitiveness. Despite these achievements, the economy is still hampered by government intervention, substantial subsidies for food, housing, and energy, and bloated public-sector payrolls. Moreover, the public sector still controls most heavy industry.

STATISTICS

GDP growth: 7% (2008)
GDP per capita: US$5,500 (2008)
CPI: 18% (2008)
Key interest rate: 12.51% (December 31, 2007)
Exchange rate versus dollar: Egyptian pounds per US dollar—5.4
Unemployment: 8.7%
FDI: US$59.03 billion
Current account surplus: US$1.483 billion
Population: 83,082,869
Source: CIA Factbook except where stated

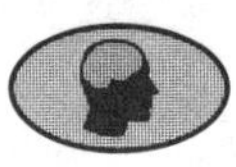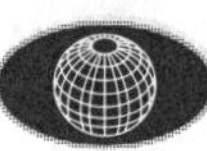

ECONOMIC POLICY OVER 12 MONTHS

Egyptians take pride in their "pharaonic heritage," and in their relationship to what they consider to be mankind's earliest civilization. However, the country today faces some very severe economic challenges. The government has struggled to meet the demands of Egypt's growing population through economic reform, and massive investment in communications and physical infrastructure. The economy was highly centralized during the rule of former president, Gamal Abdel Nasser, but opened up considerably under his successor, Anwar El-Sadat, and President Mohamed Hosni Mubarak has continued this process.

Cairo has aggressively pursued economic reforms to encourage inflows of foreign investment, and facilitate GDP growth. In 2005, Prime Minister Ahmed Nazif's government reduced personal and corporate tax rates, reduced energy subsidies, and privatized several enterprises. The stock market responded enthusiastically, and GDP grew by about 7% per annum for the next two years, until the growth momentum began to feel the effects of the global slowdown towards the end of 2008.

Despite these achievements, the government has failed to raise living standards for the average Egyptian, and has had to continue providing subsidies for basic necessities. The subsidies have contributed to a sizeable budget deficit, amounting to roughly 7% of GDP in 2007–2008. They represent a significant drain on the economy.

Foreign direct investment has increased significantly in the past two years, but the Nazif government will need to continue its aggressive pursuit of reforms in order to sustain the spike in investment and growth, and begin to improve economic conditions for the broader population. Egypt's export sectors, particularly exports of natural gas, continue to exhibit growth during the downturn.

Agriculture in Egypt is mainly in private hands, and has been largely deregulated, with the exception of cotton and sugar production. Approximately one-third of Egyptian labor is engaged directly in farming, and many others work in the processing or trading of agricultural products. Nearly all of Egypt's agricultural production takes place in some 2.5 million hectares (6 million acres) of fertile soil in the Nile valley and delta. Some desert lands are being developed for agriculture, including the ambitious Toshka project in Upper Egypt, but some other fertile lands in the Nile valley and delta are being lost to urbanization and erosion.

Construction, non-financial services, and domestic marketing are also largely private. The Egyptian economy continues to rely heavily on tourism, oil and gas exports, and revenues from managing the Suez Canal. The tourism sector suffered a severe setback following a terrorist attack in Luxor in October 1997. Tourist numbers built up again from 2000 onwards, but the sector feared a repeat of the downturn in tourist numbers, following terrorist attacks on resorts in the Sinai Peninsula in 2004 and 2005. There was some drop-off in numbers, but not on the same scale.

ECONOMIC PERFORMANCE OVER 12 MONTHS

Performance from the country's agricultural sector has been strong in recent years. Warm weather and plentiful water permit several crops a year. Further improvement is possible, but land is worked intensively, and yields are high. Cotton, rice, wheat, corn, sugarcane, sugar beets, onions, and beans are the principal crops. Increasingly, a few modern operations are producing fruits, vegetables, and flowers, in addition to cotton, for export. While the desert hosts some large, modern farms, more common traditional farms occupy one acre each, typically in a canal-irrigated area along the banks of the Nile. Many small farmers also have cows, water buffaloes, and chickens, although larger modern farms are becoming more important.

In addition to the agricultural capacity of the Nile valley and delta, Egypt's natural resources include petroleum, natural gas, phosphates, and iron ore. Crude oil is found primarily in the Gulf of Suez, and in the Western Desert. Natural gas is found mainly in the Nile delta, off the Mediterranean shore, and in the Western Desert. Oil and gas account for approximately 12% of GDP. Export of petroleum and related products (including bunker and aviation sales) amounted to US$2.7 billion in fiscal year 2003–2004.

Crude oil production has been in decline for several years, from a high of more than 920,000 bpd (barrels per day) in 1995, to fewer than 662,000 bpd as of April 2006. To minimize the growing domestic demand for petroleum products, currently estimated at 25 million tonnes per year, Egypt is encouraging the production of natural gas. Over a five-year period, production of natural gas increased by approximately 75%, to reach about 3.3 billion cubic feet per day by the end of fiscal year 2003–2004. Currently, gas accounts for almost 50% of all hydrocarbon usage in Egypt.

Over the last 22 years, more than 230 oil and gas exploration agreements have been signed, and multinational oil companies spent more than US$27 billion in exploration and production activities. As of 2005, crude oil reserves were estimated at 3.7 billion barrels, and proven natural gas reserves were estimated at 58.5 trillion cubic feet, with probable additional reserves totaling another 40–60 trillion cubic feet. Texas-based Apache Oil Company is the largest American investor in Egypt, with a total investment of more than US$2.8 billion since 1996.

The country also has three liquefied natural gas (LNG) facilities, including the Mediterranean Gas Complex in Port Said, whose main shareholders are the Italian company, AGIP, and BP. This facility involved a total cost of about US$315 million, and went on stream in late 2004. Egypt is also the largest

producer and consumer of pharmaceutical products in the Middle East, accounting for 30% of the supply to the MENA (Middle East North Africa) region.

SUPPORT FOR INWARD INVESTMENT AND IMPORTS

The Egyptian Ministry of Investment has been involved in a series of reform and promotional programs to improve both local and foreign investment in Egypt. Around 3% of all foreign direct investment in Egypt goes into the textile sector, but there are opportunities for investment across the economy. Further information can be obtained from the Ministry.

TAX EXEMPTIONS

The tax structure in Egypt is complex, and potential investors will need to seek professional advice. Further information can be obtained from the Ministry for Investment, which operates a number of exceptional incentive schemes. These schemes are aimed particularly at foreign investors who wish to take a stake in existing state-owned schemes as part of Egypt's privatization initiatives.

MORE INFO

Websites:

Egyptian Presidency: www.parliament.gov.eg

Ministry of Investment: www.investment.gov.eg

Estonia

ECONOMY AND TRADE

Estonia has a modern, market-based economy, and has one of the highest levels of GDP per capita (US$21,900) in Central and Eastern Europe. After gaining independence from the Soviet Union in 1991, successive coalition governments pursued free-market and pro-business policies. Estonia joined the European Union in 2004, and remains committed to laissez-faire policies and joining the euro. Growth exceeded 10% in 2004–2006, making Estonia one of the fastest-growing economies in the European Union. However, the economy was knocked off course by the credit crisis and is likely to be one of Europe's worst performers in 2008–2011. Government budget cuts will be necessary and greater emphasis will have to be placed on tradeable goods and services, rather than investing in sectors such as real estate, retail non-tradeable and banking. Estonia is strong in e-commerce, electronics, and telecoms, and has strong trade ties with Finland, Sweden and Germany. Services account for 69% of GDP, with industry accounting for 28% and agriculture 3%.

STATISTICS

GDP growth: −1.5% (2008, est.)

GDP per capita: US$21,900 (2008, est.)

CPI: 10.5% (2008, est.)

Key interest rate: 3% (since Dec 2008)

Exchange rate versus dollar: kroon versus US dollar—10.7 (2008)

Unemployment: 1% (2008, est.)

FDI: US$18.94bn

Current account deficit/surplus −US$3.037bn (2008, est.)

Population: 1.308 million (July 2008, est.)

Source: CIA Factbook except where stated

ECONOMIC POLICY OVER 12 MONTHS

The coalition government of Prime Minister Andrus Ansip has, like its predecessors, pursued sound fiscal policies and was more prudent than those of fellow Baltic republics, Latvia and Lithuania, during the boom times.

The government entered the recession with foreign reserves equivalent to 10% of GDP and with limited borrowings, which some analysts believe means that Estonia is better-placed to emerge more quickly from the downturn than Latvia and Lithuania. It is also seen as less likely to need emergency loans from the IMF. In December 2008, the IMF said that Estonia's foreign reserves should permit it to cope without external financing for the next two to three years.

A December 2008 IMF mission to Estonia reported that: "To cope with the current global and domestic stresses, Estonia can look to strengths in its policy and structural frameworks. First is the fixed exchange rate, underpinned by the robust currency board arrangement. This should anchor price expectations, leading to a sharp decline in inflation. Second, the banking sector is well capitalized and almost entirely owned by Nordic groups that benefit from supportive stabilization programs in their home countries. Finally, labour and product markets are flexible, which should help smooth the transition to recovery."

Rather than borrowing to restimulate its economy, Estonia's government has preferred to pursue a policy of balancing its books by raising taxes and cutting expenditure. Driven by a desire to push its budget deficit down to 3% of GDP—and thereby qualify for euro membership—the government said in January 2009 that it would cut EEK8 billion (US$668.9 million) from its 2009 budget. "The main goal of the spending cuts is to ensure the ability of the Estonian state to pay pensions, salaries to police, and teachers, also at the end of the year," said Prime Minister Ansip in January 2009.

However the picture darkened by early February 2009, when Andres Sutt, deputy governor of the central bank, said the government's cash reserves "will dwindle fast" unless it keeps its word on spending cuts and S&P put the nation's debt on "creditwatch."

In the longer term, Ansip acknowledges that the biggest barrier to Estonia's economic success is the

     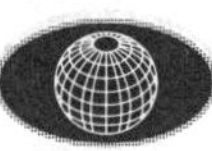   

rigidity of the country's labor laws. "We can see from various international economic reports that the old-fashioned regulation of our labor market is deemed to be the biggest problem with the Estonian economy," he said.

ECONOMIC PERFORMANCE OVER 12 MONTHS

"During the last decade, Estonia has sometimes been in the position of a wonder child. Today, we've come back to earth," said President Toomas Hendrik Ilves at an enterprise awards ceremony in September 2008.

Estonia's boom ended abruptly in mid-2007 when the country's property bubble burst and the country's banks stopped lending. Confidence and domestic demand slumped, and in 2008 the economy tumbled into recession, with an estimated GDP fall of 1.5–2.0%. The country's GDP contracted by 9.4% in the fourth quarter of 2009, the steepest decline since at least 1994, and it is expected to shrink by a further 9% in 2009 according to Andres Sutt.

The worst-hit sectors of the economy are construction, retailing, wholesale trade, and financial services. Seasonally adjusted, unemployment rose to 8.3% in November 2008, double the 4.1% level of a year earlier. Some economists believe that unemployment could peak at 10% in 2009.

Inflation reached 11% in January 2008 but by January 2009 had fallen to 4.9%, following a big fall in retail sales in 2008. The central bank predicts inflation will not exceed 2% in 2009. A decline in imports coupled with a rise in exports caused the foreign trade deficit to fall to EEK37.8 billion (US$3bn) in 2008.

The pre-2007 boom caused Estonia's current account deficit to surge to 10% of GDP, which put downward pressure on the local currency, the Estonian kroon (EEK), which remains pegged to the euro. The Estonian government sees joining the euro as a solution to many of its ills. It originally hoped to join the eurozone in 2008, but owing to difficulties in meeting the Maastricht criteria, membership now seems unlikely before 2013 at the earliest.

Prime Minister Andrus Ansip acknowledged the gravity of the situation on 22 January 2009 when he said that the economy had entered a state of crisis, as its exports had been hit by plunging currencies in neighboring countries, particularly in Scandinavia. The economy of Estonia's biggest trading partner, Finland, is heading for its biggest slump since 1992, with GDP expected to plunge by 3.7% in 2009 and by 0.7% in 2010. The Swedish krona fell by 17% against the euro in 2008 and Sweden is also in recession.

The independent economist Edward Hugh says: "The Baltic problems were created by soaring wages and a credit boom which saw funds channeled into non-tradable sectors like real estate, retail and banking. As a result, these economies became structurally distorted and they didn't diversify enough."

SUPPORT FOR INWARD INVESTORS AND IMPORTERS

Enterprise Estonia provides a wide range of services to international business including access to information on subcontractors through its extensive database of Estonian businesses, support for relocation and expansion of incoming enterprises, and support for the development of knowledge-based, skills-based, and technology investments.

TAX EXEMPTIONS

Estonia was the first country to establish a corporate income-tax system under which taxation of corporate profits is deferred until their distribution. It has flat tax rate of 22% on both personal and corporate income. Revenue reinvested in a company is tax-exempt. For further information about taxes visit the Estonian Tax and Customs Board website (www.emta.ee).

▸▸ MORE INFO

Websites:

- The Estonian Investment and Trade Agency, a division of Enterprise Estonia, has information on investing and trading with Estonia: www.investinestonia.com
- Estonian Tax and Customs Board: www.emta.ee
- Estonian Trade Council: www.etc.ee
- Bank of Estonia: www.eestipank.info
- Estonian Chamber of Commerce and Industry: www.koda.ee

Finland

ECONOMY AND TRADE

After hundreds of years of Swedish rule, Finland gained independence in 1917, only to face the threat of domination by another neighbor, the Soviet Union. Following the collapse of the Soviet regime, Finland escaped from the shadow cast by the Cold War and joined the European Union in 1995. In 2002, Finland became the only Nordic country to adopt the euro in place of its national currency, the Finnish mark. Around two-thirds of the country is covered in forest and about a tenth by water, and the forestry industry has been the backbone of Finnish industry. However, Finland has also had success in telecommunications—the Finnish firm, Nokia, is a household name around the world. One of the main economic problems facing the country is the ageing population—the working-age population will begin to decrease in

  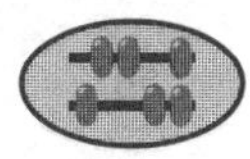    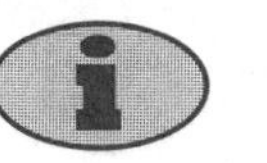  

2010. The country also has a comprehensive welfare program that has resulted in higher-than-average taxes.

ECONOMIC POLICY OVER 12 MONTHS

Finland is a well-managed economy with very healthy public finances. The government has recorded large budget surpluses in recent years—it surged to 5.25% in 2007, for example, buoyed by economic expansion, strong property revenues, and moderate spending. The level of state debt is also low (equivalent to 29% of GDP at the end of 2008). However, the economic downturn is affecting the government's finances. Although the country recorded another large surplus (of 4.1%) in 2008, the Ministry of Finance said in its spring 2009 Economic Survey that the public finances would deteriorate substantially in the next few years, and are even expected to exceed the 3% GDP deficit threshold specified in the EU's Stability and Growth Pact. In 2009, officials forecast that the government would incur a deficit equivalent to 1.8% of GDP, while in 2010 the deficit would rise to 4.8%.

The deterioration in the public finances reflects both a decline in revenues, and the government's desire to use fiscal policy to offset the impact of the global slowdown. Indeed, in its 2009 Budget, announced in January 2009, the Finnish government said that it was pursuing a highly expansionary fiscal policy during the year to bolster the economy. The budget included: tax cuts; increased benefits for families with children and low-income groups; support for housing construction and renovation; support for rental housing construction; decisions to bring forward public-sector renovation projects; and steps to improve the availability of funding for business development and export projects, as well as venture capital.

In 2009, the government also announced measures to boost exports. These include a tripling of the amount of export credit available through the financing company Finnvera, to €3.7 billion. The government also extended a €60 billion guarantee and loans scheme for financial institutions, in an attempt to reopen corporate financing. However, despite all these measures and the deterioration in the public finances, the government has said that it remains committed to reducing the overall tax burden.

Since joining the Eurozone on January 1, 2002, Finland has ceded control of its monetary policy to the European Central Bank (ECB). As one of the smaller economies in the Eurozone, Finland is unlikely to have much, if any, influence over the ECB's policy decisions. Thus, fiscal policy has assumed greater importance, while Finland no longer has the option of devaluing its currency to boost competitiveness. The ECB was slower than other central banks to loosen monetary policy amid the global financial crisis of 2008 and 2009. In March 2009, the ECB cut its key interest rate from 2.0% to 1.5%, the lowest since it started setting euro rates in January 1999. However, US and Japanese rates were, in effect, already at zero by March 2009.

ECONOMIC PERFORMANCE OVER 12 MONTHS

Finland enjoyed several years of strong growth up until 2008. The economy expanded by 4.6% in 2006, and 4.2% in 2007, but by just 0.9% in 2008. As a small, export-oriented country (Finnish exports account for 35% of GDP), Finland is vulnerable to external events. Official figures reveal that the slowdown in international trade since October 2008 has been marked. In November, exports fell by 20% year on year, while imports dropped by 14% year on year. The downward trend continued in December, with exports and imports falling by a further 15% year on year.

There are also many signs that the broader economy is slowing sharply. In January, consumer confidence remained very weak, and business confidence plunged to a new low. Industrial output has also contracted at an alarming rate, falling by 15.6% year on year in December 2008, following a 10.1% drop in November. These declines have started to feed through into job cuts, with the engineering firm, Metso, the construction group, SRV, and Nokia (the world's largest phone-maker) announcing redundancies in early 2009.

Unsurprisingly, unemployment has begun to soar, increasing to 7.6% in February 2009, from 6.4% in February 2008. Men have been harder hit by job losses, with unemployment rising to 8.1%, while unemployment for women amounted to 7%. Young people were also hard hit by job cuts. The unemployment rate among people aged 15–24 was 19.8% in February 2009—3.3 percentage points higher than in February 2008. In March 2009, Finland's Finance Ministry said that more than 100,000 jobs would be lost in 2009, pushing the jobless rate to 9% by the end of the year. Unemployment is expected to keep rising in 2010.

Certainly, Finland is expected to endure a severe recession in 2009. The Finance Ministry predicted (also in March) that GDP would shrink by 5% in 2009. The ministry also forecast that the economy would contract by a further 1.4% in 2010, and that a recovery would not take place until 2011 at the earliest. The Bank of Finland earlier said that it expected exports to collapse in 2009, taking a hit of 19.6%, while imports would drop by 17.5%. The deterioration in the global economy in 2009 appears to have surprised officials. In January 2009, the government forecast that GDP would shrink by just 2% in 2009 and that recovery would follow in 2010.

STATISTICS

GDP growth: 0.9% (2008–2009, official estimate)
GDP per capita: US$38,400 (2008, est.)
Inflation: 1.7% (February 2009, official statistics)
Key interest rate: 1.5% (March 2009, official statistics)
Exchange rate versus dollar: euro per US dollar—0.6799 (2008, est.)
Unemployment: 7.6% (February 2009, official statistics)
FDI: US$94.57 billion (2008, est.)
Current-account deficit/surplus US$10.29 billion (2008)
Population: 5,250,275 (July 2009, est.)
Source: CIA Factbook except where stated

▸▸ MORE INFO

Websites:

Invest in Finland: www.investinfinland.fi
Virtual Finland, has a wide range of information on the country: www.finland.fi
Ministry of Finance, Economic Survey spring 2009: www.vm.fi/vm/en/04_publications_and_documents/01_publications/02_economic_surveys/20090326Econom/name.jsp
EU trade policies: www.ec.europa.eu/trade/
Finnish tax authorities: www.vero.fi/default.asp?domain=VERO_ENGLISH&language=ENG

  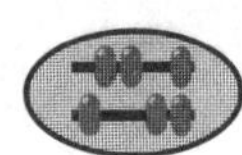      

SUPPORT FOR INWARD INVESTMENT AND IMPORTS

The Finnish government has a liberal attitude towards foreign investment, and the country offers many advantages to investors. Finland is the sixth most competitive country in the world, according to the World Economic Forum, while the World Bank ranks Finland in 13th place in terms of the ease of doing business. Invest in Finland provides information and support to investors.

Finland is part of the EU customs union. Decisions regarding quotas or customs suspensions to be applied to goods imported into Finland are currently taken at the Community level. Information on the EU's trade policies can be found on its website.

TAX EXEMPTIONS

Few tax exemptions are available in Finland. More information can be found on the website of the Finnish tax authorities, which publish a comprehensive guide to the Finnish tax system.

France

ECONOMY AND TRADE

France has the fifth-largest economy in the world and a very strong base of successful multinationals. The commanding heights of the economy have, in recent decades, been shifting from the public to the private sector, with the government disposing of stakes in Air France, France Telecom, Renault, and Thales. However, the government was criticized for displaying "economic nationalism" when in 2006 it named 11 sectors as "critical to the national interest." GDP growth has lagged behind that of other developed countries, averaging 1.9% from 2002 to 2007. However, the downturn is also expected to be less severe than in faster-growing economies. According to the OECD, public sector spending accounted for 52.4% of GDP in 2007, compared with 44.4% in the United Kingdom and 37.4% in the United States. With 75 million foreign tourists per year, France is the most-visited country in the world and has the third-largest income from tourism. Agriculture comprises 2% of GDP, industry 21%, and services 77%. The country was a founder member of the European Union and of the Eurozone.

STATISTICS

GDP growth: 0.7% (2008, est., European Commission)

GDP per capita: US$32,700 (2008, est.)

CPI: 0.8% (January 2009, government figures)

Key interest rate: 2% (February 2009) Eurozone

Exchange rate: euro per US dollar—0.6494 (2008, est.)

Unemployment: 7.8% (2008, est., European Commission)

FDI: US$1.08 trillion (2008, est.)

Current account deficit/surplus −US$47.27bn (2008, est.)

Population: 64.06m (July 2008, est.)

Source: CIA Factbook except where stated

ECONOMIC POLICY OVER 12 MONTHS

France's economy was in the throes of a painful transition from being heavily state-owned and controlled to becoming more free-market-oriented when the financial crisis intervened in 2008.

President Nicholas Sarkozy, who entered the Elysée in May 2007, pledged that he would break with the outmoded ideas and behaviors of the past, and promised to implement radical economic reform.

Initially, Sarkozy lived up to the promise, introducing reforms of the pension system, culling civil service jobs, and dismantling the country's 35-hour week. However, he found it impossible to push through other planned reforms because of the constraints of Eurozone membership, and widespread demonstrations and strikes by aggrieved trade unionists.

Even though most French banks have avoided catastrophic losses, France introduced a €21 billion bailout package for its banking sector in October 2008. Participating banks were required to boost lending by 3%, curb executive pay, and ban some severance payments. Finance minister, Christine Lagarde, unveiled a second bailout package three months later, worth a further €10.5 billion. This had more conditions attached than the first, including a requirement that participating banks should limit shareholder dividends and scrap bonuses.

The government also announced a separate €26.5 billion economic stimulus package in January 2009, mainly focused on infrastructure investment—including upgrading the national electricity grid, the Paris Metro, and SNCF railways. Fifty cathedrals are also due to be renovated.

However, Sarkozy has no intention of trying to jumpstart consumer spending through a reduction in value-added tax. He has slammed the United Kingdom government's introduction of such a scheme, saying: "It is plain to see that has brought absolutely no progress."

In February 2009, Sarkozy also unveiled a €6 billion bailout for the ailing carmakers, PSA and Renault, which have seen sales plummet as a result of the global downturn. In exchange for soft loans from the government, the carmakers pledged not to close factories in France and to use only French suppliers. However, the move has attracted criticism for being protectionist from other European countries and is being investigated by the European Commission.

France's fiscal deficit was estimated at 3.2% in 2008, just over the Eurozone's 3% limit. However, in February 2009 a minister admitted the shortfall was on course to increase to more than 4.4% in 2009. On

  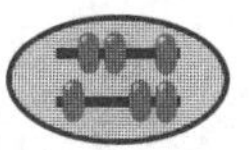 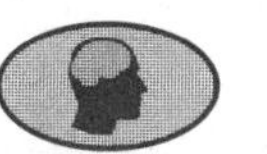  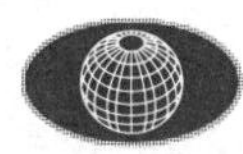   

28 January 2009, some 2.5 million people marched across France's major cities as unions coordinated a mass campaign to persuade Sarkozy to increase wages rather than fund bank bailouts.

ECONOMY OVER 12 MONTHS

Christine Lagarde, France's finance minister, said in August 2008 that it was "out of the question to talk of recession." However, by February 2009 she had admitted that France would follow neighboring countries into recession in 2009.

In 2008, the country's GDP grew by 0.7%, according to the European Commission, but Lagarde said she expects 2009 to be a "difficult" year, during which the economy will probably shrink by more than 1%. The IMF forecasts negative growth of 1% over both 2009 and 2010—half the contraction predicted for Germany and the United Kingdom. The European Commission is gloomier, expecting a contraction of 1.8% in 2009.

The official statistics office said in February 2009 that GDP shrank by 1.2% in the fourth quarter. Lagarde said: "All the countries of the Eurozone will be at about minus 2%" growth this year, adding: "We shouldn't have any illusions." She said the final quarter of 2008 had been marked by an "unheard-of collapse in industrial production."

Unemployment is expected to rise from its 2008 level of 7.8%. The number of jobless soared by 90,200 to 2.2 million in January, the biggest monthly increase since records began. This pushed the unemployment figure to more than 8%. The European Commission expects unemployment to rise to 9.8% in 2009 and 10.6% in 2010.

The stimulus packages will exert pressure on the government's finances in both 2009 and 2010. After averaging 2.9% of GDP in 2008, the fiscal deficit is expected to rise to 5% of GDP in 2009 and 5.4% in 2010, before starting to fall. This will be well above the 3% threshold set by the Stability and Growth Pact. However, economists do not believe that the overshoot will prevent the government from using fiscal policy to support the economy.

One reason for the relative robustness of the French economy is the strength of its public sector. An article published in the *Wall Street Journal* in February 2009 said that the country's long-term resistance to textbook free-market economics is enabling it to the weather the storm better than more laissez-faire countries. According to the OECD, France has 91 public jobs for every 1,000 inhabitants, compared with 49 in Germany.

Largely as a result of lower energy prices and the slowing economy, inflation has fallen from a peak of 3.6% in July 2008 to 0.8% in January 2009—its lowest rate in more than nine years. Forecasters predict inflation will have tumbled to near zero by mid-2009.

SUPPORT FOR INWARD INVESTMENT AND IMPORTS

The Invest in France Agency provides free and confidential advice to companies wishing to invest in France throughout the investment process, and serves as a central port of call, working closely with all 22 French regions to provide legal and tax advice and assistance. Once a project is underway, the agency offers follow-up services to ensure that inward investors are able to resolve unforeseen challenges. It sees this "after-care" service as a top priority. France can provide regional subsidies for investment in productive industries in regions that are underdeveloped or undergoing industrial restructuring in line with a specific map approved by the European Union.

TAX EXEMPTIONS

Business tax—a local tax levied on business activities—can be reduced or waived for periods of five years for industrial companies, and companies in the fields of science and technology. In regional zones, grants can be awarded for up to 15% of the total investment for large companies (grants of 25% are available for small companies). Business tax and property tax are adapted to the zone where the business is located, in order to attract investors. The Prime d'Aménagement du Territoire is a regional development grant of €15,000 per job created.

▸▸ MORE INFO

Websites:

Invest in France: www.invest-in-france.org

European Commission Economic Forecasts, published in January 2009: ec.europa.eu/economy_finance/pdf/2009/interimforecastjanuary/interim_forecast_jan_2009_en.pdf

OECD reports and statistics on France: www.oecd/france

Germany

ECONOMY AND TRADE

Germany—the world's fourth-largest economy and Europe's largest—is also the world's biggest exporter, with other EU countries being the biggest destination for its manufactured goods. Strong growth in 2007 caused unemployment to fall below 8% in 2008, a post-reunification low. This suggested that reforms introduced by the former chancellor, Gerhard Schroeder, were starting to take effect. His successor, Angela

 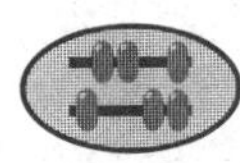      

Merkel, introduced further reforms, including raising the retirement age from 65 to 67. However, the combination of the strong euro and the credit-crisis-inspired slump in global demand means that Germany's economy has been disproportionately affected by the global economic crisis. Since late 2008, Merkel's government has focused on the introduction of policies designed to shield Germany from its worst effects. The modernization and integration of the eastern German economy—where unemployment exceeds 30% in some municipalities—has imposed a significant burden, requiring annual transfers from west to east of up to US$80 billion. Germany was a founder member of the European Union and the Eurozone.

ECONOMIC POLICY OVER 12 MONTHS

In view of the long-term goal of rebalancing the budget by 2011, the coalition government of Chancellor Angela Merkel was initially wary of adopting an expensive stimulus package. The finance minister, Peer Steinbrück, expressed his hostility towards such neo-Keynesian largesse when he labeled the tax-cutting package introduced by the United Kingdom government in November 2008 as "crass" and "breathtaking."

However, governmental hostility to such a policy response had evaporated by late 2008 and the government adopted a €80 billion (US$102 billion) two-year stimulus package in February 2009. In a debate in the Bundestag, Steinbrück said: "This stimulus package is essential."

The package—equivalent to 1.6% of Germany's GDP—includes investment in schools and roads, steps to reduce the cost of medical insurance, a cut in the basic rate of income tax, and €100 cheques for every child. The package also hands €2,500 bonuses to people who trade in old cars for newer, more environmentally friendly models.

The opposition Free Democrats had threatened to derail the package unless it included deeper tax cuts. However, Merkel managed to secure their support by proposing an overhaul of the tax system and the adoption of "further steps" to reduce the tax burden on individuals and companies.

Merkel believes the stimulus package will enable Germany to emerge from the current economic crisis in a stronger position. She describes it as "a bridge" for investment and employment until the next recovery, arguing that it will leave a lasting legacy of energy-efficient school buildings and improved communication networks.

However, Steinbrück, a member of the Social Democratic Party, has warned that the rescue packages being introduced around the world, including Germany's, could spark inflation. He warned it might be difficult to remove excess liquidity from the system once the financial crisis and recession are over.

In February 2009, Merkel's cabinet also approved a bill that will enable banks to be nationalized. If approved, the legislation will enable the federal government to take control of mortgage lender Hypo Real Estate, which has already required €100 billion of state loan guarantees. Steinbrück said that Hypo Real Estate would not be allowed to fail as it would send shockwaves across Germany's financial system.

Since winning the 2005 election, Chancellor Merkel has been governing in coalition with the leftwing Social Democrats. She has abandoned campaign pledges to introduce market-oriented reforms in Germany and instead moved towards the political center. However, there is speculation she may ally with the right-wing Free Democrats ahead of federal elections scheduled for 27 September 2009.

ECONOMIC PERFORMANCE OVER 12 MONTHS

Until early 2008, the conventional wisdom in Germany was that its economy would remain largely untouched by the credit crisis. The assumption was that the Berlin government's fiscal responsibility, the absence of a house-price bubble, and lower levels of indebtedness would ensure that the credit crisis would largely remain an Anglo-Saxon problem.

By summer 2008, that schadenfreude had evaporated. A combination of the strong euro, high oil prices, tighter credit markets, and slower growth had conspired to hammer Germany's exporters. Manufactured exports—traditionally one of Germany's greatest strengths—had become the country's Achilles heel.

The German economy contracted in both the second and third quarters of 2008 with the slump intensifying in the final three months of 2008. In the October—December quarter, the Federal Statistics Office said that GDP shrank by 2.1% compared with the third quarter. On an annualized basis, the shrinkage was 8.2%—Germany's worst economic performance since reunification in 1990.

Merkel's government has predicted that the economy will shrink by 2.25% in 2009. However, others are more pessimistic. Norbert Walter, chief economist at Deutsche Bank, believes output is more likely to collapse by more than 5% in 2009. According to a report from the European Economic Advisory Group, the German economy can be expected to shrink by a further 0.2% in 2010, signaling a more prolonged downturn in Germany than in some neighboring countries.

Exports of cars have been particularly hard hit. Volkswagen's German plants have been forced to adopt a shorter working week, as the company seeks to avoid a build-up of unsold inventories. Along with many other German companies, the carmaker has opted for shorter working hours rather than cutting jobs. The government said it would pay companies' social-insurance payments for workers who are put on short-time working. Unemployment has increased but only marginally—it climbed to 7.9% in February 2009 from 7.8% the previous month.

STATISTICS

GDP growth: 1.3% (2008, European Commission est.)
GDP per capita: US$34,800 (2008, est.)
CPI: 2.8% (2008, European Commission est.)
Key interest rate: 2.0% (since Feb. 09)
Exchange rate: euro per US$—0.6734 (2008, est.)
Unemployment: 7.9% (Feb 09, government figures)
FDI: US$924.7bn
Current account surplus/deficit US$267.1bn (2008, est.)
Population: 82.4 million (July 2008, est.)
Source: CIA Factbook except where stated

  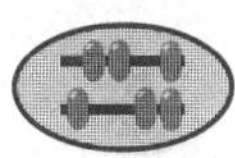   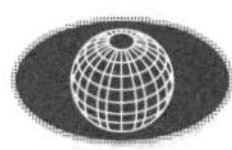   

Holger Schmieding, chief European economist at Bank of America, believes that Germany may have been unfairly penalized. "At first glance, Germany should not have been vulnerable to a credit crunch," he said. "Yet the German economy fell off a cliff in the final quarter of 2008."

He believes this is largely because the nation's exporters are struggling to access the "financial bridges" (short-term funding) they normally use to cover themselves between making a product and selling it outside Germany's borders. Schmieding believes the bridges have become harder to obtain because banks are prioritizing domestic over cross-border lending.

SUPPORT FOR INWARD INVESTMENT AND IMPORTS

Germany Trade & Invest exists to provide importers and inward investors with information about the opportunities in Germany, and the general investment and business climate in the country. It provides a central, detailed source of information about the legal, business, and tax climate in Germany, as well as information on grants and incentives. The German Business Portal provides a central portal for business information and practical information on living and working in Germany. The federal government's website provides an overview of its latest policy initiatives.

TAX EXEMPTIONS

The average nominal corporation tax of less than 30% makes Germany competitive with other European countries. All industrial imports are subject to an "import sales tax" of 19%. Equivalent to the value-added tax levied on domestically produced items, this places the same tax burden on imported and domestic products. A discounted tax of 7% is levied on food products, books, newspapers, artworks, etc.

▸▸ MORE INFO

Websites:

Federal Ministry of Economics & Technology: www.bmwi.de

Germany Trade & Invest: www.gtai.de

German Business Portal: www.german-business-portal.info

Federal Government: www.bundesregierung.de

Ghana

ECONOMY AND TRADE

Ghana, a relative economic star in Africa, is considered likely to attain its goal of middle-income status by 2015, especially given future oil revenues. It is the second-largest producer of cocoa, and Africa's no. 2 gold miner. It is relatively open to foreign investment. The domestic economy centers on agriculture. United Kingdom firm, Tullow Oil, has announced the discovery of 600 million barrels of proven reserves of light oil in the offshore Jubilee field, and additional reserves of up to 1.2 billion barrels. In September 2007, Ghana launched a US$750 million Eurobond to finance energy and infrastructure. However, escalating public spending, and a widening current-account deficit have plagued the economy, despite debt relief. The currency was revalued in July 2007 (deleting several zeros), and Ghana has been badly affected by the global economic crisis. Corruption remains an issue, yet a World Bank report in September 2008 rated Ghana as West Africa's best place for business.

ECONOMIC POLICY OVER 12 MONTHS

The focus of former president, John Kufuor's, 2008 Budget was infrastructure—roads, water, and energy. The government also launched an initiative to improve the regulatory environment for business. Foreign direct investment remains a priority. In May 2008, an emergency program to mitigate the impact of higher crude oil and food prices was launched. Import duties on rice, corn, wheat, and vegetable oil were removed, as were the debt recovery levy and excise duty on some imported fuels. A medium-term target for inflation at 5% was agreed in March 2008 by the central bank and Ministry of Finance.

In line with Ghana's policy of developing its infrastructure to sustain GDP growth, several major deals involving state companies have taken place in the past year. In August 2008, Vodafone completed the US$900 million purchase of 70% of the government-owned Ghana Telecom.

Ghana's shortage of power has led to recurring residential electricity cuts, and the government has taken various initiatives to address the problem. The Export-Import Bank of China has loaned US$562 million for building the Bui dam. The Juale and Pwalugu dams will be financed with US$550 million from Brazil's government, while the Ghanaian government is to invest US$400 million in thermal power. In February 2009, the World Bank's International Finance Corporation also approved US$215 million in loans for Dallas-based Kosmos Energy and Tullow Oil to help finance the US$3.2 billion first phase of developing the offshore Jubilee oilfield.

In February 2009, the Bank of Ghana raised its prime interest rate by 1.5% to 18.5%, a five-year high. Governor Paul Acquah said the bank had adopted a "policy bias" towards interest-rate reductions, based on expectations that inflation will fall below 10% by 2010. The central bank estimates that the budget deficit

STATISTICS

GDP growth: 6.3% (2008, EU est.)

GDP per capita: US$1,500 (2008, est.)

CPI: 20.34% (Feb 2009, Bloomberg)

Key interest rate: N/A

Exchange rate versus dollar: cedi (GHS) per US dollar—1.1 (2008, est.)

Unemployment: 11% (2000, est.)

FDI: N/A

Current account deficit/ surplus: –US$1.807 billion (2008, est.)

Population: 23.4 million (July 2008, est.)

Source: CIA Factbook except where stated

amounted to 14.9% of GDP in 2008, and that the economy will grow by 5–6% in 2009. As of February 2009, the cedi had shed nearly one-third of its value against the dollar in the preceding 12 months.

Incoming president, John Atta Mills' "Rescue Plan for a Better Ghana," unveiled in February 2009, promised austerity measures, including: monitoring the targets and dividends at state-owned companies and enterprises; "reinvigorating" revenue collection; changing the structure of public wages; and slashing the budget for official travel.

The rescue plan also included proposals for a new cocoa-processing plant in western Ghana, and plans to increase rice production for domestic consumption in order to reduce the import bill. An attempt to boost government revenue from gold mining was launched in 2008.

ECONOMIC PERFORMANCE OVER 12 MONTHS

Despite steady growth, political stability, and reform of the financial sector, Ghana has faced economic problems for several years. Provisional government statistics put GDP growth in the first nine months of 2008 at 6.2%.

However, in February 2008, Fitch downgraded its outlook on Ghana's B+ credit rating. The fiscal deficit escalated to nearly 10% of GDP in 2007, partly due to rising public wages, price subsidies for utilities, and energy investments. A report by members of the IMF Fiscal Affairs Department, in July 2008, said there had been a "loss of control over public expenditure," and called for urgent corrective measures before the oil starts to flow.

From 2010, additional oil revenues are expected to make a big difference to the economic outlook. In October 2008, Tullow Oil said that the Jubilee field will start producing in the second half of 2010. Ghana's revenues from oil and gas are expected to rise from 3% of non-oil GDP in 2011 to about 5% of non-oil GDP starting in 2013.

Following elections in January 2009, John Atta Mills, leader of the opposition center-left NDC party took over as president with a minority government. He had campaigned to rein in spending, reduce taxes, and use oil revenues for education, and to alleviate poverty. Predecessor, John Kufuor, of the center-right NPP, had completed the maximum period in the presidency of two four-year terms.

The new administration has blamed Kufuor's government for fiscal profligacy, and pushing the budget deficit to its highest level in a decade. According to Reuters, on his last day in office, Kufuor announced public-sector pay increases of 16–34%. "In a word, the government of Ghana is broke," said Mills. Paul Rawkins, an analyst at Fitch, said: "Obviously senior politicians talking about being broke is not particularly good for creditworthiness."

In February 2009, Mills outlined an austerity package, after again painting a bleak picture of the economy in his first state of the nation speech—an external deficit of 18% of GDP and inflation of almost 20%, up from 12.7% at the end of 2007.

He cited "volatility" in global commodity prices, the weakening cedi, and reductions in foreign aid and remittances. The state-owned Tema Oil Refinery and Volta River Authority together owed more than US$1.6 billion. "The picture of our economy. . . is not flattering, but this should not be cause for despair or panic," said Mills. He faces an uphill battle to fulfill his campaign promises, especially given the uncertainties of the price of crude, and the pace of Jubilee's development.

SUPPORT FOR INWARD INVESTMENT AND IMPORTS

Ghana Investment Promotion Center is the official agency that advises and monitors foreign investors, other than in mining, petroleum, and in free zones. Projects in the extractive industries must be approved or licensed by the Minerals Commission, and the Ministry of Mines and Energy, respectively. Free-zone investment is overseen by Ghana Free Zones Board.

Ghana has had non-reciprocal market access to the European Union since 1975, meaning that most of its exports enter the EU duty and quota-free. The planned integration of Ghana into the Economic Community of West African States (ECOWAS), a full customs union, will enhance its attractiveness by providing access to a larger market. Ghana also has an investment incentive agreement with the United States, and eight bilateral investment treaties (BITs) with countries including the United Kingdom, China, and Germany.

TAX EXEMPTIONS

Ghana's top corporate tax rate is 25%. Tax incentives are available for investing outside the main cities. For example, investors operating under the Free Zone Act are entitled to a 10-year corporate tax holiday. Agricultural and industrial plant, machinery, and equipment imported for investment purposes are exempt from customs duty. The Ghana Investment Promotion Center can provide more information, as can Ghana Free Zones Board.

▸▸ MORE INFO

Websites:

Ghana National Chamber of Commerce and Industry: www.ghanachamber.org

Ghana Investment Promotion Centers: www.gipc.org.gh

Ghana Free Zones Board: www.gfzb.com

  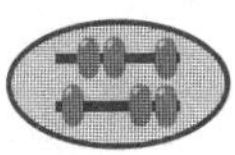      

Gibraltar

ECONOMY AND TRADE

Strategically located on the Strait of Gibraltar linking the Mediterranean Sea and the North Atlantic Ocean, Gibraltar was only ceded to Great Britain with extreme reluctance by Spain in the 1713 Treaty of Utrecht. The British garrison on the Rock was formally declared a colony in 1830. The economy of Gibraltar was adversely affected in the period from 1969 to 2006, the former date being when Spain closed its border to Gibraltar, the latter when the border was opened after the signing of the Tripartite agreement between Spain, the United Kingdom, and Gibraltar. The majority of Gibraltar's citizens voted overwhelmingly against any sharing of sovereignty with Spain in 2002. Following the signing in 2006, Spain agreed to remove restrictions on air movements, to speed up customs procedures, to implement international telephone dialing, and to allow mobile roaming agreements. Britain agreed to pay increased pensions to Spaniards who had been employed in Gibraltar before the border closed. Gibraltar has no natural resources and no arable land, and is just 6.5 square kilometers in size.

STATISTICS

GDP growth: 8% (Gibraltar Budget 2008)
GDP per capita: US$38,200 (2005)
CPI: 2.6% (2007, Gibraltar Budget 2008)
Key interest rate: N/A
Exchange rate versus dollar: GIP per US dollar—1.475 (April 2009)
Unemployment: 3%
FDI: N/A
Current account surplus: N/A
Population: 28,034
Source: CIA Factbook except where stated

ECONOMIC POLICY OVER 12 MONTHS

Gibraltar benefits from an extensive shipping trade, and from a well-developed offshore banking sector. It has also built up a reputation as an international conference center. The British military presence has been sharply reduced, and now contributes about 7% to the local economy, compared with 60% in 1984. The financial sector, tourism, shipping services fees, and duties on consumer goods also generate revenue. The financial sector, the shipping sector, and tourism each contribute some 25–30% of GDP. Telecommunications accounts for another 10%. In recent years, Gibraltar has seen major structural change from a public to a private-sector economy, but changes in government spending still have a major impact on the level of employment.

Gibraltar's economy grew at a rate of 12.7% in 2006–2007 (source: Gibraltar Budget). Gibraltar has received substantial assistance from the EU Secretariat. Some 191 separate projects were co-funded by the European Union in the period 2000–2006, and a new round of EU funding for the period 2007–2013 began on July 1, 2008. By far the largest number of these projects involved helping small-to-medium-size enterprises on Gibraltar start up, or expand business activities. One of the flagship projects for the government is the new air terminal building, which is expected to be operational by early 2010. Gibraltar is also upgrading the frontier access road and the tunnel, both of which will have a beneficial impact on tourism once the global economic downturn eases.

According to Gibraltar's 2009 Budget, public debt has stayed static at £93 million, amounting to less than 12% of GDP. This compares extremely well to the United Kingdom's debt of 40% of GDP in 2008, and the EU's convergence maximum of 60%. The government has said that it intends to take advantage of this low debt level to part-finance its extensive capital investment program for the next few years, although total debt raised will still be within prudent levels.

The government closed 2007 with a budget surplus of £15.1 million, which was broadly in line with the surplus it had predicted in last year's budget, although both spending and income levels were above those predicted. It also plans to use part of the surplus generated from the strong economic showing since 2006 to improve and expand public services, especially healthcare and care for the elderly. Accordingly, it increased the health budget by 8% for 2008–2009, and elderly care expenditure by the same amount.

ECONOMIC PERFORMANCE OVER 12 MONTHS

The Gibraltar government began the 2008 fiscal year, which ends on 31 March 2009, with a good position carried forward from 2007. Overall revenue increased by £19.5 million, from £261.2 million in 2006–2007 to 280.7 million in 2007–2008. This represents a rise of 7.5%, derived mainly from higher income-tax receipts produced from higher employment levels (despite last year's budget tax cuts), and also from higher import-duty receipts.

2007 was another good year for tourism in Gibraltar, with the number of visitors reaching almost 9.5 million (source: Gibraltar budget, June 2008). This was an increase of 15.2% on 2006. The figure slightly overstates the tourist element, in that it also includes what Gibraltar calls "frontier workers" domiciled in Spain and crossing to the Rock to work. With these persons stripped out, some 8 million visitors travelled to Gibraltar in 2007 via the land frontier with Spain. This was despite a downturn in the Spanish package tourist market. Tourist arrivals by air rose 141.12% in the period between 1996 and 2007, and arrivals by sea over the same period were up 156.7%. The total expenditure by tourists in Gibraltar in 2007 amounted to £230.58 million, an increase of 9.54% on the figures for 2006. The government has an active program of encouraging more hotels to be built, to increase the number of hotel beds available.

Gibraltar also runs an improvement and development fund, which it uses to fund a number of projects designed to benefit or beautify the country, or provide amenities. It anticipates expenditure of £25 million

     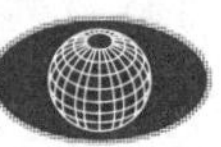   

through the I&DF fund in 2008–2009, most of which will make Gibraltar an even more appealing place for tourists to visit, and will help Gibraltar's citizens. New roads, new affordable housing schemes, a new prison, and the new air terminal are all projects underway.

Financial services, business and real estate, and government and other services are the biggest contributors to Gibraltar's economy, generating more jobs and more income than any other sectors. The government's budget was predicated on 8% growth to March 2008, generating GDP of £800 million. However, by the time the budget was presented in June 2008, it was clear that actual growth was 10%. It is extremely doubtful, though, that its assumption that this level of growth would be maintained through 2009 will turn out to be correct, given the scale of the global downturn.

The official inflation rate in Gibraltar during 2007 was 2.6%. Most of the price increases come through price inflation in the United Kingdom and Spain, which together account for around 80% of Gibraltar's non-petroleum products. The Gibraltar pound is the equivalent of the United Kingdom Pound.

SUPPORT FOR INWARD INVESTMENT AND IMPORTS

The Gibraltar government's InvestGibraltar office is the frontline organization, which acts as a bridge between the government and the private sector. It focuses both on helping Gibraltar businesses, including start-ups, and foreign investors.

TAX EXEMPTIONS

Information can be obtained from InvestGibraltar.

▸▸ MORE INFO

Websites:

Gibraltar government: www.gibraltar.gov.gi

Gibraltar Financial Services Commission: www.fsc.gi

InvestGibraltar: www.gibtour.com/investgib

Greece

ECONOMY AND TRADE

Greece became a parliamentary republic in 1974, following democratic elections. In 1981, Greece joined the European Community, now the European Union; it became the 12th member of the European Economic and Monetary Union (EMU) in 2001. Greece has a capitalist economy, with the public sector accounting for about 40% of GDP, and with per capita GDP of at least 75% of the leading Eurozone economies. Tourism provides 15% of GDP. Immigrants make up nearly one-fifth of the workforce, mainly in agricultural and unskilled jobs. Greece is a major beneficiary of EU aid, equal to about 3.3% of annual GDP. The Greek economy grew by nearly 4.0% per year between 2003 and 2007, due partly to infrastructural spending related to the 2004 Athens Olympic Games, and in part to increased availability of credit, which has sustained record levels of consumer spending. However, growth dropped to 2.8% in 2008, as a result of the world financial crisis and tightening credit conditions.

STATISTICS

GDP growth: 2.8% (2008)
GDP per capita: US$32,800
CPI: 4.4%
Key interest rate: 7.71% (December 31, 2007)
Exchange rate versus dollar: euro per US dollar—1.325 (April 2009)
Unemployment: 8%
FDI: US$55.19 billion
Current account deficit: –US$36.26 billion
Population: 10,737,428
Source: CIA Factbook except where stated

ECONOMIC POLICY OVER 12 MONTHS

Greece adopted the euro as its currency in January 2002, having joined EMU a year earlier. The adoption of the euro provided Greece (formerly a high-inflation-risk country under the drachma) with access to competitive loan rates, and also to low rates of the Eurobond market. This led to a dramatic increase in consumer spending, which gave a significant boost to economic growth. This credit also led to a more relaxed fiscal policy, starting in 2002, which, combined with expenditures associated with the preparations for the Athens 2004 Olympics, resulted in excessive deficits and debt in 2003 and 2004. The government deficit in 2004 reached 6.6% of GDP. As a result of lower post-Olympic spending, the government deficit in 2005 fell to around 4.3% of GDP, leaving Greece with a debt-to-GDP ratio of 107.9%. The government then pledged to reduce the government deficit to 2.6% of GDP in 2006, and to tighten fiscal finances, under a European Commission (EC) excessive-deficit surveillance program.

The EU's Growth and Stability Pact budget deficit criteria state that EU members must not run a budget deficit of more than 3% of GDP, which meant that Greece breached this provision for a six-year period up to 2006. However, in 2007–2008, it was able to conform to the requirement, following a sustained improvement in the economy. Public debt, inflation, and unemployment are above the Eurozone average, but were falling prior to the global economic slowdown. The Greek government continues to grapple with the task of cutting government spending, reducing the size of the public sector, and reforming the labor and pension systems. In this task, it faces considerable and vocal opposition from the country's powerful labor unions and a good section of the general public. The economy remains an important domestic political issue in Greece, and, while the ruling New Democracy government has had some success in improving economic growth and reducing the budget deficit, it faces long-term challenges in its effort to

  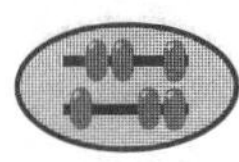   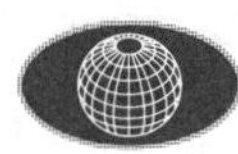   

continue its economic reforms, especially social security reform, and the privatization of state enterprises and monopolies.

Growth in the economy of around 3% between 2005 and 2007 resulted in a drop in unemployment, which fell to 9.8% in the second quarter of 2005, from 10.4% in the same period in 2004. However, unemployment still remains significantly higher among women and those under 27. Foreign direct investment (FDI) inflow has also dropped, and efforts to revive it have been only partially successful. At the same time, Greek investment in south-eastern Europe has increased, leading to a net FDI outflow in some years.

ECONOMIC PERFORMANCE OVER 12 MONTHS

Services make up the largest and fastest-growing sector of the Greek economy. About 14 million tourists are estimated to have visited Greece in 2005, with net revenues of about €10 billion. Remittances from transport (mainly shipping) are growing, and actually exceeded tourism receipts in 2004 and 2005. Receipts from tourism and transport have covered a significant portion of Greece's large trade deficit. Industrial activity has shown a mixed performance, with certain sectors, such as the food industry and high-tech/telecommunications, showing healthy increases, while textiles have declined.

Agriculture employs about 12% of the work force, and is still characterized by small farms and low capital investment, despite significant support from the European Union in structural funds and subsidies. Traditionally a seafaring nation, the Greek-owned merchant fleet totaled 3,338 ships in March 2005, 8.7% of the world merchant fleet and 16.5% of world tonnage.

Greek businesses continue to adjust to competition from EU firms, and the government has liberalized its economic and commercial regulations and practices.

Greece has been a major net beneficiary of the EU budget; in 2004, EU transfers accounted for 3.6% of GDP, and are estimated to have been approximately 3.2% of GDP in 2005. From 1994 to 1999, about US$20 billion in EU structural funds and Greek national financing were spent on projects to modernize and develop Greece's transportation network, in time for the Olympics in 2004. The centerpiece was the construction of the new international airport near Athens, which opened in March 2001 soon after the launch of the new Athens subway system.

EU transfers to Greece continued, with approximately US$24 billion in structural funds for the period 2000–2006. Unfortunately, bureaucratic obstacles have led to significant delays in Greece's absorbing these funds, leading to the real possibility that Greece may have to return a significant portion of them to the European Union. The same level of EU funding, US$24 billion, has been allocated for Greece for 2007–2013. These funds contribute significantly to Greece's current accounts balance, and further reduce the state budget deficit. EU funds will continue to finance major public works and economic development projects, upgrade competitiveness and human resources, improve living conditions, and address disparities between poorer and more developed regions of the country.

Greece's revised budget estimates for 2008, and projections for 2009, published just before the Christmas recess 2008, saw growth for 2008 confirmed at 3.2%, with a general government budget deficit of 2.5%, well inside the EU specified maximum of 3% of GDP. At the same time, inflation was said to be 4.3%, and real wage growth amounted to 3.1%. The 2009 forecast, which has been called optimistic in the press, assumes 2.7% growth and 3% inflation, with a budget deficit of just 2%. Until now, growth in the Greek economy has been driven by strong consumption and investment, and both are now in decline as a result of the global slowdown.

In January 2009, ratings agency, Standard & Poor's, cut Greece's sovereign credit ratings by one notch to A−/A−2 with a stable outlook, citing eroding economic competitiveness and a rising fiscal deficit. Reuters quoted S&P's credit analyst, Marko Mrsnik, as saying that, "the ongoing global financial and economic crisis has, in our opinion, exacerbated an underlying loss of competitiveness in the Greek economy."

SUPPORT FOR INWARD INVESTMENT AND IMPORTS

Invest in Greece Agency is the government office responsible for promoting, attracting, and supporting foreign direct investment into Greece. The agency will help potential investors identify investment targets, plus provide support and assistance in securing the necessary licenses, plus applications for cash grants for investments in excess of €15 million.

TAX EXEMPTIONS

The fiscal benefits available to investors are highly region-dependent. Larger tax exemptions are available from areas of high unemployment. Further information can be obtained from the Invest in Greece Agency.

▸▸ MORE INFO

Websites:

Office of the Greek Prime Minister, Dr Kostas Karamanlis: www.primeminister.gr

Invest in Greece Agency: www.investingreece.gov.gr

 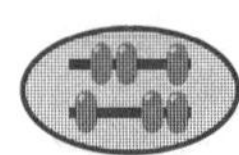      

Hong Kong

ECONOMY AND TRADE

A former British colony, Hong Kong became a special administrative region (SAR) of China in 1997, when Britain's 99-year lease of the New Territories, north of Hong Kong Island, expired. During the 150 or so years of the United Kingdom's rule, Hong Kong was transformed from a fishing and farming community into one of the world's major cities and financial centers. China has been keen to preserve Hong Kong's prosperity, and the SAR is governed under the principle of "one country, two systems," under which it retains a high degree of autonomy. China has also pledged to preserve Hong Kong's economic and social systems for 50 years from 1997.

China controls Hong Kong's foreign and defense policies, but the SAR has its own currency and customs status. Hong Kong's constitution, the Basic Law, allows for the development of democratic processes. However, Beijing can veto changes to the political system, and, according to the BBC, "pro-democracy forces have been frustrated by what they see as the slow pace of political reform." Hong Kong's economy, once based on manufacturing, is now reliant on services. As well as being a major corporate and financial center, the port of Hong Kong channels many of China's exports to the outside world. In 1997, the International Monetary Fund (IMF) reclassified the territory as an advanced economy.

STATISTICS

GDP growth: 2.5% (2008, government figures)
GDP per capita: US$22,000 (2008 est.)
CPI: 0.8% (February 2009, government figures)
Key interest rate: 0.5% (March 2009)
Exchange rate versus dollar: Hong Kong dollars (HKD) per US dollar—7.751 (2008)
Unemployment: 5.0% (Dec 2008–Feb 2009, government figures)
FDI: US$1.235 trillion (2008, est.)
Current-account deficit/surplus HK$238.4 billion (government figures)
Population: 7,008,900 (end 2008, government figures)
Source: CIA Factbook except where stated

ECONOMIC POLICY OVER 12 MONTHS

Hong Kong's open economy is dependent upon global trade, and the intermediation of capital. Consequently, economic policy has focused heavily on improving structural and institutional arrangements to maintain the territory's competitive advantage. The government has thus concentrated on improving skills, maintaining liberal policies, and containing business costs, rather than on short-term macroeconomic policies. However, the authorities have acted decisively to boost the economy during times of economic difficulty, such as the Asian 1997–1998 financial crisis. This has also proven true during the current global economic malaise.

Hong Kong entered the downturn better placed than many other economies. The IMF, in its December 2008 annual assessment of the economy, said: "The authorities' sound economic policies and steady strengthening of financial-sector regulation, and supervision in recent years have provided valuable protection in dealing with the consequences of the global financial turmoil. In addition, the various steps that the authorities have taken in recent months have bolstered stability, and buttressed the economy's resilience to spillovers."

In the latter part of 2008, the Hong Kong government implemented a range of measures to stimulate domestic demand, including a sizable fiscal package, and sought to boost liquidity in financial markets. The IMF said that the "well-targeted infrastructure investments should boost the economy's potential by further increasing skill levels and productivity."

The IMF also commended the management of the country's financial sector, which appears to have avoided the worst excesses (in terms of exposure to toxic debt) of its counterparts in Western economies. The IMF said that the SAR's banks had "managed risk prudently and provisioned for losses," and that they were "well positioned" to handle the effects of the global economic downturn.

The decision to peg the Hong Kong dollar to the US dollar in 1983 meant that the Hong Kong authorities relinquished their ability to control interest rates and the money supply. Thus, fiscal policy is of much greater importance in Hong Kong than in other economies. However, according to the IMF's December 2008 report, the peg is a "simple, transparent, exchange-rate arrangement that has, over the past 25 years, provided an anchor for monetary and financial stability in Hong Kong SAR." Fortunately, during the current global economic downturn, the business cycles in Hong Kong and the United States have also been synchronized, and thus Hong Kong has benefited from the Federal Reserve's policy of slashing interest rates in 2008 and 2009.

ECONOMIC PERFORMANCE OVER 12 MONTHS

Hong Kong endured six years of deflation, which began in 1997, before the economy embarked on a five-year-long period of expansion in mid-2003, buoyed by the rapid growth of the mainland Chinese economy. The SAR enjoyed average annual growth of more than 7% during the four years ending in 2007. According to the IMF report published in December 2008, in 2008 unemployment fell to the lowest point in more than a decade, while rising disposable incomes propelled private consumption, and productivity growth was high.

However, the IMF pointed out: "As one of the most open economies in the world and with its focus on financial and trade services, [the] Hong Kong SAR is highly exposed to the unfolding crisis in international financial markets, and to the slowdown in the global economy. There are now clear signs of economic deceleration." The economy began to falter in the first half of 2008. Net exports of goods and services fell

   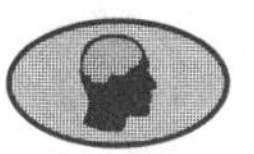  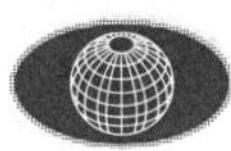   

during this period, "as the terms of trade worsened and demand from the European Union, Japan, and the United States weakened," according to the IMF.

Thus, while GDP grew by 7.3% year on year in the first quarter of 2008, this fell to 4.3% and 1.7%, respectively, in the second and third quarters, and in the last three months of the year the economy contracted by 2.5%, leaving overall growth during the year at 2.5%. The economy's descent steepened in early 2009 as domestic demand came under pressure. Retail sales of valuables and consumer durables began falling in September 2008, and this process continued into 2009.

The unemployment rate climbed to 5% in the three months ending February 2009, from 4.1% in the last three months of 2008. Analysts feared that if the rate of job losses continued at the same pace, the unemployment rate would surpass its June 2003 peak of 8.5% by the end of 2009. Certainly, the outlook for the rest of the year appears grim. In March 2009, Credit Suisse warned that Hong Kong's economy would contract by around 4% in 2009. Hong Kong's economic fortunes are highly dependent on southern China, and the neighboring province of Guangdong, which exports much of its output via the SAR. Beijing's huge US$580 billion stimulus package will help to offset the impact of plummeting global demand on Guangdong, but these measures will take time to work their way through to Hong Kong.

SUPPORT FOR INWARD INVESTMENT AND IMPORTS

The government actively encourages investment in Hong Kong, and the territory offers many advantages to investors, including very low taxes and a world-class infrastructure. According to the government, the Heritage Foundation/Wall Street Journal in the United States, and the Cato and Fraser Institutes of Canada have consistently rated the SAR as the world's freest economy. A government agency, Invest in Hong Kong, provides support to foreign investors. Information can be found on its website.

For more information on importing goods into Hong Kong, see the guide published by Invest in Hong Kong.

TAX EXEMPTIONS

Hong Kong operates a low and simple tax regime. The profit tax rate is the same for foreign and local companies, a low 16.5%. The actual tax bill is often even less after various deductions and depreciation allowances. There is no capital gains tax in Hong Kong. The Inland Revenue Department publishes a detailed guide to the tax system; see its website for more information.

▸▸ MORE INFO

Websites:

Invest in Hong Kong: www.investhk.gov.hk/pages/1/329.html

Invest in Hong Kong, import guide: www.investhk.gov.hk/pages/1/77.html

Inland Revenue Department: www.ird.gov.hk

HSBC Bank, guide to investing in Hong Kong: www.hsbc.com.hk/1/2/hsbcpremier/assistance/investing

IMF Public Information Notice, December 2008: www.imf.org/external/np/sec/pn/2008/pn08145.htm

One-stop government portal: www.gov.hk

See Also:

★ Viewpoint: Jim Rogers (pp. 232–234)

Hungary

ECONOMY AND TRADE

Hungary, which joined the European Union in 2004 but has not yet joined the euro, has made a successful transition from being a centrally planned economy to a market economy. Its per capita income is nearly two-thirds of the EU average, and the private sector accounts for more than 80% of GDP. Foreign ownership and investment in Hungarian firms is widespread, with cumulative foreign direct investment totaling more than US$60 billion since 1989. Austerity measures imposed in late 2006 have helped reduce the deficit from more than 9% of GDP in 2006 to 3.3% in 2008. However, due to an impending inability to service its short-term debt—brought on by the global credit crunch in late 2008—Hungary's government was forced to seek assistance from the IMF in October 2008. The global financial crisis, declining exports, low domestic consumption, and fixed asset accumulation—dampened by government austerity measures—will result in a negative growth rate of between 3% and 5% in 2009.

ECONOMIC POLICY OVER 12 MONTHS

During October 2008, the currency, the forint, went into freefall, slumping by 40% against the US dollar and the euro. The central bank sought to put a floor under the currency's slide by raising the benchmark interest rate to an economy-crunching 11.5% (up from 8.5%) on October 22, 2008. Protecting the forint is seen as a priority , as many Hungarian households and businesses have their borrowings in foreign currencies, including the Swiss franc and the euro.

In November 2008, Hungary received a US$25.1 billion package of loans from the International Monetary Fund, the European Union and the World Bank, largely because the country was deemed at risk of defaulting on its short-term debt.

In exchange for the rescue package, Hungary agreed to restructure its public sector finances through a series of austerity measures—including reduced public-sector pay, tax rises, and curbs on social spending. "The policies Hungary envisages justify an exceptional level of access to Fund resources," said IMF managing director, Dominique Strauss-Kahn, at the time.

STATISTICS

GDP growth: 0.5% (2008, government statistics office)

GDP per capita: US$20,500 (2008, est.)

CPI: 3% (March 2009, government statistics office)

Key interest rate: 9.5% (Central Bank)

Exchange rate versus dollar: forints per US dollar—171.8 (2008, est.)

Unemployment: 8% (2008, est.)

FDI: US$152.4bn

Current account deficit: –US$6.89 billion (2008, est.)

Population: 9.9 million (July 2008, est.)

Source: CIA Factbook except where stated

The program is unpopular, as Hungary's economic growth was already weak, and the government had already reined in spending and increased taxes under the earlier IMF-mandated austerity measures of late 2006. Furthermore, the government lacked scope to introduce any anti-cyclical fiscal stimulus, because it is struggling to meet the Maastricht criteria for euro membership, including a budget deficit of below 3% of GDP.

In November 2008, Prime Minister, Ferenc Gyurcsany, announced plans for a HUF1.4 trillion (US$6.9 billion), two-year stimulus package to kick-start economic growth. His government will raise value-added tax from 20% to 23% in July 2009, and raise corporate tax from 16% to 19% from January 2010. He has also sanctioned some tax cuts in the hope of boosting the economy.

In the first two months of 2009, the forint was Europe's worst-performing currency. In March 2009, the Hungarian National Bank took further action, saying it would use its "entire monetary policy toolkit" to ensure the currency fell no further. The bank was concerned, among other things, that a weaker forint could jeopardize its 3% medium-term inflation target, and boost defaults on overseas loans. The weakening of the currency has left the bank with little ability to cut interest rates.

In March 2009, Gyurcsany said that one of his government's core goals was to ensure Hungary meets "all criteria that are needed to enter the ERM2 regime." He also said the government was willing to consider deeper and more comprehensive reforms than those unveiled earlier, to revive the economy and stem job losses.

The government would like to reduce the budget deficit to below 3% of GDP during 2009, compared to a 3.3% deficit in 2008. It has already slashed HUF200 billion (US$809 million) off its 2009 spending. Gyurcsany has also indicated his government is willing to reduce state spending even further.

ECONOMIC PERFORMANCE OVER 12 MONTHS

In 2007, the economies of Central and Eastern Europe, including that of Hungary, were seen as the poster children of economic reform. Many seemed on course to converge with Western Europe within a few years. However, a large number of these economies have since entered deep recessions—largely because of overborrowing from overseas banks, the bursting of asset-price bubbles, weakening demand for their exports, and plummeting currencies.

By April 2008, the Hungarian economy was one of the worst affected in the region. Inflation had soared to 6.6%, more than double the central bank's target of 3%. Economists claim that the country, along with Latvia and Ukraine, would probably be bankrupt by now, had it not been for the IMF-led rescue package.

The government's 2006 austerity program meant that the economy was already weak when the global financial crisis struck. GDP growth slowed to 1.3% in 2007, and, at the time, Hungary's policymakers felt unable to raise interest rates in case they strengthened the forint, and weakened the country's important export sector. Gyurcsany's government could only meet its fiscal targets through higher taxes and expenditure cuts.

For the full year of 2008, the Hungarian economy expanded by 0.5%. However, it contracted by 2.3% in the fourth quarter of 2008, according to revised government data issued in March 2009. The figure suggests that the economy is likely to experience a deeper-than-expected recession, with some economists predicting negative growth of up to 5% in 2009, largely as a result of a collapse in exports, which has been much worse than the government's forecast of a 2.5–3.0% contraction.

On the consumption side, the paucity of credit and fears over unemployment have slowed domestic consumption, including new car sales. A survey of domestic and international banks by the central bank (published in March 2009) identified a serious decline in lending appetite in the corporate market, mainly in financing large and medium-size companies, and real-estate deals.

In the final quarter of 2008, output declined in all sectors of the economy, except for construction and agriculture, with industrial output sliding by 10.7% year-on-year, due to a sharp fall in demand from the Eurozone countries, coupled with domestic fiscal tightening. Annual consumer price inflation slowed to 3.0% in February 2009 from 3.1% in January, the KSH added.

The government expects the economy to shrink by between 3.0% and 3.5% in 2009, as a result of the collapse in demand in the Eurozone. However, some analysts believe that the downturn could be as high as 5%, especially if the recession in Western Europe turns out to be deeper than expected.

SUPPORT FOR INWARD INVESTMENT AND IMPORTS

The Hungarian Investment & Trade Development Agency (ITD Hungary) is able to provide advice and other services to foreign investors through its Invest in Hungary section. ITDH's Trade with Hungary section focuses on providing assistance to importers, and can supply comprehensive lists of current business offers from Hungarian suppliers. The organization's Enterprise Europe Network aims to promote cooperation between SMEs. The Ministry for National Development and Economy focuses on transforming Hungary's economy into a high-value-added, knowledge-based, and competitive one.

▸▸ MORE INFO

Websites:

Ministry for National Development and Economy: www.nfgm.gov.hu/en

Hungarian National Bank: www.english.mnb.hu/Engine.aspx

American Chamber of Commerce in Hungary: www.amcham.hu/usefullinks/default.aspx

ITD Hungary: www.itdh.com/engine.aspx?page=Itdh_Befektetes

Hungarian Tax and Financial Control Administration (APEH): www.en.apeh.hu

  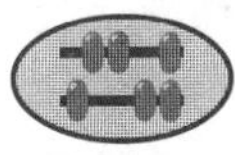 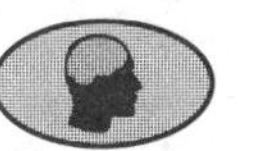  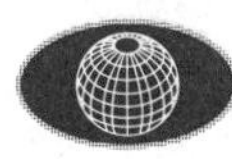   

TAX EXEMPTIONS (INCLUDING TAX BREAKS)

The Hungarian government can grant customized incentive packages for projects in sectors including manufacturing, R&D, and regional service and logistics centers. The projects must have minimum investment values ranging from €10 million to €50 million. The projects must create a certain number of jobs (more than 10, or more than 100, depending on the type of project). The grants are doubly generous in the regions of northern Hungary, the northern great Hungarian Plain and south Transdanubia. The government will raise corporate taxes from 16% to 19% in January 2010.

Iceland

ECONOMY AND TRADE

Prior to 2008, Iceland enjoyed strong growth, low unemployment, and an unusually even distribution of wealth. However, its economic "miracle"—the economy grew by more than 7% in both 2004 and 2005, before slowing to 4.4% in 2006 and 4.7% in 2007—turned to dust during 2008. The economy first faltered in early 2006, after hedge funds and other financial speculators withdrew funds from the country, forcing the central bank to raise interest rates. Pre-crisis, domestic demand had been driven by overexpansion of the country's financial sector, and massive personal and corporate borrowing. Post-crash, the króna has slumped by 70%, and Iceland has required financial support from the IMF. In the 1990s, Iceland commenced extensive free-market reforms, joining the European Economic Area in 1994. The fishing industry provides 40% of export earnings but just 5% of employment. Abundant geothermal power has attracted foreign investment into the aluminum and hydropower sectors.

STATISTICS

GDP growth: 1.6% (2008, est., IMF)
GDP per capita: US$42,600 (2008, est.)
CPI: 17.6% (March 2009, Central Bank of Iceland)
Key interest rate: 18% (since October 2008, Reuters)
Exchange rate versus dollar: króna per US dollar—ISK143 (March 2009, xe.com)
Unemployment: 9.4% (Feb 2009)
FDI: N/A
Current account deficit: –US$3.257bn (2008, est.)
Population: 304,367 (July 2008, est.)
Source: CIA Factbook except where stated

ECONOMIC POLICY OVER 12 MONTHS

The International Monetary Fund (IMF) approved a two-year US$2.1bn rescue package for Iceland in December 2008. The loans, which come from individual countries as well as from the IMF itself, will give exceptional access to the IMF's resources, equivalent to 1,190% of the country's quota.

The package aims to mitigate the effects of the crisis that has seriously destabilized the Icelandic economy, through rebuilding the value of the króna, reinventing the financial sector, reducing the current-account deficit, containing inflation, and diversifying the economy. The program imposes tight monetary and fiscal policies, and severely limits capital flows.

John Lipsky, the IMF's first deputy managing director and acting chairman, warned in December 2008: "The road ahead is difficult. The program is subject to exceptionally large uncertainty and significant risks, reflecting the unprecedented magnitude of the banking sector collapse."

The failure of Iceland's three biggest banks—Glitnir, Landsbanki, and Kaupthing—in October 2008 sparked widespread protests in the capital city of Reykjavik. In what has become known as the "saucepan revolution," protestors called for the resignations of the prime minister, Geir Haard, and of central bank chairman (and former prime minister), David Oddson.

Haard's government collapsed in January 2009, and was replaced by a new caretaker government led by Johanna Sigurdardottir, which must face elections in April 2009. Sigurdardottir's administration has pledged to adhere to the IMF-backed austerity program that was negotiated by Haard's government. In a statement outlining its priorities, the administration said: "The government will base itself on a very prudent and responsible policy in economic and fiscal matters."

The weakness of the króna has prompted a rethink of Iceland's former antipathy towards EU membership. Sigurdardottir is convinced that joining the European Union, and replacing the króna with the euro, is the best hope for Iceland's economy.

EU officials have stated that an application could progress swiftly, possibly enabling Iceland to join at the same time as Croatia, which intends to become a member in 2011. The European commissioner for enlargement, Olli Rehn, a Finn, has said that Iceland "would complement the European Union, both philosophically and economically."

However, joining the European Union would also mean Iceland would have to follow the bloc's centralized fisheries policy. This will be a big sacrifice for a nation that has jealously guarded control of its seas—which are teeming with cod, haddock, herring, and other species. Reluctance to open its waters has deterred Iceland from applying to join the European Union in the past.

ECONOMIC PERFORMANCE OVER 12 MONTHS

Iceland has been one of the most conspicuous casualties of the global credit crisis. Its banking sector,

     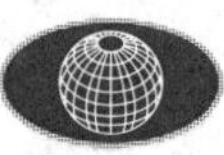   

already tottering in March 2008, collapsed under a mountain of debt in October 2008, as did high-flying local entrepreneurs, including Jon Asgeir Johannesson of the retail conglomerate, Baugur.

Successive Icelandic governments had permitted the country's banks to build up assets equivalent to almost 900% of GDP by the end of 2007. At the same time, the country's gross external indebtedness had soared to 550% of GDP, largely on account of the banks' profligacy. One commentator said: "The country was behaving like an out-of-control hedge fund."

Spooked by the collapse of Lehman Brothers in September 2008, international investors took fright and commenced a run on Iceland's banks. The three largest—Glitnir, Landsbanki, and Kaupthing—collapsed within the space of a single week the following month.

Within days of this collapse, the króna shed some 70% of its value. Other key asset prices plummeted, and the equity market fell by 80%. Severe disruptions in the external payments system threatened to spread contagion rapidly into the real economy. For a small economy that is dependent on imports, it had become a crisis of epic proportions. Icelanders were severely traumatized, and many—especially those with debts in other currencies—are suffering severe financial pain.

Poul Thomson, the IMF's mission chief for Iceland, said: "Iceland's banking system significantly outstripped the authorities' ability to act as a lender of last resort when the system ran into trouble. Only a few years ago, Iceland had a banking system that was the normal size. But after the privatization of the banking sector was completed in 2003, the banks increased their assets from being worth slightly more than 100% of GDP to being worth close to 1,000% of GDP."

By March 2009, Iceland's inflation had soared to 17% and was still rising. Unemployment was expected to climb to 8–10% by the end of 2009. Construction sites are silent, and buildings remain half-finished.

However, according to preliminary data released in March 2009, Iceland's economy shrank by only 0.9% in the fourth quarter of 2008, compared to the previous quarter, and by 1.3% from a year earlier. The króna has become virtually worthless beyond Iceland's shores, which has dramatically curtailed imports. The slump in imports helped support GDP, due to so-called net exports.

The IMF expects that Iceland's that economy will contract by 10% in 2009, which would represent the country's worst slump since it gained independence from Denmark in 1944. The severe recession is expected to continue into 2010. However, the IMF predicts that, as a result of its program, domestic demand will recover strongly in 2011.

SUPPORT FOR INWARD INVESTMENT AND IMPORTS

The government provides a range of advisory and support services to businesses considering investing in Iceland. Power-intensive industrial production, mainly focusing on metals, has led foreign direct investment in Iceland, but there are opportunities in technology, manufacturing, and services (price competitiveness is an attraction, given the króna's current weakness). The island has an investor-friendly environment, and a strong professional services base.

TAX EXEMPTIONS

Iceland offers attractive tax breaks for firms that locate holding companies and multinational headquarters with worldwide activities. Icelandic law allows non-nationals to invest in Icelandic enterprises. Substantive rules on such investments are, for the most part, the same as those in the European Union. As a member of the European Economic Area (EEA), Iceland may not impose restrictions on investments of EU or EFTA member countries.

▸▸ MORE INFO

Websites:

Government of Iceland: www.government.is

Government portal for information on investment and imports: www.iceland.org

Invest in Iceland agency: www.invest.is

Tax exemptions: www.icetradedirectory.com

Trade Council of Iceland: www.icetrade.is

India

ECONOMY AND TRADE

India is the world's largest democracy, and its second-most-populous country. India is also Asia's third-largest economy, after Japan and China. Following several decades when the economy was virtually closed to the outside world, India launched a program of reforms in the early 1990s, which have ignited rapid economic growth. These reforms included liberalizing foreign trade and investment, and significantly adjusting monetary and fiscal policy. Many analysts believe that the country has the potential to become one of the 21st century's economic superpowers. However, India still faces huge social, economic, and environmental problems. The partition of the Indian subcontinent in 1947 sowed the seeds for future conflict—there have been three wars between Hindu-majority India and Muslim-dominated Pakistan since 1947, and relations remain tense. Communal, caste, and regional tensions also continue to affect India, while the vast mass of the rural population remains illiterate and impoverished. Agriculture accounts for around one-fifth of the economy, but supports two-thirds of the population. The United States is India's largest trading partner.

  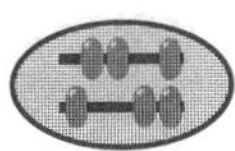      

ECONOMIC POLICY OVER 12 MONTHS

Since the Indian economy began to slow in the final months of 2008, the Indian government has announced a variety of fiscal measures to stimulate it, while the central bank has loosened monetary policy significantly. In December 2008, the government unveiled a US$4 billion spending package, and said it was also planning a substantial spending increase in the following year's budget. The measures in December included cutting various categories of value-added tax by up to 4 percentage points to encourage consumer spending, an increase in infrastructure spending, and help for businesses and for labor-intensive export sectors, such as textiles and handicrafts.

In January 2009, the government unveiled a fresh stimulus plan. Measures included allowing increased foreign investment in both Indian bonds and companies. State governments would also be allowed to borrow up to US$6 billion to fund additional infrastructure projects. In February 2009, the government announced a third stimulus package, involving a cut in excise duty to 8% from 10%, and a reduction in service tax to 10% from 12%. The 4-percentage-point reduction in central value-added tax announced in December was extended beyond March 31, 2009, when it was originally due to expire.

Also in February 2009, the government unveiled its 2009 budget, under which spending will rise by 6% to INR9.53 trillion (US$196 billion) in the year starting April 1. That, according to the government, will result in a budget gap of 5.5% of gross domestic product (GDP) by March 31, 2010. However, independent economists believe the deficit could be even larger. Rajeev Malik, a Singapore-based economist at Macquarie, told Bloomberg at the time of the budget that the shortfall could touch 8.1% of GDP by March 31, 2009, if the government included bonds sold during the year to subsidize fuel and fertilizer in its books. India regards these bonds as "off-budget" items, and doesn't show them in state accounts.

The country's rising budget deficit limited the scope for fiscal stimulus, and the authorities have focused on using monetary policy to counter the effects of the global slowdown. The central bank began cutting rates aggressively in the final quarter of 2008. By December 2008, the Reserve Bank of India's key interest rate stood at 6.5%, its lowest level since June 2006. Between mid-September and December, the central bank also injected US$60.2bn into the financial system to boost liquidity.

In January 2009, the Reserve Bank of India cut its key lending rate by a further percentage point, to an eight-year low of 5.5%, marking the fourth reduction in as many months. The central bank also cut the amount of funds that commercial lenders have to keep in reserve from 5.5% cent to 5.0%. In March 2009, rates fell yet again, this time by 50 basis points, to an all-time low of 5%.

STATISTICS

GDP growth: 7.1% (2008–2009, official estimate)
GDP per capita: US$2,900 (2008, est.)
Inflation: 2.43% (February 2009, official statistics)
Key interest rate: 5.0% (March 2009, official statistics)
Exchange rate versus dollar: Indian rupees (INR) per US dollar—43.319 (2008, est.)
Unemployment: 6.8% (2008, est.)
FDI: US$142.9 billion (2008, est.)
Current-account deficit/surplus –US$38.39 billion (2008, est.)
Population: 1,147,995,904 (July 2008, est.)
Source: CIA Factbook except where stated

ECONOMIC PERFORMANCE OVER 12 MONTHS

India's economy is largely driven by domestic demand but it has not been immune to the global financial crisis that broke in the second half of 2008. India's economy began to slow markedly in the final three months of 2008, when GDP grew by 5.3%, compared with 7.6% in the previous three months, and 8.9% in the same period of 2007. A slump in export demand was the main factor depressing growth.

Growth is likely to fall further in the first quarter of 2009. The country posted its first back-to-back decline in industrial production in 16 years in January, when output fell by 0.5%, following a 0.6% drop in December. In addition, India's exports fell at their steepest rate in a decade in January 2009, amid the global economic slump. Merchandise shipments dropped by 16% to US$12.38 billion, the fourth consecutive monthly decline.

The government expects growth to slacken to 7.1% in fiscal 2009, an outcome that would mark the weakest growth in six years, and would follow three years when the economy expanded by more than 9% a year. Some independent economists believe that growth will fall below 7%, and that it will slow further in 2010, to 5.5% or lower. That would be a strong pace of growth by global standards, but it would not be enough to raise the living standards of India's poorest citizens.

Inflation reached a 13-year high of 12.91% in August 2008, but it had fallen to a near seven-year low of 2.43% by the last week of February 2009, partly due to a sharp slide in global prices for oil and other commodities. The slowing domestic economy is also affecting inflation, with price increases expected to turn negative in 2009, according to many independent economists. Such a development would mark India's first bout of deflation since March 1976, according to central bank records. Indeed, Agence France Presse reported, in March 2009, that Goldman Sachs had said, "we think deflation will be a much bigger risk for the economy in the rest of 2009 ... due to ongoing demand destruction and commodity price collapses."

India has been chalking up large budget deficits for many years, and the poor state of the public finances has limited the government's ability to spend its way out of the slowdown (see Economic Policy). More ominously, when the government announced the 2009 budget in February 2009, the ratings agency, Standard & Poor's, put the country on watch for the loss of its investment-grade status. Meanwhile, Fitch Ratings in Hong Kong said a failure to cut the deficit "could undermine" India's economic growth prospects, and jeopardize its ability to continue to attract capital.

►► MORE INFO

Websites:

Investment Commission: www.investmentcommission.in
Ministry of Commerce and Industry: www.commerce.nic.in
Doing Business In India, guide from the US Department of Commerce: www.buyusa.gov/india/en/motm.html#_section7
The Economic Times, covering economic and financial developments in India: www.economictimes.indiatimes.com

See Also:

★ Viewpoint: Hamish McRae (pp. 789–790)
★ Viewpoint: Ravi Nedungadi (pp. 815–816)
★ Viewpoint: Rajiv Dogra (pp. 751–753)

 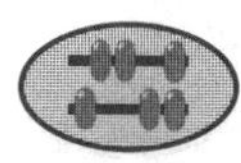 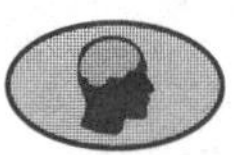     

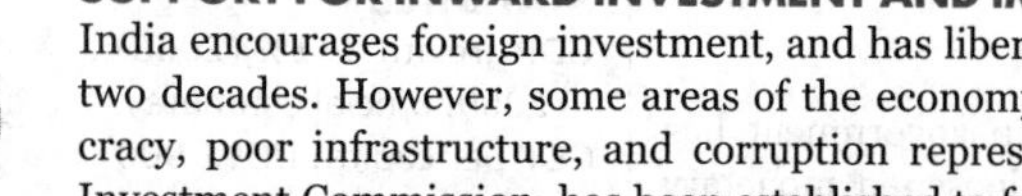

SUPPORT FOR INWARD INVESTMENT AND IMPORTS

India encourages foreign investment, and has liberalized its investment regime significantly over the past two decades. However, some areas of the economy remain off-limits to foreign investors, while bureaucracy, poor infrastructure, and corruption represent considerable barriers. A government agency, the Investment Commission, has been established to facilitate investment by foreign companies in India. The Commission recommends projects and investment proposals that should be fast-tracked and/or mentored, and promotes India as an investment destination.

India is a member of the World Trade Organization. The website of the Ministry of Commerce and Industry has information on the country's trade regime.

TAX EXEMPTIONS

Both central and state governments provide various investment incentives for domestic and foreign investors. The central government's incentives include:

- 100% tax exemption on profits related to infrastructure development and operation;
- 10-year tax exemption for exports.

Investors in the Special Economic Zones qualify for a tax exemption for the first five years, with a 50% exemption for the following five years. State governments may offer exemptions on the payment of charges for electricity, registration fees, and stamp duty.

Indonesia

ECONOMY AND TRADE

Indonesia's economy, south-east Asia's largest, has grown robustly since Asia's 1997–1999 financial crisis. Economic reforms and better fiscal management became a priority after 2004, after the succession of President Susilo Bambang Yudhoyono, following the country's first direct election, which ended decades of authoritarian rule. GDP growth rose from 5.5% in 2006 to 6.3% in 2007, the highest in a decade, but in 2008 it dipped to an estimated 5.9%. Indonesia's debt-to-GDP ratio has fallen, and, in 2003, it graduated from the International Monetary Fund (IMF) loan program. The region's main oil and gas producer, it became a net importer of oil in 2004, as a result of ageing wells and low levels of investment. Exports include oil and gas, plywood, textiles, rubber, and palm oil. Indonesia, which is Asia's third most populous country, has faced costly natural disasters, including the 2004 tsunami, and three earthquakes in 2005–2006. Its legal system remains weak, while bureaucracy and lack of infrastructure impede foreign investment.

STATISTICS

GDP growth: 5.9% (2008, est.)

GDP per capita: US$3,900 (2008, est.)

CPI: 10.5% (2008, est.)

Key interest rate: 7.75% (February 2009, BI)

Exchange rate versus dollar: rupiah per US dollar—11,500 (February 2009)

Unemployment: 8.7% (2008, ILO)

FDI: US$63.46 billion (2008, est.)

Current account deficit/surplus: US$2.485 billion (2008, est.)

Population: 237.5m (July 2008, est.)

Source: CIA Factbook except where stated

ECONOMIC POLICY OVER 12 MONTHS

The high oil price dented the Indonesian government's budget in 2008 because of high fuel subsidies. In March 2008, the fuel subsidy was forecast to cost US$11.53 billion for that year, more than double the original forecast. The government announced in May 2008 that Indonesia would leave OPEC, and focus instead on boosting its own lagging oil and gas industry. This was, in part, a political move to highlight escalating oil prices. In an unpopular development during the same month, the government also raised domestic fuel prices by 29%.

In February 2009, the government sanctioned a US$6 billion stimulus package that included tax breaks, cuts in electricity subsidies, and increased spending on transport and infrastructure. Suharso Monoarfa, deputy chairman of the parliamentary committee, said the package would curb rising unemployment, sustain consumer spending, and strengthen businesses.

Monetary policy has been conducted within an inflation-targeting regime since mid-2005, when the former policy of monetary targeting was scrapped. Following an upsurge in 2005–2006 as a result of fuel price hikes, inflation was brought under control, and ended 2007 within the desired range of 5–7%. However, it had risen to 10.5% in February 2009. Even so, the central bank felt able to reduce interest rates to 7.75% the following month.

To help ease its US$11.6 billion budget deficit, Indonesia sold US$3 billion of bonds in February 2009. The country had already raised US$4.2 billion from dollar-denominated bond sales during 2008. In February 2009, Indonesia was also one of 13 Asian nations that pooled US$120 billion of foreign-exchange reserves in an attempt to stem the flight of capital out of south-east Asia.

On March 3 2009, the World Bank approved a US$2 billion contingency loan on which the government can draw, should market liquidity or access to international or domestic credit tighten. The loan was part of

     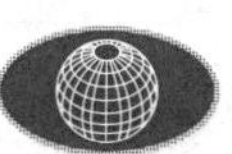   

US$5.5 billion contingency financing for Indonesia, which could include US$1.0–1.5 billion each from Australia, Japan, and the Asian Development Bank.

Joachim von Amsberg, the World Bank's Indonesia director, said that Indonesia had reduced its debt-to-GDP ratio by more than any major economy in the region—from 55% in 2004 to 30% in 2008. "The strong macroeconomic management of previous years is now paying off," he said.

The success or failure of the stimulus package is expected to be critical to the political fortunes of President Yudhoyono as he seeks re-election in July 2009, after the parliamentary polls of April 2009.

ECONOMIC PERFORMANCE OVER 12 MONTHS

Indonesia is weathering the international financial storm better than many other countries. The economy grew by 5.9% in 2008, and the government of President Yudhoyono expects it will grow by 4.5% in 2009.

The country, classed as an emerging economy, has practised prudent fiscal management, backed by reforms of its financial sector. In early 2008, however, it suffered an exogenous shock because of the rising price of food, especially staples such as wheat, soybeans, and rice, and crude oil.

In a bid to prop up the value of the rupiah, the central bank has been tapping into its foreign currency reserves. In March 2009, the currency sank to around IDR11,700 to the US dollar, well below the earlier forecast of IDR9,400. The rupiah was worth IDR2,000 to the US dollar before the Asian financial crisis of 1997–1998.

However, the weakness of the rupiah does not seem to have outweighed the slump in demand for Indonesia's key commodities. In January 2009, overseas shipments fell by 35.5% to US$7.15 billion, their biggest fall in 22 years.

The leading destination for Indonesian exports is Japan. Other big export markets include Singapore, the United States, China, South Korea, and Saudi Arabia. Indonesia's exports, however, are only equivalent to about one-third of its GDP, so it is less vulnerable to swings in global demand than some of its Asian neighbors. Indonesia is expected to become a net exporter of rice for the first time in more than 30 years during 2009, with a production of 60.93 million tonnes, up by about 1% on 2008. As a consequence, the domestic retail price of the staple did not suffer its customary first-quarter hike.

Indonesia's fiscal deficit is expected to broaden to an average of 2.8% of GDP in 2009–2010 as the country seeks to ride out the global downturn.

The country's central statistics agency said, in February 2009, that unemployment had climbed to 8.39% of the country's total workforce of 111.9 million in August 2008.

Indonesia's problems with corruption were highlighted by the conviction, in October 2008, of the central bank's ex-governor, Burhanuddin Abdullah, for embezzling some US$12.6 million from the bank. In a related case, four other former central bankers were charged with graft in February 2009. They have denied wrongdoing.

The IMF is more pessimistic about the outlook for the Indonesian economy than the government. In January 2009, it projected that GDP growth would fall to 3.5% in 2009 before recovering to 4% in 2010. The Economist Intelligence Unit is gloomier, forecasting growth will slow to 1.9% in 2009, before recovering to 2.2% in 2010.

SUPPORT FOR INWARD INVESTMENT AND IMPORTS

The Indonesia Investment Coordinating Board oversees foreign direct investment, and can provide information on incentives, and details of potential commercial partners. The board oversees Indonesia Investment Promotion Centers in cities including London, Osaka, and Los Angeles. However, foreign investors face significant restrictions. In 2007, Indonesia updated its restricted investment list of sectors in which foreign investment is prohibited or restricted. Details can be found on the board's website.

TAX EXEMPTIONS

The government said in March 2009 that it will provide additional incentives for investment in oil refineries. Indonesia needs to build new refineries and wants to encourage investment in the sector in order to reduce its dependence on imported oil. The top corporate tax rate is 30%. Other taxes include a value-added tax and a tax on interest. The March 2009 stimulus package included reduced tax tariffs, government-borne value added tax, import duties, and incentives related to income tax.

▸▸ MORE INFO

Websites:

Indonesia Investment Coordinating Board: www.bkpm.go.id

Indonesia Investment Coordinating Board (regional): www.regionalinvestment.com/sipid/en/index.php

National Agency for Export Development: www.nafed.go.id

Ministry of Industry: www.depperin.go.id/ENG2006

  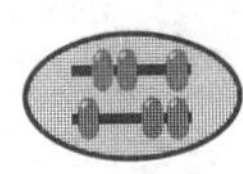      

Iran

ECONOMY AND TRADE

Iran, a theocratic Islamic republic with strained relations with the West, is a major producer of oil and gas, and has had one of the Middle East's best-performing economies. A founding member of OPEC, it has the world's third-largest proven reserves of crude oil, and the second-largest proven reserves of natural gas. Oil accounts for 80% of foreign exchange receipts, while oil and gas contribute 70% of government revenue. Iran also produces textiles, construction materials, metals, armaments, and agricultural produce. The state controls most economic activity, and spends about half of its budget subsidizing basics including fuel, electricity, bread, and rice. Bordered by Iraq to the west, and Afghanistan and Pakistan to the east, Iran is subject to UN, European Union, and US sanctions as a result of its nuclear ambitions, and as an alleged sponsor of terrorism. Its main trading partners are China, Japan, Germany, Italy, South Korea, and the UAE.

STATISTICS

GDP growth: 6.4% (2008, est.)
GDP per capita: US$13,100 (2008, est.)
CPI: 28% (2008, official Iranian estimate)
Key interest rate: 12% (December 31, 2007)
Exchange rate versus dollar: Iranian rials per US dollar—9,700 (March 2009, xe.com)
Unemployment: 12.5% (2008, official Iranian estimate)
FDI: US$6.95 billion (2008, est.)
Current account deficit/ US$27.47 billion (2008, est.)
surplus:
Population: 65.9 million (July 2008, est.)
Source: CIA Factbook except where stated

ECONOMIC POLICY OVER 12 MONTHS

Ultra-conservative President Mahmoud Ahmadinejad, elected in 2005 on a populist platform, has vowed to transform Iran into a regional economic powerhouse. With oil output limited by OPEC quotas, Iran has been striving to increase gas production, especially in the South Pars field in the Persian Gulf. In the longer term, Iran also plans to increase oil-refining capacity from 1.5 million barrels per day (bpd) in 2008 to 3 million bpd by 2012.

Iran's government has mismanaged the economy in recent times. Under Ahmadinejad, petrodollars were overspent—especially in poor and rural areas—as the price of oil climbed towards record levels in July 2008.

For the fiscal year starting March 2008, the parliament approved a budget of US$310 billion, 18% higher than a year earlier, and despite fears this surge in spending would fuel inflation. (By September 2008, inflation had reached nearly 29%). In late summer 2008, Ahmadinejad unveiled a major, five-year, economic reform plan that included a restructuring of price controls, and subsidies aimed at reducing reliance on oil revenues and boosting the economy.

Implementing the plan has proved problematic. Although the government asked for US$35 billion to fund it, only US$8.5 billion was approved. A proposal to impose a value added tax in October 2008 sparked an outcry and violent street protests. In March 2009, a day after approving the blueprint for a US$298 billion budget, Iran's parliament scrapped a key component of the plan—to raise energy prices as much as fourfold, to save US$20 billion in subsidies by March 2010.

In addition to deficit spending, the government has sought to boost the economy by expanding the money supply. In September 2008, Ahmadinejad replaced the governor of the Central Bank of Iran, Tahmasb Mazaheri, because of differences of opinion over monetary policy and inflation. Mazaheri, who was replaced by Mahmoud Bahmani, the bank's general secretary, had opposed the president and parliament by calling for a rise in interest rates.

The Oil Stabilization Fund, which holds extra oil revenue for capital investment or budgetary support, may be replaced as early as 2010 by the National Development Fund. It will be harder for the government to spend the latter on populist policies. In January 2009, Iran's supreme leader, the Ayatollah Ali Khamenei proposed that 20% of the country's oil and gas revenues should be invested in the new fund, and that the promotion of domestic and foreign investment should be prioritized.

ECONOMIC PERFORMANCE OVER 12 MONTHS

President Mahmoud Ahmadinejad has repeatedly lashed out at the West for the current financial crisis, a tactic that analysts say is intended to deflect criticism from his mismanagement of Iran's economy. However, his rhetoric has also landed him in trouble domestically, as critics have accused him of spending too much time castigating the West, and not enough fixing domestic problems.

"Iran threatened with economic melt-down," was a headline on the BBC News website in late February 2009. With income from crude accounting for 80% of foreign earnings, the world's fourth-largest crude exporter was hard hit by the slide in the oil price, from a peak of US$147 in July 2008 to a just under a third of that in early March 2009.

Even so, Iran's economic growth is likely to remain relatively stable between now and 2013. According to the Economist Intelligence Unit, real annual growth should average 4.4% over that half-decade.

In February 2009, Iran faced a budget deficit of US$44 billion for the 12 months to March 2010, according to a parliamentary research centre. At the same time, long-term unemployment among those aged under 30 was estimated at 35%.

Inflation, has climbed steadily from 11% in 2005, when Ahmadinejad became the president, to a peak of 29% in September 2008. In February 2009, it had eased to 25.9%. According to the Central Bank of Iran,

  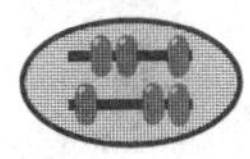 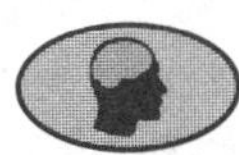  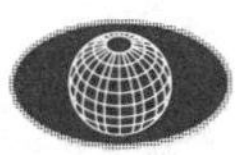   

the year-on-year rate has declined from 24% to 20.8%. However according to *The Economist*, Iranians have yet to recover from the shock of house prices tripling since 2005. The recent fall in consumer prices is a positive for Ahmadinejad, who faces reformist opponents in the June 2009 presidential elections.

Ahmadinejad's critics accuse him of squandering petrodollars when the oil price was high. Moreover, Iran's National Audit Office reported, in February 2009, that the government did not return US$1.058 billion of surplus oil revenue in its 2006–2007 budget to the national treasury, or to foreign exchange reserves, even though this is a legal requirement.

Sanctions have undermined Iran's economy. Imported commodities and technology are estimated to cost 10–20% more than they should, as a result. US sanctions, first imposed after the 1980 hostage-taking in Tehran, prohibit most business with Iran. They also make it hard for non-US oil and gas companies investing in Iran to win US business.

Despite President Barack Obama's videotaped overtures to Iran in March 2009, analysts expect any thawing of relations with the United States to take time. In a message timed for the Iranian celebration of Nowruz, a holiday marking the arrival of spring, Obama said he was keen to pursue "constructive ties" with Tehran, and engage in broad diplomacy.

France, Germany, and Britain, in February 2009, quietly proposed tougher EU sanctions on Iran's banking and military sectors. France and Britain have also pushed for sanctions targeting Iran's oil industry.

SUPPORT FOR INWARD INVESTMENT AND IMPORTS

Any business considering commercial dealings with Iran must make itself acquainted with any relevant sanctions, such as those imposed by the UN, European Union, or the United States. The Iranian government's Organization for Investment, Economic, and Technical Assistance for Iran (OIETAI) offers advice on tax and other fiscal incentives. Information about Iran's 17 Special Economic Zones and Free Zones can be obtained through the Secretariat of the High Council of Iran Free Trade-Industrial Zones (IFTIZ).

TAX EXEMPTIONS

Fiscal incentives for investing in Iran include reduced income tax rates from 65% to a flat, fixed 25% rate. See the Ministry of Economic Affairs and Finance website.

▸▸ MORE INFO

Websites:

OIETAI website: www.investiniran.ir

Ministry of Economic Affairs and Finance, tax info: www.cito.ir/site/en/download/guide.pdf

Secretariat of the High Council of Iran Free Trade-Industrial Zones: www.freezones.ir

See Also:

✔ Middle East: Regulatory Structure and Powers (p. 1041)

Iraq

ECONOMY AND TRADE

Formerly part of the Ottoman Empire, Iraq was occupied by Britain during the course of World War I; in 1920, it was declared a League of Nations mandate under United Kingdom administration. Iraq attained its independence as a kingdom in 1932. A "republic" was proclaimed in 1958, but in actuality a series of strongmen ruled the country until 2003. The last was Saddam Hussein, who was deposed following the Gulf War. In October 2005, Iraqis approved a constitution in a national referendum and, pursuant to this document, elected a 275-member Council of Representatives (CoR) in December 2005. Decreasing insurgent attacks and an improving security environment in many parts of the country are helping to spur economic activity. Iraq's economy is dominated by the oil sector, which has traditionally provided more than 90% of foreign-exchange earnings. Oil exports are around levels seen before the United States and its allies launched Operation Iraqi Freedom.

ECONOMIC POLICY OVER 12 MONTHS

Historically, Iraq's economy was characterized by a heavy dependence on oil exports, and an emphasis on development through central planning. Prior to the outbreak of the war with Iran in September 1980, Iraq's economic prospects were bright. Oil production had reached a level of 3.5 million barrels per day (bpd), and oil revenues were US$21 billion in 1979, and US$27 billion in 1980. At the outbreak of the war, Iraq had amassed an estimated US$35 billion in foreign exchange reserves.

The Iran–Iraq war depleted Iraq's foreign-exchange reserves, devastated its economy, and left the country saddled with a foreign debt of more than US$40 billion. After hostilities ceased, oil exports gradually increased with the construction of new pipelines, and the restoration of damaged facilities. Iraq's invasion of Kuwait in August 1990, subsequent international sanctions, damage from military action by an international coalition beginning in January 1991, and neglect of infrastructure drastically reduced economic activity. Government policies of diverting income to key supporters of the regime while sustaining a large

STATISTICS

GDP growth: 9.8% (2008)

GDP per capita: US$4,000

CPI: 6.8%

Key interest rate: 19.74%

Exchange rate versus dollar: New Iraqi dinars per US dollar—1.176

Unemployment: 18.2–30.0% (2008)

FDI: N/A

Current account surplus: US$22.6 billion

Population: 28,945,657

Source: CIA Factbook except where stated

 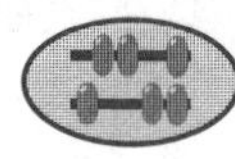    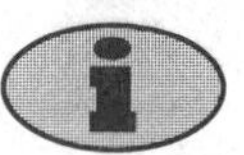  

military and internal security force further impaired finances, leaving the average Iraqi citizen facing desperate hardships.

The occupation of the US-led coalition in March–April 2003 resulted in the shutdown of much of the central economic administrative structure. The rebuilding of oil infrastructure, utilities infrastructure, and other production capacities has proceeded steadily since 2004, despite attacks on key economic facilities and continuing internal security incidents. Despite uncertainty, Iraq is making progress toward establishing the laws and institutions needed to make and implement economic policy.

Iraq's economy is dominated by the oil sector, which has traditionally provided about 95% of foreign exchange earnings. Current estimates show that oil production averages 2.1 million bpd.

The Iraqi government is seeking to pass and implement laws to strengthen the economy, including a hydrocarbon law to encourage development of this sector, a revenue-sharing law to divide oil revenues equitably within the nation in line with the Iraqi constitution, and is producing regulations to implement a new foreign investment law. Controlling inflation, reducing corruption, and implementing structural reforms, such as bank restructuring and private sector development, will be key to Iraq's economic growth.

Foreign assistance has been an integral component of Iraq's reconstruction efforts over the past three years. At a Donors Conference in Madrid in October 2003, more than US$33 billion was pledged to assist in the reconstruction of Iraq. Out of that conference, the United Nations (UN) and the World Bank launched the International Reconstruction Fund Facility for Iraq (IRFFI) to administer and disburse about US$1.7 billion of those funds. The rest of the assistance is being disbursed bilaterally. To date, US$15.3 billion has been pledged in foreign aid for 2004–2008 from outside of the United States.

ECONOMIC PERFORMANCE OVER 12 MONTHS

In December 2007, the International Monetary Fund (IMF) agreed to renew a Stand-By Arrangement (SBA) for Iraq, which provides a credit line to the Iraqi government of up to US$744 million if needed. The SBA also requires Iraq to undertake some economic policy reforms. If Iraq fulfills the terms of the SBA, the country will receive the final stage of Paris Club debt reduction. At that point, a total of 80% of Iraq's international debt will have been forgiven. The new SBA lasts for 15 months, until March 2009; the previous SBA began in December 2005 and ended in December 2007.

In July 2006, the government of Iraq and the UN began work to formulate the International Compact with Iraq (ICI), a five-year framework for Iraq to achieve economic self-sufficiency. On May 3, 2007, in Sharm el-Sheikh, the ICI was formally launched by more than 70 countries and international organizations, many represented at the ministerial level.

The Compact aims to create a mutually reinforcing dynamic of national consensus and international support. Domestically, the aim is to build a national Compact around the government's political and economic program, and to restore the Iraqi people's trust in the state, and its ability to protect them and meet their basic needs. Internationally, the Compact establishes a framework of mutual commitments to provide financial and technical assistance, and debt relief needed to support Iraq, and strengthen its resolve to address critical reforms and policies.

Despite its abundant land and water resources, Iraq remains a net food importer. Under the UN Oil-For-Food program, Iraq imported large quantities of grains, meat, poultry, and dairy products. Obstacles to agricultural development during the previous regime included labor shortages, inadequate management and maintenance, salinization, urban migration, and dislocations resulting from previous land-reform and collectivization programs. A Ba'ath regime policy to destroy the Marsh Arab culture, by draining the southern marshes and introducing irrigated farming to this region, destroyed a natural food-producing area, while concentration of salts and minerals in the soil caused by the draining left the land unsuitable for agriculture.

Through assistance from USAID and USDA, targeted efforts have begun to overcome the damage done by the Ba'ath regime in ways that will rehabilitate the agricultural sector, and confront environmental degradation. These efforts include infrastructure development, private sector development, veterinary clinic restoration, increased wheat production, and training and technical assistance in developing policies on sustainable water resources management, and building Iraqi natural resources management.

SUPPORT FOR INWARD INVESTMENT AND IMPORTS

Inward investment is handled by the Iraq Economic Development Group, via its website. It aims to develop high quality, commercially feasible projects to encourage investments into Iraq, mainly targeting critical Iraqi infrastructure to fuel economic growth, create jobs, and provide the basis for continued employment growth. Investors should have projects in mind that address these interests. The IEDG advertises projects internationally, and claims that "no project advertised has an annual return on investment of less than 30%, though this can be a five year average on larger projects. It can arrange direct investment, or take a general investment that leverages all ongoing projects. It will also help investors promote products, and will assist in getting products to market.

MORE INFO

Websites:

Official website of the multi-national force in Iraq: www.mnf-iraq.com

Iraq Economic Development Group: www.investmentsiraq.org

US Department of State country profile on Iraq: www.state.gov/r/pa/ei/bgn/6804.htm

See Also:

✔ Middle East: Regulatory Structure and Powers (p. 1041)

 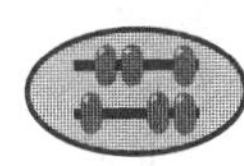      

TAX EXEMPTIONS
Further information can be obtained from IEDG.

Ireland

ECONOMY AND TRADE

Ireland was named the "Celtic Tiger" after its annual GDP growth averaged 6.5% in 1990–2007. In the first 12 years of that period, growth was largely attributable to US multinationals establishing manufacturing and service bases in the country. However, following the country's adoption of the euro in 2002, its growth was mainly fueled by a property boom that the government promoted through subsidies to the sector. Per capita GDP surged, surpassing that of the United States by 2007, which undermined the country's competitiveness. Following the bursting of its property bubble in early 2008, Ireland became the first EU member to fall into recession in summer 2008. A healthy current account surplus in the mid-1990s had become a massive deficit. In September 2008, the government of Taoiseach (prime minister) Brian Cowen offered to guarantee all bank deposits, recapitalize the banking system, and introduce new public/private venture funds. Agriculture, once the most important sector, is now dwarfed by industry and services. The export sector, dominated by overseas multinationals, remains a key component of the economy.

STATISTICS

GDP growth: −2.5% (2008, government statistics)
GDP per capita: US$47,800 (2008, est.)
CPI: 0.1% (February 2008, government statistics)
Key interest rate: 1.5% (March 2009, ECB)
Exchange rate versus dollar: euros per US dollar—0.6689 (2008, est.)
Unemployment: 11% (2009, est.)
FDI: US$216bn
Current account deficit: −US$8.621 billion (2008, est.)
Population: 4.2 million (July 2008, est.)
Source: CIA Factbook except where stated

ECONOMIC POLICY OVER 12 MONTHS

While the Irish government has expressed regret about the excesses of the housing bubble, which burst in 2008, it has no intention of abandoning the country's globalized growth model. "The key is to turn the model back to export-led growth," said finance minister Brian Lenihan in January 2009, "so we have to attend to competitiveness."

The defining moment for Taoiseach Brian Cowen came in September 2008, five months after he took office. After it emerged that Anglo-Irish Bank was at risk of collapse, and there was a danger that other Irish banks might suffer collateral damage, Cowen's government intervened with a blanket 100% guarantee to depositors. Anglo-Irish was fully nationalized in January 2009, and, the following month, the government injected €7 billion of capital into the larger Allied Irish Bank and Bank of Ireland.

The generosity of this bailout—the assets covered are worth two to three times Irish GDP—combined with a sharply reduced tax take, and a widening budget deficit, have led bond investors to fear Ireland may default on its debt. Ireland's ten-year government bonds yield 6%, double those of Germany. In March 2009, the credit rating agency Standard & Poor's, reduced Ireland's triple-A sovereign credit rating by one notch, amid concerns about the country's widening budget deficit, and the possible need for more steps to stabilize its banking system.

The government's budget has fallen into deficit because income tax cuts introduced before the bubble burst left the public finances over-dependent on "windfall" revenues from value added tax on the sale of new homes, capital gains tax, and stamp duty. When the bubble burst, revenues from such taxes collapsed. The government will, in future, rely on more stable sources of revenue, including personal income tax and excise taxes.

Rather than seek to reflate the economy through a fiscal stimulus, Cowen's government has preferred to tighten the screws on its budget. Austerity measures include an increase in value added tax, and a 7.5% cut in public-sector wages. In February 2009, 120,000 people protested against these measures, and unions have threatened a national strike if the government does not reverse his policies.

The government is not, however, contemplating any increase in the country's competitive 12.5% rate of corporate tax. This is seen as having played a key part in the country's success in attracting foreign direct investment in the 1990s, and is a shibboleth for Irish politicians.

The crisis at Ireland's leading banks has also prompted a rethink of the appropriateness of the "light touch" regulation, which fueled the growth of Dublin's international financial services center during the boom.

Even though the Irish people voted against the Lisbon Treaty in June 2008, the recession has prompted them to rediscover their enthusiasm for the European Union and the euro. The government hopes to reduce the general government deficit to below the 3% limit by 2013.

ECONOMIC PERFORMANCE OVER 12 MONTHS

The Irish Republic was once one of Europe's most dynamic and fastest-growing economies. Growth in 2005–2007 was built on the uncertain foundation of a massive property boom, which some have described as having been "out of control." The housing and construction boom was fueled by successive governments, including that of former Taoiseach Bertie Ahern, through tax breaks for property-related businesses.

After the property market crashed to earth in early 2008, the country fell into recession, and this happened faster than many other EU member states. The country officially entered recession in September 2008, and, given the number of people who had been working on building sites, unemployment has since risen sharply.

By February 2009, unemployment had jumped to 10.4%, according to official statistics. In March 2009, the governor of Ireland's central bank, John Hurley, predicted it would reach some 11% in 2009.

Hurley told a parliamentary committee at that time that, while the initial downturn in Ireland's economy could be blamed on the softening of the property and construction sectors, it has since broadened out into a marked weakening of domestic demand, as well as a slump in exports.

Exports have suffered because of weaker global demand, and because of the 15% fall in the value of the British pound against the euro between April 2008 and March 2009—the United Kingdom is a key export market. This has undermined Ireland's competitiveness. The euro gave the country interest rates that were too low in the boom years, and now the government is incapable of devaluing its currency to restore competitiveness.

Hurley admitted that the recovery some had predicted for the early part of 2009 had not materialized, and warned that Ireland faces a "very difficult year or two," and its "worst crisis in the past 40 years."

The country's GDP contracted by 2.5% during 2008, and the government expects it will shrink by a further 6.0–6.5% in 2009.

Ireland's budget deficit reached 8% of GDP in 2008. In January 2009, the government predicted it would reach 11% of GDP in 2009, and 13% of GDP the following year, which is four times the figure required under the EU's stability and growth pact.

In an interview with Bloomberg television in March 2008, finance minister, Brian Lenihan, said: "We're now at the hangover stage, as the party went a little too far." However, he believes that as Ireland was the first EU nation to enter recession, it should also be the first to experience recovery.

SUPPORT FOR INWARD INVESTMENT AND IMPORTS

The principal goal of investment promotion has traditionally been job creation, especially in technology-intensive and high-skill industries. More recently, the government has focused on Ireland's international competitiveness by encouraging foreign-invested companies to enhance research and development activities, and to deliver higher-value goods and services. IDA Ireland provides a full service to overseas firms considering locating in Ireland. It has been active in the development of infrastructure and business support services, telecoms, education, and regulatory issues, especially in relation to EU policy.

TAX EXEMPTIONS

The government would like Ireland to remain an attractive location from a fiscal perspective, within EU rules. The corporation tax rate of 12.5% is among the lowest in Europe, and the country also offers a range of other benefits, including grants to employers who create new jobs without investing in fixed assets. Irish Tax and Customs

▶▶ MORE INFO

Websites:

Enterprise Ireland: www.revenue.ie/en/index.html

IDA Ireland: www.idaireland.com/home/index.aspx?id=3

Ireland Tax and Customs: www.revenue.ie/en/index.html

Shannon Free Airport Development Company: www.irishstatutebook.ie/1986/en/act/pub/0020/index.html

Isle of Man

ECONOMY AND TRADE

The Isle of Man is often called a tax haven, but the government prefers to describe it as a "tax-efficient jurisdiction." Independence has served the economy well, with 25 years of economic growth lifting income from half the United Kingdom average in 1981 to more than 18% above, and 24% higher than the majority of countries in the European Union. Real growth has averaged 8% a year over the past decade. Offshore banking, high-tech, and e-gaming businesses have been lured to the island by a competitive tax regime, its skilled workforce, and the favorable regulatory backdrop. Traditional sectors, such as high-tech engineering, manufacturing, agriculture, and tourism—including the world famous TT Races—continue to make an important contribution to the economy. Agriculture and fishing, once the mainstays of the economy, have seen their shares of GDP diminish. The country enjoys free access to EU markets but does the bulk of its trade with the United Kingdom.

ECONOMIC POLICY OVER 12 MONTHS

Ahead of the international banking crisis of October 2008, the Isle of Man government had already instituted a policy of diversifying the island's economy away from dependence on financial and profes-

  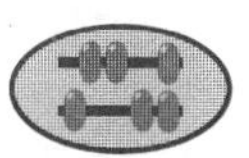      

sional services, with the space industry, e-commerce, and online gaming seen as favored sectors for growth. This is just as well, given that the Kaupthing Singer & Friedlander (KSF) debacle is perceived as having tainted the island's reputation as a safe and reliable offshore financial services center.

KSF collapsed in October 2008, leaving depositors in the Icelandic bank's Isle of Man branch at risk of large losses. The island's parliament, the Tynwald, responded by holding its first emergency session in 40 years. At this meeting, policymakers agreed to strengthen the country's deposit guarantee scheme, raising depositor protection to £50,000 for individuals and £20,000 for charities. However, the action proved insufficient for many of KSF's aggrieved customers, especially those who had entrusted larger sums to the bank. In February 2009, an Isle of Man court approved a revised "scheme of arrangement" proposal for the failed bank, under which the depositors are expected to retrieve up to 60% of their cash.

Government spending and revenue reached £600m in 2008–2009, and the government had limited room for manoeuvre when putting together its 2009–2010 Budget, given that revenues are mainly derived from a "common purse" agreement with the recession-hit United Kingdom economy. Treasury Minister, Allan Bell, said: "The revenue outlook [for the year commencing April 2009] is a difficult one, and we face problems that have not been experienced in the Isle of Man for a generation." Net government spending was increased by just 1% to £572 million.

The island's status may also suffer because tax havens and "offshore secrecy jurisdictions" are increasingly coming under attack, notably from the United Kingdom chancellor of the exchequer, Alistair Darling, who in November 2008 said that the Isle of Man's status as a "tax haven sitting in the Irish Sea" would have to be reviewed. Barack Obama supported the Stop Tax Haven Abuse Act before he became president, and if passed, this could blacklist the island and 30 other territories.

The Isle of Man has sought to preempt such measures by entering into a "constructive dialogue" with the OECD Global Forum on Taxation and establishing 12 TIEAs (tax information exchange agreements). Malcolm Couch, assessor of income tax for the Isle of Man, said: "We've quietly got on with working closely with the OECD, concluding lots of tax cooperation agreements."

ECONOMIC PERFORMANCE OVER 12 MONTHS

The island's record of economic success is testimony to its abilities to attract a diverse range of businesses to the island—including e-commerce, information technology, film production, international shipping, aircraft registry, and space and satellite businesses. In February 2007, the Internet services provider and data-hosting company, Netcetera, established a sizeable base in the island's Freeport (adjacent to the main airport at Ronaldsway), and a number of e-gaming specialists, which are locked out of the United Kingdom market, have also set up on the island.

The Isle of Man's GDP grew by 7.7% to more than £1.8 billion in 2008, but the government expects economic growth to slow to 2.5% in 2009. Unemployment among the island's 81,000 population is about 2.2%—an eighth of its 1980s level, and among the lowest levels in Europe.

However, the island remains dependent on financial and professional services for about 50% of its GDP. Its reputation in these areas suffered, following the failure of the local branch of Icelandic bank, Kaupthing Singer & Friedlander, in October 2008. The bank had more than 10,000 depositors based in the island, who had deposited more than £860m with the bank. The way in which the local regulator handled the situation attracted criticism—especially as it had earlier allowed KSF's Isle of Man branch to "upstream" assets to the United Kingdom branch. The United Kingdom government seized about £400m of KSF(IoM)'s assets when it put the Icelandic bank's United Kingdom operations into administration.

While acknowledging the Kaupthing debacle may have harmed the island's reputation as a safe haven for investors' cash, the Manx government has pointed out that funds under administration in the island have risen to US$60 billion, up from US$9.8bn in 2003.

Officials believe that the island will achieve its target of having US$150 billion of funds business by 2010. Chief minister, Tony Brown, said in January 2009: "While competitor jurisdictions have noted contraction in assets under management, we have seen continued growth year on year. In the year ahead, we expect growth will slow somewhat, but we believe we remain well placed to weather the storm."

In December 2008, rating agencies Standard & Poor's and Moody's confirmed their AAA rating on the island's government debt. Moody's noted that the £150 million earmarked by Manx Treasury for bank compensation schemes "is clearly manageable against free reserves and projected capital spending."

SUPPORT FOR INWARD INVESTORS AND IMPORTERS

The Isle of Man government positively encourages inward investment through a sympathetic tax regime and legislative framework, together with financial incentives. It is actively seeking to attract inward investment in sectors including manufacturing, tourism, e-commerce, film, space, and technology. The establishment of a "Freeport" has boosted the manufacturing sector. The Department of Trade and Industry is a good source for assistance and advice.

STATISTICS

GDP growth: 7.7% (2008, est.)

GDP per capita: US$35,000 (2005, est.)

CPI: 1.2% (Feb 2008, IoM government.)

Key interest rate: 1% (since February 2008)

Exchange rate: Manx pounds per US dollar—0.53 (2008, est.) Note: the Manx pound is on a par with the United Kingdom pound.

Unemployment: 2.2% (January 2008, IoM government)

FDI: N/A

Current account deficit/surplus: N/A

Population: 76,220 (July 2008, est.)

Source: CIA Factbook except where stated

▸▸ MORE INFO

Websites:

Isle of Man government, economic and commercial opportunities: www.gov.im/isleofman/economic.xml

Isleofman.com – official information on tourism finance and commerce: www.isleofman.com

Department of Trade and Industry website: www.gov.im/dti/

IoM Treasury website: www.gov.im/treasury/

  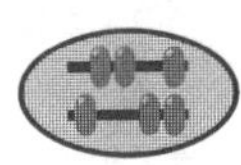      

TAX EXEMPTIONS

The island benefits from a customs union with the United Kingdom, so all rates of duty, VAT, forms, processes, etc, are familiar, giving simplified access to the United Kingdom and the rest of Europe, but in a low-tax environment. In a move to sidestep EU criticism, the government reduced corporation tax to zero for all companies from April 2007, not just offshore ones.

Israel and the Palestinian Territories

ECONOMY AND TRADE

Israel has a diversified, export-based economy with a strong high-tech bias. The main exports are software, electronics, biomedical goods, polished diamonds, military equipment, and agricultural products. Relatively isolated from its neighbors, its top trading partners are the Palestinian Territories—the West Bank and Gaza Strip, with which peace has been elusive—the United States, European Union, and China. The Territories primarily export agricultural produce to Israel. The dotcom bust and the intensified Israeli–Palestinian conflict of the early 2000s prompted a short recession. Steady growth was then promoted through structural reforms and tighter fiscal controls, although public debt remained high. In 2006, Israel registered a trade deficit, largely as a result of rising energy and commodity prices. Foreign aid and loans, mostly from the United States, are sizeable. The Territories, racked by poverty, have faced economic embargoes, and extensive damage to capital due to the conflict.

STATISTICS*

GDP growth: 4.2% (2008, est.)

GDP per capita: US$28,900 (2008, est.)

CPI: 4.7% (2008, est.)

Key interest rate: 0.75% (since February 2009, Reuters)

Exchange rate versus dollar: new Israeli shekels (ILS) per US dollar – 3.56 (2008, est.)

Unemployment: 6.1% (2008, est.)

FDI: US$68.06 billion (2008, est.)

Current account deficit –US$1.893 billion (2008, est.)

Population: 7,112,359† (July 2008, est.)

* data is for Israel only.

† includes about 187,000 Israeli settlers in the West Bank, about 20,000 in the Israeli-occupied Golan Heights, and almost 177,000 in East Jerusalem.

Source: CIA Factbook except where stated

ECONOMIC POLICY OVER 12 MONTHS

Although Israel was well-placed economically when the global financial crisis started to unfold in 2007, the country's vulnerabilities had come into sharp relief by mid-2008. A small, open economy, it had a total external gross debt of about 50% of GDP, and public debt of some 80% of GDP in the third quarter of 2008, according to the International Monetary Fund (IMF).

In June 2008, a US$92.6 billion budget for 2009 was proposed, based on projected GDP growth of 3.5% and a 1.7% cap on government expenditure growth. The long-term aim was to reduce the debt-to-GDP ratio to 58%— the OECD average—by 2015.

Between October 2008 and February 2009, the Bank of Israel reduced short-term interest rate by 3.5 percentage points to an all-time low of 0.75%. The bank also started buying up government bonds in the secondary market.

The government was dissolved ahead of the general election of February 2009, following an autumn of intense political campaigning, and Israel's military incursion into the Gaza strip of December 2008 and January 2009. After a close finish, prime minister-designate Benjamin Netanyahu (Likud Party) was still struggling to form a broad-based coalition government in mid-March 2009.

With the government in transition, the Bank of Israel took the lead in economic affairs, and in March 2009 proposed a US$1.1 billion economic stimulus plan. This revolved around channeling funds into spending on transport infrastructure and business start-ups, an earned-income tax credit, and better jobless benefits.

The plan assumed that Israel's economic decline could be limited to −1.1% in 2009, and a fiscal deficit of 5.8% of GDP, up from a previously projected 5.2%. Despite the creation of 15,000 new jobs, unemployment is projected to rise to 8% during 2009, up from a 19-year low of 6% in 2008. Bank of Israel governor Stanley Fischer warned that, if the plan were not adopted, Israel's economy could face its worst contraction since the state's inception in 1948.

The Finance Ministry's director-general, Yarom Ariav, warned that Israel might have to raise money abroad for the first time since 2006. He said that a ballooning budget deficit would mean government borrowing would escalate to US$9.4 billion in 2009, up from US$2.1 billion in 2008. Economists noted, however, that the Israeli Treasury could rely upon US$9 billion in US guarantees, dating from 2003, of which US$5.2 billion had been used.

Gaza, devastated after Israel's 22-day offensive in December 2008 and January 2009, in March 2009 received pledges from international donors of US$4.48 billion over two years—including US$900 million from the United States—for humanitarian aid, and budgetary, security, and infrastructure support. Of the total, US$1.5 billion was for the Palestinian Authority's expected budget deficit.

ECONOMIC PERFORMANCE OVER 12 MONTHS

In February 2008, an IMF report described Israel's economy as performing "exceptionally well," despite the country's large public debt. The fund predicted that economic growth would remain strong, albeit at a

  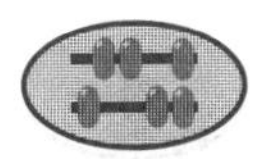 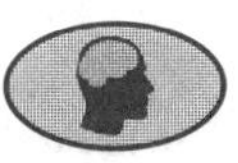   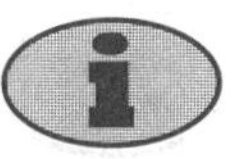  

marginally slower pace than in the preceding four years (when Israel's GDP grew by an average of 5.25%). In the same month, ratings agency Fitch upgraded Israel's foreign-currency issuer default rating to A, from A–, with a stable outlook.

Economic growth slowed to around 4% in 2008, with most of the slowdown occurring in the latter half of the year. In the fourth quarter, the economy contracted by 0.5%, largely as a result of a weakening of exports. Preliminary data suggest that there will be a further contraction in the first two quarters of 2009.

One of the main reasons for the slowdown has been economic contraction among Israel's trading partners. This caused growth in Israel's exports—which account for about 45% of its GDP—to slow to 3% in 2008, down from 8.5% growth in 2007. Growth in imports also decelerated, to 2.2%, down from 11.7% the previous year.

The current account surplus for 2008 amounted to US$1.6 billion, a significant reduction on 2007's US$4.19bn surplus. In the fourth quarter, however, the current account surplus had fallen further to US$536m, compared with a US$665m surplus in the third quarter. The central bank predicts a surplus of between US$600 million and US$2.1 billion in 2009.

Investment from overseas dropped to US$212 million in the fourth quarter of 2008, the lowest since the first quarter of 2003, which followed the dotcom bust and "first intifada." Foreign direct investment in the fourth quarter was down by 40% to US$1.84 billion, compared with a year earlier. The shekel has depreciated by 32% against a basket of other currencies between July 2008 and March 2009.

In March 2009, the Bank of Israel's governor, Stanley Fischer, painted a gloomy picture of Israel's economic outlook, as the bank trimmed its growth forecast for the fifth time in 12 months. The bank warned that the Israeli economy could contract by as much as 1.5% during 2009. A few days earlier, Merrill Lynch reduced its growth forecast for Israel in 2009 from zero to –0.7% due to weaker exports, and the worldwide slump in trading volumes. Merrill Lynch, however, retained its forecast of 1.5% growth in 2010.

SUPPORT FOR INWARD INVESTMENT AND IMPORTS

Invest in Israel, part of Israel's Ministry of Industry, Trade, and Labor, promotes investment to foreign-based individuals and companies interested in direct investment or joint ventures. The Palestinian Investment Promotion Agency similarly offers help to those interested in investing in the West Bank and Gaza Strip.

TAX EXEMPTIONS (INCLUDING TAX BREAKS)

Israel has several free trade agreements, including with the United States and European Union. The corporate tax rate is 27%, but is due to be reduced to 25% by 2010. Sizeable tax benefits are available for foreign investment, venture capital, and expenditure on research and development. In the Palestinian Territories, companies and businesses are taxed at a rate of 20%. Companies with annual revenues over US$12,000 pay 17% VAT. The Bank of Israel's website has information on tax rates for inward investors.

▸▸ MORE INFO

Websites:

Bank of Israel: www.bankisrael.gov.il/firsteng.htm

Federation of Israeli Chambers of Commerce: www.chamber.org.il/Default.aspx?lan=en-US

Invest in Israel: www.investinisrael.gov.il

Palestinian Investment Promotion Agency: www.pipa.gov.ps

See Also:

✔Middle East: Regulatory Structure and Powers (p. 1041)

Italy

ECONOMY AND TRADE

One of the founder members of the European Union, and amongst the first wave of entrants into the Eurozone in 2002, Italy is closely integrated with the European Union. The country has developed remarkably since World War II. Originally based upon agriculture, its economy is now focused upon services and manufacturing. In 2008, the International Monetary Fund (IMF) ranked Italy as the seventh-largest economy in the world in dollar terms.

However, the country faces formidable challenges. It has the lowest birth rate in Europe, and a population that is forecast to decline significantly over the next 50 years. In addition, much of the country's industrial output is generated by small and medium-sized firms, which are falling further and further behind their competitors in technological terms. The country also has a very high level of public debt, equal to 105% of GDP by the end of 2008.

ECONOMIC POLICY OVER 12 MONTHS

Italy has been more restrained than other EU countries in using fiscal pump priming to offset the impact of the global downturn on the economy. This is almost certainly because of the high level of public debt, which represents the highest indebtedness ratio in the European Union. The debt ratio will almost certainly start to rise again in 2009, even without a large stimulus package. A severe deterioration in the public finances would lead to a further sharp widening of interest-rate spreads on Italy's government debt,

  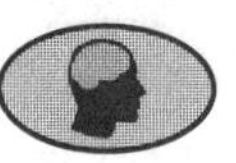  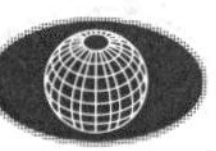   

and a hike in borrowing costs. It could also lead to a downgrade by the ratings agencies, pushing up Italy's borrowing costs still further. Indeed, *The Economist* reported, in February 2009, that the Minister of Economy and Finance, Giulio Tremonti, had insisted that, although some other governments might be able to increase their deficit and debt levels to boost their economies, Italy was not in a position to do so. Tremonti has also argued that increased borrowing will simply exacerbate a global financial crisis caused by excessive borrowing.

Rather than taking fiscal measures, the government has concentrated on encouraging the country's banks to accelerate lending. Thus, in February 2009, Italy's central bank began to underwrite collateralized interbank lending by guaranteeing the speedy repayment of loans. The central bank hoped the measure would revive interbank lending, which slumped from September 2008 onwards. Fortunately, Italy's banks have weathered the global financial crisis better than many of their European counterparts. None of the banks has failed or fallen short of regulatory requirements, and the banks have continued to fund themselves through bond issuance to domestic retail investors. The solidity of the banking system reflects its lack of exposure to toxic assets, and a relatively low dependence on wholesale funding. In February 2009, the IMF added that these factors had been supported by "a firm bank regulatory and supervisory environment, strong intervention and resolution frameworks, and pre-existing high levels of depositor protection that exceed the EU minimum."

In order to support the country's large car industry, which has seen demand plummet since the final quarter of 2008, the government announced in February 2009 that it would subsidize car purchases by providing €1,500 to every motorist who traded in a car that was least 10 years old, for a new, more fuel-efficient model.

The European Central Bank (ECB) determines monetary policy in Italy. The ECB was slower than other central banks to loosen monetary policy amid the global financial crisis of 2008–2009. In March 2009, the ECB cut its key interest rate from 2.0% to 1.5%, the lowest since it started setting euro rates in January 1999. However, US and Japanese rates were, in effect, already at zero by March 2009.

Prior to the country's entry into the Eurozone, Italy relied on devaluation to maintain its competitiveness. That option no longer exists, leading some commentators to ponder whether the Eurozone can remain intact, given that countries such as Spain and Greece face similar problems to Italy. In March 2008, Charles Dumas of Lombard Street Research in London was quoted as saying that Italy's real exchange rate—which takes inflation into account—was a third too high. Spain, he added, faced "10 years of stagnation" if it stayed in the euro.

ECONOMIC PERFORMANCE OVER 12 MONTHS

Italy's economic performance has deteriorated markedly since the late 1990s. During the current decade, economic growth in most years has been below that of comparable EU countries. In 2005, 2006, and 2007, Italy recorded growth of just 0.5%, 1.8%, and 1.5%, respectively, while in 2008 the economy contracted by 1%, according to the official statistics, the worst decline since 1975.

Furthermore, Italy's short-term prospects are worse than those of most other advanced economies. In March 2009, the Organization for Economic Co-operation and Development (OECD) said that the situation in Italy in 2009 and 2010 would be "much worse" than it had previously forecast, and that the economy's decline could be the steepest among its 30 members. Italy would not come out of its current recession until "sometime" in 2010, the OECD said. In February 2009, the IMF also said that the possibility of Italy's economic recession stretching into 2010 "cannot be ruled out." The Bank of Italy's Deputy Director General, Ignazio Visco, later said that Italy's GDP in 2009 may fall by as much as 2.6%, a figure much worse than that of 1975.

The recession has destroyed the government's plans to rein in the budget deficit. In March 2009, the IMF forecast that the shortfall in the government's finances would rise to 3.9% in 2009, from an earlier prediction of 2.5%. It added that the budget deficit would continue to increase, reaching 4.3% of GDP in 2010. The budget deficit had fallen to 1.6% of GDP in 2007, before rising to an estimated 2.7% of GDP in 2008, as the recession depressed revenues, and forced up welfare spending.

The recession is inevitably affecting employment. Officials reported a 46% increase in new unemployment claims in the first two months of 2009. At the end of 2008, the jobless rate stood at 6.7%, up from 6.1% in 2007. In February 2009, the European Commission said that it expected the jobless rate to increase to 8.2% in 2009, and to 8.7% in 2010.

As one might expect, given the deflationary forces pounding the global economy, inflation fell sharply in 2009. Inflation averaged 3.5% in 2008, up from 2% in 2007. The increase reflected sharp gains in oil and food prices in the first half of 2008. However, as the economic descent began in the final quarter of the year and international commodity prices slumped, consumer price inflation in Italy also began to ebb. By January 2009, prices were falling, declining by 1.7% from December 2008.

SUPPORT FOR INWARD INVESTMENT AND IMPORTS

Italy's investment climate remains poor, according to a US Commerce Department report published in

STATISTICS

GDP growth: −1% (Official statistics)
GDP per capita: US$31,000 (2008, est.)
CPI: 3.5% (average 2008, official statistics)
Key interest rate: 1.5% (March 2009, official statistics)
Exchange rate versus dollar: euros per US dollar—0.6689 (2008 est.)
Unemployment: 6.7% (December 2008, official statistics)
FDI: US$374.8 billion (2008, est.)
Current-account deficit/surplus −US$68.82 billion (2008, est.)
Population: 58,145,320 (July 2008, est.)
Source: CIA Factbook except where stated

►► MORE INFO

Websites:

EU trade policies: www.ec.europa.eu/trade/

Invitalia, investment guide: www.invitalia.it/flex/cm/pages/ServeBLOB.php/L/EN/IDPagina/231

Invitalia, tax guide: www.invitalia.it/flex/cm/pages/ServeBLOB.php/L/EN/IDPagina/241

US Department of Commerce Country Commercial Guide, Investment Climate chapter, published in 2009: www.buyusa.gov/italy/en/investment_climate.html

Italian newspaper, *Corriere della Sera*, published daily: www.corriere.it/english/

  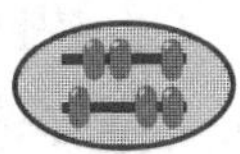 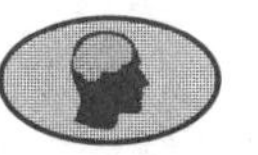     

2009 (*Italy Country Commercial Guide*, see More Info). Furthermore, the report said that "this negative assessment of Italy's investment climate is shared, in essence, by the Italian Trade Commission, by leading Italian business organizations, and by almost all of the international organizations that have examined the situation." The report added that Italy's "poor investment climate explains much of its low economic growth rate."

A government agency, Invitalia, provides assistance to companies "in all stages of the investment process."

As a member of the European Union, Italy applies the customs laws and trade regulation of the Union. Decisions regarding quotas or customs suspensions to be applied to goods imported into Italy are currently taken at the Community level.

TAX EXEMPTIONS

Invitalia publishes a guide to the Italian tax system, including all exemptions, on its website.

Japan

ECONOMY AND TRADE

Japan is the world's third-largest economy, after the United States and China, and one of its most technologically advanced. A world leader in cars, electronics, and other technologies, it is heavily dependent on manufactured exports, and imported fuel and raw materials. Economic growth averaged 10% in the 1960s, 5% in the 1970s, and 4% in the 1980s. However growth stalled after its stock-market and property bubbles burst in 1989. During the "lost decade" that followed, the authorities' mishandled the country's economic malaise, and companies were slow to cut costs. Between 2002 and 2007, the economy rebounded, as surging global demand for cars and other consumer goods strengthened the country's manufacturing sector. However, this expansionary period ended in October 2007, with Japan entering recession in 2008, and 2009 marking a return to near 0% interest rates. Japan's huge government debt, equivalent to 170% of GDP, and its ageing population are two of the country's biggest long-term problems.

STATISTICS

GDP growth: 0.7% (2008, est.)
GDP per capita: US$35,300 (2008, est.)
CPI: 1.8% (2008, est.)
Key interest rate: 0.1% (since December 2008)
Exchange rate versus dollar: Yen per US dollar—103.58 (2008, est.)
Unemployment: 4.2% (2008, est.)
FDI: US$139.7bn
Current account deficit/ surplus: −U$187.8bn (2008, est.)
Population: 127.3 million (July 2008, est.)
Source: CIA Factbook except where stated

ECONOMIC POLICY OVER 12 MONTHS

The government of former prime minister, Junichiro Koizumi, in 2006 set itself the target of getting Japan's budget into surplus by 2011. In order to achieve this, it and successor governments introduced budgetary caps, with a view to reining in spending on public works and social welfare.

However, the policy of fiscal belt-tightening, also pursued by Koizumi's successor, Shinzo Abe, was effectively overturned in December 2008 by the government of Taro Aso. Aso, who became prime minister in September 2008, declared that his government's top priority was not balancing the budget, but insulating the economy and jobs from the escalating economic crisis.

Aso has struggled to get his stimulus packages through the Diet (Japan's parliament). He has been hampered by Japan's massive public debts—a legacy of Japan's efforts to spend its way out of the 1990s recession—and by the blocking tactics of opposition parties, led the Democratic Party of Japan, which controls the Upper House. Confidence in his government suffered when his finance minister, Shoichi Nakagawa, was forced to resign after appearing to be intoxicated at a February 2009 G7 meeting in Rome.

The government finally succeeded in getting parts of its second stimulus package—a US$230bn ensemble that included controversial cash handouts to Japanese households—enacted by the Diet in early March 2009. The government secured approval despite a boycott by leading members of the ruling Liberal Democratic Party, including the popular former prime minister, Koizumi. The package also includes loans for unemployed workers, and further support for ailing banks.

Japanese interest rates were effectively held at zero from 2001 to 2006. The Bank of Japan, the central bank, reintroduced zero interest rates in December 2008, or, more accurately, it cut rates to 0.1%, and the bank's policy committee has since kept rates unchanged. The Bank of Japan has also introduced emergency measures to boost liquidity, in the hope of persuading Japanese banks to resume lending. Leading business organizations have been calling for the government to prop up the stock market, and hence bank capital ratios, by using public funds to buy stocks.

An election which must be called by September 2009 is expected to be won by the opposition Democratic Party of Japan.

ECONOMIC PERFORMANCE OVER 12 MONTHS

While Japan's banks have escaped the worst of the financial crisis, its manufacturers have been less

  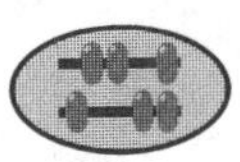 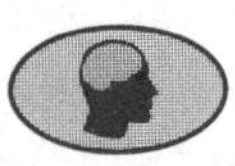   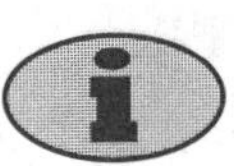  

fortunate. Locally-based multinationals, including Canon, NEC, Nissan, Panasonic, Sony, and Toyota, have all suffered a "triple whammy."

The global slump has hit demand for cars, electronics, and other manufactured goods; the strength of the yen has hampered their price competitiveness, and their focus on the premium end of the market has rendered them unusually vulnerable to the global downturn in demand. Most manufacturers have seen massive falls in earnings, been forced to reduce output, and slash domestic jobs.

Exports fell by nearly 46% in January 2009, compared with a year earlier, causing Japan's trade deficit to swell to ¥952.6 billion (US$9.7bn), the largest since records began. Unemployment climbed to 4.4% in December from 3.9%, with more than 340,000 additional Japanese joining the dole queue during December.

GDP fell at the annualized rate of 12.7% in the October–December quarter of 2008, the severest slowdown Japan has experienced since the 1974 oil shock.

"We are facing the biggest economic crisis since the second world war," said finance minister, Kaoru Yosano, in February 2009. In a statement during the same month, the Bank of Japan said: "Economic conditions have deteriorated significantly, and are likely to continue deteriorating for the time being."

Graham Turner, principal at London-based GFC Economics, believes the country has proved vulnerable because of too much exposure to emerging markets, overdependence on capital goods, and overreliance on discretionary consumer products. "Japanese industry [is] more exposed than any other major industrialized economy," he said in February 2009. There is a growing view that Japan will have to refocus towards services, to reduce its exposure to the vicissitudes of global consumer downturns.

In late February 2009, it emerged that the prices Japanese firms were paying for services had fallen to their lowest level in nearly 21 years, sparking fears that Japan was again at risk of the deflationary problems that blighted its economy in the late 1990s.

In January 2009, the International Monetary Fund issued a forecast saying that Japan's economy would shrink by 2.6% in 2009—a bigger drop than the Fund was forecasting for either the United States or European Union. However, many economists believe that a contraction of 4% is more likely in the current year. As recently as November 2008, the IMF was predicting that Japan's growth rate would outpace those of its rivals.

SUPPORT FOR INWARD INVESTORS AND IMPORTERS

The Manufactured Imports & Investment Promotion Organization (Mipro) is the agency responsible for promoting foreign direct investment, and imports into Japan. The Japan External Trade Organisation (Jetro, also known as "Invest Japan") has a particular focus on foreign direct investment. The Ministry of Economy, Trade and Industry is also worth contacting.

TAX EXEMPTIONS

Foreign Access Zones (FAZs) have been established around ports and airports to integrate import-related facilities. These offer a range of incentives to facilitate imports, including exemptions from land-holding taxes. For further information contact the National Tax Agency of Japan.

▸▸ MORE INFO

Websites:

Japan Business Federation (Nippon Keidanren): www.keidanren.or.jp

Japan External Trade Organization: www.jetro.go.jp

Ministry of Economy, Trade, and Industry: www.meti.go.jp/english/

Manufactured Imports & Investment Promotion Organization: www.mipro.or.jp/english/

National Tax Agency of Japan: www.nta.go.jp/foreign_language/index.htm

See Also:

The Art of Japanese Management (p. 1219)

Jordan

ECONOMY AND TRADE

Following World War I and the dissolution of the Ottoman Empire, the United Kingdom received a mandate to govern much of the Middle East. Britain separated out a semi-autonomous region of Transjordan from Palestine in the early 1920s, and the area gained its independence in 1946; it adopted the name of Jordan in 1950, and was ruled by King Hussein from 1953 until 1999. King Abdullah II, the son of King Hussein, assumed the throne following his father's death in February 1999. Since then, he has consolidated his power, and undertaken an aggressive economic reform program. Jordan acceded to the World Trade Organization in 2000, and began to participate in the European Free Trade Association in 2001.

ECONOMIC POLICY OVER 12 MONTHS

In November 2007, following parliamentary elections, King Abdullah instructed his new prime minister to focus on socioeconomic reform. Jordan began developing a healthcare and housing network for civilians and military personnel, and focused on improving the educational system. Jordan faces significant challenges in that it is a small country with insufficient supplies of water, oil, and other natural resources. Poverty, unemployment, and inflation are fundamental problems, but King Abdullah has undertaken some

STATISTICS

GDP growth: 4.5% (2008)
GDP per capita: US$5,000
CPI: 14.9%
Key interest rate: 8.45%
Exchange rate versus dollar: dinars per US dollar—0.709 (2008)
Unemployment: 12.9%
FDI: N/A
Current account deficit: US$4.87 billion
Population: 6,342,948
Source: CIA Factbook except where stated

  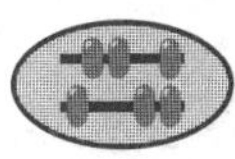 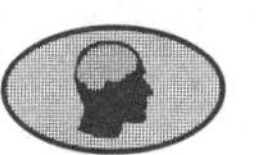     

broad economic reforms in a long-term effort to improve living standards. Jordan's continuing structural economic difficulties, burgeoning population, and more open political environment have led to the emergence of a variety of small political parties. Moving toward greater independence, Jordan's parliament has investigated corruption charges against several regime figures, and has become the major forum in which differing political views, including those of political Islamists, are expressed.

Since Jordan's graduation from its most recent IMF program in 2002, Amman has continued to follow IMF guidelines, practising careful monetary policy, making substantial headway with privatization, and opening the trade regime. Jordan's exports have significantly increased under the free trade accord between the United States and the Jordanian Qualifying Industrial Zones (QIZ), which allow Jordan to export goods with some Israeli content duty free to the United States. In 2006 and 2008, Jordan used privatization proceeds to reduce significantly its debt-to-GDP ratio. These measures have helped improve productivity, and have made Jordan more attractive for foreign investment. The government ended subsidies for petroleum and other consumer goods in 2008, in an effort to control the budget. The main challenges facing Jordan are reducing dependence on foreign grants, reducing the growing budget deficit, attracting investments, and creating jobs. Jordan is currently exploring nuclear power generation to forestall energy shortfalls. Jordan's conservative banking sector has been largely protected from the worldwide financial crisis, but many businesses, particularly in the tourism and real-estate sectors, are predicting a slowdown in 2009.

Jordan remains among the four most water-poor countries in the world, but the country is exploring ways to expand its limited water supply, and use its existing water resources more efficiently, including through regional cooperation. Lacking oil and gas reserves, Jordan depends on external sources for the majority of its energy requirements. During the 1990s, its crude petroleum needs were met through imports from neighboring Iraq, often at concessionary prices. Since early 2003, Jordan has imported oil primarily from Saudi Arabia at concessionary and market prices. In addition, a natural gas pipeline from Egypt to Jordan through the southern port city of Aqaba is now operational. The pipeline has reached northern Jordan, and construction to connect it to Syria and beyond is underway. Jordan developed a new energy strategy in 2007 that aims to develop more indigenous and renewable energy sources, including oil shale, nuclear energy, wind, and solar power.

ECONOMIC PERFORMANCE OVER 12 MONTHS

Under King Abdullah, Jordan's reforms have included taking the initiative for the phased elimination of fuel subsidies, passing legislation targeting corruption, and instituting tax reform. The Qualifying Industrial Zones (QIZ), created by the US Congress in 1996, are now driving growth in the export of light manufactured products, particularly garments. Jordan exported US$6.9 million in goods to the United States in 1997, when two-way trade was US$395 million; according to the US International Trade Commission, it exported US$1.06 billion in the first 10 months of 2008, with two-way trade at US$1.92 billion.

In 2008, Jordan's economy continued to grow, but was hurt by high inflation driven by high international oil and food prices, and the global financial crisis. Most fuel subsidies were eliminated in 2008, and barley subsidies are scheduled to be phased out. In 1996, Jordan and the United States signed a civil aviation agreement that provides for "open skies" between the two countries, and a US–Jordan Bilateral Investment Treaty (BIT) for the protection and encouragement of bilateral investment entered into force in 2003. The United States and Jordan also signed a Science and Technology Cooperation Agreement in 2007, to facilitate and strengthen scientific cooperation between the two countries, as well as a memorandum of understanding on nuclear energy cooperation. Such agreements bolster efforts to help diversify Jordan's economy and promote growth, and, at the same time, lessen reliance on exports of phosphates, potash, and, recently, textiles; overseas remittances; and foreign aid.

The government has emphasized information technology (IT), pharmaceuticals, and tourism as other promising growth sectors. The low tax and low regulation Aqaba Special Economic Zone (ASEZ) is considered a model of a government-provided framework for private-sector-led economic growth. Jordan is classified by the World Bank as a "lower-middle-income country." The per capita GDP is US$4,700. According to Jordan's Department of Statistics, 13% of the economically active Jordanian population residing in Jordan was unemployed in 2008, although unofficial estimates cite a 30% unemployment rate. Education and literacy rates, and measures of social well-being are relatively high compared to other countries with similar incomes. Jordan's population growth rate has declined in recent years, and is currently 2.2% (as reported by the Jordanian government).

One of the most important factors in the government's efforts to improve the wellbeing of its citizens is the macroeconomic stability that has been achieved since the 1990s. Jordan's 2008 and 2009 budgets emphasized increases in the social safety net to help people most affected by high inflation. The average rate of inflation in 2008 was 14.9%; the currency has been stable with an exchange rate fixed to the US dollar since 1995 at JOD0.708–0.710 to the dollar. In 2008, Jordan participated in a Paris Club debt buy-back to retire US$2.4 billion in debt using privatization proceeds. This buy-back will reduce the percentage of external debt to GDP from 46% to 32%.

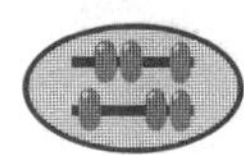
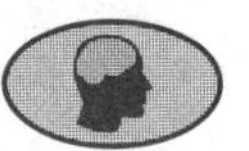

SUPPORT FOR INWARD INVESTMENT AND IMPORTS

The Jordan Investment Board (JIB) was established in 1995 as a governmental body enjoying both financial and administrative independence. Its aim is to encourage foreign direct investment into Jordan and to enhance local investment.

TAX EXEMPTIONS

Tax exemptions are at the discretion of the Jordanian Council of Ministers, and depend upon the sector being invested in, and its impact on the Jordanian economy. More information can be obtained from the JIB.

»» MORE INFO

Website:

Jordan Investment Board: www.jordaninvestment.com

See Also:

✔Middle East: Regulatory Structure and Powers (p. 1041)

Kuwait

ECONOMY AND TRADE

Kuwait is an almost entirely flat, desert plain. Britain oversaw foreign relations and defense for the ruling Kuwaiti Al-Sabah dynasty from 1899 until independence in 1961. Kuwait was attacked and overrun by Iraq on August 2, 1990. Following several weeks of aerial bombardment, a US-led, UN coalition began a ground assault on February 23, 1991 that liberated Kuwait in four days. After the liberation, Kuwait had to spend more than US$5 billion to repair oil infrastructure damage, which occurred during the Iraqi occupation. The Al-Sabah family has ruled since returning to power in 1991. It re-established an elected legislature that, in recent years, has become increasingly assertive. More than 90% of the population lives within a 500-square-kilometer area surrounding Kuwait City and its harbor. Although the majority of people residing in the State of Kuwait are of Arab origin, fewer than half are originally from the Arabian Peninsula. The discovery of oil in 1938 drew many Arabs from nearby states. Kuwait's 93.3% literacy rate, one of the Arab world's highest, is the result of extensive government support for the education system.

STATISTICS

GDP growth: 8.1% (2008)
GDP per capita: US$60,800
CPI: 11.7% (2008)
Key interest rate: 8.54%
Exchange rate versus dollar: dinars per US dollar—0.2679 (2008)
Unemployment: 2.2% (2004, est.)
FDI: US$1.2 billion (2008)
Population: 2,691,158
Source: CIA Factbook except where stated

ECONOMIC POLICY OVER 12 MONTHS

Following independence, Kuwait enjoyed an unprecedented period of prosperity under Amir Sabah al-Salim Al Sabah, who died in 1977 after ruling for 12 years. Under his rule, Kuwait and Saudi Arabia signed an agreement dividing the Neutral Zone (now called the Divided Zone), and demarcating a new international boundary. Both countries share equally the Divided Zone's petroleum, onshore and offshore. The country was transformed into a highly developed welfare state with a free market economy. Kuwait puts a great deal of emphasis on educating its citizens for the knowledge economy. Public school education, including Kuwait University, is free, but access is restricted for foreign residents. The government sponsors the foreign study of qualified students abroad for degrees not offered at Kuwait University.

Kuwait has a small, relatively open economy, dominated by the oil industry and the government sector. Approximately 90% of the Kuwaiti labor force works in the public sector, and 90% of private-sector workers are non-Kuwaitis. Kuwait's proven crude oil reserves of about 100 billion barrels—9% of world reserves—account for nearly 45% of GDP, 95% of export revenues, and 90–95% of government income. Kuwait puts 10% of its annual oil revenue in a Fund for Future Generations, in preparation for transition to the period after its oil resources are depleted. Kuwait's economy has benefited from high oil prices in recent years, as well the economic activity generated following Operation Iraqi Freedom (Kuwait is a major logistical and transit hub for Coalition operations in Iraq). Non-oil sectors such as banking, financial services, logistics, telecommunications, and construction have enjoyed strong growth in the past three to four years. The global financial crisis affected Kuwait in late 2008, with the Kuwait Stock Exchange—the region's second-largest bourse—losing almost 40% of its market capitalization during 2008.

High oil prices resulted in large budget surpluses in the period 2005–2008. Income tax reform in Kuwait has been designed to stimulate the private sector. A new set of tax laws passed in December 2007 amended a long standing tax "decree," which had set tax bands ranging from 0% to 55% of income to a single flat rate tax of 15%.

Kuwait recently began limited production from a 35 trillion cubic feet natural gas field discovered in 2006. Kuwait's current oil production capacity is estimated to be 2.8 million bpd, which it plans to increase to 3.5 million bpd by 2015. There is a further plan to extend production to 4.0 million bpd by 2020. However, there is some skepticism among oil analysts about the feasibility of these goals. Oil revenues comprise about 95% of exports and 95% of total government revenues. Kuwaiti export crude averaged about US$66/barrel in 2007.

ECONOMIC PERFORMANCE OVER 12 MONTHS

The government has sponsored many social welfare, public works, and development plans, financed with oil and investment revenues. Among the benefits for Kuwaiti citizens are retirement income, marriage bonuses, housing loans, virtually guaranteed employment, free medical services, and education at all levels. By Amiri decree, the government occasionally disburses a portion of its budget surplus as a grant to all Kuwaiti citizens. In 2006, an Amiri grant of 200 Kuwaiti dinars (approximately US$700) was paid to every citizen who applied. In 2007, the government implemented a debt-forgiveness scheme for Kuwaiti citizens, amounting to just over US$1 billion. Foreign nationals residing in Kuwait do not have access to these welfare services. The right to own stock in publicly traded companies, real estate, and banks, or a majority interest in a business are limited to Kuwaiti citizens, and citizens of Gulf Cooperation Council (GCC) states under limited circumstances. Industry in Kuwait consists of several large export-oriented petrochemical units, oil refineries, and a range of small manufacturers. It also includes large water desalinization, ammonia, desulphurization, fertilizer, brick, block, and cement plants.

The United States and Kuwaiti governments signed a Trade and Investment Framework agreement-(TIFA) in 2004. Kuwait and the other GCC nations signed a free trade agreement with Singapore in 2008. Kuwait does not attract significant foreign direct investment (FDI), largely due to bureaucratic obstacles, and a business culture that often disadvantages foreign firms. Agriculture is limited by the lack of water and arable land. The government has experimented in growing food through hydroponics and carefully managed farms. However, much of the soil that was suitable for farming in south central Kuwait was destroyed when Iraqi troops set fire to oil wells in the area, and created vast “oil lakes.” Fish and shrimp are plentiful in territorial waters, and large-scale commercial fishing has been undertaken locally and in the Indian Ocean. The Kuwait Oil Tanker Company has 24 crude oil, liquefied petroleum gas, and refined product carriers, and is the largest tanker company in an OPEC country. Kuwait also is a member of the United Arab Shipping Company.

The Kuwaiti dinar is currently pegged to an undisclosed basket of currencies; prior to 2007, the currency was pegged to the US dollar. High oil prices in 2008 ensured a budget surplus for fiscal year 2009 (ending March 31). As of January 2009, the government predicted a budget surplus of US$34.1 billion for the 2009 financial year, based on revenues of US$64.4 billion for the first nine months of the fiscal year.

The government’s two reserve funds, the Fund for Future Generations and the General Reserve Fund, are both managed by the Kuwait Investment Authority (KIA). Prior to the onset of the global financial crisis in mid-2008, the KIA’s aggregate holdings were estimated at more than a quarter of a trillion US dollars.

SUPPORT FOR INWARD INVESTMENT AND IMPORTS

Investors seeking to do business in Kuwait need to apply for a license from the Ministry of Commerce and Industry (MCI), and these are only available to Kuwaiti nationals and to GCC nationals and companies. Any joint ventures with Kuwaiti citizens have to be structured to give the Kuwaiti partners not less than 51% of the total capital. However, there is a Kuwait Free Trade Zone in Shuwaikh, which allows 100% foreign ownership of businesses within the zone, with no import duties or foreign corporate income tax

TAX EXEMPTIONS

Tax exemptions are available in the Kuwait Free Trade Zone (see above). Further information can be obtained from the Ministry of Commerce and Industry (MCI).

▸▸ MORE INFO

Website:

Kuwait site on business and restrictions: www.kuwaitiah.net

See Also:

✔Middle East: Regulatory Structure and Powers (p. 1041)

Latvia

ECONOMY AND TRADE

After gaining its independence from the Soviet Union in 1991, Latvia reoriented its economy towards the West, which involved the wholesale privatization of state-owned enterprises. After EU accession in 2004, consumers embarked on a debt-fuelled spending spree, with Scandinavian and local banks vying to offer bigger and cheaper loans. Successive coalition governments pursued loose fiscal policies. Consequently, a major house-price bubble was inflated. Economic growth peaked at 12.2% in 2006, briefly making Latvia the EU’s fastest-growing economy. However, this economic success proved short-lived and, by December 2008, the government was forced to accept a €7.5 billion rescue package from the IMF, European Union, and Nordic governments. Conditions included the need for significant cuts in government expenditure and tax increases. Agriculture accounts for 3.3% of Latvia’s GDP, industry 22.3% and services 74.4%. Forestry and wood products account for nearly one-third of exports.

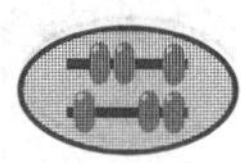

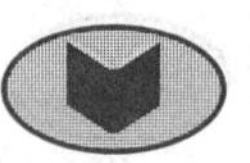

ECONOMIC POLICY OVER 12 MONTHS

In December 2008, Latvia accepted a €7.5bn rescue package from the IMF, European Union, and Nordic countries. The European Union is providing a €3.1 billion loan, the Nordic countries €1.8 billion, the World Bank €400 million, the Czech Republic €200 million, and the European Bank for Reconstruction & Development, Estonia, and Poland €100 million each.

Latvia required the loans because commercial borrowing had become prohibitively expensive, even for the government, whose credit ratings were downgraded to junk status by Standard & Poor's in February 2009. The IMF-led program is focused on maintaining the currency peg at the current exchange rate, containing the fiscal deficit, and supporting the banking system. Another goal is to enable Latvia to meet the Maastricht deficit criteria for euro adoption, a move the IMF describes as "an exit route" from severe economic crisis.

The rescue package was conditional on austerity measures, including savage cuts in expenditure and tax rises, aimed at reining in the country's current-account deficit. The package was also based on the assumption that Latvia's economy will shrink by 5% in 2009—an optimistic view given that by February 2009, the economy was expected to subside by 12% during the course of the year. The central bank governor said, in February 2009, that the Latvian economy was "clinically dead" after it shrank 10.5% in the fourth quarter of 2008.

In December 2008, parliament approved a LVL700 million (€999 million) budget cut, and raised taxes by LVL300 million, including a rise in value added tax from 18% to 21%. However, the austerity measures have proved deeply unpopular. In January 2009, scores of protesters clashed with police as they tried to storm parliament, and, on February 20, the coalition government of Ivars Godmanis was forced out of office.

There is a growing acceptance that the successor government will find it impossible to adhere to the harsh medicine prescribed by the IMF—which also includes structural policies designed to boost productivity, and help generate a shift from the production of non-tradables to tradable goods.

Days after the government's collapse, Fitch Ratings warned that any failure to maintain budgetary controls would delay the disbursement of international funds to Latvia, and bring the lats under renewed pressure.

After cutting the country's credit rating to junk status in February, Standard & Poor's said: "We believe the political commitment and public support for the current policy stance depends to a considerable degree on prospects for economic recovery in 2010, and an early Eurozone entry. . . A prolonged economic contraction would likely lead to declining public support for the current policy stance."

Some commentators, including the IMF, believe that a better solution to Latvia's economic woes would have been a devaluation of the lats, accompanied by its replacement by the euro.

ECONOMIC PERFORMANCE OVER 12 MONTHS

The global financial crisis of 2008 brought Latvia's vulnerabilities into sharp relief. Years of unsustainable growth, and large current account deficits precipitated a full-scale balance of payments crisis in 2008. Output shrank by 10.5% in the fourth quarter, compared with the same period in 2007. Unemployment climbed to 7% in December, up from 6.1% in November. Popular dissatisfaction with the government's handling of the economy prompted further crises, following the resignation of the centre-right coalition government of Prime Minister Ivars Godmanis, on February 20, 2009.

One reason for the economic crash was that locally owned banks, which make up 40% of the Latvian banking system, accepted deposits from abroad, and invested these funds in the country's booming property market. This market came under pressure in 2008 after foreign credit evaporated, and confidence in Latvian banks collapsed. In the second half of 2008, Parex Banka (the country's second largest bank, and its largest domestically owned bank) was at risk of collapse—it was nationalized in November 2008.

From August to November 2008, Latvia's reserves fell by 20% to €3.4 billion as the central bank sought to shore up the currency peg by selling foreign reserves. However, fears about a possible systemic crisis, and the sustainability of the country's external debt mounted. Despite the December 2008 €7.5bn IMF-led rescue package, the exchange-rate peg remained under pressure.

The currency peg is totemic for many Latvians, partly because of the country's desire to join the euro, and because a devaluation of the lats would worsen private-sector debt problems. Some 85% of loans to consumers and businesses in Latvia are denominated in euros, and other currencies including the Swiss franc. If the exchange-rate regime were to collapse, servicing these loans would become more expensive.

Latvia's gross domestic product contracted by 4.8% in 2008, and is expected to shrink a further 12% in 2009, and by 1–2% in 2010. Having peaked at 17.7% in May 2008, inflation had fallen to 7.7% by January 2009 on the back of lower oil prices, and the global downturn. Unveiling the IMF-led rescue package in December 2008, IMF managing director, Dominique Strauss-Kahn said: "A deep recession and a drawn-out recovery appear inevitable."

In February 2009, Latvia suffered the ignominy of having its sovereign debt reduced to junk status by

STATISTICS

GDP growth: −0.4% (2008, est.)
GDP per capita: US$18,500 (2008, est.)
CPI: 15.8% (2008, est.)
Key interest rate: N/A
Exchange rate: lats versus US dollar—0.4701 (2008)
Unemployment: 5.5% (2008, est.)
FDI: US$11.21bn
Current account deficit: −US$5.126 (2008, est.)
Population: 2.245 million (July 2008, est.)
Source: CIA Factbook except where stated

▸▸ MORE INFO

Websites:

Business co-operation database: www.trade.lv
Chamber of Trade & Industry: www.chamber.lv
Latvian Investment & Development Agency: www.liaa.gov.lv
State Regional Development Agency: www.vraa.gov.lv/en/about_us/
State Revenue Service website, for information on tax exemptions: www.vid.gov.lv/default.aspx?tabid=8&hl=2

  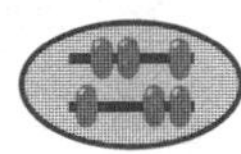      

ratings agency, Standard & Poor's. S&P reduced its rating on Latvia to BB+/B, one notch below investment grade, meaning that Latvia will have to pay more to borrow from bond markets.

SUPPORT FOR INWARD INVESTORS AND IMPORTERS

The government of Latvia regards the attraction of foreign direct investment as critical for a successful economic recovery. A range of government agencies, including the Latvian Investment & Development Agency, are on hand to provide advice and support to importers, and inward investors. Please see its website for further details:

TAX EXEMPTIONS

Corporation tax is 15%, well below the EU average of 26.3%. Pursuant to the law, "On the Liepaja Special Economic Zone," a special tax regime applies to companies operating in the Liepaja Special Economic Zone, Rezekne Special Economic Zone, Ventspils Free Port, and Riga Free Port. Companies investing in Latvia also have a high possibility of qualifying for the EU Structural Funds scheme, which runs from 2007 to 2013.

Lebanon

ECONOMY AND TRADE

Following the capture of Syria from the Ottoman Empire by Anglo-French forces in 1918, France received a mandate over this territory, and separated out the region of Lebanon in 1920. France granted this area independence in 1943. A lengthy civil war (1975–1990) devastated the country, but Lebanon has since made progress toward rebuilding its political institutions. Under the Ta'if Accord—the blueprint for national reconciliation—the Lebanese established a more equitable political system, particularly by giving Muslims a greater voice in the political process, while institutionalizing sectarian divisions in the government. Since the end of the war, Lebanon has conducted several successful elections. In July 2006, Hezbollah kidnapped two Israeli soldiers, leading to a 34-day conflict with Israel in which approximately 1,200 Lebanese civilians were killed. Army Commander Michel Sulayman was elected as president in May 2008, and a unity government was formed in July 2008, with Fuad Siniora as Prime Minister. Lebanon has a free market economy and a strong laissez-faire commercial tradition.

STATISTICS

GDP growth: 7% (2008)
GDP per capita: US$11,100
CPI: 10% (2008)
Key interest rate: 10.26%
Exchange rate versus dollar: Lebanese pounds per US dollar—1.507.5 (fixed)
Unemployment: 9.2%
FDI: N/A
Current account deficit/ surplus: N/A
Population: 4,017,095
Source: CIA Factbook except where stated

ECONOMIC POLICY OVER 12 MONTHS

The Lebanese economy is service-oriented; the main growth sectors include banking and tourism. The civil war seriously damaged Lebanon's economic infrastructure, cut national output by half, and all but ended Lebanon's position as a Middle Eastern entrepôt and banking hub. In the years since, Lebanon has rebuilt much of its war-torn physical and financial infrastructure by borrowing heavily, mostly from domestic banks. In an attempt to reduce the ballooning national debt, the government of Rafik Hariri launched an austerity program in 2000, reining in government expenditures, increasing revenue collection, and passing legislation to privatize state enterprises, but economic and financial reform initiatives stalled, and public debt continued to grow. The Israeli-Hezbollah conflict in July–August 2006 caused an estimated US$3.6 billion in infrastructure damage, and prompted international donors to pledge nearly US$1 billion in recovery and reconstruction assistance. Donors met again in January 2007 at the Paris III Donor Conference, and pledged more than US$7.5 billion to Lebanon for development projects and budget support, conditional on progress on Beirut's fiscal reform and privatization program. An 18-month political stalemate, and sporadic sectarian and political violence hampered economic activity, particularly tourism, retail sales, and investment, until the new government was formed in July 2008. Political stability since the Doha Accord of May 2008 has helped to boost investment and tourism, but economic growth is likely to slow in 2009 as a result of the global economic recession.

Lebanon's current budget deficit has to be seen in the context of the massive reconstruction program it launched back in 1992 to rebuild the country's physical and social infrastructure, following both the long civil war, and the Israeli occupation of the south (1978–2000). In addition, the delicate social balance and the near-dissolution of central government institutions during the civil war handicapped the state, as it sought to capture revenues to fund the recovery effort. Monetary stabilization, coupled with high-interest-rate policies, aggravated the debt service burden, leading to a substantial rise in budget deficits. Thus, the government accumulated significant debt, which by the end of 2008 had reached US$47 billion, or 162% of GDP. (Again, to give this figure a context, by March 25, 2009 the United Kingdom was facing a downgrading of its debt status on fears that its budget deficit might exceed 11% of GDP, a tiny fraction of

Lebanon's massive relative debt burden). Unemployment was estimated at 9.2% in 2007 by the Central Administration of Statistics.

ECONOMIC PERFORMANCE OVER 12 MONTHS

The government has maintained a firm commitment to the Lebanese pound, which has been pegged to the dollar since September 1999. The government is working toward accession to the World Trade Organization (WTO). In order to increase revenues, the government introduced a 10% value added tax (VAT), which became applicable in February 2002, and a 5% tax on interest income, which became applicable in February 2003. The Finance Ministry has submitted additional revenue-raising measures as part of the 2009 budget.

Plagued by mounting indebtedness, Lebanon submitted a comprehensive program on its financing needs at the Paris II donors' conference in November 2002, and succeeded in attracting pledges totaling US$4.4 billion, including US$3.1 billion to support fiscal adjustment, and US$1.2 billion to support economic development projects. Despite the substantial aid it had received, the government made little progress on its reform program, and, by 2006, even before the war between Hezbollah and Israel, the debt problem had grown worse. After the war, US$940 million in relief and early reconstruction aid was pledged to Lebanon on August 31, 2006 at a donors' conference in Stockholm, and was followed by the additional US$7.6 billion in assistance for reconstruction and economic stabilization, already mentioned, from the Paris Club.

Unlike the Paris II aid, however, much of the Paris III aid was contingent on Lebanon's meeting agreed benchmarks in implementing its proposed five-year economic and social reform program. The International Monetary Fund (IMF) signed an Emergency Post-Conflict Assistance (EPCA) Program with Lebanon to support the government's economic reform program in 2007, and a second EPCA for 2008–2009, to monitor the progress of reforms, and to advise donors on the timing of aid delivery.

US exports to Lebanon increased by 81% in the first nine months of 2008 to reach US$1.1 billion, compared to US$599 million during the same period in 2007, primarily due to the increase in oil prices.

According to a report published in November 2008 on the Lebanese economy by the Global Investment House of Kuwait (GIH), Lebanon's GDP growth over the last six years has been at a cumulative rate of 5.1% from a very low base, given the destruction the country has endured. However, the GIH report suggests that things are now improving, with GDP in 2008 expected to reach US$24.6 billion, with a further increase of 5% possible in 2009, despite the global slowdown. The CAGR (compound annual growth rate) of the total budget deficit over the period 2001–2007 has outstripped the growth budget very significantly at 8.4%, but the introduction of VAT in 2002 is now starting to add very substantially to government revenues.

SUPPORT FOR INWARD INVESTMENT AND IMPORTS

The Investment Development Authority of Lebanon (IDAL) was established in 1994 to spearhead Lebanon's investment promotion efforts, and, in 2001, Lebanon passed the Investment Development Law 360, which seeks to stimulate Lebanon's economic and social development by regulating investment promotion for both foreign and domestic entities.

TAX EXEMPTIONS

There is a wide range of development investment incentives, including exemption from income tax, and tax on distribution of dividends. Further information can be obtained from IDAL.

▸▸ MORE INFO

Websites:

Official site for the presidency of Lebanon: www.presidency.gov.lb

Central Bank of Lebanon: www.bdl.gov.lb

Investment Development Authority of Lebanon: www.idal.com.lb

Global Investment House of Kuwait: www.scribd.com/doc/8656152/Lebanon-Economic-Outlook-Nov-2008-by-GIH

See Also:

✔ Middle East: Regulatory Structure and Powers (p. 1041)

Libya

ECONOMY AND TRADE

The Italians took over control of the area of Libya around Tripoli from the Ottoman Turks in 1911. After World War II, Libya passed to UN administration and achieved independence in 1951. Following a 1969 military coup, Colonel Muammar Abu Minyar al-Qadhafi began to espouse his own political system, the Third Universal Theory. The system is a combination of socialism and Islam, derived in part from tribal practices, and is supposed to be implemented by the Libyan people themselves in a unique form of "direct democracy." Qadhafi has always seen himself as a revolutionary and visionary leader. His dream of changing the world through subversion and support for terrorism had Libya declared a rogue state until Qadhafi began to rebuild his relationships with Europe during the 1990s. In December 2003, Libya announced that it had agreed to reveal and end its programs to develop weapons of mass destruction, and

   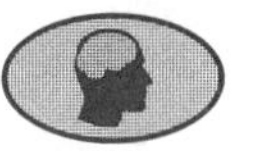     

to renounce terrorism. Since then, Qadhafi has made significant strides in normalizing relations with Western nations. He made his first trip to Western Europe in 15 years when he traveled to Brussels in April 2004. The United States rescinded Libya's designation as a state sponsor of terrorism in June 2006, which paved the way for Libya's economy to start to prosper.

STATISTICS
GDP growth: 7.3% (2008)
GDP per capita: US$14,900
CPI: 10.5%
Key interest rate: 6%
Exchange rate versus dollar: Libyan dinars per US dollar—1.2112
Unemployment: 30%
FDI: US$8.736 billion
Current account surplus: US$43.33
Population: 6,310,434
Source: CIA Factbook except where stated

ECONOMIC POLICY OVER 12 MONTHS

The Libyan economy depends primarily upon revenues from the oil sector, which contribute about 95% of export earnings, about one-quarter of GDP, and 60% of public-sector wages. The expected weakness in world hydrocarbon prices throughout 2009 will reduce Libyan government tax income, and constrain Libyan economic growth. Substantial revenues from the energy sector, coupled with a small population, give Libya one of the highest per capita GDPs in Africa, but little of this income flows down to the lower orders of society. Libyan officials have, in the past five years, made progress on economic reforms, as part of a broader campaign to reintegrate the country into the international fold. This effort picked up steam after UN sanctions were lifted in September 2003, and as Libya announced in December 2003 that it would abandon programs to build weapons of mass destruction. UN sanctions against Libya were lifted in September 2003. The process of lifting US unilateral sanctions began in spring 2004; all sanctions were removed by June 2006, helping Libya attract greater foreign direct investment, especially in the energy sector. Libyan oil and gas licensing rounds continue to draw high international interest; the National Oil Company set a goal of nearly doubling oil production to 3 million barrels per day (bpd) by 2012.

Libya faces a long road ahead in liberalizing the socialist-oriented economy, but initial steps—including applying for WTO membership, reducing some subsidies, and announcing plans for privatization—are laying the groundwork for the transition to a more market-based economy. The non-oil manufacturing and construction sectors, which account for more than 20% of GDP, have expanded from processing mostly agricultural products to include the production of petrochemicals, iron, steel, and aluminum. Climatic conditions and poor soils severely limit agricultural output, and Libya imports about 75% of its food. Libya's primary agricultural water source remains the Great Manmade River Project, but significant resources are being invested in desalinization research to meet growing water demands. The Great Manmade River Project is a US$33.69 billion project (including capital expenditure and running costs for 50 years) to pipe water from deep under the Sahara sands to Libya's coastal cities. According to Fawzi-al-Sharief Saeid, director of the project's technical centre for groundwater management, the scheme is neither "mad," nor "wasteful of resources," and is three-quarters complete. He characterized the scheme as being "some nine to 11 times better value for money, compared with desalination plants or water imported from Europe" (source: www.ymlp170.com/pubarchive_show_message. php?LibyaNews+3144).

At predicted extraction rates, there is enough water under the Sahara to serve Libya and its three neighbors—Sudan, Chad, and Egypt—for almost 5,000 years, according to Fawzi-al-Sharief Saeid. At the World Water Forum in Istanbul in March 2009, the project was hailed as "the eighth wonder of the world." Others have called it a scheme bound to stir up tension among Libya's neighbors.

ECONOMIC PERFORMANCE OVER 12 MONTHS

The government dominates Libya's socialist-oriented economy through complete control of the country's oil resources. Oil revenues constitute the principal source of foreign exchange. Much of the country's income has been lost to waste, corruption, conventional armaments purchases, and attempts to develop weapons of mass destruction, as well as to large donations made to developing countries in attempts to increase Qadhafi's influence in Africa and elsewhere. Although oil revenues and a small population give Libya one of the highest per capita GDPs in Africa, the government's mismanagement of the economy has led to high inflation, and increased import prices. These factors resulted in a decline in the standard of living from the late 1990s up to 2003.

Muammar Qadhafi's most recent economic plan for Libya is the "Wealth Distribution Plan," in terms of which the government aims to eliminate the majority of Libya's key ministries in favor of the direct distribution of oil wealth to the people. Instead of channeling oil revenues to the people through layers of bureaucracy, the idea is to streamline and transform the whole state apparatus. However, Libya has seen a number of "transformational visions" from Qadhafi, and it remains to be seen how this one will play out in 2009.

So far, despite efforts to diversify the economy and encourage private-sector participation, there remain extensive controls on prices, credit, trade, and foreign exchange, all of which act to constrain growth and discourage private investment. Import restrictions and inefficient resource allocations by government departments and agencies have caused periodic shortages of basic goods and foodstuffs.

Although agriculture is the second-largest sector in the economy, Libya imports most foods. Climatic conditions and poor soils severely limit output, while higher incomes and a growing population have caused food consumption to rise. Domestic food production meets about 25% of demand. On September 20, 2004, President George W. Bush signed an Executive Order ending economic sanctions imposed under the authority of the International Emergency Economic Powers Act (IEEPA). US persons are no longer

prohibited from working in Libya, and many US companies in diverse sectors are actively seeking investment opportunities in Libya. The Libyan government has announced ambitious plans to increase foreign investment in the oil and gas sectors, with the aim of significantly boosting production capacity from 1.2 million bpd to 3 million bpd by 2012. The government is also pursuing a number of large-scale infrastructure development projects such as highways, railways, air and seaports, telecommunications, water works, public housing, healthcare, and hotels.

SUPPORT FOR INWARD INVESTMENT AND IMPORTS

Investing in Libya is handled by the Libyan investment promotion agency, Libyan Foreign Investment Board (LFIB, telephone: +218 (21) 360-8183-360-9613).

Investment opportunities in Libya at present are limited to the oil and gas field, and associated areas. Telecommunications and the financial sector remain government monopolies, although in March 2009 news services were reporting that Libya could be opening its banks to foreign operators (source: www.animaweb.org).

TAX EXEMPTIONS

Information is available from LFIB.

▸▸ MORE INFO

Websites:

Central Bank of Libya: www.cbl.gov.ly

Great Man-Made River Authority (GMRA): www.gmmra.org

Libyan stock market: www.lsm.gov.ly

Libyan Foreign Investment Board (LFIB): www.investinlibya.com

Liechtenstein

ECONOMY AND TRADE

The Principality of Liechtenstein was established within the Holy Roman Empire in 1719. Occupied by both French and Russian troops during the Napoleonic wars, it became a sovereign state in 1806, and joined the Germanic Confederation in 1815. Liechtenstein became fully independent in 1866 when the Confederation dissolved. Until the end of World War I, it was closely tied to Austria, but the economic devastation caused by that conflict forced Liechtenstein to enter into a customs and monetary union with Switzerland. Since World War II (in which Liechtenstein remained neutral), the country's low taxes have spurred outstanding economic growth. In 1978, Liechtenstein became a member of the Council of Europe, and then joined the UN in 1990, the European Free Trade Association (EFTA) in 1991, and both the European Economic Area (EEA), and World Trade Organization (WTO) in 1995. In 2000, shortcomings in banking regulatory oversight resulted in concerns about the use of financial institutions for money laundering. However, Liechtenstein implemented anti-money-laundering legislation, and a Mutual Legal Assistance Treaty with the United States came into effect in 2003. In March 2009, Liechtenstein began talks with the United Kingdom Treasury with a view to ending its controversial privacy protection for client bank accounts, and announced it would be seeking agreements with a number of other countries.

STATISTICS

GDP growth: 3.1%
GDP per capita: US$118,000
CPI: 1%
key interest rate: N/A
exchange rate versus dollar: Swiss franc per US dollar—1.0774 (2008)
unemployment: 1.5%
FDI: N/A
Current account deficit/surplus: N/A
Population: 34,761
Source: CIA Factbook except where stated

ECONOMIC POLICY OVER 12 MONTHS

Liechtenstein has been under tremendous pressure over the last few years to end its status as a haven for foreign tax avoidance. It resisted pressure from the German government, which said it was losing millions in tax revenue because German citizens were hiding money in secret Liechtenstein bank accounts. It was blacklisted by the OECD as an "uncooperative tax haven," and a possible site for money laundering, until it implemented anti-money laundering regulations in 2003. It seems, though, that 2009 will be the year that the principality "normalizes" its relationship with tax officials around the world. On March 27, Liechenstein's government announced it was beginning talks with the United Kingdom's Revenue and Customs, saying it wanted to encourage the "voluntary disclosure of untaxed assets." At the core of Liechtenstein's new policy is the idea of a long-term process to tackle undeclared tax around the world by Liechtenstein account holders, in a way that generates benefit for tax authorities without incurring excessive penalties for its wealthy account holders. There is talk of the principality closing the bank accounts of uncooperative customers, leaving them with the considerable problem of where else they could go. Tax havens around the world have either already fallen into line with anti-avoidance and intelligence-sharing moves, or are busy doing so. Apart from financial services, Liechtenstein is a highly industrialized, free-enterprise economy, and boasts the highest per-capita income in the world. The Liechtenstein economy is widely diversified, with a large number of small businesses. Low business taxes—the maximum tax rate is 20%—and easy incorporation rules have induced many holding companies to establish nominal offices in Liechtenstein, providing 30% of state revenues. The country participates in a customs union with Switzerland, and uses the Swiss franc as its national currency. It imports more than 90% of its energy requirements. Since the signing of the Customs Treaty in 1924, Liechtenstein and Switzerland have represented one mutual

  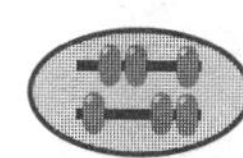   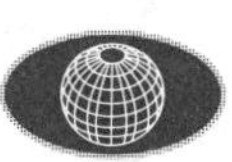   

economic area, with open borders between the two countries, and Swiss customs officers secure the principality's border with Austria. The liberal economy and tax system make Liechtenstein a safe, trustworthy, and success-oriented place for private and business purposes, especially with its highly modern, internationally laid-out infrastructure, and nearby connections to the whole world. In 2007, Liechtenstein had an obligation under the EEA treaty to harmonize its laws with EU directives 2005/36 and 1999/42, on the mutual recognition of EU and EEA university and professional diplomas. Liechtenstein is also part of the EU fund on research and technology, and is entitled to participate in EU projects and subsidies.

The Principality of Liechtenstein has gone through a process of economic and cultural development in the last 40 years like no other Western country. In this short period of time, Liechtenstein has developed from a mainly agricultural state to one of the most highly industrialized countries in the world.

ECONOMIC PERFORMANCE OVER 12 MONTHS

Besides its efficient industry, Liechtenstein also has a strong services sector. Four out of 10 employees work in the services sector, a relatively high proportion of whom are foreigners, including those who commute across the border from the neighboring states of Switzerland and Austria. Total exports increased from US$3 billion (CHF3 billion) in 2000 to US$3.6 billion (CHF3.6 billion) in 2006, while total imports increased from US$1.5 billion (CHF1.5 billion) to US$2.16 billion (CHF2.16 billion) during the same period. In 2005, about 14% of Liechtenstein's goods were exported to Switzerland, 44% to the European Union, 18% to the United States, 24% to the Asia/Pacific region, and the remainder to the rest of the world. Liechtenstein imports more than 90% of its energy requirements. The Liechtenstein industrial sector contributes 44% of the country's GDP, followed by services (26%), and agriculture (7%). Despite Liechtenstein's overall good competitive performance, there is a trend among businesses to outsource their production to low-cost countries.

In 2005, the United States was the third most important trading partner for Liechtenstein, with approximately US$521 million (CHF521 million) worth of exports, and US$72 million (CHF72 million) of imports. Germany was first, with a total trade value of US$2.1 billion (CHF2.1 billion) and Austria second with US$1.4 billion (CHF1.4 billion). Although Switzerland is an important trading partner, trade statistics are unavailable because both countries are in a customs union. Approximately 5% of the country's revenue is invested in research and development, one of the driving forces of the success of Liechtenstein's economy. The Principality of Liechtenstein is also known as an important financial center, primarily because it specializes in financial services for foreign entities. The country's low tax rate, loose incorporation and corporate governance rules, and traditions of strict banking secrecy have contributed significantly to the ability of financial intermediaries in Liechtenstein to attract funds from outside the country's borders. The same factors made the country attractive and vulnerable to money launderers, although legislation in late 2000 has strengthened regulatory oversight of illicit funds transfers.

Liechtenstein has chartered 17 banks, three non-bank financial companies, and 71 public investment companies, as well as insurance and reinsurance companies. Its 270 licensed fiduciary companies and 81 lawyers serve as nominees for, or manage, more than 75,000 entities (primarily corporations, institutions, or trusts), mostly for non-Liechtenstein residents. Approximately one-third of these entities hold the controlling interest in other entities, chartered in countries other than Liechtenstein. The principality's laws permit the corporations it charters to issue bearer shares. Until recently, the principality's banking laws permitted banks to issue numbered accounts, but new regulations require strict know-your-customer practices for all accounts.

SUPPORT FOR INWARD INVESTMENT AND IMPORTS

The Liechtenstein tax regime is the chief incentive for investing in Liechtenstein. The maximum tax on profit is 20%, but the more usual rate is between 7.5% and 15%, as the tax rate depends on the ratio of profit to capital. Assets under management of funds are tax-free.

TAX EXEMPTIONS

See above.

▸▸ MORE INFO

Website:

Official government portal for Liechtenstein: www.liechtenstein.li

Lithuania

ECONOMY AND TRADE

Today the largest and most populous of the Baltic States, the lands of Lithuania were first united in 1236. Over the next century, through alliances and conquest, Lithuania extended its territory to include most of present-day Belarus and Ukraine. By the end of the 14th century, Lithuania was the largest state in Europe. An alliance with Poland in 1386 resulted in the two states having a common ruler. Grand Duke Jogaila of Lithuania was crowned the King of Poland, which intensified Lithuania's economic and cultural development, and oriented it toward the West. In 1569, Lithuania and Poland formally united into a single dual state, the Polish-Lithuanian Commonwealth. This entity survived until 1795, when its remnants were partitioned by surrounding countries. Lithuania regained its independence following World War I, but was annexed by the USSR in 1940. On 11 March 1990, Lithuania became the first of the Soviet republics to declare its independence, which was recognized by Moscow in September 1991. The last Russian troops withdrew in 1993. Lithuania subsequently restructured its economy for integration into Western European institutions; it joined both NATO and the European Union in spring 2004.

STATISTICS

GDP growth: 3.2% (2008)
GDP per capita: US$17,700
CPI: 11% (2008)
Key interest rate: 6.86%
Unemployment: 4.8% (2008)
FDI: $16.43 billion
Current account deficit/surplus: −$6.775 billion (2008, est.)
Population: 3,555,179
Source: CIA Factbook except where stated

ECONOMIC POLICY OVER 12 MONTHS

In the second half of the 20th century, the Lithuanian economy underwent fundamental transformations. The Soviet occupation of 1940 brought Lithuania intensive industrialization and economic integration into the USSR, although the level of technology and state concern for environmental, health, and labor issues lagged far behind Western standards. Urbanization increased from 39% in 1959, to 68% in 1989. From 1949 to 1952, the Soviets abolished private ownership in agriculture, establishing collective and state farms. Production declined, and did not reach pre-war levels until the early 1960s. The intensification of agricultural production through intense chemical use and mechanization eventually doubled production, but created additional ecological problems.

The disadvantages of a centrally planned economy became evident after the collapse of the USSR in 1991, when Lithuania began its transition to a market economy. Owing to the availability of inexpensive natural resources, the industrial sector had become excessively energy-intensive, inefficient in its utilization of resources, and incapable of manufacturing internationally competitive products. More than 90% of Lithuania's trade was with the rest of the USSR, which supplied Lithuanian industry with raw materials for production, and a market for its outputs. The need to sever these trading links, and to reduce the inefficient industrial sector led to serious economic difficulties. The process of privatization and the development of new companies slowly moved Lithuania from a command economy toward a free market. By 1998, the economy had survived the early years of uncertainty and several setbacks, including a banking crisis, and seemed poised for solid growth. However, the collapse of the Russian rouble in August 1998 shocked the economy into negative growth, and forced the reorientation of trade from Russia toward the West. In 1997, exports to former Soviet states were 45% of total Lithuanian exports. In 2006, exports to the East (the Commonwealth of Independent States, or CIS) were only 21% of the total, while exports to the EU-25 (European Union 25) were 63%, and to the United States, 4.3%.

Lithuania became a member of the World Trade Organization on May 31, 2001 and joined the European Union in May 2004. Despite Lithuania's EU accession, its trade with its Central and Eastern European neighbors, and Russia in particular, accounts for a growing percentage of total trade. Privatization of the large, state-owned utilities is nearly complete. Foreign government and business support have helped in the transition from the old command economy to a market economy. It is bordered by Latvia to the north, Belarus to the southeast, Poland to the southwest, and Kaliningrad, a territory of Russia, to the west. It has 60 miles of sandy coastline, of which only 24 miles face the open Baltic Sea.

ECONOMIC PERFORMANCE OVER 12 MONTHS

Lithuania has grown on average by 8% per year over the last four years, driven by exports and domestic consumer demand. At the end of the third quarter of 2008, Lithuania had accumulated foreign direct investments (FDI) of US$12.8 billion. The current-account deficit in the second quarter of 2008 was 16.8% of GDP. However, preliminary figures show this dropping to 7.2% for the third quarter of 2008. The privatization of former state industries has gone well for the country. More than 79% of the economy's output is generated by the private sector. The share of employees in the private sector exceeds 65%. The government of Lithuania completed banking-sector privatization in 2001, with 89% of this sector controlled by foreign—mainly Scandinavian—capital.

The transportation infrastructure inherited from the Soviet period is adequate, and has been generally well maintained since independence. Lithuania has one ice-free seaport, with ferry services to German, Swedish, and Danish ports. Commercial airports at Vilnius, Kaunas, and Klaipeda operate scheduled international services. The road system is good.

     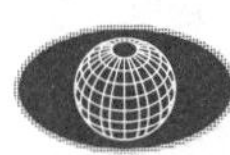   

Gross domestic product rose by 7.6% in 2005, and 7.4% in 2006. In 2007, Lithuania's GDP grew by 8.9%. GDP is predicted to grow between 3% and 5% for 2008, but the economy is expected to fall in 2009. Lithuania's economy began to slow before the worldwide financial turmoil developed in 2008, and the eventual effect of this turmoil upon the Lithuanian economy is not yet clear. In 2007, annual average inflation reached 5.8%, and the government's budget deficit stood at approximately 0.5% of GDP. The government budget deficit is predicted to be 2.35% of GDP for 2008. Inflation reached 11% in September 2008, one of the highest levels in the European Union. Real-estate prices dropped by approximately 20% in 2008, by comparison with 2007. Greater development is needed in public policy, and further progress in structural and agricultural reforms. However, the recently elected center-right coalition has a fiscal austerity plan that may implement some of these reforms. Lithuania pegged its national currency—the litas—to the euro on February 2, 2002 at the rate of LTL3.4528 to €1.

Lithuanian income levels lag behind those of older EU members. Lower wages and high income taxes may have been factors that contributed to the trend of emigration to the wealthiest EU countries after Lithuania joined the European Union in 2004. In 2008, the flat income-tax rate was reduced to 24%. It may be reduced to 20% under the newly elected government's fiscal austerity plan. Moreover, in 2008, the minimum wage increased to US$310 per month; the average wage now stands at US$820 per month, a 17.9% increase from the previous year.

The initial euro adoption target date of January 1, 2007 was postponed due to the high inflation rate of 2006. Achieving the Maastricht inflation criterion necessary to adopt the euro in 2010 will require significant fiscal tightening in Lithuania. Some commentators feel that euro adoption is unlikely before 2013.

SUPPORT FOR INWARD INVESTMENT AND IMPORTS

The Lithuanian Development Agency deals with all inward investment. The country has free economic zones with tax benefits, and a one-stop shop service provided by the LDA.

TAX EXEMPTIONS

Lithuania is particularly keen on strengthening high value-added industries, and encourages investment in R&D with a range of tax relief measures. Further information can be obtained from the LDA.

▸▸ MORE INFO

Websites:

Lithuanian government: www.lrv.lt

Lithuanian Development Agency: www.lda.lt/en

Luxembourg

ECONOMY AND TRADE

After 400 years of domination by various European nations, Luxembourg was granted the status of Grand Duchy by the Congress of Vienna on June 9, 1815. Although Luxembourg considers 1835 (Treaty of London) to be its year of independence, it was not granted political autonomy until 1839 under King William I of the Netherlands, who also was the Grand Duke of Luxembourg. In 1867, Luxembourg was recognized as independent, and received guarantees of perpetual neutrality. After being occupied by Germany in both World Wars, Luxembourg abandoned neutrality, and became a charter member of the North Atlantic Treaty Organization (NATO) in 1949. It is also one of the six original members of the European Union, formed in 1951 as the European Coal and Steel Community (ECSC). Since the end of World War II, the Christian Social Union (CSV) has been part of the governing coalitions, and usually the dominant party. The CSV leader, Prime Minister Jean-Claude Juncker, has been in power since 1995, and is the longest-serving head of government in the European Union.

STATISTICS

GDP growth: 3.6% (2008)
GDP per capita: US$85,100
CPI: 4%
Unemployment: 4.7%
FDI: N/A
Current account surplus: US$3.186 billion
Population: 491,775
Source: CIA Factbook except where stated

ECONOMIC POLICY OVER 12 MONTHS

This stable, high-income economy—benefiting from its proximity to France, Belgium, and Germany—has historically featured solid growth, low inflation, and low unemployment. The industrial sector was originally dominated by steel production, which originates from the discovery of a refining process by the English metallurgist, Sidney Thomas, in 1876 (Thomas invented a process for removing the phosphorous content from pig iron, which was very important to Luxembourg, as European pig iron is heavy in phosphorous.) This led, through a convoluted chain of events, to Luxembourg being home to Arcelor-Mittal, the largest steel-maker in the world (following the acquisition of Canada's largest steel manufacturer, Dofasco, in 2005). Arcelor-Mittal now produces some 10% of the world's steel, and the iron and steel industry in Luxembourg amounts to 11% of the economy. However, Luxembourg's economy has diversified very successfully, particularly into services, which now comprise 83.3% of GDP (source: US State Department). In 2006, there were 156 banks in Luxembourg employing 24,752 people. Political stability, good communications, easy access to other European financial centers, skilled multilingual staff, and a tradition of banking secrecy have contributed to the growth of the financial sector. German banks represent the largest number, with Italian, French, Swiss, Belgian, American, and Japanese banks also heavily represented. Total banking assets in 2005 were US$1 trillion. The funds industry is the second-largest in the world after the United States, with US$2.158 trillion in domiciled funds. In all, the financial sector now accounts for about 28% of GDP.

Agriculture is based on small, family-owned farms. The economy depends on foreign and cross-border workers for about 60% of its labor force. Although Luxembourg, like all EU members, suffered from the global economic slump in the early part of this decade, the country continues to enjoy an extraordinarily high standard of living; GDP per capita ranks third in the world, after Liechtenstein and Qatar. After two years of strong economic growth in 2006–2007, turmoil in the world financial markets slowed Luxembourg's economy in 2008, but growth remained above the European average, and is likely to remain so in 2009.

The Luxembourg budget for 2009, which went before Parliament on October 1, 2008, has a number of measures designed to further enhance Luxembourg's appeal as a preferred jurisdiction for investment. Chief among these is a proposal to reduce the corporate income-tax rate, and to abolish withholding tax on dividends paid to recipients in countries that have a tax treaty with Luxembourg (source: www.internationaltaxreview.com). This has a considerable impact for companies looking to repatriate profits from Luxembourg operations back to their home country. Commenting on the measure, a Deloitte Luxembourg tax partner, Georges Deitz, was quoted as saying that the draft bill was "very positive for the international business community."

ECONOMIC PERFORMANCE OVER 12 MONTHS

Growth in the Luxembourg economy over the past 15 years has been reflected in the way employment has grown. In the 10-year period 1991–2001, the average employment growth rate in Luxembourg was 3.6 % per year, compared to 0.5 % in Belgium, 0.5 % in France, 1.9 % in the Netherlands, and 0.4% in the EU-15 during the same period. Only Ireland recorded comparable figures. Even in the economic downturn from 2001, Luxembourg's employment growth rate was still 5.6%, the same as for 2000.

As part of a proactive policy to diversify the economy, Luxembourg adopted a number of public support schemes in the early 1990s to encourage the development of audiovisual production. The Grand Duchy is the home of two giants in the world of audiovisual communication, the European television and radio broadcaster, RTL Group, and the satellite company, Société Européenne des Satellites (SES), which operates the Astra satellites. On March 28, 2001, SES merged with GE Americom to create SES Global, the biggest satellite company in the world.

Many SMEs active in the converging fields of multimedia and telecommunications have been set up in Luxembourg around these two pillars of audiovisual communication, forming a network of skills that is driving future economic development. The Luxembourg government's policy of developing audiovisual and communication services is being pursued under the banner of the Luxembourg Mediaport. The campaign could have far-reaching effects in liberalizing the European telecommunications market.

The Luxembourg budget for 2009 (see Economic Policy above) is expected to have a very positive impact on the country's financial and banking sector, and on inward investment generally. The government knocked one percentage point off the rate of corporate income tax, down from 22% to 21%, abolished withholding tax on treaty-country profit repatriation, abolished capital duty, and encouraged companies to make jobs available to unemployed candidates by increasing subsidized income tax from 10% to 15% for three years. The government also announced that it would be diverting around 4.5% of GDP into public investment as part of a fiscal stimulus program. The projects likely to benefit include roads, rail, schools, and retirement. In addition, the government has earmarked €200 million, or 0.55% of GDP, for research on topics such as biotechnology (source: www.tax-news.com). Banks based in Luxembourg are allowed to operate as "universal banks," spanning the full range of banking activities in the home market and abroad. The country has a well-established network of private wealth managers and private banking services for high-net-worth individuals. An important part of these services is discretionary portfolio management (investing and managing asset portfolios for high-net-worth individuals).

SUPPORT FOR INWARD INVESTMENT AND IMPORTS

The Luxembourg Board of Economic Development (BED) is the Government's one-stop shop for new investment projects.

TAX EXEMPTIONS

There are favorable investment regimes for manufacturing and hi-tech companies, and for insurance, reinsurance, group treasury operations, and other financial services sectors. Further information can be obtained from BED.

» MORE INFO

Website:

Luxembourg Board of Economic Development: www.bed.public.lu

  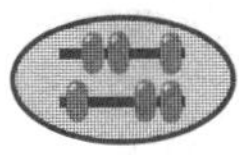      

Macau

ECONOMY AND TRADE

The Macau Special Administration Region consists of two islands, Coloane and Taipa, connected by an area of land reclaimed from the sea. The Region is on the western side of the Pearl River delta, with three bridges connecting Macau to mainland China. Macau's international airport is itself on reclaimed land jutting out into the South China Sea. The entire area is less than one-sixth the size of Washington DC. Colonized by the Portuguese in the 16th century, Macau was the first European settlement in the Far East. Pursuant to an agreement signed by China and Portugal on April 13, 1987, Macau became the Macau Special Administrative Region (SAR) of the People's Republic of China on December 20, 1999. Under this agreement, China promised that, under its "one country, two systems" formula, China's socialist economic system would not be practiced in Macau, and that Macau would enjoy a high degree of autonomy in all matters except foreign and defense affairs for the next 50 years.

STATISTICS

GDP growth: 15% (2008)
GDP per capita: US$38,000 (govt. of Macau)
CPI: 6.2%
Key interest rate: 5.25%
Exchange rate versus dollar: patacas per US dollar—8.011 (2007)
Unemployment: 3%
FDI: US$7.9 billion
Current account deficit/surplus: N/A
Population: 559,846 (July 2009, est.)
Source: CIA Factbook except where stated

ECONOMIC POLICY OVER 12 MONTHS

An essentially urban area, Macau's major growth areas have been tourism and gaming. After opening up its locally controlled casino industry to foreign competition in 2001, the territory attracted tens of billions of dollars in foreign investment, transforming Macao into the world's largest gaming center. By 2006, Macau's gaming revenue had surpassed that of the Las Vegas strip, and gaming-related taxes accounted for 75% of total government revenue. In 2008, government revenue from gaming was set to double 2006 collections. The expanding casino sector, and China's decision (beginning in 2002) to relax travel restrictions, re-energized Macau's tourism industry. In a World Tourism Organization report on international tourism statistics for 2006, Macau ranked 21st in terms of tourist arrivals, and 24th in terms of tourism receipts. From 9.1 million visitors in 2000, arrivals to Macau rose to 18.7 million visitors in 2005, and 22 million visitors in 2006, with more than 50% of the arrivals coming from mainland China, and another 30% from Hong Kong. The figure for 2007 was around 25 million visitors. Since the handover, Triad underworld violence, a deterring factor for tourists, has virtually disappeared, to the benefit of the tourism sector. This city of just over 500,000 people hosted more than 30 million visitors in 2008. Moreover, visitors from mainland China comprised 60% of total visitor numbers, despite increasing restrictions on travel to the SAR.

Macau's traditional manufacturing industry has been in a slow decline since the termination of the Multi-Fiber Agreement in 2005. In 2008, exports of textiles and garments generated only US$1.1 billion, compared to US$13.7 billion in gross gaming receipts. The Closer Economic Partnership Agreement (CEPA) between Macau and mainland China, which came into effect on January 1, 2004, offers many Macau-made products tariff-free access to the mainland. Macau's currency, the pataca, is closely tied to the Hong Kong dollar, which is also freely accepted in the territory.

Macau's casinos and gambling industry had been operating under a government-issued monopoly license going back to 1962. This ended in 2002. The ending of the monopoly license saw several Las Vegas casino operators entering the territory, with massive investments in purpose-built casino and hotel complexes. The Las Vegas Sands Corporation opened the Sands Macao, a 229,000 square feet casino with a 51-suite VIP hotel, which became a day-trip destination for millions of visitors from the Chinese mainland who do not, in general, stay over.

ECONOMIC PERFORMANCE OVER 12 MONTHS

As a region heavily dependent on tourism, Macau's economy, which had been booming since the opening up of the gambling sector in 2002, fell back in the second half of 2008. Growth in mainland China has been badly affected by the global downturn, and the number of day visitors coming across to Macau from the mainland has fallen sharply. As a result, GDP for the fourth quarter of 2008 registered the first negative growth for five years. For the whole of 2008, Macau's GDP was estimated by the Chinese government (see: www.gov.mo) to be MOP171.87 billion, up by 13.2% on GDP for 2007. Per capita GDP amounted to US$39,036. However, GDP for the fourth quarter contracted by 7.6% in real terms, with declining revenues from gambling adding to falling export demand to explain the shrinkage. However, first and second quarter growth in 2008 had been very strong, despite the fact that a number of developed economies by that stage were already going into recession. According to the government, growth in the first quarter amounted to 32.5%, and in the second quarter to 22.4%. Growth for the third quarter over the same quarter in 2007 was down to just 10.4%, creating a clear downward trend through the year, which finally turned negative in the fourth quarter.

According to the Chinese, visitor arrivals in 2008 totaled almost 23 million, with both per capita and total visitor spending rising over the previous year. More jobs and higher wages also pushed private consumption up by 7.5%, year on year, in real terms.

 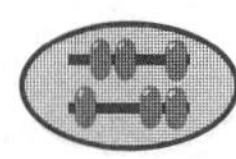      

Annual gross gaming revenues saw a growth surge to 31.0%. Net exports of goods and services (which equates to exports minus imports) outstripped Macau's GDP growth, rising from 41.4% in 2007 to 51.2% in 2008, according to Macau government statistics.

SUPPORT FOR INWARD INVESTMENT AND IMPORTS

The Macau Trade and Investment Promotion Institute is the body responsible for attracting and providing services to potential investors. Macau offers a number of fiscal incentives for inward investment.

TAX EXEMPTIONS

There is a range of possible exemptions, depending on the project being put forward and its potential relevance and benefit to Macau. Further information can be obtained from the Macau Trade and Investment Promotion Institute.

▸▸ MORE INFO

Website:

Government portal for Macau: www.gov.mo

Malaysia

ECONOMY AND TRADE

Malaysia is part of south-eastern Asia, and comprises the Malay peninsula bordering Thailand, plus the northern one-third of the island of Borneo, bordering Indonesia, Brunei, and the South China Sea. In 1826, the British settlements of Malacca, Penang, and Singapore were combined to form the Colony of the Straits Settlements. From these strongholds, in the 19th and early 20th centuries, the British established protectorates over the Malay sultanates on the peninsula. During their rule, the British developed large-scale rubber and tin production, and established a system of public administration. British control was interrupted by World War II, and the Japanese occupation from 1941 to 1945. After the war, the territories of peninsular Malaysia joined together to form the Federation of Malaya in 1948, and eventually negotiated independence from the British in 1957. In 1963, the British colonies of Singapore, Sarawak, and Sabah joined the Federation, which was renamed Malaysia. Singapore's membership, however, ended when it left in 1965, and became an independent republic. Since independence, the economy has diversified away from a near-complete dependence on the export of raw materials such as rubber and tin, with the development of a thriving manufacturing base, and a strong tourism industry.

STATISTICS

GDP growth: 5.5%
GDP per capita: US$15,700
CPI: 5.8%
Key interest rate: 6.41%
Exchange rate versus dollar: ringgits per US dollar—3.33 (2008)
Unemployment: 3.7%
FDI: US$92.76 billion
Current account deficit/surplus: US$27.44 billion
Population: 25,715,819 (July 2008, est.)
Source: CIA Factbook except where stated

ECONOMIC POLICY OVER 12 MONTHS

Malaysia is a middle-income country, and is now a fully fledged multi-sector economy. Much of the current economy owes its origins to the initiatives Malaysia undertook after 1970. In 1971, it launched The New Economic Policy, designed to benefit Malays and certain indigenous groups, and the government prioritized intercommunal harmony as one of its chief goals. Dr Mahathir Mohamad, prime minister between 1981 and 2003, attributed the success of the Asian tiger economies to the "Asian values" of its people, which he believed were superior to those of the West. Mahathir sharply criticized the International Monetary Fund (IMF), international financiers such as George Soros, and Western governments during the sharp economic and financial crisis that affected Asia in 1997–1998, and denied that the downturn was due to the failures of corruption and "crony capitalism."

Since coming to office in 2003, Prime Minister Abdullah Ahmad Badawi has tried to move the economy farther up the value-added production chain by attracting investments in high technology industries, medical technology, and pharmaceuticals. The government of Malaysia is continuing efforts to boost domestic demand, to wean the economy off of its dependence on exports. Nevertheless, exports—particularly of electronics—remain a significant driver of the economy. As an oil and gas exporter, Malaysia has profited from higher world energy prices, although the rising cost of domestic gasoline and diesel fuel forced Kuala Lumpur to reduce government subsidies.

Malaysia unpegged the ringgit from the US dollar in 2005, and the currency appreciated 6% per year against the dollar in 2006–2008. Although this helped to hold down the price of imports, inflationary pressures began to build in 2007. By 2008, inflation stood at nearly 6% year on year. The government presented its five-year national development agenda, in April 2006, through the Ninth Malaysia Plan, a comprehensive blueprint for the allocation of the national budget from 2006–2010. Prime Minister Abdullah has unveiled a series of ambitious development schemes for several regions that have had trouble attracting business investment.

Real GDP growth has averaged about 6% per year under the present administration, but regions outside Kuala Lumpur and the manufacturing hub, Penang, have not fared as well. The central bank maintains healthy foreign-exchange reserves, and the regulatory regime has limited Malaysia's exposure to riskier

  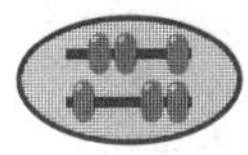 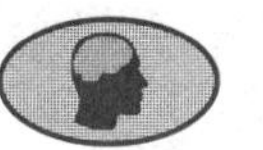  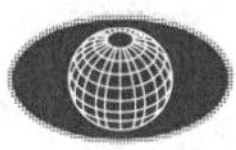   

financial instruments, and the global financial crisis. Decreasing worldwide demand for consumer goods is expected to hurt economic growth, however. Abdulla stepped down in March 2009, handing the prime minister's role to the then deputy prime minister, Najib Tun Razak.

ECONOMIC PERFORMANCE OVER 12 MONTHS

Since it became independent, Malaysia's economic record has been one of Asia's best. Real gross domestic product (GDP) grew by an average of 6.5% per year from 1957 to 2005. Performance peaked in the early 1980s through to the mid-1990s, as the economy experienced sustained rapid growth averaging almost 8% annually. High levels of foreign and domestic investment played a significant role as the economy diversified and modernized. Once heavily dependent on primary products such as rubber and tin, Malaysia today is a middle-income country, with a multi-sector economy based on services and manufacturing. Malaysia is one of the world's largest exporters of semiconductor devices, electrical goods, and information and communication technology (ICT) products.

The government continues actively to manage the economy. Malaysia's New Economic Policy (NEP), first established in 1971, was a 10-year plan that sought to rectify a situation whereby ethnic Malays and indigenous peoples (*bumiputera*), who comprised nearly 60% of the population, held less than 3% of the nation's wealth. Policy-makers implemented a complex network of racial preferences intended to promote the acquisition of economic assets by *bumiputera*. In 1981, when the racial preferences were set to expire, the government extended the NEP for another 10 years, stating that its goals had not been achieved. The policies were extended again in 1991, and in 2001.

The Malaysian economy went into sharp recession in 1997–1998 during the Asian financial crisis, which affected countries throughout the region, including South Korea, Indonesia, and Thailand. Malaysia's GDP contracted by more than 7% in 1998. Malaysia narrowly avoided a return to recession in 2001, when its economy was negatively affected by the bursting of the dotcom bubble (which hurt the ICT sector), and slow growth or recession in many of its important export markets.

In July 2005, the government removed the seven-year-old peg linking the ringgit's value to the US dollar at an exchange rate of RM3.8/US$1. The dollar peg was replaced by a managed float against an undisclosed basket of currencies. The new exchange rate policy was designed to keep the ringgit more stable, and to avoid uncertain currency swings, which could harm exports.

The Malaysian financial system has exhibited noteworthy resilience to the 2008 global financial crisis. Malaysian banks are well capitalized, and have no measurable exposure to the US subprime market. The central bank maintains high levels of foreign-exchange reserves, and a conservative regulatory environment, having prohibited some of the riskier assets in vogue elsewhere. However, decreasing demand in the United States and elsewhere is taking a toll on Malaysian exports, resulting in slower economic growth going forward.

SUPPORT FOR INWARD INVESTMENT AND IMPORTS

The Malaysian Industrial Development Authority (MIDA) is the first point of contact for investors who wish to set up projects in the manufacturing and services sector of Malaysia. Headquartered in Kuala Lumpur, MIDA has a global network of 19 overseas offices, covering Asia, Europe, the United States, and Australia to assist investors.

TAX EXEMPTIONS

Malaysia reduced corporation tax for the 2009 assessment year to 25%, and brought down the rate of individual taxation from 28% to 27%. The Promotion of Investments Act 1986 offers a range of tax incentives. More information can be obtained from MIDA.

▸▸ MORE INFO

Websites:

Malaysian Industrial Development Authority: www.mida.gov.my

Malaysian Ministry of International Trade and Industry: www.miti.gov.my

Malaysian Prime Minister's Department: www.pmo.gov.my

Malta

ECONOMY AND TRADE

Malta is highly dependent on tourism, financial services, and manufacturing, particularly electronics and pharmaceuticals. Malta produces only about 20% of its food needs, has limited fresh water supplies, and is reliant upon imported energy.

Malta was the smallest of the ten countries to join the European Union in May 2004. It joined the Eurozone in 2008. The Maltese government has implemented broad, liberalizing economic reforms since joining the European Union. The economy has enjoyed a four-year-long expansion, with an average annual growth rate of 3.2% between 2005 and 2008. Key drivers have included productivity gains, increasing

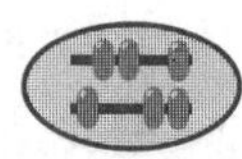

foreign direct investment, and the diversification of exports into new, dynamic sectors. Rising employment and incomes have supported domestic demand.

Malta traditionally incurs a large trade deficit, which is offset by a surplus on the services account. The country is even more closely integrated with European trading partners as a result of its membership of the European Union. Germany, France and the United Kingdom are Malta's three most important markets, with a combined share of around 36% of merchandise exports.

ECONOMIC POLICY OVER 12 MONTHS

Since joining the Eurozone on 1 January 2008, Malta has ceded control of its monetary policy to the European Central Bank (ECB). As the smallest country in the Eurozone, Malta is unlikely to have much, if any, influence over the ECB's policy decisions. Thus, fiscal policy has assumed greater importance. The government has also focused on implementing structural reforms to ensure that Malta can maintain its competitiveness—devaluing the Maltese currency to boost export performance is clearly no longer an option.

Up until 2008, the government had made good progress in improving the public finances. The budget deficit fell from 9.3% of GDP in 2003 to 1.8% in 2007, while the public debt was reduced to 61.9% of GDP from 73%. However, one-off costs related to early-retirement schemes for shipyard employees led to a jump in the budget deficit in 2008. The deficit rose to 3.5% of GDP in 2008, while the public debt rose to 63.3% (both figures are from the European Commission).

The government had aimed to balance its books by 2010, but in the 2009 budget (announced in November 2008) the authorities delayed this target to 2011, blaming the deterioration in the global economy. Prime Minister Lawrence Gonzi said that the budget would reinforce Malta as an "eco-island," with €152 million of investment in environmental projects and alternative-energy incentives. The tax regime was left largely unchanged, but the government announced plans to privatize the petroleum operations of the energy utility, Enemalta.

Earlier in 2008, the authorities adopted several expenditure retrenchment measures, including adjustments in the subsidized retail electricity tariff, with the aim of keeping the 2008 budget on track and maintaining progress towards eliminating the deficit entirely. In June 2008, the government also announced plans to privatize the state-owned Malta Shipyards, which employs around 1,700 workers. A restructuring programme (2003–2008) was intended to turn the shipyards into a self-sufficient, profitable enterprise by the end of 2008—further state aid beyond this date would not be allowed under the conditions of Malta's entry into the European Union. However, Malta Shipyards has continued to operate at a substantial loss despite the restructuring programme. By the end of 2008, the government appeared to have made little progress in selling the shipyards. It also appeared to have abandoned the sale of its remaining stake in the Bank of Valletta.

ECONOMIC PERFORMANCE OVER 12 MONTHS

Unsurprisingly, given its open, trade-oriented economy, Malta has been badly affected by the global economic slowdown. Growth slowed to 2.1% in 2008, according to the European Commission (EC), from 3.9% in 2007. In January 2009, the EC predicted that the Maltese economy would expand by just 0.7% in 2009, significantly lower than the government's 2.5% growth forecast.

Falling international demand for Maltese exports and for tourism in Malta have been the main factors undermining growth. In particular, the strength of the euro is deterring tourists from the United Kingdom, who accounted for around 35% of tourist arrivals in 2008. Economic woes in the United Kingdom, where unemployment has risen sharply, may also be a factor. Although the overall number of tourists visiting Malta increased by 3.8% in 2008, numbers fell sharply in the latter months of the year. Tourist numbers were down by 2.9% in September, 9.3% in October, 10.8% in November and 12.4% in December compared with the corresponding months in 2007.

Although economic growth has slowed sharply, Malta is faring better than other EU countries, which are likely to experience a sharp contraction in 2009. This is partly due to the health of the Maltese financial system, which appears to have avoided the problems engulfing other advanced economies. According to a report published by the International Monetary Fund (IMF) in August 2008, the banking sector's liquidity and funding profiles are healthy, and banks have remained profitable despite markdowns in security portfolios.

However, the economic slowdown has caused unemployment to rise marginally, the jobless rate increasing from 6.4% in 2007 to 6.5% in 2008, according to the EC, which is also forecasting a jump to 7.4% in 2009. Inflation surged in 2008, with the 12-month average inflation rate standing at 4.7% by the end of the year—the country's highest level since the beginning of 2005, and far above the Eurozone's 3.3% average. Malta's high dependence on fuel and commodity imports pushed up inflation in 2008, but the EC expects inflation to fall sharply in 2009, to 1.9%, reflecting the tumbling price of oil and other commodities.

However, this trend will bring little relief to the country's external finances. Malta's current-account deficit rose from 5.5% in 2007 to 6.5% in 2008, and the EC anticipates that it will continue climbing to

STATISTICS

GDP growth: 2.1% (2008 EU est.)
GDP per capita: US$24,200 (2008 est.)
CPI: 4.7% (2008 est.)
Key interest rate: 6.24% (31 December 2007)
Exchange rate versus dollar: euros per US dollar—0.6494 (2008 est.)
Unemployment: 6.4% (2007)
FDI: NA
Current account deficit/surplus –US$538 million (2008 est.)
Population: 403,532 (July 2008 est.)
Source: CIA Factbook except where stated

➤➤ MORE INFO

Websites:

Agency that promotes foreign investment and industrial development in Malta: www.maltaenterprise.com

Government portal giving links to ministries and government departments: www.gov.mt/index.asp?l=2

European Commission forecasts published in January 2009: ec.europa.eu/economy_finance/pdf/2009/interimforecastjanuary/interim_forecast_jan_2009_en.pdf

  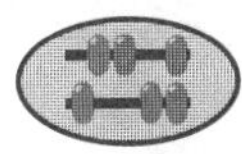      

7.0% in 2009. Falling export demand, as well as a surge in the cost of importing raw materials in 2007, is largely to blame. Malta's export competitiveness is also deteriorating, according to a Maltese newspaper report in February 2009, which quoted a "confidential" report prepared for eurozone finance ministers.

SUPPORT FOR INWARD INVESTMENT AND IMPORTS

Malta Enterprise is the agency responsible for the promotion of foreign investment and industrial development in Malta. Malta Enterprise also promotes the country's external trade by helping companies in Malta to develop new export markets. Further details are available on its website, www.maltaenterprise.com.

TAX EXEMPTIONS

Companies engaged in specific activities can benefit from tax credits on capital investment and job creation. Further details are available from Malta Enterprise.

Mauritius

ECONOMY AND TRADE

Mauritius, an Indian Ocean island of 1.3 million people, is one of Africa's most prosperous and stable economies. It has a diverse population: descendants of workers from India, who were brought to work in the sugar-cane fields, account for about 70% of the population; the remainder includes Africans, Creoles, Chinese, and Europeans. At independence in 1968, the country was poor, with a per capita income of around US$260. However, the government has successfully diversified the economy into textiles, tourism, and financial services. In recent years, information and communication technology (ICT), particularly business-process outsourcing, and seafood have emerged as important sectors of the economy. The US State Department estimates 2008 GDP at market prices at US$7.99 billion (official exchange rate) and per capita income at US$12,074 (purchasing-power parity), one of the highest in Africa. The country has benefited from its political stability (it is a multi-party parliamentary democracy), and ethnic tolerance.

ECONOMIC POLICY OVER 12 MONTHS

The Mauritian economy has been affected by changes to the world trade regime. The World Bank says that, according to one estimate, the ending of the Multi Fibre Arrangement (MFA), which governed world trade in textiles and garments, in January 2005, and the phasing out of sugar preferences in 2008 could cost Mauritius as much as 8–9% of GDP, 20% of exports, and 40% of government revenue. Increasing living standards were already undermining the country's competitive position in labor-intensive sectors such as sugar and garments.

Rising world commodity prices, especially for food and petroleum products, have also affected the island. As a result of these external shocks, export growth has dwindled and the current account deficit deteriorated to an average of 4% of GDP in the period 2004–2007. Real GDP growth has also fallen during the current decade, averaging 3.6% between 2001 and 2007, compared with 4% in the 1990s and 5% in the 1980s.

However, the government that took office in July 2005 embarked on a bold economic-reform program aimed at moving Mauritius from reliance on trade preferences to global competitiveness. The reform strategy, outlined in the past three government budgets, covering the fiscal years from 2006 to 2009, was designed to improve the government's finances, liberalize the economy, facilitate business, improve the investment climate, and mobilize foreign direct investment.

The government has also sought to restructure the textile and sugar sectors, develop the ICT sector, and promote Mauritius as a seafood hub in the region, using existing logistics and distribution facilities within the free trade zone located at the port and the airport. The government is seeking to diversify the economy by encouraging development in the following sectors:

- the land-based oceanic industry;
- hospitality and property development;
- the healthcare and biomedical industry;
- agro-processing and biotechnology;
- the knowledge industry;
- renewable energy.

In 2008, disagreements over how to counter the global economic slowdown and near double-digit inflation

STATISTICS

GDP growth: 5.2% (2008, government figures)
GDP per capita: US$12,400 (2008, est.)
CPI: 9.3% (January 2009, government figures)
Key interest rate: 6.75% (December 2008)
Exchange rate versus dollar: Mauritian rupees (MUR) per US dollar—27.973 (2008, est.)
Unemployment: 7.8% (2008, government figures)
FDI: N/A
Current account deficit/surplus –US$982 million (2008, est.)
Population: 1,274,189 (July 2008, est.)
Source: CIA Factbook except where stated

developed between the central bank and the finance ministry. While the finance ministry has sought to focus on maintaining growth, controlling inflation has been the central bank's foremost priority.

However, falling international commodity prices have eased the inflationary pressures and, in December 2008, the central bank cut its benchmark interest rate by 100 basis points, to 6.75%. During the same month, finance minister Ramakrishna Sithanen unveiled a 10.4 billion rupee (US$316.5 million) stimulus plan to bolster growth, protect jobs, and maintain purchasing power. The government hopes the package will encourage spending, and spur the struggling manufacturing and construction sectors.

ECONOMIC PERFORMANCE OVER 12 MONTHS

Prior to the global financial crisis, the government's efforts to restructure the economy were having a positive impact. Tax reform, together with improvements in the business environment and investment initiatives, spurred foreign investment to unprecedented levels and accelerated growth to between 6.5% and 7.0% in the fiscal year 2007–2008. Growth was broad-based, but it was especially strong in tourism, banking, construction, and services, according to the International Monetary Fund (IMF).

The IMF added that rising government revenues and efforts to contain government spending had cut the government deficit. Public-sector debt had also fallen. The current account was on a downward trend, caused largely by investment-driven import growth, which would eventually translate into greater export capacity.

Although the global economic slowdown has taken a toll on investment and export growth, the economy expanded by a highly respectable 5.2% in calendar 2008, down from an original prediction of 6% made at the start of the year. The government expects the economy to expand by 4% in 2009, but independent analysts believe this figure is too optimistic. Tourism is certainly feeling the effects of the global credit crunch. Tourism revenues fell by 27% in November 2008, compared with the same month in 2007. In December 2008, textile firms reported that orders had fallen by up to 15%.

The construction sector is expected to grow by just 2.5% in 2009, after recording 11.0% growth in 2008, according to a report issued by the Central Statistics Office (CSO) in January 2009. The CSO also anticipates that private-sector investment growth will fall from 24.0% to 9.2% in 2009, as investment in commercial building, hotels, luxury villas, and the financial and manufacturing sector tumbles.

Surging global commodity prices fuelled inflation on the import-dependent island in 2008. Inflation peaked at 9.9% in October, due to a sharp increase in the cost of oil and foodstuffs. However, inflation subsided in the final months of 2008 as falling global growth cut demand for commodities. By January 2009, inflation had eased to 9.3%, from 9.7% in December 2008. Unemployment fell to 7.8% in 2008, from 8.5% in 2007.

SUPPORT FOR INWARD INVESTMENT AND IMPORTS

The World Bank 2009 Doing Business Survey ranks Mauritius first in Africa and 24th in the world for ease of doing business. The government's objective is for Mauritius to rank among the 10 most investment- and business-friendly locations in the world.

The Board of Investment provides advice and information on investing in Mauritius. The Ministry of Finance and Economic Empowerment can provide advice on the country's import policy, import tariffs, and customs regulations.

TAX EXEMPTIONS

Mauritius is moving away from tax incentives and exemptions and towards the adoption of a low tax regime. The rate of corporate income tax in Mauritius is currently 15% on chargeable income, having been reduced from 25% as of 1 July 2007. Foreign investment is encouraged, and a wide range of incentives and facilities are offered in various sectors of the economy: manufacturing and light processing; textile and fashion; logistics and distribution; seafood and marine industry; hospitality and property development; the biomedical industry; the knowledge industry; and financial services.

▸▸ MORE INFO

Websites:

Board of Investment: www.boimauritius.com

Ministry of Finance and Economic Empowerment: www.gov.mu/portal/site/MOFSite/

Government portal for information on government ministries and agencies: www.gov.mu/portal/site/GovtHomePagesite/

US Department of State report on Mauritius, published in February 2009: www.state.gov/r/pa/ei/bgn/2833.htm

Mexico

ECONOMY AND TRADE

Mexico is the second-largest economy in Latin America. It is highly dependent on the US economy, which accounts for around 80% of the country's exports. Furthermore, millions of Mexicans work in the United States and the remittances they send home are a vital source of foreign exchange. Indeed, remittances are the second-biggest source of foreign-currency inflows, behind oil exports, and comprise around 3% of the country's gross domestic product. Mexico's integration with the United States has deepened since the establishment of the North American Free Trade Area (NAFTA, covering the United States, Canada and Mexico) in 1994. Trade between the three partners has increased by more than 10% a year since the agreement, which paved the way for tariffs to be cut on key products. The service sector is the largest component of GDP (70.5%), followed by the industrial sector (25.7%). Agriculture represents 3.9% of GDP. Mexico is the fifth-largest oil producer in the world (3.8 million barrels per day), although its reserves are declining.

ECONOMIC POLICY OVER 12 MONTHS

Mexico is considered one of the better-managed emerging economies and has enjoyed relatively stable economic growth during the current decade—growth averaged 3% each year between 2000 and 2007. However, there are stark divisions between rich and poor. In 2008, the OECD ranked Mexico bottom of 30 developed and developing countries in terms of economic income inequality. The wealthiest 10% of Mexicans earn more than 25 times as much as the poorest 10%. Around 40% of the population are poor and 18% are considered to live in extreme poverty, according to official estimates.

The global economic slowdown is exacerbating these divisions and the authorities have been very active in adopting measures to calm financial markets and counter the impact on the domestic economy. In October 2008, President Calderon unveiled a revised budget for 2009, which will result in the first budget deficit in several years. The budget includes a 13% spending increase on infrastructure and other projects to stimulate growth and prevent job losses.

The government plans to use 145 billion pesos (US$10 billion) saved in three stabilization funds to help cover the costs of the increased spending and to compensate for falling tax income as the economy slows. In 2008, Mexican officials at Pemex, the state-owned oil monopoly, also bought options to sell 330 million barrels of Mexican crude for US$70 a barrel—which guarantees the country at least US$9.5 billion in extra income if oil prices stay below that level.

Also in October 2008, the authorities announced various measures aimed at easing the liquidity squeeze in domestic financial markets. Critically, the Treasury announced that it would favour short-term paper over long-term bonds in order to ease constraints on long-term funding availability. In addition, and along with the central banks of Brazil, Singapore and South Korea, the Mexican authorities announced the establishment of temporary reciprocal currency swap lines with the US Federal Reserve.

The currency swaps provide each of the foreign central banks with up to US$30 billion to lend to banks in their jurisdictions to ease dollar funding conditions. The arrangement, which is set to remain in place until 30 October 2009, signals the Federal Reserve's commitment to supporting large, well-managed emerging markets that have been suffering severe contagion from global financial-market turmoil despite solid domestic fundamentals.

The Mexican central bank, Banco de México (or Banxico), has kept a tight rein on monetary policy in order to contain inflation. The central bank cut interest rates by 50 basis points in January 2009, to 7.75%. It was the first fall in borrowing costs in nearly three years. The central bank is expected to cut the key interest rate aggressively in 2009 to help the economy.

ECONOMIC PERFORMANCE OVER 12 MONTHS

The global economic slowdown and the credit crunch have had a significant impact on the Mexican economy, choking exports and investment. The economy expanded by 1.5% in 2008, according to the central bank, after recording 3.2% growth in 2007. Conditions worsened markedly in the fourth quarter of 2008, when the economy shrank by 1%. Despite the government's measures to stimulate growth, the central bank forecast in February 2009 that it expected the economy to shrink by 1.16% in 2009. The economy last contracted for a full year in 2001, when it shrank by 1.6%.

The recession in the United States is hitting remittances and exports. Money sent home by Mexican emigrants, mostly in the United States, fell by 3.6% to US$25 billion in 2008—the first drop on record, according to the central bank. The fall is thought to have been caused by a crackdown on illegal immigration and migrant job losses as the US recession leads to widespread layoffs.

Meanwhile, the Mexican Institute of Finance Executives' manufacturing index fell to 42.9 in January 2009, from 43.8 in December 2008—its seventh straight month below 50, reflecting a sharp drop in demand for exports to the United States. A slump in the price of oil has also hit export revenues. However, the decision to hedge against declining oil prices (see Economic Policy) and the government's cautious fiscal policy mean that the country has fared better than less prudent oil exporters.

Mexico has also avoided the housing speculation seen in the United States. Mexico's financial system has been stringent in extending credit. The IMF reported in December 2007 that commercial banks were well capitalized, profitable and liquid, and non-performing loans remained low.

A sharp depreciation of the peso in the latter half of 2008 fuelled inflation, which reached an eight-year high of 6.53% in 2008, above the central bank's 6.0% target. The falling peso offset the impact of a sharp drop in oil and non-oil commodity prices in the fourth quarter of 2008. Inflation exceeded the central

STATISTICS

GDP growth: 1.5% (2008 est.)
GDP per capita: $14,400 (2008 est.)
CPI: 6.5% (2008)
Key interest rate: Commercial bank prime lending rate 7.56% (31 December 2007))
Exchange rate versus dollar: Mexican pesos (MXN) per US dollar—11.016 (2008 est.)
Unemployment: 4.1% plus underemployment of perhaps 25% (October 2008)
FDI: US$278.9 billion (2008 est.)
Current account deficit/surplus −US$13.45 billion (2008 est.)
Population: 109,955,400 (July 2008 est.)
Source: CIA Factbook except where stated

bank's target of 6% in 2008. By February 2009, the central bank had spent nearly US$16.6 billion from its reserves to defend the peso since October 2008. Between August 2008 and February 2009, the peso lost 30% of its value.

SUPPORT FOR INWARD INVESTMENT AND IMPORTS

Mexico is open to foreign direct investment (FDI) in most economic sectors and has consistently been one of the largest recipients of FDI among emerging markets. ProMexico is the federal entity charged with promoting Mexican exports around the world and attracting foreign direct investment to Mexico.

The Economy Ministry maintains a bilingual website (www.economia.gob.mx) that provides information and downloadable application forms for import/export permits. Interested parties can also make online tax payments and communicate with online advisors who can answer specific investment-and trade-related questions.

TAX EXEMPTIONS

The 1993 Foreign Investment Law governs foreign investment in Mexico. The law is consistent with the foreign-investment chapter of NAFTA. US and Canadian investors generally receive national and most-favored-nation treatment when setting up operations or acquiring firms. The Mexican Federal Government has eliminated direct tax incentives, with the exception of accelerated depreciation.

MORE INFO

Websites:

Mexican government procurement portal: www.compranet.gob.mx

ProMexico has offices around the world and a multilingual website that provides information on investing in the country: www.investinmexico.com.m

The Mexican Customs Services website provides information on imports: www.aduanas.gob.mx

The Economy Ministry website for import requirements by HTS code: www.economia-snci.gob.mx

Monaco

ECONOMY AND TRADE

Monaco is the second-smallest independent state in the world, and one of the richest. Both tourists and the wealthy are drawn to the country—a constitutional monarchy—by its climate, the beauty of its setting, a world-renowned casino, and Monaco's advantageous tax regime (residents do not pay income tax). The country is surrounded on three sides by France and occupies just under two square kilometers next to the Mediterranean Sea. Customs, postal services, telecommunications, and banking in Monaco are governed by an economic and customs union with France. The official currency is the euro.

Tourism accounts for around 25% of the government's annual revenue. The country is a major banking centre and closely guards the privacy of its clients. However, Monaco's banking and taxation system has come under criticism from France and Germany. Monaco has been accused of tolerating money laundering—claims it strongly denies. Monaco remains on the Organisation for Economic Cooperation and Development's (OECD) blacklist of uncooperative tax havens, along with Andorra and Liechtenstein. They are all accused of not applying the body's voluntary standards on financial transparency and exchange of information.

ECONOMIC POLICY OVER 12 MONTHS

Monaco's prosperity has been built on tourism, and the country's status as a tax haven. Monaco has also developed a banking sector, and small, high-value-added, non-polluting industries. The government appears intent on maintaining the policies that have created its economic success, namely levying no income tax and only low business taxes. The government also retains monopolies in a number of sectors, including tobacco, the telephone network, and the postal service, which it shows no sign of relinquishing.

Monaco has refused to buckle under pressure from France, Germany and the OECD to amend its banking secrecy laws. France has been vocal in its criticism of Monaco as a haven for money laundering, even though French citizens residing there are still subject to French tax laws. The OECD, along with officials within the European Union, has been urging the principality to make commitments to transparency, and the effective exchange of information.

In December 2008, the OECD held a Financial Action Task Force (FATF) conference in Monaco. The OECD and the FATF have been leading a fight against tax havens since the early 1990s. The OECD regards tax havens as the home of speculative hedge funds, criminal money laundering, and tax evasion. At the conference, Prince Albert denied that his country is a tax haven. "I know that Monaco has to have an irreproachable conduct in its financial dealings," he told the audience.

The conference was sought by the French and German governments. "We have agreed to lend money to the banks to rescue them from bankruptcy, but at the same time they cannot continue working with tax havens," French President Nicolas Sarkozy said ahead of the OECD meeting. Tax havens must be closed, he said.

In December 2008, the government discarded a multi-billion-dollar plan to extend the densely popu-

STATISTICS

GDP growth: 0.9% (2000, est.)

GDP per capita: US$30,000 (2006, est.)

CPI: 1.9% (2000)

Key interest rate: 2% (eurozone, February 2009)

Exchange rate versus dollar: euro per US dollar—0.6734 (2008 est.)

Unemployment: 0% (2005)

FDI: N/A

Current account deficit/surplus N/A

Population: 32,796 (July 2008, est.)

Source: CIA Factbook except where stated

  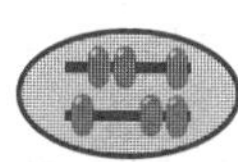   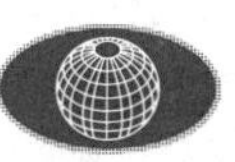   

lated principality into the sea, citing the global economic crisis and environmental concerns. The plan to build a huge artificial peninsula, which would have been the size of 20 football pitches, packed with housing, shops and tourist facilities, had drawn comparisons with the artificial islands off Dubai. The development would have increased Monaco's territory by 5%, and was expected to cost between US$5 and US$10 billion.

Monaco's ruler, Prince Albert, said that the decision to halt the landmark project did not indicate that Monaco's economy was in trouble. He added that other projects in the principality would continue, including a new hospital, two housing projects, and a yacht club.

ECONOMIC PERFORMANCE OVER 12 MONTHS

Very little information on Monaco's economy is available. Official economic statistics are not published. However, according to a US State Department report released in August 2008, which cited "2006 estimates," gross domestic product amounted to US$976.3 million, while per capita income stood at US$30,000. The State Department added that, while Monaco does not publish figures for unemployment, the jobless level was estimated at 0% in 2005.

However, there are signs that the global economic slowdown is having an impact on Monaco's economy. In February 2009, a French radio station reported that redundancies in the principality had increased in the "previous months," with five large companies cutting back on staff. It was also reported that employees had protested against what they considered inadequate severance pay.

SUPPORT FOR INWARD INVESTMENT AND IMPORTS

For information on investing and importing goods in Monaco, please contact the Department of Finance and Economy:

Ministère d'Etat
Place de la Visitation
MC 98000 Monaco
Tel: 00 377 98 98 82 56

To set up an office or a business in Monaco, it is necessary to send applications to:

Economic Development Direction
9, Rue du Gabian
MC 98000 Monaco
E-mail: expansion@gouv.mc

TAX EXEMPTIONS

Corporate tax is the only direct tax levied in Monaco. Companies of an industrial or commercial nature that make more than 25% of their turnover outside Monaco are liable for this tax. Profits from patents and royalties are subject to tax if they go to a company, but are not liable for taxation if received by a person. The taxable profit is established after the deduction of all costs, in particular, remuneration of the holder or owner, and remuneration of directors or managers carrying out a real function within the company. The scale of these deductions is established annually and allows the tax base to be reduced. A tax rate of 33.33% is then applied to the reduced profits.

Two categories of tax incentives have been established in the principality. Companies that are created in the principality, and are liable for tax on profits, but which develop a completely new business, are exempt from profits tax for a period of two years, and benefit from preferential treatment for the following three years. A start-up company pays no tax on its profits during the first and second years of operation; it pays tax on 25% of the reduced profits during the third year; pays tax on 50% of the reduced profits during the fourth year; pays tax on 75% of the reduced profits during the fifth year; and pays tax on 100% of the reduced profits in the sixth year.

There is also a research and development tax credit, under which administrative offices are not liable for tax on profits but are liable for a tax of just 2.66% levied on the running costs of the office.

▸▸ MORE INFO

Websites:

Government website listing laws and regulations, information on moving to Monaco and setting up a business in the Principality: www.monaco.gouv.mc/

Journal de Monaco, official news site: www.monaco.gouv.mc/Dataweb/journmon.nsf

Montserrat

ECONOMY AND TRADE

The British territory of Montserrat is an island in the north-eastern Caribbean. It is situated 27 miles south-west of Antigua, 30 miles south-east of Nevis and 38 miles south-east of St Kitts. It is one of the last remaining British Overseas Territories in the region and a member of the Organization of Eastern Caribbean States (OECS). Around 4,500 people live on the island, which covers 40 square miles.

  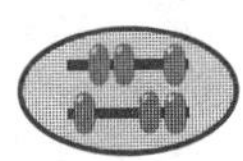   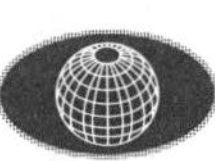   

In July 1995, the Soufrière Hills volcano erupted, destroying the capital, Plymouth, and the economy, resulting in heavy dependence on assistance from the United Kingdom. The volcano remains intermittently active; a volcanic exclusion zone covers the southern half of the island and extends two kilometers offshore. Limited economic activity is carried out on the island, including mining and quarrying, construction, financial and professional services, and tourism. Per capita income in 2006 (the latest year for which figures are available) amounted to EC$22,803 (Eastern Caribbean dollars), equivalent to around US$8,477. Eastern Caribbean dollars are issued by the Eastern Caribbean Central Bank. The states and territories that use Eastern Caribbean dollars belong to the Eastern Caribbean Currency Union. The Eastern Caribbean dollar is pegged at EC$2.70 to US$1.

ECONOMIC POLICY OVER 12 MONTHS

Montserrat is an internally governed overseas territory, whose government is run by a governor appointed by the Crown, and by Executive and Legislative Councils. The focus of the island's government has been on ensuring the safety of the population and rebuilding the island's basic infrastructure. In spite of this, the government has given much attention to improving the financial regulatory and supervisory framework for the offshore sector.

Montserrat has the smallest financial sector of the six United Kingdom overseas territories. The volume of financial services activity has fallen significantly since the volcanic eruption, but there are still 11 licensed offshore banks, down from 15 in 2000. Two banks are licensed to operate in the domestic market, providing domestic and international banking services. These banks are the Royal Bank of Canada and an indigenous bank, the Bank of Montserrat. The volcanic eruptions effectively suspended financial sector supervision in the offshore sector between 1996 and 1999, with bank records becoming irretrievable.

In 2008, the government came under pressure from the United Kingdom to improve the regulation of its financial services sector. The Public Accounts Committee of the British parliament issued a report in May 2008, which warned that the United Kingdom's remaining overseas territories were at risk of becoming centers for money laundering because of a dearth of qualified investigators to police their financial systems. The report singled out the Turks and Caicos Islands, Montserrat and Anguilla—all in the Caribbean—as most at risk from dubious financial practices because of poor quality regulatory standards. The report found that in Montserrat there are only 150 people working in the financial sector, and there is only one qualified person capable of investigating suspected fraud.

ECONOMIC PERFORMANCE OVER 12 MONTHS

In February 2009, an International Monetary Fund (IMF) mission to member countries in the Eastern Caribbean Currency Union predicted that economic activity in Montserrat would "slow considerably" in 2009 as construction and private-sector development are dampened by the global downturn. The IMF said that economic growth picked up to about 3.5% in 2008.

The IMF warned that Montserrat continues to face "a unique and challenging operating environment," with "renewed volcanic activity, declining population, and inadequate external transport linkages" continuing to limit the British dependency's growth potential. The IMF added that: "the economy relies heavily on budgetary aid from the United Kingdom and grants from donors to finance government services, and to meet its large reconstruction needs in infrastructure."

"Key policy challenges are to maintain macroeconomic stability in this difficult global environment and to minimize economic disruption from volcanic activity through strengthening the disaster-mitigation process," the IMF recommended.

The Eastern Caribbean Central Bank publishes a review of the Montserrat economy. The latest review, which covers the first half of 2008, found that economic activity had improved in the first half of 2008 relative to the corresponding period for 2007. It said that construction, mining and quarrying, and the wholesale and retail sectors drove this improvement.

The review found that the merchandise trade deficit had widened, due to an increase in import payments, but the government's finances were in surplus, in contrast to a deficit in the corresponding period for 2007. Total outstanding public-sector debt fell by 9.7%, to US$10.1 million, during the first six months of 2008. Consumer prices rose by 3.3% in the first six months of 2008.

During the first six months of 2008, the net foreign assets of the banking system rose by 9.4%, to US$185.1 million. This was attributable partly to inflows of official grants. The net foreign assets of commercial banks increased by 12.6%, reflecting growth in assets held by banks and other institutions both outside and within the currency union.

SUPPORT FOR INWARD INVESTMENT AND IMPORTS

The Montserrat Development Corporation (MDC), a limited-liability company owned by the government, establishes local and international business partnerships with the public and private sectors for improve-

STATISTICS

GDP growth: −1% (2002 est.)
GDP per capita: US$3,400 (2002 est.)
CPI: 2.6% (2002 est.)
Key interest rate: Central bank discount rate 6.5% (31 December 2007)
exchange rate versus dollar: Eastern Caribbean dollars—US dollar 2.7 (fixed)
unemployment: 6% (1998 est.)
FDI: N/A
Current account deficit/surplus N/A
Population: 5,079
Note: an estimated 8,000 refugees left the island following the resumption of volcanic activity in July 1995; some have returned (July 2008 est.)
Source: CIA Factbook except where stated

▸▸ MORE INFO

Websites:

Government website for information on Montserrat's tax system, tax administration, taxation of corporations, taxation of foreign corporations, taxation of shareholders, and taxation of foreign operations: www.devunit.gov.ms/taxes.htm

Government website for information on accounting principles and practices: www.devunit.gov.ms/accounting.htm

United Kingdom Foreign Ministry profile of Montserrat: www.fco.gov.uk/en/about-the-fco/country-profiles/north-central-america/montserrat?profile=today&pg=1

Website of the Montserrat Development Corporation: www.mdc.ms/?page_id=5

  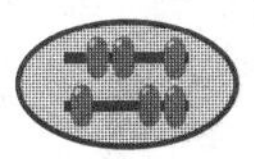 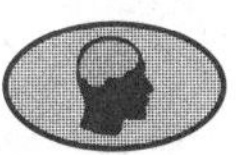  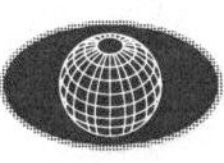   

ment of the economic status of the island. It can provide information on investment opportunities and import policy.

TAX EXEMPTIONS

The main features of Montserrat's tax system are as follows:

- The bulk of government revenue comes from direct taxation.
- Resident individuals are assessable for personal income tax.
- Capital gains are not subject to taxation.
- Tax incentives are available.

For information on the tax incentives, please see the government website in More Info, covering the tax system.

Morocco

ECONOMY AND TRADE

Morocco has achieved considerable economic progress over the past 30 years. Since the 1970s, gross national income per person has more than quadrupled from US$550 to US$2,300, while average life expectancy has increased from 55 in 1970 to 72.4 in 2007, according to the World Bank. The institution also says that Morocco is one of the leading economic reformers in the Middle East and North Africa region and that this reflects "a clear ambition to project Morocco to new heights in terms of competitiveness and growth."

Morocco has the world's biggest phosphate reserves, a large tourist industry, and a growing manufacturing sector. However, agriculture accounts for about 20% of GDP and employs roughly 40% of the labor force. Agriculture is highly dependent on rainfall, which can vary considerably from year to year. Morocco's trade is oriented towards the European Union, which buys around two-thirds of Moroccan exports. Major imports include oil, wheat, consumer goods and capital goods.

STATISTICS

GDP growth: 5.8% (2008 est.)
GDP per capita: US$4,000 (2008 est.)
CPI: 4.6% (2008 est.)
Key interest rate: Central bank discount rate 3.25% (31 December 2007)
Exchange rate versus dollar: Moroccan dirhams (MAD) per US dollar—7.526 (2008 est.),
Unemployment: 2.1% (2008 est.)
FDI: US$35.36 billion (2008 est.)
Current account deficit/ surplus –US$1.667 billion (2008 est.)
Population: 34,343,220 (July 2008 est.)
Source: CIA Factbook except where stated

ECONOMIC POLICY OVER 12 MONTHS

The government's economic strategy is to shift the economy away from its dependence upon agriculture and to create jobs and find new engines of growth. It has thus followed a policy of reform, liberalization, and modernization aimed at stimulating growth and creating jobs. Morocco needs to accelerate growth to reduce high levels of unemployment and underemployment. While overall unemployment stands at 7.7%, this figure masks significantly higher urban unemployment, as high as 33% among urban youth.

In November 2008, Parliament approved the 2009 budget, which includes a sharp increase in government investment, intended to bolster domestic demand. The state High Planning Commission expects the government to post a budget deficit of 2.9% of GDP in 2009, following a surplus in the previous two years, reflecting the increased government spending. Total government debt amounted to 54% of GDP at the end of 2007, down from 58% in 2006 (external public and publicly guaranteed debt remained at around 20% of GDP).

The government remains committed to containing the budget deficit to no more than 3% of GDP over the medium term. It aims to maintain sound expenditure controls, to reorient spending toward investment and education, to strengthen tax administration further, and to simplify the tax regime, as well as to manage its debt prudently. The authorities also intend to target subsidies at the poorest sections of the population, and thus gradually unwind universal subsidies. These reforms will be introduced in 2009.

In 2008, monetary policy remained geared toward maintaining low and stable inflation, in the context of the pegged exchange rate. Indeed, the central bank raised its benchmark interest rate by a quarter of a percentage point to 3.5% in September 2008, citing concerns about inflation, and it maintained the rate at that level for the remainder of the year. Prior to September's increase, the key policy rate had been unchanged since early 2007.

Morocco's financial system is sound and well managed, and has avoided the problems seen in many advanced economies. Banks are generally well provisioned and have little foreign exposure on either the asset or liability side, minimizing the transmission of risks from global financial markets to the real economy, the International Monetary Fund (IMF) reported in 2008. The IMF added that the authorities have continued to improve supervision, with a view to monitoring risks more closely as the economy becomes more open.

ECONOMIC PERFORMANCE OVER 12 MONTHS

The economy rebounded in 2008, growing by 5.8% after expanding by 2.7% in the previous year, when a

  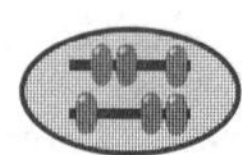      

drought afflicted the key agricultural sector. The level of rainfall doubled in 2008, boosting crop production and farm incomes over 2007. Indeed, overall private consumption grew by 7.8% in 2008, up from 3.8% in 2007. Non-agricultural sectors such as telecommunications, financial services, and construction also experienced vigorous growth.

Moroccan exports performed well in the first half of 2008 before dropping 16% in the fourth quarter from the previous three months as demand for phosphates tumbled in the face of slowing global growth. Other key exports, namely tailored clothing, hosiery and electronic parts, also fell sharply in the second half of the year. Tourism, measured by hotel occupancy, was down 2.3% in the first 11 months of 2008 after years of strong growth. Rising unemployment in key tourism markets such as the United Kingdom hit demand.

In February 2009, the state High Planning Commission said that the global economic crisis is also depressing foreign investment, which reached 31.7 billion Moroccan dirhams (US$3.72 billion) in 2008 but is expected to fall by 37% in 2009. The Commission also anticipated that tourism revenue and worker expatriate remittances, Morocco's key foreign-currency earners, would decline by 3.5% and 5.0%, respectively, in 2009. It further forecast that the country's current account deficit would widen to 5.7% as a proportion of GDP in 2009, from 4.6% in 2008.

Inflation jumped sharply in 2008 on the back of rising commodity prices. Consumer prices increased by 3.9% over the year, up two percentage points in 2007. Food price inflation amounted to 6.8% overall in 2008, after reaching a high of 9.1% in July. Policies to control domestic prices—such as food and fuel subsidies—kept inflation relatively low compared with many countries in the region. However, the cost of these subsidies has tripled in two years, reaching close to 6% of GDP in 2008.

SUPPORT FOR INWARD INVESTMENT AND IMPORTS

The government's Investment Office can help potential investors. It provides economic, financial, or statutory information needed for realising investment projects, of whatever size, in Morocco. It can also advise on the advantages of foreign investment legislation. These services, available in English, are provided free of charge. Contact details are as follows:

The Investment Office
Direction des Investissements Exterieurs
Angle Avenue Michelifen et Rue Hounain
4th Floor, Agdal
Rabat
Morocco
Tel: +212 37 673375 or +212 7 673420/1
Fax: +212 37 673417/42

The government has also established regional investment centres in 16 cities, including Casablanca, Rabat, Marrakech, Fes, Meknes, Agadir, Settat, Tangier, Oujda, Kenitra, and Safi.

For information on the government's import policy, please see the website of the Moroccan customs service: www.douane.gov.ma.

TAX EXEMPTIONS

The government has sought to reduce the plethora of tax exemptions and incentives in favor of a low corporate tax rate. Information about the numerous incentives that still exist can be obtained from the Investment Office detailed above.

MORE INFO

Websites:

Ministry of Finance: www.finances.gov.ma

US State Department report on Morocco, covering political background as well as economic and trade issues: www.state.gov/r/pa/ei/bgn/5431.htm

Nauru

ECONOMY AND TRADE

Nauru is a small, oval-shaped island in the Western Pacific Ocean, located just 42 kilometers south of the equator. A former British colony (Australia was the administering power from 1920 until independence in 1968), it is the world's smallest republic. Nauru has a total area of 21 square kilometers and a population of approximately 10,000 people. This tiny island generated enormous wealth from phosphates, created from fossilized bird droppings. In the 1980s, it had one of the highest per capita incomes in the world, but the phosphates are now close to exhaustion and the economy is in deep crisis.

Since 2000, when mining on a large-scale commercial basis ended, Nauru has relied largely on payments for fishing rights within its exclusive economic zone, and on development funding, principally from Australia, New Zealand, Japan, China, and Taiwan. Past government corruption and the disastrous mis-

  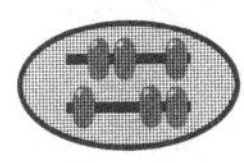 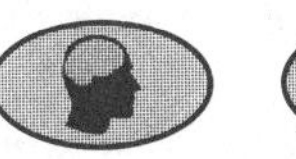 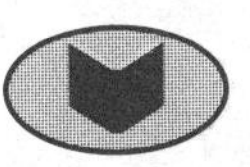 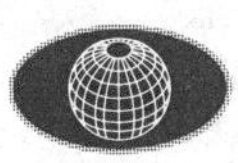 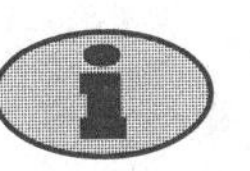  

management of trust funds that had been expected to provide post-mining revenue have exacerbated the country's decline.

ECONOMIC POLICY OVER 12 MONTHS

In August 1993, the Nauru and Australian governments signed a Compact of Settlement (NACOS), which ended litigation by Nauru against Australia in the International Court of Justice over the rehabilitation of phosphate land mined before independence. Australia agreed to pay Nauru US$57 million in cash and to provide US$50 million over a period of 20 years (paid in annual instalments of US$2.5 million indexed at 1993 values, e.g. US$3.7 million in 2008–2009). Australia and Nauru are cooperating closely on the use of NACOS funds to facilitate the mining of residual primary and, later, secondary phosphate reserves, followed by the rehabilitation of mined-out lands.

Australian officials and contracted advisers work closely with the Nauru government. An Australian finance team, comprising a secretary of finance, an economic adviser and a budget adviser, is responsible for the formulation of Nauru's budget, and for providing technical advice on economic reforms needed to improve financial management.

With the help of Australia, Nauru has implemented key financial and governance reforms. Nauru posted its fourth successive balanced budget in 2007–2008, and was removed from the Organisation for Economic Cooperation and Development's (OECD) Financial Action Taskforce (FATF) blacklist in October 2005, and from the US Treasury Financial Crimes Enforcement Network list of countries posing money-laundering concerns in April 2008. (A major shift into offshore financial services during the 1990s seemed promising, but it resulted in Nauru becoming a major haven for the financing of organized crime—and being blacklisted by both the US government and the OECD. The country was placed on the FATF blacklist of nations that are uncooperative in global efforts to tackle money laundering, and also on the tax-haven blacklist.)

Staff numbers and salary levels in the public service and state-owned enterprises (SOEs) have also been reduced to more sustainable levels and the Nauru Phosphate Corporation (NPC) has been reorganized into the RONPhos Corporation, which recommenced phosphate exports in September 2006.

Mining of primary phosphate reserves could continue until 2009 or 2010, and a recent study suggested that secondary phosphate reserves (beneath the currently exposed pinnacles) could be mined economically, in conjunction with the rehabilitation of mined lands, for up to 30 years. The export to neighbouring islands of gravel from crushed coral pinnacles (a by-product of secondary mining) is adding significantly to the island's revenues.

Nauru uses the Australian dollar as its means of exchange, giving it no control over monetary policy or interest rates, and rendering it unable to issue currency to fund deficit spending. Prices are largely influenced by those prevailing in Australia.

ECONOMIC PERFORMANCE OVER 12 MONTHS

Economic indicators for Nauru (such as GDP, inflation and GDP growth) are not available. In a report published in October 2008, the US State Department said that Nauru had a nominal per capita GDP in excess of US$2,700. Despite the lack of statistics, it is clear that the country faces enormous economic challenges. Although phosphate production has recommenced, the country lost another source of income in February 2008, when Australia closed an offshore camp for asylum seekers, which had generated millions of dollars for the Nauruan government. Officials in Nauru have voiced concern about the economic impact of the closure. Foreign Minister Kieran Keke said that about 100 people had lost their jobs and this would affect 1,000 people, or 10% of Nauru's population, who relied on these workers for support.

However, there were some positive developments in 2008. The government headed by President Stephens returned to office in snap elections in April, ending months of parliamentary deadlock over the budget. In November, the government announced plans to establish a private bank to fill the gap left by the collapse of the state-owned Bank of Nauru in 1998. Australian banks have declined an invitation to provide banking services to the country. There are no active financial institutions or services on the island.

The Asian Development Bank (ADB) issued a report on Nauru in November 2007, which said that phosphate exports had seen Nauru accumulate substantial offshore assets that peaked at approximately US$1 billion. However, the decline in phosphate mining that began in the late 1980s, combined with poor management of the country's offshore assets and public expenditure, led to a dramatic deterioration in its economic and fiscal position. By 2008, the country had built up debts approaching US$1bn.

The ADB concluded: "Deep-seated governance reforms are essential requirements for Nauru's development. The absence of accountability and transparency, particularly of public corporations, was central to Nauru's severe economic deterioration; concerted, corrective action is required to achieve a sustainable improvement in performance."

The ADB added that the government was addressing some of the structural problems the economy faces, and was making changes to establish a base for future economic growth. The prospects for phosphate mining and exports appeared good. Revenue from fishing licenses continued to support the budget. A

STATISTICS

GDP growth: N/A
GDP per capita: US$5,000 (2005 est.)
CPI: −3.6% (1993)
Key interest rate: N/A
Exchange rate versus dollar: Australian dollars (AUD) per US dollar—1.2059 (2008 est.)
Unemployment: 90% (2004 est.)
FDI: N/A
Current account deficit/surplus N/A
Population: 13,770 (July 2008 est.)
Source: CIA Factbook except where stated

▸▸ MORE INFO

Websites:

Australian Department of Foreign Affairs: www.dfat.gov.au/geo/nauru/
US State Department profile of Nauru: www.state.gov/r/pa/ei/bgn/16447.htm
Asian Development Bank report on Nauru's economy: www.adb.org/Documents/CERs/NAU/CER-NAU-2007.pdf

small revenue base had been established and the state-owned enterprises and utility services were being reformed.

SUPPORT FOR INWARD INVESTMENT AND IMPORTS

Nauru does not have a specific investment policy, nor does it offer investment incentives.

TAX EXEMPTIONS

There is no information available on tax exemptions in Nauru. Although the country was once considered a tax haven, this is no longer the case.

The Netherlands

ECONOMY AND TRADE

The Netherlands has one of the most advanced economies in the world, with a per capita income (purchasing power parity) of US$37,300 in 2006. It is home to the 16th-largest economy and the seventh-largest financial sector in the world. Financial and business services account for almost one-third of GDP, while industry and retailing together make up almost another third. Agro-food production accounts for around 10% of the economy and about 20% of exports.

In 1952, the Netherlands was a founding member of the European Coal and Steel Community, the forerunner of the European Economic Community and later the European Union. In 2002, the Netherlands was also among the 12 EU members that replaced their own individual currencies with the euro. Thus, the economy is highly integrated with the rest of the European Union. Indeed, most of the Netherlands' trade is with other EU countries.

ECONOMIC POLICY OVER 12 MONTHS

The global financial crisis dominated economic policymaking in the Netherlands in 2008. Presciently, in June 2008 the International Monetary Fund (IMF) reported that the financial system in the Netherlands was proving generally resilient to the recent market turmoil, but "some pockets of weakness warrant caution." The global financial crisis has certainly weighed heavily on the Netherlands' financial sector. In October 2008, the government took full control of the Dutch operations of the ailing European bank Fortis in a deal worth €16.8 billion. Fortis was the first European bank to fall victim to the credit crisis.

During the same month, the government pumped €10 billion into the bank ING to help it during the financial crisis, and provided a cash injection of €3 billion to the insurer Aegon. The authorities further offered a €200 billion package of loan guarantees to Dutch banks. However, financial institutions in the Netherlands were reluctant to make use of the guarantee fund set up by the government because of fears that it could damage their reputation.

The government announced its 2009 budget in September 2008. In this, it said that it would postpone a planned rise in value added tax (a tax levied on goods and services within the European Union), and would reduce the tax burden on the corporate sector and on individuals to mitigate the impact of the global economic slowdown. However, it added that it would still aim to achieve a structural budget surplus of 1% of GDP by 2011. It would also continue to pay off public debt, which it anticipated would fall to about 40% of GDP in 2009—the lowest level in percentage terms since 1815. However, the European Commission (EC) forecast in January 2009 that the government budget would fall into deficit in 2009, reflecting a rapid slowdown in economic activity in the final months of the year (see Economic Performance).

As a member of the eurozone, the Netherlands is subject to the monetary policy of the European Central Bank (ECB), which has adopted a relatively hawkish stance on inflation. In 2008, it certainly adopted a tighter monetary stance than other central banks, such as the US Federal Reserve, which slashed interest rates in the wake of the global credit crisis. By the end of 2008, interest rates in the eurozone stood at 2.5%, while the Federal Reserve had cut its key interest rate to a range of between zero and 0.25%.

ECONOMIC PERFORMANCE OVER 12 MONTHS

The Netherlands has an open economy that is highly geared towards world trade and finance. Consequently, the global financial crisis that developed in 2007 and 2008, and that has led to a slump in global economic growth and trade, has had a significant impact on the Dutch economy. GDP growth fell from 3.5% in 2007 to an estimated 1.9% in 2008, and the growth that did occur was largely due to the carry-over from strong domestic demand in the second half of 2007, according to a report published by the

STATISTICS

GDP growth: 1.9% (2008, EU est.)
GDP per capita: US$41,300 (2008, est.)
CPI: 2.2% (2008, government figures)
Key interest rate: 2% (February 2009, eurozone)
Exchange rate versus dollar: euro per US dollar—0.6494 (2008, est.)
Unemployment: 3.2% (2007)
FDI: N/A
Current account deficit/surplus US$726.9 billion (2008, est.)
Population: 16,645,313 (July 2008, est.)
Source: CIA Factbook except where stated

  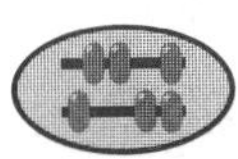   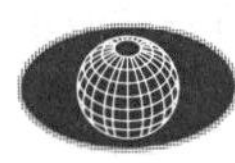   

EC in January 2009. The EC also forecast that the Dutch economy would contract by 2% in 2009, with negative growth occurring in all four quarters.

Growth was flat in the second and third quarters of 2008, and the economy is likely to have contracted in the fourth quarter. Private consumption provided only limited support in 2008—increasing inflation and rises in taxes and social premiums undermined disposable income. The recession and the financial crisis are having a negative impact on the government's finances. The EC anticipates that a budget surplus of 1.1 of GDP in 2008 will turn into a deficit of 1.4% in 2009, reflecting the impact of automatic stabilizers and lower gas revenues as a result of lower oil prices.

In 2008, average unemployment fell from 3.9% to 3.2% (one of the lowest levels in the eurozone), but the EC anticipates that the jobless level will rise sharply in the next two years—to 4.1% in 2009 and 5.5% in 2010. Unemployment has already begun to worsen, inching up to 3.9% in the fourth quarter of 2008, from 3.8% in the previous three months. Average inflation rose to 2.2% in 2008, from 1.6% in 2007. However, it should ease to 1.9%I in 2009, according to the EC, as international prices for commodities tumble.

In 2008, the country's external current-account surplus remained large (at 8.4% of GDP, down from 9.8% in 2007) and, according to an IMF report published in June 2008, "various approaches support the conclusion that Dutch competitiveness is satisfactory."

SUPPORT FOR INWARD INVESTMENT AND IMPORTS

The Netherlands Foreign Investment Agency (NFIA) is a division of the Dutch Ministry of Economic Affairs. The NFIA provides assistance to foreign companies that wish to establish, expand or reorganize operations in the Netherlands. The NFIA says it can provide help at every stage of strategic decision-making, with information, advice, and practical assistance. Services are in strict confidence, without obligation, and free of charge.

Detailed information and statistics can be provided in areas such as economics, operating costs, fiscal matters, and business locations. The NFIA service can also arrange fact-finding trips, site visits, and meetings with other companies that have chosen the Netherlands as their European base. The NFIA can offer introductions to lawyers, tax consultants, and national, regional and local organizations, as well as regional development agencies. The NFIA can also provide help to companies interested in exporting to the Netherlands.

TAX EXEMPTIONS

The government is striving to improve the investment environment in the Netherlands. The corporate tax rate is 25.5%, which is well below the EU average. Dividend tax has been reduced from 25% to 15%. The Netherlands also offers participation exemption, and a 30% tax break for highly qualified foreign employees.

▸▸ MORE INFO

Websites:

Netherlands Foreign Investment Agency: www.nfia.co.uk

The Netherlands Chamber of Commerce, which has 50 offices around the world: www.kvk.nl/english/

European Commission Economic Forecasts, published in January 2009: www.ec.europa.eu/economy_finance/pdf/2009/interimforecastjanuary/interim_forecast_jan_2009_en.pdf

IMF annual report on the Netherlands: www.imf.org/external/np/sec/pn/2008/pn0864.htm

OECD reports and statistics on the Netherlands: www.oecd.org/netherlands

New Zealand

ECONOMY AND TRADE

New Zealand is composed of two main narrow and mountainous islands, the North Island and the South Island, separated by Cook Strait, and a number of smaller outlying islands. It has a population of just 4.2 million. New Zealand has a mixed, open economy, which operates on free-market principles. In the 1980s, the country embarked upon a major reform program that deregulated the economy and improved its international competitiveness. Historically, the economy has been based on exports from a very efficient agricultural system. Leading agricultural exports include dairy products, meat, forest products, fruit and vegetables, fish, and wool.

The economy has diversified and now includes a range of manufacturing industries, although exports remain oriented around agriculture. Services account for around two-thirds of New Zealand's GDP, while manufacturing accounts for 15%. New Zealand's main export markets include Australia (which accounts for around a quarter of overseas sales), the European Union, the United States, Japan, and China. These countries also account for much of New Zealand's imports.

ECONOMIC POLICY OVER 12 MONTHS

The operation of fiscal policy in New Zealand is governed by the Public Finance Act 1989, which requires the government to outline its fiscal policy intentions in an annual Fiscal Strategy Report. The government announced an expansionary budget (including tax cuts and higher government spending) in May 2008, prior to elections in November, which saw the Labour Party lose power to a National Party-led coalition after nine years in office.

In early October 2008, the Treasury released a pre-election economic and fiscal update indicating that, after 14 years in surplus, the budget balance was set to slip into deficit. However, New Zealand is still in a strong fiscal position after recording large budget surpluses during the current decade. Thus, the new government has the scope to implement pre-election promises to cut income taxes further and increase infrastructure spending to counter the economic slowdown.

During the first half of the year, the primary concern of the central bank, the Reserve Bank of New Zealand (RBNZ), was containing inflation—despite gathering evidence that the country faced a long recession. Surging prices for fuel and other commodities fueled inflation, which rose to 3.2% in December 2007 and, throughout 2008, remained above the 1–3% range officially targeted by the central bank.

The central bank increased its Official Cash Rate to 8.25% in July 2007 and it remained at this level until July 2008, when it fell to 8%. During the remainder of the year, the RBNZ slashed rates to 3.5%, reflecting a fall in international commodity prices as well as the rapid deterioration in the global economy.

New Zealand's banks have not experienced the significant financial losses associated with housing lending that have been at the heart of the global financial meltdown. The country's banks have also benefited from effective action by the RBNZ to improve liquidity. From 2009, the RBNZ assumed responsibility for the supervision of non-bank financial institutions, with the aim of improving governance and risk management.

The government has taken a number of measures to stabilize domestic financial markets. In October 2008, the minister of finance announced the introduction of a retail deposit guarantee scheme, covering all retail deposits of participating New Zealand-registered banks and non-bank deposit-taking entities for a period of two years. In early November, the minister announced the introduction of a temporary opt-in wholesale guarantee facility, which will cover the wholesale debt of investment-grade New Zealand financial institutions.

ECONOMIC PERFORMANCE OVER 12 MONTHS

The global economic crisis has had an even more marked impact on New Zealand than on other advanced economies. This reflects the large macroeconomic imbalances that had built up over the previous decade—inflation, housing overvaluation, high household debt, and a huge current account deficit—as well as New Zealand's reliance on international trade.

Thus, New Zealand entered into a recession in the first quarter of 2008 (at a time when other advanced economies were still hopeful of avoiding a recession entirely). In February 2009, the deputy governor of the central bank, Grant Spencer, said that "the consensus" for the bottom of the economic cycle was probably in the second half of 2009 and that recovery would get underway in 2010.

The economy contracted for a third successive quarter in the three months ending in September 2008, according to an official report released in January 2009. The report added that all sectors of the economy were experiencing weakness. The economy is likely to shrink by 0.2% in the year ending 31 March 2009, after expanding by 3.2% in the previous 12 months, according to the average estimate of 11 economists surveyed by the New Zealand Institute of Economic Research in Wellington in February 2009.

Unemployment rose to a five-year high of 4.6% in the fourth quarter of 2008. The government's December *Quarterly Survey of Business Opinion* also found that businesses had reported laying off more staff in December than in previous months, while a net one in three firms expected staff numbers to decline in the March quarter, consistent with rising unemployment in 2009. In a further blow to consumer sentiment, house prices are falling fast. In January 2009, they were 8.3% lower than in the same month in 2008.

However, the recession has had a positive impact on inflation, which fell from a near two-decade high of 5.1% in September to 3.4% in December, largely due to lower fuel prices. The decline in inflation in the final quarter of 2008 was the largest in a decade. The country's Consumer Price Index actually declined by 0.5% during the three months to December 2008, raising the spectre of deflation.

In the year to the end of September 2008, the current account deficit stood at NZ$15.5 billion, equivalent to 8.6% of GDP, slightly up on the 8.4% recorded in the year to the end of June 2008. Ratings agencies have repeatedly warned that they could cut New Zealand's sovereign credit rating if the deficit does not fall.

SUPPORT FOR INWARD INVESTMENT AND IMPORTS

New Zealand encourages foreign investment without discrimination. The Overseas Investment Office (OIO) must give consent to foreign investments that would control 25% or more of businesses or property worth more than NZ$100 million. Restrictions and approval requirements also apply to certain investments in land and in the commercial fishing industry.

TAX EXEMPTIONS

New Zealand has a relatively simple, low-cost tax system compared with other countries. It operates a broad-based tax regime, designed to be comprehensive, with few exemptions and incentives.

STATISTICS

GDP growth: −0.2% (April 2008–March 2009) estimate from New Zealand Institute of Economic Research
GDP per capita: US$28,500 (2008 est.)
CPI: 3.4% (December 2008) government figures
Key interest rate: 3.5% (February 2009)
Exchange rate versus dollar: New Zealand dollars (NZD) per US dollar—1.4151 (2008 est.)
Unemployment: 4.6% (Q4 2008) government figures
FDI: US$72.41 billion (2008 est.)
Current-account deficit/surplus −US$9.047 billion (2008 est.)
Population: 4,173,460 (July 2008 est.)
Source: CIA Factbook except where stated

▸▸ MORE INFO

Websites:

Website of the Overseas Investment Office: www.linz.govt.nz/overseas-investment/
Website of the New Zealand Tax Office: www.ird.govt.nz
Australian Department of Foreign Affairs: www.dfat.gov.au/geo/new_zealand/
US State Department profile of New Zealand: www.state.gov/r/pa/ei/bgn/35852.htm
OECD report on New Zealand's economy: www.oecd.org/country/0,3377,en_33873108_33873658_1_1_1_1_1,00.html

  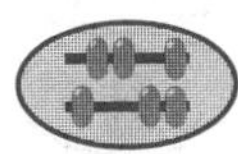 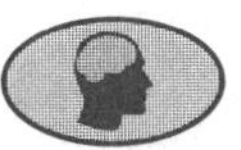     

Nigeria

ECONOMY AND TRADE

Nigeria is the most populous country in Africa, with an ethnically and religiously diverse population of 140 million. Nigeria has the second-highest GDP in Africa (US$166.78 billion in 2007), reflecting the country's substantial oil reserves. However, oil has proved a mixed blessing for the country. Much of the oil revenues has been squandered through corruption, while Nigeria neglected its strong agricultural and light manufacturing bases during the 1970s oil-price boom. Few Nigerians, including those in oil-producing areas, have benefited from the oil wealth. Nigeria is keen to attract foreign investment but it is hindered in this quest by security concerns, as well as by a shaky infrastructure troubled by power cuts. The United States is Nigeria's largest trading partner after the United Kingdom. Nigeria supplies around 11% of US oil imports. Crude oil and liquefied natural gas (LNG) account for around 98% of exports and around 80% of government revenues.

ECONOMIC POLICY OVER 12 MONTHS

The government's finances benefited from the boom in oil prices that began in 2003 and only ended in the second half of 2008, helped by a program of reforms introduced during President Olusegun Obasanjo's second term (2003–2007). These included an oil-price-based fiscal rule under which government expenditure is based on a conservative oil-price benchmark. Any revenues that accumulate above the reference prices are saved in a special excess crude account.

Thus, the 2008 budget was based on crude-oil prices of US$53 a barrel. However, the average price of crude oil during 2008 was significantly higher, reaching a peak of US$147. As a result of this fiscal rule, the government has recorded healthy budget surpluses in recent years—the budget surplus is estimated to have reached 4% of GDP in 2008, down from 5.6% in 2007.

However, the collapse in the price of oil in the final quarter of 2008 is taking a toll on the government's fiscal position. The government based its 2009 budget, passed by Parliament in December 2008, on crude selling at no less than US$45 per barrel. However, in February 2009, the government said it may scale back spending plans in 2009 as revenue from oil exports declines. The government said it may also borrow more money, or increase tax revenue from non-oil sources.

The tumbling price of oil has also undermined the Nigerian currency, the naira. In February 2009, the central bank reimposed currency controls not seen since the mid-1990s in an effort to stabilise the naira, which lost more than 20% of its value against the US dollar from mid-December 2008 to mid-February 2009.

The banking sector has not been immune to the excesses seen in other countries. Bank lending grew rapidly during the oil-price boom, much of it to finance share purchases on the stock exchange. The slump in oil prices in the latter months of 2008 caused the stock market in general and banking stocks in particular to fall sharply. The Nigerian Stock Exchange All-Share Index declined by 45.8% during the course of the year.

The central bank reacted to falling share prices and the problems in the banking sector by seeking to boost liquidity. In September 2008, it cut its key interest rate from 10.25% to 9.75%, having increased interest rates from 9.5% during the earlier part of the year. It also cut the banks' cash reserve requirement from 4% to 2% and reduced the liquidity ratio from 40% to 30%.

ECONOMIC PERFORMANCE OVER 12 MONTHS

The economy grew by 6.4% in 2008, according to official statistics, up from 6.2% in the previous year, but well below the official target of 9.8%. The slump in oil prices that occurred in the second half of 2008 has had a devastating impact on the economy. Attempts by militants in the Niger Delta to sabotage the oil business have also hit the economy. Attacks on oil infrastructure and kidnappings of oil workers have cut exports by more than 20% since 2006.

In November 2008, the government projected that the economy would grow by 8.9% in 2009. However, in February 2009, the central bank admitted that growth would slow sharply (due to falling oil prices), although the economy would avoid recession. In February 2009, JP Morgan was reported to have estimated that, at an oil price of US$43 per barrel, the Nigerian economy would grow by 4.4% in 2009 and would record a current-account surplus of 9.4%, down from an estimated 13% in 2008, and 16.4% in 2007. Other analysts, such as Dun and Bradstreet, believe that economic growth could be as low as 2.5% in 2009.

The fall in the price of oil and the consequent slump of the naira have also created powerful inflationary pressures. Year-on-year headline inflation jumped to 15.1% in December 2008, from 14.8% in November. Inflation had fallen to an annual average of 5.4% in 2007. High inflation is preventing the central bank from cutting interest rates sharply to boost the economy.

Nigeria's foreign-exchange reserves, while still healthy, are also coming under pressure. They fell to

STATISTICS

GDP growth: 6.4% (2008, government figures)

GDP per capita: US$2,200 (2008 est.)

CPI: 51.1% (December 2008, government figures)

Key interest rate: 9.75% (February 2009, Central Bank)

Exchange rate versus dollar: Pakistani rupees (PKR) per US dollar—70.64 (2008 est.)

Unemployment: N/A

FDI: US$35.75 billion (2008 est.)

Current account deficit/surplus US$7.722 billion (2008 est.)

Population: 146,255,312

Source: CIA Factbook except where stated

  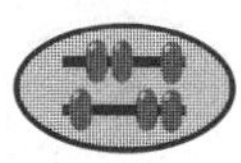 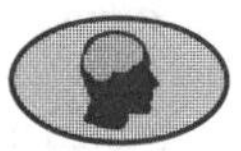     

US$52.7 billion at the end of December 2008—their lowest level in 12 months—down from US$57.8billion in late November. Earnings from crude-oil exports fell on the back of the falling price of oil. Capital inflows also declined due to a drop in foreign direct investment (FDI), reflecting the economic difficulties experienced by major investment partners such as the United States, the European Union, and China. Furthermore, the central bank intervened to support the currency, selling foreign exchange.

SUPPORT FOR INWARD INVESTMENT AND IMPORTS

The Nigerian Investment Promotion Commission (NIPC) is a one-stop federal government agency that aims to encourage, promote and coordinate investments in Nigeria. The agency provides a number of services, including business entry permits and licenses, as well as general information on the investment environment.

TAX EXEMPTIONS

Certain types of income are exempt from income tax. These include:

- the profits of any company engaged in ecclesiastical, charitable, or educational activities of a public character, in so far as such profits are not derived from a trade or business carried on by such company;
- the profits of any company formed for the purpose of promoting sporting activities, where such profits are wholly expendable for such purpose.

▸▸ MORE INFO

Websites:

Website of the Nigerian Investment Promotion Commission: www.nipc.gov.ng/

US State Department profile of Nigeria: www.state.gov/r/pa/ei/bgn/2836.htm

BBC profile of Nigeria: news.bbc.co.uk/1/hi/world/africa/country_profiles/1064557.stm

Norway

ECONOMY AND TRADE

Norway enjoys one of the highest standards of living in the world, due to the revenue generated by its offshore oil and gas deposits. It is the world's third-biggest exporter of gas and fourth-biggest exporter of oil. The government estimates its 2008 revenue from the petroleum sector at NOK413 billion (US$5.58 billion). The oil-revenue fund is the second-biggest of its kind in the world, with a value of NOK2.0 trillion (US$286 billion). The fund is designed primarily to help finance government programs once the oil and gas resources are depleted. Norway also has a large shipping fleet, while metals, pulp and paper products, chemicals, shipbuilding, and fishing are the most significant traditional industries.

Norway is not a member of the European Union, but it enjoys free trade with the European Union—with the exception of the agricultural and fisheries sectors—in the framework of the European Economic Area (EEA). Norway is not a member of the eurozone and does not have a fixed exchange rate. Its principal trading partners are in the European Union.

ECONOMIC POLICY OVER 12 MONTHS

In January 2009, the government unveiled a NOK20 billion (US$2.9 billion) stimulus package intended to dampen the impact of the global financial crisis. Finance Minister Kristin Halvorsen said that the national budget revision "is the most ambitious fiscal stimulus proposed in more than 30 years to boost growth and employment."

The package includes increased government spending of NOK16.75 billion (US$2.4 billion) for projects such as road and railway construction, maintenance and new projects in townships, and renewable-energy projects. The remaining NOK3.25 billion (US$466 million) will be provided in tax relief to businesses. Halvorsen said that Norway had anticipated a downturn after years of strong economic growth, but that "the financial crisis and the global economic downturn have intensified the turnaround."

The government has taken other measures to offset the impact of the global financial crisis on the country. In October 2008, the authorities approved a NOK350 billion (US$50 billion) bond package to help banks improve liquidity in the market, but this agreement failed to stimulate lending. Consequently, in February 2009, the government also announced NOK100 billion (US$15 billion) of measures to encourage banks to lend.

In October 2008, the government announced an expansionary budget for 2009 that was also designed to give a countercyclical boost to the economy. It was based on an oil price of US$90.50 a barrel. Although the price of oil subsequently plummeted, the government can draw on the oil-revenue fund to finance its budget. The government is expected to record a surplus of around 20% of GDP in 2008, which will fall to around 14% of GDP in 2009, according to the Organisation for Economic Cooperation and Development (OECD).

Norwegian monetary policy is aimed at maintaining a stable exchange rate for the krone against European currencies, of which the euro is a key operating parameter. It also targets annual consumer price inflation of approximately 2.5% "over time."

STATISTICS

GDP growth: 1.7% (2008) government figures

GDP per capita: US$57,500 (2008 est.)

CPI: 3.8% (2008) government figures

Key interest rate: 2.5% (February 2009)

Exchange rate versus dollar: Norwegian kroner (NOK) per US dollar—5.6361 (2008)

Unemployment: 2.5% (2008) Government figures

FDI: US$69.04 billion (2008 est.)

Current-account deficit/surplus US$84.35 billion (2008 est.)

Population: 4,644,457 (July 2008 est.)

Source: CIA Factbook except where stated

The monetary authorities were very active in using policy to stimulate the economy in the latter part of 2008. In October, the central bank cut rates by 100 basis points, ending more than three years of monetary tightening. In December, the central bank slashed its policy rate by 175 basis points, the largest cut in 22 years, to 3%. Norges Bank said that the risk of a "pronounced downturn" in the Norwegian economy had increased: the economy was likely to contract in the fourth quarter of 2008 and the first quarter of 2009, instead of the earlier forecasts for growth. In February 2009, the bank cut interest rates by a further 50 basis points, to 2.5%.

ECONOMIC PERFORMANCE OVER 12 MONTHS

The economy grew by 1.74% in 2008, compared with 3.1% in 2007. The slowdown reflects the impact of tumbling oil prices and the global financial crisis. In February 2009, the government projected that the economy would shrink by 0.5% in 2009 and that unemployment would climb to 3.5%, from 2.5% in 2008. In January 2008, Norway's unemployment rate stood at just 1.8%.

In the first half of 2008, Norway enjoyed buoyant growth—the economy expanded at a robust annual rate of 3.3% in the second quarter. But higher interest rates, weakening global growth, and tighter lending conditions had already begun to affect Norwegian households and enterprises. Interest-rate-sensitive sectors, such as construction, experienced a marked slowdown in the first half of the year.

Low interest rates between 2003 and early 2006 had led to the rapid accumulation of household debt, leaving consumers exposed in the downturn. Rising inflation and higher interest rates exacerbated the pressures facing households in 2008. Year-on-year inflation (as measured by the Consumer Price Index) peaked at 5.5% in October 2008. Higher energy, food, and transport costs were the main factors forcing up inflation in the first 10 months of the year. However, during the remainder of 2008, inflation fell sharply as international prices for commodities, including oil and food, slumped. By December 2008, the annual rate of inflation had fallen to 2.1%. Overall, inflation averaged 3.8% in 2008, up from 0.7% in 2007.

The very high oil prices that prevailed for much of 2008 supported Norway's external accounts. The OECD has estimated that the country recorded a current account surplus equivalent to 16.2% of GDP in 2008, up from 15.6% in the previous year.

High oil prices and the country's robust balance of payments position also supported the krone during the first seven months of the year: the krone gained nearly 6% against the dollar during this period. But the onset of the global financial crisis and slumping oil prices caused the krone to lose 35% of its value against the dollar during the final four months of the year.

SUPPORT FOR INWARD INVESTMENT AND IMPORTS

The government welcomes foreign investment. There is no national government agency responsible for foreign investment, which is subject to EU policy through the EEA. There are no specific incentives for the promotion of foreign investment. There is no licensing requirement for investments or limitation on degree of ownership (with some limited exceptions). Capital and earnings can be freely repatriated (subject to taxation) but there is a reporting requirement. The principal regulatory authorities are the Bank of Norway (Norges Bank), the Ministry of Finance, the Securities Commission, and the Ministry of Trade and Industry.

The import regime in Norway is liberal. Market access for non-agricultural products is all but fully open. However, domestically produced agricultural goods are heavily subsidized.

TAX EXEMPTIONS

For information on the tax exemptions available in Norway, please see this review of direct and indirect taxes on the website of the Norwegian tax authority: www.regjeringen.no/en/dep/fin/Selected-topics/Taxes-and-Duties.html?id=1359

▸▸ MORE INFO

Websites:

Website of the Customs and Excise Department: www.riksrevisjonen.no/en

US State Department profile of Norway: www.state.gov/r/pa/ei/bgn/3421.htm

OECD Economic Outlook for Norway, November 2008: www.oecd.org/dataoecd/6/33/20213253.pdf

Pakistan

ECONOMY AND TRADE

The World Bank classifies Pakistan as a low-income country, with around 33% of the population of 162 million living below the poverty line. It says that around 50% of adults are illiterate. High population growth (of around 1.81% pa), poor governance, weak security within the country, and a turbulent political environment have contributed to the country's poor economic performance.

Agriculture accounts for around 21% of GDP and provides employment for over 40% of the labor force.

Most of the population, directly or indirectly, are dependent on this sector. The most important crops are cotton, wheat, rice, sugarcane, fruits, and vegetables, which together account for more than 75% of the value of total crop output. Despite intensive farming practices, Pakistan remains a net food importer. It is also heavily dependent on oil imports, which account for around half its energy needs. Textiles account for around 70% of manufacturing output.

ECONOMIC POLICY OVER 12 MONTHS

Economic policymakers in Pakistan spent much of 2008 grappling with the latest crisis to hit the country. Surging oil prices in the first eight months of the year caused the current account deficit to increase alarmingly, triggering a plunge in the value of the rupee, as well as concerns that the country could default on its foreign debt.

In October 2008, Pakistan was forced to seek an emergency bailout from the International Monetary Fund (IMF) after key allies—China, the United States and Saudi Arabia—refused to provide funds to the country. The government had been reluctant to tap the IMF. Past IMF programmes, requiring Pakistan to agree to austerity measures, were deeply unpopular. Islamabad had hoped that, as a frontline state in the "war on terror," allies would come to its aid.

Before approaching the IMF, the government had already carried out some economic austerity measures, including the withdrawal of subsidies for fuel, electricity, and food. In November, the IMF agreed to provide US$7.6 billion in loans, conditional on the implementation of further austerity measures. These included a hike in interest rates—the central bank raised the key rate by two percentage points in November, the biggest increase in more than a decade. The government was also required to cut spending and increase taxes.

Under the IMF agreement, Pakistan was given immediate access to US$3.1bn of the loan under a 23-month facility, with the rest phased in, subject to quarterly review. In February 2009, Pakistan asked the IMF to increase its loan from US$7.6 billion to US$12.1 billion. Pakistani officials said that the country had met all the targets set by the IMF, including reducing the fiscal deficit as well as freezing borrowing from the central bank. The fiscal deficit stood at 1.9% of GDP in the latter half of calendar year 2008, against an IMF target of 2%, while central bank borrowing had undershot the IMF target.

In an attempt to contain inflationary pressures, the central bank increased its discount rate by 350 basis points, in several steps, starting in June 2007, to 13% in July 2008. Following the hike to 15% in November, the central bank left the discount rate unchanged, even though by February 2009 it was coming under pressure to ease monetary policy amid a sharp economic slowdown. However, with inflation running at well above 20%, the central bank had little scope for maneuver.

ECONOMIC PERFORMANCE OVER 12 MONTHS

Pakistan's economic statistics generally cover the country's fiscal year, which ends in June. The figures here refer to fiscal years unless otherwise stated.

Pakistan's already troubled economy came under severe pressure during calendar year 2008, due to the sharp hike in oil prices and the impact of the global financial crisis. Economic growth fell from 6.8% cent in fiscal 2007 (year ending June 2007) to 5.8% in fiscal 2008. In its December 2008 annual report on the country, the IMF forecast that growth would slow to just 3.4% in fiscal 2009.

The government's finances have deteriorated along with the economy. The budget deficit rose to 7.4% of GDP in fiscal 2008, from 4.3% in fiscal 2007. However, the IMF anticipates that the shortfall will narrow to 4.2% in fiscal 2009, reflecting the measures the government has taken to curb the deficit (see Economic Policy).

The surge in the price of oil caused the current-account deficit to increase sharply. It grew from 4.8% of GDP in fiscal 2007 to 8.4% of GDP in fiscal 2008. However, in the final months of 2008, Pakistan's external accounts began to improve. Easing global oil prices have been a major relief, while domestic demand has fallen off sharply as a result of a weak currency and tight monetary conditions. The country also benefited from a rebound in workers' remittances in November and December, after a lull in October. The IMF believes that the current account deficit will fall to 6.5% of GDP in fiscal 2009.

The aforementioned slide in the Pakistani rupee has spurred inflation to worryingly high levels. A political crisis, the increased current and trade account deficits and rising militancy in areas of Pakistan caused the currency to plummet in 2008—it lost around 28% of its value against the US dollar over the course of the year. At the end of October, it reached a record low of 87.6 rupees to the dollar, down by 41% from the start of the year.

Inflation touched an annual rate of 25% in October, fueled by surging import prices, having finished fiscal 2007 at just 7%. Despite the improvement in the rupee in the final two months of 2008, inflation has remained high, burdening consumers and businesses. In December 2008, consumer prices rose by 23.3% year-on-year, while wholesale prices increased by 17.6%.

STATISTICS

GDP growth: 5.8% (2008, government figures)
GDP per capita: US$2,600 (2008 est.)
CPI: 23.3% (2008, government figures)
Key interest rate: 15% (February 2009, Central Bank)
Exchange rate versus dollar: Pakistani rupees (PKR) per US dollar—70.64 (2008 est.)
Unemployment: 7.4% plus substantial underemployment (2008 est.)
FDI: US$25.31 billion (2008 est.)
Current account deficit/ surplus –US$10.57 billion (2008 est.)
Population: 172,800,048 (July 2008 est.)
Source: CIA Factbook except where stated

MORE INFO

Websites:

Website of the Board of Investment: www.pakboi.gov.pk/
The Ministry of Commerce website has information on trade policy: www.commerce.gov.pk/Tradepolicy.asp
US State Department profile of Pakistan: www.state.gov/r/pa/ei/bgn/3453.htm
IMF annual report on Pakistan, December 2008: www.imf.org/external/pubs/ft/scr/2008/cr08364.pdf

   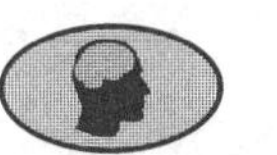  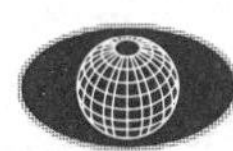   

SUPPORT FOR INWARD INVESTMENT AND IMPORTS

The government encourages foreign investment. The Board of Investment (BOI) assists firms that wish to invest in Pakistan. It offers a number of services, including the provision of information on potential investment opportunities within the country. It can also facilitate introductions to joint-venture partners.

The tariff is Pakistan's main trade policy instrument. The authorities have reduced tariffs significantly during the current decade, particularly with regional trade partners.

TAX EXEMPTIONS

Pakistan has come under pressure from the IMF to repeal tax exemptions in recent years and few now exist. For more information on the country's tax policy, please see the website of the Pakistan Federal Board of Revenue: www.cbr.gov.pk

Panama

ECONOMY AND TRADE

Panama has the highest GDP per capita in Central America, but nearly four in 10 of the population live in poverty. Services account for around 80% of Panama's GDP and include the operation of the Panama Canal—the focal point of the economy. Offshore finance, manufacturing, a shipping registry and the Colon Free Zone, the second-largest free-trade zone in the world, also generate jobs and tax revenues. The country has become a centre for medical tourism, due to its large English-speaking population and modern facilities.

Panama was once considered the world's premier tax haven. However, following military intervention by the United States in 1989 to remove former ally Manuel Noriega from power, the country has worked to rebuild its reputation as a safe haven for business, trusts, and shipping interests. The United States is the country's principal trade partner, accounting for around a third of imports and exports. Panama signed a free-trade agreement with the United States in 2007. The US Congress is expected to ratify the agreement in 2009.

STATISTICS

GDP growth: 9.2% (2008, government figures)
GDP per capita: $11,900 (2008 est.)
CPI: 8.7% (2008, government figures)
Key interest rate: 8.25% (31 December 2007)
Exchange rate versus dollar: balboas (PAB) per US dollar—1
Unemployment: 6.3% (2008 est.)
FDI: N/A
Current account deficit/surplus −US$2.536 billion (2008 est.)
Population: 3,309,679 (July 2008 est.)
Source: CIA Factbook except where stated

ECONOMIC POLICY OVER 12 MONTHS

Having instituted a number of reforms in the fiscal arena in recent years, the government took another major step forward to improve its fiscal management in 2008. A new Fiscal Responsibility Law (FRL), which sets a deficit limit of 1% of GDP for the non-financial public sector, excluding the Panama Canal Authority, and a debt target of 40% of GDP by 2015, was approved by the National Assembly in May 2009. The law will be tested in 2009, with general elections in May and a global downturn curbing revenues from the Panama Canal—which provided 22% of government income in 2007. The government says the 2009 budget has been framed to keep within the new 1% limit.

In January 2009, President Martin Torrijos presented a US$1.11 billion stimulus program intended to insulate Panama's economy from the worst effects of the global downturn. The funds will be provided by the state-owned Banco Nacional de Panama, the Andean Development Corporation, and the Inter-American Development Bank. The funds will be used to extend loans to financial institutions, which will in turn be required to offer credit to businesses and individuals.

A key plank of the government's long-term economic policy, a US$5.25 billion project to widen the Panama Canal, remained on track in 2008. The government anticipates that the project will transform Panama into a developed economy and will provide between 7,000 and 9,000 direct new jobs during the peak construction period of 2009–2011. The expansion is being financed through a combination of increased tolls and debt. The global financial crisis did not have any impact on funding for the project; in December 2008, four multilateral financial institutions and the Japan Bank for International Cooperation signed a US$2.3 billion loan deal to finance the Panama Canal expansion project.

Uniquely, Panama does not have a central bank or an independent monetary policy. The dollar is the country's de facto currency. US dollar notes are legal tender in Panama, while the local currency, the balboa, is tied to and equal to the US dollar. The market-driven system has created an extremely stable macroeconomic environment. Panama is the only country in Latin America that has not experienced a financial collapse or a currency crisis since its independence.

ECONOMIC PERFORMANCE OVER 12 MONTHS

Panama was one of the fastest-growing economies in the world in 2007, with real growth rising to 11.5%,

  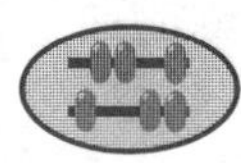 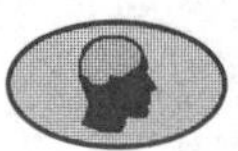     

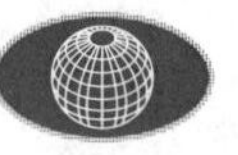

following an average growth rate of nearly 8% in 2004–2006. The economy continued to expand at a rapid pace in 2008, growing by 9.2%, according to the government. However, the country has not remained immune from the global downturn—some independent analysts are forecasting growth of just 2.5% in 2009, largely due to a drop in tourism and earnings from offshore banking. The economy certainly slowed sharply in the final quarter of 2009, expanding at an annual rate of just 3.47% in November, down from 4.75% in October.

The government recorded a budget surplus equivalent to 0.4% of GDP in 2008, down from the 3.5% surplus reported in 2007, largely as a result of higher spending intended to counter the global financial crisis. Prior to the economic downturn, the government's finances had improved significantly—the country recorded a budget deficit of around 5% of GDP in 2004. This improvement reflected fiscal reforms implemented by the government since 2004, the containment of current spending, favorable cyclical conditions, a surge in revenues from the Panama Canal, and one-off revenues.

The economic downturn has had a welcome impact on inflation. The country experienced significant inflationary pressures for much of 2008—Panama is a net importer of oil. Inflation averaged 8.7% in 2008, more than double the level seen in 2007 (4.2%). Furthermore, inflation reached a record high of 10% in September 2008. However, falling oil prices helped to subdue inflationary pressures in the latter stages of 2008. Indeed, by January 2009, Panama was experiencing deflation—consumer prices fell by 0.3% during the month, with the 12-month inflation rate falling to 4.9%.

Unemployment has fallen sharply in recent years, reaching unprecedentedly low levels—the jobless rate stood at 6.5% at the end of 2008, down from 7.8% in 2007 and above 15% in 2003. Unemployment is almost certain to rise in 2009 and probably in 2010, according to the employers' group, the National Council of Private Enterprise, reflecting a slowdown in construction and port-related activities.

SUPPORT FOR INWARD INVESTMENT AND IMPORTS

Panama encourages foreign investment in most sectors of the economy, but there are some remaining limits on foreign ownership in some areas. The fact that the dollar is the de facto currency enhances Panama's appeal to foreign investors. For more information on the foreign investment climate, please see the website of the Ministry of Finance: www.mef.gob.pa/Portal/index.html

Panama maintains an essentially liberal trade (as well as investment) regime, characterized by relatively low tariffs and few non-tariff barriers. For information on the trade regime, please see the latest report published by the World Trade Organisation: www.wto.org/english/tratop_e/tpr_e/tp287_e.htm

TAX EXEMPTIONS

Panama offers a wide range of exemptions and incentives to foreign investors. For more information, please see the website of the Ministry of Finance: www.mef.gob.pa/Portal/index.html

» MORE INFO

Websites:

US State Department profile of Panama: www.state.gov/r/pa/ei/bgn/2030.htm

IMF report on Panama, August 2008: www.imf.org/external/np/sec/pn/2008/pn08113.htm

Peru

ECONOMY AND TRADE

Peru has been home to South America's fastest-growing economy during the current decade. This partly reflects booming prices for mineral exports—Peru is the world's third-largest producer of copper, zinc, and tin, as well as the world's leading producer of silver. However, the government has also made significant progress in improving economic management, and liberalizing the economy. These measures have stimulated foreign investment, and helped to diversify the economy—exports of agricultural products, fishmeal, and textiles have also grown strongly. In recognition of the country's progress, Peru's debt was awarded an investment-grade credit rating in 2008 by Fitch, a ratings agency. However, sharp divides remain within the country. Around 13.7% of the population lived in extreme poverty in 2007, according to the government, although this figure is falling at a rapid pace. The United States is Peru's main trade partner, accounting for around one-fifth of exports. China is now Peru's second-largest trading partner.

ECONOMIC POLICY OVER 12 MONTHS

In its 2008 annual review of Peru's economy, published in February 2009, the International Monetary Fund (IMF) praised the government for establishing a sound policy framework. It said that the strong fiscal surpluses achieved in recent years had supported a significant reduction in public debt, while a sound monetary policy had been instrumental in helping to maintain macroeconomic stability and reduce dollarization. It added that structural reforms had reduced fiscal and financial vulnerabilities, and had helped to improve long-term growth prospects, and support poverty reduction.

The government is estimated to have recorded a budget surplus of 2.7% of GDP in 2008, which it expects to fall to 1% in 2009, reflecting measures to stave off the impact of the global economic slowdown, as well as lower revenues as the economy slows. In December 2008, the authorities announced a US$3 billion stimulus package of spending on infrastructure, to boost construction and create jobs. In early 2009, the Government unveiled a set of 40 measures to ease restrictions, and attract private investors.

The central bank targets annual inflation of 2%, within a tolerance band of plus or minus one percentage point. In February 2009, the central bank trimmed its benchmark interest rate from 6.5% to 6.25%, a measure aimed at mitigating the impact of the global economic crisis on the domestic economy. The central bank acted as inflationary pressures began to subside in the country (see Economic Performance below). In January 2009, the central bank also took measures to provide more liquidity for lenders. It reduced reserve requirements in local currency after bank lending slowed in December. The bank cut the minimum legal reserve requirement to 6.5% of deposits, from 7.5%.

During 2008, the central bank raised interest rates six times (each time by 25 basis points), from 5% at the start of the year, in a bid to contain inflation. The final increase (in September 2008) lifted interest rates to 6.5%, the highest level since at least July 2001. Furthermore, the central bank increased the rate of reserve requirements in 2008 to curb the growth of liquidity and credit. The central bank also intervened in foreign-exchange markets in the latter part of 2008, in an attempt to slow the dollar's gains against the local currency. It sold around US$6 billion during this process.

ECONOMIC PERFORMANCE OVER 12 MONTHS

The economy grew by 9.8% in 2008, the fastest pace in 14 years, fueled by strong commodity prices. Growth was led by a 16% increase in the construction of highways, infrastructure, private housing, and other projects, according to the government. The retail sector expanded by 12%, reflecting buoyant consumer spending. Peru enjoyed average growth of more than 6% each year between 2002 and 2008, as prices for exported metals soared.

However, the economy slowed significantly in the latter months of 2008, and in early 2009, reflecting falling international prices for metals, as well as the global economic slowdown. The economy expanded at an annual rate of just 5.6% in January 2009. In February 2009, the IMF said that economic growth would probably slow to 6% in 2009. It said this outlook reflected the slowdown in the global economy and tighter financial conditions, which would affect exports and private investment.

Fueled by high food and fuel prices, headline inflation reached 6.7% in 2008, exceeding the 1–3% target range, but remaining one of the lowest in the region. Falling international prices for commodities helped to ease inflation concerns in the final months of 2008, and this positive trend was maintained in 2009. Inflation fell to a monthly rate of just 0.11% in January 2009, the lowest monthly rate since November 2007.

Despite the strength of the economy, unemployment increased by one percentage point, to 8.8%. This rise largely reflected job losses in the final quarter, as international companies in the resources sector cut back on their operations and investment programs. Labor leaders reported in December 2008 that at least 6,000 miners had lost their jobs.

The banking sector has remained largely immune to the problems afflicting financial systems in other countries. The IMF said, in its 2008 annual review, that large foreign-exchange reserves, strong financial-soundness indicators, and the domestic banks' limited financial reliance on external funding had helped to preserve the system's stability. The authorities also introduced prudential measures in 2008, including more restrictive rules for consumer credit, new dynamic provisioning, and a strengthening of banks' minimum capital requirements.

The country recorded a current account gap of 3.2% of GDP in 2008, which the central bank expects to widen to 3.3% in 2009. The central bank said the current account gap would be more than covered by long-term foreign investment, which is expected to equal 5.3% of GDP in 2009.

SUPPORT FOR INWARD INVESTMENT AND IMPORTS

The government is eager to encourage foreign investment in Peru, and the investment environment is liberal. PROINVERSIÓN, the Peruvian Investment Promotion Agency, has been created as a strategic ally for the promotion of investments in Peru. See its website for further details on investing in Peru.

Peru has also liberalized its trade regime in recent years. The government places a high priority on preferential trade agreements with other countries. Peru has moved away from its largely uniform tariff structure, thus increasing the level of effective assistance to some sectors. For more information on the country's trade regime, see the latest World Trade Organization report (published in October 2007) on Peru.

TAX EXEMPTIONS

PROINVERSIÓN offers detailed information on the Peruvian tax regime, including information on exemptions.

STATISTICS

GDP growth: 9.8% (2008, government figures)
GDP per capita: US$8,500 (2008, est.)
CPI: 6.7% (2008, government figures)
Key interest rate: 6.5% (February 2009)
Exchange rate versus dollar: nuevo sol per US dollar—2.9322 (2008, est.)
Unemployment: 8.8% (2008, government figures)
FDI: US$32.14 billion (2008, est.)
Current-account deficit/ surplus –US$3.631 billion (2008, est.)
Population: 29,180,900 (July 2008, est.)
Source: CIA Factbook except where stated

▸▸ MORE INFO

Websites:

Central Bank of Peru; comprehensive range of statistics and reports on the economy: www.bcrp.gob.pe/home.html

PROINVERSIÓN, the Peruvian Investment Promotion Agency: www.proinversion.gob.pe/default.aspx?ARE= 1&PFL=0

PROINVERSIÓN tax exemption information: www.proinversion.gob.pe/0/0/modulos/JER/PlantillaSectorHijo.aspx?ARE=1& PFL=0&JER=2773

IMF report on Peru, February 2009: www.imf.org/external/pubs/cat/longres.cfm?sk=22668.0

World Trade Organization report on Peru, October 2007: www.wto.org/english/tratop_e/tpr_e/tp289_e.htm

The Philippines

ECONOMY AND TRADE

The Republic of the Philippines was once one of the richest countries in Asia, but economic mismanagement and corruption—most notoriously during the presidency of Ferdinand Marcos, who ruled from 1965 to 1986—reduced the archipelago to one of the poorest. The economy has enjoyed relatively strong growth rates for much of the past two decades, but agriculture still accounts for around 20% of GDP and employs around 40% of the workforce. The country does have a growing manufacturing sector, producing goods such as semiconductors and electronic microcircuits, finished electrical machinery, and garments. Like India, the country is also benefiting from the outsourcing of IT operations from developed countries. Mining is potentially one of the biggest industries—the country is rich in chromite, copper, nickel, and coal—and natural gas has been discovered. A good educational system and the fact that Filipinos are taught in English means that their services are in demand abroad—worker remittances account for more than 13% of GDP.

ECONOMIC POLICY OVER 12 MONTHS

The national government worked to reduce its fiscal deficits for five consecutive years, to 0.1% of GDP in 2007, and had hoped to balance the budget in 2008, two years ahead of its original plan. However, the global slowdown has affected these plans, and the budget deficit in 2008 is estimated at around 1% of GDP. In February 2009, government officials said they anticipated that the shortfall would increase to 2% of GDP in 2009 as revenue falls amid a slowing economy, and the government boosts spending. The government now expects to balance its budget by 2011.

The government's response to the global financial crisis has included a package of support for returning foreign workers, and increased spending on social services and community infrastructure projects, which it hopes will fuel economic activity and support growth. There have also been a number of technical measures to improve liquidity in the banking sector. The corporate income-tax rate is set to fall to 30% in 2009, from 35% in 2008, under a tax-reform law.

The government's privatization program boosted revenues in 2008 and 2009. In January 2009, the government received around US$1 billion in partial payment from a consortium that won the right to operate the country's power grid. In February 2009, the government said that it planned to negotiate the sale of a 600-megawatt, coal-fired power plant after a unit of the French utility firm Suez backed out of a deal to buy the facility. Emerald Energy Corp made a winning bid of US$786.5 million for the Calaca plant, south of Manila, through a state auction in 2007, but it said in January 2009 that it could not complete the deal after the condition of the plant deteriorated.

The Central Bank of the Philippines (Bangko Sentral ng Pilipinas) tightened monetary policy in mid-2008, raising policy rates in June, July, and August by a combined 100 basis points. However, it left rates unchanged at the October and November monetary meetings, citing an improving outlook for inflation. The central bank cut rates by a combined 100 basis points in January and February 2009, citing falling inflationary pressures, and a weakening economic performance.

ECONOMIC PERFORMANCE OVER 12 MONTHS

Following near-record growth of 7.3% in 2007, the Philippines' economy slowed in 2008 as a result of the global economic downturn, expanding by around 4.4%. The International Monetary Fund (IMF) is projecting growth of 3.5% in 2009, driven by softening external and private domestic demand, but other analysts are more pessimistic. The credit rating agency Moody's has forecast that the economy will expand by just 2–3%.

The global economic crisis, which has caused layoffs among Filipinos working overseas, has affected worker remittances to the Philippines. Remittances rose by just 0.8% in December 2008 from a year earlier, to US$1.4 billion, slowing dramatically from double-digit increases earlier in the year, according to the central bank. The central bank expected remittance growth of between 3% and 6% in 2009, but Moody's anticipates that remittances, a major driver of consumption, will drop by 5–10%.

The global slowdown is having a dramatic impact on exports, and on manufacturing sectors geared towards overseas markets, such as electronics. Philippines' exports plunged by 40.4% in December 2008 from a year earlier, the steepest fall in over two decades, and in step with export data from other countries in the region due to weak global demand. Electronics shipments alone contracted by 47.6% in December. Overall, export earnings fell by 2.86% in 2008. In February 2009, the government forecast that exports would fall by 8% in 2009 as key overseas markets fall into recession.

Unemployment rose in 2008 as the global downturn hit the manufacturing sector. The country's jobless rate stood at 6.8% in October 2008, compared with 6.3% a year earlier. In February 2009, Socioeconomic

STATISTICS

GDP growth: 4.4% (2008, government figures)
GDP per capita: US$3,400 (2008, est.)
CPI: 9.3% (2008, government figures)
Key interest rate: 5% (February 2009)
Exchange rate versus dollar: Philippine pesos (PHP) per US dollar—44.439 (2008, est.)
Unemployment: 8.8% (October 2008, government figures)
FDI: US$20.78 billion (2008, est.)
Current-account deficit/surplus US$2.687 billion (2008, est.)
Population: 96,061,680 (July 2008, est.)
Source: CIA Factbook except where stated

▸▸ MORE INFO

Websites:

Philippine Board of Investments: www.boi.gov.ph
Bureau of Customs: www.customs.gov.ph
Bureau of Internal Revenue Service: www.bir.gov.ph/home.htm
IMF annual report on the Philippines, published in February 2009: www.imf.org/external/pubs/ft/scr/2009/cr0962.pdf
Australian Department of Foreign Affairs and Trade report on the country: www.dfat.gov.au/geo/philippines/philippines_brief.html

  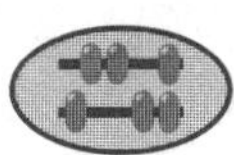      

Planning Secretary, Ralph Recto, further estimated that as many as 800,000 Filipino workers were in danger of losing their jobs in 2009—a figure which, if realized, would push the jobless rate to above 10%.

Inflation hit a 10-year high of 9.3% (annual average) in 2008. However, in February 2009, the central bank forecast that inflation would fall to 3.9% in 2009, lower than earlier estimates of 6–8%, and within the government's target of 2.5–4.5%. Tumbling commodity prices and weakening domestic demand are driving down inflation. The annual rate fell to 7.1% in January 2009, from 8% in December 2008, as prices for food and other basic commodities eased.

SUPPORT FOR INWARD INVESTMENT AND IMPORTS

The Philippine Board of Investments (BOI), an agency of the Department of Trade and Industry, is responsible for the promotion of investments in the Philippines. The Bureau of Customs regulates importing into the Philippines.

TAX EXEMPTIONS

Information on tax exemptions can be found at the Bureau of Internal Revenue Service.

Poland

ECONOMY AND TRADE

Since the collapse of Communism in 1989, Poland has adopted a free-market economy. It became a member of the European Union in 2004, and the current government aims to join the Eurozone on January 1, 2012. Over the past 20 years, Poland has attracted considerable foreign investment, while there has been a massive movement of workers to Western Europe, particularly since joining the European Union. Consequently, wage remittances constitute a significant source of capital (totaling approximately US$6 billion in 2007), much of which is invested in housing and business start-ups. Poland has enjoyed positive economic growth for the past 18 years, but remains one of the EU's least-developed countries. It still has a very large and inefficient farming sector, and poverty is particularly widespread in rural areas. The country's infrastructure remains inadequate. Trade is heavily geared towards the European Union—neighboring Germany is Poland's main trading partner.

ECONOMIC POLICY OVER 12 MONTHS

Poland's economic polices are focused on gaining entry into the Eurozone as rapidly as possible. In December 2008, Poland issued "The Convergence Program Update 2008," which sets out the measures it will adopt to meet the economic target set by the European Union as a prerequisite for entry into the Exchange Rate Mechanism-2 (ERM-2), the "ante room" for the Eurozone. The conditions (for all applicants) include: containing the budget deficit to less than 3% of GDP; limiting the government debt to no more than 60% of GDP; and achieving a rate of inflation that is no more than 1.5 percentage points above the average rate of the three EU members with the lowest inflation.

The government plans to join ERM-2 in the first half of 2009, with the goal of entering the Eurozone in 2012. It opened talks with the European Union on the issue in February 2009. However, at the same time, the governor of Poland's central bank said that there were no good economic reasons for entering ERM-2 in 2009, and that the Polish economy was not ready to do so. The Polish president, Lech Kaczynski, also voiced misgivings about entry into ERM-2. Nonetheless, the government believes that entry into ERM-2 would help to stabilize the zloty, which came under severe downward pressure during the second half of 2008 and early 2009.

In December 2008, the government adopted a stimulus plan worth U$31.4bn to kickstart the economy amid the global slowdown. However, in February 2009, it announced plans to cut government spending by US$5.6 billion in order to contain the budget deficit to within the 3% limit prescribed by the Eurozone convergence criteria. The government said that just over half the savings would come from cuts in central government spending, while the remainder would come from revamping the financing of infrastructure projects. In January 2009, the European Union estimated that the government's budget amounted to 2.5% of GDP and that it would rise to 3.6% in 2009. (The forecast was clearly made before the announcement of spending cuts in February 2009).

The central bank, the National Bank of Poland (NBP), targets an inflation rate of 2.5%. The central bank began tightening monetary policy from April 2007, raising interest rates eight times, to 6% in June 2008. Over this period, the zloty appreciated in response to a widening spread of domestic interest rates over euro and dollar interest rates. However, monetary policy began to ease in the latter part of 2008 as the

STATISTICS

GDP growth: 4.8% (2008, government figures)
GDP per capita: US$22,000 (2008, est.)
CPI: 3.3% (December 2008, government figures)
Key interest rate: 4.25% (January 2009)
Exchange rate versus dollar: zlotych (PLN) per US dollar—2.3 (2008 est.)
Unemployment: 9.5% (December 2008, government figures)
FDI: US$196.1 billion (2008, est.)
Current-account deficit/ surplus –US$29.51 billion (2008, est.)
Population: 38,500,696 (July 2008, est.)
Source: CIA Factbook except where stated

global economic slowdown intensified. Rates fell by 25 basis points in November, and by 75 basis points in both December and January 2009, leaving the benchmark reference rate at 4.25%.

ECONOMIC PERFORMANCE OVER 12 MONTHS

Poland's economic growth slowed to 4.8% in 2008, down from 6.7% a year earlier, as the global financial crisis took its toll. In January 2009, the government said that GDP growth could slow to 1.7% in 2009, while independent economists' forecasts vary from zero to 2% growth.

The European Commission forecast, in January 2009, that private consumption, fueled by cuts in personal income tax, indexation of pensions, and decelerating inflation would be the main engine of growth in 2009. However, it said that the expansion of private consumption would slow in 2009 and 2010, as unemployment rises.

The economy certainly deteriorated markedly in late 2008 and early 2009. Poland's industrial output fell for the third consecutive month in January 2009, declining at an annual rate of 15%, while unemployment surged to 9.5% in December 2008, from a record low of 8.8% in October 2008. Labor Minister, Jolanta Fedak, said in February 2009 that the jobless rate could rise to 12% by mid-2009. Workers returning home after losing their jobs in Western European countries will add to the unemployment total.

During the first six weeks of 2009, the currency weakened by more than 16% in a sell-off that also engulfed other currencies in Eastern Europe, due to worries over a collapse in the growth of their export-dependent economies and financing. Between mid-2008 and mid-February 2009, the zloty weakened by around 30 per cent against the euro.

The currency's woes are hitting homeowners and the corporate sector, raising doubts about whether they will be able to service their debts. Both have taken out large debts in foreign currencies—around 70% of all mortgages are denominated in foreign currencies, mostly Swiss francs. Furthermore, Polish borrowers need to repay about US$71 billion of debts owed to Western banks in 2009, much of it denominated in foreign currencies.

Despite the weakening currency, Polish inflation eased to an annual rate of 3.1% in January 2009, down from 3.3% in December 2008, and 3.7% in November. Inflation averaged 4.2% in 2008, up from 2.5% in 2007. Sharp hikes in food and energy costs were the main factors driving inflation in 2008. Similarly, easing commodity prices should help inflation to subside in 2009, although clearly a slump in the value of the zloty would place upward pressure on inflation.

SUPPORT FOR INWARD INVESTMENT AND IMPORTS

Poland has attracted significant levels of foreign direct investment (FDI) since the end of Communism. Poland limits foreign ownership of companies in selected strategic sectors, and also limits foreign acquisition of real estate, especially agricultural land, but in general foreign companies enjoy unrestricted access to the Polish market. In recent years, Poland has also introduced reforms to improve the climate for foreign and domestic investment. For more information on investing in Poland, see the website of the Polish Information and Foreign Investment Agency.

Following its entry into the European Union, Poland became part of the EU customs union. Currently, decisions regarding quotas or customs suspensions to be applied to goods imported into Poland are taken at the Community level.

TAX EXEMPTIONS

The government offers various tax exemptions. These include:

- Income received by taxpayers from governments of foreign states, international organizations, or international financial institutions, deriving from non-returnable aid, including funds from framework programs regarding research, development, and introduction of the European Union, and from NATO programs.
- Income earned from economic activity carried on within a Special Economic Zone on the basis of an appropriate permit.

▸▸ MORE INFO

Websites:

Polish Information and Foreign Investment Agency: www.paiz.gov.pl/index/

Information on EU trade policies: www.ec.europa.eu/trade/

US State Department profile of Poland, January 2009: www.state.gov/r/pa/ei/bgn/2875.htm

International Monetary Fund report on Poland, April 2008: www.imf.org/external/pubs/ft/scr/2008/cr08130.pdf

Portugal

ECONOMY AND TRADE

Bordered by the Atlantic Ocean to the south and west, and Spain to the north and east, Portugal has been a member of the European Union since 1986, and was among the first wave of countries to enter the

Eurozone in 2002. Living standards in Portugal are still well below those in other European countries. Agriculture remains an important sector, with 75% of production exported. Portugal is a major producer of cork, wine, olive oil, and timber, and it also has a large fishing industry. However, the EU's expansion into Eastern Europe has erased Portugal's competitive advantage, particularly in the manufacturing and agriculture sectors. The government is now focused on encouraging the growth of the high-tech sector, and is investing heavily to upgrade the country's infrastructure, particularly its transport links. Trade is geared towards the European Union—Spain, Germany, France, Italy, and the United Kingdom are Portugal's principal trading partners. Portugal depends heavily on petrol imports to meet its energy needs.

ECONOMIC POLICY OVER 12 MONTHS

Government economic policy in recent years has focused on improving the fiscal position, and addressing Portugal's competitive gap. The economy boomed in the run-up to euro entry in 2002, as real interest rates plummeted; investment, consumption, and wages surged; and fiscal policy loosened.

However, the boom quickly evaporated, and Portugal was left with wide current account and fiscal deficits, together with high household, corporate, and government debt. It also faced sanctions by the European Union for breaching the fiscal rules applied to Eurozone members. The government has since focused on reducing the deficit and public debt. The European Union requires that Portugal and other countries using the euro keep their budget deficits at 3% of GDP or lower, and public debt to less than 60% of GDP.

In its annual assessment of the Portuguese economy, published in October 2008, the International Monetary Fund (IMF) praised the government for taking decisive action to reduce the public deficit. It said that the deficit had fallen by 3.5 percentage points since 2005, to 2.6% of GDP in 2007.

However, the government's efforts to offset the impact of the global financial crisis have undone its attempts at good housekeeping. In particular, the government revised the 2009 budget in December 2008, announcing an extra US$2.8billion of spending to boost the economy. The budget deficit in 2008 amounted to 2.2%, while the total debt burden reached 65.9% of GDP. In February 2009, however, the European Commission warned that the deficit would rise to 4.6% of GDP in 2009, while the total debt burden is expected to rise to 69.7% in 2009, according to government forecasts.

Since joining the Eurozone on January 1, 2002, Portugal has ceded control of its monetary policy to the European Central Bank (ECB). As one of the smaller economies in the Eurozone, Portugal is unlikely to have much, if any, influence over the ECB's policy decisions. Thus, fiscal policy has assumed greater importance, while Portugal no longer has the option of devaluing its currency to boost competitiveness.

Furthermore, while Portugal's relatively low labor costs acted as a magnet to foreign investors seeking to establish a base within the European Union during the 1980s and 1990s, the entry of Eastern European countries to the European Union in 2004 has removed that competitive advantage. However, successive governments have failed to implement the necessary structural reforms to improve competitiveness, according to the IMF. In particular, the IMF says that it remains very difficult for employers to fire workers.

ECONOMIC PERFORMANCE OVER 12 MONTHS

The economy grew by just 0.3% overall in 2008, and entered recession in the second half of the year. The economy shrank by 2.0% in the fourth quarter, compared to the previous quarter, when it contracted by 0.1%. The figure for the last three months of 2008, when the economy shrank by twice as much as had been expected, was far worse than that for the rest of the Eurozone, where output contracted by 1.2%.

Portugal has relied heavily on exports to its Eurozone trading partners to boost economic growth in recent years. Portuguese household consumption and business investment have been depressed since a spending binge in the early 2000s led to the imposition of austerity measures, and recession. In January 2009, the government forecast that the economy would contract by 0.8% in 2009, and that the budget deficit would soar as global economic conditions deteriorate. In 2010, the economy should return to positive growth of 0.5%, the government said, while in 2011 the economy is forecast to grow by 1.3%.

The economic downturn led the ratings agency Standard & Poor's to downgrade Portugal's credit rating in January 2009. The ratings agency warned that the deepening global financial crisis had made Portuguese economic weaknesses, such as insufficient structural reforms, deteriorating public finances, and persistently low growth, harder to tackle. Standard & Poor's, which had already cut its ratings for Greece and Spain, and put Ireland on negative watch, cut Portugal's long-term rating from AA− to A+.

However, there was some positive news on the economy in 2008. Tourism, a key sector of the economy, enjoyed a bumper year. Tourism income hit a record high of US$9.45 billion, despite the economic crisis, which has affected key tourist markets such as the United Kingdom. While the number of Britons visiting Portugal fell, this was more than offset by increased numbers of Dutch, Brazilian, French, and Spanish visitors.

Furthermore, Portugal's financial system remains sound and well supervised, according to the IMF. The organization warned that threats were posed by Portuguese banks' reliance on wholesale funding, the

STATISTICS

GDP growth: 0.3% (2008, government figures)
GDP per capita: US$22,000 (2008, est.)
CPI: 2.9% (2008, est.)
Key interest rate: 7.92% (December 31, 2007)
Exchange rate versus dollar: euros per US dollar—0.6734 (2008, est.)
Unemployment: 7.6% (2008, est.)
FDI: US$118.1 billion (2008, est.)
Current-account deficit/surplus −US$23.97 billion (2008, est.)
Population: 10,676,910 (July 2008, est.)
Source: CIA Factbook except where stated

▸▸ MORE INFO

Websites:

Agência Portuguesa de Investimento (API) : www.investinportugal.pt/CmsAPI/AICEP/index.html

API tax guide: www.investinportugal.pt/NR/rdonlyres/7D5E4799-872A-45BB-84F2-911A0E77F85E/0/SistemaFfiscalINGLES.pdf

Information on EU trade policies: www.ec.europa.eu/trade/

European Commission forecasts published in January 2009: www.ec.europa.eu/economy_finance/pdf/2009/interimforecastjanuary/interim_forecast_jan_2009_en.pdf

US State Department report on Portugal, covering political background as well as economic and trade issues: www.state.gov/r/pa/ei/bgn/3208.htm

sensitivity of bank employees' pension funds and banks' own investment portfolios to stock-market returns, high household and corporate debt, and—among some banks—large exposures and a significant concentration in loans to certain sectors. However, the IMF praised the authorities for taking proactive measures to address these risks; banks with weaker capital ratios have been encouraged to raise capital.

SUPPORT FOR INWARD INVESTMENT AND IMPORTS

Investment promotion remains a high priority for the government, which has established the Agência Portuguesa de Investimento (API) to attract investment involving technology transfer in sectors such as information and communications technologies (ICT), biotechnology, and renewable sources of energy. For more information on the opportunities for foreign investors in Portugal, see the API website.

Portugal is part of the EU customs union. Decisions regarding quotas or customs suspensions to be applied to goods imported into Portugal are currently taken at the Community level.

TAX EXEMPTIONS

API publishes a guide to the tax system, which details all the tax exemptions that are available.

Qatar

ECONOMY AND TRADE

Qatar, once one of the poorest Gulf states, is now one of the world's fastest-growing economies, and the wealthiest country in the world measured by GDP per capita, due to the exploitation of large oil and gas fields since the 1940s. The country was a British protectorate until 1971, when it declared its independence, after following suit with Bahrain and refusing to join the United Arab Emirates. Oil, gas, and upstream and downstream industries are the mainstay of the Qatari economy. Qatar is already the world's largest producer of liquefied natural gas (LNG), and by 2010 it will account for one-third of the world's LNG supply. The government is seeking to exploit revenues from oil and gas to diversify the economy. It is also seeking to encourage the development of the private sector and a knowledge economy. Qatar is home to the Qatar Financial Centre (QFC), a financial and business center established by the government in 2005 to attract international financial services and multinational corporations, and develop the market for financial services in the region.

STATISTICS

GDP growth: 16% (2008, IMF)
GDP per capita: US$101,000 (2008, est.)
CPI: 15.2% (2008, est.)
Key interest rate: N/A
Exchange rate versus dollar: Qatari riyals (QAR) per US dollar—3.64 (2008, est.)
Unemployment: 0.6% (2008, est.)
FDI: US$3.627 billion (2008, est.)
Current-account deficit/surplus US$22.71 billion (2008, est.)
Population: 824,789 (July 2008, est.)
Source: CIA Factbook except where stated

ECONOMIC POLICY OVER 12 MONTHS

In its annual assessment of Qatar, published in January 2009, the International Monetary Fund (IMF) praised the authorities for their management of the Qatari economy. The organization noted Qatar's "impressive" macroeconomic performance in recent years, which had "strengthened the economy's resilience to the current global financial crisis and economic downturn." The IMF also pointed out that "prudent" macroeconomic policies had contributed to "booming" investment and exports, resulting in double-digit growth in both the hydrocarbon and non-hydrocarbon sectors, and in sizeable external and fiscal surpluses. The organization said that this had left Qatar's economy "well placed to withstand shocks."

The IMF further said that it welcomed the authorities' intention to moderate fiscal expansion, and broaden the non-oil revenue base over the medium term. It supported the government's emphasis on investing in infrastructure, and easing supply bottlenecks, while at the same time containing current government expenditure to reduce inflation.

The central bank is focusing on reducing inflation, and has said that it intends to calibrate its interest-rate and liquidity instruments carefully to ensure that this goal is achieved, while at the same time the growth of assets, credit, and deposits in the banking system is not undermined. The Qatari riyal is pegged to the US dollar (90% of the country's imports are invoiced in dollars), but the central bank did not cut interest rates in line with the US Federal Reserve in 2008 because of the need to balance the goal of reducing inflation with the need to maintain liquidity. However, the central bank did increase reserve requirements by 2 percentage points in 2008.

In June 2008, the government launched its National Vision 2030, "which aims, through sustainable development, to transform Qatar into one of the world's most advanced countries within two decades." The vision has four pillars: social, economic, environmental, and human development. In March 2009, the Qatar Science and Technology Park (QSTP) opened. QSTP is an integral part of Qatar's National Vision 2030, and involved an investment of more than US$800 million.

  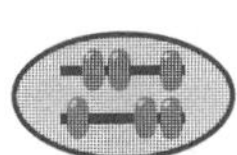 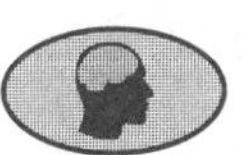     

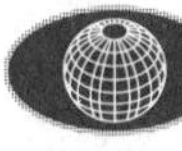

ECONOMIC PERFORMANCE OVER 12 MONTHS

In February 2009, the government said that the Qatari economy has been one of the least affected in the world by the global economic crisis. The IMF echoed these views in its annual assessment of Qatar in January 2009, saying that the country's macroeconomic performance in 2008 remained strong, with GDP growth of 16%. Increased production of oil, LNG, and condensates, and a strong performance in manufacturing, construction, and financial services were the key drivers of the economy.

However, the IMF pointed out that inflation remained high, at 15%, reflecting high rent and food prices, as well as large public outlays and a rapid expansion in private-sector credit. The organization added that the impact of the global financial crisis on the banking system had been limited, and that potential stresses were manageable. In February 2009, the *Gulf Times* reported that Finance Minister, HE Yousef Hussein Kamal, had hinted that the government might nonetheless strengthen its financial regulations to protect the economy against the global crisis.

The IMF added that the Qatari economy is expected to perform at least as strongly in 2009 as in 2008. It said that a rapid expansion in LNG production (and related industries), and in investments aimed at economic diversification would drive growth. Furthermore, it forecast that inflation would fall in 2009, reflecting the impact of declining international prices for food and raw materials, and a slower increase in domestic rents, owing to a larger supply of low- and middle-income housing.

The IMF also forecast that the country's fiscal and external current accounts would remain in surplus in 2009, despite lower oil prices. The country recorded a budget surplus equivalent to 12% of GDP in 2008, up from 11.6% in the previous year. The current-account balance amounted to 37.1% of GDP in 2008, up from 30.9% in 2008, despite an almost 50% increase in imports, which consisted mainly of capital goods.

Furthermore, the IMF said that Qatar's medium-term outlook is positive. The organization anticipates continuing strong economic growth, a gradual decline in inflation, and fiscal and external current-account surpluses. A prolonged global financial crisis, persistently low oil prices, a large decline in real-estate prices, reduced availability of financing for projects, and an escalation in geopolitical tensions pose the main risks to this outlook, according to the IMF.

SUPPORT FOR INWARD INVESTMENT AND IMPORTS

The Ministry of Economy and Commerce says that it is seeking to make the country an "ideal oasis" for investors and investment activities. The Qatar Investment Promotion Department, part of the Ministry of Economy and Commerce, provides information and support to foreign investors.

TAX EXEMPTIONS

Qatar provides a wide range of incentives to investors. These include: no custom duties on the import of machinery, equipment, and spare parts; exemption from income tax for companies for 10 years; no export duties and no taxes on corporate profits for predetermined periods.

▸▸ MORE INFO

Websites:

Qatar Investment Promotion Department: www.investinqatar.com.qa

Qatar Financial Centre Authority: www.qfc.com.qa

Qatar Financial Centre Regulatory Authority: www.qfcra.com.qa

Financial Times special report on Qatar, published in December 2008: www.ft.com/reports/qatar-2008

BBC profile of Qatar: www.news.bbc.co.uk/1/hi/world/middle_east/country_profiles/791921.stm

See Also:

✔ Middle East: Regulatory Structure and Powers (p. 1041)

Romania

ECONOMY AND TRADE

The largest of the Balkan countries, Romania experienced Communist rule following World War II, although the leadership pursued a foreign policy independent of that of the Soviet Union. The overthrow and execution of President Ceausescu in 1989 nominally ended Communism, although many of the party's hierarchy remained in government. Overall, Romania has been a slower developer than the other former Communist countries of Eastern Europe. Failure to push ahead sufficiently with reforms meant that the country was not on the list of new European Union members in 2004. However, Romania joined the European Union in January 2007. In February 2008, the European Commission warned Romania over high-level corruption, pointing to the slow pace of investigations into the activities of eight serving or former ministers.

Romania's fertile arable land, vibrant oil and gas industry, and well-educated workforce (there are more than 50,000 specialists in information technology) have attracted high levels of foreign direct investment (FDI). However, corruption and bureaucracy remain significant barriers to conducting business in the country. Trade is heavily oriented towards the European Union: Italy, Germany, Turkey, France, Hungary, the United Kingdom, and the United States are Romania's major export markets, while Germany, Italy, Russia, France, Turkey, Austria, the United Kingdom, China, Hungary, and the United States are the main sources of imports.

  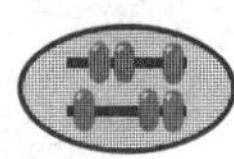      

ECONOMIC POLICY OVER 12 MONTHS

In March 2009, Romania began talks with the European Union and the International Monetary Fund (IMF) on a potential rescue package to help finance its double-digit current-account deficit, and shore up investor confidence. Officials are concerned that the central bank's hard-currency reserves and credit lines to the public sector may not be enough to finance the external deficit. Government officials said that the country needed short-term financing of around €10 billion.

The government had already announced various measures to support the economy. These included: tax relief for companies that reinvest profits (from 2010); capital injections into the state-owned banks, CEC Bank and Eximbank, to spur their lending to small and medium-sized companies; a relaxation of lending conditions for mortgages; higher rewards for replacing old cars (to support the domestic car industry); increases in old-age pensions and subsidies of medical costs for pensioners; suspension of social insurance contributions for employees affected by their company's temporary shutdown; financial support for professional training; and increases in public investment (mostly targeted at the transport infrastructure).

Inevitably, these measures have had an impact on the public finances. In December 2008, a new coalition administration, formed following inconclusive elections in November 2008, pushed through a crisis budget that slashed the budget deficit to a forecast 2% in 2009, from 5% in 2008, and froze public-sector wage growth. However, the budget was based on anticipated growth of 2.5% in 2009, which by March 2009 appeared extremely optimistic. The rating agency, Standard and Poor's, which in October 2008 downgraded Romanian debt to junk status, predicted on March 2, 2009 that the budget deficit would reach 6.2%. Budget revenue fell by 8%, year on year, in January 2009 in nominal terms, as the global crisis took its toll on the domestic economy. The budget that President Băsescu signed into law on February 25, 2009 envisaged 18% growth in revenue in 2009.

By March 2009, Romania's main interest rate stood at 10%, after a quarter-point cut earlier in the year—the first in 18 months. The central bank had been reluctant to cut rates earlier, for fear that this would accelerate the depreciation of the currency. After fluctuating in a relatively tight band of RON3.5–3.7 lei to €1 from 2005 to late 2008, the Romanian national currency fell steeply in December 2008, dropping to a record low of RON4.3 to €1 in January 2009.

Despite the economic problems facing the country, the government insisted, in March 2009, that it would stick to its goal of joining the Eurozone in 2014. In a convergence report sent to Brussels, the government said that it would seek entry into the Exchange Rate Mechanism 2 (ERM-2), which all would-be Eurozone entrants are required to join for a two-year period, in 2012. The government said that the 2012 target for ERM-2 would give the country "time to implement structural reforms that will raise the flexibility of the Romanian economy and its capacity to handle shocks." However, Standard & Poor's said that Romania was more likely to join the Eurozone in the second half of the next decade.

ECONOMIC PERFORMANCE OVER 12 MONTHS

Romania has enjoyed very rapid levels of economic growth in recent years. It expanded by 7.1% in 2008, following growth of 6% in the previous year. However, this rapid growth has created imbalances—in particular, a large current account deficit, amounting to an estimated 12% of GDP in 2008, which has left the country vulnerable to the global financial crisis.

Indeed, Romania's economic growth sank to just 2.9% on an annual basis in the fourth quarter of 2008, as the global crisis depressed consumption and industrial output. Consumption, the main driver of Romania's buoyant expansion of recent years, fell by 2.8% year on year in the final three months of 2008, after growing by 13.8% in the third quarter, as consumers and companies struggled to finance spending. Industrial production slumped by 7.7%, depressed by tumbling demand from the Eurozone, forcing many manufacturers to halt production temporarily and lay off workers.

Independent economists now expect the Romanian economy to expand by less than 1% in 2009, with many pointing to a likely contraction. A Reuters poll conducted in February found that most economists expected the economy to shrink in the first quarter of 2009.

Despite the rapid economic slowdown, inflation has accelerated in 2009, climbing to 6.8% on an annual basis in January, up from 6.4% in the previous month. The figure was four times higher than the EU average of 1.2%, and the third-highest annual inflation rate among EU member states. Curbing inflation is a key requirement for Romania if it is to switch its currency to the euro. The central bank had anticipated that inflation would fall in 2009, reflecting declining prices for oil and other commodities. However, the depreciation of the lei appears to have offset the impact of falling commodity prices.

The government anticipates that FDI will fall to €4.7 billion in 2009, down by nearly half on the level seen in 2008. However, the central bank forecast in March 2009 that the current account deficit would improve in 2009, narrowing to around 8% of GDP, from 12% in the previous year, as the economic slowdown cuts the country's appetite for imports.

SUPPORT FOR INWARD INVESTMENT AND IMPORTS

The government encourages foreign investment. In 2004, the government established the Agency for

STATISTICS

GDP growth: 7.1% (2008, government figures)
GDP per capita: US$12,500 (2008, est.)
CPI: 9.9% (2008 average, Eurostat)
Key interest rate: 10% (March 2009)
Exchange rate versus dollar: lei per US dollar—2.5 (2008, est.)
Unemployment: 4.9% (January 2009, government figures)
FDI: US$72.82 billion (2008, est.)
Current-account deficit/surplus –US$28.03 billion (2008, est.)
Population: 22,246,862 (July 2008, est.)
Source: CIA Factbook except where stated

   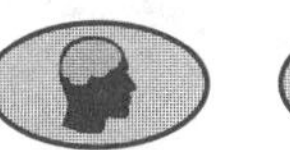     

Foreign Investment (ARIS), and took other measures to advertise Romania as an attractive investment destination, and to improve aspects of the business climate. These include strengthening the tax administration, enhancing transparency, and creating legal means to resolve contract disputes quickly. Romania's accession to the European Union in 2007 has also helped to improve the investment environment. However, judicial and legislative unpredictability remain significant problems. For more information on support for investors and the incentives available to investors, see the website of the Agency for Foreign Investment.

Romania operates an open economy, requiring no special conditions for access for importers or operation on the part of foreign companies. Since January 1, 2007, Romania has applied the common EU tariff system. Tariffs are particularly high for items such as cigarettes. Decisions regarding quotas or customs suspensions to be applied to goods imported into Romania are currently taken at the European Community level. Information on the EU's trade policies can be found on its website.

TAX EXEMPTIONS

The government made significant changes to Romanian tax legislation at the end of 2008, and in early 2009. The measures were aimed at offsetting the impact of the global financial crisis on Romania. Changes include exempting capital gains realized by companies and individuals in 2009 from share trading on the Romanian Stock Exchange. From January 1, 2009, the government abolished taxation on interest derived from deposits and other saving instruments (previously, interest on term deposits was taxable at 16%). It also introduced a tax exemption in respect of dividends reinvested for the purpose of maintaining or increasing employee numbers. The exemption also applies to dividends reinvested in the share capital of another legal entity.

In 2008 the authorities announced that IT programmers would continue to be exempt from income tax in 2009, in order to encourage the development of the IT industry.

▸▸ MORE INFO

Websites:

Agency for Foreign Investment (ARIS): www.arisinvest.ro

EU trade policy: www.ec.europa.eu/trade/

European Commission forecasts, published in January 2009: www.ec.europa.eu/economy_finance/pdf/2009/interimforecastjanuary/interim_forecast_jan_2009_en.pdf

US Department of Commerce's Romania Country Commercial Guide 2008: www.buyusa.gov/romania/en/doing_business_in_romania.html

Russia

ECONOMY AND TRADE

Following 10 years of economic pain and political instability after the collapse of the Soviet Union in 1991, Russia has enjoyed strong economic growth for much of the current decade, supported by buoyant commodity prices. For Russia is the world's largest exporter of natural gas, and, since 2007, its largest exporter of oil. Fueled by income from Russia's vast natural resources, including oil and gas, the economy grew by an average of 7% a year from 2000 to 2007. Real disposable income nearly doubled between 2002 and 2007.

Yet despite its ambitions to regain its superpower status, Russia exhibits the characteristics of a developing, rather than an advanced, economy. Resources dominate Russia's economy, and its exports. The manufacturing base is narrow, and much of the infrastructure obsolete. Excessive bureaucracy, corruption, insufficient and insufficiently enforced legislation, and selective interpretation of laws remain considerable obstacles to conducting business in the country. The European Union is Russia's largest trading partner, a relationship worth US$197 billion in 2006, and underpinned by Russia's position as the EU's major energy supplier—the European Union is dependent on Russia for approximately a quarter of both its gas and its oil imports.

ECONOMIC POLICY OVER 12 MONTHS

The government intends to maintain high public spending to support the economy. However, with tax revenues falling sharply along with international oil prices (the energy sector accounts for around half of total federal budget revenues), public finances are, inevitably, deteriorating. Indeed, officials have said that Russia faces a budget deficit of around 8% in 2009, up from 5.6% in 2008. The ratings agencies have responded by downgrading government debt. In December 2008 and February 2009, respectively, Standard & Poor's and Fitch cut their ratings on the government's foreign-currency bonds from BBB+ to BBB, with a negative outlook. The government may thus have little option but to cut public spending. The authorities have already announced that they may suspend the bailout of certain sectors other than finance.

In 2008, the government bowed to pressure from oil companies and announced wide-ranging tax cuts for the sector. Russian oil firms had complained that heavy taxes prevented them from investing in new exploration to offset declining output in mature fields in West Siberia. Russia's oil output declined for the first time in a decade in 2008, dropping by 0.7%. However, the government may be considering further tax cuts for the sector. In March 2009, energy minister Sergei Shmatko argued that if wider tax breaks were not implemented, oil production could fall further.

STATISTICS

GDP growth: 5.6% (2008, government figures)

GDP per capita: US$15,800 (2008, est.)

CPI: 13.4% (January 2009 annual, government figures)

Key interest rate: 8.3% (December 2008, interbank rate)

Exchange rate versus dollar: roubles per US dollar—24.3 (2008, est.)

Unemployment: 7.7% (December 2008, government figures)

FDI: US$491.2 billion (2007)

Current-account deficit/surplus US$98.9 billion (2008)

Population: 140,702,096 (July 2008, est.)

Source: CIA Factbook except where stated

  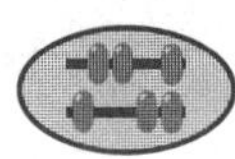    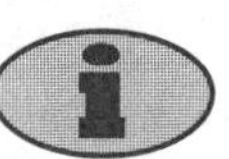  

The government's failure to press ahead with economic reforms may be exacerbating the impact of the global financial crisis on Russia. Investors have certainly turned away from Russia faster than from other former Communist countries. Russia suffered capital outflows in excess of US$130 billion in the fourth quarter of 2008, following net inflows of US$1.3 billion in the first nine months of 2008, and US$85.9 billion in 2007. The government's cavalier treatment of foreign investors may also be coming back to haunt the country. In 2008, the authorities abused tax and visa laws to eliminate the United Kingdom-based energy giant BP's hold on its Russian oil joint venture, TNK-BP, the latest in a series of examples of trampling on the rights of foreign investors.

The collapse of the rouble in the second half of 2008 prevented the authorities from using monetary policy to boost liquidity and the economy. The central bank has sought to support the rouble through high interest rates and tight liquidity, prompting criticism from industrialists, who have complained that prohibitive lending rates are stifling their enterprises. The bank has also been concerned that the falling currency would ignite inflation. In early 2009, however, inflation appeared to be stabilizing, and the central bank hinted that it might cut interest rates if the rouble's depreciation and inflation are contained. In February 2009, inflation amounted to 1.7% (month on month), higher than the 1.2% recorded in February 2008, but much lower than in January 2009, when prices jumped by 2.4%.

ECONOMIC PERFORMANCE OVER 12 MONTHS

Russia is among the emerging markets that have been hardest hit by the global financial crisis. Russia's oil- and gas-fueled economy began to slump in fall 2008, as the international price of oil began to tumble along with global growth. Capital has flowed out of the country, and export earnings have plunged, along with the price of oil (hydrocarbon exports account for two-thirds of total exports). As a consequence, the rouble depreciated by more than 50% against the US dollar between mid-July 2008 and February 2009. By March 2009, the Kremlin had spent more than US$200 billion of its reserves to defend the rouble. The remaining US$380 billion constitute the third-largest reserves in the world, but the government appears divided over how best to use them.

The prospects for 2009 appear bleak. The economy ministry believes that the economy will shrink by 2.2% in 2009, but independent economists believe that it will shrink by at least 3%. The economy contracted at an annual pace of 8.8% in January 2009. The January reading of the leading growth indicator, compiled by VTB, one of Russia's largest banks, showed its largest fall since February 1999 (in the wake of Russia's 1998 economic crisis).

The authorities' consumer confidence survey also fell to an eight-year low in the fourth quarter of 2008. Given the dire state of the labor market, this is unsurprising. Half a million workers lost their jobs in December alone, and two million had lost their jobs since September 2008, while real wages fell for the first time in nine years in December. Russia's unemployment rate rose to 7.7% during the same month, the highest rate since November 2005. The unofficial unemployment rate is, however, much higher, and many Russians with jobs are on indefinite unpaid leave. By March 2009, around 500,000 Russians were also waiting to be paid late wages.

The country's external finances remained in a healthy position in 2008, thanks to the high oil prices that prevailed for much of the year. The current account recorded a record surplus of US$98.9 billion. However, the outlook for 2009 is much bleaker. The central bank has forecast that the current account will fall into deficit if the oil price stays below US$66 a barrel, which it almost certainly will.

SUPPORT FOR INWARD INVESTMENT AND IMPORTS

Russia has an ambivalent attitude towards foreign investors. In 2008, the Organization for Economic Cooperation and Development (OECD) urged the government to adopt a more investor-friendly regime, saying that "the biggest obstacle to further domestic and foreign investment in Russia remains uncertainty over government policy, notably the risk of greater state interference in the economy and the impact of the postponement of necessary administrative and regulatory reforms." In the same year, the country's investment image was further tarnished by a fierce shareholder struggle at the TNK-BP oil venture. BP accused its Russian partners of using corporate-raider tactics to wrest control of the company. The Russian government certainly appears intent on limiting foreign participation in the energy sector. However, the OECD warned in 2008 that "stricter restrictions on foreign participation in oil and gas prospecting and extraction risk further aggravating the difficulties faced in these sectors, which are already struggling to cope with difficult exploitation conditions and growing domestic and international demand."

The Foreign Investment Promotion Center is the government agency responsible for foreign investment. For further information, see its website.

Russia maintains a number of barriers with respect to imports, including: tariffs and tariff-rate quotas; discriminatory and prohibitive charges and fees; and discriminatory licensing, registration, and certification regimes. Russia is currently negotiating to join the World Trade Organization (WTO), and will have to eliminate these measures or modify them to be consistent with internationally accepted trade policies.

▸▸ MORE INFO

Websites:

Foreign Investment Promotion Center: www.fipc.ru/fipc2001/

Hoover Institution website on Russian economy: www.hoover.org/research/russianecon

Economic Development Ministry: www.economy.gov.ru/wps/wcm/connect/economylib/mert/welcome_eng/pressservice/news/doc1124280205719

See Also:

★ Viewpoint: Hamish McRae (pp. 789–790)
★ Viewpoint: Bruce Misamore (pp. 159–161)

Non-tariff barriers are frequently used to restrict foreign access to the market, and are also a significant topic in Russia's WTO negotiations.

TAX EXEMPTIONS

Various tax exemptions are available in Russia, but, given the federal structure of the government, these vary from one region to another, and it is best to approach the local authority where you are planning to conduct business.

Saudi Arabia

ECONOMY AND TRADE

Saudi Arabia was established in 1932 by King Abd-al-Aziz. Since his death in 1953, he has been succeeded by various sons. Covering much of the Arabian peninsula, Saudi Arabia has transformed itself from an underdeveloped desert kingdom into the world's dominant oil producer, and owner of the world's largest hydrocarbon reserves. Proven reserves are estimated to be 263 billion barrels, about a quarter of world oil reserves. Despite efforts to diversify the economy, oil accounts for around one-third of GDP, more than 90% of the country's export earnings and nearly 75% of government revenues.

Saudi Arabia continues to pursue rapid industrial expansion, focusing on the petrochemical sector. The Saudi Basic Industries Corporation (SABIC), a parastatal petrochemical company, is one of the world's leading petrochemical producers. Other industries, including construction, transport, finance, and communications, are also being developed. The government is seeking to encourage privatization, liberalize foreign trade, and reform the investment regime. Saudi Arabia is a member of the Gulf Cooperation Council (GCC), which also includes the United Arab Emirates, Kuwait, Oman, Bahrain, and Qatar.

STATISTICS

GDP growth: 5.7% (2008, est.)

GDP per capita: US$21,300 (2008, est.)

CPI: 9.9% (2008 average, government figures)

Key interest rate: 2.5% (February 2008)

Exchange rate versus dollar: Saudi riyals per US dollar—3.75 (2008, est.)

Unemployment: 8.8%, among Saudi males only

FDI: N/A

Current-account deficit/ surplus US$151 billion (2008, est.)

Population: 39,817 (July 2008, est.)

Source: CIA Factbook except where stated

ECONOMIC POLICY OVER 12 MONTHS

Saudi Arabia has used revenues from the oil-price boom of recent years wisely, and thus the country has been relatively well placed to withstand the global financial crisis, and the collapse in oil prices, that began in the second half of 2008. The kingdom was certainly more cautious on spending than in past oil booms. In March 2009, Bank of America Securities-Merrill Lynch (BAS-ML) said that the government had saved 76% of the oil windfall between 2002 and 2008, and had used these funds to reduce debt to relatively low levels, and build up financial assets. Public debt fell from more than 100% of GDP in the 1990s to 13.5% in 2008. The country also benefits from strong external finances and a sound banking system.

Thus, Saudia Arabia was able to announce an expansionary budget for 2009 (unveiled in December 2008) without putting any great strain on its finances. The government hopes that a massive increase in spending will offset the impact of falling oil prices, and lay the foundations for a quick recovery by 2010. Total spending is set to grow by 16% in 2009, with capital spending rising by 36% as the government strives to support growth and employment, by funding infrastructural projects in key sectors. Revenues are projected to fall by 9%, leading to a government deficit of 3.5% of GDP and the first shortfall in the budget since 2002.

The government will spend around US$60 billion on new schools, hospitals, healthcare, agriculture, transport, and telecoms. As there is no income tax in Saudia Arabia, the government's only fiscal lever is to increase spending to boost demand—it clearly cannot cut taxes.

The monetary authorities have also sought to stimulate the economy by injecting money into the banking system to increase the availability of credit. Between November 2008 and January 2009, the central bank, Saudi Arabian Monetary Agency (SAMA), cut its repurchase rate from 4.0% to 2.5%. In its 2009 budget, the government unveiled measures to inject around US$90 billion into specialized credit institutions, in order to encourage lending.

Saudi Arabia is firmly committed to the Organization of Petroleum Exporting Countries' (OPEC) policy of cutting oil output to support oil prices. In December 2008, OPEC agreed an unprecedented cut of 2.2 million barrels per day (bpd). With this cut, oil production will have fallen by 14.5% since September 2008.

ECONOMIC PERFORMANCE OVER 12 MONTHS

The economy grew by 5.7% in 2008, supported by the high oil prices that prevailed for much of the year. The government anticipates growth of just 1.5% in 2009, but even this may be too optimistic. In March 2009, BAS-ML predicted that the kingdom's GDP would shrink by 0.2% in 2009 but that it would also be relatively unaffected by the global economic turmoil, due to its savings, lack of reliance on foreign trade, and diversified economy. BAS-ML forecast that GDP growth would rebound to 2.8% in 2010.

  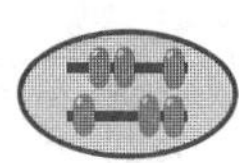      

Inflation has subsided in 2009, having jumped sharply to a record high of 9.9% in 2008. During the preceding five years, inflation averaged just 1.6% a year, according to the central bank. Annual inflation fell to 7.9% in January 2009, from 9.0% in December 2008. The Riyadh-based financial firm, Jadwa Investment, forecast in March 2009 that inflation would average around 6.7% in 2009, reflecting falling commodity prices, and a strengthening of the currency.

Saudi Arabia's balance of payments will come under pressure in 2009, having recorded large surpluses in recent years due to booming oil export revenues. In 2007 (the latest year for which official figures are available), the country recorded a current account surplus equivalent to 24.4% of GDP. Independent economists believe this figure rose to 27.5% of GDP in 2008. In its March 2009 forecast, BAS-ML said that it anticipated a current account deficit of 0.7% of GDP in 2009, as oil export earnings plunge. However, with official foreign assets in excess of 80% of GDP at the end of 2008, and a gross external debt equivalent to just 17% of GDP, the downturn in the external accounts is unlikely to pose a threat to the country's economic stability.

Despite the oil boom of the past few years, unemployment remains worryingly high. Officially, around 9% of the workforce is jobless but the true rate may be closer to 20%, according to a BBC report. The jobless rate is thought to be even higher among those aged under 30, who make up two-thirds of the population, and it is staggeringly high among women. Saudi women comprise 55% of graduates but only 5% of the workforce in the sexually segregated society. The education system, which is heavily influenced by the conservative religious establishment, may be partly to blame for the high unemployment rate according to the BBC. Around 80% of graduates study subjects such as history, geography, Arabic literature, and Islamic studies, while the country does not have enough graduates in science, engineering, or medicine.

SUPPORT FOR INWARD INVESTMENT AND IMPORTS

The government is keen to improve the investment climate as part of a broader program to liberalize the country's trade and investment regime, to diversify an economy overly dependent on oil and petrochemicals, and to boost employment levels. The government encourages investment in transport, education, health, information and communications technology, life sciences, and energy, and in six "Economic Cities" that are in various states of development. There is a list of sectors that are off-limits to foreign investors. There are also considerable barriers to investing in the country, including a formidable bureaucracy, a government insistence that companies hire Saudi workers, a conservative cultural environment, slow payment of government contracts, and a very restrictive visa policy. The Saudi Arabian General Investment Authority (SAGIA) was established in 2000 to provide information and assistance to foreign investors.

Almost all Saudi imports are covered by a general import tariff rate of 5%. Saudi "infant industries," including furniture, cooking salt, mineral water, and plastic pipes, will continue to enjoy 20% tariff protection. Imported cigarettes and tobacco products are charged 200%, wheat and flour 25%, and dates and long-life milk 40%. Despite Saudi Arabia's membership of the World Trade Organization, the US Department of Commerce says that Saudi businesses and laws still favor Saudi citizens, and Saudi Arabia still has trade barriers (mainly regulatory and bureaucratic practices) that restrict the level of trade and investment. For more information on importing goods into Saudi Arabia, see the website of the Saudi Customs Department.

TAX EXEMPTIONS

Saudi Arabia no longer offers tax holidays to foreign investors. For more information on the incentives that are available, see the SAGIA website.

▸▸ MORE INFO

Websites:

Saudi Arabian General Investment Authority (SAGIA): www.sagia.gov.sa

Saudi Customs Department: www.customs.gov.sa/CustomsNew/default_E.aspx

Ministry of Economy and Planning: www.mep.gov.sa

Australian Department of Foreign Affairs Political and Economic brief: www.dfat.gov.au/geo/saudi_arabia/saudi_brief.html

See Also:

✔Middle East: Regulatory Structure and Powers (p. 1041)

Seychelles

ECONOMY AND TRADE

The Seychelles is an archipelago of 115 tropical islands in the Indian Ocean, about 1,600 kilometers east of Kenya. The two main islands are Mahe and Praslin. About 90% of the Seychellois people live on Mahe Island. Most Seychellois are descendants of early French settlers and the African slaves brought to the Seychelles in the 19th century by the British, who freed them from slave ships on the East African coast. The country's economy depends heavily on a fishing industry, focused on tuna, and upmarket tourism. Altogether, the service sector accounts for around 70% of GDP, with manufacturing accounting for a further 20%. The country is in the World Bank's "upper middle" income bracket, and, consequently, it has received relatively little foreign aid. However, given the small size of the economy and its heavy dependence on tourism, the island remains vulnerable to external shocks.

     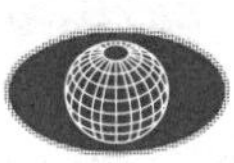   

ECONOMIC POLICY OVER 12 MONTHS

The left-wing governments that ruled the Seychelles after the country gained independence from the British in 1976 implemented generous social-service benefits, free education, free healthcare, and subsidized housing. They also kept the local currency, the rupee, pegged artificially high. At the same time, the country borrowed extensively from overseas, and consistently incurred large fiscal deficits.

In 2005 and 2006, the government implemented several measures aimed at reforming the economy, including liberalizing the trade regime, privatizing state-owned entities, and gradually liberalizing foreign-exchange restrictions. However, these limited measures were insufficient to address the long-standing macroeconomic imbalances that had developed over the previous decades.

In 2008, as global economies slowed, and oil and food prices rose, the nation's foreign-exchange reserves dwindled, while the rupee came under pressure, losing 24% of its value in the first half of the year. As foreign debt ballooned because of the plunging currency, the central bank was forced to ration foreign exchange to both public and private industry.

On July 1, 2008, the government defaulted on the repayment of one of its foreign debts. In October, the Seychelles defaulted again, and the government admitted that it was unable to service its foreign debts. It turned to the International Monetary Fund (IMF) for help, and, in an attempt to meet the conditions for a standby loan, started to implement a program of radical reforms.

The reforms included a fundamental liberalization of the exchange regime, involving the elimination of all foreign-exchange controls, and allowing the rupee to float freely. The authorities also cut spending, and sold state assets. The IMF approved a two-year, US$26 million standby loan in mid-November 2008. After the Seychelles dropped its currency peg on November 1, the rupee collapsed, tumbling to 16.51 per US dollar by 22 December, from 8.90 on November 3.

By the end of 2008, external debt stood at US$808 million, of which US$263 million was in arrears. As at September 30, 2008, the country's public debt stood at US$1.3 billion, or 153% of GDP. Only Lebanon has a higher debt ratio among B-rated emerging-market nations, at 163% of estimated 2008 GDP. In December 2008, the Seychelles government asked the Paris Club group of nations to help it reschedule its external debt. Finance minister Danny Faure said that the debt would become unsustainable if no agreement was reached. The government is hoping that around half of its foreign debt will be cancelled.

ECONOMIC PERFORMANCE OVER 12 MONTHS

The economy grew by 3.1% in 2008, but conditions deteriorated rapidly in the second half of the year after the government defaulted on its foreign debt repayments, and was forced to implemented IMF-inspired austerity measures. The IMF estimates that the economy experienced zero growth in the final quarter of 2008.

2009 is likely to prove much bleaker. In December 2008, the IMF forecast that the economy would contract by 9.5% in 2009. The global economic downturn, which is causing a slump in tourism, is compounding the archipelago's troubles. Visitor numbers fell by 15% in the first two months of 2009, compared to the same period in 2008, and the government anticipates that numbers could fall by 25% during the course of the year. The industry generated US$321 million in foreign-exchange earnings in 2008.

Layoffs in the public sector and tourism-related industries are having a dramatic impact on the jobless rate, which rose from just 1% in November 2008 to 3.6% by the end of January 2009. Meanwhile, the annual rate of inflation accelerated to 63.3% in December 2008, from 60.6% in November, the second-highest rate in Africa after Zimbabwe. Prices rose 3.5% during the month, as the cost of fish advanced 0.5% and prices for other foods jumped 6.3%.

However, in February 2009, the IMF claimed that "in early 2009, signs of success of the reform effort are beginning to appear, and the [IMF] mission believes the program will achieve its macroeconomic stabilization and reform objectives." The IMF added that "interest rates have begun to ease from their peak, and inflation is declining sharply, thanks to the tightened fiscal and monetary policies." However, it concluded that "2009 will be a challenging year, as Seychelles is being hard hit by the deterioration in the global economy."

The organization added that the government's finances had been significantly tightened, and public-sector employment was being reduced sharply, in part under a voluntary departure scheme. It also said that declining commodity prices, especially for petroleum, and higher public revenue from fisheries would partially offset the loss of tourism receipts in the balance of payments.

On an even more positive note, the Economist Intelligence Unit has forecast that 2010 will bring relief. It says that the improved global economic climate will boost tourism figures and foreign investment in 2010, lifting real GDP growth to 5%.

SUPPORT FOR INWARD INVESTMENT AND IMPORTS

The government has been consistently business-friendly, and has actively supported the development of an offshore financial-services sector. There is no discrimination against foreigners in terms of conducting business in the country, except that they need official approval to own land. The government established

STATISTICS

GDP growth: 3.1% (2008, est., government figures)
GDP per capita: US$18,700 (2008, est.)
CPI: 63.3% (December 2008, government figures)
Key interest rate: 3.6% (December 31, 2007)
Exchange rate versus dollar: Seychelles rupees per US dollar—16.51 (Bloomberg)
Unemployment: 3.6% (January 2009, government figures)
FDI: N/A
Current-account deficit/surplus −28.8% of GDP (2008, IMF estimate)
Population: 82,247 (July 2008, est.)
Source: CIA Factbook except where stated

➤➤ MORE INFO

Websites:

Seychelles Investment Bureau (SIB): www.sib.gov.sc
IMF Public Information Notice, November 2008: www.imf.org/external/np/sec/pn/2008/pn08142.htm
Official website of the Seychelles: www.virtualseychelles.sc/pages/vs_ie.htm

the Seychelles Investment Bureau (SIB) in 2004 to promote investment and support foreign investors. An import permit must be obtained from the Ministry of Finance for all imports. This is usually issued within 48 hours of application.

TAX EXEMPTIONS

In order to encourage investment, the government has provided several incentives and tax exemptions. For further details, see the website of the SIB.

Singapore

ECONOMY AND TRADE

The island republic of Singapore, which is linked to the southern tip of Malaysia by a causeway, is one of the world's most prosperous and technologically advanced cities. Although 77% of the population is Chinese, English is widely spoken, and is the language of business and administration in the former British colony. The economy has weathered various regional crises, including the 1997 Asian markets slump, and the 2003 Sars virus outbreak. An open, trade-driven economy, Singapore is highly geared towards the global economic cycle. Exports in 2007 accounted for 230% of GDP and net exports for 28% of GDP. Major industries include petroleum refining, electronics, oil-drilling equipment, rubber products, processed food and beverages, ship repair, financial services, and pharmaceutical manufacturing. The country is seeking to reduce its reliance on the manufacture and export of electronics by developing its services sector, as well as its chemical, petrochemical, and biotechnology industries. The People's Action Party has ruled the country since independence in 1959.

ECONOMIC POLICY OVER 12 MONTHS

In response to the rapidly deteriorating economic situation, the government unveiled a US$13.3 billion stimulus package in January 2009, to be partly financed by drawing upon US$3.2 billion of Singapore's vast foreign reserves (which amounted to US$177.5 billion at the end of February 2009). The government will record a budget deficit equal to 3.5% of GDP in the 2009–2010 (April–March) fiscal year, an unusual occurrence for the usually prudent Singaporean government.

Most of the fiscal package consisted of property, consumer, and business tax rebates, as well as a cut in corporation tax from 18% to 17%. However, the stimulus package is unlikely to have much impact on the economy. Domestic demand is far too small to offset lower external demand. In addition, hundreds of thousands of foreign workers are likely to leave Singapore in 2009 as the job market dries up, further cutting private spending.

The move follows a US$3.5 billion stimulus package for individuals and households in the 2008–2009 fiscal year, including a personal income-tax rebate of 20%. Key business measures included support for R&D activities, tax incentives to enhance business competitiveness, and further measures to promote Singapore's financial-services and maritime sectors.

The key objective of Singapore's monetary policy is to maintain price stability and it does this through the exchange rate. This reflects the fact that in the small and open Singapore economy, where imports and exports amount to more than twice the GDP, the exchange rate is the most effective tool in controlling inflation. The central bank (the Monetary Authority of Singapore, or MAS) manages the exchange rate against a trade-weighted basket of currencies of Singapore's major trading partners and competitors. The trade-weighted exchange rate is maintained broadly within an undisclosed target band, and is allowed to appreciate or depreciate depending on factors such as the level of world inflation, and domestic price pressures.

In its semi-annual review on October 10, 2008, MAS eased policy by shifting to neutral from a policy of allowing a gradual appreciation of the trade-weighted currency. Earlier in the year, monetary policy had been tightened. In April 2008, MAS adjusted its exchange-rate band upwards by around 2%, in response to inflation concerns and upward pressures on the exchange rate. Inflation had risen significantly on the back of international and homegrown cost pressures, reaching a 26-year high of around 7% during January–April 2008.

ECONOMIC PERFORMANCE OVER 12 MONTHS

Singapore has enjoyed strong economic growth in recent years, expanding by 7.8% in 2007, and 7.6% in 2006. However, growth slumped in 2008, reflecting the impact of the global economic slowdown on this very open and trade-dependent country. Thus, the economy expanded by just 1.1% over the course of the

STATISTICS

GDP growth: 1.1% (2008, government figures)
GDP per capita: US$52,000 (2008, est.)
CPI: 2.9% (January 2009, government figures)
Key interest rate: 10.5% (March 2009)
Exchange rate versus dollar: Singapore dollars per US dollar—1.415 (2008, est.)
Unemployment: 2.3% (2008 average, government figures)
FDI: US$225.7 billion (2008, est.)
Current-account deficit/surplus US$28.42 billion (2008, est.)
Population: 4,608,167 (July 2008, est.)
Source: CIA Factbook except where stated

  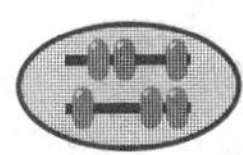   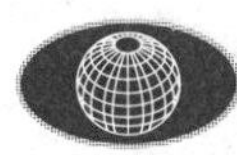   

year, and, by the end of the year was shrinking rapidly—GDP contracted by 4.2% in the fourth quarter.

All major sectors, except for construction, business services, and information and communications, saw contractions, according to the Ministry of Trade and Industry. The ministry blamed a decline in private-sector investments, and private consumption expenditure for dragging down total domestic demand. Declines in global demand for electronics products, pharmaceuticals, and chemicals are also weighing heavily on the manufacturing sector. Retail spending fell throughout the fourth quarter, while house prices declined by 6.1% from the preceding three months.

Singapore's exposure to international trade and shipping is also taking a heavy toll. Cargo throughput at the port of Singapore, a major source of income for the country, fell by 18.4% on an annual basis in December 2008. Container traffic fell by 13.1% during the same month. One of Singapore's largest shipping operators filed for bankruptcy in January 2009, while the country's largest builder of oil rigs received no new orders in the fourth quarter of 2008.

The outlook for 2009 appears bleak. In February 2009, officials forecast that the economy would contract by between 2% and 5% during the year, due to "the pessimistic global economic outlook." In March 2009, however, the country's influential former prime minister, Lee Kuan Yew, whose son, Lee Hsien Loong, is now the premier, warned that Singapore's economy may contract by as much as 10% in 2009 if exports continue to fall sharply. Between January 2008 and January 2009, Singapore's exports declined by 35%, the largest fall on record.

The recession will have a significant impact on unemployment, according to the local bank, DBS. The unemployment rate averaged 2.3% in 2008, but DBS said in March 2009 that a total of 99,000 workers could lose their jobs during the recession, with the manufacturing sector shedding around 58,000 posts. DBS forecast that unemployment would reach 4.8% by the end of 2009, and peak at about 5% by the middle of 2010, which would amount to a 20-year high. Prime Minister Loong has also accepted that the jobless rate could reach 5%.

However, inflation is on a downward path, easing to 2.9% in January 2009 (compared with the same month in 2008), its slowest pace in 16 months, as oil prices fell and the deepening economic slump hurt demand for goods and services. The consumer price index rose by 4.3% in December 2008 on an annual basis.

SUPPORT FOR INWARD INVESTMENT AND IMPORTS

The government is keen to attract foreign investment, and, with the exception of restrictions in financial services, professional services, and the media, Singapore maintains a predominantly open investment regime. The World Bank report, *Doing Business 2009*, ranked Singapore as the easiest country in the world in which to do business. A government body, the Economic Development Board of Singapore (EDB), acts as a one-stop agency for those interested in investing in the country.

Singapore is generally a free port and an open economy, and more than 99% of all imports enter the country duty-free. Information on importing goods into Singapore can be found on the website of the Singapore Customs Service.

TAX EXEMPTIONS

Singapore has range of incentives to help businesses establish and expand their operations in the country. For example, it provides full or partial exemption on withholding tax for royalty payments, or technical assistance fees payable to non-residents. This includes royalties, fees, and contributions to R&D costs paid for the transfer of technology and knowledge to Singapore. For more information on all the incentives offered by the government, see the guide published by the EDB:

For detailed information on the tax regime in Singapore, see the website of the Inland Revenue Authority of Singapore.

MORE INFO

Websites:

Economic Development Board of Singapore (EDB): www.edb.gov.sg/edb/sg/en_uk/index/about_edb/what_we_do.html

EDB Guide to Investing: www.edb.gov.sg/edb/sg/en_uk/index/why_singapore/Guide_to_Investing_in_Singapore/financial_assistance.html

Singapore Customs Service: www.customs.gov.sg/leftNav/info/Importer.htm

Inland Revenue Authority of Singapore: www.iras.gov.sg/irashome/default.aspx

World Bank, Doing Business Report 2009 on Singapore: www.doingbusiness.org/Documents/CountryProfiles/SGP.pdf

See Also:

★ Viewpoint: Jim Rogers (pp. 232–234)

Slovak Republic

ECONOMY AND TRADE

Located in Central Europe, Slovakia was part of Czechoslovakia until the "velvet divorce" in January 1993. Slovakia has escaped the shackles of its Communist past, embracing the market economy and the West. It joined both the European Union and NATO in 2004. In January 2009, it was also among the first of the former Eastern Bloc nations to join the Eurozone. Around 86% of the country's exports are now directed towards the European Union, and more than half go to countries using the single European currency.

Slovakia has felt the impact of the global financial crisis. However, thanks largely to the efforts of a centre-right government led by Prime Minister Mikulas Dzurinda, which ruled the country from 1998 to

2006, and carried out most of the painful and unpopular fiscal surgery necessary for euro adoption, the country now boasts a huge amount of foreign investment, and is better placed than many other Eastern European countries to withstand the financial maelstrom that swept across the globe in 2008 and 2009.

ECONOMIC POLICY OVER 12 MONTHS

Slovakia has undergone a remarkable economic transformation over the past 10 years. The centre-right coalition that ruled the country under Prime Minister Dzurinda between 1998 and 2006 introduced sweeping reforms to nurture the economy, and the business environment. In 2004, the government replaced its income, corporate, and sales taxes with a 19% flat rate tax. The government also reformed Slovakia's labor laws to make them more flexible than those of Western Europe, and it sold off inefficient state industries to the private sector.

As a result, foreign firms, especially in the car industry, flooded in. Slovakia's EU accession in 2004, and entry into the Eurozone in 2009, further heightened its appeal to potential investors. The country is a magnet for multinationals, which use it to produce and distribute goods cheaply and efficiently to the vast European market. The centre-left coalition that won the June 2006 general elections slowed the reform momentum, and adopted some less business-friendly changes in labor, pension, and social-insurance legislation. However, the government's commitment to the goal of adopting the euro (which the country adopted in January 2009), tempered proposals to overhaul the previous reforms, and contributed to stable macroeconomic policies.

The government has attempted to lessen the impact on Slovakia of the global economic crisis that developed in September 2008. By March 2009, the authorities had launched three stimulation packages aimed at keeping businesses afloat, helping employers maintain jobs, and giving a boost to the slowing economy. But Prime Minister Fico has insisted that the government wants to keep public spending under control, despite its crisis packages. By March 2009, the cabinet had allocated €332 million to cover the measures, a small sum in comparison with the fiscal packages being adopted by other countries. In March 2009, Fico was quoted as saying: "We want to keep the deficit under control in order to prevent it from reaching 8, 9, or even 10%, as you can see in other countries."

The European Central Bank (ECB) has determined monetary policy in Slovakia since the country joined the Eurozone on January 1, 2009. The ECB was slower than other central banks to loosen monetary policy amid the global financial crisis of 2008 and 2009. In March 2009, the ECB cut its key interest rate from 2.0% to 1.5%, the lowest since it started setting euro rates in January 1999. However, US and Japanese rates were, in effect, already at zero by March 2009.

ECONOMIC PERFORMANCE OVER 12 MONTHS

Slovakia has enjoyed robust levels of growth for much of the current decade, and has certainly been among central Europe's strongest performers. In 2007, the economy expanded by 10.4%, the highest rate in Central and Eastern Europe. The economy grew by a further 6.6% in 2008, but growth decelerated dramatically in the final quarter, reflecting the impact of the global financial crisis. Initial estimates indicate that the economy contracted by 1.8% quarter-on-quarter, taking the real GDP growth rate to 2.7% on an annual basis. By comparison, the economy expanded by 9.4% and 7.8% on a quarterly basis in the second and third quarters, respectively.

The outlook for 2009 also appears weak. Key export markets such as Germany, Italy, and Hungary are mired in recession, which will inevitably affect production in Slovakia's export-oriented industrial sector. In March 2009, the Slovak Statistics Office forecast that the economy would grow by just 0.8% in the first half of the year. The organization also anticipated that the unemployment rate would rise to 10.04% during the period. Unemployment averaged 9.6% in 2008, down from 19.3% in 2001.

Slovakia's impressive economic performance of recent years was partly due to the construction of new factories by major car producers. KIA, Peugeot-Citroën, and Volkswagen were attracted by Slovakia's central location, low wages, and attractive tax rate, and they have turned the country into the world's largest per capita producer of cars. The car industry was, to a great extent, responsible for Slovakia's strong growth figures, and the sharp reduction in its unemployment rate. However, the country that became known as the "Detroit of the East" has been affected by the global crisis that the car industry experienced in 2008 and 2009. In March 2009, the *Slovak Spectator* reported that the major car manufacturers in the country had admitted that they expected production to drop in 2009 by between 10% and 25%. The manufacturers have laid off workers, cut production, or offered severance payments to employees who agree to leave. The newspaper added that several automotive-industry suppliers had closed their factories, contributing to Slovakia's rising unemployment figures.

However, the slowdown in the Slovak economy will be accompanied by lower inflation. According to the Statistics Office, inflation should stand at 3.4% at the end of June 2009. Slovakia's annual inflation rate slowed for the fourth month in a row, and hit a 13-month low in January 2009 as the global economic downturn countered the risk of price hikes following euro adoption at the start of the year. Consumer prices rose by 2.7% during the month.

STATISTICS

GDP growth: 6.6% (2008, government figures)
GDP per capita: US$22,600 (2008, est.)
CPI: 2.7% (January 2009, government figures)
Key interest rate: 1.5% (March 2009)
Exchange rate versus dollar: euros per US dollar—0.6734 (2008, est.)
Unemployment: 9.6% (2008 average, government figures)
FDI: US$47.68 billion (2008, est.)
Current-account deficit/surplus –US$5.359 billion (2008, est.)
Population: 5,455,407 (July 2008, est.)
Source: CIA Factbook except where stated

▸▸ MORE INFO

Websites:

Slovak Investment and Trade Development Agency (SARIO): www.sario.sk/?home
Ministry of Finance: www.finance.gov.sk/en/Default.aspx?CatID=52
Slovakia Spectator, good source of current developments in the country: www.spectator.sk
Key government ministries and agencies portal: www.slovakia.org/links.htm
EU trade policies: www.ec.europa.eu/trade/

SUPPORT FOR INWARD INVESTMENT AND IMPORTS

Slovakia is very keen to attract foreign investment, and has had great success in doing so. A cheap and skilled labor force, low taxes (including a 19% flat rate tax for corporations and individuals), no dividend taxes, a relatively liberal labor code, and a favorable geographical location are Slovakia's main advantages for foreign investors. Foreign direct investment inflow (FDI) grew more than 600% from 2000, and cumulatively reached US$17.3 billion in 2006, or around US$18,000 per capita. A government agency, the Slovak Investment and Trade Development Agency (SARIO), provides assistance to foreign investors.

Slovakia is part of the EU customs union. Decisions regarding quotas or customs suspensions to be applied to goods imported into Slovakia are currently taken at the Community level. Information on the EU's trade policies can be found on its website.

TAX EXEMPTIONS

Slovakia's flat rate tax has no special rates, no exemptions, no exceptions, and almost no deductions. For more information on the tax regime in the country, a guide to the country's taxes is published on the Ministry of Finance website.

Slovenia

ECONOMY AND TRADE

Wedged between the Alps and the Adriatic Sea, Slovenia was the only one of the former Yugoslav republics to be in the first wave of candidates for membership of the European Union. It joined in May 2004, having a few months earlier become a member of NATO. Slovenia was fortunate in experiencing a relatively bloodless divorce from Yugoslavia. In addition, Slovenia was always the most prosperous region of the former Yugoslavia, and found the transition from a socialist economy to the capitalist free market relatively easy. Politically, Slovenia was the most liberal republic within Yugoslavia. In January 2007, it became the first former communist state to adopt the euro.

An open, trade-dependent economy, Slovenia exports some 70% of its production. EU states (mainly Germany, Italy, France, and Austria) account for three-quarters of its exports. The country benefits from an excellent infrastructure, and a highly educated workforce.

ECONOMIC POLICY OVER 12 MONTHS

Slovenia has pursued conservative fiscal and monetary policies in recent years in order to attain membership of the Eurozone, which it achieved in 2007. In the same year, the government embarked on an ambitious tax-reform program, which will lower revenues over a few years. The reforms included eliminating the payroll tax in 2008, and reducing the corporate tax rate from 23% in 2007, to 22% in 2008, 21% in 2009, and 20% from 2010 onwards.

In 2007, the government also committed to increase infrastructure spending. The authorities accepted that this increased spending, plus an initial decline in revenues associated with the tax-reform program, would cause the budget deficit to widen. In 2008, the budget deficit did indeed rise, to 2.2% of GDP, from 0.9% in the previous year, according to the European Commission (EC). The government planned to reduce the budget deficit to around 1% of GDP in 2009 and achieve a structural balance by 2011. However, the global economic slowdown has derailed these goals.

In December 2008, the government introduced a recovery package that will cause the deficit to widen to slightly above 3% of GDP in 2009, according to the EC, which believes that the deficit will narrow marginally to just below 3% of GDP in 2010. The recovery plan included measures worth around 2% of GDP to boost the economy, including subsidies for shorter working hours to avert mass layoffs, and tax breaks for investment in small companies.

The European Central Bank (ECB) has determined monetary policy in Slovenia since the country joined the Eurozone on January 1, 2007. The ECB was slower than other central banks to loosen monetary policy amid the global financial crisis of 2008 and 2009. In March 2009, the ECB cut its key interest rate from 2.0% to 1.5%, the lowest since it started setting euro rates in January 1999. US and Japanese rates were, in effect, already at zero by March 2009.

However, the use of the euro protects Slovenia from the dangers of a currency crisis, while the country's well-regulated financial system has not been directly affected by the global credit crunch. None of Slovakia's 19 banks has come under any pressure, and they are unlikely to do so. The financial system has generally relied on traditional, simple instruments that have shielded Slovenia from the US subprime crisis. Furthermore, in early 2009, the central bank called on commercial banks to raise additional capital, and use most of their 2008 profits to bolster their balance sheets.

STATISTICS

GDP growth: 3.5% (2008, government figures)
GDP per capita: US$30,800 (2008, est.)
CPI: 5.5% (2008, average inflation, government figures)
Key interest rate: 1.5% (March 2009)
Exchange rate versus dollar: euros per US dollar—0.6734 (2008, est.)
Unemployment: 7% (December 2008, government figures)
FDI: US$11.51 billion (2008, est.)
Current-account deficit/surplus −US$3.706 billion (2008, est.)
Population: 2,007,711 (July 2008, est.)
Source: CIA Factbook except where stated

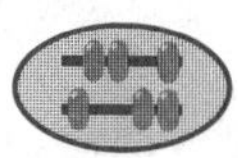

ECONOMIC PERFORMANCE OVER 12 MONTHS

The downturn in the global economy and, in particular, in the EU affected Slovenia in the latter stages of 2008. Growth moderated markedly in the third quarter of 2008, and the economy shrank by 0.8% in the final three months of the year, the first quarter of negative growth in more than 15 years. Despite this contraction, economic growth for the whole year stood at 3.5%, according to the country's statistics office.

In January 2009, the government and the EC forecast that the slowdown in economic activity would accelerate in 2009, driven mainly by declining exports as foreign demand weakens, and by a fall in investment. The EC anticipated growth of 0.6% in 2009, down from 4% in 2008 and 6.8% in 2007.

The EC also foresaw a "very gradual" recovery towards the end of 2009, while in 2010, despite a negative contribution from the external sector, the EC believed that growth would pick up to 2.3%, supported by domestic demand, and an acceleration in gross fixed-capital formation, as railway investment gathers pace.

Unemployment data confirm that the country experienced a sharp slowdown in the latter stages of 2008. The jobless rate rose to 7% in December, from 6.7% in the previous month, while industrial output fell by 17.5% year-on-year, and exports by 15.3%. Darko Kovacic, an analyst at Raiffeisen Bank, told Reuters in February 2009 that unemployment could increase by 50% during the remainder of the year, "as many companies will still have to cut jobs over the next months."

By March 2009, many firms had already announced or enforced job cuts. The country's second-largest exporter, the household-appliances maker, Gorenje, planned to lay off around 400–500 workers in 2009, out of a workforce of around 9,000 people in Slovenia. An opinion poll in March 2009 showed that more than 20% of Slovenians feared for their jobs in 2009—many construction, textile, and car firms were under pressure to cut their workforces.

However, the economic slowdown will help to quell inflation, which averaged 5.5% in 2008, up from 3.8% in 2007, and 2.5% in 2006. By January 2009, the annual rate of inflation, measured by the EC's harmonized index of consumer prices, had fallen to 2.1%. The government anticipates that average inflation will fall to 0.9% in 2009.

SUPPORT FOR INWARD INVESTMENT AND IMPORTS

Slovenia welcomes foreign direct investment that does not have a negative impact on the environment. Slovenia particularly welcomes those investments that create jobs in the high-tech sector and have links to R&D activities, for which special tax incentives are available (see Tax Exemptions). The Slovenian Public Investment Promotion Agency (JAPTI) was established to provide assistance to foreign investors.

Slovenia is part of the EU customs union. Decisions regarding quotas or customs suspensions to be applied to goods imported into Slovakia are currently taken at the European Community level.

TAX EXEMPTIONS

Corporate income tax is levied on the taxable profit of private companies at a rate of 21% for 2009 (for 2010 and beyond, the corporate-profit tax rate will fall to 20%), with a reduced rate of not less than 10% applying to corporations established in special economic zones. A special rate of 0% also applies to investment funds, pension funds, and insurance undertakings for pension plans, under certain conditions. The special rate of 0% applies also to venture-capital companies that were set up under the Venture Capital Companies Act, and that prepare a separate tax statement just for that part of their activity. The government also offers a general R&D investment incentive.

For more information on the tax regime in the country, please see the guide to the country's taxes published on the Ministry of Finance website.

▸▸ MORE INFO

Websites:

Slovenian Public Investment Promotion Agency (JAPTI): www.investslovenia.si

Official gateway to information on Slovenia: www.slovenia.si

Government portal to ministries and agencies: www.gov.si

Ministry of Finance tax guide: www.mf.gov.si/angl/dav_car/TaxationinSlovenia2009.pdf

Information on EU trade policies: www.ec.europa.eu/trade/

South Africa

ECONOMY AND TRADE

South Africa is the superpower on the African continent. It has by far the largest economy in Africa, with strong financial and manufacturing sectors, and an abundant supply of resources (such as platinum, gold, and coal). The country has a large agricultural sector, and is a net exporter of food products. South Africa is a popular tourist destination, and tourism is a key source of foreign exchange. The country also has an advanced infrastructure, and one of the world's leading stock exchanges. But there are sharp disparities in wealth, which appear to be worsening. The proportion of the population living in severe poverty doubled in the decade to 2007. Unemployment is high, and the crime rate is one of the worst in the world—an average of 50 murders take place per day. South Africa also has the second-highest number of HIV/Aids patients in the world. Around one in seven of its citizens is infected with HIV. The United States, Europe, and Japan account for around 60% of the country's exports.

ECONOMIC POLICY OVER 12 MONTHS

The South African government's main economic objectives are to accelerate growth, and reduce unemployment and poverty within a stable macroeconomic environment. Within this overall goal, the government's Accelerated and Shared Growth Initiative for South Africa (ASGISA) seeks to overcome constraints on growth, and aims to achieve average growth rates of at least 4.5% between 2005 and 2009, and 6% between 2010 and 2014, with the aim of halving the unemployment and poverty rates from 2004 levels by 2014.

The government has pursued trade liberalization and privatization as part of its attempts to overcome constraints on growth. The government is also planning to increase spending on infrastructure projects, as a means of eliminating bottlenecks and speeding growth. Fiscal policy aims to stabilize the budget balance around a chosen structural target; the government has generally achieved a budget close to balance in recent years, and has used any surpluses to pay down the public debt. South Africa's public debt stood at 23% of GDP at the end of 2008, down from 48% in 1996.

The government recorded a budget surplus of 0.9% of GDP in 2007–2008, the second surplus in a row, reflecting a large increase in tax revenue, owing to strong economic activity over most of the period, and continued collection efforts. However, the country is expected to record a surplus of just 0.1% of GDP in 2008–2009, according to independent economists, reflecting the slowdown in growth and revenues.

Overall, the government is well placed to adopt countercyclical fiscal measures to offset the impact of the global slowdown on the economy, a policy it adopted for the 2009–2010 budget, when it expects the deficit to increase to 3.8% of GDP. The government plans to reduce the shortfall to 1.9% by 2011–2012. Much of the increased spending in 2009–2010 will be focused upon a US$81 billion investment package to build infrastructure, create jobs, and prepare to host the 2010 football World Cup. But with tax revenues falling, the government will be obliged to borrow, and it may have difficulty raising all the funds it needs, given the turbulence in global financial markets.

In 2008, the government announced plans to reform the social-security regime, with the introduction of a mandatory multi-pillar scheme covering old-age pensions, unemployment insurance, and death and disability benefits. The scheme, to be introduced in 2010, will be funded by a payroll tax, while the budget will separately provide a wage subsidy for low earners, to partly offset the associated increase in labor cost.

The central bank began loosening monetary policy in December 2008, in response to an improved inflation outlook, and weakening growth. By March 2009, the main interest rate had fallen by 150 basis points. Yet for much of 2008, the government was focused on reducing inflation to within its 3–6% target. Annual inflation reached 13% in July 2008, driven by rising global food and fuel prices, and demand pressures.

The central bank raised its policy interest rate by 300 basis points between June 2007 and June 2008, to 12%. However, rates remained on hold until the December cut as the economy weakened, and inflation subsided. By March 2009, the policy rate stood at 10.5%, with further cuts anticipated unless the rand depreciates significantly. The central bank maintains a flexible exchange rate, with a publicly announced policy of purchasing foreign exchange on the market only to bolster its reserve position.

ECONOMIC PERFORMANCE OVER 12 MONTHS

Up until the second half of 2008, the South African economy had enjoyed healthy economic growth over the past decade. Growth had accelerated from 2003 onwards, supported by buoyant prices for key commodity exports. During the four years ending in 2007, economic growth averaged more than 5%. However, the slump in global growth and commodity prices in the second half of 2008 has affected the economy. Growth fell to 0.2% in the third quarter, from 5% in the second quarter, and the economy contracted by 1.8% in the final three months of the year. Overall, the economy expanded by 3.1% in 2008, down from 5.1% in the previous year.

The economy deteriorated further in 2009. Bloomberg reported in March 2009 that manufacturing had "probably" fallen at its steepest rate in more than 16 years in January, as export demand plummeted, forcing factories to scale back and lay off workers. Manufacturing production had dropped by 8% in January from the previous year, after contracting by 7% in the previous month, according to the median estimate of six economists surveyed by Bloomberg. In a further sign of the weakness of the economy, vehicle sales plunged 36% in February 2009 from a year earlier, the biggest decline seen in 25 years. All the data suggest that, in 2009, South Africa will experience its first recession in 17 years.

In February 2009, finance minister Trevor Manuel said that the government expected growth to improve in 2010, supported by public infrastructure spending, lower interest rates, the 2010 FIFA World Cup, and a recovery in the world economy. "But trading conditions are tough, and are likely to deteriorate further in the short term," said Manuel, who, according to *The Economist* (February 12, 2009), "has gained an almost mythical status for competence and integrity among foreign investors."

STATISTICS

GDP growth: 3.1% (2008, government figures)

GDP per capita: US$10,400 (2008, est.)

CPI: 8.1% (January 2009, government figures)

Key interest rate: 10.5% (March 2009)

Exchange rate versus dollar: rand per US dollar—7.9576 (2008, est.)

Unemployment: 21.9% (Q4 2008)

FDI: US$99.61 billion (2008, est.)

Current-account deficit/surplus −US$21.67 billion (2008, est.)

Population: 48,782,756

Source: CIA Factbook except where stated

   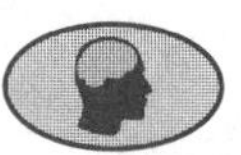     

The strong economic growth of recent years has had a positive impact on employment levels. The official jobless rate fell to 21.9% in the fourth quarter of 2008, from 23.2% in the previous quarter. However, unemployment is likely to rise in 2009, as manufacturers and mining firms lay off workers in response to weak demand.

The economic slowdown is having a positive impact on inflation, which fell to an annual rate of 8.1% in January 2009, from 9.5% in December 2008. Inflation would have fallen by more but for rising import prices, reflecting the 22% fall in the value of the rand against the dollar in the preceding six months, according to the statistics office.

The current account should also improve in 2009 on the back of lower economic growth, according to the National Treasury. It anticipates that the current account deficit will narrow to around 6% of GDP, from 8.1% in 2008, as import growth slows, and international investors receive smaller dividend payments.

SUPPORT FOR INWARD INVESTMENT AND IMPORTS

South Africa has made great progress in dismantling its old economic system, which was based on import substitution, high tariffs and subsidies, anticompetitive behavior, and extensive government intervention in the economy, according to a US State Department report published in January 2009. The government's role in the economy has been reduced, and the authorities have sought to promote private-sector investment, and competition. The government has significantly reduced tariffs and export subsidies, loosened exchange controls, cut the secondary tax on corporate dividends, and improved enforcement of intellectual-property laws.

The Department of Trade and Industry provides a one-stop shop for investors, offering a variety of services to those interested in conducting business in South Africa, including investing, and importing goods into the country.

TAX EXEMPTIONS

The Tax Exemption Unit of the South African Revenue Service can provide information on all the exemptions the country offers.

▸▸ MORE INFO

Websites:

Official gateway to the country: www.southafrica.info

Portal for government ministries and agencies: www.gov.za

Department of Trade and Industry: www.southafrica.info/business/investing/help/dti.htm

Tax Exemption Unit of the South African Revenue Service: www.sars.gov.za/home.asp?pid=1833

South Korea

ECONOMY AND TRADE

Over the past 50 years, South Korea (often referred to in financial markets as Korea) has been transformed from a largely rural and poverty-stricken country into one of the world's major economies, and a leading exporter of cars and electronic goods. South Korea's success is often called the "miracle on the Han," after the river that runs through the 23-million-strong capital, Seoul. This economic success has occurred even though South Korea remains technically at war with North Korea; the three-year civil war between the Communist North and the Western-backed South ended in 1953 without a peace agreement. The South has since lived with the threat that its unpredictable and still Communist northern neighbor, which, in 2006, successfully tested a nuclear weapon, could reignite hostilities.

The South Korean economy is now the third largest in Asia and the 13th largest in the world. However, the government must confront serious challenges if the economy is to remain prosperous. These include a rapidly ageing population, and structural problems such as a rigid labor market, and a general lack of regulatory transparency.

ECONOMIC POLICY OVER 12 MONTHS

The government of President Lee Myung-bak, who was elected in December 2007, came to power promising to roll back the influence of the state. Lee argued that "the Korean economy is too large and too complex to be managed by the government," and promised to cut corporate and personal taxation, reduce the number of government ministries, deregulate the economy, reform the labor market, privatize state-owned entities, and liberalize foreign trade. The popularity of this policy offering may have reflected widespread unease among South Koreans about the growing economic threat from China and other low-cost Asian producers. While the Lee administration has delivered on some of these pledges, the global financial crisis that broke in September 2008 has derailed others, including the government's flagship privatization program.

By the start of 2009, and following a dramatic weakening of the economy, President Lee said he was committed to finding policies that would make the recession a shallow one. The president declared a

STATISTICS

GDP growth: 3.5% (2008, official statistics)

GDP per capita: US$26,000 (2008, est.)

CPI: 4.1% (February 2008, official statistics)

Key interest rate: 2% (end-February 2009, official statistics)

Exchange rate versus dollar: South Korean won per US dollar—1,101.7 (2008, est.)

Unemployment: 3.6% (January 2009, official statistics)

FDI: US$103.7 billion (June 30, 2008)

Current-account deficit/surplus −US$6.41 billion (2008)

Population: 48,379,392 (July 2008, est.)

Source: CIA Factbook except where stated

  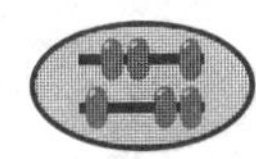      

national emergency, and said he would preside over a weekly emergency economic committee consisting of senior policy-makers to ensure that a four-year investment plan, worth US$38 billion and designed to boost the economy, was implemented. The plan is focused on environmental projects and the infrastructure, and aims to create one million jobs. However, the government may have trouble steering its plans through parliament. The opposition is opposed to a number of bills designed to liberalize the economy and improve South Korea's international competitive position, and it physically disrupted parliament for nearly two weeks during December 2008 and January 2009.

The central bank pursues an inflation-targeting monetary regime, aiming to keep inflation within a range of 2.5–3.5%. After a one-year pause, monetary policy was tightened in August 2008. Inflation had, by then, exceeded the inflation target for 10 consecutive months, and the central bank cited concerns about liquidity growth and the need to anchor inflation expectations behind the decision to raise the benchmark rate to an eight-year high of 5.25%.

Following the escalation of the global credit crunch in September 2008, the central bank embarked upon a program of cutting interest rates aggressively. By the end of February 2009, the key interest rate stood at just 2%, with further loosening anticipated by markets. However, despite these cuts, credit conditions in the country remained difficult. Risk-averse financial institutions have been conservative with new lending, and companies with low credit ratings have experienced great difficulty in raising capital.

ECONOMIC PERFORMANCE OVER 12 MONTHS

With assistance from the International Monetary Fund (IMF), South Korea recovered from the 1997–1998 Asian financial crisis to record strong growth rates for much of the current decade. In 2006 and 2007, for example, the economy expanded by 5.1% and 5%, respectively. However, the global financial crisis that developed in September 2008 hit South Korea particularly hard as a result of its open economy. According to preliminary data, the economy contracted by 5.6% in the last quarter of 2008, compared with the previous quarter. Exports declined sharply, and this fed through to weaker consumption and investment. The economy grew by 3.5% overall in 2008.

Korean financial markets were affected even more than most by external shocks during 2008. Writing for the South Korean news agency, Yonhap, in February 2009, Anoop Singh, director of the Asia and Pacific Department at the IMF, explained that "both domestic and foreign-exchange liquidity tightened for banks with large wholesale financing requirements, while foreign investors retrenched from very liquid markets such as Korea."

However, Singh argued that the economy should begin to recover during the second half of 2009, because the banking system is "well capitalized, non-performing loans are still low, and balance sheets of large corporates are generally healthy." Furthermore, Singh declared that policy-makers had taken a "comprehensive and forward-looking approach" to the global turmoil to maintain the country's fundamentals. In particular, Singh praised the loosening of monetary policy, and proactive measures taken by the authorities to ensure "that liquidity in the banking system remains ample, despite the tightening of external financing conditions." He also commended "numerous initiatives to bolster the financial and corporate sectors, and to avoid the sharp deleveraging process seen elsewhere, such as through bilateral currency-swap arrangements with the United States, Japan, and China."

In March 2009, the government said that it expected the economy to shrink by around 2% in 2009, marking the first contraction since the 1997–1998 Asian financial crisis. The finance ministry said that around 200,000 jobs would be lost during the course of the year as exports collapsed—they fell by 26% in the first two months of 2009. However, the government believed that exports would pick up later in the year, aided by a sharp fall in the currency; by March 2009, the won had lost 35% of its value against the dollar over the preceding year.

SUPPORT FOR INWARD INVESTMENT AND IMPORTS

The South Korean government has a generally positive attitude towards foreign investment, and the administration of President Lee has been particularly keen to improve the investment environment. Certainly, there are various barriers that need to be addressed. The regulatory environment remains opaque in certain areas, while labor laws are overly rigid. Labor relations are also problematic, with large numbers of days lost through strikes relative to other Organization for Economic Cooperation and Development (OECD) countries. Invest Korea can provide assistance to investors.

South Korea is a member of the World Trade Organization, and is striving to liberalize its trade regime. For information on tariffs on specific goods or for other assistance on importing goods into the country, see the website of South Korea's customs service.

TAX EXEMPTIONS

South Korea offers various tax exemptions and other incentives to companies that invest in South Korea. A guide detailing all of these incentives is published on Invest Korea's website.

▸▸ MORE INFO

Websites:

Invest Korea: www.investkorea.org

South Korean customs service: english.customs.go.kr

Website of the South Korean news agency, in English: english.yonhapnews.co.kr

Official website of South Korea: www.korea.net

 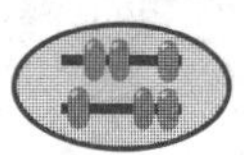      

Spain

ECONOMY AND TRADE

Spain joined the European Union in 1986, and, over the next two decades, its economy was transformed. Economically isolated until the death of General Franco in 1975, the country took advantage of €120 billion of EU funding to upgrade its infrastructure, and create some 300,000 jobs per year. Between 1994 and 2008, the economy was consistently one of the EU's best-performing. Following the bursting of the country's property and construction bubble in early 2008, however, Spain entered recession in the third quarter of that year. The Socialist prime minister, Jose Luis Rodriguez Zapatero, who has been in office since 2004 but was re-elected in March 2008, has made mixed progress in introducing structural reforms. While the global financial crisis has exacerbated the downturn, Spain's banking system is considered solid, thanks in part to conservative oversight by the Bank of Spain. The government has not needed to rescue banks on the scale seen elsewhere in Europe.

STATISTICS

GDP growth: 1.2% (2008, government statistics)
GDP per capita: US$36,500 (2008, est.)
CPI: 0.1% (February 2008, government statistics)
Key interest rate: 1.5% (March 2009, ECB)
Exchange rate versus dollar: euros per US dollar—0.6689 (2008, est.)
Unemployment: 13.9% (2009, est.)
FDI: US$606.8bn
Current account deficit −US$152.5 billion (2008, est.)
Population: 40.5 million (July 2008, est.)
Source: CIA Factbook except where stated

ECONOMIC POLICY OVER 12 MONTHS

The government of Prime Minister Zapatero, elected for a second term in March 2008, was wrong-footed by the sudden bursting of Spain's property and construction bubbles. Zapatero and his finance minister, Pedro Solbes, initially sought to downplay the situation. However, by July 2008, Solbes admitted: "This crisis is the most complex we have ever lived through."

The following month the government unveiled a package of measures aimed at cushioning the downturn, including increased government spending, tax cuts, opening up the services sector, and cutting red tape for businesses.

Constrained by its membership of the euro—which means that devaluation and monetary policy cannot be used to boost competitiveness—Zapatero contemplated using labor market reforms, and the introduction of more flexible economic regulations to cut Spanish workers' pay. However, the unions threatened to respond with a general strike, and Zapatero backed down.

The government instead introduced a €90 billion stimulus package, including tax breaks, infrastructure spending, and assistance to the financial sector, having accepted that this would require a 51% increase in borrowing in 2009.

In March 2009, the Madrid parliament approved further reforms of the service sector, which it said would create 200,000 jobs within four years, and boost GDP by 1.2 percentage points. The reforms aim to reduce red tape, and promote pan-European business in the industrial, energy, telecommunications, and transport sectors.

Ahead of the G20 summit in April 2009, Solbes and Zapatero publicly differed on whether Spain would be able to introduce further stimulus measures. Solbes said these were out of the question as a result of the EU's tight fiscal rules. He warned that the country's budget deficit would reach 5.8% in 2009—double the 3% target laid down by the EU's Stability and Growth Pact.

Zapatero, however, said that if there was no evidence of economic revival by July 2009, he would push ahead with a second round of stimulus measures. He argued this was possible since Spain's public debt, at 39% of GDP, is below the European average. He indicated he was not averse to running a public-sector deficit of up to 8% until 2011.

Spain's banks have weathered the financial crisis better than many others, and have not needed massive government interventions or nationalizations, even though their capital levels are being eroded by mounting bad debts, and the country's shrinking business base. In March, however, the savings bank, Caja Castilla-La Mancha, became the first Spanish bank to require a bailout. The Madrid government pledged a €9 billion (US$12 billion) capital injection, and to protect depositors.

ECONOMIC PERFORMANCE OVER 12 MONTHS

Spain's GDP growth slowed to 1.2% in 2008, significantly below the average growth of 3% plus seen during Spain's 1997–2007 boom. The country entered recession in the third quarter of 2008, and the government is forecasting that GDP will shrink by 1.6% in 2009, before returning to growth of 1.2% in 2010. In March 2009, Solbes warned that GDP may contract by more than these forecasts.

The causes of the slowdown included the bursting of the country's property and construction bubbles, and the ending of a debt-fueled consumer spending spree, both of which were exacerbated by the global financial crisis.

Average house prices fell by 3.2% in 2008. However, these are expected to fall by 40–45% before the recession is over, according to a Reuters poll of economists. House price falls are expected to accelerate due to the overhang of some one million unsold homes—itself a legacy of the country's protracted construction boom.

Spain was making good progress in tackling unemployment, and this fell to 8% in 2007. However, the

  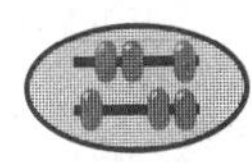    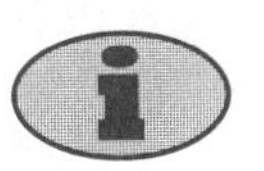  

recession, and particularly the construction sector's collapse, caused unemployment to climb sharply to 13% in 2008, the highest level of any Eurozone country. In January 2009, unemployment climbed further to 14.5%, and some forecasters warn it could reach 20% by 2010.

Spain had achieved a budget surplus equivalent to 2.2% of GDP in 2007. However, this had been transformed into a 3.8% deficit by 2008, and the government forecasts this will reach 5.8% in 2009. In January 2009, the ratings agency, Standard and Poor's, downgraded Spain's sovereign debt from "AAA" to "AA+," as spreads widened and international investors fretted about the possible risk of a default.

Inflation, which soared to 5.14% in July 2008, had fallen to −0.1% by February 2009. The government does not believe that deflation is going to become a long-term phenomenon, and is confident that 3% GDP growth will resume in 2011.

Tax collection fell by 6.1% in the first two months of 2009, partly due to a €400 income tax deduction promised by Zapatero in his 2008 election campaign. There was a sharp fall in VAT revenues in the first quarter, largely as a result of falling retail sales.

Standard & Poor's forecasts that Spain's public debt will climb to 60% of GDP by 2011, up from 40% in 2008. However, such debt levels remain low compared to some European countries, but could become difficult to contain as growth dwindles, S&P said.

SUPPORT FOR INWARD INVESTMENT AND IMPORTS

The central port of call for inquiries is Invest in Spain, an agency created in 2005, which forms part of the Ministry of Industry, Tourism, and Trade. IIS aims to provide a personal, confidential, and free service to would-be investors, and acts as a central hub for all state, regional, and local institutions engaged in promoting inward investment. It aims to provide a comprehensive and efficient service at all stages of the investment process.

TAX EXEMPTIONS

The Spanish authorities have developed a wide range of interlinked aid instruments and incentives, which place particular emphasis on encouraging projects that will create long-term employment, and on research, development, and technological innovation projects. As Spain is an EU member state, potential investors into Spain can also benefit from European aid programs.

▸▸ MORE INFO

Websites:

Ministry of Economy and Finance: www.meh.es

Bank of Spain: www.bde.es

General Directorate of Trade and Investment: www.ipyme.org

Invest in Spain: www.investinspain.org

Tax Agency: www.aeat.es

St Kitts and Nevis

ECONOMY AND TRADE

The former British colonies of St Kitts (also known as St Christopher) and Nevis have been in an uneasy federation since gaining independence in 1983. Some politicians in Nevis accuse the federal government in St Kitts—home to the majority of the population—of ignoring the needs of Nevisians. The two Caribbean islands, which lie around 150 miles to the east of Puerto Rico, are now reliant on tourism, offshore finance, and service industries. The loss-making sugar industry was wound down in 2005, with the loss of hundreds of jobs. The island's agricultural system is focused on rice, yams, bananas, cotton, peanuts, and vegetables. There is also a small fishing industry.

St Kitts and Nevis is a member of the Eastern Caribbean Currency Union (ECCU). The Eastern Caribbean Central Bank (ECCB) issues the Eastern Caribbean dollar (EC$) for all members of the ECCU. The ECCB also manages monetary policy, and regulates and supervises commercial banking activities in its member countries. The ECCB has kept the currency pegged at EC$2.7 to US$1.

ECONOMIC POLICY OVER 12 MONTHS

St Kitts and Nevis has a small and highly open economy. The economy enjoyed strong growth during much of the 1990s, but hurricanes in 1998 and 1999 and the September 11, 2001 terrorist attacks in the United States hurt the tourism-dependent country. Economic growth picked up in 2004, with a real GDP growth rate of 6.4%, followed by 4.1% growth in 2005. Economic growth accelerated to 5.8% in 2006, mostly as a result of diversification into tourism, and construction related to the Cricket World Cup. Growth is estimated to have slowed slightly in 2007, to 3.1%, as construction demand slowed following a spike in 2006.

In January 2009, the International Monetary Fund (IMF) reported on the findings of a mission to St Kitts earlier in the month. The IMF praised the government's economic management, saying that the country had enjoyed four consecutive years of sizeable primary surpluses between 2005 and 2008. How-

STATISTICS

GDP growth: 3.5% (2008, est.)

GDP per capita: US$20,000 (2008, est.)

CPI: 4.5% (2007, est.)

Key interest rate: 6.5% (December 31, 2007)

Exchange rate versus dollar: East Caribbean dollar per US dollar—2.7 (2007)

Unemployment: 4.5% (1997)

FDI: N/A

Current-account deficit/surplus −US$163 million (2007, est.)

Population: 39,817 (July 2008, est.)

Source: CIA Factbook except where stated

  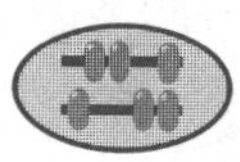   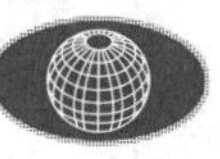 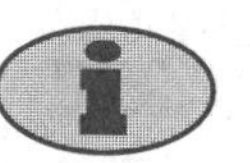  

ever, it added that, while public debt as a proportion of GDP had declined by 20 percentage points since 2005, it remained "formidably" high, at more than 170% of GDP at the end of 2008.

Tourism has shown strong growth over the past decade, and is now a major foreign-exchange earner. There were 117,300 stopover arrivals on the two islands in 2007, nearly two-thirds of which were tourists from the United States, a quarter from the rest of the Caribbean, and around 5% from Canada. There were also more than 251,000 cruise-ship passenger arrivals in 2007, well above levels in the two previous years. The government has helped to develop the industry by adopting a program of investment incentives for hoteliers who locate to the islands, including liberal tax holidays, duty-free importation of equipment and materials, and subsidies for training provided to local personnel.

In 2006, the government decided to reposition the island as a high-quality destination experience for sophisticated customers with good spending power. A new development featuring five-star hotels, luxurious restaurants, and shops is due to be finished on St Kitts in 2011. Several other development projects are underway on the islands, which should boost tourism income significantly when the global economy recovers.

In 2008, the government continued its efforts to regulate the banking sector, passing a Proceeds of Crime Act that made money laundering an extraditable offence. The islands have developed a strong offshore-banking infrastructure, particularly since St Kitts and Nevis was removed from the Organization for Economic Cooperation and Development's Financial Action Task Force (FATF) list of non-cooperative countries and territories in 2002.

ECONOMIC PERFORMANCE OVER 12 MONTHS

The islands' dependence on tourism and, in particular, on arrivals from the recession-hit US market affected the economy badly in 2008 and 2009. In March 2009, the Minister of State for Tourism, Richard Skerritt, said that hotel occupancy and revenue had declined by between 30% and 40%, compared with early 2008. The industry has also been affected by the crisis in the global aviation industry, with airlines that serve the islands cutting back on their operations. In March 2009, Windward Islands Airways International said it was considering ending its flights to St Kitts and Nevis. More positively in 2009, British Airways launched weekly direct flights to St Kitts from London. Skerritt has pointed out that St Kitts and Nevis is faring better than several of its Caribbean neighbors, which have been reporting significant job lay-offs, as well as a slowdown in foreign direct investment.

The global financial crisis has had a direct impact on the islands. In March 2009, a local newspaper reported that several of the larger institutions in the Federation have substantial investments in the struggling Trinidad-based Colonial Life Insurance Company (CLICO), and collectively could lose US$300 million. It said those at risk included high-profile financial institutions, private companies, and local investors, as well the savings, investments, and pensions of ordinary citizens. The authorities in Trinidad and Tobago have admitted that the financial problems facing CLICO are far worse than first anticipated, even though the Trinidadian government has agreed to plough billions of dollars into the company.

Hurricane Omar, which passed through the islands in October 2008, has also disrupted tourism, forcing the closure of one of the island's larger hotels, the Four Seasons Resort, until October 2009. The hotel laid off 620 employees in March 2009.

Increasing crime could pose a threat to tourism. In the first two months of 2009, seven people were murdered in the 68-square-mile country. St Kitts and Nevis, like several other Caribbean islands, has seen a spike in gang violence in recent years. To date, there have been no attacks on foreign tourists.

SUPPORT FOR INWARD INVESTMENT AND IMPORTS

The government of St Kitts is keen to encourage investment, and offers a number of incentive packages to investors. These include tax holidays, export allowances, exemption from import duties, and various packages aimed at encouraging the development of hotels.

With one exception, foreign investment in St Kitts and Nevis is not subject to any restrictions, and foreign investors receive national treatment. The only restriction is the requirement to obtain an Alien Landholders License for foreign investors seeking to purchase property for residential or commercial purposes. For more information on investing in St Kitts, see the website of the St Kitts Investment Promotion Agency.

In May 2008, the Nevis Investment Promotion Agency (NIPA) was launched as a one-stop agency to promote the island, but it does not yet appear to have a website.

For information on importing into St Kitts and Nevis, see the World Trade Organization Trade Policy Review 2007 for the islands.

TAX EXEMPTIONS

There is no personal income tax in St Kitts. Qualified companies enjoy full exemption from taxes on corporate profits for up to 15 years. Corporate tax is levied at the rate of 35% of net profits. This tax does not apply to exempt companies, or to enterprises that have been granted a tax concession.

▸▸ MORE INFO

Websites:

- Official website of the government of St Kitts and Nevis: www.gov.kn/mp.asp?mp=1
- St Kitts Investment Promotion Agency: www.stkittsipa.org
- World Bank profile of St Kitts and Nevis: www.web.worldbank.org/WBSITE/EXTERNAL/COUNTRIES/LACEXT/OECSEXTN/0,,contentMDK:20221655~pagePK:141137~piPK:217854~theSitePK:339287,00.html
- World Trade Organization Trade Policy Review 2007 for the islands: www.wto.org/english/tratop_e/tpr_e/s190kna_e.doc

  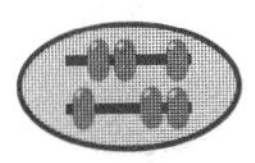      

Sweden

ECONOMY AND TRADE

Sweden is one of the world's most highly developed, post-industrial societies. Public-private partnership is at the core of "the Swedish model," which was developed by the Social Democrats, who governed for most of the 70 years until 2006. However, a center-right government elected in 2006 is committed to reducing the role of the state in the economy. Although it has been a member of the European Union since 1995, Sweden remains outside the Eurozone. In a referendum held in 2003, Swedish voters rejected membership of the Single European Currency by a clear majority.

Agriculture, which once accounted for nearly all of Sweden's economy, now employs less than 2% of the labor force. Sweden's natural resources include extensive forests, rich iron-ore deposits, and hydroelectric power. Sweden is dependent upon foreign trade, with exports accounting for around 45% of GDP. Around 75% of Sweden's foreign trade is conducted with other European nations.

ECONOMIC POLICY OVER 12 MONTHS

The center-right coalition, elected in September 2006, has focused on reducing the role of the state in the economy, adopting pro-business policies, and improving the investment climate. The government has cut taxes, and reduced benefits and active labor-market programs. The government's vast privatization program involves raising around US$31 billion from the sale of shares in six state-owned companies during the period 2007–2010, with the goal of stimulating economic growth, and raising revenue to pay down the federal debt.

By March 2009, the government had sold part or all of its stakes in four of the six companies, raising around US$20 billion, but global financial turbulence has stalled the privatization process. The government's refusal, in early 2009, to bail out the carmaker, Saab, part of the troubled General Motors empire, highlighted the government's laissez faire approach to business. The government's policy has popular backing. Opinion polls showed that only one-third of voters supported government intervention to rescue Saab. Sweden learned a hard lesson in the 1970s, when the government spent billions of krona trying to bail out a faltering ship-making industry, to no avail.

However, the government has adopted a looser fiscal policy, launching various stimulation packages in late 2008 and early 2009, to counter the impact of the global economic crisis on Sweden. Inevitably, the government's finances have deteriorated markedly as a result. In March 2009, Sweden's National Debt Office said that it expected the country's budget deficit to balloon to SEK135 billion (US$14.7 billion) in 2009, just one year after posting a SEK135 billion surplus.

In February 2009, the government announced measures to shore up confidence in the country's banks, some of which fueled a lending boom in the Baltic countries, which has left them exposed to the sharp economic downturn in that region. In February 2009, the government unveiled a bank-support scheme that would inject up to SEK50 billion (US$5.7 billion) into its financial sector as well as guaranteeing SEK1.5 trillion in new bank loans. Prime Minister, Fredrik Reinfeldt, said Swedish banks would be able to use the state aid package to prop up subsidiaries in Eastern Europe, as well as ensuring that domestic companies obtain access to capital.

Sweden's monetary policy is based upon an inflation-targeting regime (2%, with a margin of one percentage point either side), while the Swedish krona is allowed to float freely. During the first eight months of 2008, the central bank was focused upon reining in inflation, and gradually tightened monetary policy. Interest rates peaked at 4.75% in early September 2008. In October 2008, the central bank announced a cut of 50 basis points, coordinated with other central banks and prompted by a severe deterioration in the global financial system. The central bank continued to cut rates during the remainder of the year and into 2009, slashing rates by a record 175 basis points in December 2008 alone. By the end of February 2009, the country's key interest rates stood at just 1%.

ECONOMIC PERFORMANCE OVER 12 MONTHS

Sweden has enjoyed strong economic growth in recent years, with an annual average GDP growth rate of 2.7% in 2005, 4.1% in 2006, and 2.7% in 2007. However, the global economic slowdown has affected Sweden very badly. GDP shrank by an annual 4.9% in the fourth quarter of 2008, the worst performance in at least 14 years, as demand for Swedish exports slumped. Sweden is more vulnerable than many other countries to slowing world growth, as exports account for about half of its economy.

Following the announcement of the figures in February 2009, the Bloomberg news agency quoted Stefan Hoernell, a senior economist at Svenska Handelsbanken AB, as describing them as "incredibly bad." Private and public consumption were the biggest downside surprises, he said. The only positive surprise was the bigger-than-expected stock reduction. Hoernell also said the figures were among the worst in the industrialized world, and forecast that the economy would contract by 2.7% in 2009, "the weakest figure

STATISTICS

GDP per capita: US$39,600 (2008, est.)

CPI: 0.9% (December 2008, official statistics)

Key interest rate: 1% (end-February 2009)

Exchange rate versus dollar: Swedish kronor per US dollar—6.4074 (2008, est.)

Unemployment: 6.4% (December 2008, official statistics)

FDI: US$225.9 billion (2008, est.)

Current-account deficit/surplus US$35.22 billion (2008, est.)

Population: 9,045,389 (July 2008, est.)

Source: CIA Factbook except where stated

since 1940." In March 2009, Sweden's National Debt Office said that it expected the Swedish economy to contract by 2.0% in 2009, before bouncing back to see growth of 2.0% in 2010.

Unemployment had been on an improving trend until the global financial crisis broke in 2008. In 2006, the unemployment rate reached 7.1%, but in 2007 it fell to 6.2%, and, by the end of 2008, had increased slightly to 6.4%. In January 2008, the jobless rate jumped by almost a full percentage point to 7.3%, as Swedish exporters laid off thousands of workers. In February 2009, SEB AB, Scandinavia's third-largest bank by market value, forecast that the jobless rate would rise to 10.2% in 2010.

Inflation fell sharply in the second half of 2008. In December, the annual rate of inflation posted its biggest monthly decline since records began in the 1950s. Consumer prices rose by just 0.9%, the slowest pace in almost three years, reflecting weak demand, and falling prices for international commodities. The decline in inflation occurred despite the weakness of the currency. By March 2009, the Swedish krona had suffered its steepest fall since it was allowed to float in 1992, and was the worst-performing major currency during the financial crisis that began in September 2008 with the collapse of Lehmans, dropping by 20% against the euro, and 27% against the US dollar.

SUPPORT FOR INWARD INVESTMENT AND IMPORTS

Following Sweden's entry into the European Union in 1995, the investment climate has greatly improved, and the country has attracted significant foreign investment. Conditions for doing business in Sweden have also improved under the coalition government that was elected in September 2006. Corporate income taxes are now among the lowest in Europe. A government body, the Invest in Sweden Agency, provides support to foreign investors.

Following entry into the European Union in 1995, Sweden has applied the customs laws and trade regulation of the union. Decisions regarding quotas or customs suspensions to be applied to goods imported into Sweden are currently taken at the community level. Information on the EU's trade policies can be found on its website.

TAX EXEMPTIONS

Dividends paid by foreign subsidiaries in Sweden to their parent company are not subject to Swedish taxation. The Ministry of Finance has produced a guide with full information on the tax system in Sweden.

➤➤ MORE INFO

Websites:

Swedish government portal: www.sweden.gov.se

Invest in Sweden Agency: www.isa.se/templates/Startpage____2008.aspx

Ministry of Finance: www.sweden.gov.se/sb/d/9509

EU trade policies: www.ec.europa.eu/trade/

US Department of Commerce Country Commercial Guide, published in 2009: www.buyusa.gov/sweden/en/ccg.html

Switzerland

ECONOMY AND TRADE

Switzerland is an open economy with one of the highest standards of living in the world, low unemployment, and a highly skilled labor force. Switzerland's economy benefits from a highly developed services sector, led by financial services, and a manufacturing industry that specializes in high-technology, knowledge-based production. Switzerland is a net exporter. Major merchandise exports include machinery, chemicals and pharmaceuticals, watches, jewelry, and telecommunications, while the main services exports are in the banking and insurance sectors. Farm subsidies are the highest in the world, with some Swiss farmers receiving support equivalent to three-quarters of the value of production. Switzerland remains a safe haven for investors, because it has maintained a degree of bank secrecy, while the franc has traditionally been one of the world's strongest currencies.

The global financial crisis and resulting economic downturn is likely to tip Switzerland into recession in 2009, particularly given the relative size of its services sector and as global export demand stalls. Switzerland's largest banks suffered significant losses in 2008, and the country's largest bank (UBS) accepted a government rescue deal in late 2008.

ECONOMIC POLICY OVER 12 MONTHS

Faced with severe financial sector pressures in 2008, the authorities responded with broad stabilization measures commended by the IMF. The Swiss National Bank (SNB) created a fund (the StabFund) to acquire distressed assets, including a US$16.4 billion purchase of UBS's toxic assets in December 2008. The injection of government capital eased market concerns about the bank's solvency, while enhancing the deposit-protection scheme addressed the risk of a wider loss of confidence in the banking sector. The government made clear its readiness to take other measures, including guarantees, if necessary, for bank borrowing.

At the same time, the Federal Banking Commission introduced new capital-adequacy targets to encourage a further reduction in the largest banks' risks over time, although both UBS and Credit Suisse have

STATISTICS

GDP growth: 1.8% (2008, Economist Intelligence Unit)

GDP per capita: US$40,900 (2008, est.)

CPI: 2.4% (2008, est.)

Key interest rate: 0.5% (January 2009, Swiss National Bank)

Exchange rate versus dollar: Swiss franc (CHF) per US dollar—1.0774 (2008, est.)

Unemployment: 3% (December 2008)

FDI: US$333.8 billion (2008, est.)

Current account deficit/surplus: US$40.81 billion (2008, est.)

Population: 7,581,520 (July 2008, est.)

Source: CIA Factbook except where stated

until 2013 to comply. Action by the authorities has been accompanied by measures taken by banks themselves, to reduce balance sheet size and build up liquidity buffers.

Supported by recent years of strong growth, fiscal consolidation has resulted in general government surpluses, and a declining stock of public debt. In 2008, although the debt stock rose as a result of large one-off expenditures, the federal government's surplus increased again. Over 2009, however, the fiscal situation is expected to deteriorate rapidly as the recession deepens.

The Swiss government's key economic priority is to address the expected recession in 2009. The Swiss National Bank cut interest rates in December 2008, in response to company retrenchments, faltering export demand, slumping consumer confidence, and tight credit conditions. Other measures to boost GDP growth include improving competition policy, and reducing high price levels by liberalizing sectors such as electricity, energy, telecommunications, and postal services.

With a high inflation rate in the first three quarters of 2008, the SNB kept the monetary stance unchanged, offsetting the increase in risk premiums through lower repo rates. Concurrently, timely infusions of liquidity in interbank markets, use of repos with maturities up to one year, foreign exchange swaps, and new refinancing facilities lowered risk premiums, and eased upward pressure on the currency. With the economy slowing towards the end of 2008, inflationary expectations falling, and the currency appreciating, the SNB moved forcefully, relaxing the monetary policy stance by 2.25% over a period of about two months at the end of 2008. The establishment of a new integrated supervisor (FINMA) at the beginning of 2009 provided an opportunity to strengthen financial supervision further.

ECONOMIC PERFORMANCE OVER 12 MONTHS

In recent years, the Swiss economy has experienced high growth, low unemployment, and modest inflation, with strong fiscal and external positions. However, its openness, both in trade and financial relations, meant that the domestic economy could not be isolated from foreign shocks.

The global financial crisis has led to a downgrading of Switzerland's economic growth forecasts in 2008 and 2009. Switzerland's significant financial sector has exposed the Swiss economy to the global crisis, with international financial giants UBS, Swiss Re, and Credit Suisse writing down tens of billions of dollars in toxic assets. The key metals, machinery, and electronics industry saw a sharp fall in new orders, as the list of victims of the slowdown expanded beyond the banking sector.

More recently in 2009, fears have grown about Swiss banks' exposure to the growing risk of default across much of Eastern Europe, as Swiss banks lent a significant proportion of money in the region. Swiss GDP growth eased to 1.8% in 2008, and the economy is forecast to contract by around 1.8% in 2009, due to lower investment and weaker export demand (Economist Intelligence Unit, February 2009). Unemployment reached 3.4% in February 2009, the highest rate in three years. Inflation is forecast to fall to a negative 0.2% in 2009, from 2.5% in 2008. The Swiss National Bank cut official interest rates to 1% in December 2008, and to 0.5% in January 2009. The country's Swiss Market Index was dragged down by the banking sector's woes, ending down 33.5% in 2008.

The decline in economic activity has influenced demand for loans, and lending conditions have tightened in line with the deterioration of the cycle. However, the deleveraging of the two big banks has not affected domestic lending. Demand for mortgages remains high, reflecting long-term rates that are at historically low levels, as well as still-strong employment. Ample liquidity in the banking system, high credit standards, and the absence of a housing bubble have supported mortgage credit.

Economic activity is expected to contract somewhat in 2009, due to poorer export prospects, and a diminished contribution of financial services, followed by a rebound in 2010 as global financial market turbulence abates. Inflation is projected to decline further in 2009, with a few quarters of negative rates due to temporary factors. Reduced profits of Swiss multinationals abroad, including in the financial sector, are narrowing the current account surplus. As financial services contribute more than 12% to Swiss GDP, a prolonged decline in global activity in this sector would directly affect economic growth, and tax revenues.

SUPPORT FOR INWARD INVESTMENT AND IMPORTS

The Swiss authorities have a *laissez-faire* attitude towards investment. However, the government does support infrastructural investment (tourist facilities, communications, and training facilities) with subsidized loans up to 25% of a financing package. At the cantonal level, a wide variety of investment support is available. The types of support available include assistance or subsidy with land or premises, waiving of work permit requirements, tax holidays up to 10 years, cheap energy, and training subsidies.

TAX EXEMPTIONS

Most cantons grant tax holidays to companies bringing economic value-added functions and creating significant new jobs for up to ten years. Further information can be obtained from DEWS.

▸▸ MORE INFO

Websites:

Swiss Foreign Investment Agency: www.eda.admin.ch/eda/en/home/reps/nameri/vusa/ref_bufor/waecon/locswi.html

Federation of International Trade Association, information page on Switzerland: www.fita.org/countries/ch.html

Development Economic Western Switzerland (DEWS): www.dews.com/index.php?option=com_content&task=view&id=77&Itemid=93

   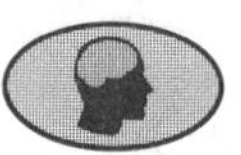     

Syria

ECONOMY AND TRADE

Syria is a lower-middle-income country with an estimated GDP per capita of US$1,365. It is led by the petroleum and agricultural sectors, which together account for about one-half of GDP. The government has implemented modest economic reforms in the past few years, including cutting lending interest rates, opening private banks, consolidating all of the multiple exchange rates, and raising prices on some subsidized items, most notably gasoline and cement. Syria has made progress in easing its heavy foreign-debt burden with its key creditors in Europe, most importantly Russia, Germany, and France. The country has also settled its debt with Iran and the World Bank.

Long-term barriers to growth include a high level of state control, declining oil production, high unemployment and inflation, rising budget deficits, and increasing pressure on water supplies caused by heavy use in agriculture, rapid population growth, industrial expansion, and water pollution.

ECONOMIC POLICY OVER 12 MONTHS

The Syrian government started its reform efforts by changing the regulatory environment in the financial sector. In 2001, Syria legalized private banking, and the sector, while still nascent, has been growing quickly since. Controls on foreign exchange continue to be one of the biggest impediments to the growth of the banking sector, although Syria has taken gradual steps to loosen those controls. The government is increasingly aware of its declining energy margin. It has recently focused on boosting the country's hydrocarbons sector through attracting foreign direct investment, and foreign technologies to improve the productivity of oil and gas fields, and substituting oil with natural gas in domestic power generation.

Syria is currently implementing its Five-Year Plan (FYP) for 2006–2010, focusing on economic and social reform. The FYP contains a number of innovative guiding principles, such as the promotion of a partnership between government, the private sector, and civil society, the principle of decentralized decision-making, and the use of indicative planning. Long-term objectives include social justice, attraction of foreign capital, and empowering women in society.

The authorities launched a program to phase out petroleum subsidies in May 2008. Gasoline and diesel prices were increased by 33% and 240%, respectively. To mitigate the impact of the diesel price increase, the authorities issued coupons. However, the cost of the explicit oil subsidy increased as a result of the sharp rise in international prices during the first eight months of 2008. Fuel oil prices were further raised by 33%, effective from December 1, 2008. The authorities aim to continue to improve the non-oil fiscal balance, in order to adjust to the reduction in oil output. To this end, they are determined to fully eliminate the fuel subsidies by 2010.

The introduction of VAT, which was initially planned for 2009, has been delayed until January 2010. This was partly to avoid contributing to inflationary pressures in view of the ongoing phasing out of fuel subsidies. There is excess liquidity in the banking system, and real interest rates have become largely negative. The Central Bank of Syria (CBS) increased its reserves requirement ratio from 5% to 10% in October 2008, to help mop up part of the excess liquidity. Advances have been made in trade liberalization by substantially reducing the tariff schedule. The export of strategic agricultural products, however, remains subject to government approval. Trade liberalization has also continued in the context of bilateral and regional trade agreements.

Syria opened a stock exchange in March 2009. The government hopes to attract new investment in the banking, tourism, insurance, and gas sectors to diversify its economy away from dependence on oil and agriculture.

ECONOMIC PERFORMANCE OVER 12 MONTHS

Syria's economic performance was strong in the first half of 2008. Non-oil growth remained robust, despite the adverse impact of a severe drought on agriculture. Inflation rose in the first half of 2008, largely due to temporary increases in food and fuel prices. The fiscal and external current deficits worsened only moderately over the past two years, despite the significant deterioration in the net oil balance. This was due to restraint on public expenditure, ongoing fuel subsidies reform, and the strong performance of non-oil exports, remittances, and tourism receipts.

However, drought, falling oil exports, and losses by state-owned industries aggravated the impact of the global credit crunch in Syria in the second half of the 2008. An economy ministry study forecast that the credit crunch would cause a 30% drop in foreign investment, especially as the slowdown intensified in the Gulf. The study also forecast a fall in remittances from Syrians working abroad (worth US$850 million in 2008). Analysts have also highlighted the plunge in the price of crude, Syria's main source of income, and a fall in all exports. These sank by half in the final months of 2008, and could weaken again in 2009. Syrian

STATISTICS

GDP growth: 5.2% (2008, est., IMF)
GDP per capita: US$4,900 (2008, est.)
CPI: 14.9% (2008, est.)
Key interest rate: 7% (November 6, 2008)
Exchange rate versus dollar: Syrian pound per US dollar—46.5281 (2008, est.)
Unemployment: 9% (2008, est.)
FDI: US$750m (2007, est., CBS)
Current account deficit/surplus: −US$192 million (2008, est.)
Population: 19,747,586
Note: in addition, about 40,000 people live in the Israeli-occupied Golan Heights: 20,000 Arabs (18,000 Druze, 2,000 Alawites), and about 20,000 Israeli settlers (July 2008, est.)
Source: CIA Factbook except where stated

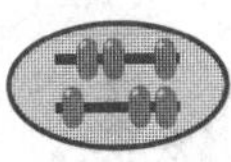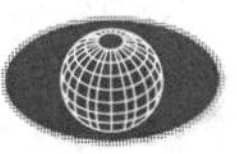

crude production dropped 2.8% in 2008, and was down 7.6% from 2007, the Middle East Economic Survey reported. GDP growth for 2008 has been estimated at 5.2% by the IMF.

The worsening of international financial conditions does not appear to have affected Syria's financial sector, given its limited integration with the global system, and with CBS regulations strictly limiting banks' foreign exposure. The Syrian economy is highly reliant on the oil sector, and, despite recent signs of resilience, remains in a precarious balance, with major structural deficiencies.

US sanctions imposed by the Bush administration in 2004 are one of the major obstacles to reforming the Syrian economy. The sanctions restrict the export of US-made products to Syria, except for some food and medicine products. Syria is also barred from importing products containing more than 10% of components made in the United States, whatever the origin of the product. However, the US sanctions did not stop bilateral trade between the United States and Syria, which grew by 7.7% in 2007.

Non-oil growth is projected to slow by about one percentage point (to around 5%) during 2009, although overall GDP growth is forecast by the IMF to slow down to 3.9%. The external current account is expected to narrow slightly, as declining oil prices should reduce the cost of net petroleum imports. The fiscal deficit is projected to narrow due to the reduction in fuel subsidies.

SUPPORT FOR INWARD INVESTMENT AND IMPORTS

Syria has only been open to external trade since 2000, although the current government is making a strong effort to attract foreign investment. More information on investing in Syria is available at the website of the Syrian Investment Agency, the government body responsible for attracting investment into the country.

TAX EXEMPTIONS

Syria has created several investment zones, and has lifted several customs and income tax levies for companies investing in the country. Further information is available from the Syrian Investment Agency.

▸▸ MORE INFO

Websites:

Syrian Investment Agency: www.investinsyria.org

Information on Syria and links to local resources: www.animaweb.org/en/pays_syrie_en.php

Taiwan

ECONOMY AND TRADE

Taiwan's economy has evolved from reliance on agriculture through manufacturing to services. Agriculture now constitutes just 1.7% of gross domestic product (GDP), down from 35% in 1952, while services now account for more than 70% of national output, and over half of all employment. The country, with a population of 23 million, is a dynamic, middle-income economy that is at the cutting edge in a number of high-technology sectors. Decreasing guidance of investment and foreign trade by the authorities has also led to some large, state-owned banks and industrial firms being privatized.

Exports have provided the primary impetus for industrialization. The island runs a large trade surplus, and its foreign reserves are among the world's largest. Recently opened cross-strait travel, transportation, and tourism links are likely to increase Taiwan's economic interdependence on China, which has overtaken the United States to become Taiwan's largest export market, and its second-largest source of imports, after Japan. With exports accounting for more than 70% of GDP, the country has been hit heavily by the global economic downturn, and officially fell into recession in the final quarter of 2008.

ECONOMIC POLICY OVER 12 MONTHS

On taking office in 2008, President Ma Ying-jeou set ambitious economic targets for his administration, as part of the process of opening up and deregulating Taiwan's economy. These targets are an annual GDP growth of 6%, an unemployment rate of less than 3%, and per capita income of US$30,000 by 2016. The focus will be on four key areas: expanding domestic demand; improving the investment environment; strengthening the economy; and increasing the quality of life. Ma plans investments totaling approximately US$140 billion, sourced from the public and private sectors, over the next eight years under the program.

Furthermore, in response to the country's export-led slowdown, the Taiwan government has announced a series of stimulus packages beginning in late 2008. The stimulus package is 3% of GDP (US$5.6bn), and comprises coupon vouchers, infrastructure spending, and tax cuts. In January 2009, the government handed out around US$100 in shopping vouchers to each of the island's residents in a US$2.3 billion program, which is estimated to contribute 0.64 percentage points to GDP in 2009.

Concerted efforts have also been made in providing financial incentives for business, increasing exports and introducing tax breaks. The economic stimulus package in Taiwan entails expenditure of NT$58.3 billion in infrastructure development, NT$20.5 billion in financial incentives for small and medium-scale

STATISTICS

GDP growth: 0.12% (2008, est., Statistics Agency)

GDP per capita: US$31,900 (2008, est.)

CPI: 3.7% (2008, est.)

Key interest rate: 1.25% (February 2009)

Exchange rate versus dollar: New Taiwan dollars per US dollar—31.53 (2008, est.)

Unemployment: 4.1% (2008, est.)

FDI: US$102.3 billion (2008)

Current account deficit/surplus: US$25 billion (2008, est.)

Population: 22,974,347 (July 2009, est.)

Source: CIA Factbook except where stated

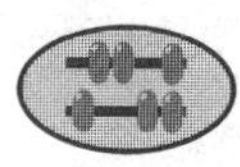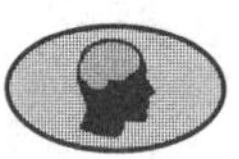

businesses, NT$37.5 billion towards tax holidays for new investments, and NT$13.5 billion in subsidies for low-income households.

After stabilization of its economy, the Taiwanese economic stimulus package has targeted streamlining exports, an important component of national revenue. To boost shipments to new overseas markets such as Russia, Brazil, and the Middle East, this Taiwan economic stimulus package has also allotted NT$1.5 billion for exports.

The economic stimulus package has also set aside NT$1.81 billion, to be provided in the form of interest subsidies to home buyers. This package is part of a preferential mortgage program, which is worth NT$200 billion. As part of this economic stimulus plan, NT$37.5 billion will also be provided as five-year tax breaks on investments made by technical service and manufacturing companies, until the end of 2009.

The Central Bank has responded to the global economic malaise by adopting a loose monetary policy, with successive interest-rate cuts since September 2008. As of February 2009, bank base rates had been cut to an all-time low of 1.25%. The continuation of an agenda of fiscal and financial reform is important to Taiwan's longer-term economic well-being, although commentators acknowledge the economy is dependent on the recovery of consumption in Taiwan export markets.

ECONOMIC PERFORMANCE OVER 12 MONTHS

As an export-led economy (exports account for more than 70% of the country's GDP), Taiwan has suffered disproportionately from the current global slowdown. It has experienced a significant decline in exports in its major export industries, such as semiconductors, memory chips, and electronic machinery, and to its major export markets, namely China and the United States. As of January 2009, exports had fallen 44% year on year, although the fall eased to 28.6% the following month. For the first two months of 2009, exports fell by 37.2%, led by a 50% fall in exports to China, the biggest buyer of Taiwanese goods.

Industrial production has correspondingly suffered, and consumer confidence is at its lowest level for some years. The unemployment rate (5.3% in January 2009) is at its highest level since 2003, and is expected to rise as students graduate from university in summer 2009. The economy shrank at an unprecedented 8.36% pace in the fourth quarter of 2008, pushing Taiwan into its first recession since the technology bubble burst in 2001. The economy expanded only a modest 0.12% over the whole of 2008, according to the statistics agency. Taiwan's benchmark TAIEX index of leading shares fell by 46% over 2008, to 4591.22.

The government has launched a US$5.6 billion economic stimulus drive, in a bid to create 150,000 new jobs, and reduce unemployment to below 4.5% in 2009. This package is not expected to return the country to positive growth. In fact, as global demand is showing no signs of improvement, analysts said Taiwan's economic contraction could tighten even further in the first quarter of 2009. The statistics agency said it expects a contraction in 2009 of almost 3%, which would be the worst since 1962, when the agency's records began. It also expects exports to slump 20% in 2009, a sharp deterioration from 2008 growth of 3.64%.

Taiwan's challenge in future economic development lies in countering the threat posed by labor-intensive economies, such as China and Vietnam. With the prospect of continued relocation of labor-intensive industries to economies with cheaper work forces, Taiwan's future development will have to rely on further transformation to a high technology and service-oriented economy, and in continued diversification of its trade markets beyond the United States and China.

SUPPORT FOR INWARD INVESTMENT AND IMPORTS

The Department of Investment Services (DOIS) promotes Taiwan as an investment destination among foreign and Taiwanese businesses, and seeks to consolidate the strength of public and private-sector businesses in Taiwan. The DOIS carries out industrial assistance programs to help Taiwanese companies operating overseas and in mainland China to develop their businesses, on both a local and international level. In addition, the DOIS plans and formulates programs to recruit science and technology personnel from abroad, while maintaining a talent search database to assist Taiwanese companies in their recruitment efforts.

TAX EXEMPTIONS

The Ministry of Economic Affairs (MOEA) offers a variety of tax incentives for industrial development aimed at encouraging corporate investment and increasing R&D, personnel training, and new equipment and technology among Taiwan companies. Information can be found on its website.

▸▸ MORE INFO

Websites:

Department of Investment Services (DOIS): investintaiwan.nat.gov.tw/en/

Ministry of Economic Affairs (MOEA), tax incentives: www.investintaiwan.nat.gov.tw/en/opp/incentives/tax_incentives/

Taiwan news portal: www.etaiwannews.com/etn/index_en.php

Taiwan investment guide: www.dois.moea.gov.tw/tig/english/page.asp?class_id=4&page=1

  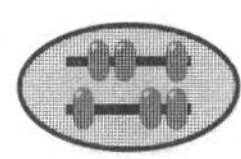 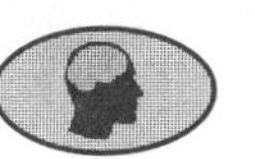     

Thailand

ECONOMY AND TRADE

With a well-developed infrastructure, a free-enterprise economy, and generally pro-investment policies, Thailand was one of East Asia's best performers from 2002–2004, averaging more than 6% annual real GDP growth.

Although the country recovered slowly from the 1997 economic crisis, domestic political uncertainty, rising violence in Thailand's four southernmost provinces, and repercussions from the devastating Indian Ocean tsunami of 2004 led to a slowing down of real GDP growth to 4–5% between 2005 and 2007. Much of this slowdown was led by falling exports, which in 2007 accounted for 70% of GDP.

The 2008 global financial crisis has further darkened Thailand's economic horizon. Continued political uncertainty will hamper the resumption of infrastructure mega-projects. Tourism—a significant contributor to the Thai economy (about 6%)—has also been hard hit. Thanks to the political protests that closed Bangkok's airports from late November to early December 2008, tourism figures declined significantly at the end of December.

Future economic performance depends on continued reform of the financial sector, attracting foreign investment, and improving domestic investment and consumption, to balance Thailand's past reliance on exports. Thailand also faces the challenge of institutionalizing social protection mechanisms to help workers and vulnerable persons, including the poor, women, children, the elderly, and the disabled.

ECONOMIC POLICY OVER 12 MONTHS

As export growth weakened in 2008, and inflationary pressure became less of a concern, the Bank of Thailand loosened monetary policy. Interest rates were reduced to 1.5% by February 2009, and the baht was allowed to depreciate relative to the dollar to stimulate exports.

In January 2009, a month after the new government was inaugurated, a US$3.3 billion economic stimulus package was approved. The funds will be used to support social security, free education programs, create jobs, and provide low-interest loans to farmers. The government will also extend a package of economic stimulus measures implemented by the previous government by another six months. These include lower water and electricity charges, free rides on some of Bangkok's public buses, and free third-class train rides nationwide. A portion of the funds will be doled out in a one-off allowance of US$57 to nine million low-income, private-sector employees and government officials.

This was supported by a US$1.2 billion economic stimulus package of tax cuts, approved later in January 2009. The package includes a new personal income-tax deduction on mortgage-loan principal payments of up to US$8,572 per year—a significant change from existing rules, where only interest payments of up to US$2,857 per year can be deducted from personal income tax. The property tax incentives will apply only to new homebuyers who make purchases this year, although existing homebuyers will still be eligible for a tax deduction of US$2,857 a year for mortgage interest payments.

Small and medium-sized enterprises (SMEs) in all sectors earning less than US$28,572 will also be exempted from income taxes. The tax allowance will benefit up to 970,000 SMEs. As part of an attempt to boost the venture capital business, the government also agreed to exempt income tax on gains arising from share transfers of SMEs, and scrap initial capital requirements for the venture capital provided. Exemptions on income tax, value-added tax, special business tax, and stamp tax on income generated from asset transfers, asset disposals, and other transactions stemming from debt restructuring were also included.

To stimulate tourism, the government allowed higher tax deductions for companies that pay for seminars or meetings. The cabinet agreed to waive visa fees for three months, cut the landing fee by 20% for regular flights, and by up to 50% for chartered flights, and waive property tax for hotel operators. An exemption on entrance fees for national parks was allowed in a bid to revive its key tourism industry.

ECONOMIC PERFORMANCE OVER 12 MONTHS

In the final quarter of 2008, the pace of GDP growth evidently weakened as various adverse factors, both domestic and global, intensified. The marked slip in global growth caused Thai exports to shrink in this quarter, both in value and volume terms. In December 2008, a coalition government, headed by Democrat Party leader, Abhisit Vejjajiva, was installed. The period immediately preceding this had been marked by increased political unrest, culminating in protesters storming Bangkok airport in November and December 2008, adversely affecting the country's tourism industry, and hammering already-soft private-sector confidence. Thailand has seen its exports particularly badly hit by the global downturn, recording a 26% fall in January 2009. Thailand's Ministry of Finance has accordingly revised its forecast for GDP growth in 2008, from September 2008's 5.1% forecast, down to 3.0%. Additionally, the GDP growth forecast for 2009 has been set at between 0% and 2.0%.

The Bank of Thailand's Inflation Report, issued on January 23, 2009, forecasts a consumer price index

STATISTICS

GDP growth: 3.0% (2008, est., Ministry of Finance)

GDP per capita: US$8,700 (2008, est.)

CPI: 5.5% (2008, est.)

Key interest rate: 1.5% (February 2009)

Exchange rate versus dollar: baht per US dollar—33.37 (2008, est.)

Unemployment: 1.2% (2008, est.)

FDI: US$80.83 billion (2007, est.)

Current account deficit/surplus: −US$1.049 billion (2008, est.)

Population: 65,905,410

Note: estimates for this country explicitly take into account the effects of excess mortality due to Aids; this can result in lower life expectancy, higher infant mortality, higher death rates, lower population growth rates, and changes in the distribution of population by age and sex than would otherwise be expected (2009, est.).

Source: CIA Factbook except where stated

(CPI) inflation rate of between –1.5% and 0.5% in 2009, and a core inflation rate of between 0.5% and 1.5%, reflecting increasing downward pressure on commodity prices.

Thailand's political scene will remain unstable in the forecast period, owing to the persistent power struggle between, on one side, the established bureaucratic and royalist elites, and the urban middle class; and on the other, the rural populations, lower income families, and other forces aligned with Thaksin Shinawatra, the former prime minister who was ousted in the September 2006 military coup.

Particularly worrisome are the country's projected exports for 2009, which are expected to decline by 10%. Commentators are urging the Thai government to accelerate the disbursement of its budgeted expenditures, promote investment in each province, find ways to end the political unrest, restore confidence among investors, and promote tourism.

According to *The Economist*, the economy will contract sharply in 2009, as the global economic slowdown will have a negative impact on exports. Ongoing concerns about political stability will also continue to prevent a major improvement in consumer and investor sentiment in the early part of the forecast period. However, as the global economy picks up, GDP growth in Thailand will accelerate to an average annual rate of 3.6% in 2011–2013.

The fall in global prices for crude oil and non-oil commodities from the highs that they reached in 2008 should also contribute to a more benign outlook for inflation in the forecast period.

SUPPORT FOR INWARD INVESTMENT AND IMPORTS

Thailand is keen to encourage inward investment, particularly in view of the slowing global economy, and has declared 2009 as the "Year of Investment." The Board of Investment is the government organization dealing with facilitating investment.

TAX EXEMPTIONS

Tax exemptions for companies setting up businesses in Thailand include corporate tax holidays for eight years, and a waiver of import/export duties on equipment used within the business. For 2008–2009, increased incentives have been introduced for six priority industries comprising alternative energy, high technology, environmentally friendly products, tourism, high-tech agricultural and mega-projects. Further information is available at: www.pwc.com/extweb/service.nsf/docid/ACFD0E3D3688819ECA257527 00354A2C

▸▸ MORE INFO

Websites:

Thai news portal: enews.mcot.net

Board of Investment website, with information and advice for companies looking to invest in Thailand: www.boi.go.th/english/

Tunisia

ECONOMY AND TRADE

Tunisia has a diverse economy, with important agricultural, mining, tourism, petroleum products, and manufacturing sectors. It also has one of Africa's highest levels of GDP per capita.

Governmental control of economic affairs, while still significant, has gradually lessened over the past decade with increasing privatization, simplification of the tax structure, and a prudent approach to debt. Progressive social policies have also helped raise living conditions in Tunisia, relative to the region.

World Bank and IMF support, coupled with prudent economic policies implemented by the Tunisian government in the mid-1980s after a balance of payments crisis, has resulted in regular stable growth. Real growth has averaged almost 5% over the past decade, although Tunisia will need to reach even higher growth levels to create sufficient employment opportunities for its population.

The challenges ahead include privatizing industry, liberalizing the investment code to increase foreign investment, improving government efficiency, reducing the trade deficit, and reducing socioeconomic disparities in the impoverished south and west.

ECONOMIC POLICY OVER 12 MONTHS

Real growth, which averaged almost 5% over the past decade, is set to decline in 2009 because of economic contraction and slowing of import demand in Europe, Tunisia's largest export market. However, development of non-textile manufacturing, a recovery in agricultural production, and strong growth in the services sector have mitigated the economic effect of slowing exports.

Tunisia's 11th development plan, called "Towards a new level of growth," covers the period 2007–2011. In terms of macroeconomic policy, it is aiming for an average budget deficit of 2.5% of GDP (not including privatizations), an average current deficit of 2.6% of GDP and external indebtedness at 39.1% of available revenue by 2011, as well as for an average inflation rate in the range of 2.8% per year.

The active, but prudent policy of opening up the country's economy, accompanied by support and

STATISTICS

GDP growth: 3.4% (2008, Central Bank)

GDP per capita: US$8,000 (2008, est.)

CPI: 4.1% (December 2008, Central Bank)

Key interest rate: 4.5% (February 2009, Central Bank)

Exchange rate versus dollar: Tunisian dinars per US dollar—1.211 (2008, est.)

Unemployment: 14% (2008, est.)

FDI: US$28.51 billion (2008, est.)

Current account deficit/surplus: –US$993 million (2008, est.)

Population: 10,383,577 (July 2008, est.)

Source: CIA Factbook except where stated

incentives for businesses and industry, made it possible to successfully establish the Tunisia–EU Free Trade Zone in January 2008. There was a significant amount of progress towards greater privatization and liberalization in 2008. In the 2009 budget, the government increased its spending plans by 12% to above US$12 billion, on the back of US$1.75 billion in foreign investment flows and a GDP growth rate of 5%.

Tunisia has also entered into a new phase of opening up its economy, in order to diversify its exports and trading partners: the European Union, with 80% of exports, is its leading partner. The global financial crisis is expected to have an impact on the real economy, and sustaining investment will be critical if the country is to achieve the growth target of 5% in 2009.

The central bank is moving from direct management of the financial sector towards a more traditional supervisory and regulatory role. Commercial banks are permitted to participate in the forward foreign-exchange market. The dinar is convertible for current account transactions, but some convertible dinar/foreign-exchange account transactions still require central bank authorization. Total convertibility of the Tunisian dinar is probably still some years away. The dinar is traded on an intra-bank market around a managed float established by the central bank (based upon a basket of the euro, the US dollar and the Japanese yen).

In 2008, Tunisia concluded agreements with the World Bank, the European Development Bank, and the African Bank to increase the amount of funding for its projects.

ECONOMIC PERFORMANCE OVER 12 MONTHS

On a macroeconomic level, Tunisia has posted healthy growth numbers while managing to keep a lid on inflation. GDP growth in 2008 stood at 3.5%, down from 6.3% in 2007, but a strong showing nonetheless, particularly given the slowdown in the Eurozone, Tunisia's largest trading bloc, and despite a disappointing agricultural season, and a decrease in hydrocarbon and mining production. Furthermore, despite massive rises in commodity prices—from building materials to foodstuffs—inflation came in at a modest 5%, compared to record price rises in excess of 12% in other countries in the region, such as Egypt or Jordan. In February 2009, the central bank said that it expected the economy to expand by 0.5% in 2009, from 3.4% in 2008.

Tunisia's domestic banking sector, which has faced a number of problems in recent years, posted impressive numbers for 2008. The banking sector's fundamentals appear to be steadily improving. An IMF report in July 2008 declared that the sector has been increasingly aggressive in improving the sustainability of its lending practices, with a decline of more than seven percentage points in bad loans since 2004. Tunisia's banking sector still often serves as the private sector's lender of first resort, but local enterprises are increasingly turning to capital markets as a source of financing. The volume of foreign investments in Tunisia increased from TND2 billion in 2007 to TND3.1 billion dinars in 2008.

Tunisia's more traditional industries have also been showing strong growth. Despite the slowdown in its European markets, tourism, one of Tunisia's key economic sectors and the country's second-largest employer after agriculture, grew steadily over the first nine months of 2008, with record revenues expected by the end of the year. Official figures released in October showed that Tunisia's tourism revenues rose by 9% year-on-year to approximately US$1.8 billion for the first nine months of 2008.

The physical appearance of the country is changing rapidly as well, with a set of colossal real-estate and infrastructure projects planned. They include a new US$700m airport, and a US$2bn deepwater port in nearby Enfidha, both of which will help increase the republic's transit links with neighboring countries. Work has also begun on a new regional railway network, as well as on numerous roads, hotels, and tourist resorts along the Mediterranean coast.

SUPPORT FOR INWARD INVESTMENT AND IMPORTS

Tunisia has made efforts to diversify its economy, to establish a stringent regulatory framework, and to improve its risk rating to attract foreign investors. Tunisia is emerging as a bridge between Europe and North Africa for many foreign investors, in particular those from the Gulf Cooperation Council. Information on investing in Tunisia is available from the Invest in Tunisia website.

TAX EXEMPTIONS

Tunisia has enacted several laws to encourage foreign investment in the industrial, services, finance, and tourism sectors. Various incentives are provided (exemptions, reduced rates, financial support, investment bonuses, a full tax allowance, etc.) through the Investment Incentives code.

MORE INFO

Websites:

Invest in Tunisia: www.investintunisia.tn/site/en/

Investment Incentives code: www.investintunisia.tn/site/en/article.php?id_article=789

Tunisia news portal: www.tunisiaonlinenews.com

Turkey

ECONOMY AND TRADE

Turkey has a dynamic economy, combining modern industry and commerce with a traditional agriculture sector that still accounts for around 9% of GDP and 27% of employment. The state still plays a major role in areas such as basic industry, banking, transport, and communication, but the private sector is strong and also growing rapidly.

A major economic crisis in 2001 led the economy to contract by 9.5%. Since then, however, the Turkish economy has grown strongly—on average by around 6% per year from 2002 to 2007. More recently, the turmoil in the financial markets and the resulting global recession has caused GDP growth to fall sharply to 1.1% in 2008.

Moderate economic growth and high levels of foreign direct investment in recent years indicate that economic fundamentals are sound. Further economic and judicial reforms, as well as the prospect of EU membership, may also boost foreign direct investment. However, the ongoing global slowdown is likely to lead to more negative figures for the Turkish economy. Unemployment—currently around 10%—and large income disparities across society as well as different regions are also still major problems.

STATISTICS

GDP growth: 1.1% (2008, Statistics Office)
GDP per capita: US$12,900 (2008, est.)
CPI: 10.2% (2008, est.)
Key interest rate: 10.5% (March 2009, Central Bank)
Exchange rate versus dollar: Turkish liras per US dollar—1.3179 (2008, est.)
Unemployment: 7.9%, plus underemployment of 4% (2008, est.)
FDI: US$124.8 billion (2008, est.)
Current account deficit/surplus: −US$51.68 billion (2008, est.)
Population: 76,805,524 (July 2009, est.)
Source: CIA Factbook except where stated

ECONOMIC POLICY OVER 12 MONTHS

The government ended its formal IMF program in May 2008, following significant falls in inflation and public-debt ratios, strong, sustained economic growth, and record levels of foreign direct investment (estimated at US$22.3 billion in the year to May 2008). However, this has also left the government with the important question of how to strike an appropriate future balance between preserving the rigorous fiscal policy stance—anchored by the IMF previously, and decisive in restoring macroeconomic stability—while still managing sustained growth in a difficult environment.

A series of large privatizations, the start of Turkey's EU membership negotiations, strong sustained growth, and structural changes in the private sector, have all contributed to the rise in foreign investment. Turkey has also taken steps to improve its investment climate further through no longer requiring foreign investments to be screened, streamlining bureaucratic processes, implementing bilateral investment and tax treaties, and strengthening intellectual property legislation. However, problems still exist, as evidenced by recent disputes involving foreign investors in Turkey. High taxation and the need to build further on the reforms already implemented, particularly with regard to intellectual property, are also potential deterrents.

Internally, the government also passed a revised social security law in early 2008, which restructures the pension system, and will be a major step forward in strengthening the long-term sustainability of Turkey's public finances. Furthermore, the decision to publish fully fledged general government accounts, according to international accounting standards, from 2009 onwards will be an important step in enhancing fiscal transparency, and government accountability,

To reverse surges in inflation in early 2008, the central bank had moved to a tightening bias, but monetary policy subsequently eased significantly as the global crisis worsened. Policymakers slashed Turkey's benchmark borrowing rate by 6.25% between November 2008 and March 2009, taking it to a record low of 10.5%.

Worryingly, negotiations with the IMF with a view to signing a new standby loan had not been concluded by March 2009. In particular, differences remain unresolved over the parameters for fiscal discipline, and the IMF's calls for continued structural fiscal reforms, including the adoption of a more rules-based fiscal framework, and strengthened tax administration. The picture is complicated by the OECD's assertion that Turkey also needs to support investor confidence, especially given the large current account deficit, and the increased volatility of the exchange rate. According to the IMF, greater fiscal transparency and the implementation of credible spending rules would facilitate the operation of automatic stabilizers without undermining confidence.

ECONOMIC PERFORMANCE OVER 12 MONTHS

By the conclusion of the last Stand-By Arrangement (SBA) with the IMF in May 2008, Turkey's economy had developed significantly: inflation had dropped from perennial double-digit numbers to its lowest levels for 35 years, public-debt ratios had declined sharply, the banking system had been restructured, and the country was enjoying a prolonged economic expansion.

Since then, the economy has slowed sharply, as weakness in domestic demand was compounded by the turbulence in financial markets, and the resulting global slowdown, which hit exports hard. Furthermore, the current-account deficit had widened considerably over the course of the economic expansion, thanks to strong capital inflows and rising commodity prices, which stoked inflationary pressures. Together, these factors weigh heavily on Turkey's economic outlook, and have heightened risks, due to the private sector's significant reliance on external financing.

The Ministry of Finance budget data up to January 2009 confirms the deterioration in the country's economic prospects. GDP growth has slowed sharply, falling by 6.2 percentage points in the final quarter of 2008, while inflation has now crept back into double figures. The rate of unemployment also rose to a record 12.3% in November 2008. The currency has also not been immune—the Turkish lira slid around 25% against the dollar in 2008, mostly in the final months of the year.

Political developments have also distracted attention from an ambitious economic agenda. In 2008, Turkish financial markets weathered significant domestic political turmoil, including the attempted closure of the ruling Justice and Development Party (AKP) over accusations of having an Islamist agenda. More recently, in local elections in March 2009, the AKP saw its vote share decline for the first time since it came to power in 2002. The move has been widely interpreted by market analysts as reflecting growing discontent over the economic downturn, which has led to calls for the government to speed up negotiations with the IMF to finalize a deal, and reinstate investor confidence.

The Economist Intelligence Unit expects the Central Bank of Turkey to cut interest rates further in 2009, as concerns over liquidity and the weakening economy mount. According to the OECD, growth is expected to decline to below 2% in 2009 before recovering to 4.25% in 2010, in line with their projected global recovery.

SUPPORT FOR INWARD INVESTMENT AND IMPORTS

The Republic of Turkey Prime Ministry Investment Support and Promotion Agency (ISPAT) is the official organization for encouraging and promoting investment in Turkey. Particular support is given to the manufacturing and energy sectors, and for investment in "priority development regions."

TAX EXEMPTIONS

There are significant tax incentives in Turkey, including those for R&D and industrial businesses. In particular, there are 20 free trade zones in Turkey, with advantages including corporate tax, income tax, and VAT exemptions.

MORE INFO

Websites:

Republic of Turkey Prime Ministry Investment Support and Promotion Agency website (ISPAT): www.invest.gov.tr

Comprehensive website on tax in Turkey, including information on tax incentives: www.gib.gov.tr/index.php?id=505

Tax exemption information: www.gib.gov.tr/index.php?id=533

News website: www.hurriyet.com.tr/english/home/

Turks and Caicos Islands

ECONOMY AND TRADE

The Turks and Caicos Islands are a British Overseas Territory. Broad policies are set by the United Kingdom, while the day-to-day management of the government and economy are the responsibility of a locally elected government.

The main drivers of the economy are tourism and offshore financial services. There is also a sizeable fishing industry, which is a valuable export earner. The only other notable industry is construction, which is largely geared towards improving tourism infrastructure. Most capital goods and food for domestic consumption are imported.

The economy was sluggish in the early part of this decade, but has expanded strongly since 2003, growing by 13.9% in 2005. However, some aid from the United Kingdom is still needed to balance the budget, and fund capital projects.

More recently, the islands have been hit by political turmoil after the Governor suspended self-government following corruption allegations, and the Queen made an order giving the Governor the power to rule directly, while an investigation took place. The move has been heavily criticized by other countries in the region.

ECONOMIC POLICY OVER 12 MONTHS

Government economic policy stresses growth and diversification, particularly focusing on tourism—seen as the key to the islands' future economic well-being, and now worth about US$500 million to the islands' economy—and the offshore sector. Under pressure from London, the European Union and global organizations such as the OECD, the government has committed to improving transparency, establishing better exchange of information in tax matters, and has introduced a tighter regulatory structure to prevent fraud and money-laundering.

The islands are currently in the midst of advanced preplanning processes for the preparation of a long-term, 10-year, sustainable development plan. The aim is to create a knowledge-driven and internationally competitive economy, with particular regard to those sectors that generate foreign exchange for the coun-

STATISTICS

GDP growth: 11.2% (2007 preliminary, Dept. of Economic Planning and Statistics)

GDP per capita: US$23,768 (2007 preliminary, Dept. of Economic Planning and Statistics)

CPI: 3.7% (2007, Dept. of Economic Planning and Statistics)

Key interest rate: N/A

Exchange rate versus dollar: N/A, the US dollar is used

Unemployment: 5.4% (2007, Dept. of Economic Planning and Statistics)

FDI: N/A

Current account deficit/surplus: N/A

Population: 36,605 (2008, Dept. of Economic Planning and Statistics)

Source: CIA Factbook except where stated

try. Specific economic goals include maintaining rates of balanced growth in the high-single digits; diversifying the economy, including with the assistance of foreign investment; greater local participation; and exploiting the islands' resources to create a sustainable economy.

The steps taken so far include: land use/zoning plan for the family of islands; population projections for the future growth, currently estimated to increase to 35,000 in 10 years, and, possibly, to above 60,000 in 20 years; sectoral development plans—some of which are currently implemented—for education, tourism, housing, solid-waste management, immigration, and citizenship law reform; and profiles reviewing the economic and social conditions on each island, their needs, and prospects.

However, there are challenges. The current lack of diversification means that the economy is heavily reliant on tourism—dangerous in a global economic slowdown—and a narrow set of export-oriented activities. Furthermore, existing tourist facilities are concentrated on one island, which potentially could lead to large disparities between different islands as the economy grows and develops. The islands are also hampered by a lack of physical infrastructure, which will need to be expanded significantly if the ambitious policy plans are to be met. This is likely to incur considerable costs, and it is unclear how much fiscal room for maneuver the state actually has, given its limited revenue base.

To combat these, the government has adopted an "Open Arms" investment policy that highlights the country's no-tax status, and offers investors a streamlined bureaucracy for licensing and immigration, access to government-owned land under long-term leases at reasonable rates, and a range of duty concessions to investors, who construct "approved" projects throughout the country, with more generous concessions for the lesser-developed islands. There is no income or company tax, which it is hoped will also help attract more offshore financial companies. There are indications that this is working, as more than 10,000 international businesses were registered in the islands in the early 21st century.

ECONOMIC PERFORMANCE OVER 12 MONTHS

The Turks and Caicos Islands underwent rapid economic growth from the mid-1980s onwards, with an average annual GDP growth rate of 8% by the early 21st century. The recent economic success is evidenced by the fact that the islands no longer receive direct grant aid from the United Kingdom. The major drivers were the rapid rise of luxury tourism and offshore financial services, two sectors on which the economy is now heavily reliant.

The islands have been hit hard on both fronts by the global slowdown, which has renewed the government's drive to diversify the economy. Visitors from the United States, Canada, and other countries are down by 15–20% because of the global slowdown, which has reduced the money flowing into tourism, and the real-estate sector. This has led to a decrease in two of the primary sources of revenue for the government—the stamp duties paid on purchases and taxes on hotels, restaurants, and departures. Local businesses such as estate agents, lawyers, the construction industry, and retail outlets have also been affected.

The problem is compounded as the overall government budget balance is not stable, showing a small surplus in 2007 before slipping back into the red in 2008. The unemployment rate has also increased over the last year, and is now 9.7% of the labor force.

The islands have also been rocked by a number of corruption and sex scandals over the last year, involving senior members of the government, including the Premier, Michael Misick. Most notably, a commission was established last year to investigate allegations of corruption among the government, following a review of the administration by members of the British parliament. Subsequently, in March 2009, the Governor invoked an order from the Queen, and suspended self-government while the investigation took place. The order will remain in place for two years, although it can also be extended or revoked. The matter has caused some controversy, with several neighboring countries heavily criticizing the decision, and the Caribbean Community (CARICOM) issuing a statement lending their support for the people of the Turks and Caicos against the suspension of the constitution.

SUPPORT FOR INWARD INVESTMENT AND IMPORTS

Attracting quality investments to create a sustainable economy for the Turks and Caicos Islands is a major objective of the TCI Government. TCInvest (Turks and Caicos Islands Investment Agency) an independent agency with a mandate to attract new offshore investment, encourages entrepreneurship among residents, and provides financing to the local population.

TAX EXEMPTIONS

TCI is a tax haven, and the government's "open arms" investment policy brings the additional advantages of an attractive package of concessions to qualified investors. These include streamlined immigration procedures, access to government land, and a variety of duty concessions. More information is available from TCInvest.

▸▸ MORE INFO

Websites:

Turks and Caicos Islands government portal: www.gov.tc

TCInvest: www.tcinvest.tc/tcinvest.htm

Weekly news website: www.tcweeklynews.com

  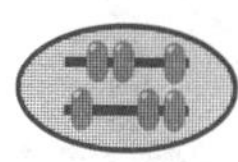      

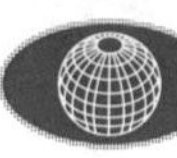

United Arab Emirates

ECONOMY AND TRADE

The United Arab Emirates (UAE) is a confederation of seven emirates, formed in 1971 by the then Trucial States after gaining independence from Britain. Each state—Abu Dhabi, Dubai, Ajman, Fujairah, Ras al Khaimah, Sharjah, and Umm al Qaiwain—maintains a large degree of independence, but the UAE is governed by the Supreme Council of Rulers made up of the seven emirs, who appoint the prime minister and the cabinet.

Before oil was discovered in the 1950s, the economy was based on fishing and a declining pearling industry. However, since 1962, when Abu Dhabi became the first of the emirates to begin exporting oil, the UAE's fortunes have been transformed. The oil industry has attracted a large influx of foreign workers, who, together with expatriates, now account for more than three-quarters of the population. The confederation's growing business sector, and its tourist industry, have helped to fuel a construction boom, with billions of dollars being pumped into showpiece schemes.

The best known of the emirates is the business center of Dubai. The largest, Abu Dhabi, covers 80% of the land mass, and holds most of the UAE's vast oil and gas reserves. The UAE has the world's third-largest conventional oil reserves, and its fifth-largest natural gas reserves. The UAE is the Middle East's second-largest economy after Saudi Arabia.

STATISTICS

GDP growth: 7.5% (2008, government figures)
GDP per capita: US$40,400 (2008, est.)
CPI: 14% (2008 average, government figures)
Key interest rate: 1% (March 2009)
Exchange rate versus dollar: Emirati dirham (AED) per US dollar—3.673 (2008 est.)
Unemployment: 2.4% (2001)
FDI: US$62.69 billion (2008, est.)
Current-account deficit/surplus US$62 billion (IIF)
Population: 4,621,399 (July 2008, est.)
Source: CIA Factbook except where stated

ECONOMIC POLICY OVER 12 MONTHS

The government of Abu Dhabi, which dominates the economy of the UAE, set out a long-term, strategic, economic development program in a document titled *Abu Dhabi Economic Vision 2030*, published in 2008. This program seeks to diversify the economy so that non-oil growth outstrips oil-sector growth within 20 years. The government aims to create a sustainable, knowledge-based, and globally integrated economy by 2030, with the non-oil sector of the economy accounting for 64% of GDP.

The role of government over this period will change: it will become a regulator, rather than a provider of public services—a goal intended to facilitate the development of the private sector. The government will seek to encourage the development of industries and services in which the emirate has a competitive advantage, including tourism and logistics, and will also focus on enhancing the quality of healthcare, education, and training in the country.

The other emirates in the UAE are similarly seeking to diversify their economies away from dependence on oil, and are investing heavily to attain this goal. This may help to offset the impact of the global financial crisis, and the collapse in oil prices on the UAE. In March 2009, the International Monetary Fund (IMF) said that the UAE planned to implement projects worth a total of US$918 billion over the next few years. The emphasis will be on the real-estate industry, which will attract US$607 billion in investment. A further US$137.5 billion will be invested in infrastructure.

However, the global economic slowdown is inflicting pain on the UAE. In March 2009, Voice of America (VOA) quoted the market-research firm Proleads as saying that more than half of the construction projects in the UAE, worth US$582 billion, had been put on hold.

Dubai has been regarded as the emirate most vulnerable to the global financial crisis. Unlike its neighbor, Abu Dhabi, Dubai does not have vast oil and gas reserves to fall back on. Dubai's growth was thus financed with debt, not oil money. It embraced globalization, and aggressively diversified its economy into non-oil sectors such as financial services, tourism, and real estate. Dubai is home to some of the most ambitious building projects on the planet, including the world's tallest tower and the world's biggest shopping mall.

However, the real-estate market in Dubai began to unravel in 2008 as the credit crisis deepened. Potential buyers could no longer raise mortgages, and prices began to tumble, leading to funding problems for some Dubai developers. Thousands of construction workers subsequently lost their jobs, while expats returned home, further undermining the property market. The tourism market is also being hit. Western tourists are cutting back on spending, and occupancy rates at many of Dubai's luxury hotels are down.

In March 2009, however, the Dubai government launched a US$20 billion bond program, and sold the first US$10 billion tranche to the UAE central bank, a move that calmed worries that Dubai could default on some US$15–20 billion in debts due for refinancing in 2009. Richard Thompson, editor of the *Middle East Economic Digest*, further told the VOA: "We are optimistic of oil prices returning. Banks should start lending in the latter half of this year, when the bailouts start filtering through. There will be a very quick rebound in Dubai."

The monetary authorities in the UAE have also been very active in taking measures to offset the impact of the credit crunch. From September 2008 onwards, the UAE central bank slashed interest rates, promised to guarantee bank deposits, and offered US$32.67 billion worth of emergency facilities for banks to bolster the financial system, and unfreeze credit markets.

  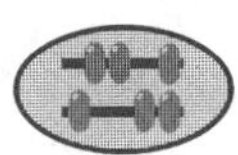   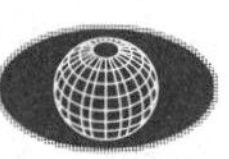   

ECONOMIC PERFORMANCE OVER 12 MONTHS

Massive investment spending by the government should help to insulate the UAE from the global economic slowdown. In March 2009, officials in Abu Dhabi said that they expected the emirate's economy to grow by 4.5% in 2009, down from around 7.5% in 2008. They also anticipate that the Abu Dhabi economy will grow by 7% a year for the six years after 2009, and by 6% a year thereafter. However, other analysts are less optimistic about the country's growth prospects in 2009.

A surge in its oil export income and other revenues boosted the UAE's fiscal surplus by 55% in 2008 but the balance is expected to decline sharply in 2009. From around US$53 billion in 2007, the surplus in the country's consolidated finances jumped to a record US$82.8 billion in 2008, according to figures from the Institute of International Finance (IIF). The surge was a result of a 41% leap in the UAE's total revenues, which hit an all-time high of US$133 billion in 2008, compared with US$93.9 billion in 2007.

The overall surplus increased despite a 22% surge in expenditure to nearly US$49.5 billion in 2008, from around US$40.5 billion in 2007. However, the UAE's investment income, mainly from assets controlled by the Abu Dhabi Investment Authority (Adia), fell to a four-year low of around US$6.5 billion in 2008, from nearly US$12.5 billion in 2007. Adia's assets are believed to have experienced sharp falls in the second half of 2008, as a result of the global financial crisis. However, according to the Saudi American Bank (Samba), Adia remains in control of an asset portfolio worth up to US$800bn.

Samba expects the UAE's fiscal and current-account surpluses to drop sharply in 2009 because of the collapse in oil prices, and a sharp cut in the country's crude output, in line with Opec's agreement to slash supplies to revive oil prices. But Samba still anticipates that the current-account balance and consolidated fiscal accounts will be in healthy surplus. The Energy Information Administration of the US Department of Energy estimates that the UAE's oil earnings hit a record US$89bn in 2008. According to the IIF, the UAE's current-account surplus also reached a record US$62bn in 2008, or around 23% of GDP, compared with US$36bn, or 19% of GDP, in 2007.

The economic slowdown and tumbling international commodity prices are having a positive impact on inflation. In March 2009, Hamad Buamin, Director-General of the Dubai Chamber of Commerce and Industry, predicted that inflation would fall to between 6% and 8% in 2009, from 14% in 2008.

SUPPORT FOR INWARD INVESTMENT AND IMPORTS

The government is keen to encourage private investment from both local and foreign investors. The government says that, to facilitate investment, it has focused on the provision of first-class industrial facilities and business support services, reducing bureaucracy and streamlining administrative procedures, as well as updating commercial laws and regulations to meet international obligations. It has also sought to increase transparency and ensure effective protection for investors. The Abu Dhabi Chamber of Commerce and Industry (ADC) can provide information and guidance on investing in the UAE.

The UAE is a member of the World Trade Organization. The UAE's applied tariff, based on the Gulf Cooperation Council's (a trade bloc of six Arab states on the Persian Gulf) common external tariff, is low, at an average of 5%; most of the UAE's applied MFN tariffs (except on alcohol and tobacco) are zero or 5%. The entire tariff is bound, but some 30 applied rates exceed bindings. Customs procedures are simple, facilitating trade. For further information on importing into the UAE, see the website of the country's Customs service.

TAX EXEMPTIONS

There is no federal tax legislation in the UAE. Each emirate has its own tax regime. For further information, see the website of the UAE's Ministry of Finance.

▸▸ MORE INFO

Websites:

Abu Dhabi Chamber of Commerce and Industry (ADC): www.adcci-uae.com

Government information on UAE's business environment: www.uae.gov.ae/government/business.htm

Portal for government ministries and agencies: www.government.ae/gov/en/index.jsp

UAE Customs: www.dxbcustoms.gov.ae/content/home

UAE's Ministry of Finance: www.mofi.gov.ae

See Also:

✔ Middle East: Regulatory Structure and Powers (p. 1041)

United Kingdom

ECONOMY AND TRADE

The United Kingdom is the fifth-largest economy in the world, with a forecast GDP of US$2.8 trillion in 2008. This highly developed, diversified, market-based economy has extensive social welfare services, and is a leading trading power and financial center.

Over the past two decades, the government has greatly reduced public ownership. Private enterprise now accounts for approximately four-fifths of employment and output. The United Kingdom has large coal, natural gas, and oil resources, but its oil and natural gas reserves are declining, and the United Kingdom became a net importer of energy in 2005. The economy is increasingly services-based, with its capital, London, a leading international financial center. The country is the world's second-largest foreign direct investment destination. Unemployment and inflation levels are among the lowest within the European

  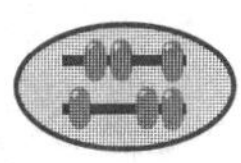      

Union. Britain remains outside the European Economic and Monetary Union (EMU) and public opinion is largely opposed to joining the euro.

London will host the 2012 Olympics, which is set to make it a focus of regeneration and improvements in transportation infrastructure.

ECONOMIC POLICY OVER 12 MONTHS

The global economic slowdown, tight credit, and falling home prices pushed Britain into recession in the latter half of 2008, and prompted the center-left government to implement a number of new measures to stimulate the economy, and stabilize the financial markets; these included part-nationalizing the banking system, cutting taxes, suspending public-sector borrowing rules, and bringing forward public spending on capital projects.

In February 2008, Northern Rock became the first British bank to be nationalized since the 1970s. This development was followed by significant bailouts of other banking institutions, and an injection of £37 billion of new capital into the Royal Bank of Scotland, Halifax Bank of Scotland, and Lloyds TSB, giving the government a significant stake in the banking sector. In October 2008, the government announced a plan to recapitalize banks, guarantee interbank lending, and extend liquidity provisions. The government offered up to £200bn in short-term lending support. The level of individual savings guaranteed by the government was also raised to £50,000.

This program of bailing out stricken banks continued into 2009. In January 2009, Prime Minister Gordon Brown announced the government would implement a capital investment program totaling £40 billion in 2009. Education, transport, and housing have been highlighted as key areas to benefit from the investment. The government also announced new measures to support the United Kingdom banking system, and increase the amount of credit available to consumers and business. Measures included an asset-protection scheme to protect financial institutions against exposure to exceptional losses on certain portfolio assets, an increased stake in the Royal Bank of Scotland, and a £50 billion Bank of England scheme to boost lending by banks through bond purchases. In March 2009, the government increased its stake in the Lloyds Group to 77%, in return for underwriting £260bn of toxic assets.

To support the government's efforts to recapitalize the banking system, the independent Bank of England slashed the key interest rate down from 5.25% in March 2008 to 0.5% in March 2009, the lowest rate on record.

In fiscal measures, the government reduced taxes to spur consumer spending. VAT was cut by 2.5% to 15% for the period of one year from November 2008, the basic rate of tax was reduced from 22% to 20%, and, after significant public pressure, the lowest rate of tax of 10% was reinstated. To support the ailing housing market, stamp duty on property purchases up to the value of £175,000 was also suspended until September 2009.

ECONOMIC PERFORMANCE OVER 12 MONTHS

The United Kingdom proved susceptible to the global economic downturn in 2008. gross domestic product (GDP) contracted by 1.5% in the fourth quarter of 2008. The contraction followed a 0.6% fall in economic growth in the third quarter, and signaled that the United Kingdom was officially in recession. Reasons attributed to this sharp decline were lower spending by businesses and consumers in the United Kingdom, its ailing financial-services sector, and the falling housing market. For 2008 as a whole, GDP rose by 0.7%, down from 3.0% in the previous year.

Output of the production industries fell 4.5% in the fourth quarter of 2008, compared with a fall of 1.7% in the previous quarter, mainly due to declining manufacturing output. Construction output fell 1.1% over the quarter. Output in the service industries fell by 0.9% in the fourth quarter. The trade deficit in real terms decreased from £9.8 billion in the third quarter of 2008, to £8.8 billion in the fourth quarter of 2008.

The second half of 2008 and the beginning of 2009 saw the pound sterling slide against the dollar, and reach new lows against the euro. Chancellor Alistair Darling's plan to increase public borrowing to help the country deal with the recession is set to leave the country's deficit at 8% of GDP—the highest level in post-war history. Rising commodity prices stoked inflation in the first half of 2008. Gas and electricity bills jumped sharply, squeezing disposable income. Inflation reached 5.2% in September—the highest since 1992, and far beyond the Bank of England's target. The subsequent fall in the price of oil helped reduce inflation to an annualized rate of 3% as of January 2009. As consumer spending fell, interest rates were reduced to 0.5%, an all time low.

House prices fell by 2.3% in February 2009, according to the Halifax House Price Index, a fall of 17.7% over the year. Prices fell 16.2% in 2008, thanks largely to the contraction of credit in the mortgage market. The United Kingdom FTSE 100 index declined as banking and mining sectors suffered, falling by 31% over the course of 2008.

Growth is projected to resume only in late 2009. Unemployment is set to rise rapidly, but is expected to

STATISTICS

GDP growth: 0.7% (2008, National Statistics)
GDP per capita: US$37,400 (2008, est.)
CPI: 3.0% (January 2009, National Statistics)
Key interest rate: 0.5% (March 2009)
Exchange rate versus dollar: pound sterling per US dollar—0.5302 (2008, est.)
Unemployment: 6.3% (2008, National Statistics)
FDI: US$1.409 trillion (2008, est.)
Current account deficit/surplus: −US$72.54 billion (2008, est.)
Population: 60,943,912 (July 2008, est.)
Source: CIA Factbook except where stated

▸▸ MORE INFO

Websites:

United Kingdom leading economic indicators: www.statistics.gov.uk/InstantFigures.asp

United Kingdom Trade and Investment, iInformation for companies looking to invest in the United Kingdom: www.ukinvest.gov.uk

Inland Revenue: www.inlandrevenue.gov.uk

See Also:

✔ United Kingdom: Regulatory Structure and Powers (p. 1055)
✔ Requirements of the UK Combined Code on Corporate Governance (p. 913)

  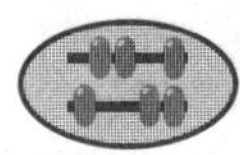   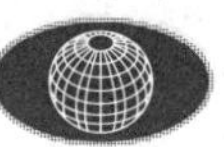 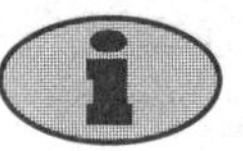  

stabilize in 2010. Fears over inflation have been receding, reflecting the recent falls in energy and food prices and the increasing output gap.

SUPPORT FOR INWARD INVESTMENT AND IMPORTS

The World Bank has ranked the United Kingdom the easiest place to set up a business in Europe, with the average business taking 13 days to set up, against an average of 32 days for the continent. United Kingdom Trade and Investment is the government body focused on maximizing foreign direct investment in the United Kingdom. More information on setting up a United Kingdom business and on support provided by the organization can be found on its website.

TAX EXEMPTIONS

In a deteriorating economy, all tax breaks have been aimed at lower-to-middle-income families, with a reduction of 2% on the second-lowest band of tax to 20%. There are few corporation-tax exemptions, though the top rate of corporation tax is a relatively low 28%. Capital gains tax has been reduced from a tapering system, capping at 40%, to a standard rate of 18%. Further information is available from the Inland Revenue.

United States of America

ECONOMY AND TRADE

The United States has the largest and most technologically powerful economy in the world, with its gross domestic product (GDP) estimated at US$14.6 trillion in 2008. This market-based economy has high levels of research and capital investment, funded by both national, and, because of decreasing saving rates, increasingly by foreign investors. The economy has benefited from the US dollar's status as the global reserve currency.

The country has a two-tier labor market, exacerbated by the development of its technology and services industries. Since 1975, practically all the gains in household income have gone to the top 20% of households.

The war in 2003 between a US-led coalition and Iraq, and the subsequent occupation of Iraq, led to massive increases in funding to the military. Soaring oil prices between 2005 and the first half of 2008 threatened inflation, as higher gasoline prices ate into consumers' budgets, which, in 2008, accounted for 72% of US economic activity. More recently, the economy has been impacted heavily by the ongoing global recession.

Long-term challenges include a low savings rate, inadequate investment in economic infrastructure, rapidly rising medical and pension costs of an ageing population, sizeable trade and budget deficits, and stagnation of family income in the lower economic groups.

ECONOMIC POLICY OVER 12 MONTHS

The past 12 months have seen the United States fighting against the adverse financial conditions that first hit the global economy in 2007. The period has been characterized by aggressive fiscal and monetary easing.

The Federal Funds rate was cut from 3% in March 2008 to a floating rate of 0–0.25% by March 2009. The Federal Reserve also participated in a simultaneous emergency interest-rate cut with the European Central Bank (ECB), the Bank of England, and the central banks of Canada, Sweden, and Switzerland of half a percentage point in October 2008. The Fed has also concentrated on "credit easing" to stimulate specific troubled markets. In November 2008, the Federal Reserve announced an injection of US$800bn into the economy in a further effort to stabilize the financial system, and encourage lending. About US$600bn is to be used to buy up mortgage-backed securities, while US$200bn is being targeted at unfreezing the consumer credit market.

Since May 2008, there have been large tax rebates to provide support to the consumer economy. Several companies have been rescued by the US government over the period, with particular attention paid to the ailing financial and property industries. In September 2008, mortgage lenders Fannie Mae and Freddie Mac—which account for nearly half of the outstanding mortgages in the United States—were taken over by the US government in one of the largest bailouts in US history. In October, lawmakers passed a package allowing the Treasury to spend up to US$700bn buying bad debts from ailing banks under the Troubled Asset Relief Program (TARP), some of which was later spent improving the flow of credit to US consumers. In November, the US government unveiled a US$250bn plan to purchase stakes in a wide variety of banks,

STATISTICS

GDP growth: 1.1% (2008, BEA)
GDP per capita: US$48,000 (2008, est.)
CPI: 0.1% (2008, US Dept of Labor)
Key interest rate: 0–0.25% (March 2009, Federal Reserve)
Exchange rate versus dollar: N/A
Unemployment: 8.1% (February 2009, Bureau of Labor Statistics)
FDI: US$237bn (2007, Department of Commerce)
Current account deficit/surplus –US$568.8 billion (2008, est.)
Population: 303,824,640 (July 2008, est.)
Source: CIA Factbook except where stated

   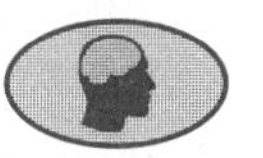     

in an effort to restore confidence in the sector. The Fed announced the purchase of mortgage-backed securities, beginning in January 2009. The government used some of these funds to purchase equity in US banks, and other industrial corporations.

In a presidential election campaign preoccupied with domestic economic malaise, Barack Obama's victory in January 2009 owed much to his focus on resuscitating the US economy. Obama has pledged that his economic recovery package will be at the centerpiece of his administration, and has announced an additional US$787 billion fiscal stimulus package—two-thirds on additional spending and one-third on tax cuts—to save or create up to 3.5 million jobs, and to help the economy recover.

ECONOMIC PERFORMANCE OVER 12 MONTHS

The US economy is going through an exceptionally difficult period after having been hit by converging adverse developments, some in reaction to excesses during the upswing, others created by financial catalysts out of the control of the government. The sharp downturn in the housing market, a financial crisis, and temporarily high commodity prices caused activity to slow sharply during 2008. GDP rose 1.1% over 2008, down from 2.0% in 2007. However, GDP fell at an annualized rate of 6.2% in the final quarter of 2008, highlighting the deepening US recession. This happened at a time when the balance of payments was persistently weak (estimated at –US$569bn for 2008), and the fiscal stance unsustainable in the long-term—making for a difficult challenge to steer policy between competing objectives.

Unemployment has also risen sharply. In February 2009, employment fell by 651,000. By then, total job losses since the recession began in December 2007 numbered almost 4.4 million, and the unemployment rate stood at 8.1%, the highest since December 1983. This, combined with December 2008 US manufacturing figures at a 60-year low (ISM) of 32.9, explain the consumer confidence level of 25 in February 2009, down from 76.4 a year earlier. The merchandise trade deficit reached a record US$847 billion in 2007, but declined to US$810 billion in 2008, as a depreciating exchange rate for the dollar against most major currencies discouraged US imports, and made US exports more competitive abroad. The currency subsequently showed relative strength as other economies across the globe succumbed to recession.

The downturn in the global economy, sparked by the collapse of two Bear Stearns hedge funds in Q3 2007, and the ensuing liquidity crisis, had an impact on the country's equity, bond, and property markets. The Dow Jones Industrials index fell 33% in 2008, bond spreads widened to levels last seen in the Great Depression, and the Case-Shiller Composite 20 Home Price Index showed an annual fall of 18.6% in 2008.

After posting a decline of 8.5% (annualized rate) in December 2008, the CPI finished the year up only 0.1% on a year-on-year basis, its lowest yearly price appreciation since 1945. This came just half a year after the 12-month growth rate of the CPI was running at a 17-year high of 5.6% (July 2008). Plummeting energy prices caused much of the headline decrease in December. While the decline in prices has reduced fears of rampant inflation, it has led to worries about a Japan-style depression and falling prices, which are partly responsible for the quantitative easing undertaken by the Federal Reserve.

SUPPORT FOR INWARD INVESTMENT AND IMPORTS

Invest in America promotes and supports foreign direct investment in the United States, contributing to US job creation, innovation, and competitiveness. Further details can be found on the website (see More Info).

TAX EXEMPTIONS

Following Hurricane Katrina in 2005, the US government instituted a series of tax incentives for companies investing in the GO (Gulf Opportunity) Zone in parts of Louisiana, Mississippi, Alabama, Florida, and Texas. Further details can be found on the US Internal Revenue Service's website.

▸▸ MORE INFO

Websites:

Useful contacts directory aimed at foreign businesses doing business in the United States, with data on performance of US economy: www.usa.gov/Business/Foreign_Business.shtml

Internal Revenue Service: www.irs.gov/newsroom/article/0,,id=152898,00.html

Invest in America: www.trade.gov/investamerica/

See Also:

★ The Impact of Demographics on Business and the World Economy (pp. 780–783)

★ Viewpoint: Brian Reading (pp. 221–224)

Ukraine

ECONOMY AND TRADE

After Russia, the Ukrainian Republic was the most important economic component of the former Soviet Union. It generated more than one-fourth of Soviet agricultural output, and its diversified heavy industry included a strong ferrous metals capability. Today, steel is the country's greatest export.

After independence in December 1991, the Ukrainian government liberalized most prices, and erected a legal framework for privatization, but widespread resistance within the government and the legislature stalled reform efforts. The loose monetary policies of the period also pushed up inflation. Prices stabilized only after the introduction of a new currency, the *hryvnia*, in 1996.

    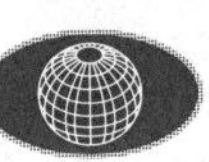   

Ukraine's dependence on Russia for energy supplies has made the Ukrainian economy vulnerable to external shocks. Further reforms are needed, including fighting corruption, developing capital markets, and improving the legislative framework. Ukraine reached an agreement with the IMF for a US$16.5 billion standby arrangement in November 2008 to deal with an economic crisis. However, political instability in Ukraine, as well as deteriorating external conditions, are likely to hamper efforts for economic recovery.

ECONOMIC POLICY OVER 12 MONTHS

The global financial crisis has exposed Ukraine's inherent macroeconomic risks. While sovereign and corporate bond spreads were already widening in the first half of 2008, due to high inflation and a widening current account deficit, the international financial crisis brought existing refinancing risks, and risks associated with the banking sector to the fore. Moreover, the slowing global economy led to a sharp fall in both the price of, and the demand for steel, Ukraine's main export.

In November 2008, Ukraine received approval for a two-year IMF loan intended to help support its banking system, and cover the country's widening current account gap. Under the terms of its agreement with the IMF, Ukraine is expected to have a balanced budget in 2009. The terms of the IMF bailout package further require Ukraine to move toward a flexible exchange rate, and limit the reduction of foreign reserves. Ukraine received the first installment of US$4.5 billion in November 2008, although the second tranche, due in February 2009, has been delayed until the IMF receives confirmation that the government has agreed a non-inflationary source of financing for its state deficit.

At the beginning of the economic crisis, Ukraine had comparatively little state debt. However, the cost of bailouts and measures to fight the recession have caused public debt to surge upwards. Total state debt increased by 37% in December 2008 to US$24.1 billion, from US$17.6 billion in December 2007, according to data from the Ukraine Finance Ministry. The government initially targeted a budget deficit of UAH18.8 billion (US$2.34 billion), or about 2% of GDP, in 2008. It later cut the gap to below 1% of GDP, in accordance with the terms of the IMF bailout. However, as a result of US$7.5 billion spent by the Ukraine central bank supporting the *hryvnia* in October and November 2008, foreign reserves have fallen significantly, jeopardizing the IMF standby arrangement.

Ukraine's governance has long been stymied by conflict between the opposing forces of Prime Minister Timoshenko and President Yushchenko. Timoshenko's response to the economic crisis has been to depreciate the currency, and try to increase government expenditure, leading to an anticipated budget deficit of 2.96% of GDP in 2009, well above the 1% level agreed with the IMF. Timoshenko has sought to correct the trade deficit by imposing an administrative tax on imports. Yushchenko has opposed all of these moves, on the grounds that they may jeopardize further tranches of the IMF loan.

In February 2009, ratings agencies S&P's and Fitch downgraded the country's rating because of political instability. By March 2009, investors were also concerned that the country might default on its debt obligations, undermining confidence in the Eastern European region.

ECONOMIC PERFORMANCE OVER 12 MONTHS

Ukraine's economy was buoyant, despite the political conflict between the prime minister and president, until mid-2008. Real GDP growth reached roughly 7% in 2006–2007, fueled by high global prices for steel, and strong domestic consumption, spurred by rising pensions and wages. A fall in steel prices and Ukraine's exposure to the global financial crisis due to aggressive foreign borrowing lowered growth in 2008, and the economy is expected to contract in 2009. A decline in industrial output, the beginning of widespread layoffs, a steep devaluation of the *hryvnia*, and loss of confidence in the banking system is only a partial list of the symptoms of Ukraine's crisis. According to the National Bank of Ukraine, the country's GDP declined at an annual rate of 20% in January 2009. The leakage of deposits from the banking system amounted to 14% over October–November 2008.

Ukraine's total state debt in 2008 increased by 37% to US$24.1 billion, from US$17.6 billion in 2007. The country, which has around US$105 billion in corporate and state debt, has the fourth-highest credit risk worldwide, according to credit-default swap data. The cost of insuring Ukraine bonds against default went up more than thirteen-fold in 2008, to an astonishing 31% of the amount of debt protected. Aggressive lending by banks that borrowed heavily from abroad has contributed to Ukraine's ballooning private-sector external debt. Official figures indicate that only some 2.5% of loans are currently problematic, but this situation is set to worsen considerably as the currency falls and the economy contracts.

Ukraine's stocks have also been falling, with the benchmark PFTS index down 74% in 2008. The *hyrvnia* has also declined significantly, losing 50% against the US dollar between June and December 2008. It is expected to drop further in 2009, given market sentiment that the IMF package effectively limits central bank intervention to halt the slide. And, as the currency slides, so too does the ability of the average Ukrainian to pay his or her debts.

Tensions with Russia also escalated towards the end of 2008, fueled by the conflict-ridden negotiations over Ukraine's gas debt. In January 2009, Russia temporarily cut off gas supplies to the country over the

STATISTICS

GDP growth: 2.1% (2008, State Statistics Committee)
GDP per capita: US$6,900 (2008 est.)
CPI: 25% (2008, est.)
Key interest rate: 12% (March 2009, National Bank of Ukraine)
Exchange rate versus dollar: hryvnia per US dollar—4.9523 (2008, est.)
Unemployment: 3% officially registered; large number of unregistered or underemployed workers (2008, est.)
FDI: US$44.08 billion (2008, est.)
Current account deficit/surplus: −US$14.22 billion (2008, est.)
Population: 45,994,288 (July 2008, est.)
Source: CIA Factbook except where stated

   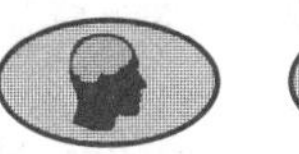     

alleged non-payment of a bill, and tensions rose again in March 2009. A wave of import restriction measures by Russia, the European Union, and the United States (on steel particularly) is likely to hamper exports, which account for roughly 60% of Ukraine's GDP growth.

In February 2009, the IMF projected that Ukraine's economy would shrink by 6% in 2009.

SUPPORT FOR INWARD INVESTMENT AND IMPORTS

InvestUkraine is an independent, non-profit investment agency of Ukraine, acting as a liaison between the government and prospective and current investors. Investment is actively welcomed, especially in agricultural sectors, and in the promotion of research and development. More information is available on its website.

TAX EXEMPTIONS

Companies involved in agricultural activities are exempt from corporation tax, those with foreign investment (Enterprises with Foreign Investments) are subject to a five-year tax holiday following a qualified foreign investment above US$50,000 in kind, or US$500,000 in cash, such that such contribution is at least 20% of the enterprise's total charter.

▸▸ MORE INFO

Websites:

InvestUkraine: www.investukraine.org

Ukrainian news portal: www.unian.net/eng/

Tax guide to Ukraine: www.ukremb.info/viewer.php?p=148

Venezuela

ECONOMY AND TRADE

Venezuela was one of three countries that emerged from the collapse of Gran Colombia in 1830 (the others being Ecuador and New Granada, which became Colombia). For most of the first half of the 20th century, Venezuela was ruled by generally benevolent military strongmen, who promoted the oil industry, and allowed for some social reforms. Democratically elected governments have held sway since 1959. However, with the election of Hugo Chávez in 1999, Venezuela has embarked on a strange course of its own, guided by Chávez's idea of "21st Century Socialism," which aims to cure social ills while countering "unhealthy" globalization. With the United States deeply unhappy at Venezuela's stance and policies, the impact on trade and regional stability has been considerable. Venezuela remains highly dependent on oil revenues, which account for roughly 90% of export earnings, about 50% of the federal budget revenues, and around 30% of GDP. The country's population of 28 million is young, growing, and urbanized, with around 90% of the population living in urban areas.

ECONOMIC POLICY OVER 12 MONTHS

A nationwide strike between December 2002 and February 2003 had far-reaching consequences on the country's economy. Real GDP declined by around 9% in 2002, and 8% in 2003, but economic output since then has recovered strongly. Fueled by high oil prices, record government spending helped to boost GDP by about 9% in 2006, 8.3% in 2007, and nearly 6% in 2008. This spending, combined with recent minimum-wage hikes, and improved access to domestic credit, has created a consumption boom, but has come at the cost of higher inflation—roughly 20% in 2007, and more than 30% in 2008. Imports also have jumped significantly. Declining oil prices in the latter part of 2008 are expected to undermine the government's ability to continue the high rate of spending. President Chávez, in 2008, continued efforts to increase the government's control of the economy, by nationalizing firms in the cement and steel sectors. In 2007, he nationalized firms in the petroleum, communications, and electricity sectors. In July 2008, Chávez issued a series of decrees, which brought in further laws to consolidate and centralize authority over the economy through his plan for "21st Century Socialism." Chávez's victory in 1998 reflected considerable anger among poorer Venezuelans about the corruption of his predecessor, President Carlos Andres Perez, who was impeached.

The Venezuelan government dominates the economy. All foreign-exchange requests must be approved by the National Exchange Control Administration (CADIVI), and the Central Bank (BCV) completes all legal purchase and sale of foreign currency. In January 2008, the Venezuelan government adopted the *bolívar fuerte* as its new currency, effectively redenominating the previous currency, the *bolívar*, by removing three zeroes (1 bolívar fuerte = 1,000 bolívars). The current exchange control regime rate for US dollar exchange is VEF2.145=US$1. Unofficial exchange rates are far higher. BCV international reserves were at US$38 billion in early December 2008.

The state oil company, PDVSA, controls the petroleum sector. Government companies control the electricity sector, and important parts of the telecommunications and media sectors. In spring 2008, the government announced the nationalization of cement and steel producers, as well as select companies in

STATISTICS

GDP growth: 5.7%

GDP per capita: US$14,000

CPI: 31%

Key interest rate: 17.11%

Exchange rate versus dollar: bolivars per US dollar—2.147 (note the currency revaluation on 1 January 2008, with 1000 old bolívars equaling 1 new bolívar)

Unemployment: 8.5%

FDI: US$44.31 billion

Current account surplus: US$48.44 billion

Population: 26,814,843

Source: CIA Factbook except where stated

the milk and meat distribution sectors. The government also unveiled its intention to nationalize Banco de Venezuela, one of the country's largest private banks, in July 2008. These and previous nationalizations, as well as other threats to property rights, and an uncertain macroeconomic environment characterized by high inflation and foreign-exchange controls, have led to reduced space for the private sector, and low levels of private investment.

There is considerable income inequality. The Gini coefficient (a measure of inequality of income distribution or inequality of wealth, whereby the lower the score between 0 and 1 the better) was 0.42 during 2007. According to government statistics, the percentages of poor and extremely poor citizens among the Venezuelan population were 27.5% and 7.6%, respectively, for the first half of 2007.

ECONOMIC PERFORMANCE OVER 12 MONTHS

Inflation has been a serious issue in Venezuela. Although real GDP growth was strong in 2007 and 2008, the consumer price index raced away in 2007, increasing by 18.7%. This followed inflation of 13.5% in 2006, and 16% in 2005. However, these were all improvements on 2004, when inflation grew by 21.7%. A combination of the global downturn and Chávez's high-spending plans are thought likely to drive inflation to above 30% in 2009.

Although economic growth has been impressive, as a result of the oil windfall, many in the Venezuelan business community remain very concerned about President Chávez' vision for "21st Century Socialism," and what it portends for the private sector. With oil prices down more than 75% between July and early December 2008, many economists believe the Venezuelan economy will struggle in 2009.

Despite political tensions between the United States and Venezuela, the United States remains Venezuela's most important trading partner. In 2007, bilateral trade topped US$50 billion. Venezuelan exports to the United States were US$40 billion (accounting for at least 60% of total Venezuelan exports), and US exports to Venezuela were US$10 billion (or 22% of total Venezuelan imports). The United States is the single most important customer for Venezuelan oil. Venezuela shipped an average of approximately 1.4 million barrels of crude oil and petroleum products per day to the United States in 2007, a figure which accounts for at least half of Venezuelan oil exports, and 10% of US oil imports. Bilateral trade is expected to reach US$70 billion in 2008, primarily due to the high oil prices that prevailed for most of the year.

The government of Venezuela has taken a vocal role against the proposed Free Trade Agreement of the Americas (FTAA). Its stated goal is to expand its Bolivarian Alternative for the Americas (ALBA) project, and develop a South American bloc.

Manufacturing contributed an estimated 17% of GDP in 2006. The manufacturing sector has continued its recovery, started in 2004, but remains hindered by a marked lack of private investment. Venezuela manufactures and exports steel, aluminum, textiles, apparel, beverages, and foodstuffs. It produces cement, tires, paper, fertilizer, and assembles cars for both domestic and export markets.

Agriculture accounts for approximately 4% of GDP, 10% of the labor force, and at least one-fourth of Venezuela's land area. Venezuela exports rice, cigarettes, fish, tropical fruits, coffee, cocoa, and manufactured products. The country is not self-sufficient in most areas of agriculture. Venezuela imports about two-thirds of its food needs. During November 2006, US firms exported US$412 million worth of agricultural products, including wheat, corn, soybeans, soybean meal, cotton, animal fats, vegetable oils, and other items to make Venezuela one of the top two US markets in South America. The United States supplies roughly one-quarter of Venezuela's food imports.

SUPPORT FOR INWARD INVESTMENT AND IMPORTS

It is extremely difficult for the private sector to invest in a country that is moving rapidly forward down a nationalization path, and where there is no certainty as to what sector will be the subject of nationalization next. Venezuela's attractiveness to inward investment is at an all-time low at present.

TAX EXEMPTIONS

With dividends paid to non-resident individuals subject to a withholding tax of 90% of the gross amount, and 95% for corporations, Venezuela is not a particularly tax-friendly place for investors. A reduced withholding tax of 4.95% applies to interest paid to financial institutions not domiciled in Venezuela.

However, in an effort to reduce reliance on oil, the Chávez government has also worked to promote growth and diversification, by implementing major tax incentives for small and mid-sized enterprises in the manufacturing, commerce, and service sectors, so as to boost employment in the most economically depressed states. In addition, industrial parks throughout the country are being revived, with significant tax breaks to encourage investment in regional areas. President Chávez has also expressed a desire to reinvigorate labor-intensive, non-oil sectors of the economy, in particular tourism, agriculture, and small business (source: Australian Government, www.dfat.gov.au).

▸▸ MORE INFO

Website:

Australian government profile of Venezuela: www.dfat.gov.au/geo/venezuela/venezuela_country_brief.html

Automobiles

MAJOR INDUSTRY TRENDS

The past year has not been a good one for many automobile manufacturers, and 2009 is shaping up to be even worse, with new car sales depressed around the world. However, an authoritative report from the accountants, PricewaterhouseCoopers (PwC), titled "Global automotive perspectives 2008," notes that there is now a real dichotomy in this sector between car manufacturers in emerging markets and those in mature markets.

Mature markets have been characterized by stagnant or falling sales, extremely low profit margins per vehicle on many models, and a desperate search for cost-cutting measures by manufacturers. This was brought into sharp focus by the three leading US motor manufacturers—Ford, General Motors, and Chrysler—which, in October 2008, had to ask for US$25 billion in government aid to help them re-equip, to meet new "fuel-efficient" standards, set by the US at 35 miles per gallon (mpg), or 6.7 liters per 100 kilometers.

This "bailout" of the big three has dominated the headlines, but few mainstream car manufacturers in the West are doing much better, and many have stopped production in key factories while they wait for demand to improve, and new car inventories to reduce.

In emerging markets, by contrast, sales prior to the global slowdown were skyrocketing, and profits per vehicle were three to five times higher than those being achieved by auto manufacturers in mature markets.

Mature-market manufacturers have had to rethink their approach to compete for market share in emerging markets, while emerging-market players, which do not have the same cost-heavy, unionized structures as, say, the big three US manufacturers, have done much better selling into mature markets. One of the major strategies of mature-market car manufacturers has been to move manufacturing and assembly to lower-cost locations. In the Americas, this has meant moving manufacturing from Detroit to Mexico. In Europe, it has meant moving from established markets to factories in the new accession countries in Central and Eastern Europe.

Asian manufacturers, such as the South Korean companies Hyundai and Kia, have been able to grow sales, not just in Asia but in mature markets as well.

PwC notes that manufacturers from both emerging and developed markets face longer-term strategic challenges on two fronts: from legislative changes, as governments seek to reduce the impact of road traffic on global warming, and from competitive innovation. Both sources of pressure on the sector add costs at a time when profits in developed markets are under tremendous pressure.

Evidence of how tough things have become for mature-market manufacturers abounds. In December, Toyota, the world's largest car maker, announced its first operating loss for 70 years, sending shock waves throughout the auto industry. Toyota was one of the pioneers of lean manufacturing techniques, and is regarded as a benchmark for efficiency in manufacturing processes. Toyota forecast an operating loss of ¥150 billion (US$1.6 billion) for the year to March 2009, completely wiping out a previous forecast of a ¥600 billion profit. In 2007, the company made a record profit of ¥2.27 trillion.

Commenting on the loss, Toyota's president, Katsuaki Watanabe, was quoted in the press as saying: "It's a kind of emergency that we've never experienced before. The environment surrounding us is extremely harsh ... The change in the world economy is of a magnitude that comes once every hundred years ... The tough times are hitting us far faster, wider, and deeper than expected." As a result, Toyota cut production at 16 of its 75 global assembly lines to one shift per day, and postponed completion of its eighth North American plant. Toyota had been aiming to become the world's first motor manufacturer to top the 10 million cars per year production mark. It now expects to produce just 7.5 million cars in 2009, and that might be overoptimistic if the crisis continues to deepen.

Emerging markets have not been immune to the effects of the global slowdown. For example, the Indian car manufacturer, Tata Motors, announced in February 2009 that, due to a severe contraction in the Indian automotive sector, for which the squeeze on consumer credit was partially responsible, the company's net revenues fell by 34.4% in the third quarter of 2008, in comparison with the same quarter in 2007.

MARKET ANALYSIS

Legislation-driven challenges for the global auto sector revolve around two needs: to maximize fuel efficiencies in engine and bodywork design, and to lower CO_2 emissions.

The sector has also had to take account of shifts in consumer preferences towards smaller, more fuel-efficient, "greener" vehicles, in response to growing concern about global warming. To protect their reputations and to be seen as good corporate citizens, manufacturers have also had to respond by "greening" their supply chains, at the same time as they move to achieve efficiencies by making greater use of outsourcing of components and assemblies.

PwC forecasts that, from now until 2015, emerging markets will enjoy some 18 times the growth in light-vehicle assembly that will be achieved in mature markets. On these figures, around 95% of light-vehicle growth will originate from emerging markets, with the BRIC countries (Brazil, Russia, India, and China) growing fastest, and accounting for some 58% of anticipated growth. PwC expects China and India to lead this growth in light-vehicle output, boosted by domestic markets that account for some 2 billion people.

During 2008, governments in emerging economies such as China, India, and South Korea took action to mitigate the effects of the credit crunch by making it easier for consumers to purchase new cars. One of the dilemmas facing the sector is how to move "gracefully" towards a future that is not based on oil. Moves to expand the use of biofuels have been blamed for diverting land away from food crops, and for the destruction of forests. This challenge remains to be solved.

Two exciting new directions for the auto sector are moves to build ever-cheaper and more-affordable small cars (to bring car purchases within the reach of greater numbers of emerging-market consumers), and a determined focus in some markets, such as the EU, on achieving more and more miles per gallon. In India, the country's leading automaker, Tata Motors, announced its "People's Car" in January 2008, with a target price of just 100,000 rupees, or US$2,500. The design makes extensive use of plastics and adhesives, instead of welding, to cut costs, and it has been produced at a price point that mature-market auto manufacturers would find impossible.

US auto manufacturers have, in the eyes of many analysts, not been helped by the very modest targets for fuel consumption set by US legislation. The US government bailout will help US auto manufacturers to produce new "fuel-efficient" engines capable of doing 35 mpg, instead of the present requirement of 25 mpg. The European Union already has legislation in place demanding that EU auto manufacturers achieve 52 mpg for new cars by 2012.

The independent research company, Plunkett Research, argues that the most important trend in developed markets over the mid-term will be the rapid growth in demand for hybrid vehicles, such as Toyota's Prius or Honda's Civic. Almost 120,000 Prius hybrids were sold in the US market in the first eight months of 2008, while Honda sold 25,577 Civic hybrids. Plug-in hybrids will become much more popular. With this technology, a petrol-driven engine is supported by battery power, or the vehicle's batteries are recharged by a petrol-fueled generator to get drivers through areas that are still without a convenient electric plug-in capability. Plunkett Research argues that consumer demand will drive tremendous improvements in battery technology, which, in turn, will lower costs, and stimulate demand in a virtuous feedback cycle.

Environmental awareness on the part of both consumers and regulators is also driving manufacturers to make further advances in diesel engine technology. Plunkett cites strong demand for clean diesel engines, such as those in new models from Volkswagen and Mercedes-Benz.

According to Plunkett Research estimates, in 2007 there were approximately 806 million cars and light trucks on the road. By 2020, the firm says, that number is expected to reach 1 billion. PwC cites International Monetary Fund estimates of close to 3 billion cars by 2050. At today's consumption rates, motorists burn some 260 billion gallons of fuel each year. PwC notes that cars emitted approximately 2.6 billion metric tons of carbon dioxide in 2000, or about 6.1% of overall global emissions. This figure could reach 6.8 billion tones or 8.1% of total emissions by 2050.

Both Plunkett Research's analysis and the PwC report point to the fact that public sensitivity to rising fuel costs around the world is already depressing sales of "gas-guzzling" sports utility vehicles (SUVs). This is particularly bad news for mature-market auto manufacturers, which have looked to this category of vehicle to sustain profitability for the past two to three years. Plunkett points out that, during the first eight months of 2008, US sales of pickup trucks, minivans, and SUVs slumped by 19.3%. Manufacturers' profit margins on SUVs can range from 15% to 20%, while profit margins on standard saloon cars struggle to reach 3%.

PwC argues, however, that environmental considerations should not be seen by auto manufacturers as just constraints on design, but rather as opening "the door to broader horizons." Opportunities for new profit sources and competitive advantages are available if the industry moves in the direction of safer, more comfortable, and simpler vehicles. Innovations such as that of Tata with the Nano (People's Car) are already dramatically altering the competitive climate, PwC argues.

Automakers' environmental initiatives are sure to win investor attention, creating both opportunities and threats for manufacturers. The EU's requirement for added use of particulate filters on diesel engines for all new cars sold in the EU from September 2009 is one obvious example of the way in which the regulatory environment is setting constraints on the industry. Emerging-market companies will not escape this trend. China, for example, aims to implement similar standards to Europe through a set of environmental and regulatory standards called the China IV Standards, which came into force in 2008.

Then there is the impact on the auto industry of environmental and waste regulatory regimes elsewhere in the economy. One example is Europe's REACH standard (Registration, Evaluation, and Authorization of Chemicals), which has an impact on the auto industry. REACH mandates transparency by suppliers and substance importers, and contributes to the "greening" of the supply chain mentioned earlier in this article.

According to the International Organization of Motor Vehicle Manufacturers (OICA, www.oica.net), just over 53 million cars were produced worldwide in 2007. (2008 statistics are not yet available). Japan was far and away the leader in terms of car production, manufacturing 9.944 million cars in 2007, but China was in second place, with 6.381 million. Germany was in third place, with 5.709 million. The US held fourth position, manufacturing 3.924 million cars in 2007, and South Korea was in fifth place, with 3.723 million. The Indian car industry is expanding rapidly; by the end of 2007, it had moved ahead of countries such as Canada and the UK, with 1.707 million cars produced during the year.

The OICA's league table of leading motor manufacturers gives the following top 10 positions. The vehicle production figures include cars, light commercial vehicles (LCVs), and heavy commercial vehicles (HCVs), and refer to the manufacturers' global production. They do not correspond to "home-country" production figures.

Table 1. OICA top 10 auto manufacturers in 2007. (*Source:* OICA. Full list online at www.oica.net)

GM	9,349,818
Toyota	8,534,690
Volkswagen	6,267,891
Ford	6,247,506
Honda	3,911,814
PSA	3,457,385
Nissan	3,431,398
Fiat	2,679,451
Renault	2,669,040
Hyundai	2,617,725

MORE INFO

Websites:

OICA: www.oica.net

PricewaterhouseCoopers: www.pwc.com

Aviation

MAJOR INDUSTRY TRENDS

This report covers the entire aviation industry, including the airline and aerospace sectors. It focuses upon the civil sector of the aerospace business. The military sector is included in the separate industry report on defense.

The Economic Cycle and Aviation

The civil aviation industry is highly cyclical, being extremely sensitive to the economic cycle. In times of economic hardship, people simply fly less often than they do in the good times. This is true of both the leisure and business sectors. This characteristic is exemplified by the industry's fortunes in 2007, 2008, and 2009. Many people in the industry described 2007 as one of the best years that they had ever experienced, with both the civil and military sectors benefiting from bulging order books. Indeed, 2007 marked the first time that a simultaneous upturn in the civil and military sectors had occurred. Factors supporting the industry included:

- Booming global growth, which supported demand for both cargo and passenger services;
- Buoyant corporate profits, which drove demand for business jets, and business travel in general;
- The rapid growth of demand in emerging economies, such as China and India;
- Conflicts in countries such as Iraq and Afghanistan, which drove demand for military equipment and services;
- Huge investment in new aircraft by the civil sector in response to environmental issues, and to the high price of oil. Fuel is the biggest operating cost facing any airline.

The fortunes of the two manufacturers that dominate the global civil aerospace market highlighted the buoyancy of the industry in 2007. The US aircraft giant, Boeing, enjoyed a record year for new orders, with 1,413 (net) orders racked up, surpassing the high set in the previous year. The European Aeronautics Defence and Space Company (EADS), which manufactures the Airbus range of airliners, also enjoyed a bumper year in terms of new orders, and said it had a backlog of 3,421 aircraft, representing about six years of production and "the highest backlog ever for the aviation industry."

In 2008, however, the industry's fortunes changed markedly due to a double whammy of rapidly increasing fuel costs in the first two-thirds of the year, and a marked deterioration in the global economy and financial system in the final third. By the time of the Farnborough Air Show (one of the most important events in the aerospace industry calendar, held every two years) in July, both Boeing and EADS remained optimistic about the outlook. The chief executive of Boeing, James McNerney, described soaring oil prices as an "opportunity" which would speed up orders for new aircraft that consume less fuel than their predecessors. Louis Gallois, the chief executive of EADS, told the BBC that he also believed that rising oil prices were encouraging airlines to buy new, more efficient airplanes.

However, independent analysts were far less sanguine about the industry's future. Nick Cunningham, an analyst at Evolution Securities in London, told aerospace-technology.com that the outlook for civil aerospace manufacturers was worse than it had been for decades. He said: "I believe that post-2010 we will see a sharp drop in deliveries—remember, in a regular recession deliveries halve—and we will see deliveries remaining depressed for a very long period of time, as they were in the 1970s, and right through the 1980s."

In December 2008, Nick Cunningham told aerospace-technology.com that, "the last few months have already been a desert as far as orders are concerned, and I think that this trend will continue for several years." He added: "The macroeconomic background has deteriorated dramatically, and that will have a very big effect. As a rule of thumb, traffic grows by around double the pace of GDP growth. Thus, if the GDP of the developed economies declines (and it looks like the US, Japan, the UK, and probably continental Europe are going to see negative GDP growth in 2009, and possibly for some of 2010), aggregate global traffic volumes will decline."

By the end of 2008, it was clear that the outlook for the global economy and the aviation industry had deteriorated even more rapidly than had been anticipated. In December 2008, global international cargo traffic plummeted by 22.6%, compared with December 2007, according to the International Air Transport Association (IATA), while international passenger traffic fell by 4.6%. The Asia-Pacific region, which accounts for 45% of global cargo, was worst hit, with a 26% drop over the preceding year, reflecting a slump in demand for the region's manufactured goods. North American carriers reported a 22% fall in their cargo business, while European airlines saw a 21.2% decline. The slump continued in 2009. In March, IATA said that the airline industry's losses could amount to US$2.5 billion during the course of the year, as traffic drops by about 3%. Civil aerospace manufacturers were forced to step up the provision of customer financing after the credit crisis hurt airlines' ability to secure financing for aircraft.

In March 2009, both Boeing and EADS reported that cancellations of existing orders had exceeded new orders since the beginning of the year. Airbus earlier cut monthly production rates for its single-aisle and wide-bodied jets, as airlines freeze or cancel orders, and passengers desert airports.

Nonetheless, once the global economic outlook improves, the prospects for the aviation industry will surely follow suit. Every year, Airbus produces a forecast (*Global Market Forecast*, see More Info) for aircraft orders over the next 20 years. In its 2008 report, Airbus identified various factors that were driving the growth of air traffic over the long term, and which are likely to come back into play when the recession ends. They include:

- The rapid growth of emerging markets, where economies and demographic developments are both being driven by, and benefiting from air travel;
- The liberalization of aviation markets around the world, which is giving greater market access to airlines, and wider choice for passengers;
- The continuing growth of low-cost carriers across the planet, but particularly in Asia;
- The emergence of megacities, and increasing congestion at airports.

Boeing also publishes an annual report on the prospects for the aviation industry over the following 20 years, called *Current Market Outlook*. In its latest review, covering the period 2008–2027, Boeing remains optimistic about long-term trends. The company says that, while air travel has grown by an average of 4.8% each year over the past 20 years, passenger travel is expected to grow by an average of 5.0% a year, and cargo is expected to grow by 5.8% a year over the next 20 years. It adds that, "the fastest-growing economies will lead the transformation into a more geographically balanced market," while more-productive new airplanes will play a greater role, and there will be a relentless pursuit of further environmental progress. Boeing also believes that, "as airlines seek better financial returns, they match the airplanes used more closely to the precise economics of the routes they fly." This means that airlines will, in general, use larger regional jets and single-aisle airplanes, and more small and medium-sized twin-aisle airplanes.

MARKET ANALYSIS

The Battle between Airbus and Boeing in the Global Civil Aerospace Market

In 2003, Airbus overtook Boeing to become the world's best-selling aircraft maker, a position it retained in 2008, when it delivered a record 483 aircraft, beating Boeing, which sold 375. Airbus sold planes worth US$100bn in 2008, giving it a market share of 54%. In January 2009, Airbus said it had total orders for 3,715 jets, which it estimated would take six years to clear, although this could be reduced to four years with cancellations. Boeing said it had 3,700 orders. The two aircraft giants are locked in a dispute over claims that they are each receiving commercial aircraft subsidies, with the issue awaiting rulings from the World Trade Organization. The EU and the US have accused each other of providing illegal subsidies to the companies. Brussels has accused the US of giving Boeing almost US$24bn in state aid, while the US says that the UK, France, Germany, and Spain have provided Airbus with US$15bn.

The two manufacturers have clearly conflicting views over the way the airline market will develop. EADS believes that the increasing problem of congestion is leading to "a clear trend towards larger aircraft." Airbus says that this is evident in all seat categories,

    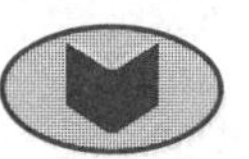    

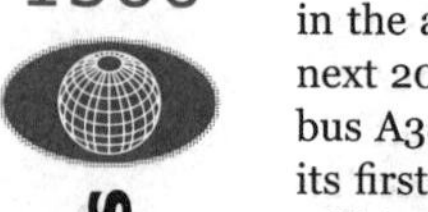

from smaller regional aircraft to very large aircraft, and will "result in the average aircraft size increasing by as much as 25% over the next 20 years." This view explains EADS's development of the Airbus A380, the largest passenger airliner in the world, which made its first commercial flight in October 2007. EADS believes airlines will increasingly require bigger planes to meet the growing numbers of passengers flying between major hubs. By the beginning of February 2009, Airbus had orders for 200 A380s.

However, Boeing has a contrary view. The US company says that the future belongs to medium-sized planes that can service smaller airports. To meet this demand, it has developed the Boeing 787 Dreamliner, an aircraft that Boeing says is much more fuel-efficient than its competitors, and produces 20% less CO_2. Boeing adopted a new manufacturing process for the 787, minimizing the work done in final assembly, simplifying tooling, and outsourcing production to a network of global suppliers. However, the 787 has been plagued by delays due to production glitches, and a two-month strike in 2008. The first delivery was initially slated for May 2008, but, in March 2009, Boeing said that it expected to make its first delivery in the final quarter of 2010. Airbus experienced similar problems with the A380—its first delivery was delayed by 18 months. By March 2009, Boeing had 878 current orders for the 787, from 57 customers.

Technological Developments

Aircraft makers are focused on reducing fuel consumption, and operating costs in general, in the battle to win orders from airlines. Fuel costs, which can account for 50% of an airline's operating costs, can make or break an airline. Boeing says that its 787 Dreamliner will cut fuel use by 20%, thanks to new engines, and the use of lightweight composite materials. Meanwhile, EADS says that the A380 is the first long-haul aircraft to consume less than three liters of fuel per passenger over 100km, a rate comparable to an economical family car. It claims that the A380's efficiency and advanced technology result in 15–20% lower seat-mile costs than those of competitor aircraft. Fuel-efficient engines and the use of advanced composite materials have played a vital role in reducing the A380's operating costs. The airframe is made up of some 25% composite material, by weight, while the Airbus A350XWB, due to enter production in 2010, will comprise around 50% composite material.

Boeing and Airbus are also engaged in developing alternative fuels. The engine makers, Pratt & Whitney, Rolls-Royce, and General Electric are all involved, and the momentum is being maintained, even though oil prices have fallen considerably from their mid-2008 peaks. In January 2009, Alan Epstein, Vice-President of Technology and Environment at Pratt & Whitney, said, "It's the first time in the history of jet aviation that the world is seriously considering going to a totally new fuel." IATA has a goal of 10% alternative fuels by 2017, while in the US, the Federal Aviation Administration is encouraging the use of new fuels. Several flights have already taken place using biofuels. In January 2009, for example, Air New Zealand flew a four-engine Boeing 747 with one engine on a 50% biofuel mix. During the same month, a Japanese Airlines 747 flew with one engine powered by a biofuel made primarily from camelina.

» MORE INFO

Websites:

Analysis and news on aerospace-industry projects: www.aerospace-technology.com

Boeing, *Current Market Outlook* 2008–27: www.boeing.com/commercial/cmo/

EADS, *Global Market Forecast*: www.airbus.com/en/corporate/gmf/

International Air Transport Association, provides statistics and information on the international aviation industry: www.iata.org

Banking and Financial Services

MAJOR INDUSTRY TRENDS

It is already clear that 2008/09 is going to be a year of unprecedented change for the global banking and financial services sector. The global banking crisis first burst into the media spotlight with the announcement by the US bank, Bear Sterns, in June 2007 that two of its more substantial hedge funds (totaling in excess of US$3 billion), both heavily invested in derivative instruments based on the US subprime mortgage market, were failing. From that point onwards, a crisis that had been gestating for around a decade in the banking sectors of the developed economies began to boil over.

The failure of the US investment bank, Lehman Brothers, in September 2008, focused attention on just how intertwined and interconnected debt had become among leading banks. Credit and interbank liquidity froze across the globe. Since then, governments around the world have been bailing out failing banks, and pumping money into the financial system in an effort to "normalize" banking activities, and to prevent a global financial meltdown.

In a report (published in February 2009) setting out a reform agenda for the European financial supervisory system, Jacques de Larosière, the former Banque de France governor (and IMF managing director), estimated the spate of write-offs and write-downs by banks and insurance companies around the world since the crisis began to be worth €1 trillion. His report presents a succinct account of how the global banking crisis came into being. It argues that excessive liquidity and low interest rates were the major underlying factors behind the crisis, but "financial innovation amplified and accelerated the consequences of excess liquidity, and rapid credit expansion."

Larosière emphasizes that strong macroeconomic growth since the mid-1990s gave an illusion that permanent and sustainable high levels of growth were not only possible, but likely, and this encouraged excessive risk-taking. Innovative financial products, based on asset-backed securities (billion-dollar parcels of residential mortgages), and termed collateralized debt obligations (CDOs), were created by major financial institutions and sold around the world. Banks mispriced the risks they were taking onto their books with these and other products, most notably, credit default swaps (essentially insurance sold by a provider which guaranteed to "make good" a debt, which could be a government debt, or a corporate or financial institution debt), in return for a premium.

Income streams were created for financial institutions, but these carried vast risks that did not appear on the balance sheets of these institutions. Securitization, a well-respected financial technique for dealing with large bundles of debt with associated income streams (repayments by debtors), such as credit card debt or mortgage debt, moved risk off the debt originator's balance sheets and dispersed it to investors around the world, often to other banks.

  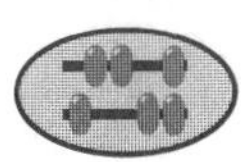 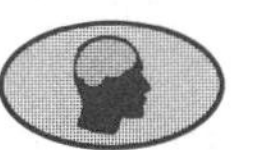  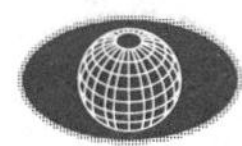   

Larosière's analysis, which has been put forward in various ways by many observers, is that although the crisis originated in the US, it is now global, deep, and (by February 2009), quite possibly, worsening.

"Significant global economic damage is occurring, strongly impacting on the cost and availability of credit; household budgets; mortgages; pensions; and big and small company financing, creating far more restricted access to wholesale funding, and now spillovers to the more fragile emerging country economies. The economies of the OECD are shrinking into recession, and unemployment is increasing rapidly," the Larosière report says.

The importance of the global banking sector to the real economy is being highlighted in the most dramatic way possible. Falls in global stock exchanges from August 2007 to March 2009 have resulted in losses in the value of listed companies amounting to €16 trillion, the report says.

Larosière, in common with other commentators, such as the European Central Bank (ECB), argues that the credit and housing bubbles in the US, and, subsequently, in Europe, were financed by massive capital inflows from emerging economies, such as China. "In this environment of plentiful liquidity and low returns, investors actively sought higher yields and went searching for opportunities. Risk became mispriced. Those originating investment products responded to this by developing more and more innovative and complex instruments designed to offer improved yields, often combined with increased leverage."

The resulting debt disaster has engulfed banks, frozen lending, and created a deep pool of "toxic assets" on bank books across the developed world. The solution many governments are adopting is both to refinance banks directly, and to create "bad banks" to buy and hold the toxic assets of banks that are judged to have a reasonable chance of survival. There is, however, a massive difficulty concerning the valuation of these complex assets. As John Mauldin, a US investment guru and market commentator, points out, if the assets are valued too cheaply and are sold on to hedge funds, the government is, in effect, handing a windfall to investors. If they are valued too dearly, taxpayers in the countries concerned bear unnecessary losses.

One thing that has already emerged with great clarity from the crisis is that the "high risk, high reward" model of banking, which US investment banks such as Citibank and JP Morgan Chase went in for, is now completely broken. There are no more investment banks—those that did not collapse have changed their status to deposit-taking banks, in order to make themselves eligible for US Federal "bailout" money.

MARKET ANALYSIS

The global banking crisis has been so broad and deep that it has virtually eclipsed other trends in banking. However, while some of these trends, such as the move to greater financial innovation, have undoubtedly been negated by the crisis, other trends persist, and will have an impact on the transformed, post-crash, global banking system going forward. These trends are summarized by Deutsche Bank Research, in a report published in April 2008 on the European banking system. They are as follows.

- Consolidation: Merger and acquisition activity has made the large banks even larger, sometimes with dire results for the acquirer. This has been spectacularly demonstrated by the acquisition of ABN AMRO by the Royal Bank of Scotland (RBS)—the acquisition was partially responsible for RBS posting a £23 billion loss, the largest loss in UK corporate history, in February 2009. However, the trend is also creating more "financial conglomerates," by matching like with unlike. From one perspective, this can be seen as making the acquiring bank more stable, by diversifying its revenue stream. From another perspective, it introduces incoherence and management difficulties that distract the acquirer from what it does well, and launches management into areas that it does not understand. Examples include the acquisition of Bank of Scotland by the Halifax Building Society in the UK in 2001, to create a financial institution known as Halifax Bank of Scotland (HBOS). Subsequently, in September 2008, Lloyds TSB acquired HBOS, after shares in the latter plummeted amid concerns over its future. However, Lloyds TSB then had to be rescued by the UK government. In March 2009, Lloyds TSB announced losses from HBOS of more than £10 billion, and the British government subsequently acquired a majority stake in Lloyds TSB in return for insuring the bank against future losses on £260 billion of toxic loans, 80% of them from the HBOS side of the banking group.
- Internationalization: European and US banks have sought higher growth by expanding outside their national boundaries, with emerging economies a favorite target.
- Greater use of technology and outsourcing of processes: IT has transformed banking processes, and, along with an accelerating use of onshore and offshore outsourcing, has helped to drive down costs, and increase profitability.
- A shift in the balance of power from West to East: The rise up the global rankings of the top Chinese banks has been spectacular, indicating the growing importance of the Asian market. The Deutsche Bank report points out that, "a deepening integration of the world economy and a surge in exports (prior to the crash) caused GDP growth in emerging markets to accelerate from an average of 3.8% from 1989 to 1998, to some 6.5% in the following decade to 2008. The report argues, too, that emerging markets do not suffer, in the main, from the ageing population syndrome of developed markets. The share of the population aged over 59 is expected to climb to 35% in Europe by 2050, compared to 24% in Asia, according to UN estimates. In a report published in January 2008, titled "What's in store for global banking?" management consultants, McKinsey, argue that banking, as an industry, is essentially a leveraged bet on national GDP growth, so the higher the GDP growth, the more prosperous the banking sector.
- The rise of *shariah*, or Islamic banking services: The target market for *shariah* banking services is the world's 1.6 billion Muslims, representing 25% of the world's population, and largely concentrated in emerging economies. The sector, just prior to the crash, had an average annual growth rate of 30%, with the expectation that funds under management would reach US$1 trillion by 2010. There are crucial differences between *shariah* banking and traditional Western banking, the most important of which, probably, is the prohibition on money earning interest. Islamic law, based on the Qur'an, requires effort to be expended if riches are to be gained. Money, in and of itself, is held to have no value, and cannot legitimately create value from itself. *Shariah* law can be applied to some major forms of traditional finance, including mortgages and leases, but has real problems with structures such as pension annuities, which are fundamentally based on interest on sovereign or corporate debt. Western banks, such as HSBC and others, have shown a strong interest in developing *shariah* offerings to try to grow market share in this sector.

Regulation Pre and Post the Crash

The integration of European financial markets is a firm EU goal, with the goal of reaching the level of integration achieved in the US under the US Federal Reserve. Prior to the crash, it was thought that Basel II, the second of the Basel accords, as set out by the Basel Committee on Banking Supervision, and embodied in the EU Directive, would provide a global standard for banking regulation.

The Basel Committee has no legislative power; it simply makes recommendations after thorough consultation with the banking industry. However, as its members are senior representatives of bank supervisory authorities, and the central banks of the G10 countries, plus Luxembourg and Spain, its views hold tremendous sway. The committee meets at the Bank of International Settlements (BIS) in Basel, which accounts for the name of the accord.

Basel II sets up rigorous risk and capital management requirements designed to ensure that banks hold sufficient capital reserves to cover the risks that they incur in trading. It uses a "three pillar" concept, based on capital adequacy requirements, usually modeled by the banks themselves (pillar 1), supervisory review (pillar 2), and market discipline (pillar 3). It is generally held that all three pillars failed, for various reasons, in the current crisis.

The Basel Committee has already issued a consultation document designed to bring all the off-balance-sheet vehicles and risks which Basel II failed to capture, back within the modeling regime used by banks to determine capital adequacy. However, while the final shape of banking regulation post the crash is still being worked through, the market in general fully expects banking regulation in future to be much tougher, with the kinds of risks that banks were formerly allowed to run being much more tightly circumscribed. A popular summary of this view is that banks, henceforth, should be seen as a kind of functional, systemically important, low-risk, low-growth utility. Just how well thought through this proposal is remains to be seen. Global merger and acquisition activity requires a rather different model, and where the liquidity is to come from to satisfy the next growth wave, if banks take on the utility model, is presently unclear.

Jacques Larosière's report argues that one of the failures of the current regulatory model was that, "too much attention was paid to individual banks, and too little to the impact of general developments on sectors or markets as a whole—insufficient attention was given to the liquidity of markets. EU supervisors failed to spot the degree to which a number of EU financial institutions had accumulated—often in off-balance-sheet constructions—exceptionally high exposure to highly complex, later to become illiquid, financial assets."

All of this was exacerbated in various ways, including by inappropriate reward structures (bonuses), mark-to-market accounting (which many now argue should be suspended in a crisis), and by inadequate cooperation between regulators.

Not surprisingly, Larosière's recommendations for the future of regulation include building much tighter links between European and other national regulators, including building a proper crisis-management infrastructure, and deepening the EU's bilateral financial relations with Asia and the US. Bankers and the entire financial services sector, including hedge funds and wealth managers, can expect much tighter regulation going forward.

▶▶ MORE INFO

Report:

European Commission. "Brief summary of the de Larosière Report." February 25, 2009. Online at: ec.europa.eu/commission_barroso/president/pdf/statement_20090225.pdf

Website:

Deutsche Bank Research: www.dbresearch.com

See Also:

- ★ The Changing Role and Regulation of Equity Research (pp. 301–302)
- ★ The Cost of Going Public: Why IPOs Are Typically Underpriced (pp. 531–533)
- ★ The Crash and the Banking Sector—Laying the Foundations (pp. 187–188)
- ★ Fair Value Accounting: SFAS 157 and IAS 39 (pp. 635–637)
- ★ How the Settlement Infrastructure Is Surviving the Financial Meltdown (pp. 211–213)
- ★ Revising Basel II—But at What Cost? (pp. 712–713)
- ★ Tripping over Prudence—Ideas for a Sensible Fix for Basel II (pp. 720–722)
- ★ Viewpoint: Viral Acharya and Julian Franks (pp. 632–634)
- ★ What the Rise of Global Banks Means for Your Company (pp. 596–597)
- ★ Why Organizations Need to be Regulated—Lessons from History (pp. 736–738)
- ✔ Achieving Success in International Acquisitions (p. 954)
- ✔ Derivatives Markets: Their Structure and Function (p. 924)
- ✔ Merchant Banks: Their Structure and Function(p. 929)
- ✔ Retail Banks: Their Structure and Function (p. 930)
- ✔ Steps for Obtaining Bank Financing (p. 1024)

Chemicals

MAJOR INDUSTRY TRENDS

With the number of "useful" chemical compound molecules approaching 10,000, and with chemicals playing a huge role in so much of what modern societies use, eat, clean, manufacture, and do each day, it might be thought that the global chemicals industry should be set for perpetual boom times. In fact, however, as the European Chemical Industry Council (Cefic), the body representing the European chemicals industry, observes in a report titled "Horizon 2015: Perspectives for the European chemical industry," things are not looking particularly encouraging for the sector, at least in Europe (see www.cefic.be).

The Cefic report sketches out the probable future of the sector to 2015, and one of its themes is that the European chemicals industry, which historically included the largest group of chemicals producers on the planet, is in danger of falling behind rival produces in Asia and the Americas, and is already trailing behind its "sister" industry, the pharmaceuticals sector.

While it is not always easy to separate the two sectors, Cefic argues that over the past decade or so, trends in pharmaceuticals and chemicals have "decoupled." "There is a strong asymmetry between the two sectors, with regard to the growth of output, trade surplus and employment. [Our] analysis shows that growth in chemicals output is lower than in pharmaceuticals," it says.

Even outside the EU, although the global chemicals trade surplus is still increasing, it shows considerably less dynamism than the growth in pharmaceuticals outputs around the world. Moreover, the number of persons directly employed by chemicals is falling dramatically, while employment in pharmaceuticals continues to show what Cefic calls "an encouraging increase."

Whereas the chemicals sector output grew at an average of 2.8% from 1996 to 2001, manufacturing output generally grew at 2.9%, and pharmaceuticals output grew at an average annual rate of 5.5%, Cefic says. It makes the point, too, that if one strips out pharmaceuticals-related growth from general chemicals growth, the picture looks even bleaker, as the share of EU pharmaceuticals trade surplus in the total chemicals surplus (which includes pharmaceuticals) has grown considerably, from 23% in 1990 to 40% in 2002.

According to Cefic, this "decoupling" between pharmaceuticals and chemicals is the result of a number of factors. These include the introduction of different technologies, changes in downstream markets, approaches to innovation, and changing shareholder expectations.

The chemicals sector itself breaks down into bulk chemicals and fine chemicals, and into a further category of petrochemicals and plastics. In 2002, total world chemicals production (excluding pharmaceuticals) was worth around €1.3 trillion, with the EU's share of that being €360 billion, followed by the USA (25.6%), and Asia (33%).

A report by Deutsche Bank Research on the Asia chemicals industry cites a turnover figure for the global chemicals industry for 2007 of €2.3 trillion, which represents a global annual growth of 5%. However, Deutsche Bank finds that Asia's growth averaged 6% (China 15%), while Europe averaged just 4%. It expects global chemicals turnover to continue to grow by 4.5% to 2020, to around €4 trillion. However, by 2020, the Bank expects Asia's share of the world chemicals market to have risen to 38%, up from its current share of 31%.

Cefic points out that with EU enlargement, the EU's share, currently 28% of global production, is set to rise, as many of the East European accession countries have their own chemicals industries. However, it points out that closer inspection shows that the EU's position is actually eroding. A decade ago, the EU's share was 32%, or 4% higher than today.

The main reasons for the decline are slow demand growth in Europe, versus high demand growth in Asia, and particularly in China, compounded by increasing imports into the EU from Asia and the Middle East, creating pressure on prices and margins. The internationalization of trade, with customer industries moving manufacturing out of Europe to low-wage economies, is also a contributing factor, as is regulatory arbitrage, with Europe constituting a highly regulated zone, versus Asia as a less highly regulated zone, and therefore a more favorable location for manufacturers. The problem for the European industry, as Cefic notes, is that as it declines, less budget is allocated to R&D, and, as the sector thrives on innovation, spending less on R&D would accelerate the decline and erode the industry's skills base in Europe.

Another issue for the European sector is that the Asian region's rate of industrial production growth is outpacing that of much of the rest of the world, creating a very strong demand for a wide range of chemicals. Moreover, Asia's greater focus on agriculture, manufacturing, and durable goods creates a more chemicals-intensive demand than developed economies, where the service sector plays a much larger role. Add to this the importance of the electronics, electrical, and textiles sectors, plus construction, leather, and plastics processing, and the result, again, is very strong and sustained demand for chemical products.

The question posed by Cefic, given all of the above, is whether Europe could still be regarded as a growth area for chemicals to 2015. Its answer, following an extensive modeling exercise, was that only in the most optimistic scenarios could the growth rates of the whole chemical industry be expected to outstrip GDP growth in Europe. The more likely scenario is that growth in demand will lag behind GDP growth, and could even become negative. If this happens, it would mean a major structural change.

"This would entail major consequences for the European chemical industry, but also, because of the leverage effects from raw materials supply and innovation, for European industry as a whole, and therefore on the whole European economy," the report warns.

MARKET ANALYSIS

In their latest report on merger and acquisition (M&A) activity in the global chemicals sector, accountants, PricewaterhouseCoopers (PwC), argue that the overall health of the global chemicals sector is tightly correlated with the state of the US and global economies. As global demand has slumped, chemical companies around the world have seen idle plants, job cuts, and falling order books.

There has been some relief as feedstock prices have declined in 2009 (to March), and are now off the record highs seen in 2008, but these price declines have not been sufficient to counterbalance the fall-off in order volumes. Companies have struggled to rationalize their production capacity as the downturn has deepened.

However, PwC argues that recessions allow companies with good balance sheets to make acquisitions that will define their business once the global economy picks up. PwC also found that chemicals CEOs as a group are more worried than in many other sectors about the possible impact on their businesses of the global liquidity crisis. PwC's 12th annual survey of global CEOs found that more than two-thirds of chemicals CEOs thought that financing costs would increase significantly, and that they would have to delay earmarked investment.

The industry is highly capital-intensive, with long product life-cycles, and the typical response of the sector to a downturn, PwC says, is to fine-tune the allocation of capital investment, rather than, as is common in some other sectors, to rethink their business model. This means that R&D spend across the sector has remained strong during the recession, as new products are seen as absolutely critical to a chemical company's long-term viability. Surprisingly, PwC found that deal activity actually increased in the chemicals sector in the fourth quarter of 2008, and the total of 869 deals completed in the sector globally, through the whole course of 2008, was higher than the total in 2007 (760 deals). What kept the M&A scoreboard ticking over during the global downturn was a large number of small and mid-sized transactions, PwC says. The volume for deals greater than US$50 million was actually lower in 2008 than for 2007 (83 deals versus 124 deals).

Regulatory Trends

The global chemicals industry has long been aware that the production and use of chemicals can have an adverse impact on both human health and the environment, and there have been a host of initiatives over the years aimed at developing coherent, industry-wide support for best practice standards on the use, production, transportation, and safe disposal of chemicals.

The industry's "Responsible Care" program has been in existence for close to two decades. As the International Council of Chemical Associations (ICCA) observes, some 15 years ago, just a handful of countries had launched Responsible Care programs in their chemicals sector. By 2002, the program had been adopted by 47 countries worldwide.

In 2009, the United Nations Environment Programme (UNEP) will hold its second international chemicals management conference in Geneva, Switzerland. The UN has been pushing for the global adoption of its strategic approach to international chemicals management (SAICM) since 2002. The SAICM concept and framework was endorsed by the World Summit on Sustainable Development in 2002, and by many global conferences since.

There is little argument against, and almost universal support for, the UN goal that, by 2020, chemicals across the world should be produced and used in ways that minimize significant adverse effects on human health and the environment (known as the Johannesburg Plan of Implementation).

SAICM objectives are grouped around five headings: risk reduction; knowledge and information; governance; capacity-building and technical assistance; and, lastly, illegal international traffic—the last being a continuing problem in the sector.

The UN's argument has a number of strands to it. The increased use of chemicals frequently accompanies economic development, and chemicals can play an important role in the improvement of living standards, including in relation to disease eradication, safe drinking water, and the alleviation of hunger. At the same time, the sound management of chemicals is essential for environmental sustainability, which, in turn, is a prerequisite for sustainable development as a whole.

UNEP says that there is increasing recognition, at the level of national governments, and by national chemical producers, of the importance of the sound management of chemicals in meeting the internationally agreed goals of the Millennium Declaration, and of the potential for exposure to toxic substances to undermine development, health, and poverty-alleviation investments.

"Many people living in poverty have weakened immune systems, leaving them more vulnerable to diseases caused or exacerbated by toxic substances and many lack knowledge of toxic substances in their community. Inadequate living conditions often leave them exposed to hazards of toxic substances and many work in occupations, such as agriculture and mining, which constantly expose them to harmful substances. Chemical exposures can also interfere with primary education by impairing children's physical growth and emotional development, and, in the case of metals such as lead and mercury, can have serious and irreversible adverse effects on children's mental development," UNEP warns.

The ICCA set up the Responsible Care Global Charter in 2006, for companies and national associations to sign up to, as part of meeting the sustainable development challenge. Cefic itself is an enthusiastic supporter of the charter.

In addition, the EU has a chemicals policy called REACH (Registration, Evaluation, and Authorization of Chemicals), which became applicable in law on June 1, 2007. REACH makes businesses responsible for the chemicals they use, and the onus is on them to show that these chemicals are safe in the way that they are being used. It also streamlines and improves the previous legislative framework on chemicals for the European Union.

The thrust of REACH is to encourage the replacement of hazardous chemicals with safer ones, and to act as a stimulus to businesses and the chemicals sector to research and develop safer products.

The United Nations has a globally harmonized system, called GHS, for identifying hazardous chemicals, and to convey information to the public and to users about these hazards, through standard symbols and phrases on packaging and labels, and through safety data sheets. GHS originated with the World Summit on Sustainable Development, held in Johannesburg in September 2002. This encouraged countries to implement GHS as a harmonized basis for providing consistent physical, environmental, and safety information on hazardous chemical substances and mixtures.

On December 16, 2008, the European Parliament and the Council adopted a new regulation on the classification, labeling, and packaging (CLP) of substances and mixtures, which aligns existing EU legislation with the UN's GHS regime. CLP was published in the Official Journal on December 31, 2008 and came into force on January 20, 2009. The deadline for substances to be classified according to CLP is December 1, 2010, and for mixtures, June 1, 2015. The CLP Regulations will ultimately replace two earlier directives, the directive on the classification, labeling, and packaging of substances, and the directive on "preparations." However, chemical companies are being given a period of time to make the transition. The deadline for substance reclassification is November 30, 2010, and for mixtures, May 31, 2015.

Companies

The ICIS Top 100 Chemical Companies includes all chemical firms around the world with sales greater than US$2.5 billion. The full table can be downloaded as a PDF from www.icis.com.

MORE INFO

Websites:

Deutsche Bank Research—see industry reports: www.dbresearch.com

European Chemical Industry Council: www.cefic.be

PricewaterhouseCoopers—see sector reports: www.pwc.com

Construction and Building Materials

MAJOR INDUSTRY TRENDS

The construction sector is in an interesting phase of its evolution, not quite yet global in nature, but with some players active in more than one national market and the largest players becoming involved in multiple projects in Europe, North America, and Asia, particularly China. The sector includes companies from the smallest to the largest. At the bottom of the scale are small house-builders, followed at the mid-range by regional and national companies capable of handling multiple projects within one country, to larger players with specialist interests, for example, in shopping mall construction, or office blocks, operating in multiple countries. The industry has a clear overlap with civil engineering on infrastructure projects, particularly where groundworks and ground preparation for site construction are concerned.

The sector, of necessity, works in partnership with a range of other professions, such as architects, quantity surveyors, and structural engineering consultants, who may be external to the construction company, or part of the company. Legal and financial advice on contracts, joint ventures, and project financing, as well as on litigation—the construction sector is associated with more than its fair share of litigation—are also essential services for the sector.

After a number of boom years, the global downturn started to have a real impact around August 2008, and is now having a severe effect on the sector across the developed world, in all areas except public works and infrastructure. The stimulus packages that are being implemented by governments globally all have as a common theme the idea of bringing forward or initiating major infrastructure projects to pump public money into the economy.

However, infrastructure is not a market that the smaller players can get involved in. Now that the housing bubble has crashed in many developed economies, smaller house-builders are going into administrative insolvency in increasing numbers, and larger construction firms are implementing layoffs, which, in many instances, will damage their ability to go forward rapidly when the upturn finally arrives.

The industry also has a clear and very close relationship with related industries specializing in building materials, including cement, plastics, wood, steel, and glass, as well as innovative new

 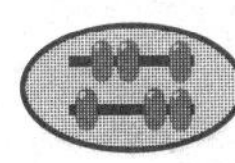 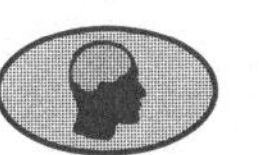  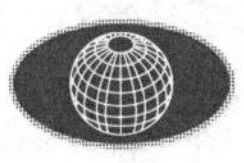    

product types, with particular strength, thermal, or low-maintenance properties.

There are huge difficulties in the way of construction companies moving outside their own national "turf." Every country has its own planning laws, building materials laws, and building regulations for residential, office, leisure, retail, and industrial building. Moreover, construction is very materials and skills-intensive, and bringing materials to the site and organizing the necessary skills, labor, and project management is a real challenge for one location, never mind for multiple locations in multiple jurisdictions.

For this reason, many cross-border construction projects are done as joint ventures until the incoming company has acquired a sufficient base of experience in the new jurisdiction's regulations and requirements, and has the necessary network of relationships to make building feasible, and tendering for local projects a practical proposition. For this reason, many international infrastructure projects tend to be project-managed by large civil engineering companies, who may use their own construction arms, or a range of large and smaller local construction companies, or some combination of all of these to get the job done.

While both the residential house-building and commercial office markets in the UK and Europe are in deep recession at present, 2009 may well turn out to be a vintage year for the launching of grand infrastructure projects in Europe and the US. Italy, for example, has revived one of Prime Minister Silvio Berlusconi's top projects, the Messina Bridge, which will have a central span of 3.3 kilometers. Once completed at a projected cost of €6.1 billion, the Messina Bridge will be the longest in the world, and will link the island of Sicily to the Italian mainland's Calabria region. It is to be part of a €17.8 billion public works program announced by the Italian government in March 2009, designed to counteract the effects of the global slowdown on Italian jobs and the Italian economy.

The new spending is a supplement to the €16.6 billion on new infrastructure spending announced by the Italian government in November 2008, to include new schools, prisons, and a flood barrier for the ancient city of Venice. Before the original Messina Bridge project was cancelled by the short-lived Socialist government, it involved a truly international consortium of construction and civil engineering companies, including Italy's Impregilo, Condotte, Aci Consorzio Stabile, Cooperativa Muratori & Cementisti (CMC), and Impresa Grassetto, alongside Spain's Sacyr Vallehermoso, and Ishikawajima-Harima Heavy Industries (IHI) from Japan.

One of the biggest construction projects in Latin America at present is the US$5.25 billion expansion of the Panama Canal to accommodate modern vessels that are longer and wider than was the case when the canal was originally built. The expansion program includes the construction of new locks on the Atlantic side, on the east side of the Gatun Locks, and on the Pacific side, to the southwest of the existing Miraflores Locks. It also involves the excavation of new access channels and the widening of existing channels, plus a modest raising of the level of Lake Gatun to accommodate the additional flows of water into the new locks at each locking. Already, three consortia of international companies have put in bids to construct the lock basins, which will take around half of the projected budget.

In the US, President Barack Obama has proposed the creation of a US$25 billion National Infrastructure Bank, as part of the US fiscal budget for 2010. A further US$60 billion to support projects funded by the bank will be raised through the issue of bonds.

One of the major expansion goals for the larger European and US construction companies is to expand their share of the burgeoning Chinese construction market. China is committed to building some 200 new cities over the next few decades. According to a study by the World Bank, cited by a report on China by the American Forest & Paper Association (AFPA), over half the house building that will take place in the world by 2015 will be in China.

Whereas 10 years ago Chinese urban living was dominated by state-provided housing, with urban residents employed in state-owned factories, from 1998 onwards the privatization of China's existing and new housing stock has moved at a pace. Today, some 40% of the Chinese population is urbanized, but by 2020, the percentage of the population living in existing and new cities is expected to reach 60%. That adds up to a building program on a truly gigantic scale.

Foreign direct investment was flowing into China, just before the current downturn, at the rate of US$1 billion a week, according to the World Bank, much of that into construction projects. The AFPA estimates that by 2020 China's housing floor area will be some 69 billion square meters. In 2004, the annual construction value of building in China amounted to between US$200 and US$300 billion, and it was growing at around 8% per annum until 2008.

In addition, the country aims to build a massive 85,000 kilometers of additional highways, plus a vast amount of infrastructure, from sewerage plants to power stations (a four-lane motorway costs around US$4 million per kilometer, double if there are bridges or tunnels involved). It is likely that Western construction companies that succeed in carving a major place for themselves in China, with the help of local Chinese construction companies, will start to achieve a real, global status.

MARKET ANALYSIS

Building Materials—Industry Trends

The building materials sector is extremely diverse and constitutes a sizeable chunk of the industrial base of developed countries. It includes a highly diverse range of suppliers, from cement manufacturers (an area that is under tremendous pressure to both innovate and to "green up"), to specialty glass and steel manufacturers, as well as providing a large market to white goods manufacturers, furniture manufacturers, paint and wiring manufacturers, and a host of other related industries.

One of the biggest boosts for the building materials sector is the seemingly endless raising of the bar by various national planning departments on "green" building. The green building materials market was worth some US$57 billion in 2008 in the US alone, with the residential market being a major driver. One of the biggest segments of this market is the green floor-coverings sector, with renewable products such as woven floor coverings, bamboo, or cork being in huge demand.

Another growth area is concrete production from recycled materials, such as ash from power furnaces (source: the Freedonia Group). Wood from proven, sustainable forests is another area that is set to boom, as are water-efficient plumbing fixtures and energy-efficient lighting fixtures, both of which should see double-digit growth every year to 2013, according to a Green Building Materials report by market analysts, the Freedonia Group.

In the residential homes sector, construction companies are often pulled and pushed in two opposing directions simultaneously by regulations, when it comes to innovations in building materials. On the one hand, anything that helps to "green" a home, by improving its thermal efficiency, or lowering its energy consumption, is regarded as good. On the other hand, local planning offices tend to be very prescriptive on the kinds of materials that are regarded as suitable, and it can be an uphill struggle for new materials to get acceptance.

There are ways around this. Australia, for example, has a Building Products Innovation Council, whose job it is to promote the

most efficient and innovative use of building products across the sector, while still seeing that construction companies adhere to a consistent regulatory framework for building. The council includes senior representation from across the spectrum of the building materials and products side of the building industry, which ensures that the council stays abreast of new product innovations.

The construction sector is, in many ways, both an ideal test bed for scientific innovation, and a powerful economic driver of innovation, as successful products can be taken up in enormous quantities on a worldwide scale. The range of innovation opportunities is as broad as the designer's imagination. One company that specializes in building product innovation, DuPont, has products on offer that range from new materials to construct "storm rooms" to keep families safe in high-risk tornado and hurricane areas, to kitchen counter tops, such as its Zodiaq range which incorporates quartz crystal to create an exceptionally durable and scratch-resistant surface. Many innovations address thermal loss from homes to make them more energy-efficient. Phase change materials, for example, release or absorb large quantities of heat when changing state from one phase to the other. Companies such as BASF and Ciba, which specialize in surface coatings, have come up with micro-encapsulation waxes that enable glass manufacturers to incorporate phase change materials into window construction (see, for example, www.esbits.com, from PCM Innovations).

Innovation need not be a matter of new building materials; it can also be innovation in the way standard materials are used. The German *Passivhaus* standard (source: www.building.co.uk) is a low-energy house, built around a set of principles applied to building design. There are some 15,000 *Passivhaus* builds in the world, and the design principle is promoted by the Passivhaus Institute in Germany. The core is a super-insulated, airtight envelope boosted by the use of glass to promote solar gain, and the result cuts heating requirements by up to 85%.

Home and buildings designers and planners have to think about both materials and the building regulations that are likely to appear in a world dominated by calls for action to cut carbon emissions. Current building requirements are likely to be further amended, almost year on year, to minimize the impact of the built environment on the planet, which means cutting emissions and energy usage. We are at the dawn of "smart" buildings, which react both to energy usage and to the needs of occupants, but many leading architects and designers are already thinking about zero-emissions buildings, or massively taller buildings, or buildings that are themselves virtual "cities"—all concepts that will provide a fertile ground for innovation in building materials.

▸▸ MORE INFO

Websites:

American Forest & Paper Association report on China's construction boom: www.cintrafor.org

Dupont, buildings materials innovation: www.dupont.com

Portland Cement Association: www.cement.org

What's New In Building, UK construction industry site: www.whatsnewinbuilding.com

Defense

MAJOR INDUSTRY TRENDS

Defense Spending and the Global Economic Downturn

Defense spending is clearly the key determinant of the health of the defense industry. It is sensitive to the economic cycle, with democratically elected governments preferring to focus their resources on politically sensitive areas such as healthcare and welfare spending, or on measures to boost employment when their revenues come under pressure during an economic slowdown. Plainly, however, when a country is at war it has little option but to maintain defense spending, regardless of the economic circumstances, and no country is willing to sacrifice its long-term security for the sake of short-term savings.

Certainly, the US will have little option but to maintain defense spending at high levels in the next few years, given its involvement in the conflicts in Iraq and Afghanistan, as well as the "war on terror." Furthermore, many countries will have difficulty cutting their defense spending by significant amounts in the short term. Defense programs can last for decades, and, if a project is already underway, it may be difficult for a government to cancel its order. Defense spending can also be politically sensitive. Cutting back on equipment orders may simply add to unemployment during a recession.

The US is by far the largest market for defense equipment. Many defense analysts argue that President Obama will have no option but to reduce the current record levels of defense spending in order to fund his big economic stimulus plans. This will clearly have a big impact on the overall defense market, for North America accounted for around 39% of global military spending in 2007, according to the research company, Frost & Sullivan. President Obama has proposed a 4% increase in defense spending, to US$534 billion, during the fiscal year beginning in October 2009. However, with a US$787 billion stimulus package, and billions more required to support banks, and possibly other companies, many defense analysts believe that the Pentagon's budget, one of the largest shares of government spending, is likely to be cut.

Given that President Obama has pledged to match the previous administration's costings for Iraq and Afghanistan until late 2010, the focus of any search for cost savings is likely to be big programs such as the US Army's plans to modernize its forces, led by Boeing, and programs such as the F-22 Raptor. Defense spending on government contracts doubled to US$500bn under the Bush administration, and Obama is reportedly looking to reform the process of awarding tenders, in a bid to save US$40bn a year. Perhaps unsurprisingly in this environment, Lockheed launched an advertising campaign in early 2009 to promote the F-22 Raptor, perhaps in a pre-emptive strike to prevent the fighter-aircraft program from being axed.

In Europe, which does not face any obvious military threats, and is not entangled in overseas conflicts on the scale of the US, the economic crisis is already having an impact on defense spending. In March 2009, the German newspaper, *Handelsblatt*, reported that Germany, the UK, Italy, and Spain want to forge a deal to reduce a third-batch delivery of Eurofighter combat aircraft to save money (the German government later denied the claims). The Eurofighter program is slated to cost the German defense budget alone around US$36 billion, according to *Handelsblatt*. The Eurofighter consortium includes Britain's BAE Systems, Airbus's parent, EADS, and Alenia, a unit of Italy's Finmeccanica. The aircraft engines are made by Rolls-Royce, MTU Aero Engines, and ITP. Also in 2009, Eastern European governments began slashing defense budgets in the wake of the economic crisis that hit the region early in the year. In March 2009, Lithuania announced a

  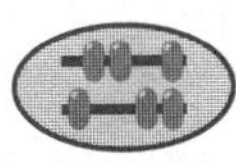   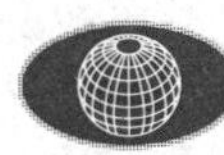   

20% cut in its defense budget, while Poland cut military spending by around US$500 million.

The recession is also having an impact on the UK, which buys more defense equipment than any other country, bar the US and China. In March 2009, a report by the UK National Defence Association warned that a shortfall in the UK's defense budget had reached such a critical point that the government would have to scrap key orders for equipment if it did not increase defense spending. The report said that the projects at risk included orders for two new aircraft carriers (HMS Queen Elizabeth and HMS Prince of Wales), which will cost US$3.5 billion each; a replacement for the Harrier jump jet, the F-35, which will cost US$25 billion; and the replacement for the submarine-borne Trident nuclear missile, which will cost US$60–100 billion over 30 years. The global financial crisis has played havoc with the UK government's finances, and it is doubtful whether London is in a position to increase defense spending—in November 2008, the government predicted that the budget deficit would reach 8% of GDP in 2008, but by March 2009, even this forecast appeared overly optimistic.

Global Financial Crisis Directly Affects Defense Companies

The global financial crisis that began in September 2008 is also hitting military suppliers. In February 2009, Lockheed Martin slashed its earnings forecast for 2009, while Northrop Grumman warned it would report a loss for 2008. In Lockheed's case, the company said it would have to make up shortfalls in its pension fund, which has been hit by the financial crisis. Northrop said the fall in the stock market had prompted it to take a US$3.0–3.4bn charge in the fourth quarter, in order to write down the book value of businesses it took over in 2001 and 2002.

MARKET ANALYSIS

Arms Race Developing in the Asia-Pacific Region

While defense spending is coming under pressure in many countries in the West, it is likely to accelerate significantly in Asia. Indeed, in March 2009, the Singapore *Straits Times* reported that Asia is expected to outstrip the rest of the world in defense spending within seven years as China and India upgrade their armed forces. The newspaper quoted the findings of Frost & Sullivan. The research consultancy had predicted that Asia's overall defense budget would account for 32% of global military spending by 2016, or US$480 billion, up from 24% in 2007, while North America's share of spending would fall from 39% to 29%.

China is certainly one country that will not be cutting back on its defense spending during the global recession. China clearly now intends to develop a military capability to match its new-found economic status. China's insatiable appetite for raw materials and energy has also widened the military's mission to protect China's strategic economic interests overseas. The country's naval and air forces certainly appear determined to impose their dominance in the South China Sea—through which vital oil supplies pass, and where several islands are in dispute—and in the East China Sea, where China and Japan are in dispute over mineral rights, and a number of contested islands.

In March 2009, Beijing announced plans to increase defense spending by 14.9% to CN¥480.7 billion (US$70.3 billion) in 2009. The increase is slightly smaller than the rises that have taken place in previous years, suggesting that Beijing is focusing its spending on boosting the wider economy. However, following increases of 17.8% in 2007 and 17.6% in 2008, China's defense budget will have increased by more than 50% between 2006 and 2009. Furthermore, the US estimates that China's defense spending is much higher than the official figures suggest because many costs, including major arms purchases, are not included in these statistics.

China has denied claims that it "hides" defense spending, and argues that its military spending is not excessive. It says that defense expenditure would amount to 6.3% of its total budget in 2009, and 1.4% of GDP, compared with 4% in the US and 2% in the UK and France. The government says that most of the increased expenditure in 2009 will be focused on improving the historically poor living conditions of soldiers in the People's Liberation Army. In addition, the authorities intend to increase spending on "informatization," in an attempt to close the gap on the US's use of "smart" technology. Defense companies in the West could benefit from China's attempts to upgrade its military technology, although it is extremely doubtful whether Washington would allow American companies to supply technology to China.

Some analysts contend that if China's economic growth remains robust, and the country is thus able to continue to expand its defense spending significantly each year, it will pose a threat to the US's military dominance of the globe by the mid-21st century, or earlier. In early 2009, Beijing confirmed plans to build aircraft carriers, with the apparent intent of projecting "blue water" naval power eastwards into the Pacific, bringing it into potential conflict with the US. For its part, Beijing fears that the US is trying to "encircle" China, by using India, and allies such as Japan and Australia, as proxies to contain China's increasing military strength. China's concerns have some validity—military ties between Washington and New Delhi, for example, are growing in a number of areas.

India is also growing into a major purchaser of US military equipment, an about-turn for a country that relied on Soviet weapons during the Cold War. In a groundbreaking deal, India agreed to buy six Lockheed C130J transport planes for around US$1bn in January 2008—New Delhi had previously procured transport aircraft from the USSR or Russia. The US is also a contender in the race to win an US$11bn deal for multi-role combat aircraft. Lockheed Martin's F-16 and Boeing's F/A-18 are up against the MiG-35 fighter from Russia, the French Rafale (Dassault Aviation), the Swedish JAS-39 Gripen (SAAB), and the European Eurofighter Typhoon (EADS).

In February 2009, India said that the global financial crisis would not affect the modernization of the Indian armed forces or other defense programs. Pradeep Kumar, secretary of state for defense production, was quoted as saying that, "there is no constraint of fund availability for the modernization of the armed forces, and these will go ahead as planned and as per the requirements of the forces." Meanwhile, in March 2009, military spokesmen said that they had plans to hand out contracts worth US$30 billion in the next three to four years.

Other Major Trends

The Environment

It might appear surprising but the US military is arguably doing more to save the planet than any other organization on earth. For the US Defense Department is investing huge sums in the search to develop renewable sources of energy, as well as improving energy efficiency. The key drivers behind this trend include: national security—the US does not want to be dependent upon energy imported from politically unstable regions; cost reasons—even a 5% cut in the fuel bill would save the Department of Defense US$635m (based on the 2007 figure); and, finally, because it makes sound military sense—many lives are lost transporting fuel to the front line in vulnerable convoys.

The US military is already one of the largest consumers of renewable energy in the world, and it has set a goal that 25% of its energy should come from renewable sources by 2025. The US Air Force's goal is that 50% of all the fuels used in domestic training flights will

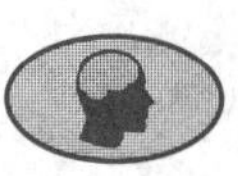

come from synthetic, or non-petroleum, sources by 2016. The US military is also investing heavily in solar and wind power.

Technological Advances

The military is one of the key drivers of technological advances. There are certainly some remarkable developments taking place. The F-35 Joint Strike Fighter, being developed by Lockheed Martin, Northrop Grumman, and BAE Systems, for example, features some extraordinary features. These include technology that allows the pilot to look through the structure of the aircraft. The aircraft also features voice commands that significantly reduce the pilot's workload.

The military is also investing heavily in information technology on land. Military units constantly transmit huge amounts of data back and forth to report their position, generate situational awareness, and share information on enemy tactics. Soldiers with access to laptops, for example, can provide vital information to military commanders. Real-time management of information enables rapid decision-making, meaning that military operations can proceed quickly, possibly providing a decisive advantage during a battle.

Cyberspace: The New Battlefield

Unsurprisingly, given the new emphasis on information technology, governments around the world are investing heavily in measures to protect their computer networks from attacks, and to launch their own cyber attacks. In 2007, the *Financial Times* reported (September 27, 2007) that, "the Chinese military is constantly trying to penetrate the defenses of US military networks, and the Pentagon is widely believed to attempt the same operations on its Chinese counterpart." The newspaper added: "Chinese military doctrine has emphasized the growing importance of cyberspace as a domain for war-fighting. While China still lags behind the US considerably in terms of capabilities on land, at sea, and in the air, in cyberspace it has the capability to impose great costs on the US." Many large defense companies have already branched out into cyber-security and information-technology services.

▸▸ MORE INFO

Websites:

DefenseLINK, official website of the US Department of Defense: www.defenselink.mil

Jane's Defence Weekly, long-established and respected source of information on developments in global defense matters: www.janes-defence-weekly.com

Stockholm International Peace Research Institute, which details trends in military spending: www.sipri.org/contents/milap/milex/mex_trends.html

E-Commerce

MAJOR INDUSTRY TRENDS

Electronic commerce, or e-commerce, involves the sale of goods and services via electronic means—principally over the internet, although sales via television (terrestrial, cable, and satellite) are also included. E-commerce can be further divided into the following sectors: business-to-business (B2B), business-to-government (B2G), consumer-to-consumer (C2C), government-to-business (G2B), government-to-citizen (G2C), and business-to-consumer (B2C). Retailers that rely primarily on e-commerce to sell goods or services are often referred to as e-tailers.

Retailing over the internet generally takes one of two forms:

- Cybermalls—the most famous cybermall is eBay, which offers access to products from a variety of independent retailers.
- Individual websites—most major retailers now have their own websites, which complement their traditional "bricks-and-mortar" outlets. Some retailers operate solely over the internet.

In terms of television sales, programs on dedicated shopping channels generally feature a presenter who demonstrates products on air. Viewers can buy these products by telephoning an order line with their credit card details or, in the case of interactive television services, by using their remote controls. Recent years have seen the development of a variety of selling techniques, including on-air auctions.

E-commerce is most closely associated with the internet, and has developed in tandem with the growth of the medium. Indeed, e-commerce initially became possible with the opening up of the internet to commercial users in the early 1990s. However, it wasn't until the latter half of the decade that companies really began to exploit the internet's commercial potential.

A number of start-up companies, such as Amazon and eBay, have exploited the power of the internet to emerge as retailing behemoths in their own right. However, e-commerce has largely been developed by established large retailers, which regard it as simply another sales channel. The gigantic grocery retailers that have expanded away from food and into a wide variety of other areas, such as clothing and electronic goods, have been particularly quick to appreciate its potential. The medium has also created opportunities for very small businesses. It is now possible to buy over the internet a wide range of specialized products that are not available in shopping malls. Thus, the internet has provided a lifeline for many small producers, and has allowed entrepreneurs to enter the retailing sector without the need to invest heavily in physical retail outlets.

E-commerce has proven so successful because it offers significant advantages to both consumers and retailers. Consumers can compare a vast array of retailers in a few minutes—something that it would be impossible to do physically. Online retailers often sell products and services at a significant discount to those offered by traditional outlets, and buying online is convenient: consumers can make their purchases from the comfort of their own home, and have them delivered to their door. Furthermore, online shopping appeals to the environmentally conscious. In March 2009, researchers at Heriot-Watt University in the UK revealed that online shopping is 24 times "greener" than taking the car to the shops, and seven times "greener" than taking the bus. The researchers compared the carbon footprint of a typical delivery from a local depot with average carbon footprints for shopping trips by car and bus, and found that home deliveries involved much lower levels of carbon emissions. For businesses, the advantages of e-commerce lie mainly in the low cost of setting up and maintaining a business. Firms do not need to invest heavily in a physical presence, or in sales staff. However, they do have to organize payment systems, distribution, and returns.

Industry Suitability

Undoubtedly, some industries are more suited to e-commerce than others. This type of retailing is most applicable to goods that are fairly simple, commoditized, and do not require on-the-spot input from knowledgeable sales staff. Thus, grocery retailing is ideally suited to e-commerce, whereas consumers generally need to try on

clothing before they make a purchase. Equally, the penetration of e-commerce may be high in some sectors of a given market, but low in others. In financial services, for example, purchasing of insurance or a loan, both highly commoditized products, is ideally suited to the internet. However, many people prefer to buy a sophisticated financial product, such as a pension, on a face-to-face basis, as they will almost certainly require advice before making their choice. Generally, it is difficult to make online sales of sophisticated goods and services that require a large amount of advice or input from the retailer.

Technological Advances

The growth of broadband internet connections around the globe has undoubtedly boosted online shopping, simply by dramatically speeding up the process of accessing websites, and buying goods. Broadband is at least ten times as fast as dial-up. Having access to broadband means that consumers are more likely to use the internet to purchase everyday items such as groceries. However, faster connection speeds also allow users to download music files, video clips, and movies, or to compete in online gaming, further boosting the potential revenues generated by e-commerce.

Traditionally, individuals and businesses have ordered goods or services online via computers, but the increasing availability of broadband on mobile phones has opened up another avenue for e-tailers. Indeed, a report published in March 2009 by ABI Research, based in New York, said that consumers are increasingly using their phones for financial transactions. ABI said that growth in e-commerce is being driven primarily by payment via SMS (short message service), mobile internet, and mobile applications. In industrialized countries, mobile users are becoming familiar and comfortable with using cell phones for more than just voice communication. In developing nations, mobile financial services are popular as an alternative to scarce local financial institutions.

Surprisingly, given that the US is generally regarded as the most advanced economy in the world, its broadband penetration rates are relatively low, according to the Organization for Economic Cooperation and Development (OECD), which publishes data on the subject (see More Info). In June 2008, Denmark had the highest penetration rate for broadband, at 36.7 per 100 inhabitants. It was followed by the Netherlands (35.5), Norway (33.4), Switzerland (32.7), and Iceland (32.3). The USA was in 15th place, with a penetration rate of 25 per 100 inhabitants.

Advances in technology are increasing the penetration of e-commerce in sectors previously regarded as unsuitable for this type of retailing, such as clothing. Currently, online sales account for just 3–5% of the total clothing market in Europe. However, innovative websites now allow consumers to "try on" clothes virtually, and analysts believe that this will cause online sales of clothing to grow rapidly.

MARKET ANALYSIS

Calculating the overall size of the global e-commerce market is complicated by the relatively high levels of cross-border sales that take place. Furthermore, few research companies measure all the various sectors of the market (B2B, B2C, etc). However, the research company eMarketer, which is based in the US, estimated worldwide e-retail sales at US$438 billion in 2008.

The US is almost certainly the largest market, reflecting the size of its economy. Total e-commerce sales in the US during 2008 were estimated at $133.6 billion, an increase of 4.6% on 2007, according to the US Commerce Department. However, according to a report by the analysts, Forrester Research, published in March 2009, UK online shoppers outspend both their American and European counterparts. More than half of all UK consumers, or about 28 million people, shop online regularly—and these shoppers estimate that they spend an average of £1,312 per year online. By comparison, German consumers spend an average of £771 per year online, while French consumers spend an average of £693. Forrester says that UK retailers are the "most sophisticated in all of Europe" when it comes to web retailing, because they realize that "the internet is their biggest opportunity."

Rapidly developing countries such as China, India, and Brazil have huge potential in terms of internet sales, according to the research firm, Key Note Ltd. The company says that "these countries are not only benefiting from fast-rising living standards, but are also spread over huge geographic distances, and thus offer great potential for online sales." The use of the internet is certainly growing rapidly in these countries. China's online population, the world's largest, grew by 41.9% in 2008, to 298 million, according to the government-linked China Internet Network Information Centre (CINIC). The number of internet users in China, which has a population of 1.3 billion, was thus almost the same as the entire population of the US. A study by CINIC said that 234 million people in China had surfed the internet to read or watch news by the end of 2008.

Varying Business Models

Companies have adopted differing business models for their e-commerce operations. Amazon operates from vast warehouses, as does Ocado, a grocery retailer based in the UK. In the Ocado model, pickers inside the warehouse service thousands of internet orders, which are stacked, packed into pods that are attached to big trucks, and then transported all over the UK to car parks, where the pods are slotted onto individual vans for street-level deliveries. Other retailers pursue different models. The UK's Tesco, the third-largest retailer in the world, bases its online shopping business at individual stores. Tesco's website sends orders to the store nearest to the shopper, and pickers visit the store's shelves to fill the orders. Tesco vans then take the orders out locally.

Amazon is regarded as one of the pioneers of e-commerce, and continues to go from strength to strength. Founded in 1995 by Jeff Bezos to sell books, Amazon now sells a wide range of consumer products, and is one of the best-known internet retailers. By the end of the 1990s, Amazon's revenue was around US$1.5 billion a

MORE INFO

Websites:

ABI Research, a supplier of technology market research: www.abiresearch.com

Key Note Ltd, provides research on a wide range of markets, including retailing: www.keynote.co.uk

OECD Broadband Portal: www.oecd.org/sti/ict/broadband

Statistical reports on internet development in China: www.cnnic.net.cn/en/index

US Census Bureau—Quarterly Retail E-Commerce Sales: www.census.gov/mrts/www/ecomm.html

See Also:

★ Avoiding the Mistakes of the Past: Lessons from the Startup World (pp. 749–750)
- Being Digital (p. 1226)
- Business @ the Speed of Thought: Succeeding in the Digital Economy (p. 1232)
- The Caring Economy: Business Principles for the New Digital Age (p. 1233)
- Digital Capital: Harnessing the Power of Business Webs (p. 1248)

  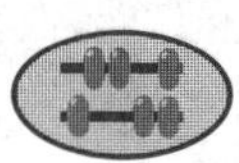      

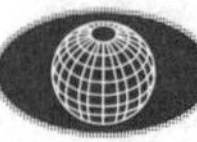

year, but it was still making a loss—it had to borrow around US$1 billion each year just to keep afloat. However, it managed to survive the financial storm, and, by the middle of the current decade, was making a healthy profit. Indeed, in 2005, on Amazon's 10th birthday, Bezos said that his aim was to turn Amazon into the Wal-Mart of electronic retailing, with a company mantra of "get big fast." In the year ending December 31, 2007, Amazon's net sales were US$14.835 billion, a 38.5% increase on the previous year. In 2008, sales continued to surge, expanding by 18%, to US$6.7 billion, in the final quarter of the calendar year.

However, another pathfinder, eBay, has encountered difficulties in recent years. Indeed, in March 2009, the company unveiled a new three-year business plan, and a change in strategy. eBay remains best known for its auction site. In recent years, it has expanded into fixed-price goods in a wide variety of product categories, with the apparent aim of taking on Amazon, but growth has slumped at its auction business, while eBay has failed to make significant progress with its fixed-price goods. The company's PayPal payment-processing division is now the fastest-growing sector of the business. eBay now plans to create a one-stop shop, where customers can make purchases in a variety of ways—from bidding in auctions to clicking on advertisements, scanning classifieds, or making outright purchases. However, the company admitted in March 2009 that even an improved site will grow more slowly than overall e-commerce during the year. eBay hopes to grow as quickly as the industry in 2010, and to once again start outpacing it in 2011. The company forecast that sales would rise from US$8.5 billion in 2008, to US$11–12 billion in 2011.

Electronics

MAJOR INDUSTRY TRENDS

If there is one sector that is changing the nature of the world we live in faster than any other, it is electronics. From mobile phones to the internet, from telecommunications to satellite TV, electronics are ubiquitous and advancing by leaps and bounds, with more power being crammed into less space year on year. It is fashionable at this point to quote Moore's Law. Geoffrey Moore was the co-founder of the PC chip company, Intel, and the man famous for predicting that the number of transistors on the same-sized piece of silicon would double every two years—without bothering even to imply an end date for this process.

A few years ago, it was thought that Moore's Law was running out of steam, as circuits were (a) becoming small enough for quantum effects to introduce instability in current flow, and (b) becoming crowded enough for the heat generated from operating the chip to start to be a real problem. However, advances in silicon substrate technology (the introduction of metal oxide gates, for example) opened up the door again, and Moore's Law still holds good. Instead of Intel merely producing one central processing unit (CPU, the calculating "heart" of a microcomputer) on a chip, it produced first two CPUs per chip, then four, then eight, and we are very close to 16-CPU chips, with higher multiples possible and planned beyond this.

Simultaneously, the software industry is on a steep learning curve as it rewrites its applications to take full advantage of the vast amounts of processing power becoming available, whether at the server, on people's desks, or on a plethora of handheld devices, from palmtop computers to mobile phones.

As the amount of cheap computer power available to engineers has increased, the power of electronics to transform the world has moved forward in leaps and bounds. No part of industry is now untouched. The ability to simulate real physics inside "the box" has allowed car-makers to stress-test both virtual parts and the whole design, long before metal goes anywhere near being machined. In advanced medicine, biosciences companies model molecules and processes to predict drug interactions on target proteins or cell constituents, before any real-world work is done. In the oil and gas sector, vast data sets from seismic and advanced scanning of reservoirs are turned into visual, three-dimensional models that geologists can "walk through," to examine reservoirs "from the inside" before any well is drilled.

The ability to create and explore real physics through virtual models increases dramatically with each new breakthrough in processing power. Advances in electronics truly have the power to change the rules for whole industries.

The electronics manufacturing sector is generally separated from the electrical manufacturing sector by a technical distinction. Under this, the term "electronics" refers to the flow of charge through non-metal conductors, such as silicon in semiconductor implementations, and "electrical" refers to the flow of charge through metal conductors. Electrical is all about wires, and electronics is all about semiconductors, broadly speaking. The latter leads to printed circuit boards (PCBs) and memory chips, while the former leads to white goods and power stations (with the proviso that almost all electrical goods these days have some PCB control circuitry somewhere).

MARKET ANALYSIS

From an industry perspective, electronics has spawned a vast range of specialist industries, from the IT industry (dominated by the likes of IBM and its competitors at the mainframe end, and Intel and AMD at the PC end), to the mobile-phone market. It includes TV-set manufacturers, video-game consoles, and, across an array of industry sectors, a vast army of specialist control-systems manufacturers, not to mention the aviation and auto sectors, both of which could not exist in their present forms without massive input from the electronics sector. Then there is the medical devices market, and so on and so forth.

Asia, today, is regarded as the powerhouse of PCB and memory-chip production, yet it all began through a combination of some breakthrough research in Japan, and US companies outsourcing first PCB assembly, then PCB fabrication, to Asia to take advantage of cheap labor rates. Today, Asia's dominance in motherboard and memory-chip manufacturing has reached the point where a US air force colonel, Charles Howe, was prompted to write a strategic study looking at the potential impact on US national security of having so much of the electronics industry outside the US.

The point is not without irony, as the semiconductor industry began in the US with innovations such as Texas Instruments' invention of the integrated circuit in 1958, and Intel's production of the first 8-bit microprocessor, the 8008, in 1972. Howe's study gives a very clear account of the integrated circuit (IC) design process. The basic design process requires electronic design automation (EDA) software in the hands of experts. Fabrication involves "etching" or imprinting the designs onto silicon wafers.

Each new generation of chip tends to require either a totally retooled fabrication plant ("fab"), or a new plant built from scratch. Each plant costs around US$3 billion, which means that each new generation of chip represents a huge bet by the manufacturer that it can sell vast numbers of its chips to the various global markets.

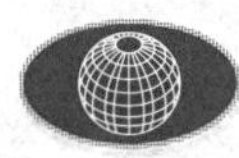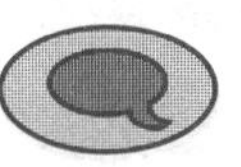

Very few companies in the world can bet on that scale and get it wrong twice, so semiconductor chip manufacturing is a game with very high entry costs, and is played for very high stakes. Asian chip companies generally play a safer game, and focus on producing not CPUs, but peripheral components, such as motherboards and memory chips.

The entire semiconductor industry is tremendously vulnerable to downturns in the economy, as in all markets, from PCs to mobile phones, the sale of new products is predicated on global growth. There is no doubt that the semiconductor industry is suffering from the global downturn. The industry recorded its first year-on-year drop in sales, at the end of 2008, since the dot.com crash in 2001.

According to the Semiconductor Industry Association (SIA), total sales for 2008 amounted to US$248.6 billion, down slightly from the $255.6 billion figure for 2007 (−2.8%). The sales for December highlighted that sharpness of the downturn, with sales falling from US$22.3 billion in December 2007, to just US$17.4 billion in December 2008, down 22%. There was also a steep decline month on month, in that November 2008 sales were US$20.9 billion, which meant that December's figure represents a fall of 16.6%.

What made the December figures worse is that the fourth quarter is traditionally a strong quarter for the industry, boosted by Christmas sales of new PCs, laptops, and handheld devices in the retail market. However, SIA president, George Scalise, commenting on the results, said that weakness was experienced across the semiconductor industry, including automotive products, PCs, cell phones, and corporate IT products. The steepest declines, though, he pointed out, were in the memory sector, where manufacturers cut prices hugely in order to boost volume.

According to the SIA, consumer demand now accounts for 50% of the worldwide drive for semiconductors, which means that the fortunes of the chip industry "are increasingly linked to macroeconomic conditions such as GDP, consumer confidence, and disposable income."

However, global demand still exists, and Asian producers, particularly, are seeing strong orders for memory for cell phones and PCs, which is driving up the total "bits shipped" figure. The reason for this is the seemingly irreversible hunger of devices of all kinds for more and more internal memory. As the world moves to more video content over mobile phones, for example, the pressure for more memory grows and grows.

Video is massively more memory-hungry than voice, which itself is more demanding on memory than text. However, price pressure on the sector is intense, and margins are being slashed.

"Over the past 12 months, DRAM [a memory chip] content in the typical PC grew by 44%, to an average of 1.8 gigabytes, while the NAND content of a typical cell phone increased by 244%," the SIA says. Yet the industry is basically making a lot more memory for a lot less money, and revenues are in decline.

The Asian Semiconductor Industry

The Asian semiconductor industry began in the 1960s, with small pockets of foreign investment. Japan established a semiconductor industry in the 1970s, and in 1979 Fujitsu became the first company to mass-produce 64 KB memory chips, with Japan cornering the world market in memory chips by the mid-1980s, passing the US in semiconductor production volumes. By the late 1980s, South Korea had developed a thriving memory-chip industry, with companies such as Samsung enjoying rapid growth. Taiwanese investment generated the world's first "on-demand, fab-for-hire" plant, and Singapore, Malaysia, and China have all developed significant chip industries.

According to Colonel Howe's study, the first US outsourcing investment in the sector was by Fairchild Semiconductor in Hong Kong in 1961. Outsourcing began with chip assembly (bringing the various components together to complete a printed circuit board), then moved to fabrication, and, later, in the 1980s, to chip design.

Asia's dominance of many aspects of the world chip industry today is illustrated by the fact that its share of the US$248 billion global sales in the sector for 2006 amounted to more than 60%. Until the current downturn, Asia was also the fastest-growing semiconductor arena, with a 12.8% compound annual growth rate (CAGR) in the years from 2002 to 2006.

By contrast, Europe's semiconductor sales grew by just 4.2% CAGR, and the US by 8.5% (source: Datamonitor). In 2006, the largest end-markets for semiconductor products were PCs (44%), consumer electronics (17%), and cell phones (17%), in all of which Asian manufacturers figure strongly.

According to the Electronic Industries Alliance (EIA), a national trade organization that includes the full spectrum of US electronics manufacturers, national paranoia about where semiconductor work is done, or who "owns" what, has the potential to be hugely counterproductive to the sector. As a sector that thrives on R&D and innovation, the greater the number of participants, and the freer and more open the semiconductor "universe" is, the better it will be for the sector, and for the global economy, the EIA argues.

In a new initiative titled "The Technology Industry at an Innovation Crossroads," the EIA argues strongly against what it sees as the possibility of protectionist policies stifling innovation in the sector. "The core value of a knowledge-based company or society should be innovation," it says. The US and other Western countries should not be worrying about the possibility of China or India dominating the semiconductor industry in years to come; they should be working to develop a vision and a strategy for the sector, the EIA says.

This opens up one of the really important themes for the sector. Electronics has enabled the globalization of business, and the electronics sector has itself, in turn, been shaped by globalization. "The resulting reorganization of manufacturing (in all sectors) along global lines, plus the creation of new, globally competitive service and knowledge-based industries (of which the semiconductor industry is a prime example) poses unprecedented challenges. . .," the EIA says.

Countries with weak science and mathematics education, and with a dearth of R&D funding, will fall behind countries that prioritize these areas. Similarly, countries that stay open to what the EIA calls "the brightest foreign minds," and that allow their companies to recruit the best from around the world, will prosper, while those that seek to restrict high-paid knowledge jobs to their own nationals will fall behind.

The semiconductor industry has already enabled software designers to go some way down the road to "virtualizing" our world, creating immensely powerful tools for solving real-world problems far faster than ever before, and enabling new products, new drugs,

MORE INFO

Report:

Spillman, Mark S. "The Asian semiconductor industry and it's potential impacts to U.S. national security." Washington, DC: Industrial College of the Armed Forces, 2007. Online at: www.ndu.edu/icaf/industry/awards/lockwood/Lockwood_Award_07.pdf

Websites:

Electronic Industry Alliance: www.eia.org

Semiconductor Industry Association: www.sia-online.org

  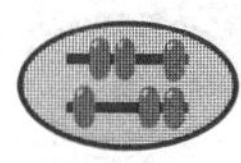      

and new forms of entertainment (of which the video-games console and the mobile phone are two stunning examples) to be brought to market extremely rapidly.

It is a safe bet that this sector is going to change life as we know it almost beyond recognition over the coming decades. As such, it is certainly a sector worth watching.

Energy

MAJOR INDUSTRY TRENDS

Energy is the lifeblood of civilized society. It is also intimately bound up with the future of the planet, in the eyes of many, in that the industrialization of the West, fueled by energy from coal for the most part, and latterly from oil and gas, has added to or brought about global warming. Now, the industrialization of emerging nations like China and India, again largely driven by coal, but with both countries having a voracious appetite for oil and gas, is adding to the pressure on energy resources, and on the environment.

According to the June 2008 report from the US Energy Information Administration (EIA), which provides official energy statistics, the total world consumption of marketed energy will increase by 50% over the period from 2005 to 2030. The largest projected increase in this growth in demand comes from non-Organization for Economic Cooperation and Development (OECD) economies, with demand from these economies outstripping that of OECD economies some time around 2012.

The EIA projection of energy demand takes into account the fact that oil prices will inevitably rise again in the near term. The rise is likely to slow the growth of energy demand, but robust economic growth, particularly in Asia, allied to expanding populations in the world's developing countries, will keep demand rising by around 2.5% year on year. By way of contrast, energy demand in the OECD economies is projected to increase at an average annual rate of only 0.7%.

In 1980, China and India together accounted for less than 8% of the world's total energy consumption. By 2005, that share had grown to 18%. By 2030, these two countries will account for 25% of total world energy consumption, the EIA projects. In stark contrast, US energy consumption, which currently dominates global consumption, is projected to fall from 22% in 2005 to around 17% by 2030.

The EIA report is good news for the "green agenda," in that it predicts that sharply rising oil prices will be far more effective than any lobbying in moving societies away from a long-term dependence on oil. The consumption of oil and gas will increase at an average annual rate of 1.2% over the period until 2030. Instead, the dominant growth will be in the use of renewable energy and coal, with consumption increasing by 2.1% and 2.0% respectively. Abundant coal reserves in large energy-consuming countries such as China, India, and the US, make coal an economical fuel choice, the EIA says.

Natural gas, however, will continue to be an important fuel for electricity generation worldwide, being more efficient and less carbon-intensive than other fossil fuels. The EIA sees total natural gas consumption increasing by 1.7% per year on average, from 104 trillion cubic feet, to 158 trillion cubic feet over the period. The share of natural gas in electricity production will go up from 20% in 2005 to 25% by 2030, it says. Coal will account for 29% of world energy consumption by 2030.

Net electricity generation worldwide will reach around 33.3 trillion kWh (kilowatt hours) in 2030, nearly double the 2005 total of 17.3 trillion kWh, with non-OECD electricity generation increasing by 4% year on year, as rising standards of living generate increased demand.

Nuclear power will continue to play an important role, the EIA says. It expects electricity generation from nuclear power to increase from 2.6 trillion kWh in 2005 to 3 trillion by 2015, and 3.8 trillion by 2030. This prediction is predicated on older nuclear plants in the OECD and non-OECD countries having their lives extended, as well as new-build programs coming on stream.

However, the EIA sees several issues that could slow the commissioning of nuclear power plants. Plant safety, disposal of radioactive waste, and concerns over nuclear weapons are all factors, it says.

Countries will also be turning to renewables, particularly hydroelectric power, but also to other grid-connected renewables. Much of the growth in renewable energy consumption is expected to come from mid-to-large-scale hydroelectric facilities in non-OECD countries. China's 18,200 MW Three Gorges Dam project, the EIA points out, is due to start generating soon. China also has the 12,600 MW Xiluodu project on the Jisha River, which is scheduled for completion in 2020, plus another project, the 6,300 MW Longtan plant on the Hongshui River.

OECD Europe is doing exceptionally well in implementing renewables, with 8,554 MW of new capacity brought on stream in 2007. The EU's target of achieving 20% of energy consumption from renewables by 2020, of which 10% will come from biofuels in cars, is very achievable.

MARKET ANALYSIS

The Future of Coal

In its report, "Technology to clean up coal for the post-oil era," Deutsche Bank Research argues that the dominant energy-generation technology for the post-oil era will be solar power. The main generating areas will be the world's deserts. Electricity will be sent via transmission lines to the world's cities. However, en route to this brave new world, coal will have a critical role in filling the gap between the end of oil (which comes about when oil is just too expensive to use, rather than when it runs out) and the arrival of solar power in sufficient quantities, the report argues. Populous emerging economies will generate more demand for energy than can be filled by oil or natural gas. The natural alternative to meeting the needs of the world's three main energy consuming arenas—power generation, the heating market, and transportation—is coal, Deutsche Bank argues.

However, as coal causes 40% of global CO_2 emissions (source: Deutsche Bank: Energy Special, February 6, 2007), mining more coal will require the deployment of new technologies to clean up coal-fired emissions.

The report points out that, at the start of 2007, there were already plans to invest some US$10 trillion in coal-fired power-generation plants. The demand is not just in China and India. Germany has passed a law mandating a move from nuclear power to "other sources." The report points out that coal accounted for 24% of Germany's primary energy consumption in 2005, a higher percentage even than natural gas (23%), and it accounted for nearly 23% of Germany's electricity generation.

According to statistics from Germany's Federal Institute for Geosciences and Natural Resources, coal comprises some 55% of the global reserves of all non-renewable sources of energy, including oil, gas, and uranium. Mapping current reserves to current usage, there are sufficient reserves of coal to continue at this pace for the

  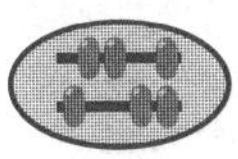 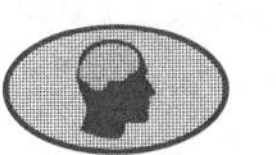   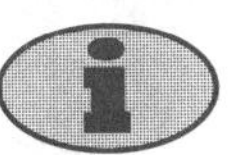  

next 153 years. By way of contrast, oil and gas would last just 42 years and 62 years, respectively, at current consumption. Using liquefaction techniques (coal to liquids), coal could even replace oil as a motor fuel, the report points out.

Wind Power

The world's wind energy capacity will nearly triple in the five years to 2014, according to the Global Wind Energy Council (GWEC), the industry forum for the global wind power sector. This development will be led by what the GWEC calls "tremendous growth in China," and steady expansion in Europe and North America. GWEC predicts that in 2013, five years from now, global wind-generating capacity will stand at 332 GW, up from 120 GW at the end of 2008. During 2013, 56.3 GW of wind-generating capacity will be added, more than double the annual market in 2008.

The year-on-year growth rates during this period will average 22%, which is modest compared to an average increase of 28% over the last ten years. Strong policy support for wind power will continue to drive growth in the three main markets of China, Europe, and the US. Steve Sawyer, Secretary General of GWEC, says: "Governments are turning the current crisis into an opportunity, putting wind power at the center of their economic stimulus and recovery programs. This will create many thousands of jobs, improve energy security, and help address the climate crisis."

For the past few years, the US and China have continuously outperformed GWEC's most optimistic expectations. However, for the next year or two, developments in the US are expected to be hampered by a lack of financing and the overall economic downturn, before the stimulus package will start having a major impact on the market. At the same time, growth in China is set to continue at a breathtaking rate, driving a substantial increase in global wind energy installations in the coming years.

According to Arthouros Zervos, GWEC's chairman: "All of the fundamental drivers that have made wind power the technology of choice for those seeking to build a secure, clean energy future are still in place. Wind power is clean, indigenous, fast to deploy, creates many jobs, uses virtually no water, and is economically competitive. Neither the threat of climate change nor the macroeconomic insecurity (in some countries) due to reliance on imported fossil fuel is going to go away because of the recession."

Biofuels and the Biofuel Controversy

The World Bank has carried out several studies into the use of biofuels, and has looked at the trade-offs between sustainability and the risk of diverting farmlands away from food production. It argues that current biofuel policies could lead to a fivefold increase in the share of biofuels in global transport, from just over 1% at present to around 6% by 2020.

The World Bank points to the crucial role of subsidies from governments in getting biofuel initiatives off the ground. "Such support includes consumption incentives (fuel tax reductions); production incentives (tax incentives, loan guarantees, and direct subsidy payments); and mandatory consumption requirements. More than 200 support measures, which cost around US$5.5 billion to US$7.3 billion a year in the United States, amount to US$0.38 to US$0.49 per liter of petroleum equivalent for ethanol," it notes.

Domestic producers in the European Union and the United States receive additional support through high import tariffs on ethanol. The World Bank argues, too, that it is now clear that biofuel production has pushed up feedstock prices. "The clearest example is maize, whose price rose by over 60% from 2005 to 2007, largely because of [demand from] the US ethanol program, combined with reduced stocks of maize in major exporting countries." Feedstock supplies are likely to remain constrained in the near term, the Bank says, but as farmers will respond to high feedstock prices by planting more land to grow maize, the price will stabilize. Moreover, as the feedstock price rises, the profit from—and, therefore, the incentives to manufacture—biofuels will diminish. However, the ethical dimension of the food or fuel debate does not look promising for the future of biofuels, the Bank suggests.

"The grain required to fill the tank of a sports utility vehicle with ethanol (240 kilograms of maize for 100 liters of ethanol) could feed one person for a year; this shows how food and fuel compete. Rising prices of staple crops can cause significant welfare losses for the poor, most of whom are net buyers of staple crops," the Bank says. However, it admits that the picture is not straightforward. Many other poor producers, who are net sellers of these crops, would benefit from the higher prices to be gained from growing maize for ethanol production. Moreover, shifting ethanol production from maize to timber waste could potentially reduce the pressure on food crops, it says. The debate still has a long way to go.

Nuclear Power

According to the International Atomic Energy Agency, debates about nuclear power generation must take into account three principal realities. The first is that as oil and gas prices rise, and as citizens in developing countries look to achieve Western standards of living, demand for energy increases and, as a corollary, expectations for nuclear power are also on the rise.

The second point, the IAEA says, is that "one size does not fit all," and questions such as "is nuclear power economic?" do not have a single, universally applicable answer. "As with just about everything else in life, the answer is 'it depends'—sometimes yes, sometimes no."

The third element, the IAEA says, is economics. Whether nuclear power lives up to the rising expectations will depend on how cheap it is compared to alternative energy sources. "Certainly, the nuclear industry can influence this issue by bringing down costs, but there are factors outside the industry's control, such as the price of natural gas or of carbon credits, that will also determine, for any particular investor, whether nuclear is a cost-effective option."

From 1960 to the mid-to-late 1980s, global nuclear capacity grew to the point where nuclear power generated some 16% of total global electricity generation. This held steady through the 1990s but fell to around 15% by 2006. The global picture is extremely varied, with some countries (for example, China) having just 2% nuclear in the mix, and others (France) having 78% of their electricity generated from nuclear.

According to the IAEA, as of March 2008, there were 439 nuclear power plants in the world, with 35 more under construction, and 20 of these are in Asia. At the same time, 28 of the last 39 nuclear plants connected to the grid are in Asia, which tells its own story. The IAEA's highest estimate of nuclear production by 2030 is 691 GW of capacity, or a 93% increase in the world's nuclear capacity.

MORE INFO

Websites:

Deutsche Bank Research: www.dbresearch.com
Energy Information Administration: www.eia.doe.gov
Global Wind Energy Council, home of the global wind power industry: www.gwec.net
International Atomic Energy Agency: www.iaea.org
World Bank: www.econ.worldbank.org

See Also:

★ Public–Private Partnerships in Emerging Markets (pp. 562–565)

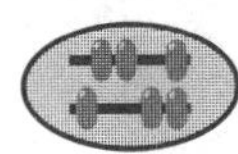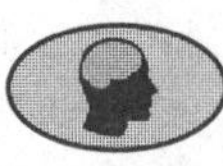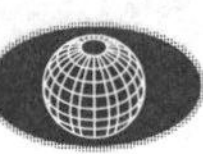

Engineering

MAJOR INDUSTRY TRENDS

The engineering sector encompasses a bewildering array of possible roles, and touches virtually all other industry segments. The discipline of engineering is generally subdivided into mechanical, electrical, and chemical engineering on the macro scale. However, with its connotations of pragmatic manipulation, as in using a body of skill and techniques to achieve a designated impact in the real world, engineering as a term is now readily applied to fields as diverse as software, genetics, and finance.

On this last point, the College of Engineering at the University of Michigan, for example, offers a financial engineering degree, teaching students how to use applied mathematics to analyze financial derivatives. In fact, the original financial engineers, whom many blame for devising some of the complex derivatives that played such a big role in the current global banking crisis, were drawn from the fields of process and operations engineering, as well as from applied mathematics backgrounds.

Understanding the behavior of complex systems, such as near-turbulent water flows, is, after all, an engineering specialty and is an essential part of propeller design. There are also numerous other classic engineering problems involving near-chaotic systems. Moving from this to spotting short-lasting, predictable trends in complex data flows, such as trades on millions of stocks, is not that big a jump.

For those concerned with educating the next generation of engineers, the way in which new fields, such as nanotechnology or genetics, are opening up rich, new seams for engineering, is not surprising. The US National Academy of Engineering (NAE) holds a symposium every year under the banner "Frontiers of Engineering—Reports on leading-edge engineering" (see www.nae.edu). In 2008, the four topics covered were: drug delivery systems, emerging nanoelectronic devices, cognitive engineering, and countering the proliferation of weapons of mass destruction.

If the proverbial man on the street were asked to guess four unlikely topics for a stereotypical engineer to be involved with, one could place a relatively safe bet that these topics would be among those on his list. Yet all four topics were extremely ably dealt with by leading young engineers.

With drug delivery systems, advances in new materials have opened up new ways of administering drugs to patients using, for example, engineered particles providing sustained release of therapies over an extended time frame. With nanoelectronic devices, the search is on to find circuit concepts and sensor functionalities, such as new switches, that can develop new technologies for information processing to create wholly new kinds of computers.

In a book, *The Engineering of 2020: Visions of Engineering in the New Century*, published in 2004 by the NAE, the Academy points out that, in the past, "changes in the engineering profession and engineering education have followed changes in technology and society. Disciplines were added and curricula were created to meet the critical challenges in society, and to provide the workforce required to integrate new developments into the economy."

However, today, technological change is occurring at a faster and faster pace. Engineering needs to apply some of its skills to anticipating future necessary advances, and adapting the education of future generations of engineers to be there "ahead of the curve," insofar as that is possible, the NAE argues.

In point of fact, this is likely to be where the real locus of competition between nations and, indeed, between multinational and multidisciplinary engineering companies will lie in a few years' time. Firms and nations that are best placed with innovative answers to emerging global challenges, be these to do with food crises, or aberrant weather patterns, or power or water shortages, will become the leaders in the field.

Simultaneously with all this, of course, established international engineering companies specializing in a huge array of disciplines, are essential generators of GDP growth in virtually all the developed, and many developing economies. This leads directly to the topic of outsourcing, which is one of the major themes in manufacturing, engineering, and design today.

MARKET ANALYSIS

A year or so ago, it was fashionable for governments in Europe and the US, and particularly in the UK, to urge manufacturers to "go up the value chain," to avoid competition from low-wage economies. The point followed logically enough from the fact that volume manufacturing, of the "pile 'em high, sell 'em cheap" variety, is essentially about price, and the lower the wages paid, the cheaper the price of the end-product.

It followed that manufacturers based in China or India, where wages were a lot lower than in advanced economies, would drive their counterparts based in high-wage economies out of business.

To counter this, the argument went, Western manufacturers should use their engineering and design know-how to focus on high-value, complex products. The problem with this argument, many people noticed, is that it presupposes that low-wage economies are trapped forever doing "grunt" low-wage jobs, and will not be able to do high-quality engineering and design work to innovate and compete on complex, high-value-added projects.

This argument began to fall away when people took account of just how many engineers and scientists low-wage economy countries such as India and China were producing. It vanished entirely when Western companies started outsourcing design and innovation to offshore centers, as Indian and Chinese engineers are also "lower wage" than their colleagues in developed economies, at least for the present.

Instead, the major themes at the start of 2009, particularly given the protectionist rhetoric that tends to follow every global downturn as countries seek to protect their own jobs for their own nationals, tend to be around concerns that Europe and the US will get "crushed" by the ability of developing economies to turn out vastly more engineers and science graduates than Western universities are managing to achieve.

A team at the Pratt School of Engineering, Duke University, US, has specialized in studying the quality and quantity of engineering graduates being produced by Indian and Chinese institutions, and the impact of globalization on the engineering profession. Their aim was to explore the factors driving the US trend to engineering outsourcing, and to look at what could be done to enable the US to retain any edge it still has in this field.

The comparative annual numbers most frequently cited for engineering graduates in the US, India, and China, they point out, are 70,000 undergraduate engineers in the US, 350,000 for India, and 700,000 for China. However, when the Duke University team checked the numbers, they found huge difficulties around semantics.

Chinese does not distinguish particularly, as far as terms go, between a motor mechanic and a nuclear engineer, both are "engineers." The team checked 200 universities in China and 100 in India. Their analysis showed that while a realistic figure for

  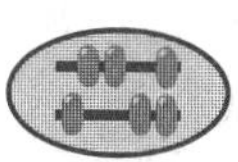      

China for 2004 was probably more like 360,000 conventionally trained engineering graduates, versus 139,000 in India, and almost 138,000 for the US, there was, nevertheless, a very real and obvious ramping-up in the number of engineers China is now producing.

This increase stems from initiatives taken by the Chinese government in 1999, and those initiatives are now bearing fruit. What has really worked for the Chinese, the Duke team found, as far as numbers at least are concerned, is to transform science and engineering education from "elite education" to "mass education," by increasing enrolment in engineering programs. The downside of this is that an improvement of 140% in numbers of students has taken place at the expense of dramatic increases in class sizes, creating some serious quality problems for qualification standards.

In other words, the quality of engineering dropped off dramatically outside some 10 to 15 Chinese engineering institutions, even as the numbers went up. The Duke team, therefore, argue that China is likely to find it at least as difficult as the US does to generate a large number of extremely well-skilled engineers over time.

India, by way of contrast, has benefited from engineering education places being offered by a number of private colleges and training institutions. Most of these face quality issues, the Duke team says, but a few are recognized as producing high-quality graduates. Indian companies told the team that they felt comfortable hiring the top graduates from a wide range of Indian institutions (a reverse of the situation in China).

A key fact that emerged from a survey of US companies carried out by the Duke University team was that the vast majority of these companies said they would move at least part of their R&D to emerging markets, in order to respond to the big opportunities in these growing markets. They also said that their units there would increasingly be catering for worldwide needs.

On the positive side, by staying open to the brightest and the best, the US—and, by implication, Europe—continues to benefit from the ability to attract very-high-caliber students from both China and India, many of whom stay in Europe after completing their studies, often making very substantial contributions in their own right to innovation and progress, and ultimately to the GDP of the host country.

The question of who will "out-innovate" whom may quite possibly prove to be irrelevant in the longer term, itself becoming a victim of the increasingly global and multinational nature of engineering operations.

Regulatory Issues

Engineering is a prime example of a discipline bounded on all sides by political and social "rules." The EU's Waste Electrical and Electronic Equipment Directive, known as WEEE, on the disposal of end-of-life electronic and electrical equipment is one obvious example. One of the goals of WEEE is to force manufacturers to think much more carefully about the way they engineer products.

By getting manufacturers to think of the waste that results at the end of a product's lifecycle, and by making them pay for the ultimate disposal of those products at expensive, special-purpose hazardous waste sites, the idea is that manufacturers will improve the recyclable content of their products (less going to landfill or hazardous waste disposal sites equals less cost per product).

In other words, the goal being set for engineers is no longer, "does this product do the job well?" The dimension, "can this product be cost-effectively disposed of at the end of its life?" has been added. From an engineer's standpoint, that is just another design challenge, and one that gives their company yet another opportunity to craft something better than their competitors have yet managed.

Equally relevant are the various moral limits on what may and may not be "engineered." The debates over genetic manipulation of crops are now familiar ground. Engineers and scientists face similar emotive debates over the topic of cloning, a subject that emerges very readily out of breakthrough research into DNA, the "blueprint" of life.

Today, and for the foreseeable future, plant cloning is "in," human cloning is "out," and the "in" and the "out" here have nothing to do with natural limits on engineering, and everything to do with the moral limits that society places on engineers.

The NAE points out that the biotechnology "revolution," for example, holds great potential but it is a field in which political and societal implications intervene to set limits on what is acceptable. In other words, there are very clear issues that have an impact on technological change that are beyond the scope of engineering.

Finally, there is much to be hoped for from the fact that engineering has a tremendous role to play in facilitating international cooperation. As the NAE notes, engineering itself "speaks through an international language of mathematics, science, and technology," and, as such, bodies of professionals across the globe very quickly find themselves on common ground when dealing with engineering concepts. It looks at least possible that the real future of engineering lies on a global, rather than on any particular merely national, stage—particularly as the challenges facing engineering are themselves increasingly global in nature.

▸▸ MORE INFO

Websites:

"Grand Challenges for Engineering" colloquium: www.engineeringchallenges.org

Prism, journal of the American Society for Engineering Education: www.prism-magazine.org

US National Academy of Engineering: www.nae.edu

Food and Agribusiness

MAJOR INDUSTRY TRENDS

Despite the accelerating industrialization of the globe over the past 100 years, and the rapid growth of manufacturing industry across the developing world over the past 20 years, around four in 10 of the total global population remain involved in agriculture, according to the latest statistics from the United Nation's Food and Agriculture Organization (FAO). The FAO says that, in 2004, 2,600 million people (out of a global population of 6,377 million) were engaged in agriculture. Clearly, the proportion of the population that is engaged in agriculture varies markedly from advanced economies such as the UK (the first country to industrialize), where agriculture accounts for just 1.7% of the population, to developing countries such as Zambia, where the figure is 66.9%.

Key Trends

Rising (and Falling) Food Prices

The FAO index of nominal food prices doubled between 2002 and 2008 and the FAO said (in its *State of Agriculture 2008* publica-

    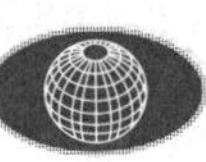   

tion) that, in 2008, "more than at any time in the past three decades, the world's attention is focused this year on food and agriculture," a comment that reflected concern about the impact of rising food prices around the world, and the potential threat to political and economic stability. For food accounts for up to 60% of household spending in many developing countries. The report warned: "World food and agriculture are facing critical challenges. Sharply higher food prices sparked riots in many countries in 2008, and have led at least 40 governments to impose emergency measures, such as food price controls or export restrictions." A number of factors caused food prices to rise sharply in 2008. These included:

- A surge in commodity prices, driven by increased energy costs (a key input in food and fertilizer production), as well as adverse weather conditions in key food-exporting countries, and strong growth in global demand, driven by robust global economic growth. At the same time, global cereal stocks fell to "historically low" levels, according to the FAO, driving market prices even higher. Cereals are not only a key ingredient in food products such as bread, but are also a key component of animal feed. Thus, higher animal feed prices inevitably result in higher meat prices.
- Government action: according to the FAO, some of the emergency measures adopted by governments to cap food prices, such as export controls, further destabilized world markets.
- The growth of biofuel production: the impact of biofuels on commodity prices is controversial, with the FAO saying that estimates range from 3% (according to the US Department of Agriculture) to 30% (from the International Food Policy Research Institute) in 2008.
- Environmental pressures: desertification is accelerating in China and sub-Saharan Africa, while proponents of climate change argue that flooding is increasing, and changing rainfall patterns are having a significant impact on agricultural production.

Prices for many commodities, including food products, came under pressure in 2008, particularly in the latter part of the year, as the global financial crisis dramatically slowed global economic growth. Despite the decline in international prices, domestic food prices remained very high in several developing countries, affecting access to food among low-income population groups. Furthermore, many of the trends identified by the FAO, as well as the growth of Western-style diets among the citizens of emerging economies (see below), are likely to re-emerge as global economic growth recovers. They will thus exert upward pressure on food prices in the long term.

Western Diets (and Health Problems) Sweep the Globe

Rising living standards and changing patterns of food consumption in fast-developing emerging countries are other key factors driving global demand for food, and putting upward pressure on commodity prices. Consumption of dairy products in countries such as India and China used to be very low, but is now surging to such an extent that it is driving up prices for dairy products around the world. Similar trends are occurring in meat, vegetable oils, and many other areas.

Meanwhile, consumers in emerging markets are adopting Western lifestyles, which tend to be fast-paced, generating enormous demand for convenience foods, such as ready meals, and canned and packaged produce. The trend towards convenience-oriented, Western-style lifestyles is exemplified by the growth of fast-food outlets in emerging markets. In February 2009, McDonald's said that it planned to open a further 500 outlets in China over the following three years. In 2008, the company opened 146 restaurants in China, one of its fastest-growing markets, increasing the number of outlets to 2,012 by the end of the year, out of more than 30,000 worldwide.

However, as consumers in developing countries adopt Western-style diets, they also encounter the health problems that are increasingly prevalent in the West. Scientists and health experts have documented alarming weight gains in recent years in China, the Middle East, Africa, Europe, and Latin America, especially in children and women, according to an article published in the *Chicago Tribune* (October 1, 2007). In the US, the obesity rate has soared to about 35% for women and 20% for men. The common factors fueling the rise in obesity are: diets rich in sweeteners and saturated fats; work and leisure activities that involve less exercise; and increasing consumption of cheap, processed foods. In the UK, the problem has grown to such an extent that fire crews are called out at least once a day to lift obese people whom staff have found too heavy to move (source: *The Guardian*, March 13, 2009). But even "desperately poor countries such as Nigeria and Uganda are wrestling with the dilemma of obesity," according to the *Chicago Tribune*. The newspaper added that the growth of another Western phenomenon in emerging economies, the supermarket, was contributing to the rise in obesity. Although these shops offer "better, cleaner food," they also supply more snacks and soft drinks, instead of local fruits and vegetables.

The Growing Power of Supermarkets and the Impact on Agribusiness

The growing power of supermarkets around the world is also having an enormous impact on agribusiness and the food chain. The phenomenon has already been well documented in Western countries. Up until the early 1960s, small, neighborhood grocery shops, independent butchers, and local fruit and vegetable shops dominated food retailing in many Western countries, such as the UK. Today, supermarkets account for more than 90% of food sales in the UK. Furthermore, four major chains—Tesco, ASDA (part of the US giant, Wal-Mart), Sainsbury's, and Morrisons—account for around 75% of sales, with Tesco alone taking more than £3 of every £10 spent on food in the UK. Similar trends can be seen in other developed countries, and, increasingly, in emerging economies around the world. Supermarkets entered Latin America in the early 1990s, and South-East Asia in the latter part of the decade. They are now sweeping across India, China, Eastern Europe, and parts of Africa. In many countries, supermarkets now account for around 50% of food sales.

While suppliers and wholesalers could once dictate prices, and even tell retailers which products they could sell, the balance of power has now shifted decisively to the retailers, which are in a position to demand ever-lower prices and improved terms. The major supermarket chains increasingly source their produce from around the world, placing further pressure on local suppliers, which either meet the demands of the major chains, or go under. Inevitably, this trend affects the person at the bottom of the supply chain: the farmer. The supermarkets are also using the increasing acceptance and popularity of their own brands to exert pressure on suppliers.

MARKET ANALYSIS

The Size of the Global Food Market

The long-established market-research publisher, Key Note Ltd of London, estimates that the global retail market for food amounted to £1,182 billion in 2008, and that growth has accelerated over the past five years, reflecting strong global economic growth (up until the latter part of 2008), and the surge in commodity prices that

  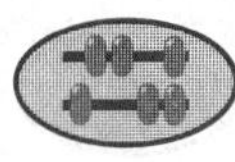      

Table 1. The global food market by sector at current prices (£bn at RSP*), 2004–2008. (*Source*: Key Note)

	2004	2005	2006	2007	2008
Meat and meat products	224	234	247	267	285
Fish and fish products	64	69	75	83	89
Fruit and vegetables	205	211	218	227	236
Dairy products, eggs, oils and fats	240	252	265	280	294
Bread, cakes, biscuits, and cereals	197	203	212	224	233
Other foods	36	38	40	43	45
Total	**966**	**1,007**	**1,057**	**1,124**	**1,182**
% change year-on-year	*3.6*	*4.2*	*5.0*	*6.3*	*5.1*

** RSP: retail selling price*

took place over the period, as well the growth of the global population and rising living standards, particularly in rapidly developing economies such as China and India.

Global Trends by Commodity

Cereals

World cereal production reached a record high in 2008, according to the FAO, reflecting clement weather conditions. But the organization anticipates that output will fall in 2009, as a result of reduced plantings and adverse weather conditions. In early 2008, wheat prices reached record highs. Extreme weather damaged crops in 2007, and US wheat inventories fell to their lowest level for 60 years in February 2008. By February 2009, however, wheat prices had fallen by around 60% from the same month in 2008, because of a rebound in world stocks.

According to Key Note, global sales of bread, cakes, biscuits, and breakfast cereals (all derived from crops such as wheat, oats, and corn, and many of which are staple foods) totaled £233 billion in 2008. Demand for products such as breakfast cereals and biscuits, which were once found only in the West, is increasing in emerging economies such as India and China, and this has helped to drive growth in global consumption over the next five years.

Rice

Rice is the staple food for around 2.5 billion people, or more than one-third of the global population. The global price of rice has been increasing for much of the current decade. According to the International Rice Research Institute (IRRI), a non-profit research and education center, this is because the world is consuming more rice than it is producing, and global stocks are becoming rapidly depleted (current stocks are at their lowest levels since 1988). A number of factors are causing this imbalance between supply and demand. They include:

- A slowdown in the growth of rice yield. In South Asia, for example, average yield growth decreased from 2.14% per year between 1970 and 1990 to 1.40% per year between 1990 and 2005, according to IRRI.
- In Asia, pressure on land is limiting the scope for increasing the area devoted to the cultivation of rice.
- Governments are devoting decreasing resources to agricultural research and development. IRRI says that declining rice prices in the 1990s led to complacency about the need for R&D among governments.
- Rice has become an increasingly popular food in Africa, leading to further pressure on global supplies.
- Population growth is outstripping growth in rice production, a problem that is projected to worsen.
- Rapid economic growth is increasing the pressure on agricultural land. IRRI says that highly productive rice land has been lost to housing and industrial development, or to the cultivation of vegetables, and other cash crops.

Meat and Meat Products

Global demand for meat has risen more than fivefold in the past 50 years, according to the FAO, and it continued to grow strongly in 2008. The FAO said that, while growth in meat consumption in developed countries is expected to remain modest in 2008, at less than 1%, stronger economic growth and growing incomes in developing countries are likely to lead to a 3% increase in global consumption in 2008.

Key Note believes that consumption of meat and meat products will continue to increase strongly. For, as the world economy grows, so does global meat consumption. The average person in the industrialized world eats more than 176 lb of meat annually, compared with around 66 lb consumed by the average resident of the developing world. As developing economies become richer, these countries' citizens spend more on meat. This is particularly true in parts of the world where consumption is relatively low, such as China and India, with their vast populations. Pork, for example, was once a rare luxury in China, but pork imports into China rose by more than 900% during the first four months of 2008 alone. In 2008, global meat production is expected to top 280 million metric tons and that figure could nearly double by 2050.

Fish and Fish Products

Fish is the main source of protein for around 1 billion people. Demand for fish is also growing rapidly, due to population growth and rising incomes. Global per capita consumption of fish has risen from 9 kg in 1961 to an estimated 17 kg in 2008, according to the FAO. Global supplies of fish in its natural environment are clearly finite—indeed, stocks of certain species are dwindling at an alarming rate. Consequently, fish from farms accounts for an increasing proportion of global supplies. According to *The Economist* (March 2, 2009), farming accounted for 6% of fish available for human consumption in the 1970s. By 2006, the most recent

▸▸ MORE INFO

Reports:

United Nations Food and Agriculture Organization (UNFAO). "Food outlook, November 2008." Rome: UNFAO, 2008. Online at: ftp://ftp.fao.org/docrep/fao/011/ai474e/ai474e00.pdf

United Nations Food and Agriculture Organization (UNFAO). "The state of food and agriculture 2008." Rome: UNFAO, 2008. Online at: ftp://ftp.fao.org/docrep/fao/011/i0100e/i0100e.pdf

Websites:

International Food Policy Research Institute: www.ifpri.org
International Rice Research Institute: www.irri.org
Key Note Publications provides research on a wide range of markets including food: www.keynote.co.uk
US Department of Agriculture: www.usda.gov

year for which figures are available, that figure had increased to 47%.

Fruit and Vegetables

Consumption of fruit and vegetables grew at a robust pace between 2003 and 2007, and it is likely to accelerate further over the next five years, according to Key Note. The company says that consumers in both the developed world and the developing world are increasingly concerned and knowledgeable about the link between health and diet, and are responding to widespread publicity about the benefits of eating fruit and vegetables. Key Note adds that the value of the market is being driven by increased prices as well as rising volume consumption.

Dairy Products, Eggs, Oils, and Fats

Prices in the dairy sector peaked in November 2007, when the FAO's index of dairy product prices (base 1998–2000 = 100) reached an all-time high of 302. In 2008 and 2009, however, dairy prices have been on a declining trend. Farmers and analysts have cited various factors for the fall in dairy prices, including increased supply, higher export subsidies by the EU, and price manipulation on global markets. However, in the long term, global dairy consumption is expected to increase, putting a floor under dairy prices. China's milk consumption, for example, rose by 9.3% in 2007 alone.

Healthcare and Pharmaceuticals

MAJOR INDUSTRY TRENDS

Healthcare and pharmaceuticals are two distinct industries, but they are interdependent and are subject to similar trends, which is why they are covered together in this report. Both are benefiting from ageing populations in many advanced economies, and various developing countries, such as China. In addition, important medical discoveries, including the decoding of the human genome, are fueling scientific advances, and the release of new drugs and treatments. Thus, these industries should weather the global economic downturn relatively well.

The Impact of the Recession

The investment community generally regards healthcare and pharmaceutical companies as "defensive" stocks, because they tend to be relatively immune to the vagaries of the economic cycle. While consumers may cut back on purchases of many discretionary items during a recession, most people regard their health as a priority. In addition, while individuals may cut back on private healthcare in time of economic hardship, this simply increases demand for healthcare services provided by the public sector. Most healthcare spending in the Western world is funded by governments, and such spending is highly sensitive in political terms. Most democratically elected governments prefer to find savings in areas other than healthcare for fear of losing votes. Clearly, however, even healthcare spending will come under pressure during a severe economic recession. In the UK, for example, the publicly funded National Health Service (NHS) is likely to see its funding cut substantially in the coming years as the government's finances are ravaged by the recession. The NHS budget rose by 5.5% in the 2008/09 fiscal year, following five years of record rises. However, in March 2009, the BBC quoted "experts" as suggesting that the NHS budget may rise by just 1% in 2009/10, which could equate to a freeze, or even a fall in funding once inflation is taken into account.

Ageing Populations

Ageing populations are driving demand for healthcare services and pharmaceutical products around the globe. Older people tend to require more healthcare, and are certainly subject to higher levels of chronic illness than younger people. In Japan, for example, the population is ageing rapidly. In 1950, 4.9% of Japanese were over the age of 65. By 2000, that figure had grown to 17.2%, and by 2050, it is expected to reach 32.3%. According to the US government, the over-65s accounted for 12.4% of the US population in 2006 (the latest year for which figures are available) but this number will rise to 20% of the population by 2030. The problem even exists in some emerging economies, such as China, which introduced a strict one-child policy in 1979 in an attempt to control its booming population. China's official Xinhua news agency reported in March 2009 that the country formally became an aged society in 2000, when the population aged 60 or above accounted for 10% of its 1.3 billion people. By the end of 2008, that proportion had increased to 12% of the whole population, and some analysts forecast that it could exceed 30% by 2050. According to a UN report published in March 2009, 22% of people in the more developed countries are aged 60 and over, and that proportion is expected to reach 33% in 2050. Furthermore, while just 9% of the population of developing countries today is aged 60 or over, that proportion will more than double to 20% by 2050.

Scientific and Technological Advances

Enormous progress has been made over the past decade in developing drugs that treat previously incurable illnesses. As the *Financial Times* (July 3, 2008) pointed out: "Little more than a decade ago, Aids was seen globally as a death sentence. Today, millions of patients, including many even in some of the poorest parts of Africa, can manage it like a chronic disease." There have also been huge advances in the treatment of cancer. In March 2009, for example, the BBC reported that nanotechnology had been used for the first time to destroy cancer cells with a highly targeted package of "tumor-busting" genes. The BBC said that the technique, which leaves healthy cells unaffected, could potentially offer hope to people with hard-to-treat cancers where surgery is not possible.

These scientific advances are adding to the pressures on health spending. However, other technological advances could help to reduce the costs of delivering healthcare. John Coulthard, UK head of Microsoft's health business, told the *Financial Times* (July 3, 2008) that productivity gains could provide a solution to the "twin time bombs" of an ageing population and a shortage of personnel. The newspaper said that Mr Coulthard believes that modern IT can provide dramatic improvements in healthcare, because manual procedures and archaic systems still dominate, even in advanced economies. However, adapting modern IT systems to healthcare systems has proved expensive and difficult. A project to computerize patient records in the UK's NHS has been dogged by delays and cost overruns. In January 2009, a parliamentary watchdog (the Committee on Public Accounts) cast fresh doubt on a 2015 deadline for the ambitious £12 billion project, and said that, even in areas of the NHS already using parts of the system, staff were unimpressed, and the cost to the NHS was uncertain. The project was originally intended to be completed by 2010, but its complexity has delayed

  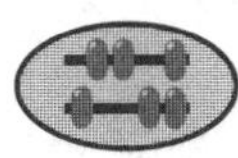      

this by up to five years. It's a similar story in the US. According to a study in the *New England Journal of Medicine*, only 4% of US physicians have a fully functional electronic health-records system. Yet the coordinators of a federal government healthcare IT initiative have said developing a national health IT network would be extremely difficult.

Pharmaceutical Industry Under Pressure from Price Caps and Generic Drugs

The pharmaceutical industry regularly tops surveys of the most profitable corporate sectors. Certainly, many of the companies involved in the industry are highly profitable. Ageing populations and scientific advances that are creating new drugs (and new demand) are propelling revenues, and profits. However, according to the Association of the British Pharmaceutical Industry (ABPI), prescription medicines "are the subject of government controls and intensive competition." The ABPI adds that pharmaceutical prices have grown at a slower rate than consumer prices as a whole and, in real terms, are 21% lower than they were 10 years ago. Similar trends can be seen in other parts of the world, where governments cap price rises for drugs. A report in the *Financial Times* (May 8, 2008) said that "some of the world's biggest pharmaceutical companies, including GlaxoSmithKline and AstraZeneca, face their worst crisis in decades, as their future revenues come under threat from shrinking drug pipelines, increased competition from generics and a slew of patent expiries."

MARKET ANALYSIS

Healthcare Spending

Healthcare spending worldwide amounts to around US$4,000 billion, according to a report by the *Financial Times* (July 3, 2008). The newspaper quoted analysis from McKinsey, the consultancy firm, which showed that healthcare spending across the members of the Organisation for Economic Cooperation and Development (OECD), the "club" of industrialized nations, had outstripped GDP by 2 percentage points each year for the past 50 years. McKinsey said that on current trends, healthcare spending would exceed 50% of GDP in the US and Switzerland by 2080. "Even if the excess growth of healthcare spending over GDP is somehow cut in half, healthcare will, by 2100, be the world's largest economic sector—and in many countries, the largest economic problem," it concluded. The rise in spending reflects the ageing of populations in OECD countries, as well as the increasing cost of healthcare, and scientific advances that are producing new drugs and treatments.

Spending on healthcare varies widely from country to country, as do outcomes. Nor is there necessarily a correlation between the amount of money spent and the effectiveness of the healthcare system. The US spends more on healthcare than any other country, in both relative and absolute terms, yet its healthcare system scores poorly in terms of its overall performance, according to the Commonwealth Fund Commission, a US private foundation that supports independent research on healthcare issues. The Fund produced a report on the performance of the US health system in 2008 (*The National Scorecard on US Health System Performance*, 2008). The scorecard aimed to measure and monitor healthcare outcomes, quality, access, efficiency, and equity in the US. It ranked the US last out of 19 countries on a measure of mortality amenable to medical care.

This poor performance may reflect the nature of healthcare provision in the US. The country has several types of privately and publicly funded insurance plans that provide healthcare services. However, the private sector dominates healthcare and the US is the "only wealthy, industrialized nation that does not ensure that all citizens have coverage" (i.e., some kind of insurance), according to the Institute of Medicine, a non-profit organization for science-based advice on matters of biomedical science, medicine, and health.

By contrast, a publicly funded healthcare system, the NHS, dominates healthcare in the UK, accounting for more than 80% of healthcare spending in the country. Founded in 1948, it aims to provide a free, comprehensive healthcare service, with delivery at the point of need, regardless of the ability to pay. It is the world's largest publicly funded health service, and claims it is also "one of the most efficient, most egalitarian, and most comprehensive." Yet it has many critics, who argue that it is inefficient and overly bureaucratic.

Other countries fund their health services in a variety of ways. According to Key Note Ltd, a UK-based market-research company, the Netherlands operates a national insurance market for its 16 million residents. Plans may operate on a for-profit or non-profit basis. The insurance market is highly concentrated, with the top five plans accounting for 82% of enrolment. Plans typically offer coverage in all areas of the country and include all providers, although selective contracting is allowed. Children are covered in full through public funds. Premiums charged for adults represent 50% of the expected annual costs. By contrast, according to Key Note, the Swiss insurance system, which covers 7.5 million people, is highly decentralized. Only non-profit insurers may participate in the scheme, and Swiss premiums vary widely according to the health risks of insured pools across the country, and within regions.

Japan spends around 8% of its GDP on healthcare, almost half the amount of the US. Yet the Japanese have the longest healthy life expectancy on the planet. Diet and lifestyle clearly play a key role, but the country's universal healthcare system may also be an

Table 1. Total Healthcare Spending as a Percentage of GDP, 2006. (*Source*: OECD, www.irdes.fr/EcoSante/DownLoad/OECDHealthData_FrequentlyRequestedData.xls)

Australia	8.7	Portugal	10.2
Canada	10.0	Spain	8.4
France	11.0	Sweden	9.2
Germany	10.6	Switzerland	11.3 (est).
Italy	8.7*	UK	8.4
Ireland	7.5	US	15.3
Japan	8.1		

(est).: estimate
* 2007

⏩ MORE INFO

Websites:

Association of the British Pharmaceutical Industry: www.abpi.org.uk

Commonwealth Fund Commission, a private foundation that supports independent research on healthcare issues: www.commonwealthfund.org

Financial Times, Special Report on Healthcare 2008: www.ft.com/reports/healthcare2008

Institute of Medicine, a US non-profit organization for science-based advice on matters of biomedical science, medicine, and health: www.iom.edu

Key Note Ltd, provides research on a wide range of markets, including healthcare and pharmaceuticals: www.keynote.co.uk

McKinsey, management consultancy, publishes regular reports on the healthcare industry: www.mckinsey.com/mgi/reports/pdfs/healthcare/

important factor. Everyone in Japan is required to take out a health-insurance policy, either at work or through a community-based insurer, according to Key Note. The firm adds: "The government pays for those who are too poor. However, 80% of Japan's hospitals are privately owned—more than in the US—and almost every doctor's office is a private business. The Japanese Health Ministry tightly controls the price of healthcare, down to the smallest detail. Every two years, the healthcare industry and the health ministry negotiate a fixed price for every procedure and every drug."

Insurance

MAJOR INDUSTRY TRENDS

Although the insurance sector has had at least one spectacular disaster during the current financial crisis, in the shape of the huge losses sustained by American International Group (AIG), it has, by and large, not been nearly as badly damaged by the crisis as the global banking sector.

In a considered paper on the impact on the sector of the crisis, Zurich Re author, Marian Bell, argues that although insurers and banks are both suppliers of financial services, and together constitute the bulk of the financial services industry, they remain very distinct businesses, with different regulatory regimes, and a different approach to risk. Thus, it is not surprising that the financial crisis has affected the two related businesses of banking and insurance differently.

The insurance sector has been exposed to the current financial crisis in several ways. It invests in equities, and, substantially, in banking stocks (which gives it exposure to bank losses through share price losses in its investment portfolio), and in corporate investment-grade bonds, about 60% of which come from the finance sector. Insurance companies have also, in recent years, become much more involved in the capital markets, with some insurance lines being securitized and sold to the capital markets.

However, this does not pose as great a risk as the banks investing in asset-backed securities, many of which turned toxic as the US subprime mortgage crisis developed. The International Association of Insurance Supervisors (IAIS), which represents insurance regulators and supervisors from some 190 jurisdictions around the world, has a clear view of the global insurance industry. In a communiqué issued on December 17, 2008, it said that the global reinsurance sector "remains resilient amid the financial crisis."

The IAIS made the remarks in the context of publishing its fifth annual overview of the financial conditions of reinsurers, the *Global Reinsurance Market Report 2008*. The overview assessed the reinsurance market's stability and interrelated risks, as well as the impact of the current turmoil on the sector's ability to transact business. The point is that reinsurers, who can be thought of as the companies to which insurance organizations hand off some of their book risk, so as to dilute their own positions, play an important role in the functioning of efficient insurance markets across the world. They act like shock absorbers, particularly in providing disaster coverage.

The reinsurance business, as is true for the whole insurance sector, is very cyclical, with good years and bad years. Another cycle in the sector is that of hard pricing versus soft pricing. Hard pricing, basically, takes over after the sector has endured one or more particularly bad years, and the cost of insurance across a whole range of lines of business rises sharply. Normally, the capacity in the industry is enough to ensure that competition for business keeps prices on the low side. Any insurance company that tries to raise prices finds its customers going elsewhere, so no single organization has the power to "harden" prices. This can only happen when capacity is taken out of the industry, again, usually after companies have made losses through massive payouts on disasters.

The IAIS points out that, following record losses in 2005, particularly hurricane losses and flood damage, both 2006 and 2007 were profitable years for the reinsurance sector. This gave the sector a solid financial base to weather the challenges of the financial crisis, the IAIS says.

Zurich Re, in its report, quotes the IAIS as saying that no insurers have, so far, experienced "liquidity difficulties as a result of the recent market turmoil." They have all remained open for business, and have been transacting business in a way that the banks clearly have not.

In all, the Zurich Re report says, insurers' exposure to the toxic asset-backed securities market amounts to no more than 1% of assets in aggregate. In effect, the report says that the upturn in the insurance industry's pricing cycle in 2008, with prices hardening in some lines of business, led insurers to start redeploying their capital away from potentially "dodgy" derivatives investments, and back into their core lines of business.

It is important to understand the difference between the types of risk run by the two sectors. As the Zurich Re report notes, the banking sector invested in products where the underlying risk is a financial or market risk (such as credit worthiness, price volatility, or exchange-rate volatility). Insurance-linked securities, on the other hand, are products where the underlying risk is a real event, such as a natural catastrophe, a fire, or a motor accident. The various types of financial risk can, in some circumstances, all turn out to be related, creating a "perfect storm." With insurance risk, however, the events are fundamentally unrelated and uncorrelated. They are non-systemic, idiosyncratic risks. This means that in financial risks the risk can be aggregated in ways that prevent hedging strategies from working (all prices fall when markets collapse). "The risks cannot be diversified away by investing in other financial and market risks," the report says. In contrast, insurance-linked securities offer the prospect of diversification and are not subject to the same degree of contagion as financial risk. Here again, this explains why the insurance sector has come out of the crash better than the banking sector.

Moreover, the sector has also benefited indirectly from the liquidity crisis. In normal times, when the capital markets are functioning efficiently, and when the insurance industry moves into a period of hard pricing (where they are able to raise premiums, often quite severely on some lines of business), new money is attracted into the sector. The capital markets fund new insurance start-ups, which compete on price, and, after a while, this competition transforms a hard cycle back into a soft cycle. In today's market, however, existing insurance companies are capital-constrained in at least two ways: one, because prudence and the regulators are dictating that companies increase their capital reserves during difficult times, which leaves them less capital with which to write business, and two, because plunging markets have wiped 40% or more off their asset portfolios. As their assets are worth less, they have to increase their reserves to make up the difference, and that draws off capital that they could otherwise use to write business. At the same time, the capital markets are more or less illiquid right now, so potential new players cannot spring up to take advantage of gaps in the market. All this adds up to less capacity to write business, and less capacity means higher prices, by the iron law of supply and demand.

MARKET ANALYSIS

Another key development in the market today is the way the industry is approaching the threat of global warming. Insurance is about covering future risk, rather than funding recovery from disasters that are certain. If sea levels start to rise beyond question, as a result of global warming and the melting of polar ice, then people on very low-lying coastal properties will not be able to buy insurance, as it is certain that their properties will suffer damage, and possible destruction. The industry is already exploring various kinds of partnering arrangements with government, which would see government stepping in where the sector cannot. It is a fact that some of the world's most valuable real estate lies on very low-lying coastal ground, or on active fault lines (California springs to mind on the latter count, Florida on the former). The sector has been very active in trying to get committed global action to mitigate the risks posed by global warming. The weather is already unpredictable enough for the industry's taste. An increase in the frequency of natural disasters would simply increase its losses, perhaps out of all proportion to the opportunities such an increase creates for the sector to write business.

However, the insurance industry has been very innovative over the years, including in relation to natural catastrophes. The instrument of this innovation is catastrophe bonds, a major branch of insurance-linked securities. In a report published on January 22, 2007, Swiss Re, one of the world's largest reinsurance companies, advocated the setting up of a European loss index based on industry-wide data. The idea is that if potential investors have access to a database that shows them a picture of the entire European claims data, they will be able to form a view of how much risk they are taking on in investing in particular catastrophe-bond instruments.

Swiss Re pointed out in the report that the issuance of European catastrophe bonds increased by 130% in 2006, bringing the total value of outstanding catastrophe bonds to US$8.1 billion. One of the drivers of this growth was the availability of US market-loss indexes for US risk. Another insurance industry derivative, industry loss warranties (ILWs) achieved US$4 billion of sales. ILWs are a product where the buyer of a US$50 million limit on an ILW at US$10 billion pays a premium, and in return, receives US$50 million if total losses to the whole insurance industry from a single event, for example a hurricane, exceed US$10 billion. It should be clear that ILWs and catastrophe bonds attract liquidity to the industry, and help it to offset losses from major disasters. At the same time, they provide money-market investors with the opportunity to make significant returns, if they call the risks correctly. Hence, better risk information makes it much easier for potential investors to decide to commit to these instruments. (The alternative way for capital markets to commit to the insurance industry, as we have seen, is to invest in new insurance start-ups after a major disaster has taken capacity out of the market). However, derivative products such as ILWs and catastrophe bonds are much more liquid, and much more specific. In essence, catastrophe bonds allow investors to enjoy premium income while taking on the risk of having to pay out specific sums, if the risk envisaged in the bond comes to pass. ILWs allow the investor to take a bet on the magnitude of an event. If it happens, but is less severe than the limit in the bond, they get nothing.

Looking at the growth of the insurance business worldwide, Swiss Re, which produces the authoritative "sigma study"[1], showed that premium incomes are growing far faster in emerging markets than mature markets—not a surprising result when one remembers that emerging markets start from a lower base, and have higher GDP growth. According to the Swiss Re study, world insurance premium income grew 3.3% in real terms in 2007, to US$4,061 billion. The growth was primarily driven by life-insurance business in both industrialized and emerging markets, and to a lesser extent by non-life business in emerging markets.

Life insurance premium growth increased by 5.4% over the figures for 2006. Non-life business in emerging markets grew even faster, at in excess of 10%, but sales actually contracted fractionally in developed markets (0.3%), according to Swiss Re.

Commenting on the report, Daniel Staib, one of the study's authors, said: "Despite a macroeconomic environment characterized by marginally slower economic growth and rising inflation, life insurance continued to expand in 2007, with world life insurance premiums increasing by 5.4% to US$2,393 billion." Sales of retirement and other wealth accumulation products spurred premium growth in the industrialized economies.

A key driver of growth in the life business is an ageing population in developed countries, where pensions and annuities business remains strong, particularly in the face of an evident pullback by governments from providing comfortable retirement safety nets for their populations. In emerging markets with relatively young populations all lines of business, from protection insurance to motor insurance and life, are seeing strong sales.

According to Swiss Re, the outlook for the coming year is for growth in life-insurance premiums to become more moderate, as capital markets and stock-market turmoil dampen demand still further. Once the upturn begins and some stability returns, life insurance is projected to resume its strong performance, Swiss Re concludes.

▸▸ MORE INFO

Websites:

IAIS: www.iaisweb.org

Swiss Re: www.swissre.com

Zurich Re report: www.zdownload.zurich.com/main/reports

See Also:

★ Climate Change and Insurance (pp. 183–184)

★ Enterprise Risk Management and Solvency II (pp. 628–631)

★ Insurance—Bruised, Not Crushed (pp. 219–220)

★ The Insurance Sector: Plenty of Silver Lining to Be Found (pp. 225–227)

★ Islamic Insurance Markets and the Structure of Takaful (pp. 242–243)

★ The Role of Institutional Investors in Corporate Financing (pp. 572–575)

✔ Captive Insurance Companies: How to Reduce Your Costs (p. 922)

✔ Corporate Insurance Cover: A Primer (p. 979)

✔ Directors' and Officers' Liability Insurance (p. 908)

✔ Stress Testing to Evaluate Insurance Cover (p. 932)

✔ Understanding and Calculating Probable Maximum Loss (PML) (p. 933)

✔ Understanding Continuity Insurance (p. 1007)

✔ Understanding the Components of an Insurance Contract (p. 934)

NOTE

1 Sigma provides comprehensive information on the international insurance markets and analyses of economic trends and strategic issues in reinsurance and financial services, covering life and non life businesses.

  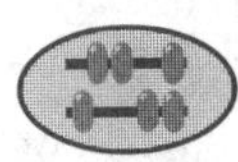   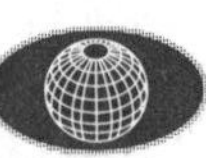   

Information Technology

MAJOR INDUSTRY TRENDS

Information technology (IT) is both a huge industry in itself, and the source of dramatic changes in business practices in all other sectors. The term IT covers a number of related disciplines and areas, from semiconductor design and production (also covered in the profile of the electronics sector), through hardware manufacture (mainframes, servers, PCs, and mobile devices), to software, data storage, backup and retrieval, networking, and, of course, the internet.

On top of this, there has been a convergence between IT and telephony, driven by transforming voice traffic from an analogue signal to a digital packet, indistinguishable from other data packets travelling through a computer network. IT in the leisure sector is already about enabling interaction with video, movies, and TV, and this trend is increasingly carrying into the business space.

Each of the major sub-areas in IT is itself capable of being divided into its component parts. Storage, for example, breaks down into disk drives, tape drives, and optical drives, and into attached storage and networked storage. PCs break down into utility-business desktop PCs, high-end work stations, and "extreme" gaming PCs for games enthusiasts—the computer and console games industry has already produced "blockbusters" that outsell top releases from Hollywood.

Software subdivides into numerous specialist areas, from relational database technologies to enterprise applications, to "horizontal" office applications characterized by Microsoft Office 2007, for example.

Somewhat off the main track of IT at present, but very much related to both increases in processor power, and to work in simulation and artificial intelligence, is the field of robotics. This lies outside the scope of this profile, but the linkages between robotics and IT are already transforming both manufacturing and defense.

In addition, the IT arena is characterized by a number of key trends and emerging technologies which, again, have the potential to transform the way businesses currently use IT, and carry out their operations. An example of a trend would be the outsourcing of IT services, such as desktop PC support, or whole IT-supported functions, such as accounts processing. An example of a technology trend would be virtualization. This refers to the ability of large servers to be subdivided into a number of virtual machines, which can be either virtual PCs or virtual servers.

Virtualization carries with it a number of benefits, including stopping what, at one stage, looked like an endless proliferation of servers inside companies. One large server can now be split into a number of virtual servers, enabling the organization to reduce the number of boxes it has to manage. Server virtualization should not be confused with another powerful trend, the creation of virtual environments inside the machine. The fact that desktop processors are now powerful enough to mimic real-world physics in computer space is transforming both design and entertainment.

All these trends have enabled the IT industry to continue to generate a strong demand for the next generation of servers, PCs, and laptops. However, in a recession, companies of all sizes generally postpone upgrading their IT, or implementing major IT projects that are not already in hand. This makes the sector vulnerable to downturns in the economy, and the current global downturn is already having a major impact on revenues in the sector worldwide.

MARKET ANALYSIS

According to the IT market analysis firm, Gartner, worldwide server shipments and revenues saw double-digit declines in the fourth quarter of 2008. By comparison with the same quarter in 2007, shipment numbers declined by 11.7% while revenue dropped by 15.1%. Commenting on the figures, Heeral Kota, a senior research analyst at Gartner, said: "The weakening economic environment had a deep impact on server market revenues in the fourth quarter, as companies put a hold on spending across most market segments. Almost all segments exhibited similar behavior, as users sought to reduce costs and spending, deferring projects where possible."

Gartner said that the fall in shipments and revenue was reported across all regions apart from Japan, which managed a 4.7% revenue increase. Europe, the Middle East, and Africa (EMEA) suffered the worst decline, with revenues falling by 20.6%. Even the emerging regions of Latin America and Asia-Pacific suffered, with declines of 12.5% and 14.8%, respectively. North America server revenue declined by 14.6%.

The scale of the IT server sector as an industry can be seen from the fact that IBM, the market leader, ended 2008 with revenues of US$4 billion from server shipments, with almost exactly one-third of the global market. However, IBM saw revenues decline by 17.4% as a result of the downturn. Hewlett-Packard was next, with revenues of just under US$4 billion and with a 30% market share.

The figures in server shipments for 2008 chart the impact of the downturn fairly starkly. The sector had been enjoying fairly strong results during the first half of 2008, but a severe decline in sales set in as the intensity of the downturn began to bite, Gartner said.

If things are bleak on the server front, the outlook is just as bad for PCs. Gartner is predicting that the PC industry will suffer its sharpest unit decline in history in 2009. Gartner expects some 257 million PCs to ship worldwide through 2009. This would represent an 11.9% contraction on the numbers sold in 2008. Even after the dot.com bubble burst in 2001, global PC unit shipments only contracted 3.2%.

To view these statistics in perspective, it is important to remember that setting up a new chip-fabrication plant to make the next generation of PCs costs some US$3 billion. With margins on PCs being at an all-time low, it is very difficult for the industry to sustain itself if companies and households stop upgrading to the latest generation of PC.

According to Gartner, both developed market economies and emerging markets are forecast to go through tremendous slowdowns. After the telecoms and dot.com crash in 2001, sales of PCs in mature markets contracted by 7.9%, Gartner says, while sales growth in emerging markets slowed to 11.1% in 2002. Both these low points will be substantially exceeded in 2009. The impact will be deepened by hardware suppliers, who will act prudently and maintain inventories at an all-time low to avoid losses.

However, all is not total gloom. The trend for corporates and home users to switch to mobile PCs, rather than desktop units, will keep growth going for worldwide mobile PC shipments. Gartner is forecasting sales of 155.6 million units, up 9% from 2008. By way of contrast, desktop PC shipments will struggle to exceed 101 million, a drop of almost 32% on 2008. The most popular form in the mobile space will continue to be the mini-notebook, Gartner says. In particular, users are moving to higher-specification notebook PCs with larger screens, of around 8.9 inches. Prices, however, will continue to fall. Gartner is predicting that the price of a mid-specification mini-notebook PC with a large screen will fall, from an average of US$450 in 2008 to under US$400 by the end of 2009.

  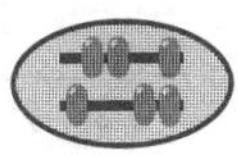      

Another plus point is that the industry as a whole learned some valuable lessons in the crash of 2001, and is already demonstrating that it is much more agile, and better able to react to changing market conditions in 2009.

Not surprisingly, with all this bad news about slowing demand on actual "built" hardware, the downturn is also hitting demand for chip production. In fact, Gartner's prediction here is that it will be at least 2013 before the semiconductor industry sees revenues comparable to those it achieved in 2008, when revenues peaked at US$256.4 billion. Over the course of 2009, the sector will see a drop in excess of 24%, with total global semiconductor revenues estimated to top out at US$194.5 billion. There is a precedent for this prediction, in that after the 2001 recession, the semiconductor industry took four years to get back to the revenues it had generated in 2000.

The contraction predicted for 2009 is considerably more gloomy than a prediction made by Gartner six months ago, when it was only predicting a contraction for the sector of 16%. On the plus side, modest single-digit growth should return in 2010.

Apart from semiconductor chip manufacturers, the other huge area in the field is memory chips, or, more specifically, DRAM chips. According to Gartner, DRAM suppliers lost more than US$13 billion in 2007 and 2008, due to massive overcapacity in the market and soft pricing. But many suppliers are now reducing supply, which should push DRAM prices back up, and put the industry on a better footing.

While the industry is absorbing all this bad news, there are positive trends that manufacturers, systems houses, value-added resellers, and consultancies can focus on. The move to replace tens or even hundreds of individual servers with large virtual servers is picking up pace, and is not going to be stopped by the recession. It is a cost-saver and efficiency driver, so companies will press ahead with virtualization programs. This, in turn, will drive sales of larger servers, and could drive applications upgrades as well. According to Gartner, worldwide virtualization software revenue will increase by 43%, from US$1.9 billion in 2008 to US$2.7 billion in 2009. Virtualization also plays well to the green agenda, and greening up IT by lowering its carbon footprint is another unstoppable trend for 2009 and 2010. Virtualization plays to this on a number of fronts. First, it is more power-efficient to run a single, large server than a number of smaller servers. Second, the manufacturing carbon footprint is lower, and, third, if the virtualization exercise extends to the desktop, then one server can replace dozens of PCs. Revenue from hosted virtual desktops (HVDs) is expected to more than triple, from US$74.1 million to US$298.6 million through 2009, Gartner says.

Storage systems in IT tend to be divided into external disk storage, where the disks are being "managed" in some way independently of processor resources, and attached storage, as in the typical PC or low-end server that comes with one or two hard drives already installed. According to the market analysis company, IDC, the worldwide external-disk storage market showed its first year-on-year fall for five years, for the last quarter of 2008. IDC reports a fall of 0.5%, with revenues totaling US$5.3 billion that quarter. Total disk-storage systems capacity shipped amounted to 2,460 petabytes, a growth of just 27.3% on the volume shipped in 2007. (The point here is that with e-mail and, now, live video, demand for storage should be vastly ahead of this figure).

Again on a positive note, one area where large and medium companies, as well as some service providers, can be expected to continue spending through the downturn is on the new IT concept known as "cloud computing." IDC expects worldwide spending on cloud computing and cloud services to reach US$42 billion by 2012. Cloud computing is a term that essentially refers to the delivery of services to communities of users over the internet, instead of via a data centre located in the same building. Access to the service is via a web browser, and everything from storage to the processor power that drives the service is located remotely. The term itself comes from the way the internet is depicted in computer network diagrams (a non-specific "cloud"), and points to the fact that all the complexity of infrastructure that makes the service possible is hidden "in the cloud."

According to a survey IDC conducted with almost 700 IT executives across the Asia-Pacific region, some 11% said they were already using cloud-based solutions. A further 41% indicated that they are either evaluating cloud-based solutions, or are piloting such solutions. Gartner, on the other hand, claims that cloud-computing application infrastructure technologies will still need some seven years to mature. It sees three phases of evolution for cloud computing going up to 2015 and beyond. Up to 2011, applications will be mostly opportunistic and tactical in nature, and will have little impact on mainstream IT, Gartner argues. By 2015, however, it expects cloud computing to have been commoditized, and to have become the preferred solution for many kinds of corporate applications that are now run in-house on standard IT equipment.

In summary, the immediate future for IT looks like being a period of tough belt-tightening. However, the underlying innovation in the sector, and its ability to transform mainstream business processes while enabling new kinds of business practice is undiminished, and should re-emerge to drive revenue growth once the global upturn starts to gain momentum.

▸▸ MORE INFO

Websites:

Gartner: www.gartner.com

IDC: www.idc.com

See Also:

★ Avoiding the Mistakes of the Past: Lessons from the Startup World (pp. 749–750)

★ Dealing with Cybersquatters (pp. 440–441)

★ Viewpoint: Hamish McRae (pp. 789–790)

Information Rules: A Strategic Guide to the Network Economy (p. 1277)

Media

MAJOR INDUSTRY TRENDS

The term "media" refers both to various forms of communication, and to the organizations behind this communication, including the press and news-reporting agencies. It can also refer to different types of data storage. This review looks at the media in all its communication activities.

One hundred years ago, the media was simply composed of the printed press. Today, there is a vast range of communication channels, including TV, radio, cinema, and the internet, as well as print. However, common industry trends can still be identified, despite the increasingly diverse nature of the market.

    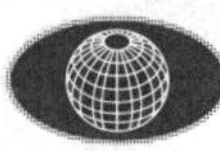   

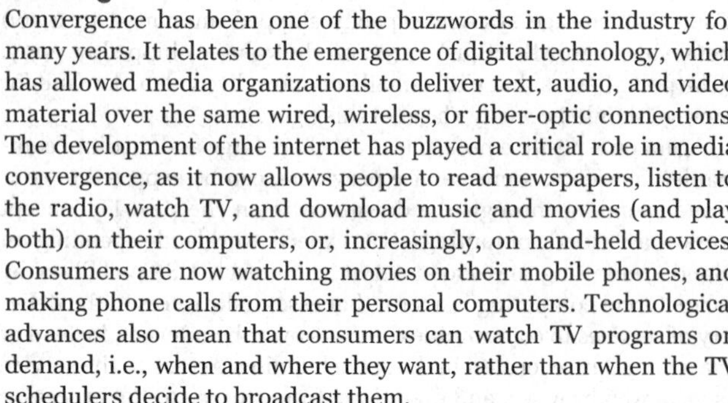

Convergence

Convergence has been one of the buzzwords in the industry for many years. It relates to the emergence of digital technology, which has allowed media organizations to deliver text, audio, and video material over the same wired, wireless, or fiber-optic connections. The development of the internet has played a critical role in media convergence, as it now allows people to read newspapers, listen to the radio, watch TV, and download music and movies (and play both) on their computers, or, increasingly, on hand-held devices. Consumers are now watching movies on their mobile phones, and making phone calls from their personal computers. Technological advances also mean that consumers can watch TV programs on demand, i.e., when and where they want, rather than when the TV schedulers decide to broadcast them.

The development of in-flight entertainment (IFE) provides a vivid illustration of the way in which the media has been transformed over the past 30 years, and of the convergence of technologies. In the 1970s, IFE consisted of a movie projected onto a screen. Today, most airlines offer personal televisions, usually located in the seat backs, featuring live satellite TV broadcasts. Some airlines offer video games and audio-visual entertainment on demand, allowing passengers to stop, start, and skip through programs, and to select movies stored in the aircraft computer system. Touch-screens and/or handsets allow passengers to choose from a variety of features and content, including feature films, news, and TV programs, as well as giving them the option to select video games and web-based content, create music playlists, etc. The more advanced IFE systems allow passengers to make hotel or rental car reservations in advance from the aircraft seat.

Back on the ground, trends over the next few years, in terms of convergence and technological developments, are likely to focus on increasing demand for personalized entertainment. In March 2009, the mobile-phone giant Motorola and the entertainment firm Virgin said they were holding discussions to provide content to customers at the time they want, and in the place they want. TMCnet.com said that both Motorola and Virgin Media "believe that the advanced multimedia services that will take over the entertainment segment in the next few years will be delivered on the next-generation, service-delivery gateway architecture," and "will include services such as multi-room TV, which provides the user with the ability to watch recorded content from any TV or PC in the house." Furthermore, the next wave of technological advances will allow for "converged entertainment services across three screens—PC, TV, and mobile—and the ability to move your content from device to device, and take it on-the-go," according to TMCnet.com.

New Media Wins Advertising Share from Traditional Broadcasters

Search Engine Marketing Professional Organization (SEMPO), a trade organization for the search-engine marketing sector, reported in March 2009 that internet search engines are continuing to steal advertising market share from traditional broadcasters. SEMPO said that more than a quarter of advertisers in its survey reported that they were shifting budgets into search-engine marketing from print magazines, while 19% said that they were moving their budgets into search from print newspaper advertising.

Part of the appeal of the new media to advertisers is that audiences can be targeted much more effectively than using traditional media. SEMPO's March 2009 survey certainly found that advertisers were expressing strong interest in new search-targeting technologies. These include "search retargeting," or targeting search ads to select groups of users based on the websites that they have previously visited, or based upon whether an individual has visited an advertiser's own website before. The search engine Google is striving to increase its advertising revenues, and is using targeted marketing as one means of achieving this. In March 2009, the company said it was starting to gather information about the websites people visit using an individual web browser, in order to target ads to their interests. "By making ads more relevant, and improving the connection between advertisers and our users, we can create more value for everyone," the company said. "Users get more useful ads, and these more relevant ads generate higher returns for advertisers and publishers." Google is also seeking to increase its advertising revenues by offering mobile advertising, including ads that appear within mobile phones' web browsers.

Other companies have been offering personalized online advertising for some time. The social networking sites, MySpace and Facebook, have targeted adverts at individual users based on their profiles since 2007, while retail sites such as Amazon and iTunes regularly recommend books and music to their users, based on their past purchases.

Technological Developments

Apart from convergence, other technological developments are likely to have a dramatic impact on the media industry over the next five to 10 years. Scientists, for example, are currently working on holographic displays that could lead to 3D TV. Indeed, in March 2009, the UK's *Daily Telegraph* newspaper reported that 3D TV could be a reality within five years. Up until now, the vast amount of information contained in holograms has meant that they require a special medium to record them, as well as vast computing power. However, the increasing cheapness of computer power, and new ways to record holograms digitally, using a sheet of laser light crafted by computer, have led to the possibility of 3D TV. The newspaper added that "leading manufacturers such as Philips, Mitsubishi, and Samsung are beginning to launch three-dimensional TVs in which objects appear to leap out at the viewer, without the need for the special glasses used in cinemas, and that can add depth to two-dimensional television."

MARKET ANALYSIS

Impact of the Recession on the Media Industry

The media industry earns a large proportion of its revenues from advertising, and is, therefore, highly influenced by the economic cycle. Advertising and marketing budgets tend to suffer first when the corporate sector comes under pressure. The recession appears to be hitting "old" media companies worse than their "new media" counterparts, although the latter are certainly not immune to the downturn. In March 2009, Italy's biggest private broadcaster, Mediaset, which is owned by the family of Italian prime minister, Silvio Berlusconi, posted a 9% fall in 2008 profit, cut its dividend, and warned that profit could slump again in 2009 as the economic downturn hits advertising revenues, according to Reuters news agency. Mediaset said that advertising revenues in its key markets of Italy and Spain saw a "marked" fall in the first two months of 2009, and were expected to be down over the entire year.

Earlier in March 2009, Michael Grade, executive chairman of British independent TV broadcaster, ITV, described the downturn as a "short-term horror." He added that conditions in the advertising market are "the most challenging I have experienced in over 30 years in UK broadcasting." Meanwhile, Germany's ProSiebenSat.1 said that revenue fell by 5.7% in 2008, to US$3.8 billion, due to a slump in advertising. Reuters said that commercial free-to-air broadcasters were among the media companies most exposed to the recession, because they usually rely almost entirely on advertising, unlike Pay TV rivals, which have subscription income to lean on.

Google contends that its business is more resilient to the downturn, because cost-conscious consumers are increasingly likely to go online to search for the best deals. In January 2009, Google reported surprisingly strong fourth-quarter results that suggested its search-advertising business and cost-cutting efforts had, indeed, enabled it to weather the recession better than rivals. But the company's chief executive said in March 2009 that the economic situation was "pretty dire," and that his company was "not immune" to current conditions. The research company, IDC, said in February 2009 that internet advertising could fall by 5% during the first quarter of 2009, marking the first contraction in online advertising spending since the collapse of the dotcom bubble in 2001. IDC forecast that first-quarter search revenue growth would continue slowing, while display and classified ads would experience worse declines than they suffered in the fourth quarter of 2008.

In March 2009, SEMPO forecast that North American search-marketing spending would increase in 2009 by 9%, to US$14.7 billion, from US$13.5 billion in 2008. However, its forecast was downgraded from estimates made in early 2008, in which it said that search-marketing spending would rise from US$15.7 billion in 2008 to US$18.8 billion in 2009. SEMPO said the value of the industry would reach US$19.8 billion in 2011, down from a previous estimate of US$25.2 billion for that year.

Pay TV Shines in the Global Media Sector

Advertising spending is undoubtedly under pressure around the globe, as economies battle against recessionary forces not seen for a generation. Yet, some pay TV companies believe that they can actually profit from the downturn. Louise Sams, head of the giant Turner Broadcasting System (TBS) of the US, said in March 2008 that around the world people were watching more TV because of the economic downturn. Sams said that free-to-air broadcasters in North America were struggling because of their reliance solely on advertising.

The *Sydney Morning Herald* quoted Sams as saying: "The US networks are not doing as many [TV show] pilots and new series, so it's going to be interesting to see how they feed their pipeline of programming. Is it going to be less-expensive reality programming, and how long will they keep people's attention? I have a hard time predicting the demise of terrestrial broadcasting in the foreseeable future, but I think right now in the US they are having a hard time justifying some of the original programming that we are continuing to do at TBS. That shows the benefit of having a dual revenue stream [subscriptions and advertising revenue]."

Growth of the Internet Hits Newspapers

The newspaper industry appears to be one of the main casualties of the growth of the internet. Certainly, the industry in the US appears in deep trouble, according to a report by Agence France Presse in March 2009. The report quoted the Pew Research Center's Project for Excellence in Journalism 2009 report, *The State of the News Media*, as saying the outlook for the industry was the "bleakest" since it began doing the annual studies six years previously. The report examined newspapers, online media, network, cable, and local television news, as well as news magazines, radio, and the ethnic press. It found that the newspaper industry "exited a harrowing 2008 and entered 2009 in something perilously close to freefall."

However, it added that "we still do not subscribe to the theory that the death of the industry is imminent," noting that the industry overall "in 2008 remained profitable." The recession is undoubtedly responsible for a significant proportion of the industry's woes, with advertising revenues falling sharply. The report noted that "audience migration to the web accelerated substantially in 2008." However, it said that while some US papers are abandoning print to go online, "going all-digital is not likely to become widespread anytime soon," as "papers still make roughly 90% of their revenue from print."

►► MORE INFO

Websites:

Pew Research Center, US research organization that studies attitudes toward politics, the press and public policy issues: www.people-press.org

Search Engine Marketing Professional Organization (SEMPO), global non-profit organization serving the search-engine marketing industry, and marketing professionals engaged in it: www.sempo.org

TMCnet.com, a good source of information on technological developments in the media: www.tmcnet.com

See Also:

★ Viewpoint: Zarin Patel (pp. 89–90)

Mining

MAJOR INDUSTRY TRENDS

The mining sector covers everything that companies extract by way of geological materials from the earth; from base and precious metals to coal, uranium, diamonds, rock salt, and potash. (Oil and gas extraction is covered in a separate sector profile and will not be considered here). This profile will focus on the commodities aspect of mining rather than on extraction techniques, while the fortunes of particular companies in the sector will be touched on collectively, through an examination of merger and acquisition deals conducted during 2008/2009.

The sector, along with agricultural products such as grain and coffee beans, constitutes the commodities sector, which is notorious for price volatility, and boom and bust cycles. However, the latest boom and bust saga in the industry, associated with the global downturn, which really hit the sector in the last quarter of 2008, has been as sharp as anything witnessed in decades.

In its survey of mining sector deals in 2008, published in January 2009, accountants PricewaterhouseCoopers (PwC) pointed out that, buoyed by the boom years of 2006/2007, the mining sector was within a whisker of making 2008 the third record year in a row for M&A deals. However, when the global crisis began to bite a number of the larger deals, as well as many smaller deals, were called off, some at the very final hurdle. One instance was BHP Billiton's decision not to pursue its US$150 billion offer for Rio Tinto in the teeth of opposition from the UK's Competition Commission. Another example was Xstrata's decision to call off its bid for Lonmin. As a result, 2008 turned out to be a record year for bids, but, after a spate of cancellations in the final quarter, deals actually done returned to 2005 levels. In all, a total of 1,668 deals (with a combined value of US$153.4 billion) were completed in the sector. This was lower than the levels seen in 2007 (1,026 deals with a combined value of US$158.9 billion), and leaves 2008 as the story of what might have been. The total deal value could easily have doubled or even trebled, had some of the largest deals gone through.

Moreover, as PwC reported, many companies that successfully

 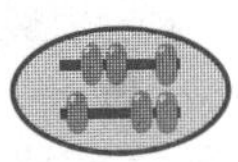 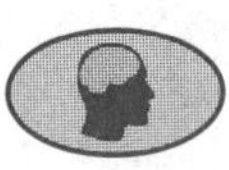     

transacted deals in 2008 found themselves facing the sudden downturn with overstretched balance sheets. "Mining shares went from rising star to plunging asteroid status," said PwC in its report.

Demand for iron ore in 2008 was massive, as global steel mills scrambled to keep abreast of rising demand from China and India, until the building frenzy was choked off by increasing concerns over falling global demand. PwC reported that the total value of deals for iron-ore assets nearly tripled in 2008, up from US$7.5 billion in 2007 to US$21.4 billion in 2008, with deal numbers rising from 40 to 107. Economic growth is also energy-hungry, and that drove demand for coal and uranium mining, with deals in both areas rising by 28%. The total value of coal and uranium mining deals in 2008 rose from US$29.9 billion to US$54.2 billion, year on year.

One of the features of the 2008 mining year, PwC pointed out, was the belief (finally abandoned in the last months of 2008) that the financial and economic downturn, which had begun to manifest itself in mid-2007, would pass without inflicting damage on the commodities sector. The hope was that demand from China and India would be strong enough to sustain the boom in the global mining sector despite falling demand in the developed economies. This continued to drive mining companies to look for mergers, as well as resource acquisitions, well after it became apparent that developed markets were in trouble. Then, in August 2008, reality caught up with the sector. Prices for copper, aluminum, and tin fell to their lowest levels in more than six months, and zinc fell back to November 2005 prices. According to the news channel Bloomberg, between May 2008 and February 2009, more than US$2 trillion was written off the global listed resources sector.

Another feature was the unexpected strength of the US dollar in the closing months of 2008 and the opening months of 2009. A rising dollar makes dollar-denominated metals extremely expensive for non-US buyers.

In January 2009, the metals desk at MFGlobal, a leading broker for exchange-traded futures and options, published its "Metals outlook 2009/2010" report, and sounded a cautiously optimistic note for the year ahead. "We suspect that markets will start to discount a far healthier supply/demand balance by the middle of 2009, at which point base metals should stabilize and work higher going into 2010," MFGlobal said.

One option for mining companies when prices fall is to build up their inventories instead of pushing product onto the market. Massive inventories, of course, both choke off supply, which pushes prices up, but also tend to act like a brake on rising prices, which can readily pull more supply into the market.

MFGlobal pointed out that, although stocks are building (copper stocks, for example, now stand at 450,000 tons), this is nowhere near the desperation levels of 1,000,000 tons of copper reached in the downturn of 2002. Zinc stocks too, are only around one-third of their 2002 peak. The two metals that are stockpiling hard, getting into "extreme territory" in MFGlobal's terms, are aluminum and nickel.

Copper is currently still being produced at close to pre-crunch levels, with copper producers being slower than other producers to cut production. The reason, MFGlobal analysts suggested, is that many copper producers are still either just making a profit or breaking even, with production costs standing at US$3,000–3,500 per metric ton. More recently though, a number of major copper producers, such as India's Hindustan Copper, and Freeport McMorRan Copper & Gold, have announced reductions. There was a surplus of copper on the market in 2008 of around 200,000 tons and estimates vary for the scale of the expected surplus in 2009, from under 300,000 tons to more than 600,000 tons. Again, a large surplus should be sufficient to check any sudden upward movement in pricing, which could fall to under US$3,000 per ton, MFGlobal suggested (its trading range for copper is US$2,640–4,250).

Aluminum stocks are currently standing at 2,700,000 tons, according to MFGlobal. This is a record high, and analysts suspect that there are at least a million tons more stockpiled in China. The International Aluminium Institute's figures for unwrought aluminum stocks stand at 1.604 million tons, as of November 2007, making the combined inventories (excluding China) equal to around 11% of global annual production. This suggests that prices could have a long way to fall before production cutbacks start to drive up pricing again, MFGlobal said.

Zinc producers are cutting back production hard, with many of them acting before the general price collapse of Fall 2008. MFGlobal estimated that, at present, some 65% of zinc producers are either operating at a loss, or are on marginal breakeven.

MARKET ANALYSIS

In an analysis titled "Commodity price moves and the global economic slowdown" (March 2008), the International Monetary Fund (IMF) pointed out that commodity price developments in 2007/2008 highlighted the dual nature of commodities. In the case of metals, they are both used as inputs in the production of other goods and, in their secondary role, they are used as financial assets. They can be used as such because they can be bought and sold, used as a store of value, and their price can be a basis for speculation, with traders taking long or short positions depending on whether they think the price is trending upwards or downwards.

In recent times, the financial side has come very much to the fore, the IMF says. Falling interest rates have forced investors to look for higher returns elsewhere, and metals have long been seen as a hedge against inflation. (Simply put, their price rises naturally with inflation in a way that investments in government gilts absolutely do not). Gold has, of course, a well-established place as a safe haven for investors when markets become turbulent. As a general rule, one can see an inverse correlation between, for example, a chart of Wall Street equities and the gold price chart, with the one falling as the other rises. In boom times, investors expect gold prices to fall (as there is more money to be made in more active investments) so they pull their money out of gold, which accelerates the price falls. When the markets become scary, investors flee back to gold, and the price pushes up sharply. As the global downturn has deepened, the price of gold has risen to record levels.

Another factor influencing metals prices was the dollar depreciation that was seen in 2007 and the opening months of 2008. By displaying a graph of the dollar and the euro plotted over time, against an index of commodity prices on the Y2 axis, the IMF makes the point that a depreciating dollar increases the cost of acquiring metals for dollar-economy producers, by comparison with euro-economy producers. It also opens the way for speculative arbitrage and hedging, and commodities have become increasingly used for portfolio diversification. "This trend has been reflected in rising inflows into commodity funds and assets," the IMF says. The increase in crude oil prices in 2008, as well as the rises in other commodity prices, are a case in point. Once this trend went into reverse and funds started flowing out of commodities, it accelerated the implosion of the commodity price bubble, and massively destabilized and complicated the market for mining companies.

Looking ahead, PwC says in its "Deals report" that depressed and, in some cases, collapsed share prices and an inability to access debt markets were causing immense distress for some mining companies in spring 2009. However, others have relatively healthy balance sheets. This kind of mixed environment is one that suggests both that acquisition activity will be muted in the short term, but with some companies under huge pressure to raise finance and with others having the means to buy, but over the medium term an increase in deal activity looks certain. The shape of the future ownership of the global mining industry looks set to change fairly dramatically over the next few years, PwC argues. As in other markets, however, those with strong balance sheets are "sitting on their hands" at present, motivated more by the belief that, if they wait, the assets they are targeting will become even cheaper, than by any faith that the market has now reached the bottom (by definition, the best time to buy).

In particular, the Chinese appetite for acquiring access to the raw materials the country sees as essential to its growth plans, seems undiminished. PwC expects to see acquirers from China being very active in the present depressed market. Chinalco's increased stake in Rio Tinto is simply the most high profile example of this. However, Chinese acquisitions of Western assets tend to generate disquiet in government, regulatory, and military strategic circles, so the response to increased acquisitiveness by China will bear watching, PwC says.

Another phenomenon PwC sees as likely in the mining sector is the possibility of both private equity (PE) and sovereign wealth funds moving into this space. Traditionally, PE has not been a big player in the mining sector, but the chance of buying in at the bottom of a market with very depressed values could well attract both sets of investors, PwC says.

"Since access to equity and debt has more or less dried up for many small to mid-cap mining companies, those with portfolios that are at the development stage or that are not sufficiently revenue generating will need to sell assets to survive," PwC says, reiterating its point that the shape of the sector, in terms of who owns what, is likely to change very substantially during 2009 and 2010.

▸▸ MORE INFO

Article:

Helbling, Thomas, and Valerie Mercer Blackman. "Commodity price moves and the global economic slowdown." *IMF Survey Magazine* (March 20, 2008). Online at: www.imf.org/external/pubs/ft/survey/so/2008/RES032008A.htm

Report:

Meir, Edward. "Metals outlook 2009/2010." London: MF Global UK, January 2009. Online at: www.mfglobalmetals.com/research/metalsoutlook2009f.pdf

Website:

PwC Global Mining Deals: www.pwc.com

See Also:

★ Public–Private Partnerships in Emerging Markets (pp. 562–565)
★ The Role of Commodities in an Institutional Portfolio (pp. 372–375)

Oil and Gas

MAJOR INDUSTRY TRENDS

Extracting Meaning from the Oil Price Roller Coaster

The oil price has had a wild ride over the last year and a half. At one point in June 2008 it was heading past US$140 a barrel, and in December 2008 it looked like the world would see the return of sub-US$30 pricing for a barrel of oil. By March 2009, it was hovering around US$51 a barrel, and giving some signs of straining at the leash to be off and away again as soon as the world's stock markets start moving reliably upward once more.

The statistics of the global oil industry provide interesting reading. There are some 687.44 billion barrels of oil (bbl) in proven reserves around the world, and exactly 40 countries have reserves in excess of 1 billion barrels (source: www.nationmaster.com). That sounds like a great deal of oil, but as Nationmaster's editor, Ian Graham, observes, the scale of those reserves diminishes when attention turns to how fast oil is being consumed.

In 1980, according to the US Energy Information Administration (EIA), worldwide consumption of oil amounted to just 63 million barrels of oil a day (mb/d). By 2009, that had risen to 83 mb/d. The International Energy Agency (IEA), which publishes the World Energy Outlook (WEO) each year, estimates that by 2030, if we continue on the same path, that total will have increased by 45% to 106 mb/d.

Dividing 687.44 billion (the total of proven reserves) by 106 million (the daily consumption rate in 2030) to get the number of days of consumption left, then dividing again by 365 to turn that into years, produces the rather surprising figure of 18 and a bit years before existing proven reserves are 100% depleted. Of course, the starting point here is 2030, which lies 21 years off from this point in time, so the whole projection is not a particularly likely scenario. The world will not be consuming 106 mb/d of oil in 2030, as the existing reserves would not support demand on that scale for that length of time. The laws of supply and demand would price oil out of reach as a source of energy well before any theoretical depletion point could be reached.

Other factors that have to be taken into account include the world's refining capacity, and the leeway—or lack of it—between productive capacity and demand. In fact, demand is already pushing at the absolute limits of existing refinery capacity. As Nobuo Tanaka, the executive director of the IEA says, "Current trends in energy supply and consumption are patently unsustainable—environmentally, economically, and socially. They can and must be altered.

"Rising imports of oil and gas into OECD regions and developing Asia, together with the growing concentration of production in a small number of countries, would increase our susceptibility to supply disruptions and sharp price hikes. At the same time, greenhouse-gas emissions would be driven up inexorably, putting the world on track for an eventual global temperature increase of up to 6°C."

To make oil last another 100 years, according to Nationmaster's Ian Graham, worldwide oil consumption would have to be cut to 6.87 billion barrels of oil per year, or just over 8% of our current rate of consumption (6.48% of the projected figure for 2030). By any standards, that looks to be an extremely difficult feat to pull off, but it may well be that pricing alone will drive the world to find alternatives or to cut back drastically on its usage.

In the short term, cutting back does not seem to be the way the world is going. In an article published in the *European Tribune*, and on www.energybulletin.net, Jerome Paris pointed out that there were some 7.3 million new car owners in China in 2008. Assuming that they each drive 5,000 miles a year at 40 miles to the gallon, this alone would generate demand for an additional 45.6 million barrels of crude. "In other words, new Chinese drivers alone

 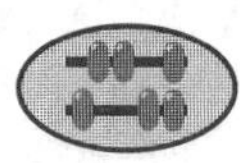      

will take up 25–30% of the Saudi 2008 production increase (before OPEC cut production to try to drive up falling oil prices)," he said.

Paris argued that the supply situation is being aggravated not just by the appearance of new consumers of oil, but by the fact that the producing nations themselves are turning into avid consumers of oil at the same time as their production is stagnating or going into reverse. "The biggest increases in oil demand, beyond the 'usual suspects' of China and India, comes from the oil producers, Saudi Arabia, Brazil, Russia, and the UAE," he argued.

MARKET ANALYSIS

Peak Oil—and Its Alternatives

The peak oil theory, formulated in the mid-1950s by one-time Shell geophysicist M. King Hubbert, is based on the Hubbert curve, which sees oil production peaking at a definite point in time, then tailing off. The curve itself works for any limited natural resource, and is frequently cited in "peak oil" debates in the sector. What makes the Hubbert curve significant for discussions about the future of oil and gas as energy reserves is that it predicts a steep fall off, or a high rate of decline of production as existing assets wind down. Peak oil debates tend to have an "Armageddon" quality to them, because they use the steep fall off predicted by the Hubbert curve to argue that global oil production will decline too fast for the world to develop sufficient alternative sources of energy to replace that gained presently from oil.

Shell itself does not subscribe to peak oil theory (see www.shell.com) but does agree that since 2000 demand for oil has accelerated. "Looking forward and assuming adoption of alternative policies, even the lowest projection shows that energy demand will continue to grow at 1.4%, while the highest projection is that demand will grow 2.5%. At that rate, demand in 2030 will be more than double what it was in 2000. While we do not subscribe to the peak oil theory, the truth is that, particularly outside the Middle East, the readily accessible sources of conventional oil are being depleted," Shell says.

The answer is not to trot out the Hubbert curve and wring one's hands, Shell says, but rather to look to some hard choices, including converting oil sands to useable oil fluids, as Shell is doing in Canada. Other options which should also be explored, according to Shell, include stepping up the progress on renewables and introducing a "cap and trade" carbon tax.

The environmental lobby, however, is massively opposed to oil sands exploitation, arguing that they are easily one of the worst (most polluting) forms of energy. WWF, for example, argues that the extraction of oil from oil sands creates "three times the carbon emissions of conventional oil production and destroys the local environment, devastating forests, and using massive amounts of river water. Oil sands production contributes to climate change, and creates dangerous waste, including poisonous water that leaks into the wider environment" (see More Info).

Oil shale is even worse, WWF argues, producing up to eight times the carbon emissions of conventional production. It quotes NASA's comment by Jim Hansen: "Squeezing oil from shale mountains is not an option that would allow our planet and its inhabitants to survive."

The Institute for Security and Development Policy (ISDP), a Stockholm-based independent research and policy institute, has done a study titled "The global race for oil and gas—Power politics and principles in Asia." It argues that whether or not global oil and gas is actually now in decline rather than on the increase, with the consequent gap between demand and production widening, it remains true that some countries and politicians are acting as if this was the case. This is creating a global "dash for oil."

In particular, the Institute argues, "Competition between consumer states over energy raw materials has already resulted in a race for oil and gas in Central Asia and Siberia."

What could this mean for the global economy? According to the ISDP, in the absence of some serious geostrategic thinking, we face some unattractive alternatives: "It is likely that China and India, ultimately even the US, the EU, and Japan, will begin to 'play hardball' in the race for raw energy materials."

The ISDP hopes that the EU's example of adhering to the Energy Charter Treaty, an international agreement that was signed in the Hague in December 1991, offers a way forward for the world, as it works its way through the traumas associated with moving from dependence on oil to other energy sources. The Treaty's essence is the peaceful implementation of non-discriminatory conditions for trade in energy materials, based on World Trade Organization rules, and provisions to ensure reliable cross-border energy transit flows. The world has already had several examples of how difficult such cross-border agreements can be, the most recent being Russia's spats with Ukraine and Belarus, both of which had the potential to have a serious impact on the supply of oil and gas to Europe.

One interesting fact that outlines the pressure that is starting to be felt on the world's oil reserves, the ISDP says, emerges from a study of the reserves declarations of four oil companies, ExxonMobil, BP, Shell, and Chevron/Texaco. Together, these four account for 15% of the world's energy production. "The annual added capacity of their collective purchasing of new oil fields as compared to their combined sales of oil was 153% in 1997 (reserves in excess of consumption). By 2000, that figure had decreased to 125%, and in 2004 it was just 70%," the ISDP says.

This dramatic decline in reserves versus consumption goes away if the view is opened up to include "unconventional assets" such as oil sands and oil shale, already discussed above, or oil from coal, a process that South Africa has used for years. Cambridge Energy Research Associates (CERA) has calculated that, by 2010, the contribution by unconventional assets to oil production could be as high as 35% of the total. The oil reserves in tar sands and bitumen match or exceed the total reserves for conventional oil. The ISDP estimates that production of oil from bitumen works out at around US$70 a barrel—not exactly attractive when the price of oil is US$53 a barrel, but very attractive at prices above US$90 a barrel. The environmental impact, though, can be expected to generate tremendous opposition to this energy source if production threatens to become mainstream.

▶▶ MORE INFO

Reports:

Energy Information Administration (EIA). "Chapter 3. Natural gas." In "International energy outlook 2008." Washington, DC: EIA, June 2008. Online at: www.eia.doe.gov/oiaf/ieo/nat_gas.html

Kiesow, Ingolf. "The global race for oil and gas: Power politics and principles in Asia." Stockholm: Institute for Security and Development Policy, October 2008. Online at: www.isdp.eu/files/publications/ap/08/ik08globalrace.pdf

Website:

WWF's oil sands arguments: www.wwf.org.uk/what_we_do/changing_the_way_we_live/oilsands.cfm

See Also:

★ The Role of Commodities in an Institutional Portfolio (pp. 372–375)

 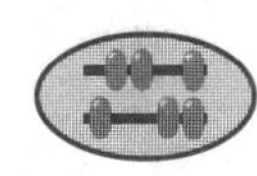 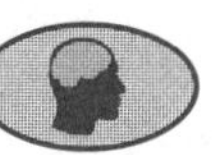  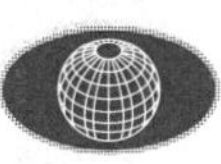   

The Global Gas Position

According to the EIA's "International energy outlook 2008," natural gas consumption is growing twice as fast in non-OECD countries as in the OECD. Moreover, the EIA expects production increases in the non-OECD region to account for more than 90% of the growth in world production between 2005 and 2030. Worldwide, natural gas consumption will increase from 104 trillion cubic feet in 2005 to 158 trillion cubic feet in 2030, about a 51% increase.

The EIA expects high and rising oil prices to cause natural gas to be used increasingly as a replacement for oil. The spin-off benefit of this, for global warming, is that natural gas produces less carbon dioxide when burned than either coal or petroleum, making it a cleaner fuel. Industry is the world's largest consumer of natural gas, and is expected to account for 43% of world usage by 2030. Electricity generation from gas-fired power plants will account for 30% of this consumption, the EIA predicts. Today, in both China and India, natural gas accounts for just 3% of the energy mix. This will grow by 5.5% per year in the case of China, and by 4.6% in the case of India, up to 2030. The Middle East is already looking to ramp up liquefied natural gas exports. In Qatar, for instance, export facilities with a total capacity of approximately 3.6 trillion cubic feet of natural gas (77 metric million tons of LNG) are expected to be in operation by 2015, compared with the country's 2005 LNG exports of 1 trillion cubic feet. The increase in exports from Qatar alone would account for 14% of the total projected increase in production from 2005 to 2015 for non-OECD countries, excluding non-OECD Europe and Eurasia, the EIA says.

Professional Services

INTRODUCTION

This report covers the market for professional services around the world. It encompasses areas such as accountancy, legal services, information technology, property management, architecture, advertising, and management consultancy. While large companies often have in-house lawyers and accountants, many small and medium-sized companies rely on the services supplied by firms that specialize in these areas, or else outsource the work to contractors. Even larger companies will outsource many functions to external suppliers. Management consultancy and services in areas such as architecture, for example, tend to be supplied by external firms or contractors that focus on these areas.

Professional services account for a large chunk of the GDP of many advanced economies, and are among the fastest-growing economic sectors. In the UK, for example, the turnover of the professional-services sector in 2007 amounted to £84.3bn (US$118.2bn), or 8% of UK output—the largest share of any sector—while professional-services firms employed 11.5% of the workforce, according to a report published by the UK Treasury in March 2009 (see More Info). The report added that professional services play a major role in UK trade, accounting for almost £16 billion of the total £29 billion trade in UK services.

MAJOR INDUSTRY TRENDS

The report written for the Treasury by the Professional Services Global Competitiveness Group, which was set up in September 2008 to look at issues affecting the professional-services sector, also identified various trends in professional services that are taking place not just in the UK, but around the globe. They include:

- *Financial stability*: Professional-services firms are likely to have an increasingly important role in promoting sound corporate governance when advising client companies, in both the financial-services sector and across the economy as a whole. Indeed, the report said that this advice would be "central to laying the foundations for a more stable and sustainable economy in the future."
- *Innovation*: The report said that "the prospect of growing demand for excellence, fierce global competition, and an ever-more-demanding client base" is likely to boost the development of innovative products and services. It added that "global professional-services centers will flourish only if they think and perform effectively and efficiently."
- *Headquartering of international firms*: The report said that there was a trend towards international and pan-European partnerships, and that, as a result, professional-services firms "will need to be flexible in order to respond to local business needs wherever they emerge in the global market." It added: "In the economy of the future, jurisdictions which provide attractive locations for international headquarters are likely to attract further business."
- *Connectivity*: "The pursuit of links and synergies between traditional clusters and emerging markets is becoming increasingly significant to the professional-services sector, offering opportunities for growth and innovation," according to the report. The authors added that "new markets tend to display high levels of innovation and creativity, often using socially responsible products and services as a growth engine."

Emergence of Global Standards in Accountancy

The drive towards global standards in areas such as accountancy appears to be gathering pace, and has been given added impetus by the global financial crisis. Indeed, more than 100 countries around the world—including the members of the European Union and China—now use international financial reporting standards, or IFRS. Around 85 of those countries require IFRS reporting for all domestically listed companies. Other countries are expected to adopt IFRS over the next few years, including Brazil in 2010, and India and Canada in 2011. The Securities and Exchange Commission (SEC), which regulates financial markets in the US, appears to favor the adoption of IFRS in place of the Generally Accepted Accounting Principles (GAAP) currently used in the country. Many US companies already use IFRS, and convergence could be completed by 2014, according to some analysts. The SEC plans to make a decision by 2011 on whether the adoption of IFRS is in the public interest and would benefit investors. However, the global financial crisis has prompted calls for the adoption of tighter global accountancy standards. Since the onset of the crisis, President Nicolas Sarkozy of France has called for a strict new international framework of accountancy standards, as well as limits on speculation in financial markets.

Legal Firms Face Paradigm Shift, As Well As Impact of Recession

The large legal firms are undoubtedly suffering under the impact of recession and the meltdown in the financial sector, once one of the major sources of income for the legal industry. However, *The Lawyer* magazine (March 31, 2009) questioned whether the sector was simply facing a cyclical downturn, or instead a paradigm shift in demand for its services. The magazine asked leading players in the industry for their views on the subject. Some said that the

    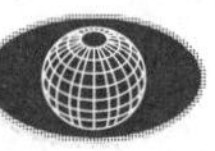   

industry was simply facing a cyclical downturn. Others believed that firms' expansion over the past decade into areas such as leveraged finance, high-yield debt, and asset-backed finance, all of which have collapsed during the global financial crisis, meant that the industry was indeed facing a paradigm shift. *The Lawyer* quoted Slaughter and May senior partner, Chris Saul, as saying: "The explosion of credit we've seen over the past 10 years or so, and the deal activity that it has helped to drive means that this downturn has a different quality of intensity about it compared with previous ones."

The magazine added that, while there might be differences of opinion in terms of the severity of the downturn facing the industry, there was a consensus that the major legal firms would have to adapt to the new world. It quoted DLA Piper's joint chief executive, Sir Nigel Knowles, as saying: "There will be fewer clients, particularly in the financial-services sector, and the clients will want to pay less. There's going to be tremendous pressure on fee rates, particularly those rates often charged by the magic circle and charmed circle." (The term "magic circle" refers to the leading law firms in London).

The economic recession may also spell the death knell for the legal profession's practice of charging by the hour. The clients of some legal firms are reportedly demanding alternative billing as a way to better predict their expenses. The American Bar Association has been urging law firms to move away from the practice for years. The *New York Times* (January 29, 2009) reported that the city's largest law firms are considering alternative billing as a way to maintain or increase revenue during the downturn. The newspaper said: "Clients have complained for years that the practice of billing for each hour worked can encourage law firms to prolong a client's problem rather than solve it. But the rough economic climate is making clients more demanding, leading many law firms to rethink their business model."

MARKET ANALYSIS

Impact of the Global Economic Downturn

The economic downturn has had an impact on all of the areas covered by this report. Clearly, as the corporate sector shrinks, demand for professional services will also contract. However, suppliers of professional services have also been adversely affected by the corporate sector's focus on cost-cutting during the downturn. Firms are either renegotiating fees downwards, or simply doing more work in-house in areas such as legal services. Despite this, some companies are benefiting from the downturn. For example, Andy Green, chief executive of the Anglo-Dutch computer-services company, Logica, said in March 2009 that demand for large outsourcing projects in the IT sector is expected to increase in 2009, as companies look for new ways to squeeze costs.

The impact of the downturn from area to area is highlighted by the following developments:

- Major law firms are making staff redundant. In January 2009, Clifford Chance announced that it would lay off up to 80 attorneys in London, while in March it laid off 24 transactional attorneys in New York. The London-based Clifford Chance also said that it was deferring the start dates of 50 law-school graduates, and paying the prospective employees' stipends during the furlough period. In March 2009, Boston-based Edwards Angell said that it was making 25 lawyers and 35 staffers across six offices in the US redundant in response to declining legal work during the recession. *The Lawyer* (March 31, 2009) summed up the prevailing mood among the big law firms, saying: "If last year was bad, the first three months of 2009 have been even worse. The weeks since 1 January have been extremely challenging for the world's largest international law firms. Certainly, for the thousands of lawyers and staff laid off by their cost-cutting firms, the first quarter of 2009 is already infamous."
- Accenture, a global management-consulting, technology-services and outsourcing company, reported in March 2009 that demand for its consultancy services shrank during the second quarter of its fiscal year (the three months ending February 28, 2009). Chief finance officer, Pam Craig, was quoted as saying: "There has been a noticeable change in the demand environment, as clients grapple with how a macroenvironment full of continuing economic challenges impacts their priorities."
- Martin Sorrell, chief executive of WPP, one of the world's major advertising groups, said in March 2009 that the company was prepared to make thousands of job cuts this year in order to counter declining revenues. Sorrell said that WPP would cut a percentage point of the 112,000 global headcount for every percentage fall in revenue. During the same month, the credit-rating agency, Standard & Poor's, revised its outlook on WPP from stable to negative, and said: "The outlook revision reflects our view that the significant deterioration of economic and advertising conditions worldwide may lead to significantly slower-than-expected deleveraging at WPP, and even to increased leverage in the short term."
- The four major global accountancy firms—KPMG, Ernst & Young, Deloitte Touche Tohmatsu, and Pricewaterhouse-Coopers—have all announced layoffs during the downturn. The companies have also encouraged staff to adopt flexible working options, such as voluntarily reducing their hours or taking sabbaticals. In January 2009, for example, KPMG offered its 11,000-strong workforce a sabbatical. The group said it was trying to avoid compulsory redundancies because it wanted to be in a strong position when the recession ended. Staff are by far the biggest expense incurred by accountants, and are an obvious target for cost-cutting measures. However, the major firms have been moving relatively cautiously in terms of job cuts, for they know that, having made significant layoffs in previous downturns, they could face difficulty in coping when the economic recovery leads to an upturn in the volume of work.
- The economic downturn has hit architecture firms around the globe. In March 2009, *Business Week* reported that "architects from Berlin to Bonn say small practices are shutting down or on life support." In the same month, the BBC reported that 400 jobs in architect practices in Northern Ireland had been lost over the previous 12 months. The figure represented 20% of the work-

▸▸ MORE INFO

Report:

PSGCG. "Professional Services Global Competitiveness Group report." London: HM Treasury, March 2009. Online at: www.hm-treasury.gov.uk/d/professional_services_group160309.pdf

Website:

The Lawyer, good source of information on the legal profession and industry: www.thelawyer.com

See Also:

★ Dispute Resolution: The Forum Selection Clause (pp. 442–444)
✔ International Comparisons of Company Law (p. 991)
✔ Islamic Commercial Law (p. 994)
✔ Islamic Law of Contracts (p. 995)
✔ Structuring, Negotiating, and Drafting Agency Agreements (p. 1005)

  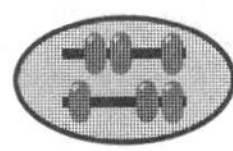 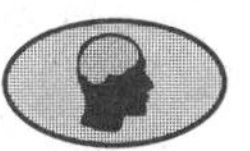     

force. In the US, the impact on architects has been particularly severe. The *San Francisco Chronicle* (March 31, 2009) reported that, while the city's national architecture convention attracted 27,000 participants in "rosier times," this figure was likely to fall to just 20,000 at the upcoming convention in April 2009. Government fiscal measures aimed at stimulating economic growth—which are often focused on infrastructure projects—could prove the saving grace for the architecture sector. President Barack Obama's multibillion-dollar economic recovery plan includes vast sums aimed at rebuilding America's highways and other infrastructure.

Real Estate

INTRODUCTION

This report covers real estate around the world, looking at the residential sector as well as the market for commercial property.

MAJOR INDUSTRY TRENDS: RESIDENTIAL MARKETS

Housing Markets Collapse Around the World

Prior to the collapse of the US housing market in 2007 and 2008, which indirectly caused the global financial crisis, some analysts had been warning for years that residential real-estate markets around the world had become overinflated. In June 2005, for example, *The Economist* warned of "the danger of a house-price collapse." However, even *The Economist* has admitted that it did not foresee that plummeting real-estate prices would rock the global financial system to its foundations, and ignite fears that the world could be heading into an economic downturn to match the Great Depression.

In its issue dated June 16, 2005, the magazine said: "We have been warning for some time that the price of housing was rising at an alarming rate all around the globe, including in America," adding that "the day of reckoning is closer at hand." Presciently, *The Economist* forecast: "It is not going to be pretty. How the current housing boom ends could decide the course of the entire world economy over the next few years. This boom is unprecedented in terms of both the number of countries involved, and the record size of house-price gains. Measured by the increase in asset values over the past five years, the global housing boom is the biggest financial bubble in history. The bigger the boom, the bigger the eventual bust."

It is certainly true that the real-estate bubble was a global phenomenon, linked by one common factor: cheap credit on lax terms. This was partly linked to the deregulation of financial markets around the globe, which helped to fuel the supply of credit, poor regulation among the relevant financial authorities in one country after another, and low interest rates, reflecting apparently subdued inflationary pressures during the latter part of the 1990s and the first half of this decade.

The party began to draw to a close in 2006 and 2007 as commodity prices spiked upwards, causing central banks around the world to hike interest rates. Countries with heavily indebted households were particularly vulnerable to the increase in interest rates. In addition, following the long boom, house prices had become stretched in many countries, with many would-be buyers simply unable to afford to enter the market. Finally, poor regulatory and banking practices in the US and other markets led to reckless lending by mortgage providers, which, when these unsound loans began to go bad, caused the financial crisis, and the credit crisis. Banks simply stopped lending to each other, as well as to individuals and corporations. This had a direct impact on the housing market, in that many people had great difficulty in remortgaging when their previous deals expired, or else were only able to do so on onerous terms. Furthermore, the drying up of liquidity in the overall economy caused unemployment to rise, which contributed to an increase in defaults on home loans, and discouraged new buyers from entering the market. (Nobody wants to take on a huge commitment such as a home loan if they fear for their job prospects).

MAJOR INDUSTRY TRENDS: COMMERCIAL MARKETS

The weakness of the global economy has inevitably affected demand for commercial property. Declining demand for office, retail, and factory space has hit occupancy rates and rental income across the planet. In the US, the problem is particularly severe. Indeed, according to the *Wall Street Journal* (March 26, 2009), "commercial real-estate loans are going sour at an accelerating pace, threatening to cause tens of billions of dollars in losses to banks already hurt by the housing downturn."

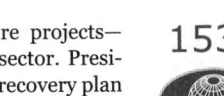

The newspaper added that "commercial real-estate debt is potentially more dangerous to the financial system than debt classes such as credit cards and student loans because of its size." It quoted figures from the Real Estate Roundtable, a trade group, that put the value of commercial real estate in the US at US$6.5 trillion, of which US$3.1 trillion is financed by debt. The newspaper also quoted Foresight Analytics of California, which estimates that the US banking sector could suffer as much as US$250 billion in commercial real-estate losses during the current recession. The research firm has predicted that more than 700 banks in the USA could fail as a result of their exposure to commercial real estate.

However, the problem is certainly not confined to the US. Jones Lang LaSalle, a global real-estate services firm, said in a report published in February 2009 ("Global market perspective," see More Info) that further weakness in the global economy had accelerated the decline in commercial-property asset values. It said that Asian markets such as Singapore and many Chinese and Indian cities were suffering from oversupply, and that the problem was particularly acute in Beijing, where around 40 million square feet of office space would come onto the market over the next five years. In Delhi, a similar volume of supply will be delivered over the next three years.

Jones Lang LaSalle added: "Efforts to raise capital for listed property groups in Australia, Singapore and Japan are accelerating at discounts of 40–50% of the current share price, compared with discounts of 10–15% just months earlier. From London to New York to Tokyo, prices for office buildings in central business districts have fallen anywhere from 30% to nearly 50%. In the United States, sellers need to entice unlevered buyers with internal rates of return of 13–16%. The value that buyers place on vacant US properties is virtually zero. The value of empty retail space in the UK also has plummeted."

Furthermore, Jones Lang LaSalle said that while credit conditions are showing some improvements, commercial real-estate lending largely is not. The firm added: "Although banks have received massive government aid, their commercial real-estate lending remains frozen amid uncertainty about nationalization and capital preservation for further loan losses. Banks are still absorbing government credit infusions rather than making significant new loans."

  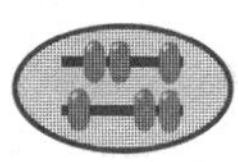      

In its March 2009 report "Global market perspective," Jones Lang LaSalle said a global property-market recovery had yet to take hold. It added: "The debt markets remain congested, and the securitization market is at a complete standstill. Restored liquidity will reset property values through asset trades that provide accurate data points on pricing floors across the globe. There are few completed transactions to analyze, which suggests the bottom of the market is still ahead and values have further to fall."

Jones Lang LaSalle concluded: "Going forward, investors likely will emphasize covenant strength, local market conditions and a deeper understanding of the outlook for specific industry sectors. For investors, 2009 will bring a return to core global markets as they look to maintain liquidity in their portfolios, and transact in markets with high levels of yield transparency and lower macroeconomic risks. For corporate occupiers, the short-term game is one of survival, and the continuous re-evaluation of property portfolios, rents, leases, and space occupation to accommodate reduced headcounts. Apart from those corporate occupiers who are currently cash-rich, more opportunistic tenant behavior will remain muted until the early part of 2010 at the earliest."

MARKET ANALYSIS

Price Falls Seen in Residential Markets Around the World

The extent of the declines seen in many economies is unprecedented. In the UK, house prices fell by a record 10.3% in the year to March 2009, according to property-data company, Hometrack. Richard Donnell, Hometrack's director of research, also predicted that, "with the expectation of continued increases in unemployment and weak economic growth, together with restricted availability of mortgages, it seems doubtful whether the increase in activity and sales will continue to gather momentum in the coming months." Other organizations have said that the decline in house prices in the UK has been even larger. The Land Registry, a government body that records data related to the housing market, said that house prices fell by 2% in February 2009 alone, pushing the annual rate of decline from 15.1% to 16.5%. Numis Securities, a City investment bank, warned in March 2009 that prices in the UK could fall by a further 40–55%.

Dubai's once-booming property sector, which boasts an indoor ski slope and the world's tallest building, has also crashed as a result of the global financial crisis. Developers have slowed or canceled projects, and thousands of jobs have been axed. In March 2009, the Reuters news agency quoted the Egyptian investment bank, EFG Hermes, as saying that house prices in the emirate had fallen by 34% on average from their peaks in 2008, and that they could fall by a further 20% in 2009. The investment bank said that prices should stabilize during the first half of 2010, and may rise in the second half of 2010 or early 2011.

Even in China, where the economy has continued to grow despite the global financial crisis, house prices have fallen. According to figures from a government body, the National Development and Reform Commission, house prices in 70 Chinese cities fell by 1.2% in the year ending February 2009—the biggest drop since records began in 2005. The price falls are unlikely to have come as a surprise to Ling Xiuli, a senior researcher with PICC Asset Management Company Ltd. In September 2008, she was reported to have warned that "house prices in big and medium-sized cities may collapse at any time," and that they could continue to fall for a further 10 years. Ling said that "the house-price-to-income ratio in China is unprecedentedly high in world economic history, and the housing price bubble has hit its peak."

The Canadian financial system avoided the toxic instruments that brought banks across the border in the US to their knees, and the country's banks followed much more responsible lending practices. Indeed, Canada's banks are regarded as among the healthiest among the advanced economies. Unlike the US, Canada also has a very low debt burden, and the government has posted big fiscal surpluses in recent years. Yet Canada, too, is suffering from falling house prices. In January 2009, Canadian home prices fell by 2.4% from a year earlier. The Teranet-National Bank National Composite House Price Index, which measures the rate of change of prices for single-family homes in six metropolitan areas, also showed that prices had fallen by 5.5% nationally from the peak hit in August 2008. The Reuters news agency said that confidence in the Canadian housing market had fallen due to the global financial crisis and the economic downturn. It added that housing activity, including resales and groundbreakings, is generally seeing a period of softness in Canada, although there has not been the same plunge in the sector that has been seen in the US.

Home sales in the US, the epicenter of the global credit crunch, have been falling since 2005, and prices peaked in 2006. The S&P/Case-Shiller home-price index of 20 metropolitan cities, one of the most respected measures of house prices in the US, declined by a record 18.5% in December 2008 from a year earlier. However, signs of hope have emerged in 2009. Sales of previously owned homes unexpectedly increased in February 2009, as low prices lured first-time buyers back into the market. Meanwhile, the Federal Housing Finance Agency reported in March that home prices increased by 1.7% in January from the previous month, the first increase seen in 10 months. Admittedly, the government noted that sales in January were "relatively low," which could have affected the data. However, US housing starts and permits also staged an unexpected rebound in February from 50-year lows, easily beating forecasts.

▸▸ MORE INFO

Websites:

Foresight Analytics, provides real-estate market analysis and projections for investors, lenders, and developers: www.foresightanalytics.com

Jones Lang LaSalle, a global real-estate services firm that publishes reports on the commercial property market, including "Global market perspective": www.joneslanglasalle.com/Pages/GlobalMarketPerspective.aspx

Retail

MAJOR INDUSTRY TRENDS

Retailing involves the sale of commodities to the public. Outlets can vary from family-run stores to global behemoths such as Wal-Mart, the world's largest retailer, with 2 million employees (or "associates," as Wal-Mart prefers to call them), and sales of US$374.5 billion during the fiscal year ending January 31, 2008. The industry also covers a wide range of sectors, from general products, such as food and clothing, to specialist goods, such as sports equipment and automobile accessories. Despite the diverse nature of the industry, a number of common trends can be identified.

  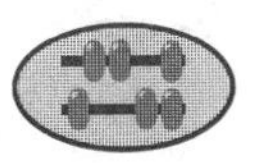 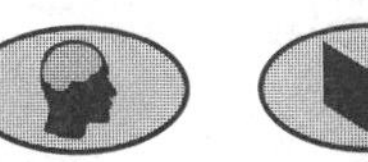     

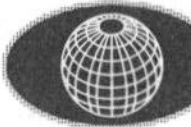

Industry Concentration

Around the world, small independent outlets, known as "Mom and Pop" stores in the US, are coming under pressure from national, and, increasingly, global giants, such as Wal-Mart, which can exploit their vast buying power to extract the best possible price from suppliers. It is often impossible for the independents, or even relatively large retail chains, to compete on price with the largest retailers.

Whereas once a consumer might have visited the butcher, the baker, and the candlestick maker on Main Street, he or she is now most likely to drive to an out-of-town retailer such as Wal-Mart in the US, Tesco in the UK, or Carrefour in France, and buy meat and bread (and candles) under one roof—a phenomenon known as one-stop shopping.

While the power of the giant retailers is already entrenched in advanced economies—the biggest four retailers account for 75% of grocery sales in the UK—these retailers are also making rapid inroads into emerging economies. This is largely because their domestic markets are close to saturation point, and because the biggest retailers account for such a large share of their own market that taking over a domestic rival could trigger opposition from the relevant competition authorities.

The pattern seen in the grocery market is being repeated in other retailing sectors, such as clothing and electronics, with sales increasingly concentrated through a relatively small number of retailers. Many of these companies are also expanding internationally. For example, the Spanish clothing retailer, Inditex, which opened its first store in 1975, now has 4,147 stores in 72 countries, and an international presence that stretches from the Americas to Asia. In 2007, its sales stood at €9.435 billion.

Brands under Pressure

The growth of the giant retailers means that they can now dictate terms to suppliers of even iconic brands. Whereas once suppliers sold their goods through a wide range of small shops, and could tell these retailers how much to charge for their goods and where they should be positioned in the store, the balance of power is now firmly in the hands of the retailer. Companies such as Tesco, which commands nearly a third of the UK grocery market, can have an enormous impact on a brand simply by refusing to stock it.

The growing popularity of own brands, also known as own labels or private labels, has given even more power to the giant retailers. Own-label goods are products sold under the retailer's brand. Some companies focus solely on supplying own-brand goods. Dailycer, which supplies own-brand breakfast cereals to European retailers, is one example. However, own brands are also supplied by companies that produce branded goods. Indeed, the own brand may be identical to its branded counterpart.

In the 1960s and 1970s, retailer own brands were focused on the "value" end of the market. In other words, retailers focused on supplying goods that offered a cheap alternative to brands, but did not try to compete on quality. That changed in the 1980s and 1990s, as retailers increased the range of own brands that they offered. During that period, many supermarkets offered goods in the value, standard, and premium segments of the market. In the late 1990s and in the current decade, supermarket own brands have become increasingly sophisticated. Now, supermarkets target consumers by lifestyle, as well as by income. Thus, in the food sector, retailers now offer "healthy" own brands, which are low in fat or sugar, as well as ethical "fair trade" products, and brands that appeal to a particular sector, such as organic foods. All this activity has inevitably strengthened the share that own brands take in the average supermarket. In the UK, which is generally thought to have the most sophisticated own-brand market, they account for around 42% of all sales, according to the market-research publisher, Key Note Ltd.

The global economic downturn appears to be giving retailers even greater power over suppliers. Hard-pressed consumers are increasingly turning to own-brand value goods to stretch their spending power. In October 2008, for example, Germany's largest retail group, Metro, said it was benefiting from a new line of value-for-money, own-brand foods in its hypermarkets, as German consumers cut back their spending in the face of mounting economic uncertainty. It's a similar story in the US, where, in 2008, the country's biggest grocery sellers—Wal-Mart, Kroger, Supervalu, and Safeway—reported that sales of their own brands were increasing as customers seek cost savings.

Technological Advances and E-Commerce

The giant retailers have been quick to exploit the benefits of advances in IT, as well as the growth of the internet. The latter medium has created new retailing giants such as Amazon, but it has largely been exploited by established retailers, which view it as simply another distribution channel, and a means to drive sales. Sales via the internet are certainly growing rapidly. ASDA, which is owned by Wal-Mart and is the UK's second-largest grocery retailer, said that its online sales grew by 40% in 2008. At present, the internet accounts for a relatively small proportion of sales in many sectors; analysts estimate, for example, that online sales of clothing represent just 3–5% of the total clothing market. However, those same analysts expect this figure to grow rapidly.

Advances in IT and communications have been exploited by retailers in a number of other ways. Inditex, for example, is credited with creating the concept of fast fashion, which gives shoppers the latest styles just a few weeks after they first appear on the catwalk, at prices that mean they can wear an outfit once or twice, and then replace it. IT enables Inditex to sell clothes in its stores two weeks after they have been designed. At Inditex, information is also continually transmitted from the company's stores to a design team of more than 200 professionals, informing them of customers' needs and concerns, allowing the company to respond very rapidly to changing tastes.

Meanwhile, companies have used IT to harness information about their customers and refine their marketing programs. In September 2008, for example, Tesco, the third-largest retailer in the world, launched an ultra-low-price Market Value range, which spans 350 lines in food, household, and personal care. It used data collected from its Clubcard loyalty scheme to identify shoppers it believed had defected to cheaper outlets, and sent them tailor-made promotions to lure them back.

Global Sourcing

The major retailers are increasingly sourcing goods from around the world, rather than just their own domestic markets. This not only allows retailers to find the cheapest suppliers in the world, but also has other advantages. Grocery retailers, for example, can now supply what were once seasonal foods all year round. In the middle of winter, a shopper in London can buy strawberries flown in from Chile.

Tesco has a global sourcing office in Hong Kong, which supplies more than 60% of all clothing and 40% of other non-food products sold in Tesco's UK stores, as well as most of the non-food items sold in the 12 other countries in which Tesco operates. The Hong Kong office is responsible for design, sourcing, overseeing production, quality control, and sorting out the customs documentation for around 50,000 Tesco product lines. Many of the goods are sourced from mainland China.

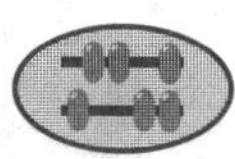

Supermarkets Expand Out of Food

The major supermarket operators around the world have expanded into a whole range of areas beyond their traditional role as suppliers of food and household goods. They now sell clothing, household equipment, music, electronics, health and beauty products, and pharmaceutical goods, as well as financial services, and even cars. This trend is being driven by various factors. For example, in many countries, there are now so many supermarkets that the market has reached saturation point. In addition, items such as electronics offer higher margins than traditional groceries.

MARKET ANALYSIS

The five largest retailers in the world are Wal-Mart (US), Carrefour (France), Tesco (UK), Ahold (Netherlands) and Delhaize (Belgium). All have long since expanded outside their domestic markets, and now operate on a global basis.

Thus, while Wal-Mart operates more than 4,100 outlets in the US, it has a further 3,100 outlets in Argentina, Brazil, Canada, China, Costa Rica, El Salvador, Guatemala, Honduras, Japan, Mexico, Nicaragua, Puerto Rico, and the UK. In January 2009, it announced that it had acquired a majority stake in Chile's largest food retailer, Distribucion y Servicio D&S SA. The company spent US$200 billion on merchandise in 2007, underlining its immense buying power.

Carrefour operates four main grocery-store formats: hypermarkets, supermarkets, hard discount stores, and convenience stores. It has more than 15,000 stores, either company-operated or franchises, and operates in 30 countries. Indeed, more than 54% of group turnover derives from outside France. The group sees strong potential for further international growth in the future, particularly in such large national markets as China, Brazil, Indonesia, Poland, and Turkey. However, in March 2009, Reuters reported that Carrefour had lost its leadership edge, especially in France, resulting in loss of market share, stalled growth, and unsatisfactory profit margins at its hypermarkets, which have seen their market share eroded by hard discounters and local supermarkets. The news agency quoted Lars Olofsson, who became CEO in January 2009, as saying that the group, which has 3 billion customers worldwide ("it's as if half the world's population buy from us"), should focus on turning around its operations in France, its home market, which accounts for 44% of sales.

Tesco operates 3,956 stores around the world, of which 2,184 are in the UK. It employs 440,000 people around the world. It is active in China, the Czech Republic, France, Hungary, Japan, Malaysia, Poland, the Republic of Ireland, Slovakia, South Korea, Thailand, Turkey, the UK, and the US. Tesco says it "has a well-established and consistent strategy for growth, which has allowed us to strengthen our core UK business and drive expansion into new markets." It is aiming to "broaden the scope of the business to enable it to deliver strong, sustainable, long-term growth by following the customer into large expanding markets at home—such as financial services, non-food, and telecoms—and new markets abroad, initially in Central Europe and Asia, and now also in the United States."

Ahold, based in Amsterdam, operates grocery stores in the US, the Netherlands, the Czech Republic, Slovakia, Sweden, Norway, and the Baltic states. In the US, Ahold owns the Stop & Shop and Giant-Landover supermarkets, and in the Netherlands it owns the Albert Heijn grocery network. In March 2009, Ahold reported a higher-than-expected 49% rise in fourth-quarter operating profit, thanks to a revamp of its US grocery stores and strong sales in its home market. The retailer said that quarterly profit excluding interest and taxes reached €365 million (US$462.6 million), against an average analyst forecast of €310 million.

Delhaize has 775 stores in Belgium, but also operates the Food Lion chain in the US. Delhaize is aiming to add between 70 and 80 stores in 2009, to bring its total to about 2,750 stores worldwide, 1,600 of which will be in the US. It has operations in various countries, including Greece, Romania, Indonesia, Luxembourg, and Germany.

▸▸ MORE INFO

Websites:

Key Note Ltd, provides research on a wide range of markets, including retailing: www.keynote.co.uk

Market-research website giving information on a wide range of reports, including those on retailing: www.marketresearchworld.net/index.php?option=com_content&task=category§ionid= 8&id=35&Itemid=48

Wal-Mart: www.walmartstores.com

Shipping

MAJOR INDUSTRY TRENDS

Before the global downturn began to cause export volumes across the world, particularly in China, to contract sharply, the global shipping sector had placed some of the biggest bets in the sector's history. These bets took the form of billions of dollars spent on a new generation of extra-large container vessels. If developed countries manage to shrug off the present deep recession and return to growth by the end of 2009, then all may yet be well for the shipping-line owners who placed these large orders. However, in March 2009, that is far from a given.

Nor is it just the huge container lines that are suffering. Bulk dry carriers, accustomed to an endless stream of orders to bring iron ore and steel from commodity-exporting countries to feed China's massive building boom (the country was, before the downturn, committed to building 200 new cities), are now also faced with collapsing demand.

Niche business sectors in shipping, a sector that is rich in niche opportunities, are faring better, but they, too, are under pressure. LNG (liquid natural gas) carriers looked like an excellent investment at the height of the boom, back at the start of 2007. The world was hungry for gas as a cleaner alternative to oil, and a major global power production program based on newly built gas-generation power plants fueled demand for security of supply.

However, by January 2009, Lloyds List was reporting that some 30 LNG carriers from a tradable fleet of about 287 were sitting idle. According to Lloyds List, this wasn't the end of the matter because advanced orders for new LNG carriers, placed in the boom times, meant that another 48 LNG carriers are due for delivery through the course of 2009. This creates a tremendous volume of spare capacity, driving shipping prices down to new lows.

For this sector, there is some hope in that cities need power, even in a downturn, and new gas-generation plants provide a greener alternative, whatever the state of the economy. Moreover, there are several major LNG projects due to come on stream in 2009. Lloyds List cites projects in Qatar, Russia, and Yemen, all of which are due to start shipping LNG to customers before the end of the year.

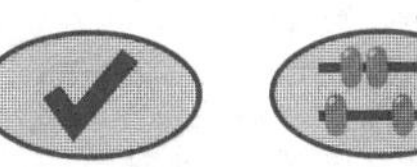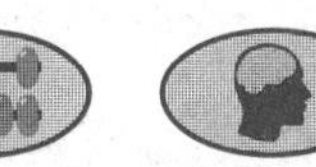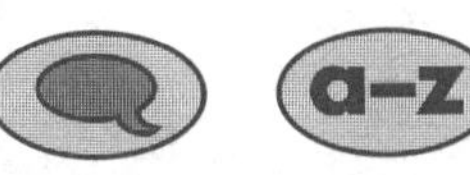

Lloyds List quotes Lorentzen & Stemoco analyst, Steve Engelen, who commented that "market utilization of LNG shipping capacity in 2008 was only 60%, which is extremely low." Engelen thought that LNG carrier owners would fare better in 2009 as the new projects came on stream. Qatar alone is scheduled to increase LNG capacity by about 24 million metric tons, which should push the global LNG carrier fleet capacity to about 75% utilization by the end of 2009.

Interestingly, the total of 30 or so idle LNG carriers at present does not include an additional 20 or so older LNG carriers which could still find demand in a buoyant market, but which are now rusting in ports around the world. In 2008, the global LNG fleet was swollen by some 50 new LNG carrier deliveries, so the scrapping of the oldest and smallest ships in the global fleet "failed to dent tonnage," according to Lloyds List.

The main drama, though, is being played out in the container market. Containers were the invention of the North Carolina entrepreneur, Malcom McLean, back in 1956, and they have completely revolutionized the transport of goods and cargo worldwide. In fact, many credit containerization for the globalization of trade, as containers make it very easy for many manufacturers to ship their specific products as part of a large, general shipment. When McLean invented the container, it cost almost US$6 a ton to hand-load a ton of cargo on to or off a ship. Using containers, that price comes down to 16¢ (source: wikipedia.org). The container was a huge step beyond the previous best "invention," namely palletted goods in break bulk cargoes.

The novel element in McLean's approach was the idea of a sealed, steel box that was never opened in transit, and that could be speedily loaded, unloaded and transshipped, or switched from rail to ship to road freight. The transformation of the whole process of shipping goods around the world was immense. Instead of having to unload ships by hand (or, in more modern times, by cranes swinging pallets of goods onshore to be checked, then warehoused until they could be freighted out), containerized goods take very little time to shift from ship to shore, or vice versa, and there is no checking of goods because the containers are sealed.

From there, the shipping industry slowly but surely moved in the direction of economies of scale. The fixed overhead costs associated with shipping a container come down when the number of containers being shipped goes up. When the world is booming, and the demand for container shipments is huge, this approach provides a fast route to superior profits. The largest of today's container ships are some 400 metres in length and 55 metres wide. They can carry 13,000 containers, or 50% more containers than the biggest ships in 2003/2004.

Ironically, in a downturn, huge container vessels lose their appeal. Instead, it is the despised, "high cost," smaller container vessels of yesterday that suddenly look much the better bet.

MARKET ANALYSIS

According to the *Financial Times*, the spot rate for moving a 40-foot container from Hong Kong to Rotterdam stood at US$2,700 in fall 2007. By December 2008, that price had fallen to US$200. Container trade between Asia and Europe has grown year on year, and the volumes for 2007 were 16.5% higher than in 2006. However, for the first time in its short history, analysts expect container traffic on this sea route to contract. For an industry accustomed to double-digit growth over the last seven years—ever since China joined the World Trade Organization (WTO)—this is a cataclysmic fall. It has placed the future of entire shipping lines in jeopardy.

The *Financial Times* quotes the view of Nick Sjoberg of Braemar Shipping Services, a London shipbroker, that, in total, ship owners around the world need to find some US$500 billion to pay for new ship purchases to which they are irrevocably committed. These ships are currently being built in shipyards around the world, and the builders will expect payment. Unfortunately for the shipping line owners, the credit crunch and the downturn have hit them with a double whammy, as both make banks and other sources of funding, including private equity, much more reluctant to finance ship purchases. Not only do the banks not have the capital to make the loans, but such loans now also look much more risky and much less compelling. There is no particular logic in investing simply to build up spare capacity that no one wants, or is likely to need for the next few years.

What is bad news for the shipping lines could be a silver lining in the current downturn for exporters, assuming they can find some demand for their goods. Shipping is now so cheap that it is probably more competitive, in many instances, for them to send containers of their goods half way around the world to new markets, than it is for them to truck their goods a few hundred miles to their own cities.

One of the peculiar features of containerized sea traffic is that it has developed as a cooperative play among shipping lines, who collaborate to ensure that ships run a week apart on a circular route. With the ships running at a good speed, it takes 56 days and eight ships to achieve the desired frequency. However, in the downturn, shipping lines are instructing their ships to lower their speed to conserve fuel, easily the single biggest overhead for a shipping line (apart from the ship itself). According to the *Financial Times*, Asia-Europe round trips utilizing fuel-saving measures take an additional week and require an additional ship. The net result for shippers is fewer options when it comes to picking sailing times, and probably fewer ports to pick from. It also means that their goods will take a week longer to get to market. On the plus side, competitive pressure has, as we have seen, pushed the rates right down.

This has become a source of concern to the industry. The chief executives of a number of shipping lines are members of an organization, a "research and discussion group," called the Transpacific Stabilization Agreement (TSA). They met in Tokyo in March 2009 to thrash out an agreement to ensure that service contracts between shipping lines and shippers are not struck at the unsustainable rates that developed as a trend during the 2008 off-peak winter season.

According to a press release issued by the TSA, ship owners agreed to ensure that the damaging practice of not charging shipping clients the full rate for fuel consumed on the journey was ended. "Lines have also indicated their intention to ensure that progress made in 2008/2009 contracting, which produced an improved level of fuel-cost recovery, continues," the TSA said.

The group represents 14 TSA carrier CEOs, and all 14 agreed that any short-term rate contracts struck over the four to five months prior to March 2009 would be terminated at the latest by 30 June 2009, giving lines a chance to reintroduce sensible pricing.

However, the TSA faces a very similar problem to OPEC, the organization of petroleum exporters, in the oil world, in that when conditions become this tight, survival becomes the name of the game, and individual owners, just like some petroleum exporters, have a tendency to break rank and strike whatever deals they can. TSA chairman, Ronald Widdows, admitted that despite an earlier, similar announcement by TSA, the behavior of carrier owners had contributed to further erosion in pricing. This had eaten into a number of different cargo segments, and affected what the industry calls "non-compensatory rates" (i.e. loss-making rates have crept in).

"Everyone involved in this trade faces the certainty of significant losses, if quick action is not taken to approach the upcoming round of contract negotiations, with a renewed focus on rates that will support continued servicing of this market. It will be evident shortly whether member lines individually can rise to the challenge," he commented.

There are some signs of potential life, however. The Baltic Dry Index is an index of freight shipping maintained by the Baltic Exchange, based in London. It provides a measure of the daily average cost of shipping bulk dry commodities such as iron ore, coal, and grain. As global growth is the major driver of increased shipping of bulk loads around the world, and as these contracts are struck months in advance of the goods actually being shipped, the Baltic Dry Index offers a very good window into whether the world's trade is contracting or expanding. In basic terms, the higher the demand is for bulk freight around the world, the higher the index rises. If it falls away, then that is a sign that trade will contract sharply some months hence. In the fourth quarter of 2008, after a near-continuous climb, the Baltic Dry Index chart plummeted, taking shipping volumes back two decades. By the end of the year, the index had dropped by more than 90%. However, the latest chart for the index in March 2009 showed substantial activity. One reading of this is that manufacturers around the world are gearing up for what they hope will be an upturn in the fourth quarter of 2009.

The Baltic Exchange's own magazine, *The Baltic*, ran an article in March 2009 titled "Light at the end of the tunnel?" on the state of the bulk dry carrier market. It pointed out that, in February 2009, "for the first time in several months, the dry-bulk market appeared to be showing signs of growth." The index itself, the article points out, recorded the biggest one-day rise in 24 years, with a 14% leap on February 4, 2009. This was not sufficient to restore the market to its old levels from its record fall, but it was encouraging. There is considerable optimism in the sector that the stimulus package that the Chinese government has put in place, amounting to close to US$1 trillion, will add an additional 1.5 percentage points of growth to China's GDP this year. That should ensure that Chinese demand for iron ore picks up again, and that will be good news for shipping lines. However, the sector badly needs global export activity to pick up, and Japan's exporting falling by 50% and more in the fourth quarter of 2008 was not good news.

MORE INFO

Websites:

The Baltic Exchange: www.thebaltic.com

Lloyds List: www.lloydslist.com

The Transpacific Stabilization Agreement: www.tsacarriers.org

See Also:

The Box: How the Shipping Container Made the World Smaller and the World Economy Bigger (p. 1231)

Steel

MAJOR INDUSTRY TRENDS

It would be easy to take a quick glance at the figures for global steel production for 2008 and conclude that the sector had come rather well out of the downturn. Total world crude steel production for 2008 reached 1.32 metric million tons, only the second year in history that world production has topped the 1.3 million metric ton mark. True, the volume produced was slightly down on the absolute record year set by 2007, but the decrease was slight, with output falling by just 1.2%, by comparison with 2007.

However, the headline figures hide a massive downturn in the fourth quarter of 2008. According to the World Steel Association (known as worldsteel), whose members produce some 85% of the world's steel, production declined in nearly all the major steel-producing countries and regions, including the EU, North America, South America, and the CIS in 2008. The one glimmer of light was that Asia in general, and China in particular, maintained positive growth.

Had it not been for the impact of the global slowdown, 2008 would have been an all-time record year. It took poor figures for October and November, and shocking figures for December to cause 2008 to fall behind the record steel production levels set in the previous year. World crude steel output for December 2008 recorded a decrease of 24.3% by comparison with volumes shipped in the same month in 2007.

The poor figures have continued into 2009. According to worldsteel, only China and Iran managed to record positive growth for February 2009. Everywhere else continued to see production declines. Iran recorded an increase of 15.9% in February 2009, producing 0.9 million metric tons of crude steel, and the Middle East is the only region showing production growth for that month.

Worldsteel points out that China's crude steel production for February 2009 was 40.4 million metric tons, an increase of 4.9% on February 2008. By contrast, Japan produced 5.5 million metric tons of crude steel in February 2009, down 44.2% compared to the same month in 2008. South Korea showed a decrease of 24.8% from February 2008, producing 3.2 million metric tons of crude steel in February 2009.

To put global production figures in context, China is far and away the world's biggest steel producer. In 2008, it became the first-ever country to produce more than 500 million metric tons in one year, topping 502 million metric tons. However, this was only marginally ahead of its performance for 2007 (2.6%), when China just failed to pass the magic 500 million metric ton barrier. In all, in 2008 China alone produced 38% of the world's total crude steel.

As a region, Asia tops the world, producing 770 million metric tons in 2008, 58% of the world's production (an increase of 1.9% on 2007). South Korea and India recorded increases of 3.8% and 3.7%, respectively. Japan, the world's second-largest steel producer, turned out a little more than a fifth of China's total production, reaching 118.7 million metric tons in 2008, a decrease of 1.2% on the 2007 figures.

North America (the world's third-largest producer) saw steeper falls in production, down 5.5% on 2007, with a maximum of 91 million metric tons being produced. Russia (fourth globally) experienced a similar decline to 68.5 million metric tons, while Ukraine (eighth in the world) did even worse, with a decline of 13.1% to 37 million metric tons.

At the same time as production is falling, the capability utilization rate, which measures actual demand for steel on a country-by-country basis, showed even more alarming falls. American Iron & Steel Industries reported that in the week ending March 28, 2009, domestic raw steel production was 1.006 net tons while the capability utilization rate was just 42.1%. By contrast, the capability utilization rate for the industry in 2008 was 89.7%, on a production of 2.14 million net tons. This represents a 53% year-on-year decline, and shows just how severely the recession is now affecting US steel usage. Adjusted year-to-date production to March 28, 2009, was 12.698 million tons, at a capability utilization of just 42.8%. During the same period in 2008, the capability utilization rate was 90.5% on more than twice the tonnage (26.841 million tons).

Turning from the raw production and capability utilization rates, beloved of the sector, to the large production items that demand vast quantities of steel, from tall buildings to automobiles to supertankers, the reason for the fall-off in demand is obvious. All these sectors are in crisis. According to Lloyds List, for example, one-fifth of all new tankers currently under construction will not make it to final delivery—often to the deep relief of the ship owners who had ordered them. Lloyds List quotes a report from the London broker, Simpson Spence & Young, which says that of the 50 vessels currently on order, representing some 56 million deadweight tonnage (DWT), which are due to enter service in 2009, only 45.2 million DWT will actually be delivered.

The problem is that shipyards are struggling to meet delivery deadlines. In the main, the problem lies with yards that have been attracted to the tanker-building market by the high demand of the boom years. In particular, a number of shipyards in China and Korea are at risk. There had been a trend of removing older tankers from the tanker market and converting them to dry bulk carriers, or for use as offshore project vessels. However, that trend, too, has dried up in 2009. "The dry bulk market has collapsed, so why spend US$30 million converting a tanker?" the brokers' report asks.

MARKET ANALYSIS

Accountants, PricewaterhouseCoopers (PwC), produce a quarterly report on the global metals sector called "Forging ahead." While a turbulent period in a sector tends to create weaknesses and distress, which then prompt heightened M&A activity, the steel sector is clearly not yet ready to resume the consolidation activity that characterized 2007 and the first half of 2008. According to PwC, the fourth quarter of 2008 saw continued deterioration for metals companies across the board, as evidenced by plummeting commodity prices.

The key trend among major producers outside China was to look for layoffs, short working, and anything that would enable them to cut costs until the market picks up again. PwC points out that because the first three quarters of 2008 were so profitable for the sector, many companies did not take the downturn as seriously as they should have, and delayed key steps in either slimming down, or in moving ahead rapidly with integration plans if they had just bought another business.

According to PwC, by the end of 2008, only 55% of deals announced during the course of the year had completed. There were 51 deals still pending, and nine had been withdrawn—seven of these in the fourth quarter alone.

PwC points out that two of the steel sector's key customer segments, automotive and construction, are among those most severely hit by the global recession. "In many cases, end-of-year steel prices were lower than they were at the start of the year," PwC points out, adding: "All of the 2008 price increases the steel sector enjoyed have been completely eroded." Not only has demand plummeted, even in regions where there is still some demand, many customers cannot access letters of credit to support their orders, as trade financing is still relatively frozen, PwC says. Many metals CEOs are running their companies in survival mode, with conservation of cash as their top priority.

However, the realities of business mean that steel company CEOs have to position their businesses not just for survival, but to be able to come out of the downturn ahead of their rivals. This means that those with stronger balance sheets are busy constructing possible deals. Some 24% of CEOs in the sector, in a survey carried out by PwC, said they were actively planning a cross-border merger or acquisition over the next 12 months. However, few CEOs thought that an acquisition would do anything for their company's short-term profitability. There is growing interest, however, in joint ventures and strategic alliances. Because the Chinese market is such a dominant part of the industry, many companies outside Asia are looking for partnering opportunities with Chinese and Asian partners.

PwC says that there are considerable parallels right now between aluminum producers and steel producers. "Major aluminum producers are significantly cutting production and thousands of jobs. Several have announced restructuring plans that include business divestments and asset disposals. Steel companies face analogous concerns, although the challenges are more severe for the integrated producers than for the mini-mill operators," PwC says.

The mini-mill operators have been benefiting from reductions in the cost of scrap metal (and there are signs that the price of scrap is now increasing again). They are also nimbler when it comes to their ability to produce to demand. PwC points out that the global benchmark hot roll price at December 31, 2008, was down 15% from the start of the year, and down 50% from the peak prices that were achieved in mid-2008.

The US and other governments' stimulus packages offer hope for the steel sector, insofar as they target infrastructure projects, such as rail and bridge-building, that rely heavily on steel. However, PwC says that industry insiders tend to see this as a buffer, which will cushion some of the impact of the slowdown, while the business cycle runs its course and demand begins to pick up again.

An indication of how quiet the fourth quarter of 2008 was can be seen from the M&A statistics for the whole metal sector. The total deal value for the sector was US$10.3 billion, whereas the figures for the fourth quarter for the last three years are US$186.5 billion, US$298.2 billion and US$77.7 billion, respectively.

Because of its scale, the eyes of the steel sector turn constantly to China, and the health or otherwise of the Chinese economy. One of the crumbs of comfort in the current downturn is that the Chinese economy grew by 9% in 2008, according to SEAISI, the South East Asia Iron and Steel Institute. Although the annual growth rate shrank continuously, from 9.9% in the first quarter to 6.8% in the fourth quarter, at least it stayed solidly in positive territory. It was, however, the first time that China's growth rate has fallen below a double-digit level since 2003.

That said, there was also plenty of gloom to be derived from the Chinese statistics. According to worldsteel, major steel demand drivers in China shrank significantly in 2008. While investment in real-estate development in urban areas grew by 20.9%—a figure that Western economies would regard as wildly overheated—it was down from the 30.2% growth seen in the sector in 2007. Auto-

▸▸ MORE INFO

Report:

PricewaterhouseCoopers (PwC). "Metals deals: Forging ahead 2008 annual review." PwC, January 2009. Online at: www.pwc.com/gx/eng/about/ind/metals/metals-deals-forging-ahead-2008.pdf

Websites:

SEAISI, South East Asia Iron and Steel Institute: www.seaisi.org

World Steel Association: www.worldsteel.org

mobile production grew by 6.5% (again, a figure that US carmakers would die for), but this was down too, from the growth figure of 8.5% achieved in 2007. Air conditioner production growth—a huge demand item in China's new cities—saw growth slashed from 17% in 2007 to just 4.9% in 2008. According to BHP Billiton, one of the world's biggest mining companies, China's destocking cycle is now almost complete, which bodes well for future orders. On the negative side, SEAISI cites the World Bank's comment that China has, as yet, made little progress in rebalancing its economy towards consumption, and away from its massive overreliance on exports to the developed world. Estimates of China's growth for 2009 by leading economists range from 5.0% to 8.0%, with Bank of China, Credit Suisse, Merrill Lynch, and Nomura International all forecasting the higher 8.0% figure. Although China's exports of finished steel products were down sharply in many categories, one area where China has had considerable success is in promoting its export of coated-steel products. This area saw a growth rate in excess of 50% in 2008, compared with 2007.

In mid-January 2009, the China State Council announced a major plan focused on the economic regeneration of the Chinese steel industry, to include favorable tax treatments of some steel products—which is already drawing protests from US and other producers—and the phasing out of obsolete facilities.

Telecoms

MAJOR INDUSTRY TRENDS

Growing Popularity of Mobile Threatens Fixed-Line Sector

The telecoms industry can be divided into two principal sectors: fixed-line services, and mobile services. The mobile sector has proved the main engine of growth over the past decade, and has proved a boon to many consumers in emerging economies who previously did not have access to fixed-line services. However, it is not just in the developing world that the growth of mobile services threatens the position of traditional fixed-line operators. In June 2008, *The Times* quoted broadband experts as predicting that the mobile-phone network could replace copper wire as the principal method by which people connect to the internet in the UK, in as little as two years.

The newspaper said that "increased sales of laptops (which can be connected to the internet via the owner's mobile-phone connection), the widespread rollout of high-speed mobile networks, and the falling price of connecting to such networks have all contributed to the uptake of mobile broadband." Similar trends can be seen in other advanced economies.

Recession Hits Sales of Handsets

After years of rapid growth, sales of mobile handsets have been dealt a blow by the global economic slowdown. In March 2009, the Reuters news agency reported that "the overall cell phone market is expected to contract by about 10% this year. . . as consumers rein in spending, and handset sellers try to clear out unsold phones." If sales were to fall in 2009, it would be only the second time this has happened in the industry's 15-year history. (In 2001, sales of mobile phones fell by 3%).

The mobile makers have responded swiftly to falling demand. Thus, the world's top cell phone maker, Nokia of Finland, announced in January 2009 that it would cut annual costs at its key handset unit alone by more than €700 million, to counter plunging demand. In March, it added that it had stopped using subcontractors to manufacture its mobile-phone engines, which include the phone, and the software that enables its basic operations. In 2008, Nokia outsourced about 17%, by volume, of the manufacturing of its mobile-phone engines.

Reuters quoted Adam Pick, an analyst at iSuppli (which provides information on the electronics-industry value chain), as saying that "this announcement clearly illustrates just how severe the situation in the mobile-handset market really is." In March 2009, another major player, Sony Ericsson, released a profit warning for the first quarter of the year. The company predicted that it would sell 37% fewer handsets in the first quarter of 2009 than it did in the same period in 2008.

Telecoms Sector in Good Overall Shape to Survive Recession

A report by PricewaterhouseCoopers (PwC), published in March 2009, found that, overall, the telecoms industry was well placed to survive the global economic slowdown. PwC said that the industry had much lower levels of debt than other sectors, despite a spate of mergers and acquisitions over the past few years. Gary Taylor, a director at PwC, was quoted as saying that "although, in terms of deal activity, the industry is seeing a return to the recent dark days, on the whole telecoms should stand up against the crippling headwind of the recession."

He added: "The dotcom crash put the industry through its paces and, as a result, we should see far less distressed debt and insolvencies than other sectors, such as banking and retailing. Telecoms companies have emerged tougher, thanks to tighter balance sheets."

PwC added that the position of the overall global industry is being aided by the fact that consumers are not cutting back on usage of mobile phones—behavior that is protecting revenue streams. Indeed, the telecoms sector traditionally does well during a recession, and this may explain why telecoms stocks have generally performed well during the current economic downturn. PwC says that, in 2008, stock prices for mobile providers fell on average by just 8.3%, while those for fixed-line providers declined by 11.1%. By contrast, the MSCI World Index fell by more than 38% in 2008. However, the impact of the global financial crisis and the economic downturn on the telecoms industry has varied around the globe, and between the fixed-line and mobile sectors.

Europe Soars. . .

In Europe, for example, the telecoms industry has proved remarkably resilient. According to a European Commission (EC) report published in March 2009, the European Union's (EU) telecoms sector, which is worth about 3% of the EU's GDP, grew by 1.3% in 2008, with revenue estimated at above €300 billion, outperforming the rest of the economy, which grew by 1%.

The EC said that Europeans are now paying far less for broadband internet access and for mobile telephone calls than in previous years, and this has contributed to an increase in usage. Lower subscriber costs have also helped to dampen inflation, the commission said. Furthermore, the EC said that the prices of most basic services, such as phone calls and internet surfing, were still falling, and that consumers were already paying around 35% less than five years ago. The average market share of the leading operators also declined by around 3% in 2008, which, the EC said, indicated that the market was becoming more competitive.

  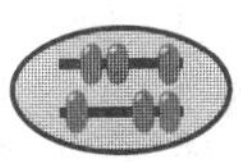      

The EC said that most broadband internet users in Europe were now paying less for speeds of above 2 megabits per second (Mbps), the minimum rate that is now generally required for video streaming. The EC said that the average monthly price for a connection rated at 1–2 Mbps fell to €31 in 2008, from €38.20 in 2007. For access speeds of 2–4 Mbps, the average monthly cost declined to €37 in 2008, from €52 a year earlier.

Mobile usage increased across the continent, with the number of subscribers increasing to 119% of the population in 2008, compared with 112% in 2007. Mobile-phone penetration is highest in Italy, where 153% of the population have a mobile phone, compared with penetration rates of 87% in the US and 84% in Japan. About 23% of European residents, representing 114 million fixed telephone lines, have broadband internet subscriptions. By contrast, around 25% of Americans have broadband internet subscriptions.

. . .While Asia Slumps

The mobile sector in Asia has been hit hard by the economic slowdown. Research released by the analysts, Informa Telecoms & Media, shows that mobile net additions in the Asia-Pacific region declined by 22.6% between the third and fourth quarters of 2008, from 87.69 million to just 67.91 million, yet the final quarter of the year is traditionally one of the strongest seasons for sales. Nicole McCormick, senior analyst at Informa, was quoted as saying that "economic woes, subscriber base clean-ups in China, Bangladesh, and Pakistan, as well as less competition in Indonesia contributed to the uncharacteristic fall in net additions" during the quarter.

MARKET ANALYSIS

China Dwarfs Other Mobile-Phone Markets

In February 2009, the total number of mobile-phone users in China reached 565 million, making the country the world's biggest cell-phone market, according to government figures. Mobile-phone use has exploded in China in recent years, on the back of falling handset prices and user charges. The two main players in the market are China Mobile, which has 450 million subscribers, and China Unicom, which has 130 million subscribers. China Telecom, the country's biggest fixed-line carrier, is also targeting the mobile-phone sector. It plans to spend CNY47 billion (US$6.88 billion) to expand its mobile-phone network in 2009, with the aim of attracting 100 million mobile subscribers by 2011. The country's three major mobile carriers are rolling out third-generation (3G) services nationwide in 2009 after obtaining licenses from the government in January. 3G networks enable faster data transmission, and easier use of services such as internet surfing and video.

In March 2009, China Mobile reported a 30% jump in net profit to CNY112.79 billion (US$16.50 billion) in 2008, up from CNY87.06 billion in 2007, but it also warned that 2009 would be a tough year for China's telecoms industry. The company's chairman and CEO, Wang Jianzhou, said: "The influence of [the] financial crisis that swept across the globe in 2008 will likely widen and deepen, and its impact on China's economy will continue. The telecommunications industry will be affected."

Wang said that the firm would be looking to boost its wireless broadband services in the coming year, and that it would also consider expansion into foreign markets. Earlier in 2009, Wang said that factory closures as a result of reduced demand for Chinese-made goods had hit the mobile market, as users had moved back to rural areas and reduced the number of calls they made.

US Market

The US may not be the largest telecoms market in the world, as measured by the number of mobile-phone users, but it remains one of the most sophisticated in terms of technological development, and market trends in the US are often later repeated in other areas of the world. The penetration of mobile-phone ownership is already high, with more than four out of five Americans owning a mobile. Thus, AT&T, Verizon Wireless, Sprint, and T-Mobile, the four main national carriers in the mobile market, are focusing on squeezing more revenue out of cell-phone users through exclusive contracts with handset makers, or other partnerships. They are also investing heavily in new network technologies, such as LTE and WiMax, which enable high-speed downloads on cell phones, and, thus, can generate further revenues by enabling users to download movies, etc. Smaller, independent phone companies will inevitably lose market share because they do not have the resources to build their own advanced technologies, leading to further consolidation in the industry.

Mobile Industry Pins Hopes on Smartphones

While sales of mobile phones are expected to fall in 2009, smartphones are expected to buck this trend, and register both volume and value growth. Smartphones are mobile phones with advanced features, such as e-mail and internet facilities, and a full keyboard. They tend to feature powerful processors and large memories. Some analysts believe that smartphones will eventually surpass laptops in popularity, and that they could account for 20% of the overall mobile-phone market within a few years.

According to the technology research firm, Gartner, smartphone sales for the whole of 2008 reached 139.3 million units, a rise of 13.9% on the previous year. The main players in the smartphone sector are Nokia, Apple (with its iPhone), Research in Motion (with its BlackBerry), HTC of Taiwan, and Samsung.

Popularity of Dongle Threatens Fixed-Line Firms

The growing popularity of the dongle—a pocket-sized USB device that provides internet access wherever there is mobile-phone coverage—was underlined in March 2009, when the leading mobile operator, 3, owned by the Hong Kong conglomerate Hutchison Whampoa, announced that it had sold 1 million of the devices. *The Times* (March 25, 2009) quoted analysts as saying that strong sales of the gadget by 3 and its rivals proved that dongles posed a significant threat to traditional landline phone companies, and to the providers of wifi hotspots.

The newspaper added that all the main UK mobile operators—Vodafone, O2, T-Mobile, and Orange, as well as 3—now offer dongles, and that 13% of the 495 million people in the EU access mobile broadband using dongles and data cards. Over the 12

▸▸ MORE INFO

Report:

PricewaterhouseCoopers (PwC). "Telecoms insights 2009." PwC, 2009. Online at: www.pwc.com/telecomsinsights

Websites:

CCS Insight, provides market information, analysis and intelligence for companies focusing on the mobile and wireless sector: www.ccsinsight.com

Gartner, supplies information-technology research: www.gartner.com

Informa Telecoms & Media, supplies business intelligence and strategic services for the global telecoms and media markets: www.informa.com/subjects/telecoms__and__media

iSuppli, provides information on the electronics-industry value chain: www.isuppli.com

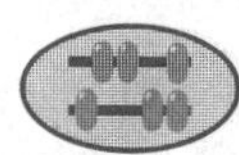

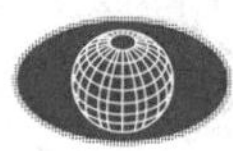

months to March 2009, the cost of dongles fell from about US$100 to less than US$50, and, in some cases, networks offer them for no cost. Users need only plug the device into a USB socket on their laptop to use it, rather than being forced to configure it. *The Times* quoted Ben Wood, of CCS Insight, a telecoms research group, as saying, "As these mobile packages and speeds get good enough, people will be starting to say 'hang on a minute, why do I need a landline again?' "

Tourism and Hotels

MAJOR INDUSTRY TRENDS

Global Financial Crisis has Significant Impact on Industry

Spending on tourism and hotels is closely related to the economic cycle. Certainly, spending on leisure activities such as holidays tends to be one of the first things that consumers cut back in times of economic hardship. The travel and hotel industry is further affected by reduced demand from the business sector, for, again, travel is one of the first areas that the corporate sector axes when the economy slows.

The United Nations World Tourism Organization (WTO) says that international tourist arrivals grew by 7% to 908 million in 2007, and that international tourist arrivals grew by an average of 4% per year between 1995 and 2007. It adds that tourism held up well during the first half of 2008, with international tourist arrivals growing by 5%. In the second half of the year, however, international tourist arrivals fell by 1%. Overall, international tourist arrivals increased by 2% in 2008. Apart from the global financial crisis, various other factors negatively affected tourism during the year. These included sky-high oil prices, which led to sharp increases in travel costs, and wild gyrations in exchange rates.

In March 2009, the WTO predicted that the tourism industry would continue its decline, at least in the short to medium term. The WTO expects international tourist arrivals to stagnate (0%) or even decline slightly (–1–2%) during 2009. However, the WTO added that the impact of the global financial crisis on tourism would vary around the world. The Americas and Europe would be most affected, "as most of their source markets are already in, or entering, recession." However, the WTO expects tourism volumes to continue to grow in the Asia-Pacific region, albeit at a slower rate than in previous years. It said that similar trends to those seen in the Asia-Pacific region would occur in Africa and the Middle East.

Spanish Experience Highlights Effect of Gyrating Exchange Rates

The impact of fluctuations in the exchange rate can be seen by the experience of Spain. The UK (which, like Spain, is a member of the European Union, but which, unlike Spain, remains outside the eurozone) has long been the main market for the Spanish tourist industry, the country's second-largest industry. In the latter half of 2008 and early 2009, however, the British pound slumped against the euro. Figures from the Spanish Tourism Ministry show that the number of British tourists visiting Spain in February 2009 dropped by almost a quarter compared with the same period in 2008. Although the recession in the UK, and rising unemployment, are undoubtedly factors, the strength of the euro against the pound has also been a major reason for the slump in the number of Britons holidaying in Spain.

Hotel Industry Battles Falling Customer Numbers and Prices

Hotels around the globe are battling for customers amid the global economic downturn. The Agence France Presse (AFP) news agency reported, in March 2009, that hotel prices around the world fell in the fourth quarter of 2008, compared with the same quarter in 2007, with the steepest declines seen in the US and Canada. AFP cited a survey by hotels.com, involving some 68,000 properties in more than 12,500 locations.

Hotel prices fell by 10% in Europe, by 7% in the Caribbean and Latin America, and by 2% in Asia, according to the survey. The slump in the hotel market in the Americas was blamed on a sharp reduction in US domestic demand, and a drop in the number of tourists from Europe. The survey said that most cities around the world had experienced falling prices, but some particularly sharp declines reflected the hotel industry's sensitivity to geopolitical and economic events. Prices in Mumbai, for example, plummeted by more than 40%, following the terrorist attacks in the Indian city in November 2008. Reykjavik, whose economy has been devastated by the global financial crisis, saw prices collapse by 36%.

Hotel Industry Faces New Corporate Age of Austerity

The hotel industry has been particularly hard hit by a slump in business travelers, who account for a large proportion of hotels' income. The outlook appears bleak, according to Amadeus, a leading provider of technology to the travel and tourism industry. Amadeus commissioned a report from the Economist Intelligence Unit, published in March 2009, which predicted that the business world was entering a new age of austerity.

The report, titled "The austere traveler—The effect of corporate cutbacks on hotels," concluded that executives would make fewer, shorter, and cheaper business trips in 2009, and that they would prefer basic efficiency and good service over ancillary services. Antoine Medawar, managing director of Amadeus Hospitality Business Group, was quoted as saying: "We are entering an age of visible austerity with regard to business travel. With the eyes of their organizations and shareholders upon them, executives are anxious to make business trips as productive as possible. Forget gyms and restaurants; instead concentrate on efficient check-in and check-out, and internet access. Good wifi connectivity is now rated above any other extra. There is a flight to trusted brands, and the expectation of a common level of good service, no matter where you are in the world."

Emergence of New Tourism Hot Spots

One of the major themes of recent decades has been the emergence of new tourism centers. While countries such as France and Spain have long been among the most popular tourism destinations, some of the major tourism centers today, such as Turkey and Thailand, barely featured on the global tourism radar just 30 years ago.

Thailand received 14.464 million international arrivals in 2007, compared with just 1.2 million in 1977, and the country is now regarded as one of the world's premier tourist destinations. Tourism is today Thailand's largest foreign-exchange earner, bringing in more than US$16 billion in 2007. It also accounts for around 6% of GDP, and generates more jobs than any other industry in the country.

It's a similar story in Turkey, which attracted 22.2 million international visitors in 2007, making it the ninth most popular tourist destination in the world, according to the WTO. Yet in 1977, the country received just 1.661 million international arrivals. Even in 1987, tourist arrivals numbered well under 3 million. The industry provides around US$20 billion in foreign-exchange earnings to Turkey, and provides employment for around 3 million Turks.

Environmental Concerns Pose Long-Term Threat to Industry

Prior to the global financial crisis, the biggest international problem grabbing the attention of the media and the political classes was that of climate change. Air travel, in particular, attracted the ire of environmentalists, and proved a useful scapegoat for politicians keen to polish their green credentials. Certainly, governments around the world were quick to impose taxes on air travel. To the cynics, this was simply an exercise in raising revenue, while environmentalists called for even higher taxes, and draconian measures to curb air travel. Given the slump in air travel that has occurred as a result of the global economic slowdown, the immediate urgency to adopt measures to discourage air travel has evaporated. In the long term, the issue may come back to haunt the industry, but the aerospace industry is investing heavily in technology to boost fuel efficiency, as well as in research to develop alternative fuels. Indeed, it is doubtful whether anything—even concern about the environment—can stop the long-term growth of the industry, given its potential in countries such as India and China as living standards rise.

MARKET ANALYSIS

The Global Market

Tourism is now one of the largest industries in the world. According to the WTO, the export income generated by international tourism ranks fourth after fuels, chemicals, and automotive products. Furthermore, the WTO points out that, for many developing countries, tourism is one of the main income sources of foreign exchange, and creates much-needed employment and opportunities for economic development. The industry has also enjoyed staggering growth over the past six decades. The WTO says that:

- From 1950 to 2007, international tourist arrivals grew from 25 million to 908 million.
- The overall export income generated by these arrivals (international tourism receipts and passenger transport) grew at a similar pace, outgrowing the world economy and exceeding US$1 trillion in 2007, or almost US$3 billion per day.
- In 1950, the top 15 destinations absorbed 98% of all international tourist arrivals, but in 1970 the proportion was 75%, and this fell to 57% in 2007, reflecting the emergence of new destinations, many of them in developing countries.

The industry is expected to continue to grow rapidly in the long term. The World Travel and Tourism Council (WTTC), a "forum for business leaders in the travel and tourism industry," says that, globally in 2009, travel and tourism employs approximately 219 million people, or 7.6% of total employment, and generates 9.4% of world GDP. The WTTC anticipates that, by 2019, travel and tourism will generate 276 million jobs, or 8.4% of total employment, and will account for 9.5% of global GDP.

Slump in Passenger Numbers Hits Airlines

The airline industry is a good barometer of the fortunes of the tourism and hotels sector. In March 2009, the International Air Transport Association (IATA) said that it anticipated a 3% fall in passenger numbers in 2009. IATA, which represents 230 airlines, including British Airways, Cathay Pacific, and United Airlines, said that the world's airlines lost up to US$8 billion in 2008, and that losses are likely to exceed US$2.5 billion in 2009, as the global economic crisis hits passenger and cargo traffic.

In January 2009, international passenger demand fell by 5.6% year-on-year, following a 4.6% decline in December 2008, according to IATA. The Association said that the fall in business traffic was particularly painful for its members. The Reuters news agency quoted Giovanni Bisignani, the director general & CEO of IATA, as saying: "Business classes are empty. The airlines make money in the front and recover the cost on economy, and when the business class disappears, it's a big problem."

Major Hotel Chains Report Impact of Downturn

The impact of the economic downturn on the hotel industry has been highlighted by results from some of the world's leading operators. In its 2008 year-end report, Rezidor, the European group that manages the Radisson SAS hotel chain, said that "the negative impact of the economic slowdown on the European hotel market escalated during the last quarter of 2008, with double-digit drops in industry RevPAR (revenue per available room)." The company added: "Industry RevPAR is expected to continue to decline further in 2009. In order to meet an increasingly weaker market we have extended our existing cost-cutting program."

In February 2009, Marriott International, which operates hotels around the globe, reported fourth-quarter 2008 adjusted income from continuing operations of US$121 million, a 49% decline on the same quarter in 2008. It said the results reflected the significant economic decline affecting worldwide lodging and timeshare demand, and the turmoil in the financial markets. Meanwhile, the France-based international hotel group, Accor, which operates hotels in 100 countries, saw a sharp decline of 34.9% in net profits, to €575 million, in 2008.

▸▸ MORE INFO

Websites:

International Air Transport Association (IATA): www.iata.org

United Nation's World Tourism Organization: www.unwto.org

World Travel and Tourism Council: www.wttc.org

Transport and Logistics

MAJOR INDUSTRY TRENDS

Slump in Global Trade Devastates Industry

The fortunes of the transport and logistics industry are closely connected to the economic cycle. When economic activity is buoyant, demand for transport and logistic services is equally strong. Consumer and business demand for goods and services inevitably translates into higher demand for transport and logistic services. Thus, the slump in global economic growth that has occurred since the second half of 2008, and that has caused global trade volumes to plummet, is having a severe impact on the transport and logistics industry.

Around the world, once-busy ports and airports are reporting sharp falls in traffic. The International Air Transport Association (IATA) reported in March 2009 that cargo volumes fell by 23.2% year-on-year in January 2009, after December 2008's 22.6% decline, the eighth consecutive month of contraction in freight

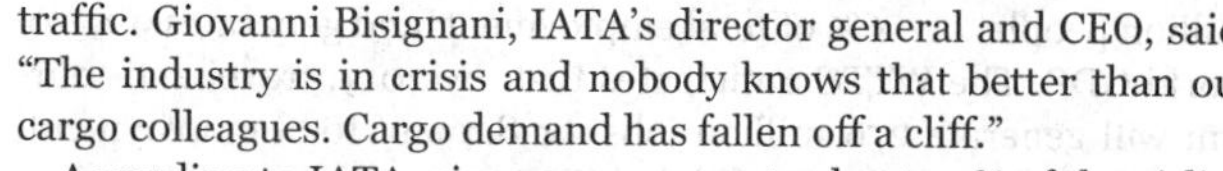

traffic. Giovanni Bisignani, IATA's director general and CEO, said: "The industry is in crisis and nobody knows that better than our cargo colleagues. Cargo demand has fallen off a cliff."

According to IATA, air cargo represents about 10% of the airline industry's revenues. As 35% of the value of goods traded internationally is transported by air, air cargo is a barometer of global economic health. "The continued decline in cargo markets is a clear sign that we have not yet seen the bottom of this economic crisis," Bisignani said in March 2009.

The shipping industry has also been badly affected by the slump in global economic growth and trade. The Baltic Dry Index provides the daily average cost to ship bulk dry commodities, such as grain products or coal, around the world. It is highly sensitive to global economic activity, as the freight costs it measures move in response to demand for shipping services. The greater the demand for raw materials around the globe, the higher the index moves.

It normally takes around six to nine months for raw materials to be delivered to customers, and made into finished products. Thus the index is also a highly accurate "leading indicator" of global economic activity—in other words, movements in the Baltic Dry Index provide a very good guide to the future direction of the global economy. In 2008, the Baltic Dry Index hit its lowest level in more than two decades, presaging the global recession. Overall, the Baltic Dry Index fell by 92% in 2008. However, it began to rise again in 2009, reaching 2298.00 on March 10, up from 773 at the beginning of the year, suggesting that global economic activity should start to pick up towards the end of 2009. This augurs well for the transport and logistics industry. Despite these encouraging signs, CC Tung, chairman of Hong Kong's Orient Overseas International, which owns the Orient Overseas Container Line (OOCL), warned in March 2009 that the shipping industry could face difficult conditions for years if government economic stimulus packages fail to revive the world economy swiftly. The shipping industry enjoyed five boom years until 2007, but the global recession has sapped demand for the transportation of Asian-made goods—much of the container shipping industry is focused on transporting manufactured goods from the Far East to markets in Europe and North America.

Furthermore, the movement of freight between Latin America and Asia has plummeted. Countries such as Brazil have been supplying many of the raw materials and commodities that have fueled Asia's industrialization. In March 2009, a port executive in Chile told CargoNewsAsia.com that "transpacific trade from Asia to the West Coast of South America has decreased by about 30–40%, while on the return journey the fall is between 10% and 15%."

In the same month, the Trans-Pacific Stabilization Agreement, a research and discussion group of major container shipping lines, warned that the industry faced a "potential catastrophic event" if prices on trans-Pacific routes did not increase. It said that freight rates from Asia to North America were unsustainably low. The *Financial Times* reported that shipping lines "desperate" to fill ships had cut spot rates on some routes to the lowest levels in the sector's 53-year history. It added that on routes between Asia and Europe, some companies had been charging "only the surcharges normally meant to cover fuel, currency changes, and terminal handling costs." Between Asia and North America, the newspaper reported that overall charges had fallen to only a few hundred dollars for each standard container, from more than US$2,000 in early 2008.

Recession Affects Logistics Industry

The global recession has also taken a toll on logistics firms. In March 2009, DHL reported that business had declined in the fourth quarter of 2009, with volumes dropping by as much as 30%, depending on the region. However, Frank Appel, chief executive of DHL's parent company, Deutsche Post, believed that firms had overreacted significantly to the bad financial news. He said: "Consumer demand hasn't dropped by that amount, so obviously, manufacturers or retail companies are drying out their supply chain, and reducing their inventory. So I would not expect that these huge double-digit volume drops will be seen for the rest of the year."

Mr Appel added: "What might happen is that we will see a turnaround pretty fast, because it can happen that demand is picking up again after the first-quarter numbers come out, and then people say, 'Oh, it's not as bad as expected, therefore let's buy supply routes now instead of waiting another three months because prices will go up.' So that means we see a lot of opportunities in Asia, as Asia has become the place for manufacturing many goods."

Protectionism and Environmental Laws Could Hit Transport Firms When Global Economy Revives

Some in the freight industry fear that even if global growth does revive, demand for transport services will never recover to the highs seen in 2007. This reflects concerns about a backlash against free trade, which could lead to rising protectionism in countries such as the US. In March 2009, CargoNewsAsia.com quoted Julian Keeling, chief executive of the forwarder Consolidators International, Inc, as saying: "I anticipate that a philosophy of looking after its own will re-emerge in the US. Globalization and free trade are things of the past."

Air freight companies may also be affected by stricter environmental regulations, according to CargoNewsAsia.com. The website said that the likely advent of more stringent global environmental regulations "would impact not only the economics of using air transport, but would also possibly result in punitive sanctions against goods produced with environmentally questionable practices." It added that the latter element would significantly erode the comparative advantage enjoyed by manufacturers in Asia, which have fueled the growth in demand for air cargo in recent years. These concerns appear to be shared by IATA. CargoNews Asia.com quoted the organization's chief economist, Brian Pearce, as saying that "the cost of protectionism and deglobalization, higher taxes, and climate-change policies will all have an impact on the industry."

MARKET ANALYSIS

Aviation Industry Cuts Jobs and Capacity

The slump in global trade and, in particular, the collapse in demand for manufactured goods from Asia is hitting the airlines and shipping companies hard. Airlines are cutting capacity, routes, and jobs. The outlook is unlikely to improve significantly in 2009, according to the German carrier, Lufthansa. The head of its cargo division, Carsten Spohr, told CargoNewsAsia.com in March 2009 that, "the 2009 business year will confront Lufthansa Cargo with the biggest challenge for many years." To offset weak demand, Lufthansa has cut working hours for pilots and ground crews in its cargo division, and has taken four cargo aircraft out of service. In the same month, American Airlines warned that cargo and other revenue is expected to decline by between 5.6% and 6.6% in the first quarter of 2009, compared with the same period in 2008.

Overcapacity Plagues Shipping Industry

The shipping sector is suffering from a combination of plummeting demand and an oversupply of ships as vessels ordered during the growth years are delivered. The shipping industry enjoyed five boom years until 2007, but the global recession has sapped demand for the transportation of Asian-made goods.

  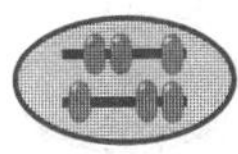   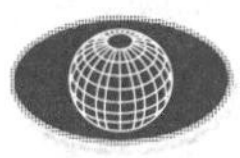 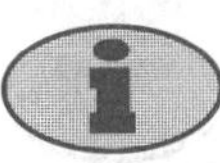  

In March 2009, *Port Strategy* magazine quoted "experts in the Far East" as saying that a third of shipping companies faced bankruptcy. It said that, since the beginning of the global financial crisis in September 2009, at least four companies "hit by a combination of falling rates and a global capacity glut" have sought bankruptcy protection in order to keep trading, and that China's diminishing need for iron-ore imports was exacerbating the lack of demand for shipping services.

Certainly, the news flowing out of the industry in 2009 has been unremittingly gloomy. In March 2009, for example:

- Orient Overseas (International) Ltd, Hong Kong's largest container line, reported a 65% plunge in second-half profit (for the six months to December 31, 2008).
- Denmark's AP Moller-Maersk, whose Maersk Line is by far the largest container shipping line, said its volumes in January 2009 were 20% lower than in 2008.
- The credit-rating agency, Standard & Poor's, warned it might cut the credit rating of France's CMA CGM, operator of the world's third-largest container shipping fleet. The agency said the company would need to generate significant amounts of cash to support its high debt level.
- Two listed owners of container lines—Singapore's Neptune Orient Lines, and Maersk—have announced that they expect their lines to be loss-making for the whole of 2009. Neptune Orient Lines, which is southeast Asia's largest shipping company and the world's seventh-largest container line, announced that container volumes plunged a huge 35% in the first six weeks of the year.

Container lines have responded to the downturn by taking vessels out of service, reducing the number of routes, and cutting jobs. Thus, Orient Overseas has said that it will cut capacity by 20% in 2009 by returning as many as 16 chartered vessels to ship owners. Orient Overseas has 10 new vessels due for delivery this year, and another 10 before 2011. In March 2009, Bloomberg said that 13% of container ships, or 575 vessels, were lying idle around the globe. *Port Strategy* said, in March 2009, that shipping lines would respond to the global slump in demand for their services by scrapping almost one-third of active vessels over the following 24 months. It said that this was because "shipping lines trying to offload vessels to reduce the size of their fleets are finding no buyers."

On top of plunging freight rates, shipping companies were also hit by soaring fuel costs in 2008. Fuel costs at Orient Overseas, for example, rose by 53% to US$1.21 billion in 2008, with the average price of fuel jumping by 45% to US$519 per metric ton. However, Orient Overseas said that fuel costs in 2009 would be around 50% lower than in 2008, reflecting the sharp fall in oil prices that took place in the second half of 2008.

Global Economic Slump Hits Logistics Specialists

Many of the major logistics firms have also reported results that reflect the impact of the global economic slump. In February 2009, for example, TNT (the Netherlands) reported a 60% fall in fourth-quarter net profit, hit by sharp volume declines at its international express unit as well as restructuring and impairment charges. The company said that 2009 would be challenging, and that it expected volumes to remain under pressure. In the same month, the US transport and logistics giant, FedEx Corporation, laid off 900 employees at its freight unit, or about 2.6% of the unit's work force. In March 2009, it added that it would make further job cuts, reduce network capacity at its express and freight segments, cut back working hours, and reduce compensation to non-US workers, where allowed. The company had already reduced salaries and other compensation for US employees.

▸▸ MORE INFO

Websites:

Cargo News Asia, provides news on transport and logistics in Asia: www.cargonewsasia.com

Drewry Shipping, independent maritime consultancy, data, and publishing: www.drewry.co.uk

The International Air Transport Association (IATA): www.iata.org

Port Strategy, good source of information on the global shipping industry: www.portstrategy.com

Water

MAJOR INDUSTRY TRENDS

Water and the Global Economic Downturn

The provision of safe water is a prerequisite of economic development and activity, and thus water utilities tend to be among the industrial sectors least affected by an economic downturn. This is partly because of the essential nature of the good that they supply, but also because water utilities tend to be heavily regulated by the state in most countries. Thus, the water sector tends to suffer from a lack of competition, and utilities can rely on regulated income streams even in times of economic hardship. Certainly, water utilities around the world have reported healthy profits and revenues despite the global financial crisis. Examples include the following:

- United Utilities (UK), which supplies water to about 7 million people across northwest England, said, in January 2009, that it was trading in line with expectations and that it was confident of a good underlying financial performance in 2008/2009.
- American Water and Aqua America are the two largest quoted water utilities in the US. In March 2009, Global Water Intelligence said that it expected both companies to report strong earnings growth in 2009, having posted robust sets of full-year results at the end of February 2009.
- In February 2009, the Spanish water utility, Aguas de Barcelona (AGBAR), reported a 13.8% rise in 2008 net profit.
- Severn Trent (UK), which supplies water and sewerage services to more than 3.7 million households and businesses in central England and mid-Wales, said, in March 2009, that it expected sales to fall by just £25 million (US$37 million) in the fiscal year ending end-December 2009, due to reduced commercial demand. Its commercial customers included the collapsed UK retailers, Woolworths Group plc and MFI Retail Ltd, but total revenues in fiscal 2008 amounted to £1,279.2 million.

Water Shortages Could Become a Serious Threat

"Water receives less attention than other environmental issues such as the climate and pollution, but the problem of water scarcity is at least as important—and, arguably, more pressing—than that of global warming," the *Financial Times* reported in December 2008. The newspaper added that a rising global population, industrialization, pollution, and climate change itself are all putting fresh-water supplies under strain.

Certainly, there has been concern for some years that lack of water could lead to conflicts in the developing world. In 2005, for

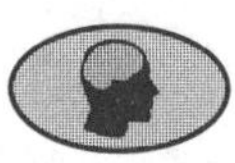

example, the former UN Secretary-General, Boutros Boutros Ghali, warned that competition for water resources could provoke wars in Africa and the Middle East. He added that military confrontation between the countries of the Nile basin was almost inevitable. Indeed, it could only be avoided if they shared water equitably, he said. The BBC reported that while Egypt had long been the greatest user of Nile water, countries upstream, including Kenya, Ethiopia, and Tanzania, on both the Blue and White Niles, were increasingly demanding a greater share. Furthermore, Boutros Ghali said that Egypt's demand for water would continue to increase rapidly because of "a demographic explosion," which had seen its population rise from 20 million people in the 1950s to 70 million today.

Water shortages are also causing problems in the developed world. The Spanish press reported on an outbreak of "water wars" in summer 2008, when the country experienced its worst drought in 40 years. The BBC reported that the growing problems caused by a lack of water had "set region against region, north against south, and government against opposition."

Furthermore, water shortages in Spain are set to worsen, according to the BBC, which said, "Climate experts warn that the country is suffering badly from the impact of climate change and that the Sahara is slowly creeping north—into the Spanish mainland." Earlier in 2008, the city of Barcelona almost ran out of water, causing the government of Catalonia Province (in which Barcelona is located) to plead for water to be transferred from rivers such as the Ebro, causing a furious row between the regions. Eventually, Barcelona shipped in millions of liters of water from France, and accelerated work on the giant desalination plant on the edge of Barcelona, which promises to provide 180,000 cubic metres of water per day. Other areas of the country are also suffering, especially already arid areas along the Mediterranean coast, from Catalonia down through Valencia, Alicante, Murcia, and Almeria.

Global Financial Crisis Threatens Development of Water Utilities in the Developing World

Water is vital for human life and economic development. Yet while access to water is taken for granted across the developed world, almost 1 billion people around the world have no access to safe water, and 2.6 billion people—out of a global population of around 6.5 billion—have no access to sanitation. The United Nations Millennium Development Goals pledged at the start of this decade to halve, by 2015, the proportion of the population without access to safe drinking water.

In March 2009, however, the World Bank said that the global financial crisis could set back development in water utilities by a decade or more as investment falters and people become increasingly unable to afford water bills. Jamal Saghir, Director of Energy, Water and Transport at the World Bank, was reported as saying that as funding dries up, a vicious circle could re-emerge of poor services, low willingness to pay, and low investment. He added that water utilities around the world would have to boost efficiency to convince cash-strapped governments they were a sound investment. Even well-run water utilities in rich countries suffer leakages of between 10% and 30%. Singapore, the most efficient country in the world in terms of water usage, loses less than 5%. However, in developing countries, wastage is above 40%, and can be even higher. In Maputo, the capital of Mozambique, 60% of water is lost before it reaches the customer.

Angel Gurria, Secretary-General of the Organisation for Economic Cooperation and Development (OECD), said that national governments must revise the way they fund water services—typically a mix of tariffs paid by users, tax revenues, and, in some countries, aid transfers. If the financial crisis makes it harder for developing countries to borrow, they must find ways of gradually moving to more tariff-based systems, which also protect those who are least able to pay, he said.

The OECD has also pointed out that population growth is adding to pressure on water resources. The global population is growing by around 80 million people per year, and by 2050 there are expected to be 9 billion people on the planet. Feeding these extra mouths, and growing more biofuels will place a major strain on water supplies, particularly by the agricultural sector, which already takes up 70% of available fresh water, according to the OECD.

MARKET ANALYSIS

The Global Market

The *Financial Times* (December 15, 2008), quoting figures from Lux Research of the US (see More Info), said that the water-services industry had a global turnover of US$385 billion in 2007, while a further US$64 billion went to companies selling water-related equipment. OOSKAnews, which publishes news and business intelligence on the global water sector, puts a higher value of around US$470 billion on the industry.

The *Financial Times* added that, while agriculture is by far the biggest user of water in the world, consuming around 70% of freshwater supplies, other activities also consume vast quantities of water. For example, it takes 2,400 liters of water to make a hamburger, and 11,000 liters to make a pair of jeans. Other industries also depend heavily on water. Semiconductor manufacturers, for instance, are among the biggest industrial users of water, while power generators "require plentiful supplies of water for cooling, and other manufacturers use water for purposes from cleaning to cutting materials."

Water Utilities Attract Huge Investment

The water industry has generally been regarded as a safe and rather boring area by investors. Prices tend to be regulated, meaning that profit growth is capped. In the past 10 years, however, privatization programs in many countries have attracted investors, and the immense growth potential of the water industry in developing countries has also caught the attention of investors. They believe that acute shortages and worsening pollution in countries such as China will support demand for clean water and sewage treatment—and the services of operators providing them—for many years to come. China opened its water industry as recently as 2004, but its plan to invest US$130 billion in water and wastewater treatment between 2006 and 2010 has ignited interest among foreign companies such as Veolia Environment, the world's largest water utility.

A similar pattern can be seen around the globe. The UN's Third World Water Development Report, issued in 2009, said that between US$92.4 and US$148 billion would need to be invested in water supplies and wastewater services each year from 2006 to 2025. In July 2007, Stenham Advisors established a fund to invest in the global water industry, saying the industry would require around US$1 trillion over the following 20 years. The company said the massive sum reflected chronic underinvestment in water infrastructure in recent years. It said that China and India alone would absorb 25% of the US$1 trillion sum.

Advanced economies, as well as the developing world, need to invest huge sums just to maintain services over the coming decades, according to the OECD. In March 2009, it said that in the United States alone, US$23 billion would be needed annually over the following 20 years, a figure that does not take into account dams, dikes, and waterway maintenance. The OECD said that France and Britain would have to boost water spending as a share of GDP by about 20% just to maintain services at current levels, while Japan and South Korea would need to make increases of more than 40%.

Climate Change to Affect Investment in Water

The water industry is likely to be one of the industries most affected by climate change. Changing weather patterns are likely to have a dramatic impact on water demand and supply, as can be seen from events in Spain (see Major Industry Trends). Unsurprisingly, therefore, the industry is paying close attention to the subject. In February 2009, for example, eight of the top US water utilities said that they were joining forces to study how rising sea levels, droughts, and other effects of global warming are taking a toll on supplies of drinking water.

According to the Reuters news agency, the coalition known as the Water Utility Climate Alliance said that water agencies need access to the best possible climate-change research as they prepare to invest hundreds of billions of dollars in infrastructure over the next 15 years. "Our systems are facing risk due to diminishing snowpack, bigger storms, more frequent drought, and rising sea levels," said Susan Leal, general manager of the San Francisco Public Utilities Commission, a member of the alliance. "We need to be organized to respond to these risks—that's why we've formed this alliance."

In January 2009, according to Reuters, scientists at the Scripps Institution of Oceanography said a water-supply crisis was looming in the western United States, thanks to human-caused climate change that has already altered the region's river flows, snowpacks, and air temperatures. The scientist said that changes over the past half-century have meant less snowpack and more rain in the mountains, rivers with greatly reduced flows by summer, and overall drier summers in the region.

▸▸ MORE INFO

Websites:

Global Water Intelligence, intelligence on the global water industry: www.globalwaterintel.com

Lux Research, independent research and advisory firm providing strategic advice and ongoing intelligence for emerging technologies: www.luxresearchinc.com

OOSKAnews, news and intelligence on the global water industry: www.ooskanews.com

FINANCE INFORMATION SOURCES

Finance Information Sources

Providing the quickest and easiest route to the best finance information available

Sometimes it's easy to grasp the basics about a topic, such as accounting, risk management, or investment. More often than not, it's difficult to know where to start—or where to go next. There is plenty of free world-class finance advice out there—but where is it?

Finance Information Sources is a highly selective and well-researched collection of sources: it's designed to give you the quickest and easiest route to the information you need, in a variety of media.

We cite thousands of sources of the best finance information from around the world, divided up into over 60 subject areas. These include the best websites, the most informative books, magazines, and journals, and the most authoritative organizations.

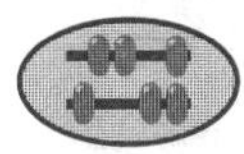
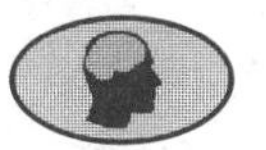

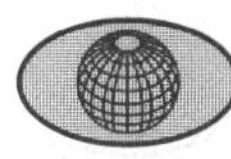

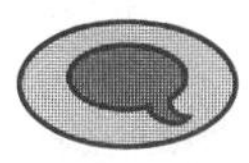
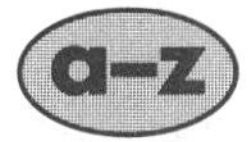

Contents

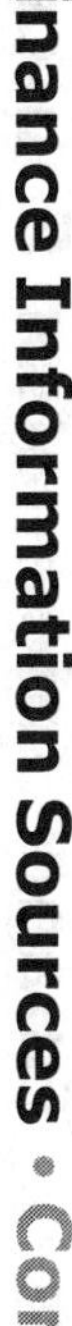
Finance Information Sources • Contents

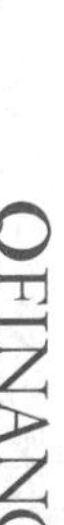
QFINANCE

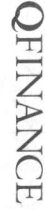

     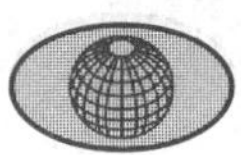   

Accounting

BOOKS

Accounting in a Nutshell: Finance for the Non-Specialist, 3rd ed

Janet Walker
Oxford: Chartered Institute of Management Accountants, 2008
368pp, ISBN: 978-0-7506-8738-6

This introductory text is designed for nonspecialist managers and students who need an understanding of the basic principles of financial and management accounting. The topics covered include accounting statements, profit and loss accounts, cost analysis, and budget planning and control.

The Best Small Business Accounts Book (Blue Version)

Peter Hingston, Stuart Ramsden
Hereford, UK: Hingston Publishing, 2004
64pp, ISBN: 978-0-906555-23-1

There are three versions of this book, all designed for the UK tax system. The blue version, which has a monthly layout, is ideal for non-VAT-registered credit-based businesses. Updated since its initial publication in 1991, this book allows the small business owner to keep the accounts in one compact book. It provides full instructions and worked examples to help the user to achieve correct and effective bookkeeping, including 16 columns to analyze checks and an easy-to-do monthly bank statement check.

CIMA Dictionary of Finance and Accounting

London: A&C Black Publishers, 2003
352pp, ISBN: 978-0-7475-6689-2

With the stamp of approval of the Chartered Institute of Management Accountants, this is an authoritative and reliable finance and accounting dictionary. It is a useful reference for both practitioners and students of all areas of business.

Corporate Financial Reporting: Text and Cases, 4th ed

E. Richard Brownlee, Kenneth R. Ferris, Mark E. Haskins
Maidenhead, UK: McGraw-Hill, 2000
944pp, ISBN: 978-0-07-118107-5

The book is written for those who require a substantial appreciation and understanding of the issues, problems, and practices of financial accounting. The topics covered are: the institutional setting and fundamental concepts of accounting; the measurement and reporting of income, financial position, and cash-flows; the measurement and reporting of assets, liabilities, and stockholders' equity; selected reporting and disclosure issues; and assessing the quality of reported earnings and financial position.

Essentials of Credit, Collections and Accounts Receivable

Mary S. Schaeffer
Chichester, UK: Wiley, 2002
272pp, ISBN: 978-0-471-22074-9

This paperback will help the reader stay up to date with the latest strategies, developments, and technologies in credit, collections, and accounts receivable. With tips, techniques, and real-world examples, the book offers practical solutions for the credit and collection professional.

FASB Current Text 2008

Financial Accounting Standards Board
Hoboken, New Jersey: Wiley, 2008
ISBN: 978-0-470-39691-9

This two-volume set is a collection of generally accepted accounting principles (GAAP) organized by topic. Material in the book is drawn from the Financial Accounting Standards Board's Statements on Financial Accounting Standards and Interpretations, the AICPA's Accounting Research Bulletins, and APB Opinions. Volume 1 is a collection of GAAP that has general applicability to all businesses. Volume 2 contains standards that apply to specific industries and nonprofit organizations. The book is updated annually to reflect new standards promulgated during the year.

Finance and Accounting for Nonfinancial Managers: All the Basics You Need to Know, 5th ed

William G. Droms
Cambridge, Massachusetts: Perseus Books Group, 2003
304pp, ISBN: 978-0-7382-0818-3

This helpful book demystifies the complex world of finance and accounting and makes it accessible to managers of all levels.

The Financial Times Guide to Using and Interpreting Company Accounts, 3rd ed

Wendy McKenzie
Harlow, UK: FT Prentice Hall, 2003
416pp, ISBN: 978-0-273-66312-6

This book is essential for any nonfinancial manager who needs to understand more about a company's accounts and wants to make more informed financial decisions. It explains what information can be found in the accounts, how to analyze accounts, and how to use the analysis.

The Green Bottom Line: Environmental Accounting for Management Current Practice and Future Trends

Martin Bennett, Peter James (editors)
Sheffield, UK: Greenleaf Publishing, 2001
432pp, ISBN: 978-1-874719-24-3

The editors have brought together a collection of papers on research and best practice in the area of environmental management accounting, with a strong focus on the analysis of financial costs and the benefits of environmentally friendly behavior in business. The papers are grouped in four sections: general concepts; empirical research; case studies of individual companies; and practical suggestions on how environment-related management accounting can be implemented.

How to Read a Financial Report, 7th ed

John A. Tracey
Chichester, UK: Wiley, 2009
216pp, ISBN: 978-0-470-40530-7

Tracey provides guidance on interpreting company accounts (with relation to US practice), paying particular attention to the three essential parts of every financial report—the balance sheet, the income statement, and the cash-flow statement. His explanations are illustrated with many examples.

Intermediate Accounting, 13th ed

Donald E. Keiso, Jerry J. Weygandt, Terry D. Warfield
Chichester, UK: Wiley, 2009
1440pp, ISBN: 978-0-470-41891-8

The book covers the conceptual framework underlying financial accounting, financial reporting standards and statements, and more complex topics and transactions that are encountered in today's business environment. Specific guidance is provided for numerous topics, including accounting for cash and receivables, inventory, intangible assets, current and long-term liabilities, income taxes, leases, shareholders' equity, and revenue recognition.

  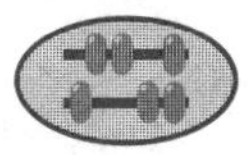   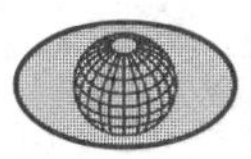   

International Financial Reporting Standards (IFRSs) 2008
International Accounting Standards Board (IASB)
London: IASB, 2008
2752pp, ISBN: 978-1-905590-54-4
The official printed edition of the IASB's authoritative pronouncements. It is comprised of the latest version of International Financial Reporting Standards (IFRSs), International Accounting Standards (IASs), IFRIC, and SIC interpretations, and supporting documents. These standards are endorsed by many countries in the European Union. Many leading companies, both inside and outside the European Union, prepare their financial statements accordingly.

Managerial Accounting, 3rd ed
James Jiambalvo
Chichester, UK: Wiley, 2007
624pp, ISBN: 978-0-470-03815-4
The author presents the fundamental concepts of managerial accounting including job-order and process costing, cost-volume-profit analysis, cost allocation and activity-based costing, capital budgeting decisions, and standard cost and variance analysis. Unlike many cost and managerial accounting texts that focus on accounting skills, the book approaches the subject matter from a manager's perspective.

The Meaning of Company Accounts, 8th ed
Walter Reid, D. R. Myddleton
Aldershot, UK: Gower Publishing, 2005
310pp, ISBN: 978-0-566-08660-1
The authors aim to help people to gain a firm grasp of what company accounts mean and to understand how they relate to business activities. Managers without formal accounting or financial training should find the book useful. It will also provide a basic introduction to company accounts for those taking formal accounting or business studies courses.

Teach Yourself Book Keeping
Andrew G. Piper, Andrew Lymer
Teach Yourself Series
London: Hodder Arnold, 2003
356pp, ISBN: 978-0-340-85942-1
This book aims to demystify the areas of bookkeeping that are essential for small business owners and managers. Offering plenty of examples to help explain key terms and concepts, it covers the double-entry system and the processes of recording purchases and different types of transactions. Profit and loss accounts and balance sheets are also explained, and the book includes helpful completed exam pages with worked examples.

Tolley's Tax Guide 2008–09
Arnold Homer, Rita Burrows
London: LexisNexis, 2008
ISBN: 978-0-7545-3285-9
Useful for both tax professionals and those who assess themselves, this book presents all the latest tax legislation accessibly. It covers the entire range of UK taxes and also features roughly 150 worked examples as well as useful checklists and planning tools. Tables of tax rates and allowances and summaries of recent changes are also included.

MAGAZINES

Accountancy
Institute of Chartered Accountants in England and Wales
Chartered Accountants' Hall, PO Box 433, Moorgate Place, London, EC2P 2BJ, UK
T: +44 (0) 20 7920 8100
F: +44 (0) 20 7920 0547
www.accountancymagazine.com
ISSN: 0001-4664
Published by Croner, but the official publication of the ICAEW, the magazine contains a wide range of news and articles relating to the practice of accountancy and fields such as auditing, taxation, finance, business, and management, as well as news about the ICAEW itself as a professional body.

Accountancy Age
Incisive Media
Haymarket House, 28–29 Haymarket, London, SW1Y 4RX, UK
T: +44 (0) 20 7316 9000
F: +44 (0) 20 7316 9250
www.accountancyage.com
ISSN: 0001-4672
Accountancy Age contains news on all aspects of accountancy practice, including financial reporting, taxation, law, business recovery, software programs, and auditing.

Accounting and Business
Association of Chartered Certified Accountants
2 Central Park Quay, 89 Hydepark Street, Glasgow, G3 8BW, UK
T: +44 (0) 141 582 2000
F: +44 (0) 141 582 2222
www.accaglobal.com/members/publications/accounting_business/
ISSN: 1460-406X
This magazine publishes articles on all aspects of, and developments in, professional accounting, and is aimed at executive agencies and professional partnerships, as well as at accounting and financial professionals.

Accounting Horizons
American Accounting Association
5717 Bessie Drive, Sarasota, FL 34233-2399, USA
T: +1 941 921 7747
F: +1 941 923 4093
aaahq.org/pubs/horizons.htm
ISSN: 0888-7993
Published quarterly, this reviewed magazine thoroughly covers all aspects of banking and finance, business, and accounting. The theory and application of business finance is paramount in this journal.

The Accounting Review
American Accounting Association
5717 Bessie Drive, Sarasota, FL 34233-2399, USA
T: +1 941 921 7747
F: +1 941 923 4093
aaahq.org/pubs/acctrev.htm
ISSN: 0001-4826
The *Review* contains news and articles on all aspects of teaching and research in the field of accounting.

Accounting Today
Accountants Media Group/Thomson
PO Box 966, Fort Worth, TX 76101, USA
T: +1 800 260 2793
F: +1 817 252 4400
www.webcpa.com/current_issue.cfm?pub=ato
ISSN: 1044-5714
Published bimonthly, this magazine is an essential resource for accounting professionals. Covering the latest trends in finance, it is a useful source of current information.

Financial Management
Chartered Institute of Management Accountants
26 Chapter Street, London, SW1P 4NP, UK
T: +44 (0) 20 8849 2251
www.cimaglobal.com/cps/rde/xchg/live/root.xsl/1673.htm
ISSN: 1471-9185
The magazine of the Chartered Institute of Management Accountants, *Financial Management* features news from the field of management accounting and articles on subjects including business performance and appraisal.

Journal of Accountancy
AICPA
1211 Avenue of the Americas, New York, NY 10036, USA
T: +1 212 596 6200
F: +1 212 596 6213

  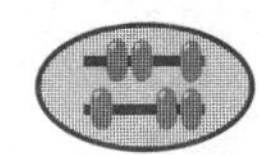 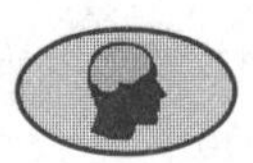  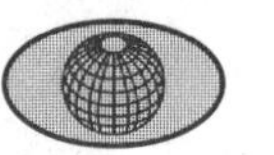   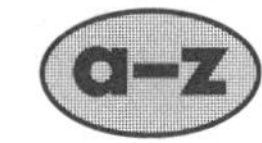

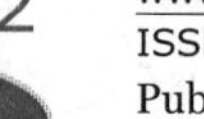

www.aicpa.org/pubs/jofa
ISSN: 1945-0729
Published monthly, this journal provides articles, interviews, and legislative updates on all aspects of accounting. The magazine is the publication of the American Institute of Certified Public Accountants.

JOURNALS

Accounting, Organizations and Society

Elsevier
The Boulevard, Langford Lane, Kidlington, Oxford, OX5 1GB, UK
T: +1 877 839 7126
F: +1 407 363 1354
www.elsevier.com/locate/inca/486
ISSN: 0361-3682
Accounting, Organizations & Society is a major international journal concerned with all aspects of the relationship between accounting and human behavior, organizational structures and processes, and the changing social and political environment of the enterprise.

Advances in Accounting, Incorporating Advances in International Accounting

Elsevier
The Boulevard, Langford Lane, Kidlington, Oxford, OX5 1GB, UK
T: +1 877 839 7126
F: +1 407 363 1354
www.elsevier.com/wps/product/cws_home/714520
ISSN: 0882-6110
This series focuses on the academic and theoretical side of the profession in the areas of financial accounting, accounting education and auditing. Articles range from empirical and analytical, to the development of new technologies.

International Journal of Accounting

Elsevier
The Boulevard, Langford Lane, Kidlington, Oxford, OX5 1GB, UK
T: +1 877 839 7126
F: +1 407 363 1354
www.elsevier.com/locate/inca/620179
ISSN: 0020-7063
The aims of the *International Journal of Accounting* are to advance the academic and professional understanding of accounting theory and practice from an international perspective and viewpoint.

International Journal of Accounting Information Systems

Elsevier
The Boulevard, Langford Lane, Kidlington, Oxford, OX5 1GB, UK
T: +1 877 839 7126
F: +1 407 363 1354
www.elsevier.com/locate/issn/1467-0895
ISSN: 1467-0895
Publishes articles that examine the rapidly evolving relationship between accounting and information technology.

Journal of Accounting Education

Elsevier
The Boulevard, Langford Lane, Kidlington, Oxford, OX5 1GB, UK
T: +1 877 839 7126
F: +1 407 363 1354
www.elsevier.com/locate/jaccedu
ISSN: 0748-5751
This is a refereed journal dedicated to promoting and publishing research on accounting education issues and to improving the quality of accounting education worldwide.

Journal of Business Finance & Accounting

Blackwell Publishing
9600 Garsington Road, Oxford, OX4 2DQ, UK
T: +44 (0) 1865 791 100
F: +44 (0) 1865 791 347
www.wiley.com/bw/journal.asp?ref=0306-686X
ISSN: 0306-686X
This journal publishes research papers in accounting and finance, relating to financial reporting, asset pricing, financial markets and institutions, market microstructure, corporate finance, corporate governance, and the economics of internal organization and management control.

Journal of International Financial Management & Accounting

Blackwell Publishing
9600 Garsington Road, Oxford, OX4 2DQ, UK
T: +44 (0) 1865 791 100
F: +44 (0) 1865 791 347
www.wiley.com/bw/journal.asp?ref=0954-1314
ISSN: 0954-1314
The *Journal of International Financial Management & Accounting* publishes original research dealing with international aspects of financial management and reporting, banking and financial services, auditing, and taxation.

INTERNET

Accountants World

www.accountantsworld.com
This is an extensive portal based in the United States with links to a wide range of websites of interest to accountants. It relates mainly to US accounting practice.

Accounting Web

www.accountingweb.co.uk
This site is an extensive online resource based in the United Kingdom. It contains material intended for accountancy and finance professionals from a number of providers. It has received an award as the New Media Business Website of the Year.

Internal Revenue Service

www.irs.gov
One of the best-known American institutions, the Internal Revenue Service (IRS) is the main body in charge of US taxes. It oversees tax laws and their enforcement, and tax collection. It also has numerous resources available online, from helpful agencies to forms for download.

Tax and Accounting Sites Directory

www.taxsites.com
Created by Dennis Schmidt, Professor of Accounting at the University of Northern Iowa, this site has numerous links to additional accounting and tax information across a broad spectrum. Easy to navigate and simple to make sense of, the directory helps businesses and individuals to find what they need quickly.

ORGANIZATIONS

Europe

Association of Accounting Technicians (AAT)

140 Aldersgate Street, London, EC1A 4HY, UK
T: +44 (0) 20 7397 3000
F: +44 (0) 20 7837 6970
E: aat@aat.org.uk
www.aat.co.uk
The AAT awards certificates in accounting at NVQ levels 2, 3, and 4. An accounting technician is qualified to a slightly lower level than a fully qualified accountant.

Association of Chartered Certified Accountants (ACCA)

2 Central Park Quay, 89 Hydepark Street, Glasgow, G3 8BW, UK
T: +44 (0) 141 582 2000
F: +44 (0) 141 582 2222
E: info@accaglobal.com
www.acca.co.uk
The Association is a professional and examining body in accountancy, recognized under the Companies Act 1989.

Chartered Institute of Management Accountants (CIMA)

26 Chapter Street, London, SW1P 4NP, UK
T: +44 (0) 20 8849 2251
www.cimaglobal.com

  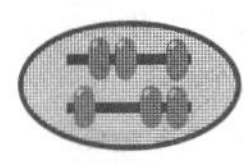 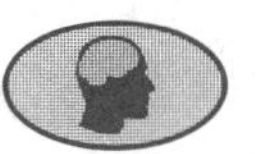  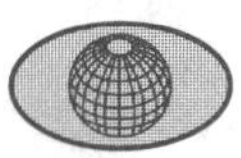   

CIMA is the leading UK professional organization for management accountants, but it also has a global reach: it represents more than 85,000 students and 65,000 members in more than 150 countries.

Chartered Institute of Public Finance and Accountancy (CIPFA)
3 Robert Street, London, WC2N 6RL, UK
T: +44 (0) 20 7543 5600
F: +44 (0) 20 7543 5700
E: corporate@cipfa.org
www.cipfa.org
CIPFA is a UK professional accountancy body whose main aim is to train managers to understand public finance and manage public money. Its members are drawn from both the public and private sectors. In addition to providing membership services, running courses, and awarding certification, it organizes conferences and produces publications.

Institute of Chartered Accountants in England and Wales (ICAEW)
Chartered Accountants' Hall, PO Box 433, London, EC2P 2BJ, UK
T: +44 (0) 20 7920 8100
F: +44 (0) 20 7920 0547
E: dsbds@icaew.co.uk
www.icaew.co.uk
This, the largest professional accountancy organization in Europe with over 120,000 members, is responsible for educating and training Chartered Accountants and maintaining standards of professional conduct among its members.

Institute of Chartered Accountants of Scotland (ICAS)
CA House, 21 Haymarket Yards, Edinburgh, EH12 5BH, UK
T: +44 (0) 131 347 0100
F: +44 (0) 131 347 0105
E: enquiries@icas.org.uk
www.icas.org.uk
The ICAS is the leading professional accounting body in Scotland, and the oldest professional body of accountants in the world.

USA

American Accounting Association (AAA)
5717 Bessie Drive, Sarasota, FL 34233-2399, USA
T: +1 941 921 7747
F: +1 941 923 4093
E: office@aaahq.org
aaahq.org
The American Accounting Association promotes worldwide excellence in accounting education, research and practice. Founded in 1916 as the American Association of University Instructors in Accounting, its present name was adopted in 1936. The Association is a voluntary organization of persons interested in accounting education and research.

American Institute of Certified Public Accountants (AICPA)
1211 Avenue of the Americas, New York, NY 10036-8775, USA
T: +1 212 596 6200
F: +1 212 596 6213
www.aicpa.org
This organization provides information, continuing education, accreditation, advocacy, and leadership to certified public accountants in the United States. The AICPA's Audit and Attest Standards team directs and develops standards for audit, attestation, and review services performed by CPAs.

Financial Accounting Standards Board (FASB)
401 Merritt 7, PO Box 5116, Norwalk, CT 06856-5116, USA
T: +1 203 847 0700
F: +1 203 849 9714
E: fasbpubs@fasb.org
www.fasb.org
Since 1973, the Financial Accounting Standards Board (FASB) has been the designated organization in the private sector for establishing standards of financial accounting and reporting in the United States.

National Society of Accountants
1010 North Fairfax Street, Alexandria, VA 22314, USA
T: +1 703 549 6400
F: +1 703 549 2984
E: members@nsacct.org
www.nsacct.org
The National Society of Accountants is a non-profit organization of some 30,000 professionals which provides accounting, tax preparation, financial and estate planning, and management advisory services to an estimated 19 million individuals and business clients. Most of the society's members are independent practitioners or partners in small to mid-size accounting and tax firms.

BRIC

Chinese Institute of Certified Public Accountants (CICPA)
6th Floor, Guangyuan Building, 5 Guangyuanzha, Haidian District, Beijing 100081, China
T: +11 8610 6872 1166
F: +11 8610 6848 3041
www.cicpa.org.cn/english
The CICPA provides services to its members, monitors the service quality and professional ethics of members, regulates the CPA profession according to relevant laws, and coordinates the relationship within and beyond the CPA profession in China.

Institute of Chartered Accountants of India (ICAI)
Bhawan, Indraprastha Marg, Post Box No. 7100, New Delhi - 110 002, India
T: +91 11 3989 3989
E: icaiho@icai.org
www.icai.org
ICAI is a statutory body for the regulation of the profession of Chartered Accountants in India. During nearly six decades of existence, ICAI has achieved recognition as a premier accounting body not only in the country but also globally, for its contribution in the fields of education, professional development, maintenance of high accounting, auditing, and ethical standards. ICAI now is the second largest accounting body in the world.

Institute of Cost and Works Accountants of India (ICWAI)
12 Sudder Street, Kolkata, 700 016, India
T: +91 33 2252 1031
F: +91 33 2252 7993
E: ceo@icwai.org
www.myicwai.com
A professional institution actively associated with the industrial and economic development of India. Cost and Works Accountants are called Management Accountants outside of India.

The Institute of Professional Accountants of Russia (IPAR)
Tverskaya Street, 22B/3, Moscow, 125009, Russia
T: +7 499 788 72 00
F: +7 495 699 46 45
E: info@ipbr.ru
www.ipbr.ru/?page=english
IPAR is professional, non-profit, self-regulatory organization of certified accountants that assists in developing standards of professional ethics as well as accounting and auditing standards. It develop the accounting profession as a key element of the governance system, arranges and conducts the training, retraining, and certification of accountants and financial managers, and aims to improve the image of accounting profession.

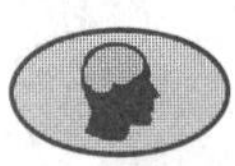

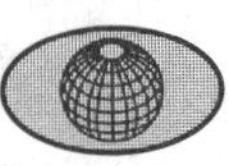

Acquisitions, Takeovers, and Mergers

BOOKS

Acquisition: Strategy and Implementation, 2nd ed
Nancy Hubbard
Basingstoke, UK: Palgrave, 2001
320pp, ISBN: 978-0-333-94548-3
The process of acquisition is explored through an in-depth look at its key stages: preacquisition planning, communication during the deal, and implementation. The book also gives an overview of the history of acquisitions, global trends, and the reasons for success and failure. Case studies demonstrate different approaches and degrees of success. The new edition includes a chapter on new technology and e-commerce acquisitions.

After the Merger: The Authoritative Guide to Integration Success, 2nd ed
Price Pritchett, Donald Robinson, Russell Clarkson
New York: McGraw-Hill, 2007
158pp, ISBN: 978-0-7863-1239-9
This book features the six main errors that managers regularly make regarding mergers, and shows how to avoid them. It also presents best practices for handling the four major categories of a merger, ways to handle cultural problems that can destroy mergers, and offers separate checklists for executives on both sides of the deal.

The Art of M&A Integration: A Guide to Merging Resources, Processes and Responsibilities, 2nd ed
Alexandra Reed Lajoux
New York: McGraw-Hill, 2006
450pp, ISBN: 978-0-07-144810-9
The Art of M&A Integration provides readers with updated facts on integration of compensation plans, new FASB and GAAP accounting rules, strategies for merging IT systems and processes, and more. This book is a comprehensive guide of post-merger integration, covering the following areas and planning and communications; integration of resources; processes and management systems; technology and innovation; and commitments to customer suppliers, shareholders and employees.

Barbarians at the Gate
Bryan Burrough, John Helyar
London: Arrow Books, 2004
536pp, ISBN: 978-0-09-946915-5
This is a classic tale of corporate greed based on the merger of RJR and Nabisco. It is as gripping a read as any work of fiction.

Capitalize on Merger Chaos: Six Ways to Profit from Your Competitors' Consolidation and Your Own
Thomas M. Grubb, Robert B. Lamb
New York: Free Press, 2001
224pp, ISBN: 978-0-684-86777-9
The authors suggest that, although merger mania is at an all-time high, up to 80% of mergers fail because of culture clashes, mismanagement, and the chaos that ensues. They examine the growth and profit opportunities that can arise from competitors' merger chaos, and identify strategies which managers can adopt to exploit them. They further illustrate their argument by considering the winning strategies devised by companies such as AOL, General Electric, Dell, and Vodafone, and the failures at Coca-Cola, Boeing, and Compaq.

Complete Guide to Mergers & Acquisitions: Process Tools to Support M&A Integration at Every Level, 2nd ed
Timothy J. Galpin, Mark Herndon
Jossey-Bass Business and Management Series
San Francisco, California: Jossey-Bass, 2007
336pp, ISBN: 978-0-7879-9460-0
The authors present an updated and expanded guide to the process of planning and managing the M&A process. The revised edition not only updates case studies and presents recent integration research, but it also adds new tools. The authors draw from their experience with numerous Fortune 500 companies; this resource will help organizations attain deal synergies more quickly and effectively. The book addresses dos and don'ts, people dynamics, common mistakes, communications strategies, and specific actions taken to create positive results throughout the integration process.

Due Diligence: Definitive Steps to Successful Business Combinations
Denzil Rankine, Graham Stedman, Mark Bomer
Harlow, UK: FT Prentice Hall, 2003
256pp, ISBN: 978-0-273-66101-6
Due diligence is a key part of the (often fraught) acquisitions process in business. Done properly, it means that potential risks are reduced and chances of success increased. This book is a useful guide to the process and offers advice, cases studies, and analysis.

Harvard Business Review on Mergers & Acquisitions
Harvard Business School Press
Boston, Massachusetts: Harvard Business School Press, 2001
224pp, ISBN: 978-1-57851-555-4
This examines current various mergers, buyouts, and joint ventures, and provides guidance on what companies should take part. From valuation to integration, it helps managers understand the importance of each strategic move for their organization.

HR Know-How in Mergers and Acquisitions
Sue Cartwright, Cary L. Cooper
Developing Practice Series
London: Chartered Institute of Personnel and Development, 2000
128pp, ISBN: 978-0-85292-634-5
The authors offer guidance on the human factors involved in mergers and acquisitions. The topics they cover include: influencing the decision to merge; establishing effective communication; handling job insecurity; pay and benefits; downsizing, early retirement, and relocation; support systems and counseling; creating a new corporate culture; and establishing new roles and training. Case studies are included.

Intelligent M&A: Navigating the Mergers and Acquisitions Minefield
Scott Moeller, Chris Brady
Chichester, UK: Wiley, 2007
328pp, ISBN: 978-0-470-05812-1
Mergers and acquisitions are essential for growing companies but most fail to reach their target. This examines the full cycle of a merger or an acquisition, identifying areas where business intelligence can result in the attainment of a specific target. It discusses techniques developed by governmental intelligence services, and includes a wide range of case studies, quotations, and anecdotes.

International Business Acquisitions: Major Legal Issues and Due Diligence, 3rd ed
Michael Whalley, Franz-Jorg Semler (editors)
Alphen aan den Rijn, The Netherlands: Kluwer Law International, 2007
568pp, ISBN: 978-90-411-2483-8
This examines aspects of international acquisitions, including accessing foreign markets, providing foreign production or marketing capacity, obtaining regulatory

  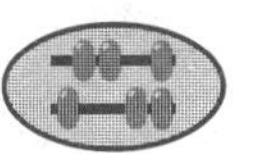   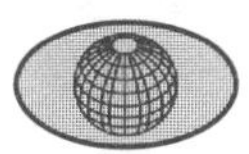   

approvals, acquiring complementary product or service lines, and spreading product, service, and market risk. It also provides useful information on the key legal issues and the process of gaining informed due diligence in each jurisdiction.

International Mergers and Acquisitions
Tony Edwards, Ali Budjanovcanin, Stuart Woollard
London: Chartered Institute of Personnel and Development, 2008
60pp, ISBN: 978-1-84398-213-5
To understand the how organizations learn from their international merger experience and how the knowledge is transferred, the involvement of HR in merger and acquisition activity is crucial. This book examines the challenges for the HR function, knowledge transfer in international mergers and acquisitions, and international policy-making and networking.

Mergers and Acquisitions: Business Strategies for Accountants, 3rd ed
William J. Gole, Joseph Morris
Hoboken, New Jersey: Wiley, 2007
416pp, ISBN: 978-0-470-04242-7
This provides a step-by-step guide to reviewing an acquisition candidate, setting up and implementing computer system transactions for the business combination, tax compilation, and regulatory considerations. It also features practical procedurals and useful examples of application.

Mergers and Acquisitions in a Nutshell, 2nd ed
Dale A. Oesterle
St Paul, Minnesota: Thomson West, 2006
313pp, ISBN: 978-0-314-15956-4
This accessible reference provides a brief description of the law on mergers and acquisitions for students and lawyers needing a reliable guide.

The Morning After: Making Corporate Mergers Work After the Deal is Sealed
Stephen J. Wall, Shannon Rye Wall
Cambridge, Massachusetts: Perseus Books Group, 2002
288pp, ISBN: 978-0-7382-0523-6
This book deals with merger management. It offers insights for recognizing when a merger is in danger, and advice on issues such as communicating effectively with stakeholders. It includes several case studies.

Reducing the M&A Risks: The Role of IT in Mergers and Acquisitions
Frank Vielba, Carol Vielba
Basingstoke, UK: Palgrave Macmillan, 2006
216pp, ISBN: 978-1-4039-4678-2
The lack of adequate and timely IT involvement in the merger and acquisition process costs companies millions of dollars every year. Current research shows that IT accounts for a growing percentage of the post-acquisition benefits in a merger or acquisition. This provides analysis of some of the key approaches by IT managers to reducing risk within the M&A process.

MAGAZINES

Acquisitions Monthly
Thomson Financial
Aldgate House, 33 Aldgate High Street, London, EC3N 1DL, UK
T: +44 (0) 20 7369 7000
F: +44 (0) 20 7369 7373
www.aqm-e.com
ISSN: 0592-3618
This monthly journal for financial executives, directors, bankers, and accountants provides information on international mergers, acquisitions, and management buyouts.

Mergers and Acquisitions: The Dealmaker's Journal
Source Media
1 State Street Plaza, 27th Floor, NY 10004, USA
T: + 1 212 803 8200
www.acg.org/maj6
ISSN: 0026-1101
This monthly journal offers complete listings of all M&A deals, including pricing, deal structure, and the sales and profit levels of merger partners. In-depth feature articles cover trends in the industry and provide practical advice.

JOURNALS

Journal of Financial Economics
Elsevier
11830 Westline Industrial Drive, St Louis, MO 63146, USA
T: +1 314 453 7076
F: +1 314 523 5153
www.elsevier.com/locate/jfec
ISSN: 0304-405X
This quarterly journal offers a section on M&A papers and case studies, which provides an outlet for events and practice. It is also a source of data that illustrates or challenges accepted theory and can lead to new insights.

INTERNET

Acquisitions Monthly
www.aqm-e.com
The site provides M&A news and data worldwide, and information on trends, industries, and sectors. Some services are subscription-based.

Antitrust Division, Department of Justice (US)
www.usdoj.gov/atr
This US government site provides information on antitrust enforcement, case filings, and links to competition authorities worldwide.

BizBuySell
www.bizbuysell.com
As well as databases of businesses for sale and e-mail notification of listings, this US-based site includes articles on how to go about buying or selling a business. Users may search for their target company by category or location.

@brint.com
www.brint.com
This extensive portal and community network for e-business, information, technology, and knowledge management contains news, articles, book reviews, and links to relevant websites in the featured areas.

Competition Matters—BERR (UK)
www.berr.gov.uk/whatwedo/businesslaw/competition
This site provides information and guidance on UK and EU legislation and procedures from the UK Department for Business Enterprise and Regulatory Reform.

Daily Deal
www.thedeal.com
This website provides up-to-date analysis on the M&A activities of various companies around the world.

European Commission—Competition
ec.europa.eu/competition
This Brussels-based site provides information on European competition policy and legislation. All material is available in a variety of languages.

FactSet Mergerstat
www.mergerstat.com
This site covers all the key concepts of M&A, as well as providing links to its publications for further coverage.

     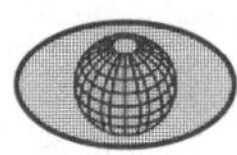   

MergerNetwork
www.mergernetwork.com
This site acts as a marketplace for buyers and sellers of companies, predominantly in North America but increasingly also in Europe, Asia, and South America. Users may search the databases of buyer profiles and businesses for sale free of charge, but must pay for contact information.

The Takeover Panel
www.thetakeoverpanel.org.uk
The Panel on Takeovers and Mergers is an independent body whose main functions are to issue and administer the City Code on Takeovers and Mergers, and to supervise and regulate takeovers and other matters to which the Code applies. Its central objective is to ensure fair treatment for all shareholders in takeover bids.

ORGANIZATIONS

Europe

Competition Commission (UK)
Victoria House, Southampton Row, London, WC1B 4AD, UK
T: +44 (0) 20 7271 0100
E: info@cc.gsi.gov.uk
www.competition-commission.org.uk
The Competition Commission (CC) is one of the independent public bodies that woks to ensure healthy competition between companies in the UK, for the benefit of companies, customers, and the economy. It concentrates on areas of concern in mergers, preventing competition in a particular market, and regulated sectors.

USA

Alliance of Merger and Acquisition Advisors (AMAA)
200 East Randolph Street, 24th Floor, Chicago, IL 60601, USA
T: +1 877 844 2535
F: +1 312 729 9800
www.amaaonline.org
This association was formed to bring together all professionals who work with mergers and acquisitions. AMAA provides national certification for members, as well as various opportunities for networking with other organization members.

Federal Trade Commission (US)
600 Pennsylvania Avenue NW, Washington, DC 20580, USA
T: +1 202 326 2222
E: antitrust@ftc.gov
www.ftc.gov
The U.S.A Fair Trade Commission practices efficient law enforcement, advances consumers' interests by sharing its expertise with federal and state legislatures and U.S. and international government agencies. It develops policy and research tools through hearings, workshops, and conferences. It also works to ensure that consumers have choices in price, selection, and service.

BRIC

Competition Commission of India
B' Wing, HUDCO Vishala, 14 Bhikaji Cama Place, New Delhi – 110 066, India
T: +91 11 2670 1619
F: +91 11 2610 3861
E: cci-bunker@nic.in
www.cci.gov.in
Established under India's Competition Act 2002, the Competition Commission of India has regulatory and quasi-judicial powers. Its duties are eliminating practices having an adverse effect on competition, promoting and sustaining competition, and protecting the interests of consumers, within the jurisdictions of anticompetitive agreements, abuse of dominant positions, M&A, and training/public awareness.

Fair Trade Commission, Taiwan
12–14 F, No. 2–2 Jinan Rd., Sec. 1, Jhongjheng (Zhongzheng) District, Taipei City 100, Taiwan (R.O.C.)
T: +886 2 2351 7588
E: ftcpub@ftc.gov.twl
www.ftc.gov.tw/internet/english
The Fair Trade Commission is the main authority in charge of competition policy and Fair Trade Law in Taiwan. Its duties include drafting fair trade policy, laws, regulations, and investigating and handling various activities impeding competition, such as monopolies, mergers, concerted actions, and other restraints on competition or unfair trade practices on the part of enterprises.

Federal Antimonopoly Service of the Russian Federation
Sadovaya Kudrinskaya, 11, Moscow, D-242, GSP-5, 123995, Russia
T: +7 495 252 70 48
E: international@fas.gov.ru
fas.gov.ru/english
The Federal Antimonopoly Service of the Russian Federation was formed in 2004, replacing the Ministry of the Russian Federation for Antimonopoly Policy and Support to Entrepreneurship in terms of its function as the federal antimonopoly body, control over the activity of natural monopolies, and observance of the legislation on advertising.

International

International Network of M&A Partners (IMAP)
6000 Cattleridge Drive, Suite 300, Sarasota, FL 34232, USA
T: +1 941 378 5500
F: +1 941 378 5505
E: info@imap.com
www.imap.com
Founded in 1971 and formerly called the International Association of Merger and Acquisition Consultants, the IMAP is a global networking organization with over 50 members. It is dedicated to helping middle-market companies obtain confidential business information on available merger and acquisition prospects. It also assists individuals in a variety of financial transactions, such as the sale of private or public companies, the purchase of product lines, leveraged buyouts, financing and investment banking services, and mezzanine financing.

M&A Source
401 North Michigan Avenue, Suite 2200, Chicago, IL 60611–4267, USA
T: +1 888 686 4222
F: +1 312 673 6599
E: admin@masource.org
www.masource.org
Founded in 1991, M&A Source proclaims itself to be the world's largest organization of middle market intermediaries. With a focus on the enhancement of the skills and abilities of its members and their professional development, this organization provides them with the guidance needed to assist clients. M&A Source also keeps them up to date with the latest issues and trends in mergers and acquisitions.

     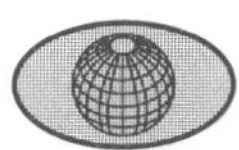   

BOOKS

Accelerated Testing: Statistical Models, Test Plans, and Data Analysis, 2nd ed

Wayne B. Nelson
Wiley Series in Probability and Statistics
Hoboken, New Jersey: Wiley, 2004
624pp, ISBN: 978-0-471-69736-7

This practical resource presents modern, statistical methods for accelerated testing including test models, analyses of data, and plans for testing. Each topic is self-contained for easy reference, and the coverage is broad and detailed enough to serve as a text or reference. It also features real test examples along with data analyses, computer programs, and references to the literature.

Basic Business Statistics: Concepts and Applications, 11th ed

Mark L. Berenson, David M. Levine
Upper Saddle River, New Jersey: Prentice Hall, 2008
936pp, ISBN: 978-0-13-500936-9

This book deals with the techniques of analyzing and presenting business data. It explains probability, normal distribution, estimation, hypothesis testing, analysis of variance, and linear and multiple regression models. It will be helpful for students to know how statistics is used in each functional area of business.

Doing Research in Business and Management: An Introduction to Process and Method

Dan Remenyi et al.
London: Sage Publications, 1998
336pp, ISBN: 978-0-7619-5950-2

After first highlighting the different contexts and purposes, strategies and tactics, and programs and processes of management research, the authors then move on to a more detailed review of the relevant research approaches and methods. They discuss the interrelationship of theoretical and empirical research and examine how these different approaches are used in practice. The implications of using quantitative and qualitative methods are reviewed, and the book also contains practical advice on available analysis techniques and software packages.

Effective Use of Statistics: A Practical Guide for Managers, 2nd ed

Tim Hannagan
Business Skills Series
London: Kogan Page, 1999
160pp, ISBN: 978-0-7494-2969-0

Hannagan provides a statistical foundation for managers, focusing on integrating statistical information into everyday work and presenting it effectively. An appendix offers basic math for managers, and the book comes with an accompanying computer disk with a data file in Microsoft Word for Windows.

Implementing Global Performance Measurement Systems: A Cookbook Approach to Evaluation

Ferdinand Tesoro, Jack Tootson
San Francisco, California: Jossey-Bass, 2000
176pp, ISBN: 978-0-7879-4744-6

This practical guide presents a step-by-step approach to evaluating and measuring ongoing business performance. Following an overview of performance measurement, it examines how to establish the business case, identify the right performance metrics, implement the performance measurement system, and leverage results to improve performance. Guidance is offered on constructing a line graph, a cause–effect diagram, and a scatter diagram.

Practical Business Statistics, 5th ed

Andrew Siegel
Maidenhead, UK: McGraw-Hill, 2002
730pp, ISBN: 978-0-07-282125-3

Though this is a college textbook, it is not simply filled with formulas and equations. It offers a less theoretical approach to statistics, focusing on examples using real data, on applications, and on the underlying reasons for using statistical analysis in business. It is especially useful because the text acknowledges that much of what is done in business statistics and analysis is now done by computer programs, rather than by unhappy, squinting workers in visors with scientific calculators.

Quantitative Approaches in Business Studies, 7th ed

Claire Morris
Harlow, UK: FT Prentice Hall, 2008
528pp, ISBN: 978-0-273-70889-6

This textbook uses a driven approach for student of business courses and management on undergraduate, Masters and professional courses. It aims to demonstrate effectiveness of quantitative methods. The four parts cover: handling numbers; numbers as a basis for deduction; and numbers as a tool of planning.

Quantitative Methods for Business, 4th ed

Donald Waters
Harlow, UK: FT Prentice Hall, 2007
648pp, ISBN: 978-0-273-69458-8

Quantitative Methods for Business has been thoroughly revised and updated for this 4th edition, and continues to provide a simple and practical introduction to an area that students can find difficult. The book takes a nonthreatening approach to the subject, avoiding excessive mathematics and abstract theory. It shows how to apply quantitative ideas to the real problems faced by managers.

Statistical Methods for Survival Data Analysis, 3rd ed

Elisa T. Lee, John Wenyu Wang
Wiley Series in Probability and Statistics
New York: Wiley, 2003
534pp, ISBN: 978-0-471-36997-4

This examines the statistical methods for analyzing survival data from laboratory studies of animals, clinical and epidemiological studies of humans, and other appropriate applications. It provides a thorough discussion of the most common parametric and nonparametric methods in survival analysis, as well as guidelines for the planning and design of clinical trials. The methods are suitable for applications in industrial reliability, the social sciences, and business.

Statistics, Data Analysis, and Decision Modeling, 3rd ed

James R. Evans
Upper Saddle River, New Jersey: Prentice Hall, 2006
576pp, ISBN: 978-0-13-188810-4

This book covers the basic concepts of business statistics, data analysis, and management science in a contemporary spreadsheet environment. It particularly emphasizes the practical applications of its approaches to business decision-making. A software package on CD is included.

Time Series Models for Business and Economic Forecasting

Philip Hans Franses
Cambridge, UK: Cambridge University Press, 1998
280pp, ISBN: 978-0-521-58641-2

Generally regarded as one of the best introductory texts on economic forecasting, this book nonetheless requires a bit more background in business and economics than the average lay-person usually possesses. Its focus is on economic time

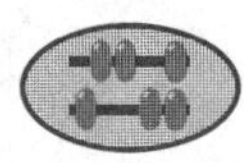
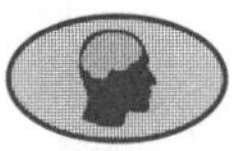

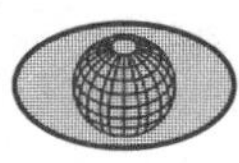

series analysis—in other words, it explains statistical analyses of trends, seasonality, and other nonlinear series. The book uses real market examples, rather than simulated data and simple equations. There is also an emphasis on model identification and diagnostics, which baffle many business forecasters. This book is definitely skewed to the academic, yet is far easier for most readers to use than standard econometrics texts.

Trend Forecasting with Intermarket Analysis: Predicting Global Markets with Technical Analysis, 2nd ed
Louis B. Mendelsohn
Columbia, Maryland: Marketplace Books, 2008
224pp, ISBN: 978-1-59280-332-3
This examines the limitations of traditional technical trading/intermarket analysis, and methods for identifying reoccuring patterns within individual financial markets and between related global markets. It shows how combining technical, fundamental, and intermarket analysis into one framework can provide an advantage in forecasting trends. It also describes trading strategies and limitations of traditional technical analysis methods, and how they can be overcome.

JOURNALS

Brazilian Journal of Probability and Statistics
Brazilian Statistical Association
Rua do Matão, 1010 sala 250A Cep, 05508-090 São Paul, Brazil
T: +55 11 3091 6261
F: +55 11 3812 5067
www.imstat.org/bjps
ISSN: 0103-0752
The *Brazilian Journal of Probability and Statistics* is an official publication of the Brazilian Statistical Association and is supported by the Institute of Mathematical Statistics (IMS). It is published twice a year, in June and December, and publishes papers in applied probability, applied statistics, computational statistics, mathematical statistics, probability theory, and stochastic processes.

Journal of Statistical Research
Institute of Statistical Research and Training
University of Dhaka, Dhaka 1000, Bangladesh
ISSN: 0256-422X
The *Journal of Statistical Research* is an official publication of the Institute of Statistical Research and Training. It is a method of transfer and communication of statistical knowledge for the developing nations across the globe, and publishes original research articles both in theoretical and applied statistics areas. The *Journal* is published twice a year, once in June and again in December.

Journal of the American Statistical Association (JASA)
American Statistical Association
732 North Washington Street, Alexandria, VI 22314–1943, USA
T: +1 703 684 1221
F: +1 703 684 2037
pubs.amstat.org/loi/jasa
ISSN: 0162-1459
JASA was established in 1888 and is published in March, June, September, and December. Subjects covered include statistical applications and statistical education.

INTERNET

Milner Library, Illinois State University
www.mlb.ilstu.edu/learn/stat
This is an online tutorial called "Finding Statistics." Via a series of Internet pages, it covers (a) finding statistics, (b) understanding them, and (c) evaluating their usefulness. A self-assessment tool, or quiz, is included in each section. On this site, the reader can find answers to a number of basic questions, such as what the general definitions and terminology are in statistical research, how to locate statistics easily, how to determine whether statistics are reliably relevant, and what statistical databases are available. This is an excellent primer on the subject.

ORGANIZATIONS

Europe

Royal Statistical Society (RSS)
12 Errol Street, London, EC1Y 8LX, UK
T: +44 (0) 20 7638 8998
F: +44 (0) 20 7614 3905
E: rss@rss.org.uk
www.rss.org.uk
Founded in 1834, the RSS has 6,500 members in the United Kingdom and internationally. It holds a number of meetings annually, including an annual international conference, and offers several professional qualifications to members. The society also publishes the *Journal of the Royal Statistical Society* (in four series), and a monthly news magazine, *RSS News*.

Staple Inn Hall
High Holborn, London, WC1V 7QJ, UK
T: +44 (0) 20 7632 2100
F: +44 (0) 20 7632 2111
E: institute@actuaries.org.uk
www.actuaries.org.uk
The Faculty's objective is to unite those practicing as actuaries in the UK, as well as those promoting actuarial education.

USA

American Statistical Association (ASA)
732 North Washington Street, Alexandria, VI 22314–1943, USA
T: +1 703 684 1221
F: +1 703 684 2037
E: asainfo@amstat.org
www.amstat.org
Founded in 1839, this is an educational society for professional statisticians that boasts Florence Nightingale, Alexander Graham Bell, and Andrew Carnegie among its former members. It now has some 16,000 members in the United States, Canada, and throughout the world. The ASA publishes or copublishes a number of journals, including the *Journal of the American Statistical Association*. The Association's website has a searchable database of relevant events.

BRIC

Indian Statistical Association
Department of Statistics, University of Poona, Poona, 411 007, India
T: + 91 212 336062
The Indian Statistical Association was formed to promote research in statistics. The General Assembly of the Association meets each year towards the end of December or early in January to elect the Governing Council.

International Chinese Association
University of Connecticut, 215 Glenbrook Road, Storrs, CT 06269–4120, USA
T: +1 860 486 6984
F: +1 860 486 4113
E: mhchen@stat.uconn.edu
The International Chinese Statistical Association (ICSA) is a non-profit organization dedicated to educational, charitable, and scientific purposes. Its membership is open to all individuals and organizations in all statistics-related areas.

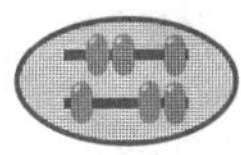

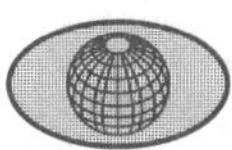

Asset and Liability Management

BOOKS

Asset and Liability Management: The Banker's Guide to Value Creation and Risk Control, 2nd ed

Jean Dermine, Youssef F. Bissada
Financial Times Series
Harlow, UK: FT Prentice Hall, 2007
187pp, ISBN: 978-0-273-71001-1

The increasing emphasis on measuring bank performance against value creation means effective ALM, and the control of value and risk, are now even more relevant. This book provides an understanding of these measures, by presenting the essential concepts, showing how to evaluate performances on a risk-adjusted basis, and price loans to ensure they create value, and covers more recent topics such Basel II and credit derivatives.

Asset and Liability Management Tools: A Handbook for Best Practice

Bernd Scherer (editor)
London: Risk Books, 2003
333pp, ISBN: 978-1-904339-06-9

This is a multi-author volume that provides a non-technical and practical overview of current ALM issues and techniques. A strong team of writers examine how to develop an enhanced understanding and competency of ALM, as well as pension finance, foundations, actuarial mathematics, fair valuation of pension liabilities, scenario simulation, and portfolio optimization.

Asset Liability Management: Individual and Institutional Approaches

Hainaut Donatien
Saarbrücken, Germany: VDM Verlag, 2008
220pp, ISBN: 978-3-8364-9178-5

This approaches ALM in terms of maximizing expected lifetime utility, focusing on both individual and institutional investors as economic agents. It analyzes asset allocation problems, such as wealth maximization under a Value at Risk constraint, and also examines the individual asset allocation decision at retirement.

Asset/Liability Management for Financial Institutions: Maximising Shareholder Value through Risk-Conscious Investing

Leo M. Tilman (editor)
London: Euromoney Books, 2003
386pp, ISBN: 978-1-84374-124-4

This is a guide to the management, techniques, and practices of ALM across financial institutions, which shows how to develop a consistent framework for risk management. A leading group of contributors examine the challenges facing the industry, and offer advice and analysis to financial and corporate executives, treasurers, portfolio managers, investment bankers, traders, actuaries, modelers, academics, and regulators.

Bank Asset and Liability Management: Strategy, Trading, Analysis

Moorad Choudhry
Wiley Finance Series
Singapore: Wiley, 2007
1,415pp, ISBN: 978-0-470-82135-0

This is a comprehensive examination of the techniques, products, and art of ALM. Aimed at anyone involved in banking and the debt capital markets, it covers bank capital, money market trading, risk management, hedging, regulatory capital, securitization and balance sheet management, yield curve analysis, structured finance products, and their role in ALM treasury operations and group transfer pricing.

Goal Programming Techniques for Bank Asset Liability Management

Kyriaki Kosmidou, Constantin Zopounidis
Applied Optimization Series
Boston, Massachusetts: Kluwer, 2004
166pp, ISBN: 978-1-4020-8104-0

A comprehensive textbook that combines an analysis of the more general concepts of bank ALM with an examination of the contribution that goal programming techniques can make to more effective asset and liability management. Aimed at academics and practitioners in operations research, management scientists, financial managers, bank managers, economists, and risk analysts.

Handbook of Asset and Liability Management, Volume 1: Theory and Methodology

S. A. Zenios, W. T. Ziemba
Amsterdam: Elsevier, 2006
508pp, ISBN: 978-0-444-50875-1

The first volume focuses on the theories and methods that align operations and business strategy with its uncertain environment. It examines the relationship between optimization tools and financial decision-making, term and volatility structures, interest rates, risk-return analysis, dynamic asset allocation strategies in discrete and continuous time, the use of stochastic programming models, and bond portfolio management.

Handbook of Asset and Liability Management, Volume 2: Applications and Case Studies

S. A. Zenios, W. T. Ziemba
Amsterdam: Elsevier, 2007
684pp, ISBN: 978-0-444-52802-5

This second volume analyzes applications, models, and case studies in a practical way, showing how the operations research and mathematical finance tools described in the first volume can be exploited profitably by pension funds, insurance companies, banks, and major and individual investors. It also presents a framework for controlling interest rate and liquidity risks.

Handbook of Asset and Liability Management: From Models to Optimal Return Strategies

Alexandre Adam
Wiley Finance Series
Chichester, UK: Wiley, 2008
550pp, ISBN: 978-0-470-03496-5

This is a comprehensive and practical guide to asset and liability management tools, techniques, and issues, which also examines balance sheet items, product modeling, and optimal returns strategies. It presents a framework based on accounting obligations (for IFRS and IAS), organization, and regulation (for both Basel II and Solvency II), and discusses the more relevant sources of risk.

The Handbook of Asset/Liability Management: State-of-the-Art Investment Strategies, Risk Controls and Regulatory Requirements, 2nd ed

Frank J. Fabozzi, Atuso Konishi (editors)
Chicago, Illinois: Irwin Professional, 1996
506pp, ISBN: 978-1-55738-800-1

This is a revised and updated reference source for practitioners needing guidance on keeping a portfolio and market risk under control, and an understanding of the benefits of effective risk management. It also examines asset securitization, how to best measure interest rate and yield curve risk, hedge with derivatives, and implement controls for managing derivative positions.

Liabilities, Liquidity, and Cash Management: Balancing Financial Risks

Dimitris N. Chorafas
New York: Wiley, 2002
316pp, ISBN: 978-0-471-10630-2

Offers guidance on how to deal with liabilities and overexposure, and implement better internal controls on liability and overexposure. It provides tools, strategies, and advice tailored to the needs of companies facing overexposure and debt risk in a volatile economy, and discusses loss of capitalization, derivatives, globalization, sensitivity analysis, gap analysis, stress testing, and real-time financial reporting.

Liquidity Risk: Managing Asset and Funding Risks
Erik Banks
Finance and Capital Markets Series
Basingstoke, UK: Palgrave Macmillan, 2005
230pp, ISBN: 978-1-4039-3399-7
This examination of liquidity risk focuses on the nature of the risk, issues that can arise in asset and funding liquidity, and mechanisms that can be developed to monitor, measure, and control such risks. It examines how to manage assets and risk, in order to avoid the problems of losses in asset/liability portfolios and off balance sheet activities, and even financial distress and insolvency.

Liquidity Risk Measurement and Management: A Practitioner's Guide to Global Best Practices
Leonard Matz, Peter Neu (editors)
Wiley Finance Series
Singapore: Wiley, 2007
395pp, ISBN: 978-0-470-82182-4
With financial crises over the last few years increasing the need for banks to operate effective systems and processes for identifying, measuring, monitoring, and controlling liquidity risks, practical guidance is important. This book offers best practice in tools and techniques for bank liquidity risk measurement and management, from day-to-day funding management to worst-case contingency planning.

Managing Financial Institutions: An Asset/Liability Approach, 4th ed
Mona J. Gardner, Dixie L. Mills, Elizabeth S. Cooperman
Dryden Press Series in Finance
Fort Worth, Texas: Dryden Press, 1999
960pp, ISBN: 978-0-03-022054-8
This provides coverage of asset and liability management tools and techniques for financial institutions such as depository institutions, finance companies, insurance companies, pension funds, mutual funds, securities firms, and diversified financial services firms, which are operating in an increasingly competitive environment. It is also suitable for courses on financial institutions and commercial bank management.

Worldwide Asset and Liability Modeling
William T. Ziemba, John M. Mulvey (editors)
Publications of the Newton Institute Series
Cambridge, UK: Cambridge University Press, 1998
665pp, ISBN: 978-0-521-57187-6
This is an introductory overview to ALM modeling, which examines the strategic and the technical issues currently facing the industry. It takes a broad approach, combining theoretical papers with practical discussions of models, and shows how to invest assets over time to achieve satisfactory returns subject to uncertainties, various constraints, and liability commitments, and presents some new techniques.

MAGAZINES

Bank Asset/Liability Management
Sheshunoff Information Services
807 Las Cimas Parkway, Suite 300, Austin, Texas 78746, USA
T: +1 512 472 2244
F: +1 512 305 6575
www.aspratt.com/store/805.php
This monthly newsletter provides practical guidance on how to reduce exposure to interest rate risks, from either the asset or liability side of the balance sheet. It covers the latest information on the full range of bank ALM topics, such as using gap analysis, duration analysis, income simulation analysis, economic value sensitivity analysis, back-testing, and management goals, policies, procedures, and systems.

JOURNALS

Journal of Asset Management
Palgrave Macmillan
Brunel Road, Houndmills, Basingstoke, Hampshire, RG21 6XS, UK
T: +44 (0) 1256 357893
F: +44 (0) 1256 328339
www.palgrave-journals.com/jam
ISSN: 1470-8272
This bimonthly journal publishes applied academic research, commercial best practice, and regulatory and legal interests, offering the latest thinking, techniques, and developments for the fund management industry. It covers new investment strategies, methodologies and techniques, new products and trading developments, and emerging trends in asset management. Core areas include asset allocation, hedge fund strategies, risk definition and management, index tracking, and performance measurement.

INTERNET

ALM Professional
www.almprofessional.com
This is a website dedicated to the ALM community, with a large global membership of industry professionals, which offers information and guidance on managing an institution's asset liability management process. Its features include articles, recommended reading, market watch, policies and procedures, calendar, newsletters, jobs listings, and a discussion board.

ORGANIZATIONS

Europe

European Fund and Asset Management Association
Chair: Mathias Bauer
18/2 Square de Meeûs, 1050 Brussels, Belgium
T: +32 2513 3969
F: +32 2513 2643
www.efama.org
EFAMA is the representative association for the European investment and asset management industry, representing its member associations and corporate members. It aims include supporting investor protection through the promotion of high ethical standards, integrity, and professionalism in the industry, promoting the completion of an effective single market for investment management, strengthening the competitiveness of the industry, and promoting relevant scientific research.

USA

The North American Asset/Liability Management Association
USA
www.nalma.net
NALMA is an industry association for senior practitioners in the field of asset and liability management and related areas of risk management. Its aim is to facilitate the exchange of ideas, to advance industry best practice, risk management problems, and to influence the development of regulatory measures.

 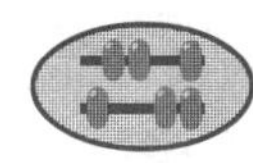  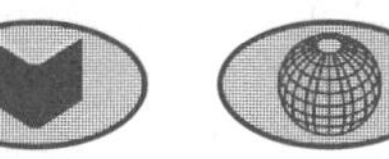 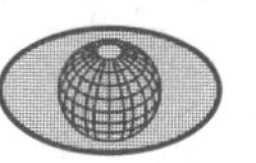   

Auditing and Management Audit

BOOKS

Auditing: A Business Risk Approach, 6th ed

Larry E. Rittenberg, Bradley J. Schwieger, Karla Johnstone
Cincinnati, Ohio: South-Western College Publishing, 2007
864pp, ISBN: 978-0-324-37558-9

This provides a thorough understanding of current auditing processes with the hands-on practice that's critical to business success. It introduces the audit process within the context of business risk–explaining why it is important to first understand the organization's business environment, and how to apply the risk model.

Auditing and Assurance Services, 12th ed

Alvin Arens, Randal Elder, Mark Beasley
Harlow, UK: Prentice Hall, 2007
888pp, ISBN: 978-0-13-245225-0

The integrated concepts approach shows students the auditing process from start to finish. It uses an illustrative example of key audit decisions for a public company audit throughout, with an emphasis on audit planning, including risk assessment processes and evaluating internal controls, and collecting and evaluating evidence in response to risks, to prepare students for real-world audit decision-making.

The Essential Handbook of Internal Auditing

K. H. Spencer Pickett
Chichester, UK: Wiley, 2005
298pp, ISBN: 978-0-470-01316-8

This shows the reader how to understand the audit context and how this context fits into the wider corporate agenda. The new context is set firmly within the corporate governance, risk management, and internal control arena.

The Internal Auditing Handbook, 2nd ed

K. H. Spencer Pickett
Hoboken, New Jersey: Wiley, 2003
802pp, ISBN: 978-0-470-84863-0

The book is a comprehensive guide to audit standards, internal controls, planning and risk analysis, statistical sampling, client interviews and flowcharting. It provides many examples of the application of audit theory by means of case studies and assignments with suggested solutions. *The Internal Auditing Handbook* also deals with special engagements and topics including computer audits, fraud investigations, establishing an audit function, and training audit staff. It is organized in four major parts that cover theory, techniques, internal audit management, and specialist auditing.

Montgomery's Auditing, 12th ed

Vincent M. O'Reilly et al.
New York: Wiley, 1999
336pp, ISBN: 978-0-471-34605-0

The book outlines all the information needed to understand and apply generally accepted auditing standards. It assists auditors in developing an enterprise plan, testing specific accounting cycles and accounts, and producing the final audit report. The book is organized in five parts that cover the audit environment, theory and concepts, auditing specific accounts, completing the audit and reporting results, and auditing specialized industries.

Quantitative Analysis for Management, 10th ed

Barry Render, Ralph M. Stair, Michael E. Hanna
Upper Saddle River, New Jersey: Prentice Hall, 2008
768pp, ISBN: 978-0-13-603625-8

This textbook for students combines coverage of traditional management science techniques with modern technology solutions. It includes a CD-ROM.

Sawyer's Internal Auditing: The Practice of Modern Internal Auditing, 5th ed

Lawrence B. Sawyer, Mortimer A. Dittenhofer, James H. Scheiner, Anne Graham, Paul Makosz
Altamonte Springs, Florida: Institute of Internal Auditors, 2003
1446pp, ISBN: 978-0-89413-509-5

This provides a new global perspective reflecting the recent transformation in the way organizations do business. It analyzes how new ideas about internal auditing are reshaping the profession, what the new competency framework means, the importance of alignment with management, the implications of outsourcing the internal audit function, and value-added approaches that are redefining the role of the internal auditor.

The Smartest Guys in the Room: The Amazing Rise and Scandalous Fall of Enron

Bethany McLean, Peter Elkind
New York: Portfolio, 2004
464pp, ISBN: 978-1-59184-053-4

Written by two *Fortune* journalists, this book attempts to lay bare the extraordinary story behind Enron's collapse in 2001. A tale of jaw-dropping corporate arrogance, it shows the impact of incompetence and greed on the notion of corporate governance.

MAGAZINES

ABI Journal

American Bankruptcy Institute
44 Canal Center Plaza, Suite 400, Alexandria, VA 22314, USA
T: +1 703 739 0800
F: +1 703 739 1060
www.abiworld.org/journal

The *ABI Journal* is published ten times a year. It is written by experts from the insolvency community and addresses issues such as consumer bankruptcy, the intersection of state laws and the Bankruptcy Code, valuation, turnaround management concerns, and recent legislative developments.

Internal Auditing

International Council for Small Business
GWU School of Business, 2201 G Street NW , Funger Hall, Suite 315, Washington, DC 20052, USA
T: +1 314 977 3628
F: +1 314 977 3627
www.iia.org.uk/en/Publications/IA_and_BR_Magazine

This magazine, the journal of the IIA-UK, covers all aspects of internal auditing and of risk assessment and risk management.

Internal Auditor

Institute of Internal Auditors
247 Maitland Avenue, Altamonte Springs, FL 32701–4201, USA
T: +1 407 937 1100
F: +1 407 937 1101
www.theiia.org/intauditor
ISSN: 0020-5745

This magazine, the journal of the IIA in the United States, covers auditing techniques and applications, internal control systems, and corporate governance, besides containing practical case studies.

JOURNALS

Accounting, Auditing and Accountability Journal

Emerald
60/62 Toller Lane, Bradford, West Yorkshire, BD8 9BY, UK
T: +44 (0) 1274 777700

  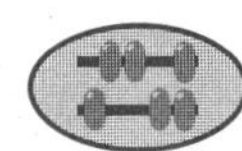   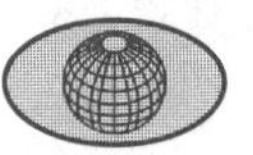   

F: +44 (0) 1274 785200
www.emeraldinsight.com/0951-3574.htm
ISSN: 0951-3574
The Accounting, Auditing & Accountability Journal is dedicated to the advancement of accounting knowledge and provides a forum for the publication of high-quality papers concerning the interaction between accounting/auditing and their socio-economic and political environments.

Auditing: A Journal of Practice & Theory

American Accounting Association
5717 Bessie Drive, Sarasota, FL 34233-2399, USA
T: +1 941 921 7747
F: +1 941 923 4093
aaahq.org/audit/ajpt.htm
ISSN: 0278-0380
This is a scholarly journal that publishes original papers on research that contributes to improvements in auditing theory or auditing methodology. It provides news and analysis of accounting and is very influential in the auditing world.

International Journal of Auditing

Blackwell Publishing
9600 Garsington Road, Oxford, OX4 2DQ, UK
T: +44 (0) 1865 791 100
F: +44 (0) 1865 791 347
www.wiley.com/bw/journal.asp?ref=1090-6738
ISSN: 1090-6738
IJA is a high-quality, specialist journal that publishes articles from the broad spectrum of auditing. Its primary aim is to communicate clearly, to an international readership, the results of original auditing research conducted in research institutions and/or in practice.

Managerial Auditing Journal

Emerald
60/62 Toller Lane, Bradford, West Yorkshire, BD8 9BY, UK
T: +44 (0) 1274 777700
F: +44 (0) 1274 785200
www.emeraldinsight.com/0268-6902.htm
ISSN: 0268-6902
The *Managerial Auditing Journal* addresses the changing function of the auditor and examines both the professional and the managerial aspects of the role. Its articles are mainly concerned with the latest developments in auditing theory and practice, research, and case studies.

INTERNET

The American Institute of Certified Public Accountants (AICPA)

www.aicpa.org
This is the website of a large membership organization that provides information, continuing education, accreditation, advocacy, and leadership to certified public accountants in the United States. The AICPA's Audit and Attest Standards team directs and develops standards for audit, attestation, and review services performed by CPAs.

Information Systems Audit and Control Association (ISACA)

www.isaca.org
This is the website of the Information Systems Audit and Control Association, a recognized leader in information technology assurance, control, and governance. With 50,000 members in more than 140 countries, the organization provides CISA (Certified Information Systems Auditor) certification and develops worldwide standards for information systems auditing and control.

The Institute of Internal Auditors (IIA)

www.theiia.org
This is the website of a nonprofit organization with more than 117,000 members from all over the world. Its purpose is to serve as the profession's international watchdog and primary resource for certification, continuing education, research, and technological issues related to internal audits.

ORGANIZATIONS

Europe

Auditing Practices Board (APB)

5th Floor, Aldwych House, 71–91 Aldwych, London, WC2B 4HN, UK
T: +44 (0) 20 7492 2300
F: +44 (0) 20 7492 2301
E: j.grant@frc-apb.org.uk
www.frc.org.uk/apb
Part of the Financial Reporting Council. The APB is committed to leading the development of auditing practice in the United Kingdom and the Republic of Ireland, to establish high standards of auditing, meet the developing needs of users of financial information, and ensure public confidence in the auditing process.

USA

Association to Advance Collegiate Schools of Business (AACSB International)

777 South Harbour Island Boulevard, Suite 750, Tampa, FL 33602–5730, USA
T: +1 813 769 6560
F: +1 813 769 6559
www.aacsb.edu
Founded in 1916, AACSB International acts as an accrediting agency for bachelor's, master's, and doctoral degree programs in business administration and accounting.

BRIC

National Audit Office of the People's Republic of China (CNAO)

No.1 Beiluyuan, Zhanlan Road, Beijing, 100830, China
F: +11 86 10 6833 0958
E: CNAO@audit.gov.cn
www.cnao.gov.cn
As the supreme audit institution of China, the CNAO, directly under the leadership of the Premier, organizes and administers audit work of the whole country, in accordance with the law and subject to no interference by any administrative organ or public organization or individual, and reports its work to the State Council. Chinese auditing standards are unique because they originated in a socialist period in which the state was the sole owner of industry.

International

The International Federation of Accountants (IFAC)

545 Fifth Avenue, 14th Floor, New York, NY 10017, USA
T: +1 212 286 9344
F: +1 212 286 9570
E: elizabethconde@ifac.org
web.ifac.org
IFAC is the global organization for the accountancy profession. It works with its 158 members and associates in 122 countries and jurisdictions to protect the public interest by encouraging high quality practices by the world's accountants. IFAC members and associates, which are primarily national professional accountancy bodies, represent 2.5 million accountants employed in public practice, industry and commerce, government, and academia.

 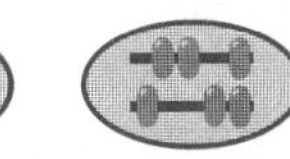   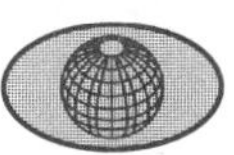   

Bankruptcy and Business Failure

BOOKS

Bankruptcy Explained: The Bankruptcy Association's Practical Guide to UK Insolvency Laws, 2nd ed

John McQueen
Lancaster, UK: Bankruptcy Association, 2005
88pp, ISBN: 978-1-905069-01-9

The Enterprise Act 2002 has introduced several amendments to the now longstanding Insolvency Act 1986. *Bankruptcy Explained* deals with the resultant changes in the various aspects of bankruptcy law. This book is the Bankruptcy Association's most popular practical guide book to the United Kingdom's insolvency legislation. It covers the law throughout the United Kingdom, and includes coverage of deals with limited companies.

The Consistency Gap: Overcoming Failure in Consistently Executing the Business Plan

Mark S. Turner
Bloomington, Indiana: iUniverse, 2005
108pp, ISBN: 978-0-595-33807-8

The Consistency Gap provides a range of practical methods and solutions to the issues of information and tolerance. The author uses imagery and outline for setting goals and explaining how to achieve those goals.

Corporate Bankruptcy: Tools, Strategies and Alternatives

Grant A. Newton
Hoboken, New Jersey: Wiley, 2003
256pp, ISBN: 978-0-471-33268-8

In its examination of the complexities of restructuring and bankruptcy, this book provides a working knowledge of the bankruptcy process and of its benefits and challenges for both companies and their creditors. Supported by actual case studies, it assesses the legal and practical problems facing both debtors and creditors. It is a useful reference tool for every bankruptcy practitioner.

Corporate Failure by Design: Why Organizations Are Built to Fail

Jonathan I. Klein
Westport, Connecticut: Quorum Books, 2000
328pp, ISBN: 978-1-56720-297-7

Despite all that has been written on the subject of making organizations succeed, the reality is that an overwhelming majority of businesses fail within five years and almost all fail within 10 years. The author suggests that this tendency is inherent in the organization and explains his theory of organizational self-destruction. Besides analyzing the causes and processes of failure, however, he also points out the lessons that can be learned from it.

Corporate Financial Distress and Bankruptcy: Predict and Avoid Bankruptcy, Analyze and Invest in Distressed Debt, 3rd ed

Edward I. Altman and Edith Hotchkiss
Wiley Finance Series
Hoboken, New Jersey: Wiley, 2006
368pp, ISBN: 978-0-471-69189-1

This 3rd edition of the most authoritative finance book on the topic updates and expands its discussion of corporate distress and bankruptcy, as well as the related markets dealing with high-yield and distressed debt, and offers state-of-the-art analysis and research on the costs of bankruptcy, credit default prediction, the post-emergence period performance of bankrupt firms, and more.

Corporate Turnaround: How Managers Turn Losers into Winners

Donald B. Bibeault
Frederick, Maryland: Beard Group, 1998
482pp, ISBN: 978-1-893122-02-4

This is a reprint of a classic book that remains a source of effective advice on financial crisis management. It distills the experiences of close to 100 managers who successfully restored companies to profitability and constitutes a practical guide to management strategies to prevent bankruptcy.

Creating Value through Corporate Restructuring: Case Studies in Bankruptcies, Buyouts, and Breakups

Stuart C. Gilson
New York: Wiley, 2001
528pp, ISBN: 978-0-471-40559-7

Management buyouts are a common form of business restructuring. This collection of recent case studies from the United States and several other countries illustrates the real-world techniques and strategies that are common to all types of restructuring. It demystifies the complex financial issues surrounding business valuation and gives the reader a better understanding of the possibilities when dealing with corporate restructuring.

Elements of Bankruptcy, 4th ed

Douglas G. Baird
New York: Foundation Press, 2005
299pp, ISBN: 978-1-59941-062-3

Baird's book gives an overview of current law and practice in the United States. Recent changes in the law and topical issues are discussed and placed in context.

The Executive Guide to Corporate Bankruptcy

Thomas J. Salerno, Jordan A. Kroop, Craig D. Hansen
Frederick, Maryland: Beard Group, 2001
736pp, ISBN: 978-1-58798-026-8

This book was written to provide a comprehensive resource for managers of financially troubled companies facing Chapter 11 bankruptcy proceedings. The authors outline the history of American bankruptcy law and explain bankruptcy terminology for the lay person, then provide a step-by-step guide to the bankruptcy and reorganization process, including sample documents.

International Insolvency Law: Themes and Perspectives

Paul J. Omar
Markets and the Law Series
Aldershot, UK: Ashgate Publishing, 2008
452pp, ISBN: 978-0-7546-2427-1

This is a new study that examines the phenomenon of cross-border incorporations and the conduct of business in more than one jurisdiction. It is a compilation of essays by academics and practitioners in the field who trace the development of the subject, and provide an account of economics, legal history and private international law. It demonstrates its relationship with finance and security issues as well as the importance of business rescue, and how new international instruments function, as well as how this area is being challenged by other areas of law.

Surviving a Downturn: Building a Successful Business. . .Without Breaking the Bank

Jeremy Kourdi
Business on a Shoestring Series
London: A&C Black Publishers, 2007
208pp, ISBN: 978-0-7136-7547-4

All businesses go through difficult times but how they react can make the difference between survival and going to the wall. Realistic but inspiring and packed with ideas that really work, this book helps small business owners face and tackle the challenges of a downturn.

     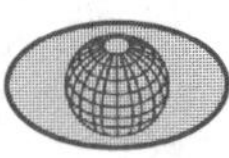   

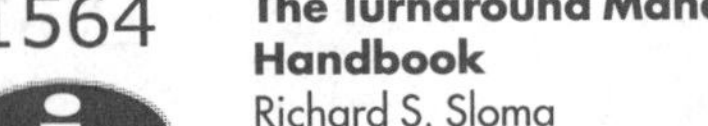

The Turnaround Manager's Handbook
Richard S. Sloma
Frederick, Maryland: Beard Group, 2000
244pp, ISBN: 978-1-893122-40-6
Designed for the corporate manager, this book provides specific details of the actions to be taken to achieve a turnaround in a failing business. The author addresses operational issues and provides recommendations and tools to restore a business to profitability.

JOURNALS

British Accounting Review
Elsevier
11830 Westline Industrial Drive, St Louis, MO 63146, USA
T: +1 314 453 7076
F: +1 314 523 5153
www.elsevier.com/locate/issn/0890–8389
ISSN: 0890-8389
The *British Accounting Review* is the official journal of the British Accounting Association. The journal is diverse and contributions are included from a wide range of research methodologies, including analytical, archival, experimental, survey, and qualitative case methods, and topics, such as financial accounting, management accounting, finance and financial management, auditing, public sector accounting, social and environmental accounting, accounting education, and accounting history.

Corporate Governance: The International Journal of Effective Board Performance
Emerald
60/62 Toller Lane, Bradford, West Yorkshire, BD8 9BY, UK
T: +44 (0) 1274 777 700
F: +44 (0) 1274 785 200
ISSN: 1472-0701
This journal publishes a range of theoretical, methodological and substantive debates, as well as practical developments in the field of corporate governance worldwide. It focuses on areas such as the impact of changes of business/corporate governance forms and practices on people, the sustainability of different governance models, how improvements in performance can be achieved through effective governance, and the legacy from contradicting governance philosophies.

Financial Analysts Journal
CFA Institute
560 Ray C. Hunt Drive, Charlottesville, VA 22903–2981, USA
T: +1 434 951 5499
F: +1 434 951 5262
ejournals.ebsco.com/direct.asp?JournalID=108977
ISSN: 0015-198X
This quarterly journal, published by the Chartered Financial Analyst Institute, is dedicated to the advancement of knowledge and understanding of the practice of investment management through the publication of high-quality, practitioner-relevant research. It serves as a bridge between academic research and practice by seeking academically rigorous papers that have direct relevance to practitioners.

Insolvency Intelligence
Sweet & Maxwell
100 Avenue Road, Swiss Cottage, London, NW3 3PF, UK
T: +44 (0) 20 7393 7000
F: +44 (0) 20 7393 7010
www.sweetandmaxwell.co.uk/Catalogue/ProductDetails.aspx?recordid=426&productid=6958
ISSN: 0950-2645
This magazine, published 10 times each year, provides immediate, concise and authoritative coverage of insolvency law, practice, and procedure.

Insolvency Law and Practice
LexisNexis
Tolley House, 2 Addiscombe Road, Croydon, CR9 5AF, UK
T: +44 (0) 20 8662 2000
F: +44 (0) 20 8662 2012
www.lexisnexis.co.uk
ISSN: 0267-0771
Aimed at legal practitioners, students, and accountants, this magazine covers all aspects of insolvency law and accountancy. It appears six times each year.

International Insolvency Review
Wiley
The Atrium, Southern Gate, Chichester, West Sussex, PO19 8SQ, UK
T: +44 (0) 1243 779 777
F: +44 (0) 1243 775 878
www.interscience.wiley.com/jpages/1180–0518
ISSN: 1180-0518
The *IIR* is published three times each year, in association with INSOL (the International Federation of Insolvency Professionals), and provides an international perspective on developments in insolvency law and practice, in addition to covering issues relating to cross-border insolvency.

International Small Business Journal
Sage Publications
1 Oliver's Yard, 55 City Road, London, EC1Y 1SP, UK
T: +44 (0) 20 7324 8500
F: +44 (0) 20 7324 8600
isb.sagepub.com
ISSN: 0266-2426
The *International Small Business Journal (ISBJ)* is a quarterly journal that aims to provide a forum for the discussion and dissemination of views and research on the small business sector. Papers published in the *ISBJ* cover theoretical, methodological, and empirical studies of small firms from a broad range of disciplines and perspectives. The papers are aimed at academics, policy makers, and analysts, in government and business, trade and business institutions, small business representative bodies, and those in support agencies.

INTERNET

ABIWorld
www.abiworld.org
ABIWorld is sponsored by the American Bankruptcy Institute and is a major source of US bankruptcy information. The site includes news and statistics, information and opinions on bankruptcy cases, information on international bankruptcy legislation, an interactive newsletter, and information on how to find a bankruptcy professional. Some sections are restricted to ABI members.

American Bankruptcy Institute
www.abiworld.org
The American Bankruptcy Institute is a nonprofit, nonpartisan organization promoting education, research, and the analysis of bankruptcy issues. Its website provides access to current news and legislation pertaining to bankruptcy and business failures, an interactive newsletter, and research and analysis.

Bankruptcy for Business
www.bankruptcyforbusiness.net
This site focuses on bankruptcy for business, providing guidance and articles on how to file and how to avoid bankruptcy, based on the premise that business turnaround is usually the cheaper alternative.

Business Bankruptcy Info
www.creditworthy.com/topics/bankruptcy.html
Hosted by Creditworthy, this website provides links to business bankruptcy information covering the United States, Canada, and the United Kingdom. It includes information on, and links to, a US bankruptcy dictionary, an overview of the US Bankruptcy Code, and statistics and research on bankruptcy filings.

  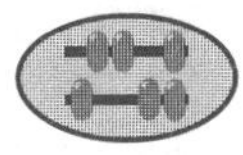   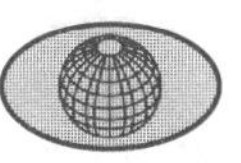   

Filing for Bankruptcy Online
www.filingforbankruptcyonline.com/businessbankruptcy.html
This US site provides practical information on bankruptcy for businesses, and a range of related areas involving legal issues, documentation, software, tax issues, mortgage, and credit.

InsolvencyAsia
www.insolvencyasia.com
This site, based in Hong Kong, provides insolvency-related news together with information on bankruptcy legislation and listings of consultants, associations, and regulatory authorities in Asian countries.

Insolvency Services
www.insolvency.gov.uk
This government-sponsored site provides practical information and advice on personal and corporate insolvency in the United Kingdom, including statistics and a database of insolvency practitioners.

InterNet Bankruptcy Library
www.bankrupt.com
Sponsored by the Bankruptcy Creditors' Service and the Beard Group, this site is aimed particularly at creditors. It includes a news archive, a database of bankruptcy professionals, information on legal rules in American states, and details of publications, as well as providing access to discussion groups.

United States Bankruptcy Courts
www.uscourts.gov/bankruptcycourts.html
Since there are specialized courts that settle bankruptcy claims in America, this site offers information about the courts themselves, offers downloadable forms, has an FAQ section, and has links to the individual courts for particular areas.

ORGANIZATIONS

Europe

Bankruptcy Association
Freepost LA1118, 4 Johnson Close,
Lancaster, LA1 5BR, UK
T: +44 (0) 1539 469 474
E: johnmcqueennospam@theba.org.uk
www.theba.org.uk
The association was founded by John McQueen in 1983 to provide information and advice to debtors and bankrupts in the United Kingdom and to campaign for reform of insolvency legislation.

Insolvency Practitioners Association (IPA)
Valiant House, 4–10 Heneage Lane, London, EC3A 5DQ, UK
T: +44 (0) 20 7623 5108
F: +44 (0) 20 7623 5127
E: secretariat@insolvency-practitioners.org.uk
www.insolvency-practitioners.org.uk
The IPA, founded in 1961, is a professional organization for insolvency practitioners. Its main objectives are to promote training and education in insolvency administration and to maintain the standards of performance and conduct of those working in the field.

R3, The Association of Business Recovery Professionals
8th Floor, 120 Aldersgate Street, London, EC1A 4JQ, UK
T: +44 (0) 20 7566 4200
F: +44 (0) 20 7566 4224
E: association@r3.org.uk
www.r3.org.uk
R3 (Rescue, Recovery, Renewal), founded in 1990 and formerly known as the Society of Practitioners of Insolvency, is a professional organization for insolvency practitioners and turnaround managers which places a growing emphasis on reconstruction, turnaround management, and corporate recovery. Its activities include courses, conferences, and producing publications–including the quarterly journal *Recovery*.

USA

American Bankruptcy Institute
44 Canal Center Plaza, Suite 400,
Alexandria, VA 22314, USA
T: +1 703 739 0800
F: +1 703 739 1060
E: support@abiworld.org
www.abiworld.org
The American Bankruptcy Institute is the largest multi-national organization dedicated to research and education on matters related to insolvency. The ABI membership includes more than 11,500 attorneys, auctioneers, bankers, judges, lenders, professors, turnaround specialists, accountants, and other bankruptcy professionals. It provides a forum for the exchange of ideas and information, and is involved in a number of publications both for the insolvency practitioner and the public.

The National Association of Bankruptcy Trustees
1 Windsor Cove, Suite 305, Columbia, SC 29223, USA
T: +1 803 252 5646
F: +1 803 765 0860
E: info@nabt.com
www.nabt.com
The association is committed to improving the administration of bankruptcy by promoting professionalism, education, and the open exchange of ideas among its members and other members of the bankruptcy community.

BRIC

Managers under the Chamber of Commerce and Industry of the Russian Federation (SOAM)
6 St Ilyinka, Moscow, 109012, Russia
T: +7 495 620 0009
F: +7 495 620 0360
E: tpprf@tpprf.ru
eng.tpprf.ru/ru/main/general/activities
The Chamber of Commerce and Industry of the Russian Federation is a non-governmental, non-profit organization which aims to meet the tasks and goal objectives set out in the Russian Federation Law on Chambers of Commerce and Industry. It represents the interests of small, medium-size, and big business, and encompasses all business sectors.

International

INSOL International
2–3 Philpot Lane, London, EC3M 8AQ, UK
T: +44 (0) 20 7929 6679
F: +44 (0) 20 7929 6678
E: heather@insol.ision.co.uk
www.insol.org
INSOL is a grouping of member associations that aims to facilitate the exchange of information and ideas and to encourage international cooperation within the insolvency profession. It participates in governmental advisory groups, supports research, and promotes the development of international guidelines and codes of practice. Its activities include the organization of seminars and conferences and the publication of newsletters, reports, and a journal.

International Association of Restructuring, Insolvency & Bankruptcy Professionals
2–3 Philpot Lane, London, EC3M 8AQ, UK
T: +44 (0) 20 7929 6679
F: +44 (0) 20 7929 6678
E: heather@insol.ision.co.uk
www.insol.org
INSOL International is a global alliance of national associations for accountants and lawyers who focus on turnaround and insolvency. It consists of 40 member associations from around the world, with over 10,000 professionals participating as members of INSOL International.

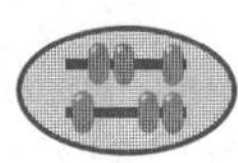

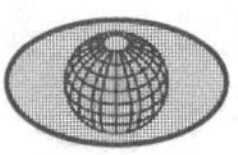

Behavioral Finance

BOOKS

Advances in Behavioral Finance, Volume I
Richard H. Thaler (editor)
New York: Russell Sage Foundation, 1993
597pp, ISBN: 978-0-87154-844-3
A groundbreaking and insightful overview of behavioral finance, the 21 papers discuss different behavioral issues and anomalies that occur in the financial markets. In the first book published on this emerging topic, the authors develop theories to help explain the effects of financial agents behaving in ways that are not fully rational.

Advances in Behavioral Finance, Volume II
Richard H. Thaler (editor)
Roundtable Series in Behavioral Economics
Princeton, New Jersey: Princeton University Press, 2005
728pp, ISBN: 978-0-691-12175-8
The second volume, published 12 years later, focuses on the large changes that have occurred in behavioral finance since the first volume was published. It shows how financial markets often fail to behave as they would if trading was undertaken by fully rational investors, and discusses the impact of behavioral finance approach on areas such as asset pricing and investor behavior.

A Behavioral Approach to Asset Pricing, 2nd ed
Hersh Shefrin
Academic Press Advanced Finance Series
Oxford: Academic Press, 2008
618pp, ISBN: 978-0-12-374356-5
Shefrin here presents a practical approach to the application of behavioral economics and finance to a range of pricing issues, such as portfolio management, trading, and the pricing of equities, bonds and options.

Behavioral Finance
Hersh Shefrin (editor)
International Library of Critical Writings in Financial Economics Series
Northampton, Massachusetts: Edward Elgar Publishing, 2001
2,088pp, ISBN: 978-1-84064-274-2
A three-volume collection of essays that examines the overlap between psychology, decision-making, and finance. It combines many of the classic approaches to both psychology and finance, and discusses the debate between the behavioral school and the efficient market school of finance.

Behavioral Finance and Wealth Management: How to Build Optimal Portfolios that Account for Investor Biases
Michael M. Pompian
Wiley Finance Series
Hoboken, New Jersey: Wiley, 2006
336pp, ISBN: 978-0-471-74517-4
This is a wide-ranging introduction to irrational investor behavior and the practical application of behavioral finance, and how to adjust portfolios for individual investors to account for behavioral biases. It also provides a history of behavioral finance, a detailed review of some of the most commonly found biases, and examines how to incorporate investor behavior into the asset allocation process.

Behavioural Finance: Insights into Irrational Minds and Markets
James Montier
Chichester, UK: Wiley, 2002
193pp, ISBN: 978-0-470-84487-8
Provides a practical overview of behavioral finance, with insights into the irrational nature of investment decisions. Montier links the underlying theory to real-life applications in financial products through an examination of measurable variables, and presents useful advice on how institutional investors can improve their decision-making through an awareness of behavioral research and finance.

Behavioural Investing: A Practitioners Guide to Applying Behavioural Finance
James Montier
Wiley Finance Series
Chichester, UK: Wiley, 2007
728pp, ISBN: 978-0-470-51670-6
This book for professional investors focuses on methods for improving investment behavior by considering behavioral decision-making biases. It reviews the applications of behavioral finance, and examines the possible errors and mental pitfalls, and discusses how to avoid them having a negative impact on returns.

Inefficient Markets: An Introduction to Behavioral Finance
Andrei Shleifer
Clarendon Lectures in Economics Series
New York: Oxford University Press, 2000
224pp, ISBN: 978-0-19-829227-2
A classic of behavioral finance, this was one of the first books published on the subject. It examines some of the most important early ideas in behavioral finance, and is aimed at financial economists who are looking for a source of empirical facts, as well as wanting to explore new ideas in this emerging area of finance.

Nudge: Improving Decisions about Health, Wealth, and Happiness
Richard H. Thaler, Cass R. Sunstein
New Haven, Connecticut: Yale University Press, 2008
293pp, ISBN: 978-0-300-12223-7
This new book on decision-making discusses how organizations can help people make better choices in their lives. Using a range of everyday activities as examples, it shows how we are susceptible to various biases, and shows how to design environments to nudge people into making better decisions.

Rumors in Financial Markets: Insights into Behavioral Finance
Mark Schindler
Wiley Finance Series
Hoboken, New Jersey: Wiley, 2007
210pp, ISBN: 978-0-470-03196-4
A new look at behavioral finance, providing insights into how finance, psychology and sociology act as the foundations for rumors in the marketplace. It integrates behavioral finance with experimental finance, to examine how rumors evolve, spread and are used, and discusses the effect this has on volatility, price movements, and herding behavior.

The Story of Behavioral Finance
Brandon Adams, Brian Finn
Bloomington, Indiana: iUniverse, 2006
82pp, ISBN: 978-0-595-39690-0
A useful primer on behavioral finance and its application to the real world. It concisely summarizes a number of related core concepts, such as the efficient market hypothesis and the Capital Asset Pricing Model, and discusses a number of key questions about the impact of behavioral finance on different market phenomena, such as investor psychology and limits to arbitrage.

The Winner's Curse: Paradoxes and Anomalies of Economic Life
Richard H. Thaler
Princeton, New Jersey: Princeton University Press, 1994
240pp, ISBN: 978-0-691-01934-5
The author, a leading figure in behavioral

economics, here analyzes a number of examples of recognizable anomalies, arguing that winners are often the real losers. He relates this to the debate over market efficiency, countering the received wisdom that economic choice rests on a foundation of rationality.

JOURNALS

Behavioral & Experimental Finance

SSRN, USA
www.ssrn.com/update/fen/fen_behav-exper-fin.html

This electronic journal publishes working and accepted paper abstracts covering all aspects of behavioral and experimental finance. It strives for greater explanation and insight into finance and investments based on research from the social sciences, and to foster a better understanding of those elements of human psychology, both cognitive and affective, that influence the decision-making process.

The Icfai University Journal of Behavioral Finance

The Icfai University Press
6-3-354/1, Stellar Sphinx, Road No. 1, Banjara Hills, Panjagutta, Hyderabad - 500 034, Andhra Pradesh, India
T: +91 40 2343 0448
F: +91 40 2343 0447
www.iupindia.org/behavioralfinance.asp
ISSN: 0972-9089

This is a quarterly journal that focuses on behavioral economics, behavior of markets, behavioral aspects influencing investment decisions of managers and behavioral aspects in corporate finance decision. It provides a platform for cutting-edge research in understanding the human behavior in relation to finance and economics.

The Journal of Behavioral Finance

The Institute of Behavioral Finance and Lawrence Erlbaum Associates
1900 Preston Road #267, Suite 310, Plano, TX 75093, USA
www.journalofbehavioralfinance.org
ISSN: 1542-7560

This journal publishes papers analyzing developments in behavioral finance, and addresses the implications of current work on individual and group emotion, cognition, and behavior in markets, aiming to foster debate among groups who have keen insights into the behavioral patterns of markets.

The Journal of Economic Behavior and Organization

Elsevier
1598 South Main Street, Room 16, JMU, MSC 5505, Harrisonburg, VA 22807, USA
F: +1 540 801 8650
www.elsevier.com/wps/find/journaldescription.cws_home/505559/description#description
ISSN: 0167-2681

This journal publishes theoretical and empirical research concerning economic decision, organization and behavior and to economic change in all its aspects. Its aim is to explore the interrelations of economics with other disciplines, such as biology, psychology, law, anthropology, sociology, and mathematics.

Journal of Risk and Uncertainty

Springer Verlag
Tiergartenstr. 17, 69121 Heidelberg, Germany
T: +49 622 1487 8575
www.springer.com/economics/economic+theory/journal/11166
ISSN: 0895-5646

This journal publishes theoretical and empirical papers that analyze risk-bearing behavior and decision-making under uncertainty, and is an outlet for research in decision analysis, economics and psychology dealing with choice under uncertainty.

INTERNET

Behavioural Finance Net

www.behaviouralfinance.net

This is an online resource on for researchers in behavioral finance. It contains key information on a large number of associated topics, and includes definitions and quotes, bibliography, people, history, links, glossary, and links topics with papers.

ORGANIZATIONS

USA

The Behavioral Finance Forum

Chair: Shlomo Benartzi, Warren Cormier
USA
www.rand.org/labor/centers/befi/

The Behavioral Finance Forum (BeFi) is a collective of academic, financial, and government leaders promoting behavioral research for practical application. It aims to help consumers worldwide make better financial decisions, and the financial industry to use this information to produce innovative product and service ideas with a unique marketing advantage. Founded in 2006, it hosts an annual conference, and conducts a number of web seminars each year; the non-profit RAND Corporation recently took on the management of its activities.

The Institute of Behavioral Finance

Harborside Financial Center, Plaza 10, Suite 800, Jersey City, NJ 07311, USA
T: +1 201 793 2015
E: vilieva@journalofbehavioralfinance.org
www.journalofbehavioralfinance.com

The Institute of Behavioral Finance was established to study the impact of psychology on investor decision-making and, through its publication, the *Journal of Behavioral Finance*, and sponsored conferences, it promotes new research in all areas of the subject. It also addresses important new issues by involving interested practitioners and academics in related fields to better explain both investor decision-making and market anomalies.

International

The Institute of Behavioral Finance

Chair: Theo Vorster
Fountain Grove Office Park, Cnr William Nicol & 2nd Road, Hyde Park, Johannesburg, South Africa
T: +27 011 888 5088
F: +27 011 888 5088
E: gerdavdl@lantic.net
www.ibfsa.co.za

The Institute of Behavioral Finance is an independent research and training institution aimed at the study and promotion of the behavioral finance discipline. It incorporates the work of researchers and academics to discuss investor decision-making and market anomalies, and add value to the professional status of the investment sector in South Africa.

  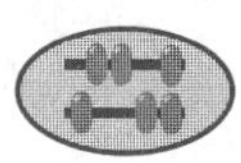   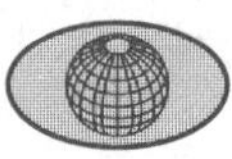   

Benchmarking

BOOKS

The Benchmarking Book

Tim Stapenhurst
Oxford: Butterworth-Heinemann, 2009
450pp, ISBN: 978-0-7506-8905-2
This essential guide to process improvement through benchmarking provides all the information you need to carry out effective benchmarking studies and improve performance. Focused on best practice across different industries, it offers crucial guidance on how to analyze data, avoid pitfalls and structure reports to achieve the best results.

Benchmarking Strategies: A Tool for Profit Improvement

Rob Reider, Harry Reider
Chichester, UK: Wiley, 2000
276pp, ISBN: 978-0-471-34464-3
This is a practical manual covering benchmarking principles, techniques, and implementation. It examines how corporations perform various tasks in identifying and implementing internal and external best practices in a program of continuous improvement.

Benchmarking: The Search for Industry Best Practices That Lead to Superior Performance

Robert C. Camp
New York: Productivity Press, 2006
299pp, ISBN: 978-1-56327-352-0
This provides a guide through the historic 10-step benchmarking process that the author developed while at Xerox, a process that is credited with reviving that company when it was floundering in 1979. It presents other examples of the process, including its dramatic application to L. L. Bean. He uses these examples to show managers how to relate benchmarking to their own circumstances, and presents strategy and tips for efficiently undertaking best performance.

Best Practices: Building Up Your Business with Customer-focused Solutions

R. Hiebeler, T. B. Kelly, C. Ketteman
Carmichael, California: Touchstone Books, 2000
240pp, ISBN: 978-0-684-84804-4
From case studies of over 40 best practice companies, this book draws lessons on how to focus on customers, create growth, reduce costs, and increase profits. It discusses new insights beyond benchmarking, best practices auditing, understanding markets and customers, involving customers in the design of products and services, selling products and services, how best to serve customers, managing customer information, and putting best practices to work.

Best Practices in Planning and Management Reporting: From Data to Decisions, 2nd ed

David A. J. Axson
Chichester, UK: Wiley, 2007
288pp, ISBN: 978-0-470-00857-7
This examines the process of improving business performance through the adoption of best practices. It introduces the technique of best practice benchmarking, and explains how best practices may be used to drive change. The issues of strategic planning, operational and financial planning, management reporting, forecasting, and the use of technology are discussed, as well as the use of benchmarking as a starting point.

Driving Your Company's Value: Strategic Benchmarking for Value

Michael J. Mard, Robert R. Dunne, Edi Osborne, James S. Rigby, Jr
Chichester, UK: Wiley, 2004
193pp, ISBN: 978-0-471-64855-0
Driving Your Company's Value is a step-by-step book presenting a valuation-oriented methodology that helps companies maximize shareholder value. It offers clear, concise, and concrete methods for management to create and preserve value, complete with case study applications.

Effective Management of Benchmarking Projects: Practical Guidelines and Examples of Best Practice

Mohamed Zairi
Oxford: Butterworth-Heinemann, 1998
348pp, ISBN: 978-0-7506-3987-3
This book begins with a profile of Rank Xerox—where the benchmarking story started. It examines the strategic application of benchmarking for best practice, as well as topics such as partner selection, the ethics of benchmarking, and the value of industrial visits and benchmarking awards. It also describes the process of benchmarking in practice.

Strategic Benchmarking Reloaded with Six Sigma: Improving Your Company's Performance Using Global Best Practice

Gregory H. Watson
Chichester, UK: Wiley, 2007
360pp, ISBN: 978-0-470-06908-0
Strategic Benchmarking Reloaded with Six Sigma updates benchmarking, by adding statistical concepts from Six Sigma. These two methodologies combine to form a powerful platform for improving any company's overall performance. This new revision reviews the first 25 years of development in benchmarking, and features new appendices, case studies, and topics.

Winning Business: How to Use Financial Analysis and Benchmarks to Outscore Your Competition

Rich Gildersleeve
Houston, Texas: Gulf Professional Publishing Company, 1999
334pp, ISBN: 978-0-88415-898-1
Financial analysis, with all its detailed measurements and calculations, is often overlooked as a benchmarking tool. This provides clear explanations of the fundamental terms used to analyze and understand financial statements, and demonstrates their value in benchmarking companies. The benchmarking indicators presented can be used to track key measurements or as a metric by which to measure your company against others.

JOURNALS

Benchmarking: An International Journal

Emerald
60/62 Toller Lane, Bradford, West Yorkshire, BD8 9BY, UK
T: +44 (0) 1274 777 700
F: +44 (0) 1274 785 200
www.emeraldinsight.com/1463-5771.htm
ISSN: 1463-5771
The journal focuses on the theory and practice of benchmarking, with articles on recent academic research as well as real-life case studies of benchmarking activities by companies. Contributors are from a wide range of countries.

Business Process Management Journal

Emerald
60/62 Toller Lane, Bradford, West Yorkshire, BD8 9BY, UK
T: +44 (0) 1274 777 700

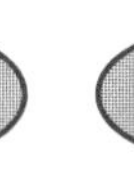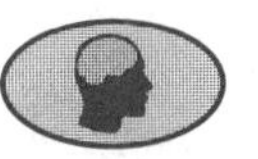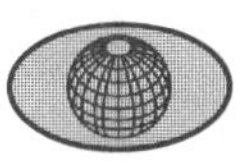

F: +44 (0) 1274 785 200
www.emeraldinsight.com/1463-7154.htm
ISSN: 1463-7154
This journal is published in association with the European Centre for Total Quality Management. Contributions from both academics and practitioners are included, and the focus is on the management of business processes for efficiency and competitive success.

Measuring Business Excellence

Emerald
60/62 Toller Lane, Bradford, West Yorkshire, BD8 9BY, UK
T: +44 (0) 1274 777 700
F: +44 (0) 1274 785 200
www.emeraldinsight.com/1368-3047.htm
ISSN: 1368-3047
Measuring Business Excellence provides international insights into non-financial methods of measuring business improvements. It shows how to apply best practice, implement innovative thinking, and learn how to use different improvement tools within an organization.

INTERNET

APQC's Benchmarking and Best Practice

www.apqc.org/best
This site summarizes the benefits of benchmarking, outlines a methodology, and lists the keys to success in the area. The "free resources" section includes articles, case studies, and white papers to guide you through the benchmarking process.

Avoid These Ten Benchmarking Mistakes

www.benchmarkingplus.com.au/mistakes.htm
Many sites tell you how to benchmark. This site lists the 10 most common mistakes in benchmarking so that you can avoid making them yourself.

Benchmarking Exchange

www.benchnet.com
This is an extremely comprehensive site with a lot of information on benchmarking practices for both members and nonmembers. Members can conduct benchmark surveys online and have the information collected and returned through the Exchange as replies are received.

Benchmarking Network

www.benchmarkingnetwork.com
This is another comprehensive site. Members share information about best practice in a wide range of operations across all industry sectors.

Best-Practice.com

www.Best-Practice.com
Providing a range of information on benchmarking, this site has links to more detailed research and tools that can be purchased direct from the various partners in the network. Membership is free.

The Business Performance Improvement Resource

www.bpir.com
The Business Performance Improvement Resource is an internet-based benchmarking and business information service. It provides access to benchmarks, best practices, performance measures, business excellence tools, self-assessments, and over 250,000 articles from around the world. It is run by the Centre for Organisational Excellence Research (COER).

Global Benchmarking Council

www3.best-in-class.com/gbc
Members have access to a benchmarking database, regular meetings, and research reports, plus a range of other services and detailed information.

ORGANIZATIONS

Europe

Best Practice Club

The Atrium, Curtis Road, Dorking, Surrey, RH4 1XA, UK
T: +44 (0) 1306 646 555
F: +44 (0) 1306 646 556
E: enquiries@bpclub.com
www.bpclub.com
With an international membership, this organization promotes organizational excellence through members networking and comparing their practice. Member companies come from both the manufacturing and the service sectors and pool their experience.

Centre for Interfirm Comparison (CIFC)

32 Thomas Street, Winchester, Hampshire, SO23 9HJ, UK
T: +44 (0) 1962 844 144
F: +44 (0) 1962 843 180
E: enquiries@cifc.co.uk
www.cifc.co.uk
The centre helps businesses of all types and in all sectors to assess their performance through confidential, detailed comparison of their financial ratios and other data with those of similar businesses, and to target improvements in specific areas of their operations. It provides a wide range of benchmarking and related consulting services.

USA

American Productivity and Quality Center (APQC)

123 North Post Oak Lane, 3rd Floor, Houston, TX 77024, USA
T: +1 713 681 4020
F: +1 713 681 1182
E: apqcinfo@apqc.org
www.apqc.org
Founded in 1977, APQC works with organizations of all sizes to improve productivity and quality. Its aim is to research and understand both emerging improvement methods and methods whose effectiveness is already proven, and it distributes its findings through education, advice, and information services. In 1992 it set up the International Benchmarking Clearinghouse to promote and facilitate the process of learning from best practice.

International

Centre for Organisational Excellence Research (COER)

Massey University, Private Bag 11 222, Palmerston North, New Zealand
T: +64 (0) 6 350 5445
E: r.s.mann@massey.ac.nz
www.coer.org.nz
The Centre for Organisational Excellence Research (COER), led by Dr Robin Mann, undertakes benchmarking and business excellence research and consultancy. They also operate the www.bpir.com site, which focuses on best practice sharing.

The Global Benchmarking Network (GBN)

c/o Informationszentrum Benchmarking (IZB), Fraunhofer IPK, Pascalstrasse 8–9, 10587 Berlin, Germany
T: +49 (0) 30 39 006
F: +49 (0) 30 393 25 03
E: gbn@ipk.fhg.de
www.globalbenchmarking.org/
The GBN is a membership-based organization for those organizations that promote and support benchmarking within their country. Currently it represents over 25 countries. The purpose of the GBN is to promote and support benchmarking worldwide and the international exchange of best practices. Its members consist of the world's leading experts in benchmarking, and its president is Dr Robert Camp, the founder of benchmarking.

 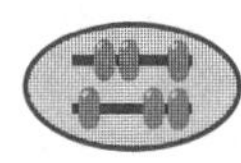   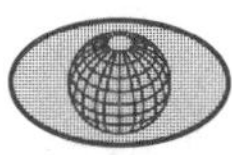   

Bonds/Fixed Income

BOOKS

The Bond Bible
Marilyn Cohen
New York: New York Institute of Finance, 2000
238pp, ISBN: 978-0-7352-0138-5
This is a comprehensive guide to bonds and fixed-income investments, discussing their characteristics, stability, equilibrium, and the benefits they bring to portfolio diversification. It demystifies bond investing, and discusses the increase in bond usage and markets, how to identify a bargain, where to buy from, and how to avoid the pitfalls of the bond market.

The Bond Book: Everything Investors Need to Know About Treasuries, Municipals, GNMAs, Corporates, Zeros, Bond Funds, Money Market Funds, and More, 2nd ed
Annette Thau
New York: McGraw-Hill, 2001
394pp, ISBN: 978-0-07-135862-0
This comprehensive introduction to bonds explains how they work, the historic returns for each type of fund, how to buy and sell them, and acts as a practical guide to safer investing and using cash flow assets. It provides useful information and tools for integrating bonds, and more recent innovations such as inflation-indexed bonds, savings bonds, CMOs, and emerging market bonds, into a portfolio.

Bond Markets, Analysis and Strategies, 7th ed
Frank J. Fabozzi
Boston, Massachusetts: Addison-Wesley, 2008
792pp, ISBN: 978-0-13-607897-5
This new textbook on fixed-income securities and bond markets shows how to understand the bond market and the necessary tools for managing bond portfolios. Taking a practical approach, it presents a detailed account of each type of bond, their investment characteristics, technology for valuing them, portfolio strategies for using them, and shows how to quantify exposure to changes in interest rates.

Charlie D.: The Story of the Legendary Bond Trader
William D. Falloon
New York: Wiley, 1997
230pp, ISBN: 978-0-471-15672-7
This biography of the famous trader, thought by many to be the greatest ever, details his life, accomplishments, and trading strategies from the Treasury bond pit at the Chicago Board of Trade, the world's largest futures trading arena. It describes his entrepreneurial style, trading integrity, and philanthropy, and looks at the risk-taking style that helped him achieve such enormous daily trading positions.

European Fixed Income Markets: Money, Bond, and Interest Rate Derivatives
Jonathan A. Batten, Thomas A. Fetherston, Peter G. Szilagyi (editors)
Wiley Finance Series
Chichester, UK: Wiley, 2004
484pp, ISBN: 978-0-470-85053-4
This analysis of fixed-income instruments and associated derivatives provides a useful overview of the euro and non-euro markets. A team of leading international academics and market practitioners examine the main features of these markets, and the increase in scope of individual national debt markets, and offer detailed country analyses, as well as discussing the post-euro landscape in these markets.

First Steps in Bonds: Successful Strategies without Rocket Science
Peter Temple
Boston, Massachusetts: FT Prentice Hall, 2002
197pp, ISBN: 978-0-273-65657-9
This is a practical bond primer that offers a comprehensive and accessible overview to the techniques and tools used by professional investors to integrate bonds into a balanced portfolio. It examines how to analyze and value bonds, key market issues, trading strategies, and discusses each of the main parts of the market, including government bonds, corporate bonds, and Eurobonds.

Fixed Income Analysis, 2nd ed
Frank J. Fabozzi (editor)
CFA Institute Investment Series
Hoboken, New Jersey: Wiley, 2007
768pp, ISBN: 978-0-470-05221-1
This practical guide provides complete coverage of fixed-income tools and techniques, and how they can be applied to the investment process and portfolio construction. It focuses on the fixed-income marketplace, the risks associated with investing in fixed-income securities, the fundamentals of valuation and interest rate risk, features of structured products, principles of credit analysis, and the valuation of fixed-income securities with embedded options.

Fixed Income Securities and Derivatives Handbook: Analysis and Valuation
Moorad Choudhry (editor)
Princeton, New Jersey: Bloomberg Press, 2005
355pp, ISBN: 978-1-57660-164-8
This comprehensive guide presents a combination of academic theory and market practice to describe the full range of methodologies, techniques, and applications used in the analysis and valuation of principal debt market instruments and their associated derivatives. It shows how bonds are structured, valued, and traded, and presents a framework for understanding fixed-income analytics in a practical way, based around individual requirements.

Fixed Income Securities: Tools for Today's Markets, 2nd ed
Bruce Tuckman
Hoboken, New Jersey: Wiley, 2002
512pp, ISBN: 978-0-471-06322-3
This describes the latest fixed-income concepts, securities, analytical techniques, and models, using a topical approach to application and risk control. As new securities are introduced that are an increasingly risky, this presents a useful framework for pricing and hedging fixed-income securities in an accessible way, backed up by a range of examples, applications, and case studies.

Fixed-Income Securities: Valuation, Risk Management and Portfolio Strategies
Lionel Martellini, Philippe Priaulet, Stéphane Priaulet
Wiley Finance Series
Chichester, UK: Wiley, 2003
631pp, ISBN: 978-0-470-85277-4
This comprehensive textbook covers all areas of bonds, including techniques for valuing them, portfolio management, and risk management in bond markets. It examines how various types of derivative securities can be used to manage the risks inherent in fixed-income securities, and presents worked examples on valuation, risk management, and portfolio strategies, as well as discussing yield curves, credit spreads, and hedging interest rate risk.

  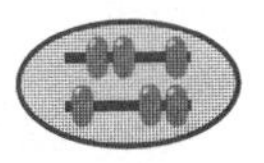 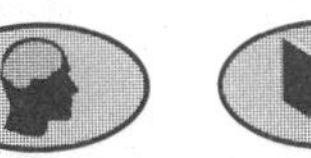  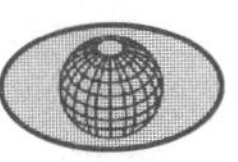   

Fixed Income Strategy: A Practitioner's Guide to Riding the Curve
Tamara Mast Henderson
Wiley Finance Series
Chichester, UK: Wiley, 2003
204pp, ISBN: 978-0-470-85063-3
This presents a practical approach to developing a successful fixed-income investing and trading strategy, combining an understanding of both theoretical models and practical market experience. It shows how to use models to your advantage, how to structure trades that are based on different strategic perspectives, and introduces the most relevant aspects of risk management necessary for practitioners.

An Introduction to Bond Markets, 3rd ed
Moorad Choudhry
Securities Institute Series
Chichester, UK: Wiley, 2006
405pp, ISBN: 978-0-470-01758-6
This bond market primer describes the different types of bonds traded in the capital markets, and the analytical techniques used by traders and fund managers. It presents the latest developments and market practice in bonds, focusing on bond yield measurement, interest rate risk, the UK gilt market and corporate debt markets, risk management, off-balance sheet instruments, including swaps and options, and the emerging markets.

The Handbook of Fixed Income Securities, 7th ed
Frank J. Fabozzi (editor)
New York: McGraw-Hill, 2005
1,495pp, ISBN: 978-0-07-144099-8
This authoritative guide to fixed-income securities, now in its seventh edition, is a popular reference, written by a team of leading academics and practitioners. It provides all the necessary details and formulas to keep pace with recent changes, focusing on applications, electronic trading, and global portfolio management, as well as containing new analysis of Eurobonds, emerging market debt, credit risk modeling, synthetics, credit derivatives, and transition management.

Investing in Fixed Income Securities: Understanding the Bond Market
Gary Strumeyer
Wiley Finance Series
Hoboken, New Jersey: Wiley, 2005
514pp, ISBN: 978-0-471-46512-6
This is a practical overview of fixed-income securities and markets for both investors and market professionals. It presents the basic bond market concepts and terminology, compares different debt instruments, and describes strategies for managing a diversified portfolio. It also offers advice on maximizing investment value, applying appropriate valuation methods to a variety of fixed-income securities, and explains macro-economic concepts and their impact on the bond market.

Naked Guide to Bonds: What You Need to Know—Stripped Down to the Bare Essentials
Michael V. Brandes
Hoboken, New Jersey: Wiley, 2003
242pp, ISBN: 978-0-471-46221-7
Using plenty of examples from the bond market, this primer for investors describes the best way to achieve a balanced, diversified portfolio. It presents insights into the full range of instruments, characteristics, structures, and strategies for the fixed-income asset class in an easy learning style, focusing on the most important factors in the investment decision process.

The Only Guide to a Winning Bond Strategy You'll Ever Need: The Way Smart Money Preserves Wealth Today
Larry E. Swedroe, Joseph H. Hempen
New York: St. Martin's Press, 2006
260pp, ISBN: 978-0-312-35363-6
This accessible guide explains the standard techniques for investing in bonds and other fixed-income securities, describing their use, how the bond market works, and how and why each security may or may not be suitable for a portfolio. It also presents useful investment tips, such as buying bonds with the highest ratings, avoiding buying hybrid securities, and not trying to time the market.

Strategic Asset Allocation in Fixed Income Markets: A Matlab Based User's Guide
Ken Nyholm
Wiley Finance Series
Hoboken, New Jersey: Wiley, 2008
186pp, ISBN: 978-0-470-75362-0
With Matlab now used by most investment banks, this guide shows how to implement financial and econometric models using applying Matlab-based computational techniques, with an emphasis on fixed-income finance. It introduces all concepts and techniques from a basic level, from fundamental aspects such as price-yield conversions to more complex topics such as term structure modeling and strategic asset allocation, with detailed descriptions of the programming steps involved.

Valuing Fixed Income Futures
David Boberski
McGraw-Hill Library Investment and Finance Series
New York: McGraw-Hill, 2007
239pp, ISBN: 978-0-07-147541-9
This is a practical assessment of the role of futures in the fixed-income marketplace, which analyzes how to measure the performance of Treasury and Eurodollar futures, and build empirical models to measure risk. It discusses major changes in trading, and explains the technology for understanding price behavior, and the development of frameworks for solving embedded option valuation in Treasury and Eurodollar futures.

JOURNALS

Journal of Fixed Income
Institutional Investor
Journals Group, 225 Park Avenue South, New York, NY 10003, USA
T: +1 212 224 3570
F: +1 212 224 3197
www.iijournals.com/JFI
ISSN: 1059-8596
This quarterly journal provides research and case studies on both bond theory and practice. Its papers are focused on the analysis of fixed-income structuring, performance tracking, and risk management, and cover bonds, municipals, ABSs, MBSs, CDOs, and credit derivatives. It also discusses relative risk and return features between different securities and markets, security performance under varying economic conditions, valuation techniques, and distressed securities.

INTERNET

Bond Market Prices
www.bondmarketprices.com
This website is for private investors, and offers access to the TRAX database of bond prices and other information produced by international bond dealers. It includes data on both sterling-denominated and foreign currency bonds trading in the international capital markets.

Bondscape
www.bondscape.net
This website is a free service that provides easy access to the bond market in the UK, and offers price and yield analysis, and

 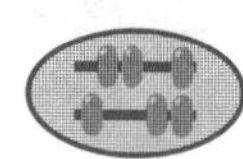   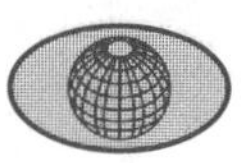   

research. It provides brokers and other professional investment advisers with the ability to trade bonds in smaller sizes, offering equity-style online dealing capabilities with multiple market makers.

Fixed Income Investor
www.fixedincomeinvestor.co.uk
This online resource provides visibility, education, and research on bonds and other sterling-denominated, fixed-income securities. It is aimed at private investors and their advisors wanting an understanding of these markets, to be able to compare and evaluate the available securities, and identify investment opportunities. It provides analysis and comment, as well as coverage of bond prices and yields, monthly bankers, and model portfolios.

InvestinginBonds.com
www.investinginbonds.com
This is a resource on bonds created by the Securities Industry and Financial Markets Association to help educate investors. It is for all level of investor wanting bond price information, and includes a wide variety of market data, news, commentary, and information about the bond markets.

Reuters Fixed Income Services Financial Glossary
www.ejv.com/bp/html/glossary3.html
This is an online glossary that provides definitions on all the main terminology relating to fixed-income products and markets.

ORGANIZATIONS

Europe

Committee of European Securities Regulators
Chair: Eddy Wymeersch
11–13 avenue de Friedland, 75008 Paris, France
T: +33 1 58 36 43 21
F: +33 1 58 36 43 30
E: secretariat@cesr.eu
www.cesr-eu.org
CESR is an independent committee that works to improve co-ordination among securities regulators, to develop effective operational network mechanisms to enhance day-to-day consistent supervision and enforcement of the single market for financial services, and act as an advisory group to assist the EU Commission.

USA

Fixed Income Analysts Society
Chair: Alex Golbin
244 Fifth Avenue, Suite L230, New York, NY 10001, USA
T: +1 212 726 8100
E: fiasi@fiasi.org
www.fiasi.org
FIASI is a non-profit, professional society of fixed-income professionals from all disciplines and all sectors, which is dedicated to the education of its membership and the fixed-income community at large. It provides a member forum on issues affecting the industry, and sponsors educational programs and workshops covering topics of current interest.

BRIC

The Fixed Income Money Market and Derivatives Association of India
Chair: V. Srikanth
52, 5th Floor, Mittal Chambers, Nariman Point, Mumbai 400021, India
T: +011 91 2202 5725
F: +011 91 2202 5739
E: fimmda@fimmda.org
www.fimmda.org
FIMMDA is a voluntary association for the bond, money, and derivatives markets, comprising of commercial banks, financial institutions, and primary dealers in India. It represents members, promotes the development of these markets, works with regulators, adopts and develops international standard practices and a code of conduct, and undertakes development, training, and the standardization of best market practices.

International

Commercial Mortgage Securities Association
Chair: J. Christopher Hoeffel
30 Broad Street, 28th Floor, New York, NY 10004-2304, USA
T: +1 212 509 1844
F: +1 212 509 1895
E: info@cmsaglobal.org
www.cmsaglobal.org
This is an international, member-driven, trade association for the commercial real estate capital markets. It acts to promote the liquidity, and viability of commercial real estate capital market finance worldwide, and in setting industry standards, and educating professionals. It represents the full range of the industry's market participants, including senior bank executives, rating agencies, insurance companies, investors, lenders, and service providers.

International Capital Market Association
Chair: Hans-Joerg Rudloff
Talacker 29, PO Box, 8022 Zurich, Switzerland
T: +41 44 363 4222
F: +41 44 363 7772
www.icmagroup.org
ICMA is a self-regulatory organization that represents a broad range of capital market interests, including global investment banks, regional banks, asset managers, exchanges, central banks, law firms, and other professional advisers. Its market conventions and standards provide a framework of rules governing market practice, it promotes the capital markets by bringing together market participants, and also undertakes educational and research programs.

The International Organization of Securities Commissions
Chair: Jean-Pierre Jouyet
C/Oquendo 12, 28006 Madrid, Spain
T: +34 91 417 55 49
F: +34 91 555 93 68
E: mail@iosco.org
www.iosco.org
This international body promotes co-operation among securities commissions to assist high standards of regulation and just, efficient and sound markets, the exchange of information to promote the development of domestic markets, efforts to establish standards and effective surveillance of international securities transactions, and mutual assistance to promote the integrity of the markets by a rigorous application of the standards and by effective enforcement.

Securities Industry and Financial Markets Association
Chair: Timothy Ryan
120 Broadway, 35th Floor, New York, NY 10271-0080, USA
T: +1 212 313 1200
F: +1 212 313 1301
E: inquiry@sifma.org
www.sifma.org
SIFMA, created through a merger of the Bond Market Association and the Securities Industry Association, is a global, member-driven organization for professionals in the financial services industry. With offices in the US, Europe and Asia, it represents investment banks, broker-dealers, and asset managers, and other institutions, such as exchanges, government-sponsored enterprises, rating agencies, service providers, industry utilities, and law firms.

     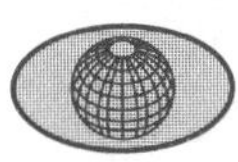   

Budgeting

BOOKS

Beyond Budgeting: How Managers Can Break Free from the Annual Performance Trap
Jeremy Hope, Robin Fraser
Boston, Massachusetts: Harvard Business School Press, 2003
256pp, ISBN: 978-1-57851-866-1
An enlightening read for all managers, not just finance specialists, this book posits that traditional budgeting processes are unproductive. Recognizing the fact that many executives are forced to spend their time "making the numbers work" rather than making the most of their company's potential, the book offers an alternative way forward. Case studies and findings from the Beyond Budgeting Roundtable are also included.

Budgeting Basics and Beyond, 3rd ed
Jae K. Shim, Joel G. Siegel
Chichester, UK: Wiley, 2008
448pp, ISBN: 978-0-470-38968-3
Budgeting Basics and Beyond provides the reader through every step to handle budgeting process. Some of the extra features include Balanced Scorecard, budgeting for nonprofit organizations, business simulations for executive and management training.

Budgeting: Technology, Trends, Software Selection and Implementation
Nils H. Rasmussen, Christopher J. Eichorn
New York: Wiley, 2000
304pp, ISBN: 978-0-471-39207-1
Describing itself as a guide to "essential budget planning for the 21st century corporation," this practically oriented book introduces and explains new trends in budgeting and budgeting software. By means of various report and contract samples, questionnaires, and interviews with leading managers, it guides the reader through the range of considerations that are crucial to streamlining the budget-planning process.

Capital Budgeting Decision: Economic Analysis of Investment Projects
Harold Bierman, Jr, Seymour Smidt
Abingdon, UK: Routledge, 2006
402pp, ISBN: 978-0-415-40004-6
This provides the corporate decision-maker with practical information on choices related to the elements of risk and time. It focuses on the theme of Net Present Value (NPV), and how it can be used as a single measure of value. It also covers areas such as distribution policy and capital budgeting, form investing in a second firm, and investing in current assets. The book is easy to understand and will enable readers to make smart capital budgeting decisions for any corporation.

Capital Budgeting: Theory and Practice
Pamela P. Peterson, Frank J. Fabozzi
New York: Wiley, 2002
243pp, ISBN: 978-0-471-21833-3
The book covers the underlying principles of capital budgeting, including discounted net cash-flows, risk assessment, and leases. It explains the importance of making wise decisions when investing in long-lived assets, and provides quantitative decision-making tools that assist managers in choosing between options.

Cash Flow Strategies: Innovation in Nonprofit Financial Management
Richard S. Linzer, Anna O. Linzer
San Francisco, California: Jossey-Bass, 2007
272pp, ISBN: 978-0-7879-8147-1
Cash Flow Strategies provides nonprofit organizations with new methods for handling financial management. It emphasizes the use of cash flow concepts that help an organization gain the working capital it needs. This book includes illustrative examples, tools, and templates which can be applied to any institution.

Cash Management: Making your Business Cash-Rich. . .Without Breaking the Bank
Tony Dalton
Business on a Shoestring Series
London: A&C Black Publishers, 2007
208pp, ISBN: 978-0-7136-7706-5
If you run your own business, keeping an eye on your cash is one of your most important tasks. Packed with ideas that really work, real-life examples, step-by-step advice and sources of further information.

Credit Risk Management: A Guide to Sound Business Decisions
H. A. Schaeffer, Jr
Chichester, UK: Wiley, 2000
288pp, ISBN: 978-0-471-35020-0
This book examines the steps leading to a sound business credit decision. It is divided into four main sections: analysis for creative credit management; building up essential business credit information; considering all factors that affect the business credit decision; and making a decision or recommendation. Detailed case studies are provided, illustrating common problems along with their solutions.

Foundations of Multinational Financial Management, 6th ed
Alan C. Shapiro, Atulya Sarin
Hoboken, New Jersey: Wiley, 2008
542pp, ISBN: 978-0-470-12895-4
This focuses on expansive practices, and provides a clear conceptual framework for analyzing key financial decisions in multinational firms. It treats international financial management as a natural and logical extension of the principles learned in the foundations course in financial management. It also builds on and extends the valuation framework provided by domestic corporate finance, to account for aspects that are unique to international finance.

Get to Grips with Budgets: How to Take the Stress Out of Working with Numbers
Steps to Success Series
London: A&C Black Publishers, 2005
96pp, ISBN: 978-0-7475-7734-8
Aimed at anyone who has to work with numbers but who feels uncomfortable with them, this is a practical and down-to-earth guide to budgeting. Featuring a special jargon-busting section, it covers a wide range of key issues including drawing up and managing budgets, keeping on top of costs, solving cash-flow problems, and interpreting balance sheets and profit and loss accounts.

Good Finance Guide for Small Businesses: How to Raise, Manage and Grow Your Company's Cash
London: A&C Black Publishers, 2007
288pp, ISBN: 978-0-7136-8209-0
Cash—or the lack of it—keeps small business owners awake at night more than anything else. This one-stop guide to small business finance is invaluable for anyone who needs to raise money to launch or grow a business, or manage the finances of one they run already. It covers five key areas: getting off the ground; managing your money; getting paid on time; company admin, tax and payroll, and coping in a crisis.

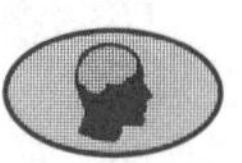

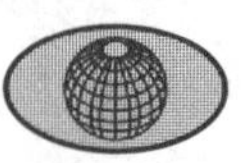

Implementing Beyond Budgeting: Unlocking the Performance Potential
Bjarte Bogsnes
Hoboken, New Jersey: Wiley, 2008
240pp, ISBN: 978-0-470-40516-1
Implementing Beyond Budgeting presents practices from real-life cases. It explains how an organization can fully utilize a performance climate with teams attaining the same target, rewards, and value creation, and examines how every organization can motivate the ambition and energy of its people under pressure from the budgeting process.

Management Accounting in Health Care Organizations, 2nd ed
David W. Young
San Francisco, California: Jossey-Bass, 2008
688pp, ISBN: 978-0-470-30021-3
This provides a clear understanding of accounting principles, concepts, and techniques that lead to managerial decision-making in health care. It also covers full-cost accounting, differential cost accounting, and responsibility accounting. Case-based problems are presented which highlight the lessons, and each chapter includes learning objectives, standard introductions, and key terms.

Managing by the Numbers
Chuck Kremer, Ron Rizzuto, John Case
Cambridge, Massachusetts: Perseus Books Group, 2000
198pp, ISBN: 978-0-7382-0256-3
In this text, Chuck Kremer and Ron Rizzuto present a practical approach to reading financial statements and to managing the three core issues of business financial performance: net profit, operating cash-flow, and return on assets. The book features numerous exercises and examples (with associated templates available on the web), a powerful new management tool known as The Financial Scoreboard, and an extensive glossary.

Mastering Spreadsheet Budgets and Forecasts: How to Save Time and Gain Control of Your Business
Malcolm Secrett
Smarter Solutions Series
Harlow, UK: FT Prentice Hall, 1999
272pp, ISBN: 978-0-273-64491-0
This step-by-step, jargon-free guide demonstrates the advantages and potential of using spreadsheets to prepare and present budgets and forecasts. It includes examples of budgets and forecasts, followed through completely from beginning to end.

Total Business Budgeting: A Step-by-Step Guide with Forms, 2nd ed
Robert Rachlin
Chichester, UK: Wiley, 1999
321pp, ISBN: 978-0-471-35103-0
Rachlin provides an introduction to a wide range of budgetary techniques and applications and shows how to analyze outside influences, develop performance targets and budgeting segments, and administer the right budgeting processes. He includes detailed instructions, forms, examples, schedules, and formats.

MAGAZINES

Business Performance Management
Penton Technology Media
221 East 29th Street, Loveland, CO 80538, USA
T: +1 847 763 9504
F: +1 913 514 3621
bpmmag.net
ISSN: 1556-813X
BPM magazine educates business, finance, and IT employees about the opportunities for changing their organization's effectiveness through the application of BPM processes. It includes analysis and advice on BPM best practices, industry trends, and research results, as well as features such as case studies where corporate users of BPM explain how they fully utilize these processes and technologies. It is published quarterly.

CMA Management
Certified Management Accountants of Canada
1 Robert Speck Parkway, Suite 1400, Mississauga, ON, L4Z 3M3, Canada
T: +1 905 949 4200
F: +1 905 949 0888
www.managementmag.com
ISSN: 1490-4225
CMA is a monthly magazine that covers all aspects of management. It includes trends, views, media, business strategies, government issues and global views.

Strategic Finance
Institute of Management Accountants
10 Paragon Drive, Suite 1, Montvale, NJ 07645, USA
T: +1 201 573 9000
F: +1 201 474 1600
www.imanet.org/publications_sfm.asp
ISSN: 1524-833X
Strategic Finance magazine provides information about practices and trends in finance, accounting, and information management that will impact members (mostly controllers, CFOs, and their staff) and their jobs. It offers advice to help financial professionals perform their jobs more effectively, advance their careers, grow personally and professionally, and make their organizations more profitable.

INTERNET

Accountants World
www.accountantsworld.com
This is an extensive portal based in the United States with links to a wide range of websites of interest to accountants. It relates mainly to US accounting practice.

Accounting Web
www.accountingweb.co.uk
This site is an extensive online resource based in the United Kingdom. It contains material intended for accountancy and finance professionals from a number of providers. It has received an award as the New Media Business Website of the Year.

CFO.com—Tools and Resources for Financial Executives
www.cfo.com
CFO.com is a great resource for anyone in a business financial setting. With multiple articles to read, CFO.com also has a newsletter, webcasts, and a magazine, which was named Magazine of the Year by the American Society of Business Publication Editors (ASBPE).

The Dyer Partnership
www.dyerpartnership.us
The site provides a wide range of information on UK tax and accounting matters and other business issues of interest to owners and managers of UK businesses.

Institute of Management Accountants
www.imanet.org
This is the website of the Institute of Management Accountants (IMA), a professional organization that promotes management accounting and financial management. The IMA is responsible for the education and certification of professionals involved in management accounting, including operational and capital budgeting responsibilities. Members of the IMA receive information and educational materials on financial budgeting and control, capital budgeting, and management accounting topics.

ORGANIZATIONS

Europe

Institute of Credit Management (ICM)
The Water Mill, Station Road, South Luffenham, Oakham, Leicestershire, LE15 8NB, UK
T: +44 (0) 1780 722 900
F: +44 (0) 1780 721 333
E: info@icm.org.uk
www.icm.org.uk
The Institute of Credit Management (ICM) is the largest organization of credit professionals in Europe, and the focal point in the United Kingdom for all matters relating to credit management and its ancillary functions. The ICM sets professional standards and tests and assesses those who wish to gain its professional qualification. It also provides advice to government and other national bodies.

Institute of Financial Accountants (IFA)
Burford House, 44 London Road, Sevenoaks, Kent, TN13 1AS, UK
T: +44 (0) 1732 458 080
F: +44 (0) 1732 455 848
E: mail@ifa.org.uk
www.ifa.org.uk
The Institute of Financial Accountants, established in 1916, is the largest professional body of its type in the world. It represents members and students in more than 80 countries around the world and provides a qualification and continuing professional development for those who want to become financial accountants. It also sets both technical and ethical standards within the profession.

BRIC

The Association of Certified Treasury Managers
52, Nagarjuna Hills, Panjagutta, Hyderabad, 500 082, India
T: +91 040 335 3411/1071/3748
E: k_seethapathi@actmindia.org
ACTM is a non-profit society that helps to develop new treasury professionals through a certification program in treasury and forex management and standards for professional practice and ethics. It develops and regulates the growth of the profession of treasury management on sound ethical lines, organizes seminars, workshops and training programs in treasury management, foreign exchange management, risk management and allied areas, undertakes research, and offers industry publications.

The National Association of Financial Market Institutions
Av. República do Chile, 230/13o andar, Centro, Rio de Janeiro 20031–170, Brazil
T: +55 21 3814 3800
F: +55 21 3814 3960
E: brazildebt@fazenda.gov.br
ANDIMA is a non-profit civil entity that brings together several financial institutions in Brazil. It is a service-provider, offering technical and operating support to these institutions, provides daily monitoring of market behavior with the dissemination of statistical data, monitoring legislation, preparing analyses, studies and reports on key economic issues, and produces a program of professional training.

     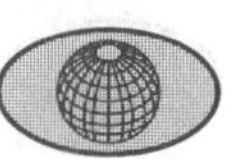   

Business Appraisal and Performance Measurement

BOOKS

Assessing Business Excellence: A Guide to Self Assessment, 2nd ed
Les Porter, Steve Tanner
Oxford: Butterworth-Heinemann, 2004
451pp, ISBN: 978-0-7506-5517-0
A strategic framework to help companies achieve business excellence and total quality management is presented in this well-informed guide. The main quality frameworks are introduced and compared, before the self-assessment process is examined.

The Balanced Scorecard
Robert S. Kaplan, David P. Norton
Boston, Massachusetts: Harvard Business School Press, 1996
322pp, ISBN: 978-0-87584-651-4
This book demonstrates to managers how to utilize their people to fulfill the company's mission. It shows how to channel the energies, abilities, and specific knowledge belonging to each individual into the achievement of long-term strategic goals for the company. The balanced scorecard is a measurement tool, but it is also a management tool for investing in the long term in customers, employees, new product development, and systems.

The Balanced Scorecard Step-by-Step: Maximizing Performance and Maintaining Results, 2nd ed
Paul R. Niven
Chichester, UK: Wiley, 2006
336pp, ISBN: 978-0-471-78049-6
This book gives valuable advice on developing a performance management system. Areas covered in this text include: the development of performance objectives and measures; the finalizing of cause and effect links; methods of embedding the balanced scorecard in the organization and sustaining its implementation; and procedures for implementing the balanced scorecard in nonprofit and public sector organizations.

Beyond Registration: Getting the Best from ISO9001 and Business Improvement, 3rd ed
Steve Tanner, Mike Bailey, Charles Pertwee
London: British Standards Institution, 2007
120pp, ISBN: 978-0-580-50363-4
The first part of this book covers ISO9001 and the Malcolm Baldrige EFQM excellence models, while the second looks at a wide range of business improvement approaches, including the balanced scorecard, benchmarking, business process reengineering, Charter Mark, failure mode effect analysis, Investors in People, kaizen/continuous improvement, Six Sigma, statistical process control, theory of constraints, total productive maintenance, and total quality management (TQM).

Business Performance Measurement: Unifying Theory and Integrating Practice, 2nd ed
Andy Neely (editor)
Cambridge, UK: Cambridge University Press, 2008
528pp, ISBN: 978-0-521-85511-2
Drawing together contributions from leading thinkers around the world, this reviews recent developments in the theory and practice of performance measurement and management. Significantly updated and modified from the first edition, it includes 10 new chapters which review performance measurement from the perspectives of accounting, marketing, operations, public services, and supply-chain management.

Corporate Valuation: Tools for Effective Appraisal and Decision Making
Bradford Cornell
Business One Series
Maidenhead, UK: McGraw-Hill, 1993
303pp, ISBN: 978-1-55623-730-0
This book illustrates the best practices for measuring and predicting value by combining the science of business appraisal with the art of perceived value. It provides a tool for comparing various valuation techniques, and shows how to rethink the investment process into the future.

Cost Benefit Analysis: Concepts and Practice
Anthony E. Boardman, David H. Greenberg, Aidan R. Vining, David Leo Weimer
Harlow, UK: Prentice Hall, 2005
560pp, ISBN: 978-0-13-143583-4
This book includes a number of up-to-date illustrations and examples to show how theories and techniques are applied to real-world situations. It provides readers with a practical orientation and introduction to cost-benefit analysis through problem solving. There are problems and exercises at the end of all chapters.

Determining Value: Valuation Models and Financial Statements
Richard Barker
Harlow, UK: FT Prentice Hall, 2001
232pp, ISBN: 978-0-273-63979-4
This is designed for members of the professional and private investment community, including stockbrokers, fund managers, corporate financiers and bankers, and advanced students of finance and accounting. It provides a comprehensive overview of valuation methods such as price-earnings ratio, dividend yield and EVA (economic value added), and analyzes the quality and availability of the financial data used in these models. It also covers stock market valuation, dividends and stock prices, price-earnings ratio, measuring earnings, measuring return on capital, and cash-flow models from stockholder value analysis to cash-flow return on investment (CFROI).

Essentials of Balanced Scorecard
Mohan Nair
Essentials Series
Chichester, UK: Wiley, 2004
248pp, ISBN: 978-0-471-56973-2
Taking simplicity as a guiding principle, this sets out to help managers understand the fundamentals of the balanced scorecard. The concept is introduced and the four perspectives that make up the methodology are outlined. The relationship of the balanced scorecard to strategy and performance management is also examined. It also identifies and describes six factors that make for success in implementing the balanced scorecard and discusses the 11 deadly sins that can lead to failure.

Essentials of Corporate Performance Measurement
George T. Friedlob, Lydia L. F. Schleifer, Franklin J. Plewa
Essentials Series
New York: Wiley, 2002
216pp, ISBN: 978-0-471-20375-9
The most common way to evaluate the success of investment is by measuring the return on investment (ROI). This practical guide explains the importance of ROI and examines its use to analyze performance. Different forms of ROI are described and its use in analyzing sales revenues, costs, and profits is considered. The techniques of return on technology investment (ROTI

  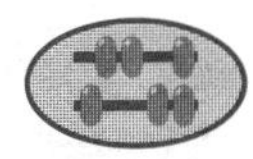   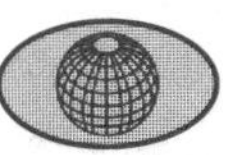   

and ROIT) are also covered, as are residual performance measures (RI and EVA).

The EVA Challenge: Implementing Value-Added Change in an Organization
Joel M. Stern, John S. Shiely, Irwin Ross
New York: Wiley, 2001
256pp, ISBN: 978-0-471-40555-9
The authors outline how to implement EVA and customize it for individual organizations. EVA, which encompasses measurement, incentives, and a financial management system, aims to measure a company's time economic performance and wealth-creating strategy. Case studies are also included.

Evaluation in Organizations: A Systematic Approach to Enhancing Learning, Performance, and Change
Darlene Russ-Eft, Hallie Preskill
Cambridge, Massachusetts: Perseus Books Group, 2001
416pp, ISBN: 978-0-7382-0268-6
This book is a guide to the context of evaluation and to its implementation in a three-phase system. It includes an audit mechanism and comprehensive resources.

Harvard Business Review on Measuring Corporate Performance
Harvard Business Review Paperbacks Series
Boston, Massachusetts: Harvard Business School Press, 1998
224pp, ISBN: 978-0-87584-882-2
A collection of articles from leading management thinkers, this book shows how to evaluate performance measures and discusses the importance of aligning corporate strategy with them. It includes discussion of the balanced scorecard, customer relationships, internal business processes, and employee learning.

How to Use The Model: Implementing the EFQM Excellence Model
British Quality Foundation
London: British Quality Foundation, 2002
48pp, ISBN: 978-1-899358-50-2
This booklet provides an introduction to the EFQM business excellence model, describes in detail the criteria used in it, and sets out the procedures that an organization needs to consider, plan, and complete. It should help anyone who is trying to raise awareness of the Excellence Model within their organization, encourage self-assessment, and improve the organization's efficiency and effectiveness.

Implementing Global Performance Measurement Systems: A Cookbook Approach to Evaluation
Ferdinand Tesoro, Jack Tootson
San Francisco, California: Jossey-Bass, 2000
176pp, ISBN: 978-0-7879-4744-6
This practical guide presents a step-by-step approach to evaluating and measuring ongoing business performance. Following an overview of performance measurement, it examines how to establish the business case, identify the right performance metrics, implement the performance measurement system, and leverage results to improve performance. Guidance is offered on constructing a line graph, a cause–effect diagram, and a scatter diagram.

Making Scorecards Actionable: Balancing Strategy and Control
Nils-Goran Olve et al.
Chichester, UK: Wiley, 2003
304pp, ISBN: 978-0-470-84871-5
Focusing on the experiences of a broad range of companies and looks at the challenges and key design issues that emerge as scorecards are put into operation. Practical guidance on operational issues is provided, which covers assigning roles and responsibilities, balancing the incentive system, and using IT. Case studies of a number of well-known companies such as Skandia, British Airways, Ericsson, Xerox, Volvo, and Hewlett Packard are included.

Natural Capitalism: Creating the Next Industrial Revolution
Paul Hawken, Amory Lovins, L. Hunter Lovins
Boston, Massachusetts: Back Bay Books, 2000
396pp, ISBN: 978-0-316-35300-7
This discusses how top companies are carrying out a modern form of industrialism which runs more smoothly, increases profits, lessens damage to the environment, and creates more jobs. They call this system "natural capitalism" and give several examples of organizations which have benefited the environment.

Oliver Wight ABCD Checklist for Operational Excellence, 5th ed
Oliver Wight International
New York: Wiley, 2000
167pp, ISBN: 978-0-471-38819-7
The Oliver Wight ABCD Checklists are a widely recognized tool used by organizations as part of an appraisal of their performance. The aim of this checklist is to become an industry standard for operational performance measurement. Beginning with an explanation of the use of the performance measures, the assessment tool then focuses on strategic planning, people and teams, total quality and continuous improvement, new product development, and planning and control.

The Organizational Measurement Manual
David Wealleans
Aldershot, UK: Gower Publishing, 2001
178pp, ISBN: 978-0-566-08349-5
Divided into three parts—the concept of measurement, establishing a process measurement program, and looking beyond the basics—this book gives a guide to performance measurements at the working level. It identifies procedures for using measurements and shows how to relate them to organizational objectives and initiatives. Wealleans demonstrates a best-practice approach, and illustrates his text with figures and tables throughout.

Performance Scorecards
Richard Y. Chang, Mark W. Morgan
San Francisco, California: Jossey-Bass, 2000
224pp, ISBN: 978-0-7879-5272-3
The authors contend that many corporations have too many performance measurements, which causes them to lose sight of the ones that are really important. They advocate customizing performance scorecards to suit an organization's strategy. The book uses a fictional storyline to illustrate the six steps that go into performance scorecards: collect, create, cultivate, cascade, connect, and confirm.

Strategy-focused Organization: How Balanced Scorecard Companies Thrive in the New Business Environment
Robert S. Kaplan, David P. Norton
Boston, Massachusetts: Harvard Business School Press, 2001
400pp, ISBN: 978-1-57851-250-8
This book presents case studies of over twenty companies that have adopted the balanced scorecard approach. Five principles for strategy-focused organizations, drawn from their experiences, are outlined in this text. These are: translating the strategy into operational terms; aligning the organization to strategy; making strategy everyone's everyday job; making strategy a continual process; and mobilizing change through effective leadership.

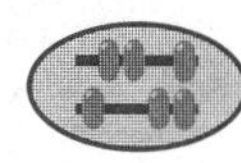

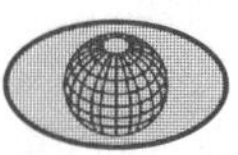

Strategy Maps: Converting Intangible Assets into Tangible Outcomes
Robert S. Kaplan, David P. Norton
Boston, Massachusetts: Harvard Business School Press, 2004
454pp, ISBN: 978-1-59139-134-0
This book explores what a strategy map is—a tool that can provide the missing link between strategy formulation and implementation. Derived from the balanced scorecard technique devised by the authors, *Strategy Maps* provides a blueprint for describing, measuring, and aligning tangible assets for superior performance. Through numerous examples of private, public, and nonprofit organizations, the process of creating customized strategy maps is explained.

Total Performance Scorecard: Redefining Management to Achieve Performance with Integrity
Hubert K. Rampersad
Oxford: Butterworth-Heinemann, 2003
336pp, ISBN: 978-0-7506-7714-1
Rampersad introduces a new concept of improvement and change management called the Total Performance Scorecard (TPS). This model integrates aspects of the balanced scorecard, total quality management and competence management. It is based around a cyclical process of continuous improvement, development, and learning and also takes account of the connections between personal and organizational development. Model appraisal forms and scorecard questions are included in appendices.

Valuation: Measuring and Managing the Value of Companies, 4th ed
Tim Koller, Marc Goedhart, David Wessels
Chichester, UK: Wiley, 2005
768pp, ISBN: 978-0-471-70218-4
At the crossroads of corporate strategy and finance lies valuation. And in today's economy, whether you're a seasoned manager or a budding business professional, it's essential to excel at measuring, managing, and maximizing shareholder and company value. This book explains how to do just that.

Valuation Workbook: Step-by-Step Exercises and Tests to Help You Master Valuation, 4th ed
Tim Koller, Marc Goedhart, David Wessels, Jeffrey P. Lessard
Chichester, UK: Wiley, 2006
200pp, ISBN: 978-0-471-70216-0
The ideal companion to *Valuation*. This comprehensive study guide provides you with an invaluable opportunity to explore your understanding of the strategies and techniques covered in the main text, before putting it to work in real-world situations.

The Value Mindset: Returning to the First Principles of Capitalist Enterprise
Erik Stern, Mike Hutchinson
Chichester, UK: Wiley, 2004
456pp, ISBN: 978-0-471-65029-4
In *The Value Mindset* the authors present their ideas as to how companies can transform themselves to deliver value and returns to shareholders. Building on their experience of EVA (Economic Value Added) programs at Stern Stewart, they explain the development of the WAI (Wealth Added Index) performance metric and illustrate the concept of the value mindset through real-world success stories, such as those of Isadore Sharp at the Four Seasons hotel chain and Roberto Goizueta at Coca-Cola. The theory and practice of strategic reconfiguration is described, and a number of related issues including financial architecture and the motivation of managers and employees are explored.

Valuing a Business: The Analysis and Appraisal of Closely-Held Companies, 5th ed
Shannon P. Pratt, Robert F. Reilly, Robert P. Schweihs
Maidenhead, UK: McGraw-Hill, 2008
1000pp, ISBN: 978-0-07-144180-3
This latest edition, originally published in 1981, includes significant revisions and ten new chapters. Its coverage now extends to topics such as credentials and standards, analyzing financial statements, control and acquisition premiums, valuing debt securities and litigation support. The book is a standard reference for defining the methodology of business valuation—for businesses of all sizes—and then arriving at an accurate and supportable estimation of value.

MAGAZINES

Balanced Scorecard Report
Harvard Business School Press
PO Box 257, Shrub Oak, NY 10588-0257, USA
T: +1 800 668 6705
F: +1 914 962 1338
hbp.harvardbusiness.org/ep
ISSN: 1526-145X
This monthly newsletter, developed in conjunction with David S. Kaplan and David P. Norton, creators of the balanced scorecard, provides the latest research and implementation news from companies using the balanced scorecard management system.

The Value Examiner
The National Association of Certified Valuation Analysts
1111 Brickyard Road, Suite 200, Salt Lake City, UT 84106-5401, USA
T: +1 801 486 0600
F: +1 801 486 7500
www.nacva.com/examiner/examiner.asp
This bimonthly magazine focuses on the latest developments regarding industry issues. It covers a variety of industry related topics, such as trends, forecasts and the latest technology resources, and provides the resources needed for business appraisal professionals.

JOURNALS

Business Valuation Review
American Society of Appraisers
555 Herndon Parkway, Suite 125, Herndon, VI 20170, USA
T: +1 703 478 2228
F: +1 703 742 8471
www.bvappraisers.org/issuestore
ISSN: 0882-2875
This quarterly journal features articles on the practice and theory of appraisal. The articles present various opinions on the latest trends in business. The journal will be beneficial for any business valuation professional.

Performance Evaluation: An International Journal
Elsevier
Radarweg 29, Amsterdam 1043 NX, The Netherlands
T: +31 20 485 3911
F: +31 20 485 2457
www.elsevier.com/locate/peva
ISSN: 0166-5316
This journal provides information relative to performance aspects, promotes interdisciplinary flow of technical information among researchers and professionals, and serves as a publication medium for various special interest groups in the performance community at large.

INTERNET

Balanced Scorecard Collaborative
www.thepalladiumgroup.com
The website of Robert Kaplan and David Norton, creators of the balanced scorecard. Their professional services company provides training, networking events, and BSC software certification. The bimonthly *Balanced Scorecard Report* magazine is also available to members through the website.

  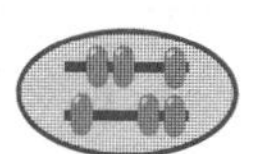 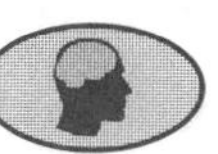  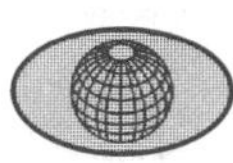   

College of Performance Management
www.pmi-cpm.org
Sponsored by a nonprofit professional organization, the site offers news, information about events and conferences, and links.

Execution Premium
hbp.harvardbusiness.org/ep/
The website of performance Gurus Robert S. Kaplan and David P. Norton, which contains their blog, publication information, and other resources.

Interthink Consulting, Inc.
www.interthink.ca
Sponsored by a Canadian consulting firm, the site includes research on topics including assessment, processes, training, and implementation, and a newsletter of industry events.

ORGANIZATIONS

Europe

British Chambers of Commerce
65 Petty France, London, SW1H 9EU, UK
T: +44 (0) 20 7654 5800
F: +44 (0) 20 7654 5819
E: info@britishchambers.org.uk
www.britishchambers.org.uk
This is an umbrella body for a national network of chambers of commerce serving local businesses and providing advice on exporting and export services to member companies.

British Quality Foundation (BQF)
32–34 Great Peter Street, London, SW1P 2QX, UK
T: +44 (0) 20 7654 5000
F: +44 (0) 20 7654 5001
www.quality-foundation.co.uk
The BQF is a nonprofit membership organization that promotes business excellence to other public and private sector organizations in the United Kingdom. It undertakes numerous activities in pursuit of this aim, most of which have the Business Excellence Model at their core. It also sponsors the UK Business Excellence Award.

European Foundation for Quality Management (EFQM)
Avenue des Pléiades 15, 1200 Brussels, Belgium
T: +33 2 775 35 11
F: +33 2 775 35 35
E: info@efqm.org
www.efqm.org
The EFQM introduced the European Excellence Model in the early 1990s to help businesses assess and improve their performance.

USA

American Society of Appraisers (ASA)
555 Herndon Parkway, Suite 125, Herndon, VI 20170, USA
T: +1 703 478 2228
F: +1 703 742 8471
E: asainfo@appraisers.org
www.appraisers.org
Founded in 1952, this organization has more than 6,000 members. ASA is a professional appraisal educator and represents all the disciplines of appraisal specialists. The society requires a mandatory certification program for all of its members, including the ASA Ethics Exam and the Uniform Standards of Professional Appraisal Practice Examination.

Institute of Business Appraisers (IBA)
PO Box 17410, Plantation, FL 33318, USA
T: +1 954 584 1144
F: +1 954 584 1184
E: ibahq@go-iba.org
www.go-iba.org
Established in 1978, the Institute of Business Appraisers is the oldest professional society devoted to the appraisal of closely held businesses. It is a nationally recognized organization with a membership of over 3,000, and seeks to educate the public in all aspects of business valuation and appraisal, and is involved in monitoring and supporting national legislation that affects the business valuation community.

MeasureNet
2115 West Lawn Avenue, Madison, WI 53711, USA
T: +1 608 256 9993
F: +1 435 304 8452
E: greg@measure.net
www.measure.net
This organization is concerned with extending and improving corporate performance measurement strategies. It provides information for measuring performance within a company, and for managing a business. To this end, it is involved in research, education and consulting services, and also conducts various seminars and courses.

The National Association of Certified Valuation Analysts (NACVA)
1111 Brickyard Road, Suite 200, Salt Lake City, UT 84106–5401, USA
T: +1 801 486 0600
F: +1 801 486 7500
E: nacva1@nacva.com
www.nacva.com
Supports the users of business and intangible asset valuation services and financial forensic services, including damages determinations of all kinds and fraud detection and prevention, by training and certifying financial professionals in these disciplines. NACVA training includes Continuing Professional Education (CPE) credit and is available to both members and non-members.

International

Foundation for Performance Measurement (FPM)
c/o Metapraxis Ltd, Hanover House, Coombe Road, Kingston-Upon-Thames, Surrey, KT2 7AH, UK
T: +44 (0) 20 8541 1696
F: +44 (0) 20 8546 2105
E: info@fpm.com
www.fpm.com
With both UK and US Chapters, this foundation serves as a source of information, a forum for research and debate, and as a link to tools and resources for organizations interested in developing practical new ways of measuring enterprise performance. It links businesses that have successfully implemented new performance measures with those that are endeavoring to do.

     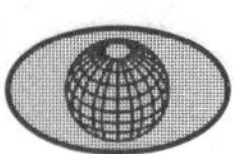   

Business Ethics and Codes of Practice

BOOKS

Absolute Honesty: Building a Corporate Culture That Values Straight Talk and Rewards Integrity

Larry Johnson, Bob Phillips
New York: AMACOM, 2003
304pp, ISBN: 978-0-8144-0781-3

This book starts out from the belief that honesty can produce economic as well as moral rewards, in terms of improved productivity, competitive advantage, morale, and public trust. It asserts the need to reestablish a culture of openness and truth in communication methods, grounded in absolute honesty. To this end it sets out a framework of six laws of absolute honesty and gives advice on implementing them within an ethical infrastructure.

Business Ethics and Ethical Business

Robert Audi
New York: Oxford University Press, 2009
176pp, ISBN: 978-0-19-536910-6

Business Ethics and Ethical Business gives a concise introduction and is organized into three parts that cover the role of business in society, the ethics of internal management, and the challenges of international business. It introduces the standards essential in business ethics, explores a wide range of issues using concrete examples, and provides analytical tools for guiding ethical decisions in the real world. Its features include short case scenarios, explanation of different ethics, and a glossary of many key terms in business ethics.

Business Ethics and Values: Individual, Corporate and International Perspectives, 3rd ed

Colin Fisher, Alan Lovell
Harlow, UK: FT Prentice Hall, 2008
640pp, ISBN: 978-0-273-71616-7

Fisher and Lovell offer the reader a comprehensive introduction to the ideas and complexities of ethics in the contemporary business world. It ensures a relevancy for today's business students through the inclusion of frequent interesting examples and activities, helping consideration of ethical questions.

Business Ethics: Ethical Decision Making and Cases, 7th ed

O. C. Ferrell, John Fraedrich, Linda Ferrell
Boston, Massachusetts: Houghton Mifflin, 2007
496pp, ISBN: 978-0-618-74934-8

Business Ethics: Ethical Decision Making and Cases consists of text and cases that offer a critically-based clear approach to workplace ethics. Its purpose is to help the reader make an informed ethical decision without depending on any particular philosophy or process. It also covers dilemmas, ethical decision-making frameworks, behavioral simulations, interactive games, e-ethics sites, and self tests.

Business Ethics: Managing Corporate Citizenship and Sustainability in the Age of Globalization, 2nd ed

Andrew Cane, Dirk Matten
Oxford: Oxford University Press, 2007
592pp, ISBN: 978-0-19-928499-3

Business Ethics covers the foundations of business ethics and applying these theories, concepts, and tools to each of the corporation's major stakeholders. It is written from a European perspective, and considers the implications of three major challenges facing the corporation: corporate citizenship, globalization and sustainability. This second edition has been thoroughly revised and updated, and includes new content on personal values and Asian perspectives.

Business Ethics: The Ethical Revolution of Minority Shareholders

Jacques Cory
Dordrecht, The Netherlands: Springer, 2005
269pp, ISBN: 978-0-387-23040-5

This book deals with the relationships between companies and minority stockholders, from the perspective of business ethics. It highlights the inefficiency of traditional safeguards of the rights of small stockholders and discusses the new "vehicles" that can bring about an ethical revolution for minority shareholders and tilt the balance in their favor. It provides cases of companies to show how minority stockholders can lose their investments. The purpose is to analyze why and how companies do not act ethically towards their minority shareholders, not how many, not which, not to what degree and not where.

Developing a Code of Business Ethics: A Guide to Best Practice including the IBE Illustrative Code of Business Ethics

Simon Webley
London: Institute of Business Ethics, 2003
64pp, ISBN: 978-0-9539517-4-1

This pamphlet provides a practical step-by-step guide to developing a code of business ethics. Webley argues the case for introducing a code, and discusses the issues involved in developing one, including ethical dilemmas and cross-cultural problems. The IBE Illustrative Code of Business Ethics, which includes checklists and sample wordings, is presented as a guide. A number of sample codes are included in an appendix.

Does Business Ethics Pay? Ethics and Financial Performance

Simon Webley, Elise More
London: Institute of Business Ethics, 2003
64pp, ISBN: 978-0-9539517-3-4

This pamphlet reports on research undertaken to measure the commitment to ethics and corporate responsibility of certain businesses and to compare the results against financial performance measures. It concludes that there is strong evidence to indicate that larger UK companies with codes of ethics outperform those without codes on the basis of both financial and other indicators. A summary of related research is also included, together with a glossary and sources of further information.

The Earthscan Reader in Business and Sustainable Development

Richard Starkey, Richard Welford (editors)
London: Earthscan, 2001
364pp, ISBN: 978-1-85383-659-6

This collection of work by leading authors in the field of business and sustainable development contains 17 chapters in sections covering business opportunities, environmental accounting, critical perspectives, and trade and sustainable development.

Just Business: Business Ethics in Action, 2nd ed

Elaine Sternberg
Oxford: Oxford University Press, 2000
320pp, ISBN: 978-0-19-829663-8

The author presents an ethical decision model that can be used as a conceptual framework for resolving questions of business ethics and corporate governance in all their variety and complexity. The book is intended for active businessmen and presupposes no knowledge of philosophy, it provides a reasoned philosophical approach to determining what constitutes ethical conduct in business.

Leading with Soul, 2nd ed
Lee G. Bolman, Terrence E. Deal
Chichester, UK: Wiley, 2001
272pp, ISBN: 978-0-7879-5547-2
This is a contemporary parable about an executive's quest for passion and purpose in work and in life. The authors draw upon many spiritual traditions, poetry, philosophy, and social science teachings on leadership and organizations. They demonstrate how to lead with soul and how to ignite the soul of an organization. This second edition has a new introduction, new material, and includes letters written by readers of the first edition.

Managing Business Ethics: Straight Talk About How to Do It Right, 4th ed
Linda K. Trevino, Katherine A. Nelson
Hoboken, New Jersey: Wiley, 2007
407pp, ISBN: 978-0-471-75525-8
Managing Business Ethics offers a practical examination of ethics in the workplace, and presents a guide to identifying and solving ethical dilemmas. It also explains why people behave in a certain way and how to design a culture that promotes ethical behavior.

Managing Values and Beliefs in Organisations
Tom McEwan
Harlow, UK: FT Prentice Hall, 2001
408pp, ISBN: 978-0-273-64340-1
This is a book, written as a student text, that summarizes the origins of corporate responsibility, business ethics, and corporate governance, and reviews the similarities and differences between them. The specific issues covered include: moral meaning and applied ethics; values, beliefs, and ideologies; individual morality in organizations; unethical behavior by individuals; international business and the developing world; ethical investment; organization culture and stakeholder theory; and corporate social performance, ethical leadership, and reputation management.

Perspectives on Corporate Social Responsibility
David Crowther, Lez Rayman-Bacchus (editors)
Aldershot, UK: Ashgate Publishing, 2004
264pp, ISBN: 978-0-7546-3886-5
This book aims to explore different perspectives on what is meant by corporate social responsibility (CSR), based on the experiences of people in different parts of the world. Contributors investigate the theoretical aspects of socially responsible behavior, its application in practice, and its ethical dimension. Specific topics covered include: assessing trust in, and the legitimacy of, the Corporate; limited liability or limited responsibility; the power of networks—organizing versus organization; and social performance in government.

Private Business, Public Battleground: The Case for 21st Century Stakeholder Companies
John Egan, Des Wilson
Basingstoke, UK: Palgrave, 2002
210pp, ISBN: 978-0-333-92939-1
The authors put forward the view that companies can no longer operate in isolation from the world around them, or ignore the concerns of their stakeholders. The relationship between business and the community is explored, covering the impact of global capitalism, environmental sustainability, the rise of the stakeholder company, and corporate citizenship. A case history of BAA (formerly the British Airports Authority) is also included.

Trust or Consequences: Build Trust Today or Lose Your Market Tomorrow
Al Golin
New York: AMACOM, 2006
248pp, ISBN: 978-0-8144-7388-7
In a climate of public skepticism toward business there is a need for organization to create a trust bank of goodwill to communicate that they are trustworthy, it is claimed. This book deals with the creation of trust strategies using the author's tried-and-tested methods in various international organizations. The book's three sections cover, respectively, an assessment of external and internal trends that have contributed to the debate; the steps organizations can take; and a framework of strategies and scenarios for action. Case studies are also included.

Value Shift: Why Companies Must Merge Social and Financial Imperatives to Achieve Superior Performance
Lynn Sharp Paine
New York: McGraw-Hill, 2003
304pp, ISBN: 978-0-07-142733-3
This book argues the case for a new style of management that will align company performance with today's ethical standards. It argues that there is now a dichotomy between traditional management and the expectations of business in contemporary society. Acknowledging it is no longer enough simply to produce goods and services and create wealth, the author discusses today's corporate leaders' need to make a shift in management values to incorporate high ethical standards along with strong financial results.

What Matters Most? Business Social Responsibility and the End of the Era of Greed
Jeffrey Hollender, Stephen Fenichell
London: Random House, 2004
240pp, ISBN: 978-1-84413-397-0
Jeffrey Hollender, CEO of Seventh Generation, a world leader in manufacturing environmentally friendly household products, is a frequent commentator on corporate responsibility. This book, coauthored with Stephen Fenichell, puts forward an approach to corporate strategy that is said to help integrate concerns related to social responsibility into an organization's culture, systems, and activities.

Working Ethics: Strategies for Decision Making and Organizational Responsibility
Marvin T. Brown
San Francisco, California: Jossey-Bass, 2000
219pp, ISBN: 978-1-889059-55-6
This book explores the role of ethics as a tool in decision-making, showing how ethical behavior can improve organizational effectiveness by fostering open communications, resolving disputes, and enhancing employee–management relations. It highlights the fact that arguments centering on an open expression of disagreements can lead to better relations, and provides examples and practical exercises for building an organization that makes morally and socially responsible decisions.

JOURNALS

Business and Professional Ethics Journal
Public Interest Enterprises
PO Box 15017, Gainesville, FL 32604, USA
T: +1 325 392 2084
F: +1 325 392 0057
ISSN: 0277-2027
Published four times each year, this journal contains articles that focus on the ethical issues encountered by business professionals working in large organizations.

Business and Society Review
Wiley Periodicals
350 Main Street, Malden, MA 02148, USA
T: +1 781 388 8598
www.wiley.com/bw/journal.asp?ref=0045-3609
ISSN: 0045-3609

  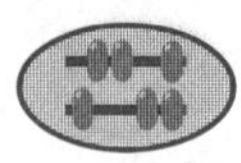   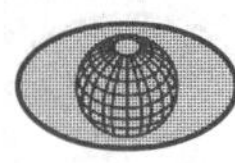   

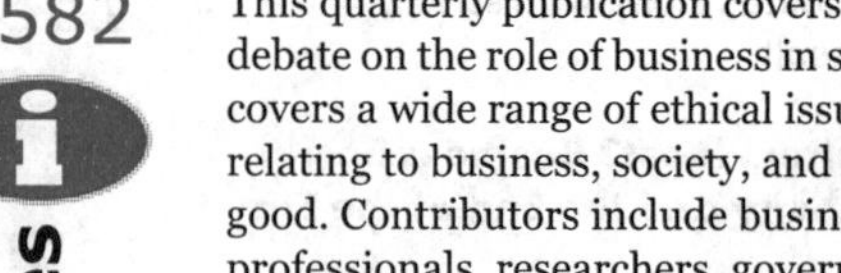

This quarterly publication covers the debate on the role of business in society and covers a wide range of ethical issues relating to business, society, and the public good. Contributors include business professionals, researchers, government administrators, and legal experts.

Business Ethics: A European Review
Blackwell Publishing
9600 Garsington Road, Oxford, OX4 2DQ, UK
T: +44 (0) 1865 791 100
F: +44 (0) 1865 791 347
www.wiley.com/bw/journal.asp?ref=0962-8770
ISSN: 0962-8770
Offering rigorous analysis of ethical issues faced by business worldwide, this quarterly is primarily an academic research journal. However, it is readable and user-friendly, and its focus is not exclusively European.

Business Ethics Quarterly: The Journal of the Society for Business Ethics
Philosophy Documentation Center
Society for Business Ethics, Philosophy Documentation Center, PO Box 7147, Charlottesville, VI 22906-7147, USA
T: +1 434 220 3300 or 800 444 2419
F: +1 434 220 3301
www.pdcnet.org/beq.html
ISSN: 1052-150X
This learned peer-reviewed journal explores the application of ethics to international business. It focuses on theoretical and methodological questions that can advance ethical inquiry and enhance the ethical performance of business organizations.

Journal of Business Ethics
Springer
PO Box 358, Dordrecht, 3300 AA, The Netherlands
T: +31 78 657 6392
F: +31 78 657 6474
www.springer.com/philosophy/ethics/journal/10551
ISSN: 0167-4544
From 2004 this monthly journal has incorporated The International Journal of Value-Based Management and Teaching Business Ethics. It covers a wide range of ethical issues related to business and includes empirical research reports. The use of specialist jargon is avoided as the publication is intended for a wide constituency including the business community, universities, government, and consumer groups.

Journal of Business Ethics and Education
Neilson Journals Publishing
151 Whitehouse Loan, Edinburgh, EH9 2EY, UK
T: +44 (0) 131 447 3300
F: +44 (0) 131 464 0300
www.neilsonjournals.com/JBEE
ISSN: 1649-5195
JBEE publishes educational materials suitable for use in ethics courses or in other business courses where ethical issues are discussed. These include case studies, lecture articles for student use, articles and ethical analyses for instructors, role-playing material, and syllabi and curricula. It covers areas such as the proper role of ethics in business education, integrating ethics into other business courses, and the relative merits of integration versus stand-alone courses.

Journal of Human Values
Sage Publications
1 Oliver's Yard, 55 City Road, London, EC1Y 1SP, UK
T: +44 (0) 20 7324 8500
F: +44 (0) 20 7324 8600
jhv.sagepub.com
ISSN: 0971-6858
Journal of Human Values focuses the effect of human values on all dimensions. Some of the dimensions are the relevance in today's world and human values at the organizational level. Its purpose is to provide an understanding of how individuals, organizations, and societies can function effectively. The journal provides an international platform for the exchange of ideas, principles and processes.

INTERNET

Business Impact
www.bitc.org.uk/index.html
This site contains information from Business in the Community's Business Impact task force, including a news directory and general information on corporate social responsibility.

Center for the Study of Ethics in the Professions
ethics.iit.edu/codes
This site makes available 850 codes of ethics from professional societies, corporations, government, and academic institutions, as well as a literature review and a user guide.

Ethics Connection
www.scu.edu/SCU/Centers/Ethics
This site, run by the Markkula Center for Applied Ethics at Santa Clara University, offers case briefings, articles, and dialogue in all fields of applied ethics, including business and technology.

Ethics Resource Center
www.ethics.org
A range of resources from this Washington-based ethics education organization can be accessed here. These include articles from *Ethics Today* magazine, useful links, book reviews, and details of training resources and events.

Global Business Society Resource Center
www.bsr.org/CSRResources/index.cfm
Business for Social Responsibility offers an introduction to issues of social responsibility and business ethics on this site. The site also includes a news archive, information about company practices and policies, award and recognition programs, and publications. A special feature is the facility it provides for creating reports on selected topics.

GlobeEthics.net
www.globethics.net
Globethics.net is a global network of people and institutions interested in different fields of applied ethics. It offers resources on ethics and collaborative web-based researches.

ORGANIZATIONS

Europe

Business in the Community
137 Shepherdess Walk, London, N1 7RQ, UK
T: +44 (0) 870 600 2482
E: information@bitc.org.uk
www.bitc.org.uk
Business in the Community was set up as a partnership between business, government, local authorities, and labor unions to promote corporate community involvement. It has a support network aimed particularly at helping new and developing businesses to become involved in the community.

Institute of Business Ethics (IBE)
24 Greencoat Place, London, SW1P 1BE, UK
T: +44 (0) 20 7798 6040
F: +44 (0) 20 7798 6044
E: info@ibe.org.uk
www.ibe.org.uk
Launched in 1986 by the then Lord Mayor of London, Alderman Sir Allan Davis, the Institute aims to emphasize the essentially ethical nature of wealth creation, to

  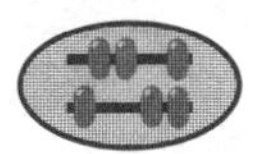 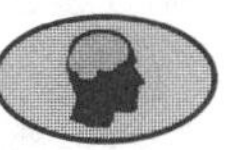  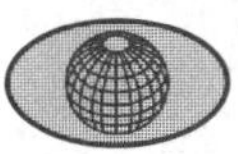   

encourage the highest standards of behavior by companies, and to publicize the best ethical practices. Its activities include research, conferences, seminars, and the development of codes of practice and resource material.

The Office of Fair Trading
Fleetbank House, 2–6 Salisbury Square, London, EC4Y 8JX, UK
T: +44 (0) 20 7211 8000
E: enquiries@oft.gsi.gov.uk.
www.oft.gov.uk
The OFT is the UK's consumer and competition authority. Their mission is to make markets work well for consumers. They encourage businesses to comply with competition and consumer law and to improve their trading practices. The OFT is a non-ministerial government department established by statute in 1973.

USA

Business for Social Responsibility (BSR)
111 Sutter Street, 11th Floor, San Francisco, CA 94104, USA
T: +1 415 984 3200
F: +1 415 984 3201
www.bsr.org
Founded in 1992, this organization provides resources–including information, news, publications, training, and consulting–designed to help member companies succeed in business while respecting ethical values. Based in the United States, BSR has developed regional networks and alliances with similar organizations worldwide.

Ethics & Compliance Officer Association
411 Waverley Oaks Road, Suite 324, Waltham, MA 02452, USA
T: +1 781 647 9333
E: msonin@theecoa.org
www.theecoa.org/AM/Template.cfm?Section=About
The Ethics & Compliance Officer Association (ECOA) is a non-consulting, member-driven association exclusively for individuals responsible for their organization's ethics, compliance, and business conduct programs. It is the largest group of business ethics and compliance practitioners in the world.

Institute for Business and Professional Ethics
1 East Jackson, Chicago, IL 60604, USA
T: +1 312 362 8000
commerce.depaul.edu/ethics
The mission of this institute is to maintain and encourage ethical deliberation by stirring the moral conscience and by developing models for ethical decision-making in business and the professions.

Society for Business Ethics (SBE)
School of Business Administration, Loyola University Chicago, 25 East Pearson Avenue, Chicago, IL 60611–2196, USA
T: +1 312 915 6112
F: +1 312 915 7207
sba.luc.edu
The SBE is an international association of scholars and professionals that aims to promote the study of business ethics, to improve the way they are taught, and to provide a forum for the exchange of ideas in the field.

International

Institute for Global Ethics
PO Box 563, Camden, ME 04843, USA
T: +1 207 236 6658
F: +1 207 236 4014
www.globalethics.org
A nonsectarian membership organization funded by private foundations, sponsors, and members, the institute fosters public discussion of and practical action on ethical issues and promotes the teaching of "ethical fitness." It has an international board of directors, an international advisory council, and branch offices in the United Kingdom and Canada. Its activities are centered on three areas: corporate services, educational programs, and public policy. Visitors to IBE's online site may register free for the weekly *Ethics Newsline* e-newsletter.

  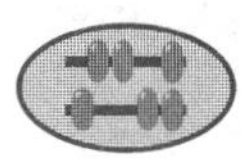 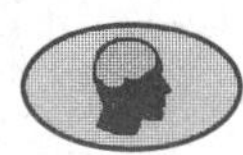  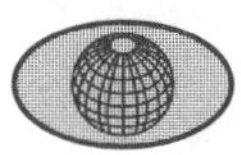   

Business Plans and Planning

BOOKS

Business Plans in a Week
Iain Maitland
In a Week Series
London: Profile Books, 2002
96pp, ISBN: 978-0-340-84963-7
This succinct guide to the process of compiling and writing a business plan explains how to identify goals, make preparatory notes, compile the financial and commercial sections, and present the finished plan effectively.

The Business Plan Workbook, 5th ed
Colin Barrow, Paul Barrow, Robert Brown
London: Kogan Page, 2005
400pp, ISBN: 978-0-7494-4346-7
The processes and procedures required to write a business plan are brought together in this workbook, and are illustrated with examples from actual business plans. The seven-phase approach focuses on: the business history and position to date; market research; competitive business strategies; operations; forecasting results; business controls; and writing up and presenting your business plan. Appendices give market research information sources and sources of finance for new and small businesses.

The Complete Book of Business Plans: Simple Steps to Writing a Powerful Business Plan
Joseph A. Covello, Brian J. Hazelgren
Naperville, Illinois: Sourcebooks, 1994
320pp, ISBN: 978-0-942061-41-3
This classic presents the key questions to bear in mind when writing a plan for a new business, and encourages the reader to look for answers to the kinds of questions that investors ask, to develop marketing strategies and financial presentations, and to find ways to stay ahead of the competition.

The Definitive Business Plan: The Fast Track to Intelligent Business Planning for Executives and Entrepreneurs, 2nd ed
Richard Stutley
Harlow, UK: FT Prentice Hall, 2006
320pp, ISBN: 978-0-273-71096-7
Written for both the newcomer and the experienced planner, this text provides a concise guide to the business planning process, and focuses attention on strategic planning and strategic and operational controls. The practical aspects of constructing various types of business plan are explained in some detail.

How to Prepare a Business Plan, 5th ed
Edward Blackwell
Sunday Times Business Enterprise Guide Series
London: Kogan Page, 2008
192pp, ISBN: 978-0-7494-4981-0
This highly recommended title takes the owner/manager through the process of developing a business plan for start-up or expansion. This book covers financial forecasting and planning and gives useful case studies of businesses preparing and following business plans.

How to Really Create a Successful Business Plan, 4th ed
David E. Gumpert
Boston, Massachusetts: Inc Publishing, 2003
236pp, ISBN: 978-0-9701181-7-2
This book provides a step-by-step method for completing a high-quality business plan. It also provides models of business plans from a number of highly successful US companies.

How to Write a Great Business Plan
William A. Sahlman
Harvard Business Review Classics
Boston, Massachusetts: Harvard Business School Press, 2008
64pp, ISBN: 978-1-4221-2142-9
Sahlman shows how to avoid creating an over-elaborate and off-the-point business plan by ensuring that your plan assesses the factors critical to every new venture: the people, the opportunity, the context, what can go wrong and right, and how the entrepreneurial team will respond.

The Mission Primer: Four Steps to an Effective Mission Statement
Richard O'Halloran, David O'Halloran
Richmond, Virginia: Mission Incorporated, 2000
130pp, ISBN: 978-0-9676635-0-0
Including an easy-to-use guide, examples of model mission statements, and a glossary of useful terms, this book will enable you to analyze your situation and create your own mission statement.

The Successful Business Plan: Secrets and Strategies, 4th ed
Rhonda M. Abrams, Paul Barrow
Palo Alto, California: Running R Media, 2008
478pp, ISBN: 978-1-84112-807-8
This book is designed to help readers create a business plan that will attract the funding they need to get started. It presents insights from some 200 business owners, venture capitalists, and CEOs, but, in addition, contains worksheets and sample business plans, provides tools to help in number-crunching, and offers guidance on the length of an ideal plan and the way it should be worded and formatted.

Your First Business Plan: A Simple Question and Answer Format Designed to Help You Write Your Own Plan, 5th ed
Brian Hazelgren
Naperville, Illinois: Sourcebooks, 2005
256pp, ISBN: 978-1-4022-0412-8
With little or no company history, the first business plan can be the most difficult. By outlining each part of the business plan and making suggestions for what to focus on and what to avoid, this book will help your writing. Also included are a glossary and a sample business plan.

JOURNALS

Long Range Planning: International Journal of Strategic Management
Elsevier
Radarweg 29, Amsterdam 1043 NX, The Netherlands
T: +31 20 485 3911
F: +31 20 485 2457
www.elsevier.com/locate/lrp
ISSN: 0024-6301
LRP, published in association with the Strategic Planning Society and the European Strategic Planning Federation, is a leading international journal in the field of strategic management. Aimed at senior managers, administrators, and academics, it includes articles from academics and practitioners.

INTERNET

Allindialive Business Planning Portal
www.allindialive.org
An Indian Blogger offering help on business planning. The site provides many links and publications on the topic.

Businessballs.com
www.businessballs.com/freebusinessplansandmarketingtemplates.htm
This section of the extensive businessballs.com site offers a useful list of key business planning terms as well as

advice on the best information to include and what to leave out. Links to sources of further help are also provided.

Business Link
www.businesslink.gov.uk
The UK Small Business Service runs this site to provide advice for small business owners and anyone thinking of setting up a small business in England. The site is packed with helpful information and easily navigable. Business Link offers a telephone support line on 0845 600 9006 and also has a network of 45 operators across the country which puts you in touch with an advisor.

Business Plan Guide
www.business-plans.co.uk
Sponsored by Miller Consultancy, this site provides information on business planning resources. It includes books, links to websites, and articles.

Business Plans
www.bplans.com
This site, created by Palo Alto Software, offers planning advice for small businesses and a substantial range of sample plans, which subscribers to bplans' software can download and edit. It also includes a resource center with links to other websites, as well as an "ask the experts" section.

More Business
www.morebusiness.com
This site has a lengthy business and marketing plans section and provides some useful sample business plans.

Planware.org
www.planware.org
This site offers free business planning software, freeware, templates, samples, and online tools, and offers advice and guides.

United States Small Business Administration
www.sba.gov
This website, run by the US government organization dedicated to helping small business owners, provides sources for technical, managerial, and financial advice and assistance. It also includes a small business planner with a model business plan.

Venture Associates
www.venturea.com/business.htm
Produced by an investment banking and management consulting firm, the site provides freely available information on various aspects of business planning. It also includes a useful business plan outline.

Venture Capital Resource Library
www.vfinance.com
This site provides a business plan template, general articles, and texts of SEC and UCC rules and regulations, as well as leads to sources of venture capital.

ORGANIZATIONS

Europe

Chartered Management Institute (CMI)
Management House, Cottingham Road, Corby, Northamptonshire, NN17 1TT, UK
T: +44 (0) 1536 204 222
F: +44 (0) 1536 201 651
E: enquiries@managers.org.uk
www.managers.org.uk
Formed in 1992, the CMI is the largest organization for professional management in the United Kingdom, representing almost 89,000 individual members and embracing 560 corporate partners. It exists to promote the art and science of management through research, publications, the provision of information services, networking opportunities, education and training, and the objective presentation of managers' views and opinions.

USA

American Management Association (AMA)
1601 Broadway, New York, NY 10019, USA
T: +1 212 586 8100
F: +1 212 903 8168
E: customerservice@amanet.org
www.amanet.org
Founded in 1923, this association has over 80,000 members. With a focus on practical training, the AMA provides business forums and seminars worldwide. Members can enhance their business skills and develop successful planning strategies by studying the best practices of various world-class organizations. Seminars are geared to every professional level, from CEO to administrative assistant. The AMA also publishes valuable print resources that cover a wide range of topics including business plans, career building, and technology.

Chief Executive Officers' Club
47 West Street, New York, NY 10013, USA
T: +1 212 925 7911
F: +1 212 925 7463
E: main@ceoclubs.org
ceoclubs.org/main/default.htm
Established in 1978, this association serves as a management resource for entrepreneurs and their professional advisers. Membership is by invitation only. Membership is restricted to CEOs of businesses that have over $2m in annual sales. The organization selects publications on developing business plans and conducts seminars on the entrepreneurial process.

United States Small Business Administration
409 Third Street, SW, Washington, DC 20416, USA
T: +1 800 827 7722
www.sba.gov
Providing multiple resources for the small business covering a wide range of topics, such as starting your business, financing your business, managing your business, and business opportunities, this link, provided by the United States government, is a handy stop for anyone interested in business planning.

BRIC

Indian Institutes of Management (IIMs)
Diamond Harbour Road, Joka, Kolkata 700104, West Bengal, India
T: +91 33 2467 9178
F: +91 33 2467 9178
E: pgpadmissions@iimcal.ac.in
www.iimcal.ac.in/
The IIMs are top business schools created by the government of India, to create a pool of highly educated managers to lead India's economy. The institutes also carry out research in emerging areas.

     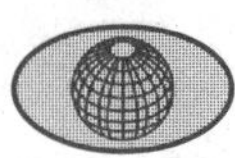   

Business Process Reengineering

BOOKS

The Aftermath of Reengineering: Downsizing and Corporate Performance

Tony Carter
Binghamton, New York: The Haworth Press, 1999
165pp, ISBN: 978-0-7890-0720-9

Carter takes a much needed, thorough look at the effectiveness of reengineering and both its positive and negative human, strategic, and societal consequences. Every chapter concludes with a case study that illustrates the topic, and the final chapter of the book provides an evaluation of reengineering best practices from a variety of companies and industries.

Beyond Reengineering: How the Process-centered Organization Is Changing

Michael Hammer
New York: HarperCollins Business, 1996
304pp, ISBN: 978-0-00-255643-9

This book explores the strategy and structure of the process-centered organization, and the consequences of reengineering.

Cases on Information Technology and Business Process Reengineering

Mehdi Khosrow-Pour
Cases on Information Technology Series
Hershey, Pennsylvania: IGI Publishing, 2006
357pp, ISBN: 978-1-59904-396-8

The technological innovation of information technology is driving businesses and organizations to reassess their structures and processes to achieve a higher level of efficiency and effectiveness using IT. In this ongoing process, the wisdom and experiences of other organizations can be a roadmap to successful IT implementation.

Making Sense of Change Management: A Complete Guide to the Models, Tools and Techniques of Organizational Change, 2nd ed

Esther Cameron and Mike Green
London: Kogan Page, 2009
304pp, ISBN: 978-0-7494-5310-7

This book is for students and professionals. It explains how change happens, and what needs to be done to make change a welcome rather than a dreaded concept. It offers considered insights in frameworks, models, and ways of approaching change, and helps the reader to apply the right approach to each unique situation.

The Reengineering Alternative: A Plan for Making Your Current Culture Work

William E. Schneider
Maidenhead, UK: McGraw-Hill, 1999
173pp, ISBN: 978-0-07-135981-8

Reengineering has virtually become business dogma, yet there are viable, and perhaps even preferable, alternatives. Mechanistic approaches to reengineering often fail to take into account one of a company's most vital and enduring resources—its culture. This book describes an approach to change management that focuses on a company's unique existing strengths and corporate objectives, and shows how to work effectively to foster improvement according to four basic corporate culture types.

Reengineering Business for Success in the Internet Age: Business-to-Business E-Commerce Strategies, 3rd ed

Debra Cameron
Charleston, South Carolina: Computer Technology Research Corporation, 2000
197pp, ISBN: 978-1-56607-084-3

The publisher is now out of business—another casualty of the e-commerce nosedive—but this report may still be purchased through online booksellers. It applies reengineering strategies to the dynamic e-business environment. Topics range from integrating legacy systems to implementing B2B security strategies, with special emphasis on the unique role of XML in reengineering for e-business.

JOURNALS

Industrial Management & Data Systems

Emerald
60/62 Toller Lane, Bradford, West Yorkshire, BD8 9BY, UK
T: +44 (0) 1274 777 700
F: +44 (0) 1274 785 200
www.emeraldinsight.com/0263-5577.htm
ISSN: 0263-5577

This journal addresses the requirements of reengineering information needed by organizations whose existence is dependent on coping with rapidly changing requirements. Reengineering examines and alters the system to reconstitute in a new form and the subsequent implementation of the new form.

Knowledge and Process Management

Wiley
The Atrium, Southern Gate, Chichester, West Sussex, PO19 8SQ, UK
T: +44 (0) 1243 779 777
F: +44 (0) 1243 775 878
www.interscience.wiley.com/jpages/1092-4604
ISSN: 1092-4604

Formerly called *Business Change and Reengineering: Journal of Corporate Transformation*, this quarterly journal aims to meet the needs of executives responsible for organizational performance improvement. Articles focus on the areas of knowledge management, organizational learning, core competences, and process management. Emphasis is placed on the practical lessons learned from the experience of organizations.

TQM Journal

Emerald
60/62 Toller Lane, Bradford, West Yorkshire, BD8 9BY, UK
T: +44 (0) 1274 777 700
F: +44 (0) 1274 785 200
www.emeraldinsight.com/1754-2731.htm
ISSN: 1754-2731

Known as The TQM Magazine until the end of 2007, this journal examines the management concept of business process reengineering (BPR), arguing that while little is really new, the need for organizations to embrace process improvement is high. It discusses some key success factors for organizations using BPR.

INTERNET

Brint.com Business Process Reengineering

www.brint.com/BPR.htm

A comprehensive collection of links to BPR resources.

Business Process Reengineering (BPR)—An Introductory Guide

www.teamtechnology.co.uk/business-process-reengineering.html

This website provides a detailed introduction to the field of business process reengineering.

  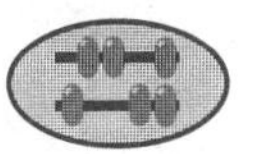   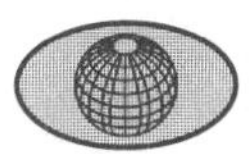   

Business Process Reengineering (BPR) Online Learning Center
www.prosci.com
This online learning center features seven series of multiple online tutorials on various aspects of business process reengineering, together with best practice benchmarking studies, a change management resource library, and a project trouble shooter.

National Center for Public Productivity
www.ncpp.us
Affiliated with Rutgers University, the website for this center is a gateway to federal, state, and international resources on productivity in the public sector, and for "citizen-driven government performance."

ORGANIZATIONS

BRIC

Business Process Industry Association of India
c/o Confederation of Indian Industry, 249-F, Phase-IV, Udyog Vihar, Sector 18, Gurgaon, 122 015 (Haryana), India
T: +91 124 410 104
F: +91 124 401 4080
E: info@bpiai.org
www.bpiai.org
The Business Process Industry Association of India (BPIAI) provides a network for members to jointly address challenges facing the call centre industry. It aims to create opportunities for networking within the industry through events and conferences, and take up policies and infrastructure-related issues with the government.

International

Business Modeling & Integration (BMI) Domain Task Force (DTF)
140 Kendrick Street, Building A, Suite 300, Needham, MA 02494, USA
T: +1 781 444 0404
F: +1 781 444 0320
E: info@omg.org
www.bpmi.org
OMG is international, open membership, non-profit computer industry consortium, which ensures that every organization, large and small, has a effective voice in their running. The membership includes hundreds of organizations, with half being software end-users in over two dozen vertical markets, and the other half representing virtually every large organization in the computer industry, as well as many smaller ones.

Business Process Management Group (BPMG)
The Manor, Haseley Business Centre, Warwick, Warwickshire, CV35 7LS, UK
T: + 44 1926 864 477
F: + 44 (0) 20 7691 7132
E: editor@bpmg.org
www.bpmg.org
The BPMG is a business interest group, established in the United Kingdom in 1992, which now has over 15,000 members worldwide. Its aims are to advance the understanding and application of business process management, to raise business awareness of BPM, and to provide a forum for the exchange of information relevant to BPM.

Workflow and Reengineering International Association (WARIA)
2436 North Federal Highway 374, Lighthouse Point, FL 33064, USA
T: +1 954 782 3376
F: +1 954 782 6365
E: waria04@waria.com
www.waria.com
WARIA is a nonprofit organization concerned with issues that arise at the intersection between BPR, knowledge management, electronic commerce, and workflow management. It encourages the sharing of information on issues common to these fields by providing networking opportunities.

Capital Markets and Stock Markets

BOOKS

Capital Market Liberalization and Development
Joseph E. Stiglitz, Jose Antonio Ocampo (editors)
New York: Oxford University Press, 2008
375pp, ISBN: 978-0-19-923844-6
This is a new examination of the impact of liberalization on the capital markets, a development that has been central to the debate on the effects of globalization. It brings together some of the leading researchers and practitioners in the field, to provide an analysis of both the risks associated with capital market liberalization and the alternative policy options available to enhance macroeconomic management.

Capital Market Revolution: The Future of Markets in an Online World
Patrick Young, Thomas Theys
Harlow, UK: FT Prentice Hall, 1999
212pp, ISBN: 978-0-273-64232-9
The book that spread an awareness of what the coming electronic age would mean for the financial markets. At a time when much trading was still done on a face-to-face basis, it predicted the move to fully automated markets and electronic trading. It presciently warned that traders and exchanges would have to change or they would be doomed.

Capital Markets
K. Thomas Liaw
Mason, Ohio: Thomson/South-Western, 2004
603pp, ISBN: 978-0-324-02420-3
A strong overview of the financial markets and institutions, with a focus on global financial centers, including the Euromarkets, European Monetary Union, and the capital markets in Japan, Asia, Russia, and Latin America. It considers the impact of globalization, deregulation, consolidation, and technology, and examines the securities markets, and current market practice.

Capital Markets: A Global Perspective
Thomas H. McInish
Boston, Massachusetts: Blackwell Publishing, 2000
429pp, ISBN: 978-0-631-21159-4
Capital Markets provides an international overview of the main financial products, principles, and operating structure of the global marketplace. It examines integration across equities, debt securities, derivatives, and foreign exchange, and focuses on market microstructure in terms of prices, risks, and transaction costs of the four product types.

Capital Markets: Institutions and Instruments, 4th ed
Frank J. Fabozzi, Franco Modigliani
Upper Saddle River, New Jersey: Prentice Hall, 2009
696pp, ISBN: 978-0-13-602602-0
This is a comprehensive and wide-ranging examination of the capital markets, by two of the most respected writers and researchers in the business. It evaluates and explains the instruments, institutions, players, and principles of valuation in a detailed and accessible way. It combines theory and practice to provide a detailed reference for professionals working in the markets.

The Complete Guide to Capital Markets for Quantitative Professionals
Alex Kuznetsov
McGraw-Hill Library of Investment and Finance Series
New York: McGraw-Hill, 2007
554pp, ISBN: 978-0-07-146829-9
Aimed at those with a technical background who are planning to enter the financial sector, and need a solid grounding in the fundamentals of how the financial sector operates. It offers advice about the type of jobs they should be contemplating, and focuses on the mechanics of trading in the markets, and the use of financial models and systems.

Financial Institutions, Markets, and Money, 10th ed
David S. Kidwell, David W. Blackwell, David A. Whidbee, Richard L. Peterson
Hoboken, New Jersey: Wiley, 2008
671pp, ISBN: 978-0-470-17161-5
This is an introduction to how the US financial system, focusing on its institutions, markets, and financial instruments, and the impact of technology and globalization. It examines the Federal Reserve System and how it conducts monetary policy, and explores the risks faced by financial institutions on interest rates, credit, liquidity, and foreign exchange, and how they can be managed effectively.

Fundamentals of the Stock Market
B. O'Neill Wyss
New York: McGraw-Hill, 2001
245pp, ISBN: 978-0-07-136096-8
A practical examination of market basics, such as how to trade, the major exchanges, different types of stock, and where to look for financial news, up to more advanced concepts, such as technical analysis, short selling, modern portfolio theory overview of stocks and mutual funds, and how trends and policies affect markets.

The Great Crash of 1929
John Kenneth Galbraith
Boston, Massachusetts: Houghton Mifflin, 1997
206pp, ISBN: 978-0-395-85999-5
An examination of the stock market crash of 1929, which heralded the Great Depression in US. Galbraith provides insights into the unbridled speculation, the high trading volumes, the market hysteria, and the inaction of the government to resolve the crisis, and records in detail the run up to the crash, and the effect it had on the US economy and society.

Handbook of World Stock, Derivatives and Commodity Exchanges
Herbie Skeete (editor)
London: GMB Publishing, 2008
1,200pp, ISBN: 978-1-84673-115-0
This is a useful directory and reference source on around 250 exchanges in over 100 countries. It contains trading, settlement and organizational information, as well as equities, futures and options traded, and contact details and a host of key facts about each exchange.

A History of the Global Stock Market: From Ancient Rome to Silicon Valley
B. Mark Smith
Chicago, Illinois: University of Chicago Press, 2004
344pp, ISBN: 978-0-226-76404-7
A thorough market history through the ages, it examines how stock markets became a focus for investment, and so integral to the global economy. Smith recounts the development of a financial market system through a series of entertaining stories, while arguing that speculative bubbles are not inevitable, and that globalization of the market is nothing new.

  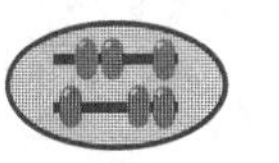 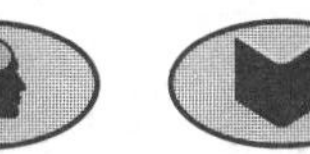 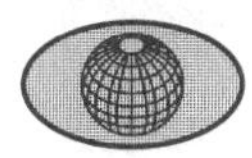   

How the Stock Market Works, 3rd ed
John M. Dalton
New York Institute of Finance Series
New York: Prentice Hall, 2001
422pp, ISBN: 978-0-7352-0183-5
Provides a comprehensive examination of the workings of the markets, and basic concepts such as market operations, understanding the financial press, initial public offerings, brokering, the mutual fund market, the globalization of the markets, and finance theory. It includes a detailed glossary as a reference tool.

An Introduction to Capital Markets: Products, Strategies, Participants
Andrew Chisholm
Wiley Finance Series
New York: Wiley, 2002
448pp, ISBN: 978-0-471-49866-7
This is a useful primer to the capital markets, which explains in easy terms the basics with the aid of real-world case studies and examples. It provides a useful overview for those entering investment banking or asset management, as it details the markets, participants, equity and debt instruments, the main derivative products, as well as risk management tools and strategies.

Money and Capital Markets, 10th ed
Peter S. Rose, Milton H. Marquis
New York: McGraw-Hill/Irwin, 2008
767pp, ISBN: 978-0-07-128432-5
Provides a thorough view of the financial sector and how it operates. All the major types of financial institutions and financial instruments are considered, as well as how the current global system of money and financial markets is evolving. Money and Capital Markets also usefully describes how interest rates and security values are determined.

Portfolio Theory and Capital Markets
William F. Sharpe
New York: McGraw-Hill, 2000
316pp, ISBN: 978-0-07-135320-5
The bible of modern portfolio theory by the Nobel Prize-winning researcher and author William Sharpe. It introduced the Capital Asset Pricing Model—which became pivotal to modern investment theory—to a wider audience and established Sharpe as a giant of financial thought, crucial as it was to the formulation of modern portfolio theory, derivatives pricing and investment.

Trading Strategies for Capital Markets
Joseph Benning
New York: McGraw-Hill, 2008
356pp, ISBN: 978-0-07-146496-3
Explains how the capital markets work in practice, what the main drivers are and how to recognize them, and the best way to develop and implement effective trading strategies for securities and derivatives. It presents real examples of successful trading strategies, guidance on how they operate, and discusses trading psychology and risk management.

Why Stock Markets Crash: Critical Events in Complex Financial Systems
Didier Sornette
Princeton, New Jersey: Princeton University Press, 2003
421pp, ISBN: 978-0-691-11850-5
A book focused on crises in the financial system; rather than the usual explanation of crashes as based on market failings in the run up to a crash, Sornette explores underlying causes months and years before the event, that can contribute to a dangerous market bubble. Also covers a range of related concepts, such as game theory, fractals, catastrophe theory, and critical phenomena.

MAGAZINES

Bloomberg Markets
Bloomberg
Bloomberg Tower, 731 Lexington Avenue, New York 10022, USA
T: +1 212 318 2000
F: +1 917 369 5000
www.bloomberg.com/news/marketsmag
ISSN: 1531-5061
This is a monthly magazine for professional investors, which provides news, articles, special reports, and commentary on the markets, companies, and hedge funds, as well as covering more general issues. It also goes out to all Bloomberg professional service subscribers.

Capital Market Magazine
Capital Market Publishers
101 Swastik Chambers, Umarshi Bappa Chowk, Sion-Trombay Road, Chembur, Mumbai 400 071, India
T: +91 022 2522 9720
F: +91 022 2522 0954
www.capitalmarket.com
This fortnightly magazine has been published since 1985, and was a pioneer in rating IPOs on a 100-point scale. It features information and commentary on the markets, analyst meetings and AGMs, market beat, market cap, bulletins, broker research, corporate results, sector trends, and company profiles.

The Stock Market Journal
Unitron Media
2605 72nd Avenue E, M/S 344, Ellenton, Florida 34222, USA
T: +1 941 932 8234
F: +1 941 870 7831
www.thestockmarketjournal.com
This financial and investment newspaper journal is aimed at traders of stocks, futures, options and forex, covering small emerging public companies and service providers in the micro-cap and small cap markets. It offers strategies, techniques, and resources related to personal investing and commentary on personal finance issues.

INTERNET

Bloomberg
www.bloomberg.com
A large-scale resource that provides a range of financial and capital market information, commentary, and analysis, as well as covering news, market data, and investment tools, and more general topics such as arts and culture, sports, and science.

Financial Times
www.ft.com
This is an international site for the *Financial Times* newspaper, that presents a wide coverage of financial news, market information, issues, and analysis, and also encompasses world events, politics, and the arts.

ORGANIZATIONS

Europe

The Federation of European Securities Exchanges
Chair: Spyros Capralos
Avenue de Cortenbergh 52, 1000 Brussels, Belgium
T: +32 2 551 01 80
F: +32 2 512 49 05
E: info@fese.eu
www.fese.be
FESE represents 42 securities exchanges in 23 different countries, and is one of the founding members of the European Capital Markets Institute. It links up with the international regulatory industry, and aims to promote the global competitiveness and recognition of European exchanges, provide a forum for debate on capital markets, advocate improved regulation and competition in securities markets, and improve the

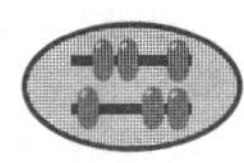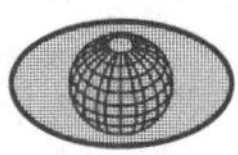

efficiency of clearing and settlement of securities.

Financial Services Authority

Chair: Lord Turner of Ecchinswell
25 North Colonnade, Canary Wharf, London, E14 5HS, UK
T: +44 (0) 20 7066 1000
F: +44 (0) 20 7066 1099
www.fsa.gov.uk

The Financial Services Authority (FSA) is an independent non-governmental body, which regulates the financial services industry in the UK. It acts as the authority for listing of shares on a stock exchange, and has four statutory objectives: market confidence, public awareness, consumer protection, and reduction of financial crime. It also has the strategic aims of promoting efficient, orderly and fair markets, helping retail consumers achieve a fair deal, and improving our business capability and effectiveness.

USA

Financial Industry Regulatory Authority

Chair: Mary L. Schapiro
1735 K Street, Washington, DC 20006, USA
T: +1 301 590 6500
www.finra.org

FINRA is the largest independent regulator for all securities firms doing business in the US, and has the role of protecting investors by maintaining the fairness of the US capital markets. It is involved in virtually every aspect of the securities business, including registering and educating industry participants, examinations of securities firms, writing rules that govern the conduct of the industry, and enforcing those rules and the federal securities laws.

Institute for Financial Markets

Chair: Peter F. Borish
2001 Pennsylvania Avenue NW, Suite 600, Washington, DC 20006, USA
T: +1 202 223 1528
F: +1 202 296 3184
E: info@theIFM.org
www.theifm.org

The IFM is a non-profit organization, and an autonomous affiliate of the Futures Industry Association. It has no members and does not engage in any lobbying or political activities, but provides unbiased information, education, ethics and data, to industry professionals, market-users, investors, and decision makers in the financial services industry.

US Securities and Exchange Commission

Chair: Christopher Cox
100 F Street NE, Washington, DC 20549, USA
T: +1 202 942 8088
E: help@sec.gov
www.sec.gov

The mission of the SEC is to protect investors, maintain fair, orderly, and efficient markets, and facilitate capital formation. It oversees the key participants in the securities world, requires public companies to disclose meaningful financial and other information to the public, and works to uncover cases of insider trading, accounting fraud, and the provision of false or misleading information about securities and the companies that issue them.

International

ACI

Chair: Manfred Wiebogen
8 Rue du Mail, 75002, Paris, France
T: +33 1 42 97 51 15
F: +33 1 42 97 51 16
E: deputymanager@aciforex.com
www.aciforex.com

The ACI is a global association for financial market professionals engaged within the financial trading or sales environment in the global financial markets, representing foreign exchange, interest rate products and other securities, banknotes and bullions, precious metals and commodities and their various kinds of derivatives.

International Association of Options Exchanges and Clearing Houses

Chair: Hugh Freedberg
www.world-exchanges.org/ioma

IOMA includes most of the major exchanges trading options on equities, equity indexes, debt instruments, currencies, futures, and commodities, and is affiliated to the World Federation of Exchanges. It conducts the annual survey of options markets, and maintains a directory of IOMA members.

World Federation of Exchanges

Chair: William J. Brodsky
France
T: +33 (0) 1 58 62 54 00
F: +33 (0) 1 58 62 50 48
E: secretariat@world-exchanges.org
www.world-exchanges.org

The WFE, formerly the International Federation of Stock Exchanges, is an international trade organization for securities and derivative markets such as stock exchanges, and its exchanges are home to over 46,000 listed companies. Membership is considered by some governments and national associations of asset managers as a criteria for preferential investment policy and taxation for these markets.

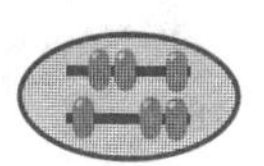

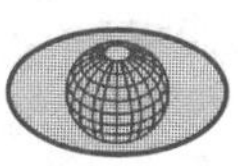

Central Banking

BOOKS

Asian States, Asian Bankers: Central Banking in Southeast Asia

Natasha Hamilton-Hart
Cornell Studies in Political Economy Series
Ithaca, New York: Cornell University Press, 2002
215pp, ISBN: 978-0-8014-3987-2

An investigation of central banks, governments, and private bankers in Southeast Asia, that shows how the development and attributes of central banks and state financial institutions shape their interactions with private bankers and affect how they manage the financial sector.

Central Bank Directory 2008

Robert Pringle (editor)
London: Central Banking Publications, 2008
290pp, ISBN: 978-1-902182-51-3

A key information resource on central banks, containing details on over 4,000 key contacts in 162 Central Banks, a short history of each bank, current legislative arrangements, terms of appointment, and past governors. Now in its 17th year, this annual directory is extensively revised every year.

Central Bank Modernisation

Peter Nicholl (editor)
London: Central Banking Publications, 2005
230pp, ISBN: 978-1-902182-38-4

A compilation of papers by leading industry experts that examine how central banks are developing their governance, strategic planning, and process reforms during a time of great upheaval in the financial sector. Uses case studies to illustrate how many leading central bankers have reformed their institutions, and are now focusing on greater efficiency and competitiveness.

Central Banking as Global Governance: Constructing Financial Credibility

Rodney Bruce Hall
Cambridge Studies in International Relations Series
Cambridge, UK: Cambridge University Press, 2009
280pp, ISBN: 978-0-521-72721-1

A new academic study that analyses central banking in terms of governance, explaining how central banking and monetary economics should be approached in the wider context of international finance. It offers an original assessment of the mechanisms of governance, arguing that they are based more on social than material processes.

Central Banking in Theory and Practice

A. S. Blinder
Lionel Robbins Lectures Series
Cambridge, Massachusetts: MIT Press, 1998
92pp, ISBN: 978-0-262-52260-1

Argues for the greater use of academic theory in the monetary policies of central banks, and offers advice for concentrating research on providing practical solutions to central banking problems. Also discusses the goals of monetary policy, the choice of monetary instrument, central bank credibility, central bank independence, and the relationship between the central bank and financial markets.

Central Banks as Economic Institutions

Jean-Philippe Touffut (editor)
Cournot Centre for Economic Studies Series
Cheltenham, UK: Edward Elgar Publishing, 2008
256pp, ISBN: 978-1-84844-108-8

A collection of papers by distinguished economists and central bankers that evaluate how central banks function, develop their policies, choose their economic instruments, and examines the implications of their increased focus on independence and inflation targeting. It also considers issues around accountability, transparency, monetary policy, and policy problems relating to globalization and financial imbalances.

Central Banks in the Age of the Euro: Europeanization, Convergence, and Power

Kenneth Dyson, Martin Marcussen (editors)
Oxford, UK: Oxford University Press, 2009
384pp, ISBN: 978-0-19-921823-3

A new study on the impact of Europeanization on central banks since the introduction of the euro, which analyses how the euro has altered the power and convergence of central banks. It also uses case studies to consider how EU central banks have evolved in terms of monetary policy, financial market supervision, accountability and transparency, and research.

Challenges for Central Banking

Anthony M. Santomero, Staffan Viotti, Anders Vredin (editors)
Boston, Massachusetts: Kluwer Academic, 2001
274pp, ISBN: 978-0-7923-7346-9

Provides a comprehensive analysis of the role and operations of central banks, and looks at the key problems that they are going to face in the future. Also discusses the challenges of financial innovations for the supervision and stability of financial institutions.

The Changing Face of Central Banking: Evolutionary Trends Since World War II

Pierre L. Siklos
Studies in Macroeconomic History Series
New York: Cambridge University Press, 2008
372pp, ISBN: 978-0-521-03449-4

This is a comprehensive and wide-ranging overview of how central banks have transformed themselves into major players in national and international policy-making over the last 60 years. It is based on a study of 20 industrial countries, and examines the economic, political and institutional influences that have affected central banks and their relationship with government.

The European Central Bank: The New European Leviathan?, 2nd ed

David J. Howarth, Peter H. Loedel
Basingstoke, UK: Palgrave Macmillan, 2005
296pp, ISBN: 978-1-4039-4159-6

Takes a comprehensive overview of the antecedents of European monetary authority, how the European Central Bank originated, its difficult first years, how it operates in the current economic climate, and explores different national perspectives on central bank independence.

Evolution and Procedures in Central Banking

David E. Altig, Bruce D. Smith (editors)
Cambridge, UK: Cambridge University Press, 2003
334pp, ISBN: 978-0-521-81427-0

A revealing overview of the institutional nature of central banking, which analyzes their overall development, operating framework, and the challenges they face in the future. Through a series of rigorous articles, this book presents a combination of historical observation and economic theory and experimentation to provide a

  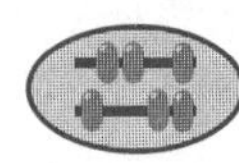 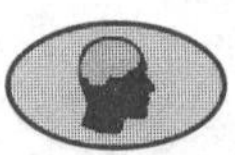  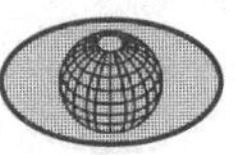   

comprehensive overview of central banking.

Financial Stability and Central Banks: A Global Perspective
Richard Brearley, Juliette Healey, Peter J. N. Sinclair, Charles Goodhart, David T. Llewellyn, Chang Shu (editors)
Central Bank Governors' Symposium Series
London: Routledge, 2001
272pp, ISBN: 978-0-415-25776-3
Written by practicing policy makers, Financial Stability and Central Banks provides an important overview of current policy issues and the legal, regulatory, managerial and economic issues that are affecting central banks. It is also a topical examination of the role of central banks in protecting the banking and payments system from risks and crises.

Handbook of Central Banking and Financial Authorities in Europe: New Architectures in the Supervision of Financial Markets
Donato Masciandaro
Elgar Original Reference Series
Cheltenham, UK: Edward Elgar Publishing, 2005
566pp, ISBN: 978-1-84376-789-3
This is a comprehensive overview of the changes in regulation and supervision of the banking and financial industry in Europe. Written by a team of industry experts, it focuses on the role of national central banks, the financial supervisory authorities, and the European Central Bank, and highlights the emerging role of new integrated financial authorities.

A History of Central Banking in Great Britain and the United States
John H. Wood
Cambridge, UK: Cambridge University Press, 2008
456pp, ISBN: 978-0-521-74131-6
Examines the early emergence of central banks and monetary policy in Great Britain and the United States in terms of the knowledge and behavior of central bankers and their interactions with economists and politicians. It focuses on how the continuity in central banking contributed to the stability of the financial markets.

International Economic Indicators and Central Banks
Anne Dolganos Picker
Wiley Finance Series
Hoboken, New Jersey: Wiley, 2007
295pp, ISBN: 978-0-471-75113-7
Discusses the importance of using the movement of international economic indicators to understand global economic events as they occur, which helps awareness of how the decisions of foreign central banks can affect market behavior. This approach can effectively improve investment decisions in international markets.

New Horizons in Central Bank Risk Management
Robert Pringle, Nick Carver
London: Central Banking Publications, 2004
269pp, ISBN: 978-1-902182-25-4
Discusses how central banks are identifying and managing the new risks they are facing, presents some of the new frameworks being introduced, and the best approach to effective risk mitigation throughout an organization. Also covers key issues such as business failure, litigation, deflation, and systemic failures, and contains a survey on the diversity and emerging trends in central bank risk management around the world.

The Origin of Financial Crises: Central Banks, Credit Bubbles and the Efficient Market Fallacy
George Cooper
Petersfield, UK: Harriman House, 2008
208pp, ISBN: 978-1-905641-85-7
A timely examination of the underlying forces behind the global economic and financial crisis; Cooper takes a contentious look at the consensus of economic theory and practice, arguing that financial markets do not actually follow the efficient market principles depicted in textbooks, but rather are inherently unstable and prone to regular upheaval and crisis.

The Past and Future of Central Bank Cooperation
Claudio Borio, Gianni Toniolo, Piet Clement (editors)
Studies in Macroeconomic History Series
Cambridge, UK: Cambridge University Press, 2008
256pp, ISBN: 978-0-521-87779-4
A timely and thoroughly researched analysis and history of central bank cooperation, demonstrating how such cooperation helps prevent or limit financial crises, as well as the potentially disastrous consequences of non-cooperation. It explores how the cooperation between central banks is crucial to maintaining monetary and financial stability, and the smooth functioning of the international financial system.

The Quiet Revolution: Central Banking Goes Modern
A. S. Blinder
Arthur M. Okum Memorial Lectures Series
New Haven, Connecticut: Yale University Press, 2004
144pp, ISBN: 978-0-300-10087-7
Looks at the evolution of central banking in the last few years, focusing on the move toward transparency, the evolution from individual to committee decision-making, and the more attentive approach to the financial markets. It is based on the author's experiences as a former vice chairman of the Federal Reserve System and member of President Clinton's Council of Economic Advisers.

MAGAZINES

The Banker
Financial Times
1 Southwark Bridge, London, SE1 9HL, UK
T: +44 (0) 20 7873 3000
www.thebanker.com
ISSN: 0005-5395
This monthly magazine, established in 1926, provides investigative comment and expert analysis on the key developments in the global banking arena. It produces articles, special reports, awards, industry rankings, database, archive, as well as free monthly electronic newsletters on cash and securities services, capital markets, FX and derivatives, news and comment, retail banking, and technology.

JOURNALS

Central Banking
Central Banking Publications, Incisive Media, Haymarket House, 28–29 Haymarket, London, SW1Y 4RX, UK
T: +44 (0) 20 7484 9700
F: +44 (0) 20 7930 2238
www.centralbanking.co.uk/publications/journals/cbj.htm
ISSN: 0960-6319
This quarterly journal is focused on reporting, analyzing, and commenting on the activities of the central banks around the world. It is aimed at senior staff and key decision-makers from central banks, and provides analysis of key developments affecting them. It also features interviews with leading central bankers, special issues on key central banks, and articles from internationally renowned academics and commentators.

   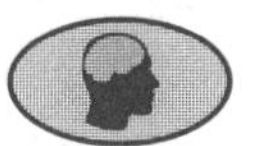  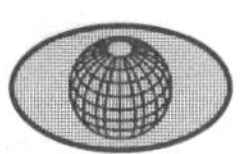   

International Journal of Central Banking
DG Research, European Central Bank, Postfach 16 03 19, D-60066 Frankfurt, Germany
T: +49 69 1344 7623
F: +49 69 1344 8553
www.ijcb.org
ISSN: 1815-4654
This quarterly international journal is an initiative of the Bank for International Settlements (BIS), the European Central Bank, the Group of Ten (G-10) central banks, and other central banks and sponsoring organizations. It features articles on central bank theory and practice, with a special emphasis on research relating to monetary and financial stability.

INTERNET

Bank for International Settlements
www.bis.org/cbanks.htm
The Bank for International Settlements (BIS) is an international organization that fosters international monetary and financial cooperation, and serves as a bank for central banks. Its website contains links to central banks of each country, listed alphabetically.

CentralBankNews.com
www.centralbanknews.com
This online resource, established in 2000, provides daily updates and an independent commentary on news and research in the fields of monetary policy and interest rates, financial regulation, reserve management, payment systems and public debt management. It also monitors the activities of the major international financial institutions such as the IMF.

ORGANIZATIONS

Europe

European Central Bank
Chair: Jean-Claude Trichet
Postfach 16 03 19, 60066 Frankfurt am Main, Germany
T: +49 69 13 44 0
F: +49 69 13 44 60 00
E: info@ecb.europa.eu
www.ecb.int
The European Central Bank is one of the most important central banks, having responsibility for monetary policy for the Eurozone. Its main task is to maintain the euro's purchasing power and price stability in the euro area, the 15 European Union countries that have introduced the euro since 1999. It works closely with the national central banks of all euro area countries, and focuses on decision-making, independence, transparency, accountability, corporate governance, and capital subscription.

USA

Federal Reserve System
Chair: Ben Bernanke
Eccles Building, Constitution Avenue, Washington, DC 20551, USA
T: +1 202 452 3000
www.federalreserve.gov
The Federal Reserve System is the central banking system of the US. It comprises the Board of Governors, the Federal Open Market Committee, 12 regional Federal Reserve Banks, many private US member banks, and a number of advisory councils. In its role as the central bank of the US, the Fed serves as both a banker's bank and the government's bank, helping to assure the safety and efficiency of the payments system, and processing a variety of financial transactions.

International

World Bank
Chair: Robert Zoellick
1818 H Street NW, Washington, DC 20433, USA
T: +1 202 473 1000
F: +1 202 477 6391
www.worldbank.org
The World Bank is a source of financial and technical assistance to developing countries for development programs with the stated goal of reducing poverty. It is made up of the International Bank for Reconstruction and Development (IBRD), and the International Development Association (IDA), which itself incorporates the International Finance Corporation, the Multilateral Investment Guarantee Agency, and the International Centre for Settlement of Investment Disputes.

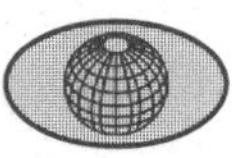

Contingency, Crisis, Disaster Management

BOOKS

Business Continuity Planning: A Step-by-Step Guide with Planning Forms on CD-ROM, 3rd ed
Kenneth L. Fulmer
Brookfield, Connecticut: Rothstein Associates, 2005
190pp, ISBN: 978-1-931332-21-7

This detailed workbook will help you build a corporate disaster plan. It covers factors such as choosing an alternate location and selecting vendors to enable your organization to resume business as soon as possible. It reviews how to choose a planning coordinator and recovery team, how to write a planning document, and stresses the need for testing the plan to be sure it works.

Business Continuity Planning: Protecting Your Organization's Life
Ken Doughty (editor)
Best Practices Series
Boca Raton, Florida: Auerbach, 2000
408pp, ISBN: 978-0-8493-0907-6

Contributions from a range of experts provide a comprehensive overview of business continuity planning. They indicate the importance of analyzing the risks to which an organization is exposed and of developing a plan for the resumption of business after a crisis. They also give detailed guidance on building, testing, maintaining, and updating a business continuity plan.

Business Continuity Strategies: Protecting Against Unplanned Disasters, 3rd ed
Kenneth N. Myers
Chichester, UK: Wiley, 2006
224pp, ISBN: 978-0-470-04038-6

Employing a thorough and practical approach, this edition provides a proven methodology for implementing a realistic and cost-efficient business contingency program. It shows corporate leaders how to prepare a logical "what if" plan that would enable an organization to retain market share, service customers, and maintain cash flow if a disaster occurs.

The Definitive Handbook of Business Continuity Management, 2nd ed
Andrew Hiles, Peter Barnes (editors)
Chichester, UK: Wiley, 2007
666pp, ISBN: 978-0-470-51638-6

This revised and updated edition tackles business continuity from two perspectives: the first part discusses the key concepts and provides an overview of the type of events which can interrupt business; the second takes the form of a practical how-to guide. Further resources, including case studies and standards for business continuity practitioners, are listed in appendices.

Disaster Management: A Guide to Management and Crisis Communication
Chris Skinner, Gary Mersham
Oxford: Oxford University Press, 2002
192pp, ISBN: 978-0-19-578313-1

This practical guidebook is about achieving a state of preparedness for all types of disaster, natural or human, that can affect a company. It provides the insights and tools required to manage the situation and any associated publicity this might incur. Relevant for students and professionals in the fields of human resource management, personnel management, public relations, and communications, it includes case studies, and offers operational guidelines and checklists for implementing a crisis management plan, and for handling media relations.

Disaster Recovery Planning: Preparing for the Unthinkable, 3rd ed
Jon William Toigo
Harlow, UK: Prentice Hall, 2002
512pp, ISBN: 978-0-13-046282-4

This volume provides the information needed to develop a plan to protect your company's data in case of an emergency. Filled with interviews with vendors and practitioners, it walks the reader through the steps that those responsible for an organization's information technology must take to ensure that organizational data will be available in the aftermath of a disaster.

Managing Communications in a Crisis
Peter Ruff, Khalid Aziz
Aldershot, UK: Gower Publishing, 2003
176pp, ISBN: 978-0-566-08294-8

This book details how crisis situations can be identified and dealt with to ensure that risks to an organization's financial well-being and reputation are minimized. Part I considers the definitions of a crisis and the theory behind dealing with crisis communications, both externally and internally. Practicalities of crisis management communications dealt with in Part II include the identification of audiences and how and by whom each should be dealt with. Checklists and supporting information on the key aspects of the communication process are also supplied, together with brief case studies.

Managing Crises Before They Happen, 2nd ed
Ian I. Mitroff, Gus Anagnos
New York: AMACOM, 2005
192pp, ISBN: 978-0-8144-7328-3

Having explained the specific features of corporate culture that enable crises to happen, the authors present a framework for preventing such crises happening and for controlling the damage they cause.

Risk Issues and Crisis Management: A Casebook of Best Practice, 4th ed
Michael Regester, Judy Larkin
PR in Practice Series
London: Kogan Page, 2008
256pp, ISBN: 978-0-7494-5107-3

This book deals with the successful handling of crisis situations so that damage and disruption are minimized. Case studies and models are included and illustrate how complex crises have been handled in practice, both successfully and unsuccessfully.

Secure Online Business Handbook: E-Commerce, IT Functionality, and Business Continuity, 4th ed
Jonathan Reuvid
London: Kogan Page, 2006
256pp, ISBN: 978-0-7494-4642-0

This practical handbook, divided into five sections, contains a collection of contributions from a range of experts in the field of information technology and e-commerce and addresses the need for effective management of business risk. Information at risk and the business case for security are considered first. Points of exposure and the range of threats to privacy and integrity are explored, and methods of software protection such as firewalls, encryption, digital signatures and biometrics are covered. In the operational management section, the need for a culture of workplace security is also discussed, and data recovery, disaster management, and forensics are covered under the heading of contingency planning.

MAGAZINES

Continuity
Business Continuity Institute
10 Southview Park, Marsack Street, Caversham, Berkshire, RG4 5AF, UK

  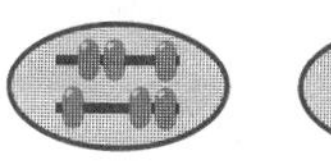  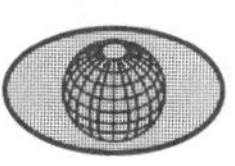   

T: +44 (0) 870 603 8783
F: +44 (0) 870 603 8761
www.thebci.org/continuity.htm
ISSN: 1460-1451
Continuity is the official journal of the Business Continuity Institute. It appears quarterly and includes articles, news, and reports of research projects.

Disaster Recovery Journal
Richard L. Arnold
PO Box 510110, St Louis, MO 63151, USA
T: +1 314 894 0276
F: +1 314 894 7474
www.drj.com
ISSN: 1079-736X
The DRJ was founded in 1987 and is published quarterly. It covers the field of business continuity and disaster recovery.

JOURNALS

Disaster Prevention and Management
Emerald
60/62 Toller Lane, Bradford, West Yorkshire, BD8 9BY, UK
T: +44 (0) 1274 777 700
F: +44 (0) 1274 785 200
www.emeraldinsight.com/0965-3562.htm
ISSN: 0965-3562
This journal appears five times a year and focuses on the latest research into the prevention and mitigation of natural and man-made disasters. Each issue includes articles by international experts in the field, news, product reviews, case studies, and details of events, conferences, and resources.

Journal of Contingencies and Crisis Management
Blackwell Publishing
9600 Garsington Road, Oxford, OX4 2DQ, UK
T: +44 (0) 1865 791 100
F: +44 (0) 1865 791 347
www.wiley.com/bw/journal.asp?ref=0966-0879
ISSN: 0966-0879
This is a quarterly journal for managers with responsibilities in the area of risk and crisis management.

Journal of Small Business and Enterprise Development
Emerald
60/62 Toller Lane, Bradford, West Yorkshire, BD8 9BY, UK
T: +44 (0) 1274 777 700
F: +44 (0) 1274 785 200
www.emeraldinsight.com/1462-6004.htm
ISSN: 1462-6004
The *JSBED* is a peerreviewed journal that disseminates research findings and best practice and aims to bridge the gap between theory and practice in the field of small business and enterprise development. The journal contains articles, case studies, and book reviews, and is aimed at those responsible for the management of SMEs, those who provide support and assistance to entrepreneurs and owner-managers, and those involved in the development of enterprise policy.

INTERNET

Crisis Management and Disaster Recovery
www.crisismanagement-disasterrecovery.com
This site provides information and links for both crisis management and disaster recovery. It links you with companies that can help with crisis management plans or disaster recovery plans, and gives information about crisis management and disaster management.

Crisis Management and Disaster Recovery Group
www.crisis-management-and-disaster-recovery.com
This site provides information on how to create and maintain a disaster recovery or crisis management plan and provides access to leading support resources.

Disaster Recovery Journal
www.drj.com
This journal's website provides access to a great deal of free material and resources including articles, a vendor directory, and chat groups.

Federal Emergency Management Agency
www.fema.gov
This US federal government site features GEMS (Global Emergency Management System), a searchable database of reviewed websites in fields related to emergency management, and a virtual library including practical guides and checklists.

globalcontinuity.com
www.globalcontinuity.com
This is a portal site for business recovery and continuity planning information, featuring a database of suppliers and including news, articles, surveys, and related links.

London Prepared
www.londonprepared.gov.uk
The UK government has launched this site to give advice and information on how to protect you business against all sorts of threats. The site is part of London Resilience, a broad project that helps people in London to prepare themselves for emergencies.

ORGANIZATIONS

Europe

Emergency Planning Society
The Media Centre, Culverhouse Cross, Cardiff, CF6 6XJ, UK
T: +44 (0) 845 600 9587
F: +44 (0) 29 2059 0396
www.the-eps.org
The society was formed in 1993 through the merger of the Emergency Planning Association and the County Emergency Planning Officers Society. Its aims are to foster effective emergency planning and management in the United Kingdom and to promote the professional interests of its members, who include representatives of the emergency services, local and central government, the health services, industry, consultants, and voluntary organizations. It is active in the areas of training, professional development, networking, representation, and publications.

USA

Contingency Planning Exchange, Inc. (CPE)
11 Hanover Square, Suite 501, New York, NY 10176-3099, USA
T: +1 212 344 4003
F: +1 212 344 2016
E: headquarters@cpeworld.org
www.cpeworld.ciom
The CPE is a professional organization for disaster recovery specialists which provides a forum for members to exchange information, and represents the views of members to government agencies and the wider business community.

Federal Emergency Management Agency (FEMA)
500 C Street S.W., Washington, DC 20472, USA
T: +1 800 621 3362
www.fema.gov
An independent agency of the federal government of the United States, FEMA was founded in 1979, but can trace its origins back to the Congressional Act of 1803. The mission of the agency is to reduce loss of life and property and to protect the national infrastructure from all types of hazard through an emergency management program that includes

  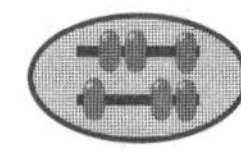   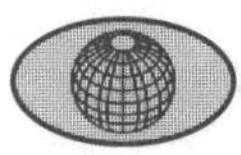   

preparation, mitigation, response, and recovery.

BRIC

BCM Institute
315 Outram Road #15-04, Tan Boon Liat Building, Singapore, 169074, Singapore
T: +65 6323 1500
F: +65 6323 0933
E: info@bcm-institute.org
www.bcm-institute.org
Covering most of Asia, including India and China, and represented in Africa, the BCM was erected to create a common base knowledge of business continuity (BC) management and disaster recovery (DR) planning, to certify qualified individuals, and to create credibility and professionalism in certified BC and DR professionals.

International

Association of Contingency Planners (ACP)
Technical Enterprises, 7044 South 13th Street, Oak Creek, WI 53154, USA
T: +1 414 768 8000
E: acp_membership@techenterprises.net
www.acp-international.com
The ACP is a nonprofit trade association for contingency planners, business continuity professionals, and emergency managers. The organization, which began informally in 1983 and was incorporated in 1985, provides an international forum for networking and information exchange. Activities include a branch network, a quarterly newsletter, and an annual international symposium.

Business Continuity Institute (BCI)
10 Southview Park, Marsack Street, Caversham, RG4 5AF, UK
T: +44 (0) 870 603 8783
F: +44 (0) 870 603 8761
E: bci@thebci.org
www.thebci.org
The BCI is a professional organization founded in 1994 to promote high standards of professional competence and ethics in the provision of business continuity planning and services. It has developed standards of competence, a code of ethics, and an accreditation scheme for continuity practitioners. Additional activities include seminars, conferences, and the Business Continuity Awards. The organization has over 1,100 members in 32 countries.

Disaster Preparedness and Emergency Response Association (DERA)
PO Box 280795, Denver, CO 80228, USA
E: dera@disasters.org
www.disasters.com
DERA is a nonprofit professional association, established in 1962, whose members include emergency management specialists, government officials, consultants, business managers, volunteers, researchers, and educators. It sponsors research projects in the field and publishes a newsletter, *DisasterCom*.

DRI International
1400 Eye Street, NW, Suite 1050, Washington, DC 20005, USA
T: +1 202 962 3979
F: +1 202 962 3939
www.drii.org
Formerly the Disaster Recovery Institute, DRI International was formed in 1988 by a group of professionals in St. Louis, Missouri, who saw a need for education in business continuity. The organization is a nonprofit one; it sets standards of competence for business continuity and has developed a certification program.

Emergency Preparedness for Industry and Commerce Council (EPICC)
9800, 140 Street, Surrey, British Columbia, V3T 4M5, Canada
T: +1 604 580 7373
F: +1 604 586 4334
E: epicc@telus.net
www.epicc.org
The aim of this organization is to help businesses and communities prepare to survive disasters through education and representation. It organizes workshops and forums, and publishes a newsletter.

International Association of Emergency Managers (IAEM)
201 Park Washington Court, Falls Church, VI 22046-4527, USA
T: +1 703 538 1795
F: +1 703 241 5603
E: info@iaem.com
www.iaem.com
The IAEM is a nonprofit educational organization; it created the Certified Emergency Manager program to maintain professional standards in emergency management. Members receive a monthly newsletter and can participate in internet discussion groups.

  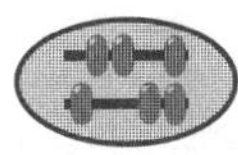 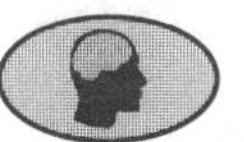  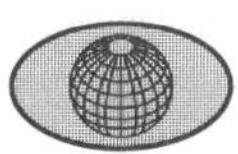   

Corporate Culture

BOOKS

Absolute Honesty: Building a Corporate Culture that Values Straight Talk and Rewards Integrity

Larry Johnson, Bob Phillips
New York: AMACOM, 2003
304pp, ISBN: 978-0-8144-0781-3

This book starts out from the belief that honesty can produce economic as well as moral rewards, in terms of improved productivity, competitive advantage, morale, and public trust. It asserts the need to reestablish a culture of openness and truth in communication methods, grounded in absolute honesty. To this end it sets out a framework of six laws of absolute honesty and gives advice on implementing them within an ethical infrastructure.

Balancing Individual and Organizational Values: Walking the Tightrope to Success

Ken Hultman, Bill Gellermann
Practicing Organization Development Series
San Francisco, California: Jossey-Bass/ Pfeiffer, 2002
240pp, ISBN: 978-0-7879-5720-9

This book is designed to help organization development (OD) practitioners create the conditions for organizational effectiveness by balancing individual and organizational values. It explores the nature and importance of beliefs, values, and norms and their relationship with behavior, and presents the Motivational System Model, a tool which can be used with individuals, teams, and organizations.

Built to Last: Successful Habits of Visionary Companies

Jim Collins, Jerry I. Porras
London: HarperCollins, 2004
368pp, ISBN: 978-0-06-056610-4

This book draws upon a six-year research project at the Stanford University Graduate School of Business, in which 18 truly exceptional and long-lasting companies were examined in depth to see what makes them so successful. It highlights factors such as their flexibility, ideology, and strong purpose. The authors then give practical guidance to those who would like to build landmark companies that similarly stand the test of time.

Business Across Cultures

Fons Trompenaars, Peter Wooliams
Culture for Business Series
Chichester, UK: Capstone, 2003
368pp, ISBN: 978-1-84112-474-2

Geared towards companies or individuals working with those from other cultures, this book is a useful overview of key issues in cross-cultural business. Accessible and engaging, it sets out to show readers how everyone working in or with a company in this situation can benefit from it.

The Character of a Corporation: How Your Company's Culture Can Make or Break Your Business, 2nd ed

Rob Goffee, Gareth Jones
London: Profile Books, 2003
256pp, ISBN: 978-1-86197-639-0

This book is based on research and consultancy in high-profile companies conducted by the authors over a period of fifteen years. It presents a methodology for assessing and transforming corporate culture, including a diagnostic test which can be used by managers to discover which of four basic cultural forms—networked, mercenary, fragmented, or communal—prevails within their organization.

Conscience and Corporate Culture

Kenneth E. Goodpaster
Malden, Massachusetts: Blackwell Publishing, 2006
336pp, ISBN: 978-1-4051-3040-0

Written for educators in the field of business ethics and practicing corporate executives, the book serves as a platform on a difficult and timely subject.

Corporate Culture and Environmental Practice: Making Change at a High-Technology Manufacturer

Jennifer A. Howard-Grenville
Cheltenham, UK: Edward Elgar Publishing, 2007
165pp, ISBN: 978-1-84720-100-3

This details how a company's culture, through its internal practices, decisions, and norms, can guide action on environmental issues. While demonstrating gaps between the main operations of the company and the demands placed by environmental considerations, it analyzes how differences are negotiated over time, offering important insights into the processes of change that can advance environmental issues within a company.

Corporate Culture and Performance

John P. Kotter, James L. Heskett
New York: Free Press, 1992
214pp, ISBN: 978-0-02-918467-7

The authors describe their research into the effects of corporate culture on economic performance in international companies. They challenge the belief that strong corporate cultures automatically create excellent business performance, arguing instead for an "adaptive" culture that takes into account the interests of stakeholders such as customers and employees to produce better results. Case studies of world-class companies are included.

Corporate Culture: Illuminating the Black Hole

Jeroma Want
New York: St Martin's Press, 2007
284pp, ISBN: 978-0-312-35484-8

Corporate Culture: Illuminating the Black Hole is a source of knowledge for understanding the new types of business culture that are required in this era of radical business change. Case studies are included to show how corporate culture has contributed to the success of such companies. It also examines how flawed corporate cultures have contributed to the failure or near failure of former industry leaders.

Corporate Culture Survival Guide

Edgar H. Schein
San Francisco, California: Jossey-Bass, 1999
224pp, ISBN: 978-0-7879-4699-9

This book provides practical advice for front-line managers and change agents. It examines business on three levels: behaviors, values, and shared assumptions. It shows how corporations can assess their own atmosphere to determine if they have the right culture for their product and organizational structure and then proceed to make real and effective changes.

Creating the Innovation Culture: Leveraging Visionaries, Dissenters and other Useful Troublemakers in Your Organization

Frances Horibe
Chichester, UK: Wiley, 2001
256pp, ISBN: 978-0-471-64628-0

This book offers practical strategies for managing creative people or dissenters and for developing processes and mechanisms to support and sustain innovation within the organization. The author gives emphasis to understanding the distinction between healthy dissent and undesirable troublemaking.

  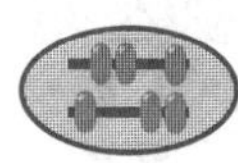   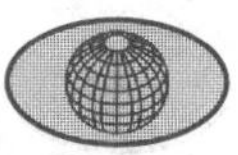   

Cultures and Organizations: Software for the Mind, 2nd ed
Geert Hofstede, Gert Jan Hofstede
Maidenhead, UK: McGraw-Hill, 2004
300pp, ISBN: 978-0-07-143959-6
The book, first published in 1991, aims to give practicing managers and students an understanding of cultural differences which will assist them in intercultural communication and cooperation in business and society. It examines the nature of culture and cultural differences and considers their implications.

Diagnosing and Changing Organizational Culture: Based on the Competing Values Framework
Kim S. Cameron, Robert E. Quinn
Addison-Wesley Series on Organization Development
Cambridge, Massachusetts: Addison-Wesley, 1998
221pp, ISBN: 978-0-201-33871-3
Written with the aim of helping managers, change agents, and scholars to understand and facilitate cultural and behavioral change within organizations, this book provides a theoretical framework for organizational culture, validated instruments for diagnosing it, and a systematic methodology for changing it.

Evolve! Succeeding in the Digital Culture of Tomorrow
Rosabeth Moss Kanter
Boston, Massachusetts: Harvard Business School Press, 2001
304pp, ISBN: 978-1-57851-439-7
An exploration of "e-culture"—a new way of living and working that will transform every aspect of today's organizations—this book is for anyone who wants to realize the potential and avoid the pitfalls of the Internet age. It draws on over 300 interviews and a global-scale company survey to provide a framework for adopting the core principles of e-culture.

Harvard Business Review on Culture and Change
Harvard Business Review Paperbacks Series
Boston, Massachusetts: Harvard Business School Press, 2002
179pp, ISBN: 978-1-57851-836-4
This text brings together a collection of articles from Harvard Business Review. It provides insights into the confusing and challenging process of changing workplace culture. The different authors examine a range of issues, including why people resist change on both the individual and corporate level and how passive aversion to cultural problems affects company performance, and provide an actionable framework for transforming corporate culture.

Managing Across Cultures, 2nd ed
Susan C. Schneider, Jean-Louis Barsoux
Harlow, UK: FT Prentice Hall, 2003
352pp, ISBN: 978-0-273-64663-1
This accessible book draws upon a broad and growing literature on culture and management to examine national differences in management practice. It relates cultural differences to daily business practice by using many and varied examples, and discusses a wide range of topics, from structure and strategy to social responsibility and ethics.

The Naked Corporation: How the Age of Transparency Will Revolutionize Business
Don Tapscott, David Ticoll
New York: Free Press, 2003
352pp, ISBN: 978-0-7432-4650-7
Transparency is a new global business issue and one of the forces of change that is revolutionizing the way business is done. Drawing on case studies such as Chiquita and Shell, the authors of this text offer a way to lead in and manage transparency as a new opportunity for business, rather than simply reacting to its requirements. The nature of transparency is discussed and the subject is explored in the contexts of the employee, business partner, customer, community, and owner. The text also considers the power of openness and leadership issues.

The New Corporate Cultures: Revitalizing the Workplace after Downsizing, Mergers, and Reengineering
Terrence E. Deal, Allan A. Kennedy
London: Texere Publishing, 2000
312pp, ISBN: 978-1-58799-026-7
This book examines how changes brought about by economic forces and management trends, such as downsizing, outsourcing, new technology, and globalization, have affected company cultures. The authors consider how companies can approach the task of rebuilding cohesive organizational cultures for greater effectiveness following the fragmentation that many have experienced.

Organisational Culture, 2nd ed
Andrew D. Brown
London: FT Pitman, 1998
320pp, ISBN: 978-0-273-63147-7
The author provides an overview of the subject and examines the link between culture and the concepts of organizational change, human resource management, and strategic issues. Examples are included throughout the text, focusing on a range of well-known European cases.

Organizational Culture and Leadership, 3rd ed
Edgar H. Schein
San Francisco, California: Jossey-Bass, 2004
464pp, ISBN: 978-0-7879-6845-8
This third edition of a classic work on the dynamics of organizational culture draws on contemporary research to show how leaders can apply the principles of culture change in order to achieve organizational goals.

Organizational Culture: Mapping the Terrain
Joanne Martin
London: Sage Publications, 2002
400pp, ISBN: 978-0-8039-7295-7
An elegant introduction to a complex topic, this book describes the main relevant theories and definitions of the subject, and the disputes that have arisen concerning them. The various methods that have evolved for studying the subject, and the ways in which these studies might develop, are also discussed. Examples and case studies are included.

Organization Development and Change, 8th ed
Christopher G. Worley, Thomas G. Cummings
Mason, Ohio: Thomson/South-Western, 2005
700pp, ISBN: 978-0-324-26060-1
Market-leading Organization Development and Change blends theory, concepts, and applications in a comprehensive and clear presentation. The authors work from a strong theoretical foothold and apply behavioral science knowledge to the development of organizational structures, strategies, and processes.

Riding the Waves of Culture: Understanding Cultural Diversity in Business, 2nd ed
Fons Trompenaars, Charles Hampden-Turner
London: Nicholas Brealey Publishing, 1997
276pp, ISBN: 978-1-85788-176-9
The authors explore cultural extremes and the incomprehension that can arise when doing business across cultures, even within the same organization. They identify five key orientations that affect how people deal with each other, do business, and manage, and propose strategies for reconciling these orientations across different cultures. They also review the concept of the "trans-national corporation," in which companies take from each culture what is best.

Understanding Organizational Culture
Mats Alvesson
Thousand Oaks, California: Sage Publications, 2002
224pp, ISBN: 978-0-7619-7006-4
This text examines the concept of culture from various perspectives, and discusses key research issues. It provides a new framework for understanding organizational culture and describes the range of advances in the area. Illustrative examples are included.

MAGAZINES

BtoB
Crain Communications, Inc
711 Third Avenue, New York, NY 10017-4036, USA
T: +1 212 210 0100
F: +1 212 210 0200
www.btobonline.com
ISSN: 1530-2369
Business Credit Magazine is published 10 times a year and targets readers who are responsible for extending business and trade credit and risk management for their companies. The magazine examines trends and important legislative, bankruptcy, business ethics, trade finance, asset protection, benchmarking, and scoring issues.

JOURNALS

Cross Cultural Management
Emerald
60/62 Toller Lane, Bradford, West Yorkshire, BD8 9BY, UK
T: +44 (0) 1274 777 700
F: +44 (0) 1274 785 200
www.emeraldinsight.com/1352-7606.htm
ISSN: 1352-7606
This quarterly journal focuses on all aspects of cross-cultural relationships at work.

International Journal of Cross-Cultural Management
Sage Publications
1 Oliver's Yard, 55 City Road, London, EC1Y 1SP, UK
T: +44 (0) 20 7324 8500
F: +44 (0) 20 7324 8600
ccm.sagepub.com
ISSN: 1470-5958
Published three times a year, this is an academic journal that acts as a medium for the dissemination of research on the cross-cultural aspects of management, work, and organization. It promotes understanding of the role of culture in management theory and practice.

Organization Studies
Sage Publications
1 Oliver's Yard, 55 City Road, London, EC1Y 1SP, UK
T: +44 (0) 20 7324 8500
F: +44 (0) 20 7324 8600
oss.sagepub.com
ISSN: 0170-8406
An international multidisciplinary journal devoted to the study of organizations, organizing, and the organized in and between societies.

INTERNET

Business.com
www.business.com
This is an extensive and helpful search engine and directory site. The home page offers over 20 topics for users to research, including small businesses, accounting, law and computing. Search results are presented as a series of useful click-through links.

Culture in the Workplace Questionnaire
www.itapintl.com
This questionnaire is based on the work of Geert Hofstede and is provided by ITAP International, a consulting company offering crosscultural services for business.

Intermundo
www.intermundo.net
This is the site for an online journal of intercultural communication.

Official Ed Schein website
web.mit.edu/scheine/www/home.html
The site gives information about publications and presentations by Edgar Schein.

Onepine
www.onepine.info
Theories and works of major thinkers are examined under the People & Theories option, which users can find when they click through on Site contents.

Teaching and Learning Resources for Business Education
tutor2u.net
This site is a publisher of e-learning resources for economic, business, and politics, and related subjects, and is useful for schools, colleges and educational institutions.

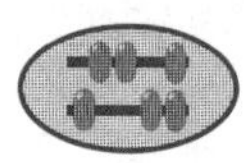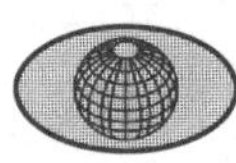

Corporate Insurance

BOOKS

Alternative Risk Strategies: A New Approach to Handling Risk
Morton Lane (editor)
London: Risk Books, 2002
684pp, ISBN: 978-1-899332-63-2

This comprehensive and wide-ranging analysis of the overlap between insurance and finance examines new areas of risk financing and their effect on traditional methods of insurance. It provides an overview of the reinsurance industry and recent developments, research, and current practice, and a detailed approach to contingent financing, terrorism risk, captives, finite risk, loss portfolio transfers, the financial impact of catastrophic natural events, and modeling techniques.

Captive Insurance Companies in Risk Management
Florian Klingenschmid
Saarbrücken, Germany: VDM Verlag, 2008
68pp, ISBN: 978-3-639-01170-8

This explores captive insurance as an innovative form of alternative risk transfer, and how companies use it to manage their risks effectively. It explains the basics of captive insurance, the different types of captives, why they are created, and the international features of the industry, as well as focusing on the influence that captives have on the risk management and credit rating of their parent company.

Dictionary of Insurance Terms, 5th ed
Harvey W. Rubin
Barron's Business Guides Series
Hauppauge, New York: Barron's Educational Series, 2008
576pp, ISBN: 978-0-7641-3884-3

This popular insurance dictionary, now in its fifth edition, provides clear definitions, descriptions, and examples of the terminology used in the industry. It is a reference for agents, brokers, actuaries, underwriters, and consumers, presenting around 4,500 key terms relevant to life, health, property, and casualty insurance, as well as to home owners' insurance, professional liability insurance, pension plans, and individual retirement accounts.

Fundamentals of Risk and Insurance, 10th ed
Emmet J. Vaughan, Therese M. Vaughan
Hoboken, New Jersey: Wiley, 2008
704pp, ISBN: 978-0-470-08753-4

This textbook addresses the principles of risk management as they relate to the insurance industry, and reviews the impact of risk on both the individual and society. It describes how insurance can effectively resolve risk management issues and problems, and discusses the key concepts of insurance theory, focusing on insurance products and the use of insurance within the risk management framework.

The Guide to Understanding Business Insurance Products: How to Safeguard Businesses from Financial Risk
A. M. Best Company
Charleston, South Carolina: BookSurge Publishing, 2007
24pp, ISBN: 978-1-4196-6635-3

This handbook on corporate insurance products provides a valuable resource, explaining what each coverage protects against, who needs it, how it works, and its key details. Produced for insurance clients, prospects, staff, brokers, agents and carriers, it describes most areas of commercial insurance coverage, including business owners' policy, commercial general liability, commercial property insurance, employment practices liability, intellectual property, and product liability.

Hide! Here Comes the Insurance Guy: A Practical Guide to Understanding Business Insurance and Risk Management
Rick Vassar
Bloomington, Indiana: iUniverse, 2006
196pp, ISBN: 978-0-595-38608-6

This is an accessible resource for reducing business and commercial insurance costs, taken from a risk management perspective. It provides understandable explanations and practical solutions, and a series of steps for reducing expenses in current insurance programs, based on understanding the language, knowing the players, developing a strategy for maximizing coverage for minimal cost, and investing the time to gain real financial benefit.

Inside the Minds: The Insurance Business
Martin D. Feinstein, Constantine Iordanou, Mark E. Watson, James J. Maguire, John W. Hayden
Inside the Minds Series
Boston, Massachusetts: Aspatore Books, 2004
128pp, ISBN: 978-1-58762-423-0

This provides insights from senior executives representing many leading insurance companies, as they explore how to be successful in this fast-changing industry. It gives an overview of current and future trends in the industry, presents strategies for revenue growth, examines the inner workings of the business, and identifies the biggest risks companies face, and how to hedge them.

Insurance: From Underwriting to Derivatives: Asset Liability Management in Insurance Companies
Eric Briys, François de Varenne
Wiley Finance Series
Chichester, UK: Wiley, 2001
165pp, ISBN: 978-0-471-49227-6

This offers a detailed examination of the convergence between the insurance industry and the capital markets, as traditional insurance is overtaken by its new role as an asset class. It discusses the main issues and trends affecting the industry, how it is responding to increasing market pressure, and how insurance risks are now being priced and exchanged on the markets.

Introduction to Risk Management and Insurance, 9th ed
Mark S. Dorfman
Upper Saddle River, New Jersey: Prentice Hall, 2008
567pp, ISBN: 978-0-13-224227-1

This primer on risk and insurance focuses on problem solving for the insurance practitioner, examining the business characteristics of risk management and insurance, as well as consumer applications. It covers professional financial planning, and insurance regulation and contracts, as well as topics such as homeowners insurance, annuities, standard life insurance contract provisions and options, commercial property insurance, general and special liability insurance, and employee benefits.

Reinsurance: Fundamentals and New Challenges, 4th ed
Ruth Gastel (editor)
New York: Insurance Information Institute, 2004
218pp, ISBN: 978-0-932387-50-9

This is a collection of essays by a number of industry experts that provides a basic introduction to reinsurance, and how it functions as a way for insurance to spread risk. It covers all the main technical aspects

  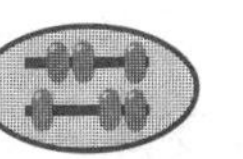 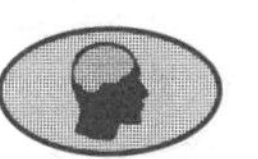  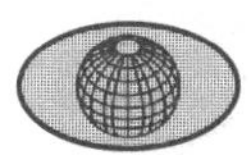   

of the subject, and the challenges currently facing the industry, and will appeal to those needing a practical overview, such as regulators and the wider financial community.

Risk Management and Insurance: Perspectives in a Global Economy
W. Jean Kwon, Harold D. Skipper
Malden, Massachusetts: Wiley, 2007
751pp, ISBN: 978-1-4051-2541-3
This examines the main aspects of risk management and insurance for both students and practitioners. It explores key aspects of international risk management and insurance, how they operate, and the economic, social, political, and regulatory landscape of the global risk and insurance markets. Using real-world case studies, discussion questions, and exercise modules, it describes the different types of risk businesses face, including financial, political, environmental, social, and health.

Risk Management for Insurers: Risk Control, Economic Capital and Solvency II
René Doff
London: Risk Books, 2007
204pp, ISBN: 978-1-904339-79-3
With the insurance industry focused on risk exposure, and the supervisory rules for regulatory capital for insurance companies being transformed, this shows how to implement risk management best practice. It presents key risk management techniques, tools, and terms, analyzes the impact of Solvency II on the regulatory framework of the industry, and explores how risk management and value creation can be integrated into the management control framework of insurance companies.

Structured Finance and Insurance: The ART of Managing Capital and Risk, 2nd ed
Christopher L. Culp
Wiley Finance Series
Hoboken, New Jersey: Wiley, 2006
892pp, ISBN: 978-0-471-70631-1
This introduction to alternative risk transfer (ART) provides an overview of the key financing and risk management innovations in both insurance and capital markets. It examines the development and benefits of this new generation of products for managing market, credit, operational, legal, and other risks, and explains the theory and practice of risk transfer through either balance sheet mechanisms or insurance.

MAGAZINES

Best's Review
A. M. Best Company
Ambest Road, Oldwick, NJ 08858, USA
T: +1 908 439 2200
www.bestreview.com
ISSN: 1527-5914
This monthly insurance magazine offers news coverage of the global insurance industry. It focuses on topical areas such as trends in the reinsurance/capital markets, new technology, health/employee benefit issues, the property/casualty sector, life insurance, agent/brokers, changes in regulation and law, and provides exclusive lists and rankings.

Business Insurance
Crain Communications
711 Third Avenue, New York, NY 10017-4036, USA
T: +1 212 210 0100
F: +1 212 210 0223
www.businessinsurance.com
ISSN: 0007-6864
This weekly newspaper on business insurance features news, comment, and analysis on the industry, as well as a number of industry directories, a knowledge center, an industry focus, details of jobs, and email news alerts.

Business Insurance Europe
Crain Communications
9–17 Perrymount Road, Haywards Heath, RH16 3DH, UK
T: +44 (0) 1444 475 650
F: +44 (0) 845 677 7804
www.bieurope.com
ISSN: 1759-1295
This fortnightly publication is a source of news, views, and analysis on the European risk and commercial insurance business. It provides coverage on the latest developments, comment on topical issues, special feature articles, case studies, regulatory updates, and the latest trends and views from leading industry professionals.

Claims
The National Underwriter Company
5081 Olympic Boulevard, Erlanger, KY 41018, USA
T: +1 859 692 2128
F: +1 859 692 2246
www.claimsmag.com
This monthly magazine focuses on the business of loss for property/casualty insurance claims professionals and corporate risk managers. It provides reports on disasters, insurance crime, emerging trends in insurance claims, regulatory, judicial and legislative changes, and expert advice and educational articles that cover techniques for handling insured losses.

Continuity Insurance & Risk
Perspective Publishing
6th Floor, 3 London Wall Buildings, London, EC2M 5PD, UK
T: +44 (0) 20 7562 2401
F: +44 (0) 20 7374 2701
www.cirmagazine.com
ISSN: 1479-862X
This professional magazine, published bimonthly, provides authoritative news and analysis for business continuity, risk management, and insurance practitioners.

Global Reinsurance
Newsquest
30 Cannon Street, London, EC4M 6YJ, UK
T: +44 (0) 20 7618 3456
F: +44 (0) 20 7618 3420
www.globalreinsurance.com
ISSN: 1358-7420
This monthly magazine provides breaking news, analysis, and industry comment on reinsurance. It offers features such as insurance agenda, catastrophe risk, research, people news, jobs, supplements, and a range of special reports covering reinsurance buying strategies, insurance-linked securities, enterprise-wide risk management, and Europe and UK market run-off.

Insurance & Technology
United Business Media
TechWeb, 11 West 19th Street, New York, NY, 10011, USA
T: +1 212 600 3000
F: +1 212 600 3060
www.insurancetech.com
ISSN: 1054-0733
This monthly magazine offers breaking news, analysis, insurance agenda, catastrophe risk, supplements, research, reinsurance jobs, and a range of special reports covering reinsurance buying strategies, insurance-linked securities, enterprise-wide risk management, and analysis of specific industry sectors.

Insurance Age
Incisive Media
32–34 Broadwick Street, London, W1A 2HG, UK
T: +44 (0) 20 8606 7516
F: +44 (0) 20 7316 9313
www.insuranceage.com
ISSN: 0143-8085
This monthly magazine is published for insurance brokers/intermediaries and companies serving the broker community,

  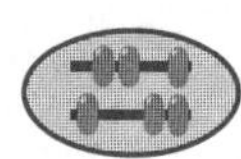   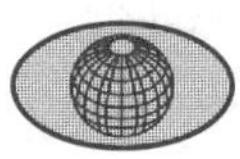   

including insurance companies, loss adjusters, claims management and IT providers. It offers news and analysis, product reviews, market sector comment, and job postings.

Insurance Day
Informa
Informa House, 30–32 Mortimer Street, London, W1W 7RE, UK
T: +44 (0) 20 7017 5000
www.insuranceday.com
This is the only daily newspaper dedicated to the international insurance, reinsurance, and risk industry. It comments on a wide range of market sectors, and provides expert comment and opinion, company profiles and results, current rates, regulation and forecasts, and technology developments, and coverage and guidelines of both the life and non-life insurance markets.

Insurance Journal
Wells Publishing
3570 Camino del Rio North, Suite 200, San Diego, CA 92108, USA
T: +1 619 584 1100
F: +1 619 584 1200
www.insurancejournal.com
ISSN: 0020-4714
This fortnightly magazine is an authoritative source of news and information on property and casualty insurance for independent insurance agents and brokers. It provides news, comment, and analysis on key industry topics, and offers features such as regional stories, classifieds, e-newsletter, forums, events, and a technology center.

Insurance Networking News
SourceMedia
550 West Van Buren Street, Suite 1100, Chicago, IL 60607, USA
T: +1 312 913 1334
F: +1 312 913 1366
www.insurancenetworking.com
ISSN: 1542-4901
This monthly magazine produces information on how technology is being implemented to support insurers' strategic business objectives, and analysis on the use of technology for automating key processes. Its coverage includes claims management, automated underwriting, fraud detection, agency automation, disaster planning, web services, business intelligence, data management, regulatory compliance, new products, and competitive strategies.

InsuranceNewsNet Magazine
InsuranceNewsNet.com
355 North 21st Street, Suite 211, Camp Hill, PA 17011, USA
T: +1 866 707 6786
www.insurancenewsnetmagazine.com
This new, free magazine for life, health, and annuity producers in the US offers analysis of annuity sales secrets, life insurance trends, and health marketing. It publishes articles by leading industry experts, and coverage of life insurance sales strategies, and health insurance marketing and business growth.

Insurance Times
Newsquest
30 Cannon Street, London, EC4M 6YJ, UK
T: +44 (0) 20 7618 3456
F: +44 (0) 20 7618 3420
www.insurancetimes.co.uk
ISSN: 1466-8149
This weekly insurance newspaper publishes breaking news, analysis, and features, including insurance agenda, comment/blogs, profiles, events, research, jobs, and a focus on regional brokers. It also offers regular supplements, including BIBA Times, Top 50 Brokers, and Top 50 Insurers.

Post
Incisive Media
Haymarket House, 28–29 Haymarket, London, SW1Y 4RX, UK
T: +44 (0) 20 7484 9700
F: +44 (0) 20 7484 9797
www.postonline.co.uk
ISSN: 1365-4284
This weekly magazine provides comprehensive and authoritative coverage of all issues of interest to the UK insurance industry, through news and analysis, comment, topical features, and technical articles, and supplements. It also features information on recruitment, and hosts conferences and annual awards.

Professional Broking
Incisive Media
32–34 Broadwick Street, London, W1A 2HG, UK
T: +44 (0) 20 7484 9700
www.professionalbroking.co.uk
ISSN: 1355-0519
This monthly magazine is produced for insurance broker managers, and delivers business intelligence on topics such as the tax implications of green strategies, and the latest employee benefits, as well as on wider economic and business issues. It also offers supplements, competitions, management events, insurance directories, ratings search, interviews, and surveys.

Property and Casualty Magazine
The National Underwriter Company
33–41 Newark Street, 2nd Floor, Hoboken NJ 07030, USA
T: +1 201 526 1230
F: +1 201 526 1260
www.propertyandcasualtyinsurancenews.com
This weekly magazine focuses on the commercial insurance business, and the wider insurance industry, covering key developments affecting buyers, sellers, and manufacturers of insurance products and related services. It discusses industry topics such as legislation, mergers and acquisitions, technology trends, compliance issues, and new product news, and publishes special reports and directories on specialty markets and technology breakthroughs.

Reinsurance
Incisive Media
Haymarket House, 28–29 Haymarket, London, SW1Y 4RX, UK
T: +44 (0) 20 7316 9000
F: +44 (0) 20 7316 9313
www.reinsurancemagazine.com
ISSN: 0048-7171
This monthly magazine presents news and analysis from the global markets and Lloyd's, as well as country reports, technical reports, statistics and surveys, views and opinions from leading industry figures, and commentary on developments in regulation, legislation and litigation.

The Review
Informa
Informa House, 30–32 Mortimer Street, London, W1W 7RE, UK
T: +44 (0) 20 7017 5000
www.thereview.biz
This monthly publication delivers reinsurance news and analysis for the global risk management industry, especially those with a responsibility for buying, distributing, or underwriting reinsurance and related risk management products.

Risk & Insurance
LRP Publications
Suite 500, 747 Dresher Road, PO Box 980, Horsham, PA 19044-0980, USA
T: +1 215 784 0910
F: +1 215 784 0275
www.riskandinsurance.com
ISSN: 1050-9232
This magazine, published 15 times each year, covers business risks and mitigation strategies, such as insurance, employee benefits, alternative risk transfer, and emerging risks. It provides features,

  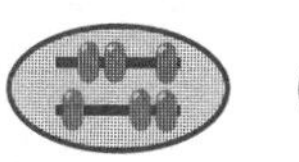   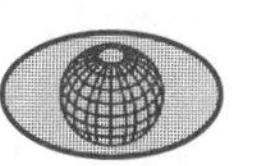   

articles, industry risk reports, in-depth series, and special reports, as well as resources and tools such as a power broker directory, risk innovators, case studies, industry events, workers' compensation forum, and vendor directories.

The Risk Retention Reporter
Insurance Communications
PO Box 50147, Pasadena, CA 91115, USA
T: +1 626 796 4972
F: +1 626 796 2363
www.rrr.com
This monthly magazine provides risk retention industry news and the latest legislative and judicial developments, and monitors hundreds of risk retention and purchasing groups. It also offers a monthly roundup, articles by industry experts, profiles, special reports, and market surveys.

JOURNALS

The Geneva Papers on Risk and Insurance
International Association of Insurance Supervisors
IAIS Secretariat, c/o Bank for International Settlements' CH-4002 Basel, Switzerland
T: +41 61 225 73 00
F: +41 61 280 91 51
www.palgrave-journals.com/gpp
ISSN: 1018-5895
This quarterly journal, sponsored by the Geneva Association, publishes papers that advance an understanding of individual and firm behavior under uncertainty. The papers tend to be theoretical, but it also publishes empirical and/or experimental research if it tests competing theories and expands knowledge of insurance economics.

Insurance: Mathematics and Economics
Elsevier
Radarweg 29, 1043 NX Amsterdam, The Netherlands
F: +31 20 485 2180
www.elsevier.com/wps/find/journaldescription.cws_home/505554/description
ISSN: 0167-6687
This bimonthly international journal is aimed at individuals and groups who produce and apply research results in insurance and finance. It publishes papers of international interest, concerned with either the theory of insurance mathematics and economics, or the inventive application of it, and focuses on the theory, models and computational methods of life and non-life insurance, reinsurance, risk management, and financial modeling.

Journal of Risk and Insurance
American Risk and Insurance Association
716 Providence Road, Malvern, PA 19355-3402, USA
T: +1 610 640 1997
F: +1 610 725 1007
www.journalofriskandinsurance.org
ISSN: 0022-4367
This quarterly academic journal publishes original theoretical and empirical research in insurance and risk management. It covers such areas as the industrial organization of insurance markets, the management of risks, insurance finance, economics of employee benefits, utility theory, asymmetric information, insurance regulation, econometric, actuarial, and statistical methodology, economics of insurance institutions, and insurance cycles and economic cycles of insurance markets.

Risk Management and Insurance Review
American Risk and Insurance Association
716 Providence Road, Malvern, PA 19355-3402, USA
T: +1 610 640 1997
F: +1 610 725 1007
www.wiley.com/bw/journal.asp?ref=1098-1616
ISSN: 1098-1616
This biannual journal publishes applied research, opinion, and discussion on risk and insurance. Its publishes original research on applications and applied techniques, perspectives on research literature, business practice, and public policy, and educational papers that provide a repository of model lectures in risk and insurance, as well as discussing and evaluating instructional techniques.

INTERNET

Insurance Day
www.insuranceday.com
This is a subscription-only service that provides the latest insurance industry news, as well as information on insurance law and insurance regulation changes.

Insurance Directories
www.insurance-directories.com
This is a useful online search facility for professional insurance services, products, and companies.

InsuranceNewsNet
www.insurancenewsnet.com
This is an online provider of focused insurance industry information, news, analysis and commentary, aimed at producers, distributors, and carriers in the insurance and financial services industry. It organizes, analyzes, and filters insurance news from sources around the world, and produces weekly industry e-newsletters.

ORGANIZATIONS

Europe

Association of British Insurers
Chair: Stephen Haddrill
51 Gresham Street, London, EC2V 7HQ, UK
T: +44 (0) 20 7600 3333
F: +44 (0) 20 7696 8999
E: info@abi.org.uk
www.abi.org.uk
The ABI is the representative body for the UK insurance industry. It speaks out on issues of common interest, participates in debates on public policy, and advocates high standards of customer service in the insurance industry. Its policy work focuses on general insurance, life and pensions, financial regulation and taxation, and investment affairs, and it also organizes conferences, and publishes research reports and policy documents.

Association of Insurance and Risk Managers
Chair: Julia Graham
6 Lloyd's Avenue, London, EC3N 3AX, UK
T: +44 (0) 20 7480 7610
F: +44 (0) 20 7702 3752
www.airmic.com
AIRMIC is the UK membership body for risk and insurance managers. Its activities include lobbying, campaigning, risk management, insurance best practice, networking, and training, as well as research into new technology and business continuity.

British Insurance Brokers' Association
Chair: Derek Thornton
8th Floor, John Stow House, 18 Bevis Marks, London, EC3A 7JB, UK
F: +44 (0) 20 7626 9676
E: enquiries@biba.org.uk
www.biba.org.uk
BIBA is a general insurance organization that represents the interests of insurance brokers, intermediaries, and their customers in the UK. It acts as the voice of the industry, advising members, regulators, government, consumer bodies, and other stakeholders on key insurance issues, and provides facilities, technical advice, guidance on regulation, business support, and works to raise and maintain industry standards.

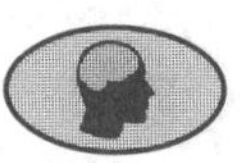

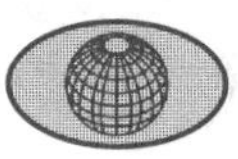

CEA
Chair: Tommy Persson
Square de Meeûs 29, 1000 Brussels, Belgium
T: +32 2 547 58 11
F: +32 2 547 58 19
www.cea.eu
The CEA is a European insurance and reinsurance federation that represents all types of insurance and reinsurance undertakings. It promotes the strategic interests of its members, raises awareness of insurers' and reinsurers' roles in providing insurance protection and security, advocates a competitive and open market, and acts as the voice of the European insurance industry at European and international level.

Chartered Insurance Institute
Chair: Alexander Scott
42–48 High Road, South Woodford, London, E18 2JP, UK
T: +44 (0) 20 8989 8464
F: +44 (0) 20 8530 3052
E: customer.serv@cii.co.uk
www.cii.co.uk
The CII is a professional and educational organization for the insurance and financial services industry in the UK. It provides accreditation and professional qualifications, and promotes competence through the provision of relevant knowledge for employees at all levels and across all sectors of the industry. It also supports fair dealing and integrity through a code of ethics and conduct to which all members subscribe.

European Federation of Insurance Intermediaries
Avenue Albert-Elisabeth 40, 1200 Brussels, Belgium
T: +32 2 735 60 48
F: +32 2 732 14 18
E: bipar@skynet.be
www.bipar.eu
BIPAR is a Europe-wide organization that promotes the interests of insurance agents and brokers in European public affairs. Its membership consists of representative national associations of professional insurance agents and brokers from within Europe, and it also represents self-employed and corporate professional insurance intermediaries.

Federation of European Risk Management Associations
Chair: Marie-Gemma Dequae
Avenue Louis Gribaumont 1, 1150 Brussels, Belgium
T: +32 2 761 94 32
F: +32 2 771 87 20
E: info@ferma.eu
www.ferma.eu
FERMA is comprised of member associations across Europe, and is dedicated to widening and raising the culture of risk management throughout Europe to its members and the risk management and insurance community. It promotes an awareness of risk management through the media, by information sharing, educational, and research projects.

Institute of Insurance Brokers
Higham Business Centre, Midland Road, Higham Ferrers, Northamptonshire, NN10 8DW, UK
T: +44 (0) 1933 410 003
F: +44 (0) 1933 410 020
E: inst.ins.brokers@iib-uk.com
www.iib-uk.com
The IIB is a non-profit, professional association dedicated to representing the interests of insurance brokers and their clients throughout the UK. It promotes their interests to government, regulatory authorities, and other relevant bodies throughout the world, and encourages debate on topical issues, through bulletins, meetings, and a professional forum.

Institute of Risk Management
Chair: Simone Wray
6 Lloyd's Avenue, London, EC3N 3AX, UK
T: +44 (0) 20 7709 9808
F: +44 (0) 20 7709 0716
E: enquiries@theirm.org
www.theirm.org
IRM is a non-profit organization that provides education, training, and qualifications at a range of levels for the risk management community. It approaches risk management as a multi-disciplinary field, and works closely with other specialist institutes and associations and represents a broad set of stakeholders, with its membership being drawn from industry, commerce, consultancy, and the public sector.

USA

American Association of Insurance Services
Chair: Paul Baiocchi
1745 South Naperville Road, Wheaton, IL 60189-8132, USA
T: +1 630 681 8347
F: +1 630 681 8356
E: info@AAISonline.com
www.aais.org
AAIS is a product development resource for insurance providers, with expertise in product research and design, actuarial analysis, and regulatory filings. It introduces new programs, product innovations, and services that respond to changes in the insurance marketplace, and offers programs of forms, rules, and rating information for personal and commercial insurance, statistical reporting plans, support services for custom product development, automation, and training.

American Insurance Association
Chair: Leigh Ann Pusey
2101 L Street, NW, Suite 400, Washington, DC 20037, USA
T: +1 202 828 7100
F: +1 202 293 1219
E: info@aiadc.org
www.aiadc.org
AIA is a property-casualty insurance trade organization, its member companies offering all types of property and liability coverage. It aims to provide constructive solutions to industry issues, and operate on promote the views of its member companies, consumers, regulators, and business leaders.

American Risk and Insurance Association
Chair: Tony Biacchi
716 Providence Road, Malvern, PA 19355-3402, USA
T: +1 610 640 1997
F: +1 610 725 1007
E: aria@cpcuiia.org
www.aria.org
ARIA is an academic organization devoted to the study and promotion of knowledge about risk management and insurance. It comprises insurance scholars, risk management and insurance professionals, and institutional sponsors, and provides resources, information, and support for professional growth and education, and offers a forum for scholarly discussion of risk management and insurance issues.

Risk & Insurance Management Society
Chair: Mary Roth
1065 Avenue of the Americas, 13th Floor, New York, NY 10018, USA
T: +1 212 286 9292
www.rims.org
RIMS is a non-profit organization dedicated to advancing the practice of risk management, and which connects risk management professionals throughout North America and the world. It represents industrial, service, non-profit, charitable, and governmental entities, and provides information, education, networking and advocacy, promotes the well-being of the industry, and supports the

integration of risk management throughout an organization.

Society of Insurance Research
Chair: Ed Budd
631 Eastpointe Drive, Shelbyville, IN 46176, USA
T: +1 317 398 3684
F: +1 317 642 0535
E: sir.mail@comcast.net
www.sirnet.org
SIR is an international, interdisciplinary organization of insurance research practitioners focused on identifying, understanding, and communicating industry trends, emerging issues, and innovations. It provides a forum for technical education, networking, and professional growth for members, who are insurance professionals with responsibilities in research, product development, competitive intelligence, actuarial science, strategic planning, marketing, and other disciplines.

BRIC

All-Russian Insurance Association
Russia
T: +7 495 956 65 87
F: +7 495 956 65 87
E: mail@ins-union.ru
www.ins-union.ru
ARIA is a national association that promotes its members interests, and the development and improvement of the Russian insurance industry. It works to improve key areas such as insurance legislation, insurance market infrastructure, conditions for insurance, and standards of professional ethics, and produces education and training programs, conferences and seminars, and industry publications.

General Insurance Council of India
Chair: K. K. Srinivasan
5th Floor, Royal Insurance Building, 14, Jamshedji TATA Road, Churchgate, Mumbai 400020, India
T: +91 22 2281 7511
F: +91 22 2281 7515
E: gicouncil@gicouncil.in
www.gicouncil.in
The GI Council represents the collective interests of the non-life insurance companies in India, provides leadership and guidance to the industry, and participates in forming public policy. It also promotes issues of common interest, works to improve the legal and regulatory framework, and act as an advocate for high standards of customer service in the industry.

International

Asia-Pacific Risk and Insurance Association
Chair: Y. U. Ziyou
The APRIA Secretariat, c/o Singapore College of Insurance, 9, Temasek Boulevard, #14-01/02/03 Suntec Tower 2, Singapore 038989, Singapore
T: +65 221 2336
F: +65 220 6684
E: apria@scidomain.org.sg
www.apria.org
APRIA is an international association for academics, executives, researchers, and government leaders interested in risk management, insurance, actuarial science, and related areas. It provides a forum for sharing ideas and engaging in collaborative research, discusses market developments, and publishes a biannual newsletter.

International Association for the Study of Insurance Economics
Chair: Jacques Aigrain
53 Route de Malagnou, 1208 Geneva, Switzerland
T: +41 22 707 66 00
F: +41 22 736 75 36
E: secretariat@genevaassociation.org
www.genevaassociation.org
Better known as The Geneva Association, this global research institution examines the growing importance of worldwide insurance activities in all sectors of the economy. It identifies trends and strategic issues in the insurance sector, and develops and encourages initiatives concerning the evolution of risk management and the notion of uncertainty. It also provides a forum for senior insurance executives to exchange ideas and discuss these issues.

International Association of Insurance Supervisors
Chair: Yoshihiro Kawai
IAIS Secretariat, c/o Bank for International Settlements, 4002 Basel, Switzerland
T: +41 61 225 73 00
F: +41 61 280 91 51
E: iais@bis.org
www.iaisweb.org
IAIS is an international organization for national insurance regulators and supervisors. It issues global insurance principles, standards and guidance papers, provides training and support on issues related to insurance supervision, and organizes meetings and seminars for insurance supervisors, as well as working with other financial sector standard setting bodies and international organizations to promote financial stability.

International Insurance Society
Chair: Brian Duperreault
101 Murray Street New York, NY 10007, USA
T: +1 212 815 9291
F: +1 212 815 9297
E: jeastmond@iisonline.org
www.iisonline.org
This is a non-profit organization that provides a resource for insurance executives, academicians, and others interested in insurance to share interests and ideas on relevant global issues. It connects the international insurance community, providing information, education, and networking opportunities for companies and individuals seeking contacts, cross-border exchanges, and knowledge on a global scale. It also produces annual seminars, insurance studies, reports, awards, and research.

World Federation of Insurance Intermediaries
Avenue Albert Elisabeth 40, 1200 Brussels, Belgium
F: +32 2 732 60 42
E: wfii@skynet.be
www.wfii.org
WFII is a non-profit federation that represents insurance agents and brokers from around the world. It works to increase the awareness of the role played by professional intermediaries with international institutions, and provides a voice for the interests of its members, innovative solutions at international level, and to enable the exchange of information on global issues and goals that all national associations of intermediaries have in common.

  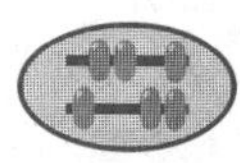   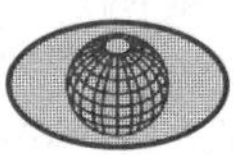   

Corporate Strategy

BOOKS

5 Kick-Ass Strategies Every Business Needs To: Explode Sales, Stun the Competition, Wow Customers and Achieve Exponential Growth
Robert Grede
Naperville, Illinois: Sourcebooks, 2006
336pp, ISBN: 978-1-4022-0640-5
This business-growth guide presents actual case studies, visual elements, and strategic steps, to help in reaching, and exceeding, growth goals. In this handbook, Robert Grede provides the essential strategies for improving each area of your business. It also examines how to create a strategic growth plan, the benefits of buying market share, ways to hunt for business, how to sell more to your current customers, and how to introduce new products.

The Boston Consulting Group on Strategy: Classic Concepts and New Perspectives, 2nd ed
Carl W. Stern, Michael S. Deimler (editors)
Chichester, UK: Wiley, 2006
432pp, ISBN: 978-0-471-75722-1
This anthology of articles on strategy and management is a companion for executives rethinking their businesses. Whether the task is to defeat new or entrenched competitors, it is often necessary to go back to the basics and to consider radical departures. It shows readers how to do both through concepts about reducing costs and gaining market share, as well as new thinking on the power of networks, pricing and segmentation, and the impact of ever cheaper communications and distribution.

Business Strategy: A Guide to Effective Decision Making
Jeremy Kourdi
London: Economist Books, 2003
256pp, ISBN: 978-1-86197-459-4
This practical guide provides help for those involved in making strategic decisions. The text also examines the decision-making process in detail. The forces shaping major decisions, including social, cultural, and commercial, are explained, and various rational and intuitive frameworks are introduced. Practical insights and techniques for handling decisions are also outlined.

Competing for the Future: How Digital Innovations Are Changing the World
Henry Kressel
Cambridge, UK: Cambridge University Press, 2007
422pp, ISBN: 978-0-521-86290-5
This offers expert personalized answers to questions such as the significance of going digital, the miniaturization of circuit boards, the role of venture capital in financing the revolution, and the importance of research and development. It explains how the technology works, why it matters, how it is financed, and what the key lessons are for public policy.

Competitive Strategy: Techniques for Analyzing Industries and Competitors
Michael E. Porter
New York: Free Press, 2004
432pp, ISBN: 978-0-684-84148-9
This work, researched by Porter during the 1970s, is regarded as a management classic and has shaped and influenced mainstream thinking on competition and strategy. The author argues that in order to retain competitive capability companies need to choose from three generic strategies (cost leadership, differentiation, and focus), which are driven by five competitive forces (customers, suppliers, the threat of similar products, existing competition, and the threat of new market entrants).

Contemporary Strategy Analysis: Concepts, Techniques, Applications, 6th ed
Robert M. Grant
Oxford: Blackwell Publishing, 2007
496pp, ISBN: 978-1-4051-6309-5
This text reflects current academic thinking and management practice and presents the tools required to formulate and implement strategies. In this edition, extra coverage is given to value creation in electronic commerce, the new economy, complexity and self-organization, and strategic innovation.

Essentials of Strategic Management, 4th ed
J. David Hunger, Thomas L. Wheelen
Harlow, UK: Pearson Education, 2006
208pp, ISBN: 978-0-13-148523-5
This text provides the essentials of the most important concepts and techniques in strategic management. The topics covered by the authors are: basics of strategic management; corporate governance and social responsibility; environmental scanning and industry analysis; internal scanning; strategy formulation; strategy implementation; evaluation and control; and suggestions for analysis.

Every Business Is a Growth Business
Noel M. Tichy, R. Charan
Chichester, UK: Wiley, 2000
352pp, ISBN: 978-0-8129-3305-5
In this title, the authors outline how to turn an ordinary company into one that grows. The book gives two main pointers for successful growth; first, to redefine your market and increase demand by seeing things from your customers' point of view, and, second, to reinvigorate the corporate culture to enable growth. The authors give many real-life examples to support these central points.

Exploring Corporate Strategy, 8th ed
Gerry Johnson, Kevan Scholes
Exploring Corporate Strategy Series
Harlow, UK: Prentice Hall, 2008
664pp, ISBN: 978-0-273-71191-9
This classic textbook provides an overview of the principles and practice of corporate strategy in a variety of contexts. The areas of strategic analysis, resource allocation, strategic choice, strategy implementation, and managing strategic change are covered. Recent developments in the field of strategy, including core competence knowledge and learning, have been incorporated into the seventh edition, which also includes a list of recommended key reading and work assignments for students.

Financial Times Guide to Strategy, 3rd ed
Richard Koch
Harlow, UK: FT Prentice Hall, 2008
334pp, ISBN: 978-0-273-70877-3
This title offers executives the help needed to build a strategic structure for a business, to organize a marketplace, and to create a business model. The book also reveals how strategy can help to raise profits and analyses the views on strategic thinking that have emerged over the last 40 years.

Good to Great: Why Some Companies Make the Leap. . .and Others Don't
Jim Collins
London: Random House Business Books, 2001
320pp, ISBN: 978-0-7126-7609-0
Written by one of the world's bestselling business writers and based on extensive research of over 1,000 businesses, this book focuses on eleven of the world's leading corporations and analyzes their successes. Concluding that an excellent corporate culture is the way forward, this

  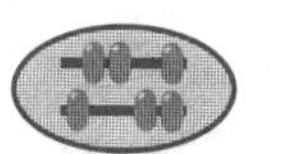   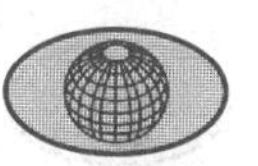   

book offers advice and useful tactics for all aspiring business builders.

Gurus on Business Strategy
Tony Grundy
London: Thorogood, 2004
224pp, ISBN: 978-1-85418-262-3
The author presents a guide to well-known writers and thinkers on business strategy and the practical lessons which can be learnt from their ideas. The work opens with an introduction to strategy as a management concept, focusing on management of the external environment, development of competitive advantage, and strategic decision-making. Subsequent sections provide introductions to the wisdom of around 40 business thinkers.

The Interactive Strategy Workout: Analyze and Develop the Fitness of Your Business Strategy, 3rd ed
Cyril Levicki
Harlow, UK: FT Prentice Hall, 2003
368pp, ISBN: 978-0-273-65912-9
This title is a step-by-step guide to creating a successful strategy, both for business purposes and for everyday life. It is accompanied by a CD-ROM.

The New Market Leaders: Who's Winning and How in the Battle for Customers
Fred Wiersema
New York: Free Press, 2002
272pp, ISBN: 978-0-7432-0466-8
This offers insights into successful customer service strategies, based on a six-year study of 5,000 global companies; it examines 100 of these companies in detail, including General Electric, Wal-Mart, Microsoft, Intel and AOL Time Warner, arguing that executives and managers can no longer blame the internet or the new economy for their customer service failings. It argues that the most successful companies focus on being at the forefront of new technology and, most importantly, try to learn from other winning companies.

One Stop Strategy
Jeremy Kourdi
One Stop Series
Hemel Hempstead, UK: ICSA Publishing, 2000
268pp, ISBN: 978-1-86072-086-4
This is a practical guide for managers looking to do more than just plan organizational activities. Key topics in a range of areas such as allocating resources, structuring the organization, controlling systems and processes, and managing people are arranged in alphabetical order. Short case studies, checklists, and summaries are included.

On the Fly: Executive Strategy in a Changing World
Stephen J. Wall
Chichester, UK: Wiley, 2004
240pp, ISBN: 978-0-471-46484-6
Businesses operate in a volatile external environment where rapid change is the norm, and it is always difficult for them to formulate a clear sense of sustained strategic direction for the future. While emphasizing the case for strong corporate identity grounded in strategic focus, this book offers a model for combining a flexible response to external factors with the analytical tools of strategic planning.

The Portable MBA in Strategy, 2nd ed
Liam Fahey, Robert M. Randall
Chichester, UK: Wiley, 2000
414pp, ISBN: 978-0-471-19708-9
This comprehensive guide features contributions from internationally recognized leaders in strategic thought and practice. Topics covered include: strategic management practices; analysis of customers, markets, and competitors; identification and assessment of strategic alternatives; and threats and opportunities facing business.

The Rise and Fall of Strategic Planning
Henry Mintzberg
New York: Free Press, 1994
464pp, ISBN: 978-0-02-921605-7
Mintzberg traces the history of strategic planning since the 1960s and gives his own perspective on past failures. The various planning models are reviewed and analyzed, the pitfalls identified, and a new approach is put forward.

Strategic Management and Organisational Dynamics: The Challenge of Complexity to Ways of Thinking about Organisations, 5th ed
Ralph D. Stacey
Harlow, UK: FT Prentice Hall, 2007
496pp, ISBN: 978-0-273-70811-7
The author of this work takes a radically different approach to strategic management. He is concerned with unpredictability and the limitations of control, factors that militate against the rational models of planning and control presented by other authors. The book explores strategy and organizational dynamics, and includes European case studies.

Strategy and Planning: A Manager's Guide, 5th ed
David Hussey
Chichester, UK: Wiley, 2000
289pp, ISBN: 978-0-471-50006-3
This work explores strategic thinking in the context of the major functional areas—marketing, manufacturing, finance, and human resources—as well as examining the major issues and steps in the development of a corporate strategy.

The Strategy-Focused Organization: How Balanced Scorecard Companies Thrive in the New Business Environment
Robert S. Kaplan, David P. Norton
Boston, Massachusetts: Harvard Business School Press, 2000
416pp, ISBN: 978-1-57851-250-8
The originators of the balanced scorecard examine how 20 companies have implemented and adapted the model and draw out five principles for strategy-focused organizations.

Strategy Process: Concepts, Contexts and Cases, 4th ed
Henry Mintzberg, James Brian Quinn
Harlow, UK: Pearson Education, 2003
1040pp, ISBN: 978-0-13-047913-6
This book is designed to support the teaching and practice of strategy formulation. A collection of readings covers the concepts and contexts of strategy and is supplemented by US and international case studies. Discussion questions for students are included.

Strategy Safari: A Guided Tour through the Wilds of Strategic Management
Henry Mintzberg, Bruce Ahlstrand, Joseph Lampel
London: Simon & Schuster, 1998
304pp, ISBN: 978-0-684-84743-6
This book provides a thorough critique of the contributions and limitations of ten different approaches to strategic planning. These include such schools of thought as entrepreneurial, cognitive, cultural, and environmental. The book then goes on to show how these alternative schools can be merged and shaped to produce one coherent approach to strategy formation.

MAGAZINES

Harvard Business Review
Harvard Business School Press
60 Harvard Way, Boston, MA 02163, USA
T: +1 800 988 0886
F: +1 617 783 7555
hbr.harvardbusiness.org
ISSN: 0017-8012

  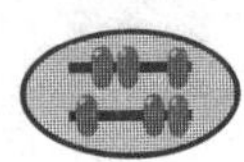 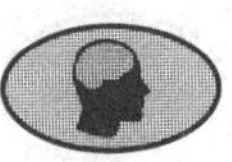  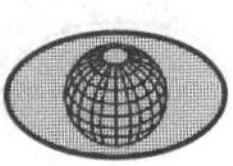  

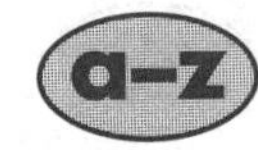

HBR is a leading magazine for business leaders and senior executives, which emphasizes current best practice and the application of leading-edge research to business problems. Coverage is wide-ranging with a strong focus on strategy. Each issue includes feature articles written by experts and an interview with a business leader.

Journal of Business Strategy
Emerald
60/62 Toller Lane, Bradford, West Yorkshire, BD8 9BY, UK
T: +44 (0) 1274 777 700
F: +44 (0) 1274 785 200
www.emeraldinsight.com/1367-3270.htm
ISSN: 0275-6668
This is a bimonthly magazine featuring practical articles on current business topics written by senior executives and strategists.

JOURNALS

Business Strategy Review
Blackwell Publishing
9600 Garsington Road, Oxford, OX4 2DQ, UK
T: +44 (0) 1865 791 100
F: +44 (0) 1865 791 347
www.wiley.com/bw/journal.asp?ref=0955-6419
ISSN: 0955-6419
Business Strategy Review is a quarterly journal published on behalf of the London Business School. It includes articles on strategic issues relevant to modern business, taking a multi-disciplinary approach, and aiming for accessibility to a wide audience, including students and academics.

Business Strategy Series
Emerald
60/62 Toller Lane, Bradford, West Yorkshire, BD8 9BY, UK
T: +44 (0) 1274 777 700
F: +44 (0) 1274 785 200
www.emeraldinsight.com/1751-5637.htm
ISSN: 1751-5637
Business Strategy Series brings 50 exclusive briefing papers to your desktop, covering all aspects of strategy development and implementation. It brings together the strategic thought leaders behind many of the world's leading corporations, including senior executives, top-flight consultants, and business school gurus.

Journal of Economics & Management Strategy
Wiley Periodicals
350 Main Street, Malden, MA 02148, USA
T: +1 781 388 8598
www.wiley.com/bw/journal.asp?ref=1058-6407
ISSN: 1058-6407
The Journal of Economics & Management Strategy provides a leading forum for interaction and research on the competitive strategies of managers and the organizational structure of firms. The journal covers theoretical and empirical industrial organization, applied game theory, and management strategy.

Journal of Strategy and Management
Emerald
60/62 Toller Lane, Bradford, West Yorkshire, BD8 9BY, UK
T: +44 (0) 1274 777 700
F: +44 (0) 1274 785 200
www.emeraldinsight.com/1755-425X.htm
ISSN: 1755-425X
The Journal of Strategy and Management is an international journal dedicated to improving the existing knowledge and understanding of strategy development and implementation globally in private and public organizations, and encouraging new thinking and innovative approaches to the study of strategy.

Long Range Planning: International Journal of Strategic Management
Elsevier
PO Box 211, 1000 AE Amsterdam, The Netherlands
T: +31 20 485 3911
F: +31 20 485 2457
www.elsevier.com/locate/lrp
ISSN: 0024-6301
LRP, published in association with the Strategic Planning Society and the European Strategic Planning Federation, is a leading international journal in the field of strategic management. Aimed at senior managers, administrators, and academics, it includes articles from academics and practitioners.

MIT Sloan Management Review
MIT Sloan School of Management
77 Massachusetts Avenue, Cambridge, MA 02139-4307, USA
T: +1 617 253 7170
F: +1 617 258 9739
sloanreview.mit.edu
ISSN: 1532-9194
Founded in 1959, this quarterly journal aims to provide senior managers with the best of current management theory and practice. It has a strong focus on corporate strategy and leadership.

Strategic Change
Wiley
The Atrium, Southern Gate, Chichester, West Sussex, PO19 8SQ, UK
T: +44 (0) 1243 779 777
F: +44 (0) 1243 775 878
www.interscience.wiley.com/jpages/1086-1718
ISSN: 1086-1718
Eight issues of *Strategic Change* are published annually. The journal aims to provide authoritative and topical research papers addressing the strategic management of change and its implementation in an increasingly globalized business environment.

Strategic Management Journal
Wiley
The Atrium, Southern Gate, Chichester, West Sussex, PO19 8SQ, UK
T: +44 (0) 1243 779 777
F: +44 (0) 1243 775 878
www.interscience.wiley.com/jpages/0143-2095
ISSN: 0143-2095
SMJ is a monthly journal devoted to the theory and practice of strategic management. It is aimed at academics and practicing managers and has a strong emphasis on research.

Strategy and Leadership
Emerald
60/62 Toller Lane, Bradford, West Yorkshire, BD8 9BY, UK
T: +44 (0) 1274 777 700
F: +44 (0) 1274 785 200
www.emeraldinsight.com/1087-8572.htm
ISSN: 1087-8572
This bimonthly journal for business leaders publishes articles describing effective practice in strategy and leadership and new theories that have the potential to advance the art of strategy development and its implementation.

INTERNET

Asian Pacific Management Forum
www.apmforum.com
This association provides a business news portal for Asia, a research center, an archive of relevant industry articles, and publishes an electronic magazine.

Business.com Strategic Planning
www.business.com
The strategic planning section (in the business directory) under "Management" includes a comprehensive collection of links to websites, associations, and publications.

Centre of Management Research (ICMR)
www.icmrindia.org
On their case studies and management resources website, which is popular in Asia, they feature many very helpful strategy case studies. The case studies focus on cases in Asia, but also cover a variety of Western countries.

Knowledge@Wharton
knowledge.wharton.upenn.edu
The section on strategic management on this site, sponsored by the Wharton School at the University of Pennsylvania, includes articles and useful links.

Strategic Management Club Online
www.strategyclub.com
This website, developed by Dr. Fred David for graduate and undergraduate students, provides links, templates, a discussion forum, and a chat facility.

Strategy + Business
www.strategy-business.com
This online version of Strategy + Business magazine offers a selection of articles on corporate strategy as well as a useful search and browse facility. Subscribers to the magazine can also sign up for a free regular e-mail newsletter on this topic.

Thinking Managers
www.thinkingmanagers.com
This is a free advice resource run by management thinkers Edward de Bono and Robert Heller. The strategy section, under business management, provides useful links and self-written blogs.

ORGANIZATIONS

Europe

Strategic Planning Society (SPS)
Buxton House, 7 Highbury Hill, London, N5 1SU, UK
T: +44 (0) 845 056 3663
F: +44 (0) 870 751 8216
E: membership@sps.org.uk
www.sps.org.uk
The SPS is a professional organization, founded in 1967, which aims to promote knowledge and understanding of strategic management through publications, training events, conferences, and special interest groups.

USA

Association for Strategic Planning
12021 Wilshire Boulevard, Suite 286, Los Angeles, CA 90025-1200, USA
T: +1 877 816 2080
F: +1 323 954 0507
E: executivedirector@strategyplus.org
www.strategyplus.org
This professional association aims to promote effective strategic thinking, planning, and action in public and private organizations.

Strategy Institute
230 Park Avenue, 10th Floor, New York, NY 10169, USA
T: +1 866 298 9343
F: +1 866 298 9344
E: info@strategyinstitute.com
www.strategyinstitute.com
A knowledge source for corporate North America, the Strategy Institute is an independent, research-based organization which monitors and communicates changes and trends in business and business strategy.

International

Global Business Network (GBN)
5900-X Hollis Street, Emeryville, CA 94608, USA
T: +1 510 547 6822
F: +1 510 547 8510
E: info@gbn.com
www.gbn.com
The GBN was founded in 1987 by Peter Schwartz, Jay Ogilvy, Napier Collyns, and Stewart Brand, with the collaboration of European colleagues Kees van der Heijden, Arie de Geus, and Bo Ekman. The founders' aim was to develop a worldwide community of individual members and subscribing organizations interested in increasing their understanding of change in the business environment and in developing ideas and tools for planning and innovation. The organization has a strong focus on the use of scenarios.

Strategic Management Society (SMS)
Purdue University, Krannert Center, 425 West State Street, West Lafayette, IN 47907-2056, USA
T: +1 765 494 6984
F: +1 765 494 1533
E: sms@exchange.purdue.edu
www.smsweb.org
The Strategic Management Society is an international organization founded in 1981 with members in more than 50 countries. It focuses on the development and dissemination of insights into strategic management, combining the contributions of practitioners and academics. It holds an international conference and smaller special interest conferences annually, and supports publications such as the *Strategic Management Journal* and a book series.

Strategos Institute
820 West Jackson Boulevard, Suite 450, Chicago, IL 60607, USA
T: +1 312 655 0826
F: +1 312 655 8334
E: contact@strategos.com
www.strategos.com
The Strategos Institute is a consortium of world-class companies working on the development of tools, processes, and metrics for strategy innovation. Business practitioners, consultants, and business school professors are involved, and the writer and thinker Gary Hamel is the chairman.

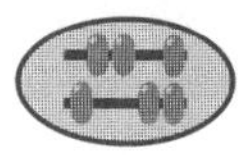

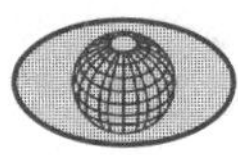

Corporate Valuation

BOOKS

Brealey & Myers on Corporate Finance: Capital Investment and Valuation

Richard A. Braeley, Stewart C. Myers
New York: McGraw-Hill, 2002
500pp, ISBN: 978-0-07-138377-6

Offers a comprehensive analysis of corporate investment and asset valuation, the best strategies for increasing value, and how they can be implemented. It explores the theory and mechanics of valuation and investing, the risks involved, the cost/benefit analyses of mergers, buyouts, issues in capital budgeting, financing and project value, the use of options, and strategies for creating shareholder value through integrated investment and operating programs.

Business Valuation: An Integrated Theory, 2nd ed

Z. Christopher Mercer, Travis W. Harms
Wiley Finance Series
Hoboken, New Jersey: Wiley, 2008
288pp, ISBN: 978-0-470-14816-7

This new, concise treatment of business valuation presents both a theoretical analysis and a guide to implementation and current modeling issues. It explains how to apply fundamental valuation concepts, how to define various levels of value, and better understand business appraisal reports, and discusses the impact of valuation on growth, risk, and reward, alternative investments, present value, and valuation premiums and discounts.

Corporate Finance: A Valuation Approach

Simon Benninga, Oded Sarig
New York: McGraw-Hill/Irwin, 1997
445pp, ISBN: 978-0-07-005099-0

This early classic on company valuation was designed for courses in corporate finance, and provides a detailed description of the valuation process, and an integrated method for valuing assets, firms, and securities across a wide variety of industries. It examines financial and accounting techniques, and assists in the development of pro-forma financial statements and their translation into values.

Corporate Finance and Valuation

Bob Ryan
London: Cengage Learning, 2007
623pp, ISBN: 978-1-84480-271-5

This textbook examines the unique challenges to business growth and valuation in an accessible way. It clearly presents the relevant theory, mathematics, key concepts and principles through practical examples, and explores the themes of value, return, and risk, offering a managerial perspective on identifying and solving financial problems in the real world.

Corporate Valuation: A Guide for Managers and Investors

Phillip R. Daves, Michael C. Ehrhardt, Ron E. Shrieves
Mason, Ohio: Thomson/South-Western, 2004
301pp, ISBN: 978-0-324-27428-8

This is an accessible handbook to company valuation, which provides guidance on how to obtain real world data, how to structure spreadsheet valuation models, and the use of spreadsheets in simplifying and standardizing accounting processes in financial statements. It offers a range of examples of valuing different types of company, and explains the fundamental economic forces that underlie a company's value.

Corporate Valuation: An Easy Guide to Measuring Value

David Frykman, Jakob Tolleryd
London: FT Prentice Hall, 2003
208pp, ISBN: 978-0-273-66161-0

This practical guide discusses the key issues of valuation, and the importance of measuring a company's health to maximize shareholder value, in the context of past results, the current situation, and prospects for the future. It covers commonly used valuation methods, and examines scenarios, ratio-based and DCF methods, techniques for reflecting industry structure and intellectual capital, and value-based management.

Creating Shareholder Value: A Guide for Managers and Investors, 2nd ed

Alfred Rappaport
New York: Free Press, 1998
205pp, ISBN: 978-0-684-84410-7

Rappaport, described as the father of shareholder value, here offers investors and corporate managers a practical guide to the practical tools needed to generate superior returns. He focuses on a shareholder value approach that uses sales/growth rates, operating profit margins, and cost of capital to measure value, rather than traditional performance metrics such as price-to-earnings ratios, return on investment, and equity measures.

Damodaran on Valuation: Security Analysis for Investment and Corporate Finance, 2nd ed

Aswath Damodaran
Wiley Finance Series
Hoboken, New Jersey: Wiley, 2006
685pp, ISBN: 978-0-471-75121-2

Written by a renowned teacher, author, and valuation expert, this is a guide to all aspects of valuation, from the valuation process, and key valuation models, to the different valuation scenarios that can be faced. It also presents techniques for assessing the effect on value of employee stock options, methodologies for using valuation models to value intangible assets, and the effect of illiquidity on value.

EVA and Value-Based Management: A Practical Guide to Implementation

S. David Young, Stephen F. O'Byrne
New York: McGraw-Hill, 2001
493pp, ISBN: 978-0-07-136439-3

This objective analysis of two key management tools discusses the advantages and disadvantages of their implementation, focusing on performance measurement, value drivers, and management compensation to increase shareholder value. It explains the main steps in their successful application for an organization, as well as providing definitions, and a practical rationale for their introduction.

The EVA Challenge: Implementing Value-Added Change in an Organization

Joel M. Stern, John S. Shiely
New York: Wiley, 2001
250pp, ISBN: 978-0-471-47889-8

This is an accessible and practical account of economic value added (EVA), which measures the financial performance of a company, and presents a strategy for creating corporate and shareholder wealth. It details what exactly EVA is, how to calculate it, what information it can provide shareholders, and how to customize and implement EVA at any level of a company.

Financial Valuation: Applications and Models, 2nd ed

James R. Hitchner (editor)
Wiley Finance Series
Hoboken, New Jersey: Wiley, 2006
1,336pp, ISBN: 978-0-471-76117-4

 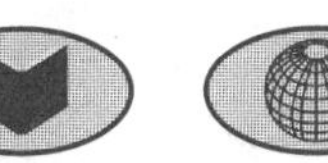   

This major practitioner resource on business valuation covers the most effective valuation procedures, and the latest in valuations for financial reporting. Written by a number of respected industry figures, it also examines the models and methods that can be used to navigate a valuation project, how to value pass-through entities, and value consulting and company analysis using the concept of strategic benchmarking for value.

Intangible Assets: Valuation and Economic Benefit
Jeffrey A. Cohen
Wiley Finance Series
Hoboken, New Jersey: Wiley, 2005
161pp, ISBN: 978-0-471-67131-2
This presents a practical framework for addressing the valuation and economics of intangibles, their treatment under current accounting rules, and how basic valuation methodologies apply to intangible assets. It examines how to identify and value intangible assets such as intellectual property, brands, patents, copyrights, trademarks, and trade secrets, and how value is created and sustained.

Principles of Private Firm Valuation
Stanley J. Feldman
Wiley Finance Series
Hoboken, New Jersey: Wiley, 2005
179pp, ISBN: 978-0-471-48721-0
This offers insights into the factors that determine private firm value for finance professionals, exploring the valuation issues, and the best tools and techniques that can be used. It also discusses the influence of taxes, the cost of capital, the size of the marketability discount, the value of control, and the importance of transparency and liquidity in establishing the value of a private firm.

The Quest for Value
G. Bennett Stewart
New York: HarperBusiness, 1991
781pp, ISBN: 978-0-88730-418-7
This bible of financial management provides a practical framework that managers can use in goal setting, resource allocation, strategy development, valuation of acquisitions, financial policy setting, incentive compensation planning, and building shareholder value. It presents corporate strategy for enhancing shareholder value, and examines issues surrounding dividends, earnings per share, and what really drives share price.

Valuation: Avoiding the Winner's Curse
Kenneth R. Ferris, Barbara S. Pecherot Petitt
Upper Saddle River, New Jersey: Prentice Hall, 2002
225pp, ISBN: 978-0-13-034804-3
This introduces and illustrates the most important valuation techniques and models, such as discounted cash flow analysis, earnings multiples analysis, adjusted present value analysis, economic value analysis, and real option analysis. It offers advice for acquiring and valuing target companies, describes key financial reporting, accounting, and tax considerations, and presents examples and case studies from many industry sectors.

Valuation: Measuring and Managing the Value of Companies, 4th ed
Tim Koller, Marc Goedhart, David Wessels
Hoboken, New Jersey: Wiley, 2005
739pp, ISBN: 978-0-471-70218-4
This classic guide to valuation has been updated to reflect the volatile global economy, and provides practical advice on how to create, manage, and measure company value, and case studies that illustrate valuation techniques in real-world situations. It also presents a framework for managers, and shows how to analyze historical performance, forecast performance, estimate the cost of capital, and interpret the results of a valuation.

Valuation: Mergers, Buyouts and Restructuring, 2nd ed
Enrique R. Arzac
Wiley Finance Series
Hoboken, New Jersey: Wiley, 2008
448pp, ISBN: 978-0-470-12889-3
This focused guide to valuation presents both a theoretical and practical overview of the valuation tools, techniques, and applications that create the foundation for mergers, buyouts and restructuring. It discusses core valuation, LBOs, options pricing, and deal structuring, as well as contract design to resolve disagreements about value, and the valuation of special offer structures.

Valuation: The Art and Science of Corporate Investment Decisions
Sheridan Titman, John Martin
Addison-Wesley Series in Finance
Boston, Massachusetts: Addison Wesley, 2008
556pp, ISBN: 978-0-321-33610-1
This textbook offers an overview of valuation and an integrated approach to both project and enterprise valuation. It moves beyond usual discounted cash flow analysis to include valuation methods such as comparables, simulations, and real options. It also discusses project analysis using DCF, cost of capital, and enterprise valuation techniques.

Valuation Workbook: Step-by-Step Exercises and Tests to Help You Master Valuation, 3rd ed
Tom Copeland, Tim Koller, Jack Murrin, William Foote
Hoboken, New Jersey: Wiley, 2006
185pp, ISBN: 978-0-471-70216-0
This successful companion workbook and practical study guide to the book, *Corporate Valuation*, can be used to test understanding of the subject and the necessary calculation skills to help apply the principles to realize shareholder value. It covers such essentials as value creation, M&As, valuation frameworks, analyzing historical information, estimating the cost of capital, forecasting performance, and calculating results.

Value Based Management: The Corporate Response to the Shareholder Revolution
John D. Martin, J. William Petty
Boston, Massachusetts: Harvard Business School Press, 2000
249pp, ISBN: 978-0-87584-800-6
Examines how a value-based management program can be used by financial managers to plan, monitor, and control a firm's operations, and to enhance shareholder value. It looks at the link between operational and financial choices and shareholder value, and discusses why maximizing shareholder value should be differentiated from maximizing earnings per share, and is based on a study of firms that have successfully implemented VBM systems

Valuing a Business: The Analysis and Appraisal of Closely Held Companies, 5th ed
Shannon P. Pratt
McGraw-Hill Library of Investment and Finance Series
New York: McGraw-Hill, 2007
1,000pp, ISBN: 978-0-07-144180-3
This respected book on business valuation principles and methods examines the full range of valuation concepts and techniques, how to analyze financial statements, and valuation standards and credentials. It also provides a useful overview of tax valuations, financial reporting and recent GAAP and FASB changes, executive compensation and lost profits analysis, and legal rulings and trends in business valuation.

  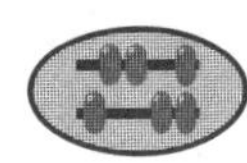   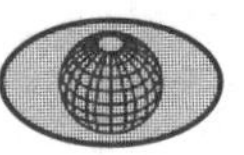   

Valuing Small Businesses and Professional Practices, 3rd ed
Shannon P. Pratt, Robert F. Reilly, Robert P. Schweihs
McGraw-Hill Library of Investment and Finance Series
New York: McGraw-Hill, 1998
1,056pp, ISBN: 978-0-7863-1186-6
The classic reference source and practical tool on small business valuation focuses on valuation theory, value estimation and analyses, and professional practices, and explains the valuation process, as well as valuation for estate plans, useful data sources for small businesses, the legal context, value drivers and their impact on valuation methods, employee stock ownership plans, and corporate partnership dissolutions/buyouts.

MAGAZINES

Business Valuation Update
Business Valuation Resources
1000 SW Broadway, Suite 1200, Portland, OR 97205, USA
T: +1 503 291 7963
F: +1 503 291 7955
www.bvlibrary.com/ProductServices/psBVU.aspx
This monthly newsletter presents a wide range of news, analyses, and expert debate on valuation issues and trends. It publishes articles by industry experts, news updates, special reports, legal and court case abstracts, data and publications notices, cost of capital updates, and a calendar of business valuation events.

CPA Expert
American Institute of Certified Public Accountants
220 Leigh Farm Road, Durham, NC 27707, USA
T: +1 888 777 7077
www.cpa2biz.com/AST/Main/CPA2BIZ_Primary/BusinessValuationandLitigationServices/LitigationServices/PRDOVR~PC-CPX-XX/PC-CPX-XX.jsp
This quarterly newsletter, published by the American Institute of Certified Public Accountants, provides news and analysis on trends, practices, concepts, and methodologies of business valuation, as well as the latest legislation and court rulings, emerging practice trends, and service and technical innovations.

Valuation Strategies
Thomson Reuters
ria.thomsonreuters.com/EStore/detail.aspx?ID=VLRP
ISSN: 1557-2919
This bimonthly journal provides information and analysis on all types of valuation issue, the tools required to ensure transactional accuracy, and valuation in a wide variety of tax planning and compliance matters. It also provides analysis of the latest appraisal techniques used for businesses, real estate, and personal property, and discusses emerging trends affecting valuation of both tangible and intangible assets.

The Value Examiner
National Association of Certified Valuation Analysts
1111 Brickyard Road, Suite 200, Salt Lake City, UT 84106-5401, USA
T: +1 801 486 0600
F: +1 801 486 7500
www.nacva.com/ecommerce/product.asp?pc=03VE
This bimonthly magazine on value offers news and articles for professionals involved in business valuation, forensic accounting, and litigation support services. It publishes substantive, peer-reviewed articles from consulting disciplines such as fraud deterrence and detection, mergers and acquisitions, exit planning strategies, intellectual property, and practice development.

JOURNALS

Business Valuation Review
American Society of Appraisers
555 Herndon Parkway, Suite 125, Herndon, VA 20170, USA
T: +1 703 478 2228
F: +1 703 742 8471
www.bvappraisers.org/IssueStore
ISSN: 0897-1781
This quarterly journal aimed at practitioners focuses on business appraisal and valuation topics. It presents academically rigorous and technical articles that analyze new concepts relevant to valuation learning, and which reiterate the teachings presented in American Society of Appraisers Business Valuation educational courses.

INTERNET

CPA2Biz
www.cpa2biz.com
CPA2Biz is a leading e-commerce site for the accounting profession, and a subsidiary of the American Institute of CPAs, the main association for certified public accountants in the US. It markets a selection of professional products and services to financial professionals across the country, and offers articles, online literature, continuing professional education, and career resources.

ValuationResources.Com
www.valuationresources.com
This free online resource for business appraisers provides a guide to business valuation, industry and company information, economic data, and offers relevant information on books and publications, financial ratios, salary surveys, economic data, cost of equity capital, public market data, M&A transaction data, valuation multiples, and legal and tax issues.

ORGANIZATIONS

USA

American Business Appraisers
USA
www.businessval.com
The ABA provides a national network business for valuation expertise and services, especially in taxation, litigation, transactions, and compliance. Their qualified members can act as either an independent and objective business appraiser or consultants for deal negotiation, supporting an unambiguous value for a business interest or asset, testifying in court, defending an audit, or participating in regulatory hearings to support conclusions.

American Institute of Certified Public Accountants
Chair: Barry C. Melancon
220 Leigh Farm Road, Durham, NC 27707, USA
T: +1 888 777 7077
E: service@aicpa.org
www.aicpa.org
AICPA is the main professional association for certified public accountants in the US. Its mission is to provide members with resources, information, and leadership, focusing on advocacy, certification and licensing, communications, recruitment and education, and standards and performance.

American Society of Appraisers
Chair: Terry J. Allen
555 Herndon Parkway, Suite 125, Herndon, VA 20170, USA
T: +1 703 478 2228
F: +1 703 742 8471
E: asainfo@appraisers.org
www.bvappraisers.org
This is an international organization for professional valuers and appraisers, representing all of the disciplines of appraisal specialists, including business valuation.

  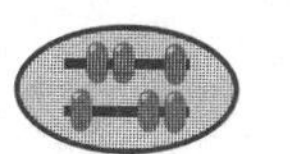   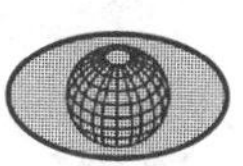   

Appraisal Foundation
Chair: Shawn McGowan
1155 15th Street NW, Suite 1111, Washington, DC 20005, USA
T: +1 202 347 7722
F: +1 202 347 7727
E: info@appraisalfoundation.org
www.appraisalfoundation.org
The Appraisal Foundation, a not-for-profit organization dedicated to the advancement of professional valuation, is main source of appraisal standards, appraiser qualifications and standards of ethical conduct in all valuation disciplines, and which aims to foster public trust in the valuation profession.

Business Valuation Association
Chair: John Worthen
500 North Plum Grove Road, Palatine, IL 60067, USA
T: +1 847 776 1976
F: +1 847 776 1980
E: info@businessvaluationassociation.org
www.businessvaluationassociation.org
BVA is a non-profit organization comprising more than 200 members in and around the Chicago area, which focuses on promoting professionalism among business valuation practitioners through continuing education. It offers a number of presentations, seminars, and special forums on the latest valuation standards and techniques by industry experts each year.

Institute of Business Appraisers
PO Box 17410 Plantation, FL 33318, USA
T: +1 954 584 1144
F: +1 954 584 1184
E: hqiba@go-iba.org
www.go-iba.org
This institute is devoted to the appraisal of closely held businesses, and the promotion of business appraisal education and professional accreditation. It focuses on increasing awareness of business valuation as a specialized profession, ensuring that the services of qualified, ethical appraisers are available, expanding the knowledge of valuation, developing and providing information, programs and services for members, and improving national policy and law affecting the valuation community.

National Association of Certified Valuation Analysts
1111 Brickyard Road, Suite 200, Salt Lake City, UT 84106-5401, USA
T: +1 801 486 0600
F: +1 801 486 7500
E: nacva1@nacva.org
www.nacva.com
NACVA supports professional education, the development of valuation software and databases, tools for providing valuation services, research support, and standards setting for the valuation industry. Its membership comprises CPAs and other valuation and consulting professionals involved in business valuation, litigation forensics consulting, fraud deterrence, and related services serving the legal and business communities.

International

International Association of Consultants, Valuators and Analysts
Chair: James P. Catty
707 Eglinton Avenue West, Suite 501, Toronto, Ontario M5N 1C8, Canada
T: +1 416 865 9665
F: +1 416 865 1249
E: info@iacva.org
www.iacva.org
IACVA provides worldwide support to professionals who either perform valuations or are engaged in fraud deterrence, with the objective of supporting best practice in both. For valuation, it promotes the uniform application of valuation theory, approaches, methods and models, and for fraud deterrence and forensic accounting it encourages the development and dissemination of consistent and demonstrable systems and techniques for the detection and prevention of fraud.

International Valuation Standards Council
12 Great George Street, London, SW1P 3AD, UK
T: +44 (0) 1442 879306
E: ivsc@ivsc.org
www.ivsc.org
The IVSC is an independent, not-for-profit, private sector organization that produces standards for many types of assets, intangible assets and businesses, and for different applications such as financial reporting and bank lending. Its objectives are to be the international voice of the valuation profession, and to create and maintain independent and transparent international valuation standards.

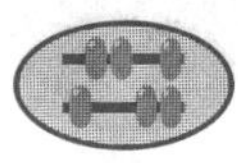

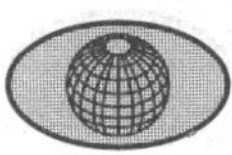

Credit and Debt Management

BOOKS

The Bank Credit Analysis Handbook: A Guide for Analysts, Bankers and Investors, 2nd ed

Jonathan Golin
Wiley Finance Series
Singapore: Wiley, 2008
800pp, ISBN: 978-0-470-82157-2

This explains the role and methodologies of bank credit analysts, and how rating agencies assign credit ratings to banks. Aimed at both investors and practitioners, it provides suggestions and insights for understanding and complying with the Basel Accords, examines the basic elements of the CAMEL model for assessing a bank's performance and financial condition, and discusses the processes of peer and trend analysis.

Credit Derivatives: Risk Management, Trading and Investing

Geoff Chaplin
Wiley Finance Series
Chichester, UK: Wiley, 2005
336pp, ISBN: 978-0-470-02416-4

This is a useful analysis of the key credit derivatives products, applications, risks, and alternative means of trading, which also provides insight into typical trades, such as basis trading, hedging, and credit structuring. It examines the industry standard 'default and recovery' and Copula models, and emphasizes the management of a portfolio or book of credit risks, and methods of correlation risk.

Credit Risk Modeling Using Excel and VBA

Gunter Loeffler, Peter N. Posch
Chichester, UK: Wiley, 2007
280pp, ISBN: 978-0-470-03157-5

This is a practical introduction to credit risk modeling, which shows how to implement analytical methods, and mathematical modeling tools and techniques, using Excel and VBA. It shows how to use option theoretic and statistical models to estimate default risk, and how portfolio models can be validated or used to access structured credit products such as CDOs.

Credit Risk Scorecards

Naeem Siddiqi
Hoboken, New Jersey: Wiley, 2005
208pp, ISBN: 978-0-471-75451-0

This is a practical guide to developing, implementing, and monitoring successful predictive credit scorecards. It presents the key steps in a straightforward way, and provides a strong grounding in the technical issues involved in building, validating, and implementing credit scoring models, making it a useful resource for scorecard specialists, credit risk managers, and other consumer credit professionals.

Euromoney Encyclopedia of Debt Finance

Tony Rhodes (editor)
London: Euromoney Books, 2007
276pp, ISBN: 978-1-84374-269-2

With contributions from leading authors and international financial institutions, this is a useful reference for both new entrants and specialists in the debt markets. It summarizes the range of debt products and markets, and provides examples of the use of these markets in practice.

Guide to Measuring and Managing Credit Risk

Arnaud de Servigny, Olivier Renault
New York: McGraw-Hill, 2004
388pp, ISBN: 978-0-07-141755-6

This is an authoritative exploration of credit risk measurement and management tools and techniques, which includes a detailed review of the most popular portfolio models. It provides practical analysis of issues such as the determinants of credit risk and loss given default, how credit risk is reflected in the prices and yields of individual securities, and how derivatives and securitization instruments can be used to transfer and repackage credit risk.

Managing Credit Risk: The Next Great Financial Challenge, 2nd ed

John B. Caouette, Edward I. Altman, Paul Narayanan, Robert Nimmo
Hoboken, New Jersey: Wiley, 2008
628pp, ISBN: 978-0-470-11872-6

This is an extensive examination of the global credit markets, exploring all the relevant topics that can influence them. It introduces some of the most effective credit risk management tools, techniques, and vehicles currently available, and offers credit risk solutions for different types of organization, including credit derivatives, and approaches that can be used to analyze counterparty credit risk.

The New Paradigm for Financial Markets: The Credit Crisis of 2008 and What It Means

George Soros
New York: PublicAffairs, 2008
208pp, ISBN: 978-1-58648-683-9

Soros examines the financial crisis in terms of how individuals and institutions manage the boom and bust cycles that dominate global economic activity, and discusses the extent of the problem in the markets around the world. He also analyzes the origins of the crisis and its implications for the future.

Standard & Poor's Fundamentals of Corporate Credit Analysis

Blaise Ganguin, John Bilardello
New York: McGraw-Hill, 2004
428pp, ISBN: 978-0-07-144163-6

This guide to the processes and tools of fundamental credit analysis focuses on credit risk, cash flow modeling, debt structure analysis, and other key risks to a company. It also explains the impact of debt instruments and debt structures on a firm's recovery prospects should it become insolvent, presenting a scoring system for assessing the ability to repay debt and evaluate recovery prospects in the event of financial distress.

The Structured Credit Handbook

Arvind Rajan, Glen McDermott, Ratul Roy
Wiley Finance Series
Hoboken, New Jersey: Wiley, 2007
496pp, ISBN: 978-0-471-74749-9

This is a comprehensive introduction to all types of credit-linked financial instruments, such as collateralized debt obligations, collateralized loan obligations, credit derivatives such as credit default swaps and swaptions, and iBoxx indexes. It provides a solid grounding in the investment rationale, risks, and rewards associated with structured credit investments, with little financial jargon or mathematical complexity

The Subprime Solution: How Today's Global Financial Crisis Happened, and What to Do About It

Robert J. Shiller
Princeton, New Jersey: Princeton University Press, 2008
208pp, ISBN: 978-0-691-13929-6

This is a forward thinking and sometimes controversial account of the subprime and credit crisis. It argues that bailouts of distressed borrowers are important for restoring confidence, that more financial

  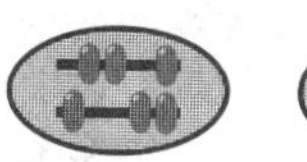 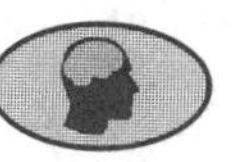  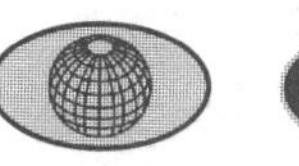   

engineering would prevent similar occurrences, and proposes a major restructuring of the institutional foundations of the financial system.

Surviving Your Business Debt: A Financial Survival Guidebook for Business Owners, Financial Managers, and CFOs
Kenneth Easton
Exeter, New Hampshire: PublishingWorks, 2007
363pp, ISBN: 978-1-933002-50-7
This is an examination of the tactics and strategies business owners need to know to attain funding, and ensure they receive credit approval. It provides guidance about personal guarantees, lender fees, interest rates, managing the problems inherent in business debt, how to re-evaluate a business' credit situation, and put in place an effective debt strategy.

MAGAZINES

Business Credit
National Association of Credit Management
8840 Columbia 100 Parkway, Columbia, Maryland 21045-2158, USA
T: +1 410 740 5560
F: +1 410 740 5574
www.nacm.org
Published 10 times a year, this magazine of the National Association of Credit Management is aimed at those responsible for extending business and trade credit and risk management for their companies. It features analysis of new trends, and important legislative, bankruptcy, business ethics, trade finance, asset protection, benchmarking, risk management, technology, and scoring issues.

Credit
Incisive Media
Haymarket House, 28–29 Haymarket, London, SW1Y 4RX, UK
T: +44 (0) 20 7484 9700
F: +44 (0) 20 7484 9797
www.creditmag.com
This monthly magazine covers the entire credit market, and includes regular features on credit derivatives, structured credit, loans and convertibles. It aims to provide a forum for bondholders, borrowers, banks, and investors to discuss the key issues of the credit market, and features industry profiles, product news, people moves, regulatory issues, events, awards, technology updates, and surveys.

Credit Today
Athene Publishing
Axe & Bottle Court, 70 Newcomen Street, London, SE1 1YT, UK
T: +44 (0) 844 477 4740
F: +44 (0) 20 7940 4843
www.credittoday.co.uk
This monthly magazine for the commercial and consumer credit industry is focused on breaking news, information, and industry debate. It also organizes a number of educational and networking events, and its website acts as a popular online credit news hub, and also features jobs and event information, and has a directory of suppliers and an industry forum.

JOURNALS

The Journal of Credit Risk
Risk Journals
Haymarket House, 28–29 Haymarket, London, SW1Y 4RX, UK
T: +44 (0) 20 7484 9700
F: +44 (0) 20 7484 9797
www.journalofcreditrisk.com
ISSN: 1744-6619
This is an international quarterly journal that publishes refereed papers on the measurement and management of credit risk, the valuation and hedging of credit products, and the promotion of greater understanding in the area of credit risk theory and practice. It features technical credit risk research from both industry and academia.

Journal of Money, Credit and Banking
Ohio State University Press
1070 Carmack Road, Columbus, Ohio 43210, USA
T: +1 614 292 7834
F: +1 614 247 7814
web.econ.ohio-state.edu/jmcb
ISSN: 0022-2879
This professional journal is published seven times a year, and is aimed at academics, researchers, and policymakers, in the areas of money and banking, credit markets, regulation of financial institutions, international payments, portfolio management, and monetary and fiscal policy.

ORGANIZATIONS

USA

National Association of Credit Management
Chair: Jim Fried
8840 Columbia 100 Parkway, Columbia, Maryland 21045-2158, USA
T: +1 410 740 5560
F: +1 410 740 5574
www.nacm.org
NACM and its network of affiliated associations are key resource for credit and financial management, and provide a full range of services, such as pre-collection services, final demand notices, industry groups, and commercial credit reports. It aims to assist members by offering accessible, products, services and programs.

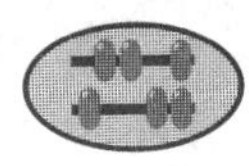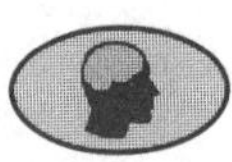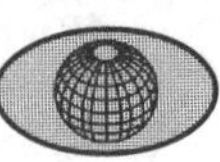

Currency and Foreign Exchange

BOOKS

Adventures of a Currency Trader: A Fable about Trading, Courage, and Doing the Right Thing

Rob Booker
Wiley Trading Series
Hoboken, New Jersey: Wiley, 2007
221pp, ISBN: 978-0-470-04948-8

An entertaining and educational guide to successful currency trading, told through the story of a fictional trader, Harry Banes. It tells of his start in the foreign currency market, learning how to trade, finding the best trading approach, avoiding the most common trading mistakes, and demonstrating in a readable way the strategies and pitfalls of currency trading.

The Complete Guide to Currency Trading & Investing: How to Earn High Rates of Return Safely and Take Control of Your Investments

Jamaine Burrell
Ocala, Florida: Atlantic Publishing, 2007
288pp, ISBN: 978-1-60138-119-4

With currency trading gaining in popularity and accessibility all the time, this guide provides practical instruction in the basics of successfully trading in the largest market in the world. Comprehensive and well-researched, it covers everything you need to know to get started, including effective investment strategies, advice on all aspects of the FX markets, and how best to avoid the main risks involved.

Currencies and Crises

Paul Krugman
Cambridge, Massachusetts: MIT Press, 1992
240pp, ISBN: 978-0-262-61109-1

This is a collection of writing on currencies by Nobel Prize winner Paul Krugman. The papers focus on his view of international monetary economics from the late 1970s onwards, and explain the role of exchange rates in balance-of-payments adjustment policy, how speculation affects the functioning of exchange-rate regimes, emerging market debt, and the development of an international monetary system.

Currency Strategy: The Practitioner's Guide to Currency Investing, Hedging and Forecasting, 2nd ed

Callum Henderson
Wiley Trading Series
Chichester, UK: Wiley, 2006
264pp, ISBN: 978-0-470-02759-2

For the more advanced reader, this takes a broad view of the currency markets, explaining the main tools for predicting, managing, and optimizing currency changes, and shows how to develop new techniques and use mathematical models to take advantage of them. This new edition also examines recent changes impacting the Chinese currency markets.

Currency Wars: How Forged Money is the New Weapon of Mass Destruction

John Cooley
New York: Skyhorse Publishing, 2008
320pp, ISBN: 978-1-60239-270-0

An investigation into the use of counterfeit money, thought to cause greater economic damage than terrorism. Cooley tells many entertaining stories of forged money through history, focusing on how counterfeiting has been used by states for political and economic reasons, to destabilize enemy governments as a sort of aggressive economic warfare.

Day Trading the Currency Market: Technical and Fundamental Strategies to Profit from Market Swings

Kathy Lien
Wiley Trading Series
Hoboken, New Jersey: Wiley, 2006
256pp, ISBN: 978-0-471-71753-9

Intended for all level of day trader, it presents all the necessary market basics and currency characteristics, and shows how to build an effective trading approach. It also discusses the emergence of the foreign exchange market, the major players, and emphasizes how to take advantage of movements in the currency market from both a technical and fundamental perspective.

A Foreign Exchange Primer, 2nd ed

Shani Shamah
Wiley Trading Series
Chichester, UK: Wiley, 2008
250pp, ISBN: 978-0-470-75437-5

This is a new edition of the accessible beginner's guide to working in the foreign exchange market, that takes you through all the practical skills necessary to trade, and examines the main products and techniques, the key institutions and players, and the terminology used.

Forex Conquered: High Probability Systems and Strategies for Active Traders

John L. Person
Wiley Trading Series
Hoboken, New Jersey: Wiley, 2007
304pp, ISBN: 978-0-470-09779-3

Provides the essentials of the foreign exchange market, the strategies and systems, and how to manage the risks involved. Written more for the experienced trader, it also explains technical topics such as candlestick charting, Elliott wave theory and Fibonacci price corrections.

Forex Patterns & Probabilities: Trading Strategies for Trending & Range-Bound Markets

Ed Ponsi
Wiley Trading Series
Hoboken, New Jersey: Wiley, 2007
272pp, ISBN: 978-0-470-09729-8

Offers practical strategies and trading methodologies based on the author's experience as a professional trader and educator. A clear presentation of how to trade like a professional, it introduces a variety of elements essential to currency trading success, from the best ways to enter, exit, and manage trades, to real-life examples of effective trading.

The Forex Trading Course: A Self-Study Guide to Becoming a Successful Currency Trader

Abe Cofnas
Wiley Trading Series
Hoboken, New Jersey: Wiley, 2007
240pp, ISBN: 978-0-470-13764-2

This is a practical and user-friendly handbook on currency trading, which teaches the trading basics, through to an understanding of the complexities of applying fundamental and technical analysis to identify patterns and trends. It also shows how to develop an effective trading plan, with appropriate strategies for different size accounts, and how to use emotional intelligence to improve trading performance.

Mastering Foreign Exchange & Currency Options: A Practical Guide to the New Marketplace, 2nd ed

Francesca Taylor
Market Editions Series
Harlow, UK: FT Prentice Hall, 2003
432pp, ISBN: 978-0-273-66295-2

Now in its second edition, this is a handbook for those involved in the market at any level, whether looking for practical guidance on forex trading, tips on how to improve your currency dealing, or how to keep appraised of new developments in this fast-changing market. It also has a useful focus on how new technology has changed the market.

  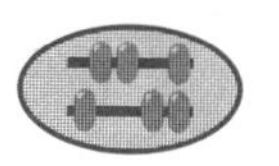  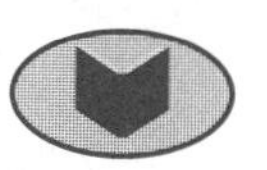 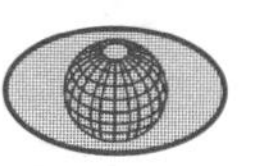   

Mathematical Methods for Foreign Exchange: A Financial Engineer's Approach
Alexander Lipton
Singapore: World Scientific, 2001
700pp, ISBN: 978-981-02-4823-9
A classic, albeit technical, examination of the mathematics that underpins a successful financial engineering approach to foreign exchange. It takes a systematic approach to financial modeling of the currency markets, and explains the mathematical, economic and trading background of this approach, and its uses in derivative pricing.

The Money Changers: A Guided Tour through Global Currency Markets
Robert G. Williams
Black Point, Nova Scotia: Fernwood Publishing, 2006
256pp, ISBN: 978-1-84277-695-7
A readable exploration of the workings of the foreign exchange markets, which provides an international perspective on the movement of currencies and exchange rates around the world. This is an important overview of the markets, systems, strategies, and people that make it work.

Technical Analysis of the Currency Market: Classic Techniques for Profiting from Market Swings and Trader Sentiment
Boris Schlossberg
Wiley Trading Series
Hoboken, New Jersey: Wiley, 2006
224pp, ISBN: 978-0-471-74593-8
A trading primer for the currency markets that focuses on using technical analysis to trade successfully in a wide range of market situations. It provides a practical approach to the use of currency trading tools and strategies, and is aimed at giving you the skill and confidence to trade in the global currency market.

MAGAZINES

Currency Trader
161 North Clark, Suite 4915, Chicago, IL 60601, USA
T: +1 312 775 5422
www.currencytradermag.com
This is a monthly magazine that covers trading strategies, systems, analysis, news, and issues of risk control and money management, for FX and currency futures traders. It includes special strategy articles that explore behavioral characteristics and tendencies in different currencies, and the relationships between currencies and economic data.

e-Forex
ASP Media
Suite 10, 3 Edgar Buildings, George Street, Bath, BA1 2FJ, UK
T: +44 (0) 1249 814466
F: +44 (0) 1249 814477
www.e-forex.net
This is an international quarterly magazine focused on electronic and online trading of FX and OTC financial instruments. Targeted at both sell-side and buy-side, it provides the latest industry news and technical developments, and evaluates the benefits of e-FX trading, and assesses the functionality and capabilities of retail or institutional online trading platforms.

Euromoney Weekly FiX
Euromoney
Nestor House, Playhouse Yard, London, EC4V 5EX, UK
T: +44 (0) 20 7779 8888
F: +44 (0) 20 7779 8602
www.euromoneyfix.com
The Weekly FiX is an online magazine that builds on Euromoney's coverage of foreign exchange, to provide news, analysis of FX market trends and regulation, commentary, Q&As with industry experts, people moves, market data and market analysis, and analysis of the institutions, people and products in the global FX business.

FX&MM
Russell Publishing
Court Lodge, Hogtrough Hill, Brasted, Kent, TN16 1NU, UK
T: +44 (0) 1959 563311
F: +44 (0) 1959 563317
www.fx-mm.com
This is a monthly magazine that examines the issues bankers, corporate treasurers, fund managers, traders' and brokers face in the international finance markets. Through in-depth global news, features, interviews and case studies on leading products and personalities in the foreign exchange and money market industry, and provides guidance on managing currency and interest rate fluctuations.

FX Week
Incisive Media
Haymarket House, 28–29 Haymarket, London, SW1Y 4RX, UK
T: +44 (0) 20 7484 9700
F: +44 (0) 20 7930 2238
www.fxweek.com
ISSN: 1050-0782
This is a monthly industry newsletter for foreign exchange and money market professionals working within banks, brokerages, institutions and corporate treasuries. It produces news stories, special reports, the latest currency forecasts index, analysis and commentary, technology news, and people moves within the industry. It also produces quarterly supplements covering CLS, emerging markets, e-FX, currency derivatives, white labeling and retail FX.

The Forex Journal
One Raffles Place, OUB Centre #18-01, Singapore 048616, Singapore
T: +65 9 788 8141
F: +65 6 312 8091
www.forexjournal.com
ISSN: 1793-2149
This is a monthly magazine designed for both advanced and novice traders in the foreign exchange markets. It covers the major Forex market basics, as well as examining issues such as factors that impact price movements in the currency market, the best times to trade for individual currency pairs, trade parameters for different market conditions, and technical and fundamental trading strategies.

INTERNET

Forex Directory
www.forexdirectory.org
The Forex Directory is an online resource for the foreign exchange and currency market, that provides listings and links to brokers, quotes, associations, training, risk management, alerts and signals, competitions, online trading and accounts, charts, magazines, accountants, legal advisors, hedge funds, and software.

Forexsites
www.forexsites.com
Provides a balanced flow of independent information for foreign exchange and currency traders around the world. It delivers real-time quotes, live news feeds, charting, technicals, fundamentals, tutorials, forums, and information specific to the major currencies.

OANDA
www.oanda.com
OANDA is one of the main internet-based forex trading and currency information services, and a market maker and a source for currency data for those involved in the market. It has access to one of the world's largest historical, high frequency, filtered currency databases; it is estimated that about a fifth of the global online spot forex transactions take place on its servers.

  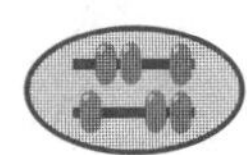   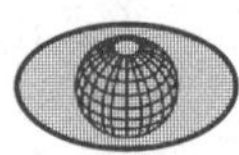   

Derivatives and Quantitative Finance

BOOKS

All About Derivatives

Michael Durbin
New York: McGraw-Hill, 2006
253pp, ISBN: 978-0-07-145147-5

This introduces you to derivatives, how they work, and how they can enhance profits and control market risk. It presents the main features and methods for all the main products, and explains their contracts, techniques for pricing and trading, terminology, the mechanics of storage, settlement, valuation, and payoff, hedging strategies, and leverage.

The Bible of Options Strategies: The Definitive Guide for Practical Trading Strategies

Guy Cohen
Upper Saddle River, New Jersey: FT Press, 2005
356pp, ISBN: 978-0-13-171066-5

This is an accessible guide to options trading that analyzes the most popular strategies, and explains how and when each one should be used, and the hazards to look out for. It covers all of the best income, volatility, leveraged, synthetic, and sideways market strategies, helping the trader to identify and implement the most effective strategy for every opportunity, trading environment, and desired outcome.

The Complete Guide to Capital Markets for Quantitative Professionals

Alex Kuznetsov
McGraw-Hill Library of Investment and Finance Series
New York: McGraw-Hill, 2007
554pp, ISBN: 978-0-07-146829-9

Offering practical advice for those with a science and technology background who need a greater understanding of how the capital markets work, this book assumes no previous knowledge of financial analytics. It explains the business models of different types of institution, and discusses the different type of job role that those with technical backgrounds can apply for.

The Complete Guide to Option Pricing Formulas, 2nd ed

Espen Gaarder Haug
New York: McGraw-Hill, 2007
536pp, ISBN: 978-0-07-138997-6

This is a comprehensive resource that contains a complete listing of nearly every options pricing formula. This practitioner-focused listing is presented in a dictionary format, and now contains more than 60 new option models and formulas, with author commentary and accompanying programming code. The new edition covers option sensitivities, discrete dividend, commodity options, and numerical methods covering trees, finite difference and Monte Carlo Simulation.

Derivatives: Markets, Valuation, and Risk Management

Robert E. Whaley
Wiley Finance Series
Hoboken, New Jersey: Wiley, 2006
930pp, ISBN: 978-0-471-78632-0

This provides an overview of derivatives products and markets, and offers guidance on using derivatives to manage the different types of risks faced by individuals, corporations, and governments. It gives a solid understanding of derivative contract valuation and risk management, as well as the structure of the markets within which they trade.

Derivatives Demystified: A Step-by-Step Guide to Forwards, Futures, Swaps and Options

Andrew M. Chishom
Wiley Finance Series
Chichester, UK: Wiley, 2004
233pp, ISBN: 978-0-470-09382-5

This describes derivative products in straightforward terms, focusing on applications and intuitive explanations of how they are used. It examines the basic building blocks of derivatives, and how they are applied to different markets and various risk management and trading problems. It also offers guidance on the underlying theory, and case studies and examples of how the products are used to solve real-world problems.

Derivatives Markets, 2nd ed

Robert L. McDonald
Boston, Massachusetts: Addison-Wesley, 2006
964pp, ISBN: 978-0-321-54308-0

A comprehensive examination of derivatives markets, which provides an in-depth treatment of the theory, institutions, and applications of derivatives, in an accessible manner. It also offers insights into derivatives pricing models, a tiered approach to the underlying mathematics, an emphasis on the application of the tools and models, and a computation-friendly approach, with pricing functions also available in accompanying spreadsheets.

Financial Derivatives: Pricing, Applications, and Mathematics

Jamil Baz, George Chacko
Cambridge, UK: Cambridge University Press, 2008
352pp, ISBN: 978-0-521-06679-2

This demonstrates the principles and mathematics of financial derivatives pricing and portfolio allocation decisions' including mean-reverting processes and jump processes, and the related tools of stochastic calculus. It also develops generic pricing techniques for assets and derivatives, and discusses key concepts such volatility and time, random walks, geometric Brownian motion, and Ito's lemma.

How I Became a Quant: Insights from 25 of Wall Street's Elite

Barry Schachter, Richard Lindsey
Hoboken, New Jersey: Wiley, 2007
386pp, ISBN: 978-0-470-05062-0

In a series of personal insights and recollections from some of the most successful names on Wall Street, they detail their backgrounds, varying career paths, and contributions to finance, as well as explaining what exactly they do and how they do it. It explains how they introduced techniques for managing risks through trading financial instruments, and the transformation of the financial markets they instigated.

An Introduction to Derivatives and Risk Management, 7th ed

Don Chance, Robert Brooks
Mason, Ohio: Thomson/South-Western, 2006
653pp, ISBN: 978-0-324-32139-5

This is a comprehensive primer to the pricing, trading, and strategy relating to the use of derivatives in trading and risk management. It combines institutional material, theory, and practical applications, and a flexible mathematical approach, to discuss options, futures, forwards, swaps, and risk management, as well as mortgage-backed securities, structured notes, derivatives accounting, and best practices benchmarks for risk management.

Mastering Derivatives Markets: A Step-by-Step Guide to the Products, Applications and Risks, 3rd ed

Francesca Taylor
Market Editions Series
Harlow, UK: FT Prentice Hall, 2007
426pp, ISBN: 978-0-273-70978-7

This comprehensive overview of derivative

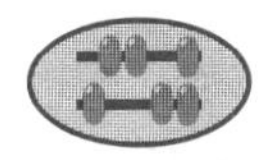
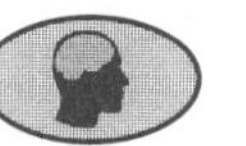

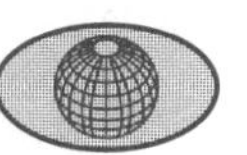

processes and instruments for the professional investor offers practical advice on the markets in an understandable way. It discusses changes in derivative trading, explains key products across the main asset classes, and covers topics such as credit derivatives, what happens after the deal is done, benchmarking, the STP market, how technology is evolving, the new accounting regulations, and the impact of MiFID.

My Life as a Quant: Reflections on Physics and Finance
Emanuel Derman
Hoboken, New Jersey: Wiley, 2004
292pp, ISBN: 978-0-470-19273-3
This is a wide-ranging and personal autobiography by one of the pioneering quants who transformed the financial markets. Derman, co-author of some of the most influential financial models, provides an entertaining account of his move to Wall Street, how the academics brought their new financial science to the business world, the incompatibility between traders and quants, and the dissimilar nature of knowledge in physics and finance.

Options, Futures, and Other Derivatives, 7th ed
John C. Hull
Prentice Hall Series in Finance
Upper Saddle River, New Jersey: Prentice Hall, 2008
821pp, ISBN: 978-1-4082-1743-6
Regarded as the classic text on derivatives, this updated and revised bestselling introduction to futures and options markets is aimed at professionals with limited mathematical background working in the markets, financial engineering, and risk management. It provides a unifying approach to the valuation of derivatives, bridging the gap between the theory and practice, supported by clear explanations and examples.

Paul Wilmott Introduces Quantitative Finance, 2nd ed
Paul Wilmott
Chichester, UK: Wiley, 2007
695pp, ISBN: 978-0-470-31958-1
This is a concise and accessible primer on the classical side of quantitative finance, adapted from Wilmott's renowned books on derivatives and quantitative finance. It presents a thorough overview of futures, options and numerical methods, and includes software to help visualize the most important ideas, and to show how techniques are implemented in practice.

Traders, Guns & Money: Knowns and Unknowns in the Dazzling World of Derivatives
Satyajit Das
Harlow, UK: FT Prentice Hall, 2006
334pp, ISBN: 978-0-273-70474-4
This is an insider's view of the business of trading and marketing derivatives, providing a sensational and controversial first-person account in the spirit of *Liar's Poker*. It details the nature of the industry, the players, the culture, games, how other people's money is made and lost, and the deceptions that underpin the entire process.

MAGAZINES

FOW
Euromoney Institutional Investor, UK
T: +44 (0) 20 7779 8219
www.fow.com
ISSN: 0953-6620
This is a monthly magazine for the global derivatives and risk management industry. it offers news and analysis on all financial asset classes and commodity derivatives, including fixed income, equity, foreign exchange, technology, new products, personal and corporate profiles, people moves, market reports and key data.

Futures
Summit Business Media
5081 Olympic Boulevard, Erlanger, KY 41018-3164, USA
T: +1 859 692 2100
www.futuresmag.com
ISSN: 0746-2468
This monthly magazine for the derivatives industry covers the futures markets, as well as the options, forex and stock markets. It publishes articles and features on fundamental and technical trading strategies, market news, managed money and fund reviews, new products, technology updates, and trader profiles.

Risk
Incisive Media
Haymarket House, 28–29 Haymarket, London, SW1Y 4RX, UK
T: +44 (0) 20 7484 9700
F: +44 (0) 20 7484 9932
www.risk.net
ISSN: 0952-8776
This is a monthly magazine that focuses on financial risk management and the global derivatives industry. It covers new developments in the derivatives markets, provides updates on the movements and activities of key players and personalities in the industry, and showcases technical papers and the latest research into derivatives tools and techniques.

Wilmott
Wiley
The Atrium, Southern Gate, Chichester, West Sussex, PO19 8SQ, UK
T: +44 (0) 1243 779777
F: +44 (0) 1243 775878
www.wilmott.com
ISSN: 1540-6962
Published every two months, *Wilmott* offers new research, innovative models, products, software, analysis, solutions, and tests the latest quantitative finance theories with practical examples. It publishes technical articles from all the functional areas of quantitative finance, derivatives, risk management, finance, and behavioral finance, usually written by quantitative analysts in banks and academia, mathematicians, econophysicists and economists.

JOURNALS

Derivatives & Financial Instruments
International Bureau of Fiscal Documentation (IBFD)
PO Box 20237, 1000HE Amsterdam, The Netherlands
T: +31 20 554 0100
F: +31 20 620 8626
www.ibfd.org/portal/Product_dfijournal.html
ISSN: 1389-1863
This bimonthly journal provides information and analysis for tax professionals and financial market experts around the world. It publishes articles on the taxation of swaps, futures, options, forward contracts, credit derivatives, synthetic equities, securitization, index-linked and unit-linked contracts and forward rate agreements, as well as on legislation, government documents, case reports, and assessments of recent events in the taxation of financial instruments.

International Journal of Theoretical and Applied Finance
World Scientific
5 Toh Tuck Link, Singapore 596224, Singapore
T: +65 6466 5775
F: +65 6467 7667
www.worldscinet.com/ijtaf
ISSN: 0219-0249
This technical journal is published eight times a year, and offers research papers, review papers, and book reviews on the quantitative tools used in finance. It focuses on the mathematical modeling of financial instruments, the application of these models to global financial markets, and the development and application of modern stochastic methods in finance.

     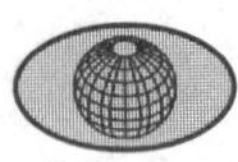   

Journal of Derivatives
Institutional Investor Journals
225 Park Avenue South, 8th Floor, New York, NY 10003, USA
T: +1 212 224 3570
F: +1 212 224 3197
www.iijournals.com/JOD
ISSN: 1074-1240

This quarterly journal, the official publication of the International Association of Financial Engineers, offers practitioner-oriented research in the area of derivatives. The articles published are academically rigorous, and focused on applicable research.

Journal of Derivatives & Hedge Funds
Palgrave Macmillan
The Macmillan Building, 4 Crinan Street, London, N1 9XW, UK
T: +44 (0) 20 7843 4684
www.palgrave-journals.com/jdhf
ISSN: 1753-9641

This is a quarterly journal that examines the derivatives market and hedge funds. Formerly known as *Derivatives Use, Trading & Regulation*, it has evolved its coverage to take into account the enormous growth in hedge funds. It focuses on trading, legal and other derivative issues, and the many challenges facing the hedge fund industry, such as transparency, liquidity risk, and risk management control.

Journal of Financial and Quantitative Analysis
Foster School of Business, University of Washington
115 Lewis, Box 353200, Seattle, WA 98195-3200, USA
T: +1 206 543 4598
F: +1 206 616 1894
www.jfqa.org
ISSN: 0022-1090

This quarterly journal publishes theoretical and empirical research in financial economics, focusing on corporate finance, investments, capital and security markets, and quantitative methods of particular relevance to financial researchers.

The Journal of Futures Markets
Wiley
989 Market Street, San Francisco, CA 94103-1741, USA
T: +1 415 433 1767
F: +1 415 951 8553
www3.interscience.wiley.com/journal/34434/home
ISSN: 0270-7314

This monthly journal presents the latest developments in financial futures and derivatives, written by leading finance academics and professionals. It covers both practical and theoretical topics, such as risk management and control, financial engineering, new financial instruments, hedging strategies, analysis of trading systems, legal, accounting, and regulatory issues, and portfolio optimization.

Quantitative Finance
Routledge
Informa House, 30–32 Mortimer Street, London, W1W 7RE, UK
T: +44 (0) 20 7017 5532
F: +44 (0) 20 7017 4781
www.tandf.co.uk/journals/rquf
ISSN: 1469-7688

This journal publishes eight issues each year, and provides an interdisciplinary forum for both theoretical and empirical approaches to quantitative methods in finance. It has a broad remit, offering technical papers from researchers and practitioners across a range of specialisms and within a variety of organizations.

Review of Derivatives Research
Springer, USA
www.springer.com/business/finance/journal/11147
ISSN: 1380-6645

Publishes three times a year, this journal is aimed at financial institutions, institutional investors, and corporations who use sophisticated quantitative techniques and financial instruments. It offers articles on the pricing and hedging of derivative assets on any underlying asset, and provides an international forum for researchers involved in the general areas of derivative assets.

Review of Quantitative Finance and Accounting
Springer, USA
www.springer.com/business/finance/journal/11156
ISSN: 0924-865X

This research-based quarterly journal focuses on presenting theoretical and methodological results with the support of empirical applications. It presents papers on the interaction of finance with accounting, economics and quantitative methods, as well as relevant topics that use finance theory and methodology, such as managerial accounting and auditing, macroeconomics, and managerial economics.

INTERNET

Derivatives Strategy
www.derivativesstrategy.com

This website, once the online presence of the monthly Derivatives Strategy magazine, now provides a forum for news and information on the global derivatives market from a US perspective. It is for users of derivatives products, rather than quants, and tries to explain complex derivatives issues in an understandable way.

DW Online
www.iiderivatives.com

An online resource for news on all derivatives types across all regions, as well as producing analysis and information on credit, equity, currencies, people and firms, regulation and documentation, conferences, and market data.

Futures and Options Intelligence
www.fointelligence.com

This website provides market data, research, news, insight, analysis, alerts, and details on volumes, exchanges, and contracts for the global exchange-traded derivatives market.

Global Derivatives
www.global-derivatives.com

This is an online resource for the quantitative finance and financial engineering industry, that offers news, forums, options databases, education, pricing models, a financial mathematics glossary, quant finance 101s, book reviews, working papers, and job postings.

ORGANIZATIONS

Europe

The Futures and Options Association
Chair: Steve Sparke
2nd Floor, 36–38 Botolph Lane, London, EC3R 8DE, UK
T: +44 (0) 20 7929 0081
F: +44 (0) 20 7621 0223
www.foa.co.uk

The FOA is a European industry trade association for firms and institutions carrying on business in futures, options and other derivatives, or which use such products in their business. Its principal role is to represent the interests of its members in the public and regulatory domain, and deliver a wide range of support services to its members.

USA

Commodity Futures Trading Commission
Chair: Walter Lukken
Three Lafayette Centre, 1155 21st Street NW, Washington, DC 20581, USA

  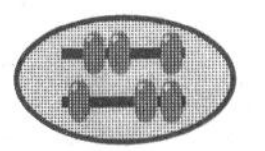 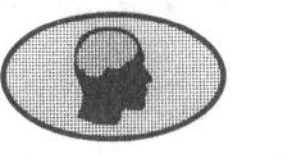  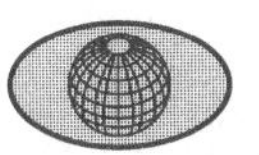   

T: +1 202 418 5000
F: +1 202 418 5521
E: questions@cftc.gov
www.cftc.gov

The mission of the CFTC is to protect market users and the public from fraud, manipulation, and abusive practices related to the sale of commodity and financial futures and options, and to foster open, competitive, and financially sound futures and option markets, and the integrity of the clearing process. It enables the futures markets to provide a means for price discovery and offsetting price risk.

Futures Industry Association

Chair: Kenneth M. Ford
2001 Pennsylvania Avenue NW, Suite 600, Washington, DC 20006, USA
T: +1 202 466 5460
F: +1 202 296 3184
www.futuresindustry.org

The FIA provides a means for the exchange of ideas, and works with commodity exchanges to promote and preserve free marketing and a high standard of ethics, a high quality of service to the public. It also examines ways of reducing the costs and increasing the volume of trading in the business, eliminating credit abuse, improving education, and protecting firms from fraudulent warehouse receipts.

International Association of Financial Engineers

Chair: David Jaffe
630 9th Avenue, Suite 802, New York, NY 10036, USA
T: +1 646 736 0705
F: +1 646 417 6378
E: main@iafe.org
www.iafe.org

This not-for-profit, professional society is dedicated to promoting quantitative finance by providing platforms to discuss key industry issues. It is composed of individual academics and practitioners from banks, broker dealers, hedge funds, pension funds, asset managers, technology firms, regulators, accounting, consulting and law firms, and universities around the world.

International Swaps and Derivatives Association

360 Madison Avenue, 16th Floor, New York, NY 10017, USA
T: +1 212 901 6000
F: +1 212 901 6001
E: isda@isda.org
www.isda.org

ISDA encourages the development of the privately negotiated derivatives industry by promoting the efficient conduct of the business, promoting the development of sound risk management practices, fostering high standards of commercial conduct, advancing international public understanding, and educating members and others on legislative regulatory, legal, accounting, tax, and other issues affecting them.

National Futures Association

Chair: W. Robert Felker
300 South Riverside Plaza, #1800, Chicago, IL 60606-6615, USA
T: +1 312 781 1300
F: +1 312 781 1467
E: information@nfa.futures.org
www.nfa.futures.org

This is an independent, self-regulatory organization for the US futures industry. It develops rules, programs and services to safeguard market integrity, protect investors and help their members meet regulatory responsibilities.

  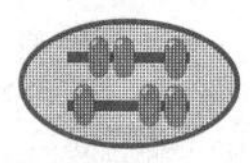   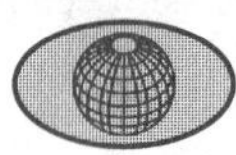   

Econometrics

BOOKS

Applied Econometrics: A Modern Approach Using Eviews and Microfit, revised ed
Dimitrios Asteriou, Stephen Hall
New York: Palgrave Macmillan, 2007
256pp, ISBN: 978-0-230-50640-4
A solid overview of current econometric thinking, it provides a practical guide to econometric data, econometrics tests and methods of estimation for those studying econometrics or quantitative economics. It also presents a step-by-step approach to using the popular software packages, and includes a section on panel data, that contains the latest developments in panel unit roots and panel cointegration.

A Concise Introduction to Econometrics: An Intuitive Guide
Philip Hans Franses
New York: Cambridge University Press, 2002
117pp, ISBN: 978-0-521-52090-4
A short and practical introduction to the subject, this guide reviews the basic econometric concepts, focusing on a select number of key methods. It emphasizes the importance of specification, evaluation, and implementation of models appropriate to the data, and also provides a series of questions in various economic disciplines, to be answered using econometric methods and models.

Econometric Analysis, 6th ed
William H. Greene
Upper Saddle River, New Jersey: Prentice Hall, 2007
1,216pp, ISBN: 978-0-13-513245-6
Provides an introduction to econometrics and its tools, as well as a resource on the professional literature on the subject that links specialized areas. Combining an applied approach with a theoretical underpinning, it covers a wide range of topics such as Classical, Bayesian, GMM, and maximum likelihood, and emphasizes new areas such a time series and panels.

Econometric Models and Economic Forecasts, 4th ed
Robert Pindyck, Daniel Rubinfeld
Boston, Massachusetts: McGraw-Hill/Irwin, 1998
634pp, ISBN: 978-0-07-913292-5
A strong textbook that focuses on modeling and model building, explaining what type of model to build, how to test it statistically, and then apply the model to practical problems in forecasting and analysis. It also analyses time series and forecasting, single-equation and the multiple regression models, and has an expanded treatment of nonlinear and maximum-likelihood estimation.

Econometrics
Fumio Hayashi
Princeton, New Jersey: Princeton University Press, 2000
690pp, ISBN: 978-0-691-01018-2
Acting as an introduction to the subject, it presents all the standard material necessary for understanding the various estimation techniques, through a mix of theory and applications. Generalized methods of moments (GMM) are helpfully used as an organizing principle throughout, and there is also a detailed analysis of stationary and non-stationary time series.

The Econometrics of Financial Markets
John Y. Campbell, Andrew W. Lo, A. Craig MacKinlay
Princeton, New Jersey: Princeton University Press, 1997
611pp, ISBN: 978-0-691-04301-2
This is a technical but accessible examination of financial econometrics by three leading researchers, presenting cutting-edge statistical techniques and the techniques of financial modeling. It examines much of empirical finance in detail, including the Random Walk Hypothesis, event analysis, the Capital Asset Pricing Model, Arbitrage Pricing Theory, statistical fractals, and chaos theory.

Essentials of Econometrics, 3rd ed
Damodar Gujarati
Boston, Massachusetts: McGraw-Hill/Irwin, 2006
553pp, ISBN: 978-0-07-313594-6
Now in its 3rd edition, this focused examination of the principles of econometrics provides an introduction to the subject for the beginner. It is accessible for those wanting a quick understanding of econometric techniques, especially linear regression analysis. It presents all the main econometric theory and techniques through extensive examples and explanations, and has an accompanying CD.

Financial Econometrics: From Basics to Advanced Modeling Techniques
Svetlozar T. Rachev, Stefan Mittnik, Frank J. Fabozzi, Sergio M. Focardi, Teo Jasic
Frank J. Fabozzi Series
Hoboken, New Jersey: Wiley, 2007
553pp, ISBN: 978-0-471-78450-0
This is a comprehensive guide to financial econometrics that uses numerous examples to help an understanding of the main issues. It provides a thorough overview of all the key topics, concepts, and theories, including background material on probability theory and statistics, and uses real-world data and the results of published research where possible.

A Guide to Econometrics, 6th ed
Peter Kennedy
Malden, Massachusetts: Blackwell Publishing, 2008
585pp, ISBN: 978-1-4051-8257-7
This is a supplement and guide to the main econometrics textbooks, which provides analysis and practical advice for all levels of econometrics classes. This new edition contains new chapters on instrumental variables and on computation considerations, and an introduction to wavelets.

A Guide to Modern Econometrics, 3rd ed
Marno Verbeek
Chichester, UK: Wiley, 2008
472pp, ISBN: 978-0-470-51769-7
The new edition of this textbook takes a practical approach to analysing some of the alternative econometric techniques available. It also introduces new material on panel data and pseudo panels, and takes a closer look at some of the more complex topics, such as multicollinearity, instrumental variables, and robust inference.

Introductory Econometrics: A Modern Approach, 4th ed
Jeffrey M. Wooldridge
Mason, Ohio: South Western, Cengage Learning, 2009
865pp, ISBN: 978-0-324-58162-1
A new edition of this guide to the fundamentals of econometrics, that focuses on current approaches and techniques, and incorporates relevant applications in many places. It includes analysis of a wide range of topics that are common in research, such as panel data, and a balance of mainstream models, equations, examples, and intuitive descriptions.

     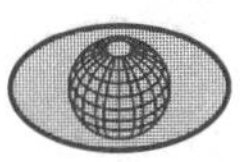   

Introductory Econometrics for Finance, 2nd ed
Chris Brooks
Information Technology & Law Series
Cambridge, UK: Cambridge University Press, 2008
648pp, ISBN: 978-0-521-69468-1
This successful textbook is a strong primer for finance students needing the basics of econometrics tailored for their learning needs. It has been updated to include new analysis of panel data and limited dependent variable models, as well as the standard topics. It assumes no prior knowledge of econometrics, and focuses more on intuitive understanding than formulae.

Practical Financial Econometrics, Volume II
Carol Alexander
Market Risk Analysis Series
Chichester, UK: Wiley, 2008
426pp, ISBN: 978-0-470-99801-4
Part of the Market Risk Analysis series, *Practical Financial Econometrics* introduces the most common econometric techniques in finance, with a unique focus on applications to asset pricing, fund management and problem solving in market risk analysis. It also covers equity factor models, volatility and correlation, GARCH, cointegration, copulas, Markov switching, forecasting, and model evaluation.

Principles of Econometrics, 3rd ed
R. Carter Hill, Wiliam E. Griffiths, Guay C. Lim
Hoboken, New Jersey: Wiley, 2008
579pp, ISBN: 978-0-471-72360-8
A rigorous overview of econometrics and how to use the basic tools for estimation, inference, and forecasting, put in the context of real-life economic problems. It offers clear descriptions of simple economic models, as well as how to estimate key economic parameters, test economic hypotheses, and predict economic outcomes, in terms of motivation, understanding, and implementation.

JOURNALS

Applied Econometrics and International Development
Euro-American Association of Economic Development Studies
Faculty of Economics, Room 119-B, Econometrics, University of Santiago de Compostela 15782, Spain
T: +34 981 563 100
www.usc.es/~econometaeid.htm
ISSN: 1578-4487
Currently publishing twice yearly, this journal places an emphasis on economic development with an international and quantitative approach, and its main aim is to foster international cooperation to development.

Econometric Reviews
Taylor & Francis
325 Chestnut Street, Suite 800, Philadelphia, PA 19106, USA
T: +1 215 625 8900
F: +1 215 625 2940
www.tandf.co.uk/journals/titles/07474938.asp
ISSN: 0747-4938
This is a bimonthly review journal that examines the limits of econometric knowledge, featuring regular refereed articles and book reviews, as well as retrospective surveys of current or developing topics. Special issues of the journal are developed on a variety of specific themes in econometrics.

Econometric Theory
Cambridge University Press
40 West 20th Street, New York, NY 10022-4211, USA
T: +1 212 924 3900
F: +1 212 691 3239
korora.econ.yale.edu/et
ISSN: 0266-4666
This is an international bimonthly journal dedicated to advancing theoretical research in econometrics. It provides an outlet for original theoretical contributions in all of the major areas of econometrics, and seeks to foster the multidisciplinary features of econometrics that extend beyond the subject of economics.

Econometrica
The Econometrics Society
Department of Economics, Princeton University, Fisher Hall, Princeton, NJ 08544-1021, USA
T: +1 609 258 4768
F: +1 609 258 8844
www.econometricsociety.org
ISSN: 0012-9682
This is a bimonthly respected journal that publishes original articles in all branches of economics—theoretical and empirical, abstract and applied. The articles explore a range of topics, from the frontier of theoretical developments in many new and important areas, to research on current and applied economic problems, to methodologically innovative, theoretical and applied studies in econometrics.

The Econometrics Journal
Royal Economic Society
Lauriergracht 123, 1016 RK Amsterdam, The Netherlands
T: +31 20 598 9898
F: +31 20 598 9899
www.ectj.org
ISSN: 1368-4221
This is a journal, published three times a year, for econometric research, open to all areas of econometrics, whether applied, computational, methodological, or theoretical. It seeks to promote the general advancement and application of econometric methods and techniques to problems of relevance to modern economics.

International Journal of Applied Econometrics and Quantitative Studies
Euro-American Association of Economic Development Studies
Faculty of Economics, Room 119-B, Econometrics, University of Santiago de Compostela 15782, Spain
T: +34 981 563 100
www.usc.es/~econometijaeqs.htm
ISSN: 1698-4153
This refereed twice-yearly journal is mainly focused on policy-oriented quantitative studies of socio-economic interest. It focuses on special topics, including key questions linking economics research and policies, studies by country, including interesting quantitative studies with special priority for articles related with education, social well-being, international trade, investment and cooperation to development in one or more countries, and reports and other studies.

Journal of Applied Econometrics
Wiley
Faculty of Economics, University of Cambridge, Sidgwick Avenue, Cambridge, CB3 9DD, UK
T: +44 (0) 1223 335291
F: +44 (0) 1223 335471
jae.wiley.com
ISSN: 0883-7252
This is a bimonthly international journal that publishes articles on the application of existing as well as new econometric techniques to a wide variety of problems in economics and related subjects, covering topics in measurement, estimation, testing, forecasting, and policy analysis.

Journal of Business and Economic Statistics
American Statistical Association
732 North Washington Street, Alexandria, VA 22314-1943, USA
T: +1 703 684 1221
F: +1 703 684 2037
www.amstat.org/publications/jbes
ISSN: 0735-0015

  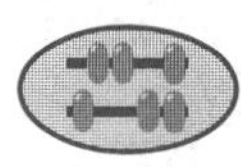   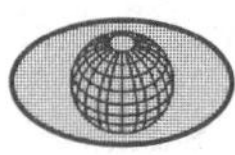   

This is a quarterly journal that publishes a range of articles, primarily applied statistical analyses of microeconomic, macroeconomic, forecasting, business, and finance related topics. It also publishes relevant papers in statistics, econometrics, computation, simulation, and graphics.

Journal of Econometrics

Elsevier
Radarweg 29, 1043 NX Amsterdam, The Netherlands
T: +31 20 485 3757
F: +31 20 485 3432
www.elsevier.com/wps/find/journaldescription.cws_home/505575/description#description
ISSN: 0304-4076

This is a monthly journal serving as an outlet for new research in both theoretical and applied econometrics. Its scope includes papers dealing with estimation and other methodological aspects of the application of statistical inference to economic data, as well as papers dealing with the application of econometric techniques to substantive areas of economics. Econometric research in the traditional divisions of the discipline, or in the newly developing areas of social experimentation, are also covered.

Journal of Financial Econometrics

Oxford University Press
Great Clarendon Street, Oxford, OX2 6DP, UK
T: +44 (0) 1865 353907
F: +44 (0) 1865 353485
jfec.oxfordjournals.org
ISSN: 1479-8409

This is a quarterly journal dedicated to this fast-growing area of research. It addresses substantive statistical issues in econometrics, and aims to reflect and advance the relationship between econometrics and finance, both at the methodological and at the empirical levels.

Review of Economics and Statistics

MIT Press
Harvard University, 79 JFK Street, Box 134, Cambridge, MA 02138, USA
T: +1 617 495 2111
F: +1 617 495 5147
www.mitpressjournals.org/loi/rest
ISSN: 0034-6535

This is a quarterly journal of applied and quantitative economics that has published some of the most important articles in empirical economics. It also publishes collections of papers or symposia devoted to a single topic of methodological or empirical interest.

INTERNET

Econometric Links

www.econometriclinks.com

This is an online journal and resource, extensively annotated, and updated monthly. It focuses on general collections and preprint sites, departments and societies, software links, books, conferences, journals and mailing lists.

Econometric-Research

www.jiscmail.ac.uk/lists/econometric-research.html

This is an online forum for applied and theoretical research in econometrics and associated statistical theory, and functions as a dissemination list for research resources such as conferences, seminars, academic jobs, and free software.

Econometric Resources on the Internet

www.oswego.edu/~kane/econometrics

Although this is a site designed to accompany an econometrics textbook, it does contain useful annotated links to econometrics resources for both students and researchers, including links to data sources, economic associations, economic journals, datasets, government sites, newsgroups and software.

Econometrics Laboratory Software Archive

elsa.berkeley.edu

This site contains links to introductory tutorials on LaTeX, Perl, SAS, TCP/IP, Maple, MATLAB, as well as links to documentation and help for other software. It also includes a large selection of links to sources of econometric data, and a software archive for GAUSS and MATLAB.

ORGANIZATIONS

Europe

The Applied Econometrics Association

Chair: Orhan Güvenen
53, rue Saint Denis, 75 001 Paris, France
T: +33 1 4221 1172
F: +33 958 888 232
E: aea08@fed-eco.org
www.aea-eu.com

The purpose of The Applied Econometrics Association is to encourage and develop econometric applications in a spirit of open-minded scientific research, and it aims to bring its proposals before public and governmental bodies, firms, teaching and professional training institutions. Its areas of speciality are employment, finance, health, sector-based analysis, macro- and microeconomics, and management.

USA

Cowles Foundation

Yale University, PO Box 208281, New Haven, CT 06520-8281, USA
T: +1 203 432 3702
F: +1 203 432 6167
E: marleen.vega-perez@yale.edu
cowles.econ.yale.edu

The Cowles Foundation, continuing the work of the Cowles Commission for Research in Economics, founded in 1932 by Alfred Cowles, conducts and encourages research in economics and related fields. It seeks to foster the development and application of rigorous logical, mathematical, and statistical methods of analysis, and provides financial support for research, visiting faculty, postdoctoral fellowships, workshops, and graduate students.

The Econometric Society

Chair: Torsten Persson
Claire Sashi, General Manager, Department of Economics, New York University, 19 West Fourth Street, 6th Floor, New York, NY 10012, USA
T: +1 212 998 3820
F: +1 212 995 4487
E: sashi@econometricsociety.org
www.econometricsociety.org

This is an international society for the advancement of economic theory in its relation to statistics and mathematics, and which promotes studies that aim at a unification of the theoretical-quantitative and empirical-quantitative approach to economic problems. The main activities of the Society are the publication of the journal, *Econometrica*, the publication of a monograph series, the organization of scientific meetings around the world, and the conduct of elections for Fellow of the Econometric Society.

     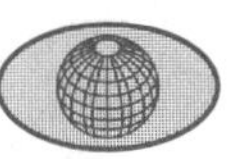   

Emerging Market Finance

BOOKS

Bailouts or Bail-Ins: Responding to Financial Crises in Emerging Economies

Nouriel Roubini, Brad Setser
Washington, DC: Institute for International Economics, 2004
348pp, ISBN: 978-0-88132-371-9

Examines the recurring economic problems and short-term financial crises in developing markets, such as a lack of foreign reserves that prevent access to international capital markets. It looks at the role of the International Monetary Fund and the G-7 countries, rescue loans, currency devaluation and default, arguing that a flexible response and a consistent framework is crucial, as every crisis is different.

Bank Risk Analysis in Emerging Markets

Howard Palmer
London: Euromoney Books, 1998
212pp, ISBN: 978-1-85564-478-6

This is designed to help build a strategic bank risk portfolio, and understand the techniques and concepts of bank risk analysis, including loan provisions, liquidity ratios, cost/income ratios, the role of correspondent banking, and the future of bank risk indicators. It shows how to appraise the risks involved in dealing with banks in emerging economies, with greater transaction risks, and less reliance on supervision and potential rescue of banks in difficulty.

Emerging Capital Markets and Globalization: The Latin American Experience

Augusto De La Torre, Sergio Schmukler
Latin American Development Forum Series
Palo Alto, California/Washington, DC: Stanford University Press/World Bank, 2007
209pp, ISBN: 978-0-8213-6543-4

This examines why the development of local capital markets in most of Latin America has not been as successful as in other emerging economies, and puts this into the context of global trends in the capital markets. It analyzes the factors for this, discusses the implications for capital market reform in Latin America, and the need for revisions to the current policy agenda.

Emerging Capital Markets in Turmoil: Bad Luck or Bad Policy?

Guillermo A. Calvo
Cambridge, Massachusetts: MIT Press, 2005
563pp, ISBN: 978-0-262-03334-3

This collection of essays analyzes the struggle of emerging markets with capital flow volatility, and the limitations and vulnerabilities these economies face. It focuses on exchange rate issues, explores the reasons why emerging market economies have been affected by such dramatic highs and lows, and the increasing role of stocks and the financial sector in containing financial crises.

Emerging Markets: A Practical Guide for Corporations, Lenders, and Investors

Jeffrey C. Hooke
New York: Wiley, 2001
283pp, ISBN: 978-0-471-36099-5

This provides both Western investors and development professionals with a guide to the opportunities and problems associated with dealing with emerging markets. It defines what emerging markets are and discusses why multinational firms should invest in them, reviews some of the obstacles to investment, and discusses patterns of business behavior and market conditions in the context of developing countries.

Emerging Markets: Lessons for Business Success and the Outlook for Different Markets, 2nd ed

Nenad Pacek, Daniel Thorniley
London: Economist, 2007
245pp, ISBN: 978-1-86197-843-1

This practical discussion on business in emerging markets examines why some firms fail and some succeed, and provides an extensive review of the outlook for different emerging markets. Based on real experiences of companies, it is aimed at both managers who are involved in emerging markets for the first time and managers already operating in them.

Emerging Markets and Financial Globalization: Sovereign Bond Spreads in 1870–1913 and Today

Paolo Mauro, Nathan Sussman, Yishay Yafeh
Oxford, UK: Oxford University Press, 2008
208pp, ISBN: 978-0-19-922613-9

This is an exploration of the development of financial globalization based on an examination and comparison of the data on sovereign bonds issued by borrowing developing countries in this earlier period and in the present day. It shows the characteristics of successful borrowers in the two periods, and informs both on how the world used to operate and on the current international financial environment.

Financial Decisions in Emerging Markets

Jaime Sabal
New York: Oxford University Press, 2002
280pp, ISBN: 978-0-19-514459-8

This examines the context and characteristics of emerging market finance and the problems they present, such as the relative lack of market efficiency. It focuses on investment and financing decisions as they relate to investors in emerging markets, and proposes relevant approaches for investment analysis in these countries. It also reviews relevant financial theory, and is aimed at practitioners, development experts, and students of finance.

Financial Markets Volatility and Performance in Emerging Markets

Sebastian Edwards, Marcio G. P. Garcia (editors)
National Bureau of Economic Research Conference Report Series
Chicago, Illinois: University of Chicago Press, 2008
287pp, ISBN: 978-0-226-18495-1

This is a collection of articles that examine the increasing globalization of the financial markets in the context of capital flows and crises, domestic credit, international financial integration, and economic policy. It discusses the balance between capital mobility and capital controls for developing countries as they operate in the complex world of private investors, hedge funds, large corporations, and international institutions.

Getting Started in Emerging Markets

Christoher Poillon
New York: Wiley, 2000
206pp, ISBN: 978-0-471-39545-4

This introduction to emerging markets describes what they are, the opportunities for high returns and portfolio diversification, the risks in each, and presents a systematic process for successful investing in the markets. It lists each country, with information about their government, markets, GDP, inflation, unemployment, and index funds, and includes a review of online investing, stock data, and investment software.

Harvard Business Review on Emerging Markets

Harvard Business Review Paperback Series
Boston, Massachusetts: Harvard Business School Press, 2008
224pp, ISBN: 978-1-4221-2649-3

This is a review of the unique challenges of

  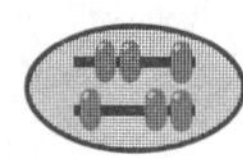   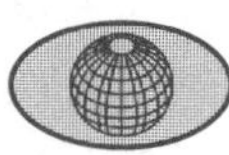   

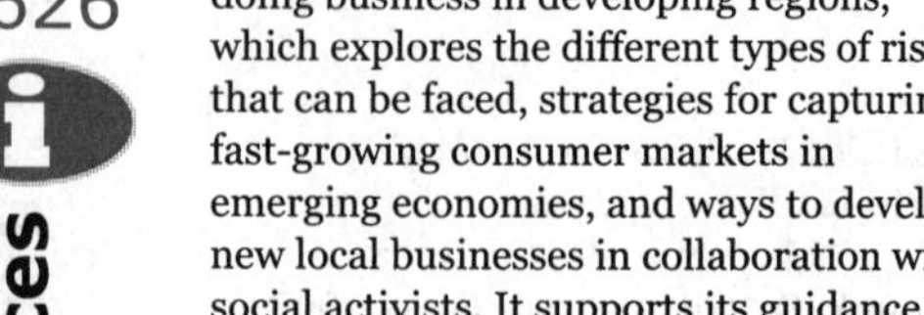

doing business in developing regions, which explores the different types of risk that can be faced, strategies for capturing fast-growing consumer markets in emerging economies, and ways to develop new local businesses in collaboration with social activists. It supports its guidance with real-world examples, to provide insight into potential issues and dangers.

Institutional Banking for Emerging Markets: Principles and Practice
Wei-Xin Huang
Wiley Finance Series
Hoboken, New Jersey: Wiley, 2007
274pp, ISBN: 978-0-470-03076-9
This explores how banks can prosper in the emerging countries, and discusses some of the unique functions of institutional banking in these markets, such as problem solving, the importance of communication, and the problems caused by the irregularity of the market and non-transparency of the financial and legal systems. It contains examples and case studies that show how institutional banking works in the real world.

Investing in Emerging Fixed Income Markets, 2nd ed
Frank J. Fabozzi, Efstathia Pilarinu (editors)
Frank J. Fabozzi Series
New York: Wiley, 2002
374pp, ISBN: 978-0-471-21836-4
This is an investor's guide to understanding and benefiting from opportunities in the fixed income markets of emerging economies. A team of leading experts analyze these markets as a potentially lucrative area of investment, addressing issues affecting the corporate bond market, valuation techniques, credit analysis, and risk management, and show how to develop an investment approach to enhance long-term returns.

Macroeconomics in Emerging Markets
Peter J. Montiel
Cambridge, UK: Cambridge University Press, 2003
445pp, ISBN: 978-0-521-78060-5
This textbook examines why emerging markets face a different set of challenges to developed economies, and provides an overview of the main issues, such as debt, high inflation, and lack of credibility, and the debate on policy reform. It combines a clear analytical framework with a comprehensive discussion of monetary, fiscal, and exchange rate policy concerns in emerging markets.

Risk Management in Emerging Markets: How to Survive and Prosper
Carl Olsson
London: FT Prentice Hall, 2002
311pp, ISBN: 978-0-273-65618-0
With understanding risk in emerging markets being a critical factor for successful businesses, this book defines risk management and related technical concepts, and offers guidance on the basics of identification, measurement and management of risk in the context of the emerging markets. It also argues that risk management is about controlled decision-making rather than risk avoidance, and that balancing risk and reward is increasingly important.

Six Sizzling Markets: How to Profit from Investing in Brazil, Russia, India, China, South Korea, and Mexico
Pran Tiku
Hoboken, New Jersey: Wiley, 2008
374pp, ISBN: 978-0-470-17888-1
This lays out the case for investing in the emerging economies of BRIC, South Korea, and Mexico, and analyzes each nation's investment opportunities and successful industries. The overview is based around the tenets of demographics, economic performance, technology, open trade, infrastructure development, transparency and rule of law, education and training, and sound financial systems and policies.

Understanding Emerging Markets: China and India
Peter Enderwick
London: Routledge, 2007
249pp, ISBN: 978-0-415-37085-1
Understanding Emerging Markets offers guidelines on the opportunities and the risks involved in doing business in large emerging markets, especially China and India, and how these countries are responding to the challenge of globalization. It discusses the challenges faced by Western businesses, the market volatility, the social and informational risk, and the implications for management and global restructuring caused by the enormous expansion of those countries.

Valuation of Companies in Emerging Markets
Luis E. Pereiro
New York: Wiley, 2002
507pp, ISBN: 978-0-471-22078-7
This is a comprehensive exploration of evaluating potential acquisitions in the emerging markets, presenting corporate and private investors with tools, data, and practical examples for valuing both new ventures and established companies. It shows how to investigate emerging economies for opportunities to expand, define the relevant features of such a market, why traditional valuation techniques prove inadequate, and assesses the importance of unsystematic risk.

MAGAZINES

Emerging Markets
Euromoney Institutional Investor
Nestor House, Playhouse Yard, London, EC4V 5EX, UK
T: +44 (0) 20 7440 6023
F: +44 (0) 20 7440 6085
www.emergingmarkets.org
This newspaper, providing analysis of finance in developing economies, is published over the course of the annual meetings of the main multilateral development banks, and is also delivered free to delegates of these meetings. It runs breaking news stories and commentary by journalists, bankers, academics and others, offering a broad range of features and analysis.

JOURNALS

Emerging Markets Finance and Trade
M. E. Sharpe
PO Box 1943, Birmingham, Alabama 35201, USA
T: +1 205 981 4007
www.mesharpe.com/mall/results1.asp?ACR=REE
ISSN: 1540-496X
Published bimonthly, this journal focuses on the financial and economic aspects of emerging economies. It provides an outlet for research that is policy oriented and interdisciplinary, employing sound econometric methods, using macro, micro, financial, institutional, and political economy data. One or two issues each year are special issues, presenting selected papers from major research conferences worldwide.

Emerging Markets Review
Elsevier
Finance and Decision Sciences Journals, Radarweg 29, 1043 NX Amsterdam, The Netherlands
F: +31 20 485 2370
www.elsevier.com/wps/find/journaldescription.cws_home/620356/description#description
ISSN: 1566-0141
This quarterly journal publishes high

impact empirical and theoretical studies in emerging markets finance. Its coverage emphasizes comparative studies with a global and regional perspective, single country studies that address critical policy issues and have significant global and regional implications, and includes papers that examine the interactions of national and international financial architecture.

Global Financial Stability Report
The International Monetary Fund
700 19th Street NW, Washington, DC 20431, USA
T: +1 202 623 7000
F: +1 202 623 4661
www.imf.org/external/pubs/ft/gfsr
These twice-yearly reports by the IMF provide comprehensive coverage of both mature and emerging financial markets as part of their tracking of financial markets. They focus on market developments and issues, assessing the global financial system and markets, structural or systemic issues relevant to international financial stability, and emerging market financing in a global context.

International Journal of Emerging Markets
Emerald Group Publishing
Howard House, Wagon Lane, Bingley, BD16 1WA, UK
T: +44 (0) 1274 777 700
F: +44 (0) 1274 785 201
info.emeraldinsight.com/products/journals/journals.htm?id=IJOEM
ISSN: 1746-8809
IJoEM publishes the latest theoretical and empirical management research from the field of management and business studies in the emerging markets. It provides this research for both the academic and business world, and also covers marketing, strategy, finance and accounting, operations and decision sciences, organizational behavior and cross-cultural management, international trade, and business economics.

Journal of Emerging Market Finance
Sage Publications
B17 Greater Kailash Enclave 2, 2nd Floor, New Delhi 110 048, India
emf.sagepub.com
ISSN: 0972-6527
This journal, with three issues each year, publishes papers on finance and economics in emerging market economies. It is aimed at the experienced practitioner, but also offers an outlet for application-oriented research, and covers models of portfolio risk management, exchange rate risks, global banking, derivative pricing, equity market structures, policy impacts on financial markets, and financial indicators.

The Journal of Emerging Markets
The Peter J. Tobin College of Business
St. John's University, 8000 Utopia Parkway, Queens, NY 11439, USA
T: +1 718 990 7305
F: +1 718 990 1868
new.stjohns.edu/academics/graduate/tobin/research/jem
ISSN: 1083-9798
This quarterly journal publishes the results of basic or applied research on the operation and structure of emerging markets, economic-financial developments in developing countries and transitional economies, and the relation between emerging and international capital markets. Articles focus on government policies, institutional frameworks and other environmental factors, and also present empirical analysis on individual countries, market sectors, or financial instruments.

INTERNET

The Emerging Markets Companion
www.emgmkts.com
This is an online financial information source on the emerging markets for the global investor. Articles from market participants and news organizations are updated throughout the day, and it provides a forum on investing in the developing economies. It offers news on asset prices, closing levels of major emerging markets, political, economic, and financial events, global research, commentary, and analysis.

ORGANIZATIONS

USA

Emerging Markets Private Equity Association
Chair: Roger S. Leeds
1055 Thomas Jefferson Street NW, Suite 650, Washington, DC 20007, USA
T: +1 202 333 8171
F: +1 202 333 3162
E: info@empea.net
www.empea.net
EMPEA is a broad-based organization that focuses on the emerging private equity markets of Africa, Asia, Central and Eastern Europe, Russia, Latin America, and the Middle East. It is comprised primarily of private equity fund managers, but also includes institutional investors, service providers, and others with an interest in the asset class, and promotes greater understanding of private equity investing in emerging markets.

EMTA
360 Madison Avenue, 18th Floor, New York, NY 10017, USA
T: +1 212 313 1100
F: +1 212 313 1016
www.emta.org
Formerly the Emerging Markets Traders Association, this trade association for the emerging markets is a not-for-profit corporation that promotes the development of fair, efficient, and transparent trading markets for emerging markets instruments, and the integration of the emerging markets into the global financial marketplace. It provides a forum for market participants to identify issues of importance to the trading and investment community.

  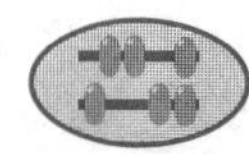   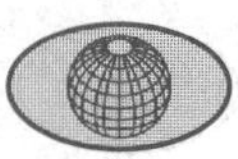   

Energy and Commodity Finance

BOOKS

Commodities and Commodity Derivatives: Modelling and Pricing for Agriculturals, Metals and Energy
Hélyette Geman
Wiley Finance Series
Chichester, UK: Wiley, 2005
396pp, ISBN: 978-0-470-01218-5

This is a technical examination of hard and soft commodities and related derivatives for academics and market professionals looking for a solid grounding in the subject. It provides an overview of the commodity markets, and a detailed analysis of commodity price and volume risk, stochastic modeling of commodity spot prices and forward curves, real options valuation, and hedging of physical assets in the energy industry.

Commodity Fundamentals: How to Trade the Precious Metals, Energy, Grain, and Tropical Commodity Markets
Ronald C. Spurga
Wiley Trading Series
Hoboken, New Jersey: Wiley, 2006
196pp, ISBN: 978-0-471-78851-5

This is an accessible primer on commodity trading, which examines the profit potential in trading precious metals, energy, grains, and tropical commodities. It offers guidance on techniques such as spread trades, and cash and carry trades, as well as trends in the global commodities market, and aspects of diversification, risks, and rewards, and how to integrate commodities into an overall trading strategy.

Commodity Investing: Maximizing Returns through Fundamental Analysis
Adam Dunsby, John Eckstein, Jess Gaspar, Sarah Mulholland
Wiley Finance Series
Hoboken, New Jersey: Wiley, 2008
290pp, ISBN: 978-0-470-22310-9

This is a detailed exploration of the investment opportunities available in the expanding commodity markets. It describes the basics of a range of commodities, and the necessary tools for integrating them effectively into a portfolio, and covers the key elements of a commodity-based trading strategy, trend following, anchor variables, the shape of the futures curve, and risk control methodologies.

Commodity Modeling and Pricing: Methods for Analyzing Resource Market Behavior
Peter Schaeffer (editor)
Wiley Finance Series
Hoboken, New Jersey: Wiley, 2008
298pp, ISBN: 978-0-470-31723-5

This is a comprehensive examination of the key issues relating to commodity price behavior and pricing. Leading industry experts and academics discuss how to apply the latest methods for analyzing, modeling, and forecasting the commodity markets, and the role that resource commodity markets play in economic development, international trade, and global economic stability.

Commodity Trader's Almanac 2008
Jeffrey A. Hirsch, Scott W. Barrie
Almanac Investor Series
Hoboken, New Jersey: Wiley, 2007
192pp, ISBN: 978-0-470-10986-1

This reference work presents information and analysis on futures and commodities, and describes the markets for those trading or hedging. It is organized in a calendar format, and features monthly almanac pages based around the three major groupings of metals, petroleum, and agriculture. It also provides market-based data and information on different market tendencies, and monthly and daily reminders of market opportunities.

Emissions Trading: Principles and Practice, 2nd ed
T. H. Tietenberg
Washington, DC: RFF Press, 2006
233pp, ISBN: 978-1-933115-31-3

This classic guide to emissions trading provides a comprehensive overview of pollution reform and the first large-scale attempt to use economic incentives in environmental policy in the US. It analyzes how the use of transferable permits to control pollution became central to the US program on acid rain and the European approach to greenhouse gases, surveys environmental policy, and identifies best practices for the design of effective programs.

Energy and Power Risk Management: New Developments in Modeling, Pricing and Hedging
Alexander Eydeland, Krzysztof Wolyniec
Wiley Finance Series
Hoboken, New Jersey: Wiley, 2003
490pp, ISBN: 978-0-471-10400-1

This is an authoritative guide to managing energy price risk in the natural gas and power markets. It examines the key issues in the development of the energy industry, the challenges for energy traders and energy risk management professionals, and presents the latest developments in modeling, pricing, and hedging the risks of the relevant derivative structures, as well as how to understand the data used in energy models.

Energy Budgets at Risk (EBaR): A Risk Management Approach to Energy Purchase and Efficiency Choices
Jerry Jackson
Wiley Finance Series
Hoboken, New Jersey: Wiley, 2008
300pp, ISBN: 978-0-470-19767-7

This new, non-technical examination of risk management and energy budgeting focuses on energy costs, price, and efficiency, and the key elements in developing a balanced approach to facility energy risk management. It introduces a new energy management framework that reduces energy costs and energy-efficiency investment risk, and increase cash flows, by applying risk management tools developed in the financial industry.

Energy Commodity Hedge Funds: A Practitioner's Guide
John P. Thompson, Erik Serrano Berntsen
Wiley Finance Series
Hoboken, New Jersey: Wiley, 2009
448pp, ISBN: 978-0-470-51940-0

This is a practical guide to energy commodity hedge funds, which examines the key factors in setting up and operating funds trading in these markets. It outlines the necessary due diligence process for evaluating and investing in the funds, and discusses the opportunities and risks of all energy commodity markets as hedge fund investments.

Energy Price Risk: Trading and Price Risk Management
Tom James
Basingstoke, UK: Palgrave Macmillan, 2003
538pp, ISBN: 978-1-4039-0340-2

This is a practical examination of methods for optimizing company performance through effective price risk strategies and tools in the energy markets. It discusses critical aspects of risk management and its impact on energy pricing, and presents the mitigation tools and strategies available in the market. It covers the full range of energy products, and offers useful worked examples and solutions.

  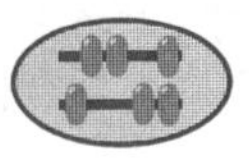 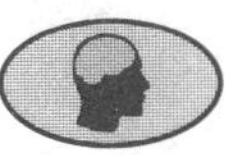  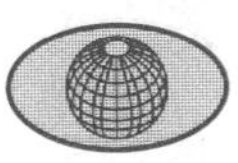   

Energy Risk: Valuing and Managing Energy Derivatives, 2nd ed
Dragana Pilipovic
New York: McGraw-Hill, 2007
400pp, ISBN: 978-0-07-148594-4
This quantitative approach to energy risk analyzes the guidelines and tools for using energy derivatives, and strategies for trading in the energy markets. It explores the main factors that influence energy risk, such as spot price behavior, volatility, and the forward price curve, market behavior, seasonal effects, how to use energy-specific models, and methods for valuing energy derivatives.

The Handbook of Commodity Investing
Frank J. Fabozzi, Roland Fuss, Dieter G. Kaiser
Frank J. Fabozzi Series
Hoboken, New Jersey: Wiley, 2008
986pp, ISBN: 978-0-470-11764-4
This guide to commodity investment examines the basic techniques, products, markets, and sectors, as well as more technical aspects such as performance measurement, risk management, and asset allocation. It explains the mechanics of the commodity market, how to understand and incorporate commodities into a portfolio, and outlines key principles for effective risk management of commodity futures portfolios.

Handbook of Financing Energy Projects
Albert Thumann, Eric Woodruff
Lilburn, Georgia: Fairmont Press, 2005
432pp, ISBN: 978-0-8493-3667-6
This practical guide to project finance in the energy sector assesses the full range of current financing, such as energy service performance contracting, rate of return analysis, and energy savings measurement and verification. It examines the importance of funding, outlines key techniques for effectively structuring a financed energy project, how to present a proposal with positive cash flow, and innovative financing methods.

Hot Commodities: How Anyone Can Invest Profitably in the World's Best Market
Jim Rogers
New York: Random House, 2004
250pp, ISBN: 978-0-8129-7371-6
This is an accessible primer on commodity investing, which explains the fundamental concepts, the relationship between the stock and commodities markets, the relative risks involved, and describes a range of techniques and strategies that can be used to trade effectively. It also offers practical advice on information sources, opening an account, index funds, industry terminology, and the place of commodities in a balanced portfolio.

Intelligent Commodity Investing: New Strategies and Practical Insights for Informed Decision Making
Hilary Till, Joseph Eagleeye (editors)
London: Risk Books, 2007
350pp, ISBN: 978-1-904339-63-2
This collection of new writing by range of investors, consultants, hedge funds, index providers, risk managers, and academics describes the range of innovative investment techniques currently being utilized in the commodity markets. It explores the characteristics, benefits, and challenges of these capital assets, and discusses asset allocation, investment strategies, and risk control, to provide a practical framework and reference on active and passive natural resources investing.

Profiting from Clean Energy: A Complete Guide to Trading Green in Solar, Wind, Ethanol, Fuel Cell, Carbon Credit Industries, and More
Richard W. Asplund
Wiley Trading Series
Hoboken, New Jersey: Wiley, 2008
370pp, ISBN: 978-0-470-11799-6
This guide to the basics of clean energy investment explains the technology and industry structure behind various sectors of this field, and discusses the opportunities available in each. It presents the full range of investment techniques that are applicable, such as individual stocks, green exchange-traded funds or mutual funds, or trading the biofuel and carbon credit markets.

Risk Management in Commodity Markets: From Shipping to Agriculturals and Energy
Hélyette Geman (editor)
Wiley Finance Series
Chichester, UK: Wiley, 2009
320pp, ISBN: 978-0-470-69425-1
This edited collection provides a guide to the main risk management issues associated with commodities such as energy, weather, agriculturals, metals and shipping. It discusses the modeling of spot and forward prices, the use of options and other derivative contract forms for hedging purposes, and the freight derivatives markets and products used to manage shipping and freight risk in the commodity markets.

Timing Strategies for Commodity Futures Markets: Effective Strategy and Tactics for Short-Term and Long-Term Traders
Colin Alexander
New York: McGraw-Hill, 2007
352pp, ISBN: 978-0-07-149601-8
This is a detailed analysis of commodity futures, which focuses on timing issues, and provides advice on setting up monthly, weekly, daily, and intraday charts with indicators for effective trading. It presents a proven approach to evaluating markets, and explores how to define a trend, avoid high-risk and marginal trades, build and read charts, and implement current market indicators.

Trading Commodities and Financial Futures: A Step-by-Step Guide to Mastering the Markets, 3rd ed
George Kleinman
Boston, Massachusetts: FT Press, 2005
258pp, ISBN: 978-0-13-147654-7
This bestselling primer shows you how to trade effectively in the commodities markets. It examines the fundamentals of each market, the best technical tools available, and how to recognize key market movements and trends. It also discusses the impact of trading psychology, electronic trading, and the latest contracts, and introduces a useful methodology, with details on its implementation.

Voluntary Carbon Markets: An International Business Guide to What They Are and How They Work
Ricardo Bayon, Amanda Hawn, Katherine Hamilton
Environmental Markets Insight Series
London: Earthscan Publications, 2007
164pp, ISBN: 978-1-84407-417-4
This guide to the international voluntary carbon markets provides a source of knowledge, information, ideas, and trends about the business potential in this new sector. It explores how business and individuals can enter the market, describes what voluntary carbon markets are, where they are, how they work, and how to capitalize on the opportunities they present for economic and environmental benefit.

MAGAZINES

Energy Risk
Incisive Media
Haymarket House, 28–29 Haymarket,
London, SW1Y 4RX, UK
T: +44 (0) 20 7484 9700
F: +44 (0) 20 7484 9797
www.energyrisk.com
ISSN: 1362-5403

This monthly magazine is dedicated to the financial, political, and legal risks in the global energy markets. It provides news, analysis, and education on the latest industry developments, and features updates on regulation issues, case studies, risk management workshops, market statistics and data, technology reviews, a regional focus, and special reports on issues facing market professionals.

Power Finance & Risk
Institutional Investor
225 Park Avenue South, New York, NY 10003, USA
T: +1 212 224 3300
www.iipower.com
PFR is a weekly magazine that provides coverage of corporate finance and restructuring, deals, mergers and acquisitions, and risk management trends and activity, and worldwide regulatory news in the power industry. It offers features such as a generation auction and sale calendar, a directory of ongoing generation asset sales, electric power indices, financing record, and a weekly recap of publicly reported power news stories.

World Energy
Loomis Publishing Services
3300 South Gessner, Suite 200, Houston, Texas 77063, USA
T: +1 713 626 5369
F: +1 713 627 1638
www.worldenergysource.com/wes/stores/1/World-Energy-Magazine-C27.aspx
Published eight times each year, this magazine provides a forum for the exchange of ideas and debate on the global energy markets. It presents a range of articles by leading industry executives, decision-makers, and energy officials, who discuss key issues such as manpower shortages, global warming, and the pricing of crude and natural gas.

JOURNALS

Energy Economics
Elsevier
Radarweg 29, 1043 NX Amsterdam, The Netherlands
F: +31 20 485 2370
www.elsevier.com/wps/find/journaldescription.cws_home/30413/description#description
ISSN: 0140-9883
This bimonthly journal provides a forum for research papers relating to the economic and econometric modeling and analysis of energy systems and issues. It takes a broad approach to the subject, covering issues related to forecasting, financing, pricing, investment, taxation, development, policy, conservation, regulation, risk management, insurance, portfolio theory, fiscal regimes, accounting, and the environment.

Journal of Energy Markets
Risk Journals
Incisive Media, Haymarket House, 28–29 Haymarket, London, SW1Y 4RX, UK
T: +44 (0) 20 7004 7531
F: +44 (0) 20 7484 9758
www.journalofenergymarkets.com
ISSN: 1756-3615
This quarterly journal publishes new empirical work on the price, risk, and investment behavior of energy commodities. It focuses on the evolution and performance of electricity, gas, oil and other energy markets, both wholesale and retail, as well as new methodologies on modeling energy markets for academics and energy professionals.

Resource and Energy Economics
Elsevier
Radarweg 29, 1043 NX Amsterdam, The Netherlands
F: +31 20 485 2370
www.elsevier.com/wps/find/journaldescription.cws_home/505569/description#description
ISSN: 0928-7655
This quarterly journal offers a forum for high-level economic analysis of the utilization and development of natural resources. This encompasses questions of optimal production and consumption affecting energy, minerals, land, air and water, and includes analysis of firm and industry behavior, environmental issues, and public policies.

INTERNET

Sustainable Alternatives Network
www.sustainablealternatives.net
SANet, a United Nations initiative, offers a tailor-made advisory service with access to local experts, one-on-one consulting, and a host of online information resources, including case studies of businesses that have successfully switched to cleaner technologies. It also provides a resource library, as well as in-person, local services in selected countries.

Sustainable Energy Finance Directory
www.sef-directory.net
This is a free online database of lenders and investors who actively provide finance to the sustainable energy sector worldwide. It is designed to help project developers and entrepreneurs identify sources of potential capital in the renewable energy and energy efficiency industry, and provides searchability on finance type, technology type, and geographic focus, as well as by criteria.

ORGANIZATIONS

International

International Association for Energy Economics
Chair: Georg Erdmann
28790 Chagrin Blvd., Ste. 350, Cleveland, Ohio 44122, USA
T: +1 216 464 5365
E: iaee@iaee.org
www.iaee.org
IAEE is an independent, global, non-profit organization that provides an interdisciplinary forum for the exchange of ideas, research, development, experiences, and issues among professionals interested in the field of energy economics. It publishes two periodicals, organizes international and regional conferences, and builds networks of energy-concerned practitioners.

The International Energy Credit Association
Chair: Denis Vermette
8325 Lantern View Lane, St. John, IN 46373, USA
www.ieca.net
IECA is an international, non-profit organization of credit and financial management professionals in the energy industry. It encourages communications between credit professionals, practitioners, and industry service providers worldwide, and provides continuing education, publications, conferences, and industry-specific seminars, with the aim of increasing recognition of the global energy credit community.

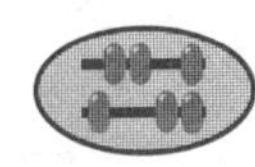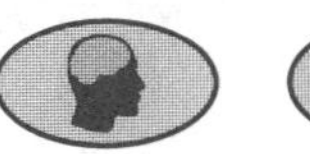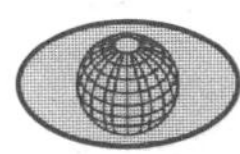

Financial Economics

BOOKS

Economic and Financial Decisions Under Risk
Louis Eeckhoudt, Christian Gollier, Harris Schlesinger
Princeton, New Jersey: Princeton University Press, 2005
234pp, ISBN: 978-0-691-12215-1
Presents an accessible introduction that bridges the gap between economic and finance theory and practice, and explains the fundamentals of risk measurement and risk aversion, and how to model risk effectively. It presents a summary of basic multi-period decision-making under risk, and how to apply these concepts to insurance decisions and portfolio choice in a one-period model.

Economics for Financial Markets
Brian Kettell
Quantitative Finance Series
Oxford, UK: Butterworth-Heinemann, 2002
359pp, ISBN: 978-0-7506-5384-8
This wide-ranging treatment covers the basics of financial economics, financial market valuation, and market behavior. It provides traders, investment managers, risk managers, and finance professionals with a sound grounding in the necessary economics, especially what type of information to concentrate on. It also examines how the new economy has changed financial market behavior, the impact of the euro on currency markets, and the actions of central banks.

Financial Accounting in an Economic Context, 7th ed
Jamie Pratt
Hoboken, New Jersey: Wiley, 2009
792pp, ISBN: 978-0-470-23398-6
This analyzes which accounting tools generate the best return on equity and create long-term shareholder value, including economic factors, measurement issues, and the principles of decision-making. It also describes how performance metrics, shareholder value creation, and market value are interwoven, and discusses methods used to account for operating, investing, and financing transactions, and new regulatory developments.

Financial Economics, 2nd ed
Zvi Bodie, Robert Merton, David Cleeton
Prentice Hall Series in Finance
Upper Saddle River, New Jersey: Prentice Hall, 2009
500pp, ISBN: 978-0-13-185615-8
This guide examines a broad range of themes, principles, and topics in financial economics, beyond the usual focus on corporate finance. It takes a balanced approach to the three key areas of optimization over time, asset valuation, and risk management, presents an overview of resource allocation over time under conditions of uncertainty, and also covers some personal finance topics, including saving and investing, and asset valuation.

Financial Economics
Chris Jones
New York: Routledge, 2008
320pp, ISBN: 978-0-415-37584-9
This is an introduction to classical finance models and financial economics, integrating both the institutional aspects of financial markets and general equilibrium analysis. It analyzes economic activity in the financial markets, focusing on how capital assets are priced and how these prices change over time, and how individuals use financial securities to choose their current and future consumption flows.

Foundations for Financial Economics
Chi-fu Huang
Englewood Cliffs, New Jersey: Prentice Hall, 1998
364pp, ISBN: 978-0-13-500653-5
This is an examination of individual consumption and portfolio decisions under uncertainty based on formal derivations of financial theory, and their implication for the valuation of securities, helping an understanding of modern financial economics. It features most of the relevant concepts, including risk aversion and stochastic dominance, capital asset pricing models and arbitrage pricing models, option pricing, and signaling models.

Global Financial Meltdown: How We Can Avoid the Next Economic Crisis
Colin Read
New York: Palgrave Macmillan, 2009
256pp, ISBN: 978-0-230-22218-2
This is new and accessible account of the problems inherent in the modern financial markets and the regulatory structure describes the reasons behind the sub prime mortgage crisis and economic downturn. It explains many of the key topics in economics, connecting them to real world financial problems, and makes recommendations for how the financial system can operate more effectively, without regular upheavals.

Handbook of the Economics of Finance: Corporate Finance, Volume 1A
George M. Constantinides, Milton Harris, René M. Stulz (editors)
Amsterdam: Elsevier, 2003
576pp, ISBN: 978-0-444-51362-5
This handbook focuses on corporate finance (Volume 1B examines the economics of financial markets), and discusses many key features relating to how economics impacts on the theory and practice of corporate finance. With contributions by many leading industry experts, it explores the financing decisions behind how businesses obtain and allocate capital, and the way in which managers can maximize the wealth of shareholders.

Intermediate Financial Theory, 2nd ed
Jean-Pierre Danthine, John B. Donaldson
Amsterdam: Elsevier, 2005
377pp, ISBN: 978-0-12-369380-8
An introductory textbook to financial asset pricing theory, this also discusses the many variations of asset pricing models, and the basic concepts of financial economics without recourse to complex mathematics. It also emphasizes the distinction between the equilibrium and the arbitrage perspectives on valuation and pricing, with this new edition including new coverage of asset management for the long-term investor.

International Financial Economics: Corporate Decisions in Global Markets, 2nd ed
Thomas J. O'Brien
New York: Oxford University Press, 2006
302pp, ISBN: 978-0-19-517504-2
This updated and revised treatment of international financial management applies the core concepts of financial economics to explaining how international corporate finance decisions are made in the real world. It takes a financial perspective rather than an economic one, offering a comprehensive discussion of economic foreign exchange exposure, hedging, and the cost of capital and accounting for overseas investments.

International Monetary and Financial Economics, 2nd ed
Joseph P. Daniels, David D. VanHoose
Mason, Ohio: Thomson/South-Western, 2002
580pp, ISBN: 978-0-324-06362-2

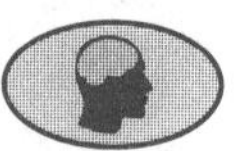

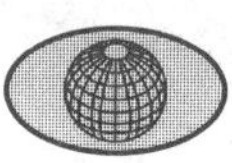

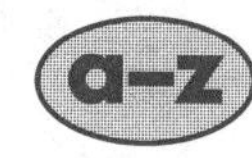

This is a comprehensive overview of all the main elements of international money and finance, open-economy macroeconomics, and international banking. It integrates theory with real-world policy and business applications, and discusses the relevance of international monetary and financial economics to international affairs and business.

Introduction to the Economics of Financial Markets
James Bradfield
Oxford, UK: Oxford University Press, 2007
489pp, ISBN: 978-0-19-531063-4
This non-technical introduction to financial theory and concepts examines all the main areas of financial economics, and shows how economists analyze the way in which financial markets allocate scarce resources. It focuses on the economics of securities markets and their operation, and explains risk-return trade-offs, the market efficiency concept, futures and options, and the economic implications of debt and equity contracts.

Microeconomics of Banking, 2nd ed
Xavier Freixas, Jean-Charles Rochet
Cambridge, Massachusetts: MIT Press, 2008
363pp, ISBN: 978-0-262-06270-1
This examines the main issues relating to the microeconomic theory of banking that has emerged over recent years, and looks at the use of the asymmetric information model for explaining the role of banks in the economy and for pinpoint structural weaknesses in the banking sector. It also covers financial intermediaries, macroeconomic consequences of financial imperfections, risk management inside the banking firm, and bank regulation.

Microfoundations of Financial Economics: An Introduction to General Equilibrium Asset Pricing
Yvan Lengwiler
Princeton, New Jersey: Princeton University Press, 2006
287pp, ISBN: 978-0-691-12631-9
This textbook explores the basics of modern asset pricing theory and microeconomic principles for masters or PhD students specializing in financial economics. It analyzes issues of general economic theory and financial economics, the consequences of heterogeneity, how welfare theorem is used in asset pricing theory, term structure models, the deficiencies in the standard asset pricing models.

Principles of Financial Economics
Stephen F. LeRoy, Jan Werner
Cambridge, UK: Cambridge University Press, 2001
280pp, ISBN: 978-0-521-58605-4
This introductory guide to financial economics focuses on the link between financial economics and equilibrium theory, describing the connection at each stage of its analysis. It avoids some of the more specific finance areas, such as the valuation of derivatives, to act as a primer for students of economics needing a better grasp of financial economics.

Quantitative Financial Economics: Stocks, Bonds and Foreign Exchange, 2nd ed
Keith Cuthbertson, Dirk Nitzsche
Chichester, UK: Wiley, 2004
720pp, ISBN: 978-0-470-09171-5
This successful introduction to the modeling of economic behavior in financial markets, now updated to take account of recent advances, focuses on theoretical innovation, model testing, and discrete time series analysis. It shows how to develop and implement an investment process, and contains new coverage of Monte Carlo simulation, and mean-variance and intertemporal asset allocation.

The Economics of Financial Markets
Roy E. Bailey
Cambridge, UK: Cambridge University Press, 2005
528pp, ISBN: 978-0-521-61280-7
This is a comprehensive textbook on the key theoretical concepts and topics in financial economics and the capital markets. It explores the underlying economic principles and theories, and describes how they relate to different financial markets. It also examines market microstructure, and the randomness of stock market prices, and discusses how the economics of uncertainty can be applied to financial decision-making.

The Economics of Financial Markets
Hendrik S. Houthakker, Peter J. Williamson
New York: Oxford University Press, 1996
361pp, ISBN: 978-0-19-504407-2
This popular financial economics textbook informs on the critical issues of increasingly complex financial markets faced by investors, traders, speculators and brokers. It shows how the concepts and tools of economics can help an understanding of the way financial markets move, and draws on data from the financial behavior of households, corporations, and governments, as well as the prices of individual securities.

The Economics of Money, Banking and Financial Markets, 8th ed
Frederic S. Mishkin
MyEconLab Series
Boston, Massachusetts: Addison Wesley, 2006
661pp, ISBN: 978-0-321-42780-9
This student textbook provides an overview and analysis of the key concepts, models, and issues in money and banking. It offers an insight into the monetary policy process, the regulation and supervision of the financial system, and the internationalization of financial markets, with an emphasis on application. It comes with an online suite of student and instructor tools built around the textbook.

The Economics of Risk and Time, 2nd ed
Christian Gollier
Cambridge, Massachusetts: MIT Press, 2004
465pp, ISBN: 978-0-262-57224-8
This treatise on the impact of risk and time on finance theory and practice presents a unified analysis of the expected utility model as applied to risk analysis, financial decision-making, macroeconomics, and environmental economics. It explores many of the key concepts of choice under uncertainty involving two different assets, and the equilibrium price of risk and time in an Arrow–Debreu portfolio.

JOURNALS

Applied Financial Economics
Taylor & Francis
4 Park Square, Milton Park, Abingdon, Oxfordshire, OX14 4RN, UK
T: +44 (0) 20 7017 6000
F: +44 (0) 20 7017 6336
www.tandf.co.uk/journals/journal.asp?issn=0960-3107&subcategory=EB050000
ISSN: 0960-3107
This journal, increasing its issue rate to 24 per year in 2009, provides an international forum for applied research on financial markets, including the bond and equity markets, derivative securities markets, the foreign exchange market, corporate finance, and market microstructure.

Applied Financial Economics Letters
Taylor & Francis
4 Park Square, Milton Park, Abingdon, Oxfordshire, OX14 4RN, UK
T: +44 (0) 20 7017 6000
F: +44 (0) 20 7017 6336
www.tandf.co.uk/journals/titles/17446546.asp
ISSN: 1744-6546
This bimonthly companion journal to

     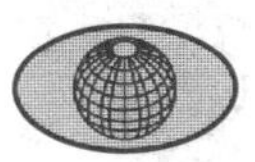   

Applied Financial Economics publishes short accounts of new and original research in financial economics. It encourages discussion of previously published letters or papers, and offers occasional special features such as software reviews, book reviews, conference reports, and industry announcements.

International Journal of Finance & Economics
Wiley
1 Oldlands Way, Bognor Regis, West Sussex, PO22 9SA, UK
T: +44 (0) 1243 843 335
F: +44 (0) 1243 843 232
www3.interscience.wiley.com/journal/15416/home?CRETRY=1&SRETRY=0
ISSN: 1076-9307
This quarterly journal publishes articles on issues in international finance that impact on national and global economies. It offers technical, empirical and theoretical papers, each prefaced by a non-technical summary, on a range of relevant issues such as exchange rates, balance of payments, financial institutions, risk analysis, international banking and portfolio management, and financial market regulation.

International Research Journal of Finance and Economics
EuroJournals
www.eurojournals.com/finance.htm
ISSN: 1450-2887
IRJFE is a bimonthly, international research journal that publishes articles and short research notes on issues in international finance and economics which impact on national and global economies. It also focuses on international banking and portfolio management, financial economics, international political economy, financial analysis, financial market regulation, financial risk analysis, and related areas.

International Review of Economics & Finance
Elsevier
Radarweg 29, 1043 NX Amsterdam, The Netherlands
F: +31 20 485 2370
www.elsevier.com/wps/find/journaldescription.cws_home/620165/description#description
ISSN: 1059-0560
IREF is a quarterly journal that publishes theoretical and empirical articles in all areas of international economics, macroeconomics and financial economics. It focuses on open economy macroeconomics, exchange rates and financial issues, and contains a book review section.

Journal of Economics and Finance
Springer
233 Spring Street, New York, NY 10013, USA
T: +1 212 460 1500
F: +1 212 460 1575
www.springer.com/economics/journal/12197
ISSN: 1055-0925
This journal, published three times each year, is the official journal of the Academy of Economics and Finance. It publishes theoretical and empirical research papers in economics and finance and related fields, such as decision sciences, marketing and accounting, with a primary focus on empirical studies with an emphasis on the policy relevance of the findings.

Journal of Economics and Finance Education
Academy of Economics and Finance
Department of Economics, Armstrong Atlantic State University, 11935 Abercorn Street, Savannah, Georgia 31419-1997, USA
T: +1 912 921 3781
F: +1 912 921 3782
www.jeandfe.org
ISSN: 1543-0464
This electronic journal, published twice yearly by the Academy of Economics and Finance, has a primary purpose of providing an outlet for scholarship in the areas of economics and finance education. It is a general interest publication, which encourages empirical and methodological contributions, as well as the occasional theoretical article.

Journal of Financial Economics
Simon School of Business
University of Rochester, Rochester, NY 14627, USA
T: +1 407 345 4020
F: +1 407 363 1354
www.jfe.rochester.edu
ISSN: 0304-405X
This monthly journal provides a forum for research on financial economics and the theory of the firm. It focuses on publishing analytical, empirical, and clinical papers on the capital markets, financial institutions, corporate finance, corporate governance, and the economics of organizations.

Journal of Financial Stability
Elsevier
Radarweg 29, 1043 NX Amsterdam, The Netherlands
F: +31 20 485 2370
www.elsevier.com/wps/find/journaldescription.cws_home/702019/description#description
ISSN: 1572-3089
This quarterly journal provides an international forum for applied research on theoretical and empirical macro and micro economic and financial analysis of the causes, management, resolution and preventions of financial crises. It also aims to publish papers that identify potential risks to financial stability, and develop means for preventing, mitigating or managing these risks both within and across countries.

Journal of Monetary Economics
Elsevier
Radarweg 29, 1043 NX Amsterdam, The Netherlands
F: +31 20 485 2370
www.elsevier.com/wps/find/journaldescription.cws_home/505566/description#description
ISSN: 0304-3932
JME, published eight times each year, offers research papers on issues in monetary economics and analysis, the operations and structure of financial institutions, the role of various institutional arrangements, the consequences of specific changes in banking structure, the workings of the credit markets, and aspects of the behavior of rates of return on assets.

Review of Financial Economics
Elsevier
Radarweg 29, 1043 NX Amsterdam, The Netherlands
F: +31 20 485 2370
www.elsevier.com/wps/find/journaldescription.cws_home/620170/description#description
ISSN: 1058-3300
This quarterly journal takes a broad approach to finance, covering corporate finance, investments, financial institutions and international finance, and economics, covering monetary theory, fiscal policy, and international economics amongst other topics. It also publishes original research on the application of economic principles to financial decision-making, as well as the behavior of security prices, and monetary and fiscal policy.

The North American Journal of Economics and Finance
Elsevier
Radarweg 29, 1043 NX Amsterdam, The Netherlands
F: +31 20 485 2370
www.elsevier.com/wps/find/journaldescription.cws_home/620163/description
ISSN: 1062-9408

  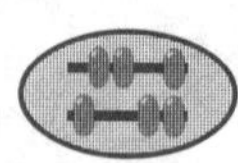   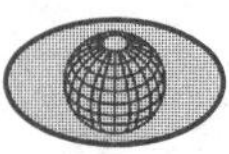   

This journal, published three times each year by the International Banking, Economics and Finance Association, focuses on the economics of integration of goods, services, financial markets, at both regional and global levels, and economic policy. It also offers theoretical and empirical papers related to globalization, and the policy implications of governments, and domestic and international institutions.

The Quarterly Review of Economics and Finance
Elsevier
Radarweg 29, 1043 NX Amsterdam, The Netherlands
F: +31 20 485 2370
www.elsevier.com/wps/find/journaldescription.cws_home/620167/description#description
ISSN: 1062-9769
QREF is a quarterly journal that covers topics in the areas of economics, financial economics, and finance. It offers theoretical, empirical, or policy related papers, and usually one special issue is published each year, devoted to a single theme with contributions by well-known authors.

INTERNET

Financial Economics Network
www.ssrn.com/fen/index.html
This major online research resource is part of the influential Social Science Research Network (SSRN). It features announcements and details on conferences, professional meetings, calls for papers, and professional job listings, and provides a research paper series, a conference management service, and a professional directory, which encourages direct communication within the SSRN community.

ORGANIZATIONS

Europe

European Economics and Finance Society
Chair: George M. Agiomirgianakis
Riga Ferreou 169 & Tsamadou, Patra 26222, Greece
T: +30 2610 367 440
F: +30 2610 367442
E: gmagios@eap.gr
www.eefs.eu
EEFS is an international association of professional economists working mainly in the area of international economics, specializing in trade theory and international macroeconomics, and international finance. It promotes scientific research and scholarly work, encourages communication among economists working in related fields, facilitates a wide dissemination of research output through its conferences and scientific meetings, and fosters the development of young economists.

International Economics and Finance Society, UK Chapter
Chair: Keith Pilbeam
Department of Economics, City University, Northampton Square, London, EC1V 0HB, UK
E: k.s.pilbeam@city.ac.uk
www.iefs.org.uk
This is an association of economists working in international economics, international macroeconomics, and international finance. It focuses on promoting research, encouraging communication in the industry, producing conferences and the publications, and providing relevant information for its members. It also encourages economists working as practitioners in government, business or other organizations to participate in events and discussions.

USA

Academy of Economics and Finance
Chair: William Sackley
USA
www.economics-finance.org
This is a scholarly association focused on economics and finance, with its membership being mostly financial economists and finance specialists. It is affiliated with both the Journal of Economics and Finance (JEF) and the Journal of Economics and Finance Education (JEFE).

Financial Economists Roundtable
Chair: George G. Kaufman
Loyola University, 820 North Michigan Avenue, Chicago, Illinois 60611, USA
T: +1 312 915 7075
F: +1 312 915 8508
E: gkaufma@luc.edu
www.luc.edu/orgs/finroundtable
FER is made up of a group of senior financial economists who have made significant contributions to financial research. It focuses on microeconomic issues in investments, corporate finance, and financial institutions and markets, and provides a forum for analysis of current policy issues in order to raise the level of public and private policy debate, and improve the quality of policy decisions.

BRIC

Association of Indian Economic & Financial Studies
Chair: Suhas L. Ketkar
Department of Economics, Vanderbilt University, VU Station B # 351819, 2301 Vanderbilt Place, Nashville, TN 37235-1819, USA
T: +1 615 343 2473
E: kwketkar@hotmail.com
www.vanderbilt.edu/econ/aiefs
AIEFS is an academic organization that promotes interest in the study of Indian economics and finance, and encourages inquiry into, and analysis of, the problems facing the Indian economy. It also facilitates communication and discussion among scholars, to reflect the growing importance of financial markets in India's economic development.

International

International Banking, Economic and Finance Association
Chair: James A. Brox
USA
T: +1 214 922 5050
F: +1 214 922 5364
E: niki.l.maas@dal.frb.org
www.ibefa.org
IBEFA is a non-profit, international organization dedicated to the study of banking, economic, and financial issues in countries and across the global economy and financial markets. It provides a framework for the exchange of research and ideas, promotes individual and collective research, and fosters friendly relationships and collaborations with other economic and finance professional associations throughout the world.

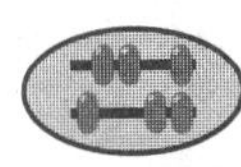

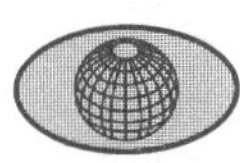

Financial Modeling

BOOKS

A Fast Track to Structured Finance Modeling, Monitoring and Valuation: Jump Start VBA

William Preinitz
Wiley Finance Series
Hoboken, New Jersey: Wiley, 2009
744pp, ISBN: 978-0-470-39812-8

This is a practical guide to structured modeling using VBA, and which works through modeling problems of differing complexity. It focuses on using monitoring and valuation models to track deal performance, shows how to implement simple tasks into VBA code using a critical subset of the features of the language, and covers general modeling concepts, and organizing and creating VBA modules to hold model code.

An Engine, Not a Camera: How Financial Models Shape Markets

Donald MacKenzie
Inside Technology Series
Cambridge, Massachusetts: MIT Press, 2008
377pp, ISBN: 978-0-262-63367-3

This new book argues that the emergence of modern economic theories had a profound impact on how the modern financial system evolved. It discusses how new structures in financial markets and the growth of derivative products was dependent on these economic theories explaining how they worked and giving them legitimacy. It also explores finance theory in terms of recent financial crises.

Building Financial Models

John S. Tjia
New York: McGraw-Hill, 2004
340pp, ISBN: 978-0-07-140210-1

This explains how to design, build, and implement core valuation/projection models for interpreting financial statements, determining company value, and projecting future performance. It provides a guide to using Excel and other spreadsheet programs for creating a dynamic financial model, and then customizing it for specific situations, and explains the underlying and accounting principles of each model.

Building Financial Models with Microsoft Excel: A Guide for Business Professionals

K. Scott Proctor
Wiley Finance Series
Hoboken, New Jersey: Wiley, 2004
347pp, ISBN: 978-0-471-66103-0

This provides a clear overview of understanding and constructing fully functioning financial models using Excel. It presents step-by-step instructions for their use in financial accounting reports, including the balance sheet, the income statement, and the statement of cash flows, and covers key topics such as budgeting, valuation, sensitivity analysis, contribution margin and financial ratios, and the basics of building and using a capitalization table.

Business Models: A Strategic Management Approach

Allan Afuah
New York: McGraw-Hill/Irwin, 2003
415pp, ISBN: 978-0-07-288364-0

This introduction to business models used in corporate finance examines the latest research in strategic management to explore how to effectively implement the most relevant models. It presents an integrated framework regarding the relationship between a company's activities, revenue model, cost structure, resources, capabilities, and competition, focusing on strategic models that benefit from the link between resources, product-market positions, and profits.

Business Models

David Watson
Petersfield, UK: Harriman House, 2005
316pp, ISBN: 978-1-897597-58-3

This is an accessible guide to investment in a company or sector, detailing a large number of models that can help an investor analyze competitive advantage. It provide scoring charts and sets of criteria for both company and sector business models, as well as other key tools such as growth at a reasonable price, technical analysis, scuttlebutting, accounting for growth, and investment axioms.

Dynamic Term Structure Modeling: The Fixed Income Valuation Course

Sanjay K. Nawalkha, Gloria M. Soto, Natalia A. Beliaeva
Wiley Finance Series
Hoboken, New Jersey: Wiley, 2007
683pp, ISBN: 978-0-471-73714-8

This is a thorough reference on modern dynamic term structure modeling and valuing fixed income derivatives, focusing on the practical implementation of the relevant models, supported by solution techniques using trees, PDE methods, Fourier methods, and approximations. It provides a description of the continuous time interest rate models, and presents equilibrium and no-arbitrage models in a new framework, and an analysis of the yield curve dynamics.

Financial Modeling, 3rd ed

Simon Benninga
Cambridge, Massachusetts: MIT Press, 2008
1,132pp, ISBN: 978-0-262-02628-4

This respected guide to financial modeling and analysis provides insight and instruction for using spreadsheets to solve real-world problems in corporate finance, investments, and derivatives. It presents a step-by-step approach to finding financial data, building programs to analyze it, and improving financial decision-making. It explains each model and how it can be solved using Microsoft Excel, with examples taken from actual company data.

Financial Modeling Using Excel and VBA

Chandan Sengupta
Wiley Finance Series
Hoboken, New Jersey: Wiley, 2004
857pp, ISBN: 978-0-471-26768-3

This comprehensive textbook provides a clear approach to developing financial models in all major areas of finance. It shows how to model a wide range of finance problems using the most common programs, Excel and VBA, and presents a toolkit for any level of application. It also explains all the relevant financial theory and concepts to aid effective implementation of real-world financial models.

Financial Modelling in Practice: A Concise Guide for Intermediate and Advanced Level

Michael Rees
Wiley Finance Series
Hoboken, New Jersey: Wiley, 2008
270pp, ISBN: 978-0-470-99744-4

This is a detailed and practical examination of financial modeling, from basic Excel functions, to designing, structuring, and building effective and appropriate models. It also explores application issues, such as modeling financial statements, cash flow valuation, risk analysis, options, and real options, the use of VBA, and discusses sensitivity analysis techniques, and the application of statistical functions.

Interest Rate Models—Theory and Practice: With Smile, Inflation and Credit, 2nd ed

Damiano Brigo, Fabio Mercurio
Springer Finance Series
Berlin: Springer, 2006
981pp, ISBN: 978-3-540-22149-4

     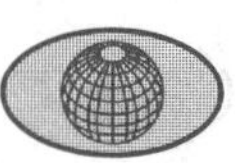   

This technical guide to interest rate modeling and derivatives combines theory and practice to provide the necessary mathematical expertise for quantitative analysts, advanced traders, and students. It analyzes the effectiveness of different models, and presents updates on hybrid products, credit derivatives, the smile issue in the LIBOR market model, calibrations to real market data, and stochastic volatility models.

Interest Rate Risk Modeling: The Fixed Income Valuation Course
Sanjay K. Nawalkha, Gloria M. Soto, Natalia A. Beliaeva
Wiley Finance Series
Hoboken, New Jersey: Wiley, 2005
396pp, ISBN: 978-0-471-42724-7
This is comprehensive introduction to interest rate risk, which details the most common models used for pricing and risk analysis of various fixed income securities and their derivatives. It explains how to measure and manage interest rate risk, how the various modeling techniques are used by fixed-income professionals, and illustrates the application of these models to a range of products.

Linear Factor Models in Finance
John Knight, Stephen Satchell (editors)
Quantitative Finance Series
Oxford, UK: Butterworth-Heinemann, 2005
282pp, ISBN: 978-0-7506-6006-8
This is a detailed exploration of one of the most widely used techniques for asset pricing, a central tenet in modern investment theory. It examines its impact on the pricing of stocks, bonds, options, futures, and derivatives, and appraises asset valuation, portfolio theory and applications, dynamic asset allocation strategies, portfolio performance measurement, risk management, international perspectives, and the use of derivatives.

Martingale Methods in Financial Modelling, 2nd ed
Marek Musiela, Marek Rutkowski
Stochastic Modelling and Applied Probability Series
Berlin: Springer, 2007
680pp, ISBN: 978-3-540-20966-9
This detailed analysis of martingales in pricing and hedging derivative securities takes a practical approach to financial modeling, focusing on the most common techniques available. It presents the latest term structure research, and provides a through overview of advanced modern financial mathematics, particularly fixed income models and stochastic volatility.

Mastering Financial Modelling in Microsoft Excel: A Practitioner's Guide to Applied Corporate Finance, 2nd ed
Alastair Day
Market Editions Series
Harlow, UK: FT Prentice Hall, 2007
497pp, ISBN: 978-0-273-70806-3
This is a guide for the professional use of Excel in corporate finance, an increasingly important tool for business managers, which explores the different ways that financial models can improve business decision-making. It explores how to use spreadsheets more effectively by quickly building and applying Excel models, how to add advanced features, and how to model more in-depth corporate finance techniques.

Microsoft Office Excel 2007: Data Analysis and Business Modeling, 2nd ed
Wayne L. Winston
Redmond, Washington: Microsoft Press, 2007
624pp, ISBN: 978-0-7356-2396-5
This describes the main techniques for using Excel for data analysis, modeling, and decision-making. It provides real-world examples and exercises to explain how to create scenarios for sales, estimate a product's demand curve, forecast using trend and seasonality, and determine which product mix will yield the greatest profit. It also covers topics such as asset allocation modeling, and how to optimize bidding strategies and portfolios.

Modeling for Insight: A Master Class for Business Analysts
Stephen G. Powell, Robert J. Batt
Hoboken, New Jersey: Wiley, 2008
466pp, ISBN: 978-0-470-17555-2
This is an introduction to building spreadsheet models and using them for effective business decision-making. It explains the problem-solving process—frame the problem, diagram the problem, build a model, and generate insights—and presents specific modeling tools, such as influence diagrams, spreadsheet engineering, parameterization, sensitivity analysis, strategy analysis, and iterative modeling, to achieve this, and describes the software packages used.

Modeling Risk: Applying Monte Carlo Simulation, Real Options Analysis, Forecasting, and Optimization Techniques
Johnathan Mun
Wiley Finance Series
Hoboken, New Jersey: Wiley, 2006
605pp, ISBN: 978-0-471-78900-0
This is a technical exploration of the main techniques for identifying, predicting, quantifying, valuing, hedging, diversifying, and managing risk. It describes modeling and analyzing risk within a business environment, applications for risk analysis, corporate strategy, and asset allocation, and covers model building, Monte Carlo simulation, real options analysis, forecasting, and optimization.

Practical Financial Modelling: A Guide to Current Practice
Jonathan Swan
London: CIMA Publishing, 2008
282pp, ISBN: 978-0-7506-8647-1
This handbook on financial modeling is aimed at finance and management professionals developing or using spreadsheets and financial models, particularly in areas such as financial budgeting and financial planning. It presents a simple approach to building and using financial models that reduces complexity, and which has been used for creating simple cash flow forecasts as well as modeling intensive transactions.

Structured Finance Modeling with Object-Oriented VBA
Evan Tick
Wiley Finance Series
Hoboken, New Jersey: Wiley, 2007
332pp, ISBN: 978-0-470-09859-2
This guide to modeling complex financial structures examines how to use object-oriented VBA in an Excel environment to produce flexible and effective models. It explains object-oriented programming for modeling structured products, and also covers stochastic models, optimization techniques, and object-oriented architecture. It presents models and their implementation, with examples of them in practice, as well as empirical studies of their sensitivities.

The Econometric Modelling of Financial Time Series
Terence C. Mills, Raphael N. Markellos
Cambridge, UK: Cambridge University Press, 2008
456pp, ISBN: 978-0-521-71009-1
This textbook on the econometrics of financial modeling presents the latest research in economic time series, and explains how it can be applied to an analysis of the financial markets. It focuses on volatility, non-linearity, non-linear models used to analyze financial data at high frequencies, the long memory characteristics found in financial time series, and the modeling of trends and structural breaks.

  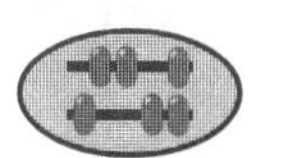   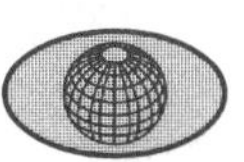   

The Mathematics of Financial Modeling and Investment Management
Sergio M. Focardi, Frank J. Fabozzi
Frank J. Fabozzi Series
Hoboken, New Jersey: Wiley, 2004
778pp, ISBN: 978-0-471-46599-7
This analyzes the overlap between mathematics and finance, focusing on financial decision-making and its economic foundations, and how key mathematical techniques can be applied in the world of modern finance. It examines mathematical tools that provide an understanding of financial econometrics and financial economics, and discuss. eg financial applications such as arbitrage pricing, interest rate modeling, derivative pricing, credit risk modeling, and risk management.

The Oxford Guide to Financial Modeling: Applications for Capital Markets, Corporate Finance, Risk Management and Financial Institutions
Thomas S. Y. Ho
Oxford, UK: Oxford University Press, 2004
735pp, ISBN: 978-0-19-516962-1
This comprehensive and applied guide to financial modeling shows how to incorporate models into corporate decision-making, problem solving, and enterprise risk management. It analyzes all the main models, including the present value model, the capital asset pricing model, interest rate models, and option models, and relates them to financial statements, risk management, and asset/liability management with illiquid instruments.

JOURNALS

Applied Stochastic Models in Business and Industry
Wiley
1 Oldlands Way, Bognor Regis, West Sussex, PO22 9SA, UK
T: +44 (0) 1243 843 335
F: +44 (0) 1243 843 232
www3.interscience.wiley.com/journal/117943444/grouphome/home.html
ISSN: 1524-1904
This bimonthly journal offers both technical and practical papers on subjects within stochastic modeling and data analysis, and their applications in business, finance, insurance, management, and production. It presents new results that solve real-life problems, and new methods for solving such problems, such as optimization, database management, knowledge acquisition, expert systems, computer-aided decision supports, and neural computing.

Economic Modelling
Elsevier
Radarweg 29, 1043 NX Amsterdam, The Netherlands
F: +31 20 485 2370
www.elsevier.com/wps/find/journaldescription.cws_home/30411/description#description
ISSN: 0264-9993
This quarterly journal publishes theoretical and applied papers on economic modeling, and complete versions of many large-scale models that have been developed for policy analysis. It also covers national macroeconomic models, growth models, optimization models, planning models, international trade models, general equilibrium modeling of national economies, modeling structural adjustments, and the sensitivity of econometric models to alternative macroeconomics policies.

Journal of Empirical Finance
Elsevier
Radarweg 29, 1043 NX Amsterdam, The Netherlands
F: +31 20 485 2180
www.elsevier.com/wps/find/journaldescription.cws_home/523106/description#description
ISSN: 0927-5398
This international journal, issued five times each year, is dedicated to empirical research in the intersection of econometrics and finance. It publishes papers on the testing of theories using financial data, the measurement of variables relevant in financial decision-making, the econometric analysis of financial market data, and the development of new econometric methodology with finance applications.

The Journal of Risk Model Validation
Incisive Media
Haymarket House, 28–29 Haymarket, London, SW1Y 4RX, UK
T: +44 (0) 20 7004 7531
F: +44 (0) 20 7484 9758
www.journalofriskmodelvalidation.com
ISSN: 1753-9579
This quarterly journal publishes technical research papers on the implementation and validation of risk models. It promotes a greater understanding of key issues, such as the empirical evaluation of existing models, pitfalls in model validation, stress testing, the development of new methods, and regulatory factors.

INTERNET

Financial Modeling Guide
www.financialmodelingguide.com
This is an online resource that provides free financial modeling tutorials, advice, tips and tricks for all levels of user. It offers simple guidelines for structuring and laying out spreadsheets for a financial model, and for managing their development and auditing results.

Financial Modelling.net
www.financialmodelling.net
This useful online resource, run by a financial modeler, has the aim of improving standards in business decision-making and financial modeling, and includes guidance on best practice, resources, links, and industry discussion.

Modelling Excel
www.westnet.net.au/balson/ModellingExcel
This is a resource on Excel modeling that provides a range of advice and practical tools and tips on its application. It includes guidance on how to modify default settings to improve the look of worksheets, tables and charts, and reduce complexity using structural templates and automation techniques.

VB Users
vbusers.com
This site provides free source code in C#, Visual Basic and VBA, as well as numerous applications and ActiveX objects. It also provides a number of resources for submitting source code and problem resolution, and features downloads, source code, report bugs, discussion groups, services, commercial software, and industry links.

     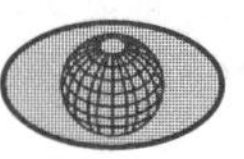   

Forecasting and Scenario Planning

BOOKS

20–20 Foresight: Crafting Strategy in an Uncertain World

Hugh Courtney
Boston, Massachusetts: Harvard Business School Press, 2001
207pp, ISBN: 978-1-57851-266-9

This book sets out to help managers understand the concept of "residual uncertainty" in today's business environment—that is, the difference between what can be known and what can't be known—so that they can develop 20/20 foresight and create competitive advantage. A five-piece management toolkit of scenario planning, game theory, decision analysis, system dynamics models, and management flight simulators can be used to plot strategy against uncertainty.

Building Financial Models: A Guide to Creating and Interpreting Financial Statements

John S. Tjia
Maidenhead, UK: McGraw-Hill, 2004
340pp, ISBN: 978-0-07-140210-1

This book provides step-by-step instructions for the design and development of financial projection models according to Generally Accepted Accounting Principles (GAAP) using Microsoft Excel software. In-depth explanations of the principles of accounting, including income statements, balance sheets, and cash-flow statements, and the concepts of model building are given. The book also describes the use of spreadsheet functions and tools and offers guidelines for making useful business forecasts.

Business Forecasting, 9th ed

John E. Hanke, Dean Wichern
Upper Saddle River, New Jersey: Pearson Education, 2008
576pp, ISBN: 978-0-13-230120-6

This book is written in a simple, straightforward style, presenting basic statistical techniques using practical business examples to teach how to predict long-term forecasts. It can also be used to teach undergraduate and postgraduate students.

The Change Game: How Today's Global Trends are Shaping Tomorrow's Companies

Peter Lawrence
London: Kogan Page, 2002
272pp, ISBN: 978-0-7494-3926-2

Based on interviews with managers from around the world, this book is an account of change in business in the West. The text provides insights into the major global trends and issues that are influencing organizations today, and what they mean for the future. The new management consensus is examined, including the gains it has made and some of the blind spots to which it has given rise. The text also addresses the ideas of competitive advantage and the unique business proposition.

Creating Futures: Scenario Planning as a Strategic Management Tool, 2nd ed

Michel Godet
London: Economica, 2006
349pp, ISBN: 978-2-7178-5244-8

This offers a collection of effective methodologies for strategic planning. It shows that with the right tools and attitude, people can learn how to create a new future. It presents these planning methods with examples and illustrative and informative case studies.

How to Forecast: A Guide for Business

James Morrell
Aldershot, UK: Gower Publishing, 2002
224pp, ISBN: 978-0-566-08492-8

Drawing on his experience as a forecaster, the author considers the key areas that affect businesses. These are divided into those that lie beyond the control of an organization and those that are under its control. The former include the national economy, government policy, the global market, population and social trends, and technological change. The latter include long-term strategy and investment, costs and prices, and profits and share prices. Each section of this book provides a set of practical conclusions and a listing of key sources of information. The book closes with a set of simple rules and guidelines for successful forecasting.

HR Forecasting and Planning

Paul Turner
Developing Practice Series
London: Chartered Institute of Personnel and Development, 2002
288pp, ISBN: 978-0-85292-933-9

The role of the human resource department in strategy formulation is widely recognized. This book offers practical step-by-step guidelines to help HR executives add value to the strategy-setting process. The author uses a three-part model: part one looks at issues surrounding forecasting, strategy, and planning, and the role of HR in these; part two presents the strategic human resources forecast; and part three outlines the human resource plan.

Learning from the Future: Competitive Foresight Scenarios

Liam Fahey, Robert Randall
New York: Wiley, 1997
288pp, ISBN: 978-0-471-30352-7

Aimed at managers, consultants, and leaders, this book comprises a selection of articles that explain how to construct and model the outcomes of a variety of strategic decisions. Four key areas are addressed: the basics of scenario learning; approaches to constructing scenarios; scenario application in diverse contexts; and managing scenario learning in the organizational context.

The Living Company: Habits for Survival in a Turbulent Business Environment

Arie de Geus
Boston, Massachusetts: Harvard Business School Press, 2002
240pp, ISBN: 978-1-57851-820-3

This book, by one of the gurus of scenario planning, focuses on his belief that businesses are like living organisms and must be managed as such if they are to survive over time and become what he calls "living companies."

The Oxford Handbook of Organizational Decision Making

Gerard P. Hodgkinson, William H. Starbuck (editors)
Oxford: Oxford University Press, 2008
720pp, ISBN: 978-0-19-929046-8

The Oxford Handbook of Decision Making surveys theory and research on organizational decision-making. It emphasizes psychological perspectives, while encompassing the insights of economics, political science, and sociology. It provides coverage at the individual, group, organizational, and inter-organizational levels of analysis, while case studies illustrate the practical implications of the work surveyed.

Quantitative Analysis for Management, 10th ed

Barry Render, Ralph M. Stair, Michael E. Hanna
Upper Saddle River, New Jersey: Prentice Hall, 2008
768pp, ISBN: 978-0-13-603625-8

This textbook for students combines

    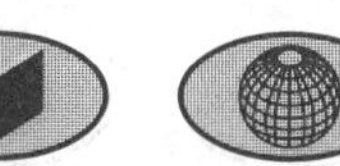   

coverage of traditional management science techniques with modern technology solutions. It includes a CD-ROM.

Scenario Planning, 2nd ed
Gill Ringland
Chichester, UK: Wiley, 2006
490pp, ISBN: 978-0-470-01881-1
Updated for this new edition, this book focuses on how scenarios can be used effectively to manage the future. It is aimed at practicing managers. The book includes extensive case studies, checklists, and practical advice.

Scenarios: The Art of Strategic Conversation, 2nd ed
Kees van der Heijden
Chichester, UK: Wiley, 2004
380pp, ISBN: 978-0-470-02368-6
Aimed at strategic managers, this book explores the relationship between the strategy process and scenario planning in order to facilitate effective decisions. Drawing on his own experiences while working for Shell, and on the experiences of the company as a whole, the author explores the principles, practices, implementation, and applications of scenario planning.

The Sixth Sense: Accelerating Organizational Learning with Scenarios
Kees van der Heijden et al.
Chichester, UK: Wiley, 2002
320pp, ISBN: 978-0-470-84491-5
The key issue of this book revolves around addressing the flaws at individual, organizational, and community levels that inhibit organizational change. The text highlights a link between organizational learning and scenario planning in order to overcome these flaws. It suggests that by motivating learners to develop a deeper perspective on the long-term business environment, and scenario planners to see their work in the context of organizational survival and development, creative limitations can be overcome and a favorable environment for multiple futures developed. This book explains why scenario thinking is important, why it is valuable as a catalyst for innovative and creative thinking, how it enhances strategic dialog, how it helps organizational learning and development, and how it can be assimilated within the strategic organizational learning framework.

Trajectory Management: Leading a Business Over Time
Paul Strebel
Chichester, UK: Wiley, 2003
222pp, ISBN: 978-0-470-86290-2
Paul Strebel believes that the search for universal best practice has given rise to the impression that there is "one true way" to business success. To work effectively, however, best practice must be adapted to the particular conditions facing the organization at the time. The author aims to help business leaders succeed over time by identifying and adapting internal business drivers to exploit changing conditions. This is the art of trajectory management, which will enable organizations to succeed in differing conditions. He considers drivers such as: governance roles, leadership styles, organization modes, and business models. He also explains the process of shaping, sustaining, and switching trajectory drivers.

MAGAZINES

Business Credit Magazine
National Association of Credit Management
8840 Columbia 100 Parkway, Columbia, MA 21045–2158, USA
T: +1 410 740 5560
www.nacm.org/bcmag/bcm_index.shtml
ISSN: 0897-0181
Business Credit Magazine is published ten times a year and targets readers who are responsible for extending business and trade credit and risk management for their companies. The magazine has up-to-date trends and important legislative, bankruptcy, business ethics, trade finance, asset protection, benchmarking, and scoring issues.

Journal of Business Forecasting
Institute of Risk Management
Lloyd's Avenue House, 6 Lloyd's Avenue, London, EC3N 3AX, UK
T: +44 (0) 20 7709 9808
F: +44 (0) 20 7709 0716
www.ibf.org/index.cfm?fuseaction=showObjects&objectTypeID=20
ISSN: 0278-6087
This is a quarterly journal aimed at business executives and managers which provides practical forecasting ideas plus guidance on recognizing and using effective forecasting models for key business decisions. The *Journal* also includes forecasts on the international economic outlook and corporate earnings.

JOURNALS

European Journal of Operational Research
Elsevier
11830 Westline Industrial Drive, St Louis, MO 63146, USA
T: +1 314 453 7076
F: +1 314 523 5153
www.elsevier.com/locate/ejor
ISSN: 0377-2217
The European Journal of Operational Research (EJOR) publishes papers that discuss the methodology of operational research and decision making. EJOR presents the following types of papers: invited reviews, innovative applications, theory and methodology papers, and short communications.

International Journal of Applied Forecasting
International Institute of Forecasters
140 Birchwood Drive, Colchester, VT 05446, USA
T: +1 781 234 4077
F: +1 509 357 5530
forecasters.org/ijf
ISSN: 0169-2070
This organization is dedicated to the research and development of forecasting techniques, with the aim of bridging the gap between forecasting theory and practice and contributing to the professional development of forecasters. The site includes information on events and conferences, its journal, time series data, and links to other forecasting sites.

International Journal of Forecasting
Elsevier
PO Box 211, 1000 AE Amsterdam, The Netherlands
T: +31 20 485 3757
F: +31 20 485 3432
www.elsevier.com/locate/ijforecast
ISSN: 0169-2070
This is the official journal of the International Institute of Forecasters, whose aims and scope it shares: to unify the field of forecasting; to bridge the gap between theory and practice; and to make forecasting useful and relevant for decision and policy makers. It publishes high-quality refereed papers on all aspects of forecasting.

Journal of Forecasting
Wiley
The Atrium, Southern Gate, Chichester, West Sussex, PO19 8SQ, UK
T: +44 (0) 1243 779777
F: +44 (0) 1243 775878
www.interscience.wiley.com/jpages/0277-6693
ISSN: 0277-6693
This international journal, published eight times each year, presents papers on theoretical, practical, and computational approaches to forecasting across a range of sectors including business, technology, and government. Individual issues include

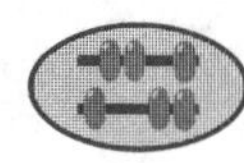

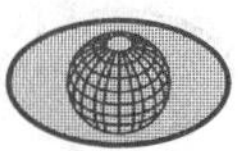

research reports, review articles, and book and software reviews.

INTERNET

Applied Forecasting

www.appliedforecasting.com

Applied Forecasting is an independent web site that contributes to the forecasting community. The focus is to serve researchers, practitioners and students worldwide with updated information and facilitating online interaction.

Forecasting: Methods and Applications

www.robhyndman.info/forecasting

This site is based on the book of the same name and offers hundreds of forecasting data sets plus links to forecasting resources and software on the internet.

Global Business Network

www.gbn.org

This is the premier site for those interested in scenario planning, including amongst its founders and members some of those who were involved in Royal Dutch/Shell's groundbreaking work in this area.

International Institute of Forecasters

www.forecasters.org

The organization is dedicated to the research and development of forecasting techniques, with the aim of bridging the gap between forecasting theory and practice and contributing to the professional development of forecasters. Its site includes information on events and conferences, information on its journal, *Foresight*, time series data, and links to other forecasting sites.

Principles of Forecasting

www.forecastingprinciples.com

This site summarizes useful knowledge about forecasting for researchers, practitioners, and educators. It features guidelines, prescriptions, rules, conditions, action statements, and advice about what to do in given situations.

Scenario Planning Resources

www.well.com/~mb/scenario_planning

This website contains references and articles about scenario planning. Some are good for orientation, while others are more technical, show how to develop method, and explore new areas of application.

World Future Society

www.wfs.org

This nonprofit educational and scientific organization provides information about the technological and social forces that shape the future—and are fundamental to scenario planning and forecasting.

ORGANIZATIONS

Europe

Lancaster University Centre for Forecasting

c/o The Management School, Lancaster University, Lancaster, Lancashire, LA1 4YX, UK
T: +44 (0) 1524 593 879
F: +44 (0) 1524 844 885
E: r.fildes@lancaster.ac.uk
www.lums.lancs.ac.uk/research/forecast.htm

This center is part of the Management School at Lancaster University. It aims to promote the development of new approaches to forecasting and business models, supports the integration of forecasting theory and practice, and offers research and consultancy services to industry, commerce, and government. Its services include corporate research, courses for practitioners, and consultancy services. The site also offers advice for special interest groups.

University of Bath Research Center

c/o School of Management, University of Bath, BA2 7AY, UK
T: +44 (0) 1225 383 594
F: +44 (0) 1225 826 473
E: p.goodwin@bath.ac.uk
www.bath.ac.uk/management/research/office/centres.html

This center is part of the Science School at Bath University. It aims to research the integration of judgment and models in forecasting and decision-making. Its aim is to design forecasting software that will provide support to managers in their use of judgment, so that these problems are reduced and greater forecast accuracy can be achieved.

USA

Institute of Business Forecasting

PO Box 670159, Flushing, New York, NY 11367–0159, USA
T: +1 516 504 7576
E: info@ibf.org
www.ibf.org

The aims of this member-based organization are to disseminate knowledge about business forecasting and planning, and to provide products and services to help business executives in their planning and forecasting efforts.

International

International Institute of Forecasters

140 Birchwood Drive, Colchester, VT 05446, USA
T: +1 781 234 4077
F: +1 509 357 5530
E: forecasters@forecasters.org
www.forecasters.org

The organization is dedicated to the research and development of forecasting techniques, with the aim of bridging the gap between forecasting theory and practice, and contributing to the professional development of forecasters. Its site includes information on events and conferences, information on its journal, time series data, and links to other forecasting sites.

  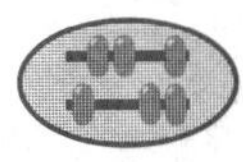   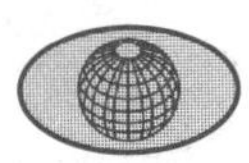   

Hedge Funds, Fund Management, and Alternative Investments

BOOKS

Absolute Returns: The Risk and Opportunities of Hedge Fund Investing

Alexander Ineichen
Wiley Finance Series
New York: Wiley, 2002
514pp, ISBN: 978-0-471-25120-0

A practical analysis of hedge fund investing, that takes a practical look at the strategies and techniques that hedge fund managers use to achieve superior investment performance, especially absolute return strategies. It also discusses methods for integrating hedge fund investment into traditional portfolios to increase returns and balance risk exposure.

The Fundamentals of Hedge Fund Management: How to Successfully Launch and Operate a Hedge Fund

Daniel A. Strachman
Wiley Finance Series
Hoboken, New Jersey: Wiley, 2007
177pp, ISBN: 978-0-471-74852-6

Teaches how to build and maintain a successful hedge fund business, presented in an accessible way. It covers all the essentials, from choosing a lawyer, and the documentation needed, to an awareness of what markets attract investors. Based on real-life cases of leading funds, it provides a practical insight into what makes a hedge fund work.

Handbook of Hedge Funds

Francois-Serge l'Habitant
Wiley Finance Series
Chichester, UK: Wiley, 2006
637pp, ISBN: 978-0-470-02663-2

A comprehensive reference on hedge funds for all those involved in the industry. It offers practical guidance on their operational, legal, and regulatory characteristics, as well as historical information, analysis of investment strategies, hedge fund indices and databases, advice on portfolio construction, and coverage of structured products and funds of hedge funds.

The Hedge Fund Handbook: A Definitive Guide for Analyzing and Evaluating Alternative Investments

Stefano Lavinio
New York: McGraw-Hill, 2000
192pp, ISBN: 978-0-07-135030-3

A guide to hedge funds, which examines the techniques and strategies used by a successful fund managers, and gives insights into how best to identify and select which funds to invest in. It gives a clear overview of the dynamics of hedge fund behavior, and the financial innovations available in alternative investments, while also discussing the risk management side of their operation.

Hedge Fund of Funds Investing: An Investor's Guide

Joseph G. Nicholas
Princeton, New Jersey: Bloomberg Press, 2004
259pp, ISBN: 978-1-57660-124-2

A concise guide, which details how to create, combine, and manage investments with multiple hedge funds as a fund of funds. It shows how to evaluate risks, estimate potential returns, and choose statistical measurement methods, as they can help to balance risks and can be incorporated into a portfolio to attain investment objectives and build diversification.

Hedge Funds: An Analytic Perspective

Andrew W. Lo
Advances in Financial Engineering Series
Princeton, New Jersey: Princeton University Press, 2008
337pp, ISBN: 978-0-691-13294-5

A new examination of the hedge fund industry by a leading financial economist, Hedge Funds discusses the need for a systematic framework for managing hedge fund investments. He outlines the basic properties of hedge fund returns, trading strategies, risk characteristics, and potential for illiquidity, and presents new tools for analyzing their dynamics.

Hedge Hunters: Hedge Fund Masters on the Rewards, the Risk, and the Reckoning

Katherine Burton
New York: Bloomberg Press, 2007
206pp, ISBN: 978-1-57660-245-4

Based on interviews with a number of rising stars in the hedge fund industry, these profiles focus on the personal and business qualities needed to build a successful asset management business, and provide revealing details into the challenges they face, and how they trade successfully.

Hedgehogging

Barton Biggs
Hoboken, New Jersey: Wiley, 2006
308pp, ISBN: 978-0-470-06773-4

Written by a legendary figure in the hedge fund industry, it provides an illuminating view of hedge fund investing, of some of the personalities involved, and what goes on behind the scenes in these funds. Biggs presents an insiders view of hedge funds, and explains how he has earned successful returns out of such a complex and risky approach.

Inside the House of Money: Top Hedge Fund Traders on Profiting in the Global Markets

Steven Drobny
Hoboken, New Jersey: Wiley, 2006
370pp, ISBN: 978-0-471-79447-9

Providing insight into the often hidden world of hedge funds, this book presents a collection of detailed interviews with a number of leading money managers. They tell of their personal trading strategies, their experiences during recent financial crises, and also examines the trend towards increased competition and specialization, and the impact this is having on their approach to investment.

An Introduction to Fund Management, 3rd ed

Ray Russell
Securities Institute Series
Chichester, UK: Wiley, 2006
178pp, ISBN: 978-0-470-01770-8

This is a primer on fund management that provides a comprehensive overview, and details the different types of fund, how they are established, their processes, performance measurement, fund administration, and their investment strategies. This updated edition provides a practical description of investment funds and fund management from a number of perspectives, and contains new material on regulatory changes and industry developments.

Investment Strategies of Hedge Funds

Filippo Stefanini
Wiley Finance Series
Hoboken, New Jersey: Wiley, 2006
315pp, ISBN: 978-0-470-02627-4

Opens up the hidden world of hedge funds to offer guidance on the opportunities for investment they provide. It details how

     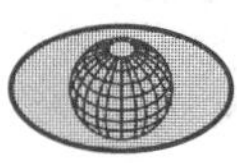   

hedge funds operate, and the tools that investors need to access these types of funds, and discusses each hedge fund strategy, with trading examples by successful hedge fund managers, to show how to create high investment returns.

MAGAZINES

Absolute Return

HedgeFund Intelligence
Nestor House, Playhouse Yard, London, EC4V 5EX, UK
T: +44 (0) 20 7779 7330
F: +44 (0) 20 7779 7331
www.hedgefundintelligence.com/ar
ISSN: 1740-4282

This is a monthly magazine that covers current events in the hedge fund industry, with an emphasis on US hedge funds. It features new fund launches, analysis of regulatory developments, interviews, industry surveys, performance data, league tables of the best performing funds, and weekly email news updates. It is available to qualified investors and industry professionals only.

Alpha

Institutional Investor
225 Park Ave South, New York, NY 10003, USA
T: +1 212 224 3300
www.iimagazine.com/alpha
ISSN: 1930-8434

Alpha is a monthly magazine that provides a link between the hedge fund industry, its users, and those who provide advisory, financial and technological services to the sector. It covers all areas of hedge fund business, including investment fund strategies, hedge fund operations, rankings, reports on tax and regulatory measures, and new fund launches.

Hedge Fund Alert

Harrison Scott Publications
5 Marine View Plaza, #400, Hoboken, NJ 07030-5795, USA
T: +1 201 659 1700
F: +1 201 659 4141
www.hfalert.com
ISSN: 1530-7832

This is a weekly newsletter that provides news and analysis for the alternative investment community. Its coverage includes fund marketing strategies, competition among prime brokers and other service providers, fund launches, new products, regulatory and legal issues, personnel moves, shifts in investor allocations, as well as developments that can affect the hedge fund industry.

The Hedge Fund Journal

31 Davies Street, London, W1K 4LP, UK
T: +44 (0) 20 7409 0888
F: +44 (0) 20 7409 0905
www.thehedgefundjournal.com
ISSN: 1756-3453

This journal is published 10 times a year, and is a major source of information on the hedge fund industry. It combines detailed profiles and interviews with news summaries, commentary, research, expert opinion and analysis, special reports, and appointments.

Hedge Funds Review

Incisive Media
Haymarket House, 28–29 Haymarket, London, SW1Y 4RX, UK
T: +44 (0) 20 7484 9700
F: +44 (0) 20 7484 9932
www.hedgefundsreview.com
ISSN: 1471-8855

This is a monthly magazine for the hedge fund industry, which aims to provide hedge fund managers, investors, and service providers with news and analysis on the trends and developments affecting their business and investment decisions. It offers news and comment, strategy analysis, interviews, trading tips, hedge fund investment mandates, fund closure lists, performance data, and special reports.

The Nordic Hedge Fund Journal

Nordic Hedge Fund Index
Kigkurren 8G, 4. tv - DK-2300 Copenhagen S, Denmark
T: +45 8 830 0000
F: +45 3 313 3730
www.hedgenordic.com/?pageid=63

This is a monthly newsletter that acts as a concise source of information on the Nordic hedge fund industry, and providing updates on the developments, performance, and challenges within the industry. It features industry interviews with asset managers, pension funds and other institutional investors.

Total Alternatives

Institutional Investor
225 Park Ave South, New York, NY 10003, USA
T: +1 212 224 3300
www.totalalternatives.com
ISSN: 1544-7596

This is an online news source for hedge funds, private equity, and other alternative investments. It contains stories on new strategies, fund launches, and reorganizations at major firms. It features the latest market news, daily email summaries, a resource of hedge fund news items in other media, and a data zone on hedge funds that includes information on strategy, rate of returns, annualized volume, and assets.

JOURNALS

Journal of Alternative Investments

Institutional Investor
225 Park Avenue South, New York, NY 10003, USA
T: +1 212 224 3570
www.iijournals.com/JAI
ISSN: 1520-3255

This quarterly journal provides research and expert analysis on managing investments in hedge funds, private equity, distressed debt, commodities, futures, energy, funds of funds, and other non-traditional instruments. It examines the growth of hedge funds and alternatives, how to measure and track portfolio performance, and includes coverage of asset allocation, risk management, indexing, regulation and taxation.

Journal of Derivatives & Hedge Funds

Palgrave Macmillan
The Macmillan Building, 4 Crinan Street, London, N1 9XW, UK
T: +44 (0) 20 7843 4684
www.palgrave-journals.com/jdhf
ISSN: 1753-9641

This is a quarterly journal that examines the derivatives market and hedge funds. Formerly known as Derivatives Use, Trading & Regulation, it has evolved its coverage to take into account the enormous growth in hedge funds. It focuses on trading, legal and other derivative issues, and the many challenges facing the hedge fund industry, such as transparency, liquidity risk, and risk management control.

INTERNET

Albourne Village

www.village.albourne.com

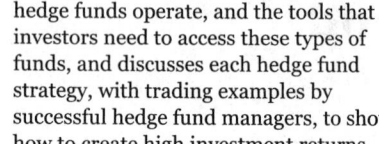

This is an online knowledge economy for

  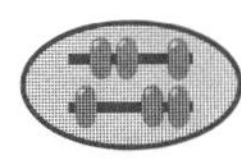   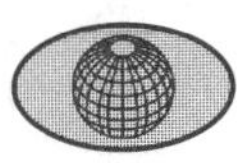   

the Alternative Investment community, designed as an environment for evolving hedge-fund news, intellectual property, content and debates on current issues. It revolves around the elements of village life—village pub, library, hedge fund mall, job centre, and data farm. There is also a conference center and Village school, and a range of shops run by financial institutions, software companies, and publishers.

The Hedge Fund Service Provider Guide

www.iihedgefundguide.com

The Hedge Fund Service Provider Guide is an Internet directory of companies serving the hedge fund industry, including accounting firms, administrators, compliance vendors, consultants and advisors, CRM, executive search, information providers, legal services, prime brokerage, risk management vendors, technology providers, and trading services. It is composed of over 550 entries, helping firms and individuals looking for service providers within their market sectors.

Hedge Funds and Compliance for Hedge Funds

www.hedge-fund-manager.net

This is a portal for information on hedge funds, which contains details on funds, managers and management, strategies, software, books, forums, compliance, certification, jobs.

HedgeWeek

www.hedgeweek.com

An online resource that provides information and reports on hedge fund news, and features jobs, events, comments and opinions, interviews, forum, and an industry directory.

HedgeWorld

www.hedgeworld.com

This is an information source for news, research, analysis, investigative reports, interviews, and profiles, aimed at individual and institutional investors and their professional advisers, fund managers and service providers in the global hedge fund industry.

HFN

www.hedgefund.net

This is resource for hedge fund news and performance data industry news, monitor existing hedge fund investments, and review fund information in anticipation of making allocations to the asset class. It is available only to accredited investors, who can access a database of information on more than 8,000 hedge funds, funds-of-funds and commodity products.

ORGANIZATIONS

USA

100 Women in Hedge Funds

331 W 57th Street, Suite 239, New York, NY 10019, USA

www.100womeninhedgefunds.org

This is an international association of more than 10,000 professional women in the hedge fund industry. It provides educational programming, professional leverage initiatives, and philanthropy. There is also a version of the association based in London, with its own Board of Directors and Executive Committee.

The Hedge Fund & Private Equity Resource Center

1225 Franklin Avenue, Suite 325, Garden City, NY 11530, USA

T: +1 516 992 3417

E: info@hfpe.net

www.hfpe.net

This is a private, non-partisan institution dedicated to independent research and education on issues of government, politics, regulatory oversight and supervision involving private investment firms. It assists in the formulation of innovative policy solutions, and its research activities involve representative members of the private investment industry, professionals, and academics.

International Association of Hedge Funds Professionals

Chair: George Lekatis

George Lekatis, Compliance LLC, 1200 G Street NW, Suite 800, Washington, DC 20005, USA

T: +1 302 342 8828

E: lekatis@hedge-funds-association.com

www.hedge-funds-association.com

This is an industry association for hedge funds manager, administrators, analysts, and others working with hedge funds. It aims to explain to the outside world what hedge funds professionals do and how their consultants operate, discuss the regulation and control of hedge funds, and also provide information on services for education and training.

International

Alternative Investment Management Association

Chair: Florence Lombard

2nd Floor, 167 Fleet Street, London, EC4A 2EA, UK

T: +44 (0) 20 7822 8380

www.aima.org

This international, not-for-profit, trade association represents nearly 1,300 corporate members worldwide, including hedge fund managers, fund of hedge funds managers, prime brokers, legal and accounting services, and fund administrators. The association influences policy development, industry initiatives, and is involved in regulation. It also focuses on developing industry skills and education standards, and is a co-founder of the Chartered Alternative Investment Analyst designation (CAIA).

The Chartered Alternative Investment Analyst Association

Chair: Peter Douglas

29 South Pleasant Street, Amherst, MA 01002, USA

T: +1 413 253 7373

F: +1 413 253 4494

E: info@caia.org

www.caia.org

The CAIA is an independent, not-for-profit, global organization that is committed to education and professionalism in the field of alternative investments. It provides information on alternative investments, promotes professional development through education, advocates high standards of professional conduct, and is the sponsoring body for the CAIA designation, the educational standard for the alternative investment industry.

The Hedge Fund Association

Chair: David Friedland

2875 NE 191st Street, Suite 900, Aventura, Florida 33180, USA

T: +1 202 478 2000

F: +1 202 478 1999

E: info@thehfa.org

www.thehfa.org

This is a not-for-profit international association for hedge fund professionals, which provides a forum for industry leaders, innovators, practitioners, and investors. It represents the industry through the education of investors, the media, regulators and legislators, lobbies at government level, and sets industry standards for fund administrators and other service providers who collect, collate, and analyze information related to hedge funds.

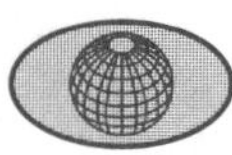

Intellectual Property

BOOKS

The Change Function: Why Some Technologies Take Off and Others Crash and Burn
Pip Coburn
London: A&C Black Publishers, 2007
240pp, ISBN: 978-0-7136-8207-6
This draws on the author's experiences to explain why some technologies are successful while others fail. It argues that consumers are only ready to change when the "pain" of their current position outweighs the potential pain of trying something new. It will be of interest to investors in new technology, and those involved in new product development.

Copyright in a Week, 2nd ed
Graham Cornish
London: Profile Books, 2002
96pp, ISBN: 978-0-340-84944-6
This introductory text will help you understand what copyright is, why it is important to respect it, and how to make use of copyright law in business, management, and everyday life.

Copyright: Interpreting the Law for Libraries, Archives and Information Services, 5th ed
Graham Cornish
London: Library Association Publishing, 2009
224pp, ISBN: 978-1-85604-664-0
Cornish's book explains the provisions of the Copyright, Designs, and Patent Act 1988 and supporting legislation, in an accessible Q&A format. New sections cover licensing schemes and developments in electronic copyright issues, including the legal deposit of electronic materials.

Essentials of Licensing Intellectual Property
Alexander I. Poltorak, Paul J. Lerner
Chichester, UK: Wiley, 2004
240pp, ISBN: 978-0-471-43233-3
Poltorak and Lerner have compiled a concise and useful primer for professionals who need answers fast and novices who would like to learn more about this subject. The book goes from the basics of the intellectual property field to copyright laws, as well as exploring current strategies and technologies.

From Ideas to Assets: Investing Wisely in Intellectual Property
Bruce M. Berman (editor)
Chichester, UK: Wiley, 2002
624pp, ISBN: 978-0-471-40068-4
Based on the experience of expert contributors, this argues that corporations need to understand what their intellectual property assets are and how to protect their rights to them. It covers such topics as maximizing returns on intellectual property assets, valuing those assets, and discerning performance variables.

Patent It Yourself, 13th ed
David Pressman
Berkeley, California: Nolo Press, 2008
592pp, ISBN: 978-1-4133-0854-9
As an experienced patent attorney and former patent examiner of the US Patent and Trademark Office, David Pressman has developed a very useful guide containing all the instructions and forms necessary to patent an invention in the United States. The book offers comprehensive and up-to-date advice for obtaining a high-quality patent and presents the information in a user-friendly, jargon-free, and well-illustrated way.

Patents, Copyrights and Trademarks for Dummies
Henri J. A. Charmasson
Chichester, UK: Wiley, 2004
348pp, ISBN: 978-0-7645-2551-3
Patents, Copyrights and Trademarks for Dummies explains, in layman's terms, the basic nature, function, and application of intellectual property (IP) rights, including how you can acquire those rights, wield them effectively against your competitors, or exploit them lucratively through licensing agreements and other rewarding adventures.

Protecting Your #1 Asset: Creating Fortunes from Your Ideas: An Intellectual Property Handbook
Michael A. Lechter
Rich Dad's Advisors Series
Boston, Massachusetts: Back Bay Books, 2003
320pp, ISBN: 978-0-446-67831-5
Placing its emphasis on protecting intellectual property (IP), this book makes the case for understanding developments in this sector. It covers topics such as identifying and benefiting from IP assets, using IP assets to build barriers to competition, licensing IP assets, and using IP assets to raise capital.

The Strategic Management of Intellectual Capital and Organizational Knowledge: A Collection of Readings
Nick Bontis, Chun Wei Choo (editors)
Oxford: Oxford University Press, 2002
748pp, ISBN: 978-0-19-513866-5
This collection of articles addresses central themes in the strategic management of intellectual capital. It is designed to assist organizations in understanding the strategic and operational roles of intellectual property, and in developing organizational infrastructures and cultures that foster the creation, development, sharing, and mentoring of intellectual capital.

Valuation of Intellectual Property and Intangible Assets, 3rd ed
Gordon V. Smith, Russell L. Parr
Intellectual Property Series
Chichester, UK: Wiley, 2000
638pp, ISBN: 978-0-471-36281-4
This book argues that intellectual property and intangible assets represent the core of most corporations' value, and offers advice on how to identify, define, and exploit these assets. It also includes a discussion of setting royalty rates based on rates of return, and recent developments in the field.

Value Driven Intellectual Capital: How to Convert Intangible Corporate Assets into Market Value
Patrick H. Sullivan
Intellectual Property Series
Chichester, UK: Wiley, 2000
240pp, ISBN: 978-0-471-35104-7
This book explores the expanding world of intellectual assets, where translating an innovative idea into bottom-line profits involves a tightly focused strategy. It offers suggestions for turning corporate knowledge, know-how, and intellectual property into a sustainable competitive weapon that will build reputation and market share.

MAGAZINES

Copyright World
Informa Law
30–32 Mortimer Street, London, W1W 7RE, UK
T: +44 (0) 20 7017 4046
F: +44 (0) 20 7453 2221
www.ipworld.com/ipwo/public/publications/article-list.htm?publication_id=copyrightworld
ISSN: 0950-2505

This publication contains international news and updates on copyright and intellectual property matters, covering both legal and practical issues.

Managing Intellectual Property
Euromoney Legal Media Group
Nestor House, Playhouse Yard, London, EC4V 5EX, UK
T: +44 (0) 20 7779 8610
F: +44 (0) 20 7779 8602
www.managingip.com
ISSN: 0960-5002
Published 10 times each year, this international magazine for intellectual property owners, especially senior in-house counsel in multinational companies. It provides news, comment, data, and analysis of the industry, and offers regular surveys and supplements on patents, trademarks, and copyright.

JOURNALS

Journal of Intellectual Property Law & Practice
Oxford Journals
Great Clarendon Street, Oxford, OX2 6DP, UK
T: +44 (0) 1865 353 907
F: +44 (0) 1865 353 485
jiplp.oxfordjournals.org
ISSN: 1747-1532
JIPLP is a peer-reviewed journal dedicated to intellectual property law and practice. Published monthly, coverage includes the full range of substantive IP topics, practice-related matters such as litigation, enforcement, drafting and transactions, plus relevant aspects of related subjects such as competition and world trade law.

Journal of World Intellectual Property
Blackwell Publishing
9600 Garsington Road, Oxford, OX4 2DQ, UK
T: +44 (0) 1865 791 100
F: +44 (0) 1865 791 347
www.wiley.com/bw/journal.asp?ref=1422-2213
ISSN: 1747-1796
This bimonthly journal is dedicated to intellectual property in relation to trade and investment, with particular focus on the WTO and TRIPS (the Agreement on Trade-Related Aspects of Intellectual Property Rights).

INTERNET

Copyright and Fair Use: Stanford University Libraries
fairuse.stanford.edu
The site provides a quick search facility and overview of copyright law, with links to internet resources, current legislation, cases, judicial opinions, regulations, treaties, and conventions.

Copyright Clearance Center
www.copyright.com
Copyright Clearance Center, Inc., the largest licenser of text reproduction rights in the world, was formed to facilitate compliance with US copyright law. It provides licensing systems for the reproduction and distribution of copyrighted materials in print and electronic formats throughout the world.

The Copyright Licensing Agency
www.cla.co.uk
The agency is the UK's reproduction rights organization—the UK equivalent of the US Copyright Clearance Center.

Franklin Pierce Law Center
www.fplc.edu
Sponsored by a law school, the site offers an extensive list of articles relating to intellectual property.

International Intellectual Property Alliance
www.iipa.com
Sponsored by a private-sector coalition formed to protect US copyrighted material around the world, this site offers articles on a variety of intellectual property topics and country-specific copyright information.

Intellectual Property Office
www.ipo.gov.uk
The website of the UK government department responsible for intellectual property—copyright, patents, designs, and trademarks—has a section of links to government, academic, and general intellectual property sites.

United States Copyright Office
www.copyright.gov
The US Copyright Office is located in the Library of Congress. The site has a section for FAQs and another for requests relating to the Freedom of Information Act, as well as material on copyright legislation, and an international section with links to the World Intellectual Property Organization.

United States Patent and Trademark Office
www.uspto.gov
The PTO promotes industrial and technological progress in the US, and strengthens the national economy by administering the laws relating to patents and trademarks, and advising the US government on patent, trademark, and copyright protection, and on trade related aspects of intellectual property.

World Intellectual Property Organization (WIPO)
www.wipo.org
WIPO is a specialized agency of the United Nations whose mandate is to promote the protection of intellectual property worldwide. With 182 countries among its member states, WIPO administers 23 treaties in the field of intellectual property. The first general group of treaties defines internationally agreed basic standards of intellectual property in each of the member states.

ORGANIZATIONS

Europe

European Patent Office
Av. de Cortenbergh 60, Brussels 1000, Belgium
T: + 49 89 2399 4636
www.epo.org
The European Patent Office (EPO) provides a uniform application procedure for individual inventors and companies seeking patent protection in up to 38 European countries. It is the executive arm of the European Patent Organisation and is supervised by the Administrative Council.

Intellectual Property Institute UK
36 Great Russell Street, London, WC1B 3QB, UK
T: +44 (0) 20 7436 3040
F: +44 (0) 20 7323 5312
E: pleonard@ip-institute.org.uk
www.ip-institute.org.uk
The purpose of the institute, a non-profit membership organization, is to increase the contribution of intellectual property to economic well-being, by timely, relevant, and authoritative research, and by informing policy makers and public debate.

Intellectual Property Office (IPO)
Concept House, Cardiff Road, Newport, South Wales, NP10 8QQ, UK
T: +44 (0) 1633 814 000
F: +44 (0) 1633 817 777
E: enquiries@ipo.gov.uk
www.ipo.gov.uk/
This is the official government body responsible for granting intellectual property (IP) rights in the United Kingdom. These rights include patents, designs, trademarks, and copyright.

USA

American Intellectual Property Law Association (AIPLA)
241 18th Street South, Suite 700, Arlington, VI 22202, USA
T: +1 703 415 0780
F: +1 703 415 0786
E: aipla@aipla.org
www.aipla.org
Founded in 1897 and having more than 16,000 members, AIPLA comprises national bar association lawyers practising in the fields of patents, trademarks, and copyrights. It also promotes the improvement of US intellectual property systems.

Intellectual Property Owners Association (IPO)
1501 M Street NW, Suite 1150, Suite 200, Washington, DC 20005, USA
T: +1 202 507 4500
F: +1 202 507 4501
E: info@ipo.org
www.ipo.org
This group comprises over 400 major corporations and lawyers that deal with intellectual property issues and concerns. The IPO works to support and strengthen the patent, trademark, copyright, and trade secret laws of the United States, and also monitors legislative activities.

United States Patent and Trademark Office (USPTO)
PO Box 1450, Alexandria, VI 22313–1450, USA
E: usptoinfo@uspto.gov
www.uspto.gov
The PTO promotes industrial and technological progress in the United States, and works to strengthen the national economy by administering the laws relating to patents and trademarks, and advising the US government on patent, trademark, and copyright protection, and on trade-related aspects of intellectual property.

BRIC

Federal Reserve for Intellectual Property, Patents and Trademarks (ROSPATENT)
30–1 Berezhkovskaya nab., Moscow G-59, GSP-5 123995, Russia
F: +7 499 240 6179
E: rospatent@rupto.ru
www.fips.ru/ruptoen
The Federal Reserve for Intellectual Property, Patents and Trademarks (ROSPATENT) in Russia is a federal executive authority performing functions of control and supervision in the area of the legal protection and exploitation of intellectual property rights, including patents and trademarks.

Institute Nacional da Propriedade Industrial (INPI)
Rua Mayrink Veiga, nº 9, Centro, Rio de Janeiro, Brazil
T: +55 21 2139 3000
www.inpi.gov.br
The Brazilian National Patent Office is responsible for the registration of brands, patents, trademarks, software programs, geographical indications, industrial design, and for transferring technology.

Intellectual Property Office India
The Patent Office, Boudhik Sampada Bhawan, Near Antop Hill Post Office, S.M.Road, Antop Hill, Mumbai 400 037, India
T: +91 22 2413 7701
F: +91 22 2413 0387
E: mumbai-patent@nic.in
www.patentoffice.nic.in
The Intellectual Property Office India registers patents, trademarks, designs and geographical indications across the country.

State Intellectual Property Office of China (SIPO)
No.6 Xitucheng Road, Haidian District, Bejing, 100088, China
SIPO organizes and coordinates intellectual property rights protection work across China, works to improve the protection system and standardize patent administration, laws, and regulations, draws up the policies of foreign-related IP work, organizes development programs for the patent work nationwide, and lays down the criteria of affirming the exclusive rights of patents, and publicizes patent laws, regulations and policies.

International

The International Intellectual Property Institute (IIPI)
4401-A Connecticut Ave NW, Box 235, Washington, DC 20008, USA
T: +1 202 544 6610
F: +1 202 478 1955
www.iipi.org
The International Intellectual Property Institute (IIPI) is a non-profit 501(c)(3) corporation located in Washington, DC. As an international development organization and think tank, IIPI is dedicated to increasing awareness and understanding of the use of intellectual property as a tool for economic growth, particularly in developing countries.

World Intellectual Property Organization (WIPO)
34, chemin des Colombettes, Geneva, Switzerland
T: +41 22 338 91 11
F: +41 22 733 54 28
www.wipo.org
WIPO is a specialized agency of the United Nations whose mandate is to promote the protection of intellectual property worldwide. Counting 182 countries among its member states, WIPO administers 23 treaties in the field of intellectual property. The first general group of treaties defines internationally agreed basic standards of intellectual property in each of the member states.

  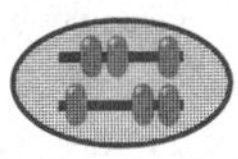   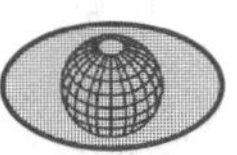   

International Finance

BOOKS

Country Risk Assessment: A Guide to Global Investment Strategy

Michel Henry Bouchet, Ephraim Clarke, Bertrand Groslambert
Wiley Finance Series
Hoboken, New Jersey: Wiley, 2003
271pp, ISBN: 978-0-470-84500-4

This is a comprehensive analysis of the various economic, financial, geopolitical, sociological, and historical factors that contribute to country risk. It examines the various sources of country risk, and details information sources and country risk service providers, strategies for international risk assessment and management, and the opportunities that have arisen from the integration of international finance markets.

Finance of International Trade

Eric Bishop
Essential Capital Markets Series
Amsterdam: Elsevier, 2004
207pp, ISBN: 978-0-7506-5908-6

This introduction to international trade finance provides a guide to each phase of a typical transaction, and examines the relationships between the various parties involved, and the facilities employed. It also explores the type of banking instruments and techniques available, when to apply a particular form of finance, the risks involved, and how they can be managed.

Fixing Global Finance

Martin Wolf
Forum on Constructive Capitalism Series
Baltimore, Maryland: Johns Hopkins University Press, 2008
230pp, ISBN: 978-0-8018-9048-2

This is a timely analysis of the structural problems impacting the global financial system. It explains the imbalances of the world economy and how they cause regular financial crises, how the current recession began, and how further disruptions to international finance can be avoided. It also explores international economics and exchange rates, and reviews various theories about market downturns.

Global Banking, 2nd ed

Roy C. Smith, Ingo Walter
Oxford, UK: Oxford University Press, 2003
438pp, ISBN: 978-0-19-513436-0

This is a practical overview of recent developments in international banking and how the financial markets operate, as well as outlining competitive strategies for the future. It focuses on international commercial banking, including issues of cross-border risk evaluation and exposure management, and regulatory oversight within the context of global competition. It also tackles international investment banking and its overlap with commercial side of the industry.

Global Corporate Finance: Text and Cases, 6th ed

Suk Kim, Seung Kim
Malden, Massachusetts: Blackwell Publishing, 2006
569pp, ISBN: 978-1-4051-1990-0

This comprehensive textbook on international finance provides a guide to global financial problems and techniques. It analyzes corporate finance and governance, international markets, global financial dynamics and strategies, and risk management techniques, with each chapter starting with a real-world case study illuminating the theories and research presented.

Global Governance of Financial Systems: The International Regulation of Systemic Risk

Kern Alexander, Rahul Dhumale, John Eatwell
Oxford, UK: Oxford University Press, 2006
320pp, ISBN: 978-0-19-516698-9

This is an examination of regulation and the system of committees, organizations, rules, and guidelines that now oversee the international financial system. It argues that the current framework fails to take account of the macroeconomic consequences that follow from the failure of financial institutions, and analyzes the role of the International Monetary Fund, the Basel committees on banking, and the Asian financial crises in financial governance.

The Global Securities Market: A History

Ranald Michie
Oxford, UK: Oxford University Press, 2006
399pp, ISBN: 978-0-19-928062-9

This is an authoritative account of the global securities market from its earliest developments to the present day. It presents a full history of the securities markets, of stocks and bonds, established and emerging markets, stock exchanges, over-the-counter trading, and its bubbles and crashes, from its beginnings in Medieval Venice, to Amsterdam and London, up to the current global market system.

Globalization and Finance

Tony Porter
Cambridge, UK: Polity, 2005
230pp, ISBN: 978-0-7456-3119-6

This comprehensive overview of the interrelationship between economic globalization and the international financial system guides the reader through the debate on the impact of a global marketplace on how we live. It discusses the structure of public-sector and non-governmental institutions and practices that influence financial globalization and offers some solutions for its regulation. It also focuses on the role of banking, securities markets, and foreign direct investment.

The Handbook of International Trade and Finance: The Complete Guide to Risk Management, International Payments and Currency Management, Bonds and Guarantees, Credit Insurance and Trade Finance

Anders Grath
London: Kogan Page, 2008
198pp, ISBN: 978-0-7494-5320-6

This practical guide to international trade and finance provides a useful discussion of the main factors involved, such as risk management, international payments, currency management, bonds and guarantees, and trade finance. It explains how to reduce risks and improve cashflow, identify the most competitive finance alternatives, structure the best payment terms, and minimize finance and transaction costs.

International Business Finance

Michael Connolly
New York: Routledge, 2007
212pp, ISBN: 978-0-415-70153-2

This textbook for foundation courses provides a useful introduction to the main building blocks of international business finance, focusing on the foreign exchange market, reviewing spot, forwards, futures and options. It also discusses the corporate aspects of international trade, presents a study of the instruments used by currency traders and hedgers, and explores the role of managers in international corporations.

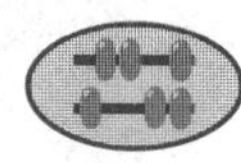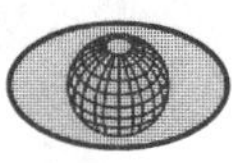

International Finance, 3rd ed
Keith Pilbeam
Basingstoke, UK: Palgrave Macmillan, 2006
497pp, ISBN: 978-1-4039-4837-3
This popular textbook provides an introduction to international finance, particularly the theories and differing policies on the balance of payments, exchange rates and the international monetary system. Various strands of research are explained in an understandable way, and related to current financial practice, aided by extensive figures, tables and graphs to illustrate the analysis.

International Finance: Transactions, Policy and Regulation, 15th ed
Hal S. Scott
University Casebook Series
New York: Foundation Press, 2008
1,115pp, ISBN: 978-1-59941-547-5
This introductory casebook to international finance, policy, and regulation focuses on the international aspects of major domestic markets, the infrastructure for financial markets, instruments and offshore markets, emerging markets, and the impact of terrorism. It discusses basic financial concepts and transactions, the expansion of US capital market regulation, and the implementation of international accounting standards.

International Financial Management, 9th ed
Jeff Madura
Mason, Ohio: Thomson/South-Western, 2008
673pp, ISBN: 978-0-324-59347-1
This abridged edition of the popular textbook balances theory with practical applications to examine the latest trends in international finance. It shows how to develop the management skills needed to succeed in the competitive financial marketplace, focusing on management decisions that maximize a firm's value, backed up by practical examples from a variety of multinational corporate projects.

International Financial Management
Geert Bekaert, Robert J. Hodrick
Prentice Hall Series in Finance
Upper Saddle River, New Jersey: Prentice Hall, 2009
810pp, ISBN: 978-0-13-116360-7
This new textbook covering the main aspects and trends of international financial management presents the necessary analytical tools for financial decision-making in the current competitive global environment. It examines the markets, their institutional aspects, and sources of risks that have an impact on them, and how they can be managed.

International Investments, 5th ed
Bruno Solnik, Dennis McLeavey
Boston, Massachusetts: Addison Wesley, 2003
760pp, ISBN: 978-0-321-22389-0
This accessible exploration of the international capital markets provides a comprehensive analysis of all the main international investment concepts and theories. It is aimed at advanced undergraduates and MBA students, but also has relevance for professionals working in the investment sector, and has been selected by the AIMR as recommended reading for the Chartered Financial Analysts exam.

International Money and Finance, 3rd ed
C. Paul Hallwood, Ronald MacDonald
Malden, Massachusetts: Blackwell Publishing, 2000
568pp, ISBN: 978-0-631-20462-6
This comprehensive and analytic textbook covers a broad range of topics relating to the international financial system. It investigates theory, evidence, policy, and institutions from a monetary, neoclassical, and neo-Keynesian perspective, to provide a resource for those studying international economy and finance. This updated edition also explores European monetary union, transition economies, and developing countries.

International Trade Finance, 8th ed
Paul Cowdell, Derek Hyde (editors)
London: Global Professional Publishing, 2003
390pp, ISBN: 978-0-85297-721-7
Now in its eighth edition, this standard text on international trade finance provides a guide for all students and practitioners wanting an introduction to the main concepts and trends, including foreign exchange, and support services, such as documentary credits, for exporters, importers and merchants.

Multinational Business Finance, 11th ed
David K. Eiteman, Arthur I. Stonehill, Michael H. Moffett
Addison-Wesley Series in Finance
Boston, Massachusetts: Addison Wesley, 2007
746pp, ISBN: 978-0-321-35796-0
This regularly updated treatment of how multinational businesses function provides a comprehensive examination of international finance, explaining how to recognize and capitalize on the unique characteristics of global markets. It offers case studies throughout to apply concepts to the real-life problems that managers of multinational firms face, and presents new analysis of multinational business finance in the emerging markets.

Multinational Financial Management, 8th ed
Alan C. Shapiro
New York: Wiley, 2006
745pp, ISBN: 978-0-471-73769-8
This respected textbook provides a conceptual framework for analyzing key financial decisions in multinational firms, and the opportunities available to them in the global marketplace. It shows how they can avoid the threats and risks of international trade, as well as examining the increase of diversification, the ability to arbitrage between imperfect capital markets, and the impact of Chinese economic expansion on the global economy.

MAGAZINES

Global Finance
Global Finance
411 Fifth Avenue, New York, NY 10016, USA
T: +1 212 447 7900
F: +1 212 447 7750
www.gfmag.com
ISSN: 0896-4181
This monthly magazine offers market intelligence, news, and analysis on the latest trends and developments in international finance. It covers corporate finance, M&A, country profiles, capital markets, e-business initiatives, investor relations, currencies, banking, risk management, custody, direct investment, and money management, and reports on how companies fund their operations, and financial groups use money and finance.

Global Money Management
Institutional Investor
FL 7, 225 Park Ave S, New York, NY 10003, USA
T: +1 212 224 3300
www.globalmoneymanagement.com
ISSN: 1529-6679
This monthly newsletter provides information, news, and analysis of new products and offerings, M&A activity, and major regulatory developments in the

  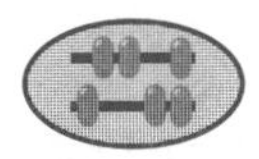   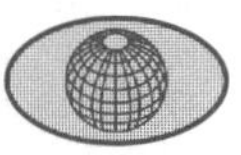   

international institutional investment sector. It also features investment manager and consultant search-and-hire activity, plan sponsor interviews, country reports, league tables, and consultant profiles, and reports on investment strategies, performance measurement, and the developing markets.

JOURNALS

Global Finance Journal

Elsevier
Radarweg 29, 1043 NX Amsterdam, The Netherlands
F: +31 20 485 2370
www.elsevier.com/wps/find/journaldescription.cws_home/620162/description#description
ISSN: 1044-0283

This journal, issued three times each year, provides a forum for the exchange of ideas, applied research, and industry techniques among academicians and practitioners in global financial management. It publishes scholarly papers that integrate theory and practice in areas such as financial management, investment, banking and financial services, accounting, and taxation.

International Finance

Wiley
PO Box 808, 1–7 Oldlands Way, Bognor Regis, PO21 9FF, UK
T: +44 (0) 1865 778315
www.wiley.com/bw/journal.asp?ref=1367-0271&site=1
ISSN: 1367-0271

This journal, published three times each year, presents scholarly, theoretical and policy research on problems in macroeconomics and finance. It offers broad coverage of key policy areas, such as exchange rates, political economy, monetary policy, financial markets, corporate finance, transition economics, and the analysis of complex market issues.

Journal of International Banking Law & Regulation

Sweet & Maxwell
100 Avenue Road, London, NW3 3PF, UK
T: +44 (0) 20 7393 7000
www.sweetandmaxwell.co.uk/Catalogue/ProductDetails.aspx?recordid=508&productid=7242
ISSN: 0267-937X

This monthly international journal on banking law and securities provides detailed, practical analysis of international legal and regulatory issues from around the world. It presents papers on topical issues and future trends, and analytical pieces that combine practical information with academic opinion, as well as expert reviews of the latest publications.

Journal of International Financial Management & Accounting

Wiley
350 Main Street, Malden, MA 02148, USA
T: +44 (0) 1865 778315
www.wiley.com/bw/journal.asp?ref=0954-1314
ISSN: 0954-1314

JIFMA, published three times each year, presents original research on international aspects of financial management and reporting, banking and financial services, auditing and taxation. It provides a forum for academics and professionals on new developments and emerging trends in the industry, including the impact of institutional, regulatory, and accounting differences across countries.

Journal of International Financial Markets Institutions and Money

Elsevier
Radarweg 29, 1043 NX Amsterdam, The Netherlands
F: +31 20 485 2370
www.elsevier.com/wps/find/journaldescription.cws_home/600113/description#description
ISSN: 1042-4431

This journal, issued five times each year, produces informed analysis of international trade, financing and investments, and the related cash and credit transactions. It also covers relevant areas such as the international financial markets, international securities markets, foreign exchange markets, international commercial and investment banking, central bank intervention, and balance of payments.

Journal of International Money and Finance

Elsevier
Radarweg 29, 1043 NX Amsterdam, The Netherlands
F: +31 20 485 2370
www.elsevier.com/wps/find/journaldescription.cws_home/30443/description#description
ISSN: 0261-5606

This journal, published eight times each year, offers theoretical and empirical research in international economics and finance for researchers and financial market professionals. It focuses on international monetary economics, international finance, and the overlap between the two, as well as research on exchange rate behavior, foreign exchange options, international capital markets, international monetary and fiscal policy, and international transmission.

 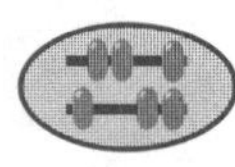   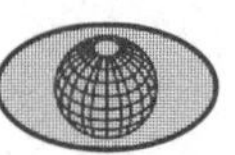   

International Management, Cross-Cultural Management

BOOKS

Breaking through Culture Shock: What You Need to Succeed in International Business
Elizabeth Marx
London: Nicholas Brealey Publishing, 2001
233pp, ISBN: 978-1-85788-221-6
This book explores the issue of culture shock, and the extent to which it affects success in today's global business environment. It stresses the importance of understanding the different motivations, behaviors, and ways of making decisions, found in other cultures. The author puts forward the culture shock triangle model as a way of helping managers to behave differently and manage their emotions so as to become truly cross-culturally effective.

Building Cross-Cultural Competence: How to Create Wealth from Conflicting Values
Charles M. Hampden-Turner, Fons Trompenaars
New Haven, Connecticut: Yale University Press, 2001
400pp, ISBN: 978-0-300-08497-9
Drawing on the results of 14 years of research, the authors examine the different cultural values of more than 40 nations and explore how managers can become successful in the global economy by being able to think in both directions and to gain cross-cultural competence. The text is illustrated with stories, cartoons, and case histories throughout.

China, Inc.: How the Rise of the Next Superpower Challenges America and the World
Ted Fishman
New York: Scribner, 2005
368pp, ISBN: 978-0-7432-5752-7
Featuring interviews with workers and managers in China, the United States, and elsewhere, this book paints a vivid picture of China, its economy, and its role in the rest of the commercial world. It provides a useful overview of China's resurgence and what that might mean for businesses elsewhere.

Cross-Cultural Management: Essential Concepts, 2nd ed
David C. Thomas
Los Angeles, California: Sage Publications, 2008
352pp, ISBN: 978-1-4129-3956-0
This examines cross-cultural management issues from a predominantly psychological perspective. As opposed to being country specific, it focuses on the interactions of people from different cultures in organizational settings. It examines the effect of culture in a way that can then be applied to a wide variety of cross-cultural interactions in a number of organizational contexts.

Cultural Dimension of International Business, 5th ed
Gary P. Ferraro
Harlow, UK: Prentice Hall, 2005
224pp, ISBN: 978-0-13-192767-4
This book explores the contribution that cultural anthropology can make to the conduct of international business. It outlines a conceptual approach to culture and international business and examines the nature of verbal and nonverbal communication patterns, as well as contrasting cultural values, cross-cultural negotiation, culture shock, and the development of global managers. Advice on sources of cultural information is appended.

Doing Business Internationally: The Guide to Cross-Cultural Success, 2nd ed
Danielle Walker, Thomas Walker
Maidenhead, UK: McGraw-Hill, 2002
288pp, ISBN: 978-0-07-137832-1
The authors aim to raise awareness of the importance of cross-cultural knowledge and understanding for the effective management of international business in the context of rapid globalization. The cultural orientations model, a framework for understanding how cultural forces influence and underpin decision-making and strategy planning, is presented and illustrated through an overview of worldwide cultural patterns. The cultural orientations approach is applied to the areas of communication, marketing, and sales. Finally, issues relevant to the management of global, multicultural teams are discussed.

Effective Organisational Communication: Perspectives, Principles and Practices, 3rd ed
Richard Blundel, Kate Ippolito
Harlow, UK: FT Prentice Hall, 2008
448pp, ISBN: 978-0-273-71375-3
Effective Organisational Communication is a comprehensive introduction to the principles of effective communication within and between organizations. It combines strong theoretical grounding and real-world examples, and encourages an exploration of fresh perspectives, while also developing practical communication skills.

Global Business Management: A Cross-Cultural Perspective
Abel Adekola, Bruno S. Sergi
Aldershot, UK: Ashgate Publishing, 2007
328pp, ISBN: 978-0-7546-7112-1
This book discusses how to manage global organizations. This helps provide a basic understanding of the influence of culture on international management and the key roles that international managers play. It clearly shows how to develop the cross-cultural expertise essential to succeed in a world of rapid and profound economic, political, and cultural changes.

Global Literacies: Lessons on Business Leadership and National Cultures
Robert H. Rosen *et al.*
London: Simon & Schuster, 2000
416pp, ISBN: 978-0-684-85902-6
In this title, the author makes a comparison between the way a child learns how to speak and the redefinition of the way top businesses work due to the arrival of a global marketplace. The authors assert that in order to achieve success organizations must educate themselves in this new language, and use numerous surveys, interviews, and studies to reveal how top companies and individuals approach both this and other challenges.

International Management: An Essential Guide to International Business, 3rd ed
John Mattock (editor)
Professional Paperbacks Series
London: Kogan Page, 2003
224pp, ISBN: 978-0-7494-3922-4
The author explores the problems and issues surrounding international and cross-cultural management, focusing on the six key steps to effective communication and negotiation: culture, company, character, tactics, timing, and talk. Each of these areas is discussed, with quizzes and exercises to illustrate how they can be approached most effectively.

     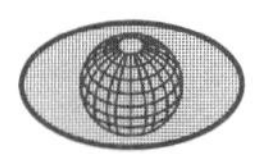   

International Management: Cross-Cultural Dimensions, 3rd ed
Richard Mead
Oxford: Blackwell Publishing, 2004
472pp, ISBN: 978-0-631-23177-6
Written for management students, this book examines how cultural factors and differences affect behavior in the workplace and the boardroom. The key skills demanded by international management are identified and discussed, their practical application is shown, and the influence and effects of culture are investigated from four viewpoints: national, organizational, strategic, and personnel.

Made in China: What Western Managers Can Learn from Trailblazing Chinese Entrepreneurs
Donald Sull, Yong Wang
Boston, Massachusetts: Harvard Business School Press, 2005
256pp, ISBN: 978-1-59139-715-1
Profiling eight of China's leading firms, this book looks at the secrets of Chinese commercial success in the 21st century. An enlightening read for any business operating in that region, hoping to begin operations there, or simply trying to keep afloat in turbulent times, the book describes the tactics of leading Chinese entrepreneurs and their key strategies.

Managing Across Borders, 2nd ed
Christopher A. Bartlett, Sumantra Ghoshal
Boston, Massachusetts: Harvard Business School Press, 2002
416pp, ISBN: 978-1-57851-707-7
Two of the leading writers in the field offer valuable lessons on running transnational companies.

Managing Cultural Differences: Leadership Strategies for a New World of Business, 6th ed
Philip R. Harris, Robert T. Moran
Houston, Texas: Gulf Professional Publishing Company, 2004
600pp, ISBN: 978-0-7506-7736-3
The book is divided into three sections: addressing the need for multicultural managerial skills, the characteristics that make up a culture, and the specifics of cultures from countries on every continent. The fifth edition contains a new chapter on women in global business.

When Cultures Collide: Managing Successfully across Cultures
Richard D. Lewis
London: Nicholas Brealey Publishing, 2000
500pp, ISBN: 978-1-85788-087-8
The author investigates how people work and communicate across cultures and explains how culture and language affect the ways in which we organize our world, think, feel, and respond. He offers insights into how different business cultures accord status and structure their organizations, reviews the role of leader, and also offers advice on negotiation, sales, and marketing.

The World is Flat: A Brief History of the Twenty-First Century, 3rd ed
Thomas L. Friedman
New York: Picador, 2007
672pp, ISBN: 978-0-312-42507-4
The winner of the inaugural Financial Times business book of the year award, *The World is Flat* focuses on how the world has "flattened" with the rise of globalization. It looks at how other events on the world stage (from 9/11 to the war in Iraq, and the democratization of technology) will impact on individuals, companies, and nations alike.

MAGAZINES

Foreign Affairs
Council on Foreign Relations
58 East 68th Street, New York, NY 10021, USA
T: +1 386 246 3386 or 800 829 5539
www.foreignaffairs.org
ISSN: 0015-7120
Published six times per year, this magazine covers current events and how they affect US relations worldwide. With a focus on international, political, commercial, and cultural relations, it has often been described as the premier journal of world affairs. This is a must-read for any corporate executive involved with international business.

Global Finance
Global Finance
411 Fifth Avenue, New York, NY 10018, USA
T: +1 212 447 7900
F: +1 212 447 7750
www.gfmag.com
ISSN: 0896-4181
This monthly magazine provides news and analysis of companies and financial institutions around the world. Coverage aimed at an international corporate audience includes corporate finance, joint ventures and M&A, country profiles, capital markets, investor relations, currencies, banking, risk management, custody, direct investment, and money management.

International Journal of Commerce and Management
International Academy of Business Disciplines
PO Box 1659, Indiana, PA 15705, USA
T: +1 724 357 5928
F: +1 724 357 7768
ecobweb.ecob.iup.edu/asc/internationaljournalof3.htm
ISSN: 1056-9219
Intended for business practitioners, academics, policy makers, and nonprofit organizations, this quarterly publication aims to promote understanding among mangers and organizations internationally and publishes articles on management theory and practice.

People Management
McMillan-Scott
9 Savoy Street, London, WC2E 7HR, UK
T: +44 (0) 20 7878 2300
F: +44 (0) 20 7379 7118
www.peoplemanagement.co.uk
ISSN: 1358-6297
This fortnightly magazine, the official magazine of the CIPD, provides information on human resources in the UK. It provides news, features, and the latest thinking and advice in HR.

JOURNALS

Cross-Cultural Research
Sage Publications
1 Oliver's Yard, 55 City Road, London, EC1Y 1SP, UK
T: +44 (0) 20 7324 8500
F: +44 (0) 20 7324 8600
ccr.sagepub.com
ISSN: 1069-3971
This is the official journal of the Society for Cross-Cultural Research, published quarterly. It is a key source for peer-reviewed articles, research reports, bibliographies, and discussion pieces on all aspects of cross-cultural and comparative studies in the fields of social and behavioral science.

International Business Review
Elsevier
PO Box 211, 1000 AE Amsterdam, The Netherlands
T: +31 20 485 3757
F: +31 20 485 3432
www.elsevier.com/locate/ibusrev
ISSN: 0969-5931
This bimonthly magazine provides a forum for the latest developments and advances in the practice of international business and includes contributions from professionals and academics. Theoretical and practical articles are included, as well as literature reviews.

     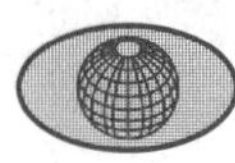   

Journal of International Business Studies
Palgrave Macmillan
Houndmills, Basingstoke, Hampshire, RG21 6XS, UK
ISSN: 0047-2506
This bimonthly journal is the official publication of the Academy of International Business at the Eli Broad College of Business, Michigan State University. The journal has a broad scope, encompassing the whole range of international business studies and encouraging an interdisciplinary approach. It includes research on: multinational business activities; strategies and managerial processes that cross national boundaries; joint ventures; strategic alliances; mergers and acquisitions; cross-national research involving innovation entrepreneurship; knowledge-based competition; judgment and decision making; bargaining; leadership; corporate governance; and new organizational forms.

Journal of International Management
Elsevier
PO Box 211, 1000 AE Amsterdam, The Netherlands
T: +31 20 485 3757
F: +31 20 485 3432
www.elsevier.com/locate/intman
ISSN: 1075-4253
This is a quarterly journal devoted to advancing the understanding of issues involved in the theory and practice of global management and focusing on international strategic management. It is aimed at business professionals working in the fields of risk management, organizational behavior, human resources, and cross-cultural management.

INTERNET

CultureGrams
www.culturegrams.com/index.htm
CultureGrams is known for collecting, organizing, and publishing information worldwide for researchers, faculty, and students in libraries and schools, and has used cultural reference products in the education, government, and non-profit arenas. CultureGrams is available in a variety of print formats and electronic media.

International Trade Data Systems
www.itds.gov
International Trade Data Systems (ITDS) has a goal to implement an integrated government-wide system for the electronic collection, use, and dissemination of international trade data. This website also provides a map of resources covering topics such as the mechanics of exporting, payment methods, customs and tariffs, and export documentation.

Learn about Cultures
www.learnaboutcultures.com
Sponsored by a consulting firm, the site offers abstracts on the cultures of different countries (for which users must pay) and free articles on aspects of cross-cultural management, including training, technology, and gender.

ORGANIZATIONS

USA

Academy of International Business (AIB)
College of Business Administration, University of Hawaii at Manoa, 2404 Maile Way, Honolulu, HI 96822, USA
T: +1 808 956 3665
F: +1 808 956 3261
E: aib@cba.hawaii.edu
www.aibworld.net
A leading body for scholars and specialists in the field of international business, this association aims to disseminate knowledge and understanding of international business issues across the globe through the exchange of information, ideas, and research, and through business cooperation.

International Association of Management (IAoM)
PO Box 64841, Virginia Beach, VI 23467–4841, USA
T: +1 757 482 2273
F: +1 757 482 0325
E: aomgt@infi.net
www.aom-iaom.org
A nonprofit professional organization for students, teachers, and practitioners of management, the IAoM is dedicated to advancing the international practice of management across professional fields through the provision of support, information, products, and services.

International Institute for Culture
6331 Lancaster Ave, Philadelphia, PA 19151, USA
T: +1 215 877 9911
F: +1 215 877 9910
E: info@iiculture.org
www.iiculture.org/index.asp
International Institute for Culture (IIC) is a nonprofit educational and research center which seeks to promote international understanding through cultural means. The IIC participates in international conferences, language and cultural programs, lectures series, educational seminars, art exhibits, and musical performances.

BRIC

China International Culture (Exchange) Association (CICA)
6/F, B3, Ziguang Building, No 11 Huixin Dongjie, China
CICA is non-profit social organization dedicated towards people-to-people cultural exchange and co-operation under the guidance and support of the Ministry of Culture of China. It develops cultural exchange and co-operation with other countries, and helps bring mutual understanding and friendship between the Chinese people and the peoples of the world.

Russian Centre for International Scientific and Cultural Co-operation
103885 GSP, Moscow, Vozdvizhenka, Russia
T: +7 95 290 6932
F: +7 95 2000 1209
www.intertec.co.at/itc2/Partners/CENTRE/default.htm#5
This organization facilitates the development of diverse international relations of the Russian Federation through the network of Russian Centres for Science and Culture and its official representatives in 63 foreign cities. Its main goals are to play an active role in the realization of the state policy of international scientific and cultural co-operation and development, promote the historic and cultural knowledge of the people of the Russian Federation, its national and foreign policies, and scientific, cultural, and intellectual potential.

International

International Association of Cross-Cultural Competence and Management
Europainstitut, Vienna University of Economics and Business Administration, Althanstraße 39–45, 1090 Vienna, Austria
T: +43 (0) 1 31 336 4310
F: +43 (0) 1 31 336 752
E: iaccm@wu-wien.ac.at
iaccm.wu-wien.ac.at
The goal of this association is to develop and explain the cross-cultural factors that have growing importance in an increasingly internationalized world, and to establish cross-cultural competence and management as a widely recognized field of research.

  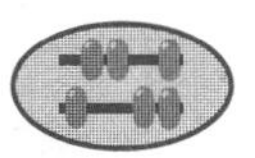   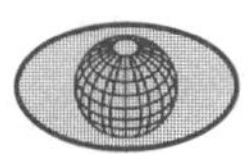   

Investment

BOOKS

The Accidental Investment Banker: Inside the Decade that Transformed Wall Street

Jonathan A. Knee
New York: Random House, 2007
260pp, ISBN: 978-0-8129-7804-9

This insider's account of investment banking takes a humorous look at the extraordinary growth of high finance during the 1990s. It describes the importance of doing deals, generating revenue, and getting noticed, and provides pen portraits of some of the characters involved. It also depicts how far professional standards have fallen, and the fundamental changes that occurred in the industry during that boom-and-bust decade.

The Business of Investment Banking: A Comprehensive Overview, 2nd ed

K. Thomas Liaw
Hoboken, New Jersey: Wiley, 2006
440pp, ISBN: 978-0-471-73964-7

This guide to investment banking describes how investment banks are dealing with the challenges of new competition, changes in regulation, the impact of globalization, and innovations in information technology. It compares financial holding companies, full-service investment banks, and boutique investment banks, and examines strategies for risk management, career opportunities, key operations, trading fundamentals, and ethics and professionalism.

Common Stocks and Uncommon Profits and Other Writings

Philip A. Fisher
Wiley Investment Classics Series
New York: Wiley, 2003
320pp, ISBN: 978-0-471-44550-0

This classic on investment techniques by a pioneer of modern investment theory introduced Fisher's investment philosophies and theories, and discussed a stock's worth in terms of potential growth for the first time. It laid the foundation for current investment practices, describing the benefits of long-term growth stocks and their emerging value, as opposed to short-term trades for quick profit.

The Financial Times Guide to Investing

Glen Arnold
London: FT Prentice Hall, 2004
410pp, ISBN: 978-0-273-66309-6

This authoritative examination of investing shows how to build a successful personal financial portfolio, and invest in the capital markets in an effective way. It explains the key information, data, facts, and comments available to the investor, describes how financial assets and markets operate, and how to invest effectively in shares, bonds, funds and derivatives, using the same tools and techniques as the professional investor.

The Four Pillars of Investing: Lessons for Building a Winning Portfolio

William J. Bernstein
New York: McGraw-Hill, 2002
316pp, ISBN: 978-0-07-138529-9

This investment guide presents the necessary concepts, tools, and processes for constructing a successful portfolio, combining market history, investing theory, and behavioral finance for achieving long-term investing success. It describes historical and market data, risk and reward in the capital markets, how to mix different asset classes in a portfolio, and the dangers of picking individual stocks.

Fundology: The Secrets of Successful Fund Investing

John Chatfeild-Roberts
Petersfield, UK: Harriman House, 2006
166pp, ISBN: 978-1-897597-77-4

This explains the essentials of fund investing, while avoiding the common mistakes that can lead to poor results. Focusing on unit trusts and open-ended investment companies, it explains how to buy and sell investment funds in a clear style, why funds are a good investment, how unit trusts and OEICs work, how to pick the best managers, and how to become an expert fund investor.

Global Perspectives on Investment Management: Learning from the Leaders

Rodney N. Sullivan (editor)
Charlottesville, Virginia: CFA Institute, 2007
352pp, ISBN: 978-1-932495-64-5

This presents a range of practical new ideas and fundamental areas of concern in investment management from some of the leading experts in the industry. It re-evaluates some key assumptions about investments, markets, and decision-making, and covers such topics as risk management and uncertainty, seeking value in equities, the corporate debt market, and the role of commodities in portfolios.

How to Create and Manage a Mutual Fund or Exchange-Traded Fund: A Professional's Guide

Melinda Gerber
Wiley Finance Series
Hoboken, New Jersey: Wiley, 2008
351pp, ISBN: 978-0-470-12055-2

This guide to mutual funds and exchange-traded funds presents a complete business plan for their launch and management, describing each stage, from initial idea to selling shares. It discusses the importance of profiling customers and identifying the competition, picking the team, producing a diverse marketing plan, and assesses new products, regulations, scandals, the inclusion of timelines, and common mistakes to avoid.

The Intelligent Investor: The Classic Text on Value Investing

Benjamin Graham
New York: HarperBusiness, 2005
269pp, ISBN: 978-0-06-075261-3

This bestselling book, first published in 1949, is written by the revered investment expert and father of value investing. It explains his methodology for shielding investors from error, buying stocks at less than their intrinsic value, and developing long-term investment strategies. This paperback edition contains a commentary that relates Graham's ideas to current market practices, as well as reinforcing some of his teachings and principles.

Investment Banking and Investment Opportunities in China: A Comprehensive Guide for Finance Professionals

K. Thomas Liaw
Hoboken, New Jersey: Wiley, 2007
560pp, ISBN: 978-0-470-04468-1

This comprehensive resource examines the Chinese investment banking industry, and the investment opportunities available in the financial services sector. It focuses on what information investors and bankers need to operate in business and the financial markets in China, and examines features of investment banking such as privatization and market reforms, growth and value investing, and financial instruments for foreign investors.

Investment Planning for Finance Professionals

Geoffrey A. Hirt, Stanley B. Block, Somnath Basu
New York: McGraw-Hill, 2006
369pp, ISBN: 978-0-07-143721-9

This comprehensive reference for financial

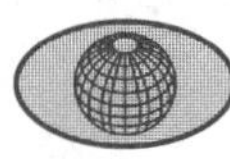

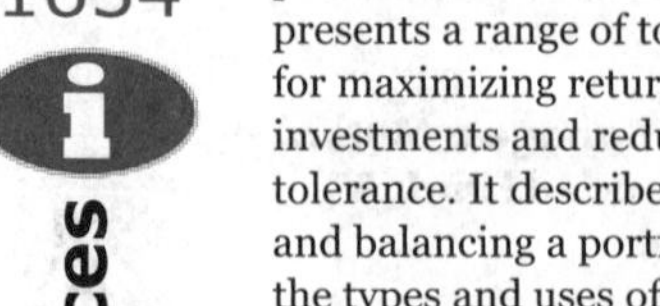

planners and investment professionals presents a range of tools, and techniques for maximizing returns on their clients' investments and reduce levels of risk tolerance. It describes ways of diversifying and balancing a portfolio of investments, the types and uses of investment vehicles, types and measures of investment risk, measures of investment returns, portfolio management and measurement concepts, and tax issues.

Investments, 8th ed
Zvi Bodie, Alex Kane, Alan J. Marcus
Boston, Massachusetts: McGraw-Hill/Irwin, 2009
1,056pp, ISBN: 978-0-07-338237-1
This is a leading textbook for graduate/MBA students of investment markets. It combines theoretical and practical coverage of the topic, and presents a unifying theme of security markets as nearly efficient, that most securities are usually priced appropriately given their risk and return attributes. It focuses on asset allocation, offering a broader treatment of futures, options, and other derivative security markets.

An Investor's Guide to Analysing Companies and Valuing Shares: How to Make the Right Investment Decision
Michael Cahill
London: FT Prentice Hall, 2003
278pp, ISBN: 978-0-273-66363-8
This analytical guide to share buying examines the decision-making process, based on a common sense investing approach, and the belief that a company's share price is determined by its fundamental value. It describes what to look for in assessing the real value of a business and its share price, emphasizing the importance of research, and how to understand the stock market's assessment of the company.

The Little Book of Common Sense Investing: The Only Way to Guarantee Your Fair Share of Stock Market Returns
John C. Bogle
Hoboken, New Jersey: Wiley, 2007
216pp, ISBN: 978-0-470-10210-7
This investment guide provides practical advice and strategies for investing in the long term, arguing that putting money into low-cost index funds is the best way to ensure greater stock market returns, and avoid investment costs, taxes, and inflation. Bogle eschews investing trends, describing how with index funds you actually own the entire market, creating a useful diversification of stocks.

Monkey Business: Swinging Through the Wall Street Jungle
John Rolfe, Peter Troob
New York: Warner Books, 2000
273pp, ISBN: 978-0-446-67695-3
Based on the authors' experiences as junior associates at a major investment bank, this exposé of life on Wall Street provides an entertaining snapshot of their daily routine, pitch book development, fee generation, and company valuation. It describes their extravagant lifestyles, as well as the mundane reality of their work, and why they could not last in that environment.

Mutual Fund Industry Handbook: A Comprehensive Guide for Investment Professionals
Lee Gremillion
Hoboken, New Jersey: Wiley, 2005
381pp, ISBN: 978-0-471-73624-0
This reference to mutual funds provides an overview of their history and structure, investment management, portfolio operations, accounting, auditing, compliance, distribution, globalization, e-commerce, and the trends affecting the industry. It also examines their benefits in offering professional management, easy diversification, liquidity, convenience, and regulatory protection, and includes real-life examples of how specific functions are performed at various firms.

One Up on Wall Street: How to Use What You Already Know to Make Money in the Market, 2nd ed
Peter Lynch
New York: Simon & Schuster, 2000
304pp, ISBN: 978-0-7432-0040-0
This classic guide to investing offers advice and effective rules for trading as a professional, explaining how investment opportunities can be discovered by observing ordinary, understandable businesses that are successful, and by reviewing a company's financial statements. It also describes how to beat the expert by identifying 'tenbaggers', stocks that appreciate tenfold or more, and provides guidelines for investing in cyclical, turnaround, and fast-growing companies.

Pioneering Portfolio Management: An Unconventional Approach to Institutional Investment, 2nd ed
David F. Swensen
New York: Free Press, 2009
432pp, ISBN: 978-1-4165-4469-2
This describes the investment process that underpins the author's own institutional investment success, and describes his often counterintuitive strategies for structuring a well-diversified equity-oriented portfolio. It analyzes asset-allocation structures, active fund management, as explores how to handle risk, select advisors, and survive market downturns, based on the key elements of trust, expertise, fortitude, and a long-term perspective.

A Random Walk Down Wall Street: The Time-Tested Srategy for Successful Investing, 9th ed
Burton G. Malkiel
New York: W. W. Norton, 2007
414pp, ISBN: 978-0-393-33033-5
This oft-updated, bestselling investment guide evaluates the full range of investment opportunities, from stocks, bonds, and money markets, to real estate investment trusts and insurance, home ownership, and tangible assets such as gold and collectibles. It presents the author's guide to investing throughout the life-cycle, with this edition including new analysis of behavioral finance, and insights into investment strategies for retirement.

Real Estate Finance & Investments, 13th ed
William B. Brueggeman, Jeffrey D. Fisher
Boston: McGraw-Hill, 2008
688pp, ISBN: 978-0-07-352471-9
This regularly revised and updated textbook on real estate finance and investments is a rigorous and practical overview of the tools needed to understand and analyze real estate markets and the investment alternatives available to both debt and equity investors. New content has been added on current trends in mortgage finance and investment techniques.

Smarter Investing: Simpler Decisions for Better Results
Tim Hale
Harlow, UK: FT Prentice Hall, 2006
371pp, ISBN: 978-0-273-70800-1
This accessible investment guide examines how to invest rationally and simply, to achieve better returns. It provides a simple and powerful approach to investing, helping you to build a balanced investment portfolio suited to your needs, emphasizing the importance of establishing what you want from your money, and how much you need to achieve your goals.

Stocks for the Long Run: The Definitive Guide to Financial Market Returns and Long Term Investment Strategies, 4th ed
Jeremy J. Siegel
New York: McGraw-Hill, 2008
380pp, ISBN: 978-0-07-149470-0
This popular guide to investing presents research, data, and analysis to support the case for an investment strategy based on understanding market forces, and building

a successful long-term portfolio that provides enhanced returns and reduced risk. It compares exchange-traded funds, mutual funds, and index options and futures, with this edition featuring new analysis of global investing, behavioral finance, and the latest index instruments.

Vault Career Guide to Investment Banking, 6th ed
Tom Lott
New York: Vault, 2008
176pp, ISBN: 978-1-58131-532-5
This handbook on working in the investment banking industry examines the fundamentals of the financial markets, such as walk-throughs of equity and fixed income offerings, and M&A private placements and reorganizations, and discusses career paths and job responsibilities in corporate finance, sales and trading, research, and syndicate.

The Warren Buffett Way, 2nd ed
Robert G. Hagstrom
Hoboken, New Jersey: Wiley, 2005
245pp, ISBN: 978-0-471-74367-5
This describes Buffett's life, business career, and investment principles, strategies, and practices, detailing the companies he has invested in and why, his value investing approach, and how he built up his fortune over the years. It also examines his perspective on long-term investing, speculation on traditional and understandable businesses, portfolio management, and the influence of investment experts such as Benjamin Graham on his investment philosophy.

When Markets Collide: Investment Strategies for the Age of Global Economic Change
Mohamed El-Erian
New York: McGraw-Hill, 2008
344pp, ISBN: 978-0-07-159281-9
This examination of the current financial turbulence argues that the upheaval is due to a collision between historical markets and future ones, and describes where the evolving economic landscape can provide investment opportunities. It shows how to differentiate between random noise and key investment signals, the increasing role of China in the global economy, and how to allocate assets on a long-term basis.

MAGAZINES

Barron's
Dow Jones & Company
200 Liberty Street, 9th Floor, New York, NY 10281, USA
T: +1 212 416 2000
online.barrons.com
ISSN: 1077-8039
This respected weekly consumer magazine provides news, commentary, market analyses, insights, and statistics on companies, industries, sectors, the economy, and financial markets for individual investors, institutional investors, financial professionals, and senior corporate decision-makers. It also features stock picks and pans, markets, technology, funds, portfolio, data and tools, and a daily stock alert.

CFA Magazine
CFA Institute
PO Box 3668, Charlottesville, VA 22903, USA
T: +1 434 951 5499
F: +1 434 951 5262
www.cfapubs.org/loi/cfm
This is a bimonthly, practice-based, professional member magazine, which updates members on CFA Institute initiatives, and presents local financial reporting and regulatory developments, industry coverage, debate, and technical articles on practical applications.

Global Investor
Euromoney Institutional Investor
Nestor House, Playhouse Yard, London, EC4V 5EX, UK
T: +44 (0) 20 7779 8610
F: +44 (0) 20 7779 8602
www.globalinvestormagazine.com
ISSN: 0951-3604
This respected monthly specialist magazine is aimed at global investment management professionals, and examines the latest developments in the financial markets from an investor's perspective. It focuses on the full range of topics related to international investment, and features a range of supplements, people moves, a summary of mandate wins and corporate activity, opinion pieces, technical challenges, interviews, and profiles.

Institutional Investor
Institutional Investor
225 Park Ave South, New York, NY 10003, USA
T: +1 212 224 3300
www.iimagazine.com
ISSN: 0020-3580
This weekly global magazine for leading financiers, corporate executives and government officials offers market analysis and intelligence, breaking stories, a newsletter, and a range of proprietary research and rankings. It focuses on the capital markets, investing and trading, research, asset management, trading technology, pensions, international markets, and opinion.

International Investment
Incisive Media
Haymarket House, 28–29 Haymarket, London, SW1Y 4RX, UK
T: +44 (0) 20 7034 2600
www.intinv.com
This monthly magazine for international financial advisers covers fund launches, banking news, cross-border life-based investment services, and the latest regulatory and tax changes facing high-net worth individuals. It also news, features, and expert opinion on stock and bond markets, portfolio construction, performance analysis, and tax and legal issues.

Investment Dealers' Digest
SourceMedia
1 State Street Plaza, 26th Floor, New York, NY 10004, USA
T: +1 212 803 8333
www.iddmagazine.com
ISSN: 0021-0080
This weekly magazine provides news and analysis for investment bankers, to help them identify market opportunities and new deal structures. It offers late-breaking news, features, and key data on the financial markets, listings of newly registered securities and new issues, and league tables.

Investment Week
Incisive Media
Haymarket House, 28–29 Haymarket, London, SW1Y 4RX, UK
T: +44 (0) 20 7484 9700
F: +44 (0) 20 7484 9994
www.investmentweek.co.uk
ISSN: 1469-1876
This weekly magazine provides news, commentary, features, fund analysis, investment strategies and product analysis on all aspects of the investment industry for investment advisers, discretionary portfolio managers, fund of funds managers, heads of investment selection, and investment researchers. It also incorporates conferences, seminars, forums, an email bulletin, and awards.

Investors Chronicle
Financial Times
1 Southwark Bridge, London, SE1 9HL, UK
T: +44 (0) 20 7775 6582
F: +44 (0) 20 7775 6501

  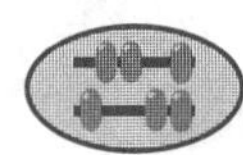   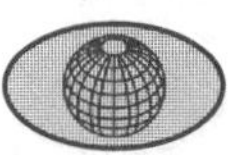   

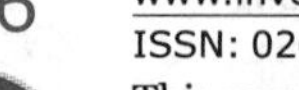

www.investorschronicle.co.uk
ISSN: 0261-3115
This respected weekly magazine provides private investors with weekly stock market analysis, offering feature articles on many aspects of successful investing, supplements on investment products, and a range of statistical and reference information.

JOURNALS

Financial Analysts Journal

CFA Institute
560 Ray C. Hunt Drive, Charlottesville, VA 22903-2981, USA
T: +1 434 951 5499
www.cfapubs.org/loi/faj
FAJ is a bimonthly publication of the CFA Institute that presents articles dedicated to the practice of investment management. It acts as a bridge between academic research and practice by offering academically rigorous papers of relevance to practitioners.

Journal of Alternative Investments

Institutional Investor
225 Park Avenue South, New York, NY 10003, USA
T: +1 212 224 3570
www.iijournals.com/JAI
ISSN: 1520-3255
This quarterly journal provides research and expert analysis on managing investments in hedge funds, private equity, distressed debt, commodities, futures, energy, funds of funds, and other non-traditional instruments. It examines the growth of hedge funds and alternatives, how to measure and track portfolio performance, and includes coverage of asset allocation, risk management, indexing, regulation and taxation.

Journal of Investing

Institutional Investor
225 Park Avenue South, New York, NY 10003, USA
T: +1 212 224 3570
F: +1 212 224 3197
www.iijournals.com/JOI
ISSN: 1068-0896
This quarterly journal for investment professionals offers research and analysis on maximizing assets and effective portfolio management, mutual funds, exchange-traded funds, asset allocation, and performance measurement. It also publishes papers on such areas as assessing the risk/return characteristics of traditional and alternative asset classes, effective strategies for structuring a global portfolio, identifying new market opportunities, and optimizing allocation in traditional and alternative investments.

Journal of Investment Compliance

Emerald Group Publishing
Howard House, Wagon Lane, Bingley, BD16 1WA, UK
T: +44 (0) 1274 777 700
F: +44 (0) 1274 785 201
www.emeraldinsight.com/Insight/viewContainer.do?containerType=JOURNAL&containerId=22667
ISSN: 1528-5812
JOIC is a quarterly professional journal that publishes articles on regulatory and compliance issues relevant to broker–dealers, investment advisers, mutual funds, hedge funds, and other types of investment companies. It offers practical advice on future directions for the industry and the compliance implications, and covers issues such as research analyst independence, employment law, registration with regulators, and preparing for regulatory examinations and investigations.

Journal of Money, Investment and Banking

EuroJournals
www.eurojournals.com/JMIB.htm
ISSN: 1450-288X
This bimonthly, international research journal publish both theoretical and empirical papers on issues relating to money, investment, international banking, and finance. It offers research papers, research notes, discussion articles, book reviews, software reviews, editorials, and letters on its core areas, as well as on financial economics, e-finance, financial analysis, risk management, financial derivatives, mathematical finance, financial accounting, financial engineering, and credit rating.

Journal of Portfolio Management

Institutional Investor
225 Park Avenue South, New York, NY 10003, USA
T: +1 212 224 3570
F: +1 212 224 3197
www.iijournals.com/JPM
ISSN: 0095-4918
This quarterly journal provides analysis and research on practical techniques in institutional investing, asset allocation, performance measurement, market trends, risk management, and portfolio optimization. It describes new and classic portfolio management techniques, with articles covering different products, equities, market behavior, international investing, and new asset classes.

Journal of Property Investment & Finance

Emerald Group Publishing
Howard House, Wagon Lane, Bingley, BD16 1WA, UK
T: +44 (0) 1274 777 700
F: +44 (0) 1274 785 201
www.emeraldinsight.com/Insight/viewContainer.do?containerType=Journal&containerId=12267
ISSN: 1463-578X
Published bimonthly, this journal provides information and ideas relating to property valuation and investment, property management, and decision-making in the commercial property market. It publishes papers by both academics and practitioners, covering the latest research, real estate law and new legislation, Internet sites and recent publications, market data, and changes in the property market.

INTERNET

Global Investor

www.global-investor.com
This is one of main online resources in the financial industry. It provides a range of investment sites, such as The Global Investor Bookshop and other branded bookshops for client websites, a popular financial glossary, information about financial events, conferences, and training, and offers courses on the investment techniques, and strategies.

Investegate

www.investegate.co.uk
This is a comprehensive online source of announcements from UK quoted companies, which presents regulatory and other published information, and offers company announcements feeds, as well as analysis of companies and sectors in the news, and a live features column.

Investing in Bonds

www.investinginbonds.com
This is a source of bond price information and other market data, news, commentary and information about bonds. It was founded by The Securities Industry and Financial Markets Association to help educate investors.

Investor Links

www.investorlinks.com
This is a financial resource website that offers a comprehensive financial directory, and links and descriptions to thousands of

  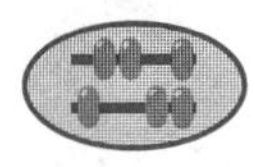 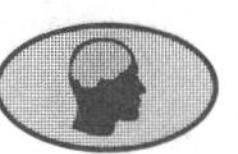  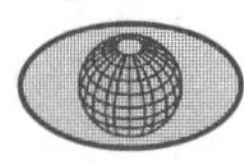   

financial websites. It also provides a portfolio tracker, e-mailed news alerts, message boards, stock quotes, and indices.

ORGANIZATIONS

Europe

Alternative Investment Management Association
Chair: Florence Lombard
2nd Floor, 167 Fleet Street, London, EC4A 2EA, UK
T: +44 (0) 20 7822 8380
www.aima.org
This is international, not-for-profit, trade association represents nearly 1,300 corporate members worldwide, including hedge fund managers, fund of hedge funds managers, prime brokers, legal and accounting services, and fund administrators. The association influences policy development, industry initiatives, and is involved in regulation. It also focuses on developing industry skills and education standards, and is a co-founder of the Chartered Alternative Investment Analyst designation (CAIA).

The Association of Investment Companies
9th Floor, 24 Chiswell Street, London, EC1Y 4YY, UK
T: +44 (0) 20 7282 5555
F: +44 (0) 20 7282 5556
E: enquiries@theaic.co.uk
www.theaic.co.uk
AIC is the trade organization for the closed-ended investment company industry. It represents a broad range of closed-ended investment companies, incorporating investment trusts, offshore investment companies, and venture capital trusts which are traded on the London Stock Exchange, AIM, and Euronext. It supports the development of the investment company market, helps directors discharge their obligations to shareholders, and works with management groups and the wider industry.

The Association of Private Client Investment Managers and Stockbrokers
Chair: David Bennett
22 City Road, Finsbury Square, London, EC1Y 2AJ, UK
T: +44 (0) 20 7448 7100
F: +44 (0) 20 7638 4636
E: info@apcims.co.uk
www.apcims.co.uk
APCIMS is the trade association of wealth management and broking firms who provide services to private investors. It promotes the interests of its members with governments, regulators, financial institutions, and all participants in financial services, and provides information and assistance to members across a wide range of regulatory, market, and business issues.

Association of Solicitors and Investment Managers
Riverside House, River Lawn Road, Tonbridge, Kent, TN9 1EP, UK
T: +44 (0) 1732 783 548
F: +44 (0) 1732 362 626
www.asim.org.uk
ASIM is a non-profit organization that supports the provision of high-quality investment management services by firms of solicitors and investment firms. It runs training programs on regulatory and investment issues, and provides a forum through which members can exchange information and experience on commonly encountered portfolio investment service issues.

The CFA Society of the UK
Chair: Joe Biernat
2nd Floor, 135 Cannon Street, London, EC4N 5BP, UK
T: +44 (0) 20 7280 9620
F: +44 (0) 20 7280 9636
E: info@cfauk.org
www.cfauk.org
CFA UK, part of the Chartered Financial Analyst Institute, leads the development of the investment profession in the UK through the promotion of the high standards of ethical behavior, and the provision of education, professional development, information, career support, and advocacy on behalf of its members.

European Fund and Asset Management Association
Chair: Mathias Bauer
Square de Meeus 18, 1050 Brussels, Belgium
T: +32 2 513 3969
F: +32 2 513 2643
www.efama.org
EFAMA is the representative association for the European investment and asset management industry, representing its member associations and corporate members. It aims include supporting investor protection through the promotion of high ethical standards, integrity and professionalism in the industry, promoting the completion of an effective single market for investment management, strengthening the competitiveness of the industry, and promoting relevant scientific research.

Investment Management Association
65 Kingsway, London, WC2B 6TD, UK
T: +44 (0) 20 7831 0898
F: +44 (0) 20 7831 9975
E: ima@investmentuk.org
www.investmentuk.org
IMA's aims are to improve the legal, regulatory and fiscal environment in which its members operate, maintain and enhance the reputation and standing of the industry, and provide a center of excellence for the development of knowledge and understanding of the industry. Its principles are based on customer focus, accountability, responsible stewardship, professionalism, efficiency, and transparency.

London Investment Banking Association
Chair: Jonathan Taylor
6 Frederick's Place, London, EC2R 8BT, UK
T: +44 (0) 20 7796 3606
F: +44 (0) 20 7796 4345
E: liba@liba.org.uk
www.liba.org.uk
LIBA is the trade association in the United Kingdom for firms active in the investment banking and wholesale securities industry. It acts to promote its members' views to legislators, regulators, and opinion-formers, works with other trade associations, provides a forum for the exchange of views, promotes London as a location for the conduct of investment banking business, and represents the London offices of investment banks from around the world.

Securities & Investment Institute
Chair: Scott Dobbie
8 Eastcheap, London, EC3M 1AE, UK
T: +44 (0) 20 7645 0600
F: +44 (0) 20 7645 0601
www.sii.org.uk
The SII is a professional body for those in the securities and investment industry in the UK and around the world. It promotes the advancement and dissemination of knowledge in securities and investments, develops high ethical standards for practitioners in securities and investments, and acts as an authoritative body for the purpose of consultation and research in matters of education or public interest concerning investment in securities.

     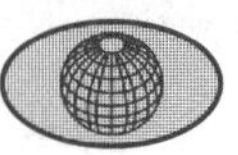   

USA

CFA Institute

Chair: John D. Rogers
560 Ray C. Hunt Drive, Charlottesville, VA 22903-2981, USA
T: +1 434 951 5499
E: info@cfainstitute.org
www.cfainstitute.org

This is a major, global, non-profit association for the global investment community. It provides a range of educational opportunities online and around the world, strives to make the financial markets equitable, free, and efficient, works on behalf of the ultimate investor, and fosters high ethical principles and self-regulatory standards.

The Chartered Alternative Investment Analyst Association

Chair: Peter Douglas
29 South Pleasant Street, Amherst, MA 01002, USA
T: +1 413 253 7373
F: +1 413 253 4494
E: info@caia.org
www.caia.org

The CAIA is an independent, not-for-profit, global organization that is committed to education and professionalism in the field of alternative investments. It provides information on alternative investments, promotes professional development through education, advocates high standards of professional conduct, and is the sponsoring body for the CAIA designation, the educational standard for the alternative investment industry.

Investment Recovery Association

638 West 39th Street, Kansas City, MO 64111, USA
T: +1 816 561 5323
F: +1 816 561 1991
E: info@invrecovery.org
www.invrecovery.org

This is the professional association for managers of surplus and idle assets, and acts as a resource for companies and individuals engaged in profit-driven asset management. It aims to assist members and their companies make the most of their past investments through strategic use of recycling, redeployment, reselling, and other techniques.

New York Society of Security Analysts

Chair: Jan Jackrel
1177 Avenue of the Americas, 2nd Floor, New York, NY 10036-2714, USA
T: +1 212 541 4530
F: +1 212 541 4677
E: staff@nyssa.org
www.nyssa.org

NYSSA is a non-profit educational organization that provides a forum for the investment community. It aims to establish and maintain a high standard of professional ethics in the security analysis field, improve analytical techniques, foster the interchange of ideas and information among security analysts, and promote proper understanding of the function of financial and security analysis and the operation of the security markets.

Professional Association for Investment Communications Resources

Chair: Lisa Bosley
191 Clarksville Road, Princeton Junction, NJ 08550, USA
T: +1 609 799 4382
F: +1 609 799 7032
www.paicr.com

PAICR is a non-profit organization that aims to empower investment marketing and communications professionals through opportunities for professional development, continuing education and networking at association events throughout North America.

International

Investment and Financial Services Association

Chair: David Deverall
Level 24, 44 Market Street, Sydney NSW 2000, Australia
T: +61 2 9299 3022
F: +61 2 299 3198
E: ifsa@ifsa.com.au
www.ifsa.com.au

IFSA is a non-profit organization that represents the retail and wholesale funds management, superannuation, and life insurance industries. It aims to assist in the development of the social, economic and regulatory framework in which their members operate, thereby assisting members to serve their customers better.

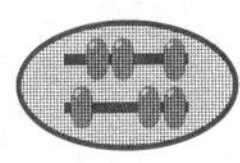

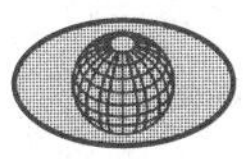

Islamic Finance

BOOKS

Critical Issues on Islamic Banking and Financial Markets: Islamic Economics, Banking and Finance, Investments, Takaful and Financial Planning

Saiful Azhar Rosly
Bloomington, Indiana: AuthorHouse, 2005
618pp, ISBN: 978-1-4184-6930-6

This is an accessible guide to modern Islamic finance, which provides a practical discussion of the underlying principles of *shariah* financial instruments, and Islamic banking, insurance, and fund management. It examines the growth of Islamic funds and transactions, and their integration into the international financial system, and explains key concepts and terms, such as *shariah, sukuk, riba, al-bay',* and *maisir*.

Financial Risk Management for Islamic Banking and Finance

Ioannis Akkizidis, Sunil Kumar Khandelwal
New York: Palgrave Macmillan, 2008
300pp, ISBN: 978-0-230-55381-1

This guide to risk management in Islamic finance presents a methodology for assessing and managing risk in *shariah*-compliant financial products and services. It details how to practically implement a risk management framework for Islamic financial institutions, to manage the increase in financial products and services, and number of Islamic financial institutions managing funds.

A Guide to Islamic Finance

Munawar Iqbal
London: Risk Books, 2007
118pp, ISBN: 978-1-904339-85-4

This focused and practical report explains the basic theory, practice, and limitations of Islamic banking and finance. It shows how to develop products that comply with Islamic principles, that perform financial intermediation functions without the involvement of interest, and explains the objectives and sources of Islamic law and the guidelines for business contracts, and offers an extensive glossary of relevant Arabic terms.

Handbook of Islamic Banking

M. Kabir Hassan, Mervyn K. Lewis (editors)
Cheltenham, UK: Edward Elgar Publishing, 2007
443pp, ISBN: 978-1-84542-083-3

This authoritative handbook examines how Islamic banking and finance operates, and assesses its role within the international banking and capital markets, as an alternative to conventional interest-based financing methods. It details the variety of financial instruments and investment vehicles, and other key topics such as governance and risk management, securities and investment, structured financing, accounting and regulation, economic development, and globalization.

The International Handbook of Islamic Banking and Finance

Elisabeth Jackson-Moore
London: Global Professional Publishing, 2009
300pp, ISBN: 978-1-906403-31-7

This comprehensive guide provides an overview of current practices in Islamic banking and finance, and the essential elements of *shariah* compliance. It examines the issues faced by bankers, scholars, regulators and others interested in understanding the objectives and challenges of Islamic finance and its growing role in the global financial markets.

Introduction to Islamic Banking and Finance

Brian Kettell
London: Islamic Banking Training, 2008
251pp, ISBN: 978-0-9558351-0-0

This comprehensive primer to Islamic banking and finance details the fundamental points of convergence and divergence between *shariah*-compliant finance and conventional interest-based finance. It analyzes the key principles, components, and techniques of the industry, the introduction of services free from interest, and the use of profit and loss sharing as a method of resource allocation and financial intermediation.

An Introduction to Islamic Finance: Theory and Practice

Zamir Iqbal, Abbas Mirakhor
Wiley Finance Series
Singapore: Wiley, 2007
332pp, ISBN: 978-0-470-82188-6

This is a concise resource on the fundamental principles of Islamic finance, an economic and financial system governed by *shariah* Islamic law. It provides guidance and insight on all of main essential topics, products, and processes, discusses the context of Islamic finance within modern finance and banking practices, and examines Islamic tenets that influence economic behavior in the fast growing Islamic financial services industry.

Islamic Economics and Finance: A Glossary, 2nd ed

Muhammad A. Khan
London: Routledge, 2003
195pp, ISBN: 978-0-415-45925-9

An updated and enlarged edition of this useful glossary, it explains terms used in Islamic banking, taxation, insurance, accounting, and auditing by Muslim scholars, historians and legal experts, from Arabic, Urdu, Turkish, Malaysian, and English sources. It provides a reference for all interested in Islamic economics and finance, including economists, bankers, accountants, students and researchers.

Islamic Finance: A Guide for International Business and Investment

Roderick Millar, Habiba Anwar (editors)
London: GMB Publishing, 2008
216pp, ISBN: 978-1-84673-078-8

This guide to Islamic financial practice aimed at banking professionals and corporate investors examines the tenets of Islamic investment that exclude areas such as gambling, alcohol, weapons, and products that are high-risk and high-return. It analyzes the differences between Islamic and conventional banking, and the reasons for investors and asset managers becoming increasingly attracted to financial products and the institutions that comply with *shariah* principles.

Islamic Finance: A Practical Guide

Rahail Ali (editor)
London: Globe Law and Business, 2008
175pp, ISBN: 978-1-905783-13-7

This practitioner approach to Islamic finance analyzes market trends, key developments and structures for sukuk, syndications, types of *shariah*-compliant fund, takaful, project financing, and Islamic liquidity management, as well as the relevant legal issues. It provides a practical guide for sovereigns, financial institutions, multinationals, and corporates on the essentials of Islamic finance, including Islamic bonds, and corporate, retail, and acquisition.

Islamic Finance in the Global Economy, 2nd ed

Ibrahim Warde
Edinburgh, UK: Edinburgh University Press, 2008
272pp, ISBN: 978-0-7486-2777-6

  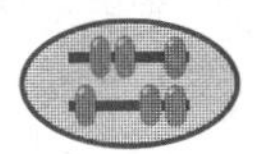   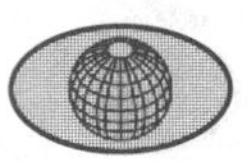   

This is a comprehensive reference to the political economy of Islamic finance, for those interested in Islamic and Middle Eastern economics, business and finance. It provides an overview of modern Islamic finance, analyzes the connection between Islamic finance and politics, explores the underlying economic, cultural, and political principles, and discusses Islamic finance in the context of the global political and economic system.

Islamic Finance: Law, Economics, and Practice

Mahmoud A. El-Gamal
Cambridge, UK: Cambridge University Press, 2006
221pp, ISBN: 978-0-521-74126-2

This is an overview of Islamic finance practices, which analyzes the constraints that Islam imposes on financial relations in attempting to replicate financial instruments, markets, and institutions, arguing that this is failing to serve the objectives of Islamic law. Instead, it proposes a fundamental reform in Islamic finance, to focus more on issues of community banking, micro-finance, and socially responsible investment.

Islamic Finance: The Regulatory Challenge

Rifaat Ahmed Abdel Karim, Simon Archer (editors)
Wiley Finance Series
Singapore: Wiley, 2007
418pp, ISBN: 978-0-470-82189-3

This examines the regulatory aspects of Islamic finance, and the development of structured regulatory, supervisory, and legal frameworks appropriate for the Islamic financial services industry worldwide. It discusses principles of Islamic commercial jurisprudence, the role of the Islamic Financial Services Board, the potential for growth in Islamic financial services, corporate governance and supervision issues, and the nature of risk in Islamic banking.

Islamic Retail Banking and Finance: Global Challenges and Opportunities

Jaffer Sohail (editor)
London: Euromoney Books, 2005
222pp, ISBN: 978-1-84374-198-5

This is an international treatment of Islamic finance and banking, which details the development of the sector over the last few years, and issues such as the increasing focus by Western banks on Islamic financial services, and Islamic retail banking in Europe. It provides an overview of the creation of Islamic mortgages, savings, insurance, and retail investment products in terms of increasing competition with conventional financial products, and their basis in Islamic law.

A Mini Guide to Islamic Banking & Finance

Centre for Research and Training
Kuala Lumpur, Malaysia: CERT Publications, 2006
123pp, ISBN: 978-983-42785-4-0

This concise introduction to Islamic banking, finance, and accountancy examines the basic requirements, obligatory prohibitions, and *shariah*-compliant transactions, as well as permissible investment and insurance alternatives. It also offers a useful set of Q&As, bibliography, and glossary.

New Issues in Islamic Finance and Economics: Progress and Challenges

Hossein Askari, Zamir Iqbal, Abbas Mirakhor
Wiley Finance Series
Hoboken, New Jersey: Wiley, 2008
320pp, ISBN: 978-0-470-82293-7

This review of the main issues and challenges facing Islamic finance focuses on governance, institutions, public finance, and economic development within an Islamic financial system. It looks at the development of Islamic finance, and argues that its future success will depend on factors such as economic and financial reform in Islamic countries, institutional reform, governance and regulatory oversight, and research into suitable financial products.

The Politics of Islamic Finance

Clement Henry, Rodney Wilson (editors)
Edinburgh, UK: Edinburgh University Press, 2004
307pp, ISBN: 978-0-7486-1837-8

This exploration of the political aspects of Islamic finance examines the experiences of Islamic banking in a range of countries, and the political implications of the increase in Islamic capital. It also explores the connections between Islamic finance and Islamic political movements, the perceived connection between Islamic finance and money laundering and terrorism, and common misconceptions about Islamic banking and finance.

Risk Analysis for Islamic Banks

Hennie van Greuning, Zamir Iqbal
Washington, DC: World Bank Publications, 2007
330pp, ISBN: 978-0-8213-7141-1

This is a focused exploration of the assessment, analysis, and management of various types of risks in the field of Islamic banking. It introduces a high-level framework that takes into account the current realities of changing economies and Islamic financial markets, and discusses the accountability of key players in the corporate governance process in terms of the management of different dimensions of Islamic financial risk.

Structuring Islamic Finance Transactions

Thomas Abdulkader, Stella Cox, Bryan Kraty (editors)
London: Euromoney Books, 2005
234pp, ISBN: 978-1-84374-213-5

This explains the fundamental principles of Islamic finance instruments and compliance with Islamic law in the context of recent financial developments and the growth of Islamic financial institutions. It discusses the complex structures and applications of Islamic transactions, such as sukuk and debt-like products, risk management and derivative-like products, and the emerging regulatory environment for Islamic finance products and transactions.

Understanding Islamic Banking: The Value Proposition that Transcends Cultures

Joseph A. DiVanna
Cambridge, UK: Leonardo and Francis Press, 2006
174pp, ISBN: 978-1-905687-00-8

This is a guide to the principles and practice of Islamic banking, which provides a framework for contemporary retail banks to be accessible for investors of any faith. It also explores the essentials of a bank's value proposition, such as brand, innovation, investment strategy, and shareholder and consumer value, as attributes of Islamic banking identifiable by Muslims and non-Muslims.

Understanding Islamic Finance

Muhammad Ayub
Wiley Finance Series
Hoboken, New Jersey: Wiley, 2007
516pp, ISBN: 978-0-470-03069-1

This introduction to Islamic finance explains all the key concepts, principles, products, and processes of this growing market. It presents a clear background and history, exploring how the concepts are rooted in Islamic law, the Islamic economic system, and *shariah* compliance. It discusses Islamic economics as a rule-base system better understood as a set of contracts, and examines how to design financial instruments compatible with Islamic jurisprudence.

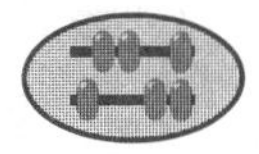

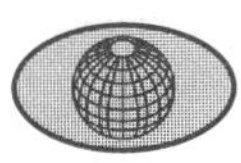

MAGAZINES

Arab Banker

The Arab Bankers Association
43 Upper Grosvenor Street, London, W1K 2NJ, UK
T: +44 (0) 20 7659 4889
F: +44 (0) 20 7659 4658
www.arab-banker.com
ISSN: 0261-2925

This journal, published twice yearly by The Arab Bankers' Association, covers current affairs, commentary, people in the news, company news, and bank results.

Islamic Banking & Finance

New Millennium Publishing
Suite 3, 20 Old Steine, Brighton, East Sussex, BN1 1EL, UK
T: +44 (0) 560 116 9695
F: +44 (0) 700 603 4010
www.islamicbankingandfinance.com
ISSN: 1814-8042

This magazine, published six times each year, reports on all aspects of Islamic banking and finance, and core topics such as takaful, law, software, and property. It features news, analysis, micro-finance, viewpoints, business scope, latest products and services, data from the latest Dow Jones Islamic Market Indices, and regular special country reports.

Islamic Finance Asia

REDmoney
21/F, Menara KUB, 12, Jalan Yap Kwan Seng, 50450 Kuala Lumpur, Malaysia
T: +603 2162 7800
F: +603 2162 7810
www.islamicfinanceasia.com

This bimonthly global magazine is distributed free to all qualified corporate individuals within the Islamic finance market. It provides research and commentary on takaful and retakaful, retails, ratings, and funds, and features information a review of Asian and global activity, as well as reviews, moves, and events.

Islamic Finance News

REDmoney
21/F, Menara KUB, 12, Jalan Yap Kwan Seng, 50450 Kuala Lumpur, Malaysia
T: +603 2162 7800
F: +603 2162 7810
www.islamicfinancenews.com

This weekly e-newsletter focuses on the global Islamic financing market and related instruments. It produces news briefs, detailed country and industry sector reports, a research review, retail news, legal updates, and information on moves and promotions, events and training courses, and league tables. Its website carries all content from the newsletter, in addition to useful supplements, books, directories, and a database.

Quantum

Qatar Financial Centre Authority, Qatar
T: +44 (0) 20 8670 1922
www.quantummagazine.com

This quarterly magazine presents a global perspective in its analysis of significant international and regional trends in the financial services industry. It encourages debate, and provides a forum for leading decision makers to present arguments and challenge conventional wisdoms. Its contributors include senior market practitioners, analysts, academics, and journalists

True Banking

Al Huda Center of Islamic Banking and Islamic Economics
Suite 9, 2nd Floor, Gohar Center, Wahdat Road, Lahore, India
T: +92 42 591 2771
F: +92 42 585 8990
www.truebanking.com.pk

This is a monthly magazine dedicated to the banking and financial services sector, focusing on industry news and analysis, new financial products, research and development, market analysis, training, and education in Islamic banking, takaful, and investment.

JOURNALS

International Journal of Islamic and Middle Eastern Finance and Management

Emerald Group Publishing
Howard House, Wagon Lane, Bingley, BD16 1WA, UK
T: +44 (0) 1274 777700
F: +44 (0) 1274 785201
info.emeraldinsight.com/products/journals/journals.htm?PHPSESSID=h9u03shl0m0hbmigiqibd1kf10&id=imefm
ISSN: 1753-8394

This quarterly journal provides original research and analysis into the growth of Islamic banking, finance and financial services, and personal finance, including hedge funds, Islamic bonds, retail and corporate lines of Islamic credit and derivatives, mortgages, auto financing, and consumer finance. It offers dedicated sections on news, new products, market/sector reports, and extended book reviews.

Islamic Economic Bulletin

4\1914, Faridi House, S. S. Nagar, Aligarh, 202002, India
T: +91 571 240 1028

This academic newsletter, published six times each year by the Indian Association for Islamic Economics, aims to create awareness of the latest development in theory and practice of Islamic economics.

Islamic Economic Studies

Islamic Research and Training Institute
PO Box 9201, Jeddah 21413, Saudi Arabia
T: +966 2636 1400
F: +966 2637 8927
www.irti.org/irj/portal/anonymous/IRTIJournal

This journal, published biannually in Muharram and Rajab, according to the Islamic calendar, offers papers that make a contribution to Islamic economics, either theoretical or applied, or discuss an economic issue from an Islamic perspective.

Journal of Islamic Banking & Finance

International Association of Islamic Banks

This quarterly journal publishes research and analysis of Islamic principles relating to banking, finance and economics, and produces reports about financial institutions and banks in Middle East and other Islamic countries.

The Review of Islamic Economics

International Association of Islamic Economics and the Islamic Foundation
Markfield Conference Centre, Ratby Lane, Markfield, Leicestershire, LE67 9SY, UK
T: +44 (0) 1530 244 944
F: +44 (0) 1530 244 946
www.islamic-foundation.org.uk
ISSN: 0962-2055

This biannual journal, published by the International Association of Islamic Economics and the Islamic Foundation, presents research articles in the field of Islamic economics, banking and finance. It focuses on theoretical issues in economics dealt with from an Islamic perspective, empirical studies about the economies of Muslim countries, applied Islamic economics, and survey articles in various fields of Islamic economics.

INTERNET

American Journal of Islamic Finance

ajif.org

American Journal of Islamic Finance is an online resource on Islamic Finance, which provides a range of useful information on the operations of Islamic banking, securities, and finance. It offers research papers on subjects such as money management, capital markets, economics, regulation, and treasury.

  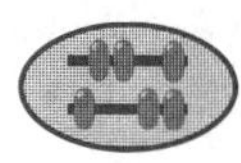   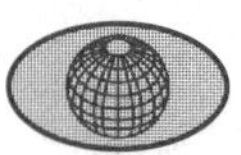   

Islam Online
www.islamonline.com/news/category.php?catid=10
This respected information resource includes a section covering the Islamic finance and banking industry, offering news from a variety of sources.

The Islamic Banker
www.theislamicbanker.com
This is a respected, professional online magazine covering the Islamic financial services industry. It focuses on promoting the Islamic banking industry, enhancing employee and organizational performance through the provision of Islamic financial news, information, and details about events and conferences.

Islamic Banking & Finance News
www.alhudacibe.com/magdetail.php
This monthly online magazine has the objective of promoting a better awareness of the Islamic banking and finance industry worldwide. It provides national and international news, analysis, research, interviews, round table discussions, product reviews, and partners with different international Islamic financial institutions to offer Islamic banking and finance information services to financial institutions.

Islamic Banking, Investment & Takaful
islamic-finance.startpagina.nl
This useful references contains more than 300 links in the field of Islamic finance, detailing news, studies, forum, shared risk/ethical banking, economics, finance index, jobs, risk management, networks, and advisors.

The Islamic Banking Portal
www.islamicbanking.com
This portal provides a comprehensive and useful list of Islamic banks and financial institutions, and gathers news from a variety of international sources.

Islamic Banks and Financial Institutions Information
www.ibisonline.net
This online portal is targeted at researchers and finance professionals working in the area of Islamic economics and finance. It provides data, information, research, and literature on the activities of Islamic finance institutions, and offers an Islamic banks database, and tools for online analysis and download.

Islamic Business & Finance Network
www.iiibf.org
IBF Net is a global network of students, researchers, bankers, and finance professionals interested in Islamic business and finance. It offers an online discussion forum, and sponsors the International Institute of Islamic Business and Finance in their educational, training, and publication programs in India and overseas.

Islamic Finance Information Source
www.securities.com/ifis
This information resource provides key Islamic research, and features newswatch, company information, Islamic bonds, Islamic banking, Islamic deals and transactions, Islamic capital markets and Islamic investments, Islamic funds, Islamic insurance, and Islamic finance league tables.

Islamic-Finance.com
www.islamic-finance.com
This is an independent online resource that features news and commentary, as well articles, research, institutional information, market updates, a glossary, and details of events, books, jobs, resources.

Islamicity
www.islamicity.com/finance
This website aims to encourage international understanding of Islam and Muslims, and offers a wide range of information and services, including financial news, products, banking, loans, investment, insurance.

ORGANIZATIONS

Europe

Academy for International Modern Studies
244 Robin Hood Lane, Blue Bell Hill, Chatham, Kent, ME5 9JY, UK
www.learnislamicfinance.com
AIMS is an international organization that promotes industry professionalism and best practice in Islamic banking and finance. Their academic partnership program, developed in response to the growth in the Islamic finance industry, is led by a committee of Islamic *shariah* scholars, and they offer customized training programs, seminars, workshops, and several certifications on areas of Islamic banking, finance and insurance.

The Arab Bankers Association
Chair: George Kardouche
43 Upper Grosvenor Street, London, W1K 2NJ, UK
T: +44 (0) 20 7659 4889
F: +44 (0) 20 7659 4658
E: arab-bankers@btconnect.com
www.arab-bankers.co.uk
This association seeks to develop ties between Arab professionals working in the financial services sector, and encourages the exchange of views, information, and expertise between the banking and financial sectors in the Arab world, and their counterparts in the United Kingdom and other countries. It also provides services to the Arab banking and financial community, and fosters an awareness of recent financial developments in the region.

Institute of Islamic Banking and Insurance
12–14 Barkat House, 116–118 Finchley Road, London, NW3 5HT, UK
T: +44 (0) 20 7245 0404
F: +44 (0) 20 7245 9769
E: iibi@islamic-banking.com
www.islamic-banking.com
This UK-based organization provides professional education, training, research, and related activities with the purpose of increasing knowledge and understanding of Islamic principles in international finance. It contributes to the education and training of people in Islamic banking and insurance through a post-graduate diploma course, publications, lectures, seminars, workshops, research, *shariah* advisory services, and a website.

International

Accounting and Auditing Organization for Islamic Financial Institutions
Block 304, Al Muthana Road, Yateem Center, Building 71, 4th Floor, Office 403, Manama, Bahrain
T: +973 244 496
F: +973 250 194
E: aaoifi@batelco.com.bh
www.aaoifi.com
AAOIFI is an Islamic independent, international, non-profit organization that prepares accounting, auditing, governance, ethics, and *shariah* standards for Islamic financial institutions and the industry, and which also offers professional qualification programs.

  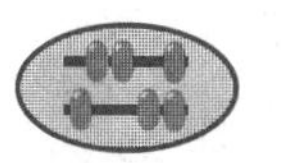  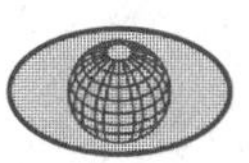   

Al Huda Center of Islamic Banking and Islamic Economics
Chair: M. Zubair Mughal
Suite 9, 2nd Floor, Gohar Center, Wahdat Road, Lahore, India
T: +92 42 591 2771
F: +92 42 585 8990
E: info@alhudacibe.com
www.alhudacibe.com
This organization provides education, training, workshops, awareness, and practice

Association of Islamic Banking Institutions Malaysia
Chair: Dato' Zukri Samat
23rd Floor, Menara Tradewinds (Menara Tun Razak), Jalan Raja Laut, 50350 Kuala Lumpur, Malaysia
T: +60 3 2694 8002
F: +60 3 2694 8012
E: admin@aibim.com
www.aibim.com
on Islamic banking, finance, takaful, and sukuk, mostly in Pakistan. It aims to train and develop bankers and finance professionals in the spiritual and intellectual heritage of Islam, and promote professional growth in this sector.

The General Council for Islamic Banks and Financial Institutions
Chair: Saleh Kamel
www.islamicfi.com
This is an international, non-profit organization formed jointly by the Islamic Development Bank and other Islamic financial institutions to improve the public awareness of Islamic *shariah* concepts, rules, and provisions related to the development of the Islamic financial industry. It works to enhance cooperation among its members, and provides information related to Islamic financial institutions.

International Association of Islamic Banks
Saudi Arabia
This association promotes links amongst Islamic financial institutions, and promotes cooperation in the industry. It also fosters the concept of Islamic banking, coordinates with Islamic banks to resolve common problems, provides assistance in manpower development, maintains a databank of all Islamic financial institutions, offers technical assistance in Islamic banking, and represents the interests of Islamic banks at all levels.

International Institute of Islamic Business & Finance
G-51/3-B Fourth Floor, Abul Fazal Enclave II, Shaheen Bagh, Okhla, New Delhi 110025, India
T: +91 989 102 9390
E: shafeeq@iiibf.org
www.iiibf.org
IIIBF, sponsored by IBF Net, offers education, training, workshops, seminars, and publication programs in India and overseas.

International Islamic Financial Market
Chair: Khalid Hamad
PO Box 11454, Bahrain Tower, Office 171, 17th Floor, Building 20, Al Khalifa Avenue Block 305, Road 385, Manama, Bahrain
T: +973 17 500 161
F: +973 17 500 171
E: iifm@batelco.com.bh
www.iifm.net
IIFM is an organization founded by the central banks and monetary agencies of several countries, which advocates the establishment, development, self-regulation, and promotion of Islamic capital and money markets. It focuses on the advancement and standardisation of Islamic financial instrument structures, contracts, product development, and infrastructure, as well as the issuance of guidelines and recommendations for the enhancement of Islamic capital and money markets globally.

Islamic Banking and Finance Institute Malaysia
Chair: Tan Sri Dato' Sri Dr. Zeti Akhtar Aziz
Malaysia
IBFIM is an industry-owned institute dedicated to improving the training and competence of those working in the Islamic finance and banking industry, with the aim of assisting the growth and professionalism of the sector.

Islamic Financial Services Board
Chair: Hamad Al- Sayari
3rd Floor, Block A, Bank Negara Malaysia Building, Jalan Dato' Onn, 50480 Kuala Lumpur, Malaysia
T: +603 2698 4248
F: +603 2698 4280
E: ifsb_sec@ifsb.org
www.ifsb.org
This organization serves as an international standard-setting body of regulatory and supervisory agencies focused on ensuring the soundness and stability of the Islamic financial services industry. It promotes the sector through international standards consistent with *shariah* principles, and ensures its work complements regulatory development by other international institutions.

Islamic International Rating Agency
Chair: Khaled M. Al-Aboodi
Al-Zamil Tower, 7th Floor, Government Avenue, Manama 305, PO Box 20582, Bahrain
T: +973 1721 1606
F: +973 1721 1605
E: iira@iirating.com
www.iirating.com
IIRA is a credit rating agency that assists the Islamic financial services industry in gaining recognition, both locally and internationally, as strong and capable financial institutions, and promotes greater standards of disclosure and transparency. It also supports the development and functioning of the regional capital market, and acts as a resource for credit ratings in accordance with *shariah* principles.

Islamic Research and Training Institute
Chair: Ahmad Mohamed Ali Al-Madani
PO Box 9201, Jeddah 21413, Saudi Arabia
T: +966 2636 1400
F: +966 2637 8927
E: irti@isdb.org
www.irti.org
IRTI undertakes research on economic, financial, and banking activities in Muslim countries, to conform to *shariah*, and offers training facilities for professionals engaged in Islamic economics and banking in IDB member countries. It also organizes and co-ordinates research on models and their application in economics, finance and banking.

  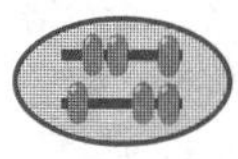   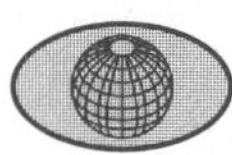   

Knowledge Management

BOOKS

Advanced Methods for Inconsistent Knowledge Management

Ngoc Thanh Nguyen
Advanced Information and Knowledge Processing Series
London: Springer, 2008
356pp, ISBN: 978-1-84628-888-3

Advanced Methods for Inconsistent Knowledge Management, aimed at researchers and students in the field of knowledge management, conflict solution, and intelligent systems, describes many random problems of inconsistent knowledge management. It provides a general overview of intelligent technologies for inconsistency resolution, as well as formal models of inconsistency and algorithms for its resolution.

Beyond Knowledge Management: Dialogue, Creativity, and the Corporate Curriculum

Bob Garvey, Bill Williamson
Harlow, UK: FT Prentice Hall, 2002
224pp, ISBN: 978-0-273-65517-6

In this book the authors explore the ways in which learning and knowledge processes link to the success of an organization. They encourage managers to think critically and offer useful frameworks for identifying and releasing tacit knowledge. They draw on a unique triad framework of strategic capability, knowledge productivity, and corporate curriculum, and stress the use of critical dialogue, learning histories, narratives, and metaphors. The implications of the knowledge economy on corporations today are explored and debated.

Building a Knowledge-Driven Organization

Robert H. Buckman
Maidenhead, UK: McGraw-Hill, 2004
272pp, ISBN: 978-0-07-138471-1

The author, chairman and CEO emeritus of Buckman Laboratories, describes how the company pioneered the development of a knowledge sharing culture as opposed to a knowledge hoarding one. The lessons learned in the process are presented with the aim of assisting others to change organizational culture and develop a knowledge-based strategy. There is a strong focus on the people aspects of implementing a knowledge system, breaking down organizational hierarchies and motivating employees to share their expertise. Aspects of knowledge management also covered include: the choice between customized and off-the-shelf information systems: the creation of communities and virtual teams; the importance of customer centricity; the development of new knowledge-based products and services; and the measurement of outcomes.

Capitalizing On Knowledge: From E-Business to K-Business

David J. Skyrme
Oxford: Butterworth-Heinemann, 2001
336pp, ISBN: 978-0-7506-5011-3

Knowledge management and e-business are rapidly converging into the emerging field of k-business. A k-business is one that turns an organization's knowledge assets into knowledge products and services, and uses the internet to market and deliver them. The book provides models and frameworks with checklists and case examples to help unravel the next phase of the knowledge and dot-com economy. Sections cover the nature of knowledge and e-business, new markets and models for conducting k-business, knowledge markets, and the 10 Ps of using the Internet for marketing. Assessment tools and checklists are provided that cover readiness for k-business, online market evaluation, website evaluation, and website project planning.

Common Knowledge: How Companies Thrive by Sharing What They Know

Nancy M. Dixon
Boston, Massachusetts: Harvard Business School Press, 2000
188pp, ISBN: 978-0-87584-904-1

Creating successful knowledge transfer systems requires matching the type of knowledge to be shared to the method best suited for transferring it effectively. Based on an in-depth study of several organizations that are leading the field in successful knowledge transfer (including Ernst & Young, Bechtel, Ford, Chevron, British Petroleum, Texas Instruments, and the US Army), *Common Knowledge* reveals groundbreaking insights into how organizational knowledge is created, how it can be effectively shared, and why transfer systems work when they do.

Cross-Cultural Management: A Knowledge Management Perspective

Nigel Holden
Harlow, UK: FT Prentice Hall, 2002
336pp, ISBN: 978-0-273-64680-8

The author treats culture as an object of knowledge management, and as an organizational knowledge resource. Previous writing on cross-cultural management is discussed, and the idea of knowledge management is described. The two are linked through four case studies, of Novo Nordisk, Matsushita Electric, LEGO, and Sulzer Infra. The final part of the book is concerned with the redesign of cross-cultural management as a knowledge domain.

Cultivating Communities of Practice: A Guide to Managing Knowledge

Etienne Wenger, Richard McDermott, William M. Snyder
Boston, Massachusetts: Harvard Business School Press, 2002
288pp, ISBN: 978-1-57851-330-7

It is argued that while knowledge drives today's marketplace, leveraging knowledge remains a challenge. Leading companies are adopting communities of practice as a keystone of an effective knowledge strategy. Such communities may form naturally, but organizations need to become proactive to develop and integrate them into their strategy. Practical methods and models for nurturing communities of practice to their full potential are described.

Effective Knowledge Management: A Best Practice Blueprint

Sultan Kermally
Chichester, UK: Wiley, 2002
208pp, ISBN: 978-0-470-84449-6

Kermally discusses best practice transfer and benchmarking and the creation of organizational knowledge of external changes. He also deals with the importance of managing knowledge, the creation and transfer of knowledge within the organization, the role of new technology, and leadership, together with intangible assets and their management. The book includes many case studies.

Enabling Knowledge Creation: How to Unlock the Mystery of Tacit Knowledge and Release the Power of Innovation

Georg von Krogh, Kazuo Ichijo, Ikujiro Nonaka
Oxford: Oxford University Press, 2000
192pp, ISBN: 978-0-19-512616-7

Written as a sequel to the authors' work *The Knowledge-Creating Company*, this book examines how organizations can encourage and enable the creation of knowledge and the generation of ideas.

  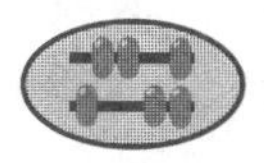   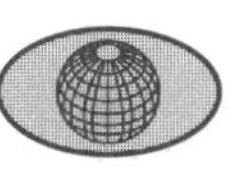   

Knowledge management, it suggests, has overemphasized information technology and measurement tools and focused on controlling rather than supporting knowledge. The authors then introduce five activities that they term "knowledge enablers": instilling a knowledge vision; managing conversations; mobilizing knowledge activists; creating the right context; and globalizing local knowledge. A case study of Gemini Consulting is included in the text.

From Know-how to Knowledge: The Essential Guide to Understanding and Implementing Knowledge Management
Bryan Gladstone
London: Thorogood, 2000
224pp, ISBN: 978-1-85835-880-2
The concept of knowledge management is defined and explored under the headings: knowledge management; better information management is not enough; knowledge creation cycle; why knowledge management is important now; process of knowledge management; being a knowledge manager; and the future of knowledge management.

Intellectual Capital: Core Asset for the Third Millennium
Annie Brooking
London: Caspian Publishing, 1996
224pp, ISBN: 978-1-86152-408-9
Brooking identifies and analyzes four primary categories of intellectual capital: market assets, intellectual property assets, human-centered assets, and infrastructure assets. This book is particularly suitable for corporations evaluating these assets prior to reengineering or downsizing, or for corporations looking to acquire a knowledge-intensive organization.

Key Issues in the New Knowledge Management
Joseph M. Firestone, Mark W. McElroy
Oxford: Butterworth-Heinemann, 2003
352pp, ISBN: 978-0-7506-7655-7
The authors present their concept of The New Knowledge Management (TNKM) as a broadening of the scope of knowledge management from a concern with the sharing, dissemination and retrieval of knowledge to a concern with its creation or production. They discuss definitions of information, data, and knowledge, introduce the knowledge life cycle, and describe its applications. They also explore the relationships between knowledge management concepts and the practical management issues of organizational learning, culture, and strategy.

The Knowing–Doing Gap: How Smart Companies Turn Knowledge into Action
Jeffrey Pfeffer, Robert I. Sutton
Boston, Massachusetts: Harvard Business School Press, 2000
320pp, ISBN: 978-1-57851-124-2
This book is all about turning knowledge to practical account. The subject headings of its main sections give a good idea of its content and approach: knowing what to do is not enough; when talk substitutes for action; when memory is a substitute for thinking; when fear prevents acting on knowledge; when measurement obstructs good judgment; when internal competition turns friends into enemies; firms that surmount the knowing–doing gap; turning knowledge into action.

The Knowledge Activist's Handbook: Adventures from the Knowledge Trenches
Victor Newman
Chichester, UK: Capstone, 2002
176pp, ISBN: 978-1-84112-320-2
The author's own consulting experiences are used to demonstrate how emotion and reflection can effectively combine to create knowledge. Rejecting an academic approach, the style is discursive and entertaining, indeed openly critical of the "tedium" of knowledge management literature. Generally structured around a collection of easy-to-read, thematically connected anecdotes of between 700 to 1500 words, each section ends with a series of punchlines or implications for the reader to consider.

Knowledge Entrepreneur: How Your Business Can Create, Manage, and Profit from Intellectual Capital
Colin Coulson-Thomas
London: Kogan Page, 2003
240pp, ISBN: 978-0-7494-3946-0
Knowledge Entrepreneur examines theories in knowledge management, and shows how to boost revenues and profit by significantly improving the performance of existing activities and creating new offerings that generate additional income. It deals with problems and makes suggestions for practical, knowledge-based, job-support tools, and provides features such as lists of possible commercial ventures, detailed checklists that can be used for identifying and analyzing opportunities for knowledge entrepreneurship, and exercises for assessing entrepreneurial potential and possible products and services.

Knowledge Management and Organizational Competence
Ron Sanchez (editor)
Oxford: Oxford University Press, 2003
264pp, ISBN: 978-0-19-925928-1
A collection of papers from notable management scholars offers a framework for understanding organizational knowledge and its role in building and leveraging competences. New insights into various kinds of knowledge that are of value to organizations are discussed.

Knowledge Management Casebook: Siemens Best Practices, 2nd ed
Thomas H. Davenport, Gilbert J. B. Probst
Munich, Germany: Publicis, 2002
336pp, ISBN: 978-3-89578-181-0
Siemens has been recognized as one of the top ten knowledge management companies worldwide. This case study describes the best of the corporation's practical applications and experiences. The six sections cover: knowledge strategy, knowledge transfer, communities of practice, added value of knowledge management, learning and knowledge management, and visualizing more of the value creation.

Knowledge Networking: Creating the Collaborative Enterprise
David J. Skyrme
Oxford: Butterworth-Heinemann, 1999
311pp, ISBN: 978-0-7506-3976-7
This book offers a comprehensive overview of the strategic application of knowledge management within global corporations. With an emphasis on good leadership practice, it shows how companies have successfully leveraged the knowledge dispersed and fragmented throughout their companies to deliver organizational benefits and create new opportunities. It gives guidance on how to innovate quickly and exploit human networks, wherever they are based, and provides examples of how global companies can harness employees' accumulated knowledge and apply it to specific problems. It also contains toolkits and checklists for individual, team, organizational, and collaborative enterprises.

Leading Organizational Learning: Harnessing the Power of Knowledge
Marshall Goldsmith, Howard Morgan, Alexander J. Ogg (editors)
New York: Jossey-Bass, 2004
368pp, ISBN: 978-0-7879-7218-9
This book brings together contributions from experts in the field of organizational learning and knowledge management including Fons Trompenaars, Jon

     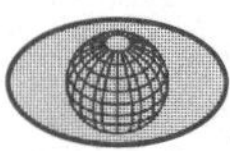   

Katzenbach, Margaret J. Wheatley, and many others. These are grouped in five sections covering: the challenges and dilemmas of knowledge management; processes for managing knowledge and learning; the role of leaders in the knowledge organization; changes for the future, including the development of new ideas and case studies and examples.

Learning to Fly: Practical Lessons from One of the World's Leading Knowledge Companies, 2nd ed
Chris Collinson, Geoff Parcell
Chichester, UK: Capstone, 2004
332pp, ISBN: 978-1-84112-124-6
Based on the authors' experiences at BP, as a detailed case study, the book sets out to provide a practical, jargon-free overview of what knowledge is, how it can be harnessed, stored, and—most importantly—shared throughout any organization. This updated edition includes a CD.

Managing Knowledge: An Essential Reader
Stephen Little, Paul Quintas, Tim Ray (editors)
Basingstoke, UK: Palgrave, 2002
400pp, ISBN: 978-0-7619-7213-6
This book provides general background on the major themes in the field. A critical overview of the theories is offered, and the four parts cover: creating knowledge; resources and capabilities; communicating and sharing knowledge; and knowledge, innovation and human resources. Some reprints of significant articles and papers are collected together to give key theoretical work, and critical case studies are included as well as newly written chapters.

Managing Knowledge: Building Blocks for Success
Gilbert Probst, Steffen Raub, Kai Romhardt
Chichester, UK: Wiley, 1999
368pp, ISBN: 978-0-471-99768-9
Based on many years of research and experience, the ideas put forward in *Managing Knowledge* result from intensive collaboration with many major organizations. The book provides a road map of the most important stages of the knowledge management process; it presents a wide range of knowledge techniques, assesses their possible effects, and addresses key questions faced by managers. It is illustrated throughout with examples from managerial practice and is designed to prompt critical thinking and assist practitioners to chart their own path through the knowledge jungle.

Managing Knowledge Security: Strategies for Protecting Your Company's Intellectual Assets
Kevin C. Desouza
London: Kogan Page, 2007
200pp, ISBN: 978-0-7494-4961-2
Managing Knowledge Security gives a clear and inclusive perspective on how to secure the physical and intangible assets owned by a business. It explains how vital it is to take measures to retain key assets and to avoid data and knowledge falling into the hands of competitors, and offers practical strategies and real-life examples from companies such as Hewlett Packard, Microsoft, Google, Boeing and Amazon.

Managing Knowledge Work
Sue Newell et al.
Basingstoke, UK: Palgrave, 2002
208pp, ISBN: 978-0-333-96299-2
This textbook looks at the nature and management of knowledge work in a wide range of organizational contexts. The introduction examines the nature of knowledge and the shifts in society that have made knowledge work central to wealth creation. The book covers the knowledge intensive organization, the importance of teamworking in knowledge creation, the impact of HRM policies in knowledge work, the relationship between knowledge and information and communication technologies (ICT), the value and management of communities of practice and the link between knowledge management and innovation. A final section draws conclusions about the key challenges in the management of knowledge work. Case studies are included.

Organizing Knowledge: An Introduction to Managing Access to Information, 4th ed
Jennifer Rowley, John Farrow
Aldershot, UK: Gower Publishing, 2008
392pp, ISBN: 978-0-7546-4431-6
This is a standard text on knowledge organization and retrieval. The different sections focus on: the nature of information and knowledge and their incorporation into documents; the use of electronic databases; the range of tools for accessing information resources, including indexing, classification, and catalogs; and the electronic contexts in which knowledge can be stored.

Profiting from Intellectual Capital: Extracting Value from Innovation
Patrick H. Sullivan
Chichester, UK: Wiley, 2001
384pp, ISBN: 978-0-471-41747-7
This volume provides examples from companies' best practices in knowledge management, with a focus on getting value from intellectual capital. The book offers an overview of essential knowledge-management concepts and detailed coverage of strategies for measuring, monitoring, and assigning value to existing knowledge assets. It provides practical advice for those familiar with the basics of knowledge generation and information sharing.

Sharing Expertise: Beyond Knowledge Management
Mark S. Akerman, Volkmar Pipek, Volker Wulf (editors)
Cambridge, Massachusetts: MIT Press, 2003
432pp, ISBN: 978-0-262-01195-2
A new approach to knowledge management (KM), "expertise sharing," focuses on what can be gained from the cognitive, social and organizational, or human expertise aspect in knowledge work. A literature review, overview, and background are provided, and expertise sharing in organizational settings is explored empirically. The tools, technology, and architectures designed for expertise management are also discussed.

Smart Things to Know about Knowledge Management
Thomas M. Koulopoulos, Carl Frappaolo
Smart Series
Oxford: Capstone, 1999
240pp, ISBN: 978-1-84112-041-6
In the new economy, say the authors, knowledge management is vital. It allows companies to leverage their most precious assets, collective know-how, talent, and experience, and only by focusing on these valuable resources can companies handle new market challenges and opportunities. The aim of this book, therefore, is to provide a framework for practical action, helping people to understand knowledge management and how it can benefit their organization, to position it at the heart of their business, to measure success in a knowledge-based economy, and to become the knowledge management champions in their organizations.

The Wealth of Knowledge: Intellectual Capital and the Twenty-First Century Organization
Thomas A. Stewart
New York: Currency/Doubleday, 2001
400pp, ISBN: 978-0-385-50072-2
This book builds on Stewart's 1997 book *Intellectual Capital*, which outlined organizational assets in a knowledge economy. It analyzes corporate practices in managing intellectual capital, providing the

  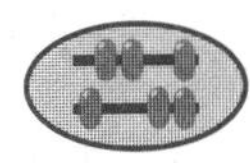   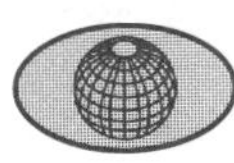   

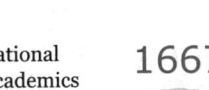

basics of knowledge organization theory and real-world examples. A four-step process is used to describe the day-to-day management of knowledge and how it can improve productivity and profitability.

Working Knowledge: How Organizations Manage What They Know
Thomas H. Davenport, Laurence Prusak
Boston, Massachusetts: Harvard Business School Press, 2000
240pp, ISBN: 978-1-57851-301-7
The authors break down knowledge management into four activities—accessing, generating, embedding, and transferring—and identify the key processes involved in each. They discuss skills and techniques, knowledge-management technologies, and best practices from their work with leading companies. They also emphasize the importance of corporate culture in fostering knowledge creation and sharing.

MAGAZINES

Knowledge Management Review
Melcrum
First Floor, Chelsea Reach, 79–89 Lots Road, London, SW10 0RN, UK
T: +44 (0) 20 7795 2205
F: +44 (0) 20 7795 2156
www.melcrum.com/products/journals/kmr.shtml
ISSN: 1369-7633
This journal provides the latest trends, techniques, and ideas in knowledge management through corporate case studies, practitioners' insights, and practical articles.

JOURNALS

European Journal of Innovation Management
Emerald
60/62 Toller Lane, Bradford, West Yorkshire, BD8 9BY, UK
T: +44 (0) 1274 777 700
F: +44 (0) 1274 785 200
www.emeraldinsight.com/1460–1060.htm
ISSN: 1460-1060
The journal aims to be a European forum for information and knowledge in the field of innovation. It publishes high-quality papers by both academics and industrialists, which capture leading developments, both in practice and theory.

International Journal of Entrepreneurship and Innovation Management
Inderscience Enterprises
World Trade Center Building, 29 route de Pre-Bois, Case Postale 896, 1215, Geneva, 15, Switzerland
T: +44 (0) 1234 240515
F: +41 22 791 08 85
www.inderscience.com/ijeim
ISSN: 1368-275X
IJEIM provides a source of information and an international platform for the field of entrepreneurship and innovation management, business corporate strategy, and government economic policy. The journal publishes theory-based empirical papers, review papers, case studies, conference reports, relevant reports and news, book reviews, and briefs.

International Journal of Innovation Management
World Scientific
ISSN: 1363-9196
The International Journal of Innovation Management (IJIM) is a quarterly publication dedicated to promoting academic research and management practice in the field of innovation management. It offers papers which integrate the management of technological, market, and organizational innovation. Contributions are based on original empirical research, as well as the observations of experienced managers, providing a platform for academics, practicing managers, and consultants.

Journal of Knowledge Management
Emerald
60/62 Toller Lane, Bradford, West Yorkshire, BD8 9BY, UK
T: +44 (0) 1274 777 700
F: +44 (0) 1274 785 200
www.emeraldinsight.com/1747–1117.htm
ISSN: 1367-3270
This quarterly, peer-reviewed publication includes original research and case studies on strategies, tools, and techniques and technologies for knowledge management. It focuses on the identification of innovative knowledge management strategies and the application of theoretical concepts to real-world situations.

Knowledge Management: Research and Practice
Palgrave Macmillan
Houndmills, Basingstoke, Hampshire, RG21 6XS, UK
ISSN: 1477-8238
KMRP is a forum for articles on all aspects of managing knowledge, organizational learning, intellectual capital, and knowledge economics, from both a theoretical and practical perspective. It places a particular emphasis on cross-disciplinary approaches, and a mix of technological, cultural, and motivational issues. Contributions from both academics and practitioners are welcomed.

INTERNET

International Knowledge Management Network
www.cibit.com
This site offers news, conference and seminar details, a discussion forum, an archive of literature resources, and weblinks. Visitors need to register to use parts of the site.

Knowledge Management Online Open Source
www.knowledge-management-online.com
This is a unique knowledge management online site offering open source KM education and open source KM consulting methods, tools and techniques.

The KNOW Network
www.knowledgebusiness.com
This site contains a knowledge management library consisting of news, summaries of trends, market research, a diary, links, and a KM resources guide to publications, reviews, and websites. It also acts as the gateway to the KNOW Network—a group of leading knowledge organizations dedicated to the identification and exchange of best practice. Some of the site can only be accessed by joining the KNOW Network.

Sveiby Knowledge Management Library
www.sveiby.com
This website provides access to Karl-Erik Sveiby's collected works on knowledge management, along with some of his favorite articles. The texts may be downloaded for research purposes and for personal viewing.

WWW Virtual Library on Knowledge Management
www.brint.com/km
This site provided by @brint.com offers full-text articles, book reviews, weblinks, and a discussion forum on various issues relating to knowledge management.

ORGANIZATIONS

Europe

International Knowledge Management Network
Secretariat, Kenniscentrum CIBIT, Arthur van Schendelstraat 570, PO Box 19210, Utrecht, 3501 AD, The Netherlands

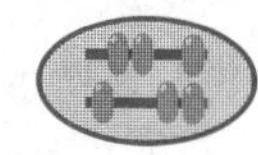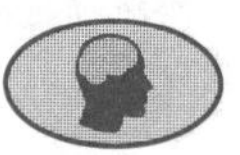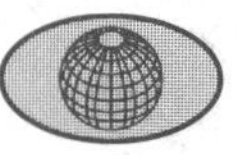

T: +31 30 230 8900
F: +31 30 230 8999
E: info@cibit.nl
www.cibit.com
Set up in 1994, the network evolved from the experiences of the Dutch Knowledge Management Network and is now a worldwide organization for exchanging ideas and experiences in the knowledge management field.

The KNOW Network
4 St George's Road, Bedford, Bedfordshire, MK40 2LS, UK
T: +44 (0) 1234 314 197
F: +44 (0) 1234 308 824
E: info@knowledgebusiness.com
www.knowledgebusiness.com
A web-based network of some of the world's foremost knowledge-based organizations, the network is dedicated to the identification and exchange of best practice for competitive advantage.

USA

Knowledge Management India
249 – F, Sector 18, Udyog Vihar, Gurgaon 122 015, India
T: +91 12 44 0140 6067
F: +91 12 44 014 080
KM India aims to create an environment that can generate economic value through knowledge and intellectual capital, within knowledge-based organizations and industries. Its intention is to create a better understanding of research and practical applications in KM.

Knowledge Management Benchmark Association
USA
T: +1 281 440 5044
F: +1 281 440 6677
www.kmba.org
The Knowledge Management Benchmarking Association assembles knowledge management professionals from a variety of companies. KMBA conducts benchmarking studies to identify practices that improve the effectiveness of Knowledge Management activities. Its objective is use the competence of the association to gain process performance data and related best practices regarding knowledge management.

Knowledge Management Consortium International
c/o Joseph M. Firestone, 309 Yoakum Parkway, #603, Alexandria, VA 22304, USA
T: +1 703 461 8823
E: help@kmci.org
KMCI was founded in 1997 as an international professional association of knowledge management practitioners. Its purpose is to enhance an organization's capacity to detect problems, solve, or dispose of them, or share or present the solutions to others. It does this by enhancing organizational learning and innovation processes.

Knowledge Management Professional Society
PO Box 16444, Alexandria, VA 22302, USA
T: +1 757 460 6500
F: +1 757 460 6672
E: support@kmpro.org
www.kmpro.org
This is a non-profit association committed to promoting knowledge management worldwide. It is created by and for KM professionals actively engaged in implementation, change management, information management, innovation, human/intellectual capital strategy, and intangible asset valuation. One of its goals is to form alliances with people who share their vision, ethics, values, and beliefs.

BRIC

Asian Knowledge Management Association
Suite 2B, Max Share Centre, 367–373 King's Road, North Point, Hong Kong
T: +852 2512 0113
F: +852 2570 4207
www.akma.com.hk/index.php
AKMA is a forum for professional learning, networking, research, and cooperation among governments, academics, business practitioners, and knowledge workers in Asia-Pacific region. The association assists companies in Asia wanting to transform and gain competitive advantage in knowledge management.

  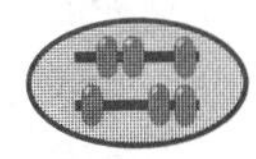 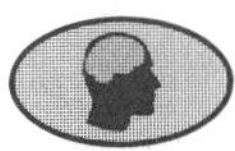  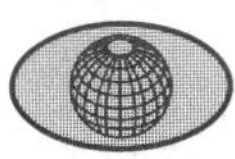   

Leadership

BOOKS

21 Leaders for the 21st Century: How Innovative Leaders Manage in the Digital Age

Fons Trompenaars, Charles Hampden-Turner
Chichester, UK: Wiley, 2005
250pp, ISBN: 978-1-84112-463-6

Leaders of global corporations, it is argued, are beset by a series of dilemmas, pairs of conflicting propositions that clamor for their attention. Successful leadership depends on the capacity to integrate these demands and create powerful strategies that unite them. 21 corporate giants reveal their personal experiences of business dilemmas and these are used to show how managers understand and use the seven dilemmas of leadership.

The Accidental Leader: What to Do When You're Suddenly in Charge

Harvey Robbins, Michael Finley
New York: Jossey-Bass, 2004
192pp, ISBN: 978-0-7879-6855-7

Written in an easy to read anecdotal style, this practical toolkit can act as a resource book and inspiration for those who have been thrust suddenly into a position of responsibility. Part one addresses self-management and areas such as coping with responsibility and meeting the team. Part two deals with technical issues such as planning and creating a learning environment; and part three explores people management.

Alpha Leadership: Tools for Business Leaders Who Want More from Life

Anne Deering, Robert Dilts, Julian Russell
Chichester, UK: Wiley, 2002
240pp, ISBN: 978-0-470-84483-0

This "how to" book is based on the authors' research that shows that the successful leader has three related strengths: anticipation, alignment, and action. Each of these areas is covered, and tools and frameworks are provided.

Arc of Ambition: Defining the Leadership Journey

James Champy, Nitin Nohria
Chichester, UK: Wiley, 2001
282pp, ISBN: 978-0-471-53020-6

Champy and Nohria explore the fascinating dimensions of ambition through the stories of dozens of achievers, past and present, who exemplify both its positive and negative qualities. From the quest of Giuseppe Garibaldi for a unified Italy to the vision of Alfred Sloan for General Motors, which changed management practice forever, and the boyhood dream of Michael Dell to have a building with a flag out front, ambition comes in many guises. Champy and Nohria outline how it can be channeled toward creative and enriching endeavors at the personal, organizational, and even national levels.

Are Leaders Born or Are They Made? The Case of Alexander the Great

Manfred F. R. Kets de Vries, Elisabet Engellau
London: Karnac Books, 2004
128pp, ISBN: 978-1-85575-315-0

In this text, the life story of Alexander the Great and how he created and administered an empire that spanned most of the ancient world is examined. The authors go on to analyze his personality and behavior from a clinical perspective, examining the psychological forces that shaped his character, the leadership qualities that brought him success, and his strengths and weaknesses as a leader. Finally, the key leadership lessons that contemporary leaders in business and politics can learn from his life are identified.

The Art and Science of Leadership, 3rd ed

Afsaneh Nahavandi
Harlow, UK: Prentice Hall, 2002
272pp, ISBN: 978-0-13-208995-1

The author presents a broad overview of the field of leadership, focusing on the history of leadership theory, popular current trends, and prospects for the future. This edition includes expanded coverage of personality traits, abilities, values, and skills. Contingency models of leadership are also examined, and separate chapters cover participative management and team leadership, change-oriented leadership, and strategic leadership. The book is intended for students of leadership and each chapter includes details of relevant research, examples of innovative practices, ethical dilemmas faced by leaders, and case studies of real-life leaders.

The Center for Creative Leadership Handbook of Leadership Development, 2nd ed

Cynthia D. McCauley, Ellen van Velsor (editors)
New York: Jossey-Bass, 2004
528pp, ISBN: 978-0-7879-7449-7

This handbook explores the essence of leadership development, reveals how individuals can effectively enhance their leadership skills, and demonstrates what organizations can do to help build leaders and leadership capacity. Part one focuses on individual leader development. Part two explores leader development across gender and race, cross-cultural issues, global roles, and lifelong adult development. Part three looks at organizational capacity for leadership and development.

Complete Leadership: A Practical Guide for Developing Your Leadership Talents

Susan Bloch, Philip Whiteley
Harlow, UK: Pearson Education, 2003
192pp, ISBN: 978-1-84304-025-5

This book is a personal coaching manual with questionnaires, guides and case studies for readers to evaluate and improve their leadership style. The book covers the following: how your style affects your staff, how it affects the organization, looking at your leadership type, how your team views you, self-awareness, personal development and progress.

Connective Leadership: Managing in a Changing World

Jean Lipman-Blumen
Oxford: Oxford University Press, 2000
432pp, ISBN: 978-0-19-513469-8

A new form of leadership is needed in an era of increasing interdependence and diversity, the author suggests. She reviews the psychological and historical foundations of leadership and develops a new model of connective leadership based around nine behavioral facets. The book draws on the results of qualitative interview research and quantitative survey research on achieving styles, conducted among over 5,000 leaders. A final section examines how the connective leadership model relates to new organizational structures and the wider social context.

Develop Your Leadership Skills

John Adair
Creating Success Series
London: Kogan Page, 2007
89pp, ISBN: 978-0-7494-4919-3

Develop your Leadership Skills is John Adair's most accessible title on leadership. Providing a useful range of exercises and checklists, it helps to boost confidence levels, and act as a guide to leadership excellence.

Effective Strategic Leadership

John Adair
Indianapolis, Indiana: PanMacmillan, 2002
352pp, ISBN: 978-0-330-48787-0

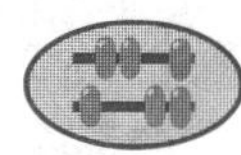

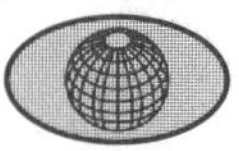

This readable and practical analysis of the nature of strategic leadership starts from a historical (ancient world) and military perspective, defining the different types of leadership with specific reference to the strategic variety. The second part of the book looks at the practical aspects of becoming a strategic leader, with many suggestions, exercises and a large number of short case studies of leaders through the ages from all walks of life.

First, Break All the Rules
Marcus Buckingham, Curt Coffman
London: Simon & Schuster, 1999
256pp, ISBN: 978-1-4165-0266-1
This book is based directly on a huge research project into the behavior of managers and how they conduct business matters to achieve success. Acknowledging that good managers are pivotal to realizing a company's potential, the authors cite instances of successful employee selection and development techniques that reflect the quality of excellent management.

The Five Most Important Questions You Will Ever Ask about Your Organization, 3rd ed
Peter F. Drucker
New York: Jossey-Bass, 2008
144pp, ISBN: 978-0-470-22756-5
This assesses Peter Drucker's five questions: What is our mission? Who is our customer? What does the customer value? What are our results? What is our plan? It provides a response to these key areas by five prominent thought leaders, and offers a close analysis of what drives their organizations.

Focus on Leadership: Servant-Leadership for the 21st Century
Larry C. Spears, Michele Lawrence (editors)
Chichester, UK: Wiley, 2002
400pp, ISBN: 978-0-471-41162-8
Focus on Leadership expands on Robert K. Greenleaf's idea of a servant-leader, an individual who seeks to improve and enhance the workplace and the community rather than focusing on company profit. This book offers writings from some of the leading thinkers on management and leadership, including Margaret Wheatley, Danah Zohar, Warren Bennis, and Stephen Covey.

The Future of Leadership: Today's Top Leadership Thinkers Speak to Tomorrow's Leaders
Warren Bennis, Gretchen M. Spreitzer, Thomas G. Cummings (editors)
New York: Jossey-Bass, 2001
320pp, ISBN: 978-0-7879-5567-0
Nineteen essays written by some of the leading thinkers in management today. The essays are arranged in the sections: including the leader of the future; how leaders stay on top of their game; insights from young leaders; and some closing thoughts. Contributors include Warren Bennis, Edward E. Lawler III, Charles Handy, Thomas H. Davenport, Tom Peters, Jeffrey Sonnenfeld, Philip Slater, and James O'Toole.

Geeks and Geezers: How Era Values and Defining Moments Shape Leaders
Warren G. Bennis, Robert J. Thomas
Boston, Massachusetts: Harvard Business School Press, 2002
224pp, ISBN: 978-1-57851-582-0
A study of two groups of leaders is presented: geeks—young leaders under 35 —and geezers—older leaders over 70. The authors interviewed both groups on their experiences of leadership and success to gain an insight into how they were shaped by the times in which they grew up and to identify the qualities that enabled them to become successful leaders. Brief biographies of geezers and geeks are included.

Improving Leadership in Nonprofit Organizations
Ronald E. Riggio, Sarah Smith Orr (editors)
New York: Jossey-Bass, 2008
320pp, ISBN: 978-0-470-40179-8
Leadership issues and challenges for nonprofit organizations are discussed by various authors, including Jay Conger. Areas covered include future challenges, ethical challenges, board leadership, pay in nonprofit organizations, succession, and assessment.

Inner Leadership: Realize Your Self-Leading Potential
Simon Smith
People Skills for Professionals Series
London: Nicholas Brealey Publishing, 2000
256pp, ISBN: 978-1-85788-271-1
The concept of the "leader in each of us" is explored here through case studies, business examples, and exercises. The author presents a four-stage model (REAL) as a method of reaching individual potential. The four stages are: recognizing the depth and diversity of resources and qualities; exploring the parts of yourself which influence decisions and actions; actualizing qualities and values to achieve leadership goals; and leading yourself.

In Search of Leaders, 2nd ed
Hilarie Owen
Chichester, UK: Wiley, 2008
384pp, ISBN: 978-0-470-22664-3
Leadership is discussed as a potential that all individuals have and can develop, rather than as a phenomenon based on hierarchical authority or a heroic chairman. The author offers a three-stage model for a journey of self-discovery. She outlines the "seven essences" of leadership and explores transformational ideas about leadership to help individuals develop their own inner leadership potential.

The Inspirational Leader: How to Motivate, Encourage, and Achieve Success
John Adair
London: Kogan Page, 2009
208pp, ISBN: 978-0-7494-5478-4
This book explores the nature and practice of leadership and reinforces the author's argument that leaders are not born but made. It takes the form of conversations between a young chief executive and the author. Each aspect of leadership is studied and discussed so that the key skills are revealed for anyone to adopt and use.

Inspiring Leadership: Learning from Great Leaders
John Adair
London: Nicholas Brealey Publishing, 2002
368pp, ISBN: 978-1-85418-207-4
This book discusses some of the great leaders in history, aiming to identify the main lessons of leadership that can be learnt from them. Each section takes a particular theme, illustrated by one or more individuals. Amongst the many individuals described are Socrates, Lao Tzu, Jesus Christ, Alexander the Great, Churchill, Machiavelli, Nelson, Shackleton, Margaret Thatcher, and Nelson Mandela.

John Adair's 100 Greatest Ideas for Effective Leadership and Management
John Adair
Chichester, UK: Capstone, 2002
192pp, ISBN: 978-1-84112-140-6
Adair offers accessible advice relating leadership to areas including time management, leadership functions, skills and team management, creativity and innovation, and communication. These are organized under the headings: getting your act together; understanding leadership; performing as a leader; thinking as a leader; power through the people; and getting the message across.

  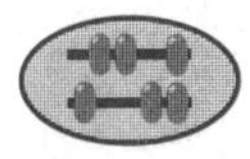 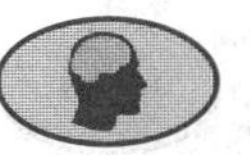  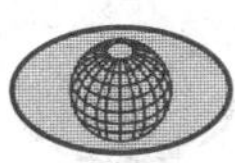   

Leadership—The Inner Side of Greatness: A Philosophy for Leaders
Peter Koestenbaum
New York: Jossey-Bass, 2002
384pp, ISBN: 978-0-7879-5956-2
The author explores how to be an exceptional and passionate leader in today's complex world. He presents his Leadership Diamond Model that challenges managers to transform their thinking and approach everything with fresh effectiveness. Insights into the characteristics great leaders have in common—vision, reality, ethics, and courage—are presented and strategies that all managers can use are described.

Leadership and the New Science
Margaret J. Wheatley
San Francisco, California: Berrett-Koehler, 2001
208pp, ISBN: 978-1-57675-344-6
This updated version of the original 1992 title discusses the effect of quantum physics on the way we organize our lives, how biology and chemistry influence the way we live, and how leadership is affected by science and chaos theory.

The Leadership Challenge, 3rd ed
James M. Kouzes, Barry Z. Posner
San Francisco, California: Jossey-Bass, 2008
416pp, ISBN: 978-0-7879-8492-2
This key title aims to help people to further their abilities to lead others to get "extraordinary" things done, presenting principles and practices that are based in solid research. It describes the five practices of exemplary leadership, discussing the characteristics that people most admire in leaders, the motives of leaders, how leaders foster collaboration and create a climate for high performance, and how leadership practices can be learnt by anyone.

The Leadership Crash Course: How to Create Personal Leadership Value, 2nd ed
Paul Taffinder
London: Kogan Page, 2006
192pp, ISBN: 978-0-7494-4638-3
The Leadership Crash Course is designed to help readers develop their skills and effectiveness. Split into seven sections, this book aims to build personal capability.

Leadership in Organizations: Current Issues and Key Trends
John Storey (editor)
London: Routledge, 2004
352pp, ISBN: 978-0-415-31033-8
This study not only strongly criticizes many currently available leadership training and development approaches, but also suggests alternatives. Areas covered include post-transformational leadership, leadership competencies, leader integrity, leadership learning, corporate university solutions, public sector leadership development, leadership and business strategy, and leadership career development.

Leadership on the Line: Staying Alive through the Dangers of Leading
Ronald A. Heifetz, Marty Linsky
Boston, Massachusetts: Harvard Business School Press, 2002
256pp, ISBN: 978-1-57851-437-3
The book describes the difficulties, risks and rewards of leadership, and discusses some strategies for surviving the dangers. It also shows how a leader may manage his or her own personal needs and vulnerabilities, and how the spirit may be sustained during difficult times. Examples are drawn from politics, business, and family life.

The Leadership Pipeline: How to Build the Leadership-Powered Company
Ram Charan, Stephen Drotter, James Noel
New York: Jossey-Bass, 2001
256pp, ISBN: 978-0-7879-5852-7
The authors show how to identify future leaders, assess their competence, plan their development, and measure the results. They also show how this process may be integrated with succession planning, so that the supply of leaders at all levels may be constantly renewed. Six critical stages in the leadership development pipeline are identified and separately addressed.

Leadership: Theory and Practice, 4th ed
Peter G. Northouse
London: Sage Publications, 2006
416pp, ISBN: 978-1-4129-4161-7
This book is a major source of insights and perspectives for all those studying on leadership courses in both the business and education sectors. It is also an excellent source for school leaders and educators who want to increase their understanding of all the key aspects of leadership.

Leadership: Theory, Application, Skill Development, 4th ed
Robert N. Lussier, Christopher F. Achua
Cincinnati, Ohio: South-Western College Publishing, 2009
544pp, ISBN: 978-0-324-59655-7
By providing new, engaging ways to learn, including role-playing and using the internet for readings and exercises, this textbook seeks to expand the user's knowledge about leadership. It is divided into three sections that focus on individual, team, and organizational leadership.

Leading at the Edge: Leadership Lessons from the Extraordinary Saga of Shackleton's Antarctic Expedition
Dennis N. T. Perkins et al.
New York: AMACOM, 2000
268pp, ISBN: 978-0-8144-0543-7
This book records the adventures of Sir Ernest Shackleton on his Antarctic expedition and examines through the lens of business the extraordinary leadership skills he displayed. Ten lessons on what it takes to be a great leader are drawn from the account. Contemporary business case studies further illustrate leadership at the edge, and the behaviors, attitudes, and ways of thinking about life that help individuals to realize their full potential as leaders are discussed.

Leading Beyond the Walls
Frances Hesselbein, Marshall Goldsmith, Iain Somerville (editors)
San Francisco, California: Jossey-Bass, 2001
320pp, ISBN: 978-0-7879-5555-7
Twenty-nine of the world's leading management thinkers explore the need for a new paradigm in leadership. In today's fast-paced global society, leaders must be adept at establishing diverse partnerships, alliances, and networks by building and maintaining relationships both within and outside their own organization. *Leading Beyond the Walls* brings together Peter Drucker, Stephen Covey, Peter Senge, Jim Collins, Noel Tichy, Regina Herzlinger, C. K. Prahalad, Sally Helgesen, and other thought leaders to describe new ways of building relationships, new approaches to strategy and marketing, new models of employee relations, and other innovative ways of thinking and acting.

Leading the Professionals: How to Inspire and Motivate Professional Service Teams
Geoff Smith
London: Kogan Page, 2004
256pp, ISBN: 978-0-7494-3996-5
This book supplies practical advice for those who lead professionals. It suggests an encouraging and supportive approach to meet the challenges of managing highly qualified or creative individuals and of developing high performing teams. Smith reviews keys to success such as objectives and values, and communication and coaching, and suggests ways to resolve performance problems and conflicts.

  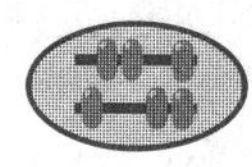   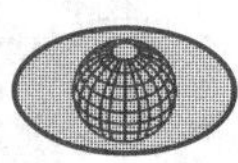   

Leading the Way: Three Truths from the Top Companies for Leaders
Robert Gandossy, Marc Effron
Chichester, UK: Wiley, 2004
224pp, ISBN: 978-0-471-48301-4
Three leadership truths are identified and these are said to be the fundamental building blocks used by top companies to build a sustainable pipeline of great leaders. Advice is given on identifying the leadership capabilities necessary for your organization and the process for building them, as well as considering the challenges, opportunities, and solutions that lie ahead.

Lead to Succeed: Creating Entrepreneurial Organisations
Colin Turner
London: Texere Publishing, 2002
240pp, ISBN: 978-1-58799-124-0
In this book the author puts forward his ideas on creating an entrepreneurial culture in established organizations. Part one examines the essential attributes of entrepreneurial leaders and how the OILS (opportunity, innovation, leadership, and service) of entrepreneurship can be applied. In part two the principles and practices of entrepreneurial leadership are outlined. Finally it looks at creating entrepreneurial people, culture, customer ethos and opportunities.

A Manager's Guide to Leadership
Mike Pedler, John Burgoyne, Tom Boydell
Maidenhead, UK: McGraw-Hill, 2004
284pp, ISBN: 978-0-07-710423-8
This is a practical self-development guide that is designed to help managers meet key leadership tasks and challenges. Part one helps you establish your leadership strengths and weaknesses and consider personal goals. Part two examines the leadership practices of power, risk taking, critical questioning, facilitation, and networking. Part three helps you develop your leadership skills by addressing the challenges to be found in the workplace.

Managing the Dream: Reflections on Leadership and Change
Warren G. Bennis
Cambridge, Massachusetts: Perseus Books Group, 2000
317pp, ISBN: 978-0-7382-0332-4
This book contains over ten of the author's most significant essays on leadership. The majority of the essays concentrate on how to make leadership possible and how to cope with change, while others discuss the character and ethics of a good leader.

The New Leaders: Transforming the Art of Leadership
Daniel Goleman, Richard E. Boyatzis, Annie McKee
Amsterdam: Time Warner, 2003
336pp, ISBN: 978-0-7515-3381-1
Psychologist Daniel Goleman is best known for his bestseller Emotional Intelligence, after which EI became a buzzword for many in the world of management. Goleman argues that our self-awareness, personal motivation, and ability to relate to others are more important than the narrow 'raw' intelligence which is measured by intelligence tests. He here unites with two academics to explore the consequences of emotional intelligence for leaders and organizations.

On Becoming a Leader, 2nd ed
Warren Bennis
Cambridge, Massachusetts: Perseus Books Group, 2003
256pp, ISBN: 978-0-7382-0817-6
In this key title, updated for the new millennium, the author outlines the characteristics that determine whether a person will become a leader and, using key figures from a range of business areas as examples, the various ways companies treat such people.

Practicing Servant-Leadership: Succeeding Through Trust, Bravery, and Forgiveness
Larry C. Spears, Michele Lawrence (editors)
New York: Jossey-Bass, 2004
336pp, ISBN: 978-0-7879-7455-8
Practicing Servant-Leadership brings together a group of exceptional thinkers, who offer a compendium of new ideas on bringing servant-leadership into the daily lives of business leaders. Each contributor focuses on their area of expertise, and explore how servant-leadership works in the real world, using examples from a variety of organizations such as businesses, nonprofit organizations, churches, schools, foundations, and leadership organizations.

Primal Leadership: Realizing the Power of Emotional Intelligence
Daniel Goleman, Richard Boyatzis, Annie McKee
Boston, Massachusetts: Harvard Business School Press, 2002
352pp, ISBN: 978-1-57851-486-1
The authors describe six styles that account for all critical management behavior: visionary, coaching, affiliative, democratic, pace-setting, and commanding. Good leaders use different styles according to the situation. They explain that the importance of these styles is that the right style used with the right team will generate "good feelings" and that style is a critical factor, not only in managing and leading but also in generating organizational profits. The book is based on studies of nearly 4,000 executives.

Ruthless Leader: Three Classics of Strategy and Power
Alistair McAlpine (editor)
Chichester, UK: Wiley, 2000
272pp, ISBN: 978-0-471-37247-9
The texts of three classic works on leadership make up this compilation: *The Prince* by Nicolò Machiavelli, *The Servant* by Alistair McAlpine, and *The Art of War* by Sun Tzu. The introduction places these texts in their contemporary contexts, and compares and contrasts them, drawing out their major themes and demonstrating their application to modern business organizations.

The Smartest Guys in the Room: The Amazing Rise and Scandalous Fall of Enron
Bethany McLean, Peter Elkind
New York: Portfolio, 2004
464pp, ISBN: 978-1-59184-053-4
Written by two *Fortune* journalists, this book attempts to lay bare the extraordinary story behind Enron's collapse in 2001. A tale of jaw-dropping corporate arrogance, it shows the impact of incompetence and greed on the notion of corporate governance.

The Snowball: Warren Buffett and the Business of Life
Alice Schroeder
London: Bloomsbury Publishing, 2008
976pp, ISBN: 978-0-7475-9191-7
This examines in detail the life, career, and financial success story of the revered investment guru.

Test Your Leadership Skills
Brian O'Neill
Test Yourself Series
London: Profile Books, 2000
95pp, ISBN: 978-0-340-78208-8
This book is intended to enable you to: discover your potential as a visionary, integration, or fulfillment type of leader; assess your leadership style—as expert, friend, guide, hero, or driver; fit your leadership to what your followers and organization require; develop outstanding teams; and anticipate future demands and opportunities.

  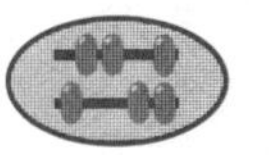 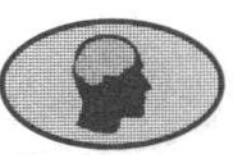  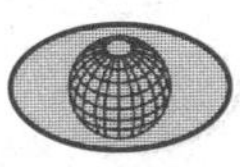   

The Transparency Edge: How Credibility Can Make or Break You in Business
Barbara Pagano, Elizabeth Pagano
Maidenhead, UK: McGraw-Hill, 2005
224pp, ISBN: 978-0-07-145884-9
This text argues that, in line with a growing culture of transparency in business, the demand for clear and transparent leadership is becoming a priority. The authors demonstrate the benefits of clear and open business policy and transparent leadership practices. This book helps leaders to develop the "transparent edge" through nine key behavioral patterns that build and enhance credibility for leaders and consequently for business.

The Trusted Leader: Bringing Out the Best in Your People and Your Company
Robert Galford, Anne Seibold Drapeau
New York: Free Press, 2003
272pp, ISBN: 978-0-7432-3539-6
The importance of trust within organizations is outlined, and the difference between being trustworthy and building trust is explained. The characteristics and competencies of the trusted leader are established, and the identification and application of the tools of trusted leaders are examined through a series of interactive exercises and diagnostic tools.

Up Your Business: 7 Steps to Fix, Build, or Stretch Your Organization, 2nd ed
Dave Anderson
Chichester, UK: Wiley, 2007
320pp, ISBN: 978-0-470-06856-4
Achieving the highest organizational performance is about quality leadership; and without the right team, vision, strategy, and values are worthless. This book encourages reflection on leadership style and strategy and discusses areas such as recruitment, culture, employee development, goal setting, and growth. Written from a nonacademic, anti-intellectual stance, it is based on real-world experience.

Why Most Things Fail: Evolution, Extinction and Economics
Paul Ormerod
London: Faber & Faber, 2008
254pp, ISBN: 978-0-470-08919-4
In what could be a wake-up call for many senior leaders, this book tackles one of the great unspoken truths of the business world: most things do not work. Drawing on the author's experience as a professor of economics and reflecting on the raft of scandals witnessed since the fall of Enron, this book sets out to equip readers with the knowledge they need to avoid a similar fate.

JOURNALS

Harvard Business Review (HBR)
Harvard Business School Press
60 Harvard Way, Boston, MA 02163, USA
T: +1 617 783 7500
F: +1 (617) 783-7555
hbr.harvardbusiness.org
ISSN: 0017-8012
The HBR is a leading magazine for business leaders and senior executives that emphasizes current best practice and the application of leading edge research to business problems. Coverage is wide-ranging with a strong focus on leadership and strategy. Each issue includes feature articles written by experts and an interview with a business leader.

Leadership and Organization Development Journal
Emerald
60/62 Toller Lane, Bradford, West Yorkshire, BD8 9BY, UK
T: +44 (0) 1274 777 700
F: +44 (0) 1274 785 200
www.emeraldinsight.com/0143-7739.htm
ISSN: 0143-7739
This bimonthly journal for business leaders publishes articles that describe effective practice in strategy and leadership, as well as new theories that have the potential to advance the art of strategy development and its implementation.

Leadership Quarterly
Elsevier
PO Box 211, 1000 AE Amsterdam, The Netherlands
T: +31 20 485 3757
F: +31 20 485 3432
www.elsevier.com/locate/leaqua
ISSN: 1048-9843
Published four times each year, this journal analyzes the many factors that contribute to outstanding leadership. Executive managers and upper-level administrators will find the information presented in this journal will enhance and improve their leadership skills. It provides current information on the latest in leadership research. There is also an annual review of leadership topics.

INTERNET

12Manage
www.12manage.com/i_l.html
Under the Leadership link, this site offers information, forums and multiple links on leadership, methods, models, and theory.

Forbes.com
www.forbes.com/leadership
Under the Leadership link, this site offers articles, special reports, links, networks, a question and answer platform, and newsletters on leadership and related topics.

Leaders Direct
www.leadersdirect.com
Offering extensive tips for managers and leaders, this site focuses on the nature and development of leadership.

Leader to Leader
www.leadertoleader.org
This site offers access to a contents listing from the *Drucker Foundation Journal* and selected articles written by today's leading thinkers from the private, public, and social sectors.

weLEAD, Incorporated
www.leadingtoday.org
weLEAD is a nonprofit organization that believes that everyone is capable of being a great leader. The site includes an online magazine, tips, and book reviews. Extra services, including access to an article archive and related useful links, are available for members.

ORGANIZATIONS

Europe

The Leadership Trust Foundation
Weston-under-Penyard, Ross-on-Wye, Herefordshire, HR9 7YH, UK
T: +44 (0) 1989 767 667
F: +44 (0) 1989 768 133
www.leadership.org.uk
The foundation provides courses, postgraduate education, grants, and bursaries for those in pursuit of excellence in leadership.

USA

Center for Creative Leadership
1 Leadership Place, PO Box 26300, Greensboro, NC 27438-6300, USA
T: +1 336 545 2810
F: +1 336 282 3284
E: info@leaders.ccl.org
www.ccl.org
The Center for Creative Leadership is a nonprofit educational institution that is an internationally recognized resource for understanding and expanding the leadership capabilities of individuals and organizations.

   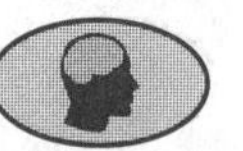  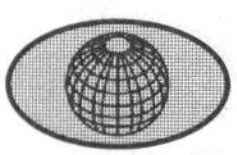   

The Global Leadership Network
The Center for Corporate Citizenship at Boston College, 55 Lee Road, Chesnut Hill, MA 02467, USA
E: info@globalleadershipnetwork.org
www.globalleadershipnetwork.org
This is an initiative of The Center for Corporate Citizenship at Boston College USA, AccountAbility in London, UK, and Rever Consulting in Brazil.

The Greanleaf Centre for Servant Leadership
770 Pawtucket Drive, Westfield, IN 46074, USA
T: +1 317 669 8050
F: +1 317 669 8055
E: lyoder@greenleaf.org
www.greenleaf.org
This international, non-profit organization promotes the understanding and practice of servant leadership worldwide. The USA-based center also has a European counterpart (http://www.servantleadershipcenter.net/) in the Netherlands.

BRIC

Brazilian Association for Leadership Development (ABDL)
Av. Prof. Almeida Prado, nº 532 prédio 31 térreo, Cidade Universitária Butantã, 05508–901 São Paulo, Brazil
T: +55 11 3719 1532
F: +55 11 3714 4222
E: abdl@abdl.org.br
ABDL is an autonomous Brazilian organization and a member of the LEAD International network (Leadership for Environment and Development), with support from several domestic and international partners who believe in the future and in the methodology of building capacity for action. ABDL is a non-profit organization with the mission of articulating leadership for a sustainable world.

Businessworld (BW)
ABP Pvt. Ltd, 3rd Floor, Express Building, 9–10, Bahadur Shah Zafar Marg, New Delhi 110 002, India
T: +11 23 7021 7079
F: +11 23 702 077
E: bwonline@bworldmail.com
www.businessworld.in/index.php/BW-Leadership
Businessworld has a separate heading for BW-Leadership, through which it offers links, a forum, listings, coaching, and news on leadership in India.

China Executive Leadership Academy Pudong (CELAP)
99 Qiancheng Road, Pudong New Area, Shanghai 201204, China
T: +86 21 2828 8888
F: +86 21 5059 5935
www.celap.org.cn
CELAP is a Shanghai-based, national institution funded by the central government. It focuses on social improvement and economic development, and provides training for leaders from government and top executives from the business community.

The Institute of Strategy, Leadership and Innovations
3 Volkhovskiy pereulok, Saint Petersburg, 199004, Russia
T: +7 812 323 8464
F: +7 812 329 3234
E: niim@gsom.pu.ru
www.gsom.pu.ru/en/niim/welcome
The institute is part of the Graduate School of Management at the St Petersburg State University, and focuses on research.

International

Association for Corporate Growth (ACG)
Suite 1, 1926 Waukegan Road, Glenview, IL 60025–1770, USA
T: +1 847 657 6730
F: +1 847 657 6819
E: acghq@tcag.com
www.acg.org
The ACG was founded in 1954 for professional managers involved in corporate growth and development in middle-market companies. The organization now has 5,000 members in the United States, Mexico, Canada, and the United Kingdom, and undertakes a range of activities including conferences. It also publishes a newsletter and offers networking opportunities.

  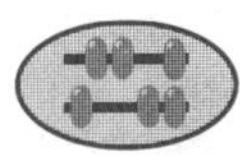   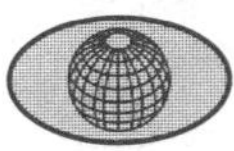   

Management Buyouts

BOOKS

The Art of M&A: A Merger Acquisition Buyout Guide, 4th ed
Stanley Foster Reed, Alexandra Reed Lajoux, H. Peter Nesvold
New York: McGraw-Hill, 2007
1100pp, ISBN: 978-0-07-140302-3
This book provides clear, in-depth answers and explanations on everything from the SEC rules and new tax guidelines to documents and key players . The authors give up-to-the-minute information on avoiding mishaps and completing the deal. It gives real-world insights through synopsis of dozens of landmark cases and includes sample forms and checklists.

Barbarians at the Gate
Bryan Burrough, John Helyar
London: Arrow Books, 2004
536pp, ISBN: 978-0-09-946915-5
This is a classic tale of corporate greed based on the merger of RJR and Nabisco. It is as gripping a read as any work of fiction.

The Buyout Book: The Insider's Guide to Buying Your Own Company
Rick Rickersten et al.
New York: AMACOM, 2001
304pp, ISBN: 978-0-8144-0626-7
This book gives you the tools and strategies you need to lead a successful management buyout. It includes everything from how to select the company you want to buy, through due diligence issues and finding equity partners, to running the company when you succeed in your buyout.

Creating Value through Corporate Restructuring: Case Studies in Bankruptcies, Buyouts, and Breakups
Stuart C. Gilson
New York: Wiley, 2001
528pp, ISBN: 978-0-471-40559-7
Management buyouts are a common form of business restructuring. This collection of recent case studies from the United States and several other countries illustrates the real-world techniques and strategies that are common to all types of restructuring. It demystifies the complex financial issues surrounding business valuation and gives the reader a better understanding of the possibilities when dealing with corporate restructuring.

How to Do a Leveraged Buyout
Christopher Jansen
Morrisville, North Carolina: Lulu.com, 2008
492pp, ISBN: 978-1-4357-1832-6
This book provides a step-by-step guide to successfully completing the leveraged buyout of any business. It offers specific advice on the key processes, techniques, and concepts involved in acquiring a business and financing its purchase.

Management Buyout: A Guide for the Prospective Entrepreneur, 2nd ed
Ian Webb
Aldershot, UK: Gower Publishing, 1990
176pp, ISBN: 978-0-566-02810-6
This book provides an introduction to the process of achieving a successful buyout and considers the financial and legal issues involved. It reviews the development of the buyout market in the United Kingdom and considers the relevance of an entrepreneurial mindset to buyout situations. Five case studies are included.

The MBO Deal: Inside the Management Buyout
Richard Westcott
Executive Briefing Series
London: Earthscan, 2001
131pp, ISBN: 978-0-273-65920-4
Management teams undertaking an MBO need to understand the complexities and risks involved. This briefing provides a detailed insight into the workings of an MBO, the processes involved, the risks, the financing, the documentation, and the negotiation of the deal itself.

Private Equity and Management Buy-Outs
Mike Wright and Hans Bruining
Cheltenham, UK: Edward Elgar Publishing, 2008
528pp, ISBN: 978-1-84720-725-8
Private Equity and Management Buy-outs provides a balanced view of the often polarized private equity debate. This careful and objective analysis of private equity in buy-out firms reviews the effects of this ownership transfer in terms of firm performance and survival, placing private equity in the broader context of its implications for value creation.

MAGAZINES

Buyouts Newsletter
Thomson Financial
195 Broadway, 10th Floor, New York, NY 10007, USA
T: +1 646 822 2000
F: +1 646 822 3230
www.buyoutsnews.com
ISSN: 1040-0990
Buyouts is a biweekly newsletter offering news, data, and analysis relating to the buyout industry. Listings of deals and funds in the United States are published quarterly. Readers can sign up for the newsletter on the website.

European Management Buyout Review
Chartered Institute of Public Finance and Accountancy
3 Robert Street, London, WC2N 6RL, UK
T: +44 (0) 20 7543 5600
F: +44 (0) 20 7543 5700
www.nottingham.ac.uk/business/cmbor/EBR.html
The *Review* focuses on trends in the European buyout market and covers 14 Western European countries.

Management Buyouts: A Quarterly Review
Chartered Institute of Public Finance and Accountancy
3 Robert Street, London, WC2N 6RL, UK
T: +44 (0) 20 7543 5600
F: +44 (0) 20 7543 5700
www.nottingham.ac.uk/business/cmbor/QR.html
This review includes feature articles on current topics as well as analyses of trends and reports on activity on the UK buyout scene.

JOURNALS

Journal of Management Studies
Blackwell Publishing
9600 Garsington Road, Oxford, OX4 2DQ, UK
T: +44 (0) 1865 791 100
F: +44 (0) 1865 791 347
www.wiley.com/bw/journal.asp?ref=0022-2380
ISSN: 0022-2380
JMS, published eight times each year, offers empirical studies, theoretical developments, and practical applications on innovation and excellence in management research organization theory and behavior, strategic and human resource management, cross-cultural comparisons of organizational effectiveness, and reviews of the latest publications in management studies.

Journal of Small Business and Enterprise Development
Emerald
60/62 Toller Lane, Bradford, West Yorkshire, BD8 9BY, UK

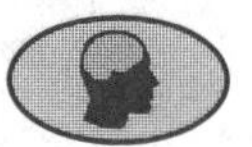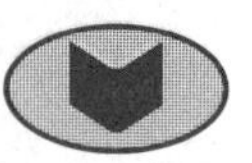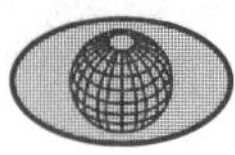

T: +44 (0) 1274 777 700
F: +44 (0) 1274 785 200
www.emeraldinsight.com/1462-6004.htm
ISSN: 1462-6004
The *JSBED* is a peer-reviewed journal that disseminates research findings and best practice and aims to bridge the gap between theory and practice in the field of small business and enterprise development. The journal contains articles, case studies, and book reviews, and is aimed at those responsible for the management of SMEs, those who provide support and assistance to entrepreneurs and owner-managers, and those involved in the development of enterprise policy.

Management Decisions

Emerald
60/62 Toller Lane, Bradford, West Yorkshire, BD8 9BY, UK
T: +44 (0) 1274 777 700
F: +44 (0) 1274 785 200
www.emeraldinsight.com/0025-1747.htm
ISSN: 0025-1747
Management Decisions consists of articles that analyze the link between management buyouts and the entrepreneurial process. It examines evidence to support the MBO-entrepreneur link, and that MBOs encourage entrepreneurial activity.

INTERNET

Are You Management Buyout Material?

www.cfo.com/Article?article=2117
Management buyouts are not for everyone. It takes the right team with appropriate backing. This checklist can help you determine whether you have what it takes to be successful.

Is a Management Buyout in Your Future?

www.imakenews.com/rcwmirus/e_article000017429.cfm
This article from the Mirus Online Newsletter describes management buyouts and identifies the characteristics of typical candidate companies. It outlines what each side is looking for and presents financing options that can be used.

Orchestrating a Management Buyout

www.southflorida.bizjournals.com/milwaukee/stories/1996/12/09/focus1.html
Describing the management buyout experience as a roller coaster ride, this article points out that perseverance is often a key element in completing the buyout successfully. It provides real-world examples of how obstacles can be overcome.

ORGANIZATIONS

Europe

The British Private Equity and Venture Capital Association

3 Clements Inn, London, WC2A 2AZ, UK
T: +44 (0) 20 7025 2950
F: +44 (0) 20 7025 2951
E: bvca@bvca.co.uk
www.bvca.co.uk/index.html
The BVCA is the industry body for the UK private equity and venture capital industry. It consists of 400 members and promotes the industry to entrepreneurs and investors, as well as provides services and best practice standards to its members.

Centre for Management Buyout Research (CMBOR)

Nottingham University Business School, Jubilee Campus, Wollaton Road, Nottingham, Nottinghamshire, NG8 1BB, UK
T: +44 (0) 115 951 5493
F: +44 (0) 115 951 5204
E: margaret.burdett@nottingham.ac.uk
www.nottingham.ac.uk/business/cmbor
CMBOR was founded by Barclays Private Equity Limited and Deloitte & Touche at the Nottingham University Business School in March 1986 to monitor and analyze management buyouts in a comprehensive and objective way. A database of MBOs in the United Kingdom and Europe has been developed, and quarterly reviews and research papers are published.

BRIC

India Venture Capital Association

301–302, Delhi Blue Apartments, Main Ring Road, New Delhi 110 029, India
T: +91 11 4162 8566
F: +91 11 4162 8863
E: info@indiavca.org
www.indiavca.org/abt_mission.aspx
Indian Venture Capital and Private Equity Association (IVCA) is a member-based, national organization that represents venture capital and private equity firms, promotes the industry within India and the rest of the world, and encourages investment in high-growth companies.

  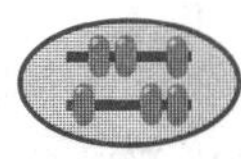   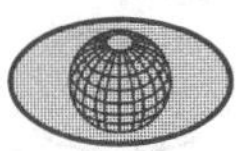   

Management Styles

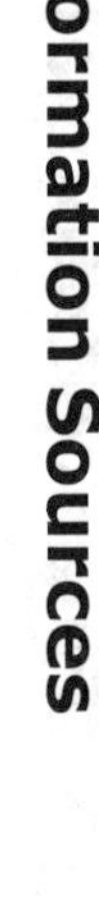

BOOKS

Brainstyles: Change Your Life Without Changing Who You Are

Marlane Miller
London: Simon & Schuster, 2004
384pp, ISBN: 978-0-9634406-2-4

This book offers a method of assessment which sorts people into four categories (deliberators, conceptors, knowers, and conciliators) and includes tips on dealing with each of the styles presented. Miller makes a strong case for people to focus on their strengths instead of working on their "nonstrengths."

Douglas McGregor, Revisited: Managing the Human Side of the Enterprise

Gary Heil, Warren Bennis, Deborah C. Stephens
Chichester, UK: Wiley, 2000
224pp, ISBN: 978-0-471-31462-2

Paying tribute to the influence of Douglas McGregor, this book updates his thinking with new concepts, fresh strategies, and modern methods of implementation. It indicates how his original thinking has reemerged in current approaches that stress distributed leadership, open-minded appraisal techniques, and employee-customer commitment. Highlighted throughout with gems of wisdom in McGregor's own words, the book emphasizes the value of his theories for the managers of today.

Jack: Straight from the Gut

Jack Welch, John A. Byrne
London: Headline, 2003
496pp, ISBN: 978-0-7472-4979-5

In this title, Welch discusses the method of management he adopted in order to turn General Electric into the hugely successful company that it has become. The book also contains a brief look at Welch's childhood and charts a career that started with him working in the plastics division of General Electric and ended with him becoming Chief Executive Officer.

Management Challenges for the 21st Century, 2nd ed

Peter F. Drucker
Oxford: Butterworth-Heinemann, 2007
224pp, ISBN: 978-0-7506-8509-2

Management Challenges for the 21st Century observes social and economic changes occurring today, and considers how management should adjust to these new realities. It is for people who care about their businesses and careers in the information age, such as CEOs, managers, and knowledge workers.

Management Worldwide: Distinctive Styles Among Globalization, 2nd ed

David J. Hickson, Derek S. Pugh
London: Penguin, 2002
352pp, ISBN: 978-0-14-100603-1

Management Worldwide is aimed at managers, students of management, and organizations who want to know how managers operate and business is conducted in different societies.

The New Imperialists

Mark Leibovich, Paul Saffo
Harlow, UK: Prentice Hall, 2002
320pp, ISBN: 978-0-7352-0317-4

This title profiles five leaders of the digital age: Bill Gates of Microsoft, AOL-Time Warner's Steve Case, Amazon.com's Jeff Bezos, Oracle's Larry Ellison, and John Chambers at Cisco. Using hundreds of interviews with friends, family, and rivals, the book charts the most significant events in these revolutionary figures' lives and reveals how they dealt with such experiences.

Primal Leadership: Realizing the Power of Emotional Intelligence

Daniel Goleman, Richard Boyatzis, Annie McKee
Boston, Massachusetts: Harvard Business School Press, 2002
352pp, ISBN: 978-1-57851-486-1

The authors describe six styles that account for all critical management behavior: visionary, coaching, affiliative, democratic, pace-setting, and commanding. Good leaders use different styles according to the situation. They explain that the importance of these styles is that the right style used with the right team will generate "good feelings" and that style is a critical factor, not only in managing and leading but also in generating organizational profits. The book is based on studies of nearly 4,000 executives.

Trump-Style Negotiation: Powerful Strategies and Tactics for Mastering Every Deal

George H. Ross
Hoboken, New Jersey: Wiley, 2008
288pp, ISBN: 978-0-470-22529-5

Explains the tactics that made Donald Trump a success, and how to use those same tactics and strategies in your daily business life and deal negotiations. It is a practical, real-world guide on effective negotiation.

Where Egos Dare: The Untold Truth about Narcissistic Leaders—and How to Survive Them

Dean B. McFarlin, Paul D. Sweeney
London: Kogan Page, 2002
272pp, ISBN: 978-0-7494-3773-2

This book explores the seamier side of leadership. Much has been written about the dynamic, focused leader, but what about the obsessive and egocentric leader? The authors investigate the psyche of such leaders and the devastating effect it can have on both individual and organizational performance. They also suggest proactive measures that can be taken to curb the excesses of a narcissistic leader.

MAGAZINES

Management Today

Haymarket Business Publications
174 Hammersmith Road, London, W6 7JP, UK
T: +44 (0) 20 8267 4610
www.managementtoday.co.uk

Management Today is a well-informed and respected magazine that focuses on the issues that trouble and inspires Britain's business leaders and managers.

Performance Management Magazine

Penton Technology Media
249 West 17th Street, New York, NY 10011, USA
T: +1 678 904 6140
www.pmezine.com
ISSN: 1556-813X

Performance Management Magazine highlights the successes of companies that use performance management as a systematic, data-oriented approach to managing people by providing positive recognition and reinforcement for individual and group performance. It explains the latest academic research in the field of behavior management, and provides links to useful sources on performance improvement.

JOURNALS

Academy of Management Journal

Academy of Management
Pace University, 235 Elm Road, Briarcliff Manor, NY 10510-8020, USA
T: +1 914 923 2607
F: +1 914 923 2615
journals.aomonline.org/amj
ISSN: 0001-4273

The Academy of Management Journal publishes tests, extends or builds management theory and contributes to management practice, and presents relevant empirical methods, including qualitative, quantitative, field, laboratory, and combination methods. It is not tied to any particular discipline, level of analysis, or national context.

Emergence: Complexity & Organization
ISCE Publishing
3810 N 188th Ave, Litchfield Park, AZ 85340, USA
T: +1 508 406 3111
F: +1 781 634 0357
iscepublishing.com/ECO/about_eco.aspx
ISSN: 1521-3250
E:CO is a quarterly journal published in print and online by The Complexity Society, the Institute for the Study of Coherence and Emergence, and Cognitive Edge in accordance with academic publishing standards and processes. It integrates multiple perspectives in management theory, research, practice, and education.

INTERNET

The Consortium for Research on Emotional Intelligence in Organizations
www.eiconsortium.org
This site has a comprehensive listing of topics related to the field of emotional intelligence. It provides downloadable reports on academic research and programs in organizations where emotional intelligence is the focus of training. It is also a useful source of information on instruments for measuring emotional intelligence.

Institute for Management Excellence
www.itstime.com
This site has many areas of information relating to management practices. It offers a number of articles on personality styles and management, an online personality test, and a monthly newsletter on various people-management topics.

Management Issues
www.management-issues.com
Management Issues is an independent, online resource that focuses on leadership, management, and people issues that are part of the changing workplace. It provides an objective platform for topical debate and informed opinion by thought leaders on management, leadership, and human resources.

ORGANIZATIONS

Europe

European Management Association
c/o Malta Institute of Management, FRCC Building, Alamein Road, Pembroke, Malta
T: +356 2145 3097
F: +356 2145 1167
E: sscerri@maltamanagement.com
www.europeanmanagement.org
EMA is an independent, professional, non-profit organization. It is also non-governmental, non-political, and non-religious, and provides an active network for bringing together management professionals and practitioners from across Europe.

International Professional Managers Association
5 Starnes Court, Union Street, Maidstone, Kent, ME14 1EB, UK
T: +44 (0) 1622 672 867
F: +44 (0) 1622 755 149
E: registrar@ipma.co.uk
www.ipma.co.uk/index.php
The International Professional Managers Association (IPMA) is an international examining, licensing, and regulatory membership qualifying professional body formed for the purpose of providing practicing managers with the opportunity to participate and to be part of the process of improving managerial performance and effectiveness in all areas of business, industry and public administration.

Project Management Institute
Avenue de Tervueren, 300, 1150 Brussels, Belgium
T: +32 2 743 15 73
F: +32 2 743 15 50
E: emea-servicecentre@pmi.org
www.pmi.org.uk/index.asp
PMI promotes the contribution of the project management profession with local businesses, educational establishments and professional associations. It has built a strong membership base of project management professionals by providing value-added membership services.

BRIC

All India Management Association
Management House, Institutional Area, Lodhi Road, New Delhi 110003, India
T: +11 24 64 5100
F: +11 24 62 6689
E: dcms@aima-ind.org
www.aima-ind.org
AIMA is a federation of local management associations (LMAs) that assists Indian managers in making the most of their opportunities. It pools management thought and practice in the country, and provides a forum to develop a national managerial culture. It affiliates 58 LMAs across the country and two co-operating management associations.

Asian Association of Management Organisations
14/F Fairmont House, 8 Cotton Tree Drive, Central, Hong Kong
T: +852 28 26 0538
F: +852 28 68 4387
E: hoo@aamo.net
www.aamo.net/default.htm
AAMO is a partner of National Management Organizations (NMO), with the purpose of sharing and leveraging resources to enhance the achievement of their respective missions. It is an independent, non-political and non-profit association, which promotes, facilitates, and supports the development of professional management in the Asia-Pacific Region.

International Association for Chinese Management Research
China
www.iacmr.org
IACMR is a professional academic organization for scholars, students, managers, and consultants who are interested in advancing knowledge on managing organizations within the Chinese context. The primary goal of the organization is to promote scholarly studies of organization and management of firms.

The Russian Project Management Association (SOVNET)
Suite 504, 7, Kibalchicha St, Moscow, 129366, Russia
T: +7 95 682 62 73
F: +7 95 682 62 73
E: sovnet@sovnet.ru
www.sovnet.ru/english
SOVNET is a non-profit, professional, international organization acting according to the Russian legislation and the associations' charter. The association unites experience, knowledge, and efforts of state and public organizations, private companies, firms, enterprises, and individual specialists in the field of project management.

  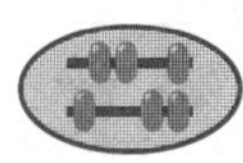  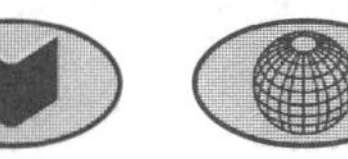 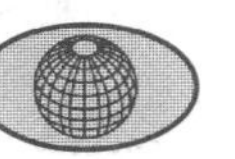   

Management Theorists

BOOKS

The Best Business Books Ever
Cambridge, Massachusetts: Perseus Books Group, 2003
256pp, ISBN: 978-0-7382-0849-7
Contained in this volume are incisive, time-saving digests of more than 100 of the finest and most influential books on business and management.

Demystifying Business Celebrity: Leaders and Gurus
Timothy Clark
New York: Routledge, 2009
224pp, ISBN: 978-0-415-32782-4
This book argues that business celebrities, including entrepreneurs, CEOs, and management gurus, are not self-made, but rather are created by a process of widespread media exposure to the point that their actions, personalities and even private lives function symbolically to represent significant dynamics and tensions prevalent in the contemporary business environment.

Essential Business Books: The World's Best Business Writing at a Glance
London: A&C Black Publishers, 2003
256pp, ISBN: 978-0-7475-6238-2
This book provides incisive, time-saving digests of more than 100 of the finest and most influential books on business and management.

The Essential Drucker: The Best of Sixty Years of Peter Drucker's Essential Writings on Management
Peter F. Drucker
London: HarperCollins, 2008
368pp, ISBN: 978-0-06-134501-2
When it comes to American management theorists, Peter Drucker tops almost everyone's list. This book is a compilation of Drucker's most important writings over the course of his lengthy and still very active career. Each article has been chosen by virtue of its contemporary relevance or its historical significance.

Guide to Management Ideas and Gurus
Tim Hindle
Economist books
London: Profile Books, 2008
322pp, ISBN: 978-1-84668-108-0
Guide to Management Ideas and Gurus gathers the most influential ideas and thinkers that have defined modern management into one compact guide. Topics covered range from active inertia and disruptive technology to triple bottom line and the long tail, while the management gurus covered include Jim Collins, Peter Drucker, Philip Kotler, Michael Porter, and Tom Peters.

The Guru Guide: The Best Ideas of the Top Management Thinkers
Joseph H. Boyett, Jimmie T. Boyett
Chichester, UK: Wiley, 2000
400pp, ISBN: 978-0-471-38054-2
The key ideas of 79 of the world's leading management experts are examined here. Presenting the gurus' works in seven subject-oriented chapters, the authors cross-link their ideas and provide critical commentaries and case study examples of the ideas in practice.

Leader to Leader 2: Enduring Insights on Leadership from the Leader to Leader Institute's Award-winning Journal
Frances Hesselbein, Paul M. Cohen (editors)
San Francisco, California: Jossey-Bass, 2008
384pp, ISBN: 978-0-470-19547-5
This collection of articles, taken from the journal *Leader to Leader*, brings together the wisdom of world renowned leaders, bestselling writers, leading thinkers, and business philosophers. These include Peter Drucker, Herb Kelleher, John P. Kotter, Rosabeth Moss Kanter, Peter Senge, and Charles Handy.

Management of Organizational Behavior: Leading Human Resources, 9th ed
Paul Hersey, Kenneth H. Blanchard, Dewey E. Johnson
Harlow, UK: Prentice Hall, 2008
550pp, ISBN: 978-0-13-144139-2
This book is primarily concerned with what many consider the soft side of management: dealing with people. The book provides a good overview of contemporary management theorists before tying their theories into Hersey and Blanchard's "situational leadership" theory. Overall, this is a lengthy but valuable book for anyone wishing to learn more about leading theories on management.

Ruthless Leader: Three Classics of Strategy and Power
Alistair McAlpine (editor)
Chichester, UK: Wiley, 2000
272pp, ISBN: 978-0-471-37247-9
The texts of three classic works on leadership make up this compilation: *The Prince* by Nicolò Machiavelli, *The Servant* by Alistair McAlpine, and *The Art of War* by Sun Tzu. The introduction places these texts in their contemporary contexts, and compares and contrasts them, drawing out their major themes and demonstrating their application to modern business organizations.

The Ultimate Business Guru Book: 50 Thinkers Who Made Management, 2nd ed
Stuart Crainer, Des Dearlove
Chichester, UK: Capstone, 2003
256pp, ISBN: 978-1-900961-59-2
Crainer discusses the ideas of 50 leading management thinkers in detail and lists their key publications. He also provides brief summaries of the work of other thinkers.

JOURNALS

Academy of Management Review
Academy of Management
Pace University, 235 Elm Road, Briarcliff Manor, NY 10510–8020, USA
T: +1 914 923 2607
F: +1 914 923 2615
journals.aomonline.org/amr
ISSN: 0363-7425
Ranked among the top 10 most influential and frequently cited management publications, AMR is a quarterly, theory development journal that publishes the highest quality conceptual work in the field. It offers articles that challenge conventional wisdom concerning all aspects of organizations and their role in society, and provide new theoretical insights. Includes reviews of relevant literature.

Chinese Management Studies
Emerald
60/62 Toller Lane, Bradford, West Yorkshire, BD8 9BY, UK
T: +44 (0) 1274 777 700
F: +44 (0) 1274 785 200
www.emeraldinsight.com/1750-614X.htm
ISSN: 1750-614X
Issued quarterly, this magazine provides a unique and insightful approach to documenting and disseminating research into Chinese processes of managing enterprises, firms and corporations. It provides in-depth analysis of Chinese managerial thinking, philosophy and processes, empirical pieces on Chinese

  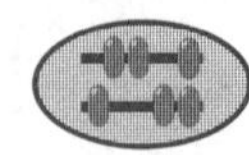 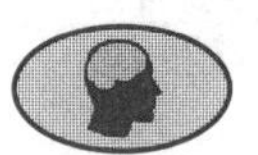  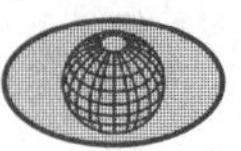   

management, and interviews that reflect current thinking on management by leading Chinese CEOs, academics, and personalities.

Euro Asia Journal of Management
Macau Foundation
Av. Repóblica, n.º 6, Macau
T: +853 2896 8658
F: +853 2896 6777
www.geocities.com/eajm2002
ISSN: 0872-8496
This is an international, peer-reviewed journal that is dedicated to the advancement of management theories and practices in Asia and Europe.

INTERNET

Business.com
www.business.com/directory/management/management_theory/management_theorists
This website offers a comprehensive list of modern management theorists in the form of links to articles by and about those theorists. With over 65 primary links and several articles in every secondary link, the coverage is extensive.

GurusOnline
gurusonline.tv
Gurusonline.tv was founded by Jorge Nascimento Rodrigues, a management and technology journalist. Over the last 15 years he has interviewed more than 100 management and technology gurus from around the world. The contents of the interviews are published here in Portuguese, Spanish, and English.

Harvard Business Blogs
discussionleader.hbsp.com
This is a useful collection of interesting blogs from business thinkers and leaders, presented by the Harvard Business School. They cover areas such as coaching, brands, marketing, global management, and innovation. A newsfeed is available for each blog.

Intute: Social Sciences
www.intute.ac.uk/socialsciences/about.html
Intute: Social Sciences provides a resource for education and research for the social sciences, including law, business, hospitality, sport, and tourism.

Thinkers50
www.thinkers50.com
This management guru website was set up by guru-spotters Stuart Crainer and Des Dearlove in 2001. The Thinkers 50 tends to appear every two years, and visitors to the page are able to vote for their favorite guru and give their reasons. The results of the most recent poll appear on the site, with concise biographies of the relevant management thinker.

ORGANIZATIONS

Europe

Academy of Management
Pace University, 235 Elm Road, Briarcliff Manor, NY 10510–8020, USA
T: +1 914 923 2607
F: +1 914 923 2615
E: mdavis@pace.edu
aomonline.org
The Academy of Management is a leading professional association for scholars dedicated to creating and disseminating knowledge about management and organizations. It is the oldest and largest scholarly management association in the world.

  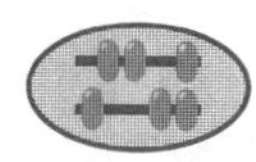   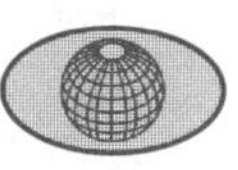   

Market Research and Competitor Intelligence

BOOKS

Competitive Intelligence and Global Business

David L. Blenkhorn, Craig S. Fleisher (editors)
Westport, Connecticut: Greenwood Publishing Group, 2005
312pp, ISBN: 978-0-275-98140-2

Competitive Intelligence and Global Business provides in-depth analysis of emerging approaches to competitive intelligence in different industry sectors, such as pharmaceuticals and automotive supply chains. It provides insights and recommendations for CI specialists, strategic planners and executives, marketers and product developers, and anyone studying competition and strategy.

Competitive Intelligence: Gathering, Analysing and Putting it to Work

Christopher Murphy
Aldershot, UK: Gower Publishing, 2005
273pp, ISBN: 978-0-566-08537-6

This book discusses financial analysis of company accounts by giving a deep coverage of UK legal forms, company filings, and how to interpret them.

Competitor Intelligence: Turning Analysis into Success

David Hussey, Per Jenster
Wiley Series in Practical Strategy
Chichester, UK: Wiley, 1999
296pp, ISBN: 978-0-471-98407-8

This book, written for managers, aims to give practical advice on how to identify and analyze intelligence relating to competitors for the purpose of gaining a competitive advantage. The authors also discuss, again in practical terms, the critical success factors involved in planning, in understanding competitors, and in sourcing information. Case studies are included.

Essentials of Marketing Research

Joseph F. Hair, Jr, Mary Wolfinbarger, Robert P Bush, David J. Ortinau
Maidenhead, UK: McGraw-Hill, 2007
400pp, ISBN: 978-0-07-338102-2

This provides an updated range of practical market research topics, including real-world experiences of the treatment of qualitative research. This book will give students and readers the tools and skills to solve business problems, and exploit business opportunities.

How Customers Think: Essential Insights into the Mind of the Market

Gerald Zaltman
Boston, Massachusetts: Harvard Business School Press, 2003
352pp, ISBN: 978-1-57851-826-5

This book offers a unique perspective on tapping into what it is exactly that your customers want. Using as a base key themes from psychology, sociology, and other sciences, it sets out to help marketers ask the right questions (and work out the right answers) so that the innovation and production cycle benefits.

Managing Frontiers in Competitive Intelligence

Craig S. Fleisher, David Blenkhorn (editors)
Westport, Connecticut: Quorum Books, 2000
328pp, ISBN: 978-1-56720-384-4

This book is a nice balance of the theoretical and the practical aspects of Competitive Intelligence (CI). While describing the best practices in the industry, the authors present the steps necessary to counter CI. They provide information on how to improve your intelligence collection process, methods, and tools. Significantly, they tie CI back to the needs of the business and point out its interface with finance, research and development, and product development.

Marketing Research, 9th ed

David A. Aaker, V. Kumar, George S. Day
Hoboken, New Jersey: Wiley, 2007
800pp, ISBN: 978-0-470-05076-7

The authors adopt a "macro-micro-macro" approach toward marketing research and its uses within organizations. They initially explore the uses and place of marketing research in managerial decision-making, as well as the industry itself (briefly examining both suppliers and users) at macro level. They also examine the processes of marketing research in more depth, including industry examples to fulfill the micro phase of the text, and provide coverage of the most recent research techniques.

Marketing Research: An Integrated Approach, 2nd ed

Alan Wilson
Harlow, UK: FT Prentice Hall, 2006
432pp, ISBN: 978-0-273-69474-8

This textbook provides an overview of research within the marketing sector, as well as describing how marketing research should be integral to business operations, rather than a marginal activity. It discusses current issues, key concepts and techniques, and their relevance for the management of customer information, new developments such as online research, multi-mode interviewing, and falling response rates, and offers cases that demonstrate real-life marketing research practice.

Marketing Research Essentials, 6th ed

Carl McDaniel, Roger Gates
Hoboken, New Jersey: Wiley, 2006
704pp, ISBN: 978-0-471-45519-6

This comprehensive manual surveys the whole process of modern market research. It deals with the role of market research in management decision-making, sources of data and primary data collection techniques, sampling and statistical analysis, and how to communicate results through effective reports. It backs up its account with many worked examples, illustrations, and case studies.

Marketing Research for Managers, 3rd ed

Sunny Crouch, Matt Housden
Oxford: Butterworth-Heinemann, 2003
400pp, ISBN: 978-0-7506-5453-1

This is one of the leading UK texts for managers seeking to understand market research. Rather than proffering over-detailed explanations of how to undertake research, this book explains enough for managers to be able to commission worthwhile research from professionals.

Market Research Matters: Tools and Techniques for Aligning Your Business

Robert Duboff, Jim Spaeth
New York: Wiley, 2000
320pp, ISBN: 978-0-471-36005-6

The authors explain the value of market research and forecasting techniques to successful business strategies. They describe the tools and techniques that enable analysts to anticipate marketplace shifts and the methods of using them. Among other topics, they discuss customer loyalty, brand management, competition, distribution channels, employee performance and loyalty, and the internet. Diagnostic material to allow readers to assess the progress of their business in each area is also included.

     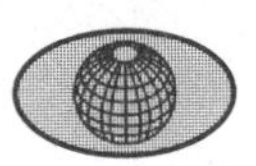   

The Market Research Toolbox: A Concise Guide for Beginners, 2nd ed
Edward F. McQuarrie
Thousand Oaks, California: Sage Publications, 2006
224pp, ISBN: 978-1-4129-1319-5
Aimed at giving a basic understanding of market research tools, this book looks at market research in the context of making a business decision. Beginning with an explanation of market research, the author goes on to describe how each of the six traditional market research techniques works, along with its costs and uses, and tips for success. Also examined are the nontraditional methods that have evolved in recent years.

Proven Strategies in Competitive Intelligence: Lessons from the Trenches
John E. Prescott, Stephen H. Miller (editors)
New York: Wiley, 2001
288pp, ISBN: 978-0-471-40178-0
This is a collection of articles that identify and explore proven practicable approaches to competitive intelligence that can be applied across a variety of business areas. Once the concept of competitive intelligence has been introduced and its legal and ethical boundaries have been explored, further contributions from leading executives and market leaders highlight the best techniques that can be used to outwit and outperform current, emerging, and potential competitors.

Qualitative Research in Intelligence and Marketing: The New Strategic Convergence
Alf H. Walle
Westport, Connecticut: Quorum Books, 2001
246pp, ISBN: 978-1-56720-366-0
This book compares and integrates the qualitative method of marketing research with competitive intelligence. It discusses how an organization can conduct an audit to take full advantage of qualitative analytical techniques, and features an appendix that discusses how to recruit and motivate researchers. This book can apply to marketing practitioners, and graduate-level students and their teachers.

Strategic and Competitive Analysis: Methods and Techniques for Analyzing Business Competition
Craig S. Fleisher, Babette Bensoussan
Upper Saddle River, New Jersey: Prentice Hall, 2002
457pp, ISBN: 978-0-13-088852-5
Strategic and Competitive Analysis examines the many ways of analyzing business and competitive data and information, including strategic, competitive, customer, environmental, evolutionary, and temporal analysis models. It shows how to make effective conclusions from limited data, and understand information that may not appear to make sense. It also offers competitive analysis techniques and a review of the literature and survey research.

MAGAZINES

Competitive Intelligence Magazine
Society of Competitive Intelligence Professionals
1700 Diagonal Road, Suite 600, Alexandria, VI 22314, USA
T: +1 703 739 0696
F: +1 703 739 2524
www.scip.org/publications/CIMagCurrent.cfm?navItemNumber=528
ISSN: 1521-5881
Competitive Intelligence Magazine examines all the key issues affecting the industry, and offers information and networking opportunities for competitive intelligence professionals.

JOURNALS

Competitive Intelligence Review
Wiley
111 River St, Hoboken, NJ 07030-5774, USA
T: +1 201 748-6000
www.interscience.wiley.com/jpages/1058-0247
ISSN: 1058-0247
The Review, which ceased publication in 2001, was the journal of the competitive intelligence (CI) profession and covered all aspects of the field, with its main emphasis on practical applications. Its target readership included CI practitioners, managers, vendors, government organizations, and academics.

Information Management Journal
ARMA International
13725 West 109th Street, Suite 101, Lenexa, KS 66215, USA
T: +1 913 217 6007
F: +1 913 341 3742
www.arma.org/imj
ISSN: 1040-1628
Information Management Journal, published bimonthly, covers all the main aspects of information management for the practitioner community.

Insolvency Law and Practice
LexisNexis
Tolley House, 2 Addiscombe Road, Croydon, CR9 5AF, UK
T: +44 (0) 20 8662 2000
F: +44 (0) 20 8662 2012
www.lexisnexis.co.uk
www.lexisnexis.co.uk
ISSN: 0267-0771
Aimed at legal practitioners, students, and accountants, this magazine covers all aspects of insolvency law and accountancy. It appears six times each year.

Journal of Competitive Intelligence and Management
Society of Competitive Intelligence Professionals
1700 Diagonal Road, Suite 600, Alexandria, VI 22314, USA
T: +1 703 739 0696
F: +1 703 739 2524
www.scip.org/publications/JCIMCurrentIssue.cfm
ISSN: 1703-5147
The Journal of Competitive Intelligence and Management aims to promote and develop competitive intelligence, and increase the level of understanding of the management of competition, by publishing scholarly papers that cover all aspects of the field, particularly practical applications. It is aimed at CI practitioners, and private and public sector managers who use CI in their decision-making.

INTERNET

Competitive Intelligence
competitive-intelligence.mirum.net
This useful website provides tools, tips, and tricks about competitive intelligence for its stakeholders. It also offers intelligence articles, resources, and information.

ECNext
www.ecnext.com
This is a site offering online access to a database of business and market intelligence from global publishers.

Esomar Glossary
www.esomar.org
This section of the useful Esomar site contains a glossary of market research terms. It seeks to explain frequently-used marketing research terms in language that someone new to the industry can easily understand.

Euromonitor International
www.euromonitor.com
In-depth strategic analysis and up-to-date market statistics and market reports are all available to purchase online from this site.

Forrester
www.forrester.com
Forrester is a leading independent research firm that conducts technology research for its clients. Its expertise is in analyzing the research results and synthesizing the critical information. Some free information is available to nonclients on its site.

Key Note Market Information Centre
www.keynote.co.uk
This site is run by suppliers of market research reports, which are available for purchase, and provides free executive summaries.

Market Research.com
www.marketresearch.com
Collecting reports from all over the world, marketresearch.com is one of the largest sources of published research on the web. Reports can be bought and managed with a personal account, and the site has other features, such as an e-mail update service.

@ResearchInfo.com
www.researchinfo.com
This site is a collection of information on the market research industry. It includes the Market Research Roundtable, a directory of research companies, software reviews, and market research calculators.

ORGANIZATIONS

Europe

Alliance of International Market Research Institutes (AIMRI)
26 Granard Avenue, London, SW15 6HJ, UK
T: +44 (0)20 8780 3343
F: +44 (0) 20 7246 6893
E: info@aimri.net
www.aimri.net
The alliance is a representative organization for market research institutes in Europe and other parts of the world.

British Market Research Association
Ealing Gateway, 26–30 Uxbridge Road, London, W5 2BP, UK
T: +44 (0) 20 8433 4000
F: +44 (0) 20 8433 4001
E: web@brmb.co.uk
www.bmrb.co.uk
The BMRA aims to represent and promote the professional and commercial interests of its members, to increase the professionalism of market research, and to promote confidence in the market research industry generally.

Institute for Competitive Intelligence
Korngasse 9, Butzbach, 35510, Germany
T: +49 60 33 971 377
F: +49 60 33 971 376
E: info@competitive-intelligence.com
The Institute for Competitive Intelligence is an association that provides post-graduate professionals with a CI training program that certifies them as competitive intelligence professionals. It offers both educational programs and in-house training.

Market Research Society
15 Northburgh Street, London, EC1V 0JR, UK
T: +44 (0) 20 7490 4911
F: +44 (0) 20 7490 0608
E: info@mrs.org.uk
www.mrs.org.uk
MRS sets and enforces the ethical standards to be observed by research practitioners. Its framework of qualifications and membership grades reflects the education, knowledge, and competence required for the effective conduct of market research.

USA

American Marketing Association
311 South Wacker Drive, Suite 5800, Chicago, IL 60606–5819, USA
T: +1 312 542 9000
F: +1 312 542 9001
E: info@ama.org
www.marketingpower.com
The American Marketing Association (AMA) has over 40,000 members worldwide, with nearly 400 chapters throughout the United States and Canada. It is an international professional organization for people involved in the practice, study, and teaching of marketing. As well as setting standards of best practice in the industry, the AMA seeks to help marketers by providing them with products, services, information, education, and resources. It has a large, informative website and publishes a wide range of journals.

Competitive Intelligence Foundation
1700 Diagonal Road, Suite 600, Alexandria, VI 22314, USA
T: +1 703 739 0696
F: +1 703 739 2524
E: bhohhof@scip.org
The CI Foundation conducts and supports research on emerging issues and key trends that affect the practice of competitive intelligence and its ability to support key decision-makers and their organizations. It also makes existing and developing competitive intelligence knowledge available and relevant for the competitive intelligence practitioner through targeted publications, such as handbooks, studies, and survey reports.

Council for Marketing and Opinion Research
110 National Drive, 2nd Floor, Glastonbury, CT 06033, USA
T: +1 860 682 1000
F: +1 860 682 1010
E: information@cmor.org
www.cmor.org
Recently merged with the Marketing Research Association, CMOR is a nonprofit trade association formed to protect the interests of the marketing and opinion research industry. Its members are research companies and their clients.

The Society of Competitive Intelligence Professionals
1700 Diagonal Road, Suite 600, Alexandria, VI 22314, USA
T: +1 703 739 0696
F: +1 703 739 2524
E: info@scip.org
www.scip.org
The society is dedicated to helping professionals develop expertise in creating, collecting, and analyzing information, in disseminating competitive intelligence, and in engaging decision makers in a productive dialogue that creates organizational competitive advantage.

International

EFAMRO
Hoek van Hollandlaan 13, 2554 EA Den Haag, The Netherlands
T: +31 70 32 38 820
E: lexolivier@efamro.com
www.efamro.com
EFAMRO is a federation of market research agency associations in the European Union, founded in 1992. Its aims are to represent the interests of its members and to maintain high standards in the industry. Members adhere to the ICC/ESOMAR International Code of Marketing and Social Research Practice.

Mathematical Finance

BOOKS

Arbitrage Theory in Continuous Time, 2nd ed

Tomas Björk
Oxford Finance Series
Oxford, UK: Oxford University Press, 2004
466pp, ISBN: 978-0-19-927126-9

This is an introduction to the classical underpinnings of mathematical finance, which combines sound mathematical principles with economic applications. It focuses on the probabilistic theory of continuous arbitrage pricing of financial derivatives, including stochastic optimal control theory and Merton's fund separation theory. It includes a solved example for every new technique presented, and contains numerous exercises.

Aspects of Mathematical Finance

Marc Yor (editor)
Berlin: Springer, 2008
80pp, ISBN: 978-3-540-75258-5

This short but insightful treatment is based on a series of public lectures given in Paris by internationally renowned experts in mathematical finance, which promoted an understanding of the fundamental ideas, techniques and new tools of the financial industries. It develops topics such as risk measures, the notion of arbitrage, and dynamic models involving fundamental stochastic processes.

The Concepts and Practice of Mathematical Finance, 2nd ed

Mark S. Joshi
Mathematics, Finance and Risk Series
Cambridge, UK: Cambridge University Press, 2008
539pp, ISBN: 978-0-521-51408-8

Written by one of the most respected figures in mathematical finance, this book is an introduction to the discipline of mathematical and quantitative finance. It provides a clear understanding of the intuition behind derivatives pricing, how models are implemented and used, and how they are used and adapted in practice.

An Elementary Introduction to Mathematical Finance: Options and Other Topics, 2nd ed

Sheldon M. Ross
Cambridge, UK: Cambridge University Press, 2003
253pp, ISBN: 978-0-521-81429-4

This primer to mathematical finance covers the basics of option pricing in an accessible way for both professional traders and undergraduates studying the fundamentals of finance. It offers explanations of arbitrage, the Black–Scholes option pricing formula, and other topics such as utility functions, optimal portfolio selections, the Capital Asset Pricing Model, and Value at Risk.

Financial Calculus: An Introduction to Derivative Pricing

Martin Baxter, Andrew Rennie
Cambridge, UK: Cambridge University Press, 1996
233pp, ISBN: 978-0-521-55289-9

One of the most respected treatments in the field, this practical introduction to the pricing of derivatives is an accessible account of the mathematics behind the pricing, construction and hedging of derivative securities. It provides real examples from stock, currency, and interest rate markets, and describes key concepts such as martingales, change of measure, and the Heath–Jarrow–Morton model.

Introduction to the Mathematics of Finance: From Risk Management to Options Pricing

Steven Roman
Undergraduate Texts in Mathematics Series
New York: Springer, 2004
354pp, ISBN: 978-0-387-21364-4

This textbook on the mathematics of financial derivatives examines discrete derivative pricing models, offering a complete derivation of the Black–Scholes option pricing formula as a limiting case of the Cox–Ross–Rubinstein discrete model. It assumes no previous experience in finance, as it explores the basics of options, and also analyzes American options, and the Capital Asset Pricing Model.

Introduction to the Mathematics of Finance

R. J. Williams
Graduate Studies in Mathematics Series
Providence, Rhode Island: American Mathematical Society, 2006
150pp, ISBN: 978-0-8218-3903-4

This is an introduction to the theory and practice of mathematical finance, which assesses the development of hedging and pricing of European and American derivatives in the discrete setting of binomial tree models. It presents tools from probability such as conditional expectation, filtration, and martingales, and describes the Black–Scholes model, for which pricing and hedging of European and American derivatives are developed.

Introduction to the Mathematics of Financial Derivatives, 2nd ed

Salih Neftci
Academic Press Advanced Finance Series
San Diego, California: Academic Press, 2000
527pp, ISBN: 978-0-12-515392-8

This is an accessible, self-contained primer on the fundamentals of mathematical finance, especially the mathematics utilized in the pricing models of derivative instruments. It is aimed at derivatives traders, risk managers, and other users and developers of derivatives models, and helps reduce the cost of entry into the mathematical world of valuation, hedging, and risk measurement for derivatives positions.

Mastering Financial Mathematics with Excel: A Practical Guide for Business Calculations

Alastair L. Day
Market Editions Series
Harlow, UK: FT Prentice Hall, 2005
350pp, ISBN: 978-0-273-68866-2

This is an examination of the use of spreadsheets tools to enable business managers to carry out financial calculations. It acts as a practical guide to the basic calculations and key financial formulas, and provides a set of tools and methods for applying Excel to solving mathematical problems. It includes a CD for working through the chapters and examples, and provides a menu of basic templates.

Mathematical Finance: Theory, Modeling, Implementation

Christian Fries
Hoboken, New Jersey: Wiley, 2007
520pp, ISBN: 978-0-470-04722-4

This is an introduction to the theoretical foundations and real-world applications of mathematical finance, aimed at students in mathematical finance, computational finance, and derivative pricing courses. It discusses the mathematical concepts and common characteristics that are the foundation of commonly used derivative pricing models, as well as providing key techniques and tips for the construction of these models.

Mathematical Techniques in Finance: Tools for Incomplete Markets

Ales Cerny
Princeton, New Jersey: Princeton University Press, 2004
378pp, ISBN: 978-0-691-08807-5

This is a comprehensive exploration of

pricing and risk measurement in incomplete markets, a key area of current research. It offers a blend of numerical applications and theoretical grounding in economics, finance, and mathematics, and focuses on asset pricing throughout the book. It also contains useful exercises, figures, worked examples, computer programs, and spreadsheets.

Mathematics for Finance: An Introduction to Financial Engineering
Marek Capinski, Tomasz Zastawniak
Springer Undergraduate Mathematics Series
London: Springer, 2003
310pp, ISBN: 978-1-85233-330-0
This is an introduction to the mathematics of derivatives, interest rates, and portfolio management. It builds on mathematical models of bonds, focusing on Black–Scholes' arbitrage pricing of options, Markowitz portfolio optimization theory and the Capital Asset Pricing Model, and interest rates and their term structure. It is designed as a textbook, containing useful worked examples and exercises.

Methods of Mathematical Finance, 3rd ed
Ioannis Karatzas, Steven E. Shreve
New York: Springer, 2001
422pp, ISBN: 978-0-387-94839-3
This technical exploration of mathematical finance methods presents techniques of practical importance, as well as advanced methods for research. It focuses on applications of stochastic analysis and optimal control theory to various problems, and provides analysis of portfolio optimization and valuation problems under constraints, as well as contingent claim pricing and optimal consumption/investment in both complete and incomplete markets.

Monte Carlo Methods in Financial Engineering
Paul Glasserman
Stochastic Modelling and Applied Probability Series
New York: Springer, 2004
596pp, ISBN: 978-0-387-00451-8
With Monte Carlo simulation now seen as a key tool in the pricing of derivative securities and in risk management, this practical guide develops the use of Monte Carlo methods in finance and uses simulation as a vehicle for presenting models and ideas from financial engineering. It also examines the foundations of derivatives pricing, and describes techniques for improving simulation accuracy and efficiency.

New Directions in Mathematical Finance
Paul Wilmott, Henrik Rasmussen (editors)
Wiley Finance Series
Chichester, UK: Wiley, 2002
192pp, ISBN: 978-0-471-49817-9
This compilation brings together the leading names in quantitative finance to discuss the modeling techniques in a variety of areas of financial engineering. It presents many new ideas on quantitative finance, including a discussion of mean-variance strategies, passport options and Value at Risk, and new techniques for risk management, equity modeling, and interest rate modeling.

Numerical Methods for Finance
John Miller, David Edelman, John Appleby
Chapman & Hall/CRC Financial Mathematics Series
Boca Raton, Florida: CRC Press, 2008
293pp, ISBN: 978-1-58488-925-0
This examination of numerical methods provides practical insights on credit risks, exotic/hybrid options, retirement plans/pensions, life insurance, portfolio selection, incentive schemes, and interest rate modeling. It presents a variety of mathematical methods involving finite-difference, Monte Carlo, and fast Fourier transform techniques, alternatives to the Value at Risk approach, and identifies the potential pitfalls of standard methodologies.

Stochastic Calculus for Finance II: Continuous-Time Models, 2nd ed
Steven E. Shreve
Springer Finance Series
New York: Springer, 2008
550pp, ISBN: 978-0-387-40101-0
The second volume in this respected and comprehensive two-volume work examines continuous-time models, and the key ideas in the mathematical theory of securities pricing based upon the ideas of classical finance. It includes a self-contained treatment of the probability theory needed for stochastic calculus, including Brownian motion and its properties, as well as technical topics including foreign exchange models, forward measures, and jump-diffusion processes.

JOURNALS

Applied Mathematical Finance
Routledge
4 Park Square, Milton Park, Abingdon, Oxfordshire, OX14 4RN, UK
T: +44 (0) 20 7017 6000
F: +44 (0) 20 7017 6336
www.tandf.co.uk/journals/routledge/1350486X.html
ISSN: 1350-486X
Published bimonthly, this journal presents theoretical and empirical research on applied mathematics and mathematical modeling in finance. It publishes papers on the modeling of financial and economic primitives, such as interest rates and asset prices, the modeling of market behavior and market imperfections, the pricing of financial derivative securities, hedging strategies, numerical methods, and financial engineering.

Finance and Stochastics
Springer
ETH Zürich, Department of Mathematics, ETH-Zentrum, CH-8092 Zürich, Switzerland
T: +41 44 63 23580
F: +41 44 63 21474
www.math.ethz.ch/~finasto
ISSN: 0949-2984
A quarterly journal that provides a forum for research in all areas of finance based on stochastic methods. It publishes papers on a range of relevant topics, such as probability theory, statistics, stochastic analysis, theory and analysis of financial markets, continuous time finance, derivatives research, portfolio selection, and term structure models, and also presents special issues and surveys in developing research areas.

The Journal of Computational Finance
Incisive Media
Haymarket House, 28–29 Haymarket, London, SW1Y 4RX, UK
T: +44 (0) 20 7004 7531
F: +44 (0) 20 7484 9758
www.journalofcomputationalfinance.com
ISSN: 1460-1559
This quarterly journal focuses on advances in numerical and computational techniques in pricing, hedging and risk management of financial instruments. It publishes technical papers on quantitative risk research, methods that provide numerical solutions of pricing equations, optimization techniques in hedging and risk management, fundamental analysis relevant to finance, and developments in free-boundary problems in finance.

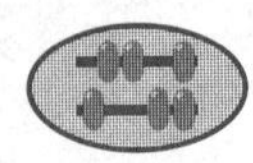
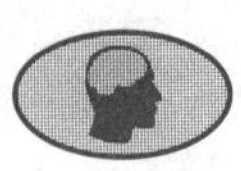

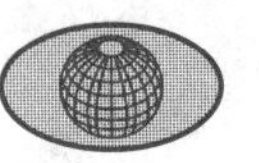

The Journal of Risk Model Validation
Incisive Media
Haymarket House, 28–29 Haymarket,
London, SW1Y 4RX, UK
T: +44 (0) 20 7004 7531
F: +44 (0) 20 7484 9758
www.journalofriskmodelvalidation.com
ISSN: 1753-9579
This quarterly journal publishes technical research papers on the implementation and validation of risk models. It promotes a greater understanding of key issues, such as the empirical evaluation of existing models, pitfalls in model validation, stress testing, the development of new methods, and regulatory factors.

Mathematical Finance
Wiley
350 Main Street, Malden, MA 02148, USA
T: +1 781 388 8598
www.wiley.com/bw/journal.asp?ref=0960-1627&site=1
ISSN: 0960-1627
This quarterly journal is devoted to the mathematical aspects of finance theory from such fields as finance, economics, mathematics, and statistics. It publishes articles on the latest theoretical developments in financial theory, financial engineering, and related mathematical and statistical techniques, and new work that assesses mathematical tools in both research and practice.

INTERNET

CQF
www.cqf.info
This is a forum dedicated to mathematical finance, quantitative finance, and related fields, including all aspects of quantitative analysis. It provides information, articles, and discussions on areas such as probability, statistics, econometrics, and optimization. It features forums, problems, literature, technical questions, mathematical finance events, computers and programming, jobs, interviews, and interview questions.

FinMath
www.finmath.com
This is an online resource for information on books relating to mathematical finance, categorized by publisher and subject area. It presents all their covers, and links to conferences, seminars, workshops, events, jobs, and relevant websites.

Mathfinance
www.mathfinance.de
This site features investment banking and academic research in mathematical finance, and information on derivative consulting, model development, implementation in C++, pricing tools in Excel, Mathematica, derivation of formulae, products, and valuation for structured products in foreign exchange or equity. It also contains details on quant jobs, courses and conferences, an industry networking forum, and a long-running fortnightly email newsletter.

ORGANIZATIONS

Europe

The Bachelier Finance Society
Chair: Ernst Eberlein
Department of Mathematical Stochastics, University of Freiburg, Eckerstraße 1, D-79104 Freiburg, Germany
T: +49 761 203 5660
F: +49 761 203 5661
E: eberlein@stochastik.uni-freiburg.de
www.bachelierfinance.com
The society encourages the advancement of finance under the application of the theory of stochastic processes, statistical and mathematical theory. It actively promotes interrelationships between industry and academia in these areas, and organizes conferences and workshops, and a prestigious world congress every two years.

 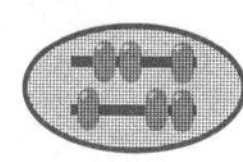 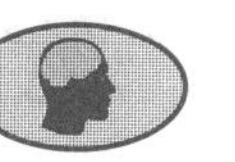  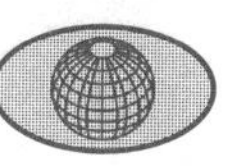   

Money Laundering

BOOKS

Anti-Money Laundering: International Law and Practice

Wouter H. Muller, Christian H. Kalin, John G. Goldsworth (editors)
Chichester, UK: Wiley, 2007
813pp, ISBN: 978-0-470-03319-7

This provides a review of international anti-money laundering rules around the world, and summarizes the approach of organizations such as the United Nations and the European Council. It examines new techniques for fighting money laundering and terrorist financing, and compares current money laundering legislation and rules in each country, and the interconnected system of regulations that international financial professionals need to understand.

Bank Secrecy Act/Anti-Money Laundering

Lilian B. Klein
New York: Nova Science Publishers, 2008
118pp, ISBN: 978-1-60456-624-6

This provides an assessment and overview of current legislation that the US government is using to prevent drug trafficking, money laundering, and related crimes. It describes in detail the Bank Secrecy Act, and its use for preventing banks from being intermediaries for criminal activity, and other laws that made money laundering a criminal activity, and help to identify money-laundering schemes in financial institutions.

Black Finance: The Economics of Money Laundering

Donato Masciandaro, Elöd Takáts, Brigitte Unger
Cheltenham, UK: Edward Elgar, 2007
257pp, ISBN: 978-1-84720-215-4

This offers a systematic analysis of the economics of money laundering and its connection with terrorism finance. It discusses money laundering in the financial markets, and national and international policies intended to combat them, techniques used in money laundering, and the similarities between the funding of terrorism and money laundering.

Capital, Payments and Money Laundering in the European Union

John Handoll
Oxford, UK: Oxford University Press, 2006
386pp, ISBN: 978-1-904501-51-0

This provides a comprehensive analysis of EU frameworks governing free movement of capital and payments, covering the definition of capital payments, the prohibition of restrictions on free movement, and permitted exceptions, derogations, and safeguard measures. In this context, it also examines the EU framework for combating money laundering, focusing on provisions, the international environment, and the impact on financial services.

Combating Money Laundering and Terrorist Financing: A Model of Best Practice for the Financial Sector, the Professions and Other Designated Businesses, 2nd ed

London: Commonwealth Secretariat, 2006
190pp, ISBN: 978-0-85092-842-6

This discusses international measures to combat money laundering and terrorist financing, focusing on global issues, national issues and strategy formulation, and financial and professional sector procedures. It examines the international standards developed by the Financial Action Task Force on Money Laundering, and systems created to help compliance with global standards.

Countering Terrorist Finance: A Training Handbook for Financial Services

Tm Parkman, Gill Peeling
Aldershot, UK: Gower Publishing, 2007
220pp, ISBN: 978-0-566-08725-7

This is a specialist resource for compliance officers in financial institutions that have responsibility for developing awareness amongst relevant employees. It provides guidance on how to train staff in the necessary processes and skills for countering terrorist financing activities, and assesses international legal responses and obligations, and the financing techniques used in recent international terrorist attacks.

Global Financial Crime: Terrorism, Money Laundering, and Off Shore Centres

Donato Masciandaro (editor)
Global Finance Series
Aldershot, UK: Ashgate Publishing, 2004
256pp, ISBN: 978-0-7546-3707-3

This is a multidisciplinary examination of money laundering, terrorism financing, and tax crime, which provides a systematic assessment of international policies on offshore countries. It focuses on ways to combat the increase in financial crime due to the globalization of the financial markets, and analyzes the economic, institutional, and political impact of offshore and onshore financial centers.

Handbook of Anti-Money Laundering

Dennis Cox
Hoboken, New Jersey: Wiley, 2009
608pp, ISBN: 978-0-470-06574-7

This practical guide takes an international approach to money laundering and money laundering deterrence, international standards and rules, and specific country rules and regulations. It examines current regulatory oversight, and its implications for banks and other financial organizations, and provides advice on how to implement the regulations, and protect against and prevent money laundering.

Money Laundering, 2nd ed

Toby Graham, Evan Bell, Nicholas Elliott
Butterworth's Compliance Series
Oxford, UK: Butterworth-Heinemann, 2003
200pp, ISBN: 978-0-406-93248-8

This is a practical guide that presents a unified examination of criminal, civil, and regulatory elements in money laundering law and practice. It examines the inherent connections between each, and discusses new laws and agencies that have been created to help deterrence, investigation, and prosecution.

Money Laundering: A Concise Guide for All Business

Doug Hopton
Aldershot, UK: Gower Publishing, 2006
182pp, ISBN: 978-0-566-08639-7

This is a practical guide to anti-money laundering regulations, international law, and standards that have been introduced by governments to combat global terrorism and criminality. It also examines the basis of money laundering and how it works, corporate responsibilities and liabilities, and what procedures businesses should establish, and how and when to report suspicious activity.

Money Laundering: A Guide for Criminal Investigators, 2nd ed

John Madinger
Boca Raton, Florida: CRC Press, 2006
530pp, ISBN: 978-0-8493-3395-8

This authoritative resource provides an overview of money-laundering practices, and explains the investigative and legislative processes that are being used for detection and prevention. It examines current legislation and how it affects money-laundering investigation, strategies needed to combat new money laundering techniques, and the increasing importance of uncovering terrorist financing.

Money Laundering Compliance, 2nd ed
Tim Bennett
Haywards Heath, UK: Tottel Publishing, 2007
559pp, ISBN: 978-1-84766-052-7
This examines the changes in UK regulatory supervision, and the role, liabilities, and obligations of trustees, practitioners and their professional advisors with regard to money laundering. It examines the range of offences and the application of principles in a number of jurisdictions, and practical issues such as know your client, reporting procedures, and the conflict between tipping-off and disclosure.

Reference Guide to Anti-Money Laundering and Combating the Financing of Terrorism, 2nd ed
Paul Allan Schott
Washington, DC: World Bank Publications, 2006
288pp, ISBN: 978-0-8213-6513-7
This is a comprehensive reference, providing practical information and guidance on combating money laundering and terrorist financing. It analyzes the effects of these crimes, how countries can work to mitigate them, and the role international organizations and international standards can play in the process, presenting tools for developing a program to effectively prevent, detect, and prosecute money laundering and terrorist financing.

The Scale and Impacts of Money Laundering
Brigitte Unger
Cheltenham, UK: Edward Elgar, 2007
228pp, ISBN: 978-1-84720-223-9
This is an overview of current money-laundering techniques and strategies, which assesses the link between money laundering and fraud, and the increasing international scope and economic impact of financial crimes. It also describes economic models that have been designed to measure money-laundering activities, and research into techniques and the potential effects of money laundering.

Suppressing Terrorist Financing and Money Laundering: The Evolution and Implementation of International Standards
Jae-myong Koh
New York: Springer, 2006
243pp, ISBN: 978-3-540-32518-5
This describes the development of international standards for countering terrorist financing from the perspective of international criminal law, as well as the theoretical and operational focus of anti-money laundering strategy since 9/11. It also assesses the functioning of organizations such as the UN Security Council, Financial Action Task Force, IMF, World Bank, and the Asia/Pacific Group on Money Laundering.

MAGAZINES

AML Compliance Alert
Eli Financial
PO Box 90324, Washington DC 20090, USA
www.elifinancial.com/aml_compliance.html
This new monthly newsletter provides information and news on the fight against money laundering and terrorism financing. It aims to assist bank professionals and their advisors increase the effectiveness of their asset liability programs, and focuses on terrorism, organized crime, and money laundering.

Anti-Money Laundering
Australian Financial Markets Association
Level 3 Plaza Building, 95 Pitt Street, Sydney 2000, NSW 2001, Australia
T: +61 2 9776 7955
F: +61 2 9776 4488
www.afma.com.au/scripts/nc.dl-l?AFMAV6.1573196:STANDARD:1648505960:pc=L1C2S2
This magazine, published by the Australian Financial Markets Association, is a source of information and education for the financial services sector on anti-money laundering and counter-terrorist financing. It provides a forum for debate and analysis on the key implementation challenges facing financial institutions across the region, and focuses on regulation, customer identification, monitoring, legal, and technology.

Money Laundering Bulletin
Informa
Telephone House, 69–77 Paul Street, London, EC2A 4LQ, UK
T: +44 (0) 20 7017 5532
www.informaprofessional.com/publications/newsletter/money_laundering_bulletin
ISSN: 1462-141X
This is a monthly newsletter that provides information and news on money-laundering schemes, methods, trends, and policing. It offers the latest legal, regulatory, and practical developments in preventing and detecting money laundering and terrorist financing for businesses.

JOURNALS

Journal of Financial Crime
Emerald Group
Howard House, Wagon Lane, Bingley, BD16 1WA, UK
T: +44 (0) 1274 777 700
F: +44 (0) 1274 785 201
info.emeraldinsight.com/products/journals/journals.htm?id=jfc
ISSN: 1359-0790
This quarterly journal is an authoritative resource for information on methods used in economic crime and the steps that can be taken to avoid and combat it. It offers a series of analyses, briefings, and updates for practitioners concerned with the prevention, detection, and prosecution of financial crime and the protection of assets.

Journal of International Money and Finance
Elsevier
Radarweg 29, 1043 NX Amsterdam, The Netherlands
F: +31 20 485 2370
www.elsevier.com/wps/find/journaldescription.cws_home/30443/description#description
ISSN: 0261-5606
Published eight times each year, this scholarly journal is devoted to theoretical and empirical research in the fields of international monetary economics, international finance, and the rapidly developing overlap area between them. It focuses on research on exchange rate behavior, foreign exchange options, international capital markets, international monetary and fiscal policy, and international transmission.

Journal of Money Laundering Control
Emerald Group
Howard House, Wagon Lane, Bingley, BD16 1WA, UK
T: +44 (0) 1274 777 700
F: +44 (0) 1274 785 201
info.emeraldinsight.com/products/journals/journals.htm?id=jmlc
ISSN: 1368-5201

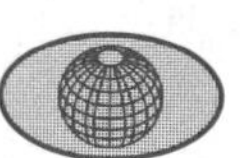

This quarterly journal publishes analysis, briefings, and updates on the latest laws, regulation, techniques, and best practice in the prevention, identification and prosecution of money laundering. It publishes on areas such as legislation in jurisdictions around the world, terrorist financing, suspicious transaction reporting requirements, monitoring patterns of suspicious payments, and new and emerging techniques in money laundering.

INTERNET

IBA Anti-Money Laundering Forum

www.anti-moneylaundering.org

This online network, run by the International Bar Association, provides a guide for lawyers in dealing with their responsibilities regarding new anti-money laundering legislation and compliance requirements. It offers detailed information, categorized by jurisdiction and region, and works to increase awareness of the difficulties in preventing and detecting money laundering among legal professionals and their clients throughout the world.

International Money Laundering Information Network

www.imolin.org

IMoLIN is an Internet-based network that works to assist governments, organizations, and individuals in the fight against money laundering and the financing of terrorism. It was developed through the cooperation of leading anti-money laundering organizations, and offers a database on legislation and regulations throughout the world, an electronic library, and a calendar of events.

MoneyLaundering.com

www.moneylaundering.com

This is a site providing money-laundering news from around the world. It covers the basics of anti-money laundering, compliance guidelines, enforcement actions, government reports, international resources, laundering cases, laws and regulations, money laundering alert, research tools, and US regulatory information, as well as conferences and seminars, products. and services.

ORGANIZATIONS

Europe

Institute of Money Laundering Prevention Officers

Chair: Steve Lock
6 Millside Place, Old Isleworth, Middlesex, TW7 6BU, UK
T: +44 (0) 20 8847 4074
E: info@imlpo.com
www.imlpo.com

IMLPO is a cross-representative forum of anti-money laundering professionals, which provides a forum for the sharing of views, experiences, and concerns on the business of combating money laundering. It also facilitates the further education and professional development of its members, and provides a broad representation for issues concerning money-laundering prevention.

USA

Association of Certified Anti-Money Laundering Specialists

Chair: John J. Byrne
Brickell Bayview Center, 80 Southwest 8th Street, Suite 2350, Miami, FL 33130, USA
T: +1 305 373 0020
F: +1 305 373 7788
E: info@acams.org
www.acams.org

ACAMS provides information, education, career development, and professional networking opportunities in the anti-money laundering sector. It promotes the development and implementation of sound anti-money laundering policies and procedures, and offers resources for financial institutions and related businesses that help train, identify, and locate practitioners in money-laundering control policies, procedures and regulations.

FIBA Anti-Money Laundering Institute

80 SW 8th Street, Suite 2505, Miami, FL 33130, USA
T: +1 305 579 0086
F: +1 305 579 0969
E: fiba@fiba.net
fiba.net/index.cfm/id/393.html

This institute, run by the Florida International Bankers Association, focuses on providing in-depth and practical professional training and courses to ensure the highest level of competency in the industry. It also organizes two certification courses for anti-money laundering compliance officers, as well as targeted professional continuing education courses in the areas of correspondent banking, private banking, outside directors, and management.

International

Asia/Pacific Group on Money Laundering

Chair: Mick Keelty, Ong Hian Sun
E: mail@apgml.org
www.apgml.org

The APG is an autonomous and collaborative international organization committed to the effective implementation and enforcement of internationally accepted standards against money laundering and the financing of terrorism. It assesses compliance, co-ordinates technical assistance and training, participates in the international anti-money laundering network, and conducts research and analysis into money laundering and terrorist financing trends and methods.

Offshore Group of Banking Supervisors

www.ogbs.net

The aims of the OGBS are to identify and discuss issues of mutual interest to its members, participate with relevant international organizations in setting and promoting the implementation of international standards for cross-border banking supervision, combating money-laundering/terrorist financing, encouraging high standards of supervision, and promoting best practice for trust and company service providers.

The Society of Anti-Money Laundering Professionals

Hong Kong
www.socamlpro.org

This global organization draws on best practice, expertise, and mentoring from senior members of the profession from around the world. It provides a forum for industry professionals, and the interchange of ideas, education and training for those engaged in combating financial crime, money laundering, and terrorist financing.

  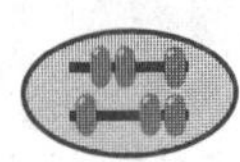   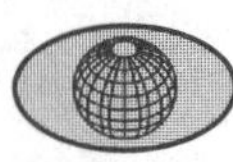   

Mortgage Finance

BOOKS

Commercial Mortgage-Backed Securitisation: Developments in the European Market

Andrew V. Petersen (editor)
London: Sweet & Maxwell, 2006
596pp, ISBN: 978-0-421-96090-9

This provides comprehensive legal and regulatory guidance on the rapidly expanding area of commercial mortgage-backed securitization in Europe. It looks at current practice, how to set up new transactions, the administration of existing arrangements, and examines related economic and technological issues. It also discusses tools such as key lending agreements, and compares European practice with that of the United States.

Commercial Real Estate Analysis and Investments, 2nd ed

David M. Geltner, Norman G. Miller, Jim Clayton, Piet Eichholtz
Mason, Ohio: Thomson/South-Western, 2007
880pp, ISBN: 978-0-324-38212-9

This presents the essential concepts, principles and tools for the analysis of commercial real estate from an investment perspective. It attempts to bridge the gap between mainstream finance and current professional real estate practice, and examines urban and financial economics, international real estate investments, real options application to real estate development, and the streamlining of data returns.

Economics of the Mortgage Market: Perspectives on Household Decision Making

David Leece
Real Estate Issues Series
Oxford, UK: Blackwell Publishing, 2004
258pp, ISBN: 978-1-4051-1461-5

This provides an organised research resource for financial analysts in real estate, as well as researchers in real estate finance, real estate economics, housing economics and urban economics. It examines the link between household behavior and issues in mortgage market economics and mortgage valuation, and emphasizes the increasing importance of the secondary mortgage market.

Financial Shock: A 360° Look at the Subprime Mortgage Implosion, and How to Avoid the Next Financial Crisis

Mark Zandi
Upper Saddle River, New Jersey: FT Press, 2009
270pp, ISBN: 978-0-13-714290-3

This new book presents an account of the economic, political, and regulatory forces behind the crisis in the subprime mortgage market. It discusses how Internet technology and access to global capital transformed the mortgage industry, the impact of housing market problems on the global financial system, and offers advice on recognizing emerging bubbles, improving oversight, and surviving downturns.

The Handbook of Mortgage-Backed Securities, 6th ed

Frank J. Fabozzi (editor)
New York: McGraw-Hill, 2006
1,238pp, ISBN: 978-0-07-146074-3

This practical guide to MBS fundamentals and trading strategies provides a resource for both private investors and professional portfolio managers. It covers the full range of MBS products and derivatives, and explores the many advantages and potential pitfalls inherent in the market. It includes new analysis of collateralized mortgage obligations, prepayment derivatives, loan level determinants of repayments, and innovative approaches to MBS valuation.

Mortgage and Real Estate Finance: Latest Innovations and Opportunities

Stefania Perrucci (editor)
London: Risk Books, 2008
350pp, ISBN: 978-1-906348-12-0

This examination of the complex structured market of mortgage and real estate finance focuses on ways of taking advantage of the current market distress, and avoiding its pitfalls. Providing a history of the market and overview of both the primary and secondary mortgage markets, it also analyses the latest innovations in the market, risk management of mortgage securities, and other relevant areas of mortgage finance.

Mortgage Markets Worldwide

Danny Ben-Shahar, Charles Ka Yui Leung, Seow Eng Ong
Real Estate Issues Series
Chichester, UK: Blackwell Publishing, 2008
312pp, ISBN: 978-1-4051-3210-7

This theoretical and empirical study of selected mortgage markets explores problems of housing finance in each country, steps taken to solve these problems, and the expected future developments of the market. It examines issues relating to housing finance efficiency and contract heterogeneity, the integration of mortgage markets with capital markets, and how particular institutional frameworks interact with mortgage markets.

Real Estate Finance and Investment Manual, 9th ed

Jack Cummings
Hoboken, New Jersey: Wiley, 2008
669pp, ISBN: 978-0-470-26040-1

This guide to financing for real estate investors covers all the financing options, new real estate investment strategies, and insider techniques available. It shows how to set realistic investment goals, practice effective negotiation, use leverage to maximize investment returns, choose between conventional and creative financing methods, understand wraparound and blanket mortgages, and uncover real estate tax loopholes.

Real Estate Finance & Investments, 13th ed

William B. Brueggeman, Jeffrey D. Fisher
Boston: McGraw-Hill, 2008
688pp, ISBN: 978-0-07-352471-9

This regularly revised and updated textbook on real estate finance and investments is a rigorous and practical overview of the tools needed to understand and analyze real estate markets and the investment alternatives available to both debt and equity investors. New content has been added on current trends in mortgage finance and investment techniques.

Real Estate Finance in a Nutshell, 6th ed

Jon W. Bruce
Mason, Ohio: Thomson/South-Western, 2008
317pp, ISBN: 978-0-314-18354-5

This primer presents a thorough overview of the law of real estate finance. It discusses the mortgage market, real estate financing devices, the underlying obligation, mortgaged property, and transfer of both the mortgagor's interest and the mortgagee's interest. It also covers rights and obligations after default and before foreclosure, and considers the legal principles underpinning real estate finance.

Real Estate Finance: Theory and Practice, 5th ed
Terrence M. Clauretie, G. Stacy Sirmans
Mason, Ohio: Thomson/South-Western, 2005
557pp, ISBN: 978-0-324-30550-0
This is a textbook that examines the techniques and strategies of real estate finance, based on sound economic and finance principles. It applies the theoretical aspects of financial economics to explain how real estate financial institutions and markets have developed over time, and examines how real estate financial markets operate in today's environment. It also discusses the impact of federal legislation on real estate finance.

Salomon Smith Barney Guide to Mortgage-Backed and Asset-Backed Securities
Lakhbir Hayre
New York: Wiley, 2001
876pp, ISBN: 978-0-471-38587-5
This provides a comprehensive guide to these fixed-income securities, now the largest sector of the bond market. It presents a framework for modeling of prepayment rates on residential mortgage loans, and discusses how the Internet has affected the mortgage origination process, option-adjusted spreads, and other types of MBS and ABS. It is useful for investment professionals, institutional investors, pension funds, and hedge funds.

Subprime Mortgage Credit Derivatives
Laurie S. Goodman, Shumin Li, Douglas J. Lucas, Thomas A. Zimmerman, Frank J. Fabozzi
Frank J. Fabozzi Series
Hoboken, New Jersey: Wiley, 2008
334pp, ISBN: 978-0-470-24366-4
This new book discusses the topical area of subprime mortgage credit derivatives, addressing areas such as mortgage credit, mortgage securitizations, and credit default swaps on mortgage securities. It outlines the origins of the subprime crisis, and examines current instruments and strategies for managing a portfolio of mortgage credits in the current volatile climate.

Your Successful Career as a Mortgage Broker
David Reed
New York: Amacom, 2007
246pp, ISBN: 978-0-8144-7370-2
This detailed and informative guide to successful mortgage broking offers practical advice on how to quote interest rates, get approved by wholesale lenders, negotiate the steps of the loan process, market and prospect effectively, licensing and educational requirements, as well as information on the different career options available as a mortgage broker, mortgage banker, and correspondent mortgage banker.

MAGAZINES

Commercial Mortgage Alert
Harrison Scott Publications
5 Marine View Plaza, #400, Hoboken, NJ 07030-5795, USA
T: +1 201 659 1700
F: +1 201 659 4141
www.CMAlert.com
ISSN: 1520-3697
This weekly newsletter provides news, analysis, and statistics on the commercial mortgage market and traditional real estate finance. It discusses financing opportunities, and key moves by big lenders and borrowers, and covers financing needs of REITs and private developers, CMBS offerings, new trends, career openings for real estate finance and securitization professionals, and the latest rankings of key players in the real estate capital markets.

Inside Mortgage Finance
Inside Mortgage Finance Publications
7910 Woodmont Avenue, Suite 1000, Bethesda, MD 20814-7019, USA
T: +1 301 951 1240
F: +1 301 656 1709
www.imfpubs.com/issues/imfpubs_imf
ISSN: 8756-0003
This weekly magazine offers statistics and analysis of legislative developments, regulatory changes, and market trends in the mortgage markets. It also produces surveys on these markets, extensive data, rankings, and charts, analysis and competitive intelligence, as well as information on the private mortgage insurance industry, the latest moves from Fannie Mae and Freddie Mac, and guidance on non-traditional loans.

Mortgage Banking
Mortgage Bankers Association
1331 L Street NW, Washington, DC 20005, USA
T: +1 202 557 2700
www.mortgagebankingmagazine.com
ISSN: 0730-0212
This monthly magazine focused on real estate finance provides coverage and analysis of the critical issues and trends affecting the industry. It features news, strategic information, research, and executive profiles for real estate finance industry leaders, senior financial services executives, mortgage bankers, and brokers.

Mortgage Finance Gazette
Metropolis Business Publishing
6th Floor, Davis House, 2 Robert Street, Croydon, CR0 1QQ, UK
T: +44 (0) 20 8253 8618
www.mfgonline.co.uk
ISSN: 0964-7988
This is a monthly magazine that provides all the latest industry news on people, jobs, products and organisations, as well as a number of special reports covering issues in the mortgage finance industry.

Mortgage Originator
Summit Business Media
1801 Park 270 Drive, Suite 550, St. Louis, MO 63146, USA
T: +1 314 824 5500
F: +1 314 824 5640
www.mortgageoriginator.com
ISSN: 1070-5708
This is a monthly magazine for mortgage originators, which acts as a resource for mortgage brokers, retail loan officers, lenders, and other mortgage professionals. It presents industry news and company highlights, and features a marketing resource center, podcasts, a resource directory, and an e-bookstore.

Mortgage Solutions
Incisive Media
Haymarket House, 28-29 Haymarket, London, SW1Y 4RX, UK
T: +44 (0) 20 7484 9700
F: +44 (0) 20 7930 2238
www.mortgagesolutions-online.com
ISSN: 1475-8008
This is a weekly magazine for mortgage intermediaries, which delivers news, editorial comment, analysis, and features on all aspects of the mortgage market. It offers articles on training, interviews with the industry figures, a regular regional housing market focus, and a market debate, and produces specialist supplements on key topics such as subprime, buy to let, and regulation.

National Mortgage News
SourceMedia
1 State Street Plaza, 27th Floor, New York, NY 10004, USA
T: +1 212 803 8333
F: +1 212 292 5216
www.nationalmortgagenews.com
ISSN: 1050-3331
A weekly newspaper that offers news and analysis, and discusses the trends and events that are affecting the mortgage industry. It is aimed at mortgage bankers,

  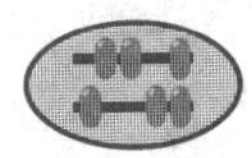 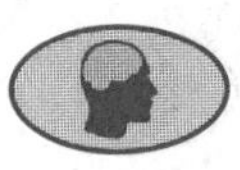  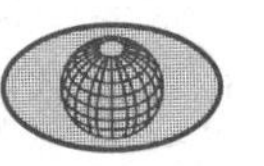   

commercial bankers, savings institutions, brokerage firms, insurance companies, and government enterprises, and covers commercial lending, mortgage servicing, technology and e-commerce, default management, B&C lending, the latest M&A developments, and industry rankings.

JOURNALS

Briefings in Real Estate Finance

Wiley
111 River Street, Hoboken, NJ 07030, USA
T: +1 201 748 6645
www3.interscience.wiley.com/journal/110484210
ISSN: 1473-1894

A quarterly publication providing a practical understanding of the processes and challenges associated with the funding of real estate. It discusses current techniques, approaches, and best practice in all aspects of the subject, and addresses such issues as risk management, structuring finance, finance for trading, development and investment, sources of funding and terms available, and changes in taxation.

Journal of European Real Estate Research

European Real Estate Society
Howard House, Wagon Lane, Bingley, BD16 1WA, UK
T: +44 (0) 1274 777 700
F: +44 (0) 1274 785 201
info.emeraldinsight.com/products/journals/journals.htm?id=jerer
ISSN: 1753-9269

This quarterly journal publishes theoretical and practical papers relating to commercial and residential property in Europe, aimed at improving property appraisal, finance and investment skills, and an understanding of the differences between the various real estate markets across the continent. Coverage includes REITs and financial derivatives, housing and residential markets, indirect property investment, cross-border portfolio diversification, and comparative market analysis.

Journal of Property Investment & Finance

Emerald Group Publishing
Howard House, Wagon Lane, Bingley, BD16 1WA, UK
T: +44 (0) 1274 777 700
F: +44 (0) 1274 785 201
www.emeraldinsight.com/Insight/viewContainer.do?containerType=Journal&containerId=12267
ISSN: 1463-578X

Published bimonthly, this journal provides information and ideas relating to property valuation and investment, property management, and decision-making in the commercial property market. It publishes papers by both academics and practitioners, covering the latest research, real estate law and new legislation, Internet sites and recent publications, market data, and changes in the property market.

The Journal of Real Estate Finance and Economics

Kluwer Academic Publishers
298B Brooks Hall, Terry College of Business, The University of Georgia, Athens, Georgia 30602-6255, USA
T: +1 706 542 3805
F: +1 706 542 4295
www.jrefe.org
ISSN: 0895-5638

This is a quarterly journal that publishes empirical and theoretical papers on real estate, finance, and economics. It covers topics such as the working and structure of markets, the role of various institutional arrangements, mortgages and asset securitization, risk management and valuation, and public policy and regulation.

The Journal of Real Estate Research

American Real Estate Society
California State University, Fullerton, College of Business & Economics, Department of Finance, Fullerton, CA 92834-6848, USA
T: +1 714 278 4363
F: +1 714 278 2161
www.business.fullerton.edu/Finance/Journal
ISSN: 0896-5803

This quarterly journal, produced by the American Real Estate Society, is devoted to promoting business decision-making applications through scholarly real estate research. It presents analytical and empirical papers on real estate development, economics, finance, investment, law, management, marketing, secondary markets, and valuation.

Real Estate Economics

American Real Estate and Urban Economics Association
PO Box 9958, Richmond, VA 23228, USA
T: +1 866 273 8321
F: +1 877 273 8323
www.areuea.org/publications/ree
ISSN: 1080-8620

This quarterly journal provides research information and ideas by academic researchers and industry professionals in the field of real estate economics. It focuses on improving the analysis of real estate decisions, and covers such areas as tax rules and the sale or leaseback of corporate real estate, and methods for measuring efficiency in the savings and loan industry.

Real Estate Finance

Aspen Publishers, USA
T: +1 301 698 7100
www.aspenpublishers.com
ISSN: 0748-318X

Published bimonthly, this journal provides tools for decision-making in real estate finance, written by investment managers and advisors, bankers and insurers, developers, property managers, tax planners, lawyers, accountants, government officials, and academics. Coverage includes volatility risk, pricing REITS and mortgage-backed securities, valuing overseas investment opportunities, and the default characteristics of real estate loans.

INTERNET

Broker Universe

www.brokeruniverse.com

This website for mortgage brokers and originators provides practical information on techniques and technologies for optimizing performance in the mortgage markets, and a daily email newsletter.

MortgageMag

www.mortgagemag.com

This online resource for mortgage industry professionals features company listings, forums, people's choice, opinions, products and services, resumé and job postings, and instant messages/email updates.

ORGANIZATIONS

Europe

The Council of Mortgage Lenders

Bush House, North West Wing, Aldwych, London, WC2B 4PJ, UK
T: +44 (0) 845 373 6771
F: +44 (0) 845 373 6778
www.cml.org.uk

This is the trade association for the mortgage lending industry, which aims to improve the operating environment in the UK housing and mortgage markets. It represents the residential mortgage lending industry, and provides economic, statistical, and legal research and other market information. Its membership comprises of banks, building societies and other mortgage lenders.

  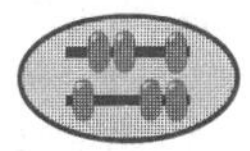   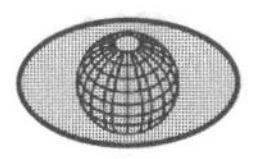   

European Mortgage Federation
Chair: Pasquale Giamboi
Avenue de la Joyeuse Entrée 14/2, 1040 Brussels, Belgium
T: +32 2 285 40 30
F: +32 2 285 40 31
E: emfinfo@hypo.org
www.hypo.org
The EMF promotes the interests of mortgage lenders at European level, uniting institutions with a special interest in the mortgage industry and the housing sector, such as mortgage banks, commercial banks, savings banks, co-operative banks, building societies, umbrella companies, and insurance companies. It encourages mortgage lending, advises EU institutions, and provides industry statistics.

European Real Estate Society
Chair: Ramon Sotelo
Hanna Kaleva, c/o KTI Kiinteistötieto Oy, KTI Finland, Eerikinkatu 28, 00180 Helsinki, Finland
T: +358 (0) 20 7430 124
F: +358 (0) 20 7430 131
www.eres.org
ERES is a non-profit organization that promotes the advancement of real estate research throughout Europe, and incorporates national property research societies, academic researchers, and real estate practitioners. It encourages professionalism in the industry, and improved communication in real estate in academia, and organizes events on real estate, including an annual conference, industry seminars, and education seminars.

USA

American Real Estate and Urban Economics Association
Chair: Frank E. Nothaft
PO Box 9958, Richmond, VA 23228, USA
T: +1 866 273 8321
F: +1 877 273 8323
E: areuea@areaue.org
www.areuea.org
The aim of AREUEA is to encourage greater information and analysis in the fields of real estate development, planning and economics. It promotes the exchange of information and opinions among academic, professional and governmental people, publishes a journal, and holds three conferences each year which promote research in the fields of real estate and urban economics.

American Real Estate Society
Chair: Mauricio Rodriguez
Clemson University, Department of Finance, 314 Sirrine Hall, Clemson, SC 29634-1343, USA
T: +1 864 656 1373
F: +1 864 656 3748
www.aresnet.org
ARES is dedicated to producing and disseminating knowledge and research related to real estate decision-making and the functioning of real estate markets. Its membership is comprised of academics in a wide variety of fields such as economics, finance, marketing, geography, and professional researchers, analysts, and appraisers. It publishes a number of industry journals, and provides listings of academic and senior research positions worldwide.

The Federal Home Loan Mortgage Corporation
Chair: David M. Moffett
8200 Jones Branch Drive, McLean, VA 22102-3110, USA
T: +1 703 903 2000
www.freddiemac.com
Commonly known as Freddie Mac, this is a stockholder-owned corporation chartered by Congress to keep money flowing to mortgage lenders in support of homeownership and rental housing. Its mission is to provide liquidity, stability and affordability to the housing market.

The Federal National Mortgage Association
Chair: Herbert M. Allison
3900 Wisconsin Avenue NW, Washington, DC 20016-2892, USA
T: +1 202 752 7000
E: headquarters@fanniemae.com
www.fanniemae.com
Commonly known as Fannie Mae, this is a stockholder-owned corporation chartered by Congress as a government-sponsored enterprise. Its purpose is to purchase and securitize mortgages in order to ensure that funds are consistently available to the institutions that lend money to home buyers, and provides services, products, and solutions to lender partners and a broad range of housing partners.

International Mortgage Lenders Association
2398 East Camelback Road, Suite 935, Phoenix, AZ 85016, USA
T: +1 602 667 3500
E: tkelley@imigrouponline.com
www.internationalmla.org
The IMLA serves the international mortgage lending community in the areas of lending, brokering, real estate, title/escrow, appraising, legal, and services. It promotes research and the exchange of ideas, the review of public policy matters, best practices, and standards to increase efficiency, and supports the educational needs of the international real estate finance industry.

The Mortgage Bankers Association
Chair: David G. Kittle
1331 L Street NW, Washington, DC 20005, USA
T: +1 202 557 2700
www.mbaa.org
This national association represents the real estate finance industry, its members comprising mortgage companies, mortgage brokers, commercial banks, thrifts, life insurance companies, and others in the mortgage-lending field. It provides news and information on strategic tools, industry trends and resources, and promotes fair lending practices and professional excellence through a wide range of educational programs and a variety of publications.

The Mortgage Insurance Companies of America
USA
E: info@micadc.org
www.privatemi.com
MICA is the trade association representing the private mortgage insurance industry. Its members help loan originators and investors make funds available to home buyers for low down payment mortgages, by protecting these institutions from a major portion of the financial risk of default. It provides information on legislative and regulatory issues, and represents the industry to government.

National Association of Mortgage Brokers
Chair: Marc S. Savitt
7900 Westpark Drive, Suite T309, McLean, VA 22102, USA
T: +1 703 342 5900
F: +1 703 342 5905
E: jotto@namb.org
www.namb.org
This is a national trade association that represents the mortgage broker industry, and promotes the industry through programs and services such as education, professional certification, and government affairs representation.

     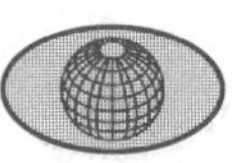   

Operations Management

BOOKS

Cases in Operations Management: Building Customer Value through World-Class Operations
Robert D. Klassen, Larry J. Menor (editors)
The Ivey Casebook Series
Thousand Oaks, California: Sage Publications, 2006
425pp, ISBN: 978-1-4129-1371-3
This approaches operations management from a real-world decision-making perspective, presenting a range of focused case studies from an international context. It describes the basic concepts while exploring economic, political, and cultural issues relating to the key areas of process design, quality, supply chain management, and customer value, and offers resources such as case notes, preparation questions, and discussion questions.

Introduction to Operations and Supply Chain Management, 2nd ed
Cecil Bozarth, Robert B. Handfield
Upper Saddle River, New Jersey: Prentice Hall, 2008
576pp, ISBN: 978-0-13-179103-9
This new textbook examines the key topics that are taught in courses on operations management, covering relevant service theory and applications, as well as manufacturing applications and theory. It assesses operations management from a cross-functional perspective, linked to other areas of an organization, and explores the impact of technology on business operations, and the integration of the value chain.

Operations Management, 10th ed
William J. Stevenson
McGraw-Hill/Irwin Series on Operations and Decision Sciences
Boston, Massachusetts: McGraw-Hill/Irwin, 2008
906pp, ISBN: 978-0-07-728409-1
This new edition presents the latest concepts and applications in operations management, as well as detailed explanations of key process to aid an understanding of how to apply the main operations management tools and methods in real-life situations.

Operations Management, 5th ed
Nigel Slack, Stuart Chambers, Robert Johnston
New York: FT Prentice Hall, 2007
728pp, ISBN: 978-1-4058-4700-1
This is a comprehensive, practical, and strategic examination of the role of operations management within business. It focuses on how organizations create and deliver products at lower cost and with higher revenue, meet the challenges posed by changes in customer preferences, Internet-based technologies and global supply networks, supply-chain planning, outsourcing, and the 'greening' of operations, and provides numerous examples of operations in practice.

Operations Management, 9th ed
Jay Heizer, Barry Render
Upper Saddle River, New Jersey: Prentice Hall, 2007
784pp, ISBN: 978-0-13-812878-4
This successful textbook emphasizes the practical elements of operations management, providing students with a sound knowledge of how companies work, and how to apply their learning to real company challenges and best practices. It does this through an extensive array of integrated problems, and examining service applications and firms and their operations activity in the real world.

Operations Management: An Integrated Approach, 3rd ed
R. Dan Reid, Nada R. Sanders
Hoboken, New Jersey: Wiley, 2007
671pp, ISBN: 978-0-471-79448-6
This integrative approach explores the critical impact that operations management now has in the business world. It provides detailed coverage of key topics, connecting these throughout, and focuses on problem solving to provide effective decision-making expertise and an understanding of the main techniques involved, and how operations management relates to every department within an organization.

Operations Management: Creating Value Along the Supply Chain, 6th ed
Roberta S. Russell, Bernard W. Taylor
Hoboken, New Jersey: Wiley, 2007
776pp, ISBN: 978-0-470-09515-7
This comprehensive textbook offers an introduction to operations management, and assesses value by analyzing the quantitative and qualitative aspects of operations and supply chain management. It presents both managerial issues and quantitative techniques, relating everything to real business methods and problems, and discusses how companies manage key processes such as inventory and forecasting.

Operations Management for Competitive Advantage, 11th ed
Richard Chase, F. Robert Jacobs, Nicholas Aquilano
Boston, Massachusetts: McGraw-Hill/Irwin, 2006
806pp, ISBN: 978-0-07-312166-6
This regularly updated textbook on using effective operations management to ensure competitive advantage provides a thorough introduction to the concepts, processes, and methods of managing and controlling operations in manufacturing or service settings. It covers all the key areas, from high-tech manufacturing to high-touch services, and integrates topical issues such as globalization, supply chain strategy, e-business, and enterprise resource planning.

Operations Management for MBAs, 3rd ed
Jack R. Meredith, Scott M. Shafer
Hoboken, New Jersey: Wiley, 2007
445pp, ISBN: 978-0-471-35142-9
This practical student textbook examines key strategic operational issues that can have a critical impact on the success of an organization, focusing on international problems and cases. It discusses the growing importance of new technologies, and the rise of service organizations, as well as Six Sigma improvement projects, project management, enterprise resource planning, lean management, outsourcing and offshoring, supply chain management, and process design and planning.

Operations Management: Goods, Service, and Value Chains, 2nd ed
David Alan Collier, James R. Evans
Mason, Ohio: Thomson/South-Western, 2007
830pp, ISBN: 978-0-324-17939-2
This textbook for business students provides coverage of the main concepts, techniques, and applications of current operations management, covering topics such as supply chain design, capacity management, quality control, and project management. It includes an assessment of contemporary and relevant service and manufacturing theory and applications, and approaches operations as linked to all other functional areas of an organization.

Operations Management: Processes and Value Chains, 8th ed
Lee J. Krajewski, Larry P. Ritzman, Manoj K. Malhotra
Upper Saddle River, New Jersey: Prentice Hall, 2007

  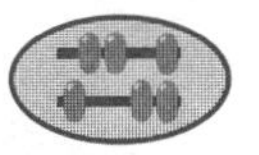 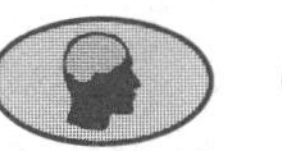  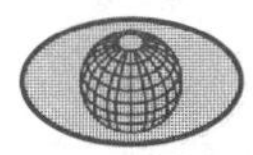   

728pp, ISBN: 978-0-13-169739-3
This examines current operational management issues, and presents a range of analytic techniques for use in operational decision-making. It offers a broad picture of the strategic operations, as well as process orientation in both service and manufacturing, and presents strategic and managerial issues, and the operations tools and techniques for problem solving, for aligning operation management activities with corporate strategy across the business.

Principles of Operations Management, 7th ed
Jay Heizer, Barry Render
Upper Saddle River, New Jersey: Prentice Hall, 2007
671pp, ISBN: 978-0-13-234328-2
This introductory textbook on operations management provides a comprehensive overview of the fundamental principles of operations and how they relate to effectively producing goods and services, and related decision-making processes. Keeping math to a minimum, it examines economic and international issues, and activities such as operations strategy for competitive advantage, forecasting, managing quality, operations technology, enterprise resource management, and supply chain management.

Quantitative Survival Guide for Operations Management, 2nd ed
Thomas Kratzer
New York: Wiley, 2005
71pp, ISBN: 978-0-471-67877-9
This is a concise reference that describes the quantitative skills and methods necessary in operations management. It analyzes the relevant mathematical concepts, and presents a series of examples of the types of problems that a student will encounter in a typical operations management textbook, as well as guidance on working through them.

Service Operations Management, 3rd ed
Robert Johnston, Graham Clark
Harlow, UK: FT Prentice Hall, 2008
533pp, ISBN: 978-1-4058-4732-2
This textbook describes the key terms, principles, tools, frameworks, and techniques for operational analysis and improvement, is aimed at students on services-orientated operations management courses. It assesses operations management within the wider business context, describes the impact of other management functions and issues, and explores the operations decisions that managers face in controlling their resources and delivering services to customers.

JOURNALS

Annals of Operations Research
Springer
233 Spring Street, New York, NY 10013, USA
T: +1 212 460 1500
F: +1 212 460 1575
www.springer.com/business/operations+research/journal/10479
ISSN: 0254-5330
Published eight times each year, this is a series of volumes dedicated to key aspects of operations research, including theory, practice, computation, and emerging trends. Each volume has a guest editor, and features research articles, short notes, expositions and surveys, reports on computational studies, and case studies that present new and innovative practical applications.

International Abstracts in Operations Research
International Federation of Operational Research Societies
Palgrave Macmillan, Brunel Road, Houndmills, Basingstoke, Hampshire, RG21 6XS, UK
T: +44 (0) 1256 357 893
F: +44 (0) 1256 328 339
www.palgrave-journals.com/iaor/index.html
ISSN: 0020-580X
IAOR, published eight times each year, offers abstracts from journals worldwide, to provide a comprehensive synopsis of current operations research literature. Further abstracts are selected from supplemental and specialized journals, if relevant to the philosophy, methodology, or practice of operations research. The topics are divided into the categories of process, application, technique, and professional.

International Journal of Operations & Production Management
Emerald Group
Howard House, Wagon Lane, Bingley, BD16 1WA, UK
T: +44 (0) 1274 777 700
F: +44 (0) 1274 785 201
info.emeraldinsight.com/products/journals/journals.htm?PHPSESSID=gc2rdmmg919cmhctpbi2cnesq0&id=ijopm
ISSN: 0144-3577
IJOPM is a monthly journal that publishes insights into the latest theoretical and practical developments and research on operations management. It provides a means of communication for all those working in the operations management field, including academics, practitioners, and consultants, and focuses on management topics, rather than technical content.

International Transactions in Operational Research
International Federation of Operational Research Societies
Wiley, 350 Main Street, Malden, MA 02148, USA
T: +1 781 388 8598
www.wiley.com/bw/journal.asp?ref=0969-6016&site=1
ISSN: 0969-6016
ITOR is a bimonthly journal that that aims to advance the understanding and practice of operational research and management science internationally. Its scope includes international problems, international work done by industry leaders, studies of worldwide interest from nations with emerging operational research communities, national or regional work which has the potential for application in other nations, and technical developments of international interest.

Journal of Operations Management
Elsevier
Radarweg 29, 1043 NX Amsterdam, The Netherlands
F: +31 20 485 2370
www.elsevier.com/wps/find/journaldescription.cws_home/523929/description
ISSN: 0272-6963
This bimonthly journal publishes high-quality research papers in the field of operations management, with the aim of furthering the understanding of the subject among researchers and practitioners, and clarifying and advancing the role of operations management within organizations.

Operations Management
The Institute of Operations Management
Earlstrees Court, Earlstrees Road, Corby, Northants, NN17 4AX, UK
T: +44 (0) 1536 740 105
F: +44 (0) 1536 740 101
www.iomnet.org.uk/control-and-news/default.aspx
ISSN: 1529-5648
This journal, published bimonthly by The Institute of Operations Management, offers technical articles, reports, and case studies by practitioners, consultants, and academics, as well as industry news, book reviews, and information on activities and forthcoming events.

  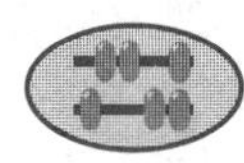   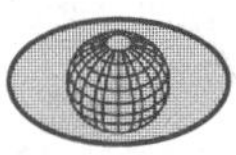   

Operations Research Letters
Elsevier
Radarweg 29, 1043 NX Amsterdam, The Netherlands
F: +31 20 485 2370
www.elsevier.com/wps/find/journaldescription.cws_home/505567/description#description
ISSN: 0167-6377

Production and Operations Management
Production and Operations Management Society, USA
www.poms.org/journal
ISSN: 1059-1478
This bimonthly journal is dedicated to research in operations management in manufacturing and services. It offers scientific research into the problems, interest, and concerns of managers, and covers all topics in product and process design, operations, and supply chain management.

INTERNET

Operations Research: The Science of Better
www.scienceofbetter.org
This online resource, run by the Institute for Operations Research and the Management Sciences, offers guidance and explanations on operations research, what it can do, and how to start using it, and features information on awards, leadership, and case studies.

ORGANIZATIONS

Europe

European Operations Management Association
Chair: Ann Vereecke
EurOMA Secretariat, c/o EIASM, Place De Brouckère Plein 31, 1000 Brussels, Belgium
T: +32 (0) 2 226 66 60
F: +32 (0) 2 512 19 29
E: euroma@eiasm.be
www.euroma-online.org
EurOMA is a leading European professional association for those involved in operations management. It comprises of an international network of academics and practitioners who are interested in the continuing development of operations management as an area of research and best practice, and offers international links for the share of knowledge, experiences, and ideas.

The Institute of Operations Management
Earlstrees Court, Earlstrees Road, Corby, Northants, NN17 4AX, UK
T: +44 (0) 1536 740 105
F: +44 (0) 1536 740 101
E: info@iomnet.org.uk
www.iomnet.org.uk
The institute provides a professional community of practitioners, consultants, academics, and thought leaders that promote the theory of, techniques for, and best practice in operations management. It is committed to excellence, continuous improvement and professionalism in operations management, and offers education and training in all its forms for the manufacturing and service industries.

USA

The Association for Operations Management
Chair: Thomas J. Krupka
8430 West Bryn Mawr Avenue, Suite 1000, Chicago, IL 60631, USA
T: +1 773 867 1777
F: +1 773 409 5576
E: service@apics.org
www.apics.org
APICS is the global association dedicated to operations management, including production, inventory, supply chain, materials management, purchasing, and logistics. It provides industry training, internationally recognized certifications, comprehensive resources, and a worldwide network of accomplished industry professionals.

Association of Business Process Management Professionals
Chair: Brett Champlin
47 West Polk Street, Suite 100-279, Chicago, IL 60605-2085, USA
www.abpmp.org
ABPMP is a non-profit, vendor-independent, professional organization dedicated to the advancement of business process management concepts and its practices. It has local chapters in several US areas, with more being formed in the US and internationally.

Institute for Operations Research and the Management Sciences
Chair: Don N. Kleinmuntz
7240 Parkway Drive, Suite 300, Hanover, Maryland 21706-1300, USA
T: +1 443 757 3500
F: +1 443 757 3515
E: onlineservices@informs.org
www.informs.org
INFORMS is a global association for professionals in the field of operations research. It serves the scientific and professional needs of operations research educators, investigators, scientists, students, managers, and consultants, as well as the organizations they serve, by publishing scholarly journals and a magazine, and organizing national and international conferences.

Production and Operations Management Society
Chair: Cheryl Gaimon
USA
E: poms@fiu.edu
www.poms.org
POMS is an international professional organization that represents the interests of industry professionals around the world. Its objectives include extending and integrating knowledge pertaining to production and operations management, disseminating information, and promoting the improvement and teaching on the subject to manufacturing and service organizations throughout the world.

International

International Federation of Operational Research Societies
Chair: Elise del Rosario
E: secretary@ifors.org
www.ifors.org
IFORS is an international umbrella organization dedicated to operational research, representing national societies around the world. It sponsors international meetings and other means for exchanging information on operational research, encourages nations to establish operational research societies, supports standards of competence in operational research, promotes operational research education, and promotes the growth of both existing and new fields of operational research.

  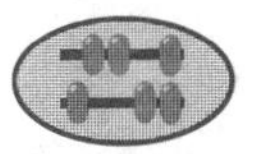 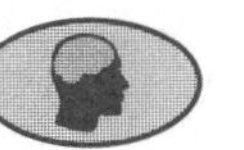  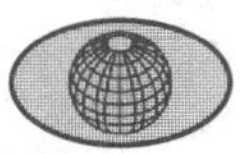   

Outsourcing

BOOKS

The Black Book of Outsourcing: How to Manage the Changes, Challenges, and Opportunities

Douglas Brown, Scott Wilson
Hoboken, New Jersey: Wiley, 2005
386pp, ISBN: 978-0-471-71889-5

This useful and comprehensive introduction to outsourcing is an essential guide to this growing (and often controversial) area. This book is as useful for those trying to carve out a career in this industry as it is for those who need to know the nuts and bolts, such as how to manage an outsourcing program.

Business Process Outsourcing: Process, Strategies, and Contracts, 2nd ed

John K. Halvey, Barbara Murphy Melby
Hoboken, New Jersey: Wiley, 2007
600pp, ISBN: 978-0-470-04483-4

In this guide for businesses looking to outsource some of their business functions, the topics dealt with address the process involved in contracting out key services, including the request for proposal (RFP) and selecting and contracting with an outsourcing vendor.

Outsourcing for Dummies

Ed Ashley
Business and Personal Finance
New York: For Dummies, 2008
367pp, ISBN: 978-0-470-22687-2

This practical, plain-English guide helps you plan an effective sourcing strategy. There are tips on negotiating with vendors, drafting a binding contract, and verifying and maintaining compliance. It also explains the importance of communicating with vendors, finding ways to measure performance, productivity, and cost-effectiveness, troubleshooting and solving outsourcing problems, and advice on ending the deal.

The Outsourcing Handbook: How to Implement a Successful Outsourcing Process

Mark J. Power, Kevin Desouza, Carlo Bonifazi
London: Kogan Page, 2006
222pp, ISBN: 978-0-7494-4430-3

The book provides detailed insight into the processes, issues, pitfalls, and successes for any type of outsourcing activity. It provides a valuable set of customer outsourcing methodology activities, and does not assume any prior knowledge of the subject.

Outsourcing IT: The Legal Aspects, 2nd ed

Rachel Burnett
Aldershot, UK: Gower Publishing, 2009
276pp, ISBN: 978-0-566-08597-0

This comprehensive guide to outsourcing the information technology function focuses on the need to obtain a properly negotiated formal contract. It discusses the structure of such a contract, and then goes on to cover the provisions that relate to staffing, location, software, costs, management liaison, allowing for change, security, duration, termination, and other matters. It also gives advice on public procurement and choosing a supplier.

The Outsourcing Process: Strategies for Evaluation and Management

Ronan McIvor
Cambridge, UK: Cambridge University Press, 2005
326pp, ISBN: 978-0-521-84411-6

This book provides a framework for an up-to-date understanding of the outsourcing process and the key issues associated with it. It integrates a number of contemporary topics, including benchmarking, buyer-supplier relationships, organizational behavior, competitor analysis, and technology influences.

What's This India Business? Offshoring, Outsourcing and the Global Services Revolution

Paul Davies
London: Nicholas Brealey Publishing, 2008
252pp, ISBN: 978-1-904838-21-0

Many businesses have outsourced some of their operations to India, and this book is a practical guide for anyone planning or simply investigating such a route. Packed with advice on how to gain competitive advantage from outsourcing to India, the books also has helpful hints on etiquette and Indian business culture.

JOURNALS

Strategic Outsourcing: An International Journal

Emerald
60/62 Toller Lane, Bradford, West Yorkshire, BD8 9BY, UK
T: +44 (0) 1274 777 700
F: +44 (0) 1274 785 200
www.emeraldinsight.com/1750-614X.htm
ISSN: 1750-614X

This journal aims to foster and lead the international debate on global sourcing and outsourcing. It provides a central, authoritative, and independent forum for the critical evaluation and dissemination of research and development, applications, processes and current practices relating to the design, implementation, and undertaking of strategic outsourcing.

INTERNET

BPO Watch India

www.bpowatchindia.com

This is a leading source for news and research on the business process outsourcing (BPO) industry.

National Outsourcing Association

www.noa.co.uk

This site provides access to recent articles by members and details of association events. It also has a members-only section.

Outsource World

www.outsource-world.com

Outsource World offers conferences, exhibitions, links, and networks through this site.

Outsourcing Center

www.outsourcing-center.com

This website provides comprehensive information and links regarding outsourcing. Its content includes industry-specific outsourcing information, research, outsourcing processes, and an online journal. It also provides material on suppliers and legal issues.

The Outsourcing Institute

www.outsourcing.com

The Outsourcing Institute is a professional association providing information and networking resources related to outsourcing. Its website offers information on the outsourcing process, including needs assessment and the selection of service providers. It also has information targeted at buyers and sellers of outsourcing services. Registration is required for some information; online membership is free.

The Outsourcing Management Zone

www.theoutsourcerzone.com

This site is aimed at both outsourcing professionals and those new to the concept. It provides numerous articles, a directory, and information on outsourcing, and also explains how and why outsourcing can affect your business.

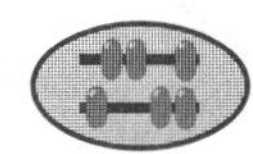

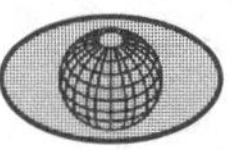

Outsourcing Research Center
www.cio.com/topic/1513/Outsourcing
The site provides online access to recent articles on outsourcing, as well as providing details of forthcoming events.

silicon.com
www.silicon.com/tags/outsourcing.htm
This business technology site offers a range of news, articles, and links on outsourcing.

TechWeb Business Technology Network
www.techweb.com
This site focuses on recent news and articles on IT outsourcing, plus links to events in its Tech Calendar.

Virtual Corporations and Outsourcing
www.brint.com
A selection of articles on outsourcing can be sourced from this site.

ORGANIZATIONS

Europe

National Outsourcing Association (NOA)
44 Wardour Street, London, W1D 6QZ, UK
T: +44 (0) 20 7292 8686
F: +44 (0) 20 7287 2905
E: admin@noa.co.uk
www.noa.co.uk
The NOA is the only outsourcing trade association in the UK. Formally established as a non-profit company, it operates as an independent organization, with a principle objective of boosting the effectiveness and success of outsourcing, through the promotion of best practice and innovation in the application and development of outsourcing.

Network Outsourcing Association
Keswick House, 44 Wardour Street, London, W1D 6QZ, UK
T: +44 (0) 20 7292 8686
F: +44 (0) 20 8778 8402
E: admin@noa.co.uk
www.noa.co.uk
The Association is an independent body, formed in the early 1990s, that acts as a forum for the business technology outsourcing community. Its membership is made up of UK and other companies with experience in outsourcing, and suppliers and consultants who support the industry.

USA

The Outsourcing Institute
Jericho Atrium, 500 North Broadway, Suite 141, Jericho, New York, NY 11753, USA
T: +1 516 681 0066
F: +1 516 938 1839
E: customerservice@outsourcing.com
www.outsourcing.com
This professional body, founded in 1993, provides outsourcing professionals worldwide with access to a business-to-business marketplace and an independent advisory network, as well as with information and education on outsourcing best practice. Membership is free.

BRIC

China Sourcing
F12 Baiyan Building, 238 Beisihuan Zhong Road, Haidian District, Beijing 100191, China
T: +86 10 823 31717
F: +86 10 823 32323
E: ruby.guan@chinasourcingguide.com
www.chinasourcingguide.com
The objective of China Sourcing is to raise awareness of China as a provider of highly skilled technology services and gain recognition for China's vibrant technology outsourcing industry. Its participants are the Beijing Municipal Science & Technology Commission, the Beijing Municipal Bureau of Commerce, and the Beijing Software Industry Productivity Center.

Export Promotion Bureau of Bangladesh (EPB)
Export Promotion Bureau, TCB Bhaban, 1–2, Kawran Bazar C/A Dhaka 1215, Bangladesh
T: +880 2 9144 821 4
F: +880 2 9119 531
E: info@epb.gov.bd
www.epb.gov.bd
This government organization, run by the Ministry of Commerce, promotes export and international trade. It is pivotal when entering into a trade agreement with a Bangladeshi company.

Outsourcing Malaysia (OM)
1106, Block B, Phileo Damansara II, 15, Jln 16/11, 46350 Petaling Jaya, Selangor Darul Ehsan, Malaysia
T: +60 3 7955 2922
F: +60 3 7955 2933
www.outsourcingmalaysia.org.my
Outsourcing Malaysia (OM) is an initiative of the outsourcing industry and a chapter of PIKOM. With the support from its institutional partners, such as the Multimedia Development Corporation and the Malaysia Debt Ventures, and senior leaders from the global services industry, it promotes the capabilities and competencies of the Malaysian outsourcing industry.

  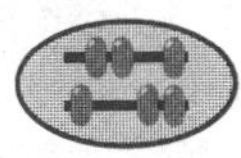   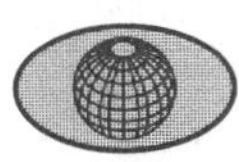   

Pension Fund Finance

BOOKS

Dealing with the New Giants: Rethinking the Role of Pension Funds
Tito Boeri, Lans Bovenberg, Benoit Coeure, Andrew Roberts
Geneva Reports on the World Economy Series
London: Centre for Economic Policy Research, 2006
140pp, ISBN: 978-1-898128-94-6
This examines the role of pension funds as major institutional investors in global financial markets, their impact of risk sharing, and imperfect markets in which they operate. It argues for a reform of public pension systems, mandatory participation in standalone, collective pension plans, a new governance structure for pension funds, the harmonization of accounting standards, and the development of innovative hybrid collective pension schemes.

Fiduciary Management: Blueprint for Pension Fund Excellence
Anton van Nunen
Wiley Finance Series
Hoboken, New Jersey: Wiley, 2008
274pp, ISBN: 978-0-470-17103-5
This practical guide examines fiduciary management as an increasingly popular strategy for organizing the management of institutional investment portfolios. It describes its rise to prominence, the benefits of fiduciary management, and the key functions of the fiduciary manager. It also analyzes it in terms of asset-liability modeling, constructing portfolios, selecting and overseeing investment managers, benchmarking and performance measurement, and reporting.

Foundation and Endowment Investing: Philosophies and Strategies of Top Investors and Institutions
Lawrence E. Kochard, Cathleen M. Rittereiser
Wiley Finance Series
Hoboken, New Jersey: Wiley, 2008
320pp, ISBN: 978-0-470-12233-4
This offers a number of profiles of top Chief Investment Officers in the foundation and endowment industry, where they discuss their investment philosophies, their strategies for improving the financial health of their organizations, and how they applied them in real-world market conditions. It also provides a practical perspective on institutional investing, and issues such as asset allocation and the emergence of alternative asset classes.

Frontiers in Pension Finance
Dirk Broeders, Sylvester Eijffinger, Aerdt Houben (editors)
Cheltenham, UK: Edward Elgar Publishing, 2008
337pp, ISBN: 978-1-84720-660-2
This is a guide to the latest insights into pension finance, pension system design, pension governance, and risk-based supervision, which attempts to meet the challenges currently faced by this fast-changing industry. A team of international experts examine the pressure of an ageing population, the shift from pay-as-you-go pension systems to pre-funded plans, the delivery of adequate pension benefits at reasonable costs, and attempts to increase the efficiency of pension systems.

How to Select Investment Managers & Evaluate Performance: A Guide for Pension Funds, Endowments, Foundations, and Trusts
G. Timothy Haight, Stephen O. Morrell, Glenn E. Ross
Frank J. Fabozzi Series
Hoboken, New Jersey: Wiley, 2007
260pp, ISBN: 978-0-470-04255-7
This is a comprehensive and accessible guide to selecting and evaluating external investment professionals, improving their effectiveness, and gauging their ability to meet clients' investment goals, objectives, and needs. It is useful for trustees of pension plans, endowments, and trusts responsible for governing and overseeing the investment of their funds, and covers such aspects as return measures, fixed income and duration, manager searches, and committee meetings.

Innovations in Pension Fund Management
Arun Muralidhar
Stanford, California: Stanford Economics and Finance, 2001
327pp, ISBN: 978-0-8047-4521-5
This is a theoretical and practical guide to current thinking on pension fund investment strategy, asset allocation, human financial resource management, risk management, and performance evaluation and implementation. It covers asset liability management, current practices of plan sponsors and investment managers, how to best measure and manage risk, and provides a framework for the use of derivatives in funds, and the benefits of leverage.

Investing in Pension Funds and Endowments: Tools and Guidelines for the New Independent Fiduciary
Russell L. Olson
New York: McGraw-Hill, 2003
409pp, ISBN: 978-0-07-141336-7
This is an accessible, practical reference to all aspects of investing for pension funds, endowments, trusts, and foundations. It analyzes the opportunities and pitfalls for fund managers, and describes how to produce superior pension management returns without sacrificing fiduciary responsibilities. It also provides practical guidance on risk, asset allocation, types of potential investments, master trustees and custodians, governance, and liabilities.

The Money Flood: How Pension Funds Revolutionized Investing
Michael J. Clowes
New York: Wiley, 2000
308pp, ISBN: 978-0-471-38483-0
This is a history of the growth of corporate pension funds over the last fifty years, which details their impact on investing, the financial markets, the labor force, corporate management, and the general economy. It also provides a warning regarding the potential consequences of these changes, the power of fund managers in the global financial markets, and the shift from defined benefit pension plans to defined contribution plans.

Pension Finance
David Blake
Chichester, UK: Wiley, 2006
465pp, ISBN: 978-0-470-05843-5
This provides a comprehensive overview of theory and practice in pension finance from a multi-disciplinary perspective. It explains the different types of investment assets, different asset classes, corporate pension finance, the financial aspects of defined contribution and defined benefit pension plans, the role of pension funds and pension fund management, pension fund performance measurement and attribution, and risk management in pension funds.

Pension Fund Governance: A Global Perspective on Financial Regulation
John Evans, Michael Orszag, John Piggott (editors)
Cheltenham, UK: Edward Elgar Publishing, 2008
269pp, ISBN: 978-1-84720-485-1
This technical treatment of pension fund governance combines original

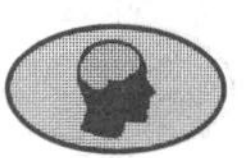

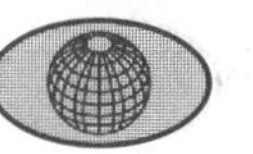

contributions from industry experts around the world, based on both theoretical analysis and empirical study. It provides frameworks for pension fund governance, and examines private and public pensions, global governance practice and experience on pension funds in the United States and Australia, and discusses the role of government guarantees.

Pension Fund Investment Management, 2nd ed
Frank J. Fabozzi
Hoboken, New Jersey: Wiley, 1997
301pp, ISBN: 978-1-883249-26-7
The new edition of this wide-ranging handbook examines the essentials of pension fund investment management, before discussing current developments and issues in pension fund governance, operations, and value creation. It is written by a team of leading industry experts, and is aimed at all investment professionals concerned with the management of pension funds.

Pension Fund Trustee Handbook, 9th ed
Roger Self
Haywards Heath, UK: Tottel Publishing, 2005
365pp, ISBN: 978-1-84592-175-0
This is a comprehensive guide to the role and duties of occupational pension fund trustees, providing a useful reference regardless of level of legal expertise. This updated edition examines both statutory and trust law, the role of the sponsoring employer, the rights of the scheme members, requirements for advisers, and looks at breaches of trust, protection for trustees, and trustee powers and discretions.

Pension Revolution: A Solution to the Pensions Crisis
Keith P. Ambachtsheer
Wiley Finance Series
Hoboken, New Jersey: Wiley, 2007
336pp, ISBN: 978-0-470-08723-7
This examination of the current failings of retirement plans offers strategic analysis of pension governance, benefit design, investment policy, funding, organizational structure, the distribution of risk, performance measurement, and results disclosure. It details the design features that have helped create the pension crisis, and explains how to bring about fundamental changes to ensure that the provision of retirement income is sustainable.

Risk-Based Supervision of Pension Funds: Emerging Practices and Challenges
Greg Brunner, Roberto Rocha, Richard Hinz (editors)
Directions in Development Series
Washington, DC: World Bank, 2008
250pp, ISBN: 978-0-8213-7493-1
This is a review of risk-based pension fund supervision and the increasing focus on risk management in both banking and insurance based on capital requirements, supervisory review, and market discipline. It examines the modifications needed to apply the method to pension funds, particularly for defined contribution funds, and presents a range of cases on the diversity of pension systems and approaches to risk-based supervision.

State and Local Pension Fund Management
Jun Peng
Public Administration and Public Policy Series
Boca Raton, Florida: Taylor & Francis, 2008
263pp, ISBN: 978-0-8493-0548-1
This is a systematic guide to the major issues facing those responsible for state and local public retirement programs. It provides a history of the public pension system, and looks at pension benefit design, actuarial valuation and funding methods, financial reporting, and pension asset investment management, before focusing on policy issues such as the management of public pension programs, and pension benefit reforms.

MAGAZINES

European Pensions & Investment News
Financial Times Group
1 Southwark Bridge, London, SE1 9HL, UK
T: +44 (0) 20 7873 3000
www.epn-magazine.com
This fortnightly magazine provides news, information, and analysis on all aspects of the investment of employer-supported retirement institutions, including traditional defined benefit and defined contribution company pension funds. It focuses on investment trends, the operation of the institutional fund management industry, analysis of regulatory changes both on a national and EU level, and analysis of the investment intentions of retirement institutions.

Global Pensions
Incisive Media
28–29 Haymarket, London, SW1Y 4RX, UK
T: +44 (0) 20 7484 9700
F: +44 (0) 20 7234 0702
www.globalpensions.com
ISSN: 1743-3312
This monthly magazine, with daily and weekly online updates, is a news-driven, campaigning publication that provides opinion and analysis of current information on institutional pension schemes worldwide. It focuses on regional pensions news, new investment products, current trends in the industry, and also offers round table discussions.

Investment & Pensions Europe
IPE International Publishers
320 Great Guildford House, 30 Great Guildford Street, London, SE1 0HS, UK
T: +44 (0) 20 7261 0666
www.ipe.com
ISSN: 1369-3727
This monthly magazine is aimed at those responsible for running pension funds in Europe. It provides coverage of the major challenges that are facing the industry in meeting the retirement needs of ageing populations, and the opportunity this provides for the asset management industry, and offers a database of pension funds country-by-country, and monthly supplements on a wide range of topics.

Pensions Age
Perspective Publishing
6th Floor, 3 London Wall Buildings, London, EC2M 5PD, UK
T: +44 (0) 20 7562 2401
F: +44 (0) 20 7374 2701
www.pensionsage.com
This monthly magazine for pensions professionals covers a wide range of topics, including personal and occupational schemes, employee benefits, investment management, legislative changes and technology. It offers news, market surveys, product developments, and features on the main issues in both the private and public sectors.

Pensions & Investments
Crain Communications
711 Third Avenue, New York, NY 10017, USA
T: +1 212 210 0100
F: +1 212 210 0117
www.pionline.com
ISSN: 1050-4974
This fortnightly international newspaper on money management provides news, research, and analysis to pension, portfolio, and investment managers in the institutional investment market. It provides coverage of events affecting the money management business, including business and financial news, legislative reports, global investments, product

development, technology, investment performance, executive changes, and corporate governance.

Pensions Management
Financial Times Group
1 Southwark Bridge, London, SE1 9HL, UK
T: +44 (0) 20 7873 3000
www.pensions-management.co.uk
This monthly magazine is source of information and debate on the UK pension and investment markets. It reports on the latest developments in the pensions sector, interviews industry experts, presents key fund statistics, and provides surveys, features, roundtables, awards, investment, people, politics/policy, and product news.

Professional Pensions
Incisive Media
28–29 Haymarket, London, SW1Y 4RX, UK
T: +44 (0) 20 7484 9700
F: +44 (0) 20 7034 2750
www.professionalpensions.com
This weekly publication for the occupational pensions industry in the UK offers news and commentary on the key issues facing schemes and their sponsors. It offers regular roundtable and panel debates on a range of investment, administrative and legal topics, industry sector reports on property investment, specialist managers, local authority schemes, group risk and consultants, as well as fund performance statistics, job opportunities, and interviews.

JOURNALS

Journal of Pension Economics and Finance
Cambridge University Press
The Edinburgh Building, Shaftesbury Road, Cambridge, CB2 8RU, UK
T: +44 (0) 1223 326 070
F: +44 (0) 1223 325 150
journals.cambridge.org/action/displayJournal?jid=PEF
ISSN: 1474-7472
JPEF is a quarterly journal that focuses on the economics and finance of pensions and retirement income. It offers research on a variety of topics, including pension fund management, the regulation of pensions, and pensions and labor markets, and current public policies, and provides a forum for international debate on the impact of demographic factors on the pensions industry.

Journal of Pension Planning and Compliance
Aspen Publishers
76 Ninth Avenue, New York, NY 10011, USA
T: +1 301 698 7100
www.aspenpublishers.com/product-.asp?catalog_name=Aspen&product_id=SS01482181
ISSN: 0148-2181
This quarterly journal publishes technical articles on major issues confronting the pension community. It covers pension compliance and design issues, plan qualification problems, new developments in employee benefits, and current legislative trends, as well as aspects of non-discrimination regulations, plan administration, tax law, and fiduciary liability.

Pensions: An International Journal
Palgrave Macmillan
Houndmills, Basingstoke, RG21 6XS, UK
www.palgrave-journals.com/pm
ISSN: 1478-5315
Pensions is quarterly journal for pensions professionals that is dedicated to the practice of pensions administration, law, compliance, and investment. It provides briefings, analyses, and updates on areas such as investment policy, benefits practices, actuarial prediction, trustee responsibility, regulation, advisory services, pensions management, government policy, accounting and reporting practices, dispute resolution, and legislation and case law.

INTERNET

IPE.com
www.ipe.com
This is a major European website that provides daily news, articles, web conferencing, white papers, and links for the pensions community. It also offers useful resources, such as a guide to managing pension funds, seminars, a real estate investment managers guide, an asset manager database, a pension funds database, and industry job information.

PensionsNet
www.pensionsnet.com
This is an online resource that presents news, features, a free weekly email service, seminars, and surveys on recent pensions and investments news.

ORGANIZATIONS

Europe

European Federation for Retirement Provision
Chair: Angel Martinez-Aldama
Koningsstraat 97 rue Royale, 1000 Brussels, Belgium
T: +32 (0) 2 289 14 14
F: +32 (0) 2 289 14 15
E: efrp@efrp.org
www.efrp.org
EFRP represents occupational/supplementary pension plans throughout the European Union, and acts as a centre of expertise within Europe. It promotes national diversity in financial vehicles to fund occupational pension schemes, the view that pension provision can be combined to form one single retirement income, the balance between the protection of pension fund beneficiaries and the efficiency of financing the liabilities, and the rights of pension funds as wholesale consumers.

National Association of Pension Funds
Chair: Joanne Segars
NIOC House, 4 Victoria Street, London, SW1H 0NX, UK
T: +44 (0) 20 7808 1300
F: +44 (0) 20 7222 7585
E: napf@napf.co.uk
www.napf.co.uk
The NAPF is an industry association dedicated to workplace pensions in the UK, representing those involved in designing, operating, advising, and investing in all aspects of pensions and other retirement provision. It offers information, conferences, seminars, and events for its members, who are pension schemes, businesses that provide services to the pensions sector, local authorities, and other organizations that provide pensions for their employees.

Pensions Institute
Chair: David Blake
Cass Business School, 106 Bunhill Row, London, EC1Y 8TZ, UK
T: +44 (0) 20 7040 8951
E: d.blake@city.ac.uk
www.pensions-institute.org
The institute undertakes high quality research in all fields related to pensions, including microeconomics, fund management and performance, contingency analysis and valuation, law and regulation, accounting, taxation and administration, and the marketing of private sector pension schemes. It also disseminates the results to academics and professionals, establishes international networks of pension researchers, and provides expert advice to the pensions industry and government.

Pensions Management Institute
Chair: Steve Delo
PMI House, 4–10 Artillery Lane, London, E1 7LS, UK
T: +44 (0) 20 7247 1452

F: +44 (0) 20 7375 0603
E: enquiries@pensions-pmi.org.uk
www.pensions-pmi.org.uk

PMI is a non-lobbying professional body that promotes professionalism amongst those working in the field of pensions. It offers four levels of membership and nine different examinations, as well as providing a range of support services for ongoing personal development, a series of national and regional events, a number of publications, and a network of nine regional groups.

Pensions Policy Institute

Chair: Baroness Greengross
King's College, Room 311, 3rd Floor, 26 Drury Lane, London, WC2B 5RL, UK
T: +44 (0) 20 7848 3744
F: +44 (0) 20 7848 1786
E: info@pensionspolicyinstitute.org.uk
www.pensionspolicyinstitute.org.uk

The PPI is an educational organization that provides non-political, independent comment and analysis on pension policy in the UK. It provides relevant and accessible information on the extent and nature of retirement provision, analysis and commentary on the policy-making process, encourages pension research and debate, acts as a sounding board for providers, policy makers and opinion formers, and informs the public debate on pensions issues.

Pensions Research Accountants Group

Chair: Jeff Highfield
c/o Deloitte & Touche, 4 Brindley Place, Birmingham, B1 2HZ, UK
E: feedback@prag.org.uk
www.prag.org.uk

PRAG is an independent research and discussion group for the development and exchange of ideas in the pensions field. It focuses on the main areas of reporting and accounting by pension schemes, and produces reports on related matters.

Society of Pension Consultants

Chair: Duncan Howorth
St Bartholomew House, 92 Fleet Street, London, EC4Y 1DG, UK
T: +44 (0) 20 7353 1688
F: +44 (0) 20 7353 9296
E: info@spc.uk.com
www.spc.uk.com

SPC is a representative body for providers of advice and services to work-based pension schemes, and their sponsors across the private pensions sector. It aims to influence policy and strategy, provide members with access to technical information on key policy debates, and helps to raise the profile of its members and address practical industry issues on their behalf.

USA

American Society of Pension Professionals & Actuaries

Chair: Brian H. Graff
4245 North Fairfax Drive, Suite 750, Arlington, VA 22203, USA
T: +1 703 516 9300
F: +1 703 516 9308
E: asppa@asppa.org
www.asppa.org

ASPPA is a national, non-profit, professional organization for career retirement plan professionals, its members being comprised of disciplines supporting retirement income management and benefits policy. Its aims are to educate retirement plan and benefits professionals, and preserve and enhance the private pension system. It offers educational programs for its members, and tracks legislative and regulatory activities affecting retirement benefits and pension policy.

National Institute of Pension Administrators

Chair: Theresa Conti
401 North Michigan Avenue, #2200, Chicago, Illinois 60611-4267, USA
F: +1 312 245 1085
E: nipa@nipa.org
www.nipa.org

NIPA is a national organization that educates and trains pension plan administrators. It encourages active participation in order to maintain our profession at the highest possible standards, and provides educational forums such as courses, workshops, and seminars on various aspects of plan administration.

The Pension Research Council

Chair: Olivia S. Mitchell
The Wharton School, 3620 Locust Walk, 3000 Steinberg Hall–Dietrich Hall, Philadelphia, PA 19104-6302, USA
T: +1 215 898 7620
F: +1 215 573 3418
E: prc@wharton.upenn.edu
www.pensionresearchcouncil.org

The Pension Research Council is a non-profit organization based at the Wharton School of the University of Pennsylvania, and is committed to generating debate on key policy issues affecting pensions and other employee benefits. It sponsors interdisciplinary research on private pension and social security programs, as well as related benefit plans worldwide. It holds conferences and symposia, research projects, and publishes books, preprints, and working papers.

International

International Federation of Pension Fund Administrators

Avda. 11 de septiembre 2155, Tower C, Office 901, Floor 9, Providencia, Santiago, Chile
T: +56 2 381 1723
F: +56 2 381 2655
E: fiap@fiap.cl
www.fiap.cl

FIAP is a non-profit organization that disseminates, promotes, defends, and publicizes the development of social security systems based on saving and individual capitalization, through pension fund administrators. Its aims include the uniting of associations, chambers, and similar institutions in countries which have legally constituted systems of pension fund administrators, the promotion of private pension fund systems, and representing the concerns of its members in an international context.

The International Organisation of Pension Supervisors

Chair: Ross Jones
c/o Andre Laboul, Secretary General, OECD Bureau Ingres 278, 2 Rue Andre Pascal, 75116 Paris, France
E: andre.laboul@oecd.org
www.iopsweb.org

IOPS is an independent international body that represents those involved in the supervision of private pension arrangements. It covers all levels of economic development and brings together all types of pension and supervisory systems. It acts as worldwide forum for policy dialogue and the exchange of information, as well as a standard setting body for promoting good practices in pension supervision.

  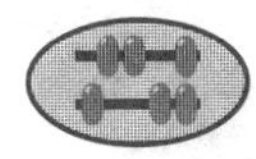 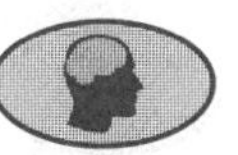  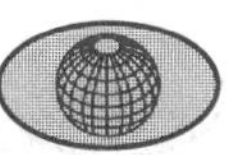   

Pricing

BOOKS

Asset Pricing
John Howland Cochrane
Princeton, New Jersey: Princeton University Press, 2001
530pp, ISBN: 978-0-691-07498-6
Asset Pricing covers the pricing of all assets, focusing on the concept of price equals expected discounted payoff. It examines empirical work using the Generalized Method of Moments, which studies sample average prices and discounted payoffs to determine whether price does equal expected discounted payoff. It also includes review of recent empirical work on return predictability and value.

International Transfer Pricing: A Study of Cross-Border Transactions
J. Elliott, C. R. Emmanuel
London: CIMA Publishing, 2000
96pp, ISBN: 978-1-85971-346-4
Directed at managers and theorists, this report is based on a research project investigating international transfer pricing (ITP) in 12 organizations. It presents the findings from interviews aimed at acquiring an in-depth understanding of single ITP transactions undertaken by participants in each of the multinational organizations involved. Key issues and trends are summarized in the last section.

Market-oriented Pricing: Strategies for Management
Michael H. Morris, Gene Morris
Lincolnwood, Illinois: Quorum Books, 2001
224pp, ISBN: 978-0-8442-3460-1
Using company case studies and examples, this manual for marketers and managers leads its readers through the steps involved in developing and implementing market-based pricing strategies. The areas covered include the psychology of pricing, market and competitor analysis, negotiating prices, using price elasticity, and computer aids in pricing.

Price Advantage
Michael V. Marn, Eric V. Roegner, Craig C. Zawada
Wiley Finance Series
Chichester, UK: Wiley, 2004
288pp, ISBN: 978-0-471-46669-7
Price advantage suggests that many companies neglect the opportunities offered by pricing strategy for increasing profitability and outperforming the competition. Drawing on their experience of advising businesses, the authors offer a practical pricing guide for managers. A three-level framework for identifying and exploiting pricing opportunities, covering industry strategy, product and market strategy, and transaction level, is set out. Pricing issues in specific contexts such as the introduction of new products, packaged offerings, price wars, post-merger pricing and practical issues such as the use of technology and the regulatory framework are also addressed. These are then placed within overall organizational strategy. The text is illustrated throughout with case studies.

The Price Advantage
Michael V. Marn, Eric V. Roegner, Craig C. Zawada
Hoboken, New Jersey: Wiley, 2006
304pp, ISBN: 978-0-471-46669-7
The Price Advantage is designed to help managers with pricing issues. It demonstrates how pricing excellence is critical to corporate success and profitability, and explains new approaches to analyzing and improving pricing strategy.

Pricing for Profitability: Activity-Based Pricing for Competitive Advantage
John L. Daly
Chichester, UK: Wiley, 2001
288pp, ISBN: 978-0-471-41535-0
The authors suggest that activity-based pricing helps companies set appropriate prices which both generate sales and result in a profit. Activity-based pricing analyzes the interdependence between price, cost and sales volume, resulting in a disciplined approach to the process of price development. Other topics included in the book are estimating customer demand, pricing law in the United States, the ethics of pricing, planning profit, and tips for successful price negotiations.

Pricing on Purpose: Creating and Capturing Value
Ronald J. Baker
Hoboken, New Jersey: Wiley, 2006
416pp, ISBN: 978-0-471-72980-8
This book explains the theory of value, and details how any business can use the various pricing strategies to create, communicate, and capture the value of their products and services. It takes a new approach by focusing on the external value as perceived by the customer, and advocates matching price to value. It can be useful for new executives, professional pricers, and marketers.

Professional's Guide to Value Pricing, 6th ed
Ronald J. Baker
Chicago, Illinois: CCH, 2005
640pp, ISBN: 978-0-7355-4806-0
This book lets readers see how pricing by the hour, instead of pricing by the value, can have a negative effect on your business. Through examples and clear and powerful writing, Baker leads the businessperson to achieve a better system of charging by the services rendered to the client.

Profitable Buying Strategies: How to Cut Procurement Costs and Buy Your Way to Higher Profits
Mike Buchanan
London: Kogan Page, 2008
256pp, ISBN: 978-0-7494-5238-4
This book gives clear and self-explanatory advice of cost reduction techniques which can be applied in any business. It examines how to improve your staff's skills in negotiation, e-procurement, market testing, and outsourcing. It also covers relevant contract laws for ensuring effective buying operations.

The Strategy and Tactics of Pricing: A Guide to Growing More Profitably, 4th ed
Thomas T. Nagle, Reed K. Holden
Harlow, UK: Prentice Hall, 2007
368pp, ISBN: 978-0-13-204358-8
The Strategy and Tactics of Pricing provides a comprehensive, practical, step-by-step guide to pricing analysis and strategy development. Ideal for MBA students, this book is a practical guide to pricing strategy. Concepts are fully illustrated with examples, and this new edition features many drawn from the world of e-commerce.

Transfer Pricing Methods: An Applications Guide
Robert Feinscreiber
Chichester, UK: Wiley, 2004
320pp, ISBN: 978-0-471-57360-9
This practical guide is designed to assist managers in mid-sized businesses with the techniques of transfer pricing. The subject is introduced and the application of specific transfer pricing techniques is explained. Also explored are various international transfer pricing issues.

  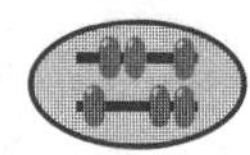 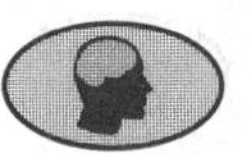  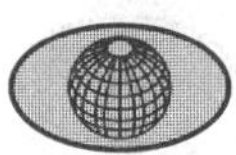   

Winning the Profit Game: Smarter Pricing and Smarter Branding
Robert G. Docters et al.
Maidenhead, UK: McGraw-Hill, 2004
320pp, ISBN: 978-0-07-143472-0
In order to improve profitability, it is argued that organizations now need to focus on the top line, and that the two fundamental tools for doing this are price and brand. The need to take a fresh look at price and brand is explained, and the process of developing an integrated price brand strategy is examined. This focuses on setting price and creating revenue, managing ongoing revenues, and building revenue capabilities.

JOURNALS

Journal of Product and Brand Management
Emerald
60/62 Toller Lane, Bradford, West Yorkshire, BD8 9BY, UK
T: +44 (0) 1274 777 700
F: +44 (0) 1274 785 200
www.emeraldinsight.com/1061-0421.htm
ISSN: 1061-0421
This academic journal, published seven times each year, explores the practice of product and brand management, as well as the understanding of product and pricing issues. It presents practical problems and solutions through case histories and examines the deployment of advertising, sales, promotion, packaging, research, consumer psychology, and other elements in branding.

Journal of Revenue and Pricing Management
Palgrave Macmillan
Houndmills, Basingstoke, Hampshire, RG21 6XS, UK
ISSN: 1476-6930
This journal, published five times each year, offers commentary and analysis on this growing sector. It focuses on revenue management, also known as yield management, and related areas, such as operations research/management science, statistics, economics, human resource management, software development, marketing, economics, e-commerce, consumer behavior, and consulting in their use for managing demand for a firm's products or services.

INTERNET

Professional Pricing Society
www.pricingsociety.com
Sponsored by a professional society dedicated to pricing management, the site offers forums, mailing list archives, products for purchase, webinars, and a bookstore for related books. Membership services are also available, as is a free newsletter.

Strategic Pricing Group
www.strategicpricinggroup.com
Sponsored by a consulting firm that specializes in strategic pricing, this site provides articles, recommended reading, a calendar of events, and information on educational services and consulting.

ORGANIZATIONS

Europe

Chartered Institute of Marketing (CIM)
Moor Hall, Cookham, Maidenhead, Berkshire, SL6 9QH, UK
T: +44 (0) 1628 427 500
F: +44 (0) 1628 427 499
E: marketing@cim.co.uk
www.cim.co.uk
The CIM is the main organization for professional marketers in the United Kingdom. It runs courses, holds examinations, produces publications, and offers information services covering all aspects of marketing.

USA

Association of Mutual Funds in India
709 Raheja Centre, Free Press Journal Marg, Nariman Point, Mumbai 400 021, India
T: +91 22 6610 1886
F: +91 22 6610 1889
www.amfiindia.com/index.asp
The Association of Mutual Funds in India focuses on developing the Indian mutual fund industry on professional and ethical lines, and enhancing and maintaining standards in all areas, to help protect and promote the interests of mutual funds and their unit holders.

National Investment Information Network
Brazil
T: +55 61 2109 7055
F: +55 61 2109 7047
E: renai@desenvolvimento.gov.br
investimentos.desenvolvimento.gov.br/renai_en/index.asp
The National Investment Information Network (RENAI) is an information network for investment activity in Brazil, supported by the Ministry of Development, Industry and Foreign Trade, with the assistance of other partners. The network aims to make such information available for wide use by investors, development incentive entities, research organisms, public bodies, and international agencies.

Fordham University Pricing Center
113 West, 60th Street, New York, NY 10023, USA
The Fordham University Pricing Center is a research institution dedicated to developing a better understanding of prices and pricing, from both academic and managerial perspectives. It conducts academic research, and sponsors research and practitioner seminars, and also acts as an advocate for pricing education in business school curricula.

Professional Pricing Society
3535 Roswell Road, Suite 59, Marietta, GA 30062, USA
T: +1 770 509 9933
F: +1 770 509 1963
E: contactus@pricingsociety.com
www.pricingsociety.com
PPS is an association for price decision makers and price management personnel; its members are primarily pricing and marketing executives. It offers its members conferences and workshops, monthly and quarterly publications, consulting services, and pricing workbooks.

  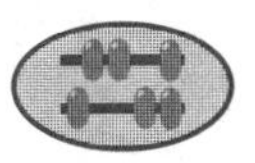   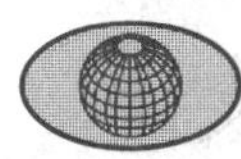   

Private Equity

BOOKS

Adding Value in Private Equity: Lessons from Mature and Emerging Markets

Eric D. Cruikshank
London: Euromoney Books, 2006
271pp, ISBN: 978-1-84374-218-0
This is a practical guide to the events and strategies that can add or undermine value in private companies throughout the investment period and exit. It explains the different stages of funding, how to determine value, the effects of globalization on private equity values, deal structuring, pre- and post-investment adding value, and adding value in the exit strategy.

Barbarians at the Gate: The Fall of RJR Nabisco

Bryan Burrough, John Helyar
HarperBusiness Essentials Series
New York: HarperBusiness, 2003
531pp, ISBN: 978-0-06-053635-0
Now hailed as a classic, this is an expose of the largest-ever leveraged buyout, of RJR Nabisco by private equity group Kohlberg Kravis Roberts. Also made into a film, its portrayal of oversized egos and greed seemed to sum up an era, and contributed greatly to the negative image of private equity in the 1980s.

Beyond the J Curve: Managing a Portfolio of Venture Capital and Private Equity Funds

Thomas Meyer, Pierre-Yves Mathonet
Wiley Finance Series
Chichester, UK: Wiley, 2005
366pp, ISBN: 978-0-470-01198-0
This is a comprehensive guide to how private equity funds operate in today's business environment, and achieve high returns. It presents a toolset for designing and managing portfolios, what it takes to select an effective fund manager, how to determine the funds' economic value, and the importance of monitoring.

Exposed to the J-Curve: Understanding and Managing Private Equity Fund Investments

Ulrich Grabenwarter, Tom Weidig
London: Euromoney Books, 2005
181pp, ISBN: 978-1-84374-149-7
This is an insightful review of the private equity fund industry, how to manage fund investments, and how institutional and private investors can safely invest into private equity funds. It discusses private equity as an asset class, how it fits into an alternative investment programme, and examines the different types of risks faced by private equity investors.

Getting a Job in Private Equity: Behind the Scenes Insight into How Private Equity Funds Hire

Brian Korb, Aaron Finkel
Glocap Guide Series
Hoboken, New Jersey: Wiley, 2008
198pp, ISBN: 978-0-470-29262-4
An insight into how the private equity hiring process works, the skills and qualifications required by hiring firms, with example interview questions, and useful case studies of successful job candidates. It shows how to improve your chances of successful employment, and how to build a long-term career in this competitive industry.

J-Curve Exposure: Managing a Portfolio of Venture Capital and Private Equity Funds

Pierre-Yves Mathonet, Thomas Meyer
Wiley Finance Series
Chichester, UK: Wiley, 2007
449pp, ISBN: 978-0-470-03327-2
A follow-up to the authors' earlier book, this presents new analysis and advanced guidance on the practical questions faced by institutions when setting up and managing a successful private equity investment program. It also examines the factors that can prevent institutions using venture capital, as well as regulatory issues, the prioritization of fund distributions, and techniques for track record analysis.

Lessons from Private Equity Any Company Can Use

Orit Gadiesh, Hugh MacArthur
Memo to the CEO Series
Boston, Massachusetts: Harvard Business School Press, 2008
126pp, ISBN: 978-1-4221-2495-6
This is a concise treatment of private equity, laid out in the format of a memo. It describes the rise of private equity in the marketplace, and its ability to maximize investor value more successfully than traditional companies, and presents a number of reasons for this, including measurement strategies, use of capital structure, and timeframe.

Private Equity and Venture Capital: A Practical Guide for Investors and Practitioners

Rick Lake, Ronald A. Lake (editors)
London: Euromoney Books, 2000
297pp, ISBN: 978-1-85564-691-9
This is an edited collection of articles from experts in private equity finance appraises this expanding asset class in the main US and UK markets, as well as in the developing markets. It focuses on the risks and returns involved in private equity investment, and discusses a number of essential features of this sector, such as investment management techniques, leveraged buyouts, and corporate governance.

Private Equity as an Asset Class

Guy Fraser-Sampson
Wiley Finance Series
Hoboken, New Jersey: Wiley, 2007
284pp, ISBN: 978-0-470-06645-4
This is a practical guide to understanding how private equity operates as an asset class. It presents basic concepts and definitions, the structure of private equity vehicles and returns, and the emerging area of total return investing. It also examines the differences between private equity and other asset classes, and the techniques used to measure and analyse performance.

Private Equity, Corporate Governance and the Dynamics of Capital Market Regulation

Justin O'Brien (editor)
London: Imperial College Press, 2007
411pp, ISBN: 978-1-86094-847-3
Examines the implications of private equity for the governance of corporations and the capital markets. It appraises the type and amount of risk posed by private equity by placing it in the wider context of the financial system, and addresses a number of key concepts, such as conflicts of interest, fiduciary duties, enforcement, systems of regulation, compliance, and accountability.

The Private Equity Edge: How Private Equity Players and the World's Top Companies Build Value and Wealth

Arthur B. Laffer, William J. Hass, Shepherd G. Pryor IV
New York: McGraw-Hill, 2009
432pp, ISBN: 978-0-07-159078-5
A new treatment of private equity, and the potential innovation and returns it brings to business. It examines value, how people can have an impact on success, the risk element, and the macroeconomic perspective, and explores the techniques that successful private equity players use to increase shareholder value and wealth for their partners.

 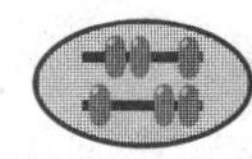   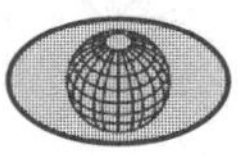   

Private Equity Exits: Divestment Process Management for Leveraged Buyouts
Stefan Povaly
Berlin: Springer, 2007
411pp, ISBN: 978-3-540-70953-4
Provides a comprehensive analysis of private equity divestment processes, or "exits," for European buyouts. It examines features of the divestment process, and the efficiency of exits, and an improved understanding of exit behavior, and also makes recommendations for integrated and exit-oriented private equity portfolio management.

Private Equity: History, Governance, and Operations
Harry Cendrowski, James P. Martin, Louis W. Petro, Adam A. Wadecki
Wiley Finance Series
Hoboken, New Jersey: Wiley, 2008
457pp, ISBN: 978-0-470-17846-1
Provides a comprehensive overview of private equity, its history and development as an asset class, the private equity process, terms of investment, and key players. It describes its ability to generate wealth for investors and the companies, and the mechanisms by which private equity achieves success, and presenting a framework for the analysis of private equity investments.

Structuring Venture Capital, Private Equity and Entrepreneurial Transactions
Jack Levin
New York: Aspen Publishers, 2008
1,326pp, ISBN: 978-0-7355-7468-7
Examines how to structure deals on a transaction-by-transaction basis, and how to ensure the tax, legal, and economic structuring consequences of deal-making works is conducted favorably. It presents practical detail on maximizing returns on transactions, controlling future rights to exit a profitable investment, and guidance on turning each transaction into a effective venture.

Venture Capital and Private Equity: A Casebook, 4th ed
Josh Lerner, Felda Hardymon, Ann Leamon
Hoboken, New Jersey: Wiley, 2009
545pp, ISBN: 978-0-470-22462-5
Now in its 4th edition, this casebook provides an overview of the industry at a time of great change in the industry, including rapid globalization. It focuses on how private equity funds are raised and structured, the interactions between private equity investors and the entrepreneurs, the process through which private equity investors exit their investments, and possible future developments.

Who's Who in Private Equity 2008, 18th ed
London: Incisive Media, 2008
An annual reference guide that contains details on over 2,300 industry professionals, from over 600 companies in 15 European countries. It provides key contact, investment and company profile information, and includes legal advisors as well as investors and corporate and leveraged finance companies.

MAGAZINES

The Elevator
HEPT
Grand Rue 114, 1820 Montreux, Switzerland
T: +41 21 944 11 80
F: +41 21 944 11 83
www.the-elevator.net
This is a quarterly up-market magazine for the private equity industry. It features a number of private equity projects and deals in each issue, discusses industry related topics with experts, and provides reviews of bespoke travel destinations and luxury products.

Emerging Private Equity
Greenland Publishing
34A Greenland Road, London, NW1 0AY, UK
T: +44 (0) 20 7870 7185
www.emergingpe.com
ISSN: 1755-3326
Aimed at private equity professionals in Africa, Asia, Central and Eastern Europe, Latin America, and the Middle East, this magazine focused on the emerging private equity markets also produces special reports, people news, and data analysis.

European Venture Capital & Private Equity Journal
Thomson Reuters
33 Aldgate High Street, London, EC3N 1DL, UK
T: +44 (0) 20 7369 7516
www.evcj.com
ISSN: 0954-1675
This magazine for the European venture capital and private equity industry is published 10 times a year, providing data and analysis on key developments in these markets. It covers every relevant activity, offers a comprehensive list of companies seeking buyers in Europe and announced deals every month, and produces supplements on issues such as mezzanine finance, MBOs, and new legal and regulatory developments.

Private Equity Europe
Incisive Media
Haymarket House, 28–29 Haymarket, London, SW1Y 4RX, UK
T: +44 (0) 20 7484 9700
F: +44 (0) 20 7004 7548
www.privateequityeurope.com
ISSN: 1465-9719
This is monthly magazine that provides fully validated pan-European coverage, statistics and analysis on the latest fundraising, buyout and exit news. It offers commentary on current issues surrounding institutional investment into the private equity asset class, as well as a deal forecast and mezzanine monitor.

Private Equity Insider
Harrison Scott Publications
5 Marine View Plaza, #400, Hoboken, NJ 07030-5795, USA
T: +1 201 659 1700
F: +1 201 659 4141
www.peinsider.com
ISSN: 1551-093X
This weekly newsletter provides the latest news and early intelligence on market developments in the private equity industry, involving operators of buyout funds, venture capital firms, funds of funds, secondaries, and other types of private equity vehicles. It covers marketing, capital raising innovations, successes and failures, infighting, fund launches, investor relations, market trends, career opportunities, valuation standards, and competition among service providers.

Private Equity International
PEI
2nd Floor, Sycamore House, Sycamore Street, London, EC1Y 0SG, UK
T: +44 (0) 20 7566 5444
www.peimedia.com/pei
This international magazine provides relevant information and insight to institutional investors and market practitioners who have an active interest in private equity. Published 10 times each year, it offers market insight and intelligence covering this global asset class, and substantive articles on the technical issues and challenges facing the market.

Private Equity News
Financial News
2nd Floor, Stapleton House, 29–33 Scrutton Street, London, EC2A 4HU, UK
T: +44 (0) 20 7426 3333
F: +44 (0) 20 7739 9954
www.penews.com
ISSN: 1741-9085
This weekly magazine provides daily news and analysis for Europe's private equity

  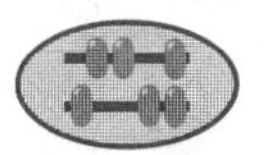  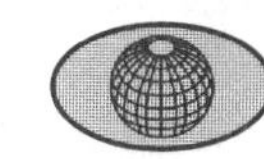   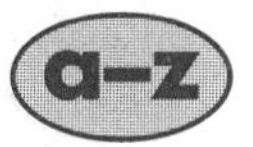

industry. It focuses on fundraising, deals, debt, advisory services, and comment, with its website also providing in-depth features, roundtables, reports and surveys on key topics and regional activity.

Real Deals Europe
Caspian Publishing
198 Kings Road, London, SW3 5XP, UK
T: +44 (0) 20 7368 7138
F: +44 (0) 20 7368 7178
www.realdeals.eu.com

This is a fortnightly magazine on the European private equity industry, which provides comment, news analysis, features, sector reports and supplements, as well as a daily news and deals email service, analysis of every European private equity deal, industry awards, and events.

Total Alternatives
Institutional Investor
225 Park Ave South, New York, NY 10003, USA
T: +1 212 224 3300
www.totalalternatives.com
ISSN: 1544-7596

This is an online news source for hedge funds, private equity, and other alternative investments. It contains stories on new strategies, fund launches, and reorganizations at major firms. It features the latest market news, daily email summaries, a resource of hedge fund news items in other media, and a data zone on hedge funds that includes information on strategy, rate of returns, annualized volume, and assets.

Unquote
Incisive Media
Haymarket House, 28–29 Haymarket, London, SW1Y 4RX, UK
T: +44 (0) 20 7484 9700
F: +44 (0) 20 7004 7548
www.unquote.com
ISSN: 1467-0062

This fortnightly newsletter presents news from the private equity and venture capital markets in the UK and Ireland, and is aimed at general partners, institutional investors, and intermediaries. It provides coverage from early-stage and expansion deals to buyouts and portfolio management, breakdowns of fundraising programs, exits, P2Ps, IPOs, and people moves, as well as in-depth analysis on key industry topics.

JOURNALS

The Journal of Private Equity
Institutional Investor
225 Park Avenue South, New York, NY 10003, USA
T: +1 212 224 3570
www.iijournals.com/JPE
ISSN: 1096-5572

This is quarterly journal presents strategies and techniques for venture investing, and practical research and analysis for the venture capital and private equity markets. It delves into each successful deal, with detailed explanations, analysis, and real-life case studies, and covers early-stage, mezzanine and later-stage private companies and financings, with articles on financial applications of structuring and exit strategies, cross-border issues, industry analyses, and management methods.

INTERNET

Albourne Village
www.village.albourne.com/private_equity

This is an online knowledge economy for the private equity community, designed as an environment for evolving news, intellectual property, content and debates on current issues. It revolves around the elements of village life—village pub, library, hedge fund mall, job centre, and data farm. There is also a conference center and village school, and a range of shops run by financial institutions, software companies, and publishers.

The International Private Equity and Venture Capital Valuation Guidelines
www.privateequityvaluation.com

This resource was developed by European private equity and venture capital associations, to reflect the need for greater comparability across the industry and for consistency with IFRS and US GAAP accounting principles. The valuation guidelines are used by the private equity and venture capital industry for valuing private equity investments, and provide a framework for fund managers and investors to monitor the value of existing investments.

NVST
www.nvst.com

This portal for the global private equity and finance community provides a broad range of private equity investment resources. It offers access to venture capital and M&A investment opportunities, online business tools, industry publications, research databases and educational resources for professional training.

Private Equity Central
www.privateequitycentral.net

This site is available to accredited individual and institutional investors, providing a source for news, data, and commentary on the fast-changing private equity market. It offers daily news about the funds, deals and people, interviews with managers, weekly market commentary, a directory of more than 1,000 private equity firms, a list of funds in the market, and searchable archives.

Private Equity Info
www.privateequityinfo.com

This is an informational resource of financial buyers, hedge funds, mezzanine investors, small business investment companies, valuation firms, M&A advisory firms, and real estate investors, and features a database of thousands of firms. It is aimed at middle market investment banks and M&A transaction-related professionals.

Private Equity Insight
www.privateequityinsight.com

This is an online database focused on the private equity industry, providing searchable data going back to 1990. This data is designed to help trend analysis, and an understanding of industry/geographic activity and competitor behavior in deal origination, portfolio management, benchmarking and strategic development, fundraising and investor relations, and performance.

Private Equity Wire
www.privateequitywire.co.uk

This site provides information on industry jobs, events, comments and opinions, interviews, and a free daily news bulletin.

ORGANIZATIONS

Europe

The British Private Equity and Venture Capital Association
Chair: Simon Walker
3 Clements Inn, London, WC2A 2AZ, UK
T: +44 (0) 20 7025 2950
F: +44 (0) 20 7025 2951
E: bvca@bvca.co.uk
www.bvca.co.uk

This is the industry body representing the UK private equity and venture capital industry. It promotes private equity for the benefit of entrepreneurs, investors, practitioners, and provides services, best practice standards to members, publications, research reports, and training courses. Its members are private equity companies active in making equity investments, and associate members who are professional firms including accountants, lawyers, and consultants.

  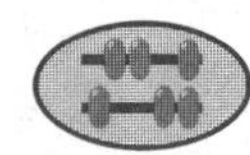 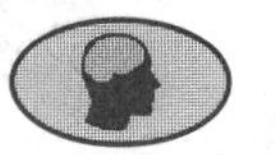  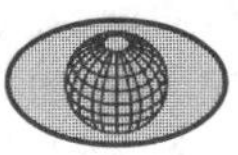   

European Private Equity and Venture Capital Association
Chair: Javier Echarri
Bastion Tower, Place du Champ de Mars 5, 1050 Brussels, Belgium
T: +32 2 715 0020
F: +32 2 725 0704
E: info@evca.eu
www.evca.eu
This is a member-based, non-profit trade association based in Brussels. It represents, promotes, and protects the interests of the European private equity and venture capital industry, and has over 1,300 members in Europe. Its activities cover the whole range of private equity, and provides network opportunities, training, co-ordination of public affairs, research initiatives, related publications, and an annual conference and seminars.

USA

The Hedge Fund & Private Equity Resource Center
1225 Franklin Avenue, Suite 325, Garden City, NY 11530, USA
T: +1 516 992 3417
E: info@hfpe.net
www.hfpe.net
This is a private, non-partisan institution dedicated to independent research and education on issues of government, politics, regulatory oversight and supervision involving private investment firms. It assists in the formulation of innovative policy solutions, and its research activities involve representative members of the private investment industry, professionals, and academics.

National Venture Capital Association
Chair: Dixon Doll
1655 North Fort Myer Drive, Suite 850, Arlington, Virginia 22209, USA
T: +1 703 524 2549
F: +1 703 524 3940
www.nvca.org
This is the main trade association representing the US venture capital industry. It is a member-based organization consisting of venture capital firms that manage pools of risk equity capital. Its mission is to foster greater understanding of the importance of venture capital to the US economy, support entrepreneurial activity and innovation, represent the public policy interests of the venture capital community, maintain professional standards, provide industry data, and sponsor professional development.

The Private Equity CFO Association
Chair: Chuck Woodard
c/o Citizens Bank, 53 State Street, 8th Floor, Boston, MA 02109, USA
E: charles.c.woodard@citizensbank.com
www.privateequitycfo.org
This association consists of over 650 private equity, venture capital and fund of funds CFOs in the New England, New York, Midwest, Mid-Atlantic and West Coast regions of the US, and provides communication, education, and networking opportunities for members. Membership is open to those responsible for the financial management in private equity, venture capital and fund of funds firms, and is not intended for asset management firms, investment bankers, industry consultants, vendors or service professionals.

BRIC

Indian Venture Capital and Private Equity Association
Chair: Saurabh Srivastava
301–302 Delhi Blue Apartments, Main Ring Road, New Delhi 110 029, India
T: +91 11 4162 8566
F: +91 11 4162 8863
E: info@indiavca.org
www.indiavca.org
This is a national organization that represents venture capital and private equity firms, promotes the industry within India and throughout the world, and encourages investment in high-growth companies. Its members comprise venture capital firms, institutional investors, banks, incubators, angel groups, corporate advisors, accountants, lawyers, government bodies, academic institutions and other service providers to the venture capital and private equity industry.

  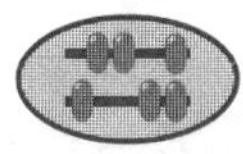   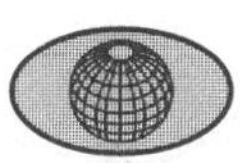   

Process Control and Statistical Process Control

BOOKS

The Desk Reference of Statistical Quality Methods, 2nd ed
Mark L. Crossley
Milwaukee, Wisconsin: ASQ Quality Press, 2007
450pp, ISBN: 978-0-87389-725-9
Arranged in alphabetical order for quick reference, this book provides the quality practitioner with a single resource that illustrates, in a practical manner, how to execute specific statistical methods frequently used in the quality sciences.

Managing Six Sigma: A Practical Guide to Understanding, Assessing, and Implementing the Strategy That Yields Bottom-Line Success
Forrest W. Breyfogle, III, James M. Cupello, Becki Meadows
London: Bantam Doubleday Dell Books, Random House, 2000
288pp, ISBN: 978-0-471-39673-4
This book provides detailed coverage of the Six Sigma techniques. Case studies describe some of the successes and pitfalls encountered in their successful implementation at Motorola and General Electric. Plans, checklists, and other materials are presented to help managers achieve a smooth and successful implementation.

The Quality Improvement Handbook, 2nd ed
John E. Bauer, Grace L. Duffy, Russell T. Westcott (editors)
Milwaukee, Wisconsin: ASQ Quality Press, 2006
242pp, ISBN: 978-0-87389-690-0
This book is for anyone who wants to improve themselves and/or their organization. It is particularly salient for those at the beginning stages of learning about the history, concepts, and tools of continual quality improvement.

The Six Sigma Handbook, 2nd ed
Thomas Pyzdek
Maidenhead, UK: McGraw-Hill, 2002
848pp, ISBN: 978-0-07-141015-1
If improving the quality of your manufacturing processes is your goal, and the extraordinarily successful Six Sigma program at GE is one you want to emulate, this book will help you implement that approach. The author examines the philosophy underlying the program and explores the management and organization of Six Sigma, then explains the statistical tools and problem-solving techniques needed to implement it.

Six Sigma Revolution: How General Electric and Others Turned Process into Profits
George Eckes
Chichester, UK: Wiley, 2000
272pp, ISBN: 978-0-471-38822-7
Presenting Six Sigma as a quantitative approach to quality that has boosted productivity and increased profits for a number of large businesses, the author explains how and why it is superior to other quality improvement methods and describes how to create and sustain a Six Sigma initiative in an organization.

Six Sigma: The Breakthrough Management Strategy Revolutionizing the World's Top Corporations
Mikel Harry, Richard Schroeder
London: Bantam Doubleday Dell Books, Random House, 2006
320pp, ISBN: 978-0-385-49437-3
This is an explanation of Six Sigma, in which the authors cite examples of companies (such as Polaroid) where the concept is currently in practice. Essentially, Six Sigma is a process that "guides companies into making fewer mistakes in everything they do—from filling out a purchase order to manufacturing airplane engines." A guide to achieving cost-effective quality within large corporations, this book is especially pertinent to managers and investors.

Statistical Methods for Quality Improvement, 2nd ed
Thomas P. Ryan
Wiley Series in Probability and Mathematical Statistics
Chichester, UK: Wiley, 2000
592pp, ISBN: 978-0-471-19775-1
Ryan provides a detailed introduction to the mathematics and statistics that form the basis of a range of fundamental quality control and statistical methods.

Statistical Process Control, 6th ed
John S. Oakland
Oxford: Butterworth-Heinemann, 2007
472pp, ISBN: 978-0-7506-6962-7
This new edition of a leading text reflects recent thinking in the field and provides a reliable reference source for statistical process control. The broad issues covered include understanding processes, process variability, process control, process capability, and process improvement.

Statistical Process Control for Quality Improvement: The Deming Paradigm and Beyond, 2nd ed
James R. Thompson, Jacek Koronacki
Boca Raton, Florida: Chapman & Hall/CRC Press, 2001
464pp, ISBN: 978-1-58488-242-8
The authors draw upon their experience of presenting short seminars to workers, foremen, and managers to create this introduction to SPC. They provide an overview of the subject for those with little knowledge of statistics, but the remaining, more detailed explanations of the analytical techniques of SPC are written for statisticians and production engineers with a higher level of mathematical understanding.

MAGAZINES

Quality Progress
World Alliance for Quality
600 North Plankinton Avenue, Milwaukee, WI 53203, USA
T: +1 414 272 8575
F: +1 414 272 1734
www.qualityprogress.com
ASQ's flagship publication, which features in-depth articles that describe the application of innovative methods. Topics include knowledge management, process improvement, and organizational behavior.

Six Sigma Forum Magazine
World Alliance for Quality
600 North Plankinton Avenue, Milwaukee, WI 53203, USA
T: +1 414 272 8575
F: +1 414 272 1734
www.asq.org/pub/sixsigma
This quarterly magazine offers feature articles focusing on companies such as Motorola and GE that have benefited from the practice of Six Sigma, and is aimed at Six Sigma professionals at all levels of experience.

JOURNALS

Total Quality Management and Business Excellence
Routledge
4 Park Square, Milton Park, Abingdon, Oxfordshire, OX14 4RN, UK
T: +44 (0) 20 7017 6000

  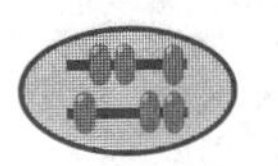   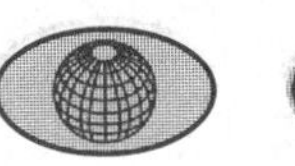   

F: +44 (0) 20 7017 6336
www.tandf.co.uk/journals/titles/14783363.asp
ISSN: 1478-3363
This international journal acts as a forum for new thinking and research in all aspects of total quality management, and provides a forum for the discussion and dissemination of research results. The journal is designed to appeal to both the academic and professional community working in this area.

INTERNET

American Society for Quality
www.asq.org
This ASQ site includes a profile of Walter A. Shewhart, the first honorary member of the Society and acclaimed father of modern quality control.

iSixSigma
www.isixsigma.com
This is an online content resource for the Six Sigma community. It offers resources to businesses at every stage of their Six Sigma maturity for professionals at all levels. It presents guidance for learning new skills, career advancement, and contributing to the success of an organization through a wide range of articles, tools, conferences, and practitioner forums.

Six Sigma Forum
www.sixsigmaforum.com
The site of this recently formed Forum provides some introductory information on Six Sigma and its application. There are links to related informative case studies and news, but you have to become a member to access these items.

ORGANIZATIONS

Europe

European Society for Quality
36–38 rue Joseph II, Brussels 1000, Belgium
T: +32 2 219 59 09
E: eoq@eoq-org.eu
www.eoq.org
The European Organization for Quality (EOQ) is an autonomous, non-profit association that acts as a forum for members of the quality industry across Europe.

USA

American Society for Quality (ASQ)
600 North Plankinton Avenue, Milwaukee, WI 53203, USA
T: +1 414 272 8575
F: +1 414 272 1734
E: cs@asq.org
www.asq.org
Founded in 1946, the ASQ is a society of individual and organizational members dedicated to the development and promotion of the concepts, principles, and techniques of quality. It has recently launched the Six Sigma Forum.

BRIC

Indian Society for Quality (ISQ)
52 Community Centre, II Floor, East of Kailash, New Delhi 110065, India
T: +91 11 4652 6000
F: +91 11 4657 2982
E: info@isqnet.org
www.isqnet.org
This is a membership-based forum on quality management. It promotes an awareness of quality management, conducts research, publishes on the subject, and awards prizes to companies that excel in the field of quality management.

Programa Gaucho da Qualidade e Produtividade (PGQP)
Rua Washington Luiz, 820, cj. 302, 90010-460, Porto Alegre, RS, Brazil
T: +55 51 3221 2663
www.mbc.org.br/mbc/pgqp/
PGQP is a non-profit organization based around voluntary work, which promotes and deploys the use of total quality management concepts and tools as a way of teaching organizational objectives and recognizing individual achievements.

Russian National Benchmarking Centre (RNBC) / The Benchmarking Club
2nd Mashinostroyeniya St., 17, 115088, Moscow, Russia
T: +7 495 771 6652
F: +7 495 771 6653
E: benchmarkingclub@mirq.ru
www.benchmarkingclub.ru
This non-profit organization is run by the Russian Organisation for Quality's (ROQ) Business Excellence Department. It aims to systematize and disseminate advanced principles of excellence and techniques for their implementation, and organize and offer practical assistance in exchange of experience between members in Russia and abroad.

Six Sigma Quality Management Research Center of RUC
School of Statistics of Renmin University, Beijing, 100872, China
T: +86 10 5198 6383
F: +86 10 6251 5246
E: hxq00@263.net
stat.ruc.edu.cn/en/research/centers/21698.html
This research center is run by the School of Statistics, Renmin University of China, and works to expand an awareness of applied statistics, and to promote the application of statistical methods and techniques in practice.

International

World Alliance for Quality (WAQ)
600 North Plankinton Avenue, Milwaukee, WI 53203, USA
T: +1 414 272 8575
F: +1 414 272 1734
waq.asq.org
The WAQ is an international organization, hosted by the American Society for Quality (ASQ), that strives to be the leader in fostering international co-operation for issues related to quality. It promotes the use of quality philosophies, principles, techniques, and tools to benefit society at large by supporting its application for activities such as resolution of global conflict and efficient use of all global resources.

Project Finance

BOOKS

Advanced Modelling for Project Finance
Charles T. Haskell
London: Euromoney Books, 2005
97pp, ISBN: 978-1-84374-214-2
This is a technical workbook that provides guidance on pricing and negotiating a project finance deal through the use of key industry models. It offers new perspectives on financial modeling, and features worked examples of how to build and analyze each step of a project finance model, to give a comprehensive understanding of the processes involved.

Advanced Project Financing
Richard Tinsley
London: Euromoney Books, 2000
294pp, ISBN: 978-1-85564-834-0
This technical overview of project finance provides timely analysis of the major risks in the sector, backed up by a range of real-world case studies where each choice of risk structure, such as currency risk and credit risk, is explained and assessed. It also describes and analyzes the impact of counterparties, joint venture documentation, and the emerging markets.

Financing Large Projects: Using Project Finance Techniques and Practices
M. Fouzul Kabir Khan, Robert J. Parra
Singapore: Prentice Hall, 2003
639pp, ISBN: 978-0-13-101634-7
This is a comprehensive examination of the techniques employed to finance large start-up projects, which addresses the financial, technical, legal, and environmental aspects of complex projects. It follows the project development cycle, from how projects are initiated, through to financial closure, and also explores the complexities of international law as it relates to project finance.

Identifying and Managing Project Risk: Essential Tools for Failure-Proofing Your Project, 2nd ed
Tom Kendrick
New York: Amacom, 2009
304pp, ISBN: 978-0-8144-1340-1
This new practical guide to project risk aims to help project managers that are time constrained, facing technical challenges, and working with inadequate resources. It describes how to minimize the possibility of project failure, by examining where possible risks can occur at each step of a project, and analyzes aspects such as project scope, scheduling, and how to use high-level risk assessment tools.

International Project Analysis and Finance
Gerald Pollio
Ann Arbor, Michigan: University of Michigan Press, 1999
235pp, ISBN: 978-0-472-11095-7
This book combines an analysis of project assessment with the necessary funding aspects needed to achieve the potential of both private and public sector investment projects. It examines concepts such as capital budgeting, limited recourse debt, and risk management, particularly in relation to natural resource projects, offering a theoretical and practical reference for economic analysts, finance specialists, lending institutions, students, and researchers.

International Project Financing, 4th ed
Ronald F. Sullivan
Huntington, New York: Juris Publishing, 2004
350pp, ISBN: 978-1-57823-193-5
This treatment of PF is aimed at lawyers practicing in the area of international project financing, and the problems counsels face when negotiating and drafting agreements relating to project finance. It integrates a discussion of particular contract provisions relevant to the topic of each chapter, as well as references to different examples of these provisions contained in the forms of agreement published at the end of the book.

Introduction to Project Finance
Andrew Fight
Essential Capital Markets Series
Boston, Massachusetts: Elsevier, 2005
208pp, ISBN: 978-0-7506-5905-5
This provides a practical grounding in the basics of project finance. It describes the key risks involved and how to mitigate them, methods of project evaluation, recourse and non-recourse funding, feasibility, the various parties involved, techniques for cash flow preparation, building cash flow statements, and the key variables impacting financial performance.

Megaprojects and Risk: An Anatomy of Ambition
Bent Flyvbjerg, Nils Bruzelius, Werner Rothengatter
Cambridge, UK: Cambridge University Press, 2003
207pp, ISBN: 978-0-521-00946-1
This is a comprehensive examination of the global megaprojects phenomenon, combining theoretical analysis with empirical research to explore the main issues—the impact of costs, revenues, the environment, and economic development—behind numerous projects around the world. It also examines how the promoters of these expensive megaprojects had them approved and built, their dealings with parliaments, the public, and the media.

Modern Project Finance: A Casebook
Benjamin C. Esty
New York: Wiley, 2004
562pp, ISBN: 978-0-471-43425-2
This financial casebook focuses on the structuring and valuing of projects, how to manage project risk, and finance projects, and is based on real cases from a range of geographic locations and industrial sectors. It explores why companies use project finance, the role of banks, how project loans should be priced, why some projects fail, and the reduction of agency costs.

Principles of Project and Infrastructure Finance
Willie Tan
London: Taylor & Francis, 2007
280pp, ISBN: 978-0-415-41577-4
This holistic approach to project finance issues provides both an introductory and analytical guide to the key areas within project finance from a project manager's perspective. It offers a range of relevant case studies that illustrate integration in selected sectors, and is aimed at students, researchers, and project finance practitioners, such as company directors, project managers, lawyers, architects, contractors, engineers, regulators, insurers, and investors.

Principles of Project Finance
Edward Yescombe
Amsterdam: Academic Press, 2002
344pp, ISBN: 978-0-12-770851-5
This introduction for project finance practitioners offers a comprehensive examination of the key concepts and techniques, integrating legal, contractual, scheduling, and other relevant aspects. It describes sources of project finance, typical commercial contracts and their impact on the project finance structure, project finance risk assessment, the structuring of project finance debt, and

issues in negotiating a project finance debt facility.

Project Finance, 3rd ed
Graham D. Vinter, Gareth Price
London: Sweet & Maxwell, 2006
473pp, ISBN: 978-0-421-90950-2
This overview of project finance focuses on the issues involved in the tendering, negotiation, financial structuring, and management of infrastructure and energy projects. It provides guidance on legal factors of typical project financing, commercial and financial planning, current market practice, as well as coverage of documentation, bid structuring, public-private partnerships, risk allocation, cover ratios, and export credit agencies.

Project Finance in Theory and Practice: Designing, Structuring, and Financing Private and Public Projects
Stefano Gatti
Academic Press Advanced Finance Series
Burlington, Massachusetts: Academic Press, 2008
414pp, ISBN: 978-0-12-373699-4
This comprehensive overview combines a discussion of project finance theory with a presentation of best practice. It examines project finance techniques, processes, and practices, creating a resource for both practitioners and researchers, explains the roles and objectives of the different parties, the legal issues, the role of advisors, and provides useful new analysis of PPPs, and credit risk measurement problems under Basel II.

Project Finance, Securitisations and Subordinated Debt, 2nd ed
Philip R. Wood
London: Sweet & Maxwell, 2007
262pp, ISBN: 978-1-84703-211-9
This is a practical guide to international project finance, which explains how the key concepts are applied in commercial situations. It examines project finance structures, securitisation contracts and financial agreements, as well as securitization issues. It describes the different international jurisdictions and relevant laws, discusses the different classes of subordination agreement, and presents a global survey of the law of subordinated debt.

Project Financing, 7th ed
Peter K. Nevitt, Frank Fabozzi
London: Euromoney Books, 2000
498pp, ISBN: 978-1-85564-791-6
This comprehensive guide to all aspects of project finance examines the key criteria for success, including the choice of financial advisers and banks, types and sources of equity and debt finance, effective project structuring, and types of risk and risk appraisal. It describes the concepts and structures that can be applied at any stage in project financing, illustrated by numerous examples and case studies.

Project Financing and the International Financial Markets
Esteban C. Buljevich, Yoon S. Park
Boston, Massachusetts: Kluwer Academic, 1999
302pp, ISBN: 978-0-7923-8524-0
This professional reference guide examines the increasing use of the global capital markets and international financing techniques for privately funding project finance initiatives. It describes the use of derivative instruments for asset and liability management, the different risk management techniques available, the impact of cross-border project financing, and reviews the various marketable debt securities actively used in the international financial markets.

Project Financing: Asset-Based Financial Engineering, 2nd ed
John D. Finnerty
Wiley Finance Series
Hoboken, New Jersey: Wiley, 2007
476pp, ISBN: 978-0-470-08624-7
This practical guide aims to provide insight into the complexities, challenges, and processes involved in project financing, and is aimed at project sponsors, regulators, host governments, and corporate financiers, as well as advisors, senior strategists, bankers, and large private investors. It examines the rationale behind project financing, the risks, security arrangements, legal structure, how to prepare the financial plan, and unsuccessful project financing cases.

Public-Private Partnerships: A Practical Analysis
Nicholas Avery
London: Globe Law and Business, 2006
199pp, ISBN: 978-1-905783-00-7
This practical textbook focuses on public-private partnership (PPP) financing, analyzing topical developments and the latest techniques in the main sectors in which it operates. It features coverage of issues such as the role of financing institutions, EU procurement, and developments in the debt and equity financial markets relevant to PPP, for lawyers, facility managers, technical advisers, and those in government departments and agencies.

Risk Management in Project Finance and Implementation
Henri L. Beenhakker
Westport, Connecticut: Quorum Books, 1997
274pp, ISBN: 978-1-56720-106-2
This offers a comprehensive examination of all the main risk management concepts involved in project finance, including financial structures and techniques, the development of efficient portfolios, and investment risks and taxes. It takes a multifaceted approach to the subject, and combines an analysis of both theory and practice, for professionals with investment responsibilities in both the public and private sectors.

MAGAZINES

Infrastructure Journal
Emap
Greater London House, Hampstead Road, London, NW1 7EJ, UK
T: +44 (0) 20 7728 5407
F: +44 (0) 20 7728 5299
www.ijonline.com
ISSN: 1460-468X
This subscription-only online news and research journal is for professionals involved in the global project finance of infrastructure transactions. It offers news and data for the international infrastructure investment market, as well as research and analysis, a projects database, league tables, awards, a global directory, forums, opinion, case studies, and a weekly review.

PPP Bulletin
Rockcliffe
20a Hillgate Place, 18–20 Balham Hill, London, SW12 9ER, UK
T: +44 (0) 20 8772 6648
F: +44 (0) 20 8675 0950
www.pppbulletin.com
ISSN: 1752-7007
This monthly subscription-based magazine provides in-depth updates on international public-private partnerships legislation, regulation, working procedure and market potential. It provides international news, interviews with the top industry figures, in-depth market reports, country reports, industry jobs, and a business leads section about new projects.

Project Finance International
Reuters Professional Publishing
Aldgate House, 33 Aldgate High Street, London, EC3N 1DL, UK
T: +44 (0) 20 7369 7000
www.pfie.com
ISSN: 0967-5914

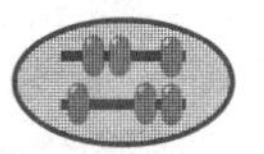

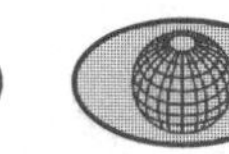
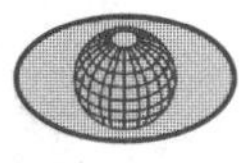

Published every two weeks, PFI offers global project finance news and information by industry sector, as well as regional news, features, people and markets, supplements, roundtables, project pipeline, completed deals, and league tables. It reports on the entire lifecycle of deals, from initial concept through to post-completion analysis.

Project Finance
Euromoney Institutional Investor
Nestor House, Playhouse Yard, London, EC4V 5EX, UK
T: +44 (0) 20 7779 8610
F: +44 (0) 20 7779 8602
www.projectfinancemagazine.com
ISSN: 1462-0014
This bimonthly magazine features in-depth articles that evaluate a range of project finance issues, from new financing instruments to deal round-ups. The industry sectors covered include telecoms, power, oil, gas, rail, roads, bridges, tunnels, water, ports, airports, property and tourism development, petrochemicals, mining, and private and public partnerships.

Public Works Financing
Public Works Financing
147 Elmer Street, Westfield, New Jersey 07090, USA
T: +1 908 654 6572
F: +1 908 654 6573
www.pwfinance.net
This monthly magazine provides project case studies, news updates, project leads, political trends, analyses of successful financings, profiles of key industry players, and a directory of the most experienced advisors. Features also examine the role played by the main parties, as well as the alignment of risks and rewards on publicly sanctioned projects.

JOURNALS

Journal of Public Works & Infrastructure
Henry Stewart Publications
Russell House, 28/30 Little Russell Street, London, WC1A 2HN, UK
T: +44 (0) 20 7404 3040
F: +44 (0) 20 7404 2081
www.henrystewart.com/jpwi
ISSN: 1755-0955
This quarterly journal publishes contributions from public works and infrastructure professionals on best practice and new thinking in the strategic management and operational delivery of public works projects and services. It offers papers on best practice, industry briefings, case studies, and empirical research that show how projects and services have been specified, designed, financed and delivered in practice.

Journal of Structured and Product Finance
Institutional Investor Journals
225 Park Avenue South, 8th Floor, New York, NY 10003, USA
T: +1 212 224 3570
F: +1 212 224 3197
www.iijournals.com/JPF
ISSN: 1082-3220
This quarterly journal offers research and commentary on all aspects of structured and project finance, including detailed analysis of the regulatory, financial and legal aspects of project finance deals. It also focuses on a range of real-life securitization deals and their investment implications, as well as environmental and political issues, to provide a strategic understanding of the products, applications, and market.

INTERNET

Project Finance Portal
www.people.hbs.edu/besty/projfinportal
This online resource, run by Harvard Business School, provides a reference guide for practitioners, researchers, and students seeking information about project finance and public-private partnerships. It presents bibliographical references for books, articles, and case studies, and hundreds of links to related sites, as well as information about particular projects and companies/organizations involved with project finance.

ORGANIZATIONS

Europe

International Project Finance Association
Chair: Geoff Haley
Linton House, 164–180 Union Street, London, SE1 0LH, UK
T: +44 (0) 20 7620 1883
F: +44 (0) 20 7620 1886
E: info@ipfa.org
www.ipfa.org
IPFA is a non-profit association that promotes and represents the interests of private sector companies involved in project finance and public-private partnerships around the world. It offers a range of information resources on current issues and developments throughout the industry, and aims to raise awareness and understanding globally about project finance and PPPs, and the role they play in infrastructure and economic development.

The Major Projects Association
Chair: Sir Robert Walmsley
Egrove Park, Kennington, Oxford, OX1 5NY, UK
T: +44 (0) 1865 422 581
F: +44 (0) 1865 326 068
E: mpa@majorprojects.org
www.majorprojects.org
This international, multi-industry association provides a forum for organizations concerned with large complex projects, with the aim of sharing knowledge, experience, and good practice. It covers all industrial, government and commercial sectors, and brings together the major players in every aspect of major projects, such as funders, promoters, designers, contractors, suppliers, operators, regulators, professional contributors, and government.

USA

INFRADEV & Infrastructure Experts Group
Chair: Barbara C. Samuels II
79 Fifth Avenue, Suite 1129B, New York, NY 10003, USA
T: +1 212 229 5901
F: +1 212 229 5903
E: infradev@globalclearinghouse.org
www.infradev.org
INFRADEV operates as an information exchange, offering a resource and financing for development tool to mobilize private capital for developing country infrastructure. It aims to enhance the capacity of developing country governments and development agencies to mobilize private sector investment and resources for infrastructure projects.

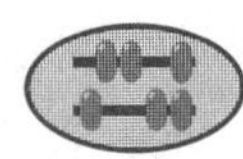

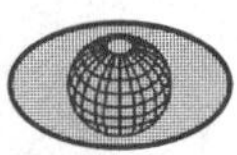

Purchasing and Supply Chain Management

BOOKS

B2B: How to Build a Profitable E-Commerce Strategy
Michael Cunningham
Cambridge, Massachusetts: Perseus Books Group, 2002
224pp, ISBN: 978-0-7382-0522-9
This book presents a definitive blueprint for creating a profitable business-to-business e-commerce strategy. Showcasing successful initiatives designed by industry leaders such as Cisco Systems and Dell Computers, as well as lesser-known trailblazers such as VerticalNet and eCredit.com, the author clearly identifies the key issues in assessing opportunities, building technological and organizational capabilities, and designing a successful business-to-business strategy using the full power of the internet.

Designing and Managing the Supply Chain, 2nd ed
David Simchi-Levi, Philip Kaminsky, Edith Simchi-Levi
New York: McGraw-Hill, 2007
544pp, ISBN: 978-0-07-334152-1
The book provides state-of-the-art models, concepts, and methods that are critical for the design, control, operation, and management of supply chain systems. In particular, the authors attempt to convey the intuition behind many key supply chain concepts, and to provide simple techniques that can be used to analyze various aspects of the supply chain.

Harvard Business Review on Supply Chain Management
Harvard Business School Press
Harvard Business Review Paperback Series
Boston, Massachusetts: Harvard Business School Press, 2006
211pp, ISBN: 978-1-4221-0279-4
Many of today's companies struggle with the task of delivering products to customers when and where they want them. Using tactics from articles in this volume, any company can learn how to beat the competition, and reduce waste in each step of their value-delivery process.

Logistics and Supply Chain Management: Creating Value-Adding Networks, 3rd ed
Martin Christopher
Harlow, UK: FT Prentice Hall, 2004
320pp, ISBN: 978-0-273-68176-2
The goal of supply chain management is to link the marketplace, the distribution network, the manufacturing process, and the procurement activity in such a way that customers are serviced at higher levels and yet at lower total cost. The author explores the role of logistics in achieving these goals. He examines the relationship between logistics and competitive strategy, the customer service dimension, measuring logistics costs and performance, and benchmarking and managing the supply chain.

Managing the Global Supply Chain, 3rd ed
Philip B Schary, Tage Skjott-Larsen
Copenhagen, Denmark: Copenhagen Business School Press, 2007
459pp, ISBN: 978-87-630-0171-7
The book shows how structure, process, and organization may build a supply network comprising distribution, production, and procurement within one integrated system. The importance of the supply chain in corporate strategy is also emphasized. This new edition stresses customer relationships and reflects recent changes in technology and practice.

New Directions in Supply Chain Management: Technology Strategy and Implementation
Tonya Boone, Ram Ganeshan
New York: AMACOM, 2002
384pp, ISBN: 978-0-8144-0637-3
This collection of 18 original essays examines the efficiencies new technology has brought to supply chain management and how new strategies and solutions based on these changes can be implemented. They are grouped into three sections covering the integration of new technologies into supply chain operations, technology-based product and service development, and knowledge management and supply-chain integration issues.

Partners.com
Michael Cunningham
Cambridge, Massachusetts: Perseus Books Group, 2002
256pp, ISBN: 978-0-7382-0687-5
Partners.com shows businesses how to forge leading-edge Internet partnerships fast with competitors, customers, employees, and other businesses. The book reveals the specifics of these new and better ways of doing business. It presents a clear picture of companies such as eBay, Altra, GoFish, Egghead, VerticalNet, and Yahoo, that are utilizing technology-driven partnerships.

Purchasing and Supply Chain Management, 7th ed
Kenneth Lysons
Harlow, UK: FT Prentice Hall, 2006
709pp, ISBN: 978-0-273-69438-0
A much revised and enlarged version of a successful textbook, this edition meets the requirements for an integrated approach to supply chain management, drawing on the many disciplines, from ethics and human resources to suppliers, sourcing, and strategy, that contribute to a full knowledge of purchasing practice and techniques.

The Sourcing Solution: A Step-by-Step Guide to Creating a Successful Purchasing Program
Larry Paquette
New York: AMACOM, 2004
224pp, ISBN: 978-0-8144-7191-3
Larry Paquette believes that, as purchasing options and technologies become more plentiful, they also become more complex. In this text, he sets out to help managers sort through alternatives, identify the strategies that make sense, and implement them in ways that complement the overall business strategy. He explains how to make the most of vendor relationships and partnerships, opportunities for cost reduction, electronic and paperless inventory management, product knowledge and company information, different production models, global sourcing opportunities, scheduling, and contracts and negotiations.

Supply Chain Excellence: A Handbook for Dramatic Improvement Using the SCOR Model, 2nd ed
Peter Bolstorff, Robert Rosenbaum
New York: AMACOM, 2007
403pp, ISBN: 978-0-8144-0926-8
The SCOR (Supply Chain Operations Reference) model, developed by the Supply-Chain Council in the United States, is introduced in this handbook, which also examines in detail the process of applying the model and describes the achieving of supply chain excellence over a 17-week period.

Supply Chain Management
John T. Mentzer (editor)
London: Sage Publications, 2001
512pp, ISBN: 978-0-7619-2111-0
A group of collaborating authors present a

     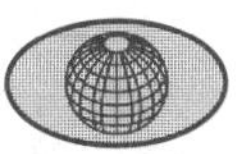   

comprehensive definition and model of supply chain management (SCM) on the basis of their interviews with top supply chain managers from 20 companies. The book distinguishes types of chain, and discusses SCM as a management philosophy and in terms of its prerequisites and its potential effects on business and channel performance.

The Supply Management Handbook, 7th ed
Joseph L. Cavinato, Ralph G. Kauffman, Anna E. Flynn
New York: McGraw-Hill, 2006
1000pp, ISBN: 978-0-07-144513-9
This successful handbook is for purchasing and supply professionals in every field and industry, and provides comprehensive updates that examine the shift from simple purchasing to a new, more technology-based imperative–identifying and managing supply chain sources and strategies.

MAGAZINES

Purchasing
Reed Business Information
8878 Barrons Boulevard, Highlands Ranch, CO 80129–2345, USA
T: +1 800 446 6551
F: +1 303 470 4280
www.purchasing.com
ISSN: 0033-4448
This is a bimonthly magazine which focuses on total supply management. It has served 93,500 professionals working in manufacturing, process, and service companies throughout the full spectrum of business for 85 years. The magazine makes available the information required by purchasing professionals to do their jobs. It provides news, identifies trends, interprets events, makes forecasts, and presents exclusive information and data sources.

Supply Management
Redactive Publishing
1 Benjamin Street, London, EC1M 5EA, UK
T: +44 (0) 20 7880 6200
F: +44 (0) 20 7814 0981
www.supplymanagement.co.uk
ISSN: 1362-2021
The journal of the Chartered Institute of Purchasing and Supply, it combines international and UK news, features, regular columns on the law and academic research, book and video reviews, news from CIPS, and a special section on key prices and economic indicators. *Supply Management* provides the essential information purchasing professionals need to carry out their jobs, together with analysis of the main strategic issues facing the profession today.

JOURNALS

Journal of Supply Chain Management
Blackwell Publishing
9600 Garsington Road, Oxford, OX4 2DQ, UK
T: +44 (0) 1865 791 100
F: +44 (0) 1865 791 347
www.wiley.com/bw/journal.asp?ref=1523-2409
ISSN: 1523-2409
This quarterly journal is aimed at supply chain management scholars, through the publication of high-quality, high-impact behavioral methodologies focusing on theory-building and empirical research.

Journal of Supply Chain Management: A Global Review of Purchasing and Supply
Institute for Supply Management
PO Box 22160, Tempe, AZ 85285–2160, USA
T: +1 480 752 6276
F: +1 480 752 7890
www.ism.ws/pubs/journalscm/index.cfm?navItemNumber=5474
ISSN: 1055-6001
A quarterly publication produced specifically for purchasing professionals, this journal provides coverage and analysis of key management issues, leading research, one-to-one interviews, and supplier relationship applications. Abstracts of the articles and the one-to-one interviews can be accessed on the web.

Supply Chain Forum: An International Journal
The Institute for Supply Chain Excellence of BEM
BEM – ISLI, 680, Cours de la Libération, 33405 Talence, France
T: +33 (0) 5 56 84 55 70
F: +33 (0) 5 56 84 55 80
www.supplychain-forum.com
ISSN: 1625-8312
Supply Chain Forum: An International Journal explores all the aspects of logistics, supply chain and operations management. It is concerned with the management and optimization of flows in the supply chain from primary supplier to final customer, and provides research articles and company case studies that enrich both the knowledge of the discipline and the practices of supply chain management.

Supply Chain Management: An International Journal
Emerald
60/62 Toller Lane, Bradford, West Yorkshire, BD8 9BY, UK
T: +44 (0) 1274 777 700
F: +44 (0) 1274 785 200
www.emeraldinsight.com/1359-8546.htm
ISSN: 1359-8546
This bimonthly journal is broad based, but with a strategic focus, covering aspects of marketing, logistics and information technology, economics, management, and organizational behavior in relation to the operation of supply chains in all sectors. It encourages the development and implementation of supply chain systems which achieve higher levels of service and substantial savings in costs.

INTERNET

CAPS Research
www.capsresearch.org
This site is offered by the Center for Advanced Purchasing Studies, a nonprofit independent research organization cosponsored by Arizona State University and the National Association of Purchasing and Supply. It provides full access to a range of recent research and benchmarking reports and their journal *Practix*. Access is free, but you must register to view articles. There are also links to related sites.

Chartered Institute of Purchasing and Supply
www.cips.org
While this site is designed to promote the training and research services and activities of CIPS, it does allow nonmembers access to its comprehensive bookstore with details of over 350 specialist publications.

Institute for Supply Management
www.ism.ws
This is the home site of the Institute for Supply Management. The amount of information available to nonmembers is limited, but there is access to selected articles or abstracts of recent articles in the institute's journals.

International Purchasing and Supply Education and Research Association
www.ipsera.com
IPSERA is an active network of academics and practitioners dedicated to the development of understanding on matters concerning the future of purchasing and supply management. The site provides general information about the association, details about membership, and advice on applying for funding.

  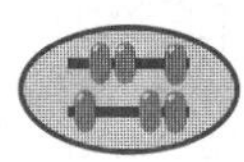   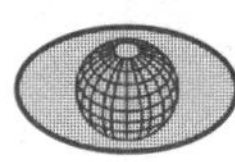   

Responsible Supply Chain Management Portal
www.csr-supplychain.org
This website offers information and advice for buyers and suppliers on corporate social responsibility in the supply chain, from a number of top companies. The site covers international standards and principles, practical guidelines, supplier training, codes of conducts for vendors, audit self-assessments, and details on how to implement supply chain programs. Topics covered include health and safety, ethics, and child labor.

Supply Chain Online
www.supplychainonline.com.br
Brazil's portal to supply chain management offers information, articles, expert opinions, news, events, software, and technological applications on supply chain management.

supplymanagement.com
www.supplymanagement.com
Managed by the Chartered Institute of Purchasing and Supply, this site offers selected content from the print magazine, breaking news stories, plus a range of online-only features, including streaming business and political news, archive of past articles, searchable events diary, e-mail news alerts, and a commodity price database.

ORGANIZATIONS

Europe

Chartered Institute of Purchasing and Supply
1 Easton House, Easton-on-the-Hill, Stamford, Lincolnshire, PE9 3NZ, UK
T: +44 (0) 1780 756 777
F: +44 (0) 1780 751 610
www.cips.org
Based in the United Kingdom, CIPS is an international education and qualification organization serving the international purchasing and supply profession. It is dedicated to promoting best practice through the provision of a wide range of services for the benefit of members and the wider business community. These include a program of continuous improvement in professional standards, and raising awareness of the contribution that purchasing and supply makes to corporate, national, and international prosperity. CIPS gained a Royal Charter in 1992.

European Supply Chain Institute (ESCI)
The European Supply Chain Institute is an international association with a mandate to research the technologies that drive the supply chain, and examine its applications. The largest research program over recent years has been regarding the application of RFID and how the technology can transform an organization's manufacturing and supply chain operations.

BRIC

China Supply Chain Council (CSCC)
Unit A, 10F, Bldg. 2, 543 Xin Hua Road, Shanghai, 200052, China
T: +86 21 5102 1617
F: +86 21 5258 3864
www.supplychain.cn
CSCC is the largest professional organization dedicated to furthering the knowledge, understanding, and career development of executives, managers, and professionals in the field of supply chain, logistics, and procurement management in China.

Indian Institute of Materials Management
Plot Nos. 102 & 104, Sector 15, Institutional Area, CBD Belapur, Navi Mumbai 400614, India
T: +91 22 2756 5741
F: +91 22 2756 5592
E: iimmedu@mtnl.net.in
www.iimm.org
This is a membership-based institute that advocates efficient supply management, provides information and research, and promotes the professional status of people working in supply management.

International

Canadian Association of Supply Chain and Logistics Management
7270 Woodbine Avenue, Suite 204, Markham, Ontario, L3R 4B9, Canada
T: +1 905 513 7300
F: +1 905 513 1248
E: members@infochain.org
www.sclcanada.org
Established in 1967, SCL is a nonprofit membership organization which aims to advance the logistics and supply chain profession in Canada. Through a range of activities, research, and informal discussion, members are encouraged to further their understanding of logistics and the art and science of its management.

Global Institute of Logistics
245 Park Avenue, 24th and 39th Floors, New York, NY 10167, US
T: +1 212 672 1846
F: +1 212 792 4001
E: ceo@globeinst.org
www.globeinst.org
The institute acts as a bridge between the academic world and business, educating the global supply chain community on the latest academic thinking on the subject.

Purchasing Management Association of Canada
777 Bay Street, Suite 2701, PO Box 112, Toronto, Ontario, ON M5G 2C8, Canada
T: +1 416 977 7111
F: +1 416 977 8886
E: info@pmac.ca
www.pmac.ca
PMAC is a national, nonprofit association and is a leading source of education, training, and development in the purchasing and supply management field in Canada. The association operates with ten provincial institutes, which can be contacted through the website.

The Supply-Chain Council (SCC)
1331 H Street NW, Suite 500, Washington, DC 20005, US
T: + 1 202 962 0440
F: + 1 202 962 3939
E: info@supply-chain.org
www.supply-chain.org
The Supply-Chain Council (SCC) is a global, non-profit trade association open to all types of organizations. It sponsors and supports educational programs, including conferences, retreats, benchmarking studies, and development of the Supply-Chain Operations Reference-Model (SCOR), as well as the Design-Chain Reference-Model (DCOR), the process reference models designed to improve users' efficiency and productivity. The council is also dedicated to improving the supply chain efficiency of its practitioner members.

  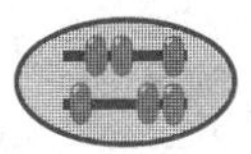 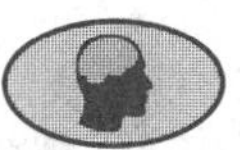  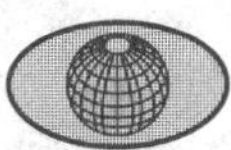   

Retail Banking

BOOKS

Analyzing and Managing Banking Risk: Framework for Assessing Corporate Governance and Financial Risk, 2nd ed

Hennie Van Greuning, Sonja Brajovic Bratanovic
Washington, DC: World Bank, 2003
384pp, ISBN: 978-0-8213-5418-6

This provides a comprehensive discussion of the assessment, analysis, and management of financial risks in banking. It considers the principles of risk management, and presents a framework for identifying the key players in the risk management and corporate governance processes. Coverage includes the treasury function, investment management, proprietary trading, asset liability management, components, and transparency in financial statements.

The Art of Better Retail Banking: Supportable Predictions on the Future of Retail Banking

Hugh Croxford, Frank Abramson, Alex Jablonowski
Chichester, UK: Wiley, 2005
276pp, ISBN: 978-0-470-01320-5

This is a wide-ranging examination of the issues facing the retail banking industry, and how it may develop over the next few years. It considers retail banking within an integrated framework, looking at how banks operate, management strategies, how they make and lose money, and how they fit into the various banking models. It emphasizes the importance of leadership, creativity, and teamwork for future success.

Bank Management, 6th ed

Timothy W. Koch, S. Scott MacDonald
Mason, Ohio: Thomson Higher Education, 2006
562pp, ISBN: 978-0-324-28927-5

Bank Management explains how managers can implement strategies to maximize stockholders wealth by balancing the trade-off between banking risks and returns. It also demonstrates how risk management decisions in different areas affect each other and the overall profitability and risk of the institution, and provides an Excel template for practising cash flow analysis and bank performance analysis.

Bank Management: Text and Cases, 5th ed

George H. Hempel, Donald G. Simonson
Hoboken, New Jersey: Wiley, 2008
700pp, ISBN: 978-0-471-16960-4

This is a comprehensive introduction to bank management that examines basic asset, liability and capital management decisions. It covers the lending function of commercial banks, such as credit analysis, loan pricing and structuring a loan, and emphasizes integrative management techniques, including a description of the use of new financial products and methods of pricing in bank management.

Commercial Banking: The Management of Risk, 3rd ed

Benton E. Gup, James W. Kolari
Hoboken, New Jersey: Wiley, 2005
548pp, ISBN: 978-0-471-46949-0

This is a practical introduction to bank management and current banking practices used to control different kinds of risk. It examines the factors that affect the value of a bank, and techniques for managing that value, and explores the principal lending activities to businesses and individuals. A comprehensive coverage of banking operations includes brokerage services, insurance, trust activities, and regulatory and legal changes.

The Economics of Banking, 2nd ed

Kent Matthews, John Thompson
Chichester, UK: Wiley, 2008
295pp, ISBN: 978-0-470-51964-6

This textbook is mathematically accessible and provides a microeconomic context, enabling students to understand contemporary trends and operations in banking. It provides a sound theoretical basis for understanding bank behavior, and focuses on bank performance, the competitive nature of the banking market, bank and financial regulation, international banking, and risk management, especially in terms of trading risk and bank book risk management.

Essentials of Banking

Deborah K. Dilley
Essentials Series
Hoboken, New Jersey: Wiley, 2008
273pp, ISBN: 978-0-470-17088-5

This guide to the banking industry explores the basic elements of banking, and is a practical resource for traditional bankers, online bankers, and finance professionals. It examines how banking has evolved from being product-centered to having a more customer-driven focus, and the increasing use of multiple channels. It covers deposit insurance, regulatory compliance, ethics, customer service, and cross-industry affiliations.

The Future of Retail Banking in Europe: A View from the Top

Oonah McDonald, Kevin Keasey
New York: Wiley, 2002
193pp, ISBN: 978-0-471-89277-9

This is an exploration of the current banking sector in Europe, and is aimed at middle managers in the banking and financial services sectors, suppliers, investors, and MBA students. It analyzes the banking structures in all the major European markets, the challenges currently being faced, and predicts future trends for retail banking in Europe through a series of insights from the CEOs of major European banks.

The Future of Retail Banking

Joseph DiVanna
New York: Palgrave Macmillan, 2003
224pp, ISBN: 978-1-4039-1126-1

This exploration of the banking and financial services industry details how the sector can develop strategic initiatives to improve operations and increase competitiveness. It also addresses current trends influencing competition, such as globalization, market structure, technology and demographics, and how these will impact upon companies and their organization, business opportunities, revenue streams, branding and customer behavior.

Introduction to Banking

Barbara Casu, Claudia Girardone, Philip Molyneux
Harlow, UK: FT Prentice Hall, 2006
560pp, ISBN: 978-0-273-69302-4

This is a comprehensive introduction to theoretical and applied issues relating to the global banking industry. It introduces banking basics, before discussing central banking and bank regulation, bank management concerns such as risk management techniques, comparative banking markets, and global trends in different banking markets.

Managing Bank Risk: An Introduction to Broad-Base Credit Engineering

Morton Glantz
Amsterdam: Academic Press, 2003
667pp, ISBN: 978-0-12-285785-0

This is an examination of the concepts of credit risk management as they relate to techniques in banking and portfolio management. It focuses on new approaches to fundamental analysis and credit administration, discusses tools for

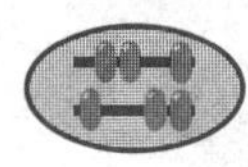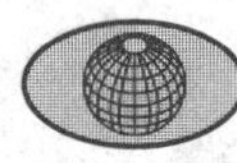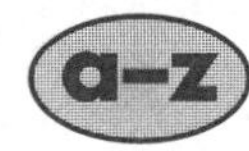

understanding and measuring credit risk, credit analysis, and new credit engineering tools for the banking sector, and shows how to assimilate these tools.

Microeconomics of Banking, 2nd ed
Xavier Freixas, Jean-Charles Rochet
Cambridge, Massachusetts: MIT Press, 2008
363pp, ISBN: 978-0-262-06270-1
This examines the main issues relating to the microeconomic theory of banking that has emerged over recent years, and looks at the use of the asymmetric information model for explaining the role of banks in the economy and for pinpoint structural weaknesses in the banking sector. It also covers financial intermediaries, macroeconomic consequences of financial imperfections, risk management inside the banking firm, and bank regulation.

Modern Banking
Shelagh Heffernan
Chichester, UK: Wiley, 2005
716pp, ISBN: 978-0-470-09500-3
This is a textbook focused on the theory and practice of banking, and its prospects for the future. It considers a number of fundamental issues, such as core banking functions, different types of banks and diversification of bank activities, issues and techniques in risk management, global regulation, banking in emerging markets, bank failure and financial crises, and competitive factors.

Retail Banking
Keith Pond
London: Financial World Publishing, 2007
192pp, ISBN: 978-0-85297-777-4
This examines the current priorities in retail banking, as well as the legal and practical environment in which they operate. It explains banking fundamentals, the main economic concepts that underpin much banking activity, and bank risk. It also reviews key banking transactions, their regulation by national and international bodies, and bank profitability from the perspective of annual accounts.

Risk Management in Banking, 2nd ed
Joël Bessis
New York: Wiley, 2002
792pp, ISBN: 978-0-471-89336-3
This classic text examines the changing nature of financial risk management in the banking sector. It emphasizes conceptual and implementation issues of risk management, and presents the latest techniques and practical issues, such as Value at Risk, asset liability management, credit risk, interest rate risk, funds transfer pricing, credit derivatives, market portfolio risk, capital management, and loan portfolio models.

MAGAZINES

ABA Banking Journal
American Banking Journal
345 Hudson Street, 12th Floor, New York, NY 10014, USA
T: +1 212 620 7200
F: +1 212 633 1165
www.ababj.com
ISSN: 0194-5947
This monthly magazine, published by the American Bankers Association, is aimed at managers and executives at commercial and savings banking institutions operating in the competitive financial services market. It provides news and commentary, and identifies and explores business and societal trends, as well as legislative and regulatory issues.

American Banker
SourceMedia
1 State Street Plaza, 27th Floor, New York, NY 10004, USA
T: +1 212 803 8200
F: +1 212 843 9600
www.americanbanker.com
ISSN: 0002-7561
American Banker is a daily paper and information resource that serves the banking and financial services community. It offers news and analysis of the issues, strategies, and people that influence events in the banking sector in the United States, as well as feature articles, data applications, and special reports.

The Asian Banker
TAB International
10 Hoe Chiang Road, #14-06 Keppel Tower, Singapore 089315, Singapore
T: +65 6236 6500
F: +65 6236 6530
www.theasianbanker.com
This magazine, published 10 times a year, covers news and developments in commercial banking and financial services in Asia. It examines critical issues, trends, and best practices, and produces a comprehensive ranking of the top 300 commercial banks in Asia Pacific by asset size and strength, as well as special reports and regular tele-consultation sessions with industry experts.

Bank Accounting & Finance
CCH, USA
T: +1 978 369 6285
www.bankaccountingandfinance.com
ISSN: 0894-3958
This bimonthly magazine for bank accounting and financial officers provides practitioners' perspectives on industry best practices and trends for financial reporting, risk management, and performance analysis. It also covers issues such as financial and management accounting, profitability measurement, asset/liability management, liquidity issues, new financial instruments and capital markets products, mergers and acquisitions, and regulation.

Bank Director
Board Member
5110 Maryland Way, Suite 250, Brentwood, TN 37027, USA
T: +1 615 309 3200
F: +1 615 371 0899
www.bankdirector.com
Bank Director is a quarterly publication that examines pertinent issues in the banking sector, such as mergers and acquisitions, technology, board accountability, and marketing and business development. It is aimed at directors and top officers in financial institutions, including chairmen, presidents, chief executives, and other directors of institutions large and small, national and international.

The Banker
Financial Times
1 Southwark Bridge, London, SE1 9HL, UK
T: +44 (0) 20 7873 3000
www.thebanker.com
ISSN: 0005-5395
This monthly magazine investigates the critical developments and trends in the global banking sector. It provides in-depth financial intelligence, and covers comments and analysis, capital markets and investment banking, securities services and payments, environments and resources, retail banking, technology, special reports, regions, and features awards, database, archive, and events.

Banking Strategies
BAI
115 South LaSalle Street, Suite 3300, Chicago, IL 60603-3801, USA
T: +1 312 683 2464
F: +1 312 683 2373
www.bai.org/bankingstrategies
ISSN: 1091-6385
This magazine is published bimonthly, and presents the latest in best practices and thought leadership, and covers and interprets strategic and managerial trends in the financial services industry.

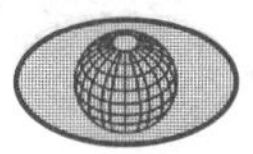

Retail Banker International
VRL KnowledgeBank
34 Porchester Road, London, W2 6ES, UK
T: +44 (0) 20 7563 5600
F: +44 (0) 20 7563 5602
www.vrlpublishing.com/retailbankerinternational.php?id=4
ISSN: 0261-1740
This newsletter is published 20 times each year, and tracks and analyzes issues related to the global retail financial services industry. It focuses on retail banking and consumer financial services on an international basis, in particular products and product innovation, marketing, distribution, technology, interim and annual results analysis, regulation and legislation, and mergers and acquisitions.

US Banker
SourceMedia
1 State Street Plaza, 27th Floor, New York, NY 10004, USA
T: +1 212 803 8200
F: +1 212 843 9600
www.americanbanker.com/usb.html
ISSN: 0148-8848
This is a monthly business management magazine that provides analysis and commentary on the industry players, financial and economic market trends, regulations, business strategies, and innovations taking place in the banking and financial services sector. It also offers guidance on improving shareholder value, business revenue and profitability, operations, and business growth, and produces rankings and series of events.

JOURNALS

Academy of Banking Studies Journal
Allied Academies
PO Box 2689, 145 Travis Road, Cullowhee, North Carolina 28723, USA
T: +1 828 293 9151
F: +1 828 293 9407
www.alliedacademies.org/Public/Journals/JournalDetails.aspx?jid=3
ISSN: 1939-2230
This journal, focused on research in the banking sector, is currently published twice yearly.

Journal of Banking & Finance
Elsevier
Radarweg 29, 1043 NX Amsterdam, The Netherlands
F: +31 20 485 2370
www.ees.elsevier.com/jbf
ISSN: 0378-4266
This is a monthly publication aimed at providing an outlet for academic research concerning financial institutions and the money and capital markets within which they function. Its emphasis is on theoretical developments and their implementation, and empirical, applied, and policy-oriented research in banking and other domestic and international financial institutions and markets.

Journal of Commercial Banking and Finance
Allied Academies
PO Box 2689, 145 Travis Road, Cullowhee, North Carolina 28723, USA
T: +1 828 293 9151
F: +1 828 293 9407
www.alliedacademies.org/Public/Journals/JournalDetails.aspx?jid=3
ISSN: 1544-0028
This practitioner-oriented journal, issued once each year, publishes theoretical and empirical papers on banking and financial management, with the aim of furthering an understanding of the discipline of banking and institutional finance.

INTERNET

Bankers Almanac
www.bankersalmanac.com
This is a major online source of reference data solutions to the banking industry for payments, due diligence, compliance, risk assessment and financial research in the banking industry.

The Islamic Banker
www.theislamicbanker.com
This is a leading professional online magazine for the Islamic financial services industry. It provides financial news and information, coverage of Islamic financial institutions, events, and conferences, and promotes Islamic banking, employee and organizational performance.

ORGANIZATIONS

Europe

British Bankers Association
Chair: Angela Knight
Pinners Hall, 105–108 Old Broad Street, London, EC2N 1EX, UK
T: +44 (0) 20 7216 8800
F: +44 (0) 20 7216 8811
E: info@bba.org.uk
www.bba.org.uk
This is the leading trade association for the UK banking and financial services sector. It speaks for 223 banking members from 60 countries on the full range of UK or international banking issues, and engages with 37 associated professional firms. Its activities include market-pricing benchmarks, such as the BBA LIBOR rates.

European Banking Federation
Chair: Michel Pebereau
10 rue Montoyer, 1000 Brussels, Belgium
T: +32 (0) 2 508 37 11
F: +32 (0) 2 511 23 28
E: ebf@ebf-fbe.eu
www.ebf-fbe.eu
The EBF represents the interests of the whole European banking sector. It provides a forum for best practice, proposes and debates legislative proposals and initiatives, helps to position the European banking industry within European and global regulatory frameworks, and promotes the interests of its members and member associations, and the development of the industry.

The Worshipful Company of International Bankers
Chair: Henry Angest
3rd Floor, 12 Austin Friars, London, EC2N 2HE, UK
T: +44 (0) 20 7374 0214
F: +44 (0) 20 7374 0207
E: tim.woods@internationalbankers.co.uk
www.internationalbankers.co.uk
This guild represents the banking and financial services sector in the City of London, and combines tradition with a modern outlook on the financial services sector. Its main aim is to promote the original purposes of the Livery Companies and Guilds, that of fellowship, charity, education, and the promotion of trades and professions.

USA

American Bankers Association
Chair: Arthur R. Connelly
1120 Connecticut Avenue NW, Washington, DC 20036, USA
T: +1 202 663 5087
www.aba.com
The ABA works to enhance the competitiveness of the nation's banking industry, strengthen the US economy and communities, and serve its members by enhancing the role of financial services institutions as providers of financial services. It does this through federal legislative and regulatory activities, legal action, communication, consumer education, research, and products and services.

BRIC

Association of Russian Banks
Chair: Garegin Ashotovich Tosunyan
Building 1, Skatertnyi per., 20, 121069, Moscow, Russia
T: +7 495 691 8098

  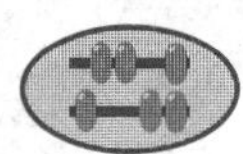   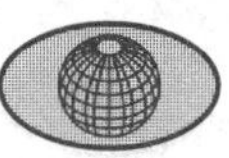   

F: +7 495 691 6666
E: arb@arb.ru
www.arb.ru
ARB is a non-governmental, non-commercial organization that unites commercial banks and other credit organizations, as well as organizations involved in the functioning of the finance-and-credit system in Russia. It represents the interests of all types and size of bank, develops the Russian banking system, and suggests and promotes amendments to legislative acts and by-laws, and improvements to tax legislation.

China Banking Association

12F China Reinsurance Mansion, 11 Jinrong Street, Beijing 100034, China
T: +86 10 6655 3358
F: +86 10 6655 3356
www.china-cba.net
CBA represents 81 full members and 37 associate members in a variety of banking institutions in China. Its aim is to best represent the interests of the industry, and actively encourage its members to self-regulate and communicate, regulate operation and management, as well as protecting the legal rights of its members, and promoting the development of the banking sector.

Indian Banks Association

Chair: T. S. Narayanasami
World Trade Centre, 6th Floor, Centre 1 Building, World Trade Centre Complex, Cuff Parade, Mumbai 400 005, India
E: webmaster@iba.org.in
www.iba.org.in
This is a trade association that represents public sector banks, private sector banks, foreign banks having offices in India, and urban co-operative banks. It promotes sound and progressive banking principles, practices, and conventions, provides services to members and the banking industry, and develops and implements new ideas and innovations in banking services, operations and procedures.

Latin Bankers Association

E: emerson.pieri@latinbankers.com
www.latinbankers.com
This is an Internet-based association focused on bringing value to professional banking networks in Latin America. It brings together Latin and international financial services professionals to connect financial people in the region and beyond, to assist in the development of their business, expertise, and knowledge.

International

The Bankers' Association for Finance and Trade

Chair: Charles H. Silverman
1120 Connecticut Avenue NW, 5th Floor, Washington, DC 20036, USA
T: +1 202 663 7575
F: +1 202 663 5538
E: baft@aba.com
www.baft.org
This is a financial trade association representing a broad range of internationally active financial institutions and companies that provide important services to the global financial community. It provides a forum for analysis, discussion and action among international financial professionals on a wide range of topics affecting international trade and finance, including legislative/regulatory issues.

The International Bankers Association

Chair: Paul Kuo
14th Floor, Ark Mori Building, 1-12-32 Akasaka, Minato-ku, Tokyo 107-6014, Japan
T: +81 3 5545 7511
F: +81 3 5545 0502
E: g-info@ibajapan.org
www.ibajapan.org
The IBA represents of the interests of the international financial community in Japan, and promotes cooperation among financial groups, banks, securities firms, and representative offices in the country. It also encourages the development of banking and capital markets, as well as the interests of its members, and works closely with government authorities, regulators, and non-governmental bodies.

The International Banking Federation

Chair: Sally Scutt
Pinners Hall, 105–108 Old Broad Street, London, EC2N 1EX, UK
E: sally.scutt@bba.org.uk
www.ibfed.org
This is the representative body for a group of key national banking associations and federations—the US, Australia, Canada, Japan, China, and India, and the European Banking Federation. Its main objective is to increase the effectiveness of the industry's response to multilateral and national government issues affecting their common interests, and functions as the main international forum for addressing legislative, regulatory and other issues of interest to the global banking industry.

   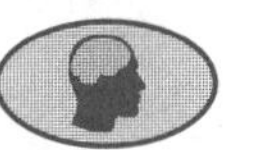  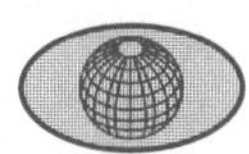   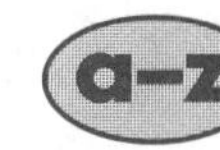

Risk Management

BOOKS

The Book of Risk

Dan Borge
Chichester, UK: Wiley, 2001
240pp, ISBN: 978-0-471-32378-5
Dan Borge breaks down the concept and application of risk management into basic ideas to facilitate a more thorough understanding. He describes the techniques professional risk managers use for determining probabilities and personal preferences, and explores their use for more effective actions. The book explains how we are all already risk managers, and the aim is to help managers become better risk managers.

Business Continuity: Helping Directors Build a Strategy for a Secure Future

Institute of Directors
Directors Guide Series
London: Kogan Page, 2000
80pp, ISBN: 978-0-7494-3563-9
In this book managing risk has been singled out explicitly as a key board responsibility. The guide introduces the crucial value of business continuity and illustrates the steps directors can take to manage the threat and reality of business interruptions. The overriding message is positive: a planned approach to risk management and business continuity will not only avoid unnecessary crisis, it will also provide a clear competitive edge.

Managing Business Risk: An Organization-Wide Approach to Risk Management

Peter C. Young, Steven C. Tippins
New York: AMACOM, 2001
448pp, ISBN: 978-0-8144-0461-4
This is a practical textbook that explains to managers the essentials of risk management. A model, called "organizational risk management," is presented to facilitate a cost saving, company-wide approach to risk management. The techniques covered include risk assessment, risk control, asset and liability exposures to risk, risk financing principles, and insurance.

Managing Environmental Risks and Liabilities

Paul Pritchard
Business and Environmental Practitioner Series
London: Earthscan, 2000
240pp, ISBN: 978-1-85383-598-8
Recent developments in environmental risk management are discussed in this book, which focuses on the nature of environmental risks and their relation to property, financial risk transfer, decision making, risk-management integration, and risk-management frameworks.

Managing Project Risk and Uncertainty

Chris Chapman, Stephen Ward
Chichester, UK: Wiley, 2002
512pp, ISBN: 978-0-470-84790-9
This focuses on the scope of recent approaches to the management of risk and uncertainty in projects and related operational strategic management. It consists of a number of real cases that explore project-related problems, including cost estimation, pricing competitive bids, risk allocation and incentive contract design, evaluation of threats and opportunities, buffer management in a supply chain, investment appraisal, portfolio management, and strategy formulation.

Managing Risk in Nonprofit Organizations: A Comprehensive Guide

Melanie L. Herman et al.
Chichester, UK: Wiley, 2004
336pp, ISBN: 978-0-471-23674-0
This practical guide shows managers in nonprofit organizations how to implement sound risk management procedures. It is divided into three sections: the nature and purposes of risk management; recognizing the context for risk management; and risk financing for nonprofits. Potential risks covered include human resource issues, fundraising, internet use, mergers, and volunteer management.

Operational Risk: Measurement and Modelling

Jack L. King
Chichester, UK: Wiley, 2001
272pp, ISBN: 978-0-471-85209-4
Operational risk, it is reported, is concerned with the risk to the performance of a firm, due to how the firm is operated as opposed to how it is financed. The authors present a new approach to measuring operational risk. This enables firms to better control the variability or risk of earnings in their operations.

Practical Risk Management: An Executive Guide to Avoiding Surprises and Losses

Erik Banks, Richard Dunn
Chichester, UK: Wiley, 2003
176pp, ISBN: 978-0-470-84967-5
This book looks at the world of financial risk management and offers practical approaches to managing financial risk based on the authors' experiences. It explores the challenges of risk management and how these can be overcome by focusing on governance and accountability. The book aims to provide an understanding of the different financial risks, the various measurement tools available, and how to construct a practical risk process that is consistent with corporate strategy.

Project Risk Assessment in a Week, 2nd ed

Donald Teale
Business in a Week Series
London: Profile Economist Books, 2003
96pp, ISBN: 978-0-340-84972-9
This book guides you step by step through the process of identifying and analyzing the key risks to a project. Guidelines are provided for identifying the risks, assessing the impact of each risk, analyzing the combined impact of the risks on the project objectives, assigning adequate contingency to the project budget and schedule, and producing a risk management plan to assist in risk mitigation.

Risk Analysis: A Quantitative Guide, 3rd ed

David Vose
Chichester, UK: Wiley, 2008
752pp, ISBN: 978-0-470-51284-5
Quantitative risk analysis (QRA), combined with Monte Carlo simulation, offers a useful method for dealing with uncertainty and variability in a problem. This focused text guides the reader through the necessary steps to produce an accurate risk analysis model, and offers general and specific techniques to cope with most modeling problems.

Risk from the CEO and Board Perspective

Mary Pat McCarthy, Timothy P. Flynn
Maidenhead, UK: McGraw-Hill, 2004
304pp, ISBN: 978-0-07-143471-3
Corporate decision-making is about navigating the business environment with one eye on the present and the other on the risks associated with each action. This text sets out to explain how corporate leaders are confronting and controlling risk in their organizations. Drawing upon their wealth of experience, the authors explore how to uncover and address sources of risk within an organization, manage risk without

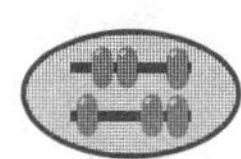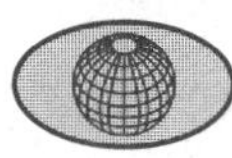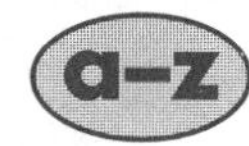

undermining ongoing initiatives, and link governance and risk management initiatives.

Risk Management: Ten Principles

Jacqueline Jeynes
Oxford: Butterworth-Heinemann, 2002
128pp, ISBN: 978-0-7506-5036-6

The ten main risk areas of a business are identified at the outset as premises, product, purchasing, people, procedures, protection, processes, performance, planning, and policy. The following sections identify and evaluate the risks and hazards relevant to each of these ten areas, and discuss ways in which the risks can be controlled. Case studies from service-based and production-based industries are included. Overall risk management strategies and policies are then described.

The Risk Management Universe: A Guided Tour, 2nd ed

David Hillson
London: British Standards Institution, 2007
424pp, ISBN: 978-0-580-50346-7

The Risk Management Universe: A Guided Tour combines the views of leading experts in the risk management field, who share their insights on various risks. It discusses the impact of new developments to maximize the effectiveness of risk management in all its diverse areas of application.

Risky Business: Corruption, Fraud, Terrorism, and Other Threats to Global Business, 2nd ed

Stuart Poole-Robb, Alan Bailey
London: Kogan Page, 2003
304pp, ISBN: 978-0-7494-4031-2

Organizations in today's world are subject to a range of risks over and above the standard expectations of terrorism and fraud, including organized crime, corruption and civil unrest. The authors' company has significant experience of these risks and the forces behind them and the book includes many case studies in areas such as Indonesia, Russia, and Asia and the Far East. Part one deals with the implications of risk for investment; part two looks at renowned trouble spots; and part three considers threats and defenses.

The Road to Audacity: Being Adventurous in Life and Work

Stephen Carter, Jeremy Kourdi
Basingstoke, UK: Palgrave Macmillan, 2003
160pp, ISBN: 978-1-4039-0617-5

The authors argue that risk-taking is an inevitable part of life and work, and that responding to uncertainty and risk is not just a matter of calculation and an attempt at objective prediction. The audacity factor is what makes the difference between caution and action. Drawing upon various examples, the book explores the way audacity can be developed and explains its importance to any individual or organization that wants to change, explore, or be different.

Secure Online Business Handbook: E-Commerce, IT Functionality, and Business Continuity, 4th ed

Jonathan Reuvid
London: Kogan Page, 2006
256pp, ISBN: 978-0-7494-4642-0

This practical handbook, divided into five sections, contains a collection of contributions from a range of experts in the field of information technology and e-commerce and addresses the need for effective management of business risk. Information at risk and the business case for security are considered first. Points of exposure and the range of threats to privacy and integrity are explored, and methods of software protection such as firewalls, encryption, digital signatures and biometrics are covered. In the operational management section, the need for a culture of workplace security is also discussed, and data recovery, disaster management, and forensics are covered under the heading of contingency planning.

Value at Risk: The Benchmark for Controlling Market Risk, 3rd ed

Philippe Jorion
Maidenhead, UK: McGraw-Hill, 2007
544pp, ISBN: 978-0-07-126047-3

This book is aimed at helping professional risk managers understand and operate within today's dynamic new risk environment. This edition updates the original book, which focused on "Value at Risk" as a financial technique to measure risks run by trading and investment operations. New developments include a chapter on liquidity risk, and information on the latest risk instruments and the expanded derivatives market.

MAGAZINES

Public Risk Magazine

Public Risk Management Association
500 Montgomery Street, Suite 750,
Alexandria, VA 22314, USA
T: +1 703 528 7701
F: +1 703 739 0200
www.primacentral.org/content.cfm?sectionid=33
ISSN: 0891-7183

Public Risk Magazine, published 10 times each year, provides risk managers in the public sector with timely, focused information in an easy-to-read format. It features articles from risk management practitioners as well as industry experts.

Risk

Incisive Media
Haymarket House, 28–29 Haymarket,
London, SW1Y 4RX, UK
T: +44 (0) 20 7316 9000
F: +44 (0) 20 7316 9250
www.risk.net
ISSN: 0952-8776

This monthly magazine covers news, analysis, and developments in financial risk management. It is aimed at financial managers, academics, bankers, and investment bankers.

Risk and Continuity

CHI Publishing
17a Everard Road, Birkdale, Southport,
Merseyside, PR8 6NN, UK
T: +44 (0) 1704 512 512
F: +44 (0) 1704 512 212
www.chi-publishing.com
ISSN: 1463-1628

This journal provides best practice information on risk and continuity management strategies. It also covers IT security, disaster management, related human factors, and legal issues, together with company and product news.

Risk Management: An International Journal

Palgrave Macmillan
Houndmills, Basingstoke, Hampshire, RG21 6XS, UK
ISSN: 1460-3799

The purpose of this quarterly journal is to generate ideas and promote good practice for all those involved in managing risk. It takes a multidisciplinary approach and aims to facilitate the exchange of information and expertise across the world.

RMA Journal

Risk Management Association
1 Liberty Place, 1650 Market Street, Suite 2300, Philadelphia, PA 19103–7301, USA
T: +1 215 446 4096
F: +1 215 446 4101
www.rmahq.org/RMA/RMAUniverse/ProductsandServices/RMABookstore/RMAJournal
ISSN: 1531-0558

Published ten times a year, this, the official journal of the Risk Management Association of the United States, covers the latest trends, techniques, and challenges that lending, credit, and

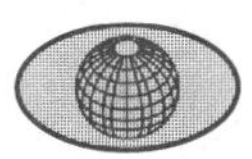

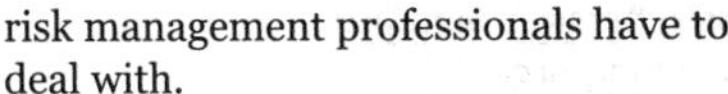

risk management professionals have to deal with.

JOURNALS

Journal of Credit Risk

Risk Journals, Incisive Media
Haymarket House, 28–29 Haymarket, London, SW1Y 4RX, UK
T: +44 (0) 20 7316 9000
F: +44 (0) 20 7316 9250
www.journalofcreditrisk.com
ISSN: 1744 6619

JCR is a quarterly journal dedicated to the measurement and management of credit risk, focusing on various aspects of portfolio credit risk and the pricing of credit products.

Journal of Operational Risk

Risk Journals, Incisive Media
Haymarket House, 28–29 Haymarket, London, SW1Y 4RX, UK
T: +44 (0) 20 7316 9000
F: +44 (0) 20 7316 9250
www.journalofoperationalrisk.com
ISSN: 1744 6740

JOP is a quarterly journal dedicated to the measurement and management of operational risk. Each issue features technical research papers and a forum to promote active discussions of current issues in operational risk, and the impact of the Basel II Accord.

Journal of Risk

Risk Journals, Incisive Media
Haymarket House, 28–29 Haymarket, London, SW1Y 4RX, UK
T: +44 (0) 20 7316 9000
F: +44 (0) 20 7316 9250
www.thejournalofrisk.com
ISSN: 1465-1211

This quarterly journal is a leading forum for research into financial risk management, which covers the latest innovations on theoretical and empirical studies in financial risk management, including the management of market and credit risk, capital allocation, and volatility estimation.

Journal of Risk Model Validation

Risk Journals, Incisive Media
Haymarket House, 28–29 Haymarket, London, SW1Y 4RX, UK
T: +44 (0) 20 7316 9000
F: +44 (0) 20 7316 9250
www.journalofriskmodelvalidation.com
ISSN: 1753-9579

JRMV is a quarterly journal that focuses on the implementation and validation of risk models, and the promotion of the greater understanding in the area of new developments in the theory and practice of risk model validation.

Risk Analysis: An International Journal

Blackwell Publishing
9600 Garsington Road, Oxford, OX4 2DQ, UK
T: +44 (0) 1865 791 100
F: +44 (0) 1865 791 347
www.wiley.com/bw/journal.asp?ref=0272-4332
ISSN: 0272-4332

The journal is an official publication of the Society for Risk Analysis. It covers new developments in risk analysis and other topics which should be of interest to scientists and managers from a wide range of disciplines.

INTERNET

The Association of Insurance and Risk Managers

www.airmic.com

This site contains membership information, details of the AIRMIC conference, a newsletter, a press release index, and a members-only section.

Business Continuity Institute

www.thebci.org

This site provides free access to various guides to continuity management, which themselves include further sources of information on business continuity and risk management. It also offers recent news items, press releases, details of conferences and training courses, and a members-only area offering networking opportunities, a worldwide contact list, details of the BCI standards, a bookstore, and the BCI forum.

Global Association of Risk Professionals

www.garp.com

Specific to financial risk management, this site offers current news items, membership information, access to detailed risk technology applications, examination information, an events calendar, a newsletter, free access to articles and other reference sources, a bookstore, and useful industry links.

Institute of Risk Management

www.theirm.org

This site provides information on the membership benefits of the IRM, gives details of its courses, certificates, and examinations, and features a careers page.

Risk and Insurance Management Society, Inc.

www.rims.org

In addition to providing information about society membership and conferences, this site also offers access to recent government-related news, a risk management newsbrief service, a job bank, education and research activities, a bookstore, an education center, a calendar of events, and related links.

RMISWEB, the Internet Resource for Risk Management Information Systems

www.rmisweb.com

This site provides access to journal and review articles and press releases on risk management. It also contains recent news items, a directory of software providers, a list of consultants, and links to other risk and insurance sites.

Society for Risk Analysis

www.sra.org

This site provides information on membership and events, recent news, a newsletter, a section on employment opportunities in this field, a journal, and related links.

ORGANIZATIONS

Europe

Alarm – The Public Risk Management Association

Ladysmith House, High Street, Sidmouth, EX10 8LN, UK
T: +44 (0) 1395 519 083
F: +44 (0) 1395 517 990
E: admin@alarm-uk.org
www.alarm-uk.org

This association creates effective risk management programs, and focuses on reducing total losses as well as explaining the effects of those which do occur and require corporate and individual commitment. They aim to provide guidance in best practices for both new and experienced risk managers.

Association of Insurance and Risk Managers

Lloyd's Avenue House, 6 Lloyd's Avenue, London, EC3N 3AX, UK
T: +44 (0) 20 7480 7610
F: +44 (0) 20 7702 3752
E: enquiries@airmic.co.uk
www.airmic.com

This membership organization, founded in 1963, brings together over 900 UK and overseas risk managers within industry, commerce, and the public sector. It offers a valuable source of contacts and practical operational support to its members, as well as assisting their self-development, technical awareness, and internal working relationships.

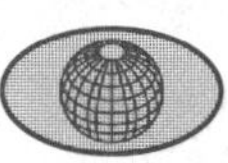

Business Continuity Institute
10 Southview Park, Marsack Street, Caversham, Berkshire, RG4 5AF, UK
T: +44 (0) 870 603 8783
F: +44 (0) 870 603 8761
E: bci@thebci.org
www.thebci.org

The BCI is a professional organization founded in 1994 to promote high standards of professional competence and ethics in the provision of business continuity planning and services. It has developed standards of competence, a code of ethics, and an accreditation scheme for continuity practitioners. Additional activities include seminars, conferences, and the Business Continuity Awards. The organization has over 1,100 members in 32 countries.

Federation of European Risk Management Associations
Avenue Louis Gribaumont, 1, 1150, Brussels, Belgium
T: +32 2 761 94 32
F: +32 2 771 87 20
E: info@ferma.eu
www.ferma.eu/Home/tabid/70/Default.aspx

FERMA's objective is to promote and raise risk management throughout Europe. It achieves its aims by promotion and raising awareness of risk management through the media, by information sharing, and educational and research projects.

Institute of Risk Management
Lloyd's Avenue House, 6 Lloyd's Avenue, London, EC3N 3AX, UK
T: +44 (0) 20 7709 9808
F: +44 (0) 20 7709 0716
E: enquiries@irmgt.co.uk
www.theirm.org

Besides providing advice and consultation, this membership organization, founded in 1986, also runs educational courses and examinations in risk management, and undertakes research.

USA

Global Association of Risk Professionals
111 Town Square Place, Suite 1215, Jersey City, New Jersey 07310, USA
T: +1 201 719 7210
F: +1 201 222 5022
E: frm@garp.com
www.garp.com
www.garp.com

Global Association of Risk Professionals is an independent association dedicated to financial risk management. Members work in regional and global banks, asset management firms, insurance companies, central banks, securities regulators, hedge funds, universities, large industrial corporations, and multinationals. It offers comprehensive programs and resources from leading financial risk professionals.

Global Association of Risk Professionals
28 East 18th Street, 2nd Floor, New York, NY 10003, USA
T: +1 212 995 0930
F: +1 212 995 0835
E: membership@garp.com

Originally an independent organization of risk management practitioners and researchers, founded by a group of risk managers from the finance industry, GARP is now a diverse association of over 15,000 professionals sharing a common interest in risk management. Its activities include facilitating the exchange of information, developing educational programs, and promoting standards in the area of financial risk management.

Public Risk Management Association
500 Montgomery Street, Suite 750, Alexandria, VA 22314, USA
T: +1 703 528 7701
F: +1 703 739 0200
E: info@primacentral.org
www.primacentral.org

The Public Risk Management Association is an industry body that provides educational programs, risk resources, and networking opportunities for public sector risk managers. It promotes effective risk management in the public interest as an essential component of public administration.

Risk and Insurance Management Society, Inc.
655 Third Avenue, 2nd Floor, New York, NY 10017, USA
T: +1 212 286 9292
www.rims.org

This is a nonprofit organization dedicated to advancing the practice of risk management. It serves its members by providing quality products, services, and information designed to manage all forms of business risk. It also offers educational opportunities and aims to develop a responsive and productive network.

Risk Management Association
1 Liberty Place, 1650 Market Street, Suite 2300, Philadelphia, PA 19103-7301, USA
T: +1 215 446 4096
F: +1 215 446 4101
E: customers@rmahq.org
www.rmahq.org

RMA is a membership organization for lending, credit, and risk management professionals in the financial services industry. Members have access to a number of benefits including professional development and networking opportunities, benchmarking tools, RMA products, and a journal. It was formerly known as Robert Morris Associates.

Society for Risk Analysis
1313 Dolley Madison Boulevard, Suite 402, McLean, VI 22101, USA
T: +1 703 790 1745
E: sra@burkinc.com
www.sra.org

Providing an open forum for those interested in risk analysis in its broadest sense, this organization devotes itself to risks of concern to individuals, the public and private sectors, and society in general. Membership is multidisciplinary and international.

BRIC

Brazalian Risk Management Association
Rua Alberto Leal, 71, São Paulo – SP, Brazil
T: +55 11 5581 3569
E: abgr@abgr.com.br
www.abgr.com.br

Risk Management Association of India
25, Baranashi Ghosh Street, Calcutta, 700 007, India
T: +91 33 239 4184
F: +91 33 233 6612
E: insurance@prgindia.com
www.prgindia.com/rsk_mgmt.php

The Risk Management Association of India promotes risk management through a forum for the exchange of views among those engaged in the risk management profession and insurance, an understanding of risk management and safety techniques, guidance and information on the latest developments in the industry, courses and lectures, and assists members in the matters of dispute.

International

International Risk Management Benchmarking Association
USA
T: +1 281 440 5044
www.irmba.com

   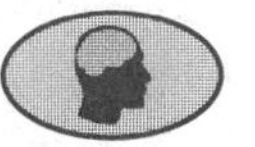  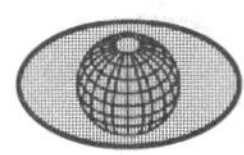   

Selling and Salesmanship

BOOKS

The 25 Sales Habits of Highly Successful Salespeople, 3rd ed

Stephan Schiffman
Avon, Massachusetts: Adams Media Corporation, 2008
128pp, ISBN: 978-1-59869-757-5

This insightful guide shows how to convert leads to sales, motivate yourself and motivate others, give killer presentations, while retaining a sense of humor. It includes new examples that use the latest advances in sales presentation technology, cases of these successful habits in action, and tips on how to overcome mistakes, set sales timetables, and reexamine processes to shore up weaknesses.

Boosting Sales: Increasing Profits. . .Without Breaking the Bank

Bob Gorton
Business on a Shoestring Series
London: A&C Black Publishers, 2007
208pp, ISBN: 978-0-7136-7541-2

Boosting your company's sales is essential if you're going to make a success of your business. Packed with ideas that really work, real-life examples, step-by-step advice and sources of further information, this book helps you to make the most of every sales opportunity.

Can I Change Your Mind?

Lindsay Camp
London: A&C Black Publishers, 2007
224pp, ISBN: 978-0-7136-7849-9

Everyone needs to be able to argue a case effectively in writing. Drawing on his long experience as a leading copywriter, Lindsay Camp shows how it's done, whether the "end product" is a magazine ad, a new business proposal, a page for the company website, or an email to your boss. Engaging, entertaining and—as you'd expect—highly persuasive, this book will change the way you think about the words you use for ever.

Clients Forever: How Your Clients Can Build Your Business for You

Doug Carter, Jenni Green
Maidenhead, UK: McGraw-Hill, 2007
256pp, ISBN: 978-0-07-140256-9

This book shows you how to build your business through solid, long-term relationships with your favorite kind of clients. It provides the know-how and confidence to focus your efforts on the people you most enjoy working with, generate better results with less effort, build relationships with clients, and develop an approach that accentuates your personal strengths.

Dalrymple's Sales Management: Concepts and Cases, 10th ed

Douglas J. Dalrymple, William L. Cron, Thomas E. DeCarlo
Chichester, UK: Wiley, 2009
500pp, ISBN: 978-0-470-16965-0

This book includes theoretical discussions and case studies covering all aspects of sales management. The topics dealt with in its various sections are strategic planning and budgeting, personal selling, territory management, estimating potentials and forecasting sales, recruiting and selecting personnel, sales training, leadership, motivating salespeople, compensating salespeople, and evaluating performance.

Delighting Your Customers: Delivering Excellent Customer Service. . .Without Breaking the Bank

Avril Owton
Business on a Shoestring Series
London: A&C Black Publishers, 2007
176pp, ISBN: 978-0-7136-7542-9

Your relationship with your customers is probably one of the most important you'll ever have. No business can survive without them, but reaching customers in the first place is a big challenge for small companies. This book will help you do just that by offering invaluable advice on a range of key issues including: understanding your customers; hiring the right people; coping with complaints; adding a personal touch; and learning from your competitors.

Global Account Management: A Complete Action Kit of Tools and Techniques for Managing Key Global Customers

Peter Cheverton
London: Kogan Page, 2008
242pp, ISBN: 978-0-7494-5227-8

This book explains the challenges of establishing a global account strategy and guides the reader through the process of decisions and actions required to manage global accounts successfully, and provides a template for all businesses with global clients. It also highlights the difference between an international company operating in different markets and one that can be considered truly global, explaining that company directors need to understand whether a client has consistent needs across different countries, possesses a global operational structure, and has the ability to implement global decisions.

Global Account Management: Creating Value

H. David Hennessey, Jean-Pierre Jeannet
Chichester, UK: Wiley, 2003
272pp, ISBN: 978-0-470-84892-0

The globalization of many industries, it is suggested, has created a unique opportunity to interact with a client on a coordinated global basis. The handling of large global customers requires special expertise, systems, and organizational alignment. This book examines the key aspects of the practice of global account management and of developing and managing global customers, and illustrates these with case studies.

How to Become a Rainmaker: The Rules for Getting and Keeping Customers and Clients

Jeffrey J. Fox
London: Vermilion, 2001
176pp, ISBN: 978-0-09-187654-8

This book is written to assist in identifying, attracting and keeping customers. It identifies "rainmakers" (people who bring revenue into organizations), who may be CEOs, owners, partners, sales representatives, or fundraisers. Jeffrey J. Fox explains how the reader can become a rainmaker, enabling him or her to attract more customers and rise above the competition in any company.

Improving Customer Satisfaction, Loyalty, and Profit: An Integrated Measurement and Management System

Michael D. Johnson, Anders Gustafsson
San Francisco, California: Jossey-Bass, 2000
240pp, ISBN: 978-0-7879-5310-2

By outlining in detail five key areas, this book offers ways to improve customer loyalty. By outlining key measures of customer satisfaction and giving suggestions for marketing strategy and product development, the book enables a more cohesive measurement and management system.

Key Account Management: A Complete Action Kit of Tools and Techniques for Achieving Profitable Key Supplier Status, 4th ed

Peter Cheverton
London: Kogan Page, 2008
368pp, ISBN: 978-0-7494-5277-3

This comprehensive textbook takes a broad perspective on key account management (KAM), starting from the premise that it is not just to do with selling but with

  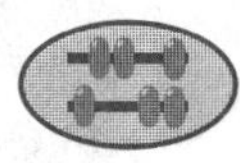   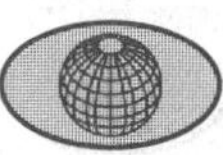   

developing profitable relationships between customers and suppliers. Peter Cheverton starts by defining KAM and explains how to understand the customer's perspective, put in place the organizational systems and processes required, identify key accounts, develop management strategies, and meet customer needs. Advice on developing key account plans and keeping track of progress and examples of good and bad practice are provided throughout.

Key Account Management and Planning: The Comprehensive Handbook for Managing Your Company's Most Important Strategic Asset
Noel Capon
London: Simon & Schuster, 2001
480pp, ISBN: 978-0-7432-1188-8
With a greater level of competition and increased costs of selling, the nature of the selling process has changed. Using research, real-life stories of successes and failures, and clarifying figures, the author presents his four-part "congruence model" of key account management. He explains: how to select the key account portfolio; how to manage key accounts; how to recruit, select, train, reward and retain key account managers, and how to formulate and execute key account strategies.

Key Account Management: Learning from Supplier and Customer Perspectives, 2nd ed
Malcolm McDonald, Beth Rogers
Oxford: Butterworth-Heinemann, 2006
416pp, ISBN: 978-0-7506-6246-8
Key account management, it is suggested, is rapidly becoming more important as purchasing power is increasingly concentrated in the hands of fewer, larger buyers. This text, based on research by Cranfield School of Management, presents a new framework for understanding the development of key account relationships. It explains the processes of identifying and targeting key accounts, key account planning, the role and skills of key account managers, and the positioning of key account activity. The book also considers the future of key account management.

Knock Your Socks Off Selling
Jeffrey Gitomer, Ron Zemke
New York: AMACOM, 1999
208pp, ISBN: 978-0-8144-7030-5
Offering an overview of sales techniques, from basic selling to developing relationships, the book is appropriate for salespeople at every level. It places emphasis on making a partnership out of the buyer-seller relationship and discusses networking, generating leads, making presentations, and following through.

Marketing and Selling Professional Services: Practical Approaches to Practice Development, 3rd ed
Patrick Forsyth
London: Kogan Page, 2003
320pp, ISBN: 978-0-7494-4090-9
With the aim of helping professionals of all kinds to develop successful strategies for marketing what are essentially intangible services, the author starts by explaining the importance and role of marketing in professional service businesses, and goes on to explore a range of practical issues, including marketing planning, promotional mix, advertising, and postal promotion. A second section deals with professional personal selling, and covers persuasive writing and communication, and systematic client development.

The New Strategic Selling: The Unique Sales System Proven Successful by the World's Best Companies, 2nd ed
Stephen E. Heiman et al.
London: Kogan Page, 2005
448pp, ISBN: 978-0-446-69519-0
Following the strategic selling process outlined in this book, the authors lay out an effective plan that leverages the key benefits of the sellers/buyers solution, and minimizes price as the principal buying criterion. The book provides a process for what successful sales people do consistently—plan.

The Sales Bible: The Ultimate Sales Resource
Jeffrey H. Gitomer
London: William Morrow & Company, 2008
304pp, ISBN: 978-0-06-137940-6
Designed as a book to be read by those within the sales industry, this book targets aspiring salesmen/women and gives them practical advice on how to reconsider and reevaluate the whole selling process. Fundamentally challenging prevailing perceptions, this text offers a comprehensive range of new ideas and strategies.

Sales Genius: A Master Class in Successful Selling
Tony Buzan, Richard Israel
Aldershot, UK: Gower Publishing, 2000
272pp, ISBN: 978-0-566-08209-2
The authors present 12 traits that can be found in professional salespeople and 12 strategies that they deploy. They then create a program of activities based on these traits.

Sales Management: Concepts and Cases, 10th ed
Douglas J. Dalrymple, William L. Cron, Thomas E. DeCarlo
Hoboken, New Jersey: Wiley, 2009
624pp, ISBN: 978-0-470-41889-5
This practical guide introduces the key issues, strategies, and relationships for managing an effective sales force. It places emphasis on developing a sales force program and managing strategic account relationships, and explores team development, diversity in the work force, problem-solving skills, and financial issues, to provide a useful guide for a career in sales management.

Selling from the Heart: The Total Success System for Mastering Business Relationships
Steven Lloyd
Arlington, Texas: Sterling & Pope, 2000
240pp, ISBN: 978-0-9678-6160-9
The main focus of the book is "emotional selling" but it also provides practical, hands-on advice on salesmanship. It covers topics including prospecting, sales presentations, customer relationships, follow-up, and building a career in sales.

Selling to Big Companies
Jill Konrath
New York: Kaplan Business, 2005
256pp, ISBN: 978-1-4195-1562-0
This presents a range of sales strategies for effectively accessing big accounts, reducing the sales cycle, and closing more business. It also provides an Account Entry Toolkit, which explains how to apply this process to your own business.

The Seven Keys to Managing Strategic Accounts
Sallie Sherman, Joseph Sperry, Samuel Reese
Maidenhead, UK: McGraw-Hill, 2003
256pp, ISBN: 978-0-07-141752-5
Offering market-proven strategies for generating competitive advantage by identifying and looking after your best customers, this book provides decision-makers with a strategy for profitably managing their largest and most critical accounts.

The SPIN Selling Fieldbook: Practical Tools, Methods, Exercises and Resources
Neil Rackham
Maidenhead, UK: McGraw-Hill, 2007
208pp, ISBN: 978-0-07-052235-0
Full of case studies and practical information, this book shows the reader how to put into practice the help and advice given in *SPIN Selling*.

  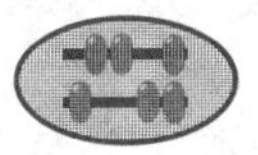 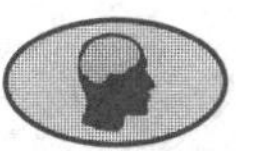  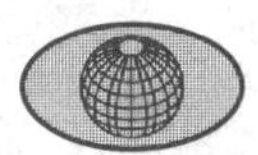   

The Ultimate Sales Letter: Attract New Customers, Get Face Time, Boost Your Sales, 3rd ed
Dan S. Kennedy, Daniel Kennedy
Avon, Massachusetts: Adams Media Corporation, 2006
224pp, ISBN: 978-1-59337-499-0
This text provides clear examples to assist in writing focused sales letters that target specific customer bases. Tips and features include creating powerful headlines, improving readability, when to use bullet points, which font to use, and which demographics to target. All this is performed within 28 structured steps, and should interest sales reps, business owners, and advertising people.

Why People Don't Buy Things: Five Proven Steps to Connect with Your Customers and Dramatically Increase Your Sales
Harry Washburn, Kim Wallace
Cambridge, Massachusetts: Perseus Books Group, 2000
208pp, ISBN: 978-0-7382-0157-3
The authors provide a methodical approach to understanding customers' motivations and show how to customize an entire sales strategy to customers' shopping patterns. In identifying different sales profiles, they reveal strategies to break out of unproductive patterns, create fresh relationships, and gain a loyal customer base.

Why We Buy: The Science of Shopping
Paco Underhill
London: Texere Publishing, 2008
320pp, ISBN: 978-1-4165-9524-3
This book is filled with retail insights, revealing, for example, how men are starting to shop like women and how women have changed the way supermarkets are designed. Looking to the future, Underhill predicts huge retail opportunities concomitant with an ageing baby-boom population, and shows how online retailing will change shopping malls.

MAGAZINES

Sales and Marketing Management
Nielsen Business Media
770 Broadway, New York, NY 10003–9595, USA
ISSN: 0163-7517
This monthly magazine features articles, profiles, and interviews written for top executives who have direct responsibility for all aspects of sales, marketing, and management. Featured topics include case studies and marketing strategies from the world's most successful companies.

Sales Leader
Dartnell Corporation
360 Hiatt Drive, Palm Beach Gardens, FL 33418, USA
T: +1 800 621 5463
F: +1 561 622 2423
www.dartnellcorp.com/sales_leader.htm
This newsletter is published 12 times each year. Written for novice and experienced sales personnel, it offers tips and advice on how to capture sales. The articles are written by expert salesmen with years of experience in closing the deal on buying decisions. Sales tactics in a variety of major industries are covered.

Sales Promotion
Market Link Publishing
The Mill, Bearwalden Business Park, Wendens Ambo, Saffron Walden, Essex, CB11 4GB, UK
T: +44 (0) 1799 544 215
F: +44 (0) 1799 544 202
www.salespromo.co.uk
ISSN: 0957-6193
Published monthly, this magazine covers promotional marketing and incentive strategy. Its target readership consists of marketing directors, brand managers, and sales promotion agencies.

Winning Edge
International Network of M&A Partners
6000 Cattleridge Drive, Suite 300, Sarasota, FL 34232, USA
T: +1 941 378 5500
F: +1 941 378 5505
www.ismm.co.uk/magazine.php
ISSN: 0264-3200
The official journal of the Institute of Sales and Marketing Management, it is published ten times a year and covers topics such as market intelligence, sales techniques, and strategies for marketing.

JOURNALS

Journal of Personal Selling and Sales Management
M. E. Sharpe
80 Business Park Drive, Armonk, NY 10504, USA
T: +1 800 541 6563
F: +1 914 273 2106
www.jpssm.org
ISSN: 0885-3134
JPSSM is a quarterly journal that seeks to advance the theory and practice of personal selling and sales management, and bridge the gap between the academic and business communities. It provides a forum for cross-talk among sales educators, researchers, and practitioners.

Journal of Selling & Major Account Management
Northern Illinois University, College of Business
College of Business, Northern Illinois University, DeKalb, IL 60115–2897, USA
T: +1 815 753 5000
www.cob.niu.edu/jsmam
ISSN: 1463-1431
The main objective of this journal is to provide a focus for collaboration between practitioners and academics for the advancement of education, research, and best practice in the areas of selling and major account management. It is aimed at both practitioners in industry and academics researching in sales.

INTERNET

BestOfSales.com
www.bestofsales.com
A list of links to sales resources on the internet is given on this site.

Just Sell
www.justsell.com
This site offers a selection of useful sales checklists and evaluation tools for sales professionals. Users must register to access the information, but registration is free.

Saleslinks.com
www.saleslinks.com/links
Run by Mentor Associates, this site is aimed at anyone who is engaged in selling for a living. It includes links to sales resources on the Internet, arranged in categories.

Salesmanship
www.dmoz.org/Business/Marketing_and_Advertising
Maintained as part of the Open Directory Project, this site contains a large list of other websites, each with a brief description, relating to all aspects of salesmanship.

Sales Rep Central
www.salesrepcentral.com
A portal for sales professionals, the site contains news, articles, a community message board, jobs, sales leads, and travel services.

SalesVault
www.salesvault.com
This site is aimed at professional salespeople. It also includes articles, news, and advice, and also advertises courses that users may wish to take up for a fee.

Selling Power
www.sellingpower.com
The online counterpart to Selling Power

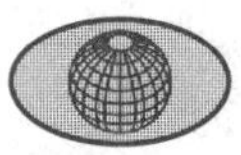

magazine, the site offers archived issues of the magazine, electronic newsletters on several sales-related topics, and advice on motivation and management. Much of the information on the site can be viewed by non-members, but to access other areas you will need to register. Registration is free.

ORGANIZATIONS

Europe

Direct Selling Association UK
29 Floral Street, London, WC2E 9DP, UK
T: +44 (0) 20 7497 1234
F: +44 (0) 20 7497 3144
E: info@dsa.org.uk
www.dsa.org.uk
The DSA aims to promote the understanding of direct selling as a distribution channel. Its benefits are potentially huge, as the site cites figures which claim that direct selling is worth more than £1.6 billion each year. The DSA's website has four major categories: protecting the consumer, direct selling today, information on the association, and "A Business of Your Own," which gives information on how direct selling can be helpful to start-up businesses.

Institute of Sales and Marketing Management
Harrier Court, Lower Woodside, Bedfordshire, LU1 4DQ, UK
T: +44 (0) 1582 840 001
F: +44 (0) 1582 849 142
www.ismm.co.uk
Established in 1966, the ISMM is a professional body for salespeople in the United Kingdom. It promotes standards of excellence in the industry and provides qualifications and training. Its members are individuals at all levels from students to sales directors. The organization holds a conference in Birmingham every October.

Institute of Sales Promotion
Arena House, 66–68 Pentonville Road, London, N1 9HS, UK
T: +44 (0) 20 7837 5340
F: +44 (0) 20 7837 5326
E: enquiries@isp.org.uk
www.isp.org.uk
The Institute of Sales Promotion was set up in 1979. It offers education, training, legal advice, and networking opportunities for members.

Society of Sales and Marketing
40 Archdale Road, East Dulwich, London, SE22 9HJ, UK
T: +44 (0) 20 8693 0555
F: +44 (0) 709 234 2170
E: info@ssam.co.uk
www.ssam.co.uk
This professional body was established in 1980. It exists to encourage the study of selling and sales management, marketing principles and practice, retail management, and international trade. It provides professional status for salespeople and accredits educational programs.

USA

Direct Selling Association
1667 K Street, NW, Suite 1100, Washington, DC 20006–1660, USA
T: +1 202 347 8866
F: +1 202 452 9010
E: info@dsa.org
www.dsa.org
DSA is a trade association for firms that manufacture and distribute goods and services sold directly to consumers. It offers its members research services, a monthly newsletter, a resource guide, conferences, networking councils, legislative lobbying, and salesforce support.

National Association of Sales Professionals
37557 Newburgh Park Circle, Livonia, MI 48152, USA
T: +1 480 951 4311
F: +1 480 483 2860
E: info@nasp.cpm
www.nasp.com
Founded in 1991, NASP states that its mission is to cater for the needs of salespersons, to help in their professional development in a changing field, and to upgrade the career status of those working in sales. It runs the Certified Professional SalesPerson program, and administers the International Registry of Accredited Salespersons.

BRIC

Direct Selling Association of Hong Kong (HKDSA)
c/o Amway Hong Kong, Amway Asia Pacific, Hong Kong Branch, 38/F, The Lee Gardens, 33 Hysan Avenue, Hong Kong, China
T: +86 852 296 96333
F: +86 852 280 73920
E: angela_keung@amway.com
www.hkdsa.org.hk
HKDSA is a trade association of person-to-person marketing companies in Hong Kong. A wide range of products and services are marketed and distributed directly to consumers through these companies' salespeople. The HKDSA is a full member of the World Federation of Direct Selling Associations.

Direct Selling Association of Russia
Ulanky Per. 4, Building 1, Moscow, Russia
T: +7 495 705 9311
F: +7 495 792 3641
E: info@rdsa.ru
www.rdsa.ru/eng.html
DSA is the national trade association of the leading firms that manufacture and distribute goods and services sold directly to consumers in Russia. Its mission is to protect, serve and promote the effectiveness of member companies and the independent business people they represent, and ensure that the marketing by member companies of products and/or the direct sales opportunity is conducted with the highest level of business ethics and service to consumers.

Indian Direct Selling Association (IDSA)
c/o Sangeet Shyamala Cultural Institute, A-12, Vasant Vihar, New Delhi 110 070, India
T: +91 11 2615 2045
F: +91 11 2615 2045
E: idsasg@idsa.co.in
www.indiandsa.co.in
The Indian Direct Selling Association is an association of companies engaged in the business of direct selling in India. Its members are of high national and international repute, having set standards in delivering quality goods and in following ethical business practices.

International

Sales and Marketing Executives International, Inc.
PO Box 1390, Sumas, Washington, DC 98295–1390, USA
T: +1 312 893 0751
F: +1 604 855 0165
E: smeihq@smei.org
www.smei.org
SME International is a worldwide association of sales and marketing managers whose members are top executives. Founded in 1935, it provides education in both sales and management, along with workshops, newsletters, meetings, and discussions.

World Federation of Direct Selling Associations (WFDSA)
1667 K Street, NW, Suite 1100, Washington, DC, 20006, USA
T: +1 202 452 8866
F: +1 202 452 9010
E: info@wfdsa.org
www.wfdsa.org
The WFDSA is a global, non-governmental, voluntary organization that represents the direct selling industry as a federation of national direct selling associations.

  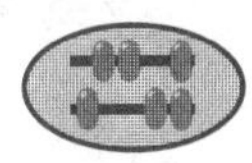   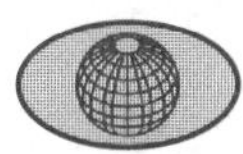   

Small and Growing Businesses

BOOKS

101 Best Businesses to Start, 3rd ed

Philip Lief Group, Russell D. Roberts, Sharon Kahn
New York: Random House, 2000
720pp, ISBN: 978-0-7679-0659-3
This popular book offers helpful, practical advice on where to start if you are looking for a new business opportunity. Each of the businesses listed is described fully and entries include profit projections, information on costs, strategies for success, and assistance on planning staff requirements.

Business Services in European Economic Growth

Luis Rubalcaba, Henk Kox (editors)
Basingstoke, UK: Palgrave, 2007
320pp, ISBN: 978-0-230-00202-9
This provides a comprehensive approach from an applied economics perspective, focusing on the contribution of business services to European economic growth, and exploring all the major mechanisms through which this contribution operates.

The E-Myth Revisited: Why Most Small Businesses Still Don't Work and What You Can Do About Yours, 2nd ed

Michael E. Gerber
London: HarperCollins, 2005
288pp, ISBN: 978-0-06-076661-0
First published in 1986, this best-selling book provides information and guidance on starting and maintaining a small business or franchise. "E-myth" stands for "entrepreneurial myth" and refers to Gerber's belief that entrepreneurs do not necessarily make good business people. The book shows the reader how to simplify the systems involved in running a business, and instead create an incredibly organized and regimented plan, so that the systems can more or less run themselves, freeing the entrepreneur's mind to focus on long-term strategy.

Enterprise Planning and Development: Small Business and Enterprise Start-Up and Growth, 2nd ed

David Butler
Oxford: Butterworth-Heinemann, 2006
432pp, ISBN: 978-0-7506-8064-6
This book aims to help owner-managers of small businesses draw up a plan for the long-term future. The subjects covered include: reviewing performance, resource implications, sales and marketing strategy, market expansion, staffing, and financial performance. The standards for business development established by the Small Firms Enterprise Development Institute (SFEDI) are appended.

Financial Management for the Small Business: A Practical Guide, 6th ed

Colin Barrow
Business Enterprise Series
London: Kogan Page, 2006
256pp, ISBN: 978-0-7494-4563-8
The author provides practical advice on proper financial planning and control for the small business. The three main sections cover key financial statements, financial analysis tools, and business plans and budgeting. A list of further reading and sources of information is included.

Finding Your Perfect Work: The New Career Guide for Making a Living, Creating a Life

Paul Edwards, Sarah Edwards
New York: Penguin Putnam, 2003
480pp, ISBN: 978-1-58542-216-6
This book is aimed at those in the crucial first phase of setting up a business: assessing yourself. Considering what you really want to do and get from your own business is explored in depth here, and the book contains worksheets to help readers pinpoint their own strengths, weaknesses, and goals.

Go It Alone: The Streetwise Secrets of Self-Employment

Geoff Burch
Chichester, UK: Capstone, 2003
336pp, ISBN: 978-1-84112-470-4
This easy-to-read, practical guide for those thinking of starting their own business is packed with anecdotal advice drawn from the author's wealth of experience in entrepreneurship and sales and conveyed in a style that is both original and humorous.

Good Finance Guide for Small Businesses: How to Raise, Manage and Grow Your Company's Cash

London: A&C Black Publishers, 2007
288pp, ISBN: 978-0-7136-8209-0
Cash—or the lack of it—keeps small business owners awake at night more than anything else. This one-stop guide to small business finance is invaluable for anyone who needs to raise money to launch or grow a business, or manage the finances of one they run already. It covers five key areas: getting off the ground; managing your money; getting paid on time; company admin, tax and payroll, and coping in a crisis.

Growing a Private Company: Commercial Strategies for Building a Business Worth Millions

Ian Smith
London: Kogan Page, 2001
192pp, ISBN: 978-0-7494-3280-5
This book is aimed at owners of private companies and provides guidance on strategy, operational efficiency, growth techniques, venture capital, acquisitions, and exit options.

Growing Business Handbook: Inspiration and Advice from Successful Entrepreneurs and Fast Growing UK Companies, 11th ed

Adam Jolly (editor)
London: Kogan Page, 2008
408pp, ISBN: 978-0-7494-5346-6
Designed to help businesses with an established market position, this handbook presents a range of practical strategies for managing growth. The contributors, who come from a variety of backgrounds, provide advice in areas including funding options, competition, managing the risks, making the most of IT, external relations, and competitive purchasing.

Growing Your Own Business: Growth Strategies for Meeting New Challenges and Maximizing Success

Gregory F. Kishel, Patricia Gunter Kishel
Lincoln, Nebraska: iUniverse, 2000
256pp, ISBN: 978-0-595-14792-2
Focusing on the key decisions needed for creating and maintaining your business from start-up to maturity, this book offers information and guidance in areas such as planning, financing, team building, marketing, expansion, taxation, and transition.

Kick Start Your Dream Business: Getting It Started and Keeping You Going

Romanus Wolter
Berkeley, California: Ten Speed Press, 2001
304pp, ISBN: 978-1-58008-251-8
This book contains practical advice for anyone thinking about starting a small business as well as supportive real-life examples of successful entrepreneurship.

  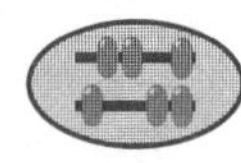   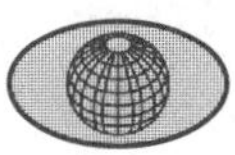   

The Loyalty Effect: The Hidden Force Behind Growth, Profits, and Lasting Value
Frederick F. Reichheld
Boston, Massachusetts: Harvard Business School Press, 2001
320pp, ISBN: 978-1-57851-687-2
Loyalty is not dead, and this book explains why, demonstrating the power of loyalty-based management as a profitable alternative to a constant flux of employees, investors, and customers.

Managing by the Numbers
Chuck Kremer, Ron Rizzuto, John Case
Cambridge, Massachusetts: Perseus Books Group, 2000
198pp, ISBN: 978-0-7382-0256-3
In this text, Chuck Kremer and Ron Rizzuto present a practical approach to reading financial statements and to managing the three core issues of business financial performance: net profit, operating cash-flow, and return on assets. The book features numerous exercises and examples (with associated templates available on the web), a powerful new management tool known as "The Financial Scoreboard," and an extensive glossary.

Marketing Your Service Business
Ian Ruskin-Brown
London: Thorogood, 2005
296pp, ISBN: 978-1-85418-316-3
This examines the key differences between the marketing of products based on goods and those which are based on services, or which use services to gain a competitive advantage. It presents current real life examples and exercises to illustrate the ideas discussed, and a sample workbook for use in training staff in Customer Service.

The Next Level: Essential Strategies for Achieving Breakthrough Growth
James B. Wood
Cambridge, Massachusetts: Perseus Books Group, 2000
224pp, ISBN: 978-0-7382-0159-7
An accessible guide to planning and managing the stages of company growth, *The Next Level* centers around the use of a powerful, field-tested diagnostic tool, the Inc Growth Strategy Analysis. James Wood carefully shows entrepreneurs and established business leaders alike how to analyze their organization's growth potential, identify the key constraints to future growth, and put into practice the strategies that will enable them to arrive at new levels of expansion and profit generation.

The On-Purpose Business: Doing More of What You Do Best More Profitably
Kevin W. McCarthy
Colorado Springs, Colorado: Navpress Publishing Group, 2002
192pp, ISBN: 978-1-57683-321-6
Written in a story format and with a spiritual backdrop, this book examines the principles of management and introduces the "On-Purpose" model, which focuses on all areas where each individual joins, belongs, and contributes to an organization.

Outsmarting Goliath: How to Achieve Equal Footing with Companies That Are Bigger, Richer, Older and Better Known
Debra Koontz Traverso
London: Kogan Page, 2000
288pp, ISBN: 978-1-57660-031-3
The author presents practical advice on how to help small businesses present a professional image, produce high quality marketing materials, and win contracts that may seem out of reach for a small company. The book also outlines innovative ways to enhance company profile.

Patent It Yourself, 13th ed
David Pressman
Berkeley, California: Nolo Press, 2008
572pp, ISBN: 978-1-4133-0516-6
As an experienced patent attorney and former patent examiner of the US Patent and Trademark Office, the author has developed a useful guide containing all the instructions and forms necessary to patent an invention in the United States. It offers comprehensive and up-to-date advice for obtaining a high-quality patent, presenting the information in a user-friendly and jargon-free manner.

Setting Up a Limited Company, 2nd ed
Mark Fairweather, Rosy Border
Pocket Lawyer Series
London: The Stationery Office, 2004
160pp, ISBN: 978-1-85941-857-4
This is a practical guide to the procedures for setting up a limited company in the United Kingdom. The text covers considering the options, roles and responsibilities, and completing the required forms. Sample letters, minutes, resolutions, and articles of association are included in the text and on disk. Listings of frequently asked questions and useful contacts are also provided.

Setting Up and Running a Limited Company: A Comprehensive Guide to Forming and Operating a Company as a Director and Shareholder, 4th ed
Robert Browning
Oxford: How To Books, 2003
192pp, ISBN: 978-1-85703-866-8
This guide is aimed at anyone thinking of establishing a limited company and addresses statutory requirements as well as advising on best practice. The book includes information on: the responsibilities of shareholders and directors; setting up your business; preparing financial records; sourcing venture capital; and retreating gracefully if things don't go to plan.

Small Business Management, 4th ed
David Stokes
London: Thomson Financial, 2002
432pp, ISBN: 978-0-8264-5679-3
This is a practical textbook, written by one of the most respected writers on small business in the United Kingdom.

Small Business Marketing Management
Ian Chaston, Terry Mangles
Basingstoke, UK: Palgrave, 2002
272pp, ISBN: 978-0-333-98075-0
This book is designed to give undergraduate and postgraduate students an understanding of the small business marketing process, including positioning, competitive advantage, product management, pricing, and distribution. The impact of e-commerce and the Internet, the marketing of services, and international marketing are also covered. The text is supported by real-life case studies and published research findings.

Small Time Operator: How to Start Your Own Business, Keep Your Books, Pay Your Taxes, and Stay Out of Trouble, 10th ed
Bernard B. Kamoroff
Willits, California: Bell Springs Publishing, 2007
240pp, ISBN: 978-0-917510-28-1
Kamoroff presents the reader with the essentials of building a business, from obtaining initial permits and licenses, to seeking financing, locating the right business area, establishing an accounts and bookkeeping system, and taking on new staff. The text is continually updated in order to reflect the very latest thinking in tax and business management.

  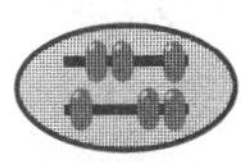   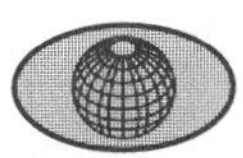   

So You Want to Start a Business: 8 Steps to Take Before Making the Leap
Edward D. Hess, Charles F. Goetz
Upper Saddle River, New Jersey: FT Press, 2008
224pp, ISBN: 978-0-13-712667-5
This identifies the main 'killer mistakes' in business services, and provides advice on the knowledge and tools to avoid them, and ensure your business thrives.

Spare Room Tycoon: Succeeding Independently—The 70 Lessons of Sane Self-Employment, 2nd ed
James Chan
London: Nicholas Brealey Publishing, 2006
224pp, ISBN: 978-1-85788-252-0
Written by a entrepreneur with over 20 years' experience of working from home, this book is aimed at anyone thinking of setting up a home-based business. It offers support and tips on how to avoid isolation and to spread the word about your business. The book focuses on "soft" skills, such as work-life balance, building confidence, and coping with the emotional demands of being your own boss, and offers reassuring anecdotal advice.

Start and Run a Creative Services Business
Susan Kirkland
Start & Run Series
Bellingham, Washington: Self-Counsel Press, 2005
192pp, ISBN: 978-1-55180-607-5
This book for creative designers shows how to make money designing anything from print ads to book jackets, logos to letter-heads, and much more. Industry specific information is presented in a logical order, appealing to the novice as well as the seasoned designer who needs advice on a particular situation.

Starting Your Own Business: The Bestselling Guide to Planning and Building a Successful Enterprise, 4th ed
Jim Green
Oxford: How To Books, 2005
304pp, ISBN: 978-1-84528-070-3
This practical guide examines the steps that need to be taken before starting a business. These include preparing a business plan, raising finance, and developing marketing strategies. The role of the Internet is also considered. The book includes a directory of sources of advice and information.

Ultimate Start-Up Directory, 2nd ed
James Stephenson
Irvine, California: Entrepreneur Press, 2006
320pp, ISBN: 978-1-932531-98-5
This book offers an extensive listing of business ideas, covering more than 1,300 potential start-ups across over 30 industries. It covers new and traditional business areas, including working from home and working via the Internet. Each entry is rated according to the following criteria: ease of start-up; estimated cost and potential income; possibility of exploiting the idea online; skills required; whether the start-up could be run part-time; and licensing/franchising opportunities.

Understanding the Small Family Business
Denise Fletcher (editor)
London: Routledge, 2002
240pp, ISBN: 978-0-415-25053-5
This book offers an overview of current research in the small family business sector, with the main focus on the relationship between work and family and the tensions and contradictions that can arise. The contributions are organized in three sections relating to rationality discourse, resource-based discourse, and critical discourse.

What No One Ever Tells You about Starting Your Own Business: Real Life Start-Up Advice from 101 Successful Entrepreneurs, 2nd ed
Jan Norman
Chicago, Illinois: Upstart Publishing, 2004
240pp, ISBN: 978-0-7931-8596-2
Drawing on the experience of, and mistakes made by, 100 businesspeople, this book contains helpful and practical advice on how to start your own business without headaches.

Working Ethically: Creating a Sustainable Business. . .Without Breaking the Bank
Business on a Shoestring Series
London: A&C Black Publishers, 2007
168pp, ISBN: 978-0-7136-7548-1
There has never been more interest in working ethically, and many small business owners are leading the way in finding positive solutions that benefit them and their community. This book helps you to do the same, by covering key issues such as: creating an ethical strategy for your business; finding suppliers who share your aims; banking ethically; and respecting and protecting the environment.

MAGAZINES

Better Business
Active Information
Cribau Mill, Chepstow, Wales, NP16 6LN, UK
T: +44 (0) 1291 641222
F: +44 (0) 1291 641777
www.better-business.co.uk
This magazine appears 10 times a year and has a practical focus. The contents include case studies of successful businesses and updates on legal, tax, and technological topics.

Entrepreneur
Entrepreneur Incorporated
2445 McCabe Way, Irvine, CA 92614, USA
T: +1 949 261 2325
F: +1 949 261 0222
www.entrepreneur.com
ISSN: 0163-3341
This monthly magazine aims to give practical information to prospective entrepreneurs. It offers readers hands-on advice on many aspects of entrepreneurship, and covers the latest developments in technology, finance, management, and marketing. Products, services, and strategies are highlighted in order to help individuals run a better business, and readers can also learn from other entrepreneurs who have successfully improved their businesses.

Inc.
Gruner & Jahr USA Publishing
38 Commercial Wharf, Boston, MA 02110-3883, USA
T: +1 617 248 8000
F: +1 617 248 8090
www.inc.com
ISSN: 0162-8968
Inc. is a US publication for entrepreneurs, and is published 14 times a year. The magazine provides advice, case studies, and overviews on the subject of small business in the United States, and also provides prospective entrepreneurs with resources and road-tested strategies for managing people, finance, sales, marketing, and technology. The magazine also looks at the personal aspects of the entrepreneurial lifestyle.

JOURNALS

Journal of Small Business Management
Blackwell Publishing
9600 Garsington Road, Oxford, OX4 2DQ, UK
T: +44 (0) 1865 791100
F: +44 (0) 1865 791347
www.wiley.com/bw/journal.asp?ref=0047-2778

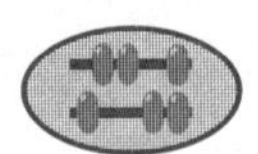
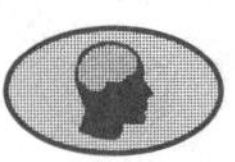

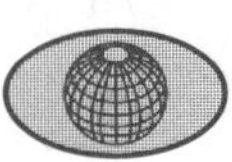

ISSN: 0047-2778

The *JSBM* is published for the International Council for Small Business and the Bureau of Business and Economic Research at West Virginia University College of Business and Economics. It is a quarterly refereed journal covering topics of interest to researchers and academics as well as practitioners.

INTERNET

BBC Business Basics—Small Business
news.bbc.co.uk/1/hi/in_depth/business/2003/small_business

The small business section of the BBC's main business pages offers articles clarifying the key issues and answering practical questions related to the running of a small business. These short articles are divided up into three subject areas: start-up support, environment issues, and bank and money matters. Many of the articles provide links to other related areas on the BBC website, such as Working Lunch (the award-winning daily business, personal finance, and consumer news program), or other organizations on the web where further information can be found.

Business.com
www.business.com

This is an extensive and helpful search engine and directory site. The home page offers over 20 topics for users to research, including small businesses, accounting, law and computing. Search results are presented as a series of useful click-through links.

Business Eye (Wales)
www.businesseye.org.uk

Launched in September 2003, Business Eye (Wales) replaces Business Connect as a free information service for all businesses in Wales. The service is managed by the Welsh Development Agency and has more than 25 offices throughout Wales. Business Eye does not provide business support or grants itself but instead aims to "signpost" users towards the best sources of help for their particular needs. The website offers a gateway to numerous resources for Welsh entrepreneurs, including links to useful sites across more than 20 key topics, a business forum, business news, information on courses and training, a support directory, and contact details of the local branches in North, Mid-, West, and South-East Wales.

Business Gateway (Scotland)
www.bgateway.com

Aimed at both start-ups and existing businesses in Scotland, Business Gateway (Scotland) operates in partnership with Scottish Enterprise, the Scottish Executive, and Scottish local authorities. There are local offices ("Gateways") in 13 regions across Scotland, but the website offers a range of help and advice to the reader, including a business information service, start-up and high-growth start-up services, and a business growth service.

Business Link
www.businesslink.gov.uk

This resource helps your business save time and money by providing instant access to clear, simple, and trustworthy information. It is developed in partnerships with subject experts within government and relevant business-support organizations to help you comply with regulations and improve your performance.

Business Owner's Toolkit
www.toolkit.cch.com

This site is packed with information for budding small business owners. Offering a series of brief guides to key aspects of starting up your own company, the site also features a selection of downloadable document templates, official government forms, and spreadsheet templates.

Community Interest Companies (CICs)
www.cicregulator.gov.uk

This site is of particular interest to anyone planning on starting a business with social, ethical, or environmental aims: a Community Interest Company (CIC). In order to register your company as a CIC you will need to gain approval by the regulator, which has a continuing monitoring and enforcement role. The CIC Regulator conducts a "community interest test" and "asset lock" to confirm that the company has indeed been established for community purposes.

Department for Business, Enterprise and Regulatory Reform
www.berr.gov.uk/bbf/smallbusiness

This site contains links to all relevant UK government departments and also offers a variety of helpful information, including taxation advice, sources of finance and legal requirements, and more generally useful "best practice" guides for small businesses from the Enterprise Directorate, formerly the Small Business Service.

Environment Agency
www.environment-agency.gov.uk/netregs

This UK government website aims to help small businesses get to grips easily with the environmental legislation with which they are legally obliged to comply.

Formationshouse.com
www.formationshouse.com

This online company-formation service guides you through the process of forming and registering a limited company.

Inc.com
www.inc.com

Inc.com is the online version of the magazine *Inc.* The website provides information, products, services, and online tools—accumulated from a variety of sources—for many business or management tasks. This information has also been organized into categories to help users quickly find what they need.

Invest in Northern Ireland
www.investni.com

This site offers practical advice on how to establish a business in Northern Ireland. It has an excellent section of sources of further information made up of weblinks to key organizations and industries in the area. The site is colorful and well-designed, and features key facts about Northern Ireland.

IRS Small Business One Stop Resource
www.irs.gov/businesses/small/index.html

The US government's Internal Revenue Service offers a broad range of tax resources for the self-employed and those running small businesses, including online workshops, forms, and publications. In addition to this, the IRS provides more general advice to those starting, operating, or closing a business, in the form of articles, checklists, tips, and extensive web links to other sources of information and help.

Jordans UK
www.jordans.co.uk

An online company-formation service that also offers additional services such as search functions and debt recovery.

Redwoods Dowling Kerr
www.redwoodsdk.com

An agency that deals in businesses for sale, from retailers to nurseries. This site offers free access to lists of businesses as well as additional fee-based services, such as finding a business that meets your specification.

SCORE
www.score.org

This site bills itself as "Counselors to America's Small Business," and is a nonprofit organization that aims to give free support and advice to entrepreneurs, both face-to-face and remotely (via e-mail). SCORE has a team of more than 10,500

  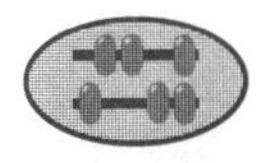   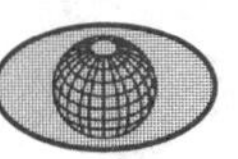   

retired and working volunteer advisors who offer guidance on a wide variety of issues, passing on the benefit of their business experience.

Scottishbusinesswomen.com
www.scottishbusinesswomen.com
Part of the Scottish Enterprise Network initiative, this website is aimed at women in Scotland who either run their own business or who are thinking about establishing one. It offers support and advice on how to grow and develop existing businesses, and also offers practical help and valuable sources of information for start-ups.

Small Business Advice Service
www.smallbusinessadvice.org.uk
Smallbusinessadvice.org.uk is a free and independent source of information and advice for entrepreneurs, owner managers, and the self-employed starting or running a business with fewer than 10 staff and based in England. The website operates a business enquiry service which links users to over 200 accredited business advisers. It also offers online guides to various aspects of business planning, a resource centre, e-business advice, discussion boards, and help for students.

Smallbusiness.co.uk
www.smallbusiness.co.uk
This website offers extensive help on variety of key small business issues. The site is divided into seven main areas (including starting up, finance, people, technology, legal, and property) that are then subdivided into more detailed sections.

Small Business Research Portal
www.smallbusinessportal.co.uk
Intended for academics, policymakers, and support agencies, the portal provides a collection of links to small business sites under categories that include news, publications, research, institutes, and conferences.

UK Company Registration
www.uk-company-registration.co.uk
Another site which helps users set up companies online. The site is easy to navigate and has a helpful list of frequently asked questions.

UK National Work-Stress Network
www.workstress.net
An informative site that aims to educate users about the causes of work-stress and various ways of coping with it. While the site does not offer stress counseling, it does feature helpful sources of, and links to, sources of further information and support.

UK Online
www.ukonline.gov.uk
UK Online is a government sponsored website run by the Office of the e-Envoy, which falls under the jurisdiction of the Cabinet Office. The UK Online site covers a variety of topics, and has a separate section on setting up and running a small business. It includes jargon-free explanations of taxes and other relevant regulations and also offers a series of checklists and sources of information about first steps.

Welcome Business USA
www.welcomebiz.com
This site is an extensive online resource for entrepreneurs and those thinking of starting their own business. It has an alliance with SCORE, who provide a team of advisors that users can contact free. The Welcome Business site offers a variety of services, including a start-up checklist, free business counseling, information on business plans, and information on tax issues for small businesses.

ORGANIZATIONS

Europe

Federation of Small Businesses
Sir Frank Whittle Way, Blackpool Business Park, Blackpool, Lancashire, FY4 2FE, UK
T: +44 (0) 1253 336 000
F: +44 (0) 1253 348 046
E: membership@fsb.org.uk
www.fsb.org.uk
The FSB, which has more than 195,000 members, represents the interests of small businesses with up to 200 employees. It organizes an annual conference, publishes a bimonthly magazine, *First Voice*, and lobbies on policy issues, while its local branches provide networking and research facilities in addition to general support services for members.

Forum of Private Business
Ruskin Chambers, Drury Lane, Knutsford, Cheshire, WA16 6HA, UK
T: +44 (0) 1565 634 467
F: +44 (0) 870 241 9570
E: info@fpb.org
www.fpb.co.uk
The FPB aims to influence laws and policies affecting private businesses in the United Kingdom and provide support for its members.

The Prince's Trust
18 Park Square East, London, NW1 4LH, UK
T: +44 (0) 800 842 842
F: +44 (0) 20 7543 1200
E: info@princes-trust.org.uk
www.princes-trust.org.uk
The Prince's Trust was established by the Prince of Wales in 1976 to help young people realize their full potential. Aimed at those aged between 14–30 (or 14–25 in Scotland), the Trust offers support and financial assistance across a range of core programs including business start-ups. Since 1983 the Trust has helped over 60,000 businesses, and its business program currently offers: a low-interest loan of up to £4,000 for a sole trader or £5,000 for a partnership; a test marketing grant of up to £250; advice lines and seminars; and access to a volunteer business mentor.

Small Business Bureau
Curzon House, Church Road, Windlesham, Surrey, GU20 6BH, UK
T: +44 (0) 1276 452 010
F: +44 (0) 1276 451 602
E: info@sbb.org.uk
www.smallbusinessbureau.org.uk
The Small Business Bureau was founded in 1976 to promote the interests of small businesses in the United Kingdom. Its activities include an annual conference and a magazine, *Small Business News*, which is published three times a year. The organization has also set up Women into Business to encourage more women to choose business and business ownership as a career.

Small Firms Enterprise Development Initiative (SFEDI)
Business Incubation Centre, Durham Way South, Aycliffe Industrial Park, County Durham, DL5 6XP, UK
T: +44 (0) 845 224 5928
F: +44 (0) 845 224 5928
E: info@sfedi.co.uk
www.sfedi.co.uk
The SFEDI has been appointed by the UK government to identify standards of best practice for small businesses and to work with providers of small business training, education, and advice to raise standards of support.

USA

American Small Business Association
P.O. Box 300777, Chicago, IL 60630–0777, USA
T: +1 877 906 2722
E: info@asbaonline.org
www.asbaonline.org/about/about.htm
ASBA is a non-profit organization dedicated to the needs of small business owners, and advocacy and education for men and women age 50 and above. They are a national association with over 500,000 members, that offers educational and consumer programs, and acts as a resource for its members and partners.

     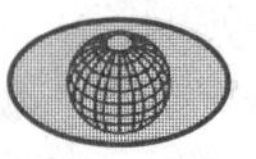   

Independent Small Business Employers (ISBE)
Ground Floor, 137 Euston Road, London, NW1 2AA, UK
T: +44 (0) 20 7554 9941
F: +44 (0) 1423 500 046
E: info@isbe.org.uk

ISBE is a network for individuals and organizations driving small business and entrepreneurship research, enterprise support and advice, entrepreneurship education, and for those who formulate, deliver, and evaluate policy in this area. It promotes the advancement of knowledge, expertise, and best practice in the area of small business and entrepreneurship.

National Business Association
PO Box 700728, Dallas, TX 75370, USA
T: +1 800 456 0440 or 972 458 0900
F: +1 972 960 9149
E: info@nationalbusiness.org
www.nationalbusiness.org

Established in 1982, the National Business Association (NBA) is a nonprofit organization, designed and managed to assist the self-employed and small business community in achieving their professional goals. The NBA uses its group buying power to provide its members with support programs, cost- and time-saving products, services, and valuable small business resource materials.

National Federation of Independent Business
53 Century Boulevard, Suite 300, Nashville, TN 37214, USA
T: +1 615 872 5800
F: +1 615 872 5353
www.nfib.org

The NFIB was founded by Wilson Harder in 1942. With 600,000 members it is the largest and probably the most influential small business lobbying group in the United States. It represents the interests of small business owners at national and state government levels and provides a range of services for its members.

Small Business Administration
409 3rd Street, SW, Washington, DC 20416, USA
T: +1 704 344 6563
F: +1 704 344 6769
E: answerdesk@sba.gov
www.sbaonline.sba.gov

The Small Business Administration was set up by the US government in 1953 to provide assistance to those starting and running their own businesses. It provides training, financial support, and advice through a network of offices in every state.

Small Business Institute Directors' Association
Miami University, Department of DSC/MIS, 311 Upham Hall, Oxford, OH 45056, USA
T: +1 513 529 4826
F: +1 513 529 4841
E: broidams@muohio.edu
www.sbida.org

The SBIDA promotes the development and improvement of educational programs for small businesses and acts as a coordinating body for Small Business Institute programs at universities and colleges in the United States. The latter were started in 1972 in cooperation with the US Small Business Administration, but became independent in 1996.

BRIC

Brazilian Micro & Small Business Support Service
SEPN 515 – Bloco C, Loja 32, Asa Norte, Brasâia, Brazil
T: +55 61 348 7218
F: +55 61 347 4120
E: paulo.alvim@sebrae.com.br
www.sebrae.com.br

This is a private, non-profit organization that supports the development and activity of small-sized businesses. It combines both public and private sectors and Brazil's main research bodies.

Enterprise Europe Network Russia
17B, Mosfilmovskaya Str, Moscow, 119330, Russia
T: +7 499 143 7320
F: +7 499 143 7321
E: eicc@siora.ru
www.euroinfocenter.ru

The Euro Info Centre Network is one of several business networks within EU that support the creation and development of an information environment for small- and medium-sized enterprises (SMEs).

Secretariat for Industrial Assistance
Udyog Bhawan, New Delhi, 110011, India
T: +91 11 2306 2626
F: +91 11 2306 1222
E: cim@nic.in
dipp.gov.in

This organization promotes the industrial development of industrially emerging areas in the North Eastern region in India. It offers international co-operation for industrial partnerships, and monitors industrial growth.

Shanghai Small Enterprises Development Coordination Office
7F, 108 Da Mu Qiao Road, Shanghai, China
T: +86 21 5452 1128
www.ssme.gov.cn

The SSE administrates and regulates roles and functions in Shanghai, including research on policy and regulations relevant to small business development, as well as collecting and analyzing information and data on SMEs.

International

International Council for Small Business
GWU School of Business, 2201 G Street NW , Funger Hall, Suite 315, Washington, DC 20052, USA
T: +1 314 977 3628
F: +1 314 977 3627
E: icsb@slu.edu
www.icsb.org

The ICSB works to increase awareness and understanding of the role of small and medium businesses worldwide through education, research, publications, management development programs, conferences, and an international exchange program. Its membership includes educators, small business owners, consultants and advisers, government officials, and trade and business associations. It also publishes the *Journal of Small Business Management*, a bulletin, a newsletter, research papers, and conference proceedings.

World Association for Small and Medium Enterprises
Plot No. 4, Sector 16A, Noida, Uttar Pradesh, 201301, India
T: +91 118 451 5238
F: +91 118 451 5243
E: wasme@vsnl.com
www.wasmeinfo.org

WASME was founded in 1980 in New Delhi, India with the aim of providing support and advice to SMEs internationally and has members and associates in 112 countries. The organization promotes technology transfer, joint ventures and cooperation between SMEs in industrialized, developing, and least-developed countries. It has set up a Technology and Trade Promotion Exchange Center (TPX) and an International Committee for Rural Industrialization (ICRI). WASME has consultative status with the Economic and Social Council of the United Nations and other UN bodies.

  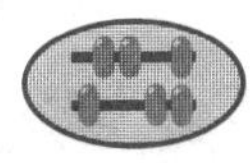 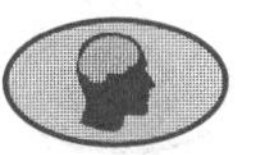  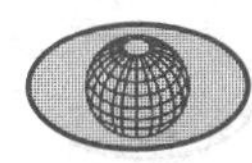   

Social Responsibility of Management

BOOKS

The Answer to How is Yes: Acting on What Matters
Peter Block
San Francisco, California: Berrett-Koehler, 2003
208pp, ISBN: 978-1-57675-271-5
The preponderance of the "how?" question in society, Block claims, is symptomatic of people living in accordance with an ethic of defense. We must strive to reclaim both our liberty and autonomy that have been radically sequestered from us. This position is to be attained for workers and managers by encouraging them to act on what they know, confronting passivity, and promoting a life where we can choose accountability and demand more compelling purpose from our work.

Awakening Social Responsibility: A Call to Action Guidebook for Global Citizens, Corporate and Nonprofit Organizations
Rossella Derickson, Krista Henley
Cupertino, California: Happy About, 2007
204pp, ISBN: 978-1-60005-065-7
The book addresses the implementation of corporate social responsibility (CSR), providing actionable step, and perspectives on how organizations can actively engage in eco initiatives, employee giving, volunteering, and savvy sustainable business practices. It acts as a guidebook to for engaging all employees in initiating CSR programs or making current programs more robust.

Building Public Trust: The Future of Corporate Reporting
Samuel A. Di Piazza, Robert G. Eccles
New York: Wiley, 2002
192pp, ISBN: 978-0-471-26151-3
In response to the global crisis in corporate reporting and its associated fallout, the authors offer their recommendations for addressing the increased levels of accountability, transparency, and integrity that are necessary in order to rebuild public trust. A three-tier model for corporate reporting is proposed that encompasses GAAP, industry standards, and company-specific information into a framework, which in turn feeds into new enabling technologies such as the internet that will assist and accelerate the process.

Business and Society: Ethics and Stakeholder Management, 7th ed
Archie B. Carroll
Cincinnati, Ohio: South-Western College Publishing, 2008
768pp, ISBN: 978-0-324-56939-1
Though the book is intended as a textbook, its managerial perspective makes it relevant for businesspeople as well. It uses case studies to illustrate relationships between business and society stakeholders and emphasizes ethical considerations in decision-making.

Business as Unusual
Anita Roddick
Chichester, UK: Anita Roddick Publishing, 2005
304pp, ISBN: 978-0-9543959-5-7
This book contains the ideas for the philosophy of Anita Roddick's Body Shop chain, detailing the unique ethos of the company, which is to maintain an operation that can be at once profitable whilst not harming the environment or violating human rights.

Citizen Brands: Putting Society at the Heart of Your Business, 2nd ed
Michael Willmott
Chichester, UK: Wiley, 2003
272pp, ISBN: 978-0-470-85358-0
Citizen Brands reflects on the need for organizations to demonstrate corporate social responsibility. The book develops this concept further, evolving the idea of corporate citizenship, the practice of which should make a business more successful.

Counting What Counts: Turning Corporate Accountability to Competitive Advantage
Bill Birchard, Marc J. Epstein
Cambridge, Massachusetts: Perseus Books Group, 2000
320pp, ISBN: 978-0-7382-0313-3
Fraud, tax evasion etc. are what the authors of this book identify as practices which obstruct managers from working efficiently. The text argues that managers should adopt the ethic of accountability, and succeed by becoming responsive and responsible. Using over 25 years of research and the experiences of a number of managers, Epstein and Birchard show that managers frequently overlook accountability and are in need of reform.

The End of Shareholder Value
Allan Kennedy
London: Orion Business, 2001
256pp, ISBN: 978-0-7382-0484-0
The main premise of Kennedy's argument is that the shareholder value ethic has signally failed to produce anything of lasting value, with the result that the future of the company as we know it is under threat. The book outlines three eras of business evolution, from the family enterprises of the 19th century to the entrepreneurs of high technology, often unfavorably, and ends with Kennedy's proposed remedies to create real, sustainable wealth for all of a company's stakeholder groups, not just the stockholders.

The Heroic Enterprise: Business and the Common Good
John Hood
New York: Free Press, 2005
272pp, ISBN: 978-1-58798-246-0
Attacking the common assertion that businesses necessarily neglect the public good at the expense of short-term profits, Hood demonstrates numerous examples of how business works to enhance the wider social good. Detailing actual examples of this happening in today's world, Hood reveals how inner-city areas have been regenerated, and how the environment, workplace, and education have all been reformed in line with business initiatives.

Mainstreaming Corporate Responsibility: Cases and Text for Integrating Corporate Responsibility Across the Business School Curriculum
N. Craig Smith and Gilbert Lenssen
Hoboken, New Jersey: Wiley, 2009
512pp, ISBN: 978-0-470-75394-1
This practical overview of corporate responsibility and its impact on the business world assesses how it is now in the economic interest of corporates to address social and environmental impacts in a manner that is integrated with their operations. It explores issues such as sustainability, stakeholder management, and corporate governance, as well as corporate philanthropy.

Managing Values and Beliefs in Organisations
Tom McEwan
Harlow, UK: FT Prentice Hall, 2001
560pp, ISBN: 978-0-273-64340-1
This is book written as a student text that summarizes the origins of corporate responsibility, business ethics, and corporate governance, and reviews the similarities and differences between them.

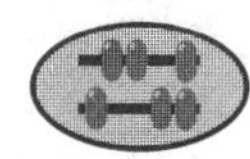
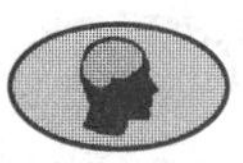

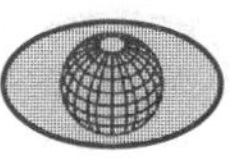

The specific issues covered include: moral meaning and applied ethics; values, beliefs, and ideologies; individual morality in organizations; unethical behavior by individuals; international business and the developing world; ethical investment; organization culture and stakeholder theory; and corporate social performance, ethical leadership, and reputation management.

The Oxford Handbook of Corporate Social Responsibility
Andrew Crane
Oxford Handbooks in Business & Management Series
Oxford: Oxford University Press, 2008
656pp, ISBN: 978-0-19-921159-3
This handbook is an authoritative review of the academic research that has both prompted, and responded to, issues involving corporate social responsibility. It examines questions about the changing relationship between business, society and government, environmental issues, corporate governance, the social and ethical dimensions of management, globalization, stakeholder debates, shareholder and consumer activism, changing political systems and values, and the ways in which corporations can respond to new social imperatives.

Perspectives on Corporate Citizenship
Jorg Andriof, Malcolm McIntosh
Sheffield, UK: Greenleaf Publishing, 2001
336pp, ISBN: 978-1-874719-39-7
Corporate citizenship is seen as one of the big issues of the 21st century. This book introduces the concept of corporate citizenship and explains the need for a fuller understanding of its impact. This collection of articles on corporate citizenship is divided into three broad sections: the evolution, context and concepts of corporate citizens; stakeholder engagement; and social accountability.

The Sustainable Company
Chris Laszlo
Washington, DC: Island Press, 2005
232pp, ISBN: 978-1-59726-018-3
Leading corporations are recognizing the changing role and expectations of business in the 21st century and the competitive advantage that can be gained in addressing the problems and challenges concerned. The gap between the interests of business and those of society and the environment have created a "triple bottom line" within organizations, resulting from associated yet conflicting sets of performance measures. This book aims to go beyond the triple bottom line. It aims to bridge the gap between shareholder concerns and stakeholder expectations, and presents an integrative business paradigm for both.

The Sustainable Company: How to Create Lasting Value through Social and Environmental Performance
Chris Laszlo
Washington, DC: Island Press, 2008
208pp, ISBN: 978-0-8047-5963-2
This illustrates how the competitive strategies of some of the world's largest businesses are changing as their leaders begin to take on a number of the world's most important social, environmental, and economic issues.

Take It Personally: How Globalization Affects You and Powerful Ways to Fight Back
Anita Roddick
London: Thorsons, 2001
256pp, ISBN: 978-0-00-712898-3
Like Naomi Klein, Roddick points to the need to concentrate on business accountability, focusing on human rights violations, environmental issues, the treatment of the developing world, and the growth of global markets. She forces her reader to ask the question: Who really controls the world—business or government?

Value Shift: Why Companies Must Merge Social and Financial Imperatives to Achieve Superior Performance
Lynn Sharp Paine
New York: McGraw-Hill, 2003
304pp, ISBN: 978-0-07-142733-3
This book argues the case for a new style of management that will align company performance with today's ethical standards. It argues that there is now a dichotomy between traditional management and the expectations of business in contemporary society. Acknowledging it is no longer enough simply to produce goods and services and create wealth, the author discusses today's corporate leaders' need to make a shift in management values to incorporate high ethical standards along with strong financial results.

What Matters Most: Business, Social Responsibility and the End of the Era of Greed
Jeffrey Hollender, Stephen Fenichell
London: Random House, 2004
320pp, ISBN: 978-1-84413-397-0
Jeffrey Hollender, CEO of Seventh Generation, a world leader in manufacturing environmentally friendly household products, is a frequent commentator on corporate responsibility. This book, which he has co-authored with Stephen Fenichell, puts forward an approach to corporate strategy that is designed to help integrate concerns related to social responsibility into an organization's culture, systems, and activities.

MAGAZINES

The Journal of Corporate Citizenship
Greenleaf Publishing
Aizlewood Business Centre, Aizlewood's Mill, Nursery Street, Sheffield, S3 8GG, UK
T: +44 (0) 114 282 3475
F: +44 (0) 114 282 3475
www.greenleaf-publishing.com/default.asp?ContentID=7
ISSN: 1470-5001
The Journal of Corporate Citizenship focuses explicitly on integrating theory about corporate citizenship with management practice. It provides a forum in which the tensions and practical realities of making corporate citizenship real are addressed in a reader-friendly, yet conceptually and empirically rigorous format.

JOURNALS

Social Responsibility Journal
Emerald
60/62 Toller Lane, Bradford, West Yorkshire, BD8 9BY, UK
T: +44 (0) 1274 777 700
F: +44 (0) 1274 785 200
www.emeraldinsight.com/1747-1117.htm
ISSN: 1747-1117
The Social Responsibility Journal, the official journal of the Social Responsibility Research Network, is interdisciplinary in its scope and encourages submissions from any relevant discipline. It encompasses the full range of theoretical, methodological and substantive debates in the area of social responsibility, and encourages contributions which address the link between different disciplines and/or implications for societal, organizational or individual behavior.

Society and Business Review
Emerald
60/62 Toller Lane, Bradford, West Yorkshire, BD8 9BY, UK
T: +44 (0) 1274 777 700
F: +44 (0) 1274 785 200
www.emeraldinsight.com/1746-5680.htm
ISSN: 1746-5680
Society and Business Review aims to cultivate and share knowledge and ideas in

order to assist businesses to enhance their commitment to society. Being international in outlook and interdisciplinary in scope, the journal seeks to provide a platform for diverse academic and practitioner communities to debate a broad spectrum of social issues and disciplinary perspectives.

INTERNET

Business Ethics

www.business-ethics.com

The online counterpart to *Business Ethics* magazine, the site offers articles, news, an events calendar, a marketplace, and a free e-mail newsletter.

Business for Social Responsibility

www.bsr.org

Sponsored by a membership organization, the site offers news, articles, a membership directory, conference and events information, and job listings.

Community Action Network

www.can-online.org.uk

This site gives access to a mutual learning and support network for social entrepreneurs.

The Corporate Social Responsibility Newswire

www.csrwire.com

This content-rich site bills itself as "the leading source of corporate responsibility and sustainability, press releases, reports, and news." It features CSR press releases, reports, an events calendar, useful resources (including an organization directory), and book recommendations.

Do-It

www.do-it.org.uk

This is a national database of voluntary work opportunities for both companies and individuals.

Ethical Corporation

www.ethicalcorp.com

Ethical Corporation is an independent media firm, launched in 2001 to encourage debate and discussion on responsible business. Ethical Corporation publishes a 60-page print magazine, a daily website, and hosts business ethics conferences all over the world.

ORGANIZATIONS

Europe

AccountAbility

250–252 Goswell Road, London, EC1V 7EB, UK
T: +44 (0) 20 7549 0400
F: +44 (0) 20 7253 7440
E: secretariat@accountability.org.uk
www.accountability21.net

Founded in 1996 as an international membership organization with the aim of improving the accountability and performance of organizations worldwide, AccountAbility (full name: the Institute of Social and Ethical Accountability) promotes best practice and ethical accounting, auditing, and reporting, and develops standards and certification for professionals in the field.

Corporate Social Responsibility (CSR) Europe

78–80 rue Defacqz, Brussels, B-1050, Belgium
T: +32 2 502 83 54
F: +32 2 502 84 58
E: info@csreurope.org
www.csreurope.org

CSR Europe helps companies achieve profitability, sustainable growth, and human progress by placing corporate social responsibility in the mainstream of business practice. It provides printed and online publications, best practices and tools, learning, benchmarking, and tailored capacity building programs.

The Prince of Wales International Business Leaders Forum (IBLF)

15–16 Cornwall Terrace, Regent's Park, London, NW1 4QP, UK
T: +44 (0) 20 7467 3600
F: +44 (0) 20 7467 3610
E: info@iblf.org
www.iblf.org

This nonprofit membership organization was established in 1990 by HRH The Prince of Wales and a group of CEOs from international companies to promote corporate social responsibility (CSR). CSR business practices are based on ethical values to help achieve socially, economically, and environmentally sustainable development.

USA

Center for Corporate Citizenship at Boston College

Wallace E. Carroll School of Management, 55 Lee Road, Chestnut Hill, MA 02467–3942, USA
T: +1 617 552 4545
F: +1 617 552 8499
E: ccc@bc.edu
www.bcccc.net

This membership organization was founded in 1985 to establish corporate citizenship as a business essential. It offers executive education, particularly the certificate program in community relations. It arranges conferences, meetings, and discussions, encourages research, oversees the standards of excellence and their companion diagnostic tools, and provides consulting services.

BRIC

Business and Social Development Institute Foundation (FIDES)

R. Santanésia, 528 – 1º ss., São Paulo, Brazil
T: +55 3726 3373
F: +55 3843 3770
E: fides@fides.org.br
www.fides.org.br

FIDES is a private, non-profit, cultural, and educational Brazilian organization dedicated to the humanization of business enterprises and to their integration with society.

Center for Business Ethics and Corporate Governance

Office 22, 2, Shvedsky pereulok, St. Petersburg, 191186, Russia
T: +7 812 324 6706
F: +7 812 327 3125
E: info@cfbe.ru
www.ethicsrussia.org

The mission of the Center for Business Ethics and Corporate Governance is to create social capital in the Russian Federation, the Independent States, and Eastern Europe by helping to institutionalize ethical and transparent business practices.

Centre for Social Markets (CSM)

3/5 Rani Jhansi Road, New Delhi, 110 055, India
T: +91 11 2352 6000
E: info@csmworld.org
www.csmworld.org

CSM promotes social, economic, political, and institutional transformation for the public interest. It is an independent, non-profit organization dedicated to making markets work for people, the planet, and for profit.

Chinese Federation for Corporate Social Responsibility

Room 801, Recourse Plaza, No.151 Zhongguancun North Street, Haidian District, Beijing, 10080, China
T: +86 10 5887 6801
F: +86 10 5887 6122
E: cfcsr@126.com
www.cfcsr.org/shehuien/index.asp

This federation aims promote the spirit and advance the development of corporate social responsibility in China.

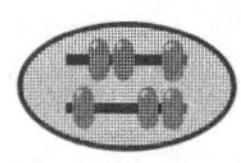

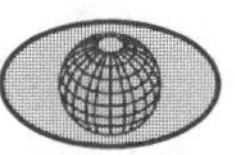

Structured Finance

BOOKS

The Analysis of Structured Securities: Precise Risk Measurement and Capital Allocation

Sylvain Raynes, Ann Rutledge
Oxford, UK: Oxford University Press, 2003
449pp, ISBN: 978-0-19-515273-9

This is a technical assessment of this expanding part of the capital markets, for practitioners looking for greater precision, efficiency, and control in managing their structured exposures. It analyzes the credit quality of structured securities, the methods used to rate asset-backed securities, collateralized debt obligations, and asset-backed commercial paper, and offers guidance on using numerical methods in cash flow modeling.

Collateralized Debt Obligations and Structured Finance: New Developments in Cash and Synthetic Securitization

Janet Tavakoli
Wiley Finance Series
Hoboken, New Jersey: Wiley, 2003
338pp, ISBN: 978-0-471-46220-0

This provides an overview of the fast-growing CDO and structured credit products market. It examines new securitization topics, such as the increase in the CDO arbitrage created by synthetics, dumping securitizations on bank balance sheets, the abuse of offshore vehicles by companies such as Enron, and securitizations made possible by new securitization techniques and the introduction of the euro.

Credit Derivatives: CDOs and Structured Credit Products, 3rd ed

Satyajit Das
Wiley Finance Series
Singapore: Wiley, 2005
800pp, ISBN: 978-0-470-82159-6

This is a comprehensive reference on credit derivative products, applications, pricing and valuation approaches, and documentation, accounting, and taxation issues. It looks in detail at the collateralized debt obligations market, presents detailed examples of applications of credit derivatives by different market participants, and discusses trading, market structures, and the regulatory framework for credit derivatives.

A Fast Track to Structured Finance Modeling, Monitoring and Valuation: Jump Start VBA

William Preinitz
Wiley Finance Series
Hoboken, New Jersey: Wiley, 2009
768pp, ISBN: 978-0-470-39812-8

This is a new, technical treatment of structured finance, which focuses on implementing simple tasks into VBA code. It helps develop the skills in an accessible way, breaking complex tasks down into simple tasks, and covers all the key issues involved, such as designing the VBA model, the VBA language, controlling the model flow, building message capabilities, and writing the main program.

FX Options and Structured Products

Uwe Wystup
Wiley Finance Series
Chichester, UK: Wiley, 2006
323pp, ISBN: 978-0-470-01145-4

This is a technical guide to the nature, risks, applications, and strategies of the main FX options and structured products. It explains how they can be used for cost savings, risk controls, and yield enhancements, and provides a grounding in the quantitative fundamentals, the basics of FX products, principles, and concepts, and a structuring view and client perspective.

The Handbook of Structured Finance

Arnaud de Servigny, Norbert Jobst (editors)
New York: McGraw-Hill, 2007
785pp, ISBN: 978-0-07-146864-0

This provides a comprehensive guide to the key issues facing investors in the structured finance market. It describes new models for identifying, measuring, pricing, and monitoring deals, and how to take advantage of leverage and market incompleteness, as well as models for debt and equity modeling.

Introduction to Structured Finance

Frank J. Fabozzi, Henry A. Davis, Moorad Choudhry
Frank J. Fabozzi Series
Hoboken, New Jersey: Wiley, 2006
385pp, ISBN: 978-0-470-04535-0

This book examines the fundamentals of structured finance, and the growing role it plays in the financial markets. It also acts as a comprehensive guide to securitization, interest rate derivatives, credit derivatives, securitized and synthetic funding structures, cash and synthetic collateralized debt obligations, credit-linked notes and structured notes, complex leasing transactions, and project financing.

Modeling Structured Finance Cash Flows with Microsoft Excel: A Step-by-Step Guide

Keith A. Allman
Wiley Finance Series
Hoboken, New Jersey: Wiley, 2007
199pp, ISBN: 978-0-470-04290-8

This book provides a guide to building a cash flow model for structured finance and securitization deals. It outlines individual functions and formulas, as well as the theory behind the spreadsheets, for practical applications of the model. It can be used as a resource for training new analysts, or help experienced cash flow modelers with their analysis of structured finance transactions.

Mortgage-Backed Securities: Products, Structuring, and Analytical Techniques

Frank J. Fabozzi, Anand K. Bhattacharya, William S. Berliner
Frank J. Fabozzi Series
Hoboken, New Jersey: Wiley, 2007
318pp, ISBN: 978-0-470-04773-6

This book provides a comprehensive introduction to the products, structures, and analytical techniques that have made such an impact on the fixed income market. Aimed primarily at investors and traders, it offers a guide to the investment characteristics, creation, and analysis of residential real estate-backed securities, and describes the methodologies and techniques used to value MBS products and assess interest-rate risk.

The Structured Credit Handbook

Arvind Rajan, Glen McDermott, Ratul Roy
Wiley Finance Series
Hoboken, New Jersey: Wiley, 2007
496pp, ISBN: 978-0-471-74749-9

This is a comprehensive introduction to all types of credit-linked financial instruments, such as collateralized debt obligations, collateralized loan obligations, credit derivatives such as credit default swaps and swaptions, and iBoxx indexes. It provides a solid grounding in the investment rationale, risks, and rewards associated with structured credit investments, with little financial jargon or mathematical complexity

  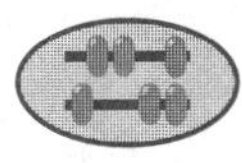 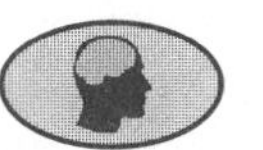  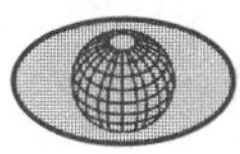   

Structured Credit Portfolio Analysis, Baskets and CDOs
Christian Bluhm, Ludger Overbeck
Chapman & Hall/CRC Financial Mathematics Series
Boca Raton, Florida: Chapman & Hall/CRC, 2007
357pp, ISBN: 978-1-58488-647-1
This is a guide to the concepts and techniques for evaluating structured credit products, and presents a review of the basic concepts of credit risk modeling. It also addresses in detail more advanced topics such as the modeling and evaluation of basket products, credit-linked notes, collateralized debt obligations, and index tranches. It is aimed at practitioners who apply mathematical concepts to structured credit products.

Structured Finance and Insurance: The ART of Managing Capital and Risk, 2nd ed
Chistopher L. Culp
Wiley Finance Series
Hoboken, New Jersey: Wiley, 2006
892pp, ISBN: 978-0-471-70631-1
This presents a comprehensive introduction to key financing and risk management innovations in both the alternative insurance and capital markets. It explores the economic and practical benefits of this new generation of products and solutions for managing market, credit, operational, legal, and other risks, and attempts to integrate these solutions and products into a unified theory of financial markets.

Structured Finance: Techniques, Products and Market
Stefano Caselli, Stefano Gatti
Springer Finance Series
Berlin: Springer, 2005
206pp, ISBN: 978-3-540-25311-2
This analyzes the characteristics of structured finance deals, such as asset-backed securitization, project finance, structured leasing and leveraged acquisitions, and discusses the state of the international financial markets for these operations. It explains new ways of financing deals based on the capacity of the operations to generate sufficient cash for the repayment of loans or bonds, and compares it to more traditional sources of funding.

Structured Finance: The Object Oriented Approach
Umberto Cherubini, Giovanni Della Lunga
Wiley Finance Series
Chichester, UK: Wiley, 2007
288pp, ISBN: 978-0-470-02638-0
This explores structured finance issues relevant to the structured finance business, for both finance professionals engaged in building, pricing and hedging products, and IT professionals engaged in designing and updating the corresponding software. It strives to share common concepts and definition within the industry, and overcome the problems of communication between these different professional functions.

Structured Products and Related Credit Derivatives: A Comprehensive Guide for Investors
Brian P. Lancaster, Glenn M. Schultz, Frank J. Fabozzi
Frank J. Fabozzi Series
Hoboken, New Jersey: Wiley, 2008
523pp, ISBN: 978-0-470-12985-2
This examines the fundamentals of structured assets and credit derivatives, describing the opportunities and risks involved in this complex financial market. It examines various consumer asset-backed securities, offers an insight on collateralized debt obligations, analyzes structured finance operating companies, and the commercial real estate sector, including ABS issues such as aircraft securitization, intermodal equipment, and life insurance reserve securitization.

Structured Products in Wealth Management
Steffen Tolle, Boris Hutter, Patrik Rüthemann, Hanspeter Wohlwend
Wiley Finance Series
Singapore: Wiley, 2008
226pp, ISBN: 978-0-470-82330-9
This describes the range of structured products in the market, as well as their characteristics and practical applications. It shows how they can be incorporated to strategically optimize an investment portfolio, explains the use of derivatives and structured products in wealth management, and is aimed at retail private investors, wealth managers, client relationship managers, and advisors.

Synthetic and Structured Assets
Erik Banks
Wiley Finance Series
Chichester, UK: Wiley, 2006
266pp, ISBN: 978-0-470-01713-5
This book analyzes many of the original classes of structured assets, including mortgage- and asset-backed securities and strips, as well as structured and synthetic instruments such as exchange-traded funds, collateralized debt obligations, and insurance-linked securities. It outlines the scope of the market, key definitions, and the financial building blocks used to create synthetic and structured assets, and reviews their risk, legal, regulatory, and accounting features.

A Wealth Manager's Guide to Structured Products
Robert Benson (editor)
London: Risk Books, 2004
257pp, ISBN: 978-1-904339-32-8
This is a comprehensive analysis of the challenges and issues that wealth managers face when using structured products into their investment strategies. It discusses the relevance of structured products for portfolio construction and risk management, the use of credit derivatives, and how the structure of products can create capital guarantees, and includes coverage of hedge funds.

MAGAZINES

SRP Magazine
Arete Consulting
12 Broadbent Close, 20–22 Highgate High Street, London, N6 5JL, UK
T: +44 (0) 20 8347 0203
F: +44 (0) 20 8347 7872
www.srpmagazine.com
This is a monthly electronic magazine for structured products professionals, which has access to a database of nearly one million products and a dedicated global news service.

Structured Products
Incisive Media
Haymarket House, 28–29 Haymarket, London, SW1Y 4RX, UK
T: +44 (0) 20 7484 9700
F: +44 (0) 20 7484 9932
www.structuredproductsonline.com
ISSN: 1745-4611
This monthly magazine on structured products provides news, features, regulatory updates, commentaries, profiles of leading companies, and analysis of new structured investment products. It covers the market for guaranteed investment products, structured notes, index products, alternative investments and funds of funds, and also produces a series of conferences and training courses.

JOURNALS

Journal of Structured Finance
Institutional Investor Journals
225 Park Avenue South, 8th Floor, New York, NY 10003, USA
T: +1 212 224 3570
F: +1 212 224 3197
www.iijournals.com/JPF
ISSN: 1082-3220

  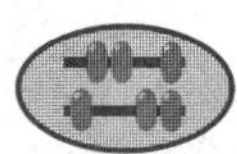   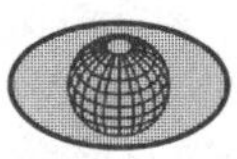   

This quarterly journal offers research and commentary on all aspects of structured finance, with a detailed analysis of structuring and investing in products such as ABSs, MBSs, CDOs, CLOs, and life settlements. It focuses on a range of real-life securitization deals and their investment implications to provide a strategic understanding of the products, applications, and market.

INTERNET

Securitization.net
www.securitization.net
This resource for the structured finance industry provides news and information from industry organizations on all aspects of securitization. It offers free email updates, links to articles and commentaries, notification of upcoming industry events, and details of relevant accounting, banking, legal, regulatory issues.

SRPAdviser.com
www.srpadviser.com
This website is aimed at financial advisers in the structured products market. It provides access to a large database of structured retail products, and features a search function for product offerings, downloadable product literature, filters, score charts, and enables the tracking of closing offers and maturing products.

Structured Retail Products
www.structuredretailproducts.com
This website focuses on the structured products market, and features a news service, analysis and research reports, portfolio, product scoring and pricing tools, and downloadable product literature. It also provides access to a large database of structured retail investment products covering the major European markets, the Americas, and the Asia-Pacific markets.

StructuredFinanceNews.com
www.structuredfinancenews.com
This online industry resource provides news and commentary on topics such as asset-backed securities, covered bonds, mortgage-backed securities, and derivatives, and offers an extensive news archive and a proprietary people database for information on the industry's top players. It also features an Asset Securitization Report and Scorecards Database.

Total Securitization
www.totalsecuritization.com
This is a news service for the global securitization markets, which provides current news and analysis, as well as aggregated stories from other sources, on significant issues in the ABS, MBS, CMBS and CDOs markets.

ORGANIZATIONS

USA

The Structured Products Association
Chair: Keith Styrcula
USA
E: keith.styrcula@structuredproducts.org
www.structuredproducts.org
The SPA is a trade group whose mission is to position structured products as a distinct asset class, promote financial innovation among member firms, develop best practices for members and their firms, and identify legal, tax, compliance and regulatory challenges to the business. Its membership comes from exchanges, self-regulatory bodies, the legal compliance community, investor networks, and both buy-side and sell-side structured product firms.

  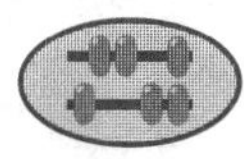   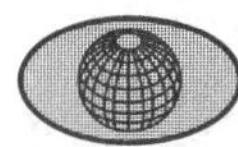   

Technical Analysis

BOOKS

The ART of Trading: Combining the Science of Technical Analysis with the Art of Reality-Based Trading

Bennet A. McDowell
Wiley Trading Series
Hoboken, New Jersey: Wiley, 2008
296pp, ISBN: 978-0-470-18772-2

This is a comprehensive introduction to technical analysis, money management, risk control, paper trading, and the psychology of trading, based on the author's own reality-based trading system. It details its benefits, use for executing trade entries and exits, identifying market direction, and ensuring consistent profits, and shows how to use price and volume to minimize distortions in financial decision-making, and select the best financial market timeframe.

Breakthroughs in Technical Analysis: New Thinking from the World's Top Minds

David Keller (editor)
New York: Bloomberg Press, 2007
227pp, ISBN: 978-1-57660-242-3

This exploration of new trends and developments in technical analysis by leading industry experts describes a number of new methods in trading. It examines their techniques and strategies, and covers key topics such as charting with candles and clouds, candlesticks, options-based technical analysis, indicators for stock trading, point-and-figure charting, deconstructing the market, and the application of market profile to global spreads.

Evidence-Based Technical Analysis: Applying the Scientific Method and Statistical Inference to Trading Signals

David R. Aronson
Hoboken, New Jersey: Wiley, 2007
544pp, ISBN: 978-0-470-00874-4

This is a focused treatment of the methodological, philosophical, and statistical foundations of evidenced-based technical analysis (EBTA), examining methods for its application, statistical tests, and the effectiveness of the data mining for evaluating technical trading signals. It shows how EBTA is based on objective rules, quantification, scrutiny, and statistical inference, and discusses the problems with interpretative methodologies, and the Efficient Market Hypothesis.

Fibonacci Analysis

Constance Brown
Bloomberg Market Essentials Series: Technical Analysis
New York: Bloomberg Press, 2008
182pp, ISBN: 978-1-57660-261-4

This is a practical overview and reference on Fibonacci analysis, and which also covers the basics of the most popular technical analysis tools. It describes trend and counter-trend movements within markets to identify the future market price, and explains how to use this analytical technique properly to achieve a higher probability of trading success.

Getting Started in Technical Analysis

Jack D. Schwager
Getting Started in Series
New York: Wiley, 1999
339pp, ISBN: 978-0-471-29542-6

This respected primer on technical analysis provides a framework for analyzing price activity to better understand market behavior and identify trading opportunities. It demystifies the subject for new investors, and details the essentials of trends such as trading ranges, types of charts, chart patterns, trading systems, charting and analysis software, the planned trading approach, with the assistance of numerous examples and explanations.

The Heretics of Finance: Conversations with the Leading Practitioners of Technical Analysis

Andrew W. Lo, Jasmina Hasanhodzic
New York: Bloomberg Press, 2009
464pp, ISBN: 978-1-57660-316-1

This is a series of extended interviews with pioneers and experts in technical analysis discuss the influence of creativity, emotion, and intuition in their work, as well as offering insights into the patterns, strategies, and applications that contributed to their success. Produced by a leading expert academic, it explains the rationale behind the rise of technical analysis as a methodology among traders and investors.

Japanese Candlestick Charting Techniques: A Contemporary Guide to the Ancient Investment, 2nd ed

Steve Nison
Paramus, New Jersey: Prentice Hall, 2001
320pp, ISBN: 978-0-7352-0181-1

This guide to Japanese candlestick charts examines their role as a technical analysis methodology that can be integrated with other tools to improve market analysis. It takes a comprehensive approach to its range of applications, and describes how they can also be used for speculation and hedging, for futures, and equities, or as a stand-alone charting method with uses in almost any market.

New Thinking in Technical Analysis: Trading Models from the Masters

Rick Bensignor (editor)
Bloomberg Professional Library Series
Princeton, New Jersey: Bloomberg Press, 2000
287pp, ISBN: 978-1-57660-049-8

This shows how to use technical analysis for predicting the price behavior of a stock, commodity, or any financial instrument, and offers advice on how create an effective trading strategy using its models based on tips from market experts. It also presents a number of tools for improving investment performance, and describes the importance of market timing for traders seeking to gain a competitive edge.

Technical Analysis Explained: The Successful Investor's Guide to Spotting Investment Trends and Turning Points, 4th ed

Martin J. Pring
New York: McGraw-Hill Professional, 2002
641pp, ISBN: 978-0-07-138193-2

This is a guidebook to understanding and implementing the tools of technical analysis, explaining the methods for improving trading and investing profits by understanding, interpreting, and forecasting movements in markets and individual stocks. It describes how individual investors can forecast price movements with the same accuracy as professionals, and presents a program for incorporating technical analysis into an overall trading strategy.

Technical Analysis for the Trading Professional: Strategies and Techniques for Superior Returns

Constance Brown
McGraw-Hill Trader's Edge Series
New York: McGraw-Hill Professional, 1999
341pp, ISBN: 978-0-07-012062-4

This guide for professional traders examines new uses of key market indicators and techniques, combinations of indicators and formulas, and techniques for combining indicators with other indicators. It also focuses on specific formulas and chart applications to improve market timing, detection of false signals, and new uses of oscillators. The formulas and

 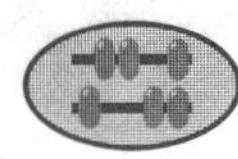 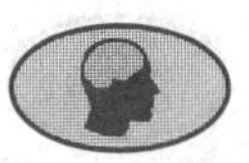  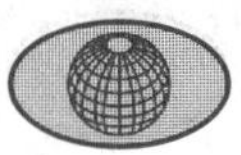   

combinations of indicators can be applied across different markets and different time frames.

Technical Analysis from A to Z, 2nd ed
Steven B. Achelis
New York: McGraw-Hill Professional, 2001
380pp, ISBN: 978-0-07-136348-8
This is a concise directory of technical analysis that presents and analyzes the vast array of technical tools and techniques available. It also serves as a comprehensive reference of current technical analysis indicators used in trading in stocks, bonds, futures, and options.

Technical Analysis of Stock Trends, 9th ed
Robert D. Edwards, John Magee, W. H. C. Bassetti
Boca Raton, Florida: CRC Press, 2007
789pp, ISBN: 978-0-8493-3772-7
This guide to stock trends presents a methodology for interpreting the behavior of investors and markets for traders and investors wanting to achieve success regardless of type of market. It offers a practical overview and reference to technical investment approaches, from the basics to less well-known chart patterns, and presents simple indicators that can be easily applied to intraday movements.

Technical Analysis of the Financial Markets: A Comprehensive Guide to Trading Methods and Applications, 2nd ed
John J. Murphy
New York Institute of Finance Series
New York: NYIF, 1998
576pp, ISBN: 978-0-7352-0066-1
This is an updated version of the classic guide to technical analysis and its application to the financial markets. It describes the fundamentals, underlying concepts, and key techniques, recent techniques in charts and charting, how to understand indicators, and the role of technical analysis in investing, as well as price patterns, methods of analysis, Elliot Wave theory, and candlestick charting.

Technical Analysis Plain and Simple: Charting the Markets in Your Language, 2nd ed
Michael N. Kahn
Harlow, UK: FT Prentice Hall, 2006
309pp, ISBN: 978-0-13-134597-3
This concise guide to technical analysis presents a general overview of theory and practice, the core concepts of chart analysis and the various aspects of the investment process, as well as more advanced topics such as candlesticks, cycles, and Elliot waves. It also shows how to read charts, follow the market effectively, understand trendlines, and corrections, and assess potential risk and reward.

Technical Analysis: The Complete Resource for Financial Market Technicians
Charles D. Kirkpatrick, Julie R. Dahlquist
Upper Saddle River, New Jersey: FT Prentice Hall, 2007
672pp, ISBN: 978-0-13-153113-0
This comprehensive reference explains technical analysis theory, and the analysis of markets and individual issues, and presents a complete investment system and portfolio management plan. It describes how to use it for identifying trading opportunities, to test sentiment, momentum indicators, seasonal affects, flow of funds, risk mitigation, and many other techniques. It also analyzes which chart patterns and indicators have been most reliable.

Technical Analysis Tools: Creating a Profitable Trading System
Mark Tinghino
New York: Bloomberg Press, 2008
295pp, ISBN: 978-1-57660-248-5
This practical guide examines how the assessment of price and volume factors to predict future price movements can be used for effective trading, and provides an assessment of the most common analytical tools available. It details the strength and weakness of each tool, which works best in which type of market, and how to integrate them into an effective trading system.

MAGAZINES

Technical Analysis of Stocks & Commodities
Technical Analysis
4757 California Avenue SW, Seattle, WA 98116-4499, USA
T: +1 206 938 0570
www.traders.com
ISSN: 0738-3355
This monthly magazine provides traders with information on how to apply charting, numerical, and computer trading methods to trade stocks, bonds, mutual funds, options, forex and futures, and examines both old and new trading methods, techniques and products.

The Technical Analyst
Global Markets Media
Jeffries House, 1–5 Jeffries Passage, Guildford, GU1 4AP, UK
T: +44 (0) 1483 573 150
www.technicalanalyst.co.uk
ISSN: 1742-8718
This quarterly magazine is devoted to technical analysis for trading and investment professionals. It offers news, features, and commentary from industry players, and presents technical trading ideas to the global markets, supported by regular events, conferences, and training courses for institutional traders, fund managers and hedge funds.

JOURNALS

The STA Market Technician
Society of Technical Analysts
Dean House, Vernham Dean, Hampshire, SP11 0JZ, UK
T: +44 (0) 20 7870 5950
F: +44 (0) 20 7900 2585
www.sta-uk.org/sta_journal.htm
This journal is published three times each year by the Society of Technical Analysts. It offers articles by expert members and guest writers on technical analysis, charting methods, book and software reviews, as well as speaker notes from some of their monthly meetings.

INTERNET

BarChart
www.barchart.com
This free resource offers a comprehensive selection of industry analysis on commodities, equities, delayed data, quotes, charts, technical analysis, and Internet applications. It also provides introductory trading newsletters, custom web content solutions, real-time charting applications, as well as access to futures prices, charts, and real-time quotes.

ChartFilter
www.chartfilter.com
This online resource for technical analysis provides a number of useful features for professional trades, such as information on technical indicators, financial content and articles, stock screeners, newsletters, e-books, educational material, and a glossary.

StockTA.com
www.stockta.com
This is a free technical analysis and stock screener website, which focuses on teaching and utilizing stock technical analysis to help optimize stock trades. It presents automated technical stock and mutual fund analysis, delayed charts, Fibonacci numbers, stock opinions, and stock profiles, as well as featuring analysis, picks, charts, a watch list, forum, book store, and educational material.

Traders Log
www.traderslog.com
The technical analysis section of this useful trading website offers detailed articles, forums, reviews, brokers, charts, newsletters, as well as featuring technical indicators, Fibonacci, trading pairs, trendlines, stochastics, and Japanese candlesticks.

ORGANIZATIONS

Europe

Society of Technical Analysts
Chair: Deborah Owen
Dean House, Vernham Dean, Hampshire, SP11 0JZ, UK
T: +44 (0) 20 7870 5950
F: +44 (0) 20 7900 2585
E: info@sta-uk.org
www.sta-uk.org
The aims of the STA are to promote greater use and understanding of technical analysis as an investment tool, and serve all members of the investment community. It provides information on education, exams and professional qualifications, meetings, reference sources, useful links, recruitment links, and charts.

USA

American Association of Professional Technical Analysts
Chair: Peter Mauthe
USA
E: membership@aapta.com
www.aapta.com
AAPTA provides a forum for its members to share research and resources, exchange ideas on technical analysis and the markets, and facilitate professionalism in the industry. It allows professional technicians to engage in networking through online forums, an annual conference, and one-day brainstorming meetings. Its members include money managers, analysts, advisors, and traders.

Association for Technical Analysis
Chair: Marv Slater
PO Box 802504, Dallas, Texas 75380-2504, USA
www.afta-dfw.com
This is an active, non-profit volunteer organization aimed at providing education, fellowship, and community to traders and investors focused on technical and investment analysis.

Market Technicians Association
Chair: Larry Berman
61 Broadway, Suite 514, New York, NY 10006, USA
T: +1 646 652 3300
F: +1 646 652 3322
www.mta.org
MTA is a global professional association devoted to those practicing technical analysis. Its CMT program and qualification is one of the industry's standards in technical analysis.

Technical Securities Analysts Association
Chair: Hank Pruden
5 Third Street, Suite 724, San Francisco, CA 94103, USA
T: +1 415 543 2111
F: +1 415 543 2112
E: staff@tsaasf.org
www.tsaasf.org
This is a non-profit, independent association committed to fellowship and development in professional technical analysis and the markets. It encourages and supports its members, providing a forum for the exchange of ideas and methodologies, leadership opportunities, and educational resources, and offers regular meetings, an annual conference, and a newsletter three times a year on topics of current interest.

BRIC

The Association of Technical Analysts
Chair: Sudarshan Sukhani
103, Chiranjeev Towers, 43 Nehru Place, New Delhi 110019, Delhi, India
T: +91 11 2646 6090
E: india1.ta@gmail.com
www.taindia.org
ATA is a trade association in India for professionals working in the technical analysis of the stock and futures markets. It promotes the art and science of technical analysis for decision making in trading and investing in stocks, futures, currencies, commodities, interest rate futures and more, and provides regular interaction for education and application of technical analysis in the real world.

International

International Federation of Technical Analysts
Chair: Elaine Knuth
9707 Key West Avenue, Suite 100, Rockville, MD 20850, USA
T: +1 240 404 6508
F: +1 301 990 9771
E: admin@ifta.org
www.ifta.org
IFTA is a non-profit affiliation of individual country societies dedicated to research, education, and dissemination of technical analysis of world markets. It supports the sharing of technical analytical methodology, high standards of professional conduct, international cooperation and scholarship, the exchange of information and data, and the standardization of education and testing.

  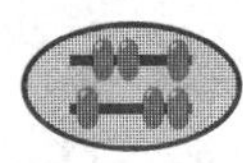   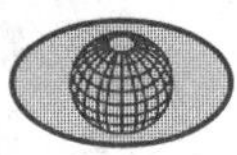   

Trading

BOOKS

Adventures of a Currency Trader: A Fable about Trading, Courage, and Doing the Right Thing

Rob Booker
Wiley Trading Series
Hoboken, New Jersey: Wiley, 2007
221pp, ISBN: 978-0-470-04948-8

An entertaining and educational guide to successful currency trading, told through the story of a fictional trader, Harry Banes. It tells of his start in the foreign currency market, learning how to trade, finding the best trading approach, avoiding the most common trading mistakes, and demonstrating in a readable way the strategies and pitfalls of currency trading.

Come into My Trading Room: A Complete Guide to Trading

Alexander Elder
Wiley Trading Series
New York: Wiley, 2002
320pp, ISBN: 978-0-471-22534-8

Practical advice on trading essentials, which outlines trading psychology, technical analysis, how to keep records and organize your time, with guidance on risk control and money management. It presents the author's own successful trading strategies, following him through several real trades, and giving an understanding of trading stocks, futures, options, and currencies.

The Disciplined Trader: Developing Winning Attitudes

Mark Douglas
New York Institute of Finance Series
New York: Prentice Hall, 1990
256pp, ISBN: 978-0-13-215757-5

This is an examination of the dynamics of trading psychology, which looks at how to analyze and limit your trading behavior, and develop the right mental approach. It argues that behavior in real life does not translate well into trading, and presents a series of insights into discipline, responsibility, and self-esteem, and the effect attitude has on potential trading success.

Exotic Options Trading

Frans de Weert
Wiley Finance Series
Chichester, UK: Wiley, 2008
188pp, ISBN: 978-0-470-51790-1

This is a practical assessment of the full range of exotic options available to the professional trader. It provides the skills for pricing and trading these complex products, and analyses the associated risks in terms of the economics and Greeks involved. It keeps the use of mathematics down to the essential pricing formulae, and explains key concepts in simple terms.

Fibonacci Trading: How to Master the Time and Price Advantage

Carolyn Boroden
New York: McGraw-Hill Professional, 2008
303pp, ISBN: 978-0-07-149815-9

A specialized book on Fibonacci trading and analyzing different patterns within the market. It explains how to identify numeric clusters and measure timing signals, to maximize profits and limit losses, using real-world trading situations. It helps a trader predict turning points in advance, improve stop–loss placement, and better identify critical support and resistance levels.

High Probability Trading Strategies: Entry to Exit Tactics for the Forex, Futures, and Stock Markets

Robert C. Miner
Wiley Trading Series
Hoboken, New Jersey: Wiley, 2009
272pp, ISBN: 978-0-470-18166-9

Shows how to recognize and profit from high-probability trading opportunities, analyze market behavior, and build a trading plan, based on four key factors that improve high-probability trade decisions. It also explains the best way to execute and managing the trades, and take them through to completion.

An Introduction to Options Trading

Frans de Weert
Securities Institute Series
Chichester, UK: Wiley, 2006
157pp, ISBN: 978-0-470-02970-1

This is a primer on options trading that presents the theory and practice of options from first principles, and provides the tools to trade options effectively. It analyzes where the profit of option traders actually comes from, the use of option structures, the hedging of options, and includes simple mathematical formulae to aid understanding, and a glossary of common terms.

Market Wizards: Interviews with Top Traders

Jack D. Schwager
Columbia, Maryland: Marketplace Books, 2008
512pp, ISBN: 978-1-59280-337-8

A series of interviews with some of the most successful traders in market history. It delves into their trading strategies, their different perspectives, and the mental approach they take to trading, and provides an insight into what it takes to become a great trader in a variety of markets.

Mastering the Trade: Proven Techniques for Profiting from Intraday and Swing Trading Setups

John F. Carter
McGraw-Hill Trader's Edge Series
New York: McGraw-Hill Professional, 2006
406pp, ISBN: 978-0-07-145958-7

Presents a practical approach to trading, focused on understanding the intricacies of the market and applying this knowledge to trading strategies and concepts. It provides chart setups, trading methodologies, money management principles, psychological guidelines, and advice on trading systems, and examines the underlying reasons price movements.

New Trading Systems and Methods, 4th ed

Perry J. Kaufman
Wiley Trading Series
Hoboken, New Jersey: Wiley, 2005
1,174pp, ISBN: 978-0-471-26847-5

Now in its 4th edition, this bestseller provides a guide to technical trading strategies and techniques, as well as information on the latest indicators, programs, spreadsheets, charts, algorithms, and systems, for choosing the right trading program. It also analyzes how much data to use, the key techniques of identifying the trend and momentum, and contains extensive risk analysis.

Quantitative Trading: How to Build Your Own Algorithmic Trading Business

Ernest P. Chan
Wiley Trading Series
Hoboken, New Jersey: Wiley, 2009
182pp, ISBN: 978-0-470-28488-9

A new guide to understanding and implementing algorithmic trading techniques—once the sole preserve of elite traders—as part of a quantitative trading strategy. It explains how to use specialized software to build algorithmic trading tools that are suited to individual needs, how to conduct quantitative research and analysis, and how to implement this highly effective approach.

  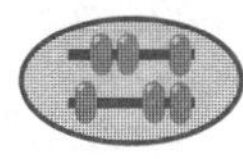 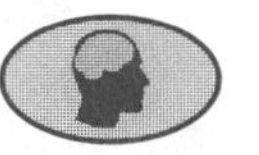  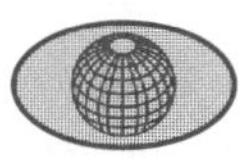   

Traders, Guns and Money: Knowns and Unknowns in the Dazzling World of Derivatives
Satyajit Das
Harlow, UK: FT Prentice Hall, 2006
334pp, ISBN: 978-0-273-70474-4
Recounts the author's career in financial derivatives, describing how derivatives originated, how they are used, their benefits, their dangers, and their impact on the financial markets. It is an insider's exposé of derivatives trading, which uncovers the theft, misrepresentation, and lies that can occur, written in a readable style.

Trading and Exchanges: Market Microstructure for Practitioners
Larry Harris
Financial Management Association Survey & Synthesis Series
Oxford, UK: Oxford University Press, 2003
643pp, ISBN: 978-0-19-514470-3
This is an overview of trading, those who trade securities and contracts, the marketplace, and the rules that govern trading operations. It examines the players such as investors, brokers, dealers, arbitrageurs, and retail traders, the different types of exchange, and looks in detail at the variety of trades, auctions, and orders available.

Trading Commodities and Financial Futures: A Step-by-Step Guide to Mastering the Markets, 3rd ed
George Kleinman
Boston: FT Prentice Hall, 2005
288pp, ISBN: 978-0-13-147654-7
Presenting a trading methodology based on the author's long experience in the markets, it assesses the fundamentals of trading commodities and futures, and offers a primer on how futures and options trading works. It also shows how traders' psychology can impact the markets, how to avoid common mistakes, and examines electronic trading, contracts, and trading techniques.

Trading for a Living: Psychology, Trading Tactics, Money Management
Alexander Elder
Wiley Finance Series
New York: Wiley, 1993
289pp, ISBN: 978-0-471-59224-2
Elder's classic book, which presents his successful trading strategy based on the three M's: mind, method, and money. It emphasizes the importance of developing discipline and avoiding emotional trading, of using analytic techniques in a trading system, and how to effectively manage money in your trading account, and shows how to trade using charts, computerized indicators, and other tools.

Trend Following: How Great Traders Make Millions in Up or Down Markets, 2nd ed
Michael W. Covel
Upper Saddle River, New Jersey: FT Prentice Hall, 2006
420pp, ISBN: 978-0-13-613718-4
An examination of the technique of following patterns and trends in the markets to create improved trading returns. Based on a tested and successful trading strategy, it presents practical guidance on applying trend following in a portfolio, and real results from leading trend followers, as well as understandable charts to aid learning.

Volatility Trading
Euan Sinclair
Wiley Trading Series
Hoboken, New Jersey: Wiley, 2008
212pp, ISBN: 978-0-470-18199-7
Offers practical guidance on the basics of option pricing, volatility measurement, hedging, money management, and trade evaluation, and presents a quantitative model for measuring volatility. It discusses the psychological aspects of trading, and emphasizes the importance of identifying and evaluating the price of implied volatility, and finding trades with a distinct statistical edge.

Way of the Turtle: The Secret Methods that Turned Ordinary People into Legendary Traders
Curtis M. Faith
New York: McGraw-Hill Professional, 2007
286pp, ISBN: 978-0-07-148664-4
The author was the youngest and most successful member of the Turtles, a group started as a bet about whether great traders were born or made. Way of the Turtle recounts the whole experiment, how 23 ordinary people were recruited and trained into effective traders in only two weeks, and explaining the selection process, rules, strategies, and how to use their system in practice.

MAGAZINES

Active Trader
161 North Clark, Suite 4915, Chicago, IL 60601, USA
T: +1 312 775 5422
F: +1 815 734 5238
www.activetradermag.com
ISSN: 1542-9466
This monthly magazine provides information and analysis on trading strategy and risk control, the buying and selling of stocks, options, futures and currencies on a (mostly) short-term basis. It also covers different aspects of the market for short-term traders, including analysis of new trading rules or regulations, new trading instruments, the impact of after-hours trading, and using different ECNs.

Technical Analysis of Stocks & Commodities
Technical Analysis
4757 California Avenue SW, Seattle, WA 98116-4499, USA
T: +1 206 938 0570
www.traders.com
ISSN: 0738-3355
This monthly magazine provides traders with information on how to apply charting, numerical, and computer trading methods to trade stocks, bonds, mutual funds, options, forex and futures, and examines both old and new trading methods, techniques and products.

Trader Monthly
Doubledown Media
240 West 35th Street, 11th Floor, New York, NY 10001, USA
T: +1 212 719 9500
F: +1 212 507 9878
www.traderdaily.com/magazine
ISSN: 1935-0279
This monthly upmarket trading magazine provides news, strategies, career information, events, and profiles of successful traders from around the world, as well as covering luxury items that traders might want to purchase. Trader Monthly is available free to professional traders and hedge fund managers.

Traders Magazine
SourceMedia
1 State Street Plaza, 27th Floor, New York, NY 10004, USA
T: +1 212 803 8333
www.tradersmagazine.com
ISSN: 0894-7295
This monthly magazine for securities industry professionals is the official publication of the Security Traders Association (STA). It publishes coverage of the entire trading process, including equities and options, major trends, financial industry news, executive profiles, and cutting edge technology developments, and is aimed at C-Level executives, senior management, head traders, managing directors, partners, and portfolio managers.

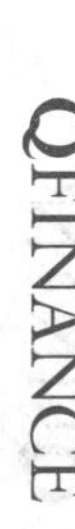

  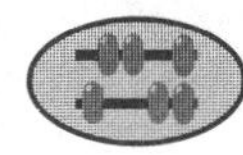 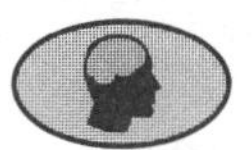  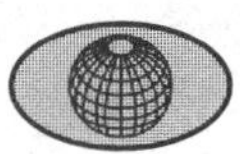   

TradersWorld.com
Halliker's
2508 West Grayrock Street, Springfield, MO 65810, USA
T: +1 417 882 9697
F: +1 417 885 5180
www.tradersworld.com
ISSN: 1045-7690
Traders World is a monthly magazine that offers a range of news, analysis, and information on the use of technical analysis by traders. It covers all the main issues in trading through stock charting, and provides detail on relevant books, software, computers, links, and conferences.

JOURNALS

The Journal of Trading
Institutional Investor
225 Park Avenue South, New York, NY 10003, USA
T: +1 212 224 3570
F: +1 212 224 3197
www.iijournals.com/JOT
ISSN: 1559-3967
This quarterly journal provides analysis of new tools and strategies in institutional trading, focusing on algorithmic trading, execution options, trading platforms, liquidity, analytical models, and multi-asset trading. It examines a number of relevant issues, such as how to review and measure trade execution performance, conduct pre- and post-trade analysis and transaction cost analysis, and achieve best execution and avoid trading pitfalls.

INTERNET

The Technical Trader
www.thetechtrader.com
A site run by veteran trader and financial commentator Harry Boxer, who has many years of experience in investment and technical analysis, this is a popular real-time diary of his trading ideas and market analysis.

Trade2Win
www.trade2win.com
This is a community website for active traders, that aims to unite and support traders around the world. It provides information, analysis, and educational content, and a range of facilities to enable members to communicate with each another, and to share their trading knowledge and views.

Traders' Resource
technical.traders.com
A site run by Technical Analysis of Stocks & Commodities magazine, this is a useful industry search area for information about products, services, and companies related to trading. It lists and links to advisory services, books, brokerages, consultants, courses and seminars, data services, exchanges, hardware, mutual funds, online trading services, publications and newsletters, software, and trading systems.

  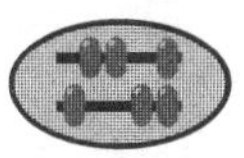 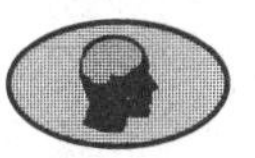  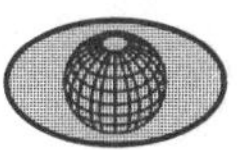   

Transport Finance

BOOKS

Air Transportation: A Management Perspective, 6th ed
John G. Wensveen (editor)
Aldershot, UK: Ashgate, 2007
568pp, ISBN: 978-0-7546-7171-8
This accessible textbook provides a comprehensive introduction to both the theory and practice of air transportation management. It explains the basics, past and present trends, and forecasts potential challenges and difficult decisions that the industry may face. It also details aspects of airline financing, as well as passenger marketing, labor relations, and security.

Airline Finance, 3rd ed
Peter S. Morrell
Aldershot, UK: Ashgate, 2007
259pp, ISBN: 978-0-7546-7000-1
This provides a fundamental understanding of airline finance, addressing each of the main techniques in financial analysis within the context of the air transport industry. It explores how these areas separately and in an integrated way, reinforcing key points with useful case studies. It also discusses financial trends and prospects for the industry, as well as topics such as low cost carriers, fuel hedging, and US Chapter 11 provisions.

Essays on Transport Economics
Pablo Coto-Millán, Vicente Inglada (editors)
Contributions to Economics Series
New York: Physica, 2007
381pp, ISBN: 978-3-7908-1764-5
This collection of articles covers a wide range of topics in transport economics, from basic analytical methods and policy analysis, to more technical discussions of industrial organization, welfare economics, general equilibrium theory, and input-output analysis. It provides theoretical introductions in each area, and presents case studies using current statistical and econometric techniques.

The Future of Pricing: How Airline Ticket Pricing Has Inspired a Revolution
E. Andrew Boyd
Basingstoke, UK: Palgrave Macmillan, 2007
192pp, ISBN: 978-0-230-60019-5
This examines the science of pricing and revenue management, and the impact it has had on the way in which airline companies approach profitable growth. Using anecdotes, interviews, and examples from the airline industry, technology, technology companies, and the history of pricing and revenue management, it provides an insight into how airline price ticketing and other related practices are transforming pricing strategies in other industries.

The Handbook of Maritime Economics and Business
Costas T. Grammenos (editor)
Maritime & Transport Law Library Series
London: LLP Professional Publishing, 2002
930pp, ISBN: 978-1-84311-195-5
This practical guide presents a thorough examination of the current state of the shipping industry, and related economic theories. It combines the original writing of a team of leading academics from around the world, to analyze an array of major maritime economic issues, and assess the research in terms of real-life applications.

Introduction to Air Transport Economics: From Theory to Applications
Bijan Vasigh, Ken Fleming, Thomas Tacker
Aldershot, UK: Ashgate, 2008
358pp, ISBN: 978-0-7546-7081-0
This comprehensive textbook applies economic theory to all technical aspects of the aviation industry. It offers an introduction to the economics of aviation, by presenting a number of articles and institutional developments that have occurred over the last few years, as well as providing new analysis of the underlying economic forces that are currently shaping the industry.

Maritime Economics, 3rd ed
Martin Stopford
London: Routledge, 2008
562pp, ISBN: 978-0-415-27558-3
This provides both an historical and an analytical account of the development of the shipping industry, and an overview of current thinking in maritime economics. It analyzes the historical roots of the industry, presents a framework for understanding modern shipping operations, and explores key issues such as markets, trade theory, shipping costs, accounts, forecasting, ship finance, return on capital, and regulation.

Modelling Transport, 3rd ed
Juan de Dios Ortúzar, Luis G. Willumsen
Chichester, UK: Wiley, 2001
499pp, ISBN: 978-0-471-86110-2
This is a comprehensive and technical guide to mathematical techniques used in transport modeling, and their use for improved decision-making, planning, and design. It examines the main modeling techniques and applications, as well as the role of theory, data, model specification, estimation, validation, and application, data collection techniques, new modeling approaches, time-of-travel and assignment modeling, and the valuation of externalities.

Principles of Transport Economics
Emile Quinet, Roger Vickerman
Cheltenham, UK: Edward Elgar, 2004
385pp, ISBN: 978-1-84542-256-1
This textbook provides a comprehensive analysis of the main areas of transportation economics and policy, including demand, costs, market structure, externalities, and investment appraisal and regulation. It explains how economic principles can be applied to problem solving, and addresses the link between transport and issues of location, urban, and regional development, and economic growth.

Project Finance: The Guide to Financing Transport Projects
Macquarie Corporate Finance
London: Euromoney Books, 2000
95pp, ISBN: 978-1-85564-752-7
This is a focused, practical report on project financing in the transport sector, which examines private financing and development of transport infrastructure. It analyzes the unique challenges posed by the sector, through a study of particular project finance deals, and discusses key issues that are common to a large number of projects, innovative approaches to funding, and risks specific to developing economies and their mitigation.

Road Pricing: Theory and Evidence
Georgina Santos (editor)
Research in Transportation Economics Series
Oxford, UK: JAI Press, 2004
324pp, ISBN: 978-0-7623-0968-9
This examines the transformation in road economic policy brought about by recent advances in road pricing as a method for reducing congestion. It discusses its role as an effective traffic demand management tool, assesses the impact of the London congestion charge, and looks at other schemes in place around the world. It also focuses on second-best congestion pricing, including the impact on the performance of the road network, and optimal locations and charge levels.

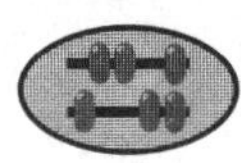

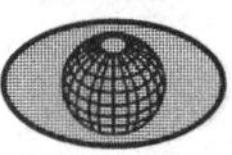

Shipping Derivatives and Risk Management

Amir Alizadeh, Nikos Nomikos
Basingstoke, UK: Palgrave Macmillan, 2009
256pp, ISBN: 978-0-230-21591-7

This is a comprehensive examination of shipping derivatives and risk management, from both a theoretical and practical standpoint. It looks at key issues such as pricing and trading different shipping derivatives instruments, the use of forward freight agreements to manage freight rate risk, basis and settlement risk, real options, and other risks such as bunker risk, interest rate risk, ship price risk, and credit risk.

Shipping Finance, 3rd ed

Stephenson Harwood
London: Euromoney Books, 2006
568pp, ISBN: 978-1-84374-265-4

This examines the shipping finance sector, and provides an explanation of ship mortgage terms, conditions, and mortgagee's rights, with a description of documentation, legislation and registration procedures across the main maritime jurisdictions. It also covers key topics such as the financing of second-hand ships, the financing of new buildings, the assignment of insurances and earnings, guarantees, indemnities, charges, debentures, and the application of Islamic finance.

Transport Economics: Theory, Application, and Policy

Graham Mallard, Stephen Glaister
Basingstoke, UK: Palgrave Macmillan, 2008
315pp, ISBN: 978-0-230-51688-5

This introductory textbook explores the key areas of the transport sector economics, and provides a concise explanation of related economic theory, as well as detailed case studies from across the European Union. It focuses on the application of microeconomic theory, and cover topics such as the theory of markets, market failure, transport policy, and future trends.

Transport Policy and Funding

Dai Nakagawa, Ryoji Matsunaka
Oxford, UK: Elsevier, 2006
208pp, ISBN: 978-0-08-044852-7

This takes an international perspective on transport policy and funding issues, comparing how different countries make capital provisions to achieve their transportation goals. It looks at a variety of funding resources and systems and how they relate to current policy, presents calculations about who is really paying transport costs, and discusses potential improvements to make transport investment and policy more effective.

Transportation Finance Review 2008/09

London: Euromoney Books, 2008
ISBN: 978-1-84374-518-1

This annual publication provides a current overview of the latest developments, trends, and funding issues in transportation and its infrastructure around the world. It offers analysis of large-scale projects for new roads, bridges, tunnels, ports and airports, and rail, and presents case studies, profiles, and discussions on the legal and risk challenges facing such projects.

Urban Transportation Economics, 2nd ed

Kenneth A. Small, Erik T. Verhoef
London: Routledge, 2006
276pp, ISBN: 978-0-415-28515-5

This textbook on the economics of transportation discusses the fundamental issues for an application of economics to transportation, including forecasting demand under alternative policies, measuring costs, price setting under practical constraints, how to choose and evaluate investments in facilities, and methods for ensuring that the private and public sectors work together in the provision of services.

Wheels Up: Airline Business Plan Development, 2nd ed

John G. Wensveen (editor)
Malabar, Florida: Krieger Publishing, 2007
130pp, ISBN: 978-1-57524-293-4

This examines airline business operations, identifying current and new trends, and exploring the importance of flexibility within the business plan. It looks at how vital this flexibility is for an airline in terms of competition, the impact of failure within the aviation environment, and how to develop an effective business plan that is suitable for airlines of any size.

MAGAZINES

Aircraft Value News

Access Intelligence
4 Choke Cherry Road, 2nd Floor, Rockville, MD 20850, USA
T: +1 301 354 2000
www.aviationtoday.com/avn
ISSN: 1071-0655

This biweekly magazine is dedicated to trends and the market analysis of aircraft values. It explores aircraft leasing and purchasing decisions, current and planned joint ventures and mergers, issues in the emerging markets, and provides useful aircraft value tabulation and analysis tables.

Airfinance Journal

Institutional Investor
Nestor House, Playhouse Yard, London, EC4V 5EX, UK
T: +44 (0) 20 7779 8999
www.airfinancejournal.com
ISSN: 0266-2132

This monthly magazine covers all the key financial aspects of commercial aviation industry, offering news on the financing of airline fleets and issues affecting commercial airlines, financiers, manufacturers, consultants, and aviation law firms. It also tracks and analyzes aircraft, airline, and aerospace finance techniques and deals, features interviews with leading industry figures, and presents relevant surveys and data tables.

Airline Fleet Management

Aviation Industry Press
2nd Floor, Ludgate House, 245 Blackfriars Road, London, SE1 9UY, UK
T: +44 (0) 20 7579 4840
F: +44 (0) 20 7579 4848
www.aviationindustrygroup.com/ME2/Audiences/Default.asp?AudID=8FB7A82C60B7404F842B557F22850190
ISSN: 1757-8833

AFM is a bimonthly, global magazine for aircraft owners, operators and lessors. It provides commentary and analysis of the main issues and challenges facing the airline industry, such as the selection, procurement, financing, operations, and management of airline fleets, and network planning, as well as forecasts and future trends.

Aviation Business Asia Pacific

Yaffa Publishing Group, Australia
T: +61 2 9281 2333
www.yaffa.com.au/btob/air.html

This bimonthly magazine is a source of news, analysis, information, and commercial intelligence for the region's airlines and airports, and the businesses that support their operations. It describes the issues and agendas of the aviation and aerospace industry, and focuses on business decision-making, and the policies that influence business investment and the business climate in the sector.

Jetrader

Naylor
401 North Michigan Avenue, Chicago, Illinois 60611, USA
www.istat.org/Media/Jetrader

This bimonthly magazine is published by the International Society of Transport Aircraft Trading and is distributed to its members. It highlights and analyzes

  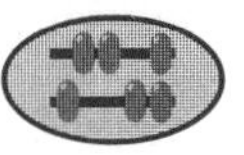 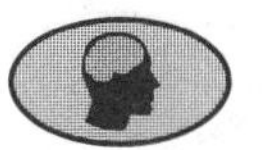  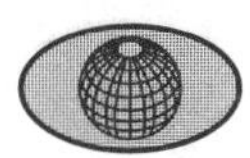  

industry news and case studies, and presents feature articles and a member focus, as well as acting as a forum for promoting communications among those involved in the aviation and supporting industries.

JOURNALS

Journal of Air Transport Management

Elsevier
www.elsevier.com/wps/find/journal description.cws_home/30438/ description#description
ISSN: 0969-6997

This bimonthly journal publishes research articles and commentary on the major policy and management issues facing the air transport industry. It offers practitioners and academics an international forum for analysis and discussion of these issues, and covers all the major sectors of the industry. Analysis focuses on air transport policy and regulation, strategic issues, operations, management, finance and economics, air law, and environmental impact.

Journal of Transport, Economics and Policy

School of Management, University of Bath
Claverton Down, Bath, BA2 7AY, UK
T: +44 (0) 1225 386 302
F: +44 (0) 1225 386 767
www.bath.ac.uk/e-journals/jtep
ISSN: 0022-5258

JTEP is published three times a year, and covers all modes of transport and a wide variety of economic themes. It acts as a source of information and debate on the economics of transport and its interface with transport policy, and offer research on the latest policy developments, as well as topics such as transport infrastructure, planning and policy, costs and pricing, productivity, economies of scale, and regulation.

Research in Transportation Economics

Elsevier
www.elsevier.com/wps/find/journal description.cws_home/714194/ description#description
ISSN: 0739-8859

Published three times each year, this journal is devoted to the dissemination of economics research in the field of transportation. It covers a wide variety of topics relating to the economics aspects of transportation, government regulatory policies regarding transportation, and issues of concern to transportation industry planners, with a focus on the application of economic theory and/or applied economic methodologies to transportation questions.

Transport Policy

Elsevier
T: +353 61 709 190
www.elsevier.com/wps/find/journal description.cws_home/30473/ description#description
ISSN: 0967-070X

This bimonthly international journal analyzes how transport policy decisions are taken, monitors their impact, and makes suggestions regarding potential improvements. Emphasizing both theory and practice, and covering all modes of transport, it reflects the concerns of policymakers in government, industry, voluntary organizations, and the public, and examines policy topics such as traffic management and control, regulation, and economic and commercial pricing policy.

INTERNET

Innovative Finance for Surface Transportation

www.innovativefinance.org

This provides guidance on innovations in all areas of surface transportation finance, and information on technical topics, projects, legislation, publications, application guidance, and institutional issues relating to all transport modes of surface transport. It describes new sources of revenue, financing mechanisms, funds management techniques, and institutional arrangements, and features news, definitions, Q&As, a resource library, an events calendar, and a glossary.

Jane's Transport Finance

jtf.janes.com

This allows viewing of the contents of the Jane's site, with a subscription providing access to full articles, news and analysis, research, and finance intelligence on debt pricing, structure, arrangers and lenders for debt deals in the aircraft, airport, shipping and rail rolling-stock sectors, as well as information on mergers and acquisitions, and financing trends.

ORGANIZATIONS

USA

International Society of Transport Aircraft Trading

Chair: Michael Platt
401 North Michigan Avenue, Chicago, Illinois 60611, USA
T: +1 312 321 5169
F: +1 312 673 6579
E: istat@istat.org
www.istat.org

ISTAT provides a forum for improved communication among those involved in aviation and supporting industries who operate, manufacture, maintain, sell, purchase, finance, lease, appraise, insure, or otherwise engage in activities related to the commercial aviation trading industry. It provides news and information, develops standards, holds lectures and demonstrations, establishes and promotes standards, certifies professional appraisers, and offers an educational program.

Transportation Research Forum

Chair: Kenneth Button
NDSU Dept 2880, PO Box 6050, Fargo, ND 58108-6050, USA
T: +1 701 231 7766
F: +1 701 231 1945
www.trforum.org

TRF is an independent organization of transportation professionals, whose aim is to provide a meeting ground for carriers, shippers, government officials, consultants, university researchers, suppliers, and others seeking an exchange of information and ideas related to both passenger and freight transportation. It offers information for researchers, holds international, national, and local meetings, and publishes professional papers related to numerous transportation topics.

International

World Conference on Transport Research Society

Chair: Tony May
LET-ISH 14, avenue Berthelot, 69363 Lyon, France
T: +33 (0) 4 72 72 64 36
F: +33 (0) 4 72 72 64 48
E: wctrs@let.ish-lyon.cnrs.fr
www.wctrs.org

WCTRS provides a forum for the interchange of ideas among transportation researchers, managers, policy makers, and educators from all over the world. It also helps to identify emerging issues and opportunities of a policy, managerial, or technical nature that will influence transportation research, policy, management and education in the future.

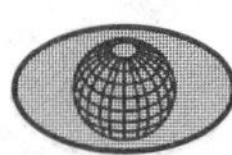

Venture Capital

BOOKS

Angel Capital: How to Raise Early-Stage Private Equity Financing
Gerald A. Benjamin, Joel B. Margulis
Hoboken, New Jersey: Wiley, 2005
373pp, ISBN: 978-0-471-69063-4
The book offers real-world advice on how to find investors and take control of the private placement process. It explains all stages of raising capital, from valuation to negotiation to due diligence, and provides a comprehensive directory of alternative capital resources, based on research of over 2,000 organizations, and a legal appendix that serves as a short course in exempt offerings, and provides the skills needed to have success with any early-stage business venture or investment.

Angel Financing: How to Find and Invest in Private Equity
Gerald A. Benjamin, Joel B. Margulis
Wiley Investment Series
New York: Wiley, 1999
320pp, ISBN: 978-0-471-35085-9
This book draws on extensive experience of the private investor market in the United States. It stresses the importance of careful planning and preparation to ensure the success of financial deals. It provides practical advice and information for entrepreneurs, investors, and intermediaries in four sections: the first focuses on how entrepreneurs can address the challenge of raising capital and finding workable strategies; the second examines the angel investor market; the third deals with the search for an investor; and the fourth provides insight into the investor's perspective on prospective deals. Detailed advice on preparing an investor-oriented business plan and an overview of securities law issues for nonlawyers are provided in appendices.

Directory of Venture Capital, 2nd ed
Kate E. Lister, Thomas D. Harnish
New York: Wiley, 2000
400pp, ISBN: 978-0-471-36104-6
The directory lists venture capital firms by state and provides detailed information on their preferences with regard to industry, stage of funding, geography, and size of company. The authors also provide information on the returns required by private equity investors, selecting the right lawyer, and important aspects of a venture partnership. Entrepreneurs will find the directory a good resource for locating the right venture capital firm to approach for funding.

Raising Venture Capital
Rupert Pearce, Simon Barnes
Hoboken, New Jersey: Wiley, 2006
258pp, ISBN: 978-0-470-02757-8
Offering a deep insight into the venture capital deal making process, this also provides a valuable introduction to the subject. It is practical in approach, although based on sound academic theory, research, and teaching materials.

Raising Venture Capital Finance in Europe: A Practical Guide for Business Owners, Entrepreneurs and Investors
Keith Arundale
London: Kogan Page, 2007
308pp, ISBN: 978-0-7494-4849-3
This book provides an outline for developing and presenting a strategic business plan, with tips on how to selectively approach venture capital in Europe, negotiate to sell or build a business, prepare for due diligence, define the benefits for investors, and plan potential exit routes.

Venture Capital and Private Equity: A Casebook, 4th ed
Josh Lerner, Felda Hardymon, Ann Leamon
Hoboken, New Jersey: Wiley, 2009
576pp, ISBN: 978-0-470-22462-5
The book explains in detail the venture capital and private equity markets. Divided into four sections, the book covers the fundraising process required to start a venture capital fund, investment selection, and the relationship between the venture capitalist and entrepreneur, the various exit strategies available, and some key issues unique to the private equity market.

Venture Capital Funding: A Practical Guide to Raising Finance
Stephen Bloomfield
London: Kogan Page, 2005
224pp, ISBN: 978-0-7494-4291-0
Written in an informal and jargon-free style, this book offers step-by-step advice on how to attract venture capital funding for your business. To make the process seem less daunting, the process is broken down into a number of manageable sections.

The Venture Capital Handbook
William D. Bygrave, Michael Hay, Jos B. Peeters (editors)
Harlow, UK: FT Prentice Hall, 1999
384pp, ISBN: 978-0-273-63899-5
This handbook, which consists of contributions from practitioners, provides an overview of the European venture capital industry and a detailed treatment of the investment process. The aspects of the process covered include fundraising and investor relations, deal generation, due diligence, deal structuring and pricing, and postinvestment venture management. Legal and ethical issues, going public, international syndication, and returns on venture capital are also dealt with.

Venture Capital Investing: The Complete Handbook for Investing in Private Businesses for Outstanding Profits, 2nd ed
David Gladstone, Laura Gladstone
Upper Saddle River, New Jersey: Prentice Hall, 2003
480pp, ISBN: 978-0-13-101885-3
This classic serves as a primer on venture capital investing. It outlines the key considerations for investing private capital, including an analysis of management, compensation, marketing and sales, financial statements and projections, and the production process. From due diligence and deal negotiation to the exit strategy, the author suggests a logical, step-by-step process that is filled with insights and actual examples from his experience as a venture capitalist. While most books are focused on how an entrepreneur can raise venture capital, this book provides an in-depth look at what it takes to be a successful investor in small private businesses.

Venture Catalyst: The Five Strategies for Explosive Corporate Growth
Don Laurie
Cambridge, Massachusetts: Perseus Books Group, 2002
288pp, ISBN: 978-0-7382-0407-9
This book presents a five-part framework for launching new initiatives, and illustrates each part with examples from industries as diverse as packaged goods and web marketing. Interviews with such pioneers as Roger Ackerman of Corning, David Wetherall of CMGI, and Mitch Kapoor of Accel provide the reader with an insider's perspective on the volatile world of corporate venturing.

MAGAZINES

Private Equity Analyst
Asset Alternatives
170 Linden Street, Wellesley, MA 02482-7919, USA
T: +1 781 304 1500

   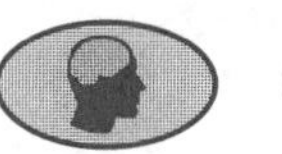  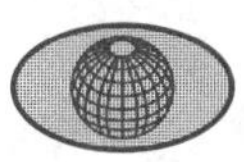   

This monthly newsletter covers the private equity market, dealing mainly with venture capital, LBOs, mezzanine investing, and turnarounds.

Private Equity Journal for India
Dickenson Intellinetics Private
266, Dr Annie Besant Road, Worli, Mumbai 25, India
T: +91 22 2625 2282
F: +91 22 2625 2282
ISSN: 0973-1636
This quarterly journal offers research and analysis from its own editorial and research team, and by participants and academics who wish to share their knowledge and research.

Private Equity Week
Thomson Financial
195 Broadway, 10th Floor, New York, NY 10007, USA
T: +1 646 822 2000
F: +1 646 822 3230
ISSN: 1099-341X
PEW is a weekly newsletter providing information on private equity deals in the venture capital market.

Real Deals Europe
National Federation of Independent Business
53 Century Boulevard, Suite 300, Nashville, TN 37214, USA
T: +1 615 872 5800
F: +1 615 872 5353
Real Deals is a private equity magazine for venture capitalists, advisors, and debt providers. Published every two weeks, it offers news, commentary, analysis, and independently compiled deal information on the European private equity and venture capital industry.

JOURNALS

European Venture Capital Journal
Venture Economics
195 Broadway, 10th Floor, NY 10007, USA
T: +1 646 822 2000
F: +1 646 822 3230
ISSN: 0954-1675
This journal, published ten times a year, provides information on the European private equity market. The *UK Venture Capital Journal* merged with it in 1999.

Venture Capital: An International Journal of Entrepreneurial Finance
Routledge
4 Park Square, Milton Park, Abingdon, Oxfordshire, OX14 4RN, UK
T: +44 (0) 20 7017 6000
F: +44 (0) 20 7017 6336
ISSN: 1369-1066
Venture Capital is a quarterly journal which publishes research-based papers from academics and practitioners on all aspects of private equity finance and on the venture capital process from decision to exit. Coverage is international, focusing on emerging venture capital markets in Eastern Europe and the Asia-Pacific area as well as established markets in Western Europe and the United States.

Venture Capital Journal
Thomson Financial
195 Broadway, 10th Floor, New York, NY 10007, USA
T: +1 646 822 2000
F: +1 646 822 3230
ISSN: 0883-2773
VCJ is a monthly journal covering the private equity and venture capital industry. It provides news and analysis of deals, company profiles, and interviews.

INTERNET

PricewaterhouseCoopers MoneyTree Report
This survey, sponsored by the accounting firm of PricewaterhouseCoopers, provides a comprehensive list of venture capital investing in the United States by industry, stage of funding, geography, and type of financing on a quarterly basis. The report tracks venture capital firm investments and the enterprises receiving capital by region/state and industry.

US Venture Partners (USVP)
Created in 1981, USVP aims to specifically help entrepreneurial ventures. In total, it has put over $1.8 billion into more than 370 companies, and their clients have gone on to become leaders in their respective fields.

vcapital
This is an action-packed site for entrepreneurs, with a distinct editorial voice. It features a "Dr VC" feature, whereby users can ask for specific advice, and encourages users to e-mail in their own stories of success and failure.

VentureSource
VentureSource is a Dow Jones database that tracks the key developments of more the 30,000 venture-backed companies in every industry and every region in the U.S., Europe, Israel, and China. It also tracks the moves and people of over 8,000 private capital firms around the world.

Venturewire
This website hosts a family of publications that are exclusively devoted to the private equity marketplace. *Venturewire Professional*, the site's flagship publication, features the latest news on fundings, acquisitions, venture capital firms, and key personnel changes in venture-backed businesses. Venturewire also publishes Lifescience, Alert, and People on a daily basis and provides the Research section as a source of in-depth coverage on specific industries.

vFinance Venture Capital Resource Library
This site is aimed at investors, entrepreneurs, and company CEOs and provides access to databases of investors, angels, and business plans. Registration is required.

ORGANIZATIONS

Europe

British Business Angels Network
New City Court, 20 St Thomas Street, London, SE1 9RS, UK
T: +44 (0) 20 7089 2305
F: +44 (0) 20 7089 2301
E: liz@bbaa.org.uk
BBAA, formerly NBAN (National Business Angels Network), is a nonprofit association sponsored by financial institutions and the Department for Business, Enterprise and Regulatory Reform in the United Kingdom. Through a network of associates across the country, it provides a service linking businesses seeking equity finance with investors seeking opportunities. A monthly bulletin of opportunities is sent to all registered investors, and an online service, BestMatch, is also provided.

British Venture Capital Association
3 Clements Inn, London, WC2A 2AZ, UK
T: +44 (0) 20 7025 2950
F: +44 (0) 20 7025 2951
E: bvca@bvca.co.uk
The BVCA was founded in 1983 and is the representative body for the UK venture capital industry. It promotes private equity and venture capital for the benefit of entrepreneurs, investors, practitioners, and the economy as a whole. Its members are venture capital companies and professional firms involved in advising on venture capital transactions. Its wide variety of activities include training, workshops, lobbying, and research, and it produces publications.

European Private Equity and Venture Capital Association (EVCA)

Bastion Tower, Place du Champ de Mars 5, Brussels, 1050, Belgium
T: +32 2 715 00 20
F: +32 2 725 07 04
E: evca@evca.com

EVCA was founded in 1983 and now has over 850 members. Its aim is to promote and facilitate the development of the European venture capital industry through lobbying and initiatives such as conferences, training, and networking opportunities. The organization was involved in the creation of EASD (European Association of Security Dealers) and the EASDAQ pan-European capital market.

USA

National Association of Investment Companies

1300 Pennsylvania Avenue NW, Suite 700, Washington, DC 20004, USA
T: +1 202 289 4336
F: +1 202 289 4329
E: naichqtrs@aol.com

NAIC is an industry association for venture capital and private equity firms. Its members are privately owned equity investment firms, small business investment companies licensed by the United States Small Business Administration, and investment companies chartered by state and local governments.

National Association of Small Business Investment Companies

666 11th Street NW, Suite 750, Washington, DC 20001, USA
T: +1 202 628 5055
F: +1 202 628 5080
E: nasbic@nasbic.org

NASBIC is a nonprofit industry association which has represented and served the SBIC industry for over 40 years. It provides educational programs for investment professionals through the Venture Capital Institute and cooperates with other business associations. Its policies and priorities are established by a board of governors.

National Venture Capital Association

1655 North Fort Myer Drive, Suite 850, Arlington, VI 22209, USA
T: +1 703 524 2549
F: +1 703 524 3940
E: lturner@nvca.org

NVCA is a trade association with a membership of over 400 venture capital firms. It aims to foster understanding of the venture capital industry in the United States, to stimulate the flow of equity capital to growth companies, to promote professional standards, facilitate networking, and provide research data for members. NVCA publishes: *NVCA Today*, a quarterly review of legislative and regulatory developments; *The Venture Capital Review*, a biannual journal which provides an overview of trends in the industry; and the *Venture Capital Yearbook.*

BRIC

Brazil Venture Capital

FINEP, Praia do Flamengo 200, 1, 2, 3, 4, 5, 7, 9, 13 e 24 andares, Rio de Janeiro, 22210-030, Brazil
T: +55 21 2555 0330
F: +55 21 2555 0402

This site is part of the INOVAR project, launched by the Brazilian ministry of Science and Technology department FINEP, to promote the development of small and medium-size businesses by designing instruments for their financing, especially venture capital.

China Venture Capital Association (CVCA)

Room 1002, 10/F, Office Tower C1, 1 East Chang An Avenue, Beijing 100738, China
T: +86 10 8515 0829
F: +86 10 8515 0835
E: cindy@cvca.com.cn

CVCA is a member-based, trade organization established to promote the interest and the development of the venture capital and private equity industry in the Greater China Region.

China Venture Capital Research Institute (CVCRI)

TU427, The Hong Kong Polytechnic University, Hung Hom, Kowloon, Hong Kong
T: +852 2766 4264
F: +852 2764 2340
E: cvcri@cvcri.com

This institute is a joint venture between The Hong Kong Polytechnic University and the China Venture Capital Company, which promotes the development of China's venture capital and hi-tech industries by providing the best services for related theoretical and practical studies and policy making. It also publishes the *China Venture Capital Journal* and the *China Venture Capital Yearbook.*

Indian Venture Capital and Private Equity Association (IVCA)

301–302, Delhi Blue Apartments, Main Ring Road, Near Safdarjung Hospital, New Delhi 110 029, India
T: +91 11 4162 8566
F: +91 11 4162 8863
E: info@indiavca.org

Indian Venture Capital and Private Equity Association (IVCA) is a member-based, national organization that represents venture capital and private equity firms, promotes the industry within India and throughout the world, and encourages investment in high-growth companies.

Russian Private Equity and Venture Capital Association (RVCA)

Office 209, 12B, pr. Engelsa 29, Saint-Petersburg, Russia
T: +7 812 326 6180
F: +7 812 326 6180
E: rvca@rvca.ru

RVCA is a member-based platform that works to create a positive political and entrepreneurial environment for investment activities, represent its members interests at the government level, in press, in financial and industrial markets within the country and abroad, provide information and support, and build a cluster of highly qualified professionals for the venture business companies.

International

Australian Venture Capital Association

Level 41, Gateway Building, 1 Macquarie Place, Sydney, New South Wales, 2000, Australia
T: +61 2 9251 3888
F: +61 2 9251 3808
E: mbrs@avcal.com.au

AVCAL was founded in 1992 to act as a forum for the venture capital industry in Australia and to encourage investment in growing businesses. Its members, numbering over 100, include venture capital firms, banks, incubators, angels, advisers, and government bodies. It organizes networking events and training courses, and sponsors a twice-yearly survey of venture capital investment.

Hong Kong Venture Capital Association

4010 Jardine House, One Connaught Place, Central, Hong Kong
T: +852 2845 6100
F: +852 2526 2713
E: enquiry@hkvca.com.hk

The HKVCA was founded in 1987 to promote and protect the interests of, and provide a forum for, the venture capital industry in Hong Kong. It organizes meetings, conferences, and seminars, and conducts research studies.

  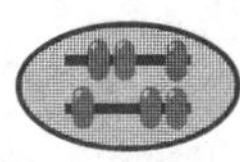   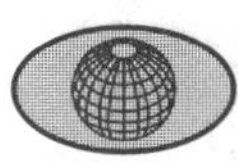   

Wealth Management

BOOKS

Behavioral Finance and Wealth Management: How to Build Optimal Portfolios that Account for Investor Biases

Michael M. Pompian
Wiley Finance Series
Hoboken, New Jersey: Wiley, 2006
317pp, ISBN: 978-0-471-74517-4

This is a comprehensive guide to irrational investor behavior, and how to build portfolios for individual investors that account for these behaviors. It focuses on improving decision-making by understanding behavioral finance research, examines an array of investor biases, and describes the impact of fear and greed in the markets, as well as good and bad investment decision-making.

Breaking Through: Building a World Class Wealth Management Business

John J. Bowen Jr., Patricia J. Abram, Jonathan Powell
San Martin, Calilfornia: CEG Worldwide, 2008
164pp, ISBN: 978-0-615-19928-3

This presents a comprehensive set of effective strategies for developing a wealth management business, with guidance on the opportunities available for financial advisors. It explains how to focus on the right affluent clients, and implement a consultative process, and explores techniques for acquiring assets and key clients, and developing useful strategic alliances.

Financial Planning and Wealth Management: An International Perspective

Louis Cheng, Tak Yan Leung, Yiu Hing Wong
New York: McGraw-Hill, 2008
520pp, ISBN: 978-0-07-124984-3

This international guide provides information and advice for those working in financial planning and wealth management. It assesses the latest developments and trends, and presents an implementable financial planning process, interviews with financial planners, and different approaches to investment management, as well as covering risk profiling and asset allocation strategies.

Global Private Banking and Wealth Management: The New Realities

David Maude
Wiley Finance Series
Chichester, UK: Wiley, 2006
346pp, ISBN: 978-0-470-85421-1

This is a comprehensive examination of the industry and the key challenges it is currently facing during a period of great change. It describes in detail the workings of the wealth management market, and the role of banks and other financial services, and covers issues such as the changing client profile, new products, pricing, and channels, competitor and business-model landscapes, and external challenges and opportunities.

Integrated Wealth Management: The New Direction for Portfolio Managers

Jean Brunel
London: Euromoney Books, 2002
335pp, ISBN: 978-1-85564-923-1

This is a thorough and authoritative examination of wealth management, which presents an integrated approach for helping portfolio managers become wealth managers. It focuses on the impact of investor psychology, maximizing tax efficiency, the implications of multiple asset locations, capital market opportunities and forecasting, strategic asset allocation, the importance of manager selection, and the multi-manager approach.

The Offshore Money Book: How to Move Assets Offshore for Privacy, Protection, and Tax Advantage

Arnold Cornez
Chicago, Illinois: Contemporary Books, 1998
280pp, ISBN: 978-0-8092-2880-5

This comprehensive and accessible resource on offshore tax havens offers practical guidance on using offshore investing as a method of asset protection. It details the practicalities of moving assets offshore, how to evaluate the best places to invest, and how to avoid offshore scams.

Private Wealth: Wealth Management in Practice

Stephen M. Horan (editor)
CFA Institute Investment Perspectives Series
Hoboken, New Jersey: Wiley, 2009
564pp, ISBN: 978-0-470-38113-7

This new collection presents the latest guidance and research on private wealth management issues, such as tax matters, lifecycle modeling, investment management for taxable private investors and the use of tax-deferred investment accounts, and after-tax performance measurement. It also presents a framework for various tax environments, and explores tax-efficient asset allocation and portfolio management techniques.

Structured Products in Wealth Management

Steffen Tolle, Boris Hutter, Patrik Rüthemann, Hanspeter Wohlwend
Wiley Finance Series
Singapore: Wiley, 2008
226pp, ISBN: 978-0-470-82330-9

This accessible guide to the use of structured products in private wealth management offers a detailed description of their emergence in the form of equity-linked derivatives, and their characteristics and practical applications. It describes how they can generate added value as part of an integrated investment process, their systematic use in portfolio management and optimization, and their overall use in achieving investment objectives.

Tax Havens Today: The Benefits and Pitfalls of Banking and Investing Offshore

Hoyt Barber
Hoboken, New Jersey: Wiley, 2007
324pp, ISBN: 978-0-470-05123-8

This is a practical guide to the effective placement of finances and investments in offshore tax havens, exploring the best investment strategies and the most common mistakes, for any type of investor. It describes 40 popular tax havens, and provides full contact details of the most important investment, banking, legal, and financial advisors, divided by tax haven or other jurisdiction, with a description of their areas of expertise.

Vault Career Guide to Private Wealth Management

John Ransom
Vault Career Library Series
New York: Vault, 2007
128pp, ISBN: 978-1-58131-448-9

This is a practical guide to finding a job or career in the private wealth management industry. It explains how the industry works, and the different job roles and career paths available, and covers the basics of equity and fixed income products, market and regulatory trends, and private wealth management at the both large and small firms.

     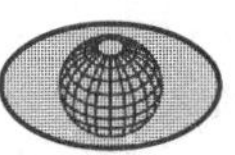   

Wealth Creation by Design: The Next Wave in Wealth Management for Financial Advisors
Goldman Sachs
Reinvented Wealth Manager Series
Hoboken, New Jersey: Wiley, 2009
320pp, ISBN: 978-0-470-28948-8
This resource for financial advisors assesses the main elements of investment and wealth management, and offers advice on how to increase value for clients and improve the effectiveness of their business. It explains prospecting, and dealing with conflicts of interest, and identifies the key challenges and opportunities open to wealth managers.

Wealth: How the World's High-Net-Worth Grow, Sustain, and Manage Their Fortunes
Merrill Lynch, Cap Gemini
Mississauga, Ontario: Wiley, 2008
236pp, ISBN: 978-0-470-15303-1
This offers advice on wealth management based on the successful strategies and techniques used by high net worth individuals. Featuring interviews with prominent HNWI individuals and advisors, it analyzes how they acquired their wealth, how they manage it to attain high investment growth. It also presents new approaches to asset allocation and alternative investments, and emerging issues such as the role of philanthropy, and inter-generational wealth transfer.

Wealth Management: A Concise Guide to Financial Planning and Investment Management for Wealthy Clients, 2nd ed
S. Timothy Kochis
Chicago, Illinois: CCH, 2006
320pp, ISBN: 978-0-8080-8949-0
This practical guide to personal wealth planning and investment management describes a wide range of strategies, and appropriate responses to decision-making issues, and examines emerging trends, such as alternative investment options. It is aimed at financial planners, accountants, lawyers, brokers, and portfolio managers serving high net worth individuals, who need assistance in effective planning and implementation.

Wealth Management in Any Market: Timeless Strategies for Building Financial Security
Bishara A. Bahbah
Hoboken, New Jersey: Wiley, 2009
300pp, ISBN: 978-0-470-40528-4
This provides accessible guidance on wealth management and financial security, which explains both the basic strategies involved, as well as more technical areas such as setting up an estate plan, managing debt, purchasing insurance, retirement planning, and employing tax-reduction techniques. It also examines how to protect assets and build wealth under different financial conditions, and how to select a wealth management team.

Wealth Management Planning: The UK Tax Principles
Malcolm James Finney
Chichester, UK: Wiley, 2008
588pp, ISBN: 978-0-470-72424-8
This presents a comprehensive summary of the UK tax rules affecting wealth management planning for UK domiciled and non-UK domiciled individuals. It describes the principles underpinning income tax, capital gains tax, and inheritance tax for financial planners, places UK tax rules in an international context, and explores topics such as the suitability of off shore financial centers, and the use of double-taxation agreements.

Wealth Management: Private Banking, Investment Decisions, and Structured Financial Products
Dimitris N. Chorafas
Oxford, UK: Butterworth-Heinemann, 2006
376pp, ISBN: 978-0-7506-6855-2
This analyzes wealth management from a practical viewpoint, and examines structured products as suitable investments for retail and institutional investors. It looks at the real risks and returns of structured financial products offered by banks, relating them to the volatility of future value of an underlying, the uncertainty of future events, and the exposure of the product.

Wealth Management Teams
Steven Drozdeck, Lyn Fisher
Logan, Utah: Financial Forum Publishing, 2005
160pp, ISBN: 978-0-9745175-4-4
This is a practical investor guide to selecting and evaluating the best financial advisors and wealth management teams. It presents detailed case studies from a series of high-level financial industry teams that explore how they deliver superior levels of advice and service to their clients.

Wealth Management: The Financial Advisor's Guide to Investing and Managing Client Assets
Harold E. Evensky
Chicago, Illinois: McGraw-Hill, 1997
481pp, ISBN: 978-0-7863-0478-3
This provides applied guidance on wealth management for financial advisors, presenting a thorough overview of current investment theories, and a range of tools and techniques for effective financial planning. It also explores an optimal asset allocation policy that can be tailored to goals and constraints of different clients, and detailed reference material for further study.

MAGAZINES

Private Wealth
Charter Financial Publishing Network
499 Broad Street, Shrewsbury, NJ 07702, USA
T: +1 732 450 8866
F: +1 732 450 8877
www.pw-mag.com
This bimonthly magazine is for professionals focused on meeting the financial, legal, and lifestyle demands of ultra-high-net-worth clients. It provides news and research on the target market, the competition, and the financial and legal strategies, and is structured around key topics such as investments, estate planning, insurance, wealth protection, lifestyle, business development, and philanthropy.

Professional Wealth Management
Financial Times
1 Southwark Bridge, London, SE1 9HL, UK
T: +44 (0) 20 7873 3000
www.pwmnet.com
ISSN: 1476-3001
This magazine is devoted to the growth in the use of third parties to distribute financial products to high-net-worth investors across Europe. It provides strategic advice and information to the key decision-makers at all levels of European distribution, and examines the new partnerships formed from banks and insurance companies contracting out the management of some of their core assets to external specialist asset management groups.

Wealth Management Review
Sovereign Publications
32 Woodstock Grove, London, W12 8LE, UK
T: +44 (0) 20 7616 0800
F: +44 (0) 20 7724 1444
www.sovereign-publications.com/wealth-management.htm
This new monthly magazine provides news and information to the super-rich and professional intermediaries advising family groups and ultra-high-net-worth individuals. It covers wealth management opportunities, issues, planning, and implementation, and effective investment strategies, as well as the basics of acquiring, growing, protecting, and using wealth, and passing it on to others.

  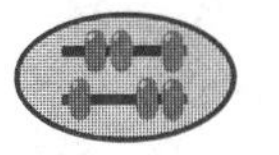 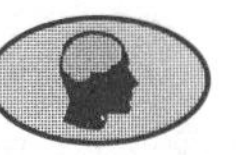 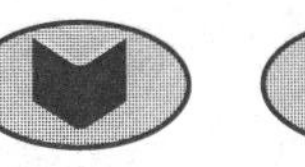 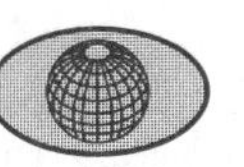   

Wealth Management
Cloughmore Media Group
Cunningham House, 130 Francis Street, Dublin 8, Ireland
T: +353 1 416 7800
F: +353 1 416 7899
www.businessandfinance.ie/publications/wealth.html

This quarterly magazine provides information and advice for the growing high-net-worth sector in Ireland. It offers news and analysis on Irish and international markets, and emerging markets, and the latest developments and trends in the investment and consumption markets.

Wealth Management
Wealth Management Information Services
Buckingham Gate, London, SW1E 6LB, UK
T: +44 (0) 20 7674 0400
F: +44 (0) 20 7674 0404
ISSN: 1462-2807

This is a quarterly electronic magazine on all aspects of wealth management. It is an online publication laid out in a magazine format, that comes with virtual page turning.

Wealth Manager
Summit Business Media
33–41 Newark Street, 2nd Floor, Hoboken, NJ 07030, USA
T: +1 201 526 1254
www.wealthmanagermag.com

This monthly magazine is a resource for investment advisors, brokers, and financial planners who manage assets for clients with high net worth. It offers guidance on investment strategies and opportunities, and news and analysis of relevant topics such as high-end investing, tax planning, practice management, legal compliance, and client relations.

Worth
Sandow Media
58 West 40th Street, 16th Floor, New York, NY 10018, USA
T: +1 212 665 6100
www.worth.com

This bimonthly magazine for high-net-worth individuals and their advisors reports on issues related to comprehensive wealth management, including investment opportunities, private banking and financial advisory services, business ownership and succession planning, and philanthropy and estate planning. It also offers features on advisors, investments/risk management, business/entrepreneurship, politics and policy, profiles, money and meaning, and cultural investments.

JOURNALS

The Journal of Wealth Management
Institutional Investor
225 Park Avenue South, 8th Floor, New York, NY 10003, USA
T: +1 212 224 3800
F: +1 212 224 3197
www.iijournals.com/JPPM
ISSN: 1520-4154

This quarterly journal is dedicated to the practical analysis of financial tools and investment strategies for investment advisors, to best service and manage high-net-worth, taxable portfolios. It covers topics such as behavioral finance, investment policy formation, investment policy execution, tax-aware investing, interdisciplinary issues, and performance measurement, as well as new investment vehicles such as hedge funds and alternatives.

Review of Income and Wealth
Wiley
c/o Faculty of Economics and Business, University of Groningen, PO Box 800, 9700 AV Groningen, The Netherlands
T: +31 50 363 8455
F: +31 50 363 8454
www.wiley.com/bw/journal.asp?ref=0034-6586
ISSN: 0034-6586

This quarterly journal aims to advance the understanding of the definition, measurement, and interpretation of national income, wealth and distribution. It covers national and social accounting, systems of economic, financial, and social statistics, and comparisons of income, wealth, inequality, poverty, well-being, and productivity.

INTERNET

TheWealthNet
www.thewealthnet.com

This is an online resource for wealth management professionals. It provides industry information, news on the latest changes and developments, such as people moves, new product launches, and M&A activity, commentary and analysis, profiles of the leading players in the market, reviews of books and reports, an industry directory, and an events calendar that features major wealth management events.

Wealth Briefing
www.wealthbriefing.com

This provides online news and analysis for wealth managers, with daily updates, weekly briefings, and in-depth features, as well as a useful search facility that contains listing of news and features, articles by professional lawyers, accountants and consultants, conferences, training and exhibitions, organizations involved in wealth management, and people moves.

ORGANIZATIONS

Europe

Association of International Wealth Management
Feldstrasse 80, 8180 Bulach, Switzerland
T: +41 44 872 35 40
F: +41 44 872 35 32
E: info@aiwm.org
www.aiwm.org

AIWM is a global, non-profit association for wealth managers, portfolio managers, investment advisors, asset managers, and trust and estate practitioners. It promotes global education in the wealth management industry, provides a set of standards for the qualification of private banking professionals, and awards the private banking designation Certified International Wealth Manager Diploma.

Association of Private Client Investment Managers and Stockbrokers
Chair: David Bennett
22 City Road, Finsbury Square, London, EC1Y 2AJ, UK
T: +44 (0) 20 7448 7100
F: +44 (0) 20 7638 4636
E: info@apcims.co.uk
www.apcims.co.uk

APCIMS is a trade association of firms who act for the private investor. Its objectives include the advancement of the interests of members across the financial services community, communicating industry changes to members, leading the debate on the development of the European securities industry, and providing information and assistance to members across a wide range of regulatory, market, and business issues.

The International Money Management Institute
26 York Street, London, W1U 6PZ, UK
T: +44 (0) 20 7553 9742
intlmmi.org

IMMI is a non-profit association that facilitates the exchange of knowledge among a global network of industry executives, and promotes the use of

  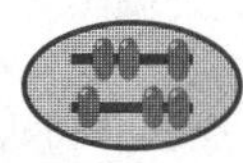 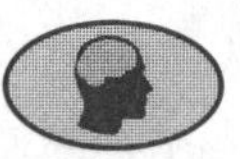  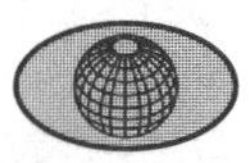   

managed solutions in a consultative environment. It serves as a forum for wealth management organizations to discuss issues of product and service development, and distribution globally, and works to identify and address operational and regulatory barriers to market entry and distribution.

USA

The Money Management Institute

Chair: Brian Jacobs
1140 Connecticut Avenue, NW Suite 1040,
Washington, DC 20036-4001, USA
T: +1 202 822 4949
F: +1 202 822 5188
www.moneyinstitute.com

MMI is a national organization for the managed solutions industry, representing portfolio manager firms and sponsors of investment consulting programs. It serves as a forum for the industry's leaders, and is a leading advocate on regulatory and legislative issues. It also educates prospective investors about the benefits of financial consulting/managed solution services, and promotes the professionalism of financial consultants who work with managed solutions.

Wealth Management Institute

Chair: Gary A. Ferraro
1200 North Federal Highway, Suite 200,
Boca Raton, Florida 33432, USA
T: +1 561 210 8504
F: +1 561 447 8724
E: info@w-m-i.org
www.w-m-i.org

This professional member and trade association offers information, education, professional resources, and expert guidance on domestic and international financial products and services for the wealth management industry. It also promotes and supports the industry in the provision of legal and ethical access to all wealth management and personal finance products, services, and subject matters for individuals and companies worldwide.

International

International Association for Research in Income and Wealth

Chair: Andrea Brandolini
IARIW Executive Director, 111 Sparks Street, Suite 500, Ottawa, Ontario K1P 5B5, Canada
T: +1 613 233 8891
F: +1 613 233 8250
E: info@iariw.org
www.iariw.org

This association is dedicated to the furthering of research on national and economic and social accounting, and focuses on international comparisons of income and wealth, the use of economic and social accounting for budgeting and policy analysis in different countries, and the experiences of different countries in the development of economic and social accounting systems.

Wealth Management Institute

Chair: Ng Kok Song
60B Orchard Road, #06-18 Tower 2, The Atrium@Orchard, Singapore 238891, Singapore
T: +65 6828 6988
F: +65 6821 1155
E: mwm@smu.edu.sg
www.wmi.com.sg

WMI is an educational institution dedicated to the wealth management industry in Asia. It caters for the rising demand for professional wealth management services, such as fund management and private banking, in the region, by providing education and research on institutional fund management, and financial and tax planning, and provides an opportunity for networking.

QUOTATIONS

  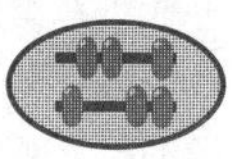  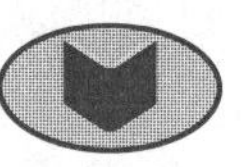 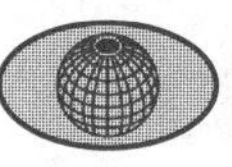 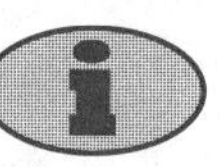  

Quotations

The **Quotations** section includes over 2,000 quotations on finance, management, leadership, money, and business in general. It is indexed by both author and theme, and provides up-to-date quotations on subjects ranging from **Accounting** and **Change** to **Power** and **Wealth**.

The entries can be viewed as perfect to enliven meetings, presentations, or conversation, and include contributions from the likes of **W. W. Rostow, Milton Friedman, Peter F. Drucker**, and **Donald J. Trump**.

The Quotations section includes:

- **Index** of people quoted, including **biographical information**
- **Full quotation** with source and date
- **Thematic headings** enabling quick identification of relevance by theme

   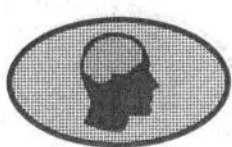  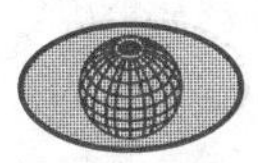   

Contents

     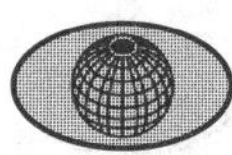 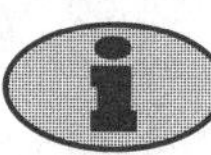  

Ability

Ability and achievement are *bona fides* no one dares question, no matter how unconventional the man who presents them. **J. Paul Getty**. *How to Be Rich* (1965)

I found that there were these incredibly great people at doing certain things, and you couldn't replace one of these people with 50 average people. They could just do stuff that no number of average people could do. **Steve Jobs**. Quoted in "Steve's Two Jobs," *Time* (Michael Krantz, October 18, 1999)

Intelligence is quickness to apprehend as distinct from ability which is capacity to act wisely on the thing apprehended. **Alfred North Whitehead**. *Dialogues* (1954)

Competence, like truth, beauty, and contact lenses, is in the eye of the beholder. **Laurence J. Peter**. *The Peter Principle: Why Things Always Go Wrong* (co-written with Raymond Hull, 1969)

If you can run one business well, you can run any business well. **Sir Richard Branson**. *New York Times* (2000)

Ability will never catch up with the demand for it. **Malcolm S. Forbes**. Attributed

A human being should be able to change a diaper, plan an invasion, butcher a hog, conn a ship, design a building, write a sonnet, balance accounts, build a wall, set a bone, comfort the dying, take orders, give orders, cooperate, act alone, solve equations, analyse a new problem, pitch manure, program a computer, cook a tasty meal, fight efficiently, die gallantly. Specialization is for insects. **Robert A. Heinlein**. *Time Enough for Love* (1973)

Accounting

One can't say that figures lie. But figures, as used in financial arguments, seem to have the bad habit of expressing a small part of the truth forcibly, and neglecting the other part, as do some people we know. **Fred Schwed**. *Where Are the Customers' Yachts?* (1940)

Accountants are the witch-doctors of the modern world and willing to turn their hands to any kind of magic. **Sir Charles Eustace Harman**. Speech (February 1964)

It sounds extraordinary, but it's a fact that balance sheets can make fascinating reading. **Mary Archer (Lady Archer of Weston-Super-Mare)**. Attributed

The system of book-keeping by double entry is, perhaps, the most beautiful one in the wide domain of literature or science. Were it less common, it would be the admiration of the learned world. **Edwin T. Freedley**. *A Practical Treatise on Business* (1853)

The pen is mightier than the sword, but no match for the accountant. **Jonathan Glancey**. Attributed

What's the difference between Enron and Fannie Mae? The guys at Enron have been convicted. **Anonymous**. Comparing accounting practices at Fannie Mae with those of the collapsed energy giant Enron. *Wall Street Journal* (June 14, 2006)

Accuracy

It is the nature of greatness not to be exact. **Edmund Burke**. Speech. "On American Taxation" (1774)

A little inaccuracy sometimes saves tons of explanation. **Saki (H. H. Munro)**. "Clovis on the Alleged Romance of Business," *The Square Egg* (1924)

I do not mind lying, but I hate inaccuracy. **Samuel Butler**. "Truth and Convenience," *Notebooks* (H. Festing-Jones, ed., 1912)

Nothing is more central to an organization's effectiveness than its ability to transmit accurate, relevant, understandable information among its members. **Saul W. Gellerman**. *The Management of Human Resources* (1976)

It's time that financial types developed a greater tolerance for imprecision, because that's the way the world is. **John C. Burton**. *Time* (January 24, 1977)

Achievement

Well, we knocked the bastard off. **Sir Edmund Hillary**. Referring to his ascent of Everest. Press comment (1953)

They have not any difficulties on the way up because they fly, but they have many when they reach the summit. **Niccolò Machiavelli**. *The Prince* (1513)

If you do it right 51 percent of the time you will end up a hero. **Alfred P. Sloan**. Quoted in *Corporate Cultures* (Deal and Kennedy, 1982)

Happiness...lies in the joy of achievement, in the thrill of creative effort. The joy and moral stimulation of work no longer must be forgotten in the mad chase of evanescent profits. **Franklin D. Roosevelt**. Presidential inaugural address (March 4, 1933)

Man grows beyond his work, walks up the stairs of his concepts, emerges ahead of his accomplishment. **John Steinbeck**. *The Grapes of Wrath* (1939)

But what those critics don't know is that these same assets that excite me in the chase often, once they are acquired, leave me bored. **Donald J. Trump**. *Trump: Surviving at the Top* (co-written with Charles Leerhsen, 1990)

Action

Chie Wen Tzu used to think thrice before acting. The Master hearing of it said, Twice is quite enough. **Confucius**. *Analects* (500? BC)

Freedom from activity is never achieved by abstaining from action. **Bhagavad Gita** 3:4 (300? BC)

I acted, and my action made me wise. **Thom Gunn**. "Incident on a Journey," *Fighting Terms* (1954)

Never confuse movement with action. **Ernest Hemingway**. Quoted in *Papa Hemingway* (A. E. Hotchner, 1966)

The world can only be grasped by action, not by contemplation. The hand is the cutting edge of man. **Jacob Bronowski**. *The Ascent of Man* (1973)

There are people who make things happen, those who watch what happens, and those who wonder what happened. **Anonymous**.

In politics if you want anything said, ask a man. If you want anything done, ask a woman. **Baroness Thatcher**. Quoted in *People* (September 15, 1975)

Do what you can, where you are, with what you have. **Theodore Roosevelt**. Quoted in *The Military Quotation Book, Revised and Expanded* (James Charlton, 2002)

A man of action forced into a state of thought is unhappy until he can get out of it. **John Galsworthy**. *Maid in Waiting* (1932)

Follow effective action with quiet reflection. From the quiet reflection will come even more effective action. **Peter F. Drucker**. Attributed

  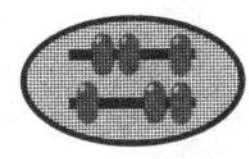 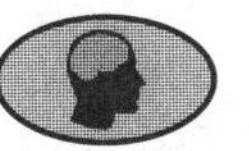  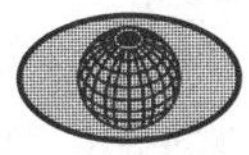 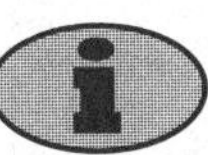  

One's objective should be to get it right, get it quick, get it out, and get it over...your problem won't improve with age. **Warren Buffett**. "Interview with Warren Buffett," *Harvard Business Review* (Norman Augustine, November–December 1995)

Action is at bottom a swinging and flailing of the arms to regain one's balance and keep afloat. **Eric Hoffer**. *The Passionate State of Mind* (1955)

When fog prevents a small-boat sailor from seeing the buoy marking the course he wants, he turns his boat rapidly in small circles, knowing that the waves he makes will rock the buoy in the vicinity. Then he stops, listens and repeats the procedure until he hears the buoy clang. By making waves, he finds where his course lies. Often the price of finding these guides is a willingness to take a few risks, to "make a few waves." **Richard Armstrong**. Attributed

Action springs not from thought, but from a readiness for responsibility. **Dietrich Bonhoeffer**. *Letters and Papers from Prison* (1953)

Adversity

Even when the universe made it quite clear to me that I was mistaken in my certainties...I did not break. The shattering of my sureties did not shatter me. **Lucille Clifton**. Quoted in *The Black Woman's Gumbo Ya-Ya* (Terri L. Jewell, 1993)

Any idiot can face a crisis; it is this day-to-day living that wears you out. **Anton Chekhov**. Quoted in *Business Babble: A Cynic's Dictionary of Corporate Jargon* (David Olive, 1991)

I believe that if ever I had to practice cannibalism, I might manage if there were enough tarragon around. **James Beard**. Quoted in "obituary," *New York Times* (January 23, 1985)

Life is truly known only to those who suffer, lose, endure adversity, and stumble from defeat to defeat. **Ryszard Kapuściński**. "A Warsaw Diary," *Granta* (1985)

There is no education like adversity. **Benjamin Disraeli (Earl of Beaconsfield)**. *Endymion* (1880), ch. 61

Hope is the power of being cheerful in circumstances which we know to be desperate. **G. K. Chesterton**. *Heretics* (1905)

Prosperity is a great teacher; adversity is a greater. **William Hazlitt**. "On the Conversation of Cards," *Essays* (1819)

He knows not his own strength who has not met adversity. **Ben Jonson**. "Explorata," *Timber, or Discoveries* (1640)

Adversity is sometimes hard upon a man; but for one man who can stand prosperity, there are a hundred that will stand adversity. **Thomas Carlyle**. "The Hero As Man of Letters," *On Heroes, Hero-Worship, and the Heroic in History* (1841)

If you warn 100 men of possible forthcoming bad news, 80 will immediately dislike you. And if you are so unfortunate to be right, the other 20 will as well. **Anthony Gaubis**. Quoted in *The Wit and Wisdom of Wall Street* (Bill Adler, 1985)

In times like these, it helps to recall that there have always been times like these. **Paul Harvey**. Quoted in *A Business Tale* (Marianne M. Jennings, 2003)

Sometimes you're the bug, sometimes you're the windshield. **Mark Knopfler**. *The Bug* (1991)

Dress your best on your execution day. Be extremely courteous to your assistant when you lose money. Try not to blame others for your fate, even if they deserve blame. Never exhibit any self-pity. Do not complain. **Nassim Nicholas Taleb**. On how to behave in adversity. *Fooled by Randomness* (2004)

Advertising

Advertising is the very essence of democracy. **Bruce Barton**. *Reader's Digest* (1955)

Don't sell the steak; sell the sizzle. It is the sizzle that sells the steak and not the cow, although the cow is, of course, mighty important. **Elmer Wheeler**. *Principles of Salesmanship* (1936?), no. 1

A desirable advertisement will be reasonable, but never dull...original, but never self-conscious...imaginative, but never misleading. **Fairfax Cone**. *Christian Science Monitor* (1963)

The Mass Audience is made up of individuals, and good advertising is written always from one person to another. When it is aimed at millions it rarely moves anyone. **Fairfax Cone**. Quoted in *The Art and Science of Marketing* (Grahame Robert Dowling, 2004)

Advertising is the ability to sense, interpret...to put the very heart throbs of a business into type, paper, and ink. **Leo Burnett**. Quoted in *Leo Burnett: Star Reacher* (Joan Kufrin, 1995)

It is pretty obvious that the debasement of the human mind caused by a constant flow of fraudulent advertising is not a trivial thing. There is more than one way to conquer a country. **Raymond Chandler**. Quoted in *Raymond Chandler Speaking* (Dorothy Gardiner and Katherine S. Walker, eds., 1962)

An advertising agency is 85 percent confusion and 15 percent commission. **Fred Allen**. *Treadmill to Oblivion* (1954)

From Those Wonderful Folks Who Gave You Pearl Harbor **Jerry Della Femina**. Book title, originally suggested as an advertising slogan for Panasonic Corporation. *From Those Wonderful Folks Who Gave You Pearl Harbor* (1970)

The modern corporation must manufacture not only goods but the desire for the goods it manufactures. **J. K. Galbraith**. *The Affluent Society* (1958), ch. 20

It is not necessary to advertise food to hungry people, fuel to cold people, or houses to the homeless. **J. K. Galbraith**. *American Capitalism* (1956)

Society drives people crazy with lust and calls it advertising. **John Lahr**. *Guardian (London)* (August 1989)

Until the rise of American advertising, it never occurred to anyone anywhere in the world that the teenager was a captive in a hostile world of adults. **Gore Vidal**. *Rocking the Boat* (1962)

Don't focus on the mink, but what's in it. **Jane Trahey**. Speaking about her famous advertising campaign for Blackglama fur. Quoted in the *New York Times* (2000)

Never stop testing, and your advertising will never stop improving. **David Ogilvy**. *Confessions of an Advertising Man* (1963)

Advertising is only evil when it advertises evil things. **David Ogilvy**. *Confessions of an Advertising Man* (1963)

When you have nothing to say, sing it. **David Ogilvy**. *Ogilvy on Advertising* (1983)

Ninety per cent of advertising doesn't sell much of anything. **David Ogilvy**. *Confessions of an Advertising Man* (1963)

What you say in advertising is more important than how you say it. **David Ogilvy**. *Confessions of an Advertising Man* (1963)

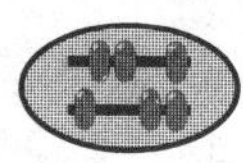
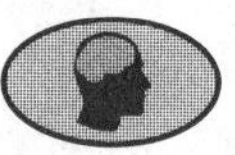
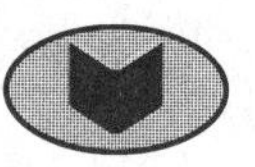
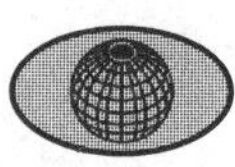

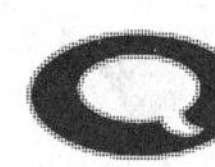

Time spent in the advertising business seems to create a permanent deformity like the Chinese habit of foot-binding. **Dean Acheson**. Quoted in *Among Friends* (David S. McLellan and David C. Acheson, 1980)

I've written books on advertising—cheque books. **Sir Alan Sugar**. *The Apprentice (UK)*

Make a Fair Product for a Fair Price, then Tell the World **William Wrigley**. "Make a Fair Product for a Fair Price, then Tell the World," *Illustrated World* (S. J. Duncan-Clark, March 1922)

Whatever happens, you get your pet back. **Anonymous**. Slogan of a Manhattan firm founded by two brothers, one a vet, the other a taxidermist. Quoted in *Architect's Journal* (July 13, 2000)

Tell me quick and tell me true, what your product's going to do, or else, my love, to hell with you. **Anonymous**. Quoted in *Marketing* (July 2000)

Of course advertising creates wants. Of course it makes people discontented, dissatisfied. Satisfaction with things as they are would defeat the American Dream. **Bernice Fitz-Gibbon**. *Macy's, Gimbels and Me* (1967)

I know half the money I spend on advertising is wasted, but I can never find out which half. **John Wanamaker**. Quoted in "How to Acquire Customers on the Web," *Harvard Business Review* (Donna L. Hoffman and Thomas P. Novak, 2000)

Advertising is the greatest art form of the twentieth century. **Marshall McLuhan**. Attributed

Good advertising can make people buy your product even if it sucks...A dollar spent on brainwashing is more cost-effective than a dollar spent on product improvement. **Scott Adams**. *The Dilbert Principle* (1996)

We read advertisements...to discover and enlarge our desires. **Daniel J. Boorstin**. *The Image* (1961)

It is far easier to write ten passably effective sonnets, good enough to take in the not too enquiring critic, than one effective advertisement that will take in a few thousand of the uncritical buying public. **Aldous Huxley**. *On the Margin* (1923)

What do you want from me? Fine writing? Or would you like to see the goddam sales curve stop going down and start going up? **Rosser Reeves**. Interview (1965)

Promise, large promise is the soul of an advertisement. **Samuel Johnson**. *The Idler* (1759), no. 40

Advertising may be described as the science of arresting human intelligence long enough to get money from it. **Stephen Leacock**. *The Perfect Salesman* (1924)

The business that considers itself immune to the necessity for advertising sooner or later finds itself immune to business. **Derby Brown**. Attributed

Ambition

When you reach for the stars, you may not quite get one, but you won't come up with a handful of mud either. **Leo Burnett**. Quoted in *Reader's Digest* (January 1985)

Man's restlessness makes him strive. **Johann Wolfgang von Goethe**. *Faust* (1832), Part 2

To him that will, ways are not wanting. **George Herbert**. *Jacula Prudentum* (1651)

If ambition doesn't hurt you, you haven't got it. **Kathleen Norris**. *Hands Full of Living* (1931)

Ambition often puts men upon doing the meanest offices; so climbing is performed in the same posture with creeping. **Jonathan Swift**. *Thoughts on Various Subjects* (1711)

At the age of six I wanted to be a cook. At seven I wanted to be Napoleon. And my ambition has been growing steadily ever since. **Salvador Dali**. *The Secret Life of Salvador Dali* (1948)

The world continues to offer glittering prizes to those who have stout hearts and sharp swords. **Frederick E. Smith (Earl of Birkenhead)**. Rectorial address (November 7, 1923)

Ambition if it feeds at all, does so on the ambition of others. **Susan Sontag**. *The Benefactor* (1963), ch. 1

The man who starts out simply with the idea of getting rich won't succeed, you must have a larger ambition. **John D. Rockefeller**. *Random Reminiscenses of Men and Events* (1909)

Focusing your life solely on making a buck shows a certain poverty of ambition. It asks too little of yourself...Because it's only when you hitch your wagon to something larger than yourself that you realize your true potential. **Barack Obama**. Knox College commencement address (June 4, 2005)

All my life, I've always wanted to be somebody, but I see now I should have been more specific. **Jane Wagner**. Comedy sketch written for Lily Tomlin

Attitude

Your attitude determines your altitude. **Stephen Covey**. Quoted in *Woodbury Reports Archives* (October 1995)

Attitudes are more important than facts. **Karl Augustus Menninger**. Attributed

A professional is a man who can do his job when he doesn't feel like it. An amateur is a man who can't do his work when he does feel like it. **James Agate**. Diary (July 19, 1945)

If you can't change your fate change your attitude. **Amy Tan**. *The Joy Luck Club* (1989)

Without the right attitude, a business with everything going for it will fail. **Robert Heller**. Referring to research into company growth carried out by consulting firm Binder Hamlyn. *Goldfinger* (1998)

Empty your mind, be formless, shapeless—like water. Now you put water into a cup, it becomes the cup. You put water into a bottle, it becomes the bottle. You put it in a teapot, it becomes the teapot. Now water can flow or it can crash! Be water my friend. **Bruce Lee**. Quoted in *Bruce Lee: Fighting Spirit* (Bruce Thomas, 1994)

You cannot control what happens to you, but you can control your attitude toward what happens to you, and in that, you will be mastering change rather than allowing it to master you. **Brian Tracy**. Attributed

Banking

A bank is a place that will lend you money if you can prove that you don't need it. **Bob Hope**. Quoted in "The Tyranny of Forms," *Life in the Crystal Palace* (Alan Harrington, 1959)

I hesitate to deposit money in a bank. I am afraid I shall never dare to take it out again. When you go to confession and entrust your sins to the safe-keeping of the priest, do you ever come back for them? **Jean Baudrillard**. *America* (1989)

Except for the con men borrowing money they shouldn't get and the widows who have to visit with the handsome young men in the trust department, no sane person ever enjoyed visiting a bank. **Martin Mayer**. *The Money Bazaars* (1984)

Our banking system grew by accident; and whenever something happens by accident, it becomes a religion. **Walter Wriston**. *BusinessWeek* (January 20, 1975)

The process by which banks create money is so simple that the mind is repelled. **J. K. Galbraith**. *Money: Whence It Came, Where It Went* (1975)

Every banker knows that if he has to *prove* that he is worthy of credit, however good may be his arguments, in fact his credit is gone. **Walter Bagehot**. *Lombard Street* (1873)

Adventure is the life of commerce but caution, I had almost said timidity, is the life of banking. **Walter Bagehot**. *Lombard Street* (1873)

Bankers regard research as most dangerous and a thing that makes banking hazardous due to the rapid changes it brings about in industry. **Charles Franklin Kettering**. Address (1927)

What is robbing a bank compared with founding a bank? **Bertolt Brecht**. *The Threepenny Opera* (1928)

I doubt if there is any occupation which is more consistently and unfairly demeaned, degraded, denounced, and deplored than banking. **William Proxmire**. Quoted in *Fortune* (October 31, 1983)

You know what the difference is between a dead skunk and a dead banker on the road? There's skid marks by the skunk. **Anonymous**. Quoted in *Final Harvest: An American Tragedy* (Andrew H. Malcolm, 1986)

It's one of life's ironies that the more you can prove that you don't need a loan, the better your chances usually are of getting one. This is especially true for start-up businesses. **Lillian Vernon**. Speech. "The Entrepreneur and the Professional Manager: Getting the Best of Both Worlds" (1998)

It has been the bankers' destiny...to find themselves on the dangerous edge of the world, pointing up the contradictions and cross-purposes. They are not often loved for it. **Anthony Sampson**. *The Moneylenders: Bankers in a Dangerous World* (1981), ch. 22

When I was young, people called me a gambler. As the scale of my operations increased I became known as a speculator. Now I am called a banker. But I have been doing the same thing all the time. **Sir Ernest Cassel**. Quoted in *Fat Cats: The Strange Cult of the CEO* (Gideon Haigh, 2005)

It is no accident that banks resemble temples, preferably Greek, and that the supplicants who come to perform the rites of deposit and withdrawal instinctively lower their voices into the registers of awe. Even the most junior tellers acquire within weeks of their employment the officiousness of hierophants tending an eternal flame. **Lewis H. Lapham**. *Money and Class in America* (1988)

I expect there will be some failures...I don't anticipate any serious problems of that sort among the large internationally active banks that make up a very substantial part of our banking system. **Ben Bernanke**. Testifying to the Senate Banking Committee (February 28, 2008)

I'm very happy to support it. And I keep my fingers crossed for the future. **Roel C. Campos**. On the Commission's fateful decision to exempt the big investment banks from capital requirements rules. Meeting of the Securities and Exchange Commission (April 28, 2004)

They took 50 sheriffs off the beat at a time when lending was becoming the Wild West. **Roy Cooper**. On the decision to block state governments from using consumer protection laws to control predatory subprime lending. Quoted in the *New York Times* (December 20, 2008)

We have a good deal of comfort about the capital cushions at these firms at the moment. **Christopher Cox**. On the big investment banks (March 11, 2008)

You have to eventually nationalize US banks, you have to take the problem by the horns. In my view actually most of the US banking system is insolvent. **Nouriel Roubini**. Interviewed on Bloomberg Television (January 29, 2009)

Less of a negotiation, more of a drive-by shooting. **Sir Fred Goodwin**. On the UK government's forced recapitalization of the banking system. Quoted in the *Evening Standard (London)* (October 15, 2008)

This is not nationalization. **Geir Haarde**. On nationalizing the country's leading banks. Quoted in the *London Review of Books* (November 20, 2008)

We are used to a less dynamic environment than we have seen in the past few months and days. **Rod Kent**. Explaining Bradford & Bingley's financial troubles. The bank was rescued by the UK government in September. Quoted in the *Independent (London)* (June 3, 2008)

If you were alive, they would give you a loan. Actually, I think if you were dead, they would still give you a loan. **Steven M. Knoebel**. On lax lending at the Washington Mutual Bank, which went into receivership in September 2008 (December 29, 2008)

I have great, great confidence in our capital markets and in our financial institutions. Our financial institutions, banks and investment banks, are strong. Our capital markets are resilient. They're efficient. They're flexible. **Henry Paulson**. Remark (March 16, 2008)

It's a safe banking system, a sound banking system. Our regulators are on top of it. This is a very manageable situation. **Henry Paulson**. On the failure of the Indymac bank. CBS News broadcast (July 20, 2008)

We're not just going to see mid-sized banks go under in the next few months, we're going to see a whopper. **Kenneth Rogoff**. Lehman Brothers filed for bankruptcy two weeks later. Remark (August 2008)

You can't overestimate what happens when you encourage regulators to believe that the goal of regulation is not to regulate. **Joseph Stiglitz**. Quoted in the *International Herald Tribune* (September 20, 2008)

Financial institutions have been merging into a smaller number of very large banks. Almost all banks are interrelated. So the financial ecology is swelling into gigantic, incestuous, bureaucratic banks—when one fails, they all fall...We have moved from a diversified ecology of small banks, with varied lending policies, to a more homogeneous framework of firms that all resemble one another. True, we now have fewer failures, but when they occur...I shiver at the thought. **Nassim Nicholas Taleb**. *The Black Swan* (2006)

If banks feel they must keep on dancing while the music is playing and that at the end of the party the central bank will make sure everyone gets home safely, then over time, the parties will become wilder and wilder. When the party ends, some innocent bystanders may lose their homes altogether. **Mervyn King**. Speech to the British Bankers' Association (June 2008)

Not since the First World War has our banking system been so close to collapse. The past few weeks have been somewhat too exciting...So let me extend an invitation to the banking industry to join me in promoting the idea that a little more boredom would be no bad thing. The long

  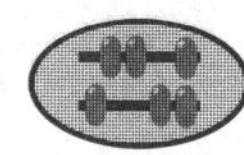 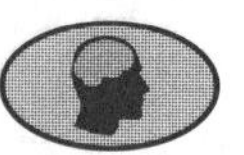 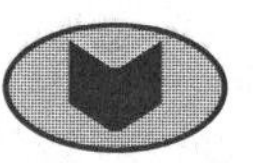 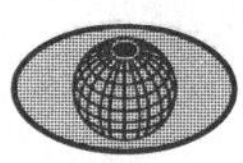 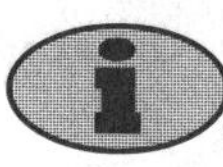  

march to boredom and stability starts tonight. **Mervyn King**. Speech (October 2008)

Blame

Everyone threw the blame on me...they nearly always do. I suppose...they think I shall be able to bear it best. **Sir Winston Churchill**. *My Early Life* (1947), ch. 17

Success is never blamed. **Thomas Fuller**. *Gnomologia* (1732), no. 4273

If we had no faults of our own, we should not take so much pleasure in noticing those of others. **François La Rochefoucauld**. *Reflections: or, Sentences and Moral Maxims* (5th ed, 1678)

One must first learn to live oneself before one blames others. **Fyodor Dostoevsky**. *Notes from the Underground* (1864)

I find that pain of a little censure, even when it is unfounded, is more acute than the pleasure of much praise. **Thomas Jefferson**. Letter to F. Hopkinson (March 13, 1789)

Our culture peculiarly honors the act of blaming, which it takes as the sign of virtue and intellect. **Lionel Trilling**. *The Liberal Imagination* (1950)

Underneath runs the main current of preoccupation, which is keeping one's nose clean at all times. This means that when things go wrong you have to pass the blame along the line, like pass-the-parcel, till the music stops. **Sir Tom Stoppard**. *Neutral Ground* (1983)

An expert is someone called in at the last minute to share the blame. **Sam Ewing**. Quoted in *Reader's Digest* (December 1992)

Boasting

If I only had a little humility, I'd be perfect. **Ted Turner**. *New York Times* (1980)

It ain't bragging if you can do it. **Babe Ruth**. Quoted in *Woodbury Reports Archives* (December 1994)

I have helped to change society in a way that is beyond presidents and is going to make the world a better and happier place. **Hugh Hefner**. *Mail and Femail* (December 18, 1989)

Some of them think they have me by the balls, but their hands aren't big enough. **Bernie Ecclestone**. Referring to negotiations with Formula 1 racing teams, when planning to float Formula 1 on the Stock Exchange. Quoted in *Formula 1, The Business of Winning* (Russell Hotten, 1998)

I don't meet competition. I crush it. **Charles Revson**. *Time* (June 16, 1958)

If you wish in this world to advance
Your merits you're bound to enhance;
You must stir it and stump it,
And blow your own trumpet,
Or trust me, you haven't a chance.
Sir W. S. Gilbert. *Ruddigore* (1887), Act 1

The only thing I have to do is look each day and see how much money came in. £50 million came in only last Friday! **Sigurjon Arnason**. Quoted in the *London Review of Books* (November 20, 2008)

Boldness

Corporate courage is usually no greater than personal courage. **Edward Teller**. Interview, *Playboy* (August 1979)

Boldness in business is the first, second, and third thing. **Thomas Fuller**. *Gnomologia* (1732)

It is better to be impetuous than circumspect. Experience shows that [fortune] is more often subdued by men who do this than by those who act coldly. **Niccolò Machiavelli**. *The Prince* (1513)

Boldness, again boldness, and always boldness! **Georges Jacques Danton**. Speech to the Legislative Committee of General Defense (September 2, 1792)

All good fortune is a gift of the gods and you don't win the favour of the ancient gods by being good but by being bold. **Anita Brookner**. Quoted in *Writers at Work* (1988)

You can be very bold as a theoretician. Good theories are like good art. A practitioner has to compromise. **Warren Bennis**. *The Director* (October 1988)

We need a readiness to enter a room in the dark and stumble over unfamiliar furniture until the pain in our shins reminds us of where things are. **Fons Trompenaars**. *Financial Times (London)* (July 1996)

If the creator had a purpose in equipping us with a neck, he surely meant us to stick it out. **Arthur Koestler**. *The Sleepwalkers* (1959)

Anything worth doing is worth doing to excess. **Edwin Land**. *Boston Globe* (March 1991)

Nothing will ever be attempted, if all possible objections must first be overcome. **Samuel Johnson**. *Rasselas, Prince of Abyssinia* (1759)

If you're going to be thinking only one thing, you might as well be thinking big. **Donald J. Trump**. Referring to the grand scale of his property deals. *Trump: The Art of the Deal* (1987)

Boom and Bust

A crash does not come knocking at the front door by appointment. **Jim Slater**. Quoted in *Treasury of Investment Wisdom* (Bernice Cohen, 1999)

A depression is a situation of self-fulfilling pessimism. **Joan Robinson**. "The Short Period," *Economic Heresies* (1970)

In a market like this, every story is a positive one. Any news is good news. It's pretty much taken for granted now that the market is going to go up. **Anonymous**. the market began to decline that day, plummeted nearly 1000 points in October, and did not regain its August peak for nearly two years. *Wall Street Journal* (August 26, 1987)

In the next economic downturn there will be an outbreak of bitterness and contempt for the supercorporate chieftains who pay themselves millions. In every major economic downturn in US history the villains have been the heroes during the preceding boom. **Peter F. Drucker**. Quoted in "Seeing Things As They Really Are," *Forbes* (Robert Lenzner and Stephen S. Johnson, 1987)

Property and stock market crashes...litter the history of capitalism. But at the same time there is no evidence that anyone has ever been successful in preventing such a crash. **Lester Thurow**. "Barking up the Wrong Tree," *www.lthurow.com* (November 2, 1999)

Nothing sedates rationality like large doses of effortless money. After a heady experience of that kind, normally sensible people drift into behavior akin to that of Cinderella at the ball the giddy participants all plan to leave just seconds before midnight. There's a problem, though: they are dancing in a room in which the clocks have no hands. **Warren Buffett**. Letter to shareholders (2000)

There is no evidence that the business cycle

  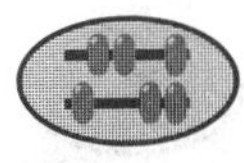 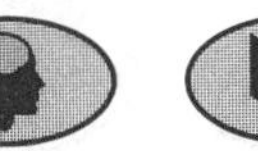 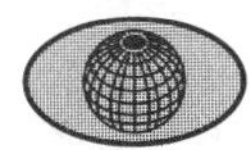   

has been repealed. **Alan Greenspan**. *Wall Street Journal* (1997)

History records no case where the bubble gracefully deflated, accompanied by a slight hiss of escaping optimism. The speculative episode always ends with a loud explosion. **Andreas Whittam Smith**. *Independent (London)* (January 28, 2008)

Bull markets are born on pessimism, grow on skepticism, mature on optimism, and die on euphoria. **Sir John Templeton**. Quoted in *Short-term Trading in the New Stock Market* (Toni Turner, 2005)

The four most expensive words in the English language are, "This time, it's different." **Sir John Templeton**. Quoted in *The Four Pillars of Investing* (William J. Bernstein, 2002)

A very powerful and durable rally is in the works. But it may need another couple of days to lift off. Hold the fort and keep the faith! **Richard Band**. *Profitable Investing Letter* (March 27, 2008)

Last year this was a financial crisis that we thought with a bit of luck would be over by Christmas... **Charles Bean**. Quoted in the *Guardian (London)* (August 26, 2008)

If Wall Street crashes, does Main Street follow? Not necessarily. **Ben Bernanke**. Remark (September 2000)

I and others were mistaken early on in saying that the subprime crisis would be contained. **Ben Bernanke**. "Anatomy of a Meltdown," *New Yorker* (December 1, 2008)

It's a crisis if everybody calls it a crisis. **Morgan Downey**. Remark (2007)

What, pray, is all the fuss about?...If this is the worst crisis since the Great Depression then we must have all been living pretty cushy, gilded lives since the 1930s. If this is all it takes to destroy capitalism...then it is a wonder why the Soviet Union failed to do so during its seven decades of existence. For the past year has actually not been very bad at all—unless you are a banker, a bank shareholder or Gordon Brown; and few will shed tears for any of those. **Bill Emmott**. *Guardian (London)* (August 12, 2008)

I think this is a case where Freddie Mac and Fannie Mae are fundamentally sound. They're not in danger of going under...I think they are in good shape going forward. **Barney Frank**. Fannie Mae and Freddie Mac were taken into government "conservatorship" in September 2008. Remark (July 14, 2008)

The final chapter of Greenspan's legacy has not been written. Maybe it will work out fine, but maybe not. **Paul Kasriel**. On Alan Greenspan's retirement as chairman of the US Federal Reserve. Quoted on *Bloomberg.com* (January 26, 2006)

The recession debate is over. It's not gonna happen...The Bush boom is alive and well. It's finishing up its sixth splendid year with many more years to come. **Lawrence Kudlow**. Kudlow's Money Politics blog (December 5, 2007)

Real estate is still a great investment opportunity for households. Price appreciation will continue. It may not be at 20%. It may...even go down to 5%. **David Lereah**. Between 2006 and 2008 US house prices fell faster than they fell during the Great Depression. Interviewed on *SmartMoney.com* (August 12, 2005)

The central problem of depression-prevention has been solved, for all practical purposes. **Robert Lucas, Jr**. Address to the American Economic Association (2003)

Anyone who says we're in a recession, or heading into one—especially the worst one since the Great Depression—is making up his own private definition of "recession." **Donald Luskin**. This was the day before Lehman Brothers filed for bankruptcy, triggering a stock-market crash. *Washington Post* (September 14, 2008)

We are in the biggest real-estate boom we've ever seen. Something is going to happen to end this. **Robert Shiller**. Between 2006 and 2008 US house prices fell faster than they fell during the Great Depression. Remark (August 2005)

It's quite possible that at some point we may get an odd quarter or two of negative growth, but recession is not the central projection at all. **Mervyn King**. Speech (May 2008)

The current financial crisis in the US is likely to be judged in retrospect as the most wrenching since the end of the Second World War. **Alan Greenspan**. *Financial Times (London)* (March 16, 2008)

We are in the midst of a once-in-a-century credit tsunami. Central banks and governments are being required to take unprecedented measures. Those of us who have looked to the self-interest of lending institutions to protect shareholders' equity are in a state of shocked disbelief. **Alan Greenspan**. Speaking before the House Committee on Oversight (October 23, 2008)

At present it is a bit like being in a country where a civil war is taking place. Away from the fighting, everything seems normal enough...Open-air cafes are full, shops are busy and the best restaurants have no spare tables. But in the combat zones, perhaps not very far away, life is hellish. **Andreas Whittam Smith**. On the deepening recession. *Independent (London)* (December 5, 2008)

The market is in the process of correcting itself. **George W. Bush**. Speech (March 14, 2008)

We can have confidence in the long-term foundation of our economy...I think the system basically is sound. I truly do. **George W. Bush**. The US financial system plunged into crisis in September. Speech (July 15, 2008)

These are not normal circumstances. The market is not functioning properly. **George W. Bush**. Speech (September 24, 2008)

This sucker could go down. **George W. Bush**. Referring to the entire US financial system at an emergency cabinet meeting. Quoted in the *New York Times* (September 25, 2008)

This thaw took a while to thaw, it's going to take a while to unthaw. **George W. Bush**. Referring to frozen credit markets. Speech given in Alexandria, Louisiana (October 20, 2008)

Global capital markets pose the same kinds of problems that jet planes do. They are faster, more comfortable, and they get you where you are going better. But the crashes are much more spectacular. **Lawrence H. Summers**. Interviewed in *Time* (June 26, 2005)

Blaming speculators as a response to financial crisis goes back at least to the Greeks. It's almost always the wrong response. **Lawrence H. Summers**. On the financial crisis in South-East Asia. Remark (1997)

Unsustainable situations usually go on longer than most economists think possible. But they always end, and when they do, it's often painful. **Paul R. Krugman**. Address given in Bangkok (September 2005)

Consumer spending is now plunging at serious-recession rate...even if the rescue now in train succeeds in unfreezing credit markets, the real economy has immense downward momentum. In addition to financial rescues, we need major stimulus programs. **Paul R. Krugman**. *New York Times* blog post entitled "Train Headed Downhill" (October 15, 2008)

  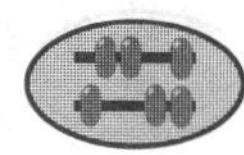   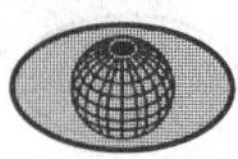   

When depression economics prevails, the usual rules of economic policy no longer apply: virtue becomes vice, caution is risky and prudence is folly. **Paul R. Krugman**. *New York Times* (November 14, 2008)

There are no atheists in foxholes and there are no libertarians in financial crises. **Paul R. Krugman**. Interview with Bill Maher on HBO television (September 19, 2008)

The fundamentals of America's economy are strong. **John McCain**. Interviewed on Bloomberg Television (April 17, 2008)

When we're talking about a trillion dollars of taxpayer money, "trust me" just isn't good enough. **John McCain**. On the US Treasury secretary's Wall Street bailout plan. Quoted in *The Times (London)* (September 25, 2008)

Brands

Brands are all about trust. You buy the brand because you consider it a friend. **Sir Michael Perry**. *Marketing* (March 2000)

You, me, all of us, must turn ourselves into distinctive one-person Brands. **Tom Peters**. "Work Matters! movement manifesto," *www.tompeters.com* (September 1999)

With the strongest brands, the CEO owns the brand. It must be owned by someone, the higher in the company the better. **Shelly Lazarus**. *Marketing News* (2000)

Truly great brands are far more than just labels for products; they are symbols that encapsulate the desires of consumers; they are standards that are held aloft under which the masses congregate. **Tony O'Reilly**. Speech, British Council of Shopping Centres. Quoted in *Granta* (Spring 1996)

Budgeting

Watch the costs and the profits will take care of themselves. **Andrew Carnegie**. Quoted in *The Entrepreneurs—An American Adventure* (R. Sobel and D. B. Silicia, 1986)

The budget is God. **Anonymous**. Slogan at Japanese optical company Topcom. Quoted in the *Economist (London)* (January 13, 1996)

Annual income twenty pounds, annual expenditure nineteen nineteen six, result happiness. Annual income twenty pounds, annual expenditure twenty pounds ought and six, result misery. **Charles Dickens**. There were twenty shillings in a pound and twelve pence in a shilling. *David Copperfield* (1849–1850), ch. 12

For as long as I can remember the slogan has been...the federal government ought to behave more like families, because families balance their budgets. It turns out that families looked around and said, "You know what? Let's behave more like the government!" **George Will**. On irresponsible borrowing. *This Week* (September 2008)

Bureaucracy

The only thing that saves us from the bureaucracy is inefficiency. An efficient bureaucracy is the greatest threat to liberty. **Eugene McCarthy**. *Time* (February 12, 1979)

Bureaucracy, safely repeating today what it did yesterday, rolls on as ineluctably as some vast computer, which, once penetrated by error, duplicates it forever. **Barbara W. Tuchman**. *The March of Folly* (1984)

The bureaucracies of the Industrial Age will appear to the new inter-corporate, transcontinental networks like old Royal typewriters do to PC owners. **Jessica Lipnack**. *St. Louis Post-Dispatch* (December 1991)

Officials are highly educated but one-sided; in his own department an official can grasp whole trains of thought from a single word, but let him have something from another department explained to him...he won't understand a word of it. **Franz Kafka**. *The Castle* (1926)

Poor fellow, he suffers from files. **Aneurin Bevan**. Referring to the administrator Sir Walter Citrine. Quoted in *Aneurin Bevan* (Michael Foot, 1962), vol. 1

Corpocracy is large-scale corporate America's tendency to be like the government bureaucracy. **Richard G. Darman**. *New York Times* (November 9, 1986)

However many people complain about the red tape, it would be sheer illusion to think for a moment that continuous administrative work can be carried out except by means of officials working in offices...The choice is only that between bureaucracy and dilettantism in the field of administration. **Max Weber**. Quoted in *Economy and Society* (Guenther Roth and Claus Wittich, eds., 1968)

A committee is an animal with four back legs. **John Le Carré**. *Tinker, Tailor, Soldier, Spy* (1974)

A memorandum is written not to inform the reader but to protect the writer. **Dean Acheson**. Quoted in *Wall Street Journal* (September 8, 1977)

Few great men could pass Personnel. **Paul Goodman**. *Growing Up Absurd* (1960)

It seems to me that there must be an ecological limit to the number of paper pushers the earth can sustain. **Barbara Ehrenreich**. "Premature Pragmatism," *The Worst Years of Our Lives* (1991)

Bureaucracy, the rule of no one, has become the modern form of despotism. **Mary McCarthy**. "The Vita Activa," *New Yorker* (October 18, 1958)

A committee is a cul-de-sac down which ideas are lured and then quietly strangled. **Barnett Cocks**. Quoted in *New Scientist* (1973)

An administrator in a bureaucratic world is a man who can feel big by merging his non-entity with an abstraction. A real person in touch with real things inspires terror in him. **Marshall McLuhan**. Letter to Ezra Pound (1951)

Guidelines for bureaucrats: (1) When in charge, ponder. (2) When in trouble, delegate. (3) When in doubt, mumble. **James H. Boren**. *New York Times* (November 9, 1970)

Bureaucratic time...slower than geologic time but more expensive than time spent with Madame Claude's girls in Paris. **P. J. O'Rourke**. *Parliament of Whores* (1991)

Muddle is the extra unknown personality in any committee. **Anthony Sampson**. *Anatomy of Britain Today* (1965)

A committee is a group of people who keep minutes and waste hours. **Milton Berle**. Attributed

Business Ethics

I believe that nicotine is not addictive. **Thomas Sandefur**. Said at the 1994 US Congressional hearings on the tobacco industry. Quoted in the *New York Times* (1997)

I ran the wrong kind of business, but I did it with integrity. **Sydney Biddle Barrows**.

  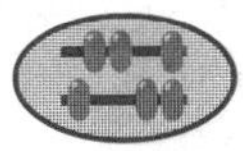   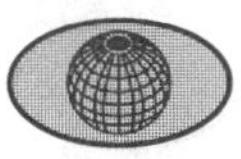   

"Mayflower Madam Tells All," *Boston Globe* (1986)

Creative swiping provides energy to an organization. **Chuck Chambers**. Quoted in *Liberation Management* (Tom Peters, 1992)

Thou shalt not steal; an empty feat when it's so lucrative to cheat. **Arthur Hugh Clough**. "The Latest Decalogue" (1862)

The meek shall inherit the earth, but not the mineral rights. **J. Paul Getty**. Quoted in *The Great Getty* (Robert Lenzner, 1985)

Always do right. This will gratify some people, and astonish the rest. **Mark Twain**. Speech to the Young People's Society, Greenpoint Baptist Church, Brooklyn, New York (1901)

The latter-day robber barons are discovering that better conditions and rewards for workers pay off in a world where consumers increasingly demand ethical standards. **Clare Short**. *Management Today* (November 1999)

Such is the brutalization of commercial ethics in this country no one can feel anything more delicate than the velvet touch of a soft buck. **Raymond Chandler**. Letter to his publisher. *Raymond Chandler Speaking* (Dorothy Gardiner and Katherine S. Walker, eds., 1962)

We have our values from the church, the temple, the mosque. Do not rob, do not murder. But our behaviour changes the minute we go into the corporate place. Suddenly all of this is irrelevant. **Dame Anita Roddick**. Interviewed in *Marketing Week* (February 24, 2000)

If you think you're too small to have an impact, try going to bed with a mosquito in the room. **Dame Anita Roddick**. Quoted in *4-D Branding* (Thomas Gad, 2001)

In business we cut each others' throats, but now and then we sit around the same table and behave—for the sake of the ladies. **Aristotle Onassis**. *Sunday Times (London)* (March 16, 1969)

If you can't pay for a thing, don't buy it. If you can't get paid for it, don't sell it. Do this, and you will have calm and drowsy nights, with all of the good business you have now and none of the bad. **Benjamin Franklin**. Quoted in *Fors Clavigera* (John Ruskin, 1873)

If you allow men to use you for your own purposes, they will use you for theirs. **Aesop**. "The Horse, Hunter, and Stag" (6th century BC)

The leader should know how to enter into evil when necessity commands. **Niccolò Machiavelli**. *The Prince* (1513)

The market has no morality. **Lord Heseltine**. Interview, Panorama, BBC Television (June 1988)

Two half truths do not make a truth. **Arthur Koestler**. *The Ghost in the Machine* (1967)

Commercialism is doing well that which should not be done at all. **Gore Vidal**. *Listener* (August 1975)

There cannot be a situation where a businessman says, "I base all my business on moral considerations." Equally, you can't say you can run a business without morality. **Sir Timothy Bevan**. Said as Chairman of Barclays Bank Ltd., when asked about Barclays' withdrawal from South Africa. *Observer (London)* (November 30, 1986)

Food comes first, then morals. **Bertolt Brecht**. *The Threepenny Opera* (1928)

As an anonymous participant in financial markets, I never had to weigh the social consequences of my actions...I felt justified in ignoring them on the grounds that I was playing by the rules. **George Soros**. *The Crisis of Global Capitalism* (1998)

Ministers and merchants love nobody. **Thomas Jefferson**. Letter to John Langdon (September 11, 1785)

Thieves respect property. They merely wish the property to become their property that they may more perfectly respect it. **G. K. Chesterton**. *The Man Who Was Thursday* (1908)

If there was a market in mass-produced portable nuclear weapons, we'd market them too. **Sir Alan Sugar**. Quoted in *The Condition of Postmodernity* (David Harvey, 1989)

We take society's capital, we take their people, we take their materials, yet without a good profit we are using precious resources that could be used better elsewhere. **Konosuke Matsushita**. *Quest for Prosperity* (1988)

A business that makes nothing but money is a poor kind of business. **Henry Ford**. Quoted in *The Arizona Republic* (1999)

We have always known that heedless self-interest was bad morals; we know now that it is bad economics. **Franklin D. Roosevelt**. Second presidential inaugural address (January 20, 1937)

Love your neighbour is not merely sound Christianity; it is good business. **David Lloyd George (Earl of Dwyfor)**. Quoted in "Sayings of the Week," *Observer (London)* (February 20, 1921)

Armaments, universal debt, and planned obsolescence—these are the three pillars of Western prosperity. **Aldous Huxley**. *Island* (1962), ch. 9

Here's the rule for bargains: Do other men, for they would do you. That's the true business precept. **Charles Dickens**. *Martin Chuzzlewit* (1843–1844), ch. 11

COMMERCE, n. A kind of transaction in which A plunders from B the goods of C, and for compensation B picks the pocket of D of money belonging to E. **Ambrose Bierce**. *The Devil's Dictionary* (1911)

Oh God, that bread should be so dear
And flesh and blood so cheap.
Thomas Hood. "The Song of the Shirt" (1843)

I find it rather easy to portray a businessman. Being bland, rather cruel and incompetent comes naturally to me. **John Cleese**. Referring to appearing in industrial training videos. *Newsweek* (June 15, 1987)

Experience teaches you that the man who looks you straight in the eye, particularly if he adds a firm handshake, is hiding something. **Clifton Fadiman**. *Enter Conversing* (1962)

If it is not right, don't do it; if it is not true, don't say it. **John A. Byrne**. *Fast Company: The Rules of Business* (2005)

A bargain is in its very essence a hostile transaction. Do not all men try to abate the price of all they buy? I contend that a bargain—even between brethren—is a declaration of war. **George Gordon, Lord Byron**. Letter (July 14, 1821)

I'll keep it short and sweet. Family. Religion. Friendship. These are the three demons you must slay if you wish to succeed in business. **Matt Groening**. Spoken by tycoon C. Montgomery Burns in *The Simpsons*

If you can take advantage of a situation in some way, it's your duty as an American to do it. **Matt Groening**. Spoken by tycoon C. Montgomery Burns in *The Simpsons*

You can't get that sort of buying opportunity very often. It's important to take advantage of it, if you have the guts and temperament. **David Lui**. On the Tiananmen Square massacre

Most men are individuals no longer so far

as their business, its activities, or its moralities are concerned. They are not units but fractions. **Woodrow T. Wilson**. Address to the American Bar Association (August 31, 1910)

There is a delicious irony in seeing private luxury jets flying into Washington, DC, and people coming off of them with tin cups in their hand, saying that they're going to be trimming down and streamlining their businesses. It's almost like seeing a guy show up at the soup kitchen in high hat and tuxedo. It kind of makes you a little bit suspicious. **Gary Ackerman**. To the chief executive officers of Ford, Chrysler, and General Motors at a hearing of the House Financial Services Committee (November 18, 2008)

When I find a short-seller, I want to tear his heart out and eat it before his eyes while he's still alive. **Richard S. Fuld, Jr**. Quoted in the *Financial Times (London)* (December 30, 2008)

I'm going to ask the three executives here to raise their hand if they flew here commercial. Let the record show, no hands went up. Second, I'm going to ask you to raise your hand if you are planning to sell your jet in place now and fly back commercial. Let the record show, no hands went up. **Brad Sherman**. To the chief executive officers of Ford, Chrysler, and General Motors at a hearing of the House Financial Services Committee (November 18, 2008)

Your company is now bankrupt, our economy is now in a state of crisis, but you get to keep $480 million. I have a very basic question for you: Is this fair? **Henry Waxman**. Questioning Lehman Brothers CEO Richard S. Fuld, Jr, over the bank's collapse. Speaking at a Congressional hearing (October 5, 2008)

Capitalism

The chief business of the American people is business. **Calvin Coolidge**. Quoted in the *New York Times* (2000)

Capitalism, wisely managed, can probably be made more efficient for attaining economic ends than any alternative system yet in sight. **John Maynard Keynes**. *The End of Laissez-Faire* (1926)

The prevailing theory of capitalism suffers from one central and disabling flaw, a profound distrust and incomprehension of capitalism. **George Gilder**. *The Spirit of Enterprise* (1984)

Capital must be propelled by self-interest; it cannot be enticed by benevolence. **Walter Bagehot**. *Economic Studies* (1880)

Our belief in salvation through the market is very much in the Utopian tradition. The economists and managers are the servants of God. Like the medieval scholastics, their only job is to uncover the divine plan. They could never create or stop it. At most they might aspire to small alterations. **John Ralston Saul**. *The Unconscious Civilization* (1995)

Capitalism, as practiced, is a financially profitable, non-sustainable aberration in human development. **Paul Hawken**. *Natural Capitalism* (co-written with Amory B. Lovins and L. Hunter Lovins, 1999)

Mr Heath talks about the unacceptable face of capitalism, but intrinsically it doesn't have an unacceptable face. **Lord Weinstock**. Referring to prime minister Edward Heath's description of Lonrho as the unacceptable face of capitalism. Quoted in the *Daily Telegraph (London)* (June 17, 1974)

The great challenge of the twentieth century...is to create a new financial architecture in which private decisions produce a less degenerate capitalism. **Will Hutton**. *The State We're In* (1995)

Capitalism works better than any of us can conceive. It is also the only truly moral system of exchange. It encourages individuals to devote their energies...to the satisfaction of others' wants and needs. **Steve Forbes**. "Three Cheers for Capitalism," *Imprimis* (September 1993)

The man who accepts the laissez-faire doctrine would allow his garden to grow wild so that roses might fight it out with the weeds and the fittest might survive. **John Ruskin**. Attributed

What breaks capitalism, all that will ever break capitalism, is capitalists. **Raymond Williams**. *Loyalties* (1985)

The system of private property is the most important guarantee of freedom, not only for those who own property, but scarcely less for those who do not. **Friedrich August von Hayek**. *The Road to Serfdom* (1944), ch. 8

We accept and welcome, therefore, as conditions to which we must accommodate ourselves, great inequality of environment, the concentration of business, industrial and commercial, in the hands of a few, and the law of competition between these, as being not only beneficial, but essential for the future progress of the race. **Andrew Carnegie**. "Wealth," *North American Review* (June 1889)

Private property is a necessary institution, at least in a fallen world; men work more and dispute less when goods are private than when they are in common. **Richard Tawney**. *Religion and the Rise of Capitalism* (1926), ch. 1, sect. 1

Capitalism without bankruptcy is like Christianity without hell. **Frank Borman**. Remark (April 21, 1986)

To speak of limits to growth under a capitalistic market economy is as meaningless as to speak of limits of warfare under a warrior society. **Murray Bookchin**. *Remaking Society* (1990)

It is just as important that business keep out of government as that government keep out of business. **Herbert Hoover**. Quoted in the *East Valley Tribune* (2000)

After a recent trip to New York one French journalist remarked that leafing through a copy of Forbes or Fortune is like reading the operating manual of a strangely sanctimonious pirate ship. **Adam Gopnik**. *Paris to the Moon* (2001)

This administration made decisions that allowed the free market to operate as a barroom brawl instead of a prize fight. **L. William Seidman**. On the Bush administration in the run-up to the financial crisis of 2008. Quoted in the *New York Times* (December 20, 2008)

The frantic scrambling that is going on in Washington marks the passing of only one type of capitalism-the peculiar and highly unstable variety that has existed in America over the last 20 years...While the impact of the collapse will be felt everywhere, the market economies that resisted American-style deregulation will best weather the storm. Britain, which has turned itself into a gigantic hedge fund, but of a kind that lacks the ability to profit from a downturn, is likely to be especially badly hit. **John Gray**. *Observer (London)* (September 28, 2008)

Capitalism versus Socialism

Less than seventy-five years after it officially began, the contest between capitalism and socialism is over: capitalism

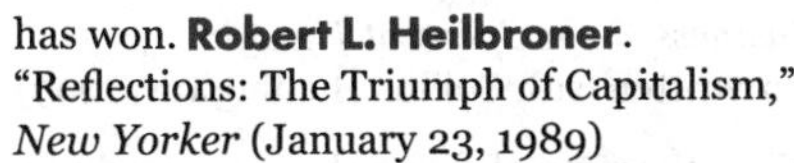

has won. **Robert L. Heilbroner**. "Reflections: The Triumph of Capitalism," *New Yorker* (January 23, 1989)

During its rule of scarce one hundred years, capitalism has created more massive and more colossal productive forces than have all preceding generations together. **Karl Marx**. *The Communist Manifesto* (co-written with Friedrich Engels, 1848)

The twentieth century marks the turning point from the old capitalism to the new, from the domination of capital in general to the domination of financial capital. **Vladimir Ilich Lenin**. *Imperialism, the Higher Stages of Capitalism* (1917)

Prosperity or egalitarianism—you have to choose. I favor freedom—you never achieve real equality anyway: you simply sacrifice prosperity for an illusion. **Mario Vargas Llosa**. *Independent on Sunday (London)* (May 5, 1991)

Communism has failed, but capitalism has not succeeded. **William Keegan**. *The Spectre of Capitalism* (1992)

The fact that global capitalism is flawed does not mean that we should turn to communism or withdraw into national isolation, just as the failure of communism does not mean that markets are perfect. **George Soros**. Speech to the Council on Foreign Relations, New York City. "The Crisis of Global Capitalism: Open Society Endangered" (December 10, 1998)

You cannot go to sleep with one form of economic system and wake up the next morning with another. **Mikhail Gorbachev**. *Guardian (London)* (December 7, 1990)

If there is a man on this earth who is entitled to all the comforts and luxuries of this life...it is the man whose labor produces them...Does he get them in the present system? **Eugene V. Debs**. Speech at Girard, Kansas. "The Issue" (May 23, 1908)

In the end we beat them with Levi 501 jeans. Seventy-two years of Communist indoctrination and propaganda was drowned out by a three-ounce Sony Walkman. **P. J. O'Rourke**. "The Death of Communism," *Rolling Stone* (November 1989)

The natural counterpart of a free market economy is a politics of insecurity. **John Gray**. *False Dawn* (1998)

Capitalism inevitably and by virtue of the very logic of its civilization creates, educates and subsidizes a vested interest in social unrest. **Joseph Alois Schumpeter**. *Capitalism, Socialism and Democracy* (1942), ch. 13

Capitalism is at its liberating best in a noncapitalist environment. The crypto-businessman is the true revolutionary in a Communist country. **Eric Hoffer**. *Reflections on the Human Condition* (1973)

Careers

No man likes to acknowledge that he has made a mistake in the choice of his profession. **Charlotte Brontë**. *The Professor* (1857), ch. 4

I'm just a guy who probably should have been a semi-talented poet on the Left Bank. I got sort of side-tracked here. **Steve Jobs**. *Fortune* (October 1, 1984)

When you retire...you go from who's who to who's that, like stepping off the pier [or] achieving statutory senility. **Walter Wriston**. On retiring as chairman of Citibank Corp. *New York Times* (1985)

Security no longer comes from being employed. It comes from being employable. **Rosabeth Moss Kanter**. *Changing Workplace Alert* (1997)

The traditional corporate career may soon share the fate of the dad-at-work-mom-at home-two-kids nuclear family: an oft-invoked ideal that applies to fewer and fewer people. **Rosabeth Moss Kanter**. *When Giants Learn to Dance: Mastering the Challenges of Strategy, Management and Careers in the 1990s* (1992), ch. 11

In many corporations managers now work with one eye on their résumé. Assignments that used to be seen in terms of their political value in the promotion game are now assessed for their résumé value. **Rosabeth Moss Kanter**. *When Giants Learn to Dance: Mastering the Challenges of Strategy, Management and Careers in the 1990s* (1992), ch. 12

I got my start by giving myself a start. **C. J. Walker**. Quoted in *On Her Own Ground: The Life and Times of Madam C. J. Walker* (A'Lelia Bundles, 2000)

Tomorrow's typical career will be neither linear nor continuous, nor will it always be upwards. Instead, one's life work will take more of a zig-zag course. **Tom Horton**. *Management Review* (1990)

Your career is literally your business. **Theodore Levitt**. *Only the Paranoid Survive* (1996)

The world's best poker players don't hanker for jobs in casino management. **Tom Peters**. *Liberation Management* (1992)

People don't choose their careers; they are engulfed by them. **John Dos Passos**. *New York Times* (October 25, 1959)

The emerging work paradox is that in a post-job world, the only viable long-term career is to be a temp. **Anonymous**. Quoted in *Management Today* (February 1995)

The stepladder is gone, and there's not even the implied structure of an industry's rope ladder. It's more like vines, and you bring your own machete. **Peter F. Drucker**. Referring to to the impact of rapid organizational change. Quoted in *How to Manage* (Ray Wild, 1995)

The best augury of a man's success in his profession is that he thinks it the finest in the world. **George Eliot**. *Daniel Deronda* (1876)

Soon the emphasis will be on getting a life instead of a career, and work will be viewed as a series of gigs or projects. **Jonas Ridderstråle**. *Funky Business* (co-written with Kjell Nordström, 2000)

Challenge

It is so tempting to try the most difficult thing possible. **Jennie Churchill**. Quoted in *Daily Chronicle* (July 8, 1909)

We specialize in the wholly impossible. **Nannie Burroughs**. Motto of the National Training School for Girls in Washington. Quoted in *Black Women in White America* (1972)

I am always doing things I can't do, that's how I get to do them. **Pablo Picasso**. Quoted in *Street-Smart Advertising* (Margo Berman, 2006)

You must do the thing you think you cannot do. **Eleanor Roosevelt**. *You Learn by Living* (1960)

The secret of life is to have a task—something you bring everything to. And the most important thing is—it must be something you cannot possibly do. **Henry Moore**. Quoted in *The Brand You 50; Reinventing Work* (Tom Peters, 1999)

Change

If you want truly to understand something, try to change it. **Kurt Lewin**. Attributed

 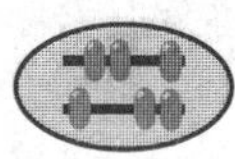   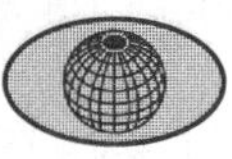 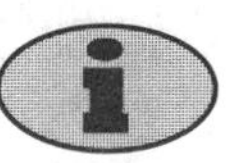  

Better never means better for everyone...It always means worse, for some. **Margaret Atwood.** *The Handmaid's Tale* (1985)

It isn't the changes that do you in, it's the transition. **Daniel Webster.** *Managing Transitions* (1991)

I want to put a ding in the universe. **Steve Jobs.** Quoted in *Made in the USA* (Phil Patton, 1992)

Changing the direction of a large company is like trying to turn an aircraft carrier. It takes a mile before anything happens. And if it was a wrong turn, getting back on course takes even longer. **Al Ries.** *Positioning: The Battle for Your Mind* (co-written with Jack Trout, 1980)

Management that wants to change an institution must first show that it loves that institution. **Sir John Tusa.** *Observer (London)* (February 1994)

The more things change, the more they are the same. **Alphonse Karr.** *Les Guêpes* (1849)

From now on, change will be the constant. The individuals best prepared to succeed are those who can learn, modify, and grow, regardless of age, experience, or ego. **Danny Goodman.** *Living at Light Speed: Your Survival Guide to Life on the Information Superhighway* (1994)

The reformer has enemies in all who profit by the old order, and only lukewarm defenders in all those who would profit by the new order. **Niccolò Machiavelli.** *The Prince* (1513)

It is only the very wisest and the very stupidest who cannot change. **Confucius.** *Analects* (500? BC)

If I were to give off-the-cuff advice to anyone trying to institute change, I would say, "How clear is the metaphor?" **Warren Bennis.** "Why Leaders Can't Lead," *Amacom* (1976)

Most of us are about as eager to be changed as we were to be born, and go through our changes in a similar state of shock. **James Baldwin.** "Every Good-Bye Ain't Gone," *New York* (December 19, 1977)

Revitalizing General Motors is like teaching an elephant to tap dance. You find the sensitive spot and start poking. **H. Ross Perot.** *International Management* (February 1987)

This extraordinary arrogance that change must start at the top is a way of guaranteeing that change will not happen in most companies. **Gary Hamel.** Interview, *Strategy + Business* (October–December 1997)

Open the windows, let in the year we're living in. **Kitty d'Alessio.** Referring to the conflict between tradition and modernity after she succeeded company founder Coco Chanel to become president of Chanel, Inc. *New York Times* (1985)

Notions of property, value, ownership, and the nature of wealth itself are changing more fundamentally than at any time since the Sumerians first poked cuneiform into wet clay and called it stored grain...few people are aware of the enormity of this shift and fewer of them are lawyers or public officials. **John Perry Barlow.** Former songwriter for the Grateful Dead, Barlow was the first to use William Gibson's science-fiction term cyberspace to describe the global electronic social space. "The Economy of Ideas," *Wired* (March 1994)

If we want everything to remain as it is, it will be necessary for everything to change. **Giuseppe di Lampedusa.** *The Leopard* (1955), ch. 1

Anyone in a large organization who thinks major change is impossible should probably get out. **John P. Kotter.** *The New Rules* (1995)

It is idle to speak of organizational transformation without individuals being transformed, especially the leader. **S. K. Chakraborty.** *Ethics in Management: Vedantic Perspectives* (1995)

When the rate of change outside exceeds the rate of change inside, the end is in sight. **Jack Welch.** *Inc.* (March 1995)

I never think of the future. It comes soon enough. **Albert Einstein.** Interview (December 1930)

To succeed at re-engineering, you have to be a missionary, a motivator, and a leg breaker. **Michael Hammer.** *Fortune* (August 1993)

What I really do is I'm reversing the Industrial Revolution. **Michael Hammer.** *Re-engineering the Corporation* (co-written with James Champy, 1993)

Unless companies change these rules, any superficial re-organizations they perform will be no more effective than dusting the furniture in Pompeii. **Michael Hammer.** *Re-engineering the Corporation* (co-written with James Champy, 1993)

If the 1980s were about quality and the 1990s were about re-engineering, then the 2000s will be about velocity. **Bill Gates.** *Business @ the Speed of Thought* (co-written with Collins Hemingway, 1999)

When the wind of change blows, some build walls, others build windmills. **Anonymous.**

To change and to improve are two different things. **Anonymous.** German proverb.

If you do what you've always done, you'll get what you've always gotten. **Anonymous.**

When you are through changing, you are through. **Percy Barnevik.** Quoted in *Financial Times Handbook of Management* (Stuart Crainer, ed, 1995)

Future shock is the disorientation that affects an individual, a corporation, or a country when he or it is overwhelmed by change and the prospect of change...we are in collision with tomorrow. **Alvin Toffler.** *Observer (London)* (1972)

Change is not merely necessary to life, it is life. **Alvin Toffler.** *Future Shock* (1970)

Change is the process by which the future invades our lives. **Alvin Toffler.** *Future Shock* (1970)

Corporations once built to last like pyramids are now more like tents. Tomorrow they're gone or in turmoil. **Peter F. Drucker.** Quoted in *How to Manage* (Ray Wild, 1995)

All great change in business has come from outside the firm, not from inside. **Peter F. Drucker.** Quoted in "Seeing Things As They Really Are," *Forbes* (Robert Lenzner and Stephen S. Johnson, 1987)

It is extremely important that you show some insensitivity to your past in order to show the proper respect for the future. **Roberto Goizueta.** Speech. Quoted in *Fortune* (December 1995)

The inevitability of gradualness. **Sidney Webb (Lord Passfield).** Speech, Labour Party conference (1920)

Change means movement. Movement means friction. **Saul Alinsky.** *Rules for Radicals* (1971)

Let chaos reign, then rein in chaos. **Andrew S. Grove.** Attributed

The new environment dictates two rules: first, everything happens faster; second, anything that can be done will be done, if not by you, then by someone else, somewhere. **Andrew S. Grove.** Attributed

The incremental approach to change is effective when what you want is more of

     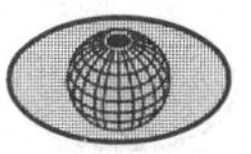  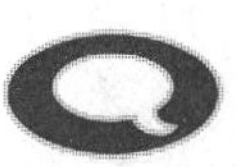 

what you've already got. **Richard Pascale**. *Managing on the Edge* (1990)

If it ain't broke, break it. **Richard Pascale**. *Managing on the Edge* (1990)

Technology changes. Economics does not. **Carl Shapiro**. *Information Rules* (co-written with Hal L. Varian, 1999)

The future is already upon us, it is just unevenly distributed. **William Gibson**. Quoted in the *Economist (London)* (June 23, 2000)

I skate to where the puck is going to be, not to where it has been. **Wayne Gretzky**. Quoted in *How to Work for an Idiot* (John Hoover, 2004)

Character

If you will think about what you ought to do for other people, your character will take care of itself. Character is a by-product, and any man who devotes himself to its cultivation in his own case will become a selfish prig. **Woodrow Wilson**. Speech, Pittsburgh, Pennsylvania (October 24, 1914)

Character is the basis of happiness and happiness the sanction of character. **George Santayana**. "Reason in Common Sense," *The Life of Reason* (1906), ch. 9

My trouble is I lack what the English call character. By which they mean the power to refrain. **Alan Bennett**. "An Englishman Abroad," *Single Spies* (1989)

I think that, as life is action and passion, it is required of a man that he should share the passion and action of his time at peril of being judged not to have lived. **Oliver Wendell Holmes, Jr**. Memorial Day address (1884)

He looked like the kind of a guy that wouldn't talk to you much unless he wanted something off you. He had a lousy personality. **J. D. Salinger**. *The Catcher in the Rye* (1951), ch. 11

Between ourselves and our real natures we interpose that wax figure of idealizations and selections which we call our character. **Walter Lippmann**. *A Preface to Politics* (1914), ch. 6

If I cannot get men who steer a middle course to associate with, I would far rather have the impetuous and hasty. For the impetuous at any rate assert themselves. **Confucius**. *Analects* (500? BC)

Talent is formed in quiet, character in the stream of human life. **Johann Wolfgang von Goethe**. *Torquato Tasso* (1790), Act 1, Scene 2

There are people whose external reality is generous because it is transparent, because you can read everything, accept everything, understand everything about them: people who carry their own sun with them. **Carlos Fuentes**. *The Old Gringo* (1985)

A woman is like a tea bag—only in hot water do you realize how strong she is. **Nancy Reagan**. *Observer (London)* (March 1981)

A man with so-called character is often a simple piece of mechanism; he has often only one point of view for the extremely complicated relationships of life. **J. August Strindberg**. *The Son of a Servant* (Claud Field, tr., 1913)

What is character but the determination of incident? What is incident but the illustration of character? **Henry James**. "The Art of Fiction," *Partial Portraits* (1888)

Though intelligence is powerless to modify character, it is a dab hand at finding euphemisms for its weaknesses. **Quentin Crisp**. *The Naked Civil Servant* (1968)

You know what charm is: a way of getting the answer yes without having asked any clear question. **Albert Camus**. *The Fall* (1956)

The perfection preached in the Gospels never yet built an empire. Every man of action has a strong dose of egotism, pride, hardness, and cunning **Charles De Gaulle**. Quoted in the *New York Times Magazine* (May 12, 1968)

We don't love qualities, we love persons; sometimes by reason of their defects as well as of their qualities. **Jacques Maritain**. *Reflections on America* (1958), ch. 3

The analysis of character is the highest human entertainment. **Isaac Bashevis Singer**. *New York Times* (November 26, 1978)

Be polite. Write diplomatically. Even in a declaration of war one observes the rules of politeness. **Otto Edward Leopold von Bismarck**. Attributed

It is with narrow-souled people as with narrow-necked bottles: the less they have in them, the more noise they make in pouring it out. **Alexander Pope**. *Thoughts on Various Subjects* (1741)

One of the best strengtheners of character and developers of stamina...is to assume the part you wish to play; to assert stoutly the possession of whatever you lack. **Orison Swett Marden**. *The Young Man Entering Business* (1903)

The best index to a person's character is (a) how he treats people who can't do him any good, and (b) how he treats people who can't fight back. **Abigail Van Buren**. Dear Abby, syndicated newspaper column (May 16, 1974)

To keep your character you cannot stoop to filthy acts. It makes it easier to stoop the next time. **Katharine Hepburn**. Quoted in the *Los Angeles Times* (November 1974)

Choice

From a narrow eitheror society with a limited range of personal choices, we are exploding into a free-wheeling multiple option society. **John Naisbitt**. *Megatrends* (1982)

Commerce is the agency by which the power of choice is obtained. **John Ruskin**. *Munera Pulveris* (1872)

Even children learn in growing up that both is not an admissible answer to a choice of which one? **Paul Samuelson**. Attributed

Any color you like as long as it's black. **Henry Ford**. Slogan advertising the mass-produced Model-T Ford. Attributed to *Ford* (Allan Nevins, 1954), vol. 2, ch. 15

Civilization

I think it would be an excellent idea. **Mahatma Gandhi**. Said when asked what he thought of Western civilization. Attributed

The meek shall inherit the earth but not the mineral rights. **J. Paul Getty**. Quoted in *BusinessWeek* (1986)

Bare-faced covetousness was the moving spirit of civilization from its first dawn to the present day; wealth, and again wealth, and for the third time wealth; wealth, not of society, but of the puny individual, was its only and final aim. **Friedrich Engels**. *The Origin of the Family* (1885)

Civilization advances by extending the number of important operations which we can perform without thinking about them. **Alfred North Whitehead**. *An Introduction to Mathematics* (1911)

If civilization has risen from the Stone Age, it can rise again from the Wastepaper Age. **Jacques Barzun**. *The House of Intellect* (1959)

  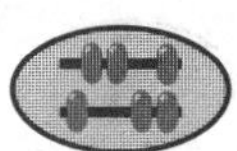   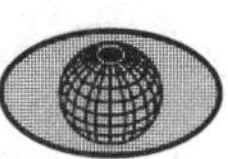   

Civilization is the progress towards a society of privacy...the process of setting man free from men. **Ayn Rand**. *The Fountainhead* (1943)

Increased means and increased leisure are the two civilizers of man. **Benjamin Disraeli (Earl of Beaconsfield)**. Speech to the Conservatives of Manchester (April 3, 1872)

A good civilisation spreads over us freely like a tree, varying and yielding because it is alive. A bad civilisation stands up and sticks out above us like an umbrella—artificial, mathematical in shape; not merely universal, but uniform. **G. K. Chesterton**. "Cheese," *Alarms and Discursions* (1910)

Civilization has developed executive powers far beyond its understanding. **Maude Meagher**. *Fantastic Traveler* (1931)

Upon the sacredness of property civilization itself depends—the right of the laborer to his hundred dollars in the savings bank, and equally the legal right of the millionaire to his millions. **Andrew Carnegie**. "Wealth," *North American Review* (June 1889)

A few suits of clothes, some money in the bank, and a new kind of fear constitute the main differences between the average American today and the hairy men with clubs who accompanied Attila to the city of Rome. **Philip Gordon Wylie**. *Generation of Vipers* (1942)

Every advance in civilisation has been denounced as unnatural while it was recent. **Bertrand Russell (Earl Russell)**. "An Outline of Intellectual Rubbish," *Unpopular Essays* (1950)

To be able to fill leisure intelligently is the last product of civilization. **Bertrand Russell (Earl Russell)**. *The Conquest of Happiness* (1930)

Ours is not so much an age of vulgarity as of vulgarization; everything is tampered with or touched up, or adulterated or watered down, in an effort to make it palatable, in an effort to make it pay. **Louis Kronenberger**. "The Spirit of the Age," *Company Manners* (1954)

A decent provision for the poor is the true test of civilization. **Samuel Johnson**. Quoted in *The Life of Samuel Johnson* (James Boswell, 1791)

In a state of nature, the weakest go to the wall; in a state of over-refinement, both the weak and the strong go to the gutter. **Elbert Hubbard**. *The Philistine* (1895–1915)

Commerce is the great civilizer. We exchange ideas when we exchange fabrics. **Robert Green Ingersoll**. Said to Indianapolis clergy. Attributed

Cooperation

Corporations can have no soul but they can love each other. **Henry Demarest Lloyd**. *Wealth Against Commonwealth* (1894)

Successful co-operation in or by formal organizations is the abnormal, not the normal, condition. **Chester Barnard**. *Organization and Management* (1948)

When you collaborate with other people, you tend to regard your own individual contribution as the most important. **Yang Jiang**. *A Cadre School Life* (1980)

The speed of the Internet provides a fundamentally different perspective on how business relationships occur...The approach relies on collaboration, not on competition...on sharing information, and understanding what we as businesses do best. **Michael Dell**. Speech to the Executives' Club of Chicago. "NetSpeed: The Supercharged Effect of the Internet" (October 23, 1998)

Only recently have people begun to recognise that working with suppliers is just as important as listening to customers. **Barry J. Nalebuff**. *Co-opetition* (co-written with Adam M. Brandenburger, 1997)

Common Sense

Common sense is a very tricky instrument; it is as deceptive as it is indispensable. **Susanne K. Langer**. *Philosophical Studies* (1962)

Common sense (which, in truth, is very uncommon) is the best sense I know of. **Lord Chesterfield**. Letter (September 27, 1748)

We seldom attribute common sense except to those who agree with us. **François La Rochefoucauld**. *Reflections: or, Sentences and Moral Maxims* (1665)

Common sense is the best distributed commodity in the world, for every man is convinced that he is well supplied with it. **René Descartes**. *Le Discours de la méthode* (1637), pt. 1

Common sense is the collection of prejudices acquired by age eighteen. **Albert Einstein**. Quoted in *Scientific American* (February 1976)

Communication

Let us write as if we were writing to a skeptical aunt. All the rest of the world can look over our aunt's shoulder. **Fairfax Cone**. *Christian Science Monitor* (1963)

The difference between the *almost* right word and the *right* word is really a large matter—it's the difference between the lightning bug and the lightning. **Mark Twain**. Letter to George Bainton (October 15, 1888)

Today, communication itself is the problem. We have become the world's first overcommunicated society. Each year we send more and receive less. **Al Ries**. *Positioning: The Battle for Your Mind* (co-written with Jack Trout, 1980)

I say what I mean, you hear what I say. That is the end of it. **Barbara Cassani**. *Management Today* (August 1999)

Toilets are great ways of giving information, whether you put things on the wall or ask for comments. You can write things on the wall anonymously. **Dame Anita Roddick**. Quoted in *The Adventure Capitalists* (Jeff Grout and Lynne Curry, 1998)

Electronic communication, as fast and efficient as it has become, does not automatically lead to better communication. **Dan Dimancescu**. *World-class New Product Development* (co-written with Kemp Dwenger, 1996)

If figures of speech based on sports and fornication were suddenly banned, American corporate communication would be reduced to pure mathematics. **Jay McInerney**. *Brightness Falls* (1992)

Through the picture I see reality; through the word I understand it. **Peter Kindersley**. Referring to the importance of both words and images in communication and publishing. Quoted in *Goldfinger* (Robert Heller, 1998)

Even the frankest and bravest of subordinates do not talk with their boss the same way they talk with colleagues. **Robert Greenleaf**. *Servant Leadership: A Journey into the Nature of Legitimate Power and Greatness* (1977)

A quotation is what a speaker wants to say, unlike a soundbite which is all that an

  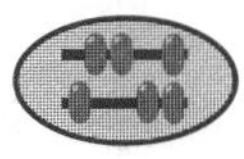   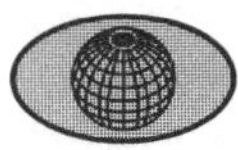   

interviewer allows you to say. **Tony Benn**. Letter (1996)

It is ironic but true that in this era of electronic communications, personal interaction is becoming more important than ever. **Regis McKenna**. Quoted in *Thriving on Chaos* (Tom Peters, 1987)

At office-managerial level...you do not read more than the first two sentences of any given report. You believe that anything which cannot be put into two sentences is not worth attending to. **Penelope Fitzgerald**. "The Axe," *The Means of Escape* (2000)

The newest computer can merely compound, at speed, the oldest problem in the relations between human beings, and in the end the communicator will be confronted with the old problem, of what to say and how to say it. **Edward R. Murrow**. Speech (October 1964)

Competition

Thou shalt not covet, but tradition
Approves all forms of competition.
Arthur Hugh Clough. "The Latest Decalogue" (1862), ll. 19–20

If we had just continued the way we were going, we would end up being nibbled to death. **Sir David Michels**. Referring to competition from smaller companies on the Internet. *Sunday Times (London)* (May 2000)

I feel sorry for those who live without competition...fat, dumb, and unhappy in cradle-to-grave security. **Donald M. Kendall**. Quoted in *How to Manage* (Ray Wild, 1995)

Competition as most of us have routinely thought of it is dead. **James F. Moore**. *The Death of Competition* (1997)

Without vassal loyalty, or abject vassal fear, the monopolist's sleep can never be secure. **Joseph Furphy**. *Such Is Life* (1903)

This is not an age of castles, moats, and armor where people can sustain a competitive advantage for very long. **Richard D'Aveni**. "The Mavericks," *Fortune* (June 1995)

In a garage somewhere, an entrepreneur is forging a bullet with your company's name on it. **Gary Hamel**. *Digital Britain* (January 2000)

When the competition is moving at 200 miles an hour, every second you're in the pits matters a lot. **Doug Nelson**. "The Mavericks," *Fortune* (June 1995)

All business sagacity reduces itself in the last analysis to a judicious use of sabotage. **Thorstein Veblen**. *An Inquiry into the Nature of Peace and the Terms of Its Perpetuation* (1917)

The goal of competitors is to prevail, not to preserve competition in the markets. **George Soros**. *Atlantic Monthly* (January 1998)

Microsoft has had clear competitors in the past. It's a good thing we have museums to document that. **Bill Gates**. Speech at the Computer History Museum (October 2001)

I believe that if you're going to take someone on, you might as well take on the biggest brand in the world. **Sir Richard Branson**. "The Mavericks," *Fortune* (June 1995)

There is no gap in the market unless you have sharp elbows. **Andrew Neil**. *Sunday Times (London)* (September 2000)

Perfect competition is a theoretical concept like the Euclidean line, which has no width and no depth. Just as we've never seen that line there has never been truly free enterprise. **Milton Friedman**. *There's No Such Thing as a Free Lunch* (1975), Introduction

Don't look back, something might be gaining on you. **Leroy Paige**. Personal saying (1952)

Men often compete with one another until the day they die; comradeship consists of rubbing shoulders jocularly with a competitor. **Edward Hoagland**. "Heaven and Nature," *Harper's Magazine* (March 1988)

So far as power is concerned, does anyone believe the premiums of insurance companies are all almost uniform by accident? **Jimmy Hoffa**. Interview *Playboy* (December 1975)

On the Internet...competitive advantage has shrunk to a few months. If they don't keep innovating, they'll be overtaken. They have to keep adding digital value, adding services, building their brand. **William (Walid) Mougayar**. Interview, *UpsideToday* (1998)

Never wrestle with a pig. You get dirty and only the pig enjoys himself. **Mark McCormack**. Quoting a proverb. *What You'll Never Learn on the Internet* (2000)

You can't measure the value of being first. **Chris Moore**. *Marketing* (June 2000)

Running other companies out of business and gaining market share is what capitalistic competition is all about. Efficiency and lower prices flow from that all-out economic life-and-death struggle. **Lester Thurow**. "Microsoft Case Is about a Good Capitalist Practice: Running Your Competitor out of Business," *www.lthurow.com* (November 3, 1999)

What do you do when your competitor's drowning? Get a live hose and stick it in his mouth. **Ray Kroc**. *Wall Street Journal* (October 1997)

Nothing focuses the mind better than the constant sight of a competitor who wants to wipe you off the map. **Wayne Calloway**. *Fortune* (March 11, 1991)

We feel the spear of the marketplace in our back. **Tony O'Reilly**. *Fortune* (April 9, 1990)

Business is becoming more and more akin to intellectual sumo wrestling. **Sir John Harvey-Jones**. *All Together Now* (1994)

A prosperous competitor is often less dangerous than a desperate one. **Barry J. Nalebuff**. *Co-opetition* (co-written with Adam M. Brandenburger, 1997)

In business, the competition will bite you if you keep running, if you stand still, they will swallow you. **William S. Knudsen**. Quoted in *The Fords: An American Epic* (Peter Collier and David Horowitz, 1987)

Computers

A sort of cognitive equivalent of a condom—it's a layer of contraceptive rubber between the direct experience and the cognitive system. **Sir Jonathan Miller**. Referring to reading from a computer screen. *Independent on Sunday (London)* (January 1996)

We no longer think of chairs as technology, we just think of them as chairs. But there was a time when we hadn't worked out how many legs chairs should have, how tall they should be, and they would often "crash" when we tried to use them. Before long, computers will be as trivial and plentiful as chairs and we will cease to be aware of the things. In fact I'm sure we will look back on this last decade and wonder how we could ever have mistaken what we were doing with them for "productivity." **Douglas Adams**. *How to Stop Worrying and Learn to Love the Internet, The Sunday Times* (August 29, 1999)

Buying the right computer and getting it to work properly is no more complicated than building a nuclear reactor from wristwatch parts in a darkened room using only your

  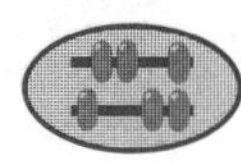   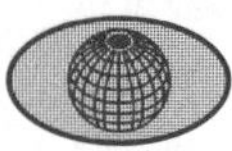   

teeth. **Dave Barry**. *Dave Barry in Cyberspace* (1996)

A computer can tell you down to the dime what you've sold, but it can never tell you how much you could have sold. **Sam M. Walton**. *Made in America* (co-written with John Huey, 1992)

The value of e-commerce is not in the e, but in the commerce. **Octavio Paz**. Quoted in *Management Today* (June 2000)

I would say that hardware is the bone of the head, the skull. The semiconductor is the brain within the head. The software is the wisdom and data is the knowledge. **Masayoshi Son**. *Harvard Business Review* (January–February 1992)

A modern computer hovers between the obsolescent and the non-existent. **Sydney Brenner**. *Society* (January 1990)

Men are going to have to learn to be managers in a world where the organization will come close to consisting of all chiefs and one Indian. The Indian, of course, is the computer. **Thomas L. Whisler**. *Christian Science Monitor* (April 21, 1964)

The search button on the browser no longer provides an objective search, but a commercial one. **Sir Tim Berners-Lee**. Referring to the commercialization of the Internet. *Weaving the Web* (1999)

The computer is a moron. **Peter F. Drucker**. Quoted in *Drucker, the Man Who Invented the Corporate Society* (John J. Tarrant, 1976)

Computers are useless. They can only give you answers. **Pablo Picasso**. Quoted in *How Breakthroughs Happen* (Andrew Hargadon, 2003)

The one thing computers have done is let us make bigger mistakes. We have to be careful not to depend on our machines. **Michael Bloomberg**. Quoted in "Terminal Velocity," *Wired* (David S. Bennahum, February 1999)

Take Wrigley's Chewing Gum. I don't think the Internet is going to change how people chew gum. **Warren Buffett**. Interview *Fortune* (July 1998)

The Weightless World **Diane Coyle**. Book title. Referring to an economy in which information is more important than physical products. *The Weightless World* (1997)

The Star Trek computer doesn't seem that interesting. They ask it random questions, it thinks for a while. I think we can do better than that. **Larry Page**. Interview, *Business Week* (May 3, 2004)

Programming today is a race between software engineers striving to build bigger and better idiot-proof programs, and the Universe trying to produce bigger and better idiots. So far, the Universe is winning. **Rick Cook**. Quoted in *Applied Choice Analysis* (David A. Hensher, John M. Rose, and William H. Greene, 2005)

There is no reason for any individual to have a computer in his home. **Kenneth H. Olson**. Speech to the convention of the World Future Society (1977)

Confidence and Self-Belief

Nothing has ever been achieved except by those who dared believe that something inside of them was superior to circumstances. **Bruce Barton**. Quoted in *Fearless Interviewing* (Marky Stein, 2002)

All you need in this life is ignorance and confidence; then success is sure. **Mark Twain**. Letter to Mrs Foote (December 2, 1887)

If you think you can, you can. And if you think you can't, you're right. **Mary Kay Ash**. *New York Times* (October 20, 1985)

One man that has a mind and knows it can always beat ten men who haven't and don't. **George Bernard Shaw**. *The Apple Cart* (1929), Act 1

I don't really see the hurdles. I sense them like a memory. **Edwin Moses**. Attributed

Whether you believe you can, or whether you believe you can't, you're absolutely right. **Henry Ford**. Attributed

We should do everything both cautiously and confidently at the same time. **Epictetus**. *Discourses* (2nd century AD), bk. 2

Attempt easy tasks as if they were difficult, and difficult as if they were easy: in the one case that confidence may not fall asleep, in the other that it may not be dismayed. **Baltasar Gracián**. *The Art of Worldly Wisdom* (1647)

Ignorance more frequently begets confidence than does knowledge. **Charles Darwin**. *The Descent of Man* (1871)

Take the place and attitude to which you see your unquestionable right, and all men acquiesce. **Ralph Waldo Emerson**. *Journals* (1836)

For a man to achieve all that is demanded of him he must regard himself as greater than he is. **Johann Wolfgang Von Goethe**. Attributed

Conscience

I've got just as much conscience as any man in business can afford to keep—just a little, you know, to swear by as 't were. **Harriet Beecher Stowe**. *Uncle Tom's Cabin* (1852), ch. 1

Most people sell their souls and live with a good conscience on the proceeds. **Logan Pearsall Smith**. "Other People," *Afterthoughts* (1931)

It is always term-time in the court of conscience. **Thomas Fuller**. *Gnomologia* (1732)

Conscience is the name which the orthodox give to their prejudices. **John Oliver Hobbes**. *A Bundle of Life* (1894)

A business must have a conscience as well as a counting house. **Sir Montague Burton**. Attributed

Conscience gets a lot of credit that belongs to cold feet. **Anonymous**. US proverb.

Conscience is the inner voice that warns us somebody may be looking. **H. L. Mencken**. *A Mencken Chrestomathy* (1948)

Sufficient conscience to bother him, but not sufficient to keep him straight. **David Lloyd George (Earl of Dwyfor)**. Referring to Ramsay MacDonald. Quoted in *Life with Lloyd George* (A. J. Sylvester, 1975)

Conscience and cowardice are really the same things. Conscience is the trade-name of the firm. **Oscar Wilde**. *The Picture of Dorian Gray* (1891), ch. 1

If we cannot be powerful and happy and prey on others, we invent conscience and prey on ourselves. **Elbert Hubbard**. *The Philistine* (1895–1915)

Be the master of your will but the servant of your conscience. **Robin S. Sharma**. *MegaLiving!: 30 Days to a Perfect Life* (1995)

Consultants and Advisers

They are the people who borrow your watch to tell you what time it is and then walk off

     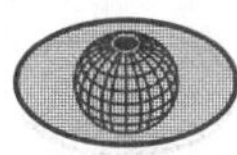   

with it. **Robert Townsend**. Referring to consultants. *Up the Organization* (1970)

What a difficult thing it is to ask someone's advice on a matter without coloring his judgment by the way in which we present our problem. **Blaise Pascal**. *Pensées* (1670)

Thinking must be the hardest job in the world. What people want to do is outsource it to a mantra or a methodology like re-engineering. **Eileen C. Shapiro**. *Fad Surfing in the Boardroom* (1998)

Get the advice of everybody whose advice is worth having—they are very few—and then do what you think best yourself. **Charles Stewart Parnell**. Quoted in *Parnell* (Conor Cruise O'Brien, 1957)

I come from an environment where, if you see a snake, you kill it. At General Motors, if you see a snake, the first thing you do is hire a consultant on snakes. **H. Ross Perot**. Speech (December 1991)

Timing; originality; forcefulness; a gift for self-promotion and perhaps above all else, the ability to encapsulate memorably what others recognize as true...are the hallmarks of the modern management guru. **Carol Kennedy**. *Guide to the Management Gurus* (1991)

It is always easier to talk about change than to make it. It is easier to consult than to manage. **Alvin Toffler**. *The Adaptive Corporation* (1985)

My greatest strength as a consultant is to be ignorant and ask a few questions. **Peter F. Drucker**. Attributed

A consultant is a person who takes your money and annoys your employees while tirelessly searching for the best way to extend the consulting contract. **Scott Adams**. *The Dilbert Principle* (1996)

Consultants eventually leave, which makes them excellent scapegoats for major management blunders. **Scott Adams**. *The Dilbert Principle* (1996)

The function of the expert is not to be more right than other people, but to be wrong for more sophisticated reasons. **David Butler**. Quoted in the *Observer (London)* (1969)

Wall Street is the only place people ride to in a Rolls Royce to get advice from people who take the subway. **Warren Buffett** *Newsday* (August 1991)

Techniques shrouded in mystery clearly have value to the purveyor of investment advice. After all, what witch doctor has ever achieved fame and fortune by simply advising "Take two aspirins"? **Warren Buffett**. Letter to shareholders (1987)

Consumption

A society in which consumption has to be artificially stimulated in order to keep production going is a society founded on trash and waste, and such a society is a house built on sand. **Dorothy L. Sayers**. *Creed or Chaos* (1947)

America is a vast conspiracy to make you happy. **John Updike**. *Problems* (1980)

Work to survive, survive by consuming, survive to consume: the hellish cycle is complete. **Raoul Vaneigem**. *The Revolution of Everyday Life* (1967)

People want economy and they will pay any price to get it. **Lee Iacocca**. *New York Times* (1974)

Our gadget-filled paradise suspended in a hell of insecurity. **Reinhold Niebuhr**. *Pious and Secular America* (1957)

Too many of us are spending money we haven't earned to buy things we don't need to impress people we don't like. **Anonymous**.

Buying is much more American than thinking and I'm as American as they come. **Andy Warhol**. *The Philosophy of Andy Warhol (from A to B and Back Again)* (1975)

What's great about this country is that America started the tradition where the richest consumers buy essentially the same things as the poorest. **Andy Warhol**. *The Philosophy of Andy Warhol (from A to B and Back Again)* (1975)

Teenagers travel in droves, packs, swarms. To the librarian, they're a gaggle of geese. To the cook, they're a scourge of locusts. To department stores they're a big beautiful exaltation of larks, all lovely and loose and jingly. **Bernice Fitz-Gibbon**. *New York Times* (1960)

Man wants but little here below but likes that little good—and not too long in coming. **Samuel Butler**. *Further Extracts from the Notebooks* (A. Bartholomew, ed, 1934)

In a consumer society there are inevitably two kinds of slaves: the prisoners of addiction and the prisoners of envy. **Ivan Illich**. *Tools for Conviviality* (1973)

Consumption is the sole end and purpose of production; and the interest of the producer ought to be attended to only so far as it may be necessary for promoting that of the consumer. **Adam Smith**. *An Inquiry into the Nature and Causes of the Wealth of Nations* (1776)

Contracts

Contract: an agreement that is binding on the weaker party. **Frederick Sawyer**. Attributed

He that payeth beforehand shall have his work ill done. **Thomas Fuller**. *Gnomologia* (1732)

There is nothing more likely to start disagreement among people or countries than an agreement. **E. B. White**. Attributed

Contracts are agreements made up of big words and little type. **Sam Ewing**. Quoted in the *Saturday Evening Post* (May 1993)

Corporate Culture

Nobody here cares which washroom you use. **Debi Coleman**. *US News & World Report* (September 1987)

I don't want to feel responsible to outsiders with financial concerns that may differ from those of the welfare of IKEA. **Ingvar Kamprad**. *Forbes* (August 2000)

Intense decentralization that gives managers the freedom usually reserved for entrepreneurs. **James W. Farnell**. *BusinessWeek* (1995)

I believe in provocative disruption. **Charlotte Beers**. *Fortune* (August 1996)

I'm forcing more men into my company to get more sexual tension into the business...I love the buzz and...sexuality of verbal foreplay. **Dame Anita Roddick**. *Marketing* (August 3, 1989)

If you look at the companies where the CEO stayed on till he's 80, those are the people who confuse themselves with the company. **Walter Wriston**. *New York Times* (April 1993)

The corporation's edict to its members could be phrased as: While you are here, you will act as though you have no other responsibilities, no other life. **Rosabeth Moss Kanter**. *When Giants Learn to Dance: Mastering the Challenges of*

Strategy, Management and Careers in the 1990s (1992), ch. 10

Companies...are likely to find hierarchies turned upside down. Juniors teach seniors, subordinates lead teams with their bosses on them...A decision-making hierarchy is replaced by an internal marketplace of ideas. **Rosabeth Moss Kanter**. "How E-Smart Are You?," *World Link* (January–February 2000)

To write down, frame, and publish your corporate values is all about self-deceit and ego. It is almost certainly bullshit. **Barry J. Gibbons**. Quoted in *How to Manage* (Ray Wild, 1995)

A company's culture is often buried so deeply inside rituals, assumptions, attitudes, and values that it becomes transparent to an organization's members only when, for some reason, it changes. **Rob Goffee**. *The Character of a Corporation* (co-written with Gareth Jones, 1998)

The way management treats their associates is exactly how the associates will then treat the customers. **Sam M. Walton**. "The Hot Ticket in Retailing," *New York Times* (Isadore Barmash, July 1984)

There is a misconception that small is always more beautiful than big. **Lou Gerstner**. *Fortune* (May 1993)

Any engineer that doesn't need to wash his hands at least three times a day is a failure. **Shoichiro Toyoda**. Referring to the importance of manufacturing in Japanese industry. Quoted in *How to Manage* (Ray Wild, 1995)

Modelers build intricate decision trees whose pretension to utility is exceeded only by the awe in which high-level managers hold the technocrats who constrain them. **Theodore Levitt**. "A Heretical View of Management Science," *Fortune* (December 1978)

Corporate totalitarianism...rules through dispensability rather than exploitation. It treats communities, people, countries, ecosystems, species as disposable and dispensable. **Vandana Shiva**. *Globalisation: Gandhi and Swadeshi* (2000)

The clichés of a culture sometimes tell the deepest truths. **Faith Popcorn**. *The Popcorn Report* (1991)

Clothes don't make the man—but they go a long way towards making a businessman. **Thomas J. Watson, Sr**. Quoted in *IBM: Colossus in Transition* (Robert Sobel, 1981)

A company needs smart young men with the imagination and the guts to turn everything upside down if they can. It also needs old figures to keep them from turning upside down those things that ought to be rightside up. **Henry Ford**. Speech (1966)

If you're not scared, you're too stupid to work here. **Lee Iacocca**. Speech (1990)

Every company has its own language, its own version of its own history (its myths), and its own heroes and villains (its legends), both historical and contemporary. **Michael Hammer**. *Beyond Re-engineering* (1996)

A corporation does seem like a family. Not necessarily that one big happy family they like to boast about...but just like every family, a hotbed of passion, rivalry, and dreams that build or destroy careers. **Paula Bernstein**. *Family Ties, Corporate Bonds* (1985)

This system sounds chaotic, can be frustrating and is, in some ways, uncontrollable. It has destroyed any semblance of corporate security. And...it has worked very well. **Ricardo Semler**. "The Mavericks," *Fortune* (June 1995)

Too many people are on boards because they want to have nice-looking visiting cards. **Utz Felcht**. *Sunday Times (London)* (October 2000)

Company cultures are like country cultures. Never try to change one. Try, instead, to work with what you've got. **Peter F. Drucker**. Attributed

Constructive confrontation. **Christopher Bartlett**. *The Individualised Corporation* (co-written with Sumantra Ghoshal, 1997)

The oppressive atmosphere in most companies resembles downtown Calcutta in summer. **Christopher Bartlett**. *The Individualised Corporation* (co-written with Sumantra Ghoshal, 1997)

Never pick up someone else's ringing phone. **Mark McCormack**. *What You'll Never Learn on the Internet* (2000)

I believe in God, family, and McDonald's and, in the office, that order is reversed. **Ray Kroc**. Quoted in *McDonald's—Behind the Arches* (John F. Love, 1986)

The software industry as a whole tends to be slightly managed chaos. It was a giant group grope in the 1970s, when this whole thing started...effectively there are no rules. **Ann Winblad**. Quoted in *Giant Killers* (Geoffrey James, 1996)

I looked for those sharp, scratchy, harsh, almost unpleasant guys who see and tell you about things as they really are. **Thomas J. Watson, Jr**. *Fortune* (August 1987)

I've often thought that after you get organized, you ought to throw away the organization chart. **David Packard**. "Lessons of Leadership," *The Nation's Business* (January 1974)

Real commitment is rare in today's organization...90 percent of the time what passes for commitment is compliance. **Peter Senge**. *The Fifth Discipline: The Art and Practice of the Learning Organization* (1990)

IBM is like the Stepford Wives. It takes the best people from the best universities and colleges and then snips out some part of the brain so that they become mindless clones. **Bill Campbell**. Quoted in *Giant Killers* (Geoffrey James, 1996)

The soul of a business is a curious alchemy of needs, desires, greed, and gratifications mixed together with selflessness, sacrifices, and personal contributions far beyond material rewards. **Harold S. Geneen**. *Managing* (co-written with Alvin Moscow, 1984)

If the washroom isn't good enough for the people in charge, then it's not good enough for the people in the store. **Lord Sieff**. Quoted in *A Passion for Excellence* (Tom Peters and Mary Austin, 1985)

It is difficult to get a man to understand something when his salary depends upon his not understanding it. **Upton Sinclair**. *I, Candidate for Governor: And How I Got Licked* (1935)

Corporate Responsibility

Business has to be a force for social change. It is not enough to avoid hideous evil—it must, we must, actively do good. If business stays parochial, without moral energy or codes of behaviour, claiming there are no such thing as values, then God help us all. If you think morality is a luxury business can't afford, try living in a world without it. **Dame Anita Roddick**. Speech, International Forum on Globalization Teach-In, Seattle, Washington. "Trading with Principles" (November 27, 1999)

The market is a mechanism for sorting the efficient from the inefficient, it is not a substitute for responsibility. **Charles**

   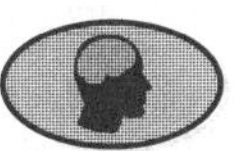  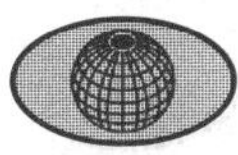 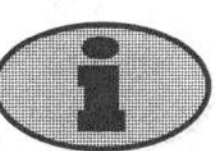  

Handy. *The Empty Raincoat: Making Sense of the Future* (1994), pt. 1, ch. 1

Increasingly, I have become concerned that the motivation to meet Wall Street earnings expectations may be overriding common sense business practices...Managing may be giving way to manipulation; integrity may be losing out to illusion. **Arthur Levitt, Jr**. Speech to the New York University Center for Law and Business, New York City. "The Numbers Game" (September 28, 1998)

I would never make a decision which might be damaging to Turin's local administration. A Texan capitalist couldn't care less about local government, he couldn't care less about the federal government. **Giovanni Agnelli**. Fiat's headquarters are based in Turin. Quoted in *Interview on Modern Capitalism* (Arrigo Levi, 1983)

Only the little people pay taxes. **Leona Helmsley**. *New York Times* (July 1989)

Few trends could so thoroughly undermine the very foundations of our free society as the acceptance by corporate officials of a social responsibility other than to make as much money for their stockholders as possible. **Milton Friedman**. *Capitalism and Freedom* (1962)

CORPORATION, n. An ingenious device for obtaining individual profit without individual responsibility. **Ambrose Bierce**. *The Devil's Dictionary* (1911)

Companies have to be socially responsible or the shareholders pay eventually. **Warren Shaw**. "The Players," *Fortune* (Eileen Gunn, April 1997)

Corporate bodies are more corrupt and profligate than individuals because they have more power to do mischief and are less amenable to disgrace or punishment. They feel neither shame, remorse, gratitude, nor goodwill. **William Hazlitt**. "On Corporate Bodies," *Table Talk* (1821–1822), Essay 27

The public be damned. I am working for my stockholders. **William Henry Vanderbilt**. Refusing to speak to a reporter. Quoted in letter from A. W. Cole, *New York Times* (August 25, 1918)

Corruption and Scandal

Greed is all right...Greed is healthy. You can be greedy and still feel good about yourself. **Ivan Boesky**. After success as a trader on Wall Street, in 1987 he was convicted of securities fraud, imprisoned for two years, and fined US$100 million. Commencement address, Berkeley, California (May 18, 1986)

It's time to make things ship-shape, to get rid of the debt, to get a bit of a cash box to work from, to enjoy life a bit more. **Lord Black of Crossharbour**. Referring to disposals from his media group. *New York Times* (April 2000)

I have no doubt that mothers in America use my name to frighten their children into finishing their vegetables. **Lord Black of Crossharbour**. Interview, *Fortune* (May 30, 2005)

If things were half as bad as some people persist in believing, I'd have retired with a bottle of Scotch and a pistol a long time ago. **Robert Maxwell**. *Daily Mail (London)* (June 1973)

If only 50 or more people were doing for the country what I have been doing, there would not be a pay freeze or a balance of payments problem. **Robert Maxwell**. Referring to his world trips to build an international scientific publishing business. Speech (December 1966)

Money you haven't earned is not good for you. **Robert Maxwell**. Quoted in *Time* (November 28, 1988)

He's a businessman...I'll make him an offer he can't refuse. **Mario Puzo**. The offer referred to is a death threat. *The Godfather* (1969), bk. 1, ch. 1

Like many businessmen of genius he learned that free competition was wasteful, monopoly efficient. And so he simply set about achieving that efficient monopoly. **Mario Puzo**. Referring to Don Vito Corleone. *The Godfather* (1969), bk. 3, ch. 14

There are two parties involved in every corrupt transaction, typically a government official and a business person. Yet those who pay bribes are often depicted as innocent victims...The reality is that both parties conspire to defraud the public. **Baroness Chalker of Wallasey**. "Public Sector Corruption from an International Perspective." Speech, University of Glasgow, Scotland (February 19, 1999)

It argues no fault in the construction of the aqueduct that the water it conveys is often dirty. **Anonymous**. Financier referring to corruption in the City. Quoted in *The City of London, Vol IV: A Club No More* (David Kynaston, 2002)

What was done was not in keeping with the values and heritage of this firm. It was wrong, there's no other word for it. **Joseph Berardino**. Referring to the part played by accountant's Arthur Andersen in the collapse of Enron. Quoted in the *Guardian (London)* (June 2002)

The business pages of American newspapers should not read like a scandal sheet. **George W. Bush**. Referring to a series of high-profile accounting scandals. Speech (July 2002)

If there is anything material and we're not reporting it, we'll be breaking the law. We don't break the law. **Kenneth Lay**. Referring to Enron's accounting practices. Quoted in *BusinessWeek* (August 24, 2001)

My aim was to make money for the bank. You lose track of the amounts involved when you are engaged in this kind of work. **Jerome Kerviel**. Referring to his loss of 4.8 bn euros through unauthorized futures trading. Quoted in the *Independent (London)* (February 6, 2008)

In today's regulatory environment, it's virtually impossible to violate rules...but it's impossible for a violation to go undetected, certainly not for a considerable period of time. **Bernard Madoff**. In 2008 Madoff was charged with the biggest investment fraud in history. Remark in an interview (October 20, 2007)

It's a proprietary strategy. I can't go into it in great detail. **Bernard Madoff**. On being asked to explain the secrets of his success. Remark (2001)

All one great big lie. **Bernard Madoff**. Confessing that his $50 billion investment fund was a total fraud. Quoted in the *Independent (London)* (December 16, 2008)

I have...spoken to the heads of various Wall Street equity derivatives trading desks and every single one of the senior managers I spoke with told me that Bernie Madoff was a fraud. Of course no one wants to take an undue career risk by sticking their head up...The fewer people who know who wrote this report the better. I am worried about the personal safety of myself and my family. **Harry Markopolos**. "The World's Largest Hedge Fund is a Fraud": document submitted to the Securities and Exchange Commission warning them about the Madoff fund (November 2005)

A super-sized fraud of this magnitude was bound to happen given the lack of regulation of these off-shore entities. **Harry Markopolos**. "The World's Largest Hedge Fund is a Fraud": document submitted to the Securities and Exchange Commission warning them about the Madoff fund (November 2005)

I've found that wherever there is one cockroach in plain sight, many more are lurking behind the corner out of view. **Harry Markopolos**. "The World's Largest Hedge Fund is a Fraud": document submitted to the Securities and Exchange Commission warning them about the Madoff fund (November 2005)

The argument that rigorous oversight will somehow stifle Wall Street's "creativity" is no longer convincing. Any system that permits a scam artist like Madoff to deceive, not just widows and orphans, but also sophisticated investors...isn't a market at all; it's a shooting gallery. **Tim Rutten**. *Los Angeles Times* (December 17, 2008)

If this were a traditional bank robbery, the eyewitness reports would say that Mr Madoff walked out with billions of dollars as someone held the door open for him. **Jeffrey Zwerling**. Quoted in the *Independent (London)* (December 17, 2008)

It looked incredibly credible! **Nicola Horlick**. On her decision to invest £10M of clients' money in the Madoff fund, subsequently exposed as entirely fraudulent. Interviewed on Today, BBC Radio 4 (December 15, 2008)

Creativity

Creativity is allowing oneself to make mistakes. Art is knowing which ones to keep. **Scott Adams**. *The Dilbert Principle* (1996)

The majority of creative acts are unplanned, and each begins with awareness of an unexpected opportunity. **Alan G. Robinson**. *Corporate Creativity* (co-written with Sam Stern, 1997)

Could Henry Ford produce the Book of Kells? Certainly not. He would quarrel initially with the advisability of such a project and then prove it was impossible. **Flann O'Brien**. *Myles Away from Dublin* (1990)

One doesn't discover new lands without consenting to lose sight of the shore for a very long time. **André Gide**. *The Counterfeiters* (1926)

When you ask creative people how they did something, they feel a little guilty because they didn't really *do* it, they just *saw* something...That's because they were able to connect experiences they've had and synthesize new things. **Steve Jobs**. Interview, "The Next Insanely Great Thing," *Wired Magazine* (February 1996)

Tap the energy of the anarchist and he will be the one to push your company ahead. **Dame Anita Roddick**. *Body and Soul* (co-written with Russell Miller, 1991)

In the middle of a hard project, I remind people to do something else. Sometimes people need to work on something completely different to get their best ideas. **Brad Fregger**. "On Achieving Excellence" (July 1991)

Creative people tend to pass the responsibility for getting down to brass tacks to others. **Theodore Levitt**. "Ideas Are Useless Unless Used," *Inc.* (February 1981)

Creativity is thinking new things. Innovation is doing new things. **Theodore Levitt**. "Ideas Are Useless Unless Used," *Inc.* (February 1981)

Minds are like parachutes. They only function when they are open. **Sir James Dewar**. Attributed

True creativity often starts where language ends. **Arthur Koestler**. *The Act of Creation* (1964)

Music is spiritual. The music business is not. **Van Morrison**. *The Times (London)* (July 1990)

Many people are inventive, sometimes cleverly so. But real creativity begins with the drive to work on and on and on. **Margueritte Bro**. *Sarah* (1949)

The majority of businessmen are incapable of original thought because they are unable to escape from the tyranny of reason. **David Ogilvy**. Quoted in *The Creative Organisation* (Gary A. Steiner, ed, 1965)

If it doesn't sell, it isn't creative. **David Ogilvy**. *Ogilvy on Advertising* (1983)

The best ideas come as jokes. Make your thinking as funny as possible. **David Ogilvy**. Quoted in *Don't Get Taken—Take Control* (Tom Sabella, 2006)

The wild, the absurd, the seemingly crazy: this kind of thinking is where new ideas come from...The people capable of such playful thought carry forward their childish qualities and childhood dreams, applying them in areas where most of us get stuck, victims of our adult seriousness. Staying a child isn't easy. **Nicholas Negroponte**. "Toys of Tomorrow," *Wired Magazine* (March 6, 1998)

Planning, by its very nature, defines and preserves categories. Creativity, by its very nature, creates categories or re-arranges established ones. **Henry Mintzberg**. *The Rise and Fall of Strategic Planning* (1994)

Creativity can be described as letting go of certainties. **Gail Sheehy**. *Speed Is of the Essence* (1971)

An artist is someone who produces things that people don't need to have but that he—for some reason—thinks it would be a good idea to give them. **Andy Warhol**. *The Philosophy of Andy Warhol (from A to B and Back Again)* (1975)

Creativity often consists of merely turning up what is already there. Did you know that right and left shoes were thought up only a little over a century ago? **Bernice Fitz-Gibbon**. Quoted in her obituary. *New York Times* (1982)

Every creative act is a sudden cessation of stupidity. **Edwin Land**. *Forbes* (June 1975)

We created an environment in which a man was expected to sit and think for two years. **Edwin Land**. *Selected Papers in Industry* (Polaroid Corporation, 1983)

Controlled accident. **Jackson Pollock**. Referring to his painting technique. Interview (1946)

All the great work comes from people's obsession and imagination, not from focus groups. **Michael Grade**. *Marketing* (June 2000)

Originality is deliberate and forced, and partakes of the nature of a protest. **Eric Hoffer**. *The Passionate State of Mind* (1955)

Criticism

I fancy it is just as hard to do your duty when men are sneering at you as when they are shooting at you. **Woodrow Wilson**. Speech (1914)

A negative judgment gives you more satisfaction than praise, providing it smacks of jealousy. **Jean Baudrillard**. *Cool Memories* (1987)

Criticism is one of the most important tasks a manager has. **Jacques Barzun**. *Emotional Intelligence* (1996)

A thick skin is a gift from God. **Konrad J. Adenauer**. *New York Times* (December 30, 1959)

Next to the joy of the egotist is the joy of the detractor. **Agnes Repplier**. "Writing an Autobiography," *Under Dispute* (1924)

No man can tell another his faults so as to benefit him, unless he loves him. **Henry**

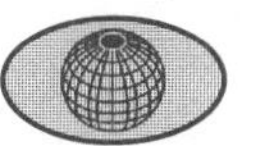

Ward Beecher. *Proverbs from Plymouth Pulpit* (1887)

Damn with faint praise, assent with civil leer,
And, without sneering, teach the rest to sneer.
Alexander Pope. "An Epistle to Dr Arbuthnot" (1735)

Cheers hearten a man. But jeers are just as essential. They help maintain his sense of balance and proportion. **Jay E. House**. "On Second Thoughts," *On Second Thoughts* (1936)

If you have bright plumage, people will take pot shots at you. **Alan Clark**. *Independent (London)* (June 25, 1994)

No one can make you feel inferior without your consent. **Eleanor Roosevelt**. *This Is My Story* (1937)

The thought pattern that keeps most people poor: they criticize instead of analyse. **Robert Kiyosaki**. *Rich Dad, Poor Dad* (2000)

Customers

It is a company's customers who effectively control what it can and cannot do. **Clayton M. Christensen**. *The Innovator's Dilemma* (1997)

Many people believe that we have entered the age of the Internet. Actually, it's more accurate to say that we're living in the age of the customer. **Anne Busquet**. "Next Stop—The 21st Century," *Fast Company* (Lucy McCauley, 1999)

You could not have got more knowledge about detergents anywhere in the world...I asked, could anyone who has washed their own clothes in the past three months put their hands up. Not one hand went up. **Niall Fitzgerald**. Referring to Unilever's problems with a detergent. *Marketing* (July 2000)

The most exciting thing happening in business is the rise of vigilante consumers. **Dame Anita Roddick**. Interview, *Marketing Week* (February 24, 2000)

Good companies will meet needs; great companies will create markets. **Philip Kotler**. *Marketing Management* (1990)

A restaurant is great if there are people queuing to get into it. It doesn't matter what the critics say. **Sir David Michels**. *Sunday Times (London)* (September 2000)

If someone thinks they are being mistreated by us, they won't tell 5 people, they'll tell 5000. **Jeff Bezos**. *Wall Street Journal* (May 1996)

Whatever the business model, it doesn't matter what anybody else thinks if customers don't like it. **Paul Gratton**. *Sunday Times (London)* (May 2000)

Customers do not care about industry boundaries; they want service and convenience. **Peter G. W. Keen**. "Basic Change," *The Process Edge* (1999)

The consumer isn't a moron; she is your wife. **David Ogilvy**. *Confessions of an Advertising Man* (1963)

The consumer is the most important part of the production line. **W. Edwards Deming**. *Out of the Crisis* (1992)

Your most unhappy customers are your greatest source of learning. **Bill Gates**. *Business @ The Speed of Thought* (1999)

Everything changes when there is a real customer yelling at you from the other end of the phone. **Percy Barnevik**. Quoted in *Liberation Management* (Tom Peters, 1992)

The customer will become so integrated into the production process that we will find it more and more difficult to tell just who is actually the consumer and the producer. **Alvin Toffler**. *The Third Wave* (1980)

A manufacturer is not through with his customer when a sale is completed. He has then only started with his customer. **Henry Ford**. *My Life and Work* (co-written with Samuel Crowther, 1922)

If you look after the customers and look after the people who look after the customers, you should be successful. **Charles Dunstone**. *Sunday Times (London)* (June 2000)

There is only one valid definition of business: to create a customer. **Peter F. Drucker**. *The Practice of Management* (1954)

Goodwill is the one and only asset that competition cannot undersell or destroy. **Marshall Field**. Attributed

The question is, then, do we try to make things easy on ourselves or do we try to make things easy on our customers, whoever they may be? **Erwin Frand**. Quoted in *Business Models* (David Watson, 2005)

When you are skinning your customers you should leave some skin on to grow again so that you can skin them again. **Nikita Khrushchev**. Speech to British businessmen (May 1961)

Consumers are statistics. Customers are people. **Stanley Marcus**. *Quest for the Best* (2001)

There is only one boss. The customer. And he can fire everybody in the company, from the chairman on down, simply by spending his money somewhere else. **Sam Walton**. Quoted in *500 of the Most Witty, Acerbic and Erudite Things Ever Said About Money* (Philip Jenks, 2002)

Debt

A debt may get mouldy, but it never decays. **Chinua Achebe**. *No Longer at Ease* (1960)

Christmas is a time when kids tell Santa Claus what they want and adults pay for it. Deficits are when adults tell the government what they want—and their kids pay for it. **Richard D. Lamm**. *US News & World Report* (1985)

Should we really let our people starve so we can pay our debts. **Julius Nyerere**. *Guardian (London)* (March 1985)

Creditors have better memories than debtors. **Benjamin Franklin**. The *Poor Richard's Almanack* series (1732–1758) were originally published under the pseudonym Richard Saunders. *Poor Richard's Almanack* (1758)

Give the Germans five deutschmarks and they will save it. But give the British £5 and they will borrow £25 and spend it. **Sir John Major**. Said while Chancellor of the Exchequer. Interview, *Daily Express (London)* (May 28, 1990)

The debt is like a crazy aunt we keep down in the basement. All the neighbors know she's there, but nobody wants to talk about her. **H. Ross Perot**. *United We Stand: How We Can Take Back Our Country* (1992)

I feel these days like a very large flamingo. No matter what way I turn, there is always a very large bill. **Joseph O'Connor**. *The Secret World of the Irish Male* (1994)

We at Chrysler borrow money the old-fashioned way. We pay it back. **Lee Iacocca**. *New York Times* (1983)

One must have some sort of occupation now-a-days. If I hadn't my debts I shouldn't have anything to think about. **Oscar Wilde**. *A Woman of No Importance* (1893), Act 1

  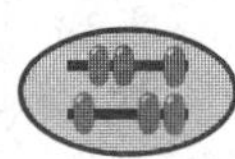   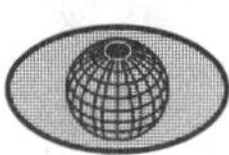   

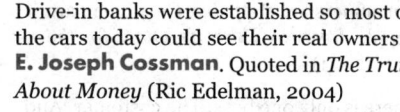

Drive-in banks were established so most of the cars today could see their real owners. **E. Joseph Cossman**. Quoted in *The Truth About Money* (Ric Edelman, 2004)

No country has ever been ruined on account of its debts. **Adolf Hitler**. Quoted in *The Face of the Third Reich* (Joachim C. Fest, 1999)

Today, there are three kinds of people: the have's, the have-not's, and the have-not-paid-for-what-they-have's. **Earl Wilson**. Quoted in *Investing Under Fire* (Alan R. Ackerman, 2003)

He is like some sherry-crazed old dowager who has lost the family silver at roulette, and who now decides to double up by betting the house as well. **Boris Johnson**. On Gordon Brown's decision to increase government borrowing to alleviate the effects of the 2008 recession. *Daily Telegraph (London)* (November 25, 2008)

Decisions

Every decision is liberating, even if it leads to disaster. Otherwise, why do so many people walk upright and with open eyes into their misfortune. **Elias Canetti**. "1980," *The Secret Heart of the Clock: Notes, Aphorisms, Fragments 1973–1985* (1991)

A complex decision is like a great river, drawing from its many tributaries the innumerable premises of which it is constituted. **Herbert A. Simon**. *Administrative Behavior* (1947)

Business today is about making decisions amid ambiguity. **Geraldine Laybourne**. Quoted in "Next Stop—The 21st Century," *Fast Company* (Lucy McCauley, 1999)

The man who is denied the opportunity of taking decisions of importance begins to regard as important the decisions he is allowed to take. **C. Northcote Parkinson**. *Parkinson's Law: The Pursuit of Progress* (1958)

Good decisions come from wisdom. Wisdom comes from experience. Experience comes from bad decisions. **Anonymous**. *Forbes* (August 10, 1987)

There is always a multitude of reasons both in favour of doing a thing and against doing it. The art of debate lies in presenting them; the art of life lies in neglecting ninety-nine hundreths of them. **Mark Rutherford**. *More Pages from a Journal* (1910)

Most discussions of decision making assume that only senior executives make decisions or that only senior executives' decisions matter. This is a dangerous mistake. **Peter F. Drucker**. *Classic Drucker* (2006)

What is important is not the decision itself but rather how committed and informed people are. The best decisions can be bungled just as the worst decisions can work just fine. **William Ouchi**. *Theory Z: How American Business Can Meet the Japanese Challenge* (1981)

A weak man has doubts before a decision, a strong man has them afterwards. **Karl Kraus**. *Half Truths and One-and-a-Half Truths* (1990)

A real decision is measured by the fact that you've taken a new action. If there's no action, you haven't truly decided. **Anthony Robbins**. *Awaken the Giant Within* (1992)

Delegating

Do not delegate an assignment and then attempt to manage it yourself—you will make an enemy of the overruled subordinate. **Wess Roberts**. *Leadership Secrets of Attila the Hun* (1991)

He liked nobody to be in any way superior to him...he chose his ministers, not for their knowledge, but for their ignorance; not for their capacity, but for their want of it. **Duc de Saint-Simon**. Referring to Louis XIV. *Memoires* (1694–1723), vol. 3

Never learn to do anything. If you don't learn, you'll always find someone else to do it for you. **Mark Twain**. Attributed

You could not maintain any illusion of direct control over a general or provincial governor...You appointed him, you watched his chariot and baggage train disappear over the hill in a cloud of dust, and that was that. **Sir Anthony Jay**. Arguing that a key reason the Roman Empire grew so large and lasted so long was the delegation necessitated by poor communications. *Management Machiavelli* (1970)

Big things and little things are my job. Middle level management can be delegated. **Konosuke Matsushita**. *Quest for Prosperity* (1988)

If you are having as much fun running a big corporation as you did running a piece of it, then you are probably interfering too much with the people who really make it happen. **James Burke**. *Fortune* (June 6, 1988)

Details

God is in the details. **Ludwig Mies van der Rohe**. *New York Times* (August 1969)

Pedantry is the dotage of knowledge. **Holbrook Jackson**. *Anatomy of Bibliomania* (1930), vol. 1

The art of being wise is the art of knowing what to overlook. **William James**. *The Principles of Psychology* (1890)

Our life is frittered away by detail... Simplify, simplify. **Henry David Thoreau**. "Where I Lived and What I Lived For," *Walden, or Life in the Woods* (1854)

A handful of men have become very rich by paying attention to details that most others ignored. **Henry Ford**. Attributed

Neglecting small things under the pretext of wanting to accomplish large ones is the excuse of a coward. **Alexandra David-Neel**. *Quest* (May–June 1978)

All knowledge is of itself of some value. There is nothing so minute or inconsiderable, that I would not rather know it than not. **Samuel Johnson**. Quoted in *The Life of Samuel Johnson* (James Boswell, 1791)

The contribution which the human mind makes to work and business is very much one of picking up information from tiny, seemingly insignificant trifles, and relating them to new ideas or concepts. **Sir John Harvey-Jones**. *Managing to Survive* (1993)

The mechanics of running a business are really not very complicated, when you get down to essentials. You have to make some stuff and sell it to somebody for more than it cost you. That's about all there is to it, except for a few million details. **John L. McCaffrey**. Speech (1953)

Determination

In some circumstances, a refusal to be defeated is a refusal to be educated. **Margaret Halsey**. *No Laughing Matter* (1977)

Never give in, never give in, never, never, never, never—in nothing, great or small, large or petty—never give in except to convictions of honour and good sense. **Sir Winston Churchill**. Address given at Harrow School (October 29, 1941)

   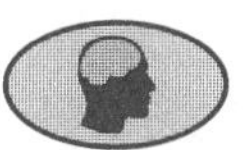  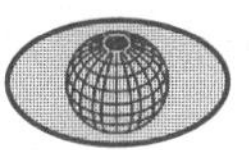   

Fanaticism consists in redoubling your effort when you have forgotten your aim. **George Santayana**. *The Life of Reason* (1905)

I shall find a way or make one. **Robert Edwin Peary**. Inscription on an expedition hut (1902)

Miracles can be made, but only by sweating. **Giovanni Agnelli**. *Corriere della Sera* (1994)

The people who get on in this world are the people who get up and look for the circumstances they want, and, if they can't find them, make them. **George Bernard Shaw**. *Mrs Warren's Profession* (1893), Act 2

Sweat is the cologne of accomplishment. **Heywood Hale Broun**. CBS television interview (July 21, 1973)

I wish to preach, not the doctrine of ignoble ease, but the doctrine of the strenuous life, the life of toil and effort, of labor and strife. **Theodore Roosevelt**. Speech, The Hamilton Club, Chicago, Illinois. "The Strenuous Life," *The Strenuous Life: Essays and Addresses* (1900)

To gain that which is worth having, it may be necessary to lose everything else. **Bernadette Devlin**. *The Price of My Soul* (1969), Preface

Discrimination

The low wages at which women will work form the chief reason for employing them at all...A woman's cheapness is, so to speak, her greatest economic asset. She can be used to keep down the cost of production. **Bureau of Labor**. "Report on Conditions of Women and Child Wage-earners in the United States" (1911), vol. 11

We don't so much want to see a female Einstein become an assistant professor. We want a woman schlemiel to get promoted as quickly as a male schlemiel. **Bella Abzug**. Quoted in *America Chronicle* (Lois Gordon and Alan Gordon, 1987)

The test for whether or not you can hold a job should not be the arrangement of your chromosomes. **Bella Abzug**. *Bella!* (1972)

Men their rights and nothing more; women their rights and nothing less. **Susan B. Anthony**.*The Revolution* was the magazine of the women's suffrage movement in the United States. *The Revolution* (1868)

Business shouldn't be like sports, separating the men from the women. **Barbara Ward (Baroness Jackson of Wadsworth)**. Speech (October 2002)

Top jobs are designed for people with wives. **Lucy Heller**. Quoted in the *Economist* (March 28, 1992)

This fellow said to me, "You know for a woman you make a lot of money. If I was you, I'd go back to my office and be happy just to have the job." **Grace Fey**. Quoted in *Women of the Street* (Sue Herera, 1997)

There are very few jobs that actually require a penis or vagina. All other jobs should be open to everybody. **Florynce R. Kennedy**. "Freelancer with No Time to Write," *Writer's Digest* (February 1974)

I regard affirmative action as pernicious—a system that had wonderful ideals when it started but was almost immediately abused for the benefit of white middle-class women. **Camille Paglia**. Interview, *Reason Magazine* (August–September 1995)

Saying that a person cannot be kept out doesn't ensure that that person can get in, and more important, stay in. **Margaret Hennig**. Discussing corporate responses to antidiscrimination legislation. *The Managerial Woman* (co-written with Anne Jardim, 1976)

The legend of the jungle heritage and the evolution of man as a hunting carnivore has taken root in man's mind...He may even believe that equal pay will do something terrible to his gonads. **Elaine Morgan**. *The Descent of Woman* (1972)

Doing Business in Africa

One of the principal reasons why genuine industrialization cannot easily be realized in Africa today is that the market for manufactured goods in any single African country is too small. **Walter Rodney**. *How Europe Underdeveloped Africa* (1972)

International finance is always looking for new opportunities. The challenge for Africa is not just to be attractive to traders and investors, but to offer opportunities which are more attractive than anywhere else in the world. **Peter Hain**. Speech, Challenges for Governance in Africa Conference, Wilton Park, England (September 13, 1999)

Here, in this realm of the spices, a market price was being created—a set of fiscal frontiers within which to reach a consensus. It was the language of the stock exchange...and it was the bourse which had obviously imitated the ways of the souk. **Douglas Kennedy**. Describing bartering for spices in the Casablanca souk. *Chasing Mammon: Travels in the Pursuit of Money* (1992)

If you look at Malaysian companies, they are not investing in Europe or the United States, they are investing in African countries, high-potential countries, where they can transfer their expertise. **Raphael Auphan**. Quoted in *International Herald Tribune* (November 4, 1997)

Doing Business in Asia-Pacific

In Sydney, you're in Asia, but not of Asia. Basing your Asian operations in Sydney is like basing your American operations in Rio. **Donald Saunders**. *Asia Inc.* (December 1996)

Never visit a Japanese company without tons of business cards. Basically, no meishi (name cards) means no existence for you on this earth. **Mark Gauthier**. *Making It in Japan: Work, Life, Leisure and Beyond* (1993)

Some people think that Japan's success is due to cartels and collaboration. It is not. In the industries in which Japan is internationally successful, it has many fiercely competitive local rivals. **Michael Porter**. *Economist* (June 9, 1990)

There is nothing Japan really wants to buy from foreign countries except, possibly, neckties with unusual designs. **Yoshihiro Inayama**. Quoted in "Sayings of the Week," *Sydney Morning Herald* (August 3, 1985)

In Japan, the best and brightest young people aspire to become bureaucrats, not businessmen, and there is intense competition for bureaucratic jobs. **Francis Fukuyama**. *Trust: The Social Virtues and the Creation of Prosperity* (1995)

The velocity of decision making in government was extraordinarily slow. It took 18 to 24 months and 15 to 20 trips to Delhi to get a license to import computers. **Narayana Murthy**. *Forbes* (June 2000)

This road of industrialization was not planned in advance by theoreticians. Rather, it has been created by the peasants

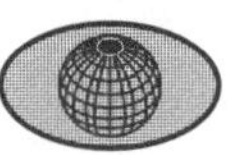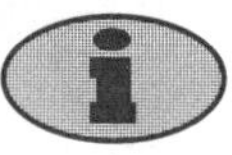

on the basis of their experience in real life. **Fei Xiaotong.** Comparing China's industrialization favorably to that of the West, where modern industry had grown at the expense of the countryside. *Beijing Review* (1985), no. 21

Indian management has to pursue processes which conform to the underlying grain of the Indian temper. **S. K. Chakraborty.** *Management by Values: Towards Cultural Congruence* (1991)

Given the economic growth and blossoming of billionaires in the region, Asia is likely to produce the world's first trillionaire. **Anonymous.** Quoted in *Asia, Inc.* (September 1996)

Five Rules for Doing Business in China: 1. Think small—focus on one region at a time. 2. Skip the manager, talk to the clerk. 3. Study the side streets. 4. Get the goods to market. 5. Above all be flexible. **Anonymous.** Quoted in the *New York Times Magazine* (February 18, 1996)

Indians in general have tended to under-market themselves. That comes because it's part of our culture...you don't go and say I have created the world's greatest software. **Subeer Bhatia.** *BusinessWeek* (September 2000)

Acts of marketing insanity such as the US firm that invested heavily in a campaign to sell cake mix to the Japanese—in profound and dismal ignorance of the fact that hardly any homes in Japan have ovens. **Robert Heller.** *The Supermarketers* (1987)

Asians save today's money for tomorrow while Americans spend tomorrow's money today. **Cheng Siwei.** Speech to the World Economic Forum (January 2008)

The dramatic modernization of the Asian economies ranks alongside the Renaissance and the Industrial Revolution as one of the most important developments in economic history. **Lawrence H. Summers.** Remark (1993)

It says something about this new global economy that *USA Today* now reports every morning on the day's events in Asian markets. **Lawrence H. Summers.** Remark (1998)

Doing Business in Europe

No one can bring together a country that has 265 kinds of cheese. **Charles De Gaulle.** Said after an electoral setback in 1953. Quoted in the *Economist* (June 27, 1992)

When an American heiress wants to buy a man, she at once crosses the Atlantic. The only really materialistic people I have ever met have been Europeans. **Mary McCarthy.** "America the Beautiful," *Commentary* (September 1947)

Lifestyles around Europe are converging, but tastes are not. **Nicholas Colchester.** *Europe Relaunched* (co-written with David Buchan, 1990)

Italy is a poor country full of rich people. **Richard Gardner.** Quoted in the *Observer (London)* (August 16, 1981)

Europe has never existed. One must genuinely create Europe. **Jean Monnet.** Quoted in *The New Europeans* (Anthony Sampson, 1968)

The rough broad difference between the American and the European business man is that the latter is anxious to leave his work, while the former is anxious to get to it. **Arnold Bennett.** *Those United States* (1926)

Propose to an Englishman any principle, or any instrument, however admirable, and you will observe that the whole effort of the English mind is directed to find a difficulty, a defect, or an impossibility in it. **Charles Babbage.** Referring to the British inability to support inventors. Quoted in *The Code Book* (Simon Singh, 1999)

Europe's strength is its diversity, not its uniformity. **Sir John Harvey-Jones.** Speech (1990)

You can tell that our economy is improving at last. For the first time someone has been arrested for counterfeiting the Hungarian currency. **Geza Jeszenszky.** Attributed

Doing Business in India

Our private enterprise is more private than enterprising. **Indira Gandhi.** Speech (December 5, 1970)

India will become the country of choice...It's already starting to happen. **Narayana Murthy.** Referring to software development. *Forbes* (October 2000)

The question is does India need dot coms? If you were to ask me this question, the answer is no, India needs infrastructure. **Subeer Bhatia.** *BusinessWeek* (September 2000)

Old India requires few tools, few skills, and many hands. **V. S. Naipaul.** *India: A Wounded Civilization* (1977)

Indian businesses often appear to be weak partners...however, they are formidable opponents who can subvert the best-laid plans of international firms. **Rajiv Desai.** *Indian Business Culture* (1999)

A company's reputation does not necessarily follow it into India, which has been a closed market for so long that established global brands have no meaning for the Indian consumer. **Rajiv Desai.** *Indian Business Culture* (1999)

Doing Business in Latin America

The United States is glad to manipulate cheap Mexican labor, chastising it in days of crisis, accepting it in boom times, and always maintaining the police fiction of an impregnable border. **Carlos Fuentes.** *A New Time for Mexico* (1994)

Multinationals are no longer immune from violence in Mexico. I personally know of seven American chief executives that have looked at the wrong end of a weapon in Mexico. **Morton Palmer.** Quoted in the *Wall Street Journal* (October 29, 1996)

The Argentinians alter their currency almost as frequently as they change their finance ministers. No people on earth has a keener interest in currency experimentation than the Argentinians. **Anonymous.** *Bankers magazine* (1889)

It is easier for a Chilean to buy a company in Argentina than it is to buy duty free. **Anonymous.** Quoted in the *New York Times* (November 17, 1996)

We may not be a tiger yet but we are already a jaguar. **Anonymous.** Referring to the Chilean economy. Quoted in *Worth* (August 1995)

What's the chance that I'd want to own this Venezuelan company for a long time because I have confidence in the company and the country? Very, very small. **Anonymous.** Said by a US emerging markets fund manager. Quoted in the *Wall Street Journal* (November 21, 1996)

Since economies in the process of organization lack resources to dynamize themselves...it is right to accept the aid of all who want to run with us the risks

     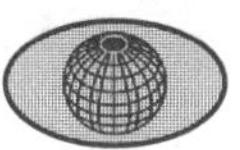   

of the marvelous adventure that is progress. **Roberto Campos**. Speech, Mackenzie University, São Paulo, Brazil (December 22, 1966)

Doing Business in North America

As a rule, from what I've observed, the American captain of industry doesn't do anything out of business hours. When he has put the cat out and locked up the office for the night, he just relapses into a state of coma from which he emerges only to start being a captain of industry again. **P. G. Wodehouse**. "Leave It to Jeeves," *My Man Jeeves* (1919)

There is no business in America...which will not yield a fair profit if it receives the unremitting, exclusive attention, and all the capital of capable and industrious men. **Andrew Carnegie**. Speech at Curry Commercial College, Pittsburgh, Pennsylvania. "The Road to Business Success" (June 23, 1885)

If it's worth doing, California will do it to excess. **Anonymous**. Comment on National Public Radio in the United States (1996)

America is still a place where most people react to seeing a man in a Ferrari by redoubling their own efforts to be able to afford one, rather than by trying to let down his tires. **Anonymous**. Let down means deflate. *Economist (London)* (January 3, 1998)

Perhaps the most revolting character that the United States ever produced was the Christian business man. **H. L. Mencken**. *Minority Report—H. L. Mencken's Notebook* (1956)

It seems to be a law in American life that whatever enriches us anywhere except in the wallet inevitably becomes uneconomic. **Russell Baker**. *New York Times* (March 24, 1968)

If there is anything of which American industry has a superfluity
It is green lights, know-how, initiative, and ingenuity.
Ogden Nash. "Ring Out the Old, Ring In the New, but Don't Get Caught In Between," *You Can't Get There from Here* (1957), 1: First Chime

E-Commerce

Fireflies throwing off sparks before the storm. **Lou Gerstner**. Referring to dot.com companies. *Sunday Times (London)* (May 2000)

I believe we can still be a footnote in the history of e-commerce. **Jeff Bezos**. *Sunday Telegraph (London)* (July 2000)

Marketing is marketing. It's easy to drape new media in magic but it comes down to whether it's a good business or not. **Carl Lyons**. *Marketing* (August 2000)

The phrase click, click you're dead focuses the mind. **Sir Martin Sorrell**. Interview (March 2000)

We're fast approaching the point at which there is really no distinction between the .com companies and traditional businesses. The only distinction will be between the winners and losers, and of course, the pace of change at which companies become winners or losers. **Michael Dell**. Speech to the DirectConnect Customer Conference, Austin, Texas. "DirectConnect" (August 25, 1999)

Any company, old or new, that does not see this technology as important as breathing could be on its last breath. **Jack Welch**. Referring to e-commerce. *Sunday Times (London)* (May 2000)

The Internet is the Viagra of big business. **Jack Welch**. Attributed

Thus, in the future, instead of buying bananas in a grocery store, you could go pick them off a tree in a virtual jungle. **Yasuhiro Fukushima**. *Wired Asia* (June 2000)

Pack lightly and carry a compass. **Raul Fernandez**. Web site (September 2000)

I am secretly looking forward to rediscovering the little pleasures of pre-electronic shopping: holding things in my hands, trying them on, and even taking them home with me after I have paid. **Anonymous**. Quoted in the *Economist (London)* (December 21, 1996)

The web site needs to be as sticky as a currant bun. **Carolyn McCall**. *Marketing* (April 2000)

The Internet is an elite organization; most of the population of the world have never made a phone call. **Noam Chomsky**. *Observer (London)* (February 1996)

Much as we talk about Internet companies today, in five years' time there won't be any Internet companies. All companies will be Internet companies or they will be dead. **Andrew S. Grove**. Speech, Los Angeles Times 3rd Annual Investment Strategies Conference, Los Angeles, California (May 22, 1999)

Stop thinking about it as the information highway and start thinking about it as the marketing superhighway. Doesn't it sound better already? **Don Logan**. Speech to the Association of National Advertisers

Secure web servers are the equivalent of heavy armoured cars. The problem is, they are being used to transfer rolls of coins and cheques written in crayon by people on park benches to merchants doing business in cardboard boxes from beneath highway bridges. Further, the roads are subject to random detours, anyone with a screwdriver can control the traffic lights, and there are no police. **Gene Spafford**. *Web Security and Commerce* (1997)

Economics

Economists can be called the worldly philosophers for they sought to embrace in a scheme of philosophy the most worldly of man's activities—his drive for wealth. **Robert L. Heilbroner**. *The Worldly Philosophers* (1953), Introduction

When the facts change, I change my mind. **John Maynard Keynes**. Quoted in *Treasury of Investment Wisdom* (Bernice Cohen, 1999)

The ideas of economists and political philosophers...are more powerful than is commonly understood. Indeed the world is ruled by little else. Practical men who believe themselves to be quite exempt from any intellectual influences, are usually the slaves of some defunct economist. **John Maynard Keynes**. *The General Theory of Employment Interest and Money* (1936)

If economists could manage to get themselves thought of as humble, competent people on a level with dentists, that would be splendid. **John Maynard Keynes**. *Essays in Persuasion* (1931)

The modern history of economic theory is a tale of evasions of reality. **Thomas Balogh**. Referring to classical economics. *The Irrelevance of Conventional Economics* (1982)

Economics is as much a study in fantasy and aspiration as in hard numbers—maybe more so. **Theodore Roszak**. *The Making of a Counter Culture* (1995), Introduction

Trickle-down theory—the less than elegant metaphor that if one feeds the horse enough oats, some will pass through to the road for the sparrows. **J. K. Galbraith**. *The Culture of Contentment* (1992)

In economics, hope and faith coexist with great scientific pretension and also a deep desire for respectability. **J. K. Galbraith**. *New York Times Magazine* (June 1970)

Economics is extremely useful as a form of employment for economists. **J. K. Galbraith**. Quoted in *The Book of Incomes* (Gerald Krefetz and Philip Gittelman, 1982)

The experience of being disastrously wrong is salutary; no economist should be denied it, and not many are. **J. K. Galbraith**. *A Life in Our Times* (1981)

Economics limps along with one foot in untested hypotheses and the other in untestable slogans. **Joan Robinson**. "Metaphysics, Morals and Science," *Economic Philosophy* (1962)

A commodity appears, at first sight, a very trivial thing, and easily understood. Its analysis shows that is is, in reality, a very queer thing, abounding in metaphysical subtleties and theological niceties. **Karl Marx**. *Das Kapital* (1867), vol. 1

Unfortunately monetarism, like Marxism, suffered the only fate that for a theory is worse than death: it was put into practice. **Ian Gilmour**. *Dancing with Dogma* (1992)

Did you ever think that making a speech on economics is a lot like pissing down your leg? It seems hot to you but it never does to anyone else. **Lyndon Baines Johnson**. Quoted in *A Life in our Times* (J. K. Galbraith, 1981)

Neoclassical economics...has uncovered important truths about the nature of money and markets because its fundamental model of rational self-interested human behavior is correct about 80 percent of the time. **Francis Fukuyama**. *Trust: The Social Virtues and the Creation of Prosperity* (1995)

As in the instances of alchemy, astrology, witchcraft, and other such popular creeds, political economy, has a plausible idea at the root of it. **John Ruskin**. "The Roots of Honour," *Unto This Last* (1862)

Everybody is always in favour of general economy and particular expenditure. **Anthony Eden (Earl of Avon)**. Quoted in "Sayings of the Week," *Observer (London)* (June 17, 1956)

We're a me-me-me generation. We're borrowing the savings of every nation in the world. We're...piling up a big tab. Now, I may think we're too big to have a run on us. You may think that. But it's possible that God does not. **Paul Samuelson**. Interview, *The New Economy?* (Online NewsHour, January 13, 2000)

As the economy gets better, everything else gets worse. **Art Buchwald**. *Time* (January 31, 1972)

One of the soundest rules to remember when making forecasts in the field of economics is that whatever is to happen is happening already. **Sylvia Porter**. Attributed

One speaks with great respect of economists, if only because they represent such a variety of opinions. **Robert Menzies**. *Sydney Morning Herald* (March 14, 1964)

If freedom were not so economically efficient it certainly wouldn't stand a chance. **Milton Friedman**. Quoted in "Sayings of the Week," *Observer (London)* (March 1, 1987)

Economists may not know how to run the economy, but they know how to create shortages or gluts simply by regulating prices below the market, or artificially supporting them from above. **Milton Friedman**. Attributed (1962)

Economists are always recommending the elimination of this or that market imperfection...no astrophysicist recommends the elimination of planets that he does not like. **Lester Thurow**. Referring to how economists relate to economic realities. *Dangerous Currents* (1983)

Humans have trouble with economics, as you may have noticed, and not just because economic circumstances sometimes cause them to starve. Humans seem to have an innate inability to pay attention to economic principles. **P. J. O'Rourke**. *Eat the Rich* (1998), ch. 1

Economists got away from really questioning how the world works, how decisions actually got made. If something doesn't conform to neoclassical models...people are not somehow behaving themselves properly. **W. Brian Arthur**. Interview, *Strategy + Business* (April–June 1998)

The invisible hand is not perfect. Indeed, the invisible hand is a little bit arthritic...I'm a believer in free markets, but I think we need to be less naïve. We need to accept that markets give us pretty good solutions, but occasionally they will lock in something inferior. **W. Brian Arthur**. Interview, *Strategy + Business* (April–June 1998)

What a country calls its vital economic interests are not the things that enable its citizens to live, but the things that enable it to make war. **Simone Weil**. *The Need for Roots* (1935)

We may be in a rapidly evolving international financial system with all the bells and whistles of the so-called new economy. But the old-economy rules of prudence are as formidable as ever. We violate them at our own peril. **Alan Greenspan**. Speech to the Financial Crisis Conference, Council on Foreign Relations, New York. "Global Challenges" (July 12, 2000)

I think there are two areas where new ideas are terribly dangerous—economics and sex. By and large, it's all been tried before, and if it's new, it's probably illegal or unhealthy. **Felix Rohatyn**. Quoted in *Business Babble: A Cynic's Dictionary of Corporate Jargon* (David Olive, 1991)

An economist is a surgeon with an excellent scalpel and a rough-edged lancet, who operates beautifully on the dead and tortures the living. **Nicholas Chamfort**. *Products of the Perfected Civilization: Selected Writings* (1969)

Inflation might be called prosperity with high blood pressure. **Arnold H. Glasgow**. Quoted in *Readers Digest* (1966)

Waiting for supply-side economics to work is like leaving the landing lights on for Amelia Earhart. **Walter Heller**. Quoted in *500 of the Most Witty, Acerbic, and Erudite Things Ever Said About Money* (Philip Jenks, 2002)

Having a little inflation is like being a little bit pregnant. **Leon Henderson**. Quoted in *Peter's Quotations: Ideas For Our Time* (Laurence J. Peter, 1977)

An economist is a man who states the obvious in terms of the incomprehensible. **Alfred A. Knopf**. Quoted in *Deflation: What Happens When Prices Fall* (Chris Farrell, 2004)

There are two things you are better off not watching in the making: sausages and econometric estimates. **Edward E. Leamer**. "Let's Take the Con Out of Econometrics," *American Economic Review* (1983)

All the great economic ills the world has known this century can be directly traced

  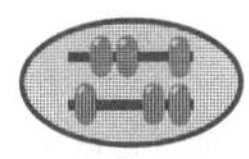   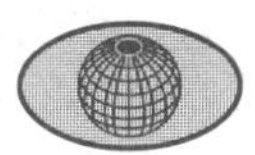   

back to the London School of Economics. **N. M. Perera**. Quoted in *500 of the Most Witty, Acerbic, and Erudite Things Ever Said About Money* (Philip Jenks, 2002)

We hate inflation, but we love everything that causes it. **William Simon**. Speech (1974)

Education

I think I'd rather have an English major than an economics major. **Michael Eisner**. Speech (June 1994)

The most important thing I would learn in school was that almost everything I would learn in school would be utterly useless. **Joseph O'Connor**. *The Secret World of the Irish Male* (1994)

Education is what survives when what has been learned has been forgotten. **B. F. Skinner**. *New Scientist* (May 21, 1964)

Education is simply the soul of a society as it passes from one generation to another. **G. K. Chesterton**. Attributed

In the Middle Ages, the rich tried to buy immortality by building cathedrals. These days they set up business schools instead. **Anonymous**. *Economist (London)* (July 20, 1996)

If Thomas Edison had gone to business school, we would all be reading by larger candles. **Anonymous**. Quoted in *What They Don't Teach You at Harvard Business School* (Mark H. McCormack, 1984)

If you think education is expensive, try ignorance. **Anonymous**.

It is the motto of the US universities that when a subject becomes totally obsolete, then a required course should be built around it. **Peter F. Drucker**. *Managing for the Future* (1992)

An art can only be learned in the workshop of those who are winning their bread by it. **Samuel Butler**. *Erewhon* (1872)

Real education must ultimately be limited to one who INSISTS on knowing, the rest is mere sheep-herding. **Ezra Pound**. *ABC of Reading* (1960)

Efficiency

If the Wright brothers were alive today, Wilbur would have to fire Orvill to reduce costs. **Charles Horton Cooley**. Quoted in *USA Today* (June 1994)

If you have someone on a job, use him. If you can't, get rid of him. **Frederick Herzberg**. *Harvard Business Review* (January–February 1968)

When two men always agree, one of them is unnecessary. **William Wrigley**. *American Magazine* (March 1920)

The pyramid, the chief organizational principle of the modern organization, turns a business into a traffic jam. **Ricardo Semler**. *Maverick!* (1993)

I make no secret of the fact that I would rather lie on a sofa than sweep beneath it. But you have to be efficient if you're going to be lazy. **Shirley Conran**. "The Reason Why," *Superwoman* (1975)

There is nothing so useless as doing efficiently that which should not be done at all. **Peter F. Drucker**. Attributed

It's pretty hard to be efficient without being obnoxious. **Kin Hubbard**. Attributed

Employees

Many organizations view people as things that are but one variable in the production equation. **David M. Noer**. *Healing the Wounds* (1993)

The inventory goes down the elevator every night. **Fairfax Cone**. Quoted in *The Trouble with Advertising* (John O'Toole, 1981)

American business long ago gave up on demanding that prospective employees be honest and hardworking. It has even stopped hoping for employees who are educated enough that they can tell the difference between the men's room and the women's room without having little pictures on the doors. **Dave Barry**. Quoted in *Really Bad Business Advice* (David Dallas and Arlen Foote, 2003)

Each employee should receive every day clear-cut definite instructions as to what he is to do and how he is to do it, and these instructions should be exactly carried out, whether they are right or wrong. **F. W. Taylor**. *The Principles of Scientific Management* (1911)

You can't look the troops in the eye and say, It's been a bad year, we can't do anything for you, but then say, By the way, we're going to pay ourselves a $1 million bonus. **H. Ross Perot**. Referring to his resignation from the General Motors board following GM's decision to freeze profit-sharing payments to workers while going ahead with executive bonus payments. Quoted in *Thriving on Chaos* (Tom Peters, 1987)

A bad reference is as hard to find as a good employee. **Robert Half**. *Half on Hiring* (1985), ch. 9

The average employee can deliver far more than his or her current job demands and far more than the terms employee empowerment, participative management, and multiple skills imply. **Tom Peters**. *The Tom Peters Seminar* (1994)

At nights and on weekends we cry out for human rights and freedom of speech, and then we go to work and become strategic and cautious about our every word for fear we will be seen as disloyal or uncommitted. **Peter Block**. *Stewardship* (1993)

Take our 20 best people away, and I will tell you that Microsoft would become an unimportant company. **Bill Gates**. *Fortune* (November 1996)

Empowerment: A magic wand management waves to help traumatized survivors of restructuring suddenly feel engaged, self-managed, and in control of their futures and their jobs. **Anonymous**. *Fortune* (February 15, 1995)

Don't be condescending to unskilled labor. Try it for a half a day first. **Brooks Atkinson**. *Theatre Arts* (1956)

How come when I want a pair of hands I get a human being as well? **Henry Ford**. *My Life and Work* (co-written with Samuel Crowther, 1922)

Few top executives can even imagine the hatred, contempt, and fury that has been created—not primarily among blue-collar workers who never had an exalted opinion of the bosses—but among their middle management and professional people. **Peter F. Drucker**. Quoted in "Seeing Things As They Really Are," *Forbes* (Robert Lenzner and Stephen S. Johnson, 1987)

I tell you, sir, the only safeguard of order and discipline in the modern world is a standardized worker with interchangeable parts. That would solve the entire problem of management. **Jean Giraudoux**. *The Madwoman of Chaillot* (1945)

You can't treat your people like an expense item. **Andrew S. Grove**. Quoted in *In the Company of Giants* (Rama Dev Jager, 1997)

  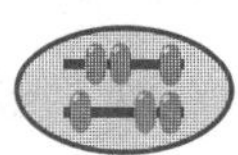   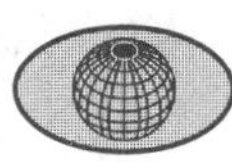   

Employers

Dear, never forget one little point. It's my business. You just work here. **Elizabeth Arden**. Said to her husband. Quoted in *Miss Elizabeth Arden* (Alfred A. Lewis and Constance Woodworth, 1972)

There could be no worse friend to labour than the benevolent, philanthropic employer...sooner or later he will be compelled to close. **Lord Leverhulme**. Quoted in *The History of Unilever* (Charles Wilson, 1951)

It might be said that it is the ideal of the employer to have production without employees and the ideal of the employee is to have income without work. **E. F. Schumacher**. Quoted in "Sayings of the Week," *Observer (London)* (May 4, 1975)

I am the proprietor. I am the boss...There can only be one boss and that is me. **Robert Maxwell**. Speech to labor leaders. Quoted in *Maxwell: The Outsider* (Tom Bower, 1988)

Enthusiasm

To run this business...you need...optimism, humanism, enthusiasm, intuition, curiosity, love, humour, magic and fun, and that secret ingredient—euphoria. **Dame Anita Roddick**. *Body and Soul* (co-written with Russell Miller, 1991)

Flaming enthusiasm, backed up by horse sense and persistence, is the quality that most frequently makes for success. **Dale Carnegie**. *How to Win Friends and Influence People* (1936)

A mediocre idea that generates enthusiasm will go further than a great idea that inspires no one. **Mary Kay Ash**. *On People Management* (1984)

There is nothing so easy but that it becomes difficult when you do it reluctantly. **Terence**. *The Self-Tormenter* (163 BC), l. 805

People who never get carried away, should be. **Steve Forbes**. *Town and Country* (November 1976)

I find that when you have a real interest in life that sleep is not the most important thing. **Martha Stewart**. Attributed

Nothing great was ever achieved without enthusiasm. **Ralph Waldo Emerson**. "Circles," *Essays: First Series* (1841)

I don't know anyone who is passionate and unsuccessful. **Jean-Pierre Garnier**. *The Times* (London) (September 26, 2005)

If you aren't fired with enthusiasm, then you will be fired with enthusiasm. **Vince Lombardi**. Quoted in *The Instant Manager* (Cyril Charney, 2004)

Entrepreneurs

Three components make an entrepreneur: the person, the idea and the resources to make it happen. **Dame Anita Roddick**. *Body and Soul* (co-written with Russell Miller, 1991)

You can never be an entrepreneur if you're afraid to lose money. It's like being a pilot who is afraid of bad weather. **Peter de Savary**. Quoted in *The Adventure Capitalists* (Jeff Grout and Lynne Curry, 1998)

If you want to understand entrepreneurs, you have to study the psychology of the juvenile delinquent. They don't have the same anxiety triggers that we have. **Abraham Zaleznik**. *US News & World Report* (October 1992)

Money isn't what motivates entrepreneurs; it is acknowledgement—a craving for your ideas to be acknowledged, **Reuben Singh**. *Management Today* (September 1999)

It's better to be the head of a chicken than the tail of a cow. **Stan Shih**. Referring to a Taiwanese proverb and the preference of entrepreneurs for running their own small business. Quoted in *Giant Killers* (Geoffrey James, 1996)

Where would the Rockefellers be today if old John D. had gone on selling short-weight kerosene...to widows and orphans instead of wisely deciding to mulct the whole country. **S. J. Perelman**. Letter (October 25, 1976)

The truth is I started my own company because I could not fill out a job application. **Terri Bowersock**. *Phoenix Business Journal* (1999)

It sounds boring, but anything is easy to start—starting a novel, starting a business...it's keeping the thing going that is difficult. **Prue Leith**. Quoted in *The Adventure Capitalists* (Jeff Grout and Lynne Curry, 1998)

Successful entrepreneurs judge correctly the need for change, then do something about it. **Lord Hanson**. *Web site* (2000)

Around Britain, thousands of young people are working from bedrooms, workshops and run-down offices, hoping that they will come up with the next Hotmail or Netscape. **Charles Leadbetter**. Quoted in the *Independent (London)* (1999)

Environment

Now there is one outstandingly important fact regarding Spaceship Earth, and that is that no instruction book came with it. **R. Buckminster Fuller**. *Operating Manual for Planet Earth* (1969)

Study how a society uses its land, and you can come to pretty reliable conclusions as to what its future will be. **E. F. Schumacher**. *Small Is Beautiful* (1973)

Conservation is business too. **Gaston Vizcarra**. *Forbes* (April 2000)

I am I plus my surroundings, and, if I do not preserve the latter, I do not preserve myself. **Jose Ortega y Gasset**. *Meditaciones del Quijote* (1914)

Excellence

If you don't do it excellently, don't do it at all. Because if it's not excellent, it won't be profitable or fun, and if you're not in business for fun or profit, what the hell are you doing there? **Robert Townsend**. *Further Up the Organization* (1984)

If you do things well, do them better. Be daring, be first, be different, be just. **Dame Anita Roddick**. Quoted in *Best Practice: Process Innovation Management* (Mohamed Zairi, 1999)

Striving for excellence motivates you; striving for perfection is demoralizing. **Harriet Beryl Braiker**. *Type E Woman: How to Overcome the Stress of Being Everything to Everybody* (1987)

No one has a greater asset for his business than a man's pride in his work. **Mary Parker Follett**. *Freedom and Co-ordination* (1949), ch. 2

The business world worships mediocrity. Officially we revere free enterprise, initiative, and individuality. Unofficially we fear it. **George Lois**. *The Art of Advertising* (1977)

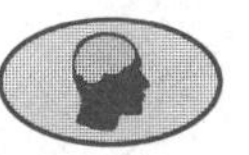

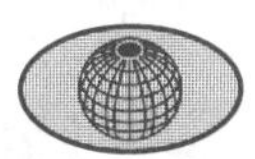

Executives

When I've had a rough day, before I go to sleep I ask myself if there's anything more I can do right now. If there isn't, I sleep sound. **L. L. Colbert**. *Newsweek* (1955)

Executives are like joggers. If you stop a jogger, he goes on running on the spot. If you drag an executive away from his business, he goes on running on the spot, pawing the ground, talking business. **Jean Baudrillard**. *Cool Memories* (1987)

Nobody should be chief executive officer of anything for more than five or six years. By then he's stale, bored, and utterly dependent upon his own clichés. **Robert Townsend**. *Up the Organization* (1970)

Regarded as a means, the businessman is tolerable. Regarded as an end, he is not so satisfactory. **John Maynard Keynes**. *Essays in Persuasion* (1978)

One lesson a man learns from Harvard Business School is that an executive is only as good as his health. **Jeffrey Archer (Lord Archer of Weston-Super-Mare)**. *Not a Penny More, Not a Penny Less* (1976)

Executive: A man who can make quick decisions and is sometimes right. **Frank McKinney Hubbard**. *The Roycroft Dictionary* (1923)

I always say to executives that they should go and see *King Lear*, because they'll be out there one day, wandering on the heath without a company car. **Charles Handy**. Interview, *The Times (London)* (April 12, 1989)

Their problem is that they play a lot of golf, which is right up there with heroin abuse as a killer of our nation's productivity. The only difference is that golf is more expensive. **Dave Barry**. Referring to executives. Interview, *Fortune* (July 7, 1997)

A molehill man is a pseudo-busy executive who comes to work at 9 a.m. and finds a molehill on his desk. He has until 5 p.m. to make this molehill into a mountain. An accomplished molehill man will often have his mountain finished before lunch. **Fred Allen**. *Treadmill to Oblivion* (1954)

The salary of the chief executive of the large corporation is not a market reward for achievement. It is frequently in the nature of a warm personal gesture by the individual to himself. **J. K. Galbraith**. *Annals of an Abiding Liberal* (1979)

Successful executives are great askers. **Warren Bennis**. *Beyond Leadership: Balancing Economics, Ethics and Ecology* (co-written with Jagdish Parikh and Ronnie Lessem, 1994)

The trouble with corporate America is that too many people with too much power live in a box (their home), travel the same road every day to another box (their office). **Faith Popcorn**. *The Popcorn Report* (1991)

There is nothing more short term than a 60-year-old CEO holding a fistful of share options. **Gary Hamel**. *Competing for the Future* (co-written with C. K. Prahalad, 1994)

Chief executives, who themselves own few shares of their companies, have no more feeling for the average stockholder than they do for baboons in Africa. **T. Boone Pickens**. *Harvard Business Review* (May–June 1986)

From now on, choosing my successor is the most important decision I'll make. It occupies a considerable amount of thought almost every day. **Jack Welch**. Quoted in *The New GE* (Robert Slater, 1993)

An overburdened, stretched executive is the best executive, because he or she doesn't have time to meddle, to deal in trivia, to bother people. **Jack Welch**. "Quotes of the Year," *Financial Times (London)* (December 30, 1989)

The heroic role of the captain of industry is that of a deliverer from an excess of business management. It is a casting out of businessmen by the chief of businessmen. **Thorstein Veblen**. *The Theory of Business Enterprise* (1904)

The chief executive...like a juggler keeps a number of projects in the air: periodically one comes down, is given a new burst of energy, and is sent back into orbit. **Henry Mintzberg**. "The Manager's Job: Folklore and Fact," *Harvard Business Review* (July–August 1975)

The biggest change in the workplace of the future will be the widespread realization that having one idiot boss is a much higher risk than having many idiot clients. **Scott Adams**. *The Dilbert Principle* (1996)

I can tell more about how someone is likely to react in a business situation from one round of golf than I can from a hundred hours of meetings. **Mark McCormack**. *What They Don't Teach You at Harvard Business School* (1984)

Some years back, a CEO friend of mine—in jest, it must be said—described the pathology of many big deals...With an impish look, he simply said: Aw, fellas, all the other kids have one. **Warren Buffett**. Chairman's letter to shareholders (March 7, 1995)

You can know a person by the kind of desk he keeps...If the president of a company has a clean desk...then it must be the executive vice president who is doing all the work. **Harold S. Geneen**. *Managing* (co-written with Alvin Moscow, 1984)

The nature of the job is you only hear problems—I guess that's what a CEO's job is. **William Clay Ford, Jr**. Interview, *Fortune* (November 2002)

Executive ability is deciding quickly and getting somebody else to do the work. **John G. Pollard**. Attributed

Expectations

Always do one thing less than you think you can do. **Bernard Baruch**. Referring to maintaining good health. *Newsweek* (May 28, 1956)

Expect nothing. Live frugally on surprise. **Alice Walker**. *Expect Nothing* (1973)

Unhappiness is best defined as the difference between our talents and our expectations. **Edward de Bono**. Quoted in the *Observer (London)* (June 12, 1997)

When I build something for somebody...My guys come in, they say it's going to cost $75 million. I say it's going to cost $125 million, and I build it for $100 million. Basically, I did a lousy job. But they think I did a great job. **Donald J. Trump**. Said to a meeting of US Football League owners. Quoted in the *New York Times* (July 1, 1986)

Experience

The way I was raised, if something wasn't tough it was not a valuable or enriching experience. **Lynn Forrester**. *Sunday Times (London)* (June 2000)

The only thing experience teaches us is that experience teaches us nothing. **André Maurois**. Attributed

A moment's insight is sometimes worth a life's experience. **Oliver Wendell Holmes**. *The Professor at the Breakfast-Table* (1860), ch. 10

Nothing ever becomes real till it is experienced...even a proverb is no proverb till your life has illustrated it. **John Keats**. Letter to George and Georgiana Keats (March 19, 1819)

  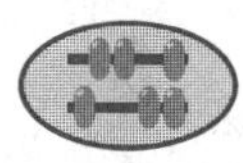 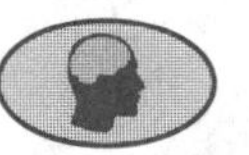  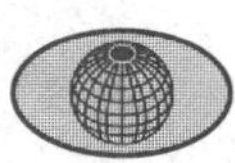   

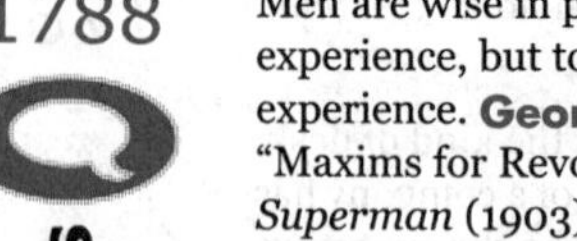

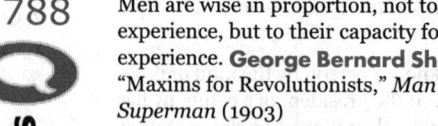

Men are wise in proportion, not to their experience, but to their capacity for experience. **George Bernard Shaw**. "Maxims for Revolutionists," *Man and Superman* (1903)

Experience is never limited, and it is never complete; it is an immense sensibility, a kind of huge spider-web...suspended in the chamber of consciousness, and catching every air-borne particle in its tissue. **Henry James**. "The Art of Fiction," *Partial Portraits* (1888)

I have learned the novice can often see things that the expert overlooks. **Tom Peters**. *Eupsychian Management* (1965)

You cannot acquire experience by making experiments. You cannot create experience. You must undergo it. **Albert Camus**. *Notebooks 1935–1942* (1962)

The process of maturing is an art to be learned, an effort to be sustained. By the age of fifty you have made yourself what you are, and if it is good, it is better than your youth. **Marya Mannes**. *More in Anger* (1958)

Experience isn't interesting until it begins to repeat itself—in fact, till it does that, it hardly is experience. **Elizabeth Bowen**. *The Death of the Heart* (1938), pt. 1, ch. 1

And the end of all our exploring
Will be to arrive where we started
And know the place for the first time.
T. S. Eliot. "Little Gidding," *Four Quartets* (1943)

Experience is a good teacher, but she sends in terrific bills. **Minna Antrim**. *Naked Truth and Veiled Illusions* (1902)

To most men, experience is like the stern lights of a ship, which illumine only the track it has passed. **Samuel Taylor Coleridge**. *Table Talk* (1836)

I try to avoid experience if I can. Most experience is bad. **E. L. Doctorow**. Interview, *Writers at Work* (1988)

EXPERIENCE, n. The wisdom that enables us to recognise as an undesirable old acquaintance the folly that we have already embraced. **Ambrose Bierce**. *The Devil's Dictionary* (1911)

a man who is so dull
that he can learn only by personal
experience
is too dull to learn
anything important by experience
Don Marquis. "archy on this and that," *archy does his part* (1935)

Experience is the name everyone gives to their mistakes. **Oscar Wilde**. *Lady Windermere's Fan* (1892), Act 3

I do not see how any man can afford...to spare any action in which he can partake. Drudgery, calamity, exasperation, want, are instructors in eloquence and wisdom. **Ralph Waldo Emerson**. Speech to the Phi Beta Kappa Society, Cambridge Divinity College, Harvard. "American Scholar" (August 31, 1837)

Education is when you read the fine print; experience is what you get when you don't. **Pete Seeger**. Quoted in *Loose Talk* (L. Botts, 1980)

In the business world, everyone is paid in two coins: cash and experience. Take the experience first; the cash will come later. **Harold S. Geneen**. *Managing* (co-written with Alvin Moscow, 1984)

Learn every day, but especially from the experiences of others. It's cheaper! **John C. Bogle**. Attributed

Failure

At some point, we all have to decide how we are going to fail: by not going far enough, or by going too far. The only alternative for the most successful (maybe even the most fulfilled) people is the latter. **Harriet Rubin**. "How Will You Fail?," *Fast Company* (1999)

In the long run, failure was the only thing that worked predictably. **Joseph Heller**. *Good As Gold* (1979)

One of the most important tasks of a manager is to eliminate his people's excuses for failure. **Robert Townsend**. *Further Up the Organization* (1984)

More strategies fail because they are overripe than because they are premature. **Kenichi Ohmae**. *The Mind of the Strategist* (1982)

It is not impossibilities which fill us with deepest despair, but possibilities which we have failed to realize. **Robert Mallet**. *Apostilles: ou, L'Utile et le Futile* (1972)

Failing is good as long as it doesn't become a habit. **Michael Eisner**. Speech (April 19, 1996)

There are few things more dreadful than dealing with a man who knows he is going under, in his own eyes and in the eyes of others. **James Baldwin**. *The Price of the Ticket* (1985), Introduction

Ever tried. Ever failed. No matter. Try again. Fail again. Fail better. **Samuel Beckett**. *Worstward Ho* (1983)

Bankruptcy is a sacred state, a condition beyond conditions...attempts to investigate it are necessarily obscene like spiritualism. One knows only he has passed into it and lives beyond us, in a condition not ours. **John Updike**. "The Bankrupt Man," *Hugging the Shore* (1983)

Failures, repeated failures, are finger posts on the road to achievement. The only time you don't fail is the last time you try something, and it works. One fails forward toward success. **Charles Franklin Kettering**. Quoted in *Reader's Digest* (May 1989)

If we do not succeed, then we run the risk of failure. **Dan Quayle**. Quoted in *Esquire* (August 1992)

We don't publicize our failures. When something doesn't work don't leave the corpse lying around. **Kenneth Iverson**. Speech (February 5, 1996)

I set a rule that people weren't allowed to send good news unless they sent around an equal amount of bad news. We had to get a balanced picture. In fact, I kind of favored just hearing about the accounts we were losing because...bad news is generally more actionable than good news. **Bill Gates**. Speech, Microsoft's Second Annual CEO Summit, Seattle, Washington (May 28, 1998)

Three failures denote uncommon strength. A weakling has not enough grit to fail thrice. **Minna Antrim**. *At the Sign of the Golden Calf* (1905)

If at first you don't succeed, try, try again. Then quit. No use being a damn fool about it. **W. C. Fields**. Attributed

It would have been cheaper to lower the Atlantic. **Lord Grade**. On the failure of his movie *Raise the Titanic*. *Sun (London)* (December 22, 1987)

The difference between failure and success is doing a thing nearly right and doing it exactly right. **Edward Emerson Simmons**. Attributed

For everything you have missed, you have gained something else. **Ralph Waldo Emerson**. "Compensation," *Essays: First Series* (1841)

I had a lot of successes, but what really made me fearless was my complete failure at Zidd-Davis. Once you've lived through that, you know you can survive, and you're not as scared...There's nothing to build confidence like real achievement, but also like real failure. **Esther Dyson**. Referring to her experience of being hired to start a newspaper, which flopped. Interview, *Reason Magazine* (November 1996)

  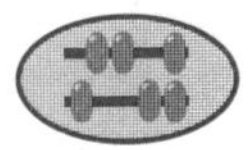 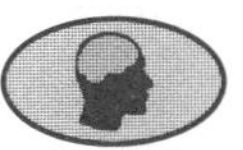  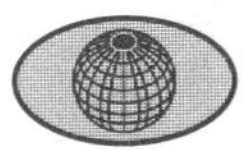   

Whenever you fall, pick up something. **Oswald Theodore Avery**. Attributed

Success requires no explanations. Failure permits no alibi. **Napoleon Hill**. *Think and Grow Rich* (1937)

Companies do not go bankrupt the way they used to, and countries are not declared in default. We talk about restructuring instead. I think this is detrimental. We cannot abolish death. **Pehr Gyllenhammar**. Attributed

When the company did well, we did well. And when the company did not do well, we did not do well, sir. **Richard S. Fuld, Jr**. Speaking before a congressional panel (October 5, 2008)

I wake up every single night wondering what I could have done differently. This is a pain that will stay with me the rest of my life. **Richard S. Fuld, Jr**. Speaking before a congressional panel (October 5, 2008)

Fear

Most people live and die with their music still unplayed. They never dare to try. **Mary Kay Ash**. *New York Times* (1985)

You know the saying, a horse always knows when the rider is afraid? That is true for business as well. **Lord Stevenson of Coddenham**. *Management Today* (April 1999)

A few yes men may be born, but mostly they are made. Fear is a great breeder of them. **William Wrigley**. *American Magazine* (March 1920)

If you aren't afraid to fail, then you probably don't care enough about success. **Mark McCormack**. *What They Don't Teach You at Harvard Business School* (1984)

We will continue to ignore political and economic forecasts, which are an expensive distraction for many investors...we have usually made our best purchases when apprehensions about some macro event were at a peak. Fear is the foe of the faddist, but the friend of the fundamentalist. **Warren Buffett**. Chairman's letter to shareholders (March 7, 1995)

Always do what you are afraid to do. **Ralph Waldo Emerson**. *Essays* (1841)

You cannot banish fear, but you can face it down, stomp on it, crush it, bury it, padlock it into the deepest recesses of your heart and soul and leave it there to rot. Refuse to acknowledge fear of failure, fear of losing your job, fear of your boss, fear of any kind. **Felix Dennis**. *How to Get Rich* (2006)

Anything that I've ever done that ended up worthwhile, initially scared me to death. You have to risk everything sometimes or you risk even more. **Danny McCrossan**. Attributed

Our deepest fear is not that we are inadequate. Our deepest fear is that we are powerful beyond measure. **Marianne Williamson**. *A Return To Love* (1996)

Finance

The City is a machine miraculously organized for extracting gold from the seas, airs, clouds, from barren lands, holds of ships, mines, plantations, cottage hearth-stones, trees and rock. **Christina Stead**. "The Sensitive Goldfish," *The Salzburg Tales* (1934)

There are two times in a man's life when he should not speculate: when he can't afford it and when he can. **Mark Twain**. *Following the Equator* (1899)

Investing is an activity of forecasting the yield over the life of the asset; speculation is the activity of forecasting the psychology of the market. **John Maynard Keynes**. Attributed (1938?)

Markets can remain irrational longer than you can remain solvent. **John Maynard Keynes**. Quoted in *Straight Talk on Investing* (Jack Brennan, 2004)

If human nature felt no temptation to take a chance there might not be much investment merely as a result of cold calculation. **John Maynard Keynes**. *The General Theory of Employment, Interest and Money* (1936)

The world of finance hails the invention of the wheel over and over again, often in a slightly more unstable form. **J. K. Galbraith**. *A Short History of Financial Euphoria* (1993)

A speculator is a man who observes the future, and acts before it occurs. **Bernard Baruch**. *Baruch: My Own Story* (1957)

I made my money by selling too soon. **Bernard Baruch**. Quoted in *The Global Trader* (Barbara Rockefeller, 2001)

We should never lose sight of the underlying essence of a market—a place where buyers and sellers come together. Every other feature—whether crafted by tradition or technology—exists only to serve that primary purpose. **Arthur Levitt, Jr**. Speech to the Columbia Law School, New York City. "Dynamic Markets, Timeless Principles" (September 23, 1999)

There is no human feeling to the US securities markets and sometimes no discernible evidence of human intelligence either. But they work. **Robert J. Eaton**. Speech (March 18, 1996)

Wall Street, runs the sinister old gag, is a street with a river at one end and a graveyard at the other. This is striking, but incomplete. It omits the kindergarten in the middle. **Fred Schwed**. *Where Are The Customers' Yachts?* (1940)

All these financiers, all the little gnomes of Zürich and the other financial centres, about whom we keep on hearing. **Harold Wilson (Lord Wilson of Rievaulx)**. Speech, House of Commons, British Parliament (November 12, 1956)

Financial markets...resent any kind of government interference but they hold a belief deep down that if conditions get really rough the authorities will step in. **George Soros**. *The Crisis of Global Capitalism* (1998)

If you must play, decide on three things at the start: the rules of the game, the stakes, and the quitting time. **Anonymous**. Chinese proverb

On Wall Street he and a few others—how many?—three hundred, four hundred, five hundred?—had become precisely that...Masters of the Universe. **Tom Wolfe**. *The Bonfire of the Vanities* (1987), ch. 1

The biggest public fallacy is that the market is always right. The market is nearly always wrong. I can assure you of that. **Jim Rogers**. Quoted in *Market Wizards* (John D. Schwager, 1989)

Take care to sell your horse before he dies. The art of life is passing losses on. **Robert Frost**. *The Ingenuities of Debt*

A group of lemmings looks like a pack of individuals compared with Wall Street when it gets a concept in its teeth. **Warren Buffett**. Quoted in *Treasury of Investment Wisdom* (Bernice Cohen, 1999)

The derivatives genieis now well and truly out of the bottle, and these instruments will almost certainly multiply in variety and number until some event makes their toxicity clear. **Warren Buffett**. Letter to shareholders (2003)

The range of derivatives contracts is limited only by the imagination of man (or sometimes, so it seems, madmen). Say you want to write a contract speculating on the number of twins to be born in Nebraska in 2020. No problem—at a price, you will

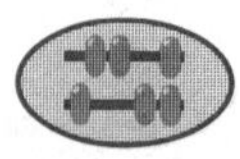
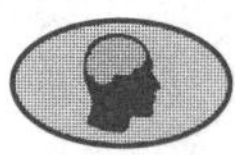

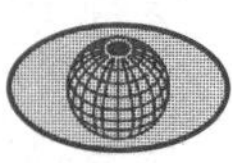

easily find an obliging counterparty. **Warren Buffett**. Letter to shareholders (2003)

In our view, derivatives are financial weapons of mass destruction carrying dangers that, while latent, are potentially lethal. **Warren Buffett**. Letter to shareholders (2003)

You only find out who is swimming naked when the tide goes out. **Warren Buffett**. Letter to shareholders (2001)

Although it's easy to forget sometimes, a share is not a lottery ticket. It's part-ownership of a business. **Peter Lynch**. *One Up On Wall Street* (1990)

Twenty years in this business convinces me that any normal person using the customary three per cent of the brain can pick stocks as well as, if not better, than the average Wall Street expert. **Peter Lynch**. *One Up On Wall Street* (1990)

If you spend more than 14 minutes a year worrying about the market, you've wasted 12 minutes. **Peter Lynch**. Quoted in *Barron's Guide to Making Investment Decisions* (Donald R. Sease and John Prestbo, 1994)

The little I know of it has not served to raise my opinion of what is vulgarly called the Monied Interest; I mean, that blood-sucker, that muckworm, that calls itself the friend of government. **William Pitt the Elder (Earl of Chatham)**. Speech to the House of Lords (November 22, 1770)

The best traders have no ego. You cannot let ego get in the way of a trade that is a loser; you have to swallow your pride and get out. **Tom Baldwin**. Quoted in *Market Wizards* (John D. Schwager, 1989)

What is high finance? It's knowing the difference between one and ten, multiplying, subtracting and adding. You just add noughts. It's no more than that. **John Bentley**. Attributed

Reversion to the mean is the iron rule of the financial markets. **John C. Bogle**. Speech given at the University of Missouri (October 22, 2002)

I used to think that if there was reincarnation, I wanted to come back as the President or the Pope or as a .400 baseball hitter, but now I would like to come back as the bond market. You can intimidate everybody. **James Carville**. Attributed

A market is the combined behaviour of thousands of people responding to information, misinformation and whim. **Kenneth Chang**. Attributed

Nobody beats the market, they say. Except for those of those of us who do. **David N. Dreman**. *Contrarian Investment Strategies* (1999)

Anybody who plays the stock market not as an insider is like a man buying cows in the moonlight. **Daniel Drew**. Quoted in *Boom and Bust* (Christopher Woo, 1989)

One market paradigm that I take exception to is: Buy low and sell high. I believe far more money is made by buying high and selling at even higher prices. **Richard Driehaus**. Quoted in *The New Market Wizards* (John D. Schwager, 1992)

It is not whether you are right or wrong that's important, but how much money you make when you're right and how much you lose when you're wrong. **Stanley Druckenmiller**. Quoted in *The New Market Wizards* (John D. Schwager, 1992)

Don't think about what the market's going to do; you have absolutely no control over that. Think about what you're going to do if it gets there. **William Eckhardt**. Quoted in *The New Market Wizards* (John D. Schwager, 1992)

Amateurs look for challenges; professionals look for easy trades. Losers get high from the action; the pros look for the best odds. **Alexander Elder**. *Come Into My Trading Room* (2002)

Patience is the hardest part of trading and investing, but also the most important, for it is in the waiting that we make bigger profits. **William F. Eng**. *Trading Rules: Strategies for Success* (1990)

A successful trader studies human nature and does the opposite of what the general public does. **W. D. Gann**. *How to Make Profits Trading in Commodities* (1942)

In the short-run, the market is a voting machine but in the long run, the market is a weighing machine. **Benjamin Graham**. *The Intelligent Investor* (1949)

To suppose that the value of a common stock is determined purely by a corporation's earnings discounted by the relevant interest rates and adjusted for the marginal tax rate is to forget that people have burned witches, gone to war on a whim, risen to the defense of Joseph Stalin and believed Orson Welles when he told them over the radio that the Martians had landed. **Jim Grant**. Quoted in *Value Investing Made Easy* (Janet Lowe, 1997)

I have noticed that everyone who has ever tried to tell me that markets are efficient is poor. **Larry Hite**. Quoted in *Market Wizards* (John D. Schwager, 1989)

The City is, in terms of its basic functioning, a far-off country of which we know little. **John Lanchester**. *London Review of Books* (January 3, 2008)

In an ideal world, one populated by vegetarians and Esperanto speakers, derivatives would be used for one thing only: reducing levels of risk. The list of individual traders who have lost more than a billion dollars at a time betting on derivatives is not short. **John Lanchester**. *London Review of Books* (January 3, 2008)

The game of speculation is the most uniformly fascinating game in the world. But it is not a game for the stupid, the mentally lazy, the person of inferior emotional balance, or the get-rich-quick adventurer. They will die poor. **Jesse Livermore**. *How To Trade in Stocks* (1940)

There is time to go long, time to go short and time to go fishing. **Jesse Livermore**. Quoted in *Come Into My Trading Room* (Alexander Elder, 2002)

Market values are fixed only in part by balance sheets and income statements; much more by the hopes and fears of humanity; by greed, ambition, acts of God, invention, financial stress and strain, weather, discovery, fashion and numberless other causes impossible to be listed without omission. **Gerald M. Loeb**. *The Battle for Investment Survival* (1935)

You can picture price fluctuations around an equilibrium level as a rubber band being stretched—if it gets pulled too far, eventually it will snap back. As a short-term trader, I try to wait until the rubber band is stretched to its extreme point. **Linda Bradford Raschke**. Quoted in *The New Market Wizards* (John D. Schwager, 1992)

Discipline allows you to trade effectively. You can take your ego out of it. You can go wrong 60, 70 percent of the time and still make a lot of money. If you ignore the discipline of managing risk, you have to be right 80 percent of the time or more, and I don't know anyone who's that good. **Larry Rosenberg**. Quoted in *500 of the Most Witty, Acerbic and Erudite Things Ever Said About Money* (Philip Jenks, 2002)

Finance is the art of passing currency from hand to hand until it finally disappears. **Robert W. Sarnoff**. Quoted in *An Introduction to International Political Economy* (Alison M. S. Watson, 2004)

I have probably purchased fifty "hot tips" in my career, maybe even more. When I put them all together, I know I am a net loser. **Charles Schwab**. *How To Be Your Own Stockbroker* (1986)

     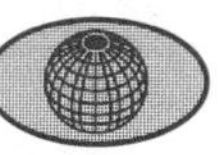 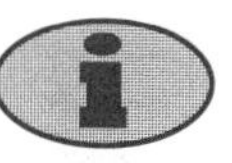  

Remember, the price that people agree to in the pit is not the price that people think is going to exist in the future. It's the price that both sides vehemently agree won't be there. **Jeffrey Silverman**. Quoted in *500 of the Most Witty, Acerbic, and Erudite Things Ever Said About Money* (Philip Jenks, 2002)

Trading has been, and always will be, a hard way to make an easy living. **Jeffrey Silverman**. Quoted in *500 of the Most Witty, Acerbic, and Erudite Things Ever Said About Money* (philip Jenks, 2002)

A good technician gets it right maybe 60% of the time. And a great technician, maybe 61% of the time. **Gary B. Smith**. on technical analysis of financial markets. Attributed

Investing in the market without knowing what stage it is in is like selling life insurance to 20 year olds and 80 year olds at the same premium. **Victor Sperandeo**. Quoted in *The New Market Wizards* (John D. Schwager, 1992)

Never ask a trader if he is profitable: you can easily see it in his gesture and gait. **Nassim Nicholas Taleb**. *Fooled by Randomness* (2004)

The time of maximum pessimism is the best time to buy and the time of maximum optimism is the best time to sell. **Sir John Templeton**. Quoted in *The Book of Investing Wisdom* (Peter Krass, 1999)

Usually God favours the people who try to do good. So, when you find that the crowd is desperately trying to sell, help them and buy. When you find that the crowd is overenthusiastically trying to buy, help them and sell. It usually works out. **Sir John Templeton**. Interview on Nightly Business Review (February 2004)

A market that slowly grinds higher is a good buy. A market that soars is usually a good sell. **Neal Weintraub**. *Tricks of the Floor Trader* (1995)

Remember this crisis began in regulated entities. This happened right under our noses. **Paul S. Atkins**. Quoted in the *Washington Post* (December 16, 2008)

It is hard for us...to even see a scenario within any kind of realm of reason that would see us losing one dollar in any of those transactions. **Joseph J. Cassano**. On trading in credit derivatives. AIG received a federal bailout of $85 billion in September 2008. (August 2007)

This proposal is stunning and unprecedented in its scope and lack of detail...It would allow the secretary of the Treasury to intervene in our economy by purchasing at least $700 billion of toxic assets. It would allow the secretary to hold onto those assets for years and to pay millions of dollars to hand-picked firms to manage those assets. It would do nothing, in my view, to help a single family save a home. **Chris Dodd**. On Henry Paulson's bailout plan for the US financial system. Senate Banking Committee hearing on the Paulson Plan (September 29, 2008)

In the past six months, our federal government has devised a dozen strategies to save America's financial markets. Each plan has been more costly, more risky, and less aligned with the principles of our country's free market economy than the last. I am disappointed to say that this latest plan puts all the rest of them to shame. **Mike Enzi**. Senate Banking Committee hearing on the Paulson Plan (September 29, 2008)

No half-measures, but a $700bn bail-out aimed at mopping up the bad debts of every lender in the land. This was...red-blooded Bolshevism, seizing the commanding heights of the financial system. You gotta love the Americans: if they do something, they do it big. **Jonathan Freedland**. On the US Treasury secretary's Wall Street bailout plan. *Guardian (London)* (October 8, 2008)

Henry Paulson is to finance what Donald Rumsfeld was to military strategy, Dick Cheney to geopolitics and Michael Chertoff to flood defence. **Anatole Kaletsky**. On the US Treasury secretary's Wall Street bailout plan. *The Times (London)* (September 25, 2008)

Recently, on the front page of Section C of the Wall Street Journal, a hedge fund manager who was also closing up shop (a $300 million fund), was quoted as saying, "What I have learned about the hedge fund business is that I hate it." I could not agree more with that statement. **Andrew Lahde**. *Wall Street Journal* (October 17, 2008)

I was in this game for the money. The low hanging fruit, i.e. idiots whose parents paid for prep school, Yale, and then the Harvard MBA, was there for the taking. These people...rose to the top of companies such as AIG, Bear Stearns and Lehman Brothers and all levels of our government. All of this...only ended up making it easier for me to find people stupid enough to take the other side of my trades. God bless America. **Andrew Lahde**. Announcing his retirement at the age of 37. *Wall Street Journal* (October 17, 2008)

The arrangement bore the same relation to actual finance as fantasy football bears to the NFL. **Michael Lewis**. On credit default swaps. *Condé Nast Portfolio* (December 2008)

Don't blow it up. **Henry Paulson**. Pleading on bended knee to House speaker Nancy Pelosi for her to back his $700bn Wall Street bailout plan. Senate Banking Committee hearing on the Paulson Plan (September 29, 2008)

The Treasury's plan has little for those outside of the financial industry. It is aimed at rescuing the same financial institutions that created this crisis with the sloppy underwriting and reckless disregard for the risk they were creating, taking or passing on to others. **Richard Shelby**. Senate Banking Committee hearing on the Paulson Plan (September 29, 2008)

To be generous, you could call it an unregulated, uncapitalized insurance market. But really, you would call it a gaming contract. **Christopher Whalen**. On credit default swaps. Quoted by Nicholas Varchaver and Katie Benner in *Fortune* (September 30, 2008)

The really scary part is that we don't have a clue. This has become essentially the dark matter of the financial universe. **Chris Wolf**. On the risk posed by credit default swaps. Quoted by Nicholas Varchaver and Katie Benner in *Fortune* (September 30, 2008)

We should probably stop trading derivatives, anything more complex than regular options...I am an options trader, and I don't understand options. How do you want a regulator to understand them? **Nassim Nicholas Taleb**. Interviewed on Bloomberg Television (January 29, 2009)

What we have found over the years in the marketplace is that derivatives have been an extraordinarily useful vehicle to transfer risk from those who shouldn't be taking it to those who are willing to and are capable of doing so. **Alan Greenspan**. Addressing the Senate Banking Committee (2003)

Not only have individual financial institutions become less vulnerable to shocks from underlying risk factors, but also the financial system as a whole has become more resilient. **Alan Greenspan**. Remark (2004)

It seems superfluous to constrain trading in some of the newer derivatives and other innovative financial contracts of the past decade. The worst have failed; investors no longer fund them and are not likely to in the future. **Alan Greenspan**. *The Age of Turbulence* (2007)

Wall Street got drunk and now it's got a hangover. And the question is, how long will it sober up and not try to do those fancy financial instruments? **George W. Bush**. Speech (July 2008)

If our laws are not extended to control the new kinds of super-powerful, super-complex and potentially super-risky investment vehicles, they will one day cause a financial disaster of global-systemic proportions. **John Lanchester**. *London Review of Books* (January 3, 2008)

Some skeptics are calling Henry Paulson's $700 billion rescue plan for the US financial system "cash for trash." Others are calling the proposed legislation the Authorization for Use of Financial Force, after the Authorization for Use of Military Force, the infamous bill that gave the Bush administration the green light to invade Iraq. **Paul R. Krugman**. *New York Times* (September 21, 2008)

Focus

The quality of your attention determines the quality of other people's thinking. **Nancy Kline**. *Time to Think* (1999)

When conscious activity is wholly concentrated on some one definite purpose, the ultimate result, for most people, is lack of balance accompanied by some form of nervous disorder. **Bertrand Russell (Earl Russell)**. Quoted in *Management by Objectives: An Integrated Approach* (S. K. Chakraborty, 1976)

I try to learn from the past, but I plan for the future by focusing exclusively on the present. **Donald J. Trump**. Quoted in *101 Best Ways to Get Ahead* (Michael E. Angier, 2004)

Focus on where you want to go, not on what you fear. **Anthony Robbins**. *Awaken the Giant Within* (1992)

I sometimes find, and I am sure you know the feeling, that I simply have too many thoughts and memories crammed into my mind. At these times I use the Pensieve. One simply siphons the excess thoughts from one's mind, pours them into the basin, and examines them at one's leisure. It becomes easier to spot patterns and links, you understand, when they are in this form. **J. K. Rowling**. Dumbledore speaking to Harry in *Harry Potter and the Goblet of Fire* (2000)

Forecasting

In a crowded room, you only have to see one inch above everyone else to notice things that others will miss. **Jim Slater**. Quoted in *Treasury of Investment Wisdom* (Bernice Cohen, 1999)

Forecast: to observe that which has passed, and guess it will happen again. **Frank McKinney Hubbard**. *The Roycroft Dictionary* (1923)

Economists are about as useful as astrologers in predicting the future (and, like astrologers, they never let failure on one occasion diminish certitude on the next). **Arthur Schlesinger, Jr**. Quoted in *New York Times* (April 15, 1993)

We have two classes of forecasters: Those who don't know—and those who don't know they don't know. **J. K. Galbraith**. Quoted in *Predicting the Future* (Nicholas Rescher, 1998)

In the mid 80s, Fortune magazine carried the prediction that, by the year 2010, North America would become the world's granary, the Pacific the world's manufacturing base and that Europe will become a discotheque. They could still be right. **Max Comfort**. *Portfolio People* (1997)

An economist is an expert who will know tomorrow why the things he predicted yesterday didn't happen today. **Laurence J. Peter**. *Peter's Quotations: Ideas For Our Time* (1977)

The future bears a resemblance to the past, only more so. **Faith Popcorn**. *The Popcorn Report* (1991)

Wall Street indexes predicted nine out of the last five recessions. **Paul Samuelson**. *Newsweek* (September 19, 1966)

The easiest way to predict the future is to invent it. **Anonymous**. Xerox Research Center, Palo Alto, California (1970)

An economic forecaster is like a cross-eyed javelin thrower: they don't win many accuracy contests, but they keep the crowd's attention. **Anonymous**. Quoted in *Demystifying Wall Street* (Bruce Fleet, 2007)

Trying to predict the future is like trying to drive down a country road at night with no lights while looking out the back window. **Peter F. Drucker**. Attributed

Among all forms of mistake, prophecy is the most gratuitous. **George Eliot**. *Middlemarch* (1871–1872)

We've long felt that the only value of stock forecasts is to make fortune tellers look good. Short-term market forecasts are poison and should be kept locked up in a safe place, away from children and also from grown-ups who behave in the market like children. **Warren Buffett**. Letter to shareholders (1992)

Business, more than any other occupation, is a continual dealing with the future; it is a continual calculation, an instinctive exercise in foresight. **Henry R. Luce**. Quoted in *The Leslie Pockell 101 Greatest Business Principles of All Time* (2004)

People who forecast simply because "that's my job," knowing pretty well that their forecast is ineffectual, are not what I would call ethical. What they do is no different from repeating lies simply because "it's my job." **Nassim Nicholas Taleb**. *The Black Swan: The Impact of the Highly Improbable* (2007)

Forecasting by bureaucrats tends to be used for anxiety relief rather than for adequate policy making. **Nassim Nicholas Taleb**. *The Black Swan: The Impact of the Highly Improbable* (2007)

The government-sponsored institution Fannie Mae, when I look at its risks, seems to be sitting on a barrel of dynamite, vulnerable to the slightest hiccup. But not to worry: their large staff of scientists deemed these events "unlikely." **Nassim Nicholas Taleb**. Fannie Mae and Freddie Mac were taken into government "conservatorship" in September 2008. *The Black Swan: The Impact of the Highly Improbable* (2007)

Getting Started

Remember that on day one, when you go in as the boss, you'll feel a mixture of exhilaration that you've made it and fatigue with all the effort. **Barbara Thomas**. *Management Today* (October 1999)

One sees great things from the valley; only small things from the peak. **G. K. Chesterton**. *The Innocence of Father Brown* (1911)

The beginning is the most important part of any work. **Plato**. *The Republic* (370? BC, 2007), bk. 2, sect. 377

Keep starting and the finishing will take care of itself. **Neil A. Fiore**. *The Now Habit* (1993)

  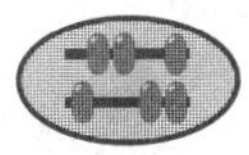 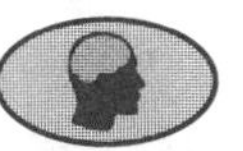  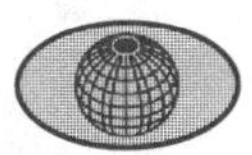   

Reading the Wall Street Journal for a week should give anyone ideas for two or three new startups. **Paul Graham**. *Why Smart People Have Bad Ideas* (2005)

That's the essence of a startup: having brilliant people do work that's beneath them. Big companies try to hire the right person for the job. Startups win because they don't—because they take people so smart that they would in a big company be doing "research," and set them to work instead on problems of the most immediate and mundane sort. Think Einstein designing refrigerators. **Paul Graham**. *Why Smart People Have Bad Ideas* (2005)

Globalization

Think globally, act locally. **Friends of the Earth**. Slogan (1985)

The United States is just one part of a global marketplace today. There isn't any offshore anymore; it's all onshore. **Walter Wriston**. *US News & World Report* (1987)

No nation was ever ruined by trade. **Benjamin Franklin**. *Essays* (1730s)

You can always buy something in English, you can't always sell something in English. **Rosabeth Moss Kanter**. *World Class* (1995)

The bigger the world economy, the more powerful its smallest player. **John Naisbitt**. *Megatrends* (1982)

Capital, technology, and ideas flow these days like quicksilver across national boundaries. **Robert H. Waterman, Jr**. *The Frontiers of Excellence* (1994)

Globalisation has in effect made the citizen disappear, and it has reduced the state into being a mere instrument of global capital. **Vandana Shiva**. *Globalisation: Gandhi and Swadeshi* (2000)

Sometimes, I'm more in the air than I am in a country. **Raoul Pinnell**. Referring to the volume of business travel for a global marketing executive. *Marketing* (June 2000)

Does it really make sense to operate on all continents? **Keiji Tachikawa**. *Forbes* (May 2000)

Today's global economic dance is no Strauss waltz. It's break dancing accompanied by street rap. **Tom Peters**. *Liberation Management* (1992)

It is better to underpromise and overdeliver than vice versa. For this one need not break the law of the land. **Narayana Murthy**. "Employee Satisfaction Crucial to Success," *Hindu Business Line* (2000)

Nationalism is an infantile sickness. It is the measles of the human race. **Albert Einstein**. Quoted in *The Human Side* (Helen Dukas and Banesh Hoffmann, 1979)

Merchants have no country. The mere spot they stand on does not constitute so strong an attachment as that from which they draw their gains. **Thomas Jefferson**. Letter to Horatio G. Spafford (March 17, 1814)

This going into Europe will not turn out to be the thrilling mutual exchange supposed. It is more like nine middle-aged couples with failing marriages meeting in a darkened bedroom in a Brussels hotel for a group grope. **E. P. Thompson**. *Sunday Times (London)* (April 1975)

We must not fall into the mistake of thinking that it is America that trades with Taiwan or Europe that trades with Asia. The truth is that it is American companies that trade with Taiwanese companies. **Baroness Thatcher**. *Far Eastern Economic Review* (September 2, 1993)

All things start in California and spread to New Jersey, then to London and then throughout Europe. **Stelios Haji-Ioannou**. *Wall Street Journal* (December 1996)

The new electronic interdependence recreates the world in the image of a global village. **Marshall McLuhan**. *The Gutenberg Galaxy* (1962)

Investing is a business that never tires. You have to work with every known thing in the world—the weather in Asia, or politics in East Europe, or the scandal of an American president. **Charles Brady**. *Sunday Times (London)* (May 2000)

These days Paris is a suburb of New York and vice-versa. **Jean-Marie Messier**. *Sunday Times (London)* (September 2000)

Global democratic capitalism is as unrealizable a condition as worldwide communism. **John Gray**. *False Dawn* (1998)

Economic modernization...spawns indigenous types of capitalism that owe little to any western model. **John Gray**. *False Dawn* (1998)

All you need is the best product in the world, the most efficient production in the world and global marketing. **Akio Morita**. Quoted in *The Financial Times Handbook of Management* (Stuart Crainer, ed, 1995)

If the whole world operates as one big market, every employee will compete with every person in the world who is capable of doing the same job. **Andrew S. Grove**. *Fortune* (September 1995)

The Death of Distance. **Frances Cairncross**. Book title. Referring to the effects of increasing globalization. *The Death of Distance* (1997)

The recent turbulence in the international markets reminds us what happens when an event in one part of the world can touch us all in just a few weeks. There was a time when a small bank in America got in trouble it was bad news for that town, or state, but nowhere else. But today, when a Florida householder defaults on his mortgage, the effects are felt, not just in America but across the world, in France, Germany, the rest of Europe and here in Britain. **Alistair Darling**. Speech at the University of Stirling, Scotland (November 8, 2007)

The raw fact is that every successful example of economic development this past century—every case of a poor nation that worked its way up to a more or less decent, or at least dramatically better, standard of living—has taken place via globalization, that is, by producing for the world market rather than trying for self-sufficiency. **Paul R. Krugman**. *The Great Unraveling: Losing Our Way in the New Century* (2007)

The United States in particular and the West in general should be feeling a little embarrassed about all that lecturing we did to the Third World. **Paul R. Krugman**. Remark made at the World Economic Forum (February 2002)

Goals and Objectives

Goals too clearly defined can become blinkers. **Mary Catherine Bateson**. *Composing a Life* (1989)

There are two things to aim at in life: first, to get what you want; and, after that, to enjoy it. Only the wisest of mankind achieve the second. **Logan Pearsall Smith**. "Life and Human Nature," *Afterthoughts* (1931)

Ah, but a man's reach should exceed his grasp,
Or what's a heaven for?
Robert Browning. "Andrea del Sarto" (1855), l. 97

If you would hit the mark, you must aim a little above it;
Every arrow that flies feels the attraction of earth.
Henry Wadsworth Longfellow. "Elegaic Verse" (1880)

A good goal is like a strenuous exercise—it makes you stretch. **Mary Kay Ash**. *On People Management* (1984)

If you don't know where you are going, you will probably end up somewhere else. **Laurence J. Peter**. *The Peter Principle: Why Things Always Go Wrong* (co-written with Raymond Hull, 1969)

Economics are the method. The object is to change the soul. **Baroness Thatcher**. *Sunday Times (London)* (April 1975)

The mantra of execute, execute, execute, speed, speed, speed seems to preclude any consideration of what we are speeding toward. That's sort of like saying, Don't bother me with the facts—I'm busy executing them. **Jay S. Walker**. Interview, *Strategy + Business* (January–March 2000)

You read a book from beginning to end. You run a business the opposite way. You start with the end, and then you do everything you must to reach it. **Harold S. Geneen**. *Managing* (1984)

Government

Government, like dress, is the badge of lost innocence...man finds it necessary to surrender up a part of his property to furnish means for the protection of the rest. **Thomas Paine**. *Common Sense* (1776)

Government does not solve problems, it subsidizes them. **Ronald Reagan**. "The Wit and Wisdom of Ronald Reagan," *Speaking My Mind* (1989)

Government's view of the economy could be summed up in a few short phrases: If it moves, tax it. If it keeps moving, regulate it. And if it stops moving, subsidise it. **Ronald Reagan**. Speech (1981)

The business of the Civil Service is the orderly management of decline. **Lord Armstrong**. Quoted in *Whitehall* (Peter Hennessey, 1990)

A government which robs Peter to pay Paul can always depend on the support of Paul. **George Bernard Shaw**. *Everybody's Political What's What?* (1944)

You can't expect a viable economy if the only object of government policy is to be re-elected every four years. **Lord Weinstock**. *Independent (London)* (December 20, 1986)

A species of tetanus where one set of muscles goes rigid pulling against another—and the patient becomes paralysed. **Sir Terence Norman Beckett**. On government interference in industry. *Daily Mail (London)* (September 28, 1979)

Governments of the Industrial World, you weary giants of flesh and steel, I come from Cyberspace...On behalf of the future, I ask you of the past to leave us alone...You have no sovereignty where we gather. **John Perry Barlow**. "A Declaration of the Independence of Cyberspace" (February 8, 1996)

Trade and commerce, if they were not made of india-rubber, would never manage to bounce over obstacles which legislators are continually putting in their way. **Henry David Thoreau**. "Resistance to Civil Government" (1849)

There's only one place where inflation is made: that's in Washington. **Milton Friedman**. Attributed (1977)

The task of government policy is not to prejudge winners but to make sure that neither private nor public restraints narrow the potential sources of innovation. **Anne K. Bingaman**. Speech, University of Kansas Law School (September 19, 1996)

There is most definitely a role for government in the innovative process. The market does not do everything well. **Anne K. Bingaman**. Speech, University of Kansas Law School (September 19, 1996)

Governments can err. Presidents do make mistakes, but...better the occasional faults of a government that lives in a spirit of charity than the consistent omissions of a government frozen in the ice of its own indifference. **Franklin D. Roosevelt**. Speech accepting re-nomination for a second presidential term, Philadelphia (June 27, 1936)

It is with government as with medicine, its only business is the choice of evils. Every law is an evil, for every law is an infraction of liberty. **Jeremy Bentham**. *Principles of Legislation* (1789)

There is no art which one government sooner learns of another than that of draining money from the pockets of the people. **Adam Smith**. *An Inquiry into the Nature and Causes of the Wealth of Nations* (1776)

It is a popular delusion that the government wastes vast amounts of money through inefficiency and sloth. Enormous effort and elaborate planning are required to waste this much money. **P. J. O'Rourke**. *Parliament of Whores* (1991)

With perfect citizens, any government is good. **Stephen Leacock**. *The Unsolved Riddle of Social Justice* (1920)

Regulation should not be at a level set to achieve the impossible task of protecting fools from their own folly— it should be no greater than that required to protect reasonable people from being made fools of. **Jim Gower**. Quoted in the *Independent (London)* (January 4, 2008)

The private market has screwed itself up and they need the government to come help them unscrew it. **Barney Frank**. On the government's bailout of insurance giant AIG. Remark (September 16, 2008)

Leave it up to the free market, and in a few generations Florida will be underwater. **Paul R. Krugman**. *New York Times* (October 15, 2008)

Greed

My father said: You must never try to make all the money that's in a deal. Let the other fellow make some money too, because if you have a reputation for always making all the money...you won't make many deals. **J. Paul Getty**. Referring to his father, George Franklin Getty, who was also a successful oil business executive. Quoted in *Getty on Getty* (Somerset de Chair, 1989), ch. 2

Greed is even more contagious than fear. **Bud Hadfield**. *Wealth within Reach: Winning Strategies for Success from the Unconventional Wisdom of Bud Hadfield* (1995)

What kind of society isn't structured on greed? **Milton Friedman**. *There's No Such Thing as a Free Lunch* (1975)

Nothing defines human beings better than their willingness to do irrational things in the pursuit of phenomenally unlikely payoffs. **Scott Adams**. *The Dilbert Principle* (1996)

The fact that people will be full of greed, fear, or folly is predictable. The sequence is not predictable. **Warren Buffett**. *Channels* (1986)

Greed—for lack of a better word—is good. Greed is right. Greed works. **Oliver Stone**. From the film satirizing some of the excesses of the 1980s. *Wall Street* (1987)

Laissez-faire, supply and demand—one begins to be weary of all that. Leave all to

  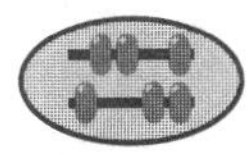   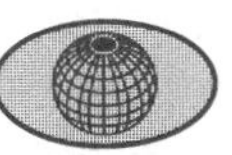   

egotism, to ravenous greed of money, of pleasure, of applause—it is the gospel of despair. **Thomas Carlyle**. *Past and Present* (1843)

If you take the greed out of Wall Street, you're left with pavement. **Anonymous**. Remark (Fall 2008)

Growth

Think small and act small, and we'll get bigger. Think big and act big, and we'll get smaller. **Herb Kelleher**. *Sales and Marketing Management* (October 1996)

There are as many foolhardy ways to grow as there are to downsize. **Gary Hamel**. *Digital Britain* (January 2000)

Growth does not always lead a business to build on success. All too often it converts a highly successful business into a mediocre large business. **Sir Richard Branson**. Speech to the Institute of Directors, London. "Growing Bigger While Still Staying Small" (May 1993)

Is your company so small you have to do everything for yourself? Wait until you're so big that you can't. That's worse. **Michael Bloomberg**. *Bloomberg by Bloomberg* (co-written with Matthew Winkler, 1997)

The strongest principle of growth lies in human choice. **George Eliot**. *Daniel Deronda* (1876)

Hiring and Firing

People in the company are almost never fired...they are encouraged to retire early or are eased aside into hollow, insignificant positions with fake functions and no authority, where they are sheepish and unhappy for as long as they remain. **Joseph Heller**. *Something Happened* (1974)

Fire the whole personnel department...Fire the whole purchasing department. They'd hire Einstein and then turn down his requisition for a blackboard. **Robert Townsend**. *Up the Organization* (1970)

Always be smart enough to hire people brighter than yourself. **Caroline Marland**. *Management Today* (September 1999)

Well sometimes you just don't like somebody. **Henry Ford**. Referring to his reasons for firing Lee Iacocca, then president of Ford, in 1978. Quoted in *Iacocca: An Autobiography* (Lee Iacocca, 1984)

Trahey's Simple Rule: Would you hire you? **Jane Trahey**. *Women in Advertising* (1979)

If each of us hires people who are smaller than we are, we shall become a company of dwarfs. But if each of us hires people who are bigger than we are, we shall become a company of giants. **David Ogilvy**. *Ogilvy on Advertising* (1983)

You do not get good people if you lay off half your workforce just because one year the economy isn't very good and then you hire them back. **Kenneth Iverson**. Speech (February 5, 1996)

Restructuring: A simple plan instituted from above in which workers are right-sized, downsized, surplused, lateralized, or in the business jargon of the days of yore, fired. **Anonymous**. *Fortune* (February 15, 1995)

I believe you can go into any traditionally centralized corporation and cut its headquarters staff by 90 percent in one year. **Percy Barnevik**. *Harvard Business Review* (March–April 1991)

Employees throughout downsized companies do not have time to think about new growth opportunities. Nor are they inclined to suggest innovations because their implicit commitment contract with the company has been severed. **Kenneth Blanchard**. "Empowerment Is the Key," *Quality Digest* (April 1996)

In a recession, people want to test me to see if I'm brave enough to have a lay-off. I'm willing to take that ridicule because it's paid off to hold on to our people. **Ken Olsen**. Speech (1982)

In the end we are all sacked and it's always awful. It is as inevitable as death following life. If you are elevated there comes a day when you are demoted. **Alan Clark**. Diary (June 21, 1983)

You're fired! No other words can so easily and succinctly reduce a confident, self-assured executive to an insecure, groveling shred of his former self. **Frank P. Louchheim**. "The Art of Getting Fired," *Wall Street Journal* (July 16, 1984)

Nothing bad's going to happen to us. If we get fired, it's not failure; it's a midlife vocational assessment. **P. J. O'Rourke**. *Rolling Stone* (November 30, 1989)

When I find an employee who turns out to be wrong for a job, I feel it is my fault because I made the decision to hire him. **Akio Morita**. Quoted in *In Search of European Excellence* (Robert Heller, 1997)

Recession isn't the fault of the workers. If management takes the risk of hiring them, we have to take the responsibility for them. **Akio Morita**. *Daily Telegraph (London)* (February 24, 1982)

Honesty

It is difficult but not impossible to conduct strictly honest business. What is true is that honesty is incompatible with the amassing of a large fortune. **Mahatma Gandhi**. *Non-Violence in Peace and War* (1948)

When in doubt tell the truth. **Mark Twain**. *Following the Equator* (1897)

If you tell the truth you don't have to remember anything. **Mark Twain**. *Notebooks* (1935)

It is not the crook in modern business that we fear, but the honest man who does not know what he is doing. **Owen D. Young**. Attributed

Total commercial honesty always costs something, but total or partial dishonesty will cost more. **Robert Heller**. *The Supermarketers* (1987)

Ideas

There is nothing so practical as a good theory. **Kurt Lewin**. *Field Theory in Social Science: Selected Theoretical Papers* (D. Cartwright, ed, 1951)

The newness of an idea matters less than its ease of use. **Mari Matsunaga**. *Fortune* (October 2000)

The empires of the future are the empires of the mind. **Sir Winston Churchill**. Speech (September 1943)

If you are possessed by an idea, you find it expressed everywhere, you even smell it. **Thomas Mann**. *Death in Venice* (1913)

For an idea ever to be fashionable is ominous, since it must afterwards always be old-fashioned. **George Santayana**. *Winds of Doctrine* (1913)

Every now and then a man's mind is stretched by a new idea and never shrinks back to its original dimensions. **Oliver**

Wendell Holmes. *The Autocrat of the Breakfast Table* (1858)

It is a far, far better thing to have firm anchor in nonsense than to put out on the troubled sea of thought. **J. K. Galbraith**. *The Affluent Society* (1958)

When an idea is not robust enough to stand expression in simple terms, it is a sign that it should be rejected. **Luc de Clapiers Vauvenargues**. *Reflections and Maxims* (1746)

One of the greatest pains to a human being is the pain of a new idea. **Walter Bagehot**. *Physics and Politics* (1872)

After the idea, there is plenty of time to learn the technology. **Sir James Dyson**. *Against the Odds* (1997)

It is as absurd to argue men, as to torture them into believing. **John Henry Newman**. Sermon (December 1831)

Never dump a good idea on a conference table. It will belong to the conference. **Jane Trahey**. *New York Times* (September 18, 1977)

It is the customary fate of new truths to begin as heresies and to end as superstitions. **Thomas Huxley**. *Science and Culture* (1887)

Nothing is more dangerous than an idea, when you only have one idea. **Émile-August Chartier**. *Propos sur la Religion* (1938)

Unless your ideas are ridiculed by experts, they are worth nothing. **Reg Revans**. *Action Learning* (1979)

Sometimes the first step is the hardest: coming up with an idea. Coming up with an idea should be like sitting on a pin—it should make you jump up and do something. **Kemmons Wilson**. "What Makes for Success?," *Imprimis* (March 1997)

It's not that we need new ideas, but we need to stop having old ideas. **Edwin Land**. Attributed

Don't worry about people stealing an idea. If it's original, you will have to ram it down their throats. **Howard Aiken**. Quoted in *Portraits in Silicon* (Robert Slater, 1987)

I can't understand why people are frightened of new ideas. I'm frightened of the old ones. **John Cage**. Quoted in *Conversing with Cage* (1988)

The ancestor of every action is a thought. **Ralph Waldo Emerson**. *Essays* (1841)

Unlike a straight academic career, you end up fully recognizing that hypotheses matter, that actions matter, and the ideas that you come up with matter. **Alan Greenspan**. Speech accepting appointment to fourth term as US Federal Reserve chairman, Washington, DC (January 4, 2000)

Owning the intellectual property is like owning land: You need to keep investing in it again and again to get a payoff; you can't simply sit back and collect rent. **Esther Dyson**. *Release 1.0* (1994)

Ours is the age of substitutes; instead of language, we have jargon; instead of principles, slogans; and, instead of genuine ideas, bright ideas. **Eric Bentley**. *New Republic* (December 1952)

We haven't got the money, so we've got to think. **Lord Rutherford of Nelson**. *Bulletin of the Institute of Physics* (1962)

Image

To be successful, keep looking tanned, live in an elegant building (even if you're in the cellar), be seen in smart restaurants (even if you only nurse one drink) and if you borrow, borrow big. **Aristotle Onassis**. Attributed

Beyond a certain point, personal media such as telephones, computers, and planners aren't just functional objects anymore, they're fashion accessories. **Michael Schrage**. Quoted in *Liberation Management* (Tom Peters, 1992)

Clothes are our weapons, our challenges, and our visible insult. **Angela Carter**. *Nothing Sacred* (1982)

Corporate identities must not be shortlived. **Clive Chajet**. "Why Corporate Identity Can't Be Designed," *The Manager* (David Uren, 2000)

We don't know how to sell products based on performance. Everything we sell, we sell based on image. **Roberto Goizueta**. *Wall Street Journal* (February 1997)

It depends entirely upon the image of you that people have in their minds whether you will climb the ladder slowly, painfully, or with a rapidity that will surprise—and appal—your friends. **Gerald Sparrow**. *How to Become a Millionaire* (1960), ch. 2

Deep down, I'm pretty superficial. **Ava Gardner**. Quoted in *Ava* (Roland Flamini, 1983), ch. 8

Imagination

The imagination of nature is far, far greater than the imagination of man. **Richard Feynman**. *The Meaning of it All* (1998)

My imagination makes me human and makes me a fool; it gives me all the world and exiles me from it. **Ursula K. Le Guin**. "Winged the Adventures on my Mind," *Harper's* (August 1990)

Imagination was given to man to compensate him for what he is not. A sense of humour was provided to console him for what he is. **Horace Walpole (Earl of Orford)**. Quoted in "The Artist," *A Kick in the Seat of the Pants* (Roger von Oech, 1986)

Live out of your imagination, not your history. **Sir Arthur Bryan**. *Seven Habits of Highly-Effective People* (1990)

The life of nations no less than that of men is lived largely in the imagination. **Enoch Powell**. Epigraph. Quoted in *English Culture and the Decline of the Industrial Spirit, 1850–1980* (Martin J. Weiner, 1981)

His imagination resembled the wings of an ostrich. It enabled him to run, though not to soar. **Lord Macaulay**. Referring to John Dryden. "John Dryden," *Essays and Biographies* (1828)

For people who live in the imagination, there is no lack of subjects. To seek for the exact moment at which inspiration comes is false. Imagination floods us with suggestions all the time, from all directions. **Federico Fellini**. *Autobiography* (1974)

I dream for a living. **Steven Spielberg**. *Time* (July 1985)

Imagination and fiction make up more than three quarters of our real life. **Simone Weil**. *Gravity and Grace* (1952)

If a man carefully examine his thoughts he will be surprised to find out how much he lives in the future. **Ralph Waldo Emerson**. Attributed

Skill without imagination is craftsmanship and gives us many useful objects such as wickerwork picnic baskets. Imagination without skill gives us modern art. **Sir Tom Stoppard**. *Artist Descending a Staircase* (1988)

We are what and where we are because we have first imagined it. **Donald Curtis**. Quoted in *Awaken the Giant Within* (Anthony Robbins, 1992)

   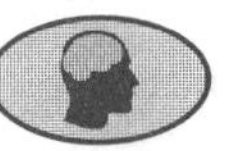  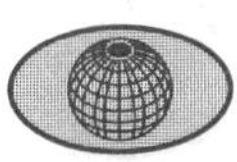  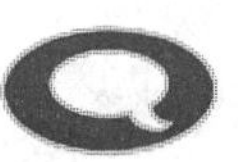 

Independence

No one can possibly achieve any real and lasting success or get rich in business by being a conformist. **J. Paul Getty**. *International Herald Tribune* (1961)

It's better to be a pirate than join the Navy. **Steve Jobs**. Quoted in *West of Eden* (Frank Rose, 1989)

You can't win without being completely different. When everyone else says we are crazy, I say, gee we really must be on to something. **Larry D. Ellison**. *Forbes* (October 2000)

I want to prevent as many men as possible from pretending that they have to do this or that because they must earn a living. *It is not true*. **Henry Miller**. The book was based on Miller's five years' experience working for Western Union; he walked out of the job in 1925 declaring, "My own master now." *Tropic of Capricorn* (1939)

Never sing in chorus, if you want to be heard. **Jules Archibald**. Attributed

Once you decide to work for yourself, you never go back to work for somebody else. **Sir Alan Sugar**. *The Apprentice (UK)*

God makes the animals, man makes himself. **Georg C. Lichtenberg**. Notebook entry

Some people have so much respect for their superiors they have none left for themselves. **Peter McArthur**. *The Best of Peter McArthur* (1967)

A man who trims himself to suit everybody will soon whittle himself away. **Charles M. Schwab**. Quoted in *The Game of Life* (Lou Harry, 2004)

Industrial Relations

All classes of society are trades unionists at heart, and differ chiefly in the boldness, ability, and secrecy with which they pursue their respective interests. **William Stanley Jevons**. *The State in Relation to Labour* (1882)

The two sides of industry have traditionally always regarded each other in Britain with the greatest possible loathing, mistrust and contempt. They are both absolutely right. **Auberon Waugh**. *Private Eye* (December 16, 1983)

When you're negotiating for a 35 hour week, remember they have only just got 66 hours in Taiwan, and you're competing with Taiwan. **Victor Kiam**. *Daily Express (London)* (June 12, 1981)

I am just a hoary old bastard who wants to win. **Sir Ian McGregor**. *Observer (London)* (March 11, 1984)

The fertility of happy invention denied its full fruit by the grimy rules of union demarcation. **Sir Harold Evans**. Referring to union opposition to new technology in the newspaper industry. *Good Times, Bad Times* (1983)

Why do people focus...on cash rewards?...We seldom create opportunities to congratulate each other. It's hard to imagine union leaders storming into a meeting, smashing their fists on the desk and demanding, We want more congratulations! **Kenneth Blanchard**. "The Gift of the Goose," *Quality Digest* (December 1997)

The strike is the weapon of the oppressed, of men capable of appreciating justice and having the courage to resist wrong and contend for principle. **Eugene V. Debs**. Speaking during the strike of engineers and firefighters on the Chicago, Burlington, and Quincy Rail Line. Quoted in *The Arizona Republic* (2000)

Industry

The successful conduct of an industrial enterprise requires two quite distinct qualifications: fidelity and zeal. **John Stuart Mill**. *Principles of Political Economy* (1848)

Properly, urban-industrialization must be regarded an experiment. And if the scientific spirit has taught us anything of value, it is that honest experiments may well fail. **Theodore Roszak**. *Where the Wasteland Ends* (1972), Introduction

It is an axiom, enforced by all the experience of the ages, that they who rule industrially will rule politically. **Aneurin Bevan**. Quoted in *Aneurin Bevan* (Michael Foot, 1962), vol. 1

The difficulty is that we have an industrial base with so many characteristics of an industrial museum or of an industrial hospital. **Barry Owen Jones**. Quoted in "Sayings of the Week," *Sydney Morning Herald* (July 12, 1986)

We have created an industrial order geared to automation, where feeble-mindedness, native or acquired, is necessary for docile productivity in the factory; and where a pervasive neurosis is the final gift of the meaningless life which issues forth at the other end. **Lewis Mumford**. *The Conduct of Life* (1951)

For years I thought what was good for our country was good for General Motors and vice versa. The difference did not exist. Our company is too big. It goes with the welfare of the country. **Charles E. Wilson**. Quoted in "Statement to US Senate committee," *New York Times* (February 24, 1953)

It takes five years to develop a new car in this country. Heck, we won World War II in four years. **H. Ross Perot**. Quoted in *Thriving on Chaos* (Tom Peters, 1987)

What will Britain's service industry be servicing when there is no hardware, when no wealth is actually being produced. We will be servicing presumably the product of wealth by others. **Lord Weinstock**. *International Management* (December 1985)

Modern industry seems to be inefficient to a degree that surpasses one's enduring powers of imagination. Its inefficiency therefore remains unnoticed. **E. F. Schumacher**. *Small Is Beautiful* (1973)

The most striking thing about modern industry is that it requires so much and accomplishes so little. **E. F. Schumacher**. *Small Is Beautiful* (1973)

It takes more than industry to industrialize. **W. W. Rostow**. *The Stages of Economic Growth* (1960), ch. 3

The spark-gap is mightier than the pen. This is not the age of the pamphleteers, it is the age of the engineers. **Lancelot Hogben**. *Science for the Citizen* (1938)

Power and machinery, money and goods are useful only as they set us free to live. **Henry Ford**. *My Life and Work* (co-written with Samuel Crowther, 1922)

Since the introduction of inanimate mechanism into British manufactories, man, with few exceptions, has been treated as a secondary and inferior machine; and far more attention has been given to perfect the raw materials of wood and metals than those of body and mind. **Robert Owen**. *A New View of Society* (1813)

Industry is the root of all ugliness. **Oscar Wilde**. *Phrases and Philosophies for the Use of the Young* (1894)

Man is a tool-using animal... Without tools he is nothing, with tools he is all. **Thomas Carlyle**. *Sartor Resartus* (1834)

  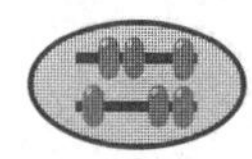   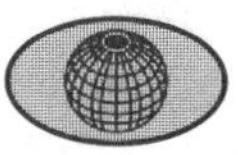   

The task of industry is continuously, year on year, to make more and better things, using less of the world's resources. **Sir John Harvey-Jones**. *Making It Happen* (1988)

Our bailout of Detroit will be remembered as the equivalent of pouring billions of taxpayers' money into the mail-order catalogue business on the eve of the birth of eBay. **Thomas Friedman**. *New York Times* (December 10, 2008)

While we're still the US sales leader, we acknowledge we have disappointed you. **General Motors**. On its financial troubles. Full-page in *Automotive News* (December 2008)

Information

The new economy favors intangible things—ideas, information, and relationships. **Kevin Kelly**. *New Rules for the New Economy: 10 Radical Strategies for a Connected World* (1998)

We don't believe it's possible to protect digital content. What's new is this amazingly efficient distribution system for stolen property called the Internet—and no one's gonna shut down the Internet. And it only takes one stolen copy to be on the Internet...You'll never stop that. So what you have to do is compete with it. **Steve Jobs**. The Rolling Stone Interview (December 2003)

Data without generalization is just gossip. **Robert M. Pirsig**. *Lila* (1992)

Information is a business in itself. It is also something that has made control impossible...you cannot get customers to accept prices in one place when they know there's a better deal elsewhere. It's a whole new world. **Walter Wriston**. Quoted in *The Financial Revolution: The Big Bang Worldwide* (Adrian Hamilton, 1986), ch. 2

Facts are available to everyone; it is interpretation and implementation that is key. **Ric Simcock**. *Marketing* (September 2000)

You can use the fanciest computers in the world and you can gather all the charts and numbers, but in the end you have to have to bring all your information together, set a timetable, and act. **Lee Iacocca**. *Iacocca: An Autobiography* (1984)

Where is all the knowledge we lost with information? **T. S. Eliot**. *The Rock* (1934)

While hard data may inform the intellect, it is largely soft data that generates wisdom. **Henry Mintzberg**. *The Rise and Fall of Strategic Planning* (1994)

If you file your waste basket for 50 years, you have a public library. **Tony Benn**. *Daily Telegraph (London)* (March 1994)

The more the data banks record about each one of us, the less we exist. **Marshall McLuhan**. Interview, *Playboy* (March 1969)

I find more and more executives less and less well informed about the outside world, if only because they believe that the data on the computer printouts are ipso facto information. **Peter F. Drucker**. Quoted in "Seeing Things As They Really Are," *Forbes* (Robert Lenzner and Stephen S. Johnson, 1987)

We can say with certainty—or 90% probability—that the new industries that are about to be born will have nothing to do with information. **Peter F. Drucker**. Quoted in *Great Writers on Organizations* (Derek S. Pugh and David J. Hickson, 2007)

An individual without information cannot take responsibility; an individual who is given information cannot help but take responsibility. **Wilbert Lee Gore**. Quoted in *Thriving on Chaos* (Tom Peters, 1987)

The highest art of professional management requires the literal ability to smell a real fact from all others. **Harold S. Geneen**. *Managing* (co-written with Alvin Moscow, 1984)

A Harvard professor told me that if there was no Gallup poll there'd be no Bill Clinton. **Jim Clifton**. *Financial Times (London)* (October 2000)

Information is costly to produce, but cheap to reproduce. **Carl Shapiro**. *Information Rules* (co-written with Hal L Varian, 1999)

The ultimate search engine would basically understand everything in the world, and it would always give you the right thing. And we're a long, long way from that. **Larry Page**. Interview, *Business Week* (May 3, 2004)

Nothing in business (or life) is more expensive than bad information. **Gary Halbert**. Quoted in *2,239 Tested Secrets For Direct Marketing Success* (Denny Hatch and Don Jackson, 1999)

Innovation

A common mistake that people make when trying to design something completely foolproof is to underestimate the ingenuity of complete fools. **Hugh Davidson**. *Mostly Harmless* (1992)

I don't think necessity is the mother of invention—invention, in my opinion arises directly from idleness, possibly also from laziness. To save oneself trouble. **Dame Agatha Christie**. *An Autobiography* (1977)

In a small company, one person's hunch can be enough to launch a new product. In a big company, the same concept is likely to be buried in committee for months. **Al Ries**. *Marketing Warfare* (co-written with Jack Trout, 1986), ch. 10

By observing California's youngsters on roller skates, a Sony engineer came up with the concept of the Walkman. **Kenichi Ohmae**. *Industry Week* (July 1985)

Everyone likes innovation until it affects himself, and then it's bad. **Walter Wriston**. Quoted in "Sayings of the Year," *Observer (London)* (December 29, 1974)

It is easy to overlook the absence of appreciable advance in an industry. Inventions that are not made, like babies that are not born, are rarely missed. **J. K. Galbraith**. *The Affluent Society* (1958), ch. 9

There is no shortage of creative people in American business. The shortage is of innovators. All too often people believe that creativity leads to innovation. It doesn't. **Theodore Levitt**. "Ideas Are Useless Unless Used," *Inc.* (February 1981)

To invent, you need a good imagination and a pile of junk. **Thomas Edison**. Quoted in "Building an Innovation Factory," *Harvard Business Review* (Andrew Hargadon and Robert I. Sutton, 2000)

Innovation! One cannot be forever innovating. I want to create classics. **Coco Chanel**. Quoted in *Coco Chanel: Her Life, Her Secrets* (1971)

Everything that can be invented has been invented. **Charles H. Duell**. Quoted in *Maxi Marketing* (Stan Rapp and Thomas L. Collins, 1995)

The artist brings something into the world that didn't exist before, and...he does it without destroying something else. **John Updike**. Quoted in *Writers at Work* (George Plimpton, ed, 1977)

Innovation will always be a mixture of serendipity, genius, and sheer bull-mindedness. But while you can't bottle lightning, you can build lightning rods. Non-linear innovation can be legitimized, fostered, supported, and rewarded. **Gary Hamel**. Interview, *Barnes & Noble* (September 2000)

Innovation is not just technical; it is also organizational and managerial. **Stewart**

  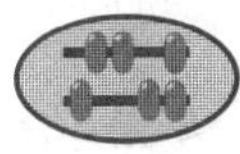   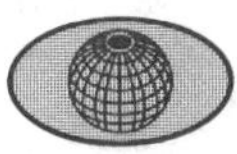   

Clegg. "Business Values and Embryonic Industry: Lessons from Australia," *Whose Business Values? Some Asian and Cross-Cultural Perspectives* (Sally Stewart and Gabriel Donleavy, eds., 1995)

Slack allows innovative projects to be pursued because it buffers organizations from the uncertain success of these projects, fostering a culture of experimentation. **Nitin Nohria**. *The Differentiated Network* (co-written with Sumantra Ghoshal, 1997)

Discovery consists of seeing what everybody has seen and thinking what nobody has thought. **Albert Szent-Györgyi**. Quoted in *The Scientist Speculates* (I. J. Good, ed, 1962)

The most successful innovators are the creative imitators, the number two. **Peter F. Drucker**. Interview, *Hot Wired* (August 1996)

Above all, innovation is not invention. It is a term of economics rather than of technology. **Peter F. Drucker**. Speech (April 1992)

Not a single, substantial, commercially-successful project had come from an adequately-funded team. They'd always come from the scrounging, scrapping, underfunded teams. **Ken Olsen**. Quoted in *A Passion for Excellence* (Tom Peters and Nancy Austin, 1985)

Sometimes I think we'll see the day when you introduce a product in the morning and announce the end of its life at the end of the day. **Al Shugart**. Quoted in *Goldfinger* (Robert Heller, 1998)

The great discoveries are usually obvious. **Philip B. Crosby**. *Quality Is Free* (1979)

One possibility for difficulties innovating is that most people really don't care about innovation. **Peter Senge**. "The Practice of Innovation," *Leader to Leader* (1998)

People are unlikely to know that they need a product which does not exist and the basis of market research in new and innovative products is limited in this regard. **Sir John Harvey-Jones**. *All Together Now* (1994)

The public does not know what is possible, we do. **Akio Morita**. *Made in Japan* (1986)

Intelligence

Brains are becoming the core of organisations—other activities can be contracted out. **Charles Handy**. Interview (February 1994)

Anti-intellectualism has long been the anti-Semitism of the businessman. **Arthur Schlesinger, Jr**. *Partisan Review* (1953)

Intellectual capital is the sum of everything everybody in a company knows that gives it a competitive edge. **Thomas A. Stewart**. *Intellectual Capital* (1997)

Intelligence...is really a kind of taste: taste in ideas. **Susan Sontag**. "Notes on Camp," *Against Interpretation* (1966)

As a human being, one has been endowed with just enough intelligence to be able to see clearly how utterly inadequate that intelligence is when confronted with what exists. **Albert Einstein**. Letter (September 1932)

The brain is a wonderful organ. It starts working the moment you get up in the morning, and does not stop until you get into the office. **Robert Frost**. Attributed

Investment

The historical data support one conclusion with unusual force: To invest with success, you must be a long-term investor. **John Clifton Bogle**. *Common Sense on Mutual Funds: New Imperatives for the Intelligent Investor* (1999), ch. 1

As time goes on, I get more and more convinced that the right method in investment is to put fairly large sums into enterprises which one thinks one knows something about and in the management of which one thoroughly believes. It is a mistake to think that one limits one's risk by spreading too much between enterprises about which one knows little and has no reason for special confidence. **John Maynard Keynes**. Letter to F. C. Scott (August 15, 1934)

Successful investing is anticipating the anticipations of others. **John Maynard Keynes**. Quoted in *Isms* (Gregory Bergman, 2006)

Those who invest only to get rich will fail. Those who invest to help others will probably succeed. **Art Fry**. Interview, *The Empty Raincoat: Making Sense of the Future* (Charles Handy, 1994)

For most individuals, the stock market is best used for investing, not trading...On-line trading may be quick and easy; on-line investing requires old-fashioned elbow grease like researching a company or making the time to appreciate the level of risk. I'm often surprised by investors who spend more time deciding what movie they'll rent than on which stock to buy. **Arthur Levitt, Jr**. Speech to the National Press Club. "Plain Talk about On-line Investing" (May 4, 1999)

Make your company stock a consumer product. When consumers buy stock in your company, they'll never buy a competitive product. You've linked their financial future to yours. **Faith Popcorn**. "Q&A with Faith Popcorn," *www.brainreserve.com* (1999)

My advice to this investor is the same that I give to the young investors in my classes...Devote the same earnest attention to investing that $50,000 as you devoted to earning it. **Ivan Boesky**. Quoted in the *Wall Street Journal* (January 2, 1985)

Speculation is an effort, probably unsuccessful, to turn a little money into a lot. Investment is an effort, which should be successful, to prevent a lot of money from becoming a little. **Fred Schwed**. *Where Are the Customers' Yachts?* (1995)

The only reason to invest in the market is because you think you know something others don't. **R. Foster Winans**. *Newsweek* (December 1, 1986)

If investing is entertaining, if you're having fun, you're probably not making any money. Good investing is boring. **George Soros**. Quoted in *The Winning Investment Habits of Warren Buffett & George Soros* (Mark Tier, 2006)

I don't invest in anything I don't understand—it makes more sense to buy TV stations than oil wells. **Oprah Winfrey**. Quoted in *Oprah Winfrey Speaks* (Janet Lowe, 1998)

Lethargy bordering on sloth remains the cornerstone of our investment style. **Warren Buffett**. *Newsweek* (May 1991)

If you aren't willing to own a stock for ten years, don't even think about owning it for ten minutes. **Warren Buffett**. Chairman's letter to shareholders (February 28, 1997)

I don't pay attention to what the stock does. If the business does well, the stock eventually follows. **Warren Buffett**. *BusinessWeek* (1994)

The true investor *welcomes* volatility...a wildly fluctuating market means that irrationally low prices will periodically be attached to solid businesses. **Warren Buffett**. Chairman's letter to shareholders (March 7, 1995)

  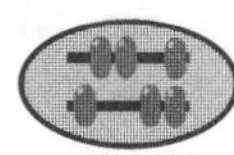   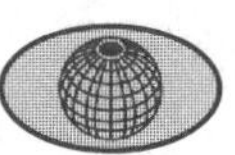   

Investing is simple, but not easy. **Warren Buffett**. Attributed

Rule no. 1: Never lose money. Rule no. 2: Never forget rule no. 1. **Warren Buffett**. Quoted in *Warren Buffett Speaks* (Janet Lowe, 1997)

Never invest in any ideas you can't illustrate with a crayon. **Peter Lynch**. *Beating the Street* (1993)

Investing in stocks is an art, not a science, and people who've been trained to rigidly quantify everything have a big disadvantage. **Peter Lynch**. *One Up On Wall Street* (1990)

I got positive feelings when I saw that Taco Bell's headquarters was stuck behind a bowling alley. When I saw those executives operating out of that grim little bunker, I was thrilled. Obviously they weren't wasting money on landscaping the office. **Peter Lynch**. On his decision to invest in Taco Bell restaurants. *One Up On Wall Street* (1990)

Go for a business that any idiot can run—because sooner or later, any idiot probably is going to run it. **Peter Lynch**. Quoted in *The Book of Investing Wisdom* (Peter Krass, 1999)

Sometimes your best investments are the ones you don't make. **Donald J. Trump**. Quoted in *Trump: The Art of the Deal* (co-written with Tony Schwartz, 1987)

Never invest your money in anything that eats or needs repainting. **Billy Rose**. *New York Post* (October 26, 1957)

Investing is not nearly as difficult as it looks. Successful investing involves doing a few things right and avoiding serious mistakes. **John C. Bogle**. *Bogle on Mutual Funds* (1993)

To achieve satisfactory investment results is easier than most people realize; to achieve superior results is harder than it looks. **Benjamin Graham**. *The Intelligent Investor* (1949)

Bond investors are the vampires of the investment world. They love decay, recession—anything that leads to low inflation and the protection of the real value of their loans. **Bill Gross**. *Bill Gross on Investing* (1998)

Whales only get harpooned when they come to the surface, and turtles can only move forward when they stick their neck out, but investors face risk no matter what they do. **Charles A. Jaffe**. Attributed

Four hundred seventy-three million to one. Those are the odds against George Soros compiling the investment record he did as manager of the Quantum Fund from 1968 through 1993. **Paul Tudor Jones**. *The Alchemy of Finance: Reading the Mind of the Market* (1994)

More money is probably lost by people who attempt to invest their money conservatively and sanely, but ignorantly, than is lost by those who enter into frank speculations. **John Moody**. Quoted in *The Book of Investing Wisdom* (Peter Krass, 1999)

You have to be intellectually honest with yourself and others. In my judgment, all great investors are seekers of truth. **Michael Steinhardt**. Quoted in *Market Wizards* (John D. Schwager, 1989)

Jobs

You ask me what I do. Well, actually, you know,
I'm partly a liaison man and partly PRO.
Essentially I integrate the export drive
And basically I'm viable from ten o'clock till five.
Sir John Betjeman. "The Executive," *A Nip in the Air* (1974)

In the past, business was the employer of all those who wanted to work. In the future, there will be lots of customers, but not lots of jobs. **Charles Handy**. *The Empty Raincoat: Making Sense of the Future* (1994)

It is just a job. Grass grows, birds fly, waves pound the sand. I beat people up. **Muhammad Ali**. Quoted in the *New York Times* (April 6, 1977)

Ninety percent of our jobs are in jeopardy, and corporations are in the middle of unprecedented change. If we simply do the job our bosses want us to do, we may soon find ourselves without any marketable skills. **Tom Peters**. "The Ominous Prediction of Tom Peters," *Small Manufacturing SIG Newsletter* (Ira Smolowitz, 2000)

Oh brave new world, said Robyn, where only the managing directors have jobs. **David Lodge**. *Nice Work* (1968)

I don't think anybody yet has invented a pastime that's as much fun, or keeps you as young, as a good job. **Frederick Hudson Ecker**. Quoted in his obituary. *New York Times* (March 20, 1964)

You don't need to interpret tea leaves stuck in a cup
To understand that people who work sitting down get paid more than those people who work standing up.
Ogden Nash. "Will Consider Situation," *The Face Is Familiar* (1940)

If you have a job without any aggravations, you don't have a job. **Malcolm S. Forbes**. Attributed

Judgements

Discrimination is the capacity to discern what is important. **Warren Blank**. *The 9 Natural Laws of Leadership* (1995)

It is at least conceivable that the 21st century business environment will be so fluid that it defies analysis, forcing executives to fall back upon hunch, or instinct. **John Elkington**. *Cannibals with Forks* (1997)

Power in a corporation becomes residual and dwells in the background. It is the ability to exercise nice matters of judgment. **Viscount Chandos**. *Memoirs of Lord Chandos: An Unexpected View from the Summit* (1963)

It takes little talent to see clearly what lies under one's nose, a good deal of it to know in what direction to point that organ. **W. H. Auden**. *The Dyers Hand* (1963)

A man with a surplus can control circumstances, but a man without a surplus is controlled by them, and often has no opportunity to exercise judgment. **Harvey Firestone**. Quoted in *The Arizona Republic* (2000)

We made a professional judgement about the appropriate accounting treatment that turned out to be wrong. **Joseph Berardino**. Referring to Enron's accounting practices. Submission to a hearing on Enron (December 12, 2002)

Knowledge

The secret of business is to know something that nobody else knows. **Aristotle Onassis**. Attributed

Knowledge resides in the heads of people. Shareholders cannot own it since owning people is not considered moral. It is also not practical. Acquisitions of intellectual capital firms therefore often fail. **Charles Handy**. Speech at the Second Workshop on Inventing the Organization of the 21st Century, Munich, Germany. "The Age of Paradox" (April 1996)

  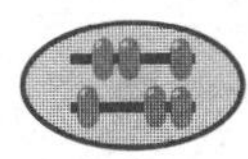   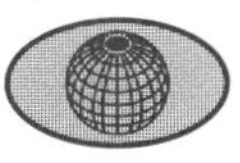 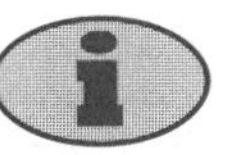  

What our competitive and careerist knowledge industry has produced already hopelessly exceeds our ability to make graceful use of it. **Theodore Roszak**. *Where the Wasteland Ends* (1972)

An expert is one who knows more and more about less and less. **Nicholas Murray Butler**. *Speed* (1901)

The person who knows how will always have a job. The person who knows why will always be his boss. **Diane Ravitch**. *Time* (June 17, 1985)

Knowledge is the only meaningful resource today. **Peter F. Drucker**. *Post-capitalist Society* (1993)

Knowledge is proportionate to being. You know in virtue of what you are. **Aldous Huxley**. *Time Must Have a Stop* (1944)

Now what is the message there? The message is that there are known knowns. There are things we know that we know. There are known unknowns. That is to say there are things that we now know we don't know. But there are also unknown unknowns. There are things we don't know we don't know. So when we do the best we can and we pull all this information together, and we then say well that's basically what we see as the situation, that is really only the known knowns and the known unknowns. And each year, we discover a few more of those unknown unknowns. **Donald Rumsfeld**. Press conference at NATO Headquarters, Brussels, Belgium (June 6, 2002)

There is no substitute for accurate knowledge. Know yourself, know your business, know your men. **Randall Jacobs**. Quoted in *How to Get from Cubicle to Corner Office* (Joel Weiss, 2005)

Law and Lawyers

As in law so in war, the longest purse finally wins. **Mahatma Gandhi**. Lecture to the Bombay Provincial Conference (September 17, 1917)

No brilliance is needed in the law. Nothing but common sense, and relatively clean finger nails. **Sir John Mortimer**. *A Voyage Round My Father* (1970)

Nothing is illegal if 100 businessmen decide to do it. **Andrew Jackson Young, Jr**. Press conference (1976)

Laws are like spider's webs: if some poor weak creature come up against them, it is caught; but a bigger one can break through and get away. **Solon**. Quoted in "Solon," *Parallel Lives* (Plutarch, 1st century AD)

A community that endures a contemptible law is itself contemptible. **Alfred G. Stephens**. *Bookfellow* (March 1, 1912)

Lawyers are like rhinoceroses: thick-skinned, short-sighted, and always ready to charge. **David Mellor**. Question Time, BBC Television (December 3, 1992)

Trying to control corporate power and abuse by American corporate law has proven about as effective as drinking coffee with a fork. **Ralph Nader**. Quoted in *The Times (London)* (October 23, 1976)

Lawyers are the only persons in whom ignorance of the law is not punished. **Jeremy Bentham**. Attributed

LAWYER, n. One skilled in circumvention of the law. **Ambrose Bierce**. *The Devil's Dictionary* (1911)

You might as well try to employ a boa constrictor as a tape-measure as to go to a lawyer for legal advice. **Oliver St. John Gogarty**. *Tumbling in the Hay* (1939)

There is no better way of exercising the imagination than the study of law. No poet ever interpreted nature as freely as a lawyer interprets truth. **Jean Giraudoux**. *Tiger at the Gates* (1935)

When the meek inherit the earth, lawyers will be there to work out the deal. **Sam Ewing**. Quoted in the *Wall Street Journal* (May 22, 1997)

Leadership

Without some element of leadership, the many at the bottom will be paralyzed with choices. **Kevin Kelly**. *New Rules for the New Economy: 10 Radical Strategies for a Connected World* (1998)

Most people in big companies are administered, not led. They are treated as personnel, not people. **Robert Townsend**. *Further Up the Organization* (1984)

The first lesson is: To hell with centralized strategic planning. If you don't have a good leader, it's all nothing; it's just a bunch of papers flying around. **Robert Townsend**. "Townsend's Third Degree in Leadership," *The Conference Board Challenge to Business: Industry Leaders Speak Their Minds* (Peter Krass and Richard E. Cavanagh, eds., 2000)

Drive thy business, let not that drive thee. **Benjamin Franklin**. The *Poor Richard's Almanack* series (1732–1758) were originally published under the pseudonym Richard Saunders. *Poor Richard's Almanack* (1758)

Managers have been brought up on a diet of power, divide and rule. they have been pre-occupied with authority, rather than making small things happen. **Charles Handy**. *The Age of Unreason* (1989)

The final test of a leader is that he leaves behind him in other men the conviction and the will to carry on. **Walter Lippmann**. "Roosevelt Has Gone," *New York Herald Tribune* (April 14, 1945)

I'll tell you what leadership is. It's persuasion and conciliation, and education, and patience. **Dwight David Eisenhower**. Quoted in *Handbook of Leadership* (R. M. Stogdill, 1974)

I have never issued an order since I have been the operating head of the corporation. **Alfred P. Sloan**. Referring to the benefits of decentralized management. "The Most Important Things I Learned About Management," *System* (August 1924)

When the effective leader is finished with his work, the people say it happened naturally. **Laozi**. *Daode Jing*

The manager does things right; the leader does the right thing. **Warren Bennis**. "Managing the Dream," *Training Management* (1990)

Leaders are almost like midwives of ideas. They really understand what is going on. You know when you come to them with an idea, they aren't going to just say, "Well, that's nice, and maybe we can use that." **Warren Bennis**. Interview, *Strategy + Business* (July–September 1997)

A leader is a man who has the ability to get other people to do what they don't want to do and like it. **Harry S. Truman**. Quoted in *Leadership Is Not a Bowler Hat* (P. Prior, 1977)

The difference between a leader and a boss is the difference between good and bad management. **Joe Klock**. *Like Klockwork: The Whimsy, Wit, and (Sometime) Wisdom of a Key Largo Curmudgeon* (1995)

I'm the boss. I'm allowed to yell. **Ivan Boesky**. Quoted in *Den of Thieves* (James B. Stewart, 1991)

They have a particular drive, a desire to bring order out of chaos, or if something is too cosy, to create chaos in order to bring

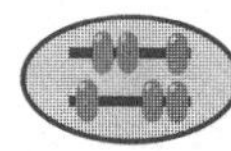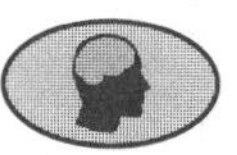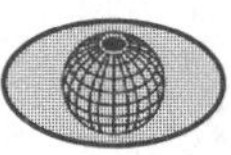

change. **Sir Michael Owen Edwardes**. On leaders. Quoted in *The New Elite* (Berry Ritchie and Walter Goldsmith, 1987)

I think you have a rocket up your ass and I want to point it in the right direction. **Harry E. Figgie, Jr**. Exemplifying Figgie's aggressive management style. Quoted in *Dangerous Company* (James O'Shea and Charles Madigan, 1997)

The most effective leader is the one who satisfies the psychological needs of his followers. **David Ogilvy**. *Ogilvy on Advertising* (1983)

Leaders with unruly, lowly minds will project and create turbulent and contaminated environments in their spheres of action. **S. K. Chakraborty**. *Ethics in Management: Vedantic Perspectives* (1995)

A leader is one who ventures and takes the risks of going out ahead to show the way and whom others follow, voluntarily, because they are persuaded that the leader's path is the right one--for them, probably better than they could devise for themselves. **Robert Greenleaf**. "Servant: Retrospect and Prospect," *The Power of Servant Leadership* (Larry Spears, ed, 1998)

Here lies one who knew how to get around him men who were cleverer than himself. **Andrew Carnegie**. Epitaph (1919)

A company is an organic, living, breathing thing, not just an income sheet and balance sheet. You have to lead it with that in mind. **Carly Fiorina**. "Secrets of the Fastest Rising Stars," *Fortune* (Patricia Sellers, 2000)

Challenge the mind and capture the heart. **Carly Fiorina**. *Forbes* (October 2000)

Either lead, follow, or get out of the way. **Anonymous**. Sign on the desk of broadcasting executive Ted Turner. *Fortune* (January 5, 1987)

Teach me to smile if it kills me. Make me a better leader...by helping develop larger and greater qualities of understanding, tolerance, sympathy, wisdom, perspective, equanimity, mind-reading, and second sight. **Anonymous**. Quoted in "A Leader's Prayer," *Understanding Organisations* (Charles Handy, 1976), pt. 1, ch. 4

Consensus is the negation of leadership. **Baroness Thatcher**. Quoted in *Woodbury Reports Archives* (June 1997)

In order for an ideal to become a reality, there must be a person, a personality to translate it. **Jesse Jackson**. Eulogy (October 1972)

At a rehearsal I let the orchestra play as they like. At the concert I make them play as I like. **Sir Thomas Beecham**. Quoted in *Sir Thomas Beecham* (Neville Cardew, 1961)

Leadership is all hype. We've had three great leaders in this century—Hitler, Stalin, and Mao. **Peter F. Drucker**. *Fortune* (February 1994)

Charisma becomes the undoing of leaders. It makes them inflexible, convinced of their own infallibility, unable to change. **Peter F. Drucker**. *The Essential Drucker* (2003)

The function of leadership is to produce more leaders, not more followers. **Ralph Nader**. *Crashing the Party* (2002)

The art of leadership is saying no, not yes. It is very easy to say yes. **Tony Blair**. *Daily Mail (London)* (October 1994)

If we're going to run this business on viscera, it's going to be my viscera. **Thomas J. Watson, Jr**. Quoted in *CEO* (Harry Levinson and Stuart Rosenthal, 1984)

The hierarchical manager of yesterday ran the Industrial Age company with Yes Sir! Yes Sir...When you're running an Information Age company, you've got to allow a lot of dissent. **Bill Campbell**. Quoted in *Giant Killers* (Geoffrey James, 1996)

The task of the leader is to get people from where they are to where they have not been. **Henry Kissinger**. *Time* (October 1980)

You just have to be the kind of guy to get people to do things. **Donald J. Trump**. *US News & World Report* (April 1987)

The leader must know, must know that he knows, and must be able to make it abundantly clear to those about him that he knows. **Clarence B. Randall**. *Making Good in Management* (1964)

A leader is a person you will follow to a place you wouldn't go by yourself. **Joel A. Barker**. *Paradigms* (1994)

Leadership comes through respect, and a large part of respect is liking someone. **Carol Leonard**. *The Times (London)* (September 26, 2005)

In essence leadership appears to be the art of getting others to want to do something you are convinced should be done. **Vance Packard**. *The Pyramid Climbers* (1962)

Learning

Bromidic though it may sound, some questions don't have answers, which is a terribly difficult lesson to learn. **Katharine Graham**. "The Power That Didn't Corrupt," *Ms.* (Jane Howard, 1974)

True learning begins with unlearning. **Fred Kofman**. *On Becoming a Leader* (1998)

Never let formal education get in the way of your learning. **Mark Twain**. Quoted in *Jump Start Your Brain* (Doug Hall, 1996)

Many organizations are now trying to walk under the banner of The Learning Organization, realizing that knowledge is our most important product...But the only place that I've seen it is in the Army. As one colonel said, "We realized a while ago that it's better to learn than be dead." **Walter Wriston**. Interview with Scott London, US National Public Radio (November 1996)

We're not in cultures which support learning; we're in cultures that give us the message consistently: "Don't mess up, don't make mistakes, don't make the boss look bad, don't give us any surprises." So we're asking for a kind of predictability, control, respect and compliance that has nothing to do with learning. **Walter Wriston**. Interview with Scott London, US National Public Radio (November 1996)

The man who views the world at fifty the same as he did at twenty has wasted thirty years of his life. **Muhammad Ali**. *Playboy* (1975)

The learning person looks forward to failure or mistakes. The worst problem in leadership is basically early success. **Warren Bennis**. Quoted in *Guide to the Management Gurus* (C. Kennedy, 1998)

Learning and performance will become one and the same thing. Everything you say about learning will be about performance. People will get the point that learning is everything. **Peter Block**. "The Future of Workplace Learning and Performance," *Training and Development* (1994)

Learning is not compulsory. Neither is survival. **W. Edwards Deming**. Quoted in *Discover Your Hidden Talents* (Bill Lucas, 2005)

I'm not an educator...I'm a learner. **Bill Gates**. *The Road Ahead* (co-written with Nathan Myhrvold and Peter N. Rinearson, 1995)

     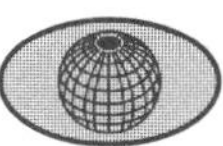  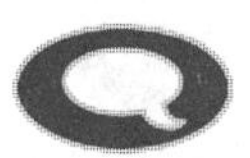 

The illiterate of the 21st century will not be those who cannot read and write but those who cannot learn, unlearn and relearn. **Alvin Toffler**. *Future Shock* (1970)

Over the long run, superior performance depends on superior learning. **Peter Senge**. "The Leader's New Work: Building Learning Organizations," *Sloan Management Review* (1990)

Individual learning is a necessary but insufficient condition for organizational learning. **Chris Argyris**. *Organizational Learning: A Theory of Action Perspective* (co-written with Donald A. Schon, 1978)

Once a company has adapted to a new environment, it is no longer the organization it used to be; it has evolved. That is the essence of learning. **Arie De Geus**. "The Living Company," *Harvard Business Review* (1997)

It's what you learn after you know it all that counts. **John Wooden**. *The Essential Wooden* (2006)

Listening

I think we have to lead people by being good listeners. That is to say, we lead in a company such as ours by drawing out ideas from people...We can't simply issue commands. **Minoru Makihara**. Interview, *Strategy + Business* (Joel Kurtzman, January–March 1996)

Sometimes listening itself may not be enough—some people must be prodded if you are to find out what they're thinking. **Mary Kay Ash**. *On People Management* (1984)

Wisdom comes with talking less frivolously and listening more seriously. The latter implies a learning attitude; the former assumes an air of omniscience that does not exist. **S. K. Chakraborty**. *Management by Objectives: An Integrated Approach* (1976)

In the industrial age, the CEO sat on the top of the hierarchy and didn't have to listen to anybody...In the information age, you have to listen to the ideas of people regardless of where they are in the organization. **John Sculley**. *Nation's Business Today* (1987)

I have often heard that the outstanding man is he who thinks deeply about a problem, and the next is he who listens carefully to advice. **Livy**. *History of Rome* (26 BC–15 AD)

Losing

'Tis better to have fought and lost,
Than never to have fought at all.
Arthur Hugh Clough. "Peschiera," *Poems* (1862)

I never thought of losing, but now that it's happened, the only thing is to do it right. That's my obligation to all the people who believe in me. We all have to take defeats in life. **Muhammad Ali**. Said after losing his first fight to Ken Norton, March 31, 1973. Quoted in the *New York Times* (1973)

There is nothing worse than a battle won except a battle lost. **Duke of Wellington**. Letter to Philip von Neumann (January 11, 1821)

If you think you are going to win, you'll lose. Moreover, if you think you are going to lose, you'll lose. **Toshihiko Seko**. Quoted in *Running with the Legends* (Michael Sandrock, 1996)

If you want to know what a man is really like, take notice how he acts when he loses money. **Anonymous**.

There is no such thing as a paper loss. A paper loss is a very real loss. **Jim Rogers**. Quoted in *Treasury of Investment Wisdom* (Bernice Cohen, 1999)

For me coming second is the same as coming last. **Lord Grade**. Interview, *You Magazine* (October 25, 1987)

If the losses don't hurt, your financial survival is tenuous. **William Eckhardt**. Quoted in *The New Market Wizards* (John D. Schwager, 1992)

Stifle that ego and learn to love small losses. If you don't have small losses, it is positively guaranteed that you will have huge losses. **John R. Hill**. *The Ultimate Trading Guide* (2000)

Loyalty

The primary rule of business success is loyalty to your employer. That's all right as a theory. What is the matter with loyalty to yourself? **Mark Twain**. Quoted in *East Valley Tribune* (2000)

I walk into all these organizations, and I'm always puzzled when I realize that people still want to be there. Most people really want to love their organizations. We need that level of commitment...Yet organizations have done very little to deserve that kind of staying-power. **Walter Wriston**. Interview with Scott London, US National Public Radio (November 1996)

What job is worth the enormous psychic cost of following a leader who values loyalty in the narrowest sense. **Warren Bennis**. *On Becoming a Leader* (1989)

Patriotism is a lively sense of collective responsibility. Nationalism is a silly cock crowing on a dunghill. **Richard Aldington**. *The Colonel's Daughter* (1931)

Loyalty saves the wear and tear of making daily decisions as to what is best to do. **Thomas J. Watson, Sr**. Quoted in *Think* (William Rogers, 1972)

Forget loyalty. Or at least loyalty to one's corporation. Try loyalty to your Rolodex—your network—instead. **Tom Peters**. *Economist* (1996)

What I want is men who will support me when I am in the wrong. **Lord Melbourne**. Quoted in *Lord M* (David Cecil, 1954), vol. 2

Today professionalism is almost a byword for loyalty towards personal mercenary aims. Yet no great achievement is ever possible without a focus of loyalty which transcends the individual self. **S. K. Chakraborty**. *Management by Values: Towards Cultural Congruence* (1991)

Men are more often bribed by their loyalties and ambitions than money. **Robert H. Jackson**. "United States v. Wunderlich" (1951)

Almost all our relationships begin and most of them continue as forms of mutual exploitation. **W. H. Auden**. *The Dyers Hand* (1963)

Make yourself necessary to someone. **Ralph Waldo Emerson**. *The Conduct of Life* (1860)

Luck

I think a lot more decisions are made on serendipity than people think. Things come across their radar screens and they jump at them. **Jay W. Lorsch**. *Wall Street Journal* (October 1, 1984)

My batting average has been good, so people ask how much luck is involved. I tell them when I work 14 hours a day, 7 days a week, I get lucky. **Armand Hammer**. *International Management* (June 1966)

We must believe in luck. For how else can we explain the success of those we don't like? **Jean Cocteau**. Attributed

  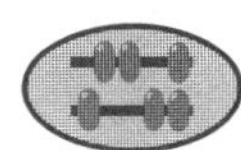   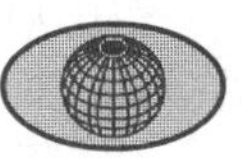   

Fortune knocks once, but misfortune has much more patience. **Laurence J. Peter**. *The Peter Principle: Why Things Always Go Wrong* (co-written with Raymond Hull, 1969)

Where observation is concerned, chance favors only the prepared mind. **Louis Pasteur**. Address (December 1854)

What we call luck is the inner man externalized. We make things happen to us. **Robertson Davies**. *What's Bred in the Bone* (1985)

With all due respect to Microsoft and Intel, there is no substitute for being in the right place at the right time. **Andrew S. Grove**. *Fortune* (June 1993)

I've found that luck is quite predictable. If you want more luck, take more chances. Be more active. Show up more often. **Brian Tracy**. Quoted in *How to Succeed in Life* (Moses Michael, 2007)

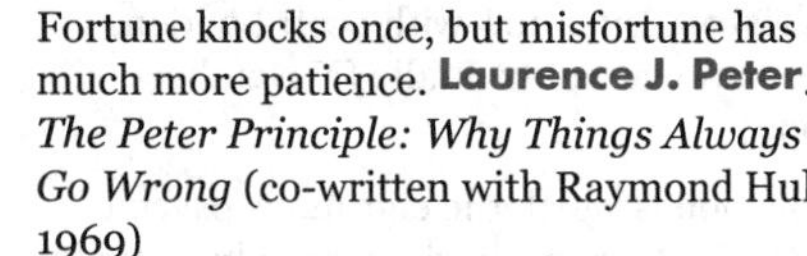

Management

The first steps to becoming a really great manager are simply common sense; but common sense is not very common. **Gerald M. Blair**. *What Makes a Great Manager* (2000)

Nobody is sure anymore who really runs the company (not even the people who are credited with running it), but the company does run. **Joseph Heller**. *Something Happened* (1974)

Top management is supposed to be a tree full of owls...hooting when management heads into the wrong part of the forest. I'm still unpersuaded they even know where the forest is. **Robert Townsend**. *Further up the Organization* (1984)

This blight is management—the dreaded four Ms, male, middle class, middle-aged and mediocre. **Janet Street-Porter**. Referring to television management in the United Kingdom. MacTaggart Lecture, Edinburgh Television Festival, Scotland (August 1995)

Management is more fun, more creative, more personal, more political and more intuitive than any textbook. **Charles Handy**. *Gods of Management* (1986)

At best we live by homely proverbs, at worst we live by pompous inanities. **Herbert A. Simon**. *Administrative Behavior* (1947)

The manager's job is to thrive in a chaotic world he cannot control. He is at last reconciled to being, openly, an intermediary. **Theodore Zeldin**. *An Intimate History of Humanity* (1994)

Of all business activities, 99% are routine...The entire 100% can be handled by managing the 1% of exceptions. **Alfred P. Sloan**. "The Most Important Things I Learned About Management," *System* (August 1924)

To be dilatory about giving orders, but to expect absolute punctuality, that is called being a tormentor. **Confucius**. *Analects* (500? BC)

Management, a science? Of course not, it's just a wastepaper basket full of recipes which provided the dish of the day during a few years of plenty and economic growth. Now the recipes are inappropriate and the companies which persist in following them will disappear. **Léon Courville**. Quoted in *The Unconscious Civilization* (John Ralston Saul, 1995)

Bad administration, to be sure, can destroy good policy; but good administration can never save bad policy. **Adlai E. Stevenson**. Speech, Los Angeles (September 11, 1952)

A good manager is a man who isn't worried about his own career but rather the careers of those who work for him. **H. S. M. Burns**. Quoted in *Men at the Top* (Osborn Elliott, 1959)

A manager is an assistant to his men. **Thomas J. Watson, Sr**. Quoted in *Father, Son & Co.: My Life at IBM and Beyond* (Thomas J. Watson, Jr, and Peter Petre, 1990)

A couple of hours in a hot kitchen can teach you as much about management as the latest books on re-engineering or total quality management. **Tom Peters**. "The Way the Cookie Crumbles" (1995)

He not only conducts his version of Beethoven and Bach, but scores it as he goes along. **Tom Peters**. Referring to the management style of Cable Network News. *Liberation Management* (1992)

Managing is getting paid for home runs someone else hits. **Casey Stengel**. Attributed

Responsibility without control is at the core of management. **Paul Corrigan**. *Shakespeare on Management* (1999)

Management today is reactive behavior. You put your hand on a hot stove and yank it off. A cat would know to do as much. **W. Edwards Deming**. Quoted in *BusinessWeek* (January 10, 1994)

Frightened, nervous managers use thick, convoluted planning books and busy slides filled with everything they've known since childhood. **Jack Welch**. *Harvard Business Review* (September–October 1989)

Society has become unmanageable as a result of management. **Henry Mintzberg**. *Mintzberg on Management* (1989)

The key managerial processes are enormously complex and mysterious, drawing on the vaguest of information and using the least articulated of mental processes. **Henry Mintzberg**. *Harvard Business Review* (July–August 1976)

People no more buy management books for their insights into epistemology than they read *Playboy* for the essays by John Updike. **Anonymous**. *Economist (London)* (May 31, 1997)

Traditional management structures were devised when information was a scarce commodity, so that knowledge about how to run the business could be communicated layer by layer. **Raymond W. Smith**. Speech (October 17, 1995)

Most of what we call management consists of making it difficult for people to get their work done. **Peter F. Drucker**. *Management: Tasks, Responsibilities and Practises* (1973)

No institution can possibly survive if it needs geniuses or supermen to manage it. It must be organized in such a way as to be able to get along under a leadership composed of average human beings. **Peter F. Drucker**. *Big Business* (1947)

Management means, in the last analysis, the substitution of thought for brawn and muscle, of knowledge for folklore and superstition, and of cooperation for force. **Peter F. Drucker**. Quoted in *The Financial Times Handbook of Management* (Stuart Crainer and Des Dearlove, 2004)

In large organizations, middle managers serve the purpose of relaying information up and down—orders down, numbers up. But with the new information technologies and more efficient forms of work, their purpose dwindles. **James Champy**. Quoted in the *New York Times* (January 7, 1996)

Controlled unreasonableness. **Gerry Robinson**. Referring to his personal management style. *Management Today* (April 1999)

Ultimately, the job of the manager is to get ordinary people to create extraordinary results. **Christopher Bartlett**. *The Individualised Corporation* (co-written with Sumantra Ghoshal, 1997)

We have a technique at Hewlett-Packard for helping managers and supervisors know their people and understand the work their people are doing...Management by Walking About. **David Packard**. *The HP Way* (1995)

Management must manage! **Harold S. Geneen**. *Managing* (co-written with Alvin Moscow, 1984)

I've spent 30 years going round factories. When you know something's wrong, nine times out of ten it's the management... people aren't being led right. And bad leaders invariably blame the people. **Sir John Harvey-Jones**. Interview, *Daily Telegraph (London)* (March 24, 1990)

The conventional definition of management is getting work done through people, but real management is developing people through work. **Hasan Abedi**. *Leaders* (July 1984)

There are three secrets to managing. The first secret is have patience. The second is be patient. And the third most important secret is patience. **Chuck Tanner**. Quoted in *Tales from the 1979 Pittsburgh Pirates* (John McCollister, 2005)

Good management to Wall Street means nothing more than a company with three consecutive quarters of rising earnings. Make it four quarters and you have great management. **Ralph Wanger**. Quoted in *500 of the Most Witty, Acerbic, and Erudite Things Ever Said About Money* (Philip Jenks, 2002)

Marketing

But markets today are moving targets. The only way to hit them is to launch your business like a cruise missile. **Harry V. Quadracci**. *Success* (June 1988)

Your company does not belong in any market where it cannot be the best. **Philip Kotler**. *Marketing Management* (1967)

Marketing takes a day to learn. Unfortunately, it takes a lifetime to master. **Philip Kotler**. *Marketing Management* (1967)

Every product has some element of service, and every service some element of product. **Aubrey Wilson**. *New Directions in Marketing* (1991)

One of the qualities I always seek in marketing people is curiosity. **Raoul Pinnell**. *Marketing* (June 2000)

The man who whispers down a well
About the goods he has to sell
Will not make as many dollars
As the man who climbs the tree and hollers!
Lord Leverhulme. Leverhulme was a consummate salesman, pioneering US mass-marketing techniques in Britain. Quoted in *Enlightened Entrepreneurs* (Ian Campbell Bradley, 1987), ch. 10

Manufacturers who don't test their products incur the colossal cost (and disgrace) of having their products fail on a national scale instead of dying inconspicuously and economically in test markets. **David Ogilvy**. *Confessions of an Advertising Man* (1963)

Half the sponsors don't know if their money is wasted or not; the other half do it in order not to be left out. **Anonymous**. Quoted in *Formula 1, The Business of Winning* (Russell Hotten, 1998)

No great marketing decisions have ever been made on qualitative data. **John Sculley**. Quoted in *The Intuitive Manager* (Roy Rowan, 1986)

The mass market has split into ever-multiplying, ever-changing sets of micromarkets that demand a continually expanding range of options. **Alvin Toffler**. *Powershift* (1990)

Marketing should focus on market creation, not market share. **Regis McKenna**. *The Regis Touch* (1986)

Marketing is not a function, it is the whole business seen from the customer's point of view. **Peter F. Drucker**. *The Practice of Management* (1954)

Business has only two functions—marketing and innovation. **Peter F. Drucker**. *The Daily Drucker* (2004)

Focus Groups are people who are selected on the basis of their inexplicable free time and their common love of free sandwiches. **Scott Adams**. *The Dilbert Principle* (1996)

Marketing is what you do when your product is no good. **Edwin Land**. Attributed

There's no business without show business. **Michael J. Wolf**. *The Entertainment Economy* (1999)

We're obviously going to spend a lot in marketing because we think the product sells itself. **Jim Allchin**. Attributed

There are three things that you should spend you time doing: marketing, marketing, marketing. If you are not prepared to do that, then everything else is irrelevant. **Emma Harrison**. *Daily Mail (London)* (November 14, 2004)

There is more similarity in the marketing challenge of selling a precious painting by Degas and a frosted mug of root beer than you ever thought possible. **A. Alfred Taubman**. Quoted in *The Virtual Handshake* (David Teten and Scott Allen, 2005)

Media

I can do more in communications than any conqueror could have done. **Ted Turner**. *Newsweek* (June 16, 1980)

One man saying that everything is wrong can command coast-to-coast attention in living color, a power not given to an absolute monarch a century ago. **Walter Wriston**. *Risk and Other Four Letter Words* (1986)

Television is simultaneously blamed, often by the same people, for worsening the world and for being powerless to change it. **Clive James**. *Glued to the Box* (1981)

A continuous clash of egomaniacal monsters, wasting more energy than dinosaurs and pouring rivers of money into the sand. **Robert Bolt**. Referring to the movie industry. *Sunday Times (London)* (June 1961)

For a politician to complain about the press is like a ship's captain complaining about the sea. **Enoch Powell**. *Guardian (London)* (December 1984)

We're in the attention getting business. **Peter Chernin**. *Forbes* (June 1998)

Television has made dictatorship impossible, but democracy unbearable. **Shimon Peres**. *Financial Times (London)* (January 1995)

No first world country has ever managed to eliminate so entirely from its media all objectivity—much less dissent. **Gore Vidal**. Referring to the United States. *A View from the Diner's Club* (1991)

Journalism—an ability to meet the challenge of filling the space. **Dame Rebecca West**. *New York Herald Tribune* (April 1956)

There is not one shred of evidence that the Internet has had any downward influence on North American or European newspaper circulation. **Lord Black of Crossharbour**. Press conference (March 2000)

The information highway will transform our culture as dramatically as Gutenberg's

  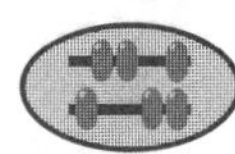   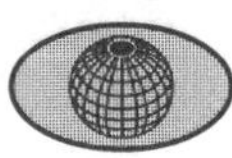   

press did the Middle Ages. **Bill Gates**. *The Road Ahead* (co-written with Nathan Myhrvold and Peter N. Rinearson, 1995)

I hate television. I hate it as much as peanuts. But I can't stop eating peanuts. **Orson Welles**. *New York Herald Tribune* (October 1956)

Freedom of the press in Britain means freedom to print such of the proprietor's prejudices as the advertisers don't object to. **Hannen Swaffer**. Quoted in *Swaff* (Tom Driberg, 1974)

No self-respecting fish would be wrapped in a Murdoch newspaper. **Mike Royko**. *Chicago Sun Times* (1984)

Gutenberg made everyone a reader. Xerox makes everybody a publisher. **Marshall McLuhan**. *Guardian (London)* (June 1977)

The medium is the message. **Marshall McLuhan**. *Understanding Media* (1964)

When I started out, people were afraid of parish priests. Now they're afraid of newspaper editors. **Michael D. Higgins**. Attributed (1997)

Government always tends to want, not a really free press, but a managed and well-conducted one. **Lord Radcliffe**. Quoted in *What the Papers Never Said* (Peter Hennessey, 1983)

A good newspaper, I suppose, is a nation talking to itself. **Arthur Miller**. *Observer (London)* (November 1961)

News is what a chap who doesn't care much about anything wants to read. **Evelyn Waugh**. *Scoop* (1938)

The media...is like an oil painting. Close up, it looks like nothing on earth. Stand back and you get the drift. **Sir Bernard Ingham**. Speech (February 1990)

Someone once described the information business as exactly the opposite of sex. When it's good, it's still lousy. **Michael Bloomberg**. *New York Times* (November 1993)

I think editors are excellent marketers. They know their audience and produce copy to appeal to them—they just don't call it marketing. **David Robinson**. *Marketing* (June 2000)

We allowed the community to tell us what was entertaining them. **Chad Hurley**. BBC News report (May 22, 2007)

Meetings

The length of a meeting rises with the number of people present and the productiveness of a meeting falls with the square of the number of people present. **Eileen Shanahan**. *Times Talk* (1963)

When committees gather, each member is necessarily an actor, uncontrollably acting out the part of himself, reading the lines that identify him, asserting his identity. **Lewis Thomas**. "On Committees," *The Medusa and the Snail* (1979)

No grand idea was ever born in a conference, but a lot of foolish ideas have died there. **F. Scott Fitzgerald**. *The Crack-Up* (1945)

A conference is a gathering of important people who, singly, can do nothing but together can decide that nothing can be done. **Fred Allen**. W. M. Martin was the president of the New York Stock Exchange. Letter to W. M. Martin (January 25, 1940)

My life has been a meeting...one long meeting. Even on the few committees I don't yet belong to, the agenda winks at me when I pass. **Gwyn Thomas**. *The Keep* (1961)

Meetings are a great trap. Soon you find yourself trying to get agreement and then the people who disagree come to think they have a right to be persuaded...However, they are indispensable when you don't want to do anything. **J. K. Galbraith**. *Ambassador's Journal* (1969), ch. 5

Outside of traffic, there is nothing that has held this country back as much as committees. **Will Rogers**. Quoted in *Will Rogers, His Life and Times* (Richard M. Ketchum, 1973)

I find that no matter how long a meeting goes on, the best ideas always come during the final five minutes, when people drop their guard and I ask them what they really think. **Michael Eisner**. *International Management* (April 1988)

A meeting is an arrangement whereby a large number of people gather together, some to say what they really do not think, some not to say what they really do. **Vladimir Voinovich**. *The Life and Extraordinary Adventures of Private Ivan Chonkin* (1969), pt. 2, ch. 6

What is a committee? A group of the unwilling, picked from the unfit, to do the unnecessary. **Richard Harkness**. *New York Herald Tribune* (1960)

Any committee that is the slightest use is a committee of people who are too busy to want to sit on it for a second longer than they have to. **Katharine Whitehorn**. "Are You Sitting Comfortably?," *Observations* (1970)

A manager's ability to turn meetings into a thinking environment is probably an organization's greatest asset. **Nancy Kline**. *Time to Think* (1999)

Whoever invented the meeting must have had Hollywood in mind. I think they should consider giving Oscars for meetings: Best Meeting of the Year, Best Supporting Meeting, Best Meeting Based on Material from Another Meeting. **William Goldman**. *Adventures in the Screen Trade* (1983), ch. 2

Mergers and Demergers

When you sell 30 percent of a business, it is like taking two limbs off a body—it's not surprising there is a negative effect on the rest of the business. **Sir Clive Thompson**. *Sunday Times (London)* (October 2000)

The very best takeovers are thoroughly hostile. I've never seen a really good company taken over. I've only seen bad ones. **Sir James Goldsmith**. *Financial Times (London)* (March 21, 1989)

You might merge with another organization, but two drunks don't make a sensible person. **Gary Hamel**. *Competing for the Future* (co-written with C. K. Prahalad, 1994)

Chief executives seem no more able to resist their biological urge to merge, than dogs can resist chasing rabbits. **Philip Coggan**. Quoted in *Treasury of Investment Wisdom* (Bernice Cohen, 1999)

The big danger in mega-mergers is that they are seen as a mating of dinosaurs. **Sir Peter Bonfield**. *Sunday Times (London)* (July 2000)

When it comes to mergers, hope triumphs over experience. **Irwin Stelzer**. Quoted in *Treasury of Investment Wisdom* (Bernice Cohen, 1999)

Dividing an elephant in half does not produce two elephants. **Peter Senge**. *The Fifth Discipline: The Art and Practice of the Learning Organization* (1990)

Leadership that's reliant on mergers and acquisitions is dangerous leadership. **John Varley**. Attributed

Mistakes

We are built to make mistakes, coded for error. **Lewis Thomas**. "To Err Is

  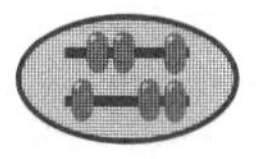   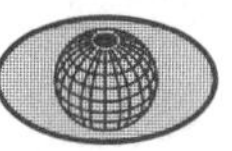   

Human," *The Medusa and the Snail* (1979)

It is a good thing to make mistakes so long as you're found out quickly. **John Maynard Keynes**. Attributed

The man who makes no mistakes does not usually make anything. **E. J. Phelps**. Speech, Mansion House, London (January 24, 1899)

If all else fails, immortality can always be achieved by a spectacular mistake. **J. K. Galbraith**. Attributed

Man errs as long as he strives. **Johann Wolfgang von Goethe**. *Faust* (1808), pt. 1

Every great mistake has a halfway moment, a split second when it can be recalled and perhaps remedied. **Pearl S. Buck**. *What America Means to Me* (1943)

I've always been able to make erroneous decisions very quickly. **Herb Kelleher**. *The Nation's Business* (October 1991)

Give me fruitful error any time, full of seeds, bursting with its own corrections. **Vilfredo Pareto**. *Mind and Society* (1916)

You can't live life without an eraser. **Tom Peters**. *The Circle of Innovation* (1998)

A man should never be ashamed to own he has been in the wrong, which is but saying, in other words, that he is wiser today than he was yesterday. **Alexander Pope**. *Thoughts on Various Subjects* (1741)

The better a man is, the more mistakes will he make—for the more new things he will try. I would never promote a man into a top level job who had not made mistakes, and big ones at that. Otherwise he is sure to be mediocre. **Peter F. Drucker**. *The Practice of Management* (1954)

We became uncompetitive by not being tolerant of mistakes. **Roberto Goizueta**. *Fortune* (May 1995)

You must learn from the mistakes of others. You can't possibly live long enough to make them all yourself. **Sam Levenson**. Attributed

If a man is both wise and lucky, he will not make the same mistake twice. But he will make any one of ten thousand brothers or cousins of the original. **Jesse Livermore**. *Reminiscences of a Stock Operator, writing as Edwin Lefèvre* (1923)

The first chance you have to avoid a loss from a foolish loan is by refusing to make it; there is no second chance. **Charlie E. Munger**. Attributed

Money

It's not how much you earn, it's how much you owe. **Ted Turner**. Speech (1986)

Money is the seed of money. The first guinea is sometimes more difficult to aquire than the second million. **Jean-Jacques Rousseau**. *Discourse Upon the Origin and Foundation of the Inequality Among Mankind* (1754)

Money is like a sixth sense without which you cannot make a complete use of the other five. **W. Somerset Maugham**. *Of Human Bondage* (1915)

To mistake money for wealth, is the same sort of error as to mistake the highway which may be the easiest way of getting to your house or lands, for the house and lands themselves. **John Stuart Mill**. *Principles of Political Economy, with Some of Their Applications to Social Philosophy* (7th ed, 1871)

Money couldn't buy you friends but you got a better class of enemy. **Spike Milligan**. *Puckoon* (1963)

Money is a singular thing. It ranks with love as man's greatest source of joy. And with death as his greatest source of anxiety. Over all history it has oppressed nearly all people in one of two ways: either it has been abundant and very unreliable, or reliable and very scarce. **J. K. Galbraith**. *The Age of Uncertainty* (1977)

To turn \$100 into \$110 is work. To turn \$100 million into \$110 million is inevitable. **Edgar Bronfman, Jr**. *Newsweek* (December 2, 1985)

Money, of course, is never just money. It's always something else, and it's always something more, and it always has the last word. **Paul Auster**. *Hand to Mouth* (1997)

Money, it turned out, was exactly like sex: you thought of nothing else if you didn't have it and thought of other things if you did. **James Baldwin**. "Black Boy Looks at the White Boy," *Esquire* (May 1961)

For the love of money is the root of all evil: which while some coveted after, they have erred from the faith, and pierced themselves through with many sorrows. **New Testament** 1 Timothy 6:10

The universal regard for money is the one hopeful fact in our civilization. **George Bernard Shaw**. *Major Barbara* (1905), Preface

I finally know what distinguishes man from the other beasts: financial worries. **Jules Renard** *Journal* (1877–1910)

Money's a horrid thing to follow, but a charming thing to meet. **Henry James**. *The Portrait of a Lady* (1881), ch. 35

Getting money is like digging with a needle; spending it is like water soaking into sand. **Anonymous**. Japanese proverb.

Money isn't everything, but it keeps the kids in touch. **Anonymous**. Quoted in *Business Wit and Wisdom* (Richard S. Zera, 2005)

There's plenty of money out there. They print more and more of it every day. But that ticket? There are only five of them, and that's all there's ever going to be. Only a dummy would give this up for something as common as money. Are you a dummy? **John August** Grandpa George persuading Charlie that he should not sell the golden ticket. Screenplay of the movie *Charlie and the Chocolate Factory* (2006)

Money is like manure. If you spread it around, it does a lot of good, but if you pile it up in one place, it stinks like hell. **Clint W. Murchison** Quoted by his son Clint Murchison, Jr. *Time* (1961)

You've heard money talking? Did you understand the message? **Marshall McLuhan** *The Mechanical Bridge* (1951)

It has been said that the love of money is the root of all evil. The want of money is so quite as truly. **Samuel Butler**. *Erewhon* (1872), ch. 20

The instinct of acquisitiveness has more perverts, I believe, than the instinct of sex. At any rate, people seem to me odder about money than about even their amours. **Aldous Huxley**. *Point Counter Point* (1928), ch. 22

There is nothing so habit forming as money. **Don Marquis**. Attributed

I'm not in Wall Street for my health. **J. P. Morgan** Quoted in *Treasury of Investment Wisdom* (Bernice Cohen, 1999)

Americans want action for their money. They are fascinated by its self-reproducing qualities if it's put to work. Gold-hoarding goes against the American grain; it fits in better with European pessimism than with America's traditional optimism. **Paula Nelson** *The Joy of Money: The Woman's Guide to Financial Freedom* (1986)

A fool and his money are soon invited everywhere. **Warren Buffett** Notice hanging in his office

In civilised society, personal merit will not serve you so much as money will. Sir, you

  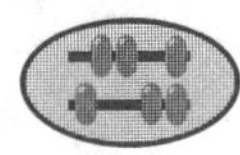   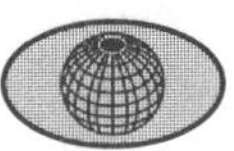   

may make the experiment. Go into the street, and give one man a lecture on morality, and another a shilling, and see which will respect you the most. **Samuel Johnson**. Quoted in *The Life of Samuel Johnson* (James Boswell, 1791)

Money, which represents the prose of life, and which is hardly spoken of in parlors without an apology, is, in its effects and laws, as beautiful as roses. **Ralph Waldo Emerson**. "Nominalist and Realist," *Essays: Second Series* (1844)

My hardest job has been to keep from being a millionaire. **Amadeo Giannini**. *American magazine* (January 1931)

We all know how the size of sums of money appear to vary in a remarkable way according as they are paid in or out. **Sir Julian Huxley**. *Essays of a Biologist* (1923)

Money is better than poverty, if only for financial reasons. **Woody Allen**. "The Early Essays," *Without Feathers* (1976)

I cannot afford to waste my time making money. **Louis Agassiz**. Quoted in *The Lazy Person's Guide to Success* (Ernie J. Zelinski, 2002)

It isn't necessary to be rich and famous to be happy. It's only necessary be rich. **Alan Alda**. Quoted in *Really Bad Business Advice* (David Dallas and Arlen Foote, 2003)

Money doesn't mind if we say it's evil, it goes from strength to strength. It's a fiction, an addiction, and a tacit conspiracy. **Martin Amis**. *Money* (1984)

A billion here, a billion there. Sooner or later it adds up to real money. **Everett Dirksen**. Attributed

What good is money if you can't inspire terror in your fellow man? **Matt Groening**. Spoken by tycoon C. Montgomery Burns in *The Simpsons*

I have never been in no situation where having money made it worse. **Clinton Jones**. Quoted in *How to License Your Million Dollar Idea* (Harvey Reese, 2002)

Money is neither my god nor my devil. It is a form of energy that tends to make us more of who we already are, whether it's greedy or loving. **Dan Millman**. Attributed

The best things in life are free
But you can give them to the birds and bees
I need money.
Barrett Strong. *Money (That's What I Want)* (1959)

Motivation

A reward once given becomes a right. **Frederick Herzberg**. *The Motivation to Work* (1959)

I can charge a man's battery and then recharge it again. But it is only when he has his own generator that we can talk about motivation. He then needs no outside stimulation. He wants to do it. **Frederick Herzberg**. *Harvard Business Review* (January–February 1968)

The common wisdom is that...managers have to learn to motivate people. Nonsense. Employees bring their own motivation. **Tom Peters**. *A Passion for Excellence* (co-written with Nancy Austin, 1985)

I do not love the money. What I do love is the getting of it...What other interest can you suggest to me? I do not read. I do not take part in politics. What can I do? **Philip D. Armour**. Quoted in *Forbes* (October 26, 1987)

Make people believe that what they think and do is important—and then get out of their way while they do it. **Jack Welch**. Quoted in *Teaching the Elephant to Dance* (James A. Belasco, 1990)

Forget socialism, capitalism, just-in-time deliveries, salary surveys, and the rest...concentrate on building organizations that accomplish that most difficult of all challenges: to make people look forward to coming to work in the morning. **Ricardo Semler**. *Maverick!* (1993)

A man always has two reasons for what he does—a good one and the real one. **J. P. Morgan**. Quoted in *Roosevelt: The Story of a Friendship* (Owen Wister, 1930)

Success is not the result of spontaneous combustion. You must set yourself on fire. **Reggie Leach**. Quoted in *Wisdom for the Soul* (Larry Chang, 2006)

Every day I get up and look through the Forbes list of the richest people in America. If I'm not there, I go to work. **Robert Orben**. Quoted in *The Winning Manager* (Julius E. Eitington, 1997)

You cannot motivate the best people with money. Money is just a way to keep score. The best people in any field are motivated by passion. **Eric S. Raymond**. Interview, *Fast Company* (1999)

The man who does not work for the love of work but only for money is not likely to make money nor find much fun in life. **Charles M. Schwab**. Quoted in *The Best Damn Book About The Profession of Selling. Period!* (Howard B. Rutstein, 2006)

The world is full of people who are waiting for someone to come along and motivate them to be the kind of people they wish they could be. The problem is that no one is coming to the rescue. **Brian Tracy**. *Eat That Frog* (2002)

Negotiation

Be careful, be cautious, do not rush into negotiations...be careful what you give away now, you may wish you had not done so should in future the balance of forces turn in your favour. **Oliver Tambo**. Advice on negotiating with the apartheid-supporting South African government. Quoted in *Mandela: The Authorised Biography* (Anthony Sampson, 2000)

Place a higher priority on discovering what a win looks like for the other person. **Harvey Robbins**. *TransCompetition* (co-written with Michael Finley, 1998)

Necessity never made a good bargain. **Benjamin Franklin**. The *Poor Richard's Almanack* series (1732–1758) were originally published under the pseudonym Richard Saunders. *Poor Richard's Almanack* (1735)

The trouble about bargaining...is that when one loses in a particular competitive negotiation, one's chances of winning the next negotiation are frequently diminished. **Theodore Zeldin**. *An Intimate History of Humanity* (1994)

A negotiator should observe everything. You must be part Sherlock Holmes, part Sigmund Freud. **Victor Kiam**. *Going For It* (1986)

Never corner an opponent, and always assist him to save his face...Avoid self-righteousness like the devil—there is nothing so self-blinding. **Sir Basil Henry Liddell Hart**. *Deterrent or Defence* (1960)

It's a well-known proposition that you know who's going to win a negotiation: it's he who pauses the longest. **Robert Holmes à Court**. *Sydney Morning Herald* (May 24, 1986)

Let us never negotiate out of fear, but let us never fear to negotiate. **John F. Kennedy**. Presidential inaugural speech (January 20, 1961)

When money is at stake, never be the first to mention sums. **Ahmed Zaki Yamani**. Quoted in *Yamani* (Jeffrey Robinson, 1988)

Anger can be an effective negotiating tool, but only as a calculated act, never as a reaction. **Mark McCormack**. *What They Don't Teach You at Harvard Business School* (1984)

Make a suggestion or assumption and let them tell you you're wrong. People also have a need to feel smarter than you are. **Mark McCormack**. *What They Don't Teach You at Harvard Business School* (1984)

Diplomacy is the art of letting someone else have your way. **Sir David Frost**. Attributed

The single and most dangerous word to be spoken in business is no. The second most dangerous word is yes. It is possible to avoid saying either. **Lois Wyse**. *Company Manners* (1987)

He knew the precise psychological moment when to say nothing. **Oscar Wilde**. *The Picture of Dorian Gray* (1891), ch. 2

Nepotism

You do not have to be the son of a rich man to be an entrepreneur. Today kids are far more willing to take risks because they've seen high rewards. **Narayana Murthy**. *Forbes* (June 2000)

The presumption that because you share a surname with someone who is good at their job, you'll be good at it too, is patently nonsense. Yet nothing seems to help you more in life than your signature. **Anonymous**. Referring to nepotism. *Guardian (London)* (July 27, 2000)

In all industries, including the media, a few names are as common as muck. This isn't talent telling, it's unashamed favoritism. **Anonymous**. Referring to nepotism. *Guardian (London)* (July 27, 2000)

I avoided the company because I wanted the opportunity to have a track record of starting a business where you are not the boss's son. **James Murdoch**. Referring to his father, Rupert Murdoch. *Forbes* (July 1998)

Office Politics

The working of great institutions is mainly the result of a vast mass of routine, petty malice, self interest, carelessness, and sheer mistake. Only a residual fraction is thought. **George Santayana**. *The Crime of Galileo* (1958)

I realized that talent would get me as far as middle management, but beyond that point it would become a matter of politics and currying favor with bosses. **Masahiro Origuchi**. *Wired Asia* (June 2000)

Weiler's Law: "Nothing is impossible for the man who doesn't have to do it himself." **Anonymous**. Quoted in *Murphy's Law and Other Reasons That Things Go Wrong* (Arthur Bloch, 1977)

There are but two means of locomotion to the top. Either people must like you so much that they push you there, or you, yourself, are so good that you push yourself there. **Gerald Sparrow**. *How to Become a Millionaire* (1960), ch. 2

He draws the bonds of his new engagements closer and tighter about him. He loses sight, by degrees, of all common sense...in the petty squabbles, intrigues, feuds, and airs of affected importance to which he has made himself accessory. **William Hazlitt**. Describing the corporate employee. "On Corporate Bodies," *Table Talk* (1821–1822), Essay 27

Opinions

It's not that I don't have opinions, rather that I'm not paid to think aloud. **Yitzhak Navon**. Quoted in the *Observer (London)* (January 16, 1983)

The more opinions you have, the less you see. **Wim Wenders**. Quoted in the *Evening Standard (London)* (April 25, 1990)

Comment is free but facts are sacred. **C. P. Scott**. *Manchester Guardian* (May 1922)

Public opinion is a weak tyrant compared with our own private opinion. **Henry David Thoreau**. *Walden, or Life in the Woods* (1854)

Some praise at morning what they blame at night;
But always think the last opinion right. **Alexander Pope**. *An Essay on Criticism* (1711)

The fact that an opinion has been widely held is no evidence whatever that it is not utterly absurd. **Bertrand Russell (Earl Russell)**. *Marriage and Morals* (1929)

The Spirit of Liberty is the spirit which is not too sure that it is right. **Learned Hand**. *The Spirit of Liberty* (1952)

Markets are never wrong—opinions often are. **Jesse Livermore**. *How To Trade in Stocks* (1940)

Opportunity

Companies worry too much about the cost of doing something. They should worry about the cost of not doing it. **Philip Kotler**. *Marketing Management* (1967)

One can present people with opportunities. One cannot make them equal to them. **Rosamond Lehmann**. *The Ballad and the Source* (1944)

Opportunities are usually disguised as hard work, so most people don't recognize them. **Ann Landers**. Attributed

Equal opportunity means everyone will have a fair chance at becoming incompetent. **Laurence J. Peter**. *Why Things Go Wrong: The Peter Principle Revisited* (1984)

A wise man will make more opportunities than he finds. **Francis Bacon (Viscount St Alban)**. "Of Ceremonies and Respects," *Essays* (1597–1625)

When written in Chinese, the word "crisis" is composed of two characters—one represents danger, and the other represents opportunity. **John F. Kennedy**. Speech in Indianapolis, Indiana (April 12, 1959)

One way of building private foresight out of public data is looking where others aren't...if you want to see the future, go to an industry confab and get the list of what was talked about. Then ask, "What did people never talk about?" That's where you're going to find opportunity. **Gary Hamel**. Interview, *Strategy + Business* (October–December 1997)

There is a tide in the affairs of men
Which, taken at the flood, leads on to fortune;
Omitted, all the voyage of their life
Is bound in shallows and in miseries.
William Shakespeare. *Julius Caesar* (1599), Act 4, Scene 3

Next to knowing when to seize an opportunity, the most important thing in life is to know when to forgo an advantage. **Benjamin Disraeli (Earl of Beaconsfield)**. *The Infernal Marriage* (1834)

I just wait until there is money lying in the corner, and all I have to do is go over there and pick it up. I do nothing in the meantime. **Jim Rogers**. On his approach to financial trading. Quoted in *The New Market Wizards* (John D. Schwager, 1992)

Only through curiosity can we discover opportunities, and only through gambling can we take advantage of them. **Clarence**

Birdseye. *American Magazine* (February 1951)

Opportunity doesn't knock. It presents itself when you beat down the door. **Kyle Chandler**. Attributed

I am far more interested in avoiding risk than I am in capturing every opportunity. My philosophy says that loss of opportunity is preferable to loss of capital. **Joseph DiNapoli**. Quoted in *Trading Systems* (Joe Krutsinger, 1997)

My first rule is not to lose money. Losing an opportunity is minor in comparison, because there are always new opportunities around the corner. **Bert Dohmen**. *Wellington Letter* (February 1999)

You never need to chase a trade. The market has plenty of opportunities. The money runs out before the opportunities do. **John Saleeby**. Attributed

Order

At the point where order and chaos most closely resemble one another, there exists the greatest possibility for broadening the human capacity to adapt to instability and uncertainty. **Daryl R. Conner**. *Leading at the Edge of Chaos* (1998)

A. A violent order is disorder; and
B. A great disorder is an order.
These two things are one.
Wallace Stevens. "Connoisseur of Chaos," *Notes Toward a Supreme Fiction* (1942)

Have a place for everything and keep the thing somewhere else. This is not advice, it is merely custom. **Mark Twain**. *Notebook* (1935)

A place for everything and everything in its place. Order is wealth. **Samuel Smiles**. *Thrift* (1875)

Confusion is a word we have invented for an order which is not understood. **Henry Miller**. "Interlude," *Tropic of Capricorn* (1939)

There is a rage to organize which is the sworn enemy of order. **Georges Duhamel**. *Vie des Martyrs* (1917)

Filing is concerned with the past; anything you actually need to see again has to do with the future. **Katharine Whitehorn**. *Sunday Best* (1976)

Large organisation is loose organisation. Nay, it would be almost as true to say that organisation is always disorganisation. **G. K. Chesterton**. "The Bluff of the Big Shops," *Outline of Sanity* (1926)

Chaos often breeds life, when order breeds habit. **Henry Brooks Adams**. *Education of Henry Adams* (1907)

Life creates order, but order does not create life. **Antoine de Saint-Exupéry**. *Letter to a Hostage* (1942)

There is a quality even meaner than outright ugliness or disorder, and this meaner quality is the dishonest mask of pretended order, achieved by ignoring or suppressing the real order that is struggling to exist and to be served. **Jane Jacobs**. *The Death and Life of Great American Cities* (1961)

Since we cannot hope for order let us withdraw with style from the chaos. **Sir Tom Stoppard**. *Lord Malaquist and Mr Moon* (1966)

There are some enterprises in which a careful disorderliness is the true method. **Herman Melville**. *Moby-Dick* (1851)

Organizations

The introduction of a new grammar, not just new words, is the key to organizational transformation. **Michael D. McMaster**. *The Intelligence Advantage* (1996)

The trouble with organizing a thing is that pretty soon folks get to paying more attention to the organization than to what they're organized for. **Laura Ingalls Wilder**. *Little Town on the Prairie* (1941)

TWIMBLE: I play it the company way
Where the company puts me, there I'll stay.
FINCH: But what is your point of view?
TWIMBLE: I have no point of view,
FINCH: Supposing the company thinks...
TWIMBLE: I think so too!
Frank Loesser. Song lyric. "The Company Way," *How to Succeed in Business without Really Trying* (1961)

In Japan, organizations and people in the organization are synonymous. **Kenichi Ohmae**. "The Myth and Reality of the Japanese Corporation," *Chief Executive* (Summer 1981)

Most of our organization tends to be arranged on the assumption that people cannot be trusted...that sort of attitude creates a paraphernalia of systems, checkers, and checkers checking checkers—expensive and deadening. **Charles Handy**. "Trust and the Virtual Organization," *Harvard Business Review* (May–June 1991)

We talk about organizations in terms not unlike those used by an Ubongi medicine man to discuss diseases. **Herbert A. Simon**. *Administrative Behavior* (1947)

Whatever the country, whatever the culture, whatever the time, when you become a big enough organization, you start to collapse and slow down. **Masayoshi Son**. Quoted in *Giant Killers* (Geoffrey James, 1996)

We're controlled by ideas and norms that have outlived their usefulness, that are only ghosts but have as much influence on our behavior as if they were alive. **Robert H. Waterman, Jr**. *Adhocracy* (1993)

Highly-adaptive, informal networks move diagonally and eliptically, skipping entire functions to get things done. **Jacques Barzun**. *Emotional Intelligence* (1996)

The core corporation is...increasingly a façade, behind which teems an array of decentralized groups and subgroups continuously contracting with similarly diffuse working units all over the world. **Robert Reich**. *The Work of Nations* (1991)

In a hierarchy every employee tends to rise to his level of incompetence. **Laurence J. Peter**. *The Peter Principle: Why Things Always Go Wrong* (co-written with Raymond Hull, 1969)

In companies whose wealth is intellectual capital, networks, rather than hierarchies, are the right organizational design. **Thomas A. Stewart**. *Intellectual Capital* (1997)

In the future the optimal form of industrial organization will be neither small companies nor large ones but network structures that share the advantages of both. **Francis Fukuyama**. *Trust: The Social Virtues and the Creation of Prosperity* (1995)

There have been seven directors or acting directors in six years. That's not an organization. That's an institutional collapse. **Daniel P. Moynihan**. Referring to the problems of managing the CIA. *Independent on Sunday (London)* (March 1997)

It can take just as much effort to run a small company as a much larger one. **Barbara Thomas**. *Management Today* (October 1999)

For a large organization to be effective, it must be simple. **Jack Welch**. Quoted in *In Search of European Excellence* (Robert Heller, 1997)

  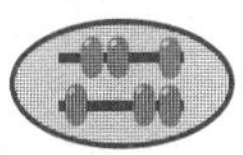   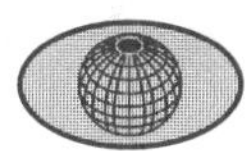   

America's business problem is that it is entering the twenty-first century with companies designed during the nineteenth century to work well in the twentieth. **Michael Hammer**. *Re-engineering the Corporation* (co-written with James Champy, 1993)

It is sobering to reflect on the extent to which the structure of our business has been dictated by the limitations of the file folder. **Michael Hammer**. *Re-engineering the Corporation* (co-written with James Champy, 1993)

Large, centralized organizations foster alienation like stagnant ponds breed algae. **Ricardo Semler**. *Maverick!* (1993)

In the knowledge economy, bureaucracy will increasingly be replaced by adhocracy, a holding unit that co-ordinates the work of numerous temporary workers. **Richard Crawford**. *In the Era of Human Capital* (1991)

Every company has two organizational structures: The formal one is written on the charts; the other is the everyday relationships of the men and women in the organization. **Harold S. Geneen**. *Managing* (co-written with Alvin Moscow, 1984)

Originality

Anyone who attempts anything original in the world must expect a bit of ridicule. **Alberto Juantorena**. Quoted in *Quick Frozen Foods* (March 1960)

Keep on the lookout for novel ideas that others have used successfully. Your idea has to be original only in its adaption to the problem you're working on. **Thomas Edison**. Quoted in *A Kick in the Seat of the Pants* (Roger von Oech, 1986)

If I have seen further, it is by standing on the shoulders of giants. **Sir Isaac Newton**. Letter to Robert Hooke (February 5,1675)

I have never avoided the influence of others. I would have considered this a cowardice and lack of sincerity toward myself. **Henri Matisse**. Interview (1907)

Original thought is like original sin: both happened before you were born to people you could not have possibly met. **Fran Lebowitz**. *Social Studies* (1981)

When people are free to do as they please, they usually imitate each other. **Eric Hoffer**. *The Passionate State of Mind* (1955)

People and Relationships

Most men are individuals no longer, so far as their business, its activities, or its moralities are concerned. They are not units but fractions. **Woodrow Wilson**. Speech (August 1910)

Get to know your people. What they do well, what they enjoy doing, what their weaknesses and strengths are, and what they want and need to get from their job. **Robert Townsend**. *Further Up the Organization* (1984)

Distinguish between the person and the behavior or performance. **Stephen Covey**. *Thirty Methods of Influence* (1991)

The more time I spend with our people, the more I find out about our business. **Herb Kelleher**. *The Nation's Business* (October 1991)

You cannot love an employee into creativity, although you can...avoid his dissatisfactions with the way you treat him. **Frederick Herzberg**. *Work and the Nature of Man* (1966), ch. 6

If future competitiveness depends on treating people as an important part of the institution, the least respectful thing I can imagine doing to a human being is asking him to urinate in a cup. **Tom Peters**. Said in testimony before the California state legislature, November 28, 1993. *New York Times* (1993)

The best way to guarantee a steady stream of new ideas is to make sure that each person in your organization is as different as possible from the others. Under these conditions, and only these conditions, will people maintain varied perspectives and demonstrate their knowledge in different ways. **Nicholas Negroponte**. "Where Do New Ideas Come From," *Wired Magazine* (January 4, 1996)

If you were to hire household staff to cook, clean, drive, stoke the fire, and answer the door, can you imagine suggesting that they not talk to each other, not see what each other is doing, not coordinate their functions? **Nicholas Negroponte**. Referring to the pressure on work relationships in an office. *Being Digital* (1995)

If you are planning for one year, plant rice. If you are planning for ten years, plant trees. If you are planning for 100 years, plant people. **Anonymous**. Indian proverb.

Develop the business around the people; build it, don't buy it; and, then, be the best. **Sir Richard Branson**. Speech to the Institute of Directors, London. "Growing Bigger While Still Staying Small" (May 1993)

The best minute I spend is the one I invest in people. **Kenneth Blanchard**. *The One Minute Manager* (1993)

No office anywhere on earth is so puritanical, impeccable, elegant, sterile or incorruptible as not to contain the yeast for at least one affair...just let a yeast raiser into the place and first thing you know—bread! **Helen Gurley Brown**. *Sex and the Office* (1964)

There is practically no area of business where the difference between rhetoric and actuality is greater than in the handling of people. **Sir John Harvey-Jones**. *All Together Now* (1994)

You can be totally rational with a machine. But, if you work with people, sometimes logic has to take a back seat to understanding. **Akio Morita**. *Made in Japan* (1986)

People are now becoming the most expensive optional component of the production process and technology is becoming the cheapest. **Michael Dunkerley**. *The Jobless Economy* (1996)

Perfection

The indefatigable pursuit of an unattainable perfection...is what alone gives a meaning to our life on this unavailing star. **Logan Pearsall Smith**. "Art and Letters," *Afterthoughts* (1931)

When you consider something ideal, you lose the opportunity to improve it. **Shoji Shiba**. Quoted in "Toyota's Fresh Look at JIT [Just-In-Time]," *Financial Times (London)* (September 10, 1990)

Perfection can be a fetish. **Bernard Leach**. *The Potter's Challenge* (1976)

An environment which calls for perfection is not likely to be easy. But aiming for it is always good for progress. **Thomas J. Watson, Jr.** *A Business and Its Beliefs* (1963)

Performance

Resolve to perform what you ought. Perform without fail what you resolve. **Benjamin Franklin**. The fourth of his 13 precepts for moral living. *Benjamin*

  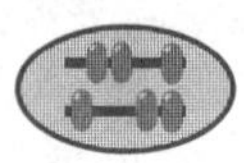 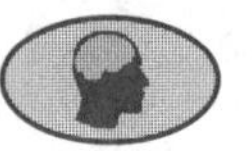  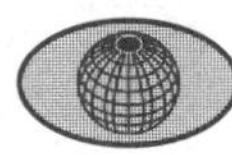 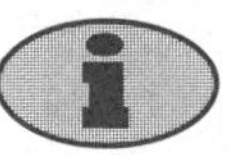  

Franklin's Autobiography (1793), pt. 2

Your legacy should be that you made it better than it was when you got it. **Lee Iacocca**. *Talking Straight* (1988)

It is an immutable law in business that words are words, explanations are explanations, promises are promises—but only performance is reality. **Harold S. Geneen**. *Managing* (co-written with Alvin Moscow, 1984)

Performance stands out like a ton of diamonds. Non-performance can always be explained away. **Harold S. Geneen**. *Managing* (co-written with Alvin Moscow, 1984)

There are no hidden genuises in large corporations. It's so obvious when someone is good and does well. **Jean-Pierre Garnier**. *The Times (London)* (September 26, 2005)

Best practices usually aren't. **Christopher Locke**. *The Cluetrain Manifesto* (2000)

The best performance improvement is the transition from the non-working state to the working state. **John Ousterhout**. Attributed

Shoulda, coulda, and woulda won't get it done. **Pat Riley**. *The Winner Within* (1993)

Persistence

Nothing in the world can take the place of persistence. Talent will not; nothing is more common than unsuccessful men of talent. Genius will not; unrewarded genius is almost a proverb. Education will not; the world is full of educated derelicts. Persistence and determination are omnipotent. **Calvin Coolidge**. Quoted at his memorial service (1933). Attributed

It's dogged as does it. It ain't thinking about it. **Anthony Trollope**. *The Last Chronicle of Barset* (1867), vol. 1, ch. 61

We're gonna stay on until the end of the world. And when that day comes we'll cover it, play Nearer My God to Thee and sign off. **Ted Turner**. Referring to his ambitions for the then fledgling Cable News Network. Quoted in *The Corporate Warriors* (Douglas K. Ramsey, 1988)

We must just KBO. **Sir Winston Churchill**. KBO stands for Keep Buggering On. Quoted in *Finest Hour* (Martin Gilbert, 1983)

You can eat an elephant one bit at a time. **Mary Kay Ash**. *Mary Kay* (1981)

How you start is important, but it is how you finish that counts. In the race for success, speed is less important than stamina. The sticker outlasts the sprinter. **Bertie Charles Forbes**. Quoted in *Reader's Digest* (1993)

Perseverance may be just as important as speed in the battle for the future. **Gary Hamel**. *Competing for the Future* (co-written with C. K. Prahalad, 1994)

Perseverance is more prevailing than violence; and many things which cannot be overcome when they are together, yield themselves up when taken little by little. **Plutarch**. "Sertorius," *Parallel Lives* (1st century AD), sect. 16

I am extraordinarily patient, provided I get my own way in the end. **Baroness Thatcher**. *Observer (London)* (April 1989)

I just love it when people say I can't do something. **David Andrews**. Quoted in *CNN: The Inside Story* (Hank Whittemore, 1990)

There are no secrets to success: don't waste time looking for them. Success is the result of perfection, hard work, learning from failure, loyalty to those for whom you work, and persistence. **Colin Powell**. *Colin Powell* (1989)

The sea does not reward those who are too anxious, too greedy, or too impatient... Patience, patience, patience, is what the sea teaches. **Anne Morrow Lindbergh**. *Gift from the Sea* (1955)

Irresolute men are sometimes very persistent in their undertakings, because if they give up their designs they would have to make a second resolution. **Giacomo Leopardi**. "Sayings of Filippo Ottonieri," *Essays, Dialogues, and Thoughts* (1827)

Saving New York City from bankruptcy is like making love to a gorilla. You don't stop when you're tired; you stop when he's tired. **Felix Rohatyn**. Quoted in *500 of the Most Witty, Acerbic, and Erudite Things Ever Said About Money* (Philip Jenks, 2002)

You have to put in many, many, many tiny efforts that nobody sees or appreciates before you achieve anything worthwhile. **Brian Tracy**. Quoted in *101 Best Ways to Get Ahead* (Michael E. Angier, 2004)

Personalities

Just look at him. He runs his company with five people in an office the size of a closet. **Katharine Graham**. Referring to Warren Buffett. *US News & World Report* (1986)

I've got a virtually limitless supply of bullshit. **Ted Turner**. Interview, *Playboy* (1978)

If a guy is over 25 percent jerk, he's in trouble. And Henry was 95 percent. **Lee Iacocca**. Referring to Henry Ford II. Said in a speech to market analysts in Detroit. Quoted in *Time* (April 1, 1985)

I'm not retiring because I'm old and tired. I'm retiring because an organization has had 20 years of me. My success will be determined by how well my successor grows it in the next 20 years. **Jack Welch**. Referring to his planned retirement on December 31, 2000. Quoted in "The Ultimate Manager," *Fortune* (November 22, 1999)

I consider that I am a revolutionary socialist. **Tiny Rowland**. Quoted in *My Life with Tiny* (Richard Hall, 1987)

There's only room for one bigmouth in my organisation, and that's me. **Sir Alan Sugar**. *The Apprentice (UK)*

For exercise, I wind my watch. **Robert Maxwell**. Quoted in *Time* (November 28, 1988)

Doing business with Alan Bond is like wrestling with a pig. You both get sprayed with mud and the pig loves it. **Anonymous**. An anonymous Texan banker on Bond's famously aggressive business strategy. *Sunday Times (London)* (February 12, 1989)

Bill Gates follows somebody's tail lights for a while then zooms past. Soon there will be no tail lights left. **Andrew S. Grove**. *BusinessWeek* (June 1994)

Philanthropy

I've been learning how to give. It's something you have to keep working on, because people like money the way they do their homes and their dogs. **Ted Turner**. *New York Times* (September 20, 1997)

The man who dies rich dies disgraced. **Andrew Carnegie**. "Wealth," *North American Review* (June 1889)

By this time two years I can so arrange all my business as to secure at least 50,000 per annum. Beyond this never earn—make no effort to increase fortune, but spend the surplus each year for benevolent purposes **Andrew Carnegie**. Carnegie's spelling was not always very good—benovelent—and, indeed, he gave financial backing to

  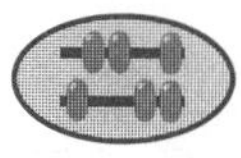   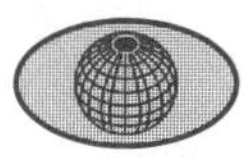   

the Simplified Spelling Board. "Private memo to himself" (December 1868)

If you show people the problems and you show people the solutions they will be moved to act. **Bill Gates**. Speech, Live 8 concert, London (July 2, 2005)

I believe it is my duty to make money and still more money and to use the money I make for the good of my fellow man according to the dictates of my conscience. **John D. Rockefeller**. Interview (1905)

The big opportunity that I see now is shepherding this wealth that has been created into our philanthropic goals. Those goals have to do with rekindling a sense of the community, reminding people that it's important to be part of your community and there's a benefit that comes with being part of your community. **Pierre M. Omidyar**. Interview, *Academy of Achievement* (October 2000)

Half the day he engages in the most ruthless financial exploitations, ruining the lives of hundreds of thousands, even millions. The other half he just gives part of it back. **Slavoj Ž ižek**. On George Soros's philanthropic activities. *The Reality of the Virtual* (2007)

Earn as much as you can. Save as much as you can. Invest as much as you can. Give as much as you can. **Revd John Wellesly**. Attributed

Planning

Managers who extensively plan the future get the timing wrong. **Shona L. Brown**. *Competing on the Edge* (co-written with Kathleen M. Eisenhardt, 1998)

There is nothing so disastrous as a rational policy in an irrational world. **John Maynard Keynes**. Quoted in *The Money Game* (Adam Smith, 1976)

Basing our happiness on our ability to control everything is futile. **Stephen Covey**. *First Things First: To Live, To Love, To Learn, To Leave a Legacy* (1994)

In preparing for battle I have always found that plans are useless, but planning is indispensible. **Dwight David Eisenhower**. Quoted in "Krushchev," *Six Crises* (Richard Nixon, 1962)

We can chart the path to the future clearly and wisely only when we know the path which has led to the present. **Adlai E. Stevenson**. Speech, Richmond, Virginia (September 20, 1952)

There was no business plan, no model. It was just guts. **Peter Chernin**. Referring to the planning style of News Corporation. *Forbes* (June 1998)

Grand business plans are all very well, but nothing beats dipping your toe in the water. **Karan Bilimoria**. *Sunday Times (London)* (October 2000)

If we had had more time for discussion we should probably have made a great many more mistakes. **Leon Trotsky**. Referring to discussions of the Soviet Communist Party's Central Committee about the Red Army. *My Diary* (1930), ch. 36

Hindsight is good, foresight is better; but second sight is best of all. **Evan Esar**. Attributed

A lot of companies...find planning more interesting than getting out a saleable product. **Ed Wrapp**. *Dunn's Review* (September 1980)

To be practical, any plan must take account of the enemy's power to frustrate it. **Karl von Clausewitz**. *On War* (1831)

Planning ahead is a matter of class. The rich and even the middle class plan for future generations, but the poor can plan ahead only a few weeks or days. **Gloria Steinem**. "The Time Factor," *Ms.* (March 1980)

Plans are only good intentions unless they immediately degenerate into hard work. **Peter F. Drucker**. Quoted in *The Definitive Drucker* (Elizabeth Haas Edersheim, 2007)

Today, if someone showed me a five-year plan, I'd toss out the pages detailing Years Three, Four, and Five as pure fantasy...Anyone who thinks he or she can evaluate business conditions five years from now, flunks. **Mark McCormack**. *Staying Street Smart in the Internet Age: What Hasn't Changed about the Way We Do Business* (2000), Introduction

Life is what happens to you while you're busy making other plans. **John Lennon**. *Beautiful Boy Double Fantasy* (1980)

It takes as much energy to wish as it does to plan. **Eleanor Roosevelt**. Quoted in *From Scratch and on a Shoestring* (Arthur A. Leidecker, 2006)

Central planning didn't work for Stalin or Mao, and it won't work for an entrepreneur either. **Michael Bloomberg**. *Bloomberg on Bloomberg* (co-written with Matthew Winkler, 1997)

You need to plan the way a fire department plans: it cannot anticipate where the next fire will be, so it has to shape an energetic and efficient team that is capable of responding to the unanticipated as well as to any ordinary event. **Andrew S. Grove**. *Only the Paranoid Survive: How to Exploit the Crisis Points That Challenge Every Company and Career* (1996), Preface

Power

Behind the screen of the ballot, the real holders of power...are the great industrial and monetary monopolies who own our national economic life. **Florence Luscomb**. Attributed

Women have so much power that even hearing the word power frightens them. **Harriet Rubin**. *www.tompeters.com* (2000)

Influence, position and wealth are not given for nothing and we must try to use them as we would wish at the last we had done. **Jeremiah James Colman**. Quoted in *Enlightened Entrepreneurs* (Ian Campbell Bradley, 1987), ch. 5

The quality of the will to power is, precisely, growth. Achievement is its cancellation. To be, the will to power must increase with each fulfillment, making the fulfillment only a step to a further one. The vaster the power gained the vaster the appetite for more. **Ursula K. Le Guin**. *The Lathe of Heaven* (1971), ch. 9

Power-worship blurs political judgement because it leads, almost unavoidably, to the belief that present trends will continue. Whoever is winning at the moment will always seem to be invincible. **George Orwell**. "Second Thoughts on James Burnham," *Shooting an Elephant* (1950)

The stronger man's argument is always the best. **Jean de La Fontaine**. "The Wolf and the Lamb," *Fables* (1668), bk. 1, fable 10

Alexander at the head of the world never tasted the fine pleasure that boys of his own age have enjoyed at the head of a school. **Horace Walpole (Earl of Orford)**. Letter (May 6, 1736)

I was allowed to ring the bell for five minutes until everyone was in assembly. It was the beginning of power. **Jeffrey Archer (Lord Archer of Weston-Super-Mare)**. Referring to his experience at school. Quoted in *Daily Telegraph (London)* (March 16, 1988)

The exercise of power is determined by thousands of interactions between the world of the powerful and that of the powerless, all the more so because these

  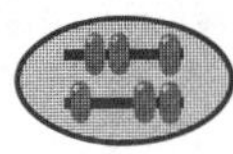   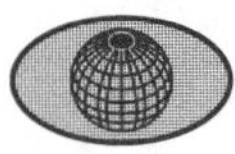   

worlds are never divided by a sharp line; everyone has a small part of himself in both. **Václav Havel**. *Disturbing the Peace* (1990), ch. 5

He did not care in which direction the car was travelling, so long as he remained in the driver's seat. **Lord Beaverbrook**. Referring to Lloyd George. *New Statesman* (June 14, 1963)

Power is the ability to get things done. **Rosabeth Moss Kanter**. *Getting It All Together: Communes Past, Present, Future* (1996)

A big man has no time really to do anything but just sit and be big. **F. Scott Fitzgerald**. *This Side of Paradise* (1920)

The purpose of getting power is to be able to give it away. **Aneurin Bevan**. Quoted in *Aneurin Bevan* (Michael Foot, 1962), vol. 1, ch. 1

Power corrupts, but lack of power corrupts absolutely. **Adlai E. Stevenson**. Referring to Lord Acton's quotation about power corrupting and absolute power corrupting absolutely. Quoted in *Observer (London)* (January 1963)

You must either conquer and rule or serve and lose, suffer or triumph, be the anvil or the hammer. **Johann Wolfgang von Goethe**. *Der Gross-Cophta* (1791), bk. 2

Real power is creating stuff. **Geraldine Laybourne**. "The 50 Most Powerful Women in American Business," *Fortune* (Patricia Sellers and Cora Daniels, October 1999)

Those who have been once intoxicated with power and have derived any kind of emolument from it, even though but for one year, never can willingly abandon it. They may be distressed in the midst of all their power; but they will never look to anything but power for their relief. **Edmund Burke**. Letter to a member of the National Assembly (January 19, 1791)

Power intoxicates men. It is never voluntarily surrendered. It must be taken from them. **James F. Byrnes**. Quoted in the *New York Times* (May 15, 1956)

But the relationship of morality and power is a very subtle one. Because ultimately power without morality is no longer power. **James Baldwin**. Conversation between James Baldwin and Nikki Giovanni. *A Dialogue* (1973)

The need to exert power, when thwarted in the open fields of life, is the more likely to assert itself in trifles. **Charles Horton Cooley**. *Human Nature and the Social Order* (1902), ch. 5

Whenever you're sitting across from some important person, always picture him sitting there in a suit of long red underwear. That's the way I always operated in business. **Joseph P. Kennedy**. Quoted in *No Final Victories* (Lawrence O'Brien, 1974)

In the new organisation, power flows from expertise, not position. **Thomas A. Stewart**. *Intellectual Capital* (1997)

You carry forever the fingerprint that comes from being under someone's thumb. **Nancy Banks-Smith**. *Guardian (London)* (January 30, 1991)

The good want power, but to weep barren tears.
The powerful goodness want: worse need for them.
...And all best things are thus confused with ill.
Percy Bysshe Shelley. *Prometheus Unbound* (1819), l. 625

Every Communist must grasp the truth. Political power grows out of the barrel of a gun. **Mao Zedong**. Speech to Central Committee, Communist Party (November 6, 1938)

Men of power have no time to read; yet the men who do not read are unfit for power. **Michael Foot**. *Debts of Honour* (1980)

An honest man can feel no pleasure in the exercise of power over his fellow citizens. **Thomas Jefferson**. Letter to John Melish (January 13, 1813)

God must have loved the People in Power, for he made them so very like their own image of him. **Kenneth Patchen**. Quoted in the *Guardian (London)* (February 1, 1972)

A friend in power is a friend lost. **Henry Brooks Adams**. *Education of Henry Adams* (1907)

The strongest poison ever known
Came from Caesar's laurel crown.
William Blake. "Auguries of Innocence" (1803?)

Monopoly is a terrible thing, till you have it. **Rupert Murdoch**. *The New Yorker* (1979)

Powerful men in particular suffer from the delusion that human beings have no memories. I would go so far as to say that the distinguishing trait of powerful men is the psychotic certainty that people forget acts of infamy as easily as their parents' birthdays. **Stephen Vizinczey**. "Commentary on a Poem," *Horizon* (October 1976)

Avoid having your ego so close to your position that, when your position fails, your ego goes with it. **Colin Powell**. Kept on his desk at the Pentagon. Attributed

The megalomaniac differs from the narcissist by the fact that he wishes to be powerful rather than charming, and seeks to be feared rather than loved. To this type belong many lunatics and most of the great men of history. **Bertrand Russell (Earl Russell)**. *The Conquest of Happiness* (1930), ch. 1

Power is the ultimate aphrodisiac. **Henry Kissinger**. *New York Times* (January 19, 1971)

Power is not only what you have but what the enemy thinks you have. **Saul Alinsky**. "Tactics," *Rules for Radicals* (1971)

The appetite for power, even for universal power, is only insane when there is no possibility of indulging it; a man who sees the possibility opening before him and does not try to grasp it, even at the risk of destroying himself and his country, is either a saint or a mediocrity. **Simone Weil**. "Cold War Policy in 1939," *Selected Essays* (Richard Rees, ed, 1962)

Life is a search after power. **Ralph Waldo Emerson**. "Power," *The Conduct of Life* (1860)

Those in possession of absolute power can not only prophesy and make their prophecies come true, but they can also lie and make their lies come true. **Eric Hoffer**. *The Passionate State of Mind* (1955)

Power tends to corrupt and absolute power corrupts absolutely. **Lord Acton**. Letter to Bishop Mandell Creighton (April 5, 1887)

Being chairman of the Senate Commerce Committee is like being a mosquito in a nudist colony. **John McCain**. Quoted in *Fortune* (March 2003)

Praise and Recognition

We find it easy to believe that praise is sincere: why should anyone lie in telling us the truth? **Jean Rostand**. *De la vanité* (1925)

There is no end to what you can accomplish if you don't care who gets the credit. **Florence Luscomb**. Quoted in *Moving the Mountain* (E. Cantorow, 1980)

If you cannot communicate your many worthwhile achievements, no one will ever know what you have done. **Jac Fitz-Enz**.

  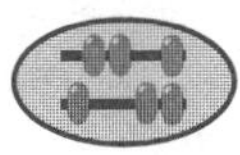   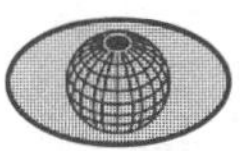   

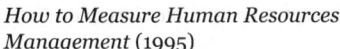

How to Measure Human Resources Management (1995)

They gave me star treatment when I was making a lot of money. But I was just as good when I was poor. **Bob Marley**. Quoted in *True Confessions* (Jon Winokar, 1992)

It is better to deserve honors and not have them than to have them and not deserve them. **Mark Twain**. Quoted in *Woodbury Reports Archives* (August 1995)

People ask you for criticism but they only want praise. **W. Somerset Maugham**. *Of Human Bondage* (1915)

It goes back to all of us wanting to be in Hollywood. We're all dying to win an Oscar. **Jerry Della Femina**. *Wall Street Journal* (1987)

Sandwich every bit of criticism between two layers of praise. **Mary Kay Ash**. Attributed

Always establish a paper trail to make sure others can't take credit for what you do. **Lord Stevenson of Coddenham**. *Management Today* (April 1999)

Watch how a man takes praise and there you have the measure of him. **Thomas Burke**. *T. P.'s Weekly* (June 8, 1928)

Congratulations offer more potential than cash. The amount of available cash is limited, but managers have an unlimited supply of congratulations. It's important to pay people fairly, but managers also should heap on congratulations and feed people's souls. **Kenneth Blanchard**. "The Gift of the Goose," *Quality Digest* (December 1997)

The world is divided into people who do things and people who get the credit. Try, if you can, to belong to the first class. There's far less competition. **Dwight Morrow**. Written in a letter to his son. Quoted in *Dwight Morrow* (Harold Nicolson, 1935)

Principles

You can't learn too soon that the most useful thing about a principle is that it can always be sacrificed to expediency. **W. Somerset Maugham**. *The Circle* (1921)

Strong men don't compromise, it is said, and principles should never be compromised. I shall argue that strong men, conversely, know when to compromise and that all principles can be compromised to serve a greater principle. **Charles Handy**. *The Age of Paradox* (1994)

It is easier to fight for one's principles than to live up to them. **Alfred Adler**. Quoted in *Alfred Adler* (Phyllis Bottome, 1939)

The Great Principles on which we will build this Business are as everlasting as the Pyramids. **Gordon Selfridge**. Preliminary announcement, opening of Selfridge's store, London. (1909)

Principles always become a matter of vehement discussion when practice is at an ebb. **George Gissing**. *Private Papers of Henry Ryecroft* (1903)

Occasionally, a man must rise above principles. **Warren Buffett**. Annual report (1991)

Priorities

My #1 job here at Apple is to make sure that the top 100 people are A+ players. And everything else will take care of itself. If the top 50 people are right, it just cascades down throughout the whole organization. **Steve Jobs**. Quoted in "Steve's Two Jobs," *Time* (Michael Krantz, October 18, 1999)

Managing intellectual assets has become the single most important task of business. **Thomas A. Stewart**. *Intellectual Capital* (1997)

Survive first and make money afterwards. **George Soros**. *Soros on Soros* (1995)

Having a sick child has put life into perspective for me. I would not care if I had no money and no material possessions if I could have Georgina's health. **Nicola Horlick**. Referring to the fact that her eldest child, Georgina, has leukemia. *Can You Have It All?* (1997)

First things first, second things never. **Shirley Conran**. *Superwoman* (1975)

Ownership is not the most important thing. IT IS THE ONLY THING THAT COUNTS. **Felix Dennis**. *How to Get Rich* (2006)

It's hard enough to make money that you can't do it by accident. Unless it's your first priority, it's unlikely to happen at all. **Paul Graham**. *Why Smart People Have Bad Ideas* (2005)

Problems and Obstacles

We live in an information economy. The problem is that information's usually impossible to get, at least in the right place, at the right time. **Steve Jobs**. Interview, "The Next Insanely Great Thing," *Wired Magazine* (February 1996)

If you eat a frog first thing in the morning, the rest of your day will be wonderful. **Mark Twain**. A "frog" being any unpleasant or difficult task that you would rather put off. Quoted in *Eat That Frog* (Brian Tracy, 2002)

Success is to be measured not so much by the position that one has reached in life as by the obstacles which one has overcome while trying to succeed. **Booker T. Washington**. *Up from Slavery* (1901)

It is characteristic of all deep human problems that they are not to be approached without some humor and some bewilderment. **Freeman Dyson**. *Disturbing the Universe* (1979)

I suppose it is tempting, if the only tool you have is a hammer, to treat everything as if it were a nail. **Abraham Maslow**. *The Psychology of Science: A Reconnaissance* (1966)

One must think until it hurts. One must worry a problem in one's mind until it seems there cannot be another aspect of it that hasn't been considered. **Lord Thomson of Fleet**. *After I Was Sixty* (1975)

Problems are the price of progress. Don't bring me anything but trouble. Good news weakens me. **Charles Franklin Kettering**. Quoted in *Strategy + Business* (1997)

It isn't that they can't see the solution. It is that they can't see the problem. **G. K. Chesterton**. *The Scandal of Father Brown* (1935)

I need problems. A good problem makes me come alive. **Tiny Rowland**. *Sunday Times (London)* (March 4, 1990)

Every solution of a problem raises new unsolved problems. **Sir Karl Raimund Popper**. *Conjectures and Refutations* (1963)

Beware of the danger signals that flag problems: silence, secretiveness, or sudden outburst. **Sylvia Porter**. Attributed

My door is always open—bring me your problems. This is guaranteed to turn on every whiner, lackey, and neurotic on the property. **Robert F. Six**. Quoted in *Money Talks* (Robert W. Kent, ed, 1986)

Work only on problems that are manifestly important and seem to be nearly impossible to solve. That way you will have

  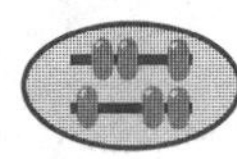   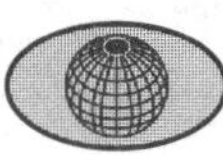   

a natural market for your product and no competition. **Edwin Land**. *Physics Today* (January 1982)

Any problem can be solved using the materials in the room. **Edwin Land**. Attributed

Problems are only opportunities in work clothes. **Henry J. Kaiser**. Quoted in obituary, *New York Times* (August 24, 1967)

The greatest risk lies in not knowing what you don't know. In a fast changing marketplace such as the Internet, this trap seems to be so open and so wide. **William (Walid) Mougayar**. Referring to the challenge to managers of traditional industries of the new economy. *Opening Digital Markets* (1997), Introduction to 2nd edition

Satisfactory under-performance is a far greater problem than a crisis. **Christopher Bartlett**. *The Individualised Corporation* (co-written with Sumantra Ghoshal, 1997)

The worst possible thing...was to lie dead in the water with any problem. Solve it, solve it quickly...If you solved it wrong, it would come back and slap you in the face, and then you could solve it right. **Thomas J. Watson, Jr**. Quoted in "The Businessmen of the Century," *Fortune* (November 22, 1999)

Problems can only be solved by the people who have them. You have to try and coax them and love them into seeing ways in which they can help themselves. **Sir John Harvey-Jones**. On his approach as a Mr. Fix-It for troubled businesses. *Independent on Sunday (London)* (March 11, 1990)

That is the trouble with prosperity—it hides the defects of a business. **Harvey Firestone**. *Men and Rubber* (co-written with Samuel Crowther, 1926)

I have yet to see any problem, however complicated, which, when you looked at it in the right way, did not become still more complicated. **Poul Anderson**. *New Scientist* (September 25, 1969)

Obstacles are things a person sees when he takes his eyes off his goal. **E. Joseph Cossman**. Quoted in *How to Turn Your Million-Dollar Idea into a Reality* (Pete Williams, 2007)

If you think the problem is bad now, just wait until we've solved it. **Arthur Kasspe**. Quoted in *How to Turn Your Million-Dollar Idea into a Reality* (Pete Williams, 2007)

There is a time in the life of every problem when it is big enough you can see it, but small enough you can still solve it. **Mike Leavitt**. Speech (May 16, 2005)

Procrastination

If you have to eat a frog, don't look at it for too long. **Mark Twain**. Quoted in *Eat That Frog* (Brian Tracy, 2002)

A wrong decision isn't forever; it can always be reversed. The losses from a delayed decision *are* forever; they can never be retrieved. **J. K. Galbraith**. *A Life in Our Times* (1981)

While we're talking, envious time is fleeing: seize the day, put no trust in the future. **Horace**. *Odes* (24–23 BC), bk. 1, no. 11, l. 7

She felt weary and careworn, in the way one often does before the big job of work is tackled; that sense of premature or projected exhaustion that is the breeding-ground of all procrastination. **William Boyd**. *Brazzaville Beach* (1990)

There is no more miserable human being than the one in whom nothing is habitual but indecision. **William James**. *The Principles of Psychology* (1890), ch. 10

Make me a beautiful word for doing things tomorrow; for that surely is a great and blessed invention. **George Bernard Shaw**. *Back to Methuselah* (1921)

Business neglected is business lost. **Daniel Defoe**. *The Complete English Tradesman* (1726), vol. 1

Defer no time; delays have dangerous ends. **William Shakespeare**. *Henry VI, Part One* (1592), Act 3, Scene 3, l. 16

Tomorrow is often the busiest day of the week. **Anonymous**. Spanish proverb.

Procrastination is the thief of time. **Edward Young**. *The Complaint, or Night Thoughts on Life, Death, and Immortality* (1742–1745)

Most executives have learned that what one postpones, one actually abandons...timing is a most important element in the success of any effort. To do five years later what would have been smart to do five years earlier, is almost a sure recipe for frustration and failure. **Peter F. Drucker**. *The Effective Executive* (1967), ch. 5

If I had eight hours to chop down a tree, I'd spend six sharpening the axe. **Abraham Lincoln**. Attributed

procrastination is the
art of keeping
up with yesterday
Don Marquis. *certain maxims of archie* (1927)

No task is a long one but the task on which one dare not start. It becomes a nightmare. **Charles Baudelaire**. *My Heart Laid Bare* (1869)

Hamlet had it wrong: he who hesitates is halfway home. **Peter Bernstein**. *Against the Gods: The Remarkable Story of Risk* (1998)

The key to productivity is to rotate your avoidance techniques. **Shannon Wheeler**. *Too Much Coffee Man* comic

Productivity

Production not being the sole end of human existence, the term unproductive does not necessarily imply any stigma. **John Stuart Mill**. *Principles of Political Economy* (1848)

In an industrial society which confuses work and productivity, the necessity of producing has always been an enemy of the desire to create. **Raoul Vaneigem**. *The Revolution of Everyday Life* (1967)

Management productivity is a more appropriate term than labor productivity. Improved productivity means less human sweat, not more. **Henry Ford**. Speech, *US News & World Report* (March 1959)

I've never seen a job being done by a five-hundred person engineering team that couldn't be done better by fifty people. **C. Gordon Bell**. *Spectrum* (February 1989)

Thanks to him, we have increased the productivity of manual work 3% to 4% compounded—which is 50-fold—and on that achievement rests all the prosperity of the modern world. **Peter F. Drucker**. Referring to Frederick W. Taylor, who inspired Henry Ford's mass-production revolution. Quoted in "The Businessman of the Century," *Fortune* (November 22, 1999)

The best balance of morale for employee productivity can be described this way: happy, but with low self-esteem. **Scott Adams**. *The Dilbert Principle* (1996)

No matter how great the talent or effort, some things just take time: you can't produce a baby in one month by getting nine women pregnant. **Warren Buffett**. Attributed

When properly administered, vacations do not diminish productivity: for every week you're away and get nothing done, there's

  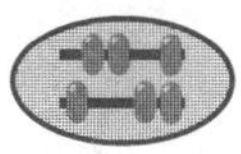   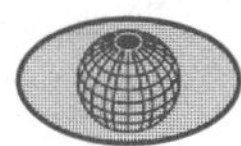   

another when your boss is away and you get twice as much done. **Daniel B. Luten**. Attributed

Products

My theory is that good furniture could be priced so that the man with a flat wallet could be attracted to it. **Ingvar Kamprad**. *Forbes* (August 2000)

Both Apple and Pixar...Their product is pure intellectual property. Bits on a disk. **Steve Jobs**. Quoted in "Steve's Two Jobs," *Time* (Michael Krantz, October 18, 1999)

Every company should work hard to obsolete its own product line before its competitors do. **Philip Kotler**. *Marketing Management* (1967)

Junk is the ideal product—the ultimate merchandise. No sales talk necessary. The client will crawl through a sewer and beg to buy. **William S. Burroughs**. *The Naked Lunch* (1959)

All products must be seen as experiments. **David Lodge**. *Relationship Marketing* (1991)

Twenty four out of twenty five new products never get out of test markets. **David Ogilvy**. *Confessions of an Advertising Man* (1963)

What makes this business difficult is that grown ups have to solve children's problems. **Horst Brandstatter**. Quoted in *Liberation Management* (Tom Peters, 1992)

No other man-made device since the shields and lances of ancient knights fulfills a man's ego like an automobile. **Lord Rootes**. Speech (1958)

I have no use for a motor car which has more spark plugs than a cow has teats. **Henry Ford**. *My Life and Work* (co-written with Samuel Crowther, 1922)

If you can't smell it, you can't sell it. **Estée Lauder**. Interview (1976)

A successful product merely gives us a head start in the race. **Sir John Harvey-Jones**. *Managing to Survive* (1993)

Anybody can cut prices, but it takes brains to produce a better article. **P. D. Armour**. Quoted in *The 101 Greatest Business Principles of All Time* (Leslie Pockell, 2004)

Profits

Civilization and profits go hand in hand. **Calvin Coolidge**. Speech (November 1920)

If there is excitement in their lives, it is contained in the figures on the profit and loss sheet. What an indictment. **Dame Anita Roddick**. Referring to companies run by accountants. *Body and Soul* (co-written with Russell Miller, 1991)

My argument is: keep the bloody bottom line at the bottom. That's where it should be. **Dame Anita Roddick**. Quoted in *The Adventure Capitalists* (Jeff Grout and Lynne Curry, 1998)

Profit has to be a means to other ends rather than an end in itself. **Charles Handy**. *The Empty Raincoat: Making Sense of the Future* (1994)

Company directors always have to prove that things are going better. They are judged like politicians, only worse, because elections are held every three months. **André Leysen**. Quoted in *Euromanagement* (H. Bloom, R. Claori, and P. de Woot, 1998)

In the foundation and development of a successful enterprise there must be a single-minded pursuit of financial profit. **C. Northcote Parkinson**. Quoted in *Famous Financial Fiascoes* (J. Train, 1995)

Where profit is, loss is hidden nearby. **Anonymous**. Japanese proverb.

Profit is like health, necessary but not the reason why we live. **Anonymous**. Statement by the London-based St. Luke's Advertising Agency. *Management Today* (April 1999)

The bottom line is in heaven. **Edwin Land**. Shareholder meeting (1977)

Short-term can be terminal. **Mark McCormack**. Referring to error of commitment to short-term profitability. *What They Don't Teach You at Harvard Business School* (1984)

Business is many things, the least of which is the balance sheet. It is a fluid, ever changing, living thing, sometimes building to great peaks, sometimes falling to crumbled lumps. **Harold S. Geneen**. *Managing* (co-written with Alvin Moscow, 1984)

I don't want to do business with those who don't make a profit, because they can't give the best service. **Lee Bristol**. Attributed

Progress

Progress, far from consisting in change, depends on retentiveness. Those who cannot remember the past are condemned to repeat it. **George Santayana**. *The Life of Reason* (1905)

If economic progress means that we become anonymous cogs in some great machine, then progress is an empty promise. **Charles Handy**. *The Empty Raincoat: Making Sense of the Future* (1994)

What we call progress is the exchange of one nuisance for another nuisance. **Havelock Ellis**. Attributed

How we feel about the evolving future tells us who we are as individuals and as a civilization: Do we search for stasis—a regulated, engineered world? Or do we embrace dynamism—a world of constant creation, discovery, and competition? **Virginia Postrel**. *The Future and Its Enemies: The Growing Conflict over Creativity, Enterprise, and Progress* (1998)

In vulgar usage, progress has come to mean limitless movement in space and time, accompanied, necessarily, by an equally limitless command of energy: culminating in limitless destruction. **Lewis Mumford**. *The Pentagon of Power* (1970)

The reasonable man adapts himself to the world; the unreasonable one persists in trying to adapt the world to himself. Therefore all progress depends on the unreasonable man. **George Bernard Shaw**. "Reason," *Maxims for Revolutionists* (1905)

Progress, therefore, is not an accident but a necessity...a part of nature. **Herbert Spencer**. *Social Statics* (1851), pt. 1, ch. 2

Progress is mostly the product of rogues. **Tom Peters**. *Liberation Management* (1992)

We have stopped believing in progress. What progress that is! **Jorge Luis Borges**. *Borges et Borges* (1969)

To go fast, row slowly. **Brendan Kennelly**. *The Power of Positive Thinking* (1972)

It's the same each time with progress. First they ignore you, then they say you're mad, then dangerous, then there's a pause and you can't find anyone who disagrees with you. **Tony Benn**. Quoted in the *Observer (London)* (October 6, 1991)

The test of our progress is not whether we add more to the abundance of those who have much; it is whether we provide enough for those who have too little. **Franklin D. Roosevelt**. Second presidential inaugural address (January 20, 1937)

All progress is based upon a universal innate desire on the part of every organism to live beyond its income. **Samuel Butler**. "Life," *Notebooks* (H. Festing-Jones, ed, 1912)

You can only stumble if you're moving. **Roberto Goizueta**. *Fortune* (May 1995)

Society never advances. It recedes as fast on one side as it gains on the other. Society acquires new arts, and loses old instincts. **Ralph Waldo Emerson**. "Self-Reliance," *Essays: First Series* (1841)

See everything. Overlook a great deal. Improve a little. **Pope John XXIII**. Quoted in *The Power of IT* (Jean De Sutter, 2004)

Much work remains to be done before we can announce our total failure to make any progress. **E. L. Kersten**. *The Art of Demotivation* (2003)

Publicity

PR cannot overcome things that shouldn't have been done. **Harold Burson**. *USA Today* (June 7, 1993)

With publicity comes humiliation. **Tama Janowitz**. Quoted in *International Herald Tribune* (September 8, 1992)

There's no such thing as bad publicity except your own obituary. **Brendan Behan**. Quoted in *My Brother Brendan* (Dominic Behan, 1965)

This famous store needs no name on the door. **Gordon Selfridge**. Referring to the fact that Selfridge removed the name from his famous London store in 1925. Quoted in *No Name on the Door* (A. H. Williams, 1957)

We must try to find ways to starve the terrorist and the hijacker of the oxygen of publicity on which they depend. **Baroness Thatcher**. Speech (July 1985)

The worst tragedy that could have befallen me was my success. I knew right away that I was through, cast out. **Jonas Salk**. Referring to other scientists' reactions to publicity surrounding his discovery of a polio vaccine. Interview (1992)

Some are born great, some achieve greatness, and some hire public relations officers. **Daniel J. Boorstin**. *The Image* (1961)

You can't shame or humiliate modern celebrities. What used to be called shame and humiliation is now called publicity. **P. J. O'Rourke**. *Give War a Chance* (1992)

The price of justice is eternal publicity. **Arnold Bennett**. *The Title* (1918)

I had worked hard for 30 years, making millions of pounds for shareholders and creating thousands of jobs for a company I loved, and I suddenly had it all taken away from me. Not for doing anything criminal. I hadn't embezzled. I hadn't lied. All I had done was say a sherry decanter was crap. **Gerald Ratner**. *Gerald Ratner: The Rise and Fall and Rise Again* (2007)

Quality

Quality is not a thing. It is an event. **Robert M. Pirsig**. *Zen and the Art of Motorcycle Maintenance* (1974)

Standards are always out of date. That's what makes them standards. **Alan Bennett**. *Forty Years On* (1969)

We have learned to live in a world of mistakes and defective products as if they were necessary to life. It is time to adapt to a new philosophy in America. **W. Edwards Deming**. *Out of the Crisis* (1992)

Don't just make it and try to sell it. But redesign it and then bring the process under control with ever-increasing quality. **W. Edwards Deming**. *Out of the Crisis* (1992)

More will mean worse. **Sir Kingsley Amis**. *Encounter* (July 1960)

Quality has to be caused, not controlled. **Philip B. Crosby**. *Quality Is Free* (1979)

The funny thing is better TV shows don't cost that much more than lousy TV shows. **Warren Buffett**. *Channels* (November 1986)

Quality control was treated as a fad here, but it's been part of the Japanese business philosophy for decades. That's why they laugh at us. **Peter Senge**. *The Fifth Discipline: The Art and Practice of the Learning Organization* (1990)

The subtle accumulation of nuances, a hundred things done a little better. **Henry Kissinger**. Quoted in *In Search of Excellence* (Tom Peters and Robert H. Waterman, 1982)

We also do cut-glass sherry decanters complete with six glasses on a silver-plated tray that your butler can serve you drinks on, all for £4.95. People say, "How can you sell this for such a low price?" I say, because it's total crap. **Gerald Ratner**. Adverse publicity for Ratner's remarks effectively destroyed his company. Speech, Institute of Directors (April 23, 1991)

Reputation

The world is not unkind, and reprobates are worse than their reputations. **Logan Pearsall Smith**. *Afterthoughts* (1931)

It took me fifteen years to discover that I had no talent for writing, but I couldn't give it up because by that time I was too famous. **Robert Benchley**. Quoted in *Robert Benchley* (Nathaniel Benchley, 1955)

Reputation, reputation, reputation—O, I ha' lost my reputation, I ha' lost the immortal part of myself, and what remains is bestial! **William Shakespeare**. *Othello* (1602–1604), Act 2, Scene 3, ll. 256–258

You can't build a reputation on what you are going to do. **Henry Ford**. Quoted in *Woodbury Reports Archives* (December 1994)

In business a reputation for keeping absolutely to the letter and spirit of an agreement, even when it is unfavorable, is the most precious of assets, although it is not entered in the balance sheet. **Viscount Chandos**. *Memoirs of Lord Chandos: An Unexpected View from the Summit* (1963)

Research

When action grows unprofitable, gather information; when information grows unprofitable, sleep. **Ursula K. Le Guin**. *The Left Hand of Darkness* (1969)

It's really hard to design products by focus groups. A lot of times, people don't know what they want until you show it to them. **Steve Jobs**. Quoted in *BusinessWeek* (May 25, 1998)

The trouble with research is that it tells you what people were thinking about yesterday, not tomorrow. It's like driving a car using a rearview mirror. **Bernard Loomis**. *International Herald Tribune* (1985)

The way to do research is to attack the facts at the point of greatest astonishment. **Celia**

  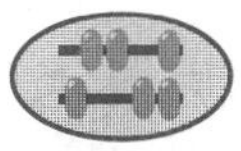   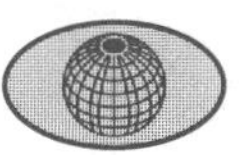   

Green. *The Decline and Fall of Science* (1977)

Basic research is what I am doing when I don't know what I am doing. **Wernher von Braun**. Quoted in *A Random Walk in Science* (R. L. Weber, 1973)

Some people use research like a drunkard uses a lamppost: for support not illumination. **David Ogilvy**. Ogilvy's advocacy of the importance of sound research reflected the experience gained during his early career selling George Gallup's innovative sampling techniques to Hollywood studios. Quoted in "Anatomies of Desire: David Ogilvy," BBC Radio 4 (September 4, 2000)

Research! A mere excuse for idleness; it has never achieved, and will never achieve any results of the slightest value. **Benjamin Jowett**. Quoted in *Unforgotten Years* (Logan Pearsall Smith, 1939)

The close relationships we form between researchers and product groups have already shown we can move the great ideas as they come along, without a schedule, into the products. **Bill Gates**. *Net News* (August 10, 1997)

My job is to help people see what I see. If it's of value, fine. And, if it's not of value, then at least I've done what I can do. **Jonas Salk**. Referring to his development of the Salk vaccine for polio. Interview (1992)

I keep six honest serving men
(They taught me all I know)
Their names
are What and Why and When
And How and Where and Who.
Rudyard Kipling. *Just So Stories* (1902)

We don't believe in market research for a new product unknown to the public. So we never do any. **Akio Morita**. Referring to his rejection of in-house engineers' concerns regarding lack of research into his idea for the Sony Walkman. *Made in Japan* (1986)

I have an simple algorithm which is, where ever you see paid researchers instead of grad students, that's not where you want to be doing research. **Larry Page**. *Lecture to the American Association for the Advancement of Science* (February 16, 2007)

Responsibility

Perhaps it is better to be irresponsible and right than to be responsible and wrong. **Sir Winston Churchill**. Party political broadcast, London (August 26, 1950)

It is impossible to get the measure of what an individual can accomplish unless the responsibility is given him. **Alfred P. Sloan**. "Modern Ideas of the Big Business World," *Work* (October 1926)

The salvation of mankind lies only in making everything the concern of all. **Aleksander Solzhenitsyn**. Nobel lecture (1970)

I don't know whether you fellows ever had a load of hay fall on you, but when they told me yesterday what had happened, I felt like the moon, the stars, and all the planets had fallen on me. **Harry S. Truman**. Said on succeeding Franklin D. Roosevelt as president. Attributed (April 1944)

The buck stops here. **Harry S. Truman**. Sign on his desk while president. Quoted in *Presidential Anecdotes* (Paul F. Boiler, 1981)

There are plenty of recommendations on how to get out of trouble cheaply and fast. Most of them come down to the same thing. Deny your responsibility. **Nancy Peretsman**. Speech (September 1967)

We are responsible for actions performed in response to circumstances for which we are not responsible. **Allan Massie**. "Etienne," *A Question of Loyalties* (1989), pt. 3, ch. 22

Whatever you blame, that you have done yourself. **Georg Groddeck**. *The Book of the It* (1923), Letter 14

Human beings were held accountable long before there were corporate bureaucracies. If the knight didn't deliver, the king cut off his head. **Alvin Toffler**. "Breaking with Bureaucracy," *Across the Board* (February 1991)

People are responsible for their opinions, but Providence is responsible for their morals. **William Butler Yeats**. Quoted in *Edward Marsh, Patron of the Arts* (Christopher Hassall, 1959), ch. 6

Responsibility is the great developer of men. **Mary Parker Follett**. *Dynamic Administration* (1941)

Responsibility is what awaits outside the Eden of Creativity. **Nadine Gordimer**. "Lecture, University of Michigan," *The Tanner Lectures on Human Values* (Sterling M. McMurrin, ed, 1985)

Those who enjoy responsibility usually get it; those who merely like exercising authority usually lose it. **Malcolm S. Forbes**. Attributed

Risk Taking

To be a leader in this new economy, you have to love risk—which means patterning your life on the heroic, not on the strategic. Acting boldly is better than acting knowingly. **Harriet Rubin**. "How Will You Fail?," *Fast Company* (1999)

There are one hundred men seeking security to one able man who is willing to risk his fortune. **J. Paul Getty**. Quoted in *The Great Getty* (Robert Lenzner, 1985)

We are pioneers and the history of pioneers is not that good. **Jeff Bezos**. *Sunday Telegraph (London)* (July 2000)

Unless you're running scared all the time, you're gone. **Michael C. Lynch**. Quoted in *Playboy* (1994)

A lot of people criticize Formula 1 as an unnecessary risk. But what would life be like if we only did what is necessary? **Niki Lauda**. Quoted in *Treasury of Investment Wisdom* (Bernice Cohen, 1999)

If you are scared to go to the brink you are lost. **John Foster Dulles**. *Life* (January 16, 1956)

Risk is what an entrepreneur eats for breakfast. It's what she slips into bed with at night. If you have no appetite for this stuff, or no ability to digest it, then get out of the game right now. **Heather Robertson**. *Taking Care of Business* (1997)

You don't go to a poker table with no money in your pocket. **Barbara Thomas**. *Management Today* (October 1999)

Eagles may soar but weasels don't get sucked into jet engines. **Anonymous**. On the dangers of ambition

People who don't take risks generally make about two big mistakes a year. People who do take risks generally make about two big mistakes a year. **Peter F. Drucker**. Quoted in *Don't Play in the Street* (George Thompson, 2003)

By definition, risk-takers often fail. So do morons. In practice it's difficult to sort them out. **Scott Adams**. *The Dilbert Principle* (1996)

A desperate disease requires a dangerous remedy. **Guy Fawkes**. Referring to the attempted destruction of Parliament. Speech (November 1605)

Risk comes from not knowing what you are doing. **Warren Buffett**. Quoted in *Treasury of Investment Wisdom* (Bernice Cohen, 1999)

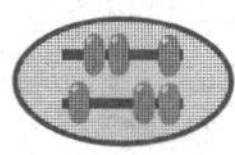
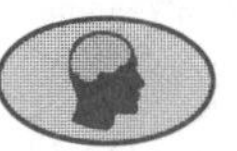

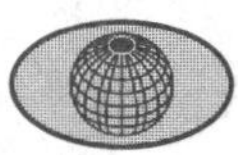

The easy way out usually leads back in. **Peter Senge**. *The Fifth Discipline: The Art and Practice of the Learning Organization* (1990)

How many millionaires do you know who have become wealthy by investing in savings accounts? I rest my case. **Robert G. Allen**. *Creating Wealth* (1986)

If we listened to our intellect, we'd never have a love affair. We'd never have a friendship. We'd never go into business. Well, that's nonsense. You've got to jump off cliffs all the time and build your wings on the way down. **Ray Bradbury**. Quoted in *Business Wit and Wisdom* (Richard S. Zera, 2005)

You want a valve that doesn't leak and you try everything possible to develop one. But the real world provides you with a leaky valve. You have to determine how much leakiness you can tolerate. **Arthur Rudolph**. Quoted in the *New York Times* (January 3, 1996)

If you only take small risks, you are only entitled to a small life. **Robin S. Sharma**. *MegaLiving!: 30 Days to a Perfect Life* (1995)

The more you seek security, the less of it you have. But the more you seek opportunity, the more likely it is that you will achieve the security that you desire. **Brian Tracy**. *Goals!: How to Get Everything You Want Faster Than You Ever Thought Possible* (2004)

Science

It is a good exercise for a research scientist to discard a pet hypothesis every day before breakfast. **Konrad Lorenz**. *On Aggression* (1966)

The aim of science is not to open the door to infinite wisdom, but to set a limit to infinite error. **Bertolt Brecht**. *The Life of Galileo* (1939)

The essence of science; ask an impertinent question, and you are on the way to a pertinent answer. **Jacob Bronowski**. *The Ascent of Man* (1973)

There are no such things as applied sciences, only applications of science. **Louis Pasteur**. Address (September 1872)

Science is a method to keep yourself from kidding yourself. **Edwin Land**. Attributed

In science, the credit goes to the man who convinces the world, not to the man to whom the idea first occurs. **Francis Darwin**. *Eugenics Review* (April 1914)

It is the tension between the scientist's laws and his own attempted breaking of them that powers the engines of science and makes it forge ahead. **W. V. O. Quine**. *Quiddities* (1987)

For a successful technology, reality must take precedence over public relations, for Nature cannot be fooled. **Richard P. Feynman**. *Report into the crash of the space shuttle Challenger* (1986)

We live in a society exquisitely dependent on science and technology, in which hardly anyone knows anything about science and technology. **Carl Sagan**. *The Sceptical Inquirer* (1990)

Selling

Inequality of knowledge is the key to a sale. **Deil O. Gustafson**. *Newsweek* (1974)

There's a sucker born every minute. **P. T. Barnum**. Attributed

If you don't listen, you don't sell anything. **Caroline Marland**. *Management Today* (September 1999)

I have heard of a man who had a mind to sell his house, and therefore carried a piece of brick in his pocket, which he showed as a pattern to encourage purchasers. **Jonathan Swift**. *The Drapier's Letters* (1724)

We sell sex. It is never going to go out of style. **Bob Guccione**. *Wall Street Journal* (1996)

Our sales representatives are like race car drivers. They can't succeed without incredible co-operation from the support team back at HQ. **Doug Nelson**. "The Mavericks," *Fortune* (June 1995)

You have to love the products if you are going to sell them. **Barbara Thomas**. *Management Today* (October 1999)

The art of salesmanship can be stated in four words: Believing something and convincing others. **William Wrigley**. "The Lowdown on Salesmanship," *American Magazine* (Neil M. Clark, October 1929)

Real salesmen stick until the buyer has used up his last No. **William Wrigley**. "The Lowdown on Salesmanship," *American Magazine* (Neil M. Clark, October 1929)

If you don't sell, it's not the product that's wrong, it's you. **Estée Lauder**. "As Gorgeous As It Gets," *New Yorker* (Kennedy Fraser, 1986)

When you stop talking, you've lost your customer. When you turn your back, you've lost her. **Estée Lauder**. "As Gorgeous As It Gets," *New Yorker* (Kennedy Fraser, 1986)

He's a man way out there in the blue, riding on a smile and a shoestring. **Arthur Miller**. *Death of a Salesman* (1949)

To found a great empire for the sole purpose of raising up a people of customers may at first sight appear a project fit only for a nation of shopkeepers. **Adam Smith**. *An Inquiry into the Nature and Causes of the Wealth of Nations* (1776)

The person who agrees with everything you say either isn't paying attention or else plans to sell you something. **Sam Ewing**. Quoted in *Reader's Digest* (1989)

In selling as in medicine, prescription before diagnosis is malpractice. **Tony Allesandra**. Attributed

Service

That's what I say about restaurants—the back part is manufacturing, the front part is retailing, the theatre is what holds the whole thing together. **Sir Terence Conran**. Quoted in *The Adventure Capitalists* (Jeff Grout and Lynne Curry, 1998)

In the best institutions, promises are kept, no matter what the cost in agony and overtime. **David Ogilvy**. *Confessions of an Advertising Man* (1963)

The decision to do that extra bit must be embedded in the company's culture. **Tom Farmer**. *Management Today* (July 1999)

Show me the business man or institution not guided by sentiment and service, by the idea that "he profits most who serves best," and I will show you a man or an outfit that is dead or dying. **B. F. Harris**. Attributed

The only certain means of success is to render more and better service than is expected of you, no matter what the task may be. This is a habit followed by all successful people since the beginning of time. Therefore the surest way to doom yourself to mediocrity is to perform only the work for which you are paid. **Og Mandino**. *The Greatest Miracle in the World* (1978)

Sincerity

The great enemy of clear language is insincerity. When there is a gap between

   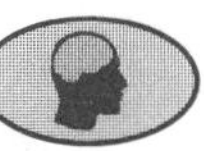  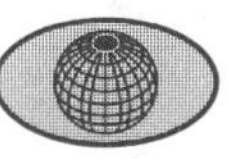   

one's real and one's declared aims, one turns as it were instinctively to long words and exhausted idioms, like a cuttlefish squirting ink. **George Orwell**. "Politics and the English Language," *Shooting an Elephant* (1950)

Weak people cannot be sincere. **François La Rochefoucauld**. *Reflections: or, Sentences and Moral Maxims* (5th ed, 1678)

Few people would not be the worse for complete sincerity. **F. H. Bradley**. *Collected Essays* (1935)

Always be sincere, even if you don't mean it. **Harry S. Truman**. Attributed

Men are always sincere. They change sincerities, that's all. **Tristan Bernard**. *Ce que l'on dit aux Femmes* (1922), Act 3

Let us say what we feel, and feel what we say; let speech harmonize with life. **Seneca**. *Letters to Lucilius* (1st century AD)

We ought to see far enough into a hypocrite to see even his sincerity. **G. K. Chesterton**. *Heretics* (1905)

Nothing in all the world is more dangerous than sincere ignorance and conscientious stupidity. **Martin Luther King**. *Strength to Love* (1963)

Some of the worst men in the world are sincere and the more sincere they are the worse they are. **Lord Hailsham**. Quoted in "Sayings of the Week," *Observer (London)* (January 7, 1968)

Sincerity has to do with the connexion between our words and thoughts, and not between our beliefs and actions. **William Hazlitt**. "On Cant and Hypocrisy," *London Weekly Review* (December 6, 1828)

A little sincerity is a dangerous thing, and a great deal of it is absolutely fatal. **Oscar Wilde**. "The Critic As Artist" (1890)

Profound sincerity is the only basis of talent as of character. **Ralph Waldo Emerson**. "Natural History of Intellect," *Essays: First Series* (1841)

Socialism and Communism

To the ordinary working man, the sort you would meet in any pub on Saturday night, Socialism does not mean much more than better wages and shorter hours, and nobody bossing you about. **George Orwell**. *The Road to Wigan Pier* (1937)

Marxian Socialism must always remain a portent to the historians of Opinion—how a doctrine so illogical and so dull can have exercised so powerful and enduring an influence over the minds of men... **John Maynard Keynes**. *The End of Laissez-Faire* (1926)

From each according to his ability, to each according to his needs. **Karl Marx**. *Critique of the Gotha Programme* (1875)

A community in which power, wealth and opportunity are in the hands of the many not the few...in which the enterprise of the market and the rigour of competition are joined with the forces of partnership and co-operation. **Labour Party**. This new version of the Labour Party Constitution's Clause Four compares with the 1918 (revised 1928) original: To secure for workers...the full fruits of their industry and the most equitable distribution thereof that may be possible upon the basis. "Clause Four," *Labour Party Constitution* (April 29, 1995)

Socialism proposes no adequate substitute for the motive of enlightened selfishness that to-day is at the basis of all human labor and effort, enterprise and new activity. **William Howard Taft**. *Popular Government* (1913)

You can't get good Chinese takeout in China and Cuban cigars are rationed in Cuba. That's all you need to know about communism. **P. J. O'Rourke**. *Give War a Chance* (1992)

Your money does not cause my poverty. Refusal to believe this is at the bottom of most bad economic thinking. **P. J. O'Rourke**. *Eat the Rich* (1999)

Society

No advance in wealth, no softening of manners, no reform or revolution has ever brought human equality a millimetre nearer. **George Orwell**. *Nineteen Eighty-Four* (1949), pt. 2, ch. 9

Freedom is a more complex and delicate thing than force. It is not as simple to live under as force is. **Thomas Mann**. Attributed

The Affluent Society. **J. K. Galbraith**. Book title. *The Affluent Society* (1958)

Economic growth may one day turn out to be a curse rather than a good, and under no conditions can it either lead to freedom or constitute a proof for its existence. **Hannah Arendt**. *On Revolution* (1963)

Idiots are always in favour of inequality of income (their only chance of eminence), and the truly great in favour of equality. **George Bernard Shaw**. *The Intelligent Woman's Guide to Socialism and Capitalism* (1928)

Which of us...is to do the hard and dirty work for the rest—and for what pay? who is to do the pleasant and clean work, and for what pay? **John Ruskin**. *Sesame and Lillies* (1865)

The trouble with a free market economy is that it requires so many policemen to make it work. **Dean Acheson**. Quoted in the *Observer (London)* (May 26, 1985)

The quality of a society will be judged by what the least privileged in it achieves. **Robert Greenleaf**. "Old Age: The Ultimate Test of the Spirit," *The Power of Servant Leadership* (Larry Spears, ed, 1998)

All men are created equal...they are endowed by their Creator with inalienable rights...among these are Life, Liberty, and the pursuit of happiness. **Thomas Jefferson**. "Declaration of Independence" (July 4, 1776)

We have an underdeveloped democracy and overdeveloped plutocracy. **Ralph Nader**. *Economist* (1996)

Years ago I recognized my kinship with all living things, and I made up my mind that I was not one bit better than the meanest on the earth. I said then and I say now, that while there is a lower class, I am in it. **Eugene V. Debs**. Statement to the Court after being convicted for violating the Sedition Act, Cleveland, Ohio. (September 18, 1918)

Speeches

If I am to speak for ten minutes, I need a week for preparation; if fifteen minutes, three days; if half an hour, two days; if an hour, I am ready now. **Woodrow Wilson**. Quoted in *The Wilson Era* (Josephus Daniels, 1946)

He is one of those orators of whom it was well said, Before they get up, they do not know what they are going to say; when they are speaking, they do not know what they are saying; and when they have sat down, they do not know what they have said. **Sir Winston Churchill**. Referring to Lord Charles Beresford (1846–1919). Quoted in *Hansard* (December 20, 1912)

     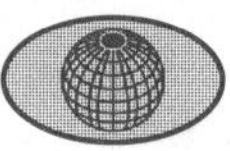  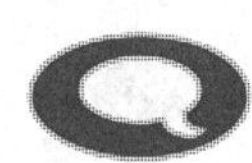 

It usually takes me more than three weeks to prepare a good impromptu speech. **Mark Twain**. Attributed

Oratory is dying; a calculating age has stabbed it to the heart with innumerable dagger-thrusts of statistics. **W. Keith Hancock**. *Australia* (1930)

Oratory is just like prostitution: you must have little tricks. **Vittorio Emanuele Orlando**. Quoted in *Time* (December 8, 1952)

Eloquence lies as much in the tone of the voice, in the eyes, and in the speaker's manner, as in his choice of words. **François La Rochefoucauld**. *Reflections: or, Sentences and Moral Maxims* (1665)

It is terrible to speak well and be wrong. **Sophocles**. *Electra* (430?–415? BC)

The object of oratory is not truth, but persuasion. **Lord Macaulay**. *The Athenian Orators* (1824)

Speak when you're angry and you'll make the best speech you'll ever regret. **Henry Ward Beecher**. Attributed

A speech is poetry and cadence, rhythm, imagery, sweep! A speech reminds us that words, like children, have the power to make dance the dullest beanbag of a heart. **Peggy Noonan**. *What I Saw at the Revolution* (1990)

The finest eloquence is that which gets things done; the worst is that which delays them. **David Lloyd George (Earl of Dwyfor)**. Speech, Paris Peace Conference (1919)

I feel like Zsa Zsa Gabor's fifth husband. I know what I'm supposed to do but I don't know if I can make it interesting. **Al Gore**. Said on being twenty-third speaker at a political dinner. Quoted in *Today* (March 1, 1989)

Nothing is so unbelievable that oratory cannot make it acceptable. **Cicero**. *Paradoxa Stoicorum* (46 BC?)

An orator can hardly get beyond commonplaces: if he does he gets beyond his hearers. **William Hazlitt**. *The Plain Speaker* (1826)

Statistics

Like dreams, statistics are a form of wish fulfilment. **Jean Baudrillard**. *Cool Memories* (1987)

There are two kinds of statistics, the kind you look up and the kind you make up. **Rex Stout**. *Death of a Doxy* (1966)

The average family exists only on paper and its average budget is a fiction, invented by statisticians for the convenience of statisticians. **Sylvia Porter**. *Sylvia Porter's Money Book* (1975)

Statistical figures referring to economic events are historical data. They tell us what happened in a nonrepeatable case. **Ludwig von Mises**. *Human Action* (1949)

Employing data bases and statistical skills, academics compute with precision the beta of a stock...then build arcane investment and capital-allocation theories around this calculation. In their hunger for a single statistic to measure risk they forget a fundamental principle: It is better to be approximately right than precisely wrong. **Warren Buffett**. Chairman's letter to shareholders (March 7, 1995)

Statistics are the triumph of the quantitative method and the quantitative method is the victory of sterility and death. **Hilaire Belloc**. *Silence of the Sea* (1941)

Never cross a river because it is on average four feet deep. **Nassim Nicholas Taleb**. Attributed

Strategy

I buy when other people are selling. **J. Paul Getty**. *International Herald Tribune* (1961)

The strategist's method is very simply to challenge the prevailing assumptions with a single question: Why? **Kenichi Ohmae**. *The Mind of the Strategist* (1982)

To stay ahead, you must have your next idea waiting in the wings. **Rosabeth Moss Kanter**. *Men and Women of the Corporation* (1977)

There is only one winning strategy. It is to carefully define the target market and direct a superior offering to that target market. **Philip Kotler**. Interview, *The Events & Awards Managers of Asia and Hamlin-Iturralde Corporation* (1999)

We like to believe we can break strategy down to Five Forces or Seven Ss. But you can't. Strategy is extraordinarily emotional and demanding. **Gary Hamel**. *Competing for the Future* (co-written with C. K. Prahalad, 1994)

Whatever you shoot is dead for a while before it starts to stink. The same goes for strategies. How many organizations carry this dead thing around with them, unaware of its irrelevancy until it is too late? **Gary Hamel**. Lecture, "Pronking and Surviving in the Age of Gazelles" (October 26, 1999)

Swing for hits, not home runs. **Michael Dell**. *Direct from Dell* (1996)

The prevailing wisdom is that markets are always right. I take the opposite position. I assume that markets are always wrong. **George Soros**. *Soros on Soros* (1995)

Mold-breaking strategies grow initially like weeds, they are not cultivated like tomatoes in a hothouse. **Henry Mintzberg**. *The Rise and Fall of Strategic Planning* (1994)

Strategy-making is an immensely complex process involving the most sophisticated, subtle, and at times subconscious of human cognitive and social processes. **Henry Mintzberg**. *The Rise and Fall of Strategic Planning* (1994)

Strategy is not the consequence of planning but the opposite, its starting point. **Henry Mintzberg**. *The Rise and Fall of Strategic Planning* (1994)

Re-engineering: The principal slogan of the Nineties, used to describe any and all corporate strategies. **Anonymous**. *Fortune* (February 15, 1995)

Long-range planning does not deal with future decisions. It deals with the future of present decisions. **Peter F. Drucker**. *Managing in Turbulent Times* (1980)

At Berkshire, our carefully-crafted acquisition strategy is simply to wait for the phone to ring. Happily, it sometimes does so, usually because a manager who sold to us earlier has recommended to a friend that he think about following suit. **Warren Buffett**. Chairman's letter to shareholders, *Berkshire Hathaway 1999 Annual Report* (March 1, 2000)

A question that often comes up at times of strategic transformation is, should you pursue a highly focused approach, betting everything on one strategic goal, or should you hedge?...Mark Twain hit it on the head when he said, Put all of your eggs in one basket and WATCH THAT BASKET. **Andrew S. Grove**. *Only the Paranoid Survive: How to Exploit the Crisis Points That Challenge Every Company and Career* (1996), ch. 8

Stress

At a certain speed, the speed of light, you lose even your shadow. At a certain speed, the speed of information, things lose their sense. **Jean Baudrillard**. *The Gulf War Did Not Take Place* (1995)

Brain cells create ideas. Stress kills brain cells. Stress is not a good idea. **Doug Hall**. *Jump Start Your Brain* (1996)

Business pressures are good for the soul: when it has unburdened itself of them, it plays all the more fully and enjoys life. **Johann Wolfgang von Goethe**. Attributed

If you want to avoid worry, do what Sir William Osler did: live in day-tight compartments. Don't stew about the future. Just live each day until bedtime. **Dale Carnegie**. *How to Stop Worrying and Start Living* (1948)

The trouble with being in the rat race is that even if you win, you're still a rat. **Lily Tomlin**. Quoted in *Slowing Down in a Speeded Up World* (Adair Lara, 1994)

Success

I am doomed to an eternity of compulsive work. No set goal achieved satisfies. Success only breeds a new goal. The golden apple devoured has seeds. It is endless. **Bette Davis**. *The Lonely Life* (1962)

The secret of success is concentration... Taste everything a little, look at everything a little; but live for one thing. **Olive Schreiner**. *The Story of an African Farm* (1883)

She knows there's no success like failure and that failure's no success at all. **Bob Dylan**. Song lyric. "Love Minus Zero, No Limits" (1965)

People who are successful simply want it more than people who are not. **Ian Schrager**. *Sunday Times (London)* (May 2000)

The common idea that success spoils people by making them vain, egotistic and self-complacent is erroneous; on the contrary, it makes them for the most part humble, tolerant and kind. **W. Somerset Maugham**. *The Summing Up* (1938)

To succeed in business it is necessary to make others see things as you see them. **Aristotle Onassis**. Attributed

If you do anything just for the money you don't succeed. **Barry Hearn**. *Sunday Telegraph (London)* (April 10, 1988)

The man of virtue makes the difficulty to be overcome his first business, and success only a subsequent consideration. **Confucius**. *Analects* (500? BC)

For a writer, success is always temporary, success is only a delayed failure. And it is incomplete. **Graham Greene**. *A Sort of Life* (1971)

A minute's success pays the failure of years. **Robert Browning**. "Apollo and the Fates" (1886), st. 42

The conduct of a losing party never appears right: at least it never can possess the only infallible criterion of wisdom to vulgar judgements—success. **Edmund Burke**. Letter to a member of the National Assembly (1791)

To burn always with this hard, gem-like flame, to maintain this ecstasy, is success in life. **Walter Pater**. *Studies in the History of the Renaissance* (1873)

To be successful you have to be lucky, or a little mad, or very talented, or to find yourself in a rapid-growth field. **Edward de Bono**. *Tactics: The Art and Science of Success* (1984)

Success is made of 99 percent failure. **Sir James Dyson**. *Management Today* (July 1999)

When you struggle hard and lose money, you're a hero. When you start making money you become a capitalist swine. **Sir Terence Conran**. Quoted in *The Risk Takers* (Jeffrey Robinson, 1985)

If at first you don't succeed, you may be at your level of incompetence. **Laurence J. Peter**. *The Peter Principle: Why Things Always Go Wrong* (co-written with Raymond Hull, 1969)

God doesn't require us to succeed; he only requires that you try. **Mother Teresa**. Quoted in *Rolling Stone* (December 1992)

It is not enough to succeed. Others must fail. **Gore Vidal**. Attributed (December 1976)

The conduct of successful business merely consists in doings things in a very simple way, doing them regularly, and never neglecting to do them. **Lord Leverhulme**. Speech, Liverpool University (1922)

I've always realised that if I'm doing well at business I'm cutting some other bastard's throat. **Kerry Packer**. *Daily Mail (London)* (November 1, 1988)

Tis not in mortals to command success
But we'll do more, Sempronius, we'll deserve it.
Joseph Addison. *Cato* (1713)

To be successful, you need leisure. You need time hanging heavily on your hands. **George Soros**. Quoted in *Becoming Rich* (Mark Tier, 2005)

The secret of the truly successful...is that they learned early in life how *not* to be busy. **Barbara Ehrenreich**. "The Cult of Busyness," *The Worst Years of Our Lives* (1991)

Success is relative: It is what we can make of the mess we have made of things. **T. S. Eliot**. *The Family Reunion* (1939)

It's possible, you can never know, that the universe exists only for me. If so, it's sure going well for me, I must admit. **Bill Gates**. *Time* (January 13, 1997)

Success is a lousy teacher. It seduces smart people into thinking they can't lose. **Bill Gates**. *The Road Ahead* (1995)

Whom the gods wish to destroy they first call promising. **Cyril Connolly**. *Enemies of Promise* (1938)

It takes years to make an overnight success. **Eddie Cantor**. Quoted in *Treasury of Investment Wisdom* (Bernice Cohen, 1999)

If you want to succeed, double your failure rate. **Samuel Butler**. *Men-Minutes-Money* (1934)

The toughest thing about success is that you've got to keep on being a success. **Irving Berlin**. Quoted in *Theater Arts* (1958)

The test of a first-rate work, and a test of your sincerity in calling it a first-rate work, is that you finish it. **Arnold Bennett**. *Things That Have Interested Me* (1921–1925)

Success is a science; if you have the conditions, you get the result. **Oscar Wilde**. Letter (1883)

I have worked without thinking of myself. This is the largest factor in whatever success I have attained. **Amadeo Giannini**. Quoted in "America's Banker," *Time 100: Heroes and Inspirations* (December 1999)

Eighty percent of success is showing up. **Woody Allen**. Quoted in *In Search of Excellence* (Thomas J. Peters and Robert H. Waterman, 1982)

I believe in the value of paranoia. Business success contains the seeds of its own destruction. The more successful you are, the more people want a chunk of your business and then another chunk and then another until there is nothing left. **Andrew S. Grove**. *Only the Paranoid Survive: How to Exploit the Crisis Points That Challenge Every Company and Career* (1996), Preface

   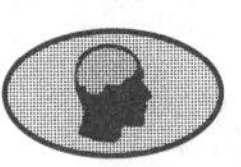  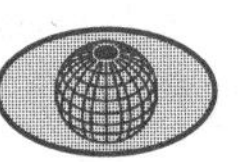 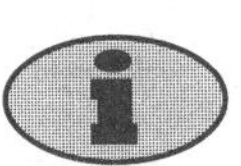 

I am successful because I have always been a tortoise. I did not come from a rich family. I was not smart in school. I did not finish school. I am not particularly talented. Yet, I am far richer than most people simply because I did not stop. **Robert Kiyosaki**. *Rich Dad's Retire Young, Retire Rich* (2002)

The secret of success is learning how to use pain and pleasure instead of having pain and pleasure use you. If you do that, you're in control of your life. If you don't, life controls you. **Anthony Robbins**. *Awaken the Giant Within* (1992)

Talent

All our talents increase in the using, and every faculty, both good and bad, strengthens by exercise. **Anne Brontë**. *The Tenant of Wildfell Hall* (1848)

Too many companies believe people are interchangeable. Truly gifted people never are. They have unique talents. Such people cannot be forced into roles they are not suited for, nor should they be. **Warren Bennis**. *Organizing Genius: The Secrets of Creative Collaboration* (co-written with Patricia Ward Biederman, 1998)

The leader...is rarely the brightest person in the group. Rather, they have extraordinary taste, which makes them more curators than creators. They are appreciators of talent and nurturers of talent and they have the ability to recognize valuable ideas. **Warren Bennis**. Interview, *Strategy + Business* (July–September 1997)

Timing and arrogance are decisive factors in the successful use of talent. **Marya Mannes**. *Out of My Time* (1971)

Talent is cheaper than table salt. What separates the talented individual from the successful one is a lot of hard work. **Stephen King**. Quoted in *Independent on Sunday (London)* (March 10, 1996)

An idea can turn to dust or magic, depending on the talent that rubs against it. **William Bernbach**. *New York Times* (October 6, 1982)

The world is filled with unsuccessful men of talent. **Ray Kroc**. Quoted in *The Fifties* (David Halberstan, 1993)

Targets

A minor invention every ten days and a big thing every six months. **Thomas Edison**. Press conference (1876)

Think nothing done while aught remains to do. **Samuel Rogers**. *Human Life* (1819)

People are ambitious and unrealistic. They set targets for themselves that are higher than what you would set for them. And because they set them, they hit them. **Liisa Joronen**. *Fast Company* (1997)

Our view was, if we could measure it, we could manage it. **Dan England**. "The Mavericks," *Fortune* (June 1995)

We build four of them a year—it's my job to sell four a year. **Robert Clifford**. Referring to the production of luxury yachts. *Australian Financial Review* (September 2000)

It is much more difficult to measure nonperformance than performance. **Harold S. Geneen**. Referring to why managers sometimes accept underachievement. *Managing* (co-written with Alvin Moscow, 1984)

Taxes

To tax and to please is no more given to man than to love and be wise. **Viscount Simon**. Budget speech, House of Commons, British Parliament (April 25, 1938)

Sex and taxes are in many ways the same. Tax does to cash what males do to genes. It dispenses assets among the population as a whole. **Steve Jones**. Speech, London (January 25, 1997)

All money nowadays seems to be produced with a homing instinct for the Treasury. **Prince Philip**. Quoted in the *Observer (London)* (May 26, 1963)

Income tax has made more liars out of the American people than golf. **Will Rogers**. *The Illiterate Digest* (1924)

Patrick Henry railed against taxation without representation. He should see it with representation. **Saul Landau**. *New York Times* (1995)

Taxes will eventually become a voluntary process, with the possible exception of real estate—the one physical thing that does not move easily and has computable value...wait until that's all there is left to tax, when the rest of the things we buy and sell come from everywhere, anywhere, and nowhere. **Nicholas Negroponte**. Referring to the prospects for taxing Internet commerce. "Taxing Taxes," *Wired Magazine* (May 6, 1998)

The hardest thing in the world to understand is income tax. **Albert Einstein**. Attributed

Inflation is one form of taxation that can be imposed without legislation. **Milton Friedman**. *Observer (London)* (September 22, 1974)

The Rich aren't like us—they pay less taxes. **Peter De Vries**. *Washington Post* (July 30, 1989)

Writing checks to the IRS that include strings of zeros does not bother me...Overall, we feel extraordinarily lucky to have been dealt a hand in life that enables us to write large checks to the government rather than one requiring the government to regularly write checks to us—say, because we are disabled or unemployed. **Warren Buffett**. Chairman's letter to shareholders, *Berkshire Hathaway 1998 Annual Report* (March 1, 1999)

President Herbert Hoover returned his salary to government. His idea caught on and now we're all doing it. **Sam Ewing**. Referring to taxation. Quoted in *Wall Street Journal* (July 23, 1996)

Teams

A good team is a great place to be, exciting, stimulating, supportive, successful. A bad team is horrible, a sort of human prison. **Charles Handy**. *Inside Organisations* (1999)

People can be themselves only in small comprehensible groups. **E. F. Schumacher**. *Small Is Beautiful* (1973)

A team of dragons doesn't need a head. **Stan Shih**. *Forbes* (September 1998)

Team player: An employee who substitutes the thinking of the herd for hisher own good judgment. **Anonymous**. *Fortune* (February 15, 1995)

Team-building exercises come in many forms but they all trace their roots back to the prison system. **Scott Adams**. *The Dilbert Principle* (1996)

One man can be a crucial ingredient on a team, but one man cannot make a team. **Kareem Abdul-Jabbar**. *Star* (1986)

Technology

We've all heard that a million monkeys banging on one million typewriters will

  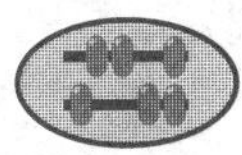 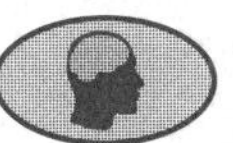  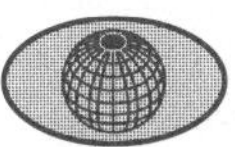 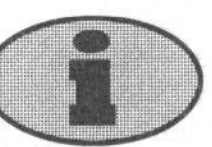  

eventually reproduce the entire works of Shakespeare. Now, thanks to the Internet, we know this is not true. **Robert Wilensky**. *Mail on Sunday* (February 1997)

The thing with high-tech is that you always end up using scissors. **David Hockney**. *Observer (London)* (July 1994)

Apple has always been, and I hope it will always be, one of the premier bridges between mere mortals and this very difficult technology. **Steve Jobs**. Quoted in "Steve's Two Jobs," *Time* (Michael Krantz, October 18, 1999)

I would trade all of my technology for an afternoon with Socrates. **Steve Jobs**. Quoted in *Newsweek* (October 29, 2001)

An important technology first creates a problem and then solves it. **Alan Kay**. Quoted in *Re-engineering the Corporation* (Michael Hammer and James Champy, 1993)

Technology is our word for something that doesn't work yet. **Douglas Adams**. *Sunday Times (London)* (June 2000)

A common mistake people make when trying to design something foolproof is to underestimate the ingenuity of complete fools. **Douglas Adams**. *Mostly Harmless* (1992)

Many executives continue to believe that they are not in the technology business and that they might just as well outsource their information technology needs. This is like an athlete saying that he is not in the strength business...these naysayers might as well say that they are not in the business of being in business. **J. William Gurley**. *Above the Crowd: Productivity Paradox* (1997)

Any sufficiently advanced technology is indistinguishable from magic. **Sir Arthur C. Clarke**. *The Lost Worlds of 2001* (1972)

If it keeps up, man will atrophy all his limbs but the push-button finger. **Frank Lloyd Wright**. Referring to advances in technology. *New York Times Magazine* (1953)

If the technocratic class often invokes technology, it is because these inanimate objects can take on a trajectory of their own and so cover for the manager's inability to give leadership. **John Ralston Saul**. *The Unconscious Civilization* (1995)

If the automobile had followed the same development as the computer, a Rolls Royce would cost $100, get a million miles per gallon, and explode once a year, killing everyone inside. **Robert X. Cringley**. *Infoworld* (March 6, 1969)

The technology of mass production is inherently violent, ecologically damaging, self-defeating in terms of non-renewable resources, and stultifying for the human person. **E. F. Schumacher**. *Small Is Beautiful* (1973)

Machines need to talk easily to one another in order to better serve people. **Nicholas Negroponte**. *Being Digital* (1995)

It's a new medium, it's a universal medium and it's not itself a medium which inherently makes people do good things, or bad things. It allows people to do what they want to do more efficiently. **Sir Tim Berners-Lee**. Talking about the World Wide Web, which he founded. Interview with Mark Lawson, BBC Newsnight (August 9, 2005)

If we hadn't put a man on the moon, there wouldn't be a Silicon Valley today. **John Sculley**. *US News & World Report* (1992)

We bet the company on that basic technology and, in 23 years, nobody else has been able to match it. **Masaru Ibuka**. *Fortune* (February 1992)

Technology will move so fast that unfortunately, or fortunately for me, you will be required to buy a new phone quite often. **Charles Dunstone**. *Management Today* (August 1999)

When this circuit learns your job, what are you going to do? **Marshall McLuhan**. *The Medium Is the Message* (1967)

Machines are worshipped because they are beautiful, and valued because they confer power; they are hated because they are hideous and loathed because they impose slavery. **Bertrand Russell (Earl Russell)**. *Sceptical Essays* (1928)

Technology—the knack of so arranging the world that we need not experience it. **Max Frisch**. *Homo Faber* (1957)

Few influential people involved with the Internet claim that it is good in and of itself. It is a powerful tool for solving social problems, just as it is a tool for making money, finding lost relatives, receiving medical advice, or, come to that, trading instructions for making bombs. **Esther Dyson**. Quoted in *IQuote: Brilliance and Banter from the Internet Age* (David L. Green, 2007)

The trouble is that all-encompassing though information technology may be, it will always convey facts and numbers...what it does not convey is perception, belief and motivation. **Sir John Harvey-Jones**. *Managing to Survive* (1993)

There are three roads to ruin; women, gambling and technicians. The most pleasant is with women, the quickest is with gambling, but the surest is with technicians. **George Pompidou**. Quoted in *Sunday Telegraph (London)* (1968)

It took 75 years for telephones to be used by 50 million customers, but it took only four years for the Internet to reach that many users. **Lori Valigra**. Attributed

Time Management

The clock not the steam engine is the key machine of the modern industrial age. **Lewis Mumford**. *Technics and Civilization* (1934)

We are speeding up our lives and working harder in a futile attempt to buy the time to slow down and enjoy it. **Paul Hawken**. *The Ecology of Commerce* (1993)

He who would make serious use of his life must always act as though he had a long time to live and must schedule his time as though he were about to die. **Émile Littré**. *Dictionnaire de la Langue Française* (1863–1873)

Time waste differs from material waste in that there can be no salvage. **Henry Ford**. *My Life and Work* (co-written with Samuel Crowther, 1922)

Do not wait; the time will never be just right. **Napoleon Hill**. *Think and Grow Rich* (1937)

What is the best use of my time right now? **Alan Lakein**. *How To Get Control of Your Time and Your Life* (1973)

If you did not look after today's business then you might as well forget about tomorrow. **Isaac Mophatlane**. Attributed

The Law of Forced Efficiency. "There is never enough time to do everything, but there is always enough time to do the most important thing." **Brian Tracy**. *The 100 Absolutely Unbreakable Laws of Business Success* (2000)

Travel

In the Middle Ages, people were tourists because of their religion, whereas now they

  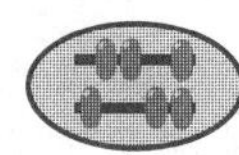 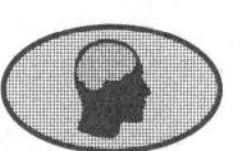  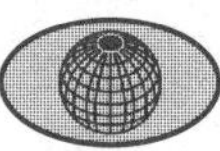 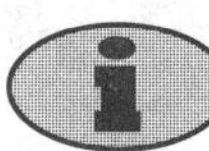  

are tourists because tourism is their religion. **Lord Runcie**. Speech (December 1988)

A man who leaves home to mend himself and others is a philosopher; but he who goes from country to country, guided by a blind impulse of curiosity, is a vagabond. **Oliver Goldsmith**. *The Citizen of the World* (1762)

They say travel broadens the mind; but you must have the mind. **G. K. Chesterton**. "The Shadow of the Shark" (1921)

Commuter—one who spends his life
In riding to and from his wife;
A man who shaves and takes a train,
And then rides it back to shave again.
E. B. White. "The Commuter" (1982)

Trust

Confidence is a thing not to be produced by compulsion. Men cannot be forced to trust. **Daniel Webster**. Speech in the Senate (1834)

Management by trust, empathy, and forgiveness sounds good. It also sounds soft. It is in practice tough. Organizations based on trust have, on occasion, to be ruthless. **Charles Handy**. *Harvard Business Review* (November–December 1992)

The superior confidence which people repose in the tall man is well merited. Being tall, he is more visible than other men and being more visible, he is much more closely watched. **J. K. Galbraith**. *The Scotch* (1964)

I am very careful about bringing people into my confidence. I want to see the color of their eyes. **E. Gerald Corrigan**. Referring to becoming president of the Federal Reserve Bank in Minneapolis. *New York Times* (December 30, 1984)

Confidence placed in another often compels confidence in return. **Livy**. *History of Rome* (26 BC–15 AD)

I've learned the perimeter of my circle of confidence. **Warren Buffett**. Quoted in *Treasury of Investment Wisdom* (Bernice Cohen, 1999)

The open bins and store rooms were symbols of trust, a trust that is central to the way HP does business. **David Packard**. "Lessons of Leadership," *The Nation's Business* (January 1974)

Our trust in those who made the financial system work has been decimated—no less than we would lose faith in the water company if the taps started dripping cyanide. **Peggy Drexler**. Huffington Post blog (December 29, 2008)

Value

Value is the most invisible and impalpable of ghosts. **William Stanley Jevons**. *Investigations on Currency and Finance* (1884)

Nothing that costs only a dollar is worth having. **Elizabeth Arden**. Quoted in *In Cosmetics the Old Mystique Is No Longer Enough* (Eleanore Carruth, 1973)

The value of a thing is the amount of laboring or work that its possession will save the possessor. **Henry George**. *The Science of Political Economy* (1897)

There are only four ways to create value in the New Economy, and they're really simple: information, entertainment, convenience, and savings. **Jay S. Walker**. Interview, *Strategy + Business* (April–June 2000)

Creating value is an inherently cooperative process, capturing value is inherently competitive. **Barry J. Nalebuff**. *Co-opetition* (co-written with Adam M. Brandenburger, 1997)

Vision

A zealous sense of mission is only possible where there is opposition to it. **D. W. Ewing**. "Tension Can Be an Asset," *Harvard Business Review* (September–October 1964)

A formal and orderly conception of the whole is rarely present, perhaps even rarely possible, except to a few men of exceptional genius. **Chester Barnard**. *The Functions of the Executive* (1938)

The last thing IBM needs right now is a vision. **Lou Gerstner**. *Fortune* (1997)

Vision is the art of seeing things invisible. **Jonathan Swift**. Attributed

Dreams have their place in management activity, but they need to be kept severely under control. **Lord Weinstock**. *Financial Times (London)* (December 30, 1989)

Effective visions are lived in details, not broad strokes. **Tom Peters**. *Thriving on Chaos* (1987)

Good business leaders create a vision, articulate the vision, passionately own the vision, and relentlessly drive it to completion. **Jack Welch**. Quoted in *10 Simple Secrets of the World's Greatest Business Communicators* (Carmine Gallo, 2006)

Vision: Top management's heroic guess about the future, easily printed on mugs, T-shirts, posters, and calendar cards. **Anonymous**. *Fortune* (February 15, 1995)

Whenever anything is being accomplished, it is being done, I have learned, by a monomaniac with a mission. **Peter F. Drucker**. *Adventures of a Bystander* (1979)

Vision without action is merely a dream. Action without vision just passes the time. Vision with action can change the world. **Joel A. Barker**. *Future Edge* (1992)

Wages

We're overpaying him, but he's worth it. **Samuel Goldwyn**. Attributed

The theory of the determination of wages in a free market is simply a special case of the general theory of value. Wages are the price of labour. **Sir John Richard Hicks**. *The Theory of Wages* (1932), pt. 1

Men work but slowly, that have poor wages. **Thomas Fuller**. *Gnomologia* (1732), no. 3407

The income men derive from producing things of slight consequence is of great consequence. The production reflects the low marginal utility of the goods to society. The income reflects the high total utility of a livelihood to a person. **J. K. Galbraith**. *The Affluent Society* (1958), ch. 21

Wages are determined by the bitter struggle between capitalist and worker. **Karl Marx**. *Early Writings* (T. B. Bottomore, ed, 1963)

When a man says he wants to work, what he means is that he wants wages. **Richard Whately**. Quoted in *Principles of Political Economy* (Henry Sidgwick, 1883)

It is but a truism that labor is most productive where its wages are largest. Poorly paid labor is inefficient labor, the world over. **Henry George**. *Progress and Poverty* (1879), bk. 9

There is no way of keeping profits up but by keeping wages down. **David Ricardo**. *On Protection to Agriculture* (1820)

  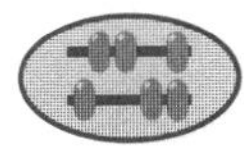   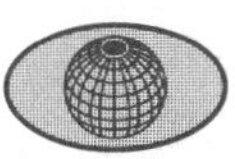   

One man's wage increase is another man's price increase. **Harold Wilson (Lord Wilson of Riveaulx)**. Speech, Blackburn, England (January 8, 1970)

No business which depends for existence on paying less than living wages to its workers has any right to continue in this country...by living wages I mean more than a bare subsistence level—I mean the wages of decent living. **Franklin D. Roosevelt**. Address (1933)

Wages are the measure of dignity that society puts on a job. **Johnnie Tillmon**. "Welfare Is a Woman's Issue," *The First Ms Reader* (Francine Klagsbrun, ed, 1972)

The trouble with the profit system has always been that it was highly unprofitable to most people. **E. B. White**. *One Man's Meat* (1942)

All wages are based primarily on productive power. Anything else would be charity. **Elbert Hubbard**. *Notebook* (1927)

Economy: cutting down other people's wages. **J. B. Morton**. Attributed

Wealth

Prosperity is only an instrument to be used, not a deity to be worshipped. **Calvin Coolidge**. Speech, Boston, Massachusetts (June 11, 1928)

If you can count your money, you don't have a billion dollars. **J. Paul Getty**. Quoted in *The Great Getty* (Robert Lenzner, 1985)

When I got my statement in January, I was worth $2.2 billion. Then I got another statement in August that said I was worth $3.2 billion. So I figure it's only nine months' earnings, who cares? **Ted Turner**. Referring to his decision to donate US$1 billion to the United Nations over a decade. Speech, United Nations Association-USA, Marriott Marquis Hotel, New York (September 19, 1997)

Wealth is like sea-water; the more we drink, the thirstier we become; the same is true of fame. **Arthur Schopenhauer**. "What a Man Has," *Parerga and Paralipomena* (1851)

As long as there are rich people in the world, they will be desirous of distinguishing themselves from the poor. **Jean-Jacques Rousseau**. *Discours sur l'Économie Politique* (1758)

Wealth is not without its advantages and the case to the contrary, although it has often been made, has never proved widely persuasive. **J. K. Galbraith**. *The Affluent Society* (1958), ch. 1

In the affluent society, no useful distinction can be made between luxuries and necessities. **J. K. Galbraith**. *The Affluent Society* (1958)

There are three ways by which an individual can get wealth—by work, by gift, and by theft. And, clearly, the reasons why the workers get so little is that the beggars and thieves get so much. **Henry George**. *Social Problems* (1883)

Short of genius, a rich man cannot imagine poverty. **Charles Pierre Péguy**. "Socialism and the Modern World," *Basic Verities* (1943)

It is easier for a camel to go through the eye of a needle, than for a rich man to enter into the kingdom of God. **New Testament**. Matthew 19:24

Purchasing power is a license to purchase power. **Raoul Vaneigem**. *The Revolution of Everyday Life* (1967)

The millionaires are a product of natural selection...the naturally selected agents of society for certain work. They get high wages and live in luxury, but the bargain is a good one for society. **William Graham Sumner**. Sumner was the leading US advocate of Herbert Spencer's Social Darwinism, the survival of the fittest. *The Challenge of Facts and Other Essays* (Albert Galloway Keller, ed, 1914)

Nothing is more admirable than the fortitude with which millionaires tolerate the disadvantages of their wealth. **Rex Stout**. Quoted in *500 of the Most Witty, Acerbic, and Erudite Things Ever Said About Money* (Philip Jenks, 2002)

What is really desired, under the name of riches, is essentially, power over men...this power...is in direct proportion to the poverty of the men over whom it is exercised, and in inverse proportion to the number of persons who are as rich as ourselves. **John Ruskin**. "The Veins of Wealth," *Unto This Last* (1862)

Not evil, but good, has come to the race from the accumulation of wealth by those who have the ability and energy that produce it. **Andrew Carnegie**. "Wealth," *North American Review* (June 1889)

Superfluous wealth can buy superfluities only. **Henry David Thoreau**. *Walden, or Life in the Woods* (1854), Conclusion

A society which reverences the attainment of riches as the supreme felicity will naturally be disposed to regard the poor as damned...if only to justify itself for making their life a hell. **Richard Tawney**. *Religion and the Rise of Capitalism* (1926), ch. 4, sect. 4

Having money is rather like being a blond. It is more fun but not vital. **Mary Quant**. Quoted in *Observer (London)* (November 2, 1986)

I have no interest in celebrities. If all the superrich disappeared, the world economy would not even notice. The superrich are irrelevant to the economy. **Peter F. Drucker**. Quoted in "Seeing Things As They Really Are," *Forbes* (Robert Lenzner and Stephen S. Johnson, 1987)

The old foundations of success are gone...The world's wealthiest man, Bill Gates, owns nothing tangible: no land, no gold or oil, no factories...For the first time in history the world's wealthiest man owns only knowledge. **Lester Thurow**. *Building Wealth: New Rules for Individuals, Companies, and Countries in a Knowledge-Based Economy* (1999), Prologue

Prosperity tries the souls even of the wise. **Sallust**. *Bellum Catilinae* (41? BC), ch. 11

In every well-governed state wealth is a sacred thing; in democracies it is the only sacred thing. **Anatole France**. *Penguin Island* (1908)

A man who has a million dollars is as well off as if he were rich. **John Jacob Astor**. Attributed

If you are not happy while getting rich, chances are that you will not be happy when you do get rich. **Robert Kiyosaki**. *Rich Dad's Rich Kid, Smart Kid* (2001)

Someone will always be getting richer faster than you. This is not a tragedy. **Charlie E. Munger**. *Annual general meeting of Berkshire Hathaway* (May 15, 2000)

It is inconceivable that anyone will divulge a truly effective get-rich scheme for the price of a book. There is ample opportunity to use wealth in this world, and neither I nor my friends, nor anyone else I have ever met, has so much of it that they are interested in putting themselves at a disadvantage by sharing their secrets. **Victor Niederhoffer**. *The Education of a Speculator* (1997)

Part of the loot went for gambling, part for horses, and part for women. The rest I spent foolishly. **George Raft**. Explaining how he spent $10 million. Quoted in *The Perfect Business* (Michael Lebeouf, 1997)

  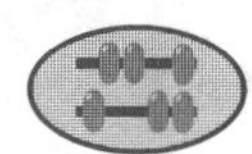 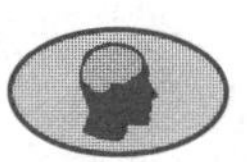  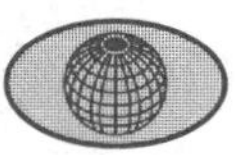   

Someday I want to be rich. Some people get so rich they lose all respect for humanity. That's how rich I want to be. **Rita Rudner**. Quoted in *Ten Commitments to Your Success* (Steve Chandler, 2005)

A nation cannot prosper long when it favors only the prosperous. **Barack Obama**. Inaugural address (January 21, 2009)

In short, it's a great economy if you're a high-level corporate executive or someone who owns a lot of stock. For most other Americans, economic growth is a spectator sport. **Paul R. Krugman**. *New York Times* (July 14, 2006)

Winners and Winning

The winner is simply someone who gets up one more time than they fall over. **Robin Sieger**. *Natural Born Winners* (1999)

One of the things I learned long ago about auctions was that it's not about ego or talent. It's simply about raising your hand for the next bid. They won. We lost. Next. **Barry Diller**. *BusinessWeek* (1994)

He who owns the most when he dies, wins. **Ivan Boesky**. *The Times (London)* (November 20, 1986)

Winners are people who have fun—and produce results as a result of their zest. **Tom Peters**. *A Passion for Excellence* (co-written with Nancy Austin, 1985)

He who does not hope to win has already lost. **José Joaquín Olmedo**. Quoted in *Reader's Digest* (June 1968)

Everyone is a potential winner. Some people are disguised as losers, don't let their appearances fool you. **Kenneth Blanchard**. *The One Minute Manager* (1993)

Winning is everything. The only ones who remember you when you come second are your wife and your dog. **Damon Hill**. *Sunday Times (London)* (December 1994)

The best way to win an argument is to begin by being right. **Jill Ruckelshaus**. Quoted in *Words of Women: Quotations for Success* (1997)

Women in Business

Men are troublesome. They complain about trifles a woman wouldn't notice. The office boys...complain that the temperature of the building is too hot or too cold...If they have a slight headache, they stay at home. **Clara Lanza**. "Women Clerks in New York," *Cosmopolitan* (1891)

Well-ventilated, well-lighted, and sanitarily kept workrooms, rest-rooms and other creature comforts provided in factories, stores, and office buildings are largely the results of women's presence in industry. **Edith Johnson**. *To Women of the Business World* (1923)

Total commitment to family and total commitment to career is possible, but fatiguing. **Muriel Fox**. Quoted in "Wait Late to Marry," *New Woman* (Barbara Jordan Moore, October 1971)

Women are naturally good motivators, good at juggling different projects and issues at the same time, and more cooperative rather than aggressive and confrontational. **Bridget A. Macaskill**. Quoted in *Women of the Street* (Sue Herera, 1997)

One of the biggest mistakes women make in business is that they aren't friendly enough. **Charlotte Beers**. *Fortune* (1996)

Running a business here in the UK, particularly being a woman, is just far too big a deal. The point at which some woman starts up a business and nobody cares about it, that's when we'll all know we made it. **Barbara Cassani**. "Mount Holyoke College: Barbara Cassani '82, Soaring to New Heights," *Vista* (2000)

It's so much easier for men. They don't have to paint their nails for a meeting. **Eve Pollard**. Quoted in *Guardian (London)* (December 30, 1995)

Women are underserved and underestimated as consumers. **Geraldine Laybourne**. "The 50 Most Powerful Women in American Business," *Fortune* (Patricia Sellers and Cora Daniels, October 1999)

Women are opening businesses at twice the rate of men...Forty percent of businesses will be owned by women. Women are saying, I don't belong in this company. I'm sick of fighting this battle. **Faith Popcorn**. Interview, *phenomeNEWS* (1999)

If you want to push something...you're accused of being aggressive, and that's not supposed to be a good thing for a woman. If you get upset and show it, you're accused of being emotional. **Mary Harney**. Attributed

Women actually do quite well on Wall Street because so much of this business is intuitive. **Elizabeth MacKay**. Quoted in *Women of the Street* (Sue Herera, 1997)

The men are always playing their own macho games. It's not really the money they want—it's beating their colleagues by making that extra phone call at night. **Anonymous**. A senior female banker on her male colleages and why women are still rare at the top of the profession. Quoted in *The Moneylenders: Bankers in a Dangerous World* (Anthony Sampson, 1981)

What kind of nation is this...nation of silk knees, slender necks, narrow fingers, and ironic mouths which has established itself upon our boundaries? **Anonymous**. A complaint about the growing number of women in the modern business office. *Fortune* (1935)

I have yet to hear a man ask for advice on how to combine marriage and a career. **Gloria Steinem**. Radio interview, LBC (April 2, 1984)

I don't play golf. I don't go to the men's room. I didn't have the ability to network the way men do. But I made myself visible. **Jill Barad**. *Wall Street Journal* (1997)

Men always try to keep women out of business so they won't find out how much fun it really is. **Vivien Kellems**. Quoted in *Women Can Be Engineers* (Alice Goff, 1946)

People assume you slept your way to the top. Frankly, I couldn't sleep my way to the middle. **Joni Evans**. Conference speech to female executives, referring to her start in publishing as a manuscript reader. *New York Times* (July 22, 1986)

Women do not win formula one races, because they simply are not strong enough to resist the G-forces. In the boardroom, it is different. I believe women are better able to marshal their thoughts than men and because they are less egotistical they make fewer assumptions. **Nicola Foulston**. Interview, *Independent (London)* (April 10, 1995)

Work and Employment

Everyone confesses in the abstract that exertion...is the best thing for us all, but practically most people do all they can to get rid of it. **Harriet Beecher Stowe**. "The

  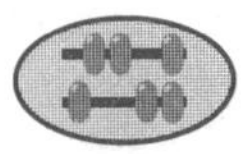   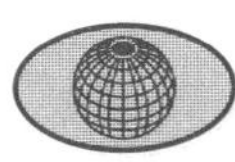   

Lady Who Does Her Own Work," *Atlantic Monthly* (1864)

The bond between a man and his profession is similar to that which ties him to his country; it is just as complex, often ambivalent, and it is understood completely only when it is broken. **Primo Levi**. *Other People's Trades* (1989)

One of the first things to be noted in business life is its imperialism. Business is exacting, engrossing, and inelastic. **Margaret Sangster**. *Winsome Womanhood* (1900)

I believe in hard work. It keeps the wrinkles out of the mind and spirit. **Helena Rubinstein**. *My Life for Beauty* (1965)

Retirement is an illusion. Not a reward but a mantrap. The bankrupt underside of success. A shortcut to death. Golf courses are too much like cemeteries. **Saul Bellow**. *The Actuel* (1997)

Work keeps us from three great evils: boredom, vice, and poverty. **Voltaire**. *Candide* (1759)

The greatest testimony to the human spirit that I'm witnessing now is the fact that people still come back to work, after all that has been done to them. They are still willing to participate for a more positive future if they would be sincerely invited. **Walter Wriston**. Interview with Scott London. US National Public Radio (November 1996)

Anyone can do any amount of work provided it isn't the work he is supposed to be doing at the moment. **Robert Benchley**. Quoted in *The Algonquin Wits* (R. E. Drennan, 1968)

One of the saddest things is that the only thing a man can do for eight hours a day, day after day, is work. You can't eat...nor make love for eight hours. **William Faulkner**. Interview, *Writers at Work (first series)* (Malcom Cowley, ed, 1958)

Work alone qualifies us for life. **Zoë Akins**. Attributed to (1924)

Work is much more fun than fun. **Sir Noël Coward**. Quoted in "Sayings of the Week," *Observer (London)* (June 21, 1963)

It's true hard work never killed anyone but I figure why take the chance? **Ronald Reagan**. *Speaking My Mind* (1990)

What is work and what is not work is a question that perplexes the wisest of men. **Bhagavad Gita** 4:16 (300? BC)

That state is a state of slavery in which a man does what he likes to do in his spare time and, in his working time, that which is required of him. **Eric Gill**. *Art—Nonsense and Other Essays* (1929)

Nothing is really work unless you would rather be doing something else. **Sir James Barrie**. Quoted in *Woodbury Reports Archives* (June 1997)

Business is like sex. When it's good, it's very, very good; when it's not so good, it's still good. **George Katona**. *Wall Street Journal* (April 9, 1969)

The one thing I know through experience...is that people don't know why they come to work until they don't have to come to work. **H. Ross Perot**. *Inc.* (January 1989)

There is nothing like employment, active, indispensable employment, for relieving sorrow. **Jane Austen**. *Mansfield Park* (1814), vol. 3, ch. 15

A perpetual holiday is a good working definition of hell. **George Bernard Shaw**. *Parents and Children* (1914)

A man who has no office to go to—I don't care who he is—is a trial of which you can have no conception. **George Bernard Shaw**. *The Irrational Knot* (1950)

Without work, all life goes rotten, but when work is soulless, life stifles and dies. **Albert Camus**. Quoted in *Good Work* (E. F. Schumacher, 1979)

I yield to no one in my admiration for the office as a social centre, but it's no place actually to get any work done. **Katharine Whitehorn**. Attributed

We're not built for free time as a species. We think we are but we aren't. **Douglas Coupland**. *Generation X* (1991)

Japanese salarymen know that for pure relaxation, nothing beats a good long day in the office. **Peter Tasker**. *Inside Japan* (1987)

I have nothing against work, particularly when performed, quietly and unobtrusively, by someone else. I just don't happen to think it's an appropriate subject for an ethic. **Barbara Ehrenreich**. "Goodbye to the Work Ethic," *The Worst Years of Our Lives* (1991)

If I were a medical man, I should prescribe a holiday to any patient who considered his work important. **Edward O. Wilson**. *Autobiography* (1967)

Labor is work that leaves no trace behind it when it is finished. **Mary McCarthy**. "The Vita Activa," *New Yorker* (October 18, 1958)

Work was like cats were supposed to be: if you disliked and feared it...it knew at once and sought you out and jumped on your lap and climbed all over you to show how much it loved you. **Sir Kingsley Amis**. *Take a Girl Like You* (1960), ch. 5

I don't like work—no man does—but I like what is in work—the chance to find yourself. Your own reality—for yourself, not for others—what no other man can ever know. **Joseph Conrad**. *Heart of Darkness* (1902)

I think many people just work as a way of not confronting themselves. **Gerry Robinson**. *Management Today* (April 1999)

Why should I let the toad *work*
Squat on my life?
...Six days of the week it soils
With its sickening poison—
Just for paying a few bills!
That's out of proportion.
Philip Larkin. "Toads," *The Less Deceived* (1955), ll. 1–2; 5–8

Nothing is more humiliating than to have to beg for work, and a system in which any man has to beg for work stands condemned. No man can defend it. **Eugene V. Debs**. Speech given at the founding of the Federal Council of Churches in Girard, Kansas. "The Issue" (May 23, 1908)

When a man tells you he got rich through hard work, ask him, "Whose?" **Don Marquis**. Attributed

I like work; it fascinates me. I can sit and look at it for hours. I love to keep it by me: the idea of getting rid of it nearly breaks my heart. **Jerome K. Jerome**. *Three Men in a Boat* (1889)

I would live my life in nonchalance and insouciance
Were it not for making a living, which is really rather a nouciance.
Ogden Nash. "Introspective Reflection," *Hard Lines* (1931)

Work is of two kinds: first, altering the position of matter at or near the earth's surface relative to other matter; second, telling other people to do so. The first kind is unpleasant and ill paid, the second is pleasant and highly paid. **Bertrand Russell (Earl Russell)**. *In Praise of Idleness* (1932)

The world is full of willing people: some willing to work, the rest willing to let them. **Robert Frost**. Attributed

Every man's work, pursued steadily, tends to become an end in itself, and so to bridge

  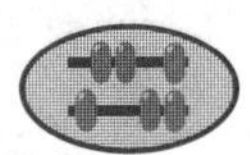   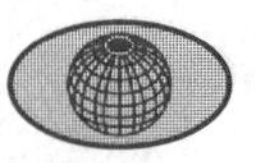   

over the loveless chasms of his life. **George Eliot**. *Silas Marner* (1861), ch. 2

Work is the grand cure of all the maladies and miseries that ever beset mankind. **Thomas Carlyle**. Speech, Edinburgh, Scotland (April 2, 1866)

If the artist does not fling himself, without reflecting, into his work as the soldier flings himself into the enemy's trenches, and if, once in this crater, he does not work like a miner on whom the walls of his gallery have fallen in; if he contemplates difficulties instead of overcoming them one by one he is simply looking on at the suicide of his own talent. **Honoré de Balzac**. *A Cousine Bette* (1846)

Some people see things that are and ask, "Why?" Some people dream of things that never were and ask, "Why not?" Some people have to go to work and don't have time for all that shit. **George Carlin**. *Brain Droppings* (1998)

Hard work often pays off after time, but laziness always pays off now. **E. L. Kersten**. *The Art of Demotivation* (2003)

We do not go to work only to earn an income, but to find meaning in our lives. What we do is a large part of what we are. **Alan Ryan**. Quoted in *If Aristotle Ran General Motors* (Tom Morris, 1997)

  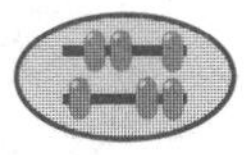   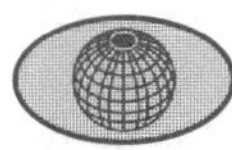   

Author Index

Abdul-Jabbar, Kareem (*b.* 1947) US basketball player **1824**
Abedi, Hasan (1922–1995) PAKISTANI banker and president of the Bank of Credit and Commerce International, Luxembourg **1805**
Abzug, Bella (1920–1998) US politician, lawyer, and campaigner **1781, 1781**
Achebe, Chinua (*b.* 1930) NIGERIAN novelist, poet, and essayist **1779**
Acheson, Dean (1893–1971) US statesman **1762, 1766, 1821**
Ackerman, Gary (*b.* 1942) US congressman **1768**
Acton, John Dalberg-, Lord (1834–1902) BRITISH historian **1814**
Adams, Douglas (1952–2001) BRITISH author **1773, 1825, 1825**
Adams, Henry Brooks (1838–1918) US historian **1810, 1814**
Adams, Scott (*b.* 1957) US cartoonist and humorist **1762, 1775, 1775, 1778, 1787, 1794, 1805, 1816, 1819, 1824**
Addison, Joseph (1672–1719) ENGLISH statesman and author **1823**
Adenauer, Konrad J. (1876–1967) GERMAN chancellor **1778**
Adler, Alfred (1870–1937) AUSTRIAN psychologist and psychiatrist **1815**
Aesop (620?–560? BC) GREEK writer **1767**
Agassiz, Louis (1807–1873) SWISS-BORN US zoologist **1808**
Agate, James (1877–1947) BRITISH critic and essayist **1762**
Agnelli, Giovanni (1921–2003) ITALIAN business executive and president of Fiat **1777, 1781**
Aiken, Howard (1900–1973) US computer engineer and mathematician **1796**
Akins, Zoë (1886–1958) US poet and playwright **1829**
Alda, Alan (*b.* 1936) US movie actor **1808**
Aldington, Richard (1892–1962) BRITISH poet and novelist **1803**
Ali, Muhammad (*b.* 1942) US boxer **1800, 1802, 1803**
Alinsky, Saul (1909–1972) US activist **1770, 1814**
Allchin, Jim (*b.* 1951) US computer scientist and former Microsoft executive **1805**
Allen, Fred (1894–1956) US comedian and satirist **1761, 1787, 1806**
Allen, Robert G. (*b.* 1948) US financial writer **1820**
Allen, Woody (*b.* 1935) US actor, humorist, producer, and director **1808, 1823**
Allesandra, Tony US marketing strategist and motivational speaker **1820**
Amis, Sir Kingsley (1922–1995) BRITISH novelist and poet **1818, 1829**
Amis, Martin (*b.* 1949) BRITISH novelist **1808**
Anderson, Poul (1926–2001) US science fiction writer **1816**
Andrews, David (*b.* 1935) IRISH politician **1812**
Anonymous **1760, 1760, 1762, 1762, 1763, 1764, 1766, 1769, 1770, 1770, 1770, 1774, 1775, 1777, 1780, 1782, 1782, 1782, 1782, 1782, 1782, 1783, 1783, 1783, 1785, 1785, 1785, 1785, 1789, 1792, 1792, 1795, 1795, 1802, 1802, 1803, 1804, 1805, 1807, 1807, 1807, 1809, 1809, 1809, 1811, 1812, 1816, 1817, 1817, 1819, 1822, 1824, 1826, 1828, 1828**
Anthony, Susan B. (1820–1906) US reformer and women's suffrage leader **1781**
Antrim, Minna (1856–1950) US writer **1788, 1788**
Archer of Western-Super-Mare, Jeffrey, Lord (*b.* 1940) BRITISH novelist and politician **1787, 1813**
Archer of Weston-Super-Mare, Mary, Lady (*b.* 1944) BRITISH chemist **1760**
Archibald, Jules (1856–1919) AUSTRALIAN journalist **1797**
Arden, Elizabeth (1884–1966) US entrepreneur and cosmetics manufacturer **1786, 1826**
Arendt, Hannah (1906–1975) US political philosopher **1821**
Argyris, Chris (*b.* 1923) US academic and organizational behavior theorist **1803**
Armour, Philip D. (1832–1901) US business executive **1808, 1817**
Armstrong, Richard (1903–1986) BRITISH author and mariner **1761**
Armstrong, William, Lord (1915–1980) BRITISH civil servant **1794**
Arnason, Sigurjon ICELANDIC manager of the Icesave high-interest savings account, which subsequently collapsed and was nationalized **1764**
Arthur, W. Brian (*b.* 1945) US economist **1784, 1784**
Ash, Mary Kay (1915–2001) US entrepreneur, business executive, and founder of Mary Kay Cosmetics **1774, 1786, 1789, 1794, 1803, 1812, 1815**
Astor, John Jacob (1763–1848) US entrepreneur and financier **1827**
Atkins, Paul S. (*b.* 1958) US former member of the Securities and Exchange Commission **1791**
Atkinson, Brooks (1894–1984) US critic and essayist **1785**
Atwood, Margaret (*b.* 1939) CANADIAN poet and novelist **1770**
Auden, W. H. (1907–1973) US poet **1800, 1803**
August, John (*b.* 1970) US screenwriter **1807**
Auphan, Raphael FRENCH business executive **1781**
Austen, Jane (1775–1817) BRITISH novelist **1829**
Auster, Paul (*b.* 1947) US novelist, short-story writer, and poet **1807**
Avery, Oswald Theodore (1877–1955) US bacteriologist **1789**
Babbage, Charles (1792–1871) BRITISH mathematician and inventor **1782**
Bacon, Francis (Viscount St Alban) (1561–1626) ENGLISH philosopher and statesman **1809**
Bagehot, Walter (1826–1877) BRITISH economist and journalist **1763, 1763, 1768, 1796**
Baker, Russell (*b.* 1925) US journalist **1783**
Baldwin, James (1924–1987) US writer **1770, 1788, 1807, 1814**
Baldwin, Tom US financial trader **1790**
Balogh, Thomas (1905–1985) BRITISH economist **1783**
Balzac, Honoré de (1799–1850) FRENCH novelist **1830**
Band, Richard US financial writer **1765**
Banks-Smith, Nancy (*b.* 1929) BRITISH journalist **1814**
Barad, Jill (*b.* 1951) US former CEO of Mattel **1828**
Barker, Joel A. US futurologist **1802, 1826**
Barlow, John Perry (*b.* 1947) US academic, lyricist, and writer **1770, 1794**
Barnard, Chester (1886–1961) US business executive and management theorist **1772, 1826**
Barnevik, Percy (*b.* 1941) SWEDISH former CEO of ABB **1770, 1779, 1795**
Barnum, P. T. (1810–1891) US showman and circus entrepreneur **1820**
Barrie, Sir James (1860–1937) BRITISH novelist and playwright **1829**
Barrows, Sydney Biddle (*b.* 1952) US brothel owner **1766**
Barry, Dave (*b.* 1947) US humorist **1773, 1785, 1787**
Bartlett, Christopher (*b.* 1945) AUSTRALIAN business writer **1776, 1776, 1804, 1816**
Barton, Bruce (1886–1967) US advertising executive and author **1761, 1774**
Baruch, Bernard (1870–1965) US financier and economist **1787, 1789, 1789**
Barzun, Jacques (*b.* 1907) FRENCH-BORN US educator, historian, and writer **1771, 1778, 1810**
Bateson, Mary Catherine (*b.* 1939) US anthropologist **1793**

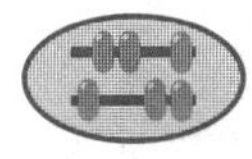

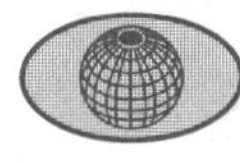

1816, 1818, 1819, 1822, 1822, 1824, 1826
Bureau of Labor US government department **1781**
Burke, Edmund (1729–1797) BRITISH philosopher and politician **1760, 1814, 1823**
Burke, James (*b.* 1925) US CEO of Johnson & Johnson **1780**
Burke, Thomas (1886–1945) BRITISH writer **1815**
Burnett, Leo (1891–1971) US advertising executive and author **1761, 1762**
Burns, H. S. M. (1900–1971) BRITISH oil industry executive, geophysicist, and president of Shell Oil Company **1804**
Burroughs, Nannie (1883–1961) US educator and journalist **1769**
Burroughs, William S. (1914–1997) US novelist **1817**
Burson, Harold (*b.* 1921) US business executive and founder of Burson-Marsteller Public Relations **1818**
Burton, John C. (*b.* 1932) US accountant and academic **1760**
Burton, Sir Montague (1885–1952) BRITISH tailor and founder of the Burton Group **1774**
Bush, George W. (*b.* 1946) US former president **1765, 1765, 1765, 1765, 1765, 1777, 1792**
Busquet, Anne (*b.* 1951?) US business executive **1779**
Butler, David (*b.* 1924) BRITISH psephologist **1775**
Butler, Nicholas Murray (1862–1947) US academic **1801**
Butler, Samuel (1835–1902) BRITISH writer **1760, 1775, 1785, 1807, 1818, 1823**
Byrne, John A. US journalist and writer **1767**
Byrnes, James F. (1879–1972) US politician **1814**
Byron, George Gordon, Lord (1788–1824) BRITISH poet **1767**
Cage, John (1912–1992) US composer **1796**
Cairncross, Frances (*b.* 1944) BRITISH journalist and author **1793**
Calloway, Wayne (1935–1998) US CEO of Pepsico **1773**
Campbell, Bill (*b.* 1940) US chairman of Intuit Corporation **1776, 1802**
Campos, Roberto (1917–2001) BRAZILIAN politician and economist **1782**
Campos, Roel C. (*b.* 1949) US member of the Securities and Exchange Commission **1763**
Camus, Albert (1913–1960) FRENCH novelist and essayist **1771, 1788, 1829**
Canetti, Elias (1905–1994) BRITISH philosopher and writer **1780**
Cantor, Eddie (1892–1964) US entertainer **1823**
Carlin, George (1937–2008) US comedian and author **1830**
Carlyle, Thomas (1795–1881) BRITISH historian and essayist **1761, 1794, 1797, 1830**
Carnegie, Andrew (1835–1919) US industrialist and philanthropist **1766, 1768, 1772, 1783, 1802, 1812, 1812, 1827**
Carnegie, Dale (1888–1955) US consultant and author **1786, 1823**
Carter, Angela (1940–1992) BRITISH novelist, short-story writer, and essayist **1796**
Carville, James (*b.* 1944) US political consultant, campaign manager to Bill Clinton **1790**
Cassani, Barbara (*b.* 1960) US former CEO of Go **1772, 1828**
Cassano, Joseph J. (*b.* 1955?) US former executive of AIG insurance **1791**
Cassel, Sir Ernest (1852–1921) BRITISH private banker to King Edward VII **1763**
Chajet, Clive (*b.* 1937) US management consultant **1796**
Chakraborty, S. K. (*b.* 1957) INDIAN academic **1770, 1782, 1802, 1803, 1803**
Chalker of Wallasey, Lynda, Baroness (*b.* 1942) BRITISH politician **1777**
Chambers, Chuck US CEO of Sara Lee Direct **1767**
Chamfort, Nicholas (1741–1794) FRENCH writer **1784**
Champy, James (*b.* 1942) US business executive **1804**
Chandler, Kyle (*b.* 1965) US movie actor **1810**
Chandler, Raymond (1888–1959) US writer **1761, 1767**
Chandos, Viscount (Oliver Lyttelton) (1893–1972) BRITISH statesman and industrialist **1800, 1818**
Chanel, Coco (1883–1971) FRENCH couturier **1798**
Chang, Kenneth US journalist **1790**
Chartier, Émile-August (1868–1951) FRENCH philosopher **1796**
Chekhov, Anton (1860–1904) RUSSIAN playwright and short-story writer **1761**
Cheng Siwei (*b.* 1935) CHINESE vice chairman of the National People's Congress of China **1782**
Chernin, Peter (*b.* 1951) US chief operating officer of News Corporation, chairman and CEO of the Fox Group **1805, 1813**
Chesterfield, Lord (Philip Dormer Stanhope) (1694–1773) ENGLISH statesman, orator, and letter writer **1772**
Chesterton, G. K. (1874–1936) BRITISH novelist, poet, and critic **1761, 1767, 1772, 1785, 1792, 1810, 1815, 1821, 1826**
Chomsky, Noam (*b.* 1928) US linguist and political activist **1783**
Christensen, Clayton M. (*b.* 1952) US writer **1779**
Christie, Dame Agatha (1891–1976) BRITISH novelist **1798**
Churchill, Jennie (1854–1921) US socialite and writer **1769**
Churchill, Sir Winston (1874–1965) BRITISH prime minister **1764, 1780, 1795, 1812, 1819, 1821**
Cicero (106–43 BC) ROMAN orator and statesman **1822**
Clark, Alan (1928–1999) BRITISH politician and diarist **1779, 1795**
Clarke, Sir Arthur C. (1917–2008) BRITISH science fiction writer **1825**
Cleese, John (*b.* 1939) BRITISH comedian, actor, and writer **1767**
Clegg, Stewart (*b.* 1947) AUSTRALIAN writer **1798**
Clifford, Robert (*b.* 1943) AUSTRALIAN business executive **1824**
Clifton, Jim (*b.* 1951) US CEO of Gallup **1798**
Clifton, Lucille (*b.* 1936) US poet and author **1761**
Clough, Arthur Hugh (1819–1861) BRITISH poet **1767, 1773, 1803**
Cocks, Barnett (1907–1989) BRITISH author **1766**
Cocteau, Jean (1889–1963) FRENCH poet, novelist, dramatist, and director **1803**
Coggan, Philip (*b.* 1959) BRITISH journalist **1806**
Colbert, L. L. (1905–1995) US chairman of Chrysler Corporation **1787**
Colchester, Nicholas (1949?–1996) BRITISH author and journalist **1782**
Coleman, Debi (*b.* 1953) US business executive and former chief financial officer of Apple Computers **1775**
Coleridge, Samuel Taylor (1772–1834) BRITISH poet **1788**
Colman, Jeremiah James (1830–1898) BRITISH food industry executive **1813**
Comfort, Max BRITISH business theorist **1792**
Cone, Fairfax (1903–1977) US advertising executive **1761, 1761, 1772, 1785**
Confucius (551–479 BC) CHINESE philosopher, administrator, and writer **1760, 1770, 1771, 1804, 1823**
Conner, Daryl R. (*b.* 1946) US management author **1810**
Connolly, Cyril (1903–1974) BRITISH critic, essayist, and novelist **1823**
Conrad, Joseph (1857–1924) POLISH-BORN BRITISH novelist and seaman **1829**
Conran, Shirley (*b.* 1932) BRITISH designer, fashion editor, and author **1785, 1815**
Conran, Sir Terence (*b.* 1931) BRITISH business executive, retailer, and founder of Habitat **1820, 1823**
Cook, Rick (*b.* 1944) US author **1774**
Cooley, Charles Horton (1864–1929) US sociologist **1785, 1814**
Coolidge, Calvin (1872–1933) US president **1768, 1812, 1817, 1827**

  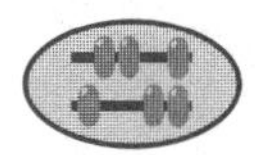   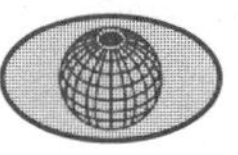   

   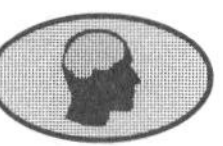  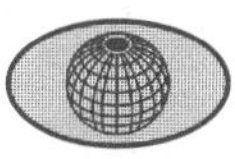   

Emmott, Bill (*b.* 1956) BRITISH economics journalist **1765**
Eng, William F. US financial trader and author **1790**
Engels, Friedrich (1820–1895) GERMAN social philosopher and political economist **1771**
England, Dan (*b.* 1948) US CEO of CR England **1824**
Enzi, Mike (*b.* 1944) US senator **1791**
Epictetus (55?–135?) GREEK philosopher **1774**
Esar, Evan (1899–1995) US humorist **1813**
Evans, Sir Harold (*b.* 1928) BRITISH newspaper editor and publisher **1797**
Evans, Joni (*b.* 1942) US publishing executive **1828**
Ewing, D. W. (*b.* 1923) US writer and editor of *Harvard Business Review* **1826**
Ewing, Sam (1920–2001) US author **1764, 1775, 1801, 1820, 1824**
Fadiman, Clifton (1904–1999) US editor and author **1767**
Farmer, Tom (*b.* 1940) BRITISH founder and former chairman of Kwik-Fit **1820**
Farnell, James W. US CEO of Illinois Tool Works, Inc. **1775**
Faulkner, William (1897–1962) US novelist **1829**
Fawkes, Guy (1570–1606) ENGLISH conspirator **1819**
Fei Xiaotong (1910–2005) CHINESE social anthropologist **1781**
Felcht, Utz (*b.* 1947) GERMAN chairman of Degussa **1776**
Fellini, Federico (1920–1993) ITALIAN movie director **1796**
Fernandez, Raul (*b.* 1966) MEXICAN IT entrepreneur **1783**
Fey, Grace US vice president and director of Frontier Capital Management **1781**
Feynman, Richard P. (1918–1988) US physicist **1796, 1820**
Field, Marshall (1834–1906) US retailer **1779**
Fields, W. C. (1880–1946) US actor and comedian **1788**
Figgie, Harry E., Jr (*b.* 1923?) US founder of Figgie International **1802**
Fiore, Neil A. US self-help writer **1792**
Fiorina, Carly (*b.* 1954) US president and CEO of Hewlett-Packard **1802, 1802**
Firestone, Harvey (1868–1938) US founder of Firestone Tire and Rubber **1800, 1816**
Fitz-Enz, Jac (*b.* 1948) US writer **1814**
Fitzgerald, F. Scott (1896–1940) US writer **1806, 1814**
Fitzgerald, Niall (*b.* 1945) IRISH former chairman and CEO of Unilever and president of the Advertising Association, current chairman of Reuters **1779**
Fitzgerald, Penelope (1916–2000) BRITISH novelist and biographer **1773**
Fitz-Gibbon, Bernice (1895?–1982) US advertising executive **1762, 1775, 1778**
Follett, Mary Parker (1868–1933) US management thinker and author **1786, 1819**
Foot, Michael (*b.* 1913) BRITISH politician and writer **1814**
Forbes, Bertie Charles (1880–1954) US publisher and writer **1812**
Forbes, Malcolm S. (1919–1990) US publisher **1760, 1800, 1819**
Forbes, Steve (*b.* 1947) US publishing executive **1768, 1786**
Ford, Henry (1863–1947) US industrialist, automobile manufacturer, and founder of Ford Motor Company **1767, 1771, 1774, 1779, 1780, 1785, 1797, 1817, 1818, 1825**
Ford, Henry (1919–1987) US automobile manufacturer and CEO of Ford Motor Company **1776, 1795, 1816**
Ford, William Clay, Jr (*b.* 1957) US business executive **1787**
Forrester, Lynn (*b.* 1954) US business executive **1787**
Foulston, Nicola (*b.* 1958?) BRITISH former CEO of the Brands Hatch group **1828**
Fox, Muriel (*b.* 1928) US business executive **1828**
France, Anatole (1844–1924) FRENCH novelist **1827**
Frand, Erwin US businessman and journalist **1779**
Frank, Barney (*b.* 1940) US chairman of the House Financial Services Committee **1765, 1794**
Franklin, Benjamin (1706–1790) US politician, inventor, and journalist **1767, 1779, 1793, 1801, 1808, 1811**
Freedland, Jonathan (*b.* 1967) BRITISH journalist **1791**
Freedley, Edwin T. (1827–1904) US manufacturer **1760**
Fregger, Brad (*b.* 1940) US CEO of 1st World Library **1778**
Friedman, Milton (1912–2006) US economist and winner of the 1976 Nobel Prize in Economics **1773, 1777, 1784, 1784, 1794, 1794, 1824**
Friedman, Thomas (*b.* 1953) US journalist and author **1798**
Friends of the Earth environmental campaign organization **1793**
Frisch, Max (1911–1991) SWISS author **1825**
Frost, Sir David (*b.* 1939) BRITISH broadcaster **1809**
Frost, Robert (1874–1963) US poet **1789, 1799, 1829**
Fry, Art (*b.* 1931) US entrepreneur and inventor of Post-it notes **1799**
Fuentes, Carlos (*b.* 1928) MEXICAN writer **1771, 1782**
Fukushima, Yasuhiro (*b.* 1948) JAPANESE business executive **1783**
Fukuyama, Francis (*b.* 1952) US economist and writer **1781, 1784, 1810**
Fuld, Richard S., Jr (*b.* 1946) US chief executive of the collapsed Lehman Brothers investment house **1768, 1789, 1789**
Fuller, R. Buckminster (1895–1983) US inventor, architect, and philosopher **1786**
Fuller, Thomas (1654–1734) ENGLISH physician and writer **1764, 1764, 1774, 1775, 1826**
Furphy, Joseph (1843–1912) AUSTRALIAN journalist, novelist, and poet **1773**
Galbraith, J. K. (1908–2006) US economist and diplomat **1761, 1761, 1763, 1784, 1784, 1784, 1784, 1787, 1789, 1792, 1796, 1798, 1806, 1807, 1807, 1816, 1821, 1826, 1826, 1827, 1827**
Galsworthy, John (1867–1933) BRITISH novelist and playwright **1760**
Gandhi, Indira (1917–1984) INDIAN prime minister **1782**
Gandhi, Mahatma (1869–1948) INDIAN nationalist leader and philosopher **1771, 1795, 1801**
Gann, W. D. (1878–1955) US trader and financial forecaster **1790**
Gardner, Ava (1922–1990) US actress **1796**
Gardner, Richard (1927–2003) US diplomat, lawyer, and educator **1782**
Garnier, Jean-Pierre (*b.* 1947) FRENCH former CEO of GlaxoSmithKline **1786, 1812**
Gates, Bill (*b.* 1955) US entrepreneur, chairman and CEO of Microsoft **1770, 1773, 1779, 1785, 1788, 1802, 1805, 1813, 1819, 1823, 1823**
Gaubis, Anthony (1902–1989) US financial analyst **1761**
Gauthier, Mark US travel writer **1781**
Gellerman, Saul W. (*b.* 1929) US psychologist and writer **1760**
Geneen, Harold S. (1910–1997) US telecommunications entrepreneur and CEO of ITT **1776, 1787, 1788, 1794, 1798, 1805, 1811, 1812, 1812, 1817, 1824**
General Motors automobile manufacturer **1798**
George, Henry (1839–1897) US economist **1826, 1826, 1827**
Gerstner, Lou (*b.* 1942) US former chairman and CEO of IBM **1776, 1783, 1826**
Getty, J. Paul (1892–1976) US entrepreneur, oil industry executive, and financier **1760, 1767, 1771, 1794, 1797, 1819, 1822, 1827**
Giannini, Amadeo (1870–1949) US banker and founder of Bank of America **1808, 1823**
Gibbons, Barry J. (*b.* 1946) US former chairman and CEO of Burger King, co-founder of Y Arriba Y Arriba, and author **1776**

  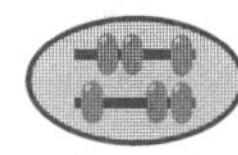   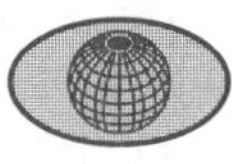   

Gibson, William (*b.* 1948) US-CANADIAN science-fiction writer **1771**
Gide, André (1869–1951) FRENCH novelist and essayist **1778**
Gilbert, Sir W. S. (1836–1911) BRITISH librettist and playwright **1764**
Gilder, George (*b.* 1939) US economist **1768**
Gill, Eric (1882–1940) BRITISH sculptor and engraver **1829**
Gilmour, Ian (1926–2007) BRITISH politician **1784**
Giraudoux, Jean (1882–1944) FRENCH diplomat, novelist, and playwright **1785, 1801**
Gissing, George (1857–1903) BRITISH novelist **1815**
Glancey, Jonathan BRITISH journalist **1760**
Glasgow, Arnold H. US psychologist **1784**
Goethe, Johann Wolfgang von (1749–1832) GERMAN poet, playwright, novelist, and scientist **1762, 1771, 1774, 1807, 1814, 1823**
Goffee, Rob (*b.* 1952) US writer, consultant, and professor at London Business School **1776**
Gogarty, Oliver St. John (1878–1957) IRISH poet and novelist **1801**
Goizueta, Roberto (1931–1997) US CEO of Coca-Cola **1770, 1796, 1807, 1818**
Goldman, William (*b.* 1931) US screenwriter and novelist **1806**
Goldsmith, Sir James (1933–1997) BRITISH entrepreneur, financier, and politician **1806**
Goldsmith, Oliver (1730–1774) BRITISH playwright, writer, and poet **1826**
Goldwyn, Samuel (1882–1974) US movie producer **1826**
Goodman, Danny (*b.* 1950) US writer **1770**
Goodman, Paul (1911–1972) US educator, psychoanalyst, and writer **1766**
Goodwin, Sir Fred (*b.* 1958) BRITISH former chairman of the Royal Bank of Scotland **1763**
Gopnik, Adam (*b.* 1956) US writer **1768**
Gorbachev, Mikhail (*b.* 1931) RUSSIAN former president **1769**
Gordimer, Nadine (*b.* 1923) SOUTH AFRICAN novelist and short-story writer **1819**
Gore, Al (*b.* 1948) US former vice president **1822**
Gore, Wilbert Lee (1912–1986) US founder of Goretex **1798**
Gower, Jim BRITISH professor of law **1794**
Gracián, Baltasar (1601–1658) SPANISH writer and priest **1774**
Grade, Lew, Lord (1906–1998) UKRAINE-BORN BRITISH entertainment entrepreneur **1788, 1803**
Grade, Michael (*b.* 1943) BRITISH television executive **1778**
Graham, Benjamin (1894–1976) US economist and investor **1790, 1800**
Graham, Katharine (1917–2001) US newspaper publisher and owner of *Washington Post* **1802, 1812**
Graham, Paul (*b.* 1964) US computer programmer, writer, and venture capitalist **1793, 1793, 1815**
Grant, Jim US investor and financial commentator **1790**
Gratton, Paul (*b.* 1960) BRITISH former CEO of Egg **1779**
Gray, John (*b.* 1948) BRITISH academic and writer **1768, 1769, 1793, 1793**
Green, Celia (*b.* 1935) BRITISH psychophysicist **1818**
Greene, Graham (1904–1991) BRITISH novelist **1823**
Greenleaf, Robert (1904–1990) US director of Management Research for AT&T and author **1772, 1802, 1821**
Greenspan, Alan (*b.* 1926) US economist and former chairman of US Federal Reserve Board **1764, 1765, 1765, 1784, 1791, 1791, 1791, 1796**
Gretzky, Wayne (*b.* 1961) CANADIAN ice-hockey player **1771**
Groddeck, Georg (1866–1934) GERMAN psychoanalyst **1819**
Groening, Matt (*b.* 1954) US animator and writer **1767, 1767, 1808**
Gross, Bill US CEO of Pimco **1800**
Grove, Andrew S. (*b.* 1936) HUNGARIAN-BORN US entrepreneur, author, and former chairman of Intel Corporation **1770, 1770, 1783, 1785, 1793, 1804, 1812, 1813, 1822, 1823**
Guccione, Bob (*b.* 1930) US magazine publisher **1820**
Gunn, Thom (1929–2004) BRITISH poet **1760**
Gurley, J. William US venture capitalist and journalist **1825**
Gustafson, Deil O. (1932–1999) US real estate executive **1820**
Gyllenhammar, Pehr (*b.* 1935) SWEDISH businessman, former chairman of Volvo **1789**
Haarde, Geir (*b.* 1951) ICELANDIC former prime minister **1763**
Hadfield, Bud (*b.* 1923) US entrepreneur and founder of Kwik Kopy **1794**
Hailsham, Lord (Quintin Hogg) (1907–1990) BRITISH politician **1821**
Hain, Peter (*b.* 1950) BRITISH politician **1781**
Haji-Ioannou, Stelios (*b.* 1967) GREEK founder of easyJet **1793**
Halbert, Gary (1942–2007) US copywriter and marketing guru **1798**
Half, Robert (*b.* 1918) US consultant **1785**
Hall, Doug (*b.* 1959) US business writer **1823**
Halsey, Margaret (1910–1997) US writer **1780**
Hamel, Gary (*b.* 1954) US academic, business writer, and consultant **1770, 1773, 1787, 1795, 1798, 1806, 1809, 1812, 1822, 1822**
Hammer, Armand (1898–1990) US industrialist, philanthropist, founder and CEO of Occidental Petroleum **1803**
Hammer, Michael (*b.* 1948) US author and academic **1770, 1770, 1770, 1776, 1811, 1811**
Hancock, W. Keith (1898–1988) AUSTRALIAN academic **1822**
Hand, Learned (1872–1961) US judge **1809**
Handy, Charles (*b.* 1932) IRISH business executive and author **1776, 1787, 1799, 1800, 1800, 1801, 1804, 1810, 1815, 1817, 1817, 1824, 1826**
Hanson, James Edward, Lord (1922–2004) BRITISH business executive and entrepreneur **1786**
Harkness, Richard (1907–1977) US radio and television journalist **1806**
Harman, Sir Charles Eustace (1894–1970) BRITISH judge **1760**
Harney, Mary (*b.* 1953) IRISH politician **1828**
Harris, B. F. (1811–1905) US businessman **1820**
Harrison, Emma BRITISH entrepreneur **1805**
Harvey, Paul (1918–2009) US broadcaster **1761**
Harvey-Jones, Sir John (1924–2008) BRITISH management adviser, author, and chairman of ICI **1773, 1780, 1782, 1798, 1799, 1805, 1811, 1816, 1817, 1825**
Havel, Václav (*b.* 1936) CZECH writer and president **1813**
Hawken, Paul (*b.* 1946?) US entrepreneur and business author **1768, 1825**
Hayek, Friedrich August von (1899–1992) AUSTRO-HUNGARIAN BORN BRITISH economist **1768**
Hazlitt, William (1778–1830) BRITISH essayist and journalist **1761, 1777, 1809, 1821, 1822**
Hearn, Barry (*b.* 1948) BRITISH sports promoter **1823**
Hefner, Hugh (*b.* 1926) US entrepreneur and publisher **1764**
Heilbroner, Robert L. (1919–2005) US economist **1768, 1783**
Heinlein, Robert A. (1907–1988) US science-fiction writer **1760**
Heller, Joseph (1923–1999) US novelist **1788, 1795, 1804**
Heller, Lucy (*b.* 1959) BRITISH business executive **1781**
Heller, Robert (*b.* 1932) BRITISH management writer **1762, 1782, 1795**
Heller, Walter (1915–1987) US economist **1784**
Helmsley, Leona (1920–2007) US hotelier **1777**
Hemingway, Ernest (1899–1961) US author **1760**

  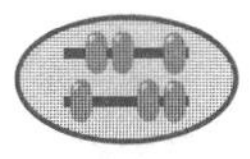   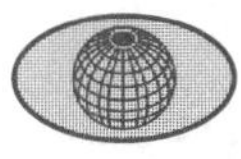 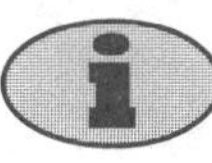  
a–z

Henderson, Leon (1895–1986) US administrator **1784**
Hennig, Margaret (*b.* 1940) US business executive and writer **1781**
Hepburn, Katharine (1907–2003) US actress **1771**
Herbert, George (1593–1633) ENGLISH poet **1762**
Herzberg, Frederick (1923–2000) US psychologist **1785, 1808, 1808, 1811**
Heseltine, Michael, Lord (*b.* 1933) BRITISH politician and publisher **1767**
Hicks, Sir John Richard (1904–1989) BRITISH economist **1826**
Higgins, Michael D. (*b.* 1941) IRISH politician **1806**
Hill, Damon (*b.* 1960) BRITISH Formula 1 racing driver **1828**
Hill, John R. US financial trader **1803**
Hill, Napoleon (1883–1970) US motivational author **1789, 1825**
Hillary, Sir Edmund (1919–2008) NEW ZEALAND explorer and mountaineer **1760**
Hite, Larry US investment manager **1790**
Hitler, Adolf (1889–1945) GERMAN dictator **1780**
Hoagland, Edward (*b.* 1932) US novelist, essayist, and naturalist **1773**
Hobbes, John Oliver (1867–1906) BRITISH novelist and dramatist **1774**
Hockney, David (*b.* 1937) BRITISH artist **1825**
Hoffa, Jimmy (1913–1975?) US labor leader **1773**
Hoffer, Eric (1902–1983) US philosopher **1761, 1769, 1778, 1811, 1814**
Hogben, Lancelot (1895–1975) BRITISH scientist **1797**
Holmes, Oliver Wendell (1809–1894) US surgeon, teacher, and writer **1787, 1795**
Holmes, Oliver Wendell, Jr (1841–1935) US jurist **1771**
Holmes à Court, Robert (1937–1990) AUSTRALIAN entrepreneur **1808**
Hood, Thomas (1799–1845) BRITISH poet **1767**
Hoover, Herbert (1874–1964) US president **1768**
Hope, Bob (1903–2003) US comedian and motion picture actor **1762**
Horace (65–8 BC) ROMAN poet and satirist **1816**
Horlick, Nicola (*b.* 1960) BRITISH fund manager **1778, 1815**
Horton, Tom (*b.* 1926) US chairman of American Management Association **1769**
House, Jay E. (1870–1936) US journalist and columnist **1779**
Hubbard, Elbert (1856–1915) US humorist **1772, 1774, 1827**
Hubbard, Frank McKinney (1868–1930) US humorist **1787, 1792**
Hubbard, Kin (1868–1930) US cartoonist and journalist **1785**
Hurley, Chad (*b.* 1977) US co-founder and CEO of YouTube **1806**
Hutton, Will (*b.* 1950) BRITISH author and newspaper editor **1768**
Huxley, Aldous (1894–1963) BRITISH novelist and essayist **1762, 1767, 1801, 1807**
Huxley, Sir Julian (1887–1975) BRITISH biologist and writer **1808**
Huxley, Thomas (1825–1895) BRITISH biologist **1796**
Iacocca, Lee (*b.* 1924) US former president of Ford Motor Company, chairman and CEO of Chrysler Corporation **1775, 1776, 1779, 1798, 1812, 1812**
Ibuka, Masaru (1908–1997) JAPANESE co-founder and chief adviser of Sony Corporation **1825**
Illich, Ivan (1926–2002) US priest and educator **1775**
Inayama, Yoshihiro (1904–1987) JAPANESE business executive **1781**
Ingersoll, Robert Green (1833–1899) US lawyer and writer **1772**
Ingham, Sir Bernard (*b.* 1932) BRITISH politician **1806**
Iverson, Kenneth (1925–2002) US industrialist, chairman and CEO of Nucor Corporation **1788, 1795**
Jackson, Holbrook (1874–1948) BRITISH writer and critic **1780**
Jackson, Jesse (*b.* 1941) US churchman, civil rights activist, and presidential candidate **1802**
Jackson, Robert H. (1892–1954) US jurist **1803**
Jacobs, Jane (1916–2006) US urban theorist and social critic **1810**
Jacobs, Randall US admiral **1801**
Jaffe, Charles A. US financial journalist **1800**
James, Clive (*b.* 1939) AUSTRALIAN writer and broadcaster **1805**
James, Henry (1843–1916) US novelist **1771, 1788, 1807**
James, William (1842–1910) US psychologist and philosopher **1780, 1816**
Janowitz, Tama (*b.* 1957) US author **1818**
Jay, Sir Anthony (*b.* 1930) BRITISH author and business consultant **1780**
Jefferson, Thomas (1743–1826) US president **1764, 1767, 1793, 1814, 1821**
Jerome, Jerome K. (1859–1927) BRITISH humorist and writer **1829**
Jeszenszky, Geza (*b.* 1941) HUNGARIAN politician and writer **1782**
Jevons, William Stanley (1835–1882) BRITISH economist and mathematician **1797, 1826**
Jobs, Steve (*b.* 1955) US entrepreneur, co-founder and CEO of Apple Computer Company, and CEO of Pixar **1760, 1769, 1770, 1778, 1797, 1798, 1815, 1815, 1817, 1818, 1825, 1825**
Johnson, Boris (*b.* 1964) BRITISH mayor of London **1780**
Johnson, Edith (1891–1954) US writer and educator **1828**
Johnson, Lyndon Baines (1908–1973) US president **1784**
Johnson, Samuel (1709–1784) BRITISH poet, lexicographer, essayist, and critic **1762, 1764, 1772, 1780, 1807**
John XXIII, Pope (originally Angelo Giuseppe Roncalli; 1881–1963) ITALIAN pope **1818**
Jones, Barry Owen (*b.* 1932) AUSTRALIAN politician **1797**
Jones, Clinton (*b.* 1945) US football player **1808**
Jones, Paul Tudor (*b.* 1954) US commodity trader **1800**
Jones, Steve (*b.* 1944) BRITISH geneticist **1824**
Jonson, Ben (1572–1637) ENGLISH playwright and poet **1761**
Joronen, Liisa (*b.* 1944) FINNISH CEO of SOL (formerly Lindstrom) **1824**
Jowett, Benjamin (1817–1893) BRITISH theologian and scholar **1819**
Juantorena, Alberto (*b.* 1950) CUBAN athlete and businessman **1811**
Kafka, Franz (1883–1924) CZECH novelist **1766**
Kaiser, Henry J. (1882–1967) US industrialist **1816**
Kaletsky, Anatole (*b.* 1952) BRITISH journalist and economist **1791**
Kamprad, Ingvar (*b.* 1926) SWEDISH business executive and founder of IKEA **1775, 1817**
Kanter, Rosabeth Moss (*b.* 1943) US management theorist, academic, and writer **1769, 1769, 1769, 1775, 1776, 1793, 1814, 1822**
Kapuściński, Ryszard (1932–2007) POLISH journalist and author **1761**
Karr, Alphonse (1808–1890) FRENCH author **1770**
Kasriel, Paul US financial analyst **1765**
Kasspe, Arthur **1816**
Katona, George (1901–1981) US academic and business analyst **1829**
Kay, Alan (*b.* 1940) US entrepreneur and personal computer developer **1825**
Keats, John (1795–1821) BRITISH poet **1787**
Keegan, William (*b.* 1938) BRITISH author and journalist **1769**
Keen, Peter G. W. (*b.* 1930) US information technology consultant **1779**
Kelleher, Herb (*b.* 1931) US businessman and founder of Southwest Airlines **1795, 1807, 1811**
Kellems, Vivien (1896–1975) US industrialist, feminist, and lecturer **1828**
Kelly, Kevin (*b.* 1958) US executive editor of *Wired* magazine **1798, 1801**

  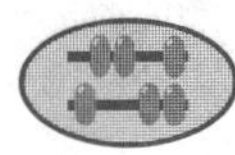 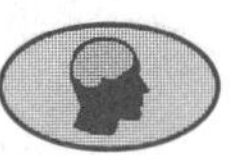  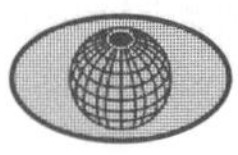   

Kendall, Donald M. (*b.* 1921) US CEO of Pepsico, Inc. **1773**
Kennedy, Carol (*b.* 1952) BRITISH business executive, editor, and author **1775**
Kennedy, Douglas (*b.* 1955) BRITISH writer, journalist and playwright **1781**
Kennedy, Florynce R. (1916–2000) US lawyer and political activist **1781**
Kennedy, John F. (1917–1963) US president **1808, 1809**
Kennedy, Joseph P. (1888–1969) US entrepreneur, government official, and diplomat **1814**
Kennelly, Brendan (*b.* 1936) IRISH poet and academic **1817**
Kent, Rod (*b.* 1947?) BRITISH former chairman of Bradford & Bingley Building Society **1763**
Kersten, E. L. US satirist, former professor of organizational communication **1818, 1830**
Kerviel, Jerome (*b.* 1977) FRENCH trader **1777**
Kettering, Charles Franklin (1876–1958) US businessman and engineer **1763, 1788, 1815**
Keynes, John Maynard (1883–1946) BRITISH economist **1768, 1783, 1783, 1783, 1787, 1789, 1789, 1789, 1799, 1799, 1807, 1813, 1821**
Khrushchev, Nikita (1894–1971) SOVIET politician **1779**
Kiam, Victor (1926–2001) US CEO of Remington Corporation **1797, 1808**
Kindersley, Peter (*b.* 1941) BRITISH publisher, co-founder of Dorling-Kindersley **1772**
King, Martin Luther (1929–1968) US pastor and civil rights leader **1821**
King, Mervyn (*b.* 1948) BRITISH governor of the Bank of England **1763, 1763, 1765**
King, Stephen (*b.* 1947) US writer **1824**
Kipling, Rudyard (1865–1936) BRITISH novelist, poet, and short-story writer **1819**
Kissinger, Henry (*b.* 1923) US diplomat **1802, 1814, 1818**
Kiyosaki, Robert (*b.* 1947) US author **1779, 1824, 1827**
Kline, Nancy (*b.* 1946) US author, educator, and consultant **1792, 1806**
Klock, Joe (*b.* 1949) US writer **1801**
Knoebel, Steven M. US founder of a real-estate appraisal company **1763**
Knopf, Alfred A. (1892–1984) US publisher **1784**
Knopfler, Mark (*b.* 1949) BRITISH rock musician **1761**
Knudsen, William S. (1879–1948) US industrialist, president of General Motors **1773**
Koestler, Arthur (1905–1983) BRITISH writer and journalist **1764, 1767, 1778**
Kofman, Fred US writer **1802**
Kotler, Philip (*b.* 1931) US marketing management thinker **1779, 1805, 1805, 1809, 1817, 1822**
Kotter, John P. (*b.* 1947) US writer **1770**
Kraus, Karl (1874–1936) AUSTRIAN writer **1780**
Kroc, Ray (1902–1984) US founder of McDonald's **1773, 1776, 1824**
Kronenberger, Louis (1904–1980) US writer **1772**
Krugman, Paul R. (*b.* 1953) US economist **1765, 1765, 1766, 1766, 1792, 1793, 1793, 1794, 1828**
Kudlow, Lawrence (*b.* 1947) US economist and right-wing commentator **1765**
Labour Party BRITISH political party **1821**
La Fontaine, Jean de (1621–1695) FRENCH writer and poet **1813**
Lahde, Andrew (*b.* 1970) US hedge fund manager **1791, 1791**
Lahr, John (*b.* 1941) US writer and critic **1761**
Lakein, Alan US self-help writer **1825**
Lamm, Richard D. (*b.* 1935) US politician **1779**
Lampedusa, Giuseppe di (1896–1957) ITALIAN writer **1770**
Lanchester, John (*b.* 1962) BRITISH journalist and novelist **1790, 1790, 1792**
Land, Edwin (1909–1991) US inventor and founder of Polaroid Corporation **1764, 1778, 1778, 1796, 1805, 1815, 1816, 1817, 1820**
Landau, Saul (*b.* 1936) US moviemaker and writer **1824**
Landers, Ann (1918–2002) US columnist **1809**
Langer, Susanne K. (1895–1985) US philosopher **1772**
Lanza, Clara (1859–1939) US journalist **1828**
Laozi (570?–490? BC) CHINESE philosopher, reputed founder of Daoism **1801**
Lapham, Lewis H. (*b.* 1935) US writer and editor **1763**
Larkin, Philip (1922–1985) BRITISH poet, critic, essayist, and librarian **1829**
La Rochefoucauld, François (1613–1680) FRENCH epigrammatist **1764, 1772, 1821, 1822**
Lauda, Niki (*b.* 1949) AUSTRIAN race car driver and founder of Lauda-Air **1819**
Lauder, Estée (1908–2004) US entrepreneur and cosmetics executive **1817, 1820, 1820**
Lay, Kenneth (1942–2006) US chairman and CEO of Enron **1777**
Laybourne, Geraldine (*b.* 1947) US chairman of Oxygen Media **1780, 1814, 1828**
Lazarus, Shelly (*b.* 1949) US chairperson of Ogilvy & Mather Worldwide **1766**
Leach, Bernard (1887–1979) BRITISH potter **1811**
Leach, Reggie (*b.* 1950) CANADIAN ice-hockey player **1808**
Leacock, Stephen (1869–1944) CANADIAN humorist, essayist, economist, and historian **1762, 1794**
Leadbeater, Charles BRITISH government adviser, journalist, and author **1786**
Leamer, Edward E. (*b.* 1944) US economist **1784**
Leavitt, Mike (*b.* 1951) US politician **1816**
Lebowitz, Fran (*b.* 1950) US writer and columnist **1811**
Le Carré, John (*b.* 1931) BRITISH novelist **1766**
Lee, Bruce (1940–1973) US-BORN HONG KONG martial arts expert **1762**
Le Guin, Ursula K. (*b.* 1929) US author **1796, 1813, 1818**
Lehmann, Rosamond (1901–1990) BRITISH novelist **1809**
Leith, Prue (*b.* 1940) BRITISH cookbook writer and business executive **1786**
Lenin, Vladimir Ilich (1870–1924) RUSSIAN revolutionary leader and political theorist **1769**
Lennon, John (1940–1980) BRITISH rock musician and songwriter **1813**
Leonard, Carol BRITISH director of Whitehead Mann **1802**
Leopardi, Giacomo (1798–1837) ITALIAN poet and scholar **1812**
Lereah, David US economist and former spokesman for the National Association of Realtors **1765**
Levenson, Sam (1911–1980) US humorist **1807**
Leverhulme, Lord (William Hesketh Lever) (1851–1925) BRITISH entrepreneur, philanthropist, and co-founder of Unilever **1786, 1805, 1823**
Levi, Primo (1919–1987) ITALIAN novelist, essayist, and chemist **1829**
Levitt, Arthur, Jr (*b.* 1931) US author and former chairman of the US Securities and Exchange Commission **1777, 1789, 1799**
Levitt, Theodore (1925–2006) US management theorist, writer, and editor **1769, 1776, 1778, 1778, 1798**
Lewin, Kurt (1890–1947) US author **1769, 1795**
Lewis, Michael (*b.* 1960) US writer and former financial trader **1791**
Leysen, André (*b.* 1927) BELGIAN chairman of Agfa-Gevaert **1817**
Lichtenberg, Georg C. (1742–1799) GERMAN scientist and writer **1797**
Liddell Hart, Sir Basil Henry (1895–1970) BRITISH military historian and strategist **1808**
Lincoln, Abraham (1809–1865) US president **1816**
Lindbergh, Anne Morrow (1906–2001) US writer **1812**

  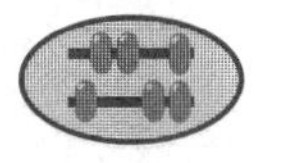 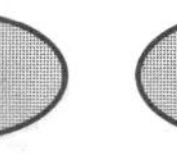 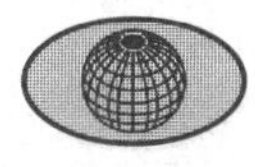   

Lipnack, Jessica (*b.* 1947) US journalist **1766**
Lippmann, Walter (1889–1974) US political commentator, editor, and writer **1771, 1801**
Littré, Émile (1801–1881) FRENCH philosopher and lexicographer **1825**
Livermore, Jesse (1877–1940) US financier **1790, 1790, 1807, 1809**
Livy (59 BC–AD 17) ROMAN historian **1803, 1826**
Lloyd, Henry Demarest (1847–1903) US journalist and reformer **1772**
Lloyd George, David (Earl of Dwyfor) (1863–1945) BRITISH prime minister **1767, 1774, 1822**
Locke, Christopher (*b.* 1947) US author and blogger **1812**
Lodge, David (*b.* 1935) BRITISH novelist and critic **1800, 1817**
Loeb, Gerald M. (1899–1975) US investor, author **1790**
Loesser, Frank (1910–1969) US composer, lyricist, and librettist **1810**
Logan, Don US president and CEO of Time, Inc. **1783**
Lois, George (*b.* 1931) US advertising executive **1786**
Lombardi, Vince (1913–1970) US football coach **1786**
Longfellow, Henry Wadsworth (1807–1882) US poet **1794**
Loomis, Bernard (1923–2006) US business executive **1818**
Lorenz, Konrad (1903–1989) AUSTRIAN zoologist **1820**
Lorsch, Jay W. (*b.* 1932) US sociologist **1803**
Louchheim, Frank P. (*b.* 1923) US business executive **1795**
Lucas, Robert, Jr (*b.* 1937) US economist **1765**
Luce, Henry R. (1898–1967) US publisher **1792**
Lui, David HONG KONG-BASED investment fund manager **1767**
Luscomb, Florence (1887–1985) US campaigner for women's suffrage, architect, and pacifist **1813, 1814**
Luskin, Donald (*b.* 1954) US investment guru **1765**
Luten, Daniel B. US **1816**
Lynch, Michael C. (*b.* 1946) BRITISH historian **1819**
Lynch, Peter (*b.* 1944) US fund manager **1790, 1790, 1790, 1800, 1800, 1800, 1800**
Lyons, Carl (*b.* 1970) BRITISH former marketing director of lastminute.com **1783**
Macaskill, Bridget A. (*b.* 1949) BRITISH non-executive director for Sainsbury's, former president and CEO of Oppenheimer Funds **1828**
Macaulay, Thomas Babington, Lord (1800–1859) BRITISH politician and historian **1796, 1822**
Machiavelli, Niccolò (1469–1527) ITALIAN historian, statesman, and political philosopher **1760, 1764, 1767, 1770**
MacKay, Elizabeth US investment strategist and managing director of Bear Stearns **1828**
Madoff, Bernard (*b.* 1938) US former fund manager and former governor of NASDAQ **1777, 1777, 1777**
Major, Sir John (*b.* 1943) BRITISH former prime minister **1779**
Makihara, Minoru (*b.* 1930) JAPANESE president of Mitsubishi Corporation **1803**
Mallet, Robert (1915–2002) FRENCH poet and playwright **1788**
Mandino, Og (1923–1996) US motivational writer **1820**
Mann, Thomas (1875–1955) GERMAN writer **1795, 1821**
Mannes, Marya (1904–1990) US essayist and journalist **1788, 1824**
Mao Zedong (1893–1976) CHINESE revolutionary leader **1814**
Marcus, Stanley (1905–2002) US businessman **1779**
Marden, Orison Swett (1848–1924) US author **1771**
Maritain, Jacques (1882–1973) FRENCH philosopher **1771**
Markopolos, Harry (*b.* 1956) US financial analyst **1777, 1777, 1778**
Marland, Caroline (*b.* 1946) IRISH former managing director of Guardian Newspapers **1795, 1820**
Marley, Bob (1945–1981) JAMAICAN musician **1815**
Marquis, Don (1878–1937) US journalist and humorist **1788, 1807, 1816, 1829**
Marx, Karl (1818–1883) GERMAN political and economic philosopher **1769, 1784, 1821, 1826**
Maslow, Abraham (1908–1970) US behavioral psychologist **1815**
Massie, Allan (*b.* 1938) BRITISH author **1819**
Matisse, Henri (1869–1954) FRENCH painter and sculptor **1811**
Matsunaga, Mari (*b.* 1954) JAPANESE IT designer **1795**
Matsushita, Konosuke (1894–1989) JAPANESE electronics executive, entrepreneur, and inventor **1767, 1780**
Maugham, W. Somerset (1874–1965) BRITISH novelist, short-story writer, and dramatist **1807, 1815, 1815, 1823**
Maurois, André (1885–1967) FRENCH biographer and critic **1787**
Maxwell, Robert (1923–1991) CZECHOSLOVAKIAN-BORN BRITISH publisher, business executive, and politician **1777, 1777, 1777, 1786, 1812**
Mayer, Martin (*b.* 1928) US author and journalist **1762**
McArthur, Peter 1797
McCaffrey, John L. (1892–1982) US president of International Harvester **1780**
McCain, John (*b.* 1936) US senator **1766, 1766, 1814**
McCall, Carolyn (*b.* 1962) BRITISH managing director of Guardian Newspapers **1783**
McCarthy, Eugene (1916–2005) US politician and writer **1766**
McCarthy, Mary (1912–1989) US author and critic **1766, 1782, 1829**
McCormack, Mark (1930–2003) US entrepreneur, founder and CEO of International Management Group **1773, 1776, 1787, 1789, 1809, 1809, 1813, 1817**
McCrossan, Danny (*b.* 1980) BRITISH comedian **1789**
McGregor, Sir Ian (1912–1998) BRITISH chairman of the National Coal Board **1797**
McInerney, Jay (*b.* 1955) US author **1772**
McKenna, Regis (*b.* 1939) US marketing entrepreneur and chairman of The McKenna Group **1773, 1805**
McLuhan, Marshall (1911–1980) CANADIAN sociologist and author **1762, 1766, 1793, 1798, 1806, 1806, 1807, 1825**
McMaster, Michael D. (*b.* 1943) US writer **1810**
Meagher, Maude (1895–1977) US writer **1772**
Melbourne, Lord (William Lamb) (1779–1848) BRITISH prime minister **1803**
Mellor, David (*b.* 1949) BRITISH politician and broadcaster **1801**
Melville, Herman (1819–1891) US novelist **1810**
Mencken, H. L. (1880–1956) US journalist, essayist, and critic **1774, 1783**
Menninger, Karl Augustus (1893–1990) US psychiatrist **1762**
Menzies, Robert (1894–1978) AUSTRALIAN prime minister **1784**
Messier, Jean-Marie (*b.* 1956) FRENCH media owner **1793**
Michels, Sir David (*b.* 1946) BRITISH former CEO of Hilton Hotels **1773, 1779**
Mies van der Rohe, Ludwig (1886–1969) GERMAN architect **1780**
Mill, John Stuart (1806–1873) BRITISH economist and philosopher **1797, 1807, 1816**
Miller, Arthur (1915–2005) US dramatist **1806, 1820**
Miller, Henry (1891–1980) US writer **1797, 1810**
Miller, Sir Jonathan (*b.* 1934) BRITISH theater director and writer **1773**
Milligan, Spike (1918–2002) IRISH comedian and writer **1807**

Millman, Dan (*b.* 1946) US former world trampoline champion and motivational writer **1808**
Mintzberg, Henry (*b.* 1939) CANADIAN academic and management theorist **1778, 1787, 1798, 1804, 1804, 1822, 1822, 1822**
Mises, Ludwig von (1881–1973) US economist **1822**
Monnet, Jean (1888–1979) FRENCH diplomat and founder of European Community **1782**
Moody, John (1868–1958) US investor and financial analyst **1800**
Moore, Chris (*b.* 1960) BRITISH CEO of Domino's Pizza **1773**
Moore, Henry (1898–1986) BRITISH sculptor **1769**
Moore, James F. (*b.* 1948) US writer and business consultant **1773**
Mophatlane, Isaac (*b.* 1943) SOUTH AFRICAN business executive **1825**
Morgan, Elaine (*b.* 1920) BRITISH playwright, screenwriter, and nonfiction author **1781**
Morgan, J. P. (1837–1913) US financier **1807, 1808**
Morita, Akio (1921–1999) JAPANESE business executive **1793, 1795, 1795, 1799, 1811, 1819**
Morrison, Van (*b.* 1945) IRISH musician **1778**
Morrow, Dwight (1873–1931) US lawyer, banker, and diplomat **1815**
Mortimer, Sir John (1923–2009) BRITISH lawyer, dramatist, and writer **1801**
Morton, J. B. (1893–1979) BRITISH writer and humorist **1827**
Moses, Edwin (*b.* 1955) US athlete **1774**
Mougayar, William (Walid) (*b.* 1959) US consultant and management theorist **1773, 1816**
Moynihan, Daniel P. (1927–2003) US politician **1810**
Mumford, Lewis (1895–1990) US social thinker and writer **1797, 1817, 1825**
Munger, Charlie E. (*b.* 1924) US investor **1807, 1827**
Murchison, Clint W. (1885–1969) US entrepreneur, oil industry executive, and financier **1807**
Murdoch, James (*b.* 1973) AUSTRALIAN chief executive and chairman of Star TV **1809**
Murdoch, Rupert (*b.* 1931) AUSTRALIAN-BORN US CEO of News Corporation **1814**
Murrow, Edward R. (1908–1965) US journalist and broadcaster **1773**
Murthy, Narayana (*b.* 1946) INDIAN founder and CEO of Infosys **1781, 1782, 1793, 1809**
Nader, Ralph (*b.* 1934) US lawyer and consumer-rights campaigner **1801, 1802, 1821**
Naipaul, V. S. (*b.* 1932) TRINIDADIAN writer and winner of the 2001 Nobel Prize in Literature **1782**
Naisbitt, John (*b.* 1929?) US business executive and author **1771, 1793**
Nalebuff, Barry J. (*b.* 1958) US author and professor of management **1772, 1773, 1826**
Nash, Ogden (1902–1971) US humorist and writer **1783, 1800, 1829**
Navon, Yitzhak (*b.* 1921) ISRAELI former president **1809**
Negroponte, Nicholas (*b.* 1943) US academic, co-founder and director of MIT Media Laboratory **1778, 1811, 1811, 1824, 1825**
Neil, Andrew (*b.* 1949) BRITISH publisher and broadcaster **1773**
Nelson, Doug (*b.* 1944) US regional vice president of Altria Group Inc. (formerly Philip Morris) **1773, 1820**
Nelson, Paula (*b.* 1944) US educator **1807**
New Testament second part of the Christian Bible **1807, 1827**
Newman, John Henry (1801–1890) BRITISH theologian **1796**
Newton, Sir Isaac (1642–1727) ENGLISH mathematician and physicist **1811**
Niebuhr, Reinhold (1892–1971) US theologian **1775**
Niederhoffer, Victor (*b.* 1943) US hedge fund manager and statistician **1827**
Noer, David M. (*b.* 1939) US writer and human resources consultant **1785**
Nohria, Nitin (*b.* 1962) US writer **1799**
Noonan, Peggy (*b.* 1950) US author and presidential speechwriter **1822**
Norris, Kathleen (1880–1966) US novelist **1762**
Nyerere, Julius (1922–1999) TANZANIAN president **1779**
Obama, Barack (*b.* 1961) US president **1762, 1828**
O'Brien, Flann (1911–1966) IRISH writer **1778**
O'Connor, Joseph (*b.* 1963) IRISH journalist and novelist **1779, 1785**
Ogilvy, David (1911–1999) BRITISH advertising executive, founder and chairman of Ogilvy & Mather **1761, 1761, 1761, 1761, 1761, 1778, 1778, 1778, 1779, 1795, 1802, 1805, 1817, 1819, 1820**
Ohmae, Kenichi (*b.* 1943) JAPANESE management consultant and theorist **1788, 1798, 1810, 1822**
Olmedo, José Joaquín (1780–1847) ECUADOREAN poet and politician **1828**
Olsen, Kenneth H. (*b.* 1926) US computer designer and co-founder of Digital Equipment Corporation **1774, 1795, 1799**
Omidyar, Pierre M. (*b.* 1967) US founder and chairman of eBay **1813**
Onassis, Aristotle (1906–1975) GREEK shipowner and financier **1767, 1796, 1800, 1823**
Orben, Robert (*b.* 1927) US writer **1808**
O'Reilly, Tony (*b.* 1936) IRISH executive chairman of Independent News & Media and former CEO of Heinz Corporation **1766, 1773**
Origuchi, Masahiro (*b.* 1962) JAPANESE business executive **1809**
Orlando, Vittorio Emanuele (1860–1952) ITALIAN statesman **1822**
O'Rourke, P. J. (*b.* 1947) US humorist and journalist **1766, 1769, 1784, 1794, 1795, 1818, 1821, 1821**
Ortega y Gasset, Jose (1883–1955) SPANISH author and philosopher **1786**
Orwell, George (1903–1950) BRITISH novelist, critic, and essayist **1813, 1820, 1821, 1821**
Ouchi, William (*b.* 1943) US writer **1780**
Ousterhout, John US computer scientist **1812**
Owen, Robert (1771–1858) BRITISH industrialist and social reformer **1797**
Packard, David (1912–1996) US entrepreneur and co-founder of Hewlett-Packard **1776, 1805, 1826**
Packard, Vance (1914–1996) US journalist and writer **1802**
Packer, Kerry (1937–2005) AUSTRALIAN entrepreneur and chairman of Consolidated Press Holdings **1823**
Page, Larry (*b.* 1973) US co-founder of Google **1774, 1798, 1819**
Paglia, Camille (*b.* 1947) US academic, educator, and writer **1781**
Paige, Leroy (1906–1982) US baseball player **1773**
Paine, Thomas (1737–1809) BRITISH politician, philosopher, and writer **1794**
Palmer, Morton US head of Palmer Associates security consultants **1782**
Pareto, Vilfredo (1848–1923) ITALIAN economist and sociologist **1807**
Parkinson, C. Northcote (1909–1993) BRITISH political scientist and author **1780, 1817**
Parnell, Charles Stewart (1846–1891) IRISH politician **1775**
Pascal, Blaise (1623–1662) FRENCH philosopher and mathematician **1775**
Pascale, Richard (*b.* 1938) US academic and author **1770, 1771**
Pasteur, Louis (1822–1895) FRENCH scientist **1804, 1820**
Patchen, Kenneth (1911–1972) US poet **1814**
Pater, Walter (1839–1894) BRITISH author and critic **1823**
Paulson, Henry (*b.* 1946) US Treasury Secretary **1763, 1763, 1791**
Paz, Octavio (1914–1998) MEXICAN writer **1774**
Peary, Robert Edwin (1856–1920) US Arctic explorer **1781**
Péguy, Charles Pierre (1873–1914) FRENCH writer **1827**

  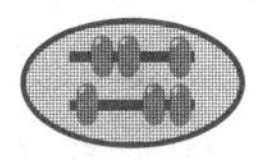 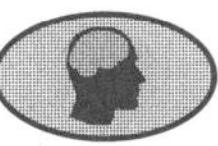  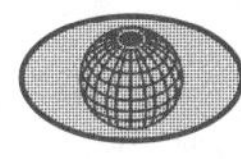   

Perelman, S. J. (1904–1979) US humorist **1786**
Perera, N. M. (1905–1979) SRI LANKAN politician **1784**
Peres, Shimon (*b.* 1923) ISRAELI former prime minister **1805**
Peretsman, Nancy (*b.* 1955) US investment banker **1819**
Perot, H. Ross (*b.* 1930) US entrepreneur, venture capitalist, and politician **1770, 1775, 1779, 1785, 1797, 1829**
Perry, Sir Michael (*b.* 1934) BRITISH business executive **1766**
Peter, Laurence J. (1919–1990) CANADIAN academic and writer **1760, 1792, 1794, 1804, 1809, 1810, 1823**
Peters, Tom (*b.* 1942) US management consultant and author **1766, 1769, 1785, 1788, 1793, 1800, 1803, 1804, 1804, 1807, 1808, 1811, 1817, 1826, 1828**
Phelps, E. J. (1822–1900) US diplomat **1807**
Philip, Prince (*b.* 1921) BRITISH consort of Queen Elizabeth II **1824**
Picasso, Pablo (1881–1973) SPANISH artist and sculptor **1769, 1774**
Pickens, T. Boone (*b.* 1928) US oil company executive and financier **1787**
Pinnell, Raoul (*b.* 1951) BRITISH former branding and marketing communications director of Shell International Petroleum **1793, 1805**
Pirsig, Robert M. (*b.* 1928) US author **1798, 1818**
Pitt the Elder, William (Earl of Chatham (1708–1778) BRITISH prime minister **1790**
Plato (428?–347? BC) GREEK philosopher **1792**
Plutarch (46?–120?) GREEK writer and philosopher **1812**
Pollard, Eve (*b.* 1945) BRITISH journalist and newspaper editor **1828**
Pollard, John G. (1871–1937) US politician **1787**
Pollock, Jackson (1912–1956) US painter **1778**
Pompidou, George (1911–1974) FRENCH politician **1825**
Popcorn, Faith (*b.* 1947) US trend expert and founder of BrainReserve **1776, 1787, 1792, 1799, 1828**
Pope, Alexander (1688–1744) ENGLISH poet **1771, 1779, 1807, 1809**
Popper, Sir Karl Raimund (1902–1994) AUSTRO-HUNGARIAN-BORN BRITISH philosopher of science **1815**
Porter, Michael (*b.* 1947) US strategist **1781**
Porter, Sylvia (1913–1991) US journalist and finance expert **1784, 1815, 1822**
Postrel, Virginia (*b.* 1960) US editor and author **1817**
Pound, Ezra (1885–1972) US poet, critic, editor, and translator **1785**
Powell, Colin (*b.* 1937) US military leader and politician **1812, 1814**
Powell, Enoch (1912–1998) BRITISH politician **1796, 1805**
Proxmire, William (1915–2005) US politician **1763**
Puzo, Mario (1920–1999) US novelist **1777, 1777**
Quadracci, Harry V. (1936–2002) US entrepreneur and founder of Quad Graphics **1805**
Quant, Mary (*b.* 1934) BRITISH fashion designer **1827**
Quayle, Dan (*b.* 1947) US former vice president **1788**
Quine, W. V. O. (1908–2000) US philosopher **1820**
Radcliffe, Cyril John, Lord (1899–1977) BRITISH lawyer **1806**
Raft, George (1895–1980) US film actor **1827**
Rand, Ayn (1905–1982) US writer **1772**
Randall, Clarence B. (1891–1967) US industrialist and government adviser **1802**
Raschke, Linda Bradford US financial trader **1790**
Ratner, Gerald (*b.* 1949) BRITISH former CEO of Ratners Group; founder of Geraldonline **1818, 1818**
Ravitch, Diane (*b.* 1938) US educator and academic **1801**
Raymond, Eric S. (*b.* 1957) US computer programmer and hacker **1808**
Reagan, Nancy (*b.* 1921) US former actress and first lady **1771**
Reagan, Ronald (1911–2004) US president and actor **1794, 1794, 1829**
Reeves, Rosser (1910–1984) US advertising executive **1762**
Reich, Robert (*b.* 1946) US economist and politician **1810**
Renard, Jules (1864–1910) FRENCH writer **1807**
Repplier, Agnes (1858–1950) US writer and historian **1778**
Revans, Reg (1907–2003) BRITISH academic **1796**
Revson, Charles (1906–1975) US entrepreneur, business executive, and founder of Revlon, Inc. **1764**
Ricardo, David (1772–1823) BRITISH economist **1826**
Ridderstråle, Jonas SWEDISH academic and author **1769**
Ries, Al (*b.* 1926) US advertising executive and chairman of Trout & Ries Advertising, Inc. **1770, 1772, 1798**
Riley, Pat (*b.* 1945) US basketball coach and motivational speaker **1812**
Robbins, Anthony (*b.* 1960) US motivational writer and speaker **1780, 1792, 1824**
Robbins, Harvey US writer on business psychology **1808**
Roberts, Wess (*b.* 1946) US writer **1780**
Robertson, Heather (*b.* 1942) CANADIAN author **1819**
Robinson, Alan G. (*b.* 1958) US author **1778**
Robinson, David (*b.* 1959) AUSTRALIAN marketing executive **1806**
Robinson, Gerry (*b.* 1948) IRISH chairman of Granada Television and of the Arts Council of England **1804, 1829**
Robinson, Joan (1903–1983) BRITISH economist **1764, 1784**
Rockefeller, John D. (1839–1937) US industrialist, philanthropist, and founder of Standard Oil **1762, 1813**
Roddick, Dame Anita (1942–2007) BRITISH entrepreneur and founder of The Body Shop **1767, 1767, 1772, 1775, 1776, 1778, 1779, 1786, 1786, 1786, 1817, 1817**
Rodney, Walter (1942–1980) GUYANESE historian and political activist **1781**
Rogers, Jim (*b.* 1935) US banker and management consultant **1789, 1803, 1809**
Rogers, Samuel (1763–1855) BRITISH poet **1824**
Rogers, Will (1879–1935) US actor, columnist, and humorist **1806, 1824**
Rogoff, Kenneth (*b.* 1953) US economist **1763**
Rohatyn, Felix (*b.* 1928) US investment company executive **1784, 1812**
Roosevelt, Eleanor (1884–1962) US reformer, author, and first lady **1769, 1779, 1813**
Roosevelt, Franklin D. (1882–1945) US president **1760, 1767, 1794, 1818, 1827**
Roosevelt, Theodore (1858–1919) US president **1760, 1781**
Rootes, William, Lord (1894–1964) BRITISH car manufacturer **1817**
Rose, Billy (1899–1966) US theatrical impresario and composer **1800**
Rosenberg, Larry US financial trader **1790**
Rostand, Jean (1894–1977) FRENCH biologist and writer **1814**
Rostow, W. W. (1916–2003) US economist **1797**
Roszak, Theodore (1933–1981) US historian, writer, and editor **1783, 1797, 1801**
Roubini, Nouriel (*b.* 1959) US financial analyst **1763**
Rousseau, Jean-Jacques (1712–1778) FRENCH philosopher and writer **1807, 1827**
Rowland, Tiny (1917–1998) BRITISH entrepreneur, co-CEO and managing director of Lonrho **1812, 1815**
Rowling, J. K. (*b.* 1965) BRITISH writer **1792**
Royko, Mike (1932–1997) US journalist **1806**
Rubin, Harriet (*b.* 1952) US author **1788, 1813, 1819**

  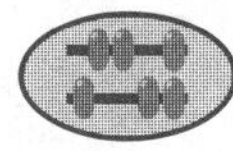 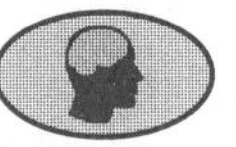  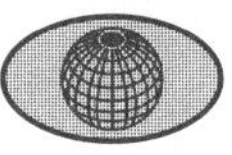   
a–z

Rubinstein, Helena (1870–1965) US entrepreneur, cosmetics manufacturer, and philanthropist **1829**
Ruckelshaus, Jill (*b.* 1937) US public official **1828**
Rudner, Rita (*b.* 1956) US comedian and writer **1828**
Rudolph, Arthur (1906–1996) GERMAN-BORN US developer of the Saturn 5 rocket **1820**
Rumsfeld, Donald (*b.* 1932) US businessman and politician **1801**
Runcie, Robert, Lord (1921–2000) BRITISH archbishop of Canterbury **1825**
Ruskin, John (1819–1900) BRITISH art critic and writer **1768, 1771, 1784, 1821, 1827**
Russell, Bertrand (Earl Russell) (1872–1970) BRITISH philosopher and writer **1772, 1772, 1792, 1809, 1814, 1825, 1829**
Ruth, Babe (1895–1948) US baseball player **1764**
Rutherford of Nelson, Ernest, Lord (1871–1937) NEW ZEALAND-BORN BRITISH physicist **1796**
Rutherford, Mark (1831–1913) BRITISH novelist **1780**
Rutten, Tim US critic and journalist **1778**
Ryan, Alan (*b.* 1940) BRITISH political philosopher **1830**
Sagan, Carl (1934–1996) US astronomer **1820**
Saint-Exupéry, Antoine de (1900–1944) FRENCH writer and aviator **1810**
Saint-Simon, Duc de (1675–1755) FRENCH writer and soldier **1780**
Saki (H. H. Munro) (1870–1916) BRITISH short-story writer **1760**
Saleeby, John US financial trader **1810**
Salinger, J. D. (*b.* 1919) US novelist **1771**
Salk, Jonas (1914–1995) US medical researcher **1818, 1819**
Sallust (86–35? BC) ROMAN historian and politician **1827**
Sampson, Anthony (1926–2004) BRITISH author and journalist **1763, 1766**
Samuelson, Paul (*b.* 1915) US economist and winner of the 1970 Nobel Prize in Economics **1771, 1784, 1792**
Sandefur, Thomas (1939–1996) US head of Brown & Williamson **1766**
Sangster, Margaret (1838–1912) US poet and writer **1829**
Santayana, George (1863–1952) US philosopher, novelist, and poet **1771, 1781, 1795, 1809, 1817**
Sarnoff, Robert W. (1918–1997) US media executive **1790**
Saul, John Ralston (*b.* 1947) CANADIAN writer **1768, 1825**
Saunders, Donald AUSTRALIAN business executive **1781**
Sawyer, Frederick (*b.* 1947) US writer **1775**
Sayers, Dorothy L. (1893–1957) BRITISH author **1775**
Schlesinger, Arthur, Jr (1917–2004) US historian, writer, and educator **1792, 1799**
Schopenhauer, Arthur (1788–1860) GERMAN philosopher **1827**
Schrage, Michael US commentator on innovation **1796**
Schrager, Ian (*b.* 1948) US entrepreneur **1823**
Schreiner, Olive (1855–1920) SOUTH AFRICAN novelist and social critic **1823**
Schumacher, E. F. (1911–1977) GERMAN-BORN BRITISH economist and conservationist **1786, 1786, 1797, 1797, 1824, 1825**
Schumpeter, Joseph Alois (1883–1950) US economist and social theorist **1769**
Schwab, Charles (*b.* 1937) US investment broker **1790**
Schwab, Charles M. (1862–1939) US industrialist **1797, 1808**
Schwed, Fred (1901–1966) US author **1760, 1789, 1799**
Scott, C. P. (1846–1932) BRITISH editor **1809**
Sculley, John (*b.* 1939) US partner of Sculley Brothers, former president of Pepsi, and CEO of Apple Computers **1803, 1805, 1825**
Seeger, Pete (*b.* 1919) US singer and songwriter **1788**
Seidman, L. William (*b.* 1921) US economist and financial commentator **1768**
Seko, Toshihiko (*b.* 1956) JAPANESE athlete **1803**
Selfridge, Gordon (1858–1947) US-BORN BRITISH retailer **1815, 1818**
Semler, Ricardo (*b.* 1959) BRAZILIAN business executive and president of Semco **1776, 1785, 1808, 1811**
Seneca (4? BC–AD 65) ROMAN politician, philosopher, and writer **1821**
Senge, Peter (*b.* 1947) US academic and author **1776, 1799, 1803, 1806, 1818, 1820**
Shakespeare, William (1564–1616) ENGLISH poet and playwright **1809, 1816, 1818**
Shanahan, Eileen (1924–2001) US journalist and author **1806**
Shapiro, Carl (*b.* 1955) US academic and author **1771, 1798**
Shapiro, Eileen C. US business consultant and author **1775**
Sharma, Robin S. (*b.* 1965) CANADIAN self-help writer **1774, 1820**
Shaw, George Bernard (1856–1950) IRISH writer and critic **1774, 1781, 1788, 1794, 1807, 1816, 1817, 1821, 1829, 1829**
Shaw, Warren (*b.* 1950) US former CEO of Chancellor LGT Asset Management **1777**
Sheehy, Gail (*b.* 1937) US journalist and author **1778**
Shelby, Richard (*b.* 1934) US senator **1791**
Shelley, Percy Bysshe (1792–1822) BRITISH poet **1814**
Sherman, Brad (*b.* 1954) US congressman **1768**
Shiba, Shoji (*b.* 1933) JAPANESE academic and author **1811**
Shih, Stan (*b.* 1945) TAIWANESE CEO of the Acer Group **1786, 1824**
Shiller, Robert (*b.* 1946) US economist and author **1765**
Shiva, Vandana (*b.* 1952) INDIAN academic **1776, 1793**
Short, Clare (*b.* 1946) BRITISH politician **1767**
Shugart, Al (1930–2006) US entrepreneur and pioneer of disk drive technology **1799**
Sieff, Marcus, Lord (1913–2001) BRITISH president of Marks & Spencer **1776**
Sieger, Robin BRITISH business executive and author **1828**
Silverman, Jeffrey US director of the Chicago Mercantile Exchange **1791, 1791**
Simcock, Ric (*b.* 1965) BRITISH advertising executive **1798**
Simmons, Edward Emerson (1852–1931) US painter **1788**
Simon, Herbert A. (1916–2001) US political scientist and economist **1780, 1804, 1810**
Simon, John, Viscount (1873–1954) BRITISH foreign secretary and chancellor of the exchequer **1824**
Simon, William (1927–2000) US Secretary of the US Treasury **1785**
Sinclair, Upton (1878–1968) US writer and political campaigner **1776**
Singer, Isaac Bashevis (1904–1991) US novelist and short-story writer **1771**
Singh, Reuben (*b.* 1976) BRITISH entrepreneur and author **1786**
Six, Robert F. (1907–1986) US airline executive **1815**
Skinner, B. F. (1904–1990) US psychologist **1785**
Slater, Jim (*b.* 1929) BRITISH business executive and author **1764, 1792**
Sloan, Alfred P. (1875–1966) US president of General Motors **1760, 1801, 1804, 1819**
Smiles, Samuel (1812–1904) BRITISH social reformer and writer **1810**
Smith, Adam (1723–1790) BRITISH economist and philosopher **1775, 1794, 1820**
Smith, Andreas Whittam (*b.* 1937) BRITISH journalist **1765, 1765**
Smith, Frederick E. (Earl of Birkenhead) (1872–1930) BRITISH politician **1762**
Smith, Gary B. US financial analyst and trader **1791**
Smith, Logan Pearsall (1865–1946) BRITISH essayist and critic **1774, 1793, 1811, 1818**

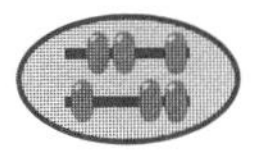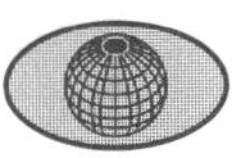
a–z

Smith, Raymond W. (*b.* 1937) US chairman of Rothschild, Inc., and former chairman of Bell Atlantic Corporation **1804**
Solon (638?–559? BC) ATHENIAN statesman, legislator, and poet **1801**
Solzhenitsyn, Aleksander (1918–2008) RUSSIAN author and winner of the 1970 Nobel Prize in Literature **1819**
Son, Masayoshi (*b.* 1957) TAIWANESE CEO of Softbank Corporation **1774, 1810**
Sontag, Susan (1933–2004) US novelist and essayist **1762, 1799**
Sophocles (496?–406 BC) GREEK tragedian **1822**
Soros, George (*b.* 1930) US financier, entrepreneur, and philanthropist **1767, 1769, 1773, 1789, 1799, 1815, 1822, 1823**
Sorrell, Sir Martin (*b.* 1945) BRITISH advertising executive **1783**
Spafford, Gene (*b.* 1956) US computer security expert **1783**
Sparrow, Gerald (1903–1988) BRITISH business executive and writer **1796, 1809**
Spencer, Herbert (1820–1903) BRITISH social theorist **1817**
Sperandeo, Victor US financial trader **1791**
Spielberg, Steven (*b.* 1946) US movie director **1796**
Stead, Christina (1902–1983) AUSTRALIAN writer **1789**
Steinbeck, John (1902–1968) US novelist **1760**
Steinem, Gloria (*b.* 1934) US entrepreneur, editor, and writer **1813, 1828**
Steinhardt, Michael (*b.* 1940) US hedge fund manager **1800**
Stelzer, Irwin (*b.* 1932) US economist **1806**
Stengel, Casey (1890?–1975) US baseball player and manager **1804**
Stephens, Alfred G. (1865–1933) AUSTRALIAN journalist and literary critic **1801**
Stevens, Wallace (1879–1955) US poet **1810**
Stevenson, Adlai E. (1900–1965) US statesman and author **1804, 1813, 1814**
Stevenson of Coddenham, Dennis, Lord (*b.* 1945) BRITISH company director **1789, 1815**
Stewart, Martha (*b.* 1941) US chairperson of Martha Stewart Living Omnimedia **1786**
Stewart, Thomas A. (*b.* 1948) US journalist and author **1799, 1810, 1814, 1815**
Stiglitz, Joseph (*b.* 1943) US economist **1763**
Stone, Oliver (*b.* 1946) US director and screenwriter **1794**
Stoppard, Sir Tom (*b.* 1937) CZECHOSLOVAKIAN-BORN BRITISH playwright and screenwriter **1764, 1796, 1810**
Stout, Rex (1886–1975) US writer **1822, 1827**
Stowe, Harriet Beecher (1811–1896) US writer **1774, 1828**
Street-Porter, Janet (*b.* 1946) BRITISH broadcaster **1804**
Strindberg, J. August (1849–1912) SWEDISH playwright and novelist **1771**
Strong, Barrett (*b.* 1941) US singer and songwriter **1808**
Sugar, Sir Alan (*b.* 1947) BRITISH entrepreneur, founder of Amstrad electronics company **1762, 1767, 1797, 1812**
Summers, Lawrence H. (*b.* 1954) US president of Harvard University, economist, and politician **1765, 1765, 1782, 1782**
Sumner, William Graham (1840–1910) US economist and sociologist **1827**
Swaffer, Hannen (1879–1962) BRITISH journalist **1806**
Swift, Jonathan (1667–1745) IRISH writer and satirist **1762, 1820, 1826**
Szent-Györgyi, Albert (1893–1986) US biochemist **1799**
Tachikawa, Keiji (*b.* 1939) JAPANESE IT executive **1793**
Taft, William Howard (1857–1930) US president **1821**
Taleb, Nassim Nicholas (*b.* 1960) LEBANESE-BORN US academic and writer, former derivatives trader **1761, 1763, 1791, 1791, 1792, 1792, 1792, 1822**
Tambo, Oliver (1917–1993) SOUTH AFRICAN political leader **1808**
Tan, Amy (*b.* 1952) US writer **1762**
Tanner, Chuck (*b.* 1929) US baseball manager **1805**
Tasker, Peter (*b.* 1955) BRITISH business author **1829**
Taubman, A. Alfred (*b.* 1924) US owner of Sotheby's **1805**
Tawney, Richard (1880–1962) BRITISH economic historian and social critic **1768, 1827**
Taylor, F. W. (1856–1915) US engineer and author **1785**
Teller, Edward (1908–2003) US nuclear scientist **1764**
Templeton, Sir John (*b.* 1912) BRITISH-BAHAMIAN investor and philanthropist **1765, 1765, 1791, 1791**
Terence (185?–159 BC) ROMAN comic playwright **1786**
Teresa, Mother (1910–1997) ALBANIAN missionary **1823**
Thatcher, Margaret, Baroness (*b.* 1925) BRITISH former prime minister **1760, 1793, 1794, 1802, 1812, 1818**
Thomas, Barbara (*b.* 1947) US banker **1792, 1810, 1819, 1820**
Thomas, Gwyn (1913–1981) BRITISH dramatist and writer **1806**
Thomas, Lewis (1913–1993) US academic, physician, and writer **1806, 1806**
Thompson, Sir Clive (*b.* 1943) BRITISH former chairman of the Confederation of British Industry and former CEO of Rentokil **1806**
Thompson, E. P. (1924–1993) BRITISH historian **1793**
Thomson of Fleet, Roy Herbert, Lord (1894–1976) CANADIAN-BORN BRITISH media entrepreneur, founder and chairman of the Thomson Organisation **1815**
Thoreau, Henry David (1817–1862) US writer **1780, 1794, 1809, 1827**
Thurow, Lester (*b.* 1938) US economist, management theorist, and writer **1764, 1773, 1784, 1827**
Tillmon, Johnnie (1926–1995) US welfare rights activist **1827**
Toffler, Alvin (*b.* 1928) US social commentator **1770, 1770, 1770, 1775, 1779, 1803, 1805, 1819**
Tomlin, Lily (*b.* 1939) US comedian and actress **1823**
Townsend, Robert (1920–1998) US business executive and author **1774, 1786, 1787, 1788, 1795, 1801, 1801, 1804, 1811**
Toyoda, Shoichiro (*b.* 1925) JAPANESE chairman of Toyota Motor Corporation **1776**
Tracy, Brian (*b.* 1944) CANADIAN businessman, author, and motivational speaker **1762, 1804, 1808, 1812, 1820, 1825**
Trahey, Jane (1923–2000) US copywriter and author **1761, 1795, 1796**
Trilling, Lionel (1905–1975) US academic, writer, and literary critic **1764**
Trollope, Anthony (1815–1882) BRITISH novelist **1812**
Trompenaars, Fons (*b.* 1952) DUTCH author and management consultant **1764**
Trotsky, Leon (1879–1940) RUSSIAN revolutionary leader and Marxist theorist **1813**
Truman, Harry S. (1884–1972) US president **1801, 1819, 1819, 1821**
Trump, Donald J. (*b.* 1946) US real estate developer **1760, 1764, 1787, 1792, 1800, 1802**
Tuchman, Barbara W. (1912–1989) US historian **1766**
Turner, Ted (*b.* 1938) US founder of Turner Broadcasting Systems **1764, 1805, 1807, 1812, 1812, 1812, 1827**
Tusa, Sir John (*b.* 1936) BRITISH broadcaster and managing director of the Barbican **1770**
Twain, Mark (1835–1910) US writer **1767, 1772, 1774, 1780, 1789, 1795, 1795, 1802, 1803, 1810, 1815, 1815, 1816, 1822**
Updike, John (1932–2009) US novelist and critic **1775, 1788, 1798**
Valigra, Lori US science writer **1825**

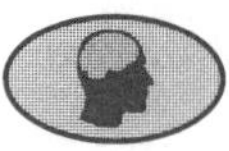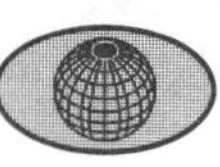

DICTIONARY

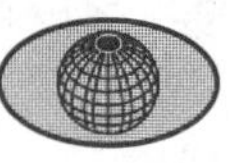

Dictionary

Defining finance and business; the most up-to-date global business and finance English dictionary

In a dynamic business and financial environment, it is essential that finance professionals keep up-to-date with the latest terms and jargon.

The Dictionary provides clear definitions to more than 9,000 international business and financial terms, abbreviations, and acronyms. It has been compiled by an international team of expert researchers and business information specialists, including over 3,000 terms from the Chartered Management Institute.

World Business and Financial English terms are included to reflect the globalization of the business world.

Abbreviations, acronyms, and their expansions are shown in full and cross-referred for ease of use.

Mini-essays to explain more complex concepts and help you get to grips with ideas quickly.

Financial and business slang from the around the world—some humorous, some serious, some baffling. If English is not your first language, these entries will help you find a **tenbagger**, avoid getting into a **big bath**, and ensure you are aware of the **witching hour**.

A

AAA[1] *abbr* ACCOUNTING American Accounting Association

AAA[2] STOCKHOLDING & INVESTMENTS top investment rating the maximum safety rating given to potential investments by Standard & Poor's or Moody's, the two best known rating agencies. *Also called* ***triple A***

AAD *abbr* CURRENCY & EXCHANGE Arab Accounting Dinar

AASB *abbr* ACCOUNTING Australian Accounting Standards Board

AAT *abbr* ACCOUNTING Association of Accounting Technicians

AB *abbr* BUSINESS Aktiebolag *or* Aktiebolaget

ABA *abbr* BANKING American Bankers Association

abacus FINANCE frame holding rods strung with beads for calculating a counting device used for making basic arithmetic calculations, that consists of parallel rods strung with beads. Still widely used in education worldwide and for business and accounting in China and Japan, its origins can be traced back to early civilizations. Australia's oldest accounting journal bears the same name.

abandonment option STOCKHOLDING & INVESTMENTS early investment-termination option the option of terminating an investment before the time that it is scheduled to end

abandonment value STOCKHOLDING & INVESTMENTS value of investment terminated early the value that an investment has if it is terminated at a particular time before it is scheduled to end

ABA routing number BANKING number allocated to US financial institution a unique, nine-digit bank code, which appears on the bottom of **negotiable instruments** such as checks, that is used to identify the US federal- or state-chartered financial institution responsible for payment. *Also called* ***routing number***

abatement FINANCE decrease in debt obligation a reduction in an amount of a liability, for example, in the amount of a person's debts, or in a company's costs of paying employee benefits

ABB *abbr* TREASURY MANAGEMENT activity based budgeting

abbreviated accounts ACCOUNTING abridged UK company accounts in the United Kingdom, a shortened version of a company's **annual accounts** that a company classified as small- or medium-sized under the **Companies Act** (1989) can file with the **Registrar of Companies**, instead of having to supply a full version

ABC *abbr* ACCOUNTING activity based costing

ABI *abbr* INSURANCE Association of British Insurers

Abilene paradox GENERAL MANAGEMENT theory of group decisions based on mistaken impressions a theory stating that some decisions that seem to be based on consensus are in fact based on misperception and lead to courses of action that defeat original intentions. The Abilene paradox was proposed by management professor Jerry Harvey in 1974 following a trip made by his family to the town of Abilene. One person suggested the visit and the others agreed, each believing that everyone else wanted to go. On their return, everyone admitted that they would rather have stayed at home. Harvey used this experience to illustrate the mismanagement of agreement, and of decision making in organizations when apparent consensus is actually founded on poor communication.

ability-to-pay principle TAX theory of tax liability a theory which holds that taxes should be paid only by those who can best afford them

ABM *abbr* GENERAL MANAGEMENT activity based management

ABN *abbr* TAX Australian Business Number

abnormal loss ACCOUNTING loss exceeding normal allowance any loss which exceeds the normal loss allowance. Abnormal losses are generally accounted for as though they were completed products.

abnormal shrinkage ACCOUNTING shrinkage contributing to abnormal loss the unexpectedly high level of reduction in inventory that has contributed to an abnormal loss

abnormal spoilage ACCOUNTING shortfall contributing to abnormal loss the unexpectedly high level of shortfall that has contributed to an abnormal loss

abnormal waste ACCOUNTING waste contributing to abnormal loss the unexpectedly high level of waste that has contributed to an abnormal loss

above par STOCKHOLDING & INVESTMENTS trading above face value used to describe a security that trades above its **nominal value** or **redemption value**

above-the-line 1. ACCOUNTING indicating exceptional items in accounts used to describe entries in a company's profit and loss accounts that appear above the line separating those entries that show the origin of the funds that have contributed to the profit or loss from those that relate to its distribution. Exceptional and extraordinary items appear above the line. *See also* ***below-the-line (sense 1)*** **2.** ECONOMICS indicating country's revenue transactions in macroeconomics, used to describe a country's revenue transactions, as opposed to its **below-the-line** or capital transactions. *See also* ***below-the-line (sense 2)*** **3.** MARKETING relating to marketing costs for advertising used to describe marketing expenditure on advertising in media such as the press, radio, television, film, and the World Wide Web, on which a commission is usually paid to an agency. *See also* ***below-the-line (sense 3)***

abridged accounts ACCOUNTING provisional UK company financial statement in the United Kingdom, financial statements produced by a company that fall outside the requirements stipulated in the **Companies Act**. Abridged accounts are often made public through the media.

ABS *abbr* **1.** STOCKHOLDING & INVESTMENTS asset-backed security **2.** STATISTICS Australian Bureau of Statistics

absolute advantage ECONOMICS favorable position of regions having low production costs an advantage enjoyed by a country or area of the world that is able to produce a product or provide a service more cheaply than any other country or area

absolute title LEGAL **1.** in UK, guaranteed right of ownership of land in the United Kingdom, an owner's guaranteed title to land, confirmed by registration with the Land Registry **2.** in UK, guaranteed right to lease in the United Kingdom, a proprietor's guaranteed valid lease on leasehold land

absorb ACCOUNTING merge production overhead costs to assign an overhead to a particular cost center in a company's production accounts so that its identity becomes lost. *See also* ***absorption costing***

absorbed account ACCOUNTING account merged with related accounts an account that has lost its separate identity by being combined with related accounts in the preparation of a financial statement

absorbed business MERGERS & ACQUISITIONS firm combined with another a

  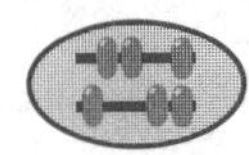   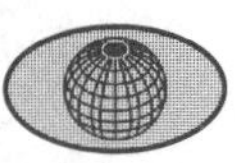   

company that has been merged into another company with which it is not on an equal footing

absorbed costs ACCOUNTING indirect manufacturing costs the indirect costs associated with manufacturing, for example, insurance or property taxes

absorbed overhead ACCOUNTING locally adjusted overhead an overhead attached to products or services by means of **absorption rates**

absorption costing ACCOUNTING method allocating overhead costs to product an accounting practice in which fixed and variable costs of production are absorbed by different cost centers. Providing all the products or services can be sold at a price that covers the allocated costs, this method ensures that both fixed and variable costs are recovered in full. However, if sales are lost because the resultant price is too high, the organization may lose revenue that would have contributed to its overhead. *See also* ***marginal costing***

absorption rate ACCOUNTING rate of merging production overhead costs the rate at which overhead costs are absorbed into each unit of production

abusive tax shelter TAX illegal tax-reduction method a tax shelter that a person claims illegally to avoid or minimize tax

ACA ACCOUNTING ICAEW Associate Chartered Accountant an Associate (member) of the Institute of Chartered Accountants in England and Wales ■ *abbr* REGULATION & COMPLIANCE Australian Communications Authority

Academy of Accounting Historians ACCOUNTING US institution for accounting history a US organization founded in 1973 that promotes "research, publication, teaching, and personal interchanges in all phases of Accounting History and its interrelation with business and economic history"

ACAS *abbr* BUSINESS Advisory, Conciliation and Arbitration Service

ACAUS *abbr* ACCOUNTING Association of Chartered Accountants in the United States

ACCA *abbr* ACCOUNTING Association of Chartered Certified Accountants

ACCC *abbr* REGULATION & COMPLIANCE Australian Competition and Consumer Commission

accelerated cost recovery system ACCOUNTING use of asset depreciation to reduce US taxes in the United States, a system used for computing the depreciation of some assets acquired before 1986 in a way that reduces taxes. *Abbr* **ACRS**

accelerated depreciation ACCOUNTING assigning higher depreciation to new assets a system used for computing the depreciation of some assets in a way that assumes that they depreciate faster in the early years of their acquisition. The cost of the asset less its residual value is multiplied by a fraction based on the number of years of its expected useful life. The fraction changes each year and charges the highest costs to the earliest years. *Also called* ***declining balance method, sum-of-the-year's digits depreciation***

acceleration clause LEGAL clause specifying conditions for early repayment of loan a section of a contract which details how a loan may be required to be repaid early if the borrower defaults on other clauses of the contract

acceptance FINANCE signature guaranteeing payment for bill of exchange the signature on a bill of exchange, indicating that the drawee (the person to whom it is addressed) will pay the face amount of the bill on the due date

acceptance bonus FINANCE bonus paid to new employee a bonus paid to a new employee on acceptance of a job. An acceptance bonus can be a feature of a golden hello and is designed both to attract and to retain staff.

acceptance credit BANKING facility for seller to draw bill of exchange a letter of credit granted by a bank to a buyer (the "applicant") against which a seller (the "beneficiary") can draw a bill of exchange

acceptance house *UK* BANKING institution guaranteeing financial instruments an institution that accepts financial instruments and agrees to honor them should the borrower default

acceptance region STATISTICS values for which null hypothesis is acceptable the set of values in a test statistic for which the null hypothesis can be accepted

acceptance sampling OPERATIONS & PRODUCTION method of checking subset to test whole group a decision-making technique for assuring quality used in a manufacturing environment, in which acceptance or rejection of a batch of parts is decided by testing a sample of the batch. The sample is checked against established standards and, if it meets those standards, the whole batch is deemed acceptable.

accepting bank BANKING bank accepting letter of credit a bank in an exporter's own country to which an issuing bank sends a **letter of credit** for the exporter

accepting house BANKING firm accepting bills of exchange a company, usually an investment bank, that accepts bills of exchange at a discount, in return for immediate payment to the issuer

Accepting Houses Committee BANKING banks linked to Bank of England for lending the main London investment banks that organize the lending of money with the Bank of England and receive favorable discount rates

acceptor FINANCE addressee of signed bill of exchange a person who has accepted liability for a bill of exchange by signing its face

access BUSINESS right to sell into particular market the right to sell goods or services into a particular market without contravening related legislation

access bond MORTGAGES S. African mortgage accepting capital against other loans in South Africa, a type of mortgage that permits borrowers to take out loans against extra capital paid into the account, home-loan interest rates being lower than interest rates on other forms of credit

ACCI *abbr* BUSINESS Australian Chamber of Commerce and Industry

accident insurance INSURANCE insurance against losses incurred in accidents insurance that will pay the insured person for loss or damages when an accident takes place

accommodation address BUSINESS address for receiving messages only an address used for receiving messages, which is not the address of the company's premises

accommodation bill FINANCE bill of exchange facilitating loan for another company a bill of exchange where the drawee who signs it is helping another company (the drawer) to raise a loan. The bill is given on the basis of trade debts owed to the borrower.

account 1. FINANCE arrangement for deferred payment a business arrangement involving the exchange of money or credit in which payment is deferred **2.** FINANCE record of financial dealings a record maintained by a financial institution itemizing its dealings with a particular customer **3.** ACCOUNTING record of monetary value of transactions a structured record of transactions in monetary terms, kept as part of an accounting system. This may take the form of a simple list or that of entries on

     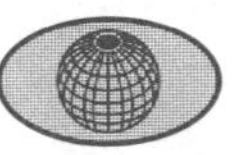   

a credit and debit basis, maintained either manually or as a computer record.
4. MARKETING advertising firm's client a client of an advertising or public relations agency
◇ on account FINANCE used to describe a transaction where something is received that is to be paid for later

accountability CORPORATE GOVERNANCE responsibility for actions the allocation or acceptance of responsibility for one's own actions or those of others lower in the hierarchy

accountancy ACCOUNTING professional activities of accountants the work and profession of accountants

accountancy bodies *UK* ACCOUNTING = ***accounting bodies***

accountancy profession *UK* ACCOUNTING = ***accounting profession***

accountant ACCOUNTING somebody responsible for financial records a professional person who maintains and checks the business records of a person or organization and prepares forms and reports for financial purposes

accountant's letter ACCOUNTING independent statement about financial report a written statement by an independent accountant that precedes a financial report, describing the scope of the report and giving an opinion on its validity

accountant's opinion ACCOUNTING audit report on firm's accounts a report of the audit of a company's books, carried out by a certified public accountant

account day ACCOUNTING day of settlement of executed order the day on which an executed order is settled by the delivery of securities, payment to the seller, and payment by the buyer. This is the final day of the **accounting period**.

account debtor ACCOUNTING body responsible for paying for something a person or organization responsible for paying for a product or service

account director MARKETING advertising firm employee in charge of client's business a senior person within an advertising agency responsible for overall policy on a client's advertising account

account executive MARKETING senior employee in charge of specific client's business an employee of an organization such as a bank, public relations firm, or advertising agency who is responsible for the business of a specific client

accounting ACCOUNTING range of activities undertaken by accountants a generic term for the activities such as bookkeeping and financial accounting conducted by accountants. Accounting involves the classification and recording of monetary transactions; the presentation and interpretation of the results of those transactions in order to assess performance over a period and the financial position at a given date; and the monetary projection of future activities arising from alternative planned courses of action. Accounting in larger businesses is typically carried out by financial accountants, who focus on formal, corporate issues such as taxation, and management accountants, who provide management reports and guidance.

Accounting and Finance Association of Australia and New Zealand ACCOUNTING organization for accountancy and financial professionals an organization for accounting and finance academics, researchers, and professionals. The Association has a variety of objectives, including the promotion of information on accounting to the public, and the provision of programs in continual professional development to both members and nonmembers. The Association's name was changed in 2002 to incorporate the Accounting Association of Australia and New Zealand and the Australian Association of University Teachers in Accounting. *Abbr* **AFAANZ**

accounting bases ACCOUNTING fundamental accounting methods the methods used for applying fundamental accounting concepts to financial transactions and items; preparing financial accounts; determining the accounting periods in which revenue and costs should be recognized in the profit and loss account; and determining the amounts at which material items should be stated in the balance sheet

accounting bodies *US* ACCOUNTING professional organizations for accountants professional institutions and associations for accountants. These include such bodies as the Accounting Standards Board in the United Kingdom and the American Institute of Certified Public Accountants in the United States. *UK term* ***accountancy bodies***

accounting concept ACCOUNTING accepted basis for preparing accounts any of the general assumptions on which accounts are prepared. The main concepts are: that the business is a going concern; that revenue and costs are noted when they are incurred and not when cash is received or paid; that the present accounts are drawn up following the same principles as the previous accounts; and that the revenue or costs are only recorded if it is certain that they will be received or incurred.

accounting cost ACCOUNTING cost of proper financial records the cost of maintaining and checking the business records of a person or organization and of preparing forms and reports for financial purposes

accounting cycle ACCOUNTING process of regularly updating financial records the regular process of formally updating a firm's financial position by recording, analyzing, and reporting its transactions during the accounting period

accounting date ACCOUNTING end date of accounting period the date on which an accounting period ends. This can be any date, though it is usually 12 months after the preceding accounting date.

accounting department *US* ACCOUNTING company department dealing with finance the department in a company which deals with money paid, received, borrowed, or owed. *UK term* ***accounts department***

accounting equation ACCOUNTING formula relating assets, liabilities, and equity a formula in which a firm's assets must be equal to the sum of its liabilities and the owners' equity. *Also called* ***balance sheet equation***

accounting exposure ACCOUNTING risk from changing exchange rates the risk that foreign currency held by a company may lose value because of exchange rate changes when it conducts overseas business

accounting fees ACCOUNTING fees for preparing accounts fees paid to an accountant for preparing accounts. Such fees are tax-deductible.

accounting insolvency ACCOUNTING condition of liabilities exceeding assets the condition that a company is in when its liabilities to its creditors exceed its assets

accounting manager *US* ACCOUNTING manager of accounting department the manager of the accounting department in a business or institution. *UK term* ***accounts manager***

accounting manual ACCOUNTING set of instructions for keeping accounts a collection of accounting instructions governing the responsibilities of persons, and the procedures, forms, and records relating to the preparation and use of accounting data. There can be separate manuals for the constituent parts of the accounting system, for example, budget manuals or cost accounting manuals.

   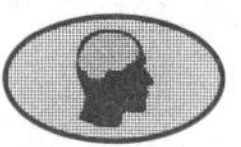  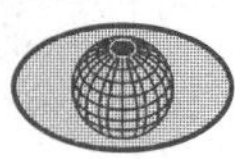   

accounting period ACCOUNTING time between financial reports a length of time for which businesses may prepare internal accounts so as to monitor progress on a weekly, monthly, or quarterly basis. Accounts are generally prepared for external purposes on an annual basis.

accounting policies ACCOUNTING options for financial reporting the specific accounting methods selected and consistently followed by an entity as being, in the opinion of the management, appropriate to its circumstances and best suited to present fairly its results and financial position. For example, from the various possible methods of **depreciation**, the accounting policy may be to use **straight line depreciation.**

accounting principles ACCOUNTING rules of financial reporting the rules that apply to accounting practices and provide guidelines for dealing appropriately with complex transactions

Accounting Principles Board ACCOUNTING former US organization with oversight of accounting in the United States, the professional organization which issued opinions that formed much of **Generally Accepted Accounting Principles** until 1973, when the Financial Accounting Standards Board (FASB) took over that role. *Abbr* **APB**

accounting procedure ACCOUNTING method of keeping financial records an accounting method developed by a person or organization to deal with routine accounting tasks

accounting profession *US* ACCOUNTING set of organizations overseeing accountants collectively, the professional bodies of accountants that establish and regulate training entry standards and professional examinations, as well as ethical and technical rules and guidelines. These bodies are organized on national and international levels. *UK term* ***accountancy profession***

accounting profit ACCOUNTING difference between revenue and costs the difference between total revenue and explicit costs. Accounting profits exclude costs such as **opportunity costs.**

accounting rate of return ACCOUNTING ratio of unadjusted profit to capital employed the ratio of profit before interest and taxation to the percentage of capital employed at the end of a period. Variations include using profit after interest and taxation, equity capital employed, and average capital for the period. *Abbr* **ARR**

accounting ratio ACCOUNTING ratio of one accounting result to another an expression of accounting results as a ratio or percentage, for example, the ratio of **current assets** to **current liabilities**

accounting records ACCOUNTING materials for preparing financial statements all documentation and books used during the preparation of financial statements. *Also called* ***books of account***

accounting reference date ACCOUNTING last day included in financial record the nominal last day of a company's **accounting reference period**, which ends on that date or on one no more than seven days on either side of it

accounting reference period ACCOUNTING 12 months that annual accounts cover the period covered by a company's annual accounts, which is usually one full year

accounting software ACCOUNTING programs for electronic accounts computer programs used to help maintain **accounting records** electronically. Such software can be used for a variety of tasks, including preparing statements and recording transactions.

accounting standard ACCOUNTING approved method of presenting financial information an authoritative statement of how specific types of transaction and other events should be reflected in financial statements. Compliance with accounting standards will usually be necessary for financial statements to give a true and fair view.

Accounting Standards Board ACCOUNTING UK standard-setting organization in the United Kingdom, a standard-setting organization established on August 1, 1990, to develop, issue, and withdraw accounting standards. Its objectives are "to establish and improve standards of financial accounting and reporting, for the benefit of users, preparers, and auditors of financial information." *Abbr* **ASB**

accounting system ACCOUNTING everything used in producing accounting information the means, including staff and equipment, by which an organization produces its accounting information

accounting technician ACCOUNTING qualified person working in finance industry a qualified person who works in accounting and finance alongside **certified public accountants.** Accounting technicians have a variety of jobs, including accounts clerk, credit controller, and financial manager. Their professional body is the **AAT**.

accounting year *UK* ACCOUNTING = ***fiscal year***

account reconciliation ACCOUNTING **1.** comparing balances of transactions a procedure for ensuring the reliability of accounting records by comparing balances of transactions **2.** comparing checkbook records with bank statement a procedure for comparing the register of a checkbook with an associated bank statement

accounts ACCOUNTING record of monetary value of transactions a structured record of transactions in monetary terms, kept as part of an accounting system. This may take the form of a simple list or that of entries on a credit and debit basis, maintained either manually or as a computer record.

accounts department *UK* ACCOUNTING = ***accounting department***

accounts manager *UK* ACCOUNTING = ***accounting manager***

accounts payable ACCOUNTING amount owed through credit the amount that a company owes for goods or services obtained on credit. *Abbr* **AP**

accounts receivable ACCOUNTING amount owed by customers the money that is owed to a company by those who have bought its goods or services and have not yet paid for them. *Abbr* **AR**

accounts receivable aging ACCOUNTING money owed grouped by month and customer a periodic report that classifies outstanding receivable balances according to customer and month of the original billing date

accounts receivable factoring ACCOUNTING buying of discounted invoiced debts the buying of **accounts receivable** at a discount with the goal of making a profit from collecting them

accounts receivable financing ACCOUNTING using money owed as collateral for loan a form of borrowing in which a company uses money that it is owed as collateral for a loan it needs for business operations

accounts receivable turnover ACCOUNTING ratio indicating length of time before customers pay a ratio that shows how long the customers of a business wait before paying what they owe. This can cause cash flow problems for small businesses.

The formula for accounts receivable turnover is straightforward. Simply divide

  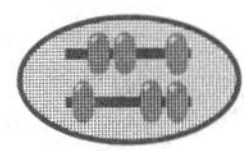 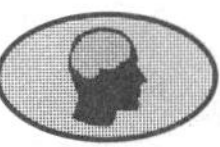  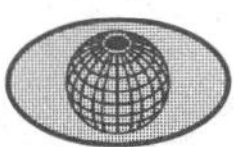   

the average amount of receivables into annual credit sales:

$$\frac{\text{Sales}}{\text{Receivables}} = \text{Receivables turnover}$$

If, for example, a company's sales are $4.5 million and its average receivables are $375,000, its receivables turnover is:

$$\frac{4{,}500{,}000}{375{,}000} = 12$$

A high turnover figure is desirable, because it indicates that a company collects revenues effectively, and that its customers pay bills promptly. A high figure also suggests that a firm's credit and collection policies are sound. In addition, the measurement is a reasonably good indicator of cash flow, and of overall operating efficiency.

accredited investor STOCKHOLDING & INVESTMENTS investor with income of specific size an investor whose wealth or income is above a specific amount. It is illegal for an accredited investor to be a member of a private limited partnership.

accreted value STOCKHOLDING & INVESTMENTS bond's value at present interest rate the theoretical value of a bond if interest rates remained at the current level

accretion MERGERS & ACQUISITIONS firm's asset growth the growth of a company through additions or purchases of plant or value-adding services

accrual ACCOUNTING unpaid charge in accounting results a charge that has not been paid by the end of an accounting period but must be included in the accounting results for the period. If no invoice has been received for the charge, an estimate must be included in the accounting results.

accrual basis or **accrual concept** or **accrual method** ACCOUNTING recording transactions for period they refer to an accounting method that includes income and expense items as they are earned or incurred irrespective of when money is received or paid out. *See also* ***cash accounting*** *(sense 1)*

accrual bond STOCKHOLDING & INVESTMENTS = ***zero coupon bond***

accrual of discount STOCKHOLDING & INVESTMENTS annual gain for bond bought below face value the annual gain in value of a bond owing to its having been bought originally for less than its **nominal value**

accrual of interest FINANCE addition of interest to principal the automatic addition of interest to the original amount loaned or invested. Accrual of interest costs match the cost of capital with the provision of capital.

accruals basis or **accruals concept** ACCOUNTING *see* ***accrual basis***

accrue 1. FINANCE increase with time to increase and be due for payment at a later date, for example, interest **2.** ACCOUNTING include item when earned or incurred to include an income or expense item in transaction records at the time it is earned or incurred

accrued dividend STOCKHOLDING & INVESTMENTS dividend earned since previous dividend payment a dividend earned since the date when the last dividend was paid

accrued expense ACCOUNTING expense incurred but not paid an expense that has been incurred within a given accounting period but not yet paid

accrued income FINANCE income due income that has been earned or accumulated over a period of time but not yet received

accrued interest STOCKHOLDING & INVESTMENTS interest accumulated since previous interest payment the amount of interest earned by a bond or similar investment since the previous interest payment

accrued liabilities FINANCE recorded but unpaid liabilities liabilities which are recorded, although payment has not yet been made. This can include liabilities such as rent and utility payments.

accruing FINANCE increasing with time added as a periodic gain, for example, as interest on an amount of money

accumulated depreciation ACCOUNTING cumulative depreciation claimed as expense the cumulative annual depreciation of an **asset** that has been claimed as an expense since the asset was acquired. *Also called* ***aggregate depreciation***

accumulated dividend STOCKHOLDING & INVESTMENTS dividend earned since previous dividend payment the amount of money in dividends earned by a stock or similar investment since the previous dividend payment

accumulated earnings tax TAX tax in place of dividends the tax that a company must pay because it chose not to pay dividends that would subject its owners to higher taxes

accumulated profit ACCOUNTING profit carried over into next year profit which is not paid as dividend but is taken over into the accounts of the following year

accumulated reserves FINANCE annual reserves put aside reserves which a company has put aside over a period of years

accumulating shares STOCKHOLDING & INVESTMENTS common stock issued in place of dividend common stock issued by a company equivalent to and in place of the net dividend payable to holders of common stock

accumulation unit STOCKHOLDING & INVESTMENTS unit with dividends used for more units a share in a mutual fund for which dividends accumulate and form more units, as opposed to an **income unit**, where the investor receives the dividends as **income**

accuracy STATISTICS closeness of data match the degree to which data conforms to a recognized standard value

ACH *abbr* E-COMMERCE, BANKING automated clearing house

acid test 1. ACCOUNTING test of organization's liquidity a test used to measure an organization's liquidity. *See also* ***acid-test ratio*** **2.** GENERAL MANAGEMENT decisive test a stringent test of the worth or reliability of something

acid-test ratio ACCOUNTING measure of organization's liquidity an accounting ratio used to measure an organization's liquidity. The most common expression of the ratio is:

$$\frac{\text{Current assets} - \text{Inventory}}{\text{Current liabilities}} = \text{Acid-test ratio}$$

If, for example, current assets total $7,700, inventory amounts to $1,200, and current liabilities total $4,500, then:

$$\frac{7{,}700 - 1{,}200}{4{,}500} = 1.44$$

A variation of this formula ignores inventories altogether, distinguishes assets as cash, receivables, and short-term investments, then divides the sum of the three by the total current liabilities, or:

$$\frac{(\text{Cash} + \text{Accounts receivable} + \text{Short-term investments})}{\text{Current liabilities}} = \text{Acid-test ratio}$$

If, for example, cash totals $2,000, receivables total $3,000, short-term investments total $1,000, and liabilities total $4,800, then:

$$\frac{2{,}000 + 3{,}000 + 1{,}000}{4{,}800} = 1.25$$

In general, the ratio should be 1:1 or better. It means a company has a unit's worth of easily convertible assets for each unit of its current liabilities.

ACP *abbr* INTERNATIONAL TRADE African Caribbean and Pacific States

acquirer **1.** FINANCE buyer an organization or individual that buys a business or asset **2.** E-COMMERCE institution handling credit card transactions a financial institution, commonly a bank, that processes a merchant's credit card authorizations and payments, forwarding the data to a credit card association, which in turn communicates with the issuer. *Also called* ***clearing house (sense 3)***

acquisition MERGERS & ACQUISITIONS when one organization buys another the process of one organization taking control of another, by the direct purchase of the net assets or liabilities of the other. *See also* ***merger***

acquisition accounting MERGERS & ACQUISITIONS, ACCOUNTING = ***purchase acquisition***

acquisition integration MERGERS & ACQUISITIONS merging of new company into existing company the process by which a company plans for and implements a successful integration of a newly acquired company

ACRS *abbr* ACCOUNTING accelerated cost recovery system

ACT *abbr* TAX advance corporation tax

action-centered leadership GENERAL MANAGEMENT model of actions of effective leaders a leadership model that focuses on what leaders actually have to do in order to be effective. The action-centered leadership model is illustrated by three overlapping circles representing the three key activities undertaken by leaders: achieving the task, building and maintaining the team, and developing the individual.

action research GENERAL MANAGEMENT study of results of researcher's own changes research that involves conducting experiments by making changes while simultaneously observing the results. The researcher takes an involved role as a participant in planning and implementing change.

active account BANKING account regularly used for transactions an account such as a bank account or investment account that is used to deposit and withdraw money frequently

active asset FINANCE asset in daily use an asset that is used in the daily operations of a business

active fund management STOCKHOLDING & INVESTMENTS proactive managing of mutual fund the managing of a mutual fund by making judgments about stock valuations instead of relying on automatic adjustments such as indexation. *See also* ***passive investment management***

active partner HR & PERSONNEL working partner in partnership firm a partner who gives a significant amount of working time to a company that is a partnership

active portfolio strategy STOCKHOLDING & INVESTMENTS proactive managing of investment portfolio the managing of an investment portfolio by making judgments about stock valuations instead of relying on automatic adjustments such as indexation

activist fiscal policy TREASURY MANAGEMENT institutional intervention to affect exchange rate the policy of a government or national bank that tries to affect the value of its country's money by such measures as changing interest rates for loans to banks and buying or selling foreign currencies

activity based budgeting TREASURY MANAGEMENT allocation of resources to individual activities the determination of which activities incur costs within an organization, establishing the relationships between them, and then deciding how much of the total budget should be allocated to each activity. *Abbr* **ABB**

activity based costing ACCOUNTING calculating business's cost from cost of activities a method of calculating the cost of a business by focusing on the actual cost of activities, thereby producing an estimate of the cost of individual products or services.

An ABC cost-accounting system requires three preliminary steps: converting to an **accrual method** of accounting; defining cost centers and cost allocation; and determining process and procedure costs.

Businesses have traditionally relied on the cash basis of accounting, which recognizes income when received and expenses when paid. ABC's foundation is the accrual-basis income statement. The numbers this statement presents are assigned to the various procedures performed during a given period. Cost centers are a company's identifiable products and services, but also include specific and detailed tasks within these broader activities. Defining cost centers will of course vary by business and method of operation. What is critical to ABC is the inclusion of all activities and all resources.

Once cost centers are identified, management teams can begin studying the activities each one engages in and allocating the expenses each one incurs, including the cost of employee services.

The most appropriate method is developed from time studies and direct expense allocation. Management teams who choose this method will need to devote several months to data collection in order to generate sufficient information to establish the personnel components of each activity's total cost.

Time studies establish the average amount of time required to complete each task, plus best- and worst-case performances. Only those resources actually used are factored into the cost computation; unused resources are reported separately. These studies can also advise management teams how best to monitor and allocate expenses that might otherwise be expressed as part of general overheads, or go undetected altogether. *Abbr* **ABC**

activity based management TREASURY MANAGEMENT management based on cost of activities a management control technique that focuses on the resource costs of organizational activities and processes, and the improvement of quality, profitability, and customer value. This technique uses **activity based costing** information to identify strategies for removing resource waste from operating activities. Main tools employed include: **strategic analysis**, **value analysis**, **cost analysis**, **life-cycle costing**, and **activity based budgeting**.

activity cost pool TREASURY MANAGEMENT total cost of activity a grouping of all of the cost elements associated with an activity

activity driver analysis TREASURY MANAGEMENT assessing financial demands of activity the identification and evaluation of the activity drivers used to trace the cost of activities to cost objects. It may also involve selecting activity drivers with potential to contribute to the cost management function, with particular reference to cost reduction.

activity indicator ECONOMICS measure of economic productivity a calculation used to measure labor productivity or manufacturing output in an economy

act of God INSURANCE unforeseen event not covered by insurance an unexpected and unavoidable event or occurrence such as a storm or a flood that is not covered by an insurance policy

actual cash value INSURANCE cost of replacing something damaged beyond repair the amount of money, less **depreciation**, that it would cost to replace something damaged beyond repair with a comparable item

actual price MARKETS price for immediate delivery a price for a commodity that is to be delivered immediately

  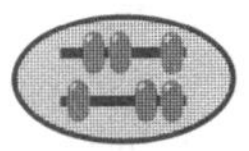   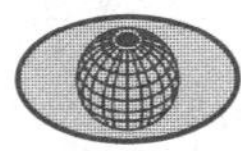   

actuals 1. FINANCE commodities immediately available commodities that can be bought and used, as contrasted with commodities traded on a **futures contract** 2. ACCOUNTING past earnings and expenses earnings and expenses that have occurred rather than being only projected

actual to date ACCOUNTING cumulative value already realized the cumulative value realized by something between an earlier date and the present

actual turnover FINANCE times person spends average available sum the number of times during a specific period that somebody spends the average amount of money that he or she has available to spend during that period

actuarial age INSURANCE person's statistically derived life expectancy the statistically derived life expectancy for any given person's age, used, for example, to calculate the periodic payments from an annuity

actuarial analysis INSURANCE calculation carried out by actuary a life expectancy or risk calculation carried out by an actuary

actuarial science INSURANCE statistics for calculating risk and life expectancy the branch of statistics used in calculating risk and life expectancy for the administration of pension funds and life insurance policies

actuarial tables INSURANCE lists of life expectancy by age lists showing how long people of specific ages are likely to live, used in calculating life assurance premiums

actuary INSURANCE statistician calculating life expectancy a statistician who calculates probable life spans so that the insurance premiums to be charged for various risks can be accurately determined

ACU *abbr* CURRENCY & EXCHANGE Asian Currency Unit

adaptive control OPERATIONS & PRODUCTION automatic changes to industrial process a system of automatic monitoring and adjustment, usually by computer, of an industrial process. Adaptive control allows operating parameters to be changed continuously in response to a changing environment in order to achieve optimum performance.

adaptive learning GENERAL MANAGEMENT method of modifying behavior to repeat successes a style of organizational learning that focuses on prior successes and the use of these as the basis for developing future strategies and successes. Organizations use adaptive learning to make incremental improvements to existing products, services, and processes in response to the changing business environment. **Generative learning** is a contrasting approach to organizational learning.

adaptive measure STATISTICS choosing best statistical method a means of choosing the most appropriate method for a statistical analysis

ADB *abbr* BANKING 1. African Development Bank 2. Asian Development Bank

ad click rate E-COMMERCE = ***click-through rate***

ADDACS *abbr* BANKING Automated Direct Debit Amendment and Cancellation Service

added value 1. GENERAL MANAGEMENT = ***value added*** 2. MARKETING addition to product that increases attractiveness an increase in the attractiveness to customers of a product or a service achieved by adding something to it

addend FINANCE number added to complete sum the initial number added to an **augend** in order to complete an **addition**

addition FINANCE adding together numbers to make sum an arithmetical operation consisting of adding together two or more numbers to make a sum

additional premium INSURANCE payment for extra insurance cover a payment made to cover extra items added on to existing insurance

additional principal payment *US* ACCOUNTING making larger than necessary loan payment the payment of a lump sum to reduce the capital borrowed on a mortgage or other loan, thereby reducing the term of the loan and saving a large amount of interest expense, or the amount paid. *UK term* ***overpayment***

additional voluntary contributions PENSIONS beneficiary's extra payments into company pension extra money that an individual chooses to pay into an **occupational pension** plan to improve the benefits he or she will receive on retirement. *Abbr* **AVCs**

address verification E-COMMERCE matching credit card customer's stated address to records a procedure used by the processor of a credit card to verify that a customer's ordering address matches the address in the customer's record

ADF *abbr* PENSIONS Approved Deposit Fund

adhocracy GENERAL MANAGEMENT organizational system with no set rules a system of organization that emphasizes informality and flexibility and does not employ fixed rules or standard procedures for dealing with problems

adjudication of bankruptcy LEGAL legal statement of bankruptcy a legal order officially stating that somebody is bankrupt

adjustable rate mortgage MORTGAGES mortgage with fluctuating interest rate a mortgage where the interest rate changes according to the current market rates. *Abbr* **ARM**

adjustable rate preferred stock STOCKHOLDING & INVESTMENTS preferred stocks linked to Treasury interest rate preferred stocks on which dividends are paid in line with the interest rate on Treasury bills. *Abbr* **ARPS**

adjusted book value ACCOUNTING current value of firm's assets and liabilities the value of a company in terms of the current market values of its assets and liabilities. *Also called* ***modified book value***

adjusted futures price STOCKHOLDING & INVESTMENTS current value of futures contract the current value of a futures contract to buy a commodity at a fixed future date

adjusted gross income ACCOUNTING income after adjustments for tax purposes the amount of annual income that a person or company has after various adjustments for income or corporation tax purposes. *Abbr* **AGI**

adjusted present value ACCOUNTING separated discounted cash flows for operations and finance where the capital structure of a company is complex, or expected to vary over time, discounted cash flows may be separated into (i) those that relate to operational items, and (ii) those associated with financing. This treatment enables assessment to be made of the separate features of each area. *Abbr* **APV**

adjuster *US* INSURANCE assessor of insurance claims a professional person acting on behalf of an insurance company to assess the value of an insurance claim. *UK term* ***loss adjuster***

adjustment FINANCE change in financial condition a change, often a significant downward turn, in the financial condition of a business, business sector, stock market, economy, etc.

adjustment credit BANKING short-term loan from US Federal Reserve a short-term loan from the US Federal Reserve to a commercial bank and the most common borrowing method to meet reserve requirements

  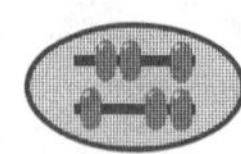   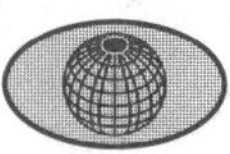   

adjustment trigger CURRENCY & EXCHANGE factor triggering adjustment in exchange rates a factor such as a specific level of inflation that triggers an adjustment in exchange rates

adminisphere GENERAL MANAGEMENT part of firm dealing with administration the part of an organization that deals with administrative matters, often perceived negatively by employees because of the apparently unnecessary nature of decisions made by its members (*slang*)

administered price OPERATIONS & PRODUCTION retail price fixed by manufacturer the price of a good or service which is fixed by a manufacturer and which cannot be varied by a retailer

administration 1. FINANCE = ***receivership*** 2. GENERAL MANAGEMENT management of firm's operations the management of the affairs of a business, especially the planning and control of its operations

administration costs TREASURY MANAGEMENT management costs costs of management, not including production, marketing, or distribution costs

administration school GENERAL MANAGEMENT attitude to business management a school of thought that defines management activities as a set of processes: organizing, coordinating, commanding, and controlling. *See also* ***business administration***

administrative receiver FINANCE receiver representing long-term creditor a receiver appointed by a **debenture** holder to liquidate the assets of a company on his or her behalf

administrator GENERAL MANAGEMENT, HR & PERSONNEL somebody appointed to return firm to solvency a licensed **insolvency practitioner** who is appointed by a court, the company itself, or somebody owed money to bring the company back to solvency

admissibility STATISTICS when procedure performs better than all others the property of a procedure if, and only if, there is no other of its class that performs as well or better in at least one case

ADR *abbr* STOCKHOLDING & INVESTMENTS American depository receipt

ADS *abbr* STOCKHOLDING & INVESTMENTS American depository share

adspend MARKETING = ***advertising expenditure***

ad valorem duty or **ad valorem tax** TAX sum based on something's value a tax such as Value Added Tax or duty that is calculated on the value of the products or services provided, rather than on their number or size

advance FINANCE 1. money loaned or paid before due date money paid as a loan or as a part of a payment scheduled to be made later 2. rise in price or rate an increase in the price, rate, or value of something 3. pay money as loan or part payment to pay an amount of money to somebody as a loan or as a part of a payment scheduled to be made later 4. become higher in price or rate to increase in price, rate, or value

advance corporation tax TAX former UK company tax formerly, in the United Kingdom, a tax paid by a company equal to a percentage of its dividends or other distributions of profit to its stockholders. It was abolished in 1999. *Abbr* **ACT**

advance-decline ratio MARKETS ratio of rising stocks to falling stocks a ratio used for indicating the strength of a stock market, calculated by dividing the number of securities whose price rose by the number whose price fell. A positive result indicates a rising market and a negative result, a falling market.

advance payment FINANCE prepaid amount an amount paid before it is earned or incurred, for example, a prepayment by an importer to an exporter before goods are shipped, or a cash advance for travel expenses

advance payment guarantee or **advance payment bond** FINANCE guarantee for recovery of advance payment a guarantee that enables a buyer to recover an advance payment made under a contract or order if the supplier fails to fulfill its contractual obligations

adverse action FINANCE refusal of credit the action of refusing somebody credit or of canceling somebody's credit

adverse balance ACCOUNTING deficit on account a deficit on an account

adverse balance of trade INTERNATIONAL TRADE level of imports higher than exports a situation where a country has more visible imports than it has exports

adverse opinion ACCOUNTING auditor's statement that accounts are misleading a statement in the auditor's report of a company's annual accounts indicating a fundamental disagreement with the company to such an extent that the auditor considers the accounts misleading

adverse selection MARKETING poor quality items sell faster the theory that poor quality goods are more likely to sell than good, because some sellers want to get rid of products, and buyers are unable to judge whether the quality or price is too low. This applies in many spheres, such as the stock market or insurance industry, as well as in the buying and selling of merchandise. Three factors come into play: (i) the variable quality of similar products on the market; (ii) the fact that buyers and sellers do not possess the same information about the product (usually the seller knows more than the buyer); (iii) sellers are more likely to want to get rid of bad quality products than good quality products.

advertisement MARKETING firm's paid announcement to sell product a public announcement by a company in a newspaper, on television or radio, or over the Internet, intended to attract buyers for a product or service

advertising MARKETING using paid announcements to try to sell products the promotion of goods, services, or ideas, through paid announcements. Advertising aims to persuade or inform the general public and can be used to induce purchase, increase brand awareness, or enhance product differentiation. An advertisement has two main components: the message, and the medium by which it is transmitted. Advertising forms just one part of an organization's total marketing strategy.

advertising agency MARKETING firm that creates paid product announcements for clients an organization that, on behalf of clients, drafts and produces advertisements, places advertisements in the media, and plans advertising campaigns. Advertising agencies may also perform other marketing functions, including market research and consulting.

advertising campaign MARKETING planned series of paid product announcements a planned program using advertising aimed at a particular target market or audience over a defined period of time for the purpose of increasing sales or raising awareness of a product or service

advertising department MARKETING part of firm that creates paid product announcements the department within an organization which is responsible for advertising its products or services. The advertising department is also the name given to the section of a publishing house that coordinates the placing of advertisements in its magazines, newspapers, or other publications. It is involved in the sale of advertising space to clients.

  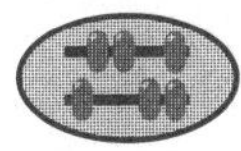 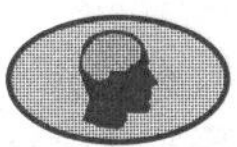  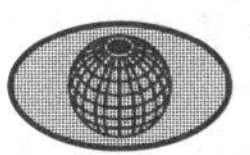   

advertising expenditure MARKETING money spent by firm on paid product announcements the amount spent by an organization on advertising, usually per year. Advertising expenditure is analyzed by breaking it down into the main advertising channels used by companies, such as newspapers, magazines, television, radio, movie theaters, and outdoor advertising. Expenditure can show the total spending nationally, by sector, or by type and size of company, or may relate to one company's spend on advertising, including the proportion spent on specific brands. *Also called* ***adspend***

advertising manager MARKETING employee in charge of firm's paid product announcements an employee of a business who is responsible for planning and controlling its advertising activities and budgets

advertising media MARKETING TV, radio, newspapers, etc. used for product announcements the communication channels used for advertising, including television, radio, the printed press, and outdoor advertising

advertising research MARKETING gathering information about effectiveness of product announcements research carried out before or after advertising to ensure or test its effectiveness

advertorial MARKETING article influenced by advertisers a combination of an advertisement and an editorial article. The content of an advertorial is significantly influenced, and may even be entirely written, by the advertisers. Examples of advertorials include travel or leisure supplements in newspapers or magazines that are designed to attract advertisements from suppliers of relevant goods or services. A criticism of advertorials is that it is sometimes difficult to distinguish between an advertising article and ordinary journalistic articles, particularly when they appear in the same typeface as the other contents of the newspaper or magazine. To overcome this, some advertorials are headed "Advertisement."

advice of fate BANKING notification as to whether check will be honored immediate notification from a drawer's bank as to whether a check is to be honored or not

advid MARKETING promotional video a video used to promote a product or service

advising bank BANKING, INTERNATIONAL TRADE bank facilitating firm's overseas credit a bank in an exporter's own country to which an issuing bank sends a letter of credit. *Also called* ***notifying bank***

Advisory, Conciliation and Arbitration Service BUSINESS UK organization resolving workplace disputes in the United Kingdom, a public body, funded by taxpayers, that aims to prevent and resolve problems between employers and their workforces. The government established the first voluntary conciliation service in 1896, but the modern ACAS was founded in 1974 when the organization moved away from government control and became independent. It hosted talks between opposing sides in many of the high-profile labor disputes in the 1970s and 1980s, including the miners' strike in 1984. *Abbr* **ACAS**

advisory funds STOCKHOLDING & INVESTMENTS funds invested at intermediary's discretion funds placed with a financial institution to invest on behalf of a client as the institution sees fit

advisory management STOCKHOLDING & INVESTMENTS stockbroker's provision of investment advice an advisory service offered by some stockbrokers through which clients are able to discuss a variety of investment options with their broker and receive appropriate advice. No resulting action may be taken, however, without a client's express approval.

AEO *abbr* INTERNATIONAL TRADE Authorized Economic Operator

AER *abbr* FINANCE Annual Equivalent Rate

AEX *abbr* MARKETS Amsterdam Stock Exchange

AFAANZ *abbr* ACCOUNTING Accounting and Finance Association of Australia and New Zealand

AFBD *abbr* MARKETS Association of Futures Brokers and Dealers

AfDB *abbr* BANKING African Development Bank

affiliate BUSINESS **1.** firm legally linked to another a company that is controlled by another or is a member of a larger group **2.** firm owning some voting stock of another either of two companies where one owns a minority of the voting stock of the other

affiliated enterprise BUSINESS firm partly owned by another a company that is partly owned, though less than 50%, by another, and in which the stock-owning company exerts some management control or has a close trading relationship with the associate. *Also called* ***associate company***

affiliate directory E-COMMERCE list of websites with affiliate programs a directory that indexes sites belonging to **affiliate programs**. Affiliate directories offer information for companies seeking to subscribe to a program, as well as for those wanting to establish affiliate programs of their own.

affiliate marketing E-COMMERCE advertising through Internet partnerships the use of **affiliate programs** providing advertising links on websites

affiliate partner E-COMMERCE firm that advertises another firm's products on Internet a company that markets a product or service on the Internet for another company

affiliate program E-COMMERCE Internet advertising partnership between firms an advertising program in which one merchant induces others to place their banners and buttons on its website in return for a commission on purchases made by their customers.

There is no better example of the success of affiliate marketing than that of Amazon.com. The company has links on literally hundreds of thousands of external websites, linking through to its own site, from where it offers books and other products. It is a win-win situation: the external vendors can offer their visitors extra services that are easy to establish, and receive revenue from Amazon. At the same time, Amazon opens up a new channel for marketing each time a new visitor links through to its website. *Also called* ***associate program***

affinity card MARKETING credit card offering benefits a credit or debit card co-issued by a bank and another organization whose logo appears on the card. The other organization may be a charity or a commercial enterprise. If it is a charity, the issuing bank makes a donation each time the card is used. A commercial enterprise may get a portion of the revenues that the card generates and may offer benefits in the form of discounts or frequent flyer miles to the cardholder to encourage use of the card.

affirmative action HR & PERSONNEL favoring appointments from disadvantaged groups preferential treatment, usually through a quota system, to prevent, or correct, discriminatory employment practices, particularly relating to recruitment and promotion. The term is widely used in the United States, whereas in the United Kingdom, **positive discrimination** is the preferred term.

affluent society wealthy community a community in which material wealth is widely distributed

     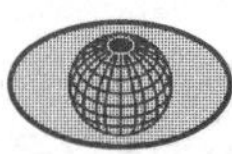   

affluenza bad feelings associated with being rich feelings of unhappiness, stress, and guilt induced by the pursuit and possession of wealth (*slang*)

AFP *abbr* FINANCE Association for Financial Professionals

African Caribbean and Pacific States INTERNATIONAL TRADE nations grouped for trade purposes a set of independent states that are treated in a similar way for the purposes of trade preferences. *Abbr* **ACP**

African Development Bank BANKING bank supporting development in African countries a bank set up by African countries to provide long-term loans to help agricultural development and improvement of the infrastructure. *Abbr* **ADB**

Afrikaanse Handelsinstituut GENERAL MANAGEMENT S. African business organization the South African national chamber of commerce for Afrikaans businesses. *Abbr* **AHI**

AFTA *abbr* INTERNATIONAL TRADE ASEAN Free Trade Area

after-acquired collateral FINANCE collateral obtained after loan agreed collateral for a loan that a borrower obtains after making the contract for the loan

after date FINANCE after date stated on bill after the date specified on a bill of exchange. Wording on a bill will state when payment has to be made, for example, "60 days after date, we promise to pay. . ." means 60 days after the date of the bill. *See also* ***bill of exchange***

after-hours buying MARKETS deals done after close of stock exchange buying, selling, or dealing in stock after a stock exchange has officially closed for the day, such deals being subject to normal stock exchange rules. In this way, dealers can take advantage of the fact that, because of time differences and the various stock exchanges around the world, there is almost always at least one stock exchange open throughout 24 hours.

aftermarket MARKETS trade in newly launched stock a market in new shares of stock that starts immediately after trading in the shares begins

after-sales service MARKETING help for customers after buying product customer support following the purchase of a product or service. In some cases, after-sales service can be almost as important as the initial purchase. The manufacturer, retailer, or service provider determines what is included in any warranty or guarantee package. This will include the duration of the warrant, traditionally one year from the date of purchase but increasingly two or more years, maintenance and/or replacement policy, items included/excluded, labor costs, and speed of response. In the case of a service provider, after-sales service might include additional training or help desk availability. Of equal importance is the customer's perception of the degree of willingness with which a supplier deals with a question or complaint, speed of response, and action taken.

after sight FINANCE after bill's acceptance after acceptance of a bill of exchange. Wording on a bill will state when payment has to be made, for example, "60 days after sight, we promise to pay. . ." means 60 days after acceptance of the bill. *See also* ***bill of exchange***

after-tax TAX after deduction of tax relating to earnings or income from which tax has already been deducted

AG FINANCE public limited company in German-speaking country used after the name of a German, Austrian, or Swiss business to identify it as a public limited company. *Full form* ***Aktiengesellschaft***

against actuals STOCKHOLDING & INVESTMENTS relating to futures trade in cash relating to a trade between owners of futures contracts that allows both to reduce their positions to cash instead of commodities

aged debt FINANCE debt that is overdue a debt that is overdue by one or more given periods, usually increments of 30 days

aged debtor FINANCE somebody with overdue debt a person or organization responsible for a debt that is overdue

agency GENERAL MANAGEMENT authority to represent somebody else a relationship between two people or organizations in which one is empowered to act on behalf of the other in dealings with a third party

agency bank BANKING bank that is foreign bank's agent a bank that does not accept deposits, but acts as an agent for another, usually foreign, bank

agency bill BANKING bill of exchange drawn on local bank a bill of exchange drawn on the local branch of a foreign bank

agency broker STOCKHOLDING & INVESTMENTS dealer trading in shares for commission a dealer who acts for a client, buying and selling stock for a commission

agency commission MARKETING money given to advertising firm for delivering business a percentage of advertising expenditure rebated to an advertising agency, media buyer, or client organization by a media owner

agency markup MARKETING additional management fee charged by advertising firm a management fee charged by an advertising agency in addition to the cost of external services that it buys on behalf of a client

agenda GENERAL MANAGEMENT list of subjects to deal with at meeting a list of topics to be discussed or business to be transacted during the course of a meeting, usually sent prior to the meeting to those invited to attend

agent GENERAL MANAGEMENT representative for somebody else a person or organization empowered to act on behalf of another when dealing with a third party

agent bank BANKING **1.** bank participating in partner bank's credit card program a bank that takes part in another bank's credit card program, acting as a depository for merchants **2.** bank acting on foreign bank's behalf a bank that acts on behalf of a foreign bank

agent's commission FINANCE money paid for agent's services money, often a percentage of sales, paid to an agent

age pension ANZ PENSIONS government money received by retired person a sum of money paid regularly by the government to people who have reached the age of retirement

agflation ECONOMICS rapidly rising food prices an economic situation occurring when the cost of food rises rapidly

aggregate demand ECONOMICS total money spent or invested in economy the sum of all expenditures in an economy that makes up its **GDP**, for example, consumers' expenditure on goods and services, investment in **capital stock**, and government spending

aggregate depreciation ACCOUNTING = ***accumulated depreciation***

aggregate income FINANCE total of all incomes in economy the total of all incomes in an economy without adjustments for inflation, taxation, or types of **double counting**

aggregate output ECONOMICS all goods and services produced in economy the total value of all the goods and services produced in an economy. *Also called* ***aggregate supply***

  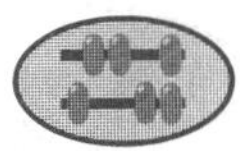   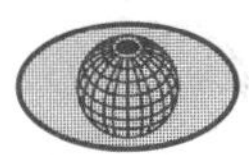   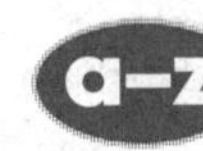

aggregate planning OPERATIONS & PRODUCTION planning for manufacture of related products medium-range capacity planning, typically covering a period of 3 to 18 months. Aggregate planning is used in a manufacturing environment and determines not only the overall output levels planned but the appropriate resource input mix to be used for related groups of products. Generally, planners focus on overall or aggregate capacity rather than on individual products or services. Aggregate planning can be used to influence demand as well as supply, in which case variables such as price, advertising, and the product mix are taken into account.

aggregate supply ECONOMICS = ***aggregate output***

aggregator 1. FINANCE firm selling product packages a company that combines similar products or services into larger packages, making a profit by cost savings, by reaching a larger market, or by charging more for the combined package. In the secondary mortgage market, aggregators buy individual mortgages from financial institutions and turn them into **mortgage-backed securities**, pooling them and selling them on at a higher price.
2. E-COMMERCE middleman between producers and online customers an organization that acts as an intermediary between producers and customers in an Internet business web. The aggregator selects products, sets prices, and ensures fulfillment of orders.

aggressive STOCKHOLDING & INVESTMENTS describing high-risk investment strategy used to describe an investment strategy marked by willingness to accept high risk while trying to realize higher than average gains. Such a strategy involves investing in rapidly growing companies that promise capital appreciation but produce little or no income from dividends and de-emphasizes income-producing instruments such as bonds.

aggressive accounting ACCOUNTING deliberately inaccurate accounting to improve firm's position inaccurate or unlawful accounting practices used by an organization in order to make its financial position seem healthier than it is in reality (*slang*)

aggressive growth fund STOCKHOLDING & INVESTMENTS mutual fund pursuing large profits riskily a mutual fund that takes considerable risks in the hope of making large profits

AGI *abbr* ACCOUNTING adjusted gross income

agile manufacturing OPERATIONS & PRODUCTION flexible method for producing goods to meet demand a manufacturing method that focuses on meeting the demands of customers by adopting flexible manufacturing practices. Agile manufacturing emerged as a reaction to **lean production**. It differs by focusing on meeting the demands of customers without sacrificing quality or incurring added costs. Based on the idea of the **virtual organization**, agile manufacturing aims to develop flexible, often short-term, relationships with suppliers, as market opportunities arise. Stock control is considered less important than satisfying the customer, and so customer satisfaction measures become more important than output measures. Agile manufacturing requires an adaptable, innovative, and empowered work force.

agility GENERAL MANAGEMENT ability to quickly respond and adapt to change the organizational capability to be flexible, responsive, adaptive, and show initiative in times of change and uncertainty. Agility has origins in manufacturing and has been cited as a source of competitive advantage by many management gurus. For others, the key to agility lies in what the organization is, as opposed to what it does. Agility grew as a reaction against the slowness of bureaucratic organizations to respond to changing market conditions. The **virtual organization** has been quoted as one extreme example of an agile organization.

agio 1. FINANCE difference between two related values the difference between two values, for example, between the interest charged on loans made by a bank and the interest paid by the bank on deposits, or between the values of two currencies
2. CURRENCY & EXCHANGE charge for exchanging currency a charge made for changing money of one currency into another, or for changing paper money into coins

AGM *UK* CORPORATE GOVERNANCE = ***annual meeting***

agreed price OPERATIONS & PRODUCTION price agreed on by buyer and seller a price for a product or service that has been accepted by both the buyer and seller

agreement among underwriters STOCKHOLDING & INVESTMENTS document forming syndicate of underwriters a document which forms a syndicate of underwriters, linking them to the issuer of a new stock issue

agreement of sale LEGAL formal contract between buyer and seller a written contract specifying the terms under which the buyer agrees to buy particular real estate and the seller agrees to sell it

agreement to sell LEGAL contract to sell at future date a contract between two parties in which one agrees to sell something to the other at a date in the future

agricultural produce ACCOUNTING slaughtered animals and harvested plants farm animals and plants once they have been slaughtered or harvested. Before this they are classified as **biological assets**.

AHI *abbr* BUSINESS Afrikaanse Handelsinstituut

AIA *abbr* ACCOUNTING Association of International Accountants

AIB *abbr* BANKING American Institute of Banking

AIC *abbr* STOCKHOLDING & INVESTMENTS Association of Investment Companies

AICPA *abbr* ACCOUNTING American Institute of Certified Public Accountants

AIFA *abbr* FINANCE Association of Independent Financial Advisers

aim GENERAL MANAGEMENT goal of effort an end toward which effort is directed and on which resources are focused, usually to achieve an organization's strategy. There is considerable discussion on whether aim, goal, target, and objective are the same. In general usage, the terms are often interchangeable, so it is important that, if an organization has a particular meaning for one of these terms, it must define it in its documentation. Sometimes an aim is seen as the desired final end result, while a goal is a smaller step on the road to it.

AIM *abbr* MARKETS Alternative Investment Market

air bill *US* FINANCE documents accompanying shipments by air the documentation issued by an airline for the shipment of goods by air freight. *UK term* ***air waybill***

air cover GENERAL MANAGEMENT support and protection from high-ranking employee support from a senior member of staff, usually during a time of change, upheaval, or unpopular decisions (*slang*)

airtime MARKETING amount of time that advertisement is broadcast the amount of time given to an advertisement on television, radio, or in movie theaters

air waybill *UK* FINANCE = ***air bill***. *Abbr* **AWB**

  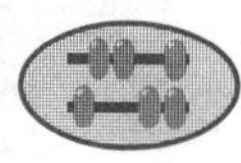   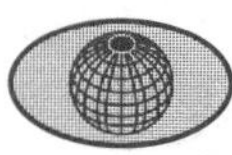   

AITC *abbr* FINANCE Association of Investment Companies

Aktb *abbr* BUSINESS Aktiebolag

Aktiebolag or **Aktiebolaget** BUSINESS Incorporated the Swedish equivalent of Inc. *Abbr* **Aktb**

Aktiengesellschaft FINANCE *see* ***AG***

alien corporation BUSINESS firm registered in another country a company that is based in one country, but registered in another

all equity rate FINANCE interest rate charged for high-risk project the interest rate that a lender charges because of the apparent risks of a project that are independent of the normal market risks of financing it

alligator spread MARKETS unprofitable spread in good market conditions in the US options market, a **spread** that remains unprofitable even with good market conditions, usually as the result of high commissions paid to brokers or agents (*slang*)

All Industrials Index MARKETS Australian index of non-mining companies a subindex of the Australian **All Ordinaries Index** which includes all the companies from that index that are not involved in resources or mining

All Mining Index MARKETS Australian index of mining companies a subindex of the Australian **All Ordinaries Index** which includes all the companies from that index that are involved in the mining industry

allocate **1.** FINANCE assign item to single cost unit to assign a whole item of **cost**, or of **revenue**, to a single cost unit, center, account, or time period **2.** STOCKHOLDING & INVESTMENTS choose between different investments to assign assets to different investment types such as equities, bonds, or cash

allonge FINANCE attachment to bill of exchange allowing more signatures a piece of paper attached to a bill of exchange, so that more endorsements can be written on it

All Ordinaries Accumulation Index MARKETS measure of change in Australian stock prices a measure of the change in stock prices on the Australian Stock Exchange, based on the **All Ordinaries Index**, but assuming that all dividends are reinvested

All Ordinaries Index MARKETS major index of Australian stocks the major index of Australian stocks, comprising more than 300 of the most active Australian companies listed on the Australian Stock Exchange. *Abbr* **AO**

all-or-none underwriting MARKETS option of canceling public stock issue the option of canceling a public offering of stock if the underwriting is not fully subscribed. *Abbr* **AON**

allotment STOCKHOLDING & INVESTMENTS UK issue of new company's stock to applicants in the United Kingdom, the act of selling shares of stock in a new company to people who have applied for them

allowable deductions TAX legitimate deductions from UK taxable income in the United Kingdom, deductions from income that are allowed by HM Revenue & Customs, reducing the total on which tax is payable

allowable expenses TAX business expenses offset against tax business expenses that can be used to reduce the amount of income on which tax is paid

allowable losses ACCOUNTING losses rightly offset against gains losses such as those on the sale of assets that can be used to reduce the amount of income on which tax is paid

allowance for bad debt ACCOUNTING accounting arrangement covering unpaid debt a provision made in a company's accounts for potentially unrecoverable debts

All Resources Index MARKETS Australian index of companies in resources industry a subindex of the Australian **All Ordinaries Index** which includes all the companies from that index that are involved in the resources industry

all-risks policy INSURANCE insurance policy covering all likely claims an insurance policy that covers risks of any kind, with no exclusions

alpha STOCKHOLDING & INVESTMENTS number measuring price increase a number representing an estimate of the anticipated price increase of a stock. A high alpha suggests a stock is likely to produce a good return. *See also* ***beta***

alpha rating STOCKHOLDING & INVESTMENTS expected return when market's rate is zero the return a security or a portfolio would be expected to earn if the market's rate of return were zero. Alpha expresses the difference between the return expected from a stock or mutual fund, given its beta rating, and the return actually produced. A stock or trust that returns more than its beta would predict has a positive alpha, while one that returns less than the amount predicted by beta has a negative alpha. A large positive alpha indicates a strong performance, while a large negative alpha indicates a dismal performance.

To begin with, the market itself is assigned a beta of 1.0. If a stock or trust has a beta of 1.2, this means its price is likely to rise or fall by 12% when the overall market rises or falls by 10%; a beta of 7.0 means the stock or trust price is likely to move up or down at 70% of the level of the market change.

In practice, an alpha of 0.4 means the stock or trust in question outperformed the market-based return estimate by 0.4%. An alpha of −0.6 means the return was 0.6% less than would have been predicted from the change in the market alone.

Both alpha and beta should be readily available upon request from investment firms, because the figures appear in standard performance reports. It is always best to ask for them, because calculating a stock's alpha rating requires first knowing a stock's beta rating, and beta calculations can involve mathematical complexities. *See also* ***beta rating***

alpha value STOCKHOLDING & INVESTMENTS money given to departing employee for investment in Australia and New Zealand, a sum paid to an employee when he or she leaves a company that can be transferred to a concessionally taxed investment account such as an **Approved Deposit Fund**

alternate director CORPORATE GOVERNANCE absent director's representative at board meeting a person who is allowed to act for an absent named director of a company at a board meeting

alternative investment STOCKHOLDING & INVESTMENTS investment not in bonds or stock an investment other than in bonds or stock of a large company or one listed on a stock exchange

Alternative Investment Market MARKETS London market trading in smaller firms' stock the London market trading in stock of emerging or small companies not eligible for listing on the London Stock Exchange. It replaced the Unlisted Securities Market (USM) in 1995. *Abbr* **AIM**

alternative minimum tax TAX US system to ensure that wealthy pay tax in the United States, a way of calculating income tax that is intended to ensure that wealthy individuals, corporations, trusts, and estates pay at least some tax regardless of deductions, but that is increasingly targeting the middle class because the threshold was never indexed for inflation. This has turned the AMT into an important political issue, with the possibility that the

   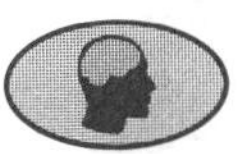  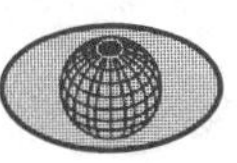   

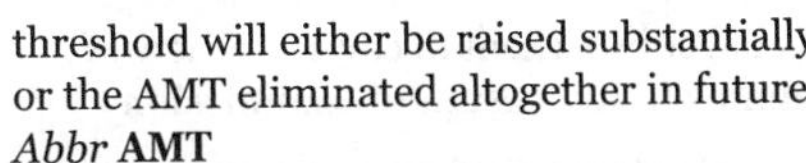

threshold will either be raised substantially or the AMT eliminated altogether in future. *Abbr* **AMT**

alternative mortgage instrument MORTGAGES open-ended non-amortizing mortgage any form of mortgage other than a fixed-term amortizing loan

alternative order STOCKHOLDING & INVESTMENTS instruction for either of two specified actions an order given to a broker to do one of two things, for example, to sell a stock either when it goes up to a specified price or down to a specified price, thereby limiting gains and losses

AM *abbr* STOCKHOLDING & INVESTMENTS asset management

amalgamation MERGERS & ACQUISITIONS joining of organizations for mutual benefit the process of two or more organizations joining together for mutual benefit, either through a **merger** or **consolidation**

amanah FINANCE trust arrangement between parties in Islamic financing, an arrangement in which one person holds funds or property in trust for another

ambit claim ANZ FINANCE excessive arbitration claim anticipating compromise a claim made to an arbitration authority for higher pay or improved conditions that is deliberately exaggerated because the claimants know that they will subsequently have to compromise

American Accounting Association ACCOUNTING organization promoting accounting research a voluntary organization for those with an interest in accounting research and best practice. Its mission is "to foster worldwide excellence in the creation, dissemination, and application of accounting knowledge and skills." The association was founded in 1916. *Abbr* **AAA**

American Bankers Association BANKING US association representing banks an association that represents banks in the United States and promotes good practice. *Abbr* **ABA**

American depository receipt STOCKHOLDING & INVESTMENTS document indicating ownership of foreign stock a document that indicates a US investor's ownership of stock in a foreign corporation. *Abbr* **ADR**

American depository share STOCKHOLDING & INVESTMENTS foreign stock owned by US investor a share of stock in a foreign corporation, whose ownership by a US investor is represented by an **American depository receipt**. *Abbr* **ADS**

American Institute of Banking BANKING US association training bankers the part of the American Bankers Association that organizes training for people who work in the banking industry. *Abbr* **AIB**

American Institute of Certified Public Accountants ACCOUNTING US association for certified public accountants in the United States, the national association for certified public accountants, founded in New York in 1887. *Abbr* **AICPA**

American option or **American style option** STOCKHOLDING & INVESTMENTS option contract running to expiration date an option contract that can be exercised at any time up to and including the expiration date. Most exchange-traded options are of this style. *See also* ***European option***

American Stock Exchange or **AMEX** MARKETS New York exchange listing smaller firms a New York stock exchange listing smaller and less mature companies than those listed on the larger New York Stock Exchange

amortization FINANCE **1.** method of recovering costs of assets a method of recovering (deducting or writing off) the capital costs of intangible assets over a fixed period of time.

For tax purposes, the distinction is not always made between amortization and depreciation, yet amortization remains a viable financial accounting concept in its own right.

It is computed using the straight-line method of depreciation: divide the initial cost of the intangible asset by the estimated useful life of that asset.

$$\frac{\text{Initial cost}}{\text{Useful life}} = \text{Amortization per year}$$

For example, if it costs $10,000 to acquire a patent and it has an estimated useful life of 10 years, the amortized amount per year is $1,000.

The amount of amortization accumulated since the asset was acquired appears on the organization's balance sheet as a deduction under the amortized asset.

While that formula is straightforward, amortization can also incorporate a variety of noncash charges to net earnings and/or asset values, such as depletion, write-offs, prepaid expenses, and deferred charges. Accordingly, there are many rules to regulate how these charges appear on financial statements. The rules are different in each country, and are occasionally changed, so it is necessary to stay abreast of them and rely on expert advice.

For financial reporting purposes, an intangible asset is amortized over a period of years. The amortizable life, or "useful life," of an intangible asset is the period over which it gives economic benefit.

Intangibles that can be amortized can include:

Copyrights, based on the amount paid either to purchase them or to develop them internally, plus the costs incurred in producing the work (wages or materials, for example). At present, a copyright is granted to a corporation for 75 years, and to an individual for the life of the author plus 50 years. However, the estimated useful life of a copyright is usually far less than its legal life, and it is generally amortized over a fairly short period.

Cost of a franchise, including any fees paid to the franchiser, as well legal costs or expenses incurred in the acquisition. A franchise granted for a limited period should be amortized over its life. If the franchise has an indefinite life, it should be amortized over a reasonable period not to exceed 40 years.

Covenants not to compete: an agreement by the seller of a business not to engage in a competing business in a certain area for a specific period of time. The cost of the not-to-compete covenant should be amortized over the period covered by the covenant unless its estimated economic life is expected to be less.

Easement costs that grant a right of way may be amortized if there is a limited and specified life.

Organization costs incurred when forming a corporation or a partnership, including legal fees, accounting services, incorporation fees, and other related services. Organization costs are usually amortized over 60 months.

Patents, both those developed internally and those purchased. If developed internally, a patent's "amortizable basis" includes legal fees incurred during the application process. A patent should be amortized over its legal life or its economic life, whichever is the shorter.

Trademarks, brands, and trade names, which should be written off over a period not to exceed 40 years.

Other types of property that may be amortized include certain intangible drilling costs, circulation costs, mine development costs, pollution control facilities, and reforestation expenditures.

Certain intangibles cannot be amortized, but may be depreciated using a straight-line approach if they have "determinable" useful life. Because the rules are different in each country and are subject to change, it is essential to rely on specialist advice.

2. equal payment of principal and interest the payment of the principal and interest on a loan in equal amounts over a period of time

amortize FINANCE gradually repay debt or reduce value of assets to reduce the value of an **asset** gradually by systematically writing off its cost over a period of time, or to repay a **debt** in a series of regular installments or transfers

amortized mortgage *US* MORTGAGES mortgage with combined principal and interest payments a long-term loan, usually for the purchase of real estate, in which the borrower makes monthly payments, part of which cover the interest on the loan and part of which cover the repayment of the principal. In the early years, the greater proportion of the payment is used to cover the interest charged but, as the principal is gradually repaid, the interest portion diminishes and the repayment portion increases. *UK term **repayment mortgage***

amortized value FINANCE value of amortized financial instrument the value at a specific time of a financial instrument that is being amortized

amortizing swap STOCKHOLDING & INVESTMENTS interest rate swap with decreasing notional principal amount an **interest rate swap** in which the **notional principal amount** declines over the period of the contract

amount paid up MARKETS money paid for new stock an amount paid for a new issue of shares of stock, either the total payment or the first installment, if the shares are offered with installment payments

AMPS *abbr* STOCKHOLDING & INVESTMENTS auction market preferred stock

AMT *abbr* TAX alternative minimum tax

analysis STOCKHOLDING & INVESTMENTS evaluation of markets a systematic examination and evaluation of the financial markets and the performance of securities

analysis of variance STATISTICS isolation of one cause of statistical variation the process of separating the statistical variation caused by a particular factor from that caused by other factors

analysis of variance table STATISTICS table showing variation in statistical data a table that shows the total variation in the observations in a statistical data set

analyst STOCKHOLDING & INVESTMENTS somebody who evaluates investments a person whose job is to analyze the performance of securities and make recommendations about buying and selling

analytical review TREASURY MANAGEMENT examination of trends between financial periods the examination of ratios, trends, and changes in balances from one period to the next, to obtain a broad understanding of the financial position and results of operations and to identify any items requiring further investigation

angel investing FINANCE investing in unproven business venture willingness of an individual or network of individuals to invest in an unproven but well-researched startup business, taking an advisory role without making demands

angel investor or **angel** FINANCE investor in unproven business venture an individual or group of individuals willing to invest in an unproven but well-researched startup business. Angel investors are typically the first port of call for Internet startups looking for financial backing, because they are more inclined to provide early funding than **venture capital** firms are. After investing in a company, angel investors take an advisory role without making demands.

angel network or **angel investment group** FINANCE network of potential investors for entrepreneurs a network of backers, organized through a central office which keeps a database of suitable investors and puts them in touch with entrepreneurs who need financial backing

angular histogram STATISTICS circular chart showing data a histogram that represents data in a circular form. *Also called **pie chart***

ANN *abbr* E-COMMERCE artificial neural network

announcement STOCKHOLDING & INVESTMENTS statement of company's trading prospects a statement that a company makes to provide information on its trading prospects, which will be of interest to its existing and potential investors

announcement date STOCKHOLDING & INVESTMENTS = ***declaration date***

annual accounts CORPORATE GOVERNANCE, ACCOUNTING document showing company's financial performance a profit and loss account and balance sheet, and, where a company has subsidiaries, the company's group accounts, included in the **annual report and accounts** for stockholders. *See also **annual report***

annual charge STOCKHOLDING & INVESTMENTS management fee covering administrative costs a management fee paid yearly to a stockbroker or collective fund manager by a client to cover a variety of administrative costs and **commission**

annual depreciation ACCOUNTING reduction in book value of asset a reduction in the book value of a fixed asset at a specific rate per year, based on the estimated useful life of that asset. *See also **straight line depreciation***

annual depreciation provision ACCOUNTING allocation of cost of asset to specific year the allocation of the cost of an asset to a single year of the asset's expected lifetime

Annual Equivalent Rate FINANCE UK notional annual compound interest rate in the United Kingdom, a way of expressing different interest rates charged over different periods as an annual rate equivalent to a single payment of interest made on the anniversary of the loan and each subsequent year to repayment. *Abbr* **AER**. *See also **compound annual return***

annual general meeting *UK* CORPORATE GOVERNANCE = ***annual meeting***

annual income FINANCE money received in one year the money received from earnings or investments during a calendar year

annualized percentage rate FINANCE monthly rate times twelve the percentage rate over a year, calculated by multiplying the monthly rate by twelve. It is not as accurate as the **annual percentage rate**, which includes fees and other charges. *Abbr* **APR**

annual management charge STOCKHOLDING & INVESTMENTS charge made for managing investment account a charge made by the financial institution that is managing an investment account

annual meeting *US* CORPORATE GOVERNANCE stockholders' yearly business meeting a yearly meeting at which a company's management reports the year's results and stockholders have the opportunity to vote on company business, for example, the appointment of directors and auditors. Other business, for example, voting on dividend payments, and board- and stockholder-sponsored resolutions, may also be transacted. *Also called **annual stockholders' meeting**. UK term **AGM***

annual percentage rate FINANCE hypothetical rate based on simple interest the interest rate that would exist if it were calculated as simple rather than compound interest.

Different investments typically offer different compounding periods, usually quarterly or monthly. The APR allows them

  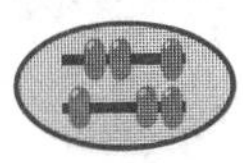 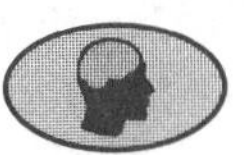  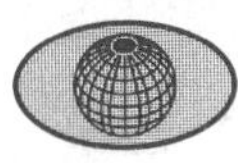   

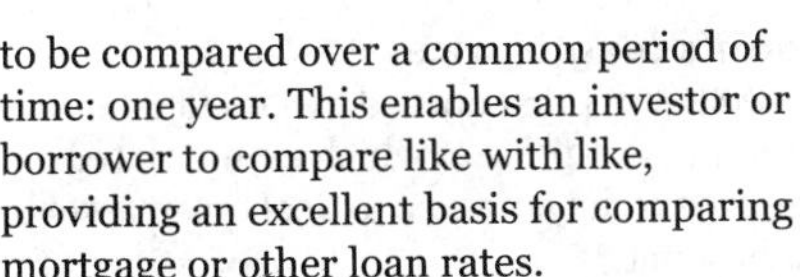

to be compared over a common period of time: one year. This enables an investor or borrower to compare like with like, providing an excellent basis for comparing mortgage or other loan rates.

APR is calculated by applying the formula:

$$APR = \left[\frac{1+i}{m}\right] m - 1.0$$

In the formula, *i* is the interest rate quoted, expressed as a decimal, and *m* is the number of compounding periods per year.

The APR is usually slightly higher than the quoted rate, and should be expressed as a decimal, that is, 6% becomes 0.06. When expressed as the cost of credit, other costs should be included in addition to interest, such as loan closing costs and financial fees. *Abbr* **APR**

annual percentage yield FINANCE effective annual return on investment the effective or true annual rate of return on an investment, taking into account the effect of **compounding**. For example, an annual percentage rate of 6% compounded monthly translates into an annual percentage yield of 6.17%. *Abbr* **APY**

annual report or **annual report and accounts** CORPORATE GOVERNANCE, ACCOUNTING document reporting company's business performance a document prepared each year to give a true and fair view of a company's state of affairs.

Annual reports are issued to shareholders and filed at the Securities and Exchange Commission in accordance with the provisions of company legislation. Contents include a **profit and loss account** and **balance sheet**, a **cash flow statement**, **auditor's report**, directors' report, and, where a company has subsidiaries, the company's group accounts. The **financial statements** are the main purpose of the annual report, and usually include notes to the accounts. These amplify numerous points contained in the figures and are critical for anyone wishing to study the accounts in detail.

annual rest system MORTGAGES system crediting overpayments once a year a system in which extra payments or overpayments made to reduce the amount borrowed on a mortgage are credited to the account only once a year

annual return ACCOUNTING in UK, firm's report to Registrar of Companies in the United Kingdom, an official report that a registered company has to make each year to the Registrar of Companies

annual stockholders' meeting US CORPORATE GOVERNANCE = ***annual meeting***

annuitant PENSIONS recipient of annuity income a person who receives income from an **annuity**

annuity PENSIONS contract for regular payments from one-off investment a contract under which a person pays a lump-sum premium to an insurance company and in return receives periodic payments, usually yearly, often beginning on retirement.

There are several types of annuities. They vary both in the ways they accumulate funds and in the ways they dispense earnings. A **fixed annuity** guarantees fixed payments to the individual receiving it for the term of the contract, usually until death; a **variable annuity** offers no guarantee but has potential for a greater return, usually based on the performance of a stock or mutual fund; a **deferred annuity** delays payments until the individual chooses to receive them; a **hybrid annuity**, also called a **combination annuity**, combines features of both the fixed and variable annuity.

annuity certain PENSIONS contract paying for set period an **annuity** that provides payments for a specific number of years, regardless of whether the annuitant remains alive

annuity contract INSURANCE contract providing lifelong regular payments an **annuity** that provides payments of a fixed sum regularly while the annuitant is alive

annuity in arrears INSURANCE annuity with delayed first payment an **annuity** whose first payment is due at least one payment period after the start date of the annuity's contract

anonymizer E-COMMERCE website that hides user's identity a website through which a person browsing can visit the World Wide Web without leaving any identity traces

ANSI X.12 standard E-COMMERCE accepted method of electronic business transactions an American National Standards Institute-supported protocol for the electronic interchange of business transactions. *Also called* ***X.12***

antedate UK GENERAL MANAGEMENT = ***predate***

anticipation note STOCKHOLDING & INVESTMENTS bond repaid with future receipts or borrowings a bond that a borrower intends to pay off with money from taxes due or money to be borrowed in a later and larger transaction

anticipatory hedging STOCKHOLDING & INVESTMENTS hedging before relevant transaction occurs hedging conducted before the transaction to which the **hedge** applies has taken place. *See also* ***hedge*** *(sense 2)*

anti-dumping INTERNATIONAL TRADE preventing cheap sale of products overseas intended to prevent the sale of goods on a foreign market at a price lower than is usually charged in the home market

anti-dumping duty TAX, INTERNATIONAL TRADE import tax offsetting subsidized price of import a tax imposed by a country on imported goods, when the price of the goods includes a subsidy from the government in the country of origin. *Also called* ***countervailing duty***

anti-inflationary ECONOMICS restricting inflation restricting or trying to restrict an increase in inflation

anti-trust laws LEGAL US laws preventing monopolies in the United States, laws that prevent the formation of monopolies. Antitrust laws also attempt to curb **trusts** and **cartels** and to keep them from employing monopolistic practices to make unfair profits. They are intended to encourage competitive behavior.

ANZCERTA *abbr* INTERNATIONAL TRADE Australia and New Zealand Closer Economic Relations Trade Agreement

AO *abbr* MARKETS All Ordinaries Index

AON MARKETS *see* ***all-or-none underwriting***

AP *abbr* ACCOUNTING accounts payable

APACS *abbr* BANKING Association for Payment Clearing Services

APB *abbr* ACCOUNTING Accounting Principles Board

APEC *abbr* INTERNATIONAL TRADE Asia-Pacific Economic Cooperation

application server E-COMMERCE host computer network allowing dynamic information exchange an advanced type of server used to run programming languages that help websites to deliver dynamic information such as the latest news headlines, stock quotes, personalized information, or shopping carts

applied economics ECONOMICS use of economic theories for practical policies the practical application of theoretical economic principles, especially in formulating national and international economic policies

     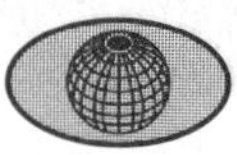   

apportionment ACCOUNTING distribution of costs the sharing of costs between different internal parties, cost centers, etc.

appreciation **1.** ACCOUNTING value that asset accrues over time the value that some assets such as land and buildings accrue over time. Directors of companies are obliged to reflect this in their accounts. **2.** CURRENCY & EXCHANGE relative increase in currency value the increase in value of a currency with a **floating exchange rate** relative to another

appropriation ACCOUNTING sum set aside a sum of money that has been allocated for a specific purpose

appropriation account ACCOUNTING section of account showing treatment of profits the part of a **profit and loss account** that shows how a company's profit has been dealt with, for example, how much has been given to the stockholders as dividends and how much is being put into the reserves

approved accounts ACCOUNTING accounts agreed on by company directors accounts that have been formally accepted by a company's board of directors

Approved Deposit Fund PENSIONS fund accepting payments from superannuation fund in Australia and New Zealand, a concessionally taxed fund managed by a financial institution into which **eligible termination payments** can be transferred from a superannuation fund. *Abbr* **ADF**

approved securities STOCKHOLDING & INVESTMENTS state bonds as bank reserves state bonds that can be held by banks to form part of their reserves

APR *abbr* FINANCE **1.** annual percentage rate **2.** annualized percentage rate

APRA *abbr* REGULATION & COMPLIANCE Australian Prudential Regulation Authority

APV *abbr* ACCOUNTING adjusted present value

APY *abbr* FINANCE annual percentage yield

AR *abbr* FINANCE accounts receivable

Arab Accounting Dinar CURRENCY & EXCHANGE accounting unit of Arab Monetary Fund a bookkeeping unit used between member states of the Arab Monetary Fund, equal to three IMF **Special Drawing Rights**. *Abbr* **AAD**

arbitrage MARKETS trade profiting from variations in market price the buying and selling of foreign currencies, products, or financial securities between two or more markets in order to make an immediate profit by exploiting the differences in market prices quoted

arbitrage fund MARKETS fund capitalizing on variations in market price a fund which tries to take advantage of price discrepancies for the same **asset** in different **markets**

arbitrage pricing theory MARKETS model used for assessing return and risk a model of financial instrument and portfolio behavior that provides a benchmark of return and risk for capital budgeting and securities analysis. It can be used to create portfolios that track a market index, estimate the risk of an asset allocation strategy, or estimate the response of a portfolio to economic developments.

arbitrage syndicate MARKETS group raising capital for arbitrage deals a group of people formed to raise the capital to invest in arbitrage deals

arbitrageur MARKETS somebody buying stock for windfall profit a firm or individual who purchases stock or financial securities to make a windfall profit

arbitration GENERAL MANAGEMENT, HR & PERSONNEL process of resolving disagreement by unbiased person the settlement of a dispute by an independent third person, rather than by a court of law. Arbitration allows for claims or grievances to be settled quickly, cost-effectively, privately, and by somebody who is suitably qualified. A contract may include an arbitration clause to be invoked in the case of a dispute. *See also* ***mediation***

arbitrator GENERAL MANAGEMENT unbiased person who resolves other people's disagreements an impartial person accepted by both parties in a dispute to hear both sides and make a judgment

arbun FINANCE nonrefundable deposit allowing buyer right to cancel in Islamic financing, a nonrefundable down payment paid by a buyer to a seller upon the signing of a sale contract in which the buyer has the right to cancel the contract at any time

area sampling STATISTICS randomly selecting subregions for inspection a form of sampling in which a region is subdivided and some of the divisions are then selected at random for a complete survey

arithmetic mean STATISTICS simple average a simple average calculated by dividing the sum of two or more items by the number of items

ARM *abbr* MORTGAGES adjustable rate mortgage

armchair economics ECONOMICS casual economic opinion economic forecasting or theorizing based on insufficient data or knowledge of a subject (*informal*)

arm's-length price OPERATIONS & PRODUCTION price agreed by unrelated seller and buyer a price at which an unrelated seller and buyer agree to deal on an asset or a product

ARPS *abbr* STOCKHOLDING & INVESTMENTS adjustable rate preferred stock

ARR *abbr* ACCOUNTING accounting rate of return

arrangement fee BANKING bank charge for arranging credit a charge made by a bank to a client for arranging credit facilities

arrears FINANCE money owed but unpaid money that is owed, but that has not been paid at the time when it was due ◇ in arrears FINANCE still owing money that should have been paid, especially in a series of payments

articles of association *UK* CORPORATE GOVERNANCE = ***bylaws***

articles of incorporation CORPORATE GOVERNANCE legal document creating US corporation in the United States, a legal document that creates a corporation and sets forth its purpose and structure according to the laws of the state in which it is established. *Also called* ***charter***

articles of partnership CORPORATE GOVERNANCE = ***partnership agreement***

artificial intelligence GENERAL MANAGEMENT computer systems thinking like humans a branch of computer science concerned with the development of computer systems capable of performing functions that normally require human intelligence, for example, reasoning, problem solving, learning from experience, and speech recognition. Artificial intelligence research combines aspects of computer science and cognitive psychology. Artificial intelligence has applications in business and management, for example, in **expert systems**.

artificial neural network GENERAL MANAGEMENT information processing system allowing computers to learn an information processing system with interconnected components analogous to neurons, based on mathematical models that mimic some features of biological nervous systems and the ability to learn through experience. *Abbr* **ANN**

ASB *abbr* ACCOUNTING Accounting Standards Board

ascending tops MARKETS market chart pattern showing series of ascending peaks a term used to refer to an upward trend in the

  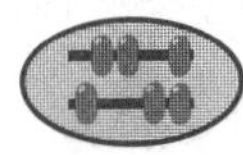 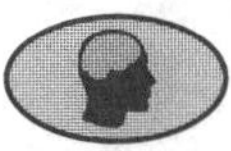  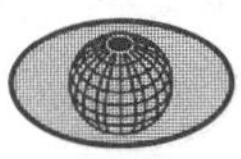   

market as shown on a chart, in which each peak in the chart is higher than the preceding one

ASEAN Free Trade Area INTERNATIONAL TRADE conceptual agreement fostering trade around Singapore a conceptual regional free trade agreement supported by Singapore to foster trade within the region covered by the Association of Southeast Asian Nations. *Abbr* **AFTA**

A share STOCKHOLDING & INVESTMENTS share issued to raise additional capital in the United States, a share of stock in a company issued to raise additional capital without diluting control of the company. *Also called* ***nonvoting share****. See also* ***B share***

Asian Currency Unit ACCOUNTING unit for recording transactions in Asian Dollar market a bookkeeping unit used for recording transactions made by approved financial institutions operating in the Asian Dollar market. *Abbr* **ACU**

Asian Development Bank BANKING bank supporting development in Asia a bank set up by various Asian countries, with other outside members, to assist countries in the region with money and technical advice. *Abbr* **ADB**

Asian dollar BANKING, CURRENCY & EXCHANGE US dollar deposited in Asian bank a dollar deposited in a bank in Asia or the Pacific region

Asian option STOCKHOLDING & INVESTMENTS, RISK = ***average option***

Asia-Pacific Economic Cooperation INTERNATIONAL TRADE forum promoting trade in Pacific region a forum designed to promote trade and economic cooperation among countries bordering the Pacific Ocean. It was established in 1989. Members include Australia, Indonesia, Thailand, the Philippines, Singapore, Brunei, and Japan. *Abbr* **APEC**

ASIC *abbr* REGULATION & COMPLIANCE Australian Securities and Investments Commission

ask 1. US MARKETS security's selling price the price at which a security is offered for sale. *UK term* ***asked price*** **2.** STOCKHOLDING & INVESTMENTS value of mutual fund the net asset value of a mutual fund plus any sales charges

asked price UK MARKETS = ***ask*** *(sense 1)*

asking price OPERATIONS & PRODUCTION original price the price that a seller puts on something before any negotiation

ask price US MARKETS = ***ask*** *(sense 1)*

assay precious metal purity test a test used for determining the purity of a precious metal such as gold or silver

assembly OPERATIONS & PRODUCTION putting product parts together the process of joining components together to make a complete product

assembly line OPERATIONS & PRODUCTION system for putting parts together in specific order a line of production in which a number of assembly operations are performed in a set sequence. The speed of movement of an assembly line has to be matched with the skills and abilities of the workers and the complexity of the assembly process to be performed. The assembly line emerged from the ideas of **scientific management** and was popularized by a number of entrepreneurs, including Henry Ford in the car production industry.

assembly plant OPERATIONS & PRODUCTION factory for assembling products the factory building in which an **assembly line** is housed

assessed loss TAX in S. Africa tax-deductible expenses exceeding taxable income the excess of tax-deductible expenses over taxable income as confirmed by the South African Revenue Service. It may be carried forward and deducted in determining the taxpayer's taxable income in subsequent years of assessment.

assessed value FINANCE value calculated by professional adviser a value for something that is calculated officially by somebody such as an investment adviser

assessor FINANCE somebody who establishes something's worth a person who determines the value of something such as real estate for tax or insurance purposes

asset ACCOUNTING item to which value is assigned any tangible or intangible item to which a value can be assigned. Assets can be physical, such as machinery and consumer durables, or financial, such as cash and accounts receivable, or intangible, such as brand value and goodwill.

Assets are typically broken down into five different categories. **Current assets** include cash, cash equivalents, marketable securities, inventories, and prepaid expenses that are expected to be used within one year or a normal operating cycle. All cash items and inventories are reported at historical value. Securities are reported at market value. **Noncurrent assets**, or long-term investments, are resources that are expected to be held for more than one year. They are reported at the lower of cost and current market value, which means that their values will vary. **Fixed assets** include property, plant and facilities, and equipment used to conduct business. These items are reported at their original value, even though current values might well be much higher. **Intangible assets** include legal claims, patents, franchise rights, and accounts receivable. These values can be more difficult to determine. **Accounts receivable**, for example, reflect the amount a business expects to collect, such as, say, $9,000 of the $10,000 owed by customers. Deferred charges include prepaid costs and other expenditures that will produce future revenue or benefits.

asset allocation STOCKHOLDING & INVESTMENTS strategy maximizing return while minimizing risk an investment strategy that distributes investments in a portfolio so as to achieve the highest investment return while minimizing risk. Such a strategy usually apportions investments among cash equivalents, stock in domestic and foreign companies, fixed-income investments, and real estate.

asset-backed security STOCKHOLDING & INVESTMENTS security backed by loans a security based on the collateral of outstanding loans for which the investor receives the payments

asset backing STOCKHOLDING & INVESTMENTS assets supporting stock price support for a stock price provided by the value of the company's assets

asset base STOCKHOLDING & INVESTMENTS tangible assets of firm or person the **tangible assets** held by a company or individual investor at any point in time

asset-based lending FINANCE loans repaid with proceeds from acquired assets the lending of money with the expectation that the proceeds from an asset or assets will allow the borrower to repay the loan

asset class STOCKHOLDING & INVESTMENTS investment category a category into which an investment falls, for example, stocks, bonds, commodities, or real estate

asset conversion loan FINANCE loan repaid with proceeds from sale of asset a loan that the borrower will repay with money raised by selling an asset

asset cover or **asset coverage** FINANCE ratio showing company's solvency a ratio, derived from the net assets of a company divided by its debt, that indicates the company's solvency

asset demand ECONOMICS assets held in cash the amount of assets held as cash, which will be low when interest rates are high and high when interest rates are low

asset financing FINANCE borrowing that uses assets as collateral the borrowing of money by a company using its assets as collateral

asset for asset swap FINANCE exchange of bankrupts' debts an exchange of one bankrupt debtor's debt for that of another

asset management STOCKHOLDING & INVESTMENTS investment service combining banking and brokerage an investment service offered by some financial institutions that combines banking and brokerage services. *Abbr* **AM** —**asset manager**

asset play STOCKHOLDING & INVESTMENTS stock purchase assuming unknown assets the purchase of a company's stock in the belief that it has assets that are not properly documented and therefore unknown to others

asset pricing model FINANCE pricing model determining asset's future profit a pricing model that is used to determine the profit that an asset is likely to yield

asset protection trust FINANCE trust protecting funds from creditors a trust, often established in a foreign country, used to make the trust's principal inaccessible to creditors

asset restructuring FINANCE purchase or sale of valuable assets the purchase or sale of assets worth more than 50% of a listed company's total or net assets

asset side ACCOUNTING side of balance sheet showing assets the side of a balance sheet that shows the economic resources a firm owns, for example, cash in hand or in bank deposits, products, or buildings and fixtures

assets requirements FINANCE assets needed to trade the tangible and intangible assets needed for a business to continue trading

asset stripping MERGERS & ACQUISITIONS practice of selling acquired firm's assets piecemeal the purchase of a company whose market value is below its asset value, usually so that the buyer can sell the assets for immediate gain. The buyer usually has little or no concern for the purchased company's employees or other **stakeholders**, so the practice is generally frowned upon. —**asset stripper**

asset substitution FINANCE purchase of risky assets undisclosed to lender the purchase of assets that involve more risk than those a lender expected the borrower to buy

asset swap 1. FINANCE exchange of assets allowing easy diversification an exchange of assets between companies so that they may dispose of parts no longer required and enter another product area **2.** STOCKHOLDING & INVESTMENTS exchange of fixed for varying payment in capital markets, the exchange of a fixed coupon payment associated with a bond for a floating rate payment, usually based on LIBOR

asset turnover ACCOUNTING measure of firm's business efficiency the ratio of a company's sales revenue to its total assets, used as a measure of the firm's business efficiency

asset valuation ACCOUNTING total value of firm's assets the aggregated value of the assets of a firm, usually the capital assets, as entered on its balance sheet

asset value MERGERS & ACQUISITIONS firm's value as combined value of assets the value of a company calculated by adding together all its assets

assign FINANCE transfer ownership of asset to transfer ownership of an **asset** to another person or organization

assignable cause of variation OPERATIONS & PRODUCTION apparent reason that something is different an evident reason for deviation from the norm. An assignable cause exists when variation within a process can be attributed to a particular cause that is a fundamental part of the process. Once identified, the assignable cause of the errors must be investigated and the process adjusted before other possible causes of variation are examined.

assignation *UK* LEGAL = ***assignment***

assigned risk INSURANCE poor risk that company must insure for a poor insurance risk that a company is required by law to insure itself against

assignee LEGAL somebody receiving property or rights a person to whom property or the rights to something have been transferred

assignment *US* LEGAL transfer of property or rights a legal transfer of property or the rights to something. *UK term* ***assignation***

assignor LEGAL person transferring property or rights a person who transfers property or the rights of something to somebody else

associate *ANZ* MARKETS stock exchange member without seat a member of a stock exchange who does not have a seat on it

associate company BUSINESS = ***affiliated enterprise***

associated company BUSINESS firm partly owned and controlled by another a company in which another company owns less than 50% and either has some management control over it or has a close trading relationship with it

associate director CORPORATE GOVERNANCE unelected director attending board meetings a director who attends board meetings, but has not been elected by the stockholders

associate program E-COMMERCE = ***affiliate program***

Association for Financial Professionals FINANCE US organization for professionals in finance industry in the United States, an organization for corporate financial managers that provides training and certification to members and represents their interests to government. *Abbr* **AFP**

Association for Payment Clearing Services BANKING UK organization for payments industry the professional organization for providers of payment services to customers in the United Kingdom. *Abbr* **APACS**

Association of Accounting Technicians ACCOUNTING UK accounting organization a professional organization founded in the United Kingdom in 1980 and offering qualifications in subjects related to accounting. It now has members and students worldwide. *Abbr* **AAT**

Association of British Insurers INSURANCE association representing UK insurance companies an association that represents over 400 UK insurance companies to the government, the regulators, and other agencies, as well as providing a wide range of services to its members. *Abbr* **ABI**

Association of Chartered Accountants in the United States ACCOUNTING association representing US chartered accountants a nonprofit professional and educational organization that represents over 5,000 chartered accountants based in the United States. The Association was founded in 1985. *Abbr* **ACAUS**

Association of Chartered Certified Accountants ACCOUNTING international organization representing accountants an international accounting organization with over 300,000 members in more than 160 countries. It was formed in 1904 as the London Association of Accountants. *Abbr* **ACCA**

  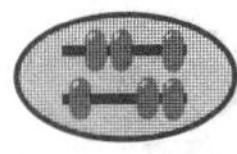   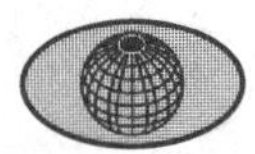   

Association of Futures Brokers and Dealers MARKETS organization overseeing futures and options trading a self-regulating organization that oversees the activities of dealers in the futures and options markets. *Abbr* **AFBD**

Association of Independent Financial Advisers FINANCE UK trade association for financial advisers a UK trade association that represents the interests of independent financial advisers to the UK government and in the European Union. *Abbr* **AIFA**

Association of International Accountants ACCOUNTING organization for accountants a professional accounting organization founded in the United Kingdom in 1928 and offering qualifications in international accounting. *Abbr* **AIA**

Association of Investment Companies STOCKHOLDING & INVESTMENTS UK organization for investment industry the professional organization for UK investment trust companies. It was founded in 1932 and until 2006 was called the Association of Investment Trust Companies. *Abbr* **AIC**

Association of Unit Trusts and Investment Funds STOCKHOLDING & INVESTMENTS *see* ***Investment Management Association***

assumable mortgage MORTGAGES mortgage that buyer can take over from seller a mortgage that the buyer of a property can take over from the seller

assumed bond STOCKHOLDING & INVESTMENTS bond for which new firm takes responsibility a bond for which a company other than the issuer takes over responsibility

assumption STATISTICS condition for statistical method to work accurately the conditions under which valid results can be obtained from a statistical technique

assurance *UK* INSURANCE *see* ***life insurance***

assure *UK* INSURANCE = ***insure*** *(sense 2)*

assured shorthold tenancy *UK* REAL ESTATE tenancy for fixed short period a tenancy for a fixed period of at least six months during which the tenant cannot be evicted other than by court order. Any new tenancy without a written agreement is an assured shorthold tenancy.

assured tenancy *UK* REAL ESTATE tenancy for indefinite period a tenancy for an indefinite period in which the tenant cannot be evicted other than by court order

assurer or **assuror** *UK* INSURANCE = ***insurer***

AST *abbr* MARKETS automated screen trading

ASX *abbr* MARKETS Australian Stock Exchange

ASX 100 MARKETS Australian index of companies a measure of the change in stock prices on the **Australian Stock Exchange** based on changes in the stocks of the top 100 companies. Similar indexes include the ASX 20, ASX 50, ASX 200, and ASX 300.

asymmetrical distribution STATISTICS uneven distribution of data around central point a frequency or probability distribution of statistical data that is not symmetrical about a central value in the data

asymmetric information BUSINESS information that differs between parties to transaction a situation in which consumers, suppliers, and producers do not all have the same information on which to base their decisions

asymmetric risk RISK investment risk where gains and losses differ widely the risk an investor faces when the gain realized from the move of an **underlying asset** in one direction is significantly different from the loss incurred from its move in the opposite direction

asymmetric taxation TAX difference in tax status between parties to transaction a difference in tax status between parties to a transaction, typically making the transaction attractive to both parties because of taxes that one or both can avoid

asynchronous transmission E-COMMERCE method of sending intermittent data the transmission of data in which the end of the transmission of one unit denotes the start of the next, rather than transmission at fixed intervals

at best MARKETS instruction to buy or sell immediately an instruction to a stockbroker to buy or sell securities immediately at the best possible current price in the market, regardless of adverse price movements. It is also applicable to the commodity or currency markets. *See also* ***at limit***

at call FINANCE repayable on demand used to describe a short-term loan that is repayable immediately upon demand

at limit MARKETS instruction to buy or sell security within limits an instruction to a stockbroker to buy or sell a security within specific limits, usually not to sell below or to buy above a set price. A time limit is stipulated by the investor, and, if there has been no transaction within that period, the instruction lapses. It is also applicable to the commodity or currency markets. *See also* ***at best***

ATM BANKING electronic machine for withdrawing money an electronic machine at which bank customers can withdraw money or access an account using an encoded plastic card. *Full form* ***automated teller machine***

ATM card *US* BANKING plastic card used in ATM a plastic card used to withdraw money or access an account at an ATM. *UK term* ***cash card***

ATO *abbr* TAX Australian Taxation Office

atomize GENERAL MANAGEMENT subdivide firm to split a large organization into smaller operating units

at par MARKETS, STOCKHOLDING & INVESTMENTS describing security sold at face value used to describe a security that sells at a price equal to its face value

ATS *abbr* BANKING automatic transfer service

at sight FINANCE immediately as soon as presented. A negotiable instrument which is payable at sight is called a **sight draft**. *See also* ***bill of exchange***

attachment LEGAL process enabling creditor to secure debtor's repayment a legal process that enables a creditor to secure dues from a debtor. A debtor's earnings and/or funds held at his or her bankers may be attached.

attachment order LEGAL court order preventing sale of debtor's property an order from a court to hold a debtor's property to prevent it from being sold until debts are paid

attention economy ECONOMICS theory that website viewing is tradable commodity a view of the economy in the late 20th century that suggests that people's attention to websites is a valuable and tradable commodity

attention management GENERAL MANAGEMENT making sure employees focus on work and goals a method of ensuring that employees are focused on their work and on organizational goals, as inattentiveness results in wasted time. An important factor in winning and sustaining attention is tapping into people's emotions.

attestation clause FINANCE clause showing that signature has been witnessed a clause showing that the signature of the person signing a legal document has been witnessed

at-the-money STOCKHOLDING & INVESTMENTS describing option where trading price

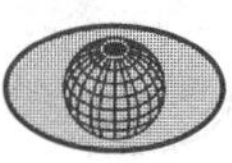

matches stock price used to describe an option with a **strike price** roughly equivalent to the price of the underlying stock

attitude GENERAL MANAGEMENT feeling or belief about situation a mental position consisting of a feeling, emotion, or opinion evolved in response to an external situation. An attitude can be momentary or can develop into a habitual position that has a long-term influence on somebody's behavior. Attempts can be made to modify attitudes that have a negative effect in the workplace, for example, through education and training.

attitude survey MARKETING questions about people's feelings toward firm or product a piece of research carried out to assess the feelings of a target audience toward a product, brand, or organization

attributable profit ACCOUNTING profit generated by specific business activity a profit that can be shown to come from a specific area of the company's operations

attribute sampling OPERATIONS & PRODUCTION method of quality testing through random samples a random testing method for determining the quality of a finished product by inspecting a sample number of the items in each batch. The items selected are examined for a selected attribute, which is usually an abnormal or negative characteristic—for example, a sample of cars from one production run might be inspected for poor paintwork, and the number of sampled cars found with this attribute used to calculate the number of defective items in the whole batch.

auction FINANCE sale of goods by competitive bidding a sale of goods or property by competitive bidding on the spot, by mail, by telecommunications, or over the Internet

auction market preferred stock STOCKHOLDING & INVESTMENTS UK stock with dividends tracking money-market index stock in a company owned in the United Kingdom that pays dividends which track a money-market index. *Abbr* **AMPS**

AUD *abbr* CURRENCY & EXCHANGE Australian dollar

audience MARKETING everyone who reads, sees, or hears advertisement the total number of readers, viewers, or listeners who are exposed to an advertisement

audience research MARKETING research concerning target group of advertising research carried out to measure the size or composition of the target audience for a piece of advertising

audit ACCOUNTING systematic examination of firm's activities and records a systematic examination of the activities and status of an entity, based primarily on investigation and analysis of its systems, controls, and records

audit committee ACCOUNTING, GENERAL MANAGEMENT committee monitoring firm's finances a committee of a company's board of directors, from which the company's executives are excluded, that monitors the company's finances

audited accounts ACCOUNTING accounts passed by auditor a set of accounts that have been thoroughly scrutinized, checked, and approved by a team of auditors

auditing ACCOUNTING official examination of firm's accounts the work of officially examining the books and accounts of a company to see that they follow generally accepted accounting practices

audit of management GENERAL MANAGEMENT = ***operational audit***

auditor ACCOUNTING person auditing accounts a person who audits companies' accounts or procedures

Auditor-General FINANCE official responsible for legality of Australian government expenditure an officer of an Australian state or territory government who is responsible for ensuring that government expenditure is made in accordance with legislation

auditors' fees ACCOUNTING approved payment to firm's auditors fees paid to a company's auditors, which are approved by the stockholders at an annual meeting

auditors' qualification ACCOUNTING auditors' statement that firm's financial position is misrepresented a form of words in a report from the auditors of a company's accounts, stating that in their opinion the accounts are not a true reflection of the company's financial position. *Also called* ***qualification of accounts***

auditor's report ACCOUNTING auditor's confirmation of firm's financial records a certification by an auditor that a firm's financial records give a true and fair view of its profit and loss for the period

audit report ACCOUNTING official summary of audit the summary submission made by auditors of the findings of an **audit**. An audit report is usually of the financial records and accounts of a company. An auditor's report normally takes one of the forms approved by the accountancy professional organizations to cover all requirements imposed by law on the auditor. If reports do not support the company's records, they may be termed "qualified." A report is qualified if it contains any indication that the auditor has failed to satisfy himself or herself on any of the points that the law requires. The qualification may, for example, add a rider stating that the appointed auditor has had to rely on secondary information supplied by other auditors under circumstances in which it has been inappropriate to do otherwise. Qualifications may also refer to the inadequacy of information or explanations supplied, or to the fact that the auditor is not satisfied that proper books or other records are being kept.

audit risk ACCOUNTING, RISK danger of auditors' mistaken view the risk that auditors may give an inappropriate audit opinion on financial statements

audit trail ACCOUNTING record of steps in transaction the records of all the sequential stages of a transaction. An audit trail may trace the process of a purchase, a sale, a customer complaint, or the supply of goods. Tracing what happened at each stage through the records can be a useful method of problem solving. In financial markets, audit trails may be used to ensure fairness and accuracy on the part of the dealers.

augend FINANCE number added to complete sum the number added to an **addend** in order to complete an addition

Aussie Mac MORTGAGES Australian security backed by mortgages a mortgage-backed certificate issued in Australia by the National Mortgage Market Corporation. The corporation has been issuing such certificates since 1985.

austerity budget TREASURY MANAGEMENT budget to discourage consumer spending a budget imposed on a country by its government with the goal of reducing the national deficit by way of cutting consumer spending

Austrade FINANCE Australian government organization promoting trade Australian Trade Commission, a federal government body responsible for promoting Australian products abroad and attracting business to Australia. It currently has 108 offices in 63 countries.

Australia and New Zealand Closer Economic Relations Trade Agreement INTERNATIONAL TRADE intergovernmental agreement to foster trade an accord between Australia and New Zealand designed to

  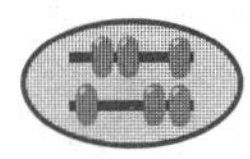 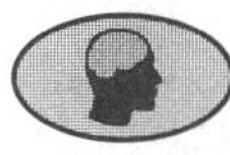  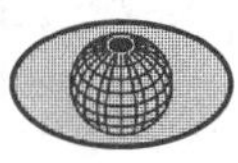   

facilitate the exchange of goods between the two countries. It was signed on January 1, 1983. *Abbr* **ANZCERTA**

Australian Accounting Standards Board ACCOUNTING agency overseeing accounting standards the body that is responsible for setting and monitoring accounting standards in Australia. It was established under Corporations Law in 1988, replacing the Accounting Standards Review Board. *Abbr* **AASB**

Australian Bureau of Statistics STATISTICS Australian government agency collecting data on population an Australian federal government body responsible for compiling national statistics and conducting regular censuses. It was established in 1906. *Abbr* **ABS**

Australian Business Number TAX tax code of Australian business a numeric code that identifies an Australian business for the purpose of dealing with the Australian Tax Office and other government departments. ABNs are part of the new tax system that came into operation in Australia in 1998. *Abbr* **ABN**

Australian Chamber of Commerce and Industry BUSINESS national organization for businesses a national council of business organizations in Australia. It represents around 350,000 businesses and its members include state chambers of commerce as well as major national employer and industry associations. *Abbr* **ACCI**

Australian Communications Authority REGULATION & COMPLIANCE government organization overseeing communications industries the government body responsible for regulating practices in the communications industries. It was established in 1997 as a result of the merger of the Australian Telecommunications Authority and the Spectrum Management Agency. *Abbr* **ACA**

Australian Competition and Consumer Commission REGULATION & COMPLIANCE body monitoring Australian trade practices in Australia, an independent statutory body responsible for monitoring trade practices. It was established in November 1995 as a result of the merger of the Trade Practices Commission and the Prices Surveillance Authority. *Abbr* **ACCC**

Australian Prudential Regulation Authority REGULATION & COMPLIANCE organization overseeing solvency of financial institutions a federal government body responsible for ensuring that financial institutions are able to meet their commitments. *Abbr* **APRA**

Australian Securities and Investments Commission REGULATION & COMPLIANCE organization overseeing financial dealings of businesses an Australian federal government body responsible for regulating Australian businesses and the provision of financial products and services to consumers. It was established in 1989, replacing the Australian Securities Commission. *Abbr* **ASIC**

Australian Stock Exchange MARKETS principal Australian stock market the principal market for trading stock and other securities in Australia. It was formed in 1987 as a result of the amalgamation of six state stock exchanges and has offices in most state capitals. *Abbr* **ASX**

Australian Taxation Office TAX organization overseeing federal tax system a statutory body responsible for the administration of the Australian federal government's taxation system. It is based in Canberra and is also responsible for the country's superannuation system. *Abbr* **ATO**

AUT *abbr* STOCKHOLDING & INVESTMENTS authorized unit trust

authentication E-COMMERCE procedure for verifying authenticity of online sales messages a software security verification procedure to acknowledge or validate the source, uniqueness, and integrity of an e-commerce message to make sure data is not being tampered with. The verification is typically achieved through the use of an electronic signature in the form of a key or algorithm that is shared by the trading partners.

authority GENERAL MANAGEMENT right to be in charge the right to act or command. People willingly obey a person in authority, because they believe he or she has a legitimate entitlement to exercise power.

authority chart CORPORATE GOVERNANCE diagram of organization's hierarchical relationships a diagram showing the hierarchical lines of authority and reporting within an organization. Organization charts are similar.

authority to purchase FINANCE bill bearing authorization for bank to buy it a bill drawn up and presented with shipping documentation to the purchaser's bank, allowing the bank to purchase the bill

authorization FINANCE giving approval for financial transaction the process of assessing a financial transaction, confirming that it does not raise the account's debt above its limit, and allowing the transaction to proceed. This would be undertaken, for example, by a credit card issuer. A positive authorization results in an authorization code being generated and the relevant funds being set aside. The available credit limit is reduced by the amount authorized.

authorized capital FINANCE firm's money raised from selling shares the money made by a company from the sale of authorized shares of common and preferred stock. It is measured by multiplying the number of authorized shares by their par value.

Authorized Economic Operator INTERNATIONAL TRADE internationally recognized EU trader an internationally recognized certification that an EU trader's role in the international supply chain is secure and that customs controls and procedures are compliant. *Abbr* **AEO**

authorized share STOCKHOLDING & INVESTMENTS share issued legitimately a share that a company issued with the authority to do so

authorized share capital *UK* STOCKHOLDING & INVESTMENTS stock firm has approval to issue the type, class, number, and amount of the stocks that a company may issue, as empowered by its memorandum of association. *See also* ***nominal share capital***

authorized signatory STOCKHOLDING & INVESTMENTS issuer of documents approving financial transactions the most senior issuer of authorization certificates in an organization, recognized by a signatory authority and designated in a signatory certificate

authorized stock *US* STOCKHOLDING & INVESTMENTS stock firm has approval to issue the number of shares of stock that a corporation is allowed to issue, as stated in its articles of incorporation. *See also* ***authorized share***

authorized unit trust STOCKHOLDING & INVESTMENTS US mutual fund in the United Kingdom, a mutual fund that complies with the regulations of the Financial Services Authority. Different rules apply to different categories of mutual fund. *Abbr* **AUT**

AUTIF STOCKHOLDING & INVESTMENTS *see* ***Investment Management Association***

autocorrelation STATISTICS = ***serial correlation***

automated clearing house BANKING, E-COMMERCE computerized network for interbank transactions **ATM** systems for

interbank clearing and settlement of financial transactions. The network is also used for electronic fund transfers from a checking or savings account. *Abbr* **ACH**

Automated Direct Debit Amendment and Cancellation Service BANKING UK computerized system for changing direct debits in the United Kingdom, a **BACS** service that allows paying banks to inform direct debit payees of a change of instruction, for example, an amendment to the customer's account details or a request to cancel the instructions. *Abbr* **ADDACS**

automated handling OPERATIONS & PRODUCTION using computers to move goods in warehouses the use of computers to control the moving and positioning of materials in a warehouse or factory. Automated handling may involve the use of robots.

Automated Order Entry System MARKETS US system of direct access to exchange floor in the United States, a system that allows small orders to bypass the floor brokers and go straight to the specialists on the exchange floor

automated screen trading MARKETS computerized system for trading securities an electronic trading system for the sale and purchase of securities. Customers' orders are entered via a keyboard; a computer system matches and executes the deals; and prices and deals are shown on monitors, thus dispensing with the need for face-to-face contact on a trading floor. *Abbr* **AST**

automated storage and retrieval systems OPERATIONS & PRODUCTION using computers to manage storage in warehouses the use of computerized vehicles to store, select, and move pallets around a large warehouse

automated teller machine BANKING *see* ***ATM***

automatic debit US BANKING bank customer's instruction for regular payments an instruction given by an account holder to a bank to make regular payments on given dates to the same payee. *Also called* ***banker's order***. *UK term* ***standing order***

automatic execution MARKETS computerized matching of buy and sell orders a trade of a security that is executed electronically by a computerized trading system that matches buy and sell orders

automatic rollover MARKETS in US, automatic repetition of fixed-term investment on the London Money Market, the automatic reinvestment of a maturing fixed term deposit for a further identical fixed term, an arrangement that can be canceled at any time

automatic transfer service BANKING automatic funds transfer protection an arrangement by which money from a depositor's savings account can be transferred automatically to his or her checking account to cover an overdraft or maintain a minimum balance. *Abbr* **ATS**

Auto Pact INTERNATIONAL TRADE Canadian and US agreement about automobile imports an agreement between Canada and the United States, by which duties were reduced on imported cars for US automakers assembling vehicles in Canada. Subsequent provisions of the North American Free Trade Agreement reduced its effect (*informal*).

autopoiesis E-COMMERCE process of replacing own parts a process whereby a system, organization, or organism produces and replaces its own components and distinguishes itself from its environment

availability float ACCOUNTING money representing checks written but not cashed money that is available to a company because checks that it has written have not yet been charged against its accounts

aval FINANCE guarantee of payment of bill or note in Europe, an endorsement by a third party guaranteeing the payment of a bill or promissory note

AVCs *abbr* PENSIONS additional voluntary contributions

average 1. STATISTICS arithmetic mean the arithmetic mean of a sample of observations **2.** STOCKHOLDING & INVESTMENTS purchase stock regularly over period of changing prices to purchase additional shares of a stock whose price is rising or falling at intervals during the period of changing prices, in order to affect the average price paid for the stock

average accounting return ACCOUNTING percentage return of asset based on recorded value the percentage return realized on an asset, as measured by its **book value**, after taxes and depreciation

average adjuster INSURANCE insurer determining shared losses a person who calculates how much of an insurance is to be borne by each party

average adjustment INSURANCE insurer's determination of shared losses the calculation of the share of cost of damage to or loss of a ship

average collection period ACCOUNTING average time for cashing accounts receivable the mean time required for a firm to liquidate its accounts receivable, measured from the date each receivable is posted until the last payment is received.

Its formula is:

$$\frac{\text{Accounts receivable}}{\text{Average daily sales}} = \text{Average collection period}$$

For example, if accounts receivable are $280,000, and average daily sales are 7,000, then:

$$\frac{280{,}000}{7{,}000} = 40$$

average cost of capital FINANCE average cost of getting money the average of what a company is paying for the money it borrows or raises by selling stock

average deviation STATISTICS difference between actual and average values the spread of a sample of observations, measured by calculating their mean, specifying the distance between each observation and that mean, then calculating the mean of these distances

average down STOCKHOLDING & INVESTMENTS purchase stock regularly over period of falling prices to purchase additional shares of a security whose price is falling at intervals during the price drop period, in order to lower the average price paid for the stock

average due date FINANCE date around which several payments are due the average date when several different payments fall due

average nominal maturity FINANCE average time for mutual fund to provide return the average length of time until the **financial instruments** of a mutual fund mature

average option or **average price option** STOCKHOLDING & INVESTMENTS, RISK option determined by commodity's average price an **option** whose value depends on the average price of a commodity during a specific period of time. *Also called* ***Asian option***

average up STOCKHOLDING & INVESTMENTS purchase stock regularly over period of rising prices to purchase additional shares of a security whose price is rising at intervals during the price rise period, in order to raise the average price paid for the stock

Average Weekly Earnings STATISTICS in Australia, official measure of wages a measure of wage levels in the Australian workforce that is calculated regularly by the Australian Bureau of Statistics. The

  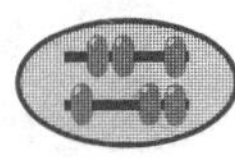  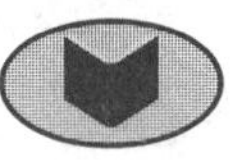 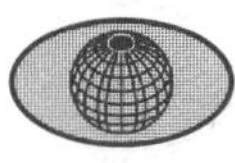   

measure is considered one of Australia's key **economic indicators**. *Abbr* AWE

Average Weekly Ordinary Time Earnings STATISTICS in Australia, official measure of wages without overtime a measure of wage levels in the Australian workforce that excludes overtime payments, published by the Australian Bureau of Statistics

averaging STOCKHOLDING & INVESTMENTS stock trading at intervals to get average price the buying or selling of stocks at different times and at different prices to establish an average price

AWB *abbr* FINANCE air waybill

AWE *abbr* STATISTICS Average Weekly Earnings

"aw shucks" REGULATION & COMPLIANCE US strategy for denying responsibility for financial irregularities in the United States, a defense strategy adopted by senior executives involved in financial scandals before the **Sarbanes-Oxley Act**, affecting corporate governance, came into effect in 2005. Under this strategy the accused maintained that they were simply not aware of the distortion of financial reporting that took place on their watch. The new law aimed to overhaul corporate financial reporting by improving its accuracy and reliability. Accountability standards have also been considerably tightened, and chief executives are to take full responsibility for the accuracy of all financial results by signing a statement to that effect (*informal*). *See also* ***Sarbanes-Oxley Act***

ax STOCKHOLDING & INVESTMENTS expert in a particular investment a financial adviser who is the current expert on a particular security or market sector

B

B2B E-COMMERCE relating to Internet commerce between businesses used to describe an advertising or marketing program aimed at companies doing business with other companies as opposed to consumers. The term is most commonly used in reference to commerce or business that is conducted over the Internet between commercial enterprises. *Full form* ***business-to-business***

B2B advertising MARKETING advertising directed at firms advertising that is aimed at buyers for organizations rather than domestic consumers

B2B agency MARKETING advertising firm for businesses selling to other businesses an advertising agency that specializes in planning, creating, and buying advertising aimed at buyers for organizations rather than domestic consumers

B2B auction E-COMMERCE Internet site where suppliers compete for sales a Web marketplace that provides a mechanism for negotiating prices and bidding for services. Web-based B2B auctions reverse the traditional auction formula in which the goal is to help the seller get the best price. B2B Web auctions involve suppliers competing with one another by bidding down the price of their service. This inevitably benefits the buyer, as, instead of having to bid higher for a specific service or product, he or she can wait until the suppliers have bid themselves down to a reasonable price. Typically, online auctions require companies to follow a registration process in order to take part. During this process, users have to provide their credit card information and shipping preferences as well as agree to the site's code of conduct. Some sites also manage secure auctions, which restrict potential bidders to specific firms or individuals.

B2B commerce MARKETS business involving firms only, not individual customers the business conducted between companies, rather than between a company and individual consumers

B2B exchange MARKETS place for businesses to trade with each other the business-to-business marketplace that enables suppliers, buyers, and intermediaries to come together and offer products to each other according to a set of criteria

B2B marketing MARKETING = ***industrial marketing***

B2B web exchange MARKETS, E-COMMERCE marketplace adjusting prices the business-to-business marketplace that provides constant price adjustments in line with fluctuations of supply and demand

B2C MARKETS connected with Internet commerce between businesses and consumers relating to an advertising or marketing program aimed at businesses doing business directly with consumers as opposed to other businesses. The term is most commonly used in reference to commerce or business that is conducted over the Internet between a commercial enterprise and a consumer. *Full form* ***business-to-consumer***

BAA *abbr* ACCOUNTING British Accounting Association

baby bonds *US* STOCKHOLDING & INVESTMENTS bonds with low values bonds in small denominations, usually less than $1,000, which small investors can afford to buy (*informal*)

backdate GENERAL MANAGEMENT **1.** put earlier date on document to put an earlier date than the current date on a document such as a check or an invoice **2.** make something apply from earlier date to make something effective from an earlier date than the current date

backdoor selling FRAUD **1.** illegal wholesaler selling directly to consumers the practice by wholesalers of selling products directly to consumers in violation of contracts with retailers **2.** selling tactic bypassing competitive bid requirement the practice by salespeople of persuading buyers who are required to obtain competitive bids to purchase goods and services without them

back duty TAX tax unpaid because information was withheld tax relating to a past period that has not been paid because of the taxpayer's failure to disclose relevant information through negligence or fraud. If back duty is found to be payable, the relevant authorities may instigate an investigation and penalties or interest may be charged on the amount.

back-end loading STOCKHOLDING & INVESTMENTS sales fee paid by investor a management charge or commission that is levied when an investor sells some types of investments such as funds and annuities. *See also* ***front-end loading***

backer FINANCE provider of financial or moral support a person or company that gives somebody financial or moral support

back interest FINANCE interest not yet paid interest that is due but has not yet been paid

backlink checking E-COMMERCE way of discovering which websites are linked a means of finding out which web pages are linked to a specific website. Backlink checking enables e-business and website managers to keep track of their own and their competitors' online popularity.

backlog OPERATIONS & PRODUCTION list of orders not yet filled the buildup of unfulfilled orders for a product or process that is behind schedule. A backlog can result from bad scheduling, production delays, an unanticipated demand for a product or process, or where the capacity of the process is not able to keep up with

  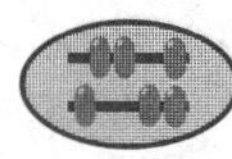 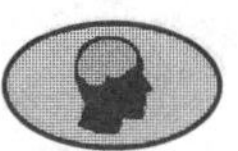  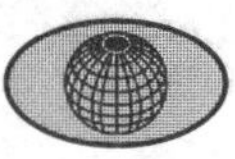   

demand. Some large products, for example, aircraft and ships, have to be built to a backlog of orders, as it is not feasible to supply them on demand.

backlog depreciation ACCOUNTING extra depreciation on revalued asset the additional depreciation required when an asset is revalued to make up for the fact that previous depreciation had been calculated on a now out-of-date valuation

back office GENERAL MANAGEMENT staff without direct dealings with customers the administrative staff of a company who do not have face-to-face contact with the company's customers. *See also* ***front office, middle office***

back pay FINANCE overdue pay from earlier time period pay that is owed to an employee for work carried out before the current payment period and is either overdue or results from a backdated pay increase

back payment FINANCE payment due but not yet paid a payment that is due to somebody but has not yet been paid

back tax TAX tax due but not yet paid tax that is owed to a government and that is overdue

back-to-back loan FINANCE, CURRENCY & EXCHANGE arrangement for two matching loans in different currencies an arrangement in which two companies in different countries borrow offsetting amounts in each other's currency and each repays their loan at a specific future date in its domestic currency. Such a loan, often between a company and its foreign subsidiary, eliminates the risk of loss from fluctuations in exchange rates.

backup MARKETS **1.** when yields rise and prices fall a period in which the yields from bonds rise and prices fall, moving inversely to each other **2.** when market trends reverse a sudden reversal in a stock market trend, so that a **bear market** becomes a **bull market** or vice versa

backup credit BANKING secondary source of credit a **line of credit** to be used as a standby should the primary credit source become unavailable. *Also called* ***standby credit*** *(sense 1)*

backup facility GENERAL MANAGEMENT substitute copy to be used if original fails a secondary system, record, or contract intended to take the place of another that fails

backup withholding TAX tax payable on miscellaneous income in the United States, a withholding tax that a payer sends to the Internal Revenue Service so that somebody who has received certain types of income such as dividends or interest, or who has not provided a correct taxpayer identification number, cannot avoid all taxes on that income

backwardation MARKETS **1.** penalty paid for late delivery of stock a penalty paid by the seller when postponing delivery of stock to the buyer **2.** when cash price exceeds forward price a situation in which the **spot price** is higher than the **forward price**. *See also* ***forwardation***

backward compatible E-COMMERCE usable with previous software or computers describes a computer hardware or software product that is compatible with its predecessors to the extent that it can use interfaces and data from earlier versions

backward integration OPERATIONS & PRODUCTION forming alliance with supplier to protect supply the building of relationships with suppliers in order to secure the supply of raw materials. Backward integration can involve taking control of supply companies.

backward scheduling OPERATIONS & PRODUCTION determining scheduling plan based on due date a technique for scheduling production, planning work on the basis of when the completed work is due. By using backward scheduling, managers are able to assign work to particular workstations so that the overall task is completed exactly when it is due. The technique allows potential bottlenecks and idle time for particular workstations to be identified in advance.

BACS BANKING UK electronic clearing system for straightforward payments in the United Kingdom, an electronic bulk clearing system generally used by banks and building societies for low-value and/or repetitive items such as standing orders, direct debits, and automated credits such as salary payments. It was formerly known as the Bankers Automated Clearing Service.

bad bank BANKING government bank accepting other banks' risky loans a government-owned bank created to buy and hold risky assets from other banks, in order to re-activate lending and stimulate economic activity

BADC *abbr* REGULATION & COMPLIANCE Business Accounting Deliberation Council

bad check or **bad cheque** BANKING check returned unpaid a check that is returned uncashed for any reason to the person who wrote it

bad debt FINANCE debt that has to be written off a debt that is or is considered to be uncollectable and is, therefore, written off either as a charge to the **profit and loss account** or against an existing doubtful debt provision

bad debt provision ACCOUNTING estimate of uncollectable debts an accounting estimate of the amount of debts thought likely to have to be written off

bad debt reserve FINANCE firm's money set aside for uncollectable debts an amount of money that a company sets aside to cover bad debts

bad debts recovered FINANCE money written off then recovered money formerly written off as uncollectable debt that has since been recovered either wholly or in part

badwill FINANCE negative goodwill a situation in which the value of the **separable net assets** of a company is greater than the total value of the business *(slang)*

bai al-bithaman ajil FINANCE installment sale of goods arranged by bank in Islamic financing, a sale of goods in which a bank purchases the goods on behalf of the buyer from the seller and sells them to the buyer at a profit, allowing the buyer to make installment payments. *Also called* ***bai muajjal***

bailment FINANCE delivery of something on loan the delivery of goods from the owner to another person on the condition that they will eventually be returned

bail out FINANCE give help to firm in financial difficulty to provide sufficient financial support to a company that is having financial difficulties to ensure its survival

bailout FINANCE financial backing for firm in crisis the provision of sufficient financial support to a company that is having financial difficulties to ensure its survival

bai muajjal FINANCE = ***bai al-bithaman ajil***

bait and switch MARKETING advertising one product but selling more expensive one a marketing practice whereby customers are encouraged to enter a store by an advertisement for one product and are then persuaded to buy another more expensive product *(slang)*

balance **1.** BANKING money in bank account the state of a bank account at any one time, indicating whether money is owed (a debit) or owing (a credit balance) **2.** ACCOUNTING discrepancy between debit and credit figures in double-entry bookkeeping, the amount

     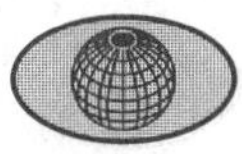   

required to make the debit and credit figures in the books equal each other **3.** ACCOUNTING difference between money paid and received the difference between the totals of the debit and credit entries in an account

balance billing FINANCE charging person for own insurance shortfall the practice of requesting payment from a receiver of a service such as medical treatment for the part of the cost not covered by the person's insurance

balance brought down ACCOUNTING figure in account to balance income and expenditure an amount entered in an account at the end of a period to balance income and expenditure

balanced budget ACCOUNTING spending plan in which income equals expenses a budget in which planned expenditure on goods and services and debt interest can be met by current income

balanced design STATISTICS experimental design with equal observations for each combination an experimental design in which the same number of observations is used for each combination of the experimental factors

balanced fund STOCKHOLDING & INVESTMENTS mutual fund with diversified investments a mutual fund that invests in a variety of types of companies and financial instruments to reduce the risk of loss through poor performance of any one type

balanced investment strategy STOCKHOLDING & INVESTMENTS spreading types of investment the practice of investing in a variety of types of companies and financial instruments to reduce the risk of loss through poor performance of any one type

balanced line OPERATIONS & PRODUCTION production system with equalized workstation times an assembly line in which the cycle time for all the workstations is equal. A balanced line is achieved by allocating the right amount of work and the correct amount of operators and machinery to produce a given flow of product over a set period, taking into account the fact that each workstation will have a different capacity and that each process involved has a different cycle time.

balanced quantity OPERATIONS & PRODUCTION materials needed by workstation to produce agreed amount an inventory measure of the quantity of materials and parts required by a workstation to achieve a planned level of output

balanced scorecard approach GENERAL MANAGEMENT emphasis on providing management with strategic information an approach to the provision of information to management in order to assist strategic policy formulation and implementation to build the long-term value of the business. It emphasizes the need to provide the user with information that addresses all relevant areas of performance in an objective and unbiased fashion. The information provided may include financial and non-financial items and cover areas such as profitability, customer satisfaction, internal efficiency, and innovation. The term originates from the best-selling business book, *The Balanced Scorecard*, written by Robert Kaplan and David Norton and published by Harvard Business School Press in 1996. Their approach applies the concept of **shareholder value analysis**, and is based on the premise that the traditional measures used by managers to see how well their organizations are performing, such as business ratios, productivity, unit costs, growth, and profitability, are only a part of the picture. Traditional measures are seen as providing a narrowly focused snapshot of how an organization performed in the past, and give little indication of likely future performance. In contrast, the balanced scorecard offers a measurement and management system that links strategic objectives to comprehensive performance indicators.

balance off ACCOUNTING find balance by adding up totals to add up and enter the totals for both sides of an account at the end of an accounting period in order to determine the balance

balance of payments INTERNATIONAL TRADE country's trade transactions over time period a list of a country's credit and debit transactions with international financial institutions and foreign countries over a specific period. *Abbr* **BOP**

balance of payments capital account INTERNATIONAL TRADE non-domestic items in country's balance of payments items in a country's balance of payments which refer to capital investments made in or by other countries

balance of payments current account INTERNATIONAL TRADE record of trade between countries a record of imports and exports of goods and services and the flow of money between countries arising from investments

balance of payments deficit INTERNATIONAL TRADE extent to which imports exceed exports the shortfall in income that arises when a country buys more from other countries than it sells as exports

balance of payments on capital account INTERNATIONAL TRADE record of country's non-domestic investment transactions a system of recording a country's investment transactions with the rest of the world during a given period, usually one year. Among the included transactions are the purchase of physical and financial assets, intergovernmental transfers, and the provision of economic aid to emerging nations.

balance of payments on current account INTERNATIONAL TRADE record of imports and exports a system of recording a country's imports and exports of goods and services during a given period, usually one year

balance of payments surplus INTERNATIONAL TRADE extent to which exports exceed imports the increase in income that arises when a country sells more to other countries than it buys as imports

balance of trade INTERNATIONAL TRADE gap between imports and exports the difference between a country's imports and exports of goods and services. *Abbr* **BOT**

balance sheet ACCOUNTING statement of total assets, liabilities, and owners' equity a financial report stating the total assets, liabilities, and owners' equity of an organization at a given date, usually the last day of the accounting period. The credit side of the balance sheet states assets, while the debit side states liabilities and equity, and the two sides must be equal, or balance.

Assets include cash in hand and cash anticipated (receivables), inventories of supplies and materials, properties, facilities, equipment, and whatever else the company uses to conduct business. Assets also need to reflect depreciation in the value of equipment such as machinery that has a limited expected useful life.

Liabilities include pending payments to suppliers and creditors, outstanding current and long-term debts, taxes, interest payments, and other unpaid expenses that the company has incurred.

Subtracting the value of aggregate liabilities from the value of aggregate assets reveals the value of owners' equity. Ideally, it should be positive. Owners' equity consists of capital invested by owners over the years and profits (net income) or internally generated capital, which is referred to as "retained earnings"; these are funds to be used in future operations. *Abbr* **B/S**

balance sheet audit ACCOUNTING partial audit to check compliance with rules a limited audit of the items on a company's balance sheet in order to confirm that it complies with the relevant standards and requirements. Such an audit involves checking the value, ownership, and existence of assets and liabilities and ensuring that they are correctly recorded.

balance sheet date ACCOUNTING annual date for balance sheet preparation the date, usually the end of a financial or accounting year, when a company's balance sheet is drawn up

balance sheet equation ACCOUNTING = ***accounting equation***

balance sheet total ACCOUNTING total at bottom of UK firm's balance sheet in the United Kingdom, the total of assets shown at the bottom of a balance sheet and used to classify a company according to size

balancing item or **balancing figure** ACCOUNTING number making one total equal another a number added to a series of numbers to make the total the same as another total. For example, if a debit total is higher than the credit total in the accounts, the balancing figure is the amount of extra credit required to make the two totals equal.

ball ◇ take the ball and run with it GENERAL MANAGEMENT to take an idea and implement it

balloon FINANCE **1.** = ***balloon loan*** **2.** = ***balloon payment***

balloon loan FINANCE loan with large final payment a loan repaid in regular installments with a single larger final payment including interest

balloon mortgage MORTGAGES mortgage with large final payment a mortgage for which the final payment including interest, called a **balloon payment**, is larger than the others

balloon payment FINANCE large final payment on loan a large final payment including interest on a loan, after a number of periodic smaller payments have been made

ballpark or **ballpark figure** FINANCE rough total a rough, estimated figure. The term was derived from the approximate assessment of the number of spectators at a sporting event that might be made on the basis of a glance around (*slang*).

BALO FINANCE French financial publication a French government publication that includes financial statements of public companies. *Full form* ***Bulletin des Annonces Légales Obligatoires***

BAN *abbr* STOCKHOLDING & INVESTMENTS bond anticipation note

bang for the/your buck FINANCE financial benefit the leverage provided by an investment (*slang*)

bangtail MARKETING order form attached to envelope an order form for a new product that is attached by a perforated line to an envelope flap (*slang*)

bank BANKING institution holding and lending money a commercial institution that keeps money in accounts for individuals or organizations, makes loans, exchanges currencies, provides credit to businesses, and offers other financial services

bankable BANKING acceptable as security for loan acceptable by a bank as security for a loan

bankable paper BANKING document accepted by bank as security a document that a bank will accept as security for a loan

bank account BANKING facility for depositing and withdrawing money at bank an arrangement that a customer has with a bank, by which the customer can deposit and withdraw money

bank advance BANKING = ***bank loan***

bank balance BANKING money in bank account the state of a bank account at any one time, indicating whether money is owed (a debit) or owing (a credit balance)

bank base rate BANKING interest rate determining bank's rate to customers the basic rate of interest on which the actual rate a bank charges on loans to its customers is calculated

bank bill BANKING **1.** US = ***banknote*** **2.** = ***banker's bill***

bank book BANKING booklet recording deposits and withdrawals a small booklet formerly issued by banks and some other financial institutions to record deposits, withdrawals, interest paid, and the balance on savings and deposit accounts. In most cases, it has now been replaced by statements. *Also called* ***passbook***

bank card BANKING payment card issued by bank a plastic card issued by a bank and accepted by merchants in payment for transactions. The most common types are **credit cards** and **debit cards**. Bank cards are governed by an internationally recognized set of rules for the authorization of their use and the clearing and settlement of transactions.

bank certificate BANKING confirmation of firm's bank balance a document, often requested during an audit, that is signed by a bank official and confirms the balances due to or from a company on a specific date

bank charge BANKING = ***service charge***

bank confirmation BANKING verification of firm's bank balances verification of a company's balances requested by an auditor from a bank

bank credit BANKING maximum credit the maximum credit available to somebody from a specific bank

bank deposits BANKING money deposited in banks all money placed in banks by private or corporate customers

bank discount basis BANKING income from US Treasury bills expressed over 360 days the expression of yield that is used for US Treasury bills, based on a 360-day year

bank draft BANKING = ***banker's draft***

bank-eligible issue BANKING US Treasury bonds available to commercial banks US Treasury obligations with a remaining maturity of ten years or less, eligible for purchase at any time by commercial banks

banker BANKING owner or senior executive of bank somebody who owns or is an executive of a bank or group of banks

banker's acceptance BANKING = ***banker's credit***

Bankers Automated Clearing Service BANKING *see* ***BACS***

banker's bill BANKING bank's order to another bank to pay money an order by one bank telling another bank, usually in another country, to pay money to somebody. *Also called* ***bank bill***

banker's check BANKING = ***banker's draft***

banker's credit BANKING financial instrument guaranteed by bank a financial instrument, typically issued by an exporter or importer for a short term, that a bank guarantees. *Also called* ***banker's acceptance***

banker's draft BANKING check drawn by bank on itself a **bill of exchange** payable on demand and drawn by one bank on another. Regarded as being equivalent to cash, the draft cannot be returned unpaid. *Also called* ***bank draft, banker's check.*** *Abbr* **B/D**

bankers' hours BANKING short working day short hours of work. The term refers to

  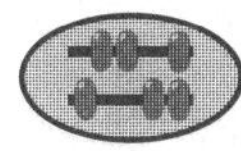 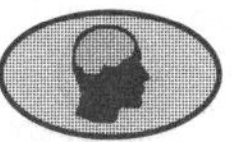  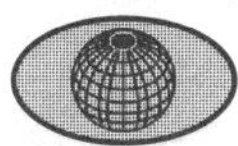   

the relatively short time that a bank is open to customers in some countries (*informal*).

banker's lien BANKING bank's right to hold client's property as security the right of a bank to hold some property of a customer as security against payment of a debt

banker's order BANKING = ***automatic debit***

banker's reference BANKING bank's report on customer's creditworthiness a report issued by a bank regarding a particular customer's creditworthiness

bank fee BANKING administrative charge for transaction a charge that is either paid in advance or is included in the gross capitalized cost, usually covering administrative costs such as the costs of obtaining a credit report, verifying insurance coverage, and checking documentation

Bank for International Settlements BANKING bank dealing with international finance a bank that promotes cooperation between central banks, provides facilities for international financial operations, and acts as agent or trustee in international financial settlements. The 17-member board of directors consists of the governors of the central banks of Belgium, Canada, France, Germany, Italy, Japan, the Netherlands, Sweden, Switzerland, the United Kingdom, and the United States. *Abbr* **BIS**

bank giro BANKING = ***giro***

bank guarantee BANKING bank's undertaking to pay debt a commitment that a bank will pay a debt if the debtor defaults, for example, a bank may guarantee to pay an exporter for goods shipped if the buyer defaults

bank holding company BANKING firm owning bank or banks a company that owns one or more banks as part of its assets

bank holiday *UK* BANKING public holiday on weekday a weekday, especially a Monday, that is a public holiday when the banks are closed

bank identification number BANKING international number identifying individual bank n internationally agreed six-digit number that formerly identified a bank for credit card purposes. *Abbr* **BIN**. *See also* ***issuer identification number***

banking account BANKING facility for depositing and withdrawing money at bank an arrangement that a customer has with a bank, by which the customer can deposit and withdraw money

Banking Code BANKING UK banks' voluntary code of practice a voluntary code of best practice for the banking and financial services industry, which is developed and revised by the **British Bankers' Association**

banking house BANKING financial institution providing banking services a financial organization such as a bank or **credit union** that is in the business of providing banking services to the public

banking insurance fund INSURANCE US fund insuring banks' deposits in the United States, a fund maintained by the Federal Deposit Insurance Corporation to provide deposit insurance for banks other than savings banks and savings and loan associations

Banking Ombudsman BANKING Australian or New Zealand official handling banking complaints an official of the Australian or New Zealand government responsible for dealing with complaints relating to banking practices

banking passport BANKING passport for holding assets abroad a second passport in another name used to hold assets confidentially and for banking transactions in another country

banking products BANKING items provided by banks for customers goods and services that banks provide for their customers, for example, statements, direct debits, and automatic debits

banking syndicate BANKING investment banks jointly offering new security a group of investment banks that jointly underwrite and distribute a new security offering

banking system BANKING network of banks providing financial services a network of commercial, savings, and specialized banks that provide financial services, including accepting deposits and providing loans and credit, money transmission, and investment facilities

bank investment contract BANKING contract between bank and investors a contract that specifies what a bank will pay its investors

bank line FINANCE = ***line of credit***

bank loan BANKING loan made to bank's customer a loan made by a bank to a customer, usually against the security of a property or asset. *Also called* ***bank advance***

bankmail BANKING agreement by bank not to finance customer's rival an agreement by a bank not to finance any rival's attempt to take over the same company that a particular customer is trying to buy (*slang*)

bank mandate BANKING written order for opening bank account a written order to a bank that asks the bank to open an account, names the person(s) allowed to sign checks on behalf of the account holder, and provides specimen signatures, etc.

banknote BANKING **1.** item of paper money a piece of paper money printed by a bank and approved as legal tender. *Also called* ***bank bill*** **2.** note from Federal Reserve Bank usable as cash in the United States, a non-interest bearing note, issued by a Federal Reserve Bank, that can be used as cash

Bank of England BANKING UK central bank the central bank of the United Kingdom, established in 1694. Originally a private bank, it became public in 1946 and increased its independence from government in 1997, when it was granted sole responsibility for setting the base rate of interest.

bank rate BANKING **1.** central bank's discount rate the discount rate offered by a country's central bank **2.** formerly, Bank of England's lending rate formerly, the rate at which the Bank of England lent to other banks. It was then also called the minimum lending rate. *See also* ***base rate***

bank reconciliation BANKING comparison of bank statement with firm's ledger the process of comparing a bank statement with a company's ledger to verify that the balances are the same

bank reserve ratio BANKING = ***required reserve ratio***

bank reserves BANKING bank's ready money the money that a bank has available to meet the demands of its depositors

bankroll FINANCE **1.** finance for project the money used for financing a project or business **2.** give money to support something to provide the financing for a project or business

bankrupt LEGAL **1.** entity legally recognized as unable to pay debts a person or corporation that has been declared by a court of law as unable to meet their financial obligations **2.** unable to pay debts legally declared unable to meet financial obligations

bankruptcy LEGAL when unable to pay debts the condition of being unable to pay debts, with liabilities greater than assets. There are two types of bankruptcy: involuntary bankruptcy, where one or more creditors bring a petition against the debtor; and voluntary bankruptcy, where

  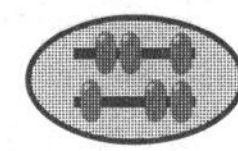 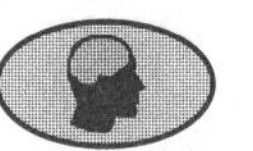  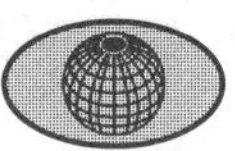   

the debtor files a petition claiming inability to meet his or her debts.

bankruptcy-remote RISK not likely to risk bankruptcy used to describe a strategy or business structure designed to isolate a valuable asset or entity from financial risk

bank statement BANKING statement of transactions on customer's bank account a written statement from a bank showing the balance of an account and transactions over a period of time

bank term loan BANKING bank loan lasting at least one year a loan from a bank that has a term of at least one year

bank transfer BANKING transference of money to another account an act of moving money from one bank account to another

bar *UK* CURRENCY & EXCHANGE £1,000,000 one million pounds sterling, used by traders (*slang*)

barbell STOCKHOLDING & INVESTMENTS portfolio with no medium-term bonds a portfolio that concentrates on very long-term and very short-term bonds only

bar chart GENERAL MANAGEMENT informational graph using colored bars the presentation of data in the form of a graph using blocks or bars of color or shading. A bar chart is especially useful for showing the impact of one factor against another, for example, income over time, or customer calls against sales.

barefoot pilgrim *US* STOCKHOLDING & INVESTMENTS inexperienced and unsuccessful investor an unsophisticated investor who has lost everything trading in securities (*slang*)

bargain MARKETS stock-market transaction a transaction on a stock market, especially the London Stock Exchange (*slang*)

bargaining chip FINANCE useful factor in negotiation something that can be used as a concession or inducement in negotiation

bargain tax date MARKETS date of stock-market transaction the date of a transaction on a stock market, especially the London Stock Exchange

barometer FINANCE indicator of trend an economic or financial indicator that forecasts a trend in the economy or in financial markets

barometer stock MARKETS popular security typical of market a widely held security such as a **blue chip** that is regarded as an indicator of the state of the market

barren money STOCKHOLDING & INVESTMENTS = ***idle capital***

barrier option STOCKHOLDING & INVESTMENTS option with trigger for trading in others an option that includes automatic trading in other options when a commodity reaches a specific price

barrier to entry MARKETS obstacle to free entry into market any impediment to the free entry of new competitors into a market

barrier to exit MARKETS obstacle to withdrawal from market any impediment to the exit of existing competitors from a market

barter FINANCE exchange of goods or services the direct exchange of goods or services between two parties without the use of money as a medium

BAS *abbr* TAX Business Activity Statement

base currency CURRENCY & EXCHANGE way of expressing income from investment the currency used for measuring the return on an investment, usually the currency of the country in which the investment is made

base date MARKETS benchmark date for index calculations the reference date from which an index number such as the **retail price index** is calculated

base interest rate FINANCE US minimum expected interest rate in the United States, the minimum interest rate that investors will accept for investing in a non-Treasury security. *Also called* ***benchmark interest rate***

base pay *US* FINANCE basic salary before additional benefits a guaranteed sum of money given to an employee in payment for work, disregarding any fringe benefits, allowances, or extra rewards from an **incentive plan**. *UK term* ***basic pay***

base period FINANCE period against which current financial period is measured a period of time against which financial or economic comparisons are made

base rate BANKING **1.** US Federal Reserve's interest rate the interest rate set by the US **Federal Reserve** that dictates the rate at which money is lent to other banks and which they in turn charge their customers **2.** Bank of England's interest rate the interest rate at which the Bank of England lends to other UK banks and which they in turn charge their customers

base rate tracker mortgage MORTGAGES mortgage with varying interest rate a mortgage whose interest rate varies periodically, usually annually, so as to remain a specific percentage above a standard rate

base-weighted index ECONOMICS price index comparing prices against standard time period a price index that is weighted according to prices from the base period

base year ECONOMICS benchmark year for index calculations the reference year from which an index is calculated

basic balance FINANCE relationship of current and long-term capital accounts the balance of current and long-term capital accounts in a country's balance of payments, which by implication must be financed with short-term **capital flows** such as short-term securities, money funds, and bank deposits

basic pay *UK* FINANCE = ***base pay***

basic rate TAX lower UK rate of income tax in the United Kingdom, the lower of the two bands of income tax, paid by the majority of people. **Her Majesty's Revenue & Customs** is responsible for the administration of income tax and publishes information on current tax rates and allowances on its website. *See also* ***higher rate***

basic wage FINANCE in Australia, minimum allowable pay for particular job in Australia, the minimum rate of pay set by an industrial court or tribunal for a specific occupation

basic wage rate FINANCE minimum pay in UK job in the United Kingdom, the wages paid for a specific number of hours' work per week, excluding overtime payments and any other incentives

basis FINANCE starting point for calculations a point, price, or number from which calculations are made. For example, the purchase price of a security would be used as the basis for calculating gains or losses.

basis of assessment TAX way of deciding time of tax assessment a method of deciding in which year financial transactions should be assessed for taxation

basis period TAX time when transactions are assessed for taxation the period during which financial transactions occur, used for the purpose of deciding when they should be assessed for taxation

basis point STOCKHOLDING & INVESTMENTS in bond interest rates, one hundredth of 1% one hundredth of 1%, used in relation to changes in bond interest rates. Thus a change from 7.5% to 7.4% is 10 basis points.

basis price STOCKHOLDING & INVESTMENTS **1.** price on which investment return is based the price used for calculating the gain on any investment when selling it, based on purchase price and any other costs **2.** price

  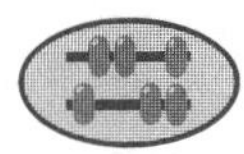   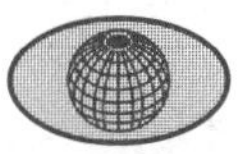   

of bond given as yield to maturity the price of a bond shown as its annual percentage yield to maturity rather than being quoted in a currency **3.** over-the-counter securities price the price agreed between a buyer and seller on the over-the-counter market

basis risk MARKETS danger from price or interest-rate changes the risk that price variations in the cash or futures market will diminish revenue when a futures contract is liquidated, or the risk that changes in interest rates will affect the repricing of interest-bearing liabilities

basis swap MARKETS exchange of financial instruments with different interest rates the exchange of two financial instruments, each with a variable interest calculated at a different rate

basket case BUSINESS firm or person beyond recovery a company or individual considered to be in such dire circumstances as to be beyond help (*slang*)

basket of currencies CURRENCY & EXCHANGE group of currencies providing benchmark a group of currencies, each of which is weighted, calculated together as a single unit in establishing a standard of value for another unit of currency. *Also called* ***currency basket***

basket of prices FINANCE group of prices used as benchmark a group of prices used as a standard for measuring value over time

basket of securities STOCKHOLDING & INVESTMENTS set of securities traded together a group of securities that is treated as a single unit and traded together

basket of shares *US* STOCKHOLDING & INVESTMENTS set of shares of stock sold together a fixed number of shares of stock that is treated as a single unit and traded together. *UK term* ***parcel of shares***

batch E-COMMERCE credit card transactions submitted together a collection of credit card transactions including authorizations, payments, and credits saved for electronic submission to an **acquirer** for settlement. The merchant is encouraged to submit one large batch rather than several small ones by being charged a fee for each batch submitted.

batch production OPERATIONS & PRODUCTION producing goods in groups through individual stages a production system in which a process is broken down into distinct operations that are completed on a batch or group of products before moving to the next production stage. As batch sizes can vary from very small to extremely large quantities, batch production offers greater flexibility than other production systems.

bath ◇take a bath FINANCE to experience a serious financial loss

Bayesian theory or **Bayes' theorem** STATISTICS statistical technique for predicting future based on past a statistical theory and method for drawing conclusions about the future occurrence of a given parameter of a statistical distribution by calculating from prior data on its frequency of occurrence. The theory is useful in the solution of theoretical and applied problems in science, industry, and government, for example, in econometrics and finance.

BBA *abbr* BANKING British Bankers' Association

BC *abbr* TREASURY MANAGEMENT budgetary control

BCA *abbr* BUSINESS Business Council of Australia

BCC *abbr* BUSINESS British Chambers of Commerce

BCCS *abbr* CURRENCY & EXCHANGE Board of Currency Commissioners

B/D *abbr* BANKING banker's draft

bean counter ACCOUNTING accountant an accountant, used to refer in a derogatory way especially to an accountant who works in a large organization (*slang*)

bear STOCKHOLDING & INVESTMENTS exploiter of unfavorable business conditions somebody who anticipates unfavorable business conditions, especially somebody who practices **short selling**, or selling stocks or commodities expecting their prices to fall, with the intention of buying them back cheaply later. *See also* ***bull***

bear CD STOCKHOLDING & INVESTMENTS CD paying more in falling market a **certificate of deposit** that pays a higher interest rate when an underlying market index falls in value

bear covering MARKETS buying back stock at lower prices the point in a market at which dealers who sold stock short now buy back at lower prices to cover their positions

bearer BANKING person holding check or certificate a person who holds a check or certificate that is redeemable for payment

bearer bond STOCKHOLDING & INVESTMENTS bond owned by physical possessor of it a negotiable bond or security whose ownership is not registered by the issuer, but is presumed to lie with whoever has physical possession of the bond

bearer check *US* BANKING blank check a check with no name written on it, so that the person who holds it can cash it. *Also called* ***check to bearer***. *UK term* ***cheque to bearer***

bearer instrument FINANCE financial document entitling its presenter to payment a financial instrument such as a check or bill of exchange that entitles the person who presents it to receive payment

bearer security STOCKHOLDING & INVESTMENTS security owned by physical possessor of it a stock or bond that is owned by the person who possesses it

bearish MARKETS of markets with falling prices relating to unfavorable business conditions or selling activity in anticipation of falling prices. *See also* ***bullish***

bear market MARKETS market with falling prices a market in which prices are falling and in which a dealer is more likely to sell securities than to buy them. *See also* ***bull market***

bear raid STOCKHOLDING & INVESTMENTS = ***raid***

bear spread MARKETS transactions to make profit when price falls a combination of purchases and sales of options for the same commodity or stock with the intention of making a profit when the price falls. *See also* ***bull spread***

bear tack MARKETS downward market movement a downward movement in the value of a stock, a part of the market, or the market as a whole

bear trap MARKETS reversing trends in market a situation in which a market reverses its upward trend, leading **short investors** to believe the trend will then continue downward and encouraging them to get into the market, at which time the market reverses again, forcing short investors to cover their positions and lose money

beauty contest *US* GENERAL MANAGEMENT situation where competing firms try to attract business a situation in which several organizations in turn compete in order to persuade another organization to use their services. *UK term* ***beauty parade***

beauty parade *UK* GENERAL MANAGEMENT = ***beauty contest***

bed ◇get into bed with somebody GENERAL MANAGEMENT to begin a business association with a person or organization

bed and breakfast deal STOCKHOLDING & INVESTMENTS selling and buying back security overnight a transaction in which somebody sells a security at the end of one trading day and repurchases it at the beginning of the next. This is usually done to formally

     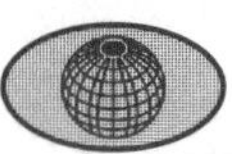   

establish the profit or loss accrued to this security for tax or reporting purposes.

bed and spouse STOCKHOLDING & INVESTMENTS method for couples to reduce capital gains tax in the United Kingdom, a method used by married taxpayers to reduce capital gains tax. A spouse who has a capital gain and has not used all their capital gains tax allowance may sell a security, and the other spouse may buy the same security back the next day, thereby allowing the spouse who sold to offset all or part of the gain with their tax allowance, while still holding onto the stock.

before-tax profit margin TAX income before tax minus expenditure the amount by which the net income of a company before tax exceeds its expenditure

beginning inventory *US* ACCOUNTING inventory carried over to next balance sheet the closing inventory at the end of the balance sheet from one accounting period that is transferred forward and becomes the opening inventory in the one that follows. *UK term* ***opening stock***

behavioral accounting *US* ACCOUNTING accounting emphasizing psychological and social aspects an approach to the study of accounting that emphasizes the psychological and social aspects of the profession in addition to the more technical areas

behavioral science *US* HR & PERSONNEL science studying how people act academic disciplines such as sociology and psychology that relate to the study of the way in which humans conduct themselves. In the field of management, the behavioral sciences are used to study the behavior of organizations.

bells and whistles (*slang*) **1.** FINANCE features appealing to investors or producers special features attached to a derivatives instrument or securities issue that are intended to attract investors or reduce issue costs **2.** MARKETING extra unnecessary features peripheral features of a product that are unnecessary but desirable

bellwether STOCKHOLDING & INVESTMENTS security with representative price a security whose price is viewed by investors as an indicator of future developments or trends

belly ◇ go belly up FINANCE to fail financially or go bankrupt

below par STOCKHOLDING & INVESTMENTS selling at less than face value describes a stock with a market price that is lower than its par value

below-the-line 1. ACCOUNTING showing profit distribution or sources of bottom line used to describe entries in a company's **profit and loss account** that show how the profit is distributed, or where the funds to finance the loss originate. *See also* ***above-the-line*** *(sense 1)* **2.** ECONOMICS showing country's capital transactions in macroeconomics, used to describe a country's capital transactions, as opposed to its **above-the-line** or revenue transactions. *See also* ***above-the-line*** *(sense 2)* **3.** MARKETING connected with marketing costs for everything but advertising relating to the proportion of marketing expenditure allocated to activities that are not related to advertising, such as public relations, sales promotion, printing, presentations, sponsorship, and sales force support. *See also* ***above-the-line*** *(sense 3)*

belt and braces man FINANCE lender wanting extra safeguards a very cautious lender who asks for extra collateral as well as guarantees for a loan (*slang*)

benchmark GENERAL MANAGEMENT standard used for measuring performance a point of reference or standard against which to measure performance. Originally used for a set of computer programs to measure the performance of a computer against similar models, benchmark is now used more generally to describe a measure identified in the context of a **benchmarking** program against which to evaluate an organization's performance in a specific area.

benchmark accounting policy ACCOUNTING one of two possible approved policies one of a choice of two possible policies within an International Accounting Standard. The other policy is marked as an "allowed alternative," although there is no indication of preference.

benchmark index MARKETS significant index an influential index for a particular market or activity

benchmarking GENERAL MANAGEMENT establishment of baselines and targets for assessing performance the establishment, through data gathering, of targets and comparators, through whose use relative levels of performance, and particularly areas of underperformance, can be identified. By the adoption of identified best practices it is hoped that performance will improve.

There are various types of benchmarking. **Internal benchmarking** is a method of comparing one operating unit or function with another within the same industry. **Functional benchmarking** compares internal functions with those of the best external practitioners of those functions, regardless of the industry they are in (also known as operational benchmarking or generic benchmarking). **Competitive benchmarking** gathers information about direct competitors, through techniques such as reverse engineering. **Strategic benchmarking** is a type of competitive benchmarking aimed at strategic action and organizational change.

benchmark interest rate FINANCE = ***base interest rate***

beneficial interest FINANCE benefiting from house as if its owner an arrangement whereby somebody is allowed to occupy or receive rent from a house without owning it

beneficial occupier REAL ESTATE occupier not owning property a person who occupies a property but does not own it fully

beneficial owner STOCKHOLDING & INVESTMENTS receiver of benefits of another's stock a person who receives all the benefits of a stock such as dividends, rights, and proceeds of any sale but is not the registered owner of the stock

beneficiary FINANCE somebody who will receive assets or proceeds a person who is designated to receive assets or proceeds from, for example, an estate or insurance policy

beneficiary bank BANKING bank dealing with gift a bank that handles a gift such as a bequest

benefit 1. FINANCE something extra offering improvement or reward something that improves the profitability or efficiency of an organization or reduces its risk **2.** HR & PERSONNEL nonmonetary reward for employee any nonmonetary reward such as a paid vacation or employer contribution to a pension that is given to employees

benefit-cost ratio ACCOUNTING = ***cost-benefit analysis***

benefit in kind *UK* HR & PERSONNEL = ***fringe benefits***

BEP *abbr* OPERATIONS & PRODUCTION break-even point

bequest FINANCE item left in will a gift that has been left to somebody in a will

Berhad BUSINESS Malay equivalent of plc a Malay term for "private." Companies can use "Sendirian Berhad" or "Sdn Bhd" in their name instead of "plc." *Abbr* **Bhd**

Berne Union FINANCE = ***International Union of Credit and Investment Insurers***

BERR *abbr* Department for Business, Enterprise and Regulatory Reform

  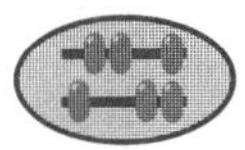 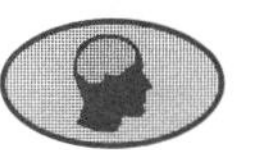  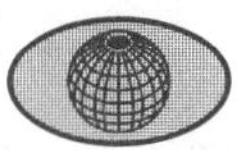   

Besloten venootschap BUSINESS limited company the Dutch term for a limited liability company. *Abbr* **BV**

best-in-class GENERAL MANAGEMENT leading in best practice leading a market or industrial sector in efficiency. A best-in-class organization exhibits exemplary **best practice**. Such an organization is clearly singled out from the pack and is recognized as a leader for its procedures for dealing with the acquisition and processing of materials and the delivery of end products or services to its customers. The concept of best in class is closely allied with **total quality management**, and one tool that can help in achieving this status is **benchmarking**.

best-of-breed MARKETING best available among computer products in marketing, sales, and competitive analysis, a computer product that is the best available software, hardware, or system in its class

best practice GENERAL MANAGEMENT most effective way of doing something the most effective and efficient method of achieving any objective or task. What constitutes best practice can be determined through a process of **benchmarking**. An organization can move toward achieving best practice, either across the whole organization or in a specific area, through **continuous improvement**. In production-based organizations, **world class manufacturing** is a related concept. More generally, a market or sector leader may be described as best-in-class.

best value GENERAL MANAGEMENT UK program encouraging local government efficiency a UK government initiative intended to ensure cost efficiency and effectiveness in the delivery of public services by local authorities. The best value initiative was announced in early 1997 to replace compulsory competitive tendering, and pilot schemes in selected local authorities began in April 1998. The Local Government Act 1999 requires councils, as part of the best value process, to review all services over a five-year period, setting standards and performance indicators for each service, comparing performance with that of other bodies, and undertaking consultation with local taxpayers and service users.

beta or **beta coefficient** STOCKHOLDING & INVESTMENTS number measuring changes in value a number representing an estimate of the fluctuations in value of a stock in relation to the market as a whole. A high beta indicates that a stock is likely to be more sensitive to market movements and therefore has a higher risk. *See also* ***alpha, beta rating***

beta rating STOCKHOLDING & INVESTMENTS means of measuring market risk a means of measuring the volatility (or risk) of a stock or fund in comparison with the market as a whole.

The beta of a stock or fund can be of any value, positive or negative, but usually is between +0.25 and +1.75. Stocks of many utilities have a beta of less than 1. Conversely, most high-tech NASDAQ-based stocks have a beta greater than 1; they offer a higher rate of return but are also risky. Both alpha and beta ratings should be readily available upon request from investment firms, because the figures appear in standard performance reports. *See also* ***alpha rating***

b/f *abbr* ACCOUNTING brought forward

BFH *abbr* TAX Bundesfinanzhof

Bhd *abbr* BUSINESS Berhad

bias STATISTICS distortion of statistical results inaccuracy or deviation in inferences, results, or a statistical method

bid 1. FINANCE highest realistic price the highest price a prospective buyer for a good or service is prepared to pay **2.** STOCKHOLDING & INVESTMENTS offer for most of firm's capital shares an offer to buy all or the majority of the capital shares of a company in an attempted takeover **3.** OPERATIONS & PRODUCTION statement outlining acceptable price for job a statement of what a person or company is willing to accept when selling a product or service. *Also called* ***quote***. *See also* ***tender***

bid-ask price MARKETS price charged for security in some markets, the price charged to buyers and sellers of a security, based on the **bid-offer spread**. *See also* ***bid-offer price***

bid-ask quote MARKETS statement of amounts being offered and asked a statement of the prices that are being offered and asked for a security or option contract

bid bond FINANCE guarantee of finance for international tender offer a guarantee by a financial institution of the fulfillment of an international tender offer

bid costs MERGERS & ACQUISITIONS professional fees paid during takeover costs incurred during the takeover of a company as a result of professional advice to the purchasing company from, for example, lawyers, accountants, and bankers

bidder OPERATIONS & PRODUCTION person submitting quote a person or company that submits a quotation. *UK term* ***tenderer***

bidding war MARKETS when buyers compete for same stock or security a competition between prospective buyers for the same stock or security, during which it rises in price

bid form MARKETS form detailing offer to underwrite US municipal bonds in the United States, a form containing details of an offer to underwrite municipal bonds

bid market MARKETS market for price of stocks a market for bids (the price at which a dealer will buy stocks)

bid-offer price MARKETS price charged for security in some markets, the price charged to buyers and sellers of a security, based on the **bid-offer spread**. *See also* ***bid-ask price***

bid-offer spread MARKETS gap between buyer's offer and seller's price the difference between the highest price that a buyer of a security is prepared to offer and the lowest price that a seller is prepared to accept

bid price MARKETS what stock exchange dealer will pay the price a stock exchange dealer will pay for a security or option contract

bid rate FINANCE, CURRENCY & EXCHANGE interest rate on Eurocurrency deposits a rate of interest paid on Eurocurrency deposits

bid-to-cover ratio MARKETS ratio of would-be and actual purchasers a number that shows how many more people wanted to buy Treasury bills than actually did buy them

bid up MARKETS **1.** make offer to raise price to bid for something merely to increase its price, not with the intention of acquiring it **2.** repeatedly increase bid price to make successive increases to the **bid price** for a security so that unopened orders do not remain unexecuted

Big Bang MARKETS 1980s restructuring of London Stock Exchange radical changes to practices on the London Stock Exchange implemented in October 1986. Fixed commission charges were abolished, leading to an alteration in the structure of the market, and the right of member firms to act as market makers as well as agents was also abolished (*slang*).

big bath ACCOUNTING deliberately making bad income statement worse the practice of making a particular year's poor income statement look even worse by increasing

  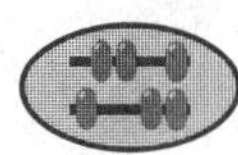   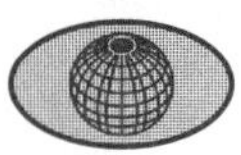   

expenses and selling assets. Subsequent years will then appear much better in comparison (*slang*).

big beast UK powerful person or firm a person or a company that has a lot of financial or political power and is able to influence events (*informal*)

Big Board MARKETS New York Stock Exchange the New York Stock Exchange, where the stocks of the largest US corporations are traded. *See also* ***Little Board***

big business BUSINESS large firms with a lot of power powerful business interests or companies in general. The term is particularly used when referring to **large-sized businesses** or **multinational businesses**.

Big Four 1. BANKING largest UK banks the United Kingdom's four largest commercial banks: Barclays, HSBC, Lloyds Banking Group, and NatWest (owned by Royal Bank of Scotland) **2.** ACCOUNTING largest accounting firms the four largest international auditors: PricewaterhouseCoopers, Deloitte Touche Tohmatsu, Ernst & Young, and KPMG **3.** BANKING largest Australian banks Australia's four largest banks: the Commonwealth Bank of Australia, Westpac Banking Corporation, National Australia Bank, and the Australia and New Zealand Banking Group Limited

Big GAAP ACCOUNTING in US, accounting principles for large firms in the United States, the **Generally Accepted Accounting Principles** that apply to large companies. It is sometimes felt that they are unnecessarily complex for smaller companies (*slang*).

big money lots of money a very large amount of money

big picture GENERAL MANAGEMENT overview of situation and context a broad perspective on an issue that encompasses its surrounding context and long-term implications (*slang*)

Big Three BUSINESS largest US automobile manufacturers before 1998 before the merger of Chrysler and Mercedes in 1998, the three largest automobile manufacturers in the United States: Chrysler, Ford, and General Motors

big-ticket FINANCE expensive used to describe something that costs a lot of money (*slang*)

big uglies BUSINESS established manufacturing and industrial firms traditional manufacturing and industrial companies, thought to be unglamorous but good long-term investments (*informal*)

Bilanzrichtliniengesetz ACCOUNTING German law covering accounting the 1985 German accounting directives law. *Abbr* **BiRiLiG**

bilateral clearing BANKING central banks' settling of accounts between countries the system of annual settlements of accounts between some countries, where accounts are settled by the central banks

bilateral credit BANKING credit to banks during clearing of checks credit allowed by banks to other banks in a clearing system to cover the period while checks are being cleared

bilateral facility BANKING arrangement for lending to single borrower a facility for making loans from one bank to one borrower, especially a corporate borrower

bilateral monopoly ECONOMICS market with one seller and one buyer a market in which there is a single seller and a single buyer

bilateral netting BANKING significant settling of contracts between banks the settling of contracts between two banks to give a new position

bilateral trade INTERNATIONAL TRADE special trade arrangement between two countries trade between two countries which give each other specific privileges such as favorable import quotas that are denied to other trading partners

bill 1. FINANCE document promising payment a written paper promising to pay money **2.** US FINANCE piece of paper money a piece of paper currency printed by a bank and approved as legal tender. *UK term* ***note*** **3.** LEGAL draft of new law a draft of a new law that will be discussed in a legislature **4.** OPERATIONS & PRODUCTION list of charges payable to supplier a written list of charges to be paid by a customer to a supplier **5.** OPERATIONS & PRODUCTION give bill to customer for payment to present a bill to a customer so that it can be paid

bill broker FINANCE dealer in bills of exchange an agent who buys and sells **promissory notes** and **bills of exchange**

bill discount BANKING Federal Reserve's interest rate to banks the interest rate that the Federal Reserve charges banks for short-term loans. This establishes a de facto floor for the interest rate that banks charge their customers, usually a little above the **discount rate**.

bill discounting rate FINANCE reduction in cost of US Treasury bill the amount by which the price of a Treasury bill is reduced to reflect expected changes in interest rates

billing cycle FINANCE time between requests for payment the period of time, often one month, between successive requests for payment

billion FINANCE **1.** thousand millions a sum equal to one thousand millions **2.** UK one million millions a sum equal to one million millions (*dated*)

billionaire FINANCE person with income over one billion a person whose net worth or income is more than one billion dollars, pounds, or other unit of currency

bill of entry INTERNATIONAL TRADE statement about imports or exports for customs a statement of the nature and value of goods to be imported or exported, prepared by the shipper and presented to a customhouse

bill of exchange FINANCE negotiable instrument a negotiable instrument, drawn by one party on another, for example, by a supplier of goods on a customer, who, by accepting (signing) the bill, acknowledges the debt, which may be payable immediately (a **sight draft**) or at some future date (a **time draft**). The holder of the bill can thereafter use an accepted time draft to pay a bill to a third party, or can discount it to raise cash.

bill of goods FINANCE **1.** in US, batch of goods in the United States, a consignment of merchandise for transportation and delivery **2.** in US, statement about batch of goods in the United States, a statement of the nature and value of a consignment of goods to be transported and delivered

bill of lading FINANCE document acknowledging shipment of goods a document prepared by a consignor by which a carrier acknowledges the receipt of goods and which serves as a document of title to the goods consigned

bill of sale FINANCE document confirming purchase a document confirming the transfer of goods or services from a seller to a buyer

bills payable FINANCE bills that firm must pay to creditors bills, especially bills of exchange, that a company will have to pay to its creditors. *Abbr* **B/P**

bills receivable FINANCE bills that firm's debtors will pay bills, especially bills of exchange, that are due to be paid by a company's debtors. *Abbr* **B/R**

BIN *abbr* FINANCE bank identification number

   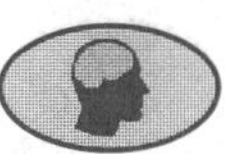  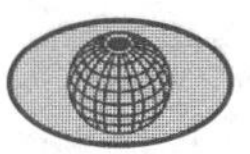   

binary thinker GENERAL MANAGEMENT somebody who thinks "it's all or nothing" a person who thinks only in absolute, black-and-white terms and is incapable of appreciating the subtleties and complexities of a situation (*slang*)

binder US INSURANCE temporary insurance certificate a document that an insurance company issues to a customer to serve as a temporary insurance certificate until the issue of the policy itself. *UK term* ***cover note***

biological assets ACCOUNTING live animals and growing plants farm animals and plants classified as assets. International Accounting Standards require that they are recorded on balance sheets at market value. Once they have been slaughtered or harvested, the assets become **agricultural produce**.

bionomics ECONOMICS economics considered as ecosystem a theory suggesting that economics can usefully be thought of as similar to an evolving ecosystem

BiRiLiG *abbr* ACCOUNTING Bilanzrichtliniengesetz

birth-death ratio STATISTICS birth count compared to death count the ratio of the number of births to the number of deaths in a population over a specific period of time

BIS *abbr* BANKING Bank for International Settlements

bivariate data STATISTICS information involving two variables data in which two variables are involved in each subject

bivariate distribution STATISTICS distribution involving two variables a form of distribution in which two random variables are involved

black ◇ in the black FINANCE making a profit, or having more assets than debt

black chip *S. Africa* BUSINESS firm with black owners or stockholders a South African company that is owned or managed by black people, or is controlled by black stockholders (*slang*)

black economic empowerment ECONOMICS encouraging S. African black economic participation the promotion of black ownership and control of South Africa's economic assets

black economy ECONOMICS unofficial, untaxed economic activity economic activity that is not declared for tax purposes and is usually carried out in exchange for cash

black hole GENERAL MANAGEMENT project using resources without producing profit a project that consumes unlimited amounts of resources without yielding any profit (*slang*)

black knight MERGERS & ACQUISITIONS former friendly firm involved in takeover a former **white knight** that has disagreed with the board of the company to be acquired and has established its own hostile bid. *See also* ***knight***

black market MARKETS illegal market for scarce goods an illegal **market**, usually for goods that are in short supply, but also for currency. Black market trading breaks government regulations or legislation and is particularly prevalent during times of shortage or rationing, or in industries such as pharmaceuticals or armaments that are highly regulated. *Also called* ***shadow market***

black market economy **1.** ECONOMICS illegal trading a system of illegal trading in officially controlled goods **2.** CURRENCY & EXCHANGE illicit parallel currency market an illicit secondary currency market that has rates markedly different from those in the official market

Black Monday MARKETS 10.28.1927 or 10.19.1987 when financial markets dropped either of two Mondays, October 28, 1929 or October 19, 1987, that were marked by the largest stock market declines of the 20th century. Although both market crashes originated in the United States, they were immediately followed by similar market crashes around the world.

black money ECONOMICS untaxed money earned unofficially or illegally money circulating in the **black economy** in payment for goods and services

Black-Scholes model STOCKHOLDING & INVESTMENTS formula for determining option call price a complex mathematical formula for calculating an option's **call price** using the current price of the security, the **strike price**, volatility, time until expiration, and the risk-free interest rate

Black Tuesday MARKETS 10.29.1929 when financial markets dropped Tuesday, October 29, 1929, a day on which values of stocks fell precipitously

Black Wednesday ECONOMICS 09.16.1992 when sterling crashed Wednesday, September 16, 1992, when the pound sterling left the European Exchange Rate Mechanism and was devalued against other currencies

blame culture GENERAL MANAGEMENT group's tendency to blame others for mistakes a set of attitudes, for example, within a business or organization, characterized by an unwillingness to take risks or accept responsibility for mistakes because of a fear of criticism or prosecution

blank check or **blank cheque** BANKING signed check with amount left blank a check with the amount of money and the name of the payee left blank, but signed by the drawer

blanket bond INSURANCE insurance against losses caused by employees an insurance policy that covers a financial institution for losses caused by the actions of its employees

blanket lien LEGAL right to somebody's property a legal right to all a person's property, including their personal effects

blended rate FINANCE intermediate interest rate an interest rate charged by a lender that is between an old rate and a new one

blind certificate E-COMMERCE computer file with user's name omitted a cookie from which the user's name is omitted so as to protect his or her privacy while making collected data available for marketing studies

blind entry **1.** ACCOUNTING uninformative bookkeeping entry a bookkeeping entry that records a debit or credit but fails to show other essential information **2.** *ANZ* FINANCE statement of cost of goods and tax a document issued by a supplier that stipulates the amount charged for goods or services as well as the amount of **Goods and Services Tax** payable

blind pool BUSINESS limited partnership without details of purposes a limited partnership in which the investment opportunities the general partner plans to pursue are not specified

blindside MARKETING attack somebody without warning to attack somebody in a way that he or she cannot anticipate (*slang*)

blind trust STOCKHOLDING & INVESTMENTS trust without participation of beneficiary a trust that manages somebody's business interests, with contents that are unknown to the beneficiary. People assuming public office use such trusts to avoid conflicts of interest.

block STOCKHOLDING & INVESTMENTS 10,000 or more shares of stock a very large number of shares of stock, typically 10,000 or more

block diagram STATISTICS presentation of statistical data in blocks a diagram that represents ranges of statistical data by vertical rectangular blocks

  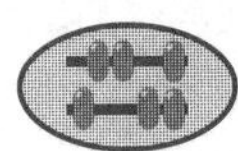   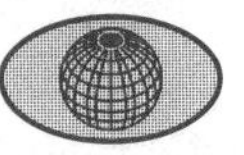   

blocked account BANKING frozen bank account a bank account from which funds cannot be withdrawn for any of a number of reasons, for example, bankruptcy proceedings, liquidation of a company, or government order when freezing foreign assets

blocked currency CURRENCY & EXCHANGE currency hard to exchange a currency that people cannot easily trade for other currencies because of foreign **exchange controls**

blocked funds CURRENCY & EXCHANGE money frozen in one place money that cannot be transferred from one place to another, usually because of foreign **exchange controls** imposed by the government of the country in which the funds are held

block grant FINANCE **1.** in US, federal money for local government in the United States, money that the federal government gives to a local government to spend in ways that the recipient determines **2.** in UK, government money for local authorities in the United Kingdom, money that the government gives to local authorities to fund local services

blockholder STOCKHOLDING & INVESTMENTS investor with large stake in firm an individual or institutional investor who holds a large number of shares of stock or a large dollar amount of bonds in a given company

block investment *ANZ* STOCKHOLDING & INVESTMENTS taking or having large stake in firm the purchase or holding of a large number of shares of stock or a large dollar amount of bonds in a given company

block trade STOCKHOLDING & INVESTMENTS sale of many stocks or bonds the sale of a large round number of stocks or large amount of bonds

block trading MARKETS bulk trading in securities buying and selling in very large numbers of securities

blow-off top MARKETS rapid price rise then fall a rapid increase in the price of a financial stock followed by an equally rapid drop in price (*slang*)

blowout *US* MARKETS immediate sale of complete stock issue the rapid sale of the whole of a new stock issue (*slang*)

Blue Book FINANCE UK national statistics of incomes and expenditure national statistics of personal incomes and spending patterns in the United Kingdom, published annually

blue chip STOCKHOLDING & INVESTMENTS profitable and low risk used to describe an equity or company which is of the highest quality and in which an investment would be considered as low risk with regard to both dividend payments and capital values

blue-chip stocks STOCKHOLDING & INVESTMENTS common stock in safe firm common stock in a company that is considered to be well established, highly successful, and reliable, and is traded on a stock market

blue-collar job HR & PERSONNEL job involving manual labor a position that involves mainly physical labor. With the decline in manufacturing and an increase in **harmonization** agreements, the term blue collar is now rarely used. Blue collar refers to the blue overalls traditionally worn in factories in contrast to the white shirt and tie supposedly worn by an office worker, known as a **white-collar worker**.

blue-collar worker HR & PERSONNEL manual laborer a person whose job involves mainly physical labor

Blue Dogs FINANCE fiscally conservative democrats in US Congress members of a coalition of fiscally conservative Democrats in the House of Representatives of the US Congress

Blue List MARKETS information about municipal bonds in the United States, a daily list of municipal bonds and their ratings, published by Standard & Poor's

blue-sky ideas GENERAL MANAGEMENT unrealistically optimistic plans extremely ambitious, idealistic, or unrealistic proposals, apparently unconfined by conventional thinking (*slang*)

blue-sky laws FRAUD, REGULATION & COMPLIANCE US state laws protecting investors from fraudulent deals in the United States, state laws designed to protect investors against fraudulent traders in securities

blue-sky securities STOCKHOLDING & INVESTMENTS worthless stocks and bonds stocks and bonds that have no value, being worth the same as a piece of "blue sky" (*slang*)

blur GENERAL MANAGEMENT when big changes in firm happen quickly a period of transition for a business in which changes occur at great speed and on a large scale

BO *abbr* BANKING branch office

board CORPORATE GOVERNANCE = ***board of directors***

board dismissal CORPORATE GOVERNANCE removal of firm's whole board the dismissal and removal from power of an entire board or **board of directors**

board meeting CORPORATE GOVERNANCE directors' meeting a meeting of the board of directors of a company

Board of Currency Commissioners CURRENCY & EXCHANGE issuer of Singaporean currency the sole currency issuing authority in Singapore, established in 1967. *Abbr* **BCCS**

Board of Customs and Excise INTERNATIONAL TRADE *see* ***Her Majesty's Revenue & Customs***

board of directors CORPORATE GOVERNANCE firm's highest management board the people selected to sit on an authoritative standing committee or governing body, taking responsibility for the management of an organization. Members of the board of directors are officially chosen by stockholders, but in practice they are usually selected on the basis of the current board's recommendations. The board usually includes major stockholders as well as directors of the company. *Also called* ***board***

Board of Inland Revenue TAX *see* ***Her Majesty's Revenue & Customs***

board of trustees STOCKHOLDING & INVESTMENTS group managing funds, assets, or property for others a committee or governing body that takes responsibility for managing – and holds in trust – funds, assets, or property belonging to others, for example, charitable or pension funds or assets

boardroom CORPORATE GOVERNANCE room for board meetings a room in which board meetings are held. A boardroom may be a room used only for board meetings or can be a multiuse room that becomes a boardroom for the duration of a board meeting.

boardroom battle CORPORATE GOVERNANCE struggle between board members a conflict or power struggle between individual board members or between groups of board members

board seat CORPORATE GOVERNANCE position on firm's board a position of membership of a board, especially a **board of directors**

board secretary CORPORATE GOVERNANCE organization's senior administrative officer a senior employee in a public organization, with a role similar to that of a **company secretary**

body corporate CORPORATE GOVERNANCE group acting as individual an entity such as a company or institution that is legally authorized to act as if it were one person

  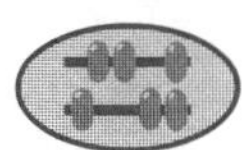   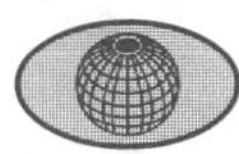   

body of creditors BUSINESS creditors regarded as single unit the creditors of a company or individual treated as a single creditor in dealing with the debtor

body of shareholders STOCKHOLDING & INVESTMENTS shareholders regarded as single unit the shareholders of a company treated as a single shareholder in dealing with the company

bogey *US* MARKETS performance benchmark for fund managers a benchmark, often the Standard and Poor's 500 Index, against which mutual fund managers or portfolio managers measure their performance (*slang*)

boilerplate LEGAL reusable contract language standard language that can be used for the same purpose from contract to contract (*slang*)

boiler room MARKETING room for selling financial products by phone a room from which sales personnel using high-pressure sales tactics try to sell financial products or real estate of questionable value, usually by telephone and often using illegal tactics

boiler room fraud FRAUD illegal selling of worthless stock the illegal practice of calling people and pressing them to buy worthless stock in companies that do not exist or are virtually bankrupt

Bolivarism ECONOMICS socialist vision of Venezuelan president the new socialist and pan-South American vision of President Hugo Chávez of Venezuela, named for Simón Bolívar, the South American revolutionary leader who fought against Spanish colonial rule

bolsa MARKETS stock exchange a **stock exchange** in a Spanish-speaking country

bona fide FINANCE undertaken in good faith used to describe a sale or purchase that has been conducted in good faith, without collusion or fraud

bona vacantia FINANCE goods of intestate person with no heirs the goods of somebody who has died intestate and has no traceable living relatives. In the United Kingdom, these goods become the property of the state.

bond **1.** FINANCE money given as deposit a sum of money paid as a deposit, especially on rented premises **2.** STOCKHOLDING & INVESTMENTS contract promising loan repayment with interest a certificate issued by a company or government that promises repayment of borrowed money at a set rate of interest on a particular date **3.** *S. Africa* MORTGAGES = ***mortgage bond***

bond anticipation note STOCKHOLDING & INVESTMENTS loan repaid through bonds issued later a loan that a government agency receives to provide capital that will be repaid from the proceeds of bonds that the agency will issue later. *Abbr* **BAN**

bond covenant STOCKHOLDING & INVESTMENTS promise by lender to limit activities part of a bond contract whereby the lender promises not to do some things such as borrow beyond a specified limit

bond discount STOCKHOLDING & INVESTMENTS gap between price and higher face value the difference between the face value of a bond and the lower price at which it is issued

bonded warehouse INTERNATIONAL TRADE warehouse for dutiable or taxable goods a warehouse that holds goods awaiting duty or tax to be paid on them

bond equivalent yield STOCKHOLDING & INVESTMENTS compound interest conversion for bond comparison the interest rate on a Treasury bill, commercial paper, or discount note, usually quoted as simple interest, converted to compound interest in order to compare it with the interest on a bond. *Also called* ***equivalent bond yield***. *See also* ***compound annual return***

bond fund STOCKHOLDING & INVESTMENTS mutual fund with bonds a mutual fund with an investment **portfolio** made up of bonds

bondholder STOCKHOLDING & INVESTMENTS entity owning bonds an individual or institution owning bonds issued by a government or company. Bondholders are entitled to payments of the interest as due and the return of the **principal** when the bond matures.

bond indenture STOCKHOLDING & INVESTMENTS document describing bond a document that specifies the terms and conditions of a bond

bond indexing STOCKHOLDING & INVESTMENTS matching yield from bonds and specific index the practice of investing in bonds in such a way as to match the yield of a designated index

bond issue STOCKHOLDING & INVESTMENTS sale of bonds to investors an occasion when a company or government offers **bonds** to investors in order to raise funding

bond market MARKETS market for government or municipal bonds a financial market in which participants trade in government or municipal bonds

bond premium STOCKHOLDING & INVESTMENTS gap between price and lower face value the difference between the face value of a bond and a higher price at which it is issued

bond quote STOCKHOLDING & INVESTMENTS up-to-date statement of bond's price a statement of the current price of a bond when traded on the open market

bond rating STOCKHOLDING & INVESTMENTS assessment of bond-issuer's reliability the rating of the reliability of a company, government, or local authority that has issued a bond. The highest rating is AAA (triple A).

bond swap STOCKHOLDING & INVESTMENTS simultaneous sale and purchase of bonds an exchange of some bonds for others, usually to gain a tax advantage or to diversify a portfolio

bond value ACCOUNTING value stated in accounts the value of an **asset** or **liability** as recorded in the accounts of a person or organization

bond-washing STOCKHOLDING & INVESTMENTS avoidance of tax on dividend income the practice of selling a bond before its dividend is due and buying it back later in order to avoid paying tax on the dividend

bond yield STOCKHOLDING & INVESTMENTS yield of bond in relation to market price the annual return on a bond (the rate of interest) expressed as a percentage of the current market price of the bond. Bonds can tie up investors' money for periods of up to 30 years, so knowing their yield is a critical investment consideration.

bonus FINANCE extra money given as reward to employee a financial incentive given to employees in addition to their **base pay** in the form of a one-time payment or as part of a **bonus plan**

bonus dividend STOCKHOLDING & INVESTMENTS irregular additional dividend a one-time extra dividend in addition to the usual payment

bonus issue STOCKHOLDING & INVESTMENTS proportionate issue of new shares to stockholders the capitalization of the reserves of a company by the issue of additional shares to existing stockholders, in proportion to their holdings. Such shares are usually fully paid up with no cash called for from the stockholders.

bonus offer MARKETING sales offer of extra product for same price a sales promotion technique offering consumers an additional amount of product for the basic price

bonus plan *US* FINANCE program for rewarding employees with extra money a form of **incentive plan** under which a

  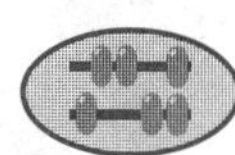   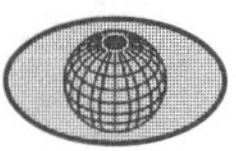   

bonus is paid to employees in accordance with rules concerning eligibility, performance targets, time period, and size and form of payments. A bonus plan may apply to some or all employees and may be determined on organization, business unit, or individual performance, or on a combination of these. A bonus payment may be expressed as a percentage of salary or as a flat-rate sum. *UK term* ***bonus scheme***

bonus scheme *UK* FINANCE = ***bonus plan***

bonus shares STOCKHOLDING & INVESTMENTS **1.** increased number of shares not affecting total value shares issued to stockholders in a **stock split**, with at least one more share for every share owned, without affecting the total value of each holding. *See also* ***stock split*** **2.** UK government reward to loyal founding stockholders in the United Kingdom, extra shares paid by the government as a reward to founding stockholders who did not sell their initial holding within a specific number of years

book STOCKHOLDING & INVESTMENTS record of trader's investments and amounts owed a statement of all the holdings of a trader and the amount he or she is due to pay or has borrowed ◇ cook the books FRAUD to use accounting methods to hide aspects of a company's financial dealings such as losses or illegal activities ◇ do the books ACCOUNTING to keep records of expenditure and income

book-building STOCKHOLDING & INVESTMENTS gathering information to determine offering price the research done among potential institutional investors to determine the optimum offering price for a new issue of stock

book cost STOCKHOLDING & INVESTMENTS total cost of stocks the price paid for a stock, including any payments to intermediaries such as brokers

book entry ACCOUNTING account entry unsupported by documentation an accounting entry indicated in a record somewhere but not represented by any document

book-entry security STOCKHOLDING & INVESTMENTS security without paper certificate a security that is recorded as a **book entry** but is not represented by a paper certificate

book inventory ACCOUNTING stock level recorded in accounts the number of items in stock according to accounting records. This number can be validated only by a physical count of the items.

bookkeeper ACCOUNTING maintainer of business's financial records a person who is responsible for maintaining the financial records of a business

bookkeeping ACCOUNTING recording income and expenditure the activity or profession of recording the money received and spent by an individual, business, or organization

bookkeeping barter ACCOUNTING exchange of goods treated as money transaction the direct exchange of goods between two parties without the use of money as a medium, but using monetary measures to record the transaction

book of original entry or **book of prime entry** ACCOUNTING chronological and classified record of transactions a chronological record of a business's transactions arranged according to type, for example, cash or sales. The books are then used to generate entries in a double-entry bookkeeping system.

books ACCOUNTING record of sales and receipts the set of records that a business keeps, showing what has been spent and earned

book sales OPERATIONS & PRODUCTION recorded sales sales as recorded in a company's sales book

books of account *UK* ACCOUNTING = ***accounting records***

book-to-bill ratio ACCOUNTING relationship between orders received and bills issued the ratio of the value of orders that a company has received to the amount for which it has billed its customers

book transfer STOCKHOLDING & INVESTMENTS recorded change in security's ownership without transfer documents a transfer of ownership of a security without physical transfer of any document that represents the instrument

book value **1.** ACCOUNTING recorded value of asset the value of an asset as recorded in a company's balance sheet, usually the original cost with an allowance made for depreciation. Book value is not usually the same as **market value** (the amount it could be sold for). **2.** STOCKHOLDING & INVESTMENTS, ACCOUNTING firm's own valuation of its stock the value of a company's stock according to the company itself, which may differ considerably from the **market value**. Book value is calculated by subtracting a company's liabilities and the value of its debt and **preferred stock** from its total assets. All of these figures appear on a company's balance sheet. For example:

	$
Total assets	1,300
Current liabilities	–400
Long-term liabilities, preference shares	–250
Book value	**= 650**

Book value represents a company's net worth to its stockholders. When compared with its market value, book value helps reveal how a company is regarded by the investment community. A market value that is notably higher than the book value indicates that investors have a high regard for the company. A market value that is, for example, a multiple of book value suggests that investors' regard may be unreasonably high. *Also called* ***carrying amount, carrying value***

book value per share STOCKHOLDING & INVESTMENTS, ACCOUNTING firm's own valuation of each share the value of one share of a stock according to the company itself, which may differ considerably from the market value. It is calculated by dividing the **book value** by the number of shares in issue.

boom FINANCE significant increase in business a period of time during which business activity increases significantly, with the result that demand for products grows, as do prices, salaries, and employment

boom and bust or **boom or bust** FINANCE extreme economic or market upswings and downswings a regular pattern of alternation in an economy or market between extreme growth and collapse and recession

BOP *abbr* INTERNATIONAL TRADE balance of payments

border tax adjustment INTERNATIONAL TRADE taxing imported but not exported goods the application of a domestic tax on imported goods while exempting exported goods from the tax in an effort to make the exported goods' price competitive both nationally and internationally

borrow **1.** FINANCE arrange to use another's assets for a time to be given money by a person or financial institution for a fixed period of time, usually paying it back in installments and with interest **2.** STOCKHOLDING & INVESTMENTS buy at delivery price and sell forward simultaneously to buy a commodity or security at the present spot price and sell forward at the same time

  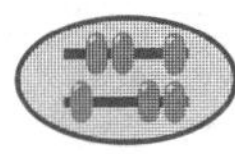 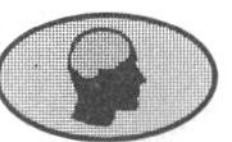  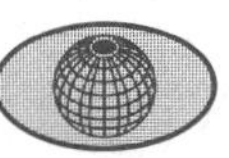   

borrower FINANCE somebody borrowing money from lender a person who receives money from a lender with the intention of paying it back, usually with interest

borrowing FINANCE receipt of money from lender the act of borrowing money from a lender

borrowing capacity or **borrowing power** FINANCE amount firm can borrow in loans the amount of money available as a loan to a company at a particular time, based on the company's financial situation

borrowing costs FINANCE expense of taking out loan expenses such as interest payments incurred from taking out a loan or any other form of borrowing. In the United States, such costs are included in the total cost of the asset whereas in the United Kingdom, and in International Accounting Standards, this is optional.

borrowings FINANCE money borrowed money borrowed, usually in the form of long-term loans

boss GENERAL MANAGEMENT person managing group or process the person in charge of a job, process, department, or organization, more formally known as a manager or supervisor

Boston Box or **Boston matrix** BUSINESS plotting market share against growth rate a model used for analyzing a company's potential by plotting market share against growth rate. The Boston Box was conceived by the Boston Consulting Group in the 1970s to help in the process of determining which businesses a company should invest in and which it should divest itself of. A business with a high market share and high growth rate is a **star**, and one with a low market share and low growth rate is a **dog**. A high market share with low growth rate is characteristic of a **cash cow**, which could yield significant but short-term gain, and a low market share coupled with high growth rate produces a **question mark company**, which offers a doubtful return on investment. To be useful, this model requires accurate assessment of a business's strengths and weaknesses, which may be difficult to obtain.

BOT *abbr* INTERNATIONAL TRADE balance of trade

bottleneck **1.** FINANCE process that holds up others an activity within an organization which has a lower capacity than preceding or subsequent activities, thereby limiting throughput. Bottlenecks are often the cause of a buildup of work in progress and of idle time. **2.** OPERATIONS & PRODUCTION somebody or something that slows down process a limiting factor on the rate of an operation. A workstation operating at its maximum capacity becomes a bottleneck if the rate of production elsewhere in the plant increases but throughput at that workstation cannot be increased to meet demand. An understanding of bottlenecks is important if the efficiency and capacity of an assembly line are to be increased. The techniques of **fishbone charts**, **Pareto charts**, and **flow charts** can be used to identify where and why bottlenecks occur.

bottom fisher MARKETS financial bargain hunter an investor who searches for bargains among stocks that have recently dropped in price (*slang*)

bottom line ACCOUNTING firm's net profit or loss the net profit or loss that a company makes at the end of a specific period of time, used in the calculation of the earnings-per-share business ratio

bottom-of-the-harbor scheme *ANZ* TAX tax avoidance involving asset-stripping a tax avoidance strategy that involves stripping a company of assets and then selling the company a number of times so that it is hard to trace

bottom out MARKETS stabilize at low level to reach the lowest level in the downward trend of the market price of securities or commodities before the price begins an upward trend again

bottom-up approach **1.** STOCKHOLDING & INVESTMENTS describing investment on individual potential independent of trends used to describe an approach to investing that seeks to identify individual companies that are fundamentally sound and whose stock will perform well regardless of general economic or industry-group trends **2.** GENERAL MANAGEMENT involving employee participation at all levels used to describe a consultative leadership style that promotes employee participation at all levels in decision making and problem solving. A bottom-up approach to leadership is associated with **flat** organizations and the empowerment of employees. It can encourage creativity and flexibility. *See also* ***top-down approach***

bottom-up budgeting TREASURY MANAGEMENT = ***participative budgeting***

bought day book ACCOUNTING record of items bought on credit a book used to record purchases for which cash is not paid immediately

bought deal STOCKHOLDING & INVESTMENTS purchase of new issue for resale to investors a method of selling stock in a new company or selling an issue of new shares in an existing company, in which an underwriter purchases all the shares at a fixed price for resale to investors

bought-in goods FINANCE goods from outside supplier components and subassemblies that are purchased from an outside supplier instead of being made within the organization

bought ledger ACCOUNTING firm's book recording expenditure a book in which all of a company's expenditure is logged

bought ledger clerk *UK* HR & PERSONNEL employee dealing with bought ledger an office employee who deals with the bought ledger or the sales ledger

bounce BANKING **1.** fail to honor check to refuse payment of a check because the account for which it is written holds insufficient money (*slang*). *Also called* ***dishonor*** **2.** be refused by bank (of a check) to be returned by a bank because there are insufficient funds in the account to meet the demand (*informal*)

bounced check BANKING check that bank fails to honor a draft on an account that a bank will not honor, usually because there are insufficient funds in the account

boundaryless organization GENERAL MANAGEMENT organizational model whose goal is flexibility a model that views organizations as having permeable boundaries. An organization has external boundaries that separate it from its suppliers and customers, and internal boundaries that provide demarcation to departments. This rigidity is removed in boundaryless organizations, where the goal is to develop greater flexibility and responsiveness to change and to facilitate the free exchange of information and ideas. The boundaryless organization behaves more like an organism encouraging better integration between departments and closer partnerships with suppliers and customers. The concept was developed at General Electric and described in the book *The Boundaryless Organization: Breaking the Chains of Organizational Structure* by Ron Ashkenas and others, which was published in 1995.

bourse MARKETS French stock exchange a European stock exchange, especially the one in Paris

boutique **1.** STOCKHOLDING & INVESTMENTS small specialist firm a small firm that offers a limited number of investments or services. *See also* ***boutique investment house*** **2.** BANKING small investment bank a small investment banking firm

boutique investment house STOCKHOLDING & INVESTMENTS specialist broker a brokerage that deals in securities of only one industry. *Also called* ***niche player*** *(sense 2)*

Bowie bond STOCKHOLDING & INVESTMENTS, RISK bond backed by intellectual property an **asset-backed security** for which the right to royalties from intellectual property is the collateral

box ◇ think outside the box GENERAL MANAGEMENT to think imaginatively about a problem

box spread MARKETS trading in single thing an arbitrage strategy that eliminates risk by buying and selling the same thing

B/P *abbr* FINANCE bills payable

BPR *abbr* GENERAL MANAGEMENT, OPERATIONS & PRODUCTION business process reengineering

B/R *abbr* FINANCE bills receivable

bracket creep US TAX incremental movement into higher tax bracket the movement of a taxpayer into increasingly higher tax brackets in a progressive tax system, usually as a result of incremental pay increases to keep pace with inflation

Brady bond STOCKHOLDING & INVESTMENTS emerging country's bond backed by Treasury bonds a bond issued by an emerging nation that has US Treasury bonds as collateral. It is named for Nicholas Brady, banking reformer and former Secretary of the Treasury.

brain drain GENERAL MANAGEMENT relocation of experts overseas for better working environment the overseas migration of specialists, usually highly qualified scientists, engineers, or technical experts, in pursuit of higher salaries, better research funding, and a perceived higher quality of working life

brainstorming GENERAL MANAGEMENT activity for generating free flow of ideas a technique for generating ideas, developing creativity, or problem solving in small groups, through the free-flowing contributions of participants. To encourage the free flow of ideas, brainstorming sessions operate according to a set of guidelines, and the production and evaluation of ideas are kept separate. Several variations of brainstorming and related techniques have emerged such as **brainwriting**, where ideas are written down by individuals, and **buzz groups**.

brainwriting GENERAL MANAGEMENT writing down flow of ideas a variation of **brainstorming** in which ideas are written down by individuals

branch accounts ACCOUNTING financial records for firm's subsidiary operations the **accounting records** or **financial statements** for the component parts of a business, especially those that are located in a different region or country from the main enterprise

branch office BANKING organization in different location from headquarters a bank or other financial institution that is part of a larger group and is located in a different geographic area from the parent organization. *Abbr* **BO**

branch tax TAX S. African tax on some foreign companies a South African tax imposed on nonresident companies that register a branch rather than a separate company

brand MARKETING name or symbol identifying product or service the distinguishing proprietary name, symbol, or **trademark** that differentiates a particular product or service from others of a similar nature

brand architecture MARKETING strategy for using brand on products and services the naming and structuring of **brands** within the product portfolio of an organization. Brand architectures may be monolithic (the corporate name is used on all products and services), endorsed (subordinate brands are linked to the corporate brand by means of either a verbal or visual endorsement), or freestanding (each product or service is individually branded for its target market). Brand architecture is influenced by the overall brand management and brand positioning strategy of the organization.

brand awareness MARKETING measure of consumers' familiarity with specific brand name the level of **brand recognition** that consumers have of a specific brand and its specific product category. Brand awareness examines three levels of recognition: whether the brand name is the first to come to mind when a consumer is questioned about a specific product category; whether the brand name is one of several that come to mind when a consumer is questioned about a specific product category; and whether or not a consumer has heard of a specific brand name.

brand building MARKETING efforts to gain consumer confidence in brand the establishment and improvement of a brand's identity, including giving the brand a set of values that the consumer wants, recognizes, identifies with, and trusts. Values developed in the process of brand building include psychological, physical, and functional properties that consumers desire and should always identify a property that is unique to that brand.

brand champion MARKETING employee responsible for developing and marketing brand an employee of an organization who is responsible for the development, performance, and communication of a particular brand

brand equity MARKETING brand's perceived value the estimated value that a particular brand name brings

brand extension MARKETING using known brand name to enter new market the exploitation, diversification, or stretching of a brand to revive or reinvigorate it in the marketplace. Products developed in the brand extension process may be directly recognizable derivatives or may look and feel completely different.

brand image MARKETING consumer's opinion of brand the perception that consumers have of a brand. Brand image is usually carefully developed by the brand owner through marketing campaigns or product positioning. Occasionally, the image of a brand may develop spontaneously through customer responses to a product. The image of a brand can be seriously tarnished through inappropriate advertising or association with somebody or something that has fallen from public favor.

branding MARKETING process of creating identity for brand a means of distinguishing one firm's products or services from another's and of creating and maintaining an image that encourages confidence in the quality and performance of that firm's products or services

brand leader MARKETING best-selling brand the brand that has the largest **market share**

brand life cycle MARKETING stages from brand introduction to withdrawal from market the three phases through which brands pass as they are introduced, grow, and then decline. The three stages of the brand life cycle are the introductory period, during which the brand is developed and is introduced to the market; the growth period, when the brand faces competition from other products of a similar nature; and, finally, the maturity period, in which the brand either extends to other products or its image is constantly updated. Without careful **brand management**, the maturity period can lead to decline and result in the brand being withdrawn. Similar stages can be observed in the **product life cycle**.

  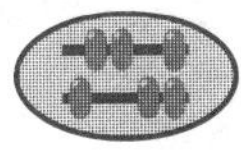 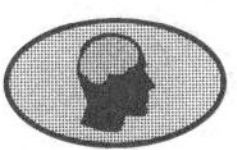  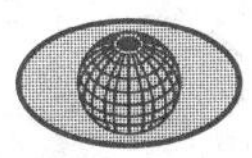   

brand loyalty MARKETING customer's inclination to stay with specific brand a long-term customer preference for a specific product or service. Brand loyalty can be produced by factors such as customer satisfaction with the performance or price of a specific product or service, or through identifying with a brand image. It can be encouraged by advertising.

brand management MARKETING responsibility for advertising, promoting, and selling product the marketing of one or more proprietary products. Brand managers have responsibility for the promotion and marketing of one or more commercial brands. This includes setting targets, advertising, and retailing, as well as coordinating all related activities to achieve those targets. In the case of multiple brand management, consideration needs be to given to questions relating to the treatment of the brands as equal or as having some differentiating value. This may affect the amount of resources committed to each brand. *See also* ***product management***

brand positioning MARKETING Identifying place in market to compete effectively the development of a brand's position in the market by heightening customer perception of the brand's superiority over other brands of a similar nature. Brand positioning relies on the identification of a real strength or value that has a clear advantage over the nearest competitor and is easily communicated to the consumer.

brand recognition MARKETING measurement of consumer's awareness of brand a measurement of the ability of consumers to recall their experience or knowledge of a particular brand. Brand recognition forms part of **brand awareness**.

brand value MARKETING benefit to firm of brand the amount that a brand is worth in terms of income, potential income, reputation, prestige, and market value. Brands with a high value are regarded as considerable assets to a company, so that when a company is sold a brand with a high value may be worth more than any other consideration.

brand wagon MARKETING increasing use of branding the trend toward using branding in marketing concepts and techniques (*slang*)

brandwidth MARKETING measurement of awareness of product the degree to which a brand of product or service is recognized (*slang*)

breach of contract LEGAL not performing according to contract a refusal or failure to fulfill an obligation imposed by a **contract**

breach of trust LEGAL instance of betraying people's trust a situation in which somebody does not act correctly or honestly when people expect him or her to

breadth-of-market theory MARKETS significance of relationship of rising and falling prices the theory that the health of a market is measured by the relative volume of items traded that are going up or down in price

break 1. MARKETS sharp price drop in stocks a sudden or sharp fall in prices on a financial market **2.** LEGAL fail to honor contract to fail to carry out the duties of a contract **3.** LEGAL end contract to cancel a contract

breakdown GENERAL MANAGEMENT list of individual items a detailed list or analysis of something item by item

break even ACCOUNTING make neither profit nor loss to balance income and expense, so as to show neither a net gain nor a loss

break-even MARKETING when revenue equals costs the point at which revenue from a product or project cancels out its costs

break-even analysis OPERATIONS & PRODUCTION establishing point of profit and loss balance a method for determining the point at which fixed and variable production costs are equaled by sales revenue and where neither a profit nor a loss is made. Usually illustrated graphically through the use of a **break-even chart**, break-even analysis can be used to aid decision making, set product prices, and determine the effects of changes in production or sales volume on costs and profits.

break-even chart 1. GENERAL MANAGEMENT chart showing break-even point a management aid used in conjunction with **break-even analysis** to calculate the point at which fixed and variable production costs are met by incoming revenue. Lines are plotted to indicate expected sales revenue and production costs. The point at which the lines intersect marks the **break-even point**, where no profit or loss is made. **2.** OPERATIONS & PRODUCTION chart comparing sales volumes and income a chart that indicates approximate profit or loss at different levels of sales volume within a limited range

break-even point OPERATIONS & PRODUCTION balance of profit and loss the point or level of financial activity at which expenditure equals income, or the value of an investment equals its cost, so that the result is neither a profit nor a loss. *Abbr* **BEP**

breakout 1. MARKETS significant movement in security's price a rise in a security's price above its previous highest price, or a drop below its former lowest price, taken by technical analysts to signal a continuing move in that direction **2.** GENERAL MANAGEMENT analysis of collected data a summary or breakdown of data that has been collected

breakpoint 1. FINANCE investment size that triggers reduced charges the size of investment at which the **front-end loading** on larger investments in a mutual fund starts to be reduced **2.** BANKING account balance that causes interest rate change a balance reached in an account that triggers the payment of either a higher or lower interest rate

breakthrough strategy GENERAL MANAGEMENT successful new strategy a strategy that achieves significant new results in business or management

break-up value MERGERS & ACQUISITIONS value of company's assets sold individually the combined market value of a firm's assets if each were sold separately, as contrasted with selling the firm as an ongoing business. Analysts look for companies with a large break-up value relative to their market value to identify potential takeover targets.

Bretton Woods ECONOMICS agreement establishing IMF and IBRD an agreement signed at a conference at Bretton Woods, in the United States, in July 1944, that established the **IMF** and the **IBRD**

bribery FRAUD offer of gift or cash to gain advantage the act of persuading somebody to exercise his or her business judgment in your favor by offering cash or a gift and thereby gaining an unfair advantage. Many organizations have **codes of conduct** that expressly forbid the soliciting or payment of bribes.

brick ◇ hit the bricks GENERAL MANAGEMENT to go out on strike

bricks-and-mortar E-COMMERCE relating to firms not operating online used to describe a traditional business not involved in e-commerce and incurring the cost of physical structures such as retail stores

bridge financing FINANCE borrowing in expectation of later loans short-term borrowing that the borrower expects to

  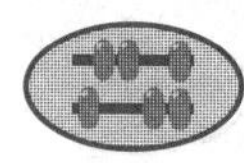  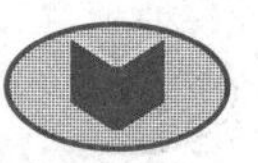 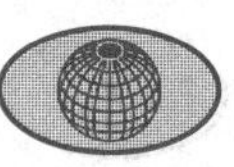 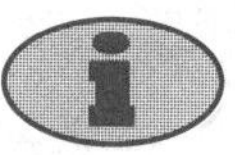  

repay with the proceeds of later, larger loans. *See also* ***takeout financing***

bridge loan US FINANCE temporary loan while waiting for money a short-term loan providing funds until further money is received, for example, for buying one property while trying to sell another. *UK term* ***bridging loan***

bridging FINANCE borrowing short-term until finance is arranged the obtaining of a short-term loan to provide a continuing source of financing in anticipation of receiving an intermediate or long-term loan. Bridging is routinely employed to finance the purchase or construction of a new building or property until an old one is sold.

bridging loan *UK* FINANCE = ***bridge loan***

bring forward ACCOUNTING carry sum to next column or page to carry a sum from one column or page to the next, or from one account to the next

Brisch system OPERATIONS & PRODUCTION coding system for all firm's resources a coding system, developed principally for the engineering industry by E. G. Brisch and Partners, in which a code is assigned to every item of resources, including materials, labor, and equipment.

British Accounting Association ACCOUNTING association for accountancy education and research an organization for the promotion of accounting education and research in the United Kingdom. *Abbr* **BAA**

British Bankers' Association BANKING nonprofit financial organization a not-for-profit trading association for the financial services and banking industries. The Association was established in 1919 and has 260 members, including 57 associate members. It addresses a variety of industry issues, including the development and revision of the voluntary **Banking Code**, which aims to set standards of best practice. *Abbr* **BBA**

British Chambers of Commerce BUSINESS association of accredited chambers of commerce a national network of accredited **chambers of commerce**. The BCC represents over 135,000 businesses in the United Kingdom. *Abbr* **BCC**

British pound = ***pound sterling*** (*informal*)

British Private Equity and Venture Capital Association FINANCE UK organization for equity and venture firms the official organization representing UK-based private equity and venture capital firms and their advisers. *Abbr* **BVCA**

broad tape MARKETS news service reporting financial information a news service that reports general information about securities and commodities

broken lot MARKETS = ***odd lot***

broker 1. FINANCE, GENERAL MANAGEMENT intermediary in transaction an agent who arranges a deal, sale, or contract **2.** STOCKHOLDING & INVESTMENTS = ***stockbroker* 3.** FINANCE, GENERAL MANAGEMENT act as intermediary in transaction to act as an agent in arranging a deal, sale, or contract

brokerage 1. FINANCE fee for arranging deal a fee paid to somebody who acts as an agent for somebody else. For example, brokers who arrange deals for the purchase and sale of real estate, those who execute orders for securities, and those who sell insurance receive commissions. *Also called* ***broker's commission* 2.** STOCKHOLDING & INVESTMENTS broker's business the business of being a broker, trading on a stock exchange on behalf of clients **3.** *US* STOCKHOLDING & INVESTMENTS firm trading in securities for others a company whose business is buying and selling stocks and other securities for its clients. *Also called* ***brokerage firm, brokerage house***. *UK term* ***broking house***

broker-dealer STOCKHOLDING & INVESTMENTS broker who also holds stocks for resale a dealer who buys stocks and other securities and holds them for resale, and also deals on behalf of investor clients

brokered market MARKETS where brokers introduce traders a financial market in which brokers bring buyers and sellers together

brokering *US* MARKETS securities the business or job of dealing in securities. *UK term* ***broking***

broker loan rate BANKING interest charged for buying derivatives the interest rate that banks charge brokers on money that they lend for purchases **on margin**

broker recommendation STOCKHOLDING & INVESTMENTS advice to trade or hold security a recommendation to buy, hold, or sell a stock, made by an analyst who is employed by a brokerage firm to research specific companies' strengths and weaknesses

broker's commission STOCKHOLDING & INVESTMENTS = ***brokerage (sense 1)***

broking *UK* STOCKHOLDING & INVESTMENTS = ***brokering***

broking house *UK* STOCKHOLDING & INVESTMENTS = ***brokerage***

brought forward ACCOUNTING carried to next column or page indicating a sum carried from one column or page to the next, or from one account to the next. *Abbr* **b/f**. *See also* ***bring forward***

brownfield REAL ESTATE unused urban development site an urban development site that has been previously built on but is currently unused. *UK term* ***brownfield site***

brownfield site *UK* REAL ESTATE = ***brownfield***

brown goods *UK* MARKETING audio, video, computing, and telecommunications consumer goods electronic consumer goods such as televisions, radios, and CD players, used primarily for home entertainment. *See also* ***white goods***

B/S *abbr* ACCOUNTING balance sheet

B share STOCKHOLDING & INVESTMENTS **1.** US share with limits on voting in the United States, a share that has limited voting power. *See also* ***A share* 2.** Australian mutual fund share with fee payable on redemption in Australia, a share in a mutual fund that has no front-end sales charge but carries a redemption fee, or **back-end loading**, payable only if the share is redeemed. This load, called a **contingent deferred sales charge**, declines every year until it disappears, usually after six years.

BTI *abbr* MARKETS Business Times Industrial index

bubble MARKETS rapid rise followed by fall in asset price a rapid rise in the price of any type of asset, due mainly to people's belief that the price will continue to rise. When it rises above the real value of the asset, the price falls rapidly, analogous to a bubble bursting. *Also called* ***speculative bubble***

bubble economy ECONOMICS booming economic activity before crash an unstable boom based on speculation in any market, often followed by a financial crash

buck *US* CURRENCY & EXCHANGE (*slang*) **1.** US dollar a United States dollar **2.** one million one million of any currency unit, used by traders

bucket shop MARKETS broker engaging in delayed trades to customer's disadvantage in the United States, a firm of brokers or dealers that accepts customers' orders but does not execute the transactions until it is financially advantageous to the broker, at the customers' expense

bucket trading MARKETS broker's illegal delay of transactions for own benefit in the United States, an illegal practice in which a

  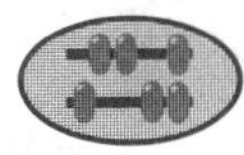 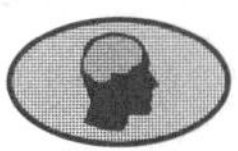  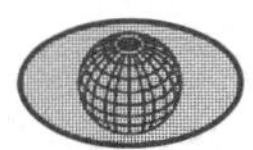   

broker or dealer accepts customers' orders but does not execute the transactions until it is financially advantageous to the broker, at the customers' expense

budget TREASURY MANAGEMENT statement of predicted income and expenditure a quantitative statement, for a defined period of time, that may include planned revenues, expenses, assets, liabilities, and cash flows. A budget provides a focus for an organization, as it aids the coordination of activities, allocation of resources, and direction of activity, and facilitates control. Planning is achieved by means of a fixed master budget, whereas control is generally exercised through the comparison of actual costs with a flexible budget.

Budget FINANCE UK government's annual statement of financial plans in the United Kingdom, the government's annual spending plan, which is announced to the House of Commons by the Chancellor of the Exchequer. The government is legally obliged to present economic forecasts twice a year, and since the 1997 general election the main Budget has been presented in the spring while a **pre-Budget report** is given in the autumn. This outlines government spending plans prior to the main Budget, and also reports on progress since the last Budget.

budget account *UK* BANKING bank account for regular expenses a bank account established to control a person's regular expenditure, such as the payment of insurance premiums, mortgage, utilities, or telephone bills. The annual expenditure for each item is paid into the account in equal monthly installments, bills being paid from the budget account as they become due.

budgetary TREASURY MANAGEMENT of future financial plans relating to a detailed plan of financial operations, with estimates of both revenue and expenditure for a specific future period

budgetary control TREASURY MANAGEMENT regulation of spending regulation of spending according to a planned budget

budget committee TREASURY MANAGEMENT committee that prepares budgets the group within an organization responsible for drawing up budgets that meet departmental requirements, ensuring they comply with policy, and then submitting them to the board of directors

budget deficit ACCOUNTING amount expenditure exceeds income the extent by which expenditure exceeds revenue, especially that of a government. *Also called* ***deficit***

budget director TREASURY MANAGEMENT person responsible for budget preparation the person in an organization who is responsible for running the budget system

budgeted capacity TREASURY MANAGEMENT output level in budget an organization's available output level for a budget period according to the budget. It may be expressed in different ways, for example, in machine hours (the number of hours for which a machine is in production) or standard hours.

budgeted revenue TREASURY MANAGEMENT expected income in budget the income that an organization expects to receive in a budget period according to the budget

budgeting TREASURY MANAGEMENT preparation of budget the preparation of a budget in planning the management of income and expenditure

budget management TREASURY MANAGEMENT adjusting activities to meet budgets the comparison of actual financial results with the estimated expenditures and revenues for the given time period of a budget and the taking of corrective action as necessary

budget surplus ACCOUNTING amount income exceeds expenditure the extent by which revenue exceeds expenditure, especially that of a government. *Also called* ***surplus***

budget variance ACCOUNTING difference between budget estimate and reality the difference between the financial value of something estimated in the budget, such as costs or revenues, and its actual financial value

buffer inventory OPERATIONS & PRODUCTION items available to cope with changes the products or supplies of an organization maintained on hand or in transit to stabilize variations in supply, demand, production, or lead time

buffer stock OPERATIONS & PRODUCTION items available to cope with supply failure a stock of materials, or of work in progress, maintained in order to protect user departments from the effect of possible interruptions to supply

building and loan association BANKING = ***savings and loan association***

Building Societies Ombudsman REGULATION & COMPLIANCE UK official protecting customers of building societies a UK official whose duty is to investigate complaints by members of the public against building societies

building society BANKING UK financial institution supporting real estate purchases in the United Kingdom, a financial institution that offers interest-bearing savings accounts, the deposits being reinvested by the society in long-term loans, primarily mortgage loans for the purchase of real estate

bulge MARKETS sudden trend of rising prices a rapid increase in prices in the commodities market

bulk buying OPERATIONS & PRODUCTION purchase of goods cheaply in quantity the act of buying large quantities of goods at low prices

bulk handling FINANCE financing of moneys due in bulk the financing of a group of receivables together to reduce processing costs

bull STOCKHOLDING & INVESTMENTS exploiter of favorable business conditions somebody who anticipates favorable business conditions, especially somebody who buys specific stocks or commodities in anticipation that their prices will rise, often with the expectation of selling them at a large profit at a later time. *See also* ***bear***

bull CD STOCKHOLDING & INVESTMENTS CD paying more in rising market a **certificate of deposit** that pays a higher interest rate when an underlying market index rises in value. *See also* ***bear CD***

bulldog bond STOCKHOLDING & INVESTMENTS foreign sterling bond in UK market a bond issued in sterling in the UK market by a non-British corporation

bullet FINANCE final large loan repayment a single large repayment of the outstanding **principal** of a loan at maturity

bullet bond STOCKHOLDING & INVESTMENTS bond repaid with single payment a bond that can be redeemed only when it reaches its maturity date

Bulletin des Annonces Lgales Obligatoires FINANCE *see* ***BALO***

bullet loan FINANCE loan with only interest payments until maturity a loan that involves specific payments of interest until maturity, when the **principal** is repaid

bullion FINANCE precious metal in bars gold, silver, or platinum produced and traded in the form of bars

bullish 1. MARKETS of markets with rising prices conducive to or characterized by buying stocks or commodities in anticipation of rising prices. *See also* ***bearish*** **2.** GENERAL MANAGEMENT optimistic about business anticipating favorable

  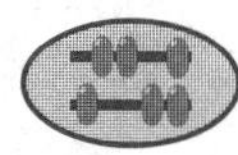   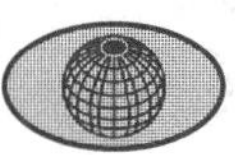   

business conditions and optimistic about taking advantage of them

bull market MARKETS market with rising prices a market in which prices are rising and in which a dealer is more likely to be a buyer than a seller. *See also* ***bear market***

bull spread MARKETS transactions to make profit when price rises a combination of purchases and sales of options for the same commodity or stock, intended to produce a profit when the price rises. *See also* ***bear spread***

bunching MARKETS combining orders for same security from different clients a process by which brokers combine orders for the same security, so that the orders can be executed together and save clients who have placed orders for **odd lots** of fewer than 100 shares of stock from paying extra fees

Bund STOCKHOLDING & INVESTMENTS, RISK German government bond a bond issued by the German government with a maturity of 8.5 to 10 years

Bundesfinanzhof TAX German tax court in Germany, the supreme court for issues concerning taxation. *Abbr* **BFH**

bundle FINANCE combination of products or services a package of financial products or services offered to a customer

buoyant MARKETS showing a continuous rise in prices describes a financial market or a security with continuously rising prices

buoyant market MARKETS market with rising prices a market that experiences plenty of trading activity and on which prices are rising, rather than falling

bureaucracy GENERAL MANAGEMENT rigid organizational structure an organizational structure with a rigid hierarchy of personnel, regulated by set rules and procedures. The term bureaucracy has gradually become a pejorative synonym for excessive and time-consuming paperwork and administration. Bureaucracies fell subject to **delayering** and **downsizing** from the 1980s onward, as the flatter organization became the target structure to ensure swifter market response and organizational flexibility.

burn rate FINANCE rate at which firm's capital is used the rate at which a new business spends its initial capital before it becomes profitable or needs additional funding, used by investors as a measure of a company's ability to survive, or the rate at which a mature business spends its accumulated cash and liquid securities. *Also called* ***cash burn***

bush telegraph GENERAL MANAGEMENT quick informal communication method a method of communicating information or rumors swiftly and unofficially by word of mouth or other means

business BUSINESS **1.** activity carried out for profit work such as buying, selling, or producing goods or services that a person or organization does to make a profit **2.** commercial organization a company or other organization that buys, sells, or produces goods or services to make a profit **3.** commercial transactions commercial dealings or discussions carried on between people or organizations

Business Accounting Deliberation Council REGULATION & COMPLIANCE Japanese body making accounting rules in Japan, a committee controlled by the Ministry of Finance that is responsible for drawing up regulations regarding the consolidated financial statements of listed companies. *Abbr* **BADC**

Business Activity Statement TAX Australian document giving firm's tax details in Australia, a standard document used to report the amount of **GST** and other taxes paid and collected by a business. *Abbr* **BAS**

business address BUSINESS address of firm's premises the details of number, street, and city or town where a company is located

business administration GENERAL MANAGEMENT procedures involved in operating successful business the establishment and maintenance of procedures, records, and regulations in the pursuit of a commercial activity. Business administration involves the conduct of activities leading to, and resulting from, the delivery of a product or service to the customer. Administration is often seen as paperwork and form-filling, but it reaches more widely than that to encompass the coordination of all the procedures that enable a product or service to be delivered, together with the keeping of records that can be checked to identify errors or opportunities for improvement.

business angel FINANCE investor in new company an individual who is prepared to invest money in a startup company. The amount offered by angels is typically much less than that offered by **venture capitalists**, but angels are often willing to take greater risks.

business case GENERAL MANAGEMENT proposal showing tangible value to organization the essential value to an organization of a proposal. A business case is made through the preparation and presentation of a business plan and is used to prevent blue-sky ideas taking root without justifiable or provable value to an organization.

business center BUSINESS **1.** area where city's main businesses are the part of a city or town where the main banks, stores, and offices are located **2.** independent office providing business services an office that provides business services such as Internet access, photocopying, meeting rooms, etc., for example, to travelers in a hotel

business cluster BUSINESS cooperative of small related firms a group of small firms from similar industries that team up and act as one body. Creating a business cluster enables firms to enjoy economies of scale usually only available to bigger competitors. Marketing costs can be shared and goods can be bought more cheaply. There are also networking advantages, allowing small firms to share experiences and discuss business strategies.

business combinations MERGERS & ACQUISITIONS acquisitions or mergers in the United States, acquisitions or mergers involving two or more business enterprises

Business Council of Australia BUSINESS organization of chief executives a national association of chief executives, designed as a forum for the discussion of matters pertaining to business leadership in Australia. *Abbr* **BCA**

business cycle ECONOMICS regular repeating pattern of economic activity a regular pattern of fluctuation in national income, moving from upturn to downturn in about five years

business day BUSINESS normal weekday a weekday when banks, businesses, and stock exchanges are open for business

business efficiency GENERAL MANAGEMENT maximizing output while minimizing input a situation in which an organization maximizes benefit and profit, while minimizing effort and expenditure. Maximization of business efficiency is a balance between two extremes. Managed correctly, it reduces costs, waste, and duplication. The greater the efficiency, the more impersonal, rational, and emotionally detached a bureaucracy becomes. The flatter organizations more prevalent today attempt to be more customer-responsive than efficient in this sense, and the notion of such an ordered and impersonal efficiency has lost favor in an era when creativity and innovation are valued as a competitive advantage.

  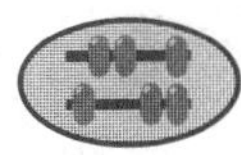 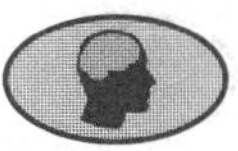  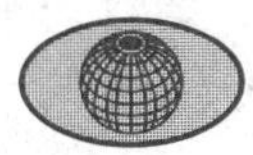   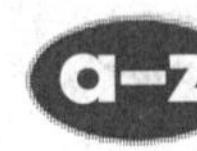

business expenses ACCOUNTING money spent on firm's running costs money spent on running a business, not on stock or assets

business failure GENERAL MANAGEMENT bankrupt organization an organization that has gone bankrupt. A business that is at risk of failure may be saved by **turnaround management**, which identifies and deals with the reasons for decline. *Also called* ***failure***

business gift MARKETING gift presented to customer a present, usually from a supplier to a customer, often used to maintain good relations. Business gifts may range from a pen to a gift basket and are often a form of **merchandising**. The acceptance of a business gift is often governed by an organization's **code of conduct** and is often forbidden on the grounds that business gifts, particularly high value ones, may be seen as an attempt to bribe.

business hours BUSINESS period when most firms are open the time during which a business is available to be in contact with customers, usually 9:00 a.m. to 5:00 p.m.

business intelligence GENERAL MANAGEMENT collection of business data the information and information gathering techniques used by businesses

business interruption insurance INSURANCE insurance protection against interruptions to business a policy indemnifying an organization for loss of profits and continuing fixed expenses when some insurable disaster, for example, a fire, causes the organization to stop or reduce its activities. *Also called* ***consequential loss policy***

business manager GENERAL MANAGEMENT somebody responsible for firm's operations a person who is responsible for implementing the policies and procedures of a business or part of a business

business model GENERAL MANAGEMENT description of business operations a description of the way in which a specific business or type of business operates, including its structure, policies, products, services, customers, and market strategies

business name BUSINESS in UK, name that organization uses in the United Kingdom, the legal term for the name under which an organization operates

business objective GENERAL MANAGEMENT organization's goal as basis for operational policies a goal that an organization sets for itself, for example, profitability, sales growth, or return on investment. These goals are the foundation upon which the strategic and operational policies adopted by the organization are based.

business plan GENERAL MANAGEMENT outline of firm's intentions for achieving goals a document describing the current activities of a business, setting out its goals and objectives and how they are to be achieved over a set period of time. A business plan may cover the activities of an organization or a group of companies, or it may deal with a single department within the organization. In the former case, it is sometimes referred to as a corporate plan. The sections of a business plan usually include a market analysis describing the target market, customers, and competitors, an operations plan describing how products and services will be developed and produced, and a financial section providing profit, budget, and cash flow forecasts, annual accounts, and financial requirements. Businesses may use a business plan internally as a framework for implementing strategy and improving performance or externally to attract investment or raise capital for development plans. A business plan may form part of the overall corporate planning process within an organization and be used for the implementation of a company's strategy.

business process reengineering GENERAL MANAGEMENT, OPERATIONS & PRODUCTION review and change to benefit organization the initiation and control of the change of processes within an organization, in order to derive competitive advantage from improvement in the quality of products. Business process reengineering requires a review and imaginative analysis of the processes currently used by the organization. BPR, therefore, has similarities to **benchmarking**, as this review of processes can reveal critical points where significant improvements in quality can be made. Business process reengineering was at the height of its popularity in the early to mid-1990s. It has been criticized as one of the root causes of the bouts of **downsizing** and **delayering** that have affected many parts of industry. It has also received a negative press because few BPR projects have delivered the benefits expected of them. *Abbr* **BPR**

business property relief TAX reduction in UK inheritance tax on business property in the United Kingdom, a reduction in the amount liable to inheritance tax on some types of business property

business rate TAX UK tax on business premises in the United Kingdom, a tax on businesses calculated on the value of the property occupied. Although the rate of tax is set by central government, the tax is collected by the local authority.

business risk RISK possible risk to firm's standing the uncertainty associated with the unique circumstances of a particular company which might affect the price of that company's securities, for example, the introduction of a superior technology by a competitor

business segment ACCOUNTING distinct part of business or enterprise a distinguishable part of a business or enterprise which is subject to a different set of risks and returns from any other part. Listed companies are required to declare in their annual reports information such as sales, profits, and assets, for each segment of an enterprise.

business strategy GENERAL MANAGEMENT firm's intended means of achieving long-term goals a long-term approach to implementing a firm's business plans to achieve its business objectives

Business Times Industrial index MARKETS Asian index of stocks an index of 40 Singapore and Malaysian stocks, sponsored by the *Business Times*. *Abbr* **BTI**

business-to-business E-COMMERCE *see* ***B2B***

business-to-consumer E-COMMERCE *see* ***B2C***

business transaction OPERATIONS & PRODUCTION instance of buying or selling an act of buying or selling goods or services in order to make a profit

business transfer relief TAX UK tax benefit in takeovers the UK tax advantage gained when selling a business for shares of stock in the company that buys it

business unit ACCOUNTING distinct part of business organization a part of an organization that operates as a distinct function, department, division, or stand-alone business. Business units are usually treated as a separate **profit center** within the overall business.

bust ◇ go bust FINANCE to become bankrupt (*informal*)

bust up MERGERS & ACQUISITIONS divide or subdivide firm to split up a company or a division of a company into smaller units

bust-up proxy proposal MERGERS & ACQUISITIONS approach to stockholders for leveraged buyout an overture to a company's stockholders for a **leveraged buyout** in which the acquirer will sell some of the company's assets in order to repay the debt used to finance the takeover

  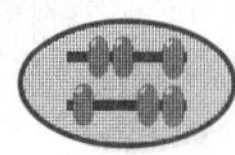   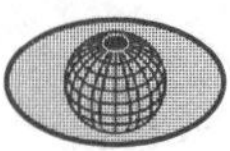   

butterfly spread STOCKHOLDING & INVESTMENTS simultaneously buying and selling variety of options a complex option strategy based on simultaneously purchasing and selling calls at different exercise prices and maturity dates, the profit being the premium collected when the options are sold. Such a strategy is most profitable when the price of the underlying security is relatively stable.

buy FINANCE **1.** pay to get something to get something in exchange for money **2.** something you pay for something that you pay for relative to its being worth or not worth the amount you pay

buy and hold STOCKHOLDING & INVESTMENTS investment for long term an investment strategy based on retaining securities for a long time

buy and write STOCKHOLDING & INVESTMENTS buying stock and selling options as safeguard an investment strategy involving buying stock and selling options to eliminate the possibility of loss if the value of the stock goes down

buyback 1. MARKETS purchase by firm of its own stock an arrangement whereby a company buys its own stock on the stock market. *Also called* ***stock buyback*** **2.** STOCKHOLDING & INVESTMENTS agreed repurchase of bonds or stock the repurchase of bonds or stock, as agreed by contract. The seller is usually a **venture capitalist** who helped finance the forming of the company.

buydown 1. FINANCE initial payment to secure favorable interest rate an initial lump-sum payment made on a loan in order to get a more favorable ongoing rate, especially a loan secured by a mortgage **2.** MORTGAGES partial repayment of principal on mortgage the payment of principal amounts which reduces the monthly payments due on a mortgage

buyer 1. BUSINESS person buying or intending to buy somebody who is in the process of buying something or who intends to buy something **2.** OPERATIONS & PRODUCTION professional acquirer of items needed somebody whose job is to choose and buy goods, merchandise, services, or media time or space for a company, factory, store, or advertiser

buyer expectation MARKETING = ***customer expectation***

buyer's guide MARKETING information helping consumer choose from variety of products a document that offers information on a variety of related products, usually from a number of different organizations

buyer's market MARKETS when supply exceeds demand a situation in which supply exceeds demand, prices are relatively low, and buyers therefore have an advantage

buy in STOCKHOLDING & INVESTMENTS acquire controlling interest in firm to buy stock in a company so as to have a controlling interest. This is often done by or for executives from outside the company.

buying department *UK* OPERATIONS & PRODUCTION = ***purchasing department***

buying economies of scale FINANCE lower cost involved in large transactions a reduction in the cost of purchasing raw materials and components or of borrowing money due to the increased size of the purchase

buying manager OPERATIONS & PRODUCTION = ***purchasing manager***

buying power FINANCE assessment of ability to purchase products and services the assessment of a person's or organization's disposable income, regarded as determining the quantity and quality of products and services that person or organization can afford to buy

buy on close MARKETS purchase late in day a purchase of securities or insurance policies made at the end of the trading day

buy on margin STOCKHOLDING & INVESTMENTS, RISK borrow to pay for part of security purchase to purchase securities by paying cash for part of the purchase and borrowing, using the security as collateral, for the remainder

buy on opening MARKETS purchase early in day a purchase of securities or insurance policies made at the beginning of the trading day

buy or make OPERATIONS & PRODUCTION = ***purchasing versus production***

buy out MERGERS & ACQUISITIONS **1.** buy and take over business to purchase the entire stock of, or controlling financial interest in, a company **2.** buy all somebody's share to pay somebody to relinquish his or her interest in a property or other enterprise

buyout 1. MERGERS & ACQUISITIONS buying and taking over of business the purchase and **takeover** of an ongoing business. It is more formally known as an **acquisition**. If a business is purchased by managers or staff, it is known as a **management buyout**. **2.** MERGERS & ACQUISITIONS buying all of somebody's stock ownership the purchase of somebody else's entire stock ownership in a firm. It is more formally known as an **acquisition**. **3.** PENSIONS leaver's ability to move pension assets an option to transfer benefits of a pension plan on leaving a company

buy stop order MARKETS instruction to buy stock at specific price an order to buy stock when its price reaches a specific level, above the current offering level

buy-to-let *UK* FINANCE = ***buy-to-rent***

buy-to-let mortgage *UK* MORTGAGES = ***buy-to-rent mortgage***

buy-to-rent *US* FINANCE purchase of property for rental purposes an investment in property with the intention of renting it to produce income, often to pay the original mortgage used to purchase it. *UK term* ***buy-to-let***

buy-to-rent mortgage *US* MORTGAGES mortgage to purchase property for rental a mortgage used to buy property that you intend to rent. It differs from a mortgage on property that you intend to live in, in that the mortgagee takes into consideration the income the property will produce in deciding how much to lend. *UK term* ***buy-to-let mortgage***

buzz group GENERAL MANAGEMENT small group for discussing specific issue a small discussion group formed for a specific task such as generating ideas, solving problems, or reaching a common viewpoint on a topic within a specific period of time. Large groups may be divided into buzz groups after an initial presentation in order to cover different aspects of a topic or maximize participation. Each group appoints a spokesperson to report the results of the discussion to the larger group. Buzz groups are a form of brainstorming.

BV *abbr* BUSINESS Besloten venootschap

BVCA *abbr* FINANCE British Private Equity and Venture Capital Association

by-bidder FINANCE somebody bidding at auction to benefit seller somebody who bids at an auction solely to raise the price for the seller

bylaws *US* CORPORATE GOVERNANCE rules for corporation's internal procedures rules governing the internal running of a corporation, such as the number of meetings, the appointment of officers, and so on. *UK term* ***articles of association***

bypass trust TAX trust saving tax by increasing beneficiaries a trust that leaves money in a will in trust to people other than the prime beneficiary in order to gain tax advantage

byproduct OPERATIONS & PRODUCTION secondary product sold for profit a secondary product, made as a result of manufacturing a main product, that can be sold for profit

C

CA *abbr* ACCOUNTING **1.** chartered accountant **2.** certified accountant

c/a *abbr* BANKING current account

C/A *abbr* FINANCE capital account

cable CURRENCY & EXCHANGE exchange rate between US dollar and pound a spot exchange rate between the US dollar and the pound sterling

CAC 40 MARKETS French stock market index of 40 top stocks an index of prices on the Paris Stock Exchange, based on the prices of the 40 leading stocks

CAD *abbr* OPERATIONS & PRODUCTION computer-aided design

cafeteria plan or **cafeteria employee benefit plan** HR & PERSONNEL US employee benefit plan allowing choice of benefits in the United States, an employee benefit plan that allows employees to select a number of benefits such as contributions to a retirement plan, insurance, or cash to pay for medical expenses not covered by insurance, all or some of which may be exempt from payroll tax. *Also called* ***flexible benefit plan***

cage *US* MARKETS department of brokerage firm handling paperwork the part of a brokerage firm where the paperwork involved in the buying and selling of stocks is processed (*slang*)

calendar spread STOCKHOLDING & INVESTMENTS, RISK = ***horizontal spread***

calendar variance ACCOUNTING accounting difference from calendar months versus working days a variance that occurs if a company uses calendar months for the financial accounts but uses the number of actual working days to calculate overhead expenses in the cost accounts

calendar year January 1 to December 31 a year between the calendar dates January 1 and December 31

call STOCKHOLDING & INVESTMENTS **1.** option to buy stock an **option** to buy stock at an agreed price or before a particular date. *Also called* ***call option*** **2.** demand for agreed partial payment of share capital a request made to the holders of partly paid-up share capital for the payment of a predetermined sum due on the share capital, under the terms of the original subscription agreement. Failure on the part of the stockholder to pay a call may result in the forfeiture of the relevant holding of partly paid shares. *Also called* ***call up***

callable STOCKHOLDING & INVESTMENTS able to be repurchased before maturity used to describe a security that the issuer has the right to buy back before its maturity date. *See also* ***noncallable***

callable bond STOCKHOLDING & INVESTMENTS bond able to be bought back a bond that may be bought back by the issuer prior to its maturity date

callable capital FINANCE capital from unpaid sale of stock the part of a company's capital from the sale of stock for which the company has not yet received payment

callable preferred stock *US* STOCKHOLDING & INVESTMENTS = ***redeemable preferred stock***

call center GENERAL MANAGEMENT department or business providing information by telephone a department or business wholly focused on telephone inquiries. Call centers usually provide a centralized point of contact for an organization and support telemarketing, after-sales service, telephone helplines, or information services, either for a parent organization or on a contract basis for other businesses.

call date STOCKHOLDING & INVESTMENTS pre-maturity deadline for repurchase of bond the date before maturity on which the issuer of a **callable bond** has the right to buy it back

called-up share capital STOCKHOLDING & INVESTMENTS stock not paid for by stockholders the proportion of the of stock issued by a company that has not yet been paid for. *See also* ***fully paid share capital***

call in BANKING request payment of debt to ask for a debt to be paid at once

call loan BANKING bank loan repayable on demand a bank loan that must be repaid as soon as repayment is requested

call option STOCKHOLDING & INVESTMENTS = ***call*** *(sense 1)*

call payment STOCKHOLDING & INVESTMENTS sum in partial payment for stock an amount that a company demands in partial payment for stock such as a rights issue that is not paid for at one time

call price STOCKHOLDING & INVESTMENTS early redemption cost of US bond a price to be paid by an issuer for the early redemption of a US bond

call provision STOCKHOLDING & INVESTMENTS clause allowing bond to be redeemed early a clause in an **indenture** that lets the issuer of a bond redeem it before the date of its maturity

call purchase FINANCE purchase where either party can establish price a transaction where either the seller or purchaser can fix the price for future delivery

call risk STOCKHOLDING & INVESTMENTS, RISK risk of premature repurchase of bond the possibility that the issuer of a **callable bond** will buy back the bond and the bondholder will be forced to reinvest at a lower interest rate

call rule MARKETS fixing of commodity price at end of trading a commodities exchange rule whereby the price of a commodity is fixed at the end of a day's trading and remains valid until the next trading day begins

calls in arrears STOCKHOLDING & INVESTMENTS outstanding money for shares money called up for shares, but not paid at the correct time. The shares may be forfeited or a special calls in arrears account is established to debit the sums owing.

call up STOCKHOLDING & INVESTMENTS = ***call*** *(sense 2)*

CAM *abbr* OPERATIONS & PRODUCTION computer-aided manufacturing

campaign MARKETING advertising and marketing plan a program of advertising and marketing activities with a specific objective

Canadian Institute of Chartered Accountants ACCOUNTING main professional body for accountants in Canada, the principal professional accountancy body that is responsible for setting accounting standards. *Abbr* **CICA**

cancellation price STOCKHOLDING & INVESTMENTS price at which mutual fund will redeem securities the lowest value possible in any one day of a mutual fund. In the United Kingdom, it is regulated by the **Financial Services Authority**.

cap FINANCE upper limit an upper limit such as on a rate of interest for a loan

CAPA *abbr* ACCOUNTING Confederation of Asian and Pacific Accountants

capacity OPERATIONS & PRODUCTION measure of production capability the measure of the capability of a workstation or a plant to produce output. Capacity measures can focus on a variety of factors, which typically include quantity (the number of items

  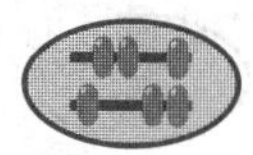 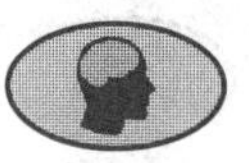  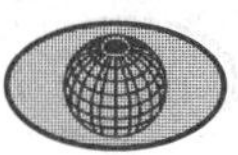   

produced over a given period) and scope (the range of items produced by type or size).

capacity planning OPERATIONS & PRODUCTION estimation of organization's requirements to meet workload the process of measuring the amount of work that can be completed within a given time and determining the necessary physical and human resources needed to accomplish it. Capacity planning uses **capacity utilization** to ensure that the maximum amount of product is made and sold. The planning involves a regulation process that identifies deviations from the plan, allowing corrective action to be taken. A **capacity requirements planning** program can aid in the process of capacity planning.

capacity requirements planning OPERATIONS & PRODUCTION computerized system for planning resource requirements a computerized tracking process that translates production requirements into practical implications for manufacturing resources. Capacity requirements planning is part of manufacturing resource planning and is carried out after a manufacturing resource planning program has been run. This produces an **infinite capacity plan**, as it does not take account of the capacity constraints of each workstation. Where the process is extended to cover capacity requirements, a **finite capacity plan** is produced. This enables **loading** at each workstation to be smoothed and determines the need for additional resources.

capacity usage variance FINANCE difference in result caused by working hours the difference in gain or loss in a given period compared to budgeted expectations, caused because the hours worked were longer or shorter than planned

capacity utilization 1. OPERATIONS & PRODUCTION measure of equipment actually used for production a measure of the plant and equipment of a company or an industry that is actually being used to produce goods or services. Capacity utilization is usually measured over a specific period of time, for example, the average for a month, or at a given point in time. It can be expressed as a ratio, where utilization = actual output divided by design capacity. This measure is used in both **capacity planning** and **capacity requirements planning** processes. **2.** ECONOMICS degree of production capability being used the output of an economy, firm, or plant divided by its output when working at full capacity

Caparo case ACCOUNTING English ruling on auditors' responsibilities in England, a court decision made by the House of Lords in 1990 that auditors owe a duty of care to present, not prospective, stockholders as a body but not as individuals

CAPEX *abbr* ACCOUNTING capital expenditure

capital FINANCE investment money money that is available to be invested by a person, business, or organization in order to make a profit

capital account FINANCE firm's total capital the sum of a company's **capital** at a specific time. *Abbr* **C/A**

capital adequacy ratio FINANCE percentage of bank's assets represented by capital an amount of money which a bank has to hold in the form of stockholders' equity, shown as a proportion of its risk-weighted assets, agreed internationally not to fall below 8%. *Abbr* **CAR**. *Also called* ***capital to risk-weighted assets ratio***

capital allowance TAX tax allowance for new plant and machinery in the United Kingdom and Ireland, an allowance against income or corporation tax available to businesses or sole traders who have purchased plant and machinery for business use. The rates are set annually and vary according to the type of fixed asset purchased, for example, whether it is machinery or buildings. This system effectively removes subjectivity from the calculation of depreciation for tax purposes.

capital appreciation FINANCE increase in wealth the increase in a company's or individual's wealth at market values

capital appreciation fund STOCKHOLDING & INVESTMENTS mutual fund concentrating on capital not income a mutual fund that aims to increase the value of its holdings without regard to the provision of income to its owners

capital asset ACCOUNTING real estate owned but not traded real estate that a company owns and uses but that the company does not buy or sell as part of its regular trade

capital asset pricing model STOCKHOLDING & INVESTMENTS theory about relationship between cost and expected return a model of the market used to assess the cost of capital for a company based on the rate of return on its assets.

The capital asset pricing model holds that the expected return on a security or portfolio equals the rate on a risk-free security plus a risk premium. If this expected return does not meet or beat a theoretical required return, the investment should not be undertaken. The formula used for the model is:

Risk-free rate + (Market return – Risk-free rate) × Beta value = Expected return

The risk-free rate is the quoted rate on an asset that has virtually no risk. In practice, it is the rate quoted for 90-day US Treasury bills. The market return is the percentage return expected of the overall market, typically a published index such as Standard & Poor's. The beta value is a figure that measures the volatility of a security or portfolio of securities compared with the market as a whole. A beta of 1, for example, indicates that a security's price will move with the market. A beta greater than 1 indicates higher volatility, while a beta less than 1 indicates less volatility.

Say, for instance, that the current risk-free rate is 4%, and the S&P 500 index is expected to return 11% next year. An investment club is interested in determining next year's return for XYZ Software, Inc., a prospective investment. The club has determined that the company's beta value is 1.8. The overall stock market always has a beta of 1, so XYZ Software's beta of 1.8 signals that it is a more risky investment than the overall market represents. This added risk means that the club should expect a higher rate of return than the 11% for the S&P 500. The CAPM calculation, then, would be:

4% + (11% – 4%) × 1.8 = 16.6% expected return

What the results tell the club is that, given the risk, XYZ Software, Inc. has a required rate of return of 16.6%, or the minimum return that an investment in XYZ should generate. If the investment club does not think that XYZ will produce that kind of return, it should probably consider investing in a different company. *Abbr* **CAPM**

capital base FINANCE funding structure as basis of firm's worth the funding structure of a company (**stockholders' equity** plus loans and retained profits) used as a way of assessing the company's worth

capital bonus INSURANCE extra payment arising from capital gain a bonus payment by an insurance company that is produced by **capital gain**

capital budget ACCOUNTING part of firm's budget concerned with capital expenditure a subsection of a company's master budget that deals with expected capital expenditure within a defined period. *Also called* ***capital expenditure budget, capital investment budget***

  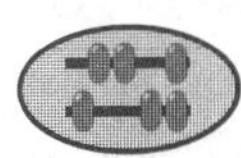   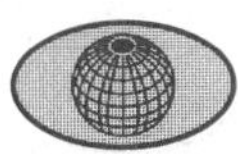   

capital budgeting TREASURY MANAGEMENT preparing budget for capital expenditure the process concerned with decision making with respect to the following issues: the choice of specific investment projects, the total amount of **capital expenditure** to commit, and the method of financing the investment portfolio

capital commitments ACCOUNTING authorized but unspent capital expenditure expenditure on assets which has been authorized by directors, but not yet spent at the end of a financial period

capital consumption FINANCE depreciation of fixed assets in a given period, the total depreciation of the fixed assets of a company or national economy, based on replacement costs

capital controls REGULATION & COMPLIANCE government restrictions on asset ownership regulations placed by a government on the amount of capital people may hold. Sometimes there are restrictions only on share ownership, at other times on bank accounts; also controls may apply to non-residents as well as residents.

capital cost allowance TAX Canadian tax benefit for capital depreciation in Canada, a tax advantage given for the depreciation in value of **capital assets**

capital costs ACCOUNTING expenses on buying fixed assets expenses associated with the purchase of fixed assets such as land, buildings, and machinery

capital deepening ECONOMICS increase in country's capital-to-labor ratio the process whereby capital increases but the number of employed people falls or remains constant

capital employed FINANCE stockholders' funds plus long-term loans an amount of **capital** consisting of **stockholders' equity** plus the long-term loans taken out by a business. *See also* ***return on assets***

capital equipment ACCOUNTING equipment used for everyday operations the equipment that a factory or office uses in operating its business

capital expenditure ACCOUNTING spending on fixed assets the cost of acquiring, producing, or enhancing fixed assets such as land, buildings, and machinery. *Abbr* **CAPEX**. *Also called* ***capital investment***

capital expenditure budget ACCOUNTING = ***capital budget***

capital expenditure proposal ACCOUNTING application for capital expenditure a formal request for authority to undertake **capital expenditure**. This is usually supported by the case for expenditure in accordance with capital investment appraisal criteria. Levels of authority must be clearly defined and the reporting structure of actual expenditure must be to the equivalent authority level.

capital flight STOCKHOLDING & INVESTMENTS withdrawal of investments from country the transfer of large sums of money between countries to seek higher rates of return or to escape a political or economic disturbance

capital flow STOCKHOLDING & INVESTMENTS international movement of money the movement of investments from one country to another. *Also called* ***capital movement***

capital formation STOCKHOLDING & INVESTMENTS adding to capital by investment the creation of long-term assets, such as long-dated bonds or shares

capital funding planning TREASURY MANAGEMENT determining of means to finance capital expenditure the process of selecting suitable funds to finance long-term assets and **working capital**

capital gain ACCOUNTING money made from disposing of asset the financial gain made upon the disposal of an asset. The gain is the difference between the cost of its acquisition and the net proceeds upon its sale.

capital gains distribution STOCKHOLDING & INVESTMENTS allocation of capital gains to investors a sum of money that a body such as a mutual fund pays to its owners in proportion to the owners' share of the organization's capital gains for the year

capital gains expenses ACCOUNTING cost of buying or selling assets expenses incurred in buying or selling assets, which can be deducted when calculating a capital gain or loss

capital gains reserve TAX Canadian tax benefit for customers' unpaid bills in Canada, a tax advantage given for money not yet received in payment for something that has been sold

capital gains tax TAX tax on difference between buying and selling price a tax on the difference between the gross acquisition cost and the net proceeds when an asset is sold. *Abbr* **CGT**

capital gearing STOCKHOLDING & INVESTMENTS firm's debt per share the amount of debt of all kinds that a company has for each share of its common stock

capital goods ECONOMICS assets used for producing other goods physical assets that are used in the production of other goods

capital growth FINANCE increase in value of assets an increase in the value of assets in a fund, or of the value of stock

capital inflow FINANCE money entering country from services overseas the amount of capital that flows into an economy from services rendered abroad

capital instrument FINANCE means of raising money a security such as stocks or **debentures** that a business uses to raise finance

capital-intensive FINANCE requiring money rather than labor used to describe economic activities that primarily require a high proportion of **capital** as opposed to needing labor. *See also* ***labor-intensive***

capital investment ACCOUNTING = ***capital expenditure***

capital investment budget ACCOUNTING = ***capital budget***

capitalism ECONOMICS economic system where citizens own means of production an economic and social system in which individuals can maximize profits because they own the means of production

capitalist FINANCE investor in business a person who invests **capital** in trade and industry, for profit

capitalist economy ECONOMICS economy giving great commercial and financial freedom an economy in which each person has the right to invest money, to work in business, and to buy and sell products and services, without major government restrictions

capitalization **1.** FINANCE raising funds through stock split the conversion of a company's reserves into **capital** through a stock split **2.** STOCKHOLDING & INVESTMENTS amount invested in firm the amount of money that is invested in a company **3.** STOCKHOLDING & INVESTMENTS firm's worth the worth of the bonds and stocks issued by a company

capitalization issue *UK* STOCKHOLDING & INVESTMENTS = ***stock split***

capitalization rate FINANCE rate of raising capital through stock split the rate at which a company's **reserves** are converted into **capital** by way of a **stock split**

capitalization ratio FINANCE proportion of firm's value in capital the proportion of a company's value represented by debt, stock, assets, and other items.

By comparing debt to total capitalization, these ratios provide a glimpse of a company's long-term stability and ability to withstand losses and business downturns.

A company's capitalization ratio can be expressed in two ways:

$$= \frac{\text{Long-term debt}}{\text{Long-term debt + Owners' equity}}$$

and

$$= \frac{\text{Total debt}}{\text{Total debt + Preferred + Common equity}}$$

For example, a company whose long-term debt totals $5,000 and whose owners hold equity worth $3,000 would have a capitalization ratio of:

$$\frac{5{,}000}{5{,}000 + 3{,}000} = \frac{5{,}000}{8{,}000} = 0.625$$

Both expressions of the ratio are also referred to as **component percentages**, since they compare a firm's debt with either its total capital (debt plus equity) or its equity capital. They readily indicate how reliant a firm is on debt financing. Capitalization ratios need to be evaluated over time, and compared with other data and standards. Care should be taken when comparing companies in different industries or sectors. The same figures that appear to be low in one industry can be very high in another.

capitalize **1.** FINANCE invest money in business to provide investment money for a business, in expectation of making a profit **2.** ACCOUNTING enter cost of asset in balance sheet to include money spent on the purchase of an **asset** as an element in a **balance sheet**

capital lease *US* REAL ESTATE lease treated as though leased assets were purchased a lease that is treated as though the lessee had borrowed money and bought the leased assets.

If a lease agreement does not meet any of the criteria below, the lessee treats it as an **operating lease** for accounting purposes. If, however, the agreement meets one of the following criteria, it is treated as a capital lease:

1. The lease agreement transfers ownership of the assets to the lessee during the term of the lease.

2. The lessee can purchase the assets leased at a bargain price (also called a bargain purchase option), such as $1, at the end of the lease term.

3. The lease term is at least 75% of the economic life of the leased asset.

4. The present value of the minimum lease payments is 90% or greater of the asset's value.

Capital leases are reported by the lessee as if the assets being leased were acquired and the monthly rental payments as if they were payments of principal and interest on a debt obligation. Specifically, the lessee capitalizes the lease by recognizing an asset and a liability at the lower of the present value of the minimum lease payments or the value of the assets under lease. As the monthly rental payments are made, the corresponding liability decreases. At the same time, the leased asset is depreciated in a manner that is consistent with other owned assets having the same use and economic life. *UK term* ***finance lease***

capital levy TAX tax on fixed assets a tax on fixed assets or property, rather than income. Capital levies are usually collected only once.

capital loss ACCOUNTING loss on sale of fixed asset a loss made through selling a **capital asset** for less than its market price

capital maintenance concept ACCOUNTING principle underpinning inflation accounting a concept used to determine the definition of profit, which provides the basis for different systems of **inflation accounting**

capital market MARKETS market for longer-term securities a financial market dealing with securities that have a life of more than one year

capital movement STOCKHOLDING & INVESTMENTS = ***capital flow***

capital outlay ACCOUNTING = ***capital expenditure***

capital profit ACCOUNTING profit from sale of asset a profit that a company makes by selling a **capital asset**

capital project OPERATIONS & PRODUCTION project requiring capital investment a project that involves expenditure of an organization's monetary resources for the purpose of creating capacity for production. Capital projects are usually large scale, complex, need to be completed quickly, and involve **capital expenditure**. *See also* ***capital project management***

capital project management GENERAL MANAGEMENT control of project requiring capital expenditure control of a project that involves expenditure of an organization's monetary resources for the purpose of creating capacity for production. Capital project management often involves the organization of major construction or engineering work. Different techniques have evolved for capital project management from those used for normal **project management**, including methods for managing the complexity of such projects and for analyzing return on investment afterward.

capital property ACCOUNTING, TAX type of asset under Canadian tax law under Canadian tax law, assets that can depreciate in value or be sold for a capital gain or loss

capital ratio ACCOUNTING firm's income as fraction of fixed assets a company's income expressed as a fraction of its **tangible assets**. These assets include leases and company stock, as well as physical assets such as land, buildings, and machinery.

capital rationing FINANCE **1.** firm's limiting of new investment the restriction of new investment by a company because of a shortfall in its capital budget **2.** imposition of limit on capital expenditure a restriction on an organization's ability to invest capital funds, caused by an internal budget ceiling being imposed by management (**soft capital rationing**), or by external limitations being applied to the company, as when additional borrowed funds cannot be obtained (**hard capital rationing**)

capital reconstruction MERGERS & ACQUISITIONS closing down then reconstituting firm the act of placing a company into voluntary liquidation and then selling its assets to another company with the same name and same stockholders, but with a larger capital base

capital redemption reserve ACCOUNTING in UK, firm's account underpinning trade in own stock in the United Kingdom, an account required by law to prevent a reduction in capital, where a company purchases or redeems its own stock out of **distributable profits**

capital reduction FINANCE withdrawal of capital funds the **retirement** or redemption of capital funds by a company

capital reorganization STOCKHOLDING & INVESTMENTS restructuring firm's share holdings the act of changing the capital structure of a company by amalgamating or dividing existing shares to form shares of a higher or lower nominal value

capital reserves FINANCE **1.** *UK* funds unavailable for dividend payments reserves not legally available for distribution to stockholders as dividends according to the Companies Act (1985) **2.** *US* funds for future investment money that a company holds in reserve for future investment or expense

capital resource planning TREASURY MANAGEMENT assessing assets for strategic

   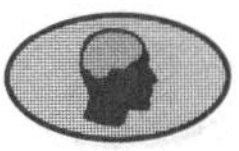  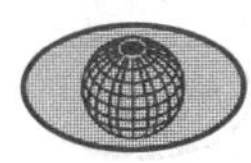   

purposes the process of evaluating and selecting long-term assets to meet established strategies

capital shares STOCKHOLDING & INVESTMENTS shares with increasing value but no income shares in a mutual fund that rise in value as the capital value of the individual stocks rises, but do not receive any income

capital stock STOCKHOLDING & INVESTMENTS stock authorized by US firm's charter in the United States, the stock authorized by a company's charter, including **common stock** and **preferred stock**. *See also* ***share capital***

capital structure ACCOUNTING relationship of equity capital and debt capital the relative proportions of **equity capital** and **debt capital** in a company's **balance sheet**

capital sum INSURANCE lump sum from insurance an amount of money that an insurer pays as a **lump sum** on the death of an insured person or some other agreed occurrence

capital surplus STOCKHOLDING & INVESTMENTS difference between current and nominal value of stock the value of all of the stock in a company that exceeds the **nominal value** of the stock

capital tax TAX tax on firm's capital a tax levied on the capital owned by a company, rather than on its spending. *See also* ***capital gains tax***

capital-to-asset ratio or **capital/asset ratio** FINANCE = ***capital adequacy ratio***

capital to risk-weighted assets ratio FINANCE = ***capital adequacy ratio***

capital transaction FINANCE transaction bearing on non-current items a transaction affecting non-current items such as fixed assets, long-term debt, or share capital, rather than revenue transactions

capital transfer tax TAX former UK tax on asset transfers in the United Kingdom, a tax on the transfer of assets, which was replaced in 1986 by inheritance tax

capital turnover FINANCE annual sales in relation to stock value the value of annual sales as a multiple of the value of a company's stock

capital widening ECONOMICS increase in country's capital per person employed the process whereby capital is increased as a result of an increase in the number of people being employed

CAPM *abbr* **1.** OPERATIONS & PRODUCTION computer-aided production management **2.** STOCKHOLDING & INVESTMENTS capital asset pricing model

capped floating rate note FINANCE floating rate note with limited interest rate a **floating-rate note** that has an agreed maximum rate of interest

capped rate FINANCE variable interest rate with upper limit an interest rate on a loan that may change, but cannot be greater than an amount fixed at the time when the loan is taken out by a borrower

captive finance company FINANCE provider of credit for customers of parent company an organization that provides credit and is owned or controlled by a commercial or manufacturing company, for example, a retailer that owns its store card operation or a car manufacturer that owns a company for financing the vehicles it produces

captive insurance company INSURANCE provider of insurance for customers of parent company an insurance company that has been established by a parent company to underwrite all its insurance risks and those of its subsidiaries. The benefit is that the premiums paid do not leave the organization. Many captive insurance companies are established offshore for tax purposes.

captive market MARKETS market with one supplier operating monopoly a market in which one supplier has a monopoly and the buyer has no choice over the product that he or she must purchase

capture E-COMMERCE transfer of funds in credit card transaction the submission of a credit card transaction for processing and settlement. Capture initiates the process of moving funds from the **issuer** to the **acquirer**.

CAR *abbr* FINANCE capital adequacy ratio

cardholder BANKING named user of credit card an individual or company that has an active credit card account with an **issuer** with which transactions can be initiated

card-issuing bank BANKING = ***issuer***

card-not-present merchant account E-COMMERCE account permitting online processing of credit card transactions an account that permits e-merchants to process credit card transactions without the purchaser being physically present for the transaction

cards ◇ get your cards *UK* HR & PERSONNEL = ***get your pink slip*** (*informal*)

careline MARKETING customer assistance telephone service a telephone service allowing customers to obtain information, advice, or assistance from retailers

caring economy ECONOMICS friendly relationships between firms and individuals an economy based on amicable and helpful relationships between businesses and people

carriage free *UK* OPERATIONS & PRODUCTION sent without charge to customer sent without making a charge to the customer for shipping

carriage inward OPERATIONS & PRODUCTION cost of having purchase delivered delivery expenses incurred through the purchase of goods. These may be separately itemized in financial statements.

carriage outward OPERATIONS & PRODUCTION cost of delivering purchase delivery expenses incurred through the sale of goods. These may be separately itemized in financial statements.

carriage paid *UK* OPERATIONS & PRODUCTION with shipping charge paid by seller sent by a seller who has paid for the shipping

carried interest FINANCE profit paid to private equity partners the profit that partners in a private equity enterprise receive for the services they provide

carrier OPERATIONS & PRODUCTION provider of network services to customers a telecommunications company that provides network infrastructure services and charges customers for carrying their communications over the network. Carriers do not necessarily own their own network, but may rent time on a number of networks.

carry FINANCE = ***carrying charge***

carry forward ACCOUNTING use as opening balance for next accounting period to use an account balance at the end of the current period or page as the starting point for the next period or page

carrying amount STOCKHOLDING & INVESTMENTS = ***book value*** (*sense 2*)

carrying charge FINANCE interest paid on money borrowed the interest expense on money borrowed to finance a purchase. *Also called* ***carry***

carrying cost OPERATIONS & PRODUCTION cost of temporarily holding stock any expense associated with holding stock for a given period, for example, from the time of delivery to the time of dispatch. Carrying costs will include storage and insurance.

carrying value STOCKHOLDING & INVESTMENTS = ***book value*** (*sense 2*)

carryover STOCKHOLDING & INVESTMENTS amount of commodity at beginning of fiscal year the amount of a commodity that is

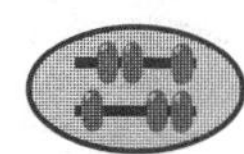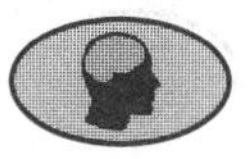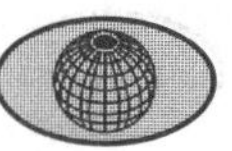

being held at the beginning of a new fiscal year, to be added to the next year's supply. The amount of carryover may have an impact on price.

carryover day MARKETS new account's first day on London Stock Exchange the first day of trading on a new account on the London Stock Exchange

carry trade MARKETS, CURRENCY & EXCHANGE borrowings in one currency purchasing assets in another the practice of borrowing at low interest rates in one currency and using the loan to buy assets offering higher yields in another country

cartel BUSINESS association to regulate competition an alliance of business companies formed to control production, competition, and prices

cartogram STATISTICS map showing statistical data a diagrammatic map on which statistical information is represented by shading and symbols

carve-out STOCKHOLDING & INVESTMENTS = ***equity carve-out***

cash BANKING **1.** exchange check for cash to present a check and receive banknotes and coins in return **2.** banknotes and coins money in the form of banknotes and coins that are legal tender. This includes cash in hand, deposits repayable on demand with any bank or other financial institution, and deposits denominated in foreign currencies.

cash account **1.** ACCOUNTING record of money transactions a record of receipts and payments of cash, checks, or other forms of money transfer **2.** STOCKHOLDING & INVESTMENTS type of brokerage account an account with a broker that does not allow **buying on margin**

cash accounting **1.** ACCOUNTING recording money transactions as they occur an accounting method in which receipts and expenses are recorded in the period when they actually occur. *See also* ***accrual basis*** **2.** TAX UK system giving automatic VAT relief on debts in the United Kingdom, a system for **value-added tax** that enables the taxpayer to account for tax paid and received during a given period, thus allowing automatic relief for bad debts

cash advance BANKING **1.** loan of cash against future payment a loan given in cash as early part payment of a larger sum to be received in the future **2.** loan on credit card a sum of money taken as a loan on a credit card account

cash at bank BANKING money in bank accounts the total amount of money held at the bank by a person or company

cash available to invest STOCKHOLDING & INVESTMENTS total amount available for investment with broker the amount, including cash on account and balances due soon for outstanding transactions, that a client has available for investment with a broker

cashback FINANCE **1.** giving purchaser cash refund a sales promotion technique offering customers a cash refund after they buy a product **2.** service allowing debit card payment to include cash a facility that allows consumers who pay for items by debit card in a supermarket or some other stores to add a small amount of money to the amount of their purchase and receive that amount in cash

cash balance ACCOUNTING account balance representing held cash only an account balance that represents cash alone, as distinct from an account balance that includes money owed but as yet unpaid

cash basis ACCOUNTING recording money in account only for actual transactions the bookkeeping practice of accounting for money only when it is actually received or spent

cash bonus STOCKHOLDING & INVESTMENTS extra dividend payment an unscheduled dividend that a company declares because of unexpected income

cashbook ACCOUNTING account book for cash transactions a book in which all cash payments and receipts are recorded. In a double-entry bookkeeping system, the balance at the end of a given period is included in the trial balance and then transferred to the balance sheet itself.

cash budget TREASURY MANAGEMENT estimate of cash transactions a detailed budget of estimated cash inflows and outflows incorporating both revenue and capital items. *Also called* ***cash flow projection***

cash burn FINANCE = ***burn rate***

cash card *UK* BANKING = ***ATM card***

cash contract OPERATIONS & PRODUCTION contract for delivery of product a contract for actual delivery of a commodity, by which the seller receives the **spot price** on the day of delivery

cash conversion cycle ACCOUNTING period between buying materials and selling product the time between the acquisition of a raw material and the receipt of payment for the finished product. *Also called* ***cash cycle***

cash cow **1.** FINANCE mature product generating cash a product characterized by a high market share but low sales growth, whose function is seen as generating cash for use elsewhere within the organization **2.** MARKETING very profitable product requiring little investment a product that sells well and makes a substantial profit without requiring much advertising or investment (*slang*) **3.** GENERAL MANAGEMENT slow-growing firm with high market share in the **Boston Box** model, a business with a high market share with low growth rate, which could yield significant but short-term gain. *See also* ***Boston Box***

cash crop ECONOMICS plants grown in quantity and sold for cash a crop such as tobacco, that is typically sold for cash rather than used by the producer

cash cycle ACCOUNTING = ***cash conversion cycle***

cash deficiency agreement FINANCE agreement to supply cash shortfall a commitment to supply whatever additional cash is needed to complete the financing of a project

cash discount FINANCE discount for paying promptly or in cash a discount offered to a customer who pays for goods or services with cash, or who pays an invoice within a particular period

cash dispenser *UK* BANKING = ***ATM***

cash dividend STOCKHOLDING & INVESTMENTS dividend in cash not shares a share of a company's current earnings or accumulated profits distributed to stockholders in cash, not in the form of **bonus shares**

cash economy ECONOMICS sector of economy avoiding tax an unofficial or illegal part of the economy, where goods and services are paid for in cash, and therefore not declared for tax

cash equivalents STOCKHOLDING & INVESTMENTS investments convertible into cash immediately short-term investments that can be converted into cash immediately and that are subject to only a limited risk. There is usually a limit on their duration, for example, three months.

cash float FINANCE banknotes and coins for giving change banknotes and coins held by a retailer for the purpose of supplying customers with change

cash flow ACCOUNTING money from sales the movement through an organization of money that is generated by its own operations, as opposed to borrowing. It is the money that a business actually receives from sales (the cash inflow) and the money that it pays out (the cash outflow).

  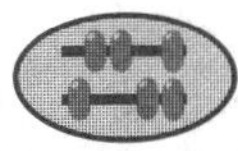   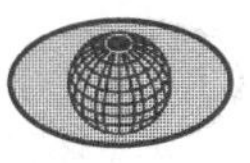   

cash flow accounting ACCOUNTING accounting that considers only cash receipts and payments the practice of measuring the financial activities of a company in terms of cash receipts and payments, without recording **accruals**, advance payments, debtors, creditors, and stocks

cash flow coverage ratio ACCOUNTING ratio of cash received and required the ratio of income to outstanding obligations which must be paid in cash

cash flow forecast TREASURY MANAGEMENT estimate of money coming in and going out a prediction of the amount of money that will move through an organization. This is an important tool for monitoring its solvency. *See also* ***cash budget***

cash flow life HR & PERSONNEL lifestyle dependent on income from project fees a lifestyle characterized by working for individual project fees rather than a regular salary

cash flow per common share STOCKHOLDING & INVESTMENTS cash generated for each share of common stock the amount of cash that a company derives from its activities, less any dividends paid, for each share of its common stock

cash flow projection TREASURY MANAGEMENT = ***cash budget***

cash flow risk RISK danger of receiving less cash than required the risk that a company's available cash will not be sufficient to meet its financial obligations

cash flow statement ACCOUNTING account of cash transactions a record of a company's cash inflows and cash outflows over a specific period of time, typically a year.

It reports funds on hand at the beginning of the period, funds received, funds spent, and funds remaining at the end of the period. Cash flows are divided into three categories: cash from operations; cash investment activities; and cash-financing activities. Companies with holdings in foreign currencies use a fourth classification: effects of changes in currency rates on cash.

cash fraction STOCKHOLDING & INVESTMENTS cash sum for allocation of part of share a small amount of cash paid to a stockholder to make up the full amount of part of a share which has been allocated in a **stock split**

cash-generating unit FINANCE smallest set of assets involved in cash transactions the smallest identifiable group of assets generating cash inflows and outflows that can be measured

cash hoard FINANCE, MERGERS & ACQUISITIONS = ***cash reserves*** *(informal)*

cashier *UK* BANKING = ***teller***

cashier's check BANKING check drawn by bank on itself a bank's own check, drawn on itself and signed by the cashier or other bank official

cash in STOCKHOLDING & INVESTMENTS sell investments for cash to sell stock or other property for cash

cash in hand FINANCE, ACCOUNTING available money money that is held in coins and banknotes, not in a bank account

cashless pay HR & PERSONNEL payment directly into bank account the payment of a weekly or monthly wage through the electronic transfer of funds directly into the bank account of an employee

cashless society ECONOMICS community in which all payments are electronic a society in which all bills and debits are paid by electronic money media such as bank and credit cards, direct debits, and online payments

cash limit 1. FINANCE fixed sum available to spend a fixed amount of money that can be spent during a specific period or on a specific project **2.** BANKING limit on single ATM withdrawal a maximum amount somebody can withdraw at one time from an ATM using an ATM card

cash loan company FINANCE S. African provider of unsecured short-term loans in South Africa, a **microcredit** business that provides short-term loans without collateral, usually at high interest rates

cash machine *UK* BANKING = ***ATM***

cash management OPERATIONS & PRODUCTION strategy for having cash available to produce income a strategy used by businesses to manage their cash flow in order to have more cash available for short-term investment. The strategy would include such things as accelerating cash receipts, prioritizing cash disbursements, and maintaining a cash balance to cover emergencies.

cash market MARKETS securities market based on immediate payment the market in **gilt-edged securities** where purchases are paid for almost as soon as they are made

cash offer FINANCE **1.** offer to buy firm for cash an offer to buy a company for cash rather than for stock **2.** offer of cash payment an offer to pay for something in cash

cash payments journal BANKING chronological record of payments from firm's bank account a chronological record of all the money paid out from a company's bank account

cashpoint *UK* BANKING = ***ATM***

cash position 1. ACCOUNTING amount of cash currently available to firm a statement of the amount of cash that a company currently has available to spend **2.** STOCKHOLDING & INVESTMENTS holdings in short-term debt the extent to which a portfolio of assets includes short-term debt securities

cash price FINANCE **1.** better deal offered to customer paying cash a lower price or better terms that apply to a sale if the customer pays cash rather than using credit **2.** = ***spot price***

cash ratio FINANCE liquid assets divided by total liabilities the ratio of a company's liquid assets such as cash and securities divided by total liabilities. *Also called* ***liquidity ratio***

cash receipts journal BANKING chronological record of deposits into firm's bank account a chronological record of all the receipts that have been paid into a company's bank account

cash reserves FINANCE, MERGERS & ACQUISITIONS available cash a large amount of cash that a company holds in order to facilitate an expected project. Cash reserves are often attractive to a company looking to make an acquisition. *Also called* ***cash hoard***

cash sale FINANCE sale paid for in cash a sale in which payment is made immediately in cash rather than put on credit

cash settlement STOCKHOLDING & INVESTMENTS **1.** early payment on options contract an immediate payment on an options contract without waiting for expiration of the normal, usually five-day, settlement period **2.** paying for securities bought the completion of a transaction by paying for securities, rather than physical delivery of them

cash surrender value INSURANCE sum received on cancellation of insurance policy the amount of money that an insurance company will pay to terminate a policy at a specific time if the policy does not continue until its normal expiration date

cash transaction FINANCE dealing involving cash payment a transaction in

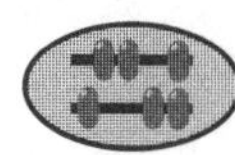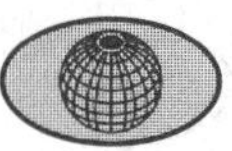

which the method of payment is cash, as distinct from a transaction paid for by means of a transfer of a **financial instrument**

cash voucher FINANCE document exchangeable for cash a piece of paper that can be exchanged for cash

casual worker HR & PERSONNEL worker who is not regular employee somebody who provides labor or services under an irregular or informal working arrangement. A casual worker is usually considered as an independent contractor rather than as an employee. Consequently, there is no obligation on the part of an employer to provide work, and there is no obligation on the part of the casual worker to accept all offers of work made by an employer.

catastrophe bond STOCKHOLDING & INVESTMENTS bond with lower value in event of disaster a bond with a very high interest rate which may be worth less or give a lower rate of interest if a disaster occurs, whether it be natural or otherwise

catastrophe future STOCKHOLDING & INVESTMENTS, RISK futures contract covering insurance losses from catastrophes a futures contract used by insurers to hedge their risk for low-probability catastrophic losses due to natural causes

catastrophe swap STOCKHOLDING & INVESTMENTS, RISK option contract covering insurance losses from catastrophes an option contract in which an investor exchanges a fixed periodic payment for part of the difference between an insurance company's premiums and its losses caused by claims due to a catastrophe

catch-up contribution PENSIONS extra payment to US pension in the United States, an additional contribution that somebody over the age of 50 is allowed to contribute to a personal retirement plan such as a **401(k) plan** or an **IRA**

category killer BUSINESS large business destroying competition a major organization that puts out of business smaller or more specialized companies in a given field by offering goods or services at a lower price, or by using its brand to attract more consumer interest (*slang*)

category management MARKETING product development involving both manufacturers and retailers the process of manufacturers and retailers working together to maximize profits and enhance customer value in any given product category. Category management has developed from **brand management** and the techniques of efficient consumer response, and is most prevalent in the fast moving consumer goods sector. It is founded on the assumption that consumer purchase decisions are made from a variety of products within a category and not merely by brand. It has gained in prominence, as it is believed to meet customer needs better than standard brand management. *Abbr* **CM**

cats and dogs *US* STOCKHOLDING & INVESTMENTS stocks with doubtful origins speculative stocks with dubious sales histories (*slang*)

cause and effect diagram GENERAL MANAGEMENT **1.** aid to identifying causes of variation a diagram that aids the generation and sorting of the potential causes of variation in an activity or process **2.** = ***fishbone chart***

caveat emptor BUSINESS buyer should check condition of goods purchased a Latin phrase meaning "let the buyer beware," which indicates that the buyer is responsible for checking that what he or she buys is in good condition

CBI *abbr* BUSINESS Confederation of British Industry

CBO *abbr* STOCKHOLDING & INVESTMENTS, RISK collateralized bond obligation

CC *abbr* BUSINESS close corporation (sense 2)

CCA *abbr* ACCOUNTING current cost accounting

ccc *UK* FINANCE public limited company the Welsh term for a public limited company. *Full form* ***cwmni cyfyngedig cyhoeddus***

CD *abbr* BANKING certificate of deposit

CDO *abbr* STOCKHOLDING & INVESTMENTS collateralized debt obligation

CDS *abbr* STOCKHOLDING & INVESTMENTS credit default swap

CDSC *abbr* STOCKHOLDING & INVESTMENTS contingent deferred sales charge

CEIC *abbr* BUSINESS closed-end investment company

ceiling upper limit the highest point that something can reach, for example, the highest rate of a pay increase

ceiling effect STATISTICS when statistical data groups near upper limit in a statistical study, the occurrence of clusters of scores near the upper limit of the data

cellular organization GENERAL MANAGEMENT independently functioning members of single organization a form of organization consisting of a collection of self-managing firms or cells held together by mutual interest. A cellular organization is built on the principles of self-organization, member ownership, and entrepreneurship. Each cell within the organization shares common features and purposes with its sister cells but is also able to function independently.

center *US* ACCOUNTING chargeable unit of organization a department, area, or function to which costs and/or revenues are charged

central bank ECONOMICS, BANKING bank controlling country's monetary system a bank that controls the credit system and money supply of a country

central bank discount rate BANKING central bank's rate for discounting bills the rate at which a central bank discounts bills such as **Treasury bills**

centralization FINANCE concentration of shared functions at main office the gathering together, at a corporate headquarters, of specialist functions such as finance, personnel, centralized purchasing, and information technology. Centralization is usually undertaken in order to effect economies of scale and to standardize operating procedures throughout the organization. Centralized management can become cumbersome and inefficient, and may produce communications problems. Some organizations have shifted toward **decentralization** to try to avoid this.

centralized purchasing OPERATIONS & PRODUCTION concentration of purchasing in single department the control by a central department of all the purchasing undertaken within an organization. In a large organization centralized purchasing is often located in the headquarters. Centralization has the advantages of reducing duplication of effort, pooling volume purchases for discounts, enabling more effective inventory control, consolidating transport loads to achieve lower costs, increasing skills development in purchasing personnel, and enhancing relationships with suppliers.

central planning ECONOMICS economy planned by government the use of an economic system in which the government plans all business activity, regulates supply, sets production targets, and itemizes work to be done

Central Provident Fund PENSIONS Singapore's retirement benefit plan in Singapore, a retirement benefit plan to which all employees and employers make

  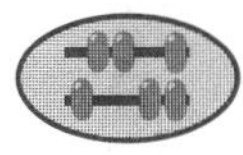 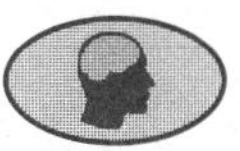  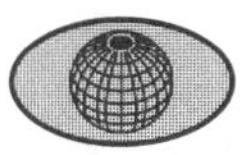   

compulsory contributions each month. *Abbr* **CPF**

central purchasing OPERATIONS & PRODUCTION purchasing through firm's main office purchasing organized by a company's main office on behalf of all its departments or branches

Central Registration Depository STOCKHOLDING & INVESTMENTS US searchable database of investment advisers and brokers a computerized database of brokers, investment advisers, and brokerage firms that is maintained by the US Securities and Exchange Commission and is accessible to the public. *Abbr* **CRD**

CEO *abbr* CORPORATE GOVERNANCE chief executive officer

CEO churning GENERAL MANAGEMENT, HR & PERSONNEL speed at which chief executive officers lose jobs the rapid rate at which chief executive officers are often removed from their positions (*slang*)

certain annuity PENSIONS annuity payable for limited number of years an annuity that will be paid for a specific number of years only

certificate STOCKHOLDING & INVESTMENTS document of share ownership a document representing partial ownership of a company which states the number of shares that the document is worth and the names of the company and the owner of the shares

certificate authority E-COMMERCE organization verifying identities of parties in online transactions an independent organization that verifies the identity of a purchaser or merchant and issues a **digital certificate** attesting to this for use in e-commerce transactions

certificate of deposit BANKING document giving guaranteed interest rate for deposit a document from a bank showing that money has been deposited at a guaranteed interest rate for a specific period of time. *Abbr* **CD**

certificate of incorporation LEGAL registration document of new company in UK in the United Kingdom, a written statement by the Registrar of Companies confirming that a new company has fulfilled the necessary legal requirements for incorporation and is now legally constituted

certificate of origin INTERNATIONAL TRADE document declaring origin of imported goods a document showing where imported goods come from or were made

certificate of tax deducted TAX UK statement of tax paid on interest in the United Kingdom, a document issued by a financial institution showing that tax has been deducted from interest payments on an account

certificate to commence business LEGAL authorizing document for UK public limited company in the United Kingdom, a written statement issued by the Registrar of Companies confirming that a public limited company has fulfilled the necessary legal requirements regarding its authorized minimum share capital

certified accountant ACCOUNTING UK accountant qualified by practical training in the United Kingdom, an accountant trained in industry, the public service, or in the offices of practicing accountants, who is a member of the **Association of Chartered Certified Accountants**. Such an accountant fulfills much the same role as a **chartered accountant** and is qualified to audit company records. *Abbr* **CA**

certified check BANKING check bank guarantees to pay a check that a bank guarantees is good and will be paid out of money put aside from the payer's bank account

certified public accountant ACCOUNTING US professional licensed accountant in the United States, an accountant who has passed the exam administered by the American Institute of Certified Public Accountants and has met all other educational and experience requirements to be licensed by the state in which he or she practices. Certified public accountants fulfill much the same role as **chartered accountants** in the United Kingdom and are qualified to audit company records. *Abbr* **CPA**

cessation LEGAL closing down of business the discontinuation of a business for tax purposes or of its trading on the stock market

ceteris paribus STATISTICS indicator of effect of one variable on another a Latin phrase meaning "all other things being equal", used to indicate that when considering the effect of one economic variable on another, all other factors that may affect the second variable remain constant

CFD *abbr* **1.** STOCKHOLDING & INVESTMENTS contract for difference (sense 1) **2.** CURRENCY & EXCHANGE contract for difference (sense 2)

CFO *abbr* TREASURY MANAGEMENT chief financial officer

CFR *abbr* OPERATIONS & PRODUCTION cost and freight

CFTC *abbr* REGULATION & COMPLIANCE Commodity Futures Trading Commission

CGT *abbr* TAX capital gains tax

CH *abbr* REGULATION & COMPLIANCE Companies House

chain of command GENERAL MANAGEMENT hierarchical structure for passing down instructions the line of authority in a hierarchical organization through which instructions pass. The chain of command usually runs from the most senior personnel, through all reporting links in an organization's or department's structure, to a targeted person or to frontline employees. **Line management** relies on the chain of command in order for instructions to pass throughout an organization.

chair CORPORATE GOVERNANCE *see* ***chairman***

chairman CORPORATE GOVERNANCE organization's highest executive the most senior executive in an organization, responsible for running the **annual meeting** and meetings of the **board of directors**. He or she may be a figurehead, appointed for prestige or power, and may have no role in the day-to-day running of the organization. Sometimes the roles of chairman and **chief executive officer** are combined, and the chairman then has more control over daily operations; sometimes the chairman is a retired chief executive. In the United States, the person who performs this function is often called a **president**. Historically, the term **chairman** was more common. The terms **chairwoman** or **chairperson** are later developments, although **chair** is now the most generally acceptable. Chairman, however, remains in common use, especially in the corporate sector.

chairman's report or **chairman's statement** CORPORATE GOVERNANCE chair's review of year's performance and prospects a statement included in the annual report of most large companies in which the chair of the board of directors gives an often favorable overview of the company's performance and prospects

chairperson CORPORATE GOVERNANCE *see* ***chairman***

chairwoman CORPORATE GOVERNANCE woman who is organization's highest executive a woman who is the most senior executive in an organization, responsible for running the **annual meeting**, and meetings of the **board of directors**. *See also* ***chairman***

chamber of commerce BUSINESS association of local businesspeople an

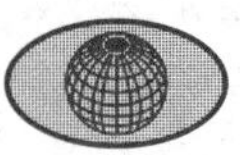

organization of local businesspeople who work together to promote trade in their area and protect common interests

Chancellor of the Exchequer FINANCE UK's chief finance minister the United Kingdom's senior finance minister, based at **HM Treasury** in London. The office of Chancellor dates back to the 13th century. Some of the most famous names in British politics have served in this very senior government position, including William Gladstone and Lloyd George.

change agent GENERAL MANAGEMENT administrator of major and minor changes in organization a person in an organization who is a leader in the process of change. *See also* ***change management***

change management GENERAL MANAGEMENT administration of major and minor changes in organization the coordination of a structured period of transition from situation A to situation B in order to achieve lasting change within an organization. Change management can be of varying scope, from **continuous improvement**, which involves small ongoing changes to existing processes, to radical and substantial change involving organizational strategy. Change management can be reactive or proactive. It can be instigated in reaction to something in an organization's external environment, for example, in the realms of economics, politics, legislation, or competition, or in reaction to something within the processes, structures, people, and events of the organization's internal environment. It may also be instigated as a proactive measure, for example, in anticipation of unfavorable economic conditions in the future. Change management usually follows five steps: recognition of a trigger indicating that change is needed; clarification of the end point, or "where we want to be"; planning how to achieve the change; accomplishment of the transition; and maintenance to ensure the change is lasting. Effective change management involves alterations on a personal level, for example, a shift in attitudes or work routines, and thus personnel management skills such as motivation are vital to successful change. Other important influences on the success of change management include leadership style, communication, and a unified positive attitude to the change among the workforce. **Business process reengineering** is one type of change management, involving the redesign of processes within an organization to raise performance. With the accelerating pace of change in the business environment in the 1990s and 2000s, change has become accepted as a fact of business life and is the subject of books on management.

channel MARKETING way of selling products directly or through others a method of selling and distributing products to customers, directly or through intermediaries. Channels include direct sales, retail outlets, the Internet, and wholesalers.

channel communications MARKETING communications targeting customer sales organizations communications aimed at organizations that sell and distribute products to customers, for example, retailers, sales teams, or wholesalers

channel management MARKETING process of identifying, reaching, and satisfying customers the organization of the ways in which companies reach and satisfy their customers. Channel management involves more than just distribution, and has been described as management of how and where a product is used and of how the customer and the product interact. Channel management covers processes for identifying key customers, communicating with them, and continuing to create value after the first contact.

channel of distribution OPERATIONS & PRODUCTION = ***distribution channel***

channel strategy MARKETING plan for effectively getting products to customers a management technique for determining the most effective method of selling and distributing products to customers

channel stuffing FINANCE making special offers at end of fiscal year the artificial boosting of sales at the end of a fiscal year by offering distributors and dealers incentives to buy a greater quantity of goods than they actually need (*slang*)

channel support MARKETING marketing or financial support for customer sales organizations marketing or financial support aimed at improving the performance of organizations that sell and distribute products to customers, for example, retailers, sales teams, or wholesalers

chaos GENERAL MANAGEMENT situation in which change happens quickly and unexpectedly a situation of unpredictability and rapid change

chaos theory GENERAL MANAGEMENT belief in randomness of change the theory that behavior is essentially random. It emerged in the 1970s as a mathematical concept that defied the theory of cause and effect. Writers have applied the theory to management, arguing that attempts to plan and control management processes are fundamentally doomed to failure and that, instead, managers should embrace change and flexibility in order to cope with an environment that is altering at an ever-increasing rate.

CHAPS BANKING means of rapid electronic transfer of substantial funds a method for the rapid electronic transfer of funds between participating banks on behalf of large commercial customers, where transfers tend to be of significant value. *Full form* ***Clearing House Automated Payment System***

Chapter 7 LEGAL part of US Bankruptcy Act regulating liquidation process a section of the US Bankruptcy Reform Act 1978, that sets out the rules for liquidation, a choice available to individuals, partnerships, and corporations

Chapter 11 LEGAL US act protecting potential bankrupts the US Bankruptcy Reform Act (1978) that entitles enterprises experiencing financial difficulties to apply for protection from creditors and thus have an opportunity to avoid bankruptcy

charge LEGAL legal interest in land as surety to creditor a legal interest in land or real estate created in favor of a creditor to ensure that the amount owing is paid off

chargeable asset TAX type of asset liable to capital gains tax an asset that will produce a **capital gain** when sold. Assets that are not chargeable include family homes, cars, and some types of investments such as government stocks.

chargeable gain *UK* TAX = ***taxable gain***

chargeable transfer TAX gifts liable to UK inheritance tax in the United Kingdom, gifts that are liable to **inheritance tax**

charge account FINANCE arrangement for customer to buy on credit a facility with a retailer that enables the customer to buy goods or services on credit rather than pay in cash. The customer may be required to settle the account within a month to avoid incurring interest on the credit. *Also called* ***credit account***

charge and discharge accounting ACCOUNTING former bookkeeping system formerly, a bookkeeping system in which a person charges himself or herself with receipts and credits himself or herself with payments. This system was used extensively before the advent of double-entry bookkeeping.

charge card FINANCE card used for buying store items on account a card issued to

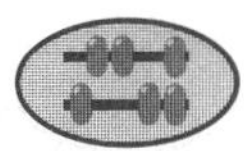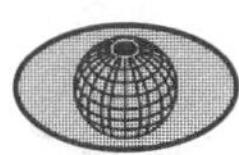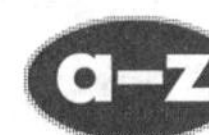

customers by a store, bank, or other organization, used to charge purchases to an account for later payment. *See also* ***credit card***

chargee FINANCE **1.** creditor with legal interest in land a person who holds a **charge** over a property, and who therefore has first claim on proceeds from the sale of the property **2.** person with enforcement rights a person who has the right to force a debtor to pay

charge off ACCOUNTING unrepeated expense or bad debt an uncollectable debt or a one-time expense that appears on a company's income statement

charitable contribution ACCOUNTING firm's gift to charity a donation by a company to a charity, deductible against tax

charity accounts ACCOUNTING records of charity's financial activities the accounting records of a charitable institution, which include a statement of financial activities rather than a profit and loss account. In the United Kingdom, the accounts should conform to the requirements stipulated in the Charities Act (1993).

charter LEGAL legal document creating US corporation in the United States, a legal document that creates a corporation and sets forth its purpose and structure according to the laws of the state in which it is established. *Also called* ***articles of incorporation***

chartered accountant ACCOUNTING UK accountant qualified by professional examination in the United Kingdom, a qualified professional accountant who is a member of an Institute of Chartered Accountants. Chartered accountants are qualified to audit company accounts and some hold management positions in companies. *Abbr* **CA**

Chartered Association of Certified Accountants ACCOUNTING formerly, UK certified accountants' association the former name of the **Association of Chartered Certified Accountants** in the United Kingdom

chartered bank BANKING N. American bank established by government charter in the United States and Canada, a bank that has been set up by government charter

chartered company or **chartered entity** BUSINESS UK organization founded by royal charter in the United Kingdom, an organization formed by the grant of a royal charter. The charter authorizes the entity to operate and states the powers specifically granted.

Chartered Institute of Management Accountants ACCOUNTING *see* ***CIMA***

Chartered Institute of Public Finance and Accountancy ACCOUNTING *see* ***CIPFA***

Chartered Institute of Taxation TAX UK organization for tax professionals in the United Kingdom, an organization for professionals in the field of taxation

charter value BANKING worth of bank's capacity to continue operating the value of a bank being able to continue to do business in the future, reflected as part of its share price

charting MARKETS stock market analysis based on charts the use of charts to analyze stock market trends and to forecast future rises or falls

chartist MARKETS stock market analyst employing charts an analyst who studies past stock market trends, the movement of stock prices, and changes in the accounting ratios of individual companies. The chartist's philosophy is that history repeats itself: using charts and graphs, he or she uses past trends and repetitive patterns to forecast the future. Although the chartist approach is considered narrower than that of a traditional analyst, it nevertheless has a good following.

chase demand plan OPERATIONS & PRODUCTION plan for matching output to customer demand a production control plan that attempts to match capacity to the varying levels of forecast demand. Chase demand plans require flexible working practices and place varying demands on equipment requirements. Pure chase demand plans are difficult to achieve and are most commonly found in operations where output cannot be stored or where the organization is seeking to eliminate stores of finished goods.

chattel mortgage MORTGAGES money borrowed using personal items as security money that is borrowed using an item of personal property, not land or buildings, as collateral

cheap money FINANCE money lent at low interest money that is lent at low interest rates, used as a government strategy to stimulate an economy either at the initial signs of, or during, a recession. *Also called* ***easy money***. *See also* ***dear money***, ***expansionary monetary policy***

check *US* BANKING written instruction to bank to pay money an order in writing requiring the banker to pay on demand a specific sum of money to a specified person or bearer. Although a check can theoretically be written on anything (in a P. G. Woodhouse story, one was written on the side of a cow), banks issue preprinted, customized forms for completion by an account holder who inserts the date, the name of the person to be paid (the payee), the amount in both words and figures, and his or her signature. The customer is the drawer. *UK term* ***cheque***

checkbook *US* BANKING book of blank cheques a booklet with new blank checks for a bank's customer to complete. *UK term* ***cheque book***

check card *US* BANKING = ***debit card***

check digit BANKING reference number for validating transactions the last digit of a string of computerized reference numbers, used to validate a transaction

checking account *US* BANKING flexible bank account with easy withdrawal a bank account in which deposits can be withdrawn at any time by writing checks but do not usually earn interest, except in the case of some online accounts. It is the most common type of bank account. *Abbr* **c/a**. *UK term* ***current account***

check register *US* BANKING record of check transactions a control record of checks issued or received, maintained by a person or organization. *UK term* ***cheque register***

check routing symbol BANKING number on US check identifying Federal Reserve district a number shown on a US check that identifies the Federal Reserve district through which the check will be cleared

check stub *US* BANKING part of check left in checkbook a piece of paper left in a checkbook after a check has been written and taken out. *UK term* ***cheque stub***

check to bearer *US* BANKING = ***bearer check***

cheque *UK* BANKING = ***check***

cheque book *UK* BANKING = ***checkbook***

cheque card BANKING UK card guaranteeing payment of check a plastic card from a UK bank that guarantees payment of a check up to some amount, even if the user has no money in his or her account

cheque register *UK* BANKING = ***check register***

cheque stub *UK* BANKING = ***check stub***

cheque to bearer *UK* BANKING = ***bearer check***

  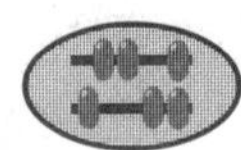   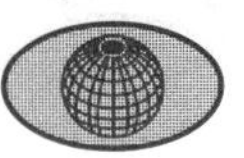   

cherry picking GENERAL MANAGEMENT selecting the best of available options the selection of what is perceived to be the best or most valuable from a series of ideas or options

Chicago Mercantile Exchange MARKETS Chicago exchange trading in futures a leading exchange for futures contracts based in Chicago. Its main product areas are interest rates, stock indexes, foreign exchange, and commodities. *Abbr* **CME**

Chicago School ECONOMICS school of conservative economic thought a school of conservative economic thought, promoting free markets and capitalism and relying heavily on mathematical analysis. It is associated with the University of Chicago and was for many years led by Professor Milton Friedman.

chief executive officer or **chief executive** CORPORATE GOVERNANCE executive ultimately responsible for firm's management the person with overall responsibility for ensuring that the daily operations of an organization run efficiently and for carrying out strategic plans. The chief executive of an organization normally sits on the **board of directors**. In a limited company, he or she is usually known as a managing director. *Abbr* **CEO**

chief financial officer TREASURY MANAGEMENT executive responsible for firm's financial management the officer in an organization responsible for handling funds, signing checks, the keeping of financial records, and financial planning for the company. *Abbr* **CFO**

chief information officer GENERAL MANAGEMENT executive responsible for firm's internal information systems the officer in an organization responsible for its internal information systems and sometimes for its e-business infrastructure. *Abbr* **CIO**

chief operating officer GENERAL MANAGEMENT executive responsible for firm's day-to-day operations the officer in a corporation responsible for its day-to-day management, usually reporting to the chief executive officer. *Abbr* **COO**

Chief Secretary to the Treasury FINANCE UK government minister controlling public expenditure in the United Kingdom, a government minister responsible to the Chancellor of the Exchequer for the control of public expenditure

Chinese wall STOCKHOLDING & INVESTMENTS obstacle to exchange of inside information the procedures enforced within a securities firm to prevent the exchange of confidential information between the firm's departments so as to avoid the illegal use of inside information

CHIPS BANKING US international wire transfer system in the United States, the computerized domestic and international wire transfer system that also serves to convert all pending payments into a single transaction. *Full form* ***Clearing House Interbank Payments System***

CHIS *abbr* FRAUD covert human intelligence source

chit GENERAL MANAGEMENT **1.** official note an official note or document, usually signed by somebody in authority **2.** receipt a receipt for something or a statement of money owed

chose in action FINANCE personal right treated like property a personal right such as a patent, copyright, debt, or check that can be enforced or claimed as if it were property

chose in possession FINANCE object that can be owned a physical item such as a piece of furniture that can be owned

churn 1. STOCKHOLDING & INVESTMENTS encourage investor to change portfolio frequently to encourage an investor to change stock frequently because the broker is paid every time there is a change in the investor's portfolio (*slang*) **2.** INSURANCE encourage somebody to change insurance policy to encourage a client to change his or her insurance policy solely to earn the salesperson a commission **3.** GENERAL MANAGEMENT successive purchases of different brands of products to purchase a quick succession of products or services without displaying loyalty to any of them, often as a result of competitive marketing strategies that continually undercut rival prices, thus encouraging customers to switch brands constantly in order to take advantage of the cheapest or most attractive offers **4.** HR & PERSONNEL experience high employee turnover to suffer a high turnover rate of executives or other employees

churn rate 1. STOCKHOLDING & INVESTMENTS measure of change in investment portfolio a measure of the frequency and volume of trading of stocks and bonds in a brokerage account **2.** GENERAL MANAGEMENT rate at which customers abandon new product the rate at which new customers try a product or service and then stop using it

CICA *abbr* ACCOUNTING Canadian Institute of Chartered Accountants

CIF *abbr* OPERATIONS & PRODUCTION cost, insurance, and freight

CIFAS *abbr* FRAUD Credit Industry Fraud Avoidance System

CIMA ACCOUNTING UK institution awarding financial degree to businesspeople a UK organization that is internationally recognized as offering a financial degree for business, focusing on strategic business management. Founded in 1919 as the Institute of Cost and Works Accountants, it has offices worldwide, supporting over 128,000 members and students in 156 countries. *Full form* ***Chartered Institute of Management Accountants***

CIO *abbr* GENERAL MANAGEMENT chief information officer

CIPFA ACCOUNTING UK professional accountancy organization in the United Kingdom, one of the leading professional accountancy bodies and the only one that specializes in the public services, for example, local government, public service bodies, and national audit agencies, as well as major accounting firms. It is responsible for the education and training of professional accountants and for their regulation through the setting and monitoring of professional standards. CIPFA also provides a variety of advisory, information, and consulting services to public service organizations. It is the leading independent commentator on managing accounting for public money. *Full form* ***Chartered Institute of Public Finance and Accountancy***

circuit breaker MARKETS US provision for stopping trading a rule created by the major US stock exchanges and the **Securities and Exchange Commission** by which trading is halted during times of extreme price fluctuations (*slang*)

circular file GENERAL MANAGEMENT office wastebasket a wastebasket in an office (*slang*)

circular flow of income ECONOMICS model of relationship between income and spending a model of a country's economy showing the flow of resources when consumers' wages and salaries are used to buy goods and so generate income for manufacturing firms

circularization of debtors ACCOUNTING auditors' approach to debtors to identify assets the sending of letters by a company's auditors to debtors in order to verify the existence and extent of the company's assets

circular letter of credit BANKING bank's authorization of payment to every branch a letter of credit sent to all branches of the bank which issues it

  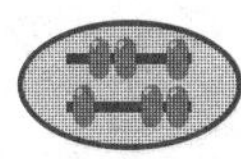 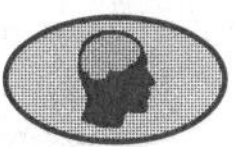  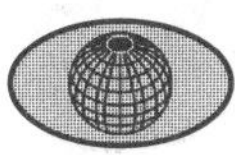   

circular merger MERGERS & ACQUISITIONS joining of firms sharing distribution channels a merger involving firms that have different products but similar distribution channels. *See also* ***merger***

circulating capital FINANCE = ***working capital***

circulation MARKETING number of copies of newspaper or magazine sold the number of copies sold or distributed of a single issue of a newspaper or magazine

circulation of capital FINANCE transfer of capital between investments the movement of **capital** from one investment to another, or between one country and another

City or **City of London** FINANCE area of London containing UK financial center the United Kingdom's financial center found in the historic center of London, where most banks and many large companies have their main offices. *See also* ***Wall Street***

City bonus FINANCE annual financial reward for UK employee a very large sum of money, in addition to salary, paid to an employee in London's financial industry for effective performance in increasing his or her company's profits. *See also* ***Wall Street bonus***

City Code on Takeovers and Mergers MERGERS & ACQUISITIONS UK code for fairness in takeovers in the United Kingdom, a code issued on behalf of the **City Panel on Takeovers and Mergers** that is designed principally to ensure fair and equal treatment of all stockholders in relation to **takeovers**. The Code also provides an orderly framework within which takeovers are conducted. It is not concerned with the financial or commercial advantages or disadvantages of a takeover, nor with issues such as competition policy which are the responsibility of the government. The Code represents the collective opinion of those professionally involved in the field of takeovers on how fairness to stockholders can be achieved in practice.

City Panel on Takeovers and Mergers MERGERS & ACQUISITIONS independent UK group supervising takeovers in the United Kingdom, an independent nonstatutory group whose job is to supervise and regulate **takeovers** according to the **City Code on Takeovers and Mergers**. *Also called* ***Takeover Panel***

City watchdog REGULATION & COMPLIANCE = ***Financial Services Authority*** *(informal)*

claim LEGAL statement of entitlement to money an official request for money, usually in the form of compensation, from a person or organization

claimant FINANCE somebody who makes benefit claim to government a person who claims a government benefit such as an unemployment or disability benefit

claim form INSURANCE form completed to make insurance claim a form that has to be filled in giving details of the reason for making an insurance claim

claims adjuster *US* INSURANCE assessor of insurance claims somebody who determines the value of a claim made under an insurance policy. *UK term* ***loss adjuster***

claims manager INSURANCE person responsible for insurance claims the person responsible for dealing with claims in an insurance company

class STOCKHOLDING & INVESTMENTS classification for common stock a type of common stock issued by a company, usually with the designations A and B, and conferring different voting rights

class action LEGAL joint civil law action a civil law action taken by a group of individuals who have a common grievance against an individual, organization, or legal entity

classical economics ECONOMICS economic theory stressing importance of free enterprise a theory focusing on the functioning of a market economy and providing a rudimentary explanation of consumer and producer behavior in particular markets. The theory postulates that, over time, the economy would tend to operate at full employment because increases in supply would create corresponding increases in demand.

classical system of corporation tax TAX system doubly taxing firm's income a system in which companies and their owners are liable for **corporation tax** as separate entities. A company's taxed income is therefore paid out to stockholders, who are in turn taxed again. This system operates in the United States and the Netherlands. It was replaced in the United Kingdom in 1973 by an **imputation system**.

classified stock STOCKHOLDING & INVESTMENTS US firm's common stock divided into classes in the United States, a company's **common stock** divided into classes such as Class A and Class B

class interval STATISTICS division of statistical frequency distribution in a set of statistical observations, any of the intervals of the frequency distribution

class of assets ACCOUNTING categorization of assets the grouping of similar assets into categories. This is done because, under International Accounting Standards Committee rules, **tangible assets** and **intangible assets** cannot be revalued on an individual basis, only within a class of assets.

claw back FINANCE take back money previously allocated to recover money that has already been assigned to a specific use, especially money given in grants or tax incentives

clawback 1. FINANCE money reclaimed money taken back, especially money taken back by the government from grants or tax incentives which had previously been made **2.** MARKETS allocation of new stock to existing stockholders the allocation of new shares of stock to existing stockholders, so as to maintain the value of their holdings

clean float CURRENCY & EXCHANGE exchange rate unrestricted by government a **floating exchange rate** that is allowed to vary without any intervention from the country's monetary authorities

clean opinion or **clean report** ACCOUNTING auditor's report without reservations an auditor's report that is not qualified because of concern about the scope or treatment of some matter

clean price MARKETS bond price not including interest the price of a bond excluding accrued interest

clean surplus concept FINANCE advocating statements showing all gains and losses the idea that a company's income statement should show the totality of gains and losses, without any of them being taken directly to equity

clear OPERATIONS & PRODUCTION sell cheaply to get rid of merchandise to sell goods at a discounted price in order to dispose of inventory

clearance certificate INTERNATIONAL TRADE document giving goods customs clearance a document showing that goods have been passed by customs

clearing 1. BANKING process of passing check through banking system an act of passing of a check through the banking system, including the transfer of money from one account to another **2.** MARKETS completion of transactions and payments the process of verifying and settling orders between buyers and sellers in securities transactions

clearing bank BANKING in UK, bank employing clearing house in the United

  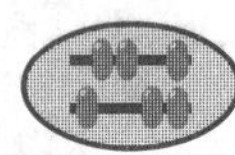   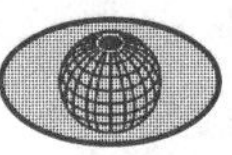   

Kingdom, a bank that deals with other banks through a **clearing house**

clearing house or **clearing firm** or **clearing corporation** 1. BANKING institution handling bank transactions an institution that settles accounts between banks, using the **clearing system** 2. MARKETS institution handling securities transactions an organization that coordinates the confirmation, delivery, and settlement of securities transactions on behalf of exchanges 3. E-COMMERCE = ***acquirer*** *(sense 2)*

Clearing House Automated Payment System BANKING *see* ***CHAPS***

Clearing House Interbank Payments System BANKING *see* ***CHIPS***

clearing system BANKING system for handling bank transactions the system of settling accounts among banks through **clearing houses**. It allows member banks to offset claims against each other.

clear profit FINANCE profit after paying expenses the profit remaining after all expenses have been paid

clear title LEGAL = ***good title***

clerical error mistake in preparing documents a mistake made in the preparation of documents such as reports or financial accounts

clickable corporation E-COMMERCE firm operating online a company that operates on the Internet. The term was popularized by a 1999 book by Jonathan Rosenoer, Douglas Armstrong, and J. Russell Gates.

click rate E-COMMERCE = ***click-through rate***

clicks-and-bricks or **clicks-and-mortar** E-COMMERCE organization with physical facility that also operates online combining a traditional **bricks-and-mortar** organization with the click technology of the Internet. Such an organization has both a virtual and a physical presence. Examples include retailers with physical stores and also websites where their goods can be bought online.

clickstream E-COMMERCE record of activity left by user surfing Web the virtual trail that a user leaves behind while surfing the Internet. A clickstream is a record of a user's activity on the Internet, including every Web page visited, how long each page is visited for, and the order in which the pages are visited. Both Internet service providers and individual websites are able to track an Internet user's clickstream.

click-through rate E-COMMERCE using click-throughs as measure of success of ad the percentage of viewings of an advertisement that result in a click on an on-screen device to take the user to the advertiser's website, which is a measure of the success of the advertisement. *Also called* ***ad click rate, click rate***

click wrap agreement or **click wrap license** E-COMMERCE contract agreed to online a contract presented entirely over the Internet, the purchaser indicating assent to be bound by the terms of the contract by clicking on an "I agree" button. The term stems from "shrink wrap" agreements, licenses that become enforceable when the user removes designated packaging containing a copy of the agreement. *Also called* ***point and click agreement***

client MARKETING 1. somebody hiring professional services a person or organization that employs the services of a professional person or organization 2. customer a person or organization to whom goods or services are provided or sold

client base MARKETING professional's steady clients the group of regular clients of a professional person or organization

clientele effect STOCKHOLDING & INVESTMENTS influence of investors on choice of securities the preference of an investor or group of investors for buying a particular type of security

Clintonomics ECONOMICS Clinton's policy of economic intervention the policy of former President Clinton's Council of Economic Advisers to intervene in the economy to correct market failures and redistribute income

CLO *abbr* STOCKHOLDING & INVESTMENTS collateralized loan obligation

CLOB International MARKETS Singaporean facility for trading in foreign stocks in Singapore, a mechanism for buying and selling foreign stocks, especially Malaysian stocks

clone fund STOCKHOLDING & INVESTMENTS mutual fund matching established fund by using derivatives a mutual fund that, by the use of derivatives, is able to duplicate the strategy and performance of a successful established mutual fund

close 1. MARKETS end of stock trading for day the end of a day's trading on a stock exchange 2. MARKETS have a particular price at end of trading of a stock, to end the day's trading at a particular price 3. US REAL ESTATE pay balance on real estate to pay off the balance owed on real estate in exchange for a deed showing ownership of the real estate. *UK term* ***complete*** ◇ close a position MARKETS to arrange affairs so that there is no longer any liability to pay, for example, by selling all securities held ◇ close the accounts FINANCE to come to the end of an accounting period and make up the profit and loss account

close company or **closed company** *UK* BUSINESS = ***close corporation***

close corporation or **closed corporation** BUSINESS 1. *US* public corporation controlled by few shareholders a public corporation in which all of the voting stock is held by a few stockholders, for example, management or family members. Although it is a public company, stock would not normally be available for trading because of a lack of liquidity. *UK term* ***close company*** 2. S. African business controlled by 10 or fewer in South Africa, a business registered in terms of the Close Corporations Act of 1984, consisting of not more than 10 members who share its ownership and management. *Abbr* **CC**

closed economy ECONOMICS economic system isolated from international trade an economic system in which little or no external trade takes place

closed-end credit FINANCE credit with fixed date for full repayment a loan, plus any interest and finance charges, that is to be repaid in full by a specific future date. Loans that have real estate or motor vehicles as collateral are usually closed-end. *See also* ***open-end credit***

closed-end fund or **closed-end investment company** STOCKHOLDING & INVESTMENTS investment company with fixed number of shares an investment company such as an investment trust that has a fixed number of shares that can be bought and sold in the marketplace. *See also* ***open-end fund***

closed-end mortgage MORTGAGES mortgage that cannot be paid off early a mortgage with an **indenture** disallowing repayment before it comes to maturity. *See also* ***open-end mortgage***. *Also called* ***closed mortgage***

closed fund STOCKHOLDING & INVESTMENTS mutual fund in US closed to new investors in the United States, a mutual fund that is no longer accepting new investors, because it has become too large

closed-loop production system OPERATIONS & PRODUCTION system of recycling industrial output into new product an environmentally friendly production

     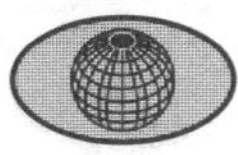   

system in which any industrial output is capable of being recycled to create another product

closed-loop system GENERAL MANAGEMENT management control system allowing correction a management control system which includes a provision for corrective action, taken on either a feed forward or a feedback basis

closed market OPERATIONS & PRODUCTION market with supplier dealing exclusively with agent or distributor a market in which a supplier deals only with one agent or distributor and does not supply any others direct

closed mortgage MORTGAGES = ***closed-end mortgage***

closely held corporation BUSINESS US public company with few stockholders in the United States, a company whose stock is publicly traded but held by very few people

closely held shares STOCKHOLDING & INVESTMENTS publicly traded US stock with few holders in the United States, stock that is publicly traded but held by very few people

Closer Economic Relations agreement INTERNATIONAL TRADE = ***Australia and New Zealand Closer Economic Relations Trade Agreement***

closing *US* REAL ESTATE act of transferring ownership in real estate the point at which a buyer pays off the balance owed on real estate in exchange for a deed showing ownership of the real estate. *UK term* ***completion***

closing balance **1.** ACCOUNTING amount carried forward to next accounting period the difference between credits and debits in a ledger at the end of one accounting period that is carried forward to the next **2.** BANKING bank balance at end of business day the amount in credit or debit in a bank account at the end of a business day

closing bell MARKETS end of period of trading the end of a trading session at a stock or commodities exchange when a bell is rung

closing costs REAL ESTATE expenses of transferring real estate ownership the charges and fees paid by buyers and sellers in a real estate or mortgage transaction at the time of closing

closing-down sale OPERATIONS & PRODUCTION sale of goods by store closing down a sale of goods that follows a store's decision to cease trading

closing entries ACCOUNTING entries at very end of accounting period in a double-entry bookkeeping system, entries made at the very end of an **accounting period** to balance the expense and revenue ledgers

closing out **1.** MARKETS sale of commodity that ends futures contract the ending of a **futures contract** by the sale of the relevant commodity **2.** OPERATIONS & PRODUCTION sale of goods cheaply to offload them the act of selling goods cheaply to try to get rid of them, usually because they have not been selling well or because the seller is going out of business

closing price MARKETS last price paid during trading session the price of the last transaction for a specific security or commodity at the end of a trading session

closing quote MARKETS last price bid or offered during trading session the last bid and offer prices for a specific security or commodity recorded at the close of a trading session

closing rate CURRENCY & EXCHANGE exchange rate at end of accounting period the exchange rate of two or more currencies at the close of business at the end of an accounting period, for example, at the end of the fiscal year

closing rate method CURRENCY & EXCHANGE currency conversion method in accounts a technique for translating the figures from a set of financial statements into a different currency using the **closing rate**. This method is often used for the accounts of a foreign subsidiary of a parent company.

closing sale FINANCE sale that reduces seller's risk a sale that reduces the risk that the seller has through holding a greater number of shares or a longer term contract

closing statement REAL ESTATE statement of expenses of transferring real estate ownership a statement of all charges and fees paid by buyers and sellers in a real estate or mortgage transaction at the time of closing

closing stock ACCOUNTING inventory at end of accounting period a business's remaining stock at the end of an **accounting period**. It includes finished products, raw materials, or work in progress and is deducted from the period's costs in the balance sheets.

cluster analysis STATISTICS statistical analysis using groupings that share characteristics a statistical method used to analyze complex data and identify groupings that share common features. Cluster analysis is a form of **multivariate analysis** that attempts to explain variability in a set of data. It involves finding unifying elements that enable identification of groups or clusters displaying common characteristics. It could be used, for example, to analyze results of market research and delineate groups of respondents that share specific attitudes.

clustered data STATISTICS statistical information grouped according to shared features data in which sampling units in a study are grouped into clusters sharing a common feature, or longitudinal data in which clusters are defined by repeated measures on the unit

cluster sampling STATISTICS *see* ***random sampling***

CM *abbr* GENERAL MANAGEMENT category management

CMBS *abbr* STOCKHOLDING & INVESTMENTS, MORTGAGES commercial mortgage-backed securities

CME *abbr* MARKETS Chicago Mercantile Exchange

CML *abbr* MORTGAGES Council of Mortgage Lenders

CMO *abbr* MORTGAGES collateralized mortgage obligation

CN or **C/N** *abbr* FINANCE credit note

CNCC *abbr* REGULATION & COMPLIANCE Compagnie Nationale des Commissaires aux Comptes

CNS *abbr* MARKETS continuous net settlement

COB *abbr* MARKETS Commission des Opérations de Bourse

co-branding MARKETING, E-COMMERCE display of multiple logos to suggest joint venture the display of two or more corporate logos on a product or website in order to give the impression that the product or site is a joint enterprise

co-creditor FINANCE one of several people to whom firm owes money one of two or more people or organizations that are owed money by the same company

code of conduct GENERAL MANAGEMENT standard of ethical and social behavior and responsibility a statement and description of required behaviors, responsibilities, and actions expected of employees of an organization or of members of a professional body. A code of conduct usually focuses on ethical and socially responsible issues and applies to individuals, providing guidance on how to act in cases of doubt or confusion.

     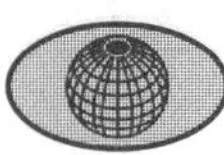   

code of practice GENERAL MANAGEMENT statement of preferred organizational procedures a policy statement and description of preferred methods for organizational procedures.

Codes of practice may govern procedures for industrial relations, health and safety, and, more recently, customer service and professional development. An agreed code of practice enables activities to be carried out to a required organizational standard and provides a basis for dispute resolution.

co-director CORPORATE GOVERNANCE person involved in controlling firm one of two or more people who direct the same company

coefficient of variation STATISTICS measure of dispersion of statistical information a measure of the spread of a set of statistical data, such as a set of investment returns, calculated as the mean or standard deviation of the data multiplied by 100

co-financing FINANCE joint provision of finance the provision of money for a project jointly by two or more parties

COGS *abbr* OPERATIONS & PRODUCTION cost of goods sold

cohesion fund FINANCE EU fund to equalize members' economies in the European Union, the main financial instrument for reducing economic and social disparities within by providing financial help for projects in the fields of the environment and transport infrastructure

cohort STATISTICS group of study participants with shared characteristic a group of individuals in a statistical study who have a common characteristic such as age or income

cohort study STATISTICS long-term study of people with shared characteristic a study in which a group of individuals who have a common characteristic such as age or income are observed over several years

coincident indicator ECONOMICS indicator of current economic activity a factor that provides information on economic activity taking place at the current time

COLA *abbr* FINANCE cost-of-living adjustment

cold call MARKETING call strangers to sell something to make unsolicited calls to customers or consumers in an attempt to sell products or services. **Cold calling** is disliked, particularly by individual consumers, and is an inefficient way of selling, as the take-up rate is very low. *Also called* ***dial and smile***

cold start OPERATIONS & PRODUCTION new operation unsupported by previous turnover the act of beginning a new business or opening a new store with no previous turnover to base it on

Collaborative Planning, Forecasting, and Replenishment *see* ***CPFR®***

collar STOCKHOLDING & INVESTMENTS, RISK preset limit a contractually imposed lower limit on a **financial instrument**

collateral FINANCE resources providing security against loan property or goods used as security against a loan and forfeited to the lender if the borrower defaults

collateralize FINANCE provide loan with security to secure a loan by pledging assets. If the borrower defaults on loan payments, the pledged assets can be taken by the lender. —**collateralization**

collateralized bond obligation STOCKHOLDING & INVESTMENTS, RISK investment grade pool of bonds carrying risk an **investment grade asset-backed security** that consists of a portfolio of bonds, some of which may carry high risk. Pooling bonds with different degrees of risk is thought to provide enough diversification to qualify the security for an investment grade rating. *Abbr* **CBO**

collateralized debt obligation STOCKHOLDING & INVESTMENTS investment combining bonds and loans a complex investment vehicle based on a portfolio of bonds and loans, which may include assets with an underlying risk. *Abbr* **CDO**. *Also called* ***debt obligation***

collateralized loan obligation STOCKHOLDING & INVESTMENTS asset-backed security formed when loan is repackaged an asset-backed security that is created by repackaging loans, usually commercial loans made by a bank, at an attractive rate of interest. *Abbr* **CLO**

collateralized mortgage obligation STOCKHOLDING & INVESTMENTS, MORTGAGES instrument with mortgages on property a financial instrument that has mortgages on property given as security in case of default. CMOs are issued against the collective value of pooled mortgages, offering interest payments based on the overall cash flow. *Abbr* **CMO**

collateral trust certificate STOCKHOLDING & INVESTMENTS bond with stock in another firm as security a bond for which stock in another company, usually a subsidiary, is used as collateral

collecting bank BANKING bank receiving check for processing a bank into which a person has deposited a check, and which has the duty to collect the money from the account of the writer of the check

collection FINANCE collecting payments on unpaid debts the process of collecting payments on unpaid loans or bills

collection agency FINANCE business collecting outstanding payments a business that collects payments on unpaid loans or on bills

collection ratio ACCOUNTING average time for invoice to be paid the average number of days it takes a firm to convert its accounts receivable into cash.

Ideally, this period should be decreasing or constant. A low figure means the company collects its outstanding receivables quickly. Collection ratios are usually reviewed quarterly or yearly.

Calculating the collection ratio requires three figures: total accounts receivable, total credit sales for the period analyzed, and the number of days in the period (annual, 365; six months, 182; quarter, 91). The formula is:

$$\left(\frac{\text{Accounts receivable}}{\text{Total credit sales for the period}}\right) \times \text{Number of days in the period}$$

For example: if total receivables are $4,500,000, total credit sales in a quarter are $9,000,000, and number of days is 91, then:

$$\frac{4{,}500{,}000}{9{,}000{,}000} \times 91 = 45.5$$

Thus, it takes an average of 45.5 days to collect receivables.

Properly evaluating a collection ratio requires a standard for comparison. A traditional rule of thumb is that it should not exceed a third to a half of selling terms. For instance, if terms are 30 days, an acceptable collection ratio would be 40 to 45 days.

Companies use collection ratio information with an **accounts receivable aging** report. This lists aged categories of receivables, for example, 0–30 days, 30–60 days, 60–90 days, and over 90 days. The report also shows the percentage of total accounts receivable that each group represents, allowing for an analysis of delinquencies and potential bad debts. *Also called* ***days' sales outstanding***

collusive tendering FINANCE when job offerers share inside information the illegal practice among companies making offers for a job of sharing privileged information between themselves, with the objective of fixing the end result

colocation E-COMMERCE sharing of hosting center with other Internet clients the sharing of the facilities of a hosting center with other Internet clients

     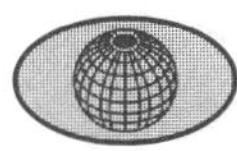   

combination annuity INSURANCE = ***hybrid annuity***

combination bond STOCKHOLDING & INVESTMENTS bond secured by project's revenue and government credit a government bond for which the collateral is both revenue from the financed project and the government's credit

combined financial statement FINANCE summary of financial position of related firms a written record covering the assets, liabilities, net worth, and operating statement of two or more related or affiliated companies

COMEX *abbr* MARKETS commodity exchange

comfort letter **1.** FINANCE parent company's support for subsidiary's loan a letter from the parent company of a subsidiary that is applying for a loan, stating the intention that the subsidiary should remain in business **2.** ACCOUNTING in US, endorsement of financial statement in the United States, a statement from an accounting firm provided to a company preparing for a public offering, which confirms that the unaudited financial information in the **prospectus** follows **Generally Accepted Accounting Principles**

command economy ECONOMICS economic system controlled by government an economy in which all economic activity is regulated by the government, as formerly in China or the Soviet Union

commerce FINANCE trading on large scale the large-scale buying and selling of goods and services, usually applied to trading between different states or countries

commerce integration FINANCE marrying of old and new ways of trading the blending of Internet-based commerce capabilities with the **legacy systems** of a traditional business to create a seamless transparent process

commerce server E-COMMERCE **1.** computer storing e-commerce data for website a computer in a network that maintains all transactional and back-end data for an e-commerce website **2.** computer containing programs for processing online transactions a networked computer that contains the programs required to process transactions via the Internet, including dynamic inventory databases, shopping cart software, and online payment systems

commerce service provider E-COMMERCE organization providing service to firm involved in e-commerce an organization or company that provides a service to a company to facilitate some aspect of electronic commerce, for example, by functioning as an Internet **payment gateway**. *Abbr* **CSP**

commercial FINANCE of trading relating to the buying and selling of goods and services

commercial bank BANKING privately owned bank offering range of facilities a bank that provides financial services such as checking and savings accounts and loans to individuals and businesses. *See also* ***investment bank***

commercial bill FINANCE bill of exchange not issued by government a **bill of exchange** issued by a company (a **trade bill**) or accepted by a bank (a **banker's bill**), as opposed to a **Treasury bill**, which is issued by a government

commercial directory BUSINESS book listing local businesses a book that lists all the businesses and businesspeople in a town

commercial hedger STOCKHOLDING & INVESTMENTS producer investing in commodities it needs a company that holds **options** in the commodities it uses or produces, usually in order to ensure the price stability of the commodity

commercialization FINANCE conversion of something into business the application of business principles to something in order to run it as a business

commercial law LEGAL law dealing with trade the body of law that deals with the rules and institutions of commercial transactions, including banking, commerce, contracts, copyrights, insolvency, insurance, patents, trademarks, shipping, storage, transportation, and warehousing

commercial loan FINANCE short-term renewable loan to firm a short-term renewable loan or line of credit used to finance the seasonal or cyclical working capital needs of a company

commercial mortgage-backed securities MORTGAGES stocks with cash flow from commercial mortgage stocks that are backed by the security of a mortgage on commercial rather than residential property. *Abbr* **CMBS**

commercial paper FINANCE unsecured short-term loan note an unsecured loan note issued by a company for a short period, generally maturing within nine months

commercial property REAL ESTATE buildings and land used by business buildings and land used for the performance of business activities. Commercial property can include single offices, buildings, factories, and hotels.

commercial report FINANCE background financial report on applicant an investigative report made by an organization such as a **credit bureau** that specializes in obtaining information regarding a person or organization applying for something such as credit or employment

commercial substance FINANCE economic reality behind piece of business the economic reality that underlies a transaction or arrangement, regardless of its legal or technical denomination. For example, a company may sell an office block and then immediately lease it back: the commercial substance may be that it has not been sold.

commercial year FINANCE 12 months of 30 days an artificial year treated as having 12 months of 30 days each, used for calculating such things as monthly sales data and inventory levels

commission **1.** FINANCE sum paid to intermediary a payment made to an intermediary, often calculated as a percentage of the value of goods or services provided. Commission is most often paid to sales staff, brokers, or agents. **2.** *US* MARKETS broker's fee for sale a fee that a broker receives for a sale of securities. *Also called* ***placement fee***

commission agent FINANCE agent paid percentage of sales an agent whose payment is based on a specific percentage of the sales made

Commission des Oprations de Bourse MARKETS institution overseeing French stock exchanges the agency, established by the French government in 1968, that is responsible for supervising France's stock exchanges. *Abbr* **COB**

commission house FINANCE firm charging commission on futures contracts a business that buys or sells **futures contracts** for clients and charges a commission for this service

Commission of the European Community = ***European Commission***

commitment STOCKHOLDING & INVESTMENTS agreement to underwrite credit an agreement by an underwriting syndicate to underwrite a **note issuance facility** or other credit facility

commitment document LEGAL document with contractual force confirming transaction a contract, change order, purchase order, or letter of intent pertaining to the supply of

  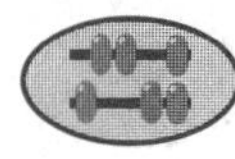 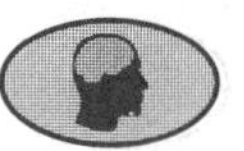  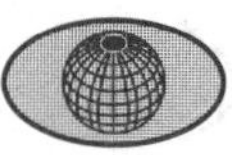   

goods and services that commits an organization to legal, financial, and other obligations

commitment fee FINANCE payment to fix interest rate on forthcoming loan a fee that a lender charges to guarantee a rate of interest on a loan a borrower is soon to make. *Also called* ***establishment fee***

commitment letter FINANCE official confirmation of US loan in the United States, an official notice from a lender to a borrower that the borrower's application has been approved and confirming the terms and conditions of the loan

commitments basis FINANCE way of recording expenditure before outlay the method of recording the expenditure of a public sector organization at the time when it commits itself to it rather than when it actually pays for it

commitments for capital expenditure FINANCE amount committed to fixed assets in future the amount a company has committed to spend on fixed assets in the future. In the United Kingdom, companies are legally obliged to disclose this amount, and any additional commitments, in their **annual report**.

committee GENERAL MANAGEMENT group of people delegated to consider particular matter a group of people appointed and authorized to study, investigate, or make recommendations on a particular matter

Committee on Accounting Procedure ACCOUNTING former US committee establishing accounting principles in the United States, a committee of the American Institute of Certified Public Accountants that was responsible between 1939 and 1959 for issuing accounting principles, some of which are still part of the **Generally Accepted Accounting Principles**

Committee on Uniform Securities Identification Procedures REGULATION & COMPLIANCE committee that codes US securities a committee set up by the American Bankers Association to assign a code to all securities approved for trading in the United States. *Abbr* **CUSIP**

commodities exchange MARKETS market for bulk raw materials a market in which raw materials are bought and sold in large quantities as **actuals** or **futures**

commodities market MARKETS = ***commodity market***

commodity MARKETS product that can be traded an item that can be bought or sold, especially a raw material or something that has been manufactured

commodity-backed bond STOCKHOLDING & INVESTMENTS bond linked to price of commodity a bond tied to the price of an underlying commodity such as gold or silver, often used as a hedge against inflation

commodity contract MARKETS contract for transferring commodity a legal document for the delivery or receipt of a commodity

commodity exchange MARKETS exchange where commodity futures are traded an exchange where futures are traded, for example, the commodity exchange for metals. *Abbr* **COMEX**

commodity future MARKETS fixed contract to buy or sell commodity a contract to buy or sell a commodity at a predetermined price and on a specific delivery date

Commodity Futures Trading Commission REGULATION & COMPLIANCE US agency monitoring futures trading an independent agency set up by the US government to monitor trading in **futures contracts**. *Abbr* **CFTC**

commodity market MARKETS market for bulk raw materials a market in which raw materials are bought and sold in large quantities as **actuals** or **futures**. *Also called* ***commodities market***

commodity paper FINANCE loan secured by commodities a loan or advance for which commodities or financial documents relating to them are collateral

commodity pool FINANCE group trading in commodity options a group of people who join together to trade in **options** on commodities

commodity-product spread FINANCE trading in commodity and product coordinated trades in both a commodity and a product made from it

commodity trader MARKETS somebody buying and selling commodities a person whose business is buying and selling commodities

common cost 1. ACCOUNTING cost recorded in more than one center a cost that is allocated to two or more cost centers within a company **2.** OPERATIONS & PRODUCTION cost associated with multiple items cost relating to more than one product or service and unable to be allocated to any individual one

common equity STOCKHOLDING & INVESTMENTS common stock in a company the ownership interest in a company that consists only of the common stock

common market INTERNATIONAL TRADE group of trading partners with few trade barriers an economic association, typically between nations, with the goal of removing or reducing trade barriers

common ownership BUSINESS ownership by employees collectively a situation in which a business is owned by the employees who work in it

common pricing OPERATIONS & PRODUCTION illegal price-fixing the illegal fixing of the price of a good or service by several businesses so that they all charge the same price

common seal LEGAL = ***company seal***

common-size financial statements ACCOUNTING statements with everything in percentages statements in which all the separate parts are expressed as percentages of the total. Such statements are often used for making performance comparisons between companies.

common stock *US* STOCKHOLDING & INVESTMENTS stock without first call on dividends a stock that provides voting rights but only pays a dividend after dividends for preferred stock have been paid. *UK term* ***ordinary share***

common stock ratio STOCKHOLDING & INVESTMENTS in US, proportion of capital represented by share in the United States, a measure of the interest each stockholder has in the company's capital

commorientes LEGAL people who die at same time the legal term for two or more people who die at the same time. For the purposes of inheritance law, in the event of two people dying at the same time, it is assumed that the older person died first.

communication GENERAL MANAGEMENT exchange of messages, information, ideas, etc. the exchange of messages conveying information, ideas, attitudes, emotions, opinions, or instructions between individuals or groups with the objective of creating, understanding, or coordinating activities. Communication is essential to the effective operation of an organization. It may be conducted informally through a grapevine or formally by means of letters, reports, briefings, and meetings. Communication may be verbal or nonverbal and include spoken, written, and visual elements.

communications GENERAL MANAGEMENT systems or technologies used for communicating systems or technologies such as postal, telephone, and e-mail networks, used for the communication of messages or for communicating within an organization

communications channel GENERAL MANAGEMENT methods by which people communicate a medium through which a message is passed in the process of **communication**. Communications channels include the spoken, written, and printed word, and electronic or computer-based media such as radio and television, telephones, videoconferencing, and e-mail. The most effective channel for a specific message depends on the nature of the message and the audience to be reached, as well as the context in which the message is to be transmitted.

communications envelope E-COMMERCE = ***electronic envelope***

communication skills HR & PERSONNEL skills required for effective communication skills that enable people to communicate effectively with one another. Effective communication involves the choice of the best **communications channel** for a specific purpose, the technical knowledge to use the channel appropriately, the presentation of information in an appropriate manner for the target audience, and the ability to understand messages and responses received from others. The ability to establish and develop mutual understanding, trust, and cooperation is also important. More specifically, communication skills include the ability to speak in public, make presentations, write letters and reports, chair committees and meetings, and conduct negotiations.

communications management GENERAL MANAGEMENT job of ensuring effective communications the management, measurement, and control activities undertaken to ensure the effectiveness of communications

communications strategy MARKETING deciding best way to communicate with marketplace a management technique for determining the most effective method of communicating with the marketplace

communication technology GENERAL MANAGEMENT electronic systems for communicating electronic systems used for communication between individuals or groups. Communication technology facilitates communication between individuals or groups who are not physically present at the same location. Systems such as telephones, telex, fax, radio, television, and video are included, as well as more recent computer-based technologies, including **electronic data interchange** and e-mail.

community E-COMMERCE group of people with shared interest communicating online a group of Internet users with a shared interest or concept who interact with each other in newsgroups, mailing-list discussion groups, and other online interactive forums

community of interest GENERAL MANAGEMENT diverse group united for common cause a group of diverse people or organizations with a shared concern who have united to campaign for a common cause

community property FINANCE asset to be shared equally on divorce any asset that is acquired during marriage by either spouse and that, in some states of the United States, must be divided equally between them if they should divorce. *Also called* ***marital property***

Compagnie Nationale des Commissaires aux Comptes REGULATION & COMPLIANCE French regulatory body in France, an organization that regulates auditing by external, independent auditors. *Abbr* **CNCC**

Companies Act REGULATION & COMPLIANCE UK legislation governing activities of firms in the United Kingdom, an Act of Parliament that regulates the working of companies. Although the first one was passed in 1844, the Acts of 1985 and 1989 consolidated previous legislation and incorporated directives from the European Union.

Companies House REGULATION & COMPLIANCE building where UK firms are registered in the United Kingdom, the office of the **Registrar of Companies**. It has three main functions: the incorporation, re-registration, and dissolving of companies; the registration of documents that must be filed under company, insolvency, and related legislation; and the provision of company information to the public. *Abbr* **CH**

Companies Registration Office REGULATION & COMPLIANCE office where UK firms are registered the office of the Registrar of Companies, an official UK organization at which companies' records must be deposited so that they can be inspected by the public. *Abbr* **CRO**

companion bond STOCKHOLDING & INVESTMENTS US bond secured by mortgages in the United States, a class of a **collateralized mortgage obligation** that is paid off first when interest rates fall, leading to the underlying mortgages being prepaid. Conversely, the **principal** on these bonds will be repaid more slowly when interest rates rise and fewer mortgages are prepaid.

company BUSINESS organized group trading goods or providing services a group of people organized to buy or sell goods or to provide a service, usually for profit

company director CORPORATE GOVERNANCE somebody appointed to help run company a person appointed by the stockholders to help run a company

company law CORPORATE GOVERNANCE legislation governing firms the body of legislation that relates to the formation, status, conduct, and **corporate governance** of companies as legal entities

company limited by guarantee BUSINESS incorporated organization whose members have pre-agreed liability a type of organization, normally formed for nonprofit purposes, in which each member of the company agrees to be liable for a specific sum in the event of liquidation

company limited by shares BUSINESS UK organization with share holdings determining liability in the United Kingdom, a type of organization in which each member of the company is liable only for the fully paid value of the shares they own

company pension PENSIONS = ***occupational pension***

company policy CORPORATE GOVERNANCE firm's guidelines for behavior or procedure a statement of desired standards of behavior or procedure applicable across an organization. Company policy defines ways of acting for staff in areas where there appears to be latitude in deciding how best to operate. This may concern areas such as time off for special circumstances, drug or alcohol abuse, workplace bullying, personal use of Internet facilities, or business travel. Company policy may also apply to customers, for example, policy on complaints, customer retention, or disclosure of information. Sometimes a company policy may develop into a **code of practice**.

company promoter BUSINESS somebody establishing new firm a person who organizes the setting up of a new company

company registrar CORPORATE GOVERNANCE person maintaining firm's share register the person who is responsible for maintaining the share register records of a company

company report CORPORATE GOVERNANCE statement of firm's activities and performance a document giving details of the activities

     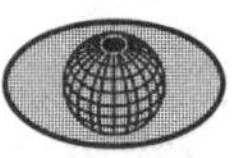   

and performance of a company. Companies are legally required to produce specific reports and submit them to the competent authorities in the country of their registration. These include **annual reports** and financial reports. Other reports may cover specific aspects of an organization's activities, for example, environmental or social impact.

company seal LEGAL firm's authenticating stamp or signature the impression of a company's official signature on paper or wax. Certain documents, such as stock certificates, have to bear this seal. *Also called* ***common seal***

company secretary CORPORATE GOVERNANCE UK firm's senior administrative officer a senior employee in an organization with director status and administrative and legal authority. The appointment of a company secretary is a legal requirement for most limited companies, except the smallest. A company secretary can also be a **board secretary** with appropriate qualifications. In the United Kingdom, many company secretaries are members of the Institute of Chartered Secretaries and Administrators.

comparative advantage ECONOMICS, BUSINESS benefit of higher, more efficient production an instance of higher, more efficient production in a particular area. A country that produces far more cars than another, for example, is said to have the comparative advantage in car production. It has been suggested that specialization in activities in which individuals or groups have a comparative advantage will result in gains in trade.

comparative advertising MARKETING advertising comparing firm's product with competitors' products a form of advertising that gives carefully selected details of competitor products for comparison with a company's own product, usually to the detriment of competitors. Comparative advertising is frequently used to advertise cars, where the availability of features such as a sun roof, air conditioning, advanced braking systems, fuel efficiency, safety features, and warranty terms in similarly priced cars is given.

comparative balance sheet TREASURY MANAGEMENT financial statement compared with one of different date one of two or more financial statements prepared on different dates that lend themselves to a comparative analysis of the financial condition of an organization

comparative credit analysis RISK assessment of financial risk an analysis of the risk associated with lending to different companies

compensating balance BANKING **1.** money required in bank account the amount of money a bank requires a customer to maintain in a non-interest-bearing account, in exchange for which the bank provides free services **2.** money required in bank account allowing credit the amount of money a bank requires a customer to maintain in an account in return for holding credit available, thereby increasing the true rate of interest on the loan

compensating errors ACCOUNTING mistakes after which accounts still balance two or more errors that are set against each other so that the accounts still balance

compensation FINANCE payment for work pay given to somebody in recompense for work performed

compensation fund STOCKHOLDING & INVESTMENTS fund compensating investors when stock exchange members default a fund operated by a stock exchange to compensate investors for losses incurred when members of the stock exchange default (lose more on their trading positions than they hold in capital)

compensation package HR & PERSONNEL overall employee pay and benefits offered by US employer in the United States, a bundle of rewards including pay, financial incentives, and **fringe benefits** offered to, or negotiated by, an employee

compensatory financing FINANCE IMF financial assistance financing from the **International Monetary Fund** to help a country in economic difficulty

competence GENERAL MANAGEMENT, HR & PERSONNEL ability to perform duties at level required an acquired personal skill that is demonstrated in an employee's ability to provide a consistently adequate or high level of performance in a specific job function. Competence should be distinguished from **competency**, although in general usage the terms are used interchangeably. Early attempts to define the qualities of effective managers were based on lists of the personality traits and skills of the ideal manager. This is an input model approach, focusing on the skills that are needed to do the job. These skills are competencies and reflect potential ability to do something. With the advent of scientific management, people turned their attention more to the behavior of effective managers and to the outcomes of successful management. This approach is an output model, in which a manager's effectiveness is defined in terms of actual achievement. This achievement manifests itself in competences, which demonstrate that somebody has learned to do something well. There tends to be a focus in the United Kingdom on competence, whereas in the United States, the concept of competency is more popular. Competences are used in the workplace in a variety of ways. Competences are also used in reward management, for example, in competence-based pay. The assessment of competence is a necessary process for underpinning these initiatives by determining what competences an employee shows. At an organizational level, the idea of **core competence** is gaining in popularity.

competency GENERAL MANAGEMENT, HR & PERSONNEL innate personal ability an innate skill or ability that somebody has. *See also* ***competence***

competition ECONOMICS, BUSINESS struggle between firms to win business rivalry between companies to achieve greater **market share**. Competition between companies for customers will lead to product innovation and improvement and, ultimately, lower prices. The opposite of market competition is either a **monopoly** or a **controlled economy**, where production is governed by quotas. A company that is leading the market is said to have achieved **competitive advantage**.

Competition Commission REGULATION & COMPLIANCE UK regulator of competition in the United Kingdom, an independent public body with the role of ensuring healthy competition between companies. It conducts in-depth inquiries into mergers, markets, and the regulation of the major regulated industries. It replaced the Monopolies and Mergers Commission in April 1999.

competitive advantage ECONOMICS, BUSINESS benefit of being more competitive a factor giving an advantage to a nation, company, group, or individual in competitive terms

competitive analysis BUSINESS evaluation of competitors' ability to compete analysis carried out for marketing purposes, which can include industry, customer, and **competitor analysis**. A thorough competitive analysis done within a strategic framework can provide in-depth evaluation of the capabilities of key competitors.

competitive bid STOCKHOLDING & INVESTMENTS selling new securities at competing prices or terms a method of auctioning new securities whereby various underwriters offer the stock at competing prices or terms

competitive devaluation CURRENCY & EXCHANGE currency devaluation to increase competitiveness the devaluation of a currency to make a country's goods more competitive on the international markets

competitive equilibrium price BUSINESS price resulting in balance of buyers and sellers the price at which the number of buyers willing to buy a good equals the number of sellers prepared to sell it

competitive forces ECONOMICS, BUSINESS external factors forcing organization to become more competitive the external business and economic factors that compel an organization to improve its competitiveness

competitive intelligence BUSINESS information gathered that improves organization's competitive ability data gathered to improve an organization's competitive capacity. Competitive intelligence may include, for example, information about competitors' plans, activities, or products, and may sometimes be gained through **industrial espionage**. Such information can have a significant impact on a company's own plans: it could limit the effectiveness of a new product launch, or identify growing threats to important accounts, for example. Unless organizations monitor competitor activity and take appropriate action, their business faces risk.

competitive local exchange carrier BUSINESS telecommunications provider competing with established provider a company that offers an alternate service to the established telephone service provider in a particular area

competitiveness index ECONOMICS, BUSINESS ranking of countries in order of competitive advantage an international ranking of states which uses economic and other information to list countries in order of their competitive performance. A competitiveness index can show which countries have overall or industry sector **competitive advantage**.

competitive position BUSINESS situation in relation to competitors the market share, costs, prices, quality, and accumulated experience of an entity or product relative to competition

competitive pricing BUSINESS determining price by checking others setting a price by reference to the prices of comparable competitive products

competitive trader MARKETS = ***floor trader***

competitor BUSINESS person, company, or product competing with another a person, company, or product that is in commercial competition with another

competitor analysis or **competitor profiling** BUSINESS comparing firm's products with competitors' in developing strategy the identification and quantification of the relative strengths and weaknesses of a product or service compared with those of competitors or potential competitors that could be of significance in the development of a successful competitive strategy

complaint GENERAL MANAGEMENT customer's expression of dissatisfaction an expression of dissatisfaction with a product or service, either orally or in writing, from an internal or external customer. A customer may have a genuine cause for complaint, although some complaints may be made as a result of a misunderstanding or an unreasonable expectation of a product or service. How a complaint is handled will affect the overall level of **customer satisfaction** and may affect long-term customer loyalty. It is important for providers to have clear procedures for dealing rapidly with any complaints, to come to a fair conclusion, and to explain the reasons for what may be perceived by the customer as a negative response. *Also called* ***customer complaint***

complaints management GENERAL MANAGEMENT technique for handling complaints a management technique for assessing, analyzing, and responding to customer complaints

complementary goods MARKETING products depending on each other for sales goods sold separately, but dependent on each other for sales. Examples of complementary goods include toothbrushes and toothpaste or computers and computer desks.

complementor BUSINESS firm selling product that complements another firm's product a company that supplies a product that complements a product supplied by another company, for example, computers and software

complete *UK* REAL ESTATE = ***close***

completion *UK* REAL ESTATE = ***closing***

completion date BUSINESS date when something will finish the date when a financial or business transaction is due to be finalized

complex adaptive system GENERAL MANAGEMENT self-regulating system without controls a system that overrides conventional human controls because those controls will subdue inevitable change and development within that system. Complex adaptive systems are a product of the application of **chaos theory** and **complexity theory** to the world of organizations. It has been suggested that organizations that are subject to too much control are at risk of failure. Bureaucracy and the **top down approach** to management have been cited as examples of extreme control. However, if a bureaucracy is left to adapt naturally, it could become capable of self-organization and of creating new methods of operating.

complexity costs OPERATIONS & PRODUCTION business costs relating to changing economy the costs of operating a business which are difficult to quantify and relate to remaining competitive in a rapidly changing and increasingly complex economic environment. *Also called* ***costs of complexity***

complexity theory GENERAL MANAGEMENT theory that events will develop in random and complex fashion the theory that random events, if left to happen without interference, will settle into a complicated pattern rather than a simple one. Complexity theory is a development of **chaos theory**. In a business context, it suggests that events within organizations and in the wider economic and social spheres cannot be predicted by simple models but will develop in a seemingly random and complex manner.

compliance REGULATION & COMPLIANCE fulfillment of requirements action to do what is required to meet official or agreed standards or regulations, or to do what is ordered by a court

compliance audit REGULATION & COMPLIANCE check to establish if obligations are being met an audit of specific activities in order to determine whether performance conforms with a predetermined contractual, regulatory, or statutory requirement

compliance department
1. STOCKHOLDING & INVESTMENTS, REGULATION & COMPLIANCE department in stockbroking firm enforcing stock exchange rules a department in a stockbroking firm that makes sure that the stock exchange rules are followed and that confidentiality is maintained in cases when the same firm represents rival clients **2.** REGULATION & COMPLIANCE department in firm enforcing

  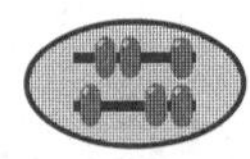 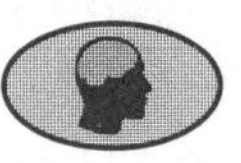  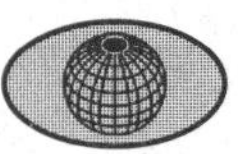   

business regulations a department that ensures that the company it is part of is adhering to any relevant laws and regulations relating to its business

compliance documentation STOCKHOLDING & INVESTMENTS, REGULATION & COMPLIANCE documents required for stock issues documents that a stock-issuing company publishes in line with regulations on stock issues

compliance officer REGULATION & COMPLIANCE officer ensuring that financial regulations are observed an employee of a financial organization who ensures that regulations governing its business are observed

component percentage FINANCE proportion of firm's value in capital the proportion of a company's value represented by debt, stock, assets, and other items. *See also* ***capitalization ratio***

composite index MARKETS index combining equities, indices, or averages an index of various equities, indices, or averages, mainly used as an indicator of the performance of the market or a specific sector of the market

compound FINANCE **1.** pay part of debt in the United Kingdom, to agree with creditors to settle a debt by paying part of what is owed **2.** calculate compound interest to calculate compound interest, based on the initial sum plus any interest that has accrued

compound annual return or **compounded annual return** STOCKHOLDING & INVESTMENTS return on investment including reinvestment returns the annual return on an investment after allowing for the return on reinvested intermediate **cash flows**

compounding FINANCE **1.** calculating compound interest the calculation of **compound interest**, based on the initial sum plus any interest that has accrued **2.** using compound interest the making of a transaction involving the payment or receipt of **compound interest**

compound interest FINANCE interest calculated after inclusion of accrued interest interest calculated on the sum of the original borrowed amount and the accrued interest. *See also* ***simple interest***

compound option STOCKHOLDING & INVESTMENTS, RISK option with underlying asset another option an option that has a second option as the underlying asset. If the first option is exercised, the second option acts like an ordinary option.

compound rate FINANCE rate using compound interest the interest rate of a loan based on its **principal**, the amount remaining to be paid, or any interest payments already received

comprehensive auditing ACCOUNTING = ***value for money audit***

comprehensive income FINANCE firm's income reflecting any changes in owner equity a company's total income for a given accounting period, including all gains and losses, not only those included in a normal income statement but also any that reflect a change in the value of an owner's interest in the business. In the United States, comprehensive income must be declared, whereas in the United Kingdom it appears in the statement of total recognized gains and losses.

comprehensive insurance or **comprehensive policy** INSURANCE insurance policy covering all likely risks an insurance policy that covers you against all risks that are deemed likely to happen

comptroller ACCOUNTING organization's senior accountant an accountant who is responsible for maintaining an organization's accounts

Comptroller of the Currency BANKING US official responsible for federal banks an official of the government responsible for the regulation of banks that are members of the Federal Reserve

compulsory acquisition STOCKHOLDING & INVESTMENTS purchasing last 10% of stocks at original price in the United Kingdom, the purchase by a bidder of the last 10% of stocks in an issue by right, at the offer price

compulsory liquidation BUSINESS enforced sale of assets to pay liabilities the closing of a business and selling its assets to pay off its liabilities, which is ordered by a court

compulsory purchase annuity PENSIONS annuity purchased from UK personal pension plan in the United Kingdom, an annuity that must be purchased with the fund built up in a personal pension plan before age 75

compulsory winding up *UK* BUSINESS = ***compulsory liquidation***

computational error ACCOUNTING calculation mistake a mistake that was made in doing a calculation

computer-aided design or **computer-assisted design** OPERATIONS & PRODUCTION product design using computers the use of a computer to assist with the design of a product. Computer graphics, modeling, and simulation are used to represent a product on screen, so that designers can produce more accurate drawings than is possible on paper alone, and to perform calculations easily, thereby optimizing designs for production. *Abbr* **CAD**. *Also called* ***computer-assisted design***

computer-aided manufacturing or **computer-assisted manufacturing** OPERATIONS & PRODUCTION product manufacturing controlled by computer a system in which the manufacture and assembly of a product are directed by a computer. Computer-aided manufacturing can be integrated with **computer-aided design** to create a CAD/CAM system. *Abbr* **CAM**. *Also called* ***computer-assisted manufacturing***

computer-aided production management OPERATIONS & PRODUCTION use of computers to direct production management functions a system that enables all functions within an organization that are associated with production management to be directed by computer. **MRP II** is a well-known form of computer-aided production management. *Abbr* **CAPM**

computer-assisted design OPERATIONS & PRODUCTION = ***computer-aided design***

computer-assisted manufacturing OPERATIONS & PRODUCTION = ***computer-aided manufacturing***

computer model STOCKHOLDING & INVESTMENTS training using Internet, intranet, or standalone computer a system for calculating investment opportunities, used by fund managers to see the right moment to buy or sell

computer telephony integration BUSINESS combining of telephone technology and computer technology the combining of computer and telephone technology to allow a computer to dial telephone numbers, route calls, and send and receive messages. One product of computer telephony integration is the process of **caller identification**, or caller ID. Caller ID identifies the telephone number a customer is calling from, searches the customer database to identify the caller, and pops up the customer account on the receiver's computer screen, using the facility known as **screen popping**, before the call is answered. *Abbr* **CTI**

concealment of assets FRAUD hiding of assets from creditors the dishonest act of hiding assets so that creditors do not know they exist

  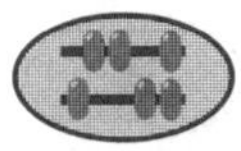   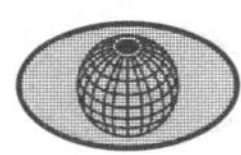   

concentration ratio MARKETS ratio indicating composition of market a ratio showing the proportion of a market that is dominated by a few large companies. This is calculated according to information about the size distribution of firms.

concentration risk RISK risk related to lack of variety in lending the risk of loss to a financial institution as a result of having too many outstanding loans concentrated in a particular instrument, with a particular type of borrower, or in a particular country

concentration services BANKING moving money into single account the placing of money from various accounts into a single account

concept board MARKETING large board for displaying advertising ideas a board used for presenting creative advertising ideas, usually a large one that members of a group can see easily

concept product MARKETING innovative product not yet on market a highly advanced and innovative product that is not yet in commercial production

concepts ACCOUNTING principles of accounting principles and abstract ideas underpinning the preparation of accounting information. *See also* ***fundamental accounting concepts***

concept search E-COMMERCE online search returning documents relating to word an online search for documents related conceptually to a word, rather than specifically containing the word itself

concept statement MARKETING summary of project's goals or nature an explanation or summary of the overall goals or nature of a project

concept testing MARKETING test of effectiveness of advertising idea research carried out to test the effectiveness of a creative advertising idea

concern BUSINESS firm and its staff a business or company and the people involved in it

concert party MERGERS & ACQUISITIONS secret plan to acquire company an arrangement by which several people or companies work together in secret, usually to acquire another company through a takeover bid

concession **1.** FINANCE price reduction for selected group a reduction in price for a specific group of people, not for everyone **2.** BUSINESS right to operate in another's premises the right of a retail outlet to operate within the premises of another establishment **3.** GENERAL MANAGEMENT agreement to ignore product's nonconformity to specification an agreement to ignore the failure of a product or service to conform to its specification, with a possible resultant deterioration in the quality of the product or service **4.** GENERAL MANAGEMENT compromise a compromise in opinion or action by a party to a dispute

concessionaire BUSINESS somebody with exclusive right to sell product a person or business that has the right to be the only seller of a product in a place

concessionally taxed TAX taxed at low rate being liable to tax at a preferential rate. Savings or benefits, for example, may be concessionally taxed.

conciliation HR & PERSONNEL dispute resolution by independent negotiator action taken by an independent negotiator to bring disputing sides together with the goal of restoring trust or goodwill and reaching an agreement or bringing about a reconciliation

concurrent engineering OPERATIONS & PRODUCTION product development by teams working in parallel a team-based cooperative approach to product design and development, in which all parties involved in **new product development** work in parallel. Concurrent engineering reduces or removes the time lag between the different stages of a product's development, and earlier entry into a market is therefore possible. Product quality is improved, development and product costs are minimized, and competitiveness is increased. *Also called* ***parallel engineering, simultaneous engineering***

conditional distribution STATISTICS probability distribution of specific random variable the probability distribution of a random variable while the values of one or more random variables are fixed

conditions of employment HR & PERSONNEL contract containing terms of employment terms agreed to by an employer and employee, which are legally enforceable through a **contract of employment**. Conditions of employment include conditions that may be unique to the individual, such as notice period, remuneration, fringe benefits, and hours of work, as well as those that form organization-wide policies, such as discipline and grievance procedures and those dictated by legislation.

conditions of sale OPERATIONS & PRODUCTION agreements about how something is sold agreed ways in which a sale may take place, including information on discounts and credit terms

condominium REAL ESTATE combination of private and joint real estate ownership in the United States, a type of real estate ownership in which the owner has title to a dwelling unit, especially an apartment or town house, in a building or on land that is owned jointly with the owners of the other units

conduit IRA PENSIONS = ***rollover IRA***

Confederation of Asian and Pacific Accountants ACCOUNTING Asia-Pacific organization for accountants an umbrella organization for a number of accounting associations. *Abbr* **CAPA**

Confederation of British Industry BUSINESS organization supporting UK businesses a corporate membership organization that aims to promote the interests of UK business. The CBI's headquarters are in London, but it has regional offices throughout the United Kingdom, a European office in Brussels, and a US base in Washington, DC. *Abbr* **CBI**

conference GENERAL MANAGEMENT meeting for members of organizations with shared interests a type of meeting held between members of often disparate organizations to discuss matters of mutual interest. Conferences are held for a variety of reasons, including resolving problems, making decisions, developing cooperation, and publicizing ideas, products, and services. They may take place within an organization but often draw people together regionally, nationally, or internationally, and involve a large number of speakers and delegates. Many conferences are organized for commercial profit.

conference call GENERAL MANAGEMENT telephone call connecting three or more people a telephone call that connects three or more lines so that people in different locations can communicate and exchange information by voice. Conference calls reduce the cost of meetings by eliminating travel time and expenditure. Public switched telephone networks or dedicated private networks and a centrally located device called a bridge are used to connect the participants. Microphones and loudspeakers may also be used to make group-to-group communication possible. Conference calls are a type of **teleconferencing**.

confidence indicator ECONOMICS, MARKETS number that shows how economic market will

  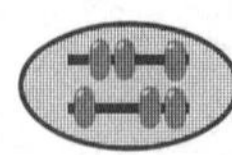 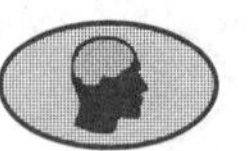  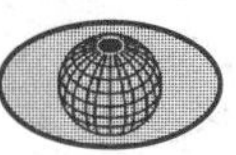   

perform a number that gives an indication of how well a market or an economy will fare

confidence interval STATISTICS expected range of possible outcomes in a statistical study, the range of values of sample observations that contain the true parameter value within a given probability

confidentiality agreement GENERAL MANAGEMENT agreement to treat information as private and confidential an agreement whereby an organization that has access to information about the affairs of another organization makes an undertaking to treat the information as private and confidential. A potential buyer of a company who requires further information in the process of due diligence may be asked to sign a confidentiality agreement stating that the information will only be used for the purpose of deciding whether to go ahead with the deal and will only be disclosed to employees involved in the negotiations. Such agreements are also used where information is shared in the context of a partnership or **benchmarking** program.

confirmation STOCKHOLDING & INVESTMENTS, OPERATIONS & PRODUCTION document confirming transaction or agreement a written acknowledgment of a transaction or agreement, for example, from a broker confirming and detailing a securities transaction

conflict management GENERAL MANAGEMENT discovering and controlling conflict within organization the identification and control of conflict within an organization. There are three main philosophies of conflict management: all conflict is bad and potentially destructive; conflict is inevitable and managers should attempt to harness it positively; conflict is essential to the survival of an organization and should be encouraged.

conflict of interest or **conflict of interests** GENERAL MANAGEMENT situation in which somebody's opposing interests prejudice objectivity a situation in which a person or institution is caught between opposing concerns, loyalties, or objectives that prejudice impartiality. A conflict of interest may be between self-advantage and the benefit of an organization for which somebody works, or it could arise when somebody is connected with two or more companies that are competing. The correct course of action in such cases is for the person concerned to declare any interests, to make known the way in which those interests conflict, and to abstain from participating in the decision-making process involving those interests. A conflict of interest may also arise when an institution acts for parties on both sides of a transaction and could derive an advantage from a specific outcome.

conglomerate company BUSINESS organization owning different types of companies an organization that owns a diverse range of companies in different industries. Conglomerates are usually **holding companies** with subsidiaries in wide-ranging business areas, often built up through mergers and takeovers and operating on an international scale.

conglomerate diversification MERGERS & ACQUISITIONS starting different types of subsidiaries the **diversification** of a **conglomerate company** through the setting-up of **subsidiary companies** with activities in various areas

conglomerate merger MERGERS & ACQUISITIONS merger of companies in unrelated industries a merger of organizations that belong to different types of industry

connectivity GENERAL MANAGEMENT ability of devices or people to connect electronically the ability of electronic products to connect with others, or of individuals, companies, and countries to be connected with one another electronically

connexity GENERAL MANAGEMENT being electronically connected worldwide the condition of being closely and intricately connected by worldwide communications networks

consequential loss policy INSURANCE = ***business interruption insurance***

consideration FINANCE payment for service a sum of money paid in return for a service

consignee OPERATIONS & PRODUCTION somebody receiving goods a person who receives goods from somebody for their own use or to sell for the owner

consignment OPERATIONS & PRODUCTION goods to be sold or returned a quantity of goods given to somebody for sale, with the provision that any unsold goods will be returned

consignment stock STOCKHOLDING & INVESTMENTS stock held by dealer for somebody stock held by one party (the "dealer") but legally owned by another (the "manufacturer") on terms that give the dealer the right to sell the stock in the normal course of its business, or, at its option, to return it unsold to the legal owner

consignor OPERATIONS & PRODUCTION somebody handing goods over a person who gives goods to somebody else for sale, safekeeping, or disposal

consistency ACCOUNTING using same accounting rules every year the concept that a company should apply the same rules and standards to its accounting procedures for similar items and from one year to the next. In the United Kingdom, deviation from consistency must be noted in the company's **annual report**.

consolidate ACCOUNTING combine accounts of holding company and its subsidiaries to combine the accounts of several subsidiary companies as well as their **holding company** in a single financial statement

consolidated accounts ACCOUNTING = ***consolidated financial statement***

consolidated balance sheet ACCOUNTING outline of firm's finances a balance sheet containing the most significant details of a company's finances, including those of subsidiaries

consolidated debt FINANCE debt incorporating smaller debts a single large debt into which smaller ones have been subsumed

consolidated financial statement ACCOUNTING outline of finances of parent company and subsidiaries a listing of the most significant details of the finances of a company and of all its subsidiaries. *Also called* ***consolidated accounts***

consolidated fund TAX public money for paying national debt a fund of public money, especially from taxes, used by the government to make interest payments on the national debt and other regular payments

consolidated invoice OPERATIONS & PRODUCTION combined invoice for items sent to buyer separately an invoice that covers all items shipped by one seller to one buyer during a particular period

consolidated loan FINANCE large loan for paying off smaller loans a large loan, the proceeds of which are used to eliminate smaller ones

consolidated stock STOCKHOLDING & INVESTMENTS *see* ***consols***

consolidated tape MARKETS ticker tape listing all US stock exchange activity a ticker tape that lists all transactions of the New York and other US stock exchanges

consolidated tax return TAX joint tax return for several firms a tax return that

  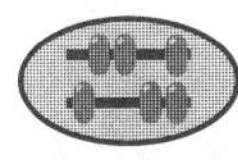 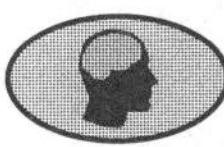  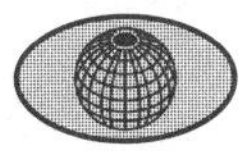   

covers several companies, typically a parent company and all of its subsidiaries

consolidation 1. MERGERS & ACQUISITIONS joining several firms together the uniting of two or more businesses into one company **2.** STOCKHOLDING & INVESTMENTS creating fewer but costlier shares the combination of a specific number of lower-priced shares into one higher-priced one

consolidation accounting ACCOUNTING combining financial statements for parent firm and subsidiaries the process of adjusting and combining financial information from the individual financial statements of a parent undertaking and its subsidiary undertakings to prepare consolidated financial statements that present financial information for the group as a single economic entity

consols STOCKHOLDING & INVESTMENTS UK government bonds with no maturity date in the United Kingdom, government bonds that pay interest but do not have a maturity date. *Full form* ***consolidated stock***

consortium BUSINESS group of independent organizations allied for specific goal a group of independent organizations that join forces to achieve a particular goal, for example, to bid for a project or to conduct cooperative purchasing. A consortium goes on to complete the project if its bid is successful and is often dissolved on completion. This form of temporary alliance allows diverse skills, capabilities, and knowledge to be brought together.

consultant GENERAL MANAGEMENT specialist brought in to give advice to organization an expert in a specialized field brought in to provide independent professional advice to an organization on some aspect of its activities. A consultant may advise on the overall management of an organization or on a specific project, such as the introduction of a new computer system. Consultants are usually retained by a client for a set period of time, during which they will investigate the matter in hand and produce a report detailing their recommendations. Consultants may be established in business independently or be employed by a large consulting firm. Specific types of consultants include **management consultants** and **internal consultants**.

consulting actuary PENSIONS actuary advising pension funds an independent actuary who gives mathematical and statistical advice to large pension funds

consumer ECONOMICS somebody using product or service somebody who uses a product or service. A consumer may not be the purchaser of a product or service and should be distinguished from a customer, who is the person or organization that purchased the product or service.

consumer advertising MARKETING advertising aimed at consumer market advertising aimed at individuals and the domestic and family market as opposed to industrial advertising, which is aimed at businesses

consumer behavior MARKETING consumer buying behavior the factors that affect people's decision-making on whether to buy something and what to buy. *See also* ***consumer demand***

consumer confidence ECONOMICS how people feel about economic future a measure of how people feel about the future of the economy and their own financial situation, obtained through polling

consumer council BUSINESS group representing consumers' interests a group that represents the interests of consumers

consumer credit FINANCE credit provided for purchase of goods credit given by stores, banks, and other financial institutions to consumers so that they can buy goods

Consumer Credit Act, 1974 FINANCE UK legislation regulating provision of loans in the United Kingdom, an Act of Parliament that licenses lenders and requires them to state clearly the full terms of loans that they make, including the APR

consumer demand MARKETING consumer buying behavior the patterns of **consumer behavior** that affect buying decisions. Consumer demand is influenced in various ways. Psychologists and marketers have identified three important factors affecting buying decisions: needs, which are things we must have, such as food; wants, which are nice to have but not essential, such as a new car; and motives, such as keeping up appearances. These factors form part of a profile which includes motivations, personality, perceptions, cognition, attitudes, and values. Other factors that influence demand include gender, age, social grouping, education, location, income, culture, and the seasons. Consumers can therefore be divided into discrete segments, each of which has a specific pattern of buying behavior. Products and services can then be targeted at specific segments of the market.

consumer durables BUSINESS purchased items intended for long-term use items that are bought and used by the public and intended to last a long time, for example, washing machines, refrigerators, or stoves

consumer-facing GENERAL MANAGEMENT **1.** engaging directly with consumers involved with or involving direct contact with consumers **2.** directly accessible by consumers able to be directly accessed by consumers, and often being the first point of contact

consumer goods marketing MARKETING promotion of products to end users the promotion of products to members of the public. Consumer goods marketing is aimed at individuals rather than organizations and promotes products directly to the end user rather than to intermediaries. Marketing strategies will be different from those used in **industrial goods marketing**.

consumerism MARKETING influence of consumers on product manufacturing and sale the influence of the general public, as end users of products and services, on the way companies manufacture and sell their goods. Consumers exert considerable power over companies as organizations become more customer-focused. Demand is rising for products that are of high quality, ethically produced, well priced, and safe, and consumerism pressures companies to operate and produce goods and services in accordance with the public's wishes. In fact, the goals of consumerism are not at odds with those of marketing, as both have the end goal of pleasing the consumer. In practice, however, marketing does not always succeed, and there is still a need for legislation to back up the right of consumers to demand products that are of good quality and for consumer protection bodies that influence the commercial world on consumers' behalf. A particular form of consumer pressure, motivated by environmental concerns, is **green consumerism**, which campaigns for environmentally friendly goods, services, and means of production.

consumer market research MARKETING market research focusing on consumers **market research** that focuses on gathering and analyzing data on individual or domestic consumers, as opposed to industrial or business customers. *Also called* ***consumer research***

consumer panel MARKETING selected consumers whose purchasing habits are tracked a carefully selected group of people whose purchasing habits are regularly monitored. A consumer panel usually consists of a large cross-section of the population so as to provide meaningful data. There are two types of panel: **diary panels**, where members fill in a regular detailed diary of purchases, and, less commonly, **home audit panels**, where visits are made to the homes of members to check purchases, packaging, and used cartons. These panels run over a period of time to gain a broad overview of purchasing habits. A **focus group** is similar to a consumer panel, but is usually used to determine customers' views of a specific product or range of products. Members of a group meet together under the guidance of a facilitator to discuss their opinions on a face-to-face basis.

consumer price index ECONOMICS benchmark of basic retail prices an index of the prices of goods and services purchased by consumers, used to measure the cost of living or the rate of inflation in an economy. *Abbr* **CPI**

consumer profile MARKETING detailed analysis of similar consumers for market research a detailed analysis of the purchasing habits of a group of **consumers**, assessing influences such as age, gender, education, occupation, income, and personal and psychological characteristics. Consumer profiles are built up from extensive **market research** and are used for **market segmentation** purposes.

consumer protection MARKETING regulations protecting consumers' interests the safeguarding of consumers' interests in terms of quality, price, and safety, usually within a statutory framework. The growing purchasing power of consumers and the rise in **consumerism** from the late 1950s onward led to increased demands for protection against unsafe goods and services and unscrupulous trading practices.

consumer research MARKETING = ***consumer market research***

consumer services marketing MARKETING promotion and sale of services to domestic consumers the marketing of services to domestic consumers. Consumer services marketing may promote such services as banking, insurance, travel and tourism, leisure, telecommunications, and services provided by local authorities. Strategies to market these services to business constitute **industrial services marketing**.

consumer spending MARKETING total amount of household and personal expenditure the total value of household and personal expenditure measured at macro and micro levels. At the macro level, consumer confidence can be measured by the overall levels of consumer spending; if earnings have increased at a faster rate than prices, then disposable income, or spending power, increases. At a micro level, there are market reports on the value of actual and predicted spend on a large range of consumer goods, including food, pharmaceuticals, clothing, cars, and vacations. **Consumer demand** is a related concept.

consumer-to-consumer commerce E-COMMERCE electronic transactions between consumers e-business transactions conducted between two individuals. The auction site eBay is a facilitator of consumer-to-consumer commerce.

consumption ECONOMICS amount of products and services used the quantity of resources used by consumers to satisfy their current needs and wants, measured by the sum of the current expenditure of the government and individual consumers

consumption tax TAX tax to encourage less use of something a tax used to encourage people to buy less of a particular good or service by increasing its price. This type of tax is often levied in times of national hardship.

contact card E-COMMERCE card that physically touches card reader a **smart card** in which the microprocessor chip is visible and can make physical contact with the reading device

contactless card E-COMMERCE card with chip read by radio signals a **smart card** in which the microprocessor chip is not visible and is accessed by the reading device by radio signals rather than by physical contact. An increasingly common use of this technology is in such applications as toll collection, where the card is accessed as the motorist displays it to the reading device in passing.

contagion ECONOMICS spreading effect of downturn across economies a situation in which a weakening economy in one country causes economies in other countries to weaken

contango MARKETS future delivery costing more than delivery now a situation where the price of commodities is higher for future delivery than it is for immediate delivery

content management E-COMMERCE dealing with words and pictures on website the means and methods of managing the textual and graphical content of a website

contestable market MARKETS economic market that any firm can participate in a market in which there are no barriers to entry, as when there is **perfect competition**

contested takeover bid MERGERS & ACQUISITIONS takeover bid resisted by board of target firm a takeover bid where the board of the target company does not recommend it to the stockholders and tries to fight it. *Also called* ***hostile bid***

contingency LEGAL condition to be met in contract a condition in a contract which must be met before the contract becomes legally binding

contingency fund ACCOUNTING money held for unplanned expenditure money set aside from normal expenditure in case it is needed for unplanned expenses

contingency management GENERAL MANAGEMENT skill of adapting to changing situation the capacity for flexibility in varying responses and attitudes to meet the needs of different situations. Contingency management may be practiced by both individuals and organizations. Within the latter, it may be formalized through a **contingency plan** linked to **risk** or **crisis management** strategies, or be derived from the results of **scenario planning**.

contingency plan GENERAL MANAGEMENT **1.** secondary plan prepared in case of situational changes a plan, drawn up in advance, to ensure a positive and rapid response to a changing situation. A contingency plan often results from **scenario planning** and may form part of an organization's strategy for coping with disasters. **2.** plan if situation does not progress as hoped action to be implemented only upon the occurrence of anticipated future events other than those in the accepted forward plan

contingency table STATISTICS table classifying data by variables a table in which observations on data are classified according to a number of variables

contingency tax TAX new tax to deal with particular problem a one-time tax levied by a government to deal with a particular economic problem, for example, too high a level of imports coming into the country

contingency theory GENERAL MANAGEMENT idea that management method should match situation in management, the theory that there is no single best way to organize or manage and that each firm should be organized and structured to suit the technology used and the environment around it

contingent beneficiary LEGAL person who inherits if main beneficiary is dead a person

  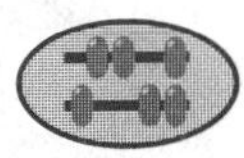   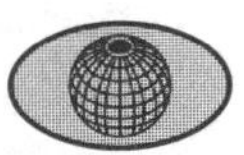   

who is designated to receive assets or proceeds such as those from an insurance policy or estate, if the primary beneficiary has died

contingent deferred sales charge STOCKHOLDING & INVESTMENTS fee payable on redemption a redemption fee, or **back-end loading**, payable on a share in a mutual fund only if the share is redeemed. It declines every year until it disappears, usually after six years. *Abbr* **CDSC**. *See also* ***B share***

contingent liability ACCOUNTING potential liability provided for in company's accounts a liability that may or may not occur, but for which provision is made in a company's accounts, as opposed to "provisions," for which money is set aside for an anticipated expenditure

continuous budget TREASURY MANAGEMENT = ***rolling budget***

continuous compounding ACCOUNTING continuous calculation and addition of interest a system in which interest is continuously calculated and added to the initial sum plus any interest that has already accrued on a debt

continuous disclosure STOCKHOLDING & INVESTMENTS in Canada, providing full information about public firm in Canada, the practice of ensuring that complete, timely, accurate, and balanced information about a public company is made available to shareholders

continuous improvement GENERAL MANAGEMENT making frequent small changes to improve quality the seeking of small improvements in processes and products, with the objective of increasing quality and reducing waste. Continuous improvement is one of the tools that underpin the philosophies of **total quality management** and **lean production**. Through constant study and revision of processes, a better product can result at reduced cost.

continuous inventory or **continuous stocktaking** ACCOUNTING comparing actual inventory to accounting records throughout year regular and consistent stocktaking throughout the fiscal year in order to ensure that the physical reality of the stock situation at any given time tallies with the accounting records. Any discrepancies will highlight errors or losses of stock and the accounts are adjusted to reflect this. Continuous inventory may preclude the need for an annual inventory.

continuous net settlement MARKETS automated system of tracking securities and cash balances an automated accounting system that uses a central clearing house to clear and settle securities transactions, maintaining complete records of companies' money balances. *Abbr* **CNS**

continuous operation costing or **continuous process costing** OPERATIONS & PRODUCTION basing costs on process not product a costing method in which costs are first charged to the process of production, then averaged over the units produced during the relevant period. It is used where production consists of a sequence of continuous or repetitive operations.

contra account ACCOUNTING account offsetting another account an account that offsets another account, for example, when a company's supplier is not only a creditor in that company's books but also a debtor because it has purchased goods on credit

contract 1. MARKETS securities transaction an agreement to buy or sell **securities** or other **financial instruments 2.** GENERAL MANAGEMENT legal agreement a mutually agreed, legally binding agreement between two or more parties

contract broker MARKETS broker trading for other brokers a broker who buys or sells stock on behalf of other brokers

contract costing ACCOUNTING attributing costs to individual contracts a form of **specific order costing** in which costs are attributed to individual contracts

contract for difference 1. STOCKHOLDING & INVESTMENTS swapping of fixed-price assets for floating-price assets an exchange of a fixed-price asset for one that has a price that varies **2.** CURRENCY & EXCHANGE currency exchange contract a **forward exchange rate** contract for currency ▶ *Abbr* **CFD**

contract hire GENERAL MANAGEMENT when firm leases resources from another firm an arrangement whereby an organization enters into a **contract** for the use of assets owned by another organization, as an alternative to purchasing the assets itself. Contract hire agreements usually cover a period shorter than the useful economic life of the assets concerned and often include arrangements for maintenance and replacement. Organizations frequently use contract hire arrangements for the provision of company cars or office equipment.

contracting GENERAL MANAGEMENT process of making legal supply agreement the process of making an agreement governed by a **contract** for the provision of goods or services to an organization

contracting out 1. GENERAL MANAGEMENT = ***outsourcing* 2.** PENSIONS moving employees from former UK state pension plan formerly in the United Kingdom, the withdrawal of employees by an employer or voluntarily from **SERPS** and their enrollment in a government-approved employer-sponsored pension plan or in a **personal pension**

contracting party LEGAL party to formal agreement a person or organization that signs a formal agreement to do or not do something

contract manufacturing OPERATIONS & PRODUCTION having another firm produce product or part the **outsourcing** of a requirement to manufacture a particular product or component to a third party. Contract manufacturing enables companies to reduce the level of investment in their own capabilities to manufacture, while retaining a product produced to a high quality, at a reasonable price, and delivered to a flexible schedule.

contract month MARKETS month when goods must be delivered the month in which an option expires and goods covered by it must be delivered. *Also called* ***delivery month***

contract note MARKETS full description of transaction a document with the complete description of a stock transaction

contract of employment LEGAL, HR & PERSONNEL legal agreement between employer and employee a legally enforceable agreement, either oral or written, between an employer and an employee which defines terms and **conditions of employment** to which both parties must adhere. Express terms of the contract are agreed between the two parties and include the organization's normal terms and conditions in addition to those that relate specifically to the individual. These terms can only be changed by employee agreement, if the contract itself allows for variation, or by terminating the contract. Terms are also implied in the contract by custom and practice or by common law. *Also called* ***employment contract***

contract purchasing OPERATIONS & PRODUCTION process of buying product through leasing a mechanism for buying leased goods. In contract purchasing, a purchaser agrees to buy goods or equipment to be paid for in a series of installments, each comprising a proportion of the capital and an interest element. After a final payment, legal ownership passes to the user.

 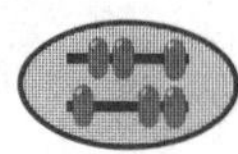   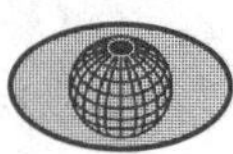   

contractual liability LEGAL legal responsibility stated in contract a legal responsibility for something as set out formally in a written agreement

contractual obligation LEGAL course of action required by contract the legal duty to take a specific course of action, as imposed by a commercial **contract** or a **contract of employment**

contractual savings STOCKHOLDING & INVESTMENTS money saved regularly in long-term investments savings in the form of regular payments into long-term investments such as pension plans

contract work HR & PERSONNEL work done under contract work done according to the terms of a written agreement

contra entry ACCOUNTING account entry offsetting earlier entry an entry made in the opposite side of an account to offset an earlier entry, for example, a debit against a credit

contrarian STOCKHOLDING & INVESTMENTS investing against market trends used to describe an investor who purchases securities in opposition to the current market trend, buying when most others are selling and vice versa

contrarian research STOCKHOLDING & INVESTMENTS investigation of purchases against market trends research on market trends resulting in advice to potential buyers to purchase stocks against the current trend

contrarian stockpicking STOCKHOLDING & INVESTMENTS choosing stocks against market trends the practice of purchasing stocks against the current market trend

contributed surplus FINANCE money from sources other than earnings the part of company profits that comes from sources other than earnings, for example, from selling stock above its **nominal value**

contribution 1. FINANCE, PENSIONS money paid into fund an amount of money placed in a fund of any kind, for example, money paid regularly into a pension **2.** FINANCE amount extra unit gains or loses the amount of money gained or lost from selling an additional unit of a product

contribution center FINANCE profitable section of business a **profit center** in which marginal or direct costs are equal to or less than revenue

contribution margin FINANCE profit from individual product the amount of money that an individual product or service contributes to net profit

contribution of capital FINANCE money paid as additional capital money paid to a company as additional capital

contributions holiday PENSIONS period when firm stops payments to pension plan a period during which a company stops making contributions to its pension plan because the plan is considered to be sufficiently well funded

contributory pension plan *US* PENSIONS pension provision requiring employees' contribution a pension plan into which employees must pay a portion of their salary on a regular basis. *UK term* ***contributory pension scheme***

contributory pension scheme *UK* PENSIONS = ***contributory pension plan***

control CORPORATE GOVERNANCE power to run organization the authority to direct an organization's operations and activities

control environment CORPORATE GOVERNANCE organization's management style the corporate culture of the directors and senior management of an organization

controlled company BUSINESS firm where one stockholder holds majority of voting stock a company in which a decisive proportion of the stock belongs to one owner. In the United States this is more than 25%, and in the United Kingdom, more than 50%.

controlled disbursement FINANCE payment once daily the practice of presenting checks for payment only once each day

controlled economy ECONOMICS economy with production quotas an economy in which production is governed by quotas. Controlled economies and **monopolies** are the opposite of market competition. *See also* ***competition***

controller ACCOUNTING organization's senior accountant an accountant who is responsible for maintaining an organization's accounts

control procedures CORPORATE GOVERNANCE rules for running organization the policies and procedures in addition to the **control environment** which are established to achieve an organization's specific objectives. They include procedures designed to prevent or to detect and correct errors.

control risk RISK likelihood of firm's control system allowing errors the part of an **audit risk** that relates to a client's internal control system

control security STOCKHOLDING & INVESTMENTS security held by somebody with management power a security held by a person who has an affiliation with the issuing company and the power to direct its management and policies, and whose resale must meet US Securities and Exchange Commission conditions

convergence 1. ECONOMICS movement toward similarity in countries' economies a situation in which the economic factors in two countries become more alike, for example, when basic interest rates or budget deficits become more similar **2.** MARKETS coming together of futures and spot prices a situation in which the price of a commodity on the futures market moves toward the **spot price** as settlement date approaches

conversion 1. MARKETS trading one investment product for another a trade of one convertible financial instrument for another, for example, a bond for shares of stock **2.** MARKETS trading one mutual fund's shares for another's a trade of shares of one mutual fund for shares of another in the same family **3.** PENSIONS transfer of assets to Roth IRA the process of transferring assets to a **Roth IRA** from another type of **IRA**

conversion costs FINANCE expense of changing raw materials into products the cost of changing raw materials into finished or semi-finished products. Conversion costs include wages, other direct production costs, and the production overhead.

conversion discount or **conversion premium** STOCKHOLDING & INVESTMENTS price difference between convertible and common stock the difference between the price of convertible stock and the common stock into which it is to be converted

conversion issue STOCKHOLDING & INVESTMENTS offer of new bonds as older bonds expire the issue of new bonds, timed to coincide with the date of maturity of older bonds, with the intention of persuading investors to reinvest

conversion of funds FRAUD improper use of somebody else's money the act of using money that does not belong to you for a purpose for which it is not supposed to be used

conversion period STOCKHOLDING & INVESTMENTS period for converting loan stock into common stock a time during which convertible loan stock may be changed into common stock

conversion price 1. CURRENCY & EXCHANGE exchange rate for currency the price at

     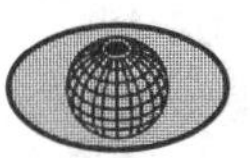   

which a currency is changed into a foreign currency. *Also called* ***conversion rate*** *(sense 2)* **2.** STOCKHOLDING & INVESTMENTS price offered for converting preferred stock the price at which preferred stock is converted into common stock

conversion rate **1.** STOCKHOLDING & INVESTMENTS = ***conversion price*** **2.** MARKETING how many people buy after consideration the percentage of inquiries by potential customers or sales calls by sales staff that results in actual sales

conversion ratio **1.** STOCKHOLDING & INVESTMENTS relative value of two convertible investment products an expression of the quantity of one security that can be obtained for another, for example, shares for a **convertible bond**.

The conversion ratio may be established when the convertible is issued. If that is the case, the ratio will appear in the indenture, the binding agreement that details the convertible's terms.

If the conversion ratio is not set, it can be calculated quickly by dividing the nominal value of the convertible security (typically $1,000) by its conversion price.

$$\frac{\$1{,}000}{\$40 \text{ per share}} = 25$$

In this example, the conversion ratio is 25:1, which means that every bond held with a $1,000 nominal value can be exchanged for 25 shares of common stock.

Knowing the conversion ratio enables an investor to decide whether convertibles (or a group of them) are more valuable than the shares of common stock they represent. If the stock is currently trading at 30, the conversion value is $750, or $250 less than the nominal value of the convertible. It would therefore be unwise to convert.

A convertible's indenture can sometimes contain a provision stating that the conversion ratio will change over the years. **2.** MERGERS & ACQUISITIONS number of shares traded for others during merger the number of shares of one common stock to be issued for each outstanding ordinary share of a different type when a merger takes place

conversion value STOCKHOLDING & INVESTMENTS value of investment if changed for another type the value that a security would have if converted into another type of security

convertibility CURRENCY & EXCHANGE ease of currency exchange the ability of one currency to be easily exchanged for another currency

convertible ARM MORTGAGES adjustable-rate mortgage that can be made fixed-rate an adjustable-rate mortgage that the borrower can convert into a fixed-rate mortgage under specific terms

convertible bond STOCKHOLDING & INVESTMENTS bond that can be traded for another investment a bond that the owner can convert into another asset, especially common stock

convertible currency CURRENCY & EXCHANGE easily exchanged currency a currency that can easily be exchanged for another

convertible debenture STOCKHOLDING & INVESTMENTS debenture exchangeable for stock a debenture or **loan stock** that can be exchanged for stock at a later date

convertible loan stock STOCKHOLDING & INVESTMENTS in UK, money loaned and redeemable as stock in the United Kingdom, money lent to a company which can be converted into shares at a later date

convertible preference shares *UK* STOCKHOLDING & INVESTMENTS = ***convertible preferred stock***

convertible preferred stock *US* STOCKHOLDING & INVESTMENTS stock that can be traded for another investment stocks that give the holder the right to exchange them at a fixed price for another security, usually common stock.

Preferred stocks and other convertible securities offer investors a hedge: fixed-interest income without sacrificing the chance to participate in a company's capital appreciation.

When a company does well, investors can convert their holdings into common stock that is more valuable. When a company is less successful, they can still receive interest and principal payments, and also recover their investment and preserve their capital if a more favorable investment appears.

Conversion ratios and prices are important facts to know about preferred stocks. This information is found on the indenture statement that accompanies all issues. Occasionally the indenture will state that the conversion ratio will change over time. For example, the conversion price might be $50 for the first five years, $55 for the next five years, and so forth. Stock splits can affect conversion considerations.

In theory, convertible preferred stocks (and convertible exchangeable preferred stocks) are usually perpetual. However, issuers tend to force conversion or induce voluntary conversion for convertible preferred stocks within ten years. Steadily increasing common stock dividends is one inducement tactic used. As a result, the conversion feature for preferred stocks often resembles that of debt securities. Call protection for the investor is usually about three years, and a 30 to 60-day call notice is typical.

About 50% of convertible equity issues also have a "soft call provision." If the common stock price reaches a specified ratio, the issuer is permitted to force conversion before the end of the normal protection period. *UK term* ***convertible preference shares***

convertibles STOCKHOLDING & INVESTMENTS securities convertible to common stock corporate bonds or shares of preferred stock that can be converted into common stock at a set price on set dates

convertible security STOCKHOLDING & INVESTMENTS investment product that can be converted to another a bond, warrant, or share of preferred stock that can be converted into another type of security, especially common stock

convertible term assurance *UK* INSURANCE = ***convertible term insurance***

convertible term insurance *US* INSURANCE extendable life insurance life insurance with an agreed termination date that the policyholder can convert to insurance until death under specific conditions

convexity ECONOMICS, FINANCE relationship of values the convex shape of a curve. The theory is that if points in a set are connected and the line between any two points is included in the set, then the set is convex. In economics, this corresponds to diminishing **marginal utility**. In finance it can represent a convex curve in the price yield relationship of a bond or any non-linear price function, for example, that of an option.

conveyance *US* REAL ESTATE transfer of title to real estate the legal transfer of real estate from the seller to the buyer. *UK term* ***conveyancing***

conveyancing *UK* REAL ESTATE = ***conveyance***

COO *abbr* GENERAL MANAGEMENT chief operating officer

cooling-off period **1.** LEGAL time allowed for reconsidering agreement a period during which somebody who is about to enter into an agreement may reflect on all aspects of the arrangement and change his or her mind if necessary **2.** HR & PERSONNEL break in negotiations allowing parties to calm down an agreed pause in a dispute, especially a labor dispute, to allow the tempers of the negotiating parties to cool before the

     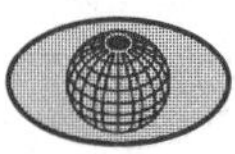   

resumption of negotiations **3.** *UK* INSURANCE period allowing cancellation of insurance a period of ten days during which somebody who has signed a life insurance policy may cancel it

cooperative BUSINESS jointly owned organization a business that is jointly owned by the people who operate it, with all profits shared equally

cooperative advertising MARKETING joint advertising by different groups with same goals a joint advertising campaign between groups with a shared objective, for example, retailer groups, or manufacturer and retailer

cooperative movement BUSINESS organized effort to share profits from joint business a movement that aims to share profits and benefits from jointly owned commercial enterprises among members. The movement was begun in Rochdale, Lancashire, England, in 1844 by 28 weavers and developed to include manufacturing and wholesale businesses as well as insurance and financial services. The Co-op in the United Kingdom and the Mondragon cooperative in Spain are two of the best-known examples.

cooperative society BUSINESS organization with customers and employees as joint partners an organization in which customers and employees are partners and share the profits

coproperty BUSINESS co-ownership of property the ownership of property by two or more people together

coproprietor BUSINESS sharer in ownership of property a person who owns a property with one other person or more

copyright LEGAL legal protection for creative material the legal protection for creative ideas, trademarks, and other brand-related material

copy testing MARKETING investigating effectiveness of advertising content research carried out to test the effectiveness of creative advertising material

copywriter MARKETING somebody who writes advertising material a person who devises the wording of an advertisement or promotional material. A copywriter may be employed by an advertising agency or, in scientific or technical areas, directly by a manufacturing or distribution company. Many copywriters also work freelance.

core business BUSINESS firm's most important activities the central, and usually the original, focus of an organization's activities which differentiates it from others and makes a vital contribution to its success. The concept of core business became prominent in the 1980s when **diversification** by large companies failed to generate the anticipated degree of commercial success. It was later suggested that organizations should avoid diversifying into areas beyond their field of expertise. An organization's core business should be defined by its **core competences**.

core capability GENERAL MANAGEMENT = ***core competence***

core competence GENERAL MANAGEMENT, HR & PERSONNEL firm's important ability that makes it different a key ability or strength that an organization has acquired that differentiates it from others, gives it **competitive advantage**, and contributes to its long-term success. Core competence is a resource-based approach to corporate strategy. The terms core competence and core capability are often used interchangeably, but some writers make distinctions between the two concepts. *Also called* ***core capability***

core values 1. GENERAL MANAGEMENT firm's important guiding principles the guiding principles of an organization, espoused by senior management, and accepted by employees, often reflected in the **mission statement** of the organization. Core values often influence the culture of an organization and are usually long-standing beliefs. *Also called* ***shared values*** **2.** HR & PERSONNEL person's important guiding principles a small set of key concepts and ideals that guide somebody's life and help him or her to make important decisions

corner MARKETS control market and price to control enough of a specific good or service to be able to manipulate the price

corporate action STOCKHOLDING & INVESTMENTS firm's action that affects its shares a measure that a company takes that has an effect on the number of shares outstanding or the rights that apply to shares

corporate bond STOCKHOLDING & INVESTMENTS bond issued by firm a long-term bond with fixed interest issued by a corporation

corporate culture GENERAL MANAGEMENT shared values of organization the combined beliefs, values, ethics, procedures, and atmosphere of an organization. The culture of an organization consists of largely unspoken values, norms, and behaviors that become the natural way of doing things. An organization's culture may be more apparent to an external observer than an internal practitioner. There can be several subcultures within an organization, for example, defined by hierarchy, e.g.shop floor or executive, or by function, e.g. sales, design, or production. Changing or renewing corporate culture in order to achieve the organization's strategy is considered one of the major tasks of organization leadership, as it is recognized that such a change is hard to achieve without the will of the leader.

corporate finance FINANCE financial affairs of businesses the financial affairs of companies and institutions

corporate fraud FRAUD dishonest behavior at company level a type of fraud committed by large organizations rather than individuals, for example, auditing irregularities. Since the collapse of Enron and WorldCom in 2001 and 2002, respectively, auditing practice around the world, but especially in the United States, has come under much scrutiny. Both companies had overstated their profits, but the auditors, Arthur Andersen, had approved accounts in each case.

corporate giving GENERAL MANAGEMENT donations by firm to community monetary or in-kind donations by organizations as part of the process of community involvement

corporate governance CORPORATE GOVERNANCE system for running firm the system by which companies are directed and controlled. Boards of directors are responsible for the governance of their companies. The stockholders' role in governance is to appoint the directors and the auditors and to satisfy themselves that an appropriate governance structure is in place. The responsibilities of the board include setting the company's strategic goals, providing the leadership to put them into effect, supervising the management of the business, and reporting to the stockholders on their stewardship. The board's actions are subject to laws, regulations, and the wishes of the stockholders in the general meeting.

corporate hospitality GENERAL MANAGEMENT meals and entertainment paid for by firm entertainment provided by an organization. Corporate hospitality was originally designed to help sales people build relationships with customers, but it is now increasingly used as a staff incentive and in employee team building and training exercises.

corporate identity CORPORATE GOVERNANCE firm's distinctive features as expressed to outsiders the distinctive characteristics or personality of an organization, including

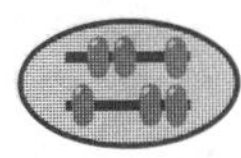

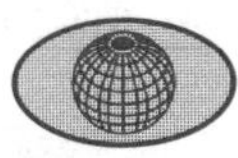

corporate culture, values, and philosophy as perceived by those within the organization and presented to those outside. Corporate identity is expressed through the name, symbols, and logos used by the organization, and the design of communication materials, and is a factor influencing the **corporate image** of an organization. The creation of a strong corporate identity also involves consistency in the organization's actions, behavior, products, and brands, and often reflects the **mission statement** of an organization. A positive corporate identity can promote a sense of purpose and belonging within the organization and encourage employee commitment and involvement.

corporate image CORPORATE GOVERNANCE public's ideas about what firm is like the perceptions and impressions of an organization by the public as a result of interaction with the organization and the way the organization presents itself. Organizations have traditionally focused on the design of communication and advertising materials, using logos, symbols, text, and color to create a favorable impression on target groups, but a variety of additional activities contribute to a positive corporate image. These include public relations programs such as community involvement, sponsorship, and environmental projects, participation in quality improvement schemes, and good practice in industrial relations.

corporate planning CORPORATE GOVERNANCE process of making plans to achieve firm's objectives the process of drawing up detailed action plans to achieve an organization's goals and objectives, taking into account the resources of the organization and the environment within which it operates. Corporate planning represents a formal, structured approach to achieving objectives and to implementing the corporate strategy of an organization. It has traditionally been seen as the responsibility of senior management. The use of the term became predominant during the 1960s but has now been largely superseded by the concept of **strategic management**.

corporate raider MERGERS & ACQUISITIONS somebody buying stake prior to hostile takeover a person or company that buys a stake in another company with a view to making a **hostile takeover** bid

corporate resolution CORPORATE GOVERNANCE document saying who can manage firm's money a document signed by the officers of a corporation naming those persons who can sign checks, withdraw cash, and have access to the corporation's bank account

corporate restructuring GENERAL MANAGEMENT major change in firm's activities a fundamental change in direction and strategy for an organization, which affects the way in which the organization is structured. Corporate restructuring may involve increasing or decreasing the layers of personnel between the top and the bottom of an organization, or reassigning roles and responsibilities. Invariably, corporate restructuring has come to mean reorganizing after a period of unsatisfactory performance and poor results, and is often manifested in the divestment or closure of parts of the business and the outplacement, or shedding, of personnel. In this case, corporate restructuring is used as a euphemism for delayering, rationalization, downsizing, or rightsizing.

corporate spinoff BUSINESS small firm formed from larger parent firm a small company that has been split off from a larger, parent organization

corporate strategy GENERAL MANAGEMENT firm's plans for future the direction an organization takes with the objective of achieving business success in the long term. Recent approaches have focused on the need for companies to adapt to and anticipate changes in the business environment. The formulation of corporate strategy involves establishing the purpose and scope of the organization's activities and the nature of the business it is in, taking the environment in which it operates, its position in the marketplace, and the competition it faces into consideration.

corporation US BUSINESS firm owned by stockholders an organization in which a number of people provide financing in return for stock. The principle of **limited liability** limits the maximum loss a stockholder can make if the company fails. *UK term* ***limited liability company***

corporation tax TAX tax on profits and gains a tax on profits and capital gains made by companies, calculated before dividends are paid. *Abbr* **CT**

correction FINANCE adjustment in valuation of something a change in the valuation of something that is thought to be overvalued or undervalued which results in its being more realistically valued

correlation STATISTICS relatedness of variables the interdependence between pairs of variables in data

correlation coefficient STATISTICS measure of relatedness of variables an index of the linear relationship between two variables in data

correspondent bank BANKING bank operating as foreign bank's agent a bank that acts as an agent for a foreign bank

cost FINANCE **1.** money paid for product the amount of money that is paid to secure a good or service. Cost is the amount paid from the purchaser's standpoint, whereas the price is the amount paid from the vendor's standpoint. **2.** calculate cost of something to ascertain what must be paid to acquire a specific thing or engage in a specific activity

cost, insurance, and freight OPERATIONS & PRODUCTION including product, shipping, and insurance costs indicates that a quoted price includes the costs of the merchandise, transportation, and insurance. *Abbr* **CIF**

cost account ACCOUNTING accounting record of section of business a record of revenue and/or expenditure of a cost center or cost unit

cost accountant ACCOUNTING accountant advising on business costs an accountant who gives managers information about their business costs

cost accounting ACCOUNTING preparation of accounts detailing business costs the process of preparing special accounts of manufacturing and sales costs

cost allocation ACCOUNTING assignment of fixed expenses to cost centers the way in which overhead expenses are assigned to different cost centers

cost analysis OPERATIONS & PRODUCTION calculation of cost of new product the process of calculating in advance how much a new product will cost

cost and freight OPERATIONS & PRODUCTION including product and shipping costs, but not insurance indicates that a quoted price includes the costs of the merchandise and the transportation but not the cost of insurance. *Abbr* **CFR**

cost audit ACCOUNTING check on cost records and accounts the verification of cost records and accounts, and a check on adherence to prescribed **cost accounting** procedures and their continuing relevance

cost basis ACCOUNTING price paid including purchase costs the price paid for an asset plus any expenses such as commissions associated with it at the time of purchase

cost-benefit analysis ACCOUNTING comparison of activity's costs against results

     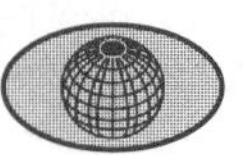   

a comparison between the cost of the resources used, plus any other costs imposed by an activity, for example, pollution or environmental damage, and the value of the financial and non-financial benefits derived, to establish whether there is a positive outcome. *Also called **benefit-cost ratio***

cost center ACCOUNTING section of business that costs firm money a department, function, section, or individual whose cost, overall or in part, is an accepted overhead of a business in return for services provided to other parts of the organization. A cost center is usually an **indirect cost** of an organization's products or services.

cost cutting OPERATIONS & PRODUCTION actions to reduce organization's expenses the reduction of the amount of money spent on the operations of an organization or on the provision of products and services. Cost-cutting measures such as budget reductions, salary freezes, and layoffs may be taken by an organization at a time of recession or financial difficulty or in situations where inefficiency has been identified. Alternative approaches to cost cutting include modifying organizational structures and redesigning organizational processes for greater efficiency. Excessive cost cutting may affect **productivity** and quality or the organization's ability to add value.

cost driver ACCOUNTING something that affects cost of activity a factor that determines the cost of an activity. Cost drivers are analyzed as part of **activity based costing** and can be used in **continuous improvement** programs. They are usually assessed together as multiple drivers rather than singly. There are two main types of cost driver: the first is a **resource driver**, which refers to the contribution of the quantity of resources used to the cost of an activity; the second is an **activity driver**, which refers to the costs incurred by the activities required to complete a specific task or project.

cost-effective OPERATIONS & PRODUCTION giving best results for least expense offering the maximum benefit for a given level of expenditure. When limited resources are available to meet specific objectives, the cost-effective solution is the best that can be achieved for that level of expenditure and the one that provides good value for money. The term is also used to refer to a level of expenditure that is perceived to be commercially viable.

cost-effectiveness analysis TREASURY MANAGEMENT measurement of how much positive results cost a method for measuring the benefits and effectiveness of a particular item of expenditure. Cost-effectiveness analysis requires an examination of expenditure to determine whether the money spent could have been used more effectively or whether the resulting benefits could have been attained through less financial outlay.

cost factor ACCOUNTING activity or item incurring business cost an activity or item of material, equipment, or personnel that incurs a cost

cost function ECONOMICS ratio of total cost to quantity produced a mathematical function relating a firm's or an industry's total cost to its output and factor costs

cost inflation ECONOMICS = ***cost-push inflation***

costing OPERATIONS & PRODUCTION calculating total expenses related to product the determination of the total cost of a product, from the purchase of **raw materials** to delivery to the consumer. There are a large number of costing techniques, including **life-cycle costing**, **activity based costing**, and **operating costing**.

cost of appraisal OPERATIONS & PRODUCTION money spent to check quality of products the costs incurred in order to ensure that outputs produced meet required quality standards

cost of capital TREASURY MANAGEMENT interest paid on operating capital interest paid on the capital used in operating a business

cost of conformance OPERATIONS & PRODUCTION money spent on quality requirements the costs of achieving specific quality standards for a product or service. *See also **cost of appraisal**, **cost of prevention***

cost of entry OPERATIONS & PRODUCTION expense of bringing out new product the costs of introducing a new product to the market. Cost of entry calculations include the cost of all research, development, production, testing, marketing, advertising, and distribution of the new product.

cost of external failure OPERATIONS & PRODUCTION cost of correcting quality of products after sale the costs arising from inadequate quality which are identified after the transfer of ownership from supplier to purchaser. *See also **cost of internal failure***

cost of goods sold OPERATIONS & PRODUCTION **1.** money spent on products to sell for a retailer, the cost of buying and acquiring the goods it sells to its customers **2.** money spent on supplying services for a service firm, the cost of the employee services supplied **3.** money spent manufacturing products to sell for a manufacturer, the cost of buying the raw materials and manufacturing finished products ► *Abbr* **COGS**

cost of internal failure TREASURY MANAGEMENT cost of correcting quality of products before sale the costs arising from inadequate quality which are identified before the transfer of ownership from supplier to purchaser. *See also **cost of external failure***

cost of living FINANCE money spent on housing, food, and basics the average amount spent by somebody on accommodations, food, and other basic necessities. In the United States, a broad definition might sometimes include education and healthcare. Salaries are usually increased annually to cover rises in the cost of living.

cost-of-living adjustment or **cost-of-living increase** FINANCE, HR & PERSONNEL extra pay to cover price rises a small increase in salaries made to account for rises in the **cost of living**

cost-of-living index FINANCE, HR & PERSONNEL information on changes in prices over time an index that shows changes in the cost of living by comparing current prices for a variety of goods with the prices paid for them in previous years

cost of nonconformance OPERATIONS & PRODUCTION money lost by not meeting quality requirements the cost of failure to deliver the required standard of quality for a product or service. *See also **cost of external failure**, **cost of internal failure***

cost of prevention OPERATIONS & PRODUCTION money spent to avoid producing low-quality products the costs incurred prior to or during production in order to prevent substandard or defective products or services from being produced

cost of sales OPERATIONS & PRODUCTION = ***cost of goods sold** (sense 3)*

cost per click-through E-COMMERCE system paying online advertiser for each ad click a pricing model for online advertising, where the seller gets paid whenever a visitor clicks on an ad

cost-plus pricing OPERATIONS & PRODUCTION deciding price by adding amount to product's cost a standard **markup** added to the cost of a product or service to establish

  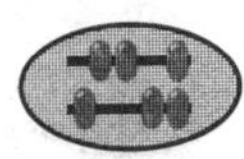   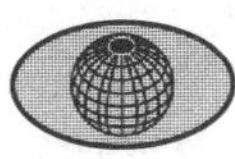   

a selling price. Many companies simply add a percentage of production costs to arrive at a selling price. The degree of markup depends on the level of anticipated sales. It may incorporate a desired return on investment. Low volume luxury goods may have a high markup; high volume goods may have a relatively lower markup.

cost price OPERATIONS & PRODUCTION selling price yielding no profit to seller a selling price that is the same as the price paid by the seller, which results in no profit being made

cost-push inflation ECONOMICS price increases caused by rise in production costs inflation in which price rises result from increased production costs or similar factors rather than from customer demand

cost reduction OPERATIONS & PRODUCTION cutting costs to increase profits the process of identifying and eliminating unnecessary costs to improve the profitability of a business

costs ACCOUNTING amounts of money paid out for something amounts of money that are paid out for something, especially on a regular basis

cost savings OPERATIONS & PRODUCTION benefits from reducing costs the benefits to an organization derived from reducing expenditures

costs of complexity OPERATIONS & PRODUCTION = ***complexity costs***

cottage industry BUSINESS commercial activity performed by individuals or small businesses an industry made up of small businesses, often run from the home of the proprietor

Council of Mortgage Lenders MORTGAGES UK association for mortgage industry in the United Kingdom, the trade association for the mortgage industry, whose members account for about 98% of UK residential mortgage lending. *Abbr* **CML**

council tax TAX local tax paid in UK in the United Kingdom, a tax paid by individuals or companies to a local authority. Introduced in April 1993, the rate of council tax depends on the estimated value of the residential or commercial property occupied.

counterbid FINANCE **1.** higher bid competing with another bid a higher bid made in reply to a previous bid by another bidder **2.** make counterbid to make a higher bid in reply to a previous bid

counter-claim LEGAL **1.** claim for damages responding to another a claim for damages made in reply to a previous claim **2.** make counter-claim to put in a counter-claim for something

countercyclical stock STOCKHOLDING & INVESTMENTS stock price moving against economic trend a stock that tends to rise as the economy weakens and fall as it strengthens

counterfeit FRAUD **1.** illegally produce imitation goods or money to produce forged or imitation goods or money intended to deceive or defraud. Counterfeited goods of inferior quality are often sold at substantially lower prices than genuine products and may bear the **brand** or **trade name** of the company. Counterfeiting violates **trademark** and **intellectual property** rights and may damage the reputation of producers of authentic goods. National and international legislation provides some recourse to companies against counterfeiters, but strategies such as consumer warnings and labeling methods are also used to minimize the impact of counterfeiting. Efforts to eliminate counterfeiting are coordinated by the International Anti-Counterfeiting Coalition. **2.** also **counterfeited** relating to illegally produced imitations used to describe goods or money illegally produced but appearing authentic

counterfoil BANKING small paper record of transaction a slip of paper kept after writing a check, an invoice, or a receipt, as a record of the deal that has taken place

countermand GENERAL MANAGEMENT cancel order given earlier to say that an order must not be carried out

counter-offer BUSINESS higher or lower offer responding to another a higher or lower offer made in reply to another offer

counterparty LEGAL other person in legal agreement a person or organization with whom the person or organization in question is entering into a contract

counterparty risk RISK risk associated with other party to contract the possibility that the person or persons with whom a contract exists will fail to fulfill the terms of their side of the contract

counterpurchase INTERNATIONAL TRADE import bartered for exporter's commitment to further trade a reciprocal trading practice involving a traditional export transaction plus the commitment of the exporter to buy additional goods or services from that country. *See also* ***countertrade***

countersign FINANCE sign document after other signatory to sign a document that has already been signed by somebody else

countertrade INTERNATIONAL TRADE system of trade between two parties a variety of reciprocal trading practices. This umbrella term encompasses practices ranging from the direct exchange of goods for goods where no cash changes hands (**barter**) to more complex variations: **counterpurchase**, which involves a traditional export transaction plus the commitment of the exporter to buy additional goods or services from that country; and **buyback**, in which the supplier of a plant or equipment is paid from the future proceeds resulting from the use of the plant. Countertrade conditions vary widely from country to country and can be costly and administratively cumbersome.

countervailing duty TAX, INTERNATIONAL TRADE = ***anti-dumping duty***

country risk INTERNATIONAL TRADE risk of doing business in particular country the risk associated with undertaking transactions with, or holding assets in, a particular country. Sources of risk might be political, economic, or regulatory instability affecting overseas taxation, repatriation of profits, nationalization, currency stability, etc.

coupon STOCKHOLDING & INVESTMENTS **1.** paper requesting bond payment a piece of paper attached to a government bond certificate which a bondholder presents to request payment **2.** interest rate of bond the rate of interest paid on a bond issued at a fixed rate. *Also called* ***coupon rate***. **3.** interest payment on bond an interest payment made to a bondholder, originally on presentation of a dated coupon to the company or an agent of the issuer ◇ clip coupons FINANCE to collect periodic interest on a bond

coupon rate STOCKHOLDING & INVESTMENTS = ***coupon*** *(sense 2)*

coupon security STOCKHOLDING & INVESTMENTS government security carrying coupon and paying interest a government security that carries a coupon and pays interest, as opposed to a **zero-coupon security**, that pays no interest but is sold at a discount from its face value. *See also* ***zero-coupon security***

covariance STATISTICS measure of two variables' tendency to change together the value that is predicted from the product of the deviations of two variables from each of their means

covariate STATISTICS less important variable affecting important variable a variable that is not crucial in an investigation but may

     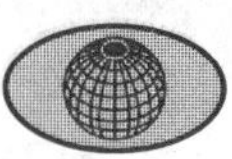   

affect the crucial variables from which a model is being built

covenant FINANCE legal financial agreement a financial agreement conditional on future events, for example, changes in the capital structure and rating of a firm, or fundamental changes in business strategy such as to divest of a major asset or to acquire another company. Covenants are frequently included in bond offerings or bank loan/syndication terms. In the United Kingdom, when payments are made by an individual under covenant to a charity, the charity can reclaim the tax paid by the donor.

cover *UK* INSURANCE = ***coverage***

coverage **1.** MARKETING how many customers reached the percentage of a target audience reached by different media **2.** *US* INSURANCE level of insurance protection the amount or type of protection guaranteed by an insurance policy. *UK term* ***cover***

covered bond STOCKHOLDING & INVESTMENTS bond with loan as security a bond that has mortgage or other loans given as security in case of default

covered option STOCKHOLDING & INVESTMENTS option backed by actual stock an **option** whose owner holds the stock for the option. A covered option can be either a **call option** or a **put option**.

covered warrant STOCKHOLDING & INVESTMENTS futures contract a type of **futures contract** issued by a financial institution allowing the holder to buy or sell a quantity of its **financial instruments**

cover note *UK* INSURANCE = ***binder***

covert human intelligence source FRAUD somebody providing information about illegal activity in the United Kingdom, a person who supplies information about somebody being investigated, for example, for fraud, without the knowledge of the person being investigated. *Abbr* **CHIS**

CP *abbr* FINANCE commercial paper

CPA *abbr* ACCOUNTING certified public accountant

CPF *abbr* PENSIONS Central Provident Fund

CPFR® OPERATIONS & PRODUCTION business practice encouraging collaboration between buyers and sellers a business practice that uses information sharing among buyers and sellers throughout the supply chain to make products available to customers when they need them, while reducing suppliers' costs such as inventory and transportation. *Full form* ***Collaborative Planning, Forecasting, and Replenishment***

CPI *abbr* ECONOMICS consumer price index

CPI inflation ECONOMICS inflation rate of economy using consumer price index the rate of **inflation** in an economy calculated using data from a **consumer price index**

CPIX *ANZ* ECONOMICS consumer price index the **consumer price index** excluding interest costs, on the basis that these are a direct outcome of monetary policy

crack E-COMMERCE disable copy protection on software, CD, or DVD to defeat the copy protection that is intended to prevent somebody from illegally copying and distributing a software product, music CD, or DVD

crash **1.** MARKETS very large drop in stock price a precipitous drop in value, especially of the stocks traded in a market **2.** ECONOMICS large and sudden economic decline a sudden and catastrophic downturn in an economy. While there were several in the 20th century, the crash in the United States in 1929 is one of the most famous. However, the events of 2008 have had even more severe global consequences.

crawling peg CURRENCY & EXCHANGE incremental control on exchange rates a method of controlling exchange rates, allowing them to move up or down slowly

CRD *abbr* STOCKHOLDING & INVESTMENTS Central Registration Depository

creative accounting FRAUD accounting methods used to conceal firm's true state the use of accounting methods to hide aspects of a company's financial dealings in order to make the company appear more or less successful than it is in reality (*slang*). *See also* ***corporate fraud***

creative destruction MERGERS & ACQUISITIONS process of new firms and products replacing old a way of describing the endless cycle of innovation, which results in established goods, services, or organizations being replaced by new models. The term was first mentioned by Joseph Schumpeter in *Capitalism, Socialism and Democracy* (1942), but used heavily during the dot-com boom of the late 1990s and early 2000s.

creative thinking or **creativity** GENERAL MANAGEMENT coming up with original interesting ideas the generation of new ideas by approaching problems or existing practices in innovative or imaginative ways. Psychologists have disagreed on the nature of creative thinking. Until about 1980, research concentrated on identifying the personality traits of creative people, but more recently psychologists have focused on the mental processes involved. Creative thinking involves reexamining assumptions and reinterpreting facts, ideas, and past experience. A growing interest in creative thinking as a source of **competitive advantage** has developed in recent years, and creative thinking is considered important, not just for the development of new products and services, but also for its role in organizational decision making and problem solving. Many organizations actively seek a corporate culture that encourages creative thinking. There are a number of techniques used to foster creative thinking, including brainstorming. Creative thinking is linked to innovation, the process of taking a new idea and turning it into a market offering.

credit FINANCE **1.** positive amount of assets after liabilities are deducted the amount of money left over when a person or organization has more **assets** than **liabilities**, and those liabilities are subtracted from the total of the assets **2.** lender's belief that borrower will repay loan the trust that a lender has in a borrower's ability to repay a loan, or a loan itself **3.** arrangement to pay later for product bought now a financial arrangement between the vendor and the purchaser of a good or service by which the purchaser may buy what he or she requires, but pay for it at a later date ◇ post a credit ACCOUNTING in bookkeeping, to enter a credit item in a ledger

credit account FINANCE = ***charge account***

credit availability FINANCE ease of borrowing the ease with which money can be borrowed at a given time

credit balance FINANCE sum owed on credit account the amount of money that a customer owes on a **charge account**

credit bureau FINANCE US firm evaluating people's ability to repay loans a company that assesses the creditworthiness of people for businesses or banks. *See also* ***mercantile agency***

credit capacity FINANCE total amount somebody can borrow and repay the amount of money that a person or organization can borrow and be expected to repay

credit card BANKING card from bank used to pay for things a card issued by a bank or financial institution and accepted by a merchant in payment for a transaction for which the cardholder must subsequently reimburse the issuer. *See also* ***charge card***

credit ceiling FINANCE = ***credit limit***

credit column ACCOUNTING accounting column recording money received the right-hand column in accounts showing money received

credit committee RISK group assessing creditworthiness a committee that evaluates a potential borrower's credit status and ability to repay loans

credit company FINANCE firm that lends money a company that extends credit to people. It may be an independent company or a subsidiary of a parent company such as an automobile manufacturer whose products are being bought.

credit control RISK monitoring of customers' credit management a system of checks designed to ensure that customers pay on time and do not owe more than their credit limit

credit controller FINANCE employee who manages payment of overdue invoices a member of staff whose job is to expedite the payment of overdue invoices

credit cooperative FINANCE group borrowing together an organization of people who join together to gain advantage in borrowing

credit creation FINANCE ability of banks to lend more money the collective ability of finance companies, banks, and other lenders of money to make money available to borrowers. While a central bank can create money, it cannot create credit.

credit crunch FINANCE inability or reluctance of banks to lend money the collective inability or unwillingness of finance companies, banks, and other lenders to make money available to borrowers (*informal*). *Also called* ***credit squeeze, liquidity squeeze***

credit default swap STOCKHOLDING & INVESTMENTS, RISK assumption of credit risk in return for payments a **derivative instrument** similar in structure to an insurance policy, in which the buyer of the instrument agrees to make payments to the seller in return for a guarantee that the seller will assume the credit risk of a third party. *Abbr* **CDS**

credit deposit E-COMMERCE credit card transaction amount put in seller's bank the value of the credit card purchases deposited in a merchant's bank account after the acquirer's fees are deducted

credit derivative STOCKHOLDING & INVESTMENTS, RISK contract transferring lender's risk a **financial instrument** or **derivative** by which the lender's risk is devolved to a third party and separately traded

credit entity FINANCE person borrowing or lending a borrower from a finance company, bank, or other lender of money, or the lender of the funds

credit entry ACCOUNTING entry for income or value an item in a financial statement recording money received or the value of an asset

credit exposure RISK lender's risk that borrower will not repay the risk to a lender that a borrower will default and not fulfill their contractual payment

credit facility BANKING arrangement to supply credit an arrangement with a bank or supplier that enables a person or organization to be given credit or borrow money when it is needed, for example, a **letter of credit, revolving credit** or a **term loan.** *Also called* ***lending facility***

credit freeze FINANCE period when government limits banks' lending a period during which lending by banks is restricted by government

credit granter FINANCE lender a person or organization that lends money

credit history FINANCE record of somebody's repayment of loans a potential borrower's record of debt repayment. Individuals or organizations with a poor credit history may find it difficult to find lenders who are willing to give them a loan.

Credit Industry Fraud Avoidance System FRAUD UK fraud prevention service in the United Kingdom, a nonprofit membership organization established for the purpose of preventing financial crime. *Abbr* **CIFAS**

crediting rate STOCKHOLDING & INVESTMENTS interest rate on insurance policy the interest rate paid on an insurance policy which is an investment

credit limit FINANCE total amount somebody is allowed to borrow the highest amount that a lender will allow somebody to borrow, for example, on a credit card. *Also called* ***credit ceiling***

credit line FINANCE = ***line of credit***

credit-linked note RISK fixed-income security with embedded credit default swap a fixed-income security with an embedded **credit default swap** which is sold to investors willing to take the risk of default in return for a high yield on their investment

credit market MARKETS market trading in debt securities the market in which debt securities such as loans, corporate bonds, commercial paper, and **credit default swaps** are bought and sold

credit note FINANCE *abbr* **c/n.** = ***credit slip***

creditor FINANCE somebody you owe money for goods or services a person or an entity to whom money is owed as a consequence of the receipt of goods or services in advance of payment

creditor days FINANCE number of days firm takes to pay creditors the number of days on average that a company requires to pay its creditors.

To determine creditor days, divide the cumulative amount of unpaid suppliers' bills (also called trade creditors) by sales, then multiply by 365. If suppliers' bills total \$800,000 and sales are \$9,000,000, the calculation is:

$$\frac{800{,}000}{9{,}000{,}000} \times 365 = 32.44 \text{ days}$$

The company takes 32.44 days on average to pay its bills.

Creditor days is an indication of a company's creditworthiness in the eyes of its suppliers and creditors, since it shows how long they are willing to wait for payment. Within reason, the higher the number the better, because all companies want to conserve cash. At the same time, a company that is especially slow to pay its bills (100 or more days, for example) may be a company having trouble generating cash, or one trying to finance its operations with its suppliers' funds. *See also* ***debtor days***

creditor nation INTERNATIONAL TRADE country with balance of payments surplus a country where payments received exceed those made over the same period

creditors' committee FINANCE lenders' group seeking money from bankrupt borrower a group that directs the efforts of creditors to receive partial repayment from a bankrupt person or organization. *Also called* ***creditors' steering committee***

creditors' meeting FINANCE meeting of bankrupt's creditors a meeting of those to whom a bankrupt person or organization owes money

creditors' settlement FINANCE agreement for partial repayment by bankrupt borrower an agreement on partial repayment to those to whom a bankrupt person or organization owes money

creditors' steering committee FINANCE = ***creditors' committee***

credit rating or **credit ranking** FINANCE **1.** evaluation of creditworthiness an

  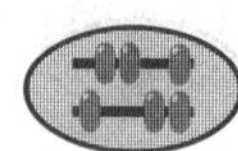   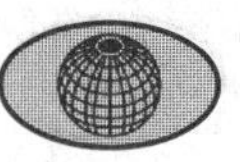   

assessment of a person's or an organization's ability to pay back money that they owe according to the terms on which it was borrowed, based on a broad assessment of financial health including previous loans and other outstanding financial obligations **2.** process of evaluating creditworthiness the process of assessing a person's or an organization's ability to pay back money that they owe according to the terms on which it was borrowed

credit rating agency US FINANCE firm evaluating creditworthiness a company that assesses a person's or an organization's ability to pay back money that they owe according to the terms on which it was borrowed, on behalf of businesses or banks. *UK term **credit-reference agency***

credit rationing FINANCE, RISK process of making it harder to borrow money the process of making credit less easily available or subject to high interest rates

credit receipt US FINANCE = ***credit slip***

credit-reference agency UK FINANCE = ***credit rating agency***

credit references FINANCE list of previous lenders when opening credit account details of individuals, companies, or banks who have given credit to a person or company in the past, supplied as references when somebody is opening a credit account with a new supplier

credit report FINANCE information concerning person's or organization's creditworthiness information about the ability of a person or organization to pay back money that they owe, used by financial institutions in determining decisions relevant to granting credit

credit risk RISK possibility that debtor will default the possibility that a person or an organization will not be able to pay back money that they owe according to the terms on which it was borrowed

credit sale FINANCE sale for which buyer can pay later a sales transaction by which the buyer is allowed to take immediate possession of the purchased goods and pay for them at a later date

credit scoring FINANCE calculation during credit rating a calculation done in the process of assessing a person's or an organization's ability to pay back money that they owe according to the terms on which it was borrowed

credit side ACCOUNTING part of financial statement with assets the section of a financial statement that lists assets. In **double-entry bookkeeping**, the right-hand side of each account is designated as the credit side. *See also **debit side***

credit slip US FINANCE statement that store owes customer money a receipt saying that a store owes a customer an amount of money for returned goods and entitling the person to goods of that value. *UK term **credit note***

credit spread RISK difference between debt yield of firm and benchmark the difference between the yield on the debt of a particular company and the yield on a risk-free asset such as a US **Treasury bond** having the same maturity

credit spread option STOCKHOLDING & INVESTMENTS, RISK option contract based on firm's credit spread an option contract on the **credit spread** of the debt of a particular company whose payoff is based on changes in the credit spread

credit spread swap STOCKHOLDING & INVESTMENTS, RISK exchange of fixed for credit-spread payment a **swap** in which one party makes a fixed payment to the other on the swap's settlement date and the second party pays the first an amount based on the actual credit spread

credit squeeze FINANCE = ***credit crunch***

credit standing FINANCE somebody's reputation for repaying debt the reputation that somebody has with regard to meeting financial obligations

credit system FINANCE means of making loans a set of rules and organizations involved in making loans on a commercial basis

credit union BANKING financial institution providing banking services to members a cooperative financial organization that provides banking services, including loans, to its members at relatively low rates of interest

creditworthiness FINANCE reliability in repaying debt the extent to which a person or organization is financially reliable enough to borrow money or be given credit

creditworthy FINANCE reliable in repaying debt regarded as being reliable in terms of ability to pay back money owed according to the terms on which it was borrowed

creeping takeover MERGERS & ACQUISITIONS takeover through gradual acquisition a takeover of a company achieved by the gradual acquisition of small amounts of stock over an extended period of time (*slang*)

creeping tender offer MERGERS & ACQUISITIONS gradual acquisition of firm's stock an acquisition of many shares in a company by gradual purchase, especially to avoid US restrictions on tender offers

CREST MARKETS UK electronic transaction system in the United Kingdom, the paperless system used for settling stock transactions electronically

crisis management GENERAL MANAGEMENT firm's methods of dealing with unexpected negative situation actions taken by an organization in response to unexpected events or situations with potentially negative effects that threaten resources and people or the success and continued operation of the organization. Crisis management includes the development of plans to reduce the risk of a crisis occurring and to deal with any crises that do arise, and the implementation of these plans so as to minimize the impact of crises and assist the organization to recover from them. Crisis situations may occur as a result of external factors such as the development of a new product by a competitor or changes in legislation, or internal factors such as a product failure or faulty **decision making**, and often involve the need to make quick decisions on the basis of uncertain or incomplete information. *See also **risk management**, **disaster management***

criticality OPERATIONS & PRODUCTION evaluation of ways something can fail a ranking of the severity of the various ways in which a system, device, or process can fail, their frequency of occurrence, and the consequences of their failure

critical mass GENERAL MANAGEMENT when firm or project becomes clearly worth continuing the point at which an organization or project has gained sufficient momentum or **market share** to be either self-sustaining or worth the input of extra investment or resources

critical-path method or **critical-path analysis** GENERAL MANAGEMENT way of determining activities necessary for success a planning technique used especially in project management to identify the activities within a project that are critical for its success. In critical-path method, individual activities within a project and their duration are recorded in a diagram or flow chart. A critical path is plotted through the diagram, showing the sequence in which activities must be completed in order to complete the project in the shortest amount of time, incurring the least cost.

critical region STATISTICS set of test results causing rejection of hypothesis the range of values of a test statistic that lead a researcher to reject the null hypothesis

critical restructuring GENERAL MANAGEMENT very large changes in firm's organization major economic or social changes that fundamentally reshape traditional patterns of organization

critical success factor GENERAL MANAGEMENT aspect essential to firm's success any of the aspects of a business that are identified as vital for successful targets to be reached and maintained. Critical success factors are usually identified in such areas as production processes, employee and organization skills, functions, techniques, and technologies. The identification and strengthening of such factors may be similar to identifying **core competences**, and is considered an essential element in achieving and maintaining **competitive advantage**.

critical value STATISTICS standard against which hypothesis is rejected the value with which a researcher compares a statistic from sample data in order to determine whether or not the null hypothesis should be rejected

CRM *abbr* MARKETING customer relationship management

CRO *abbr* REGULATION & COMPLIANCE Companies Registration Office

crony capitalism ECONOMICS system in which well-connected people control wealth a form of capitalism in which business contracts are awarded to the family and friends of the government in power rather than by open-market tender

cross MARKETS transaction with shared broker a transaction in securities in which one broker acts for both parties

crossborder services ACCOUNTING accounting services for client in another country accounting services provided by an accounting firm in one country on behalf of a client based in another country

crossborder trade INTERNATIONAL TRADE trade between neighboring countries the buying and selling of goods and services between two countries that have a common frontier

cross currency swap CURRENCY & EXCHANGE = ***currency swap*** *(sense 1)*

cross-docking OPERATIONS & PRODUCTION immediately matching items between incoming and outgoing shipments a procedure used in **logistics** to reduce handling and warehousing costs by immediately matching items from incoming shipments on the loading dock with outgoing shipment requirements and transferring them to the outgoing vehicles

crossed cheque *UK* BANKING check that can only be deposited a check with two lines across it showing that it can only be deposited at a bank and not exchanged for cash

crossed market MARKETS where price to buy exceeds price to sell a situation in which a bid to buy a stock or option is higher than the offer to sell

cross-functional OPERATIONS & PRODUCTION working as team with different functions toward goal used to describe a group of employees who have different functions within an organization and who work together as a team to achieve an objective

cross-hedging MARKETS hedging with related futures contract a form of hedging using an option on a different but related commodity, especially a currency

cross holdings STOCKHOLDING & INVESTMENTS, MERGERS & ACQUISITIONS reciprocal stockholdings designed to combat takeovers a situation in which two companies own stock in each other in order to stop either from being taken over

cross listing OPERATIONS & PRODUCTION trying to sell same thing in multiple places the practice of offering the same item for sale in more than one place

cross rate CURRENCY & EXCHANGE exchange rate of two currencies against third currency the rate of exchange between two currencies expressed in terms of the rate of exchange between them and a third currency, for example, sterling and the peso in relation to the dollar. *Also called* ***exchange cross rate***

cross-sectional study STATISTICS survey collecting various information at once a statistical study in which a variety of information is collected at the same time, for example, in a single telephone call

cross-sell OPERATIONS & PRODUCTION sell range of complementary products at same time to sell customers a range of products or services offered by an organization at the same time, for example, offering insurance services while selling somebody a mortgage

crowding out or **crowding out effect** MARKETS effect of major borrowing by government on credit markets the effect on credit markets produced by extremely large borrowing by a national government, causing an increase in interest rates and a reduction in some areas of investment

Crown Agent INTERNATIONAL TRADE UK government representative on international board a person appointed by the UK government to sit on a board that provides financial, commercial, and other services to some foreign governments and international organizations

crown jewels FINANCE company's most valuable properties an organization's most valuable **assets**, often the motivation behind **takeover bids**

cryptography E-COMMERCE method of restricting who can access website a powerful means of restricting access to part or all of a website, whereby only a user with an assigned "key" can request and read the information

CSP *abbr* E-COMMERCE commerce service provider

CT *abbr* TAX corporation tax

CTI *abbr* BUSINESS computer telephony integration

culture shock GENERAL MANAGEMENT confusion on exposure to unfamiliar situation the effects on an employee or organization when faced with new, unfamiliar, or rapidly changing circumstances. Symptoms of culture shock include uncertainty, stress, confusion, disorientation, or simply not knowing how to act in the circumstances. Culture shock can occur in a number of scenarios, for example, when expatriates come across new cultures and customs in a foreign country; when new staff are thrown into the deep end of a busy department; when two organizations merge with poor strategic, operational, or cultural synergy; or when public sector organizations adopt private sector practices. The degree of shock can be reduced through careful analysis, planning, training, and consequent preparedness.

cum FINANCE with the Latin word for "with." Its opposite is "ex-."

cum-all STOCKHOLDING & INVESTMENTS including all normal benefits of stock ownership including all of the entitlements that are attached to owning a share of stock. *See also* ***ex-all***

cum coupon STOCKHOLDING & INVESTMENTS with coupon attached or before payment of interest with a coupon attached or before interest due on a security is paid

cum dividend or **cum div** STOCKHOLDING & INVESTMENTS including unpaid dividend including the next dividend still to be paid

cum rights STOCKHOLDING & INVESTMENTS including rights an indication that the buyer

     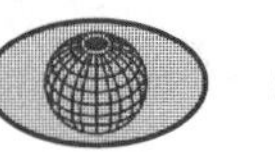   

of the stock is entitled to participate in a forthcoming **rights issue**

cumulative increasing over time added to regularly and becoming increasingly larger over a period of time

cumulative interest FINANCE total interest the total interest added to capital originally invested

cumulative method GENERAL MANAGEMENT system of adding things together a system in which items are added together, used, for example, in some forms of electing officers to a number of posts

cumulative preference share *UK* STOCKHOLDING & INVESTMENTS = ***cumulative preferred stock***

cumulative preferred stock *US* STOCKHOLDING & INVESTMENTS preferred stock whose dividends accumulate if not paid a type of **preferred stock** that will have the dividend paid at a later date even if the company is not able to pay a dividend in the current year. *UK term* ***cumulative preference share***

cumulative voting CORPORATE GOVERNANCE system of election of directors a voting system that allows a stockholder one vote per share of stock owned multiplied by the number of directors to be elected. Stockholders may distribute these votes among the candidates in any way they choose.

currency CURRENCY & EXCHANGE money of particular country the system of money in general circulation in a particular country

currency backing CURRENCY & EXCHANGE gold or securities supporting currency gold, other valuable metal, or government securities, that support the strength of a country's currency

currency band CURRENCY & EXCHANGE allowable range of variation in exchange rate exchange rate levels between which a **currency** is allowed to move without full revaluation or devaluation

currency basket CURRENCY & EXCHANGE = ***basket of currencies***

currency clause CURRENCY & EXCHANGE clause fixing exchange rate for contract a clause in a contract that avoids problems of payment caused by exchange rate changes by fixing in advance the exchange rate for the various transactions covered by the contract

currency future STOCKHOLDING & INVESTMENTS option on currency a contract for buying or selling currency at a particular exchange rate within a set period

currency hedging STOCKHOLDING & INVESTMENTS, RISK reducing risk by diversifying currency holdings a method of reducing **exchange rate risk** by diversifying currency holdings and adjusting them according to changes in exchange rates

currency mismatching CURRENCY & EXCHANGE depositing low-interest loan in country with high-interest the practice of borrowing money in the currency of a country where interest rates are low and depositing it in the currency of a country with higher interest rates. The potential profit from the interest rate margin may be offset by changes in the exchange rates, which increase the value of the loan in the company's balance sheet.

currency note CURRENCY & EXCHANGE paper money a piece of paper money, representing a promise to pay the bearer a specific sum on demand

currency reserves CURRENCY & EXCHANGE government's reserves of foreign currency foreign money held by a government to support its own currency and to pay its debts

currency risk CURRENCY & EXCHANGE, RISK likelihood of adverse exchange rate the possibility of a loss due to future changes in exchange rates

currency swap CURRENCY & EXCHANGE **1.** agreement to use one currency for another an arrangement between two parties to exchange an amount of one currency for another currency, later returning the original amounts. This is useful, for instance, where both parties hold a currency other than the one they need at a specific time. *Also called* ***cross currency swap*** **2.** selling and buying same amount of foreign currency the selling or buying of a particular amount of a foreign currency for immediate delivery, accompanied by selling or buying the same amount of the same currency on the **futures market**

currency unit CURRENCY & EXCHANGE coin or bill in specific monetary system each of the notes and coins that are the medium of exchange in a country

current account BANKING **1.** record of transactions between two parties a record of transactions between two parties, for example, between a bank and its customer, or a branch and head office, or two trading nations. *Abbr* **c/a** **2.** *UK* = ***checking account***

current account equilibrium INTERNATIONAL TRADE balance of country's imports and exports a country's economic circumstances when its expenditure equals its income from trade and **invisible earnings**

current account mortgage MORTGAGES long-term real estate loan a long-term loan, usually for the purchase of real estate, in which the borrower pays interest on the sum loaned in monthly installments and repays the principal in one lump sum at the end of the term. When calculating the interest payments, the lender takes into account the balance in the borrower's checking and/or savings accounts. It is the borrower's responsibility to make provisions to accumulate the required capital during the period of the mortgage, usually by contributing to tax efficient investment plans or by relying on an anticipated inheritance. *See also* ***mortgage***

current assets FINANCE cash, or asset to be converted to cash cash or other assets, such as stock and long-term investments, held for conversion into cash in the normal course of trading

current assets financing FINANCE using current assets to back loan the use of current assets such as cash, debtors, and stock as collateral for a loan

current cash balance STOCKHOLDING & INVESTMENTS money that broker's client has available to invest the amount, which excludes balances due soon for outstanding transactions, that a client has available for investment with a broker

current cost accounting ACCOUNTING accounting based on current replacement cost of assets a method of accounting that notes the cost of replacing assets at current prices, rather than valuing assets at their original cost. *Abbr* **CCA**. *See also* ***historical cost accounting***

current earnings FINANCE firm's most recent annual earnings the annual earnings most recently reported by a company, which exclude interest and tax

current liabilities FINANCE debt to be repaid within one year liabilities which fall due for payment within one year. They include that part of any long-term loan due for repayment within one year.

current principal factor FINANCE part of original loan left to be paid the portion of the initial amount of a loan that remains to be paid

current ratio FINANCE ratio of current assets to current liabilities a ratio of **current assets** to **current liabilities**, used to measure a company's liquidity and its ability to meet its short-term debt obligations.

  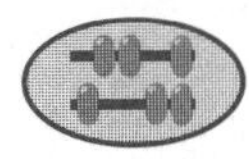   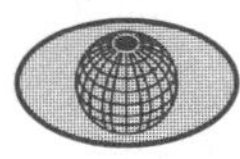   

The current ratio formula is a simple one:

$$\frac{\text{Current assets}}{\text{Current liabilities}} = \text{Current ratio}$$

Current assets are the ones that a company can turn into cash within 12 months during the ordinary course of business. Current liabilities are bills due to be paid within the coming 12 months.

For example, if a company's current assets are $300,000 and its current liabilities are $200,000, its current ratio would be:

$$\frac{300{,}000}{200{,}000} = 1.5$$

As a rule of thumb, the 1.5 figure means that a company should be able to get hold of $1.50 for every $1.00 it owes.

The higher the ratio, the more liquid the company. Prospective lenders expect a positive current ratio, often of at least 1.5. However, too high a ratio is cause for alarm too, because it indicates declining receivables and/or inventory, which may mean declining liquidity. *Also called* ***working capital ratio***

current stock value STOCKHOLDING & INVESTMENTS value of all stock held the value of all stock in an investor's set of holdings, including stock in transactions that have not yet been settled

current value FINANCE current assets minus current liabilities a ratio indicating the amount by which **current assets** exceed **current liabilities**

current yield STOCKHOLDING & INVESTMENTS interest on bond divided by market price the interest being paid on a bond divided by its current market price, expressed as a percentage. *Also called* ***income yield***

curriculum vitae *UK* HR & PERSONNEL = ***résumé***

cushion FINANCE firm's surplus money money left after a company has serviced its debts and therefore available to meet unexpected demands

cushion bond STOCKHOLDING & INVESTMENTS high-interest bond a bond that pays a high rate of interest and so depreciates less when interest rates rise but is at risk of being called if interest rates fall

CUSIP *abbr* REGULATION & COMPLIANCE Committee on Uniform Securities Identification Procedures

custodial account BANKING bank account for child in the United States, a bank account opened, normally by a parent or guardian, in the name of a minor who is too young to control it

custodian BANKING manager of trust funds a legal guardian, whether a person or an institution, whose principal function is to maintain and grow the assets contained in a trust

customer MARKETING somebody who buys product or service a purchaser of a product or service. A customer is a person or organization that purchases or obtains goods or services from other organizations such as manufacturers, retailers, wholesalers, or service providers. A customer is not necessarily the same person as the **consumer**, as a product or service can be paid for by one party, the customer, and used by another, the consumer.

customer capital FINANCE value of firm's customer relationships the value of an organization's relationships with its customers, which involves factors such as market share, customer retention rates, and profitability of customers

customer care MARKETING = ***customer relations***

customer-centric model GENERAL MANAGEMENT emphasis on customers a business model organized around the needs of the customer

customer complaint GENERAL MANAGEMENT *see* ***complaint***

customer demand MARKETING amount of product customers will and can buy the quantity of a product or service that customers are willing and able to purchase at a given price during a given period of time

customer equity FINANCE value of firm's customer relationships the total asset value of the relationships that an organization has with its customers. The term was coined by Robert C. Blattberg and John Deighton in their article "Manage Marketing by the Customer Equity Test," *Harvard Business Review*, Jul/Aug, vol. 74 no. 4, pp. 136–144. Customer equity is based on **customer lifetime value**, and an understanding of customer equity can be used to optimize the balance of investment in the acquisition and retention of customers. It is also known as **customer capital** and forms one component of the **intellectual capital** of an organization.

customer expectation MARKETING what potential buyer thinks or feels about product the needs, wants, and preconceived ideas of a customer about a product or service. Customer expectation will be influenced by his or her perception of the product or service and can be created by previous experience, advertising, hearsay, awareness of competitors, and brand image. The level of customer service is also a factor, and a customer might expect to encounter efficiency, helpfulness, reliability, confidence in the staff, and a personal interest in his or her patronage. If customer expectations are met, then customer satisfaction results. *Also called* ***buyer expectation***

customer flow MARKETING how many customers pass through store, airport, etc. the number and pattern of customers coming into a store or passing through a train or bus station, airport, or other large service, retail, or leisure area. Customer flow can be monitored by observation, time lapse or normal closed circuit television, or, less satisfactorily, by analysis of purchase data. This provides useful information about the number of customers, flow patterns, bottlenecks, areas not visited, and other aspects of consumer behavior.

customer focus GENERAL MANAGEMENT firm's attention to what customers want or need an organizational orientation toward satisfying the needs of potential and actual **customers**. Customer focus is considered to be one of the keys to business success. Achieving customer focus involves ensuring that the whole organization, and not just frontline service staff, puts its customers first. All activities, from the planning of a new product to its production, marketing, and after-sales care, should be built around the customer. Every department and every employee should share the same customer-focused vision. This can be aided by practicing good **customer relationship management** and maintaining a **customer relations** program.

customer knowledge management GENERAL MANAGEMENT use of information from customers to improve firm the acquisition and use of customer-related knowledge to create value for both the organization and the purchasers of its products and services. Customer knowledge management is a form of **knowledge management** which focuses on the human aspects of customer knowledge acquired through direct interaction with the customer as well as quantitative transactional data. Some writers restrict the concept to the use of knowledge residing in, or acquired from, customers as opposed to information *about* customers collected by **customer relationship management** systems. Interactive technologies, conversations with customers, and user groups may be used to create knowledge-sharing and

  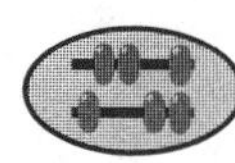 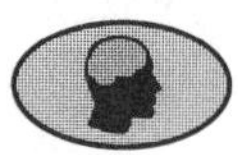  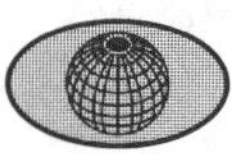   

partnership between the organization and its customers.

customer lifetime value FINANCE expected profit from customer over time the **net present value** of the profit an organization expects to realize from a customer for the duration of their relationship. Customer lifetime value focuses on customers as assets rather than sources of revenue; the volume of purchases made, customer retention rates, and profit margins are factors taken into account in calculations. Strategies for increasing customer lifetime value aim to improve customer retention and lengthen the life of the relationship with the customer. It is a key factor in the customer equity of an organization.

customer profitability FINANCE amount of firm's profits due to customers the degree to which a **customer** or segment of customers contributes toward an organization's profits. Customer profitability has been shown to be produced primarily by a small proportion of customers, perhaps 10% to 20%, who generate up to 80% of a company's profits. Up to 40% of customers may generate only moderate profits, and the other 40% may be loss making. Such data enables companies to focus efforts on the most profitable segments.

customer recovery MARKETING attempts to win back firm's customers activities intended to win back customers who no longer buy from an organization

customer relations MARKETING how firm deals with buyers of its products the approach of an organization to winning and retaining customers. The most critical activity of any organization wishing to stay in business is its approach to dealing with its customers. Putting customers at the center of all activities is seen by many as an integral part of quality, pricing, and product differentiation. On one level, customer relations means keeping customers fully informed, turning complaints into opportunities, and genuinely listening to customers. On another level, being a customer-focused organization means ensuring that all activities relating to trading – for example, planning, design, production, marketing, and after-sales of a product or service – are built around the customer, and that every department and individual employee understands and shares the same vision. Only then can a company deliver continuous **customer satisfaction** and experience good customer relations. *Also called* ***customer care***

customer relationship management MARKETING development of connections with buyers of firm's products the cultivation of meaningful relationships with actual or potential purchasers of goods or services. Customer relationship management aims to increase an organization's sales by promoting customer satisfaction, and can be achieved using tools such as relationship marketing.

CRM is particularly important in the sphere of e-commerce, as there is no personal interaction between the vendor and the customer. A website therefore has to work hard to develop the relationship with customers and demonstrate that their business is valued. A CRM system generally includes some or all of the following components: customer information systems, **personalization** systems, **content management** systems, **call center** automation, **data warehousing**, **data mining**, sales force automation, and campaign management systems. All these elements combine to provide the essentials of CRM: understanding customer needs; anticipating their information requirements; answering their questions promptly and comprehensively; delivering exactly what they order; making deliveries on time; and suggesting new products that they will be genuinely interested in. *Abbr* **CRM**

customer retention MARKETING maintaining connections with buyers of firm's products the maintenance of the patronage of people who have purchased a company's goods or services once and the gaining of repeat purchases. Customer retention occurs when a customer is loyal to a company, a brand, or a specific product or service, expressing long-term commitment and refusing to purchase from competitors. A company can adopt a number of strategies to retain its customers. Of critical importance to such strategies are the wider concepts of customer service, customer relations, and relationship marketing. Companies can build loyalty and retention through the use of a number of techniques, including **database marketing**, the issue of loyalty cards redeemable against a variety of goods or services, preferential discounts, free gifts, special promotions, newsletters or magazines, members' clubs, or customized products in limited editions. It has been argued that customer retention is linked to employee loyalty, since loyal employees build up long-term relationships with customers.

customer satisfaction MARKETING how happy buyers are with firm's products the degree to which **customer expectations** of a product or service are met or exceeded. Corporate and individual customers may have widely differing reasons for purchasing a product or service and therefore any measurement of satisfaction will need to be able to take into account such differences. The quality of after-sales service can also be a crucial factor in influencing any purchasing decision. More and more companies are striving, not just for customer satisfaction, but for customer delight, that extra bit of added value that may lead to increased customer loyalty. Any extra added value, however, will need to be carefully costed.

customer service MARKETING how firm helps buyers of its products the way in which an organization deals with its **customers**. Customer service is most evident in sales and **after-sales service**, but should infuse all the processes in the **value chain**. Good customer service is the result of adopting **customer focus**. Poor customer service can be a product of poor **customer relations**.

customization GENERAL MANAGEMENT changing products for individual customers the process of modifying products or services to meet the requirements of individual customers

customs barrier INTERNATIONAL TRADE measure designed to restrict trade a provision intended to make trade more difficult, for example, a high level of duty

customs broker INTERNATIONAL TRADE shipper's agent clearing goods through customs a person or company that takes goods through customs for a shipping company

customs clearance INTERNATIONAL TRADE **1.** passage granted to imports or exports by customs the act of passing goods through customs so that they can enter or leave the country **2.** document proving payment of customs duty a document given by customs to a shipper to show that customs duty has been paid and the goods can be shipped

customs declaration INTERNATIONAL TRADE form stating dutiable imports a statement showing goods being imported on which duty will have to be paid

customs duty INTERNATIONAL TRADE tax on imports and exports tax paid on goods brought into or taken out of a country

customs entry point INTERNATIONAL TRADE border point for declaring goods to customs a place at a border between two countries where goods are declared to customs

customs formalities INTERNATIONAL TRADE procedures followed by customs officials a declaration of goods by the shipper and examination of them by the customs authorities

customs seal INTERNATIONAL TRADE seal showing contents not examined by customs officials a seal attached by a customs officer to a box, to show that the contents have not passed through customs

customs tariff INTERNATIONAL TRADE list of import taxes a list of taxes to be paid on imported goods

customs union INTERNATIONAL TRADE agreement allowing goods to cross borders without duties an agreement between several countries that goods can travel between them without **duty** being paid, while goods from other countries are subject to duties

cutthroat BUSINESS extremely competitive aggressively ruthless, especially in dealing with competitors

cutting-edge GENERAL MANAGEMENT technologically advanced at the forefront of new technologies or markets

CV *UK* HR & PERSONNEL = ***résumé***

cwmni cyfyngedig cyhoeddus *UK see* ***ccc***

cybermarketing E-COMMERCE advertising via the Internet the use of Internet-based promotions of any kind. This may involve targeted e-mail, bulletin boards, websites, or sites from which the customer can download files.

cybersales E-COMMERCE electronic sales sales made electronically through computers and information systems

cyberspace E-COMMERCE Internet as imagined world of electronic data the online world and its communication networks

cyberterrorism E-COMMERCE terrorist methods to disrupt information systems the use of techniques that disrupt or damage computer-based information systems to cause fear, injury, or economic loss

cyberwar E-COMMERCE using Internet to damage other's computer networks the use of information systems such as the Internet to exploit or damage an adversary's computer-based network processes

cycle time OPERATIONS & PRODUCTION **1.** time taken to get product to market the total time taken from the start of the production of a product or service to its completion. Cycle time includes processing time, move time, wait time, and inspection time, only the first of which creates value. **2.** = ***lead time*** *(sense 3)*

cyclical factors BUSINESS effects of trade cycle on businesses the way in which a **trade cycle** affects businesses

cyclical stock STOCKHOLDING & INVESTMENTS stock affected by business cycles a stock whose value rises and falls in line with economic cycles

cyclical unemployment ECONOMICS recurring temporary lack of employment unemployment, usually temporary, caused by a lack of **aggregate demand**, for example, during a downswing in the business cycle

cyclic variation STATISTICS regular recurrence of change the repeatable systematic variation of a variable over time

D/A *abbr* BANKING deposit account (sense 1)

daily price limit MARKETS daily allowable change in option price the amount by which the price of an **option** is allowed to rise or fall during a single trading day

daily trading limit MARKETS permitted daily futures or options price range the highest and lowest prices that are allowed for a futures or options contract during a single trading day

Daimyo bond CURRENCY & EXCHANGE Japanese bond for European investors a Japanese **bearer bond** that can be cleared through European clearing houses

daisy chaining MARKETS illegal practice to inflate price of security an illegal financial practice whereby traders create artificial transactions in order to make a particular security appear more active than it is in reality *(slang)*

daman FINANCE contract whereby one person underwrites obligation of another in Islamic financing, a contract of guarantee in which the guarantor agrees to be responsible for a debt or obligation of another. *Also called* ***dhaman***

D&B *abbr* BUSINESS Dun and Bradstreet

data STATISTICS information from statistical survey the measurements made and observations collected during a statistical investigation

database GENERAL MANAGEMENT organized collection of information a structured collection of related information held in any form, especially on a computer. The creation of a database assists organizations in keeping records and facilitates the retrieval of specific facts or different categories of information as and when required. Databases of various kinds may form part of an organization's **MIS**.

database management system STATISTICS computer program for managing information a dedicated computer program designed to manipulate a collection of information

database marketing MARKETING collecting information about customers to target advertising the collection and analysis of information about customers and their buying habits, lifestyles, and other such data. Database marketing is used to build profiles of individual customers, who are then targeted with customized mailings, special offers, and other incentives to encourage spending.

data capture MARKETING collecting customer information through response forms the acquisition of information through advertisement coupons, inquiry forms, or other means that require a customer response

data cleansing MARKETING making sure information is accurate the process of ensuring that data is up to date and free of duplication or error

data dredging STATISTICS using information from outside study to draw conclusions the process of making comparisons with, and drawing conclusions from, data which was not part of the original basis of a study

data fusion E-COMMERCE merging information from different sources into consistent system the integration of data and knowledge collected from disparate sources by different methods into a consistent, accurate, and useful whole

data mining **1.** E-COMMERCE using software to find patterns in online databases the process of using sophisticated software to identify commercially useful statistical patterns or relationships in online databases **2.** MARKETING pulling information from firm's databases for management decisions the extraction of information from a **data warehouse** to assist managerial decision making. The information obtained in this way helps organizations gain a better understanding of their customers and can be used to improve customer support and marketing activities.

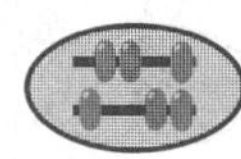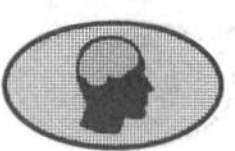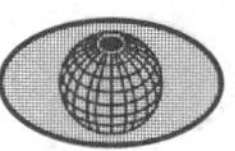

data protection MARKETING methods of keeping personal information in databases safe the safeguards that govern the storage and use of personal data held on computer systems and in paper-based filing systems. The growing use of computers to store information about individuals has led to the enactment of legislation in many countries designed to protect the privacy of individuals and prevent the disclosure of information to unauthorized persons.

data reduction STATISTICS summarizing large data sets the process of summarizing large data sets into histograms or frequency distributions so that calculations such as means can be made

data screening STATISTICS checking data for significant anomalies the process of assessing a set of observations to detect significant deviations such as **outliers**

data set STATISTICS collection of statistical information all of the measurements or observations collected in a statistical investigation

data smoothing algorithm STATISTICS method for removing meaningless data a procedure for removing meaningless data from a sequence of observations so that a pattern can be detected

Datastream MARKETS online financial data system a data system available online that gives financial information, for example, about securities, prices, and stock exchange transactions

data transfer E-COMMERCE how much information is downloaded from website the amount of data downloaded from a website. This information can be useful, particularly for measuring the number of visitors to a website.

data warehouse GENERAL MANAGEMENT information database used for business analysis a collection of subject-orientated data collected over a period of time and stored on a computer to provide information in support of managerial decision making. A data warehouse contains a large volume of information selected from different sources, including operational systems and organizational databases, and brought together in a standard format to facilitate retrieval and analysis **Data mining** techniques are used to access the information in a data warehouse.

dated date STOCKHOLDING & INVESTMENTS start date for calculation of interest the date on which interest begins to accrue on a fixed-income security, which is also the date the security is issued

date of maturity = ***maturity date***

dawn raid STOCKHOLDING & INVESTMENTS large morning purchase of firm's stock a sudden, planned purchase of a large amount of a company's stock at the beginning of a day's trading. Up to 15% of a company's stock can be bought in this way, and the purchaser must wait for seven days before buying more. A dawn raid may sometimes be the first step toward a **takeover**.

DAX MARKETS main German stock exchange the principal German stock exchange, based in Frankfurt. *Full form* ***Deutscher Aktienindex***

day book ACCOUNTING book for recording daily sales and purchases a book in which an account of sales and purchases made each day can be recorded

dayn FINANCE debt obligation in Islamic financing, a debt incurred as the result of any contract or financial transaction

Day of the Jackal Fraud FRAUD UK identity fraud using dead child's birth certificate in the United Kingdom, a form of identity fraud in which a person obtains the birth certificate of a dead child and uses it to acquire a false identity and passport

day order CURRENCY & EXCHANGE in dollar trading, order with one day's validity an order that is valid only during one trading day

days' sales outstanding ACCOUNTING = ***collection ratio***

day trader MARKETS trader operating by the day a trader who turns holdings into cash at the end of each day

day trading MARKETS operating by the day the practice of turning holdings into cash at the end of each day

DC *abbr* BANKING documentary credit

D/C *abbr* BANKING documentary credit

DCF *abbr* FINANCE discounted cash flow

DCM *abbr* MARKETS Development Capital Market

DD *abbr* **1.** BANKING direct debit **2.** ACCOUNTING due diligence (sense 1)

dead account BANKING inactive account an account that is no longer used

dead cat bounce MARKETS brief rise in stock price after large drop a short-term increase in the value of a stock following a precipitous drop in value (*slang*)

deadweight loss ECONOMICS inefficiency caused by imbalance economic inefficiency caused by a fall in quantities of a product produced, for example, when a monopoly producer keeps production low to maintain high prices, or by a tax

deal 1. BUSINESS business transaction a business arrangement or agreement between two or more people, usually to their mutual benefit **2.** BUSINESS trade in something as business to buy and sell something as a business **3.** MARKETING bargain something offered for sale on favorable terms ◇ cut somebody a deal BUSINESS to agree on terms for a business arrangement with somebody

dealer 1. BUSINESS person who buys and sells something a person engaged in the purchase and sale of goods or services **2.** MARKETS person trading for self, not clients a person or firm that buys or sells on their own account, not as a broker on behalf of clients

dealership MARKETING business selling products for specific manufacturer a retail outlet distributing, selling, and servicing products such as cars on behalf of a manufacturer

deal flow STOCKHOLDING & INVESTMENTS presentation of new investments the rate at which new offers of investments are being presented to underwriters

dealing room MARKETS area in stock exchange used for trading securities a room at a stock exchange where the buying and selling of stocks takes place

dealings BUSINESS business between people or organizations business activities conducted between people or organizations

dear money FINANCE money lent at high interest to restrict spending money that is lent at a high interest rate and will therefore restrict a borrower's expenditure. *See also* ***cheap money***

death benefit INSURANCE payment made when insured person dies insurance benefit paid to the family of somebody who dies in an accident at work

death by committee GENERAL MANAGEMENT termination of proposal by committee inertia the prevention of serious consideration of a proposal by assigning a committee to look at it

death duty *UK* TAX = ***estate tax***

death tax *US* TAX = ***estate tax*** (*informal*)

debenture BUSINESS acceptance by firm of debt obligation the written acknowledgment of a debt by a company, usually given under its seal and containing provisions as to payment of interest and

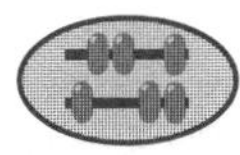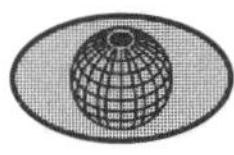

principal. A debenture may be secured on some or all of the assets of the company or its subsidiaries.

debenture bond FINANCE
1. documentation of unsecured bond a certificate showing that a **debenture** has been issued, and giving its terms and conditions 2. US loan without security in the United States, a long-term unsecured loan, a common type taken out by companies

debenture capital FINANCE loan that company secures with assets money borrowed by a company, using its fixed assets as security

debenture holder FINANCE somebody holding a bond a person who holds a bond or certificate of debt for money lent

debenture stock FINANCE stock paying fixed interest on fixed schedule a form of debt instrument in which a company guarantees payments on a fixed schedule or at a fixed rate of interest

debit ACCOUNTING charge against account in bookkeeping a bookkeeping entry that shows an increase in assets or expenses, or a decrease in liabilities, revenue, or capital. It is entered in the left-hand side of an account in **double-entry bookkeeping**.

debit balance ACCOUNTING balance showing more money owed than received the difference between debits and credits in an account where the value of **debits** is greater

debit card BANKING bank card that functions like check a card issued by a bank or financial institution and accepted by a merchant in payment for a transaction. Unlike the procedure with a **credit card**, purchases are deducted from the cardholder's account at the time when the transaction takes place. *Also called* ***check card***

debit column ACCOUNTING left side of double-entry bookkeeping system the left-hand side of an account, showing increases in a company's assets or decreases in its liabilities

debit entry ACCOUNTING entry for expenditure an item in a financial statement recording money spent

debit note FINANCE document showing that customer owes money a document that shows how much money a person or company owes. *Abbr* **D/N**

debits and credits ACCOUNTING record of firm's financial transactions figures entered in a company's accounts to record increases and decreases in **assets**, expenses, liabilities, revenues, or capital

debit side ACCOUNTING accounting column for money owed or paid out the section of a financial statement that lists payments made or owed. In **double-entry bookkeeping**, the left hand side of each account is designated as the debit side. *See also* ***credit side***

debt FINANCE 1. money owed an amount of money owed to a person or organization 2. money borrowed money borrowed by a person or organization to finance personal or business activities

debt bomb ECONOMICS economic volatility caused by default of major institution instability in an economy as a result of a major financial institution defaulting on its obligations

debt capital FINANCE money raised as loan capital that is raised that carries an obligation to pay back the principal together with interest

debt collection agency FINANCE business specializing in getting debts repaid a business that secures the repayment of debts for third parties on a commission or fee basis

debt-convertible bond STOCKHOLDING & INVESTMENTS bond convertible from variable to fixed interest a floating-rate bond that can be converted to a fixed rate of interest. *See also* ***droplock bond***

debt counseling FINANCE guidance for people in financial difficulty a service offering advice and support to individuals who are financially stretched

debt/equity ratio MARKETS relationship between firm's debts and value the ratio of what a company owes to the value of all of its outstanding shares of stock

debt factoring FINANCE purchase of firm's accounts receivable at discount the business of buying debts at a discount. A factor collects a company's debts when due, and pays the creditor in advance part of the sum to be collected, thus "buying" the debt.

debt finance *UK* FINANCE = ***debt financing***

debt financing *US* FINANCE raising of capital by long-term borrowing the activity of raising capital from long-term borrowing such as the sale of bonds or notes. *UK term* ***debt finance***

debt forgiveness FINANCE lender's canceling of debt the writing off of all or part of a nation's debt by a lender

debt instrument FINANCE written agreement between borrower and lender any document used or issued for raising money, for example, a bill of exchange, bond, or promissory note

debt market FINANCE market trading in debts a market in which corporate or municipal, government, or public debts are bought and sold

debtnocrat BANKING person in position to make very large loans a senior bank official who specializes in lending extremely large sums, for example, to emerging nations (*slang*)

debt obligation STOCKHOLDING & INVESTMENTS = ***collateralized debt obligation***

debtor FINANCE person owing money a person or organization owing money to another. *Also called* ***obligor***

debtor days FINANCE average time it takes to collect payment the number of days on average that it takes a company to receive payment for what it sells.

To determine debtor days, divide the cumulative amount of accounts receivable by sales, then multiply by 365. If accounts receivable total $600,000 and sales are $9,000,000, the calculation is:

$$\frac{600{,}000}{9{,}000{,}000} \times 365 = 24.33 \text{ days}$$

The company takes 24.33 days on average to collect its debts.

Debtor days is an indication of a company's efficiency in collecting monies owed. Obviously, the lower the number the better. An especially high number is a telltale sign of inefficiency or worse. *See also* ***creditor days***

debtor nation INTERNATIONAL TRADE country owing more money than it is owed a country whose foreign debts are larger than money owed to it by other countries

debtors' control FINANCE systems for prompt repayment strategies used to ensure that borrowers pay back loans on time

debt ratio FINANCE relationship between firm's debts and assets the debts of a company shown as a percentage of its **equity** plus loan capital

debt rescheduling FINANCE negotiation of new terms for debt repayment the renegotiation of debt payments. Debt rescheduling is necessary when a company can no longer meet its debt payments. It can involve deferring debt payments, deferring payment of interest, or negotiating a new loan. It is usually undertaken as part of **turnaround management** to avoid **business failure**. Debt rescheduling is also undertaken in less developed countries that encounter national debt difficulties. Such arrangements are usually overseen by the **International Monetary Fund**.

debt security STOCKHOLDING & INVESTMENTS security issued as evidence of debt to purchaser a security issued by a company or government which represents money borrowed from the security's purchaser and which must be repaid at a specified maturity date, usually at a specified interest rate

debt service FINANCE combined interest and principal due on money borrowed the payments due under a loan agreement, i.e. interest payable and payments of principal

debt/service ratio ECONOMICS measurement of debt against gross income the ratio of a country's or company's borrowing to its equity or **venture capital**

debt swap FINANCE exchange of country's debt for local currency a method of reducing exposure to long-term debt of nations with undeveloped economies by purchasing the debt at a discount and exchanging it with the central bank for local currency

decentralization GENERAL MANAGEMENT giving decision-making power to larger group the dispersal of decision-making control. Decentralization involves moving power, authority, and decision-making control within an organization from a central headquarters or from high managerial levels to subsidiaries, branches, divisions, or departments. As an organizational concept, decentralization implies delegation of both power and responsibility by top management in order to promote flexibility through faster decision making and improved response times. Decentralization is, therefore, strongly related to the concept of empowerment, though the latter is perhaps more focused on direct working front-line staff.

decile STATISTICS value representing one-tenth of frequency distribution one of the nine values that divide the total number of items in a **frequency distribution** into ten groups, each containing an equal number of items

decision analysis GENERAL MANAGEMENT = ***decision theory***

decision maker GENERAL MANAGEMENT somebody authorized to make important decisions for firm somebody with the responsibility and authority to make decisions within an organization, especially those that determine future direction and strategy. **Decision theory** is used to assist decision makers in the process of **decision making**.

decision making GENERAL MANAGEMENT process of determining what to do the process of choosing between alternate courses of action. Decision making may take place at an individual or organizational level. The process may involve establishing objectives, gathering relevant information, identifying alternatives, setting criteria for the decision, and selecting the best option. The nature of the decision-making process within an organization is influenced by its culture and structure, and a number of theoretical models have been developed. **Decision theory** can be used to assist in the process of decision making. Specific techniques used in decision making include heuristics and decision trees. Computer systems designed to assist managerial decision making are known as decision support systems.

decision-making unit MARKETING group of employees responsible for purchase decisions a group of people within an organization who directly or indirectly influence the purchase of a product or service

decision support system GENERAL MANAGEMENT computer system containing information used for management decisions a computer system designed to collect, store, process, and provide access to information to support managerial decision making. Decision support systems were developed in the 1970s to facilitate unstructured and one-off decision making, as the standard reporting capabilities of **MIS**s were perceived to be more suitable for routine day-to-day decisions. Data on an organization's external operating environment, as well as internal operational information, is included and an interactive interface allows managers to retrieve and manipulate data. Modeling techniques are used to examine the results of alternative courses of action.

decision theory GENERAL MANAGEMENT analysis of how people determine course of action a body of knowledge that attempts to describe, analyze, and model the process of **decision making** and the factors influencing it. Decision theory encompasses both formal mathematical and statistical approaches to solving decision problems, using quantitative techniques such as probability and **game theory**, and more informal behavioral approaches. It is used to inform and assist decision making in organizations. *Also called* ***decision analysis***

decision tree GENERAL MANAGEMENT chart helping people determine course of action a diagram designed to help decision makers by representing available options and possible outcomes as branches of a tree. Decision trees provide an overview of multiple-stage **decision making** by showing successive decision points arising from previous choices. Values representing the relative probability of individual outcomes may be assigned to each branch of the tree in order to compare strategies and select the most favorable.

declaration date STOCKHOLDING & INVESTMENTS day when firm sets next dividend in the United States, the date when the directors of a company meet to announce the proposed dividend per share that they recommend be paid

declaration of dividend STOCKHOLDING & INVESTMENTS firm's official announcement of next dividend a formal announcement by a company's directors of the proposed dividend per share that they recommend be paid. It is subsequently put to a stockholders' vote at the company's annual meeting.

declaration of income TAX = ***income tax return***

declaration of solvency BUSINESS official notice of UK firm's creditworthiness in the United Kingdom, a document, filed with the **Registrar of Companies**, that lists the assets and liabilities of a company seeking voluntary liquidation to show that the company is capable of repaying its debts within 12 months

declared value TAX figure on customs form the value of goods as entered on a customs declaration

declining balance method ACCOUNTING = ***accelerated depreciation***

deconstruction GENERAL MANAGEMENT breaking up old-fashioned business systems the breaking up of traditional business structures to meet the requirements of the modern economy

decreasing term life insurance or **decreasing term life assurance** INSURANCE life insurance with death benefit decreasing over time life insurance that is in effect for a specified period of time and provides a death benefit that decreases incrementally during the period the policy is in effect

de-diversify BUSINESS sell off firm's marginal interests to sell off parts of a company or group that are not considered directly relevant to its main area of interest

  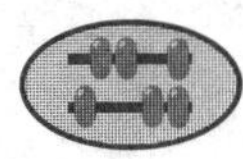   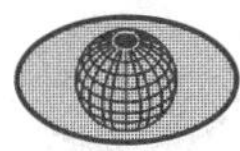   

deductible US INSURANCE portion of insurance claim paid by policyholder the part of a commercial insurance claim that has to be met by the policyholder rather than the insurance company. A deductible of $1,000 means that the company pays all but $1,000 of the claim for loss or damage. *UK term* ***excess***

deduction FINANCE deducting from total, or amount deducted a subtraction of money from a total, or an amount of money subtracted from a total

deduction at source TAX taking taxes directly from salary in the United Kingdom, the collection of taxes from an organization or individual paying an income, rather than from the recipient of the income, for example, from an employer paying wages, a bank paying interest, or a company paying dividends

deed LEGAL legal evidence of real estate sale a legal document, most commonly one that details the transfer or sale of real estate

deed of arrangement LEGAL agreement to terms of repayment by insolvent debtor in the United Kingdom, a legal document that sets out the agreement between an insolvent person and his or her **creditors**

deed of assignment LEGAL document transferring real estate to creditor in the United Kingdom, a legal document detailing the transfer of real estate from a **debtor** to a **creditor**

deed of covenant LEGAL legal promise to make payments in the United Kingdom, a legal document in which a person or organization promises to pay a third party a sum of money on an annual basis, with tax advantages. A deed of covenant was often used for making regular payments to a charity before the introduction of **Gift Aid**.

deed of partnership LEGAL legal agreement for partnership in the United Kingdom, a legal document formalizing the agreement and financial arrangements between the parties that make up a partnership

deed of transfer STOCKHOLDING & INVESTMENTS documentation of transfer of stock ownership in the United Kingdom, a legal document that attests to the transfer of stock ownership

deed of variation LEGAL procedure for changing deceased person's will in the United Kingdom, an arrangement that allows the will of a deceased person to be amended, provided specific conditions are met and the amendment is signed by all the original beneficiaries

deep-discount bond STOCKHOLDING & INVESTMENTS bond selling at far less than value a bond offered at a large discount on the face value of the debt so that a significant proportion of the return to the investor comes by way of a capital gain on redemption, rather than through interest payments

deep-discounted rights issue STOCKHOLDING & INVESTMENTS new shares priced below market value a rights issue where the new shares are priced at a very low price compared to their current market value to ensure that stockholders take up the rights

deep-in-the-money call option STOCKHOLDING & INVESTMENTS profitable contract to buy securities a **call option** that has an exercise price below the market price of the underlying asset and has therefore become very profitable. *See also* ***deep-out-of-the-money call option***

deep-in-the-money put option STOCKHOLDING & INVESTMENTS profitable contract to sell securities a **put option** that has an exercise price above the market price of an underlying asset and has therefore become very profitable. *See also* ***deep-out-of-the-money put option***

deep market MARKETS market in which volume will not affect price a commodity, currency, or stock market in which the volume of trade is such that a considerable number of transactions will not influence the market price

deep-out-of-the-money call option STOCKHOLDING & INVESTMENTS unprofitable contract to buy securities a **call option** that has an exercise price above the market price of the underlying asset and has little intrinsic value. *See also* ***deep-in-the-money call option***

deep-out-of-the-money put option STOCKHOLDING & INVESTMENTS unprofitable contract to sell securities a **put option** that has an exercise price below the market price of an underlying asset and has little intrinsic value. *See also* ***deep-in-the-money put option***

deep pocket BUSINESS firm giving financial assistance to another a company that provides much-needed funds for another company (*slang*)

de facto standard GENERAL MANAGEMENT successful product's recognized standing in market a standard set in a given market by a highly successful product or service

defalcation FINANCE misuse of money entrusted to somebody's care the improper and illegal use of funds by a person who does not own them, but who has been charged with their care

default **1.** STOCKHOLDING & INVESTMENTS be unable to cover loss on trades as a member of an exchange, to lose more on a trading position than is held in capital **2.** LEGAL not do what you have contracted to do to fail to comply with the terms of a contract, especially to fail to pay back a debt

defaulter FINANCE person failing to make scheduled payments a person who defaults, for example, somebody who fails to make scheduled payments on a loan

default notice LEGAL = ***notice of default***

default risk STOCKHOLDING & INVESTMENTS, RISK risk of non-payment the possibility that the issuer of a bond will be unable to make payments of principal and interest when they are due

defeasance LEGAL clause specifying how contract might be broken a clause in a collateral deed that says a contract or bond will be revoked if something happens or if some act is performed

defended takeover bid MERGERS & ACQUISITIONS offer to buy firm that opposes being sold a bid for a company takeover in which the directors of the target company oppose the action of the bidder

defensive security STOCKHOLDING & INVESTMENTS security providing earnings despite falling market a security that has very little risk and provides a return even when the stock market is weak

defensive stock STOCKHOLDING & INVESTMENTS stock not affected by external factors stock that prospers predictably regardless of external circumstances such as an economic slowdown, for example, the stock of a company that markets a product everyone must have

deferment FINANCE putting off of something a postponement of something, for example, taxes or interest on a loan, until a later date

deferred annuity STOCKHOLDING & INVESTMENTS investment offering return 12+ months after last premium an investment that does not pay out until at least one year after the final premium has been paid

deferred common stock US STOCKHOLDING & INVESTMENTS stock paying dividends only after others are paid a type of stock usually held by founding members of a company, often with a higher dividend that is only paid after other shareholders have received their dividends and, in some cases, only when a specific level of profit

  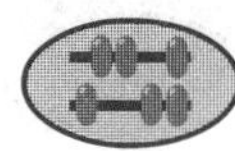 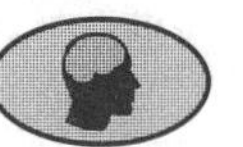  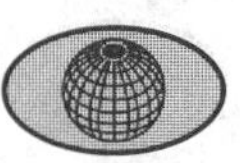   

has been achieved. This type of stock is rarely issued in the United States. *Also called* ***deferred share***. *UK term* ***deferred ordinary share***

deferred consideration BUSINESS purchase in which final payment has conditions attached installment payments for the acquisition of new subsidiaries, usually made in the form of cash and stock, where the balance due after the initial deposit depends on the performance of the business acquired

deferred coupon STOCKHOLDING & INVESTMENTS bond that delays interest payments a **coupon** that pays no interest at first, but pays relatively high interest after a specific date

deferred credit or **deferred income** ACCOUNTING money received but not yet recorded as income revenue received but not yet reported as income in the profit and loss account, for example, payment for goods to be delivered or services provided at a later date, or government grants received for the purchase of assets. The deferred credit is treated as a credit balance on the balance sheet while waiting to be treated as income. *See also* ***accrual basis***

deferred creditor FINANCE creditor paid after all others a person who is owed money by a bankrupt person or organization but who is paid only after all other creditors

deferred interest bond STOCKHOLDING & INVESTMENTS bond that delays interest payments a bond that pays no interest at first, but pays relatively high interest after a specific date

deferred month STOCKHOLDING & INVESTMENTS distant month for option a month relatively late in the term of an **option**

deferred ordinary share *UK* STOCKHOLDING & INVESTMENTS **1.** stock paying no dividend in early years a type of stock that pays no dividend for a specific number of years after its issue date but then is treated the same as the company's common stock **2.** = ***deferred common stock***

deferred payment 1. FINANCE money to be repaid later money owed that will be repaid at a later date **2.** OPERATIONS & PRODUCTION payment in installments payment for goods by installments over a period of time

deferred revenue ACCOUNTING income carried into next accounting period revenue carried forward to future accounting periods

deferred share STOCKHOLDING & INVESTMENTS = ***deferred common stock***

deferred tax TAX tax payable later a tax that may become payable at some later date

deficiency FINANCE amount of shortfall the amount by which something such as a sum of money is less than it should be

deficit ACCOUNTING = ***budget deficit***

deficit financing FINANCE covering shortfall the borrowing of money because expenditure will exceed receipts

deficit spending FINANCE spending financed by borrowing government spending financed through borrowing rather than through taxation or other current revenue

defined contribution pension plan PENSIONS employer's retirement plan with specific investments in the United States, a retirement plan arranged by an employer in which the money contributed by both the employer and employee is invested, so that the retirement benefit is not fixed but is dependent on how well the investments do

deflation ECONOMICS long-term decline in prices a reduction in the general level of prices sustained over several months, usually accompanied by declining employment and output

deflationary ECONOMICS causing drop in prices causing a decline in the prices of goods and services

deflationary fiscal policy ECONOMICS government policy of raising taxes and reducing spending a government policy that raises taxes and reduces public expenditure in order to reduce the level of **aggregate demand** in the economy

deflationary gap ECONOMICS failure in exploiting economic potential a gap between **GDP** and the potential output of the economy

deflator ECONOMICS inflation-related reduction in national income the amount by which a country's **GDP** is reduced to take into account **inflation**

degearing BUSINESS reduction in firm's long-term debt a reduction in a company's loan capital in relation to the value of its common stock plus reserves. *See also* ***leverage***

degressive tax TAX tax decreasing as taxable amount increases a tax for which the amount to be paid decreases as the amount that is liable for taxation increases. *See also* ***progressive tax***

delayed settlement processing E-COMMERCE storing credit card transactions online until shipment a procedure for storing authorized transaction settlements online until after the merchant has shipped the goods to the purchaser

delayering GENERAL MANAGEMENT removing layers of firm's management the removal of supposedly unproductive layers of middle management to make organizations more efficient and customer-responsive. The term came into vogue during the 1980s.

del credere FINANCE extra charge to protect against nonpayment an amount added to a charge to cover the possibility of its not being paid

del credere agent FINANCE sales agent who guarantees purchaser's payment an agent who agrees to sell goods on commission and pay the principal even if the buyer defaults on payment. To cover the risk of default, the commission is marginally higher than that of a general agent.

delegatee GENERAL MANAGEMENT person being allocated task a person who is given the responsibility and authority to undertake a specific activity

delegation GENERAL MANAGEMENT putting somebody else in charge of activity the process of entrusting somebody else with the appropriate responsibility and authority for the accomplishment of a specific activity. Delegation involves briefing somebody else to perform a task for which the delegator holds individual responsibility, but which need not be executed by him or her. There are various degrees of delegation: for example, a manager may delegate responsibility, but not necessarily full authority, and continue to supervise the activity. Delegation should be a positive activity, for example, as an aid to employee development, rather than a negative one, for example, passing on an unpopular task. It should be accompanied by support and encouragement from the delegator to the delegatee. An extension of delegation is empowerment, in which complete authority for a task is passed to somebody else, who takes full responsibility for its objectives, execution, and results.

delegator GENERAL MANAGEMENT person allocating task a person who gives somebody else the responsibility and authority to undertake a specific activity

deleverage FINANCE pay off debt to reduce the size of a company's debt, possibly by selling off some assets

  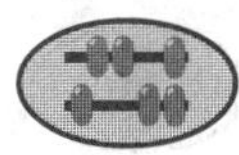   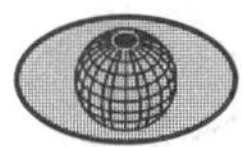   

delinquent BUSINESS late in repaying money owed used to describe a person or organization that is late in paying an account, or a debt that remains unpaid

delisting REGULATION & COMPLIANCE removal of firm from stock exchange the action of removing a company from being traded on a recognized stock exchange —**delist**

delivered price OPERATIONS & PRODUCTION price that includes shipping and handling a price that includes any expenses incurred during packing and transportation of the item to its final destination

delivery 1. FINANCE handing over of bill of exchange for payment the transfer of a bill of exchange or other negotiable instrument to the bank that is due to make payment **2.** OPERATIONS & PRODUCTION act of delivering commodity to buyer the transportation of a commodity by a seller to a purchaser as set out in a futures contract

delivery date MARKETS date for delivery of commodity the date on which a commodity bought or sold in a futures contract must be delivered

delivery month MARKETS = ***contract month***

delivery notice MARKETS notification of details of handover a written notice to the buyer of a commodity on a **futures contract** of its delivery and terms of settlement

Delphi technique GENERAL MANAGEMENT forecasting method avoiding group pressure a qualitative forecasting method in which a panel of experts respond individually to a questionnaire or series of questionnaires, before reaching a consensus. The Delphi technique requires individual submission of, and response to, the questionnaire on the topic under investigation, in order to avoid the effect of a dominant personality influencing a group discussion. A summary of the written replies is then distributed so that responses can be revised in the light of the views expressed. This cycle is repeated until the coordinator of the group is satisfied that the best possible consensus has been reached. The Delphi technique was developed at the Rand Corporation during the late 1940s and 1950s and owes its name to the Greek oracle at Delphi, which was believed to make predictions about the future.

delta STOCKHOLDING & INVESTMENTS option price change compared with associated asset the amount of change in the price of an option as compared to a corresponding change in the price of its underlying asset

demand 1. FINANCE request for payment an act of asking somebody for payment of money owed **2.** MARKETING measure of consumers' willingness to buy the need that consumers have for a product or their eagerness and ability to buy it

demand bill FINANCE bill of exchange payable on demand a **bill of exchange** that must be paid when payment is asked for

demand deposit BANKING account balance available for writing checks money in a deposit account that the holder can withdraw at any time by writing a check

demand forecasting FINANCE estimation of consumer demand for product or service the activity of estimating the quantity of a product or service that consumers will purchase. Demand forecasting involves techniques including both informal methods such as educated guesses and quantitative methods such as the use of historical sales data or current data from test markets. Demand forecasting may be used in making pricing decisions, in assessing future capacity requirements, or in making decisions on whether to enter a new market.

demand management OPERATIONS & PRODUCTION predicting and meeting customer demand the **supply chain** activity of **forecasting**, effectively planning for, and meeting **customer demand** for a product

demand note FINANCE promissory note that is payable on demand a promissory note that has no specific date for payment but instead must be paid when it is presented

demand price FINANCE price buyer is willing to pay the price that purchasers are willing to offer to pay for a given quantity of goods

demand-pull inflation ECONOMICS inflation caused by increased demand inflation caused by rising demand that cannot be met

demand risk RISK risk of customer demand not matching firm's forecast the risk for a company that demand for a product will either exceed their expectations and ability to meet the demand or fall short of their expectations and leave them with product they cannot sell

demassifying GENERAL MANAGEMENT tailoring mass medium to customers' needs the process of changing a mass medium to a medium that is customized to meet the requirements of individual consumers

demerge MERGERS & ACQUISITIONS separate parts of firm to split up an organization into a number of separate parts

demerger MERGERS & ACQUISITIONS separation of company into independent parts the separation of a company into several distinct entities, especially used of companies that have grown by acquisition

demographics STATISTICS characteristics and statistics of human population the characteristics of the size and structure of a human population, including features such as its distribution and age range

demography STATISTICS study of human population statistics the study of the size and structural characteristics of human populations

demonetize CURRENCY & EXCHANGE discontinue coin or note to withdraw a coin or note from a country's currency

demurrage BUSINESS payment made to compensate for late shipment compensation paid to a customer when shipment of a good is delayed at a port or by customs

demutualization BANKING conversion of mutual society to public corporation the process by which a mutual society becomes a publicly owned corporation

Denial of Service Attack E-COMMERCE attempt to prevent Internet use an attempt to limit or prevent a user or users from accessing the Internet, a network, or using their e-mail, for example, by flooding it with more requests than it can handle

denomination CURRENCY & EXCHANGE value on coin, banknote, or stamp a unit of money imprinted on a coin, banknote, or stamp

department GENERAL MANAGEMENT section of firm responsible for particular function a section of an organization, usually centered on a specialized function, under the responsibility of a head of department or team leader

departmental budget ACCOUNTING budget for department a budget of income and/or expenditure applicable to a specific department. *See also* ***functional budget***

departmentalization GENERAL MANAGEMENT dividing firm into sections the division of an organization into sections. Departmentalization is usually based on operating function, and organizations will commonly have departments for, for example, finance, personnel, or marketing. Such organizational structure is typical of a **bureaucracy**. It may be used in **centralization**, when a particular activity is undertaken by one department in one location on behalf of the whole

  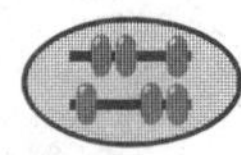   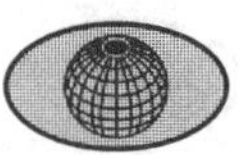   

organization, but may equally be a feature of a **decentralized** organization, in which departments are used as individual operating units responsible for their own management.

Department for Business, Enterprise and Regulatory Reform British government department a British government department dealing with areas such as enterprise, business law, markets, energy policy, and business regulation. It was created in 2007 to bring together the functions of the **Department of Trade and Industry** and regulatory functions formerly performed within the Cabinet Office. *Abbr* **BERR**

Department of Trade and Industry former British government department the former British government department that dealt with areas such as commerce, international trade, and the stock exchange. Its functions are now taken over by the **Department for Business, Enterprise and Regulatory Reform**. *Abbr* **DTI**

dependency ratio ECONOMICS proportion of society economically dependent on work force a measure of the proportion of a population that is too young or too old to work and is therefore economically dependent on that part of the population that is productively working. *Also called* ***support ratio***

dependent variable STATISTICS variable that changes in response to another a variable or factor whose value changes as a result of a change in another (the **independent variable**)

deposit 1. BANKING money added to bank account money placed in a bank for safekeeping or to earn interest **2.** BUSINESS partial payment to reserve something part of the price of an item given by a customer in advance so that the item will not be sold to somebody else before the full price is paid **3.** OPERATIONS & PRODUCTION add money to bank account to pay money into a bank account

deposit account BANKING **1.** interest-paying account requiring prior notice for withdrawal a bank account that pays interest on deposited funds but on which prior notice must be given in order to withdraw money. *Abbr* **D/A 2.** interest-paying UK building society account in the United Kingdom, a building society account that is held by somebody who is not a member of the society. Deposit accounts are generally paid a lower rate of interest, but in the event of the society going into liquidation deposit account holders are given preference. *See also* ***share account***

depositary BUSINESS somebody who entrusts valuable items to institution a person or organization that has placed money or documents for safekeeping with a **depository**

depositor BANKING somebody who deposits money in financial institution a person or business that places money in a bank, savings and loan, or other type of financial institution

depository BANKING institution responsible for keeping valuable items safe a bank or organization with whom money or documents can be placed for safekeeping

Depository Trust and Clearing Corporation BUSINESS US company for handling securities transactions in the United States, a holding company with several subsidiaries, which is set up to efficiently handle clearance, settlement, and depository services for the securities industry. *Abbr* **DTCC**

deposit protection INSURANCE insurance against loss of deposits insurance that depositors have against loss by a financial institution. In the United States, the Federal Deposit Insurance Corporation (FDIC) provides this.

deposit slip or **deposit receipt** *US* BANKING receipt for deposits made in bank account the slip of paper that accompanies money or checks being paid into a bank account. *UK term* ***paying-in slip***

deposit-taking institution BANKING banking institution serving general public an institution that is licensed to receive money on deposit from private individuals and to pay interest on it, for example, a bank or savings and loan

depreciable cost ACCOUNTING expense spread over several accounting periods an expense that may be set against the profits of more than one accounting period

depreciate 1. FINANCE lose value over time to lose value, or decrease the value of something, usually over a period of time **2.** ACCOUNTING make allowance for asset's progressive loss of value to make an allowance in business accounts for the loss of value of an asset over time

depreciation 1. ACCOUNTING loss of value an allocation of the **cost** of an **asset** over a period of time for accounting and tax purposes. Depreciation is charged against earnings, on the basis that the use of capital assets is a legitimate cost of doing business. Depreciation is also a non-cash expense that is added into net income to determine cash flow in a given accounting period.

To qualify for depreciation, assets must be items used in the business that wear out, become obsolete, or lose value over time from natural causes or circumstances, and they must have a useful life beyond a single tax year. Examples include vehicles, machines, equipment, furnishings, and buildings, plus major additions or improvements to such assets. Some intangible assets also can be included under certain conditions. Land, personal assets, stock, leased or rented property, and a company's employees cannot be depreciated.

Straight line depreciation is the most straightforward method. It assumes that the net cost of an asset should be written off in equal amounts over its life. The formula used is:

$$\frac{\text{Original cost} - \text{Scrap value}}{\text{Useful life in years}}$$

For example, if a vehicle cost $30,000 and can be expected to serve the business for seven years, its original cost would be divided by its useful life:

$$\frac{30{,}000 - 2{,}000}{7} = 4{,}000 \text{ per year}$$

The $4,000 becomes a depreciation expense that is reported on the company's year-end income statement under "operation expenses."

In theory, an asset should be depreciated over the actual number of years that it will be used, according to its actual drop in value each year. At the end of each year, all the depreciation claimed to date is subtracted from its cost in order to arrive at its **book value**, which would equal its market value. At the end of its useful business life, any portion not depreciated would represent the salvage value for which it could be sold or scrapped.

For tax purposes, some accountants prefer to use the **declining balance method** to record larger amounts of depreciation in the asset's early years in order to reduce tax bills as soon as possible. In contrast to the straight-line method, this assumes that the asset depreciates more in its earlier years of use. The table below compares the depreciation amounts that would be available, under these two methods, for a $1,000 asset that is expected to be used for five years and then sold for $100 as scrap.

  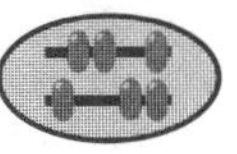     

Straight-line method of depreciation

Year	Annual depreciation	Year-end book value
1	$900 × 20% = $180	$1,000 – $180 = $820
2	$900 × 20% = $180	$820 – $180 = $640
3	$900 × 20% = $180	$640 – $180 = $460
4	$900 × 20% = $180	$460 – $180 = $280
5	$900 × 20% = $180	$280 – $180 = $100

Declining-balance method of depreciation

Year	Annual depreciation	Year-end book value
1	$1,000 × 40% = $400	$1,000 – $400 = $600
2	$600 × 40% = $240	$600 – $240 = $360
3	$360 × 40% = $144	$360 – $144 = $216
4	$216 × 40% = $86.40	$216 – $86.40 = $129.60
5	$129.60 × 40% = $51.84	$129.60 – $51.84 = $77.76

The depreciation method to be used for a particular asset is fixed at the time that the asset is first placed in service. Whatever rules or tables are in effect for that year must be followed as long as the asset is owned.

Depreciation laws and regulations change frequently over the years as a result of government policy changes, so a company owning property over a long period may have to use several different depreciation methods. **2.** CURRENCY & EXCHANGE decrease in value of currency a reduction of a currency's value in relation to the value of other currencies

depreciation rate ACCOUNTING annual rate at which asset loses value the rate at which the value of an asset decreases each year in business accounts

depressed market MARKETS market where supply outweighs demand a market in which there are more goods available than there are customers who are willing to buy them, leading to lower prices. A stock market that is depressed, with falling prices, is called a **bear market.**

depression ECONOMICS long-term decline in economic activity a prolonged slump or downturn in the business cycle, marked by a high level of unemployment

deprival value FINANCE = ***value to the business***

deregulation REGULATION & COMPLIANCE lessening of government controls a reduction in government controls over a specific business activity with the intention of stimulating competition

deregulatory model REGULATION & COMPLIANCE belief in less government regulation the theory that less government regulation in the economy will result in more competition and a more efficient marketplace

derivative STOCKHOLDING & INVESTMENTS security with price link to underlying asset a **security** such as an **option**, the price of which has a strong correlation with an underlying commodity, currency, or **financial instrument**

derivative instruments or **derivatives** STOCKHOLDING & INVESTMENTS securities based on other securities or market conditions forms of traded securities, such as option contracts, which are derived from ordinary bonds and shares, exchange rates, or stock market indices

Derivative Trading Facility MARKETS Australian computer system for trading options a computer system and associated network operated by the Australian Stock Exchange to facilitate the purchase and sale of exchange-traded options. *Abbr* **DTF**

descending tops MARKETS chart pattern with each successive peak lower a term used to refer to a chart pattern that shows falling market, in which each high is lower than the previous one

designated account BANKING account requiring second person for extra identification an account opened and held in one person's name, but that also includes another person's name for extra identification purposes

design for manufacturability or **design for assembly** or **design for production** OPERATIONS & PRODUCTION designing products for ease of manufacture the process of designing products to optimize the manufacturing process while assuring the product's highest quality, performance, and reliability for the price

design for supply OPERATIONS & PRODUCTION designing desirable products that keep costs low the process of designing products that will meet **customer demand** without sacrificing quality or customer service, while minimizing costs throughout the **supply chain**

design protection MARKETING = ***copyright***

de-skilling HR & PERSONNEL replacing need for particular job skills with technology the removal of the need for skill or judgment in the performance of a task, often because of new technologies. While it can be argued that de-skilling has adversely affected some manual workers in traditional manufacturing industries, the technologies used in modern production systems require a wider range and higher level of skill among the workforce as a whole.

desk research MARKETING investigation conducted from office research carried out in an office, using documents, telephone interviews, or the Internet

Deutscher Aktienindex MARKETS *see* ***DAX***

devaluation ECONOMICS reduction of official currency exchange rate a reduction in the official fixed rate at which one currency exchanges for another under a fixed-rate regime, usually to correct a balance of payments deficit

developing country ECONOMICS poor nation with little industrial development a country, often a producer of primary goods such as cotton or rubber, that cannot generate investment income to stimulate growth and that possesses a national income that is vulnerable to change in commodity prices

development area or **development zone** BUSINESS area receiving government aid to attract commercial development a geographic area that has been given special help from a government to encourage businesses and factories to be set up there

development capital FINANCE money for expansion financing acquired or provided for the expansion of an established business

Development Capital Market MARKETS closed sector of Johannesburg exchange for developing companies a sector on the South African stock exchange for listing smaller developing companies which was closed to new listings in 2004 due to low liquidity. *Abbr* **DCM**

development cycle MARKETING *see* ***new product development***

dhaman FINANCE = ***daman***

Diagonal Street *S. Africa* FINANCE financial district of Johannesburg the financial center of Johannesburg or, by extension, South Africa (*informal*)

     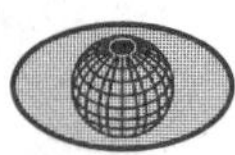   

dial and smile US MARKETING call strangers to sell something to call potential customers of a product or service to try to make a sale (*slang*)

DIAMONDs STOCKHOLDING & INVESTMENTS shares in selected firms on American Stock Exchange shares in a fund, traded on the American Stock Exchange, that is made up of the 30 companies represented in the **Dow Jones Industrial Average**

dicing and slicing MARKETING analyzing information in different ways the analysis of raw data to extract information under different categories (*slang*)

dictum meum pactum MARKETS my word is my bond Latin for the phrase "My word is my bond," the motto of the London Stock Exchange

differential costing FINANCE way to determine costs based on production levels a costing method that shows the difference in costs that results from different levels of activity such as making one thousand or ten thousand extra units of a product

differential pricing MARKETING selling product at different prices in different places a method of pricing that offers the same product at different prices, for example, in different markets, countries, or retail outlets

differential tariff TAX charge that varies by class or source a tax on goods or services which varies according to their class or source

differentiation MARKETING = ***product differentiation***

digital cash E-COMMERCE form of electronic cash carrying no user information an anonymous form of **digital money** which can be linked directly to a bank account or exchanged for physical money. As with physical cash, there is no way to obtain information about the buyer from it, and it can be transferred by the seller to pay for subsequent purchases. *Also called* ***e-cash, electronic cash***

digital certificate E-COMMERCE electronic document that shows buyer is authentic an electronic document issued by a recognized authority which validates a purchaser. It is used much as a driver's license or passport is used for identification purposes in a traditional business transaction.

digital coins E-COMMERCE form of electronic cash for small payments a form of electronic payment authorized for instant transactions which facilitates the purchase of items priced in small denominations of **digital cash**. Digital coins are transferred from customer to merchant for a transaction such as the purchase of a newspaper using a **smart card** for payment.

digital coupon E-COMMERCE online form used for obtaining lower product price a voucher or similar form that exists electronically, for example, on a website, and can be used to reduce the price of goods or services

digital divide E-COMMERCE inequality of access to information technology the difference in opportunities available to people who have access to modern information technology and those who do not. Factors such as urban living, education level, economic class, and industrialization affect the digital divide.

digital economy ECONOMICS economic system based on online business transactions an economy in which the main productive functions are in electronic commerce, for example, trade on the Internet

digital goods E-COMMERCE products sold and delivered electronically merchandise that is sold and delivered electronically, for example, over the Internet

digital hygienist GENERAL MANAGEMENT employee who inspects other employees' Internet usage somebody within a company who is responsible for checking employees' e-mails and surfing habits for non-work-related activity (*slang*)

digital money E-COMMERCE electronic cash related to real-world currency a series of numbers with an intrinsic value in some physical currency. Online digital money requires electronic interaction with a bank to conduct a transaction; offline digital money does not. Anonymous digital money is synonymous with **digital cash**. Identified digital money carries with it information revealing the identities of those involved in the transaction. *Also called* ***e-money, electronic money***

digital strategy GENERAL MANAGEMENT plan based on information technology a business strategy that is based on the use of information technology

digital wallet E-COMMERCE shopper's software used for making online payments software stored on the hard drive of an online shopper's computer allowing the user to pay for purchases electronically. The wallet can hold in encrypted form such items as credit card information, digital cash or coins, a digital certificate to identify the user, and standardized shipping information. *Also called* ***electronic wallet***

digitizable E-COMMERCE able to be converted to electronic form capable of being converted to digital form for distribution via the Internet or other networks

dilution levy FINANCE charge to compensate for effect of investors' transactions an extra charge levied by fund managers on investors buying or selling units in a fund, designed to offset any potential effect on the value of the fund of such purchases or sales

dilution of equity US STOCKHOLDING & INVESTMENTS sale of additional stock resulting in reduced value a situation in which a company makes more shares of common stock available without an increase in its assets, with the end result that each share is worth less than before. *UK term* ***dilution of shareholding***

dilution of shareholding UK STOCKHOLDING & INVESTMENTS = ***dilution of equity***

dip MARKETS small temporary fall in securities prices a slight temporary fall in the price of securities after a long-term gain

direct action marketing MARKETING = ***direct response marketing***

direct channel MARKETING way of selling and delivering directly to buyers a method of selling and distributing products direct to customers. Direct channels include direct selling, mail order, and the Internet.

direct cost OPERATIONS & PRODUCTION cost relating to production a variable cost directly attributable to production. Items that are classed as direct costs include materials used, labor deployed, and marketing budget. Amounts spent will vary with output. *See also* ***indirect cost***

direct debit BANKING arrangement for charging customer's account automatically a system by which a customer allows a company to make charges to his or her bank account automatically and where the amount charged can be increased or decreased with the agreement of the customer. *Abbr* **DD**. *See also* ***automatic debit***

directive LEGAL **1.** official order an official or government instruction that something should happen **2.** new law in EU in the EU, a decision made centrally that is applied through the domestic law of member states

direct labor HR & PERSONNEL employees who actually make products or perform services personnel directly involved in the manufacturing of products or the provision of services. Direct labor includes **blue-collar workers**.

  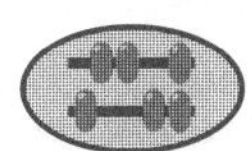   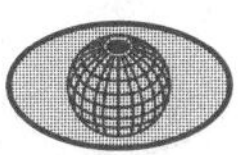 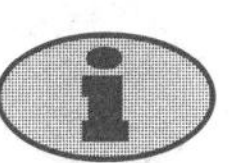  

direct labor cost percentage rate FINANCE product overhead attributed to labor costs an **overhead absorption rate**, based on labor costs, which can readily be allocated to individual units of production

direct labor hour rate FINANCE product overhead attributed to labor hours an **overhead absorption rate**, based on labor hours, which can readily be allocated to individual units of production

direct mail MARKETING sending advertising directly to potential customers the sending by mail, fax, or e-mail of advertising communications addressed to specific prospective customers. Direct mail is one tool that can be used as part of a marketing strategy. The use of direct mail is often administered by third-party companies that own databases containing not only names and addresses, but also social, economic, and lifestyle information. It is sometimes seen as an invasion of personal privacy, and there is some public resentment of this form of advertising. This is particularly true of e-mailed direct mail, known as spam. By enabling advertisers to target a specific type of potential customer, however, direct mail can be more cost-efficient than other advertising media. It is frequently used as part of a relationship marketing strategy.

direct mail preference service MARKETING arrangement for removing name from firm's mailing list an arrangement that allows individuals and organizations to refuse direct mail by having participating organizations remove them from their mailing lists

direct marketing MARKETING = ***direct response marketing***

director HR & PERSONNEL **1.** person elected by stockholders to help run company a person appointed by the stockholders to be one of the people with the responsibility of running the company. A director is usually in charge of one or other of its main functions, for example, sales or human resources, and is usually a member of the board of directors. **2.** person in charge of something the person who is in charge of a project, an official institute, or other organization

directorate CORPORATE GOVERNANCE group directing firm's course the governing or controlling body of an organization responsible for the organization's corporate strategy and accountable to its stakeholders for business results. A directorate may also be known as a **board of directors** or council, or, at an inner level, the executive or management committee.

director's dealing STOCKHOLDING & INVESTMENTS stock transactions by firm's director the purchase or sale of a company's stock by one of its directors

director's fees FINANCE money paid to company director money paid to a director of a company for attendance at board meetings

directors' report CORPORATE GOVERNANCE board of directors' annual report the annual report prepared by the board of directors and distributed to the company's stockholders

direct response marketing or **direct response advertising** MARKETING methods for trying to sell directly to consumers the use of direct forms of advertising to elicit inquiries or sales from potential customers directly to producers or service providers. Direct response marketing aims to bypass intermediaries such as wholesalers or retailers. Forms of communication used include direct mail, home shopping channels, and television and press advertisements. *Also called **direct action marketing, direct marketing***

direct selling MARKETING selling products to consumers without intermediate steps the selling of products or services directly to customers without the use of intermediaries such as wholesalers, retailers, or brokers. Direct selling offers many advantages to the customer, including lower prices and shopping from home. Potential disadvantages include lack of after-sales service, an inability to inspect products prior to purchase, lack of specialist advice, and difficulties in returning or exchanging goods. Methods of direct selling include mail order catalogs and door-to-door and telephone sales. Direct selling has increased with the growth of the Internet, which enables producers to make direct contact with potential customers.

direct share ownership *UK* STOCKHOLDING & INVESTMENTS = ***direct stock ownership***

direct stock ownership *US* STOCKHOLDING & INVESTMENTS ownership of stock by private individuals the ownership of stock by private individuals, buying or selling through brokers, and not via holdings in mutual funds. *UK term **direct share ownership***

direct tax TAX tax paid directly by producer or provider a tax on income or capital that is paid directly rather than added to the price of goods or services

dirty float CURRENCY & EXCHANGE exchange rate influenced by central bank's actions abroad a floating exchange rate that cannot float freely because a country's central bank intervenes on foreign exchange markets to alter its level

dirty price FINANCE cost of debt plus unpaid interest the price of a debt instrument that includes the amount of accrued interest that has not yet been paid

disaggregation MERGERS & ACQUISITIONS breaking up group of allied firms the breaking apart of an alliance of companies to review their strengths and contributions as a basis for rebuilding an effective business web

disaster management GENERAL MANAGEMENT firm's response to major unexpected negative events the actions taken by an organization in response to unexpected events that are adversely affecting people or resources and threatening the continued operation of the organization. Disaster management includes the development of **disaster recovery plans**, for minimizing the risk of disasters and for handling them when they do occur, and the implementation of such plans. Disaster management usually refers to the management of natural catastrophes such as fire, flooding, or earthquakes. Related techniques include **crisis management**, **contingency management**, and **risk management**.

disaster recovery plan GENERAL MANAGEMENT plan for firm's response to disaster a plan for minimizing the risk of disasters and for handling them when they do occur. It usually refers to natural catastrophes such as fire, flooding, or earthquakes. *See also **disaster management***

disbursement FINANCE paying out of money the payment of money, for example, as an expense or to get rid of a debt

disbursing agent FINANCE = ***paying agent***

discharged bankrupt LEGAL person released from bankruptcy a person who has been released from being bankrupt because his or her debts have been paid

discipline HR & PERSONNEL rules of expected behavior or performance standards of required behavior or performance. Good practice requires an organization to establish a disciplinary procedure in order to ensure just decisions. A disciplinary procedure should consist of a formal system of documented warnings and hearings, with rights of representation and appeal at each stage.

   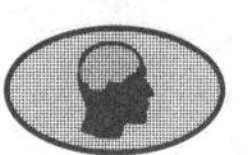 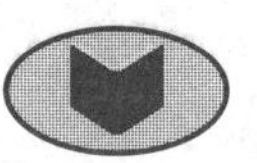 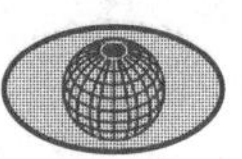 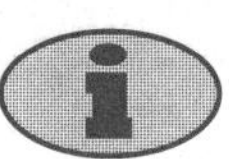  

disclaimer LEGAL statement denying legal responsibility for something a statement expressing a refusal to accept legal responsibility for something such as the outcome of an event or the validity of a claim

disclosure REGULATION & COMPLIANCE legal obligation to reveal pertinent facts the act of declaring facts that were previously unknown, such as share ownership which might affect business decisions, especially to comply with legal requirements

disclosure of information LEGAL giving potentially confidential information to outsiders the release of information to a third party or parties which may be considered confidential. The disclosure of information in the public interest may be prohibited, permitted, or required, by legislation in a variety of contexts. For example: **data protection** legislation restricts the disclosure of personal data held by organizations; **company law** requires the publication of certain financial and company data; and **whistleblowing** legislation entitles employees to divulge information relating to unethical or illegal conduct in the workplace. **Restrictive covenants** and **confidentiality agreements** also regulate the information that may be disclosed to third parties.

disclosure of shareholding STOCKHOLDING & INVESTMENTS public disclosure of holdings in firm a public announcement of a shareholding in a company, required by the regulatory authorities and stock exchanges if a shareholding exceeds a given percentage

discount 1. FINANCE price reduction to encourage buying a reduction in the price of goods or services in relation to the standard price. A discount is a selling technique that is used, for example, to encourage customers to buy in large quantities or to make payments in cash. It can also be used to improve sales of a slow-moving line. The greater the purchasing power of the buyer, the greater the discounts that can be negotiated. Some companies inflate original list prices to give the impression that discounts offer value for money; conversely too many genuine discounts may harm profitability. 2. STOCKHOLDING & INVESTMENTS reduced share price offered by investment trust the difference between the share price of an investment trust and its **net asset value**

discount allowed BUSINESS amount of seller's price reduction the amount by which the seller agrees to reduce his or her price to the customer

discount broker STOCKHOLDING & INVESTMENTS broker with lower fees offering fewer services a broker who charges relatively low fees because he or she provides restricted services

discount brokerage *US* FINANCE finance firm offering fewer, cheaper services a brokerage that offers fewer services for a reduced commission than a standard brokerage

discounted bond STOCKHOLDING & INVESTMENTS low-yield bond priced below face value a bond that is sold for less than its face value because its yield is not as high as that of other bonds

discounted cash flow FINANCE forecast return on investment subject to cost-of-funds adjustment a calculation of the forecast return on capital investment by discounting future cash flows from an investment, usually at a rate equivalent to the company's minimum required rate of return. *Abbr* **DCF**

discounted dividend model STOCKHOLDING & INVESTMENTS calculation of stock's value by discounting future dividends a method of calculating a stock's value by reducing future dividends to the present value. *Also called* ***dividend discount model***

discounted value STOCKHOLDING & INVESTMENTS = ***present value***

discount house FINANCE firm trading in discounted bills of exchange in the United Kingdom, a financial company that specializes in buying and selling **bills of exchange** at a reduced price

discount loan FINANCE loan issued with interest payments deducted a loan that amounts to less than its face value because payment of interest has been subtracted

discount market MARKETS market for borrowing and lending money a market for borrowing and lending money, through certificates of deposit, Treasury bills, etc.

discount rate 1. BANKING interest rate banks pay for loans the rate charged by a central bank on any loans it makes to other banks 2. E-COMMERCE fee seller pays for credit card transaction settlement a percentage fee that an e-commerce merchant pays to an account provider or independent sales organization for settling an electronic transaction

discount received BUSINESS amount of customer's price reduction the amount by which the purchaser receives a reduction in price from the seller

discount security FINANCE low-priced security not paying interest a security that is sold for less than its face value in lieu of bearing interest

discount window BANKING Federal Reserve loans to member banks in the United States, the system by which the Federal Reserve grants loans to a member bank by giving advances on the security of Treasury bills that the bank is holding

discrete variable STATISTICS statistical variable with whole-number value in a statistical study, a variable such as the number of deaths in a population which has only a whole-number value

discretionary account STOCKHOLDING & INVESTMENTS account allowing broker to make trading decisions a securities account in which the broker has the authority to make decisions about buying and selling without the customer's prior permission. *Also called* ***managed account***

discretionary client STOCKHOLDING & INVESTMENTS client who lets broker manage funds without consultation a client whose funds are managed at the discretion of a broker without the broker needing to refer to the client for prior permission

discretionary funds STOCKHOLDING & INVESTMENTS funds broker can manage without consulting client funds managed at the discretion of a broker without the broker needing to refer to the owner for prior permission

discretionary management STOCKHOLDING & INVESTMENTS investment agreement allowing broker to make decisions an arrangement between a stockbroker and his or her client whereby the stockbroker makes all investment decisions. It is the opposite of an **advisory management** arrangement.

discretionary order STOCKHOLDING & INVESTMENTS transaction handled by broker alone a security transaction in which a broker controls details such as the time of execution

discretionary spend *UK* FINANCE = ***discretionary spending***

discretionary spending *US* FINANCE money for things you want but don't need the amount of money available after direct taxation to an individual or family to spend on items other than necessities such as food, clothing, and homes. *UK term* ***discretionary spend***

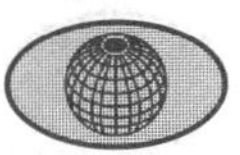

discretionary trust FINANCE trust arrangement giving trustee full decision-making power a trust where the trustees decide how to invest the income and when and how much income should be paid to the beneficiaries

discriminant analysis STATISTICS statistical method of identifying variables that differentiate groups a statistical technique designed to predict the groups or categories into which individual cases will fall on the basis of a number of independent variables. Discriminant analysis attempts to identify which variables or combinations of variables accurately discriminate between groups or categories by means of a scatter diagram or classification table called a "confusion matrix." Discriminant analysis has applications in finance, for example, credit risk analysis, or in the prediction of company failure, and in the field of marketing, for market segmentation purposes.

discriminating monopoly ECONOMICS sole producer tailoring prices to markets a company able to charge different prices for its output in different markets because as the only producer it has power to influence prices for its goods

discrimination HR & PERSONNEL unfairly treating people differently because of prejudice unfavorable treatment in employment based on prejudice. Major forms of outlawed discrimination include those based on sex, race, disability, and, in some countries, age.

diseconomies of scale OPERATIONS & PRODUCTION increased unit cost with increased production a situation in which increased production increases, rather than decreases, unit costs

disequilibrium FINANCE imbalance in economy, as between supply and demand an imbalance in the economy when supply does not equal demand, or when a country's balance of payments is in deficit

disequilibrium price ECONOMICS product price causing supply and demand imbalance the price of a good set at a level at which demand and supply are not in balance

dishonor BANKING not pay check because funds are inadequate to refuse payment of a check because the account for which it is written does not contain enough money. *Also called* ***bounce*** *(sense 1)*

disinflation ECONOMICS removal of inflation through monetary policies the elimination or reduction of inflation or inflationary pressures in an economy by fiscal or monetary policies

disintermediation **1.** FINANCE direct trading in money market the process of savers and borrowers making transactions directly in the money market rather than by making deposits and taking loans from banks **2.** E-COMMERCE removing middlemen to sell directly to customer the elimination of intermediaries, for example, the wholesalers found in traditional retail channels, in favor of direct selling to the consumer. *See also* ***reintermediation***

disinvest **1.** FINANCE reduce investment by non-replacement of capital assets to reduce investment by not replacing capital assets when they wear out **2.** STOCKHOLDING & INVESTMENTS reduce investment by selling stock to reduce investment overall or in a specific area by selling stock

disinvestment FINANCE **1.** reduction in investment through non-replacement of capital assets a process of reducing investment by not replacing capital assets when they wear out **2.** reduction in investment by selling stock a process of reducing investment overall or in a specific area by selling stock

dismissal HR & PERSONNEL firing employee the termination of somebody's employment by his or her employer

dispensation TAX UK employer's tax allowance for business expenses in the United Kingdom, an arrangement between an employer and **Her Majesty's Revenue & Customs** in which business expenses paid to an employee are not declared for tax

dispersion STATISTICS degree of deviation from mean the amount by which a set of observations deviates from its mean

disposable income or **disposable personal income** TAX income after tax and other deductions income that is left for spending after taxes and other deductions have been made from the income of a person or organization. *See also* ***net pay***

dispute HR & PERSONNEL disagreement between parties a disagreement. An **industrial dispute** is a disagreement between an employer and an employees' representative, usually a labor union, over pay and conditions and can result in industrial action. A **commercial dispute** is a disagreement between two businesses, usually over a contract. There are three main types of dispute resolution: litigation, arbitration, and alternative dispute resolution.

disqualification LEGAL court decision disallowing person from becoming company director a court order that prevents somebody from being a director of a company. A variety of offenses, even those termed as "administrative," can result in some people being disqualified for up to five years.

distrain BUSINESS take control of assets to pay debt to seize **assets** belonging to a person or organization in order to pay off a debt

distressed property FINANCE property subject to repossession property originally purchased with the aid of a loan on which payments have stopped and the borrower has defaulted

distress merchandise OPERATIONS & PRODUCTION goods sold cheaply to pay company's debts goods that are sold at sharply reduced prices in order to settle a company's debts

distress sale OPERATIONS & PRODUCTION sale of goods cheaply to pay company's debts a sale of goods at sharply reduced prices in order to settle a company's debts

distributable profit STOCKHOLDING & INVESTMENTS profit usable as dividends profit that can be distributed to stockholders as dividends if the directors decide to do so

distributed profit STOCKHOLDING & INVESTMENTS profit passed on as dividends profit passed to stockholders in the form of dividends

distribution OPERATIONS & PRODUCTION supplying of manufactured goods to retailers the act of sending goods from the manufacturer to the wholesaler and then to retailers

distribution center OPERATIONS & PRODUCTION place for holding products to be sent out a warehouse or storage facility where the emphasis is on processing and moving goods on to wholesalers, retailers, or consumers rather than on storage

distribution channel OPERATIONS & PRODUCTION means of moving products from suppliers to customers the route by which a product or service is moved from a producer or supplier to customers. A distribution channel usually consists of a chain of intermediaries, including wholesalers, retailers, and distributors, which is designed to transport goods from the point of production to the point of consumption in the most efficient way. *Also called* ***channel of distribution***

distribution list E-COMMERCE named group of e-mail addresses a list of e-mail addresses given one collective name. Internet users can send a message to all the addresses on the list simultaneously by referring to the list name.

     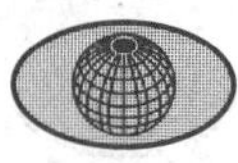   

distribution management OPERATIONS & PRODUCTION handling movement of goods from production to sale the management of the efficient transfer of goods from the place of manufacture to the point of sale or consumption. Distribution management encompasses such activities as warehousing, materials handling, packaging, stock control, order processing, and transportation.

distribution of income 1. STOCKHOLDING & INVESTMENTS payment of dividends to stockholders the payment of accumulated dividends to stockholders on record, usually on an annual basis **2.** ECONOMICS wealth range in society the way income is spread across society as a whole, as a measure of the equality or inequality of wealth

distribution resource planning OPERATIONS & PRODUCTION computerized system managing needs for finished products a computerized system that integrates distribution with manufacturing by identifying requirements for finished goods and producing schedules for **inventory** and its movement within the distribution process. Distribution resource planning systems receive data on sales forecasts, customer order and delivery requirements, available inventory, **logistics**, and manufacturing and purchasing **lead times**. This data is analyzed to produce a time-phased schedule of resource requirements that is matched against existing supply sources and production schedules to identify the actions that must be taken to synchronize supply and demand. The effective integration of material requirements planning and distribution resource planning systems leads to the more effective and timely delivery of finished goods to the customer, and to reduced inventory levels and lower material costs. *Abbr* **DRP**

distributions STOCKHOLDING & INVESTMENTS income from investment any income arising from a bond fund or an equity

distributive network E-COMMERCE interconnected system for moving products a system or infrastructure that enables products and services to move around. Offline distributive networks include roads, telephone companies, electrical power grids, and the mail service. In the new economy, distributive networks include online banks and Web-enabled mobile telephones.

distributor MARKETING intermediary between manufacturer and seller an organization that distributes products to retailers on behalf of a manufacturer

distributor support MARKETING aid from manufacturer to firm that distributes products marketing or financial support by manufacturers aimed at improving the performance of organizations that distribute their products

District Bank BANKING member bank of Federal Reserve in the United States, one of the 12 banks that make up the **Federal Reserve**. Each District Bank is responsible for all banking activity in its assigned region.

divergence MARKETS contradictory indications of trends a situation in which two or more indicators such as a stock price and an index move in opposite directions, showing a shift in a trend

diversification GENERAL MANAGEMENT, MERGERS & ACQUISITIONS developing new areas for growth or risk reduction a strategy to increase the variety of business, service, or product types within an organization. Diversification can be a growth strategy, taking advantage of market opportunities, or it may be aimed at reducing risk by spreading interests over different areas. It can be achieved through **acquisition** or through internal research and development, and it can involve managing two, a few, or many different areas of interest. Diversification can also be a corporate strategy of investment in acquisitions within a broad portfolio range by a large **holding company**. One distinct type is **horizontal diversification**, which involves expansion into a similar product area, for example, a domestic furniture manufacturer producing office furniture. Another is **vertical diversification**, in which a company moves into a different level of the **supply chain**, for example, a manufacturing company becoming a retailer.

diversified investment company FINANCE varied mutual fund a mutual fund with a range of types of investments

divestiture FINANCE firm's sale of asset the sale by a company of an asset, for example, to get money to pay off a debt

divestment 1. MERGERS & ACQUISITIONS selling or closing part of firm the sale or closure of one or several businesses, or parts of a business. Divestment often takes place as part of a rationalization effort to cut costs or to enable an organization to concentrate on core business or competences, and may take the form of a **management buyout**. **2.** STOCKHOLDING & INVESTMENTS giving up ownership in firm the proportional or complete reduction in an ownership stake in an organization

dividend STOCKHOLDING & INVESTMENTS profits paid to stockholders part of a company's net profits paid out to qualified stockholders at a fixed amount per share

dividend check US STOCKHOLDING & INVESTMENTS check in payment of dividend a check issued to qualified stockholders that makes payment of a dividend. *UK term* ***dividend warrant***

dividend clawback STOCKHOLDING & INVESTMENTS arrangement for reinvestment of dividends an agreement that dividends will be reinvested as part of the financing of a project

dividend cover STOCKHOLDING & INVESTMENTS ability of net profit to pay firm's dividend the number of times a company's dividends to ordinary stockholders could be paid out of its net after-tax profits. This measures the likelihood of dividend payments being sustained, and is a useful indication of sustained profitability.

If the figure is 3, a firm's profits are three times the level of the dividend paid to stockholders.

Dividend cover is calculated by dividing earnings per share by the dividend per share:

$$\frac{\text{Earnings per share}}{\text{Dividend per share}} = \text{Dividend cover}$$

If a company has earnings per share of $8, and it pays out a dividend of 2.1, dividend cover is

$$\frac{8}{2.1} = 3.80$$

An alternative formula divides a company's net profit by the total amount allocated for dividends. So a company that earns $10 million in net profit and allocates $1 million for dividends has a dividend cover of 10, while a company that earns $25 million and pays out $10 million in dividends has a dividend cover of 2.5:

$$\frac{10{,}000{,}000}{1{,}000{,}000} = 10 \quad \text{and} \quad \frac{25{,}000{,}000}{10{,}000{,}000} = 2.5$$

A dividend cover ratio of 2 or higher is usually adequate, and indicates that the dividend is affordable. A dividend cover ratio below 1.5 is risky, and a ratio below 1 indicates a company is paying the current year's dividend with retained earnings from a previous year's, a practice that cannot continue indefinitely. On the other hand, a high dividend cover figure may disappoint an investor looking for income, since the figure suggests directors could have

  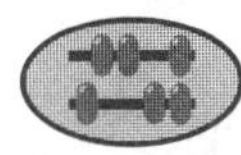   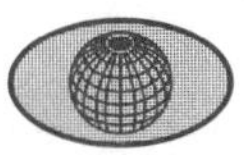   

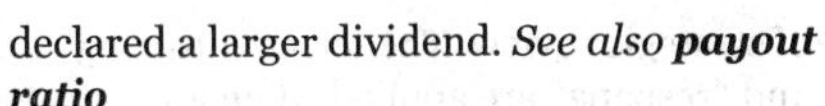

declared a larger dividend. *See also* ***payout ratio***

dividend discount model STOCKHOLDING & INVESTMENTS = ***discounted dividend model***

dividend forecast STOCKHOLDING & INVESTMENTS predicted amount of next dividend a prediction of the amount that an expected dividend will pay per share

dividend limitation STOCKHOLDING & INVESTMENTS restriction on dividend payments for bond a provision in a bond limiting the dividends that may be paid

dividend mandate STOCKHOLDING & INVESTMENTS permission to directly deposit dividends in bank account an authorization by a stockholder to the company in which he or she has a holding to pay dividends directly into his or her bank account

dividend payout STOCKHOLDING & INVESTMENTS money paid as dividends to stockholders money distributed by a company in the form of dividends to qualified stockholders

dividend payout ratio STOCKHOLDING & INVESTMENTS = ***payout ratio***

dividend per share STOCKHOLDING & INVESTMENTS amount of dividend per share of stock held an amount of money paid by a company as dividend for each share of stock held

dividend reinvestment plan STOCKHOLDING & INVESTMENTS arrangement for reinvesting dividends in firm's stock a plan that provides for the reinvestment of dividends in the stock of the company paying the dividends. *Abbr* **DRIP**

dividend rights STOCKHOLDING & INVESTMENTS rights to receive dividends the entitlement of a stockholder to receive a share of the company's profits

dividends-received deduction STOCKHOLDING & INVESTMENTS, TAX tax break on dividends from subsidiary company a tax advantage on dividends that a company receives from a company it owns

dividend warrant *UK* STOCKHOLDING & INVESTMENTS = ***dividend check***

dividend yield STOCKHOLDING & INVESTMENTS relative size of dividend dividends paid out expressed as a percentage of a stock's price

D/N *abbr* FINANCE debit note

documentary credit or **documentary letter of credit** BANKING provision for payment in international transactions an arrangement, used in the finance of international transactions, whereby a bank undertakes to make a payment to a third party on behalf of a customer. *Abbr* **D/C**

dog GENERAL MANAGEMENT firm with low market share and growth in the **Boston Box** model, a business with a low market share and low growth rate. *See also* ***Boston Box***

dog-eat-dog MARKETING extremely competitive ruthlessly willing to harm competitors, especially in the marketplace (*slang*)

dogs of the Dow MARKETS stocks with smallest yield according to Dow Jones in the United States, the stocks in the **Dow Jones** Industrial Average that pay the smallest dividends as a percentage of their prices (*informal*)

dollar CURRENCY & EXCHANGE currency unit in US and some other countries a unit of currency used in the United States and other countries such as Australia, Bahamas, Barbados, Bermuda, Brunei, Canada, Fiji, Hong Kong, Jamaica, New Zealand, Singapore, and Zimbabwe

dollar area CURRENCY & EXCHANGE region using US dollar for trading an area of the world where the US dollar is the main trading currency

dollar cost averaging *US* FINANCE regular repeating of investment the regular periodic purchase of the same amount in dollars of the same security regardless of its price. *UK term* ***pound cost averaging***

dollar gap CURRENCY & EXCHANGE shortage of US dollars a situation in which the supply of US dollars is not enough to satisfy the demand for them from overseas buyers

dollar roll MARKETS arrangement to sell then repurchase stock in the United States, an agreement to sell a stock and buy it back later for a specified price

dollars-and-cents *US* FINANCE influenced by money used to describe a situation in which cost and return are considered the determining factors

dollar stocks STOCKHOLDING & INVESTMENTS stocks in US companies stocks issued by companies incorporated in the United States

domestic consumer ECONOMICS user of product for personal purposes a **consumer** who uses a product for personal, domestic, or household purposes

domestic currency CURRENCY & EXCHANGE money legally accepted in home country the legal **currency** of the jurisdiction that issued it

domestic economy ECONOMICS economy of home country the production, consumption, and distribution of wealth within a specific country

domestic market MARKETS market in home country the market for goods and services in the country where a company is based

domestic production OPERATIONS & PRODUCTION production of goods for home country use the production of goods and services for internal consumption in the producer country rather than for export

domestic tax TAX tax on residents and businesses in home country tax levied on companies doing business and individuals living in a specific country

domestic trade BUSINESS trade inside firm's home country trade by a company within the country in which it is based

domicile LEGAL country of somebody's residence or firm's registration the country in which somebody has his or her permanent residence or where a company's office is registered

domicilium citandi et executandi *S. Africa* FINANCE address for delivering legal documents the address where a summons or other official notice should be served if necessary, which must be supplied by somebody applying for credit or entering into a contract

dominant influence TREASURY MANAGEMENT undisputed influence over financial policy influence that can be exercised to achieve the operating and financial policies designed by the holder of the influence, notwithstanding the rights or influence of any other party

donor FINANCE giver of gift a person who gives a gift, especially money

dormant account BANKING inactive bank account a bank account that is no longer used by the account holder

dormant company ACCOUNTING firm not doing business for a while a company that has not made any transactions during a specific **accounting period**

dot.com E-COMMERCE firm selling on Internet an e-commerce enterprise, marketing its products only through the Internet

double bottom MARKETS bullish chart pattern with *W* shape a chart pattern in which the price of a security drops, recovers moderately, drops again, then recovers a second time and continues its upward trend, regarded as an indicator of a bullish market

  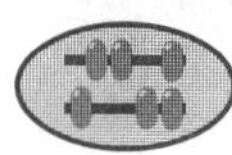   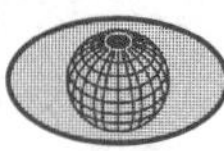   

double counting ACCOUNTING using same cost or benefit twice in calculation the counting of a cost or benefit element twice when carrying out analysis. This can happen when the total sales in a market is calculated as the sum of all sales made by companies, without deducting the purchases companies make from other firms in the market.

double digit growth ECONOMICS rapid growth of firm or economy an increase of between 10% and 99% in the productivity or size of a company, business activity, or economy within a specific period of time

double digit inflation ECONOMICS rapid growth of inflation rate a rate of inflation between 10% and 99%, usually calculated on an annual basis

double dipping FRAUD fraudulently receiving two incomes from government in the United States, the illegal practice of receiving income from a government pension as well as social security payments, or of holding a government job while receiving a government pension

double-entry bookkeeping ACCOUNTING type of bookkeeping system used by most businesses the most commonly used system of **bookkeeping**, based on the principle that every financial transaction involves the simultaneous receiving and giving of value, and is therefore recorded twice

double indemnity INSURANCE commitment to pay double insurance for accidental death a provision in an insurance policy that guarantees payment of double its face value on the accidental death of the holder

double taxation TAX having to pay tax twice on same income the taxing of something twice, usually the combination of corporation tax and tax on the dividends that stockholders earn

double taxation relief TAX tax break between countries on taxes already paid a reduction of tax payable in one country by the amount of tax on income, profits, or capital gains already paid in another country

double top MARKETS bearish chart pattern with *M* shape a chart pattern in which the price of a security rises, drops moderately, rises again, then drops a second time and continues its downward trend, regarded as an indicator of a bearish market

Dow Jones FINANCE provider of business and financial news Dow Jones and Company, Inc., a US corporation that provides business and financial news worldwide and compiles the **Dow Jones Averages**.

Dow Jones Averages MARKETS stock price listing of selected US traded stocks an index of the prices of selected stocks on the New York Stock Exchange compiled by Dow Jones & Company, Inc

Dow Jones Industrial Average or **Dow Jones Index** MARKETS index of stocks in major industrial firms an index of 30 predominately industrial stocks actively traded on the New York Stock Exchange, used as an indicator of the performance of stocks in the United States

downgrade MARKETS **1.** reduce projection for stock price to change the forecast for a stock price to a lower one **2.** reduce bond rating to change the credit rating for a **bond** to a lower one

down payment FINANCE partial payment at time of purchase a part of the full price of something paid at the time it is bought, with the remaining part to be paid later

downshifting GENERAL MANAGEMENT reducing work and income for simpler, better life the concept of giving up all or part of your work commitment and income in exchange for improved quality of life Downshifting is integral to the idea of **portfolio working**, in which individuals opt out of a formal employee relationship to sell their services at a pace and at a price to suit themselves

downside factor or **downside potential** STOCKHOLDING & INVESTMENTS possibility of loss in value the possibility of incurring a loss when an investment declines in value

downside risk STOCKHOLDING & INVESTMENTS risk of loss in value the risk that an investment will decline in value. *See also* ***upside potential***

downsizing **1.** BUSINESS expense cuts to make organization more efficient organizational restructuring involving outsourcing activities, replacing permanent staff with contract employees, and reducing the number of levels within the organizational hierarchy, with the intention of making the organization more flexible, efficient, and responsive to its environment **2.** HR & PERSONNEL reducing number of firm's employees the reduction of the size of a business, especially by laying staff off. Downsizing may be part of a rationalization process, or corporate restructuring, with the removal of hierarchies or the closure of departments or functions either after a period of unsatisfactory results or as a consequence of strategic review. The terms "upsizing" and "resizing" are applied when an organization increases the number of staff employed.

downstream OPERATIONS & PRODUCTION at later stage at a point later in the production process

downstream progress GENERAL MANAGEMENT easy advancement toward goals movement by a company toward achieving its objectives which is easy because it involves riding a wave or trend and benefiting from favorable conditions. *See also* ***upstream progress***

downswing MARKETS decline in stock prices a downward movement in stock prices following a period of steady or rising prices

downtick MARKETS trade at price lower than in previous trade a transaction in which the price of a particular security is lower than the price in the transaction immediately preceding it

downtime OPERATIONS & PRODUCTION period when machinery is not working a period of time during which a machine is not available for use because of maintenance or breakdown

downturn FINANCE, MARKETS downward trend a downward trend in sales, profits, a stock market, or an economy

Dow Theory MARKETS idea that movements in selected stocks predict prices the theory that stock market prices can be forecast on the basis of the movements of selected industrial and transportation stocks

draft BANKING document ordering payment a written order to pay a particular sum from one account to another, or to a person. *See also* ***sight draft, time draft***

drawback TAX tax rebate on imports that produce exports a rebate on customs duty for imported goods that are used in producing exports

drawdown FINANCE decision to use money made available earlier the act of obtaining money that has previously been made available under a credit agreement

drawee BANKING payer of bill of exchange or check the individual or institution to whom a bill of exchange or check is addressed, who will pay the sum indicated

drawer BANKING person who writes check or bill the person who writes a check or a bill asking an individual or institution to pay money to the payee indicated

drawing account BANKING account for tracking money withdrawn an account that permits the tracking of withdrawals, used,

  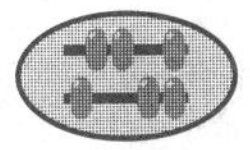 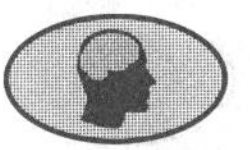  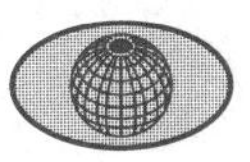   

for example, by a **sole proprietor** or **partner**

drawing rights FINANCE member country's right to borrow from IMF fund **a right of a member country of the International Monetary Fund to borrow money from the fund in a foreign currency.** *See also* ***Special Drawing Right***

drilling down MARKETING investigating more detailed subject information **a technique for managing data by arranging it in hierarchies that provide increasing levels of detail**

DRIP *abbr* STOCKHOLDING & INVESTMENTS dividend reinvestment plan

drip feed 1. FINANCE gradual provision of capital **a method of providing capital to a small startup company in which investors contribute capital as needed over a period of time 2.** STOCKHOLDING & INVESTMENTS regular increase in investment **a method of investing in securities in which investors invest a specific amount of money on a regular basis**

drip method MARKETING calling potential customers repeatedly until they buy **a marketing method that involves calling potential customers at regular intervals until they agree to make a purchase (*slang*)**

drive time MARKETING time when people drive to or from work **the time of the day when most people are likely to be in their cars, usually early in the morning or late in the afternoon, considered to be the optimum time to broadcast a radio commercial (*slang*)**

drop a bundle MARKETS spend or lose large sum of money **to spend or lose a lot of money, especially on the stock market (*slang*)**

drop lock FINANCE change from floating to fixed interest rate **the automatic conversion of a debt instrument with a floating rate to one with a fixed rate when interest rates fall to an agreed percentage**

droplock bond STOCKHOLDING & INVESTMENTS bond becoming fixed rate if interest rate falls **a floating-rate bond that will convert to a fixed rate of interest if interest rates fall to a specific level.** *See also* ***debt-convertible bond***

DRP *abbr* OPERATIONS & PRODUCTION distribution resource planning

dry goods textiles and housewares **textiles, clothing, and general housewares**

DTCC *abbr* BUSINESS Depository Trust and Clearing Corporation

DTF *abbr* MARKETS Derivative Trading Facility

DTI *abbr* Department of Trade and Industry

dual currency bond CURRENCY & EXCHANGE bond issued and paying interest in different currencies **a bond that pays interest in a currency other than the one used to buy it**

dual economy ECONOMICS different growth rates for manufacturing and services **an economy in which the manufacturing and service sectors are growing at different rates**

dual listing MARKETS listing of stock on two exchanges **the listing of a stock on two or more stock exchanges, often including a regional exchange in addition to a nationwide exchange**

dual pricing MARKETS selling product at different prices in different markets **the practice of setting different prices for the same product in the different markets in which it is sold**

dual trading FINANCE working as agent for buyer and seller **the practice of acting as agent for both a broker's firm and its customers**

duck ◇ get your ducks in a row **or** line up your ducks GENERAL MANAGEMENT **1. to get everything properly organized 2. to get all concerned parties to agree to a plan of action**

dud check BANKING check not honored because of insufficient funds **a check that cannot be cashed because the person writing it does not have enough money in the account to pay it**

due bill STOCKHOLDING & INVESTMENTS notice of transfer from seller to buyer **a notification that a security has been transferred from the seller to the buyer, giving details of the amounts such as cost, dividends, or interest owed either the seller or buyer**

due date FINANCE deadline for payment of debt **the date on which a debt is required to be paid**

due diligence 1. ACCOUNTING detailed check of firm's accounts before sale **the examination of a company's accounts prior to a potential takeover by another organization. This assessment is often undertaken by an independent third party.** *Abbr* **DD 2.** GENERAL MANAGEMENT investigation of firm before purchase or investment **the collection, verification, analysis, and assessment of information about the operations and management of a company undertaken by a potential purchaser or investor. Due diligence aims to confirm that the purchaser or investor has an accurate picture of the target company and to identify risks and benefits associated with the prospective deal. Due diligence usually starts after the signing of a letter of intent by both parties and information disclosed during the process is normally protected by the signing of a confidentiality agreement. Due diligence often leads on to negotiations on the detailed terms of the agreement. The process may cover the financial, legal, commercial, technical, cultural, and environmental aspects of the organization's operations as well as its assets and liabilities, and may be conducted with the assistance of professional advisers.**

due-on-sale clause MORTGAGES obligation to pay off mortgage upon property sale **a provision requiring a homeowner to pay off a mortgage upon sale of the property**

dumping INTERNATIONAL TRADE selling commodity abroad at greatly reduced price **the selling of a commodity on a foreign market at a price below its marginal cost, either to dispose of a temporary surplus or to achieve a monopoly by eliminating competition —dump**

Dun and Bradstreet BUSINESS organization that collects and provides credit information **an international organization that sources credit information from companies and their creditors which it then makes available to subscribers.** *Abbr* **D&B**

duopoly ECONOMICS market with only two sellers of product **a market in which only two sellers of a good exist. If one decides to alter the price, the other will respond and influence the market's response to the first decision.**

durable power of attorney LEGAL power to act for another **a power of attorney that allows one person to act on behalf of another if that person should become unable to act on their own behalf, for example, because of mental incompetence**

duration STOCKHOLDING & INVESTMENTS time to receive current value of payments **the time in years that it will take to receive the present value of all the payments from a fixed-income investment, calculated using the effect that a 1% change in the interest rate will have on the investment. This calculation is mainly used to measure the sensitivity of changes in bond prices to changes in interest rates.**

Dutch auction FINANCE auction in which price bidding goes down **an auction in which the lot for sale is offered at an initial**

  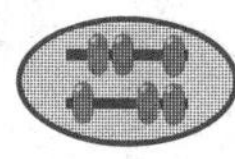 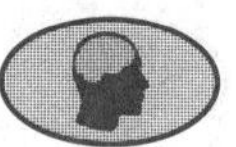  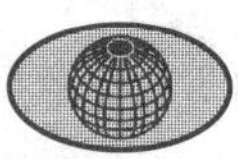   

price that, if there are no bidders, is then reduced until there is a bid

duty TAX tax on goods, especially imports and exports a tax that must be paid on goods, especially on imported and exported goods

duty-free TAX exempt from customs duty sold without the requirement for any customs duties to be paid

dynamic pricing FINANCE pricing from demand pricing that changes in line with patterns of demand

dynamic programming GENERAL MANAGEMENT mathematical approach to solving production and inventory problems a mathematical technique used to solve complex problems in the fields of production planning and inventory control. Dynamic programming divides the problem into steps or decision stages that can be addressed sequentially, usually by working backward from the last stage. Applications of the technique include maintenance and replacement of equipment, resource allocation, and process design and control.

E

EAA *abbr* ACCOUNTING European Accounting Association

EAI *abbr* OPERATIONS & PRODUCTION enterprise application integration

e-alliance E-COMMERCE union of organizations for Internet commerce a partnership forged between organizations in order to achieve business objectives for enterprises conducted over the web. There has been a surge in such alliances since the Internet took off in the mid-1990s, and studies show that the most successful have been those involving traditional offline businesses and online entities, known as the clicks-and-mortar strategy, for example, that between Amazon.com and Toys 'R' Us. Toys 'R' Us had the physical infrastructure and brand, while Amazon.com had the online infrastructure and experience of making e-commerce work.

E&O *abbr* ACCOUNTING errors and omissions

early adopter GENERAL MANAGEMENT one of first users of new technology an individual or organization that is among the first to make use of a new technique, strategy, technology, etc.

early withdrawal BANKING taking money out of time deposit account early the removal of money from a deposit account before the due date. Early withdrawal often incurs a penalty that the account holder must pay.

earned income FINANCE money earned for work performed money generated by a person's or organization's labor, for example, wages, salaries, fees, royalties, and business profits. *See also* ***unearned income***

Earned Income Credit TAX US tax credit for low paid in the United States, a federal income tax credit for low-income individuals and families with income generated from employment. *Abbr* **EIC**

earning potential **1.** BUSINESS amount person can earn the amount of money somebody should be able to earn in his or her professional capacity **2.** STOCKHOLDING & INVESTMENTS potential dividend earnings the amount of dividend that a share potentially can produce

earnings **1.** FINANCE money obtained through work a sum of money gained from paid employment, usually quoted before tax, including any extra rewards such as **fringe benefits**, allowances, or incentives **2.** ACCOUNTING money available to business after expenses income or profit from a business, quoted gross or net of tax, which may be retained and distributed in part to the stockholders

earnings before interest, tax, depreciation, and amortization ACCOUNTING *see* ***EBITDA***

earnings before interest and taxes ACCOUNTING *see* ***EBIT***

earnings cap PENSIONS in UK, maximum earnings for pension purposes in the United Kingdom, the top limit of earnings that can be used in calculating a retirement pension paid from an **occupational pension** plan

earnings credit BANKING in US, amount offsetting bank charges in the United States, an allowance that reduces bank charges on checking accounts

earnings drift FINANCE pay increases outstripping official rates a situation in which an increase in pay is greater than that of officially negotiated rates

earnings growth STOCKHOLDING & INVESTMENTS increase in profit per share of stock an increase in the profit a company earns as expressed on a per-share basis

earnings momentum STOCKHOLDING & INVESTMENTS change in profit per share of stock an increase or decrease in a company's earnings per share as compared to the same period of time in the previous year, used by investors as a measure of how its stock will perform

earnings performance STOCKHOLDING & INVESTMENTS dividend-yielding pattern of stock a measure of how well a specific stock does in providing dividends

earnings per share STOCKHOLDING & INVESTMENTS profit allotted to each share of common stock a financial ratio that measures the portion of a company's profit allocated to each outstanding share of common stock. It is the most basic measure of the value of a share, and also is the basis for calculating several other important investment ratios.

EPS is calculated by subtracting the total value of any preferred stock from net income (earnings) for the period in question, then dividing the resulting figure by the number of shares outstanding during that period.

$$\frac{\text{Net income} - \text{Dividends on any preferred stock}}{\text{Average number of shares outstanding}}$$

Companies usually use a weighted average number of shares outstanding over the reporting period, but shares outstanding can either be "primary" or "fully diluted." Primary EPS is calculated using the number of shares that are currently held by investors in the market and able to be traded. Diluted EPS is the result of a complex calculation that determines how many shares would be outstanding if all exercisable warrants and options were converted into shares at the end of a quarter.

Suppose, for example, that a company has granted a large number of share options to employees. If these options are capable of being exercised in the near future, that could significantly alter the number of shares in issue and thus the EPS, even though the net income is the same. Often in such cases, the company might quote the EPS on the existing shares and the fully diluted version. *Abbr* **EPS**

earnings-related contributions FINANCE payments into social security fund based on earnings contributions to social security that rise as the person's earnings rise, especially **National Insurance** contributions in the United Kingdom

earnings-related pension PENSIONS in UK, pension linked to salary in the United Kingdom, a pension that is linked to the size of the beneficiary's salary

  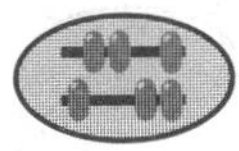   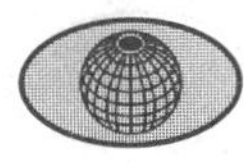   

earnings report US STOCKHOLDING & INVESTMENTS published financial report of US firm a company's financial statements, which must be published according to US law. *UK term **published accounts***

earnings retained ACCOUNTING = ***retained profits***

earnings season STOCKHOLDING & INVESTMENTS time when firms announce earnings the time of year when major companies declare their results for the previous period

earnings surprise STOCKHOLDING & INVESTMENTS gap between actual and expected earnings a considerable difference in size between a company's actual and anticipated earnings

earnings yield FINANCE earnings as percentage of stock price money earned by a company during a year, expressed as a percentage of the price of one of its shares

EASDAQ MARKETS European stock exchange for technology and growth companies a stock exchange for technology and growth companies based in Europe and modeled on the **NASDAQ** in the United States. *Full form **European Association of Securities Dealers Automated Quotations***

eased UK MARKETS describes stock market that is slightly down used in stock market reports to describe a market that has experienced a slight fall in prices

easy market MARKETS stock market with few buyers a market in which fewer people are buying, with the effect that prices are lower than hoped

easy money FINANCE = ***cheap money***

easy money policy FINANCE government policy to encourage borrowing a government policy that aims to expand the economy by making money more easily accessible to the public. This is done by strategies such as lowering interest rates and offering easy access to credit.

easy terms UK FINANCE = ***installment plan***

EBIT ACCOUNTING income minus costs revenue minus the cost of goods sold and normal operating expenses. *Full form **earnings before interest and taxes***

EBITDA ACCOUNTING use of earnings to measure firm's performance the earnings generated by a business's fundamental operating performance, frequently used in accounting ratios for comparison with other companies. Interest on borrowings, tax payable on those profits, depreciation, and amortization are excluded on the basis that they can distort the underlying performance.

It is calculated as follows:

Revenue – Expenses (excluding tax and interest, depreciation, etc.) = EBITDA

It is important to note that EBITDA ignores many factors that impact on true cash flow, such as working capital, debt payments, and other fixed expenses. Even so, it may be useful for evaluating firms in the same industry with widely different capital structures, tax rates, and depreciation policies. *Full form **earnings before interest, tax, depreciation, and amortization***

EBQ OPERATIONS & PRODUCTION size cheapest and easiest to produce the optimum batch size for the manufacture of an item or component, at the lowest cost. The batch size is a tradeoff between unit costs that increase with batch size and those that decrease. The point of lowest combined or total cost indicates the most economic batch size for production. *Full form **economic batch quantity**. Also called **economic lot quantity**. See also **economic order quantity***

EBRD BANKING European bank helping to develop market economies A bank, established in 1991, to develop programs to tackle a variety of issues. These included the creation and strengthening of infrastructure; industry privatization; the reform of the financial sector, including the development of capital markets and the privatization of commercial banks; the development of productive competitive private sectors of small and medium-sized enterprises in industry, agriculture, and services; the restructuring of industrial sectors to put them on a competitive basis; and the encouragement of foreign investment and cleaning up the environment. The EBRD had 41 original members: the European Commission, the European Investment Bank, all the then EU countries, and all the countries of Eastern Europe except Albania, which finally became a member in October 1991, followed by all the republics of the former USSR in March 1992. *Full form **European Bank for Reconstruction and Development***

e-business E-COMMERCE **1.** carrying out of business over Internet the conduct of business on the Internet, including the electronic purchasing and selling of goods and services, servicing customers, and communications with business partners. *Also called **electronic business*** **2.** firm operating over Internet a company that conducts the main part of its business on the Internet

EC *abbr* INTERNATIONAL TRADE European Community

e-cash E-COMMERCE = ***digital cash***

ECB BANKING bank responsible for EU monetary policy the financial institution that replaced the European Monetary Institute in 1998 and that is responsible for carrying out EU monetary policy and administering the Euro. *Full form **European Central Bank***

ECBC *abbr* FINANCE European Covered Bond Council

ECGD *abbr* INTERNATIONAL TRADE Export Credit Guarantee Department

ECML *abbr* E-COMMERCE electronic commerce modeling language

ECN *abbr* MARKETS Electronic Communications Network

ECOA *abbr* FINANCE Equal Credit Opportunity Act

e-collaboration E-COMMERCE cooperation using Internet collaboration among people or organizations made possible by means of electronic technologies such as the Internet, videoconferencing, and wireless devices

e-commerce E-COMMERCE business conducted electronically, especially via Internet the exchange of goods, information products, or services via an electronic medium such as the Internet. Originally limited to buying and selling, it has evolved to include such functions as customer service, marketing, and advertising. *Also called **electronic commerce, web commerce***

e-commerce processes E-COMMERCE stages of trading over Internet the flow of information through planning, design, manufacture, sales, order processing, distribution, and quality in an e-business

e-company E-COMMERCE e-commerce business a company engaged in e-commerce or that conducts the main part of its business on the Internet

econometric model ECONOMICS set of mathematical equations representing economic relationships a way of representing the relationship between economic variables as an equation or set of equations with statistically precise parameters linking the variables

econometrics ECONOMICS study of mathematical equations for representing economic relationships the branch of

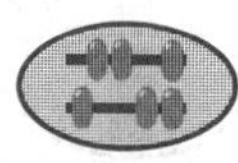

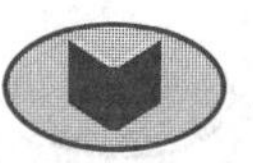
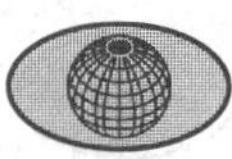

economics concerned with using mathematical models to describe relationships in an economy, for example, between wage rates and levels of employment

economic assumption ECONOMICS belief on which economic model is based an assumption built into an economic model, for example, that output will grow at 2.5% in the next tax year

economic batch quantity OPERATIONS & PRODUCTION *see* ***EBQ***

economic benefit FINANCE benefit measurable in money a benefit to a person, business, or society that can be measured in financial terms

economic cycle ECONOMICS recurrent expansion and slowdown of trade a repeated sequence of business activity expanding, then slowing down, and then expanding again

economic development ECONOMICS rise in country's living standards improvements in the living standards and wealth of the citizens of a country

Economic Development Board BUSINESS organization promoting foreign investment in Singapore's economy an organization established in 1961 that works to promote investment in Singapore by providing various services and assistance programs to foreign and local companies. *Abbr* **EDB**

economic efficiency BUSINESS *see* ***efficiency***

economic forecaster ECONOMICS person predicting future economic performance a person whose job is to predict how a country's economy will perform in the future

economic goods ECONOMICS products or services sold in market services or physical objects that can command a price in the market

economic growth ECONOMICS increase in country's economic activity and income an increase in the national income of a country created by the long-term productive potential of its economy

economic indicator ECONOMICS statistical measurement of country's economy a statistic that may be important for a country's long-term economic health, for example, rising prices or falling exports

economic life ECONOMICS country's manufacturing and trade conditions the conditions of trade and manufacture in a country that contribute to its prosperity or poverty

economic lot quantity OPERATIONS & PRODUCTION *see* ***EBQ***

economic miracle ECONOMICS dramatic rebuilding of economies after World War II the rapid growth after 1945 in countries such as Germany and Japan, where in ten years economies shattered by World War II were regenerated

economic model ECONOMICS computerized forecast of economic trends a computerized plan of a country's economic system, used for forecasting economic trends

economic order quantity OPERATIONS & PRODUCTION amount for best inventory control the most economic inventory replenishment order size, which minimizes the sum of inventory ordering costs and holding costs. *Abbr* **EOQ**

economic paradigm ECONOMICS fundamental economic belief a basic unchanging economic principle, one that governs the way economists view the world

economic planning ECONOMICS government's plans for future of economy plans made by a government for the financial state of a country over different future time periods

Economic Planning and Advisory Council REGULATION & COMPLIANCE advisory group for Australia's economic policies a committee of businesspeople and politicians appointed to advise the Australian government on economic issues

economic pressure ECONOMICS country's negative economic conditions a condition in a country's economy in which economic indicators are unfavorable

economic profit ACCOUNTING total revenue less total cost the difference between the total revenue and total cost associated with a specific business

economic relations INTERNATIONAL TRADE trade and finance interactions between countries the arrangements for cooperation in international trade, finance, and investment existing between individual countries and sets of countries

economics ECONOMICS study of society's wealth the study of the consumption, distribution, and production of wealth in societies

economic sanctions INTERNATIONAL TRADE trade restrictions to bring about political changes restrictions on trade with a country in order to influence its political situation or to make its government change its policy

economic surplus ECONOMICS positive balance of costs against output the positive difference between an economy's output and the costs incurred in factors such as wages, raw materials, and depreciation

economic theory of the firm ECONOMICS idea that firm's responsibility is to serve stockholders the theory that the only duty that a company has to those external to it is financial. The economic theory of the firm holds that stockholders should be the prime beneficiaries of an organization's activities. The theory is associated with **top-down leadership** and **cost cutting** through rationalization and **downsizing.** With immediate stock price dominating management activities, the economic theory of the firm has been criticized as being too short-term, as opposed to the longer-term thinking behind **stakeholder theory**.

economic value added FINANCE evaluating performance by comparing earnings to capital investment a way of judging financial performance by measuring the amount by which the earnings of a project, an operation, or a corporation exceed or fall short of the total amount of capital that was originally invested by its owners.

EVA is conceptually simple: from net operating profit, subtract an appropriate charge for the opportunity cost of all capital invested in an enterprise (the amount that could have been invested elsewhere). It is calculated using this formula:

Net operating profit less applicable taxes –
Cost of capital = EVA

If a company is considering building a new plant, and its total weighted cost over ten years is $80 million, while the expected annual incremental return on the new operation is $10 million, or $100 million over ten years, then the plant's EVA would be positive, in this case $20 million:

$100 million – $80 million = $20 million

An alternative but more complex formula for EVA is:

(% Return on invested capital – % Cost of capital) ×
Original capital invested = EVA

EVA is frequently linked with shareholder value analysis, and an objective of EVA is to determine which business units best utilize their assets to generate returns and maximize shareholder value; it can be used to assess a company, a business unit, a single plant, office, or even an assembly line. This same technique is equally helpful in evaluating new business opportunities. *Abbr* **EVA**

     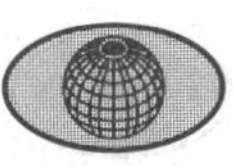   

economic welfare ECONOMICS society's well-being in economic terms the level of prosperity in an economy, as measured by employment and wage levels

economies of scale ECONOMICS savings achieved by mass production the cost advantages of a company producing a product in larger quantities so that each unit costs less to make. *See also* ***diseconomies of scale***

economies of scope ECONOMICS savings achieved when multiple products share same technology the cost advantages of a company producing a number of products or engaging in a number of profitable activities that use the same technology

economist ECONOMICS somebody who studies society's wealth a person who studies the consumption, distribution, and production of wealth in societies

economy ECONOMICS production, consumption, and distribution of society's wealth the distribution of wealth in a society and the means by which that wealth is produced and consumed

economy drive BUSINESS effort to save money or materials a concerted effort to save money or materials, as by reducing expenditures or avoiding waste

economy efficiency principle ECONOMICS theory about relationships in efficient economy the principle that if an economy is efficient, no one can be made better off without somebody else being made worse off

ecopreneur BUSINESS environmentalist entrepreneur an entrepreneur who is concerned with environmental issues

ECP *abbr* MARKETS Eurocommercial paper

EDB *abbr* BUSINESS Economic Development Board

EDC *abbr* E-COMMERCE electronic data capture

EDI *abbr* E-COMMERCE electronic data interchange

EDI envelope E-COMMERCE = ***electronic envelope***

EEA *abbr* INTERNATIONAL TRADE European Economic Area

EEC *abbr* INTERNATIONAL TRADE European Economic Community

e-economy ECONOMICS economy based largely on online business transactions an economy that is characterized by extensive use of the Internet and information technology

effect STATISTICS result of change of statistical variable the change in a response that is created by a change in one or more of the explanatory **variables** in a statistical study

effective annual interest rate FINANCE average annual interest rate on deposit the average interest rate paid on a deposit for a period of a year. It is the total interest received over 12 months expressed as a percentage of the principal at the beginning of the period.

effective capacity OPERATIONS & PRODUCTION output under normal operating conditions the volume that a workstation or process can produce in a given period under normal operating conditions. Effective capacity can be influenced by the age and condition of the machine, the skills, training, and flexibility of the workforce, and the availability of **raw materials**.

effective date FINANCE, OPERATIONS & PRODUCTION actual starting date the date when an action such as the issuing of new stock is effective

effective demand FINANCE demand for product by those able to buy demand for a product made by people and organizations with sufficient wealth to pay for it

effective exchange rate CURRENCY & EXCHANGE exchange rate of one currency against others a rate of exchange for a currency calculated against a group of currencies whose values have been weighted

effectiveness BUSINESS *see* ***efficiency***

effective price STOCKHOLDING & INVESTMENTS stock price adjusted for rights issue the price of a stock adjusted to take into account the effects of existing stockholders being offered a rights issue. *See also* ***rights issue***

effective rate FINANCE true interest rate including all factors the real interest rate to be paid on a loan or deposit, which includes compounding and other factors

effective sample size STATISTICS size of sample with extraneous factors removed the remaining size of a sample after irrelevant or excluded factors have been removed

effective spread STOCKHOLDING & INVESTMENTS difference between new issue price and underwriter's price the difference between the price of a newly issued stock and what the underwriter pays, adjusted for the effect of the announcement of the offering

effective strike price STOCKHOLDING & INVESTMENTS actual price paid when option is exercised the price of an option at a specific time, adjusted for fluctuation since the initial offering

effective tax rate TAX actual tax rate paid by taxpayer after adjustments the average tax rate applicable to a given transaction, whether it is income from work undertaken, the sale of an asset, or a gift, taking into account personal allowances and scales of tax. It is the amount of money generated by the transaction divided by the additional tax payable because of it.

effective yield *UK* STOCKHOLDING & INVESTMENTS = ***yield to maturity***

efficiency BUSINESS meeting goals economically the achievement of goals in an economic way. Efficiency involves seeking a good balance between economy in terms of resources such as time, money, space, or materials, and the achievement of an organization's goals and objectives. A distinction is often made between technical and economic efficiency. **Technical efficiency** means producing maximum output with minimum input, while **economic efficiency** means the production and distribution of goods at the lowest possible cost. In management, a further distinction is often made between efficiency and **effectiveness**, with the latter denoting performance in terms of achieving objectives.

efficiency ratio FINANCE measure of relationship between income and overhead expenses a way of measuring the proportion of operating revenues or fee income spent on overhead expenses.

Often identified with banking and financial sectors, the efficiency ratio indicates a management's ability to keep overhead costs low. In banking, an acceptable efficiency ratio was once in the low 60s. Now the goal is 50, while better-performing banks boast ratios in the mid-40s. Low ratings usually indicate a higher return on equity and earnings.

This measurement is also used by mature industries, such as steel manufacture, chemicals, or car production, that must focus on tight cost controls to boost profitability because growth prospects are modest.

The efficiency ratio is defined as operating overhead expenses divided by turnover. If operating expenses are \$100,000, and turnover is \$230,000, then

$$\frac{100{,}000}{230{,}000} = 0.43 \text{ efficiency ratio}$$

However, not everyone calculates the ratio in the same way. Some institutions include all non-interest expenses, while others exclude certain charges and intangible asset amortization.

     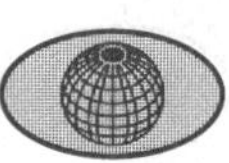   

A different method measures efficiency simply by tracking three other measures: accounts payable to sales, days' sales outstanding, and stock turnover. This indicates how fast a company is able to move its merchandise. A general guide is that if the first two of these measures are low and the third is high, efficiency is probably high; the reverse is likewise true.

To find the stock turnover ratio, divide total sales by total stock. If net sales are $300,000, and stock is $140,000, then

$$\frac{300,000}{140,000} = 2.14 \text{ stock turnover ratio}$$

To find the accounts payable to sales ratio, divide a company's accounts payable by its annual net sales. A high ratio suggests that a company is using its suppliers' funds as a source of cheap financing because it is not operating efficiently enough to generate its own funds. If accounts payable are $50,000, and total sales are $300,000, then

$$\frac{50,000}{300,000} = 0.14 = 14\% \text{ accounts payable to sales ratio}$$

efficiency variance FINANCE disparity between actual and standard cost of production the difference between the standard cost of making a product and actual costs of production. A separate variance can be calculated for materials, labor, and overhead.

efficient capital market MARKETS stock market in which prices quickly reflect information a market in which stock prices reflect all the information available to the market about future economic trends and company profitability

efficient markets hypothesis ECONOMICS theory on limitations of financial information the hypothesis that exploiting stock market information cannot bring an investor unexpected returns because stock prices already reflect all the information available to the market about future economic trends and company profitability. *Abbr* **EMH**

EFT *abbr* E-COMMERCE electronic funds transfer

EFTA *abbr* INTERNATIONAL TRADE European Free Trade Association

EFTPOS *abbr* E-COMMERCE electronic funds transfer at point of sale

EGM *abbr* CORPORATE GOVERNANCE extraordinary general meeting

EIB BANKING organization that finances EU development a financial institution whose main task is to further regional development within the EU by financing capital projects, modernizing or converting undertakings, and developing new activities. *Full form* ***European Investment Bank***

EIC *abbr* TAX Earned Income Credit

EIS *abbr* GENERAL MANAGEMENT **1.** environmental impact statement **2.** electronic information system. *See also* ***MIS***

either-way market CURRENCY & EXCHANGE currency market buying and selling at same price a currency market with identical prices for buying and selling, especially for the Euro

elastic ECONOMICS sensitive to price changes responsive to changes in the price of a product

elasticity ECONOMICS relationship between supply, demand, and price a measurement of the relationship between supply, demand, and price

In practical terms, elasticity indicates the degree to which consumers respond to changes in price. It is obviously important for companies to consider such relationships when contemplating changes in supply, demand, and price.

Demand elasticity measures how much the quantity demanded by a customer changes when the price of a product or service is increased or lowered. This measurement helps companies to find out whether the quantity demanded will remain constant despite price changes. Supply elasticity measures the impact on supply when a price is changed. The reverse can also be calculated, that is, how much the market clearing price for a good or service changes in response to changes in the supply or demand function. This is called the price elasticity, or demand or supply elasticity, respectively.

The general formula for elasticity is:

$$\text{Elasticity} = \frac{\%\text{ change in x}}{\%\text{ change in y}}$$

In theory, x and y can be any variable. However, the most common application measures price and demand. If the price of a product is increased from $20 to $25, or 25%, and demand in turn falls from 6,000 to 3,000, elasticity would be calculated as:

$$\frac{-50\%}{25\%} = -2$$

A value greater than 1 means that demand is strongly sensitive to price, while a value of less than 1 means that demand is not price-sensitive.

elected officers HR & PERSONNEL officials chosen in election officials such as directors or union representatives who are chosen by a vote of the members or stockholders of an organization and who hold a **decision making** position on a committee or board

electronic banking BANKING remote bank transactions by computer the use of computers to carry out banking transactions such as withdrawals through ATMs or transfer of funds at point of sale

electronic business E-COMMERCE = ***e-business***

electronic cash E-COMMERCE = ***digital cash***

electronic check *US* E-COMMERCE means of paying electronically a payment system in which fund transfers are made electronically from the buyer's checking account to the seller's bank account. *UK term* ***electronic cheque***

electronic cheque *UK* E-COMMERCE = ***electronic check***

electronic commerce E-COMMERCE = ***e-commerce***

electronic commerce modeling language E-COMMERCE standardized format for electronic purchases a standardization of field names to streamline the process by which e-merchants electronically collect information from consumers about order shipping, billing, and payment. *Abbr* **ECML**

Electronic Communications Network MARKETS system for direct securities trading a computerized securities trading system that allows investors who have accounts with brokers with access to the system to trade directly and anonymously. *Abbr* **ECN**

electronic data capture E-COMMERCE use of computers for card transactions the use of a point-of-sale terminal or other data-processing equipment to validate and submit credit or debit card transactions. *Abbr* **EDC**

electronic data interchange E-COMMERCE standardized way of transmitting business documents a standard for exchanging business documents such as invoices and purchase orders in a standard form between computers through the use of electronic networks such as the Internet. *Abbr* **EDI**

electronic envelope E-COMMERCE opening and closing data in electronic transmission the header and trailer information that precedes and follows the data in an electronic transmission to provide routing information and security. *Also called* ***communications envelope, EDI envelope, envelope***

  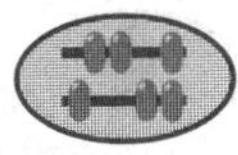   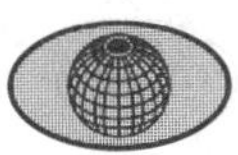   

electronic funds transfer E-COMMERCE payment system using electronic medium a payment system that processes financial transactions between two or more parties or institutions. *Abbr* **EFT**

electronic funds transfer at point of sale E-COMMERCE payment by card swipe, immediately transferring funds the payment for goods or services by a bank customer using a card that is swiped through an electronic reader on the register, thereby transferring the cash from the customer's account to the retailer's or service provider's account. *See also* ***debit card***

electronic information system GENERAL MANAGEMENT information collection system supporting decision making a management information system designed specifically to collect and store information from both internal and external sources for use by senior managers in making strategic decisions. *Abbr* **EIS**. *See also* ***MIS***

electronic money E-COMMERCE = ***digital money***

electronic payment system E-COMMERCE method for payments over Internet a means of making payments over an electronic network such as the Internet

electronic point of sale E-COMMERCE automated checkout system a computerized checkout system in stores that records sales by scanning bar codes, automatically updates the retailer's inventory lists, and provides a printout of the customer's purchases. *Abbr* **epos**

electronic procurement E-COMMERCE = ***e-procurement***

electronic retailer E-COMMERCE = ***e-retailer***

electronic shopping E-COMMERCE making purchases over Internet the process of selecting, ordering, and paying for goods or services over an electronic network such as the Internet. *Also called* ***online shopping***

electronic software distribution E-COMMERCE making computer programs available over Internet a form of electronic shopping in which computer programs can be purchased and downloaded directly from the Internet

electronic store E-COMMERCE website for selling goods a website that is specifically designed to provide product information and handle transactions, including accepting payments

electronic trading STOCKHOLDING & INVESTMENTS securities trading using computers the buying and selling of investment instruments using computer systems

electronic wallet E-COMMERCE = ***digital wallet***

elephant FINANCE financial institution whose high-volume trading increases prices a very large financial institution such as a bank that makes trades in high volumes, thereby increasing prices (*slang*)

eligible liabilities BANKING liabilities considered when calculating bank's reserves liabilities that must be taken into account in the calculation of a bank's reserves

eligible paper FINANCE **1.** US financial instruments accepted for rediscounting in the United States, first class paper, such as a bill of exchange or a check, acceptable for rediscounting by the Federal Reserve System **2.** UK financial instruments accepted as loan security in the United Kingdom, bills of exchange or securities accepted by the Bank of England as security for loans to discount houses ► *See also* **lender of last resort**

eligible reserves BANKING total amount of money held by US bank the sum of the cash held by a US bank plus the money it holds at its local Federal Reserve Bank

eligible termination payment TAX in UK, termination pay eligible for concessional tax in the United Kingdom, a sum paid to an employee when he or she leaves a company, that can be transferred to a concessionally taxed investment account, such as an **Approved Deposit Fund**. *Abbr* **ETP**

e-mail blast MARKETING e-mail appeal to large group a single instance of sending out an e-mail to a large group to reach potential customers

e-marketplace E-COMMERCE place on Internet for trading an Internet-based environment that brings together business-to-business buyers and sellers so that they can trade more efficiently online.

The key benefits for users of an e-marketplace are reduced purchasing costs, greater flexibility, saved time, better information, and better collaboration. However, the drawbacks include costs in changing procurement processes, cost of applications, set-up, and integration with internal systems, and transaction/subscription fees.

There are three distinct types of e-marketplace: independent, in which public environments seek simply to attract buyers and sellers to trade together; consortium-based, in which sites are established on an industry-wide basis, typically when a number of key buyers in a particular industry get together; and private, in which e-marketplaces are established by a particular organization to manage its purchasing alone.

embargo INTERNATIONAL TRADE government order stopping trade with foreign country a government order that stops a type of trade, such as exports to, or imports from, a specific country

embezzlement FRAUD illegal use of money for personal benefit the illegal use of somebody else's money for personal benefit by the person to whom it has been entrusted

emergency credit FINANCE special credit given by US Federal Reserve in the United States, credit given by the **Federal Reserve** to an organization that has no other means of borrowing capital

emerging country or **emerging nation** ECONOMICS country experiencing development and economic growth a country in the early stages of becoming industrialized and undergoing economic growth and foreign investment

emerging economy ECONOMICS *see* ***emerging market*** *(sense 1)*

emerging market **1.** ECONOMICS country experiencing development and economic growth a country that is becoming industrialized and undergoing economic growth. *Also called* ***emerging economy*** **2.** MARKETS financial market in emerging nation a financial market in a newly industrialized country, often with a high growth rate but with some risks

EMH *abbr* ECONOMICS efficient markets hypothesis

emoluments FINANCE payments from employment wages, salaries, fees, or any other monetary benefit derived from employment

e-money E-COMMERCE = ***digital money***

emotional capital GENERAL MANAGEMENT interaction of employees the intangible organizational asset created by employees' cumulative emotional experiences that give them the ability to successfully communicate and form interpersonal relationships. Emotional capital is increasingly being seen as an important factor in company performance. Low emotional capital can result in conflict between staff, poor teamwork, and poor **customer relations**. By contrast, high emotional capital is evidence of emotional intelligence and an ability to think and feel in a positive way, which results in good interpersonal communication and self-

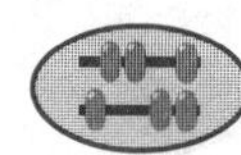

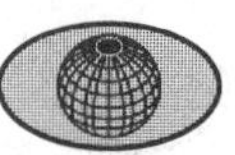

motivation. A related concept is **intellectual capital**.

employability HR & PERSONNEL possession of useful skills the potential for obtaining and keeping fulfilling work through the development of skills that are transferable from one employer to another. Employability is affected by market demand for a particular set of skills and by personal circumstances. Employees may take responsibility for developing their own employability through learning and training, or, as part of the **psychological contract**, employers may assist their employees in enhancing their employability. An important factor in employability is the concept of learning throughout life.

employee HR & PERSONNEL person contracted to work for another somebody hired by an employer under a **contract of employment** to perform work on a regular basis at the employer's behest. An employee works either at the employer's premises or at a place otherwise agreed, is paid regularly, and enjoys **fringe benefits** and employment protection.

employee ownership STOCKHOLDING & INVESTMENTS when shares are in employees' hands the possession of shares in a company, in whole or in part, by the workers. There are various forms of employee ownership that give employees a greater or lesser stake in the business. These include: **employee stock ownership plans**, employee **buyouts**, **cooperatives**, and employee trusts. Ownership does not necessarily lead to greater **employee participation** in decision making, although the evidence suggests that where employees are involved in this, the company is more successful.

employee participation HR & PERSONNEL inclusion of employees in decision making the involvement of employees in decision making. Employee participation can take either a representational or direct form. Representation takes place through bodies such as consultative committees. Direct participation can be achieved through communication methods such as letters, employee attitude surveys, and team briefing, or through initiatives such as self-managed teams and suggestion programs.

Employee Retirement Income Security Act LEGAL US law setting benefit plan standards in the United States, a federal law that sets the minimum requirements for retirement and health benefit plans in the private sector. *Abbr* **ERISA**

employee share ownership plan *UK* STOCKHOLDING & INVESTMENTS = ***employee stock ownership plan***. *Abbr* **ESOP**

employee share scheme STOCKHOLDING & INVESTMENTS making stock available to employees in the United Kingdom, a plan to give, or encourage employees to buy, a stake in the company that employs them by awarding free or discounted stock. Such plans may be available to some or all employees, and plans approved by HM Revenue & Customs enjoy tax advantages. Types of plan include **employee share ownership plans**, **stock options**, **Save as You Earn**, and employee share ownership trusts. Among the potential benefits are improved employee commitment and productivity, but the success of a plan may depend on linking it to employee performance and the performance of the price of stock.

employee stock fund STOCKHOLDING & INVESTMENTS US firm's fund for buying stock for employees in the United States, a fund from which money is taken to buy shares of a company's stock for its employees

employee stock ownership plan *US* STOCKHOLDING & INVESTMENTS system of allocating stock to employees a plan sponsored by a company by which a trust holds stock in the company on behalf of **employees** and distributes that stock to employees. In the United States, stock can only be sold when an employee leaves the organization, and is thus thought of as a form of pension provision. In the United Kingdom, stock can be disposed of at any time. There are two types of employee stock ownership plans in the United Kingdom: the case-law employee stock ownership plan, which can benefit all or some employees but may not qualify for tax benefits; and the employee stock ownership trust. *UK term* ***employee share ownership plan***. *Abbr* **ESOP**

employee stock purchase plan STOCKHOLDING & INVESTMENTS making stock available to employees in the United States, a plan to encourage employees to buy a stake in the company that employs them by awarding free or discounted stock. Such plans may be available to some or all employees, and plans approved by the Internal Revenue Service enjoy tax advantages. Among the potential benefits are improved employee commitment and productivity, but the success of a plan may depend on linking it to employee performance and the performance of the price of stock. *Abbr* **ESPP**

employer HR & PERSONNEL person or organization with employees a person or organization that pays people to perform specific activities. An employer usually contracts an **employee** to fill a permanent or temporary position to perform work on a regularly paid basis within the relevant legal framework of the country of residence.

employers' association BUSINESS organization assisting employers a body that regulates relations between employers and employees, represents members' views on public policy issues affecting their business to national and international policymakers, and supplies support and advice. An employers' association represents companies within one or many sectors at regional, national, or international level and is usually a nonprofit, nonparty political organization, funded by subscriptions paid by its members.

employer's contribution PENSIONS employer's payments into employee's pension money paid regularly by an employer toward an employee's retirement pension

employers' liability insurance INSURANCE insurance covering employee accidents insurance to cover accidents that may happen to employees at work, and for which the company may be responsible

employment contract HR & PERSONNEL = ***contract of employment***

employment equity *S. Africa* HR & PERSONNEL offering opportunities to qualified people from disadvantaged groups the policy of giving preference in employment opportunities to qualified people from sectors of society that were previously discriminated against, for example, black people, women, and physically challenged people

employment law LEGAL, HR & PERSONNEL rules regulating employers and employees the collection of statutes, common law rules, and decisions in court or employment tribunal cases that govern the rights and duties of employers and employees. The **contract of employment** forms the cornerstone of employment law, which also embraces **discrimination** and **severance** rights, collective bargaining, health and safety, union membership, and industrial action.

employment pass HR & PERSONNEL in S. Africa, work permit for professionals in South Africa, a visa issued to a foreign national who is a professional with a qualifying salary level

     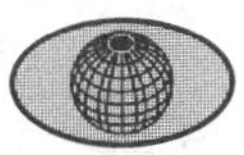  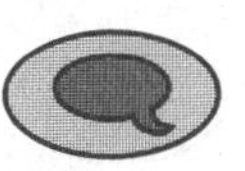 

empowerment GENERAL MANAGEMENT, HR & PERSONNEL conferring authority on employees the redistribution of power and decision-making responsibilities, usually to employees, where such authority was previously a management prerogative. Empowerment is based on the recognition that employee abilities are frequently underused, and that, given the chance, most employees can contribute more. Empowered workplaces are characterized by managers who focus on energizing, supporting, and coaching their staff in a blame-free environment of trust.

EMS CURRENCY & EXCHANGE first stage in European monetary union the first stage of economic and monetary union of the EU, which came into force in March 1979, giving stable, but adjustable, exchange rates. *Full form* ***European Monetary System***

EMU ECONOMICS movement toward common European currency a program for the integration of European economies and the introduction of a common currency. The timetable for European monetary union was outlined in the Maastricht Treaty in 1991. The criteria were that national debt must not exceed 60% of GDP; budget deficit should be 3% or less of GDP; inflation should be no more than 1.5% above the average rate of the three best performing economies of the EU in the previous 12 months; and applicants must have been members of the **ERM** for two years without having realigned or devalued their currency. The ERM was abandoned with the introduction of the **euro** in 12 countries in 2002. *Full form* ***European Monetary Union***

encash *UK* CURRENCY & EXCHANGE = ***cash*** *(sense 1)*

encryption E-COMMERCE putting information in code for transmission over Internet a means of encoding information, especially financial data, so that it can be transmitted over the Internet without being read by unauthorized parties.

Within an Internet security system, a secure server uses encryption when transferring or receiving data from the Web. Credit card information, for example, that could be targeted by a hacker, is encrypted by the server, turning it into special code that will then be decrypted only when it is safely within the server environment. Once the information has been acted on, it is either deleted or stored in encrypted form.

encryption key E-COMMERCE system for encoding and decoding information a sequence of characters known to both or all parties to a communication, used to initiate the **encryption** process

encumbrance MORTGAGES debt using real estate as collateral a liability such as a mortgage or charge that is attached to a property or piece of land

end consumer MARKETING somebody using product or service a person who uses a product or service. An end consumer may not be the purchaser of a product or service and should be distinguished from a customer.

endogenous variable STATISTICS dependent variable in an econometric study, the dependent variable, such as the stock price of a company, that is acted on by an independent variable, such as the company's earnings growth rate

endorse BANKING sign reverse side of check to sign a bill or check on the back to show that its ownership is being passed to another person or company

endorsement MARKETING explicit approval of product the public approval of a product by a person or organization. The endorsement can be used to promote the product to other organizations that may be more cautious in their approach to adopting new products.

endowment FINANCE donation of money for specified purpose a gift of money, especially to a nonprofit organization, to be used for a specific purpose

endowment assurance *UK* INSURANCE = ***endowment insurance***

endowment fund FINANCE fund for nonprofit organization a mutual fund established to provide income for a nonprofit institution

endowment insurance *US* INSURANCE insurance paying on policy's maturity or death an insurance policy that pays a set amount to the policyholder when the policy matures, or to a beneficiary if the policyholder dies before it matures. Part of the premium paid is for the life coverage element, while the remainder is invested in real estate and stocks (either a "with-profits" or "without-profits" policy) or, in the case of a share-linked policy, is used to purchase shares in a life fund. The sum the policyholder receives at the end of the term depends on the size of the premiums and the performance of the investments. *See also* ***term insurance***. *UK term* ***endowment assurance***

endowment mortgage MORTGAGES loan with both interest and endowment policy payments a long-term loan, usually for the purchase of real estate, in which the borrower makes two monthly payments, one to the lender to cover the interest on the loan, and the other as a premium paid into an endowment insurance policy. At the end of the loan's term, the proceeds from the endowment policy are used to repay the principal. *See also* ***mortgage***

endowment policy INSURANCE *see* ***endowment insurance***

endpoint STATISTICS when final event in study happens a point at which a definable event in a study takes place

energy audit GENERAL MANAGEMENT investigation of sourcing and employment of energy a review, inspection, and evaluation of sources and uses of energy within an organization to ensure efficiency and lack of waste

energy conservation GENERAL MANAGEMENT prevention of overuse of fuel the minimization of fuel consumption. Energy conservation, through the monitoring and control of the amounts of electricity, gas, and other fuels used in the workplace, can help reduce costs and damage to the environment. An energy management plan provides a systematic method of assessing, evaluating, and improving an organization's energy usage. This forms part of an organization's approach to environmental management.

engagement letter BUSINESS letter formalizing business relationship between professional and client a letter, usually required by professional standards, sent by a professional such as an accountant to a client, setting out the work the accountant is to do and further administrative matters such as any limit on the accountant's liability

entail LEGAL restriction on somebody inheriting real estate a legal condition that passes ownership of a property to specific persons only

enterprise 1. GENERAL MANAGEMENT bold undertaking a venture characterized by innovation, creativity, dynamism, and risk. An enterprise can consist of one project, or may refer to an entire organization. It usually requires several of the following attributes: flexibility, initiative, problem-solving ability, independence, and imagination. Enterprises flourish in the environment of delayered, nonhierarchical organizations but can be stifled by bureaucracy. **2.** BUSINESS firm a commercial business or company

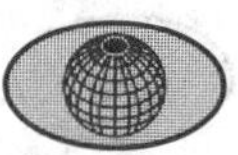

enterprise application integration OPERATIONS & PRODUCTION sharing of information and proceedings using software the unrestricted sharing of data and business processes via integrated and compatible software programs. As businesses expand and recognize the need for their information and applications to be shared between systems, they are investing in enterprise application integration in order to streamline processes and keep all the parts of their organizations, for example, human resources and inventory control, connected. *Abbr* **EAI**

enterprise culture GENERAL MANAGEMENT attitudes and behavior fostering bold undertakings an organizational or social environment that encourages and makes possible initiative and innovation. An organization with an enterprise culture is usually more competitive and more profitable than a bureaucracy. Such an organization is believed to be more rewarding and stimulating to work in. A society with an enterprise culture facilitates individuality and requires people to take responsibility for their own welfare. Conservative governments in the United Kingdom during the 1980s and 1990s promoted an enterprise culture by introducing market principles into all areas of economic and social life. These included policies of deregulation of financial services, privatization of utilities and national monopolies, and commercialization of the public sector. The enterprise culture is now supported by both main political parties.

enterprise investment scheme TAX tax incentives for investors in unquoted UK firms in the United Kingdom, a plan to promote investment in unquoted companies by which qualifying gains are exempt from capital gains tax

enterprise portal E-COMMERCE website collating useful information a website that assembles a wide range of content and services for employees of a particular organization, with the goal of bringing together all the key information they need to do a better job. The key difference between an enterprise portal and an intranet is that an enterprise portal contains not just internal content, but also external content that may be useful, such as specialized news feeds, or access to industry research reports. Ensuring that content is relevant, current, and frequently refreshed is essential for such sites to succeed, and enterprise portals are thus expensive to maintain.

Enterprise Risk Management RISK procedure for reducing risk to organization the process of planning and establishing control systems in order to minimize the risks that an organization faces, including financial, strategic, operational, and hazard risks. *Abbr* **ERM**

enterprise zone FINANCE, BUSINESS district where government gives incentives for economic development an area in which the government offers financial incentives such as tax relief to encourage new business activities. *Abbr* **EZ**

entertainment expenses HR & PERSONNEL reclaimable money spent on customers or suppliers costs, reimbursable by an employer, that are incurred by an employee in hosting social events for clients or suppliers in order to obtain or maintain their patronage or goodwill

entitlement GENERAL MANAGEMENT assumption of deserving reward the expectation that an organization or individual will make large profits regardless of their contribution to the economy or company

entitlement offer FINANCE nontransferable offer an offer that cannot be transferred to anyone else

entrepot port OPERATIONS & PRODUCTION international port dealing in re-exports a town with a large international commercial port dealing in re-exports

entrepreneur BUSINESS somebody who starts and operates new business somebody who sets up a business or enterprise. An entrepreneur typically demonstrates effective application of a number of enterprising attributes, such as creativity, initiative, risk taking, problem-solving ability, and autonomy, and will often risk his or her own capital to establish a business.

entropy STATISTICS measure of system's information transfer rate a measure of the rate of transfer of the information that a system such as a computer program or factory machine receives or outputs

entry ACCOUNTING item written in accounts ledger an item of written information put in an accounts ledger

entry barrier MARKETING hindrance to entering market a perceived or real obstacle preventing a competitor from entering a market

envelope E-COMMERCE = ***electronic envelope***

environmental accounting ACCOUNTING including costs to environment in decision making the practice of including the indirect costs and benefits of a product or activity, for example, its environmental effects on health and the economy, along with its direct costs when making business decisions. *Also called* ***full cost accounting, green accounting***

environmental audit GENERAL MANAGEMENT assessment of success of environmental policies the regular systematic gathering of information to monitor the effectiveness of environmental policies. An environmental audit is concerned with checking conformity with legislative requirements and environmental standards, as well as with company policy. The audit may also cover potential improvements in environmental performance and systems.

environmental impact assessment GENERAL MANAGEMENT study of effect on environment of proposed project a study, undertaken during the planning phase before an investment is made or an operation started, to consider any potential environmental effects

environmental impact statement GENERAL MANAGEMENT findings of environmental impact assessment a report on the results of a particular environmental impact assessment. *Abbr* **EIS**

environmental management GENERAL MANAGEMENT control of organization's impact on environment a systematic approach to minimizing the damage created by an organization to the environment in which it operates. Environmental management has become an issue in organizations because consumers now expect them to be environmentally aware, if not environmentally friendly. Senior managers and directors are increasingly being held liable for their organizations' environmental performance, and the onus is on them to adopt a **corporate strategy** that balances economic growth with environmental protection. Environmental management involves reducing pollution, waste, and the consumption of natural resources by implementing an environmental action plan. This plan brings together the key elements of environmental management, including an organization's **environmental policy** statement, an **environmental audit**, environmental management system, and external standards.

environmental policy GENERAL MANAGEMENT intentions regarding minimizing harm to environment a statement of organizational intentions regarding the safeguarding of the environment

EOQ *abbr* FINANCE, OPERATIONS & PRODUCTION economic order quantity

epos or **EPOS** or **EPoS** *abbr* E-COMMERCE electronic point of sale

e-procurement E-COMMERCE purchasing of products over Internet the business-to-business sale and purchase of goods and services over an electronic network such as the Internet. *Also called* ***electronic procurement***

EPS *abbr* STOCKHOLDING & INVESTMENTS earnings per share

Equal Credit Opportunity Act FINANCE US law ensuring equal treatment for borrowers in the United States, a federal law that gives all consumers an equal opportunity to obtain credit by requiring creditors to follow specific rules regarding the information they can obtain from applicants. *Abbr* **ECOA**

equal opportunities HR & PERSONNEL provision of same chances to all the granting of equal rights, privileges, and status regardless of gender, age, race, religion, disability, or sexual orientation. Equality in employment is regulated by law in most Western countries. An organizational equal opportunities policy works to go farther than the regulatory framework demands. Such a policy should focus on preventing discriminatory or harassing behavior in the workplace and achieving equal access to training, job, and promotion opportunities. **Affirmative action**, referred to as positive discrimination in the United Kingdom, is a controversial approach to encouraging the advancement of minorities. **Diversity management** builds on and goes beyond equal opportunities by looking at the rights of individuals rather than groups.

equal pay HR & PERSONNEL paying men and women at same rate the principle and practice of paying men and women in the same organization at the same rate for like work, or work that is rated as of equal value. Work is assessed either through an organization's job evaluation plan or by the judgment of an independent expert appointed by an industrial committee. Although many countries have legislation on equal pay, a gap still exists between men's pay and women's pay and is attributed to sexual discrimination in job evaluation and payment systems.

equal treatment HR & PERSONNEL avoidance of discrimination at work a principle of the European Union that requires member states to ensure that there is no **discrimination** with regard to employment, vocational training, and working conditions. The principle of equal treatment is applied through Europe-wide directives and national legislation of the member states.

equilibrium ECONOMICS balance in economy the state of balance in the economy where supply equals demand or a country's balance of payments is neither in deficit nor in excess

equilibrium price ECONOMICS product price causing balanced supply and demand the price at which the supply of and the demand for a good are equal. Suppliers increase prices when demand is high and reduce prices when demand is low.

equilibrium quantity ECONOMICS amount regulating supply and demand the quantity that needs to be bought for supply to match demand at a specific price. Suppliers increase quantity when demand, and therefore the price, is high and reduce quantity when demand or price is low.

equilibrium rate of interest ECONOMICS when expected and actual interest rates match the rate at which the expected interest rate in a market equals the actual rate prevailing

equipment trust certificate STOCKHOLDING & INVESTMENTS US bond issued to pay for equipment in the United States, a bond sold for a 20% down payment and collateralized by the equipment purchased with its proceeds

equities STOCKHOLDING & INVESTMENTS stock in corporation a stockholder's holdings in a corporation

equity 1. FINANCE value of asset minus outstanding loans the value of an asset minus any loans outstanding on it **2.** FINANCE value of company owned by stockholders the value of a company that is the property of its stockholders, calculated as the value of the company's assets minus the value of its liabilities, not including the ordinary share capital **3.** STOCKHOLDING & INVESTMENTS ownership of company's stock ownership in a company in the form of stock **4.** STOCKHOLDING & INVESTMENTS stockholder's right to share in company's profit the right of a stockholder to receive dividends from the profit of a company in which the shares of stock are owned

equity accounting ACCOUNTING listing subsidiary's profits on parent company's books a method of accounting that puts part of the profits of a subsidiary into the parent company's books

equity capital STOCKHOLDING & INVESTMENTS stock owned by stockholders the part of the nominal value of the stock owned by the stockholders of a company. *See also* ***share capital***

equity carve-out STOCKHOLDING & INVESTMENTS sale of shares of stock to fund spin-off a situation in which an established company sells off shares of stock to investors in order to create an independent company from a subsidiary part of the business. *Also called* ***carve-out***

equity claim FINANCE claim on residual earnings a claim on earnings that remain after debts are satisfied

equity contribution agreement FINANCE agreement to contribute equity an agreement to buy a proportion of the **capital stock** of a company in order to provide funds for a project

equity derivative STOCKHOLDING & INVESTMENTS derivative instrument based on stock a **derivative instrument** whose **underlying asset** is a stock. The most common equity derivative is an **option**.

equity dilution STOCKHOLDING & INVESTMENTS decrease in percentage of ownership in firm the reduction in the percentage of a company represented by each share for an existing stockholder who has not increased his or her holding in the issue of new common stock

equity dividend cover *UK* ACCOUNTING calculation of firm's ability to pay dividend an accounting ratio, calculated by dividing the distributable profits during a given period by the actual dividend paid in that period, that indicates the likelihood of the dividend being maintained in future years

equity finance *UK* FINANCE = ***equity financing***

equity financing *US* FINANCE money contributed for share in business the money introduced into a business by its owners. If it is a for-profit company, then the equity is introduced in exchange for shares and investors can expect a share of any profit. In the case of limited companies, it takes the form of dividends. *UK term* ***equity finance***

equity floor MARKETS payment agreement based on market drop an agreement for one party to pay another whenever some indicator of a stock market's value falls below a specific limit

equity fund STOCKHOLDING & INVESTMENTS mutual fund that is invested in equities a mutual fund that is invested mainly in stocks, not in government securities or other funds

  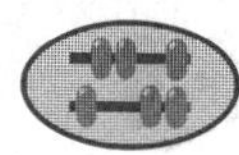   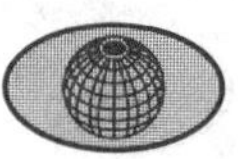   

equity gearing FINANCE relationship of borrowings to equity the ratio between a company's borrowings and its **equity**

equity kicker MARKETS investment incentive promising share of future revenue an incentive given to people to lend a company money, in the form of a warrant to share in future earnings

equity multiplier FINANCE US firm's worth as multiple of stock price in the United States, a measure of a company's worth, expressed as a multiple of each dollar of its stock's price

equity risk premium STOCKHOLDING & INVESTMENTS extra return expected on equities compared to bonds an extra return on equities over the return on bonds, because of the risk involved in investing in equities

equity swap STOCKHOLDING & INVESTMENTS, RISK agreement between parties to exchange cash flows an agreement in which one party agrees to exchange its cash flow, which is linked to a benchmark such as the **London Interbank Offered Rate** or the rate of return on an **index**, for another party's fixed or floating rate of interest

equity sweetener FINANCE incentive for people to lend firm money an incentive to encourage people to lend a company money. The sweetener takes the form of a warrant that gives the lender the right to buy stock at a later date and at a specific price.

equivalent annual cash flow FINANCE return on annuity compared to other investment the value of an annuity required to provide an investor with the same return as some other form of investment

equivalent bond yield STOCKHOLDING & INVESTMENTS = ***bond equivalent yield***

equivalent taxable yield TAX return on taxable investment compared to other investment the value of a taxable investment required to provide an investor with the same return as some other form of investment

ERDF *abbr* FINANCE European Regional Development Fund

e-retailer E-COMMERCE retail business operating over Internet a business that uses an electronic network such as the Internet to sell its goods or services. *Also called* ***electronic retailer, e-tailer***

ergonomics GENERAL MANAGEMENT, HR & PERSONNEL study of efficient working environments the study of workplace design and the physical and psychological impact it has on workers. Ergonomics is about the fit between people, their work activities, equipment, work systems, and environment to ensure that workplaces are safe, comfortable, efficient, and that productivity is not compromised. Ergonomics may examine the design and layout of buildings, machines, and equipment, as well as aspects such as lighting, temperature, ventilation, noise, color, and texture. Ergonomic principles also apply to working methods such as systems and procedures, and the allocation and scheduling of work.

ERISA *abbr* LEGAL Employee Retirement Income Security Act

ERM CURRENCY & EXCHANGE former system for stabilizing European Community exchange rates a system to maintain exchange rate stability used in the past by member states of the European Community. *Full form* ***Exchange Rate Mechanism*** ■ *abbr* RISK Enterprise Risk Management

ERR *abbr* STOCKHOLDING & INVESTMENTS expected rate of return

error account BANKING account for recording transactions made in error an account for the temporary placement of funds involved in a financial transaction known to have been executed in error

error rate ACCOUNTING proportion of errors made the number of mistakes per thousand entries or per page

errors and omissions ACCOUNTING bookkeeping mistakes mistakes arising from incorrect record keeping or accounting. *Abbr* **E&O**

ESC *abbr* GENERAL MANAGEMENT, HR & PERSONNEL European Social Charter

escalator clause LEGAL contract clause permitting price increases a clause in a contract that allows for regular price increases for a product or service to cover projected cost increases

escape clause LEGAL clause specifying conditions under which contract is void a clause in a contract that allows one of the parties to avoid carrying out the terms of the contract under specific conditions

escheat LEGAL government claim on property in absence of heirs the reversion of real or personal property to the government upon the death of a person who has no legal heirs

escrow LEGAL safe keeping by third party of valuable item an agreement between two parties that holds that something such as a good, document, or amount of money should be held for safe keeping by a third party until specific conditions are fulfilled

escrow account BANKING account holding money until contract conditions are met an account where money is held until specific conditions, such as a contract being signed, or a consignment of goods being safely delivered, are met

e-shock E-COMMERCE unstoppable advance of e-commerce the forward momentum of electronic commerce, considered as powerful and irresistible

ESOP *abbr* STOCKHOLDING & INVESTMENTS employee stock ownership plan

ESPP *abbr* STOCKHOLDING & INVESTMENTS employee stock purchase plan

essential industry ECONOMICS industry necessary to nation's economy an industry regarded as crucial to a country's economy and often supported financially by a government by way of tariff protection and tax breaks

establishment fee FINANCE = ***commitment fee***

estate FINANCE deceased person's assets the net assets of somebody who has died

estate duty TAX former tax paid on estate before distribution in the United Kingdom until 1975, a tax paid on the property left by a dead person before it is passed to the heirs. *See also* ***inheritance tax***

estate tax TAX tax paid on estate before distribution to heirs in the United States, a tax paid on the property left by a dead person before it is passed to the heirs

estimate FINANCE **1.** approximation of something's value an approximate calculation of an uncertain value. An estimate may be a reasonable guess based on knowledge and experience or it may be calculated using more sophisticated techniques designed to forecast projected costs, profits, losses, or value.
2. approximation of cost of work a written statement of an approximate price for work to be undertaken by a business

estimation STATISTICS predicted numerical value the provision of a numerical value for a parameter of a population that has been sampled

estimator FINANCE person who calculates expected job costs a person whose job is to calculate the likely cost for carrying out work

estoppel LEGAL ruling denying somebody right to give evidence a rule of evidence whereby somebody is prevented from denying or asserting a fact in legal proceedings

     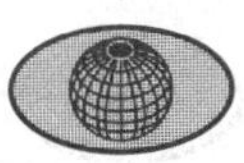   

e-tailer E-COMMERCE = ***e-retailer***

e-tailing E-COMMERCE operating retail business over Internet the practice of doing business over an electronic network such as the Internet

ETF *abbr* MARKETS exchange-traded fund

ethical fund FINANCE fund providing money to firms having moral practices a fund that invests in companies that operate by moral standards approved of by their investors, such as not manufacturing or selling weapons, not trading with countries with poor human rights records, or using only environmentally acceptable sources of raw materials

ethical index STOCKHOLDING & INVESTMENTS list of stock in conscientious firms a published index of stock in companies that operate by moral standards approved of by their investors

ethical investment STOCKHOLDING & INVESTMENTS investing only in socially responsible firms investment only in companies whose policies meet the ethical criteria of the investor. *Also called* ***socially conscious investing***

Ethical Investment Research Service STOCKHOLDING & INVESTMENTS organization determining which firms have moral practices an organization that does research into companies and recommends those that follow specific ethical standards

ETP *abbr* TAX eligible termination payment

EU *abbr* ECONOMICS European Union. *See also* ***single market***

Euribor *abbr* MARKETS Euro Interbank Offered Rate

euro or **Euro** CURRENCY & EXCHANGE currency of nations belonging to EU the currency of 12 member nations of the European Union. The euro was introduced in 1999, when the first 11 countries to adopt it joined together in an Economic and Monetary Union and tied their currencies' exchange rate to the euro. Notes and coins were brought into general circulation in January 2002, although banks and other financial institutions had before that time carried out transactions in euro. The official plural of euro is "euro," although "euros" is widely used.

euro account BANKING account operated in euro a checking account or savings account in euro

Eurobank BANKING US bank dealing in Eurocurrency a bank that handles transactions in **Eurocurrency**

Eurobond STOCKHOLDING & INVESTMENTS bond issued and traded in different currencies a bond issued in the currency of one country and sold to investors from another country. *Also called* ***global bond***

Eurocheque BANKING check good in any European bank a check that can be cashed at any bank in the world displaying the European Union crest. The Eurocheque system is based in Brussels.

Euroclear MARKETS European payment system for securities a user-owned system for routing and settling securities transactions throughout Europe

Eurocommercial paper MARKETS form of short-term loan short-term loans without collateral obtained by companies in foreign countries. *Abbr* **ECP**

Eurocredit BANKING, CURRENCY & EXCHANGE credit in currency of another country a loan made in a currency other than that of the lending institution

Eurocurrency BANKING, CURRENCY & EXCHANGE deposits in currency of another country money deposited in one country but denominated in the currency of another country, for example, dollars deposited in a British bank

Eurodeposit BANKING, CURRENCY & EXCHANGE deposit in Eurocurrency a short-term deposit of **Eurocurrency**. Eurodeposits have a variable interest rate based on the Euro Interbank Offered Rate.

Eurodollar BANKING, CURRENCY & EXCHANGE US dollar deposited in foreign bank a dollar deposited in a European bank or other bank outside the United States

Euroequity MARKETS European stock not traded domestically a stock in an international company that is traded outside its country of origin

Euroequity issue MARKETS security for foreign country a capital issue in a currency and a country other than that of the issuer

Euro Interbank Offered Rate MARKETS lending rate for euro the **Interbank Offered Rate** for loans in euro. *Abbr* **Euribor**

euroland ECONOMICS = ***eurozone***

euro LIBOR MARKETS LIBOR denominated in euros the **London Interbank Offered Rate** denominated in euro rather than US dollars

Euro-note CURRENCY & EXCHANGE security in Eurocurrency market a form of **Eurocommercial paper** in the Eurocurrency market

Euro-option MARKETS option to buy European bonds an option to buy European bonds at a later date

European Accounting Association ACCOUNTING European organization for accounting academics an organization for accounting academics. Founded in 1977 and based in Brussels, the EAA aims to be a forum for European research in accounting. It holds an annual congress and since 1992 has published a journal, *European Accounting Review*. *Abbr* **EAA**

European Association of Securities Dealers Automated Quotations MARKETS *see* ***EASDAQ***

European Bank for Reconstruction and Development BANKING *see* ***EBRD***

European Central Bank BANKING *see* ***ECB***

European Commission EU executive body the main executive body of the European Union, made up of members nominated by each member state. *Also called* ***Commission of the European Community***

European Community INTERNATIONAL TRADE former organization of European nations the name of the immediate precursor of the **EU**. *Abbr* **EC**

European Covered Bond Council FINANCE representative organization for various financial institutions the official organization bringing together bond issuers, analysts, investment bankers, rating agencies, and a wide range of interested market participants. *Abbr* **ECBC**

European Economic Area INTERNATIONAL TRADE EU and EFTA member countries an area comprising the countries of the European Union and the members of EFTA, formed by an agreement on trade between the two organizations. *Abbr* **EEA**

European Economic Community INTERNATIONAL TRADE former organization of European nations the name of the precursor of the **European Community** before it became the **EU**. *Abbr* **EEC**

European Free Trade Association INTERNATIONAL TRADE free-trade group linked with EU a group of countries (Iceland, Liechtenstein, Norway, and Switzerland) formed to encourage free trade between its members, and linked with the European Union in the European Economic Area. *Abbr* **EFTA**

European Investment Bank BANKING *see* ***EIB***

European Monetary System CURRENCY & EXCHANGE *see* ***EMS***

European Monetary Union CURRENCY & EXCHANGE *see* ***EMU***

  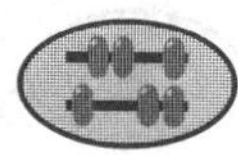   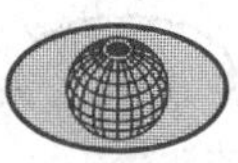   

European option STOCKHOLDING & INVESTMENTS option exercisable only on expiration date an option that the buyer can exercise only on the day that it expires. *See also* ***American option***

European Private Equity and Venture Capital Association FINANCE group providing information for investors an organization that provides information and networking opportunities for investors, entrepreneurs and policymakers in the **equity financing** industry. *Abbr* **EVCA**

European Regional Development Fund FINANCE fund supporting less developed European areas a fund set up to provide grants to less industrially developed parts of Europe. *Abbr* **ERDF**

European Social Charter ECONOMICS charter containing rights of EU members a charter adopted by the European Council of the EU in 1989. The 12 rights it contains are: freedom of movement, employment, and remuneration; social protection; improvement of living and working conditions; freedom of association and collective bargaining; worker information; consultation and participation; vocational training; equal treatment of men and women; health and safety protection in the workplace; pension rights; integration of those with disabilities; and protection of young people. *Abbr* **ESC**

European Union ECONOMICS organization of European nations a social, economic, and political organization involving 27 European countries. It came into effect in 1993 as a result of the signing of the Maastricht Treaty by 15 countries; other countries joined later. Precursors were the European Community (EC), and the European Economic Community (EEC). *Abbr* **EU**

Euroyen CURRENCY & EXCHANGE yen deposited in bank abroad a Japanese yen deposited in a bank outside Japan

Euroyen bond STOCKHOLDING & INVESTMENTS Eurobond in yen a Eurobond denominated in yen but issued outside of Japan by a non-Japanese company

eurozone ECONOMICS countries using euro the area of Europe comprising those countries that have adopted the euro as a common currency. *Also called* ***euroland***

EVA *abbr* FINANCE economic value added

EVCA *abbr* FINANCE European Private Equity and Venture Capital Association

event marketing MARKETING promotion of social functions the promotion and marketing of a specific event such as a conference, seminar, exhibition, or trade fair. Event marketing may encompass **corporate hospitality** activities, business or charity functions, or sporting occasions. The planning, marketing, and managing of the function on the day are sometimes entirely **outsourced** to companies specializing in event management.

event risk STOCKHOLDING & INVESTMENTS chance of loss on bond the possibility that a bond rating will drop because of an unexpected event such as a takeover or restructuring

evergreen loan FINANCE loan supplying flow of capital a series of loans providing a continuing stream of capital for a project

exact interest ACCOUNTING annual interest calculated over 365 days annual interest calculated on the basis of a full 365 days, as opposed to ordinary interest that is calculated on 360 days

ex-all STOCKHOLDING & INVESTMENTS without rights to anything pending having no right with respect to stocks in any pending transaction such as a split or the issuance of dividends. *Abbr* **xa.** *See also* **cum-all**

excellence GENERAL MANAGEMENT, OPERATIONS & PRODUCTION attainment of highest standards a state of organizational performance achieved through the successful integration of a variety of operational and strategic elements which enables an organization to become one of the best in its field. Excellence is initially evident when an organization rises above its competitors, and it is usually measured by the ability to sustain a leading or significant market share. The strategic and operational elements contributing to excellence include the organization's approach to **total quality management**, core competency, **benchmarking**, **customer service**, the **balanced scorecard approach**, and **leadership**. Taken all together, these components should produce an organizational approach to the generation, development, and delivery of products and services which is better, cheaper, and smarter than that of the competition. Attempts at becoming an excellent organization have spawned terms such as **best practice** and **world class manufacturing** and are usually associated with a holistic approach to **competitive advantage**.

exceptional items ACCOUNTING **1.** ordinary business costs of unusual size or nature costs that arise from normal business dealings, but that must be recorded because of their unusual size or nature **2.** unusual items included in pre-tax balance sheet items in a balance sheet that do not appear there each year and that are included in the accounts before the pre-tax profit is calculated, as opposed to **extraordinary items** that are calculated after the pre-tax profit

exception reporting GENERAL MANAGEMENT providing only significant information the passing on of information only when it breaches or transcends agreed norms. Exception reporting is intended to reduce information overload by minimizing the circulation of repetitive or old information. Under this system, only information that is new and out of the ordinary will be transmitted.

excess **1.** FINANCE assets less liabilities in a financial institution, the amount by which assets exceed liabilities **2.** *UK* INSURANCE = ***deductible***

excess capacity OPERATIONS & PRODUCTION underutilized manufacturing capability spare manufacturing capability that is not being used

excess liquidity BANKING cash in bank exceeding required amount cash held by a bank above what is required by the regulatory authorities

excess profit FINANCE unusually high profit a level of profit that is higher than a level regarded as usual

excess profits tax TAX tax levied in unusual situation a tax levied by a government on a company that makes extraordinarily large profits in times of unusual circumstances, for example, during a war. An excess profits tax was imposed in both the United States and the United Kingdom during World War II.

excess reserves BANKING reserves in financial institution exceeding required amount reserves held by a financial institution that are higher than those required by the regulatory authorities. As such reserves may indicate that demand for loans is low, banks often sell their excess reserves to other institutions.

excess return FINANCE profit from investment the amount received from an investment in excess of the basic interest rate or the cost of capital by which an activity is financed

exchange **1.** MARKETS place for buying and selling a **market** where goods, services, or financial instruments are bought and sold **2.** STOCKHOLDING & INVESTMENTS converting one form of security to another the conversion of one type of security for another, for example, the exchange of a bond for stock **3.** E-COMMERCE environment

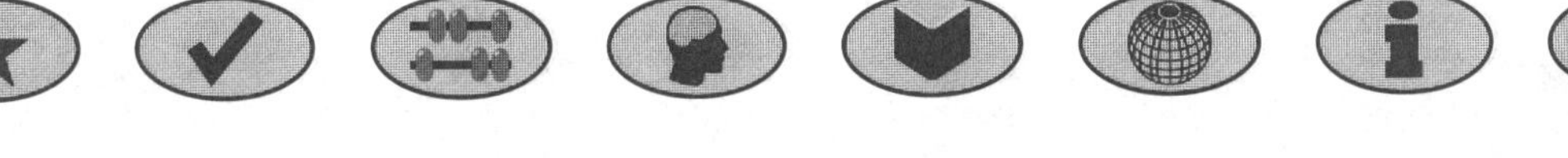

for conducting business the main type of business-to-business marketplace. The **B2B exchange** enables suppliers, buyers, and intermediaries to come together and offer products to each other according to a set of criteria. **B2B Web exchanges** provide constant price adjustments in line with fluctuations of supply and demand. In E2E or "exchange-to-exchange" e-commerce, buyers and sellers conduct transactions not only within exchanges but also between them. **4.** FINANCE barter to trade goods and services for other goods and services **5.** CURRENCY & EXCHANGE trade one country's currency for another to trade the currency of one country or economic zone for that of another

exchange controls CURRENCY & EXCHANGE regulations governing foreign exchange dealings the regulations by which a country's banking system controls its residents' or resident companies' dealings in foreign currencies and gold

exchange cross rate CURRENCY & EXCHANGE = ***cross rate***

exchange dealer CURRENCY & EXCHANGE foreign currency trader a person who buys and sells foreign currency

exchange equalization account CURRENCY & EXCHANGE bank account for regulating value of British pound the Bank of England account that sells and buys sterling for gold and foreign currencies to smooth out fluctuations in the exchange rate of the British pound

exchange offer STOCKHOLDING & INVESTMENTS offer of one security for another an offer to trade one security for another, usually to stockholders of a company in financial trouble and at less favorable terms

exchange option STOCKHOLDING & INVESTMENTS option allowing holder to exchange assets an option that allows the holder to trade one asset for another. The option may be either a **European option**, which can be exercised only on the expiration date, or an **American option**, which can be exercised at any time up to and including the expiration date. *Also called* ***Margrabe option***

exchange premium CURRENCY & EXCHANGE surcharge for buying foreign currency an extra cost above the usual rate for buying a foreign currency

exchange rate CURRENCY & EXCHANGE rate for converting one currency to another the rate at which one country's currency can be exchanged for that of another country

Exchange Rate Mechanism CURRENCY & EXCHANGE *see* ***ERM***

exchange rate movements CURRENCY & EXCHANGE changes in value between currencies the fluctuations in value between currencies that can result in losses to businesses that import and export goods and to investors

exchange rate parity CURRENCY & EXCHANGE relative value of currencies the relationship between the value of one currency and another

exchange rate risk CURRENCY & EXCHANGE, RISK chance of incurring loss on converting currencies the risk of suffering loss on converting another currency to the currency of a company's own country.

Exchange rate risks can be arranged into three primary categories. (1) Economic exposure: operating costs will rise due to changes in rates and make a product uncompetitive in the world market. Little can be done to reduce this routine business risk that every enterprise must endure. (2) Translation exposure: the impact of currency exchange rates will reduce a company's earnings and weaken its balance sheet. To reduce translation exposure, experienced corporate fund managers use a variety of techniques known as **currency hedging**. (3) Transaction exposure: there will be an unfavorable move in a specific currency between the time when a contract is agreed and the time it is completed, or between the time when a lending or borrowing is initiated and the time the funds are repaid. Transaction exposure can be eased by **factoring** (transferring title to foreign accounts receivable to a third-party factoring house).

Although there is no definitive way of forecasting exchange rates, largely because the world's economies and financial markets are evolving so rapidly, the relationships between exchange rates, interest rates, and inflation rates can serve as leading indicators of changes in risk. These relationships are as follows. Purchasing Power Parity theory (PPP): while it can be expressed differently, the most common expression links the changes in exchange rates to those in relative price indices in two countries:

Rate of change of exchange rate = Difference in inflation rates

International Fisher Effect (IFE): this holds that an interest-rate differential will exist only if the exchange rate is expected to change in such a way that the advantage of the higher interest rate is offset by the loss on the foreign exchange transactions. Practically speaking, the IFE implies that while an investor in a low-interest country can convert funds into the currency of a high-interest country and earn a higher rate, the gain (the interest rate differential) will be offset by the expected loss due to foreign exchange rate changes. The relationship is stated as:

Expected rate of change of the exchange rate = Interest-rate differential

Unbiased Forward Rate Theory: this holds that the forward exchange rate is the best unbiased estimate of the expected future spot exchange rate.

Expected exchange rate = Forward exchange rate

exchange rate spread CURRENCY & EXCHANGE difference in buying and selling price of currencies the difference between the price at which a broker or other intermediary buys and sells foreign currency

exchange-traded MARKETS traded on exchange bought and sold on an exchange, as opposed to over-the-counter

exchange-traded fund MARKETS fund traded like stocks a group of stocks that can be traded on a stock exchange like a single stock and is linked to a specific market index. *Abbr* **ETF**

Exchequer BANKING UK government's bank account in the United Kingdom, the government's account at the Bank of England into which all revenues from taxes and other sources are paid

Exchequer stocks STOCKHOLDING & INVESTMENTS UK government stocks UK government stocks used to finance government expenditure. They are regarded as a very safe investment.

excise duty TAX tax on specific goods a tax on goods such as alcohol or tobacco produced and sold within a specific country

excise license TAX license permitting sale of specific products a license issued against payment to allow somebody to trade in products such as wine that are subject to excise duty

excise tax TAX tax on specific goods a tax levied for a particular purpose

exclusion clause LEGAL clause listing items not covered by agreement a clause in an insurance policy or warranty that states which items or events are not included in the cover provided

exclusive agency *US* BUSINESS exclusive agreement to operate an agreement to be the only person to represent a company or

  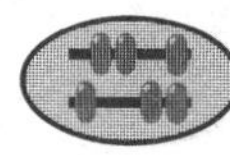   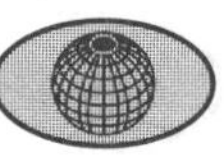   

to sell a product in a particular area. *UK term* ***sole agency***

exclusive agreement MARKETING sole right to sell product an agreement by which a person or company is made sole agent for selling a product in a market

exclusive economic zone ECONOMICS area in country with special economic conditions a zone in a country in which specific economic conditions apply. The Special Economic Zone in China, where trade is conducted free of state control, is an example.

ex coupon STOCKHOLDING & INVESTMENTS without interest coupons without the interest coupons or after interest has been paid

ex dividend STOCKHOLDING & INVESTMENTS giving buyer no dividend right used to describe bonds or stocks that, when they are sold, do not provide the buyer with the right to a forthcoming dividend

execution **1.** STOCKHOLDING & INVESTMENTS completion of securities trade the process of completing an order to buy or sell securities **2.** LEGAL carrying out contract the process of carrying out the terms of a legal order or contract

execution only MARKETS handling security transaction without giving advice used to describe a stock market transaction undertaken by an intermediary who acts on behalf of a client without providing advice. *See also* ***active fund management, discretionary management***

executive CORPORATE GOVERNANCE **1.** person in senior management an employee in a position of senior responsibility in an organization. An executive is involved in planning, strategy, policy making, and **line management**. **2.** any person with responsible job a person with a significant role in an organization or project, for example, a **manager**, **consultant**, **executive officer**, or **agent**

executive chairman CORPORATE GOVERNANCE organization's highest executive the most senior executive in an organization when the roles of chair and chief executive are combined, and the executive chairman has some control over daily operations. *See also* ***chairman***

executive director CORPORATE GOVERNANCE director in senior management position a senior employee of an organization, usually with responsibility for a specific function and usually, but not always, a member of the **board of directors**

executive officer CORPORATE GOVERNANCE = ***executive*** *(sense 2)*

executive pension plan PENSIONS UK pension plan for firm's top executives in the United Kingdom, a pension plan for senior executives of a company. The company's contributions are a tax-deductible expense but are subject to a cap. The plan does not prevent the executive from being a member of the company's group pension plan although the executive's total contributions must not exceed a specific percentage of his or her salary.

executive share option scheme *UK* STOCKHOLDING & INVESTMENTS = ***executive stock option plan***

executive stock option plan *US* STOCKHOLDING & INVESTMENTS stock purchase arrangement for top employees an arrangement whereby some directors and employees are given the opportunity to purchase stock in the company at a fixed price at a future date. In some jurisdictions, such arrangements can be tax efficient if specific local tax authority conditions are met. *UK term* ***executive share option scheme***

executive summary GENERAL MANAGEMENT statement outlining main points of business plan a concise summary at the beginning of a business plan of the objectives, products and/or services, marketing plans, operations, etc. of the proposed business, designed to attract investors

executor LEGAL person responsible for distribution of deceased person's assets a person appointed under a will to ensure the deceased's estate is distributed according to the terms of the will

exempt gift TAX in US, untaxed gift in the United States, a gift that is not subject to **gift tax**

exempt investment fund TAX UK investment for people having certain tax advantages in the United Kingdom, a collective investment, usually a mutual fund, for investors, such as charities or contributors to pension plans, who have tax privileges

exemption TAX allowance per person subtracted from taxable income an amount per family member that somebody can subtract when reporting income to be taxed

exempt purchaser STOCKHOLDING & INVESTMENTS institutional investor exempt from securities commission filing requirements an institutional investor who may buy newly issued securities without filing a prospectus with a securities commission

exempt security STOCKHOLDING & INVESTMENTS security exempt from legal requirement a security that is not subject to a provision of law such as margin or registration requirements

exempt supply TAX in UK, item exempt from VAT in the United Kingdom, an item or service on which **VAT** is not levied, for example, the purchase of, or rent on, real estate and financial services

exercise STOCKHOLDING & INVESTMENTS to use the right to act to put into effect a right to carry out a transaction with previously agreed terms, especially in trading **options**

exercise date STOCKHOLDING & INVESTMENTS date when option may be taken the date on which the holder of an option can put its terms into effect

exercise notice STOCKHOLDING & INVESTMENTS option holder's notice of wish to exercise option an option holder's notification to the option writer of his or her desire to exercise the option

exercise of warrants STOCKHOLDING & INVESTMENTS using warrant to buy stock the process of activating the right given by a warrant to purchase stock at a specific date

exercise price STOCKHOLDING & INVESTMENTS **1.** price at which option is taken the price at which an option will be put into effect **2.** = ***strike price***

exercise value STOCKHOLDING & INVESTMENTS profit from cashing in option the amount of profit that can be realized by cashing in an **option**

ex-gratia payment HR & PERSONNEL exceptional extra payment a one-time extra payment in addition to normal pay, made out of gratitude or courtesy, or in recognition of a special contribution

exhibition MARKETING large event for displaying goods an event organized to bring together buyers and sellers at a single venue

Eximbank BANKING US bank lending money to foreign importers a bank founded in 1934 that provides loans direct to foreign importers of US goods and services. *Full form* ***Export-Import Bank***

existential culture GENERAL MANAGEMENT attitudes and behavior fostering individuals a form of corporate culture in which the organization exists to serve the individual, rather than individuals being servants of the organization. Existential culture was identified by Charles Handy. It typically consists of a group of professionals who work together, but have no leader.

  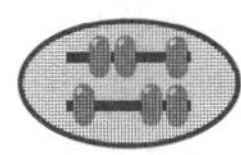      

exit STOCKHOLDING & INVESTMENTS termination of investment the way in which an investor can realize the gains or losses of an investment, for example, by selling the company they have invested in

exit charge or **exit fee** STOCKHOLDING & INVESTMENTS fee charged to sell out of investment a charge sometimes made by a trust when selling shares in a mutual fund

exit fee STOCKHOLDING & INVESTMENTS = ***exit charge***

exit P/E ratio FINANCE final price/earnings ratio the **price/earnings ratio** when a company changes hands, as by a takeover or sale

exit price MARKETS price at which investment is sold the price at which an investor sells an investment or at which a firm sells all its merchandise and leaves a market

exit strategy BUSINESS planned disposal of business a plan for disposing of a business and realizing the value of the investment made in it. The development of an exit strategy involves establishing the value of the business, identifying and selecting exit options, identifying and removing obstacles, and preparing and implementing a plan. Exit options include the sale of the business, **merger**, flotation or public listing, **management buyout**, **franchising**, family succession, ceasing to trade, or **liquidation**.

ex-legal STOCKHOLDING & INVESTMENTS US bond not displaying legal opinion in the United States, a municipal bond that is issued without the legal opinion of a law firm printed on it

ex officio CORPORATE GOVERNANCE by virtue of one's office because of an office held. An officeholder such as a treasurer may attend a committee meeting "ex officio" because of the office held in the wider organization, even if they are not otherwise a member of that committee.

exogenous variable STATISTICS variable from outside study in an econometric study, any variable that has an impact on it from outside

exotic option STOCKHOLDING & INVESTMENTS, RISK complicated option traded in over-the-counter market a complex option contract whose underlying asset or terms of payoff differ from those of either a standard **American option** or **European option**. Exotic options are usually traded in the **over-the-counter market**.

expansionary monetary policy FINANCE lending at low interest to stimulate economy a government strategy of lending money at low interest rates to stimulate an economy that is entering or experiencing a recession

expected rate of return or **expected return** STOCKHOLDING & INVESTMENTS probable return on investment the projected percentage return on an investment, based on the weighted probability of all possible rates of return.

It is calculated by the following formula:

$$ERR = \sum_{i=1}^{n} (P(i) \times r_i)$$

where P(*i*) is the probability of outcome *i* and r_i is the return for outcome *i*.

The following example illustrates the principle that the formula expresses:

The current price of ABC, Inc. stock is trading at \$10. At the end of the year, ABC shares are projected to be traded:

- 25% higher if economic growth exceeds expectations—a probability of 30%;
- 12% higher if economic growth equals expectations—a probability of 50%;
- 5% lower if economic growth falls short of expectations—a probability of 20%.

To find the expected rate of return, simply multiply the percentages by their respective probabilities and add the results:

$$(30\% \times 25\%) + (50\% \times 12\%) + (25\% \times -5\%) = 7.5 + 6 + -1.25 = 12.25\% \text{ ERR}$$

A second example:

- if economic growth remains robust (a 20% probability), investments will return 25%;
- if economic growth ebbs, but still performs adequately (a 40% probability), investments will return 15%;
- if economic growth slows significantly (a 30% probability), investments will return 5%;
- if the economy declines outright (a 10% probability), investments will return 0%.

Therefore:

$$(20\% \times 25\%) + (40\% \times 15\%) + (30\% \times 5\%) + (10\% \times 0\%) = 5\% + 6\% + 1.5\% + 0\% = 12.5\% \text{ ERR}$$

Abbr **ERR**. *See also* ***capital asset pricing model***

expected value FINANCE future value based on probability of an occurrence the future value of a course of action, weighted according to the probability that the course of action will actually occur. If the possible course of action produces income of \$10,000 and has a 10% chance of occurring, its expected value is 10% of \$10,000 or \$1,000.

expenditure FINANCE amount spent an amount of money spent on a particular thing, or the total amount spent

expenditure switching ECONOMICS switching government spending from one area to another government action to divert domestic spending from one sector to another, for example, from imports to home-produced goods

expense ACCOUNTING **1.** cost required a cost incurred in buying goods or services **2.** money spent a charge against a company's profit

expense account HR & PERSONNEL **1.** money allowed for business travel and entertainment money that businesspeople are allowed by their companies to spend on traveling and entertaining clients in connection with business **2.** facility to draw or reclaim money for expenses an amount of money that an employee or group of employees can draw on to reclaim personal **expenses** incurred in carrying out activities for an organization

expense ratio STOCKHOLDING & INVESTMENTS percentage of management costs passed on the percentage of the assets held in a mutual fund that includes management fees and other costs of operating the fund and that are passed on to stockholders

expenses HR & PERSONNEL money spent by employee as part of work personal costs that are reimbursed by the employer to any employee carrying out activities for an organization

experience curve GENERAL MANAGEMENT = ***learning curve***

experiential learning HR & PERSONNEL learning through experience and analysis a model that views learning as a cyclical process in four stages: concrete experience, reflective observation, abstract conceptualization, and active experimentation. Experiential learning relates to participants' activities and reactions to a training event, in contrast to passive learning. Proposed by David A. Kolb in 1971, the model was later expanded by other practitioners including Peter Honey and Alan Mumford.

experimental design STATISTICS how experiment is set up the planning of the procedures to be used in an experimental study

expert system GENERAL MANAGEMENT computer program providing expert knowledge and procedures a computer program that emulates the reasoning and decision making of a human expert in a particular field. The main components of

     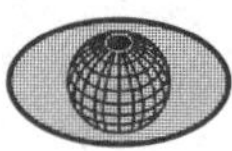   

an expert system are the knowledge base, which consists of facts and rules about appropriate courses of action based on the knowledge and experience of human experts; the inference engine, which simulates the inductive reasoning of a human expert; and the user interface, which enables users to interact with the system. Expert systems may be used by nonexperts to solve well-defined problems when human expertise is unavailable or expensive, or by experts seeking to find solutions to complex questions. They are used for a wide variety of tasks, including medical diagnostics and financial decision making, and are an application of **artificial intelligence**.

expiration cycle MARKETS system showing stock option's expiration date in options trading, a way of designating the month on which a stock option expires. An option is assigned to one of three cycles, January (with expiration dates in January, April, July, and October), February (with expiration dates in February, May, August, and November), and March (with expiration dates in March, June, September, and December).

expiration date *US* STOCKHOLDING & INVESTMENTS last day on which to exercise an option the last day on which somebody who holds an option to buy or sell an asset can exercise that option. *UK term* ***expiry date***

expiry date *UK* STOCKHOLDING & INVESTMENTS = ***expiration date***

explicit cost FINANCE cost of using resources not owned by producer the cost of resources that are bought from outside the company producing the good or service. *See also* ***implicit cost***

exploding bonus FINANCE potential recruits' bonus that diminishes with time a bonus offered to recent graduates that encourages them to sign for a job as quickly as possible as it reduces in value with every day of delay (*slang*)

exponential smoothing STATISTICS statistical method of identifying long-term trends a statistical technique used in quantitative **forecasting**, particularly in the areas of inventory control and **sales forecasting**, that adjusts data to give a clearer view of trends in the long term. In exponential smoothing, values are calculated using a formula that takes all previous values into account but assigns greatest weight to the most recent data.

exponential trend STATISTICS trend in statistics over time a statistical trend that is revealed as observations are collected at uniformly spaced intervals over a period of time

export INTERNATIONAL TRADE **1.** sending goods abroad for sale the practice or business of sending goods from one country to another to be sold. *See also* ***exports*** **2.** send goods abroad for sale to send goods from one country to another to be sold

export agent INTERNATIONAL TRADE facilitator of trade abroad an intermediary who acts on behalf of a company to open up or develop a market in a foreign country. Export agents are often paid a commission on all sales and may have exclusive rights in a particular geographic area. A good agent will know or get to know local market conditions and will have other valuable information that can be used to mutual benefit.

exportation INTERNATIONAL TRADE act of sending goods abroad for sale the act of sending goods to foreign countries for sale

Export Credit Guarantee Department INTERNATIONAL TRADE UK government department helping exporters with finances a UK government department that provides financial and insurance assistance for exporters. The Export Credit Guarantee Department works to benefit organizations exporting UK goods and services and sets up insurance for UK companies investing overseas. *Abbr* **ECGD**

exporter INTERNATIONAL TRADE firm sending goods abroad for sale a company that sends goods from one country to another to be sold

Export-Import Bank BANKING, INTERNATIONAL TRADE *see* ***Eximbank***

exporting INTERNATIONAL TRADE selling products abroad the process of selling goods to other countries. Exporting provides access to nondomestic markets and can be coordinated by an export manager. As with all business activities, careful market research needs to be undertaken. This can be conducted by the company itself or through an experienced export agent. Many companies produce goods almost entirely for export. Services also can be exported, but require different delivery mechanisms through subsidiary offices, or local **franchise** or **licensing agreements**.

export-led growth ECONOMICS increase in economy based on exports growth in which a country's main source of income is from its export trade

export license LEGAL government permit allowing exportation of something a government permit allowing goods to be sent to another country for sale

exports INTERNATIONAL TRADE goods sent abroad for sale goods sent to another country to be sold. *See also* ***export***

ex-rights STOCKHOLDING & INVESTMENTS sold without rights for sale without rights such as voting or conversion rights. The term can be applied to transactions such as the purchase of new shares.

ex-rights date MARKETS date of first ex-rights trade the date when a stock first trades ex-rights, with the rights remaining with the seller rather than transferring to the buyer

extendable bond STOCKHOLDING & INVESTMENTS bond whose maturity can be postponed a bond whose maturity can be delayed by either the issuer or the holder

extendable note STOCKHOLDING & INVESTMENTS note whose maturity can be postponed a note whose maturity can be delayed by either the issuer or the holder

extended credit FINANCE **1.** credit with long repayment terms credit that allows the borrower a long time before payment is required **2.** long repayment term offered by US Federal Reserve in the United States, an extra long period of credit offered to commercial banks by the Federal Reserve

extended fund facility ECONOMICS time allowance for repaying IMF a credit facility operated by the **International Monetary Fund** that allows a country up to eight years to repay money it has borrowed from the fund

Extensible Business Reporting Language FINANCE *see* ***XBRL***

extension GENERAL MANAGEMENT extra time granted for something an additional period of time allowed for something, for example, the repayment of a debt or the filing of a tax return

external account BANKING account of overseas resident in UK bank an account held at a United Kingdom-based bank by a customer who is an overseas resident

external audit ACCOUNTING periodic independent audit of firm's accounts a periodic examination of the books of account and records of an entity conducted by an independent third party (an auditor) to ensure that they have been properly maintained; are accurate and comply with established concepts, principles, and accounting standards; and give a true and fair view of the financial state of the entity. *See also* ***internal audit***

   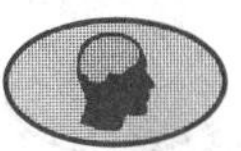  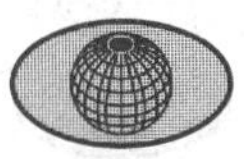   

external communication GENERAL MANAGEMENT informal exchange of information the exchange of information and messages between an organization and other organizations, groups, or individuals outside its formal structure. The goals of external communication are to facilitate cooperation with groups such as suppliers, investors, and stockholders, and to present a favorable image of an organization and its products or services to potential and actual customers and to society at large. A variety of channels may be used for external communication, including face-to-face meetings, print or broadcast media, and electronic communication technologies such as the Internet. External communication includes the fields of PR, media relations, advertising, and marketing management.

external debt ECONOMICS country's debts to nonresidents the part of a country's debt that is owed to creditors who are not residents of the country

external finance FINANCE investors' money money that a company obtains from investors, for example, by loans or by issuing stock

external funds FINANCE third-party money money that a business obtains from a third party rather than from its own resources

external growth BUSINESS growth as result of joining with another firm business growth as a result of a merger, a takeover, or through a partnership with another organization

external market INTERNATIONAL TRADE international market for securities issued outside single country a securities market in which securities issued outside the jurisdiction of any one country are offered simultaneously to investors in a number of countries

external trade INTERNATIONAL TRADE trade with other countries commercial activity carried out with foreign countries. *See also* ***internal trade, crossborder trade***

extraordinary general meeting CORPORATE GOVERNANCE general meeting other than regular annual meeting any general meeting of an organization other than the **annual meeting**. Directors can usually call an extraordinary general meeting at their discretion, as can company members who either hold not less than 10% of the paid-up voting shares, or who represent not less than 10% of the voting rights. Directors are obliged to call an EGM if there is a substantial loss of capital. Fourteen days' written notice must be given, or 21 days' written notice if a special resolution is to be proposed. Only special business can be transacted at the meeting, the general nature of which must be specified in the convening notice. *Abbr* **EGM**

extraordinary item ACCOUNTING exceptional inclusion in firm's accounts an item, such as an acquisition or a sale of assets,that is included in a company's accounts but is not likely to occur again. These items are not taken into account when a company's **operating profit** is calculated.

extraordinary resolution CORPORATE GOVERNANCE vote held on exceptional issue in the United Kingdom, an exceptional issue that is put to the vote at a company's general meeting, for example, a change to the company's articles of association, requiring 14 days' notice

extrapolate STATISTICS estimate value beyond set of known values to estimate from a set of values that lies beyond the range of the data collected

extreme value STATISTICS smallest or largest values in statistical study either of the smallest or largest variate values in a sample of observations from a statistical study

EZ *abbr* FINANCE, BUSINESS enterprise zone

F

face value 1. FINANCE amount on banknote the amount printed on a banknote, showing its value **2.** STOCKHOLDING & INVESTMENTS value displayed the value shown on a **financial instrument** such as bonds or stocks, often different than the actual value

facilitation HR & PERSONNEL making it easier for others to do something the process of helping groups, or individuals, to learn, find a solution, or reach a consensus, without imposing or dictating an outcome. Facilitation works to empower individuals or groups to learn for themselves or find their own answers to problems without control or manipulation. Facilitators need good communication skills, including listening, questioning, and reflecting. Facilitation is used in a variety of contexts including training, conflict resolution, and negotiation.

facility FINANCE total credit offered the total amount of credit that a lender will allow a borrower under a specific agreement

facility fee FINANCE charge for arranging credit a charge made by a lender to a borrower for arranging credit facilities

facility takeover *UK* FRAUD type of identity theft a type of fraud in which a person impersonates another person and falsely claims a change of address in order to gain access to and control that person's financial accounts

factor 1. FINANCE collector of corporate debt a business that purchases or lends money on **accounts receivable** based on an evaluation of the **creditworthiness** of prospective customers of the business, for a small percentage of the debt amount **2.** STATISTICS statistical variable in a statistical study, a variable such as one affecting the price of an asset which can be isolated and modeled separately

factor analysis STATISTICS study of relationships between variables the examination of the relationships existing between the variables observed in a statistical study

factor four OPERATIONS & PRODUCTION quadrupling productivity to reduce waste a concept of environmentally friendly production based on increasing the productivity of resources by a factor of four to reduce waste

factoring FINANCE **1.** transferring of foreign debts the practice of transferring title to foreign **accounts receivable** to a third-party **factor** that assumes responsibility for collections, administrative services, and any other services requested. Major exporters use factoring as a way of reducing exchange rate risk. The fee for this service is a percentage of the value of the receivables, anywhere from 5% to 10% or higher, depending on the currencies involved. Companies often include this percentage in selling prices to recoup the cost. **2.** selling firm's debts at discount the sale of **accounts receivable** to a third party (the **factor**) at a discount, in return for cash. A factoring service may be "with recourse," in which case the supplier takes the risk of the debt not being paid, or "without recourse," when the factor takes the risk. *See also* ***invoice discounting*** **3.** buying of debts the practice of buying up a business's **accounts receivable**, providing it with **working capital**

factoring charges FINANCE cost of selling debts to third party the cost of selling **accounts receivable** to an agent for a commission

factor market ECONOMICS place where capital or labor is traded a market in which

factors of production are bought and sold, for example, the capital market or the labor market

factors of production OPERATIONS & PRODUCTION land, labor, and capital the three things needed to produce a product: land, labor, and capital

factory OPERATIONS & PRODUCTION place for manufacturing goods a building or set of buildings housing workers and equipment for the sole purpose of manufacturing goods, often on a large scale

factory gate price OPERATIONS & PRODUCTION manufacturing cost of goods the actual cost of manufacturing goods before any additional charges are added to give a profit. The factory gate price includes direct costs such as labor, raw materials, and energy, and indirect costs such as interest on loans, plant maintenance, or rent.

failure GENERAL MANAGEMENT = ***business failure***

Failure Mode and Effects Analysis RISK way of identifying and dealing with potential failures a method for identifying and ranking the seriousness of ways in which a product, process, or service could fail, and finding ways in which to minimize the risk of those potential failures. *Abbr* **FMEA**

fair dealing MARKETS legal trading in stock the buying and selling of stock in a legal and open manner

fair market value or **fair value** FINANCE asset's or liability's worth in arm's length transaction the amount for which an asset or liability could be exchanged in an arm's length transaction between informed and willing parties, other than in a forced or liquidation sale

fair price OPERATIONS & PRODUCTION good price for both buyer and seller a price that is favorable for both buyer and seller

fair trade INTERNATIONAL TRADE agreement waiving duties on some imports an international business system by which countries agree not to charge import duties on some items imported from their trading partners

fair value accounting *UK* ACCOUNTING = ***historical cost accounting***

fair wear and tear OPERATIONS & PRODUCTION, INSURANCE damage caused by normal use the acceptable and expected level of damage caused by normal use

fallen angel STOCKHOLDING & INVESTMENTS highly rated security whose value has dropped a stock that was once very desirable but has now dropped in value (*slang*)

falling knife STOCKHOLDING & INVESTMENTS stock whose price has taken steep drop a stock whose price has fallen at a rapid rate over a short time period

false accounting ACCOUNTING, FRAUD criminal accounting practices the criminal offense of changing, destroying, or hiding accounting records for a dishonest purpose

false market MARKETS, FRAUD market influenced by illegal manipulation of stock prices a market in stocks caused by persons or companies conspiring to buy or sell and so influence the stock price to their advantage

falsification FRAUD making false accounting entries the activity of making false entries in financial accounts

family business BUSINESS business owned and run by family a small or medium-sized business that is controlled and operated by members of a family. It may be organized as a sole proprietorship, partnership, corporation, or limited liability company.

family of funds STOCKHOLDING & INVESTMENTS related group of mutual funds a selection of mutual funds with different objectives that is offered by one investment company, allowing investors to easily transfer money from one fund to another with little cost. *Also called* ***fund family***

Fannie Mae MORTGAGES US institution financing housing the largest source of financing for housing in the United States, which funds mortgages by issuing debt securities in US and international securities markets. Fannie Mae was created in 1938 as a federal agency and chartered in 1968 by the US Congress as a stockholder-owned private company. On September 7, 2008, after Fannie Mae reported billions of dollars in losses from **subprime loans**, its government regulatory agency, the Federal Housing Finance Agency put Fannie Mae under its conservatorship. In addition, the US Treasury agreed to provide up to $100 billion of capital as needed to ensure Fannie Mae's continued operation. *Full form* ***Federal National Mortgage Association***. *See also* ***Freddie Mac***

FAQ E-COMMERCE commonest questions about something FAQ pages are often included on websites to provide first-time visitors with answers to the most likely questions they may have. FAQ pages are also used in newsgroups and software applications. *Full form* ***frequently asked question***

far month MARKETS most distant month in futures trading the latest month for which there is a futures contract for a particular commodity. *See also* ***nearby month***

FAS ACCOUNTING US accounting standards in the United States, the standards of financial reporting and accounting established by the FASB. *Full form* ***Financial Accounting Standards***

FASB ACCOUNTING US accounting organization in the United States, an institution responsible for establishing the standards of financial reporting and accounting for companies in the private sector. The **Securities and Exchange Commission** performs a comparable role for public companies. *Full form* ***Financial Accounting Standards Board***

FASTER MARKETS New Zealand Stock Exchange's computerized trading system a computer-based clearing, settlement, registration, and information system operated by the New Zealand Stock Exchange. *Full form* ***Fully Automated Screen Trading and Electronic Registration***

fast track GENERAL MANAGEMENT route providing rapid results a rapid route to success or advancement. The fast track involves competition and a race to get ahead, and is associated with high ambition and great activity. An employee can be on a fast track, for example, to promotion, but an activity also can be said to take the fast track, for example, to rapid product development.

fat cat BUSINESS highly paid chief executive a derogatory term used to describe a chief executive of a large company or organization who secures extremely large pay, pension, and termination packages, and may receive large bonuses

FCA ACCOUNTING ICAEW Fellow Chartered Accountant a Fellow (long-term member) of the Institute of Chartered Accountants in England and Wales

FCCA ACCOUNTING ACCA Fellow, Chartered Certified Accountant a Fellow (long-term member) of the Association of Chartered Certified Accountants

FCM *abbr* STOCKHOLDING & INVESTMENTS futures commission merchant

FCMA ACCOUNTING CIMA Fellow Chartered Management Accountant a Fellow (long-term member) of the Chartered Institute of Management Accountants

FDI *abbr* STOCKHOLDING & INVESTMENTS foreign direct investment

  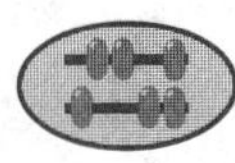   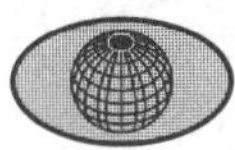   

FDIC *abbr* INSURANCE Federal Deposit Insurance Corporation

feasibility study GENERAL MANAGEMENT assessment of ease of doing something an investigation into a proposed plan or project to determine whether and how it can be successfully and profitably carried out. Frequently used in **project management**, a feasibility study may examine alternative methods of reaching objectives or be used to define or redefine the proposed project. The information gathered must be sufficient to make a decision on whether to go ahead with the project, or to enable an investor to decide whether to commit finances to it. This will usually require analysis of technical, financial, and market issues, including an estimate of resources required in terms of materials, time, personnel, and finance, and the expected return on investment.

Fed BANKING = ***Federal Reserve***

Federal Deposit Insurance Corporation INSURANCE US agency insuring deposits in commercial banks the US federal agency that manages insurance funds that insure deposits in commercial banks and in savings and loans associations. *Abbr* **FDIC**

Federal Funds FINANCE US reserves deposits held in reserve at the Federal Reserve by the US banks. The **Federal Funds rate**, the rate that the Federal Reserve charges banks for borrowing reserves, is the key US monetary policy rate.

Federal Home Loan Mortgage Corporation MORTGAGES, RISK *see* ***Freddie Mac***

federal income tax TAX deductions from employees' pay funding US government in the United States, money deducted from employees' salaries in order to fund Federal services and projects

Federal Insurance Contributions Act HR & PERSONNEL *see* ***FICA***

Federal National Mortgage Association MORTGAGES, RISK *see* ***Fannie Mae***

Federal Open Market Committee ECONOMICS committee that oversees US monetary policy the 12-member committee of the **Federal Reserve Board** that meets eight times a year to determine US monetary policy by setting interest rates or by buying and selling government securities. *Abbr* **FOMC**

federal organization GENERAL MANAGEMENT combining of subsidiaries for benefits of scale a form of organization structure in which subsidiaries federate to gain benefits of scale. In a federal organization, the leader provides coordination and vision, and initiatives are generated from the component subsidiary organizations. Federal organization is one of the many ways in which organizations restructure in order to deal with the dilemmas of power and control. Federal organization offers an enabling framework for autonomy to release corporate energy for people to do things in their own way, provided that it is in the common interest, and for people to be well informed so as to be able to interpret that common interest. Royal Dutch Shell, Unilever, and ABB are exemplars of federalism.

Federal Reserve BANKING system of federal government control of US banks the central banking system of the United States, founded in 1913 by an Act of Congress. The board of governors, made up of seven members, is based in Washington, DC, and 12 Reserve Banks are located in major cities across the United States. It regulates money supply, prints money, fixes the discount rate, and issues bonds for government debt. *Also called* ***Federal Reserve System, Fed***

Federal Reserve bank BANKING major US bank any of the 12 banks that are members of the US **Federal Reserve**

Federal Reserve Board BANKING supervisory board of the US Federal Reserve the seven-member Board of Governors, appointed by the President of the United States and confirmed by the Senate, that supervises the **Federal Reserve** and formulates monetary policy. Appointees to the Board of Governors serve for 14 years. *Abbr* **FRB**

Federal Reserve note CURRENCY & EXCHANGE US paper money a piece of paper money issued by the Federal Reserve Bank and approved as the legal tender of the United States

Federal Reserve System BANKING = ***Federal Reserve***

Federation of Small Businesses BUSINESS organization representing UK small businesses in the United Kingdom, a not-for-profit membership organization representing the interests of small businesses. The FSB was established in 1974 and has over 174,000 members. *Abbr* **FSB**

Fed funds rate BANKING interest rate on interbank loans in Federal Reserve the rate charged by US banks for lending money deposited with the **Federal Reserve** to other banks

Fed pass BANKING US Federal Reserve's easing of credit the addition of reserves to the **Federal Reserve** in order to increase availability of credit

Fedwire BANKING US electronic transfer system the US **Federal Reserve**'s electronic system for transferring funds

fee FINANCE payment to professional for services money paid for work carried out by a professional person such as an accountant

feedback GENERAL MANAGEMENT information about performance to facilitate improvement the communication of responses and reactions to proposals and changes, or of the findings of appraisals of performance, with the goal of enabling improvements to be made. Feedback can be either positive or negative.

feedback control GENERAL MANAGEMENT identification and regulation of outputs the measurement of differences between planned outputs and actual outputs achieved, and the modification of subsequent action and/or plans to achieve future required results

feeding frenzy MARKETS frantic buying in a financial market, a period of extremely active buying *(slang)*

fee work FINANCE work done for organization by non-employees work on a project carried out by independent workers or contractors, rather than employees of an organization

FHLMC MORTGAGES *see* ***Freddie Mac***

fiat money FINANCE government-recognized money coins or banknotes that have little intrinsic value in the material of which they are made but that are recognized by a government or other other issuing authority, such as the European Central Bank, as having value

FICA HR & PERSONNEL in US money deducted for Social Security and Medicare in the United States, a federal law that requires employers to deduct a percentage of their employees' income for payment into the trust fund that provides Social Security and Medicare benefits. Employers and employees are each responsible for half the payment, while self-employed individuals are responsible for the entire payment but are allowed a tax deduction for half. *Full form* ***Federal Insurance Contributions Act***

FICO score FINANCE US system for assessing credit rating a score used by lenders in the United States to assess a person's ability to pay back a loan, based on the person's payment history, current debt, types of credit used, length of credit history, and new credit. Scores range from 300 to 850. The system was devised by the Fair Isaac Corporation (FICO).

fictitious assets ACCOUNTING book assets with no resale value assets such as prepayments that do not have a resale value but are entered as assets on a company's **balance sheet**

FID *abbr* TAX Financial Institutions Duty

fiduciary LEGAL **1.** person acting for another a person who controls property or acts on behalf of or for the benefit of another person **2.** on behalf of another controlled or managed for another person

fiduciary deposit BANKING bank-managed deposit a bank deposit that is managed for the depositor by the bank

field research MARKETING direct contact with customers to gain information the collection of data directly from contact with customers and potential customers through surveys, interviews, and other forms of **market research**

field trial MARKETING test of product in actual use a limited pilot test of a product under real conditions. A field trial is undertaken to test the physical or engineering properties of a product in order to identify and iron out any technical shortcomings prior to marketing. Customers may be involved in some trials, for example, in testing a new laundry detergent. Field trials should not be confused with test marketing, which is used to determine the likely market for, and likely consumer response to, a new product or service.

field work MARKETING work in real environment practical work, study, or research carried out in the real world away from the desk. In a marketing context, field work forms primary **market research** and involves obtaining customers' views and opinions on a face-to-face basis or through mail questionnaires or telephone surveys.

FIFO OPERATIONS & PRODUCTION inventory control system a method of inventory management in which the stock of a given product first placed in store is used before more recently produced or acquired goods or materials. *Full form* ***first in first out***

FIF Tax *abbr* TAX Foreign Investment Funds Tax

figures ACCOUNTING financial results a company's financial results calculated for a particular period of time

filing date *UK* TAX = ***filing deadline***

filing deadline *US* TAX due date for income tax returns the date by which income tax returns must be filed with the relevant taxation authority. *UK term* ***filing date***

fill STOCKHOLDING & INVESTMENTS buy or sell an investment upon client's order to carry out a client's instructions to buy or sell a security or commodity

filter GENERAL MANAGEMENT extracting useful information from large amounts of data a process for analyzing large amounts of incoming information to identify any material that might be of interest to an organization

FIMBRA *abbr* REGULATION & COMPLIANCE Financial Intermediaries, Managers and Brokers Regulatory Association

final average monthly salary PENSIONS earnings on which most US pensions are based the earnings on which most defined benefit pensions are based. *UK term* ***pensionable earnings***

final closing date MERGERS & ACQUISITIONS final day for acceptance of takeover the last date for the acceptance of a **takeover bid**, when the bidder has to announce how many stockholders have accepted the offer

final demand FINANCE last reminder before legal action of debt a last reminder from a supplier to a customer to pay an outstanding debt. Suppliers often begin legal proceedings if a final demand is ignored.

final discharge FINANCE last debt payment the final payment on the amount outstanding on a debt

final dividend STOCKHOLDING & INVESTMENTS year-end dividend payment the **dividend** paid at the end of a year's trading. The final dividend must be approved by a company's stockholders.

final salary pension PENSIONS in UK, benefit on retirement based on earnings in the United Kingdom, a retirement benefit regularly paid to employees or their survivors by an employer, based on salary at or near retirement. Employers set up pension plans by depositing an amount of money in the employee's name into a pension fund, which may be contributed to by the employer or both the employer and the employee. The fund is invested and benefits are paid to the employee from the fund upon retirement. Either the employer or employee may assume the risk of investment failure depending upon the type of pension.

final sale *US* FINANCE sale of nonreturnable items a sale that does not allow the purchaser to return the goods. *UK term* ***firm sale***

finance FINANCE **1.** supply money for business or project to provide an amount of money for a particular purpose. *See also* ***fund*** **2.** *UK* = ***financing***

Finance Act TAX legislation granting British government power of taxation an annual Act of the British Parliament that gives the government the power to obtain money from taxes as proposed in the **Budget**

Finance and Leasing Association FINANCE financing and leasing firms' UK organization in the United Kingdom, an organization representing firms engaged in business financing and the leasing of equipment and cars

finance bill TAX public-spending bill a proposal for legislation giving a government the power to obtain money from taxes

finance company FINANCE business lending money for purchases a business that lends money to people or companies against **collateral**, especially to make purchases of some kind

finance house *UK* FINANCE = ***finance company***

finance lease *UK* FINANCE = ***capital lease***

finance market MARKETS = ***money market***

finances FINANCE money available for spending the financial status of a person or organization

financial FINANCE of finance relating to the management of money

financial accountant TREASURY MANAGEMENT UK accountant acting as adviser or financial director a qualified accountant, a member of the Institute of Financial Accountants, who advises on accounting matters or who works as the financial director of a company

financial accounting **1.** TREASURY MANAGEMENT financial reports for investors and external parties the form of accounting in which financial reports are produced to provide investors or others outside a company with information on a company's financial status. *See also* ***management accounting*** **2.** ACCOUNTING process of producing financial statements the process of classifying and recording a company's transactions and presenting them in the form of profit and loss accounts, balance sheets, and cash flow statements, for a given **accounting period**

     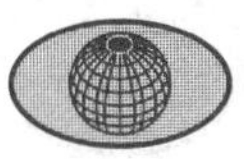   

Financial Accounting Standards ACCOUNTING *see* ***FAS***

Financial Accounting Standards Board ACCOUNTING *see* ***FASB***

financial adviser FINANCE investment adviser somebody whose job is to give advice about investments

financial aid FINANCE money provided to help somebody or something monetary assistance given to an individual, organization, or nation. International financial aid, from one country to another, is often used to fund educational, health-related, or other humanitarian activities.

financial analyst STOCKHOLDING & INVESTMENTS = ***investment analyst***

financial capital FINANCE funds for buying physical assets funds that can be used for the purchase of assets such as buildings and equipment. *See also* ***real capital***

financial control TREASURY MANAGEMENT management of firm's finances the policies and procedures established by an organization for managing, documenting, and reporting its financial transactions

financial correspondent FINANCE reporter who covers money matters a reporter who writes articles on money matters or reports on them on television or radio

financial distress FINANCE situation close to bankruptcy the condition of being in severe difficulties over money, especially being close to **bankruptcy**

financial economies of scale FINANCE benefits gained by increasing scale of activity financial advantages gained by being able to do things on a large scale

financial engineering STOCKHOLDING & INVESTMENTS converting or creating financial instruments the conversion of one form of financial instrument into another, such as the swap of a fixed-rate instrument for a floating-rate one, or the creation of a new type of financial instrument —**financial engineer**

financial futures or **financial futures contract** MARKETS contract to purchase financial instrument for future delivery a contract for the purchase of a specific **basket of securities**, such as interest rates, exchange rates, share prices, or indices, for delivery at a date in the future. *Also called* ***financials***

financial futures market MARKETS market in financial instruments for future delivery the market in **basket of securities**, such as interest rates, exchange rates, share prices, or indices, for delivery at a date in the future

financial incentive scheme FINANCE in UK, money rewarding improved performance in the United Kingdom, a program offering employees a cash bonus, share options or other monetary reward for improved commitment and performance and as a means of motivation. *See also* ***non-financial incentive scheme***

financial institution FINANCE organization investing large sums of money an organization, such as a bank, savings and loan, pension fund, or insurance company, that invests large amounts of money in securities

Financial Institutions Duty TAX Australian tax on money deposited in financial institutions a tax on monies paid into financial institutions imposed by all state governments in Australia except for Queensland. Financial institutions usually pass the tax on to customers. *Abbr* **FID**

financial instrument STOCKHOLDING & INVESTMENTS contract that is evidence of financial transaction any contract that gives rise to both a financial asset of one entity and a financial liability or equity instrument of another entity. Financial instruments include both primary financial instruments such as bonds, currency, and stocks, and derivative financial instruments, whose value derives from the underlying assets.

Financial Intermediaries, Managers and Brokers Regulatory Association REGULATION & COMPLIANCE former UK financial regulator a former UK financial regulatory authority, now incorporated into the **Financial Services Authority**. *Abbr* **FIMBRA**

financial intermediary FINANCE financial institution handling deposits and/or loans an institution that accepts deposits or loans from individuals and lends money to clients. Banks, **savings and loan associations**, and finance companies are all financial intermediaries.

financial leverage FINANCE relationship between firm's borrowings and stockholders' funds the relationship between a company's borrowings (which includes both prior charge capital and long-term debt) and its stockholders' funds (common share capital plus reserves). Calculations can be made in a number of ways, and may be based on capital values or on earnings/interest relationships. Overdrafts and interest paid thereon may also be included:

$$\frac{\text{Profit before interest and tax}}{\text{Profit before tax}}$$

shows the effect of interest on the operating profit.

$$\frac{\text{Profit before interest and tax}}{\text{Interest expense}}$$

shows the number of times that profit will cover interest expense.

$$\frac{\text{Total long-term debt}}{\text{Shareholders' funds + long-term debt}}$$

shows the proportion of long-term financing which is being supplied by debt.

$$\frac{\text{Total long-term debt}}{\text{Total assets}}$$

a measure of the capacity to redeem debt obligations by the sale of assets.

$$\frac{\text{(Operating cash flows – Taxation paid – Returns on investment and servicing of finance)}}{\text{Repayments of debt due within one year}}$$

measures ability to redeem debt.

A company with a high proportion of prior charge capital to shareholders' funds is highly leveraged, and is lowly or lightly leveraged if the reverse situation applies.

financial market MARKETS market for buying and selling financial instruments a market in which financial instruments are traded. The financial markets are stock exchanges, commodity exchanges, bond markets, and the foreign exchange market.

financial obligation FINANCE something you must pay a sum of money that you are committed to pay, especially a debt. *See also* ***collateralized debt obligation***

financial obligations FINANCE things you must spend money on things that you must use your money to pay for, such as rent, household expenses, dependent family members, etc.

Financial Ombudsman REGULATION & COMPLIANCE UK organization handling complaints against financial institutions in the United Kingdom, an organization responsible for investigating and resolving complaints involving money from members of the public against a company, institution, or other organization. The Ombudsman is not a governmental body, but it does operate under an Act of Parliament in the form of the Financial Services and Markets Act 2000.

financial performance FINANCE firm's ability to generate revenue a measure of a company's ability to generate income over a given period of time

financial planner FINANCE somebody giving advice about money a professional investment adviser who analyzes a person's financial situation and goals and prepares

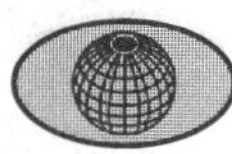

a plan to meet those goals. *See also* ***independent financial adviser***

financial planning FINANCE money management for future the activity of producing strategies for the acquisition of funds to finance activities and meet established goals

Financial Planning Association of Australia FINANCE Australian organization for financial planners a national organization representing companies and individuals working in the Australian financial planning industry. Established in 1992, the Association is responsible for monitoring standards among its members. *Abbr* **FPA**

financial position FINANCE value of firm's assets and liabilities the amount of money that a person or organization has in terms of assets and liabilities

financial pyramid STOCKHOLDING & INVESTMENTS, RISK investment pattern tapering from safe to risky an investment strategy, typically having four levels of risk. The first and largest percentage of assets are in safe, liquid investments; the second, in investments that provide income and long-term growth; the third, in riskier investments with a chance of greater return; and the fourth and smallest percentage, in the riskiest investments with the chance of greatest return.

financial report ACCOUNTING document detailing firm's financial position a document that gives the financial position of a company or other organization

Financial Reporting Review Panel ACCOUNTING UK group for examining questionable accounting practices in the United Kingdom, a review panel established to examine contentious departures from accounting standards by large companies

Financial Reporting Standards Board ACCOUNTING New Zealand accounting organization in New Zealand, an organization that is responsible for setting and monitoring accounting standards. *Abbr* **FRSB**

financial resources FINANCE money available for spending the money that is available for a person or organization to spend

financial review FINANCE examination of organization's finances an examination of the state of an organization's finances

financial risk FINANCE, RISK investors' chance of loss the possibility of financial loss in an investment or speculation

financials MARKETS = ***financial futures***

Financial Services Act REGULATION & COMPLIANCE UK legislation regulating providers of financial services in the United Kingdom, an Act of Parliament that regulates the offering of financial services to the general public and to private investors

Financial Services Authority REGULATION & COMPLIANCE UK organization overseeing financial system in the United Kingdom, an independent non-governmental organization formed in 1997 following reforms in the regulation of financial services. Banking and investment services supervision was merged into the remit of the previous regulator, the **Securities and Investments Board**, which then changed its name to become the Financial Services Authority. The FSA's four statutory objectives were specified by the Financial Services and Markets Act 2000: maintaining market confidence; increasing public knowledge of the finance system; ensuring appropriate protection for consumers; and reducing financial crime. *Abbr* **FSA**. *Also called* ***City watchdog***

Financial Services Compensation scheme FINANCE fund compensating customers of insolvent UK financial firm in the United Kingdom, an independent organization set up by law to pay compensation to customers who have made claims against an authorized financial services firm in the event that the firm is unable, or likely to be unable, to pay the claims

financial services industry FINANCE financial institutions dealing in money management the business activity of the financial institutions that offer money management services such as banking, investment, brokerage, and insurance

financial statements ACCOUNTING documents reporting company's financial performance summaries of accounts to provide information for interested parties. The most important financial statements are the balance sheet, income statement, statement of cash flows, and the shareholders' equity statement. *See also* ***annual report***

financial supermarket FINANCE firm providing many different financial services a company that offers a variety of financial services. For example, a bank may offer loans, mortgages, retirement plans, and insurance alongside its existing range of normal banking services.

Financial Times FINANCE British financial newspaper a respected British financial daily newspaper, printed in 23 cities across the world and available in 140 countries, as well as online. *Abbr* **FT**

Financial Times Index or **Financial Times Ordinary Index** MARKETS UK market index of thirty blue chip companies an index based on the market prices of thirty **blue chip** companies. This index is the oldest of the Financial Times indices, and is now considered too narrow to have much relevance.

financial year *UK* **1.** ACCOUNTING = ***fiscal year*** **2.** TAX for UK corporations, April 1 to March 31 in the United Kingdom, for corporation tax purposes, the period from 1 April of a given year to 31 March of the following year

financier FINANCE somebody who provides financing a person who specializes in the provision of financing to other people or organizations

financing *US* FINANCE money required to pay for something the money needed by an individual or company to pay for something, for example, a project or inventory. *UK term* ***finance***

financing gap **1.** FINANCE difference between money available and money needed a shortfall between the funds available and the funds needed for a project. For example, a company planning expansion is able to finance some of this activity from internally generated cash and some from existing finance agreements but any shortfall requires the raising of new funds. **2.** ECONOMICS funding shortfall from canceling poorer countries' debts a gap in funding for institutions such as the **International Monetary Fund** caused by canceling the debts of poorer countries such as those in West Africa

financing vehicle FINANCE product providing funds for activity a method or product used to provide the funds for an activity

finder's fee FINANCE fee for finding new client a fee paid to somebody who finds a client for another person or company, for example, somebody who introduces a new client to a brokerage firm

fine-tuning ECONOMICS making small changes to improve economic position the process of making small adjustments in areas such as interest rates, tax bands, or the money supply, to improve a nation's economy

  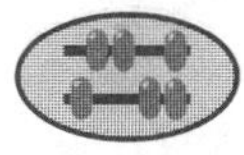   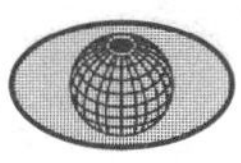   

finish MARKETS end of stock trading for day the end of a day's trading on a stock exchange

finished goods OPERATIONS & PRODUCTION items ready for sale completed goods that are available for distribution or sale to customers

finite capacity plan OPERATIONS & PRODUCTION plan for resource requirements a plan produced where **capacity requirements planning** covers capacity requirements, enabling **loading** at each workstation to be smoothed and determining the need for additional resources. *See also* ***capacity requirements planning***

finite population STATISTICS fixed-size group a statistical population that has a limited size

FIRB *abbr* REGULATION & COMPLIANCE Foreign Investment Review Board

fire sale **1.** FINANCE sale of anything at a large discount a sale of anything at a very low price, usually because the seller is facing **bankruptcy** **2.** OPERATIONS & PRODUCTION sale of fire-damaged goods a sale of goods that have been damaged during a fire

firm BUSINESS **1.** company a business or company. This wide sense is the one in which the word is used in this dictionary. **2.** partnership a business run by **partners**

firm order MARKETS order to broker to sell or buy an order to a broker to sell or buy a security on a specific date or at a specific price

firm quote MARKETS bid to trade with time limit a bid to buy or offer to sell a security that a **market maker** is obligated to meet within a specified period of time

firm sale *UK* FINANCE = ***final sale***

first call MARKETS firm processing earnings forecasts a company that gathers and reports brokerage analysts' earnings forecasts for use by brokers and investors in making investment recommendations and decisions

first in first out OPERATIONS & PRODUCTION *see* ***FIFO***

first mover MARKETING innovating firm the company that first introduces a new type of product or service to a market. Those organizations that follow a first mover to market are known as **followers** or **laggards**—terms that also describe companies that are not the recognized leaders in a sector.

first mover advantage GENERAL MANAGEMENT advantage of being first with new product the benefit produced by being the first to enter a market with a new product or service. First mover advantages include becoming a market leader in a new area; establishing a new leading **brand**; being able to charge a premium until competitor products appear; enhanced reputation, design, and copyright protection; and possibly setting an industry standard to which other competitors may have to aspire. Disadvantages include cheaper, and possibly better, **follower** products; the possibility of having to reduce prices or continuously having to add value to stay ahead; first mover development costs; a possible shift in consumer tastes away from the product; obsolescence; and a follower product being accepted as the industry standard.

first quarter ACCOUNTING first part of fiscal year the period of three months from January to the end of March, or the period of three months at the start of any fiscal year. *Abbr* **Q1**

first-round financing FINANCE initial funding the first infusion of capital into a project

fiscal TAX relating to finance, especially to tax relating to financial matters, especially in respect of governmental collection, use, and regulation of money through taxation

fiscal agent BANKING agent in finance matters a bank or trust that takes over the fiscal responsibilities of another party

fiscal balance ECONOMICS balance of income and expenditure the extent to which government receipts differ from government outlay. If outlays exceed receipts then the fiscal balance is negative or in deficit; if receipts exceed outlays then the balance is positive or in surplus.

fiscal drag *UK* TAX increase in tax paid as inflation rises the effect that inflation has on taxation in that, as earnings rise, the amount of tax collected increases without a rise in tax rates

fiscal measures TAX tax changes introduced for economic reasons tax changes made by a government to improve the working of the economy

fiscal policy ECONOMICS, TAX government's methods for managing economy the central government's policy on lowering or raising taxation or increasing or decreasing public expenditure in order to stimulate or depress **aggregate demand**

fiscal year *US* ACCOUNTING, TAX firm's 12-month accounting period a twelve-month period used by a company for accounting and tax purposes. A fiscal year is not necessarily the same as a calendar year. *UK term* ***financial year***. *Abbr* **FY**

fishbone chart GENERAL MANAGEMENT diagram for investigation of causes of problems a diagram that is used to identify and categorize the possible causes of problems. Within such a chart, which resembles the shape of the skeleton of a fish, the topic or problem to be discussed is placed in a box at the right-hand side that corresponds to the fish's head, and the major items to be investigated are shown as branches at an angle to the horizontal spine. Questions are asked to identify possible causes of problems in each area and the results are added to the diagram as additional layers of branches. This ensures that all aspects of the problem are considered systematically. The fishbone chart is also known as a **cause and effect diagram**. It is frequently used in brainstorming and problem solving.

fixation MARKETS setting of commodity's price on options market the act by a government of stating the price of a commodity on an options market

fixed annuity INSURANCE *see* ***annuity***

fixed asset ACCOUNTING asset that firm keeps long-term a long-term business asset such as a machine or building that will not usually be traded

fixed assets register ACCOUNTING register of tangible assets a record of individual tangible fixed assets belonging to a company or organization

fixed-asset turnover ratio ACCOUNTING measure of how firm uses its assets a measure of the use a business makes of its capital assets. It is calculated by dividing sales by net fixed assets.

fixed capital FINANCE durable assets such as buildings and machinery assets in the form of buildings and machinery, that are long-lasting and can be used repeatedly for production

fixed charge FINANCE creditor's right to specific asset the right of a creditor to a claim on a specific asset, as opposed to a **floating charge** that applies to all a company's assets. *Also called* ***specific charge***

fixed cost ACCOUNTING cost that remains fixed when sales fluctuate a cost that does not change according to sales volumes, for example, overhead such as rent or production costs

fixed deduction TAX agreed UK tax deduction for general expenses in the United Kingdom, a deduction agreed by HM Revenue & Customs and a group of employees which covers general expenditure on clothes or tools used in the course of employment

fixed deposit BANKING deposit paying fixed interest over set period a deposit that pays a fixed rate of interest over a defined period

fixed exchange rate CURRENCY & EXCHANGE set rate of exchange between currencies a rate of exchange of one currency against another that cannot fluctuate, and can only be changed by devaluation or revaluation

fixed exchange rate system CURRENCY & EXCHANGE currency exchange system with unchanging rates a system of currency exchange in which there is no change of rate

fixed expenses FINANCE unvarying overhead costs costs that do not vary with different levels of production, for example, rent, staff salaries, and insurance

fixed income FINANCE income that remains unchanged each year income that does not change from year to year, for example, from an annuity

fixed interest FINANCE **1.** with unvarying interest rate used to describe a loan or financial product that has an interest rate that does not go up or down **2.** interest rate that stays the same interest that is paid at a rate that does not vary over a period of time

fixed-interest loan FINANCE loan with unchanging interest rate a loan whose rate of interest stays the same over the whole period of the loan

fixed-interest security STOCKHOLDING & INVESTMENTS investment paying constant interest an investment such as a government bond that produces an amount of interest that does not change with changes in short-term interest rates. *Also called* ***fixed-rate security***

fixed interval re-order system OPERATIONS & PRODUCTION = ***periodic inventory review system***

fixed-price agreement OPERATIONS & PRODUCTION contract setting prices for period of time an agreement whereby a company provides a service or a product at a price that stays the same for the whole period of the agreement

fixed rate FINANCE unchanging interest rate an interest rate for loans that does not change with fluctuating conditions in the market and stays the same for the whole period of the loan

fixed-rate loan FINANCE loan with unchanging interest rate a loan with an interest rate that is set at the beginning of the term and remains the same throughout

fixed-rate mortgage MORTGAGES mortgage with unchanging interest rate a mortgage for which the interest rate on the loan it secures is set at the beginning of the term and remains the same throughout

fixed-rate security STOCKHOLDING & INVESTMENTS = ***fixed-interest security***

fixed scale of charges FINANCE range of standard charges a set of charges that does not vary according to individual circumstances but is applied consistently in all cases of the same kind

fixed yield FINANCE constant percentage return on investment a percentage return on an investment which does not change over a period of time

fixtures and fittings REAL ESTATE items sold along with property the objects in a property that are sold with the property, both those which cannot be removed and those which can. Fixtures and fittings are a category of **fixed assets**.

flag MARKETS chart pattern that confirms price trend a pattern on a chart showing a period during which securities prices consolidate a previous advance or fall

flat **1.** MARKETS steady market price due to low demand used to describe market prices that do not fall or rise, because of low demand **2.** GENERAL MANAGEMENT without hierarchy used to describe a management structure that is not strongly hierarchical

flat rate FINANCE unvarying standard rate a price, payment or interest rate that remains the same regardless of other factors which may change

flat tax TAX tax unrelated to income a tax levied at one unchanging rate regardless of the level of somebody's income. *See also* ***progressive tax***

flat yield STOCKHOLDING & INVESTMENTS interest rate as percentage of fixed-interest security price an interest rate that is a percentage of the price paid for a **fixed-interest security**

flat yield curve FINANCE graph using unified interest rate for bonds a visual representation of relative interest rates that shows the same interest rates for long-term bonds as for short-term bonds. As investors are assumed to prefer shorter maturities to longer ones, other factors being equal, a flat yield curve is normally assumed to imply that investors can expect lower short-term rates in future.

flexed budget FINANCE budget responsive to changes in trade a budget that changes in response to changes in sales turnover and output

flexible benefit plan HR & PERSONNEL = ***cafeteria plan***

flexible exchange rate system CURRENCY & EXCHANGE currency exchange system with fluctuating rates a system of currency exchange in which rates change from time to time

flexible manufacturing system OPERATIONS & PRODUCTION **1.** various stages of production under central computer control an integrated system of computer-controlled machine tools and transport and handling systems under the control of a larger computer. Flexibility is achieved by having an overall method of control that coordinates the functions of both the machine tools and the handling systems. **2.** computer-controlled system producing variety of parts an integrated, computer-controlled production system that is capable of producing any of a variety of parts, and of switching quickly and economically between them ► *Abbr* **FMS**

flexible spending account HR & PERSONNEL US employee benefit based on voluntary salary deductions in the United States, an employee benefit plan, a type of **cafeteria plan**, funded by voluntary salary reduction, that the employee may use for specific expenses that are exempt from payroll taxes. *Also called* ***salary reduction plan***

flight of capital FINANCE removal of investment money because of economic uncertainty the rapid movement of investment money out of one country because of lack of confidence in that country's economic future

flight to quality STOCKHOLDING & INVESTMENTS movement of investors to low-risk securities a tendency of investors to buy safe well-established securities when the economic outlook is uncertain

flip **1.** BUSINESS new company run for short-term success a startup company that works to build market share quickly and generate short-term personal wealth for its founders through flotation or sell-off **2.** REAL ESTATE develop property for quick profit to buy a property, fix it up, and then resell it in a short period in order to make a profit

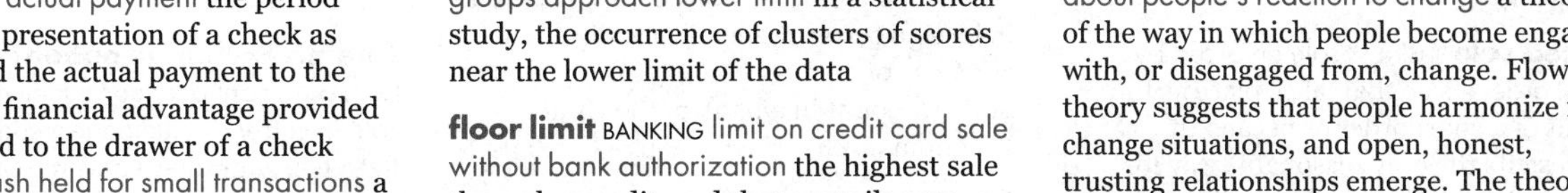

float **1.** FINANCE delay between presentation of check and actual payment the period between the presentation of a check as payment and the actual payment to the payee or the financial advantage provided by this period to the drawer of a check **2.** FINANCE cash held for small transactions a small cash balance maintained to facilitate low-value cash transactions. Records of these transactions should be maintained as evidence of expenditure, and periodically a float or petty cash balance will be replenished to a predetermined level. **3.** STOCKHOLDING & INVESTMENTS sell stocks or bonds to sell stocks or bonds. *See also* ***new issue***

floater FINANCE variable-rate loan a loan with an interest rate that varies over time

floating asset FINANCE short-term asset replaced by another an asset that it is assumed will be consumed during the company's normal trading cycle and then replaced by the same type of asset

floating capital FINANCE amount of company's money invested in current assets the portion of a company's money that is invested in current assets, as distinct from that invested in **fixed assets** or **capital assets**

floating charge FINANCE charge linked to company's assets overall a charge linked to any of the company's assets in a category, but not to a specific item

floating debenture FINANCE debenture running for lifetime of firm a **debenture** secured on all of a company's assets which runs until the company is closed down

floating debt FINANCE loan frequently renewed a borrowing for less than one year that is repeatedly renewed

floating exchange rate CURRENCY & EXCHANGE currency exchange rate that is allowed to vary an exchange rate for a specific currency that can vary according to market demand, and is not fixed by a government

floating rate FINANCE interest rate fluctuating as market fluctuates an interest rate that is not fixed and which changes according to fluctuations in the market

floating-rate note FINANCE, CURRENCY & EXCHANGE Eurocurrency loan with variable interest rate a Eurocurrency loan that is not given at a fixed rate of interest. *Abbr* **FRN**

floor **1.** FINANCE lower limit a lower limit on an interest rate, price, or the value of an asset **2.** MARKETS = ***trading floor***

floor broker MARKETS = ***pit broker***

floor effect STATISTICS when statistical data groups approach lower limit in a statistical study, the occurrence of clusters of scores near the lower limit of the data

floor limit BANKING limit on credit card sale without bank authorization the highest sale through a credit card that a retailer can accept without having to obtain authorization from the issuing bank

floor price MARKETS lowest possible price the lowest possible price that something can be sold for

floor trader MARKETS exchange member trading for own account a member of an exchange who buys and sells securities mainly for their own account on the **trading floor** of an exchange. *Also called* ***competitive trader***

flotation MARKETS funds raised by sale of stock the financing of a company by selling stock in it or a new debt issue, or the offering of stock and bonds for sale on the stock exchange. *See also* ***initial public offering***

flow chart or **flow diagram** GENERAL MANAGEMENT diagrammatic representation of stages a graphic representation of the stages in a process or system, or of the steps required to solve a problem. A flow chart is commonly used to represent the sequence of functions in a computer program or to model the movement of materials, money, or people in a complex process. Two primary symbols used in flow charts are the **process box**, indicating a process or action taking place, and the **decision lozenge**, indicating the need for a decision.

flow line production or **flow production** OPERATIONS & PRODUCTION processing in stages in single direction a production method in which successive operations are carried out on a product in such a way that it moves through the factory in a single direction. Flow line production is most widely used in mass production on production lines. More recently, it has been linked with batch production. Under flow line production, inventory is often kept to the minimum necessary to ensure continued activity. Stoppages and interruptions to the flow indicate a fault, and corrective action can be taken. Assembly line production is an extreme version of flow line production.

flow on BUSINESS pay raise awarded to match another a pay increase awarded to one group of employees as a result of a pay raise awarded to another group working in the same field

flow theory GENERAL MANAGEMENT idea about people's reaction to change a theory of the way in which people become engaged with, or disengaged from, change. Flow theory suggests that people harmonize in change situations, and open, honest, trusting relationships emerge. The theory recognizes the unpredictability and rigidity of human nature when faced with change. *See also* ***change management***

fluff it and fly it MARKETING make product look good, then sell it to enhance a product's appearance and then put it on the market (*slang*)

FMA *abbr* STOCKHOLDING & INVESTMENTS Fund Managers' Association

FMEA *abbr* RISK Failure Mode and Effects Analysis

FMS *abbr* OPERATIONS & PRODUCTION flexible manufacturing system

FNMA MORTGAGES *see* ***Fannie Mae***

FOB or **f.o.b.** *abbr* FINANCE free on board (sense 1)

focus group MARKETING group giving reactions and opinions a carefully selected representative variety of consumers or employees used for the purposes of providing feedback on preferences and responses to a selected range of issues. A focus group usually operates with a facilitator to guide discussion.

folio ACCOUNTING numbered page in account book a page with a number, especially two facing pages in an account book which have the same number

followback survey STATISTICS follow-up check on statistical population a further survey of a statistical population carried out a period of years after an original survey

follower MARKETING firm moving into area created by another a company that follows the first company to introduce a new type of product or service to a market. *See also* ***first mover***

FOMC *abbr* ECONOMICS Federal Open Market Committee

footfall MARKETING how many people walk past store a measure of the number of people who walk past a store

Footsie MARKETS *see* ***FTSE 100 Share Index***

Forbes 500 FINANCE list of largest US public companies a list of the 500 largest public companies in the United States, ranked

  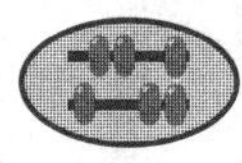   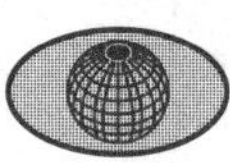   

according to various criteria by *Forbes* magazine

forced sale BUSINESS sale enforced by court order a sale that takes place as the result of a court order or because it represents the only reasonable way for a company or individual to avoid a financial crisis

force field analysis GENERAL MANAGEMENT means of making change more acceptable a technique for promoting change by identifying positive and negative factors and by working to lessen the negative forces while developing the positive ones

force majeure LEGAL incident that contractual parties cannot predict or control something that happens that is out of the control of the parties who have signed a contract, for example, a strike, war, or storm

forecast STATISTICS estimation of value of variable a prediction of the value of a variable in a statistical study

forecast dividend STOCKHOLDING & INVESTMENTS expected year-end dividend a dividend that a company expects to pay at the end of the current trading year. *Also called* ***prospective dividend***

forecasting GENERAL MANAGEMENT estimation or prediction of future the prediction of outcomes, trends, or expected future behavior of a business, industry sector, or the economy through the use of statistics. Forecasting is an **operational research** technique used as a basis for management planning and decision making. Common types of forecasting include trend analysis, **regression analysis, Delphi technique, time series** analysis, **correlation**, and **exponential smoothing.**

foreclose *US* FINANCE acquire mortgaged property when owner defaults to acquire a property because the owner cannot or will not repay money that he or she has borrowed to buy the property. *UK term* ***repossess***

foreclosure *US* FINANCE act of recovering security on unpaid loan the acquisition of property when an owner cannot or will not repay the loan that was taken out to buy the property. *UK term* ***repossession***

foreign bill FINANCE bill of exchange payable only overseas a bill of exchange that is not payable in the country where it is issued

foreign currency CURRENCY & EXCHANGE other country's money the currency or interest-bearing bonds of a foreign country

foreign currency account BANKING, CURRENCY & EXCHANGE bank account operated in foreign currency a bank account in the currency of another country, for example, a dollar account in a bank in the United Kingdom

foreign currency reserves CURRENCY & EXCHANGE foreign money held by government foreign money held by a government to support its own currency and pay its debts. *Also called* ***foreign exchange reserves, international reserves***

foreign debt CURRENCY & EXCHANGE debt owed to other country hard-currency debt owed to a foreign country in payment for goods and services

foreign direct investment STOCKHOLDING & INVESTMENTS investment in firm by foreign company or government investment in a company outside the country of the investor, who sets up subsidiaries or acquires usually about 10% of the stock with voting rights, thus gaining influence in the foreign company's management. *Abbr* **FDI**

foreign dividend STOCKHOLDING & INVESTMENTS in UK, dividend paid from overseas in the United Kingdom, a dividend paid from another country, possibly subject to special rules under UK tax codes

foreign draft CURRENCY & EXCHANGE check drawn and payable in different countries a check that is drawn in one country and payable in another

foreign equity market MARKETS market equities of overseas companies the market in one country for equities of companies in other countries

foreign exchange CURRENCY & EXCHANGE **1.** foreign currencies currencies and financial instruments used to buy goods abroad or as investments. *Also called* ***forex*** **2.** dealings in foreign currencies dealings in the currencies of other countries, on foreign-exchange markets

foreign exchange broker or **foreign exchange dealer** CURRENCY & EXCHANGE trader in foreign currencies a person whose business is to buy and sell foreign currencies

foreign exchange dealing CURRENCY & EXCHANGE trade in foreign currencies the business of buying and selling currencies of other countries

foreign exchange market CURRENCY & EXCHANGE **1.** market for trading foreign currencies a market where people buy and sell foreign currencies **2.** dealings in foreign currencies dealings in the currencies of other countries

foreign exchange option CURRENCY & EXCHANGE contract guaranteeing minimum rate in currency exchange a contract that, for a fee, guarantees a worst-case exchange rate for the future purchase of one currency for another. Unlike a **forward transaction**, the option does not obligate the buyer to deliver a currency on the settlement date unless the buyer chooses to. These options protect against unfavorable currency movements while preserving the ability to participate in favorable movements.

foreign exchange reserves CURRENCY & EXCHANGE = ***foreign currency reserves***

foreign exchange transfer CURRENCY & EXCHANGE sending of money abroad the process of sending money from one country to another

foreign income dividend STOCKHOLDING & INVESTMENTS dividend from earnings abroad a dividend paid from earnings in countries other than the one in which the investment was made

Foreign Investment Funds Tax TAX Australian tax on offshore investments a tax imposed by the Australian government on **unrealized capital gains** made by Australian residents from offshore investments. It was introduced in 1992 to prevent overseas earnings from being taxed at low rates and never brought to Australia. *Abbr* **FIF Tax**

Foreign Investment Review Board REGULATION & COMPLIANCE Australian institution regulating foreign investment in Australia, a non-statutory body that regulates and advises the federal government on foreign investment. It was established in 1976. *Abbr* **FIRB**

foreign investments STOCKHOLDING & INVESTMENTS money invested abroad money invested in countries other than your own

foreign money order CURRENCY & EXCHANGE money order for somebody abroad a money order in a foreign currency that is payable to somebody living in a foreign country

foreign reserve CURRENCY & EXCHANGE centrally held foreign currency the currency of other countries held by an organization, especially a country's central bank

foreign subsidiary company BUSINESS *see* ***subsidiary company***

foreign tax credit TAX tax benefit for taxes paid abroad a tax advantage for taxes that are paid to or in another country

  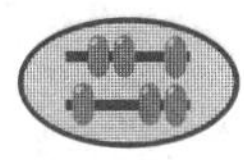   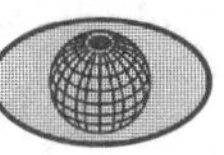   

forensic accounting 1. ACCOUNTING, FRAUD accounting that assists in identifying financial fraud an accounting practice that specializes in investigating and presenting expert court testimony concerning crimes involving financial matters 2. ACCOUNTING reference to accounts to check legality of activities the use of accounting records and documents in order to determine the legality or otherwise of past activities

forex or **Forex** CURRENCY & EXCHANGE = ***foreign exchange***

forfaiting INTERNATIONAL TRADE purchase of exporter's goods by third party the purchase of an exporter's goods by a third party at a discount. This party then collects payment from the importer with the shipped goods serving as collateral.

forfeit clause LEGAL contractual clause stating forfeit if contract not fulfilled a clause in a contract which states that goods or a deposit will be taken if the contract is not fulfilled by one of the signers

forfeiture LEGAL punitive loss of property or right loss of property or the right to something, usually because of an unlawful act

form 3 STOCKHOLDING & INVESTMENTS US form for reporting first securities transactions in the United States, a form that must be filed with the Securities and Exchange Commission within 10 days of the first securities transaction by officers, directors, or 10% shareholders in a company reporting their holdings in the company

form 4 STOCKHOLDING & INVESTMENTS US form for reporting changes in securities holdings in the United States, a form that must be filed with the Securities and Exchange Commission reporting any changes in the securities holdings of officers, directors, or 10% shareholders in a company

formal documents MERGERS & ACQUISITIONS documents detailing takeover bid documents that provide the full details of a takeover bid

form letter GENERAL MANAGEMENT identical letter sent to different people a letter that can be sent without any change to several correspondents

form T STOCKHOLDING & INVESTMENTS US form for reporting transactions after market close in the United States, a required form used by brokers to report to the National Association of Securities Dealers all securities transactions that have taken place after the markets have closed

Fortune 500 FINANCE list of largest US industrial companies a list of the 500 largest industrial companies in the United States, compiled annually by *Fortune* magazine

forwardation MARKETS when cash price is lower than forward price a situation in which the spot price of a futures product is lower than the **forward price**

forward contract MARKETS contract for future delivery a private contract for delivery of a commodity at a later date

forward cover FINANCE cash purchase of commodity fulfilling futures contract the purchase for cash of the quantity of a commodity needed to fulfill a futures contract

forward delivery MARKETS, OPERATIONS & PRODUCTION delivery at agreed future date a delivery at some date in the future that has been agreed to by the buyer and seller

forwarder OPERATIONS & PRODUCTION agent who handles shipping and customs for clients a person or company that arranges shipping and customs documents for several shipments from different companies, putting them together to form one large shipment

forward exchange rate CURRENCY & EXCHANGE rate for future foreign currency purchase a rate for purchase of foreign currency at a fixed price for delivery at a later date. *Also called* ***forward rate*** *(sense 2)*

forwarding agent BUSINESS somebody preparing shipping and customs documents a person or company that arranges shipping and customs documents for clients

forward integration OPERATIONS & PRODUCTION way to ensure products will be distributed a means of guaranteeing **distribution channels** for products and services by building relationships with, or taking control of, **distributors**. Forward integration can free the supplier from the threat or influence of major buyers and can also provide a barrier to market entry by potential rivals. **Backward integration** can provide similar guarantees on the supply side.

forward interest rate FINANCE interest rate set for future loan an interest rate specified for a loan to be made at a future date

forward-looking study STATISTICS ongoing statistical survey a survey of a statistical population carried out for a period such as a year after an original survey

forward margin MARKETS difference between current and future price the difference between the current price (**spot price**) and the future price (**forward price**)

forward market MARKETS market for purchases delivered at future date a market for the buying of foreign currency, stocks, or commodities for delivery at a later date at a prearranged price

forward price MARKETS contracted price for future delivery the price set in an **option** contract for a security or commodity to be delivered at a future date

forward pricing STOCKHOLDING & INVESTMENTS setting of investment price using future valuation the establishment of the price of a share in a mutual fund based on the next asset valuation

forward rate 1. FINANCE rate for loan the rate at which there is no economic arbitrage between receiving an interest rate today and receiving an interest rate starting at some point in the future 2. CURRENCY & EXCHANGE = ***forward exchange rate***

forward rate agreement STOCKHOLDING & INVESTMENTS, RISK contract trading fixed interest for variable interest a contract traded in the **over-the-counter market** in which parties agree to exchange a fixed interest rate or currency exchange rate for a variable rate on an agreed amount of money for an obligation beginning at a future time

forward sales MARKETS sale for future delivery sales of stock, commodities, or foreign exchange for delivery at a later date

forward scheduling OPERATIONS & PRODUCTION way of establishing when each stage must start a method for determining the start times for the various operations involved in a particular **job**. Forward scheduling is most often used when the operations department sets the delivery date for a job, rather than the sales or marketing departments. Jobs are scheduled for the various operations as the workstations are expected to become available. The customer can then be informed of the projected delivery date. *See also* ***backward scheduling***

forward trading MARKETS buying or selling for future delivery the activity of buying or selling stock, commodities, or foreign exchange for delivery at a later date

forward transaction MARKETS agreement to buy and sell currency in future an agreement to buy one currency and sell another on a date some time beyond two business days. This allows an exchange rate on a given day to be specified for a future payment or receipt, thereby eliminating exchange rate risk.

  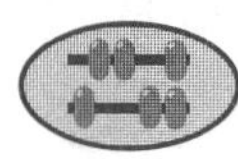   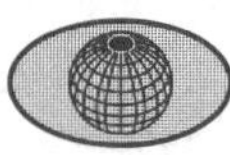   

founders' shares UK STOCKHOLDING & INVESTMENTS stock issued to firm's founders stock held by founding members of a company, often with a higher dividend that is only paid after other stockholders have received their dividends and, in some cases, only when a specific level of profit has been achieved. *See also* ***deferred common stock***

401(k) plan PENSIONS type of US retirement plan in the United States, a personal retirement plan arranged by an employer for an employee, invested in bonds, mutual funds, or stock. The employee contributes a proportion of salary, on which tax can be deferred; the employer can also make contributions.

fourteen hundred MARKETS warning of stranger in London Stock Exchange formerly, an exclamation used as a warning when a stranger walked onto the **trading floor** of the London Stock Exchange

fourth level of service GENERAL MANAGEMENT high level of increased value a very high rating in a system of measuring the value added to a product or service

fourth market MARKETS direct trading, without brokers trading conducted directly without brokers, usually by large institutions

fourth quarter ACCOUNTING last period of fiscal year the period of three months from October to the end of the year, or the period of three months at the end of a fiscal year. *Abbr* **Q4**

FPA *abbr* FINANCE Financial Planning Association of Australia

fractional certificate STOCKHOLDING & INVESTMENTS certificate relating to part of share a certificate for less than a full share (**fractional share**)

fractional currency CURRENCY & EXCHANGE paper money in very small denominations the paper money that is in denominations smaller than one unit of a standard national currency

fractional share STOCKHOLDING & INVESTMENTS less than full share of stock one part of a full share of stock, usually created as the result of a dividend reinvestment plan or a **stock split**

franchise MARKETING authorization to provide another's products an agreement enabling a third party to sell or provide products or services owned by a manufacturer or supplier. A franchise is granted by the manufacturer, or **franchisor**, to a **franchisee**, who then retails the product. The franchise is regulated by a **franchise contract**, or **franchise agreement**, that specifies the terms and conditions of the franchise. These may include an obligation for the franchisor to provide national advertising or training for sales staff in return for the meeting of agreed sales targets by the franchisee. The franchisee usually retains a percentage of sales income. In other cases, a franchise may involve the **licensing** of a franchisee to manufacture a product to the franchisor's specification, and the sale of this product to retailers. Franchises can also be organized by issue of a **master franchise**.

franchise agreement or **franchise contract** MARKETING *see* ***franchise***

franchise chain MARKETING group of stores with same franchise a number of retail outlets operating the same **franchise**. A franchise chain may vary in size from a few to many thousands of outlets and in coverage from a small local area to worldwide.

franchisee MARKETING holder of franchise a third party with a contract to sell or provide products or services owned by a manufacturer or supplier. The franchisee usually retains a percentage of sales income. *See also* ***franchise***

franchisor MARKETING granter of franchise a manufacturer or supplier who has made an agreement enabling a third party to sell or provide products or services that it owns. *See also* ***franchise***

franco FINANCE free available at no cost

franked payment STOCKHOLDING & INVESTMENTS **1.** dividends with tax credits dividends carrying tax credits paid by a company to stockholders **2.** dividend free of UK corporation tax in the United Kingdom, a dividend received by a company from another UK company, exempt from corporation tax

fraud FRAUD dishonest methods used for personal benefit the use of dishonesty, deception, or false representation in order to gain a material advantage or to injure the interests of others. Types of fraud include false accounting, theft, third party or investment fraud, employee collusion, and computer fraud. *See also* ***corporate fraud***

fraud ring FRAUD group organized to defraud others an organized group of people or companies who defraud others, for example, by stealing identities to gain access to financial information, by forging mortgage documents, or by filing false insurance claims

fraudulent misrepresentation LEGAL making false statements to deceive the action of making a false statement with the intention of deceiving a customer

FRB *abbr* BANKING Federal Reserve Board

Freddie Mac MORTGAGES, RISK US institution financing housing a stockholder-owned private company chartered in 1970 by the US Congress to fund home mortgages by issuing debt securities in US and international securities markets. On September 7, 2008, after Freddie Mac reported more than $2 billion in losses from **subprime loans**, its government regulatory agency, the Federal Housing Finance Agency, put Freddie Mac under its conservatorship. *Full form* ***Federal Home Loan Mortgage Corporation***. *Abbr* **FHLMC**. *See also* ***Fannie Mae***

freebie MARKETING something given away free a product or service that is given away, often as a business promotion

free coinage CURRENCY & EXCHANGE minting from donated metals a government's minting of coins from precious metals provided by citizens

free competition BUSINESS unregulated competition for business between companies a situation in which companies are allowed to compete with each other to win business without government intervention or restrictions

free currency CURRENCY & EXCHANGE currency that can be traded without restriction a currency that is allowed by the government to be bought and sold without restriction

free enterprise ECONOMICS freedom to trade without government control the trade carried on in a free-market economy, where resources are allocated on the basis of supply and demand

free gold FINANCE government gold not part of national reserve gold held by a government but not pledged as a reserve for the government's currency

freeholder REAL ESTATE person who owns property a person who owns a property legally and unconditionally, with rights to grant leases

freehold property REAL ESTATE property held free and clear property that the owner holds legally and unconditionally, with rights to grant leases

free issue STOCKHOLDING & INVESTMENTS = ***bonus issue***

  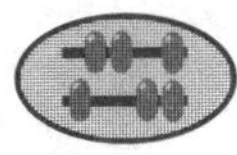   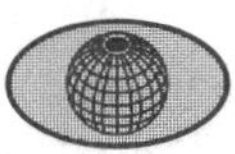   

freelance GENERAL MANAGEMENT, HR & PERSONNEL self-employed working on the basis of being self-employed, and possibly working for several employers at the same time, perhaps on a temporary basis. Freelance workers have been described as ideally suited to **portfolio working**.

freelancer HR & PERSONNEL self-employed person somebody who works on a **freelance** basis, offering skills and expertise to different employers anywhere in the world. A freelancer works independently and may follow a pattern of **portfolio working**.

free market ECONOMICS system of trade without government controls a market in which supply and demand are unregulated, except by the country's competition policy, and rights in physical and intellectual property are upheld

free market economy ECONOMICS economic system operating without government controls an economic system in which the government does not intervene or unduly regulate business activity

free on board OPERATIONS & PRODUCTION **1.** including all costs till goods are on carrier including in the price all the seller's costs until the goods are on the ship for transportation **2.** including all costs to point of delivery including in the price all the seller's costs until the goods are delivered to a place ► *Abbr* **f.o.b.**

free period BANKING permitted delay between credit card purchase and payment the period allowed to credit card holders before payment for credit card purchases is requested

free port INTERNATIONAL TRADE port without customs duties a port where no customs duties are charged

free reserves BANKING bank reserves without restrictions the part of a bank's reserves that are above the statutory level and so can be used for various purposes as the bank wishes

free-standing additional voluntary contributions plan PENSIONS additional personal pension a separate pension plan taken out by somebody in addition to an **occupational pension**

free trade INTERNATIONAL TRADE unrestricted trade between nations a system in which trading of goods between one country and another takes place without any restrictions or customs barriers

free trade area or **free trade zone** INTERNATIONAL TRADE group of countries trading without restrictions a group of countries engaged in trading between themselves without restrictions or customs barriers

free trader INTERNATIONAL TRADE person favoring free trade a person who is in favor of free trade

freeze-out STOCKHOLDING & INVESTMENTS compulsory purchase of minor stockholdings in acquired company the exclusion of minority stockholders in a company that has been taken over. A freeze-out provision may exist in a **takeover** agreement, which permits the acquiring organization to buy the noncontrolling shares held by small stockholders. A fair price is usually set, and the freeze-out may take place at a specific time, perhaps two to five years after the takeover. A freeze-out can still take place, even if provision for it is not made in a corporate charter, by applying pressure to minority stockholders to sell their shares to the acquiring company.

freight OPERATIONS & PRODUCTION goods being transported goods loaded for onward transport, most often by sea or by air

freight forwarder OPERATIONS & PRODUCTION firm consolidating shipments of freight an organization that collects shipments from a number of businesses and consolidates them into larger shipments for economies of scale. A freight forwarder often also deals with route selection, price negotiation, and documentation of distribution, and can act as a distribution agent for a business. By consolidating loads, a freight forwarder can negotiate cheaper rates of transportation than the individual businesses and can prebook space to ensure a more rapid delivery schedule.

frequency analysis MARKETING way of comparing chances of reaching target audience a technique for comparing the number of opportunities to reach the same target audience in different media

frequency distribution STATISTICS classifying statistical data and recording frequencies in a statistical study, the process of dividing a sample of observations into classes and listing the number of observations in each class

frequency polygon STATISTICS representation of frequency a diagrammatic representation showing the values in a **frequency distribution**

frequently asked question E-COMMERCE *see* ***FAQ***

frictional unemployment ECONOMICS temporarily between jobs a situation in which people are temporarily out of the labor market. They could be seeking a new job, incurring search delays as they apply, attending interviews, and relocating.

friction-free market MARKETS market in which competing products are very similar a market in which there is little differentiation between competing products, so that the customer has exceptional choice

friendly society BANKING in UK, association whose dues help members in need in the United Kingdom, a group of people forming an association to pay regular subscriptions to a fund that is used to help members of the group when they are in financial difficulties

fringe benefits HR & PERSONNEL supplements to main pay from employer rewards given or offered to employees in addition to their wages or salaries and included in their employment contract. Fringe benefits range from share options, company cars, expense accounts, cheap loans, medical insurance, and other types of **incentive plan** to discounts on company products, subsidized meals, and membership of social and health clubs. Many of these benefits are liable for tax. In the United States, a **cafeteria plan** permits employees to select from a variety of such benefits, although usually some are deemed to be core and not exchangeable for others. Minor benefits, sometimes appropriated rather than given, are known as **perks**.

FRN *abbr* FINANCE, CURRENCY & EXCHANGE floating-rate note

front company BUSINESS, FRAUD firm hiding illegal activities of controlling firm a company established as a legitimate business to conceal the illegal activities of the business controlling it

front end GENERAL MANAGEMENT section of firm dealing directly with customers the part of an organization that deals with customers on a face-to-face basis

front-end loading FINANCE early deduction of charges and commission the practice of taking the commission and administrative expenses from the early payments made to an investment or insurance plan. *See also* ***back-end loading***

front office GENERAL MANAGEMENT staff that interacts with customers and clients the members of staff in a financial institution or brokerage who deal directly with customers and clients. *See also* ***back office, middle office***

  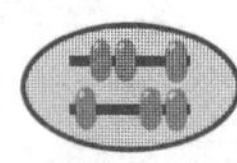   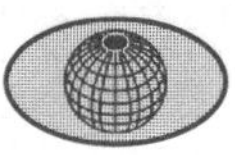   

frozen account BANKING bank account made inoperable by court order a bank account whose funds cannot be used or withdrawn because of a court order

frozen credits BANKING credits that are not movable credits in an account which cannot be moved, usually owing to a legal dispute

FRSB *abbr* ACCOUNTING Financial Reporting Standards Board

FSA *abbr* REGULATION & COMPLIANCE Financial Services Authority

FSB *abbr* BUSINESS Federation of Small Businesses

FT *abbr* FINANCE Financial Times

FTASI *abbr* MARKETS FTSE Actuaries Share Indices

FTSE MARKETS Financial Times-Stock Exchange an abbreviation of "Financial Times-Stock Exchange," used in the name of various indices of the London Stock Exchange published in the Financial Times

FTSE 30 Share Index or **FTSE 30** MARKETS index of influential UK companies an index showing the stock prices of 30 influential companies on the London Stock Exchange. Although in existence since 1935, the FTSE 30 Share Index is now one of the less popular indices.

FTSE 100 Share Index or **FTSE 100** MARKETS index of most-highly capitalized UK public companies an index, established in 1984, that is based on the stock prices of the 100 most highly capitalized public companies in the United Kingdom

FTSE 250 Index or **FTSE 250** MARKETS index of medium-capitalized UK UK companies an index of medium-capitalized companies not included in the **FTSE 100 Share Index**. It represents over 17% of UK market capitalization.

FTSE Actuaries Share Indices MARKETS several indices based on London stock prices several indices based on prices on the London Stock Exchange, which are calculated by and published in the Financial Times in conjunction with the Actuaries Investment Research Committee. *Abbr* **FTASI**

FTSE All-Share Index MARKETS average of UK stock prices an average of the stock prices of all the companies listed on the London Stock Exchange. As this encompasses over 1,000 companies, this index is often used as a reliable barometer of the performance of different companies. This index aggregates the FTSE 100, FTSE 250, and FTSE Small Cap Indices.

FTSE Small Cap Index MARKETS index of UK companies with smallest capitalization an index that indicates the performance of companies with the smallest market capitalization, representing roughly 2% of market capitalization in the United Kingdom

FTSE TMT Index MARKETS index of UK companies in technology, media, and telecommunications an index which indicates the performance of companies in the United Kingdom in three key business areas: technology, media, and telecommunications. *Abbr* **FTSE TMT**

fulfillment MARKETING dealing with approaches from customers the process of responding to customer inquiries, orders, or sales promotion offers

fulfillment house MARKETING firm handling approaches from customers for others an organization that specializes in responding to inquiries, orders, or sales promotion offers on behalf of a client

full bank BANKING bank offering full domestic and international services a local or foreign bank permitted to engage in the full range of domestic and international services

full cost accounting ACCOUNTING = ***environmental accounting***

full coupon bond STOCKHOLDING & INVESTMENTS bond with competitive interest rate a bond whose interest rate is competitive in the current market

full cover *UK* INSURANCE = ***full coverage***

full coverage *US* INSURANCE insurance for most risks insurance that provides coverage against a wide range of risks. *UK term* ***full cover***

full employment HR & PERSONNEL situation in which all capable workers have jobs a situation in which all the people who are fit to work have jobs

full faith and credit FINANCE US government debt repayment guarantee an unconditional guarantee by the US government to repay the principal and interest on all its debt

full price OPERATIONS & PRODUCTION standard price with no discounts the regular price for a product, with no special discounts applied

full rate OPERATIONS & PRODUCTION standard charge with no discounts the standard charge for a service, with no special discounts applied

full-service banking BANKING provision of banking and financial services a type of banking that offers a whole range of services including mortgages, loans, and pension plans

full-service broker FINANCE broker managing portfolios and giving financial advice a broker who manages portfolios for clients, and gives advice on stocks and financial questions in general

full time HR & PERSONNEL standard working hours the standard hours of attendance expected in an organization. *See also* ***part time***

Fully Automated Screen Trading and Electronic Registration MARKETS *see* ***FASTER***

fully connected world GENERAL MANAGEMENT population in touch by networks a world in which most people and organizations are linked by networks such as the Internet

fully diluted earnings per share STOCKHOLDING & INVESTMENTS earnings per share taken over all ordinary shares the amount earned per share calculated over the whole number of shares on the assumption that convertible shares and options have been converted to ordinary shares

fully diluted earnings per (common) share STOCKHOLDING & INVESTMENTS earnings including commitments to issue more stocks the amount earned per share taking into account commitments to issue more shares, for example, as a result of convertibles, stock options, or warrants

fully diluted shares STOCKHOLDING & INVESTMENTS total shares, including convertible shares and stock options total number of shares that would be outstanding assuming that convertible shares have been converted to ordinary shares and that stock options have been exercised

fully distributed issue STOCKHOLDING & INVESTMENTS issue fully sold out to investors an issue of stocks sold entirely to investors rather than being held by dealers

full year ACCOUNTING 12 months a 12-month period, especially with reference to financial information such as earnings, sales, profits, and outlook for the future

full-year forecast ACCOUNTING prediction of future 12 months' earnings or losses a prediction of the expected earnings or losses of a business for the future over a 12-month period

full-year results ACCOUNTING past 12 months of financial data the financial

  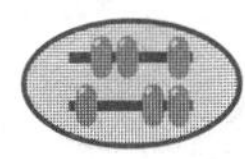   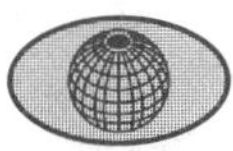   

information of a business, especially its profits or losses, calculated for the preceding 12-month period

fully paid share capital or **fully paid-up capital** STOCKHOLDING & INVESTMENTS total paid by investors for capital holdings the amount of the share capital when all calls have been paid on all issued shares. *See also* ***called-up share capital, paid-up capital***

functional budget TREASURY MANAGEMENT budget for activity or department a budget of income and/or expenditure applicable to a specific function. A function may refer to a process or a department. Functional budgets frequently include the following: production cost budget (based on a forecast of production and plant utilization); marketing cost budget; sales budget; personnel budget; purchasing budget; and research and development budget. *See also* ***departmental budget***

functional relationship STATISTICS relationship between statistical variables the relationship between variables in a statistical study in which there is no bias or any other distorting factor

fund FINANCE **1.** money earmarked for something an amount of money set aside for a particular purpose **2.** money invested money invested in an investment trust as part of a mutual fund, or given to a financial adviser to invest on behalf of a client. *See also* ***funds*** **3.** supply money for purpose to provide an amount of money for a particular purpose. *See also* ***finance***

fundamental accounting concepts ACCOUNTING basic assumptions for accounts broad basic assumptions that underlie the periodic financial accounts of business enterprises. *See also* ***concepts***

fundamental analysis STOCKHOLDING & INVESTMENTS assessment of influences affecting firm's performance an assessment of how the external and internal influences on a company's activities should affect investment decisions. *See also* ***technical analysis***

fundamentals BUSINESS, MARKETS most basic business components the basic components such as assets, profitability, and dividends of a company or a stock market

funded FINANCE **1.** backed by long-term loans supported by money in the form of long-term loans **2.** based on a fund a future financial commitment,such as the payment of a pension, that is supported by an existing fund of money

funded debt FINANCE long- or medium-term debt long-term debt or debt that has a maturity date in excess of one year. Funded debt is usually issued in the public markets or in the form of a private placement to qualified institutional investors.

fund family STOCKHOLDING & INVESTMENTS = ***family of funds***

funding FINANCE **1.** finance for business or project the financial support that is available for a business or project **2.** changing short-term debt into long-term loan the conversion of a short-term debt into a loan that has a maturity date in excess of one year

funding risk RISK likelihood of difficulty in raising funds the risk that it might be difficult to realize assets or otherwise raise funds to meet commitments associated with **financial instruments**. *See also* ***liquidity risk***

fund management STOCKHOLDING & INVESTMENTS business of investing clients' money the business of dealing with the investment of sums of money on behalf of clients

fund manager STOCKHOLDING & INVESTMENTS manager of investments somebody who manages the investments of a mutual fund or other financial institution. *Also called* ***investment manager***

Fund Managers' Association STOCKHOLDING & INVESTMENTS UK organization for fund managers an association representing the interests of UK-based institutional fund managers. It now forms part of the **Investment Management Association**. *Abbr* **FMA**

fund of funds STOCKHOLDING & INVESTMENTS mutual fund investing in several underlying mutual funds a registered mutual fund that invests in a variety of underlying mutual funds. Subscribers own units in the fund of funds, not in the underlying mutual funds.

funds FINANCE money available to spend money that is available to a person, business, or organization for spending. *See also* ***insufficient funds***

fungibility BUSINESS, FINANCE interchangeability of product the ability to be easily substituted for or combined with another similar product

fungible **1.** FINANCE substitutable indistinguishable for business purposes from other items of the same type. Such products may be easily combined in making up shipments. **2.** STOCKHOLDING & INVESTMENTS interchangeable used to describe an asset, especially a security, that can be exchanged for a similar asset

funny money **1.** CURRENCY & EXCHANGE forged currency money that is counterfeit or forged **2.** FRAUD questionable money money obtained from a legally or morally suspect source

future STOCKHOLDING & INVESTMENTS contract for future delivery a contract to deliver a commodity at a future date at a fixed price. *Also called* ***futures contract***

future delivery OPERATIONS & PRODUCTION delivery at prearranged future date a delivery at some date in the future that has been arranged by the buyer and seller

future option STOCKHOLDING & INVESTMENTS contract for future trade at set price a contract in which somebody agrees to buy or sell an option for purchasing or selling a commodity, currency, or security at a prearranged price for delivery in the future. *Also called* ***futures option***

futures STOCKHOLDING & INVESTMENTS items traded now for later delivery stock, currency, or commodities that are bought or sold now for delivery at a later date

futures commission merchant STOCKHOLDING & INVESTMENTS broker for futures somebody who acts as a broker for **futures contracts**. *Abbr* **FCM**

futures contract STOCKHOLDING & INVESTMENTS *see* ***future***

futures exchange CURRENCY & EXCHANGE exchange for futures an exchange on which **futures contracts** are traded

futures market MARKETS market for trade in items with fluctuating prices a market for buying and selling securities, commodities, or currencies that tend to fluctuate in price over a period of time. The market's goal is to reduce the risk of uncertainty about prices in the period ahead.

futures option STOCKHOLDING & INVESTMENTS *see* ***future option***

futures research GENERAL MANAGEMENT consideration of what could happen in future the identification of possible future **scenarios** with the goal of anticipating and perhaps influencing what the future holds. Futures research is important to the process of **issues management**. It usually identifies several possible scenarios for any set of circumstances, and enables an informed decision to be made.

future value FINANCE projected value of sum of money the value that a sum of money

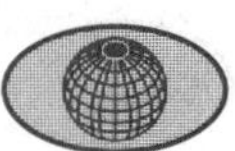

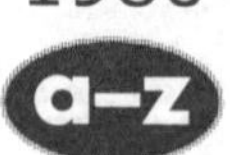

will have in the future, taking into account the effects of inflation, interest rates, or currency values.

Future value calculations require three figures: the sum in question, the percentage by which it will increase or decrease, and the period of time. In this example, these figures are $1,000, 11%, and two years.

At an interest rate of 11%, the sum of $1,000 will grow to $1,232 in two years:

$\$1,000 \times 1.11 = \$1,110 \text{ (first year)} \times 1.11 = \$1,232 \text{ (second year, rounded to whole dollars)}$

Note that the interest earned in the first year generates additional interest in the second year, a practice known as compounding. When large sums are in question, the effect of compounding can be significant.

At an inflation rate of 11%, by comparison, the sum of $1,000 will shrink to $812 in two years:

$$\frac{\$1,000}{1.11} = \frac{\$901 \text{ (first year)}}{1.11} = \$812 \text{ (second year, rounded to whole dollars)}$$

In order to avoid errors, it is important to express the percentage as 1.11 and multiply and divide by that figure, instead of using 11%; and to calculate each year, quarter, or month separately. *See also* ***present value***

futuristic planning GENERAL MANAGEMENT planning for potentially radically different future planning for a period that extends beyond the planning horizon in the form of future expected conditions that may exist in respect of the entity, products/services, and environment, but that cannot usefully be expressed in quantified terms. An example would be working out the actions needed in a future with no automobiles.

futurize GENERAL MANAGEMENT keep technologically up to date to ensure that an organization is taking full advantage of the latest technologies

fuzzy accounting ACCOUNTING, FRAUD accounting practices that mislead investors company accounting practices designed to inflate earnings or earnings estimates in order to attract investors

fuzzy search E-COMMERCE computer search giving near and exact matches a computer search that returns not only exact matches to the search request, but also close matches that include possibilities and allow for such things as spelling errors

FY *abbr* ACCOUNTING fiscal year

G

G7 FINANCE group of seven major industrial nations the group of seven major industrial nations established in 1985 to discuss the world economy, consisting of Canada, France, Germany, Italy, Japan, the United Kingdom, and the United States. *Full form* ***Group of Seven***

G8 FINANCE G7 countries plus Russia the group of eight major industrial nations consisting of the G7 plus Russia. *Full form* ***Group of Eight***

G10 FINANCE nations contributing to General Arrangements to Borrow fund the group of ten countries who contribute to the General Arrangements to Borrow fund: Belgium, Canada, France, Germany, Italy, Japan, the Netherlands, Sweden, the United States, and the United Kingdom. Switzerland joined in 1984. *Full form* ***Group of Ten***. *Also called* ***Paris Club***

G20 ECONOMICS group of industrial and emerging countries a forum for discussion between 20 industrialized and emerging-market countries on issues related to global economic stability. *Full form* ***Group of Twenty***

GAAP *abbr* ACCOUNTING Generally Accepted Accounting Principles

GAB FINANCE international fund providing large loans to countries a fund financed by the **G10** that is used when the IMF's own resources are insufficient, for example, when there is a need for large loans to one or more industrialized countries. *Full form* ***General Arrangements to Borrow***

gain FINANCE increase in amount or value an increase in the amount or level of something, for example, in a company's profit or in the value of stocks on a stock exchange

gain sharing FINANCE sharing profits from efficiency improvements with employees a group-based **bonus plan** to share profits from improvements in production efficiency between employees and the company

galloping inflation ECONOMICS very rapid inflation inflation that increases rapidly by large amounts

game theory GENERAL MANAGEMENT technique for investigating consequences of strategies and conflicts a mathematical technique used in **operational research** to analyze and predict the outcomes of games of strategy and conflicts of interest. Game theory is used to represent conflicts and problems involved in formulating marketing and organizational strategy, with the goal of identifying and implementing optimal strategies. It involves assessing likely strategies to be adopted by players in a given situation under a particular set of rules.

gamma STOCKHOLDING & INVESTMENTS rate of change in option price the rate of change in the **delta** of an option for a unit change in the price of the underlying asset. It is a measure of **convexity**.

gap analysis **1.** FINANCE analyzing shortfall between current results and ultimate goals a method of improving a company's financial performance by analyzing the reasons for the gap between current results and long-term objectives **2.** MARKETING investigation of gaps in market or availability a marketing technique used to identify gaps in market or product coverage. In gap analysis, consumer information or requirements are tabulated and matched to product categories in order to identify product or service opportunities or gaps in product planning.

gap financing FINANCE short-term loan arrangement the process of arranging an extra loan such as a **bridge loan** in order to make a purchase not fully covered by an existing loan

garage **1.** MARKETS part of New York Stock Exchange the annex to the main floor of the New York Stock Exchange **2.** *UK* TAX move assets or liabilities for tax advantage to transfer assets or liabilities from one financial center to another to take advantage of a tax benefit

garbatrage *US* STOCKHOLDING & INVESTMENTS stocks benefiting from unrelated takeover stocks that rise because of a **takeover** but that are not connected to the target company (*slang*)

garden leave GENERAL MANAGEMENT full pay without working in a **contract of employment**, a clause that allows the employer to keep an employee on full pay, but not require him or her to work, during the employee's contractual **notice period**. Garden leave thereby prevents the employee from working for another employer until the notice period has expired, by which time any confidential information the employee holds is likely to have become commercially out of date.

garnishee FINANCE person ordered to redirect debt payment to another a person who owes money to a creditor and is ordered by a court to pay that money to a creditor of the original creditor, and not to the actual creditor

garnishee order LEGAL order requiring debt payment to third party a court order, making somebody pay money not directly to a creditor, but to a third party. For example, a court may order an employer to take money from an employee's pay and pay it to somebody to whom the employee owes money. *Also called* ***garnishment*** *(sense 2)*

garnishment **1.** FINANCE withholding of income to repay debt a procedure by which wages or salary are withheld from an employee in order to pay off the employee's debt **2.** LEGAL = ***garnishee order***

GAS *abbr* ACCOUNTING Government Accountancy Service

gatekeeper GENERAL MANAGEMENT controller of dissemination of information somebody within an organization who controls the flow of information and therefore influences policy

gateway E-COMMERCE where computer networks meet and exchange data a point where two or more computer networks meet and can exchange data

GATT INTERNATIONAL TRADE international treaty promoting multilateral trade a treaty signed in Geneva in 1947 that aimed to foster multilateral trade and settle trading disputes between adherent countries. Initially signed by 23 nations, it started to reduce trade tariffs and, as it was accepted by more and more countries, tackled other barriers to trade. It was replaced on January 1, 1995, by the World Trade Organization. *Full form* ***General Agreement on Tariffs and Trade***

gazump *UK* REAL ESTATE accept higher offer, negating earlier verbal agreement to agree verbally to sell to one buyer, but before the agreement becomes legally binding, to accept a higher offer from another buyer. Gazumping is usually associated with the real estate market, although it can occur in any market where the prices are rising rapidly.

gazunder *UK* REAL ESTATE undercut price verbally agreed earlier to agree verbally to buy at one price, but before the agreement becomes legally binding, to offer a lower price. Gazundering is usually associated with the real estate market, although it can occur in any market where the prices are falling rapidly.

GBE *abbr* GENERAL MANAGEMENT Government Business Enterprise

GB pound CURRENCY & EXCHANGE = ***pound sterling***

GDP ECONOMICS all goods and services produced by economy the total flow of goods and services produced by an economy over a quarter or a year, measured by the aggregate value of goods and services at market prices. *Full form* ***gross domestic product***

GDP per capita ECONOMICS total economic output divided by population **GDP** divided by the country's population so as to achieve a figure per person in the population

GEAR ECONOMICS redistributive economic program in S. Africa the macroeconomic reform program of the South African government, intended to foster economic growth, create employment, and redistribute income and opportunities in favor of the poor. *Full form* ***Growth, Employment, and Redistribution***

geared investment trust *UK* STOCKHOLDING & INVESTMENTS = ***leveraged investment company***

gearing FINANCE, RISK = ***leverage***

gearing ratios FINANCE = ***leverage ratios***

geisha bond STOCKHOLDING & INVESTMENTS = ***shogun bond***

general account MARKETS account with investment broker who lends money the US Federal Reserve Board's term for a **margin account** set up for a brokerage customer

General Agreement on Tariffs and Trade INTERNATIONAL TRADE *see* ***GATT***

General Arrangements to Borrow FINANCE *see* ***GAB***

general audit ACCOUNTING comprehensive examination of firm's accounts an examination of all books and accounts belonging to a company

general average INSURANCE sharing of insured loss by all policyholders a process by which the cost of lost goods is shared by all parties to an insurance policy, as in cases when some goods have been lost in an attempt to save the rest of the cargo

General Commissioners TAX in UK, officials appointed to hear tax appeals in the United Kingdom, an independent group of people from a variety of backgrounds appointed by the Lord Chancellor to hear appeals from taxpayers against Her Majesty's Revenue & Customs. In Scotland, Commissioners are appointed by Scottish ministers.

general expenses ACCOUNTING routine costs of running business minor expenses of various kinds incurred in the running of a business

general fund FINANCE mutual fund with wide-ranging investments a mutual fund that has investments in a variety of stocks

general insurance INSURANCE insurance against losses excluding life insurance insurance relating to various potential losses such as theft or damage, but excluding life insurance

general ledger ACCOUNTING book listing firm's financial transactions a book that lists all of the financial transactions of a company

general lien LEGAL **1.** right to hold property until debt paid a right to hold the goods or property of a debtor until a debt has been paid **2.** right to hold debtor's personal property only a right to hold the personal possessions of a debtor until a debt is paid, but not his or her house or land. *See also* ***banker's lien***

Generally Accepted Accounting Principles ACCOUNTING guidelines relating to fair accounting practices a summary of best practice in respect to the form and content of financial statements and auditors' reports, and of accounting policies and disclosures adopted for the preparation of financial information. GAAP has statutory or regulatory authority in the United States and Canada and some other countries, but not in the United Kingdom. *Abbr* **GAAP**

general manager GENERAL MANAGEMENT manager involved in all aspects of organization a **manager** whose work encompasses all areas of an organization. A general manager is traditionally a nonspecialist, has a working knowledge of all aspects of an organization's activities, and oversees all operating functions. In large companies and the public sector, specialist managers with expert knowledge may control departments, while a general manager provides unifying **leadership** from the top.

general meeting CORPORATE GOVERNANCE meeting of company's stockholders a meeting of all the stockholders of a company or of all the members of an organization

General National Mortgage Association MORTGAGES *see* ***Ginnie Mae***

general obligation bond STOCKHOLDING & INVESTMENTS municipal bond financing public undertakings a municipal or state bond that is repaid out of general funds. *Abbr* **GO bond**

general partner BUSINESS partner in firm who has no limited liability a partner in a

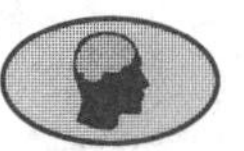

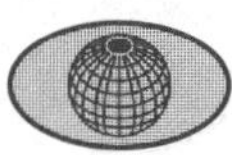

business whose responsibility for its debts is not limited and whose personal assets may be at risk if the company's assets are not sufficient to discharge its debts

general partnership BUSINESS business where all partners share profits and liabilities a business in which each partner has a share in the administration, profits, and losses of the operation

general undertaking REGULATION & COMPLIANCE directors' undertaking to obey Stock Exchange regulations an agreement, signed by all the directors of a company applying for Stock Exchange listing, that promises that they will work within the regulations of the Stock Exchange

generative learning GENERAL MANAGEMENT learning that fosters experimentation and open-mindedness a style of organizational learning that encourages experimentation, risk taking, openness, and system-wide thinking. Organizations have successfully used this style of learning to transform themselves in the face of technological, social, and market change. **Adaptive learning** is a contrasting approach.

generic strategy MARKETING marketing strategy any of three strategies for marketing products or services: cost leadership, differentiation, and focus. The first implies supplying products in a more cost-effective way than competitors; the second refers to adding value to products or services; and the third focuses on a specific product market segment with the goal of establishing a monopoly.

gensaki STOCKHOLDING & INVESTMENTS bond sale incorporating repurchase agreement the Japanese term for a bond sale incorporating a repurchase agreement at a later date

gentleman's agreement GENERAL MANAGEMENT reliable unwritten agreement a verbal agreement between two people who trust each other to keep the agreement without a formal contract

Gesellschaft mit beschrnkter Haftung BUSINESS *see* ***GmbH***

gharar FINANCE uncertainty prohibited in Islamic business dealings in Islamic financing, excessive uncertainty in a business transaction of any type. It is one of three prohibitions in Islamic law, the others being **maysir** and **riba**.

ghosting MARKETS, FRAUD illegal price fixing of stock an illegal practice in which two or more market makers, who are required by law to compete, join to influence the price of a stock

Giffen good ECONOMICS = ***inferior good***

Gift Aid TAX in UK, tax advantage on gifts to charity in the United Kingdom, a system through which a charity receiving a gift of money from a taxpayer can also directly receive the tax that had been paid on the sum at the standard rate

gift inter vivos TAX gift between living persons a gift that is made to another living person. *Abbr* **GIV**

gift-leaseback TAX leasing back of gifted property the practice of giving somebody a property and then leasing it back, usually for tax advantage or charitable purposes

gift tax TAX in US, tax paid by giver on gift in the United States, a tax on money or property given to another living person, which is to be paid by the giver. Exemptions exist for gifts below a specific value, gifts between spouses, etc.

gift with reservation FINANCE gift that benefits donor in some way in the United Kingdom, a gift with some benefit retained for the donor, for example, the legal transfer of a dwelling when the donor continues in residence

gilt STOCKHOLDING & INVESTMENTS *see* ***gilt-edged security***

gilt-edged STOCKHOLDING & INVESTMENTS issued by blue-chip company used to describe a security issued by a blue-chip company, which is therefore considered very secure (*informal*)

gilt-edged security STOCKHOLDING & INVESTMENTS UK government security paying regular fixed interest in the United Kingdom, a security issued by the government that pays a fixed rate of interest on a regular basis for a specific period of time until the redemption date, when the principal is returned. Their names, for example, Exchequer 10½% 2005 (abbreviated to Ex 10½% '05) or Treasury 11¾% 2003–07 (abbreviated to Tr 11¾% '03–'07) indicate the rate and redemption date. Thought to have originated in the 17th century to help fund the war with France, today they form a large part of the **national debt**. *Also called* ***gilt***. *See also* ***index-linked gilt, short-dated gilts***

gilt repos MARKETS UK market in trading gilts in the United Kingdom, the market in prearranged sales and repurchase of gilt-edged securities, launched in 1996 by the Bank of England to make gilts more attractive to overseas investors

gilt strip STOCKHOLDING & INVESTMENTS UK bond yielding single cash payment at maturity in the United Kingdom, a **zero coupon bond** created by splitting the interest payments from a gilt-edged security so that it produces a single cash payment at maturity

gilt unit trust STOCKHOLDING & INVESTMENTS UK mutual fund investing in gilts in the United Kingdom, a mutual fund where the underlying investments are **gilt-edged securities**

Ginnie Mae MORTGAGES US securities agency in the United States, a government agency that issues mortgage-backed bonds. *Full form* ***General National Mortgage Association***

giro BANKING UK bank transfer in the United Kingdom, a system of transferring money from one bank account to another. *Also called* ***bank giro***

GIV *abbr* TAX gift inter vivos

give up MARKETS three-way trade a transaction involving three brokers in which broker A, who is busy, asks broker B to execute a trade for a client with broker C. The trade is recorded as broker A's transaction, so broker A receives a commission, and broker B, who actually executed the trade, gives up the transaction.

glamour stock STOCKHOLDING & INVESTMENTS fashionable investment a currently fashionable and popular security (*slang*)

Glass-Steagall Act REGULATION & COMPLIANCE US law separating banking and brokerage industries in the United States, a law enacted in 1933 that enforces the separation of the banking and brokerage industries. Some provisions have since been repealed, most notably: (1) allowing the Federal Reserve to regulate interest rates in savings accounts, and (2) prohibiting a bank holding company from owning other financial companies.

global bank BANKING bank with worldwide business a bank that is active in the international markets and has a presence in several continents

global bond STOCKHOLDING & INVESTMENTS = ***Eurobond***

global bond issue STOCKHOLDING & INVESTMENTS bond issue allowing transfer of titles between markets an issue of a bond that incorporates a settlement mechanism allowing for the transfer of titles between markets

global brand MARKETING brand name known everywhere the brand name of a product that has worldwide recognition. A

  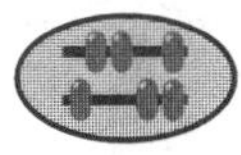 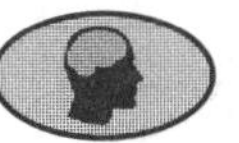  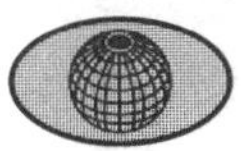   

global brand has the advantage of economies of scale in terms of production, recognition, and packaging. *Also called* ***global product***

global coordinator STOCKHOLDING & INVESTMENTS overall manager of global stock issue the lead manager of a global offering who is responsible for overseeing the entire issue and is usually supported by regional and national coordinators

global custody FINANCE bundle of financial services for institutional investors a financial service, usually available to institutional investors only, that includes the safekeeping of securities certificates issued in markets across the world, the collection of dividends, dealing with tax, valuation of investments, foreign exchange, and the settlement of transactions

global depositary receipt STOCKHOLDING & INVESTMENTS certificate for shares of stock traded abroad a certificate held by a bank in one country representing shares of stock that are traded on an exchange in a foreign country but can be purchased through various banks worldwide

global economy ECONOMICS, INTERNATIONAL TRADE international trade relations the economic relations between countries in a world where markets in individual countries have now spread beyond national boundaries and are more integrated with those of other countries. *Also called* ***world economy***

global hedge STOCKHOLDING & INVESTMENTS = ***macrohedge***

globalization GENERAL MANAGEMENT expanding operations worldwide the creation of international strategies by organizations for overseas expansion and operation on a worldwide level. The process of globalization has been precipitated by a number of factors, including rapid technology developments that make global communications possible, political developments such as the fall of communism, and transportation developments that make traveling faster and more frequent. These produce greater development opportunities for companies with the opening up of additional markets, allow greater customer harmonization as a result of the increase in shared cultural values, and provide a superior competitive position with lower operating costs in other countries and access to new raw materials, resources, and investment opportunities.

global marketing MARKETING marketing to sell products worldwide a marketing strategy used mainly by multinational companies to sell goods or services internationally. Global marketing requires that there be harmonization between the marketing policies for different countries and that the marketing mix for the different countries can be adapted to the local market conditions. Global marketing is sometimes used to refer to overseas expansion efforts through **licensing**, **franchises**, and **joint ventures**.

global marketplace ECONOMICS, INTERNATIONAL TRADE market encompassing whole world a worldwide trading system that has grown up since the 1970s, in which goods can be produced wherever the production costs are cheapest wherever they are ultimately sold

global offering STOCKHOLDING & INVESTMENTS worldwide offering of securities the offering of securities in several markets simultaneously, for example, in Europe, the Far East, and North America

global pricing contract OPERATIONS & PRODUCTION contract for single worldwide price a contract between a customer and a supplier whereby the supplier agrees to charge the customer the same price for the delivery of parts or services anywhere in the world. As **globalization** increases, more customers are likely to press their suppliers for global pricing contracts. Through such contracts suppliers can benefit by gaining access to new markets and growing their business, achieving economies of scale, developing strong relationships with customers, and thereby gaining a **competitive advantage** that is difficult for competitors to break. There are risks involved, too, for example, being in the middle of a conflict between a customer's head office and its local business units, or being tied to one customer when there are more attractive customers to serve.

global product MARKETING *see* ***global brand***

glocalization GENERAL MANAGEMENT expanding and adapting operations worldwide the process of tailoring products or services to different local markets around the world. Glocalization is a combination of globalization and localization. Improved communications and advances in technology have made worldwide markets accessible to even small companies but, rather than being homogenous, the global market is in fact made up of many different localities. Success in a globalized environment is more likely if products are not globalized or mass marketed, but glocalized and customized for individual local communities that have different needs and different cultural approaches.

glue GENERAL MANAGEMENT unifying factor a common factor such as information that unifies organizations, supply chains, and other commercial groups (*informal*)

GM *abbr* FINANCE gross margin

GmbH BUSINESS corporation the German term for a corporation. *Full form* ***Gesellschaft mit beschränkter Haftung***

GNMA MORTGAGES *see* ***Ginnie Mae***

gnomes of Zurich BANKING Swiss bankers bankers and currency dealers based in Switzerland, who have a reputation for secrecy. The term is often used to refer in a derogatory way to unknown currency speculators who cause upheavals in the currency markets (*informal*).

GNP ECONOMICS country's total economic output plus foreign investment income the **GDP** plus domestic residents' income from investment abroad less income earned in the domestic market accruing to noncitizens abroad. *Full form* ***gross national product***

GNP per capita ECONOMICS GNP divided by population the **GNP** divided by the country's population so as to achieve a figure per person in the population

goal GENERAL MANAGEMENT target of effort an end toward which effort is directed and on which resources are focused, usually to achieve an organization's strategy. There is considerable discussion on whether objective, goal, target, and aim are the same. In general usage, the terms are often interchangeable, so it is important that, if an organization has a particular meaning for one of these terms, it must define it in its documentation. Sometimes an objective is seen as the desired final end result, while a goal is a smaller step on the road to it.

GO bond STOCKHOLDING & INVESTMENTS = ***general obligation bond***

go-go fund STOCKHOLDING & INVESTMENTS, RISK high-risk mutual fund a mutual fund that trades heavily and predominantly in high-return, high-risk investments

going concern BUSINESS company currently trading a company that is actively trading and making a profit

going short FINANCE selling asset for repurchase at lower price borrowing and then selling an asset one does not own with the intention of acquiring it at a later date at a lower price for delivery to the purchaser. *See also* **bear**

  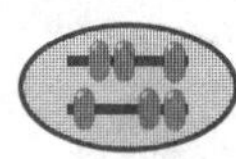   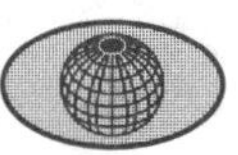   

gold bond STOCKHOLDING & INVESTMENTS bond with gold as collateral a bond for which gold is collateral, often issued by mining companies

gold bug STOCKHOLDING & INVESTMENTS investor who believes gold prices will rise a person who believes that gold is the best investment

gold bullion FINANCE gold bars gold in the form of bars

gold card BANKING credit card for wealthy customer a gold-colored credit card, generally issued to customers with above average incomes, that may include additional benefits such as an overdraft at an advantageous interest rate. It may require an annual fee.

gold certificate LEGAL document stating ownership of gold a document that shows ownership of gold that the owner may not be storing

golden handcuffs FINANCE financial incentive to remain in organization a financial incentive paid to encourage employees to remain in an organization and dissuade them from leaving for a rival business or to start their own company (*informal*)

golden handshake or **golden goodbye** FINANCE generous payment for departing senior executive a sum of money given to a senior executive on his or her involuntary departure from an employing organization as a form of severance pay. A golden handshake can be offered when an executive is required to leave before the expiration of his or her contract, for example, because of a **merger** or corporate restructuring. It is intended as compensation for loss of office. It can be a very large sum of money, but often it is not related to the perceived performance of the executive concerned (*informal*).

golden hello FINANCE **1.** generous financial arrangement for new employee a welcome package for a new employee which may include a bonus and stock options. A golden hello is designed as an incentive to attract employees. Some of the contents of the welcome package may be contingent on the performance of the employee. **2.** support for employer hiring new employee a payment from a government to an employer who takes on new staff when jobs are hard to find in a recession

golden parachute or **golden umbrella** FINANCE generous financial package on dismissal from employment a clause inserted in the contract of employment of a senior employee that details a financial package payable if the employee is dismissed. A golden parachute provides an executive with a measure of financial security and may be payable if the employee leaves the organization following a **takeover** or **merger**, or is dismissed as a result of poor performance.

golden share STOCKHOLDING & INVESTMENTS government's controlling interest in newly privatized company a controlling interest retained by a government in a company that has been privatized after having been in public ownership

gold fix or **gold fixing** FINANCE twice-daily setting of gold price a system by which the world price for gold is set twice a day in US dollars on the London Gold Exchange and in Paris and Zurich

gold point CURRENCY & EXCHANGE price variation in gold-backed currency an amount by which a currency that is linked to gold can vary in price

gold reserve CURRENCY & EXCHANGE central bank's gold holdings gold coins or bullion held by a central bank to support a paper currency and provide security for borrowing

gold standard CURRENCY & EXCHANGE system valuing currency against gold a system in which a currency unit is defined in terms of its value in gold

good faith deposit FINANCE sum given to confirm deal a deposit made by a buyer to a seller to show a firm intention to complete the transaction

good for the day MARKETS describing instructions valid only on specific day used to describe instructions to a broker that are valid only for the specific day indicated

good for this week or **good for this month** *UK* MARKETS = ***good this week***

goods OPERATIONS & PRODUCTION things that are bought and sold items, materials, and products that can be transported and are for sale

goods and chattels FINANCE movable personal property movable personal possessions, as opposed to land and buildings

Goods and Services Tax TAX **1.** Australian tax on goods and services in Australia, a government-imposed consumption tax, currently of 10%, added to the retail cost of goods and services **2.** former Canadian tax on goods and services a former Canadian tax on goods and services. It was a value-added tax and was replaced by the **harmonized sales tax**. *Abbr* **GST**

goods received note OPERATIONS & PRODUCTION receipt for goods a record of goods issued at the point of receipt

good this week or **good this month** *US* STOCKHOLDING & INVESTMENTS describes instructions valid only during particular week/month used to describe instructions to a broker that are valid only for the duration of the week/month given. *Abbr* **GTM**. *UK terms* ***good for this week, good for this month***

good 'til cancel MARKETS describing order effective up to 60 days used to describe an order to buy or sell a security that is effective until an investor cancels it, up to a maximum of 60 days. *Abbr* **GTC**

good title LEGAL unquestionable property ownership ownership of a property that cannot be legally challenged successfully. *Also called* ***clear title***

goodwill ACCOUNTING business assets such as reputation and expertise an **intangible asset** of a company which includes factors such as reputation, contacts, and expertise, for which a buyer of the company may have to pay a premium.

Goodwill becomes an intangible asset when a company has been acquired by another. It then appears on a balance sheet in the amount by which the price paid by the acquiring company exceeds the net tangible assets of the acquired company. In other words

Purchase price – Net assets = Goodwill

If an airline is bought for $12 billion and its net assets are valued at $9 billion, $3 billion of the purchase would be allocated to goodwill on the balance sheet.

go private STOCKHOLDING & INVESTMENTS change to private status without stock market listing to revert from being a public limited company quoted on a stock exchange to a private company without a stock market listing

go public STOCKHOLDING & INVESTMENTS become public corporation to place stock of a private company for sale on a stock exchange in order to raise funds

gourde CURRENCY & EXCHANGE Haitian currency unit a unit of currency used in Haiti

governance CORPORATE GOVERNANCE management of firm the process of managing a company, especially with respect to the soundness or otherwise of its management

Government Accountancy Service ACCOUNTING body monitoring accounting practice in UK Civil Service in the United

     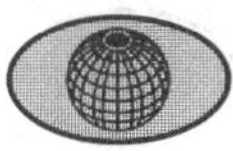   

Kingdom, a part of **HM Treasury** whose remit is to ensure that best accounting practice is observed and conducted across the whole of the Civil Service. *Abbr* **GAS**

government bond STOCKHOLDING & INVESTMENTS investment product issued by government a bond or other security issued by a government on a regular basis as a method of borrowing money for government expenditure

government borrowing FINANCE money government borrows to fund public spending the total amount of money that a country's central government has borrowed to fund its spending on public services and benefits. *See also* ***national debt***

Government Business Enterprise GENERAL MANAGEMENT partly nationalized Australian business an Australian business that is fully or partly owned by the state. *Abbr* **GBE**

Government National Mortgage Association MORTGAGES *see* ***Ginnie Mae***

government securities/stock STOCKHOLDING & INVESTMENTS securities or stock issued by government securities or stock such as US Treasury bonds or UK gilt-edged securities that are issued by a government

GPM *abbr* MORTGAGES graduated payments mortgage

graduated payments mortgage MORTGAGES US mortgage with initial low payments in the United States, a mortgage with a fixed interest rate but with low payments that gradually increase over the first few years. *Abbr* **GPM**

graduated pension scheme PENSIONS former UK government pension linking benefits to individual salaries in the United Kingdom, a government pension arrangement where the benefit was calculated as a percentage of a person's salary. Former contributors still receive payments but there are no new contributors.

graduated tax TAX = ***progressive tax***

grand total FINANCE sum of all subtotals the final total, which is a result of adding several subtotals

granny bond *UK* STOCKHOLDING & INVESTMENTS savings type for older people a long-term savings opportunity for older people, with a tax advantage or a return linked to the rate of inflation (*informal*). *See also* ***index-linked savings certificate***

grant 1. FINANCE money given to fund something money given by a government or other organization to help pay for something such as education or research **2.** LEGAL transfer something legally to somebody else to transfer money, property, or rights to somebody in a legal transaction

grant of probate LEGAL in UK, document certifying validity of will in the United Kingdom, a document that states the validity of a will and upholds the appointment of the executor(s)

grantor STOCKHOLDING & INVESTMENTS seller of option a person who sells an **option** to another person

grapevine GENERAL MANAGEMENT unofficial means of communication an informal communication network within an organization that conveys information through unofficial channels independent of management control. Information travels much more quickly through the grapevine than through formal channels and may become distorted. A grapevine may reinterpret official corporate messages or spread gossip and rumor in the absence of effective organization channels. It can, however, also complement official communication, provide feedback, and strengthen social relationships within the organization.

graph STATISTICS representation of relationship between variables a diagram depicting the relationship between dependent and independent variables through the use of lines, curves, or figures on horizontal and vertical axes. Time is the most common independent variable, showing how the dependent variable has altered over a defined period.

graveyard market MARKETS **1.** market for infrequently traded stocks a market for stock that is infrequently traded either through lack of interest or because of little or no value **2.** market where sellers face large losses a **bear market** where investors who dispose of their holdings are faced with large losses, as potential investors prefer to stay liquid until the market shows signs of improving

gravy train BUSINESS business activity yielding large profits easily any type of business activity in which a person or organization makes a large profit without much effort

gray knight *US* MERGERS & ACQUISITIONS unreliable friendly firm involved in takeover a **white knight** that does not have the confidence of the company to be acquired in a **takeover**. *UK term* ***grey knight***. *See also* ***knight***

gray market *US* **1.** MARKETS unofficial market for stock before official trading an unofficial market run by dealers, in which new issues of stock are bought and sold before they officially become available for trading on a stock exchange, even before the stock allocations become known **2.** MARKETS market for imported goods a **market** in which goods are sold that have been manufactured abroad and imported. A gray market product is one that has been imported legally, in contrast to one on the **black market**, which is illegal. Such markets arise when there is a supply shortage, usually for exclusive goods, and the goods are offered for sale at lower prices than the equivalent goods manufactured in the home country. **3.** MARKETING older people's shopping preferences the market segment occupied by older members of a population ► *UK term* **grey market**

gray marketing *US* MARKETING targeting older people marketing aimed at older age groups such as the middle-aged and elderly. *UK term* ***grey marketing***

gray wave *US* BUSINESS describing companies with good prospects for distant future used to describe a company that is thought likely to have good prospects in the distant future. It gets its name from the fact that investors are likely to have gray hair before they see their expectations fulfilled (*slang*).

Great Depression ECONOMICS 1930s global economic crisis the world economic crisis that began after the US stock market collapsed in 1929 and continued through the 1930s, resulting in mass unemployment and poverty, especially in North America

greater fool theory STOCKHOLDING & INVESTMENTS strategy assuming overpriced stock will attract buyer the investing strategy that assumes it is wise to buy a stock that is not worth its current price. The assumption is that somebody will buy it from you later for an even greater price.

green accounting ACCOUNTING = ***environmental accounting***

greenback CURRENCY & EXCHANGE US paper money a piece of US paper money of any denomination

green card HR & PERSONNEL work permit for noncitizens in US an identity card and work permit issued by the US government to a person living and working in the United States who is not a US citizen. It is officially known as a "United States Permanent Resident Card."

green chips BUSINESS promising small companies small companies considered to have potential for growth

     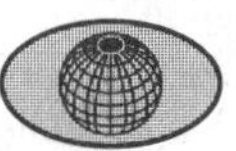   

green currency CURRENCY & EXCHANGE former EU currency for agricultural prices in the European Union, currency formerly used for calculating agricultural payments. Each country had an exchange rate fixed by the Commission, so before the introduction of the euro there were currencies such as "green francs" and "green marks."

green dollar *US* FINANCE spending and investment based on environmental awareness money spent on environmentally sound products and services and investing in companies with environmentally sound policies and practices. *UK term* ***green pound***

green investing STOCKHOLDING & INVESTMENTS investment in green technologies investing in companies developing environmentally sound technologies and products to counter the economic effects of climate change

greenmail MARKETS stock purchase threatening takeover to prompt profitable resale the purchase of enough of a company's stock to threaten it with **takeover**, so that the company is forced to buy back the stock at a higher price to avoid the takeover (*slang*)

Green Paper UK government report on proposed law in the United Kingdom, a report from the government on proposals for a new law to be discussed in Parliament. *See also* ***White Paper***

green pound **1.** *UK* FINANCE = ***green dollar*** **2.** CURRENCY & EXCHANGE monetary unit used for converting EU agricultural prices in the European Union, a currency unit formerly used for converting agricultural prices into pounds sterling

green shoe or **greenshoe option** STOCKHOLDING & INVESTMENTS option in stock issue covering potential shortfall an option offered by a company raising the capital for the issue of further shares of stock to cover a shortfall in the event of overallocation. It gets its name from the Green Shoe Manufacturing Company, which was the first to include the feature in a public offering (*slang*).

green taxes TAX taxes that discourage environmental damage taxes levied to discourage behavior that will be harmful to the environment

Gresham's Law ECONOMICS theory that cheaper money replaces more valuable money the principle that "bad money will drive out good." If two forms of money with the same denomination exist in the same market, the form with the higher metal value will be driven out of circulation because people hoard it and use the lower-rated form to spend.

grey knight *UK* MERGERS & ACQUISITIONS = ***gray knight***

grey market *UK* MARKETS = ***gray market***

grey marketing *UK* MARKETING = ***gray marketing***

grey wave *UK* BUSINESS = ***gray wave***

gross ACCOUNTING without deductions before taxes and other deductions have been taken into account

gross borrowings ACCOUNTING total of firm's loans and overdrafts the total of all money borrowed by a company including items such as overdrafts and long-term loans but without deducting cash in bank accounts and on deposit

gross domestic product ECONOMICS *see* ***GDP***

gross earnings FINANCE total pay before deductions a person's salary or wage before subtracting payroll deductions such as taxes and retirement savings

gross income FINANCE total income before deductions a person's salary or wage plus any other money received from other sources, before subtracting payroll deductions, such as taxes and retirement savings, and any other taxes

gross income yield ACCOUNTING yield before tax the yield of an investment before tax is deducted

gross interest ACCOUNTING interest earned before tax is deducted the interest earned on a deposit or security before the deduction of tax. *See also* ***net interest***

gross lease FINANCE lease that exempts lessee from some payments a lease that does not require the lessee to pay for things the owner usually pays for. *See also* ***net lease***

gross margin **1.** FINANCE difference between borrower's interest payments and lender's costs the difference between the interest rate paid by a borrower and the cost of the funds to the lender **2.** ACCOUNTING percentage difference between income and costs the difference between revenue and cost of revenue expressed as a percentage **3.** OPERATIONS & PRODUCTION difference between unit's manufacturing cost and sale price the difference between the manufacturing cost of a unit of output and the price at which it is sold ► *Abbr* **GM**

gross national product ECONOMICS *see* ***GNP***

gross negligence GENERAL MANAGEMENT failure to act responsibly a breach of a duty to act with expected care in conducting activities. *See also* ***negligence***

gross profit ACCOUNTING difference between total sales revenue and production costs the difference between an organization's sales revenue and the cost of goods sold. Unlike **net profit**, gross profit does not include distribution, administration, or finance costs. *Also called* ***trading profit***

gross profit margin ACCOUNTING *see* ***profit margin***

gross receipts ACCOUNTING total revenue the total revenue received by a business, before tax and other deductions have been taken into account. *See also* ***net receipts***

gross redemption yield *UK* STOCKHOLDING & INVESTMENTS = ***yield to maturity***

gross sales ACCOUNTING sales before discounts the total of all sales before discounts

gross spread MARKETS difference between public's and underwriter's price for security the difference between the price of a security offered to the public and the price the underwriter pays

gross turnover ACCOUNTING total turnover all of a business's income less statutory allowances

gross yield STOCKHOLDING & INVESTMENTS income derived from securities before tax the income return derived from securities before the deduction of tax

gross yield to redemption *UK* STOCKHOLDING & INVESTMENTS = ***yield to maturity***

ground rent REAL ESTATE **1.** rent paid to owner of land under building a rent paid by the main tenant to the owner of the ground on which a building sits **2.** rent paid on vacant land in the United States, a rent paid on land by a tenant to the owner of the land

group BUSINESS firm with subsidiaries a commercial organization consisting of a parent company and subsidiaries under common ownership

group balance sheet ACCOUNTING = ***consolidated balance sheet***

group investment STOCKHOLDING & INVESTMENTS shared investment an investment made by more than one person

group life assurance *UK* INSURANCE = ***group life insurance***

group life insurance *US* INSURANCE life insurance policy covering several individuals a life insurance policy that covers a number

     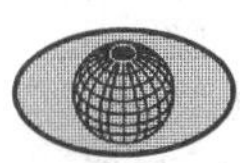   

of people such as members of an association or club, or employees at a company. *UK term* ***group life assurance***

Group of Eight FINANCE *see* ***G8***

Group of Seven FINANCE *see* ***G7***

Group of Ten FINANCE *see* ***G10***

Group of Twenty FINANCE *see* ***G20***

groupthink GENERAL MANAGEMENT desire for agreement that compromises judgment a phenomenon that occurs during **decision making** or **problem solving** when a team's desire to reach an agreement overrides its ability to appraise the problem properly. It is similar to the **Abilene paradox** in that it is based on people's desire to conform and please others.

growth **1.** FINANCE firm's economic increase an increase in productivity, sales, or earnings that an organization experiences **2.** OPERATIONS & PRODUCTION increase in demand for product the second stage in a product life cycle, following the launch, when demand for the product increases rapidly

Growth, Employment, and Redistribution INTERNATIONAL TRADE *see* ***GEAR***

growth and income fund STOCKHOLDING & INVESTMENTS mutual fund seeking capital increase with large dividends a mutual fund that tries to maximize growth of capital while paying significant dividends

growth capital FINANCE funding that firm uses to expand funding that allows a company to accelerate its growth. For new startup companies, growth capital is the second stage of funding after **seed capital**.

growth company BUSINESS firm increasing in size or output a company whose contribution to the economy is growing because it is increasing its workforce or earning increased foreign exchange for its exported goods

growth curve STATISTICS line on graph showing increase over time a line plotted on a graph that shows a statistical increase over a period of time

growth equity STOCKHOLDING & INVESTMENTS promising investment product an equity that is thought to have good prospects of growth, usually with a high price/earnings ratio. *Also called* ***growth stock***

growth fund STOCKHOLDING & INVESTMENTS mutual fund focusing on capital increase a mutual fund that tries to maximize growth of capital without regard to dividends

growth index BUSINESS numerical scale representing firm's economic increase an index showing the growth in a company's revenues, earnings, dividends, or other figures

growth industry FINANCE area of business expanding quickly an industry that is developing and expanding at a faster rate than other industries

growth prospects FINANCE potential for economic increase the likelihood that something such as a specific stock or a country's economy will considerably improve its performance

growth rate ECONOMICS how much and how fast economy is growing the rate of an economy's growth as measured by its technical progress, the growth of its labor force, and the increase in its **capital stock**

growth stock STOCKHOLDING & INVESTMENTS = ***growth equity***

GST *abbr* TAX Goods and Services Tax

GTC *abbr* MARKETS good 'til cancel

GTM *abbr* MARKETS good this month

GTW *abbr* MARKETS good this week

guarantee FINANCE promise to cover another person's contractual duties a promise made by a third party, or guarantor, that he or she will be liable if one of the parties to a contract fails to fulfill their contractual obligations. A guarantee may be acceptable to a bank as security for borrowing, provided the guarantor has sufficient financial means to cover his or her potential liability.

guaranteed bond STOCKHOLDING & INVESTMENTS bond with guaranteed principal and interest a bond on which the principal and interest are guaranteed by an institution other than the one that issues it, or a stock in which the dividends are similarly guaranteed. *Also called* ***guaranteed stock***

guaranteed fund STOCKHOLDING & INVESTMENTS investment whose losses third party promises to cover a fixed term investment where a third party promises to repay the investor's principal in full should the investment fall below the initial sum invested

guaranteed income bond INSURANCE UK life insurance bond providing fixed income a bond issued by a UK life insurance company designed to provide an investor with a fixed rate of income for a specific period of time. Only those policies with an independent third party guarantee can receive this denomination.

guaranteed investment contract *US* INSURANCE investment guaranteeing interest but not principal an investment instrument issued by an insurance company that guarantees interest but not principal

guaranteed renewable policy INSURANCE policy valid as long as payments continue an insurance policy that remains in effect as long as the premiums are paid

guaranteed stock STOCKHOLDING & INVESTMENTS = ***guaranteed bond***

guarantor BUSINESS somebody promising to repay borrower's loan if necessary a person or organization that guarantees repayment of a loan if the borrower defaults or is unable to pay

guarantor of last resort FINANCE person or entity guaranteeing bad debt repayment a person, organization, or government that guarantees repayment of a debt that cannot otherwise be repaid

guardian LEGAL court-appointed person managing affairs of another a person appointed by law to act on behalf of somebody, especially a child, who cannot act on his or her own behalf

guardian ad litem LEGAL somebody representing child in court case a person who acts on behalf of a minor who is a defendant in a court case

gun jumping FINANCE profitable trading based on inside information trading that takes place on the basis of privileged information (*slang*)

gunslinger STOCKHOLDING & INVESTMENTS investment manager investing in high-risk stocks a portfolio manager who invests in high-risk stocks hoping that they will yield high returns (*slang*)

GW *abbr* E-COMMERCE payment gateway

H

haggle FINANCE discuss to agree on price of item to reach a price with a buyer or seller by the gradual raising of offers and lowering of the price asked until a mutually accepted figure is obtained

haircut **1.** FINANCE difference between loan amount and value of collateral the difference between the market value of a security and the amount lent to the owner using the security as collateral **2.** STOCKHOLDING & INVESTMENTS estimate of investment loss an estimate of possible loss in investments

     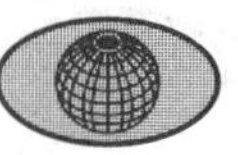   

half-life MORTGAGES years it takes to repay half of mortgage the number of years needed to repay half the principal borrowed on a mortgage

half-normal plot STATISTICS plot of statistical data to identify anomalies a way of plotting statistical data which is used to check for the presence of values in the data that fall outside the expected range

half-stock STOCKHOLDING & INVESTMENTS $50 stock a stock that has a nominal value of fifty US dollars

half-year ACCOUNTING half of accounting period six months for which accounts are presented

hammer MARKETS take firm off London Stock Exchange to remove a business from trading on the London Stock Exchange because it has failed ◇ hammering the market MARKETS the practice of **short selling** by speculators who think prices are about to drop so they can buy back before delivery and make a profit

handle **1.** BUSINESS to deal in particular product, service, or market to buy, sell, or trade in a particular product, service, or market **2.** STOCKHOLDING & INVESTMENTS whole-number price of share of stock or currency the price of a stock or foreign currency, quoted as a whole number

handling charge OPERATIONS & PRODUCTION money charged for preparing goods for dispatch money to be paid for packing, invoicing, or dealing with goods which are being shipped

hand off *US, Canada* GENERAL MANAGEMENT transfer responsibility for project to give responsibility for a project to another person or organization

hand signals MARKETS signs made with hands in stock exchange the signs used by **traders** on the **trading floors** at exchanges for futures and options to overcome the problem of noise

hands-off GENERAL MANAGEMENT without constant supervision characterized by an absence of close and constant management attention

hands-on GENERAL MANAGEMENT closely involved characterized by first-hand personal involvement in the management of an activity

hang out loan FINANCE outstanding amount on loan the amount of a loan that is still outstanding after the termination of the loan

Hang Seng index MARKETS Hong Kong Stock Exchange indicator an index of the prices of selected stocks on the Hong Kong Stock Exchange

hara-kiri swap FINANCE exchange of interest rates with no profit margin an interest rate swap made without a profit margin

hard capital rationing FINANCE *see* ***capital rationing*** *(sense 2)*

hard cash CURRENCY & EXCHANGE money in bills money in the form of bills and coins, as opposed to checks or credit cards

hard commodities MARKETS nonperishable raw materials metals such as copper, zinc, mercury, tin, aluminum, and lead, and other solid raw materials. *See also* ***commodity, soft commodities***

hard currency CURRENCY & EXCHANGE money traded in foreign exchange market a currency that is traded in a foreign exchange market and for which demand is persistently high relative to its supply. *See also* ***soft currency***

hardening FINANCE **1.** stabilizing after changes becoming stable after a period of fluctuation **2.** describing prices that are slowly rising used to describe prices that are slowly moving upward

hard landing ECONOMICS sudden economic recession after growth period the rapid decline of an economy into recession and business stagnation after a sustained period of growth

harmonization **1.** FINANCE equality of financial and social regulation the convergence of financial and social regulation in the countries of the European Union **2.** GENERAL MANAGEMENT equalizing pay and conditions the resolution of inequalities in the pay and conditions of employment between different categories of employees **3.** GENERAL MANAGEMENT equalizing benefits of related companies the alignment of the systems of pay and benefits of two companies that become one by merger, acquisition, or takeover **4.** GENERAL MANAGEMENT equalizing treatment of full- and part-time employees the process of removing differences between groups of employees, such as full- and part-time staff, with regard to terms and conditions of employment such as rates of pay, pension rights, and vacation entitlement

harmonized sales tax TAX Canadian tax on goods and services a Canadian tax on goods and services. It is a value-added tax that replaced the Goods and Services Tax. *Abbr* **HST**

harvesting strategy MARKETING slowing marketing activity before sale of product ends a reduction in or cessation of marketing for a product prior to it being withdrawn from sale, resulting in an increase in profits on the back of previous marketing and advertising campaigns

head and shoulders MARKETS graph showing three rallies in firm's stock price a pattern in a graph plotting a company's stock price which resembles the silhouette of a person's head and shoulders (three rises and falls, with the most pronounced rise and fall in the middle). Analysts see this pattern as an indication of an impending larger fall in price.

headcount reduction HR & PERSONNEL reducing number of employees a reduction in the number of people employed by a company in circumstances such as a drop in the amount of sales

headline rate of inflation ECONOMICS inflation measure including wide range of costs a measure of inflation that attempts to take account of most costs and services. In the United States, the headline rate is based on the Consumer Price Index. In the United Kingdom, it is based on the Retail Price Index, which takes account of homeowners' mortgage costs.

head of household TAX US tax status for somebody with dependents in the United States, a federal tax filing status that qualifies a person to pay less income tax if they are unmarried or considered unmarried on the last day of the year, have paid more than half of the cost of keeping a home for the year, and have had a dependent child or other qualified dependent such as a parent living with them for more than half the year

headquarters or **head office** BUSINESS firm's main office the main office of an organization where most of the administrative work is done and where the board of directors meets

heads of agreement GENERAL MANAGEMENT key items agreed on the most important subjects or items dealt with in a commercial agreement

head tax TAX tax on each adult a tax paid by all adult inhabitants of a country, regardless of their income

health saving account FINANCE US savings plan for medical expenses in the United States, a savings plan with tax benefits that is designed to help individuals accumulate money for qualified medical expenses. *Abbr* **HSA**

health warning STOCKHOLDING & INVESTMENTS message on UK advertisements

  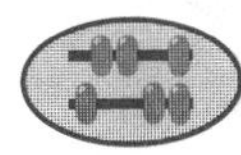   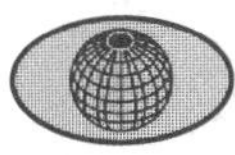   

about risks of investing in the United Kingdom, a legally required warning message printed on advertisements for investments, stating that the value of investments can fall as well as rise (*slang*)

heavy 1. MARKETS experiencing more activity than usual used to describe a market in which trading is more active than usual 2. STOCKHOLDING & INVESTMENTS investing too much in one type of stock having too many investments in related industries or stock 3. STOCKHOLDING & INVESTMENTS high-priced used to describe a stock that has such a high price that small investors are reluctant to buy it. In this case the company may decide to split the stock so as to make it more attractive.

heavy industry OPERATIONS & PRODUCTION manufacturing sector making large products a manufacturing industry that requires a lot of resources, uses heavy raw materials such as coal, and makes large products such as ships or engines

hedge STOCKHOLDING & INVESTMENTS 1. method of protecting against possible loss a protection against a possible loss on an investment which involves taking an action that is the opposite of an action taken earlier 2. take action to reduce risk of investment loss to take measures to offset risk of loss on an investment, especially by investing in counterbalancing securities as a guard against price fluctuations

hedge fund STOCKHOLDING & INVESTMENTS, RISK risky type of investment fund an investment fund that takes considerable risks, including investment in unconventional instruments, in the hope of generating great profits. There are many types of hedge funds, using very different strategies. Some are highly geared and some use arbitrage, futures, and options to achieve their objectives.

hedging STOCKHOLDING & INVESTMENTS, RISK strategy for protecting against possible financial losses financial transactions intended to protect against possible losses from existing financial activities or investments, for example, buying investments at a fixed price for delivery later or investing in counterbalancing securities ◇ hedging against inflation STOCKHOLDING & INVESTMENTS investing in order to avoid the impact of inflation, thus protecting the purchasing power of capital. Historically, equities have generally outperformed returns from savings accounts in the long term and beaten the **retail price index**. They are thus considered as one of the best hedges against inflation, although no stock market investment is without risk.

held order STOCKHOLDING & INVESTMENTS large order that seller waits to process an order that a dealer does not process immediately, often because of its large size

hereditament LEGAL property that can be inherited any property, including personal, land, and buildings, that somebody can inherit

Her Majesty's Revenue & Customs TAX, INTERNATIONAL TRADE UK government department that collects tax in the United Kingdom, the government department responsible for the administration and collection of all forms of tax, including VAT, income tax, and excise duties. HMRC combines the duties of two formerly separate departments, the Inland Revenue and HM Customs and Excise. *Abbr* **HMRC**

Herstatt Risk CURRENCY & EXCHANGE, RISK risk of delivery failure in foreign currency transaction the risk in foreign currency exchange transactions that one party to the exchange will fail to make payment after having received payment from the other party

heuristics GENERAL MANAGEMENT exploration of possible solutions in problem solving a method for problem solving or decision making that arrives at solutions through exploratory means such as experimentation, trial and error, or evaluation

hidden asset ACCOUNTING firm's property recorded at lower than actual value an asset that is shown in a company's accounts as being worth much less than its true market value

hidden economy ECONOMICS = ***black economy***

hidden reserves ACCOUNTING firm's unrecorded reserves funds that are set aside but not declared in the company's balance sheet

hidden tax TAX tax that not everyone is aware of a tax that is not immediately apparent. For example, while a consumer may be aware of a tax on retail purchases, a tax imposed at the wholesale level, which consequently increases the cost of items to the retailer, will not be apparent.

high concept GENERAL MANAGEMENT succinct idea a compelling idea that is expressed clearly and concisely

high-end GENERAL MANAGEMENT of most expensive, advanced, or powerful kind relating to the most expensive, most advanced, or most powerful in a variety of products such as computers

higher rate TAX upper UK income tax rate in the United Kingdom, the higher of the two bands of income tax. **Her Majesty's Revenue & Customs** is responsible for the administration of income tax and publishes information on current tax rates and allowances on its website. *See also* ***basic rate***

high finance FINANCE dealing with very large amounts of money the lending, investing, and borrowing of very large sums of money organized by financiers

high-flier or **high-flyer** STOCKHOLDING & INVESTMENTS stock that increases quickly in price a heavily traded stock that increases in value considerably over a short period

high gearing FINANCE when firm borrows a lot of money a situation in which a company has a high level of borrowing compared to its stock price

high-income STOCKHOLDING & INVESTMENTS describing fund yielding high returns used to describe a fund that yields a high rate of return

highly geared company or **highly-geared company** *UK* BUSINESS = ***highly leveraged company***

highly leveraged company *US* BUSINESS firm with relatively large debts a company that has a large amount of debt in proportion to its equity. *UK term* ***highly geared company***

high net worth individual FINANCE somebody with at least $4 million a person whose net assets, excluding the value of a home, are worth more than $4 million, by some classifications. It is estimated that some 10 million worldwide fall into this category. *Abbr* **HNWI**

high-powered GENERAL MANAGEMENT able and dynamic having, showing, or requiring great dynamism and ability

high-premium convertible debenture STOCKHOLDING & INVESTMENTS bond unlikely to be converted a convertible bond with an exercise price that makes it unlikely to be converted in the foreseeable future. It therefore has a low option premium.

high-pressure MARKETING forceful and persistent used to describe a selling technique in which the sales representative attempts to persuade a buyer forcefully and persistently

high-risk company BUSINESS, RISK firm running high business risks a company that is exposed to high levels of business risk

  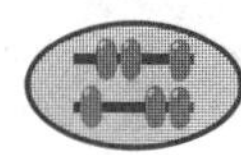 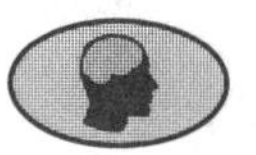  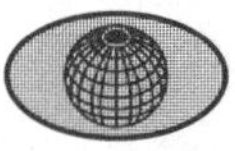   

High Street bank BANKING major UK bank with local offices a UK bank that provides **retail banking** services and has many local offices for customers to visit, as distinguished from an **investment bank** or a bank that provides services only on the Internet

high-tech crime FRAUD crime committed using computer technologies illegal activities using the Internet or other computer technologies. *Also called* ***hi-tech crime***

high yield STOCKHOLDING & INVESTMENTS, RISK higher than usual yield a higher rate of return than is usual for a particular type of investment or company

high-yield bond STOCKHOLDING & INVESTMENTS, RISK = ***junk bond***

high yielder STOCKHOLDING & INVESTMENTS, RISK high-performing but risky investment product a security that has a higher than average rate of return and is consequently often a higher risk investment

hire 1. HR & PERSONNEL give job to somebody to employ somebody new to work for you or your organization **2.** *UK* FINANCE = ***rent***

hire purchase *UK* FINANCE = ***installment plan***

historical cost or **historic cost** ACCOUNTING original cost of item bought in past the record of the value of a firm's asset reflecting its original price when it was purchased

historical cost accounting ACCOUNTING record keeping based on original cost of items the preparation of accounts on the basis of historical cost, with assets valued at their original cost of purchase. *UK term* ***fair value accounting***. *See also* ***current cost accounting***

historical cost depreciation ACCOUNTING discounting asset's value based on original cost the accounting practice of depreciating a firm's asset based on its original cost

historical figures ACCOUNTING figures or values correct at the time figures or values that were correct at the time of purchase or payment, as distinct from a current value

historical summary ACCOUNTING UK report of firm's results in past in the United Kingdom, an optional synopsis of a company's results over a period of time, often five or ten years, featured in the annual accounts

historical trading range MARKETS = ***trading range***

historic pricing STOCKHOLDING & INVESTMENTS basing mutual fund prices on most recent holdings the establishment of the price of a share in a mutual fund on the basis of the most recent values of its holdings

hi-tech crime FRAUD = ***high-tech crime***

HMCE INTERNATIONAL TRADE *see* ***Her Majesty's Revenue & Customs***

HM Customs and Excise INTERNATIONAL TRADE *see* ***Her Majesty's Revenue & Customs***

HMRC *abbr* TAX, INTERNATIONAL TRADE Her Majesty's Revenue & Customs

HM Revenue & Customs TAX, INTERNATIONAL TRADE = ***Her Majesty's Revenue & Customs***. *See* ***IRS***

HM Treasury FINANCE UK government department that manages public funds the UK government department responsible for managing the country's public revenues. While the incumbent prime minister holds the title of First Lord of the Treasury, the department is run on a day-to-day basis by the **Chancellor of the Exchequer**.

HNWI *abbr* FINANCE high net worth individual

hockey stick BUSINESS performance curve that falls then rises sharply a performance curve, typical of businesses in their early stages, that descends then rises sharply in a straight line, creating a shape similar to that of a hockey stick

hold STOCKHOLDING & INVESTMENTS own security for long time to own a security over a long period of time

holdback E-COMMERCE reserve funds covering possible disputed charges funds from a merchant's credit card transactions held in reserve for a predetermined time by the merchant account provider to cover possible disputed charges. *Also called* ***reserve account***

holder FINANCE owner of financial obligation the person who is in possession of a **bill of exchange** or **promissory note**

holder of record STOCKHOLDING & INVESTMENTS official owner of stock the person who is registered as the owner of stock in a company

holding or **holdings** STOCKHOLDING & INVESTMENTS investment owned by somebody an investment, or set of investments, that a person owns at a specific time

holding company BUSINESS parent firm that owns other firms a parent organization that owns the majority of share capital in other companies in order to gain control of them. A holding company may have no other business than the holding of stock in other companies.

holding period STOCKHOLDING & INVESTMENTS period between purchase and sale of asset the length of time an asset was held from the time of purchase to the time of sale, used for determining whether a capital gain or loss is taxed as short-term (less than one year) or long-term (one year or more)

home banking BANKING using computer at home for banking services a system of banking using a personal computer at home to carry out various financial transactions such as paying invoices or checking transactions in a bank account

home loan MORTGAGES money used for house purchase a loan of money to enable the purchase of a house

homeowner's insurance policy *US* INSURANCE insurance for house and contents an insurance policy that protects homeowners against loss of or damage to a home or its contents and provides coverage for personal liability if somebody is injured while on the premises. *UK term* ***household policy***

home policy *UK* INSURANCE = ***homeowner's insurance policy***

home run FINANCE investment with rapid returns an investment that produces a high rate of return in a short time

home trade *UK* BUSINESS = ***domestic trade***

homogenization INTERNATIONAL TRADE imposition of uniformity on separate markets and cultures the removal of characteristic differences between separate markets and cultures. Globalization is frequently blamed for homogenization.

honorarium FINANCE modest payment for simple duties a payment made to somebody for performing a specific service, often a token amount

horizontal diversification BUSINESS developing new but related areas expansion into a related but different product area, for example, a domestic furniture manufacturer producing office furniture. *See also* ***diversification***

horizontal equity ECONOMICS belief in similar taxation for similar incomes the theory that individuals in similar financial situations should be taxed at the same rate

horizontal integration BUSINESS merging of similar functions or organizations the merging of functions or organizations that operate on a similar level. Horizontal integration involves the amalgamation of

  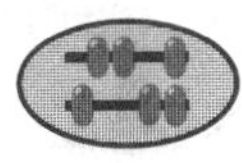 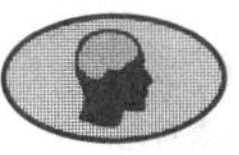  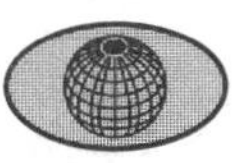   

companies producing the same types of goods or operating at the same stage of the supply chain. It may also describe the merging of departments within an organization that perform similar tasks. *See also* ***vertical integration***

horizontal merger MERGERS & ACQUISITIONS combining of firms in same industry the amalgamation of two or more organizations from the same industry under single ownership, through the direct **acquisition** by one organization of the net assets or liabilities of the other. *See also* ***merger***

horizontal spread STOCKHOLDING & INVESTMENTS, RISK simultaneous buying and selling of two options a purchase of one **option** accompanied by the sale of another with the same **exercise price** but a different date of maturity. *Also called* ***calendar spread***

horse-trading GENERAL MANAGEMENT shrewd bargaining bargaining in which the goods are not directly comparable and the valuations are frequently subjective

hostile bid MERGERS & ACQUISITIONS = ***contested takeover bid***

hostile takeover MERGERS & ACQUISITIONS unwelcome acquisition of firm the acquisition by a company of a controlling interest in the voting share capital of another company whose directors or stockholders are opposed to the action. *See also* ***takeover***

hot card BANKING stolen credit card a credit card that has been stolen and might be used fraudulently

hot issue STOCKHOLDING & INVESTMENTS new investment product expected to perform well a new security that is expected to trade at a significant premium to its issue price. *See also* ***hot stock***

hot money **1.** FRAUD stolen money money that has been obtained by dishonest means. *See also* ***money laundering*** **2.** STOCKHOLDING & INVESTMENTS funds transferred for short-term gain money that is moved on short notice from one financial center to another to secure the best possible return

hot stock MARKETS stock whose price rises rapidly a stock, usually a new issue, that rises quickly on the stock market. *See also* ***hot issue***

house FINANCE finance firm a business organization, especially a financial institution that handles the purchase and sale of securities to investors

house call STOCKHOLDING & INVESTMENTS warning by brokerage firm of low margin account notice from a brokerage firm that the amount of money in a client's margin account is less than the required amount

household policy *UK* INSURANCE = ***homeowner's insurance policy***

house journal GENERAL MANAGEMENT periodic bulletin giving internal information an informal publication issued periodically by an organization or agency to aid the internal communication process

house poor FINANCE with all money invested in house a situation in which the cost of owning a home is too high in proportion to the homeowner's income

HSA *abbr* FINANCE health saving account

HST *abbr* TAX harmonized sales tax

human asset accounting HR & PERSONNEL = ***human capital accounting***

human capital HR & PERSONNEL staff the **employees** of an organization. The term builds on the concept of capital as an asset of an organization, implying recognition of the importance and monetary worth of the skills and experience of its employees. It is measured through **human capital accounting.**

human capital accounting HR & PERSONNEL attempted valuation of employee knowledge and skills an attempt to place a financial figure on the knowledge and skills of an organization's **employees** or **human capital**. *Also called* ***human asset accounting, human resource accounting*** *(sense 1)*

human resource accounting HR & PERSONNEL **1.** = ***human capital accounting*** **2.** record keeping of value of firm's employees the identification, recording, and reporting of the investment in, and return from the employment of, the personnel of an organization

human resource forecasting GENERAL MANAGEMENT estimates of future employment needs and supply the prediction of future levels of demand for, and supply of, workers and skills at organizational, regional, or national level. A variety of techniques are used in manpower forecasting, including the statistical analysis of current trends and the use of mathematical models. At national level, these include the analysis of census statistics; at organizational level, projections of future requirements may be made from sales and production figures. Human resource forecasting forms part of the human resource planning process. *Also called* ***manpower forecasting***

human resource management HR & PERSONNEL management of employees as individuals a model of **personnel management** that focuses on the individual rather than taking a collective approach. It is characterized by an emphasis on strategic integration, employee commitment, workforce flexibility, and quality of goods and services.

human resource planning GENERAL MANAGEMENT efforts to balance employment needs with supply the development of strategies to match the supply of workers to the availability of jobs at organizational, regional, or national level. Human resource planning involves reviewing current personnel resources, forecasting future requirements and availability, and taking steps to ensure that the supply of people and skills meets demand. At a national level, this may be conducted by government or industry bodies, and at an organizational level, by human resource managers. *Also called* ***manpower planning***

hurdle rate **1.** BANKING rate above which loan is profitable for bank a minimum rate of return needed by a bank to fund a loan, representing the rate below which a loan is not profitable for the bank **2.** STOCKHOLDING & INVESTMENTS minimum return before fees due the minimum rate of return required on a fund before the fund manager can begin taking fees **3.** *UK* STOCKHOLDING & INVESTMENTS growth rate needed to repay stock's redemption price the rate of growth in a portfolio required to repay the final fixed redemption price of zero dividend preference shares

hurricane bond STOCKHOLDING & INVESTMENTS, RISK catastrophe bond for hurricane insurance risk a type of **catastrophe bond** that transfers some of the insurance risk from insurers to investors in the event of a hurricane

hybrid STOCKHOLDING & INVESTMENTS combination of investment types a combination of financial instruments, for example, a bond with warrants attached, or a variety of cash and derivative instruments designed to mirror the performance of a financial market

hybrid annuity INSURANCE part fixed part variable annuity a type of **annuity** that combines features of both a fixed annuity (guaranteeing fixed payments to the individual receiving it for the term of the contract, usually until death) and a variable annuity (offering no guarantee but having potential for a greater return, usually based on the performance of a stock or mutual fund). *Also called* ***combination annuity***

  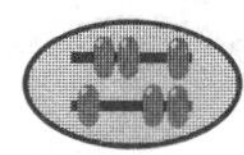  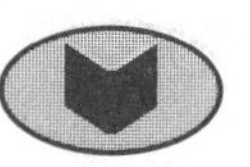 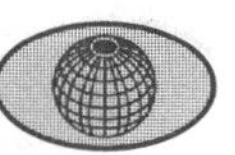   

hybrid financial instrument STOCKHOLDING & INVESTMENTS investment type with features of other types a **financial instrument** such as a convertible bond that has characteristics of multiple types of instruments, often convertible from one to another

hyperinflation ECONOMICS extremely high rate of inflation a very rapid growth in the rate of inflation so that money loses value and physical goods replace currency as a medium of exchange. This happened, for example, in Latin America in the early 1990s and in Zimbabwe in the 2000s.

hyperpartnering E-COMMERCE temporary commercial partnerships using Internet technology a form of commerce in which companies use Internet technology to form partnerships and execute transactions at high speed and low cost in order to take advantage of business opportunities as soon as they appear

hypothecate FINANCE **1.** use real estate to back loan to use the mortgage on real estate as collateral for a loan **2.** use money for defined purpose to designate money, especially public funds, to be used for a specific purpose only

hypothecation FINANCE **1.** using assets as loan collateral without transferring ownership an arrangement in which assets such as securities are used as collateral for a loan but without transferring legal ownership to the lender **2.** designating money for specific purpose the process of earmarking money derived from specific sources for related expenditure, for example, using taxes collected on gasoline sales solely on public transportation

hypothesis testing STATISTICS checking sample data against knowledge of sample the process of testing sample data from a statistical study to determine whether it is consistent with what is known about the sample population

hysteresis ECONOMICS dependency of equilibrium on change the way in which equilibrium is dependent on the changes that take place as an economy experiences change

I

IAS *abbr* TAX, STOCKHOLDING & INVESTMENTS installment activity statement

IASB *abbr* ACCOUNTING International Accounting Standards Board

IASC *abbr* ACCOUNTING International Accounting Standards Committee

IB *abbr* BANKING investment bank

IBOR or **IBR** *abbr* MARKETS Interbank Offered Rate

IBR MARKETS *see* ***Interbank Offered Rate***

IBRC INSURANCE former association of UK insurance brokers in the United Kingdom, a statutory body established under the Insurance Brokers Registration Act of 1977 which was deregulated following the establishment of the Financial Services Authority and the General Insurance Services Council. Its complaints and administration functions passed to the Institute of Insurance Brokers. *Full form* ***Insurance Brokers Registration Council***

IBRD BANKING UN bank that helps poorest nations a United Nations organization that provides funds, policy guidance, and technical assistance to facilitate economic development in its poorer member countries. *Full form* ***International Bank for Reconstruction and Development***

ICA *abbr* INSURANCE Insurance Council of Australia

ICAEW *abbr* ACCOUNTING Institute of Chartered Accountants in England and Wales

ICAI *abbr* ACCOUNTING Institute of Chartered Accountants in Ireland

ICANZ *abbr* ACCOUNTING Institute of Chartered Accountants of New Zealand

ICAS *abbr* ACCOUNTING Institute of Chartered Accountants of Scotland

ICC BUSINESS association to support private business an organization that represents business interests to governments, working to improve trading conditions and foster private enterprise. *Full form* ***International Chamber of Commerce***

ICSA *abbr* UK FINANCE Institute of Chartered Secretaries and Administrators

ICSID *abbr* BANKING International Centre for Settlement of Investment Disputes

IDA *abbr* FINANCE International Development Association

identity theft FRAUD use of another's identity for criminal purpose the use of another person's personal and financial information, such as credit card numbers, Social Security numbers, or passport information, without their knowledge, to commit a crime

idle capital or **idle cash** FINANCE firm's unused money and property the money and assets of a business that are not being invested productively. *Also called* ***barren money, sideline cash***

IDR *abbr* STOCKHOLDING & INVESTMENTS International Depository Receipt

IFA *abbr* **1.** FINANCE independent financial adviser **2.** ACCOUNTING Institute of Financial Accountants

IFAD *abbr* FINANCE International Fund for Agricultural Development

IFC *abbr* FINANCE International Finance Corporation

IFRS *abbr* ACCOUNTING International Financial Reporting Standards

IHT *abbr* US TAX inheritance tax

IIB *abbr* INSURANCE Institute of Insurance Brokers

IIN *abbr* BANKING issuer identification number

ijara or **ijarah** FINANCE agreement by bank to purchase then lease item in Islamic financing, a leasing arrangement in which a bank or financier purchases an item for a customer, then leases it to the customer at a profit

ijara wa-iqtina FINANCE agreement by customer to buy item after leasing it in Islamic financing, a leasing arrangement with a bank similar to ijara in which the customer agrees to purchase the item at a prearranged price at the end of the lease term

ILG *abbr* STOCKHOLDING & INVESTMENTS index-linked gilt

illegal parking STOCKHOLDING & INVESTMENTS, FRAUD concealing true ownership an illegal stock market practice of using another company's name when purchasing securities (*slang*)

illiquid FINANCE **1.** lacking easy access to cash used to describe a person or business that lacks cash or assets such as securities that can readily be converted into cash **2.** not easily convertible to cash used to describe an asset that cannot be easily converted into cash

illiquid market STOCKHOLDING & INVESTMENTS securities market with low trading volume a securities market in which very little trading is taking place

IMA *abbr* STOCKHOLDING & INVESTMENTS **1.** investment management agreement **2.** Investment Management Association

imaginization GENERAL MANAGEMENT business approach encouraging creativity and innovation an approach to creativity

  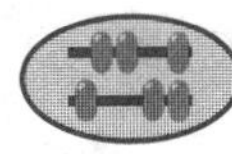   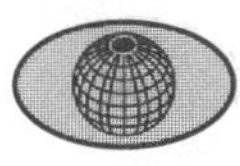   

concerned with improving our ability to see and understand situations in new ways, with finding new ways of organizing, with creating shared understanding and personal empowerment, and with developing a capability for continuing self-organization

IMF FINANCE international lending organization an international organization based in Washington, DC, that was established by industrialized nations to monitor economic and financial developments, lend to countries with balance of payments difficulties, and provide expert policy advice and technical assistance. *Full form* ***International Monetary Fund***

immediate annuity PENSIONS single-premium annuity with immediate payments a type of **annuity** that is purchased with a single premium and whose payments begin immediately

immediate holding company BUSINESS subsidiary UK firm with its own subsidiaries in the United Kingdom, a company with one or more subsidiaries that is itself a subsidiary of another company (the holding company)

immovable property REAL ESTATE land and buildings land and permanent structures such as buildings

impact day MARKETS first day of trading the day when the terms of a new issue of stock are announced

impaired capital FINANCE firm's total capital lower than stock value a company's capital that is worth less than the nominal value of its stock

impaired credit FINANCE when somebody's credit rating is reduced a situation in which a person becomes less creditworthy than before

impairment of capital FINANCE how much firm's stock value exceeds total capital the extent to which the value of a company is less than the nominal value of its stock

imperfect competition MARKETS = ***monopolistic competition***

impersonation of the deceased fraud FRAUD fraud using deceased person's identity in the United Kingdom, a situation in which a person uses the identity of somebody who has recently died to commit a crime such as accessing financial information or obtaining a passport. *Abbr* **IOD fraud**

implicit cost FINANCE cost of using resources owned by producer the cost of using resources that are owned by a company that is producing a good or service. *See also* ***explicit cost***

import INTERNATIONAL TRADE product or service introduced from abroad a product or service brought into another country from its country of origin either for sale or for use in manufacturing

import duty INTERNATIONAL TRADE, TAX tax on imported products a tax on goods imported into a country. Although it may simply be a measure for raising revenue, it can also be used to protect domestic manufacturers from overseas competition.

importer INTERNATIONAL TRADE firm bringing goods into country for sale a company that brings goods from one country to another to be sold

import license INTERNATIONAL TRADE government-issued document allowing importation of goods a document issued by a government which allows goods that are to be sold to be brought into the country from another country

import penetration INTERNATIONAL TRADE proportion of foreign goods in domestic market the degree to which one country's imports dominate the **market share** of those from other industrialized countries

import quota INTERNATIONAL TRADE set amount of product allowed into country a fixed quantity of a particular type of goods, which the government allows to be brought into the country from another country

import restriction INTERNATIONAL TRADE government action limiting goods brought into country an action by a government to reduce the level of imported goods, for example, by setting quotas and imposing duties

import surcharge INTERNATIONAL TRADE, TAX extra tax on imported goods to discourage imports an extra duty levied on imported goods in an attempt to limit imports in general and to encourage local manufacture

imprest account ACCOUNTING type of petty cash record in the United Kingdom, a record of the transactions of a type of petty cash system. An employee is given an advance of money, an imprest, for incidental expenses and, when most of it has been spent, he or she presents receipts for the expenses to the accounts department and is then reimbursed with cash to the total value of the receipts.

imprest system ACCOUNTING petty cash system involving written receipts in the United Kingdom, a system of controlling a petty cash fund, in which cash is paid out against a written receipt, and the receipt is used to get more cash to bring the fund up to the original level

improvement curve GENERAL MANAGEMENT = ***learning curve***

imputation system TAX dividend tax credit for tax paid by firm a system in which recipients of dividends gain tax advantage for taxes paid by the company that paid the dividends

imputed interest FINANCE, TAX taxable interest considered paid but not paid interest that is considered to be paid and may be taxed, even though it has not yet been paid

IMRO *abbr* REGULATION & COMPLIANCE Investment Management Regulatory Organisation

inactive account BANKING bank account that is not in use a bank account that is not used over a particular period of time

inactive market MARKETS market with little trading taking place a stock or commodities market in which there is little interest shown by potential investors, resulting in few trades

'inan BUSINESS business partnership where partners contribute money and work in Islamic financing, a type of partnership in which the partners contribute both capital and work to a business

Inc. *abbr* BUSINESS incorporated

incentive plan *US* FINANCE program rewarding improved performance a program set up to give benefits to employees to reward them for improved commitment and performance and as a means of motivation. An incentive plan is designed to supplement **base pay** and **fringe benefits**. A **financial incentive plan** may offer stock options or a cash bonus, whereas a **nonfinancial incentive plan** offers benefits such as additional paid vacations. Awards from incentive plans may be made on an individual or team basis. *UK term* ***incentive scheme***

incentive scheme *UK* FINANCE = ***incentive plan***

incentive stock option STOCKHOLDING & INVESTMENTS US plan allowing employees to buy stock in the United States, an employee stock option plan that gives each qualifying employee the right to purchase a specific number of the corporation's shares at a set price during a specific time period. Tax is only payable when the stocks are sold.

incestuous share dealing STOCKHOLDING & INVESTMENTS stock trading among firms in same group stock trading by companies

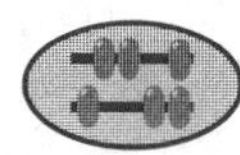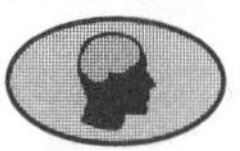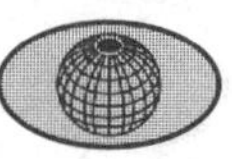

within a group in the stock of the other companies within that group. The legality of such transactions depends on the objective of the deals.

inchoate instrument FINANCE incomplete monetary contract a **negotiable instrument** that is incomplete because, for example, the date or amount is missing. The person to whom it is delivered has the authority to complete it in any way he or she considers fit.

incidence of tax TAX indicating who must pay tax used to indicate where the final burden of a tax lies. For example, although a retailer pays any sales tax to the tax collecting authority, the tax itself is ultimately paid by the customer.

incidental expenses FINANCE small amounts spent on unplanned items small amounts of money spent at various times in addition to the usual larger budgeted amounts

income **1.** FINANCE money received money received by a company or individual **2.** FINANCE money created money generated by a business **3.** STOCKHOLDING & INVESTMENTS interest or dividends received from investments money received from savings or investments, for example, interest on a bank account or dividends from stock

income bond STOCKHOLDING & INVESTMENTS bond repaid from profits a bond that a company repays only from its profits

income distribution **1.** FINANCE, HR & PERSONNEL levels of earnings across group or area the distribution of income across a specific group such as a company or specific area such as a region or country, showing the various wage levels and the percentage of individuals earning at each level **2.** *UK* STOCKHOLDING & INVESTMENTS = ***income dividend***

income dividend *US* STOCKHOLDING & INVESTMENTS money paid to investors from group investment earnings payment to investors of the income generated by a collective investment, less management charges, tax, and expenses. It is distributed in proportion to the number of shares held by each investor. *UK term* ***income distribution***

income elasticity of demand FINANCE demand changing with income a proportional change in demand in response to a change in income

income fund STOCKHOLDING & INVESTMENTS fund focused on high income a fund that attempts to provide high income rather than capital growth

income gearing FINANCE ratio of firm's loan interest payments to profits the ratio of the interest a company pays on its borrowing shown as a percentage of its pre-tax profits

income redistribution ECONOMICS government policy to balance income levels through taxation a government policy to redirect income to a targeted sector of a country's population, for example, by lowering the rate of tax paid by low-income earners

income shares *UK* STOCKHOLDING & INVESTMENTS = ***income stock***

income smoothing ACCOUNTING accounting method to make income appear steady a form of **creative accounting** that involves the manipulation of a company's financial statements to show steady annual profits rather than large fluctuations

incomes policy ECONOMICS UK government policy to limit wage and price increases in the United Kingdom, any government policy that seeks to restrain increases in wages or prices by regulating the permitted level of increase

income statement ACCOUNTING = ***profit and loss account***

income stock *US* **1.** STOCKHOLDING & INVESTMENTS stock expected to pay high dividends common stock sought because of its relatively high yield as opposed to its potential to produce capital growth **2.** MARKETS split fund shares receiving income, not capital appreciation certain funds, for example, investment trusts, that issue split level funds where holders of the income element receive all the income (less expenses, charges, and tax), while holders of the capital element receive only the capital gains (less expenses, charges, and tax) ▶ *UK term* **income shares**

income stream FINANCE money received from product or activity the income received by a company from a particular product or activity

income support FINANCE UK government subsidy for people with low incomes in the United Kingdom, a government benefit paid to low-income earners who are working less than 16 hours per week, and may be disabled or have family care responsibilities. *Abbr* **IS**

income tax TAX tax on money received a tax levied directly on the income of a person or a company and paid to a local, state, or federal government. *Abbr* **IT**

income tax allowance TAX untaxed part of person's income in the United Kingdom, a proportion of somebody's income that is not subject to tax. Allowances are announced each year by the **Chancellor of the Exchequer** in the **Budget**. *See also* ***income tax***

income tax return TAX report of earnings for tax purposes a standard format used for reporting income and computing the tax due on it. *Also called* ***declaration of income***

income unit STOCKHOLDING & INVESTMENTS in UK, share in mutual fund in the United Kingdom, a share in a mutual fund that makes regular dividend payments to its stockholders

income yield STOCKHOLDING & INVESTMENTS = ***current yield***

inconvertible CURRENCY & EXCHANGE describing currency not easily converted used to describe a currency that cannot be easily converted into other currencies

incorporated BUSINESS set up as corporation in the United States, legally established as a corporation. *Abbr* **inc.**

incorporation LEGAL process of forming corporation the legal process of creating a corporation or company. Incorporated entities have a legal status distinct from that of their owners, and limited liability.

incorporeal chattels LEGAL intellectual properties intangible properties such as patents or copyrights

incremental scale *UK* HR & PERSONNEL system of salaries increasing by regular yearly amounts a scale that includes standard increases, especially a salary scale that increases by regular annual amounts

indebted FINANCE owing money to somebody else used to describe a person, company, or country that owes money to another person, a financial institution, or another country

indemnity FINANCE agreement to pay compensation an agreement by one party to make good the losses suffered by another. *See also* ***indemnity insurance, letter of indemnity***

indemnity insurance INSURANCE insurance paid to reimburse damages or losses an insurance contract in which the insurer agrees to cover the cost of losses suffered by the insured party. Most insurance contracts take this form except personal accident and life insurance policies, where fixed sums are paid as compensation, rather than reimbursement, for a loss that cannot be quantified in monetary terms.

indenture STOCKHOLDING & INVESTMENTS agreement about bond a formal document showing the terms of agreement on a **bond issue**

independent authenticator BUSINESS firm that guarantees other firms are genuine a company that has the authority, either from the government or a controlling body, to issue certificates of authentication when they are sure that a company is who it claims to be

independent company BUSINESS firm not owned by another firm a company that is not owned or controlled by any another company

independent financial adviser FINANCE somebody giving unbiased advice about money a person who gives impartial advice to clients on financial matters and who is not employed by any financial institution, although commission for the sale of products may be received. *Abbr* **IFA**. *See also* ***financial planner***

independent variable STATISTICS factor whose change in value affects other factors a factor whose value, when it changes, influences one or more other variables

index **1.** FINANCE amount representing value of group an amount calculated to represent the relative value of a group of things **2.** MARKETS number indicating value of stocks in market a standard that represents the value of stocks in a market, for example, the Hang Seng, Dow Jones Index, or Nikkei average

index arbitrage MARKETS simultaneously trading stocks and stock index futures the buying or selling of a basket of stocks against an index option or future

indexation FINANCE connecting rate to standard price index the linking of a rate to a standard index of prices, interest rates, stock prices, or similar items

indexed portfolio STOCKHOLDING & INVESTMENTS stock in all firms in stock exchange index a portfolio of stock in all the companies that form the basis of a specific stock exchange index

index fund STOCKHOLDING & INVESTMENTS mutual fund linked to stock exchange index a mutual fund composed of companies listed in an important stock market index in order to match the market's overall performance. *Also called* ***index tracker***, ***tracker fund***. *See also* ***managed fund***

index futures STOCKHOLDING & INVESTMENTS futures contract on stock exchange index a **futures contract** trading in one of the major stock market indices such as the **Standard & Poor's 500 Index**. *See also* ***Dow Jones Averages***

index-linked FINANCE changing in relation to numerical scale varying in value in relation to an index, especially the **consumer price index**, or the **retail price index** for index-linked securities in the United Kingdom

index-linked bond STOCKHOLDING & INVESTMENTS investment product with index tied to index a security where the income is linked to an index such as a financial index. *See also* ***index-linked gilt***, ***index-linked savings certificate***

index-linked gilt STOCKHOLDING & INVESTMENTS UK bond with payments linked to retail prices in the United Kingdom, an inflation-proof government bond, first introduced for institutional investors in 1981 and then made available to the general public in 1982. It is inflation-proof in two ways: the dividend is raised every six months in line with the **retail price index** and the original capital is repaid in real terms at redemption, when the indexing of the repayment is undertaken. The nominal value of the stock, however, does not increase with inflation. Like other gilts, ILGs are traded on the market. Price changes are principally dependent on investors' changing perceptions of inflation and real yields. *Abbr* **ILG**

index-linked savings certificate STOCKHOLDING & INVESTMENTS UK savings type with payments linked to inflation rate a certificate issued by the UK National Savings & Investments organization, with a return linked to the **retail price index**. *See also* ***granny bond***

index-linked security *UK* STOCKHOLDING & INVESTMENTS = ***inflation-proof security***

index number ECONOMICS number indicating relative economic change a weighted average of a number of observations of an economic attribute, for example, retail prices expressed as a percentage of a similar weighted average calculated at an earlier period

index of leading economic indicators ECONOMICS predictor of future economic performance a statistical measure that uses a set of economic variables to predict the future performance of an economy

index option STOCKHOLDING & INVESTMENTS option to purchase shares in market index an option to purchase shares in a stock market index. This allows an investor to trade within a particular sector and eliminates some of the risk of investing in individual stocks.

index tracker STOCKHOLDING & INVESTMENTS = ***index fund***

index tracking MARKETS managing stocks to match stock exchange performance an investment technique whereby a portfolio is maintained in such a way as to match the growth in a stock market index

indicated dividend STOCKHOLDING & INVESTMENTS predicted annual dividends if current rate stays same the forecast total of all dividends in a year if the amount of each dividend remains as it is

indicated yield STOCKHOLDING & INVESTMENTS predicted annual income the forecast yield at the current dividend rate

indication price *UK* MARKETS approximate price of investment product an approximation of the price of a security as opposed to its firm price

indicative price MARKETS investment product price as shown on trading screen the price shown on a screen-based system for trading securities such as the UK Stock Exchange Automated Quotations system. The price is not firm, as the size of the bargain will determine the final price at which market makers will actually deal.

indicator STATISTICS something that shows situation's trend over time a variable that, followed over time, gives an indication of a trend with regard to a particular situation

indifference curve ECONOMICS curve on graph representing customers' product satisfaction a line on a graph showing how consumers view different combinations of products. The line joins various points, each point representing a combination of two products, and each combination giving the customer equal satisfaction.

indirect channel MARKETING selling and distribution via intermediary the selling and distribution of products to customers through intermediaries such as wholesalers, distributors, agents, dealers, or retailers

indirect cost ACCOUNTING unchanging expense not directly related to production a fixed or overhead cost that cannot be attributed directly to the production of a particular item and is incurred even when there is no output. Indirect costs may include the **cost center** functions of finance and accounting, information technology, administration, and personnel. *See also* ***direct cost***

indirect labor costs OPERATIONS & PRODUCTION pay for staff not directly involved in production the cost of paying employees such as cleaners or cafeteria staff who are

     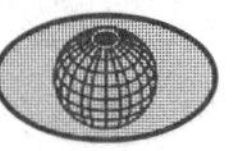   

not directly involved in making a product. Such costs cannot be allocated to a **cost center**.

indirect tax TAX tax not paid directly to government a tax such as sales tax that is not paid directly to the government that levies it but is collected and paid by a third party

indirect taxation TAX process of collecting taxes paid through third party the process of levying taxes that are not paid directly to a government, but are paid through a third party. A sales tax, for example, is paid by the purchaser of a product to the seller, who then pays the tax to the government.

individual retirement account PENSIONS see ***IRA***

Individual Savings Account STOCKHOLDING & INVESTMENTS see ***ISA***

Individual Voluntary Arrangement LEGAL UK payment agreement between debtors and lenders in the United Kingdom, a legally binding arrangement between debtors and creditors by which debtors offer the creditors the best deal they can afford by realizing their assets, thus avoiding the expense of bankruptcy proceedings

induction UK HR & PERSONNEL = ***orientation***

industrial action UK GENERAL MANAGEMENT = ***job action***

industrial dispute UK GENERAL MANAGEMENT = ***labor dispute***

industrial espionage GENERAL MANAGEMENT underhand methods of obtaining rival's commercial secrets the practice of spying on a business competitor in order to obtain its trade or commercial secrets. Information sought through industrial espionage will often refer to new products, designs, formulas, manufacturing processes, marketing surveys, research, or future plans. The goal of industrial espionage is either to injure the business prospects or market share of the target company, or to use the secrets discovered for another organization's commercial benefit.

industrial goods OPERATIONS & PRODUCTION goods produced for industry goods used in industrial processes, including processed or raw materials, machinery, components, and equipment

industrial goods marketing MARKETING marketing of goods to organizations marketing directed at organizations, businesses, and other institutions, rather than at the individual end user of a product. It may require different marketing strategies from those used in **consumer goods marketing** to be effective.

industrial marketing MARKETING marketing of goods or services to organizations the marketing of goods or services to companies, as opposed to individual consumers. Industrial marketing involves a number of key differences from selling to consumers. These include a smaller customer base with higher value or larger unit purchases, more technically complex or specially tailored products, professionally qualified purchasers, closer buyer--seller relationships, and possible group-purchasing decision making. *Also called* ***B2B marketing***

industrial market research MARKETING research into marketing of products to organizations research into the marketing of services and goods to industry, businesses, and other institutions. Industrial market research is used as an aid to **decision making** and concerns the manufacture, selling, and distribution of products with the goal of reducing costs and increasing profits. It considers factors such as the available labor force, location of the firm, export market potential, and use of resources.

industrial production ECONOMICS total output of factories and mines the output of a country's productive industries. Until the 1960s, this commonly related to iron and steel or coal, but since then lighter engineering in automobile or robotics manufacture has taken over.

industrial revenue bond STOCKHOLDING & INVESTMENTS bond to pay for building a bond that a private company uses to finance construction

industrial services marketing MARKETING marketing of services to organizations the marketing of services such as maintenance contracts, insurance, training, transportation, office cleaning, and advertising to industry, businesses, and other institutions. Many services offered to industry are also offered to the consumer, but promoting them to consumers requires strategies derived from **consumer services marketing**.

industrial tribunal HR & PERSONNEL UK court deciding employment disagreements in the United Kingdom, a court that can hear and decide disputes involving employment. These include disputes relating to discrimination, unfair dismissal, breach of contract, and pay.

industry BUSINESS **1.** all components of manufacturing process all factories, companies, or processes involved in the manufacturing of products **2.** companies providing similar products or services a group of companies making the same type of product or offering the same type of service

ineligible bills FINANCE bills unacceptable for discounting those **bills of exchange** that cannot be **discounted** by a central bank

inertia selling MARKETING selling by sending unsolicited goods in the United Kingdom, a method of selling, regarded by some as unethical, that involves the sending of unsolicited goods on a sale or return policy. Inertia selling relies on the passive reaction of a potential purchaser to choose to pay for the goods received rather than undertake the effort to send them back. The receiver of the goods is not bound by law to pay for them but must keep them in good condition until they are collected or returned.

infant industry BUSINESS new area of business an industry in the early stages of development

inference STATISTICS conclusion about statistical population based on observation a conclusion drawn by a researcher about a statistical population after observing individuals in the population

inferior good ECONOMICS item demanded less as income rises a good that a consumer buys in decreasing quantities as his or her income rises. *Also called* ***Giffen good***

infinite capacity plan OPERATIONS & PRODUCTION plan for resource requirements disregarding workstation limitations a plan produced where **capacity requirements planning** does not take account of the capacity constraints of each workstation. *See also* ***capacity requirements planning***

inflation ECONOMICS increase in prices over time a sustained increase in a country's general level of prices which devalues its currency, often caused by excess demand in the economy

inflation accounting ACCOUNTING record-keeping method including effects of inflation the adjustment of a company's accounts to reflect the effect of inflation and provide a more realistic view of the company's position

inflationary ECONOMICS tending to cause increase in prices characterized by excess demand or high costs creating an excessive increase in the country's money supply

  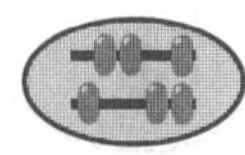   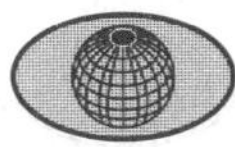   

inflationary gap ECONOMICS situation where demand is greater than production capacity a gap that exists when an economy's resources are utilized and **aggregate demand** is more than the full-employment level of output. Prices will rise to remove the excess demand.

inflationary spiral ECONOMICS cycle of rising prices and wages a situation in which, repeatedly, in inflationary conditions, excess demand causes producers to raise prices and employees to demand wage rises to sustain their living standards. *Also called* ***wage-price spiral***

Inflation linked bond STOCKHOLDING & INVESTMENTS, RISK government bond with inflation protection a bond issued by a government that is indexed to protect against inflation

inflation-proof ECONOMICS indexed to inflation so as to preserve value used to describe a pension, wage, or investment that is indexed to inflation so that its value is preserved in times of inflation

inflation-proof security US STOCKHOLDING & INVESTMENTS security growing with inflation a security that is indexed to inflation or a cost-of-living index. *UK term* ***index-linked security***

inflation rate ECONOMICS rate at which prices increase over time the rate at which general price levels increase over a period of time

inflation target ECONOMICS central bank's goal for increase in prices a range or figure for the rate of increase in prices that the central bank of a country aims to reach at a specific date in the future

inflation tax TAX **1.** government gain from inflation the decrease in buying power imposed by inflation on holders of currency and fixed-return assets, to the government's gain as it inflates the money supply **2.** tax on firms that give large pay raises an income policy that taxes companies that grant pay raises above a specific level

infomediary E-COMMERCE website providing industry information for companies a website that provides and aggregates relevant customer or industry information for other companies

infomercial MARKETING commercial including helpful information a television or cinema commercial that includes helpful information about a product as well as advertising content

info rate MARKETS provisional rate a money market rate quoted by dealers for information only

informal economy ECONOMICS untaxed, unofficial economic activity the economy that runs in parallel to the formal economy but outside the reach of the tax system, most transactions being paid for in cash or goods

information management GENERAL MANAGEMENT acquisition and organization of information the acquisition, recording, organizing, storage, dissemination, and retrieval of information. Good information management has been described as getting the right information to the right person in the right format at the right time.

information space E-COMMERCE Web as information source the abstract concept of all the knowledge, expertise, and information accessible on the Web

infrastructure GENERAL MANAGEMENT basic support system the basic parts of a system that function together to support something, for example, the network and systems that support computing or the public services and facilities that support business activity

ingot CURRENCY & EXCHANGE gold or silver bar a bar of gold or silver

inheritance FINANCE property received from somebody who has died property that is received from somebody through a will or by legal succession

inheritance tax TAX **1.** US tax paid on inherited property in some states of the United States, tax paid on property received by inheritance or legal succession, calculated according to the value of the property received **2.** UK tax paid on estate before distribution to heirs in the United Kingdom, tax payable on wealth or property worth above a specific amount and inherited after somebody's death. The threshold in 2008–9 was £312,000, and the estate is liable for 40% tax on the excess amount. *Abbr* **IHT**

initial capital FINANCE money used for starting firm the money that is used to start a business. Sources of initial capital might include personal funds, bank loans, grants, or credit from suppliers.

initial margin STOCKHOLDING & INVESTMENTS required deposit on open positions the deposit required of members of the **London Clearing House** on all open positions, long or short, to cover short-term price movements. It is returned to members when the position is closed. *See also* ***variation margin***

initial offer STOCKHOLDING & INVESTMENTS in UK, first offer on another firm's stock in the United Kingdom, the first offer that a company makes to buy the stock of another company

initial public offering STOCKHOLDING & INVESTMENTS first time firm's stock are sold the first instance of making particular stock available for sale to the public. *Abbr* **IPO**. *See also* ***flotation***

initial sales OPERATIONS & PRODUCTION product sales when product is new to market the sales of a new product or service immediately after its introduction to the market

initial yield STOCKHOLDING & INVESTMENTS expected yield of new investment fund the yield that an investment fund is estimated to provide at its launch

injunction LEGAL court ruling preventing specific action a court order preventing a person or organization from doing something

inland bill CURRENCY & EXCHANGE in UK, bill belonging to one country in the United Kingdom, a bill of exchange that is payable and drawn in the same country

inland freight charge OPERATIONS & PRODUCTION fee for transporting products within country a charge for transporting goods from one part of a country to another part of the same country

Inland Revenue TAX, INTERNATIONAL TRADE *see* ***Her Majesty's Revenue & Customs***

Inland Revenue Department TAX New Zealand government agency responsible for taxes the New Zealand government body responsible for the administration of the national taxation system. *Abbr* **IRD**

innovation GENERAL MANAGEMENT creation of new product or service the creation, development, and implementation of a new product, process, or service with the goal of improving efficiency, effectiveness, or **competitive advantage**. Innovation may apply to products, services, manufacturing processes, managerial processes, or the design of an organization. It is most often viewed at a product or process level, where product innovation satisfies a customer's needs, and process innovation improves efficiency and effectiveness. Innovation is linked with creativity, and involves taking new ideas and turning them into reality through invention, research, and new product development.

inputs OPERATIONS & PRODUCTION things needed for producing products and services resources such as materials, staff, equipment, and funds that are required to produce a product or service

  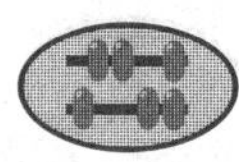 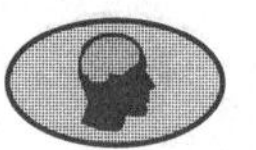  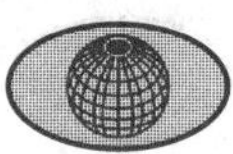   

input tax TAX *see* ***VAT***

input tax credit TAX refund of Canadian Goods and Services Tax in Canada, an amount paid as **Goods and Services Tax** on supplies purchased for business purposes, which can be offset against Goods and Services Tax collected

inside director CORPORATE GOVERNANCE full-time director of firm a director who works full-time in a corporation. *See also* ***outside director***

inside information or **insider information** STOCKHOLDING & INVESTMENTS secret knowledge about firm information that is of advantage to investors but is only available to people who have personal contact with a company

inside quote MARKETS range of buyers' and sellers' prices a range of prices for a security, from the highest offer to buy to the lowest offer to sell

insider BUSINESS somebody with secret information about firm somebody who has access to information that is privileged and unavailable to most members of the public

insider dealing or **insider trading** MARKETS, FRAUD trading stock using secret information profitable, usually illegal, trading in securities carried out using information not available to the public

insolvency FINANCE lacking money to pay debt the inability to pay debts when they become due. Insolvency will apply even if total assets exceed total liabilities, if those assets cannot be readily converted into cash to meet debts as they mature. Even then, insolvency may not necessarily mean **business failure. Bankruptcy** may be avoided through **debt rescheduling** or **turnaround management.**

insolvency practitioner FINANCE UK insolvency specialist in the United Kingdom, a licensed professional who advises on or acts in all formal insolvency procedures

insolvent FINANCE unable to pay debts used to describe a person or business that is unable to pay debts, because the debts are more than the amount of assets that can be readily turned into cash

insourcing GENERAL MANAGEMENT use of internal staff, not external contractor or consultant the use of in-house personnel or an internal department to meet an organization's need for specific services. Insourcing is seen as a reaction to the growing popularity of **outsourcing**, a practice that has not always met expectations.

inspector of taxes TAX UK government tax official in the United Kingdom, an official who reports to HM Revenue & Customs and is responsible for issuing tax returns and assessments, determining tax liabilities, and conducting appeals on tax matters

installment FINANCE one of several payments for initial public offering one of two or more payments made for the purchase of an initial public offering

installment activity statement TAX, STOCKHOLDING & INVESTMENTS Australian form for reporting payments on investment income a standard form used in Australia to report **pay-as-you-go** installment payments on investment income. *Abbr* **IAS**

installment loan *US* FINANCE fixed-interest loan with regular payments a loan that is repaid with fixed regular installments, and with a rate of interest fixed for the duration of the loan. *UK terms* ***instalment credit***

installment plan *US* FINANCE method of paying for purchase with regular payments a method of buying something by paying for it in regular equal amounts over a period of time. *UK terms* ***hire purchase, easy terms***

instalment credit *UK* FINANCE = ***installment loan***

instant access account BANKING UK savings account with easily accessible funds in the United Kingdom, a savings account that pays interest, but from which the account holder can withdraw money immediately whenever he or she needs it

Institute of Chartered Accountants in England and Wales ACCOUNTING UK accounting organization the largest professional accounting body in Europe, providing certification by examinations, ensuring high standards of education and training, and supervising professional conduct. *Abbr* **ICAEW**

Institute of Chartered Accountants in Ireland ACCOUNTING Ireland-wide accounting organization the oldest and largest professional body for accountants in Ireland, the ICAI was founded in 1888. Its many objectives include promoting best practice in chartered accountancy and maintaining high standards of professionalism among its members. It publishes a journal, *Accountancy Ireland*, and has offices in Dublin and Belfast. *Abbr* **ICAI**

Institute of Chartered Accountants of New Zealand ACCOUNTING New Zealand accounting organization the only professional accounting body in New Zealand, representing over 26,000 members in that country and abroad. ICANZ has overseas branch offices in Fiji, London, Melbourne, and Sydney. *Abbr* **ICANZ**

Institute of Chartered Accountants of Scotland ACCOUNTING Scottish accounting organization the world's oldest professional body for accountants, based in Edinburgh. *Abbr* **ICAS**

Institute of Chartered Secretaries and Administrators *UK* FINANCE association of administrators and administrative assistants an organization that works to promote the efficient administration of commerce, industry, and public affairs. Founded in 1891 and granted a royal charter in 1902, it represents the interests of its members to government, publishes journals and other materials, promotes the standing of its members, and provides educational support and qualifying programs. *Abbr* **ICSA**

Institute of Directors CORPORATE GOVERNANCE UK organization for directors of firms in the United Kingdom, an individual membership association whose stated objective is to "serve, support, represent, and set standards for directors." Founded in 1903 by Royal Charter, the IoD it is an independent, nonpolitical body. It is based in London, but also has offices in Belfast, Birmingham, Bristol, Edinburgh, Manchester, and Nottingham. *Abbr* **IoD**

Institute of Financial Accountants ACCOUNTING UK organization for accountants a UK professional organization, established in 1916, that works to set technical and ethical standards in financial accounting. *Abbr* **IFA**

Institute of Financial Services BANKING UK organization for financial education in the United Kingdom, the trading name of the Chartered Institute of Bankers, especially when involved with education

Institute of Insurance Brokers INSURANCE UK association of insurance brokers in the United Kingdom, the professional body for insurance brokers and the caretaker for the deregulated Insurance Brokers Registration Council's complaints program. *Abbr* **IIB**

institutional buyout MERGERS & ACQUISITIONS purchase of firm by financial institution the **takeover** of a company by a financial institution that backs a group of managers who will run it

institutional investor STOCKHOLDING & INVESTMENTS organization that invests an institution such as an insurance company,

     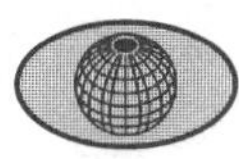   

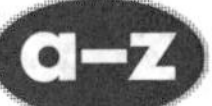

bank, or labor union that makes investments

institutional survey STATISTICS statistical analysis of firms a statistical investigation in which an institution such as a company is the unit of analysis

instrument **1.** FINANCE way of achieving something a means to an end, for example, a government's expenditure and taxation in its quest for reducing unemployment **2.** STOCKHOLDING & INVESTMENTS investment product a generic term for either securities or derivatives. Instruments can be negotiable or nonnegotiable. *See also* ***financial instrument, negotiable instrument*** **3.** LEGAL legal document an official or legal document

insufficient funds FINANCE too little money in bank account for check a lack of enough money in a bank account to pay a check drawn on that account

insurable interest INSURANCE personal interest in insured property a relationship between a person insuring something and the thing insured that would cause the person financial loss if the thing insured were damaged or destroyed

insurable risk INSURANCE quantifiable risk a risk that can be accurately assessed on the basis of past experience and for which insurance policy may be acquired. *See also* ***risk***

insurance **1.** INSURANCE contract to pay for others' losses a legally binding arrangement in which individuals or companies pay another company to guarantee them compensation if they suffer loss resulting from risks such as fire, theft, or accidental damage **2.** MARKETS any method of reducing investment risk in financial markets, hedging or any other strategy that reduces risk while permitting participation in potential gains

Insurance and Superannuation Commission INSURANCE Australian government insurance agency an Australian federal government body responsible for regulating the superannuation and insurance industries. *Abbr* **ISC**

insurance broker INSURANCE somebody who sells insurance a person or company that acts as an intermediary between companies providing insurance and individuals or companies that need insurance

Insurance Brokers Registration Council INSURANCE *see* ***IBRC***

insurance company INSURANCE firm that pays for damage or injury a company whose business is guaranteeing people compensation if they suffer financial loss as a result of events such as death, fire, and accidental damage

Insurance Council of Australia INSURANCE Australian organization supporting insurance firms an independent body representing the interests of businesses involved in the insurance industry. It was established in 1975 and currently represents around 110 companies. *Abbr* **ICA**

insurance coverage INSURANCE guaranteed compensation for specified risks the type and amount of compensation against specific risks that is guaranteed by an **insurance policy**

insurance intermediary INSURANCE somebody that gives insurance advice and arranges policies a person or company that provides advice on insurance and can arrange policies. *See also* ***IIB, IBRC***

insurance policy INSURANCE contract specifying terms of insurance a document that sets out the terms and conditions for providing compensation against specific risks

insurance premium INSURANCE regular payment to insurance firm a regular payment made by a person or a company to a company for a specific **insurance policy**

insurance premium tax TAX UK tax on general insurance in the United Kingdom, a tax on household, motor vehicle, travel, and other general insurance

insurance reserves *US* INSURANCE insurance firm's funds in reserve the assets that an insurance company maintains to meet future claims or losses. *UK term* ***technical reserves***

insure INSURANCE **1.** agree to compensate in declared circumstances to make a contract to pay compensation if a particular loss or event occurs **2.** *US* insure somebody's life to insure somebody's life, so that the insurance company will pay compensation when that person dies. *UK term* ***assure***

insured INSURANCE protected by insurance covered by a contract of insurance for specific risks such as loss, damage, illness, or death

insured account INSURANCE US bank account protected by insurance in the United States, an account with a bank or savings institution that belongs to a federal or private insurance organization

insured bond STOCKHOLDING & INVESTMENTS bond protected by insurance a bond whose principle and interest payments are insured against default

insurer INSURANCE insurance provider a company that provides insurance for a variety of risks

intangible asset FINANCE non-material resource an asset such as intellectual property or **goodwill**. *Also called* ***invisible asset***. *See also* ***tangible asset***

intangibles FINANCE non-material costs and benefits to business the benefits to a business such as customer goodwill and employee loyalty, and costs such as training time and lost production, that cannot easily be quantified

integrated implementation model GENERAL MANAGEMENT product development with simultaneous stages a model of **new product development** that strives to achieve both flexibility and acceleration of development. All activities such as design, production planning, and test marketing are performed in parallel rather than going through a sequential linear progression. *See also* ***new product development***

integration BUSINESS joining business under central authority the act of bringing several businesses together under a central control

intellectual assets FINANCE knowledge, experience, and skills of workers the knowledge, experience, and skills of its staff that an organization can make use of

intellectual capital FINANCE firm's combined intangible assets the combined intangible assets owned or controlled by a company or organization that provide **competitive advantage**. Intellectual capital assets can include the knowledge and expertise of employees, brands, customer information and relationships, contracts, **intellectual property** such as patents and copyright, and organizational technologies, processes, and methods. Intellectual capital can be implicit and intangible, stored in people's heads, or explicit and documented in written or electronic format.

intellectual property FINANCE ownership of items such as copyrights and patents the ownership of rights to ideas, designs, and inventions, including **copyrights**, **patents**, and **trademarks**. Intellectual property is protected by law in most countries, and the World Intellectual Property Organization is responsible for harmonizing the law across different countries and promoting the protection of intellectual property rights.

intellectual property crime FRAUD crime involving counterfeiting and copyright piracy illegal activities involving the manufacture and distribution of counterfeit and copyrighted products

intellectual property rights LEGAL rights to ownership of intellectual property the legal rights a person or company has to the ownership of their ideas, designs, and inventions, including **copyrights**,**patents**, and **trademarks**. *Abbr* **IPRs**

interactive planning GENERAL MANAGEMENT process allowing participation in futures design and achievement a process that promotes participation in both the design of a desirable future and the developments that enable this future to be achieved rather than waiting for it to happen. Interactive planning is associated with Russell Ackoff, and was outlined in *Creating the Corporate Future* (1981).

interbank loan BANKING loan made to another bank a loan that one bank makes to another bank

interbank market MARKETS, BANKING lending of money amongst banks a market in which banks lend money to or borrow money from each other for short periods

Interbank Offered Rate or **Interbank Rate** MARKETS interest rate that banks charge each other the rate of interest at which banks lend to each other on the **interbank market**. *Abbr* **IBOR**

interchange E-COMMERCE, BANKING transaction between issuing and acquiring banks a transaction between an **acquirer** and an **issuer**

interchangeable bond STOCKHOLDING & INVESTMENTS bond whose form can be changed a bond whose owner can change it at will between registered and coupon form, sometimes for a fee

interchange fee E-COMMERCE, BANKING charge on interchange, paid by acquiring bank the charge on a transaction between the acquiring bank and the issuing bank, paid by the acquirer to the issuer

intercommodity spread STOCKHOLDING & INVESTMENTS options for purchase and sale of related goods a combination of purchase and sale of options for related commodities with the same delivery date

intercompany pricing OPERATIONS & PRODUCTION setting prices for product sales between firms the setting of prices by companies within a group to sell products or services to each other, rather than to external customers

inter-dealer broker STOCKHOLDING & INVESTMENTS intermediary between dealers a broker who arranges transactions between dealers in government securities

interest FINANCE borrowing charge or payment the rate that a lender charges for a loan or **credit facility**, or a payment made by a financial institution for the use of money deposited in an account

interest arbitrage *UK* FINANCE switching funds between countries for higher interest rates transactions in two or more financial centers in order to make an immediate profit by exploiting differences in interest rates. *See also* ***arbitrage***

interest assumption FINANCE predicted amount of interest the expected rate of return on a portfolio of investments

interest-bearing FINANCE paying or requiring interest used to describe a deposit, account, shares, etc., that pay interest, or a loan that requires interest

interest-bearing account or **interest-bearing deposit** BANKING money in bank account that earns interest a deposit of money, or a bank account, that receives interest

interest charge BANKING fee paid for borrowing money an amount of money paid by a borrower as interest on a loan

interest cover FINANCE amount of money available for payment of interest the amount of earnings available to make interest payments after all operating and nonoperating income and expenses, except interest and income taxes, have been accounted for.

Interest cover is regarded as a measure of a company's creditworthiness because it shows how much income there is to cover interest payments on outstanding debt.

It is expressed as a ratio, comparing the funds available to pay interest (earnings before interest and taxes, or EBIT) with the interest expense. The basic formula is

$$\frac{\text{EBIT}}{\text{Interest expense}} = \text{Interest coverage ratio}$$

If interest expense for a year is $9 million, and the company's EBIT is $45 million, the interest coverage would be

$$\frac{45\text{ million}}{9\text{ million}} = 5{:}1$$

The higher the number, the stronger a company is likely to be. A ratio of less than 1 indicates that a company is having problems generating enough cash flow to pay its interest expenses, and that either a modest decline in operating profits or a sudden rise in borrowing costs could eliminate profitability entirely. Ideally, interest coverage should at least exceed 1.5; in some sectors, 2.0 or higher is desirable.

Variations of this basic formula also exist. For example, there is:

$$\frac{\text{Operating cash flow + Interest + Taxes}}{\text{Interest}} = \text{Cash flow interest coverage ratio}$$

This ratio indicates the firm's ability to use its cash flow to satisfy its fixed financing obligations. Finally, there is the fixed-charge coverage ratio, that compares EBIT with fixed charges:

$$\frac{\text{EBIT + Lease expenses}}{\text{Interest + Lease expenses}} = \text{Fixed-charge coverage ratio}$$

"Fixed charges" can be interpreted in many ways, however. It could mean, for example, the funds that a company is obliged to set aside to retire debt, or dividends on preferred stock.

interested party BUSINESS somebody with financial relationship to firm a person or company that has a financial interest in a company

interest-elastic investment STOCKHOLDING & INVESTMENTS investment with variable rate of return an investment with a rate of return that varies with the rise and fall of interest rates

interest expense FINANCE cost of borrowing money the cost of the interest payments on borrowed money

interest-free credit FINANCE loan for which no fee is charged credit or a loan on which no interest is paid by the borrower

interest group GENERAL MANAGEMENT group promoting members' interests a group that is concerned with promoting the economic interests of its members, for example, a business association, professional association, or labor union

interest-inelastic investment STOCKHOLDING & INVESTMENTS investment with fixed rate of return an investment with a rate of return that does not vary with the rise and fall of interest rates

interest in possession trust FINANCE UK trust whose income can be distributed immediately in the United Kingdom, a trust that gives one or more beneficiaries an immediate right to receive any income generated by the trust's assets. It can be used for real estate, enabling the beneficiary either to enjoy the rent generated by the property or to reside there, or as a life policy, a common arrangement for inheritance tax planning.

interest-only mortgage MORTGAGES loan on which interest is paid before principal a long-term loan, usually for the purchase of

  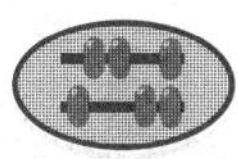 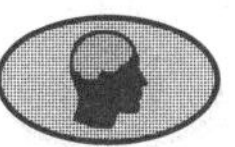  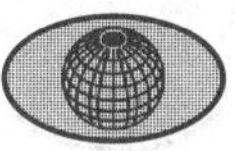 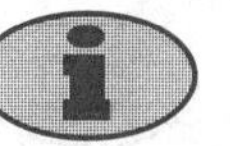  

real estate, in which the borrower only pays interest to the lender during the term of the mortgage, with the principal being repaid at the end of the term. It is thus the borrower's responsibility to make provisions to accumulate the required capital during the period of the mortgage. *See also* ***mortgage***

interest payment FINANCE borrowing or lending charge an amount of money paid by a financial institution for the use of money deposited in an account, or money paid by a borrower as interest on a loan

interest rate FINANCE percentage of money charged for borrowing the amount of interest charged for borrowing a sum of money over a specific period of time

interest rate cap MORTGAGES highest allowed interest rate an upper limit on a rate of interest, for example, in an adjustable-rate mortgage

interest rate effect ECONOMICS interest rate change leading to increased investment the increase in investment that takes place when companies take advantage of lower interest rates to invest more

interest rate exposure *UK* FINANCE possible loss related to changes in interest rates the risk of a loss associated with movements in the level of interest rates. *See also* ***bond***

interest rate floor MORTGAGES lowest allowed interest rate a lower limit on a rate of interest, for example, in an adjustable-rate mortgage

interest rate future MARKETS futures contract for interest a **futures contract** with an underlying asset that bears interest. *See also* ***future***

interest rate guarantee FINANCE **1.** limit on fluctuation a limit that is set to prevent interest rates moving outside a specific range **2.** legal protection from interest-rate changes a tailored indemnity protecting the purchaser against future changes in interest rates

interest rate option STOCKHOLDING & INVESTMENTS contract for interest a contract conferring the right but not an obligation to pay or receive a specific interest rate under stated terms. *See also* ***option***

interest rate risk FINANCE risk of investment loss due to rising interest the risk that the value of a fixed-income investment will decrease if interest rates rise

interest rate swap FINANCE trade of loans with different interest rates an exchange of two debt instruments with different rates of interest, made to tailor cash flows to the participants' different requirements. Most commonly a longer-term fixed rate is swapped for a shorter-term floating one.

interest-sensitive FINANCE affected by changes in interest rates used to describe assets, generally purchased with credit, that are in demand when interest rates fall but considered less attractive when interest rates rise

interest yield FINANCE set rate of return paid on investment a rate of gain generated by an investment that pays a fixed rate of return, usually a percentage of the amount invested

interfirm cooperation GENERAL MANAGEMENT agreement between firms to collaborate commercially a formal or informal agreement between organizations to collaborate in achieving common or new goals more efficiently or effectively. Interfirm cooperation may take the form of a **joint venture**.

interim certificate LEGAL document showing partial stock ownership a **certificate of deposit** certifying partial ownership of stock that is not totally paid for at one time

interim dividend STOCKHOLDING & INVESTMENTS dividend for part of tax year a dividend whose value is determined on the basis of a period of time of less than a full **fiscal year**

interim financial statement FINANCE financial statement for part of tax year only a financial statement that covers a period other than a full **fiscal year**. Although UK companies are not legally obliged to publish interim financial statements, those listed on the London Stock Exchange are obliged to publish a half-yearly report of their activities and a profit and loss account that may either be sent to stockholders or published in a national newspaper. In the United States, the practice is to issue quarterly financial statements. *Also called* ***interim statement***

interim financing FINANCE providing of temporary finance financing by means of bridge loans, between the purchase of one asset and the sale of another

interim payment STOCKHOLDING & INVESTMENTS partial payment of dividend early in year a distribution to stockholders of part of a dividend in the first part of a financial year

interim statement FINANCE = ***interim financial statement***

intermarket spread MARKETS trading in similar options in different markets a combination of purchase and sale of options for the same commodity with the same delivery date on different markets

intermediary FINANCE agent for financial transactions a person or organization that arranges financing, insurance, or investments for others

intermediate goods OPERATIONS & PRODUCTION items for producing other items goods bought for use in the production of other products

intermediation FINANCE acting as agent in financial transaction the process of arranging financing through an intermediary. Financial institutions act as intermediaries when they lend depositors' money to borrowers.

internal audit RISK audit by firm's own employees an audit of a company undertaken by its employees, usually to check on its internal controls. *See also* ***external audit***

internal benchmarking GENERAL MANAGEMENT *see* ***benchmarking***

internal consultant GENERAL MANAGEMENT expert within company advising colleagues an employee who uses knowledge and expertise to offer advice or business solutions to another department or business unit within an organization

internal consulting GENERAL MANAGEMENT advising colleagues elsewhere in firm the activity of offering advice or business solutions to another department or business unit within an organization. *See also* ***internal consultant***

internal control GENERAL MANAGEMENT management system for controlling firm's activities a system set up by the management of a company to monitor and control the company's activities

internal cost analysis ACCOUNTING investigation into organization's activities to establish profitable areas an examination of an organization's value-creating activities to determine sources of profitability and to identify the relative costs of different processes. Internal cost analysis is a tool for analyzing the **value chain**. Principal steps include identifying those processes that create value for the organization, calculating the cost of each value-creating process against the overall cost of the product or service, identifying the cost components for each process, establishing the links between the processes, and working out the opportunities for achieving relative cost advantage.

internal differentiation analysis GENERAL MANAGEMENT assessment of what makes product or service distinctive an examination of processes in the **value chain** to determine which of them create differentiation of the product or service in the customer's eyes, and thus enhance its value. Internal differentiation analysis enables an organization to focus on improving the identified processes to maximize **competitive advantage**. Steps involve identification of value-creating activities, evaluation of strategies that can enhance value for the customer, and assessment of which differentiation strategies are the most sustainable.

internal growth BUSINESS growth by developing existing business organic growth created within a business, for example, by inventing new products and so increasing its market share, producing products that are more reliable, offering a more efficient service than its competitors, or being more aggressive in its marketing. *See also* ***external growth***

internal marketing MARKETING implementation of marketing principles within organization the application of the principles of marketing within an organization. Internal marketing involves the creation of an internal market by dividing departments into business units, with control over their own operations and expenditure, with attendant impacts on corporate culture, politics, and power. Internal marketing also involves treating employees as internal customers with the goal of increasing employees' motivation and focus on customers.

internal rate of return FINANCE interest rate indicating worthwhile profit in a discounted cash flow calculation, the rate of interest that reduces future income streams to the cost of the investment; practically speaking, the rate that indicates whether or not an investment is worth pursuing.

Let's assume that a project under consideration costs $7,500 and is expected to return $2,000 per year for five years, or $10,000. The IRR calculated for the project would be about 10%. If the cost of borrowing money for the project, or the return on investing the funds elsewhere, is less than 10%, the project is probably worthwhile. If the alternative use of the money will return 10% or more, the project should be rejected, since from a financial perspective it will break even at best.

Typically, managements require an IRR equal to or higher than the cost of capital, depending on relative risk and other factors.

The best way to compute an IRR is by using a spreadsheet (such as Excel) or financial calculator.

If using Excel, for example, select the IRR function. This requires the annual cash flows to be set out in columns and the first part of the IRR formula requires the cell reference range of these cash flows to be entered. Then a guess of the IRR is required. The default is 10%, written 0.1.

If a project has the following expected cash flows, then guessing IRR at 30% returns an accurate IRR of 27%, indicating that if the next best way of investing the money gives a return of –20%, the project should go ahead.

Now	–2,500
Year 1	1,200
Year 2	1,300
Year 3	1,500

IRR can be misleading, especially as significant costs will occur late in the project. The rule of thumb "the higher the IRR the better" does not always apply. For the most thorough analysis of a project's investment potential, some experts urge using both IRR and net present value calculations, and comparing their results. *Abbr* **IRR**

Internal Revenue Code TAX US federal tax laws the complex series of federal tax laws in the United States

Internal Revenue Service TAX *see* ***IRS***

internal trade BUSINESS trade within one country commercial activity that is carried out within a specific country. *Also called* ***home trade***. *See also* ***external trade***

internal versus external sourcing OPERATIONS & PRODUCTION = ***purchasing versus production***

International Accounting Standards Board ACCOUNTING organization that sets accounting standards an independent and privately funded standard-setting organization for the accounting profession, based in London. The Board, whose members come from nine countries and a variety of backgrounds, is committed to developing a single set of high quality, understandable, and enforceable global standards that require transparent and comparable information in general purpose financial statements. It also works with national accounting standard setters to achieve convergence in accounting standards around the world. *Abbr* **IASB**

International Accounting Standards Committee ACCOUNTING former organization promoting international agreement on accounting standards formerly, an organization based in London that worked toward achieving global agreement on accounting standards, replaced by the **International Accounting Standards Board**. *Abbr* **IASC**

International Bank for Reconstruction and Development BANKING *see* ***IBRD***

International Centre for Settlement of Investment Disputes BANKING part of World Bank Group one of the five institutions that comprise the World Bank Group, based in Washington, DC. It was established in 1966 to undertake the role previously undertaken in a personal capacity by the president of the World Bank in assisting in mediation or conciliation of investment disputes between governments and private foreign investors. The overriding consideration in its establishment was that a specialist institution could help to promote increased flows of international investment. Although ICSID has close links to the World Bank, it is an autonomous organization. *Abbr* **ICSID**

International Chamber of Commerce BUSINESS *see* ***ICC***

International Depository Receipt STOCKHOLDING & INVESTMENTS outside US, document indicating ownership of stock the equivalent of an **American depository receipt** in the rest of the world, an IDR is a negotiable certificate issued by a bank that indicates ownership of stock. *Abbr* **IDR**

International Development Association FINANCE agency helping poorest nations an agency administered by the International Bank for Reconstruction and Development to provide assistance on concessionary terms to the poorest countries. Its resources consist of subscriptions and general replenishments from its more industrialized and developed members, special contributions, and transfers from the net earnings of the International Bank for Reconstruction and Development. *Abbr* **IDA**

International Finance Corporation FINANCE UN agency encouraging private investment in developing nations a United Nations organization promoting private sector investment in developing countries to reduce poverty and improve the quality of people's lives. It finances private sector projects that are profit-oriented and environmentally and socially sound, and helps to foster development. The

  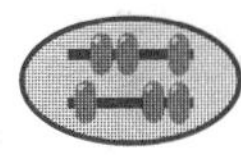   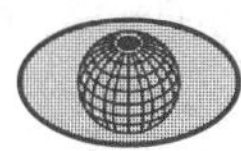   

International Finance Corporation has a staff of 2,000 professionals around the world who seek profitable and creative solutions to complex business issues. *Abbr* **IFC**

International Financial Reporting Standards ACCOUNTING standards for preparing financial statements a set of rules and guidelines established by the **International Accounting Standards Board** for standardizing the preparation of financial statements so that investors, organizations, and governments have a basis for comparison. *Abbr* **IFRS**

international fund FINANCE mutual fund with domestic and foreign investments a mutual fund that invests in securities both inside and outside a country

International Fund for Agricultural Development FINANCE UN agency in poor countries a specialized United Nations agency with a mandate to combat hunger and rural poverty in countries with developing economies. Established as an international financial institution in 1977 following the 1974 World Food Conference, it has financed projects in over 100 countries and independent territories, to which it has committed US$7.7 billion in grants and loans. It has three sources of finance: contributions from members, loan payments, and investment income. *Abbr* **IFAD**

International Monetary Fund FINANCE *see* ***IMF***

international money market MARKETS, CURRENCY & EXCHANGE exchange of foreign currencies a market in which currencies can be borrowed and lent and converted into other currencies

International Organization of Securities Commissions REGULATION & COMPLIANCE institution overseeing international securities transactions an organization of securities commissions from around the world, based in Madrid. Its objectives are to promote high standards of regulation, exchange information, and establish standards for, and effective surveillance of, international securities transactions. *Abbr* **IOSCO**

international reserves CURRENCY & EXCHANGE = ***foreign currency reserves***

International Securities Market Association MARKETS association concerned with international securities market the self-regulatory organization and trade association for the international securities market. Its primary role is to oversee the fast-changing marketplace through the issuing of rules and recommendations relating to trading and settlement practices. Established in 1969, the organization has over 600 members from 51 countries. *Abbr* **ISMA**

International Swaps and Derivatives Association STOCKHOLDING & INVESTMENTS organization for derivative traders a professional association for international traders in derivatives, founded in 1985. *Abbr* **ISDA**

international trade INTERNATIONAL TRADE buying and selling activity between countries the sale and purchase of goods and services that takes place between trading partners in different countries

International Union of Credit and Investment Insurers INSURANCE association concerned with exports and foreign investments an organization that works for international acceptance of sound principles of export credit and foreign investment insurance. Founded in 1934, the London-based Union has 51 members in 42 countries that play a role of central importance in world trade, both as regards exports and foreign direct investments. *Also called* ***Berne Union***

Internet merchant E-COMMERCE businessperson selling over Internet a businessperson who sells a product or service over the Internet

Internet payment system E-COMMERCE fund transfer system using Internet any mechanism for fund transfer from customer to merchant or business to business via the Internet. There are many payment options available, including credit card payment, credit transfer, electronic checks, direct debit, smart cards, prepaid plans, loyalty plan points-based approaches, person-to-person payments, and cellphone plans.

Getting the online payment system right is critical to the success of e-commerce. Currently, the most common form of online consumer payment is by credit card (90% in the United States; 70% in Europe). The most common business-to-business payments, however, are still offline, probably because such transactions often involve large sums of money.

Good online payment systems share key characteristics: ease of use; robustness and reliability; proper authentication (to combat fraud); efficient integration with the vendor's own internal systems; and security and assurance procedures that check that the seller gets the money and the buyer gets the goods.

Internet security E-COMMERCE protection of computer files from unauthorized access the means used to protect websites and other electronic files from attack by hackers and viruses. The Internet is, by definition, a network; networks are open, and are thus open to attack. A poor Internet security policy can result in a substantial loss of productivity and a drop in consumer confidence.

interpolation STATISTICS way of calculating approximate value a method of estimating an unknown value such as a return on an investment using values that are known

interquartile range STATISTICS difference between first and third quartiles the difference between the first and third quartiles of a statistical sample, used to measure the spread of variables in the data

interstate commerce BUSINESS trade between US states in the United States, commerce that involves more than one state and is therefore subject to regulation by Congress. *See also* ***intrastate commerce***

intervention ECONOMICS government action to influence market forces government action to manipulate market forces for political or economic purposes

intervention mechanism CURRENCY & EXCHANGE central banks' means of maintaining fixed exchange rates a method such as buying or selling of foreign currency used by central banks in maintaining equivalence between exchange rates

inter vivos trust FINANCE trust set up between living people a legal arrangement for managing somebody's money or property, set up by one living person for another living person

in the money STOCKHOLDING & INVESTMENTS having intrinsic value used to describe an option that, if it expired at the current market price, would have significant **intrinsic value**. *See also* ***out of the money***

intraday MARKETS during one trading day within a single day of trading

intrapreneur GENERAL MANAGEMENT worker deploying entrepreneurial skills within firm an employee who uses the approach of an entrepreneur within an organizational setting. An intrapreneur must have freedom of action to explore and implement ideas, although the outcome of such work will be owned by the organization rather than the intrapreneur, and it is the organization that will take the associated risk. Managers of organizations in which intrapreneurs are allowed to operate subscribe to the view that innovation can be achieved by encouraging creative and exploratory activity in semiautonomous units.

intrastate commerce BUSINESS trade within US state in the United States, commerce that occurs within a single state. *See also* ***interstate commerce***

intrinsic value STOCKHOLDING & INVESTMENTS gap between share price and option price with reference to an option or convertible, the value at which a security would trade if there were no **option premium**, i.e. the share price less the option price

introducing broker STOCKHOLDING & INVESTMENTS broker not paid directly by customers a person or organization acting as a broker but not able to accept payment from customers

introduction 1. MARKETING making product available for first time an act of bringing something into existence or operation for the first time, for example, bringing a new product onto the market for sale for the first time **2.** MARKETS initially listing established company on stock exchange the act of bringing an established company to the Stock Exchange. It is done by getting permission for the shares to be traded on the Stock Exchange, and is used when a company is formed by splitting from an existing larger company and no new shares are being offered for sale.

inventory 1. OPERATIONS & PRODUCTION firm's supply of finished and unfinished products the supply of finished goods, raw materials, and work in progress held by a company **2.** BUSINESS all commercial assets owned in the United States, the sum total of the commercial assets of an organization

inventory control OPERATIONS & PRODUCTION keeping optimal level of merchandise on hand the process of making sure that the correct level of inventory is maintained, to be able to meet demand while keeping the costs of holding inventory to a minimum

inventory depreciation ACCOUNTING reduction in value of stored stock a reduction in value of inventory that is held in a warehouse for some time

inventory financing FINANCE obtaining loans against product inventory a method by which manufacturers of consumer products obtain a loan by using their inventory as collateral

inventory record OPERATIONS & PRODUCTION firm's record of inventory a record of the **inventory** held by an organization. An inventory record forms an important part of material requirements planning systems. Such records usually make use of some form of part numbering or classification system, and include a description of the part, the quantity held, and the location of all the holdings. A **transaction file** keeps track of inventory use and replenishment.

inventory turnover 1. ACCOUNTING replacement rate of commercial assets an accounting ratio of the number of times **inventory** is replaced during a given period. The ratio is calculated by dividing net sales by average inventory over a given period. Values are expressed as times per period, most often a year, and a higher figure indicates a more efficient manufacturing operation.

It is calculated as follows:

$$\frac{\text{Cost of goods sold}}{\text{Inventory}}$$

If COGS is $2 million, and inventory at the end of the period is $500,000, then

$$\frac{2{,}000{,}000}{500{,}000} = 4$$

Also called ***stock turns***.

2. *US* STOCKHOLDING & INVESTMENTS measure of how quickly inventory needs replacing the total value of inventory sold in a year divided by the average value of goods held in stock. This checks that cash is not tied up in inventory for too long, losing its value over time. *UK term* ***stock turnover***

inventory valuation *US* ACCOUNTING estimation of stock value an estimation of the value of inventory at the end of an accounting period. *UK term* ***stock valuation***

inverse floating rate note STOCKHOLDING & INVESTMENTS security with interest varying inversely with base rate a security whose interest rate varies inversely with a **base interest rate**, rising as it falls and vice versa

inverted market MARKETS when near-term futures are dearest a situation in which near-term **futures contracts** cost more than long-term futures for the same commodity. *See also* ***backwardation***

inverted yield curve STOCKHOLDING & INVESTMENTS showing lower interest rates for long-term bonds a visual representation of relative interest rates that shows lower interest rates for long-term bonds than for short-term bonds. *See also* ***yield curve***

invested capital FINANCE firm's stock, retained earnings plus debt the total amount of a company's stock, retained earnings, and long-term debt

investment 1. FINANCE expenditure on assets and securities the spending of money on stocks and other securities, or on assets such as plant and machinery **2.** FINANCE something invested in something such as stocks, real estate, or a project in which money is invested in the expectation of making a profit **3.** STOCKHOLDING & INVESTMENTS money invested an amount of money invested in something in the expectation of making a profit

investment analyst STOCKHOLDING & INVESTMENTS researcher into investment possibilities an employee of a stock exchange company who researches other companies and identifies investment opportunities for clients. *Also called* ***financial analyst***

investment appraisal STOCKHOLDING & INVESTMENTS assessment of future value of new assets analysis of the future profitability of capital purchases as an aid to good management

investment bank BANKING **1.** bank for corporate borrowers a bank that specializes in providing funds to corporate borrowers for startup or expansion **2.** *US* bank for investors and their backers a bank that does not accept deposits but provides services to those who offer securities to investors, and to those investors. *See also* ***commercial bank***. *UK term* ***merchant bank*** ▶ *Abbr* **IB**

investment bond INSURANCE UK investment in life insurance policy in the United Kingdom, a product where the investment is paid as a single premium into a life insurance policy with an underlying asset-backed fund. The bondholder receives a regular income until the end of the bond's term when the investment (the current value of the fund) is returned to the bondholder. *Also called* ***life insurance bond***

investment borrowing ECONOMICS borrowing money to promote economic growth the borrowing of funds intended to encourage a country's economic growth or to support the development of particular industries or regions by adding to physical or human capital

investment center STOCKHOLDING & INVESTMENTS section responsible for profitable investment a profit center with additional responsibilities for capital investment, and possibly for financing, whose performance is measured by its return on investment

investment club STOCKHOLDING & INVESTMENTS group combining to invest in securities a group of people who join together to make investments in securities

investment committee BANKING bank employees assessing proposals for investment in the United States, a group of

  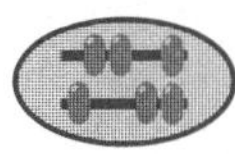   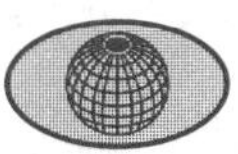   

employees of an investment bank who evaluate investment proposals

investment company STOCKHOLDING & INVESTMENTS firm investing money of several investors a company that pools for investment the money of several investors. *See also* ***investment fund***

investment dealer *Canada* STOCKHOLDING & INVESTMENTS securities broker a broker dealing in stock, bonds, debentures, and other securities. *Also called* ***broker***

investment fund STOCKHOLDING & INVESTMENTS savings plan that makes investments a savings plan that invests its clients' funds in, for example, corporate start-up or expansion projects. *See also* ***investment company***

investment grade STOCKHOLDING & INVESTMENTS refers to highly rated bond relating to a bond issued by a company, government, or local authority with a rating of BBB or higher, carrying relatively little risk. Trusts or pension funds may be restricted to investing in investment grade securities.

investment grade rating STOCKHOLDING & INVESTMENTS opinion of quality of bond as safe investment an assessment by a **rating agency** that a bond carries little risk for the investor. Bonds with ratings between AAA and BBB are considered investment grade.

investment grant STOCKHOLDING & INVESTMENTS government money given to firms for capital assets a government grant to a company to help it invest in capital assets such as buildings, equipment, or new machinery

investment horizon STOCKHOLDING & INVESTMENTS period of time for holding investment the length of time an investor expects to hold an investment, or the holding period over which an investment is analyzed

investment income STOCKHOLDING & INVESTMENTS money earned on investments revenue paid to investors that is derived from their investments, for example, dividends and interest on securities. *See also* ***earned income***

investment management agreement STOCKHOLDING & INVESTMENTS contract between investor and fund manager a contract between an investor and an investment manager. *Abbr* **IMA**

Investment Management Association STOCKHOLDING & INVESTMENTS association for UK investment professionals the trade body for the UK investment industry, formed in February 2002 following the merger of the Association of Unit Trusts and Investment Funds and the Fund Managers' Association. *Abbr* **IMA**. *See also* ***Fund Managers' Association***

Investment Management Regulatory Organisation REGULATION & COMPLIANCE UK group regulating investment fund managers in the United Kingdom, an organization that regulated managers of investment funds such as retirement funds, now part of the Financial Services Authority. *Abbr* **IMRO**

investment manager STOCKHOLDING & INVESTMENTS = ***fund manager***

investment objective STOCKHOLDING & INVESTMENTS long-term financial goal of investments the financial goal that determines how an individual or institution invests its assets, for example, for long-term growth or income

investment portfolio STOCKHOLDING & INVESTMENTS = ***portfolio***

investment professional STOCKHOLDING & INVESTMENTS somebody legally qualified to give investment advice a person who is licensed to offer advice on, and sell, investment products

investment properties FINANCE buildings bought to rent out either commercial buildings such as stores, factories, or offices, or residential dwellings such as houses or apartments, that are purchased by businesses or individuals for renting to third parties

investment revaluation reserve *UK* FINANCE reserve created by firm investing in property the capital reserve where changes in the value of a business's investment properties are disclosed when they are revalued

Investment Services Directive STOCKHOLDING & INVESTMENTS former EU regulations governing investment and market conduct formerly, an EU directive regulating the conduct and operation of investment companies and markets, replaced by the **Markets in Financial Instruments Directive**. *Abbr* **ISD**

investment tax credit TAX former US tax advantage in the United States, a tax advantage for investment that was available until 1986

investment trust STOCKHOLDING & INVESTMENTS investment firm with limited shares an investment company with a fixed number of shares available. Investment trusts are **closed-end investment companies**.

investment vehicle STOCKHOLDING & INVESTMENTS product or firm to invest in a financial product such as stocks, bonds, funds, or futures, or a company, in which somebody can invest money

investomer BUSINESS combined customer and investor a customer of a business who is also an investor (*slang*)

investor STOCKHOLDING & INVESTMENTS person or organization spending money for financial return a person or organization that invests money in something, especially in the stock of publicly owned corporations

investor relations research STOCKHOLDING & INVESTMENTS research into how financial markets view firm research carried out on behalf of an organization in order to gain an understanding of how financial markets regard the organization, its stock, and its sector

invisible asset FINANCE = ***intangible asset***

invisible earnings INTERNATIONAL TRADE foreign currency from services not commodities foreign currency earned by a country in providing services such as banking and tourism, rather than in selling goods

invisible exports INTERNATIONAL TRADE money generated by selling services overseas the profits, dividends, interest, and royalties received from selling a country's services abroad

invisible hand ECONOMICS power of market forces according to the 18th century British economist Adam Smith, the force of the market which drives the economy

invisible imports INTERNATIONAL TRADE money paid to foreign service firms the profits, dividends, interest, and royalties paid to foreign service companies based in a country

invisibles INTERNATIONAL TRADE services that are traded items such as financial and leisure services that are traded by a country, rather than physical goods

invisible trade INTERNATIONAL TRADE buying and selling services between countries trade in items such as financial and other services that are listed in the current account of the **balance of payments**

invoice FINANCE document requesting payment a document that a supplier sends to a customer detailing the cost of products or services supplied and asking for payment

invoice date FINANCE official date of sending of invoice the date on which an

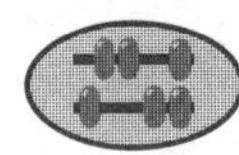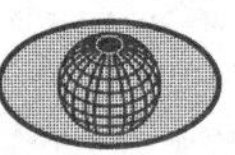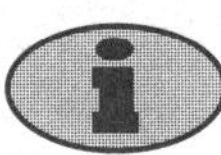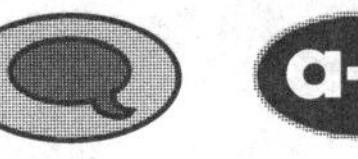

invoice is issued. The invoice date may be different from the delivery date.

invoice discounting FINANCE sale of invoices for less than stated value the selling of invoices at a discount for collection by the buyer, or the payment of invoices at a discount by an intermediary with the customer's eventual payment routed through the intermediary, who takes a fee

invoice price OPERATIONS & PRODUCTION total price as listed on bill the price as given on an invoice, including any discount and sales tax

invoice register ACCOUNTING record of invoices for things bought a list of purchase invoices recording the date of receipt of the invoice, the supplier, the invoice value, and the person to whom the invoice has been passed to ensure that all invoices are processed by the accounting system

invoicing FINANCE requesting payment the process of sending out invoices to customers

involuntary bankruptcy LEGAL bankruptcy petitioned for by creditors a situation in which a petition is filed with the creditors to have a person or corporation declared bankrupt

involuntary liquidation preference STOCKHOLDING & INVESTMENTS payment to particular stockholders before liquidation a payment that a company must make to holders of its preferred stock if it is forced to sell its assets when facing bankruptcy

inward bill INTERNATIONAL TRADE list of merchandise being brought into country a bill of lading for goods arriving in a country from a foreign country

inward investment STOCKHOLDING & INVESTMENTS investment in local area investment by a government or company in its own country or region, often to stimulate employment or develop a business infrastructure

IoD *abbr* CORPORATE GOVERNANCE Institute of Directors

IOD fraud *abbr* FRAUD impersonation of the deceased fraud

IOSCO *abbr* REGULATION & COMPLIANCE International Organization of Securities Commissions

IOU FINANCE note of money borrowed personally a representation of "I owe you" that can be used as legal evidence of a debt, although it is most commonly used as an informal reminder of a minor transaction

IP-backed STOCKHOLDING & INVESTMENTS, RISK describes securities backed by intellectual property used to describe securities whose underlying assets are intellectual property such as patents, copyrights, and trademarks

IPO *abbr* STOCKHOLDING & INVESTMENTS initial public offering

IPRs *abbr* LEGAL intellectual property rights

IRA PENSIONS personal pension plan allowing tax-free deposits in the United States, a pension plan, designed for individuals without a company pension plan, that allows annual sums, subject to limits dependent upon employment income, to be set aside from earnings tax-free. Individuals with a company pension may invest in an IRA, but only from their net income. IRAs, including the Education IRA, designed as a way of saving for children's education, may invest in almost any financial security except real estate. *Full form* ***individual retirement account***

IRA rollover PENSIONS transfer of assets between retirement plans in the United States, a transfer of assets from a tax-deferred qualified retirement plan to a tax-deferred IRA managed by the plan's owner

IRD *abbr* TAX Inland Revenue Department

IRD number TAX New Zealand income tax code for employees a numeric code assigned to all members of the New Zealand workforce for the purpose of paying income tax

IRR *abbr* FINANCE internal rate of return

irrecoverable debt FINANCE loan that will never be repaid a debt that will never be paid to the person to whom it is owed and must be written off, either as a charge to the profit and loss account or against an existing doubtful debt provision

irredeemable bond STOCKHOLDING & INVESTMENTS indefinite government bond a government bond that has no date of maturity but provides interest

irrevocable letter of credit BANKING permanent credit authorization a **letter of credit** that cannot be canceled

irrevocable trust FINANCE unalterable trust a trust that cannot be canceled or revised without the agreement of its beneficiary

IRS TAX US government agency for tax collection in the United States, the branch of the federal government charged with collecting the majority of federal taxes. *Full form* ***Internal Revenue Service***

IS *abbr* FINANCE income support

ISA STOCKHOLDING & INVESTMENTS UK tax-free account for savings and investment in the United Kingdom, a tax-free savings account in which up to £7,200 a year can be invested. £3,600 of which can be in cash and the remainder in stocks, or all the investment can be in stocks. Formerly, there were Maxi ISAs and Mini ISAs, each with two components: cash and stocks. *Full form* ***Individual Savings Account***

ISC *abbr* INSURANCE Insurance and Superannuation Commission

ISD *abbr* STOCKHOLDING & INVESTMENTS Investment Services Directive

ISDA *abbr* STOCKHOLDING & INVESTMENTS International Swaps and Derivatives Association

Islamic law LEGAL Muslim religious law the law as interpreted by trained Islamic legal scholars. In strict Islamic countries, all businesses, financial institutions, and products must meet the requirements of Islamic law. *Also called* ***sharia, shariah***

ISMA *abbr* MARKETS International Securities Market Association

issuance costs FINANCE money spent issuing debt the underwriting, legal, and administrative fees required to issue a debt. These fees are significant when issuing debt in the public markets, such as the bond market. However, other types of debt, such as private placements or bank loans, are cheaper to issue because they require less underwriting, legal, and administrative support.

issue STOCKHOLDING & INVESTMENTS stocks or bonds for sale at one time a set of stocks or bonds that a company offers for sale at one time

issue by tender STOCKHOLDING & INVESTMENTS = ***sale by tender***

issued capital STOCKHOLDING & INVESTMENTS = ***share capital***

Issue Department BANKING part of Bank of England issuing currency the department of the Bank of England that is responsible for issuing currency

issued price STOCKHOLDING & INVESTMENTS price of firm's first stock issue the price of shares of stock in a company when they are offered for sale for the first time

issued share capital STOCKHOLDING & INVESTMENTS amount representing shares the type, class, number, and amount of the shares held by stockholders. *See also* ***stockholders' equity***

issued shares STOCKHOLDING & INVESTMENTS shares held by investors those shares that comprise a company's authorized capital that has been distributed to investors. They

     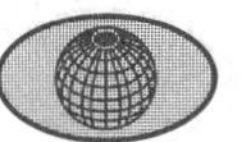   

may be either fully paid or partly paid shares.

issue price STOCKHOLDING & INVESTMENTS original price of securities the price at which securities are first offered for sale

issuer E-COMMERCE organization providing payment cards a financial institution that issues payment cards such as credit or debit cards, pays out to the merchant's account, and bills the customer or debits the customer's account. The issuer guarantees payment for authorized transactions using the payment card. *Also called* ***card-issuing bank, issuing bank***

issuer bid STOCKHOLDING & INVESTMENTS offer to buy own securities an offer made by an issuer for its own securities when it is disappointed by the offers of others

issuer identification number BANKING international number identifying individual bank an internationally agreed six-digit number that uniquely identifies a bank in electronic transactions. *Abbr* **IIN**

issues management GENERAL MANAGEMENT process of anticipating trends for commercial gain the anticipation and assessment of key trends and themes of the next decade, and the relation of these to the organization. Issues management is informed by **futures research** in order to formulate strategic plans and actions.

issuing bank E-COMMERCE = ***issuer***

issuing house FINANCE UK financial institution that launches private companies in the United Kingdom, a financial institution that specializes in the flotation of private companies. *See also* ***investment bank, merchant bank***

istisna'a or **istisnah** OPERATIONS & PRODUCTION product manufacturing contract with agreed delivery and price in Islamic financing, a contract for manufacturing a product in which the manufacturer agrees to produce a specified product to be delivered at a specified time for a specified price

IT *abbr* TAX income tax

item ACCOUNTING unit of accounting information a single piece of information included in a company's accounts

itemized deductions TAX expenses allowed to reduce US income tax in the United States, amounts paid by individual taxpayers for expenses that can be deducted to reduce taxable income, for example, medical and dental expenses, charitable contributions, mortgage interest, and losses due to theft

J

J curve CURRENCY & EXCHANGE line representing falling exchange rate's effect on trade a line on a graph shaped like a letter "J," with an initial short fall, followed by a longer rise, used to describe the effect of a falling exchange rate on a country's balance of trade

Jensen's measure FINANCE = ***risk-adjusted return on capital***

JEPI *abbr* E-COMMERCE joint electronic payment initiative

jikan MARKETS Japanese rule for choosing between identical instructions in Japan, the priority rule relating to transactions on the Tokyo Stock Exchange whereby the earlier of two buy or sell orders received at the same price prevails

JIT *abbr* OPERATIONS & PRODUCTION just-in-time

job BUSINESS assignment a customer order or other piece of work

job action *US* GENERAL MANAGEMENT action to force resolution of dispute a temporary action such as a strike or lockout taken by one side in a labor dispute in an attempt to bring pressure on the other side to settle. *UK term* ***industrial action***

jobber's turn MARKETS UK dealer's profit on transaction formerly, a term used on the London Stock Exchange for a **spread**, the difference between the buying and selling price that a dealer arranges and takes as profit

jobbing backward *UK* STOCKHOLDING & INVESTMENTS review of actions the analysis of an investment transaction with the benefit of hindsight

job cost ACCOUNTING describes accounting allowing determination of profit per job used to describe a method of accounting whereby a project-oriented business allocates costs to a specific project, thereby having the ability to determine the profitability of individual projects

job lot FINANCE varied items bought or sold together a miscellaneous assortment of items, including securities, that are offered as a single deal

Johannesburg Stock Exchange MARKETS former name of JSE Limited until November of the year 2000, the official name of the JSE Limited, the South African stock exchange

joint account BANKING account shared by two or more people an account, such as one held at a bank or by a broker, that two or more people own in common and can access

joint and several liability LEGAL obligation to meet payment together or individually a legal liability that applies to a group of individuals as a whole and each member individually, so that if one member does not meet his or her liability, the shortfall is the shared responsibility of the others. Most guarantees given by two or more individuals to secure borrowing are joint and several. It is a typical feature of most partnership agreements.

joint bond STOCKHOLDING & INVESTMENTS bond guaranteed by third party a bond that is guaranteed by a party other than the company or government that issued it

joint electronic payment initiative E-COMMERCE proposed protocol for electronic payment a proposed industry standard protocol for electronic payment in e-commerce transactions. *Abbr* **JEPI**

joint float CURRENCY & EXCHANGE shared exchange relationship within set of currencies a group of currencies that maintains a fixed internal relationship and moves jointly in relation to another currency

joint life annuity INSURANCE annuity lasting until death of both parties an annuity that continues until both parties have died. They are attractive to married couples as they ensure that the survivor has an income for the rest of his or her life.

joint management GENERAL MANAGEMENT running of firm by more than one person the overseeing and control of the affairs of an organization shared by two or more people

joint ownership BUSINESS ownership by several people or organizations ownership by more than one party, each with equal rights in the item owned. Joint ownership is often applied to property or other assets.

joint return TAX single tax return covering spouses in the United States, a tax return filed jointly by a husband and wife

joint stock bank BANKING formerly, commercial bank a term that was formerly used for a commercial bank that is a partnership, as opposed to one that is a **publicly held corporation**

joint-stock company BUSINESS formerly, public limited company in UK formerly in the United Kingdom, a public company whose stock was owned by many people. Now such a company is called a public limited company or Plc. *See also* ***company limited by shares***

  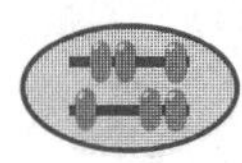 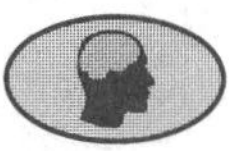  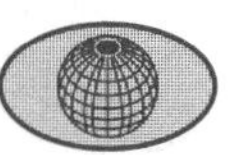   

joint venture BUSINESS enterprise undertaken by two or more firms a business project in which two or more independent companies collaborate and share the risks and rewards. *Abbr* **JV**

journal ACCOUNTING consolidated record of transactions a record of original entry, into which transactions are usually transferred from source documents. The journal may be subdivided into: sales journal/day book for credit sales; purchases journal/day book for credit purchases; cash book for cash receipts and payments; and the journal proper for transactions which could not appropriately be recorded in any of the other journals.

JSE MARKETS *see* ***JSE Limited***

JSE Limited MARKETS South African Stock Exchange the largest stock exchange in Africa, located in Johannesburg, South Africa. *Abbr* **JSE**

JSE Securities Exchange South Africa MARKETS name of JSE Limited between 2000 and 2005 from 2000 to 2005, the official name of the JSE Limited, the South African stock exchange

ju'alal FINANCE contract for payment for services performed in Islamic financing, a contract for performing a specified act for a specified fee

judgment creditor LEGAL plaintiff in court case for debt in a legal action, the individual or business who has brought the action and to whom the court orders the judgment debtor to pay the money owed. In the event of the judgment debtor not conforming to the court order, the judgment creditor must return to the court to request that the judgment be enforced.

judgment debtor LEGAL defendant in court case for debt in a legal action, the individual or business ordered to pay the judgment creditor the money owed

jumbo mortgage MORTGAGES US mortgage too large for favorable terms in the United States, a mortgage that is too large to qualify for favorable treatment by a government agency

junior capital STOCKHOLDING & INVESTMENTS capital representing stockholders' equity capital in the form of stockholders' equity which is repaid only after the secured loans forming the senior capital have been paid if the firm goes into liquidation

junior debt FINANCE debt with low priority for repayment a debt that has no claim on a debtor's assets, or less claim than another debt. *See also* ***senior debt***. *Also called* ***subordinated debt***

junior mortgage MORTGAGES mortgage with low priority for repayment a mortgage whose holder has less claim on a debtor's assets than the holder of another mortgage. *See also* ***senior mortgage***

junior partner BUSINESS member of business partnership with limited involvement a person whose participation in management and share in the profits of a partnership are very limited

junior security STOCKHOLDING & INVESTMENTS security that is subordinate to another a security whose interest or dividend payment has a lower priority than that of another security issued by the same company

junk bond STOCKHOLDING & INVESTMENTS, RISK high-interest but high-risk bond a high-yielding bond issued on a low-grade security. The issue of junk bonds has most commonly been linked with takeover activity.

junk-rated STOCKHOLDING & INVESTMENTS, RISK describes bond that is risky investment used to describe a bond that is considered by a **rating agency** to not be **investment grade** and therefore has a higher than average risk. Junk-rated bonds have a rating of BB or less.

just-in-time OPERATIONS & PRODUCTION production method reducing inventory stockpiling a production method that requires necessary materials to be at the place of manufacture or assembly at the appropriate time to minimize holding excess inventory, reducing wastage and expense. *Abbr* **JIT**

JV *abbr* BUSINESS joint venture

K

K FINANCE 1,000 one thousand: used especially after numbers expressing a sum of money. It derives from kilo-.

kafalah FINANCE agreement to pay debt of another who defaults in Islamic financing, an agreement in which one party assumes responsibility for the debt of another if the debtor should fail to pay

kakaku yusen MARKETS Japanese rule for choosing between differing instructions in Japan, the price priority system operated on the Tokyo Stock Exchange whereby a lower price takes precedence over a higher price for a sell order, and vice versa for a buy order. *See also* ***jikan***

kangaroo MARKETS Australian stock an Australian stock traded on the London Stock Exchange (*slang*)

Kansas City Board of Trade MARKETS specialized US commodities exchange a commodities exchange, established in 1856, that specializes in futures and options contracts for red winter wheat, the Value Line® Index, natural gas, and the ISDEX® Internet Stock Index

kappa STOCKHOLDING & INVESTMENTS relationship between option price change and asset's volatility a ratio between the expected change in the price of an option and a one percent change in the expected volatility of the underlying asset. *Also called* ***lambda, vega***

Keidanren BUSINESS Japan Federation of Economic Organizations the Japanese abbreviation for the Japan Federation of Economic Organizations. Established in 1946, it works toward a resolution of the major problems facing the Japanese and international business communities and the sound development of their economies. Its members include over 1,000 of Japan's leading corporations, including over 50 foreign companies, and over 100 industry-wide groups representing such major sectors as manufacturing, trade, distribution, finance, and energy.

Keough Plan PENSIONS US pension benefiting specific groups in the United States, a pension subject to tax advantage for somebody who is self-employed or has an interest in a small company. *See also* ***stakeholder pension***

kerb market UK MARKETS unofficial stock market a stock market that exists outside the stock exchange. The term originates from markets held in the street.

ker-ching FINANCE expression suggesting financial success an expression suggesting that something will be very successful financially (*slang*)

key account management MARKETING management of most important customer relationships the management of the customer relationships that are most important to a company. Key accounts are those held by customers who produce most **profit** for a company or have the potential to do so, or those who are of strategic importance. Development of these **customer relations** and **customer retention** is important to business success. Particular emphasis is placed on analyzing which accounts are key to a company at any one time, determining the needs of these particular customers, and implementing

  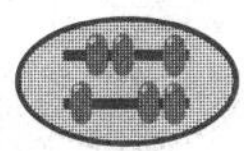 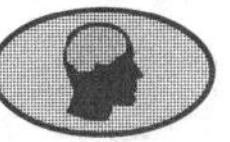  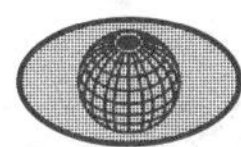   

procedures to ensure that they receive premium **customer service** and to increase **customer satisfaction.**

Keynes, John Maynard British economist with influential theories on macroeconomics economics a British economist who lived from 1883–1946. He is best known for his theories regarding ***macroeconomics***. He believed that in a ***recession***, the only way to reduce unemployment and improve the economy was for the government to increase spending, even if it meant running a deficit, and to reduce interest rates to encourage borrowing.

Keynesian economics ECONOMICS economic philosophy of John Maynard Keynes the economic teachings and doctrines associated with **John Maynard Keynes**

key rate FINANCE interest rate on which other rates are based an interest rate that gives the basic rate on which other rates are calculated, for example, the Bank of England's bank rate or the Federal Reserve's discount rate in the United States

kickback FRAUD illicit payment to facilitator in transaction a sum of money paid illegally to somebody in order to gain concessions or favors (*slang*)

kicker STOCKHOLDING & INVESTMENTS attractive extra to standard security an addition to a standard security that makes it more attractive, for example, options and warrants (*slang*). *See also* ***bells and whistles, sweetener***

kiddie tax TAX US tax on youth income in the United States, a tax on the investment income of children and young people up to the age of 24. The amount of the tax is calculated based on their student status and/or earned income.

kill FINANCE stop instruction to stop an instruction or order from being carried out (*slang*)

killer bee BUSINESS facilitator in averting takeover somebody, especially a banker, who helps a company avoid being taken over

killing ◇ make a killing FINANCE to make a lot of money very quickly

kimono ◇ open the kimono GENERAL MANAGEMENT to inspect something that has not been open for examination before, especially a company's accounts

kitchen sink bond STOCKHOLDING & INVESTMENTS, RISK bond created from collection of collateralized mortgage obligations a high-risk bond created by combining **tranches** of existing collateralized mortgage obligations

kite 1. FRAUD fraudulent check, bill, or receipt a fraudulent financial transaction, for example, a bad check that is dated to take advantage of the time interval required for clearing **2.** FINANCE sign fraudulent checks to write bad checks in order to take advantage of the time interval required for clearing ◇ fly a kite **1.** FRAUD to use a fraudulent financial document such as a bad check **2.** GENERAL MANAGEMENT to make a suggestion in order to test people's opinion of it

kiwibond CURRENCY & EXCHANGE Eurobond in NZ dollars a **Eurobond** denominated in New Zealand dollars

knight MERGERS & ACQUISITIONS firm involved in takeover a term borrowed from chess strategy to describe a company involved in the politics of a **takeover** bid. There are three main types of knights. A **white knight** is a company that is friendly to the board of the company to be acquired. If the white knight gains control, it may retain the existing **board of directors.** A **black knight** is a former white knight that has disagreed with the board of the company to be acquired and has established its own hostile bid. A **gray knight** is a white knight that does not have the confidence of the company to be acquired.

knock-for-knock *UK* INSURANCE with each insurer paying own customer's repair bill used to describe a practice between insurance companies whereby each will pay for the repairs to the vehicle it insures in the event of an accident

knockout option STOCKHOLDING & INVESTMENTS option with condition attached an option to which a condition relating to the underlying security's or commodity's present price is attached so that it effectively expires when it goes **out of the money**

knowledge capital FINANCE knowledge applicable for profit knowledge that a company possesses and can put to profitable use

knowledge management GENERAL MANAGEMENT use of organization's knowledge for competitive advantage the coordination and exploitation of an organization's knowledge resources, in order to create benefit and competitive advantage

Korea Composite Stock Price Index MARKETS index of traded Korean stocks the index of all the common stocks traded on the Korean stock exchanges. *Abbr* **KOSPI**

KOSPI *abbr* MARKETS Korea Composite Stock Price Index

krona CURRENCY & EXCHANGE Swedish and Icelandic currency unit a unit of currency used in Sweden and Iceland

Krugerrand CURRENCY & EXCHANGE South African gold coin a South African coin consisting of one ounce of gold, first minted in 1967, bearing the portrait of 19th-century South African president Paul Kruger on the obverse

kurtosis STATISTICS distribution around mean a statistical measure of the distribution of data around a mean, as used in charts that assess the volatility of an investment

L

L ECONOMICS measurement of money supply a measure of the money supply, calculated as the broad money supply plus short-term Treasury securities, savings bonds, and commercial paper

labor HR & PERSONNEL all workers considered as group all the people employed in work, especially those doing manual labor, in a country, company, or industry considered as a group

labor dispute *US* GENERAL MANAGEMENT conflict between workers and management a disagreement or conflict between an **employer** and **employees** or between the **employers' association** and **labor union**. *UK term* industrial dispute (see **dispute**)

labor force survey STATISTICS quarterly survey of UK workforce a survey carried out every quarter in the United Kingdom, covering such topics as unemployment and hours of work

labor-intensive OPERATIONS & PRODUCTION requiring many people involving large numbers of workers or high labor costs. *See also* ***capital-intensive***

labor-intensive industry OPERATIONS & PRODUCTION business requiring many workers an industry that needs large numbers of employees and in which labor costs are high in relation to other costs

labor union *US* GENERAL MANAGEMENT organization representing employees' interests an organization of **employees** within a trade or profession that has the objective of representing its members' interests, primarily through improving pay and conditions, and provides a variety of services. *UK term* ***trade union***

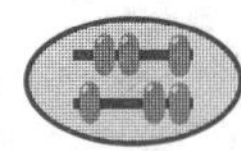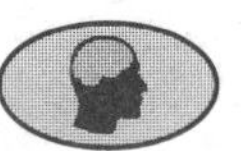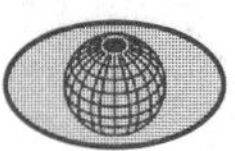

laddering **1.** STOCKHOLDING & INVESTMENTS selling after raising stock price by continued buying **the investment strategy of repeatedly buying shares in a newly launched corporation so as to force up the price, then selling the whole investment at a profit** **2.** STOCKHOLDING & INVESTMENTS, RISK timed purchase, sale, and reinvestment strategy reducing risk **the action of making a series of investments that mature at different times, cashing each one at maturity, then reinvesting the proceeds, thereby reducing the risk of losing large amounts all at once**

ladder option STOCKHOLDING & INVESTMENTS, RISK option whose profit is locked in set level **an option whose strike price is reset when the underlying asset breaks through a specified level, locking in the profit between the old and new strike price**

Lady Macbeth strategy BUSINESS change in which white knight becomes black knight **a change of approach on the part of a presumed white knight, in which it becomes a black knight. A Lady Macbeth strategy is usually associated with takeover battles and has connotations of treachery.**

Laffer curve ECONOMICS, TAX graph showing effects of tax rate changes **a graph showing that cuts in tax rates increase output in the economy and thus increase overall tax revenues**

laggard MARKETING firm that does not innovate **an organization that follows a first mover to market, or a company that is not the recognized leader in a sector.** *See also* ***first mover***

lagging indicator ECONOMICS economic factor confirming change in economic trend **a measurable economic factor, for example, corporate profits or unemployment, that changes after the economy has already moved to a new trend, which it can confirm but not predict**

laissez-faire economy ECONOMICS economic system in which government does not intervene **an economy in which the government does not interfere because it believes that market forces should determine the course of the economy**

lambda STOCKHOLDING & INVESTMENTS relationship of option price to underlying asset's volatility **a ratio between the expected change in the price of an option and a one percent change in the expected volatility of the underlying asset.** *Also called* ***kappa, vega***

lame duck BUSINESS firm with financial problems **a company that is in financial difficulties**

land bank FINANCE undeveloped land owned by builder or developer **the land that a builder or developer has that is available for development**

land banking FINANCE acquiring land for future development **the practice of buying land that is not needed immediately, but with the expectation of using it in the future**

landed costs INTERNATIONAL TRADE costs of shipping and customs clearance **costs of goods that have been delivered to a port, unloaded, and passed through customs**

landing order INTERNATIONAL TRADE permit to hold goods in bonded warehouse **a permit that allows goods to be unloaded into a bonded warehouse without paying customs duty**

landlord BUSINESS owner of rented property **a person or company that owns a property that is rented**

land register REAL ESTATE record of UK property and its owners **in the United Kingdom, a list of pieces of land, showing who owns each and what buildings are on it**

land tax TAX Australian tax on residential land **a form of wealth tax imposed in Australia on the value of residential land. The level and conditions of the tax vary from state to state.**

lapping *US* ACCOUNTING way of concealing missing funds **an attempt to hide missing funds by delaying the recording of cash receipts in a business's books.** *UK term* ***teeming and lading***

lapse STOCKHOLDING & INVESTMENTS expiry of option without trading **the termination of an option without trade in the underlying security or commodity**

lapsed option STOCKHOLDING & INVESTMENTS expired right to buy or sell investment **an option to buy or sell a security or commodity that is no longer valid because it has expired**

lapse rights STOCKHOLDING & INVESTMENTS rights of somebody allowing offer to lapse **rights, such as those to a prearranged premium, owned by the person who allows an offer to lapse**

large-sized business BUSINESS organization with 250 or more employees **an organization that has grown beyond the limits of a medium-sized business and has 250 or more employees. This definition of a large-sized enterprise is the one adopted by the United Kingdom's Department for Business Enterprise and Regulatory Reform for statistical purposes It is usually from the ranks of large-sized businesses that multinational businesses arise.**

last quarter ACCOUNTING final period of fiscal year **a period of three months from October to the end of the year, or the period of three months at the end of the fiscal year**

last survivor policy INSURANCE life insurance policy for two or more **an insurance policy covering the lives of two or more people. The sum insured is not paid out until all the policyholders are deceased.** *See also* ***joint life annuity***

last trading day MARKETS final trading day in futures or options contract **the last day in which trading takes place in a futures or options contract relating to a certain delivery month, after which the contract must be settled**

latent market MARKETING group of potential consumers of proposed product **a group of people who have been identified as potential consumers of a product that does not yet exist**

launch MARKETING making new product available **the process of introducing a new product to the market**

laundering FRAUD concealing illegal origins of money **the process of passing the profits of illegal activities such as tax evasion into the normal banking system via apparently legitimate businesses**

LAUTRO REGULATION & COMPLIANCE former UK regulator **a former UK financial authority regulating life insurance and mutual funds. It was brought to an end in 1995.** *Full form* ***Life Assurance and Unit Trust Regulatory Organization***

law of diminishing marginal utility ECONOMICS increased consumption of product decreases consumer's satisfaction **a general theory in economics stating that each unit of a product consumed adds less satisfaction to the consumer than the previous one, i.e., the marginal utility of any good or service diminishes as each new unit of it is consumed**

law of diminishing returns ECONOMICS increase in one area has limited effect **a rule stating that as one factor of production is increased, while others remain constant, the extra output generated by the additional input will eventually fall. The law of diminishing returns therefore means that extra workers, extra capital, extra machinery, or extra land may not necessarily raise output as much as expected. For example, increasing the supply of raw materials to a production line may allow additional output to be produced by using any spare capacity workers have. Once this capacity is fully used, however, continually increasing the amount of raw**

  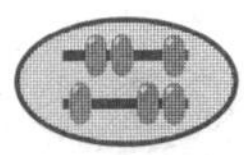   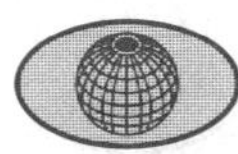   

material without a corresponding increase in the number of workers will not result in an increase of output.

law of supply and demand ECONOMICS *see* ***supply and demand***

lay-away *US* FINANCE paying for product in installments before taking ownership the reservation of an article for purchase by the payment of an initial deposit followed by regular interest-free installments, on completion of which the article is claimed by the buyer

lay off HR & PERSONNEL **1.** terminate somebody's employment because of too little work to dismiss an employee or employees permanently because there is insufficient work to occupy them **2.** temporarily stop somebody's employment to suspend an employee or employees temporarily because there is insufficient work to occupy them

layoff *US* HR & PERSONNEL termination of employment because of too little work dismissal, often temporarily, from work because a job ceases to exist or because of lack of work. Employees who are laid off may qualify for severance pay. If the layoff process is handled incorrectly, the employer may be faced with claims for unfair dismissal. *UK term* ***redundancy***

LBO *abbr* MERGERS & ACQUISITIONS leveraged buyout

LC or **L/C** *abbr* BANKING letter of credit

LCH *abbr* BANKING London Clearing House

LCM *abbr* ACCOUNTING lower of cost or market

LDC *abbr* ECONOMICS **1.** less developed country **2.** least developed country

LDT *abbr* FINANCE licensed deposit-taker

lead INSURANCE first underwriter of Lloyd's policy in an insurance policy from Lloyd's, the first named underwriting syndicate

lead bank BANKING main bank in loan syndicate the primary bank in a loan syndicate, which organizes the transaction in question

leader **1.** GENERAL MANAGEMENT, HR & PERSONNEL firm's executive who motivates others well a business executive who possesses exceptional leadership qualities as well as management skills **2.** MARKETING top performing thing the most successful product or company in a marketplace

leadership GENERAL MANAGEMENT, HR & PERSONNEL ability to guide and motivate others well the capacity to establish direction and to influence and align others toward a common goal, motivating and committing them to action and making them responsible for their performance. Leadership theory is one of the most discussed areas of management, and many different approaches are taken to the topic. Some notions of leadership are related to types of **authority** delineated by Max Weber. It is often suggested that leaders possess innate personal qualities that distinguish them from others. Other theories, such as Behaviorist theories of leadership, suggest that leadership is defined by action and behavior, rather than by personality. A related idea is that leadership style is not fixed but should be adapted to different situations, and this is explored in **contingency theory**. Perhaps the most simple model of leadership is action-centered leadership, which focuses on what an effective leader actually does. These many approaches and differences of opinion illustrate the complexity of the leadership role and the intangibility of the essence of good leadership.

leading economic indicator or **leading indicator** ECONOMICS early indication of change in economic trends an economic variable, such as private-sector wages, that tends to show the direction of future economic activity earlier than other indicators. *See also* ***lagging indicator***

leading edge BUSINESS most modern and innovative situated at the forefront of **innovation**. A leading edge company is ahead of others in such areas as inventing or implementing new technologies, and in entering new markets.

lead manager *UK* STOCKHOLDING & INVESTMENTS = ***lead underwriter***

lead partner BUSINESS dominant partner the organization that takes the lead role in an alliance

leads and lags CURRENCY & EXCHANGE adjusting speed of transactions with exchange rates in businesses that deal in foreign currencies, the practice of speeding up the receipt of payments (leads) if a currency is going to weaken, and slowing down the payment of costs (lags) if a currency is thought to be about to strengthen, in order to maximize gains and reduce losses

lead time **1.** FINANCE, OPERATIONS & PRODUCTION time between starting and finishing the time interval between the start of an activity or process and its completion, for example, the time between ordering goods and their receipt, or between starting manufacturing of a product and its completion **2.** OPERATIONS & PRODUCTION period between order placement and delivery in inventory control, the time between placing an order and its arrival on site. Lead time differs from delivery time in that it also includes the time required to place an order and the time it takes to inspect the goods and receive them into the appropriate store. Inventory levels can afford to be lower and orders smaller when purchasing lead times are short. **3.** OPERATIONS & PRODUCTION, MARKETING period from new product idea to sales readiness in **new product development** and manufacturing, the time required to develop a product from concept to market delivery. Lead time increases as a result of the poor sequencing of dependent activities, the lack of availability of resources, poor quality in the component parts, and poor plant layout. The technique of **concurrent engineering** focuses on the entire concept-to-customer process with the goal of reducing lead time. Companies can gain a **competitive advantage** by achieving a lead time reduction and so getting products to market faster. *Also called* ***cycle time*** *(sense 2)*

lead underwriter *US* STOCKHOLDING & INVESTMENTS institution in charge of new issue the financial institution with overall responsibility for a new issue of shares of stock including its coordination, distribution, and related administration. *UK term* ***lead manager***

lean enterprise OPERATIONS & PRODUCTION efficient business structure with little waste an organizational model that strategically applies the key ideas behind **lean production**. A lean enterprise is viewed as a group of separate individuals, functions, or organizations that operate as one entity. The goal is to apply lean techniques that create individual breakthroughs in companies and to link these up and down the supply chain to form a continuous value stream to raise the whole chain to a higher level.

lean manufacturing OPERATIONS & PRODUCTION = ***lean production***

lean operation OPERATIONS & PRODUCTION business with little waste a company following the methodology of **lean production**, with low **inventories**. *See also* ***lean production***

lean production OPERATIONS & PRODUCTION efficient manufacturing method with little waste a methodology aimed at reducing waste in the form of overproduction, excessive **lead time**, or product defects in order to make a business more effective and more competitive. Lean production

  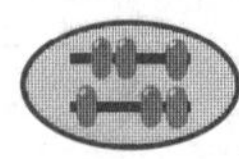   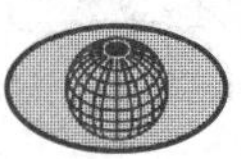   

originates in the production systems established by Toyota in Japan in the 1950s. In the early 1980s there was a significant increase in the application of lean production in Western companies. Lean production is characterized by **lean operations** with low **inventories**; **quality management** through prevention of errors; small batch runs; **just-in-time** production; high commitment human resource policies; team-based working; and close relations with suppliers. Concepts that can help an organization move toward lean production include **continuous improvement** and **world class manufacturing**. *Also called* ***lean manufacturing***

LEAPS STOCKHOLDING & INVESTMENTS options with one- to three-year expiry date options that expire between one and three years in the future. *Full form* ***long-term equity anticipation securities***

learning by doing GENERAL MANAGEMENT finding out about job by performing it the acquisition of knowledge or skills through direct experience of carrying out a task. Learning by doing often happens under supervision, as part of a training or **orientation** process, and is closely associated with the practical experience picked up by **"sitting with Nellie."** It is an outcome of the research into learning of David Kolb and Reg Revans. A more formalized approach to learning by doing is **experiential learning**.

learning curve **1.** GENERAL MANAGEMENT rate at which new information must be acquired a graphic representation of the acquisition of knowledge or experience over time. A steep learning curve reflects a substantial amount of learning in a short time, and a shallow curve reflects a slower learning process. The curve eventually levels out to a plateau, during which time the knowledge gained is being consolidated. **2.** OPERATIONS & PRODUCTION proportional reduction in effort when production doubles the proportional decrease in effort when production is doubled. The learning curve has its origin in productivity research in the airplane industry of the 1930s, when T. P. Wright discovered that in assembling an aircraft, the time and effort decreased by 20% each time the cumulative number of planes produced doubled. ▶ *Also called* **experience curve**

learning opportunity GENERAL MANAGEMENT mistake to learn from a positive way of referring to a mistake that somebody has made at work, presenting it as a chance to gain new knowledge

learning organization GENERAL MANAGEMENT customer-focused firm with little hierarchy an organizational model characterized by a flat structure and **customer-focused** teams, that engenders the collective ability to develop shared visions by capturing and exploiting employees' willingness, commitment, and curiosity. The concept of the learning organization was proposed by Chris Argyris and Donald Schön as part of their work on organizational learning, but was brought back to public attention in the 1990s by Peter Senge. For Senge, a learning organization is one with the capacity to shift away from views inherent in a traditional hierarchical organization, toward the ability of all employees to challenge prevailing thinking and gain a balanced perspective. Senge believes the five major characteristics of a learning organization are mental models, personal mastery, systems thinking, shared vision, and team learning. Because of the requirement for an open, risk-tolerant culture, which is the opposite of the corporate culture of most organizations today, the learning organization remains, for many, an unattainable ideal.

learning style GENERAL MANAGEMENT way that somebody best acquires knowledge and skills the way in which somebody approaches the acquisition of knowledge and skills. Learning styles have been divided into four main types by Peter Honey and Alan Mumford, in their *Manual of Learning Styles* (1982). The types of learners are the activist, who likes to get involved in new experiences and enjoys the challenges of change; the theorist, who likes to question assumptions and methodologies and learns best when there is time to explore links between ideas and situations; the pragmatist, who prefers practicality and learns best when there is a link between the subject matter and the job in hand and when he or she can try out what he or she has learned; and the reflector, who likes to take his or her time and think things through, and who learns best from activities where he or she can observe and conduct research. One person can demonstrate more than one learning style, and the category or categories that best describe somebody can be determined through use of a learning styles questionnaire.

lease LEGAL **1.** written contract for renting something a written contract for renting a building, a piece of land, or a piece of equipment for a fixed period of time in return for payment of a fee **2.** rent offices, land, or equipment to somebody to rent offices, land, or equipment to a person or business for a fixed period of time specified in a written contract **3.** rent offices, land, or equipment from somebody to use offices, land, or equipment for a fixed period of time specified in a written contract and pay a fee

leaseback LEGAL, FINANCE *see* ***sale and leaseback***

leasehold LEGAL, REAL ESTATE **1.** right to rent property for fixed period the right to possess a property on a lease, for a fixed period of time **2.** piece of property that is rented a property held on a lease granted by the legal owner of the property

leaseholder LEGAL, REAL ESTATE somebody renting piece of property under lease a person who is in possession of a property by way of a lease

least developed country ECONOMICS very poor country with little economic development a country that is not economically advanced, especially a country that borrowed heavily from commercial banks in the 1970s and 1980s to finance its industrial development, and so helped to create an international debt crisis. *Abbr* **LDC**

leave HR & PERSONNEL paid time away from work work time when an employee is paid, but is not required to be at work. Leave takes several forms and includes time off for vacation. The number of days of vacation is set out in the contract of employment and may be dependent on the employee's length of service. It may also take the form of sick leave, educational leave, or maternity or paternity leave.

ledger ACCOUNTING **1.** book for accounts a book in which account transactions are recorded **2.** book with record of account transactions a collection of accounts, or book of accounts. Credit sales information is recorded, for example, by debtor, in the sales ledger. **3.** book of consolidated accounts a collection of accounts, maintained by transfers from the books of original entry. The ledger may be subdivided as follows: the sales ledger/debtors' ledger contains all the personal accounts of customers; the purchases ledger/creditors' ledger contains all the personal accounts of suppliers; the private ledger contains accounts relating to the proprietor's interest in the business such as capital and drawings; the general ledger/nominal ledger contains all other accounts relating to assets, expenses, revenue, and liabilities.

  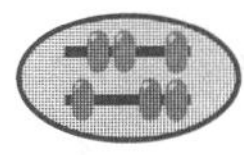   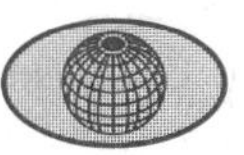   

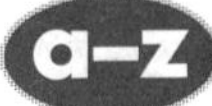

leg STOCKHOLDING & INVESTMENTS price for security either the highest price offered for a security or the lowest price a seller will accept for a security

legacy system BUSINESS computer system with long-term function an existing computer system that provides a strategic function for a specific part of a business. Inventory management systems, for example, are legacy systems.

legal charge LEGAL legal document showing ownership of UK property in the United Kingdom, a legal document held by the Land Registry showing who has a claim on a property

legal charges LEGAL = ***legal costs***

legal claim LEGAL lawful right or statement of ownership a legally recognized right to the ownership of something, or a statement of such a right

legal costs LEGAL money spent on lawyers' fees the amount of money spent on legal matters, particularly lawyers' fees. *Also called* ***legal charges, legal expenses***

legal currency LEGAL, CURRENCY & EXCHANGE legally accepted money money that is recognized by a government to be legally acceptable for payment of a debt

legal expenses LEGAL = ***legal costs***

legal list LEGAL, STOCKHOLDING & INVESTMENTS securities that financial institutions can legally invest in a list of blue-chip securities in which banks and financial institutions are allowed to invest by the state in which they are based

legal loophole LEGAL legal flaw allowing people to get around law an area in the law that is insufficiently explicit or comprehensive and allows the law to be circumvented

legal tender LEGAL, CURRENCY & EXCHANGE legally accepted paper money and coins paper money and coins that have to be accepted within a given jurisdiction when offered as payment of a debt. *See also* ***limited legal tender***

lemon BUSINESS unsatisfactory product a product that is defective in some way, for example, an investment that is performing poorly (*slang*)

lender FINANCE somebody who lends money a person or financial institution that lends money

lender of last resort BANKING bank lending to troubled commercial banks a central bank that lends money to banks that cannot borrow elsewhere

lending facility BANKING = ***credit facility***

lending limit BANKING maximum amount of money bank can lend a restriction placed on the amount of money a bank can legally lend

lending margin BANKING spread above base rate borrowers agree to pay an agreed spread for lending paid by borrowers, based on a reference rate such as the London Interbank Offered Rate

length of service HR & PERSONNEL how long employee has worked for firm the period in which somebody has been continually employed in an organization, without breaks in the **contract of employment**. Length of service may determine entitlement to employment rights or **fringe benefits**, for example, the amount of annual leave allocated.

less developed country ECONOMICS poorer country with limited economic development a country whose economic development is held back because it lacks the technology and capital to make use of its natural resources to produce goods demanded on world markets. *Abbr* **LDC**

lessee LEGAL user of something leased the person who has the use of a leased asset

lessor LEGAL provider of something on lease the person who provides an asset being leased

let *UK* REAL ESTATE = ***rent***

letter of acknowledgment GENERAL MANAGEMENT letter saying something has been received a letter written to somebody to say that something that he or she sent has been received

letter of agreement LEGAL simple contract a document that constitutes a simple form of contract

letter of comfort *UK* BANKING = ***letter of moral intent***

letter of credit BANKING letter of authorization from one bank to another a letter issued by a bank that can be presented to another bank to authorize the issue of credit or money. *Abbr* **L/C**

letter of indemnity LEGAL statement accepting loss from replaced stock certificate a statement that a stock certificate has been lost, destroyed, or stolen and that the stockholder will indemnify the company for any loss that might result from its reappearance after the company has issued a replacement to the stockholder

letter of intent BUSINESS written commitment to do something a document that indicates an intention to do something such as buy a business, grant somebody a loan, or participate in a project. The intention may or may not depend on specific conditions being met and the document is not legally binding. *See also* ***letter of moral intent***

letter of license LEGAL, FINANCE letter giving debtor more time for repayment a letter from a creditor to a debtor who is having problems repaying money owed, giving the debtor a specific period of time to raise the money and an undertaking not to bring legal proceedings to recover the debt during that period

letter of moral intent *US* BANKING parent company's support for subsidiary's loan a letter from a holding company addressed to a bank where one of its subsidiaries wishes to borrow money. The purpose of the letter is to support the subsidiary's application to borrow funds and offer reassurance – although not a guarantee – to the bank that the subsidiary will remain in business for the foreseeable future, often with an undertaking to advise the bank if the subsidiary is likely to be sold. *UK term* ***letter of comfort***

letter of renunciation STOCKHOLDING & INVESTMENTS document transferring new stock a form used to transfer an allotment of shares in a **rights issue** to another person

letter security STOCKHOLDING & INVESTMENTS unregistered security salable under certain conditions in the United States, a security that has not been registered with the **SEC** but can be sold privately if the buyer signs a letter of intent stating that the security is for investment, not resale, or can be traded publicly if the owner files a Form 144 with the SEC showing that the sale meets conditions that exempts it from registration with the SEC

letters patent LEGAL official document conferring commercial rights on inventor an official document giving somebody the exclusive right to make and sell something that he or she has invented

level load STOCKHOLDING & INVESTMENTS decreasing annual fee an annual fee that is deducted from the assets in a mutual fund to cover management costs and that decreases gradually over time

level term insurance INSURANCE life insurance policy for fixed period a life insurance policy in which an agreed lump sum is paid if the policyholder dies before a specific date. A joint form of this life cover is popular with couples who have children.

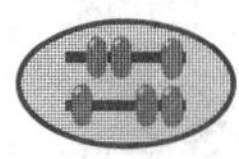

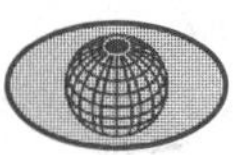

leverage FINANCE corporate funding mainly through borrowing a method of corporate funding in which a higher proportion of funds is raised through borrowing than through stock issue. *Also called* ***gearing****. See also* ***financial leverage***

leveraged bid MERGERS & ACQUISITIONS takeover bid with borrowed finance a takeover bid financed by borrowed money, rather than by a stock issue

leveraged buyout MERGERS & ACQUISITIONS takeover with borrowed finance a takeover using borrowed money, with the purchased company's assets as collateral. *Abbr* **LBO**

leveraged investment company *US* STOCKHOLDING & INVESTMENTS investment company using borrowed money to expand an investment company that borrows money in order to increase its portfolio. When the market is rising, stocks in a leveraged investment trust rise faster than those in an unleveraged trust, but they fall faster when the market is falling. *UK term* ***geared investment trust***

leveraged required return STOCKHOLDING & INVESTMENTS income from investment exceeding cost of loan the rate of return from an investment of borrowed money needed to make the investment worthwhile

leverage ratios FINANCE, RISK means of quantifying risk from capital ratios that indicate the level of risk taken by a company as a result of its capital structure. A number of different ratios may be calculated, for example, debt ratio (total debt divided by total assets), debt-to-equity or leverage ratio (total debt divided by total equity), or interest cover (earnings before interest and tax divided by interest paid). *Also called* ***gearing ratios***

levy TAX tax that raises money for specific purpose a type of tax on a specific product or service by which a government raises money for a specific purpose

liabilities FINANCE firm's debts the debts of a business, including dividends owed to stockholders

liability FINANCE money lent without guarantee of repayment a debt that has no claim on a debtor's assets, or less claim than another debt

liability insurance INSURANCE insurance against incurring costs insurance against legal liability that the insured might incur, for example, from causing an accident

liability management FINANCE investigation of impact of liabilities on profitability any exercise carried out by a business with the objective of controlling the effect of liabilities on its profitability. This will typically involve controlling the amount of risk undertaken, and ensuring that there is sufficient liquidity and that the best terms are obtained for any funding needs.

LIBID *abbr* MARKETS London Interbank Bid Rate

LIBOR *abbr* MARKETS London Interbank Offered Rate

license *US* LEGAL contract to do or use something for payment a contractual arrangement, or a document representing this, in which one organization gives another the rights to produce, sell, or use something in return for payment

licensed deposit-taker FINANCE UK institution that took deposits and paid interest formerly in the United Kingdom, a type of **deposit-taking institution** that was licensed to receive money on deposit from private individuals and to pay interest on it, for example, a bank or savings and loan. *Abbr* **LDT**

licensed institution FINANCE = ***licensed deposit-taker***

licensing LEGAL making contract to do or use something the transfer of rights to manufacture or market a particular product to another individual or organization through a legal arrangement or contract. Licensing usually requires that a fee, commission, or royalty is paid to the licensor.

licensing agreement LEGAL permission for firm to do or use something an agreement permitting a company to market or produce a product or service owned by another company. A licensing agreement grants a license in return for a fee or royalty payment. Items licensed for use can include patents, trademarks, techniques, designs, and expertise. This kind of agreement is one way for a company to penetrate overseas markets in that it provides a middle path between direct export and investment overseas.

lien LEGAL legal right to hold property against debt a legal right to hold somebody's goods or property until a debt that is secured by the goods or property has been repaid

life annuity INSURANCE annuity with fixed monthly payment until death an annuity that pays a fixed amount per month until the holder's death

life assurance *UK* INSURANCE = ***life insurance***

Life Assurance and Unit Trust Regulatory Organization REGULATION & COMPLIANCE *see* ***LAUTRO***

life assured INSURANCE = ***life insured***

lifeboat 1. FINANCE = ***lifeboat scheme* 2.** *S. Africa* BANKING loan to rescue commercial bank a low-interest emergency loan made by a central bank to rescue a commercial bank in danger of becoming insolvent

lifeboat scheme FINANCE rescue measure for business or fund a measure designed to protect or rescue a failing business or fund. *Also called* ***lifeboat*** *(sense 1)*

life cover INSURANCE = ***life insurance***

life cycle MARKETING course of product's development and sales over time the sales pattern of a product or service over a period of time. Typically, a life cycle falls into four stages: introduction, growth, maturity, and decline.

life-cycle costing ACCOUNTING way of assessing asset's cost over time a method of calculating the total cost of a physical asset throughout its life. Life-cycle costing is concerned with all costs of ownership and takes account of the costs incurred by an asset from its acquisition to its disposal, including design, installation, operating, and maintenance costs.

life-cycle fund STOCKHOLDING & INVESTMENTS mutual fund linked to investor's age a mutual fund whose investments vary according to the age of the investor

life-cycle savings motive ECONOMICS reason for saving money over lifetime a reason that a household or individual has for saving at specific times in life so as to have sufficient funds available to spend on anticipated expenses, for example, when starting a family or nearing retirement

life expectancy INSURANCE, PENSIONS how long average person lives the number of years that somebody of a given age is expected to live

life insurance *US* INSURANCE insurance paying others on insured's death insurance that pays a specified sum to the insured person's beneficiaries after the person's death. *Also called* ***life cover****. UK term* ***life assurance***

life insurance bond INSURANCE = ***investment bond***

life insured *US* INSURANCE person with life insurance policy the person or persons covered by a life insurance policy. The insurance company pays out on the death of the policyholder. *UK term* ***life assured***

life interest REAL ESTATE lifetime right to benefit from property a situation where somebody benefits from a property for the entirety of his or her lifetime

life office INSURANCE, PENSIONS firm offering life insurance in the United Kingdom, a company that provides life insurance and sometimes pension plans

life policy INSURANCE, PENSIONS life insurance contract a contract for insurance that pays a specific sum to the insured person's beneficiaries after the person's death

lifestyle audit TAX comparison of taxpayer's living standards to reported income a study of a taxpayer's living standards and spending to determine if it is consistent with that person's reported income

lifestyle business BUSINESS business run by enthusiasts a typically small business run by individuals who have a strong interest in the product or service offered, for example, handmade greeting cards or jewelry, antique dealing or restoring. Such businesses tend to operate during hours that suit the owners, and generally provide them with a comfortable living.

life table STATISTICS table listing expected life spans by age a table that shows the probabilities of death, survival, and remaining years of life for people of given ages

lifetime customer value BUSINESS = ***lifetime value***

lifetime transfer TAX = ***chargeable transfer***

lifetime value BUSINESS person's accumulated expenditure on brand a measure of the total value to a supplier of a customer's business over the duration of their transactions.

In a consumer business, customer lifetime value is calculated by analyzing the behavior of a group of customers who have the same recruitment date. The revenue and cost for this group of customers is recorded, by campaign or season, and the overall contribution for that period can then be worked out. Industry experience has shown that the benefits to a business of increasing lifetime value can be enormous. A 5% increase in customer retention can create a 125% increase in profits; a 10% increase in retailer retention can translate to a 20% increase in sales; and extending customer life cycles by three years can treble profits per customer. *Also called **lifetime customer value***

LIFFE *abbr* MARKETS London International Financial Futures and Options Exchange

lightning strike HR & PERSONNEL strike that happens with little warning in the United Kingdom, a stoppage of work as protest that occurs at very short notice. It may be of short duration and may not be sanctioned by a labor union.

LIMEAN *abbr* BANKING London Interbank Mean Rate

limit STOCKHOLDING & INVESTMENTS specified minimum or maximum price for transaction an amount above or below which a broker is not to conclude the purchase or sale of a security for the client who specifies it

limit down MARKETS maximum daily price fall in option the most that the price of an option may fall in one day on a particular market

Limited BUSINESS part of name of UK limited company when placed at the end of the company's name, used to indicate that a UK company is a limited company

limited company BUSINESS UK firm with individual liability related to investment a British-registered company in which each stockholder is responsible for the company's debts only to the amount that he or she has invested in the company. Limited companies must be formed by at least two directors. *See also **private company, publicly held corporation**. Abbr* **Ltd**

limited legal tender LEGAL, CURRENCY & EXCHANGE bills and coins only usable in small transactions in some jurisdictions, low denomination bills and all coins that may only be submitted up to a specific sum as legal tender in any one transaction

limited liability BUSINESS obligation to pay limited to size of investment the restriction of an owner's loss in a business to the amount of capital he or she has invested in it

limited liability company *UK* BUSINESS = ***corporation***

limited market MARKETS market with few of each security a market in which dealings for a specific security are difficult to transact, for example, because it has only limited appeal to investors or, in the case of stock, because institutions or family members are unlikely to sell it

limited partnership BUSINESS firm with partners responsible for proportion of debts a registered business in which the liability of the partners is limited to the amount of capital they have each provided for the business, and in the running of which the partners may not take part

limit order STOCKHOLDING & INVESTMENTS order to buy or sell security an order to a broker to sell a security at or above an agreed price, or to buy a security at or below an agreed price

limit up MARKETS maximum daily price rise in option the most that the price of an option may rise in one day on a particular market

linear programming GENERAL MANAGEMENT method for optimizing production a mathematical technique used to identify an optimal solution for the deployment of resources to meet organizational objectives. Linear programming uses graphic and algebraic means to calculate which combination of resources, subject to predicted constraints, is most likely to fulfill a given objective.

line management GENERAL MANAGEMENT hierarchy where each employee reports to single manager a hierarchical **chain of command** from executive to front-line level. Line management is the oldest and least complex management structure, in which top management have total and direct authority and employees report to only one supervisor. Managers in this type of organizational structure have direct responsibility for giving orders to their subordinates. Line management structures are usually organized along functional lines, although they increasingly undertake a variety of cross-functional duties such as employee development or strategic direction. The lowest managerial level in an organization following a line management structure is supervisory management.

line manager GENERAL MANAGEMENT employee's direct boss an employee's immediate superior, who oversees and has responsibility for the employee's work. A line manager at the lowest level of a large organization is a supervisor, but a manager at any level with direct responsibility for employees' work can be described as a line manager.

line of credit FINANCE means of borrowing money an agreed finance facility that allows a company or individual to borrow money. *Also called **bank line, credit line***

line organization GENERAL MANAGEMENT hierarchy with line managers an organizational structure that is based on **line management**

liquid FINANCE easy to convert to cash describes an asset that is easily converted to cash

liquid asset ratio FINANCE ratio of liquid to total assets the ratio of liquid assets to total

  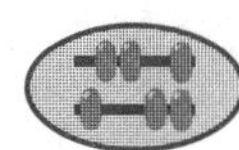   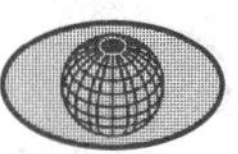   

assets. This is an indicator of a company's solvency.

liquid assets FINANCE possible sources of cash cash, and other assets readily convertible into cash without significant loss of capital

liquidate **1.** BUSINESS end existence of firm to close a company by selling its assets, paying off any outstanding debts, distributing any remaining profits to the stockholders, and then ceasing trading **2.** STOCKHOLDING & INVESTMENTS convert into cash to sell assets in order to be able to have cash

liquidated damages LEGAL penalty for breaking contract an amount of money somebody pays for breaching a **contract**

liquidated damages clause LEGAL clause stating penalty for breaking contract a clause in a **contract** that sets out the compensation to be paid in the event of a breach or a default of the terms of the contract. The compensation set out in a liquidated damages clause should be a genuine preestimate of the loss suffered as a result of the noncompletion of the contract. An example would be an amount payable per day in the event of the noncompletion of a building project. If the amount specified is not considered a genuine estimate of the losses incurred, and the clause is perceived to be solely an incentive for the completion of the contract, the clause is deemed a penalty clause and is not legally enforceable. However, liquidated damages clauses are often inaccurately referred to as penalty clauses. *See also* ***breach of contract***

liquidation BUSINESS process of ending existence of firm the winding-up of a company, a process during which assets are sold, liabilities settled as far as possible, and any remaining cash returned to the members. Liquidation may be voluntary or compulsory.

liquidation value BUSINESS yield from quick sale of firm's assets the amount of money that a quick sale of all of a company's assets would yield

liquidator BUSINESS seller of insolvent firm's assets the person appointed by a company, its creditors, or its stockholders to sell the assets of an insolvent company. The proceeds of the sale are used to discharge debts to creditors, with any surplus distributed to stockholders.

liquidity FINANCE ability to obtain cash from assets an assessment of the ease with which assets can be converted to cash

liquidity agreement FINANCE agreement to cash in asset an agreement to allow a company to convert an asset into cash

liquidity event FINANCE exit strategy of startup business the means by which founders and initial investors in a new company are able to obtain the money the business has earned by changing their **equity** into cash. The company may be sold or there may be a public offering of stock.

liquidity preference FINANCE desire for cash over other investments a choice made by people to hold their wealth in the form of cash rather than bonds or stocks. A general increase in liquidity preference is symptomatic of a financial crisis whereas a general decrease is associated with increased appetite for risk.

liquidity ratio FINANCE = ***cash ratio***

liquidity risk RISK danger of inability to cash in assets the risk that an entity will encounter difficulty in realizing assets or otherwise raising funds to meet commitments associated with financial instruments. *See also* ***funding risk***

liquidity squeeze FINANCE time when money is hard to borrow a situation or period in which money for borrowing is unavailable from finance companies, banks, and other lenders of money. *Also called* ***credit squeeze***

liquidity trap BANKING inability to push interest rates lower a central bank's inability to lower interest rates once investors believe rates can go no lower

liquid market MARKETS market with brisk trading a market in which a large number of trades are being made

liquid savings FINANCE money saved money held in deposit and savings accounts that is easily available if needed and not usually subject to large fluctuations in value

list broker BUSINESS intermediary arranging shared mailing lists a person or organization that makes the arrangements for one company to use another company's direct mail list

listed company BUSINESS firm with stock trading on exchange a company whose stock is quoted on a recognized stock exchange. *Also called* ***quoted company***

listed security STOCKHOLDING & INVESTMENTS, MARKETS security traded on exchange a security that is quoted on a recognized stock exchange

Listing Agreement MARKETS agreement when firm's stock are listed a document that a company signs when being listed on the Stock Exchange, in which the company promises to abide by stock exchange regulations

listing details MARKETS **1.** information published before firm's UK stock exchange listing in the United Kingdom, detailed information about a company, which is published when the company applies for a listing on a stock exchange. The US equivalent is the **registration statement**. **2.** information about institutions backing issue detailed information published about the institutions that are backing a stock issue

listing requirements MARKETS conditions for security to be traded on exchange the conditions that have to be met before a security can be traded on a recognized stock exchange. Although exact requirements vary from one exchange to another, the two main ones are that the issuing company's assets should exceed a minimum amount and that the required information about its finances and business should have been published.

list price BUSINESS product price given by supplier the price of goods or services published by a supplier. The list price of an item may be discounted to regular customers or for bulk purchases.

list renting BUSINESS making firm's direct mail list available for fee an arrangement in which a company that owns a direct mail list lets another company use it for a fee

litigation LEGAL process of dealing with lawsuit the process of bringing a lawsuit against a person or organization

Little Board MARKETS American Stock Exchange for small firms the New York exchange for lesser companies' stocks and bonds. *Also called* ***American Stock Exchange***. *See also* ***Big Board***

lively market MARKETS stock market with brisk trading an active stock market in which many stocks are being bought or sold

livery MARKETING symbol on corporate property a mark of corporate identity used on something belonging to a company

living wage FINANCE amount of pay needed for normal life a level of pay that provides enough income for normal day-to-day basic requirements

living will LEGAL instructions for allowing death a legal document that specifies the measures you want or do not want taken to prolong your life in the event of a terminal illness or injury. It may also designate a person to make healthcare decisions on your behalf.

     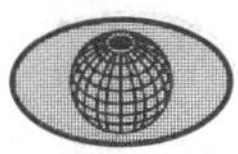   

Lloyd's INSURANCE = ***Lloyd's of London***

Lloyd's broker INSURANCE agent arranging insurance through Lloyd's an agent who represents a client who wants insurance, and who arranges this insurance for him through a **Lloyd's underwriting syndicate**

Lloyd's of London INSURANCE London-based insurance market an insurance market based in London made up of a group of member underwriting syndicates that underwrite most types of insurance policy. *Also called* **Lloyd's**. *See also* ***Lloyd's underwriting syndicate***

Lloyd's underwriting syndicate INSURANCE London-based syndicate underwriting insurance an underwriting syndicate in membership with **Lloyd's of London**

LME *abbr* MARKETS London Metal Exchange

load STOCKHOLDING & INVESTMENTS administration charge for investment a charge in some investment funds to cover administration, profit, and incidentals. When the primary cost is paid at the beginning this is **front-end loading**; at the end it is **back-end loading**. *See also* ***load fund***

load fund STOCKHOLDING & INVESTMENTS mutual fund requiring payment for transactions a mutual fund that charges a fee for the purchase or sale of shares. *See also* ***no-load fund***

loading 1. OPERATIONS & PRODUCTION giving particular jobs to workstation the assignment of tasks or jobs to a workstation. The loading of jobs is worked out through the use of **master production scheduling**. **2.** *ANZ* FINANCE extra pay for exceptional skills or work environment a payment made to employees over and above the basic wage in recognition of special skills or unfavorable conditions, for example, for overtime or shiftwork

loan FINANCE borrowing arrangement with fixed schedule a borrowing either by a business or a consumer where the amount borrowed is repaid according to an agreed schedule at an agreed interest rate, typically by regular installments over a set period of years. However, the principal may be repayable in one installment. *See also* ***balloon loan, fixed-rate loan, interest-only mortgage, variable interest rate***

loanable funds theory ECONOMICS interest rates are determined by supply and demand the theory that interest rates are determined solely by supply and demand. It assumes that consumers must be offered interest on their savings to induce them not just to spend their income and to make funds available for investment.

loanback 1. FINANCE in US, return of money to lender in the United States, the return to somebody of money that has been given as a loan, often as a way of illegally masking the money's true owner **2.** PENSIONS in UK, arrangement to borrow from pension fund in the United Kingdom, the ability of a holder of a pension fund to borrow money from it

loan capital FINANCE money firm borrows for operations a part of a company's capital that is a loan to be repaid at a later date

loan committee FINANCE group considering nonstandard loan applications a committee that examines applications for special loans, such as higher loans than usually allowed by a bank

loan constant ratio FINANCE ratio of annual payments to original balance the total of annual payments due on a loan as a fraction of the amount of the principal

Loan Council FINANCE Australian federal committee overseeing borrowing by states an Australian federal body, made up of treasurers from the states and the Commonwealth of Australia, that monitors borrowing by state governments

loan loss reserves BANKING sum held by bank to cover bad debts the money a bank holds to cover losses through defaults on loans that it makes

loan note FINANCE written details of loan a written agreement between parties describing the terms of repayment, interest if applicable, and due date of a loan

loan participation BANKING collaboration by banks to make single large loan the grouping together by several banks to share a very large loan to one single customer

loan production cycle FINANCE time between loan application and lending of money the period that begins with an application for a loan and ends with the lending of money

loan schedule FINANCE details of loan payments a list of the payments due on a loan and the balance outstanding after each has been made

loan shark FINANCE lender charging excessively high interest rates somebody who lends money at excessively, often illegally, high rates of interest (*informal*)

loan stock STOCKHOLDING & INVESTMENTS bonds and debentures a fixed-income security given in exchange for a loan

loan to value ratio FINANCE ratio of worth of loan to collateral the ratio of the amount of a loan to the value of the collateral for it. *Abbr* **LTV ratio**

loan value FINANCE sum available to borrower the amount that a lender is willing to lend a borrower

lobby GENERAL MANAGEMENT group trying to influence decisions of politicians a group that seeks to influence government or legislators on behalf of a specific cause or interest

local MARKETS independent trader in futures or options a trader in futures or options, who occasionally makes trades on behalf of clients, but usually trades on his or her own account

local authority bond STOCKHOLDING & INVESTMENTS UK local government's fixed-interest bond in the United Kingdom, a loan raised by a local authority in the form of a fixed-interest bond, repayable at a specific date. Local authority bonds are similar to US **Treasury bonds**.

local authority deposits FINANCE money lent to UK local government in the United Kingdom, money deposited with a local authority to earn interest for the depositor

localization MARKETING customizing to geographic audience adapting products, websites, and marketing to the needs of target users in different parts of the world. Studies have shown that if a vendor is serious about selling to foreign marketplaces, localizing is essential. Without localization, sales will be minimal, and returns very high.

lockbox BANKING banking service for checks sent by mail a banking system in which checks sent to a Post Office box rather than to a company are picked up by a bank and deposited in a bank account

lock limit MARKETS market limit on price change per session an occasion in which the trading price of a contract in a **futures market** reaches an exchange's specified upward or downward limit during a trading session, causing trading to halt. Lock limits are set to protect investors from large losses in a volatile market.

lockup period MARKETS time when investors cannot sell a specified period of time during which investors, especially insiders and employees of an initial public offering, are unable to sell their shares of stock

logistics OPERATIONS & PRODUCTION controlling flow of materials through firm's processes the management of the movement, storage, and processing of materials and information in the **supply chain**. Logistics encompasses the

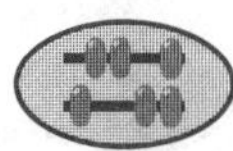

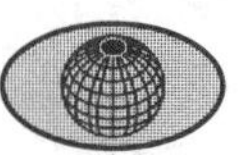

acquisition of raw materials and components, manufacturing or processing, and the distribution of finished products to the end user. Each organization focuses on a different aspect of logistics, depending on its area of interest. For example, one might apply logistics to find a way of linking **physical distribution management** with earlier events in the supply chain, another to plan its acquisition and storage, while a third might use logistics as a support operation.

logistics management OPERATIONS & PRODUCTION handling of delivery the management of the distribution of products to the market

logo GENERAL MANAGEMENT firm's recognizable symbol a graphic device or symbol used by an organization as part of its corporate identity. A logo is used to facilitate instant recognition of an organization and to reinforce **brand** expectations and public image.

Lombard loan RISK loan with securities pledged as collateral a loan granted by a financial institution against pledged collateral in the form of securities

London Bullion Market MARKETS market for gold and silver the world's largest market for gold, where silver is also traded. It is a wholesale market, where the minimum trades are generally 1,000 ounces for gold and 50,000 ounces for silver. Members typically trade with each other and their clients on a principal-to-principal basis so that all risks, including those of credit, are between the two parties to the transaction.

London Chamber of Commerce and Industry BUSINESS UK's largest chamber of commerce in the United Kingdom, the largest chamber of commerce, that strives "to help London businesses succeed by promoting their interests and expanding their opportunities as members of a worldwide business network." *See also* ***ICC***

London Clearing House MARKETS organization trading in contracts for members an organization that acts on behalf of its members as a central counterparty for contracts traded on the London International Financial Futures and Options Exchange, the International Petroleum Exchange, and the London Metal Exchange. When the LCH has registered a trade, it becomes the buyer to every member who sells and the seller to every member who buys, ensuring good financial performance. To protect it against the risks assumed as central counterparty, the LCH establishes margin requirements. *Abbr* **LCH**. *See also* ***margining***

London Commodity Exchange MARKETS *see* ***London International Financial Futures and Options Exchange***

London Interbank Bid Rate MARKETS UK rate for banks' bidding for deposits on the UK money markets, the rate at which banks will bid to take deposits in Eurocurrency from each other. The deposits are for terms from overnight up to five years. *Abbr* **LIBID**

London Interbank Mean Rate MARKETS average of two inter-bank interest rates the average of the London Inter Bank Offered Rate and the London Inter Bank Bid Rate, occasionally used as a reference rate. *Abbr* **LIMEAN**

London Interbank Offered Rate MARKETS UK rate for bank's offering to take deposits on the UK money markets, the rate at which banks will offer to make deposits in Eurocurrency from each other, often used as a reference rate. The deposits are for terms from overnight up to five years. *Abbr* **LIBOR**

London International Financial Futures and Options Exchange MARKETS exchange for financial futures and options an exchange for trading financial futures and options. Established in 1982, it offered contracts on interest rates denominated in most of the world's major currencies until 1992, when it merged with the London Traded Options Market, adding equity options to its product range. In 1996 it merged with the London Commodity Exchange, adding a variety of soft commodity and agricultural commodity contracts to its financial portfolio. From November 1998, trading gradually migrated from the floor of the exchange to screen-based trading. *Abbr* **LIFFE**

London Metal Exchange MARKETS market for aluminum, tin, and nickel one of the world's largest nonferrous metal exchanges, that deals in aluminum, tin, and nickel. The primary roles of the exchange are hedging, providing official international reference prices, and appropriate storage facilities. Its origins can be traced back to 1571, though in its present form it dates from 1877. *Abbr* **LME**

London Traded Options Market MARKETS *see* ***London International Financial Futures and Options Exchange***

long STOCKHOLDING & INVESTMENTS having more shares than wanted having a positive holding as a trader in a security

long bond or **long coupon bond** STOCKHOLDING & INVESTMENTS bond that matures after 10 years or more a bond which will mature in more than ten years' time, usually a 30-year bond issued by the US Department of the Treasury

long credit FINANCE loan that borrower can repay over long time credit terms which allow the borrower a long time to pay back the money he or she has borrowed

long-dated STOCKHOLDING & INVESTMENTS maturing after 15 years or more used to describe securities such as bonds that mature after fifteen years or more. *See also* ***short-dated***

long-dated bill STOCKHOLDING & INVESTMENTS bill payable after three or more months a bill that is payable at a date that is not less than three months away

long-dated gilt STOCKHOLDING & INVESTMENTS UK government security maturing in 15 years or more a security issued by the UK government that pays a fixed rate of interest on a regular basis until the redemption date, in 15 years or more, when the principal is returned. *See also* ***gilt-edged security***

long-dated stocks STOCKHOLDING & INVESTMENTS = ***longs***

long firm fraud FRAUD crime of business buying on credit, then disappearing in the United Kingdom, a criminal activity in which somebody sets up an apparently legitimate wholesaling business, obtains fake credit references, trades on credit with wholesale suppliers with no intention of paying for the goods, and then disappears

longitudinal study STATISTICS statistical investigation over period of time a statistical study that produces data gathered over a period of time

long lease REAL ESTATE over 21-year lease in UK in the United Kingdom, a rental agreement that runs at least 21 years

long position MARKETS when dealers avoid selling a situation in which dealers hold securities, commodities, or contracts, expecting prices to rise. *See also* ***short position***

longs STOCKHOLDING & INVESTMENTS long-term government stocks government stocks that will mature more than15 years after the date of purchase

long-term balance of payments INTERNATIONAL TRADE record of money used in overseas investments a record of movements of capital relating to overseas investments and the purchase of companies overseas

long-term bond STOCKHOLDING & INVESTMENTS bond maturing in 7 years or more a bond that has at least seven years before its redemption date, or, in some markets, a bond with more than seven years until its redemption date

long-term borrowings FINANCE borrowings repayable in several years' time money that is borrowed that does not have to be repaid for a number of years

long-term care insurance INSURANCE insurance against need for costly care insurance that provides coverage for a person who needs ongoing care in a nursing home or their own home

long-term debt FINANCE loans for more than one year loans and debentures that are not due until after at least one year

long-term equity anticipation securities STOCKHOLDING & INVESTMENTS *see* ***LEAPS***

long-term financing FINANCE provision of funding with extended credit forms of funding, such as loans or stock issue, that do not have to be repaid immediately

long-term lease REAL ESTATE lease of 10 years plus a lease that does not expire for at least ten years

long-term liabilities FINANCE debts with extended credit forms of debt such as loans that do not have to be repaid immediately

lookback option MARKETS option with price selected from past prices an option whose price the buyer chooses from all of the prices that have existed during the option's life

loose change CURRENCY & EXCHANGE coins of little value money in the form of coins, especially when the value is small

loose credit ECONOMICS easily available credit to encourage growth a central banking policy to make borrowing easier by lowering interest rates in order to stimulate economic activity

loss ACCOUNTING when costs of activity exceed income from it a financial position in which the **costs** of an activity exceed the **income** derived from it

loss adjuster *UK* INSURANCE = ***adjuster***

loss assessor INSURANCE in UK, person who assists with insurance claims in the United Kingdom, somebody appointed by an insurance policyholder to assist with his or her claim. *See also* ***claims adjuster***

loss carryback ACCOUNTING application of current-year loss to prior year the process of applying a net operating loss to a previous accounting year in order to reduce tax liability in that year

loss carryforward ACCOUNTING application of current-year loss to future year the process of applying a net operating loss to a following accounting year in order to reduce tax liability in that year

loss control FINANCE, RISK methods of limiting impact of loss of asset the implementation of safety procedures to prevent or limit the impact of a complete or partial loss of an organization's physical assets. Loss control is based on safety audit and prevention techniques. It is concerned with reduction or elimination of losses caused by accidents and occupational ill health. The extent to which it is implemented is usually decided by calculating the total organizational asset cost and weighing this against the likelihood of failure and its worst possible effects on the organization. Loss control was developed in the 1960s as an approach to **risk management**.

loss leader MARKETING product sold cheaply to attract customers for others a product or service that is sold below the cost of producing it in order to attract more customers to other associated products for purchase

lossmaker BUSINESS product or firm that loses money a product or company that fails to make a profit or break even

loss-making BUSINESS losing money used to describe a business or business activity that is losing money

loss relief TAX in UK, tax relief on previous year's loss in the United Kingdom, an amount of tax not to be paid on one year's profit to offset a loss in the previous year

lot **1.** MARKETS smallest quantity traded on exchange the minimum quantity of a commodity that may be purchased on an exchange, for example, 1,000 ounces of gold on the London Bullion Market **2.** BUSINESS unit for sale at auction an item or a collection of related items being offered for sale at an auction **3.** MARKETS group of shares treated together in the United States, a group of shares held or traded together, usually in units of 100 **4.** *US, Canada* REAL ESTATE land for sale a piece of land assigned to be sold. *UK term* ***plot***

lottery GENERAL MANAGEMENT random selection of successful applicants the random method of selecting successful applicants for something, occasionally used when a new stock issue is oversubscribed

lower level domain E-COMMERCE sublevel name at beginning of Internet address the main part of a domain name. For most e-business sites this is usually the company or brand name.

lower of cost or market ACCOUNTING accounting method treating stocks at lower value a method used by manufacturing and supply firms when accounting for their homogenous stocks which involves valuing them either at their original cost or the current market price, whichever is lower. *Abbr* **LCM**

low gearing *UK* FINANCE low ratio of firm's debt to assets a situation in which a company has only a small amount of debt in proportion to its assets

low start mortgage MORTGAGES loan with only interest repayment at first a long-term loan, usually for the purchase of real estate, in which the borrower only pays the interest on the loan for the first few years, usually three. After that, the payments increase to cover the interest and part of the original loan, as in an **amortized mortgage**. Low start mortgages are popular with first-time buyers, as the lower initial costs may free up funds for furnishings or home improvements. *See also* ***mortgage***

loyalty bonus STOCKHOLDING & INVESTMENTS extra shares given after UK privatizations in the United Kingdom in the 1980s, a number of extra shares, calculated as a proportion of the shares originally subscribed, given to original subscribers of privatization issues providing the shares were held continuously for a given period of time

Ltd *abbr* *UK* BUSINESS limited company

LTV ratio *abbr* FINANCE loan to value ratio

lump sum FINANCE **1.** repaid in one installment used to describe a loan that is repayable with one installment at the end of its term. *See also* ***balloon loan, interest-only mortgage*** **2.** money received in single payment an amount of money received in one payment, for example, the sum payable to the beneficiary of a life insurance policy on the death of the policyholder

luxury tax TAX tax on inessential items a tax on goods or services that are considered nonessential

M

M0 ECONOMICS money available to public for spending an estimate of the amount of money in public circulation, available for use as a means of exchange. *Also called* ***narrow money*** *(sense 2)*

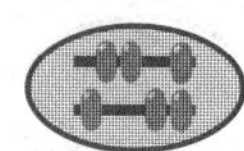

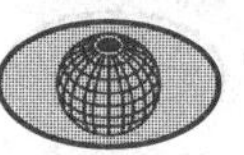

M1 ECONOMICS cash plus bank accounts an estimate of the amount of money held by the public in coins, banknotes, and checking accounts. *Also called* ***narrow money*** *(sense 1)*

M2 ECONOMICS cash plus easily available deposits an estimate of the amount of money held by the public in coins, currency, checking and savings accounts, and deposits

M3 ECONOMICS M1, M2 plus international money an estimate of the amount of money in M1, M2 and large denomination repurchase agreements, institutional money market accounts, and some Eurodollar time deposits

ma and pa shop UK BUSINESS = ***mom-and-pop operation***

Macaulay duration MARKETS, RISK measure of interest-rate risk in owning bonds a measure of a bond's sensitivity to changes in interest rates. It is calculated by dividing the present value of the cash flows received by the current market value of the bond. *See also* ***modified duration***

machine hour rate FINANCE proportion of overhead costs an **overhead absorption rate** based on the number of hours a machine is used in production

macroeconomics ECONOMICS study of national economic systems the study of national income and the economic systems of nations. *See also* ***microeconomics***

macroeconomy ECONOMICS national economy as whole the broad sectors of a country's economic activity, for example, the financial or industrial sectors, that are aggregated to form its economic system as a whole. *See also* ***microeconomy***

macrohedge RISK reduction of risk on whole portfolio a **hedge** that aims to cover the overall risk to an entire investment **portfolio**. *Also called* ***global hedge***. *See also* ***microhedge***

mail ballot US FINANCE election accepting votes returned by mail an election of officers of a company in which the voters send in their ballot papers by mail. *UK term* ***postal vote***

mail form E-COMMERCE webpage for inputting data sent as e-mail a webpage that requires the user to input data such as name, address, or order or shipping information, that is transmitted to an e-merchant via e-mail

mailing US MARKETING appeal to specific group through mail a speculative targeting of a specific group of people by mail. A mailing normally contains information, advertising, fundraising requests, or press releases.

mailing house MARKETING firm dealing in direct mail projects an organization that specializes in planning, creating, and implementing direct mail campaigns for clients

mailing list MARKETING names and addresses for marketing purposes the names and addresses of a specific group of people compiled for marketing purposes. A mailing list may be compiled internally or bought or rented from an outside agency, and can be used for advertising, fundraising, news releases, or for direct mail or a mailshot. A mailing list is usually compiled for a selected group using one or more criteria, such as men between the ages of 25 and 30, or retired people.

mail order MARKETING method of requesting products from catalog for delivery a form of retailing in which consumers order products from a catalog for delivery to their home

mail-out MARKETING = ***mailing***

mailshot MARKETING = ***mailing***

mailsort MARKETING UK sorting service for direct mail in the United Kingdom, a sorting service offered to organizations by the Post Office, intended to reduce the cost and time spent on direct mail

mainstream corporation tax TAX main UK tax on corporations the principal UK tax on resident companies, paid on profits after deduction of allowable expenses. This was formerly reduced by the amount of **advance corporation tax** already paid.

maintenance bond STOCKHOLDING & INVESTMENTS guarantee for period after complete transaction a bond that provides a guarantee against defects for some time after a contract has been fulfilled

majority decision or **majority vote** GENERAL MANAGEMENT decision of most people made by voting a decision that represents the wishes of the largest group as shown by a vote, for example, in a board meeting or a shareholders' meeting

majority shareholder STOCKHOLDING & INVESTMENTS stockholder with controlling interest a shareholder with a controlling interest in a company. *See also* ***minority interest***

majority shareholding STOCKHOLDING & INVESTMENTS stockholding in excess of 50% a group of shares of stock that are more than half the total and enough to give control to the person or entity holding them

make or buy GENERAL MANAGEMENT *see* ***purchasing versus production***

maladministration GENERAL MANAGEMENT incompetent management of public affairs failure on the part of an administration to act in a competent manner, especially in public affairs

managed account STOCKHOLDING & INVESTMENTS = ***discretionary account***

managed currency fund CURRENCY & EXCHANGE managed fund investing in currencies a managed mutual fund that makes considered investments in foreign exchange

managed derivatives fund STOCKHOLDING & INVESTMENTS fund investing in derivatives a fund that uses mainly **futures** and **options** instead of investing in the underlying securities

managed economy ECONOMICS economy controlled by government an economy directed by a government rather than the free market

managed float ECONOMICS exchange rate affected by government action the position when the exchange rate of a country's currency is influenced by government action in the foreign exchange market

managed fund STOCKHOLDING & INVESTMENTS mutual fund investing after research a mutual fund with professional managers who make considered investments, as opposed to an **index fund**. *Also called* ***managed mutual fund***

managed mutual fund US STOCKHOLDING & INVESTMENTS = ***managed fund***

managed rate BANKING financial institution's independently established interest rate a rate of interest charged by a financial institution for borrowing that it sets itself from time to time, rather than following a prescribed margin over base rate

managed unit trust STOCKHOLDING & INVESTMENTS = ***managed fund***

management GENERAL MANAGEMENT, HR & PERSONNEL using firm's resources effectively to achieve goals the use of professional skills for identifying and achieving organizational objectives through the deployment of appropriate resources. Management involves identifying what needs to be done, and organizing and supporting others to perform the necessary tasks. A manager has complex and ever-changing responsibilities, the focus of which shifts to reflect the issues, trends, and preoccupations of the time. At the beginning of the 20th century, the emphasis was both on supporting the organization's administration and managing **productivity** through increased efficiency. At the beginning of the 21st century, those original drivers are still much in evidence, although the emphasis has moved to key areas of competence such as people management. Although management is a profession in its own right, its skill set often applies to professionals of other disciplines.

management accountant TREASURY MANAGEMENT financial adviser on management decisions a person who contributes to management's decision-making processes by, for example, collecting and processing data relating to a business's costs, sales, and the profitability of individual activities

management accounting TREASURY MANAGEMENT use of accounting principles to benefit organization the application of the principles of accounting and financial management to create, protect, preserve, and increase value so as to deliver that value to the stakeholders of profit and nonprofit enterprises, both public and private. Management accounting is an integral part of management, requiring the identification, generation, presentation, interpretation, and use of information relevant to formulating business strategy; planning and controlling activities; decision making; efficient resource usage; performance improvement and value enhancement; safeguarding tangible and intangible assets; and corporate governance and internal control.

management accounts TREASURY MANAGEMENT financial report prepared for manager financial information prepared for a manager so that decisions can be made, including monthly or quarterly financial statements, often in great detail, with analysis of actual performance against the budget

management audit GENERAL MANAGEMENT = ***operational audit***

management buyin MERGERS & ACQUISITIONS purchase of business by external managers the purchase of an existing business by an individual manager or management group outside that business. *Abbr* **MBI**

management buyout MERGERS & ACQUISITIONS takeover of business by its management the purchase of an existing business by an individual manager or management group from within that business. *Abbr* **MBO**

management by objectives or **management by results** GENERAL MANAGEMENT method for achieving goals through series of objectives a method of managing an organization by setting a series of **objectives** that contribute toward the achievement of its goals. *Abbr* **MBO**

management charge *UK* STOCKHOLDING & INVESTMENTS = ***annual management charge***

management company BUSINESS firm that manages aspects of another firm's business a company that takes over responsibility from internal staff for managing facilities such as computer systems, telecommunications, or maintenance. The process is known as **outsourcing**.

management consultancy *UK* GENERAL MANAGEMENT = ***management consulting***

management consultant GENERAL MANAGEMENT person who gives advice about management methods a person professionally engaged in advising on, and providing, a detached, external view of a company's management techniques and practices. A management consultant may be self-employed, a partner, or employed in a specialist firm. Consultants can be called in for many reasons, but are employed particularly for projects involving business improvement, **change management**, information technology, and long-term planning.

management consulting *US* GENERAL MANAGEMENT giving advice about management methods the activity of advising on management techniques and practices. Management consulting usually involves the identification of a problem, or the analysis of a specific area of one organization, and the reporting of any resulting findings. The consulting process can sometimes be extended to help put into effect the recommendations made. *UK term* ***management consultancy***

management consulting firm GENERAL MANAGEMENT firm giving management advice a firm of **management consultants**, offering professional advice on ways to improve efficiency

management fee STOCKHOLDING & INVESTMENTS fee for managing mutual fund a fee paid to a mutual fund manager by a client to cover their services and a variety of administrative costs

management information system OPERATIONS & PRODUCTION *see* ***MIS***

management process GENERAL MANAGEMENT management of human, financial, and material resources the process of planning, implementing, and controlling activities that involve human, financial, and material resources

management team GENERAL MANAGEMENT, HR & PERSONNEL = ***senior management***

management trainee HR & PERSONNEL low-ranking manager learning management methods an employee who holds a low-level management position while undergoing formal training in management techniques

management training HR & PERSONNEL courses teaching management methods planned activities for developing management skills. Management training methods include public or in-company training courses and on-the-job training designed to improve managerial **competences**. Management training tends to be practical and to focus on specific management techniques. It does not result in a formal degree.

manager GENERAL MANAGEMENT, HR & PERSONNEL employee responsible for part of firm's activities a person who identifies and achieves organizational objectives through the deployment of appropriate resources. A manager can have responsibilities in one or more of five key areas: managing activities; managing resources; managing information; managing people; and managing him- or herself while working within the context of the organizational, political, and economic business environments. There are managers in all disciplines and activities, although some may not bear the title of manager. Some specialize in areas such as personnel, marketing, production, finance, or project management, while others are **general managers**, applying management skills across all business areas. Very few jobs are entirely managerial, and very few exist without any management responsibilities. It is the capability to harness resources that largely distinguishes a manager from a non-manager.

managerialism GENERAL MANAGEMENT firm's focus on effective management emphasis on efficient management, and the use of systems, planning, and management practice. Managerialism is often used in a critical sense, especially from the perspective of the public sector, to imply overenthusiasm for efficiency, or private sector management techniques and systems, possibly at the expense of service or quality considerations. The term is also used to describe confrontational attitudes,

  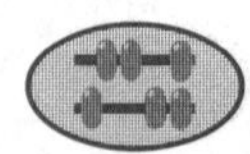   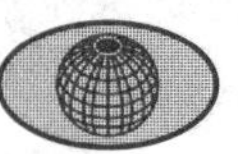   

or actions displayed by management toward labor unions.

managing agent INSURANCE administrator of Lloyd's syndicate a person who runs the day-to-day activities of a Lloyd's syndicate

managing director CORPORATE GOVERNANCE limited company's director in charge of daily business the **chief executive officer** of a **limited company** in the United Kingdom and other countries, who has overall responsibility for its day-to-day operations. *Abbr* **MD**

managing for value GENERAL MANAGEMENT focusing on long-term value of business an approach to building the long-term value of a business. The term is most frequently used by businesses that are implementing the **balanced scorecard approach** and emphasizes the need to make financial and commercial decisions that build the value of the business for its stockholders.

M&A *abbr* MERGERS & ACQUISITIONS mergers and acquisitions

mandarin GENERAL MANAGEMENT important government adviser a high-ranking and influential adviser, especially in government circles

mandatory bid STOCKHOLDING & INVESTMENTS compulsory bid for remaining stock an offer to purchase the remaining shares of a company that a stockholder has to make if he or she acquires at least 30% of that company's stock

mandatory quote period MARKETS time when security prices must be displayed on the London Stock Exchange, the period of time during which prices of securities must be displayed

manpower forecasting GENERAL MANAGEMENT = ***human resource forecasting***

manpower planning GENERAL MANAGEMENT = ***human resource planning***

manufacture OPERATIONS & PRODUCTION making products in factory the large-scale production of goods from raw materials or parts

manufacturer OPERATIONS & PRODUCTION maker of factory products a person or organization involved in the large-scale production of goods from raw materials or parts

manufacturer's agent OPERATIONS & PRODUCTION representative of product-maker for getting contracts a person or organization with authority to act for a **manufacturer** in obtaining a **contract** with a third party

manufacturing OPERATIONS & PRODUCTION process by which product is made the processes and techniques used in making a product from raw materials or parts

manufacturing account ACCOUNTING accounts showing only production costs a financial statement that shows production costs only, as opposed to a **profit and loss account**, which shows sales and costs of sales. A manufacturing account will include direct materials and labor costs and the production overhead.

manufacturing cost OPERATIONS & PRODUCTION money needed to make products the expenditure incurred in carrying out the production processes of an organization. The manufacturing cost includes **direct costs**, for example, labor, materials, and expenses, and indirect costs, for example, subcontracting and overhead.

manufacturing information system OPERATIONS & PRODUCTION computer system for production process a management information system designed specifically for use in a production environment

manufacturing resource planning OPERATIONS & PRODUCTION *see* ***MRP II***

manufacturing system OPERATIONS & PRODUCTION organization of firm's production process a method of organizing production. Manufacturing systems include assembly and **batch production**, **flexible manufacturing systems**, **lean production**, and **mass production**.

manufacturing to order OPERATIONS & PRODUCTION producing goods to fill requests not for stockpile a production management technique in which goods are produced to meet firm orders, rather than being produced for inventory

Marché des Options Négotiables de Paris MARKETS French traded options market in France, the market that deals in options that can be traded at any time. *Abbr* **MONEP**

Marché International de France MARKETS French international exchange in France, the international futures and options exchange

margin FINANCE **1.** gap between cost and selling price the difference between the cost and the selling price of a product or service **2.** ANZ extra pay for employees' special skills a payment made to workers over and above the basic wage in recognition of special skills

margin account FINANCE account with investment broker who lends money an account with a broker who lends money for investments, held in the name of an investor who pays only a percentage of the price of purchases

marginal 1. FINANCE not worth money spent producing very little benefit in relation to the amount of money spent (*informal*) **2.** OPERATIONS & PRODUCTION barely covering production cost nearly unable to cover the cost of production when selling goods or when goods are being sold

marginal analysis ECONOMICS investigation into economic effects of small changes the study of how small changes in an economic variable will affect an economy

marginal cost OPERATIONS & PRODUCTION extra cost of producing additional item the part of the cost of one unit of product or service that would be avoided if that unit were not produced, or that would increase if one extra unit were produced

marginal costing ACCOUNTING accounting system treating variable and fixed costs differently the accounting system in which variable costs are charged to cost units and fixed costs of the period are written off in full against the aggregate contribution. Its special value is in recognizing cost behavior, and hence assisting in decision making. *Also called* ***variable costing***

marginal costs and benefits ECONOMICS losses and gains resulting from incremental changes the losses or gains to a person or household arising from a small change in a variable, such as food consumption or income received

marginalization ECONOMICS process of becoming less important in world economy the process by which countries lose importance and status because they are unable to participate in mainstream activities such as industrialization or the Internet economy

marginal lender FINANCE lender with lower limit on interest rate a lender who will make a loan only at or above a particular rate of interest

marginal pricing OPERATIONS & PRODUCTION setting prices between variable cost and full cost the practice of basing the selling price of a product on its variable costs of production plus a margin, but excluding fixed costs

marginal revenue OPERATIONS & PRODUCTION money from producing more the revenue generated by additional units of production

  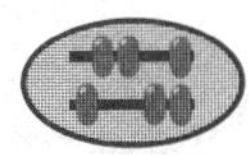 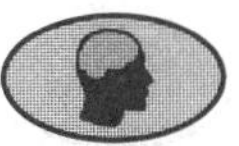  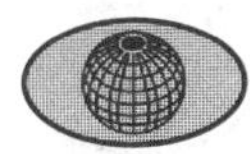   

marginal tax rate TAX tax rate on income after business expenses the rate of tax payable on a person's income after business expenses have been deducted

marginal utility ECONOMICS satisfaction in using one additional unit satisfaction gained from using one more unit of a product or service

margin call STOCKHOLDING & INVESTMENTS request for additional deposit to margin account a request for a purchaser of a futures contract or an option to deposit more money in his or her **margin account**, since the fall in the price of the securities or commodity has brought the value of the original deposit below the minimum required

margining STOCKHOLDING & INVESTMENTS, RISK way London Clearing House controls risk the system by which the London Clearing House controls the risk associated with the position of a member of the London International Financial Futures and Options Exchange on a daily basis. To achieve this, members deposit cash or collateral with the London Clearing House in the form of initial and variation margins. The initial margin is the deposit required on all open positions, long or short, to cover short-term price movements and is returned to members by the London Clearing House when the position is closed. The variation margin is the members' profits or losses, calculated daily from the marked-to-market-close value of their position, whereby contracts are revalued daily for the calculation of variation margin and credited to or debited from their accounts.

margin of error GENERAL MANAGEMENT amount allowed for miscalculation an allowance made for the possibility that something has been miscalculated or that conditions change

margin of safety TREASURY MANAGEMENT level of firm's performance above break-even point the difference between the level of activity at which an organization breaks even and the level of activity greater than this point. For example, a margin of safety of $300,000 is achieved when the break-even point is $900,000 and sales reach $1,200,000. This measure can be expressed as a proportion of sales value, as a number of units sold, or as a percentage of **capacity**.

Margrabe option STOCKHOLDING & INVESTMENTS, RISK = ***exchange option***

marital deductions TAX spouse's nontaxable part of inheritance the part of an estate which, after a death, is not subject to estate tax because it goes to the spouse of the deceased

marital property FINANCE = ***community property***

mark down OPERATIONS & PRODUCTION reduce price of something to make the price of something lower

mark-down OPERATIONS & PRODUCTION **1.** reduction in price an act of reducing the price of something to less than its usual price **2.** percentage reduction in price the percentage amount by which a price has been reduced

marked cheque *UK* BANKING = ***certified check*** *(slang)*

marked price OPERATIONS & PRODUCTION price displayed on product for sale the original displayed price of a product in a store. In a sale, customers may be offered a savings on the marked price.

market 1. FINANCE rate of financial sales the rate at which financial commodities or securities are being sold **2.** ECONOMICS group of consumers with shared need a group of people or organizations unified by common requirements **3.** ECONOMICS group of buyers and sellers trading goods a gathering of sellers and purchasers to exchange commodities ◇ make a market MARKETS to be prepared as a dealer to buy or sell a particular security at the quoted bid or ask price

marketable MARKETING able to be sold successfully possessing the potential to be commercially viable. To determine whether a new product or service is marketable, an assessment needs to be conducted to see if it is likely to make a profit. The assessment is often based on detailed **market research** analyzing the potential market, and the projected financial returns and any other benefits for the company.

marketable security STOCKHOLDING & INVESTMENTS security easily sold or exchanged a security that can easily be sold and converted into cash, or exchanged for a different type of security

market analysis MARKETING study of particular market the study of a market to identify and quantify business opportunities

market area MARKETING where market is the geographic location of a particular group of consumers with shared needs

market-based pricing OPERATIONS & PRODUCTION charging what customer will pay setting a price based on the value of the product in the perception of the customer. *Also called* ***perceived value pricing***

market bubble MARKETS short period of inflated prices a stock market phenomenon in which values in a particular sector become inflated for a short period. If the bubble bursts, stock prices in that sector collapse.

market capitalization MARKETS full market value of firm the total market value of a company, calculated by multiplying the price of its shares on the Stock Exchange by the number of shares outstanding. *Abbr* **market cap**. *Also called* **market valuation** *(sense 1)*

market coverage MARKETS how well product satisfies customers' needs the degree to which a product or service meets the needs of a market

market cycle MARKETS sequence of market expansion, contraction, and expansion a period during which a market expands, then slows down, and then expands again

market development MARKETING activities to expand demand for particular product type marketing activities designed to increase the overall size of a market through education and awareness

market driven or **market-driven** MARKETING strongly influenced by needs of potential customers using market knowledge to determine the corporate strategy of an organization. A market-driven organization has a customer focus, together with awareness of competitors, and an understanding of the market.

market economist MARKETS specialist in investment a person who specializes in the study of financial structures and the return on investments in the stock market

market economy ECONOMICS economic system not controlled by government an economy in which a **free market** in goods and services operates

marketeer MARKETING small firm competing with larger firms a small company that competes in the same market as larger companies. Examples of marketeers are restaurants, travel agents, computer software providers, garages, and insurance brokers.

marketer MARKETING promoter of sales a person who is responsible for developing and implementing marketing policy

marketface MARKETS where suppliers and customers meet the interface between suppliers of goods or services and their customers

market-facing enterprise BUSINESS firm focusing on marketplace and customers an organization that aligns itself with its markets and customers and makes them its priority concern

market-focused organization BUSINESS organization responsive to market needs an organization whose strategies are determined by market requirements rather than organizational demands

market forces MARKETS factors affecting prices influences on sales which bring about a change in prices

market fragmentation MARKETS market consisting of small-scale buyers and sellers a situation in which the buyers or sellers in a market consist of a large number of small organizations

market gap MARKETS situation where no producer is meeting market need an opportunity in a market where no supplier provides a product or service that buyers need

market if touched STOCKHOLDING & INVESTMENTS instruction to trade at specific price an order to trade a security if it reaches a specific price. *Abbr* **MIT**

marketing MARKETING efforts to promote products the process of building long-term relationships with customers and with other interested parties and to provide value to them. This begins with market research, which analyzes needs and wants in society, and continues with attracting customers and the cultivation of mutually beneficial exchange processes with them. Tools used in this process are diverse and include market segmentation, brand management, PR, logistics, direct response marketing, sales promotion, and advertising. ◇ 4 Ps of marketing MARKETING the variety of integrated decisions made by a marketing manager to ensure successful marketing, in four key areas—product, price, place, and promotion—covering issues such as the type of product to be marketed, brand name, pricing, advertising, publicity, geographic coverage, retailing, and distribution

marketing agreement MARKETING agreement to market another firm's product a contract by which one company agrees to market another company's products

marketing audit MARKETING evaluation of firm's marketing approach an analysis of either the external marketing environment or a company's internal marketing goals, objectives, operations, and efficiency. An external marketing audit covers issues such as economic, political, infrastructure, technological, and consumer perspectives; market size and market structure; and competitors, suppliers, and distributors. An internal marketing audit covers aspects such as the company's mission statement, goals, and objectives; its structure, corporate culture, systems, operations, and processes; product development and pricing; profitability and efficiency; advertising; and deployment of the sales force.

marketing consultancy MARKETING firm creating marketing plan for other firms an organization that plans and develops marketing strategies and programs on behalf of clients

marketing information system MARKETING computer system for managing firm's marketing program an information system concerned with the collection, storage, and analysis of information and data for marketing decision-making purposes. Information for use in marketing information systems is gathered from customers, competitors, and their products, and from the market itself.

marketing management MARKETING responsibility for firm's efforts to promote products one of the main management disciplines, encompassing all the strategic planning, operations, activities, and processes involved in achieving organizational objectives by delivering value to customers. Marketing management focuses on satisfying customer requirements by identifying needs and wants, and developing products and services to meet them.

marketing manager MARKETING person responsible for promoting firm's products somebody who is responsible for planning and controlling marketing activities and budgets for a company

marketing mix MARKETING mixture of techniques for promoting products the variety of integrated decisions made by a marketing manager to ensure successful marketing. These decisions are made in four key areas known as the **4 Ps of marketing**—product, price, place, and promotion—and cover issues such as the type of product to be marketed, brand name, pricing, advertising, publicity, geographic coverage, retailing, and distribution.

marketing myopia MARKETING mistake of forgetting customers' needs the theory that some organizations ignore the fact that to be successful, the wants of customers must be their central consideration

marketing planning MARKETING process of deciding plan for promoting firm's products the process of producing a marketing plan incorporating overall marketing objectives and the strategies and programs of action designed to achieve those objectives. Marketing planning requires a careful examination of all strategic issues, including the business environment, the markets themselves, competitors, the corporate **mission statement**, and organizational capabilities. The resulting marketing plan should be communicated to appropriate staff through an oral briefing to ensure it is fully understood.

market intelligence MARKETING information about particular area of commercial activity a collection of internal and external data on a given market. Market intelligence focuses particularly on competitors, customers, consumer spending, market trends, and suppliers.

market leader MARKETING one with highest market share the product, service, or company that has a dominant **market share**

market logic MARKETS circumstances governing firm's stock market performance the prevailing forces or attitudes that determine a company's success or failure on the stock market

market maker MARKETS **1.** provider of market for unlisted security a broker or bank that maintains a market for a security that does not trade on any exchange **2.** securities dealer who both buys and sells a securities dealer who offers either to buy or sell stock on the stock market at a guaranteed price **3.** *UK* promoter of trading in one particular firm somebody who works in a stock exchange to facilitate trades in one particular company

market neutral funds STOCKHOLDING & INVESTMENTS hedge funds exploiting temporary fluctuations **hedge funds** that are not related to general market movements but that are used to find opportunities to take advantage of temporary slight changes in the relative values of particular financial assets

market order MARKETS instruction to trade security at best available price an order to trade a security at the best price the broker can obtain

market penetration MARKETING percentage of potential sales that firm has made a measure of the percentage or potential percentage of the market that a product or company is able to capture,

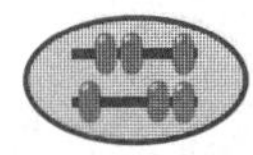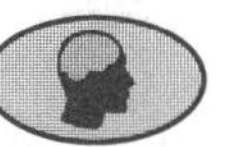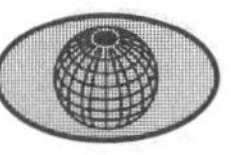

expressed in terms of total sales or turnover. Market penetration is often used to measure the level of success a new product or service has achieved.

market penetration pricing MARKETING practice of setting prices low to increase sales the policy of pricing a product or service very competitively, and sometimes at a loss to the producer, in order to increase its **market share**

market position MARKETS product's portion of total sales in market the place held by a product or service in a **market**, usually determined by its percentage of total sales. An ideal market position is often predefined for a product or service. Analysis of potential customers and competing products can be used with product differentiation techniques to formulate a product to fill the desired market position.

market potential MARKETS predictions about product's sales and earning possibilities a forecast of the size of a market in terms of revenue, numbers of buyers, or other factors

market power MARKETS buyers' or sellers' ability to control market the dominance of a market either by customers, who create a buyer's market, or by a particular company, which creates a seller's market. Individuals or companies retain control of the market by fixing the pricing and number of products available.

market price **1.** MARKETS price consumers are paying the price that buyers are currently paying for a good, service, commodity, etc. **2.** ECONOMICS price at which supply equals demand the theoretical price at which supply equals demand

market quote MARKETS current best stock market price the most up-to-date highest price being offered for a security on a stock exchange

market research MARKETING investigation of commercial activity research conducted to assess the size and nature of a market

market risk MARKETS, RISK risk inherent in securities market or economy investment risk that is attributable to the performance of the stock market or of the economy and cannot be removed by diversification

market risk premium STOCKHOLDING & INVESTMENTS return needed to compensate for risk the extra return required from a high-risk investment to compensate for its higher-than-average risk

market sector or **market segment** MARKETS distinctive subsection of consumers a subdivision of a **market** with distinctive characteristics. Market sectors are usually determined by market segmentation, which divides a market into different categories. Car buyers, for example, could be put into sectors such as car fleet buyers, private buyers, buyers under 20 years old, and so on. The smaller the sector, the more its members will have in common. Sellers may decide to compete in the whole market or only in segments that are attractive to them or where they have an advantage.

market segmentation MARKETS categorization of buyers by buying habits the division of the market or consumers into categories according to their buying habits

market sentiment MARKETS general feeling among brokers and traders the mood of those participating in exchange dealings that can range from absolute euphoria to downright gloom and despondency and tends to reflect recent company results, economic indicators, and comments by politicians, analysts, or opinion formers. Optimism increases demand and therefore prices, while pessimism has the opposite effect.

market share MARKETING firm's or product's proportion of total sales the proportion of the total market value of a product or group of products or services that a company, service, or product holds. Market share is shown as a percentage of the total value or output of a market, usually expressed in US dollars, pounds sterling, or euros, by weight (tons or tonnes), or as individual units, depending on the commodity. The product, service, or company with a dominant market share is referred to as the **market leader**.

Markets in Financial Instruments Directive MARKETS, REGULATION & COMPLIANCE EU directive governing conduct of investment companies an EU directive that sets out detailed requirements governing the organization and conduct of business of investment companies, and how regulated markets and multilateral trading facilities should operate. It came into force on November 1, 2007, replacing the Investment Services Directive (ISD), and made significant changes to the regulatory framework to reflect developments in financial services and markets since the ISD was implemented. *Abbr* **MiFID**

market site E-COMMERCE website shared by several Internet firms a website shared by multiple e-commerce vendors, each having a different specialty, to conduct business over the Internet

market size MARKETS **1.** maximum number of shares traded together the largest number of shares that a market will handle in one trade of a specific security **2.** number of consumers in specific group the size of a group of consumers with shared needs and their buying power

market structure MARKETS organization of particular area of commercial activity the makeup of a particular **market**. Market structure can be described with reference to different characteristics of a market, including its size and value, the number of providers and their **market share**, consumer and business purchasing behavior, and growth forecasts. The description may also include a demographic and regional breakdown of providers and customers and an analysis of pricing structures, likely technological impacts, and domestic and overseas sales.

market targeting MARKETING promoting products to specific group of consumers the selection of a particular market sector toward which all marketing effort is directed. Market targeting enables the characteristics of the chosen sector to be taken into account when formulating a product or service and its advertising.

market timing STOCKHOLDING & INVESTMENTS trading determined by market trends an investing strategy of buying and selling securities based on indicators of market trends over relatively short periods of time

market trend MARKETS rising or falling price movements a period during which stock market prices are moving in a particular direction

market valuation MARKETS **1.** = ***market capitalization*** **2.** worth of portfolio on selling the value of a portfolio if all its investments were to be sold at current market prices **3.** professional assessment of current value of real estate the opinion of an expert professional as to the current worth of a piece of real estate

market value FINANCE worth of asset if sold the value of an asset based on what price would be received for it if it were sold

market value added MARKETS difference between market and book value the difference between a company's market value (derived from the stock price), and its economic book value (the amount of capital that stockholders have committed to the firm throughout its existence, including any retained earnings). *Abbr* **MVA**

marking down MARKETS lowering of price required the reduction by market makers in

     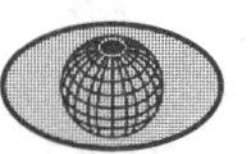   

the price at which they are prepared to deal in a security, for example, because of an adverse report by an analyst, or the announcement or anticipated announcement of a profit warning by a company

mark to market MARKETS securities valuation that reflects current prices daily valuation of the price of securities held in an account at the closing price, or the **market quote** if the last sale falls outside the market quote, so that the equity fully reflects current prices

mark up OPERATIONS & PRODUCTION increase price of something to make the price of something higher, especially in order to provide the seller with a profit

markup OPERATIONS & PRODUCTION amount added to make selling price the addition to the cost of goods or services which results in a selling price. The markup may be expressed as a percentage or as an absolute monetary amount.

massaging ACCOUNTING presentation to suggest better performance the adjustment of financial figures to create the impression of better performance (*slang*)

mass market MARKETING area of commercial activity involving much of population a market that covers substantial numbers of the population. A mass market may consist of a whole population or just a segment of that population. Mass customization of products has allowed a greater number of single products to satisfy a mass market.

mass production OPERATIONS & PRODUCTION manufacturing large numbers of same product at once large-scale manufacturing, often designed to meet the demand for a particular product. Mass production methods were developed by Henry Ford, founder of the Ford Motor Company. Mass production involves using a moving production or assembly line on which the product moves while operators remain at their stations carrying out their work on each passing product. Mass production is now challenged by methods including **just-in-time** and **lean production**.

master franchise MARKETING arrangement allowing franchisee to permit further franchises a license issued by the owner of a product or service to another party or master franchisee allowing them to issue further **franchise** licenses. A master franchise can benefit the original franchisor, as the master franchisee effectively develops the **franchise chain** on their behalf. A master franchise usually grants further licenses within a defined geographic area, and several master franchises may cover a country.

master limited partnership BUSINESS partnership with benefits in tax and liquidity a partnership of a type that combines tax advantages and advantages of liquidity

Master of Business Administration GENERAL MANAGEMENT *see* ***MBA***

master production scheduling OPERATIONS & PRODUCTION method of developing detailed manufacturing plan a technique used in material requirements planning systems to develop a detailed plan for product manufacturing. The **master production schedule**, compiled by a master scheduler, takes account of the requirements of various departments, including sales (delivery dates), finance (inventory minimization), and manufacturing (minimization of setup times), and it schedules production and the purchasing of materials within the capacity of and resources available to the production system.

matador bond STOCKHOLDING & INVESTMENTS foreign bond in Spain a foreign bond issued into the Spanish domestic market by a non-Spanish company (*slang*)

matched bargain *UK* STOCKHOLDING & INVESTMENTS connected sale and rebuying the linked sale and repurchase of the same quantity of the same security. *See also* ***bed and breakfast deal***

matching convention ACCOUNTING accounts basis with matching of sales with costs the basis for preparing accounts that says that profits can only be recognized if sales are fully matched with costs accrued during the same period

material cost OPERATIONS & PRODUCTION price paid for product's raw materials the cost of the raw materials that go into a product. The material cost of a product excludes any **indirect costs**, for example, overhead or wages, associated with producing the item.

material facts MARKETS **1.** compulsory information for prospectus information about a company that has to be disclosed in a **prospectus**. *See also* ***listing requirements*** **2.** information insurer must be told in an insurance contract, information that the insured has to reveal at the time that the policy is taken out, for example, that a house is located on the edge of a crumbling cliff. Failure to reveal material facts can result in the contract being declared void.

material information *US* MARKETS information firm must tell exchange price-sensitive developments in a company, for example, proposed acquisitions, mergers, profit warnings, and the resignation of directors, that most stock exchanges require a company to announce immediately to the exchange. *UK term* ***material news***

material news *UK* MARKETS = ***material information***

materials returned note OPERATIONS & PRODUCTION record of unused material a record of the return to stores of unused material

matrix management GENERAL MANAGEMENT managing through both horizontal and vertical reporting structures management based on two or more reporting systems that are linked to the vertical organization hierarchy, and to horizontal relationships based on geographic, product, or project requirements

matrix organization GENERAL MANAGEMENT way of structuring firm both horizontally and vertically organization by both vertical administrative functions and horizontal tasks, areas, processes, or projects. Matrix organization originated in the 1960s and 1970s, particularly within the US aerospace industry, when **organization charts** showing how the management of a given project would relate to **senior management** were often required to win government contracts. A two-dimensional matrix chart best illustrates the dual horizontal, and vertical, reporting relationships. Matrix organization is closely linked to **matrix management**.

matrix structure GENERAL MANAGEMENT firm's organization with both horizontal and vertical relationships a form of organizational structure based on horizontal and vertical relationships. The matrix structure is linked closely to **matrix management**, and is related to **project management**. It emerged on an improvised rather than a planned basis as a way of showing how people work with or report to others in their organization, project, geographic region, process, or team.

matrix trading STOCKHOLDING & INVESTMENTS trading taking advantage of differences in yields a **bond swap** strategy that takes advantages of discrepancies in yields of bonds of different classes

mature FINANCE due for payment having reached maturity

  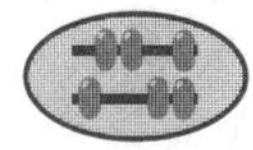   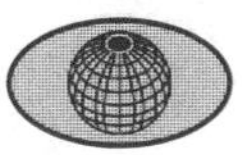   

mature economy ECONOMICS economy that has slowed down an economy that is no longer developing or growing rapidly. Such economies tend to have increased consumer spending rather than industrial and manufacturing investment.

maturity STOCKHOLDING & INVESTMENTS period before repayment date of financial instrument the period that will elapse before a financial instrument such as a bond becomes due for repayment or an option expires

maturity date STOCKHOLDING & INVESTMENTS expiration date of option the date on which a financial instrument such as a bond becomes due for repayment or an option expires

maturity value STOCKHOLDING & INVESTMENTS amount payable on mature financial instrument the amount payable when a bond or other financial instrument matures

maturity yield STOCKHOLDING & INVESTMENTS = ***yield***

Maxi ISA STOCKHOLDING & INVESTMENTS former UK tax-free investment formerly, in the United Kingdom, an **ISA** in which savers invested tax-free mainly in stocks with a limited cash component. Savers could own only one Maxi ISA. *See also* ***Mini ISA, ISA***

maximize FINANCE increase financial gain as much as possible to take measures to increase something such as your gain on an investment or profit in a business as much as possible

maximum **1.** greatest possible amount the largest number, price, quantity, or degree possible or allowed **2.** greatest possible of the largest possible or allowed amount or value

maximum inventory level *US* OPERATIONS & PRODUCTION size above which inventory must not increase an inventory level, set for control purposes, which actual holdings should never exceed. It is calculated as follows:

Reorder level + Economic order quantity – Minimum rate of usage × Minimum lead time

UK term ***maximum stock level***

maximum stock level *UK* OPERATIONS & PRODUCTION = ***maximum inventory level***

maysir FINANCE gambling or speculation prohibited by Islamic law in Islamic financing, gambling with the intention of making an easy profit. It is one of three prohibitions in Islamic law, which is extended to such financial practices as speculation, insurance, futures, and options; the others are **gharar** and **riba**.

MBA GENERAL MANAGEMENT master's degree in business administration a postgraduate degree awarded after a period of study of topics relating to the strategic management of businesses. A Master of Business Administration course can be taken at a business school or university, and covers areas such as finance, personnel, and resource management, as well as the wider business environment and skills such as information technology use. The course is mostly taken by people with experience of managerial work, and is offered by universities worldwide. Part-time or distance learning MBAs are available, so that students can study while still working. There is an increasing number of MBA graduates, as an MBA is seen as a passport to a better job and higher salary. For many positions at a higher level within organizations, an MBA is now a prerequisite. *Full form* ***Master of Business Administration***

MBI *abbr* MERGERS & ACQUISITIONS management buyin

MBIA INSURANCE US firms insuring high-rated municipal bonds a large US-based insurance company whose core business is in high-rated municipal bonds. *Full form* ***Municipal Bond Insurance Association***

MBO *abbr* **1.** MERGERS & ACQUISITIONS management buyout **2.** GENERAL MANAGEMENT management by objectives

MBS *abbr* MORTGAGES, STOCKHOLDING & INVESTMENTS mortgage-backed security

m-commerce E-COMMERCE sales transactions conducted with portable electronic devices electronic transactions between buyers and sellers using mobile communications devices such as cellphones, personal digital assistants (PDAs), or laptop computers

MD *abbr* CORPORATE GOVERNANCE managing director

mean STATISTICS average statistical value a central value or location for a continuous variable in a statistical study

mean reversion STATISTICS pattern of returning to average value the tendency of a variable such as price to return toward its average value after approaching an extreme position

means **1.** resources required to accomplish something the amount of money or resources that are needed to achieve something **2.** way of accomplishing something a method, action, or thing that makes it possible for somebody to do something

means test FINANCE **1.** examination of somebody's eligibility for government aid an inquiry into how much money somebody earns or has in savings to see if they are eligible for government benefits **2.** bankruptcy test in US courts a test used by US courts to see whether somebody wishing to file for bankruptcy has enough income to repay some of the debt, determining which type of bankruptcy that person is eligible for

means-test FINANCE determine if somebody is eligible for government aid to find out how much money somebody earns or has in savings and assets to see if they are eligible for government benefits

measurement error STATISTICS numerical mistake in statistical analysis an error in the recording, calculating, or reading of a numerical value in a statistical study

media independent MARKETING firm that buys advertising for clients an organization that specializes in planning and buying advertising for clients or advertising agencies

median STATISTICS midpoint in set of statistical values the value that divides a set of ranked observations into two parts of equal size

media plan MARKETING evaluation of communication channels for advertising an assessment and outline of the various advertising media to be used for a campaign

media planner MARKETING employee who organizes advertising an employee of an advertising agency or media independent who chooses the media, timing, and frequency of advertising

media schedule MARKETING document detailing advertising plan a document that sets out the choice of media, timing, and frequency of advertising

mediation GENERAL MANAGEMENT effort by outsider to solve disagreement intervention by a third party in a dispute in order to try to reach agreement between the disputing parties. Where a commitment or award is imposed on either party the process is known as **arbitration**. *Also called* ***conciliation***

medical insurance INSURANCE insurance covering medical expenses arrangement by which a firm promises to pay all or part of the cost of medical treatment

Medicare INSURANCE **1.** US government health insurance for seniors a health

  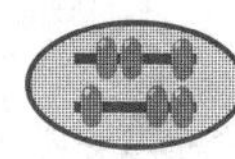   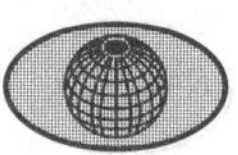   

insurance program in which the US government pays part of the cost of medical care and hospital treatment for people over 65 **2.** Australia's public health insurance system the Australian public health insurance system. It was created in 1983 and is funded by a levy on income.

medium-dated STOCKHOLDING & INVESTMENTS maturing in 5–10 years used to describe securities such as bonds that mature in five to ten years. *See also* ***long-dated, short-dated***

medium-dated gilt STOCKHOLDING & INVESTMENTS UK government security with 5–10 years' maturity a security issued by the UK government that pays a fixed rate of interest on a regular basis for at least five but no more than ten years until the redemption date, when the principal is returned. *See also* ***gilt-edged security***

medium of exchange FINANCE means of paying for goods anything that is used to pay for goods. Nowadays, this usually takes the form of money (banknotes and coins), but in ancient societies it included anything from cattle to shells.

medium-sized business BUSINESS *see* ***small and medium-sized enterprise***

medium-term bond STOCKHOLDING & INVESTMENTS bond redeemed in 5 to 10 years a bond that has at least five but no more than ten years before its redemption date. *See also* ***long-term bond***

medium-term note FINANCE borrowing repaid within 5 years borrowing arranged over a period of up to five years. *Abbr* **MTN**

medium-term noteholder FINANCE investor repaying borrowings within 5 years an investor who borrows money over a period of up to five years

megacorporation or **megacorp** US BUSINESS extremely large, powerful firm an extremely large and powerful business organization (*informal*)

meltdown MARKETS stock market crash an incidence of substantial losses on the stock market. Black Monday, October 19, 1987, was described as Meltdown Monday in the press the following day.

member 1. STOCKHOLDING & INVESTMENTS shareholder in firm somebody who owns stock in a limited liability company **2.** BUSINESS organization belonging to larger group a business organization that is part of a larger group

member bank BANKING bank in US Federal Reserve System a bank that is a member of the US Federal Reserve System

member firm MARKETS member of London Stock Exchange a firm of brokers or market makers that is a member of the London Stock Exchange

member of a company STOCKHOLDING & INVESTMENTS in UK, registered stockholder in the United Kingdom, a stockholder whose name is recorded in the register of members

members' voluntary liquidation BUSINESS in UK, decision to close down solvent firm in the United Kingdom, a special resolution passed by the members of a solvent company for the closing-down of the organization. Prior to the resolution the directors of the company must make a declaration of solvency. Should the appointed liquidator have grounds for believing that the company is not solvent, the winding-up will be treated as compulsory liquidation. *See also* ***voluntary liquidation***

memorandum of association LEGAL document officially registering UK firm in the United Kingdom, an official company document, registered with the **Registrar of Companies**. A memorandum of association sets out company name, status, address of the registered office, objectives of the company, statement of **limited liability**, amount of guarantee, and the amount of authorized share capital.

mentee GENERAL MANAGEMENT somebody being helped to develop professionally a person who, with the help of a **mentor**, develops their skills and improves their performance so that they can achieve their goals

mentor GENERAL MANAGEMENT experienced person helping another to develop professionally a person experienced in a particular area who helps and encourages a less experienced person to learn and develop

mentoring GENERAL MANAGEMENT more-experienced employees' training of less-experienced employee a form of employee development whereby a trusted and respected person, the **mentor**, uses his or her experience to offer guidance, encouragement, career advice, and support to another person, the **mentee**. The aim of mentoring is to facilitate the mentee's learning and development and to enable him or her to discover more about his or her potential. Mentoring can occur informally or it can be arranged by means of an organizational program.

Mentor/mentee relationships can take any form that suits the individuals involved, but in practice there are a few rules that apply to most such arrangements, the most important of which is that anything discussed remains confidential. The relationship also needs to be based on trust and candid communication. A mentor does not have to belong to the same organization as the mentee, but can come from any sphere of the mentee's life (professional association, a community center, your alumni organization, for example) just as long as he or she is not the mentee's direct supervisor or working in the same department. Mentoring does not have to be paid for; in fact it is usually seen as an honor by the mentor. Many accomplished individuals consider it good professional citizenship to participate in the process of helping those coming up after them. It can also frequently be beneficial to volunteer to be a mentor, as many organizations consider mentoring a valuable hallmark of leadership material.

mercantile ECONOMICS relating to trading relating to trade or commercial activity

mercantile agency BUSINESS firm assessing credit status a company that evaluates the creditworthiness of potential corporate borrowers on behalf of other companies. *See also* ***credit bureau***

mercantile paper STOCKHOLDING & INVESTMENTS = ***commercial paper***

mercantilism ECONOMICS economic theory based on importance of international trade the body of economic thought developed between the 1650s and 1750s, based on the belief that a country's wealth depended on the strength of its foreign trade

merchandising MARKETING **1.** activities promoting quick sale of products the process of increasing the market share of a product in retail outlets using display, stocking, and sales promotion techniques **2.** promoting products in connection with movie, celebrity, etc. the promotion and display of goods associated with a specific **brand**, movie, or celebrity. Merchandising based on a specific movie, for example, may significantly add to its total revenues through appropriate **licensing** opportunities. Merchandising may include clothing, toys, food products, or music and often extends well beyond the **core business** of the producer of the original product.

merchantable quality OPERATIONS & PRODUCTION UK standard of acceptable product quality in UK law, a minimum standard to which goods being sold must conform. It requires that the goods be reasonably priced given their description,

  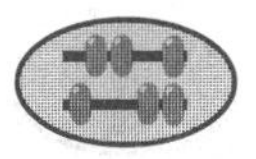   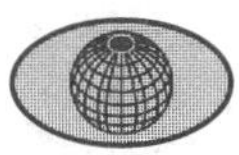   

be fit for the purpose for which they were purchased, and be free of defects.

merchant account E-COMMERCE seller's bank account for credit card transactions an account established by a trader to receive the proceeds of credit card transactions

merchant bank 1. E-COMMERCE bank accepting proceeds from seller's credit card transactions a financial institution at which a trader has opened a **merchant account** into which the proceeds of credit card transactions are credited after the institution has subtracted its fee **2.** *UK* BANKING = ***investment bank***

merchant number E-COMMERCE identification number for credit card merchant a number that identifies a merchant, printed at the top of the report slip when depositing credit card payments

merger MERGERS & ACQUISITIONS when one organization buys and combines with another the amalgamation of two or more organizations under single ownership, through the direct acquisition by one organization of the net assets or liabilities of the other. A merger can be the result of a friendly **takeover**, which results in the combining of companies on an equal footing. After a merger, the legal existence of the acquired organization is terminated. There is no standard definition of a merger, as each is different, depending on what is expected from the merger, and on the negotiations, strategy, stock and assets, human resources, and stockholders of the players. Four broad types of mergers are recognized. A **horizontal merger** involves firms from the same industry, while a **vertical merger** involves firms from the same supply chain. A **circular merger** involves firms with different products but similar distribution channels. A **conglomerate company** is produced by the union of firms with few or no similarities in production or marketing but that come together to create a larger economic base and greater profit potential. *See also* ***acquisition, consolidation, joint venture, partnership***

merger accounting ACCOUNTING accounting treating combined firm as result of merger a method of accounting that regards a business combination as the acquisition of one company by another. The identifiable assets and liabilities of the company acquired are included in the consolidated balance sheet at their fair value at the date of acquisition, and its results included in the profit and loss account from the date of acquisition. The difference between the fair value of the consideration given and the fair values of the net assets of the entity acquired is accounted for as **goodwill**.

mergers and acquisitions MERGERS & ACQUISITIONS ways in which organizations change ownership a blanket term covering the main ways in which organizations change hands. *Abbr* **M&A**

merit rating or **merit pay** HR & PERSONNEL system for increasing pay based on employees' performance a payment system in which the personal qualities of an employee are rated according to organizational requirements, and a pay increase or bonus is made against the results of this rating. Merit rating has been in use since the 1950s, and examines an employee's input to the organization (for example, their attendance, adaptability, or aptitude) as well as the quality or quantity of work produced. In merit rating programs, these factors may be weighted to reflect their relative importance and the resultant points score determines whether the employee earns a bonus or pay increase.

method study GENERAL MANAGEMENT evaluation of existing techniques to find best one the systematic recording, examination, and analysis of existing and proposed ways of conducting work tasks in order to discover the most efficient and economical methods of performing them. The basic procedure followed in method study is as follows: select the area to be studied; record the data; examine the data; develop alternative approaches; install the new method; maintain the new method. The technique was initially developed to evaluate manufacturing processes but has been used more widely to evaluate alternative courses of action.

metrics GENERAL MANAGEMENT measures of organization's effectiveness the standards used to measure or quantify the activities and success of an organization

mezzanine finance *UK* FINANCE = ***mezzanine financing***

mezzanine financing FINANCE firm's financing following initial investments financing provided to a company after it has received start-up financing. *UK term* ***mezzanine finance***

MFN *abbr* INTERNATIONAL TRADE most favored nation

microbusiness BUSINESS firm with 1–9 employees a very **small business** that directly employs fewer than ten people. This definition of small and medium-sized enterprises is the one adopted by the United Kingdom's Department for Business Enterprise and Regulatory Reform for statistical purposes.

microcash E-COMMERCE type of electronic money allowing sub-denomination payments a form of electronic money with no denominations, permitting sub-denomination transactions of a fraction of, for example, a cent

microcredit BANKING financing those not eligible for standard bank loans the extension of credit to entrepreneurs and **microbusinesses** that are too poor to qualify for conventional bank loans. *Also called* ***microlending***

microeconomic incentive ECONOMICS financial encouragement to improve market performance a tax benefit or subsidy given to a business to achieve a specific objective such as increased sales overseas

microeconomics ECONOMICS study of consumers' and firms' roles in economy the branch of economics that studies the contribution of groups of consumers or firms, or of individual consumers, to a country's economy. *See also* ***macroeconomics***

microeconomy ECONOMICS individual areas of economy that influence whole economy the narrow sectors of a country's economic activity that influence the behavior of the economy as a whole, for example, consumer choices. *See also* ***macroeconomy***

microfinance *UK* FINANCE = ***microfinancing***

microfinancing *US* FINANCE providing variety of financial services to poor the provision of a range of financial resources such as small loans, insurance, and savings to low-income families in order to help them build businesses and increase their income. *UK term* ***microfinance***. *See also* ***microcredit***

microhedge STOCKHOLDING & INVESTMENTS hedge for one asset or liability a **hedge** that relates to a single asset or liability in an investment **portfolio**. *See also* ***macrohedge***

microlending BANKING = ***microcredit***

microloan FINANCE small loan to low-income borrower a very small loan made to somebody who has a low or no income and nothing to offer as collateral, or to the owner of a small unprofitable business

micromanagement GENERAL MANAGEMENT too close control of subordinate employees' work a style of management where a

  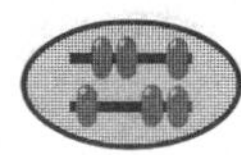 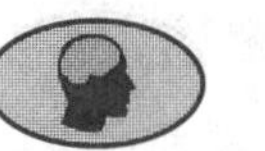  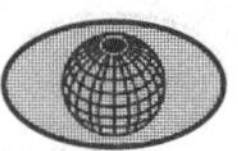   

manager becomes over-involved in the details of the work of subordinates, resulting in the manager making every decision in an organization, no matter how trivial. Micromanagement is a euphemism for meddling, and has the opposite effect to **empowerment**. Micromanagement can retard the progress of organizational development, as it robs employees of their self-respect.

micromarketing MARKETING promoting products to very small groups marketing to individuals or very small groups. It targets the specific interests and needs of individuals by offering customized products or services. Rather than targeting one large niche market, a micromarketing company targets a large number of very small niches. *See also* ***mass market, niche market***

micromerchant E-COMMERCE online seller accepting microcash a provider of goods or services on the Internet in exchange for electronic money, including **microcash**

micropayment E-COMMERCE means of paying small sums electronically a payment protocol for small amounts of electronic money, ranging from a fraction of a cent to no more than ten US dollars or euros

micro-profits FINANCE profits after microfinancing the profits made by businesses that have been financed by **microfinancing**

middleman GENERAL MANAGEMENT go-between in interactions between others an intermediary in a transaction. With direct sales models, manufacturers cut out the middleman by dealing directly with end customers.

middle management HR & PERSONNEL level of managers neither at top nor bottom the position held by managers who are considered neither senior nor junior in an organization. Middle managers were subject to **delayering** and **downsizing** in the 1980s as organizations sought to reduce costs by removing the layer of managers between those who had direct interface with customers and senior decision-makers.

middle office GENERAL MANAGEMENT staff that works with front and back offices staff who do not interact directly with customers but are involved in making business decisions. Risk management is an example of a middle office function. *See also* ***back office, front office***

middle price or **mid-price** UK STOCKHOLDING & INVESTMENTS price between bid price and offer price a price, halfway between the bid price and the offer price, that is generally quoted in the press and on information screens

mid-range STATISTICS average of maximum and minimum values the mean of the largest and smallest values in a statistical sample

MiFID *abbr* MARKETS, REGULATION & COMPLIANCE Markets in Financial Instruments Directive

MIGA *abbr* BANKING Multilateral Investment Guarantee Agency

million FINANCE thousand thousands a sum equal to one thousand thousands

millionaire FINANCE person with income over one million a person whose net worth or income is more than one million dollars, pounds, or other unit of currency

mindshare MARKETING public goodwill the attitude toward a product or organization that has been generated among the general public

Mini-Case BUSINESS technique for training business and finance students a set of circumstances used as the basis for solving a business or financial problem, used as a technique for training college students in business and finance

Mini ISA STOCKHOLDING & INVESTMENTS former UK tax-free cash savings account formerly, in the United Kingdom, an **ISA** in which savers held cash tax-free. Savers could also have a second Mini ISA in which they held stocks. *See also* ***Maxi ISA, ISA***

minimax regret criterion GENERAL MANAGEMENT choosing course with minimum regret or loss an approach to decision making under uncertainty in which the opportunity cost (regret) associated with each possible course of action is measured, and the decision-maker selects the activity that minimizes the maximum regret, or loss. Regret is measured as the difference between the best and worst possible payoff for each option.

minimum **1.** least possible amount the smallest number, price, quantity, or degree possible or allowed **2.** least possible of the smallest possible or allowed amount or value

minimum balance BANKING least amount of money required in account the smallest amount of money which must be kept in an account to qualify for the services provided

minimum inventory level US OPERATIONS & PRODUCTION size below which inventory must not decrease an inventory level, set for control purposes, below which holdings should not fall without being highlighted. It is calculated as follows:

Re-order level – Average rate of usage × Average lead time

UK term ***minimum stock level***

minimum lending rate BANKING lowest UK central bank interest rate formerly, the rate at which the Bank of England lent to other banks, now replaced by **base rate**. *Abbr* **MLR**

minimum quote size MARKETS minimum number of shares for one transaction the smallest number of shares that a market must handle in one trade of a particular security

minimum reserves BANKING least amount that bank must have in reserve the smallest amount of reserves which a commercial bank must hold with a central bank

minimum stock level *UK* OPERATIONS & PRODUCTION = ***minimum inventory level***

minimum subscription STOCKHOLDING & INVESTMENTS minimum bid for new issue the smallest number of shares or securities that may be applied for in a new issue

minimum wage FINANCE least hourly pay rate legally allowed the lowest hourly rate of pay, usually set by government, to which all **employees** are legally entitled

minority interest or **minority ownership** CORPORATE GOVERNANCE holding less than half of firm's common stock ownership of less than 50% of a company's common stock, which is not enough to control the company

minority shareholder STOCKHOLDING & INVESTMENTS stockholder with less than 50% of firm's stock a person who owns a group of shares of stock but less than half of the stock in a company. *Also called* ***minority stockholder***

minority shareholding STOCKHOLDING & INVESTMENTS less than 50% of firm's stock a group of shares of stock that somebody has which account for less than half the total shares in a firm

minority stockholder STOCKHOLDING & INVESTMENTS = ***minority shareholder***

minus factor GENERAL MANAGEMENT negative aspect of situation a factor that is unfavorable in some way, for example, because it reduces profitability

minutes CORPORATE GOVERNANCE official notes from meeting an official written record of the proceedings of a meeting. Minutes usually record points for action, and indicate who is responsible for implementing decisions. Good practice requires that the minutes of a meeting be

  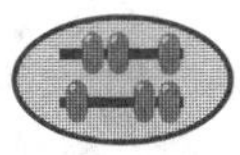   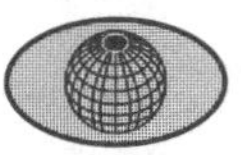   

circulated well in advance of the next meeting, and that those attending that meeting read the minutes in advance. Registered companies are required to keep minutes of meetings and make them available at their registered offices for inspection by company members and shareholders.

mirror fund STOCKHOLDING & INVESTMENTS investment trust and mutual fund under same control an investment trust where the manager also runs a mutual fund with the same objectives

MIS OPERATIONS & PRODUCTION computer system with information for management decisions a computer-based system for collecting, storing, processing, and providing access to information used in the management of an organization. Management information systems evolved from early electronic data processing systems. They support managerial decision making by providing regular structured reports on organizational operations. Management information systems may support the functional areas of an organization such as finance, marketing, or production. **Decision support systems** and **EISs** are types of MIS developed for more specific purposes. *Full form* ***management information system***

misappropriation FRAUD fraudulent use of somebody else's money the illegal use of money by somebody who is not the owner but who has been trusted to look after it

mismanagement GENERAL MANAGEMENT incompetent or illegal handling of firm's resources functional or ethical dereliction of duty due to ignorance, negligence, incompetence, avoidance, or criminality

missing value STATISTICS expected statistical observation that is missing an observation that is absent from a set of statistical data, for example, because a member of a population to be sampled was not at home when the researcher called

mission statement GENERAL MANAGEMENT formal statement of firm's goals a short memorable statement of the reasons for the existence of an organization. *See also* ***vision statement***

MIT *abbr* STOCKHOLDING & INVESTMENTS market if touched

Mittelstand BUSINESS mid-sized German companies a German term that incorporates the meaning of "medium-sized enterprise"

mixed economy ECONOMICS combination of government and private business ownership an economy in which both public and private enterprises participate in the production and supply of goods and services

MLR *abbr* BANKING minimum lending rate

MMC *abbr* REGULATION & COMPLIANCE Monopolies and Mergers Commission

MMDA *abbr* BANKING money market deposit account

MNC *abbr* BUSINESS multinational corporation

mobile money FINANCE use of cell phones for financial transactions a facility that allows people to use their cell phones and other hand-held devices to handle financial transactions

mobile office GENERAL MANAGEMENT setup of portable office equipment a set of conditions allowing working on the move. Mobile office equipment would typically include a cell phone, laptop computer, and a modem to link the computer to the Internet or a company's main office.

mode STATISTICS most frequent statistical observation in a statistical study, the most frequently occurring value in a set of ranked observations

model building STATISTICS creating structure for statistical observations the process of providing an adequate fit to the data in a set of observations in a statistical study

model risk MARKETS danger of inadequacy of computer modeling the possibility that a computer model on which investment decisions are based may be unreliable in extreme market conditions

modernization GENERAL MANAGEMENT replacing outdated equipment with new investing in new equipment or upgrading existing equipment to bring resources up to date or improve efficiency

modern portfolio theory STOCKHOLDING & INVESTMENTS = ***portfolio theory***

modified accounts ACCOUNTING = ***abbreviated accounts***

modified ACRS TAX US method of assessing asset depreciation in the United States, a system used for computing the depreciation of some assets acquired after 1985 in a way that reduces taxes. The ACRS applies to older assets. *See also* ***accelerated cost recovery system***

modified book value ACCOUNTING = ***adjusted book value***

modified cash basis ACCOUNTING different accounting for short- and long-term assets the bookkeeping practice of accounting for short-term assets on a cash basis and for long-term assets on an accrual basis

modified duration MARKETS, RISK measure of interest-rate risk in owning bonds a measure of a bond's sensitivity to changes in interest rates, based on the assumption that interest rates and bond prices move in opposite directions

mom and pop investors US STOCKHOLDING & INVESTMENTS inexperienced investors people who hold or wish to purchase stock but have little experience with or knowledge of the stock market (*slang*)

mom-and-pop operation *US, Canada* BUSINESS small family business a small family-run business, especially in the retail sector. *UK term* ***ma and pa shop***

momentum investor STOCKHOLDING & INVESTMENTS buyer of stock rising in price an investor who buys stock that seems to be moving upward in price

MONEP *abbr* MARKETS Marché des Options Négotiables de Paris

monetarism ECONOMICS belief that increased money causes inflation an economic theory that states that inflation is caused by increases in a country's money supply

monetarist ECONOMICS **1.** believer in monetarism a person who believes that inflation is caused by increases in a country's money supply and that the money supply should remain fairly steady **2.** according to monetarism according to the economic theory of **monetarism**

monetary FINANCE of money, cash, or liquid assets relating to or involving cash, currency, or assets that are readily convertible into cash

monetary assets ACCOUNTING assets corresponding to amounts in accounts assets such as accounts receivable, cash, and bank balances that are realizable at the amounts stated in the accounts. Other assets such as facilities and machinery, inventories, and marketable securities will not necessarily realize the sum stated in a business's balance sheet.

monetary base ECONOMICS nation's total cash supply the stock of a country's coins, notes, and bank deposits held by the central bank

monetary base control ECONOMICS government restrictions on cash availability the restricting of the amount of **liquid**

  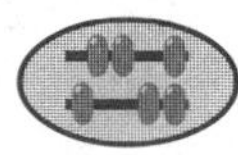   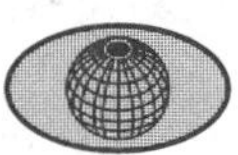   

assets in an economy through government controls

monetary items ACCOUNTING items worth the same regardless of inflation monetary assets, such as cash and debtors, and monetary liabilities, such as overdrafts and creditors, whose values stay the same in spite of inflation

monetary policy ECONOMICS government policy regarding money and currency government economic policy concerning a country's rate of interest, its exchange rate, and the amount of money in the economy

Monetary Policy Committee ECONOMICS Bank of England committee that sets interest rates a committee of the Bank of England, chaired by the Governor of the Bank, that has responsibility for setting UK interest rates independently of the British government. Its goal is to set rates with a view to keeping inflation at a defined level and avoiding deflation. *Abbr* **MPC**

monetary reserve BANKING currency and bullion in central bank the foreign currency and precious metals that a country holds, that provide a cushion for central banking functions

monetary standard CURRENCY & EXCHANGE value on which currency system is based the value underlying the currency in a specific country's monetary system, for example, the **gold standard**, which in the past many countries used to set the value of their currencies

monetary system ECONOMICS set of government rules controlling nation's money the set of government regulations concerning a country's monetary reserves and its holdings of notes and coins

monetary targets FINANCE government financial targets figures that are given as targets by the government when setting out its budget for the forthcoming year

monetary unit CURRENCY & EXCHANGE standard unit of nation's currency the standard unit of a country's currency, such as the dollar in the United States, the pound sterling in the United Kingdom, or the euro in many other countries of the European Union

monetary working capital adjustment ACCOUNTING adjustment in accounts for inflation an adjustment in **current cost accounting** to the historical cost balance sheet to take account of the effect of inflation on the value of debtors, creditors, and stocks of finished goods. *Abbr* **MWCA**

monetize CURRENCY & EXCHANGE designate as official currency to establish a currency as a country's legal tender

money CURRENCY & EXCHANGE current medium of exchange a medium of exchange that is accepted throughout a country as payment for services and goods and as a means of settling debts ◇at the money STOCKHOLDING & INVESTMENTS, RISK a situation in which the price an option holder must pay to exercise an option is the same as the current **market price** of the underlying security or commodity ◇at the money forward STOCKHOLDING & INVESTMENTS, RISK a situation in which the price an option holder must pay to exercise an option is the same as the **forward price** of the underlying security or commodity

money at call and short notice BANKING **1.** in UK, advances repayable on demand or soon in the United Kingdom, advances made by banks to other financial institutions, or corporate and personal customers, that are repayable either upon demand (call) or within 14 days (short notice) **2.** in UK, balances available on demand or soon in the United Kingdom, balances in an account that are either available upon demand (call) or within 14 days (short notice)

money broker MARKETS in UK, arranger of loans in the United Kingdom, an intermediary who works on the money market, arranging loans between banks, discount houses, and dealers in government securities

moneyer CURRENCY & EXCHANGE coiner of money an archaic term for somebody who is authorized to mint money

money laundering LEGAL concealing illegal origins of money the process of making money obtained illegally appear legitimate by passing it through banks or businesses

moneylender FINANCE lender of money at interest a person whose business is lending money to others for interest

money lying idle FINANCE uninvested money producing no interest money that is not being used to produce interest and that is not invested in business

money management FINANCE, STOCKHOLDING & INVESTMENTS business of investing clients' money the activity of making decisions about income and expenditure, including budgeting, banking arrangements, making investments, and tax payments, either for yourself or on behalf of clients

money manager STOCKHOLDING & INVESTMENTS specialist in investment management a person or company that manages an investment **portfolio**, usually of **money market instruments**, on behalf of investors. *See also* ***portfolio manager***

money market MARKETS market for buying and selling financial instruments a market in which short-term financial instruments such as certificates of deposit, Treasury bills, commercial papers, and bank deposits are traded. New York is the major money market, followed by London and Tokyo. *Also called* ***finance market***

money market account BANKING account with high interest rate an account with a financial institution that requires a minimum deposit, and pays a rate of interest, related to the wholesale money market rates, generally higher than retail rates. Most institutions offer a variety of term accounts, with either a fixed rate or variable rate, and notice accounts, with a variety of notice periods at variable rates.

money market deposit account BANKING US savings account in the United States, a type of savings account with deposits invested in the money market and having a high yield. There is often a high minimum deposit and withdrawals require notice. *Abbr* **MMDA**

money market fund STOCKHOLDING & INVESTMENTS mutual fund investing in short-term securities a mutual fund that invests in short-term debt securities. In the United States these are strictly regulated by the **Securities and Exchange Commission**.

money market instruments STOCKHOLDING & INVESTMENTS financial products traded on money markets short-term assets and securities, usually maturing within 12 months, that are traded on money markets, for example, certificates of deposit, commercial papers, and Treasury bills

money men FINANCE people working in finance industry the people who provide finance for a venture, campaign, etc.

money national income ECONOMICS unadjusted value of nation's annual output **GDP** measured using money value, not adjusted for the effect of inflation

money of account ACCOUNTING unit for accounting purposes a monetary unit that is used in keeping accounts but is not necessarily an actual currency unit

money order BANKING instruction to make payment to someone a written order to pay somebody a sum of money, issued by a bank or post office

  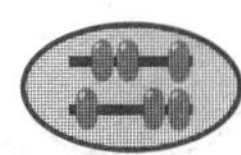 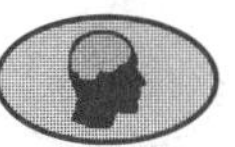  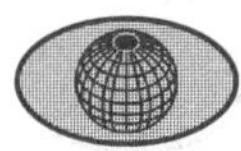   

money purchase pension or **money purchase scheme** PENSIONS UK pension plan to buy annuity in the United Kingdom, a pension plan where the fund that is built up is used to purchase an annuity. The retirement income that the beneficiary receives therefore depends on his or her contributions, any employer contributions, the performance of the investments those contributions are used to buy, the annuity rates, and the type of annuity purchased at retirement.

money purchase plan PENSIONS US pension plan with employer and employee contributing in the United States, a pension plan (a defined benefit plan) in which the participant contributes part and the firm contributes at the same or a different rate

money substitute CURRENCY & EXCHANGE trading goods used to replace currency any goods used as a medium of exchange because of the degree of devaluation of a country's currency

money supply ECONOMICS nation's cash available for purchases the stock of **liquid assets** in a country's economy that can be given in exchange for services or goods

monies or **moneys** CURRENCY & EXCHANGE sums of money amounts of money, especially those that come from a specific place or have a specific purpose

Monopolies and Mergers Commission REGULATION & COMPLIANCE former UK commission for competition in the United Kingdom, a commission that was replaced by the Competition Commission in April 1999. *Abbr* **MMC**

monopolistic competition MARKETS situation blocking new competition in market a situation that exists in a market in which there are strong barriers to the entry of new competitors. *Also called* ***imperfect competition***

monopoly ECONOMICS economic situation in which one firm controls market a **market** in which there is only one producer or one seller. A company establishes a monopoly by entering a new market or eliminating all competitors from an existing market. A company that holds a monopoly has control of a market and is able to fix prices. For this reason, governments usually try to avoid monopoly situations. However, some monopolies such as government-owned utilities are seen as beneficial to **consumers**.

monopsony MARKETS situation where only one customer needs product a situation in which there is only one buyer for a specific product or service

Monte Carlo method or **Monte Carlo simulation** STATISTICS statistical method of deciding based on uncertainties a statistical method of reducing the uncertainty in estimating future outcomes by running repeated calculations using current and historical data, used in business decision-making that involves a number of uncertain variables such as capital investment and resource allocation. The name of the Monte Carlo method derives from the use of random numbers as generated by a roulette wheel. The numbers are used in repeated simulations, often performed by spreadsheet programs on computers, to calculate a range of possible outcomes, using current and historical data. The technique was developed by mathematicians in the early 1960s for use in nuclear physics and **operational research** but has since been used more widely.

month-end ACCOUNTING of end of month relating to the end of each month when financial transactions for the current month are finalized

Moody's Investors Service STOCKHOLDING & INVESTMENTS US firm that rates credit risk of investments a US organization that rates the reliability of a debtor organization on a scale from AAA to C. It also issues ratings on municipal bonds, running from MIG1, the highest rating, to MIG4. *See also* ***Standard & Poor's***

moonlighting HR & PERSONNEL doing second job in addition to main job undertaking a second job, often for cash and in the evenings, in addition to a full-time permanent job

moral hazard RISK danger through protection from consequences of actions a risk that somebody will behave immorally because insurance, the law, or some other agency protects them against loss that the immoral behavior might otherwise cause

moratorium FINANCE postponement a period of delay, for example, additional time agreed on by a creditor and a debtor for recovery of a debt

more bang for your buck *US* FINANCE greater financial benefit greater leverage provided by an investment (*slang*)

Morgan Stanley Capital International Indexes MARKETS worldwide stock market indexes a group of indexes that track stocks traded on stock markets worldwide and are considered benchmarks for international investment portfolios

mortality and expense risk charge INSURANCE charge for annuity guaranteeing benefit and compensating insurer an extra charge paid on some annuities to guarantee that if the policyholder dies, his or her heirs will receive a benefit, and also that the insurance company will be compensated for an annuitant who lives longer than he or she should according to the mortality tables

mortgage MORTGAGES **1.** agreement to lend money for property a financial lending arrangement enabling somebody to borrow money from a bank or other lending institution in order to buy property or land. The original amount borrowed, the **principal**, is then repaid with interest to the lender over a fixed number of years. *See also* ***amortized mortgage***, ***current account mortgage***, ***endowment mortgage***, ***interest-only mortgage***, ***low start mortgage*** **2.** grant of right to asset of defaulting borrower a borrowing arrangement whereby the lender is granted a legal right to an asset, usually a piece of real estate, should the borrower default on the payments. *See also* ***second mortgage***

mortgage-backed security STOCKHOLDING & INVESTMENTS, MORTGAGES security backed by mortgages a security for which the collateral is the principal and interest on a set of mortgages

mortgage bank BANKING bank dealing in mortgages a financial institution that trades in mortgages

mortgage bond STOCKHOLDING & INVESTMENTS, MORTGAGES debt backed by real estate especially in the United States, a debt secured by real estate

mortgage broker MORTGAGES intermediary between seekers and offerers of mortgages a person or company that acts as an agent between people seeking mortgages and organizations that offer them

mortgage debenture MORTGAGES long-term loan secured against firm's fixed assets a debenture in which the loan is secured against a company's **fixed assets**

mortgagee MORTGAGES lender in mortgage agreement a person or organization that lends money to a borrower under a mortgage agreement. *See also* ***mortgagor***

mortgage equity analysis MORTGAGES calculation of value of property minus mortgages owed a computation of the difference between the value of a property and the amount owed on it in the form of mortgages

mortgage famine MORTGAGES when house buyers unable to get mortgages a situation where there is not enough money available to offer mortgages to house buyers

mortgage insurance INSURANCE mortgagee's insurance against borrower's default insurance that provides somebody holding a mortgage with protection against default

mortgage lien MORTGAGES claim against mortgaged property a claim against a property that is mortgaged. Mortgagees often own the mortgage lien to secure the loan.

mortgage note MORTGAGES record of mortgage a note that documents the existence and terms of a mortgage

mortgage pool MORTGAGES mortgages on sale together a group of mortgages with similar characteristics packaged together for sale

mortgage portfolio MORTGAGES in US, bank's holdings in mortgages in the United States, the group of mortgages held by a **mortgage bank**

mortgage rate MORTGAGES interest rate on mortgage the interest rate charged on a mortgage by a lender

mortgage securitizer STOCKHOLDING & INVESTMENTS firm creating and selling groups of mortgage loans as securities a company that collects residential mortgage loans into a package for sale to investors

mortgage tax TAX US tax on mortgage in the United States, a one-time tax paid when a mortgage is taken out

mortgagor MORTGAGES borrower in mortgage agreement somebody who has taken out a mortgage to borrow money. *See also* ***mortgagee***

most distant futures contract MARKETS futures option with longest term a futures option with the latest delivery date of those being considered. *See also* ***nearby futures contract***

most favored nation INTERNATIONAL TRADE foreign country given very good trade terms a foreign country allowed very favorable trade terms by another country. *Abbr* **MFN**

motion study GENERAL MANAGEMENT evaluation of efficiency of physical work patterns the observation of physical movements involved in the performance of work, and investigation of how these can be made more effective and cost efficient

motivation GENERAL MANAGEMENT giving employees reason to perform their best the creation of stimuli, incentives, and working environments which enable people to perform to the best of their ability in pursuit of organizational success. Motivation is commonly viewed as the magic driver that enables managers to get others to achieve their targets. In the 20th century, there was a shift, at least in theory, away from motivation by dictation and discipline toward motivation by creating an appropriate corporate climate and addressing the needs of individual employees. Although it is widely agreed to be one of the key management tasks, it has frequently been argued that one person cannot motivate others but can only create conditions for others to self-motivate.

mousetrap ◇ build a better mousetrap MARKETING to create a new or better product

mover and shaker GENERAL MANAGEMENT powerful person who initiates things an influential and dynamic person within an organization or group of people

moving average MARKETS average of stock prices that is continually recalculated an average of stock prices on a stock market, in which the calculation is made over a period which moves forward regularly

MPC *abbr* ECONOMICS Monetary Policy Committee

MRP II OPERATIONS & PRODUCTION computer-based system used in manufacturing a computer-based manufacturing, inventory planning, and control system that broadens the scope of production planning by involving other functional areas that influence production decisions. Manufacturing resource planning evolved from material requirements planning to integrate other functions in the planning process. These functions may include engineering, marketing, purchasing, production scheduling, business planning, and finance. *Full form* ***manufacturing resource planning***

MSB *abbr* BANKING mutual savings bank

MTF *abbr* MARKETS multilateral trading facility

MTN *abbr* FINANCE medium-term note

mudaraba or **mudarabah** BUSINESS Islamic partnership between investor and entrepreneur in Islamic financing, a type of partnership in which one partner provides the capital while the other provides expertise and management. Each gets a prearranged percentage of the profits, but the partner providing the capital bears any losses.

mudarib BUSINESS entrepreneur in mudaraba partnership in Islamic financing, the entrepreneurial partner in a **mudaraba** partnership who provides the expertise and management

multichannel E-COMMERCE using Internet and traditional methods using a combination of online and offline communication methods to conduct business

multicurrency FINANCE offering number of currencies used to describe a loan that gives the borrower a choice of currencies

multifunctional card BANKING plastic card with more than one use a plastic card that may be used for two or more purposes, for example, as an ATM card, a check card, and a debit card

Multilateral Investment Guarantee Agency BANKING part of World Bank Group one of the five institutions that constitute the World Bank Group. MIGA was created in 1988 to promote foreign direct investment into emerging economies by insuring against political risk, with the objective of improving people's lives and reducing poverty. Apart from offering political risk insurance to investors and lenders, MIGA assists emerging countries to attract and retain private investment. *Abbr* **MIGA**

multilateral netting CURRENCY & EXCHANGE consolidating sums from various sources into one currency a method of putting together sums from various international sources to reduce currency transaction costs, used by groups of companies or banks trading in several currencies at the same time

multilateral trading facility MARKETS system combining third-party commercial interests under the provisions of the **Markets in Financial Instruments Directive**, a system of bringing together multiple third-party buying and selling interests in financial instruments. *Abbr* **MTF**

multilevel marketing MARKETING = ***network marketing***

multinational business or **multinational** or **multinational company** or **multinational corporation** BUSINESS firm operating in more than one country a company that operates internationally, usually with subsidiaries, offices, or production facilities in more than one country

multiparty auction E-COMMERCE Internet selling with buyers making online bids a method of buying and selling on the Internet in which prospective buyers make electronic bids

multiple application STOCKHOLDING & INVESTMENTS more than one application for new share issue the submission of more than one share application for a new issue that is expected to be oversubscribed. In most jurisdictions, this practice is illegal.

multiple exchange rate CURRENCY & EXCHANGE exchange rate varying with transaction's purpose a two-tier rate of exchange used in some countries where the more advantageous rate may be for tourists or for businesses proposing to build a factory

multiple ownership BUSINESS when group owns something together a situation in which something is owned by several parties jointly

multiple regression analysis STATISTICS *see* ***regression analysis***

multiple sourcing OPERATIONS & PRODUCTION using more than one supplier a **purchasing** policy of using two or more suppliers for products or services. Multiple sourcing prevents reliance on any one supplier. It encourages competition between suppliers, and ensures access to a wide variety of goods or services. Dealing with more than one supplier can improve access to market information but can also entail more administration.

multiple time series STATISTICS sets of data observed together over time two or more sets of data that are observed simultaneously

multiplier FINANCE factor that multiplies another number or value a number that multiplies another, or a factor that tends to multiply something, for example, the effect of new expenditure on total income and reserves

multiplier effect ECONOMICS effect of increased investment or spending on income a situation in which a small initial change in investment or spending produces a proportionately larger change in national income

multiskilling HR & PERSONNEL training in a variety of skills a process of training employees to do a variety of tasks rather than focusing on single tasks. Employees are therefore available to undertake a number of different jobs and have better general employability.

multitasking E-COMMERCE conducting several tasks together the practice of doing more than one activity or task at a time

multivariate analysis STATISTICS investigation of characteristics of multiple variables any of a number of statistical techniques used in **operational research** to examine the characteristics and relationships between multiple variables. Multivariate analysis techniques include **cluster analysis, discriminant analysis,** and multiple **regression analysis**.

multivariate data STATISTICS statistical observations involving multiple variables data for which each observation involves values for more than one random variable

mum and dad investors ANZ STOCKHOLDING & INVESTMENTS = ***mom and pop investors*** *(slang)*

municipal bond or **muni** or **muni-bond** STOCKHOLDING & INVESTMENTS US government security in the United States, a security issued by states, local governments, and municipalities

municipal bond fund STOCKHOLDING & INVESTMENTS fund investing in municipal bonds a fund that is invested in municipal bonds

Municipal Bond Insurance Association INSURANCE *see* ***MBIA***

murabaha or **murabahah** FINANCE when Islamic bank purchases item for customer in Islamic financing, an arrangement in which a bank purchases an item for a customer provided the customer agrees to purchase it from the bank at a prearranged higher price. *See also* ***tawarruq***

Murphy's Law GENERAL MANAGEMENT anything that can go wrong will the principle that if something can go wrong, it will

musharaka or **musharakah** BUSINESS Islamic partnership in which all partners invest money in Islamic financing, a type of partnership in which all partners contribute capital to an enterprise, share profits in a prearranged way, and share losses equally

mutual BUSINESS relating to financial organization with members not stockholders used to describe an organization that is run in the interests of its members and that does not have to pay dividends to its stockholders, so surplus profits can be plowed back into the business. In the United Kingdom, building societies and friendly societies were formed as mutual organizations, although in recent years many have demutualized, either by becoming public limited companies or by being bought by other financial organizations, resulting in members receiving cash or share windfall payments. In the United States, **mutual associations**, a type of savings and loan association, and state-chartered mutual savings banks are organized in this way.

mutual company BUSINESS firm owned by its customers a company that is owned by its customers who share in the profits

mutual fund *US* STOCKHOLDING & INVESTMENTS firm trading in investments for clients an investment company that holds a range of stocks in which investors can buy units. *UK term* ***unit trust***

mutual insurance INSURANCE insurance firm owned by policyholders an insurance company that is owned by its policyholders who share the profits and cover claims with their pooled premiums

mutual recognition directive REGULATION & COMPLIANCE EU directive about recognizing other members' practices a directive of the European Union that each country's accounting firms and cross-border services should be recognized by other member states

mutual savings bank BANKING US savings bank run by trustees in the United States, a state-chartered savings bank run in the interests of its members. It is governed by a local board of trustees, not necessarily the legal owners. Most of these banks offer accounts and services that are typical of full-service banks. *Abbr* **MSB**

muzara'a or **muzara'ah** FINANCE payment for land rent by crop share in Islamic financing, an agreement in which a landowner lets somebody farm an area of land in return for part of the crop

MVA *abbr* MARKETS market value added

MWCA *abbr* ACCOUNTING monetary working capital adjustment

N

NAIC *abbr* **1.** INSURANCE, REGULATION & COMPLIANCE National Association of Insurance Commissioners **2.** STOCKHOLDING & INVESTMENTS National Association of Investors Corporation

naked debenture BUSINESS unsecured debt obligation a debt acknowledged by a company that is without security for the interest or the amount of principal. *See also* ***debenture***

naked option STOCKHOLDING & INVESTMENTS = ***uncovered option***

naked position STOCKHOLDING & INVESTMENTS holding with unhedged securities a situation in which an investor holds securities some of which are not **hedged**

  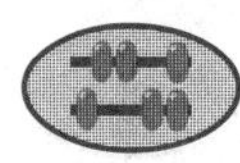 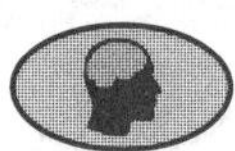  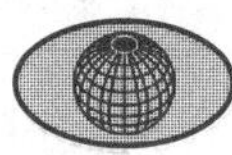   

naked writer STOCKHOLDING & INVESTMENTS offerer of option on another's shares a person selling an option who does not own the underlying shares

name INSURANCE member of Lloyd's insurance group an individual who is a member of the **Lloyd's underwriting syndicate**, an insurance group based in London

named perils insurance INSURANCE insurance for specific types of risk a type of insurance that provides coverage for only those losses that occur as a result of specifically named risks

NAO *abbr* REGULATION & COMPLIANCE National Audit Office

narrowcasting E-COMMERCE targeting information to restricted group targeting information to a niche audience. Owing to its ability to personalize information to the requirements of individual users, the Internet is generally viewed as a narrowcast rather than a broadcast medium.

narrow market MARKETS market with little trading a market where the trading volume is low. A characteristic of such a market is a wide spread of bid and offer prices.

narrow money ECONOMICS **1.** US = ***M1*** **2.** UK = ***Mo***

NASD *abbr* STOCKHOLDING & INVESTMENTS National Association of Securities Dealers

NASDAQ[1] *abbr* MARKETS NASDAQ Composite Index

NASDAQ[2] or **Nasdaq** MARKETS computerized trading system a computerized quotation system that supports market making in over-the-counter and listed securities. It was established by the **National Association of Securities Dealers** in 1971. NASDAQ International has operated from London since 1992.

NASDAQ Composite Index MARKETS US index of high-tech stock prices a specialist US stock price index covering stock of high-technology companies

National Association of Insurance Commissioners INSURANCE, REGULATION & COMPLIANCE US group of insurance regulators in the United States, an organization that brings together the state regulators of insurance. *Abbr* **NAIC**

National Association of Investors Corporation STOCKHOLDING & INVESTMENTS US organization promoting investment clubs in the United States, an organization that fosters the creation and development of **investment clubs**. *Abbr* **NAIC**

National Association of Securities Dealers STOCKHOLDING & INVESTMENTS, REGULATION & COMPLIANCE US organization for traders in securities in the United States, the self-regulatory organization for securities dealers that develops rules and regulations, conducts regulatory reviews of members' business activities, and designs and operates marketplace services facilities. It is responsible for the regulation of the NASDAQ securities market. Established in 1938, it operates subject to the Securities Exchange Commission oversight and has a membership that includes virtually every US broker or dealer doing securities business with the public. *Abbr* **NASD**

National Audit Office REGULATION & COMPLIANCE UK organization monitoring public spending an independent nongovernmental body in the United Kingdom that examines public spending. The NAO audits the accounts of government agencies and departments, reporting back to Parliament with the results. An officer of the House of Commons, the Comptroller and Auditor General, runs the NAO. It has offices in London, Newcastle, Cardiff, and Blackpool. *Abbr* **NAO**

national bank BANKING **1.** central bank of state a bank owned or controlled by the state that acts as a bank for a government and implements its monetary policies **2.** US bank in Federal Reserve in the United States, a bank that operates under federal charter and is legally required to be a member of the **Federal Reserve**

National Credit Union Administration REGULATION & COMPLIANCE US government organization overseeing credit unions in the United States, a federal agency that charters and supervises federal **credit unions** and insures savings in federal and most state-chartered credit unions through a fund backed by the US government

national debt ECONOMICS amount of government borrowing the total amount of money that a country's central government has borrowed and is still unpaid

national demand ECONOMICS overall need for products in country's economy the total demand for goods and services made by consumers in an economy

National Guarantee Fund MARKETS insurance fund of Australian Stock Exchange a supply of money held by the Australian Stock Exchange which is used to compensate investors for losses incurred when an exchange member fails to meet its obligations

national income ECONOMICS country's total earnings from goods and services the total earnings from a country's production of goods and services in a specific year

national income accounts FINANCE statistical information on country's economy economic statistics that show the state of a nation's economy over a given period of time, usually a year. *See also* ***GDP, GNP***

National Insurance PENSIONS UK social insurance plan for all adults in the United Kingdom, a compulsory state social insurance plan to which employees and employers contribute. *Abbr* **NI**. *See also* ***Social Security***

National Insurance contributions PENSIONS money paid into UK social insurance plan in the United Kingdom, payments made by both employers and employees to the government. The contributions, together with other government receipts, are used to finance pensions given by the government and other benefits such as welfare. *Abbr* **NIC**

National Insurance number PENSIONS person's identifying number for UK social insurance plan a unique number allocated to each UK citizen at the age of 16. It allows HM Revenue & Customs and the Department for Work and Pensions to record contributions and credit them to each person's account. *See also* ***Social Security number***

nationalization GENERAL MANAGEMENT transferring of private firms to state ownership the taking over of privately owned companies by government. Nationalization has strong political connotations. Recent global political trends had moved away from nationalization by introducing more competition and liberalization into markets before the banking crisis of 2008 caused governments to take considerable holdings in financial institutions to save them from collapse. *See also* ***privatization***

National Market System MARKETS system encouraging competition between US stock exchanges in the United States, an inter-exchange network system designed to foster greater competition between domestic stock exchanges. Legislated for in 1975, it was implemented in 1978 with the **Intermarket Trading System** that electronically links eight markets: American, Boston, Cincinnati, Chicago, New York, Pacific, Philadelphia, and the

   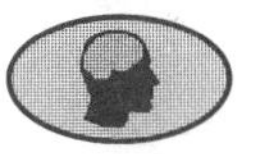  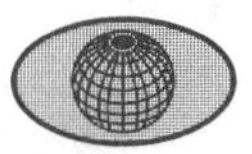   

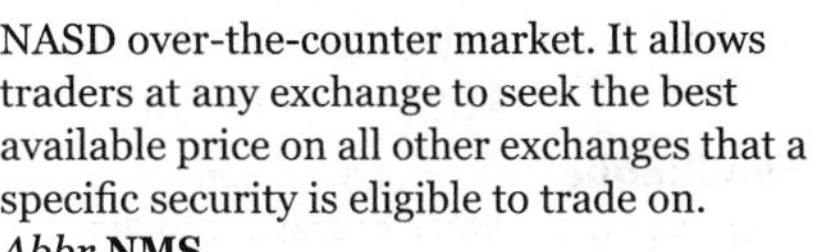

NASD over-the-counter market. It allows traders at any exchange to seek the best available price on all other exchanges that a specific security is eligible to trade on. *Abbr* **NMS**

National Savings & Investments STOCKHOLDING & INVESTMENTS UK government agency for savings and investment in the United Kingdom, a government agency accountable to the Treasury that offers a variety of savings and investment products directly to the public or through post offices. The funds raised finance government borrowing (the **national debt**).

National Savings Bank BANKING UK savings plan in the United Kingdom, a savings plan established in 1861 as the Post Office Savings Bank and now operated by National Savings & Investments. *Abbr* **NSB**

National Savings Certificate STOCKHOLDING & INVESTMENTS UK investment providing tax-free income in the United Kingdom, either a fixed-interest or an index-linked certificate issued for two- or five-year terms by National Savings & Investments with returns that are free of income tax. *Abbr* **NSC**

National Society of Accountants ACCOUNTING US association of financial professionals in the United States, a non-profit organization of some 17,000 professionals who provide accounting, tax preparation, financial and estate planning, and management advisory services to an estimated 19 million individuals and business clients. Most of the NSA's members are individual practitioners or partners in small to mid-size accounting and tax firms. *Abbr* **NSA**

natural capitalism ECONOMICS capitalism incorporating environmentalism an approach to capitalism in which protection of the Earth's resources is a strategic priority

natural disaster INSURANCE disaster caused by forces of nature a catastrophe that occurs as a result of forces of nature. Natural disasters include hurricanes, tornados, severe storms, floods, tsunamis, earthquakes, and volcanic eruptions.

NAV *abbr* STOCKHOLDING & INVESTMENTS net asset value

NBV *abbr* ACCOUNTING net book value

NDA *abbr* HR & PERSONNEL **1.** nondisclosure agreement **2.** nondisparagement agreement

NDP *abbr* ECONOMICS net domestic product

nearby futures contract STOCKHOLDING & INVESTMENTS option with closest delivery date a futures option with the earliest delivery date of those being considered. *See also* ***most distant futures contract***

nearby month STOCKHOLDING & INVESTMENTS next month with futures contract available the earliest month for which there is a **futures contract** for a specific commodity. *Also called* **spot month**. *See also* ***far month***

near-cash STOCKHOLDING & INVESTMENTS easy to convert to cash used to describe an investment that can be quickly converted to cash

near money STOCKHOLDING & INVESTMENTS assets easily cashed in assets such as some types of bank deposit, short-dated bonds, and certificates of deposit that can quickly be turned into cash. *See also* ***quick asset***

negative amortization FINANCE addition to principal following incomplete interest payments an increase in the **principal** of a loan due to the inadequacy of payments to cover the interest

negative carry FINANCE when interest payments exceed income on loan interest that is so high that the borrowed money does not return enough profit to cover the cost of borrowing

negative cash flow FINANCE higher expenditures than income a cash flow in which expenditures are higher than income

negative equity FINANCE when property is worth less than it cost a situation in which a fall in prices leads to a property being worth less than was paid for it

negative gearing FINANCE, TAX borrowing money that earns less than interest payments the practice of borrowing money to invest in property or stocks and claiming a tax deduction on the difference between the income and the interest payments

negative goodwill MERGERS & ACQUISITIONS value of company's assets above price paid the gain that a company has when a company it acquires has assets with a market value greater than the price the acquiring company paid for them

negative income tax TAX US tax credits to raise income levels in the United States, payments such as tax credits made to households or individuals to increase their income to a guaranteed minimum level

negative pledge clause STOCKHOLDING & INVESTMENTS condition preventing bond issuer from disadvantaging holders a provision in a bond agreement that prohibits the issuer from doing something that would give an advantage to holders of other bonds

negative yield curve STOCKHOLDING & INVESTMENTS graph plotting interest rates against different maturities a visual representation of relative interest rates showing that they are higher for short-term bonds than they are for long-term bonds

negligence GENERAL MANAGEMENT failure to act responsibly a breach of a duty to act with expected care in conducting activities, resulting in harm to one or more people. Negligence occurs when an organization causes harm or injury through carelessness or inattention to the needs of the groups to which it owes a duty of care. These can include its customers, consumers of its product or service, shareholders, or the local community. Victims of negligence are entitled to claim compensation. Negligence is considered to be **gross negligence** if it is the result of excessively careless behavior.

negotiable FINANCE transferable or cashable able to be transfered from one person to another or exchanged for cash

negotiable certificate of deposit FINANCE certificate of deposit that can change hands freely a certificate of deposit with a very high value that can be freely traded

negotiable instrument or **negotiable paper** FINANCE document promising to pay cash to holder a document that can be exchanged for cash, for example, a bill of exchange or a check

negotiable order of withdrawal BANKING in US, check drawn on savings account in the United States, a check drawn on a type of savings account that bears interest but allows withdrawals

negotiable order of withdrawal account BANKING = ***NOW account***

negotiable security STOCKHOLDING & INVESTMENTS security that can change ownership a security that can be freely traded to bring its owner some benefit

negotiate FINANCE **1.** sell financial instruments to transfer ownership of financial instruments such as bearer securities, bills of exchange, checks, and promissory notes to somebody else in exchange for money **2.** discuss to agree price of item to reach an agreed price with a buyer or seller by the gradual raising of offers and lowering of the price asked until a mutually agreeable price is reached

negotiated commission FINANCE brokers' commission discussed and agreed with customers a commission that results from bargaining between brokers and their customers, typically large institutions

negotiated issue STOCKHOLDING & INVESTMENTS = ***negotiated offering***

negotiated market MARKETS market where buyers and sellers bargain over prices a market in which each transaction results from negotiation between a buyer and a seller

negotiated offering STOCKHOLDING & INVESTMENTS offer at price negotiated with underwriting syndicate a **public offering** of stock, the price of which is determined by negotiations between the issuer and an **underwriting syndicate**. *Also called* ***negotiated issue***

negotiated sale FINANCE offer at price negotiated with one underwriter a **public offering** of stock, the price of which is determined by negotiations between the issuer and a single underwriter

negotiation GENERAL MANAGEMENT attempt to reach agreement a discussion with the goal of resolving a difference of opinion or dispute, or to settle the terms of an agreement or transaction

neoclassical economics ECONOMICS economic theory emphasizing free markets an economic theory that emphasizes the need for the free operation of market forces through supply and demand

nest egg FINANCE savings for retirement savings, usually other than a pension plan or retirement account, that have been set aside for use in somebody's retirement (*informal*)

nester MARKETING person not easily affected by advertising in advertising or marketing, a consumer who is not influenced by advertising hype but prefers value for money and traditional products (*slang*)

net 1. FINANCE remaining after deductions have been made used to describe the amount of something such as a price or salary remaining after all deductions have been made **2.** ACCOUNTING earn amount as profit to make a profit after all expenses have been taken into account

net advantage of refunding ACCOUNTING money raised by replacing debt the amount gained by renewing the funding of debt after interest rates have fallen

net advantage to leasing ACCOUNTING cost difference between leasing and borrowing to buy the amount by which leasing something is financially better than borrowing money and purchasing it

net advantage to merging MERGERS & ACQUISITIONS value gained after merging firms the amount by which the value of a merged enterprise exceeds the value of the preexisting companies, minus the cost of the merger

net assets ACCOUNTING value of assets minus liabilities the amount by which the value of a company's assets exceeds its liabilities, representing its capital

net asset value STOCKHOLDING & INVESTMENTS firm's net market value the value of a company's stock assessed by subtracting any liabilities from the market value. *Abbr* **NAV**

net asset value per share ACCOUNTING, STOCKHOLDING & INVESTMENTS firm's net market value divided by share number the value of a company's stock assessed by subtracting any liabilities from the market value and dividing the remainder by the number of shares of stock issued

NetBill E-COMMERCE means of buying digital goods over Internet a micropayment system developed at Carnegie Mellon University for purchasing digital goods over the Internet. After the goods are delivered in encrypted form to the purchaser's computer, the money is debited from the purchaser's prefunded account and the goods are decrypted for the purchaser's use.

net book value ACCOUNTING original cost of asset minus depreciation the historical cost of an asset less any accumulated depreciation or other provision for diminution in value, for example, reduction to net realizable value, or asset value which has been revalued downward to reflect market conditions. *Abbr* **NBV**. *Also called* ***written-down value***

net borrowings ACCOUNTING borrowings minus cash available the total of all borrowings less the cash in bank accounts and on deposit

net capital ACCOUNTING net assets minus noncash assets the amount by which net assets exceed the value of assets not easily converted to cash

net cash balance ACCOUNTING value of ready cash on a balance sheet, the amount of cash recorded as on hand

net cash flow ACCOUNTING difference between cash inflows and outflows the difference between the amount of money coming in and going out of an organization

net change MARKETS difference between prices on successive days the difference between the price of a security at the close of business from one day to the next

net change on the day MARKETS difference between opening and closing prices the difference between the opening price of a stock at the beginning of a day's trading and the closing price at the end

NetCheque™ E-COMMERCE means of exchanging electronic checks a trademark for an electronic payment system developed at the University of Southern California to allow users to write electronic checks to one another

net current assets ACCOUNTING assets minus liabilities the amount by which the value of a company's current assets exceeds its current liabilities. *Also called* ***net working capital***

net dividend STOCKHOLDING & INVESTMENTS worth of dividend after tax the value of a dividend after the recipient has paid tax on it

net domestic product ECONOMICS total national economic output with factors deducted the figure produced after factors such as depreciation have been deducted from **GDP**. *Abbr* **NDP**

net errors and omissions ACCOUNTING size of discrepancies in accounting the net amount of the discrepancies that arise in the calculation of a balance of payments

net exports FINANCE total exports minus total imports a figure showing the total value of exports less the total value of imports

net fixed assets ACCOUNTING worth of fixed assets after depreciation the value of fixed assets after depreciation as shown on a balance sheet

net foreign factor income FINANCE gross national minus gross domestic product income from outside a country, constituting the amount by which a country's gross national product exceeds its gross domestic product

net income ACCOUNTING **1.** income minus expenditures an organization's income less the costs incurred to generate it **2.** income after tax gross income less tax that has been deducted **3.** earnings after tax and other deductions a salary or wage less tax and other statutory deductions. *See also* ***disposable income***

net interest FINANCE interest after tax gross interest less tax that has been deducted

net investment STOCKHOLDING & INVESTMENTS capital invested minus estimated capital consumption an increase in the total capital invested. It is calculated as gross capital invested less an estimated figure for capital consumption or depreciation.

net lease REAL ESTATE lease where lessee pays operating costs a lease that requires

     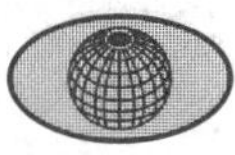   

the lessee to pay for things that the owner usually pays for. *See also* ***gross lease***

net liquid funds ACCOUNTING money plus salable investments minus short-term borrowings an organization's cash plus its marketable investments less its short-term borrowings such as overdrafts and loans

net loss ACCOUNTING loss taking all expenses into consideration a loss calculated after the deduction of overhead and other expenses

net margin ACCOUNTING percentage of income that is profit the percentage of revenues that is profit, often used an an indicator of cost control

net national product FINANCE national income a country's **GNP** adjusted to deduct capital depreciation during the period in question. *Abbr* **NNP**

net operating income ACCOUNTING income minus expenses the amount by which income exceeds expenditure, before considering taxes, interest, and other expenses

net operating margin ACCOUNTING income minus expenses as percentage of revenues **net operating income** as a percentage of revenues. It is an indicator of profitability.

net pay FINANCE total pay minus deductions the amount of pay an employee receives after all deductions such as income tax, social security, or pension contributions. *Also called* ***take-home pay***. *See also* ***disposable income***

net position STOCKHOLDING & INVESTMENTS balance of long and short positions the difference between an investor's long and short **positions** in the same security

net present value ACCOUNTING cash inflows minus cash outflows the value of an investment calculated as the sum of its initial cost and the **present value** of expected future cash flows

A positive NPV indicates that the project should be profitable, assuming that the estimated cash flows are reasonably accurate. A negative NPV indicates that the project will probably be unprofitable and therefore should be adjusted, if not abandoned altogether.

NPV enables management to consider the time-value of money it will invest. This concept holds that the value of money increases with time because it can always earn interest in a savings account. When the time-value-of-money concept is incorporated in the calculation of NPV, the value of a project's future net cash receipts in "today's money" can be determined. This enables proper comparisons between different projects.

For example, if Global Manufacturing Inc. is considering the acquisition of a new machine, its management will consider all the factors: initial purchase and installation costs; additional revenues generated by sales of the new machine's products, plus the taxes on these new revenues. Having accounted for these factors in its calculations, the cash flows that Global Manufacturing projects will generate from the new machine are:

Year 1	–100,000 (initial cost of investment)
Year 2	30,000
Year 3	40,000
Year 4	40,000
Year 5	35,000
Net Total	145,000

At first glance, it appears that cash flows total 45% more than the $100,000 initial cost, a sound investment indeed. But the time-value of money shrinks the return on the project considerably, since future dollars are worth less than present dollars in hand. NPV accounts for these differences with the help of present-value tables, which list the ratios that express the present value of expected cash flow dollars, based on the applicable interest rate and the number of years in question.

In the example, Global Manufacturing's cost of capital is 9%. Using this figure to find the corresponding ratios on the present value table, the $100,000 investment cost and expected annual revenues during the five years in question, the NPV calculation looks like this:

Year	Cash flow	Table factor (at 9%)	Present value
1	($100,000) ×	1.000000 =	($100,000)
2	$30,000 ×	0.917431 =	$27,522.93
3	$40,000 ×	0.841680 =	$33,667.20
4	$40,000 ×	0.772183 =	$30,887.32
5	$35,000 ×	0.708425 =	$24,794.88
NPV =	$16,873.33		

NPV is still positive. So, on this basis at least, the investment should proceed. *Abbr* **NPV**

net price OPERATIONS & PRODUCTION price actually paid the price paid for goods or services after all relevant discounts have been deducted

net proceeds ACCOUNTING gains from transaction minus its cost the amount received from a transaction minus the cost of making it

net profit ACCOUNTING income after expenses an organization's income as shown in a **profit and loss account** after all relevant expenses have been deducted. *Also called* ***profit after tax***

net profit margin ACCOUNTING, OPERATIONS & PRODUCTION *see* ***profit margin***

net profit ratio ACCOUNTING ratio of net profit to net sales the ratio of an organization's net profit to its total net sales. Comparing the net profit ratios of companies in the same sector shows which are the most efficient.

net realizable value ACCOUNTING selling price minus costs the value of an asset if sold, allowing for costs

net receipts ACCOUNTING income after all deductions have been made receipts calculated after the deduction of commission, tax, discounts, and other associated expenses. *See also* ***gross receipts***

net relevant earnings TAX income for pension-contribution purposes earnings which qualify for calculating pension contributions and against which relief against tax can be claimed. Such earnings can be income from employment which is not pensionable, for example, the profits of a self-employed sole trader.

net residual value ACCOUNTING value of asset being disposed of the anticipated proceeds of an asset at the end of its useful life, less the costs such as transportation and the commission associated with selling it. It is used when calculating the annual charge for **straight line depreciation**. *Abbr* **NRV**

net return ACCOUNTING profit from investment after expenditures the amount received from an investment, taking taxes and transaction costs into account

net salary FINANCE earnings after all deductions have been made the salary remaining after deductions for taxes, social security, medicare, and any employee share of insurance premiums. *See also* ***disposable income***

net sales ACCOUNTING actual value of sales a company's total sales less any relevant discounts such as those given to retailers

net salvage value ACCOUNTING value of project being abandoned, after tax the amount of money remaining after a project has been terminated, taking tax consequences into consideration

net tangible assets ACCOUNTING firm's total assets minus intangible assets the total assets of a company less its intangible assets such as goodwill or intellectual property. *Abbr* **NTA**

netting MARKETS carrying only net result forward a method of settling financial transactions in which only the net result in a transaction is carried forward

network culture GENERAL MANAGEMENT attitudes and behavior of global networks cultural patterns that are heavily influenced by communication using global networks

net working capital ACCOUNTING = ***net current assets***

network management GENERAL MANAGEMENT supervision of functioning of computer network the coordinated control of computer systems and programs to allow access to and delivery of information to a number of users

network marketing MARKETING trading through independent agents the selling of goods or services through a network of self-employed agents or representatives. Network marketing usually involves several levels of agents, each level on a different commission rate. Each agent is encouraged to recruit other agents. In genuine network marketing, in contrast to **pyramid selling**, there is an end product or service sold to customers. Another version of network marketing is the loose cooperative relationship between a company, its competitors, collaborators, suppliers, and other organizations affecting the overall marketing function. *Also called* ***multilevel marketing***

network organization GENERAL MANAGEMENT loose association of teams a company or group of companies that has a minimum of formal structures and relies instead on the formation and dissolution of teams to meet specific objectives. A network organization utilizes information and communications technologies extensively, and makes use of knowledge across and within companies along the **value chain**. *See also* ***virtual organization***

network revolution GENERAL MANAGEMENT dramatic change arising from global networks the fundamental change in business practices triggered by the growth of global networks

network society GENERAL MANAGEMENT society dependent on global networks a society in which patterns of work, communication, and government are characterized by the use of global networks

net worth ACCOUNTING assets minus liabilities the difference between the assets and liabilities of a person or company

net yield ACCOUNTING rate of return after costs and tax the amount produced by an investment after deducting all costs and taxes

new economy ECONOMICS economic system based on e-commerce a term used in the late 1990s and 2000s to describe the e-commerce sector and the **digital economy**, in which firms mostly trade online rather than in the bricks and mortar of physical premises

new entrant MARKETING new arrival in market or sector an organization or product that has recently come into a market or sector

new issue STOCKHOLDING & INVESTMENTS **1.** new security on sale for first time a new security, such as a bond or stock, being offered to the public for the first time. *See also* ***float, initial public offering*** **2.** issue of new security an additional issue of an existing security, for example, a **rights issue**

new issue market or **new issues market** MARKETS market into which new stock is launched a market where companies can raise finance by issuing additional shares or by a flotation. *See also* ***float, initial public offering, primary market***

newly acquired business BUSINESS business recently bought by another a business in the early stages of the changes caused by having been bought by another company

newly industrialized economy ECONOMICS nation benefiting from industrialization a country whose industrialization has recently started to develop. Mexico and Malaysia are examples of newly industrialized economies.

new metrics GENERAL MANAGEMENT nontraditional standards for measuring business performance standards for measuring or quantifying the activities and success of an organization that incorporate nontraditional approaches

new money FINANCE financing from a new source financing provided by an issue of new shares of stock or by the transfer of money from one account to another

new product development MARKETING stages of bringing something new to market the processes involved in getting a new product or service to market. The traditional **product development cycle**, the **stage-gate model**, embraces the conception, generation, analysis, development, testing, marketing, and commercialization of new products or services. Alternative models of new product development fall into two broad categories: **accelerating time to market models** and **integrated implementation models**. These strive to achieve both flexibility and acceleration of development. All activities such as design, production planning, and test marketing are performed in parallel rather than going through a sequential linear progression. *Abbr* **NPD**

new time MARKETS when stock exchange sales are carried over the period on a stock exchange when sales in the last few days of the previous account are credited to the following account

New York Mercantile Exchange MARKETS US exchange for energy and precious metals the world's largest physical commodity exchange and North America's most important trading exchange for energy and precious metals. It deals in crude oil, gasoline, heating oil, natural gas, propane, gold, silver, platinum, palladium, and copper. *Abbr* **NYMEX**

New York Stock Exchange MARKETS stock exchange in New York the leading stock exchange in New York, which is self-regulatory but has to comply with the regulations of the US Securities and Exchange Commission. *Abbr* **NYSE**

New York Stock Exchange Composite Index MARKETS New York stock price index an index designed to track the change in the market value of all common stocks listed on the New York Stock Exchange

New Zealand Stock Exchange MARKETS New Zealand's main market for securities the principal market in New Zealand for trading in securities. It was established in 1981, replacing the Stock Exchange Association of New Zealand and a number of regional trading floors. *Abbr* **NZSE**

New Zealand Trade Development Board FINANCE New Zealand agency promoting exports and inward investment a government body responsible for promoting New Zealand exports and facilitating foreign investment in New Zealand. *Also called* ***TRADENZ***

next futures contract STOCKHOLDING & INVESTMENTS option for following month an **option** to buy or sell for the month after the current month

NI *abbr* PENSIONS National Insurance

NIC *abbr* PENSIONS National Insurance contributions

niche bank or **niche banker** BANKING specialist banker a bank or banker specializing in a specific field such as management buyouts

niche company BUSINESS specialist firm a company that produces a product or service that fills a specialized gap in the overall provision of a market

niche market MARKETING specialized market segment a very specialized market segment within a broader segment. A niche market involves specialist goods or services with relatively few or no competitors. Customers may look for exclusiveness or some other differentiating factor such as high status. Alternatively, they may have a specific requirement not satisfied by standard products. *See also* ***micromarketing***

niche player (*informal*) **1.** BANKING = ***niche bank*** **2.** STOCKHOLDING & INVESTMENTS = ***boutique investment house***

nickel *US* FINANCE small margin five hundredths of one percent, expressing a fine margin (*slang*)

NIF *abbr* FINANCE note issuance facility

Nifty Fifty *US* MARKETS institutional investors' favorite stocks the 50 most popular stocks among institutional investors on the New York Stock Exchange from the 1960s until the early 1970s (*informal*)

Nikkei 225 or **Nikkei Index** MARKETS Japanese stock price index an index of stock prices on the Tokyo Stock Exchange, the largest stock exchange in Japan

nil paid STOCKHOLDING & INVESTMENTS nothing paid yet with no money yet paid. In the United Kingdom, the term is used in reference to the purchase of newly issued stocks, or to the stocks themselves, when the stockholder entitled to buy new stocks has not yet made a commitment to do so and may sell the rights instead.

nil return *UK* TAX report of no taxable income a report filed with a tax authority showing no transactions or income on which tax is owed

ninja loan FINANCE loan made to somebody with poor credit rating a loan made to somebody who has No INcome, No Job, and no Assets (*slang*). *See also* ***subprime loan***

NMS *abbr* MARKETS National Market System

NNP *abbr* FINANCE net national product

no-claims bonus or **no-claims discount** INSURANCE reduced insurance price because no claims are made a reduction of premiums on an insurance policy because no claims have been made

noise GENERAL MANAGEMENT distracting unimportant data irrelevant or insignificant data which overload a feedback process. The presence of noise can confuse or divert attention from relevant information; efficiency in a system is enhanced as the ratio of information to noise increases.

noise trader MARKETS uninformed market participant a participant in the stock market who does not have much knowledge about the securities being traded (*slang*)

no-load fund STOCKHOLDING & INVESTMENTS mutual fund with no fee for trading a mutual fund that does not charge a fee for the purchase or sale of shares. *See also* ***load fund***

nominal **1.** FINANCE very much lower than usual level very small when compared with what would be considered usual, especially with reference to a sum of money **2.** ACCOUNTING relating to current prices considered in terms of the stated or original value only, without adjustment for inflation and other changes **3.** GENERAL MANAGEMENT assigned by name assigned to a specific name or category

nominal account ACCOUNTING account recording items according to category a record of revenues and expenditures, liabilities and assets classified by their nature, for example, sales, rent, rates, electricity, wages, or share capital

nominal annual rate FINANCE = ***annual percentage rate***

nominal capital STOCKHOLDING & INVESTMENTS = ***nominal share capital***

nominal cash flow ACCOUNTING cash flow disregarding inflation cash flow in terms of currency, without adjustment for inflation

nominal exchange rate CURRENCY & EXCHANGE stated exchange rate the exchange rate as specified, without adjustment for transaction costs or differences in purchasing power

nominal interest rate FINANCE stated interest rate the interest rate as specified, without adjustment for compounding or inflation

nominal ledger *UK* ACCOUNTING ledger recording money values a record of revenue, operating expenses, assets, and capital

nominal price OPERATIONS & PRODUCTION price disregarding value the price of an item being sold when the price is lower than the full value

nominal share capital STOCKHOLDING & INVESTMENTS maximum amount of firm's share capital the total value of all of a corporation's stock at **nominal value**. *Also called* ***nominal capital***. *See also* ***authorized share capital***

nominal value STOCKHOLDING & INVESTMENTS original value of new stock the original value officially given to a newly issued stock. *Also called* ***par value***. *See also* ***capitalization***, ***reserves***

nominal yield STOCKHOLDING & INVESTMENTS dividend as percentage of face value the dividend paid on a share of stock expressed as a percentage of its face value

nominee **1.** FINANCE in US, somebody acting for another in the United States, a person who is appointed to deal with financial matters on your behalf **2.** *US* STOCKHOLDING & INVESTMENTS holder of security on another's behalf a financial institution, or an individual employed by such an institution, that holds a security on behalf of the actual owner. While this may be to hide the owner's identity, for example, in the case of a celebrity, it is also to allow an institution managing any individual's portfolio to conduct transactions without the need for the owner to sign the required paperwork. *UK term* ***nominee name***

nominee account BANKING account not in owner's name an account held not in the name of the real owner of the account, but instead in the name of another person, organization, or financial institution. Stocks can be bought and held in nominee accounts so that the owner's identity is not disclosed.

nominee name *UK* STOCKHOLDING & INVESTMENTS = ***nominee***

nonacceptance BANKING rejection of bill of exchange on presentation a refusal to accept a bill of exchange when it is presented, by the person on whom it is drawn

nonbranded goods MARKETING items from unidentified source generic goods such as food produce, pharmaceuticals, or computer keyboards that are not linked to a specific **brand** name, manufacturer, or producer. Nonbranded goods are often widely available in street markets or by mail order and are often perceived to be of low quality.

nonbusiness days BANKING days when banks are closed those days when banks are not open for business, for example, public holidays, or Saturdays and Sundays in Western countries

noncallable STOCKHOLDING & INVESTMENTS not able to be repurchased before maturity used to describe a security that the issuer cannot buy back before its maturity date. *See also* ***callable***

noncash item **1.** ACCOUNTING entry in income statement not representing cash an item, such as a gain or loss from an investment or depreciation expenses, that occurs on an income statement and is not a receipt of actual money **2.** BANKING financial instruments representing money checks, drafts, and similar items that have money value but are not money themselves

noncompetitive bid MARKETS purchasing US Treasury security at average competitive bid price a method of purchasing US Treasury securities through member banks of the **Federal Reserve** in which a buyer agrees to pay a price equal to the average of all competitive bids for that particular week's issue of securities

nonconformance costs OPERATIONS & PRODUCTION = ***quality costs***

nonconforming loan TAX loan not meeting usual conditions a loan that does not conform to the lender's standards, especially those of a US government agency

noncontributory pension plan *US* PENSIONS pension plan financed by employer a pension plan to which the employee makes no payments. *UK term* ***non-contributory pension scheme***

non-contributory pension scheme *UK* PENSIONS = ***noncontributory pension plan***

noncurrent assets FINANCE long-term investments resources that are expected to be held for more than one year. They are reported at the lower of cost and current market value, which means that their values will vary.

nondeductible ACCOUNTING not admissible as deduction not allowed to be deducted from a payment, especially not acceptable as an allowance against income tax

nondisclosure agreement HR & PERSONNEL agreement not to give away company secrets a legally enforceable agreement preventing present or past employees from disclosing commercially sensitive information belonging to the employer to any other party. A nondisclosure agreement can remain in force for several years after an employee leaves a company. In the event of a dispute, a company may be required to prove that the information in question belongs to the company itself, is not in the public domain, or cannot be obtained elsewhere. *Abbr* **NDA**

nondisparagement agreement HR & PERSONNEL agreement not to criticize employer an agreement that prevents present or past employees from criticizing an employing organization in public. Nondisparagement agreements are a relatively new type of agreement and have arisen primarily to prevent employees putting comments about their employing organization onto the Internet. Case law has yet to determine whether such agreements are legally binding. *Abbr* **NDA**

nondom or **nondomicile** TAX person not paying tax on earnings abroad a person who is exempt from paying tax on foreign earnings because his or her permanent home is in another country

nonexecutive director CORPORATE GOVERNANCE board member without day-to-day involvement a part-time, nonsalaried member of the **board of directors,** involved in the planning, strategy, and policy making of an organization but not in its day-to-day operations. The appointment of a nonexecutive director to a board is usually made in order to provide independence and balance to that board, and to ensure that good **corporate governance** is practiced. A nonexecutive director may be selected for the prestige they bring or for their experience, contacts, or specialist knowledge. *Also called* ***part-time director***. *See also* **outside director**

nonfinancial asset ACCOUNTING not money or financial contract an asset such as real estate or personal property that is neither money nor a financial instrument

non-financial incentive scheme FINANCE UK program rewarding performance other than with money in the United Kingdom, a program offering benefits such as additional paid vacations, set up to reward employees for improved commitment and performance and as a means of motivation. *See also* ***financial incentive scheme***

noninterest-bearing bond STOCKHOLDING & INVESTMENTS bond with discount rather than interest a bond that is sold at a discount instead of with a promise to pay interest

nonjudicial foreclosure LEGAL in US, reclamation of property without using court in the United States, a foreclosure on real estate without recourse to a court. The mortgage lender issues a notice of mortgage default to the owner, along with a notice of intent to sell the property.

nonline E-COMMERCE not online not provided with an Internet connection, or not done via the Internet

nonlinear programming STATISTICS using some nonlinear equations a process in which the equations expressing the interactions of variables are not all linear but may, for example, be in proportion to the square of a variable

nonline community E-COMMERCE people not using e-mail or Internet the people who do not use e-mail or the Internet for communications, information, or purchasing

nonnegotiable instrument FINANCE financial contract that cannot change hands a financial instrument that cannot be signed over to anyone else. These include **bills of exchange** and **crossed checks.**

nonoperational balances BANKING Bank of England deposits that cannot be withdrawn accounts that banks maintain at the Bank of England without the power of withdrawal

nonparticipating preferred stock STOCKHOLDING & INVESTMENTS preferred stock paying fixed dividend the most common type of preferred stock that pays a fixed dividend regardless of the profitability of the company. *See also* ***participating preferred stock***

nonperforming asset STOCKHOLDING & INVESTMENTS asset providing no income an asset that is not producing income, for example, one that is no longer accruing interest

nonperforming loan FINANCE loan made to borrower likely to default a loan made to a borrower who is not likely to pay any interest nor to repay the principal

nonprofit organization or **nonprofit** BUSINESS organization not operated solely for profit an **organization** that does not have financial profit as a main strategic objective. Nonprofit organizations include charities, professional associations, labor unions, and religious, arts, community, research, and campaigning bodies. These organizations are not situated in either the **public** or **private sectors**, but in what has been called the **third sector**. Many have paid staff and working capital but their

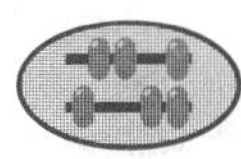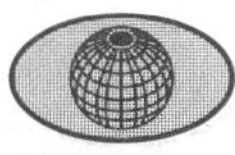

main purpose is not to provide a product or service, but to effect change. They are led by values rather than financial commitments to shareholders. *Abbr* **NPO**. *See also* ***third sector***

nonqualified annuity PENSIONS US annuity bought with taxed income in the United States, a type of annuity that can be purchased with after-tax income to provide retirement income. Taxes on earnings from the annuity are deferred until money is withdrawn.

nonrandom sampling OPERATIONS & PRODUCTION sampling with unequal chances of selection a **sampling** technique that is used when it cannot be ensured that each item has an equal chance of being selected, or when selection is based on expert knowledge of the population. *See also* ***random sampling***

nonrecourse debt FINANCE debt with no liability a debt for which the borrower has no personal responsibility, typically a debt of a limited partnership

nonrecoverable FINANCE that will never be paid back used to describe a debt that will never be paid, for example, because of the borrower's bankruptcy

nonrecurring charge ACCOUNTING unique charge a charge that is made only once

nonrecurring item ACCOUNTING unique item in account in a set of accounts an item that is included on only one occasion

nonresident TAX working abroad used to describe somebody who has left his or her native country to work overseas for a period. Nonresidency has tax advantages, such as exemption from tax on overseas earning. While a US citizen is working overseas for a period of 11 out of 12 months, a limited amount of his or her earned income generated overseas is exempt from US income tax. During a period of nonresidency, many expatriates choose to bank offshore.

Non-Resident Withholding Tax TAX New Zealand levy on nonresidents' investment income a duty imposed by the New Zealand government on interest and dividends earned by a nonresident from investments. *Abbr* **NRWT**

nonstore retailing E-COMMERCE selling over Internet without building to visit the selling of goods and services electronically without actually establishing a physical store

nonstrategic BUSINESS not related to achievement of long-term goals not related to the long-term objectives of an organization or the resources used to achieve those objectives

non-sufficient funds *UK* BANKING = ***insufficient funds***

nonsystematic risk RISK risk related to particular firm investment risk that is attributable to the performance of a specific company, not to the performance of the stock market or economy, and can be reduced by diversification

nontariff barrier INTERNATIONAL TRADE regulations that make imports more difficult a country's economic regulation on something such as safety standards that impedes imports, often from emerging markets. *Abbr* **NTB**

nontaxable TAX not liable to tax not subject to tax. In the United Kingdom, interest from **ISAs**, prize winnings, and statutory redundancy pay are among non-taxable sources of income.

nonvoting share STOCKHOLDING & INVESTMENTS common stock receiving dividend but not voting rights common stock that is paid a dividend from the company's profits, but that does not entitle the stockholder to vote at any meeting of stockholders. Such stock is unpopular with institutional investors. *Also called* ***A share***

norm STATISTICS expected range of values for set in a statistical study, a range of values that is normal for a population or other set

normal distribution STATISTICS expected distribution of random variable in a statistical study, the probability distribution of a random variable

normal profit ECONOMICS minimum profit required for business **the minimum level of** profit that will attract an entrepreneur to begin a business or remain trading

normal yield curve STOCKHOLDING & INVESTMENTS showing lower yields for short-term bonds a visual representation of interest rates showing higher yields for long-term bonds than for short-term bonds. *See also* ***yield curve***

no-strike agreement HR & PERSONNEL arrangement with union not to call strike a formal understanding between an employer and a labor union that the union will not call its members out on strike. A no-strike agreement is usually won by the employer in exchange for improved terms and conditions of employment, including pay, and sometimes guaranteed employment.

nostro account BANKING account with bank abroad an account that a bank has with a **correspondent bank** in another country

notary public LEGAL somebody with authority to officially witness documents a person who has been authorized by a state to witness documents, making them legally accepted, and to administer oaths

notch *S. Africa* HR & PERSONNEL point on scale a position on a scale such as an incremental salary scale

note 1. CURRENCY & EXCHANGE item of paper money a piece of paper money printed by a bank and approved as legal tender. *Also called* ***banknote (sense 1), bill (sense 2)*** **2.** FINANCE document promising to repay borrowed money a written promise to repay money that has been borrowed

note issuance facility FINANCE facility for buying and reselling Eurocurrency notes a credit facility where a company obtains a loan underwritten by banks and can issue a series of short-term **Eurocurrency** notes to replace others that have expired. *Abbr* **NIF**

note of hand FINANCE = ***promissory note***

notes to the accounts or **notes to the financial statements** ACCOUNTING information supporting account entries an explanation of specific items in a set of accounts

not-for-profit FINANCE not operated to generate income organized typically for a charitable, humanitarian, or educational purpose and not generating profits for shareholders. In the United States, not-for-profit corporations can apply for tax-exempt status at both the federal and state levels of government. *See also* ***nonprofit organization***

notice of coding TAX information about another's tax code a notice that informs a third party of the code number given to indicate the amount of tax allowances to which somebody is entitled

notice of default *US* LEGAL official notification to defaulter a formal document issued by a lender to a borrower who is in default. *UK term* ***default notice***

notice period HR & PERSONNEL time between resignation or dismissal and leaving the amount of time specified in the terms and **conditions of employment** that an **employee** must work between resigning from an organization and leaving the employment of that organization

notifying bank BANKING, INTERNATIONAL TRADE = ***advising bank***

notional income ACCOUNTING income not physically received invisible benefit that is not actual money, goods, or services

  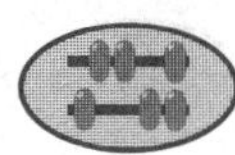 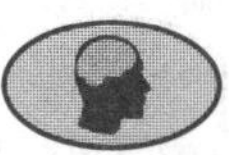  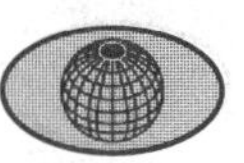   

notional principal amount FINANCE value of loan the value used to represent a loan in calculating **interest rate swaps**

notional rent ACCOUNTING theoretical rent for firm's own premises an amount of money noted in accounts as rent where the company owns the building it is occupying and so does not pay an actual rent

not negotiable FINANCE not able to change hands absolutely used to describe a check or bill of exchange that cannot be transferred to somebody else. If such a document is given by one person to another, the recipient obtains no better title to it than the signatory. *See also* ***negotiable instrument***

not sufficient funds *UK* BANKING = ***insufficient funds***

novation LEGAL agreed replacement of one party to contract an agreement to change a contract by substituting a third party for one of the two original parties

NOW account BANKING interest-paying US account with checks in the United States, an interest-bearing account with a bank or savings and loan association, on which checks (called **negotiable orders of withdrawal**) can be drawn. *Full form* ***negotiable order of withdrawal account***

NPD *abbr* MARKETING new product development

NPO *abbr* BUSINESS nonprofit organization

NPV *abbr* ACCOUNTING net present value

NRV *abbr* ACCOUNTING net residual value

NRWT *abbr* TAX Non-Resident Withholding Tax

NSA *abbr* ACCOUNTING National Society of Accountants

NS&I *abbr* STOCKHOLDING & INVESTMENTS National Savings & Investments

NSB *abbr* BANKING National Savings Bank

NSC *abbr* STOCKHOLDING & INVESTMENTS National Savings Certificate

NSF *abbr* BANKING non-sufficient funds *or* not sufficient funds

NTA *abbr* ACCOUNTING net tangible assets

NTB *abbr* INTERNATIONAL TRADE nontariff barrier

nuisance parameter STATISTICS unimportant but necessary variable in a statistical model, a parameter that is insignificant in itself but whose unknown value is needed to make inferences about significant variables in a study

null hypothesis STATISTICS lack of significant effect the assumption that there is no relationship between variables that has produced a significant difference

numbered account BANKING bank account without holder's name a bank account identified by a number to allow the holder to remain anonymous

numerical control OPERATIONS & PRODUCTION automation using numerical data the use of numerical data to influence the operation of equipment. It allows the operation of machinery to be automated and usually involves the use of computer systems. Data is generated, stored, manipulated, and retrieved while a process is in operation.

nuncupative will LEGAL oral will a will that is made orally in the presence of a witness, rather than in writing

NYMEX *abbr* MARKETS New York Mercantile Exchange

NYSE *abbr* MARKETS New York Stock Exchange

NZSE *abbr* MARKETS New Zealand Stock Exchange

NZSE10 Index MARKETS index of 10 largest New Zealand firms a measure of changes in stock prices on the New Zealand Stock Exchange, based on the change in value of the stocks of the ten largest companies. *Abbr* **NZSE10**

NZSE30 Selection Index MARKETS index of 30 largest New Zealand firms a measure of changes in stock prices on the New Zealand Stock Exchange, based on the change in value of the stocks of the 30 largest companies. *Abbr* **NZSE30**

NZSE40 Index MARKETS index of 40 largest New Zealand firms the principal measure of changes in stock prices on the New Zealand Stock Exchange, based on the change in value of the stocks of the 40 largest companies. The composition of the index is reviewed every three months. *Abbr* **NZSE40**

OBI *abbr* E-COMMERCE open buying on the Internet

object and task technique GENERAL MANAGEMENT budgeting by costing each task in the United States, a method of budgeting that involves assessing a project's objectives, determining the tasks required for their accomplishment, and then estimating the cost of each task

objective GENERAL MANAGEMENT goal of effort an end toward which effort is directed and on which resources are focused, usually to achieve an organization's strategy. There is considerable discussion on whether objective, goal, target, and aim are the same. In general usage, the terms are often interchangeable, so it is important that, if an organization has a particular meaning for one of these terms, it must define it in its documentation. Sometimes an objective is seen as the desired final end result, while a goal is a smaller step on the road to it.

obligation LEGAL legal agreement, especially to pay debt a binding legal agreement, by which somebody is bound to do something, especially to pay an amount of money

obligor FINANCE = ***debtor***

OBSF *abbr* FINANCE off-balance-sheet financing

obsolescence 1. FINANCE loss through becoming out of date the loss of value of a fixed asset due to advances in technology or changes in market conditions **2.** MARKETING becoming out of date the decline of products in a market due to the introduction of better competitor products or rapid technology developments. Obsolescence of products can be a planned process, controlled by introducing deliberate minor cosmetic changes to a product every few years to encourage new purchases. It can also be unplanned, however, and in some sectors the pace of technological change is so rapid that the rate of obsolescence is high Obsolescence is part of the product life cycle, and if a product cannot be turned around, it may lead to product abandonment.

occupational pension PENSIONS in UK, pension plan maintained by employer in the United Kingdom, a pension plan run by an organization for its employees. Occupational pensions are regarded as deferred pay and form part of the total compensation package. Until recently, most plans were based on final salary but there has been a shift toward **money purchase pensions**, particularly among smaller companies. Alternatively, employers may choose to contribute to an employee's **personal pension**. *Also called* ***company pension***

OCF *abbr* ACCOUNTING operating cash flow

OCR *abbr* BANKING official cash rate

O/D *abbr* BANKING overdraft

  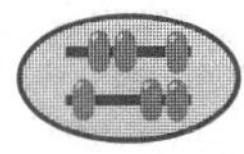   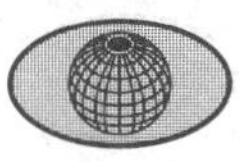   

odd lot MARKETS fewer than 100 shares traded together a group of fewer than 100 shares of stock bought or sold together. *Also called* ***broken lot, uneven lot***

OECD INTERNATIONAL TRADE association of nations promoting democracy and free market a group of 30 member countries, with a shared commitment to democratic government and the market economy, that has active relationships with some 70 other countries via nongovernmental organizations. Formed in 1961, its work covers economic and social issues from macroeconomics to trade, education, development, and scientific innovation. Its goals are to promote economic growth and employment in member countries in a climate of stability; to assist the sustainable economic expansion of both member and nonmember countries; and to support a balanced and even-handed expansion of world trade. *Full form* ***Organisation for Economic Co-operation and Development***

OEIC *abbr* STOCKHOLDING & INVESTMENTS open-ended investment company

OEM *abbr* OPERATIONS & PRODUCTION original equipment manufacturer

off-balance-sheet financing FINANCE raising money through items not on balance sheet financing obtained by means other than debt and equity instruments, for example, by partnerships, joint ventures, and leases. *Abbr* **OBSF**

off-board MARKETS of trading between dealers used to describe the trade of listed securities that does not take place on the stock exchange, or that takes place in the **over-the-counter market**

offer STOCKHOLDING & INVESTMENTS **1.** *see* ***offering price*** **2.** net value of mutual fund the **net asset value** of a mutual fund plus any sales charges. It is the price investors pay when they buy a security.

offer by prospectus STOCKHOLDING & INVESTMENTS UK means of selling securities to public in the United Kingdom, one of the ways available to a **lead underwriter** of offering securities to the public. *See also* ***float, initial public offering, new issue, offer for sale***

offer document STOCKHOLDING & INVESTMENTS = ***prospectus***

offered market *UK* MARKETS market with more sellers than buyers a market in which sellers outnumber buyers, giving an advantage to buyers

offer for sale STOCKHOLDING & INVESTMENTS invitation to buy stock an invitation to apply for stock in a company, based on information contained in a prospectus

offering MARKETS security offered for sale an issue of a security that is offered for sale

offering circular STOCKHOLDING & INVESTMENTS = ***prospectus***

offering date MARKETS first day of stock sale the date on which a company offers its stock for sale to the public for the first time

offering price *US* STOCKHOLDING & INVESTMENTS selling price of share of stock the price at which somebody offers a share of a stock, especially a new issue, for sale. *Also called* ***offer price***

offeror STOCKHOLDING & INVESTMENTS maker of bid somebody who makes a bid to buy a **financial obligation** such as a debt

offer period MERGERS & ACQUISITIONS time span when takeover bid is open the time after a **takeover bid** for a company is first announced until the deal is closed or the offer lapses

offer price *UK* STOCKHOLDING & INVESTMENTS = ***offering price***

Office of Fair Trading REGULATION & COMPLIANCE UK government department protecting consumers a department of the UK government that protects consumers against unfair or illegal business practices. *Abbr* **OFT**

Office of Management and Budget REGULATION & COMPLIANCE US government office that helps prepare federal budget the US government office, part of the executive branch of the government, that helps the President to prepare the federal budget. *Abbr* **OMB**

Office of Thrift Supervision REGULATION & COMPLIANCE US agency regulating savings and loan associations an agency within the United States Department of the Treasury that regulates the savings and loan associations to ensure that they operate in a way that protects people's savings. *Abbr* **OTS**

officer GENERAL MANAGEMENT = ***executive***

official books of account ACCOUNTING institution's financial records the official financial records of an organization set up for educational, professional, religious, or social purposes

official cash rate BANKING government interest rate the current interest rate as set by a central bank. *Abbr* **OCR**

official development assistance FINANCE money made available to emerging country money that the **OECD's** Development Assistance Committee gives or lends to an emerging country

official intervention CURRENCY & EXCHANGE government action to affect exchange rate an attempt by a government to influence the exchange rate by buying or selling foreign currency

official list MARKETS list of securities traded on London Stock Exchange in the United Kingdom, the list maintained by the **Financial Services Authority** of all the securities traded on the London Stock Exchange

official receiver LEGAL UK court agent managing bankruptcy in the United Kingdom, an officer of the court who is appointed to wind up the affairs of an organization that goes bankrupt. An official receiver is appointed by the Department for Business, Enterprise & Regulatory Reform and often acts as a **liquidator**. The job involves realizing any assets that remain to repay debts, for example, by selling property. *Abbr* **OR**

official return ACCOUNTING legally required financial report a financial report or statement required by law and made by a person or company, for example, a tax return

off-line transaction processing E-COMMERCE recording of credit or debit card transactions the receipt and storage of order and credit or debit card information through a computer network or point-of-sale terminal for subsequent authorization and processing

offset STOCKHOLDING & INVESTMENTS counterbalancing transaction in security a transaction that balances all or part of an earlier transaction in the same security

offset clause INSURANCE insurance condition allowing counterbalancing of credits and debits a provision in an insurance policy that permits the balancing of credits against debits so that, for example, a company can reduce or omit payments to another company that owes it money and is bankrupt

offshore INTERNATIONAL TRADE **1.** send jobs overseas to get cheaper labor to hire workers in foreign countries in order to take advantage of a supply of skilled but relatively cheap labor **2.** located in another country based outside a specific country, especially in a place where taxes are low

offshore account TAX account located in low-tax country an account maintained in a place where taxes are low, to reduce a person's or company's liability to tax where their income originates

  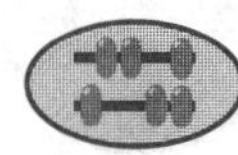 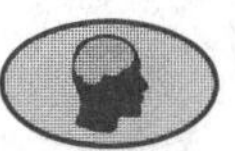  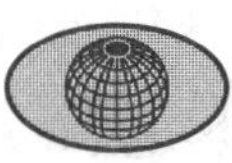   

offshore banking BANKING banking in foreign banks banking in a foreign country, especially one that has favorable taxation regulations and is considered as a **tax haven**

offshore company BUSINESS firm registered abroad for financial benefits a company that is registered in a country other than the one in which it conducts most of its business, usually for tax purposes. For example, many **captive insurance companies** are registered in the Cayman Islands.

offshore finance subsidiary *UK* BUSINESS = ***offshore financial subsidiary***

offshore financial center FINANCE finance hub in foreign country a country or other political unit that has banking laws intended to attract business from industrialized nations

offshore financial subsidiary *US* BUSINESS firm abroad handling parent company's finances a company created in another country to handle financial transactions, giving the owning company tax and legal advantages in its home country. *UK term* ***offshore finance subsidiary***

offshore fund STOCKHOLDING & INVESTMENTS fund based abroad a fund that is based in a foreign country, usually a country that has favorable taxation regulations

offshore holding company BUSINESS firm abroad owning firms at home a company created in another country to own other companies, giving the owning company legal advantages in its home country

offshore production INTERNATIONAL TRADE making goods abroad for import the manufacture of goods abroad for import to the home market

offshore trading company BUSINESS firm abroad handling parent company's commercial transactions a company created in another country to handle commercial transactions, giving the owning company legal advantages in its home country

offshoring INTERNATIONAL TRADE moving service operations abroad the transfer of service operations to foreign countries in order to take advantage of a supply of skilled but relatively cheap labor

off-the-shelf company BUSINESS UK firm available for purchase in the United Kingdom, a company for which all the legal formalities, except the appointment of directors, have been completed so that a purchaser can transform it into a customized new company with relative ease and low cost

OFT *abbr* REGULATION & COMPLIANCE Office of Fair Trading

OI ACCOUNTING *see* ***EBIT***

oil economy ECONOMICS **1.** economy based on oil revenues an economy that is funded by the revenues from oil resources **2.** economy based on oil an economy that depends on oil supplies for its transportation, agricultural, and energy needs

Old Lady of Threadneedle Street *UK* BANKING Bank of England the Bank of England, which is located in Threadneedle Street in the City of London (*informal*)

oligarch FINANCE rich powerful businessman one of a small group having financial and political power, especially nowadays somebody with extreme personal wealth (*slang*)

oligarchy GENERAL MANAGEMENT control by small group an organization in which a small group of managers exercises control. Within an oligarchy, the controlling group often directs the organization for its own purposes, or for purposes other than the best interests of the organization.

oligopoly MARKETS market with few major sellers a market that is controlled by a few, very large, suppliers

oligopsony MARKETS market with few customers a market in which there are only a few buyers for a specific product or service

OMB *abbr* REGULATION & COMPLIANCE Office of Management and Budget

ombudsman REGULATION & COMPLIANCE independent investigator of complaints a public official who investigates complaints against public departments, large organizations, or business sectors

omitted dividend STOCKHOLDING & INVESTMENTS unpaid regular dividend a regularly scheduled dividend that a company does not pay

omnibus account STOCKHOLDING & INVESTMENTS combined account for broker's convenience an account of one broker with another that combines the transactions of multiple investors for the convenience of the brokers

omnibus survey MARKETING wide-ranging survey a survey covering a number of topics, usually undertaken on behalf of several clients who share the cost of conducting the survey

on account FINANCE by advance payment used to describe an amount of money paid that represents part of a sum of money due to be paid in the future

oncost ACCOUNTING general cost of running business a business cost that cannot be charged directly to a particular good or service and must be apportioned across the business

on demand 1. BANKING allowing immediate withdrawals used to describe an account from which withdrawals may be made without giving a period of notice **2.** FINANCE allowing demand for immediate repayment used to describe a loan, usually an overdraft, that the lender can request the borrower to repay immediately **3.** FINANCE payable immediately to holder used to describe a bill of exchange that is paid upon presentation

one-stop shopping FINANCE provision of complete variety of financial services the ability of a single financial institution to offer a full variety of financial services

one-to-one marketing MARKETING emphasis on individual customers a marketing technique using detailed data, personalized communications, and customized products or services to match the requirements of individual customers

one-way trade INTERNATIONAL TRADE when seller does not buy in return an economic situation in which one country sells to another, but does not buy anything in return

one-year money STOCKHOLDING & INVESTMENTS investment for fixed period of one year money placed on a money market for a fixed period of one year, with either a fixed or variable rate of interest. It can be removed during the fixed term only upon payment of a penalty.

on-hold advertising MARKETING advertising to telephone callers waiting for service telephone advertising aimed at consumers who are being kept on hold while waiting to speak to somebody

online banking E-COMMERCE, BANKING banking service accessible by computer over Internet a system by which customers have bank accounts that they can access directly from their home computers, using the Internet, and can carry out operations such as checking on their account balances, paying invoices, and receiving their salaries electronically

online capture E-COMMERCE means of initiating payment after shipment a payment transaction generated after goods have

  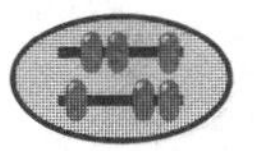   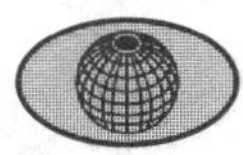   

been shipped, in which funds are transferred from the issuing bank to the acquiring bank and into the merchant account

online catalog E-COMMERCE consolidated catalog on Internet a business-to-business marketplace that collects the catalog data of every supplier in a specific industry and places it on one central Web resource. *Also called* ***procurement portal***

online community E-COMMERCE user network for Internet communication a means of allowing Web users to engage with one another and with an organization through use of interactive tools such as e-mail, discussion boards, and chat systems. They are a means by which a website owner can take the pulse of consumers to find out what they are thinking, and to generate unique content. As stand-alone businesses, online communities have been found to be weak; they work best when they are supporting the need for an organization to collect ongoing feedback.

online shopping E-COMMERCE = ***electronic shopping***

online trading MARKETS trading securities via Internet the process of buying and selling securities over the Internet

onshore FINANCE located in home country based in the home country, especially referring to a company that is registered in the country in which it conducts most of its business, or to funds or activities that are held or located in the home country. *See also* ***offshore***

on-target earnings FINANCE commission equaling amount aimed at the amount earned by somebody working on **commission** who has achieved the targets set. *Abbr* **OTE**

OPEC INTERNATIONAL TRADE association of oil-producing countries an international organization of 11 countries, each one largely reliant on oil revenues as its main source of income, that tries to ensure there is a balance between supply and demand by adjusting the members' oil output. OPEC's headquarters are in Vienna. The current members, Algeria, Indonesia, Iran, Iraq, Kuwait, Libya, Nigeria, Qatar, Saudi Arabia, the United Arab Emirates, and Venezuela, meet at least twice a year to decide on output levels and discuss recent and anticipated oil market developments. *Full form* ***Organization of the Petroleum Exporting Countries***

open account FINANCE **1.** credit offered to buyer without requiring security a credit account offered by a supplier to a purchaser for which the supplier does not require security **2.** unpaid credit an account offered by a business to a customer that is as yet unpaid

open buying on the Internet E-COMMERCE protocol for Internet trading a standard built around a common set of business requirements for electronic communication between buyers and sellers that, when implemented, allows different e-commerce systems to talk to one another. *Abbr* **OBI**. *See also* ***open trading protocol***

open check US BANKING blank signed check a signed check where the amount payable has not been indicated

open cheque UK BANKING uncrossed check a check that is not crossed and so may be cashed by the payee at the branch of the bank where it is drawn. *See also* ***crossed cheque***

open credit FINANCE credit offered without requiring security credit given by a supplier to a good customer without requiring security

open economy INTERNATIONAL TRADE economic system with unrestricted international trade an economy that places few restrictions on the movement of capital, labor, foreign trade, and payments into and out of the country

open-end credit US FINANCE arrangement allowing borrowing and repaying at will a credit facility that allows the borrower, within an overall credit limit and for a set period, to borrow or repay debt as required. *Also called* ***revolving credit***. *UK term* ***open-ended credit***

open-ended credit UK FINANCE = ***open-end credit***

open-ended fund UK STOCKHOLDING & INVESTMENTS = ***open-end fund***

open-ended investment company UK STOCKHOLDING & INVESTMENTS **1.** = ***open-end fund*** **2.** = ***open-end investment company***

open-ended management company UK STOCKHOLDING & INVESTMENTS = ***open-end management company***

open-ended mortgage UK MORTGAGES = ***open-end mortgage***

open-end fund US STOCKHOLDING & INVESTMENTS mutual fund with varying share numbers a mutual fund that has a variable number of shares. *UK term* ***open-ended fund***. *See also* ***closed-end fund***

open-end investment company US STOCKHOLDING & INVESTMENTS firm pooling funds for mutual funds a company with a variable number of shares that it sells to investors and pools for investment in mutual funds. *UK term* ***open-ended investment company***. *See also* ***open-end fund***

open-end management company US STOCKHOLDING & INVESTMENTS firm selling mutual funds a company that sells mutual funds. *UK term* ***open-ended management company***

open-end mortgage US MORTGAGES mortgage permitting prepayment a mortgage that can be paid off before the closing date originally agreed on. *UK term* ***open-ended mortgage***

opening balance ACCOUNTING amount at beginning of record the value of a financial quantity at the beginning of an accounting period

opening balance sheet ACCOUNTING record of opening balances a record giving details of an organization's financial balances at the beginning of an accounting period

opening bell MARKETS start of day's trading the beginning of a day of trading on a market

opening entry ACCOUNTING first record in account the first entry recorded in an account, for example, the first entry when starting a new business

opening price MARKETS price at start of day's trading the price for a security at the beginning of a day of trading on a market

opening purchase STOCKHOLDING & INVESTMENTS first in series of option purchases the first of a series of purchases to be made in options of a specific type for a specific commodity or security

opening stock UK ACCOUNTING = ***beginning inventory***

open interest STOCKHOLDING & INVESTMENTS total of options not yet closed the number of **options** contracts that have not yet been exercised, offset, or allowed to expire

open loop system GENERAL MANAGEMENT system with no facility for intervention a management control system that includes no provision for corrective action to be applied to the sequence of activities

open market MARKETS market with unlimited competition a market in which anyone is allowed to buy or sell and compete without restrictions

open market operation MARKETS government transaction in public market a transaction conducted by a central bank in a public market

  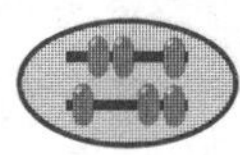 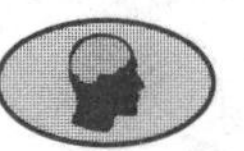  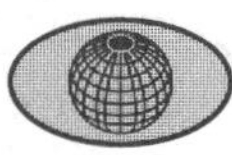   

open market value MARKETS potential price if available to all the price that an asset or security would realize if it was offered on a market open to all

open order MARKETS order remaining open until executed or canceled an order to buy or sell a security that is effective until it is executed or an investor cancels it. *See also* ***good 'til cancel***

open outcry MARKETS verbal exchanges to complete sale the method of making verbal bids and offers used by buyers and sellers on the **trading floor** of some exchanges such as the London Metal Exchange

open trading protocol E-COMMERCE e-commerce standard a standard designed to support Internet-based retail transactions, that allows different systems to communicate with each other for a variety of payment-related activities. The **open buying on the Internet** protocol is a competing standard. *Abbr* **OTP**. *See also* ***open buying on the Internet***

operating budget ACCOUNTING plan for firm's income and expenses a forecast of income and expenses that result from the day-to-day activities of a company over a period of time

operating cash flow ACCOUNTING money used and generated in firm's operations the amount used to represent the money moving through a company as a result of its operations, as distinct from its purely financial transactions. *Abbr* **OCF**

operating costing OPERATIONS & PRODUCTION way of costing output of continuous operation a costing system that is applied to continuous operations in mass production or in the service industries. In the simplest form of operating costing, the costing period is set at a specific length of time, usually a calendar month or four weeks. The costs incurred over the period are related to the number of units produced, and the division of the first by the second gives the average unit cost for the period.

operating costs or **operating expenses** ACCOUNTING expenses for firm's ordinary business activities the costs arising from the day-to-day activities of running a company. *Also called* ***running costs***

operating cycle OPERATIONS & PRODUCTION process between investment and income from product the cycle of business activity in which cash is used to buy resources that are converted into products or services and then sold for cash

operating environment OPERATIONS & PRODUCTION combination of external factors affecting business the combination of economic, social, and political factors that affect an organization's activities

operating income ACCOUNTING = ***EBIT***

operating lease GENERAL MANAGEMENT lease treated as rent in accounts a lease that is regarded by accountants as rental rather than as a **capital lease**. The monthly lease payments are simply treated as rental expenses and recognized on the income statement as they are incurred. There is no recognition of a leased asset or liability.

operating leverage ACCOUNTING ratio of fixed to total costs the ratio of a business's fixed costs to its total costs. Fixed costs have to be paid regardless of output, the higher the ratio, the higher the risk of losses in an economic downturn.

operating loss ACCOUNTING firm's loss during ordinary business activities a loss incurred by a company during the course of its usual business

operating margin ACCOUNTING = ***profit margin***

operating profit ACCOUNTING standard income minus standard costs the difference between a company's revenues and any related costs and expenses, not including income or expenses from any sources other than its normal methods of providing a good or service

operating risk ACCOUNTING poor ratio of fixed to total costs the risk of a high **operating leverage**, when each sale makes a significant contribution to fixed costs

operational audit GENERAL MANAGEMENT assessment of systems and procedures of organization a structured review of the systems and procedures of an organization in order to evaluate whether they are being conducted efficiently and effectively. An operational audit involves establishing performance **objectives**, agreeing the standards and criteria for assessment, and evaluating actual performance against targeted performance. *Also called* ***management audit, operations audit***

operational costs ACCOUNTING costs of running business the costs incurred by a company during the course of its usual business

operational disciplines OPERATIONS & PRODUCTION activities supporting ongoing operation of business the activities and systems within an organization that ensure that the daily operations required to produce goods and services are running smoothly

operational gearing ACCOUNTING ratio of fixed to total costs the relationship between a company's fixed costs and its total costs. Fixed costs have to be paid before profit can be made, so high operational gearing increases a company's risk.

operational manager OPERATIONS & PRODUCTION manager of goods and services production the person in an organization who is in charge of the activities required to produce goods and services

operational research GENERAL MANAGEMENT analysis of managerial and administrative procedures the application of scientific methods to the solution of managerial and administrative problems, involving complex systems or processes. Operational research strives to find the optimum plan for the control and operation of a system or process. It was originally used during World War II as a means of solving logistical problems. It has since developed into a planning, scheduling, and **problem solving** technique applied across the industrial, commercial, and public sectors.

operational risk OPERATIONS & PRODUCTION, RISK risk of loss from internal or external failures the risk of economic loss that an organization faces, resulting from failed or inadequate controls, processes, or systems, or from human or external events

operations OPERATIONS & PRODUCTION production processes activities that are required to produce goods or services for consumers. *See also* ***operations management***

operations audit GENERAL MANAGEMENT = ***operational audit***

operations management OPERATIONS & PRODUCTION overseeing of production processes the maintenance, control, and improvement of organizational activities that are required to produce goods or services for consumers. Operations management has traditionally been associated with manufacturing activities but can also be applied to the service sector.

opinion leader MARKETING influencer of public opinion a high-profile person or organization that can significantly influence public opinion. An opinion leader can be a politician, a religious, business or community leader, a journalist, or an educator. Show business and sports personalities can exert a great deal of influence on young people's leisure lifestyles and buying habits and are consequently frequently used in advertising campaigns.

  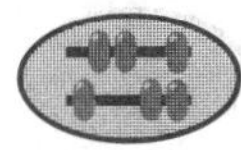   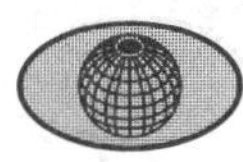 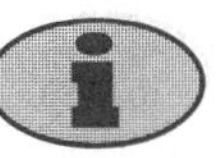  

opinion leader research MARKETING inquiry into top people's views the investigation of the perceptions of **corporate image** and reputation among the people at the top of a company, industry, or profession

opinion survey GENERAL MANAGEMENT set of questions to discover people's attitudes a survey conducted to determine what members of a population think about a specific topic

opportunity cost STOCKHOLDING & INVESTMENTS loss through choice of investment an amount of money lost as a result of choosing one investment rather than another

opportunity score MARKETING measure of salability of product before production a measure of the potential marketability of a product or service while it is still in the development stage

optimal portfolio STOCKHOLDING & INVESTMENTS best possible investments a theoretical set of investments that would be the most profitable for an investor

optimize GENERAL MANAGEMENT use resources in best way to allocate such things as resources or capital as efficiently as possible

optimum best best or most desirable out of a number of possible options or outcomes

optimum capacity OPERATIONS & PRODUCTION cheapest quantity to produce the level of output at which the minimum cost per unit is incurred

option 1. STOCKHOLDING & INVESTMENTS contract for trading rights a contract for the right to buy or sell an asset, typically a commodity, under agreed terms. *Also called* ***option contract, stock option*** **2.** BUSINESS opportunity to buy or sell on agreed terms an agreement that somebody may buy or sell a specific asset on predetermined terms on or before a future date

option account STOCKHOLDING & INVESTMENTS account for buying and selling options an account that an investor holds with a broker and uses for trading in **options**

optionaire STOCKHOLDING & INVESTMENTS millionaire in terms of stock options a millionaire whose wealth consists of or is derived from stock **options** (*slang*)

optional redemption provision STOCKHOLDING & INVESTMENTS bond early redemption clause the terms in a bond agreement that allow the issuer (usually) or the lender (less frequently) to redeem it before the final redemption date

option buyer STOCKHOLDING & INVESTMENTS buyer of option an investor who acquires an **option** to buy or sell a security, currency, or commodity

option class STOCKHOLDING & INVESTMENTS group of options of same type a set of **options** that are identical with respect to type and underlying asset

option contract STOCKHOLDING & INVESTMENTS = ***option***

option dealing MARKETS trading in stock options the activity of buying and selling stock **options**

option elasticity STOCKHOLDING & INVESTMENTS relative changing values of option and underlying asset the relative change in the value of an **option** as a function of a change in the value of the underlying asset

option income fund STOCKHOLDING & INVESTMENTS mutual fund with options a mutual fund that derives income from investing in **options**

option premium STOCKHOLDING & INVESTMENTS cost of each share in option the amount per share that a buyer pays for an **option** to buy or sell a security, currency, or commodity above the exercise price

option price STOCKHOLDING & INVESTMENTS price of option the price of an **option** to buy or sell a security, currency, or commodity

option pricing model STOCKHOLDING & INVESTMENTS means of establishing value of options a model that is used to determine the fair value of **options**. *See also* ***Black-Scholes model***

options clearing corporation REGULATION & COMPLIANCE US organization overseeing trades in options in the United States, an organization responsible for the listing of options and clearing trades in them

option seller STOCKHOLDING & INVESTMENTS = ***option writer***

option series STOCKHOLDING & INVESTMENTS group of options representing same thing a collection of options that are identical in terms of class, **exercise price**, and date of maturity

options market MARKETS **1.** trading options the trading in options to buy or sell securities, currencies, or commodities **2.** place for trading options a venue where traders engage in buying and selling **options**

options on physicals STOCKHOLDING & INVESTMENTS options on physical assets a type of **option** that is on real assets rather than financial assets

option trading MARKETS trading in stock options the business of buying and selling stock **options**

option writer STOCKHOLDING & INVESTMENTS seller of option a person, institution, or other organization that sells an **option** to buy or sell a security, currency, or commodity. *Also called* ***option seller***

OR *abbr* LEGAL official receiver

order 1. OPERATIONS & PRODUCTION arrangement between customer and supplier a **contract** made between a customer and a supplier for the supply of a variety of goods or services in a determined quantity and quality, at an agreed price, and for delivery at or by a specific time **2.** STOCKHOLDING & INVESTMENTS instruction to trade for investor's own account an occasion when a broker is told to buy or sell a financial product for an investor's own account

order book OPERATIONS & PRODUCTION record of orders waiting to be fulfilled a record of the outstanding orders that an organization has received. An order book may be physical, with the specifications and delivery times of orders recorded in it, or the term may be used generally to describe the health of a company. A full order book implies a successful company, while an empty order book can indicate an organization at risk of business failure.

order confirmation E-COMMERCE e-mail acknowledgment of order an e-mail message informing a purchaser that an order has been received

order-driven system or **order-driven market** MARKETS system where stock prices change according to orders on a stock exchange, a price system where prices vary according to the level of orders. *See also* ***quote-driven system***

order imbalance MARKETS backlog in trading of security a situation in which there are more orders to buy or sell a security than can be executed, sometimes resulting in a halt to trading until the situation is resolved

order picking OPERATIONS & PRODUCTION extraction of items requested selecting and withdrawing goods or components from a store or warehouse to meet production requirements or to satisfy customer orders

  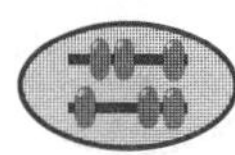  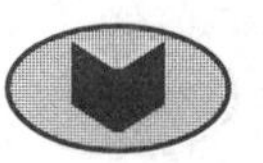 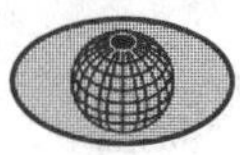   

order point OPERATIONS & PRODUCTION amount triggering reordering the quantity of an item that is on hand when more units of the item are to be ordered

order processing OPERATIONS & PRODUCTION keeping track of orders the tracking of orders made with suppliers and received from customers

orders pending STOCKHOLDING & INVESTMENTS, OPERATIONS & PRODUCTION unfulfilled orders orders that have not yet resulted in transactions

ordinary interest FINANCE interest based on 360-day year interest calculated on the basis of a year having only 360 days

ordinary resolution CORPORATE GOVERNANCE general issue put to vote at annual meeting a resolution put before an annual meeting, usually referring to some general procedural matter, that requires a simple majority of votes to be accepted

ordinary share *UK* STOCKHOLDING & INVESTMENTS = ***common stock***

organic growth BUSINESS = ***internal growth***

organigram GENERAL MANAGEMENT = ***organization chart***

Organisation for Economic Co-operation and Development INTERNATIONAL TRADE *see* ***OECD***

organization GENERAL MANAGEMENT collection of people and resources with specific purpose an arrangement of people and resources working in a planned manner toward specific strategic goals. An organization can be any structured body such as a business, company, or firm in the private or public sector, or in a nonprofit association.

organization chart GENERAL MANAGEMENT diagram of organization's structure a graphic illustration of an organization's structure, showing hierarchical authority and relationships between departments and jobs. The horizontal dimension of an organization chart shows the nature of job function and responsibility and the vertical dimension shows how jobs are coordinated in reporting or authority relationships. *Also called* ***organigram, org chart***

Organization of the Petroleum Exporting Countries INTERNATIONAL TRADE *see* ***OPEC***

org chart GENERAL MANAGEMENT = ***organization chart***

orientation *US* HR & PERSONNEL formal introduction to new job a process through which a new employee is integrated into an organization, learning about its **corporate culture**, policies and procedures, and the specific practicalities of his or her job. An orientation program should not consist of a one-day introduction, but should be planned and paced over a few days or weeks. There is a growing use of boot camps, which work to assimilate a new employee rapidly into the culture of the employing organization. *UK term* ***induction***

original cost ACCOUNTING total cost of asset the total cost of acquiring an asset

original equipment manufacturer OPERATIONS & PRODUCTION firm making product from bought-in parts a company that assembles components from other suppliers to produce a complete product. *Abbr* **OEM**

original face value MORTGAGES amount originally borrowed the amount of the principal of a mortgage on the day it is created

original issue discount STOCKHOLDING & INVESTMENTS discount at bond's first sale the discount offered on the day of sale of a debt instrument

original maturity STOCKHOLDING & INVESTMENTS date for payment of bond a date on which a **debt instrument** is due to mature

origination fee MORTGAGES charge for providing mortgage a fee charged by a lender for providing a mortgage, usually expressed as a percentage of the principal

orthogonal STATISTICS statistically unrelated statistically independent

OTC *abbr* FINANCE over-the-counter

OTC bulletin board MARKETS electronic system for quoting unlisted securities an electronic real-time quoting system for unlisted securities that are traded in the over-the-counter market but not traded on the NASDAQ. *Full form* ***over-the-counter bulletin board***

OTC market *abbr* MARKETS over-the-counter market

OTE *abbr* FINANCE on-target earnings

other capital ACCOUNTING uncategorized capital capital that is not listed in specific categories

other current assets ACCOUNTING non-cash assets maturing within year assets that are not cash and are due to mature within a year

other long-term capital ACCOUNTING uncategorized long-term assets long-term capital that is not listed in specific categories in accounts

other long-term liabilities FINANCE obligations with no interest charge in next year obligations such as deferred taxes and employee benefits with terms greater than one year and on which there is no charge for interest in the next year

other prices FINANCE unlisted prices prices that are not listed in a catalog

other short-term capital ACCOUNTING uncategorized short-term assets a residual category in the balance of payments that includes financial assets of less than one year such as currency, deposits, and bills

OTP *abbr* E-COMMERCE open trading protocol

OTS *abbr* REGULATION & COMPLIANCE Office of Thrift Supervision

outgoings *UK* ACCOUNTING = ***costs***

outlay ACCOUNTING money spent for specific purpose money spent on something such as capital assets or operating costs

outlier STATISTICS statistic that is very different from others a statistical observation that deviates significantly from other members of a sample

out-of-pocket expenses ACCOUNTING amount of employee's own money spent on business an amount of an employee's personal money that he or she has spent on company business, especially when considered for reimbursement

out of the money STOCKHOLDING & INVESTMENTS having no intrinsic value used to describe an **option** that, if it expired at the current market price, would have no intrinsic value. *See also* ***in the money***

outperform MARKETS do better than other companies to achieve better results in the stock market than other similar companies

output OPERATIONS & PRODUCTION goods produced anything that a company produces, usually referring to physical products but also to services

output gap ECONOMICS difference between economy's production capacity and actual production the difference between the amount of activity that is sustainable in an economy and the amount of activity actually taking place

output method ACCOUNTING accounting technique categorizing costs by output purpose an accounting system that classifies costs according to the outputs for

  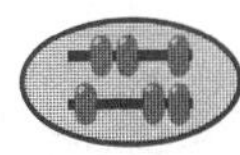   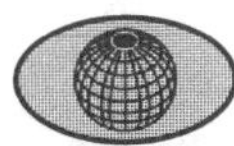   

which they are incurred, not the inputs they have bought

output per hour OPERATIONS & PRODUCTION how much is produced each hour the amount of something produced in one hour, especially the amount of a company's product or service

output tax TAX tax due from trader in Australia and New Zealand, the amount of Goods and Services Tax paid to the tax office after the deduction of **input tax credits**

outside director CORPORATE GOVERNANCE director not employed by firm a member of a company's **board of directors** neither currently nor formerly in the company's employment. An outside director is sometimes described as being synonymous with a **nonexecutive director**, and as usually being employed by a holding or associated company. In the United States, an outside director is somebody who has no relationships at all to a company. In US public companies, compensation and audit committees are generally made up of outside directors, and use of outside directors to select board directors is becoming more common.

outsourcing GENERAL MANAGEMENT **1.** switching from in-house personnel to outside supplier the transfer of the provision of services previously performed by in-house personnel to an external organization, usually under a **contract** with agreed standards, costs, and conditions. Areas traditionally outsourced include legal services, transport, catering, and security. An increasing variety of activities, including IT services, training, and public relations are now being outsourced. Outsourcing, or **contracting out**, is often introduced with the goal of increasing efficiency and reducing costs, or to enable the organization to develop greater flexibility or to concentrate on core business activities. The term **subcontracting** is sometimes used to refer to outsourcing. **2.** obtaining goods or services from outside suppliers the use of external suppliers as a source of finished products, components, or services

outstanding check ACCOUNTING check issued but not cashed a check which has been written and therefore has been entered in the company's ledgers, but which has not been presented for payment and so has not been debited from the company's bank account

outstanding share STOCKHOLDING & INVESTMENTS share allotted to applicant a share that a company has issued and somebody has bought

outstanding share capital STOCKHOLDING & INVESTMENTS value of stock available to trade the value of all of the stock of a company minus the value of retained shares

outwork GENERAL MANAGEMENT in UK, work done away from premises in the United Kingdom, work performed for a company away from its premises

outworker HR & PERSONNEL in UK, person working away from premises in the United Kingdom, a subcontractor or employee carrying out work for a company away from its premises

overall capitalization rate FINANCE income minus most costs divided by value **net operating income** other than debt service divided by value

overall market capacity ECONOMICS amount of product that market can absorb the amount of a service or good that can be absorbed in a market without affecting the price

overall rate of return or **overall return** STOCKHOLDING & INVESTMENTS return relative to investment the aggregate of all the dividends received over an investment's life together with its capital gain or loss at the date of its realization, calculated either before or after tax. It is one of the ways an investor can look at the performance of an investment.

overbid FINANCE **1.** bid too much to bid more than necessary to make a successful purchase **2.** too high a bid an amount that is offered that is unnecessarily high for a successful purchase to be made

overborrowed FINANCE having too much debt in comparison to assets used to describe a company that has very high borrowings compared to its assets, and has difficulty in meeting its interest payments

overbought MARKETS inflated by too many buyers used to describe a market or security considered to have risen too rapidly as a result of excessive buying

overbought market MARKETS market with overinflated prices a market where prices have risen beyond levels that can be supported by fundamental analysis. The market for Internet companies in 2001 was overbought and subsequently collapsed when it became clear that their trading performance could not support such price levels.

overcapacity OPERATIONS & PRODUCTION more capacity than needed an excess of capability to produce goods or provide a service over the level of demand

overcapitalized FINANCE having surplus capital used to describe a business that has more capital than can profitably be employed. An overcapitalized company could buy back some of its own stock in the market; if it has significant debt capital it could repurchase its bonds in the market; or it could make a large one-time dividend to stockholders.

overdraft BANKING **1.** deficit in bank account the amount by which the money withdrawn from a bank account exceeds the balance in the account. *Abbr* **O/D** **2.** = ***overdraft facility***

overdraft facility BANKING agreement for deficit in bank account a credit arrangement with a bank, allowing a person or company with an account to use borrowed money up to an agreed limit when nothing is left in the account

overdraft line BANKING agreed amount of overdraft an amount in excess of the balance in an account that a bank agrees to pay in honoring checks on the account

overdraft protection BANKING guarantee of payment from overdrawn account a bank service, amounting to a **line of credit**, that assures that the bank will honor overdrafts, up to a limit and for a fee

overdraw BANKING create deficit in bank account to withdraw more money from a bank account than it contains or than was agreed could be withdrawn

overdrawn BANKING having deficit in bank account in debt to a bank because the amount withdrawn from an account exceeds its balance

overdue FINANCE still owing still to be paid after the date due

overfunding ECONOMICS when UK government sells more stock than necessary in the United Kingdom, a situation in which the government borrows more money than it needs for expenditure, as a result of selling too much government stock

overgeared FINANCE with greater financial commitments than common stock capital describing a company with debt capital and preferred stock that outweigh its common stock capital

overhang MARKETS **1.** large remaining block of one investment, depressing price a large quantity of shares of unsold stock or of a commodity available for sale, which has the effect of depressing the market price **2.** to depress market prices to put downward pressure on stock or commodity prices

overhead *US* ACCOUNTING = ***overhead costs***

  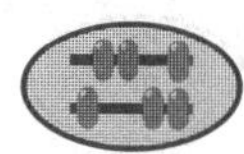 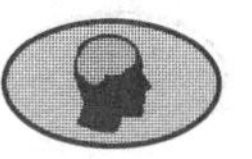  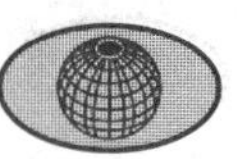   

overhead absorption rate ACCOUNTING proportion of overhead attributed to product or service a means of attributing overhead to a product or service, based for example on direct labor hours, direct labor cost, or machine hours (the number of hours for which a machine is in production). The choice of overhead absorption base may be made with the objective of obtaining "accurate" product costs, or of influencing managerial behavior; for example, overhead applied to labor hours or part numbers appears to make the use of these resources more costly, thus discouraging their use.

overhead capacity variance ACCOUNTING gap between budgeted and required overhead the difference between the overhead absorbed, based on budgeted hours, and actual hours worked

overhead costs ACCOUNTING costs incurred in upkeep or running the indirect costs of the day-to-day running of a business, i.e. not money spent on producing goods, but money spent on such things as renting or maintaining buildings and machinery. *Also called* ***overhead, overheads***

overhead expenditure variance ACCOUNTING misjudgment of indirect costs the difference between the budgeted **overhead costs** and the actual expenditure

overheads *UK* ACCOUNTING = ***overhead costs***

overinsuring INSURANCE obtaining excessive insurance cover insuring an asset for a sum in excess of its market or replacement value. It is unlikely that an insurance company will pay out more in a claim for loss than the asset is worth or than the cost of replacing it.

overinvested 1. STOCKHOLDING & INVESTMENTS with too much invested having a higher than desired amount invested in a security, or having a higher amount committed to tracking an index or matching a model portfolio than the index or model suggests **2.** BUSINESS with investment predicated on higher demand used to describe a business that invests heavily during an economic boom only to find that when it starts to produce an income, the demand for the product or service has fallen

overlap profit ACCOUNTING profit assignable to two accounting periods profit that arises in two overlapping accounting periods and on which tax relief can be claimed

overnight position MARKETS trader's commitments at end of trading day a trader's holdings in a security or option at the end of a trading day

overnight rate MARKETS, RISK interest rate on interbank overnight loans the interest rate charged by financial institutions on overnight loans to each other

overnight repo BANKING arrangement for temporary sale for cash a repurchase agreement where banks sell securities for cash and repurchase them the next day at a higher price. This type of agreement is used by central banks as a means of regulating the **money markets**.

overpayment 1. FINANCE paying too much an act of paying more than is required or reasonable, or the sum paid in such a situation **2.** *UK* ACCOUNTING = ***additional principal payment***

overprice MARKETING charge too high price for something to set the price of a product or service too high, with the result that it is unacceptable to the market

overrated FINANCE with value set too high used to describe something that is valued more highly than it should be

overriding commission or **override** or **overrider** FINANCE further additional commission a special extra commission which is above all other commissions

overseas company BUSINESS part of firm incorporated abroad a branch or subsidiary of a business that is incorporated in another country

overseas funds FINANCE investment products in foreign countries investment funds that are based in other countries and are not subject to regulation in the home country

Overseas Investment Commission REGULATION & COMPLIANCE New Zealand organization overseeing investment from abroad in New Zealand, an independent body reporting to the government that regulates foreign investment. It was established in 1973 and is funded by the Reserve Bank of New Zealand.

oversold MARKETS depressed by too many sellers used to describe a market or security that is considered to have fallen too rapidly as a result of excessive selling. *See also* ***bear market***

overspend ACCOUNTING **1.** spend more than planned to spend more money than was budgeted or planned or than can be afforded **2.** excess amount spent an amount that is more than was budgeted for spending

overstocked OPERATIONS & PRODUCTION having surplus inventory used to describe a business that has more inventory than it needs

oversubscription MARKETS when investors want more stock than are available a situation in which investors are interested in buying more shares of stock in a new issue than are being made available

over-the-counter FINANCE of trading between dealers used to describe the trade of securities directly between licensed dealers, rather than through an auction system. *Abbr* **OTC**

over-the-counter market MARKETS market conducted directly between dealers a market in which trading takes place directly between licensed dealers, rather than through an auction system as used in most organized exchanges. *Abbr* **OTC market**

over-the-counter security STOCKHOLDING & INVESTMENTS security traded directly between dealers a security that is traded directly between licensed dealers on the **over-the-counter market**

overtrading OPERATIONS & PRODUCTION when firm increases sales and production too rapidly a situation in which a company increases sales and production too much and too quickly, so that it runs short of cash

overvalue FINANCE, GENERAL MANAGEMENT give something too high a value to give a higher value to something or somebody than is justified

own brand *UK* MARKETING = ***private label***

owner 1. LEGAL possessor of legal title to something a person or organization that has legal title to products or services **2.** BUSINESS person having own firm the person who has legal control of a private company

owner-occupier REAL ESTATE somebody who owns home a person who owns the property in which he or she lives

owner-operator BUSINESS = ***sole proprietor***

owner's equity ACCOUNTING total assets minus total liabilities a business's total assets less its total liabilities, being the funds provided by the owners. *See also* ***capital, common stock***

ownership of companies BUSINESS holding of stock in firms the possession of stock in companies. Company ownership structures can differ widely. Owners of public companies may be institutions, or individuals, or a mixture of both. Directors are often offered company stock as incentives and more participative

  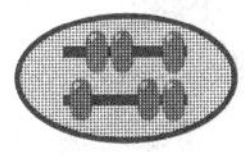 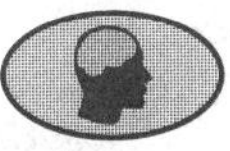  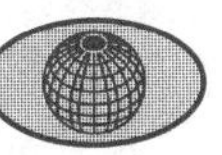 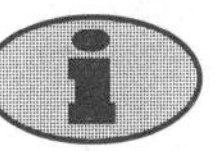  

companies may offer stock to employees through **employee ownership** plans. Private companies are usually owned by individuals, families, or groups of individual stockholders. Nationalized industries are publicly owned. Cooperatives are wholly owned by employees. A separation between the ownership and control of companies became a widely discussed issue during the 20th century, especially in the United States and the United Kingdom where stockholders have tended to be more passive. Managers were viewed as having come to occupy controlling positions as the scale of industry grew. From the 1980s, this position changed to some extent as **privatization**, **management buyouts**, restructuring, and **stock incentive plans** led to greater stock ownership among managers and produced less passive stockholders.

own label *UK* MARKETING = ***private label***

P

paced line OPERATIONS & PRODUCTION production line moving at steady speed a production line that moves at a constant speed

package and sell STOCKHOLDING & INVESTMENTS sell combined loans to combine a number of loans and sell them to investors as **mortgage-backed securities**

package deal GENERAL MANAGEMENT agreement including several aspects simultaneously an agreement that covers several different things at the same time

packaging MARKETS combining securities for trade the practice of combining different securities in a single trade

Pac Man defense MERGERS & ACQUISITIONS offer to purchase buyer to avoid firm's takeover a strategy by a company seeking to avoid a hostile takeover, in which the target company makes an offer to purchase the prospective buyer

paid-in capital STOCKHOLDING & INVESTMENTS firm's capital received from investors for stock capital in a business that has been provided by its stockholders

paid up FINANCE fully paid having paid all the money owed

paid-up capital or **paid-up share capital** STOCKHOLDING & INVESTMENTS stock issued and paid for an amount of money paid for the issued capital shares of stock, which does not include **called-up share capital**. *See also* ***fully paid share capital, partly paid capital***

paid-up policy INSURANCE **1.** policy providing life insurance after policyholder stops paying in the United Kingdom, an **endowment insurance** policy that continues to provide life insurance while the cost of the premiums is covered by the underlying fund after the policyholder has decided not to continue paying premiums. If the fund is sufficient to pay the premiums for the remainder of the term, the remaining funds will be paid to the policyholder at maturity. **2.** insurance policy with premiums paid in the United States, an insurance policy on which all the premiums have been paid

paid-up share STOCKHOLDING & INVESTMENTS stock paid for in full a stock for which stockholders have paid the full contractual amount. *See also* ***call, called-up share capital, paid-up capital, share capital***

painting the tape MARKETS illegal splitting of orders into smaller units an illegal practice in which traders break large orders into smaller units in order to give the illusion of heavy buying activity. This encourages investors to buy, and the traders then sell as the price of the stock goes up (*slang*).

panda CURRENCY & EXCHANGE Chinese gold or silver collector coin one of a series of Chinese gold and silver bullion collector coins, each featuring a panda, that were first issued in 1982. Struck with a highly polished surface, the smallest gold coin weighs 0.05 ounces, the largest 12 ounces.

P&L *abbr* ACCOUNTING profit and loss

Panel on Takeovers and Mergers MERGERS & ACQUISITIONS UK group overseeing fairness in takeovers in the United Kingdom, the group that issues the **City Code on Takeovers and Mergers**, a code designed principally to ensure fair and equal treatment of all stockholders in relation to takeovers. *See also* ***City Code on Takeovers and Mergers***

panel study MARKETING study of small group's opinions over time a study that surveys a selected group of people over a period of time

panic buying FINANCE exceptional buying because of fear of shortages an unusual level of buying caused by fear or rumors of product shortages or by severe price rises

panic dumping CURRENCY & EXCHANGE selling currency because of devaluation fears a rush to sell a currency at any price because of fears of a possible devaluation

paper **1.** FINANCE record of holdings a certificate of deposits and other securities **2.** STOCKHOLDING & INVESTMENTS issue of stock or bonds to raise capital a rights issue or an issue of bonds launched by a company to raise additional capital **3.** FINANCE all debt issued by firm all funding instruments issued by a company, other than **equity**

paper company BUSINESS firm without physical presence a company that only exists on paper and has no **physical assets**

paper gain STOCKHOLDING & INVESTMENTS = ***paper profit***

paper loss STOCKHOLDING & INVESTMENTS drop in value of unsold investment a loss made when an asset has fallen in value but has not been sold. *Also called* ***unrealized loss***

paper millionaire STOCKHOLDING & INVESTMENTS person owning stock valued currently at one million an individual who owns stock that is worth in excess of a million in currency at a specific date, but which may fall in value. In 2001 many of the founders of dot-com companies were paper millionaires. *See also* ***paper profit***

paper money **1.** CURRENCY & EXCHANGE bills currency that is not coins **2.** BANKING checks payments in paper form such as checks

paper offer MERGERS & ACQUISITIONS takeover bid with stock rather than cash a takeover bid in which the purchasing company offers its stock in exchange for stock in the company being taken over, as opposed to a cash offer

paper profit ACCOUNTING increase in value on investment not yet sold an increase in the value of an investment that the investor has no immediate intention of realizing

PAR *abbr* BANKING prime assets ratio

paradigm shift GENERAL MANAGEMENT fundamental change a basic change in an accepted pattern of thought or behavior

paradox of saving or **paradox of thrift** ECONOMICS cutbacks in expenditure lead to increased expenditure elsewhere the observation that savings made by individuals in their consumption lead to a drop in overall demand which in turn leads to increased spending by a business or government

parafiscal tax TAX tax levied for specific purpose a tax on a specific product or service by which a government raises money for a specific purpose. The money raised is usually paid to a body other than the national tax authority.

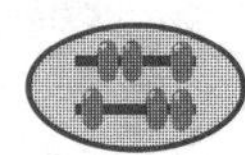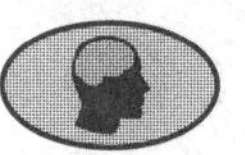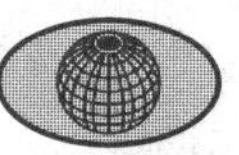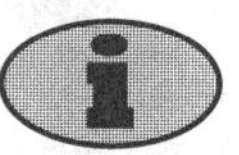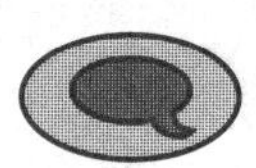

parallel economy ECONOMICS = ***black economy***

parallel engineering OPERATIONS & PRODUCTION = ***concurrent engineering***

parallel loan FINANCE = ***back-to-back loan***

parallel pricing OPERATIONS & PRODUCTION competitors' changing of prices together the practice of varying prices in a similar way and at the same time as competitors

paralysis by analysis GENERAL MANAGEMENT substitution of background work for decision making the inability of managers to make decisions as a result of a preoccupation with attending meetings, writing reports, and collecting statistics and analyses. Paralysis of effective **decision making** in organizations can occur in situations where there is horizontal conflict, disagreement between different hierarchical levels, or unclear objectives.

parameter STATISTICS quantity relating to entire statistical set a quantity that is numerically characteristic of a whole model or population

parameter design STATISTICS method of limiting variability a process aimed at reducing variation in processes or products

parcel STOCKHOLDING & INVESTMENTS set of securities sold together a group of related securities that are sold at one time

parcel of shares *UK* STOCKHOLDING & INVESTMENTS = ***basket of shares***

parent company BUSINESS firm with subsidiaries a main company in a group that also has one or more subsidiary undertakings

Pareto's Law ECONOMICS idea that income will be distributed similarly everywhere a theory of income distribution that states that regardless of political or taxation conditions, income will be distributed in the same way across all countries

pari passu GENERAL MANAGEMENT ranking equally a Latin phrase that means being of equal rank

Paris Club FINANCE = ***G10***

Paris Interbank Offered Rate BANKING bank releasing money against check the French equivalent of the **London Interbank Offered Rate**. *Abbr* **PIBOR**

parity MARKETS price equivalence in different markets a situation when the price of a commodity, foreign currency, or security is the same in different markets. *See also* ***arbitrage***

parity bit E-COMMERCE digit used as check an odd or even digit used to check binary computer data for errors

parity value STOCKHOLDING & INVESTMENTS = ***conversion value***

park STOCKHOLDING & INVESTMENTS (*slang*) **1.** illegally disguise ownership of stock to place owned stock with third parties to disguise their ownership, usually illegally **2.** invest money safely for short time to put money into safe investments while deciding where to invest it in the longer term

parking STOCKHOLDING & INVESTMENTS (*slang*) **1.** illegal transfer of stock to nominee the transfer of stock in a company to a third party such as a nominee or the name of an associate, often illegally **2.** temporarily keeping money in safe investments the practice of putting money into safe investments while deciding where to invest it in the longer term

Parkinson's Law HR & PERSONNEL work expands to fill time available the facetious assertion that work will expand to fill the time available

Parquet MARKETS Paris stock exchange the Bourse, or stock exchange, in Paris, France (*slang*)

part exchange *UK* FINANCE = ***trade-in***

participating bond STOCKHOLDING & INVESTMENTS bond yielding dividends and interest a bond that pays the holder dividends as well as interest

participating insurance INSURANCE insurance offering dividends a form of insurance in which policyholders receive a dividend from the insurer's profits

participating preference share *UK* STOCKHOLDING & INVESTMENTS = ***participating preferred stock***

participating preferred stock *US* STOCKHOLDING & INVESTMENTS stock yielding dividend and share of surplus profit a type of **preferred stock** that entitles the holder to a fixed dividend and, in addition, to the right to participate in any surplus profits after payment of agreed levels of dividends to holders of **common stock** has been made. *See also* ***nonparticipating preferred stock***. *UK term* ***participating preference share***

participative budgeting TREASURY MANAGEMENT system allowing budget holders to draft own budgets a budgeting system in which all budget holders are given the opportunity to participate in setting their own budgets. *Also called* ***bottom-up budgeting***

partly paid capital or **partly paid share capital** STOCKHOLDING & INVESTMENTS capital not paid in full capital composed of shares for which the stockholders have not paid the full value at once, but have paid in installments. *See also* ***fully paid share capital, paid-up capital***

partly paid share STOCKHOLDING & INVESTMENTS stock not paid in full a stock for which stockholders have not paid the full value at once, but have paid in installments. *See also* ***call, partly paid capital***

partner BUSINESS member of business partnership a person who works in a business partnership and shares with one or more other people in the profits or losses of the business

partnership BUSINESS legal relationship between business partners the relationship which exists between persons carrying on business in common with a view to profit. In the United Kingdom, this is regulated by the Partnership Act of 1890, and the liability of the individual partners is unlimited unless provided for by the partnership agreement. The Limited Partnership Act of 1907 allows a partnership to contain one or more partners with limited liability so long as there is at least one partner with unlimited liability. A partnership consists of not more than 20 persons.

partnership accounts 1. BANKING accounts of business partners the capital and checking accounts of each partner in a partnership **2.** ACCOUNTING record of financial activities accounts that record the business activities of each partner in a partnership

partnership agreement LEGAL legal basis for partnership the document that establishes a partnership, detailing the capital contributed by each partner; whether an individual partner's liability is limited; the apportionment of the profit; salaries; and possibly procedures to be followed, for example, in the event of a partner retiring or a new partner joining. *Also called* ***articles of partnership***

part-owner BUSINESS somebody owning something jointly with others a person who owns something jointly with one or more other people

part-ownership BUSINESS shared ownership of business or property a situation in which two or more people share in the ownership of a business or property

part payment FINANCE amount paid to cover part of debt a partial payment that leaves a balance to pay at some future time

     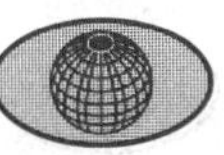   

part time HR & PERSONNEL some of standard working hours a proportion of the standard working hours expected in an organization. *See also* ***full time***

part-time director CORPORATE GOVERNANCE = ***nonexecutive director***

party LEGAL somebody involved in legal dispute or agreement a person or organization involved in a legal dispute or legal agreement

par value STOCKHOLDING & INVESTMENTS = ***nominal value***

passbook BANKING = ***bank book***

passing off FRAUD intentionally making one product appear to be another a form of fraud in which a company tries to sell its own product by deceiving buyers into thinking it is another product

passive investment management STOCKHOLDING & INVESTMENTS managing investment portfolio by automatic adjustments the managing of a **mutual fund** or other investment portfolio by relying on automatic adjustments such as tracking an index instead of making personal judgments. *See also* ***active fund management***

passive portfolio strategy STOCKHOLDING & INVESTMENTS relying on automatic adjustments to manage investments a plan for managing an investment portfolio that relies on automatic adjustments such as tracking an index

passportable BUSINESS describing financial activities permitted in another European state used to describe activities set out in the relevant EU directives for banking, insurance, insurance mediation, management, and investment services that permit a company registered in the European Economic Area to carry on business in another EEA state

passporting BUSINESS doing business in another European state the exercise by a company registered in the European Economic Area of a right to carry on business in another EEA state

passport in/out BUSINESS do business in another European state to exercise the right to carry on business in another state of the European Economic Area

pass-through security STOCKHOLDING & INVESTMENTS security made up of pool of securities a security that represents an interest in a pool of securities, most commonly **mortgage-backed securities**, in which the earnings are passed through to investors

patent LEGAL government licence giving sole right to something a type of **copyright** granted as a fixed-term monopoly to an inventor by a government to prevent others copying an invention or improvement to a product or process.

The granting of a patent requires the publication of full details of the invention or improvement. The use of the patented information is restricted to the patent holder or any organizations licensed by them.

A patent's value is usually the sum of its development costs, or its purchase price if acquired from someone else. It is generally to a company's advantage to spread the patent's value over several years. If this is the case, the critical time period to consider is not the full life of the patent (17 years in the United States), but its estimated useful life.

For example, in January 2000 a company acquired a patent issued in January 1995 at a cost of $100,000. It concludes that the patent's useful commercial life is ten years, not the 12 remaining before the patent expires. In turn, patent value would be $100,000, and it would be spread (or amortized in accounting terms) over 10 years, or $10,000 each year.

patent attorney LEGAL specialist in law of patents a lawyer who specializes in patents

path analysis STATISTICS method of showing relationships between statistical variables in a statistical study, a method for showing the correlation between variables

pathfinder prospectus *UK* STOCKHOLDING & INVESTMENTS preliminary prospectus to test market a preliminary prospectus used in initial public offerings to gauge the reaction of investors. *US term* ***red eye***

pawnbroker FINANCE person lending money against personal items a person who lends money against the security of a wide variety of chattels, from jewelry to cars. The borrower may recover the goods by repaying the loan and interest by a specific date. Otherwise, the items pawned are sold and any surplus after the deduction of expenses, the loan, and interest is returned to the borrower.

pay FINANCE money paid for work done a sum of money given in return for work done or services provided. Pay, in the form of salary or wages, is generally provided in weekly or monthly fixed amounts, and is usually expressed in terms of the total sum earned per year. It may also be allocated using a **piece rate** system, where employees are paid for each unit of work they perform.

payables ledger *US* ACCOUNTING record of accounts to be paid a ledger in which a company records its **accounts payable**. *UK term* ***purchase ledger***

payable to order FINANCE indicating that payee may be changed the statement on a bill of exchange or check, used to indicate that the payee is able to endorse it to a third party

Pay As You Earn TAX in UK, payment of employees' taxes through employer in the United Kingdom, a system for collecting direct taxes that requires employers to deduct taxes from employees' pay before payment is made. *Abbr* **PAYE**

pay-as-you-go PENSIONS financing of current pensions by current employees in Canada, a means of financing a pension system whereby benefits of current retirees are financed by current workers

Pay-As-You-Go TAX Australian payment system for business and investment taxes in Australia, a system used for paying income tax installments on business and investment income. PAYG is part of the new tax system introduced by the Australian government on July 1, 2000. *Abbr* **PAYG**

payback FINANCE **1.** repayment of borrowed money the act of paying back money that has been borrowed **2.** time taken for investment project to break even the time required for the cash revenues from a capital investment project to equal the cost

payback clause LEGAL rules in contract about loan repayment a clause in a contract that states the terms which govern the repayment of a loan

payback period ACCOUNTING time needed to recover project investment costs the length of time it will take to earn back the money invested in a project.

The straight payback period method is the simplest way of determining the investment potential of a major project. Expressed in time, it tells a management how many months or years it will take to recover the original cash cost of the project. It is calculated using the formula:

$$\frac{\text{Cost of project}}{\text{Annual cash revenues}} = \text{Payback period}$$

Thus, if a project cost $100,000 and was expected to generate $28,000 annually, the payback period would be:

$$\frac{100{,}000}{28{,}000} = 3.57 \text{ years}$$

If the revenues generated by the project are expected to vary from year to year, add the revenues expected for each succeeding

  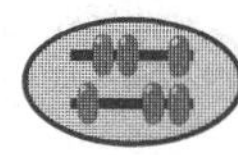 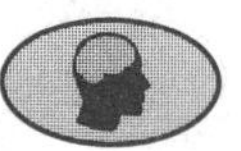  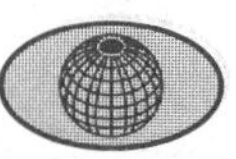   

year until you arrive at the total cost of the project.

For example, say the revenues expected to be generated by the $100,000 project are:

Revenue	Total	Cum. total
Year 1	$19,000	$19,000
Year 2	$25,000	$44,000
Year 3	$30,000	$74,000
Year 4	$30,000	$104,000
Year 5	$30,000	$134,000

Thus, the project would be fully paid for in Year 4, since it is in that year the total revenue reaches the initial cost of $100,000. The precise payback period would be calculated as:

$$\frac{100{,}000 - 74{,}000}{1000{,}000 - 74{,}000} \times 365 = 316 \text{ days} + 3 \text{ years}$$

The picture becomes complex when the time-value-of-money principle is introduced into the calculations. Some experts insist this is essential to determine the most accurate payback period. Accordingly, the annual revenues have to be discounted by the applicable interest rate, 10% in this example. Doing so produces significantly different results:

Revenue	Present value	Total	Cum. total
Year 1	$19,000	$17,271	$17,271
Year 2	$25,000	$20,650	$37,921
Year 3	$30,000	$22,530	$60,451
Year 4	$30,000	$20,490	$80,941
Year 5	$30,000	$18,630	$99,571

This method shows that payback would not occur even after five years.

Generally, a payback period of three years or less is desirable; if a project's payback period is less than a year, some contend it should be judged essential.

pay down FINANCE reduce loan amount through payments to reduce the amount of the **principal** on a loan by making payments

paydown FINANCE partial repayment of loan a repayment of part of a sum which has been borrowed

PAYE *abbr* TAX Pay As You Earn

payee 1. FINANCE person being paid the person or organization to whom a payment has to be made **2.** BANKING person to whom check is payable the person or organization to whom a check is specified as payable. *Also called* ***drawee***

payer BANKING person paying the person or organization making a payment

PAYG *abbr* TAX Pay-As-You-Go

paying agent FINANCE institution paying interest or repaying capital the institution responsible for making interest payments on a security and repaying capital at redemption. *Also called* ***disbursing agent***

paying banker *UK* BANKING bank releasing money against check the bank on which a bill of exchange or check is drawn

paying-in book *UK* BANKING book of slips for listing bank deposits a book of detachable slips that accompany money or checks being paid into a bank account

paying-in slip *UK* BANKING = ***deposit slip***

payload OPERATIONS & PRODUCTION cargo capacity the amount of cargo that a form of transport can carry

paymaster FINANCE person issuing pay the person responsible for paying an organization's employees or the members of a country's armed services

payment FINANCE **1.** giving of money for goods or services the act of giving an amount of money in exchange for goods or services **2.** money paid for goods or services an amount of money paid in exchange for goods or services

payment by results FINANCE making pay dependent on work output a system of pay that directly links an employee's salary to his or her work output

payment gateway E-COMMERCE intermediary in card payment system a company or organization that provides an interface between a merchant's point-of-sale system, **acquirer** payment systems, and **issuer** payment systems. *Abbr* **GW**

payment in advance FINANCE payment made before goods are delivered a payment made for goods when they are ordered and before they are delivered. *See also* ***prepayment***

payment in due course FINANCE payment on fixed future date the payment of a bill of exchange on a fixed date in the future

payment in kind FINANCE something of equivalent value instead of money an alternative form of pay given to employees in place of monetary reward but considered to be of equivalent value. A payment in kind may take the form of use of a car, purchase of goods at cost price, or other nonfinancial exchange that benefits the employee. It forms part of the total pay package rather than being an extra benefit. *See also* ***PIK note***

payment-in-lieu FINANCE money as substitute payment that is given in place of an entitlement

payment terms OPERATIONS & PRODUCTION firm's conditions for reimbursement for goods and services the stipulation by a business as to when it should be paid for goods or services supplied, for example, cash with order, payment on delivery, or within a particular number of days of the invoice date

payoff FINANCE **1.** final repayment a final payment for something that is owed, for example, the outstanding balance of principal and interest on a mortgage or loan **2.** profit or reward of some sort a profit or reward, for example, from a plan or project that is financially successful

payout FINANCE **1.** money given to somebody in difficulties money that is given to help a company or person experiencing difficulties **2.** amount paid a particular sum of money offered, for example, in compensation, or from an insurance policy

payout ratio STOCKHOLDING & INVESTMENTS amount of firm's earnings paid as dividends an expression of the total dividends paid to stockholders as a percentage of a company's net profit in a specific period of time. This measures the likelihood of dividend payments being sustained, and is a useful indication of sustained profitability. The lower the ratio, the more secure the dividend, and the company's future.

The payout ratio is calculated by dividing annual dividends paid on common stock by earnings per share:

$$\frac{\text{Annual dividend}}{\text{Earnings per share}} = \text{Payout ratio}$$

Take the company whose earnings per share are $8 and its dividend payout is 2.1. Its payout ratio would be:

$$\frac{2.1}{8} = 0.263 \text{ or } 26.3\%$$

A high payout ratio clearly appeals to conservative investors seeking income. When coupled with weak or falling earnings, however, it could suggest an imminent dividend cut, or that the company is short-changing reinvestment to maintain its payout. A payout ratio above 75% is a warning. It suggests the company is failing to reinvest sufficient profits in its business, that the company's earnings are faltering, or that it is trying to attract investors who otherwise would not be interested. *Also called* ***dividend payout ratio***. *See also* ***dividend cover***

PayPal™ E-COMMERCE means of paying over Internet a Web-based service that enables

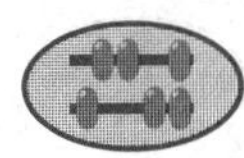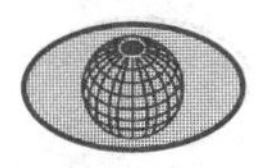

Internet users to send and receive payments electronically. To open a PayPal™ account, users register and provide their credit card or checking account details. When they decide to make a transaction via PayPal™, their card or account is charged for the transfer.

payroll ACCOUNTING record of pay and deductions for each employee a record showing for each employee his or her gross pay, deductions, and net pay. The payroll may also include details of the employer's associated employment costs.

payroll giving plan *US* TAX system for deducting money from salary for charity a plan by which an employee pays money to a charity directly out of his or her salary. The money is deducted by the employer and paid to the charity, and the employee gets tax relief on such donations. *UK term* ***payroll giving scheme***

payroll giving scheme *UK* TAX = ***payroll giving plan***

payroll tax TAX tax on money paid to employees a tax on salary and wages of the people employed by a company

payslip HR & PERSONNEL statement of employee's pay a document given to employees when they are paid, providing a statement of pay for that period. A payslip includes details of deductions such as income tax, social security contributions, pension contributions, and labor union dues.

PBR *abbr* FINANCE pre-Budget report

PBT *abbr* ACCOUNTING profit before tax

P/C *abbr* ACCOUNTING petty cash

PDR *abbr* STOCKHOLDING & INVESTMENTS price/dividend ratio

P/E STOCKHOLDING & INVESTMENTS *see* ***price/earnings multiple, price/earnings ratio***

peak MARKETS highest point or rate the highest price, value, or point reached in a cycle

pecuniary FINANCE of money relating to or involving money

peg 1. CURRENCY & EXCHANGE fix exchange rate of currency against others to fix the exchange rate of one currency against that of another or of a basket of other currencies **2.** FINANCE fix wages and salaries to control inflation to fix wages and salaries during a period of inflation to help prevent an inflationary spiral

P/E multiple *abbr* STOCKHOLDING & INVESTMENTS price/earnings multiple

penalty FINANCE money paid for breaking contract an arbitrary prearranged sum that becomes payable if one party breaks a term of a contract or an undertaking. A common penalty is a high rate of interest on an unauthorized **overdraft**. *See also* ***overdraft***

penalty clause LEGAL clause stating exaggerated penalty for breaking contract a clause in a **contract** that sets out the compensation to be paid in the event of a breach or a default of the terms of the contract when the amount specified is not considered a genuine estimate of the losses incurred, and the clause is perceived to be solely an incentive for the completion of the contract. However, genuine **liquidated damages clauses** are often inaccurately referred to as penalty clauses. *See also* ***liquidated damages clause***

penalty rate *ANZ* FINANCE high rate of overtime pay a higher than normal rate of pay awarded for work performed outside normal working hours

penetrated market MARKETING existing customers the customers who already exist within a well-established market

penetration pricing OPERATIONS & PRODUCTION setting low prices to break into market setting prices low, especially for new products, in order to maximize **market penetration**

pennant MARKETS chart pattern showing converging high and low prices a triangular chart pattern that is formed when a stock's high and low points begin to converge

penny share *UK* STOCKHOLDING & INVESTMENTS = ***penny stock***

penny stock *US* STOCKHOLDING & INVESTMENTS very low-priced stock very low-priced stock, typically under one dollar, that is a speculative investment. *UK term* ***penny share***

pension PENSIONS money received regularly after retirement from paid work money received regularly after retirement, from a government or through a **personal pension** or **occupational pension**. *Also called* ***retirement pension***

pensionable earnings *UK* PENSIONS = ***final average monthly salary***

pension benefit guaranty corporation PENSIONS, INSURANCE US corporation insuring pension benefits for retirees in the United States, a corporation set up by the federal government to insure the retirement benefits of employees of private-sector companies that have established pension plans

pension entitlement PENSIONS amount of retirement income due the amount of income that someone has the right to receive when he or she retires

pension fund PENSIONS **1.** organization investing money to provide future pensions an organization that receives money from employers and employees in order to provide pensions at a later date. The pension funds of large companies and organizations are significant investors in the financial markets. **2.** *UK* = ***retirement fund***

Pension Protection Fund PENSIONS UK fund compensating people when pension providers fail in the United Kingdom, a fund set up by government to compensate people whose pension providers fail. It is funded by a levy on all pension funds. *Abbr* **PPF**

pension provider PENSIONS firm selling pension products a company **pension fund**, or company that sells different investment plans that will build up savings for retirement

PEP *abbr* STOCKHOLDING & INVESTMENTS Personal Equity Plan

PER *abbr* STOCKHOLDING & INVESTMENTS price/earnings ratio

per annum FINANCE in a year in one year

P/E ratio *abbr* STOCKHOLDING & INVESTMENTS price/earnings ratio

per capita FINANCE per person average for each person

per capita income ECONOMICS average income of group of people the average income of each of a specific group of people, for example, the citizens of a country

perceived value pricing OPERATIONS & PRODUCTION = ***market-based pricing***

percentage increase STATISTICS increase expressed as percentage an increase calculated on the basis of a rate for one hundred

percentile STATISTICS one of 99 equal divisions of total one of a series of ninety-nine figures below which a percentage of the total falls

perception of risk RISK = ***risk perception***

per diem FINANCE, HR & PERSONNEL rate allowed for each day an amount of money paid per day, for example, for expenses when an employee is working away from the office

perfect capital market ECONOMICS when buying and selling do not affect prices a

  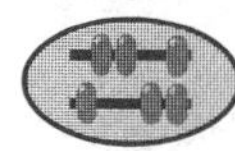 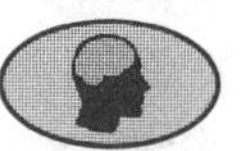  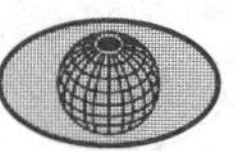   

situation in which the decisions of buyers and sellers have no effect on market price in a **capital market**

perfect competition ECONOMICS when no single buyer or seller affects price a situation in which no individual buyer or seller can influence prices. In practice, perfect markets are characterized by few or no barriers to entry and by many buyers and sellers.

perfect hedge STOCKHOLDING & INVESTMENTS investment with balanced risks an investment that exactly balances the risk of another investment

performance bond BANKING guarantee against third party failure to perform a guarantee given by a bank or insurance company to a third party stating that it will pay a sum of money if its customer, the account holder, fails to complete a specific contract

performance criteria GENERAL MANAGEMENT standards for judgment the standards used to evaluate a product, service, or employee

performance fund STOCKHOLDING & INVESTMENTS higher-risk investment fund expecting high returns an investment fund designed to produce a high return, reflected in the higher risk involved

performance indicator GENERAL MANAGEMENT criterion for assessing firm's performance a key measure designed to assess an aspect of the qualitative or quantitative performance of a company. Performance indicators can relate to operational, strategic, confidence, behavioral, and ethical aspects of a company's operation and can help to pinpoint its strengths and weaknesses. They are periodically monitored to ensure the company's long-term success.

performance management GENERAL MANAGEMENT helping employees to be successful the facilitation of high achievement by employees. Performance management involves enabling people to perform their work to the best of their ability, meeting and perhaps exceeding targets and standards. For successful performance management, a culture of collective and individual responsibility for the continuing improvement of business processes needs to be established, and individual skills and contributions need to be encouraged and nurtured Where organizations are concerned, performance management is usually known as company performance and is monitored through business appraisal.

performance rating MARKETS, GENERAL MANAGEMENT assessment of stock or firm's performance a judgment of how well a stock or a company has performed

performance-related pay FINANCE payment related to the quality of work a payment system in which the level of pay is dependent on the employee's performance. Performance-related pay can be entirely dependent or only partly dependent on performance. There are usually three stages to a performance-related pay system: determining the criteria by which the employee is assessed, establishing whether the employee has met the criteria, and linking the employee's achievements to the pay structure. Performance measures can incorporate skills, knowledge, and behavioral indicators. The system can be compared to **payment by results**, which is based solely on quantitative productivity measures.

performance share *UK* STOCKHOLDING & INVESTMENTS = ***performance stock***

performance stock *US* STOCKHOLDING & INVESTMENTS higher-risk stock showing capital growth a stock which is likely to show capital growth rather than income, which is a characteristic of stocks with a higher risk. *UK term* ***performance share***

period bill *UK* FINANCE bill of exchange with specific payment date a bill of exchange payable on a specific date rather than on demand. *Also called* ***term bill***

period-end ACCOUNTING of end of accounting period relating to the end of an accounting period when financial transactions for that period are finalized

periodic inventory review system OPERATIONS & PRODUCTION means of regularly re-ordering inventory a system for placing orders of varying sizes at regular intervals to replenish inventory up to a specified or target level. A periodic inventory review system sets a specific re-order period, but the re-order quantity can vary according to need. The quantity re-ordered is calculated by subtracting existing inventory and on-order inventory from the target level. *Also called* ***fixed interval re-order system***

period of account ACCOUNTING time span covered by UK firm's accounts the period covered by a UK firm's accounts, sometimes coinciding with the firm's **accounting period**

period of qualification time required to become qualified the time that has to pass before somebody becomes eligible or suitable for something

perk HR & PERSONNEL small supplement to pay a minor benefit that an employee receives in addition to pay, such as the opportunity to buy products cheaply or an interest-free loan for a season ticket (*informal*). *See also* ***fringe benefits***

permanent interest-bearing shares STOCKHOLDING & INVESTMENTS UK stock issued by credit union in the United Kingdom, stock issued by the UK equivalent of a credit union to raise capital because the law prohibits it from raising capital in more conventional ways. *Abbr* **PIBS**

perpetual bond STOCKHOLDING & INVESTMENTS bond without maturity date a **bond** that has no date of maturity and pays interest in perpetuity

perpetual debenture FINANCE debenture without maturity date a **debenture** that has no date of maturity and pays interest in perpetuity

perpetual inventory OPERATIONS & PRODUCTION daily inventory check the daily tracking of inventory in order to keep its recorded amount and value up to date

perpetuity PENSIONS annuity that continues indefinitely a form of annuity that entitles the person holding it to receive payments without setting an end date

perquisites HR & PERSONNEL = ***fringe benefits***

per se GENERAL MANAGEMENT as such a Latin phrase meaning by itself or in itself

personal account **1.** ACCOUNTING record of amounts for or from individual a record of amounts receivable from or payable to a person or an entity. In the United Kingdom, a collection of these accounts is known either as a sales/debtor ledger or a purchases/creditors ledger, or, more simply, as a **revenue ledger** or a **purchase ledger**. In the United States, the terms **receivables ledger** and **payables ledger** are used. **2.** BANKING bank account for individual a bank account designed for a private individual rather than a business entity

personal allowance *UK* TAX = ***personal exemption***

personal brand GENERAL MANAGEMENT distinctive way somebody wishes to be seen the public expression and projection of a person's identity, personality, values, skills, and abilities. It aims to influence the perceptions of others, emphasizing personal strengths and differentiating the individual from others.

personal contract HR & PERSONNEL individualized contract of employment a

  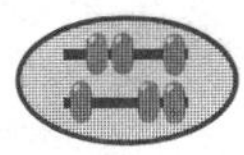   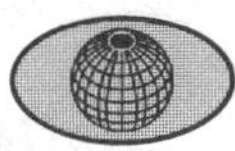   

contract of employment that is negotiated on an employee by employee basis, rather than using a traditional structured system that gives identical contracts to groups of workers

Personal Equity Plan STOCKHOLDING & INVESTMENTS former UK stock-based investment in the United Kingdom, a share-based tax-effective investment replaced by the ISA in 1999. *Abbr* **PEP**

personal exemption US TAX amount somebody can earn without paying income tax the amount of money that an individual can earn without having to pay income tax. *UK term* ***personal allowance***

personal financial planning FINANCE person's short- and long-term financial arrangements short- and long-term financial planning by somebody, either independently or with the assistance of a professional adviser. It will include the use of tax-efficient plans such as Individual Retirement Accounts, ensuring adequate provisions are being made for retirement, and examining short- and long-term borrowing requirements such as overdrafts and mortgages.

Personal Identification Number BANKING *see* ***PIN***

personal income FINANCE money person receives from earnings and other payments the income received by somebody from various sources such as earnings, retirement funds, disability benefits, and dividends from investments

Personal Investment Authority REGULATION & COMPLIANCE UK organization regulating financial service providers in the United Kingdom, a self-regulatory organization that regulates the activities of financial advisers, insurance brokers, and others who give financial advice or arrange financial services for small clients. *Abbr* **PIA**

personalization E-COMMERCE individualized selection of information by website the process by which a website presents customers with selected information on their specific needs. To do this, personal information is collected on the individual user and employed to customize the website for that person.

personal loan FINANCE loan used for personal purpose a loan from a financial institution to somebody for a personal use such as making home improvements or purchasing an automobile

personal pension PENSIONS pension independent of employer a pension taken out by somebody with a private sector insurance company or bank. A personal pension usually takes the form of a program in which money is paid regularly to a pension provider, who invests it in a pension fund. On retirement, a lump sum is available for the purchase of an annuity that provides weekly or monthly payments.

personal pension plan PENSIONS pension provision covering one person not group a pension plan that is set up for one specific person rather than covering a group of employees

personal property FINANCE things belonging to somebody property other than real estate that a person owns

personnel management HR & PERSONNEL appointment, training, and welfare of employees the part of management that is concerned with people and their relationships at work. Personnel management is the responsibility of all those who manage people, as well as a description of the work of specialists. Personnel managers advise on, formulate, and implement personnel policies such as recruitment, conditions of employment, performance appraisal, training, industrial relations, and health and safety. There are various models of personnel management, of which **human resource management** is the most recent.

person-to-person lending FINANCE = ***social lending***

per stirpes LEGAL distribution of estate between remaining heirs a method of distributing the assets of an estate, in which the share of assets that would have gone to an heir who predeceases the maker of the will are divided equally among that heir's descendants

PERT *abbr* OPERATIONS & PRODUCTION program evaluation and review technique

petites et moyennes entreprises GENERAL MANAGEMENT small and medium-sized businesses the French for small and medium-sized businesses. *Abbr* **PME**

petroleum revenue tax TAX UK tax on North Sea oil firms in the United Kingdom, a tax on revenues from companies extracting oil from the North Sea. *Abbr* **PRT**

petty cash ACCOUNTING amount kept for small payments a small accessible store of cash used for minor business expenses. *Abbr* **P/C**

petty cash account ACCOUNTING record of small cash receipts and payments a record of relatively small cash receipts and payments, the balance representing the cash in the control of an individual, usually dealt with under an **imprest system**

petty cash voucher ACCOUNTING document recording petty cash payments a document supporting payments of small amounts of cash to employees under a petty cash system

petty expenses ACCOUNTING small amounts spent on small items small sums of money spent on such items as postage, taxi fares, or copying charges

phantom bid MERGERS & ACQUISITIONS rumored company purchase a reported but nonexistent attempt to buy a company

phantom income TAX income subject to tax though never received income that is subject to tax even though the recipient never actually gets control of it, for example, income from a limited partnership

pharming E-COMMERCE, FRAUD fraudulent poaching of online bank customers the hijacking of online bank customers by infecting web browsers and redirecting them to fake websites, where they are asked to disclose their account details

Phillips curve STATISTICS relationship between unemployment and inflation rate a visual representation of the relationship between unemployment and the rate of inflation

phishing E-COMMERCE, FRAUD fraud to obtain financial information the fraudulent use of e-mail and fake websites to obtain financial information such as credit card numbers, passwords, and bank account information

phoenix company BUSINESS firm formed from identical failed firm a company formed by the directors of a company that has gone into **receivership**, trading in the same way as the first company and, except in name, appearing to be exactly the same

physical asset ACCOUNTING asset that is not cash or securities an asset such as a building or equipment that has a physical presence, as opposed to cash or securities

physical distribution management OPERATIONS & PRODUCTION overseeing of distribution of manufactured goods the planning, monitoring, and control of the distribution and delivery of manufactured goods

physical market MARKETS futures market involving delivery of commodities a market dealing in **futures contracts** that involves physical delivery of the commodities traded, rather than purchases that will be set off against sales in cash transactions and never actually delivered

  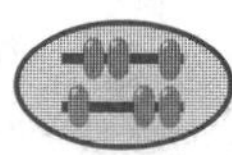   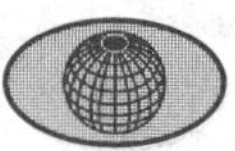   

physical price MARKETS price of commodity for immediate delivery the price of a commodity that is available for immediate delivery, rather than just representing a purchase that will be set off against a sale in a cash transaction and never actually delivered

physicals MARKETS commodities that can be bought and used commodities that are bought and delivered, rather than commodities traded on a **futures contract**

PIA *abbr* REGULATION & COMPLIANCE Personal Investment Authority

PIBOR *abbr* BANKING Paris Interbank Offered Rate

PIBS *abbr* STOCKHOLDING & INVESTMENTS permanent interest-bearing shares

picture MARKETS details of particular Wall Street stock the price and trading quantity of a specific stock on Wall Street used, for example, in the question to a specialist dealer "What's the picture on ABC?" The response would give the bid and offer price and number of shares for which there would be a buyer and seller (*slang*)

piece rate FINANCE payment according to units completed payment of a predetermined amount for each unit of output by an employee. The rate of pay is usually fixed subjectively, rather than by more objective techniques. Rates are said to be tight when it is difficult for an employee to earn a bonus and loose when bonuses are easily earned. Piece-rate systems are a form of **payment by results** or **performance-related pay**.

piecework FINANCE work paid according to items produced work for which employees are paid in accordance with the number of products produced or pieces of work done and not at an hourly rate

pie chart STATISTICS circle graph divided into sections a chart drawn as a circle divided into proportional sections like portions of a pie

piggyback advertising MARKETING free secondary advertising with another campaign an offer or promotion that runs in parallel with another campaign and incurs no costs

piggyback loan FINANCE loan against same security as existing loan a loan that is raised against the same security as an existing loan

piggyback rights STOCKHOLDING & INVESTMENTS permission to sell existing shares with new shares permission to sell existing shares in conjunction with the sale of similar shares in a new offering

PIK note FINANCE debt finance paying interest on note redemption a form of **debt financing** that pays interest only when the note is redeemed, although the interest rate is usually much higher than on ordinary debt. The issue of PIK notes constitutes the payment of interest for tax purposes, so if the notes are issued in the accounting period in which the interest accrues, the interest is tax deductible on an **accrual basis** and does not affect cash flow. *Full form* ***payment-in-kind note***

pilot or **pilot survey** MARKETING trial to test methodology a preliminary piece of work conducted before full implementation of an activity or process to test its effectiveness

PIN BANKING number verifying card transaction a set of numbers that is used to access an account at an ATM, a computer, or a telephone system, or to verify a credit or debit card at an electronic point of sale. *Full form* ***Personal Identification Number***

pink dollar *US* FINANCE money spent by gays and lesbians money spent by gays and lesbians on goods and services that appeal to them. *UK term* ***pink pound***

pink form STOCKHOLDING & INVESTMENTS in the UK, stock application form for employees in the United Kingdom, a preferential application form for an **initial public offering** that is reserved for the employees of the company being floated. *Also called* ***preferential form***

pink paper *UK* FINANCE = ***Financial Times*** (*informal*)

pink pound *UK* FINANCE = ***pink dollar***

pink sheets MARKETS publication giving unlisted securities prices a daily publication of the prices of unlisted securities traded in the **over-the-counter market** but that are not traded on the NASDAQ exchange

pink slip ◇ get your pink slip *US* HR & PERSONNEL to be dismissed from employment (*informal*). *UK terms* ***get your cards, get the sack***

Pink 'Un *UK* FINANCE Financial Times an informal name for the London-based newspaper *The Financial Times*. It is printed on pink paper (*informal*).

pip CURRENCY & EXCHANGE smallest unit in currency price the smallest unit of change in the bid or ask price of a currency

pipeline MARKETS SEC procedure for new security issue the procedure required by the US Securities and Exchange Commission before a new security can be issued for sale to the public

piracy FRAUD illegal copying illegal copying of a product such as software or music

pit MARKETS trading area of financial exchange the area of an exchange where trading takes place. It was traditionally an octagonal stepped area with terracing so as to give everyone a good view of the proceedings during the verbal trading called **open outcry**. *See also* ***ring*** *(sense 1)*

pit broker MARKETS trader in pit of financial exchange a broker who transacts business in the **pit** of a futures or options exchange. *Also called* ***floor broker***

pitch MARKETING attempt to persuade somebody to buy an attempt to win business from a customer, especially a presentation by a sales person

PITI MORTGAGES four items in monthly mortgage payment the four items included in a monthly mortgage payment. Lenders use PITI to determine the amount they will lend based on the relationship between monthly income and PITI. *Full form* ***principal, interest, taxes, and insurance***

placement *US* STOCKHOLDING & INVESTMENTS = ***private placement***

placement fee *UK* STOCKHOLDING & INVESTMENTS = ***commission***

placing *UK* MARKETS = ***private offering***

plain vanilla FINANCE standard form of financial product a basic or standard form of a **financial instrument** such as an **option**, **bond**, or **swap** (*slang*)

plank ◇ make somebody walk the plank HR & PERSONNEL to dismiss somebody from employment

planned economy ECONOMICS economic system completely controlled by government an economic system in which the government plans all business activity, regulates supply, sets production targets, and itemizes work to be done. *Also called* ***command economy***. *See also* ***central planning***

planned obsolescence OPERATIONS & PRODUCTION deliberate designing of products to require replacing a policy of designing products to have a limited life span so that customers will have to buy replacements regularly

plan participant HR & PERSONNEL employee in benefit plan an employee enrolled in a employer-sponsored benefit plan

plant ACCOUNTING fixed assets producing goods the capital assets used to produce

  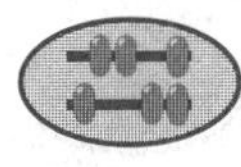   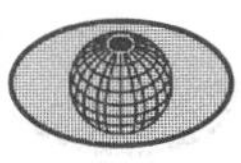   

goods, typically factories, production lines, and large equipment

plastic or **plastic money** BANKING debit or credit card a payment system using a debit or credit card, not cash or checks (*informal*). *See also* ***credit card, debit card, multifunctional card***

platform GENERAL MANAGEMENT product supporting others a product used as a basis for building more complex products or delivering services, for example, a communications network is a platform for delivering knowledge or data

platinum MARKETS precious metal traded as commodity a rare precious metal traded on bullion markets

plc or **PLC** *abbr* BUSINESS public limited company

plenitude ECONOMICS hypothetical situation with abundant supply of products a hypothetical condition of an economy in which manufacturing technology has been perfected and scarcity is replaced by an abundance of products

plot *UK* REAL ESTATE = ***lot** (sense 4)*

plough back *UK* FINANCE = ***plow back***

ploughed back profits *UK* FINANCE = ***plowed back profits***

plow back *US* FINANCE reinvest earnings instead of paying dividends to reinvest a company's earnings in the business instead of paying them out as dividends. *UK term* ***plough back***

plowed back profits *US* FINANCE retained profits the amount of profit kept within the company for reinvestment, not distributed. *UK term* ***ploughed back profits***

plug MARKETING advertise something to publicize or advertise a product or service

plum *UK* STOCKHOLDING & INVESTMENTS successful investment an investment that yields a good return (*slang*)

plus tick MARKETS = ***uptick***

PME *abbr* GENERAL MANAGEMENT petites et moyennes entreprises

PN *abbr* FINANCE promissory note

PO *abbr* OPERATIONS & PRODUCTION purchase order

point FINANCE **1.** unit used in calculating a value a unit used for calculation of a value, such as a hundredth of a percentage point for interest rates **2.** unit on scale a single unit on any scale of measurement, such as a salary scale or range of prices

point and click agreement E-COMMERCE = ***click wrap agreement***

poison pill MERGERS & ACQUISITIONS deterrent measure taken to avoid hostile takeover a measure taken by a company to avoid a hostile takeover, for example, the purchase of a business interest that will make the company unattractive to the potential buyer (*slang*). *Also called* ***show stopper***

policyholder INSURANCE person or organization with insurance policy a person or business that has taken out a specific insurance policy

political economy ECONOMICS study of government and economics the study of the ways in which the politics and economic organization of a country interact

political price ECONOMICS bad effect on government of decision the negative impact on a government of a policy decision such as raising interest rates

political risk ECONOMICS possible bad effect on government of decision the potential negative impact on a government of a policy decision such as raising interest rates

Ponzi scheme FRAUD banking fraud a fraudulent pyramid selling activity that offers investors high returns which are paid directly from the money deposited by new investors. When new deposits cannot match payments, the organization fails. The fraud is named after Charles Ponzi, who first set up such a scheme in the United States in 1920.

pool FINANCE collateral underpinning loan a group of mortgages and other collateral that is used to back a loan

poop *US* FINANCE somebody with privileged information a person who has **inside information** on a financial deal (*slang*)

pooping and scooping *US* MARKETS illegally spreading rumor to lower stock price an illegal financial practice in which a person or group of individuals attempts to drive down the price of a stock by spreading false unfavorable information. The advent of the Internet has allowed pooping and scooping to become more widespread (*slang*).

population STATISTICS set of people, things, or events in a statistical study, the entire collection of units such as events or people from which a sample may be observed

population pyramid STATISTICS representation of group by sex and age a graphical presentation of data in the form of two histograms with a common base, showing a comparison of a human population in terms of sex and age

pork bellies FINANCE meat of pigs traded as commodity meat from the underside of pig carcasses used to make bacon, traded as **futures** on some US commodities exchanges

portable pension *UK* PENSIONS pension savings transferring with employee to new job a **personal pension** that moves with an employee when he or she changes employer, as opposed to an **occupational pension** that usually does not. *See also* ***stakeholder pension***

portfolio STOCKHOLDING & INVESTMENTS investments held by one owner a set of investments, such as stocks and bonds, owned by one person or organization. *Also called* ***investment portfolio***

portfolio career HR & PERSONNEL work pattern of several employments followed simultaneously an employment pattern that involves working part-time on several different jobs at any one time, rather than on a succession of single full-time jobs. *See also* ***portfolio working***

portfolio immunization STOCKHOLDING & INVESTMENTS measures to maintain investment value measures taken by traders to protect their holdings against loss or undue risk

portfolio insurance STOCKHOLDING & INVESTMENTS options protecting portfolio the use of **options** that provide **hedges** against the set of investments held

portfolio investment STOCKHOLDING & INVESTMENTS investment seeking spread of assets a form of investment that attempts to achieve a mixture of securities in order to minimize risk and maximize return

portfolio management STOCKHOLDING & INVESTMENTS trading to maximize investor's profit the professional management of investment portfolios with the goal of minimizing risk and maximizing return

portfolio manager STOCKHOLDING & INVESTMENTS specialist in investment management a person or company that specializes in managing an investment portfolio on behalf of investors. *See also* ***money manager***

portfolio theory STOCKHOLDING & INVESTMENTS idea that variety of investments bring best results a strategy for managing a portfolio of investments in order to minimize risk and maximize return by having a variety of types of investments. *Also called* ***modern portfolio theory***. *See also* ***CAPM***

portfolio working HR & PERSONNEL having several employments simultaneously a way of

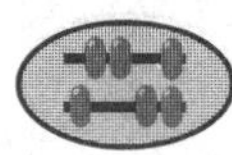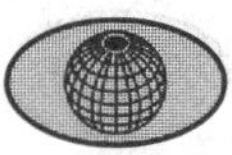

working in which a person follows several simultaneous career pursuits at any one time rather than working full-time for one employer. *See also* ***downshifting, portfolio career***

position STOCKHOLDING & INVESTMENTS size of holding of one owner the number of shares of a security that are owned by a person or organization

position limit STOCKHOLDING & INVESTMENTS maximum holding for individual or group the largest amount of a security that any group or individual may own

positive carry STOCKHOLDING & INVESTMENTS when investment return is greater than cost a situation in which the cost of financing an investment is less than the return obtained from it

positive cash flow FINANCE when firm's income is greater than outflow a situation in which more money is coming into a company than is going out

positive discrimination HR & PERSONNEL favoring appointments from disadvantaged groups preferential treatment, usually through a quota system, to prevent or correct discriminatory employment practices, particularly relating to recruitment and promotion

positive economics ECONOMICS study of verifiable economic theories the study of economic propositions that can be verified by observing the real economy

positive yield curve STOCKHOLDING & INVESTMENTS when long-term investment return exceeds short-term a visual representation of a situation in which the yield on a short-term investment is less than that on a long-term investment. In a long-term investment, an investor expects a higher return because his or her money is tied up and at risk for a longer period of time.

possessor in bad faith REAL ESTATE holder of land not asserting legal right somebody who occupies land even though they do not believe they have a legal right to do so

possessor in good faith REAL ESTATE holder of land asserting legal right somebody who occupies land believing they have a legal right to do so

possessory action REAL ESTATE legal action about land rights a lawsuit over the right to own a piece of land

postal account BANKING account operated only by mail an account for which all dealings are done by post, thereby reducing **overhead costs** and allowing a higher level of **interest** to be paid

postal vote *UK* FINANCE = ***mail ballot***

post-balance sheet event ACCOUNTING incident affecting accounts after balance sheet completed something that happens after the date when a balance sheet is completed but before it is officially approved by the directors, that affects a company's financial position

Post Big Bang MARKETS describing current London Stock Exchange trading system used to describe the trading mechanism on the London Stock Exchange after the market liberalization changes effected in October 1986. *See also* ***Big Bang***

post-completion audit GENERAL MANAGEMENT independent appraisal of success of project an objective and independent appraisal of the measure of success of a capital expenditure project in progressing the business as planned. The appraisal should cover the implementation of the project from authorization to commissioning and its technical and commercial performance after commissioning. The information provided is also used by management as feedback, which helps the implementation and control of future projects.

postdate GENERAL MANAGEMENT date document or check later than date signed to put a later date on a document or check than the date when it is signed, with the effect that it is not valid until the later date

postindustrial society ECONOMICS economy not reliant on heavy industry a society in which the resources of labor and capital are replaced by those of knowledge and information as the main sources of wealth creation. The postindustrial society involves a shift in focus from manufacturing industries to service industries and is enabled by technological advances.

pot **1.** STOCKHOLDING & INVESTMENTS unreleased portion of stock issue the part of a new stock issue that is not released to the public and is only available for purchase by institutional investors **2.** *US* FINANCE amount collected for specific use an amount of money collected from the members of a group for a specific purpose ◇ pot of gold FINANCE a large amount of money, especially one that is achieved by accident or good luck ◇ pot of money FINANCE an amount of money assigned to a specific purpose ◇ pots of money FINANCE an extremely large amount of money

potential GDP ECONOMICS full value of country's production capacity a measure of the real value of the services and goods that can be produced when a country's factors of production are fully employed. *See also* ***GDP***

potentially exempt transfer TAX gift conditionally exempt from UK inheritance tax in the United Kingdom, an outright gift made during a lifetime to a person or to some types of trusts that does not affect the standard of living of the donor. There is no **inheritance tax** to be paid on such a gift, but a liability arises if the donor dies within seven years, with that liability decreasing the longer the donor survives. *See also* ***chargeable transfer***

pot trust FINANCE trust for group of people a trust, typically created in a will, for a group of beneficiaries

pound CURRENCY & EXCHANGE main currency unit in UK and other countries a unit of currency used in the United Kingdom and many other countries including Cyprus, Egypt, Lebanon, Malta, Sudan, and Syria

pound cost averaging *UK* STOCKHOLDING & INVESTMENTS = ***dollar cost averaging***

pound sterling CURRENCY & EXCHANGE official UK currency the official term for the currency used in the United Kingdom

poverty trap TAX disadvantage occurring when pay rise reduces total income a situation whereby low-income families are penalized by a progressive tax system: an increase in income is either counteracted by a loss of social benefit payments or by an increase in taxation

power center GENERAL MANAGEMENT most influential section of organization the part of an organization that has the strongest influence on policy

power of appointment LEGAL power of trustee to dispose of real estate the power of a trustee to dispose of interests in real estate to another person

power of attorney LEGAL legal agreement for acting for another a legal document granting one person the right to act on behalf of another in legal and financial matters and, in the United Kingdom since 2007, in decisions on healthcare and welfare

power structure GENERAL MANAGEMENT relative location of influence the way in which power is distributed among different groups or individuals in an organization

pp GENERAL MANAGEMENT on behalf of derived from the Latin "per pro," used beside a signature at the end of a letter, meaning "on behalf of"

PPF *abbr* PENSIONS Pension Protection Fund

  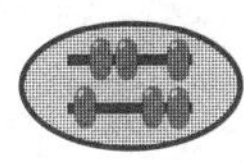 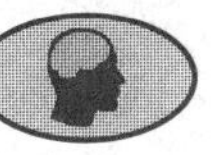  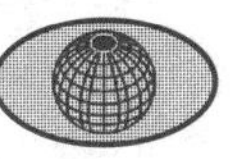  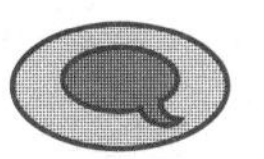 

PPP *abbr* **1.** CURRENCY & EXCHANGE purchasing power parity **2.** BUSINESS public private partnership

preauthorized electronic debit *US* BANKING agreed transfer between bank accounts a system in which a payer agrees to let a bank make payments from an account to somebody else's account. *UK term* ***direct debit***

prebilling OPERATIONS & PRODUCTION submitting bill before delivery the practice of submitting a bill for a product or service before it has actually been delivered

pre-Budget report FINANCE fall forecast of UK government's economic plans in the United Kingdom, an economic forecast the government has to present in the fall of each year, reporting on progress since the Budget in the spring and outlining government spending plans prior to the next Budget. *Abbr* **PBR**

preceding year ACCOUNTING previous fiscal year the year before the **fiscal year** in question

preceding year basis ACCOUNTING using previous year's accounts the principle of assessing income or profits based on the figures for the year before the **fiscal year** in question. *Abbr* **PYB**

precious metals FINANCE high value metals rare metals with a high economic value, especially gold, silver, and platinum

predate *US* GENERAL MANAGEMENT **1.** put earlier date on document to put an earlier date than the current date on a document **2.** make something apply from earlier date to make something effective from an earlier date than the current date ▶ *UK term* **antedate**

predatory lending FINANCE unfair lending practices the practice of encouraging people to borrow in an unfair or unprincipled way, especially if the loan is greater than a borrower can reasonably be expected to repay, or is based on personal property such as a house or car which will be lost if the borrower defaults

predatory pricing OPERATIONS & PRODUCTION setting prices lower than competitors the practice of setting prices for products that are designed to win business from competitors or to damage competitors

pre-emption right *UK* STOCKHOLDING & INVESTMENTS = ***pre-emptive right***

pre-emptive right *US* STOCKHOLDING & INVESTMENTS right of stockholder to first purchase of new stock the right of a stockholder who already owns stock in a company to maintain proportional ownership by being first to purchase stock in a new issue. *UK term* ***pre-emption right***

preference share *UK* STOCKHOLDING & INVESTMENTS = ***preferred stock***

preferential creditor FINANCE creditor who must be paid before others a creditor who is entitled to payment, especially from a bankrupt, before other creditors

preferential form STOCKHOLDING & INVESTMENTS = ***pink form***

preferential issue STOCKHOLDING & INVESTMENTS stock for specific buyers an issue of stock available only to designated buyers

preferential payment FINANCE payment to priority creditor a payment to a **preferential creditor**, whose debt has first claim on a bankrupt or company that is winding up

preferred risk INSURANCE somebody not regarded as a poor insurance risk somebody considered by an insurance company to be less likely to collect on a policy than the average person, for example, a nonsmoker

preferred stock *US* STOCKHOLDING & INVESTMENTS stock receiving dividend or repayment before others stock that entitles the owner to preference in the distribution of dividends and the proceeds of liquidation in the event of bankruptcy. *UK term* ***preference share***

pre-financing FINANCE securing funding before project begins the practice of arranging funding in advance of the start date of a project

prelaunch MARKETING preparation for product launch the activities that precede the introduction of a new product to the market

preliminary announcement ACCOUNTING initial announcement of firm's financial results an announcement of a company's full-year financial results, which are given out to the press before the detailed annual report is released

preliminary prospectus STOCKHOLDING & INVESTMENTS details about firm given before initial public offering a document issued prior to an **initial public offering** that provides details about the company and its financial situation. *Also called* ***red herring***

premarket MARKETS describing transactions before official opening of market used to describe transactions between market members conducted prior to the official opening of the market. *Also called* ***pretrading***

Premiers' Conference FINANCE annual meeting of Australian federal and state heads an annual meeting at which the premiers of the states and territories of Australia meet with the federal government to discuss their funding allocations

premium 1. FINANCE extra cost for scarcity a higher price paid for a scarce product or service **2.** FINANCE extra charge for high quality a pricing method that uses high price to indicate high quality **3.** STOCKHOLDING & INVESTMENTS price paid for option the price a purchaser of a traded **option** pays to its seller **4.** STOCKHOLDING & INVESTMENTS difference between futures price and cash price the difference between the futures price and the cash price of an underlying asset **5.** INSURANCE price of insurance contract the amount paid for an insurance contract, which is needed before the contract is valid ◇ at a premium **1.** FINANCE of a fixed interest security, at an issue price above its nominal value **2.** FINANCE at a price that is considered expensive in relation to others **3.** STOCKHOLDING & INVESTMENTS of a new issue, at a trading price above the one offered to investors

Premium Bond STOCKHOLDING & INVESTMENTS non-interest-bearing UK security eligible for prize draw in the United Kingdom, a nonmarketable security issued by National Savings & Investments at £1 each that pays no interest but is entered into a draw every month to win prizes from £50 to £1 million. There are many lower value prizes, but only one £1 million prize. The bonds are repayable upon demand.

premium income INSURANCE insurance firm's income from premiums the income earned by an insurance company from the money paid for its contracts

premium offer MARKETING offer of free gift with sale a sales promotion technique in which customers are offered a free gift

premium pay plan FINANCE higher pay scale for top employees an enhanced pay scale for high performing employees. A premium pay plan can be offered as an incentive to motivate employees, rewarding such achievements as high productivity, long service, or completion of training with an increased pay package.

premium pricing MARKETING charging high price for high quality the deliberate setting of high prices for a product or service to emphasize its quality or exclusiveness. *Also called* ***prestige pricing***

premoney valuation or **premoney value** FINANCE firm's value before capital investors contribute the assessed value of a

  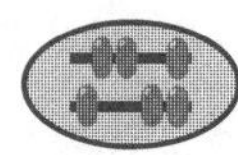 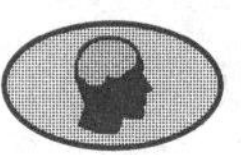  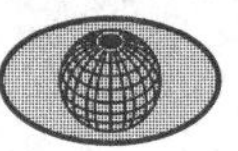 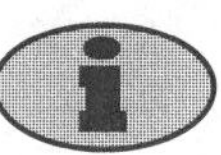  

business before **venture capital** or other capital investors make their investment

prepaid interest FINANCE interest paid early interest paid in advance of the date on which it is due

prepayment FINANCE payment of debt before due date the payment of a debt before it is due to be paid

prepayment penalty FINANCE charge made for early payment a charge that may be levied if a payment, such as one on a mortgage or loan, is made before it is due to be paid. The penalty compensates the lender or seller for potential lost interest.

prepayment privilege FINANCE payment before due date without penalty the right to make a payment, such as one on a loan or mortgage, before it is due to be paid, without penalty

prepayment risk FINANCE, RISK risk that prepayment will reduce interest income the risk that a debtor will avoid interest charges by making partial or total payment in advance on a mortgage or loan, especially when interest rates fall

prequalification **1.** FINANCE, MORTGAGES evaluation of likely borrower the process of establishing the financial circumstances of a borrower or mortgage customer before a loan is formally applied for **2.** MARKETING evaluation of likely customer a sales technique in which the potential value of a prospect is carefully evaluated through research

prerefunding STOCKHOLDING & INVESTMENTS using funds from new bond to repay another the process of issuing a longer-term bond in order to take advantage of a drop in interest rates and use the funds to pay off another bond issued earlier

prescribed payments system TAX deduction of tax from Australian casual workers' payments in Australia, a system under which employers are obliged to deduct a specific amount of tax from cash payments made to casual workers

present value FINANCE **1.** future value of asset, discounted for inflation the amount that a future interest in a financial asset is currently worth, discounted for inflation. *Also called* ***discounted value*** **2.** current value of future income, minus accruing interest the value now of an amount of money that somebody expects to receive at a future date, calculated by subtracting any interest that will accrue in the interim

preservation of capital STOCKHOLDING & INVESTMENTS cautious investment strategy an approach to financial management that protects a person's or company's capital by arranging additional forms of finance

pressure group GENERAL MANAGEMENT group formed to lobby for something a body of people who have banded together to campaign on one or more issues of importance to them. A pressure group usually has a formal constitution and coordinates its activities to influence the attitudes or activities of business or government.

prestige pricing MARKETING = ***premium pricing***

pre-syndicate bid STOCKHOLDING & INVESTMENTS advance bid on NASDAQ exchange in the **NASDAQ** system, a bid made before a public offering in order to stabilize the price of the stock on offer

pretax TAX before tax before taxes are deducted

pretax profit TAX profit before tax the amount of profit a company makes before taxes are deducted

pretax profit margin TAX profit as a percentage of sales, before tax the profit made by a company, calculated as a percentage of sales and before taxes are considered

pretrading MARKETS = ***premarket***

prevalence STATISTICS how many individuals show same feature in a statistical study, a measure of the number of individuals involved who have a specific characteristic

previous balance ACCOUNTING closing balance of previous accounting period a balance in an account at the end of the **accounting period** before the current one

price OPERATIONS & PRODUCTION amount charged to customer an amount of money that a seller charges a customer for a good or service

price-book ratio STOCKHOLDING & INVESTMENTS = ***price-to-book ratio***

price cartel OPERATIONS & PRODUCTION set of firms illegally coordinating prices a group of businesses who make an agreement, often illegally, to maintain prices for a product at a specific level

price ceiling OPERATIONS & PRODUCTION highest price on offer the highest price that a buyer is willing to pay

price change MARKETS price movement of specific stock during day an amount by which the price of a specific share of stock moves during a day's trading

price competition OPERATIONS & PRODUCTION competition on price only a form of competition that is based only on price rather than factors such as quality or design

price controls ECONOMICS government limits on prices to control inflation measures used by a government to set prices in order to protect consumers from rapidly rising prices. Many economists believe that price controls actually hurt the economy by creating shortages and should only be used in an emergency.

price cutting OPERATIONS & PRODUCTION reducing prices to encourage sales a sudden lowering of prices below normal levels in order to boost sales and outsell competitors

price-cutting war OPERATIONS & PRODUCTION = ***price war***

price differential OPERATIONS & PRODUCTION difference in price between similar products a difference in price between products in a range. A basic digital camera, for example, will have a relatively low price compared to the same camera with additional features.

price differentiation OPERATIONS & PRODUCTION pricing same product differently in different markets a pricing strategy in which a company sells the same product at different prices in different markets

price discovery ECONOMICS establishment of price in free market the process by which price is determined by negotiation in a free market

price discrimination OPERATIONS & PRODUCTION selling to different buyers at different prices the practice of selling the same product to different buyers at different prices

price/dividend ratio STOCKHOLDING & INVESTMENTS price of stock divided by annual dividend paid a ratio derived from the price of a stock divided by the annual dividend paid on a share, which gives an indication of how much has to be paid to receive $1 of dividends. *Abbr* **PDR**

price/earnings multiple STOCKHOLDING & INVESTMENTS stock price divided by its earnings the number of times by which the price of stock is greater than the earnings per share, or **EPS**. *Abbr* **P/E multiple**. *See also* ***price/earnings ratio***

price/earnings ratio STOCKHOLDING & INVESTMENTS price of stock divided by earnings per share a company's stock price divided by earnings per share.

While earnings per share (EPS) is an actual amount of money, usually expressed in cents per share, the P/E ratio has no units, it is just a number. Thus if a quoted company has a stock price of $100 and EPS of $12 for the last published year, then it

  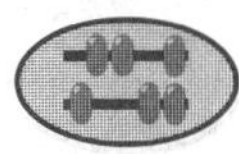   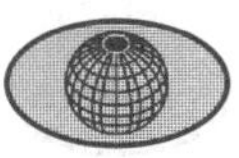   

has a historical P/E ratio of 8.3. If analysts are forecasting for the next year EPS of, say, $14, then the forecast P/E ratio is 7.1.

The P/E ratio is predominantly useful in comparisons with other stocks rather than in isolation. For example, if the average P/E ratio in the market is 20, there will be many stocks with P/E ratios well above and well below this, for a variety of reasons. Similarly, in a particular sector, the P/E ratios will frequently vary from the sector average, even though the constituent companies may all be engaged in similar businesses. The reason is that even two businesses doing the same thing will not always be doing it as profitably as each other. One may be far more efficient, as demonstrated by a history of rising EPS compared with the flat EPS picture of the other over a series of years, and the market might recognize this by awarding the more profitable stock a higher P/E ratio. *Abbr* **PER**

price effect ECONOMICS how price changes affect economy the impact of price changes on a market or economy

price elasticity of demand ECONOMICS how demand responds to price changes the percentage change in demand divided by the percentage change in price of a good

price elasticity of supply ECONOMICS how supply responds to price changes the percentage change in supply divided by the percentage change in price of a good

price escalation clause LEGAL provision permitting seller to cover increased costs a contract provision that permits the seller to raise prices in response to increased costs

price fixing OPERATIONS & PRODUCTION illegal agreement by producers to coordinate prices an often illegal agreement between producers of a good or service in order to maintain prices at a particular level

price floor OPERATIONS & PRODUCTION lowest price acceptable the lowest price at which a seller is prepared to do business

price index ECONOMICS index measuring inflation an index such as the consumer price index that measures inflation

price indicator ECONOMICS measure of general price trends a measurable variable that can be used as an indicator of the price of something, for example the number of home loans arranged can be an indicator for rising or falling house prices

price-insensitive ECONOMICS describing essential goods or services with unvarying sales used to describe a good or service for which sales remain constant no matter what its price because it is essential to buyers

price instability ECONOMICS situation in which prices change frequently a situation in which the prices of goods alter daily or even hourly

price leadership OPERATIONS & PRODUCTION setting of prevailing market price the establishment of price levels in a market by a dominant company or brand

price ring OPERATIONS & PRODUCTION set of traders illegally coordinating prices a group of individual traders who make an agreement, often illegally, to maintain the price of a product at a specific level

prices and incomes policy ECONOMICS government regulations on prices and wages a policy that limits price or wage increases through government regulations

price-sensitive ECONOMICS describing goods or services with price-dependent sales used to describe a good or service for which sales fluctuate depending on its price, often because it is a nonessential item

price-sensitive information MARKETS information affecting firm's stock price if published as yet unpublished information that will affect a company's stock price. For example, the implementation of a new manufacturing process that will substantially cut production costs would have a positive impact, whereas the discovery of harmful side effects from a recently launched drug would have a negative impact.

price slashing OPERATIONS & PRODUCTION making very large price reduction sudden extreme lowering of a price in order to boost sales

price stability ECONOMICS insignificant changes in prices a situation in which there is little fluctuation in the price of goods or services overall

price support ECONOMICS government spending to keep prices from falling government assistance designed to keep market prices from falling below a minimum level

price-to-book ratio STOCKHOLDING & INVESTMENTS ratio of firm's market value to theoretical value the ratio of the value of all of a company's stock to its **book value**. *Also called* ***price-book ratio***

price-to-cash-flow ratio STOCKHOLDING & INVESTMENTS ratio of firm's market value to cash flow the ratio of the value of all of a company's stock to its cash flow for the most recent complete fiscal year

price-to-sales ratio STOCKHOLDING & INVESTMENTS ratio of firm's market value to sales the ratio of the value of all of a company's stock to its sales for the previous twelve months, a way of measuring the relative value of a stock when compared with others.

The P/S ratio is obtained by dividing the **market capitalization** by the latest published annual sales figure. So a company with a capitalization of $1 billion and sales of $3 billion would have a P/S ratio of 0.33.

P/S will vary with the type of industry. You would expect, for example, that many retailers and other large-scale distributors of goods would have very high sales in relation to their market capitalizations—in other words, a very low P/S. Equally, manufacturers of high-value items would generally have much lower sales figures and thus higher P/S ratios.

A company with a lower P/S is cheaper than one with a higher ratio, particularly if they are in the same sector so that a direct comparison is more appropriate. It means that each share of the lower P/S company is buying more of its sales than those of the higher P/S company.

It is important to note that a stock which is cheaper only on P/S grounds is not necessarily the more attractive stock. There will frequently be reasons why it has a lower ratio than another similar company, most commonly because it is less profitable.

price war OPERATIONS & PRODUCTION cycle of cost cutting to undercut competitors a situation in which two or more companies each try to increase their own share of the market by lowering prices. A price war involves companies undercutting each other in an attempt to encourage more customers to buy their goods or services. In the long term, this can devalue a market and lead to loss of profits, but it can sometimes have short-term success.

price-weighted index ECONOMICS index adjusted for price changes an index of production or market value that is adjusted for changes that occur in prices

pricing model OPERATIONS & PRODUCTION computerized multifactorial system for calculating prices a computerized system for calculating prices, based on a variety of factors including costs and anticipated margins

pricing policy or **pricing strategy** OPERATIONS & PRODUCTION way in which

  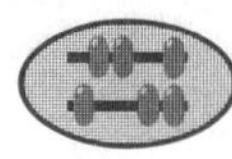   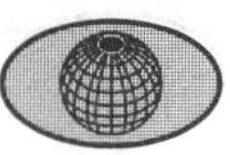   

businesses determine prices the method of **decision making** used for setting the prices for a company's products or services. A pricing policy is usually based on the costs of production or provision with a margin for profit, for example, **cost-plus pricing**.

primary account number BANKING credit card identifier an identifier for a credit card used in secure electronic transactions

primary commodities MARKETS agricultural bulk produce farm produce that is grown in large quantities, for example corn, rice, or cotton

primary data or **primary information** MARKETING information from original research original data derived from a new research study and collected at source, as opposed to previously published material

primary earnings per (common) share STOCKHOLDING & INVESTMENTS profit from each current share of common stock a measure of earnings per share calculated on the basis of the number of shares of **common stock** actually held by investors, not including exercisable warrants and options. *See also* ***fully diluted earnings per (common) share, earnings per share***

primary industry BUSINESS type of business involved in obtaining natural resources an industry that deals with obtaining basic raw materials such as coal, wood, or farm products

primary liability FINANCE, INSURANCE responsibility as first payer of financial claims a responsibility to pay before anyone else who also has financial responsibility for financial claims such as damages covered by insurance

primary market MARKETS market for securities offered to investors by issuer the part of the market on which securities are first offered to investors by the issuer. The money from this sale goes to the issuer, rather than to traders or investors as it does in the secondary market. *See also* ***secondary market***

primary product MARKETS natural resource, often used in other products a product which is a basic raw material, for example, wood, milk, or fish

primary sector ECONOMICS part of economy involved in production businesses operating in the sector of a country's economy that is involved in producing goods

prime BANKING = ***prime rate***

prime assets ratio BANKING Australian banks' obligatory holding in secure assets in Australia, the proportion of total liabilities that banks are obliged by the Reserve Bank to hold in highly secure assets such as cash and government securities. *Abbr* **PAR**

prime bill FINANCE risk-free bill of exchange an agreement that involves no risk of default, setting out an instruction to pay a particular person a fixed sum of money on a particular date or when the person requests payment

prime broker STOCKHOLDING & INVESTMENTS investment bank servicing hedge fund an investment bank that provides borrowing, lending, and settlement services to a **hedge fund**. Such financial services are often considered the most profitable activity for a major bank but great losses can be incurred if the hedge fund fails.

prime cost OPERATIONS & PRODUCTION cost of producing product, not including overhead the cost involved in producing a product, excluding the general recurring costs of running a business

prime rate or **prime interest rate** BANKING in US, best interest rate on offer in the United States, the lowest interest rate that commercial banks offer on loans to well-regarded customers. It is analogous to the **base rate** in the United Kingdom. *Also called* ***prime***

priming FINANCE = ***pump priming***

principal FINANCE original amount lent the original amount of a loan or investment, not including any **interest**. *See also* ***mortgage***

principal shareholders *UK* STOCKHOLDING & INVESTMENTS = ***principal stockholders***

principal stockholders *US* STOCKHOLDING & INVESTMENTS owners of majority of stock the people who own the largest percentage of stock in a business or organization. *UK term* ***principal shareholders***

principles-based regulation REGULATION & COMPLIANCE financial industry regulation relying on good practice regulation of the financial industry that relies more on desired regulatory outcomes and principles and less on detailed rules

prior charge percentage STOCKHOLDING & INVESTMENTS = ***priority percentage***

priority percentage STOCKHOLDING & INVESTMENTS share of profit paid to priority stockholders the proportion of a business's net profit that is paid in interest to holders of **debt capital** and **preferred stock**. *Also called* ***prior charge percentage***

prior lien bond STOCKHOLDING & INVESTMENTS bond giving priority claim on debtor's assets a bond whose holder has more claim on a debtor's assets than holders of other types of bonds

prior year adjustment ACCOUNTING alteration to accounts of previous years an adjustment made to accounts for previous years, because of changes in accounting policies or because of errors

private bank BANKING **1.** bank owned by individual or small group a bank that is owned by a single person or a limited number of private stockholders **2.** bank for wealthy clients a bank that provides banking facilities to high net worth individuals. *See also* ***private banking*** **3.** independent bank in country with state-owned institutions a bank that is not state-owned in a country where most banks are owned by the government

private banking BANKING banking services offered to wealthy clients a service offered by some financial institutions to high net worth individuals. In addition to standard banking services, it will typically include portfolio management and advisory services on taxation, including estate planning.

private company BUSINESS company whose stock is not publicly traded a company that is privately owned and whose stock is not offered for sale to the public

private cost ECONOMICS cost to individual consumer or firm of consumption the cost incurred by individuals or companies when they consume resources

private debt FINANCE nongovernmental borrowings money owed by individuals and organizations other than governments

private enterprise ECONOMICS businesses not controlled by government business or industry that is controlled by companies or individuals rather than the government

private equity company BUSINESS private firm funding profitable projects a company not quoted on a public stock market that provides long-term equity finance to unquoted companies by investing money in the form of shares of stock or shares and shareholder loans. Private equity companies provide money for both **venture capital funds** and **buyout** or **growth funds**.

private equity financing FINANCE = ***venture capital***

private income FINANCE income separate from salary income from dividends, interest, or rent which is not part of a salary

private investor STOCKHOLDING & INVESTMENTS ordinary person investing money

an ordinary person who makes investments and who is not in the business of investing other people's money

private label US MARKETING generic product sold under retailer's name a product or range of products offered by a retailer under its own name in competition with branded goods. Private label products, like **nonbranded goods**, are normally cheaper than branded items but are often perceived to be of lower quality. *Also called **own label**. UK term **own brand***

private label MBS BUSINESS US finance company creating and selling bonds in the United States, a finance company other than Fannie Mae, Ginnie Mae, and Freddie Mac that creates and sells mortgage-backed securities or other bonds and is often collateralized by loans which are not eligible for purchase by Freddie Mac

private limited company BUSINESS private UK firm with small number of stockholders in the United Kingdom and some other countries, a company that has a small number of stockholders and whose stock is not traded on the stock exchange

private mortgage insurance INSURANCE insurance to cover default on mortgage an insurance policy that will cover the risk of a mortgagee defaulting on payments, in the case of loss of job, long-term illness, or other financial difficulty

private offering US MARKETS finding buyer for many shares in new firm the act of finding a single buyer or a group of institutional buyers for a large number of shares in a new company or a company that is going public. *UK term **placing***

private ownership BUSINESS ownership by citizens not by government a situation in which a company is owned by private stockholders, as opposed to being owned by a government

private placement US STOCKHOLDING & INVESTMENTS sale of securities directly to investors the sale of securities directly to institutions for investment rather than resale. *UK term **private placing***

private placing UK STOCKHOLDING & INVESTMENTS = ***private placement***

private property FINANCE property not for general public use property or assets that are owned by a person or group and not for use by the general public

private sector ECONOMICS part of economy not controlled by government the section of the economy that is financed and controlled by individuals or private institutions such as companies, stockholders, or investment groups. *See also **public sector***

private sector investment ECONOMICS non-government investment investment by the private enterprise sector of an economy

private treaty FINANCE land sale without auction the sale of land arranged by seller and buyer without a public auction

privatization GENERAL MANAGEMENT transfer from state to private ownership the transfer of a company from ownership by either a government or a few individuals to the public via the issuance of stock

probability STATISTICS how likely it is something will happen the quantitative measure of the likelihood that a given event will occur

probability distribution STATISTICS formula representing probability of values of variables in a statistical study, a mathematical formula showing the probability for each value of a variable

probability measure RISK, STATISTICS evaluation of chance of event occurring in a statistical study, a calculation of the likelihood that a given event will occur

probability plot STATISTICS graph comparing two probability distributions in a statistical study, a graphic plot of data that compares two probability distributions

probability sampling STATISTICS creating statistical sample that could include any individual in a statistical study, a way of sampling in which every individual in a finite population has a known, but not necessarily equal, chance of being included in the sample, which is known as a **probability sample**

probate LEGAL legal acceptance of validity of will the legal process by which a will is accepted as valid

problem child 1. US BUSINESS troublesome subsidiary company a subsidiary company that is not performing well or is damaging the **parent company** in some way (*slang*) 2. MARKETING underperforming product with high potential a product with a low market share but high growth potential. Problem children often have good long-term prospects, but high levels of investment may be needed to realize the potential, thereby draining funds that may be needed elsewhere. *See also **Boston Box***

problem solving GENERAL MANAGEMENT methodology for dealing with management problems a systematic approach to overcoming obstacles or problems in the management process. Problems occur when something is not behaving as it should, when something deviates from the norm, or when something goes wrong. A number of problem-solving methodologies exist, but the most widely used includes these steps: recognizing a problem exists and defining it; generating a variety of solutions; evaluating the possible solutions and choosing the best one; implementing the solution and evaluating its effectiveness in solving the problem.

proceeds FINANCE income from sale the money derived from a sale or other commercial transaction

process box GENERAL MANAGEMENT symbol representing action a primary symbol used in a **flow chart** that indicates a process or action taking place. *See also **flow chart***

process costing OPERATIONS & PRODUCTION costing method dividing manufacturing cost by units produced a method of costing something that is manufactured from a series of continuous processes, where the total costs of those processes are divided by the number of units produced

processor E-COMMERCE = ***acquirer***

procurement OPERATIONS & PRODUCTION = ***purchasing***

procurement exchange OPERATIONS & PRODUCTION group of companies with combined buying power a group of companies that act together to buy products or services they need at lower prices

procurement manager OPERATIONS & PRODUCTION = ***purchasing manager***

procurement portal E-COMMERCE = ***online catalog***

producer price index ECONOMICS statistical measure of wholesale prices the **weighted average** of the prices of commodities that firms buy from other firms

product OPERATIONS & PRODUCTION, MARKETING marketable good or service anything that is offered to a market that customers can acquire, use, interact with, experience, or consume, to satisfy a want or need. Early **marketing** tended to focus on tangible physical goods and these were distinguished from **services**. More recently, however, the distinction between products and services has blurred, and the concept of the product has been expanded so that in its widest sense it can now be said to cover any tangible or intangible thing that satisfies the consumer. Products that are marketed can include services, people, places, and ideas.

     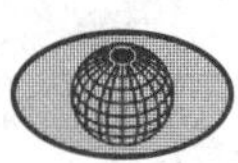   

product abandonment OPERATIONS & PRODUCTION, MARKETING discontinuation of particular good or service the ending of the manufacture and sale of a product. Products are abandoned for many reasons. The market may be saturated or declining, the product may be superseded by another, costs of production may become too high, or a product may simply become unprofitable. Product abandonment usually occurs during the decline phase of the **product life cycle**.

product assortment OPERATIONS & PRODUCTION, MARKETING = ***product mix***

product churning OPERATIONS & PRODUCTION, MARKETING launch of multiple products hoping one will succeed the flooding of a market with new products in the hope that one of them will become successful. Product churning is especially prevalent in Japan, where prelaunch test marketing is often replaced by multiple product launches. Most of these products will decline and disappear, but one or more of the new products churned out may become profitable.

product development OPERATIONS & PRODUCTION, MARKETING modification of product for renewed consumer appeal the revitalization of a product through the introduction of a new concept or consumer benefit. Product development is part of the **product life cycle**. The concepts or benefits that can be implemented range from modification of the product to simply introducing new packaging.

product development cycle OPERATIONS & PRODUCTION, MARKETING *see **new product development***

product differentiation MARKETING promotion of product as different from competition a marketing technique that promotes and emphasizes a product's difference from other products of a similar nature. *Also called **differentiation***

product family MARKETING group of similar goods or services a group of products or services that meet a similar need in the market

production versus purchasing OPERATIONS & PRODUCTION = ***purchasing versus production***

productive capacity OPERATIONS & PRODUCTION maximum output achievable at any one time the maximum amount of output that an organization or company can generate at any one time

productive capital FINANCE assets producing income the part of a company's assets that generate an income

productivity OPERATIONS & PRODUCTION measure of production efficiency a measurement of the efficiency of production, taking the form of a ratio of the output of goods and services to the input of factors of production. Labor productivity takes account of inputs of employee hours worked; capital productivity takes account of inputs of machines or land; and marginal productivity measures the additional output gained from an additional unit of input. Techniques to improve productivity include greater use of new technology, altered working practices, and improved training of the workforce.

productivity measurement OPERATIONS & PRODUCTION *see **productivity***

product launch MARKETING introduction of new product to market the introduction of a new product to a market. A product launch progresses through a number of important stages: internal communication, which encourages high levels of awareness and commitment to the new product; prelaunch activity, which secures distribution and makes sure that retailers have the resources and knowledge to market the product; launch events at national, regional, or local level; post-event activity, which helps sales forces and retailers make the most of the event; and launch advertising and other forms of customer communication.

product leader MARKETING = ***brand leader***

product liability OPERATIONS & PRODUCTION obligation to accept responsibility for defects in products a manufacturer's, producer's, or service provider's obligation to accept responsibility for defects in their products or services. Faulty products may result in personal injury or damage to property, in which case product liability may result in the payment of compensation to the purchaser.

product life cycle OPERATIONS & PRODUCTION, MARKETING time from development through decline of product the life span of a product from development, through testing, promotion, growth, and maturity, to decline and perhaps regeneration. A new product is first developed and then introduced to the market. Once the introduction is successful, a growth period follows with wider awareness of the product and increasing sales. The product enters maturity when sales stop growing and demand stabilizes. Eventually, sales may decline until the product is finally withdrawn from the market or redeveloped.

product line OPERATIONS & PRODUCTION family of related products a family of related products. Products within a line may be the same type of product, they may be sold to the same type of customer or through similar outlets, or they may all be within a specific price range.

product management OPERATIONS & PRODUCTION control of manufacturing process the process of producing a specification or chart of the manufacturing operations to be carried out by different functions and workstations over a specific time period. Production scheduling takes account of factors such as the availability of plant and materials, customer delivery requirements, and maintenance schedules.

product manager OPERATIONS & PRODUCTION, MARKETING person with oversight of product at all stages a person in charge of **product management**, who focuses on the marketing of the product but may also be responsible for pricing, packaging, branding, research and development, production, distribution, sales targets, and product performance appraisal

product market OPERATIONS & PRODUCTION, MARKETING selling to business rather than consumer the market in which products are sold to companies rather than directly to consumers. The product market is concerned with purchasing by organizations for their own use, and includes such items as raw materials, machinery, and equipment, which may in turn be used to manufacture items for the consumer market.

product mix OPERATIONS & PRODUCTION, MARKETING variety of products sold by business the variety of product lines that a company produces, or that a retailer stocks. Product mix usually refers to the length (the number of products in the product line), breadth (the number of product lines that a company offers), depth (the different varieties of product in the product line), and consistency (the relationship between products in their final destination) of product lines. *Also called **product assortment***

product portfolio OPERATIONS & PRODUCTION, MARKETING products that company handles the range of products manufactured or supplied by an organization

product positioning MARKETING = ***brand positioning***

product range *UK* OPERATIONS & PRODUCTION, MARKETING complete list of products all of the types of products made by one company

     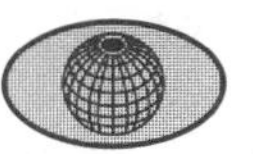   

product recall OPERATIONS & PRODUCTION removal of defective product from market the removal from sale of products that may constitute a risk to consumers because of contamination, sabotage, or faults in the production process. A product recall usually originates from the product manufacturer but retailers may act autonomously, especially if they believe their outlets are at risk. *See also* ***brand positioning***

profile BUSINESS description of firm a description of the activities of a company, including information on its products or business activities and its finances

profit FINANCE **1.** difference between higher selling price and lower purchase price the difference between the selling price and the purchase price of a product when the selling price is higher. In the case of a security or financial instrument the profit will include any accrued interest. **2.** income exceeding expenditure in business transactions, the amount by which income is greater than expenditure **3.** money made by activity the amount of money that is made from a business undertaking or transaction ◇turn a profit FINANCE to make a profit from a business activity

profitability FINANCE **1.** extent of profit the degree to which an individual, company, or single transaction achieves financial gain **2.** generation of profit the ability to achieve financial gain from a sale or other commercial transaction

profitability index FINANCE current value of investment divided by original investment the present value of the amount of money an investment will earn divided by the amount of the original investment

profitability threshold FINANCE start point of making profit the point at which a business begins to make profits from its activities or from a specific product

profitable FINANCE producing a profit used to refer to a product, service, or business that achieves financial gain

profit after tax ACCOUNTING = ***net profit***

profit and loss ACCOUNTING difference between income and costs the difference between a company's income and its costs as shown in its accounts. *Abbr* **P&L**

profit and loss account or **profit and loss statement** ACCOUNTING record of firm's external financial transactions the summary record of a company's sales revenues and expenses over a period, providing a calculation of profits or losses during that time. *Also called* ***trading account***

profit before tax ACCOUNTING amount of profit before tax the amount that a company or investor has made, before tax is deducted. *Abbr* **PBT**

profit center ACCOUNTING business unit responsible for own costs and profits a person, unit, or department within an organization that is considered separately when calculating profit. Profit centers are used as part of management control systems. They operate with a degree of autonomy with regard to marketing and pricing, and have responsibility for their own costs, revenues, and profits.

profit distribution STOCKHOLDING & INVESTMENTS, FINANCE allocation of profits the allocation of profits to different categories of recipients such as stockholders and owners, or for different purposes such as research or investment

profiteering BUSINESS making high profit unethically the practice of making an excessive profit, often in a way that is thought to be unethical or dishonest, or has a detrimental effect on others

profit from ordinary activities ACCOUNTING profits gained from usual business profits earned in the normal course of business, as opposed to profits from extraordinary sources such as windfall payments

profit margin ACCOUNTING, OPERATIONS & PRODUCTION amount by which revenues exceed expenses the amount by which income is greater than expenditure. The profit margin of an individual product is the sale price minus the cost of production and associated costs such as distribution and advertising. The **net profit margin** or **return on sales** is net income after taxes divided by total sales. On a larger scale, the profit margin is an accounting ratio of company income compared with sales. The profit margin ratio can be used to compare the efficiency and profitability of a company over a number of years, or to compare different companies. The **gross profit margin** or **operating margin** of a company is its operating, or gross, profit divided by total sales. The level of profit reported is also influenced by the extent of the application of accounting conventions, and by the method of product costing used, for example, **marginal costing** or **absorption costing**.

profit motive BUSINESS desire to make a profit the desire of a business or service provider to make a profit

profit sharing FINANCE allocation of some profit to employees the allocation of a proportion of a company's profit to employees by an issue of stock or other means

profit-sharing debenture STOCKHOLDING & INVESTMENTS employee debenture linking payouts to company performance a **debenture** held by an employee, the payments from which depend on the employing company's financial success

profit squeeze BUSINESS reduced profitability compared with the past the inability to maintain a person's or business's profit in a venture, in comparison to previous ventures

profits tax *UK* TAX tax on firm's profit any tax on a company's profits, for example, UK corporation tax (*informal*)

profits warning STOCKHOLDING & INVESTMENTS firm's prediction of low profits an announcement by a company of lower than expected profits for a specific period. *Also called* ***profit warning***

profit-taking STOCKHOLDING & INVESTMENTS sale of investments the act of selling investments in order to receive money for the profit they have made

profit warning STOCKHOLDING & INVESTMENTS = ***profits warning***

pro-forma GENERAL MANAGEMENT preliminary document issued before final version a document issued before all relevant details are known, usually followed by a final version

pro forma balance sheet ACCOUNTING statement of projected financial position after planned transaction in the United States, a projection showing a business's financial statements after the completion of a planned transaction

pro-forma financial statement *UK* ACCOUNTING statement of projected financial position after planned transaction a projection showing a business's likely financial statements after the completion of a planned transaction

pro-forma invoice ACCOUNTING initial basic invoice an invoice that does not include all the details of a transaction, often sent before goods are supplied and followed by a final detailed invoice

program evaluation and review technique *US* OPERATIONS & PRODUCTION way of managing major project a way of planning and controlling a large project, concentrating on scheduling individual activities and completing the project on time. *Abbr* **PERT**. *UK term* ***programme evaluation and review technique***

  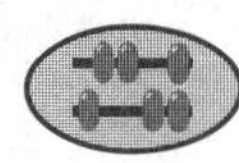 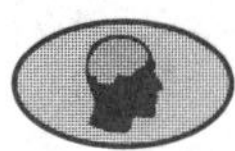  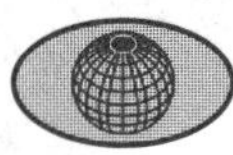   

programme evaluation and review technique UK OPERATIONS & PRODUCTION *abbr* PERT. = ***program evaluation and review technique***

program trading STOCKHOLDING & INVESTMENTS electronic trading of securities the trading of securities electronically, by sending messages from the investor's computer to a market

progressive tax TAX tax with rate rising with income a tax with a rate that increases proportionately with taxable income. *See also* ***proportional tax, regressive tax, flat tax***

progress payment FINANCE payment of project work in stages a payment of a portion of the total contracted price of a project that is made at a agreed stage of completion

project creep GENERAL MANAGEMENT gradual extension of deadlines and targets the gradual alteration of deadlines and expansion of targets as a project progresses

project finance FINANCE funds raised for specific venture money raised for a specific self-contained venture such as a construction or development project

projection FINANCE financial forecast a forecast of conditions that will occur in the future, especially the ways in which they are likely to affect business operations

project management GENERAL MANAGEMENT management of operation and outcome of project the integration of all aspects of a project in order to ensure that the proper knowledge and resources are available when and where needed, and above all to ensure that the expected outcome is produced in a timely, cost-effective manner. The primary function of a **project manager** is to manage the trade-offs between performance, timeliness, and cost.

project risk analysis or **project risk assessment** GENERAL MANAGEMENT, RISK assessment of risks to activities the identification of **risks** to which a project is exposed, and the assessment of the potential impact of those risks on the project. Project risk analysis forms part of the process of **project management** and is a specialized type of **risk analysis**.

promissory note FINANCE agreement to pay for something received a written contract to pay money to a person or organization for a good or service received. *Abbr* **PN**

promotion MARKETING = ***sales promotion***

property FINANCE asset owned by somebody **assets**, such as real estate or goods, that a person or organization owns

property bond STOCKHOLDING & INVESTMENTS bond with property as collateral a bond for which real estate is collateral

property damage insurance INSURANCE insurance for real property insurance against the risk of damage to or on one's real estate

property developer UK REAL ESTATE = ***real estate developer***

property tax TAX local tax on real estate a tax that is based on the value of a piece of real estate and paid to a local government

proportional tax TAX tax proportional to value of taxed item a tax that is strictly proportional in amount to the value of the item being taxed, especially income. *See also* ***progressive tax, regressive tax***

proprietary company ANZ, S. Africa BUSINESS private limited liability company in Australia and South Africa, a private limited liability company. *Abbr* **Pty**

proprietary drug OPERATIONS & PRODUCTION patented drug marketed exclusively under brand name a patented drug that is made by a specific company and marketed only by that company under a brand name

proprietors' interest FINANCE owners' investment in business an amount of money which the owners of a business have invested in the business

pro rata FINANCE at a proportional rate at a rate that is in proportion to something. For example, several investors in a company may share the profits of that company in proportion to their ownership interest.

ProShare MARKETS group representing private investors on London Stock Exchange a group that acts in the interests of private investors in securities on the London Stock Exchange

prospect MARKETING potential client or customer a person or organization considered likely to buy a product or service

prospecting MARKETING identification of potential clients or customers the process of identifying people or organizations that are likely to buy a product or service

prospective dividend STOCKHOLDING & INVESTMENTS = ***forecast dividend***

prospective P/E ratio STOCKHOLDING & INVESTMENTS P/E ratio forecast on expected dividends an assessment of the **price/earnings ratio** that can be expected for the future on the basis of forecast dividends

prospect theory GENERAL MANAGEMENT analysis of why individuals make nonrational decisions a branch of decision theory that attempts to explain why individuals make decisions that deviate from rational decision making by examining how the expected outcomes of alternative choices are perceived. The theory is based on the premise that people treat risks associated with perceived losses differently from risks associated with perceived gains. Prospect theory has applications in a wide range of fields, including marketing management, where it is relevant to the way in which choices are presented to the consumer.

prospectus STOCKHOLDING & INVESTMENTS document accompanying sale of securities a description of a company's operations, financial background, prospects, and the detailed terms and conditions relating to an offer for sale or placing of its stock by notice, circular, advertisement, or any form of invitation which offers securities to the public

protectionism INTERNATIONAL TRADE government protection of domestic firms by limiting imports a government economic policy of restricting the level of imports by using measures such as **tariffs** and **nontariff barriers** in order to protect a country's domestic industries

protective put buying STOCKHOLDING & INVESTMENTS purchase of options to sell something already owned the purchase of **options** to sell **financial instruments** that are the same as some the purchaser already owns

protective tariff INTERNATIONAL TRADE tax on imports to protect domestic firms a tariff imposed to restrict imports into a country

protest FINANCE proof that bill of exchange is unpaid an official document that proves that a bill of exchange has not been paid

protocol GENERAL MANAGEMENT rules regulating a process a set of rules that govern and regulate a process

prototype GENERAL MANAGEMENT working model of new product or invention an initial version or working model of a new product or invention. A prototype is constructed and tested in order to evaluate the feasibility of a design and to identify problems that need to be corrected. Building a prototype is a key stage in **new product development**.

provident INSURANCE paying benefits for illness or other need providing benefits in case of illness, old age, or other cases of need

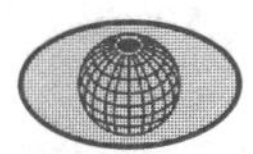

provision ACCOUNTING money earmarked for potential future expense a sum set aside in the accounts of an organization in anticipation of a future expense, often for doubtful debts. *See also* ***bad debt***

provisional tax TAX tax payment based on previous year's income tax paid in advance on the following year's income, the amount being based on the actual income from the preceding year

proxy CORPORATE GOVERNANCE surrogate voter at company meeting somebody who votes on behalf of another person at a company meeting

proxy fight CORPORATE GOVERNANCE consideration of proxy votes in settling disagreement the use of **proxy votes** to settle a contentious issue at a company meeting

proxy form or **proxy card** CORPORATE GOVERNANCE form that stockholders use to appoint proxy a form that stockholders receive with their invitations to attend an annual meeting, and that they fill in if they want to appoint somebody to vote for them on a resolution

proxy statement CORPORATE GOVERNANCE firm's notification to stockholders of voting rights a notice that a company sends to stockholders, allowing them to vote and giving them all the information they need to vote in an informed way

proxy vote CORPORATE GOVERNANCE vote made by somebody authorized by absent person a vote given by somebody who is present at a company meeting and has been authorized by a person who is not present to vote on his or her behalf

PRT *abbr* TAX petroleum revenue tax

prudence TREASURY MANAGEMENT *see* ***prudence concept***

prudence concept TREASURY MANAGEMENT principle of not anticipating profits in accounts the principle that revenue and profits are not anticipated but are included in the **profit and loss account** only when realized in the form either of cash or of other assets, the ultimate cash realization of which can be assessed with reasonable certainty. Provision is made for all known liabilities (expenses and losses) whether the amount of these is known with certainty or is a best estimate in the light of the information available.

prudent FINANCE careful and sensible about money careful and exercising good judgment, especially in financial matters

prudential ratio BANKING, REGULATION & COMPLIANCE in EU, ratio of capital to assets in the European Union, the regulations covering the ratio of capital to assets that a bank should have

prudent man rule FINANCE rule requiring trustees to act carefully the assumption that trustees who make financial decisions on behalf of other people will act carefully, as any prudent person usually would

PSBR *abbr* FINANCE public sector borrowing requirement (see **public sector cash requirement**)

psychic income HR & PERSONNEL job satisfaction independent of salary the level of satisfaction derived from a job rather than the salary earned doing it (*slang*)

psychological contract HR & PERSONNEL tacit understanding between employee and employer the set of unwritten expectations concerning the relationship between an employee and an employer. The psychological contract addresses factors that are not defined in a written contract of employment such as levels of commitment, productivity, quality of working life, job satisfaction, attitudes to working flexibly, and the provision and take-up of suitable training. Expectations of both employer and employee can change, so the psychological contract must be reevaluated at intervals to minimize misunderstandings.

Pty *abbr* ANZ, *S. Africa* BUSINESS private limited liability company

Public Accounts Committee FINANCE UK House of Commons committee monitoring government spending in the United Kingdom, a committee of the House of Commons that examines the spending of each department and ministry

public company BUSINESS = ***publicly held corporation***

public corporation BUSINESS government-owned organization especially in the United Kingdom, a state-owned organization established to provide a specific service, for example, the British Broadcasting Corporation

public debt FINANCE money owed by government the money that a government or a group of governments owes

public deposits FINANCE money of UK government departments in the United Kingdom, the balances to the credit of the government held at the Bank of England

public expenditure FINANCE government spending on citizens' needs spending by the government of a country on items such as pension provision and infrastructure enhancement

public finance law REGULATION & COMPLIANCE financial legislation regulating public-sector organizations legislation relating to the financial activities of government or public-sector organizations

public financing FINANCE money that governments raise and spend the money raised by means of taxation and borrowing, and spent by governments, or the process of raising and spending this money

public funds FINANCE money that government spends money that a government has available for expenditure

public issue STOCKHOLDING & INVESTMENTS offer of stock to public offering a new issue of stock for sale to the public. An issue of this type is often advertised in the press. *See also* ***offer for sale, offer by prospectus***

public-liability insurance INSURANCE insurance against financial liability for injury insurance against the risk of being held financially liable for injury to somebody

public limited company *UK* BUSINESS = ***publicly held corporation***. *Abbr* **plc** or **PLC**

publicly held corporation *US* BUSINESS organization listed on exchange an organization with common stock listed on a stock exchange. *UK term* ***public limited company***

public monopoly BUSINESS when government is sole supplier of good a situation of limited competition in the public sector, usually relating to nationalized industries

public offering STOCKHOLDING & INVESTMENTS raising of funds via offer of stock a method of raising money used by a company in which it invites the public to apply for shares

public ownership BUSINESS ownership by national government a situation in which a government owns and operates a business

public placement *US* STOCKHOLDING & INVESTMENTS restricted selling of stock in public company the selling of stock in a **publicly held corporation** to a limited number of designated buyers. *UK term* ***public placing***. *See also* ***private placement***

public placing *UK* STOCKHOLDING & INVESTMENTS = ***public placement***. *See also* ***private placement***

   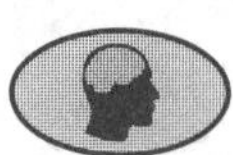  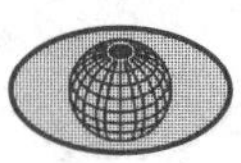   

public private partnership BUSINESS private-sector involvement in traditionally public-sector service a partnership between government and the private sector for the purpose of more effectively providing services and infrastructure traditionally provided by the public sector. *Abbr* **PPP**

public sector BUSINESS organizations financed and controlled by government the organizations in the section of the economy that is financed and controlled by central government, local authorities, and publicly funded corporations. *See also* ***private sector***

public sector borrowing requirement FINANCE *see* ***public sector cash requirement***

public sector cash requirement FINANCE difference between revenue and expenses of public sector the difference between the income and the expenditure of the public sector. It was formerly called the **public sector borrowing requirement**.

public spending ECONOMICS government expenditure spending by the government of a country on publicly provided goods and services

public utility BUSINESS company providing basic service to community a company that provides a service such as electricity, gas, telecommunications, or water that is used by the whole community

published accounts *UK* ACCOUNTING = ***earnings report***

puff MARKETING exaggerate merits of something to overstate the virtues of a product or a service (*informal*)

puffery MARKETING exaggerated claims regarding product or service exaggerated claims made for a product or service. In general, puffery does not constitute false advertising under law (*slang*).

puff piece MARKETING press item for promotional purposes an article in a newspaper or magazine promoting a product or service (*slang*)

pullback MARKETS price drop after rise a fall in the price of a security after it has reached a high

pull strategy MARKETING *see* ***push and pull strategies***

pull system OPERATIONS & PRODUCTION production of goods only as needed by customer a production planning and control system in which the specification and pace of output of a delivery, or supplier, workstation is set by the receiving, or customer, workstation. In pull systems, the customer acts as the only trigger for movement. The supplier workstation can only produce output on the instructions of the customer for delivery when the customer is ready to receive it. Demand is therefore transferred down through the stages of production from the order placed by an end customer. Pull systems are far less likely to result in work-in-progress inventory, and are favored by just-in-time or **lean production** systems. *See also* ***push system***

pump-and-dump STOCKHOLDING & INVESTMENTS illegal exaggeration of value of stock for profit an illegal practice in which the owner of a stock makes false claims about the stock, exaggerating its value, then sells it at a profit (*slang*)

pump priming FINANCE injection of funds to boost business the injection of further investment in order to revitalize a company or economy in stagnation, or to help a **startup** business over a critical period. Pump priming has a similar effect to the provision of **seed capital**.

punter STOCKHOLDING & INVESTMENTS speculator in stock market a person who hopes to make a quick profit in a stock market (*slang*)

purchase FINANCE **1.** something bought a product or service that somebody is going to buy or has bought **2.** to buy something to buy a product or service

purchase acquisition MERGERS & ACQUISITIONS, ACCOUNTING accounting procedures for mergers the standard accounting procedures that must be followed when one company merges with another. *Also called* ***acquisition accounting***

purchase contract OPERATIONS & PRODUCTION agreement to buy at stated price a form of agreement to buy specific products at an agreed price

purchase ledger *UK* ACCOUNTING = ***payables ledger***

purchase money mortgage MORTGAGES mortgage used to buy property that is collateral in the United States, a mortgage whose proceeds the borrower uses to buy the property that is collateral for a loan

purchase order OPERATIONS & PRODUCTION document specifying terms of purchase of goods or services a written order for goods or services specifying quantities, prices, delivery dates, and contract terms. *Abbr* **PO**

purchase price OPERATIONS & PRODUCTION price paid the price that somebody pays to buy a good or service

purchase requisition OPERATIONS & PRODUCTION internal request to purchase goods or services an internal instruction to a buying office to purchase goods or services, stating their quantity and description and generating a **purchase order**

purchase tax TAX in UK, forerunner of VAT in the United Kingdom, a former tax paid when purchasing nonessential items that was replaced by VAT

purchasing OPERATIONS & PRODUCTION acquisition of goods and services by organization the acquisition of goods and services needed to support the various activities of an organization, at the optimum cost and from reliable suppliers. Purchasing involves defining the need for goods and services; identifying and comparing available supplies and suppliers; negotiating terms for price, quantity, and delivery; agreeing contracts and placing orders; receiving and accepting delivery; and authorizing the payment for goods and services. *Also called* ***procurement***

purchasing by contract OPERATIONS & PRODUCTION = ***contract purchasing***

purchasing department OPERATIONS & PRODUCTION department of firm responsible for purchasing the department in a company that buys raw materials or goods for use in the company. *Also called* ***buying department***

purchasing manager OPERATIONS & PRODUCTION employee responsible for purchasing an individual with responsibility for all activities concerned with purchasing. The responsibilities of a purchasing manager can include ordering, commercial negotiations, and delivery chasing. *Also called* ***buying manager***

purchasing power FINANCE measure of ability to buy goods and services a measure of the ability of a person, organization, or sector to buy goods and services

purchasing power parity CURRENCY & EXCHANGE theory linking exchange rate to purchasing power a theory that the exchange rate between two currencies is in equilibrium when the purchasing power of currency is the same in each country. If a basket of goods costs £100 in the United Kingdom and $150 for an equivalent in the United States, for equilibrium to exist, the exchange rate would be expected to be £1 = $1.50. If this were not the case, **arbitrage** would be expected to take place until equilibrium was restored. *Abbr* **PPP**

purchasing routine OPERATIONS & PRODUCTION stages in purchase of product or service the various stages involved in organizing the purchase of a product or service

purchasing versus production OPERATIONS & PRODUCTION choice between making or buying needed item a decision on whether to produce goods internally or to buy them in from outside the organization. The goal of purchasing versus production is to secure needed items at the best possible cost, while making optimum use of the resources of the organization. Factors influencing the decision may include: cost, spare **capacity** within the organization, the need for tight quality and scheduling control, flexibility, the enhancement of skills that can then be used in other ways, volume and economies of scale, utilization of existing personnel, the need for secrecy, capital and financing requirements, and the potential reliability of supply. *Also called* ***buy or make, make or buy, internal versus external sourcing***

pure competition MARKETS situation in which many sellers compete in market a situation in which there are many sellers in a market and there is free flow of information

pure endowment FINANCE gift with conditions attached a gift that can only be used in the way laid down by its donor

purpose credit STOCKHOLDING & INVESTMENTS credit for purchasing securities credit obtained with the intention of buying and selling securities

push and pull strategies MARKETING contrasting marketing strategies targeting either distributor or customer approaches used as part of a marketing strategy to encourage customers to purchase a product or service. Push and pull strategies are contrasting approaches and tend to target different types of consumers. A **pull strategy** targets the end consumer, using advertising, sales promotions, and direct response marketing to pull the customer in. This approach is common in consumer markets. A **push strategy** targets members of the distribution channel, such as wholesalers and retailers, to push the promotion up through the channel to the consumers. This approach is more common in industrial markets.

push system OPERATIONS & PRODUCTION production of goods to be sold from inventory a production control and planning system in which demand is predicted centrally and each workstation pushes work out without considering if the next station is ready for it. While the central control aspect of a push system can achieve a balance across workstations, in practice a specific station can experience any one of a number of problems that delay work flow, so affecting the whole system. Push systems are characterized by work-in-progress inventory, lines, and idle time. *See also* ***pull system***

push the envelope GENERAL MANAGEMENT take risk of overstepping normal limits to exceed normal limits, implying a sense of risk at transcending the normal safe limits of operation

put or **put option** STOCKHOLDING & INVESTMENTS option to sell stock an option to sell stock within an agreed time at a specific price

put bond STOCKHOLDING & INVESTMENTS bond redeemable at specific date before maturity a bond that can be redeemed at face value at a specified time before its maturity date

put-call ratio MARKETS volume of puts divided by calls a ratio of the volume of puts to calls, often used as an indicator of the best time to buy or sell stocks

PV *abbr* FINANCE present value

PYB *abbr* ACCOUNTING preceding year basis

pyramiding 1. FINANCE illegal payment of interest from new deposits the illegal practice of using new investors' deposits to pay the interest on the deposits made by existing investors **2.** MERGERS & ACQUISITIONS process of acquiring increasingly large companies the process of building up a major group by acquiring controlling interests in many different companies, each larger than the original company

pyramid selling MARKETING chain selling of goods from distributor to distributor the sale of the right to sell products or services to distributors who in turn recruit other distributors. Sometimes ending with no final buyer, pyramid selling is a form of multilevel marketing, and often involves a system of franchises. It is similar to **network marketing**, but in many cases no end products are actually sold. Unscrupulous sellers of a pyramid marketing plan profit from the initial fees paid to them by distributors in advance of promised sales income. Pyramid selling is illegal in the United Kingdom.

Q

Q1 *abbr* ACCOUNTING first quarter

Q2 *abbr* ACCOUNTING second quarter

Q3 *abbr* ACCOUNTING third quarter

Q4 *abbr* ACCOUNTING fourth quarter

qard or **qard hassan** FINANCE interest-free loan in Islamic financing, a loan, which under Islamic law is always free of profit. A qard may also be a bank deposit, which is considered a loan to a bank for its use but which must be returned to the depositor upon request.

qualification of accounts ACCOUNTING = ***auditors' qualification***

qualification payment FINANCE financial reward for academic qualification an additional payment sometimes made to employees of New Zealand companies who have gained an academic qualification relevant to their job

qualified auditor's report ACCOUNTING = ***adverse opinion***

qualified domestic trust FINANCE trust giving benefits to non-US spouse in the United States, a trust established by a US citizen for a noncitizen spouse that affords tax advantages to the spouse at the time of the citizen's death

qualified lead MARKETING good potential customer a prospective customer whose potential value has been carefully researched

qualified listed security STOCKHOLDING & INVESTMENTS security that can be purchased by regulated entity a security that is eligible for purchase by a regulated entity such as a trust

qualified plan PENSIONS IRS-approved retirement or benefit plan in the United States, a retirement plan or employee benefit plan that meets the requirements of the IRS for special tax consideration

qualified valuer FINANCE professional person conducting valuation a person conducting a valuation who holds a recognized and relevant professional qualification. The person must also have recent post-qualification experience and sufficient knowledge of the state of the market with reference to the location and category of the tangible fixed asset being valued.

qualifying distribution STOCKHOLDING & INVESTMENTS former UK dividend payment formerly in the United Kingdom, the payment to a stockholder of a dividend on which **advance corporation tax** was paid

qualifying period FINANCE period needed for eligibility a period of time that has to pass before somebody is eligible for something, for example, a grant or subsidy

  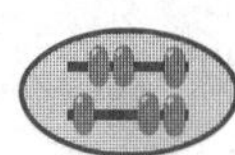   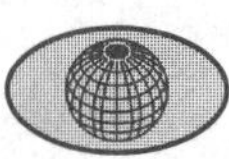   

qualifying ratio MORTGAGES calculation of mortgage affordability a calculation of how much mortgage a borrower can afford, by comparing his or her monthly income against monthly outgoings

qualifying shares STOCKHOLDING & INVESTMENTS stockholding required before rights are granted the number of shares of stock somebody needs to hold to be eligible for something such as a bonus issue

qualitative analysis GENERAL MANAGEMENT appraisal of project with no quantifiable data the subjective appraisal of a project or investment for which there is no quantifiable data. *See also* ***chartist, quantitative analysis, technical analysis***

qualitative research GENERAL MANAGEMENT research using data that is not measurable research that focuses on "soft" data, for example, attitude research or focus groups. *See also* ***quantitative research***

quality bond STOCKHOLDING & INVESTMENTS bond issued by safe firm a bond issued by an organization that has an excellent credit rating

quality costs OPERATIONS & PRODUCTION costs associated with failure to meet standards costs associated with the failure to achieve conformance to requirements. Quality costs accrue when organizations waste large sums of money because of carrying out the wrong tasks, or failing to perform the right tasks correctly the first time. *Also called* ***nonconformance costs***

quality equity STOCKHOLDING & INVESTMENTS equity with good performance history an equity with a good track record of earnings and dividends. *See also* ***blue chip***

quango *UK* GENERAL MANAGEMENT semi-governmental organization an acronym derived from quasi-autonomous nongovernmental organization, a body outside the civil service but established by the government, answerable to a government minister, and with responsibility in a specific area

quantitative analysis GENERAL MANAGEMENT assessment of investment using various numerical standards the appraisal of a project or investment using econometric, mathematical, and statistical techniques. *See also* ***chartist, qualitative analysis, technical analysis***

quantitative easing FINANCE central bank's issue of money to other banks the release by a central bank of sufficient funds to stimulate activity in a banking system that has become sluggish and generate an improvement in the economy. This sometimes means printing money in order to give banks more capital.

quantitative research GENERAL MANAGEMENT analysis of numerical data the gathering and analysis of data that can be expressed in numerical form. Quantitative research involves data that is measurable and can include statistical results, financial data, or demographic data. *See also* ***qualitative research***

quantity discount OPERATIONS & PRODUCTION price reduction for bulk buying a reduction in price given to people who buy large quantities of a product

quantum meruit FINANCE as much as has been earned a Latin phrase meaning "as much as has been earned." A claim for quantum meruit can be for reasonable payment for work that has been done without a full estimate.

quarter 1. ACCOUNTING three-month period a three-month calendar period, often used as a period for reporting earnings, paying taxes, or calculating dividends **2.** CURRENCY & EXCHANGE US coin worth 25 cents a US coin worth one-fourth of a dollar or 25 cents

quarter day *UK* OPERATIONS & PRODUCTION day when some payments become due a day at the end of a quarter, when rents, fees, and other payments become due

quarter-end ACCOUNTING of end of three-month period relating to the end of a three-month **accounting period** when financial transactions for that period are finalized

quarterly 1. GENERAL MANAGEMENT happening every three months taking place once in every period of three months **2.** ACCOUNTING company's financial results the results of a corporation, produced each quarter

quarterly report ACCOUNTING financial statement for quarter of tax year a financial statement that covers a quarter of a full fiscal year. In the United States the general practice is to issue quarterly reports. *See also* ***interim financial statement***

quartile STATISTICS one of four equal ranges of values any of the values in a frequency or probability distribution that divide it into four equal parts

quasi-contract LEGAL in UK, court order stipulating legal obligation a decree by a UK court stipulating that one party has a legal obligation to another, even though there is no legally binding contract between the two parties

quasi-loan FINANCE arrangement to pay somebody else's debt an arrangement whereby one party pays the debts of another, on the condition that the sum of the debts will be reimbursed by the indebted party at some later date

quasi-money *UK* STOCKHOLDING & INVESTMENTS = ***near money***

quasi-public corporation BUSINESS firm partly owned by government in the United States, an organization that is owned partly by private or public stockholders and partly by the government

quasi-rent FINANCE difference between production cost and selling cost excess earnings made by a company representing the difference between production cost (the cost of labor and materials) and selling cost

qubes STOCKHOLDING & INVESTMENTS fund tracking NASDAQ-100 an exchange-traded fund that tracks the stocks in the NASDAQ-100 index, which consists mainly of the largest nonfinancial companies traded on the NASDAQ

question mark company STOCKHOLDING & INVESTMENTS uncertain investment prospect a company that offers a doubtful return on investment

quick asset FINANCE asset easily cashed in cash or any asset that can quickly be turned into cash, for example, a bank deposit of some types, a short-dated bond, or a certificate of deposit. *See also* ***near money***

quick ratio FINANCE **1.** measure of somebody's short-term borrowing potential a measure of the amount of cash a potential borrower can acquire in a short time, used in evaluating creditworthiness **2.** ratio of liquid assets to current debts the ratio of a company's liquid assets to its current liabilities, used as an indicator of **liquidity**

quid pro quo FINANCE something in exchange a Latin phrase meaning "something for something," something given or done in exchange for something else. To be valid, a contract must involve a quid pro quo.

quorum CORPORATE GOVERNANCE minimum number of attendees required for decision-making the minimum number of people required in a meeting for it to be able to make decisions that are binding on the organization. For a company, this number is stated in its **bylaws**; for a partnership, in its partnership agreement.

quota 1. FINANCE limit of investment by party in joint venture the maximum sum to be contributed by each party in a joint venture or joint business undertaking

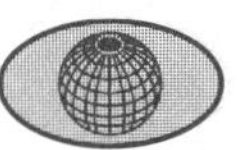

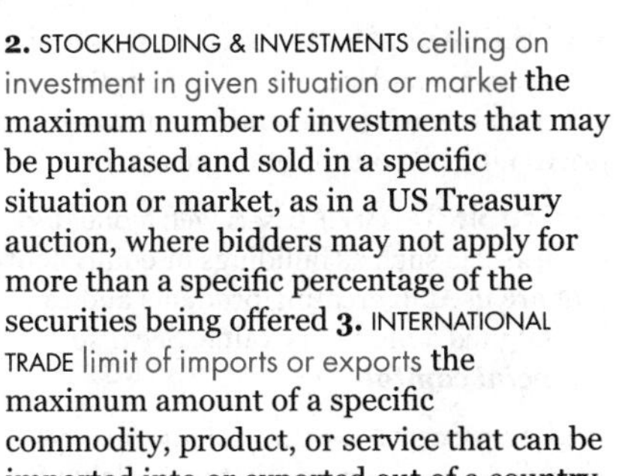

2. STOCKHOLDING & INVESTMENTS ceiling on investment in given situation or market the maximum number of investments that may be purchased and sold in a specific situation or market, as in a US Treasury auction, where bidders may not apply for more than a specific percentage of the securities being offered **3.** INTERNATIONAL TRADE limit of imports or exports the maximum amount of a specific commodity, product, or service that can be imported into or exported out of a country

quota system **1.** OPERATIONS & PRODUCTION, INTERNATIONAL TRADE system that limits imports or supplies a system in which imports or supplies of a commodity, for example, are limited to fixed maximum amounts **2.** OPERATIONS & PRODUCTION distribution system allocating items evenly among distributors an arrangement for distribution which allows each distributor only a specific number of items

quote or **quotation** FINANCE estimate of price a statement of what a person or company is willing to accept when selling a product or service. *Also called* **bid**

quoted company BUSINESS, MARKETS = ***listed company***

quote-driven system MARKETS system fixing initial stock price by quotes a price system on a stock exchange in which prices are generated by dealers' and market makers' quotes before market forces come into play and prices are determined by the interaction of supply and demand. The London Stock Exchange's dealing system, as well as those of many **over-the-counter markets**, have quote-driven systems. *See also* ***order-driven system***

quoted securities MARKETS securities listed on exchange securities or stocks that are listed on a recognized stock exchange

R

racket FRAUD illegal money-making deal an illegal business deal that makes a lot of money, involving such activities as bribery or intimidation

raid MARKETS illegal selling of stock the illegal practice of taking a **short position** in a large number of shares of stock of a particular company in order to drive the price down. *Also called* ***bear raid***

raider MERGERS & ACQUISITIONS maker of hostile takeover bids a person or company that makes hostile takeover bids, wanted neither by directors nor stockholders

rake it in BUSINESS make large amount of money to make a great deal of money relatively easily (*slang*)

rake-off BUSINESS commission a payment made to an intermediary, often calculated as a percentage of the value of goods or services provided (*slang*)

rally MARKETS price rise after fall a rise in stock prices after a significant fall

ramp MARKETS buy stock to raise price to buy stock with the objective of raising its price rather than as an investment. *See also* ***rigged market***

ramp up GENERAL MANAGEMENT greatly increase efforts or interest to increase significantly your interest or efforts in a particular area

rand CURRENCY & EXCHANGE S. African currency unit the standard unit of currency of the Republic of South Africa, equal to 100 cents

Randlord BUSINESS wealthy businessman in Johannesburg originally a Johannesburg-based mining magnate or tycoon of the late 19th or early 20th centuries, now used informally for any wealthy or powerful Johannesburg businessman

random STATISTICS equally likely to occur relating to a set in which all the members have the same probability of occurrence

random sampling STATISTICS statistical technique for sampling individuals at random an unbiased **sampling** technique in which every member of a population has an equal chance of being included in the sample. Based on probability theory, random sampling is the process of selecting and canvassing a representative group of individuals from a specific population in order to identify the attributes or attitudes of the population as a whole. Related sampling techniques include: **stratified sampling**, in which the population is divided into classes, and random samples are taken from each class; **cluster sampling**, in which a unit of the sample is a group such as a household; and **systematic sampling**, which refers to samples chosen by any system other than random selection. *See also* ***nonrandom sampling***

random walk **1.** MARKETS unpredictable movement in stock prices a movement that cannot be predicted, used to describe movements in stock prices that cannot be forecast **2.** STATISTICS sampling method producing random selection a sampling technique that allows for random selection within specific limits set up by a non-random technique

range STATISTICS spread from smallest to largest value the difference between the smallest and the largest observations in a data set

range pricing BUSINESS logical pricing of products in range the pricing of individual products so that their prices fit logically within a variety of connected products offered by one supplier, differentiated by a factor such as weight of pack or number of product attributes offered

ranking STATISTICS order in which values are arranged the ordered arrangement of a set of variable values

ratchet effect ECONOMICS adjusting more easily to income increases than decreases the result when households adjust more easily to rising incomes than to falling incomes, as, for example, when their consumption drops by less than their income in a recession

rate FINANCE assess value to calculate or assess the value of something, for example, real estate for tax purposes

rateable value FINANCE value calculated according to rule the value of something calculated with reference to a rule. An example is the value of a commercial property taken as a basis for calculating local taxes.

rate cap FINANCE = ***cap***

rate of exchange CURRENCY & EXCHANGE = ***exchange rate***

rate of inflation ECONOMICS percentage increase in prices over year the percentage increase in the price of goods and services calculated over a twelve-month period

rate of interest FINANCE percentage charged on loan or paid on investment a percentage charged on a loan or paid on an investment for the use of the money

rate of return ACCOUNTING, STOCKHOLDING & INVESTMENTS ratio of investment profit to investment cost an accounting ratio of the income from an investment to the amount of the investment, used to measure financial performance.

There is a basic formula that will serve most needs, at least initially:

$$\frac{\text{(Current value of amount invested} - \text{Original value of amount invested)}}{\text{Original value of amount invested}} \times 100\% = \text{Rate of return}$$

If $1,000 in capital is invested in stock, and one year later the investment yields $1,100, the rate of return of the investment is calculated like this:

$$\frac{1{,}100 - 1{,}000}{1{,}000} = \frac{100}{1{,}000} \times 100\% = 10\%$$

Now, assume $1,000 is invested again. One year later, the investment grows to $2,000 in value, but after another year the value of the investment falls to $1,200. The rate of return after the first year is:

$$\frac{2{,}000 - 1{,}000}{1{,}000} \times 100\% = 100\%$$

The rate of return after the second year is:

$$\frac{1{,}200 - 2{,}000}{2{,}000} \times 100\% = -40\%$$

The average annual return for the two years (also known as average annual arithmetic return) can be calculated using this formula:

$$\frac{\text{Rate of return for year 1} + \text{Rate of return for year 2}}{2} = \text{Average annual return}$$

Accordingly:

$$\frac{100\% + -40\%}{2} = 30\%$$

The average annual rate of return is a percentage, but one that is accurate over only a short period, so this method should be used accordingly.

The geometric or compound rate of return is a better yardstick for measuring investments over the long term, and takes into account the effects of compounding. This formula is more complex and technical.

The real rate of return is the annual return realized on an investment, adjusted for changes in the price due to inflation. If 10% is earned on an investment but inflation is 2%, then the real rate of return is actually 8%. *Also called* **return**

rates TAX in UK, forerunner of council tax in the United Kingdom, local UK taxes formerly levied on property and now replaced by **council tax**

rate tart FINANCE somebody often changing to accounts with better rates somebody who changes loan providers or savings accounts regularly to benefit from better interest rates (*slang*)

rating FINANCE relative assigned value the value or quality that something is assessed as having, for example, the status of a person or company in terms of creditworthiness, or a company or product in terms of suitability for investment. *See also* ***credit rating***

rating agency STOCKHOLDING & INVESTMENTS organization rating firms issuing bonds an organization that gives a **rating** to companies or other organizations issuing bonds

ratio analysis FINANCE using ratios in financial analysis the use of ratios to measure a company's financial performance, for example, the **current ratio** or the **leverage ratios**

rationalization GENERAL MANAGEMENT measures taken to increase organization's efficiency the application of efficiency or effectiveness measures to an organization. Rationalization can occur at the onset of a downturn in an organization's performance or results. It usually takes the form of cutbacks intended to bring the organization back to profitability and may involve layoffs, plant closures, and cutbacks in supplies and resources. It often involves changes in organization structure, particularly in the form of **downsizing**. The term is also used in a cynical way as a euphemism for mass layoffs.

raw materials OPERATIONS & PRODUCTION materials from which products are manufactured items bought for use in the manufacturing or development processes of an organization. While most often referring to bulk materials, raw materials can also include components, subassemblies, and complete products.

RBA *abbr* BANKING Reserve Bank of Australia

RBNZ *abbr* BANKING Reserve Bank of New Zealand

RD or **R/D** *abbr* UK BANKING refer to drawer

RDG *abbr* ECONOMICS regional development grant

RDP FINANCE government policies addressing economic aftermath of apartheid a policy framework by means of which the South African government intends to correct the socioeconomic imbalances caused by apartheid. *Full form* ***Reconstruction and Development Program***

RDPR *abbr* BANKING refer to drawer please re-present

ready money FINANCE money immediately available cash or money that is immediately available for use

Reaganomics ECONOMICS 1980s economic policies of Ronald Reagan the economic policy of former US President Reagan in the 1980s, who reduced taxes and social security support and increased the national budget deficit to an unprecedented level

real FINANCE after considering inflation after the effects of inflation are taken into consideration

real asset FINANCE physical asset an asset with a physical presence such as land or a building. *See also* ***tangible asset***

real balance effect ECONOMICS results of falling prices and increased consumption the effect on income and employment when prices fall and consumption increases

real capital FINANCE assets with monetary value assets such as buildings or equipment that are used in creating products and can be assigned a monetary value. *See also* ***financial capital***

real earnings FINANCE available income after deductions income that is available for spending after tax and other contributions have been deducted, adjusted for inflation. *Also called* ***real income, real wages***

real economy ECONOMICS goods, services, and jobs the production of goods and services on which jobs, incomes, and consumer spending depend

real estate REAL ESTATE land and improvements in the United States, property that consists of land and anything attached to it, for example, trees and buildings. *Also called* ***realty***

real estate developer *US* REAL ESTATE somebody who develops land or buildings a person or company that develops land or buildings to increase their value. *UK term* ***property developer***

real estate investment trust REAL ESTATE, STOCKHOLDING & INVESTMENTS trust investing in properties and mortgages a publicly traded **investment trust** that uses investors' money to invest in properties and mortgages. *Abbr* **REIT**

real exchange rate CURRENCY & EXCHANGE exchange rate adjusted for inflation a current exchange rate that has been adjusted for inflation

real GDP ECONOMICS GDP adjusted for prices a measure of **GDP** adjusted for changes in prices

real growth ECONOMICS economic growth adjusted for prices the increase in productivity, sales, or earnings of a country or a household adjusted for changes in prices

real income FINANCE = ***real earnings***

real interest rate FINANCE interest rate adjusted for inflation an interest rate after a deduction for inflation has been made

real investment FINANCE purchase of real estate or plant, not securities the purchase of assets such as land, real estate, and plant and machinery, as opposed to the acquisition of securities

realize FINANCE sell asset for cash to change an **asset** into an amount of money by selling it

     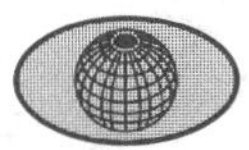   

realized profit FINANCE profit from sale of something profit made when something has been sold, as opposed to **paper profit**

real money FINANCE **1.** capital from investors who have not borrowed investment capital provided by investors such as pension funds, some insurance companies, retail mutual funds, and high net worth individuals who are not borrowing it from other sources **2.** bills and coins money available as bills and coins to spend, rather than existing only as items on financial accounts **3.** lots of money a very large amount of money (*informal*)

real option STOCKHOLDING & INVESTMENTS, RISK choice available to investor in tangible investment the opportunity to choose a course of action that an investor has when investing in something tangible such as a business project

real property REAL ESTATE land and permanent improvements in the United States, land and the permanent structures on it

real purchasing power ECONOMICS how much consumer is able to buy the purchasing power of a country or a household adjusted for changes in prices

real rate of return FINANCE rate of return allowing for inflation the rate of return received after a deduction for inflation

real return after tax FINANCE, TAX net income or profit the income or profit made after deductions for taxes and inflation

real time company BUSINESS firm providing immediate response to customers over Internet a company that uses the Internet and other technologies to respond immediately to customer demands

real time credit card processing E-COMMERCE immediate authorization of credit card during online transaction the online authorization of a credit card indicating that the credit card has been approved or rejected during the transaction

real time EDI E-COMMERCE online transactions between businesses and customers online **electronic data interchange**: the online transfer and processing of business data, for example, purchase orders, customer invoices, and payment receipts, between suppliers and their customers

real time manager E-COMMERCE service manager for Internet customers a manager who is responsible for delivering the immediate service that customers expect, using the Internet and other technologies

real time transaction E-COMMERCE online payment immediately approved or rejected an Internet payment transaction that is approved or rejected immediately when the customer completes the online order form

Realtor REAL ESTATE real estate agent belonging to professional body in the United States, a licensed real estate agent who is a member of the National Association of Realtors

realty REAL ESTATE land and buildings property that consists of land and anything attached to it, for example, trees and buildings. *Also called* ***real estate***

real value FINANCE value of investment in real terms a value of an investment that is maintained at the same level, for example, by making it **index-linked**

real wages FINANCE = ***real earnings***

rebadge MARKETING sell another company's product under your name to buy a product or service from another company and sell it as part of your own product range

rebate 1. FINANCE money returned when payment is excessive money returned because a payment exceeded the amount required, for example, a tax rebate **2.** FINANCE discount a reduction in the price of goods or services in relation to the standard price **3.** STOCKHOLDING & INVESTMENTS reduce client's commission charge of a broker, to reduce part of the commission charged to the client as a promotional offer

recapitalization FINANCE reorganization of firm's capital the process of changing the way a company's capital is structured, in terms of the balance between debt and equity, usually in response to a major financial problem such as **bankruptcy**

recapture 1. FINANCE sale with right to buy back a situation in which a seller of an asset retains the right to buy back part or all of the asset **2.** TAX, ACCOUNTING treatment of past deduction as income a situation in which a deduction taken in a previous tax year must be reported as income, for example, when a depreciated asset is sold at a gain

recd or **rec'd** *abbr* FINANCE received

receipt BUSINESS acknowledgment of transfer a document acknowledging that something has been received, for example, a payment

receipts FINANCE money from sales the total amount a retailer takes from sales. *Also called* ***takings***. *See also* ***gross receipts***, ***net receipts***

receivables ACCOUNTING money owing but not paid money that has been billed to customers or clients but has not yet been received

receivables ledger US ACCOUNTING record of accounts receivable a ledger in which a company records its **accounts receivable**. *See also* ***payables ledger***. *UK term* ***purchase ledger***

received FINANCE referring to money taken in used in recording payments or sums of money. *Abbr* **recd**, **rec'd**

receiver LEGAL person selling firm's assets in insolvency a person appointed to sell the assets of a company that is insolvent. The proceeds of the sale are used to discharge debts to creditors, with any surplus distributed to **shareholders**.

Receiver of Revenue TAX **1.** S. African tax office a local office of the South African Revenue Service (**SARS**) **2.** S. African Revenue Service the South African Revenue Service (**SARS**) as a whole (*informal*)

receivership LEGAL management of insolvent company by court-appointed official a state of **insolvency** prior to **liquidation**. During receivership, receivers may attempt to undertake **turnaround management** or decide that the company must go into liquidation.

recession ECONOMICS slowdown of economic activity a stage of the **business cycle** in which economic activity is in slow decline. Recession usually follows a boom, and precedes a **depression**. It is characterized by rising unemployment and falling levels of output and investment.

recessionary gap ECONOMICS shortfall of demand needed to ensure full employment a shortfall in the amount of **aggregate demand** in an economy needed to create full employment

recharacterization PENSIONS movement of US retirement contributions in the United States, the process of transferring a contribution made to one type of Individual Retirement Account (**IRA**) to another type, or reversing a prior conversion such as from a **traditional IRA** to a **Roth IRA**

reciprocal holdings STOCKHOLDING & INVESTMENTS mutual stockholdings that prevent takeover bids a situation in which two companies own stock in each other to prevent takeover bids

reciprocal trade INTERNATIONAL TRADE trade between countries trade between two countries, usually based on an agreement that benefits both countries

  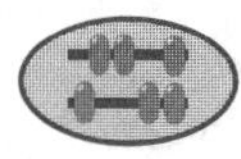   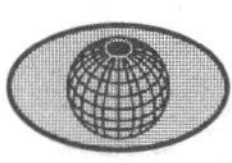   

recognized investment exchange MARKETS in UK, financial exchange recognized by FSA in the United Kingdom, a stock exchange, futures exchange, or commodity exchange recognized by the **Financial Services Authority**. *Abbr* **RIE**

recognized professional body BUSINESS in UK, organization recognized by FSA in the United Kingdom, a professional organization that regulates its members and is recognized by the **Financial Services Authority**. *Abbr* **RPB**

recommended retail price *UK* BUSINESS = ***suggested retail price***

reconciliation ACCOUNTING accounting adjustment in line with authoritative information adjustment of a record, such as somebody's own record of bank account transactions, to match more authoritative information

reconciliation statement ACCOUNTING document verifying date of independently recorded transaction a document used to verify that two independent records of the same financial transactions agree as of a particular date

Reconstruction and Development Program FINANCE *see* ***RDP***

record date GENERAL MANAGEMENT date of computer data entry the date when a computer data entry or record is made

recourse FINANCE right of lender to demand repayment of loan a right of a lender to compel a borrower to repay money borrowed, or, in some cases, to take assets belonging to the borrower if the money is not repaid

recourse agreement FINANCE installment plan agreement allowing retailer to repossess an agreement in an installment plan whereby the retailer repossesses the goods being purchased in the event that the purchaser fails to make regular payments

recoverable ACT TAX former part of UK corporation tax formerly in the United Kingdom, **advance corporation tax** that could be set against the **corporation tax** payable for the period

recoverable amount ACCOUNTING value of asset if sold or when used the value of an asset, either the price it would bring if sold, or its value to the company when used, whichever is the larger figure

recovery ECONOMICS return to normal economic activity after downturn the return of a country to economic health after a crash or a depression

recovery fund STOCKHOLDING & INVESTMENTS fund investing in recovery stock a fund that invests in **recovery stock** that it considers likely to return to a previous higher price

recovery stock STOCKHOLDING & INVESTMENTS underperforming stock now recovering a stock that has fallen in price because of poor business performance, but is now expected to climb as a result of an improvement in the company's prospects

rectification note OPERATIONS & PRODUCTION authorization to improve poor product the authorization for more work to be done to improve a product that did not originally meet the required standard

recurring billing transaction E-COMMERCE automatic rebilling of customer's credit card a means of electronic payment based on the automatic charging of a customer's credit card in each payment period

recurring payments E-COMMERCE series of automatic payments preauthorized by customer a means of electronic payment that permits a merchant to process multiple authorizations by the same customer either as multiple payments for a fixed amount or recurring billings for varying amounts

red BANKING color for debits the color of debit or overdrawn balances in some bank statements ◇ in the red FINANCE, BANKING, ACCOUNTING in debt, or losing money

Red Book FINANCE copy of UK finance minister's Budget speech a copy of the Chancellor of the Exchequer's speech published on the day of the Budget. It can be regarded as the United Kingdom's financial statement and report.

Red chips STOCKHOLDING & INVESTMENTS good Chinese companies Chinese companies that are considered risk-free and worth investing in

red day *US* FINANCE unprofitable day a day on which no profit has been made (*slang*)

redeem 1. FINANCE pay off loan or debt to carry out the repayment of a loan or a debt **2.** BUSINESS exchange voucher for something to exchange a voucher, coupon, or stamp for a gift or a reduction in price **3.** STOCKHOLDING & INVESTMENTS exchange security for cash to exchange a security for cash

redeemable bond STOCKHOLDING & INVESTMENTS bond that will be repaid a bond that is redeemable

redeemable gilt STOCKHOLDING & INVESTMENTS gilt that will be repaid a gilt that is redeemable

redeemable government stock STOCKHOLDING & INVESTMENTS stock redeemable for cash government stock that can be redeemed for cash at some time in the future

redeemable preference share *UK* STOCKHOLDING & INVESTMENTS = ***redeemable preferred stock***

redeemable preferred stock *US* STOCKHOLDING & INVESTMENTS preference share that firm may buy back a type of preferred stock that a company has the right to buy back at a specific date and for a specific price. *Also called* ***callable preferred stock***. *UK term* ***redeemable preference share***

redeemable security STOCKHOLDING & INVESTMENTS security redeemable at face value a security that can be redeemed at its face value at a specific date in the future

redeemable shares STOCKHOLDING & INVESTMENTS shares of stock that may be repurchased stock that is issued on terms that may require it to be bought back by the issuer at some future date, at the discretion either of the issuer or of the holder

redemption STOCKHOLDING & INVESTMENTS ending of financial obligation repayment of a financial obligation, frequently used in connection with preferred stock, debentures, and bonds

redemption date STOCKHOLDING & INVESTMENTS date for repayment of redeemable security the date on which a redeemable security is due to be repaid

redemption value STOCKHOLDING & INVESTMENTS value of security at redemption the value of a security at the time it is redeemed

redemption yield STOCKHOLDING & INVESTMENTS yield on security up to redemption a yield on a security including interest and its value up to the time it is redeemed. *See also* ***yield to maturity***

red eye *US* STOCKHOLDING & INVESTMENTS preliminary prospectus to test market information in the form of a **preliminary prospectus** used in **initial public offerings** to gauge the reaction of investors (*slang*). *UK term* ***pathfinder prospectus***

red herring STOCKHOLDING & INVESTMENTS = ***preliminary prospectus***

rediscount FINANCE discount bill of exchange for second time to discount a bill of exchange that has already been discounted by a commercial bank

redistribution of wealth ECONOMICS sharing of wealth across population the

     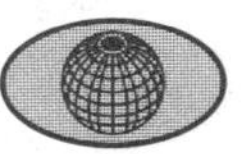   

process of sharing wealth among the entire population, often through taxation

redistributive effect ECONOMICS, TAX wealth equalization resulting from taxes and benefits the tendency toward equalization of people's wealth that results from a **progressive tax** or selective benefit

redlining FINANCE, LEGAL discrimination against borrowers because of neighborhood of residence the illegal practice by financial institutions of discriminating against prospective borrowers because of the area of the town or city in which they live

red screen market MARKETS in UK, market with low prices in the United Kingdom, a market where the prices are down and are being shown as red on the dealing screens

red tape GENERAL MANAGEMENT excessive bureaucracy excessive bureaucracy or unwillingness to depart from rules and regulations

reducing balance depreciation CURRENCY & EXCHANGE *see* ***depreciation***

reducing balance method ACCOUNTING = ***accelerated depreciation***

redundancy *UK* HR & PERSONNEL = ***severance***

redundancy package *UK* HR & PERSONNEL = ***severance package***

redundancy payment *UK* FINANCE, HR & PERSONNEL = ***severance pay***

redundant capacity OPERATIONS & PRODUCTION = ***surplus capacity***

reengineering GENERAL MANAGEMENT *see* ***business process reengineering***

reference BANKING = ***banker's reference***

reference population STATISTICS standard set for statistical comparison a standard against which a statistical population under study can be compared

reference rate FINANCE rate used as benchmark a benchmark interest rate, for example, a bank's own set rate or the **London Interbank Offered Rate**. Lending rates are often expressed as a margin over a reference rate.

reference site E-COMMERCE customer website showcasing new technology a customer website where a new technology is being used successfully

referred share STOCKHOLDING & INVESTMENTS ex dividend stock a stock that is **ex dividend**, the right to dividends remaining with the vendor

refer to drawer *UK* BANKING refuse to pay check from underfunded account to refuse to pay a check because the account from which it is drawn has too little money in it. *Abbr* **RD, R/D**

refer to drawer please re-present BANKING shown on refused UK check in the United Kingdom, marked on a check by the paying banker to indicate that there are currently insufficient funds to meet the payment, but that the bank believes sufficient funds will be available shortly. *See also* ***refer to drawer***. *Abbr* **RDPR**

refinance FINANCE replace loan to replace one loan with another, especially at a lower rate of interest or at a longer maturity

refinancing FINANCE **1.** replacing one loan with another the process of taking out a loan to pay off other loans **2.** new loan that repays old loan a loan taken out for the purpose of repaying another loan or loans

reflation ECONOMICS increasing employment by increasing demand a method of reducing unemployment by increasing an economy's **aggregate demand**. *See also* ***recession***

refugee capital FINANCE resources entering country through necessity people and other financial resources that come into a country because they have been forced to leave their own country for economic or political reasons

refund BUSINESS return of purchase price to buyer the reimbursement of the purchase price of a good or service, for reasons such as manufacturing flaws or dissatisfaction with the service provided

refundable BUSINESS able to be repaid able or liable to be paid back

refunding FINANCE issuance of new bonds to replace old the process of a government's renewing of the funding of a debt by issuing new bonds to replace those that are about to mature

regeneration ECONOMICS revitalization of rundown industrial or business areas the redevelopment of industrial or business areas that have suffered decline, in order to increase employment and business activity

regional development grant ECONOMICS grant encouraging business in UK regions in the United Kingdom, a grant given to encourage a business to establish itself in a specific part of the country. *Abbr* **RDG**

regional fund STOCKHOLDING & INVESTMENTS mutual fund investing in geographic region a mutual fund that invests in the markets of a particular geographic region

regional stock exchange MARKETS stock exchange outside country's main financial center a stock exchange that is not in the main financial center of a country

registered bond STOCKHOLDING & INVESTMENTS bond with ownership recorded by issuer a bond the ownership of which is recorded on the books of the issuer

registered broker MARKETS broker registered on exchange a broker who is registered as a member of a particular stock exchange

registered capital FINANCE = ***authorized capital***

registered check BANKING check written on temporary bank account a check written on a bank's account on behalf of a customer who does not have a bank account but who gives the bank funds to hold to cover the check

registered company REGULATION & COMPLIANCE UK firm registered with Companies House in the United Kingdom, a company that has filed official documents with the **Registrar of Companies** at Companies House. A registered company is obliged to conduct itself in accordance with company law. All organizations must register in order to become companies.

registered investment advisor STOCKHOLDING & INVESTMENTS professionally recognized US financial manager a person or company that is registered with the US Securities and Exchange Commission and usually manages the portfolios of others

registered name REGULATION & COMPLIANCE name of UK firm registered with Companies House in the United Kingdom, the name of a company as it is registered at Companies House. It must appear, along with the company's registered number and office, on all its letterheads and orders. *See also* ***company, corporation***

registered number REGULATION & COMPLIANCE number assigned to registered UK firm in the United Kingdom, a unique number assigned to a company registered at Companies House. It must appear, along with the company's registered name and office, on all its letterheads and orders. *See also* ***company, corporation***

registered office REGULATION & COMPLIANCE in UK, company's official mailing address in the United Kingdom, the official address of a company, which is reproduced on its letterheads and registered with Companies House, to which all legal correspondence and documents must be delivered

registered representative STOCKHOLDING & INVESTMENTS qualified US seller of securities a person who is licensed by the US Securities and Exchange Commission to sell securities, after having passed the required examinations

registered security or **registered share** STOCKHOLDING & INVESTMENTS security with holder's name recorded by issuer a security for which the holder's name is recorded in the books of the issuer. *See also **nominee***

registered share capital STOCKHOLDING & INVESTMENTS = ***authorized share capital***

registered trademark LEGAL unique mark identifying product with producer a unique legally registered mark on a product, that may be a symbol, words, or both, connecting the product to the trader or producer of that product

register of companies REGULATION & COMPLIANCE in UK, list of registered firms in the United Kingdom, the list of companies maintained at Companies House. *See also **company, corporation***

register of directors and secretaries REGULATION & COMPLIANCE firm's record of directors and secretaries a record that every **registered company** in the United Kingdom must maintain of the names and residential addresses of directors and the company secretary together with their nationality, occupation, and details of other directorships held. Public companies must also record the date of birth of their directors. The record must be kept at the company's registered office and be available for inspection by stockholders without charge and by members of the public for a nominal fee.

register of directors' interests REGULATION & COMPLIANCE, STOCKHOLDING & INVESTMENTS firm's record of directors' holdings a record that every **registered company** in the United Kingdom must maintain of the stocks and other **securities** that have been issued by the company and are held by its directors. It has to be made available for inspection during the company's **annual meeting.**

registrar CORPORATE GOVERNANCE keeper of official records a person or organization responsible for keeping official records, for example, the person who keeps a record of stockholders in a company

Registrar of Companies LEGAL, CORPORATE GOVERNANCE official holding record of registered UK companies the person charged with the duty of holding and registering the official startup and constitutional documents of all **registered companies** in the United Kingdom

registration REGULATION & COMPLIANCE **1.** official listing or recording of information the process of recording something such as names, data, or other required information on an official list **2.** provision of required documentation before selling company stock in the United States, the process by which a company files documents with the **SEC** prior to offering stock for sale to the public. The document must contain detailed financial information that has been certified by an outside accountant, information about the company's management, and details of the public offering.

registration fee **1.** REGULATION & COMPLIANCE money paid to have something registered money paid to cover the cost of having something, such as a company, registered **2.** GENERAL MANAGEMENT fee for attending event money paid to take part in an event or activity, for example, a conference or training session

registration statement REGULATION & COMPLIANCE document produced by US corporation issuing securities in the United States, a document that corporations planning to issue securities to the public have to submit to the **SEC**. It features details of the issuer's management, financial status, and activities, and the purpose of the issue. *See also **shelf registration***

regression analysis STATISTICS method of determining relationships between variables a **forecasting** technique used to establish the relationship between quantifiable variables. In regression analysis, data on dependent and independent variables is plotted on a scatter graph or diagram, and trends are indicated through a line of best fit. The use of a single independent variable is known as **simple regression analysis**, while the use of two or more independent variables is called **multiple regression analysis**.

regressive tax TAX tax where rate falls as income increases a tax with a rate that decreases proportionally as the value of the item being taxed, especially income, rises. Social security taxes are regressive. *See also **progressive tax, proportional tax***

regulated superannuation fund TAX Australian superannuation fund regulated by legislation an Australian superannuation fund that is regulated by legislation and therefore qualifies for tax concessions. To attain this status, a fund must either show that its main function is the provision of pensions, or adopt a corporate trustee structure.

regulation REGULATION & COMPLIANCE control of activities using laws and rules the use of laws or rules stipulated by a government or regulatory body, such as the **Securities and Exchange Commission** in the United States or the **Financial Services Authority** in the United Kingdom, to provide orderly procedures and to protect consumers and investors

regulation D REGULATION & COMPLIANCE rule allowing sale of securities without SEC registration in the United States, a regulation that allows some smaller companies to offer their securities for sale without having to register them with the **Securities and Exchange Commission**

regulation S-X REGULATION & COMPLIANCE US rules on financial reports in the United States, a regulation that controls the form and content of financial reports filed with the **Securities and Exchange Commission**

regulation T REGULATION & COMPLIANCE rule on extensions of credit in the United States, a federal law that regulates extensions of credit by brokers and dealers and specifies initial margin requirements and payment rules on some securities transactions

regulation Z REGULATION & COMPLIANCE rule requiring transparency in loans in the United States, a federal law requiring that all lenders and credit card issuers disclose in writing all the costs and terms associated with obtaining the loan or credit

regulator REGULATION & COMPLIANCE government official who monitors businesses and markets a government official or body that monitors the behavior of companies and the level of competition in particular markets, for example, telecommunications or energy

regulatory body or **regulatory agency** REGULATION & COMPLIANCE organization regulating firms' activities an independent organization, usually established by government, that regulates the activities of companies in an industry

regulatory framework REGULATION & COMPLIANCE system of regulations and enforcement a system of regulations and the means to enforce them, usually established by a government to regulate a specific activity. *Also called **regulatory regime***

regulatory pricing risk INSURANCE, RISK risk that government will regulate insurance company's prices the risk an insurance company faces that a government will regulate the prices it can charge

  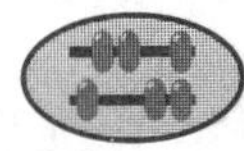   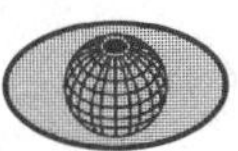   

regulatory regime REGULATION & COMPLIANCE = ***regulatory framework***

rehypothecation FINANCE pledge of client's securities as loan collateral an arrangement in which a broker pledges securities in a client's margin account as collateral for a loan from a bank

reimbursement FINANCE repayment of expense incurred repayment of money spent for an agreed or official purpose or taken as a loan, or money paid as compensation for a loss

reinsurance INSURANCE reduction of insurance risk by transferring policy a method of reducing risk by transferring all or part of an insurance policy to another insurer

reinsurer INSURANCE provider of insurance to insurers an insurer to whom another insurer transfers all or part of an insurance policy to reduce risk

reintermediation E-COMMERCE reintroduction of intermediaries in traditional retail channels the reintroduction of intermediaries found in traditional retail channels. *See also* ***disintermediation***

reinvestment STOCKHOLDING & INVESTMENTS **1.** investing of money again the act of investing money again in the same securities **2.** firm's investing of earnings in own business the act of investing a company's earnings in its own business by using them to create new products for sale

reinvestment rate FINANCE interest rate available for reinvested income the interest rate at which an investor is able to reinvest income received from an investment

reinvestment risk FINANCE, RISK risk that reinvestment will be at lower rate the risk that an investor will be unable to earn the same rate of return on the proceeds of an investment as he or she earns on the investment as a result of declining interest rates

reinvestment unit trust STOCKHOLDING & INVESTMENTS mutual fund using dividends to buy more stock in the United Kingdom a mutual fund that uses dividends to buy more shares in the company issuing them. *See also* ***accumulation unit***

REIT *abbr* REAL ESTATE, STOCKHOLDING & INVESTMENTS real estate investment trust

rejects OPERATIONS & PRODUCTION inferior products or merchandise units of output that fail a set quality standard and are subsequently rectified, sold as substandard, or disposed of as scrap

related company BUSINESS firm that other firm invests in a company in which another company makes a long-term capital investment in order to gain control of it or influence its decisions

relationship management MARKETING effort to maintain good customer relations the process of fostering good relations with customers to build loyalty and increase sales

relative income hypothesis ECONOMICS belief that people care about others' incomes the theory that consumers are concerned less with their absolute living standards than with consumption relative to other consumers

relevant interest ANZ STOCKHOLDING & INVESTMENTS legal position enabling investor to buy and sell the legal status held by stock investors who can legally dispose of, or influence the disposal of, stocks

relocation GENERAL MANAGEMENT transfer of business to new location the transfer of a business from one location to another. Relocation occurs for a variety of reasons, including the need for more space, the desire to centralize operations, or to be nearer to suppliers, customers, or raw materials.

reminder BUSINESS, FINANCE letter reminding of obligation to pay invoice a letter to remind a customer that he or she has not paid an invoice

remittance BUSINESS, FINANCE money sent as payment money that is sent to pay a debt or to pay an invoice

remittance advice or **remittance slip** BUSINESS, FINANCE detailed document accompanying payment a document sent with payment, giving details of what invoices are being paid and credits, if any, being taken

remitting bank BANKING = ***collecting bank***

remuneration FINANCE, HR & PERSONNEL = ***earnings***

remuneration package HR & PERSONNEL employee's total pay, including bonuses and benefits the salary, pension contributions, bonuses, and other forms of payment or benefits that an employer gives an employee

renewal notice INSURANCE document advising of need to renew insurance a document, usually in the form of an invoice, sent by an insurance company asking the insured person to renew the insurance for a particular period of time

renewal premium INSURANCE payment to renew insurance a payment to an insurance company to renew insurance for a particular period of time

renounceable document LEGAL evidence of temporary ownership in the United Kingdom, written proof of ownership for a limited period, for example, a letter of allotment of shares of stock in a **rights issue**. *See also* ***letter of renunciation***

rent **1.** FINANCE arrangement to use equipment for money an arrangement whereby customers pay money to be able to use a car, boat, or piece of equipment owned by another person or firm for a period of time **2.** REAL ESTATE arrangement to use buildings or land for money money paid to use an office, building, or piece of farmland, for example, owned by another person for a period of time **3.** FINANCE allow somebody use of something for money to use or allow somebody to use, an office, building, or piece of farmland, for example, in return for a regular payment. *Also called* ***let***

rental value REAL ESTATE level of rent at current market rate a full value of the rent for a property if it were charged at the current market rate, usually calculated between rent reviews

rent control LEGAL, REAL ESTATE limit on amount chargeable as residential rent regulation by a government restricting the amount somebody can charge to rent a residential property

renting back FINANCE = ***sale and leaseback***

rent review LEGAL, REAL ESTATE increase in rent during term of lease an increase in rents that is carried out during the term of a lease. Most leases allow for rents to be reviewed every three or five years.

renunciation STOCKHOLDING & INVESTMENTS = ***letter of renunciation***

reorder level OPERATIONS & PRODUCTION fixed limit triggering new order of inventory a level of inventory at which a replenishment order should be placed. Traditional "optimizing" systems use a variation on the computation of maximum usage multiplied by maximum lead, which builds in a measure of safety.

reorganization bond STOCKHOLDING & INVESTMENTS US bond for creditors of firm being reorganized in the United States, a bond issued to creditors of a business that is undergoing a form of **Chapter 11** reorganization. Interest is normally only paid when the company can make the payments from its earnings.

     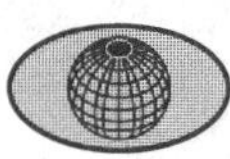   

repatriation FINANCE return of foreign investment earnings to home country the act of sending money earned on foreign investments to the home country of their firm or owner

repayable FINANCE to be repaid used to describe money that is to be paid back, usually in a particular way, for example, in monthly installments

repayment FINANCE **1.** repaying of money the act of paying money back, usually in a particular way, for example, in monthly installments **2.** money repaid money that is paid back, usually in a particular way, for example, in monthly installments

repayment mortgage *UK* MORTGAGES = ***amortized mortgage***

repeat business BUSINESS, MARKETING continuing orders from same supplier the placing of order after order with the same supplier. Repeat business can be implemented by an agreement between the customer and supplier for purchase on a regular basis. It is often used where there are small numbers of customers, or high volumes per product and low product variety. There is market competition for the first order only, and customization is usually available for the initial purchase only. Sales and marketing have a diminished role once the business has been gained.

replacement cost or **replacement price** ACCOUNTING today's cost of replacing something the cost of replacing an asset or service with its current equivalent

replacement cost accounting ACCOUNTING means of evaluating firm's assets a method of valuing company assets based on their replacement cost

replacement cost depreciation ACCOUNTING depreciation based on current replacement cost depreciation based on the actual cost of replacing the asset in the current year

replacement ratio ECONOMICS difference between wages and unemployment benefits the ratio of the total resources received when unemployed to those received when in employment

replacement value INSURANCE today's cost of replacing something the cost of replacing an insured asset with its current equivalent

repo 1. FINANCE = ***repurchase agreement*** **2.** MARKETS open-market buying and selling by US Federal Reserve in the United States, an open-market operation undertaken by the **Federal Reserve** to purchase securities and agree to sell them back at a stated price on a future date **3.** BANKING Bank of England's repurchase agreement in the United Kingdom, a Bank of England repurchase agreement with **market makers** in **gilt-edged securities**. It is used to provide securities for **short positions**.

reporting entity CORPORATE GOVERNANCE organization providing financial information to stockholders any organization such as a limited company that reports its accounts to its stockholders

repositioning MARKETING marketing old product in new ways a marketing strategy that changes aspects of a product or brand in order to change **market position** and alter consumer perceptions

repossession FINANCE return of merchandise after default on time payments the return of goods purchased through an installment plan when the purchaser fails to make the required regular payments. *See also* ***recourse agreement***

repudiation FINANCE refusing to honor debt a refusal to pay or acknowledge a debt or similar contract

repurchase FINANCE buy back shares in mutual fund to buy back shares, for example, when a fund manager buys back the shares in a mutual fund after an investor sells, or when companies repurchase shares instead of or in addition to paying a dividend to shareholders

repurchase agreement MARKETS agreement to both sell and buy back security in the bond and money markets, a spot sale of a security combined with its repurchase at a later date and pre-agreed price. In effect, the buyer is lending money to the seller for the duration of the transaction and using the security as collateral. Dealers finance their positions by using repurchase agreements. *Also called* ***repo (sense 1)***

request form E-COMMERCE Web page with blanks for user data an interactive Web page that accepts user-provided data—for example, name, address, or shipping information—that can be saved for recurring use or sent by e-mail to the page owner

required beginning date PENSIONS, TAX date to start pension payments in the United States, the date on which the **IRS** requires that distributions to a participant in a **qualified retirement plan** begin

required rate of return FINANCE lowest acceptable return the minimum return for a proposed project investment to be acceptable. *See also* ***discounted cash flow***

required reserve ratio or **required reserves** BANKING ratio of bank's reserves to deposits the proportion of a bank's deposits that must be kept in reserve.

In the United Kingdom and in certain European countries, there is no compulsory ratio, although banks will have their own internal measures and targets to be able to repay customer deposits as they forecast they will be required. In the United States, specified percentages of deposits—established by the Federal Reserve Board—must be kept by banks in a non-interest-bearing account at one of the twelve Federal Reserve Banks located throughout the country.

In Europe, the reserve requirement of an institution is calculated by multiplying the reserve ratio for each category of items in the reserve base, set by the European Central Bank, with the amount of those items in the institution's balance sheets. These figures vary according to the institution.

The required reserve ratio in the United States is set by federal law, and depends on the amount of checkable deposits a bank holds. Up to $9.3M the required reserve ratio is 0%, from $9.3M to $43.9M it is 3% and above $43.9M it is 10%. These breakpoints are reviewed annually in accordance with money supply growth. No reserves are required against certificates of deposit or savings accounts.

The reserve ratio requirement limits a bank's lending to a certain fraction of its demand deposits. The current rule allows a bank to issue loans in an amount equal to 90% of such deposits, holding 10% in reserve. The reserves can be held in any combination of till money and deposit at a Federal Reserve Bank. *Also called* ***bank reserve ratio***, ***reserve ratio***, ***reserve requirement***

requisition OPERATIONS & PRODUCTION firm's purchase order an official order form used by companies when purchasing a product or service

resale price maintenance MARKETING UK agreement with supplier restricting retail price formerly in the United Kingdom, an agreement between suppliers or manufacturers and retailers, restricting the price that retailers can ask for a product or service. Resale price maintenance was designed to enable all retailers to make a profit. The Resale Prices Act now prevents this practice on the grounds that it is uncompetitive. Now, unless they can prove that resale price maintenance is in the public interest, manufacturers can only recommend a retail price. *Abbr* **RPM**

  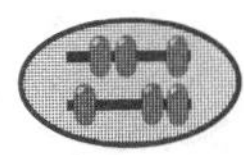   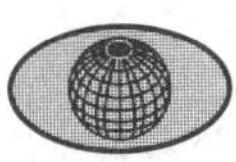   

reschedule FINANCE arrange new payment schedule for debt to arrange a new payment schedule and new conditions for the repayment of a debt

rescission LEGAL cancellation of contract an act of rescinding or annulling a contract

research STOCKHOLDING & INVESTMENTS evaluation of information to aid investing the examination of statistics and other information regarding past, present, and future trends or performance that enables analysts to recommend to investors which stocks to buy or sell in order to maximize their return and minimize their risk. It may be used either in the top-down approach (where the investor evaluates a market, then an industry, and finally a specific company) or the bottom-up approach (where the investor selects a company and confirms his or her findings by evaluating the company's sector and then its market). Careful research is likely to help investors find the best deals, in particular **value shares** or **growth equities**. *See also* ***technical analysis***

reserve FINANCE business profits withheld to cover unexpected costs profits in a business that have not been paid out as dividends but have been set aside in the business to cover any unexpected costs. *Also called* ***reserve fund***

reserve account E-COMMERCE = ***holdback***

reserve bank BANKING bank that holds money for other banks in the United States, a bank such as a Federal Reserve bank that holds the reserves of other banks

Reserve Bank of Australia BANKING central bank of Australia Australia's central bank, which is responsible for managing the Commonwealth's monetary policy, ensuring financial stability, and printing and distributing currency. *Abbr* **RBA**

Reserve Bank of New Zealand BANKING central bank of New Zealand New Zealand's central bank, which is responsible for managing the government's monetary policy, ensuring financial stability, and printing and distributing currency. *Abbr* **RBNZ**

reserve currency CURRENCY & EXCHANGE foreign currency kept for international trading foreign currency that a central bank holds for use in international trade

reserve for fluctuations CURRENCY & EXCHANGE money to absorb exchange rate differences money set aside to allow for changes in the values of currencies

reserve fund FINANCE = ***reserve***

reserve price FINANCE minimum price in auction a price for a particular lot, set by the vendor, below which an auctioneer may not sell

reserve ratio BANKING = ***required reserve ratio***

reserve requirement BANKING = ***required reserve ratio***

reserves 1. FINANCE money held for contingencies and opportunities a sum of money held by a person or organization to finance unexpected business opportunities. *See also* ***war chest*** **2.** BANKING money that bank holds for withdrawals the money that a bank holds to ensure that it can satisfy its depositors' demands for withdrawals **3.** ACCOUNTING, STOCKHOLDING & INVESTMENTS profit not distributed plus stock subscriptions in a company balance sheet, the total of profits not yet distributed to shareholders and the amount subscribed for stock in excess of the **nominal value**

residential property REAL ESTATE dwellings houses, apartments, or other dwellings in which people and their families live

residual value ACCOUNTING value of asset after depreciation a value of an asset after it has been depreciated in the company's accounts

residuary legatee LEGAL person inheriting after specific bequests the person to whom a testator's estate is left after specific bequests have been made

residue FINANCE money left over money that has not been spent or paid out

resizing HR & PERSONNEL = ***upsizing***

resolution CORPORATE GOVERNANCE proposal to be voted on at meeting a proposal put to a meeting, for example, an **annual meeting** of shareholders, on which those present and eligible can vote. *See also* ***extraordinary resolution, special resolution***

resource driver ACCOUNTING **1.** *see* ***cost driver*** **2.** unit for measuring usage and assignment of resources a measurement unit that is used to assign resource costs to **activity cost pools** based on some measures of usage. For example, it may be used to assign office occupancy costs to purchasing or accounting services within a company.

resources OPERATIONS & PRODUCTION total means by which organization achieves its purpose anything that is available to an organization to help it achieve its purpose. Resources are often categorized into finance, property, premises, equipment, people, and raw materials.

response bias STATISTICS difference between answer given and actual fact the disparity between information that a survey respondent provides and data analysis, for example, a person claiming to watch little television but giving answers showing 30 hours' weekly viewing

response rate STATISTICS how many people respond to survey the proportion of subjects in a statistical study who respond to a researcher's questionnaire

responsibility accounting ACCOUNTING record-keeping that shows individual responsibilities the keeping of financial records with an emphasis on who is responsible for each item

responsibility center GENERAL MANAGEMENT organizational center for which manager is completely accountable a department or organizational function whose performance is the direct responsibility of a specific manager

restated balance sheet ACCOUNTING accounts reorganized to emphasize selected feature a balance sheet reframed to serve a specific purpose such as highlighting depreciation on assets

restatement ACCOUNTING revised financial statement a revision of a company's earlier financial statement

restraint of trade GENERAL MANAGEMENT, HR & PERSONNEL restriction of right to compete against former employer a term in a contract of employment that restricts a person from carrying on their trade or profession if they leave an organization. Generally illegal, it is usually intended to prevent key employees from leaving an organization to establish a competing organization.

restricted security STOCKHOLDING & INVESTMENTS security bought in unregistered sale a security acquired in an unregistered private resale from the issuer or an affiliate of the issuer, and whose sale must meet certain conditions laid down by the **Securities and Exchange Commission**

restricted surplus US FINANCE funds unavailable for dividend payments reserves that are not legally available for distribution to stockholders as dividends. *UK term* ***undistributable reserves***

restricted tender STOCKHOLDING & INVESTMENTS conditional offer for stock an offer to buy stock only under specific conditions

restrictive covenant FINANCE agreement to retain loan collateral an agreement by a

   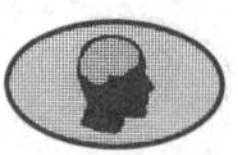  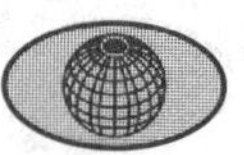   

borrower not to sell an asset that he or she has used as collateral for a loan

restructure BUSINESS reorganize firm's financial basis to reorganize the financial basis of a company

result ACCOUNTING account produced at end of trading period a profit or loss account for a company at the end of a trading period

result-driven GENERAL MANAGEMENT focused on outcome rather than process used to describe a type of corporate strategy focused on outcomes and achievements. A result-driven organization concentrates on meeting objectives, delivering to the required time, cost, and quality, and holds performance to be more important than procedures.

résumé *US* HR & PERSONNEL document summarizing job history and skills a document that provides a summary of personal career history, skills, and experience. A résumé is usually prepared to aid in a job application. A job advertisement may ask either for a résumé or instead may require a candidate to complete an application form.

Every résumé should include the following: the jobseeker's name and contact details; a clear and concise description of his or her career objective; some kind of outline of work experience; and a list of education and degrees. It is important to customize a résumé to the type of job or career being applied for, and to make sure it has impact: a hiring manager receives an average of over 120 résumés for every job opening.

There are four basic types of résumé: the chronological, the functional, the targeted, and the capabilities résumé. A chronological résumé is useful for people who stay in the same field and do not make major career changes. They should start with and focus on the most recent positions held. A functional résumé is the preferred choice for those seeking their first professional job, or those making a major career change. It is based around 3–5 paragraphs, each emphasizing and illustrating a particular skill or accomplishment. A targeted résumé is useful for jobseekers who are very clear about their job direction and need to make an impressive case for a specific job. Like a functional résumé, it should be based around several capabilities and accomplishments that are relevant to the target job, focusing on action and results. A capabilities résumé is used for people applying for a specific job within their current organization. It should focus on 5–8 skills and accomplishments achieved with the company.

The format of a résumé should also be considered—whether it is to be printed out, incorporated into an e-mail, posted on a website, or burned onto a CD-ROM. Different layout and design elements, such as the choice of fonts or inclusion of multimedia, are suitable for each medium, and should be thought through carefully. *UK term* ***CV***

retail BUSINESS **1.** sale of goods to general public the sale of small quantities of goods to the general public **2.** sell goods to general public to sell goods in small quantities to the general public

retail banking BANKING financial services for individuals services provided by commercial banks to individuals as opposed to business customers that include current accounts, deposit and savings accounts, as well as credit cards, mortgages, and investments. In the United Kingdom, although this service was traditionally provided by high street banks, separate organizations, albeit offshoots of established financial institutions, more recently began to provide Internet and telephone banking services, though the credit crunch of 2008 has set back their operations. *See also* ***wholesale banking***

retail cooperative BUSINESS retailers who cut costs by purchasing collectively an organization for the collective purchase and sale of goods by a group who share profits or benefits. Retail cooperatives were the first offshoot of the **cooperative movement** and profits were originally shared among members through dividend payments proportionate to a member's purchases.

retail deposit BANKING money held in bank on somebody's behalf a sum of money held in a bank on behalf of an individual

retail depositor BANKING individual bank customer an individual who deposits money in a bank, as opposed to a business customer

retailer BUSINESS store selling directly to customer an outlet through which products or services are sold to customers. Retailers can be put into three broad groups: independent traders, multiple stores, or **retail cooperatives**.

retailer number BANKING retailer's identification number for depositing credit card payments the identification number of the retailer, printed at the top of the report slip when depositing credit card payments

retail investor STOCKHOLDING & INVESTMENTS small investor a private investor who buys and sells stock

retail price BUSINESS price for small quantity a price charged to customers who buy in limited quantities *Also called* ***shop price***

retail price index ECONOMICS list of average prices charged to consumers a listing of the average levels of prices charged by retailers for goods or services. The retail price index is calculated on a set variety of items, and usually excludes luxury goods. It is updated monthly, and provides a running indicator of changing costs. *Abbr* **RPI**

retained earnings *US* ACCOUNTING = ***retained profits, retensions***

retained profits ACCOUNTING firm's profits kept as reserves, expansion, or investment the amount of profit remaining after tax and distribution to stockholders that is retained in a business and used as a reserve or as a means of financing expansion or investment. *Also called* ***retained earnings, retentions***

retainer FINANCE money advanced to retain somebody's services money paid in advance to somebody so that they will work for you and not for someone else

retention **1.** FINANCE withholding of payment the holding back of money due until a condition has been fulfilled **2.** HR & PERSONNEL keeping existing employees the process of keeping the loyalty of existing employees and persuading them not to work for another company

retentions ACCOUNTING = ***retained profits***

retire **1.** FINANCE pay off loan to pay the balance owed on a loan **2.** HR & PERSONNEL stop working at end of career to leave a job or career voluntarily at the usual age or time for doing so

retirement **1.** FINANCE payment of loan balance the act of paying the balance owed on a loan **2.** HR & PERSONNEL act of retiring the act of leaving a job or career voluntarily at the usual age or time for doing so **3.** HR & PERSONNEL time after retiring the time that follows the end of a person's working life

retirement annuity PENSIONS pension paid as annuity to retired person an annuity paid to a person when they reach a specific age, derived from a fund built up over time

retirement benefits PENSIONS pension payments to retired person benefits that are payable by a pension plan to somebody who retires

retirement fund *US* PENSIONS money set aside to pay pensions of retirees a large sum of money made up of contributions from employees and their employer which

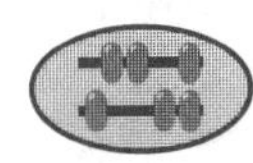

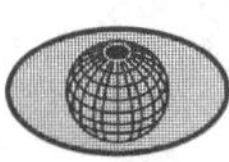

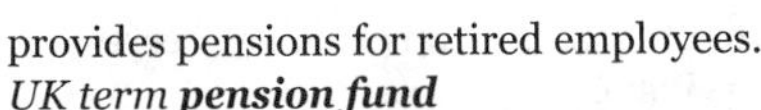

provides pensions for retired employees. *UK term* ***pension fund***

retirement pension PENSIONS = ***pension***

retrenchment FINANCE cost reductions to improve profitability the reduction of costs or spending in order to maintain or improve profitability, especially in response to changed economic circumstances

return 1. ACCOUNTING, STOCKHOLDING & INVESTMENTS = ***rate of return* 2.** TAX = ***tax return***

return date ACCOUNTING in UK, date for required annual return in the United Kingdom, a date by which a company's annual return has to be made to the **Registrar of Companies**

return on assets ACCOUNTING net income as percentage of total assets a measure of profitability calculated by expressing a company's net income as a percentage of total assets. *Abbr* **ROA**

return on capital or **return on capital employed** ACCOUNTING ratio used for measuring profitability by UK firms in the United Kingdom, a ratio of the net profit made in a fiscal year in relation to the **capital employed.** It is used as a measure of business profitability. *Abbr* **ROC, ROCE**

return on equity FINANCE relationship between net income and stockholders' funds the ratio of a company's net income as a percentage of shareholders' funds.

Return on equity is easy to calculate and is applicable to the majority of industries. It is probably the most widely used measure of how well a company is performing for its shareholders.

It is calculated by dividing the net income shown on the income statement (usually of the past year) by shareholders' equity, which appears on the balance sheet:

$$\frac{\text{Net income}}{\text{Owners' equity}} = \text{Return on equity}$$

For example, if net income is \$450 and equity is \$2,500, then:

$$\frac{450}{2{,}500} = 0.18 \times 100\% = 18\% \text{ return on equity}$$

Return on equity for most companies should be in double figures; investors often look for 15% or higher, while a return of 20% or more is considered excellent. Seasoned investors also review five-year average ROE, to gauge consistency. *Abbr* **ROE**

return on invested capital or **return on investment** FINANCE profit as percentage of investment a ratio of the profit made in a financial year as a percentage of an investment

The most basic expression of ROI can be found by dividing a company's net profit (also called net earnings) by the total investment (total debt plus total equity), then multiplying by 100 to arrive at a percentage:

$$\frac{\text{Net profit}}{\text{Total investment}} = \text{ROI}$$

If, say, net profit is \$30 and total investment is \$250, the ROI is:

$$\frac{30}{250} = 0.12 \times 100\% = 12\%$$

A more complex variation of ROI is an equation known as the Du Pont formula:

$$\frac{\text{Net profit after taxes}}{\text{Total assets}} = \frac{\text{Net profit after taxes}}{\text{Sales}} \times \frac{\text{Sales}}{\text{Total assets}}$$

If, for example, net profit after taxes is \$30, total assets are \$250, and sales are \$500, then:

$$\frac{30}{250} = \frac{30}{500} \times \frac{500}{250} = 12\% = 6\% \times 2 = 12\%$$

Champions of this formula, which was developed by the Du Pont Company in the 1920s, say that it helps reveal how a company has both deployed its assets and controlled its costs, and how it can achieve the same percentage return in different ways.

For shareholders, the variation of the basic ROI formula used by investors is:

$$\frac{\text{Net income} + (\text{Current value} - \text{Original value})}{\text{Original value}} = \text{ROI}$$

If, for example, somebody invests \$5,000 in a company and a year later has earned \$100 in dividends, while the value of the shares is \$5,200, the return on investment would be:

$$\frac{100 + (5{,}200 - 5{,}000)}{5{,}000} = \frac{100 + 200}{5{,}000} = \frac{300}{5{,}000} = 0.06 \times 100\% = 6\% \text{ ROI}$$

It is vital to understand exactly what a return on investment measures, for example, assets, equity, or sales. Without this understanding, comparisons may be misleading. It is also important to establish whether the net profit figure used is before or after provision for taxes. *Abbr* **ROI, ROIC**

return on net assets FINANCE profit as percentage of firm's assets a ratio of the profit made in a fiscal year as a percentage of the assets of a company. *Abbr* **RONA**

return on sales ACCOUNTING profit or loss as percentage of sales a company's operating profit or loss as a percentage of total sales for a given period, typically a year. *Abbr* **ROS.** *See also* ***profit margin***

returns to scale ECONOMICS increase in output related to increases in inputs the proportionate increase in a country's or company's output as a result of increases in all its inputs

revaluation CURRENCY & EXCHANGE increase in value of nation's currency a rise in the value of a country's currency in relation to other currencies

revaluation method ACCOUNTING asset depreciation using change in value over year a method of calculating the depreciation of assets by which the asset is depreciated by the difference in its value at the end of the year over its value at the beginning of the year

revaluation of assets ACCOUNTING asset depreciation using change in value since acquisition the revaluation of a company's **assets** to take account of inflation or changes in value since the assets were acquired. The change in value is credited to the **revaluation reserve account.**

revaluation of currency CURRENCY & EXCHANGE altering currency value to affect balance of payments an increase in the value of a currency in relation to others. In situations where there is a **floating exchange rate,** a currency will usually find its own level automatically but this will not happen if there is a **fixed exchange rate.** Should a government have persistent **balance of payments** surpluses, it may exceptionally decide to revalue its currency, making imports cheaper but its exports more expensive.

revaluation reserve CURRENCY & EXCHANGE money held to cover fluctuations in foreign currencies money set aside to account for the fact that the value of assets may vary as a result of accounting in different currencies

revaluation reserve account ACCOUNTING account for asset depreciation an account to which the change in value of a company's assets is credited during a **revaluation of assets**

revalue ACCOUNTING reassess value of something to value something again, usually setting a higher value on it than before

revenue FINANCE income from product or service the income generated by a product or service over a period of time

revenue account ACCOUNTING business account for recording income an account in a business used for recording receipts from sales, services, commissions, and other income associated with the business's activities

revenue anticipation note STOCKHOLDING & INVESTMENTS, TAX government means of raising money a government-issued **debt instrument** for which expected income from taxation is collateral

revenue bond STOCKHOLDING & INVESTMENTS US government bond a bond that a US state or a local government issues, to be repaid from the money made from the project financed with it

revenue center FINANCE center for generating income without costs a part of a business that raises revenue but has no responsibility for costs, for example, a sales center

revenue expenditure ACCOUNTING money spent on inventory purchases for current-year sale expenditure on purchasing stock, but not on capital items, which is then sold during the current accounting period

revenue ledger ACCOUNTING record of total income a record of all the income received by an organization. *Also called* ***sales ledger***

revenue officer TAX employee in tax office a person working in the government tax offices

revenue recognition ACCOUNTING determination of when income becomes revenue an accounting principle that determines when income is recognized as revenue. In **cash accounting**, revenue is recognized not when services were performed or products delivered but when payment is actually received. Following the **accrual concept**, revenue is recognized when payment is earned no matter when it is actually received.

revenue reserves FINANCE, ACCOUNTING undistributed earnings held as stockholders' funds **retained profits** that are shown in the company's balance sheet as part of the stockholders' funds

revenue sharing 1. TAX distribution of US federal taxes to states distribution to states by the federal government of money that it collects in taxes **2.** BUSINESS income sharing within limited partnerships the distribution of income within **limited partnerships**, where there are both general and limited partners

revenue stamp TAX stamp certifying receipt of tax payment a stamp that a government issues to certify that somebody has paid a tax

revenue tariff TAX national tax on imports or exports a tax levied on imports or exports to raise revenue for a national government

reversal FINANCE change in status a change to the opposite, for example, from being profitable to unprofitable, or, in the case of a stock price from rising to falling

reversal stop MARKETS price that triggers change between buying and selling a price at which a trader stops buying and starts selling a security, or vice versa

reverse leverage FINANCE **1.** higher expenditures than income a cash flow in which expenditures are higher than income **2.** borrowing at higher interest rate than investments pay the borrowing of money at a rate of interest higher than the expected rate of return on investing the money borrowed

reverse mortgage MORTGAGES arrangement using mortgage as collateral for annuity payment a financial arrangement in which a lender such as a bank takes over a mortgage and then pays an annuity to the homeowner

reverse split STOCKHOLDING & INVESTMENTS exchange of fewer new shares for old shares the issuing to stockholders of a fraction of one share for every share that they own. *See also* ***stock split***

reverse takeover MERGERS & ACQUISITIONS takeover by lesser company the **takeover** of a large company by a smaller one, or the takeover of a public company by a private one

reverse yield gap FINANCE, STOCKHOLDING & INVESTMENTS amount by which expenditure exceeds yield or income the amount by which bond yield exceeds equity yield, or interest rates on loans exceed rental values as a percentage of the costs of properties

reversing entry ACCOUNTING final debit or credit entry reversing earlier entry a debit or credit entry in a chart of accounts that is made at the end of an accounting period to reverse an entry

reversionary annuity PENSIONS annuity paid on person's death an annuity paid to somebody on the death of another person

reversionary bonus INSURANCE annual bonus on life assurance policy an annual bonus on a life assurance policy, declared by the insurer

revocable trust FINANCE trust that can be revoked a trust whose provisions can be amended or canceled

revolving charge account FINANCE account with renewable credit for buying goods a charge account with a company for use in buying that company's goods with **revolving credit**

revolving credit FINANCE = ***open-end credit***

revolving fund FINANCE fund receiving revenue from projects it finances a fund the resources of which are replenished from the revenue of the projects that it finances

revolving loan BANKING loan allowing money repaid to be borrowed again a loan facility whereby the borrower can choose the number and timing of withdrawals against their bank loan and any money repaid may be reborrowed at a future date. Such loans can be made available to both businesses and personal customers.

riba FINANCE interest charge or unfair profit in Islamic financing, interest or any unjust profit made by a lender in a financial transaction. It is one of three prohibitions in Islamic law, the others being **gharar** and **maysir**.

rider INSURANCE additional provision added to contract an additional clause or provision added to an insurance policy, which becomes part of the policy

RIE *abbr* MARKETS recognized investment exchange

rigged market MARKETS illegal trading practice to attract investors a market where two or more parties are buying and selling securities among themselves to give the impression of active trading with the intention of attracting investors to purchase the stocks. This practice is illegal in most jurisdictions.

right of survivorship LEGAL joint owner's right after death of other the right of a surviving joint owner of property to acquire the interest of a deceased joint owner

rights issue STOCKHOLDING & INVESTMENTS raising capital by offering existing stockholders additional stock the raising of new capital by giving existing stockholders the right to subscribe to new shares or **debentures** in proportion to their current holdings. These shares of stock are usually issued at a discount to market price. A stockholder not wishing to take up a rights issue may sell the rights. *Also called* ***rights offer***

  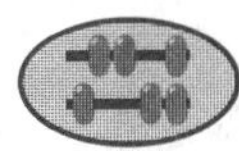   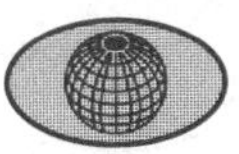 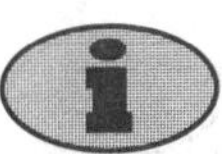  

rightsizing GENERAL MANAGEMENT restructuring of company to most effective size corporate restructuring, or rationalization, with the goal of reducing costs and improving efficiency and effectiveness. Rightsizing is often used as a euphemism for **downsizing**, or **delayering**, with the suggestion that it is not as far-reaching. Rightsizing can also be used to describe increasing the size of an organization, perhaps as an attempt to correct a previous downsizing, or delayering, exercise.

rights offer STOCKHOLDING & INVESTMENTS = ***rights issue***

rights offering STOCKHOLDING & INVESTMENTS offering additional stock to existing stockholders an offering for sale of a **rights issue**, in proportion to the holdings of existing stockholders

ring MARKETS **1.** trading floor a trading area at an exchange, especially a commodity exchange. *See also* ***pit*** **2.** session on London Metal Exchange a trading session on the **London Metal Exchange**, which deals in copper, lead, zinc, aluminum, tin, and nickel

ring-fence **1.** FINANCE separate profitable elements to safeguard business to separate valuable assets or profitable businesses from others in a group that are unprofitable and may make the whole group collapse **2.** FINANCE use money for specific projects to identify money from specific sources and only use it in agreed areas or for specific projects. *See also* ***hypothecation*** **3.** BUSINESS not let firm's liquidation affect others in group to allow one company within a group to go into liquidation without affecting the viability of the group as a whole or any other company within it

ring member MARKETS member of London Metal Exchange a member of the **London Metal Exchange**, dealing in copper, lead, zinc, aluminum, tin, and nickel

ring trading MARKETS business conducted on trading floor business conducted in the trading area of a commodity exchange

rising bottoms MARKETS graph showing stock's rising price following low prices a pattern on a graph of the price of a security or commodity against time that shows an upward price movement following a period of low prices (*slang*). *See also* ***chartist***

risk RISK **1.** possibility of suffering harm or loss the possibility of suffering damage or loss in the face of uncertainty about the outcome of actions, future events, or circumstances. Organizations are exposed to various types of risk, including damage to property, injury to personnel, financial loss, and legal liability. These may affect profitability, hinder the achievement of objectives, or lead to business interruption or failure. Risk may be deemed high or low, depending on the probability of an adverse outcome. Risks that can be quantified on the basis of past experience are insurable and those that cannot be calculated are uninsurable. **2.** potential for negative outcome a condition in which there exists a quantifiable dispersion in the possible outcomes from any activity

risk-adjusted return on capital STOCKHOLDING & INVESTMENTS, RISK return on capital evaluated in terms of risks return on capital calculated in a way that takes into account the risks associated with income. *Also called* ***Jensen's measure, Treynor ratio***

risk analysis RISK determination of how risks might affect organization the identification of risks to which an organization is exposed and the assessment of the potential impact of those risks on the organization. The goal of risk analysis is to identify and measure the risks associated with different courses of action in order to inform **decision making**. In the context of business decision making, risk analysis is especially used in investment decisions and capital investment appraisal. Risk analysis may be used to develop an organizational **risk profile**, and also may be the first stage in a **risk management** program.

risk arbitrage MARKETS, RISK trading without guaranteed profit simultaneous buying and selling without certainty of profit, though at relatively low risk. It is particularly employed by **hedge fund** managers.

risk arbitrageur RISK somebody engaged in risk arbitrage a person whose business is **risk arbitrage**

risk assessment RISK determination of how risky something is the determination of the level of risk in a specific course of action. Risk assessments are an important tool in areas such as health and safety management and environmental management. Results of a risk assessment can be used, for example, to identify areas in which safety can be improved. Risk assessment can also be used to determine more intangible forms of risk, including economic and social risk, and can inform the scenario planning process. The amount of risk involved in a specific course of action is compared to its expected benefits to provide evidence for decision making.

risk asset ratio BANKING, RISK proportion of assets that carry risk the proportion of a bank's total capital assets that carry risk. *See also* ***risk-weighted asset***

risk-averse STOCKHOLDING & INVESTMENTS, RISK having desire to avoid risk in investment wanting to achieve the best return that can be had on an investment while taking the least possible risk

risk aversion STOCKHOLDING & INVESTMENTS, RISK desire to avoid risk in investment a desire to achieve the best return that can be had on an investment while taking the least possible risk

risk-based capital assessment BANKING, RISK bank's value based on risk attached to assets an internationally approved system of calculating a bank's capital value by assessing the risk attached to its assets. Cash deposits and gold, for example, have no risk, while loans to less-developed countries have a high risk.

risk-bearing economy of scale BUSINESS, RISK employing diversification to reduce risk conducting business on such a large scale that the risk of loss is reduced because it is spread over so many independent events, as in the issuance of insurance policies

risk capital FINANCE, RISK = ***venture capital***

risk factor RISK degree of risk in enterprise the degree of risk in a project or other business activity

risk-free return STOCKHOLDING & INVESTMENTS, RISK money from safe investment the profit made from an investment that involves no risk

risk management RISK **1.** actions intended to reduce or eliminate risks the variety of activities undertaken by an organization to control and minimize threats to the continuing efficiency, profitability, and success of its operations. The process of risk management includes the identification and analysis of risks to which the organization is exposed, the assessment of potential impacts on the business, and deciding what action can be taken to eliminate or reduce risk and deal with the impact of unpredictable events causing loss or damage. Risk management strategies include taking out insurance against financial loss or legal liability and introducing safety or security measures. **2.** understanding and dealing with inevitable risks the process of understanding and managing the risks that an organization is inevitably subject to in attempting to achieve its corporate objectives. For management purposes, risks are usually divided into categories such as operational,

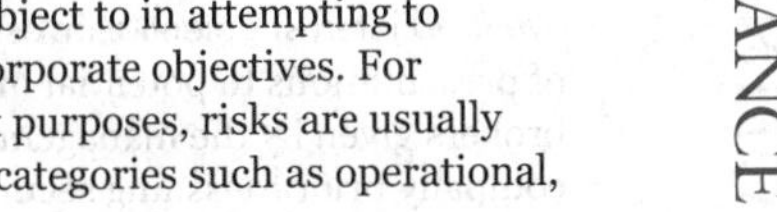

  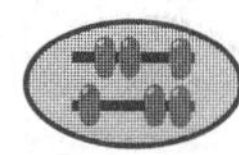 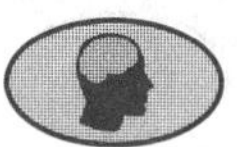  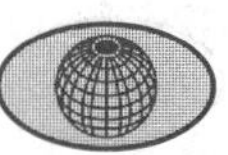   

financial, legal compliance, information, and personnel.

risk manager GENERAL MANAGEMENT, HR & PERSONNEL, RISK employee managing business risk the person in an organization who is in charge of assessing and managing business risks

risk perception RISK nonobjective view of risk the way in which people and organizations view risk, based on their concerns and experiences, but not necessarily on objective data. Risk perceptions can influence such things as business policies and investment decisions. *Also called* ***perception of risk***

risk premium FINANCE, RISK extra payment received by somebody taking risks an extra payment, for example, increased dividend or higher than usual profits, for taking risks

Risk Priority Number RISK number used to quantify risk a measure used in **Failure Mode and Effects Analysis** to quantify risk. It is a product of the severity, probability of occurrence, and ability to detect failure. *Abbr* **RPN**

risk profile RISK **1.** description of risks facing organization an outline of the risks to which an organization is exposed. An organizational risk profile may be developed in the course of **risk analysis** and used for **risk management**. It examines the nature of the threats faced by an organization, the likelihood of adverse effects occurring, and the level of disruption and costs associated with each type of risk. **2.** analysis of willingness to take risks an analysis of the willingness of individuals or organizations to take risks. A risk profile describes the level of risk considered acceptable by an individual or by the leaders of an organization, and considers how this will affect decision making and corporate strategy.

risk tolerance STOCKHOLDING & INVESTMENTS, RISK ability to withstand stress of investing the ability of an investor to handle the uncertainty and money losses inherent to investing

risk-weighted asset FINANCE, RISK asset weighted by its riskiness an asset weighted by factors relating to its riskiness, used by financial institutions in managing their capital requirements. *See also* ***risk asset ratio***

ROA *abbr* ACCOUNTING return on assets

road show STOCKHOLDING & INVESTMENTS events to interest potential investors a series of presentations to potential investors and brokers given by the management of a company prior to issuing securities, especially in an **initial public offering**, intended to create interest in the offering

ROC *abbr* ACCOUNTING return on capital

ROCE *abbr* ACCOUNTING return on capital employed

rocket scientist FINANCE innovative finance worker an employee of a financial institution who creates innovative securities that usually include derivatives (*slang*)

rodo kinko FINANCE Japanese provider of loans to small businesses in Japan, a financial institution that specializes in providing credit for small businesses

ROE *abbr* FINANCE return on equity

rogue trader MARKETS stock dealer acting illegally a dealer in stocks who uses illegal methods to make profits

ROI *abbr* FINANCE return on investment

ROIC *abbr* FINANCE return on invested capital

roll down MARKETS close then open option position at lower price to close a position on one option and open another at a lower **strike price**

rolled-up coupon *UK* STOCKHOLDING & INVESTMENTS interest coupon added to capital value of security an interest coupon on a security that is not paid out, but added to the capital value of the security

rolling account MARKETS stock exchange system with no fixed settlement days a system in which there are no fixed settlement days, but stock exchange transactions are paid at a fixed period after each transaction has taken place, as opposed to the UK system, in which a settlement day is fixed each month

rolling budget ACCOUNTING budget that moves with time a budget that moves forward on a regular basis, for example, a budget covering a twelve-month period that moves forward each month or quarter

roll-out MARKETING launch of program the full-scale implementation of an advertising campaign or marketing program

rollover FINANCE extension of credit or period of loan an extension of credit or of the period of a loan, though not necessarily on the same terms as previously

rollover IRA PENSIONS US personal retirement plan transferred to individual control in the United States, an **IRA** that is created when the assets of a **qualified retirement plan** arranged by an employer are transferred out of the employer-sponsored plan into an IRA managed by the owner of the plan. *Also called* ***conduit IRA***. *See also* ***traditional IRA***

roll up FINANCE loan payments including interest the addition of interest amounts to principal in loan payments

Romalpa clause LEGAL clause withholding title to goods pending full payment a clause in a contract whereby the seller provides that title to the goods does not pass to the buyer until the buyer has paid for them

RONA *abbr* FINANCE return on net assets

rort *ANZ* GENERAL MANAGEMENT (*slang*) **1.** dishonest practice an illegal or underhand strategy **2.** work a system to manipulate or break the rules of a system for personal gain

ROS *abbr* ACCOUNTING return on sales

Roth 401(k) PENSIONS employee plan with taxed contributions and untaxed payments in the United States, a qualified employee retirement plan, to which the employee contributes after-tax dollars but whose distributions are tax-exempt

Roth IRA PENSIONS personal plan with taxed contributions and untaxed payments in the United States, an **IRA** whose contributions unlike **traditional IRAs** are not tax-deductible, but whose distributions are tax-exempt

round figures FINANCE numbers adjusted to nearest 10, 100, 1,000, etc. figures that have been adjusted up or down to the nearest 10, 100, 1,000, and so on

rounding STATISTICS expressing number as simpler estimated value the practice of reducing the number of significant digits in a number, for example, expressing a figure that has four decimal places with only two decimal places

round lot MARKETS 100 shares of stock traded together a group of 100 shares of stock bought or sold together in one transaction

routing number BANKING = ***ABA routing number***

royalties FINANCE share of income paid to creator of product a proportion of the income from the sale of a product paid to its creator, for example, an inventor, author, or composer

RPB *abbr* BUSINESS recognized professional body

RPI *abbr* ECONOMICS retail price index

RPIX ECONOMICS indicator of inflation excluding mortgages in the United Kingdom, an index based on the **retail**

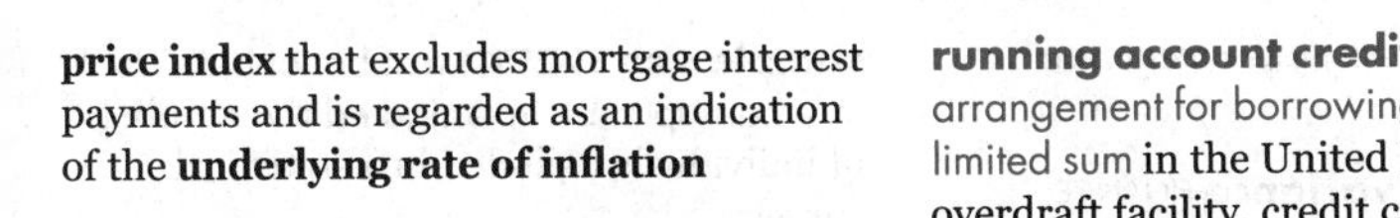
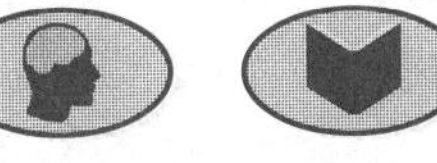
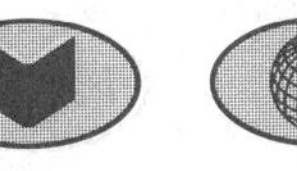
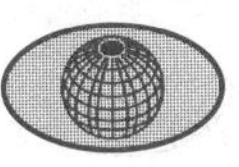
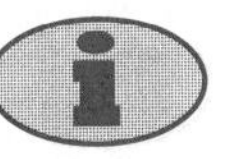

price index that excludes mortgage interest payments and is regarded as an indication of the **underlying rate of inflation**

RPIY ECONOMICS indicator of inflation excluding indirect tax and mortgages in the United Kingdom, an index based on the **retail price index** that excludes mortgage interest payments and indirect taxation

RPM *abbr* MARKETING resale price maintenance

RPN *abbr* RISK Risk Priority Number

R-squared STOCKHOLDING & INVESTMENTS benchmarked measure of investment performance a measure of how much of the performance of an investment can be explained by the performance of a **benchmark index**

rubber check BANKING check returned because of insufficient funds a check that cannot be cashed because the person writing it does not have enough money in the account to pay it (*slang*)

rule 144 REGULATION & COMPLIANCE rule on selling certain securities an **SEC** rule that specifies the conditions under which somebody holding **restricted** or **control securities** can sell them to the public

rule of 72 STOCKHOLDING & INVESTMENTS method of calculating growth of investment a calculation that an investment will double in value at compound interest after a period shown as 72 divided by the interest percentage, so interest at 10% compounded will double the capital invested in 7.2 years

rule of 78 STOCKHOLDING & INVESTMENTS calculation of interest rebate on loan repaid early a method used to calculate the rebate on a loan with front-loaded interest that has been repaid early. It takes into account the fact that as the loan is repaid, the share of each monthly payment related to interest decreases, while the share related to principal increases.

rumortrage *US* MARKETS securities trading based on rumor of takeover speculation in securities issued by companies that are rumored to be the target of an imminent takeover attempt (*slang*)

run 1. BANKING, CURRENCY & EXCHANGE simultaneous withdrawal of money by bank customers an incidence of bank customers, or owners of holdings in a specific currency, simultaneously withdrawing their entire funds because of a lack of confidence in the institution **2.** STATISTICS unbroken sequence in statistical series an uninterrupted sequence of the same value in a statistical series

running account credit BANKING UK arrangement for borrowing and reborrowing limited sum in the United Kingdom, an overdraft facility, credit card, or similar system that allows customers to borrow up to a specific limit and reborrow sums previously repaid by either writing a check or using their card

running costs ACCOUNTING = ***operating costs***

running total ACCOUNTING total carried over to next column a total carried from one column or set of figures to the next

running yield STOCKHOLDING & INVESTMENTS = ***current yield***

runoff MARKETS display of closing prices the process of displaying the closing prices of every stock on an exchange on the **ticker**

run-off STOCKHOLDING & INVESTMENTS reduction in value of mortgage-backed securities a decline in the value of **mortgage-backed securities**, caused by borrowers refinancing at lower interest rates or defaulting on their loans, resulting in losses by investors in the securities

SA *abbr* BUSINESS **1.** Sociedad Anónima **2.** Sociedade Anónima **3.** Société Anonyme

sack ◇ get the sack *UK* HR & PERSONNEL = ***get your pink slip*** (*informal*)

SADC or **SADEC** INTERNATIONAL TRADE organization for economic development in southern Africa an organization that aims to harmonize economic development in southern Africa. The member countries are Angola, Botswana, the Democratic Republic of the Congo, Lesotho, Malawi, Mauritius, Mozambique, Namibia, Seychelles, South Africa, Swaziland, Tanzania, Zambia, and Zimbabwe. *Full form **Southern African Development Community***

safe custody STOCKHOLDING & INVESTMENTS = ***safe keeping***

safe hands STOCKHOLDING & INVESTMENTS **1.** investors buying securities to hold for longer term investors who buy securities and are unlikely to sell in the short- to medium-term **2.** securities held by friendly investors securities held by investors who are not likely to sell them

safe investment STOCKHOLDING & INVESTMENTS investment unlikely to lose value an investment such as a bond that is not likely to fall in value

safe keeping STOCKHOLDING & INVESTMENTS holding by financial institutions of customers' valuable documents a service provided by a financial institution in which stock certificates, deeds, wills, or a locked deed box are held by it on behalf of customers. Securities are often held under the customer's name in a locked cabinet in the vault so that if the customer wishes to sell, the bank can forward the relevant certificate to the broker. A will is also usually held in this way so that it may be handed to the executor on the customer's death. Deed boxes are always described as "contents unknown to the bank." Most institutions charge a fee for this service. *Also called **safe custody***

safety margin OPERATIONS & PRODUCTION extra time or space allowed for safety an extra amount of time or space allowed to make sure that something can be done safely

SAIF *abbr* INSURANCE Savings Association Insurance Fund

salam FINANCE agreement to pay now for goods delivered later in Islamic financing, a contract for the purchase of goods to be delivered at a specified time in the future. Payment for the goods is made in advance.

salaried partner BUSINESS partner paid regular salary a partner, often a junior one, who receives a regular salary that is detailed in the partnership agreement

salary FINANCE monthly payment for work a form of pay given to employees at regular intervals in exchange for the work they have done. Traditionally, a salary is a form of remuneration given to professional employees on a monthly basis. In modern usage, the word refers to any form of pay that employees receive on a regular basis. A salary is usually paid straight into an employee's account.

salary ceiling HR & PERSONNEL **1.** top of relevant pay range the highest level in a pay range that an employee can achieve under his or her contract **2.** restriction on size of pay an upper limit on pay imposed by government or fixed according to labor union and employer agreements

salary reduction plan HR & PERSONNEL = ***flexible spending account***

salary reduction simplified employee pension PENSIONS voluntary pay deductions for pension in the United States, a **simplified employee pension plan** that is funded by voluntary employee salary reductions

salary review HR & PERSONNEL regular reconsideration of employee's pay a reassessment of an individual employee's

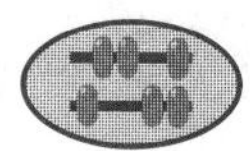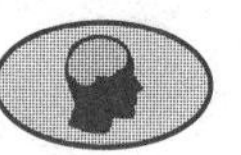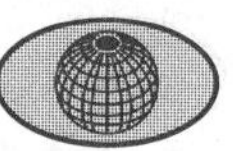

rate of pay, usually conducted on an annual basis

salary sacrifice scheme HR & PERSONNEL exchange of future pay rise for other benefit in the United Kingdom, an agreement between **employer** and **employees** by which the employees relinquish a right to future cash in exchange for a noncash benefit of some sort

sale and leaseback FINANCE seller's leasing of previously sold asset the leasing back by the former owner of an asset, usually buildings, that has been sold to a third party. *Also called* ***leaseback, renting back***

sale by tender FINANCE sale to party invited to make offer the sale of an asset to interested parties who have been invited to make an offer. The asset is sold to the party that makes the highest offer. *See also* ***tender***

sales MARKETING **1.** selling the activity of selling a company's products or services **2.** income from selling the income generated by selling a company's products or services **3.** department for selling the department within a company that deals with selling its products or services

sales analysis MARKETING examination of reports of poor sales an examination of the reports of sales to discover why items have or have not sold well

sales charge STOCKHOLDING & INVESTMENTS purchase fee on some mutual funds a fee charged to the purchaser of some types of mutual funds

sales figures MARKETING total amount of money spent by consumers the total amount of money spent by consumers, for example, in a particular product category, a particular region of the country, or within a particular time period. Sales figures are often used by analysts to judge how well an economy is doing.

sales force MARKETING team responsible for selling a group of salespeople or sales representatives responsible for the sales of either a single product or the entire range of an organization's products. *Also called* ***sales team***

sales forecast MARKETING estimation of future sales a prediction of future sales, based mainly on past sales performance. Sales forecasting takes into account the economic climate, current sales trends, company capacity for production, company policy, and **market research**. A sales forecast can be a good indicator of future sales in stable market conditions, but may be less reliable in times of rapid market change.

sales ledger ACCOUNTING = ***revenue ledger***

sales mix profit variance FINANCE varying profitability of products in range the differing profitability of different products within a product range

sales promotion MARKETING concentrated activities to sell product activities, usually short-term, designed to attract attention to a particular product and to increase its sales, using advertising and publicity. Sales promotion usually runs in conjunction with an advertising campaign that offers free samples or money-off coupons. The product may be offered at a reduced price and the campaign may be supported by additional telephone or door-to-door selling or by competitions. *Also called* ***promotion***

sales revenue FINANCE income from sales the income generated by sales of goods or services

sales tax US TAX tax on item sold, collected at purchase a tax that is paid on each item sold and is collected when the purchase is made. *UK term* ***VAT***. *Also called* ***turnover tax***

sales team MARKETING = ***sales force***

sales turnover FINANCE amount of sales in specific period the total amount sold within a specific time period, usually a year. Sales turnover is often expressed in monetary terms but can also be expressed in terms of the total amount of stock or products sold.

sales volume FINANCE number of items sold the number of units of a product sold

sales volume profit variance FINANCE difference between actual and forecast profits the difference between the profit on the number of units actually sold and the forecast figure

Sallie Mae FINANCE US company investing in student loans the largest source of student loans and administrator of college savings plans in the United States. Created in 1972 as a government-sponsored entity, it became completely privatized in 2004 and is a stockholder-owned company traded on the New York Stock Exchange. Sallie Mae purchases loans from lenders, pools them, and sells them to investors. *Full form* ***Student Loan Marketing Association***

salvage value ACCOUNTING = ***scrap value***

sample STATISTICS representative subgroup of larger group to be investigated a subset of a population in a statistical study chosen so that selected properties of the overall population can be investigated

sample size STATISTICS number of individuals in subgroup to be investigated the number of individuals included in a statistical survey

sample survey STATISTICS statistical analysis of subgroup of larger population a statistical study of a sample of individuals designed to collect information on specific subjects, such as buying habits or voting behavior

sampling 1. MARKETING providing free samples a sales promotion technique in which customers and prospects are offered a free sample of a product **2.** STATISTICS selecting representative subgroup from population under investigation the selection of a small proportion of a set of items being studied, from which valid inferences about the whole set or population can be made. Sampling makes it possible to obtain valid research results when it is impracticable to survey the whole population. The size of the sample needed for valid results depends on a number of factors, including the uniformity of the population being studied and the level of accuracy required. The technique is based on the laws of probability, and a number of different sampling methods can be used, including **random sampling** and **nonrandom sampling**.

sampling design STATISTICS plan for selecting representative subgroup the procedure by which a particular sample is chosen from a population

sampling error STATISTICS discrepancy between whole population and subgroup investigated the difference between the population characteristic being estimated in a statistical study and the result produced by the sample investigated

sampling units STATISTICS items chosen from whole population for investigation the items chosen for sampling from a larger population by a sampling design

sampling variation STATISTICS differences between various subgroups of same population variation between different samples of the same size taken from the same population

samurai bond STOCKHOLDING & INVESTMENTS bond sold by foreign institution in Japan a bond issue denominated in yen and issued in Japan by a foreign institution. *See also* ***shibosai bond, shogun bond***

sandbag MERGERS & ACQUISITIONS prolong negotiations in hostile takeover in a hostile **takeover** situation, to enter into talks with the bidder and attempt to prolong them as long as possible, in the hope that a **white knight** will appear and rescue the target company (*slang*)

     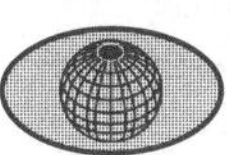   

S&L *abbr* BANKING savings and loan association

S&P *abbr* STOCKHOLDING & INVESTMENTS Standard & Poor's

S&P 500 *abbr* MARKETS Standard & Poor's 500 Index

S&P Index *abbr* MARKETS Standard & Poor's 500 Index

Santa Claus rally MARKETS year-end stock price rise a rise in stock prices in the last week of the year (*slang*). *Also called* ***year-end bounce***

Sarbanes-Oxley Act REGULATION & COMPLIANCE US law covering financial reporting and accountability a corporate governance law that came into effect in the United States in 2005. Created in the aftermath of a series of high-profile financial scandals, including Enron and WorldCom, Sarbanes-Oxley seeks to overhaul corporate financial reporting by improving its accuracy and reliability. Though it is an American law, its reach is global and has affected the way that large companies and audit firms do business. Chief executives are to take full responsibility for the accuracy of all financial results by signing a statement to that effect, thereby putting paid to the so-called "aw shucks" defense strategy adopted by senior executives involved in earlier financial scandals. Under this strategy, the accused maintained that they were simply not aware of the distortion of financial reporting that took place under their governance. *Abbr* **SOX**

sarf CURRENCY & EXCHANGE currency trading in Islamic financing, the buying and selling of currencies

SARL *abbr* BUSINESS société á responsabilité limitée

SARS *abbr* TAX South African Revenue Service

saucer MARKETS chart shape showing stock price rising from low a dish-shaped chart that indicates that the price of a stock has reached its low and is beginning to rise

Save as You Earn STOCKHOLDING & INVESTMENTS method of saving attracting tax relief in the United Kingdom, a system for employees to save on a regular basis toward buying shares in their company that is encouraged by the government through tax concessions. *Abbr* **SAYE**

savings FINANCE money reserved for future use money set aside by consumers for various purposes such as meeting contingencies or providing an income during retirement. Savings (money in deposit and savings accounts) differ from investments such as stocks in that they are not usually subject to price fluctuations and are thus considered safer. *Also called* ***liquid savings***

savings account BANKING account paying interest an account with a bank or savings and loan association that pays interest. *See also* ***fixed rate, gross interest, net interest***

savings and loan association BANKING chartered bank offering services for consumers in the United States, a **chartered bank** that offers savings accounts, pays dividends, and invests in new mortgages. *Abbr* **S&L**. *Also called* ***building and loan association***. *See also* ***thrift institution***

Savings Association Insurance Fund INSURANCE insurance for federal and state savings in the United States, an insurer of deposits in federal savings banks and federal and state savings and loan associations operated by the Federal Deposit Insurance Corporation. *Abbr* **SAIF**

savings bank BANKING bank managing small investments a bank that specializes in managing small deposits from customers with personal savings. *See also* ***thrift institution***

savings bond STOCKHOLDING & INVESTMENTS = ***US savings bond***

savings certificate STOCKHOLDING & INVESTMENTS = ***National Savings Certificate***

savings function ECONOMICS measurement of how much people will save an expression of the extent to which people save money instead of spending it

savings ratio ECONOMICS measurement of proportion of income saved the proportion of the income of a country or household that is saved in a particular period

savings-related share option scheme STOCKHOLDING & INVESTMENTS arrangement allowing UK employees to buy stock in the United Kingdom, an arrangement that allows employees of a company to buy company shares of stock with money which they have contributed to a savings scheme

SAYE *abbr* STOCKHOLDING & INVESTMENTS Save as You Earn

SC *abbr* REGULATION & COMPLIANCE Securities Commission

scale GENERAL MANAGEMENT system of graded levels a system that is graded into various levels

scalp MARKETS make profits on many quick trades to make many quick trades in a single day for many small gains

scarce currency CURRENCY & EXCHANGE money traded in foreign exchange market a currency that is traded in a foreign exchange market and for which demand is persistently high relative to its supply

scarcity ECONOMICS situation in which demand exceeds supply a situation in which the demand for something exceeds the supply. This can apply to anything from consumer goods to raw materials.

scarcity value FINANCE value of rare item in great demand the value something has because it is rare and a large demand exists for it

scatter STATISTICS how much observations differ from average observation the amount by which a set of observations deviates from its mean

scatter chart or **scatter diagram** or **scatter plot** STATISTICS graph showing relationship between variables a chart or diagram that plots a sample of values for two variables for a set of data, in two dimensions

scenario GENERAL MANAGEMENT postulated state of affairs or sequence of events a possible future state of affairs or sequence of events. Scenarios are imagined or projected on the basis of current circumstances and trends and expectations of change in the future.

scenario planning GENERAL MANAGEMENT imagining future conditions or events for planning strategy a technique that requires the use of a scenario in the process of strategic planning to aid the development of corporate strategy in the face of uncertainty about the future The process of identifying alternative scenarios of the future, based on a variety of differing assumptions, can help managers anticipate changes in the business environment and raise awareness of the frame of reference within which they are operating. The scenarios are then used to assist in both the development of strategies for dealing with unexpected events and the choice between alternative strategic options.

schedule 1. FINANCE long-term plan a plan of how an activity will be carried out over a period of time, drawn up in advance. For example, a repayment schedule sets out how debts will be paid. **2.** FINANCE list of interest rates a list of rates of interest that apply to a range of investments **3.** LEGAL list attached to contract a list, especially a list forming an additional document attached

   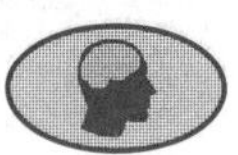  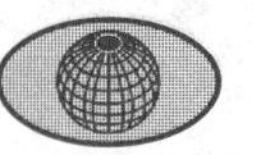   

to a contract **4.** TAX form relating to UK income tax in the United Kingdom, a form relating to a particular kind of income liable for income tax **5.** INSURANCE details of insurance cover details of the items covered by insurance, sent with the policy

scheme *UK* arrangement or method a plan, arrangement, or way of working

scheme of arrangement FINANCE UK plan for avoiding bankruptcy proceedings in the United Kingdom, a plan offering ways of paying debts, drawn up by a person or company to avoid bankruptcy proceedings

scientific management GENERAL MANAGEMENT, HR & PERSONNEL managing using systematic approaches an analytical approach to managing activities by optimizing efficiency and productivity through measurement and control. Scientific management theories were dominant in the 20th century, and many management techniques such as **benchmarking**, **total quality management**, and **business process reengineering** result from a scientific management approach.

scrap value ACCOUNTING value of asset if scrapped the value of an asset if it is sold for scrap. *Also called* ***salvage value***

screening study STATISTICS statistical investigation of prevalence of particular disease a medical statistical study of a population, conducted to investigate the prevalence of a disease

scrip MARKETS security or certificate for it a security, for example, a share or bond, or the certificate issued to show that somebody has been allotted such a security

scrip dividend STOCKHOLDING & INVESTMENTS dividend paid with stock a dividend paid by the issue of additional company shares, rather than by cash

scrip issue *UK* STOCKHOLDING & INVESTMENTS = ***stock split***

scripophily STOCKHOLDING & INVESTMENTS collecting of old stocks and bonds the collecting of stock or bond certificates that have been canceled, for their historical, aesthetic, or rarity value

Sdn *abbr* BUSINESS Sendirian

SDR *abbr* CURRENCY & EXCHANGE Special Drawing Right

SEAQ MARKETS London Stock Exchange's system for UK securities transactions the London Stock Exchange's system for UK securities. It is a continuously updated computer database of quotations that also records prices at which transactions have been struck. *Full form* ***Stock Exchange Automated Quotations system***

SEAQ International MARKETS London Stock Exchange's system for overseas securities transactions the London Stock Exchange's system for overseas securities. It is a continuously updated computer database of quotations that also records prices at which transactions have been struck. *Full form* ***Stock Exchange Automated Quotations system International***

seasonal adjustment ACCOUNTING accounts adjustment for seasonal distortion of figures an adjustment made to accounts to allow for any short-term seasonal factors such as Christmas sales that may distort the figures

seasonal business BUSINESS trade influenced by time of year trade that is affected by seasonal factors, for example, trade in goods such as suntan products or Christmas trees

seasonality OPERATIONS & PRODUCTION situation in which business varies between seasons variations in production or sales that occur at different but predictable times of the year

seasonal products MARKETING items sold at particular time of year products that are only marketed at particular times of the year, for example, Christmas trees or fireworks

seasonal unemployment HR & PERSONNEL unemployment that changes with seasons unemployment that rises and falls according to the season

seasonal variation STATISTICS changes in data based on time of year the variation of data according to specific times of the year such as the winter months or a tourist season

seasoned equity STOCKHOLDING & INVESTMENTS stocks traded for 90 days stocks that have traded for more than 90 days on a regulated market, long enough to be purchased by **retail investors**

seasoned issue STOCKHOLDING & INVESTMENTS offering from established company a stock issue that has traded for more than 90 days on a regulated market, long enough to be purchased by **retail investors**. *See also* ***unseasoned issue***

seat MARKETS stock exchange membership membership in a stock exchange

SEATS MARKETS Australian Stock Exchange's electronic trading system the electronic screen-trading system operated by the Australian Stock Exchange. It was introduced in 1987. *Full form* ***Stock Exchange Automatic Trading System***

SEC *abbr* REGULATION & COMPLIANCE Securities and Exchange Commission

SEC fee STOCKHOLDING & INVESTMENTS US SEC trading fee in the United States, a small fee that the Securities and Exchange Commission charges for the sale of securities listed on a stock exchange

secondary bank BANKING finance company funding installment-plan deals a finance company that provides money for installment-plan deals

secondary industry OPERATIONS & PRODUCTION industry manufacturing goods from raw materials an industry that uses basic raw materials to produce manufactured goods

secondary issue STOCKHOLDING & INVESTMENTS offer of already traded stock an offer of listed stocks that have previously been publicly traded

secondary market MARKETS market buying and selling other than new issues a market that trades in existing stocks rather than new stock issues, for example, a stock exchange. The money earned from these sales goes to the dealer or investor, not to the issuer. *See also* ***primary market***

secondary offering MARKETS offering of securities already on market an offering of securities of a kind that is already on the market

secondary product OPERATIONS & PRODUCTION product made from raw materials a product that has been processed from raw materials. *See also* ***primary product***

Secondary Tax on Companies TAX *see* ***STC***

second half ACCOUNTING second 6-month period in fiscal year the period of six months that is the second part of any fiscal year

secondment HR & PERSONNEL temporary assignment to work elsewhere in the United Kingdom, the temporary transfer of a member of staff to another organization for a defined length of time, usually for a specific purpose. Secondment has grown in popularity in recent years, primarily for career development purposes. Secondments between the public and private sectors have been used as a mechanism to share management techniques and to disseminate best practice.

second mortgage MORTGAGES loan using already-mortgaged property as collateral a loan that uses the equity on a mortgaged property as security and is taken out with a

  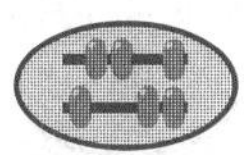   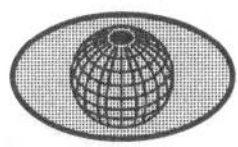   

different lender from the first mortgage. The second mortgagee has to record its interest and cannot be paid off on foreclosure until the first mortgagee is paid off.

second quarter ACCOUNTING second of four divisions of fiscal year the period of three months from April to the end of June, or the period of three months following the first quarter of the fiscal year. *Abbr* **Q2**

second-tier market MARKETS more informal financial market than main market a market in stocks where the listing requirements are less onerous than for the main market, as in, for example, London's **Alternative Investment Market**

secretary of the board CORPORATE GOVERNANCE *see* ***company secretary***

Secretary of the Treasury FINANCE US government official overseeing finance a senior member of the US government in charge of financial affairs

secret reserves FINANCE = ***hidden reserves***

Section 21 company BUSINESS S. African nonprofit organization in the Republic of South Africa, a company established as a nonprofit organization

sector 1. ECONOMICS businesses in economy providing similar products or services a part of the economy in which businesses produce the same type of product or provide the same type of service
2. STOCKHOLDING & INVESTMENTS securities in particular industry or market a group of securities in one type of industry or market, for example, the banking sector or the industrial sector

sector fund STOCKHOLDING & INVESTMENTS fund invested in a particular sector a fund that is invested in only one sector of the stock market

sector index MARKETS list of firms specializing in specific markets an index of companies specializing in specific markets whose stocks are listed on a general or specialist stock exchange

secular STOCKHOLDING & INVESTMENTS developing over many years underlying movement over a long period, usually a number of years

secular trend STATISTICS pattern of change in data collected over time the underlying development of a series of measurements collected over a time period of several years to assess long-term trends and seasonal fluctuations

secured FINANCE *see* ***collateral, security***

secured bond STOCKHOLDING & INVESTMENTS bond with asset as collateral a bond for which real estate or goods have been pledged as collateral

secured creditor FINANCE creditor with legal claim on defaulting debtor's assets a person or organization that is owed money and has a legal claim to some or all of the borrower's assets if the borrower fails to repay the money owed

secured debt FINANCE debt backed by assets a debt that is guaranteed by assets that have been pledged. *See also* ***unsecured debt***

secured loan FINANCE loan guaranteed by borrower's assets as security a loan that is guaranteed by the borrower giving assets as security

secure server E-COMMERCE computer system protecting card transactions over Internet a combination of hardware and software that secures e-commerce credit card transactions so that there is no risk of unauthorized people gaining access to credit card details online

securities account TREASURY MANAGEMENT account record of financial assets an account that shows the value of financial assets held by a person or organization

securities analyst FINANCE professional studying effectiveness of firms and their securities a professional person who studies the performance of securities and the companies that issue them

Securities and Exchange Commission REGULATION & COMPLIANCE US agency overseeing financial transactions of public companies the US government agency responsible for establishing standards of financial reporting and accounting for public companies. *Abbr* **SEC**

Securities and Futures Authority REGULATION & COMPLIANCE US organization for supervising financial advisers and facilitators in the United States, a self-regulatory organization responsible for supervising the activities of institutions advising on corporate finance activity, or dealing or facilitating deals in securities or derivatives. *Abbr* **SFA**

Securities and Investments Board REGULATION & COMPLIANCE former UK organization regulating securities markets in the United Kingdom, the organization that formerly had the responsibility of regulating the securities markets, now superseded by the FSA. *Abbr* **SIB**

Securities Commission REGULATION & COMPLIANCE New Zealand monitoring organization for securities market a statutory body responsible for monitoring standards in the New Zealand securities markets and for promoting investment in New Zealand. *Abbr* **SC**

securities deposit account BANKING electronic deposit account for securities a brokerage account in which deposits of securities are registered electronically, without receipt of an actual certificate

Securities Institute of Australia FINANCE organization of Australian financial industry professionals a national professional body that represents people involved in the Australian securities and financial services industry. *Abbr* **SIA**

Securities Investor Protection Corporation INSURANCE US corporation insuring clients of securities firms in the United States, a corporation created by Congress in 1970 that is a mutual insurance fund established to protect clients of securities firms. In the event of a firm being closed because of bankruptcy or financial difficulties, the corporation will step in to recover clients' cash and securities held by the firm. Its reserves are available to satisfy cash and securities that cannot be recovered up to a maximum of $500,000, including a maximum of $100,000 on cash claims. *Abbr* **SIPC**

securities lending FINANCE lending of securities between brokers the loan of securities from one broker to another in the process of **selling short**

securitization MORTGAGES, STOCKHOLDING & INVESTMENTS changing debt into securities the process of changing financial assets such as mortgages and loans into securities. The practice of selling mortgages to investors by repackaging the loans as **loan notes** paying a rate of interest that international banks and fund managers found attractive became widespread and eventually contributed to the financial difficulties experienced by banks and other financial institutions worldwide in 2008.

securitized mortgage STOCKHOLDING & INVESTMENTS mortgage exchanged for securities a mortgage that has been converted into securities. *See also* ***securitization***

securitized paper STOCKHOLDING & INVESTMENTS documents representing securitization the **bond** or **promissory note** resulting from changing financial **assets** such as mortgages and loans into **securities**

  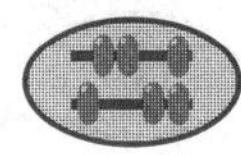 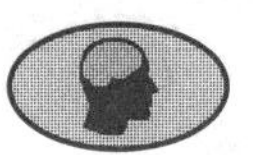  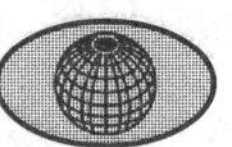   

security **1.** STOCKHOLDING & INVESTMENTS financial asset that can be bought and sold a tradable financial asset, for example, a bond, stock, or a warrant **2.** FINANCE guarantee of payment of debt an asset pledged as collateral for a loan or other borrowing

security deposit FINANCE deposit forfeited in transaction if buyer backs out an amount of money paid before a transaction occurs to compensate the seller in the event that the transaction is not concluded because the buyer defaults

security investment company MARKETS firm engaged in securities trading a financial institution that specializes in the analysis and trading of securities

security printer FINANCE printer of valuable documents a printer who prints paper money, stock prospectuses, and confidential government documents

seed capital or **seed money** FINANCE money needed to start new business a usually modest amount of money used to convert an idea into a viable business. Seed capital is a form of **venture capital**.

segmentation STATISTICS separating statistical data into categories the division of the data in a study into categories

seigniorage CURRENCY & EXCHANGE difference between money's production cost and its value the difference between the cost of producing a currency and the face value of the currency. If the money is worth more than it cost to produce, the government makes a profit.

selection bias STATISTICS distortion of data by unmeasured variables in a statistical study, the distorting effect on variables of the methods that have been used to collect the data

selective pricing FINANCE pricing according to market setting different prices for the same product or service in different markets. This practice can be broken down as follows: category pricing, which involves cosmetically modifying a product such that the variations allow it to sell in a number of price categories; customer group pricing, which involves modifying the price of a product or service so that different groups of consumers pay different prices; peak pricing, setting a price which varies according to the level of demand; and service level pricing, setting a price based on the specific level of service chosen from a range.

self-assessment TAX UK system allowing taxpayers to estimate taxes owed in the United Kingdom, a system that enables taxpayers to assess their own income tax and capital gains tax payments for the fiscal year

self-certification FINANCE borrower's unconfirmed statement of income a statement by a borrower of their income, without confirmation by an employer or accountant, made in order to obtain a loan

self-certified mortgage MORTGAGES mortgage granted based on borrower's statement of income a mortgage granted on the basis of a borrower's statement of their income rather than an employer's or accountant's statement. Self-certified mortgages are usually granted to self-employed people whose income varies during the year but who have good credit ratings.

self-employed HR & PERSONNEL working but not on any firm's payroll working for yourself, or not on the payroll of a company

self-financing FINANCE financing of project from own resources the process by which a company finances a project or business activity from its own resources, rather than by applying for external financing

self-insurance INSURANCE setting money aside for possible loss the practice of saving money to pay for a possible loss rather than taking out an insurance policy against it

Self Invested Personal Pension Plan PENSIONS UK pension plan with great freedom of investment in the United Kingdom, a pension plan that allows the holder a much wider choice of investments than a conventional plan, and allows the investments to be held directly rather than by a third party. The plan holder can control the investment strategy or can appoint a fund manager or stockbroker to manage the fund. *Abbr* **SIPP**

self-liquidating FINANCE paying for itself providing enough income to pay off the amount borrowed for financing

self-liquidating premium MARKETING self-financing promotional technique a sales promotion technique that pays for itself, in which customers send money and vouchers or proof of purchase to obtain a premium gift

self-liquidating promotion MARKETING self-financing sales activity a sales promotion in which the cost of the campaign is covered by the incremental revenue generated by the promotion

self-regulation REGULATION & COMPLIANCE regulation of industry by own members the regulation of an industry by its own members, usually by means of a committee that issues guidance and sets standards that it then enforces

self-regulatory organization REGULATION & COMPLIANCE **1.** in US, organization that is its own authority in the United States, an organization that polices its own members, for example, a stock exchange **2.** in UK, professional body responsible for financial activities in the United Kingdom, a professional body licensed by the **FSA** and responsible for policing the range of investment activities undertaken by its members, ensuring that compensation is available in cases of negligence or fraud, and ensuring that there is sufficient professional indemnity ► *Abbr* **SRO**

self-tender STOCKHOLDING & INVESTMENTS US firm's offer to buy back stock in the United States, the repurchase by a corporation of its stock by way of a tender

sell and build GENERAL MANAGEMENT practice of only producing when order paid for an approach to manufacturing in which the producer creates a product only when a customer has placed an order and paid for it, rather than creating and stocking products that have not been ordered

seller's market MARKETS market in which sellers can get top price a market in which sellers can dictate prices, typically because demand is high or there is a product shortage

selling costs or **selling overhead** OPERATIONS & PRODUCTION expenses involved in selling something the amount of money needed for the advertising, sales representatives' commissions, and other expenses involved in selling something

selling price OPERATIONS & PRODUCTION price at which something is sold the price at which somebody is willing to sell something

selling price variance OPERATIONS & PRODUCTION discrepancy between actual and planned selling prices the difference between the actual selling price and the budgeted selling price

selling season MARKETS good time for selling a period in which market conditions are favorable to sellers

sell-off MARKETS wave of selling that lowers security's price rapid or widespread selling that causes a sudden drop in the price of a security or a drop in a market

sell short MARKETS sell borrowed security anticipating price drop to sell commodities, currencies, or securities that have been borrowed from a third party in the

   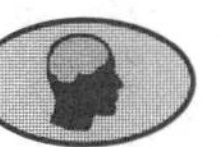  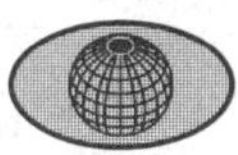   

expectation that prices will fall before the commodities, currencies, or securities are bought back and the loan redeemed, so ensuring a profit *Also called* ***short*** *(sense 3)*

semiannual FINANCE paying or payable twice a year paying, or requiring payment, every six months

semi-variable cost or **semi-fixed cost** OPERATIONS & PRODUCTION production costs that vary somewhat according to quantity the amount of money paid to produce a product, which increases, though less than proportionally, with the quantity of the product made

Sendirian BUSINESS "Limited," in company name the Malay term for "limited." Companies can use "Sendirian Berhad" or "Sdn Bhd" in their name instead of "plc." *Abbr* **Sdn**

senior capital FINANCE loan capital with priority for payment capital in the form of **secured loans** to a company that, in the event of liquidation, is repaid before **junior capital** such as stockholders' equity

senior debt FINANCE debt with higher claim on assets than others a debt whose holder has more claim on the debtor's assets than the holder of another debt. *See also* ***junior debt***

senior management GENERAL MANAGEMENT, HR & PERSONNEL those at top level of organization the managers and executives at the highest level of an organization. Senior management includes the **board of directors**. Senior management has responsibility for **corporate governance**, **corporate strategy**, and the interests of all the organization's **stakeholders**. *Also called* ***management team***

senior mortgage MORTGAGES mortgage with higher claim on assets than others a mortgage whose holder has more claim on the debtor's assets than the holder of another mortgage with the same mortgagee. *See also* ***junior mortgage***

sensitivity analysis ACCOUNTING analysis of effect of small adjustments to calculation the analysis of the effect of a small change in a calculation on the final result

SEP *abbr* PENSIONS simplified employee pension plan

separable net assets ACCOUNTING assets that can be sold separately assets that can be separated from the rest of the assets of a business and sold off

sequestration LEGAL act of seizing property by court order the act of taking and keeping property on the order of a court, especially of seizing property from somebody who is in contempt of court

sequestrator LEGAL person seizing property by court order a person who takes and keeps property on the order of a court

serial correlation STATISTICS correlation of variable over period of time the correlation of a variable with itself over different points in time, used as an indicator of the future performance of something such as a security or economy. *Also called* ***autocorrelation***

serial entrepreneur BUSINESS person who repeatedly starts new enterprises an **entrepreneur** who sets up a string of new ventures, one after the other

seriation STATISTICS arrangement of objects in series the process of arranging a set of objects in a series on the basis of similarities or dissimilarities

series STOCKHOLDING & INVESTMENTS bonds or savings certificates issued over time a group of bonds or savings certificates, issued over a period of time but all bearing the same interest

Serious Fraud Office REGULATION & COMPLIANCE UK government department investigating major commercial fraud in the United Kingdom, a government department in charge of investigating major fraud in companies. *Abbr* **SFO**

SERPS PENSIONS UK plan for earnings-related pensions in the United Kingdom, a state program that was designed to pay retired employees an additional pension to the standard state pension. It was replaced by the **State Second Pension.** *Full form* ***State Earnings-Related Pension Scheme***

service MARKETING system or activity meeting need any activity with a mix of tangible and intangible outcomes that is offered to a market with the goal of satisfying a customer's need or desire. Early marketing tended to distinguish a service from a physical good, but more recently these two have been seen as interrelated because service delivery frequently has physical aspects. For example, in a restaurant, service is provided by a waiter but physical goods, such as the food and the dining room, are also involved. In modern marketing, all forms of services and goods can be seen as products.

service charge **1.** FINANCE, BANKING sum or additional sum paid for service a fee for any service provided, or an additional fee for any improvements to an existing service. For example, residents in apartment buildings may pay an annual maintenance fee, or banks may charge a fee for operating an account or obtaining foreign currency for customers (also called a **bank charge**). **2.** MARKETING payment to serving staff a gratuity usually paid in restaurants and hotels. A service charge may be voluntary or may be added as a percentage to the bill.

service contract HR & PERSONNEL employment contract for senior executive a contract of employment for executive directors that lays down the conditions of employment and details of any bonus that may be paid, and outlines the procedure for ending employment

service cost center FINANCE cost center serving other cost centers in organization a cost center providing services to other cost centers. When the output of an organization is a service rather than goods, an alternative name is usually used, for example, support cost center or utility cost center.

service/function costing ACCOUNTING cost accounting for services within organization **cost accounting** for services or functions, for example, canteens, maintenance, or personnel

service industry BUSINESS industry specializing in service not products an industry that does not make products, but instead offers a service such as banking, insurance, or transport

service level agreement LEGAL contract giving details of service to be performed a contract between a service provider and a customer that specifies in detail the level of service (quality, frequency, flexibility, charges, etc.) to be provided over the contract period, as well as the procedures to implement in the case of default

servicing borrowing FINANCE paying interest the process of paying the interest that is due on a loan

set-aside ACCOUNTING = ***reserves***

set-off FINANCE offset of debts or loss against gain an agreement between two parties to balance one debt against another or a loss against a gain

settle STOCKHOLDING & INVESTMENTS finalize security sale to transfer property such as securities from a seller to a buyer in return for payment

settlement **1.** FINANCE payment the payment of an outstanding debt, invoice, account, or charge **2.** STOCKHOLDING & INVESTMENTS finalizing security sale the transfer of property such as securities from a seller to a buyer in return for payment

3. E-COMMERCE transfer of payment to account of e-business the portion of an electronic transaction during which the customer's credit card is charged for the transaction and the proceeds are deposited into the **merchant account**

settlement date FINANCE due date for paying debt or charge the date on which an outstanding debt or charge is due to be paid, or when cash offered for securities or derivatives of them must be delivered

settlement day MARKETS **1.** in UK, final day for paying for stock in the United Kingdom, the day on which shares of stock bought must be paid for. On the London Stock Exchange the account period is three business days from the day of trade. **2.** in US, day when securities become purchaser's property in the United States, the day on which securities bought actually become the property of the purchaser

setup costs ACCOUNTING amount spent to make equipment usable the costs associated with making a workstation or equipment available for use. Setup costs include the personnel needed to set up the equipment, the cost of downtime during a new setup, and the resources and time needed to test the new setup to achieve the specification of the parts or materials produced.

setup fees E-COMMERCE amount spent arranging to accept Internet payments the costs associated with establishing a **merchant account**, for example, application and software licensing fees and point-of-sale equipment purchases

setup time OPERATIONS & PRODUCTION time spent to make equipment fully productive the time it takes to prepare, calibrate, and test a piece of equipment to produce a required output

seven-day money MARKETS money-market funds with seven-day term funds that have been placed on the money market for a term of seven days

severally LEGAL not jointly as separate individuals or entities, not jointly

severance *US* HR & PERSONNEL dismissal or discharge from employment dismissal from employment because the job or worker is considered no longer necessary. *UK term* ***redundancy***

severance package *US* HR & PERSONNEL benefits for dismissed or discharged employee a package of benefits that an employer gives to an employee who is dismissed. *UK term* ***redundancy package***

severance pay *US* FINANCE payment to dismissed or discharged employee a payment made by an employer to an employee when the employee who has been dismissed or discharged leaves the organization. *Also called* ***unemployment compensation***. *UK term* ***redundancy payment***

SFA *abbr* REGULATION & COMPLIANCE Securities and Futures Authority

SFAS *abbr* REGULATION & COMPLIANCE Statement of Financial Accounting Standards

SFE *abbr* MARKETS Sydney Futures Exchange

SFO *abbr* REGULATION & COMPLIANCE Serious Fraud Office

SGX *abbr* MARKETS Singapore Exchange

shadow economy ECONOMICS = ***black economy***

shadow market MARKETS = ***black market***

shadow price ECONOMICS estimated cost of new economic activity the amount that engaging in a new economic activity is likely to cost a person or an economy. *See also* ***opportunity cost***

shakeout MARKETS exiting of timid investors during financial crisis the elimination of weak or cautious investors during a crisis in the financial market (*slang*)

share STOCKHOLDING & INVESTMENTS = ***stock***

share account **1.** STOCKHOLDING & INVESTMENTS account with credit union paying dividends in the United States, an account with a credit union that pays dividends rather than interest **2.** BANKING member's account in UK building society in the United Kingdom, an account at a building society where the account holder is a member of the society. Account holders who are not members are offered a deposit account. *See also* ***deposit account***

share at par STOCKHOLDING & INVESTMENTS stock valued at face value a share whose value on the stock market is the same as its face value

share buyback STOCKHOLDING & INVESTMENTS = ***buyback***

share capital STOCKHOLDING & INVESTMENTS capital from sale of stock the amount of **nominal share capital** that a company raises by issuing shares of stock. Share capital does not reflect any subsequent increase or decrease in the value of stock sold; it is capital raised, irrespective of changes in stock value in the secondary markets. *Also called* ***issued capital***. *See also* ***stockholders' equity, reserves***

share certificate *UK* STOCKHOLDING & INVESTMENTS = ***stock certificate***

shared drop MARKETING delivery of simultaneous promotional offers a sales promotion technique in which a number of promotional offers are delivered by hand to **prospects** at the same time

shared values GENERAL MANAGEMENT = ***core values***

share exchange STOCKHOLDING & INVESTMENTS exchange of individual stockholdings for shares in fund a service provided by some collective investment plans whereby they exchange investors' existing individual stockholdings for shares in their funds. This saves the investor the expense of selling holdings, which can be uneconomical when dealing with small stockholdings.

share-for-share offer STOCKHOLDING & INVESTMENTS bidder's offer of shares as payment for company a type of **takeover bid** where the bidder offers its own shares, or a combination of cash and shares, for the target company

shareholder STOCKHOLDING & INVESTMENTS **1.** somebody owning stock in corporation a person or organization that owns shares in a limited company or partnership. A shareholder has a stake in the company and becomes a member of it, with rights to attend the **annual meeting**. Since shareholders have invested money in a company, they have a vested interest in its performance and can be a powerful influence on company policy; they should consequently be considered **stakeholders** as well as shareholders. Some pressure groups have sought to exploit this by becoming shareholders in order to get a particular viewpoint or message across. At the same time, in order to maintain or increase the company's market value, managers must consider their responsibility to shareholders when formulating strategy. It has been argued that on some occasions the desire to make profits to raise returns for shareholders has damaged companies, because it has limited the amount of money spent in other areas (such as the development of facilities, or health and safety). *Also called* ***stockholder*** **2.** participant in pooled investment a person who owns shares of a fund or **investment trust**

shareholders' equity or **shareholders' funds** STOCKHOLDING & INVESTMENTS = ***stockholders' equity***

shareholders' perks STOCKHOLDING & INVESTMENTS benefits for stockholders besides dividends benefits offered to stockholders in addition to dividends, often in the form of discounts on the company's products

   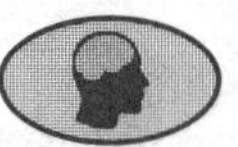  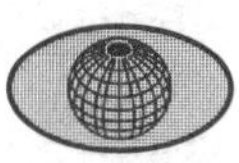   

and services. *Also called* ***stockholder perks***

shareholder value STOCKHOLDING & INVESTMENTS total return to stockholders including dividends and appreciation the total return to the stockholders in terms of both dividends and share price growth, calculated as the present value of future free cash flows of the business discounted at the weighted average cost of the capital of the business less the market value of its debt. *Also called* ***stockholder value***

shareholder value analysis STOCKHOLDING & INVESTMENTS firm's value based on return to stockholders a calculation of the value of a company made by looking at the returns it gives to its stockholders. *Abbr* **SVA**. *Also called* ***stockholder value analysis***

shareholding *UK* STOCKHOLDING & INVESTMENTS = ***stockholding***

share incentive scheme *UK* HR & PERSONNEL = ***stock incentive plan***

share index *UK* MARKETS = ***index***

share issue STOCKHOLDING & INVESTMENTS offer to sell shares in business the offering for sale of shares in a business. The capital derived from share issues can be used for investment in the core business or for expansion into new commercial ventures.

share of voice MARKETING comparative amount spent on advertising an individual company's proportion of the total advertising expenditure in a sector

share option *UK* STOCKHOLDING & INVESTMENTS = ***stock option***

share option scheme *UK* STOCKHOLDING & INVESTMENTS = ***stock option plan***

shareowner STOCKHOLDING & INVESTMENTS = ***shareholder***

share premium STOCKHOLDING & INVESTMENTS amount paid for share above declared value the amount payable for a share above its **nominal value**. Most shares are issued at a **premium** to their nominal value. Share premiums are credited to the company's **share premium account**.

share premium account ACCOUNTING account where firms credit share premiums the special reserve in a company's balance sheet to which **share premiums** are credited. Expenses associated with the issue of shares may be written off to this account.

share register STOCKHOLDING & INVESTMENTS list of stockholders a list of the stockholders in a particular company

share shop STOCKHOLDING & INVESTMENTS office where stock is traded the name given by some financial institutions to an office open to the public where stock may be bought and sold

shares of negligible value STOCKHOLDING & INVESTMENTS worthless shares in defunct firm shares that are considered as having no value in income tax terms because the company has ceased to exist. The shares of companies in receivership are not deemed to be of negligible value, although they may eventually end up as such.

share split STOCKHOLDING & INVESTMENTS = ***stock split***

share tip *UK* STOCKHOLDING & INVESTMENTS = ***stock tip***

Share Transactions Totally Electronic MARKETS *see* ***STRATE***

shareware E-COMMERCE program available free but chargeable for continued use software distributed free of charge, but usually with a request that users pay a small fee if they like the program

share warrant STOCKHOLDING & INVESTMENTS document stating right to hold stock a document stating that somebody has the right to a number of shares of stock in a company

sharia or **shariah** LEGAL = ***Islamic law***

sharia-compliant FINANCE in accordance with Islamic law used to describe financial activities and investments that comply with Islamic law, which prohibits the charging of interest and involvement in any enterprise associated with activities or products forbidden by Islamic law

shark watcher *US* MARKETS firm that identifies takeover targets a firm that specializes in monitoring the stock market for potential takeover activity (*slang*)

Sharpe ratio STOCKHOLDING & INVESTMENTS formula for calculating relationship between risk and return a method of determining the relationship between investment risk and return, calculated by subtracting the return on a risk-free investment from the rate of return on a portfolio of investments and dividing the result by the standard deviation of the return

sharp practice FRAUD underhand business methods business methods that are not illegal but are not entirely open and honest

shelf registration STOCKHOLDING & INVESTMENTS in US, statement registering future securities sale in the United States, a **registration statement** filed with the **Securities and Exchange Commission** two years before a corporation issues securities to the public. The statement, which has to be updated periodically, allows the corporation to act quickly when it considers that the market conditions are right without having to start the registration procedure from scratch.

shelfspace MARKETING area available for product in store the amount of space allocated to a product in a retail outlet

shell company BUSINESS registered firm whose shares no longer trade a company that has ceased to trade but is still registered, especially one sold to enable the buyer to begin trading without having to establish a new company

shibosai STOCKHOLDING & INVESTMENTS sale of securities direct to investors the Japanese term for a **private placement**, which is the sale of securities direct to institutions for investment rather than resale

shibosai bond STOCKHOLDING & INVESTMENTS yen-denominated bond sold direct by issuing company a bond denominated in yen sold direct to investors by the foreign issuing company. *See also* ***samurai bond, shogun bond***

shift differential FINANCE extra pay for working unpopular shift payment made to employees over and above their basic rate to compensate them for the inconvenience of working in shifts. A shift differential usually takes account of the time of day when the shift is worked, the duration of the shift, the extent to which weekend working is involved, and the speed of rotation within the shift.

shingle ◇ hang out your shingle GENERAL MANAGEMENT to start a business or announce the startup of a new business

shinyo kinku BANKING Japanese bank financing small businesses in Japan, a financial institution that provides financing for small businesses

shinyo kumiai BANKING Japanese credit union financing small businesses in Japan, a credit union that provides financing for small businesses

shirkah FINANCE contract between people going into business for profit in Islamic financing, a contract between two or more people who launch a business or financial enterprise in order to make a profit. *Also called* ***musharaka***

shogun bond STOCKHOLDING & INVESTMENTS non-yen bond sold in Japan by non-Japanese institution a bond denominated in a currency other than the yen that is sold on the Japanese market by a non-Japanese

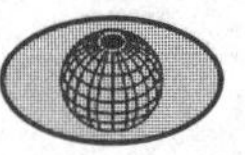

financial institution. *Also called* **geisha bond**. *See also* **samurai bond**, **shibosai bond**

shop price OPERATIONS & PRODUCTION = ***retail price***

short 1. FINANCE asset behind security benefiting from asset's fall an asset underlying a security in which a dealer has a **short position** and so gains by a fall in the asset's value **2.** MARKETS investor selling short an investor who is holding a **short position** **3.** MARKETS = ***sell short***

short bill FINANCE bill payable at short notice a bill of exchange that becomes payable at short notice

short-change FRAUD give customer too little change to give a customer less change than is right, either by mistake or in the hope that it will not be noticed, or to treat somebody less than fairly

short covering MARKETS purchase of security benefiting from asset's fall the buying back of foreign exchange, commodities, or securities by a firm or individual that has been **selling short**. Such purchases are undertaken when the market has begun to move upward, or when it is thought to be about to do so.

short credit FINANCE credit terms demanding repayment soon terms of borrowing that allow the customer only a little time to pay

short-dated STOCKHOLDING & INVESTMENTS maturing in 5 years or less used to describe securities such as bonds that mature in five years or less. *See also* ***long-dated***, ***medium-dated***

short-dated bill FINANCE bill payable almost immediately a bill that is payable within a few days

short-dated gilts STOCKHOLDING & INVESTMENTS UK government security maturing within 5 years fixed-interest securities issued by the UK government that mature in less than five years from the date of purchase. *Also called* **shorts**. *See also* ***gilt-edged security***

shortfall FINANCE amount missing from expected total an amount that is missing that would make the total expected sum

shorting MARKETS = ***short selling***

short interest STOCKHOLDING & INVESTMENTS quantity of security sold and not repurchased the total number of shares of a specific security that investors have sold short and have not repurchased in anticipation of a price decline

short investor MARKETS seller of securities expecting to repurchase them somebody who sells shares they have borrowed in order to buy expecting to be able to buy them back later at a lower price

short position STOCKHOLDING & INVESTMENTS selling unbought security hoping price will decline a situation in which somebody sells commodities, currencies, or securities they have borrowed for a fee in the expectation that they will be able to buy them back and return the loan at a lower price, so making a profit. *See also* ***long position***

shorts STOCKHOLDING & INVESTMENTS = ***short-dated gilts***

short sale STOCKHOLDING & INVESTMENTS sale of borrowed security anticipating cheap repurchase a sale of borrowed commodities, currencies, or securities in the expectation that prices will fall before they have to be bought back and then returned to the original owner

short selling MARKETS selling borrowed security anticipating cheap repurchase the practice of selling borrowed commodities, currencies, or securities in the expectation that prices will fall before they have to be bought back and then returned to the original owner. *Also called* **shorting**

short-term bond STOCKHOLDING & INVESTMENTS bond maturing within 2 years a bond on the corporate bond market that has an initial maturity of less than two years

short-term capital FINANCE money on short-term loan funds raised for a period of less than 12 months, for example, by a bank loan, to cover a short-term shortage. *See also* ***working capital***

short-term debt FINANCE debt due within year debt that has a term of one year or less

short-term economic policy ECONOMICS economic planning for near future an economic policy with objectives that can be met within a period of months or a few years

short-term forecast MARKETS forecast covering few months only a forecast that covers a period of a few months

short-termism GENERAL MANAGEMENT emphasis on quick results not long-term goals an approach to business that concentrates on short-term results rather than long-term objectives

short-term loan FINANCE loan repayable in weeks a loan that has to be repaid within a year, usually within a few weeks

short-term security STOCKHOLDING & INVESTMENTS security maturing within 5 years a security that matures in less than five years

show stopper MERGERS & ACQUISITIONS = ***poison pill*** *(slang)*

shrinkage OPERATIONS & PRODUCTION **1.** reduction in firm's inventories a reduction in the amount of inventory held by a company, often caused by production processes **2.** goods lost to theft or damage a term used to describe goods that leave a retail outlet but are not logged as sales. Shrinkage can include goods that are stolen by shoplifters, or are damaged or broken.

SI *abbr* LEGAL statutory instrument

SIA *abbr* FINANCE Securities Institute of Australia

SIB *abbr* REGULATION & COMPLIANCE Securities and Investments Board

SIC *abbr* BUSINESS Standard Industrial Classification

SICAV *abbr* BUSINESS société d'investissement à capital variable

sickness and accident insurance INSURANCE policy paying creditors during sickness or injury a form of insurance for ill health that may be sold with some form of credit, for example, a credit card or personal loan. In the event of the borrower being unable to work because of accident or illness, the policy covers the regular payments to the credit card company or lender.

sideline cash FINANCE = ***idle capital***

sight bill FINANCE bill of exchange payable immediately a bill of exchange payable when it is presented, rather than at a given length of time after presentation or after a date indicated on the bill

sight deposit BANKING bank deposit withdrawable immediately a bank deposit against which the depositor can immediately make a withdrawal

sight draft FINANCE bill of exchange payable immediately a bill of exchange that is payable on delivery. *See also* ***time draft***

sight letter of credit FINANCE letter of credit presented along with required documents a **letter of credit** that is paid when the necessary documents have been presented

signatory LEGAL somebody signing contract or document a person who signs a contract or other legal document

signature guarantee BANKING stamp or seal validating signature a stamp or seal, usually from a bank or a broker, that vouches for the authenticity of a signature

  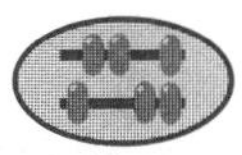   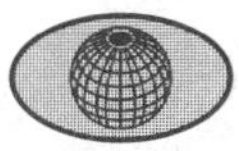   

signature loan FINANCE = ***unsecured loan***

silent partner *US* BUSINESS investment partner with no active management role a person or organization that invests money in a company but takes no active part in the management of the business. Although silent partners are inactive in the operation of the business, they have legal obligations and benefits of ownership, and are therefore fully liable for any debts. *UK term* ***sleeping partner***

silly money FINANCE excessively high or low sum an amount of money that is regarded as excessively large or, occasionally, small (*informal*)

silver MARKETS precious metal traded as commodity a precious metal traded on commodity markets such as the London Metal Exchange

simple interest FINANCE interest paid on principal only interest charged simply as a constant percentage of the principal and not compounded. *See also* ***compound interest***

simple moving average STATISTICS method of sampling giving every unit equal chance the selection of units from a population in such a way that every possible combination of selected units is equally likely to be in the sample chosen

simplified employee pension plan PENSIONS IRA funded by employer a type of **qualified plan** that provides employers with a way of making contributions toward their employees' and their own retirement. Contributions are paid directly into an **IRA** set up for each person. *Abbr* **SEP**

simulation GENERAL MANAGEMENT representation of possible situation or system the construction of a mathematical model to imitate the behavior of a real-world situation or system in order to test the outcomes of alternative courses of action. Simulation techniques are used in situations where real-life experimentation would be impossible, costly, or dangerous, and for training purposes.

simultaneous engineering OPERATIONS & PRODUCTION = ***concurrent engineering***

Singapore dollar CURRENCY & EXCHANGE Singapore's unit of currency Singapore's unit of currency, whose exchange rate is quoted as S$ per US$

Singapore Exchange MARKETS Singapore stock and monetary exchange the institution resulting from the merger in 1999 of the Stock Exchange of Singapore and the Singapore International Monetary Exchange. It provides securities and derivatives trading, securities clearing and depository, and derivatives clearing services. *Abbr* **SGX**

single-currency CURRENCY & EXCHANGE denominated in same currency used to describe an international transaction denominated entirely in one currency

single customs document INTERNATIONAL TRADE standardized customs form a standard, universally used form for the passage of goods through customs

single entry ACCOUNTING book-keeping system using only one entry per transaction a type of bookkeeping where only one entry, reflecting both a credit to one account and a debit to another, is made for each transaction

single-figure inflation ECONOMICS inflation below 10% inflation that is rising at less than 10% per annum

single market MARKETS organization of European nations the European Union in its role as an economic organization. *See also* ***EU***

single-payment bond STOCKHOLDING & INVESTMENTS bond redeemed with single payment at maturity a bond redeemed with a single payment combining principal and interest at maturity

single premium assurance *UK* INSURANCE = ***single premium insurance***

single premium deferred annuity TAX deferred annuity funded with single initial payment an annuity that is paid for with a single payment at inception and pays returns regularly after a set date. It gives a tax advantage.

single premium insurance *US* INSURANCE life insurance paid for with single initial premium life coverage where the premium is paid in one lump sum when the policy is taken out, rather than in installments. *UK term* ***single premium assurance***

single tax TAX tax to cover everything one major tax that supplies all revenue, especially on land

sinker STOCKHOLDING & INVESTMENTS bond paid from debt repayment reserve a bond whose principal and interest payments are paid out of the issuer's **sinking fund**

sinking fund FINANCE money set aside for debt payments money put aside periodically to settle a liability or replace an asset. The money is invested to produce a required sum at an appropriate time.

SIPC *abbr* INSURANCE Securities Investor Protection Corporation

SIPP *abbr* PENSIONS Self Invested Personal Pension Plan

sister company BUSINESS company belonging to same group a company that belongs to the same group of companies as another

SIV *abbr* STOCKHOLDING & INVESTMENTS structured investment vehicle

six-month money MARKETS money invested for 6 months funds invested on the money market for a period of six months

size of firm BUSINESS relative size of company for government records a method of categorizing companies according to size for the purposes of government statistics. Divisions are typically **microbusiness**, **small business**, **medium-sized business**, and **large-sized business**.

skewness STATISTICS lack of statistical symmetry a lack of symmetry in a **probability distribution**

skimming FRAUD stealing small amounts from customer accounts the unethical and usually illegal practice of taking small amounts of money from accounts that belong to other individuals or organizations

skin in the game FINANCE amount of entrepreneur's money invested in business the amount of an entrepreneur's own money that they have invested in their business, considered by **venture capitalists** as an indication of the entrepreneur's commitment to making the business successful

sleeper 1. STOCKHOLDING & INVESTMENTS stock with potential to rise in value a stock that has not risen in value for some time, but may suddenly do so in the future **2.** BUSINESS product that sells after period of sluggish sales a product that does not sell well for some time, then suddenly becomes very popular

sleeping partner *UK* BUSINESS = ***silent partner***

slippage STOCKHOLDING & INVESTMENTS discrepancy between estimated and actual costs the difference between the estimated costs of buying or selling a security and the actual costs of the transaction

slowdown ECONOMICS minor decrease in economic activity a fall in demand that causes a lowering of economic activity, less severe than a **recession** or **slump**

slow payer FINANCE somebody slow to pay debts a person or company that does not pay debts on time

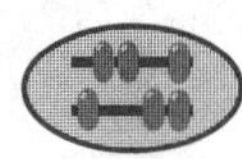

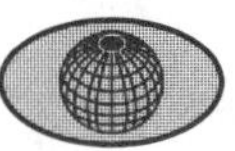

slump ECONOMICS major decrease in economic activity a severe downturn phase in the business cycle

slumpflation ECONOMICS decrease in economic activity with increased inflation a collapse in all economic activity accompanied by wage and price inflation. This happened, for example, in the United States and Europe in 1929 (*slang*).

slush fund FINANCE fund used for bribery or corruption a fund used by a company for illegal purposes such as bribing officials to obtain preferential treatment for planned work or expansion

small and medium-sized enterprise BUSINESS firm with under 250 employees an organization that is in the **startup** or growth phase of development and has fewer than 250 employees. This definition of a small and medium-sized enterprise is the one adopted by the United Kingdom's Department for Business Enterprise and Regulatory Reform for statistical purposes. *Abbr* **SME**

small business BUSINESS firm with under 50 employees managed by owner an organization that is small in relation to the potential market size, is managed by its owners, and has fewer than 50 employees. This definition of a small business is the one adopted by the United Kingdom's Department for Business Enterprise and Regulatory Reform for statistical purposes.

small change FINANCE money in coins a small quantity of coins of mixed value that somebody might carry, often used to suggest a sum of no significance

small claim LEGAL in UK, claim for less than £5,000 in the United Kingdom, a claim for less than £5,000 in the County Court

Small Order Execution System MARKETS NASDAQ system for trading small lots automatically on the NASDAQ, an automated execution system for bypassing brokers when processing small order agency executions of NASDAQ securities up to 1,000 shares

small print GENERAL MANAGEMENT details and conditions printed smaller than main text details in an official document such as a contract that are usually printed in a smaller size than the rest of the text and, while often important, may be overlooked. Items often referred to as "small print" may include deliberately hidden charges, unfavorable terms, or loopholes.

smart card E-COMMERCE plastic card with built-in microprocessor a small plastic card containing a microprocessor that can store and process transactions and maintain a bank balance, thus providing a secure, portable medium for electronic money. Financial details and personal data stored on the card can be updated each time the card is used.

smart market E-COMMERCE market only using electronic communications a market in which all transactions are performed electronically using network communications

SME *abbr* BUSINESS small and medium-sized enterprise

smoothing methods STATISTICS ways of removing irregularities in statistical data procedures used in fitting a set of observations in a study into a statistical model, often by creating a graph of the data

smurf FRAUD somebody involved in money-laundering someone who passes money obtained illegally through banks or businesses in order to make it appear legitimate

snake CURRENCY & EXCHANGE currencies formerly in European Exchange Rate Mechanism formerly, the group of currencies within the European Exchange Rate Mechanism whose exchange rates were allowed to fluctuate against each other within specific bands or limits

snowball sampling STATISTICS method of creating samples based on existing samples a form of sampling in which existing sample members suggest potential new sample members, for example, personal acquaintances

snowflake STATISTICS graph of multiple variables a graph that shows **multivariate data**

social business or **social enterprise** BUSINESS business run for positive social change a business whose main objective is to make positive social change in areas such as poverty, education, health, the environment, etc.

social lending FINANCE direct lending between people the practice of one person offering to lend money to another, without the involvement of a bank or other institution, especially through the Internet. *Also called* ***person-to-person lending***. *See also* ***ZOPA***

socially conscious investing STOCKHOLDING & INVESTMENTS = ***ethical investment***

social marginal cost ECONOMICS cost to society of change in economic variable the additional cost to a society of a change in an economic variable, for example, the price of gas or bread

social security INSURANCE, PENSIONS government financial support system a system of financial support in a variety of areas of personal need provided by a government, for example for retired people, those with young children, or those unemployed or unable to work

Social Security INSURANCE, PENSIONS US government assistance program for elderly and disabled in the United States, the federal insurance program that provides income for retirees and their dependents and survivors, disability income, and healthcare for seniors. The program is funded by required contributions from employers and working individuals.

Social Security number INSURANCE, PENSIONS, TAX person's identifying number for US social insurance plan in the United States, a unique nine-digit number assigned to each person within the Social Security system, which is used for taxation and identification purposes and does not change throughout the person's life. *Abbr* **SSN**

Sociedad Annima BUSINESS Spanish public corporation a Spanish company with a status comparable to a public corporation. *Abbr* **SA**

Sociedade Annima BUSINESS Portuguese public corporation a Portuguese company with a status comparable to a public corporation. *Abbr* **SA**

Societ a responsabilit limitata BUSINESS Italian private corporation an Italian unlisted company with a status comparable to a private corporation. *Abbr* **Srl**

Societ per Azioni BUSINESS Italian public corporation an Italian company with a status comparable to a public corporation. *Abbr* **SpA**

Socit Anonyme BUSINESS French public corporation a French company with a status comparable to a public corporation. *Abbr* **SA**

socit responsabilit limite BUSINESS French unlisted corporation a French unlisted company with a status comparable to a private corporation. *Abbr* **SARL**

socit d'investissement capital variable BUSINESS French investment company a French company managing an investment fund with capital varying according to the number of investors at any one time. *Abbr* **SICAV**

Society for Worldwide Interbank Financial Telecommunication BANKING *see* ***SWIFT***

socioeconomic ECONOMICS relating to social and economic factors involving both social and economic factors. Structural unemployment, for example, has socioeconomic causes.

socioeconomic segmentation MARKETING separation of market into socioeconomic groups the division of a market according to the different socioeconomic categories within it

Sod's Law *UK* GENERAL MANAGEMENT = ***Murphy's Law***

soft capital rationing ACCOUNTING management's imposition of limit on capital investment a restriction on an organization's ability to invest capital funds caused by an internal budget ceiling being imposed by management. *See also* ***capital rationing***

soft commissions FINANCE brokerage commissions rebated to institutional customer brokerage commissions that are rebated to an institutional customer in the form of, or to pay for, research or other services

soft commodities MARKETS commodities other than solid raw materials commodities such as foodstuffs that are neither metals nor other solid raw materials. *Also called* ***softs***. *See also* ***future, hard commodities***

soft-core radicalism MARKETING exploitation of customers' environmental and ethical concerns a marketing technique that plays on people's concerns about environmental and ethical issues in order to sell them a product (*slang*)

soft currency CURRENCY & EXCHANGE currency that is weak or expected to fall a currency that is weak, usually because there is an excess of supply and a belief that its value will fall in relation to others. *See also* ***hard currency***

soft dollars MARKETS payment by brokers for management firms' business rebates given by brokers to money management firms in return for funds' transaction business

soft landing ECONOMICS slowdown of economic activity without recession the situation when a country's economic activity has slowed down but demand has not fallen far enough or rapidly enough to cause a recession

soft loan FINANCE loan on highly favorable terms a loan on exceptionally favorable terms, for example, for a project that a government considers worthy

soft market MARKETS market with falling prices a market in which prices are falling because there are more sellers than buyers

softs MARKETS = ***soft commodities***

sold short STOCKHOLDING & INVESTMENTS borrowed and sold anticipating price drop used to refer to commodities, currencies, or securities that somebody borrows and sells, then buys back and repays in the expectation that prices will have fallen. *See also* ***sell short***

sole agency *UK* BUSINESS = ***exclusive agency***

sole distributor BUSINESS retailer with exclusive right to sell something a retailer who is the only one in an area who is allowed by the manufacturer to sell a specific product or service

sole practitioner BUSINESS professional practicing alone the proprietor of a professional practice, who is personally responsible for all its debts

sole proprietor BUSINESS person operating business alone somebody who owns and runs an unincorporated business by himself or herself. Sole proprietors are taxed at the personal income level and are personally liable for all business losses or debts; in the event of bankruptcy personal possessions may be forfeited. *Also called* ***sole trader, owner-operator***

sole proprietorship BUSINESS business of one person a business operated by a sole proprietor, who is personally responsible for all its debts

sole trader BUSINESS = ***sole proprietor***

solicit FINANCE request money to ask another person or company for money

solvency FINANCE situation of being able to pay all debts a situation in which a person or organization is able to pay all debts on their due date. *See also* ***insolvency***

solvency margin FINANCE business's assets minus liabilities a business's **liquid assets** that exceed the amount required to meet its liabilities

solvency ratio **1.** FINANCE ratio of assets to liabilities a ratio of assets to liabilities, used to measure a company's ability to meet its debts **2.** INSURANCE in UK, measure of insurance company's financial condition in the United Kingdom, the ratio of an insurance company's net assets to its non-life premium income

solvent FINANCE able to pay all one's debts used to refer to a situation in which the assets of an individual or organization are worth more than their liabilities

sort code *UK* BANKING number identifying UK bank branch a combination of numbers that identifies a bank branch on official documentation such as bank statements and checks. *See also* ***ABA routing number***

source and application of funds statement ACCOUNTING = ***cash flow statement***

sources and uses of funds statement ACCOUNTING = ***cash flow statement***

South African Revenue Service TAX S. African tax authority the government body that is responsible for collecting taxes and ensuring compliance with tax law in South Africa. *Abbr* **SARS**

Southern African Development Community INTERNATIONAL TRADE *see* ***SADC***

sovereign bond STOCKHOLDING & INVESTMENTS government bond in foreign currency a bond issued by a national government denominated in a foreign currency

sovereign loan FINANCE bank loan to foreign government a loan by a financial institution to an overseas government, usually of an emerging country. *See also* ***sovereign risk***

sovereign money STOCKHOLDING & INVESTMENTS money in sovereign wealth funds the money that is invested in **sovereign wealth funds**

sovereign risk FINANCE risk that foreign government may default on loan the risk that an overseas government may refuse to repay or may default on a **sovereign loan**

sovereign wealth fund STOCKHOLDING & INVESTMENTS very wealthy state investment fund an investment fund owned by a government with very large amounts of money at its disposal. There is concern that such a fund would be able to buy stakes in another country's strategic industries. *Abbr* **SWF**

SOX *abbr* REGULATION & COMPLIANCE Sarbanes-Oxley Act

SpA *abbr* BUSINESS Società per Azioni

spam MARKETING unwanted e-mailed advertising e-mailed direct mail regarded as an invasion of personal privacy. *See also* ***direct mail***

special clearing BANKING = ***special presentation***

Special Commissioner TAX UK Treasury official who hears income tax appeals in the United Kingdom, an official appointed by the Treasury to hear cases where a taxpayer is appealing against an income tax assessment

special damages FINANCE damages awarded for calculable loss damages awarded by a court to compensate for a loss that can be calculated, for example, the expense of repairing something

special deposit **1.** MORTGAGES in US, mortgage money for home improvements in the United States, an amount of money set aside for the renovation or improvement of a property as part of a mortgage **2.** BANKING commercial bank's required deposit in Bank of England a large sum of money that a commercial bank has to deposit with the Bank of England

Special Drawing Right CURRENCY & EXCHANGE country's entitlement to receive IMF loans an accounting unit used by the **International Monetary Fund**, allocated to each member country for use in loans and other international operations. The value is calculated daily on the weighted values of a group of currencies shown in dollars. *Abbr* **SDR**

Special Economic Zone INTERNATIONAL TRADE Chinese free trade region in China, an area where trade is conducted under special conditions and largely free of state control

specialist **1.** BUSINESS person or company specializing in one thing a person or company that deals with one particular type of product, or with one subject **2.** MARKETS stock exchange member acting as market maker a member of a stock exchange who maintains an inventory of particular stocks, selling to or buying from brokers in order to maintain a stable market for those stocks

special notice STOCKHOLDING & INVESTMENTS late announcement of proposal for stockholder meeting notice of a proposal to be put before a meeting of the stockholders of a company that is issued less than 28 days before the meeting

special presentation BANKING direct delivery of check to paying banker the sending of a check directly to the paying banker rather than through the clearing system. *Also called* ***special clearing***. *See also* ***advice of fate***

special purpose bond STOCKHOLDING & INVESTMENTS bond for one particular project a bond for one particular project, financed by levies on the people who benefit from the project

special resolution CORPORATE GOVERNANCE vote held on exceptional issue in the United Kingdom, an exceptional issue that is put to the vote at a company's general meeting, for example, a change to the company's articles of association, requiring 21 days' notice

special situation STOCKHOLDING & INVESTMENTS expectation of stock price rise the expectation that a stock will increase in value as a result of a change in the company such as a merger

specie CURRENCY & EXCHANGE coins that are legal tender coins, as opposed to pieces of paper money, that are legal tender

specific charge FINANCE = ***fixed charge***

specific order costing ACCOUNTING way to track costs billed by separate contractors the basic cost accounting method used where work consists of separately identifiable contracts, jobs, or batches

speculation FINANCE purchase made on basis of large anticipated gain a purchase made solely to make a profit when the price or value of something increases

speculative bubble MARKETS = ***bubble***

speculator MARKETS somebody taking risks to make quick profit somebody who buys goods, stock, or foreign currency with a higher-than-average risk in the hope that it will rise quickly in value

spending money CURRENCY & EXCHANGE personal money money that is available for small ordinary personal expenses

spinning MARKETS offering stock to preferred customers a practice of questionable legality in which brokerage firms offer stock in **initial public offerings** that are in high demand to preferred customers, in order to obtain or keep their business

spin-off GENERAL MANAGEMENT firm formed from larger one a company or subsidiary formed by splitting away from a parent company. A spin-off company can, for example, be created when research and development yields a new product that does not fit into the company's current portfolio, or when a company wants to explore a new venture related to its current activities. It can also be formed from a demerger, in which acquired companies or parts of a business are separated in order to create a more streamlined parent organization. A spin-off is often entrepreneurial in spirit, but the backing of the parent company can provide financial stability.

split STOCKHOLDING & INVESTMENTS = ***stock split***

split-capital investment trust or **split-capital trust** STOCKHOLDING & INVESTMENTS = ***split-level investment trust***

split commission FINANCE transaction fee divided among multiple parties commission that is divided between two or more parties in a transaction

split coupon bond STOCKHOLDING & INVESTMENTS = ***zero coupon bond***

split-level investment trust or **split-level trust** STOCKHOLDING & INVESTMENTS investment trust combining income shares and capital shares an investment trust with two categories of shares: income shares, which receive income from the investments, but do not benefit from the rise in their capital value, and **capital shares**, which increase in value as the value of the investments rises. Income shareholders receive all or most of the income generated by the trust and a predetermined sum at liquidation, while capital shareholders receive no interest but the remainder of the capital at liquidation. *Also called* ***split trust, split-capital investment trust, split-capital trust***

split payment FINANCE payment greatly subdivided a payment that is divided into small units

split trust STOCKHOLDING & INVESTMENTS = ***split-level investment trust***

sponsor **1.** FINANCE person or company giving money for venture a person or company that pays money to help with an activity or to pay for a business venture **2.** FINANCE firm giving money to sport for advertising rights a company that pays to help a sport, in return for advertising rights **3.** STOCKHOLDING & INVESTMENTS backer of an initial public offering an organization such as an investment bank that backs an initial public offering **4.** BUSINESS somebody giving job recommendation somebody who recommends another person for a job **5.** MARKETING company purchasing advertising on TV program a company that pays part of the cost of making a television program by taking advertising time on the program

sponsorship **1.** FINANCE financial support financial backing for an activity or business venture **2.** MARKETING financial support as means of advertising a form of advertising in which an organization provides funds for something such as a television program or sports event in return for exposure to a target audience

spot MARKETING broadcast advertisement a commercial broadcast on television or radio

spot cash CURRENCY & EXCHANGE cash paid on the spot cash paid immediately for something bought

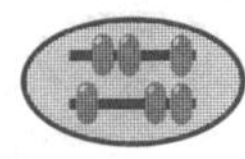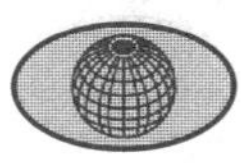

spot currency market CURRENCY & EXCHANGE, MARKETS market for currency deliverable at time of sale a market that deals in foreign exchange for immediate rather than future delivery. *See also* ***spot market***

spot exchange rate CURRENCY & EXCHANGE, MARKETS current exchange rate the exchange rate used for immediate currency transactions

spot goods MARKETS commodity deliverable immediately a commodity traded on the **spot market**, for immediate delivery

spot interest rate MARKETS current interest rate an interest rate that is determined when a loan is made

spot market MARKETS market for items deliverable at time of sale a market that deals in commodities or foreign exchange for immediate rather than future delivery. *See also* ***spot currency market***

spot month MARKETS = ***nearby month***

spot price MARKETS current price the price for immediate delivery of a commodity or currency

spot rate MARKETS current rate of interest to maturity on security the rate of interest to maturity currently offered on a particular type of security

spot transaction MARKETS transaction for immediate delivery a transaction in commodities or foreign exchange for immediate delivery

spread 1. MARKETS difference between buying and selling price for security the difference between the buying and selling price of a security achieved by a **market maker** on a stock exchange **2.** STOCKHOLDING & INVESTMENTS mix of investments the range of the investments in a particular portfolio

spread betting STOCKHOLDING & INVESTMENTS betting on stock movements within specified range betting on the movement of a stock price in relation to a range of high and low values. If the price moves outside the range on a specific day, the bettor wins a multiple of the original stake times the number of points outside the range.

spreadsheet GENERAL MANAGEMENT software organizing data in columns a computer program that provides a series of ruled columns in which data can be entered, manipulated, and analyzed

sprinkling trust STOCKHOLDING & INVESTMENTS trust in which trustees have discretion over distributions a trust with multiple beneficiaries where the trustees have discretion over how the trust's income is distributed

Square Mile FINANCE British financial center an area of London where the British financial center is located. *Also called* ***City of London***

squeeze ECONOMICS government restriction of available credit a government policy of restriction, commonly affecting the availability of credit in an economy

Srl *abbr* BUSINESS Società a responsabilità limitata

SRO *abbr* REGULATION & COMPLIANCE self-regulatory organization

SSAPs *abbr* REGULATION & COMPLIANCE, ACCOUNTING Statements of Standard Accounting Practice

SSN *abbr* INSURANCE, PENSIONS, TAX Social Security number

stabilization fund ECONOMICS government reserve for international financial support a fund created by a government for use in maintaining its official exchange rate when necessary

stag STOCKHOLDING & INVESTMENTS somebody buying new stock for immediate resale somebody who buys **initial public offerings** at the offering price and sells them immediately to make a profit

staged payments FINANCE payments made in stages payments that are made in stages over a period of time

stage-gate model MARKETING way of bringing something new to market the traditional model of **new product development**, comprising the conception, generation, analysis, development, testing, marketing, and commercialization of new products or services. *See also* ***new product development***

stagflation ECONOMICS situation with high unemployment and inflation a situation in which both inflation and unemployment exist at the same time in an economy. There was stagflation in the United Kingdom and the United States in the 1970s, for example.

stagnation ECONOMICS situation with no economic progress a situation in which no progress is being made, especially in economic matters

stakeholder BUSINESS party with vested interest in firm's success a person or organization with a legitimate interest in the successful operation of a company or organization. A stakeholder may be an employee, customer, supplier, partner, or even the local community within which an organization operates.

stakeholder pension PENSIONS in UK, low-cost pension supplementing state plan a pension bought from a private company in which the retirement income depends on the level of contributions made during a person's working life. Stakeholder pensions are designed for people without access to a pension from their employment, and are intended to provide a low-cost supplement to a pension from the government. A stakeholder pension plan can either be trust-based, like an occupational pension plan, or contract-based, similar to a personal pension. Employers must provide access to a stakeholder pension plan for employees, subject to some exceptions, although they are not required to establish a stakeholder pension plan themselves. Membership of a stakeholder pension plan is voluntary. *See also* ***Keough Plan***

stakeholder theory STOCKHOLDING & INVESTMENTS theory that stockholders' interests needn't harm stakeholders the theory that an organization can enhance the interests of its stockholders without damaging the interests of its wider **stakeholders**. Stakeholder theory grew in response to the **economic theory of the firm**. One of the difficulties of stakeholder theory is allocating importance to the values of different groups of stakeholders, and a solution to this is proposed by **stakeholder value analysis**.

stakeholder value analysis STOCKHOLDING & INVESTMENTS assessment of stakeholders' views for corporate planning purposes a method of determining the values of the **stakeholders** in an organization for the purposes of making strategic and operational decisions. Stakeholder value analysis is one method of justifying an approach based on **stakeholder theory** rather than the **economic theory of the firm**. It involves identifying groups of stakeholders and eliciting their views on particular issues in order that these views may be taken into account when making decisions.

stale bull STOCKHOLDING & INVESTMENTS investor seeking to sell nonperforming security an investor who bought stocks hoping that they would rise, and now finds that they have not risen and wants to sell them

stamp duty LEGAL in UK, duty verified with postage stamp in the United Kingdom, a duty that is payable on some legal documents and is shown to have been paid by a stamp being affixed to the document

standard OPERATIONS & PRODUCTION benchmark measurement a benchmark

     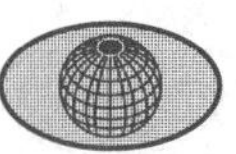   

measurement of resource usage, set in defined conditions on the basis of expected, potentially attainable, prior or comparable performance standards. Standards may be set at attainable levels, which assume efficient levels of operation but include allowances for normal loss, waste, and machine downtime, or at ideal levels, which make no allowance for the above losses and are only attainable under the most favorable conditions.

standard agreement or **standard contract** LEGAL contract containing usual language a printed contract form that contains the usual language applicable to a particular situation

Standard & Poor's STOCKHOLDING & INVESTMENTS major US bond-rating corporation in the United States, a corporation that rates bonds according to the credit-worthiness of the organizations issuing them. Standard & Poor's also issues several stock market indices, for example, the Standard & Poor's Composite Index. *Abbr* **S&P**

Standard & Poor's 500 Index MARKETS US index of 500 stock prices a US index of 500 general stock prices selected by the Standard & Poor agency. *Abbr* **S&P Index**

Standard & Poor's rating STOCKHOLDING & INVESTMENTS US stock rating service a stock rating service provided by the US agency Standard & Poor's

standard cost FINANCE calculated future cost as basis of estimates a future cost that is calculated in advance and against which estimates are measured

standard costing ACCOUNTING comparison of standard and actual costs a control procedure that compares standard costs and revenues with actual results to obtain variances, which are used to stimulate improved performance

standard deduction TAX untaxed part of person's income in the United States, a proportion of personal income that is not subject to tax for people who do not itemize their deductions. It is calculated based on marital status, number of children or dependents, and whether or not a person is aged 65 or older. *See also* ***itemized deductions***

standard deviation STATISTICS quantity expressing difference from mean a measure of how dispersed a set of numbers are around their mean

standard hour OPERATIONS & PRODUCTION amount of work expected per hour the amount of work achievable, at standard efficiency levels, in an hour

Standard Industrial Classification BUSINESS US system for identifying businesses with their activity in the United States, a system used for categorizing and coding businesses according to the type of activity in which they are engaged. *Abbr* **SIC**

standard letter GENERAL MANAGEMENT letter sent to several correspondents a letter that is sent without change to a number of correspondents

standard of living ECONOMICS people's ability to buy desired goods and services a measure of economic well-being based on the ability of people to buy the goods and services they desire

standard rate TAX in UK, usual rate of VAT in the United Kingdom, the rate of **VAT** usually payable on goods or services

standby credit 1. BANKING = ***backup credit*** **2.** ECONOMICS credit that can be used by emerging countries credit drawing rights given to an emerging country by an international financial institution, to fund industrialization or other growth policies

standby fee FINANCE fee for additional loan a fee paid to obtain **standby credit**

standby loan ECONOMICS loan to emerging country for specific purposes a loan given to an emerging country by an international financial institution, to fund technology hardware purchase or other growth policies

standing instructions GENERAL MANAGEMENT procedural instructions normally in effect instructions, which may be revoked at any time, for a specific procedure to be undertaken in the event of a specific occurrence; for example, an instruction that money in a savings account for a fixed term should be placed on deposit for a further period when the term expires

standing order *UK* BANKING = ***automatic debit***

standing room only MARKETING illusion of high demand to encourage sales a sales technique whereby customers are given the impression that there are many other people waiting to buy the same product at the same time (*slang*)

staple commodity FINANCE basic item of trade any basic food or a raw material that is important in a country's economy

star 1. BUSINESS fast-growing business with high market share in the **Boston Box** model, a business with a high market share and high growth rate. *See also* ***Boston Box*** **2.** STOCKHOLDING & INVESTMENTS outstanding investment an investment that is performing extremely well

startup BUSINESS new business, especially in technology sector a relatively new, usually small business, particularly one supported by venture capital and within those sectors closely linked to new technologies

startup costs FINANCE money required to launch new business the initial sum required to establish a business or to get a project under way. The costs will include the capital expenditure and related expenses before the business or project generates revenue.

startup financing or **start-up financing** FINANCE first stage in financing new project the first stage in financing a new project, which is followed by several rounds of investment capital as the project gets under way

state bank BANKING bank chartered by US state in the United States, a commercial bank chartered by one of the states rather than having a federal charter

state capitalism ECONOMICS capitalistic system where government controls most production a way of organizing society in which the state controls most of a country's means of production and capital

State Earnings-Related Pension Scheme PENSIONS *see* ***SERPS***

state enterprise BUSINESS nationalized or largely nationalized firm an organization in which the government or state has a controlling interest

statement BANKING list of bank account transactions a summary of all transactions, for example, deposits or withdrawals, that have occurred in an account at a bank or savings and loan association over a given period of time

statement of account ACCOUNTING **1.** list of recent transactions a summary of transactions that have occurred between two parties over a given period of time **2.** list of commercial transactions a list of sums due, usually comprising unpaid invoices, items paid on account but not offset against particular invoices, credit notes, debit notes, and discounts

statement of affairs ACCOUNTING list of assets and liabilities showing financial condition a statement in a prescribed form, usually prepared by a receiver, showing the estimated financial position of a debtor or a company that may be unable to meet its debts. It contains a summary of the debtor's assets and liabilities, with the assets shown at their estimated realizable values. The various classes of creditors, such as preferential, secured, partly secured, and unsecured, are shown separately.

     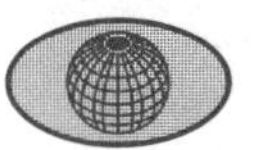   

statement of cash flows ACCOUNTING list of cash transactions a statement that documents actual receipts and expenditures of cash

statement-of-cash-flows method ACCOUNTING accounting system based on business's cash flow a method of accounting that is based on flows of cash rather than balances on accounts

statement of changes in financial position ACCOUNTING list of business's income and expenditures a financial report of a company's incomes and outflows during a period, usually a year or a quarter

Statement of Financial Accounting Standards REGULATION & COMPLIANCE in US, declaration of standards governing financial reporting in the United States, a statement detailing the standards to be adopted for the preparation of financial statements. *Abbr* **SFAS**

statement of source and application of funds ACCOUNTING = ***cash flow statement***

statement of total recognized gains and losses ACCOUNTING list of changes in stockholders' equity a financial statement showing changes in stockholders' equity during an accounting period

Statements of Standard Accounting Practice REGULATION & COMPLIANCE, ACCOUNTING UK rules for preparation of financial statements rules laid down by the UK Accounting Standards Board for the preparation of financial statements. *Abbr* **SSAPs**

state of indebtedness FINANCE situation of owing money the situation that exists when somebody owes money

state ownership BUSINESS ownership of industry by government a situation in which an industry is taken over from private ownership and run by a government

state pension PENSIONS UK government pension in the United Kingdom, the basic pension entitlement provided by the government for a retired person

State Second Pension PENSIONS additional UK government pension in the United Kingdom, an additional pension entitlement over and above the basic pension provided by the government, available to people who had caring responsibilities or long-term illness or disability as well as to those who were employed

statistic STATISTICS item of numerical data a piece of information in numerical form, obtained from analysis of a large quantity of numerical data

statistical discrepancy STATISTICS discrepancy arising from different calculation methods the amount by which sets of figures differ, usually because of a difference in the methods of calculation

statistical expert system STATISTICS computer program for performing statistical analysis a computer program used to conduct a statistical analysis of a set of data

statistical model STATISTICS techniques for analyzing data in statistical study the particular methods used to investigate the data in a statistical study

statistical quality control STATISTICS methods for checking consistency of statistical samples the process of inspecting samples of a product to check for consistent quality according to given parameters

statistical significance STATISTICS status as statistical pointer in a statistical study, a value assigned to the likelihood that something has occurred by chance

statistics STATISTICS **1.** numerical data information in numerical form, obtained from analysis of a large quantity of numerical data **2.** study of numerical data the collection, analysis, and presentation of large quantities of numerical data

status inquiry FINANCE credit check the act of checking on a customer's credit rating

statute-barred debt FINANCE debt that is uncollectable after time limit a debt that cannot be pursued as the time limit laid down by law has expired

statute of limitations LEGAL time limit for bringing lawsuit a law that allows only a fixed period of time during which somebody can start legal proceedings to claim property or compensation for damage

statutory auditor ACCOUNTING, REGULATION & COMPLIANCE in UK, officially qualified auditor in the United Kingdom, a professional person qualified to conduct an audit required by the Companies Act

statutory body BUSINESS group created by law an organized group with a particular function that has been established by government legislation

statutory instrument LEGAL in UK, legislation not needing full Parliamentary approval in UK law, a form of legislation that allows the provision of an Act of Parliament to be brought into force or altered without full Parliamentary approval. *Abbr* **SI**

statutory regulations REGULATION & COMPLIANCE UK financial regulations based on Parliamentary acts in the United Kingdom, regulations covering financial dealings that are based on Acts of Parliament, for example, the Financial Services Act, as opposed to the rules of self-regulatory organizations, which are non-statutory

statutory voting CORPORATE GOVERNANCE system granting one vote per share a system of voting in which stockholders in a company have one vote per share of stock owned

STC TAX S. African tax on dividends in South Africa, a tax that is levied on corporate dividends. *Full form* ***Secondary Tax on Companies***

stealth tax TAX initially unnoticed tax a new tax or tax increase, especially an indirect tax, that is introduced without much public attention, or an additional charge that is effectively a tax although not officially classed as one

sterling CURRENCY & EXCHANGE UK currency the standard currency (pounds and pence) used in the United Kingdom

sterling area CURRENCY & EXCHANGE formerly, countries using sterling as trading currency formerly, the area of the world where the pound sterling was the main trading currency

sterling balances CURRENCY & EXCHANGE trade balances expressed in sterling a country's trade balances expressed in pounds sterling

sterling index CURRENCY & EXCHANGE index measuring sterling against other currencies an index that shows the current value of sterling against a group of other currencies

stipend FINANCE regular payment to office-holder a regular remuneration or allowance paid as a salary to an office-holder such as a member of the clergy

stock 1. STOCKHOLDING & INVESTMENTS fixed interest investment a form of security issued in fixed units at a fixed rate of interest. The technical difference between stocks and shares is that a company that fixes its capital in terms of a monetary amount and then sells different proportions of it to investors creates stock, while a company that creates a number of shares of equal nominal value and sells different numbers of them to investors creates shares. For all practical purposes they are the same. In the United States, all equity instruments are called stocks, whereas in the United Kingdom, they are called shares. **2.** UK OPERATIONS & PRODUCTION = ***inventory***

  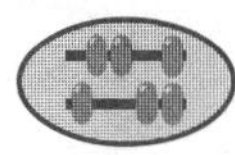   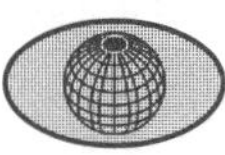   

stockalypse STOCKHOLDING & INVESTMENTS collapse in stock prices a sudden and dramatic drop in the price of stock (*slang*)

stockbroker STOCKHOLDING & INVESTMENTS professional agent for securities a person or company that arranges the sale and purchase of stocks and other securities, usually for a commission. *Also called* ***broker***

stockbroking STOCKHOLDING & INVESTMENTS dealing in stock the business of dealing in stocks and other securities for clients

stock buyback STOCKHOLDING & INVESTMENTS = ***buyback***

stock certificate *US* STOCKHOLDING & INVESTMENTS document representing ownership in firm a document that certifies ownership of stock in a company. *UK term* ***share certificate***

stock control *UK* OPERATIONS & PRODUCTION = ***inventory control***

stock depreciation *UK* ACCOUNTING = ***inventory depreciation***

stock dividend STOCKHOLDING & INVESTMENTS dividend paid as additional shares of stock a dividend paid to a stockholder in the form of additional stock rather than cash

stock exchange MARKETS market for securities a registered place where securities are bought and sold. *Also called* ***stock market*** *(sense 2)*

Stock Exchange Automated Quotations system MARKETS *see* ***SEAQ***

Stock Exchange Automated Quotations system International MARKETS *see* ***SEAQ International***

Stock Exchange Automatic Trading System MARKETS *see* ***SEATS***

stock exchange listing MARKETS presence on official stock list the fact of being on the official list of stocks that can be bought or sold on a stock exchange

stockholder *US* STOCKHOLDING & INVESTMENTS somebody with shares in company a person or organization that owns one or more shares of stock in a company. *UK term* ***shareholder***

stockholder perks *US* STOCKHOLDING & INVESTMENTS = ***shareholders' perks***

stockholders' equity *US* FINANCE firm's share capital and reserves the part of a company's financial assets consisting of **share capital** and **retained profits**. *Also called* ***shareholders' equity, shareholders' funds***

stockholder value *US* STOCKHOLDING & INVESTMENTS = ***shareholder value***

stockholder value analysis *US* STOCKHOLDING & INVESTMENTS = ***shareholder value analysis***

stockholding *US* STOCKHOLDING & INVESTMENTS ownership of shares in firm the stock in a **corporation** owned by a stockholder. *Also called* ***shareholding***

stock incentive plan *US* HR & PERSONNEL offering shares in firm to employees a type of financial **incentive plan** in which employees can acquire shares in the company in which they work and so have an interest in its financial performance. A stock incentive plan is a type of **employee stock ownership plan**, in which employees may be given stock by their employer, or stock may be offered for purchase at an advantageous price, as a reward for personal or group performance. *UK term* ***share incentive scheme***

stockjobber MARKETS former UK dealer in securities the equivalent of a **market maker** on the London Stock Exchange before the **Big Bang** of October 1986. Stockjobbers could not deal directly with private investors. *See also* ***market maker***

stockjobbing MARKETS former trading activities on stock exchange formerly, the business of buying and selling shares from other traders on a stock exchange

stock level OPERATIONS & PRODUCTION quantity of goods in inventory the quantity of goods kept in inventory. *Also called* ***inventory level***

stock market MARKETS **1.** trading in securities the activity or profession of trading in securities **2.** = ***stock exchange***

stock market crash MARKETS = ***crash***

stock market index MARKETS = ***index***

stock market manipulation MARKETS efforts to influence stock prices an attempt or series of attempts to influence the price of stocks by buying or selling in order to give the impression that the stocks are widely traded

stock market rating MARKETS stock price indicating firm's value the price of a stock on the stock market, which shows how investors and financial advisers generally consider the value of the company

stock market valuation MARKETS firm's value based on stock price the value of a company based on the current market price of its stock

stock option STOCKHOLDING & INVESTMENTS right to buy or sell on agreed terms the right of an option holder to buy or sell a specific stock on predetermined terms on, or before, a future date. *Also called* **option**. *UK term* ***share option***

stock option plan *US* STOCKHOLDING & INVESTMENTS employees' right to buy company stock a program in which an employee is given the option to buy a specific number of shares of stock at a future date, at an agreed price. Stock options provide a financial benefit to the recipient only if the stock price rises over the period the option is available. If the stock price falls over the period, the employee is under no obligation to buy. There may be a tax advantage to the employees who participate in such a program. Share options may be available to all employees or operated on a discretionary basis. *UK term* ***share option scheme***

stockout OPERATIONS & PRODUCTION unavailability of part from stock the situation where the stock of a particular component or part has been used up and has not yet been replenished. Stockouts result from poor stock control or the failure of a **just-in-time** supply system. They can result in delays in the delivery of customer orders and can damage the reputation of the business.

stockpicker STOCKHOLDING & INVESTMENTS buyer choosing stock somebody who is choosing which stock to buy. *See also* ***bottom-up approach***

stock quote MARKETS current price of stock trading on stock exchange the highest **bid price** or lowest **ask price** of a share of stock at any point in time during a trading day

stocks and shares STOCKHOLDING & INVESTMENTS firms' capital owned by public the units of ownership in public companies. The technical difference between stocks and shares is that a company that fixes its capital in terms of a monetary amount and then sells different proportions of it to investors creates stock, while a company that creates a number of shares of equal nominal value and sells different numbers of them to investors creates shares. For all practical purposes they are the same. In the United States, all equity instruments are called stocks, whereas in the United Kingdom, they are called shares.

stock split *US* STOCKHOLDING & INVESTMENTS numerical increase of shares without affecting total value an act of issuing stockholders with at least one more share for every share owned, without affecting the total value of each holding. A stock split usually occurs because the stock price has become too high for easy trading. *Also*

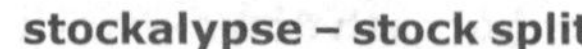

  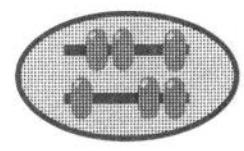   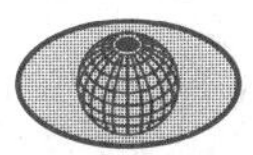   

*called **share split, split**. See also **bonus shares, reverse split**. UK term **scrip issue***

stock symbol MARKETS short form of firm's name a shortened version of a company's name, usually made up of two to four letters, used in screen-based trading systems and newspaper listings

stocktaking OPERATIONS & PRODUCTION counting items held in stock the process of measuring the quantities of stock held by an organization. Inventory can be held both in stores and within the processes of the operation.

stock tip US STOCKHOLDING & INVESTMENTS expert's recommendation on stock a recommendation about a stock published in the financial press, usually based on research published by a financial institution. *UK term **share tip***

stock turnover UK STOCKHOLDING & INVESTMENTS = ***inventory turnover***

stock turns ACCOUNTING = ***inventory turnover***

stock valuation UK ACCOUNTING = ***inventory valuation***

stokvel BANKING S. African savings association in South Africa, an informal, widely used cooperative savings program that provides small-scale loans

stop-go ECONOMICS alternately tightening and loosening economic policies the alternate tightening and loosening of fiscal and monetary policies, characteristic of the UK economy in the 1960s and 1970s

stop limit order MARKETS order to trade stock above specific price an order to trade only if and when a security reaches a specified price

stop loss MARKETS = ***stop-loss order***

stop-loss order or **stop-loss** or **stop order** MARKETS instruction to sell stock if price falls an instruction to a stockbroker to sell a stock if the price falls to a specified level

stop price MARKETS specified trading price the price at which to sell or buy a security specified in a **stop-loss order**

store card FINANCE credit card used exclusively in department store a credit card issued by a large department store, which can only be used for purchases in that store

story stock STOCKHOLDING & INVESTMENTS stock reported on in press a stock that is the subject of a press or financial community story that may affect its price

straddle STOCKHOLDING & INVESTMENTS simultaneous security purchase of put and call options the act of buying a **put option** and a **call option** for the same number of shares of the same security at the same time with the same **strike price** and expiration date. This allows the buyer to make a profit if the price rises or falls. *See also **strangle***

straight line depreciation ACCOUNTING reducing value of asset evenly over its lifetime a form of **depreciation** in which the cost of a fixed asset is spread equally over each year of its anticipated lifetime

Straits Times Industrial Index MARKETS Singapore stock exchange indicator an index of 30 Singapore stocks, the most commonly quoted indicator of stock market activity in Singapore

strangle MARKETS simultaneously trading differently priced put and call options a strategy in which a **put option** and a **call option** with the same expiration date but different **strike prices** on the same asset are either bought or sold. *See also **straddle***

STRATE MARKETS S. African electronic exchange system the electronic stock transactions system of the South African stock exchange, JSE Limited. *Full form **Share Transactions Totally Electronic***

strategic analysis GENERAL MANAGEMENT assessment of business procedures and environment the process of evaluating the business environment within which an organization operates and the organization itself as part of a process of formulating long-term objectives

strategic business unit GENERAL MANAGEMENT section with own marketing strategy a division within a large organization that shares the organization's market and customer focus but has responsibility for the development of its own marketing strategy. A single overall strategic approach is often inappropriate in large diversified organizations or multinational companies.

strategic financial management FINANCE handling firm's money to achieve firm's goals the identification of the strategies capable of maximizing an organization's net present value, the allocation of scarce capital resources, and the implementation and monitoring of a particular strategy

strategic management GENERAL MANAGEMENT management for longer-term objectives the development of corporate strategy, and the management of an organization according to that strategy. Strategic management focuses on achieving and maintaining a strong competitive advantage. It involves the application of corporate strategy to all aspects of the organization, and especially to decision making. As a discipline, strategic management developed in the 1970s, but it has evolved in response to changes in organization structure and corporate culture. With greater empowerment, strategy has become the concern not just of directors but also of employees at all levels of the organization.

strategic marketing MARKETING direct selling to customers a method of selling products directly to customers, bypassing traditional retailers or distributors

strategy GENERAL MANAGEMENT structured course of action for longer-term objectives a planned course of action undertaken to achieve the goals and objectives of an organization. The overall strategy of an organization is known as corporate strategy, but strategy may also be developed for any aspect of an organization's activities such as environmental management or manufacturing strategy.

stratified random sampling STATISTICS selecting random subgroups from stratified statistical population sampling carried out at random from each stratum of a stratified population. *See also **random sampling***

stratified sampling STATISTICS *see **random sampling***

street US MARKETS describing person with market awareness used to describe somebody who is considered to be well informed about the market (*slang*)

Street MARKETS US financial industry the financial industry in the United States, located in and around Wall Street

street name MARKETS brokerage house holding customer's investments in the United States, a way of registering a customer's security in which a broker or brokerage holds the security in the brokerage house's name to facilitate transactions

strike price STOCKHOLDING & INVESTMENTS price fixed by seller the price for a security or commodity that underlies an **option**. *Also called **exercise price** (sense 2)*

strip STOCKHOLDING & INVESTMENTS separation of coupons from bond for sale individually the separation of the coupons from the principal of a bond in order to sell them separately as a package of interest coupons and a bond that repays principal without interest. *See also **strips***

strippable bond STOCKHOLDING & INVESTMENTS bond separable into principal

  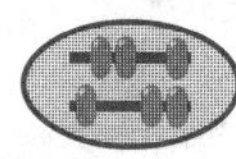 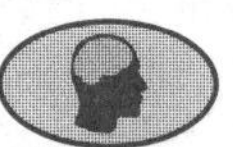  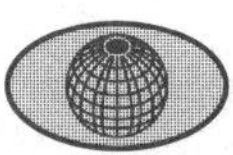   

and interest payments a bond that can be divided into separate zero-coupon bonds, representing its principal and interest payments, which can be traded independently

stripped bond STOCKHOLDING & INVESTMENTS bond separated into principal and interest payments a bond that has been divided into separate zero-coupon bonds, representing its principal and interest payments, which can be traded independently

stripped stock STOCKHOLDING & INVESTMENTS stock without dividend rights stock for which the rights to dividends have been split off and sold separately

stripping STOCKHOLDING & INVESTMENTS splitting bond into two parts for separate trading the process of separating the coupons from the principal of a bond in order to sell them separately as a package of interest coupons and a bond that repays principal without interest. *See also* ***strips***

strips STOCKHOLDING & INVESTMENTS bond parts allowing interest or principal payments only the parts of a **stripped bond** that entitle the owner to interest payments only, or to the payment of principal only

strong currency CURRENCY & EXCHANGE currency with relatively high value a currency that has a high value against other currencies

structural adjustment ECONOMICS change in basic framework of economy the reallocation of resources in response to alterations in the composition of the output of an economy as it experiences changes between the contribution of different business sectors. *Also called* ***structural change***

structural change ECONOMICS = ***structural adjustment***

structural fund STOCKHOLDING & INVESTMENTS mutual fund invested in EU economic development a type of **mutual fund** that invests in projects that contribute to the economic development of poorer nations in the European Union

structural inflation ECONOMICS inflation with no specific cause inflation that naturally occurs in an economy, without any particular triggering event

structural unemployment ECONOMICS unemployment caused by change in basic economic framework unemployment resulting from a change in demand or technological advances, which cause a surplus of labor in a particular location or skills area

structured investment vehicle STOCKHOLDING & INVESTMENTS product with short-term borrowing funding high-yielding securities a product that borrows money in the short-term credit market to invest in high-yielding, longer-dated securities. *Abbr* **SIV**

structured product STOCKHOLDING & INVESTMENTS customized investment a type of investment designed to meet an investor's specific needs

stub equity STOCKHOLDING & INVESTMENTS **1.** money from high risk bond sales the money raised through the sale of large quantities of high risk bonds, as in a **leveraged buyout** **2.** stock with greatly reduced price a stock whose price has seriously fallen due to major financial problems. Stub stock is a risky investment with great potential if the company regains its strength.

Student Loan Marketing Association FINANCE *see* ***Sallie Mae***

subcontracting GENERAL MANAGEMENT, OPERATIONS & PRODUCTION employing another to fulfill part of contract the delegation to a third party of some or all of the work that somebody has contracted to do. Subcontracting usually occurs where the contracted work such as the construction of a building requires a variety of skills. Responsibility for the fulfillment of the original contract remains with the original contracting party. Where the fulfillment of a contract depends on the skills of the person who has entered into the contract, as in the painting of a portrait, then the work cannot be subcontracted to a third party. The term subcontracting is sometimes used to describe **outsourcing** arrangements.

subject to collection FINANCE depending on repayment dependent upon the ability to collect the amount owed

subordinated debt FINANCE = ***junior debt***

subordinated loan FINANCE debt whose repayment ranks after all others a loan that ranks below all other borrowings with regard to both the payment of interest and principal. *See also* ***pari passu***

subprime loan FINANCE loan made to borrower unlikely to repay a loan made to somebody who does not meet the usual or standard qualifications for borrowing the amount in question. In 2007–8, a world financial crisis was precipitated by defaults on subprime mortgage loans.

subscribed capital or **subscribed share capital** STOCKHOLDING & INVESTMENTS = ***issued share capital***

subscriber **1.** STOCKHOLDING & INVESTMENTS somebody who buys stocks in new firm a buyer, especially one who buys stocks in a new company or new issues **2.** BUSINESS original stockholder a person who signs a company's **memorandum of association**

subscription price STOCKHOLDING & INVESTMENTS price of new stock offered for sale the price at which new shares of stock in an existing company are offered for sale

subscription share STOCKHOLDING & INVESTMENTS share of stock in new firm a stock purchased by a subscriber when a new company is formed

subsidiary BUSINESS = ***subsidiary company***

subsidiary account BANKING individual account for one owner of joint account an account for one of the individual people or organizations that jointly hold another account

subsidiary company BUSINESS firm controlled by another a company that is controlled by another. A subsidiary company operates under the control of a parent or **holding company**, which may have a majority on the subsidiary's **board of directors**, or a majority shareholding in the subsidiary—giving it majority voting rights—or it may be named in a contract as having control of the subsidiary. If all of the stock in a company is owned by its parent, it is known as a **wholly-owned subsidiary**. A subsidiary that is located in a different country from the parent is a **foreign subsidiary company**.

subsidized FINANCE having financial assistance for which a **subsidy** has been paid

subsidy FINANCE financial assistance for activity or firm financial assistance to a company or group of people, usually given by a government, to encourage new developments of benefit to the public or to support an industry for a period of time. Subsidies are regarded as restrictive in international trade if by supporting a domestic industry they make imports more expensive.

subsistence allowance FINANCE money for living expenses away from home **expenses** paid by an employer, usually within preset limits, to cover the cost of accommodations, meals, and incidental expenses incurred by employees when away on business

  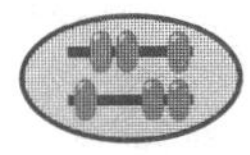   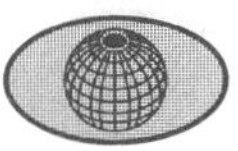   

subtreasury FINANCE subordinate treasury a place where some of a nation's money is held

sub-underwriter MARKETS firm underwriting stock issue a company that underwrites an issue, taking shares of stock from the main underwriters

subvention FINANCE financial support given officially money given by a government or official body to support an activity

suggested retail price US BUSINESS sale price suggested by manufacturer the price at which a manufacturer suggests a product should be sold on the retail market, though this may be reduced by the retailer. *UK term* ***recommended retail price***

suit GENERAL MANAGEMENT employee in formal role a business executive who works for a large corporation, especially in a relatively faceless management role (*slang*)

suitability rules REGULATION & COMPLIANCE rules ensuring that client can afford an investment guidelines that brokers and others selling or recommending investments are required to follow to ensure that investors are financially able to handle the risks involved in investing

sukuk FINANCE asset-backed interest-free bond in Islamic financing, the equivalent of a bond, which represents undivided shares in ownership of tangible assets. Under Islamic law it cannot earn interest.

sum FINANCE **1.** money a particular amount of money **2.** total amount of something the total amount of any given item, such as stocks or securities **3.** total of added numbers the total arising from the addition of two or more numbers

sum at risk FINANCE, RISK how much of something investors might lose an amount of any given item, such as money, stocks, or securities, that an investor might lose

sum insured INSURANCE largest amount insurance firm will pay the maximum amount that an insurance company will pay out in the event of a claim

sum of digits method or **sum-of-the-year's-digits depreciation** ACCOUNTING = ***accelerated depreciation***

sums chargeable to the reserve ACCOUNTING sums debited to company's reserves sums that can be debited to a company's reserves

sunk cost ACCOUNTING completed cost unrelated to future decisions a cost that has been irreversibly incurred or committed prior to a decision point, and cannot therefore be considered relevant to subsequent decisions

sunshine law REGULATION & COMPLIANCE US law requiring openness in the United States, a law that requires public disclosure of a government act or government proceedings

superannuation PENSIONS money yielding income, usually in retirement money providing an income for somebody who no longer works, usually because they are older than the normal age for retirement

superannuation plan PENSIONS Australian pension plan in Australia, a pension plan that may be personal or operated by an employer

superannuation scheme PENSIONS New Zealand pension plan in New Zealand, a pension plan that may be personal or operated by an employer

supplementary benefit HR & PERSONNEL formerly in UK, government payments for poor people formerly, in the United Kingdom, payments from the government to people with very low incomes. It was replaced by **income support**.

supplier OPERATIONS & PRODUCTION firm providing what another firm needs a company that provides materials, components, goods, or services for another company

supply and demand ECONOMICS quantity of available goods and desire for them the quantity of goods available for sale at a given price, and the level of consumer need for those goods. The balance of supply and demand fluctuates as external economic factors—for example, the cost of materials and the level of competition in the marketplace—influence the level of demand from consumers and the desire and ability of producers to supply the goods. Supply and demand is recognized as an economic force, and is often referred to as the **law of supply and demand**.

supply chain GENERAL MANAGEMENT, OPERATIONS & PRODUCTION network of firms involved in production process the network of manufacturers, wholesalers, distributors, and retailers, who turn raw materials into **finished goods** and services and deliver them to consumers. Supply chains are increasingly being seen as integrated entities, and closer relationships between the organizations throughout the chain can bring competitive advantage, reduce costs, and help to maintain a loyal customer base.

supply chain management OPERATIONS & PRODUCTION overseeing of relationships between firms in supply chain the management of the movement of goods and flow of information between an organization and its suppliers and customers, to achieve strategic advantage. Supply chain management covers the processes of managing materials, physical distribution, purchasing, information, and logistics.

supply price OPERATIONS & PRODUCTION price at which something is provided the price at which goods or services are supplied

supply shock ECONOMICS event causing reduced supply of necessity an event that causes a sudden reduction, or perceived reduction, in the production or availability of a product or resource necessary to an economy

supply-side economics ECONOMICS economic theory stressing incentives for suppliers a branch of economics that emphasizes the production of goods through incentives as a means of stimulating economic growth

support price ECONOMICS product price subsidized by government the price of a product that is fixed or stabilized by a government so that it cannot fall below a specific level

support ratio ECONOMICS = ***dependency ratio***

surcharge OPERATIONS & PRODUCTION charge added to standard charge a charge added to the standard charge for a specific product or service

surety FINANCE **1.** guarantor somebody who promises to cover another person's obligations **2.** guarantee for loan the **collateral** given as security when a person, business, or organization takes out a loan

surplus ACCOUNTING = ***budget surplus***

surplus capacity OPERATIONS & PRODUCTION ability to produce more than customers require the capability of a factory or workstation to produce output over and above the level required by consumers or subsequent processes. Surplus capacity is a product of materials, personnel, and equipment that are superfluous, or not working to maximum **capacity**. Some surplus capacity is required in any production system to deal with fluctuations in demand, and as a backup in case of failure. Excessive surplus capacity, however, adds to the cost of the production process as work-in-process inventory or finished-goods storage increases, and can

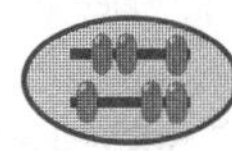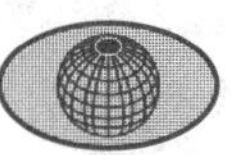

result in **overcapacity**. If a workstation has no surplus capacity its workloads cannot be increased, so it is at risk of becoming a **bottleneck**. *Also called* ***redundant capacity***

surrender INSURANCE relinquish insurance policy before maturity to cancel an insurance policy before the contracted date for maturity

surrender charge FINANCE penalty for early withdrawal of invested money a charge levied when somebody withdraws money invested before the date allowed

surrender value INSURANCE money paid by insurance firm for canceled policy the sum of money offered by an insurance company to somebody who cancels a policy before it has completed its full term

surtax TAX tax paid on top of other taxes a tax paid in addition to another tax, typically levied on a corporation with very high income

survey MARKETING, STATISTICS collection of data from group on particular topic the collection of data from a given population for the purpose of analysis of a particular issue. Data is often collected from only a sample of a population, and this is known as a **sample survey**. Surveys are used widely in research, especially in **market research**.

survivalist enterprise *S. Africa* BUSINESS small firm with no paid workers a business that has no paid employees, generates income below the poverty line, and is considered the lowest level of microbusiness

sushi bond STOCKHOLDING & INVESTMENTS Japanese bond a bond that is not denominated in yen and is issued in any market by a Japanese financial institution. This type of bond is often bought by Japanese institutional investors (*slang*).

suspended trading MARKETS halt in trading of stock a period when trading in a specific stock or on an exchange is stopped, usually in response to information about a company, or concern about rapid movement of the stock price. *See also* ***trading halt***

suspense account BANKING temporary holding account an account in which debits or credits are held temporarily until sufficient information is available for them to be posted to the correct accounts

sustainable advantage GENERAL MANAGEMENT lasting competitive advantage a competitive advantage that can be maintained over the long term, as opposed to one resulting from a short-term tactical promotion

sustainable development GENERAL MANAGEMENT development that does not disadvantage future generations development that meets the needs of the present without compromising the ability of future generations to meet their own needs. The concept of sustainable development was introduced by the Brundtland Report, the first report of the World Commission on Environment and Development, established by the United Nations in 1983. It advocates the integration of social, economic, and environmental considerations into policy decisions by business and government. Particular emphasis is given to social, cultural, and ethical implications of development. Sustainable development can be achieved through **environmental management** and is a feature of a socially responsible business.

SVA *abbr* STOCKHOLDING & INVESTMENTS shareholder value analysis

swap 1. FINANCE, STOCKHOLDING & INVESTMENTS trade of payment terms between two firms an arrangement whereby two organizations contractually agree to exchange payments on different terms, for example, in different currencies, or one at a fixed rate and the other at a floating rate. *See also* ***asset swap, bond swap, interest rate swap*** **2.** FINANCE exchange an exchange of credits or liabilities

swap book STOCKHOLDING & INVESTMENTS list of exchanges wanted a broker's list of stocks or securities that clients wish to swap

swaption STOCKHOLDING & INVESTMENTS right to exchange an **option** giving the right but not the obligation to enter into a **swap** contract (*slang*)

sweat equity FINANCE unpaid work by firm's founder work done for little or no pay by the owner or partners of a new company in the early stages of the company's activities

sweep facility BANKING automatic service moving money to different account the automatic transfer of sums from a checking account to a deposit account, or from any low interest account to a higher one. For example, a personal customer may have the balance transferred just before receipt of their monthly salary, or a business may stipulate that when a balance exceeds a specific sum, the excess is to be transferred.

sweetener 1. GENERAL MANAGEMENT incentive an incentive offered to somebody to take a particular course of action **2.** STOCKHOLDING & INVESTMENTS attractive extra feature on investment product a feature added to a security to make it more attractive to investors **3.** STOCKHOLDING & INVESTMENTS high-yield investment added to lower yield collection a security with a high yield that has been added to a portfolio to improve its overall return. *See also* ***kicker***

SWF *abbr* STOCKHOLDING & INVESTMENTS sovereign wealth fund

SWIFT BANKING society supporting common global financial transactions network a nonprofit cooperative organization with the mission of creating a shared worldwide data processing and communications link and a common language for international financial transactions. Established in Brussels in 1973 with the support of 239 banks in 15 countries, it now has over 7,000 live users in 192 countries, exchanging millions of messages valued in trillions of dollars every business day. *Full form* ***Society for Worldwide Interbank Financial Telecommunication***

swing trading MARKETS buying and selling stock after sudden price changes the trading of stock in order to take advantage of sudden price movements that occur especially when large numbers of traders have to cover short sales

switch 1. STOCKHOLDING & INVESTMENTS replace one investment product in set with another to exchange a specific security with another within a portfolio, usually because the investor's objectives have changed **2.** STOCKHOLDING & INVESTMENTS swap involving exchange rates a type of **swap** that involves different currencies and interest rates. *See also* ***swap*** **3.** OPERATIONS & PRODUCTION move goods elsewhere to move a commodity from one location to another

Switch BANKING UK debit card a debit card formerly used in the United Kingdom

switching STOCKHOLDING & INVESTMENTS buying and selling different futures contracts simultaneously the simultaneous sale and purchase of contracts in futures with different expiration dates, as, for example, when a business decides that it would like to take delivery of a commodity earlier or later than originally contracted

switching discount STOCKHOLDING & INVESTMENTS lower charge to existing customers for exchanging funds the discount available to holders of collective investments who move from one fund to another offered by the same fund manager.

   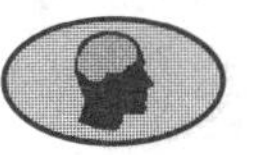  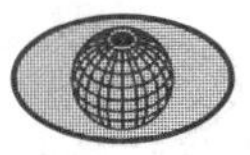 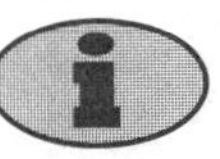  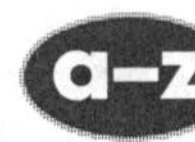

The discount is usually a lower initial charge compared to the one made to new investors, or to existing investors who make a further investment.

SWOT analysis GENERAL MANAGEMENT, MARKETING assessment of strengths, weaknesses, opportunities, and threats an assessment of the "Strengths, Weaknesses, Opportunities, and Threats" in an organization. SWOT analysis is used in the early stages of strategic and **marketing planning**, in **problem solving** and **decision making**, or for making staff aware of the need for change. It can be used at a personal level when determining possible career development.

SYD *abbr* ACCOUNTING sum-of-the-years'-digits depreciation = ***accelerated depreciation***

Sydney Futures Exchange MARKETS main Australian commodity exchange the principal market in Australia for trading financial and commodity futures. It was established in 1962 as a wool futures market, the Sydney Greasy Wool Futures Exchange, but adopted its current name in 1972 to reflect its widening role. *Abbr* **SFE**

symmetrical distribution STATISTICS even distribution of statistical data around central value a distribution of statistical data that is symmetrical about a central value

syndicate 1. BUSINESS group joining together for business activity a group of people or companies that come together for a specific business activity, especially when they jointly contribute capital to a project **2.** GENERAL MANAGEMENT distribute item to several outlets to agree to distribute an article, a cartoon, a television show, or other work to several different outlets, publications, or broadcasting companies **3.** BANKING get large loan underwritten by international banks to arrange for a large loan to be underwritten by several international banks

syndicated research MARKETING data on commercial trends trend data supplied by research agencies from their regularly operated retail audits or consumer panels

systematic risk RISK risk related to securities market or economy investment risk that is attributable to the performance of the stock market or the economy

systematic sampling STATISTICS *see* ***random sampling***

systematic withdrawal STOCKHOLDING & INVESTMENTS regular payment from mutual fund to shareholder an arrangement in which a mutual fund pays out a specific amount to the shareholder at regular intervals. *See also* ***withdrawal plan***

systems analysis GENERAL MANAGEMENT assessment of efficiency of business operation the examination and evaluation of an operation or task in order to identify and implement more efficient methods, usually through the use of computers. Systems analysis can be broken down into three main areas: the production of a statement of objectives; determination of the best methods of achieving these objectives in a cost-effective and efficient way; and the preparation of a **feasibility study**. *Also called* ***systems planning***

systems approach GENERAL MANAGEMENT use of computers in business organization a technique employed for organizational **decision making** and **problem solving** involving the use of computer systems. The systems approach uses **systems analysis** to examine the extent to which a system's components are interrelated and interdependent. When working together, these components produce an effect greater than the sum of the parts. System components might comprise departments or functions of an organization or business which work together for an overall objective.

systems audit GENERAL MANAGEMENT auditing approach an approach to **auditing** that utilizes a **systems approach**. By using a systems audit to assess the internal control system of an organization, it is possible to assess the quality of the accounting system and the level of testing required from the financial statements. One shortcoming of systems audit is that it does not consider audit risk.

systems planning GENERAL MANAGEMENT = ***systems analysis***

T

T+ FINANCE number of days for completing business deal an expression of the number of days allowed for settlement of a transaction

tactical plan GENERAL MANAGEMENT short-term plan a short-term plan for achieving the objectives of a person, business, or organization

tail 1. MARKETS difference between acceptable yields in US Treasury auction the spread between the average yield accepted in an auction of US government securities and the highest yield accepted **2.** STOCKHOLDING & INVESTMENTS numbers after decimal point in bond price the figures that come after the decimal point in the quoted price of a bond

tailgating MARKETS broker trading stock immediately after client does the practice by a broker of buying or selling a security immediately after a client's transaction, in order to take advantage of the impact of the client's deal

takaful INSURANCE insurance comprised of pool of funds Islamic insurance in which all participants are members and contribute to a pool of funds that provide assistance in the event of loss on the part of any of the participants. An Islamic insurance arrangement avoids the prohibitions against gambling and interest in Islamic law.

take a flier FINANCE guess to speculate about what might happen (*slang*)

take a hit FINANCE lose money to make a loss on an investment (*slang*)

take a view MARKETS form expectation of how market will perform to form an opinion on the likely direction a market will take, and take a position that will be of benefit if the opinion proves correct

takeaway MARKETING customer's impressions of product the impressions that a consumer forms about a product or service

take-home pay FINANCE = ***net pay*** (*informal*)

takeout STOCKHOLDING & INVESTMENTS selling stock in firm the act of removing capital that was originally invested in a new company by selling stock

takeout financing FINANCE long-term borrowing long-term loans taken out to replace short-term financing

takeover MERGERS & ACQUISITIONS **1.** when one firm takes control of another the acquisition by a company of a controlling interest in the voting share capital of another company, usually achieved by the purchase of a majority of the voting stocks **2.** = ***takeover bid***

takeover approach *UK* MERGERS & ACQUISITIONS = ***tender offer***

takeover battle MERGERS & ACQUISITIONS result of firm's resistance to acquisition the activities surrounding a **contested takeover bid**. The bidder may raise the offer price and write to the stockholders extolling the benefits of the takeover. The board may contact other companies in the same line of business, hoping that a **white**

  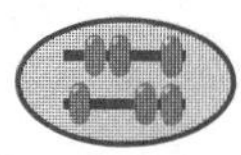   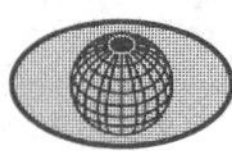   

knight may appear. It could also take action to make the company less desirable to the bidder. *See also* ***poison pill***

takeover bid MERGERS & ACQUISITIONS firm's attempt to buy another an attempt by one company to acquire another. A takeover bid can be made either by a person or an organization, and usually takes the form of an approach to shareholders with an offer to purchase. The bidding stage is often difficult and fraught with politics, and various forms of **knight** may be involved.

Takeover Panel MERGERS & ACQUISITIONS, REGULATION & COMPLIANCE = ***City Panel on Takeovers and Mergers***

takeover ratio *UK* MERGERS & ACQUISITIONS indicator of likelihood that firm is acquisition target the **book value** of a company divided by its market capitalization. If the resulting figure is greater than one, then the company is a candidate for a takeover. *See also* ***appreciation, asset stripping***

takeover target MERGERS & ACQUISITIONS firm another company wants to purchase a company that another company has chosen to acquire by buying enough of its stock to control it

taker 1. STOCKHOLDING & INVESTMENTS buyer of option the buyer of an **option** to buy or sell at a particular price and time **2.** FINANCE borrower somebody who takes out a loan

take-up rate STOCKHOLDING & INVESTMENTS percentage of stockholders agreeing to buy more stock the percentage of acceptances of an offer to existing stockholders to buy more stock in a specific company

takings FINANCE = ***receipts***

talon STOCKHOLDING & INVESTMENTS form for ordering bond coupons a form attached to a **bearer bond** that the holder of the bond uses to order new coupons when those attached to the bond have been depleted

tangible asset ACCOUNTING firm's material resource an asset that has a physical presence, for example, buildings, cash, and stock. Leases and securities, although not physical in themselves, are classed as tangible assets because the underlying assets are physical. *See also* ***intangible asset***

tangible asset value or **tangible net worth** ACCOUNTING asset value expressed per share the value of all the assets of a company less its intangible assets such as goodwill, shown as a value per share

tangible book value ACCOUNTING value of all firm's material resources the book value of a company after intangible assets, patents, trademarks, and the value of research and development have been subtracted

tank STOCKHOLDING & INVESTMENTS drop steeply in price to fall suddenly and steeply, especially with reference to stock prices (*slang*)

tap CD FINANCE certificate of deposit issued on demand an issue of a **certificate of deposit**, normally in a large denomination, at the request of a specific investor

tape ◇ don't fight the tape STOCKHOLDING & INVESTMENTS don't go against the direction of the market

taper relief TAX UK system for adjusting capital gains tax payable in the United Kingdom, a system of reduction in the capital gains tax payable on the disposal of assets by relating the proportion of the capital gain charged to tax to the length of time the asset has been owned. The reduction differs for business assets and non-business assets.

tap stock STOCKHOLDING & INVESTMENTS UK government stock issued over time in the United Kingdom, a government stock that is made available over a period of time in varying amounts

target 1. GENERAL MANAGEMENT goal of effort an end toward which effort is directed and on which resources are focused, usually to achieve an organization's strategy **2.** MERGERS & ACQUISITIONS = ***target company***

target audience MARKETING likely consumers of product or service a group of people considered likely to buy a product or service

target cash balance FINANCE amount of money firm wants available the amount of cash that a company would like to have readily available

target company MERGERS & ACQUISITIONS firm subject to acquisition a company that is the object of a **takeover bid**

targeted repurchase MERGERS & ACQUISITIONS buying back stock from firm's potential buyer a company's purchase of its own stock from somebody attempting to buy the company

target population STATISTICS group to be investigated in statistical study in a statistical study, a sample set of units such as events or people that is to be observed

target savings motive ECONOMICS desire to save money for particular goal the wish to have a specific item or to achieve a specific goal that gives people a reason to save

target stock level OPERATIONS & PRODUCTION supply of stored goods that meets likely customer demand the level of inventory that is needed to satisfy all demand for a product or component over a specific period

tariff 1. INTERNATIONAL TRADE government tax on imports or exports a government duty imposed on imports or exports to stimulate or dampen economic activity **2.** OPERATIONS & PRODUCTION list of prices a list of prices at which goods or services are supplied

Tariff Concession Scheme TAX Australian program for reduced duties on some imports a system operated by the Australian government in which imported goods that have no locally produced equivalent attract reduced duties. *Abbr* **TCS**

tariff office INSURANCE UK insurance firm charging regulated premiums in the United Kingdom, an insurance company whose premiums are based on a scale set collectively by several companies

tawarruq FINANCE sale for cash of item purchased by installments in Islamic financing, an arrangement in which somebody purchases an item from a bank on a deferred payment plan, then sells it immediately to obtain money. *See also* ***murabaha***

tax TAX government charge on people and firms a charge levied by a government on individuals and companies to pay for public services. Tax may be taken directly from income or indirectly through a sales tax or other indirect tax.

tax abatement TAX temporary reduction in tax owed a reduction in the amount of tax owed, usually for a short period of time

taxability TAX liability to tax the extent to which a good or individual is subject to a tax

taxable base TAX amount that can be taxed the amount of income that is subject to taxation, after allowances and deductions have been made

taxable gain *US* TAX profit liable to capital gains tax a profit from the sale of an asset that is subject to **capital gains tax**. *UK term* ***chargeable gain***

taxable income TAX income that can be taxed the proportion of the income of a person, business, or organization that is subject to taxes

taxable matters TAX products that can be taxed goods or services that fall into a category of things that is subject to a tax

     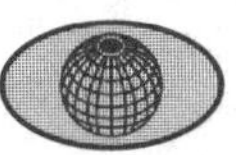   

taxable supply TAX goods subject to VAT a supply of goods that are subject to tax in countries that have **VAT**

tax adjustment TAX change to amount of tax owed a change made to the amount of tax owed

tax adviser TAX = ***tax consultant***

tax allowance TAX portion of UK income not taxed in the United Kingdom, a part of somebody's income that is not taxed. There are different reasons for receiving a tax allowance and they vary according to age and personal circumstances.

tax and price index ECONOMICS, TAX UK measure of household buying power in the United Kingdom, an index number showing the percentage change in gross income that taxpayers need if they are to maintain their real **disposable income**

tax assessment TAX calculation of property value for tax an official calculation of the value of property for the purposes of taxation

taxation TAX **1.** system of raising public revenue the system of raising revenue for public funding by taxing individuals and organizations **2.** amount raised by tax the amount of money raised by imposing a tax

tax auditor US TAX official checking tax returns a government employee who investigates taxpayers' returns. *UK term* ***tax inspector***

tax avoidance TAX way of managing finances to pay less tax the organization of a taxpayer's affairs so that the minimum tax liability is incurred. Tax avoidance involves making the maximum use of all legal means of minimizing liability to taxation. *See also* ***tax evasion, tax break***

tax base TAX value of things taxed the taxable value of all property, goods, and activities taxed by a government

tax bracket TAX group of incomes with same tax rate a range of income levels subject to marginal tax at the same rate

tax break TAX special reduction in taxes an investment that is tax-efficient or a legal arrangement that reduces the liability to tax. *See also* ***tax avoidance, tax shelter***

tax code TAX **1.** number indicating UK tax allowance in the United Kingdom, a number given to indicate the amount somebody can earn before tax has to be paid **2.** US laws on tax in the United States, the system of laws and regulations regarding taxation

tax concession UK TAX tax reduction encouraging investment a tax reduction allowed, for example, to encourage investment in a particular type of industry

tax consultant TAX professional adviser on taxes a professional who advises on all aspects of taxation from tax avoidance to estate planning. *Also called* ***tax adviser***

tax court TAX US court deciding cases involving federal taxes in the United States, a court that deals with disputes between taxpayers and the Internal Revenue Service

tax credit TAX **1.** sum offset against tax a sum of money that can be offset against tax **2.** portion of UK dividend already taxed in the United Kingdom, the part of a dividend on which the company has already paid tax, so that the stockholder is not taxed on it **3.** deduction from individual's income tax liability an amount that can be subtracted directly to reduce somebody's income tax liability

tax-deductible TAX subtracted before tax calculation allowed to be removed from the total of income that will be subject to tax

tax-deferred TAX taxed later not to be taxed until a later time

tax deposit certificate TAX UK certificate showing advance payment of tax in the United Kingdom, a certificate showing that a taxpayer has deposited money in advance of an expected tax payment. The money earns interest while on deposit.

tax dodge TAX illegal way of avoiding taxes any illegal method of paying less tax than a person or company is obliged to pay (*informal*)

tax dollars TAX US taxes funding government the income taxes paid in the United States to fund the government

tax domicile TAX somebody's legal home for tax purposes a place that a government levying a tax considers to be somebody's home

tax-efficient TAX reducing tax due financially advantageous by leading to a reduction of the taxes that have to be paid

tax evasion TAX illegally not paying taxes the illegal practice of paying less money in taxes than is due. *See also* ***tax avoidance***

tax evasion amnesty TAX official forgiveness by government for not paying taxes a government measure that gives freedom from punishment to people who have evaded a tax

tax-exempt TAX **1.** not subject to expected tax not subject to tax though falling into a category of things that are usually subject to tax **2.** tax-free falling into a category of things that is legally exempted from a tax

tax exemption TAX **1.** freedom from specific tax liability freedom from having to pay specific taxes that would ordinarily be collected **2.** portion of income not taxed a part of somebody's income on which tax does not have to be paid

Tax-Exempt Special Savings Account STOCKHOLDING & INVESTMENTS *see* ***TESSA***

tax exile TAX **1.** living abroad to avoid tax residence in another country in order to avoid paying taxes in the home country **2.** person or firm moving abroad to avoid taxes a person or business that leaves a country to avoid paying taxes

tax-favored asset TAX resource taxed at lower rate an asset that receives more favorable tax treatment than some other asset

tax file number TAX Australian taxpayer's number in Australia, a unique identification number assigned to each taxpayer. *Abbr* **TFN**

Tax File Number Withholding Tax TAX *see* ***TFN Withholding Tax***

tax-free TAX not subject to tax not subject to an expected tax

tax harmonization TAX making tax laws in different areas similar the enactment of taxation laws in different jurisdictions, such as neighboring countries, provinces, or states of the United States, that are consistent with one another

tax haven TAX place with attractively low tax rates a country that has generous tax laws, especially one that encourages noncitizens to base operations in the country to avoid higher taxes in their home countries

tax holiday UK TAX period when tax is waived an exemption from tax granted for a specific period of time, for example, when just starting out in business (*informal*)

tax incentive TAX lowering of taxes on specific activities a tax reduction given to encourage or support specific courses of action

tax inspector UK TAX = ***tax auditor***

tax invoice TAX in Australia and New Zealand, invoice specifying tax in Australia and New Zealand, a document issued by a supplier which stipulates the amount charged for goods or services as well as the amount of **Goods and Services Tax** payable

 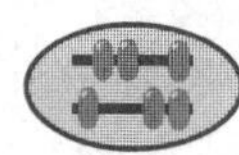   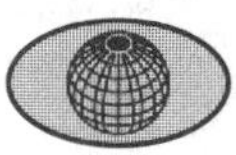   

tax law TAX legislation regulating taxation the body of laws on taxation, or a specific law on an aspect of taxation

tax liability TAX tax payable by person or organization the amount of tax that a person or organization has to pay

tax lien TAX legal notice to recover tax a legal order to hold somebody's goods or property until a debt that is secured by the goods or property has been repaid

tax loophole TAX flaw in law allowing tax avoidance an ambiguity in a tax law that enables some individuals or companies to avoid or reduce taxes

tax loss TAX financial loss claimable against tax a transaction that results in a reduced tax liability, even though it may not be associated with an actual cash loss, for example, a loss associated with depreciation

tax loss carry back TAX using current losses to lower past year's taxes the reduction of taxes in a previous year, by subtraction from income for that year of losses suffered in the current year

tax loss carry forward TAX using current losses to lower future taxes the reduction of taxes in a future year, by subtraction from income for that year of losses suffered in the current year

tax obligation TAX how much tax is owed the amount of tax that a person, business, or organization owes

tax on capital income TAX tax on selling assets a tax on a business's income from sales of capital assets

tax payable TAX how much tax is due the amount of tax a person or company has to pay

taxpayer TAX somebody paying tax a person, business, or organization that pays a tax

tax planning TAX planning of tax avoidance the process of planning how to avoid paying too much tax, for example by investing in tax-exempt bonds

tax rate TAX percentage of income due in tax the rate at which a tax is payable, usually expressed as a percentage

tax refund TAX overpaid tax money returned to taxpayer an amount that a government gives back to a taxpayer who has paid more taxes than were due

tax relief TAX reduction in taxes deductions and exemptions allowed taxpayers for specific expenses or losses they may have incurred, or because of their age or status as a caregiver, etc.

tax return TAX form for calculating and reporting taxes owed an official form on which a company or individual enters details of income and expenses, used to assess tax liability. *Also called* ***return***

tax revenue FINANCE, TAX money from taxes the money that a government receives in taxes from any source

tax sale TAX government's sale of property for unpaid tax in the United States, the sale of an item by a government to recover overdue taxes on a taxable item

tax shelter TAX arrangement to avoid tax a financial arrangement designed to avoid or reduce tax liability. *See also* ***abusive tax shelter, tax break***

tax subsidy TAX special lowering of taxes for business a tax reduction that a government gives a business for a particular purpose, usually to create jobs

tax system TAX processes for taxation an organized and integrated method for imposing and collecting taxes

tax threshold *UK* TAX point at which tax rate changes a point at which another percentage of tax is payable

tax treaty TAX agreement between nations concerning taxes an international agreement that deals with taxes, especially taxes by several countries on the same individuals

tax year TAX period for which taxes are calculated a 12-month period covered by a statement for taxation purposes about income, spending, and allowable deductions

T-bill *abbr* STOCKHOLDING & INVESTMENTS Treasury bill

T-bond *abbr* STOCKHOLDING & INVESTMENTS Treasury bond

TCO *abbr* GENERAL MANAGEMENT total cost of ownership

T-commerce E-COMMERCE business via TV business that is conducted by means of interactive television

TCS *abbr* TAX Tariff Concession Scheme

TDB *abbr* FINANCE Trade Development Board

teaser MARKETING advertising that interests customers in learning more an advertisement that gives a little information about a product in order to attract customers by making them curious to know more

teaser rate MORTGAGES special temporary interest rate to attract customers a temporary concessionary interest rate offered on mortgages or credit cards in order to attract new customers (*informal*)

technical analysis STOCKHOLDING & INVESTMENTS examination of changes in investment prices the analysis of past movements in the prices of financial instruments, currencies, commodities, etc., with a view to predicting future price movements by applying analytical techniques. *See also* ***fundamental analysis, qualitative analysis, quantitative analysis***

technical correction MARKETS when stock price changes to match true value a situation where a stock price or a currency moves up or down because it was previously too low or too high, due to technical factors

technical rally MARKETS short-term price increase against prevailing market decrease a temporary rise in security or commodity prices while the market is in a general decline. This may be because investors are seeking bargains, or because analysts have noted a support level.

technical reserves *UK* INSURANCE = ***insurance reserves***

Technology and Human Resources for Industry Programme FINANCE *see* ***THRIP***

technology stock STOCKHOLDING & INVESTMENTS shares in technology firms stock issued by a company that is involved in new technology

TED spread MARKETS yield difference between LIBOR and US Treasury bills the difference in yield between commercial **LIBOR** rates and US **Treasury bills.** *Full form* ***Treasury Eurodollar spread***

teeming and lading *UK* ACCOUNTING = ***lapping***

telebanking BANKING = ***telephone banking***

telecommuter GENERAL MANAGEMENT, HR & PERSONNEL = ***teleworker***

teleconferencing GENERAL MANAGEMENT meetings conducted via telephones or TV channels the use of telephone or television channels to connect people in different locations in order to conduct group discussions, meetings, conferences, or courses

telegraphic transfer BANKING means of moving money abroad a method of transferring funds from a bank to a financial institution overseas, using telephone or cable. *Abbr* **TT**

  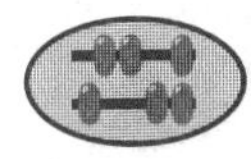   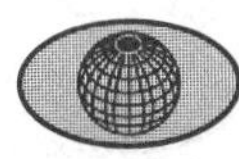   

teleimmersion GENERAL MANAGEMENT advanced teleconferencing creating impression of physical immediacy an enhanced teleconferencing technology that uses banks of video cameras linked to computers, enabling users in remote locations to collaborate as if they were in the same room

telephone banking BANKING accessing bank account by telephone a system in which customers can access their accounts and a variety of banking services 24 hours a day by telephone. *Also called* ***telebanking***

telephone number salary FINANCE very high salary a six- or seven-figure salary, especially one aspired to or considered undeserved (*informal*)

teleworker GENERAL MANAGEMENT, HR & PERSONNEL employee who works largely remotely an employee who spends a substantial amount of working time away from the employer's main premises and communicates with the organization through the use of computing and telecommunications equipment. *Also called* ***telecommuter***

teller *US* BANKING bank employee dealing with customers face to face an employee in a bank or savings and loan association who deals in person with customers' deposits and withdrawals. *UK term* ***cashier***

tenancy in common LEGAL joint ownership without right to inherit other's share a type of ownership in property in which two or more people each have the right to enjoy the entire property but have no right to automatically inherit other owners' shares

tenant REAL ESTATE somebody renting place to live or work a person or company that rents a house, apartment, or office to live or work in

tenbagger STOCKHOLDING & INVESTMENTS investment with big increase in value an investment that increases in value ten times over its purchase price (*slang*)

tender **1.** STOCKHOLDING & INVESTMENTS make offer for investment product at auction to bid for securities at auction. The securities are allocated according to the method adopted by the issuer. In the standard auction style, the investor receives the security at the price they tendered. In a Dutch style auction, the issuer announces a strike price after all the tenders have been examined. This is set at a level where all the issue is sold. Investors who submitted a tender above the strike price just pay the strike price. The Dutch style of auction is increasingly being adopted in the United Kingdom. US Treasury bills are also sold using the Dutch system. *See also* ***offer for sale, sale by tender*** **2.** GENERAL MANAGEMENT submit price to do work to offer to undertake work or supply goods at a specific price, usually in response to an invitation to bid for a work contract in competition with other suppliers **3.** OPERATIONS & PRODUCTION statement outlining acceptable price for job a statement of what a person or company is willing to accept when offering to undertake a major piece of work or supply goods, given in response to request to bid competitively for the work

tenderer *UK* OPERATIONS & PRODUCTION = ***bidder***

tender offer *US* MERGERS & ACQUISITIONS price offered for takeover the price at which a prospective buyer offers to purchase a controlling interest in a business or corporation. *UK term* ***takeover approach***

10-K ACCOUNTING US firm's official yearly financial statement the filing of a US company's annual accounts with the New York Stock Exchange

tenor FINANCE period before bill of exchange can be paid the period of time that has to elapse before a bill of exchange becomes payable

10-Q ACCOUNTING US firm's official quarterly financial statement the filing of a US company's quarterly accounts with the New York Stock Exchange

term STOCKHOLDING & INVESTMENTS period before investment product is fully payable the period of time that has to elapse from the date of the initial investment before a security or other investment such as a term deposit or endowment insurance becomes redeemable or reaches its maturity date

term assurance *UK* INSURANCE = ***term insurance***

term bill FINANCE = ***period bill***

term deposit BANKING savings held for a specified period in the United Kingdom, a deposit account held for a fixed period. Withdrawals are either not allowed during this period, or they involve a fee payable by the depositor.

terminal bonus INSURANCE bonus received at policy maturity date in the United Kingdom, a bonus received when insurance comes to an end

terminal market MARKETS place for trading futures contracts an exchange on which futures contracts or spot deals for commodities are traded

termination clause LEGAL clause detailing termination of contract a clause that explains how and when a contract can be terminated

term insurance INSURANCE insurance that is valid for specified period insurance, especially life insurance, that is in effect for a specified period of time. *UK term* ***term assurance***

term loan FINANCE debt arrangement for specified period a loan for a fixed period, usually called a **personal loan** when it is for non-business purposes. While a personal loan is usually at a fixed rate of interest, a term loan to a business may be at either a fixed or variable rate. Term loans may be either secured or unsecured. An early payment fee is usually payable when such a loan is repaid before the end of the term. *See also* ***balloon loan, bullet loan***

terms STOCKHOLDING & INVESTMENTS conditions attached to new issue the conditions that apply to an issue of shares of stock

term share BANKING building society account for specified period in the United Kingdom, a share account in a building society that is for a fixed period of time. Withdrawals are usually not allowed during this period. However, if they are, then a fee is usually payable by the account holder.

terms of sale OPERATIONS & PRODUCTION agreed conditions attached to sale the conditions attached to a sale and agreed to by buyer and seller, for example, payment due dates, method of payment, and delivery date

term structure of interest rates STOCKHOLDING & INVESTMENTS discount pattern for each year to maturity a set of interest rates for each year to maturity of fixed-rate securities such as bonds of differing **term**. *See also* ***yield to maturity***

terotechnology OPERATIONS & PRODUCTION techniques designed to optimize life of assets a multidisciplinary technique that combines the areas of management, finance, and engineering with the goal of optimizing life-cycle costs for physical assets and technologies. Terotechnology is concerned with acquiring and caring for physical assets. It covers the specification and design for the reliability and maintainability of plant, machinery, equipment, buildings, and structures, including the installation, commissioning, maintenance, and replacement of this plant, and also incorporates the feedback of information on design, performance, and costs.

tertiary industry BUSINESS business providing a service an industry that does not produce raw materials or manufacture

  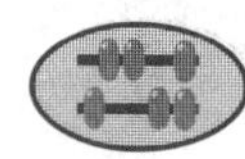 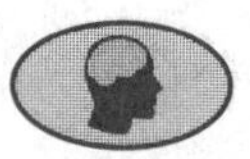 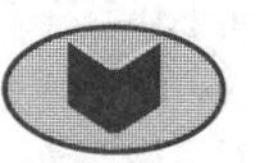 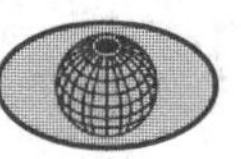   

products but offers a service such as banking, retailing, or accountancy

tertiary sector ECONOMICS part of economy involving nonprofit organizations the part of the economy made up of nonprofit organizations such as consumer associations

TESSA STOCKHOLDING & INVESTMENTS former untaxed UK bank account a former UK savings account in which investors could save up to £9,000 over a period of five years and not pay any tax, provided they made no withdrawals over that time. *Full form* ***Tax Exempt Special Savings Account***

test STOCKHOLDING & INVESTMENTS assessment of likely stock price movements in technical analysis, a way of determining whether to buy or sell a stock by observing if it is likely to rise above or drop below specific price levels that it has had difficulty breaking through in the past

testacy LEGAL possession of valid will at death the legal position of somebody who has died leaving a valid will

testate LEGAL having valid will at death used to refer to somebody who has died leaving a valid will

testator LEGAL somebody with valid will a person who has made a valid will or left a legacy

testatrix LEGAL woman with valid will a woman who has made a valid will or left a legacy

test level STOCKHOLDING & INVESTMENTS barrier price level a specific price level that a stock has had difficulty breaking through in the past. In technical analysis, it is used in determining whether to buy or sell a stock.

TFN *abbr* TAX tax file number

TFN Withholding Tax TAX Australian tax when information missing in Australia, a levy imposed on financial transactions involving somebody who has not disclosed his or her tax file number. *Full form* ***Tax File Number Withholding Tax***

theta STOCKHOLDING & INVESTMENTS ratio of option's decreasing value to decreasing time a ratio between the rate of decrease in the value of an option and the decrease in time as it approaches expiration. *Also called* ***time decay***

thin market MARKETS exchange where little trading is happening a market where the trading volume is low. A characteristic of such a market is a wide spread of bid and offer prices.

third market MARKETS secondary stock exchange a market other than the main stock exchange in which stocks are traded

third party LEGAL person other than two main parties to contract a person other than the two main parties involved in a contract, for example, in an insurance contract, anyone who is not the insurance company nor the person who is insured

third-party network or **third-party service provider** E-COMMERCE = ***value-added network***

third quarter ACCOUNTING third of four divisions of fiscal year the period of three months from July to the end of September, or the period of three months following the second quarter of the fiscal year. *Abbr* **Q3**

third sector ECONOMICS part of economy involving nonprofit organizations the part of the economy made up of **nonprofit organizations** such as charities, professional associations, labor unions, and religious, arts, community, research, and campaigning bodies. *See also* ***nonprofit organization***

three-dimensional management or **3-D management** GENERAL MANAGEMENT theory of management styles a theory outlining eight styles of management that differ in effectiveness, four that are effective and four that are less effective. Different styles may be used in different types of work settings and managers modify their style to suit different circumstances.

3i BANKING bank-owned group providing company finance a finance group owned by the big British commercial banks which provides finance to other companies, especially small ones

360 degree branding LEGAL, STOCKHOLDING & INVESTMENTS supporting brand identity by all marketing activity taking an inclusive approach in branding a product by bringing the brand to all points of consumer contact

three steps and a stumble MARKETS if interest rates increase three times, stocks fall a rule of thumb used on the US stock market that if the Federal Reserve increases interest rates three times consecutively, stock market prices will go down

threshold GENERAL MANAGEMENT starting point the point at which something begins or changes

threshold agreement FINANCE UK contract promising pay raise in specific situation in the United Kingdom, a contract that says that if the cost of living goes up by more than an agreed amount, pay will go up to match it

threshold company BUSINESS emerging company a company that is on the verge of becoming well established in the business world

threshold price OPERATIONS & PRODUCTION lowest sale price for imports into EU in the European Union, the lowest price at which farm produce imported into the EU can be sold

thrift **1.** FINANCE care in managing money a cautious attitude toward the management of money, shown by saving, or spending it carefully and looking for good value
2. BANKING private local US bank for small investors in the United States, a private local bank, savings and loan association, or credit union, that accepts and pays interest on deposits from small investors

thrift institution BANKING US institution acting like savings bank in the United States, an institution that is not a bank but accepts savings deposits and makes loans to savers. *See also* ***savings and loan association, savings bank***

THRIP FINANCE S. African program supporting industry research and development in South Africa, a collaborative program involving industry, government, and educational and research institutions, which supports research and development in technology, science, and engineering. *Full form* ***Technology and Human Resources for Industry Programme***

TIBOR *abbr* MARKETS Tokyo Interbank Offered Rate

tick STOCKHOLDING & INVESTMENTS smallest amount price or rate can change the least amount by which a value such as the price of a stock or a rate of interest can rise or fall, for example, a hundredth of a percentage point or an eighth of a dollar
◇ have ticks in all the right boxes GENERAL MANAGEMENT to be on course to meet a series of objectives

ticker or **ticker tape** MARKETS continuous display of stock prices the electronic display of stock prices that stream across a computer or television screen. The information was formerly produced on continuous paper tape.

ticker symbol MARKETS letters representing stocks traded on stock exchange letter or letters used to identify the stocks or funds listed for trade on a stock exchange

tied loan FINANCE loan to foreign country to buy lender's products a loan made by one national government to another on the condition that the funds are used to purchase goods from the lending nation

tiger MARKETS Hong Kong, S. Korea, Singapore, or Taiwan any of the key markets in the Pacific Basin region except Japan, i.e. Hong Kong, South Korea, Singapore, and Taiwan

tight money ECONOMICS situation where borrowing money is difficult a situation where it is expensive to borrow because of restrictive government policy or high demand

tight money policy ECONOMICS government policy restricting money supply a government policy to restrict money supply, usually by raising interest rates, making it more difficult to borrow and spend money

TILA *abbr* LEGAL Truth in Lending Act

time and material pricing FINANCE determining price based on work and materials a form of **cost-plus pricing** in which price is determined by reference to the cost of the labor and material inputs to the product or service

time bargain MARKETS stock exchange trade for future date a stock market transaction in which the securities are deliverable at a future date beyond the exchange's normal settlement day

time decay STOCKHOLDING & INVESTMENTS = ***theta***

time deposit BANKING US savings arrangement for specified period a US savings account or a certificate of deposit, issued by a financial institution. While the savings account is for a fixed term, deposits are accepted with the understanding that withdrawals may be made subject to a period of notice. Banks are authorized to require at least 30 days' notice. While a certificate of deposit is equivalent to a term account, passbook accounts are generally regarded as funds readily available to the account holder.

time draft BANKING type of US bill of exchange a bill of exchange drawn on and accepted by a US bank. It is either an **after date** bill or **after sight** bill.

times covered STOCKHOLDING & INVESTMENTS ability of net profit to pay firm's dividend the number of times a company's dividends to ordinary stockholders could be paid out of its net after-tax profits. This measures the likelihood of dividend payments being sustained, and is a useful indication of sustained profitability. *Also called* ***dividend cover***

time series STATISTICS collection of data at intervals a series of measurements collected at uniformly spaced intervals of time, sometimes over a period of several years, used to assess long-term trends and seasonal fluctuations

time spread MARKETS simultaneously buying and selling options with different maturities the purchase and sale of options in the same commodity or security with the same price and different **maturities**

time value MARKETS market value minus face value the premium at which an option is trading relative to its **intrinsic value**

time value of money FINANCE potential growth in value over time the principle that a specific amount of money is worth more now than it will be at a date in the future, because the sum available now can be invested and will have grown in value by the date in the future

tip STOCKHOLDING & INVESTMENTS recommendation given by expert a piece of useful expert information, for example, a recommendation about a product or a **stock tip**

tip-off STOCKHOLDING & INVESTMENTS confidential information a piece of confidential information about something that is going to happen, or a warning based on confidential financial or commercial information. *See also* ***insider dealing, money laundering***

title LEGAL right of ownership a legal right to the ownership of property. If somebody has good title to a property, proof of ownership is beyond doubt.

title deed LEGAL document showing real estate ownership a document showing who is the owner of real estate

title insurance INSURANCE protection from problems in legal title an insurance policy that protects a purchaser or lender from loss of real property due to defects in the **title**

toasted FINANCE having suffered financial losses used to refer to someone or something that has lost money (*slang*)

toehold purchase or **toehold** MERGERS & ACQUISITIONS small stake in corporation in the United States, the acquisition of less than 5% of the outstanding stock in a company that is targeted for a takeover. At the 5% level, the acquiring company must notify the Securities and Exchange Commission and the targeted company of its plans.

token charge OPERATIONS & PRODUCTION small charge levied as token gesture a small charge that does not cover the real costs of providing the goods or services

token payment FINANCE small payment made as token gesture a small payment made only so that a payment of some sort is seen to be made

Tokyo Interbank Offered Rate MARKETS in Japan, rate for banks' offers of deposits on the Japanese money markets, the rate at which banks will offer to make deposits in yen with each other, often used as a reference rate. The deposits are for terms from overnight up to five years. *Abbr* **TIBOR**

tombstone FINANCE newspaper notice detailing large loan for business a notice in the financial press giving details of a large lending facility, or large equity or debt securities offerings, to a business. It may relate to a management buyout or to a package that may include an **interest rate cap** and **collars** to finance a specific package. More than one bank may be involved. Although it may appear to be an advertisement, technically in most jurisdictions it is regarded as a statement of fact and therefore falls outside the advertisement regulations. The borrower generally pays for the advertisement, though it is the financial institutions that derive the most benefit.

top-down approach GENERAL MANAGEMENT leadership style with managers driving changes an autocratic style of leadership in which strategies and solutions are identified by senior management and then cascaded down through an organization. The top-down approach can be considered a feature of large bureaucracies. A number of management gurus have criticized it as an out-of-date style that leads to stagnation and business failure. *See also* ***bottom-up approach***

top management HR & PERSONNEL senior members of firm the upper-level managers of an organization or company, especially the **senior management** or a **board of directors** (*informal*)

top slicing **1.** STOCKHOLDING & INVESTMENTS sale of holding yielding original cost of investment selling part of a stockholding that will realize a sum that is equal to the original cost of the investment. What remains therefore represents potential pure profit. **2.** TAX in UK, assessment of tax on mature investments in the United Kingdom, a complex method used by HM Revenue & Customs for assessing what tax, if any, is paid when some investment bonds or endowment policies mature or are cashed in early

  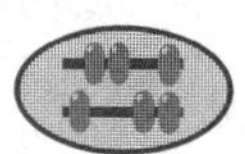   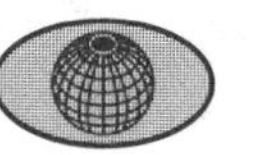   

total absorption costing ACCOUNTING accountant's method of pricing goods and services a method used by a cost accountant to price goods and services, allocating both direct and indirect costs. Although this method is designed so that all of an organization's costs are covered, it may result in opportunities being missed because of high prices. Consequently sales may be lost that could contribute to overheads. *See also* ***marginal costing***

total assets FINANCE sum of assets owned by person or organization the total value of all current and long-term assets owned by a person or organization

total cost OPERATIONS & PRODUCTION sum of costs of producing amount of something all the costs of producing a specific amount of something, including fixed costs and variable costs

total cost of ownership GENERAL MANAGEMENT cost including all aspects of ownership a structured approach to calculating the **costs** associated with buying and using a product or service. Total cost of ownership takes the purchase cost of an item into account but also considers related costs such as ordering, delivery, subsequent usage and maintenance, supplier costs, and after-delivery costs. Originally designed as a process for measuring IT expense after implementation, total cost of ownership considers only financial expenses and excludes any **cost-benefit analysis**. *Abbr* **TCO**

total overhead cost variance ACCOUNTING difference between actual and absorbed overhead costs the difference between the overhead costs absorbed and the actual overhead costs incurred, both fixed and variable

total quality management GENERAL MANAGEMENT integrated system of business planning an integrated and comprehensive system of planning and controlling all business functions so that products or services are produced which meet or exceed customer expectations. TQM is a philosophy of business behavior, embracing principles such as employee involvement, continuous improvement at all levels, and customer focus, as well as being a collection of related techniques, such as full documentation of activities, clear goal-setting, and performance measurement from the customer perspective, that are aimed at improving quality. *Abbr* **TQM**

total responsibility management GENERAL MANAGEMENT procedures ensuring responsible business practices systems and procedures to ensure responsible business practices and management. It is used to describe the codes of practice and systems that organizations are developing to manage their social, environmental, and ethical responsibilities in response to pressures from stakeholders, emerging global standards, general social trends, and institutional expectations. Some issues, linked to labor, ecology, and community, are included because they are subject to increasing assessment or regulation, while others are raised intermittently as a result of public controversies.

total return STOCKHOLDING & INVESTMENTS percentage change in overall value of investment the total percentage change in the value of an investment over a specified time period, including capital gains, dividends, and the investment's appreciation or depreciation.

The total return formula reflects all the ways in which an investment can earn or lose money, resulting in an increase or decrease in the investment's **net asset value** (NAV):

$$\frac{\text{(Dividends + Capital gains distributions +/- Change in NAV)}}{\text{Beginning NAV}} = \text{Total return}$$

If, for instance, you buy a stock with an initial NAV of $40, and after one year it pays an income dividend of $2 per share and a capital gains distribution of $1, and its NAV has increased to $42, then the stock's total return would be:

$$\frac{2+1+2}{40} = \frac{5}{40} = 0.125 \times 100\% = 12.5\%$$

The total return time frame is usually one year, and it assumes that dividends have been reinvested. It does not take into account any sales charges that an investor paid to invest in a fund, or taxes they might owe on the income dividends and capital gains distributions received.

total revenue FINANCE total income from all sources all income from all sources

total utility ECONOMICS consumer's total satisfaction from good or service the overall satisfaction that a consumer receives from consuming a particular quantity of a specific good or service

touch MARKETS difference between best bid and offer prices the difference between the best bid and the best offer price quoted by all market makers for a specific security

touch price MARKETS best gap between bid and offer prices the largest available difference between the bid and offer prices of a security

toxic FINANCE, STOCKHOLDING & INVESTMENTS adversely affecting financial status damaging to financial health. The term as applied to loans, debt, assets, and financial instruments such as mortgages, bonds and other securities refers to finance that is risky and potentially seriously damaging not only to the owner but to the financial system as a whole (*informal*).

toxic waste STOCKHOLDING & INVESTMENTS high-risk securities new securities with unusually high risk, often notes that have as collateral the riskiest portions of numerous issues of otherwise relatively low-risk debt (*slang*)

TQM *abbr* GENERAL MANAGEMENT total quality management

tracker fund STOCKHOLDING & INVESTMENTS = ***index fund***

tracking 1. STOCKHOLDING & INVESTMENTS investing to match a market index the practice of buying investments in order to achieve the same or a similar return to a market index **2.** MARKETING research into changing perception of product or organization research designed to monitor changes in the public perception of a product or organization over a period of time

tracking error STOCKHOLDING & INVESTMENTS degree to which fund fails to track index the deviation by which an **index fund** fails to replicate the index it is aiming to mirror

tracking stock STOCKHOLDING & INVESTMENTS stock with dividends linked to performance of subsidiary a stock whose dividends are tied to the performance of a subsidiary of the corporation that owns it

trade OPERATIONS & PRODUCTION **1.** carry on a business to buy and sell products, or carry on a business **2.** buying and selling the business of buying and selling goods or, in some situations, bartering goods **3.** particular type of business a particular type of business, or the people or companies dealing in the same type of product **4.** one transaction a single activity of buying or selling that is carried out

trade agreement INTERNATIONAL TRADE trading agreement between countries an international agreement between countries over general terms of trade

trade association OPERATIONS & PRODUCTION organization promoting interests of particular trade a membership organization of businesses in the same trade that promotes the interests of the businesses

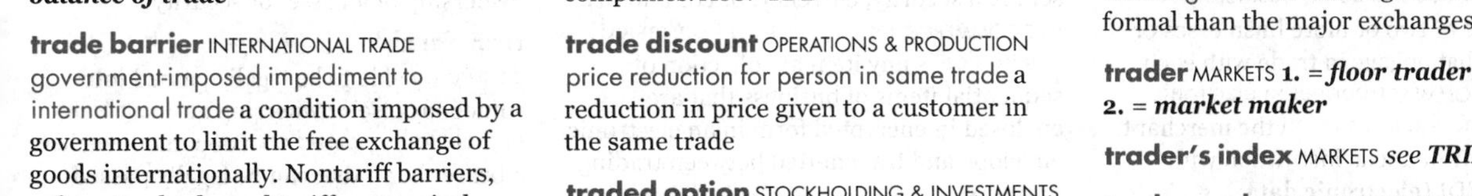

trade balance INTERNATIONAL TRADE = ***balance of trade***

trade barrier INTERNATIONAL TRADE government-imposed impediment to international trade a condition imposed by a government to limit the free exchange of goods internationally. Nontariff barriers, safety standards, and tariffs are typical trade barriers.

trade bill FINANCE bill of exchange between trading partners a bill of exchange between two businesses that trade with each other. *See also* ***acceptance credit***

trade credit FINANCE credit offered to trading partner credit offered by one business when trading with another. Typically this is for one month from the date of the invoice, but it could be for a shorter or longer period.

trade cycle INTERNATIONAL TRADE period of cyclical fluctuations in trade a period during which trade expands, then slows down, then expands again

trade date STOCKHOLDING & INVESTMENTS date of a purchase or sale the date on which a buyer and seller reach an agreement for the purchase and sale of an asset

trade debt FINANCE debt from normal trading a debt that originates during the normal course of trade

trade debtor FINANCE debtor with debt incurred through normal trading a person or company that owes money to a company as a result of the normal activities of trading

trade deficit INTERNATIONAL TRADE extent to which imports exceed exports the difference in value between a country's imports and exports when its imports exceed its exports. *Also called* ***balance of payments deficit***. *See also* ***trade gap***

trade description REGULATION & COMPLIANCE legal description of product a description of a product provided by the manufacturer and controlled for accuracy by the **Trade Descriptions Act**

Trade Descriptions Act REGULATION & COMPLIANCE UK legislation governing product description in the United Kingdom, an act that limits the way in which products can be described so as to protect customers from wrong descriptions made by manufacturers

Trade Development Board INTERNATIONAL TRADE agency promoting trade with Singapore companies a Singapore government agency that was established in 1983 to promote trade and explore new markets for Singapore products, and offers various programs of assistance to companies. *Abbr* **TDB**

trade discount OPERATIONS & PRODUCTION price reduction for person in same trade a reduction in price given to a customer in the same trade

traded option STOCKHOLDING & INVESTMENTS option bought and sold on exchange an option that can be continuously traded on an exchange

trade gap INTERNATIONAL TRADE gap between imports and exports the difference between the value of a country's imports and that of its exports. *See also* ***trade deficit***

trade-in *US* FINANCE using old product as partial payment for new the act of giving an old product as part of the payment for a new one. *UK term* ***part exchange***

trade investment STOCKHOLDING & INVESTMENTS investment of one business in another the action or process of one business making a loan to another, or buying stock in another. The latter may be the first stages of a friendly **takeover bid**.

trademark GENERAL MANAGEMENT unique mark identifying product with producer an identifiable mark on a product that may be a symbol, words, or both, that connects the product to the trader or producer of that product and gives the producer or trader protection from fraudulent use. Any use of the trademark without permission gives the owner the right to sue for damages. In the United States, trademarks are controlled by the United States Patent and Trademark Office. In the United Kingdom, a trademark can be registered at the Register of Trademarks maintained by the Intellectual Property Office.

trade mission INTERNATIONAL TRADE foreign visit for purpose of discussing trade a visit by businesspeople from one country to another for the purpose of discussing trade between their respective nations

trade name MARKETING proprietary name of product or service the proprietary name given by the producer or manufacturer to a product or service. A trade name occasionally becomes the generic name for products of a similar nature, for example, "Thermos" is often applied to all insulated flasks, and "Kleenex" to all tissues.

TRADENZ *abbr* BUSINESS New Zealand Trade Development Board

tradeoff OPERATIONS & PRODUCTION exchange of items or concessions in business deal an act of exchanging one thing for another as part of a business deal

trade point MARKETS informal, minor stock exchange a stock exchange that is less formal than the major exchanges

trader MARKETS **1.** = ***floor trader*** **2.** = ***market maker***

trader's index MARKETS *see* ***TRIN***

trade surplus INTERNATIONAL TRADE extent to which exports exceed imports the difference in value between a country's imports and exports when its exports exceed its imports. *Also called* ***balance of payments surplus***

trade union *UK* GENERAL MANAGEMENT, HR & PERSONNEL = ***labor union***

trade war INTERNATIONAL TRADE competition between countries for market share a competition between two or more countries for a share of international or domestic trade

trade-weighted index CURRENCY & EXCHANGE measure of country's currency against trading partners' currencies an index that measures the value of a country's currency in relation to the currencies of its trading partners

trading MARKETS buying and selling goods the business of buying and selling goods or assets

trading account ACCOUNTING = ***profit and loss account***

trading area BUSINESS area where business is concentrated the area in which a company does most of its business, or the area around a city that is the main center of a region

trading company BUSINESS firm that buys and sells goods a company that specializes in buying and selling goods

trading floor MARKETS where dealers trade face to face an area in a stock exchange or similar market where dealers meet to trade with each other personally

trading halt MARKETS cessation of trade in firm's stock a stoppage of trading in a stock on an exchange, usually in response to information about a company, or concern about rapid movement of the stock price. *See also* ***suspended trading***

trading limit MARKETS maximum amount allowed to single trader the maximum amount of a product that can be traded by a single trader

trading loss FINANCE sales income lower than expenditure a situation in which the amount of money an organization receives in sales is less than its expenditure

  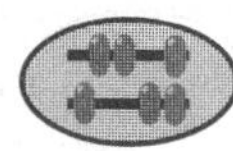 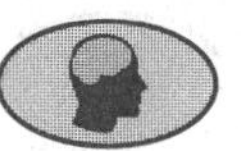  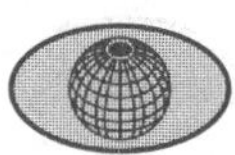   

trading partner 1. BUSINESS, INTERNATIONAL TRADE firm or country doing business with another one of two or more businesses or countries that engage in trade with each other 2. E-COMMERCE partner in electronic data interchange transaction the merchant, customer, or financial institution with whom an EDI (**electronic data interchange**) transaction takes place. Transactions can be either between senders and receivers of EDI messages or within distribution channels in an industry, for example, financial institutions or wholesalers.

trading pit MARKETS *see* ***pit***

trading profit ACCOUNTING = ***gross profit***

trading range MARKETS difference between highest and lowest prices the difference between the highest and lowest price for a stock or bond over a period of time. *Also called* ***historical trading range***

trading session MARKETS one trading day in stock or commodities market a period of one day of buying and selling at a stock or commodities exchange from the opening bell to the closing bell

trading stamp OPERATIONS & PRODUCTION stamp exchanged for goods in store a special stamp given away by a store, which the customer can collect and exchange later for free goods

traditional IRA PENSIONS retirement savings facility in the United States, the original **IRA**, that allows individuals to set up retirement accounts, contributions to which are tax-deductible up to a specific amount depending on income. *See also* ***rollover IRA, Roth IRA***

training levy TAX UK tax funding government's training programs in the United Kingdom, a tax to be paid by companies to fund the government's training programs

tranche STOCKHOLDING & INVESTMENTS one installment in series one of a series of installments, used, for example, when referring to loans to companies, government securities that are issued over a period of time, or money withdrawn by a country from the IMF

tranche CD BANKING certificate of deposit sold in series over time a **certificate of deposit** that is part of a set that is sold by the issuing bank over a period of time. Each of the CDs in a tranche has the same maturity date.

transaction 1. BUSINESS business negotiation an act of negotiating something or carrying out a business deal 2. MARKETS instance of trading an instance of buying or selling a security, currency, or commodity 3. E-COMMERCE item of business transmitted electronically any item or collection of sequential items of business that are enclosed in encrypted form in an electronic envelope and transmitted between trading partners

transaction costs STOCKHOLDING & INVESTMENTS direct costs of buying or selling asset incremental costs that are directly attributable to the buying or selling of an asset. Transaction costs include commissions, fees, and direct taxes.

transaction e-commerce E-COMMERCE electronic selling the electronic sale of goods and services, either business-to-business or business-to-customer

transaction exposure CURRENCY & EXCHANGE, RISK risk in international trade from changing exchange rates the risk that an organization may incur major losses from the effects of foreign exchange rate changes during the time it takes to arrange the export or import of goods or services. Transaction exposure is present from the time a price is set.

transaction file OPERATIONS & PRODUCTION means of tracking inventory a file for keeping track of inventory use and replenishment. *See also* ***inventory record***

transaction history STOCKHOLDING & INVESTMENTS record of trades with broker a record of all of an investor's transactions with a broker

transaction message or **transaction set** E-COMMERCE electronic document exchanged in e-commerce transaction the EDI (**electronic data interchange**) equivalent of a paper document, exchanged as part of an e-commerce transaction, comprising at least one data segment representing the document sandwiched between a header and a trailer. It is called a transaction message in the UN/EDIFACT protocol and a transaction set in the ANSI X.12 protocol.

transactions motive ECONOMICS desire to keep cash for upcoming purchases the motive that consumers have to hold money for their likely purchases in the immediate future

transfer 1. BANKING movement of money between banks the movement of money through the domestic or international banking system, between banks in a **clearing system**, or between particular bank accounts. *See also* ***BACS, Fedwire, SWIFT*** 2. STOCKHOLDING & INVESTMENTS change of ownership the change of ownership of an asset or security

transferable LEGAL 1. legally able to be passed on able to be legally passed into somebody else's ownership 2. document eligible to be passed on a document such as a bearer bond that can be legally passed into somebody else's ownership

transfer agent STOCKHOLDING & INVESTMENTS agent handling transfers of ownership an agent employed by a corporation to keep a record of the owners of securities and handle transfers of ownership

transferee LEGAL somebody to whom an asset is transferred a person who receives ownership of an asset that is being transferred

transferor LEGAL somebody transferring asset to another a person who transfers the ownership of an asset or security to another person

transfer out fee STOCKHOLDING & INVESTMENTS fee for closing broker's account a fee payable when an investor closes an account with a broker

transfer price OPERATIONS & PRODUCTION price for goods or services within firm the price at which goods or services are transferred between different units of the same company. If those units are located in different countries, the term **international transfer pricing** is used.

The extent to which the transfer price covers costs and contributes to (internal) profit is a matter of policy. A transfer price may, for example, be based upon marginal cost, full cost, market price, or negotiation. Where the transferred products cross national boundaries, the transfer prices used may have to be agreed with the governments of the countries concerned.

transfer pricing OPERATIONS & PRODUCTION pricing method used between departments of organization a pricing method used when supplying products or services from one part of an organization to another. The transfer pricing method can be used to supply goods either at cost or at profit if profit targets are to be achieved. This can cause difficulties if an internal customer can buy more cheaply outside the organization. Multinational businesses have been known to take advantage of this pricing policy by transferring products from one country to another in order for profits to be higher in the country where corporation tax is lower.

transfer stamp REAL ESTATE, TAX mark on UK deeds showing payment of stamp duty in the United Kingdom, the mark embossed onto

   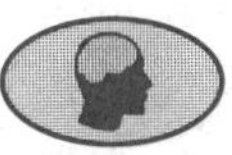  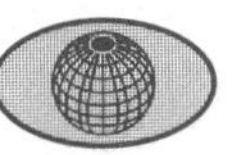   

title deeds when property is transferred to signify that **stamp duty** has been paid

transfer value PENSIONS in UK, value of somebody's pension rights in the United Kingdom, the value of a person's rights in a pension when they are given up on acquiring rights in a new pension, for example, when somebody changes the company providing the pension. *See also* ***vested rights***

transit time OPERATIONS & PRODUCTION delay after completing operation the period between the completion of an operation and the availability of the material at the next workstation

translation exposure CURRENCY & EXCHANGE, RISK risk on business from changing exchange rates the risk that the balance sheet and income statement may be adversely affected by foreign exchange rate changes

transmission E-COMMERCE electronic data sent between trading partners digital data sent electronically from one trading partner to another, or from a trading partner to a **value-added network**

transmission control standards E-COMMERCE format for exchanging electronic business data the defined format by which to address the **electronic envelopes** used by trading partners to exchange business data

transnational business or **transnational company** or **transnational corporation** or **transnational** BUSINESS = ***multinational business***

transparency MARKETS when information is freely available the condition in which nothing is hidden. This is an essential condition for a free market in securities. Prices, the volume of trading, and factual information must be available to all.

trash and cash MARKETS driving stock price down to repurchase more cheaply a trade of a security in which a trader sells a stock, then spreads negative information about the company whose stock they just sold, causing the stock's price to decline and enabling the trader to buy it back at a low price and make a profit

travel accident insurance INSURANCE travel insurance provided by credit card company a form of insurance coverage offered by some credit card companies when the whole or part of a travel arrangement is paid for with the card. In the event of death resulting from an accident in the course of travel, or the loss of eyesight or a limb, the credit card company will pay the cardholder, or his or her estate, a pre-stipulated sum. *See also* ***travel insurance***

traveler's checks BANKING checks for cashing in foreign country checks bought by a traveler that are valid for use at home or abroad, but are generally cashed in a foreign country. Only a countersignature is required from the holder for verification. *UK term* ***traveller's cheques***

travel insurance INSURANCE insurance for various risks associated with travel a form of insurance coverage that provides medical cover while abroad as well as covering the policyholder's possessions and money while traveling. Many travel insurance policies also reimburse the policyholder if a holiday has to be canceled and pay compensation for delayed journeys. *See also* ***travel accident insurance***

traveller's cheques BANKING = ***traveler's checks***

treasurer TREASURY MANAGEMENT officer responsible for money a person who is responsible for the funds and other assets of an organization

Treasurer FINANCE Australian government minister responsible for financial and economic matters in Australia, the minister responsible for financial and economic matters in a national, state, or territory government

treasuries STOCKHOLDING & INVESTMENTS US government securities negotiable debt instruments issued by the US government. *See also* ***Treasury bill, Treasury bond, Treasury note***

treasury TREASURY MANAGEMENT section of firm responsible for financial matters the department of a company or corporation that deals with all financial matters

Treasury FINANCE government department responsible for finance and economy in some countries, the government department responsible for the nation's financial policies as well as the management of the economy

Treasury bill STOCKHOLDING & INVESTMENTS discounted short-term security a short-term security issued by the US or UK government that is sold at a discount from face value and pays no interest but can be redeemed for full face value at maturity. *Abbr* **T-bill**

Treasury bill rate STOCKHOLDING & INVESTMENTS effective interest earned from holding Treasury bill the rate of interest obtainable by holding a **Treasury bill.** Although Treasury bills are non-interest bearing, by purchasing them at a discount and holding them to redemption, the discount is effectively the interest earned by holding these instruments. The Treasury bill rate is the discount expressed as a percentage of the issue price. It is annualized to give a rate per annum.

Treasury bond STOCKHOLDING & INVESTMENTS US government bond a bond issued by the US government that bears fixed interest. *Abbr* ***T-bond***

treasury direct STOCKHOLDING & INVESTMENTS trading system for US Treasury bills in the United States, a system offered through Federal Reserve banks that allows investors to buy and sell **Treasury bills** directly from the Federal Reserve

Treasury Eurodollar spread MARKETS *see* ***TED spread***

treasury inflation protected security STOCKHOLDING & INVESTMENTS US government security protected from inflation a security issued by the US government with principal and coupon payments that are increased automatically to protect against inflation

treasury management TREASURY MANAGEMENT firm's handling of all financial matters the corporate handling of all financial matters, the generation of external and internal funds for business, the management of currencies and cash flows, and the complex strategies, policies, and procedures of corporate finance

Treasury note STOCKHOLDING & INVESTMENTS **1.** US 2–10-year government security a fixed-interest security issued by the US government that can mature within two to ten years **2.** short-term debt instrument issued by Australian government a short-term debt instrument issued by the Australian federal government. Treasury notes are issued on a tender basis for periods of 13 and 26 weeks.

treasury stock STOCKHOLDING & INVESTMENTS shares of firm's stock bought back by firm shares of a company's stock that have been bought back by the company and not canceled. In the United States, these shares are shown as deductions from equity; in the United Kingdom, they are shown as assets in the balance sheet.

treaty 1. LEGAL written agreement between nations a written agreement between nations, such as the Treaty of Rome (1957), that was the foundation of the European Union **2.** INSURANCE contract in which reinsurer accepts insurer's risks a contract between an insurer and the reinsurer whereby the latter is to accept risks from the insurer **3.** REAL ESTATE = ***private treaty***

   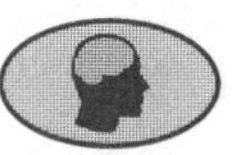  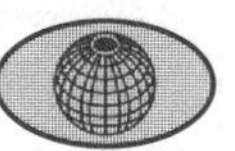   

trend STATISTICS regular movement of variable values over time the movement in a specific direction of the values of a variable over a period of time

trendline STATISTICS pattern of change in variable values over time a visual representation of the direction of change shown by variables over a period of time

Treynor ratio ECONOMICS = ***risk-adjusted return on capital***

trial balance ACCOUNTING draft balance in bookkeeping in a double-entry bookkeeping system, a draft calculation of debits and credits to see if they balance

trickle-down theory ECONOMICS belief that benefits spread downward in economy the theory that financial and other benefits received by big businesses and wealthy people eventually spread down through an economy to the rest of society

trillion one million millions a sum equal to one million millions (1 plus 12 zeros). An older use in the United Kingdom was a larger number, 1 plus 18 zeros.

TRIN MARKETS measure of rising to falling stocks a market indicator calculated by dividing the advancing stocks by declining stocks and comparing it to the volume of advances to declines. A result less than one is considered bullish, and a result greater than one is considered bearish. *Full form* ***trader's index***

tripartite authority REGULATION & COMPLIANCE UK system of financial regulators in the United Kingdom, the financial regulatory system composed of the Treasury, Financial Services Authority, and the Bank of England

triple A STOCKHOLDING & INVESTMENTS = ***AAA***

triple bottom line GENERAL MANAGEMENT firm's environmental and social behavior, together with profitability environmental sustainability and social responsibility used as criteria when judging the overall performance of a company, in addition to purely financial considerations

triple I organization GENERAL MANAGEMENT corporate culture focusing on information, intelligence, and ideas a type of **corporate culture** in which the focus is on three areas: information, intelligence, and ideas. The triple I organization recognizes the value of information and learning. It minimizes the distinction between managers and workers, concentrating instead on people and the need to pursue learning, including personal, lifelong, and organizational learning, in order to keep up with the pace of change.

triple tax exempt TAX exempt from US tax at all levels in the United States, used to describe bonds, interest payments, and other sources of income that are exempt from federal, state, and local taxes

triple witching hour MARKETS joint maturity date for futures and options a time when stock options, stock index futures, and options on such futures all mature at once. Triple witching hours occur quarterly and are usually marked by highly volatile trading.

troubleshooter FINANCE consultant employed by firm in difficulty an independent person, often a consultant, who is called in by a company in difficulties to help formulate a strategy for recovery

trough ECONOMICS low point in economic cycle the lowest point or period in an economic cycle before the situation begins to improve

troy ounce FINANCE unit of weight for precious metals the traditional unit used when weighing precious metals such as gold or silver. It is equal to approximately 1.097 ounces avoirdupois or 31.22 grams.

true and fair view *UK* ACCOUNTING auditor-confirmed statement of firm's financial position a correct statement of a company's financial position as shown in its accounts and confirmed by the auditors

true copy LEGAL copy of legal document attested by notary an exact copy of a legal document, as declared before a **notary public**

true interest cost FINANCE real interest rate paid on debt security the effective rate of interest paid by the issuer on a debt security that is sold at a discount

trump MARKETING make competitor's product appear useless by comparison to make something such as a competitor's product appear useless because what you have is so much better (*slang*)

trust 1. FINANCE assets held for somebody else money or property held by one person or a group of people (the trustees) with a legal obligation to administer them for another person's benefit. *See also* ***blind trust*** **2.** *US* BUSINESS cartel a group of companies that act together with the effect of reducing competition and controlling prices

trust account BANKING account held for somebody else money held by one person (the trustee), often a professional, on behalf of the owner of the funds in it, for example, a minor

trust bank BANKING Japanese bank offering banking and trustee services a Japanese bank that acts commercially in the sense of accepting deposits and making loans and also in the capacity of a trustee

trust company BUSINESS firm administering trusts a company whose business is administering trusts on behalf of trustees

trust corporation BANKING US institution sometimes performing banking activities a US state-chartered institution that may undertake banking activities

trust deed LEGAL document outlining trust a document that sets out the regulations governing a trust

trustee FINANCE somebody holding assets in trust a person who, either individually or as a member of a board, has a legal obligation to administer assets for another person's benefit

trustee in bankruptcy FINANCE somebody managing bankrupt's finances somebody appointed by a court to manage the finances of a bankrupt person or company

trustee investment STOCKHOLDING & INVESTMENTS investment made by trustee an investment that is made by a trustee and is subject to legal restrictions

trusteeship FINANCE **1.** status of trustee the position of a **trustee** with a legal obligation to administer assets for another person's benefit **2.** time as trustee the term during which somebody acts as a **trustee**

trust fund FINANCE set of assets held in trust assets held in trust by a **trustee** or board of trustees for the trust's beneficiaries

trust officer FINANCE manager of assets of trust somebody who manages the assets of a trust, especially for a bank that is acting as a **trustee**

Truth in Lending Act LEGAL US law requiring transparent disclosure of credit terms in the United States, a law requiring lenders to disclose the terms of their credit offers accurately so that consumers are not misled and are able to compare the various credit terms available. The Truth in Lending Act requires lenders to disclose the terms and costs of all loan plans, including the following: annual percentage rate, points, and fees; the total of the principal amount being financed; payment due date and terms, including any balloon payment where applicable and late payment fees; features of variable-rate loans, including the highest rate the lender would charge, how it is calculated and the resulting monthly payment; total finance charges; whether the loan is assumable; the existence of any application fees or any annual or one-time service fees; and whether there are any pre-payment penalties. Where applicable, it also requires the lender to confirm the address of the property securing the loan. *Abbr* **TILA**

TT *abbr* BANKING telegraphic transfer

turbulence GENERAL MANAGEMENT sudden changes affecting performance unpredictable and swift changes in an organization's external or internal environments, or in an economy, that affect its performance. The late 20th century was considered a turbulent environment for business because of the rapid growth in technology and globalization, and the frequency of restructuring and merger activity. 2008 was an especially turbulent period for financial markets, when banks worldwide could not meet their loans and had to receive government support.

turkey FINANCE poor performer an investment or business that is performing badly (*informal*)

turn MARKETS market maker's profit the difference between the bid and offer prices of a **market maker**

turnaround *US* **1.** FINANCE return of profitability a term for the act of making a company profitable again **2.** OPERATIONS & PRODUCTION value of sales divided by value of inventory a term for the value of goods sold during a year divided by the average value of goods held in stock **3.** OPERATIONS & PRODUCTION preparation of vehicle for another commercial trip a term for the process of emptying a ship, plane, etc., and getting it ready for another commercial trip **4.** OPERATIONS & PRODUCTION processing and dispatching of orders a term for the time it takes to process orders and send out the goods ► *UK term* **turnround**

turnaround management GENERAL MANAGEMENT implementation of rescue measures for failing organization the implementation of a set of actions required to save an organization from business failure and return it to operational normality and financial solvency. Turnaround management usually requires strong leadership and can include restructuring and job losses, an investigation of the root causes of failure, and long-term programs to revitalize the organization.

turnkey contract GENERAL MANAGEMENT agreement to control project until handover to client an agreement in which a contractor designs, constructs, and manages a project until it is ready to be handed over to the client and operation can begin immediately

turnover 1. ACCOUNTING firm's total sales revenue the total sales **revenue** of an organization for an accounting period. This is shown net of **VAT**, trade discounts, and any other taxes based on the revenue in a **profit and loss account**. **2.** MARKETS total value of stocks traded during year the total value of stocks bought and sold on an exchange during the year. This covers both sales and purchases, so each transaction is counted twice. **3.** HR & PERSONNEL rate of change of staff the rate at which staff leave and are replaced in an organization

turnover ratio OPERATIONS & PRODUCTION frequency of firm's changes in inventory during year a measure of the number of times in a year that a business's inventory changes completely. It is calculated as the cost of sales divided by the average book value of inventory.

turnover tax TAX **1.** *US* = ***sales tax*** **2.** *UK* = ***VAT***

turnround *UK* FINANCE = ***turnaround***

twenty-four hour trading MARKETS constant financial trading the possibility of trading in currencies or securities at any time of day or night, because there are always trading floors open at different locations in different time zones. A financial institution with offices in the Far East, Europe, and the United States can offer its clients 24-hour trading—either by the client contacting their offices in each area, or by the customer's local office passing the orders on to another center.

20-F BUSINESS document giving detailed information about non-US companies a document compiled by non-US companies listed on the New York Stock Exchange for the Securities and Exchange Commission that gives detailed corporate information

two-tier tender offer MERGERS & ACQUISITIONS offering premium for initial stock in acquisition attempt in the United States, a **takeover bid** in which the acquirer offers to pay more for shares bought early than for those acquired at a later date, in order to encourage stockholders to accept the offer, thus gaining control quickly. This form of bidding is outlawed in some jurisdictions, including the United Kingdom.

U

UBR *abbr* TAX uniform business rate

UCC *abbr* REGULATION & COMPLIANCE uniform commercial code

UCITS STOCKHOLDING & INVESTMENTS EU rules for mutual funds a set of directives that regulate mutual funds throughout all the countries of the European Union. *Full form* ***Undertakings for Collective Investment in Transferable Securities***

UGMA *abbr* REGULATION & COMPLIANCE Uniform Gifts to Minors Act

UHNWI *abbr* FINANCE ultra high net worth individual

UIF *abbr* INSURANCE Unemployment Insurance Fund

UIT *abbr* STOCKHOLDING & INVESTMENTS unit investment trust

ultra high net worth individual FINANCE person with $30 million plus a person whose net assets, excluding the value of a home, are worth more than $30 million. About 100,000 people worldwide fall into this category. *Abbr* **UHNWI**

ultra vires LEGAL beyond scope of organization's authority a Latin phrase meaning "beyond the powers," used to refer to an activity that normally falls beyond the scope of the instrument from which an organization's authority is derived, and thus may be challenged by the courts. A corporation's powers are limited by the objectives in its charter. Most objectives tend to be wide-ranging, but, should a corporation's directors act outside of these objectives, any resulting agreement may be unenforceable.

ultra vires activity FINANCE something disallowed by rules an act that is not permitted by applicable rules such as those of a corporate charter. Such acts may lead to contracts being void.

umbrella fund STOCKHOLDING & INVESTMENTS offshore investment in other offshore concerns a collective investment based offshore that invests in other offshore collective investments

umbrella organization BUSINESS organization embracing several member organizations a large organization that includes a number of member organizations and works to protect their shared interests

unbalanced growth ECONOMICS different parts of economy growing at different rates

  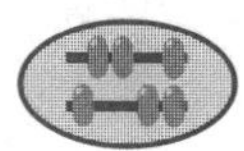   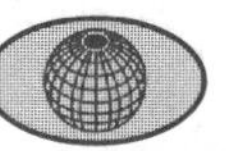   

the situation that occurs when some sectors of an economy grow at different rates from others

unbundling 1. MERGERS & ACQUISITIONS dividing of firm before selling it off the dividing of a company into separate constituent companies, often to sell all or some of them after a takeover 2. STOCKHOLDING & INVESTMENTS splitting returns on security for separate sale the separation of the components of a security in order to sell them separately

uncalled share capital STOCKHOLDING & INVESTMENTS unpaid proportion of stock value the amount of the **nominal value** of shares for which the company has not requested payment. It may not be intended that this payment should be requested unless the company goes into **liquidation**.

uncollectable FINANCE describing debt that is written off used to describe a debt that must be written off, either as a charge to the **profit and loss account** or against an existing doubtful debt provision

uncollected funds BANKING value residing in deposit that bank cannot negotiate money deriving from the deposit of an instrument that a bank has not been able to negotiate

unconditional bid MERGERS & ACQUISITIONS takeover bid offering payment irrespective of stock volume in a takeover battle, a situation in which a bidder will pay the offered price irrespective of how many shares are acquired, typically after the acquisition of a majority of the shares

unconsolidated STOCKHOLDING & INVESTMENTS not grouped together used to describe shares, holdings, loans, or subsidiaries that are not combined into a single unit

uncontested bid GENERAL MANAGEMENT offer of contract to single bidder the offering of a contract by a government or other organization to one bidder only, without competition

uncovered bear STOCKHOLDING & INVESTMENTS person selling stock not yet acquired a person who sells stock which he or she does not hold, hoping to be able to buy stock back at a lower price when it is time to settle

uncovered option STOCKHOLDING & INVESTMENTS option whose seller does not own associated asset a type of **option** in which the underlying asset is not owned by the seller, who risks considerable loss if the price of the asset falls. *Also called* ***naked option***

UNCTAD INTERNATIONAL TRADE UN department dealing with development and finance a part of the United Nations system dealing with the integrated treatment of development and interrelated issues in trade, finance, technology, and investment. *Full form* ***United Nations Conference on Trade and Development***

undated bond STOCKHOLDING & INVESTMENTS bond without maturity date a bond to which no maturity date has been assigned

underbanked STOCKHOLDING & INVESTMENTS describing new issue with few sellers used to describe a new issue without enough brokers to sell it

undercapitalized FINANCE with insufficient capital used to describe a business that has insufficient capital for its requirements

underemployed capital FINANCE capital not producing enough income capital that is not being used effectively to produce income

underlying asset STOCKHOLDING & INVESTMENTS asset with option an asset that is associated with an **option** or other derivative or structured note

underlying inflation or **underlying rate of inflation** MORTGAGES inflation rate not considering mortgage costs a measure of inflation that does not take mortgage costs into account

underlying security STOCKHOLDING & INVESTMENTS security with option a security that is associated with an **option**

undermargined account BANKING account with funds insufficient for margin requirements an account that does not have enough funds to cover its margin requirements, resulting in a **margin call**

underspend FINANCE 1. spend less than intended or allowed to spend less than the amount that was budgeted for spending 2. smaller amount spent than expected an amount that is less than the amount that was budgeted for spending

undersubscribed STOCKHOLDING & INVESTMENTS describing stock issue with some stock unsold used to describe a new issue in which not all shares are sold, and part of the issue remains with the underwriters

undertaking 1. BUSINESS business a commercial business or company 2. LEGAL formal promise a promise, especially a legally binding one

Undertakings for Collective Investment in Transferable Securities STOCKHOLDING & INVESTMENTS *see* ***UCITS***

underused liquidity FINANCE cash not being optimally used available capital that is not being put to effective use in developing a business

undervaluation FINANCE valuation at less than true worth the assessment of an asset as having a value that is less than its expected value or worth

undervalued FINANCE describing asset available for less than value used to describe an asset that is offered for sale at a price lower than its expected value or worth

undervalued currency CURRENCY & EXCHANGE currency available cheaply a currency that costs less to buy with another currency than it is worth in goods

underwrite STOCKHOLDING & INVESTMENTS, INSURANCE, RISK be liable for potential losses to assume risk, especially for a new issue or an insurance policy. *Also called* ***write***

underwriter 1. STOCKHOLDING & INVESTMENTS guarantor of public offering an institution or group of institutions who, for a fee, guarantee a public offering from a corporation and, if it fails to find enough buyers, will purchase the remaining shares 2. INSURANCE insurance risk assessor a person who establishes insurance risk and issues insurance policies for an **insurance company** or syndicate, paying the insured party if a specified loss occurs. *Also called* ***writer*** *(sense 1). See also* ***Lloyd's underwriting syndicate***

underwriters' syndicate STOCKHOLDING & INVESTMENTS group guaranteeing public offering a group of institutions who, for a fee, guarantee a public offering from a corporation and, if it fails to find enough buyers, will purchase the remaining shares

underwriting STOCKHOLDING & INVESTMENTS guaranteeing of public offering the activity of guaranteeing a public offering from a corporation for a fee, agreeing to buy any shares that remain unsold

underwriting commission or **underwriting fee** STOCKHOLDING & INVESTMENTS fee guaranteeing purchase of new stock a fee paid by a company to the **underwriters** for guaranteeing the purchase of new shares in that company

underwriting income INSURANCE profit from insurance premiums the money that an insurance company makes because the premiums it collects exceed the claims it pays out

underwriting spread STOCKHOLDING & INVESTMENTS difference between stock costs and income from sale an amount that is the

  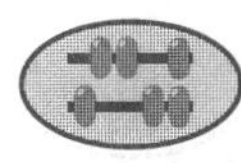   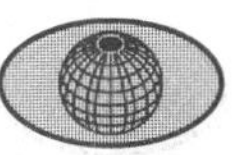 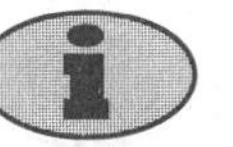  

difference between what an organization pays for an issue and what it receives when it sells the issue to investors

underwriting syndicate STOCKHOLDING & INVESTMENTS group of institutions selling new securities to investors a group of financial institutions who join to sell new securities to investors, and agree to buy any that are unsold themselves

undischarged bankrupt LEGAL somebody still officially classed as bankrupt a person who has been declared bankrupt and has not yet been released from that status by a court

undistributable reserves *UK* FINANCE = ***restricted surplus***

undistributed profit STOCKHOLDING & INVESTMENTS profit not paid out as dividend profit that has not been distributed as dividends to stockholders

UNDP ECONOMICS UN agency providing human development grants a part of the United Nations system with goals that include the elimination of poverty, environmental regeneration, job creation, and advancement of women. It is the world's largest source of grants for sustainable human development. *Full form* ***United Nations Development Program***

unearned income FINANCE money not received from employment income received from sources such as investments or interest on savings rather than from employment. *See also* ***earned income***

unearned increment REAL ESTATE increase in property value not created by owner an increase in the value of a property that arises from causes other than the owner's improvements or expenditure

unearned premium INSURANCE money repaid from terminated insurance policy the amount of money repaid by an insurance company when a policy is terminated

uneconomic FINANCE not producing profits not profitable for a country, firm, or investor in the short or long term

unemployment ECONOMICS people wanting to work but not finding jobs the situation in which some members of a country's labor force are willing to work but cannot find employment

unemployment compensation *US* HR & PERSONNEL = ***severance pay***

Unemployment Insurance Fund INSURANCE employee insurance against potential unemployment in South Africa, a system administered through payroll deductions that insures employees against loss of earnings through being made unemployed by such causes as retrenchment, illness, or maternity. *Abbr* **UIF**

unencumbered REAL ESTATE property with no mortgage used to describe a property that is not subject to a mortgage

uneven lot MARKETS = ***odd lot***

unfair competition BUSINESS dubious way of gaining competitive advantage the practice of trying to do better than another company by using underhand techniques such as importing foreign goods at very low prices or wrongly criticizing a competitor's products

unfunded debt FINANCE debt to be repaid within a year short-term debt requiring repayment within a year of being issued

ungeared *UK* FINANCE = ***unleveraged***

ungluing MERGERS & ACQUISITIONS splitting up established networks the process of breaking up traditional supply chains or groups of cooperating organizations after taking control of the element of mutual interest that holds them together

uniform business rate TAX tax on UK local businesses in the United Kingdom, the rate of tax set by central government that is to be collected from businesses by local government. *Abbr* **UBR**

uniform commercial code REGULATION & COMPLIANCE US laws regulating commercial transactions in the United States, a set of laws governing commercial transactions that has been adopted totally or in part by all 50 states. *Abbr* **UCC**

uniform costing OPERATIONS & PRODUCTION identical approach to costing the use by several businesses of the same costing methods, principles, and techniques

Uniform Gifts to Minors Act REGULATION & COMPLIANCE US standards protecting assets given to children in the United States, a set of standards for protecting financial assets that have been given to minors. *Abbr* **UGMA**

Uniform Transfers to Minors Act REGULATION & COMPLIANCE US regulations protecting noncash gifts to children in the United States, a set of standards for protecting noncash assets that have been given to minors. *Abbr* **UTMA**

unincorporated BUSINESS describing business without status of company used to describe a business that is operating as a partnership or sole trader and has not been made into a company

uninsurable risk INSURANCE risk for which insurance is unavailable an event that is met with so rarely that it is impossible to calculate a probability of occurrence and therefore impossible to calculate a suitable price for insurance. *See also* ***insurable risk, risk***

unique selling point or **unique selling proposition** MARKETING *see* ***USP***

unissued share capital or **unissued capital** *UK* STOCKHOLDING & INVESTMENTS = ***unissued stock***

unissued stock *US* STOCKHOLDING & INVESTMENTS capital stock not yet issued the proportion of a company's **capital stock** that is authorized but has not been issued. *UK term* ***unissued share capital***

unit STOCKHOLDING & INVESTMENTS **1.** securities traded together a collection of securities traded together as a single item **2.** single mutual fund share of stock a share in a mutual fund

unitary taxation TAX taxing of international firm based on worldwide income a method of taxing a corporation based on its worldwide income rather than on its income in the country of the tax authority

unit cost OPERATIONS & PRODUCTION cost of producing single item the cost of one item, calculated on the basis of production and overhead costs for a number of such items produced together

United Nations Conference on Trade and Development INTERNATIONAL TRADE *see* ***UNCTAD***

United Nations Development Program ECONOMICS *see* ***UNDP***

unit investment trust STOCKHOLDING & INVESTMENTS investment company offering units in unmanaged portfolio an investment company that offers an unmanaged portfolio of securities to investors through brokers, typically in units of $1,000 each. *Abbr* **UIT**

unit-linked insurance INSURANCE insurance policy linked to unit trust in the United Kingdom, an insurance policy that is linked to the security of units in a unit trust or fund

unit of account CURRENCY & EXCHANGE currency unit used for payments a unit of a country's currency that can be used in payment for goods or in a firm's accounting

unit of trade STOCKHOLDING & INVESTMENTS smallest amount that can be traded the smallest quantity that can be bought or sold

  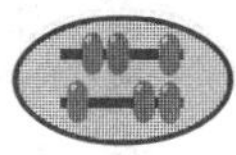   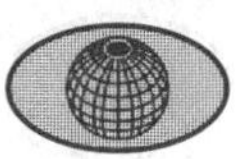   

of a share of stock, or a contract included in an **option**

unit price OPERATIONS & PRODUCTION price of single item the price of one item, calculated on the basis of the cost of production and overhead costs for a number of such items produced together

unit trust *UK* STOCKHOLDING & INVESTMENTS = ***mutual fund***

universal life insurance INSURANCE life insurance that accrues savings a type of life insurance policy that builds up savings and allows the insurer to change the amount of premiums and the coverage

unleveraged *US* FINANCE describing firm with no borrowings used to describe a company that has no borrowed money. *UK term* ***ungeared***

unlimited liability FINANCE full responsibility for debts full responsibility for the obligations of a **general partnership**. This may include the use of personal assets to pay debts.

unlimited risk RISK risk with unlimited potential loss a risk whose potential loss is unlimited, for example, in futures trading

unlisted company BUSINESS, MARKETS company with stock not listed on exchange a company whose shares are not listed on an exchange

unlisted securities STOCKHOLDING & INVESTMENTS stocks not listed on exchange stocks that are not listed on an exchange. *Also called* ***unquoted investments***, ***unquoted shares***

unlisted securities market MARKETS market for minor stocks a market for stocks that are not listed on a recognized exchange. *Abbr* **USM**

unprofitable FINANCE not profitable not producing a profit

unquoted MARKETS having no publicly stated price used to describe a security that has no publicly stated price because it is not listed on an exchange

unquoted investments STOCKHOLDING & INVESTMENTS = ***unlisted securities***

unquoted shares STOCKHOLDING & INVESTMENTS = ***unlisted securities***

unrealized capital gain ACCOUNTING profitable investment not yet sold a profit from the holding of an asset worth more than its purchase price, but not yet sold

unrealized profit/loss ACCOUNTING profit or loss from asset not yet sold a profit or loss that need not be reported as income, for example, deriving from the holding of an asset worth more or less than its purchase price, but not yet sold

unreason GENERAL MANAGEMENT unorthodox approaches that bring business success the process of thinking the unlikely and doing the unreasonable that can be a means by which an organization or individual achieves success

unremittable gain ACCOUNTING in UK, capital gain that cannot be imported in the United Kingdom, a capital gain that cannot be imported into the taxpayer's country, especially because of currency restrictions

unseasoned issue STOCKHOLDING & INVESTMENTS issue of stocks to SEC-approved investors an issue of stocks that a dealer may only sell to specific qualifying investors as agreed by the US Securities and Investment Commission. *See also* ***seasoned issue***

unsecured creditor FINANCE creditor making unsecured loans a creditor who is owed money, but has no security from the debtor for the debt

unsecured debt FINANCE money borrowed without collateral an amount of money borrowed without the borrower providing **collateral** to the lender

unsecured loan FINANCE loan provided without collateral a loan made without **collateral** provided to the lender by the borrower. *Also called* ***signature loan***

unstable equilibrium ECONOMICS easily disrupted balance of supply and demand a market situation in which, if there is a movement of price or quantity away from the equilibrium, existing forces will push the price even further away

unsubsidized FINANCE without financial assistance for which no **subsidy** has been paid. *See also* ***subsidized***

up market MARKETS rising stock market a stock market that is rising or is at its highest level

upside potential STOCKHOLDING & INVESTMENTS potential for value of security to go up the possibility that a security will increase in value. *See also* ***downside risk***

upsizing HR & PERSONNEL increase in activities and staff expansion and restructuring of business activities, including an increase in the number of staff employed. *Also called* ***resizing***. *See also* ***downsizing***

upstairs market MARKETS area of exchange where major institutions trade the place where traders for major brokerages and institutions do business at an exchange

upstream OPERATIONS & PRODUCTION at earlier stage at a point earlier in the production process. *See also* ***downstream***

upstream progress GENERAL MANAGEMENT commercial progress in difficult conditions advancement against opposition or in difficult conditions. A company or project can make upstream progress if it moves toward achieving its objectives despite impediments. *See also* ***downstream progress***

upswing MARKETS rise in stock prices following fall an upward movement in stock prices following a period of steady or falling prices

uptick MARKETS trade at price higher than in previous trade a transaction in which the price of a specific security is higher than the price in the transaction immediately preceding it. *Also called* ***plus tick***

upturn ECONOMICS upward trend an upward trend in sales, profits, a stock market, or an economy

urbun FINANCE forfeitable deposit paid by buyer to seller in Islamic financing, money paid by a buyer to a seller at the time of execution of a contract that will be forfeited if the contract is canceled by the buyer

used credit FINANCE used part of offered credit the portion of a **line of credit** that is no longer available for use

use of proceeds FINANCE details of intended investment use detailed information for investors on how money invested in an undertaking will be put to use

USM *abbr* MARKETS unlisted securities market

USP MARKETING feature distinguishing specific product a specific feature that differentiates a product from similar products. *Full form* ***unique selling point***

US savings bond STOCKHOLDING & INVESTMENTS US Federal government savings product in the United States, a bond that can be bought from the Federal government. *Also called* ***savings bond***

usury FINANCE lending money at high rates the practice of lending money at a rate of interest that is either unlawful or considered to be excessively high

utility **1.** BUSINESS company that provides a service to community a public service company, for example, one that supplies water, gas, or electricity or that runs public

  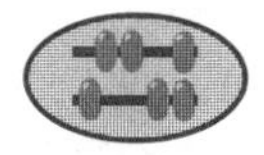   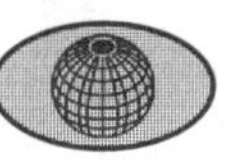   

transportation **2.** ECONOMICS customer satisfaction the usefulness or satisfaction that a consumer gets from a product

UTMA *abbr* REGULATION & COMPLIANCE Uniform Transfers to Minors Act

valuation FINANCE estimate of worth an estimate of how much something is worth

value FINANCE **1.** worth measured in money the amount of money that something is worth **2.** estimate worth of something in money to estimate how much money something is worth

value added GENERAL MANAGEMENT **1.** difference between cost of materials and selling price the difference between the cost of bought-in materials and the eventual selling price of the finished product **2.** valuable distinguishing features of product or service the features that differentiate one product or service from another, and thus create value for the customer. Value added is a customer perception of what makes a product or service desirable over others and worth a higher price. Value added is more difficult to measure without a physical end product, but value can be added to services as well as physical goods, through the process of **value engineering**. *Also called **added value** (sense 1)*

value-added network E-COMMERCE organization providing messaging and communications services an organization that provides messaging-related functions and EDI (**electronic data interchange**) communications services, for example, protocol matching and line-speed conversion, between trading partners. *Abbr* **VAN**. *Also called **third-party network**, **third-party service provider***

value-added reseller BUSINESS trader selling repackaged items bought at retail a merchant who buys products at retail and packages them with additional items for sale to customers. *Abbr* **VAR**

value-added tax TAX *see **VAT***

value-adding intermediary GENERAL MANAGEMENT distributor adding value to product before sale a distributor who adds value to a product before selling it to a customer, for example, by installing software or a modem in a computer

value analysis OPERATIONS & PRODUCTION technique of eliminating unnecessary costs a cost reduction and problem-solving technique that analyzes an existing product or service in order to reduce or eliminate any costs that do not contribute to value or performance. Value analysis usually focuses on design issues relating to the function of a product or service, looking at the properties that make it work, or which are **USPs**.

value-at-risk STOCKHOLDING & INVESTMENTS, RISK *see **Var***

value chain BUSINESS business activities adding value to products or services the sequence of business activities by which, in the perspective of the end user, value is added to products or services produced by an organization

value date FINANCE transfer date a date on which a transaction takes place

value driver FINANCE something adding value to product or service an activity or organizational focus that enhances the value of a product or service in the perception of the consumer and which therefore creates value for the producer. Advanced technology, reliability, or reputation for customer relations can all be value drivers.

value engineering OPERATIONS & PRODUCTION activity that aids design of product an activity that helps to design products that meet customer needs at the lowest cost while assuring the required standards of quality and reliability

value for customs purposes only INTERNATIONAL TRADE declared value of item imported into US what somebody importing something into the United States declares that it is worth

value for money audit ACCOUNTING examination of firm's effectiveness in using resources an investigation into whether proper arrangements have been made for securing economy, efficiency, and effectiveness in the use of resources. *Abbr* **VFM**. *Also called **comprehensive auditing***

value innovation GENERAL MANAGEMENT approach to business growth concentrating on new markets a strategic approach to business growth, involving a shift away from a focus on the existing competition to one of trying to create entirely new markets. Value innovation can be achieved by implementing a focus on innovation and creation of new market possibilities.

value investing STOCKHOLDING & INVESTMENTS investing based on company's value an investment strategy based on the value of a company rather than simply on its stock price

value map MARKETING extra value differentiating product or service the level of value that the market recognizes in a product or service and that helps to differentiate it from competitors

value proposition FINANCE proposed profit-making plan a proposed plan for making a profit, presented, for example, to a potential investor

value share or **value stock** STOCKHOLDING & INVESTMENTS currently underpriced stock a stock that is considered to be currently underpriced by the market, and therefore an attractive investment prospect

value to the business or **value to the owner** FINANCE asset's minimum assessable value the lower of the figures for the **recoverable amount** and the **replacement cost** of an asset. *Also called **deprival value***

VAN *abbr* E-COMMERCE value-added network

Var or **VAR** STOCKHOLDING & INVESTMENTS assessment of likely depreciation of asset or investment a risk assessment measure that is used to establish how much the market value of an asset or a portfolio is likely to decrease over a specific period of time. *Full form **value-at-risk***

VAR *abbr* BUSINESS value-added reseller

variable STATISTICS piece of data studied in statistical analysis an element of data whose changes are the object of a statistical study

variable annuity INSURANCE annuity without fixed payments an **annuity** that offers no guarantee but has potential for a greater return, usually based on the performance of a stock or mutual fund. *See also **annuity***

variable costing ACCOUNTING = ***marginal costing***

variable interest rate FINANCE interest rate that fluctuates during loan period an interest rate that changes, usually in relation to a standard index, during the period of a loan

variable life assurance *UK* INSURANCE = ***variable life insurance***

variable life insurance *US* INSURANCE life insurance where benefits vary with investment performance a type of whole-life insurance policy providing a death benefit that varies according to the performance of an investment portfolio managed by the insurance company. *UK term **variable life assurance***

variable rate FINANCE interest rate that fluctuates a rate of interest on a loan that is

 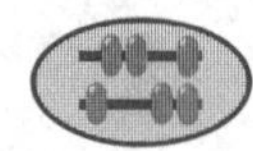   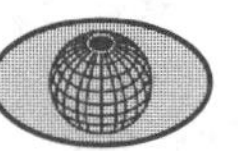   

not fixed, but can change with the current bank interest rates. *Also called* ***floating rate***

variable rate note FINANCE note with interest rate linked to index a note whose interest rate is tied to an index, such as the prime rate in the United States or the London Interbank Offering Rate in the United Kingdom. *Abbr* **VRN**

variance **1.** GENERAL MANAGEMENT difference between actual and predicted performance a measure of the difference between actual performance and forecast, or standard, performance **2.** ACCOUNTING difference between planned and actual cost the difference between a planned, budgeted, or standard cost and the actual cost incurred. The same comparisons may be made for revenues.

variation margin STOCKHOLDING & INVESTMENTS, RISK daily profits or losses the profits or losses of members of the **London Clearing House**, calculated daily from the marked-to-market-close value of their position. *See also* ***initial margin***

VAT TAX tax added at each manufacturing stage a tax added at each stage in the manufacture of a product. It acts as a replacement for a **sales tax** in almost every industrialized country outside North America. It is levied on selected goods and services, paid by organizations on items they buy, and then charged to customers. *Full form* ***value-added tax***

VAT declaration TAX in UK, statement of VAT income in the United Kingdom, a statement to **Her Majesty's Revenue & Customs** declaring that proportion of a business's income that is liable to **VAT**

VAT inspector TAX UK government official checking payment of VAT a UK government official who examines VAT returns and checks that VAT is being paid

VAT paid TAX in UK, with VAT paid in the United Kingdom, indicating an item on which **VAT** has already been paid

VAT receivable TAX with VAT not yet collected with the VAT for an item not yet collected by a taxing authority

VAT registration TAX listing as firm eligible for some refunding of VAT the process of listing with a European government as a company eligible for the return of VAT in some cases

vault cash BANKING cash used for bank's everyday needs cash held by a bank in its vaults, used for day-to-day needs

VC *abbr* FINANCE venture capitalist

VCM *abbr* MARKETS Venture Capital Market

VCT *abbr* BUSINESS venture capital trust

vega STOCKHOLDING & INVESTMENTS relationship of option price to underlying asset's volatility a ratio between the expected change in the price of an option and a 1% change in the expected volatility of the underlying asset. *Also called* ***kappa, lambda***

velocity of circulation of money ECONOMICS how quickly money moves around economy the rate at which money circulates in an economy

vendor FINANCE seller a person or organization that sells goods, services, shares, or property

vendor placing STOCKHOLDING & INVESTMENTS business vendor's exchanging of acquired stock for cash the practice of issuing stock to acquire a business, where an agreement has been made to allow the vendor of the business to place the stock with investors for cash

venture capital FINANCE finance for new businesses or projects money used to finance new companies or projects, especially those with high earning potential and high risk. *Also called* ***risk capital***

venture capital fund FINANCE fund providing venture capital a fund that invests in finance houses providing **venture capital**

venture capitalist FINANCE firm or individual providing venture capital a finance company or private individual specializing in providing venture capital. *Abbr* **VC**

Venture Capital Market MARKETS closed sector of Johannesburg exchange for developing companies a sector on the South African stock exchange for listing smaller developing companies that was closed to new listings in 2004 due to low liquidity. *Abbr* **VCM**. *See also* ***Development Capital Market***

venture capital trust BUSINESS in UK, trust investing in smaller firms in the United Kingdom, a trust that invests in smaller firms that need capital to grow. *Abbr* **VCT**

venture funding FINANCE second round of funding for new firm the round of funding for a new company that follows the provision of seed capital by venture capitalists

venture management GENERAL MANAGEMENT collaboration encouraging entrepreneurism and innovation the collaboration of various sections within an organization to encourage an **entrepreneurial** spirit, increase innovation, and produce successful new products more quickly. Venture management is used within large organizations to create a small-firm, entrepreneurial atmosphere, releasing innovation and talent from promising employees. It cuts out bureaucracy and bypasses traditional management systems. The collaboration is generally between research and development, corporate planning, marketing, finance, and purchasing functions.

venturer FINANCE partner in joint venture one of two or more parties involved in a **joint venture**

verbal contract GENERAL MANAGEMENT oral, not written, agreement an agreement that is oral and not written down. It remains legally enforceable by the parties who have agreed to it.

verification ACCOUNTING in-depth examination of firm's assets and liabilities in an audit, a substantive test of the existence, ownership, and valuation of a company's assets and liabilities

vertical diversification GENERAL MANAGEMENT, MERGERS & ACQUISITIONS developing new areas in supply chain **diversification** in which a company moves into a different level of the **supply chain**, for example, a manufacturing company becoming a retailer. *See also* ***diversification***

vertical equity TAX principle that tax rates vary with income the principle that people with different incomes should pay different rates of tax

vertical form ACCOUNTING presentation of debits and credits in single column the presentation of a financial statement in which the debits and credits are shown in one column of figures

vertical integration GENERAL MANAGEMENT combining of operations in supply chain the practice of combining some or all of the sequential operations of the **supply chain** between the sourcing of **raw materials** and sale of the final product. Vertical integration can be pursued as a strategy through the acquisition of **suppliers**, **wholesalers**, and **retailers** to increase control and reliability. It can also be achieved when a company gains strong control over suppliers or distributors, usually by exercising purchasing power.

vertical market MARKETS market geared toward one product type a market that is oriented to one particular specialty, for

   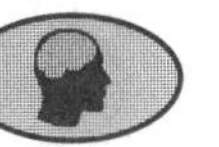  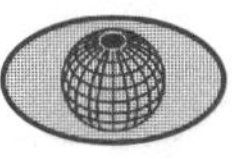   

example, plastics manufacturing or transportation engineering

vertical merger MERGERS & ACQUISITIONS combining of firms in same supply chain the amalgamation of two or more organizations from the same **supply chain** under single ownership, through the direct **acquisition** by one organization of the net assets or liabilities of the other. *See also* ***merger***

vested employee benefits HR & PERSONNEL benefits not linked to job employee benefits that are not conditional on future employment by the company in question, for example, a pension plan

vested interest FINANCE personal interest in maintaining status quo a special interest in keeping an existing state of affairs for personal gain

vested rights PENSIONS in US, value of pension on leaving job the value of somebody's rights in a pension if he or she leaves a job

vesting HR & PERSONNEL in US, continuing right to receive employer contributions the right of an employee participating in a benefit plan to employer contributions to the plan, whether or not the employee continues working for the company

VFM *abbr* ACCOUNTING value for money audit

v-form FINANCE graph line showing value falling then rising a graphic representation of something that had been falling in value and is now rising

viatical settlement INSURANCE proceeds from sale of terminal patient's insurance policy the proceeds received from the sale of a life insurance policy to a third party by somebody who is terminally ill

virement *UK* ACCOUNTING transfer of money between accounts or budgets a transfer of money from one account to another or from one section of a budget to another

virtual bank BANKING, E-COMMERCE bank only accessible electronically a financial institution that offers banking services via the Internet, ATMs, and telephone but does not have a physical location for customers to visit

virtual hosting E-COMMERCE hosting option with user responsible for software a type of hosting suitable for small and medium-sized businesses, in which the customer uses space on a network vendor's server that is also used by other organizations. The hosting company agrees to deliver minimum access speeds and data transfer rates, and to conduct basic hardware maintenance, but the customer is responsible for managing the content and software.

virtualization E-COMMERCE creation of product or service with electronic existence the creation of a product, service, or organization that has an electronic rather than a physical existence

virtual organization E-COMMERCE temporary partnerships between firms via communications technologies a temporary network of companies, suppliers, customers, or employees, linked by information and communications technologies, with the purpose of delivering a service or product. A virtual organization can bring together companies in partnering or outsourcing arrangements, enabling them to share expertise, resources, and cost savings until objectives are met and the network is dissolved. Such organizations are virtual not only in the sense that they exist largely in cyberspace, but also in that they are unconstrained by the traditional barriers of time and place. A greater level of trust is required between employer and employee or coworkers, or partner organizations, because they will be working out of one another's sight for most of the time. *See also* ***network organization, virtual team***

virtual team GENERAL MANAGEMENT remote employees collaborating via communications technologies a group of employees using information and communications technologies to collaborate from different work bases. Members of a virtual team may work in different parts of the same building or may be scattered across a country or around the world.

visible INTERNATIONAL TRADE describing tangible goods imported or exported used to describe real products or goods that are imported or exported

visible trade INTERNATIONAL TRADE buying and selling physical goods trade in physical goods and merchandise

vision statement GENERAL MANAGEMENT statement of organization's aims a statement giving a broad, aspirational image of the future that an organization is aiming to achieve

voetstoots FINANCE in S. Africa, at buyer's risk in South Africa, used to describe a sale or purchase for which there is no warranty or guarantee

volume discount OPERATIONS & PRODUCTION discount to customer for quantity purchase the discount given to a customer who buys a large quantity of goods

volume of retail sales BUSINESS how much consumers buy the amount of trade in goods conducted in the retail sector of an economy in a particular period

volume of trade MARKETS number of stocks sold during trading day the number of shares sold on a stock exchange during a day's trading

volume variances ACCOUNTING monetary differences when actual and budgeted activity diverges differences in costs or revenues compared with budgeted amounts, caused by differences between the actual and budgeted levels of activity

voluntary arrangement FINANCE agreement with terms not legally binding an agreement the terms of which are not legally binding on the parties

voluntary bankruptcy LEGAL bankruptcy declared by debtor **bankruptcy** in which the debtor files a petition claiming inability to meet his or her debts, as opposed to involuntary bankruptcy, where one or more creditors bring a petition against the debtor. *See also* ***bankruptcy***

voluntary liquidation BUSINESS unforced liquidation supported by stockholders liquidation of a solvent company that is supported by the stockholders

voluntary registration TAX in UK, optional VAT registration by small company in the United Kingdom, registration for **VAT** by a trader whose turnover is below the registration threshold. This is usually done in order to reclaim tax on inputs.

vostro account BANKING local bank account held for foreign bank an account held by a local bank on behalf of a foreign bank

votes on account FINANCE extra money for UK government department in the United Kingdom, money granted by Parliament to allow government departments to continue spending in a fiscal year before final authorization of the totals for the year

voting shares *UK* STOCKHOLDING & INVESTMENTS = ***voting stock***

voting stock *US* STOCKHOLDING & INVESTMENTS stock giving voting rights stock whose owners have the right to vote at the company's annual meeting and any extraordinary meetings. *UK term* ***voting shares***

voting trust STOCKHOLDING & INVESTMENTS group with voting rights from stockholders

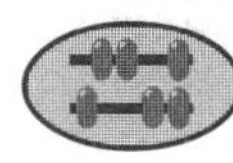
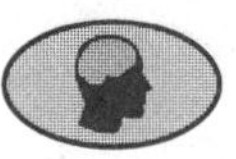
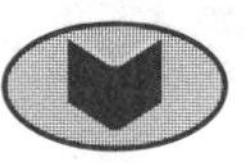
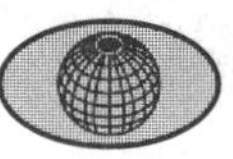

a group of individuals who have collectively received voting rights from stockholders

voucher ACCOUNTING evidence for accounting entry a document supporting an entry in a company's accounts

vouching ACCOUNTING auditor's matching of vouchers with accounting entries an auditing process in which documentary evidence is matched with the details recorded in an accounting record in order to check for validity and accuracy

Vredeling Directive GENERAL MANAGEMENT proposal requesting multinational firms to consult employees a proposal, presented to the European Council of Ministers in 1980, for obligatory information, consultation, and participation of employees at headquarters level in multinational enterprises

VRN *abbr* FINANCE variable rate note

vulture capitalist FINANCE venture capitalist benefiting investors, not entrepreneur client a **venture capitalist** who exploits entrepreneurs by structuring deals on their behalf in such a way that the investors benefit rather than the entrepreneurs (*slang*)

vulture fund STOCKHOLDING & INVESTMENTS investment fund specializing in discounted items a mutual fund that specializes in acquiring investments such as bonds that have been downgraded or **distressed property**

W

wage FINANCE money regularly paid for work done the money paid to an employee in return for work done, especially when it is based on an hourly rate and is paid weekly

wage drift FINANCE = ***earnings drift***

wage freeze ECONOMICS government restraints on wage increases a government policy of preventing pay raises in order to combat inflation

wage incentive FINANCE monetary reward for employee's performance a monetary benefit offered as a reward to those employees who perform well in an agreed way

wage indexation ECONOMICS linking of pay raises to cost of living the linking of increases in wages to the percentage rise in the cost of living

wage policy *US* ECONOMICS government policy on wage levels a government policy setting wages and wage increases for workers, for example, setting minimum wage requirements. *UK term* ***wages policy***

wage-price spiral ECONOMICS = ***inflationary spiral***

wage restraint FINANCE curbs on pay raises the act of keeping increases in wages under control and in proportion to increases in workers' productivity

wages FINANCE money in return for work a form of pay given to employees in exchange for the work they have done. Traditionally, the term wages applied to the weekly pay of manual, or nonprofessional workers. In modern usage, the term is often used interchangeably with salary.

wages costs ACCOUNTING costs of paying employees the costs of paying employees for their work. Along with other costs such as pension contributions, these costs typically form the largest single cost item for a business.

wages payable account ACCOUNTING in UK, account showing expenditure on employees in the United Kingdom, an account showing the gross wages and employer's **National Insurance** contributions paid during a specific period

wages policy *UK* ECONOMICS = ***wage policy***

waiting time OPERATIONS & PRODUCTION period of inactivity enforced by machine breakdown the period for which an operator is available for production but is prevented from working by shortage of material or tooling, or by machine breakdown

waiver LEGAL avoidance of legal condition an act of giving up a right or removing the conditions of a rule

waiver of premium INSURANCE policy provision to suspend premium payments a provision of an insurance policy that suspends payment of premiums, for example, if the insured receives a disabling injury

wakalah FINANCE contract appointing agent in Islamic financing, a contract in which one person appoints another person to act as an agent on their behalf in a transaction

wallet technology E-COMMERCE software facilitating payment by digital cash a software package providing **digital wallets** or purses on the computers of merchants and customers to facilitate payment by digital cash

wallflower STOCKHOLDING & INVESTMENTS unappealing investment an investment that does not attract a lot of interest from potential investors (*slang*)

wallpaper STOCKHOLDING & INVESTMENTS major stock issue financing takeovers a disparaging term used to describe a situation where a company issues and sells many new shares in order to finance a series of takeovers (*slang*)

Wall Street MARKETS **1.** US financial markets a collective name for the financial industry in the United States **2.** financial district of New York City a street in Manhattan in and around which the **New York Stock Exchange** and other important financial institutions are located

Wall Street bonus FINANCE large financial reward for US employee a very large sum of money, in addition to annual salary, paid to an employee in New York's financial industry for effective performance in increasing his or her company's profits. *See also* ***City bonus***

Wall Street Journal FINANCE US financial newspaper a respected daily newspaper published by Dow Jones & Company in New York City, with Asian and European editions, that covers US and international business and financial news and topics

war babies STOCKHOLDING & INVESTMENTS defense industry securities securities in companies that work as contractors in the defense industry (*slang*)

war chest MERGERS & ACQUISITIONS reserves for financing takeovers a large amount of money held by a person or a company in **reserves** that can be used to finance the **takeover** of other companies (*slang*)

warehouse capacity OPERATIONS & PRODUCTION available storage space in warehouse the space available in a warehouse for storing goods

war loan STOCKHOLDING & INVESTMENTS UK government bond paying fixed interest a UK government bond that pays a fixed rate of **interest** and has no final **redemption date**. War loans were originally issued to finance military expenditure.

warrant STOCKHOLDING & INVESTMENTS contract to buy stocks in future a contract that gives the right to buy a predetermined number of shares of stock in the future

warrantee LEGAL somebody given warranty a person who is given a warranty by a **warrantor**

     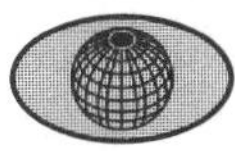   

warrantor LEGAL somebody giving warranty a person who gives a warranty to a **warrantee**

warrant premium STOCKHOLDING & INVESTMENTS extra paid for buying and exercising warrant a premium paid to buy and exercise a warrant, above the price of buying the shares of stock directly without the warrant

warrants risk warning notice STOCKHOLDING & INVESTMENTS broker's statement of risks of options trading a statement that a broker in the United Kingdom gives to clients to alert them to the risks inherent in trading in options

warranty 1. INSURANCE insured person's statement that information provided is correct a statement made by somebody who is being insured that the facts stated by that person are true **2.** LEGAL legal document promising quality of goods a legal document that promises that a machine will work properly or that an item is of good quality **3.** LEGAL promise in contract a promise explicitly stated in a contract

wash sale STOCKHOLDING & INVESTMENTS sale and repurchase of same stock the sale and then immediate repurchase of a block of stock. In the United States it may be used as a means of creating fictitious trading volume. *See also* ***bed and breakfast deal***

wasting asset ACCOUNTING asset that is consumed to earn income a **fixed asset** that is consumed or exhausted in the process of earning income, for example, a mine or a quarry

watchdog REGULATION & COMPLIANCE organization regulating particular industry an independent organization set up to police a particular industry, ensuring that member companies do not act illegally

watch list MARKETS list of securities to be monitored a list of securities that a brokerage firm, exchange, or regulatory agency is watching closely. These may be securities of firms targeted for takeovers, those planning to issue new securities, or those suspected of rules violations.

watered stock STOCKHOLDING & INVESTMENTS stock with value lower than capital invested stock in a company that is worth less than the total **capital** invested

watermark LEGAL symbol in document proving authenticity a design inserted into documents to prove their authenticity. For example, banknotes all carry watermarks to prevent forgery.

WC *abbr* FINANCE working capital

WDA *abbr* ACCOUNTING, TAX writing-down allowance

WDV *abbr* ACCOUNTING written-down value = ***net book value***

weak market MARKETS stock market with falling prices a stock market in which prices tend to fall because there are no buyers

wealth ECONOMICS real estate or investments physical assets such as a house or financial assets such as stocks and bonds that can yield an income for their holder

wealth tax TAX tax on accumulated wealth a tax on somebody's accumulated wealth, as opposed to their income

wear and tear ACCOUNTING degeneration of asset owing to normal use the deterioration of a tangible **fixed asset** as a result of normal use. This is recognized for accounting purposes by **depreciation.**

web commerce E-COMMERCE = ***e-commerce***

web marketplace E-COMMERCE online community for commercial trade a business-to-business web community that brings business buyers and sellers together. Although their exact nature can vary considerably, there are essentially three types of web-based B2B marketplace: online catalogs, auctions, and exchanges.

wedge MARKETS representation of converging highs and lows in market analysis, a chart pattern in which the lines that connect the highs and lows are gradually converging while moving in the same direction

WEF *abbr* ECONOMICS World Economic Forum

weighted average STATISTICS average reflecting relative importance of individual values an average of quantities that have been adjusted by the addition of a statistical value to allow for their relative importance in a set of items

weighted average cost of capital FINANCE average cost of firm's capital the average cost of a company's financing (equity, debentures, bank loans) weighted according to the proportion each element bears to the total pool of capital. Weighting is usually based on market valuations, current yields, and costs after tax. The weighted average cost of capital is often used as the **hurdle rate** for investment decisions, and as the measure to be minimized in order to find the optimal capital structure for the company.

weighted average cost price FINANCE cost of each item in inventory a value for the cost of each item of a specific type in an inventory, taking into account what quantities were bought at what prices

weighted average number of ordinary shares *UK* STOCKHOLDING & INVESTMENTS = ***weighted average number of shares outstanding***

weighted average number of shares outstanding *US* STOCKHOLDING & INVESTMENTS figure used for calculating earnings per share the number of shares of common stock at the beginning of a period, adjusted for shares canceled, bought back, or issued during the period, multiplied by a time-weighting factor. This number is used in the calculation of **earnings per share.** *UK term* ***weighted average number of ordinary shares***

weighted index ECONOMICS index with importance affecting value an index in which some important items are given more value than less important ones

weighting STATISTICS giving more importance to some values the assigning of greater importance to particular items in a data set

weightlessness GENERAL MANAGEMENT quality ascribed to knowledge economy a quality considered to characterize an economy that is based on knowledge or other intangibles rather than on physical assets

Wheat Report ACCOUNTING report examining principles and methods of US accounting a report produced by a committee in 1972 that set out to examine the principles and methods of accounting in the United States. Its publication led to the establishment of the **FASB.**

whisper number or **whisper estimate** FINANCE rumored earnings an estimate of a company's earnings that is based on rumors

whisper stock STOCKHOLDING & INVESTMENTS stock predicted to rise in value a stock about which there is talk of a likely change in value, usually upward and often related to a takeover

whistle ◇ blow the whistle on somebody or something GENERAL MANAGEMENT to engage in **whistleblowing** with regard to some malpractice, misconduct, corruption, or mismanagement

whistleblowing GENERAL MANAGEMENT exposure of misconduct within organization speaking out to the media or the public on malpractice, misconduct, corruption, or mismanagement witnessed in an organization. Whistleblowing is usually undertaken on the grounds of morality or conscience, or because of a failure of business ethics on the part of the organization being reported.

white-collar crime FRAUD crime by white-collar worker a crime committed by somebody in the course of doing a **white-collar job**, for example, embezzlement

white-collar job HR & PERSONNEL job involving no physical labor a position of employment that does not involve physical labor, for example, a job in an office. The term refers to the white shirt and tie supposedly worn by office workers. *See also* ***blue-collar job***

white-collar worker HR & PERSONNEL office worker a person whose job involves working in an office

white elephant BUSINESS product or service underperforming against development costs a product or service that has not sold well, despite large amounts of money being pumped into its development

white goods MARKETING large household appliances large household electrical appliances such as ranges, refrigerators, and freezers

white knight MERGERS & ACQUISITIONS preferred buyer whose action thwarts takeover a person or company liked by a company's management, who buys the company when a hostile company is trying to buy it. *See also* ***knight***

whitemail MERGERS & ACQUISITIONS issue of cheap shares of stock to prevent takeover a method used by a company that is the target of a takeover bid to prevent the takeover, in which the target company issues a large number of shares of stock below the market price to friendly investors. The company wanting to acquire the target must buy the shares in order to be successful.

White Paper BUSINESS report stating UK government's policy a report issued by the UK government as a statement of government policy on a particular problem. *See also* ***Green Paper***

white squire MERGERS & ACQUISITIONS shareholder whose stock purchases prevent takeover bid somebody who purchases a significant, but not controlling, number of shares of stock in order to prevent a **takeover bid** from succeeding. A white squire is often invited to purchase the shares by the company to be acquired, and may be required to sign an agreement to prevent him or her from later becoming a **black knight**.

whiz kid BUSINESS young person enjoying huge business success a young, exceptionally successful person, especially one who makes a lot of money in large financial transactions, including takeovers (*informal*)

whole-life assurance UK INSURANCE = ***whole-life insurance***

whole-life insurance or **whole-life policy** US INSURANCE insurance policy paying out on death an insurance policy in which the insured person pays a fixed premium each year and the insurance company pays a sum when he or she dies. *UK term* ***whole-life assurance***

whole loan MORTGAGES mortgage sold in entirety a mortgage loan that is sold to an investor along with all of its rights and responsibilities

wholesale BUSINESS describing business of selling goods to retailers relating to the business of buying goods from manufacturers and selling them in large quantities to retailers who then sell in smaller quantities to the general public

wholesale banking BANKING banking services provided by merchant banks banking services between investment banks and other financial institutions. *See also* ***retail banking, commercial bank***

wholesale funded BANKING funded by short-term borrowing used to describe a bank whose funds come from other banks and financial institutions in the form of short-term loans rather than from long-term deposits

wholesale funding BANKING funding of banks through short-term borrowing a method of funding banks by short-term borrowing from other banks and financial institutions

wholesale market MARKETS, BANKING = ***interbank market***

wholesale price BUSINESS price for bulk purchases of items for resale a price charged to customers who buy large quantities of an item for resale in smaller quantities to others

wholesale price index ECONOMICS government indicator of inflation level a government-calculated index of wholesale prices, indicative of inflation in an economy

wholesaler OPERATIONS & PRODUCTION intermediary between producer and retailer a business that purchases goods from a manufacturer or producer and sells them to a retailer or distributor

wholly-owned subsidiary BUSINESS firm completely owned by another a company that is completely owned by another company. A wholly-owned subsidiary is a **registered company** with board members who all represent one **holding company** or corporation. Board members may be directly from the holding company or acting as its nominees, or they may be from other wholly-owned subsidiaries of the holding company.

whoops US FINANCE disparaging name for Washington state power company a disparaging way of referring to the Washington Public Power Supply System, a municipal corporation in the US state of Washington that built and operated power plants. Delays, cost overruns, and mismanagement in the construction of nuclear power plants caused the company to default on the $2.25 billion in bonds, the largest bond default in US history before the events of 2008.

widow-and-orphan stock US STOCKHOLDING & INVESTMENTS dependable stock a stock considered extremely safe as an investment

will LEGAL document stating distribution of property after death a legal document in which a person says what should happen to his or her property after he or she dies

wimbledonization UK BUSINESS migration of ownership of British industry the process of the ownership of British industry gradually moving out of the country. The term derives from the major tennis tournament of Wimbledon, where the contest is still played in the UK but the high-profile players are from other countries (*slang*).

windfall gains and losses FINANCE unforeseen gains and losses large financial gains and losses that occur unexpectedly

windfall profit FINANCE large unexpected profit a large profit that is made unexpectedly and may be subject to extra tax

windfall tax UK TAX = ***excess profits tax***

winding-up LEGAL dissolving firm the legal process of closing down a company

winding-up petition LEGAL petition to court to liquidate company a formal request to a court for the compulsory liquidation of a company

window dressing GENERAL MANAGEMENT artificial inflation of firm's success the practice of making a business seem more profitable or more efficient than it really is

  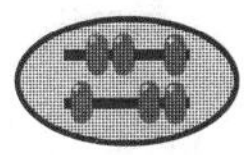 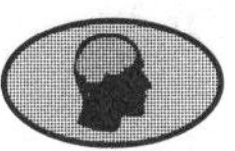  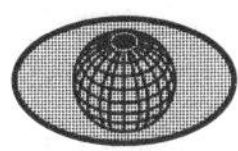   

wind up LEGAL close business down to close down a business or organization and sell its assets

WIP *abbr* OPERATIONS & PRODUCTION work in process

wire house MARKETS brokerage with electronically connected branch offices a brokerage firm whose branch offices are linked by a communications system that allows them to rapidly share data relating to financial markets and individual securities

wire room **1.** BANKING bank department dealing with payment orders the department in a financial institution that originates, receives, and transmits payment orders **2.** MARKETS brokerage department dealing with securities orders the department in a brokerage firm that receives and transmits securities orders to the floor of the exchange or the trading department

wire transfer E-COMMERCE electronic transfer of funds a transfer of money from one account to another electronically

witching hour *US* MARKETS time when financial instrument becomes due the time when a type of derivative financial instrument such as a **put**, a **call**, or a contract for advance sale becomes due (*slang*)

withdraw **1.** BANKING take money from account to remove money from an account **2.** FINANCE rescind offer to retract an offer that has been made

withdrawal STOCKHOLDING & INVESTMENTS income disbursement from open-end mutual fund the regular disbursement of dividend or capital gain income from an open-end mutual fund

withdrawal plan STOCKHOLDING & INVESTMENTS regular payment to shareholder from mutual fund an arrangement in which a mutual fund pays out a specific amount to a shareholder at regular intervals. *See also* ***systematic withdrawal***

withholding or **withholding tax** TAX **1.** US employee's income tax deducted at source in the United States, the money that an employer pays directly to the government as a payment of the income tax of the employee **2.** tax on dividend or interest paid directly to government the money deducted from a dividend or interest payment that a financial institution pays directly to the government as a payment of the income tax on the recipient **3.** tax in place of dividends the tax that a company must pay because it chose not to pay **dividends** that would subject its owners to higher taxes

with profits INSURANCE describing insurance policy paying share of profits used to describe an insurance policy that guarantees the policyholder a share in the profits of the fund in which the premiums are invested

working capital FINANCE firm's money available for trading the funds that are readily available to operate a business.

Working capital comprises the total net **current assets** of a business minus its **current liabilities.**

Current assets – Current liabilities

Current assets are cash and assets that can be converted to cash within one year or a normal operating cycle; current liabilities are monies owed that are due within one year.

If a company's current assets total $300,000 and its current liabilities total $160,000, its working capital is:

$300,000 – $160,000 = $140,000

Abbr **WC**

working capital productivity FINANCE measure of firm's productivity a way of measuring a company's efficiency by comparing working capital with sales or turnover.

It is calculated by first subtracting **current liabilities** from **current assets,** which is the formula for working capital, then dividing this figure into sales for the period.

$$\frac{\text{Sales}}{\text{Current assets} - \text{Current liabilities}} = \text{Working capital productivity}$$

If sales are $3,250, current assets are $900, and current liabilities are $650, then:

$$\frac{3250}{900 - 650} = \frac{3250}{250} = 13 \text{ working capital productivity}$$

In this case, the higher the number the better. Sales growing faster than the resources required to generate them is a clear sign of efficiency and, by definition, productivity.

The working capital to sales ratio uses the same figures, but in reverse:

$$\frac{\text{Working capital}}{\text{Sales}} = \text{Working capital to sales ratio}$$

Using the same figures in the example above, this ratio would be calculated:

$$\frac{250}{3250} = 0.077 \times 100\% = 7.7\%$$

For this ratio, obviously, the lower the number the better.

Some experts recommend doing quarterly calculations and averaging them for a given year to arrive at the most reliable number.

working capital ratio ACCOUNTING = ***current ratio***

working capital turnover FINANCE sales divided by average working capital a figure equal to sales divided by average working capital

Working Time Directive or **Working Hours Directive** HR & PERSONNEL EU directive concerning maximum working hours a European Union directive concerning the maximum number of hours an employee can work. The directive currently limits weekly working hours to a maximum of 48, but employees can choose to opt out and work more hours than this.

work in process *US* OPERATIONS & PRODUCTION products currently being made any product that is in the process of being made. Such items are included in inventories and usually valued according to their production costs. *Abbr* **WIP**. *UK term* ***work in progress***

work in progress *UK* OPERATIONS & PRODUCTION = ***work in process***

work simplification GENERAL MANAGEMENT elimination of nonessential tasks the streamlining of business practices that attempts to eliminate tasks that do not add value to an idea or process. Tasks in a procedure are analyzed to see if unnecessary steps can be eliminated, thereby reducing complexity as much as possible, enabling workers to complete tasks more quickly. Work simplification is most suited to manufacturing processes and low-skilled jobs. It can lead to cost savings and better use of resources, but it has been criticized for resulting in workers specializing in only one task and for making work repetitive and monotonous.

World Bank BANKING group of institutions funding less developed countries one of the largest sources of funding for the less industrially developed countries in the world. It is made up of five organizations: the International Bank for Reconstruction and Development, the International Development Association, the International Finance Corporation, the Multilateral Investment Guarantee Agency, and the International Centre for Settlement of Investment Disputes. The World Bank was founded at the 1944 Bretton Woods Conference and has over 180 member countries. Its head office is located in Washington, DC, but the Bank has field

  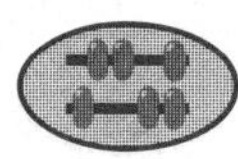   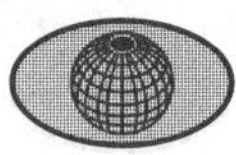   

offices in over 100 countries. Its focus has shifted dramatically since the 1980s, when over one-fifth of its lending was made up of investment in the energy industry. Its current priorities are education, health, and nutrition in the most economically challenged countries of the world.

world class manufacturing GENERAL MANAGEMENT level of manufacturing excellence recognized internationally a position of international manufacturing excellence, achieved by developing a culture based on factors such as continuous improvement, problem prevention, zero defect tolerance, customer-driven **just-in-time** production, and **total quality management**

World Economic Forum ECONOMICS organization seeking to effect global economic improvement an independent economic organization whose goal is to "improve the state of the world." Based in Switzerland, the WEF was formed in the 1970s by Professor Klaus Schwab, who set out to bring together the CEOs of leading European companies in order to discuss strategies that would enable Europe to compete in the global marketplace. Since then, over 1,000 companies around the world have become members of the WEF and its interests have diversified to cover health, corporate citizenship, and peace-building activities. However, it has attracted criticism from some quarters, and antiglobalization protesters gather regularly at its meetings. *Abbr* **WEF**

world economy ECONOMICS = ***global economy***

World Trade Organization INTERNATIONAL TRADE international organization established to reduce trade restrictions an international organization set up with the goal of reducing restrictions in trade between countries. *Abbr* **WTO**

wrap account STOCKHOLDING & INVESTMENTS brokerage account charging periodic fee a client account with a broker in which the broker charges a set quarterly or annual fee covering transaction and management costs instead of charging per transaction

wrap fund STOCKHOLDING & INVESTMENTS fund investing in various underlying mutual funds a registered fund that, while not itself a mutual fund, has similar status to that of a stockbroker's portfolio and invests in a variety of underlying mutual funds, each of which is treated as a discrete holding, often in the form of an insurance bond. *Also called* ***wrapper***

wrapper STOCKHOLDING & INVESTMENTS = ***wrap fund***

writ LEGAL document starting legal process an official document issued by a judge requiring a specific action

write STOCKHOLDING & INVESTMENTS, RISK = ***underwrite***

write-down ACCOUNTING assignment of lower value to asset the recording of an asset at a lower value than previously

write-off **1.** ACCOUNTING reduction in recorded value of asset a reduction in the recorded value of an asset, usually to zero **2.** INSURANCE cancellation of debt the total loss or cancellation of a bad debt **3.** INSURANCE something damaged beyond repair for insurance claims, something that is so badly damaged that it cannot be repaired and will have to be replaced

writer **1.** INSURANCE = ***underwriter*** **2.** STOCKHOLDING & INVESTMENTS seller of traded option somebody who is selling a **traded option**

write-up ACCOUNTING increase in book value of asset an increase made to the book value of an asset to adjust for an increase in market value

writing-down allowance ACCOUNTING, TAX tax relief on acquired assets that lose value in the United Kingdom, a form of capital allowance giving tax relief to companies acquiring **fixed assets** that are then depreciated. This allowance forms part of the system of **capital allowances.** *Abbr* **WDA**

written-down value ACCOUNTING = ***net book value***

wrongful trading LEGAL continued trading by directors aware of impending insolvency in the United Kingdom, the continuation of trading when a company's directors know that it cannot avoid insolvent liquidation

WTO *abbr* INTERNATIONAL TRADE World Trade Organization

X

X STOCKHOLDING & INVESTMENTS with no dividend right a symbol used in newspapers to designate a stock or bond that is trading **ex dividend**

X.12 E-COMMERCE = ***ANSI X.12 standard***

xa *abbr* STOCKHOLDING & INVESTMENTS ex-all

XBRL FINANCE computer language for financial reporting a computer language used for financial reporting. It allows companies to publish, extract, and exchange financial information through the Internet and other electronic means. *Full form* ***Extensible Business Reporting Language***

xd *abbr* STOCKHOLDING & INVESTMENTS ex dividend

xr *abbr* STOCKHOLDING & INVESTMENTS ex-rights

xw STOCKHOLDING & INVESTMENTS trading without a warrant to buy shares a symbol used in newspapers to designate a stock that is trading without a **warrant** to buy shares of stock

Y

Yankee bond STOCKHOLDING & INVESTMENTS foreign bond in US market a bond issued in the US domestic market by a non-US company

yard CURRENCY & EXCHANGE one billion currency units used by traders for one billion units of any currency *(slang)*

year end ACCOUNTING end of fiscal year the end of the financial year, when a company's accounts are prepared

year-end ACCOUNTING of end of fiscal year relating to the end of a fiscal year

year-end bounce MARKETS = ***Santa Claus rally*** *(slang)*

year-end closing ACCOUNTING statements at end of firm's fiscal year the financial statements issued at the end of a company's fiscal year

year to date ACCOUNTING period from start of fiscal year to now the period from the start of a fiscal year to the current time. A variety of financial information, such as a company's profits, losses, or sales, may be displayed on this basis. *Abbr* **YTD**

yen CURRENCY & EXCHANGE Japanese currency the basic unit of currency used in Japan

yield STOCKHOLDING & INVESTMENTS percentage that is annual income from investment a percentage of the amount invested that is the annual income from an investment.

Yield is calculated by dividing the annual cash return by the current share price and expressing that as a percentage.

Yields can be compared against the market average or against a sector average, which in turn gives an idea of the relative value of the share against its peers. Other things being equal, a higher yield share is

  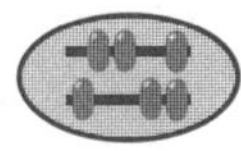   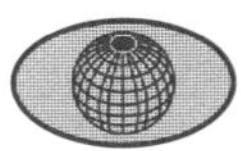   

preferable to that of an identical company with a lower yield.

An additional feature of the yield (unlike many of the other share analysis ratios) is that it enables comparison with cash. Cash placed in an interest-bearing source like a bank account or a government stock produces a yield—the annual interest payable. This is usually a safe investment. The yield from this cash investment can be compared with the yield on shares, which are far riskier. This produces a valuable basis for share evaluation.

Share yield is less reliable than bank interest or government stock interest yield, because, unlike banks paying interest, companies are under no obligation at all to pay dividends. Frequently, if they go through a bad patch, even the largest companies will cut dividends or abandon paying them altogether.

yield curve STOCKHOLDING & INVESTMENTS graph showing comparable interest on bonds a visual representation of relative interest rates of short- and long-term bonds. It can be normal, flat, or inverted.

yield gap STOCKHOLDING & INVESTMENTS difference in return between equities and bonds an amount representing the difference between the yield on a safe equity investment and the yield on a riskier bond investment. *See also* ***reverse yield gap***

yield management FINANCE price adjustment that secures maximum profits securing maximum profits from available capacity by manipulating pricing to gain business at different times, and from differing market segments. Yield management is used particularly in service industries such as the airline, hotel, and equipment rental industries, where there are heavy fixed overheads and additional revenue has a big impact on bottom line profitability. Increasing computing power has enabled organizations to integrate complex information from different sources (for example, customer travel histories and current information on bookings) and use mathematical models to analyze the possibility of increasing profitability. Hotel businesses, for example, can use price offers to increase “revenue per available room,” or “RevPAR,” on the basis of yield management analysis.

yield to call STOCKHOLDING & INVESTMENTS yield on bond at potential call date the yield on a bond at a date when the bond can be called

yield to maturity *US* STOCKHOLDING & INVESTMENTS investor’s total return if security held to maturity the total return to an investor if a fixed interest security is held to maturity, in other words, the aggregate of gross interest received and the capital gain or loss at redemption, annualized. *Abbr* **YTM**. *UK term* ***gross redemption yield***

yield to worst MARKETS lowest possible bond yield the lowest possible yield from a bond, calculated using the lower of the yield to maturity or any **yield to call**

YK *abbr* BUSINESS yugen kaisha

YTD *abbr* ACCOUNTING year to date

YTM *abbr* STOCKHOLDING & INVESTMENTS yield to maturity

yugen kaisha BUSINESS private limited liability corporation in Japan in Japan, a private limited liability corporation. Usually, the number of stockholders must be under 50. The minimum capital of a limited liability corporation is 3 million yen. The nominal value of each share must be 50,000 yen or more. *Abbr* **YK**

Z

ZBB *abbr* ACCOUNTING zero-based budgeting

Z bond STOCKHOLDING & INVESTMENTS bond paying interest after paying all other holders a bond whose holder receives no interest until all of the holders of other bonds in the same series have received theirs

zero-balance account BANKING bank account for outgoings, holding no residual funds a bank account that does not hold funds continuously, but has money automatically transferred into it from another account when claims arise against it

zero-based budgeting ACCOUNTING budgeting method requiring costs to be justified a method of budgeting that requires each cost element to be specifically justified, as though the activities to which the budget relates were being undertaken for the first time. Without approval, the budget allowance is zero. *Abbr* **ZBB**

zero coupon bond STOCKHOLDING & INVESTMENTS discounted bond paying no interest a bond that pays no interest and is sold at a large discount. *Also called* ***accrual bond***, ***split coupon bond***

zero-coupon security STOCKHOLDING & INVESTMENTS government security without interest a government security that pays no interest but is sold at a discount from its face value

zero-fund FINANCE provide no money for project to assign no money to a business project without actually canceling it *(slang)*

zero growth ECONOMICS no increase in output a lack of increase in the output of a business or economy between one period, such as one quarter, and the next. *See also* ***recession***

zero-rated TAX on which no sales tax is paid used to describe an item on which a buyer pays no sales tax

zero-rated supplies or **zero-rated goods and services** TAX goods or services not liable for VAT in the United Kingdom, taxable items or services on which **VAT** (Value Added Tax) is charged at zero rate, for example, food, books, public transport, and children’s clothes

zero-rating TAX sales tax rating of 0% the rating of a product or service at 0% sales tax

zero-sum game FINANCE gain by one results in loss by another a situation in which a gain by one participant results in another participant’s equivalent loss

zombie *US* BUSINESS firm still trading although insolvent a business that continues to trade supported by its bank even though it is insolvent and unlikely to recover *(slang)*

ZOPA BANKING website facilitating loans between users a personal loan exchange website that allows web users to lend to and borrow from each other directly. *Full form* ***Zone of Possible Agreement***

Z score STATISTICS, FINANCE measure of bankruptcy risk a statistical measure used to determine the likelihood of bankruptcy from a company’s credit strength

   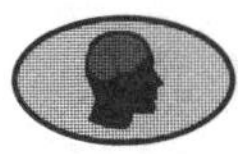  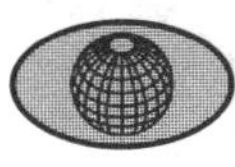   

Index

  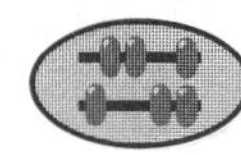   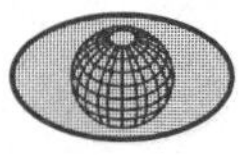   

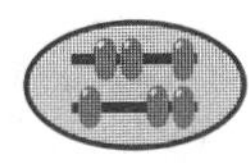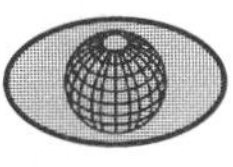

    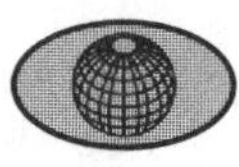   

     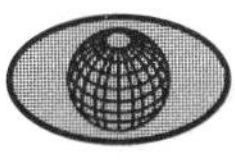   
a–z

  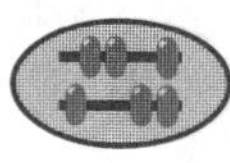   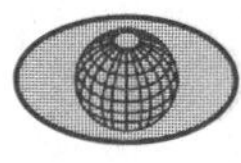   

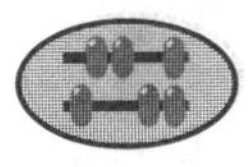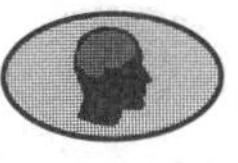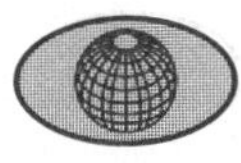

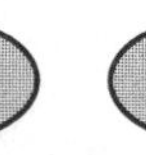 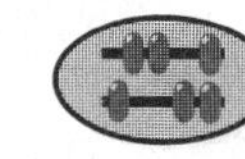   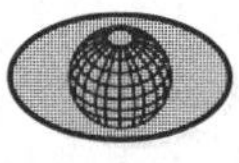   

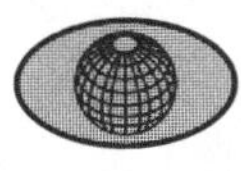
a–z

  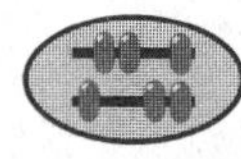   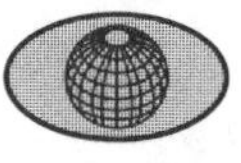 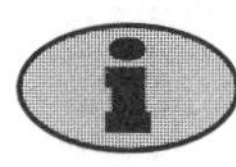  

 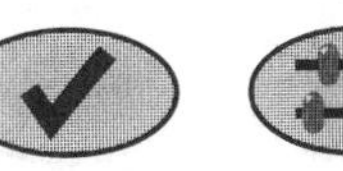 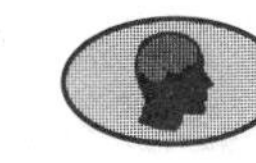  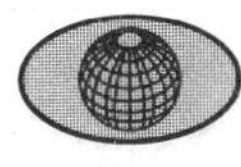   

  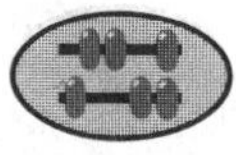 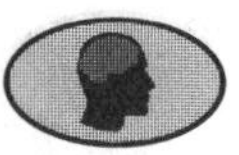  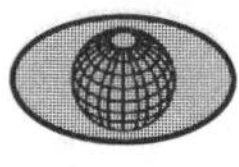   

  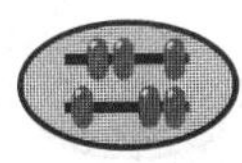   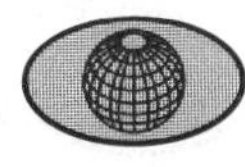   

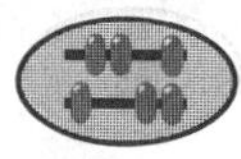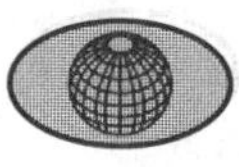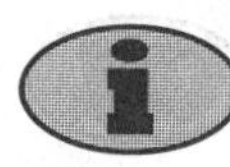

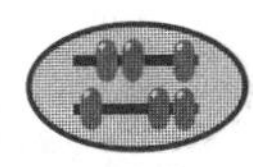
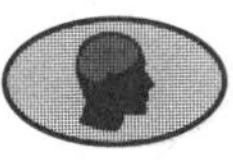

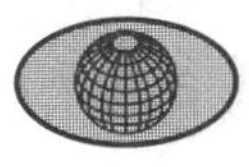

  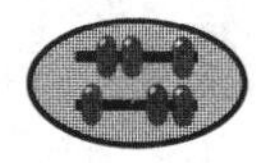   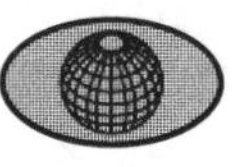   

  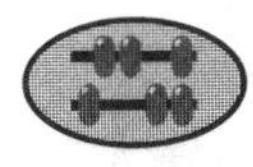   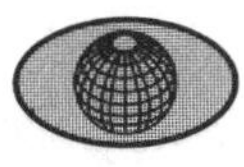   

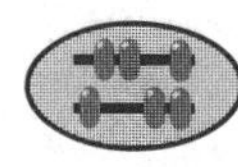

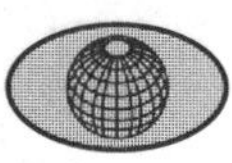

a–z

QFINANCE

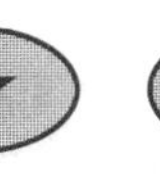  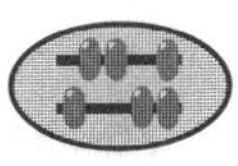   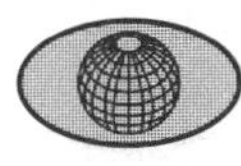   

  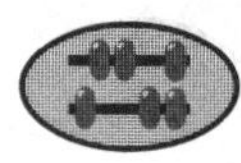 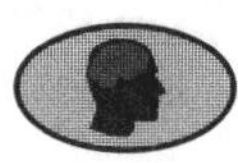  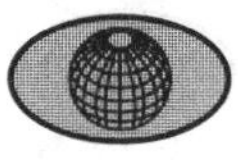   

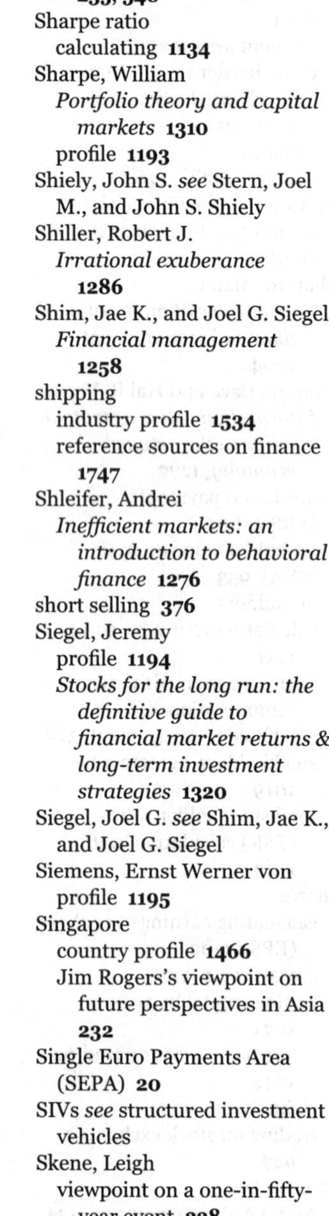

     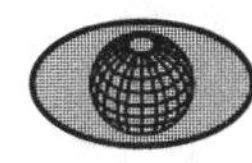   

 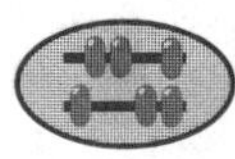   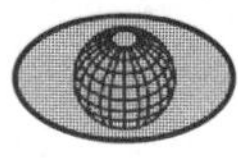  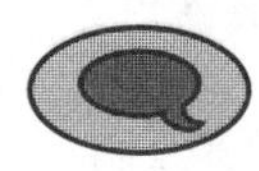 

  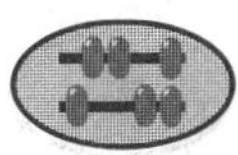 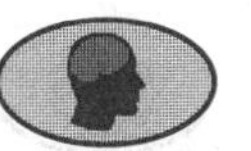  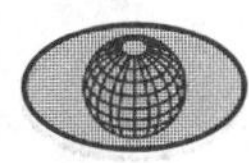   

Credits

Best Practice
pp. 569–571, "Raising Capital in the United Kingdom" copyright © Lauren Mills

Calculations and Ratios
61 Calculations and Ratios copyright © A&C Black Publishers Ltd

Country and Sector Profiles
Many statistics copyright © Central Intelligence Agency

Finance Information Sources
34 Finance Information Sources copyright © Chartered Management Institute

Dictionary
Management terms copyright © Chartered Management Institute

Photographs
Prince Al-Walid bin Talal copyright © AFP Photo/Gerard Cerles
Igor Ansoff copyright © Oxford University Press
Gary Becker copyright © Ralf-Finn Hestoft/CORBIS
Peter L. Bernstein copyright © Peter Bernstein
Fischer Black copyright © The MIT Museum
Gary Brinson copyright © Michael L. Abramson/Time Life Pictures/Getty Images
Warren Buffet copyright © Paul White/AP/Press Association Images
Andrew Carnegie copyright © AP/Press Association Images
Ronald Harry Coase copyright © Coase Institute
John C. Cox copyright © MIT Sloan
Gottlieb Daimler copyright © AP/Press Association Images
Joseph de la Vega copyright © Sonsbeek Publishers
Marc Faber copyright © Marc Faber
Eugene Fama copyright © Eugene Fama
Irving Fisher copyright © Robert Kradin/AP/Press Association Images
John Kenneth Galbraith copyright © AP/Press Association Images
Louis Gerstner copyright © Stuart Ramson/AP/Press Association Images
Benjamin Graham copyright © AP/Press Association Images
Alan Greenspan copyright © AP/Press Association Images
Friedrich Hayek copyright © HL/AP/Press Association Images
Daniel Kahneman copyright © Daniel Hulshizer/AP/Press Association Images
John Maynard Keynes copyright © Walter Sanders/Time Life Pictures/Getty Images
Edwin Lefèvre copyright © Condé Nast Archive/CORBIS
Burton Malkiel copyright © Don Heiny/AP/Press Association Images
Harry Markowitz copyright © AP/Press Association Images
Robert Merton copyright © KUNI/AP/Press Association Images
Merton Miller copyright © Charles Bennett/AP/Press Association Images
Franco Modigliani copyright © Mark Lennihan/AP/Press Association Images
J. P. Morgan copyright © AP/Press Association Images
Nicholas Negroponte copyright © William B. Plowman/AP/Press Association Images
Paul O'Neill copyright © Paul Goguen/LANDOV/Press Association Images
Michael Eugene Porter copyright © Lou Krasky/AP/Press Association Images
C. K. Prahalad copyright © Susana Gonzalez/LANDOV/Press Association Images
David Ricardo copyright © Hulton Archive/Stringer/Getty Images. From an engraving by Hodgetts after a portrait by T. Phillips
John D. Rockefeller copyright © AP/Press Association Images
Stephen A. Ross copyright © Daniel Acker/LANDOV/Press Association Images
Nouriel Roubini copyright © Mark Lennihan/AP/Press Association Images

  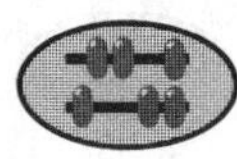 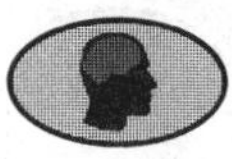  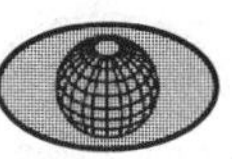   

Paul Samuelson copyright © Daniel Lippitt/AP/Press Association Images
Jean-Baptiste Say copyright © The Warren J. Samuels Portrait Collection at Duke University
Myron Scholes copyright © Daniel Acker/LANDOV/Press Association Images
Ernst Friedrich Schumacher copyright © The Schumacher Society
Joseph Schumpeter copyright © Imagno/Getty Images
William F. Sharpe copyright © AP/Press Association Images
Jeremy Siegel copyright © Matt Rourke/AP/Press Association Images
Ernst Werner von Siemens copyright © Time Life Pictures/Mansell/Time Life Pictures/Getty Images
Adam Smith copyright © Hulton-Deutsch Collection/CORBIS. From an engraving by Robert Graves
George Soros copyright © Koji Sashara/AP/Press Association Images
Joseph Stiglitz copyright © Virginia Mayo/AP/Press Association Images
Sun Tzu copyright © Steve Allen/Brand X/Corbis
Richard Thaler copyright © Ralf-Finn Hestoft/CORBIS
James Tobin copyright © Joel Page/AP/Press Association Images
Jean-Claude Trichet copyright © Mr M. Joppen. (*Source*: European Central Bank/Frankfurt)
Amos Tversky copyright © Barbara Tversky
Arnold, Lord Weinstock copyright © PA/PA Archive/Press Association Images
Jack Welch copyright © Elise Amendola/AP/Press Association Images
Mohammed Yunus copyright © Franka Bruns/AP/Press Association Images
Robert Zoellick copyright © Gregorio Borgia/AP/Press Association Images

We extend our grateful thanks to all of the following who donated photographs for use in *QFINANCE*:
Viral Acharya, Amjid Ali, Jacques Attali, Wim Bartels, Jagdish Bhagwati, Anthony Bolton, Roger Bootle, Todd Buchholz, Sir Howard Davies, Rajiv Dogra, Javier Estrada, Frank Feather, Julian Franks, Bill Hambrecht, Stewart Hamilton, Tim Hindle, Fred Hu, Jonathan M. Karpoff, Graeme Leach, Ernst Ligteringen, Justin Yifu Lin, Augusto Lopez-Claros, Jay W. Lorsch, Thierry Malleret, Aldo Mareuse, Hamish McRae, Bruce Misamore, Maureen J. Miskovic, Mark Mobius, James Montier, Mike Moore, Jon Moulton, Ravi Nedungadi, Nenad Pacek, Michael J. Panzner, Zarin Patel, Lawrence Phillips, Brian Reading, Ricardo Rebonato, Jim Rogers, John Schaetzl, Leigh Skene, Bernhard Speyer, Roger Steare, Achim Steiner, Sir John Stuttard, Pavan Sukdhev, Jean-Claude Trichet, Norbert Walter, Richard A. Werner, Paul Wilmott, Linda Yueh, Muhammad Yunus, Peter Zollinger.